THE CATHOLIC STUDY BIBLE

EDITORS AND CONTRIBUTORS

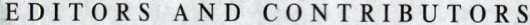

Dianne Bergant
Lawrence Boadt
Richard J. Clifford
John J. Collins
Mary Ann Getty
Daniel J. Harrington
Leslie J. Hoppe
Luke Timothy Johnson
Kevin Madigan
Carolyn Osiek
Pheme Perkins
Eileen Schuller
Donald Senior
Ronald A. Simkins
Ronald D. Witherup

The Catholic Study Bible

Donald Senior • John J. Collins • Mary Ann Getty

EDITORS

The New American Bible

Revised Edition

OXFORD
UNIVERSITY PRESS

OXFORD
UNIVERSITY PRESS

Oxford University Press, Inc., publishes works that further Oxford University's objective of excellence in research, scholarship, and education.

Oxford New York
Auckland Cape Town Dar es Salaam Hong Kong Karachi Kuala Lumpur Madrid
Melbourne Mexico City Nairobi New Delhi Shanghai Taipei Toronto

With offices in
Argentina Austria Brazil Chile Czech Republic France Greece
Guatemala Hungary Italy Japan Poland Portugal Singapore
South Korea Switzerland Thailand Turkey Ukraine Vietnam

Published by Oxford University Press, Inc.
198 Madison Avenue, New York, New York 10016

http://www.oup.com

Oxford is a registered trademark of Oxford University Press

Nihil Obstat
Reverend John G. Lodge, S.S.L., S.T.D.
Censor Deputatis
Reverend Robert L. Schoenstene, M.A., S.S.L.
Censor Deputatis
September 13, 2005

Imprimatur
Reverend John F. Canary, S.T.L., D.Min.
Vicar General
Archdiocese of Chicago
September 14, 2005

The *Nihil Obstat* and *Imprimatur* are official declarations that a book is free of doctrinal and moral error. No implication is contained therein that those who have granted the *Nihil Obstat* and *Imprimatur* agree with the content, opinions, or statements expressed. Nor do they assume any legal responsibility associated with publication.

Scripture texts, prefaces, introductions, footnotes, and cross references used in this work constitute

The New American Bible
Nihil Obstat
Stephen J. Hartdegen, O.F.M., S.S.L.
Christian P. Ceroke, O. Carm., S.T.D.

Imprimatur
†Patrick Cardinal O'Boyle, D.D.
Archbishop of Washington
July 27, 1970

Revised New Testament
Nihil Obstat
Stephen J. Hartdegen, O.F.M., S.S.L.
Censor Deputatis

Imprimatur
† James A. Hickey, S.T.D., J.C.D.
Archbishop of Washington
August 27, 1986

Revised Psalms
Imprimatur
Most Rev. Daniel E. Pilarczyk, President, National Conference of Catholic Bishops, October 10, 1991

RESCRIPT

In accord with canon 825 §1 of the Code of Canon Law, the United States Conference of Catholic Bishops hereby approves for publication The New American Bible, Revised Old Testament, a translation of the Sacred Scriptures authorized by the Confraternity of Christian Doctrine, Inc.

The translation was approved by the Administrative Committee of the United States Conference of Catholic Bishops in November 2008 and September 2010. It is permitted by the undersigned for private use and study.

Given in the city of Washington, the District of Columbia, on the Feast of Saint Jerome, Priest and Doctor of the Church, the 30th day of September, in the year of our Lord 2010.

Francis Cardinal George, O.M.I.
Archbishop of Chicago
President, USCCB

Interior typesetting by Blue Heron Bookcraft, Battle Ground, WA

Printed in Korea

1 3 5 7 9 8 6 4 2

CONTENTS

List of Sidebar Essays, Charts, and Drawings ix
List of Maps xi
About the Editors and Contributors xiii
Alphabetical Listing of the Books of the Bible xv
Abbreviations of the Books of the Bible xvii
Key to References xix

General and Introductory Articles

General Introduction *Donald Senior* RG 3
The Biblical Texts and Their Background *Donald Senior* RG 10
The Catholic Study Bible *Donald Senior* RG 13
The Bible in Catholic Life *Daniel J. Harrington* RG 16
Biblical History and Archaeology *Ronald A. Simkins* RG 30
Catholic Interpretation of the Bible *Kevin Madigan* RG 54
The Challenges of Biblical Translation *Ronald D. Witherup* RG 68
The Bible in the Lectionary *Eileen Schuller* RG 76

Reading Guides

The Pentateuch *Lawrence Boadt* RG 85
Genesis, RG 100 Exodus, RG 115 Leviticus, RG 125 Numbers, RG 133
Deuteronomy, RG 141

The Deuteronomistic History *Leslie J. Hoppe* RG 149
Joshua, RG 149 Judges, RG 156 Ruth, RG 164 1 and 2 Samuel, RG 169
1 and 2 Kings, RG 183

The Chronicler's History and the Later Histories *Leslie J. Hoppe* RG 199
1 Chronicles, RG 199 2 Chronicles, RG 203 Ezra, RG 207 Nehemiah, RG 211

Tobit, RG 215 Judith, RG 218 Esther, RG 222 1 Maccabees, RG 226
2 Maccabees, RG 231

The Wisdom Books *Dianne Bergant* RG 235
Job, RG 236 Psalms, RG 243 Proverbs, RG 254 Ecclesiastes, RG 262
The Song of Songs, RG 267 The Book of Wisdom, RG 272 Sirach, RG 276

The Major Prophets, Baruch, and Lamentations *Richard J. Clifford* RG 280
Isaiah, RG 280 Jeremiah, RG 296 Lamentations, RG 310 Baruch, RG 315
Ezekiel, RG 320

Daniel and the Minor Prophets *John J. Collins* RG 336
Daniel, RG 336 The Twelve Minor Prophets, RG 344 Hosea, RG 346
Joel, RG 349 Amos, RG 351 Obadiah, RG 356 Jonah, RG 357 Micah, RG 359
Nahum, RG 361 Habakkuk, RG 362 Zephaniah, RG 363 Haggai, RG 364
Zechariah, RG 365 Malachi, RG 369

The Gospels and Acts *Donald Senior and Pheme Perkins* RG 371
The Synoptic Gospels, RG 371 Matthew, RG 373 Mark, RG 387 Luke, RG 397
John, RG 412 Acts, RG 423

Paul and His Writings *Mary Ann Getty and Carolyn Osiek* RG 351
Romans, RG 441 1 Corinthians, RG 450 2 Corinthians, RG 458
Galatians, RG 464 Ephesians, RG 471 Philippians, RG 475 Colossians, RG 478
1 Thessalonians, RG 482 2 Thessalonians, RG 484 1 Timothy, RG 487
2 Timothy, RG 489 Titus, RG 491 Philemon, RG 493

The General Letters and Revelation *Luke Timothy Johnson* RG 496
Hebrews, RG 496 James, RG 501 1 Peter, RG 506 2 Peter, RG 510 1 John, RG 513
2 John, RG 516 3 John, RG 517 Jude, RG 519 Revelation, RG 520

The Old Testament of the *New American Bible, Revised Edition*
Preface to the *New American Bible*: Old Testament 3
Preface to the Revised *New American Bible*: Old Testament 5

The Pentateuch 7
The Book of Genesis, 9 The Book of Exodus, 81 The Book of Leviticus, 133
The Book of Numbers, 172 The Book of Deuteronomy, 222

The Historical Books 267
The Book of Joshua, 268 The Book of Judges, 296 The Book of Ruth, 326
The First Book of Samuel, 332 The Second Book of Samuel, 370
The First Book of Kings, 399 The Second Book of Kings, 440
The First Book of Chronicles, 474 The Second Book of Chronicles, 508
The Book of Ezra, 548 The Book of Nehemiah, 561

Biblical Novellas 578
The Book of Tobit, 578 The Book of Judith, 595 The Book of Esther, 614
The First Book of Maccabees, 628 The Second Book of Maccabees, 664

The Wisdom Books 690
The Book of Job, 691 The Book of Psalms, 727 The Book of Proverbs, 834
The Book of Ecclesiastes, 879 The Song of Songs, 890 The Book of Wisdom, 899
The Wisdom of Ben Sira (Ecclesiasticus), 924

The Prophetic Books 987
The Book of Isaiah, 988 The Book of Jeremiah, 1071
The Book of Lamentations, 1142 The Book of Baruch, 1151
The Book of Ezekiel, 1161 The Book of Daniel, 1220 The Book of Hosea, 1245
The Book of Joel, 1259 The Book of Amos, 1265 The Book of Obadiah, 1276
The Book of Jonah, 1278 The Book of Micah, 1281 The Book of Nahum, 1289
The Book of Habakkuk, 1293 The Book of Zephaniah, 1297
The Book of Haggai, 1301 The Book of Zechariah, 1304 The Book of Malachi, 1317

The New Testament of the *New American Bible, Revised Edition*

Preface to the *New American Bible*: First Edition of the New Testament 1325
Preface to the Revised Edition 1326

The Gospels 1331
The Gospel According to Matthew, 1332 The Gospel According to Mark, 1400
The Gospel According to Luke, 1433 The Gospel According to John, 1486
The Acts of the Apostles, 1526

The New Testament Letters 1576
The Letter to the Romans, 1577 The First Letter to the Corinthians, 1600
The Second Letter to the Corinthians, 1624 The Letter to the Galatians, 1643
The Letter to the Ephesians, 1654 The Letter to the Philippians, 1662

The Letter to the Colossians, 1670 The First Letter to the Thessalonians, 1676
The Second Letter to the Thessalonians, 1680 The First Letter to Timothy, 1684
The Second Letter to Timothy, 1691 The Letter to Titus, 1696
The Letter to Philemon, 1699 The Letter to the Hebrews, 1700

The Catholic Letters 1721
The Letter of James, 1721 The First Letter of Peter, 1728
The Second Letter of Peter, 1735 The First Letter of John, 1740
The Second Letter of John, 1746 The Third Letter of John, 1747
The Letter of Jude, 1749 The Book of Revelation, 1751

Glossary 1781
Measures and Weights 1806
Lectionary 1809
The New 3-Year Cycle of Readings for Sunday Mass 1809
Readings for the Major Feasts of the Year 1814
Weekday Readings 1815

Index to Reading Guide 1821

Collaborators on the Old Testament of the *New American Bible* 1970 1849
Collaborators on the Revised Psalms of the *New American Bible* 1991 1850
Collaborators on the Revised New Testament of the *New American Bible* 1986 1851
Collaborators on the Old Testament of the *New American Bible* 2010 1852
Collaborators on the Book of Psalms of the *New American Bible* 2010 1853

A Concordance to the *New American Bible* 1854

New Oxford Bible Maps

LIST OF SIDEBAR ESSAYS, CHARTS, AND DRAWINGS

The Major Divisions of Genesis 13
The *Toledoth* ("Generations") Lists 19
The Family Tree of Abraham 42
Calendar 113
Structure of the Tabernacle 116
Purity, Cleanliness, and Ritual 147
Tribal Lists in Genesis, Numbers, and Deuteronomy 175
"Hear, O Israel" 232
The Temple and Palace of Solomon 409
Chronology of the Two Kingdoms 424
The Temple of Solomon according to 2 Chronicles 512
The Kings of Persia 550
The Four Stages of Return from Exile 562
The Structure of the Book of Psalms 729
Hebrew Poetry 841
Acrostic Poems in Hebrew 1146
Rulers during New Testament Times 1411
Parables in the Synoptic Gospels 1425

LIST OF MAPS

Table of Nations 25
Geography of Ancestral Narratives 29
Probable Exodus Route according to the Bible 97
Journey from the Wilderness to Canaan 219
Conquest of Canaan according to the Book of Joshua 273
Levitical Cities 291
Important Cities Mentioned in Judges 302
Battles of Gideon 306
The Twelve Judges 311
Five Cities of the Philistines 317
Sites Mentioned in Benjaminite War 324
Places in Ruth 327
The Activity of Samuel 337
Wanderings of the Ark 338
The Kingdom of Saul according to 1 Samuel 347
The Kingdom of David according to 2 Samuel 375
Solomon's Twelve Administrative Districts 407
The Divided Monarchy 422
Places Associated with Elijah 431
Places Associated with Elisha 442
Campaign of Tiglath-pileser III 463
Campaign of Sennacherib 466
Nebuchadnezzar's Campaign 474
The Levitical Cities according to 1 Chronicles 484
The Kingdom of David according to 1 Chronicles 490
The Kingdom of Solomon according to 2 Chronicles 518
The Divided Monarchy according to 2 Chronicles 522
Exile of Northern Kingdom 541

(List of Maps, continued)

Exile of Southern Kingdom 547
The Return from Exile 551
The Persian Empire 616
The Campaigns of the Maccabees and Hasmoneans 632
The Jerusalem Vicinity 633
Places Mentioned in the Oracles against the Nations 1006, 1129, 1189
The Assyrian Empire 1033
Jeremiah's Journey to Egypt 1127
Tribal Territories in the Restored Israel 1218
The Neo-Babylonian Empire 1223
Alexander's Empire 1235
The Ptolemaic and Seleucid Kingdoms 1240
Jerusalem in the Time of Jesus 1377
Site of Jesus' Travels in Galilee and Vicinity 1416
Sites of Jesus' Journey to Jerusalem and within It 1470
Geography of the Gospel of John 1491
The Native Lands of Pentecost Pilgrims 1529
Sites of Early Christian Missionary Activities 1540
First Missionary Journey of Paul 1549
Second Missionary Journey of Paul 1554
Third Missionary Journey of Paul 1560
Paul's Journey to Rome 1573
Paul's Journeys to Asia Minor 1645
The Seven Churches 1756

New Oxford Bible Maps follow the last page of text

ABOUT THE EDITORS AND CONTRIBUTORS

Dianne Bergant, C.S.A. Reading Guides to the Wisdom and Poetical Books: Job, Psalms, Proverbs, Ecclesiastes, Song of Songs, Wisdom, Sirach.
Dianne Bergant is Professor of Old Testament Studies at Catholic Theological Union, Chicago.

Lawrence Boadt, C.S.P., S.S.D. General Introduction to the Pentateuch. Reading Guides to Genesis, Exodus, Leviticus, Numbers, Deuteronomy.
Lawrence Boadt is Professor Emeritus of Hebrew Scriptures at Washington Theological Union.

Richard J. Clifford, S.J. Reading Guides to Isaiah, Jeremiah, Lamentations, Baruch, Ezekiel.
Richard J. Clifford is Professor of Old Testament at the Weston Jesuit School of Theology in Cambridge, Massachusetts, and is on the board of trustees and editorial board of the Catholic Biblical Association of America.

John J. Collins. Editor. Reading Guides to Daniel and the Twelve Minor Prophets: Hosea, Joel, Amos, Obadiah, Jonah, Micah, Nahum, Habakkuk, Zephaniah, Haggai, Zechariah, Malachi.
John J. Collins is Holmes Professor of Old Testament Criticism and Interpretation at Yale University. He is currently serving as president of the Society of Biblical Literature.

Mary Ann Getty. Editor. Paul and His Writings. Reading Guides to Romans, 1 Corinthians, 2 Corinthians, Galatians, Ephesians, Philippians, Colossians, 1 Thessalonians, 2 Thessalonians, 1 Timothy, 2 Timothy, Titus, Philemon.
Mary Ann Getty is Associate Professor of New Testament, St. Vincent College, Latrobe, Pennsylvania.

Daniel J. Harrington, S.J. The Bible in Catholic Life.
Daniel J. Harrington is Professor of New Testament and Chair of Biblical Studies at the Weston Jesuit School of Theology in Cambridge, Massachusetts. He is also editor of New Testament Abstracts.

Leslie J. Hoppe, O.F.M. Reading Guides to Joshua, Judges, Ruth, 1 and 2 Samuel, 1 and 2 Kings, 1 Chronicles, 2 Chronicles, Ezra, Nehemiah, Tobit, Judith, Esther, 1 Maccabees, 2 Maccabees.
Leslie J. Hoppe is Professor of Old Testament Studies at Catholic Theological Union in Chicago.

(Editors and Contributors, continued)

Luke Timothy Johnson. Reading Guides to Hebrews, James, 1 Peter, 2 Peter, 1 John, 2 John, 3 John, Jude, Revelation.
Luke Timothy Johnson is R.W. Woodruff Professor of New Testament and Christian Origins at Candler School of Theology at Emory University in Atlanta, Georgia. He is also a senior fellow at Emory's Center for the Study of Law and Religion.

Kevin Madigan. Catholic Interpretation of the Bible.
Kevin Madigan is Professor of the History of Christianity at Harvard Divinity School, Cambridge, Massachusetts.

Carolyn Osiek. Paul and His Writings. Reading Guides to Romans, 1 Corinthians, 2 Corinthians, Galatians, Ephesians, Philippians, Colossians, 1 Thessalonians, 2 Thessalonians, 1 Timothy, 2 Timothy, Titus, Philemon.
Carolyn Osiek is Charles Fischer Catholic Professor of New Testament at Brite Divinity School at Texas Christian University in Fort Worth, Texas.

Pheme Perkins. Reading Guides to Luke, John, Acts.
Pheme Perkins is Professor of Theology (New Testament) at Boston College.

Eileen Schuller. The Bible in the Lectionary.
Eileen Schuller is Professor of Religious Studies at McMaster University in Hamilton, Ontario.

Donald Senior, C.P. Editor. General Introduction. The Biblical Texts and Their Backgrounds. The Catholic Study Bible Reading Guide. Reading Guides to the Synoptic Gospels, Matthew, Mark.
Donald Senior is President and Professor of New Testament at Catholic Theological Union in Chicago.

Ronald A. Simkins. Biblical History and Archaeology.
Ronald Simkins is Director of the Center for the Study of Religion and Society at Creighton University and Associate Professor of both Theology and Classical & Near Eastern Studies at Creighton.

Ronald D. Witherup, S.S. The Challenges of Biblical Translation.
Ronald Witherup is Provincial Superior of the United States Province of Sulpicians.

ALPHABETICAL LISTING OF THE BOOKS OF THE BIBLE

Acts	1526
Amos	1265
Baruch	1151
Ben Sira (Ecclesiasticus)	924
1 Chronicles	474
2 Chronicles	508
Colossians	1670
1 Corinthians	1600
2 Corinthians	1624
Daniel	1220
Deuteronomy	222
Ecclesiastes	879
Ecclesiasticus (Ben Sira)	924
Ephesians	1654
Esther	614
Exodus	81
Ezekiel	1161
Ezra	548
Galatians	1643
Genesis	9
Habakkuk	1293
Haggai	1301
Hebrews	1700
Hosea	1245
Isaiah	988
James	1721
Jeremiah	1071
Job	691
Joel	1259
John	1486
1 John	1740
2 John	1746
3 John	1747
Jonah	1278
Joshua	268
Jude	1749
Judges	296
Judith	595
1 Kings	399
2 Kings	440
Lamentations	1142
Leviticus	133
Luke	1433
1 Maccabees	628
2 Maccabees	664
Malachi	1317
Mark	1400
Matthew	1332
Micah	1281
Nahum	1289
Nehemiah	561
Numbers	172
Obadiah	1276
1 Peter	1728
2 Peter	1735
Philemon	1699
Philippians	1662
Proverbs	834
Psalms	727
Revelation	1751
Romans	1577
Ruth	326
1 Samuel	332
2 Samuel	370
Sira (Ecclesiasticus)	924
Song of Songs	890
1 Thessalonians	1676
2 Thessalonians	1680
1 Timothy	1684
2 Timothy	1691
Titus	1696
Tobit	578
Wisdom	899
Zechariah	1304
Zephaniah	1297

ABBREVIATIONS OF THE BOOKS OF THE BIBLE

Old Testament

Gn	Genesis	Neh	Nehemiah	Lam	Lamentations
Ex	Exodus	Tb	Tobit	Bar	Baruch
Lv	Leviticus	Jdt	Judith	Ez	Ezekiel
Nm	Numbers	Est	Esther	Dn	Daniel
Dt	Deuteronomy	1 Mc	1 Maccabees	Hos	Hosea
Jos	Joshua	2 Mc	2 Maccabees	Jl	Joel
Jgs	Judges	Jb	Job	Am	Amos
Ru	Ruth	Ps(s)	Psalms	Ob	Obadiah
1 Sm	1 Samuel	Prv	Proverbs	Jon	Jonah
2 Sm	2 Samuel	Eccl	Ecclesiastes	Mi	Micah
1 Kgs	1 Kings	Song (or Sg)	Song of Songs	Na	Nahum
2 Kgs	2 Kings	Wis	Wisdom	Hb	Habakkuk
1 Chr	1 Chronicles	Sir	Sirach (Ecclesiasticus)	Zep	Zephaniah
2 Chr	2 Chronicles	Is	Isaiah	Hg	Haggai
Ezr	Ezra	Jer	Jeremiah	Zec	Zechariah
				Mal	Malachi

New Testament

Mt	Matthew	Eph	Ephesians	Heb	Hebrews
Mk	Mark	Phil	Philippians	Jas	James
Lk	Luke	Col	Colossians	1 Pt	1 Peter
Jn	John	1 Thes	1 Thessalonians	2 Pt	2 Peter
Acts	Acts of the Apostles	2 Thes	2 Thessalonians	1 Jn	1 John
Rom	Romans	1 Tm	1 Timothy	2 Jn	2 John
1 Cor	1 Corinthians	2 Tm	2 Timothy	3 Jn	3 John
2 Cor	2 Corinthians	Ti	Titus	Jude	Jude
Gal	Galatians	Phlm	Philemon	Rev	Revelation

KEY TO REFERENCES

For greater clarity and convenience, the footnotes and cross references are printed at the bottom of each page and cross-indexed in the text itself. An *asterisk* (*) in the text indicates that there is a footnote to the text in question. Each footnote is in turn clearly marked with the number of the chapter and the verse to which it pertains. Similarly a *superior letter* ([a]) in the text indicates that there is a cross-reference to a particular verse. The reference itself is also clearly marked with the same letter. Hence, the reader is always aware of a footnote or a cross-reference simply by *reading the text.*

Key to Scripture References

Gn 1:1	refers to Genesis, chapter one, verse one.
Gn 1:1a	refers to Genesis, chapter one, first part of verse one.
Gn 1:1f(f)	refers to Genesis, chapter one, verse one and the following verse (verses).
Gn 1:1–10	refers to Genesis, chapter one, verses one through ten.
Gn 1:1–10, 24	refers to Genesis, chapter one, verses one through ten and verse twenty-four.
Gn 1–5	refers to Genesis, chapters one through five inclusive.
Gn 1:1–2:3	refers to Genesis, chapter one, verse one through chapter two, verse three inclusive.
Gn 1:1; 2:3	refers to Genesis, chapter one, verse one and chapter two, verse three.

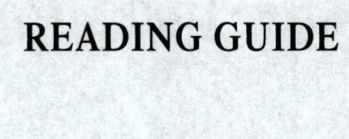

READING GUIDE

GENERAL INTRODUCTION

The book you hold in your hand contains one of humanity's greatest treasures. No one can deny that the Bible has had a profound impact on world civilization. Its epic stories, its powerful language and images have left their imprint on human history, especially in cultures touched by Judaism and Christianity.

For the Christian, the Bible has an importance far more profound than its impact on culture. The Christian believes that through the turbulent and wonderful chapters of biblical history, God speaks to us. Although expressed in genuinely human terms and through very human authors, the Bible is, at the same time, the Word of God for us. Therefore, as Christians we reverence and love the Scriptures and seek to understand them as much as we can.

The purpose of this *Catholic Study Bible* is to enable the reader to read the Scriptures with new understanding and depth. The primary audience of this Study Bible is Roman Catholic. Some of the comments in the notes to the text, the Articles, and the Reading Guides deliberately reflect Catholic experience and Catholic interests. However, the editors do not wish to exclude other Christian readers from the focus of this book. In most instances, the materials included here will be useful for all Christians who want to enter deeply into the mysteries and marvels of the Bible.

In this general introduction and the two following articles, we hope to: (1) Provide a general introduction to the Bible as a whole: the nature and diversity of its contents, and how it came to be; (2) introduce the reader to the special resources for understanding the Bible provided in this *Catholic Study Bible* edition and to suggest more profitable ways of using them.

INTRODUCING THE BIBLE

Although it is bound under one cover and bears a single title, the Bible is not a single, unified book. It is, in fact, a collection of some seventy-three different works by different authors, using very different styles and perspectives, composed over a span of several centuries, and in three different languages (Hebrew, Aramaic, Greek). Most of the Old Testament (forty-six books) was written in Hebrew, but parts of the books of Daniel (2:4–7:28), Ezra (4:6–6, 18:7, 12–26), and one verse from Jeremiah (10:11) were originally composed in Aramaic, a Middle Eastern language related to but different from Hebrew. All twenty-seven of the New Testament books were composed in Greek.

The rich diversity of the Bible is one of its glories because it allows the story of God's people to be told from various perspectives. It also presents a challenge to the reader who should be aware of the different cultural, historical, and literary contexts of each biblical book. But there is a deeper unity to the Bible that binds together these individual pieces of literature. Through the many biblical books flows the continuing saga of God's love for Israel and for the church. Each of the biblical authors, no matter how much separated in time, culture, and literary style, shares a conviction that God's presence is felt in human history and that God invites the human family to respond with faith and integrity.

The Writing of the Bible

As its diverse makeup implies, the Bible was not written at a single point in history. The events covered in the Old Testament span nearly two thousand years of history, from the time of Abraham and the patriarchs (around 1800 BC) to the period of the Maccabean wars (140 BC). If one includes the epic accounts of the creation and prepatriarchal stories such as Noah and the flood, then the reach of the biblical saga goes back to the beginning of time. But the actual formulation of the biblical accounts, although making use of earlier stories and traditions, is confined to a narrower period of time, probably beginning with the monarchy (around 1000 BC) and concluding in the century before the birth of Christ.

The New Testament books were all written during the latter half of the first century AD. The letters of Paul were probably the earliest New Testament works to be put in writing, dating mainly from the decade of the fifties. The sayings of Jesus and the many stories about his ministry circulated in the Christian community all during these early decades of the church but were probably not put in writing until shortly after AD 70, with Mark the first Gospel to be written. Matthew, Luke (and his second volume, the Acts of the Apostles), and John follow, with the compositions of their Gospels taking place sometime during the last quarter of the first century. The other non-Pauline letters and writings, including the book of Revelation or the Apocalypse, also date from this period.

Forming a "Bible" from Diverse Books: The Story of the Canon

The gathering of these diverse writings into a single collection or "book" (the literal meaning of the word *Bible*) was itself a long-term and laborious process. The technical term for designating which books belong to the Bible is the *canon* (measurement). Both Judaism and Christianity had to make choices about which books to include and which books to exclude from their respective Bibles. Judaism would not make any official decision about which books belonged to its Bible until the end of the first century AD, but that does not mean it was without a Bible for so much of its history. There was little or no dispute about the major books of the Old Testament, books which were constantly used in Jewish liturgy and teaching, but there was debate about the inclusion of later and less central works such as Tobit or the Wisdom of Solomon.

The Jewish or Hebrew canon ultimately recognizes thirty-nine books, divided into three major categories:

1. The Law (sometimes referred to as the Pentateuch, or first five books of the Bible): Genesis, Exodus, Leviticus, Numbers, Deuteronomy.

2. The Prophets: Subdivided into the "Former Prophets": Joshua, Judges, 1 and 2 Samuel, 1 and 2 Kings; and the "Latter Prophets": Isaiah, Jeremiah, Ezekiel, and the "Twelve" (=Hosea, Joel, Amos, Obadiah, Jonah, Micah, Nahum, Habakkuk, Zephaniah, Haggai, Zechariah, Malachi).

3. The Writings: Psalms, Proverbs, Job, Song of Songs, Ruth, Lamentations, Ecclesiastes, Esther, Daniel, Ezra-Nehemiah, 1 and 2 Chronicles.

As we shall explain below, not included in the official Jewish or Hebrew canon are seven other books that Roman Catholics (and Orthodox Christians) consider part of their Scriptures. Judaism reverences these books and considers them sacred, but they are not part of their canon or official list. These books are: Tobit, Judith, 1 and 2 Maccabees, Wisdom, Sirach/Ecclesiasticus, and Baruch. There are also some additional passages in the books of Daniel and Esther.

The formation of the Christian canon also took place over a considerable period of time. In fact, the official Roman Catholic decision about the canon did not come until the Council of Trent in the sixteenth century, but by that time the choice of which writings were to be included in the Bible was well established. There were many sacred writings in the early decades of the church that presumably could have been included in the Bible. We cannot always tell what criteria or decision-making processes were used to establish the canon. Some "gospels" evidently portrayed Jesus in a way unacceptable to the vast majority of Christians and so were not included. Other early writings, however, such as the *Didache* (Greek for "teaching")—a short handbook of moral behavior and church practice—seem perfectly acceptable in content and tone but were still not included. Probably the early church considered a work's content, its authorship, and the frequency of its usage in the liturgy and teaching of the churches as important criteria for judging if a sacred writing was inspired by God and worthy of inclusion in its official canon or Scriptures.

All Christians agree on the twenty-seven books to be included in the New Testament, but there is a dispute about some of the books in the Old Testament. As noted above, Roman Catholics and Orthodox Christians agree on the forty-six books that make up the Old Testament (the Orthodox include additional books in their canon: 1 and 2 Esdras; the Prayer of Manasseh; Psalm 151; 3 Maccabees). Judaism and Protestant Christians hold for the shorter list of thirty-nine books sketched above; the remaining seven are designated as the "apocryphal" books.

The reason for this divergence is that earliest Christianity used an ancient Greek translation of the Old Testament (called the Septuagint) as its Bible. This Greek version of the Bible included forty-six books. Since most of the early Christians were Greek-speaking, this is the Bible they preferred. But when Judaism officially set out to determine its canon at the end of the first century, it drew up a shorter list of thirty-nine books: those written in Hebrew. In the Reformation period, Protestants went back to this shorter, Hebrew canon, considering it more authentic.

Today, many of the doctrinal tensions that separated Catholics and Protestants have eased. Some Protestant editions of the Bible include the seven apocryphal (what Roman Catholics call *deuterocanonical*) books in an appendix of their Bibles or in a special section between the Old and New Testaments. Following usual Catholic practice, the *New American Bible* integrates the deuterocanonical books into the order of the Old Testament canon.

THE DIVERSE LITERARY FORMS AND HISTORICAL VALUE OF THE BIBLE

The broad span of biblical history and the fact that the Bible is a collection of various books signal its rich diversity. The reader of the Bible needs to be attentive not only to the historical context of a particular passage but to the varieties of literary forms and the specific style and intent of each biblical author. The prophetic oracles of Isaiah or Jeremiah are very different in literary style from the legal codes of Leviticus or the narratives of Exodus. The long lists of wise sayings in Proverbs are dramatically different in tone, style, and theology from the sweeping liturgical poetry of the Psalms. So, too, do the parables of the Gospels differ greatly from the letters of Paul or the dramatic apocalyptic scenes in the book of Revelation. The notes and Reading Guides found in this Study Bible help the reader to understand more about these various literary forms and their implications for interpreting the meaning of a particular biblical passage.

The presence of various literary forms or means of expression in the Bible also complicates the issue of the historical value of the Bible. Some Christians, particularly fundamentalist Christians, fear that admitting the Bible contains poetry, stories, and other literary forms is somehow an attack on the veracity of the Bible and dilutes its witness to history. They prefer to regard the story of creation in Genesis, or the episode of Jonah's sojourn in the belly of a great fish, as literally true.

Roman Catholic teaching—and that of many other Christian denominations—sees no incompatibility between recognizing the truth of the biblical witness and the fact that it is expressed in many forms of literary expression characteristic of human communication. Credible witness to the truth of history is not confined to an "objective" reporting of the facts in the manner of a police report or a mere "factual" description of what happened. All reporting of history involves a degree of interpretation, and such means as poetry, hymns, stories, myths, and other literary forms can also communicate historical truth about past events and the perspectives of our ancestors.

Undoubtedly, both the Old and New Testaments contain many accurate historical facts and descriptions reflecting the times and events of biblical history. But the biblical writers also wanted to interpret the *meaning* of that history and present it unabashedly from their perspectives. Previous traditions are given new interpretations and adapted to the circumstances of a different generation. In most instances their intent was not to provide a historical archive for subsequent generations but to see in the events of this history the presence of God's grace, and to communicate that conviction to their readers. The

Bible is a witness to the vitality of the people who lived its events and pondered their meaning in a spirit of faith. Each biblical passage, therefore, must be evaluated on its own terms in attempting to distinguish between factual historical data and the theological and historical interpretation provided by the biblical writer.

THE TRANSMISSION OF THE BIBLICAL TEXT AND ITS MODERN TRANSLATIONS

Each modern reader of the Bible is in debt to countless numbers of people—Jewish and Christian—who lovingly handed on to the next generations the treasures of the Bible. For much of biblical history, such transmission of the biblical tradition was done orally, not in written form. Stories, sayings of great teachers and leaders, hymns, and poetry were lovingly memorized and handed down from parents to children, teacher to disciple, from leader of prayer to congregation, and, thereby, formed the growing body of the biblical heritage.

In ancient (and some modern) cultures, oral transmission of important literature was not a casual, haphazard affair. For our modern culture, so dependent on written means of communicating information, it is hard to realize that in oral cultures subtle and often unspoken rules govern how information is shaped, retained, and transmitted from one person and one generation to another. But as styles of writing and writing materials became more sophisticated in Israel, and when it had the social organization under the monarchy to have archives and develop an educated class of scribes, then undoubtedly some parts of the Bible were preserved in written form as well.

In the New Testament, many of the Gospel materials were first preserved in oral form. Sayings of Jesus, his parables, the stories about his healings, his conflicts with opponents, and the narrative of his Passion would have been preserved and transmitted in a variety of settings such as the liturgy, instruction within the home or small Christian communities, or, perhaps even more formally, in some early centers of Christian learning. But eventually these oral materials were gathered and put in written form by the evangelists. It is likely that the oral transmission of the biblical materials, both Old and New Testaments, continued to exist and be employed even after the biblical text had been put into writing. Paul's letters and other New Testament texts such as the Catholic Epistles and the book of Revelation were composed or dictated into written form immediately.

No original manuscript of any biblical book exists. Copyists from one generation to the next transcribed the biblical materials and enabled them to be available for subsequent generations. The earliest written manuscripts we have of some Old Testament biblical materials date from the first century BC. These were part of the wealth of written materials discovered in 1948 on the northwest shore of the Dead Sea and thereafter called the "Dead Sea Scrolls." Most of the other early written materials for both the Old and the New Testaments would be papyrus fragments of biblical passages dating from the early second century AD and more complete manuscripts of the Bible on parchment from the third and fourth centuries AD.

The biblical texts of the ancient church did not have the neat format of our modern Bible. Division into the present system of chapters and verses was introduced only in the Middle Ages. Prior to that, demarcations between individual sentences and sections of a particular biblical book were much more casual and fluid. The hands of many copyists, with different personal interests and levels of skill, inevitably introduced some variations and errors into the numerous editions of the biblical text. Ancient translations or versions of manuscripts into other languages, such as Latin or Syriac or Coptic, could also introduce errors or varying interpretations not found in the original biblical language.

The science of textual criticism attempts to trace the relationships of ancient manuscripts to each other and to reestablish the most reliable form of the biblical text. The discovery of biblical texts among the Dead Sea Scrolls rolled back the age of extant biblical manuscripts several centuries. Surprisingly, although some variants exist, there is still remarkable correspondence between the state of the biblical text in the first century BC and the third or fourth century AD—testimony to the accuracy and care with which ancient peoples handed on the biblical tradition.

The *New American Bible* Translation

Most modern translations, including that found in the NAB, are based on the most reliable texts of the Bible we have and are translated from the original biblical languages rather than using any intervening translations. Many previous Catholic translations had been based on the Vulgate, or Latin version of the Bible, first prepared by Jerome in the fifth century.

As the preface to the NAB states (see pp. 3–4 of the Old Testament section), its translation was a collaborative achievement of some fifty Catholic biblical scholars, determined to use the best of modern scholarship to bring a fresh and accurate translation of the Bible to the American Catholic community.

The first full edition of the Old and New Testaments appeared in 1970. A revision of the New Testament appeared in 1986, and a revision of the Psalms in 1991. It is this fully revised edition that is used in the *Catholic Study Bible*.

Every translation, no matter how accurate and faithful, falls short in attempting to communicate the subtlety and meaning of another language. All translators have to make decisions about the purpose and audience of their translation, and the consequent principles they will use in translating the Bible from its original languages to a modern language such as American English. And, to some degree, every translation is a subtle "interpretation" of the biblical text.

The translators of the NAB wanted as much as possible to accurately reflect the nuance and form of biblical Hebrew and Greek, while recasting the language to make it compatible with the rules and style of modern English and in harmony with traditional Catholic interpretations of Scripture. The translators, however, wanted to avoid making the NAB a "paraphrase" or quasi-interpretation of the biblical text. Some modern translations attempt this. While such paraphrases perhaps make the biblical texts more palatable to a modern audience, they also risk a high degree of subjectivity in recasting the contents of the Bible. The NAB translation is faithful to the biblical text and takes its place alongside rigorously literal translations such as the Revised Standard Version. This makes it particularly suitable for deeper study of the biblical message, as well as its use in prayer and liturgy.

Accuracy of translation from one language to another also involves issues that are more than linguistic. For instance, the editors of the revised New Testament translation had to struggle with the question of inclusive language. This is a sensitive issue in modern American culture and in the Catholic Church in particular. The translators adopted a compromise stance here. Where the original biblical language clearly intended a generic reference to human beings, the translation is careful to use inclusive language. Where the original text uses a gender specific reference, however, such as many references to God through male pronouns, the translation does not attempt to use inclusive language.

Modern political issues can also cause difficulties for the translator. Such geographical terms as *Israel* or *Palestine* have highly charged meanings in the political arena of today's Middle East. But their appearance in the biblical translation of the NAB implies no endorsement of any modern political stance on these difficult issues. So, too, can modern religious sensitivities come into play. Judaism in all its modern forms, out of reverence, avoids the use of the name *Yahweh* for God. Readers in the synagogue, for example, will substitute *Adonai* (My Lord) wherever the divine name appears in the biblical text. The modern translator and commentator have to make a decision on whether to try to respect this understandable religious sensitivity.

It should be noted that the Reading Guides and major Articles included in the *Catholic Study Bible* attempt throughout to use inclusive language, and, wherever possible, to avoid offense to modern religious, cultural, or political sensitivities. The editors believed that such a spirit is in accord with both the biblical witness and sound Catholic tradition. Some use of the geographical terms *Israel* and *Palestine* was unavoidable in some of the Reading Guides, but no reference to modern geopolitical realities is intended.

READING, STUDYING, AND PRAYING THE SCRIPTURES

From the beginning of its existence, the Bible has been the object of intense study, prayerful reading, and even heated debate. The Bible is not meant to be a coffee-table book.

One could say that the Bible was formed in a

context of prayer and reflection. The various biblical authors reflected on significant events in the life of Israel, of Jesus, and of the early church. Their discovery of God's presence working within history gives the Bible its force. For all Christians the Bible has unique authority as writings inspired by God's Spirit working within the communities of Israel and the Church, and impelling the biblical writers to give expression in human words to their faith perspective. (For a Catholic view of biblical inspiration, see "The Bible in Catholic Life," RG 16–29).

Judaism has always maintained a rich tradition of reflection on its Scriptures. The rabbis lovingly studied every detail of the biblical text and saw an infinite possibility of applications to everyday life. The Scriptures were reverenced as God's Word and took a central place within the prayer life of the synagogue. Christian tradition has had the same character. Until the late Middle Ages, almost all of the Church's theology and teaching was little more than an elaboration of the biblical text.

Some of this biblical focus was lost in the Catholic Church when philosophical analysis—always important—became overdominant and theological reflection could often be far distant in focus and spirit from our biblical foundations: While biblical symbols remained dominant in Catholic liturgical life and architecture, in popular preaching and much popular piety, the Bible was a more distant echo. In the past fifty years, that trend has been radically reversed. The Second Vatican Council gave a strong impetus to a biblical renewal in every dimension of Catholicism (see "The Bible in Catholic Life," RG 16–29).

One can approach reading and study of the Bible from several vantage points.

The Historical Approach. One purpose in reading the Bible is to comb through the biblical books, seeking leads to the historical context of a given period or culture. While this is a legitimate historical enterprise, it does not correspond to the fundamentally religious character of the Bible. The Bible does have strong historical value; but its purpose is not simply to inform the reader about history but to probe the meaning of past history for the life of faith.

The Theological Approach. Another way of entering the biblical world is to seek what the Bible, or a particular biblical book, has to say on a specific doctrinal or moral issue. What, for example, does the Bible say about violence? Or what is the biblical perspective on justice? Because the Bible is such a rich and diverse body of literature, we soon discover that the Bible will yield many perspectives on such important issues. There is seldom a single biblical viewpoint on any specific theological or moral issue. Only by first understanding the context of each biblical period and biblical book, and then interrelating the Bible's varied approaches to profound questions of faith, can one weave together a biblical theology.

The Inspirational Approach. For most Christians, reading the Bible has a more modest, yet still important goal. They turn to the Scriptures for inspiration in living out their life of faith. Such inspiration can be gained in many different ways.

For some, the Scriptures are an important stimulant for prayer. The words of the Psalms, the challenge of the prophets, the compassionate mission of Jesus, the soaring words of Paul—all of these give form and expression to the longing of our own hearts as we seek the face of God. Very often the biblical words are able to express the feelings and fears and hopes we could not put into words ourselves. And in reaching out to the Bible we unite ourselves with the faith of countless generations of Christians who found the same solace and strength in the Scriptures.

For others, probing the Scriptures either in private or with a group of fellow Christians helps guide and illumine their daily life. Study of the biblical text and discussion of its meaning with other thoughtful Christians can help us understand our own experience of faith and expand our perspective on what it means to be a believer in the modern world. This approach works best when the participant is not afraid to reflect on his or her own experience, and can then relate that reflection to the ideas and images of the Bible. Very often the Bible opens its treasures when we bring to it questions and hopes that spring from our life of faith. Then, in turn, the biblical message can give new insight and nourishment to our faith experience.

A profound sense of grief or loss, for example, might lead a Christian to read with new understanding the lament psalms of the Old Testament

(RG 243–44) or the Passion of Jesus. And these biblical passages, in turn, can bring new strength to the one who suffers.

Whatever approach one takes to reading and praying the Bible, it is important from a Catholic perspective that it not be done in isolation. The Bible is the Church's book, not a private library. Only in the context of the Church's faith and tradition as a whole can the full meaning of the Bible be discovered. Some Christians who isolate themselves from common sense and from the sound wisdom of the Church community can interpret the Scriptures in a bizarre and even destructive manner. That is why the effort to understand the biblical text in its context, to sound out its possible meaning with other thoughtful Christians, and to be open to the guidance of the Church and its teaching forms the best context for full integration of the Bible into our lives (on this see the 1993 statement of the Pontifical Biblical Commission, *The Interpretation of the Bible in the Church,* which fully endorses the use of modern biblical methods).

The *Catholic Study Bible* is designed to open the beauty and power of the Bible to the reader. The editors and the Oxford University Press hope that the guides, articles, and other resources provided in this unique volume will serve you well as you step into the marvelous world of the Bible.

Donald Senior, C.P.
General Editor

THE BIBLICAL TEXTS AND THEIR BACKGROUND

DONALD SENIOR

The biblical writings were created over a wide expanse of time. That broad historical and cultural canvas is one important cause for the Bible's rich diversity. In this Study Bible, the Reading Guides provided for each biblical book, and the introductions provided in the notes to the biblical text itself, offer specific information about the historical background of the individual books of the Bible. A clear and succinct historical summary is provided in the article "Biblical History and Archaeology" (RG 30–53). The following paragraphs sketch the relationship of the biblical books to that evolving history.

The accounts of creation and the stories about the first ancestors of the human family, such as the tragic rivalry between Cain and Abel and the story of Noah and the flood, obviously do not have the same historical grounding that later traditions could. These stories answer the question about the origin of humanity and its plight in history. Firm historical traditions begin only with the forging of Israel into an identifiable people, an event that did not begin until probably around 1250 BC. Traditions about the earlier patriarchal period starting around 1850 BC are much less certain historically, and even events from the time of Israel's sojourn in Egypt and during the period of the Exodus and early settlement in the land are sketchy since there were few means of preserving historical archives.

THE MAJOR PERIODS OF BIBLICAL HISTORY

The Time of the Patriarchs (1850–1250 BC)

The period from Abraham to Joseph is recounted in Genesis 12–50. Historically, this was a period of vast migrations in the Middle East, with clans of herders moving freely from Mesopotamia down through the Fertile Crescent into present-day Israel. Egypt had been a dominant power in the Middle East for more than two thousand years prior to that time. Egypt's might was counterbalanced by a succession of powerful dynasties at the eastern end of the Fertile Crescent, including the Persians, Assyrians, and Babylonians. Israel, located geographically between those two areas, would often be the battleground for those opposing forces. (See map #6.)

Few firm historical traditions exist from this period, but the general picture provided in the biblical traditions about the patriarchs does reflect something of the nomadic lifestyle and familial religion typical of the period.

The Exodus, Wilderness Wandering, and Settlement in the Land (1250–1130 BC)

This period is covered in Exodus, Deuteronomy, Numbers, and Joshua. The story of Israel as a unified people begins in Egypt with the stories about Moses and the miraculous exodus from Egypt. During a period of wandering in the desert, the covenant was formed with Yahweh, the LORD, the God of Israel. Under the leadership of Joshua, Israel finally breaks through into the Promised Land, driving the native Canaanites before them.

There is considerable debate about the historical background to this period. Some scholars, particularly conservative ones, are willing to accept the biblical portrayal at face value: namely that there was a mass migration of Hebrews from Egypt and that they invaded the regions of Israel with military force and thereby gained possession of the land.

The lack of clear archaeological evidence supporting such a vast military conquest, and some ambiguity in the biblical traditions themselves, have led other historians to surmise that both the migration from Egypt and the possession of the land took place over a longer period of time. Some Hebrew tribes may have already settled in Israel prior to the Exodus, and joined with the incoming tribes at a later period. While some Canaanite cities may have been taken by force, some of the land was probably settled in a peaceful fashion.

In any event, the Bible sees this process as a dramatic act of deliverance by God and as the historic beginning of the story of Israel.

The Period of the Judges (1130–1020 BC)

This early period of Israelite history is narrated in the book of Judges. It is clear that the Israelites at first resisted the idea of a strong central government. They preferred a loosely organized federation of clans or tribes ruled by charismatic leaders called judges. Only the Lord could claim the right to be called King. This independent spirit and aversion to the monarchy goes deep into the consciousness of Israel.

The Monarchy (1020–587 BC)

This long, but in fact highly diverse, period of Israel's history is taken up in the books of 1 and 2 Samuel, 1 and 2 Kings, and a parallel account in 1 and 2 Chronicles.

The transition from the more informal and charismatic leadership under the judges to the more institutional form of the monarchy begins with Saul (about 1020–1000 BC) but reaches its zenith with David (1000–960 BC) and Solomon (960–930 BC). Threats from surrounding peoples and the need for more complex social organization gradually led Israel to adopt a monarchical form of government. David eventually unified diverse groups of people under a single government system, ruled from his new centrally located capital of Jerusalem. Under David and his son Solomon, Israel's territories greatly expanded.

The united kingdom forged by David did not last very long. Solomon strained it by increasing taxation and by lack of sensitivity to the old tribal loyalties. When Solomon's son Rehoboam ascended to the throne, the seams between north and south split and the separate kingdoms of Judah in the south and Israel in the north began. This divided monarchy would last until 724 BC, when the Assyrian empire would crush the Northern Kingdom. Judah would survive until the Babylonian invasion of 587 BC.

The biblical account has little respect for the northern rulers and takes a critical view of most of the kings of Judah as well, considering them unfaithful to the covenant. During this period the great prophetic movement would ignite in Israel. Elijah, Elisha, Amos, and Hosea were prophets in the northern kingdom. Isaiah served as court prophet to the kings of Judah.

Exile and Return (587–332 BC)

This crucial period of Israelite history is narrated in 2 Kings 24–25 and in the books of Ezra and Nehemiah.

The Babylonian captivity would last almost fifty years. Systematic deportation as a way of subduing conquered peoples had been used first by Assyrians and then by the Babylonians. Only a small remnant of Israelites was left behind under the firm control of Babylonian officials. When the exiled Jews eventually returned, they considered the people who had stayed behind as somehow corrupt and would not allow them to take part in the reconstruction of Israel, a source of bitterness that would lead to the sharp divisions between Jews and Samaritans so obvious in the New Testament period.

Under the leadership of Ezra and Nehemiah, Jerusalem and its Temple were rebuilt. But Israel was now only a small and fragile nation, clustered around Jerusalem and very concerned with preserving its identity.

The Greek Conquest and the Rise of the Hasmoneans (332–39 BC)

This is a turbulent part of Israelite history, reflected in 1 and 2 Maccabees and Daniel.

Alexander conquered Palestine in 332 BC, beginning a period in which Greek culture would have a strong impact on the life of Israel. After his death, the Middle Eastern portion of Alexander's empire was divided between the Seleucid dynasty, which ruled from Syria, and the Ptolemies who ruled from Egypt. The Ptolemaic dynasty controlled Israel from approximately 332 to 199 BC. Their generally benign rule gave way to the Seleucids, who attempted to impose Greek culture and taxation in a more rigorous fashion. Seleucid ruthlessness eventually triggered the Maccabean revolt, which by 160 BC had thrown off the yoke of the Seleucids against incredible odds.

The Jewish dynasty of the Hasmonean family now begins a hundred-year reign. The Hasmonean kings proved to be as corrupt and ruthless as the foreigners who had preceded them. Reactions by pious Jews to the compromises of the Hasmoneans and their Jerusalem aristocracy would give rise to protest groups such as the Essenes and Pharisees. By 60 BC, Roman influence was growing in the Middle East and brought pressure on Israel itself. The Hasmonean period came to an end with the emergence of Herod the Great, a vassal of the Romans, who would unify the country and hold it in his grip.

The Roman Period (39 BC–AD 100)

The New Testament writings emerge during this period of biblical history. With the death of Herod in 4 BC, the Romans divided Israel among his three sons. Eventually the Romans removed the cruel and incompetent Archaelaus, taking over direct rule of Judah and Samaria. Herod Philip and Herod Antipas would continue to govern in the regions of Upper Galilee, Lower Galilee, and the Transjordan (see map #12).

Roman rule and its heavy taxation proved intolerable to the Jewish people. Tensions mounted all during the first half of the first century, exploding into revolution in AD 66. That revolt would be violently suppressed by the Romans, climaxing with the destruction of Jerusalem and its great Temple in AD 70. That event would change the complexion of Judaism forever. Another short-lived revolt would break out in AD 132. The Romans would continue to occupy Palestine until the time of the Byzantine empire. All of these events have left a profound impression on the writings of the New Testament.

THE CATHOLIC STUDY BIBLE

DONALD SENIOR

HOW TO USE THIS STUDY BIBLE

This one-volume Study Bible offers a full range of aids to help the reader discover the meaning of the Bible. The following description of its contents, and suggestions for using the book, might help you take full advantage of its unique resources.

The Resources of the Study Bible

There are seven major sections in this volume:

The *New American Bible*

Beginning on page 7 of the Old Testament section, you will find the full text and notes of the NAB. Each major section of the Bible and each biblical book has a brief introduction. Extensive notes explaining words or individual verses are found at the bottom of the page. An asterisk (*) alongside a particular word or verse signals to you that an explanatory note is provided for that biblical text. These notes are the official notes that were prepared by the editors of the NAB, and they provide a wealth of information for the studious reader.

The NAB also provides cross-references to other related biblical passages. These cross-references are signaled by a small italic letter printed within specific verses. The cross-reference is found at the bottom of the page.

Finally, along the side margins there is another set of cross-references, directing you to the Reading Guides and Articles found in other sections of the *Catholic Study Bible*. These cross-references are indicated by page numbers enclosed within a shaded box. Page numbers referring to the Reading Guides and Articles are preceded by the letters RG.

The Reading Guides

One of the special features of this Study Bible is the Reading Guides found in the front section beginning on page RG 85. There are Guides for each book of the Bible, and their purpose is precisely to lead the reader through the structure and basic message of each biblical book.

The notes found at the bottom of the page with the NAB translation provide information on specific details of a given verse. The Reading Guides add a new perspective by taking a broader look at each biblical book, tracing its major sections and themes, and making suggestions about its meaning for today. Each of them also provides references to other books and articles for readers who want to continue their study of specific issues.

The Articles

Another helpful feature of the *Catholic Study Bible* is that it provides extensive and detailed studies of key issues for understanding and using the Bible. These essays will prove especially valuable for those who want to probe deeper into a particular question. In addition to this introduction, the reader will find the following Articles:

• "The Bible in Catholic Life" explains the Roman Catholic view of Scripture and the meaning of biblical inspiration.

• "Biblical History and Archaeology" offers a succinct overview of the major periods of biblical history along with a helpful explanation of the methods and major discoveries of biblical archaeology.

• "Catholic Interpretation of the Bible" traces the history of the Church's approach to the meaning of Scripture.

• "The Challenges of Biblical Translation" shows how taking a text from one language to another is both an art and a science.

• "The Bible in the Lectionary" explains the role of the Bible in liturgy and, in particular, shows the rationale for the selection of biblical passages in the Lectionary. This will be useful for preachers or those who prepare liturgies.

Sunday and Weekday Lectionaries

The lectionaries give up-to-date cycles of readings for public services.

The Glossary

The glossary provides clear explanations of the less familiar or more technical terms used in the Bible or in the Reading Guide.

Concordance

The concordance, or word index, provides key citations for important biblical names and terms.

New Oxford Bible Maps

These extensive maps provide the reader with the entire geographical canvas on which the biblical drama is portrayed.

Suggestions for Use

The resources of the *Catholic Study Bible* enable the reader to use it in a variety of ways and settings.

For Individual Reading or Study

If your goal is to read and reflect on a single biblical book or major passage of the Bible, the two key sections of the Study Bible to use are the biblical text itself and the Reading Guides. Both should be used in tandem.

You may wish to read through the introductions to the biblical book first, both the one found in the Reading Guide and in the NAB text. In turning to the Gospel of Luke, for example, one would read the introduction in the Reading Guide on RG 397–412 and then turn to the Bible section on pp. 1349–50. After that the reader can pick his or her way through the Gospel, noting the major characteristics of the biblical passage and its major motifs by attentive reading of the biblical text and its accompanying notes, and by referring to the information provided in the Reading Guide.

For the more ambitious reader, the "Suggested Readings" at the end of the Reading Guides and in the Articles offer leads to further study.

For Group Study

The *Catholic Study Bible* lends itself well to group use. If each member of the group has a copy, then the leader could suggest the reading of a specific biblical text and the accompanying section from the Reading Guide as a good means of preparing for the group session. Preparation always enhances group Bible study. Often the Reading Guide will provide some points of reflection that a group might find helpful as a starting point for discussion about the meaning of a passage.

Some of the articles, such as the ones on "The Bible in Catholic Life" and "The Bible in the Lectionary," could also be fruitful sources for group study and discussion. Where the group itself does not have access to individual copies, the *Catholic Study Bible* can serve as a resource for the leader or can be on hand for reference when the group discussion generates a question that needs further information.

Teaching Resource

The *Catholic Study Bible* is particularly useful for the college or religious education classroom. It provides virtually a one-volume textbook and reference library on the Bible. Experienced and imaginative teachers will find their own way to best utilize a book like this. A few suggestions might help.

The Study Bible can certainly serve as a textbook for a course on the Bible as a whole or for introductions to the Old or New Testaments. Here again interplay between pertinent sections of the Reading Guides and the biblical text and notes is very important.

Teachers in a Catholic setting may want to give special attention to the article on "The Bible in Catholic Life" as an important summary of Catholic teaching on the role of the Bible in the Church's life and thought. "The Bible in the Lectionary" will help Catholics (and Christians from other mainline denominations) understand how the liturgy is a major source of biblical inspiration for Roman Catholic tradition.

The volume will also support a course on the history and geography of the Bible. The article on the history and archaeology of the Bible provides clear and useful information. The accompanying maps enable the teacher to discuss the geography of the Bible in detail. The maps can especially be a useful illustration when studying such narratives as Exodus, the historical books, the Gospels, Acts, and Paul's letters.

Sermon and Liturgy Preparation

The thematic approach of the Reading Guides and the attempt they make to relate the biblical message to spirituality and Church teaching should prove useful for sermon and liturgy preparation.

The article on "The Bible in the Lectionary" provides important and often neglected information on the rationale for the selection and arrangement of biblical passages in the Lectionary, and offers good suggestions about relating the Bible to the liturgical year.

THE BIBLE IN CATHOLIC LIFE

DANIEL J. HARRINGTON

CHURCH LIFE TODAY

One of the great achievements of the Second Vatican Council (1962–65) has been the renewal of interest in the Bible among Catholics. How dramatic this renewal has been can be grasped by comparing Catholic practice around 1950 and the situation in the early years of the twenty-first century.

At mid-twentieth century the Scriptures were read at Mass in Latin. There were few selections from the Old Testament, and a rather small number of New Testament passages dominated the one-year cycle. In response to the mandate of the Second Vatican Council we now have a three-year cycle of Sunday readings and a two-year weekday cycle. (See "The Bible in the Lectionary," RG 76–84.) The Old Testament is very prominent, and almost the entire New Testament (Gospels and Epistles) is represented. The passages, of course, are read in the vernacular (English, Spanish, or whatever is the dominant local language).

In the 1950s study of Bible texts was not an integral part of the primary- or secondary-school curriculum in Catholic schools. At best Bible content was conveyed through summaries of the texts. Catholic college students might work through parts of the Bible with the aid of cautious and approved textbooks as guides. But now the texts of the Bible form a primary resource for Catholic religious education at all levels. And Bible courses and Bible study groups have become especially popular forums for adult education.

At mid-twentieth century Catholic seminarians took most of their Scripture courses toward the end of their theology programs. In comparison with dogma and moral theology, Scripture study was considered a minor course. Now biblical studies are a major component of the seminary curriculum at all stages. And such courses are very popular. Students in Catholic seminaries assume that much of their preaching and teaching in the future will be devoted to the Bible, and so they study it with eagerness. There is also a lively dialogue and interdisciplinary cooperation between professors of Scripture and their theological colleagues.

Since Vatican II the Bible has become prominent not only in Catholic liturgy and education but also in popular piety. The revised prayers for the sacraments and other liturgical actions use biblical language almost entirely. Charismatic groups and base communities have found biblical reflection and prayer to be the source of great spiritual energy. Even traditional Catholic observances like the Rosary are (and always have been) thoroughly biblical. The language of Catholic prayer in almost every instance derives from the Bible.

The Scriptures have also been a major element in the ecumenical movement since the Council. The serious historical and theological differences between the Christian churches remain, but the most progress has been made where the different church groups have focused on the Bible as their common heritage and have reexamined their differences in light of the Bible's language and thought patterns. When this has occurred, the usual result has been the recognition that what unites the Christian churches is more important and fundamental than what divides them. In the new and more positive relationship that has emerged between Christians and Jews in recent years, Bible study has been a vital force toward greater mutual understanding and respect.

Catholic theology since the Council gives far more attention to biblical sources and is likely to express itself more in biblical than in philosophical language. Official church documents on theological matters or current problems almost always begin from Scripture and try to ground their arguments in biblical texts. The Catholic Church today is far more biblical than it was in the mid-1950s.

BIBLE STUDY IN HISTORY

In order to understand the Bible's place in Catholic thinking today, it can be helpful to see how Christians in other times and places thought about and interpreted the Bible. The Bible has not always been studied according to the principles of modern historical criticism. Nor should scientific study of the Bible be understood as superseding, and thus making obsolete, all earlier approaches. A brief history of biblical interpretation will reveal important insights that remain valid today.

The Old Testament constituted the Bible for Jesus and the early Christians. According to the Gospels, Jesus sometimes quoted or alluded to Old Testament texts in order to establish a theological point or to suggest a way of acting. He clearly accorded these texts a certain degree of authority. Nevertheless, Jesus emerges from the New Testament as displaying flexibility toward the Old Testament and even asserting his authority over it. He distinguishes what comes from God and what comes from Moses (see Mk 10:1–12), goes beyond certain scriptural teachings (Mt 5:21–48), and rates love of God and neighbor (Mk 12:28–31) over strict observance of the Sabbath.

New Testament writers such as Paul and Matthew looked upon the Old Testament Scriptures as "fulfilled" in Jesus Christ. Basing themselves on what apparently was a widespread early Christian understanding, they interpreted the Old Testament Scriptures in the light of the life, death, and resurrection of Jesus. Like other Jews of the time, they understood the Old Testament to be a "mystery"—that is, something that could not be understood without guidance or explanation. Whereas the Qumran community (the Jewish group that gave us the Dead Sea Scrolls) found the key to the Scriptures in their own sect's history and life, the early Christians discovered Jesus to be the key that opened up the mystery of the Hebrew Bible.

By the time of the Fathers of the Church (the patristic period), the Christian Bible contained two Testaments—Old and New. These early theologians generally adopted one or the other of two basic approaches to the reading and interpretation of Scripture: the allegorical and the literal methods.

The allegorical method, favored particularly by those theologians who lived in Alexandria in Egypt, emphasized uncovering the spiritual truths beneath the surface of the biblical stories. This method had been developed by Greek thinkers who interpreted the stories in Homer's *Iliad* and *Odyssey* as symbolizing emotional or spiritual struggles within the individual. It had also been adopted by Jewish interpreters, like Philo of Alexandria, who used the method on the Hebrew Bible in order to appeal to non-Jews and especially to Jews who had come under the influence of Greek philosophy and culture. Christian theologians who used this method included Origen and Clement of Alexandria.

In contrast to this method was the more literal reading of the Bible, favored by those Christian thinkers who lived in Antioch, the capital of Syria in Roman times. The literal approach focused more on the historical realities described in Scripture, and insisted that any higher or deeper sense should be based firmly on the literal sense of the text. John Chrysostom and Theodore of Mopsuestia were among those who favored this approach.

It is important to recognize that these different emphases were not completely opposed to each other. Thus the allegorical method did not deny the historical truth of events in Scripture, nor did the literal method deny the spiritual meaning of those events. Later theologians tended to blend the two approaches, though favoring one tendency or the other. Augustine, for instance, tended toward the allegorical and Jerome toward the literal.

Medieval interpreters, building on both these approaches, distinguished four senses in a scriptural text: literal (what took place), allegorical (the hidden theological meaning), anagogical (the heavenly sense), and moral or tropological (the significance for the individual's behavior). The classic example was the word *Jerusalem* (see Gal 4:22–31), which can refer to a city in Palestine (literal), the church (allegorical), the heavenly home of us all (anagogical), and the human soul (moral). Since this wide-ranging approach to Scripture could easily degenerate into subjectivity, careful interpreters like Thomas Aquinas insisted that "nothing necessary to faith is contained under the spiritual sense that is not elsewhere put forward by Scripture in its literal sense." Thomas Aquinas also used human reason as a tool in explaining the Scriptures and tried to bring together philosophical truth (especially as proposed by Aristotle) and biblical truth.

With the Renaissance and the rise of Humanism came a new interest in studying the Scriptures in their original languages and their historical settings. Erasmus produced a new edition of the Greek New Testament to go along with his revision of the Latin Vulgate translation. He also used the Greek and Roman classics of paganism along with the writings of the Church Fathers to interpret the biblical texts. Catholic enthusiasm for the study of the Scriptures cooled, however, in response to the claims for the Bible (*sola scriptura* or Scripture alone) made by Martin Luther and other Protestant Reformers, especially their statements about the clarity of Scripture (so that there is no need for the church as the final interpreter) and its sufficiency (so that there is no need for church tradition).

The rationalist claims of the European Enlightenment made matters even more complicated for Catholic interpreters of the Bible. For example, the philosopher Baruch Spinoza maintained that when Scripture and philosophy come into conflict (as in the case of miracles), then Scripture is to be rejected in favor of "reason." Thus the Catholic Church was backed into being the defender of biblical "truth," sometimes with unfortunate consequences.

This survey reveals some abiding principles of Catholic biblical interpretation: the central significance of Christ; the struggle to be faithful to the literal meaning while searching for spiritual meaning; the conviction that faith and reason are not opposed; the insistence that the Bible should be interpreted in the Church; and the emphasis on biblical truth against the attacks of rationalism.

MODERN DEVELOPMENTS

The gradual Catholic acceptance of scientific biblical criticism (or the historical-critical method) while remaining true to the Church's heritage can be traced with reference to a series of official Roman documents issued during the late nineteenth and the twentieth centuries. For a full collection of official Roman Catholic documents pertaining to the study of the Bible, see *The Scripture Documents: An Anthology of Official Catholic Teachings* (Dean R. Bechard, ed., Collegeville, MN: Liturgical Press, 2002).

A cautious beginning was made with the papal encyclical *Providentissimus Deus* by Pope Leo XIII in 1893, only to be blunted by fears of Modernism under Pius X and by Benedict XV's encyclical *Spiritus Paraclitus* issued in 1920. A new age dawned with the encyclical titled *Divino Afflante Spiritu* that was promulgated by Pius XII in 1943, in which the historical study of the Bible was given official approbation. The approach outlined by Pius XII was put into practice by the Pontifical Biblical Commission in its 1964 *Instruction Concerning the Historical Truth of the Gospels.*

The culmination of official Catholic pronouncements on biblical studies was the Second Vatican Council's *Dogmatic Constitution on Divine Revelation*. The nature of these documents is cumulative; that is, the latest document generally restates the teachings contained in previous documents and clarifies matters not discussed earlier in detail. However, the document of an ecumenical council has far more official weight than a papal encyclical or an instruction from the Pontifical Biblical Commission. Moreover, the Council's document on Scripture was a "dogmatic constitution," the most authoritative kind issued by Vatican II. Thus Vatican II's *Dogmatic Constitution on Divine Revelation* can be taken as the authoritative climax of a long series of developments in the Church's attitude toward the Bible.

Vatican II was a pastoral council. It sought to

address the needs of the Church and the world in the twentieth century and beyond. Its constitution on divine revelation (also known by its Latin title, *Dei verbum*)was addressed not so much to scholars or theologians as to the Church at large. In effect, the bishops were saying, "This is what the Catholic Church thinks and believes about the Bible and related matters." The document had a rocky history from its first draft in 1962 to its final form in 1965. Pope John XXIII's rejection of the initial draft, which favored a propositional understanding of revelation (revelation consists of statements of abstract truths) and a theory of two sources of revelation (Scripture and tradition), set the Second Vatican Council on its path of *aggiornamento* (Italian for "bringing up to date"). (All quotations are from the translation by Liam Walsh and Wilfrid Harrington in *Vatican Council II: The Conciliar and Post-Conciliar Documents* [Austin Flannery, ed., Northport, NY: Costello, 1975] 750–65.)

The six chapters in *Dei verbum* treat divine revelation itself, the transmission of divine revelation, Sacred Scripture—its divine inspiration and its interpretation—the Old Testament, the New Testament, and Sacred Scripture in the life of the Church. What the constitution teaches on these topics will be taken up in the remaining parts of this essay. Here, only what it teaches about scientific biblical criticism will concern us.

The conciliar statement about biblical criticism appears in paragraph 12, which is part of the chapter on the inspiration and interpretation of Scripture. It is prefaced by an acknowledgment that since God speaks in Scripture through human beings, and so in human fashion, interpreters should give careful attention to the ways in which the sacred writers thought and expressed themselves:

> In determining the intention of the sacred writers, attention must be paid, *inter alia,* to literary forms for the fact is that truth is differently presented and expressed in the various types of historical writing, in prophetical and poetical texts, and in other forms of literary expression. Hence the exegete must look for that meaning which the sacred writer, in a determined situation and given the circumstances of his time and culture, intended to express and did in fact express, through the medium of a contemporary literary form. Rightly to understand what the sacred author wanted to affirm in his work, due attention must be paid both to the customary and characteristic patterns of perception, speech and narrative which prevailed at the age of the sacred writer, and to the conventions which the people of his time followed in their dealings with one another.

The statement, which is really a condensation of Pius XII's 1943 encyclical *Divine Afflante Spiritu,* makes three points. First, it insists that we take into account the various literary forms in which the Bible is written, and it warns us against confusing historical, prophetic, and poetic texts. Next, it urges us to pay attention to the historical setting in which the sacred author wrote, suggesting that such historical awareness is necessary for grasping what the author intended. Finally, it recommends that we learn about the literary conventions and cultural assumptions that people accepted at the time when the biblical books were composed. Thus the conciliar document encourages the literary, historical, and sociological study of biblical texts.

The acceptance of biblical criticism, of course, does not reduce the Sacred Scriptures to the status of other, strictly human books. In fact, the very next sentence in the document affirms the divine authorship of the biblical texts and urges biblical interpreters to take that into consideration:

> But since sacred Scripture must be read and interpreted with its divine authorship in mind, no less attention must be devoted to the content and unity of the whole of Scripture, taking into account the Tradition of the entire Church and the analogy of faith, if we are to derive their true meaning from the sacred texts.

In this way the conciliar document achieves a balance between the human and the divine contributions to Scripture. Interpreters are thereby encouraged to apply all the tools of biblical criticism, while bearing in mind the Church's longstanding conviction that the Bible contains "the Word of God in the words of men."

In 1993, to mark the one hundredth anniversary of *Providentissimus Deus* and the fiftieth anniversary of *Divino Afflante Spiritu,* the Pontifical Biblical Commission, with the full approval of Pope John Paul II, issued a document titled "The Interpretation of the Bible in the Church." Prepared by an international team of distinguished Catholic biblical scholars, this document describes various methods of and approaches to biblical interpretation, examines certain questions of a hermeneutical nature, reflects on the characteristic features of a Catholic interpretation of the Bible, and considers the place that biblical interpretation has in the life of the church. This document spells out in some detail many of the directions recommended in the papal encyclicals and in Vatican II's *Dei verbum.*

The Pontifical Biblical Commission's document describes the historical-critical method as "the indispensable method for the scientific study of the meaning of ancient texts." While giving attention to the many possible contributions from certain "new" literary and social-scientific approaches, it criticizes fundamentalism as "dangerous" and even as inviting people to "a kind of intellectual suicide." And it insists on the pastoral significance of the whole exegetical enterprise when it states: "Exegesis produces its best results when it is carried out in the context of the living faith of the Christian community, which is directed toward the salvation of the entire world."

Methods of Biblical Interpretation

The term *biblical criticism* refers to various methods of scientific biblical study that have as their goal establishing the text, understanding the content and the literary style of biblical books, and determining their origin and authenticity. This undertaking is sometimes called the "historical-critical method"—"historical" because it focuses on the original historical settings of the biblical texts and the historical processes that gave rise to them, and "critical" because it applies reason to the texts and makes judgments about them in the effort to be as objective as possible. Biblical criticism aims to understand what a text was saying to its original audience and to make clear its significance then (and now).

Textual criticism (sometimes called "lower criticism") seeks to establish the wording of the biblical text as the biblical authors wrote it. Since we no longer have direct access to the manuscripts written by the biblical authors (autographs), textual critics try to come as close as possible to the original form of the texts by gathering all the pertinent manuscript evidence (Hebrew and Aramaic for the Old Testament, Greek for the New Testament, ancient translations for both Testaments). When the evidence has been assembled, textual critics determine where the ancient manuscripts differ and proceed to decide which reading is original and to explain how the other readings arose. The rejected readings may have been unconscious mistakes (for example, confusing similar letters of the alphabet, omitting words or phrases, inserting marginal comments into the main text) or deliberate modifications (for example, harmonizing with parallel texts, correcting grammar or style, removing "offensive" material). The accepted readings should be consistent with the content and style of the document and follow the rules of grammar and good sense.

Literary criticism attends to the words and images, the characters and their relationships, the structure and progress of thought, the literary form, and the meaning. These processes are used today in studying all kinds of literature; they are by no means confined to biblical study. Bible concordances, dictionaries, and encyclopedias make it possible to trace the development of a word (for example, *faith*) or a theme (for example, *covenant*) and to locate a particular occurrence within such a framework. Careful inspection of a text enables one to chart out the interactions among the characters or to outline the progress of the argument. The biblical writers used many different literary forms. The Old Testament consists of law codes, narratives, psalms, prophecies, proverbs, visions, and even love poetry. The New Testament contains stories of Jesus' words and deeds (Gospels), the actions of some apostles (Acts), letters (Epistles), and visions (Revelation). Rather than stating theological truths in the form of theses or propositions, the biblical authors conveyed their message in artistic and memorable ways. Literary criticism helps us to read the biblical books on their own terms and thus to appreciate their artistry and their truth.

Historical criticism concerns the world behind the biblical texts; that is, the origin and growth of the biblical documents. Scholars assume that sometimes a complicated process of composition lies behind a finished book of the Bible. Smaller literary units—for example, a saying from Jesus, or a hymn—were told and retold, or used orally in worship. Later, perhaps, a collection of sayings or hymns was generated. Still later, a writer created a longer narrative into which various sayings were fitted, or which quoted a hymn in order to make a point. At each stage, the original small unit was being used in a slightly different context, and it may have been changed in small ways in order to fit its new use better.

Scholars have various names for this sort of investigation of a biblical text, depending on what level they are examining. *Source criticism* attempts to establish where previously existing material (for example, a hymn, a saying, or a vision account) has been used by a later author in a longer work, either by accepting what is stated in the work itself or by noticing differences in content, vocabulary, and literary style. *Form criticism* seeks to classify literary genres or forms, and to isolate the historical settings in which the forms developed and functioned before they became part of the main text. A sermon, for instance, will have characteristics that are different from those of a letter or a story. *Redaction criticism* deals with the ways in which a biblical author or editor (*redactor* means editor) used sources, and sometimes changed them, to address problems and concerns facing his readers. So biblical criticism takes account of historical settings at three levels: the sources, the small units, and the finished document.

Archaeological excavations and textual discoveries such as the Ugaritic texts and the Dead Sea Scrolls can shed light on the material world and culture in which the biblical books were written. For example, ancient epics outside the Bible have helped us to appreciate the creation stories in the book of Genesis. And the Dead Sea Scrolls, besides providing the earliest extant manuscripts of the Hebrew Bible, have illumined the thought and organization of the early church.

The interpretive process can also be enriched by the application of concepts and methods used in the social sciences such as sociology, cultural anthropology, and psychology. These approaches help in exposing the cultural assumptions about the human condition and the world that people in biblical times took for granted, and in explaining the development of ancient Israel into a nation and the early Christian communities into what we call the church.

Historical criticism is sometimes defined narrowly to refer to the reality of the event behind the text, to determining what actually occurred at (for example) the first Passover or the first Easter. What really happened in detail is sometimes hard to discern, since the biblical authors were often more interested in the meaning of the events than in their precise details. Some historical critics (in the narrow sense) rule out the miraculous and divine intervention on philosophical grounds and make negative judgments about the communities that handed on the biblical texts. But this is not true of all historical critics, nor is it at all consistent with the Catholic approach to Scripture, which assumes that the biblical texts tell the "honest truth" about the events described in the texts.

While the classic historical-critical method is oriented mainly to illumining the history of the text and the world behind the text, certain new methods of literary analysis focus more on the text as it now stands (the world of the text) and on its effects on the reader today (the world before or in front of the text). *Rhetorical analysis* explores the capacity of a biblical text to persuade and convince the reader, while *narrative analysis* investigates how a text works in the sense of its success in telling a story involving plot, characters, and point of view. *Structuralist analysis* and *semiotic analysis* are modern linguistic methods that examine the various temporal and spatial relationships in a text, with an eye toward revealing the deeper patterns of meaning underlying the text.

Another set of approaches to biblical interpretation privileges the interpreter and the social location of the interpreter. *Liberation theology* takes as its starting point the lived experience of poor people today and enters into conversation with biblical texts (e.g., Israel's exodus from Egypt, or Mary's *Magnificat* in Lk 1:46–55) as a way of illumining both the biblical text and the present situation of the poor. *Feminist interpretation* calls attention to the prominence of certain women in the Bible, exposes the patriarchal or male-centered assumptions of the cultures in which the Bible was originally produced, and challenges interpreters to recognize the liberating contributions of women to the biblical story of salvation.

Other reader-oriented resources in biblical interpretation include the *history of interpretation* (how a text has been understood by Jewish and Christian readers throughout the centuries) and the *history of effects* (the impact or influence that a text has exercised in the course of history). *Canonical criticism* focuses on the final canonical form of a biblical text, explores its place within the biblical canon as a whole, and considers its significance for the church's faith and way of life. *Hermeneutics* is concerned with discerning the present significance of a biblical text. While this is what preachers have always done, the hermeneutical phase of the interpretive task is open to and incumbent upon all Bible readers. It involves the fusion of horizons between the ancient text and the reader in the present, and envisions a process by which the reader is changed intellectually and spiritually by encounter with the biblical text.

Two terms that have recently become prominent with regard to Catholic biblical interpretation and its practical impact in church life are *actualization* and *inculturation.* The Christian Scriptures are ancient texts, and so they need to be presented in ways in which they can speak to peoples of different times (actualization) and places or cultures (inculturation). The Scriptures are made "actual" whenever their spiritual insights are presented in such a way that they can address the problems and possibilities of the present day. Likewise, the Scriptures are "inculturated" whenever they are translated, interpreted, and applied in terms that peoples from outside the ancient Mediterranean world can understand and so live out their challenges and opportunities.

One traditional way of bringing together all these different methods in a simple and coherent framework is through the traditional Catholic approach developed in monastic circles and known as *lectio divina* (divine or spiritual reading). There are four steps. The first step is *lectio* (reading); that is, a careful reading of the text from various critical perspectives (literary, historical, and theological) and the assimilation or appropriation of the text on both intellectual and emotional levels. The second step is *meditatio,* which explores what this text may be saying to me (or us) now. One can open up the text by focusing on a theme or a few phrases, by applying the senses (sight, hearing, smell, taste, touch) to the biblical scene, and by trying to make connections between the text and one's present situation. The third step is *oratio* (prayer) in which on the basis of reading and meditating one may speak words of praise, petition, adoration, and/or thanksgiving to God. The fourth step may take the form of *contemplatio* (relishing the religious experience generated by the encounter with the text and resting in the mystery of God) and/or *actio* (coming to a decision about one's life, or finding new ways to express what one has learned—through dance, drama, artwork, group sharing, homily, etc.).

Catholic Biblical Research

Catholic institutions and scholars make important contributions to scientific biblical research. The Vatican Museum and other such institutions conserve and make available important manuscript evidence. The publishing programs of the Pontifical Biblical Institute (Rome), the Catholic Biblical Association (Washington), and the Studium Biblicum Franciscanum (Jerusalem) are among the most ambitious and respected. The research of Catholic scholars appears in prestigious journals published under Catholic auspices: *Biblica, Biblische Zeitschrift, Catholic Biblical Quarterly, Estudios Biblicos, Revue Biblique,* and *Rivista Biblica Italiana.* Of course, non-Catholic scholars are welcome to publish in these Catholic scientific journals. Catholic scholars routinely write for periodicals not under Church auspices: *Journal of Biblical Literature, New Testament Studies, Novum Testamentum, Vetus Testamentum, Zeitschrift für Neutestamentliche Wissenschaft,* and so forth. The major bibliographical services—*Old Testament Abstracts, New Testament Abstracts,* the *Elenchus of Biblica,* and the *International Review of Biblical Studies*—emanate from Catholic institutions. Articles on biblical topics frequently appear in Catholic theological journals, and popular periodicals *(The Bible Today)* and books make available to a general audience the results of scientific biblical research.

Many Catholic biblical scholars have received their professional training at the Pontifical Biblical Institute in Rome, the Ecole Biblique in Jerusalem, the Studium Biblicum Franciscanum in Jerusalem, as well as at European Catholic universities such as Louvain, the Catholic theological faculties at German universities, and the departments of theology at Catholic universities in the United States (Boston College, Catholic University in Washington, Notre Dame, Loyola of Chicago, etc.). Others have gotten philological and archaeological training at Harvard, Yale, Johns Hopkins, University of Chicago, Emory, and many other institutions. A major professional organization for biblical scholars in the United States is the Catholic Biblical Association. Catholic scholars are also heavily involved in the non-denominational Society of Biblical Literature, the American Schools of Oriental Research, and the Society of New Testament Studies.

Modern biblical scholarship is an international and interconfessional enterprise. The Catholic Church contributes to this dialogue by providing well-trained scholars and channels for publishing research. Some good examples of Catholic biblical scholarship in the United States are the *New American Bible,* the *New Jerome Biblical Commentary,* and the Sacra Pagina series of New Testament commentaries published by Liturgical Press.

Scripture as Tradition

The official Catholic emphasis on attention to the literary forms, historical settings, and cultural assumptions of the biblical writings flows from the nature of the books themselves. Far from being individual creations generated in solitude, the biblical books include many ideas, traditions, and even small pieces that already existed before being integrated into the texts in which they now stand. Biblical literature is thoroughly and deliberately traditional.

The traditional character of the Old Testament has long been acknowledged. The first five books, which are customarily called the Pentateuch or Torah, are generally recognized to incorporate material from at least four different sources (Yahwist, Elohist, Deuteronomist, Priestly; see "Introduction to the Pentateuch"). The historical books (Joshua to 2 Kings, Chronicles, Ezra, and Nehemiah) include earlier accounts, memoirs, genealogies, and the like. The prophetic books are anthologies of short pieces of poetry and prose, and the wisdom books contain ideas and sayings that circulated in the ancient Near East for centuries. The Psalms are a collection of varied kinds of songs used mainly in the Jerusalem Temple; in the Psalms there may even be remnants of non-Jewish hymns (see Psalm 29). So complicated and so rich is the process of transmission that it is difficult in most cases to speak of *the* author of a biblical book as one may speak of an author today. The situation is further complicated by the fact that in biblical times personal creativity and originality were not important values. One displayed real creativity by using traditional ideas and expressions in new settings and in new combinations.

Given the nature of the Old Testament and the ancient concept of creativity, one would expect the New Testament to be thoroughly traditional also—and it is. The earliest complete documents in the New Testament are Paul's letters. Even these highly original and occasional pieces rely at key points on preexisting material (for example, Rom 1:3–4; 1 Cor 13:1–13; 15:3–5; Phil 2:6–11). Those epistles whose direct Pauline composition is doubtful (for example, the Pastorals, Ephesians, Colossians, 2 Thessalonians) are best understood as later attempts to bring the figure and teaching of Paul to bear on situations facing the churches in the late first century. We often regard Paul as a creative genius. However, not only did he use some traditional material, but also almost all his undisputed letters contain some indication of joint authorship (see 1 Thes 1:1; 1 Cor 1:1; Rom 16:22; etc.). Moreover, throughout his letters Paul gives credit to his co-workers and encourages the collection for the Jerusalem community as a sign of solidarity with the mother church there.

The complicated process of tradition and composition also applies to the Gospels. Most scholars today place the final composition of the four canonical Gospels in the late first century: Mark around AD 70, Matthew and Luke around AD 80–90, and John around AD 90–100. Yet all scholars acknowledge that the evangelists used already existing material in their Gospels. For example, Matthew and Luke each seem to have read both Mark's Gospel and a collection of Jesus' sayings that modern scholars call *Q* (from the German word *Quelle,* meaning "source"). John utilized a collection of miracle stories (signs) and perhaps also some revelation discourses. The Markan and Johannine Passion narratives surely contain much traditional information, accounts that had been passed from one person to another.

The Gospels and the traditions incorporated in

them tell the story of Jesus of Nazareth, who was crucified around AD 30. Like other Jewish teachers of his time, Jesus taught by word (parables, proverbs, debates, other sayings) and deed (example, healings, symbolic gestures). His disciples remembered and retold his words and deeds, thus providing the basic materials for what became the Gospel tradition. Jesus did not write books. What we know of Jesus comes to us through the process of tradition from Jesus to the early church and finally to the evangelists.

The nature of the Gospels demands that interpreters attend to three stages in their development. The *Dogmatic Constitution on Divine Revelation* (*Dei verbum* 19) captures that development in this marvelously concise statement:

> The sacred authors, in writing the four Gospels, selected certain of the many elements which had been handed on, either orally or already in written form, others they synthesized or explained with an eye to the situation of the churches, the while sustaining the form of preaching, but always in such a fashion that they have told us the honest truth about Jesus.

The council's document affirms that the Gospels tell us the "honest truth" about Jesus. It recognizes that there was an intermediary stage in which traditions about Jesus circulated in oral and written forms as "preaching" about the significance of Jesus. It acknowledges that the evangelists give us only a selection (see Lk 1:1–4; Jn 20:30–31; 21:25) of the traditions about Jesus. It also recognizes that the evangelists used the traditions about Jesus to address the situations of their own day. Therefore Catholics must read the Gospels as traditional documents (because they are such) and attend to three stages in their development: Jesus, the early church, and the evangelists.

Although in the past there has been some Catholic resistance to accepting the traditional character of the biblical books, this emphasis is perfectly compatible with the principles of Catholicism. There is no obligation for Catholics to be conservative historians of early Christianity (nor is there any obligation for them to be reckless or indifferent). As long as Catholic scholars make clear the link from Jesus through the early church to the evangelists, they remain faithful to their theological heritage.

In fact, an emphasis on the traditional nature of the biblical writings is fully consistent with certain distinctively Catholic principles. The Catholic stress on the communal character of our way to God and God's way to us sensitizes Catholics to the complexity of early Christian tradition and to the role of the Church in shaping it and being formed by it. The Catholic emphasis that encounter with God is rooted in history and is a mediated experience helps us to see the continuity between Jesus and the early reflections on him, as well as the significance and correctness of those reflections. The Catholic sacramental approach, which sees God in and through all things, leads us to view the very human process of tradition as a vehicle for expressing, safeguarding, and adapting divine revelation.

Scripture and Tradition

The Catholic Church does not restrict divine revelation to the biblical text. Against the Protestant Reformation's slogan of "Scripture alone," Catholic theologians insisted on "Scripture and tradition." The term *tradition* recognizes the fact that the living reality of the Church has the task of preserving the Gospel as well as interpreting and applying it in new situations. Catholic Christianity is not simply a "religion of the Book."

While acknowledging the twofold reality of Scripture and tradition, Catholic theologians have long debated the precise relation between the two. One way of approaching the problem was to assume that Scripture and tradition constitute two separate sources of divine revelation. The Second Vatican Council rejected this view in the second chapter of its *Dogmatic Constitution on Divine Revelation* (*Dei verbum* 10): "Sacred Tradition and sacred Scripture make up a single sacred deposit of the Word of God, which is entrusted to the Church." In other words, the Word of God (or divine revelation) is the source of both tradition and Scripture.

How exactly Scripture and tradition are related remains a problem. The conciliar document uses the analogy of a wellspring or fountain to insist on their unity while preserving their diversity in *Dei verbum* 9:

> Sacred Tradition and sacred Scripture then, are bound closely together, and communicate one with the other. For both of them, flowing out from the same divine wellspring, come together in some fashion to form one thing, and move to-

> wards the same goal. Sacred Scripture is the speech of God as it is put down in writing under the breath of the Holy Spirit. And Tradition transmits in its entirety the Word of God which has been entrusted to the apostles by Christ the Lord and the Holy Spirit.

The same paragraph rejects the "Scripture alone" principle of the Reformation and preserves the Catholic approach of "Scripture and tradition" by insisting that the Church does not draw certainty about all revealed truths from the holy Scriptures alone. Hence, both Scripture and tradition must be accepted and honored with equal feelings of devotion and reverence. Thus the Second Vatican Council insisted that Scripture and tradition flow from the same divine wellspring and that both must be accepted and honored. Without endorsing any one theological approach to their relation, the council rejected the opinion of those who wished to keep the two separate.

The same tension appears when the *Dogmatic Constitution* addresses the issue of authoritative interpretation of the Scriptures in *Dei verbum* 10:

> . . . the task of giving an authentic interpretation of the Word of God, whether in its written form or in the form of Tradition, has been entrusted to the living teaching office of the Church alone. Its authority in this matter is exercised in the name of Jesus Christ. Yet this Magisterium is not superior to the Word of God, but is its servant. It teaches only what has been handed on to it. At the divine command and with the help of the Holy Spirit, it listens to this devotedly, guards it with dedication and expounds it faithfully. All that it proposes for belief as being divinely revealed is drawn from this single deposit of faith.

On the one hand, this statement entrusts authentic interpretation to the magisterium (the bishops with the pope). On the other hand, it insists that the magisterium is the servant of divine revelation and can teach only what is drawn from the single deposit of faith constituted by divine revelation.

The precise relation between Scripture and tradition also remains a problem. As a pastoral council, Vatican II avoided becoming an arbiter of theological disputes. Its insistence on the oneness of Scripture and tradition, however, did have a pastoral dimension. While not conceding to the "Scripture alone" position, it insisted that the Bible take again its rightful place in the center of Catholic life and that appeals to tradition be judged according to their consistency with Scripture.

The Nature of the Bible

What is this book that it should be studied so intensely and guarded so carefully? The *Dogmatic Constitution on Divine Revelation* made its own a theological formula that had become prominent before Vatican II: "the words of God, expressed in the words of men" (*Dei verbum* 13). That formula derives from the classical theological definitions of the divine and human natures in the person of Jesus Christ. In speaking about the Bible in this way, the Second Vatican Council sought to hold together the transcendent nature of Scripture and its human form. Although the Bible may look like other books and may be studied profitably as other books are studied (that is, with the techniques of biblical criticism), the Bible is different with regard to its origin and its nature. The different character of the Bible is expressed by means of some rather complicated terms: revelation, inspiration, inerrancy, and canon. As with "Scripture and tradition," the Second Vatican Council used these terms without adjudicating the theological disputes surrounding them. As a pastoral council it sought to express the significance of the words for the way in which the Bible is read within the Church.

Revelation is fundamentally God's self-revelation; it is the communication of the mystery of God to the world: "It pleased God, in his goodness and wisdom, to reveal himself and to make known the mystery of his will" (*Dei verbum* 2). The Christian theological tradition affirms that God's self-revelation comes to us through creation, history, persons, society, and reason. It is also customary to refer to the Bible as a privileged revealer of God—that is, a place where the divine revelation is particularly clear. This tradition appears prominently in *Dei verbum* 6:

> By divine Revelation God wished to manifest and communicate both himself and the eternal decrees of his will concerning the salvation of mankind.

The order adopted in this statement ("both himself and the eternal decrees") is significant, for it gives pride of place to the personal character of divine revelation without denying the content and the consequences. Although this point may seem obvious today, the council's emphasis on the personal dimension of revelation was correctly taken as a major step in clarifying Catholic attitudes toward Scripture. Through the Bible we encounter the mystery of God, not simply lists of commandments or interesting stories. The personal God makes those commandments and stories meaningful.

Two other theological terms for talking about the difference of the Bible from other books are *inspiration* and *inerrancy*. Again the *Dogmatic Constitution on Divine Revelation* asserts the basic point expressed by these terms without arbitrating the very complicated theological debates surrounding them. On inspiration *Dei verbum* 11 states:

> The divinely revealed realities which are contained and presented in the text of sacred Scripture have been written down under the inspiration of the Holy Spirit. For Holy Mother Church relying on the faith of the apostolic age, accepts as sacred and canonical the books of the Old and the New Testaments, whole and entire, with all their parts, on the grounds that, written under the inspiration of the Holy Spirit (cf. Jn 20:31; 2 Tm 3:16; 2 Pt 1:19–21; 3:15–16), they have God as their author, and have been handed on as such to the Church herself. To compose the sacred books, God chose certain men who, all the while he employed them in this task, made full use of their powers and faculties so that, though he acted in them and by them, it was as true authors that they consigned to writing whatever he wanted written, and no more.

The same paragraph treats inerrancy:

> Since, therefore, all that the inspired authors, or sacred writers, affirm should be regarded as affirmed by the Holy Spirit, we must acknowledge that the books of Scripture firmly, faithfully and without error teach that truth which God, for the sake of our salvation, wished to see confided to the sacred Scriptures. Thus "all Scripture is inspired by God, and profitable for teaching, for reproof, for correction and for training in righteousness, so that the man of God may be complete, equipped for every good work" (2 Tm 3: 16–17, Greek text).

The key expression in this statement is "that truth which God, for the sake of our salvation, wished to see confided to the sacred Scriptures." Without explicitly embracing the theory of only limited inerrancy, that statement suggests that the Bible's inerrancy consists primarily in its being a trustworthy guide on the road to salvation. Thus it expresses "inerrancy" in a positive way and avoids conceiving it as a defensive program of protecting the Bible against accusations of scientific or historical error.

The council's statement on inspiration refers to the books of the Bible as "sacred and canonical." The word *canon* (reed or measuring stick) originally meant the rule or characteristics that decided whether a particular book was judged to be part of Sacred Scripture. It now usually refers to the collection of books that are acknowledged to be authoritative in the Church and by which the Church's faith can be measured. The canon of Old Testament books traditional in Catholicism contains all the books of the Hebrew Bible (which is the same as the Protestant Old Testament canon) together with seven others that were part of the Greek and Latin Bible tradition (Judith, Tobit, Baruch, 1 and 2 Maccabees, Sirach/ Ecclesiasticus, Wisdom). All Christians today share the same canon of twenty-seven New Testament books. The history of the canon's development is quite complex. The final definitive list of biblical books (including the seven additional Old Testament books) for the Catholic Church was drawn up only at the Council of Trent in 1546, though there was little disagreement about the substance of the canon from the early centuries of the Christian era.

The Bible is different. How it is different has been expressed with the help of some traditional words: revelation, inspiration, inerrancy, and canon. The Second Vatican Council in its authoritative declaration on Scripture *(Dei verbum)* took over those hallowed terms. In interpreting the Council's use of these words we must take account of the pastoral orientation of the council as a whole. Rather than working out theological subtleties or choosing among theological schools, the *Dogmatic Constitution on Divine Revelation* used those words to convey basic attitudes about how the Bible differs from other books. It affirmed that God's self-revelation comes to us through the Bible, that in some mysterious way God entered into the composition of these writings and inspired them, that the biblical books provide reliable guidance (inerrancy) for those who walk the way toward salvation with God, and that these books constitute the norm or rule (canon) by which the life of the Church is to be guided and measured in all ages. These are the basic pastoral meanings of revelation, inspiration, inerrancy, and canon.

The Authority of the Bible

The terms by which Christians express the difference of the Bible indicate that it possesses great authority for them. The Bible is the "words of God, expressed in the words of men." It is revealed, inspired, inerrant, and canonical. The *Dogmatic Constitution on Divine Revelation* goes beyond the general assertions conveyed by the traditional theological vocabulary and speaks about the authority of various parts of the Bible.

The Old Testament (see *Dei verbum* 15) prepares for and declares in prophecy the coming of Christ. It conveys our basic understanding of God and the human situation: "how a just and merciful God deals with mankind." It provides "sound wisdom" and "a wonderful treasury of prayers." The document also mentions "matters imperfect and provisional" in the Old Testament, without specifying precisely what these are (presumably legislation about sacrifices and ritual purity, "vengeful" psalms, and other such material). The unity of the two Testaments is traced back to God who "in his wisdom has so brought it about that the New should be hidden in the Old and that the Old should be made manifest in the New" (*Dei verbum* 16).

The Council accorded the Gospels a special place within the Bible "because they are our principal source for the life and teaching of the Incarnate Word, our Saviour" (*Dei verbum* 18). It insisted on the historicity and apostolicity of the Gospels, while recognizing the complex process of their composition from Jesus through the early church to the Gospel texts. Catholics find a basic continuity between Jesus and the Gospel tradition under the guidance of the Spirit working in the church. Their tendency is to insist that the tradition is basically historical. They assume that the modifications and reinterpretations made necessary by changing circumstances do not do violence to the original teaching or event. The "apostolic" character of the Gospels refers not so much to their direct composition by apostles as it does to the faithful transmission of the material in them by those who had experienced the risen Lord and bore witness to his resurrection. The term *apostolic* describes the generation between Jesus' death (about AD 30) and the composition of the New Testament books. The claim implied by the term is that those witnesses have told us the "honest truth" about Jesus.

The New Testament also contains Paul's letters and other writings (Hebrews, the Catholic Epistles, Revelation). After affirming their composition under the inspiration of the Holy Spirit, *Dei verbum* 20 describes the contributions that these writings make in the following way:

> In accordance with the wise design of God these writings firmly establish those matters which concern Christ the Lord, formulate more and more precisely his authentic teaching, preach the saving power of Christ's divine work and foretell its glorious consummation.

It would be a mistake, however, to conclude from this description that the Epistles have a secondary status as supplements to the Gospels. In fact, Paul's authentic letters (1 Thessalonians, Galatians, 1 and 2 Corinthians, Philippians, Philemon, Romans) are the earliest complete documents in the New Testament from the standpoint of their dates of composition. Thus they give us precious information about how Paul and other early Christians in the fifties of the first century AD (some twenty-five years after the death of Jesus) understood the significance of Jesus' life, death, and resurrection. They show us how early Christians struggled to articulate their new faith in an environment that was often hostile and foreign to them. They reveal the kinds of problems that early Christians faced within their own communities (see especially 1 Cor) and so warn us against too easily viewing the apostolic period as a trouble-free and conflictless "golden age."

Enough has been said about the Bible in general (revelation, inspiration, inerrancy, and canon) and about its major parts (Old Testament, Gospels, Epistles) to indicate that it possesses great authority. But what kind of authority does the Bible have? It is surely not the coercive authority of a parent or the state or the police, which have the power to enforce a law or decision and to punish the uncooperative. It is not even the persuasive authority of the lawyer or the mathematician who convinces another by logic, arguments, proofs, and so forth. At some points in his epistles (for example, in 1 Cor 15) Paul does labor to make a convincing case on the basis of logic. But that is not his usual mode of presentation, nor is it the customary idiom of other biblical writers.

The authority that the Bible possesses can perhaps be best described as compelling. Compelling authority is the authority of the witness, the expert, the participant. Much of the Bible concerns what God's people say about God's action on their behalf. Without narrowing the testimony of the Bible to the concept of an eyewitness, it is possible to describe the Scriptures as a collection of testimonies to God. The biblical descriptions of creation, exodus, monarchy, exile, and return from exile all stress God's relatedness to Israel and Israel's responses of praise, confession, thanksgiving, and so forth. The New Testament writers portray Jesus as the revelation of God's power (and weakness). The proper response is faith, hope, and love. Thus the biblical documents contain the proclamation and articulation of people's faith about God and God's ways with creation.

God is the real basis of the Bible's authority. Insofar as the biblical books bear witness to God and thus enable us to understand better who God is and how God acts, and to grow in love for and trust in the God of the Scriptures, the Bible can be aptly called the "word of God." And so Vatican II's *Dogmatic Constitution on Divine Revelation,* which so emphasizes God's self-communication, is appropriately titled from its initial two words *Dei verbum* (Latin for "word of God").

Scripture in Church Life

This essay began with a comparison regarding the Bible's place in church life of the 1950s and today. A look at Catholic liturgy, education, piety, and theology led to the conclusion that the Catholic Church today is far more biblical than it was in the 1950s. This development mirrors some powerful statements made in the final chapter of Vatican II's *Dogmatic Constitution on Divine Revelation.*

The centrality of Scripture in Catholic liturgy involves both preaching and sacramental practice. *Dei verbum* 21 insists that "all the preaching of the Church, as indeed the entire Christian religion, should be nourished and ruled by sacred Scripture." The same paragraph directly confronts and dissolves the opposition between word and sacrament that had been prominent since the Protestant Reformation. It does so with reference to the celebration of the Eucharist:

> The Church has always venerated the divine Scriptures as she venerated the Body of the Lord, in so far as she never ceases, particularly in the sacred liturgy, to partake of the bread of life and to offer it to the faithful from the one table of the Word of God and the Body of Christ.

The council document insists that word and sacrament belong together in the Eucharist, to the point of asserting that they form "one table."

The popularity of Scripture in Catholic education and piety responds to a very strong statement in *Dei verbum* 22: "Access to sacred Scripture ought to be wide open to the Christian faithful." The document goes on to urge the production of modern-language translations made from the ancient biblical texts. It also encourages biblical exegetes to examine and explain the sacred texts so that preachers, teachers, and catechists "may be able to distribute fruitfully the nourishment of the Scriptures to the People of God" (*Dei verbum* 23).

The importance of Scripture for Catholic theology is stated in no uncertain terms: "The 'study of the sacred page' should be the very soul of sacred theology" (*Dei verbum* 24). The document mandates that all those officially engaged in the ministry of the word should "immerse themselves in the Scriptures by constant sacred reading and diligent study" (*Dei verbum* 25). The same paragraph recommends the preparation of volumes such as the present one: "translations of the sacred texts which are equipped with necessary and really adequate explanations." There is overwhelming evidence that in response to the Second Vatican Council the Catholic Church has become much more biblical. One of its most important documents was the *Dogmatic Constitution on Divine Revelation,* which has served as our principal guide in this article. At nearly every point the post-Vatican II Church has fulfilled the mandates of that council document and thus become more biblical.

The challenge facing the Catholic Church today is to look upon *Dei verbum* not only as the end of a long development (which it was) but also as the beginning of a process that has taken us into the twenty-first century and beyond. A still more biblical church will paradoxically be better able to adjust to the rapid changes that the new millennium is already bringing upon us. A still more biblical church will be better prepared to make common cause with other Christians, with Jews and Muslims, and with all truly religious people. A still more biblical church will preserve its spiritual heritage and open its riches to others. An obvious step in the process toward a more biblical church is an increase in knowledge and love of the Scriptures.

FURTHER READING

Bechard, Dean R., ed. *The Scripture Documents: An Anthology of Official Catholic Teachings.* Collegeville, MN: Liturgical Press, 2002.

Brown, Raymond E. *Biblical Exegesis and Church Doctrine.* New York and Mahwah, NJ: Paulist Press, 1985.

——. *Responses to 101 Questions on the Bible.* New York and Mahwah, NJ: Paulist Press, 1990.

Brown, Raymond E., Joseph A. Fitzmyer, and Roland E. Murphy, eds. *The New Jerome Biblical Commentary.* Englewood Cliffs, NJ: Prentice Hall, 1990.

Fitzmyer, Joseph A. *Scripture, the Soul of Theology.* New York and Mahwah, NJ: Paulist Press, 1994.

——. *"The Interpretation of the Bible in the Church": Text and Commentary.* Rome: Editrice Pontificio Istituto Biblico, 1995.

Hagen, Kenneth and others. *The Bible in the Churches: How Various Christians Interpret the Scriptures.* 3rd ed. Milwaukee, WI: Marquette University Press, 1998.

Harrington, Daniel J. *Interpreting the Old Testament.* Collegeville, MN: Liturgical Press, 1981.

——. *Interpreting the New Testament.* Rev. ed. Collegeville, MN: Liturgical Press, 1988.

Lienhard, Joseph T. *The Bible, the Church, and Authority.* Collegeville, MN: Liturgical Press, 1995.

Schneiders, Sandra M. *The Revelatory Text. Interpreting the New Testament as Sacred Scripture.* Rev. ed. Collegeville, MN: Liturgical Press, 1999.

Williamson, Peter S. *Catholic Principles for Interpreting Scripture. A Study of the Pontifical Biblical Commission's "The Interpretation of the Bible in the Church."* Rome: Editrice Pontificio Istituto Biblico, 2001.

BIBLICAL HISTORY AND ARCHAEOLOGY

RONALD A. SIMKINS

HISTORY IN THE BIBLICAL LITERATURE

The Bible as a Historical Source

To what extent is history—a record of actual past events—embedded in the diverse literature of the Bible? The Bible is composed of many different formal types of literature (genres), and although many of the genres present a past, no literature in the Old Testament claims or presents itself to be a work of history. History, as first practiced by the classical historians Hecataeus, Herodotus, and Thucydides, entails not only the collecting of tales and traditions about the past, but also the inquiry (which is what *historia* means) into the reliability of the traditions and plausibility of the tales. Although ancient historians used different standards to judge their source materials from those modern historians would use, the important point is that they did make *critical judgments* about their sources. In the New Testament, only the writer of Luke-Acts claims to present a work of history (Lk 1:1–4). Whereas the writer of Luke-Acts claims to have investigated his sources in order to present a reliable account to Theophilus, the Old Testament writers made no such critical judgments. They were not historians in either the modern or classical sense.

Although the Bible is not itself a work of history, the Old Testament authors did write about Israel's past. The narrative genres present the story of the people of Israel from the creation of the world through the days of Ezra and Nehemiah. The biblical writers drew upon tales and traditions of Israel's past in order to communicate an idea to their contemporaries. They were not concerned about whether the tales and traditions were reliable or plausible. Even when some attempt was made to communicate factual information, such as in the books of Kings, the writing of history was secondary to other purposes of the biblical writers. The non-narrative genres of the Bible—laws, songs, prophetic oracles, proverbs, and wisdom literature—attest to the story of Israel only indirectly. These texts too are ideological, though they also served ritual, educational, moral, and other functions in ancient Israelite society. (The various genres of biblical literature are discussed in the relevant sections of the Reading Guide.)

The extent of history embedded in the biblical texts is also questioned because of the chronological gap between the biblical writers and the events that they purport to narrate. In most cases, the biblical writers did not witness the events they describe. They often lived centuries later and were dependent upon oral traditions and perhaps some written sources (the Bible refers to a number of written sources, discussed on RG 44–46) for the composition of their narratives of the past. The reliability of these sources and their use by the biblical writers is unknown. When no source material was available—for private events, for example—the biblical writers would simply fill in the historical void in their presentation of the past one way or another, ultimately by pure invention.

Many of the biblical stories are shaped according to traditional literary or mythic patterns that make their reliability suspect. For example, the common Near Eastern myth popularly known as the conflict myth—a tale which describes a young warrior-god's rise to kingship by defeating an old god or force who poses a threat to the order and stability of the world—is transformed by the biblical writers into a literary pattern that shapes the stories of the Exodus, Joshua's conquest of Canaan, and Saul's election as king. Many other stories utilize such literary patterns. The traditional motif of the barren mother of an important person, for example, is used in the stories of Sarai and Isaac, Rachel and Joseph, and Hannah and Samuel.

The biblical writers' use of traditional literary and mythic patterns to tell their stories of Israel calls into question not only the narrative of the events but also the historical value of many details of the stories. This writing style of the biblical writers does not necessarily mean that no actual events lie beneath the narrative, but at the very least it indicates that the presentation of such events has been shaped to conform to a traditional interpretive framework. In other words, the meaning of such events as indicated by their presentation in the stories of Israel is more significant to the biblical writers than the historical reality of the events.

The Contribution of Archaeology

Archaeology is the scientific study of the material remains of past human life and activities. The material remains are discovered through excavations and surveys, and include both unwritten and written discoveries. Among the unwritten discoveries are architectural features such as temples, palaces, fortifications, public buildings, and houses; industrial features such as oil presses, wine presses, silos, ovens, and pottery kilns; and artifacts such as pottery, tools, jewelry, weapons, and statues and figurines. The written material, usually discovered during the process of excavation, is ordinarily studied by epigraphists and paleographers and includes literary documents (such as the Dead Sea Scrolls), inscriptions on stone or clay tablets, seals (bullae), and ostraca (broken pieces of pottery with words inscribed on them).

The year 1890 marks the beginning of the scientific study of Syro-Palestinian archaeology, when W. M. Flinders Petrie conducted the first systematic excavation in Palestine at Tell el-Hesi in the northern Negev. The Arabic word tell (*tel,* in Hebrew) is used to designate the artificial mounds in the shape of truncated cones that dominate the landscape of Palestine. They are sites of ancient settlements, built up by successive levels of human occupation and destruction over the centuries. The oldest occupancy, of course, is at the bottom of the mound, and the most recent at the top. At Tell el-Hesi, Petrie laid the foundations of stratigraphy and ceramic typology, the basic interpretative principles of archaeological field method. Stratigraphy is the technique of excavating a mound (tell) layer by layer, and at the same time isolating the contents of each occupational layer (stratum). Typology is the study and classification of groups of objects (artifacts) on the basis of shared characteristics (shape, material, decoration). By correlating stratigraphy and typology archaeologists can construct a relative chronology. Using distinctive types of pottery as his dating tool, Petrie constructed a chronological framework for Palestine.

Except for a few excavations, like George Reisner's at Samaria (Sebaste) in 1909–10, archaeological excavations in Palestine before World War I resembled treasure hunts. Between World Wars I and II there was a significant advance in field techniques, largely due to William F. Albright, distinguished American archaeologist and biblical scholar. He refined pottery chronology through excavation and survey; he identified several mounds as biblical sites; he related many of the biblical episodes to archaeological contexts. Archaeological field methods advanced rapidly after World War II. Three archaeologists contributed meaningfully to this development: a Briton, Kathleen Kenyon, an Israeli, Yigael Yadin, and an American, G. Ernest Wright. At Jericho Kenyon used precise stratigraphic method to clarify the chronology of the fortification walls that had been dated incorrectly to the Late Bronze Age (1550–1200 BC). Yadin directed the first large-scale dig in modern Israel at Hazor in Upper Galilee, the largest biblical city in Palestine. In keeping with the Israeli method, Yadin concentrated on broad exposure of the monumental architecture of the site. G. Ernest Wright excavated Shechem in the central hill country, the first capital of the kingdom of Israel. Wright gave special attention to the pottery of the site as one of the most accurate indicators of ancient chronology; also, he trained a new generation of archaeologists at Shechem.

Since 1970 there has been a striking change in field method as archaeologists borrow from both the natural and the social sciences. In the first place, almost all excavation staffs are interdisciplinary: such specialists as paleobotanists, zooarchaeologists, geologists, ecologists, and, especially, physical and cultural anthropologists collaborate with archaeologists in the field. Also, the technologies of modern science, such as carbon-14 (for dating organic substances), thermoluminescence (for dating pottery), magnetometry (for detecting the presence of metal objects), potassium argon (for dating geological samples), and neutron activation analysis (for tracing the origin of clay), are being used to analyze the data with greater precision. The purpose of this comprehensive approach, at least in theory, is to reconstruct the daily life of the people whose remains are being excavated, including their social structure and economic development, as well as their religious practices. Archaeologists' earlier interest in digging isolated tells is now also combined with regional surveys as a way of studying a tell's relationship with the surroundings. Regional study is indispensable in determining town planning, settlement patterns, and population expansion, to mention some of the concerns of modern archaeologists.

Because archaeology provides a different *kind* of evidence than that from the Bible, archaeology cannot be expected to make definitive contributions to several basic problems in the history of Israel. For example, archaeology cannot determine chronology beyond the broad limits determined by ceramic or radiocarbon dating. Archaeology addresses chronology through typologies of material remains that lack the precision of the chronological framework established by texts. The basis of typology is that human culture changes gradually and within limits. When a broad range of features and artifacts from stratified archaeological contexts are compared, a typological sequence can be established into which new features and artifacts can be placed. This typological sequence then becomes a means for dating the material uncovered in a new excavation. The major artifact used in typological dating is pottery. Pottery sherds are virtually indestructible and are found at every site in Syria-Palestine for every period since the Neolithic period. Moreover, whole pottery vessels were easily broken, leading to the production of more pottery and to rapid changes in the pottery repertoire. As a result, a large database of pottery has enabled archaeologists to establish a typological sequence by which they are able to date layers of human occupation in an excavation. Although this pottery typology is tied to an absolute chronology by occasional dated inscriptions that are found in sealed archaeological contexts, the changes within the pottery sequence provide a chronological precision of no greater than a few decades.

Other historical issues to which archaeology cannot make a definitive contribution include the problem of ethnicity. Archaeology can provide much of the material content of ethnicity, but it cannot finally define the ethnic groups because such a definition also involves shared cultural values and self-perceptions. Ethnicity involves both material and ideological components. The identification of the early Israelites in the archaeological record has been a continual problem in this regard, for the early Israelites appear to share the same material culture as the Canaanites. Some interpreters attempt to get around this problem by identifying the inhabitants of the new settlements in the central hill country at the beginning of the Iron I period as early Israelites and those inhabitants who continue to occupy the Late Bronze cities and towns as Canaanites. However, such an interpretation cannot be supported by the archaeological evidence, and in any case is only possible because of the implications of the biblical text (e.g., see Jos 17:14–18).

The interrelation of particular human events in a political history is also beyond the scope to which archaeology can contribute. Archaeology can demonstrate that the city of Hazor in northern Israel was destroyed near the end of the Late Bronze Age, and that the city of Lachish in Judah was destroyed approximately a century later. It cannot answer the questions: Who destroyed the cities? Was the same agent responsible for the destruction of each city? Why were they destroyed? What were the causes of the cities' destruction? What happened to the inhabitants of the cities after they were destroyed? Archaeology does not deal with the evidence necessary to answer these questions. For many of the problems of political history, archaeology can only remain silent.

Finally, archaeology cannot demonstrate the truth or confirm the meaning of the biblical texts. The meaning of the biblical texts is not found in the degree to which the texts correspond to what really happened in the past. Rather, the meaning of the texts is found in the message that the biblical writers were communicating to their ancient readers, and this message is beyond the scope of archaeological research.

The focus of archaeology is on the material world, and in this regard archaeology can contribute to the historical study of ancient Israel. Archaeology provides the material context for understanding this history by presenting the material remains of a broad spectrum of Middle Eastern peoples and places. This material provides the general setting for the history of Israel, and through cross-cultural comparison is able to shed light on the Israelite material culture. For example, archaeology can provide information about the distinctive cultures of those peoples who lived near and interacted with the Israelites, such as the Philistines, Edomites, Phoenicians, Arameans, and Assyrians. Regional surveys allow us to reconstruct settlement patterns and the demographics of particular regions. The faunal and floral remains gathered from excavations enable us to reconstruct Israel's environmental setting and its changes over time.

Archaeology also provides the specific material context for many of the events narrated in the Bible, much of which the biblical narratives themselves do not address. The biblical description of King Hezekiah's rebellion against the Assyrian empire focuses primarily on the diplomatic maneuvers of the Rabshakeh of Assyria to coerce Hezekiah into submission (2 Kgs 18–19). The archaeological evidence, however, presents a picture of Hezekiah's preparations for revolt and its tragic consequences.

Ultimately, archaeological remains illuminate the daily life of the ancient Israelites, which supplements the biblical narratives. Only from archaeology can we learn about the planning and defenses of the Israelite and Judean towns and cities; the architecture of palaces, houses, temples, and public buildings; figurines, altars, and other cult objects; tombs and the Israelites' treatment of their dead; luxury items such as jewelry, carved ivories, metal and stone vessels, and imported items; and common tools and weapons. Archaeology enables us to reconstruct aspects of the society, economy, and religion of the ancient Israelites that are neglected by the biblical tradition. Furthermore, because archaeological evidence is random—its preservation is by chance, unaffected by human selection—it provides an alternative perspective from which to view the biblical narratives. This is especially true regarding aspects of the Israelites' religious practices and beliefs. The widespread abundance of terracotta female figures, for example, attests to a dominant concern for female fertility that is given little attention in the biblical texts. Similarly, the graffiti found at Kuntillet ʿAjrud refers to "Yahweh and his asherah." The meaning of this phrase is debated, referring to a consort or a symbol of Yahweh. In either case, the phrase attests to a view of Yahweh that has been excluded from the Bible.

The Bronze Age

Chronology

Archaeologists divide the Bronze Age into three major periods, tied to the chronology of Egypt, based on changes in material culture. The Early Bronze Age (3300–2000 BC) is the first period of urbanization in Palestine. This period corresponds to the Early Dynastic period and Old Kingdom in Egypt. The Early Bronze Age is further divided into four sub-periods. Only the beginnings of urbanization are evident in Early Bronze I (3300–3000 BC). By Early Bronze II and III (3000–2200) Palestine is characterized by numerous large fortified cities. Notable excavated sites include Megiddo and Beth Yerak (Khirbet Kerak) in the north, Tell el-Far'ah (perhaps biblical Tirzah) and Ai in the central hill country, and Tel Yarmuth and Arad in the south. With the weakening of the Old Kingdom at the end of the Sixth Dynasty, Egypt entered the First Intermediate Period. Similarly, most of the urban centers in Palestine were abandoned or destroyed, with much of the population subsisting on pastoralism. This final rural period is known alternatively as Early Bronze IV, Middle Bronze I, or Intermediate Bronze (2200–2000 BC).

The Middle Bronze Age (2000–1550 BC) marks the height of prosperity and power in

Palestine with a resurgence of urbanization. The numerous large fortified cities during this period are characterized by massive fortifications consisting of ramparts, mudbrick walls, and large fortress-style gates. The large temples and palaces constructed inside the city walls attest to the prosperity of the period, and many luxury items of foreign origin give evidence of a vibrant international trade. Excavated sites of note for this period include, from north to south, Dan, Hazor, Megiddo, Aphek, Shechem, Jericho, Gezer, Ashkelon, and Tell el-ʿAjjul. The Middle Bronze Age corresponds to the Middle Kingdom and Second Intermediate Period in Egypt. In contrast to the end of the Early Bronze Age, however, the cities of Palestine continued to flourish with the collapse of the Middle Kingdom and during the rule of the foreign Hyksos kings of the Second Intermediate Period. Only when the native Egyptian kings of the Seventeenth Dynasty succeeded in driving out the Hyksos did the Middle Bronze Age come to an end, with numerous cities in Palestine being destroyed.

The Late Bronze Age (1550–1200/1150 BC) corresponds to the New Kingdom in Egypt. This largely urban period lacks the prosperity of the Middle Kingdom as the cities of Palestine became subject to the Egyptian empire. Nevertheless, the period is also characterized by internationalism, with material culture from Egypt, Greece, Cyprus, Turkey, Lebanon, and Syria found at several of the sites in Palestine. Important excavated sites for this period include, from north to south, Hazor, Megiddo, Beth Shan, Aphek, Shechem, Gezer, Lachish, Tell el-Farʾah (south), and Timna. The Late Bronze Age comes to an end with the weakening of Egypt in the Twentieth Dynasty and the withdrawal of Egypt from Palestine.

In the chronology supplied by the Bible, the Israelites' ancestors—the patriarchs Abraham, Isaac, and Jacob—are placed in the period from the end of the Early Bronze Age through the beginning of Middle Bronze Age. The exodus from Egypt is placed at the beginning of the Late Bronze Age. 1 Kings 6:1 claims that the construction of Solomon's Temple began 480 years after the Israelites came out of Egypt in the Exodus. A conservative date for the beginning of Solomon's reign would be around 960 BC, placing the exodus event around 1440 BC. In Exodus 12:40, the text claims that the Israelites lived in Egypt for 430 years. Thus, Joseph would have brought his father, his brothers, and their families into Egypt around 1870 BC. Further references establish a chronology for the ancestors: Abraham was 100 years old when Isaac was born (Gn 21:5); Isaac was 60 years old when Jacob was born (Gn 25:26); and Jacob lived 130 years before Joseph brought him to Egypt (Gn 47:28). According to this chronology, Abraham would have been born around 2160 BC.

Although the biblical chronology is indicated fairly precisely, critical examination indicates a number of problems. First, setting aside historical problems that will be discussed below, the figure of 480 years for the period between the Exodus and the construction of the Temple is a suspiciously round number. It translates into twelve times forty, the latter being the traditional biblical length for a generation. In other words, the biblical writer is stating that the Temple was constructed twelve generations after the Exodus. The number twelve, of course, is suspicious, especially in the context of the Temple—the single most significant building in Israel—because the number often represents "all Israel." Solomon is also the twelfth generation from Judah according to some genealogies (e.g., 2 Chr 2:1–17; 3:1–9), and this might have served as the basis for the 480 years. The figure of 430 years for the duration of the Israelites' stay in Egypt is also problematic, but for a different reason. In Genesis 15:13–16 the figure of 400 years is used for the same period, and this is equated with three generations. Indeed, Moses and Aaron belong to the third generation after Levi. Finally, the extremely long lives attributed to the ancestors—Abraham lived to be 175 years old, Isaac surpassed his father with 180 years, and Jacob died at the age of 147—cannot be accepted. The great ages of the ancestors reflect their proximity to the antediluvian period. Those who lived before the flood had life spans of 900 years or more, but after the flood the life spans of the people gradually diminished (indeed, Joseph only lived to be 110 years old). In the end, the biblical chronology cannot be taken simply as historical in the modern sense of the term.

The Patriarchs in History

The story of the Israelites' ancestors in Genesis is composed of numerous, originally independent, folktales. Scholars usually assume that these tales had an oral prehistory, but their written form dates from 900 BC to 400 BC (the date depends on how they understand the composition of Genesis, and there is wide disagreement on this issue). Unfortunately, there is little conclusive evidence determining the date and nature of the book's composition. Nevertheless, many anachronisms in the story indicate that it was written many centuries after the time it purports to describe. Also, as is typical of folktales, many parts of the story were written, and perhaps originally told, according to fixed patterns of storytelling in the ancient world. For example, all three of the major women in the story—Sarah, Rebekah, and Rachel—are initially barren. This is a common motif (it may reflect the social and physical reality of young girls who are married soon after their first menstruation, but unable to conceive for a few years) used in the story of the ancestors to demonstrate the providence of God. Other fixed patterns include: the rivalry between a barren, favored wife and a fertile co-wife or concubine (Sarah and Hagar, Rachel and Leah); encounter of the future betrothed at a well (Rebekah, Rachel); journey in the desert and the discovery of a well (Ishmael); revelations of a deity in a dream (Jacob); and the testament of a dying ancestor (Jacob). One fixed pattern that is found repeated in the story of the ancestors but not elsewhere is the motif of an ancestor telling a king that his wife is his sister. Abraham does this twice and Isaac once, and in each case the common motif is told in a slightly different way to fit a different context regarding whether the wife is barren, promised a child, or already has children.

Does the story of Israel's ancestors preserve any recoverable traces of actual events that took place in the Bronze Age? Some scholars have thought so. W. F. Albright placed Abraham's migration from Haran to Canaan within the context of the Amorite migrations that are attested in texts from Mesopotamia. The Amorites, known as "Amurru" in the Mesopotamian texts, were interpreted as a distinct, semi-nomadic people who migrated into southern Mesopotamia from eastern Syria and Turkey, and contributed to the collapse of the Akkad Dynasty and the rise of the First Dynasty of Babylon (whose most important king was Hammurapi). The Amorites were also given credit for the collapse of the Early Bronze city-states in Palestine. Albright further argued that documentary evidence from texts discovered at Mari and Nuzi indicates the historicity of the patriarchal figures. Dating to the Middle Bronze Age, the Mari texts attest to many of the personal and place names mentioned in the ancestor stories; the later Nuzi texts corroborate many of the social and legal practices in the Genesis narratives. Finally, the picture in Genesis of the ancestors living a seminomadic life in the midst of fortified urban centers fits the general situation of the Middle Bronze Age.

Kathleen Kenyon, who excavated at Jericho, thought she could identify the Amorites in the archaeological record. During the Intermediate Bronze Age, Jericho was characterized by a period of occupation (perhaps in tents) prior to the construction of any permanent structures. The buildings that were built on the tell during this period were characterized by thin, rather flimsy walls. Nevertheless, the inhabitants carved hundreds of large shaft tombs out of the bedrock, in which one individual was buried in each tomb with a bronze dagger or with a few small pots. Because she also identified many foreign elements in the material culture, Kenyon argued that the evidence from Jericho attests to the arrival of nomadic invaders, whom she associated with the Amorites.

Although widely influential, Kenyon's interpretation is no longer credible. First, it is worth noting that the biblical stories do not identify the ancestors as Amorites. Abraham begins his journey not from Haran but from Ur of the Chaldeans in southern Mesopotamia; his journey goes "upstream" against the flow of Amorites into Mesopotamia. Outside Genesis, Abraham is called an Aramean (Dt 26:5). The Amorites in the biblical tradition are presented as the native inhabitants of the land of Canaan ("Amorite" is often used synonymously with "Canaanite"), whose land would be given to Abraham's descendants. In Mesopotamian texts, the term *Amurru* simply denoted the west Semitic population of the Bronze Age. Although some groups of Amurru were nomadic, others were urbanized, occupying a wide range of socio-economic roles in the society. Second, the correspondences between the names and social and legal customs of the ancestors and those presented in the Mari and Nuzi texts are not unique to the second millennium.

Many of these names and customs can be identified in first-millennium texts during the period in which the ancestor stories themselves were written. Finally, the social situation of the ancestors as seminomads living in the midst of urban centers is also not unique to the Middle Bronze Age. In fact, this social situation is typical of virtually every period in the history of Palestine, from the Early Bronze Age through the Ottoman period. In the end, the ancestor narratives reflect the period of the Iron Age in which they were written.

The Exodus in History

The historical value of the Exodus narrative is much more difficult to assess than the story of the patriarchs. On the one hand, the Exodus narrative presents a spectacular story in which the God of Israel fights and defeats Pharaoh and his army in order to rescue his people from bondage and humiliate the Egyptians who dared to challenge the honor and kingship of God. The story is told in accordance with the widely recognized mythic pattern of the conflict myth, and many aspects of the story have a supernatural rather than a historical character. Indeed, some aspects of the story cannot be historical. The sheer magnitude of the event—that the firstborn male of every Egyptian household died (Ex 12:29); that the entire Egyptian army pursued the Israelites to the sea and were subsequently drowned (Ex 14: 9, 28); that the number of Israelites who escaped from Egypt were 603,550 men of fighting age, not counting Levites, old men, women, and children (Nm 1:44–47), renders it historically impossible. Other aspects of the story also exceed the bounds of a purely historical description. For example, the story does not record the name of the Egyptian king, the primary adversary of God and the Israelites. This is extremely odd since elsewhere the biblical writers mention the names of most other foreign kings—the two notable exceptions being the Egyptian king who married Sarai in Genesis 12 and the Egyptian king in the Joseph story, both of whom are known simply as Pharaoh. The depiction of the plagues is also not historically plausible. Although many of the individual plagues are natural events that can occur in Egypt, the combination of all the plagues, the scope and severity of the plagues, and the references to the plagues not affecting the Israelites or their animals affirm a theological conviction and challenge a purely literal and historical reading of the story.

The Exodus story, on the other hand, gives evidence of the writer's familiarity with Egypt. The story is set in the context of the family of Jacob migrating into Egypt during a famine in Palestine and after Joseph had risen to the rank of vizier. Ample evidence indicates that Asiatics migrated to and lived in Egypt during all periods and especially during the Second Intermediate Period. In fact, during this period a group of Asiatics living in the eastern Delta region, known as the Hyksos, succeeded in establishing their rule over all of Lower Egypt and parts of Upper Egypt. Many scholars have noted that Joseph's ascendancy in the court of Pharaoh fits in the Hyksos period, but Asiatics also rose to prominence in later periods as well. Moreover, some parts of the Joseph story have parallels in Egyptian literature, such as the Tale of Two Brothers. Many of the names in the Exodus narrative are Egyptian. *Moses* is the Egyptian word for birth, and occurs with theophoric elements in the names of Thutmose and Ramesses. The names of Hophni, Phinehas, Shiphrah, and Puah are also Egyptian. The narrative claims that the Israelites were forced to build the store-cities Pithom and Ramesses. Ramesses can be identified with Pi-Ramesses, the capital city of Ramesses II in the eastern Delta at Tell el-Dabʿa. *Pithom* is Hebrew for Egyptian *Per-Atum,* (House of Atum,) and can be identified with either Tell el-Retabeh or nearby Tell el-Maskhuta in the eastern Delta. Evidence also indicates that foreigners living in Egypt were conscripted into the corvée labor groups used to work on the state building projects during the New Kingdom.

How do we reconcile these two opposing views of the historicity of the Exodus story? Two characteristics of biblical story telling are important in this regard. First, the biblical writers responsible for this narrative are not attempting to write a *history* of the event, in either the modern or the classical Greek sense of history. The biblical writers did not investigate or critically examine their sources, nor did they necessarily invent the story. They simply took the traditions about the past that were present in their day (probably in oral form) and constructed from them a dramatic and persuasive written narrative. The traditions might have been generated in response to actual events of the past, but, as is often the case with oral tradition, the actual events no longer resembled the traditions and cannot be reconstructed from them. Second, the biblical writers describe the significance of the event *for Israel.* The biblical writers present the Exodus as one of the most significant events in the history of Israel, yet no reference to the Israelites or the Exodus can be found in any of the Egyptian records. We would not necessarily expect the Egyptians to record what would have been a disaster for their king and army at the sea—rarely do royal scribes record the failures of their king—but we would expect to find some record of the Israelites' presence in the Delta (the "land of Goshen") or their role in state building projects. The absence of any reference to the Israelites suggests that whatever actual events might lie behind the narrative, they were insignificant from the perspective of the Egyptians. Therefore, although we might acknowledge that the Exodus narrative does preserve some traces of past events, the present form of the narrative does not provide us with any evidence from which to reconstruct those events.

Whatever events might underlie the Exodus narrative must be set in the context of what we do know about Egypt and Palestine in the Late Bronze Age. Palestine in the Late Bronze Age had a material culture that was continuous with the Middle Bronze Age, but the society itself was much poorer and less organized. This is attested in the settlement pattern. Most of the large fortified Middle Bronze cities in Palestine were destroyed at the end of the period. Many of the sites were not immediately reinhabited. Gradually, the old sites were reinhabited and new sites were settled, but the total settled area remained stable due to the abandonment of several large sites. The central hill country, which had been widely settled in the Middle Bronze Age, was now largely devoid of settlement. Most of the sites in the Late Bronze Age were small (less than twelve acres) and unfortified. The massive Middle Bronze ramparts continued to exist, but often no city wall was built on top of the ramparts. Instead, buildings were placed along the edge of the tell in a continuous line so that the outer wall of the structures offered modest protection. Few public buildings have been uncovered. The large fortress-style temples of the Middle Bronze Age (at Shechem and Megiddo) continued to be used, but on a diminished scale. The large city of Hazor alone continued to flourish during the Late Bronze Age, perhaps due to its orientation toward the large cities in Syria rather than toward Egypt.

The Egyptian kings of Thebes, who had been ruled by the Asiatic Hyksos during the latter part of the Middle Bronze Age, now sought to extend their rule into Palestine. When Ahmose (1550–1525 BC) drove the Hyksos out of Egypt, he campaigned into Palestine to provide a buffer against further Asiatic incursions into Egypt. By the reign of Thutmose III (1492–1425 BC), all of Palestine was incorporated into the Egyptian empire. He set up an administrative system over Palestine that would endure through the remainder of the Late Bronze Age. (It is worth noting that the biblical chronology places the Exodus during the reign of Thutmose III—an impossible scenario.) Although Egypt faced opposition from the kingdoms of Mitanni (Hurrians) and Hatti (Hittites), Egypt maintained control over Palestine through the reign of Ramesses III (1184–1153 BC). Then a series of weak kings and political turmoil across the Mediterranean forced Egypt to withdraw from Palestine after approximately 350 years of control.

Evidence of the Egyptian presence and control of Palestine is found in numerous Egyptian artifacts (scarabs, jewelry, statues, stelae, anthropoid coffins) and buildings (temples and residences), especially from the end of the Late Bronze Age. Egyptian-style temples differ in distinct ways from the Syrian-style temples in Palestine that continued the Middle Bronze tradition. The Egyptian temple at Beth Shan (Strata VIII–VII), for example, consisted of a broadroom entrance hall, with benches along its walls and two pillars to support its roof. The cella in the back of the temple was raised above the floor and reached by seven steps. A platform in the cella probably held a statue of the deity. A similar temple was found at Lachish. This temple had a large central hall supported by two pillars inside an entrance chamber. From the central hall a monumental stone staircase led to a small raised chamber interpreted as the cella. Remnants of cedar beams supporting the roof and colored (Egyptian blue) plaster from the walls have survived. An Egyptian temple of a different plan was found near the copper mines at Timna in the southern Arabah. The shrine consists of a small room abutting a rock scarp. Opposite the entrance is a small niche carved into the rock face. Archaeologists have suggested that in its final phase of use the shrine was probably covered only with a cloth canopy, which is attested by the many textile fragments found on the floor. The deity worshipped at this shrine was undoubtedly Hathor, for her image has been found repeatedly carved into stones and pillars.

A number of new buildings constructed at the end of the Late Bronze Age appear to attest to the strategic concerns of the Egyptians. The buildings are similar to the private dwellings in Egypt, and thus are called "Egyptian residences." Most of these residences were built at existing sites—Beth Shan, Tell el-Farʿah (south), Megiddo, Tel Seraʿ, Aphek, Jaffa, Tell es-Saʿidiyeh—but a few were built at uninhabited sites such as Tel Mor (near Ashdod) and Deir el-Balah (west of Gaza) and thus served as fortified outposts. The buildings are typically square with corner entrances. A square courtyard is at the center of the structure. Small chambers were built surrounding the center court, and a corner staircase would lead to a second floor. The construction of the buildings also demonstrated Egyptian techniques. The walls were thick and made of mudbrick either on a mudbrick foundation or without a foundation. The T-shaped stone doorjambs and thresholds found in the buildings are also indicative of Egyptian style.

Two episodes during the Late Bronze Age are often connected to the Bible. During the reigns of Amenhotep III (1390–1352 BC) and Akhenaten (1352–1336 BC) numerous letters sent from the local rulers of the Canaanite cities to the Egyptian court (known as the Amarna letters) refer to groups of people known as *ʿApiru* (or *Habiru),* who seem to be responsible for some of the regional turmoil. The letters imply that the ʿApiru were mercenaries or bandits, and were employed by some local rulers to promote their self-interests against other rulers. Because the term *ʿApiru* is etymologically similar to *Hebrew,* some scholars have suggested the Amarna letters give evidence of Hebrews—i.e., the early Israelites—in the land of Canaan. It is possible that *ʿApiru* is related to *Hebrew,* but at the most they probably designate a similar social category rather than an ethnic group. In any case, if the Amarna letters refer to groups of people that can be identified as Hebrews or early Israelites, the information about them does not correspond to the biblical tradition and thus little is known about them.

The second episode occurred during the reign of Merneptah (1213–1203 BC), the son of Ramesses II. In the fifth year of his reign, he defended Egypt against a Libyan assault, and commemorated his victory on a stela where he also refers to his campaign into Palestine against Ashkelon, Gezer, Yanoam, and Israel. Whereas Ashkelon, Gezer, and Yanoam are designated in the Egyptian inscription as cities, Israel is designated as a people or tribe. This is the first reference to Israel in any Middle Eastern text, and the only reference to Israel in an Egyptian text. Unfortunately, we learn nothing about Israel, its geographic location, or its relationship to the Canaanite cities from this text. We can be certain, however, that by the reign of Merneptah a group of people known as Israel is living in the land of Canaan.

The Iron I Age

The Israelites in the Biblical Tradition

The end of the Late Bronze Age and beginning of the Iron I Age (1200/1150–1000 BC) was characterized by political turmoil. Across the Mediterranean prominent civilizations—the Mycenaeans, Minoans, Hittites—were brought to ruin, many of the Syrian and Palestinian cities were destroyed, and Egypt was forced to retreat to the Nile valley. The causes of the turmoil are many and not fully understood. One group that emerged from the turmoil was the Philistines. Originating in the Mycenaean world, they settled along the southern coast of Palestine, from Tell Qasile on the Yarkon River to Gaza, after losing a series of land and sea battles against Ramesses III in the eighth year of his reign (as recorded on the walls of his mortuary temple at Medinet Habu and in the Harris Papyrus I). They brought with them a distinct Mycenaean-style pottery that allows archaeologists to identify their settlements. The Israelites are another group that emerge during this period, but their identification in the archaeological record is not as clear as that of the Philistines.

The biblical presentation of the Israelites' conquest of Canaan and the period of the Israelite judges should presumably be set in the Iron I Age. The political vacuum that resulted from Egypt's withdrawal from Palestine would have enabled the settlement of the Israelite tribes in Canaan and the formation of new political structures, culminating in the Israelite state. The Bible's presentation of this period, however, is riddled with literary, historical, and archaeological problems.

The bulk of the stories of Israel's settlement of the land of Canaan comes from Joshua 1–12. They describe the military invasion of the land by a unified people under the leadership of Joshua. The conquest was largely successful. All the Canaanite cities were destroyed except for Gibeon, whose inhabitants deceived the Israelites into making peace with them. In its present form, the book of Joshua is part of what has come to be known as the Deuteronomistic History (along with the books of Judges, Samuel, and Kings). In the story of the conquest given in Joshua and Judges, the Deuteronomistic Historian presents an ideological tale that focuses on the Israelites' faithfulness to God as demonstrated by their fidelity to the laws of God, especially the laws of Deuteronomy. According to this ideology, the Israelites would succeed in their conquest and possession of the land of Canaan as long as they were faithful to God's covenant (Jos 1:3–8). If they were unfaithful to the covenant—if they turned their back on Yahweh and served other gods—they would fail in taking and keeping the land. Instead, God would leave the Canaanites in the land to oppress the Israelites and to be a test of their covenant fidelity. Thus, in the story of Joshua the Israelites are faithful to the covenant and succeed in conquering the land. However, upon the death of Joshua, the people turned away from Yahweh and worshipped the Baals, and as a result God gave the Israelites over to their enemies and they were unable to stand against them (Jgs 2:11–15). The book of Judges then describes how the people of Israel struggled in the midst of the Canaanites. The book presents the rule of each judge according to the following cycles of events: the people would suffer under the oppression of their more powerful Canaanite neighbors because they had worshipped other gods; the people would eventually turn to Yahweh and plead for help; God would then raise up a judge who would deliver them by defeating their enemies in battle; peace would endure throughout the life of the judge, when the people would once again reject Yahweh and the whole cycle would repeat.

From a literary perspective, numerous problems result from the Deuteronomistic Historian's presentation of the Israelite settlement. One arises from a glaring inconsistency regarding the fate of King Jabin of Hazor. In Joshua 11, the Israelites fight and defeat Jabin, put to the sword all the inhabitants of Hazor, and then burn the city. In Judges 4, however, King Jabin of Canaan who reigns in Hazor is oppressing the Israelites until they, under the leadership of Deborah and Barak, defeat his army and eventually destroy him. Although it is possible that multiple kings, especially within a dynasty, would bear the same name, it is unlikely that the king and entire population of Hazor could be killed and the city destroyed, yet emerge as a powerful force in a following generation. A more likely scenario is that the book of Judges refers to King Jabin anachronistically.

More substantial literary problems exist with the presentation of the conquest in Joshua 1–12, for the Bible preserves alternative accounts of this story. A brief tale in Joshua 17:14–18 presents a picture in which the Israelites were militarily incapable of driving out the Canaanites because the valley-dwelling Canaanites had iron chariots. The tribes of Ephraim and Manasseh must therefore resort to clearing the forests in the inhospitable hill country in order to find enough land to subsist on. Exodus 23:23–33 presents a situation in which the Israelites are too few in number to conquer the land of Canaan. The land can only be conquered little by little until the Israelites have sufficient population to occupy it, presumably after several generations. In Judges 1 the Israelites do not conquer the land as a unified people, but each tribe acts independently. Although the tribe of Judah has a measure of success, all of the tribes fail to drive out the Canaanite inhabitants of the land. The accounts of the allotment of the land also challenge the literary presentation of the conquest in Joshua 1–12. In Joshua 18:2–5 Joshua divides the land among seven tribes that had failed to take possession of their land (the hill country was already occupied by the tribes of Judah and Joseph). In this account, the tribe of Benjamin had failed to take possession of its land, but the stories in Joshua 1–12 emphasize clearly that the land of Benjamin is conquered. Finally, the general picture of Israel during the lifetime of Joshua is at odds with the picture of Israel during the period of the judges. In the stories of Joshua, the Israelites are a unified people made up of twelve clearly defined tribes under the leadership of a single individual. In the stories of Judges, the Israelites are not unified. In fact, intertribal conflict is presented on more than one occasion. The judges rule over individual tribes, and the number and composition of the tribes remains fluid.

Do the books of Joshua and Judges preserve traces of events of the past? For the stories of the conquest in Joshua 1–12, the answer is probably "no," as we will explain in the following sections. The tribal allotments and boundary lists in Joshua 13–21 probably do preserve historical records of tribal boundaries, but the period to which they attest is uncertain. We should note that none of the boundary lists are given in their entirety, and the descriptions of the allotment of the land are inconsistent. The historical value of the book of Judges is a little more complicated. The overall form of the individual stories has been shaped to correspond to the ideology of the Deuteronomistic Historian, and is thus clearly secondary. Nevertheless, many biblical scholars suggest that the content of the stories preserves at least some social history and perhaps also some political history. The stories do seem to attest to early Israelite customs and social configurations, but many of these customs and social configurations may have endured well into the period of the Israelite and Judean states. Reference to conflicts with other peoples might reflect longstanding antagonism (such as with the Philistines), though some might be anachronistic for the Iron I period (such as Moab). It is possible that the text preserves the names of early tribal leaders, especially in the lists of so-called minor judges (Jgs 3:31; 10:1–5; 12:7–15). The references to these judges are short, simply naming the judge, the location from where he judged, how long he judged, and often referring to his sons and where he is buried. Perhaps these lists formed part of the writer's source material. The names of the so-called major judges—Ehud, Deborah, Gideon, Jephthah, Samson—probably also would have been included in this source material, but their stories were filled out from other, presumably oral, traditions.

Models of the Israelite Settlement

Over the last century, biblical scholars formulated three competing historical models in order to explain the settlement of the Israelites in Palestine during the Iron I Age. The Nomadic Infiltration model was first developed by Albrecht Alt and his student Martin Noth in the first half of the twentieth century. This model posits that the early Israelites were nomads or seminomads in a process of gradual sedentarization in the sparsely inhabited central hill country. The settlement was a two-stage process: The early Israelites first entered the land of Canaan in the process of changing pastures; slowly they began to settle permanently in the sparsely populated parts of the country and extended their territory as occasion offered. The whole process began by peaceful means without the use of military force. As the settlers increased in numbers, they gradually moved into the lowlands where they came into conflict with the Canaanite urban centers. This model views Joshua 1–12 as etiologically generated traditions with little historical value. Some cities such as Hazor and Bethel were destroyed by the Israelites as they moved into the lowlands, but the bulk of Joshua 1–12 is fictional. This model emphasizes the uncoordinated movements of Israelites into Canaan from different directions and at different times. If there ever was an exodus event, only a fraction of later Israel was involved.

This model is flawed in several respects. First, the model is unable to demonstrate that the Israelites originated from outside Palestine. As indicated above, all material evidence indicates that the early Israelites resembled their Canaanite neighbors. This would not be the case if the Israelites, like the Philistines, had entered Palestine from elsewhere. Second, the model presents an inadequate understanding of nomadism. Pastoral nomadism cannot be viewed as an evolutionary interval between hunting and gathering and agricultural societies. It is rather a marginal specialization of animal husbandry. The relationship between agriculturalists and pastoralists was symbiotic. Moreover, early Israelites appear to have practiced both pastoralism and agriculture.

The Military Invasion model was created in response to the Nomadic Infiltration model. The main proponents of this model—W. F. Albright, G. Ernest Wright, and John Bright—argued that archaeology has vindicated the essential historicity of the narratives in Joshua 1–12 by demonstrating that the numerous cities stated in the text to have been destroyed do in fact provide evidence of massive destruction. They acknowledge that the ancient sites of Jericho, Ai, Gibeon, and Arad pose problems to this model because they provide no evidence of occupation at the end of the Late Bronze Age. Nevertheless, they also note that the overwhelming evidence for the many other sites is decisive. Moreover, the destruction levels of most of these sites are followed by poor unfortified occupations. There is also a large number of sites with new occupation or occupation that followed centuries of abandonment. In other words, this model suggests, building on the integration of the biblical and archaeological records, that a large group of people rapidly moved into Palestine from outside the land, and their conflict with the native Canaanite inhabitants was primarily political.

The Military Invasion model has been challenged in many respects. First, the application of archaeology to Joshua 1–12 is selective. The evidence is absent for much of the text, and it is embarrassing with regard to Jericho, Ai, Gibeon, and Arad. The sites of Kadesh-Barnea, Hormah, Heshbon, Dibon, and Hebron could also be added to the list of sites in which the archaeological record does not support the biblical tradition. Second, this model has been challenged on its very assumption that archaeology could be used to verify the biblical texts in this regard, for archaeological data are inherently ambiguous. A destroyed city does not indicate the agents of destruction. Although the early Israelites could have been responsible for a site's destruction, more likely scenarios would point to the Egyptians or the Philistines (or other so-called sea peoples) as the agents of the destructions. Archaeology also raises a chronological problem for the model because not all the Late Bronze cities that give evidence of destruction were destroyed during the same time period. The destructions of Hazor and Lachish, for example, were separated by over a century. Many of the large sites that give evidence of massive destruction were in areas in which the native Canaanite inhabitants remained dominant. In other words, the material culture after the destruction of the site was similar to the material culture beforehand. Finally, the Military Invasion model also implies that the material culture of early Israel would be intrusive into the native Canaanite culture, but this is not the case.

The Peasant Revolt model was first put forward by George Mendenhall and subsequently modified by Norman Gottwald. According to this model, the Amarna letters—which refer to the internal struggles in Palestine caused by the ʿApiru—and the biblical events (especially as presented in Judges) represent the same political process: the withdrawal of large population groups from an obligation to existing political regimes, and therefore, the renunciation of any protection from these sources. There was no significant invasion of Palestine; no displacement of population; no genocide; no large scale driving out of the population, only of royal administrators. Instead, there was a peasants' revolt against the network of interlocking Canaanite city-states. The catalyst for this movement might have been the Exodus group: corvée-labor captives who escaped from Egypt and made a covenant with God at Sinai. This group espoused an ideology attractive to those oppressed in Canaan, who immediately joined them. Many of the biblical texts suggest that the people of Israel were unable to conquer the cities of the plains until David's time. Therefore, the early Israelites had geographically removed themselves from the Canaanite cities by retreating into the wooded hill country. The early Israelite settlements were in fact opening this previously uninhabited frontier; such frontiers often attract the socially disenfranchised. Credit should be given to several technological improvements—iron tools, rock terraces, lined cisterns—which made this achievement possible.

Although this model takes into account the similarities between Israelite and Canaanite material culture, it has been criticized for failing to demonstrate the existence of a true peasants' revolt in ancient Palestine and imposing modern, especially Marxist, ideologies on the early Israelites. The Peasant Revolt model overemphasizes the uniqueness of the Israelite settlement. The early highland villages of Israel are identical to other highland villages outside of Palestine; the Israelite settlement does not appear to depend on a unique religious experience or a political ideology.

The Archaeology of the Settlement

A number of new models explaining the Israelite settlement have emerged in recent years, but none has risen to the paradigmatic status of the earlier models. Rooted heavily in the new evidence gleaned from excavations and surveys, especially in the central hill country and the northern Negev, these models share numerous similarities: the Israelites emerged largely from the indigenous population of Canaan, the settlement was primarily peaceful, and the population was engaged in agricultural and pastoral activities. The models differ in their explanation of the causes of the settlement. Some models emphasize the disruption of international trade or the collapse of the Late Bronze cities; others emphasize environmental factors or long-term social processes. Undoubtedly, multiple causes are responsible for the emergence of the Israelites. The new models simply provide interpretive frameworks for the growing body of archaeological evidence of the Israelite settlement.

An explosion of new settlements in the central hill country characterizes the archaeology of the Iron I period. During the Late Bronze Age the hill country held only twenty-nine settlements (down from 220 during the preceding Middle Bronze Age). During the Iron I period, the settlements in the hill country increased to 254. The size of the settlements was quite small, averaging 4.25 acres, but most were less than 2.5 acres in size (the Late Bronze settlements on average were twice as large). Most of the settlements were founded on previously unoccupied sites, although many were founded on abandoned sites that had been occupied during the Early or Middle Bronze Ages. Except for a few major sites that show continuous settlement from the Late Bronze Age, such as Shechem and Jerusalem, most of the settlements were poor hamlets with no fortifications or public buildings.

The central hill country has gone through periods of settlement and abandonment from the Early Bronze Age through the Iron Age, and during each period the settlement pattern is fairly similar. The northern hill country (Shechem and north) is more conducive to settlement with its large valleys, moderate topography, and fertile eastern slope. The southern Judean hill country is less hospitable. As a result, more settlements are found in the north. During periods of settlement decline such as the Late Bronze Age, the percentage of settlements shifts to the north. However, during the waves of settlement such as the Iron I period, the percentage of settlements increases in the southern hill country. Similarly, an east to west settlement shift can be detected. Because the eastern side of the hill country is closer to the desert fringe, it is the location of the early wave of settlement. During settlement declines, only the eastern flank is settled. The western side of the hill country is ideal for horticulture, but it is also more mountainous and demands more permanent commitment for settlement. Thus it is not occupied until later during the waves of settlement.

This settlement pattern might be interpreted in terms of the shift from pastoral to sedentary life. The eastern and southern regions are where pastoralism is primarily practiced, and where the people would be able to make the transition from pastoral to a primarily agricultural life. The economy of these small settlements appears to be dependent primarily upon agriculture and supplemented with pastoralism. The building of many terraces throughout the hill country attests to the agricultural economy of the region. Also, pits for holding grain and cisterns for holding water are characteristic features of the Iron I sites. The domestic structures, however, attest to the importance of pastoralism, for they were adapted to serve as shelter also for the flocks. The mixed economy of farming and herding served to minimize the risks inherent in the establishment of new settlements.

Although most of the settlements simply consist of a group of houses, some of the settlements attest to planning. The common plan was the arrangement of the houses along the perimeter so that the external walls of the houses formed a defensive wall, or the ring of houses could also have created a pen for gathering the inhabitants' flocks of sheep and goats. At ʿIzbet Sartah, for example, twenty-two broad-room houses formed an oval enclosure, a half-acre in area, surrounding a central open area. At Beersheba the first built-up settlement (Stratum VII, dating to the end of the Iron I period; Strata IX–VIII contained mostly pit dwellings) consisted of a ring of houses built around the perimeter of the mound, with their external walls forming a defensive barrier.

The material culture of these sites is simple and plain, and is characterized by the pillared house and the collared-rim storage jar. The pillared house is the most common architectural feature of the Iron I Age. The pillars consisted of large stone monoliths, unworked stone drums, or wooden posts placed on stone socles. Rows of pillars served to divide courtyards into roofed and unroofed areas, as well as define multiple rooms within buildings. The pillared houses followed a variety of plans, but the most common and enduring plan was the four-room house.

The basic plan of the four-room house consisted of three long rooms backed by a broad room. Pillars were usually used to separate the three long rooms; solid walls are also employed to separate the long rooms. In modified plans, the long rooms themselves (or the broad room in back) could be further subdivided. The center long room typically served as a courtyard, with ovens and food processing equipment in this room. There is debate over whether it was roofed. The side rooms separated by pillars were used to house animals, with troughs placed between the pillars. The back broad room served as the main living room. Based on the amount of charred debris in the buildings, many of these houses supported a second story. The bedrooms would have been located in the upper story over the side and back rooms. In a number of villages, the pillared houses appear in clusters or compounds in which several houses shared walls and a common courtyard. These compounds probably reflect the kinship structures of the settlers (such as the extended family). They also might attest to the economic and labor needs that the settlers faced. The shared walls of the compounds would have minimized the labor and resource needs of the settlement.

The pottery repertoire of the hill country settlements is characterized by numerous large storage jars *(pithoi),* including the collared-rim storage jar. Other utilitarian vessels are also found in lesser quantities. Painted decoration is rare, although applied or impressed decoration can be found. All of the pottery has antecedents in the pottery of the Late Bronze Age. Only a few cultic items have been found—a bronze bull at an open-air site near Mount Gilboa, a bronze figurine of a seated deity in a cult room at Hazor, pottery incense stands and small stone four-horned altars at Megiddo and Lachish—and in every case they stand firmly within the Canaanite tradition.

Who were these settlers in the central hill country? The biblical tradition, of course, would identify many of these settlers as Israelite, and indeed they became part of the states of Israel and Judah. Many of the settlers, however, might not have identified themselves as Israelites, at least not initially. In any case, the archaeological and historical evidence suggests that the settlers were a mixture of several population groups. One group undoubtedly consisted of those who left the Late Bronze urban centers in the lowlands. The settlers' knowledge of dry farming and other technological skills such as terracing, digging of cisterns, and house construction argues in favor of their origin in the Late Bronze cities. The continuities of the material culture that the settlers share with the earlier Canaanites further support this interpretation. Another group consisted of pastoralists living on the desert fringe. This group lived in a symbiotic relationship with the urban centers throughout the history of Palestine. During periods of settlement decline, the pastoral population increased and their mode of subsistence became more diverse. During periods of settlement as in the Iron I period, many in this group chose a predominantly agricultural lifestyle while others would revert to a strictly pastoral lifestyle. Finally, the settlers could have consisted of groups that are mentioned in historical texts such as the ʿApiru and the Shasu (the latter is a nomadic group mentioned in the Egyptian texts), and, perhaps, also a group of refugees who had escaped the corvée in Egypt.

Iron II Age

Historical Sources

For the Iron II Age (1000–539 BC) the historian of ancient Israel finally has at hand numerous literary and documentary sources in addition to the biblical literature. The primary and most important sources are the annals of the Assyrian kings. Beginning with Shalmaneser III (858–824 BC), the Assyrian kings began to encounter the kings of Israel in their campaigns toward the Mediterranean, and hence began to include reference to Israel in their annals and inscriptions. The annals of Shalmaneser, for example, record his battles with an Aramean coalition in which the Israelite kingdom participated. Ahab is presented as one of the stronger members, supplying the coalition with 2,000 chariots and 10,000 foot soldiers. In a later inscription on the Black Obelisk, Shalmaneser records the tribute of Jehu, the son of Omri [*sic*], and includes a relief representation of the king kneeling in submission to him. With the reign of Tiglath-pileser III (744–727 BC) the Assyrian kings also had encounters with the kings of Judah, who are now mentioned in the Assyrian annals and inscriptions. The Assyrian records are important sources for understanding Israel's relations with Damascus and other Aramean states, the events that culminated in the destruction of Samaria and the end of the Israelite kingdom, and the political events surrounding the reigns of Ahaz and Hezekiah.

The Babylonians also kept annals that shed light on the political events in the Middle East at the end of Assyrian domination. Few texts refer to Judah directly, but one chronicle does record Nebuchadnezzar's battles in Palestine, including his destruction of Jerusalem.

The Egyptian records during this period shed little light on the events involving the Israelites, for they are largely preoccupied with internal matters. During the Late Period, Egypt under the Twenty-fifth and the Twenty-sixth Dynasties is once again involved in the political affairs of Palestine, but records that attest to this involvement are few. The most notable Egyptian record of Egypt's interaction with Israel and Judah during the Iron II period is the list of conquered cities in Israel and Judah by Sheshonq I (945–924 BC; identified as the biblical Shishak), which is carved on the walls of the Karnak temple. Unfortunately, Sheshonq did not include a narrative description of his campaign, and thus his inscription offers little historical insight.

Numerous Hebrew and Aramaic inscriptions that provide important first-hand information on the events of this period have been uncovered in Palestine. The most famous of these inscriptions is the Moabite Stela, erected by King Mesha of Moab in dedication of a temple. The inscription describes how Mesha freed his land from Israelite vassalage during the reign of Omri's "son" (usually interpreted to mean Omri's grandson, Joram). The recently discovered Tel Dan inscription celebrates an unnamed king's defeat of the kings of Israel and the "house of David." The inscription was presumably erected by Hazael, king of Damascus, but the fragmentary and incomplete condition of the inscription make such an interpretation tentative. The Siloam Tunnel Inscription describes the construction of the tunnel that brought water from the Gihon spring into a pool inside the walls of Jerusalem. The inscription describes the events from the perspective of the workers, but the tunnel probably was dug at the command of Hezekiah in preparation for his rebellion against Assyria. The Lachish Letters describe diplomatic and military maneuvers during the final days of the kingdom of Judah as it was being assaulted by the Babylonians. From the same period, the Arad Letters record the provisioning of the Judean fort at Arad, but also record conflict with the Edomites who live south of Judah.

Other inscriptions attest to economic, social, and religious conditions of the Iron II period. The Gezer Calendar describes the agricultural cycle of the year. Because of the content, some scholars have interpreted this inscription to be a practice text, attesting to scribal activity. The Samaria Ostraca are a series of tax receipts that also attest to kinship structures in Israel. The Yavneh-yam Letter records the complaint of a farm worker to the commander of a fort who has deprived him of his cloak. The Kuntillet ʿAjrud Inscriptions attest to forms of Yahwism that have not been preserved in the Bible.

The primary sources in the Bible for the Iron II Age are the books of Samuel, Kings, and Chronicles (some of the prophetic books, especially Isaiah and Jeremiah, also provide historical information for this period). The stories of Samuel and Saul in 1 Samuel 1–15 are similar in kind to the stories in the book of Judges. They probably record real historical figures, and perhaps also early conflicts between the Israelites in the central hill country and the Philistines on the coastal plain. No earlier source material other than oral traditions can be recognized behind the narrative. The story of Saul and David's conflict in 1 Samuel 16—2 Samuel 1 has been shaped by an apologist on behalf of the Davidic Dynasty. Saul is presented as one driven mad by an evil spirit, whereas David is a loyal servant who refuses to raise his hand against Saul. Some of this material probably preserves traces of real historical events, such as Saul's death in battle against the Philistines, but whatever historical sources might have lain beneath the narrative are now difficult to ascertain.

The stories of 2 Samuel 2—1 Kings 11 address the period of the "United Monarchy," the reigns of David and Solomon. The historical value of these stories is currently the subject of intense debate by biblical scholars and archaeologists. This debate is compounded by the fact that this period (often labeled Iron IIA, or in some circles Iron IC) is not addressed in any nonbiblical sources, and the material remains of this period give at best an ambiguous picture. At issue is the nature and scope of the "kingdom" of David and Solomon: Was there a United Monarchy? Did David and Solomon rule over a territorial state? What was the relationship of this "kingdom" to the other "kingdoms"—Ammon, Aram, Edom, Philistia, Phoenicia—in the region? Many of the stories of David and Solomon are either legendary tales or creations of the biblical writer, perhaps based on brief historical records. Whereas the death notice of Solomon (1 Kgs 11:41–43) refers to the "book of the chronicles of Solomon," no such source is listed in the stories of David. Texts that appear to be based on earlier sources might include the lists of David's administrators (2 Sm 8:16–18; 20:23–26) and his warriors (2 Sm 23:8–39). The references to David's battles (2 Sm 8:1–15) might also be based on an earlier source. A longer list of historical sources might be extracted from the story of Solomon: list of Solomon's officials (1 Kgs 4:1–6); list of officials responsible for supplying food for the court (1 Kgs 4:7–19); Solomon's use of forced labor (1 Kgs 5:13–18); cities that Solomon built and fortified with forced labor (1 Kgs 9:15–19); dealings with King Hiram of Tyre (1 Kgs 9:26–28; 10:11–12:22); Solomon's trade in horses and chariots (1 Kgs 10:28–29); and conflicts with Hadad of Edom, Rezon of Damascus, and Jeroboam of Ephraim (1 Kgs 11:14–40). Many other aspects of the stories, such as David's conquering of Jerusalem, Solomon's wisdom and wealth, and his building of the Temple, are legendary and might have been widely known oral traditions.

The stories of the separate kingdoms of Israel and Judah are found in 1 Kings 12–25. These stories are based on two groups of sources. The first source has been called the "Tales of the Prophets." This source consists of stories of prophets and especially their dealings with kings, their prophecies and their fulfillments. The source includes, for example, the story of Ahijah's prophecy that Jeroboam will become the king of the northern ten tribes of Israel (1 Kgs 11:26–40) and his subsequent prophecy that the house of Jeroboam will be destroyed (1 Kgs 14:1–18). Other stories are about Shemaiah (1 Kgs 12:1–24), Jehu (1 Kgs 16:1–4, 7), Micaiah (1 Kgs 22:1–38), Jonah (2 Kgs 14:25–27), Isaiah (2 Kgs 18:13–20:19), and a number of unnamed prophets (1 Kgs 12:25–13:32; 1 Kgs 20; 2 Kgs 21:10–15). The best known and largest group of stories focus on Elijah and Elisha and their interaction with the house of Ahab (1 Kgs 17–19; 21; 2 Kgs 1–10; 13). Although many of these stories are largely legendary and often reflect a later situation, they appear to have preserved some reliable historical information, particularly regarding the political situation of the period. However, it should be noted that the focus of the stories is primarily religious; the political and social context of the stories is often the backdrop for a religious message regarding the king's (and the people's) faithfulness to Yahweh.

The second major source for the book of Kings is the Israelite and Judean chronicles, which provides the framework for the story of each king. The reign of each king is introduced with a reference to his father, the age at which he began to reign and the length of his reign, and his mother's name. The reigns of the kings of Judah are synchronized with the reigns of the kings of Israel. The story of the king's reign ends with a reference to his death and the place of his burial. Mixed in with this framework are references to deeds accomplished by the king and a statement that other deeds are recorded in either the "Books of the Annals of the Kings of Israel" or the "Books of the Annals of the Kings of Judah." Although the Deuteronomistic Historian adds his own evaluation of each king's reign, the Historian does not appear to have edited or omitted information from the chronicles of the Judean kings. Less information is preserved about the Israelite kings—the king's father and mother are not listed—but this might reflect the nature of the Israelite chronicle rather than the Deuteronomistic Historian's bias. The chronicles preserve fairly reliable historical information. This information, however, is not without its problems. The chronology and synchronization of the Israelite and Judean kings, for example, does not fit within the absolute dates that can be fixed from Assyrian, Babylonian, and Egyptian records. Part of the problem might be that we are not certain how regnal years were counted in each case or whether a king's reign included a co-regency with his father. In other cases, the numbers supplied by the chronicles are incorrect. It seems impossible that Pekah could have reigned for twenty years or that Uzziah (Azariah) reigned for fifty-two years (though the latter's reign could be accounted for with a co-regency).

Other sources that could have been used by the writer of the book of Kings might be dedicatory building inscriptions (similar to the Moabite Stone) or inscriptions associated with votive dedications or biographic stelae that would have been set up in the Temple, the king's palace, or a prominent public location in Jerusalem. The existence of such inscriptions is likely and many texts in the books of Kings could be based on such inscriptions, but in the end their existence must remain speculative.

The book of Chronicles is also a source for the Iron II Age. For the stories of David and Solomon, the book of Chronicles is largely dependent upon the books of Samuel and Kings and offers little independent material. For the stories of the later kings, however, Chronicles offers some material that is not found in Kings. For example, the book of Chronicles records how the Assyrians took Manasseh as a captive to Babylon, where he repented to God who restored him to Jerusalem (2 Chr 33:10–13). This episode is absent from the book of Kings, probably because it does not fit the ideology of the Deuteronomistic Historian, who blames the sins of Manasseh for the eventual destruction of Jerusalem by the Babylonians. In such cases, the book of Chronicles gives us insight into sources that were not accessible to or rejected by the Deuteronomistic Historian. Moreover, this particular example should caution against placing too much confidence in the sources used by the Chronicler or other biblical writers. It is unlikely that Manasseh was ever taken to Babylon, which was a center of repeated revolt against the Assyrian empire. It is possible, however, that Manasseh was taken to Nineveh—an inscription of Esarhaddon records that Manasseh and twenty-one other kings were forced to bring building materials to Nineveh. A number of sources are named in Chronicles—History of the Prophet Nathan, Prophecy of Ahijah the Shilonite, Visions of the Seer Iddo (2 Chr 9:29), Records of the Prophet Shemaiah and Seer Iddo (2 Chr 12:15), Midrash of the Book of Kings (2 Chr 24:27), Acts of Uzziah by Isaiah (2 Chr 26:22), and Acts of Hezekiah by Isaiah (2 Chr 32:32)—but the nature of these sources or whether they are included in the book of Kings is unknown.

The Tenth Century

The beginning of the Iron II Age is imperceptible in the archaeological record. The similarities of the tenth century with the material culture of the Iron I period have led some scholars to label the tenth century as Iron IC. The tenth century is associated with the Iron II Age primarily because the Bible claims that it is the period of statehood—the formation of the United Monarchy. Unfortunately, the United Monarchy is not clearly evident in the archaeological record. No archaeological remains can be associated with David's kingdom. There is archaeological evidence attributed to the reign of Solomon, but the significance of this evidence for understanding the history of Israel is debated.

The archaeological foundation for the United Monarchy has been the large, fortress-style, six chamber city gates and massive casemate walls at Hazor, Megiddo, and Gezer (1 Kgs 9:15 claims that Solomon built up the walls of these cities). The gates and walls at Hazor and Gezer do appear to date to the tenth century, but the gate of Megiddo should now be dated to the ninth century (the first phase of Stratum IVA), and there is no evidence of a casemate wall surrounding the city. Instead, tenth century Megiddo (Stratum VA–IVB) consists of two large monumental palaces—palace 6000 in the north and palace 1723 in the south. No wall surrounds Megiddo at this period, though the exterior walls of the houses and two palaces built along the edge of the mound provide some protection. The palaces have foundations made of ashlars (cut stones), as does the gate of Gezer. The gate and walls of Hazor are constructed of fieldstones. The Gezer gate is also associated with guard quarters (palace 10,000) and perhaps an outer gate and solid wall. Inside the gates of Hazor and Gezer only a few buildings can be dated to the tenth century, and none is monumental or impressive. Moreover, both Hazor and Gezer are small settlements, covering only part of the tell. Elsewhere, the gradual process of urbanization is detectable in the material culture, though no monumental architecture has been found.

The significance of these archaeological remains for understanding the political structures of the tenth century is fiercely debated. For those who follow the biblical tradition and argue for a large United Monarchy, these remains provide significant, yet limited, evidence of the veracity of the tradition. For others, the material culture of the tenth century attests to some centralized building activity, but not a state, let alone a United Monarchy. A key site in this debate would presumably be Jerusalem, where the Bible claims Solomon built a Temple, a palace, and many other administrative public buildings. Unfortunately, virtually nothing from the tenth century has been uncovered in the numerous excavations of the city. Two reasons are generally given to account for this lack of evidence. First, Jerusalem was continuously occupied until Nebuchadnezzar II destroyed it in 586 BC. Evidence of tenth century Jerusalem was destroyed by later rebuilding and occupation of the city. Second, the remains of many of the Solomonic buildings would be beneath the present Temple Mount *(Haram esh-Sharif)*, which is impossible to excavate due to the religious and political situation in the city.

The Kingdom of Israel

The short-lived kingdom of Israel (931–722/1 BC) is well attested in the archaeological record. Its capital Samaria was founded in the ninth century on top of several olive-oil installations. An independently fortified royal acropolis, consisting of a large platform supported by massive retaining walls, was built on the rounded summit of a hill. The platform contained a couple of palaces and a number of administrative buildings. Most of the construction utilized finely cut ashlars. In one of the palaces a large cache of carved ivories, many imported from Phoenicia, attests to the wealth of the kingdom—the cache is usually attributed to the reign of Ahab (873–852 BC), who the Bible claims built a house of ivory (1 Kgs 22:39). The Samaria Ostraca were found in one of the administrative buildings, and were inscribed during the reign of Jeroboam II (784–744 BC). The city was destroyed in a conflagration by Sargon II (721–705 BC), though the Assyrian assault might have begun during the reign of Shalmaneser V (726–722 BC).

Megiddo was one of the major administrative cities of the kingdom of Israel. The Israelite city (limited to Stratum IVA) was surrounded by a large wall and entered though a six-chamber gate (later rebuilt as a four-chamber gate) on its north side. A palace (380) was located on the eastern side of the city, but most of the city was dedicated to two large complexes of tripartite-pillared buildings. The southern complex consisted of five connected tripartite-pillared buildings fronted by a large walled yard. The northern complex consisted of three groups of five, two, and five connected buildings surrounding a walled yard. The interpretation of these buildings has been debated. Most commonly they are interpreted as stables for the royal chariot force. Other interpretations argue that the buildings were used for storerooms in a state-run redistribution center, or functioned as markets and fair grounds. The large water tunnel on the western side of the city, which leads to the spring outside the city wall, was constructed during this period. Tiglath-pileser III destroyed Megiddo in 732 BC and rebuilt the city (Stratum III) as an Assyrian provincial capital. The city was filled with residential buildings in an orthogonal pattern, with several Assyrian-style palaces built near the gate.

Unlike Megiddo, both Hazor and Dan in the northern Jordan Valley give evidence of several strata of occupation during this period, attesting to Israel's conflicts with Damascus and Assyria. Israelite Hazor covers the entire acropolis (the lower city was not inhabited after the Late Bronze Age). The tenth-century casemate wall is filled in to form a solid fortification wall, and another solid wall is constructed to surround the new eastern half of the city. Inside the six-chamber gate, now in the middle of the city, a single tripartite-pillared building was uncovered. Two large halls attached to the building could have functioned as a granary or storerooms to support the function of the pillared building (as a stable or market). A large citadel was built on the western end of the acropolis. Administrative buildings resembling those of Samaria were found immediately to the north and south of the citadel. The massive walls of the citadel (over six feet thick) initially served as the western fortification of the city, but at the height of the Assyrian threat at the end of the Israelite period, a new wall was added to the north, west, and south of the citadel, covering over the administrative buildings. New administrative buildings were constructed on the east side of the citadel. On the southern side of the city an enormous shaft and tunnel were dug into the aquifer beneath the city in order to supply the populace with water during a siege.

Dan was Israel's northernmost city and so often at the center of conflict with Israel's northern neighbors. The complex set of gates with multiple building phases on the southern side of the city attests to this conflict. On the north side of the tell, Avraham Biran, the excavator, uncovered a large series of structures that he identified with the high place initially built by Jeroboam I (931–911 BC; see 1 Kgs 12:26–31). In the earliest stratum, the structure consisted of a large podium constructed of ashlars. The excavator assumed that the podium served as an open-air high place, but traces of foundations on the podium have led others to suggest that it supported a large superstructure, probably a temple. In front of the podium on the south is a large altar platform built of ashlars, with storage rooms on the west and an oil press farther south. A second phase of the temple is not well preserved. The third phase of the temple complex, dating to the eighth century, is the most developed. The podium now supported a temple. A monumental staircase made of ashlars was added to the south side of the podium. A large four-horned altar that was approached by steps and surrounded by an enclosure was constructed in front of the podium. A row of rooms on the west side of the temple and altar functioned in support of the temple cult. Tiglath-pileser III, presumably, destroyed the temple at the end of the eighth century with the rest of the city.

The Kingdom of Judah

Judah was Israel's poorer and weaker sibling, and the material culture of Judah generally reflects this distinction. Although there were periods of friendly relations between the two kingdoms—with Judah often submitting to a more powerful Israel such as during the Omride Dynasty, and perhaps also during parts of the Jehu Dynasty—the Bible also attests to strained relations and military conflicts. The material evidence of these relations can be seen in the early fortification of some of the towns of Judah. One such site was Tell en-Nasbeh, which has been identified with biblical Mizpah and is situated at the border between Israel and Judah. At this site a massive solid inset-offset wall was built outside an earlier (tenth century) casemate wall. The wall was roughly nineteen hundred feet in length, stood forty feet above bedrock, and had an average thickness of more than twelve feet. Eleven towers fortified the wall. The wall was made from uncut fieldstones, but ashlars were used in corners and on the face of the towers. A stone glacis further protected several towers and long sections of the wall. The city was entered through a two-chamber outer gate and a four-chamber inner gate. It appears that the inner gate was the original gate, but in the ninth century the fortifications were strengthened with the construction of a new outer gate that was fortified by a massive tower. The heavy fortifications at this site attest to political tensions and perhaps military conflict between Israel and Judah.

Although the kingdom of Judah developed under relatively peaceful conditions—despite the construction of some new fortifications, few destruction levels are attested—the Assyrian threat in the eighth century led to the fortification of Judah. Unlike Israel, which had several large urban centers, the kingdom of Judah developed primarily around Jerusalem. By the end of the eighth century, Jerusalem had swelled to a large fortified city of 150 acres, larger than any city in Israel. Lachish, the second largest city in Judah, covered an area of only twenty acres. The other Judean towns averaged only five to eight acres in size. The generally peaceful conditions of Judah also enabled it to rapidly increase in population. In addition to natural population growth, the population of Judah increased due to the migration of refugees from the north, especially during the second half of the eighth century, which culminated in Israel's destruction by the Assyrians. The population increase was felt prominently in Jerusalem but also across the Judean hill country. Numerous small settlements were established during this period, many of which were unfortified and roughly two miles apart.

At the end of the eighth century, archaeology is able to provide a material context for one of the more crucial events recorded in the biblical texts: the archaeological evidence provides a picture of Hezekiah's revolt against Assyria (1 Kgs 18–19). Hezekiah fortified an enlarged Jerusalem with a massive, seven-meter thick city wall (the so-called broad wall uncovered in the Jewish Quarter). Recent excavations in the Kidron Valley have uncovered a second, outer wall around the eastern side of the city. This wall might also have been constructed by Hezekiah. In order to secure drinking water for the inhabitants of the city in case of siege, he diverted the water from the Gihon spring to a pool inside the city wall through the excavation of the Siloam tunnel. Further evidence of Hezekiah's preparation against an Assyrian assault is attested in the distribution of royal storage jars that are impressed with the inscription *lamelech* (belonging to the king). The impressions are applied to the loop handles of large ovoid jars that are 60 centimeters high, have four handles, a narrow mouth, and a short upright neck. The jars were apparently used to store liquids rather than dry goods. The seal impressions have either a winged solar disk or a four-winged scarab. The word *lamelech* is inscribed above the design. Below the design one of four towns is named: Hebron, Socoh, Ziph, and *mmsht* (the last name is unknown). These jars and seals have been securely dated to the end of the eighth century. They have been found throughout Judah, but mostly at Jerusalem and Lachish. Some scholars have argued that the jars were used to gather taxes in the form of agricultural produce such as wine and oil. Others argue that the jars represent four centers of royal wine production. Another interpretation is that the four cities inscribed on the seals represent four military divisions and that the jars conveyed provisions to military units posted by Hezekiah throughout his kingdom. In any case, the jars attest to the king's provisioning of his cities in preparation for his revolt.

Although Jerusalem was never sacked, Hezekiah's rebellion was a complete failure. Most of the cities of Judah were destroyed, and part of Judah was placed under the domain of the Philistine king of Ekron. Hezekiah himself was forced to pay a large tribute to Sennacherib. The consequences of Hezekiah's revolt are illustrated in the Lachish reliefs found in Sennacherib's palace at Nineveh and in the excavations at Lachish. The Lachish reliefs depict in graphic detail the Assyrian assault, defeat, and plunder of Lachish. The excavations of Lachish revealed the violent destruction of Stratum III. At the southern corner of the city, the Assyrians built a massive siege ramp. Inside the city wall, the inhabitants of the city built a counterramp over their own houses in order to hold the Assyrians back. The hundreds of arrowheads and spherical slingstones attest to the intensity of the battle. The discovery of a mass grave with more than fifteen hundred bodies is grim evidence of the slaughter of the people of Lachish.

The southern border of Judah was along the Beersheba Valley and was fortified by Arad on the east and Beersheba on the west. Beersheba was a small, fortified town from the tenth century through the eighth century (Strata V–II). It provides the best example of a complete and regular city plan from the Iron II period. Although the city only occupied an area of three acres, it probably served as the major administrative center in the south. The city was fortified by a casemate wall, and entered through a four-chamber gate. Surrounding the city a stone glacis was constructed against the rampart supporting the wall. Inside the city gate was a large open square that probably served a variety of public functions. The street plan of the city was composed of concentric ovals connected by radial lanes, with the entire system converging on the plaza inside the gate. A water system was uncovered in the northeastern corner of the city. The city contained approximately seventy-five houses, most of which were designed according to a special four-room type. The back rooms of those houses that abutted the city wall along the peripheral road were incorporated into the casemates of the wall. Some of the houses have stairs preserved indicating that they had a second story. Three tripartite-pillared buildings were built east of the city gate and open onto the plaza. Together they cover an area of 600 square meters. A large building located near the city plaza at the juncture of the outer road and a radial road has been called the "governor's house." It contained three large reception halls whose entrances were built of ashlars. Beersheba was destroyed at the end of the eighth century, presumably by the Assyrians in response to Hezekiah's revolt.

The fortress of Arad was built on top of a small settlement in the ninth century (though the excavator initially dated the first fortress to the tenth century). The fortress was destroyed and rebuilt five times before finally being destroyed early in the sixth century with the destruction of the kingdom of Judah by the Babylonians. A number of letters inscribed on pottery sherds found in the fort suggest that the fort functioned primarily as a Judean bastion against the encroachment of the Edomites. The pressure of the Edomites on Judah's southern border is attested at numerous other sites in this region. At ʿEin Hatzeva in the Arabah (southeast of Arad), the large eighth century Judean fortress is replaced by a smaller Edomite fortress in the seventh century. At Horvat Qitmit in the Arad Valley (southwest of Arad) a small Edomite shrine-complex was built late in the seventh century. The fortress of Horvat ʿUza on the eastern end of the Arad Valley (southeast of Arad) was destroyed by the Edomites (as suggested by an Edomite letter found in a gate chamber) at the beginning of the sixth century. Both Aroer and Tel Malhata in the Negev (between Arad and Beersheba) present evidence of Edomite occupation by the beginning of the sixth century.

Jerusalem was destroyed in 586 BC by the Babylonian army in order to crush the rebellion by Zedekiah, Judah's last king. The archaeological remains of the City of David primarily attest to this period. Heavy ash layers in several buildings give evidence of the destruction, and numerous Babylonian iron arrowheads hint at the presumable human slaughter. One of the buildings on the eastern slope of the City of David that was destroyed in the conflagration appears to have been an archive. Dubbed the "House of the Bullae," this building contained fifty-one clay bullae that had sealed papyrus or parchment scrolls. Many of the names inscribed on the bullae are mentioned in the Bible, especially in the book of Jeremiah. The most notable bulla, found elsewhere in the city, records the name of "Baruch, son of Neriah, the scribe"—the companion of Jeremiah.

The Period of the Great Empires

The Persian Period

It is ironic that although most of the biblical books were written or compiled during the Persian period, few books actually attest to the period. The books of Ezra and Nehemiah provide the main narrative source for this period. The numerous prophetic books that attest to this period include Haggai, Zechariah, Malachi, and Isaiah 56—66, but unfortunately, these books attest to little more than the social and religious situation of the period. The books of Ezra and Nehemiah are particularly valuable for understanding this period because they seem to preserve primary sources. Each book preserves a first-hand report that has been labeled a memoir. The Nehemiah memoir is found in Nehemiah 1:1–7, 73a; 12: 31–43; 13:4–31; the Ezra memoir is found in Ezra 7:27–9:15. The book of Ezra also contains several letters from correspondence with the Persian administration. These letters also might be based on primary texts. Because many scholars have argued that Ezra is a fiction, an ideal lawgiver, his memoirs are not usually given the same status as the Nehemiah memoirs. Although Ezra has been idealized in later tradition, the presentation of him in the book of Ezra has a realistic basis and probable historical source. In any case, in their present context the memoirs and letters have been shaped by the ideological concerns of the biblical writer.

Other sources for the Persian period include the *Jewish Antiquities* of Josephus (a first-century Jewish historian). Although Josephus largely follows the biblical text, he adds information concerning the relationship between the Judeans and the Samaritans. Many Greek sources contribute to writing the history of Persia, most notably, the History of Herodotus and the works of Diodorus Siculus, but these texts give little attention to the events of Judah. The archaeological evidence for this period has not been investigated well. In terms of material culture, the spread of Phoenician and Greek influence along the coastal plain can be detected. The hill country demonstrates cultural continuities with the Iron Age. Destruction layers at numerous cities attest to military conflicts, but the dating of these destruction layers to specific events is problematic. Inscriptions and papyri, such as the Elephantine Papyri, provide evidence of the administration of the province of Judea, but they attest to little more than names of governors and high priests.

The biblical evidence refers to only two periods during the long Persian rule of Judah, and in both cases its presentation of the events is less than clear. The first period focuses on the rebuilding of the Temple by the exiles who returned to Judah from Babylon. Once Cyrus defeated Babylon (539 BC), he sought to consolidate the empire under his rule by restoring the gods and the peoples that the Babylonians had exiled. Thus Cyrus issued an edict for the Judeans to return to their homeland and rebuild the Temple of Yahweh (Ezr 6:3–5; compare this text to an edict that has survived in the so-called Cyrus Cylinder). The book of Ezra gives a conflated presentation of who initially returned to Babylon. Sheshbazzar, who is called a prince over Judah, is credited with leading the initial return, bringing the Temple vessels from Babylon (Ezr 1:8–11), and laying the Temple foundation (Ezr 5:16). Yet Zerubbabel is also listed as the leader of the people, under whose direction the foundation of the Temple was laid in the second year of the return (537 BC; Ezr 3:8–13). After a delay of several years, the rebuilding of the Temple resumed under Zerubbabel in the second year of Darius (520 BC). The Temple was completed in Darius's sixth year (515 BC).

Little is known about Sheshbazzar; no genealogy is given about him. He is often identified with Shenazzar, a son of Jehoiachin (1 Chr 3:18), but this identification has little support. As a prince over Judah he could have been a member of the royal family, as Zerubbabel probably was, but he could simply be a leader of the people. He is called a governor just as Zerubbabel is later called. What happened to Sheshbazzar is also unknown. He probably did begin to rebuild the Temple, laying only the foundation. His leadership might have come to an end with his failure to rebuild the Temple, or in the wake of the turmoil associated with Darius's usurpation of the Persian throne. Zerubbabel is the grandson of Jehoiachin, Judah's last king, though some scholars suggest that this is a fiction of the biblical writer. Like Sheshbazzar, he was appointed governor of Judah. When he was appointed governor is never stated in the text, although Haggai first mentions him in reference to Darius's second year (520 BC). Although he was the civil administrator of Judah, only his work in rebuilding the Temple is recorded. Once the Temple is rebuilt, no more is heard about him.

The second period that the biblical evidence addresses is the period of Ezra and Nehemiah. The relationship of these two reformers poses a significant historical problem. The stories of Ezra and Nehemiah have been artificially joined. Part of the story of Ezra has been inserted into the middle of Nehemiah's story (Neh 8–9). The biblical text places Ezra first, followed by Nehemiah, but this relationship could be artificial. The text claims that Ezra's mission began in the seventh year of Artaxerxes, whereas Nehemiah's mission began in Artaxerxes' twentieth year, but several kings by this name ruled Persia. The date of Nehemiah's mission is fairly certain. He became governor over Judah in the twentieth year of Artaxerxes I (465–424 BC), thus in 445 BC. This date is independently confirmed by a letter from the Judean community in Elephantine, Egypt, dated 25 November 407 BC, at which time a certain Bagoas was governor over Judah, referring to Delaiah and Shelemiah, the sons of Sanballat, a contemporary of Nehemiah. Nehemiah's term of office lasted until 433 BC, at which time he was recalled to the Persian court. He was appointed for a second term some time before 424 BC, the end of Artaxerxes' reign, and served as governor until some time before 411 BC, at which time Bagoas is governor.

If Ezra's mission is to be dated to the seventh year of Artaxerxes I, then his mission began in 458 BC. This relationship, however, poses several problems. The high priest Jehohanan, the grandson of Eliashib who was a contemporary of Nehemiah, is mentioned in relation to Ezra, but the Elephantine texts place him in Judah around 407 BC. The names of the high priests in the preserved lists have been corrupted because of repetition (several men named Jehohanan son of Eliashib served as high priest), thus this evidence is not conclusive. If Ezra preceded Nehemiah, then his reform does not appear to have been successful, for when Nehemiah comes on to the scene the problems addressed by Ezra continue to exist. Moreover, Nehemiah never mentions Ezra and blames his predecessors for the corrupt situation in Judah (in Neh 8:9 the two are mentioned together, but this is clearly the result of editorial activity). Scholars have also noted that during Ezra's time Jerusalem is occupied and surrounded by a wall (Ezr 9:9), but in Nehemiah's time Jerusalem is unoccupied and its wall has been torn down. From Nehemiah's perspective, Jerusalem could have recently been destroyed during the revolt of Megbyzus, the satrap of Abar-nahara (of which Judah was a part) in 449/8 BC, but no evidence clearly attests to this. As a result of these problems, many scholars prefer to date Ezra to the reign of Artaxerxes II (404–358 BC). Ezra's mission would then have begun in 398/7 BC, after Nehemiah. However, the biblical order of placing Ezra's mission during the reign of Artaxerxes I cannot be ruled out.

The Hellenistic and Roman Periods

The sources for understanding the history of Israel during the Hellenistic (332–63 BC) and Roman (63 BC–AD 70) periods are many, though few texts in the Bible provide much information regarding the political history of the periods. The primary biblical source for the Hellenistic period is 1 Maccabees. This book, written in the style of the book of Kings, tells of the struggle of Mattathias and his sons against the Seleucid king Antiochus IV Epiphanes and his heirs, which has come to be known as the Maccabean revolt after the name of Mattathias's eldest son, Judah Maccabee. The book is clearly biased on behalf of the Hasmoneans (as the descendants of Mattathias are known), and it seeks to legitimate the rule of John Hyrcanus and his sons, but it nevertheless preserves much historical information about the period. The other biblical books that address the period of the Maccabean revolt are Daniel and 2 Maccabees. The visions of Daniel (7–12) were composed during the revolt and thus provide the most immediate view of the events. The historical contribution of the visions, however, is in places obscured by figurative and cryptic language. 2 Maccabees, an abridgement of a five-volume history by Jason of Cyrene, covers a more limited period of time than 1 Maccabees (it ends with the death of Judas), but provides a greater depth of coverage and includes material not mentioned in 1 Maccabees. Second Maccabees is particularly valuable for its description of the Hellenistic reform, the events leading up to the revolt, especially the life and murder of Onias III, and the relations between Jerusalem and the Egyptian Diaspora.

All the books of the New Testament were written during the Roman period, but their focus is on the teaching and ministry of Jesus (Gospels) and the early church (Epistles), and they give an uneven picture of the larger Judean and Roman world in which they are set. The Gospels do not present a life of Jesus; the specific framework of the story of Jesus has been shaped by the particular focus of each evangelist. Jesus' cleansing of the Temple, for example, occurs early in his ministry in John, but during the Passion Week in Matthew, Mark, and Luke. Nevertheless, the Gospels provide information about the historical geography of Palestine, the local administration, and numerous social customs. The Epistles present an incomplete picture of the local churches to which they were written, but rarely do they address events or issues of the larger Roman world. Only the Acts of the Apostles, which presents a history of the early church, provides substantial information on the Judean and Roman world. The Acts of the Apostles also presents interesting details about a number of persons who are known from other sources: Herod Agrippa I, Herod Agrippa II, the Roman procurators Felix and Festus, and the proconsul Gallio of Achaia.

The classical authors who provide information on Judea during this period include Diodorus Siculus, Polybius, Nicholas of Damascus, Strabo, Pliny the Elder, Tacitus, Suetonius, and Dio Cassius. Two significant Jewish authors are Philo of Alexandria and Flavius Josephus. In *In Flaccum* and *Legatio ad Gaium,* Philo describes the persecutions of the Jews during the reign of Gaius Caligula, which he personally witnessed. Josephus' works, *The Jewish War* and *Jewish Antiquities,* give detailed information about the Hasmoneans, the Herodians, and the events leading up to and the consequences of the Judean revolt against Rome. Other notable sources for this period are the Zenon papyri, which attest to the administration of Judea when it was under Ptolemaic control, and the Dead Sea Scrolls, which attest to the religious diversity of the Roman period.

The archaeology of this period is dominated by the many monumental building projects sponsored by Herod the Great. In addition to the rebuilding and expansion of the Temple in Jerusalem, for which he is most known, Herod founded the port city of Caesarea Maritima on the coast south of Carmel. He rebuilt Samaria, renaming it Sebaste in honor of Augustus. He rebuilt Jericho. Both Caesarea and Sebaste included Roman-style temples dedicated to the emperor. Herod built palaces at Caesarea and at Herodian Jericho. Herod also built or rebuilt several fortresses in the Judean wilderness: Machaerus, the Herodium, and Masada. Although Herod's temple in Jerusalem was thoroughly destroyed by the Romans in AD 70 in the wake of the Judean revolt, the present Temple Mount preserves much of the platform on which Herod's temple was built. South and west of the Temple Mount, Herodian construction associated with the Temple has been uncovered: stone-paved streets with shops and piers supporting staircases to the Temple, a royal stoa, and a monumental staircase leading up to the western Double Gate and the eastern Triple Gate. West of the Temple, in the present Jewish Quarter, excavations have uncovered several large, well-decorated houses with mosaic floors and luxurious stone objects (tables, bowls, and jars). The houses were destroyed by the Romans when Titus sacked Jerusalem in AD 70. These houses attest to the affluence of Jerusalem during this period and to the violence of the Judean revolt.

Other notable archaeological sites during this period include Capernaum, Chorazin, Bethsaida, Sepphoris, and Qumran. At Capernaum and Chorazin, two towns on the northern side of the Sea of Galilee in which Jesus taught, early examples of Jewish synagogues have survived. The synagogues date to the first or second century AD, but at Capernaum traces of an earlier synagogue that dates to the period of Jesus lie beneath the later well-preserved synagogue. Also, at Capernaum the excavators have uncovered a house that Byzantine Christians identified as the house of Peter, for they built on the site a large octagon-shaped church (similar in form to the Byzantine church built at Caesarea on top of the ruins of Herod's temple to Augustus and to the Dome of the Rock on the Temple Mount). At Bethsaida, the Galilean home of several of Jesus' disciples, the excavators have uncovered several large first-century homes. In one of the homes numerous fishing implements were discovered. Sepphoris is a large Roman city with a theatre approximately four miles from Nazareth. The city was rebuilt by Antipas during Jesus' youth, and Joseph, perhaps accompanied by Jesus, would probably have been employed in its construction (the Greek term used for Joseph's occupation, *tekton,* may refer to someone who works with either wood or stone). Although it is never mentioned in the New Testament, the cultural life of Sepphoris would have been well known to Jesus. The use of the word *hypocrite* by Jesus in the Gospels, which refers to a stage actor who plays a role for an audience's approval, perhaps derives from Jesus' familiarity with the theatre of Sepphoris. The identification of the community that lived at Qumran has been debated by scholars. Although some would identify the buildings as part of a large Roman villa, the site is generally recognized as the remains of the Essene community responsible for authoring and preserving the Dead Sea Scrolls.

CATHOLIC INTERPRETATION OF THE BIBLE

KEVIN MADIGAN

The Early Church (ca. AD 100–500)

The early Catholic interpretation of the Bible, like Christianity itself, did not emerge or develop in a religious, cultural, or intellectual void. Instead, it was formed and influenced by two antecedent interpretive traditions, one Greco-Roman, the other Jewish.

The Greco-Roman tradition traces its origins back at least to the sixth century BC. This tradition originated with the followers of the brilliant Pythagoras of Samos. The Pythagoreans focused their interpretive attention upon the epic poetry of Homer, and their Platonic and Stoic successors on other classics of the Greco-Roman tradition. Confident that the poets had written under inspiration as theologians, so to speak, these interpreters concluded that great poetry was about deep cosmological and ethical realities. Accordingly, they developed a philosophy or method of interpretation called *allegoria* (allegory). Using this technique, Greek and Roman interpreters of classical literature claimed to find the deep meaning intended by the author. This meaning was usually hidden by the surface language of the poet, which could be crudely literal, enigmatic, superficially trivial, or otherwise intellectually or morally offensive. All assumed, in fact, that the literal meaning was an impediment to the "real," deep, and true (or truer) meaning of the text.

Similar assumptions and methods passed over into Diaspora Judaism no later than the turn of the first century BC and were used in the interpretation of the Septuagint, notably with the ascetic Therapeutae. Without doubt, the preeminent practitioner of the allegorical method in Hellenistic Judaism was Philo of Alexandria (20 BC–AD 50). With non-Jewish Hellenistic interpreters, he shared several crucial assumptions: that the text (the Septuagint) was divinely inspired and thus permanently normative; that it contained deeper truths than those expressed superficially and contained a spiritual sense above or beyond the literal-historical; that the deeper truths were present especially where the text was, or seemed, irrational, ambiguous, absurd, sacrilegious, or otherwise difficult; and that such truths could be understood by the interpreter skilled in allegory. In addition, it was Philo's conviction that such truths were consistent with the highest insights of Stoic and Platonic thought, so that the allegorist in some sense "rewrote" the sacred text so as to harmonize it with these insights. Yet Philo insisted on literal adherence to Torah. He also observed that some texts (e.g., Nm 23:19: "God is not like a man") were literally clear and therefore required no allegorical gloss. On several very important Christian exegetes also from Alexandria, especially Clement and Origen (who was very conscious of and explicit about his debt to Philo), Philonic hermeneutics would exercise a profound influence, which would then be felt for more than a millennium in both Eastern and Western Christianity.

With Philo and, indeed, with all contemporary Jews, the earliest Christian community agreed that "the Scriptures" referred to a collection of authoritative Jewish writings, namely that collection of writings Christians today refer to as the Old Testament. With Hellenistic Jews, early

Christians also shared the methodological conviction that the Scriptures could be (and sometimes should be) permitted to say things other than that which the words seemed to suggest or require.

In the application of this principle, of course, early Christians parted company with contemporary Jews. This is because the earliest Christians rapidly took those authoritative Jewish writings to attest typologically to the eschatological events that had occurred in the life, death, and resurrection of Jesus of Nazareth. That is, early Christians interpreted the events of Israelite history as *types*—intentional figural prophecies expressed in the spiritual sense of the text and recognized as prophetic only in the light of later events—of the decisive redemptive actions taken by God in the life of Jesus. Thus, typology (a form of allegory) grew up with Christianity as a hermeneutical method. (Such a hermeneutic is in evidence no later than the letters of Paul, e.g., in 1 Cor 10:6 and Rom 5:4). Indeed, it enabled Christians to understand the events of Christ, especially the problem of a crucified Messiah, in terms prefigured in the Hebrew Scriptures. Accordingly, it was crucial to the project of emerging Christian and ecclesiastical self-definition. That Christian typology required a thoroughgoing reinterpretation of the Scriptures the community shared with contemporary Jewish exegetes and practitioners goes without saying.

This is not to say that all early Christians, or all who so identified themselves, were comfortable with the typological method and the practical exegetical results its application effected. Some were not. Few were more uncomfortable than Marcion of Pontus, a layman of formidable wealth and missionary zeal. After having worked among the Roman Christians (ca. 144), Marcion founded a church based, exegetically, on the rejection of the typological method and of the Hebrew Scriptures and of the God revealed therein. He composed a *canon,* perhaps the first composed by any Christian, consisting solely of an expurgated version of the Gospel of Luke and a collection of ten Pauline letters. Had Marcion's position carried the day, the Old Testament would have ceased to be an arsenal of proof text to be used, in conjunction with the words of the evangelists and Paul, to establish the messiahship of Jesus. However quaint and occasionally even disrespectful typological exegesis sounds to a postcritical and ecumenical age, it did preserve the Hebrew Scriptures for the use of the church.

Eventually, Marcion's views (as well as those of Gnostic Christians who also rejected the Hebrew Scriptures) were condemned by the mainstream or emerging "Catholic" Church. But Marcion's views gave considerable impetus to the formation within this Catholic Church of an authoritative list of scriptural writings. Within decades of Marcion's death—certainly no later than AD 180—the Catholic Church had composed a list, a canon, of authoritative Scriptures that resembled very closely the contents of this Study Bible. It included an "Old Testament," understood now as a collection of writings pointing typologically beyond itself to Christ, and a "New Testament." The former was the Greek Septuagint, which included the Apocrypha, books not allowed by the rabbis into the Jewish canon in the first two centuries after Jesus' birth. The contents of the latter were very much like those of our Greek New Testament, though writings later listed in the canon (e.g., James, Hebrews) were not then included.

For the remainder of the second century, the Bible was exploited above all in polemical writing against Jewish and heretical interlocutors (sometimes imaginatively configured). While these Catholic polemicists hardly ignored the New Testament, the Hebrew Bible was, as it were, the turf on which such battles were fought. Typology was the most frequently wielded arrow in the Catholic exegete's quiver. In his *Dialogue with Trypho the Jew* (ca. 160), for example, Justin Martyr attempted to demonstrate that Christ's life and especially crucifixion had been copiously, almost ubiquitously, foreshadowed in the Hebrew Scriptures. So intent was Justin on proving that the cross had been prefigured there that he found types of it in virtually any reference or allusion to wood, beginning with the Tree of Life in Genesis.

Aside from being an accomplished practitioner of the typological method, Bishop Irenaeus of Lyons (fl. 170–80) established a crucially influential principle of correct interpretation of the Bible. Dubbed by R. M. Grant "the father of authoritative exegesis in the church" and often recognized to be a father of early Catholicism,

Irenaeus argued (particularly against heretics) that only bishops in an unbroken line of succession from the apostles were to be counted as trusted interpreters. From this principle, it followed that authoritative interpretation was to be found solely within the walls of the churches and, more precisely, in those churches that could trace their origins to the apostles and whose episcopal successors had, in addition, produced short creeds to summarize the main events of salvation history contained in the Scriptures. These creeds (or rules of faith) could then be used (circularly, it might be observed) to test the orthodoxy of any scriptural interpretation.

In the Catholic interpretation of Scripture and above all in hermeneutical theory, Origen of Alexandria (ca. 185–253) towers over the third century. The fourth book of his masterwork, *On First Principles,* is dedicated solely to a theory of biblical interpretation; it is a deeply influential manifesto of Christian allegoresis. Origen's basic presumption, like that of his fellow Alexandrians, not least of all Philo, is that the Scriptures are intended to reveal not simply the historical events of salvation history but deep spiritual, theological, and cosmological truths. Such truths are revealed above all where the literal sense says things unworthy of the Deity (God planting a garden, for example), or impossible (three "days" of creation without any natural body of light), or inconsistent. (Origen was deeply impressed with the inconsistency of, among other things, the Passion and Resurrection accounts, from which he concluded they must each intend a deeper spiritual meaning.) In some cases, a biblical passage will have no literal sense. But *all* passages have a deeper spiritual sense, to which the interpreter is clued by the "stumbling blocks" of an illogical or absurd "letter." Such texts invite the skilled exegete to unearth the spiritual treasure buried below, and Origen gives quite specific rules about how to uncover this camouflaged meaning. He encourages the exegete to "search the scriptures" (Jn 5:39) and establish the meaning of difficult passages by clear ones (a method that of course presupposed the unity of the biblical witness) and by paying attention to context and to etymology. Echoing Irenaeus, he also adds (perhaps less enthusiastically than the Bishop of Lyon) that the meaning of Scripture can be established by use of the church's Rule of Faith. These reflections made Origen by far the most sophisticated theoretician of interpretation in ancient Christianity. He was, in addition, an enormously prolific exegete. Not to be overlooked is his *Hexapla* (sixfold), an edition of the Hebrew Scriptures which contained, in six parallel columns, one version of the Old Testament in Hebrew, one of the transliterated Hebrew, and four, including the Septuagint, in Greek. This might be called the first attempt in ecclesiastical history at textual criticism of the Hebrew Scriptures. His influence on late-antique and medieval exegetes, especially those sympathetic to allegorical interpretation (like the fourth-century Cappadocian fathers, Gregory of Nyssa and Basil), would be, if indirect, immense.

Not all were sympathetic. (We remember here Marcion.) If Alexandria nourished its scholars on allegoresis, the biblical exegetes in the important city of Antioch tended to stress the fundamental importance of the literal and historical sense of the text. According to Eusebius, the Antiochene exegetes, represented typically by John Chrysostom (407), interpreted the text "with moderation"—that is, unallegorically. This is not to say Antiochene exegetes denied that the sacred text had a higher meaning. It is to say that they were nervous about allegory. In their view, allegory simply made the text a springboard for unrestrained flights of speculation that left the natural, obvious, or contextual meaning of the text far from view. For the deeper meaning of the text, they preferred the term *theoria*. Their leader, Diodore of Tarsus (d. 390), actually composed a text titled *On the Difference between Theoria and Allegoria.* Two others, Eustathius, Bishop of Antioch, and Diodore's pupil Theodore of Mopsuestia (d. 428), wrote tracts on the same topic with the same unambiguous title—*Against Origen.*

As it turns out, the difference is largely one of emphasis, with the Antiochene school typically stressing the need to ground the higher meaning of the text in its foundational historical meaning, or at least not be opposed to it. Both men were concerned that allegoresis actually robbed the text of the meaning it purported to uncover by plunging and thus dissolving it into the murky, seemingly undisciplined universe of discourse of "spiritual understanding." (The Antiochenes would have vibrated sympathetically to von Harnack's complaint about Origen's "biblical alchemy.") Neither Antiochene was as apprehensive about, in his understandable preoccupation with the historicity of the text, what was for Origen and his Alexandrian peers the sometimes disturbingly anthropomorphic, mythical fabric of the biblical narrative. Looking ahead, one could say, somewhat simply, that in the early Latin West, the Alexandrian tradition would certainly carry the day, while in the high Middle Ages, with the reintroduction of Aristotle, the Antiochene tradition asserted its supremacy.

Even as no scholar of the fourth century did as much to explicate and make available the Bible to contemporaries, no figure exemplified ambivalence to the allegorical approach more than the great Jerome (ca. 340–420). His early commentarial efforts are highly allegorical. Later, he came under the influence of the Antiochene school through Apollinaris of Laodicea (d. ca. 390), who was later condemned for Christological heresy at the second ecumenical council of Constantinople (381). At that point, Jerome stated his desire to avoid excessive allegoresis, going so far as to claim he allegorized only when he could not determine the literal sense of a passage. However, this claim was purely theoretical, as his voluminous commentaries are replete with allegorical interpretation, about much of which, at the end of his life, he finally expressed regret.

It is difficult to imagine that such a man as Jerome could look back on his career at all ruefully. He was without doubt the greatest scholar of the fourth century. His knowledge of the history, geography, and philology of Palestine was simply unrivaled. He wrote capaciously on the Bible; indeed, he was the most prolific commentator of his day. In 382 Pope Damasus commissioned him to translate the Bible into Latin. The result was the Vulgate *(editio vulgata)*, a Latin Bible translated from the original languages. To this day, it remains the edition of the Bible that has perhaps been most widely read in the West, where it had tremendous influence on language, liturgy, art, architecture, literature, politics, and theology.

One can hardly make mention of the Latin West without speaking of the importance of the North African tradition. It was there, probably by the end of the second century, that the first translation of the Bible into Latin was made, and we know there were several such translations. Tertullian quotes from these old Latin versions as, in the mid-third century, does Bishop Cyprian of Carthage (d. 258) and as Augustine would as well. A contemporary of Jerome, Tyconius (d. ca. 400) authored the first tract on the theory of interpretation in the West worthy of comparison to Origen's. This *Liber Regularum* (Book of Rules) set out, as its title suggests, a set of principles (seven in all) for interpreting Scripture. One of the most important is that when Scripture speaks of the *head* of the church, it refers also to its *body.* In this way, statements made about Christ could be understood to refer to the church in the present age as well. Tyconius also authored a very influential commentary on the Apocalypse, which shifted the exegetical tradition away from the historic millenarian reading of the book.

Tyconius's influence was nowhere more deeply felt than in the writings of his fellow North African, Augustine of Hippo (354–430). Indeed, the influence of Tyconius on the greatest of Latin doctors has not always been recognized or conceded, because the former was a member of the schismatic Donatist church, which Augustine spent much of his life quite fiercely denouncing. But upon inspection of Augustine's own hermeneutical theory as it is expressed in his classic *On Christian Doctrine,* it will be obvious that Tyconius's influence was profound. It was felt in the wide circulation in the Middle Ages not only of Augustine's book on Christian teaching but of his own *Book of Rules,* both of which were recommended by no less a figure than Cassiodorus (d. 580).

When speaking of Augustine, it is impossible not to mention the decisive influence in his life as well as work of the allegorical method. Indeed, it might easily be said that, but for that method, Augustine might never have been baptized. It was only in the wake of hearing the Old Testament interpreted allegorically by Bishop Ambrose of Milan (ca. 339–97) that Augustine felt ready to convert. Until then, Augustine, nurtured on the classics of Roman literature, had regarded the Old Testament with a feeling bordering on contempt. Allegory enabled him to understand the Hebrew Scriptures in a new way and to harmonize them, as had Ambrose, with the Neoplatonic philosophy on which he had also been nourished. Like Origen, he offered copious guidance on how to treat difficult passages (and his advice is remarkably like Origen's). Augustine insists, as had Irenaeus, Tertullian, and Origen, on the utility of the church's Rule of Faith. But he also adds that all Scripture is to be interpreted in light of the Law of Love, so that *any* interpretation that contributed to the Reign of Charity should command assent. Augustine is also capable of sounding eerily modern, as when, in his *Harmony of the Gospels,* he is prepared to concede that the narratives in the Gospels reflect recorded community memory rather than accurate chronological narrative history. Augustine also acknowledged that Jesus' words were not always recorded verbatim; it was their sense that was communicated accurately to posterity.

The question of how many senses of Scripture there were, and what each meant, achieved authoritative definition at the end of the ancient period in Christianity in the writings of the monk John Cassian (360–435). Most ancient commentators worked with the practical distinction between literal and spiritual senses. Origen had theoretically designated three senses: literal, moral, and spiritual (*On First Principles* 4.2.4), though scrutiny of his surviving commentaries indicates he did not follow this principle slavishly. In his *Conferences,* Cassian became the first to argue that, theoretically, Scripture contained or expressed four senses: literal, allegorical, moral or tropological, and anagogical or eschatological. Eventually, this understanding was versified as follows:

Littera gesta docet, quid credas allegoria,
Moralia quid agas, quo tendas anagogia.

This little couplet basically meant that the literal sense has to do with the history of God's redemptive activity, the allegorical level with articles of belief, the moral with ethical behavior, and the anagogical with one's eternal destiny. Thus, for example, when Jerusalem is mentioned in the Bible, it would refer literally to the earthly city, allegorically to the church, morally to the soul, and anagogically to the heavenly city. Cassian's *Conferences* was one of the few texts recommended in the *Rule of Benedict.* As a consequence, his theory was absorbed in Benedictine cloisters in the early Middle Ages and passed on to interpreters for a millennium. Again, few interpreters applied this principle mechanically; many were content to distinguish in their commentaries between two or sometimes three senses.

When we survey the history of the Catholic use of Scripture in early Christianity, two important truths emerge. First, theology and scriptural interpretation were virtually one and the same activity. At the least, theology invariably began as exegesis. Second, the allegorical method, which the church did not invent, had been appropriated and baptized by it. All Christian interpreters recognized that allegory (or, with the Antiochenes, *theoria*) gave the church access to a meaning that was not frozen in time or fixed. With the allegorical method, the church had inherited, and had brilliantly exploited, a way of making the Scriptures inexhaustible. To it the ancients had bequeathed a means by which, until the modern era, it could make the Scriptures perennially relevant, above all, perhaps, in preaching.

The Medieval Era (ca. 500–1500)

One can hardly mention Benedict and early medieval monasticism without at least noting how central was the role of the Bible in the monastic life. Monastic prayer began with the *lectio divina* (divine reading) of Scripture and continued with meditation upon it. Monks were utterly immersed in the language, imagery, and thought-world of the Scriptures. So often and so carefully did they read and so assiduously ruminate upon certain parts of Scripture (the Psalter, for example) that such texts became a fundamental mark of their spiritual and mental experience. As Jean Leclercq has shown, monastic culture was a profoundly scriptural one. Monastic education was oriented almost exclusively to the ability to read and understand Scripture. In addition, early medieval scholarship on Scripture was produced almost exclusively in monastic scriptoria and by monks. One thinks of the Venerable Bede (ca. 673–735) in Northumbria, Pope Gregory the Great (590–604) in Rome, and a whole succession of eighth- and ninth-century Frankish monks, including Rabanus Maurus, Walafrid Strabo, Alcuin, Haimo, and Remigius of Auxerre, Paschasius Radbertus, to mention only a few of the most accomplished. In short, Catholic scholarship on the Bible took place almost exclusively in the setting of the monastic cloister.

It would be difficult to exaggerate the awe with which such monks beheld the patristic tradition of exegesis. Few would have dared to think of a scriptural book other than *in sensu patrum*—"in the sense of the Fathers." So understood, scholarship was prized not for novelty but for fidelity to the received tradition. Early medieval biblical scholarship was therefore traditionalist and conservative in nature. The early medieval period was, in terms of biblical scholarship, an age of compilation, not innovation. In the eighth and ninth centuries, Frankish biblical scholars produced commentaries that were, by and large, syntheses of venerable authorities. Very few dared personal commentary on the received wisdom of the Fathers. The main objective, particularly in the Carolingian era, was the transmission of patristic extracts (technically known as *florilegia*) that were authentic and otherwise reliable. Such collections are dominated by the Latin fathers, especially by Jerome, Ambrose, Augustine, and Gregory the Great. Such exposure to the Greek fathers (especially Origen) as was communicated to Western readers was achieved, largely, by presentation of the Latin fathers (like Hilary of Poitiers, Ambrose, Jerome, and Gregory) by whom they were influenced.

Most ages in church history can be identified by their interest in some discrete collection of scriptural writings, usually reflecting the theological and ecclesiological interests of the time. In the early Middle Ages, the Scriptures most used and commented were those holding a central role in monastic liturgy and thought and, to a lesser extent, doctrinal theology: the Psalter, the Song of Songs, Genesis, Paul, and Matthew (the one Gospel, curiously, that received widespread commentarial attention in the early Middle Ages). Leclercq has rightly emphasized that, for the entirety of the early Middle Ages, there is a strong and consistent link between the Bible and prayer (private and public) and, indeed, that such a link is *the* common characteristic of the use of the Bible in this period.

One of the great achievements in biblical scholarship in the early Middle Ages was the production of a standard or *Ordinary Gloss (Glossa Ordinaria)* of patristic commentary on the entire Bible. Nonetheless, its origins, authorship, and history of the *Gloss* have long remained obscure. Thanks to the researches of Beryl Smalley and others, we are now better informed about such questions. First of all, none of the *Gloss* was produced in a Carolingian monastic setting—the so-called marginal gloss had long been attributed to the monk Walafrid of Strabo (d. ca. 850)—as had long been presupposed. Instead, it was begun in the cathedral school of Laon in the early twelfth century, at which time it, and the theological scene in Europe, was dominated by the brothers Anselm (d. 1117) and Ralph (d. ca. 1135), though the very earliest glosses on the Bible appeared in the late eighth century in England and Ireland. The former probably glossed the Psalter, Paul, and the Gospel of John; the latter the Gospel of Matthew. Others, including Gilbert the Universal, glossed much of the Hebrew Scriptures, including the Pentateuch. The entire collaborative project was completed no later than the first quarter of the thirteenth century. It usually appeared with the biblical text as a "glossed Bible," with short interlinear comments and longer marginal comments, usually of patristic origin, a form that is similar to contemporary Jewish commentary on the Talmud. Distributed in large numbers from a center in Paris, it was probably the most widely read and influential commentary on the Bible from the time of its widespread circulation ca. 1220 until the seventeenth century.

Over the course of the century that produced these two textbooks, running commentaries on the Bible came more and more to be disrupted by the introduction of theological issues or questions *(quaestiones)*. Eventually, these questions were grouped together and finally broke off from their original commentarial context altogether to form textbooks of doctrinal theology. The classic in this genre is, without doubt, Peter Lombard's *Book of Sentences*. Late in the twelfth century, scholastic masters began lecturing on the Lombard independently of the sacred page *(sacra pagina)*—the Vulgate page that had been established as a set text in the schools. This is a development of some moment. Aside from signaling the growing hegemony of the schools and the eclipse of monastic biblical scholarship and emerging universities in theological discourse, it indicates the beginning of the separation of biblical and theological studies, heretofore conceived as a single discipline.

It was, however, in the famous house of canons of St. Victor in Paris that hermeneutical and exegetical developments of great importance occurred in the twelfth century. In Hugh (d. 1141) and Andrew of St. Victor (d. 1175), the Middle Ages are sometime said to have received, respectively, their own Augustine (the former for his *Didascalicon,* often called a reworking of Augustine's *De Doctrina Christian*) and Jerome (the latter for his immense erudition, knowledge of Hebrew, and concentration on the literal-historical sense). From these men came important new reflections on the primacy and content of the primary or literal sense of Scripture, reflections that would gesture toward the ways in which biblical scholarship would change in the schools and universities and in a time during which Aristotle was being reabsorbed in Western Europe.

Like some of the Antiochenes, Hugh wrote a tract (in his case an imaginative debate) on the relationship of the literal and allegorical sense. There he described the operation of the allegorical sense with considerable precision. It was not, he argued, the language or words of Scripture that expressed the allegorical meaning, but those things to which the words pointed; the figurative meaning of the text, if such it has, belongs to the literal sense. (This was to be an issue taken up, and resolved definitively for Catholic exegesis for centuries, by St. Thomas Aquinas.) It was, he argued, on this spiritual plane or level of exegesis that the unity of Scripture was contained. It could not be on the level of the literal sense, for it was all too plain that the literal sense contradicted itself in scores of places in the Scriptures.

However, Hugh was adamant that the literal sense was of foundational importance for the allegorical sense, and he rebukes unrestrained allegorists with some sarcasm. In his book *De Scripturis,* he observes:

> I wonder how people have the face to boast themselves teachers of allegory, when they do not know the primary meaning of the letter. . . . How do you read Scripture then, if you don't read the letter? Subtract the letter and what is left?

Hugh even dares to deny Christological interpretations of texts that had long received such interpretations. Given his preoccupation with the importance of the literal sense, it is interesting to observe that Hugh was among those exegetes in twelfth-century Europe that were first to have forged ties with the Jewish exegetical community. Hugh was convinced that Jewish exegesis of the Hebrew Scriptures furnished the most literal sense of the text, and for that reason often quoted the great Jewish exegete Rabbi Solomon bar Isaac of Troyes ("Rashi," 1040–1105) as an authoritative guide to the literal sense.

If the Victorine Richard (d. 1173) undertook to refute some of Hugh's ideas, Hugh's promise was, as Beryl Smalley observed, fulfilled in the Victorine Andrew, whose obscurity she did much to overcome and on whose significance she wrote a long chapter in her groundbreaking (if not uncontroversial) book, *The Study of the Bible in the Middle Ages* (finished in 1940), which, as it were, invented the field of the study of medieval exegesis.

Andrew is without question the hero of Smalley's book, and it is because he concentrates on the historical and literal sense to the explicit exclusion of the doctrinal and moral. In this, he was quite aware that he was embarking on something new in the Middle Ages. Or, to put it another way, he saw himself continuing the work of St. Jerome. Of Andrew, Smalley observes, "No western commentator before him had set out to give a purely literal interpretation of the Old Testament." For his access to the literal truth of the Hebrew Scriptures (Andrew commented on the Pentateuch, Joshua, Judges, many of the Prophets, and some of the wisdom literature), he, too, relied on the school of Rashi. Like Hugh, he simply felt that the "Jewish explanation" of the text *was* the literal sense of the text. To the extent that he was preoccupied with establishing the literal sense of Scripture, he made extraordinary and unprecedented use of Jewish exegesis by making contact with the communities most influenced by Rashi.

One of the several other twelfth-century exegetes worthy of mention alongside Hugh of St. Victor, by whom he was influenced, is Peter Comestor or Manducator (d. ca. 1179), dean of the cathedral of Troyes and chancellor of the University of Paris. The name means "Peter the Eater," which he earned for having absorbed all of the Scriptures. His most enduring contribution to the understanding of the Scriptures was a work titled the *Historia scholastica.* This was an epitome (depending on some non-Christian authors, like Josephus) of biblical history from Creation to the events narrated in the Acts of the Apostles. As such, it fulfilled the requirements of Hugh of

St. Victor's *Didascalicon,* which called for a foundational knowledge of biblical history. It also relied heavily (though anonymously) on the commentaries of Andrew and so was in a double sense a child of the great abbey of St. Victor. Like the *Gloss,* it became a standard textbook. Judging from the number of manuscripts and early printed editions made of it, it remained very popular through the fifteenth century.

Another disciple of Andrew, perhaps the finest biblical scholar of the twelfth century, was Stephen Langton (d. 1228). Perhaps his most important contribution to biblical scholarship was the production of a new edition of the Bible. This edition was important because it divided the entire Bible into chapters (ca. 1200); Thomas Gallus (d. 1246) would later divide it into verses. This was the edition that was to become standard at Paris, and, as such, became the one used in the new university setting of the thirteenth century. The early thirteenth century was, among other things, an age in which several aids to biblical study were produced. Once Langton's Bible had been produced, with its chapter references, it was possible to produce a concordance, and indeed a concordance to the Latin of the Vulgate was produced ca. 1235 in the new Dominican priory of St. Jacques in Paris.

It was in the very different monastic setting of southern Italy that the highly innovative exegesis of Joachim of Fiore set exegesis on a radically different path—deplored once by Smalley, an enthusiast for Andrew and literal exegesis, as an attack of "senile dementia" in the spiritual sense, a prime example of the "spiritual sense in decline"—than that recommended by the great Victorines and early friars of Paris. Born in 1135 in Celico, Joachim entered the Benedictine abbey at Corazzo in 1171, of which he became prior, then abbot (ca. 1176–77). Multiple visions at the Cistercian Abbey of Casamari in 1183–84 revealed to him the fullness and harmony *(concordia)* of the Scriptures and the mystery of the Trinity. Convinced that the inner mystery of God's existence as a Trinity of Persons was linked with the structure of history, Joachim, pondering the Scriptures, saw salvation history unfolding in terms of three successive, overlapping ages *(status),* each primarily under the aegis of one of the persons of the Trinity. Thus Joachim postulates a status of the Father, of the Son, and of the Holy Spirit, the last about to dawn.

This intricate theology of history is based on an equally complex hermeneutical theory. For Joachim, one of the major objectives of scriptural exegesis was to demonstrate the numerous literal parallels or concordances *(concordiae)* between Old Testament history and New. These *concordiae* not only shed light on the past but were also capable of revealing the future. The gifted exegete could see in both Testaments (above all in the book of Revelation) sets of concordances, which enabled him not merely to understand the first two *status* more fully but to predict the structure and meaning of the dawning third *status* of history. Joachim's exegesis was to have profound influence not only on the Franciscans of the subsequent century, who saw in Francis a herald in the new age of history just then dawning, but on many exegetes and many secular thinkers down to the twentieth century.

If Bonaventure and other Franciscan exegetes such as Peter Olivi (d. 1298) enthusiastically capitalized on Joachite hermeneutics in their own exegetical works, their Dominican confreres emphatically did not. Probably the greatest early Dominican exegete was the prolific Hugh of St. Cher (d. 1263). Intended to supplement the *Glossa Ordinaria,* his massive *Postillae in Totam Bibliam*—which relied heavily on Stephen Langton and his moralizing exegesis—was almost certainly compiled as the work of a Dominican "team" of exegetes at St. Jacques. Nonetheless, the postilla (or commentary, from the words *post illa* [*verba?*] "after those [scriptural] words"), which was a continuous gloss on every book of the Bible, bore his signature. This postilla would exercise enormous influence on contemporary exegetes (such as Bonaventure and his fellow Dominicans Albert the Great and St. Thomas Aquinas). Hugh and his collaborators also produced a *Correctorium Bibliae*. In this work, alternative readings of the Vulgate were established in an attempt to establish an authoritative text.

Hugh's fellow Dominican Thomas Aquinas is today renowned as the author of the *Summa Theologiae* and the scholastic theologian whose work was declared normative by Pope Leo XIII in 1879. Less well known is that, as part of his duties, first at Cologne, then later at Paris, he was required to lecture on the Bible. The result was a series of commentaries on Job, the Psalter, the Song of Songs, Isaiah, Jeremiah, Lamentations, Matthew, John, and the Pauline letters. Some of these exist as versions edited by Thomas, others in student lecture-notes *(reportationes),* while others still (like the commentary on the Canticum) have been lost. Thomas also produced, at the behest of Pope Urban IV, a continuous gloss on all four Gospels. This *Catena Aurea* (Golden Chain) of mostly patristic excerpts, including an extraordinary number of Greek ones, had influence on commentaries on the Gospels down to the nineteenth century, when it was edited by Cardinal Newman, though it had its greatest impact in the Middle Ages. One of its warmest admirers would be Erasmus.

Though he commented extensively on the Bible, it was probably in the area of theory or hermeneutics that Thomas exercised the profounder influence. Thomas heightened the emphasis, begun among the twelfth-century Victorines, on the primacy of the literal sense. Indeed, he argued that upon its authority alone could a necessary theological argument be constructed *(Summa Theologiae* 1.1.10 *ad 1um).* The literal or first sense is that intended by the author; like Augustine, Thomas agreed that this literal sense could have more than one meaning. Thomas is also clear that the literal sense could include figurative and poetic language. The spiritual sense is threefold—Thomas accepted the traditional medieval division of allegorical, moral, and anagogical spiritual senses. This threefold spiritual sense is based on the literal and presupposes it. It has to do with those spiritual realities signified by things expressed in the literal sense. Only revelation has this property, since the author of holy Scripture is God, who intends this threefold spiritual sense to be expressed by the literal sense and apprehended by the reader. In short, the literal sense for Thomas is the meaning communicated by the words; the spiritual sense is the meaning conveyed by the things *(res)* to which the literal words refer (see *Quodlibetales* 7.16.4).

In a real sense, Thomas's insistence on the primacy of the literal sense and his clear definition of it were applied to the entire Bible by a late-medieval exegete whom many have compared, for the breadth of his work, with Jerome. Whatever the merit of that analogy, the Franciscan Nicholas of Lyra (d. 1349) is without question the dominant biblical exegete of the late Middle Ages and author, in his *Literal Postill on the Whole Bible,* of one of the most impressive works of biblical scholarship in all of ecclesiastical history.

After taking the Franciscan habit in 1300 and studying theology in Paris, Nicholas became Regent Master in Theology there in 1309. In 1322, after having been elected, three years earlier, Minister of the Province of Paris, he began his *Literal Postill,* which he finished in about a decade. From 1333 to 1339, he wrote his *Moral Commentary on the Whole Bible,* a shorter commentary that emphasized the moral and mystical meanings of the text. This was intended as a practical handbook for preachers and teachers. Unlike the postills written under the name of Hugh of St. Cher, these were all composed by Nicholas himself. The *Postilla* was the first biblical commentary to be printed (Rome, 1471–72).

Unlike most contemporary Christian exegetes, Lyra was able to read at least some Hebrew, and he knew the Talmud, the Midrash and the works of Rashi, who influenced him deeply. Lyra's great hermeneutical innovation was his teaching on the "double literal sense" *(duplex sensus literalis),* which held that citations from the Hebrew Scriptures found in the New Testament had two literal meanings. The first and more perfect meaning referred to Christ, the second and less perfect to pre-Christian history.

Lyra's influence was enormous. More than 200 manuscripts of his *Postilla Literalis* exist. Since the late fifteenth century, it has been printed 176 times. It ranks, along with the *Glossa Ordinaria,* the *Sentences* of Peter Lombard and Thomas's *Summa,* as one of the most influential theological works of the Middle Ages. Moreover, some of his commentaries are known to have influenced Luther, at least indirectly, an influence immortalized, with pardonable exaggeration, in a famous early modern couplet: *Si Lyra non lyrasset / Lutherus non saltasset* ("Had Lyra not lyred, Luther would not have danced"). Whatever the degree of his influence on Luther, Lyra did share with the reformer a revulsion for what he took to be the over-allegorization of the Bible and an emphasis on the plain, clear sense of the biblical text, an exegetical emphasis which has caused him to be known as "the clear and plain doctor."

Looking back over a millennium of the use of the Bible in medieval Catholic history, the historian is hindered by the length of the era and the complex use of the Bible from easily summarizing the main developments of the period. Nonetheless, there are certain elements of the use of the Bible, and certain trends in how and in what contexts it was interpreted, that deserve to be underscored. First of all, as we pass from the early to the high Middle Ages, we observe that biblical scholarship becomes more professionalized. Fewer and fewer Benedictine monks rank among great biblical scholars (with the exception of the great Rupert of Deutz, almost none in the twelfth century and following). Biblical scholarship moves from cloister to the schools and universities and their classrooms. It thus becomes less exclusively oriented to prayer and spiritual experience. Dominance of the field passes from the Benedictines to the new school and secular university masters, first at Laon and Paris and then to Dominicans and Franciscan friars at the University of Paris. With this development, emphasis is placed on glossing the entire Bible, often carried out in "teams." (In the late Middle Ages, we witness the reemergence of the virtuoso solo performer—Nicholas of Lyra is the primary example—who himself comments upon the entire Bible.) At the same time, a whole host of aids to Bible study are produced. These include histories of the biblical world and its geography, verbal concordances and editions of the Bible with chapters.

In terms of hermeneutics, we see an increasing emphasis, beginning in the twelfth century, on the literal and historical sense of Scripture, an emphasis reflected in many commentaries in the high and late Middle Ages. With the absorption of Aristotle in the twelfth and thirteenth centuries, the nature of each sense, and specifically how the literal is distinguished from the spiritual, received more precise definition. This hermeneutical project also boosted the ascendancy of the literal sense. Indeed, although Henri de Lubac is surely correct to insist that medieval authors never relinquished the allegorical sense to the extent argued by Smalley—it enjoyed something of a renaissance in the late Middle Ages—it was perhaps in the high- and late-medieval emphasis on the primacy of the literal sense of Scripture that, in principle, had the most profound effect on the sixteenth-century reformers, even if, in the application of that principle, they came to radically different exegetical conclusions than their Catholic forerunners. Their efforts to translate the Bible into the vernacular made reflection on the literal sense not just desirable but imperative.

The Early Modern Period (ca. 1500–1650)

Dominating the early medieval period and contemporaneous with the reformer Martin Luther is the outstanding biblical humanist Erasmus (d. 1536). In Erasmus, we see the union of superior classical learning, the desire to reform the church by learning, and excellent biblical scholarship. His greatest contribution to the use of the Bible was his publication of the first Greek critical edition in 1516. This was a two-columned work, which contained not only the Greek New Testament but Erasmus's own Latin translation of the Greek (which corrected many perceived errors of Jerome), as well as extensive annotations at the back of the edition. For the Greek edition, Erasmus used five manuscripts he had discovered in Basel, relying especially on two of them. In later editions, his Latin translation became more and more different than Jerome's. Some of his changes, which he thought reflected the sense of the Greek more precisely, were to undermine key Catholic dogma, especially sacramental claims. For example, where Jerome translated Matthew 4:17 *"poenitentiam agite"* (do penance), Erasmus translated it simply as "repent." This seemed to subvert the biblical foundation for the sacrament of penance. Other translations would seem to undermine other key elements of Catholic doctrine, including aspects of Mariology. Luther would make use of the 1519 edition of Erasmus's edition of the New Testament for his German translation (1522), as Tyndale would for his English version (1525). It would also serve, indirectly, as the basis for the King James version (1611) and the Textus Receptus (1633). Hundreds of commentators, well into the seventeenth century, would use his edition as well.

Erasmus also wrote a *Paraphrase on Romans*, published at virtually the same time (1517)

Luther would arrive at his own revolutionary understanding of that book. For the next seven years, he wrote paraphrases of every other book of the New Testament, save the Apocalypse. These would have special influence on the Swiss reformers. In 1547 they were placed in every parish in England and in the library of every aspiring divine. Together with the enormous influence of his edition, they easily made Erasmus the most influential Catholic biblical scholar of the early sixteenth century.

One of Luther's great theological opponents, Thomas de Vio, Cardinal Cajetan (1469–1534), certainly agreed with the Reformer and with Erasmus that reliable exegesis depended on the availability of good Hebrew and Greek texts. Although Cajetan is probably best known for his anti-Lutheran polemics and as a great admirer of Thomas (his is the commentary on the Angelic Doctor that appears in the authoritative Leonine edition of Thomas's works), he was also an accomplished exegete. Indeed, shortly after engaging in examinations of Luther's writings, he began dedicating himself to biblical translation and interpretation, producing, finally, commentaries on the Pentateuch, the historical books of the Hebrew Bible, Job, Ecclesiasticus, the Gospels, and the Epistles. Similarly, Jacopo Sadoleto, while known primarily as an opponent of Calvin, was an accomplished humanist, who also dedicated much of his life to biblical interpretation. He produced commentaries on Paul, the Gospels, and Acts. In the middle of the sixteenth century Isidorus Clarius (d. 1555) produced a revision of the Vulgate New Testament on the basis of his translation from the Greek.

The status and the authority of the Vulgate was one of the issues taken up at the Council of Trent (1545–63). At the council, it was decreed that the Vulgate was authoritative for dogma. The reason for making it so was explicitly not its proximity to the original sense of the Hebrew and Greek Scriptures but, rather, that it had been normatively so used for a millennium. Against the notion that any individual could interpret the Scripture, Trent explicitly declared:

> No one, relying on his own skill, shall, in matters of faith and of morals pertaining to the edification of the structure of Christian doctrine, wresting the sacred Scripture to his own senses, presume to interpret the said sacred Scripture contrary to that sense which holy mother church, whose it is to judge the true sense and interpretation of the holy Scriptures, has held and does hold.

It will be perceived that, again, this is in effect a reassertion of the ancient authoritative principle found in the writings of Irenaeus. Reacting against the reformed emphasis on "scripture alone" *(sola scriptura),* Trent defined *both* Scripture *and* tradition as sources of revelation to be received *pari affectu*—i.e., with the same reverence. This phrasing leaves it ambiguous whether the Scriptures, presumed of course to have a divine author, were a higher and more authoritative form of revelation than the writings included under the rubric "tradition."

Trent is thus largely conservative and backward-looking in its main dogmatic decrees on Scripture and interpretation. But not all Catholics in the sixteenth century were looking backward. The Catholic exegete in the sixteenth century who most anticipates modern interpretive concerns is undoubtedly Sixtus of Siena *(Senensis)* (d. 1569). A convert from Judaism, Sixtus brilliantly postulated, in a guide to the Bible entitled *Bibliotheca Sancta,* that the Psalter had multiple authors and in other ways foreshadowed the insights of modern biblical criticism.

Still, it must be conceded that Sixtus was something of an exception. Indeed, while much Catholic exegesis was absorbed in polemic with Reformed exegetes, it still shared premodern assumptions with them. Both Protestant and Catholic exegetes, however radically they differed in their dogmatic interpretation of Scriptures, shared certain crucial assumptions. Both agreed that the Scriptures were inerrant; that they were inspired; that they were heaven-sent; that revelation did not change or develop and, above all, that the Scriptures were not influenced by the cultural or historical matrices in which they were produced. At the end of the period, however, Catholic exegesis began to point to developments that would revolutionize our understanding of the original meaning of the Scriptures.

The Emergence and Development of Modern Catholic Biblical Criticism (1650–1943)

Probably no Catholic exegete so anticipated the discoveries of modern Catholic biblical criticism as Richard Simon (1638–1712). Originally a member of the French Congregation of the Oratory, Simon—like many Europeans writing under the influence of rationalistic or empirical movements and scientific discoveries, which would revolutionize Western thought in the Enlightenment—published a pathbreaking three-volume book, *Historical Criticism of the Old Testament* (1678). Simon was an immensely learned man; he knew rabbinic as well as patristic literature, and he was an accomplished patrologist. Among other things, he denied that the Pentateuch had been authored only by Moses; in fact, he maintained that Moses kept some sort of notes or annals that were later worked up by another author. Simon also argued that oral traditions usually precede their codification in written form—a crucial insight all but ignored then. Eleven years later, he followed up this daring study with a similarly bold examination of the New Testament. For these studies he paid a dear price. He felt he had to leave the Congregation on the publication of his first book. In addition, his books were condemned by the Parliament of Paris; others of his writings were later attacked by no less a figure than Louis XIV, and Jacques-Benigne Bossuet (1627–1704) was among his fiercest critics. In 1682, Simon's study of the Old Testament was placed on the Index, owing to the influence of Bossuet and his former Congregation. Nonetheless, it would be translated into English the same year and later into German. A copy of it was eventually discovered in the library of Friedrich Schleiermacher (1768–1834).

Simon's work was perfectly illustrative of the ways in which historical criticism would threaten cherished, historic dogmatic assumptions, and its condemnation a hint of how the new criticism would be received in ecclesiastical circles. For nearly two centuries after the death of Simon, Catholic biblical scholarship felt content to ignore Simon's insights. These were centuries of desiccation and dreariness in Catholic biblical scholarship practically unprecedented. Even when Julius Wellhausen (1844–1916) masterfully set out his documentary theory, many Catholic exegetes remained in a state of siege, rejecting the theory because of the rationalistic and empirical assumptions that underlay it.

In this gloomy context, the Dominican M.-J. Lagrange (1855–1938) stands out as a shining example of exegetical vigor and enlightenment. In 1890 Lagrange founded the École Biblique in Jerusalem in order to encourage analysis of the word of God with the assistance of the historical-critical method. Two years later, he founded the first important journal in Catholic biblical studies, *Revue biblique*. At a Catholic conference in Fribourg in 1897, he urged his fellow Catholic biblical scholars to take more seriously than they heretofore had the Pentateuchal criticism. On this question, he felt, the historical evidence had to trump the literary tradition. In 1902 he started an important series of biblical commentaries titled *Etudes bibliques*. His *Historical Criticism and the Old Testament* (1905) championed the use of the historical method. In all of these endeavors, Lagrange strove to demonstrate that the historical-critical method was not necessarily destructive of immutable truth of the Catholic faith. In addition, he did pioneering work on the study of biblical genres and forms.

Not surprisingly, Lagrange failed to convince everyone that the historical-critical enterprise was compatible with the maintenance of historic dogma, and he did not emerge unscathed. After a warning from the Sacred Congregation, he turned his attention to the New Testament. Meanwhile, Pius X established the Pontifical Biblical Institute as a rival to the Ecole, and he removed Lagrange from his position there. Nonetheless, Lagrange's legacy certainly lives on, not least of all in the continuing vitality of Catholic biblical study at the École Biblique.

Shortly after Lagrange founded the École Biblique, Pope Leo XIII, who had seemed once to express the opinion that the higher criticism and Catholic dogma were compatible, issued the encyclical *Providentissimus Deus* (1893), which left a very different impression. In that encyclical, Leo demanded that the Vulgate version be used, though he allowed that other versions ought not to be neglected. He also argued that a biblical text could not contradict the sense given it by the magisterium or by the unanimous consent of the fathers, and no exegete was allowed to interpret the text so as to contradict church dogma. In a very real sense, this is again simply a modern reassertion of the ancient principle of authoritative interpretation, heard expressed in the second century by Irenaeus, that the supreme arbiter of interpretation is the church's doctrine as taught by the magisterial authority.

No Catholic interpreter of Scripture in the twentieth century ran so directly against the grain of this idea than the French biblical critic and "Modernist" Alfred Loisy (1857–1940). Loisy was a talented philologist and interpreter who taught Scripture at the Institut Catholique in Paris from 1884 to 1893. He fully accepted the methods, insights, and implications of the historical-critical method. In 1902 he wrote his classic book, *The Gospel and the Church.* In it, he concluded that many New Testament texts were ahistorical and were, in fact, produced by the early church. He dismissed the typological method and denied that the church developed in a way that Jesus could have foreseen. In later works, he sharply distinguished between the Jesus recoverable by historical method and the Christ known by faith, and argued that Jesus was unconscious of his divinity.

By the time Loisy had published these works, he had been dismissed from the Catholic Institute. More severe retribution was to follow. In 1907 his "errors" were condemned by the Holy Office in its encyclical *Lamentabili.* In the following year, Pius X issued the decree *Pascendi dominici gregis,* which condemned sixty-five "Modernist" propositions. Many of these were from Loisy's work on the New Testament (or were epitomes, more or less tendentious, of his positions). *Pascendi* denied that the authority of the church was incompetent to judge the meaning of Scripture; that the exegete could or should ignore the supernatural origin of the Bible; and that the Scriptures contained error. Classically, it denied the proposition that:

> No chapter of scripture from the beginning of Genesis to the end of Revelation contains a teaching absolutely identical with that which the church sets forth on the same subject; and consequently no chapter of scripture has the same meaning for the critic as for the theologian (Proposition 61).

Not surprisingly, Loisy was excommunicated. Still, he had identified a problem that still awaits satisfactory resolution: the relationship of the truth discovered by the exegete to the dogmatic truth proclaimed magisterially by the church. Even if many Catholic exegetes have not wanted to go as far as Loisy theoretically, none of any repute has denied the reality, or the problem, of the gap he so clearly perceived. The debate has centered, rather, on the dimensions of the gap and the possibility and peril of attempting to bridge it.

The Coming of Age of Catholic Biblical Scholarship (1943–2000)

Catholic biblical scholarship, which in some sense had been plunged into a dark age with these papal pronouncements, was, in 1943 reliberated to do its work by another papal encyclical, Pope Pius XII's *Divino Afflante Spiritu.* Issued on the fiftieth anniversary of *Providentissimus Deus,* it announced its intentions to "ratify" what had been "wisely laid down" by Leo XIII. In fact, it reverses or radically recasts much of what he had to say. Where, for example, Leo had designated the Vulgate the authoritative text, Pius commanded scholars to translate and explain the original Hebrew and Greek texts. Much emphasis was laid upon determining the *literary form* the human author employed. Pius also encouraged scholars, as Leo emphatically did not, to examine the original intention and circumstances of the authors of Scripture and thus to understand the context in which they wrote. Remarkably, Pius also encouraged scholars to harmonize their conclusions with those of the profane sciences.

Even at the time, Catholic scholars recognized that *Divino Afflante Spiritu* had opened up a new epoch in the Catholic interpretation of the Bible, and its publication was hailed by the editors of *Revue biblique.* Ironically, Pius XII, who has recently been excoriated by some for his passivity in the face of the Holocaust, has been lionized by scholars as a grand patron of Catholic biblical studies. It was his pontificate that marked an about-face in Catholic attitudes toward the Bible in the twentieth century, so that so sensible an authority as Raymond Brown could once observe that *Divino Afflante* represented the Catholic Magna Charta for progress in biblical study.

Nonetheless, a renewed atmosphere of chill prevailed in Rome in the wake of Pius's death in 1958, as several professors were removed from their teaching office at the Pontifical Biblical Institute for displeasure with their historical conclusions. They were restored to their positions, however, under John XXIII and Paul VI, as the warming winds of *aggiornamento* (modernization) swept through Rome during the Second Vatican Council. The Council's dogmatic constitution on revelation (*Dei Verbum,* November 18, 1965) takes a largely positive, if cautious, attitude (reflective of the fact that it went through multiple revisions and had to reflect diplomatic compromise) toward the program laid out by Pius XII.

The efflorescence of Catholic biblical scholarship in the forty years since the Council is so great as to defeat any attempt to summarize it easily. Still, a number of crucial developments may be noted. First of all, since the Council, Protestant and Catholic interpretations of the Scriptures have been methodologically indistinguishable. Roman Catholic scholarship has accepted modern biblical criticism. Having accepted modern approaches, Roman Catholics have now produced some of the most accomplished biblical scholars in the world. As the center of gravity in biblical scholarship has shifted from the European Continent to North American, and as an increasing number of women have entered the academy since the Council, the number of outstanding Catholic women biblical scholars who have trained or who teach in the United States has soared. Adela Yarbro Collings, Margaret Mitchell, Carolyn Osiek, Pheme Perkins, and Elizabeth Schüssler-Fiorenza, to mention only a few, all have made signal contributions to the field which are recognized worldwide. Their male counterparts—among others, R. E. Brown, J. Collins, J. Donahue, J. Fitzmeyer, D. Harrington, J. Meier, D. Senior—rank at the top of their field internationally and belong to, and in many cases have led, the most important international societies of biblical studies (e.g., Society of Biblical Literature). In addition, numerous new approaches—literary-critical, liberation, feminist, structural, rhetorical, social-scientific—have given us new insight into the original meaning of the Scriptures and the communities to which they were addressed. Meanwhile, the "search for the historical Jesus" seems to have lost none of its vigor, and the renowned "Jesus seminar" includes a number of important Catholic participants, including John Dominic Crossan.

The overall picture, then, since Vatican II has been an overwhelmingly positive one. It will be left to twenty-first-century Catholic interpreters to address three questions, which the Catholic acceptance of modern biblical approaches has generated or made more acute. First, to what extent do new approaches involve retrojection of modern concerns and imperatives, legitimate in themselves, into the ancient biblical texts? Second, modern biblical criticism has, for those with ears to hear, only widened the gap between historical analysis of the biblical text and the historic dogmatic claims of the church. Some eminent biblical scholars, such as R. E. Brown, have heroically attempted to bridge that gap, but the results have been mixed and not inevitably convincing. How and even if the Bible and theology can be brought together is a question that, it must be admitted, has yet to receive an authentically convincing Catholic response. Finally, once the original, contextual, historical meaning of the text has been by and large established, what is left for the exegete or even the ordinary readers of Scripture? As we have seen, for the ancients and medievals, that was merely the first job of the interpreter. But we live now in an age in which the practice of allegoresis and the Platonic assumptions on which it rested have lost credibility. Few have any desire to repristinate the allegorical method. Yet the postallegorical questions linger: does the biblical text have any genuine meaning beyond or above that established by historical analysis and allied disciplines? If so how is it established and verified? Through most of the two millennia surveyed in this article, Catholic exegetes could answer those questions with confidence. Part of the pathos in the otherwise happy acceptance in Catholic biblical scholarship in the late twentieth century is that Catholic exegetes no longer know how, or even if, those questions can be answered.

THE CHALLENGES OF BIBLICAL TRANSLATION

RONALD D. WITHERUP, S.S.

For the average person in the pew, the need for new biblical translations can be bewildering. "Why do we need *new* translations?" or "What translation is the best one?" are common questions. The task of biblical translation is, however, quite complicated. There is no one biblical translation that is the best and serves all purposes equally. The translation used in this Study Bible is the *New American Bible* (revised), and special attention will be given to it. But first, one should have a general overview of the challenges posed by translating the Bible into modern English.

Presuppositions

The need for biblical translation should be self-evident. The Bible has come down to us in ancient Hebrew, Aramaic, and Greek, languages that few but scholars can use today. The Bible itself witnesses to the necessity of translation. After the Babylonian exile (sixth century BC), when the Jews dispersed throughout the ancient world and began to lose command of their native Hebrew tongue, the need arose to produce a translation of their Hebrew Bible into the vernacular of the empire, which at the time was Greek. Thus was produced one of the great translations of all time, the Septuagint (LXX), which had a major influence on the writers of the New Testament. Without translation, many of the traditions of Israel may have been lost over time, as the Jewish people struggled to retain their identity in the midst of the multiple influences of the Greco-Roman world.

No translation is perfect, however. Scholars frequently quote the adage that every translation is an interpretation. There is no such thing as a purely objective translation, yet there are some guiding presuppositions that modern translators acknowledge. The following list of five orients the discussion.

1. Language is a living reality. By nature it changes with usage and experience. No translation stands forever. The following quotation from Ronald Knox, one of the great translators of the Bible into English, affirms this reality:

> Words are living things, full of shades of meaning, full of associations; and, what is more, they are apt to change their significance from one generation to the next. The translator who understands his job feels, constantly, like Alice in Wonderland trying to play croquet with flamingoes for mallets and hedgehogs for balls; words are for ever eluding his grasp. (*The Trials of a Translator* [New York: Sheed & Ward, 1949] 13)

Because living languages change, translations—even of ancient texts—must take this growth into account.

2. The task of translating from one language to another involves primarily two interrelated values: (*a*) preserving faithfully the meaning of the original text, and (*b*) enunciating the original text in clearly understood terms of the receptor language. Generally, the one cannot take absolute precedence over the other because this can lead to distorted translation. A literal translation could, for instance, lead to a total misreading of the original text because the *words* were translated but not the *meaning*. Fidelity to the original might well require a less literal translation in the receptor language. One must also consider the range of meaning of words in both the original and receptor languages.

A related value in the task of translation is the need to preserve in the receptor language as much as possible the form and structure of the original. Poetic and narrative forms are quite different, for example, and require separate attention. Literary form and genre is as important for translation as the actual words. Some might approach this task more loosely than others, since every language employs unique formal conventions that may or may not appear in other languages. Hebrew, for instance, has certain tendencies for repetition and simple, staccato expressions that, when translated literally into English, can seem stilted. The careful translator attempts to bridge this gap in a way that respects the linguistic uniqueness of both languages.

3. In the recent past there has been a tendency to bifurcate the task of translation into two categories: (*a*) formal equivalence (word-for-word), and (*b*) dynamic equivalence (thought-for-thought). The first is the more literal style of translation in which each word is produced as nearly as possible to preserve both the sense and the form of the original. The second approach translates more fluidly, not by replicating words and form but by conveying the *meaning* of the original in the proper form of the receptor language (that is, thought-for-thought rather than word-for-word). A third category not included in this twofold division is commonly called a *paraphrase*. This is not a translation as such but a total rephrasing of the text. It is strongly interpretive.

Recent translation theory has recognized that this duality can be misleading. Instead, translation is better viewed as a continuum ranging from a formal, one-to-one literal translation on one end to a totally free form translation or paraphrase on the other, with a range of options in between. This continuum allows for many more diverse approaches to biblical translation, which are in fact seen in the wide variety of English translations currently available. It also recognizes that the complexity of biblical translation requires more than a choice between two mutually exclusive opposites.

4. Every translation involves some interpretative moves, even if the goal is to capture as accurately as possible the original intention of the author of the text. If this principle is acknowledged, then it must be seen that not even a literal word-for-word translation constitutes the same reality as the source text. As Eugene A. Nida, a notable Bible translator, indicates, translation always involves three realities: (*a*) loss of information; (*b*) addition of information; and (*c*) alteration of information ("Principles of Translation as Exemplified by Bible Translating," in *On Translation* [Reuben A. Brower, ed.; NY: Oxford University, 1966], 13). Words in any given language have a multiplicity of meanings and shades of nuance that do not permit one-to-one correspondence into other languages. Thus, fidelity to a biblical text does not necessarily involve an overly literal approach. This is particularly true of idioms. By their very nature idioms cannot generally be translated in literal fashion but must be compared to an appropriate, corresponding idiom in the receptor language.

The Pontifical Biblical Commission, an international body of professional consultants who provide expert advice to the Congregation for the Doctrine of the Faith in Rome, reinforces this point.

> The literal sense is not to be confused with the "literalist" sense to which fundamentalists are attached. It is not sufficient to translate a text word for word in order to obtain its literal sense. One must understand the text according to the literary conventions of the time. When a text is metaphorical, its literal sense is not that which flows immediately from a word to word translation (e.g., "Let your loins be girt": Lk 12, 35), but that which corresponds to the metaphorical use of these terms ("Be ready for action"). (*The Interpretation of the Bible in the Church* [Boston: St. Paul Books & Media, 1993], 82)

5. Translation must also take into account the influence of culture. This is a controversial point. Some believe that only a literal, word-for-word, translation is authentic to the original text. This position, however, denies that the value of all translation is to communicate faithfully the sense of the text in other cultures and contexts. If fidelity to the original text is always viewed as the ultimate value, serious mistranslation can occur. One need only ask the experience of expert Bible translators who have undertaken the task of translating biblical texts for very foreign cultures (African, Asian, indigenous peoples, etc.) to know how serious this challenge is. For example, one cannot utilize properly the biblical image of

sheep and goats and shepherds in a culture that only has experience of cattle, as in the case of some African tribes. The culture(s) represented in the biblical text are not the only ones that must be respected if the Word of God is to be communicated in modern contexts.

Again, the Pontifical Biblical Commission emphasized this point when they wrote:

> A translation, of course, is always more than a simple transcription of the original text. The passage from one language to another necessarily involves a change of cultural context: concepts are not identical and symbols have a different meaning, for they come up against other traditions of thought and other ways of life. (*The Interpretation of the Bible in the Church,* 122)

Similarly, Pope John Paul II, in an Italian address to the United Bible Societies (November 26, 2001), spoke of a threefold requirement for translators.

> A good translation is based on the three pillars that must contemporaneously support the entire work. First, there must be a deep knowledge of the language and the cultural world at the point of origin. Next, there must be a good familiarity with the language and cultural context at the point where the work will arrive. Lastly, to crown the work with success, there must be an adequate mastery of the contents and meaning of what one is translating.

Taking into account at least these five presuppositions helps to see the complexity of the translation process. It also implies that the act of translation is as much an art as it is a science. Balancing the different factors and remaining true to both the original and receptor languages and cultures is an enormous challenge.

Multiple Translations

The availability of so many modern English translations can be confusing to people. How does one choose? There are, in fact, different goals for different translations. Some are intentionally directed to a specific denominational audience, be it Catholic, mainstream Protestant, evangelical, Orthodox, or fundamentalist. Some are intended for private study, others for public reading or worship services. Many modern English translations are available in Catholic editions; they purposefully include the Old Testament apocrypha, which are often excluded from Protestant editions of the Bible.

The table below and opposite lays out some of the choices among the most well known contemporary English translations.

Now we will take a closer look at some differences of approach among these translations.

Mark 2:1 narrates Jesus' return to his hometown. The NAB translates: "When Jesus returned to Capernaum after some days, it became known that he was *at home.*" The italicized phrase literally reads "in (the) house" (e.g., NJB), but most translations use the expression "at home" (RSV, NRSV, NIV). The NLT pro-

Translation, Date	Brief Description	Sample Text: Ps 86:14
New American Bible (NAB) 1970 (Revised New Testament, 1986; Psalms, 1991)	The basic American Catholic translation intended for study, prayer, and use in liturgy; uses modern American English with an attempt to balance literal and thought-for-thought translation suitable for oral proclamation as well as private reading	O God, the arrogant have risen against me; a ruthless band has sought my life; to you they pay no heed.
New Revised Standard Version (NRSV) 1989	Based upon the classic Revised Standard Version (RSV), which remains a good literal translation but with sensitivity to inclusive language; uses modern idiomatic English intended for a broad appeal	O God, the insolent rise up against me; a band of ruffians seeks my life, and they do not set you before them.

Translation, Date	Brief Description	Sample Text: Ps 86:14
New International Version (NIV) 1984	Intended for broad ecumenical appeal; attempts a balance between literal and thought-for-thought translation	The arrogant are attacking me, O God; a band of ruthless men seeks my life—men without regard for you.
New Jerusalem Bible (NJB) 1985, 1990	A more poetic translation from a French edition, noted for its extensive explanatory footnotes and some sensitivity to gender-inclusive language issues	Arrogant men, God, are rising up against me, a brutal gang is after my life, in their scheme of things you have no place.
Revised English Bible (REB) 1989	A modern English version utilizing spellings and idioms of English common to the United Kingdom (Great Britain, etc.)	Violent men rise to attack me, a band of ruthless men seeks my life; they give no thought to you, my God.
New Living Translation (NLT) 1996, 2004	A thorough revision of an earlier paraphrase, The Living Bible (TLB), but now based upon a translation from the original languages; leans toward explanatory translations of ambiguous passages	O God, insolent people rise up against me; a violent gang is trying to kill me. You mean nothing to them.
Contemporary English Version (CEV) 1995	Uses simple, modern, colloquial American English intended for the broadest American audience, especially young people	Proud and violent enemies, who don't care about you, have ganged up to attack and kill me.
New King James Version (NKJV) 1982	Based upon the traditional King James Version (1611) but with some refinement of the antiquated Elizabethan language; largely retains the structure and some familiar terms of seventeenth-century English	O God, the proud have risen against me, And a mob of violent *men* have sought my life, And have not set You before them.
New American Standard Bible (NASB) 1997	An updated edition of a very literal and conservative translation in contemporary English, aimed primarily at evangelical Christians	O God, arrogant men have risen up against me, And a band of violent men have sought my life, And they have not set You before them.
NET Bible (NET) 1996–2003	A totally new concept in Bible translation, making use of the Internet (www.netbible.com) and allowing for frequent changes in translation and extensive explanatory notes as new information emerges; uses contemporary American English	O God, arrogant men attack me; a gang of ruthless men, who do not respect you, seek my life.

vides a freer translation: "When Jesus returned to Capernaum several days later, the news spread quickly that he was back home."

The Greek text of Mark 2:19 uses an expression that is an obvious Hebraism, namely, "sons of the wedding hall." Virtually all translations recognize that this is an idiom that cannot be accurately translated in literal fashion. There is a divergence in the terms that are used, however. Some use "wedding guests" (RSV, NRSV, NAB, RSV, NLT, NET), while others use "the bridegroom's attendants" (e.g., NJB).

More serious issues arise when the text is somewhat ambiguous. Hebrews 12:2 provides an example. Many translations follow the RSV: "looking to Jesus the pioneer and perfecter of *our faith. . . ,*" assuming that the text refers to the faith of believers (e.g., NRSV, NJB, NIV, NLT, NET). However, the context indicates that Jesus' faith is most likely the object of attention in the text; the modifier "our" is not found in the Greek text. Thus the NAB translation preserves the ambiguity of the text: "keeping our eyes fixed on Jesus, the leader and perfecter *of faith.*" It is left to the reader to decide whether our faith or Jesus' faith is intended. An earlier version of the NLT read: "Keeping our eyes on Jesus, on whom our faith depends from start to finish." This is overly interpretive and exceeds the import of the text. The revised NLT reads: "Jesus, the champion who initiates and perfects our faith."

At times a more literal translation whose meaning is obscure is best left literally, even when it is universally recognized as a saying whose meaning is not intended to be taken literally. An example is found in Romans: "if your enemy is hungry, feed him; if he is thirsty, give him something to drink; for by so doing you will *heap burning coals upon his head*" (Rom 12:20 NAB; cf. RSV, NRSV, NJB, NET). The saying is a proverb from the Old Testament (Prv 25: 21–22), the exact meaning of which has been debated through history. The text is not likely meant to be taken literally to pour live coals on someone's head. Rather, it appears to be an expression of bringing shame or humiliation to one's enemy by paradoxically providing a kindness.

This is the way the NLT takes the passage, which it renders: "Instead, 'If your enemies are hungry, feed them. If they are thirsty, give them something to drink. In doing this, you will heap burning coals of shame on their heads.' " While this interpretive translation may communicate the meaning of the text, this is not self-evident from the passage. Since Patristic times, various interpretations of the passage have been proposed from which one can choose an acceptable option. Thus the majority of translations simply retain the reference to burning coals. Footnotes, commentaries, or study Bibles can then offer a variety of interpretations that lie beyond the scope of the translation itself.

The Case of Inclusive Language

In the late twentieth century modern English translations have had to confront a special translating challenge that became a politically charged issue, namely, the question of "inclusive language."

Inclusive language means language that includes rather than excludes. It is usually identified with feminist concerns that traditional English translations of the Bible exhibit a vocabulary that is too patriarchally oriented and excludes the viewpoint of women. Thus, some speak of "gender-inclusive language," but the concept of inclusive language, as we will see below, actually is not restricted to feminist concerns. Yet we must acknowledge that the Bible grew out of a patriarchal culture, one in which men were dominant and women generally secondary. Thus it is not surprising to find a dominant male perspective expressed in biblical texts.

Inclusive language is divided into two categories, "horizontal inclusive language" (i.e., concerned with human beings) or "vertical inclusive language" (i.e., language about God). Bible translators have had to deal with this question directly. The NAB, for instance, has taken the stance that moderate attention to horizontal inclusive language is appropriate for a contemporary English translation. Where possible the translators avoid using the words *man* or *mankind* where the text is meant to embrace all human beings, because these terms have become increasingly more restrictive in modern English than in previous eras. Also, the literal term *sons of Israel* (an idiomatic Hebrew expression) is translated *Israelites,* since that is what the term means in most contexts. When the Pauline letters address the audience as "brothers" (Greek *adelphoi),* the NRSV utilizes the translation "brothers and sisters" (e.g., Rom 1:13; 7:1; 1 Cor 1:10; etc.) because the word clearly applies to the entire community Paul is addressing. The NAB recognizes the principle (see footnote for Rom 1:13) but has chosen to stick with the literal translation "brothers" in deference to convention. When the NAB translation was adapted for use in Roman Catholic lectionary, however, the more inclusive "brothers and sisters" has been employed where appropriate.

While the expression "inclusive language" is most frequently tied to feminist sensitivities, it has also been applied to other categories. Some translators, for instance, object to traditional expressions like "the lame" or "the blind" because they overly emphasize the handicap of an individual or class of people rather than their human dignity. They propose alternative translations like "the one who is lame" or "the one whose sight is impaired." A similar concern has arisen regarding the biblical contrasts between light and darkness (Mt 10:27), day and night (Jn 11: 9–10; 1 Thes 5:5), or white and black (Ps 51:9, "whiter than snow"), because such contrasts allegedly denigrate people of color. An even more aggressive position is taken regarding a biblical title like "the Son of Man," which has Christological significance (e.g., Mk 10:45; Jn 8:28). They translate the phrase "child of the human one," an odd and clumsy translation that ignores the Christological implications of the title. (See *New Testament and Psalms: An Inclusive Language Version* [New York: Oxford University Press, 1989].) Most translators view such attempts as excesses that are overly intrusive in the translation process. These are examples of the imbalance of allowing modern cultural concerns to dictate absolutely how to communicate ancient texts. Such instances do not respect the integrity of the biblical text.

The principle of inclusivity has also been applied to biblical language about God (e.g., vertical inclusive language). Some object to the overabundance of masculine terminology for God in the Bible, although it is an understandable outgrowth of a patriarchal culture. They attempt to counteract this by avoiding the masculine pronouns *he* or *him* or by repeating the word *God* frequently or designing other circumlocutions for the Deity. Theologically, since God is a spirit and is neither male nor female, biblical language about God, in fact, has its limitations. As the *Catechism of the Catholic Church* points out:

> We must therefore continually purify our language of everything in it that is limited, image-bound or imperfect, if we are not to confuse our image of God—"the inexpressible, the incomprehensible, the invisible, the ungraspable"—with our human representations. Our human words always fall short of the mystery of God. (#42)

To refer to God as "he" or to call God a rock or a fortress (2 Sm 22:2; Ps 18:3), a shepherd (Ps 23:1; 80:1), etc., is to use metaphorical and analogous language to describe how God acts toward people or how we experience God. These are not literal descriptions of God's identity. There are also feminine images for God in the Bible that should be remembered and that can provide some counterbalance to the predominance of masculine images (e.g., the image of God as a woman in labor [Is 46:3–4] or as a tender mother [Is 49:15; 66:13]).

Another aspect of inclusive language is the limitation of English when utilizing singular forms of pronouns. Unlike some languages (e.g., French or Spanish), English has a limited form of third-person pronouns. For example, in French the same expression *"sa croix"* (or Spanish *"su cruz"*) can mean *his* or *her* cross, depending upon who is envisioned as the antecedent. But English requires the use of *both* modifying pronouns if one wants to apply the expression to men and women alike.

Let's take a biblical example. Jesus' saying about the necessity of taking up one's cross (Mt 10:38) obviously applies to all Jesus' disciples, male and female. The NAB translates: *"whoever* does not take up *his cross* and follow after me is not worthy of me." The NRSV tries to make the saying more inclusive by deleting the modifying pronoun: *"whoever* does not take up *the cross* and follow me is not worthy of me." This solution, however, has the unfortunate side effect of making it seem that each disciple is to take up Jesus' cross rather than his or her own cross. The NLT avoids the problem by transposing the saying into second person: "If *you* refuse to take up *your cross* and follow me, *you* are not worthy of being mine."

Another example is the translation of Jesus' famous saying in Matthew 6:24, which also applies to all followers of Jesus: *"No one* can serve two masters. *He* will either hate one and love the other, or be devoted to one and despise the other. You cannot serve God and mammon." The NRSV attempts to solve the more restrictive phrasing by inserting an implied word that is not literally present in the biblical text: "*No one* can serve two masters; for *a slave* will either hate the one and love the other, or be devoted to the one and despise the other. You cannot serve God and wealth." One also notes in this latter example the difference between the NAB's retention of the original word *mammon*—an Aramaic or Hebrew word for money or goods—and the NRSV's *wealth,* which presumably is intended to be better understood by a broad audience (cf. also NJB, NIV).

In short, English poses a peculiar problem for inclusivity that can be quite vexing for translators who wish to preserve the meaning of the original text and to remain sensitive to modern concerns. While this is not the only contemporary issue affecting biblical translation theory, it has become one of the more controversial.

Translation and Interpretation

It was noted above that all translations are essentially an interpretation. Regardless of how objective translators attempt to be, biases exist that can enter into the process. This accounts for the oft-quoted Italian saying attributed to Dante, "*Traduttore traditore*" (A translator is a traitor). Inevitably, in the history of Bible translation there have been many instances of external issues that creep into the translation process.

One example is the tendency at times for translations to make up for perceived or real mistakes in the biblical text. Matthew 1:17 provides an example. The RSV text translates in a fairly literal fashion (see also NAB, NRSV, NIV):

> So *all the generations* from Abraham to David were *fourteen generations,* and from David to the deportation to Babylon *fourteen generations,* and from the deportation to Babylon to the Christ *fourteen generations.*

While the text is clear, anyone with a knowledge of the history of Israel recognizes that Matthew's genealogy has telescoped that history into an artificial construct and has left out of the list numerous kings and generations. This is for theological reasons. The genealogy is likely based upon a symbolic number (fourteen) that alludes to King David and reinforces Jesus' background as the Davidic Messiah. The NLT, noting this deficiency, consequently translates the passage more loosely to rectify the apparent mistake, in a way that glosses over Matthew's theological intention:

> *All those listed above* include *fourteen generations* from Abraham to David, *fourteen* from David to the Babylonian exile, and *fourteen* from the Babylonian exile to the Messiah.

Critical questions arise also when passages of profound Christological significance are considered. A passage in the Letter to the Hebrews provides an example, especially because it quotes an Old Testament Psalm that it then applies to Jesus Christ. The NAB sticks with a fairly literal translation of Hebrews 2:6, quoting Psalm 8:5:

> Instead, someone has testified somewhere: "What is *man* that you are mindful of him, or *the son of man* that you care for him?"

In the context of Hebrews, the text's use of "the son of man" is meant to evoke the mysterious Christological title that the New Testament associates with Jesus (e.g., Mt 8:20; 9:6, etc.). At issue is not what the original meaning of Psalm 8 was, but what use was made of it by the author of the Letter to the Hebrews. The more literal translation preserves the Christological connection. The NRSV translation, however, in an effort to make the passage more inclusive, obscures the meaning of the text and glosses over its Christological significance by use of plural expressions and the substitution of "mortals" for "son of man":

> But someone has testified somewhere, "What are *human beings* that you are mindful of them, or *mortals,* that you care for *them*?"

In instances such as this, good translation requires careful attention to the context as well as the words.

Characteristics of the NAB Translation

Since the NAB is the basis for this study Bible, it is appropriate to highlight some of the characteristics of this translation.

1. The NAB falls in the middle of the continuum mentioned on RG 69 yet leans toward a more formal translation. It seeks to offer an exact rendering of the biblical text in good, modern,

American English that is not overly literal. For instance, no attempt is made to duplicate fully the Hebraisms of the Old Testament, although the parallelism of many poetic passages is retained.

2. The NAB takes into account recent finds in ancient manuscripts, such as the Dead Sea Scrolls, and more current decisions about the various families of manuscripts that are in existence. Textual critics are always attempting to ascertain the most authentic reading of ancient manuscripts based upon the latest scholarship. This is one reason why new translations are needed on a periodic basis as our knowledge of ancient texts grows.

3. Unlike its predecessor, the proposed Old Testament of the revised NAB would leave the verse order of the Masoretic text (the authoritative received text of the Hebrew Bible) intact instead of attempting a reorganization based upon scholarly theories of a more original word order.

4. A common flaw in translations can be the unevenness of translating the same word in the original text with a different English word. Unless the meaning is clearly otherwise, the NAB tries to translate the original terms with the same English equivalent consistently throughout its translation.

5. The NAB utilizes modest horizontal inclusive language wherever possible and where it would not distort the text. As much as possible, where the text necessarily requires an inclusive reading, such is rendered in the English translation. The translation does not employ vertical inclusive language.

6. The proposed NAB takes into account modern American English in its rendering of the biblical text. There is an avoidance of terms that might confuse or offend modern readers, such as *holocaust* (which can be confused with the Holocaust—the Nazi atrocity of attempting to exterminate the Jews during World War II) and *cereal offerings* (which can be confused with breakfast food rather than "grain" offerings).

7. The exegetical notes, essential for clarification and interpretation, have been thoroughly revised in the proposed NAB Old Testament to bring them more in line with the approach taken in the earlier NAB New Testament translation.

8. For Catholics, it should be noted that the NAB is published with full ecclesiastical approval and has followed the required principles for Bible translation that are standard in the Roman Catholic Church. It is thus a reliable and faithful translation that is useful for both spiritual and scholarly purposes.

The Future of Biblical Translation

In conclusion, there will always be a need for new translations. Every translation has strengths and weaknesses. In as much as translation is both a science and an art, there will always be room for improvements as time goes on. The fund of knowledge about the Bible and its world, about the ancient languages and cultures out of which it emerged, grows daily. In order for the Word of God to seep into the very lifeblood of modern English-speaking peoples, new English translations will have to take into account not only the results of scientific investigations but also the changes that continue to occur at a rapid rate within the English language. This reality ensures that Bible translation will remain an exciting field for succeeding generations who will continue to seek ways to communicate the Word of God effectively in their time and place.

FURTHER READING

Catholic International 13:4 (November 2002). Entire issue devoted to "Translation and Interpretation."

de Waard, J., and E. A. Nida. *From One Language to Another: Functional Equivalence in Bible Translating*. Nashville: Nelson, 1986.

Metzger, B. M. *The Bible in Translation: Ancient and English Versions*. Grand Rapids, MI: Baker Academic, 2001.

Nowell, Irene. "The Making of Translations: A Dilemma." *Worship* 75, 1 (2001): 58–68.

Porter, S. E., and R. E. Hess. "Translating the Bible: Problems and Prospects." *Journal of the Study of the New Testament Supplement Series,* no. 173; Sheffield: Sheffield Academic Press, 1999.

Sheeley, S. M., and R. N. Nash, Jr. *The Bible in English Translation: An Essential Guide*. Nashville: Abingdon Press, 1997.

Soukup, P. A., and R. Hodgson, eds. *Fidelity and Translation*. Franklin, WI: Sheed & Ward, 1999.

Witherup, R. D. *A Liturgist's Guide to Inclusive Language*. Collegeville, MN: Liturgical Press, 1996.

THE BIBLE IN THE LECTIONARY

EILEEN SCHULLER

One of the enduring results of the Second Vatican Council has been a renewed emphasis on the place of the Bible within Catholic life, and greater attention to its use in worship, study, and devotion. As a Church and as individuals we are discovering anew the truth of St. Jerome's insight that "ignorance of the Scriptures is ignorance of Christ." Most Catholics now own a Bible; there are Bible study groups in many parishes; children are introduced to biblical stories and actual biblical texts from the first stages of their religious education; many new hymns and much contemporary folk music are biblically based; Services of the Word (which often include a solemn enthronement of the Bible) and parish celebrations of the Liturgy of the Hours are slowly finding a place in Catholic piety.

Still, for most Catholics, their main exposure to the Bible comes at those times when the Church gathers for liturgy, to offer together praise and worship to God through Jesus. Each time the Mass is celebrated there are two or three readings from the Bible, always one from the Gospel and others from the book of Acts, the Epistles, or the Old Testament. Whenever the sacraments are celebrated (even when baptisms, marriages, and the sacrament of penance are celebrated apart from the Mass), readings from the Word of God are an integral part of the ritual. The first reading from Scripture is regularly followed by a psalm so that we might give our response in the words of Scripture. The Gospel Acclamation, the Entrance, and Communion antiphons are usually taken directly from Scripture; other prayers and texts of the Mass reflect or are based on scriptural sources (for instance, the Glory to God in the Highest, the Lamb of God, the Lord's Prayer).

It is instructive to reflect on why the Christian tradition is so insistent that we read the Word of God whenever we gather to pray as Church. The *Constitution on the Sacred Liturgy,* one of the foundational documents of the Second Vatican Council, puts it this way: "Christ is present in His Word since it is He Himself who speaks when the holy Scriptures are read in the church" (*CSL,* 7). The *Eucharistic Instruction* of 1967 elaborates at greater length "the principal modes by which the Lord is present to his Church in liturgical celebrations. First of all, Christ is present in the assembly of the faithful gathered in his name; He is also present in his word for it is He who is speaking as the sacred Scriptures are read in the Church; in the eucharistic sacrifice, He is present both in the person of the minister . . . and above all under the eucharistic elements" (*CSL,* 9).

Roman Catholicism has traditionally placed primary emphasis (at times, almost the sole emphasis) on the eucharistic presence of Christ under the appearances of bread and wine. More recent theological reflection has emphasized that Christ is present from the moment when the people gather together in the Christian Assembly, and that He is present especially during the proclamation of the Word of God, both in the reading of Scripture and in its unfolding in the homily. The *Eucharistic Instruction* brings this all together with the beautiful imagery of food: "The Church is nourished by the bread of life, which she finds at the table both of the Word of God and the Body of Christ" (10).

The Revision of the Lectionary

Very early on in the Second Vatican Council, the Bishops of the Church, recognizing that "Sacred Scripture is of paramount importance in the celebration of the liturgy" (*Constitution on the Sacred Liturgy,* 24), called for certain reforms and changes so that this truth might become a living and pastoral reality in the Church. They said there should be "more reading from holy Scripture" and it should be "more varied and suitable" (*CSL,* 35); or, to put it in more poetic fashion, "the treasures of the Bible are to be opened up more lavishly, so that richer fare may be provided for the faithful at the table of God's Word" (*CSL,* 51). Thus, one of the first major reforms following on the Council was a revision of the Lectionary, that is, the biblical readings that are set down for each Sunday and weekday of the year, and also for use in the celebration of the sacraments, on Feast Days, at funerals, and for Votive Masses and Masses for Special Occasions.

The reforms envisaged by the Council meant not only that the readings would be in English, but that new and previously unheard sections of the Bible would need to be introduced both on Sundays and at weekday Masses. In the centuries since the Council of Trent, the *Roman Missal* of Pius V (1570) had prescribed a set series of Gospel passages on a yearly basis, and a second reading usually from the Epistles; very few passages from the Old Testament were ever heard at Sunday Mass.

To fulfill the Council's mandate, a committee was established by Rome in 1964; liturgical, scriptural, and pastoral experts, along with bishops around the world, were consulted. The work was completed in 1969 with the publication of the *Lectionary for Mass,* and introduced in all churches throughout the world on the First Sunday of Advent, 1971. In January of 1981 a second edition of the Lectionary was published with a few minor additions and changes, plus an expanded and very helpful Introduction, which explains more fully the goals and purpose of the Lectionary.

The revision of the Lectionary has been one of the most extensive and significant reforms of the Council. Unfortunately, it has not always been given the attention it deserves, nor are some of its fundamental principles always well understood, either by the clergy who preach on these readings or by the laity who hear them. Our appreciation of the Scriptures in the liturgy can be greatly enriched by a more careful examination of the Lectionary.

Why a Lectionary at All?

Before we look at more specific questions about how the Lectionary is put together and exactly which passages are chosen, it is helpful to step back and ask the more fundamental questions: "Why a lectionary at all? What do we gain by using a lectionary?"

The decision to use a lectionary means that the readings for a given Sunday or weekday are predetermined; they are a given, and therefore they are the starting point for the planning of the liturgy as a whole and the homily. On certain other occasions (for instance, celebrations of marriages, funerals) there are more options given for Scripture readings, and a choice is to be made of what is most appropriate to the pastoral needs of a given congregation. When a special group gathers for a one-time occasion (a Retreat Day, a meeting), it is recognized that the given readings for the day may not be appropriate, and provision is made for using readings "that are more suited to the particular celebration, provided that they are chosen from the texts of an approved lectionary" (*Masses with Special Groups,* 6e). Interestingly, the greatest flexibility is allowed in choosing readings for Masses with children, although a reading from the Gospels is always to be included (*Directory for Masses with Children,* 43).

The norm in the Roman Catholic tradition is that the Scripture readings are set; they are not the choice of the priest or anyone else in the congregation. Certainly a case can be made (and has been made in the Reform and Free Church traditions) for the freedom and spontaneity to choose readings suitable to a specific community and occasion. But the Catholic tradition has opted for a structured and planned system of readings that "provides the faithful with a knowledge of the whole of God's Word, in a pattern suited to the purpose" (*CSL: Introduction,* 60).

The imposition of a lectionary seeks to lessen the temptation (although it can never remove it entirely!) to pick and choose, to listen only to those parts of the Bible that we find readily helpful and to omit those that we find difficult to understand or accept—but which may be the ones we most need to hear. For instance, if I am readily inclined to look upon God as one who is loving, merciful, kind, and forgiving, the Lectionary will certainly provide my favorite passages, but it will also force me to read those difficult passages (from both the Old and the New Testament) that speak of the wrath of God, judgment, and punishment. Or again, if I am a person with a strong social-justice orientation, firmly convinced that "actions on behalf of justice . . . are a constitutive dimension of the preaching of the gospel-message" (1971 Synod of Bishops), the Lectionary will show many of the key biblical texts both from the prophets and the Gospels; but it will also include passages that speak of the personal dimension of union with God, of a world that is passing away, even passages in praise of the monarchy and the established realm. The gift and challenge of the Lectionary is that it places before each of us passages that we might otherwise not choose to read; unrelentingly it nudges us to open ourselves to the totality of God's Word.

Foundational Principles of the Lectionary

On a first examination of the Lectionary, it is easy to get bogged down in a mass of details about different cycles and lists of what is read when, so that the whole thing can seem somewhat intimidating. Rather than trying to determine why certain texts are read on a certain day, it is more important to get an overall sense of the arrangement and rationale of the whole. The general principles and foundational decisions that have determined the basic shape and ordering of the Roman Lectionary will then be clear.

The Paschal Mystery

The focal point of the whole Lectionary is Jesus Christ, especially "the paschal mystery of his blessed passion, resurrection from the dead and glorious ascension" (*CSL,* 5). Throughout the cycle of the Church's Year, the Lectionary sets before us the totality of this central mystery of the Christian life, a mystery that was not only accomplished in Jesus, but a mystery in which we now share through Baptism and faith.

Thus, primacy is given to readings from the Gospels, which speak most directly of the person of Jesus. Furthermore, we read these texts not as individuals but as a people gathered for praise and thanksgiving. "Within the Christian assembly the proclamation of the word inevitably has a Christian aura . . . the God whom we worship in our liturgy is not, first of all, the God of the Book (which is why we freely interpret the Book by arranging it in a lectionary). Our God is the God of the Gathering" (R. Keifer, *To Hear and To Proclaim,* 115). At Mass, every passage of Scripture, whether from the Old or New Testament, is set in relationship to the Passion and Resurrection of Jesus as made present to us in the Eucharist.

The Church Year

Not everything in the Lectionary is of equal importance. The Lectionary is divided into six parts: the major section (and the one that will be the main focus of our attention) is the Temporal Cycle, that is, the readings for Sundays and weekdays throughout the Church Year; the rest of the Lectionary contains the readings for special occasions (Proper of the Saints, Commons, Ritual Masses [for examples, readings for sacraments, funerals], Masses for Various Occasions, and Votive Masses).

Within the Temporal Cycle, not all days of the year are of equal importance. Sundays have special importance, since they are the weekly celebration of the Lord's Resurrection and the occasion for the gathering of the whole community; thus, "the more important biblical passages" (*CSL: Introduction,* 65) are assigned to Sundays and the Solemnities of the Lord. The Sunday cycle is set up independent from the weekday cycle, which, in a sense, complements it.

The Church Year as a whole has its own rhythm. "The solemnity of Easter has the same kind of preeminence [in the year] . . . that Sunday has in the week" (*Norms for the Liturgical Year,* 18); there are six Sundays in Easter season, followed by Pentecost and Trinity Sundays. Then, next to Easter, the Church "holds most sacred the memorial of Christ's birth and early manifestation" (*Norms,* 32). There are two Sundays after Christmas, followed by Epiphany and the Sunday after that. These two major feasts, each with their preparatory period (Lent, with six Sundays, before Easter, and Advent, with four Sundays, before Christmas) are the primary seasons of the Church Year; the other thirty-four

Sundays, which celebrate "the mystery of Christ in all its aspects" (*Norms,* 43), form what is called simply Ordinary Time. (The Lectionary provides for more than fifty-two Sundays to allow for variations in the length of time after Easter, since Easter can fall anywhere from March 22 to April 25.)

Lectio Semicontinua* and *Lectio Electa

There are many different ways in which we could go about reading the Bible in a systematic fashion. We could start with the story of Creation and work through the events of the Old Testament chronologically, then move on to the New Testament and conclude with the book of Revelation; this would be a kind of salvation-history approach. Another option would be to organize the Scripture readings around certain great themes (grace, salvation, forgiveness, creation) or moral principles; the traditional name for this approach is *lectio electa,* "readings chosen" to suit a predetermined theme. Or, we could adopt *lectio continua,* a "continuous reading" of the Bible from beginning to end. This is the system of the Jewish synagogue in which the Torah, the first five books, are read continuously through a year; on the same day that the last chapter of Deuteronomy is finished the first chapter of Genesis is begun, so that the reading of Torah is unceasing.

The Roman Lectionary has opted for a combination of *lectio electa* (particularly in the major seasons of the Church Year) and *lectio continua* (particularly during Ordinary Time and in the weekday cycle); in fact, it is really more correct to talk of *lectio semicontinua* since no biblical book is read through in its entirety.

Although a "harmony" (to use the term from the *CSL: Introduction,* 66) exists between the different readings during Advent, Lent, and Easter, for most Masses there is no one theme in the three (Sunday) or two (weekday) readings. Thus, attempts (whether by a homilist or by musicians) to discover or impose a theme for every Mass can result in a misleading or artificial approach to the Scriptures.

Readings of Suitable Length; Omission of Difficult Sections

In the early church the custom was to read "the memoirs of the apostles or the writings of the prophets as long as there is time" (Justin Martyr, *Apol.* 67). That, however, is not the norm today; within the Mass, particularly when there are three readings, none can be too long. Narrative texts (Gospel stories, parables) are often longer (ten to fifteen verses) so that they can be complete and because they more easily hold people's attention. Other texts, particularly Sunday readings from the Epistles, are shorter (between four and eight verses) "because of the profundity of their teaching" (*CSL: Introduction,* 75). Occasionally an option is given for reading either a long or a short version of a text (for example, the story of Jesus and the Samaritan woman on the Third Sunday of Lent, A).

The Roman Lectionary also recognizes that not every passage in the Bible is either suitable or helpful for public reading in the liturgy. Decisions were made to omit entirely certain passages with "complex literary, critical, or exegetical problems" (*CSL: Introduction,* 76) that would make them difficult for most people to understand. Similarly, following the long-established practice in Roman lectionaries, at times selected verses within a reading are omitted because the passage would otherwise be too long or because a verse is "unsuitable pastorally or . . . involves truly difficult problems" (*CSL: Introduction,* 77).

Basic Arrangement of the Sunday Lectionary

After examining the possibility of spreading the readings over as little as two years or as many as four, the planners of the Sunday Lectionary decided on a three-year cycle. That is, there are different readings for each Sunday in Years A, B, and C (as they are commonly designated) and then the cycle begins over again. (Years where the sum of all the digits are divisible by three, for instance 1989, 1992, are always Year C. The year begins on the First Sunday of Advent.)

For each Sunday there are three readings: one from the Old Testament (with a few exceptions, as we will note in the Sundays after Easter), one from the Epistles or the book of Revelation, and one from the Gospels. Although provision is made for an individual Conference of Bishops to allow only two readings "for pastoral reasons" (*General Instruction,* 318), three is clearly the norm.

Since there is considerable divergence in the shape of the Lectionary during the major seasons of Advent–Christmas and Lent–Easter as compared with the Sundays of Ordinary Time, it is easier and less confusing to look at each separately, beginning with Ordinary Time.

The Gospels in Ordinary Time

One of the three Synoptic Gospels forms the central focus of each of the thirty-three (occasionally thirty-four) Sundays of each year of Ordinary Time. Year A is always the Gospel of Matthew; Year B, the Gospel of Mark; and Year C, the Gospel of Luke. The Gospel of John is not neglected, even though it does not form the core of a specific year. In accord with an ancient tradition of the Church, John has always been read during the Lent and Easter seasons "because it is the 'spiritual' Gospel in which the mystery of Christ is sounded out to greater depths" (*CSL: Introduction,* 7); in addition, because of the shortness of the Gospel of Mark, chapter 6 of John (the Bread of Life discourse) is taken up on five Sundays during Year B.

This particular arrangement of the Lectionary allows us to hear each of the Gospels in its own right; over the course of a year we come to know the distinctive picture of Jesus presented by Matthew or Mark or Luke.

The Epistles in Ordinary Time

Over the Sundays of Ordinary Time, passages are selected from the Epistles for the second reading, according to the following outline:

Year A
1 Corinthians 1–4 (Sundays 2–8)
Romans (Sundays 9–24)
Philippians (Sundays 25–28)
1 Thessalonians (Sundays 29–33)

Year B
1 Corinthians 6–11 (Sundays 2–6)
2 Corinthians (Sundays 7–14)
Ephesians (Sundays 15–21)
James (Sundays 22–26)
Hebrews 2–10 (Sundays 27–33)

Year C
1 Corinthians 12–15 (Sundays 2–8)
Galatians (Sundays 9–14)
Colossians (Sundays 15–18)
Hebrews 11–12 (Sundays 19–22)
Philemon (Sunday 23)
1 Timothy (Sundays 24–26)
2 Timothy (Sundays 27–30)
2 Thessalonians (Sundays 31–33)

Though individual passages are quite short and there is no attempt to read the Epistles in their entirety, over the three years the Lectionary gives a rich and varied exposure to the main themes and emphases of this part of Scripture. As already noted, in the Sundays in Ordinary Time there is no direct correlation between the Gospel reading and the Epistle reading; although at times they may touch on similar aspects of the Christian mystery, they have not been picked to provide a common theme.

The Old Testament Reading in Ordinary Time

In contrast to the selection of the Epistle, the first reading from the Old Testament has been carefully chosen to correlate with the Gospel text of the day. Although the intent is to highlight the unity between the Old and New Testaments, in fact there is considerable variety in how this "harmony" (*CSL: Introduction,* 67) is achieved. Sometimes it is a common theme that binds the two readings together; at other times the Old Testament will foreshadow or suggest something that is more fully developed in the Gospel (for example, on Sunday 16, Year C, the story of Martha and Mary giving hospitality to Jesus is paired with the story from Genesis of Abraham receiving his three guests). Often, if the Gospel quotes a verse from the Old Testament or refers to a specific incident, this passage will be the first reading (for example, on the Third Sunday, Year A, Matthew quotes Isaiah 8:23–9:1, and that Isaianic text services as the first reading). At times, the single lines given before the readings in the Lectionary are most helpful (though they are not meant to be read publicly) to indicate the point of correspondence that led to the choice of a particular reading.

While the desirability of a weekly Old Testament reading is undisputed, it is probably fair to say that the selection of Old Testament passages has been the single most controversial aspect of the Lectionary. The decision to link the first reading so closely with the Gospel imposes certain limitations. Many of the most important Old Testament passages simply do not readily lend themselves to correlation with a particular Gospel passage, and so are never heard in the Sunday assembly; often, such a brief or peripheral section of a major Old Testament story is read that it is difficult to get a sense of the whole picture. Furthermore, relatively little ever appears from the corpus of Wisdom literature (only three selections from Proverbs and two, both truncated, from the book of Job). The passages selected from the prophets are those that are readily seen to be fulfilled in Jesus, or which at least have Christological implications, but other aspects of the prophetic message are given less prominence (for example, the relatively few "social justice" passages read over the three years).

The Lent–Easter Season

As noted above, the seasons of Lent–Easter and Advent–Christmas form independent units; both cycles (the Advent even more so than the Lent) are carefully crafted so that through the Scripture readings we may be more closely initiated into the Church's understanding of these great feasts.

Easter, especially the Easter Triduum (Holy Thursday, Good Friday, and Easter Vigil on Saturday), is "the culmination of the entire liturgical year" (*Norms,* 18); Lent serves as a time of preparation, especially as a period of "closer attention to the Word of God" (*CSL,* 109). During Lent, "those important passages from the Gospels which were read to catechumens in the early centuries to prepare them for Baptism are proclaimed. These readings are directed to *all* the faithful because during Lent the whole Church, along with those about to be baptized, calls to mind the mystery of its initiation into Christ." Though it is not possible to examine closely all the readings for the Lent–Easter season, a few examples will illustrate the care and theological insight that finds expression in the arrangement of the Lectionary for this season.

The baptismal thrust is seen most clearly in Year A on the final three Sundays of Lent, where the great themes of water, light, and life are proclaimed through the reading from John's Gospel of the Samaritan woman at the well (Third Sunday), the curing of the man born blind (Fourth), and the raising of Lazarus from the dead (Fifth); so pivotal are these particular texts to the process of Christian initiation that they can be used in any of the three years, especially when there are candidates preparing for Baptism.

The readings for the first two Sundays of Lent are always the account of the Temptation and the Transfiguration respectively, read according to the Gospel being followed in a given year. In Year B, the Gospels for the rest of Lent focus on the Crucifixion and Resurrection; in Year C, on the process of conversion.

At first glance, the choice of Old Testament readings for the Sundays of Lent might look entirely diverse and random; certainly they are not specifically linked to the Gospel. Rather, each year, they are meant to lead us through the Old Testament, presenting "the main elements of salvation history from its beginning until the promise of the New Covenant" (*CSL: Introduction,* 97):

Year A

First Sunday: Creation and fall
Second Sunday: The call of Abraham
Third Sunday: Water from the rock in the desert
Fourth Sunday: The anointing of David as king
Fifth Sunday: Promise of the restoration

Year B

First Sunday: Flood and covenant
Second Sunday: Abraham's sacrifice of his son
Third Sunday: The ten commandments
Fourth Sunday: Exile and destruction of the Temple
Fifth Sunday: Promise of the new covenant

Year C

First Sunday: Retelling the deliverance from Egypt
Second Sunday: The covenant with Abraham
Third Sunday: The call of Moses
Fourth Sunday: The Passover celebrated in the Promised Land
Fifth Sunday: Promise of a new exodus

The Epistle readings during Lent highlight themes such as faith, repentance, and baptismal motifs, and often are related to the first reading (for example, on the First Sunday of Lent, A, the passage from Romans about Christ as the Second Adam corresponds to the reading about the sin of Adam in Genesis 2).

The reading of the Gospel of John continues on most of the Sundays after Easter in all three years with texts about the Good Shepherd (Fourth Sunday) and from John's presentation of the Farewell Discourse and Prayer of Jesus (the Fifth to Seventh Sundays). This is the only time when there are no Old Testament readings; in keeping with a very ancient tradition, the Church turns to the Acts of the Apostles in all three years so that we ponder the work of the Spirit in the early Church. For the second reading, semicontinuous selections are taken from 1 Peter in Year A, 1 John in Year B (both rich in baptismal allusions), and from the book of Revelation (with its emphasis on heavenly worship) in Year C.

Advent–Christmas Season

The Lectionary for Advent is very carefully planned, with a definite movement as we progress toward the celebration of Christmas. The First Sunday emphasizes the Second Coming of Christ, picking up on a theme already sounded in the final Sunday of the Church Year (the feast of Christ the King). On the Second and Third Sundays, the Gospel is always about John the Baptist, so that the focus of attention moves more to the historical coming of a Messiah. On the Fourth Sunday, we turn to the first chapters of Matthew and Luke for events immediately prior to the birth of Jesus (the Annunciation to Mary and Joseph, and the Visitation).

In keeping with a long tradition in the Church, the Book of Isaiah with its messianic prophecies has a special place in both the Advent and Christmas readings. The Epistle readings are more general, offering exhortations and reflections; often, as the Advent focus moves to the birth of Jesus in time, the second reading serves to remind us of the Coming, which still awaits us in the future.

Throughout the Christmas season, the Lectionary preserves many of the readings that have been traditional in the Roman Church. On the Octave of Christmas, the Solemnity of Mary, Mother of God (New Year's Day), the first reading is the priestly blessing from Numbers 6, and the other two speak more specifically of Mary.

The Lectionary for Weekdays

The readings for weekdays throughout the year form a separate cycle, independent of the Sunday cycle. Even with only two readings, obviously more of the Bible can be covered on weekdays, although still only portions of many of the longer Old Testament books are included. The seasons of Advent–Christmas and Lent–Easter follow an annual cycle, that is, the readings are repeated every year; in Ordinary Time, the same Gospel passages are read every year, while the first reading follows a two-year cycle (designated as Year I and Year II).

The following will give a brief outline of the weekday cycle:

Advent–Christmas Season.

During the first nine days of Advent, the Lectionary follows a very ancient custom of the Church and reads (in sequence) selected passages from the prophet Isaiah; on these days, contrary to usual practice, the Gospel is chosen to relate to this first reading. After the Thursday of the second week of Advent, the Gospel consistently speaks of John the Baptist, while the first reading is still from Isaiah or chosen to relate to the Gospel. From December 17 to 24, passages are selected from the first chapters of Matthew and Luke of events leading up to the birth of Christ; the first reading presents some of the major Old Testament messianic prophecies.

From December 27 on throughout the Epiphany season, there is a virtually continuous reading of 1 John. The Gospels relate various manifestations of Jesus; the whole of the first chapter of John's Gospel is read between December 31 and January 5.

Lent–Easter Season

Throughout Lent, the Gospel and Old Testament are rather closely related to each other and present to us different aspects of the major Lenten themes of Baptism and penance. In accord with an ancient custom in the Church, the Gospel of John is read from the fourth week on; in Holy Week the focus is more specifically on Christ's Passion.

During the Easter season, on weekdays as on Sundays, the Lectionary maintains the ancient custom of reading semicontinuously from the Acts of the Apostles. During the Octave of Easter, the Gospel selections recount the different occasions on which Christ appeared; over the next weeks there is semicontinuous reading of the teaching and prayer of Jesus at the Last Supper from John 13 through John 17.

Ordinary Time

Over the course of the year, the Gospels are read on a semicontinuous basis: Mark 1–12 in weeks 1–9, Matthew 5–25 in weeks 10–21, and Luke 4–21 in weeks 22–34. The Church Year ends with those passages from Luke that talk specifically of the Second Coming.

The first reading is completely independent from the Gospel and provides the opportunity to read selections from the majority of the Old Testament books and Epistles. Longer books are sometimes divided (for example, Genesis 1–11 is read in weeks 5–6 of Year I, Genesis 12–50 in weeks 12–14). At the very end of the Church Year, we read from Daniel in Year I and the book of Revelation in Year II with their eschatological themes.

The Responsorial Psalm

The Lectionary also introduces us to the psalms in the Bible; in fact, more than eighty psalms (or verses thereof) are used in the Sunday Lectionary and some 130 of the 150 psalms appear somewhere in the complete Lectionary. The psalm comes between the first and second reading, and is considered as "an integral part of the Liturgy of the Word" (*General Instruction,* 36).

The psalms are poetry, the majority of them certainly originally composed to be sung with musical accompaniment. The introduction to the Lectionary strongly encourages singing the psalm at Mass, preferably by a soloist (cantor) with the congregation joining in with a refrain; if the psalm is spoken, it is "to be recited in a manner conducive to meditation on the Word" (*CSL: Introduction,* 22).

Although the psalm always serves in some way as a response to the Word of God, there is considerable diversity in terms of its precise relationship to other readings. If the first reading or the Epistle or even the Gospel quotes a particular psalm verse, that psalm is usually taken up as an echo or anticipated response (for example, the use of Psalm 91 on the First Sunday of Lent, C, when a verse from this psalm, "He has put his angels in charge of you," is quoted during the temptation story in the Gospel). Often a psalm simply picks up and carries on the mood of the first reading, whether lamentation, thanksgiving, or praise. Some psalms have a long tradition of usage on particular feasts (Psalm 47, "God goes up with shouts of joy" for the Ascension; Psalm 72, "the kings of Arabia and Seba shall bring tribute. All Kings shall pay him homage, all nations shall serve him" for Epiphany). According to Lucien Deiss (a member of the committee involved in the choice of psalms when the Lectionary was compiled), some psalms that would not otherwise be used were introduced primarily so that the Christian community could become more familiar with the entire Psalter (*Spirit and Song of the New Liturgy,* 110–11).

Ecumenical Import of the Lectionary

One of the unexpected and unforeseen results of the revision of the Roman Lectionary has been its adoption (with some modifications) by many Protestant churches, including Anglican/Episcopalian, Methodist, Presbyterian, Lutheran, and United Church of Canada. James White, a Methodist minister, in a much-quoted statement remarked that the Lectionary has become "Catholicism's greatest gift to Protestant preaching, just as Protestant biblical scholarship has given so much impetus to Catholic preaching" (*Christian Worship in Transition,* 139).

In recent years, many of these churches came together under the auspices of the Consultation on Common Texts and developed the *Common Lectionary,* an order of readings for use on Sundays and a few special days of the Christian year. The *Common Lectionary* basically follows the Roman Lectionary, with some significant changes in the choice of Old Testament passages in order to deal with some of the problem areas we have noted.

Although Catholics and Protestants do not share exactly the same Lectionary, tremendous progress has been made toward common reading of Scripture. The ecumenical import, even on a practical level, is significant; in many places ministers of different churches now gather together to reflect and prepare their Sunday sermons. And, although we are still not at the point of being able to be united at the table of the Lord's banquet, we can be united and nourished at the common table of his Word.

Using the Lectionary for Prayer and Study

Many people, both clergy and lay, today use the Lectionary as a basic resource for daily prayer, whether or not they are able to celebrate liturgy with the Christian community every day. Consistent use of the Lectionary over a period of years will necessarily expose us to a broad expanse of Scripture and protect us against the subjective reading of the Bible spoken about earlier. The Lectionary puts us in touch with the Church's understanding of the mysteries of our faith as presented through the Church year, helping us to recover dimensions which may have been lost in popular piety (for example, the baptismal dimension of the season of Lent as opposed to a solely ascetic focus).

Many religious educators are discovering the Lectionary as a valuable resource in catechetics; reflection on the readings as appropriate to various age groups provides a common focus when the whole community gathers in prayer. Parish study groups or Bible studies often take the Gospel of a given year as their text for study. More and more the Lectionary is being used as the core of the RCIA program to introduce the new catechumens to the life of faith and community.

Though the Lectionary contains the Word of God, the particular selection of material is a human endeavor and thus only more or less perfect. It is recognized that some choices of specific readings could have been more auspicious, and certainly revisions will probably be made in time.

In particular, two areas are surfacing that seem to call for further discussion and reflection. As we ponder the role of women today in church and society, we bring certain questions to the Lectionary; we need to ask why certain texts have been omitted (for example, the story of courageous midwives who defy Pharaoh and ensure the survival of the Hebrew people in Egypt) and whether it is either necessary or helpful pastorally to include other texts that are open to being interpreted in a way derogatory to women (for example, Eph 5:20). The second concern is in the area of our relationship to the Jewish people; as we become more aware of "the continuity of our faith with that of the earlier covenant" (*Vatican Guidelines,* 1974), we are more sensitive to the fact that the Lectionary must "promote among the Catholic people a genuine appreciation of the special place of the Jewish people as first chosen in the history of salvation, and in no way slight the honor and dignity that is theirs" (*American Bishops' Statement on Catholic-Jewish Relations,* 1975).

The revision of the Lectionary stands as one of the most tangible and permanent implementations of the vision and challenge of the Second Vatican Council. In the Lectionary, "the treasures of the Bible are . . . opened up more lavishly so that a richer share in God's Word may be provided for the faithful" (*CSL,* 51). The Lectionary has the potential to shape the life of the Christian community, not only as the Word of God is proclaimed in the celebration of the liturgy but also as it is broken open for us in the homily, in catechetics, and in private and group study and prayer, which is rooted in Scripture. As the Lectionary is used over the cycle of years and even generations, "there is reason to hope for a new awakening of the spiritual life deriving from an increased dedication to God's word which 'abides forever' (Is 40:8)" (*Dei Verbum,* 26).

FURTHER READING

The text of the *Constitution on the Sacred Liturgy: Introduction to the Lectionary* has been published by the United States Catholic Conference, *Lectionary for Mass: Introduction, Liturgy Documentation* Series 1, 1982.

Canadian Conference of Bishops. *National Bulletin on Liturgy,* no. 50, 1975.

Proclaim the Word: the Lectionary for Mass. Liturgy Study Text Series 8. Washington, DC: United States Catholic Conference, 1982.

Fitzsimmons, John H. *Guide to the Lectionary.* London: Mayhew-McCrimmon, 1981.

Keifer, Ralph. *To Hear and To Proclaim: Introduction, Lectionary for Mass with Commentary for Musicians and Priests.* Washington, DC: National Association of Pastoral Musicians, 1983.

Skudlarek, William. *The Word in Worship: Preaching in a Liturgical Context.* Abingdon's Preacher's Library. Nashville: Abingdon, 1981.

For discussion of some of the issues around the Bible and our relationship to the Jewish people, see Pawlikowski, John J., and James A. Wilde. *When Catholics Speak About Jews.* Chicago: Liturgy Training Program, 1987.

THE PENTATEUCH

LAWRENCE BOADT

The Nature of the Pentateuch

What Is the Pentateuch?

Beginnings are important. If we want to know what kind of a book we are reading, we skim over the first few pages to see how it starts and what point of view the author adopts. For this reason it is vital to recognize the special character of the first five books of the Old Testament. They stand apart as an introduction to the rest of the Bible and, more importantly, both the Jewish and the Christian faiths recognize them as the foundation on which the rest of the Scriptures are built. They might be called a blueprint or a constitution that becomes the standard by which all other revelation is interpreted. The name *Pentateuch* comes from the title given in the earliest Greek translation that dates to the second century BC and means a "five-part" writing. This confirms that even from biblical times the Pentateuch has always been understood as a single work. Jewish tradition calls it *Torah,* which does not so much mean "law" as "teaching." This five-book Torah contains the basic teaching of the Jewish faith.

The Pentateuch as a Part of the Canon of Scripture

A "canon" means a rule of arrangement. Biblical books are in a certain order. We do not always know clearly just when or why the Bible was ordered in exactly its present lineup, but we can be sure of one thing—it was never accidental. The order of some books changed over the centuries, but gradually each book was positioned intentionally to be read in its present order; and how we interpret the message of a book is determined at least in part by where it stands in relation to other books. So, when we begin to study the Old Testament, we must look for the clues that tell us why Genesis, Exodus, Leviticus, Numbers, and Deuteronomy are divided into five books and are lined up as they are. This must be done on two levels: (1) the religious and theological meaning of the books for our Jewish and Christian faiths today; and (2) the background of what the text and words meant to those who wrote it and put it together. This latter task also involves several other aspects: (1) the *historical* development of how the books came together and what pieces were added to them as they grew to their final size; (2) the literary shape or form of the books alone and together that give them such qualities as a plot, dramatic power, connected narrative story, and the like; and (3) whatever knowledge of Israel's *actual history* that we can discover. Thus, in all, when we set out to study the Pentateuch, we ask four questions: (1) What kind of literature is it? (2) What is it saying to us? (3) What really happened to Israel behind this account? and (4) How did this literature reach this form? It is far easier to answer the first two questions about the literary qualities and the message of the text than to rediscover after more than two thousand years how accurately all the stories from Israel's history were transmitted, or the actual way the text itself was put together by generations of biblical editors.

Reading through the Pentateuch in the *New American Bible*

The text of the NAB already provides us with several helpful tools with which we can deepen our understanding of the text of the first five books of the Old Testament. There is a brief introduction to the Pentateuch itself at the beginning, as well as specific introductions placed before the opening chapter of each individual book. These introductions sketch for the reader some of the key structures in the outline of a book and some of the major religious themes that play a crucial role in the text's message for us. They also raise a few of the major concerns of biblical scholarship for the reader to consider. In addition, there are the valuable notes at the bottom of each page of text that give us historical and scholarly information about difficult or confusing words in the text, or about the customs of ancient peoples, or about the meanings of obscure references. They sometimes also explain doctrinal beliefs of our faith that are rooted in particular biblical verses, or refer us to similar passages in other books of the Bible that throw further light on the subject under discussion.

As important as all these helps are, they are very brief. It is the purpose of this study guide to do several things to supplement them so that a serious reading of the Pentateuch will be possible without getting lost in the forest because we cannot see past all the trees. First of all, these study aids will expand the points mentioned in the introductions and notes of the NAB about the scholarly interpretation of the text's background and development so that they can be understood as part of the larger picture that the Pentateuch paints. And second, they will explore the literary unity and artistic shaping so that the harmony of its inspired message will stand out more clearly to the modern reader. We will hopefully better appreciate how the five books all relate to one another both historically and literarily to form the foundational source of biblical faith.

The contents pages of the NAB (see p. v) include eight books in all under the title "Pentateuch." This is an unusual division, and it may be more helpful for us to look at the biblical arrangement in the threefold way that the Jewish Bible does rather than in the fourfold groupings that the NAB and other modern Christian Bibles follow. Thus, for the Jewish tradition there is the Torah (or "Law"), the Prophets, and the Writings. See diagram below.

The Catholic Bible also includes seven other books under the Writings, which are lacking in Jewish and Protestant Bibles, and are often called *deuterocanonical* because they were written in Greek and not Hebrew: Tobit, Judith, Wisdom of Solomon, Sirach/Ecclesiasticus, Baruch, and 1 and 2 Maccabees.

When ordered in columns like this, it becomes evident that prophecy includes both historical books and prophetic speakers. That is, both types are considered to call people back prophetically to the message in the Pentateuch and to show how that message was lived out or not lived out in history. The Writings, in turn, are a further

The Law (Torah)	*The Prophets*	*The Writings*
Genesis	FORMER PROPHETS	Psalms
Exodus	Joshua	Job
Leviticus	Judges	Proverbs
Numbers	1 Samuel	Ruth
Deuteronomy	2 Samuel	Song of Songs
	1 Kings	Ecclesiastes
	2 Kings	Lamentations
		Esther
	LATTER PROPHETS	Daniel
	Isaiah	Ezra–Nehemiah
	Jeremiah	1 Chronicles
	Ezekiel	2 Chronicles
	The Book of the Twelve	

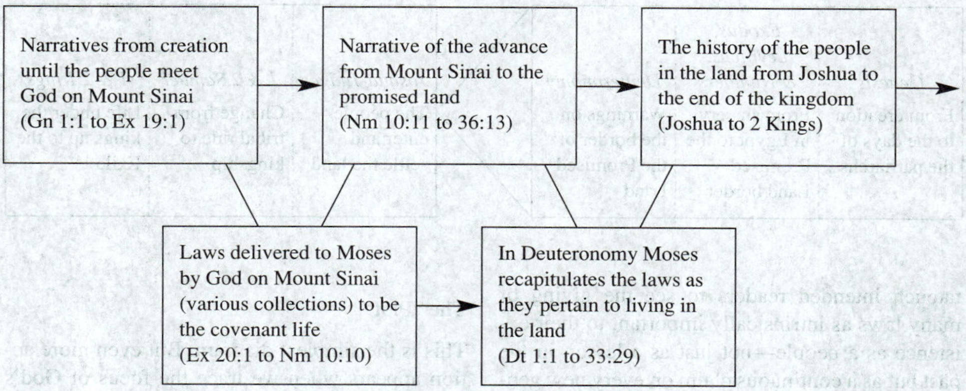

grouping that should be understood primarily as books of reflection, piety, or additional explanation to help us live the message of Torah day by day. In short, all the other books of the Old Testament flow from reflection on the Torah five.

What Kind of Literature Is It?

Story and Law

Before we begin to read the text closely, several preliminary issues must be discussed more deeply in order to answer our four questions. The first is: What kind of literature is it? At first glance, the NAB reveals that it is prose rather than poetry, except in a few places (for example, Ex 15; Dt 32). But what kind of prose? A quick survey of all five books reveals a mixture of two types: *laws* and *narratives*. Generally, they are separated into large sections of each, carefully alternated, but not completely. Every narrative part contains scattered commands and laws, and every collection of laws has a healthy episode or two of story. The books break down as follows (in rough divisions):

Genesis All Narrative (Genesis 1–50);
Exodus Part Narrative (Exodus 1–19; 24; 32–34); Part Law (20–31; 35–40);
Leviticus All Law (Leviticus 1–27);
Numbers Part Narrative (Numbers 11–17; 20–26; 31–33); Part Law (Numbers 1–10; 18–19; 27–30; 34–36);
Deuteronomy Part Narrative (Deuteronomy 1–4; 31–34); Part Law (Deuteronomy 5–30).

One could illustrate this dramatically by the diagram above.

Jewish religious tradition generally identifies 613 divine commandments within the Pentateuch. The rabbis and sages have divided the breakdown of these laws as follows:

Genesis 3 laws
Exodus 111 laws
Leviticus 247 laws
Numbers 52 laws
Deuteronomy 200 laws

As shown above, the laws are contained inside a story framework that traces the "history" events from the moment of creation in Genesis 1 down to the moment when Israel stands at the edge of the Promised Land, but before it has been entered in Deuteronomy 34. But this story is really part of a much larger historical narrative that combines the Pentateuch with the so-called Deuteronomistic History (the books of Joshua, Judges, 1 and 2 Samuel, and 1 and 2 Kings) and goes from Creation to the fall of Judah, the last independent part of Israel as a nation, before the Babylonians in the sixth century BC.

What the Pentateuch proposes as a way of life through Law and Story is then narrated and judged as lived or rejected in the history of the national life on the land. 2 Kings 25 ends with a vague openness to a possible new start after the people have been defeated and exiled for their failure to obey the Word of God that was given in the Pentateuch and then proclaimed by God's prophets (see 2 Kgs 17). Because of this greater scope, we can be sure that the authors of the Pen-

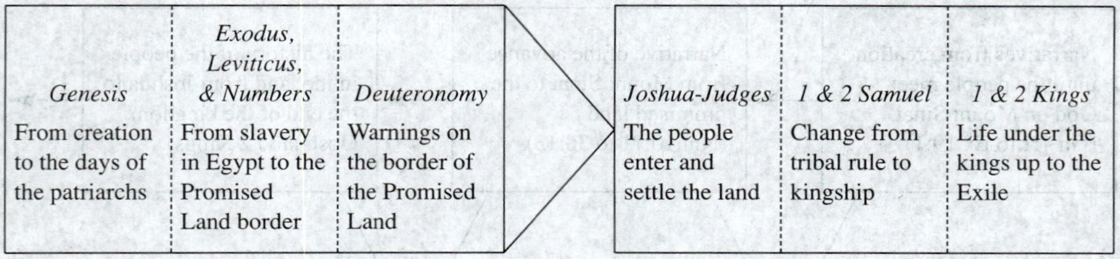
Genesis
From creation to the days of the patriarchs
Exodus, Leviticus, & Numbers
From slavery in Egypt to the Promised Land border
Deuteronomy
Warnings on the border of the Promised Land
Joshua-Judges
The people enter and settle the land
1 & 2 Samuel
Change from tribal rule to kingship
1 & 2 Kings
Life under the kings up to the Exile

tateuch intended readers to see the giving of many laws as intrinsically important to their existence as a people—not just as a lesson in the past but as a continuous claim on every new generation of Israel (see diagram above).

The mixture of law and story narrative may seem boring to modern ears since we are not used to hearing long lists of regulations recited inside a good story. But to the ancient believer, knowing and accepting such laws expressed a continuity with the stories of how God dealt with their ancestors. They might say, "Our ancestors did *those* things, and we obey *these* laws, and as a result we are one and the same people of God!"

The Overall Structure

The present structure of the Pentateuch has a distinct shape to it. Not only is it story and law, it is also drama. Each book has its own subject matter that can be studied by itself, but only if the reader does not forget the larger movement of all five books. One way to look at this interlocking action among the books is to see three distinct stages:

1. The preparation period (Genesis)
2. The time of Moses in Egypt and Sinai (Exodus to Numbers)
3. The new preparation for life in the land (Deuteronomy)

This can be diagrammed as a forward movement, as shown below.

The "Plot"

This is the simplest diagram. But even more action appears when we trace the focus of God's "plan" through the developing plot. God creates the world for all peoples to praise the divine goodness, but humanity fails the divine hopes (Gn 1–11); so God chooses a single family or people that will prove faithful and teach all other nations (Gn 12–50). These in turn must learn the lesson of God's goodness through hardship and then deliverance (Ex) and become obedient and formed as truly God's holy people (Lv and Nm 1–10). Then God will lead them to a Promised Land (Nm 10–36), which they will keep only if obedient and loyal (Dt). This new articulation can be diagrammed also. See diagram at top of next page.

The Symmetrical and Artistic Unity

The Pentateuch has been divided into five books by ancient editors who found that they had so much material they needed five separate scrolls to copy it all down. They made the divisions as naturally as possible, choosing about the same lengths for each scroll and breaking between obvious changes in place or topic. But the five divisions also reveal a very carefully balanced symmetry in which the ends and middles balance

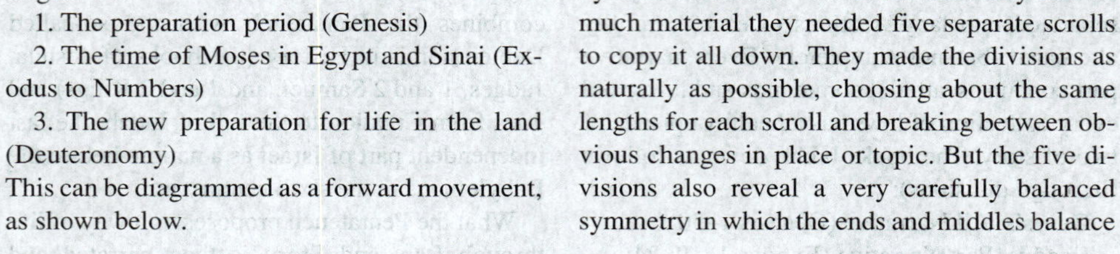
Genesis
On beginnings: God deals with the forbears in promise and person.
Exodus
God rescues and covenants with the people.
Leviticus
Laws are given for a holy people.
Numbers
Desert journey of God's guidance to the Promised Land.
Deuteronomy
A "second law" that both sums up, and looks to the land ahead.

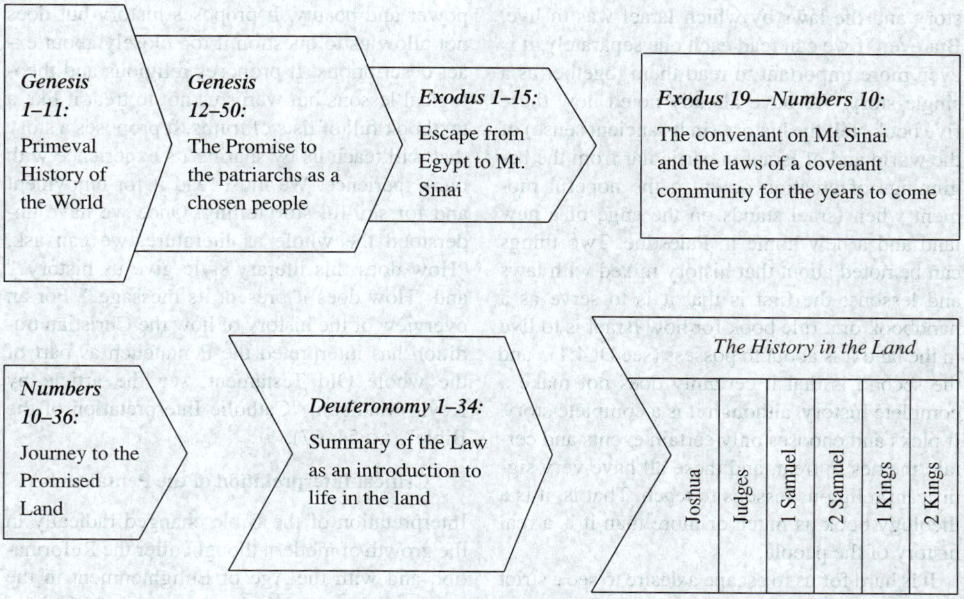

one another in a chiastic (or ladderlike) construction that can be called an ABCBA pattern. (See diagram below.)

Many themes of call and response, promise and rescue are echoed between Genesis and Deuteronomy and between Exodus and Numbers, and key themes of obedience and faith resound in all five books.

Key Theological Themes

Certain key themes flow through the five books, sometimes limited to only one book, sometimes found in several books. The most important are:

1. The primeval history of the world before Israel's own remembered history began (Gn 1–11).

2. The promises and blessings to the great tribal ancestors, the patriarchs and matriarchs (Gn 12–50).

3. The rescue and exodus out of Egypt (Ex 1–18).

4. The giving of a covenant and laws (Ex 19:1–Nm 10, 10).

5. Guidance in the wilderness (Ex 13–18; Nm 10:11–36:13).

6. The conditional warnings to guide Israel through its "salvation history" in the land (Dt).

7. The conquest of the land (Gn passim; Nm and Dt).

These all interact. Note, for example, that the promise of land is announced as God's plan of action in Exodus 3:7–10; but it has been foreshadowed to Abraham in Genesis 12:1–3 and then noted as fulfilled in Deuteronomy 34:1–3, just as the conquest is to begin.

Reading the Pentateuch without Being a Fundamentalist

Each book of the Pentateuch has its own unique flavor, and each deals with a different part of the

A. Genesis	(the preface in which God calls and forms the ancestors)
B. Exodus	(the wilderness journey to the mountain of Sinai to meet God)
C. Leviticus	(the center at the top of Sinai where God gives Covenant and Law)
B. Numbers	(the wilderness journey from Sinai to the Promised Land)
A. Deuteronomy	(the epilogue in which God calls and forms Israel for the land)

story and the laws by which Israel was to live. But even if we can read each one separately, it is even more important to read them together as a single story. We have already noted how these five books tell the history (in its ancient sense) of the world and of Israel in particular from the beginnings of creation down to the hopeful moment when Israel stands on the edge of a new land and a new home in Palestine. Two things can be noted about that history mixed with laws and lessons: the first is that it is to serve as a handbook or a rule book for how Israel is to live in the land it is about to possess (see Dt 4:1), and the second is that it certainly does not make a complete history, although it is a complete story. It picks and chooses only certain events and certain themes to treat, and these all have very significant religious lessons to teach. That is, it is a theology book as much or more than it is a real history of the people.

It is hard for us to escape a desire to see a strict modern scientific history in the stories of the Pentateuch, but let's look at one illustration to help us. In Genesis 4, Cain kills Abel when they are the only two living children of Adam and Eve according to the story. Cain is punished by God and sent far to the East. Then the text says that "Cain had relations with his wife" in Genesis 4:17. But what wife was possible in a real history? Up to this point, the story has moved from the world's first killing to a new theme—how the world was populated—and it doesn't seem to bother the author that the second cannot fit this history just related. The only concern for the writer is to make a series of religious lessons that we can all learn from.

But the Pentateuch is not an idle story, either. It is very carefully crafted and put together to tell of the crucial things that happened in the past that we need to know in order to discover God. It tells of human weaknesses and urgings toward sin, about the failure of most of the world to know God, and the divine choice of Israel to witness the loving concern of God to others, and how God was revealed in a number of central events: (1) the choice of the patriarchs, (2) the giving of a covenant, (3) the law to be obeyed, and (4) the guidance through the wilderness to a promised land.

The Pentateuch is a great work of art. It tells a vital story of God's relationship to the world with power and beauty. It proposes history but does not allow us to question it too closely about exact descriptions. It proposes religious and theological lessons but warns us not to treat it like a textbook full of lists of truths. It proposes a story that will teach us by sharing its experience with our experience. We must read it for enjoyment and for skillful storytelling. Once we have understood the whole as literature, we can ask, "How does this literary style give us history?" and "How does it present its message?" For an overview of the history of how the Christian tradition has interpreted the Pentateuch as part of the whole Old Testament, see the article by Kevin Madigan, "Catholic Interpretation of the Bible" (RG 54–67).

Critical Interpretation of the Pentateuch

Interpretation of the Bible changed radically in the growth of modern thought after the Reformation and with the Age of Enlightenment in the seventeenth and eighteenth centuries. Much of the early efforts at a critical and historical interpretation of the Scriptures began with work on the Pentateuch. Before we look at how those scholars tried to recover the actual historical development of the Pentateuchal texts and what methods they proposed for understanding its meaning, we need to note briefly how the New Testament itself makes use of texts from the Pentateuch in order to have a point of comparison.

The New Testament

Jesus himself and the various authors of New Testament writings often cite texts from the Bible, which of course was simply the Old Testament in their day. Almost always, they cite passages from the narratives and rarely refer to the legal materials in Leviticus and Numbers, although the laws first given on Mount Sinai in Exodus 20—23 and then the speech of Moses on the law in Deuteronomy were known to them. Often the stories are cited as proofs for something that Jesus taught or that the apostles were preaching. An example is found in Jesus' teaching on divorce that is found in Matthew 19:5 (and Mark 10:7f). Jesus refers to Genesis 2:24 when he says "a man shall leave his father and mother and be joined to his wife, and the two shall become one flesh."

A few stories from the Pentateuch are treated

as a *type case*. Paul in Romans 4:9–22 cites the story of Abraham recorded in Genesis 15:1–6 and 17:1–5 as a forerunner of a chosen people having faith without having the law of Moses to live by. Abraham is viewed as a forerunner of the Christian believer; but in a general sense this usage may be seen as a type of prophecy—the Old Testament person foreshadows God's revelation to the Gentiles; like Abraham, they are called without living under the Law. Elsewhere, the authors of the Gospels and Acts quote Old Testament passages from the prophets and psalms as predictions of Jesus as Messiah and to help explain his death and resurrection. But occasionally, Paul uses an almost allegorical method of interpreting biblical texts. In Galatians 4:21–31, he treats the children of Hagar and Sarah, that is, Ishmael and Isaac from Genesis 16–21, as prototypes of Jews and Christians. Hebrews 7:1–10 does the same with the story of Melchizedek and Abraham from Genesis 14:18–20. The author wants to show that Melchizedek represents a fore-type of Christ, who is the new and eternal high priest. To do this, however, he plays on the etymology of the name Melchizedek as "king of righteousness" and Melchizedek's position as king of Salem ("king of peace") and fancifully builds up a case that since no mention is made in the text of the king's parents, his birth, or his death after the event, he prefigures the eternal character of Jesus as divine high priest.

Overall, however, New Testament use of the Bible is nearly always focused on showing the deep connection between the meaning of earlier revelation and the person and role of Jesus. A good source for all the quotations of the Old Testament in the New is R. Bratcher, *Old Testament Quotations in the New Testament* (United Bible Societies, 1987).

The Post-Reformation Interest in Sources

The Protestant Reformation stressed the return to the study of the original texts of the Old Testament in Hebrew and other languages. This soon led to the keen observation that the vocabulary and style of passages were not consistent within the Pentateuch itself and perhaps showed signs of combining different (and older) traditions together.

The first (1678) truly modern Pentateuchal scholar was a French priest, Richard Simon. Simon noted after careful analysis that Genesis 1 and 2 seemed to differ in style, and that this was found elsewhere in Genesis and probably showed that Moses used several different sources in writing the five books of the Pentateuch. For such a modest insight, his work was condemned by church authorities and put on the index. But it opened the door. He was followed in the next century by many others who gradually explored the differences between passages that constantly called God by the proper name *Yahweh,* and those that called God by the more general term *Elohim.* The NAB always renders *Yahweh* by the English word "LORD," and *Elohim* by "God."

These could be traced as two complete parallel stories interwoven throughout the Pentateuch up to the book of Numbers. Arguments developed over whether these had been originally two separate written works that told the same history of Israel, or whether there was one original version that was supplemented or added to over many centuries to make two variants with time. In the early nineteenth century, scholars began to note that the so-called Elohist passages really represented two separate accounts themselves, one more narrative and interested in the great interventions of God, the other more concerned with priestly and ritual actions. These were named in turn the Elohist and the Priestly strands.

By the mid-nineteenth century it was commonly agreed that there had indeed been three independent versions of the Pentateuch's basic story, which could be titled by the initials J (for German *Jahwist),* E (for Elohist), and P (for Priestly). At the same time, the book of Deuteronomy was acknowledged to be a fourth and totally separate source of its own that could be labeled D naturally enough. In 1878 Julius Wellhausen published his *Prolegomena to the History of Israel,* in which he laid out the arguments for the postexilic composition of the P source. In the process he not only analyzed the arguments for the "four-source theory," as it was now called, but he supported the basic sequence of JE as monarchic, followed by D in the early exilic period, and then by P in the postexilic period, and he identified the four historical situations that led to each different telling of the history.

The Development of Form Criticism

Shortly after Wellhausen's great summary of the theory of four separate documents was published, attention turned to getting behind the four sources to the original units that comprised them. Where did all the individual incidents and poems and stories and laws come from? Thus, at the beginning of the twentieth century was born form criticism, the search for the earliest and the smallest units of the tradition. The founder of this method was Hermann Gunkel, who wrote extensively on the form-critical analysis of Genesis and the Psalms. These scholars were interested in the literary *genres* that made up the four sources. If scholars could identify the special form of a poem or a hymn or a law or a narrative, they could probably identify the situation out of which it came. Thus the victory hymn of Israel over the Egyptians in Exodus 15 can be further specified as praise of God as a divine warrior who battles alongside Israel's troops and guarantees the defeat of the enemy. This helps us realize it originates in a tribal setting before the people were settled in a kingdom, and perhaps was sung at an annual festival of God's victory.

Form criticism can even help distinguish different types of law. The Ten Commandments in Exodus 20:1–17 are simple and direct commands to do or not to do something. They differ completely from most of the laws in the Pentateuch that specify "if you do such and such, then the penalty will be the following." Because the laws had these two differing styles, scholars assume that the first kind was more like a catechetical instruction for children to help them memorize and summarize the law; while the second type came from actual court cases in which a decision had to be made.

It can honestly be said that the work of form-critical study of the Pentateuch was the dominant task of scholarly study of the Bible in the first half of the twentieth century. As scholarship has developed in the last forty years, both source and form criticism have given way before new concerns and the new methods needed to deal with them. Before noting such shifts, what can be said of the accomplishment of these older methods?

The Fruits of Source Criticism

When scholarly criticism was born in the seventeenth and eighteenth centuries, it first noted the difficulties in the text, which suggested more than one style or author. Examples included the different names for God in the two creation stories of Genesis 1:1–2:4a; and 2:4b–3:24. The first always calls the divine name "God," the second always uses the title "LORD God." The first is extremely formal and shows great reverence for God's transcendence, while the second makes God almost like a human being, working in clay to build a body and conferring in person with his creature. Many other places in the text show the same clear differences. Also, they noted many examples of double accounts which, except for some small differences, looked like exactly the same story being told twice. Compare Genesis 12 and 20 on Abraham passing his wife Sarah off as his sister; or the two accounts on how Hagar had to flee to the wilderness with Ishmael in Genesis 16 and 21.

After three centuries of study, scholars reached a general consensus in the late nineteenth century that there were indeed the four sources described in the section above. They can be briefly described in the following manner to reveal their individual characters and the probable date and historical situation from which they came:

The Yahwist (J)

This is the earliest and most comprehensive source of the whole story. It was written in Judah, probably Jerusalem. It was long believed to have been written under King Solomon or one of his successors in the late tenth century or early ninth century BC, but now many scholars are convinced that it was done much later in the monarchy or even in the Exile, while others believe that at least many additions can be found in the present J text that were added much later to an early version. The authors wished to show that the promises to Abraham were fulfilled in the empire founded by David. It uses the name *Yahweh* for God and has a frank and earthy language about God's closeness to those he chooses. It naturally favors strong leaders of the type of David.

The Elohist (E)

When Solomon's kingdom fell apart and the north went its own way, it needed an official account of the tradition that reflected its anti-Jerusalem view. Early source critics believed it was written shortly after the founding of the Northern Kingdom just after 900 BC, but many scholars today wonder if there ever was such an independent document; the majority perhaps believe the unique E elements are simply revisions or additions to the basic J text over the centuries. However, many of its characteristics are strong in certain sections of the Pentateuch, such as the Jacob stories or the Exodus narrative. These passages prefer the name *Elohim* for God and strongly emphasize Jacob and northern places such as Bethel, Shechem, and the like.

The Deuteronomist (D)

Deuteronomy and those books influenced by it, the so-called Deuteronomistic History (Joshua, Judges, Samuel, and Kings), are generally understood today to reflect the Exile in their final form. Many scholars trace their origins to the eighth and seventh centuries BC as a reassessment of the J and E traditions in light of pagan inroads and unfaithful kings. It has affinities to the Elohist in its stress that the covenant with Moses is more important than kingship, and on the need for total loyalty to Yahweh; and it has affinities to J with its emphasis on Jerusalem. Unlike J, the D source restricts worship of Yahweh to Jerusalem as the only legitimate center for north and south alike.

The Priestly Source (P)

Much of the P material on cult and law probably dates to the same time as Deuteronomy, but its ordering and some new materials are clearly reflective of the needs of the exilic community in the sixth century BC. It stresses obedience to the law and the permanence of God's blessing no matter how desperate the situation, and it demands personal commitment to God. Most probably the P editors arranged all four of the sources into our present Pentateuch around 500 BC. Some commentaries date it to as much as a century later. Both P and the Pentateuch as a whole reflect a definite Judean point of view in their final shapes.

J and E went along side by side as long as the two kingdoms lasted from 930 to 722 BC. When the northern kingdom fell, its E story was carried down to Judah by refugees and there combined at some point around 700 BC with J into a single account. Still later, in the time of the fall of Judah itself in 587 BC and during its exile, D and P were also combined with JE to make our final JEDP. Editors and teachers from the Priestly circles put it into final shape, and possibly it was this work that Ezra the Scribe made all the people accept as the Book of the Law of God about 458 BC (see Neh 8–9).

Form Criticism and the Process of Tradition

Although the results of source criticism have largely stood the test of time, the interest in going back behind these written sources led to the dominant role of form criticism in this century. The heart of the form-critical method is recognition of the various literary genres and types used in biblical books. Each genre has a certain style and way of being expressed that corresponds to its purpose or function. So a letter always has a heading and salutation because a person who receives it will feel this personal touch and more likely pay attention to its message than if one just writes someone a list of facts on a page. In the opposite fashion, a telephone book always uses columns, alphabetic order, and a listlike format because a continuous letterlike paragraph would make it impossible to locate a name, which after all is the sole purpose of the directory.

Form criticism assumes that communication is socially determined by rules that reveal what kind of thing someone is trying to say. Scholars recognized that, in ancient society especially, most people depended on oral recitation and memory aids because knowledge of writing was reserved to a few, and writing materials were scarce. Thus ancient ways of speaking were stereotyped—that is, they stuck to certain well-known patterns of saying things that were used according to their intended purpose—and these genres lasted over many centuries with little variation in form. Actually, each time something was said or passed on, speakers gave it a slightly different emphasis or touch. Only when it was written down and became fixed did it stop changing altogether, yet the basic form remained constant.

To understand Pentateuch texts from a form-critical viewpoint, first see if you can find the beginning and end of a single section (what are the limits of a unit?). Then attempt to name the genre or form (is it a hymn? law? temple lament? historical narrative? fable? myth?). Next, guess at what might have been its original purpose or setting in the ancient life situation (is it part of a long epic of great heroic ancestors? Is it from the temple liturgy? Is it part of a catechism for children? Is it propaganda?). Finally, ask what purpose it plays in this narrative or section (Does it add a new episode to the plot? Does it support a line of argument? Does it explain the character of the hero?).

Our interest in the original form of a unit of biblical literature, and our investigation of where it came from in the life of ancient Israel, should draw our attention to a final critical consideration: to question the entire process of how traditions get passed on and grow or change. Both form and source criticism fall under a more general interest in the *transmission* history of the text (often called its tradition history or redaction criticism). Each original statement or story or law goes through a process of being combined with other units and then combined again in still larger works. Thus collections grow and stories are put in a new order or used in a different way for a new purpose. At the same time, each age looks at the old stories and laws and often rewrites or changes them to fit modern times.

The redaction critic tries to trace this history of transmission, editing, and adapting from the earliest stages right up to the final form as we have it in the Pentateuch today. It is a complex and difficult process that can only be done by those who know Hebrew as well as the history and literary works of the Near East. But even the new reader can get some flavor of it by carefully looking at a text, noting its structures and development, enjoying it as literature, and using the commentaries and other available tools.

Current Trends in Critical Study

Both source and form criticism work directly from what we can know of the text by comparing it with other literary styles and literary works. Much of the inspiration for form criticism, for example, came from the great work on the origins and development of fairy tales and folk stories by the brothers Grimm and Hans Christian Anderson in the early nineteenth century. But these methods have been mostly analytical; that is, they break down the narratives and laws into smaller and smaller units, and assign dates and origins to each piece. This makes it harder to read the biblical books as single works. There has been a definite movement to counterbalance this with rediscovery of methods that can be used to read the Pentateuch more fully as a whole story or literary work.

Some of these are *rhetorical criticism,* which tries to show the literary artistry in the combination of pieces into a whole and how the whole story is structured for effect; *structural analysis,* which searches for the language patterns and levels of meaning that control both the plot and the underlying message by word clues; *reader-response criticism,* which studies a text by paying attention to what the audience would hear and expect and how an author tries to reach that audience—this requires imagining ourselves in the world of the text. All of these are under the broad category of modern literary theory, and they have become very important new directions for biblical study, especially of the early books. Closely connected to these is *canonical criticism,* which tries to understand how a book like Genesis or Exodus is read as part of the larger collection of sacred books. Is there importance in Genesis being first? What happens when we read the wisdom books before the prophets in the order of our present canon?

Still another major area of new study focuses on the contributions of the social sciences. Sociology gives us models for how various types of social groupings interact together that might throw light on how ancient tribal or town or small-kingdom forms of life were lived in biblical times. Anthropology and ethnology let us study people who are still living more like the ancients did than like the way we live. Archaeology as well discovers and re-creates life as it was from stones and human remains.

Truly, Bible study today employs all the tools made available by cooperative sharing of scholarly knowledge among different sciences. At the same time, none of the gains of one movement, such as those of the early source critics, are ever thrown away as useless, but they need to be supplemented and refined by later research. And whenever one branch of study concentrates too much on just a part of the picture, we can be sure that other scholars will arise to call us back to what we have neglected.

The Historical Background of the Pentateuch

A Wide Diversity of Materials

The Pentateuch as a historical narrative begins with the creation of the earth and follows human history up to the time the Israelites enter the land of Canaan. In fact, however, few passages in the five books really reflect historical records of the past. First of all, many sections are made up of laws that have been included from collections dating to different periods in Israel's history. In a very loose way we could say they all belong under the name of Moses, the first lawgiver, because he founded the way of defining the covenant by means of religious laws.

Second, some stories are clearly not about ordinary time in history at all. All of Genesis 1–11 treats the creation of the world and the first events of human existence without any historical concreteness. As a literary genre, they do not fit the category of history telling. Instead, they are about why things are the way they are—why God made humans this way, why we sin, why we die, why it is hard to obey God, why men and women are different, why the earth is plagued with floods, how God deals with evil. Such stories about the divine purposes at the beginning of creation, and about the nature of human life as we experience it, are usually called *myths* if they are told in story form. Genesis 1–11 is almost entirely based on the myth genre. And even the stories of the patriarchs and matriarchs in Genesis 12–50 are not a modern type of recalling history but largely model hero stories built around folktale types of storytelling. Even though they are based on real history, it is often hard to pin them down to exact locations and events.

The View of the Ancient Historian

This special character of the Pentateuch as both law and story alerts us to a fundamental problem that plagues most modern believers who read the Bible. Contemporary understanding of history differs greatly from that of the ancient world. Modern people expect proof through documents, witnesses, electronic records such as audio tapes or video recordings, and careful digging to find out just what happened, without all the propaganda and personal bias of a particular interest group. This is a difficult order to fill in any case, since all of us, even trained historians, have special points of view that color what we find. It is, however, an impossible order to demand of the ancient historian. They never thought this way, and as a result did not record the events of their time with such neutral objectivity, nor did they ever believe in telling the past as a simple and objective search for exactly what happened.

First, of course, they had no ways of getting much of the historical record. There were fewer written accounts and documents, there were no electronic or permanent ways of storing information in large and easy-to-produce books like we have, and there were no schools of science that valued exact observation as a primary end. Thus little or nothing was preserved for its own sake. Second, everything that went on told us about something important for our lives. This meant that most history was seen as a lesson for humans to learn by. History was written largely to persuade people of a certain type of behavior or a certain outlook on the world. It was viewed much as we would understand propaganda for a good cause, perhaps like newspaper editorials that take sides to explain major events or argue for their favorite causes.

The bottom line, therefore, is that ancient history was more interested in explaining *why* something happened than *what* precisely took place, and it was more interested in the message it communicated for the audience than in a record of accurate details for future study.

This insight will help us understand why the ancient historians felt no awkwardness in adding long lists of laws to a good story. The laws were vital parts of the "message" that the story was supposed to tell.

Moses as the Author of the Pentateuch

Traditionally, Moses has been considered the author of the Pentateuch. Orthodox Jews and Conservative Christians still hold this position strongly, but historical scholarship does not. Nowhere do these books actually mention an author, but frequently they state that Moses taught the people their contents, especially the laws (see Lv 23:1–25). If Moses is the actual author, then all the laws at least would have their origin in a direct revelation from God on Mount Sinai. The book of Nehemiah relates how Ezra brought forth "the book of the law of Moses which the LORD prescribed for Israel" (Neh 8:1), and insisted on a total commitment to its words. This passage has generally been understood to mark the beginning of a concept of canon, that is, that the book of the law of Moses was sacred and not to be revised or added to in the future. Ezra made his proclamation sometime after 458 BC, far removed from the days of Moses in the late second millennium BC. Moreover, the response of the people, and Ezra's efforts to explain it to them, suggest that they certainly did not already know this book as it was read out loud. Although they all recognized the teaching, they did not seem to be aware of this particular collection as a single work (read Neh 8–10).

For this reason, and for many others, including the fact that many of the laws belong to situations much later than the time of Moses and the people in the desert (see, for example, the laws on worshipping at the one sanctuary in Jerusalem in Deuteronomy 12), modern scholars do not try to prove that Moses was the author of the *written* books of the Pentateuch. Rather, Moses was the founder of Israelite faith as we find it in the Bible. The Pentateuch, however, contains many, many traditions, laws, stories, hymns, and reflections added by later generations from earliest times right down to the time when it was completed and Ezra declared it sacred so that further additions were no longer permitted.

Historical Dating of the Pentateuchal Traditions

Despite the difficulties in locating the exact historical events and pinning the materials to firm dates, the discoveries of other ancient tablets and chronicles, and the findings of archaeologists digging in ancient sites have given us some idea of what each different period in the second millennium BC was like. Scholars who hold a more conservative view generally situate the patriarchal narratives somewhere between 2000 and 1500 BC, the Exodus event between 1450 and 1250 BC, and the invasion of the land of Palestine around 1250 to 1200 BC. As doubts have arisen about the accuracy of the portrayal of the invasion of Canaan as recounted in the accounts of Exodus and Numbers, many scholars are expressing caution about whether the descriptions accurately reflect genuine memories of such early periods, or are rather the creations of later writers, who used some earlier materials and memories but more likely reflected the life of their own times. Many anachronisms occur in the patriarchal narratives for example, such as use of the domesticated camel, or the presence of the Philistines, neither of which were known in the first half of the second millennium.

Arguments for some early dates are more likely than others. Thus, because Egypt had foreign rulers between 1750 BC and 1550 BC, scholars have argued that the Joseph story fits best into this time frame; because Exodus 1:11 says the enslaved Israelites built the cities Pithom and Raamses, they would date the Exodus to the reign of Ramesses II (about 1295 to 1235 BC). On the other hand, lack of evidence for the violent destruction of Canaanite cities in the twelfth century BC can be used to argue for later tradition idealizing the past. For further discussion of dates and times, consult an introduction to the Old Testament or a short history of Israel listed in the bibliography.

A brief chart of comparative events may also be helpful (see RG 97).

Reflecting on the Message of the Pentateuch

The Theological Themes that Unite the Pentateuchal Books

In reading the Pentateuch with its vast array of materials that reflect a world of thought so different from our own, we need some guideposts. We can generally find them in those themes and topics to which the books return over and over again. The demand for obedience to the divine will would be one such example. From Adam and Eve and their failure to obey, down to Moses' own failure when striking the rock for water in Numbers 20, great stress is laid on obedience. Another way of identifying central topics is to follow the dramatic action that focuses on a certain moment or specific action. The conferring of a covenant in Exodus 19–24 is an example of this type of guidepost. The biblical tradition is so rich that there may be trouble trying to limit such important topics to ten or twenty or even thirty. Nor would it be wise to do so, since every time we read we will discover new aspects of revelation that speak to us today.

Before listing any of the major theological themes of the Pentateuch, it will help us to understand them all if we remember that the Bible is not only a book of God but about God. The central thread that weaves together all the other strands in these books tells of that God who acts in human history. More particularly, the Bible al-

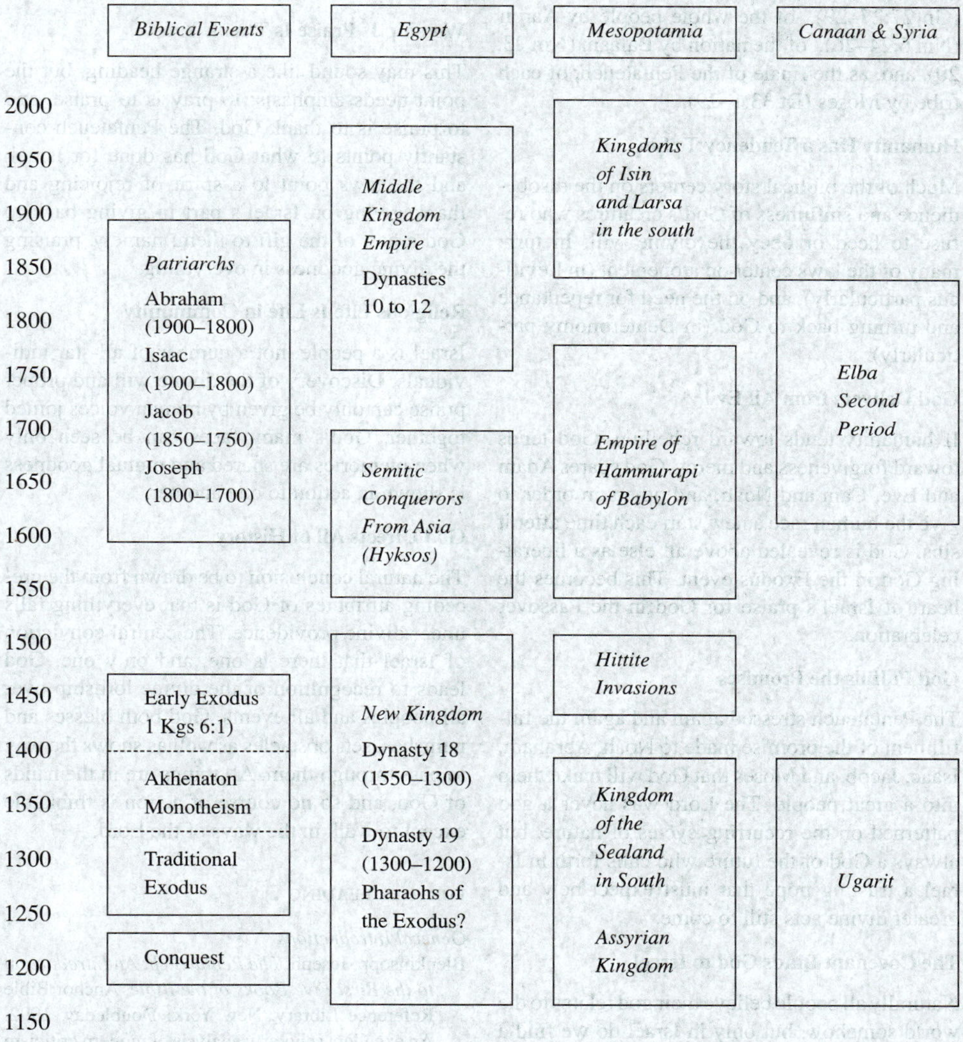

most never worries about the general need for a divine principle in the world, or about the gods of other peoples, but only about this God who has been revealed as the one God and who chooses to be known to Israel in a special way. In short, the following themes all flow from the Lord's conversation with the people—and their responses!

Ten Central Themes

Creation Establishes a Good World

When Genesis 1 affirms that God created all things by speaking a word, it really means that all is ordered by the divine plan and works together in harmony. After creation was completed, God looked and "found it very good" (Gn 1:31). Thus, no matter what evil and failure will follow in world history, we are to recall that goodness will prevail.

God Has Blessed Human Life

An important corollary of a good world is divine blessing upon it. Twice Genesis tells us that God blessed the human race (Gn 1:28; 9:1). Later, much is made of the blessing of Abraham (Gn 12:2), of Sarah and Isaac (Gn 17:16), of Jacob

(Gn 27:27–29), of the whole people by Aaron (Nm 6:24–26), of the nation by Balaam (Nm 23:20), and, as the finale of the Pentateuch, of each tribe by Moses (Dt 33:1–29).

Humanity Has a Tendency To Sin

Much of the biblical story centers on the disobedience and sinfulness of God's creatures who refuse to heed or obey the divine will. In turn, many of the laws center on atonement (in Leviticus particularly), and on the need for repentance and turning back to God (in Deuteronomy particularly).

God Delivers from All Evil

If humanity tends toward rebellion, God tends toward forgiveness and mercy. God spares Adam and Eve, Cain and Noah, and others in order to give the human race a new start each time after it sins. God is revealed above all else as a liberating God in the Exodus event. This becomes the heart of Israel's praise for God in the Passover celebration.

God Fulfills the Promises

The Pentateuch stressed again and again the fulfillment of the promise made to Noah, Abraham, Isaac, Jacob, and Moses that God will make them into a great people. The Lord was never a god patterned on the recurring cycles of nature, but always a God of the future who calls forth in Israel a trusting hope that must expect new and greater divine acts still to come.

The Covenant Binds God to Israel

Naturally all people believe their god relates to the world somehow, but only in Israel do we find a union based on love and loyalty pledged to each other in a permanent union that actually respects the role of the human partner. The covenant is the heart of biblical faith because it expresses a unique bond between God and people, built on past deeds but committed to future collaboration.

The Law Expresses Israel's Bond to God

The covenant establishes a relationship, but the laws of the Pentateuch show how that relationship can be lived out by the people—they are not restrictive rules but a dynamic way of life that expresses faithfulness to God in actions as well as words, always with a touch of joy for flavoring.

Worship Is Praise Is Thank You

This may sound like a strange heading, but the point needs emphasis: to pray is to praise, and to praise is to thank God. The Pentateuch constantly points to what God has done for Israel, and the laws point to a spirit of rejoicing and thanksgiving on Israel's part in giving back to God a part of the gift to them: namely, praising the divine goodness in everything.

Religious Life Is Life in Community

Israel is a people, not a number of all-star individuals. Discovery of the divine will and proper praise can only be given by human voices joined together. God's many faces can be seen only when memories are shared and mutual goodness is shown in action to one another.

God Directs All of History

The natural conclusion to be drawn from the preceding attributes of God is that everything falls under divine providence. The central conviction of Israel that there is one, and only one, God leads to recognition of the divine lordship over all peoples and all events. God both blesses and punishes, sets obstacles as well as shows the way to pass through them. All things are in the hands of God, and so no course of action is thinkable except to walk in the ways of the Lord.

FURTHER READING

General Introductions

Blenkinsopp, Joseph. *The Pentateuch: An Introduction to the First Five Books of the Bible*. Anchor Bible Reference Library. New York: Doubleday, 1992. An excellent scholarly analysis of modern criticism and its difficulties and achievements.

Boadt, Lawrence, C.S.P. *Reading the Old Testament: An Introduction*. Mahwah, NJ: Paulist Press, 1985. A readable overview of all the critical and theological issues of Old Testament study.

Campbell, Anthony, and Mark O'Brien. *Sources of the Pentateuch*. Minneapolis: Fortress, 1993. The authors provide texts and notes on the various documents that supposedly stand behind the Pentateuch and its growth.

Childs, Brevard. *Introduction to the Old Testament as Scripture*. Minneapolis: Fortress, 1979. A very technical but excellent introduction to each book of the Bible as it developed through the process of transmission and redaction.

General Commentaries

Barton, John, and John Muddiman. *The Oxford Bible Commentary.* Oxford and New York: Oxford University Press, 2001.

The Collegeville Old Testament Commentary. Collegeville, MN: Liturgical Press, 1985, 1987. Short, handy series written for Catholics.

The International Bible Commentary. Collegeville, MN: Liturgical Press, 1998. Scholars from every continent contribute to this work that emphasizes a literary approach to interpretation of each book, combining literary theory, historical criticism, and the history of how the book was used and interpreted throughout the centuries.

The Message of the Old Testament. Wilmington, DE: Michael Glazier, 1980, 1984. Readable middle-level commentaries on the theology of each book of the Bible.

The New Interpreter's Bible. Nashville: Abingdon Press, 1994. The combination of modern scholarship and theological reflection in a very readable format make this an excellent resource for parish libraries.

The New Jerome Biblical Commentary. Englewood Cliffs, NJ: Prentice Hall, 1990. A superb one-volume commentary on all of Scripture with fine background articles for study of the Pentateuch.

Biblical Criticism

Brueggemann, Walter, and Hans Walter Wolff. *The Vitality of Old Testament Traditions.* 2nd ed. Atlanta: John Knox, 1982. Readable essays on each of the four sources.

Friedman, Richard Elliott. *Who Wrote the Bible?* New York: Summit Books, 1987. Most readable account ever of the excitement of discovering the four sources in the Pentateuch.

Ralph, Margaret Nutting. *"And God Said What?"* Mahwah, NJ: Paulist Press, 1986. A very understandable introduction to literary forms in the Bible.

Bible Dictionaries

Achtemeier, Paul, ed. *Harper's Bible Dictionary.* New York: Harper & Row, 1985. Another excellent, up-to-date resource book.

Freedman, David Noel, ed. *Anchor Bible Dictionary.* New York: Doubleday, 1991. Comes in six large volumes and is the most complete resource tool available.

McKenzie, John L. *Dictionary of the Bible.* Milwaukee: Bruce Publishing, 1965. A superb work on almost every facet of Bible study but somewhat dated in its information on the latest trends in criticism. Its strength lies in McKenzie's incisive insights into the Catholic biblical tradition.

Metzger, Bruce M., and Michael D. Coogan. *The Oxford Companion to the Bible.* New York and Oxford: Oxford University Press, 1993.

The Individual Books of the Pentateuch

Bailey, Lloyd. *Leviticus.* Atlanta: John Knox, 1987. Simple but useful handbook to the various laws in Leviticus.

Boadt, Lawrence. *Genesis.* The International Bible Commentary. Collegeville, MN: Liturgical Press, 1998.

Childs, Brevard. *The Book of Exodus.* Old Testament Library. Philadelphia: Westminster Press, 1974. A very detailed treatment of Exodus and the origins of its traditions and its history of use in the Church.

Craighie, Peter. *The Book of Deuteronomy.* New International Commentary on the Old Testament. Grand Rapids: Eerdmans, 1976. A readable and thorough explanation of the theology of Deuteronomy.

Levine, Baruch. *Numbers 1–20.* Anchor Bible. New York: Doubleday, 1993.

Milgrom, Jacob. *Leviticus 1–16.* Anchor Bible. New York: Doubleday, 1994.

———. *Leviticus 17–22.* Anchor Bible. New York: Doubleday, 2000.

———. *Leviticus 23–27.* Anchor Bible. New York: Doubleday, 2002.

Sarna, Nahum. *Understanding Genesis: The Heritage of Biblical Israel.* New York: Schocken Books, 1966. Very fine explanation of the message and background of Genesis from a Jewish viewpoint.

———. *Exploring Exodus.* New York: Schocken Books, 1986. The follow-up to *Understanding Genesis* and just as readable, just as informative.

Weinfeld, Moshe. *Deuteronomy 1–11.* Anchor Bible. New York: Doubleday, 1991.

Westermann, Claus. *Genesis 1–11; Genesis 12–36; Genesis 37–50.* 3 vols. Minneapolis: Augsburg Press, 1984, 1987.

Other Literatures of Biblical Times

Matthews, Victor, and Don Benjamin. *Old Testament Parallels.* Rev. ed. Mahwah, NJ: Paulist Press, 1998.

Pritchard, James. *Ancient Near Eastern Texts Relating to the Old Testament.* Princeton: Princeton University Press, 1969. An excellent anthology. Referred to as ANET.

GENESIS

[see pages 9–81 of the Old Testament]

An Overview of the Book of Genesis

If we begin our study of the Bible with Genesis, it is important to remember that this is clearly *the beginning*. Whatever it contains has been chosen and put into place to provide the foundation for all that will follow in the Bible. Although it makes a great story in its own right, it also requires attention to the key themes that it develops if we are to fully understand its purpose. In order to do this effectively, first read quickly the entire fifty chapters, just glancing over them to get the drift of the "plot." After you have the basic story in mind and have gotten a small taste of its style, or better, its varied styles that change throughout the book, a second detailed study of each section will reveal much more.

The Major Divisions of Genesis

Traditionally scholars have divided Genesis into two parts: chapters 1 through 11 and 12 through 50. This is based on their subject matter and the type of literature that is found in each part. Both parts appear at first to be a single continuous story, but closer examination reveals strong differences between them. Simply put, the first eleven chapters discuss the process of creation and ideas about the earliest human ancestors as ancients understood them. The second part describes the unique traditions about the concrete clans or tribal ancestors of Israel itself. As literature, Genesis 1–11 is defined as *myth,* which is a story that attempts to explain some mystery of the relation of the gods (whom we do not know) to the world of humans (which we do know). Every myth is really also a model pattern, either bad or good, of human behavior. Although a myth in form, Genesis 1–11 is often simply called the "primeval history." In contrast, the stories of the patriarchs and matriarchs in Genesis 12–50 are more like legends, in which people recognize events from their past, although they may not have happened exactly the way they are described. They relate individual events as they have been passed down, and which have shaped the special identity of Israel.

Both types of writing give us models to follow but, of course, not in the same way. The world of the primeval history has little in common with what we ourselves experience in the world. It is a special world when things were different and the laws of time and intimacy with the gods were different from our own time. On the other hand, Abraham, Isaac, Jacob, and the others in chapters 12 to 50 wrestle with the same world that we do, and their decisions have consequences, which are concrete and very much part of the later history of a people.

We can perhaps note some differences between them in table at top of next page.

Subdivisions of Genesis 1–50

This two-part structure can be broken down further into smaller narratives that carry the story forward and are themselves joined by a variety of means that explain how they relate to one another. See table at bottom of next page.

This is only a general sketch. Note how the four major sections of the primal history match four sections of the great founding leaders of Israel. In each the editors were skilled storytellers who wove the parts together to make one whole. But they hardly disguised their intention to show that there are stages in the history of humanity, and in the history of Israel in particular. Each period can have a major impact on the next. For world history, it was the constant spread of sin; for Israel, it was the constant development of blessing.

We could also organize the book around the stages of major figures whom God has summoned forth. Many commentators break the book down into four large blocs or stages:

• The prologue: all humankind is called to blessing; but sin prevails (Gn 1–11)

• The story of Abraham and his call, blessing, and promise (Gn 12–25)

• The stories of his son Isaac and grandson Jacob and how they carry on the blessing (Gn 26–36)

• The story of Joseph in Egypt in preparation for God's great self-revelation in the Exodus (Gn 37–50)

These four sections indicate clearly enough that the plot of Genesis focuses on major deci-

Genesis 1–11	*Genesis 12–50*
1. It is set in time that is before human history	1. It is set in historical times well known to ancient records
2. Its exact place is vague—somewhere to the the East	2. It is set in Palestine and Egypt and northern Mesopotamia exactly
3. The persons seem like symbols—nothing is known of their lives	3. The persons have names and engage in actions typical of the second millennium BC
4. Many of the stories have the form of myths like those known from Mesopotamia	4. The stories are largely sagalike or epic narratives similar to oral lore of tribal groups
5. Most of the events seem to take place in a supernatural setting unlike our own	5. The major stories keep events close to the type of experience all human eras share
6. The purpose deals only with the beginnings of humanity long before Israel's time	6. The purpose is to trace the direct tribal and clan ancestors of Israel itself

sions by key individuals. The unlikely conclusion of the story finds this people apparently in prosperity and blessing somewhere else than where they were promised. In this sense, the book of Genesis can be read as an unfinished plot of a mystery story.

Division by the Special *Toledoth* Name Lists

The NAB points out in its introduction to Genesis that the book is divided into separate sections by genealogical notices, each of which begins "These are the descendants of . . ." In the list of eleven below, it should be noted that the NAB is not always consistent in the way it translates the same Hebrew phrase, nor should this particular method of dividing be considered necessarily the most important. It did serve one of the editor's purposes, namely to show that generations come and generations go, but God's plan moves ahead no matter what. Nevertheless, these lists are truly dividers since they often group all the members of a single family line or tribe in one place to mark a break with what has just gone before. Sometimes, however, the list is given before the events, and sometimes at the end. This can easily be discovered by looking up each example:

Gn 2:4a "The descendants of heaven and earth," that is, the second story of creation, begins after this statement. (Here the NAB refers to it as "the *story* of the heavens."

Genesis 1–3 The story of God's creation and the first human sin	*Genesis 12–25* Abraham is chosen to receive God's blessing and give witness to others
Genesis 4–5 The evil of sin grows and spreads through the world	*Genesis 21–27* The son, Isaac, inherits the promise and passes it on
Genesis 6–9 Evil overwhelms the world; God must begin again with a new blessing	*Genesis 27–36; 48–50* Jacob in turn receives the promise; he is blessed with and bears the twelve sons who will become Israel
Genesis 10–11 People again multiply across the earth but sin persists	*Genesis 37–50* Joseph brings the promise to Egypt while remaining completely faithful

Gn 5:1 "[T]he record of the descendants of Adam," introduces the long break between the first family and the days of Noah.

Gn 6:9 "[T]he descendants of Noah," introduces the story of the flood.

Gn 10:1 "[T]he descendants of Noah's sons," marks the great expansion of peoples all over the world.

Gn 11:10 "[T]he descendants of Shem," marks the addition of a new list of the nations of the world by the P source.

Gn 11:27 "[These are] the descendants of Terah," begins the story of Abraham.

Gn 25:12 "[T]he descendants of Abraham's son Ishmael," closes off the life of Abraham's "other" family through Hagar and Ishmael.

Gn 25:19 "[T]he family history of Isaac," opens the story of Jacob's birth and destiny.

Gn 36:1 "[T]he descendants of Esau," ends the role of the second brother, Esau, and directs us to Jacob's children, especially Joseph.

Gn 36:9 This is a repetition within the Esau list, which marks its conclusion.

Gn 37:2 "This is his [Jacob's] family history," marks the opening of the story of Joseph and his brothers, which goes to the end of Genesis.

The Primeval History in Genesis 1–11

We can now move to a more detailed analysis of the book. In studying these early chapters, several aspects should be noted: (1) They are generally described by form criticism as a combination of myths and genealogical tables. (2) They are described by source criticism as a combination of passages from the Yahwist (J) and the Priestly (P) sources. (3) Many of the individual stories have parallel narratives that are known from other ancient Near Eastern peoples, often much older than the biblical version. (4) The final masterpiece has its own purpose and beauty that makes it much more than just a collection of myths and genealogy lists.

J and P Sources

If we remember that the J stories are probably much older than the P stories, and at first stood alone as the basic proclamation of the beginnings of the world, we can first glance at each group separately. See chart on RG 103.

It might be noted that there are several duplications in these lists: both J and P have a list of great ancestors between Adam and Noah (4:17–26 vs. 5:1–32); both have a flood story, which is now hopelessly intermixed as a single account; and both have a Table of Nations that spread over the earth in Genesis 10–11, which is also interwoven as a single narrative list.

The Theology of the Yahwist Source

If we look at the incidents chosen by the J source to tell its story of creation and the first humans, we find that they generally center on the tension between God's goodness given to the earth and the human response of disobedience. Each story—Adam and Eve, Cain and Abel, the angels and the women, the wicked generation of the flood, the sons of Noah, those who build the tower of Babel—all are given ample signs of God's love and bountiful providence as they fill the earth. Even so, each generation rises in disobedience according to one of the deadly vices: greed, envy, lust, pride.

The author uses a general pattern that structures the stories:

- God acts lovingly toward humanity,
- people disobey God and sin,
- God announces punishment,
- the punishment is given,
- God ends in compassion by bestowing mercy and a new blessing.

In the repetition of the pattern over and over again, J emphasizes how humanity as a whole has failed to respond to the intimate relationship of a God who once spoke to them face to face. Instead they have spread the practice of sin until it contaminated all people. Even after a new beginning following the flood, they continued to sin boldly, as is evident by the fact that God ended up confusing their languages in Gn 11:1–9. God's hope for faithfulness and obedience from the humans in his image and likeness, and his desire to speak with them face to face, will have to take a new form; that form will be the choice of a single family or nation, through Abraham, which will respond to God's goodness and teach other people. That new promise will open chapter 12.

J **(tenth century BC)**	**P** **(seventh to sixth centuries BC)**
	Gn 1:1–2:4a The creation of the world
Gn 2:4b–3:24 The human condition at creation, and sin	
Gn 4:1–26 Cain and Abel: even the children sin but God continues to care	
	Gn 5:1–32 The list of long-lived ancestors from Adam to Noah
Gn 6:1–4 More evil caused by the sin of angels and humans	
Gn 6:5–9:29 The flood story with 40 days and 7 pairs of clean animals, etc.	**Gn 6:5–9:29** The flood story based on 365 days and one pair of each animal only, etc.
	Gn 10:1–7, 20–24 Table of all the nations
Gn 10:8–19, 25–30 Table of Nations from a different source	
Gn 11:1–9 The story of the tower of Babel	
	Gn 11:10–32 The continuation of the Table of Nations down to Abraham

The Theology of the Priestly Source

We can assume that the priestly writers knew and accepted the basic J account of sin, punishment, and grace in the ages before Abraham. But they also knew that the later J promises to the ancestors Abraham, Isaac, and Jacob might be interpreted as a promise of international power and rule over other peoples, such as David and his family had exercised. Since P wrote in the sixth century BC, after Israel had known the defeat and loss of ten of the twelve tribes in 722, and the other two were in exile in Babylon from 598 to 539, they wished to refocus even the creation stories to emphasize the sovereign rule of God guiding the entire universe and constantly giving blessings much larger in scope than merely to Israel. Thus in chapters 1 and 9, when God first establishes and then reestablishes the order and purpose of creation, P writes in solemn proclamations, such as the litany of the days of creation in chapter 1, the great dignity of humans created as the image of God (1:27 and 9:6) to populate (sharing in creation?) and govern the earth, the arbitrary and majestic creation by God's word alone, the description of the flood in terms of the solar year, and even the mighty signs in nature like the rainbow. P places the story of humankind against a vast cosmic setting as a preface to the sordid and messy succeeding history of the world and even of Israel itself.

The very neatly ordered genealogies of chapters 5 and 10–11, which record the enormous life spans of the early heroes of the earth, are also part of P's insistence that God has a plan that is not subject to human whims nor even upset by human sin. God's rule is so vast that humans must learn trust! P stresses that divine blessing can always be relied on, even as it includes the J story in which punishment follows all sin. P has enlarged the J vision from finding God anew in every crisis to reassurance that God's providence was always at work—a perfect answer to an exiled Israel, despairing that God really stood by them in their times of defeat.

The Overall Message of Genesis 1–11

The act of combining J and P, as well as all the additions and refinements made by others, including the final editors who put it all together, provided a double emphasis: (1) the eternal goodness of the creator, and (2) the moral demand on humans to obey the divine plan and come to know God. It is no accident that God begins creation by speaking the world into being and seeing that all of it is good. Nor is it accidental that God then speaks to each of the first generations—Adam and Eve, Cain and Abel, Noah, and finally Abraham—with directives. In turn, these stories and directives now stand as a prologue to the whole body of Torah teaching that fills the latter part of the Pentateuch.

The pattern of divine goodness and moral imperative established in Genesis 1–11 also demand that proper worship be given to God alone. Both J and P use familiar Near Eastern myths in order to slyly attack pagan practices (such as the way J ridicules the excessive worship of the supposed supernatural power of serpents in Gn 3). Each story intends to show that only the moral goodness of God is an adequate basis for worship, and that most Canaanite religious practices and beliefs pervert God's plan.

Some Particular Helps in Reading Individual Passages

Genesis is a literary masterpiece as well as an inspiring theological message. To appreciate it better, here are a few examples of what to note about sections as we read:

Genesis 1:1–2:4a

The six days of creation are divided into two panels of three days each that are matched. See chart at top of RG 105.

A comparison of the two panels reveals that in the first three days God builds a stage of heavens, water, and land; and in the corresponding second three days fills this stage with its primary actors, each in turn. The last day in each panel, days three and six, have a double task. This serves to emphasize how especially fertile the land is. Moreover, the climactic seventh day is a celebration of the goodness of this creation and becomes the model for human rest and celebration of divine goodness each week.

The pattern of creation was not invented by the P authors. The same order is followed in the ancient creation myth from Babylon called the *Enuma Elish* in which Marduk, the chief god of Babylon and young king of all the gods, fashions the world from the body of Tiamat, the mother goddess whom he had slain in battle. The *Enuma Elish* describes Marduk's creative actions in a sequence with many parallels to the account in Genesis 1. See chart at bottom of RG 105.

Genesis 2:4b–3:24

This is an independent account of the creation that is older than Genesis 1 and uses a number of mythic story themes known also in Mesopotamia, although the biblical version is unique as a whole and far more sophisticated in its vision than anything else we have found in the ancient world. However, similarities exist between parts of Genesis 2–3 and the following:

1. *The Myth of Etana* (ANET 114–118). A great eagle eats the young of a serpent who, in turn, catches the eagle and traps it in a pit with the help of the gods. Meanwhile, Etana, a first human being, is childless, and he prays to the gods to get to heaven to eat of the plant of birth. The sun god Shamash leads Etana to the eagle, who promises to fly him to heaven to reach the plant of birth (or new life). The story breaks off, but it seems that he gets there.

2. *The Myth of Adapa* (ANET 101–102). The gods create a first man, Adapa, who has great wisdom. He catches and breaks the wings of the south wind one day because it prevents him from fishing. When the gods begin to miss the breeze, they find out that Adapa has caused this, and so Anu, the head of the gods, summons him to heaven to account for himself. He is warned not to accept Anu's offer of the bread and water of life, because it is really the food of death. When

Prologue: Introductory Statement that God Can Control Chaos	
Day 1 Heavens and light are made	**Day 4** Specific lights fashioned in the sky
Day 2 Waters established on their own	**Day 5** Fish and sea creatures made to fill the water
Day 3 Dry land made and vegetation added	**Day 6** The animals are created for the land, and then, finally, humans
Day 7 Epilogue: God rests after completing all creation and is in total control	

Anu extends the offer, Adapa refuses what really does turn out to be the bread and water of life, and thus loses the chance for immortality for human beings.

3. *The Myth of Atrahasis* (ANET 104). This is also a story of the creation of human beings as servants to the gods to keep the world running and save the gods from laboring. In time, they also revolt against the heavy labor; when plagues fail to diminish their numbers, the gods send a flood to punish them. Only Atrahasis and his family on their ark manage to escape and restart the human race.

4. *The Myth of Baal* (ANET 129–142). Baal is the chief ruling god of the Canaanites and is known from written tablets found at Ugarit, a town in northern Syria. It tells of El, the father of the gods who lives as ruler of the heavens and the earth at the "source of the two rivers," and the struggles of Baal, one of his younger sons, the god of the Mediterranean rainstorm and the resulting fertility for the earth, to rule the earth. Baal must battle against the gods Sea and Death for the kingship. Many themes resemble those of the Enuma Elish.

4. *Ezekiel 28:11–19*. This is an important version of creation related by Ezekiel about the king of Tyre, which possibly reflects Canaanite beliefs that the first man was a king, paradise was a sacred mountain, that it was covered with precious stones, and that the king was known for great wisdom. Then he sinned and was driven from the mountains by means of cherubim, a kind of protective animal god.

5. *Gilgamesh* (ANET 72–99). This Babylonian myth tells the story of two great god-men heroes who challenge the gods themselves for rule of the earth. For example, the hero Gilgamesh and his friend Enkidu cut down the sacred trees in the cedar forest of the gods, which is forbidden. When the gods punish Enkidu by death, Gilgamesh searches for the key to immortality by finding the hero of the flood (which corresponds to Noah), one Utnapishtim. When Gilgamesh fails the test for immortality, he is given a second chance when given the plant of continued rejuvenation, but he loses even that to a serpent. In the end, he must return home fully mortal and learn to bear his lot.

More ancient parallels can also be found, but these should be enough to help us read the accounts of human origins and sin in the light of the pressing questions faced by all the ancient religious stories: why are the gods immortal but not

Enuma Elish		Genesis 1
1. It begins with a conquest of chaos by order	=	The opening statement of Gn 1:1–2
2. Heavens created and separated from the water	=	Day 2, the creation of heavens and separation of the waters
3. The earth is set over the waters	=	Day 3, the land appears from the waters
4. Creation of sun and moon	=	Day 4, sun and moon are set in heaven
5. (No mention of plants or animals)	=	(Days 5–6, the creation of fish, birds, and animals)
6. Creation of human beings	=	Day 6, the creation of humans
7. The gods rest and celebrate	=	Day 7, God rests

we humans? Why do we receive punishment from the gods in life? What is our fate? The major differences between the biblical accounts and the stories of other religions center on the clear connection in the Bible between a single God's loving care for humanity, the moral refusal of people to obey God, and the justified reason that God imposed a sentence of mortality upon us together with a change in our relation to the land that now requires backbreaking labor to make it a blessing.

Genesis 4:1–16

The story of Cain and Abel offers a moral about how when evil flourishes it leads even to fratricide. But it also builds on an age-old theme of the conflict between the farmer and the herder. The musical *Oklahoma* sings how the farmer and the cowman should be friends, but their interests conflict—the farmer wants to fence in and protect his plot of land, and the cowman requires wide-open spaces over which the cattle or sheep can move to new pastures. This was a conflict well known to the early Israelites, who as nomadic shepherds came up against the protected and settled lands of the Canaanite farmers.

Genesis 4:17–22; 5:1–32

The genealogies of Genesis 4–5 with the enormous ages of the patriarchs are not intended to be understood as literally exact. We can compare them to the enormous ages given to the primeval kings of Sumeria who lived before the great flood in an ancient list (ANET 265):

A-lu-lim	28,800 years
Alalgar	36,000 years
En-men-lu-anna	43,200 years
En-men-gal-anna	28,800 years
Dumuzi	36,000 years
En-sipa-zi-anna	28,800 years
En-men-dur-anna	21,000 years
Ubar-tutu	18,600 years
The flood	

Such genealogy lists are typical of many peoples who keep largely oral traditions. The parallel lists in Genesis 4 and 5 show signs of such an oral tradition. They contain some identical and many similar names, so they probably both go back to a single core list. But they differ in length, with eight generations in chapter 4 and ten in chapter 5. In oral tradition, the first and last names in a list are carefully preserved, but the middle names tend to change from place to place, depending on where those lists are recited. Such lists are an exciting and mysterious device for imagining how far back our ancestors go and how long the world has existed. And they serve the biblical authors well as a way of linking the wondrous events of ancient days to the more historical times we all know about.

Genesis 6:1–9:27

Two observations should preface serious study of what the flood story means. First, this story must have been very important, because both the Yahwist and the Priestly traditions had separate versions of the flood and both were considered important enough to save. Second, it has a very strong resemblance to similar flood stories told in both Babylon and Syria, although it has some differences from both.

The more famous parallel is in the Gilgamesh myth where the hero, Utnapishtim, is warned to build an ark and take some of every kind of animal on earth aboard before the gods destroy the world with a flood. After the flood has killed all living things left on the land, the hero sends out birds (just as in Gn 8:6–12) after the ark becomes stuck on a mountain peak. When the hero finally leaves the ark, he offers a sacrifice to the gods. They are so grateful that they bless him and make him immortal. This is quite close to the plot of Genesis except that in the pagan versions, no real cause of human evil is given for why the gods decreed a flood; in the biblical version, Noah does not receive immortality as a gift at the end. In still another ancient flood myth, Atra-Hasis, the authors retain the same basic plot, but suggest that the gods were tired of the human noise that disturbed their sleep, and so decided to do away with humans.

Again, Genesis 6–9 must be read through the eyes of the ancient Israelite who knew of the pagan versions and their account of strained relations between the divine and human worlds. The author insists that the God of Israel acted entirely out of justice and in response to moral evil in humans but still continued to love them and hold out the promise of blessing at the end. This is confirmed by restoring the earlier blessing of Genesis 1 in 9:1–17. It is made specific to Israel as a chosen people in the final story of 9:18–27 where the descendants of Noah's son Shem will be blessed over the peoples that stem from his other sons, Ham and Japheth.

Genesis 9:28–10:32

A new genealogical list is placed after the flood story to confirm that the renewed divine blessing multiplied to reconstruct an entire world of peoples and nations. This section is made up of two separate traditional lists of names for the world's peoples, one from the P school, and the other from J. The earlier list of J can be generally recognized right away in 10:8–30 by its more narrative flavor; the P list in 9:28–10:7 and 10: 21–24 (and continued in 10:31f) is much drier, simply presented as a list of names. But the editors of Genesis 1–11 have skillfully put them together to form a montage of different peoples spreading from the family home of Noah after the flood to fill the far corners of the earth.

Genesis 11:1–9

The tower of Babel story is an excellent example of the J writer at work. It is told with humor and irony, and it makes a very pointed attack against pagan religious ideas. It is a story about words and speaking, but it is the misuse of words that is at stake. The plot pictures all people speaking the same language, which leads them to an enormous sin of pride. They seek to build a temple high enough to reach heaven so that they might have "a name for themselves," that is, to be like God. But note that as they build this tremendous monument, God looks down from heaven and can barely make it out because it is so puny by God's standards. He must come down to see it. As punishment, he halts their sinful ambition by confusing their languages. The author then ends with a bit of sharp humor. The city of such arrogance was called *Babel,* but God made it *balal,* the verb in Hebrew for "confused in language." Thus verse 9 is a pun and as such mocks the claims of Babylon and its god Marduk to rule over other peoples.

Genesis 11:10–32

The primeval history now closes with a P list parallel to that of Genesis 5:1–32. It links the primeval events of chapters 1 through 11 with the concrete call of Abraham in the very real towns of Ur and Harran in Mesopotamia. Like Genesis 5:1–32 it bridges the time between major moments or stages of divine intervention. Each patriarch is recorded with the age at which he died. The lengths are much less than those of the ten before the flood, descending from 600 years for Shem, the son of Noah, down to the four hundreds for Arpachshad, Shelah, and Eber, and rapidly down to the two hundreds for the remaining names. Of course, like the ages in chapter 5, these are not to be taken as actual ages, but as a device for showing that the "golden age" of olden times was rapidly coming to an end as the people became more and more like ourselves.

Name lists were important in the ancient world for remembering who was related to whom. And it will seem obvious, by the time we have looked at many of these lists, that the names do not really represent individuals at all, but whole tribes or peoples. This can be direct, as in 10, 22 where P writes that Shem was the father of Elam, Assyria, and the Arameans; or indirect, when a nation is identified by a famous founder or hero, such as Ishmael, the son of Abraham, who is listed as the father of the Arabs in Genesis 25:12–18.

Structure of the Genealogies in Genesis 1–11

The name lists in Genesis 1–11 are very important parts of the overall story by highlighting the passage of time between crucial moments of sin and grace, and by serving as times of blessing between the particular stories of sin and punishment. Thus, it can be charted as shown on RG 108.

Church Use of the Genesis Story of Human Creation

It is well to note that the account of making humanity in the divine image and likeness figures significantly in a number of official Catholic church documents. For example, Pope Paul VI looked to Genesis 1:28 as a significant reference in his development of the responsibility to subdue the earth and its resources intelligently (*Populorum Progressio* #22). And along the same vein, John Paul II went to Genesis 1:26–30 to ground the fundamental "goodness" of creation in the Creator's eyes, which thereby also grounds the claim that redemption is possible *(Redemptor Hominis).* Likewise, the American bishops in their pastoral *Economic Justice for All* used Gen-

Key Moments of Sin, Punishment, Blessing	*Genealogy Lists*
Genesis 1:1–4:16 The story of creation and the blessings and sins of the first generations	
	Genesis 4:17–5:32 The long age of blessing of the ten great patriarchs before Noah's time
Genesis 6:1–9:27 Sin, flood as punishment and blessing on Noah, followed by further sin by his sons	
	Genesis 9:28–10:32 The list of all the nations known to ancient Israel to show the divine blessing of fertility and having dominion over the earth
Genesis 11:19 Sin again rises up out of human pride after blessing	
	Genesis 11:10–32 God's blessing continues, now focusing on one family, that of Terah and Abraham
Genesis 12:1–? The story of Abraham and the new direction of divine blessing	

esis 1, 26f to show that all human relations must be based on the acknowledgment of the dignity of those created in God's image. This helps form the economic reflections of the letter.

The Great Ancestor Narratives in Genesis 12–50

As already noted above, the second major part of Genesis is arranged around the lives of four patriarchal figures: Abraham, Isaac, Jacob, and Joseph. Each of these represents a forward step in the divine plan to bring about recognition of the divine blessing promised to the world—if only humanity would obey and honor God. Since humans as a whole proved very stubbornly unresponsive to God's self-revelation through long ages, God decided to turn to a new plan and work through a single chosen people who would respond and witness God's blessings to all nations.

And where is this plan laid out? Why, right at the beginning of course, in Genesis 12:1–3. When we read this call of Abraham by God, all the subsequent themes are present:

verse 1 the promise of a land for his family
verse 2 the promise of blessing through empire and fame, and probably children ("a great nation")
verse 3 the promise to rule other nations and to mediate God's blessing to them.

These themes will echo throughout the narratives to follow, especially the combination of a son to carry on the name and a specific land. But they will not be fulfilled easily. It is very important to understand that God never promised anyone a rose garden. The narrators have constructed a story of failure and success, obedience and disobedience, a lesson of deep faith in some stories, and of a sinful lack of trust in others. Along the way, divine providence and guidance overcome all the obstacles to bringing about the promise, maintaining blessing on this small family even in the unlikely land of their enemy, Egypt.

The Literary Questions of Genesis 12–50

Scholars have identified many individual passages of both J and P throughout the patriarchal stories, and have added one more source, the Elohist (E), which is quite close to J in spirit but does not yet use the name of Yahweh to refer to God. These sources can be identified by their parallel structures, which treat the same chief events in order. If we look just at the Abraham and Sarah story of Genesis 12–25, we can get a good idea of this overlapping (table on RG 110).

Each source stresses a different aspect of the person of Abraham. J stresses his faith and trust in the promise of land and a son; E stresses his obedience even to sacrificing his heir; P stresses his fidelity in fulfilling all the divine religious prescriptions, especially circumcision.

But scholars have sought for more than these written sources alone; they wished to uncover the underlying traditions that existed before J, E, or P ever wrote a word. The form critics have noted that for the cycles of Abraham, Isaac, and Jacob, most of the incidents described are self-contained. That is, you could leave one or another of the events out, and the story could still go on. This suggests that a long history of oral stories existed about the patriarchs and matriarchs before they were finally used in written sources. The father of form criticism was Hermann Gunkel, and he pointed to many characteristics of these particular stories that were similar to the characteristics of the Icelandic sagas of the Middle Ages. Some of these elements are:

• the stories are hero-centered around a major ancestor of a family or group;

• they don't really tell of private lives as much as of the national fortunes of their group in the past;

• they use many standard formulas, themes, and literary motifs common to folktales and hero legends;

• they are told with a highly dramatic, often poetic style of description, and not in simple narrative chronicle fashion;

• they identify major themes or beliefs of the group or tribe *today* that this ancestor initiated or began;

• they often delight in *etiological,* or causal, explanations of events or things (that is, in the why or how of the way things are). See Genesis 17:5, where the editor explains the meaning of Abraham's name, or 21:31, which explains how Beersheba got its name.

However, even with so many similarities between the biblical stories and medieval hero legends or family sagas, we must not forget that they only hint at the way the oldest traditions about the founding ancestors were probably originally passed down. The actual passages that we now read in the book of Genesis were carefully composed by each of the literary sources with a special religious note, and they were combined and revised numerous times to point more clearly to the lessons in the stories for the faith of later generations of Israelites. We must try to read them with an eye both to the level of their original description of the experience of God and to the complete picture painted by the finished text that sees a clear guiding hand of God through history.

The Historical Setting of the Patriarchal Stories

The general consensus of the scholarly world has been in the past that the customs and movements described in Genesis 12–50 best fit the first half

	J	E	P
Abraham receives a promise of land and/or a son	12:1–3	15:1–6	12:4–9
God makes a covenant with Abraham	15:7–12	15:13–16	17:1–14
A son is born and the line of the promise is secured	16:1–16 18:1–19	21:1–21	17:15–27
The final note of closing the life of Abraham	25:1–6	(22:1–13)	23:1–20

of the second millennium BC, that is, from 1900 to 1500 BC. Some of the main reasons for this view are:

- the names of the patriarchs are not used in later periods but are known before 1500 BC;
- the wanderings from Mesopotamia to Canaan to Egypt coincide with the periods of Amorite migrations in the Near East and the time of the Middle Kingdom in Egypt (2000–1750 BC);
- customs such as the adoption of an heir (Gn 15:1–3) and marrying a sister (12:10–20) reflect known legal procedures from Nuzi and other towns in the second millennium;
- the story of Joseph as a prime minister in Egypt would fit well the period in Egypt when it was ruled by the Hyksos, a group of Semitic invaders from Palestine and farther East that controlled northern Egypt from about 1750 to 1500 BC;
- Abraham and Isaac and Jacob are described as seminomadic clans that settled near urban centers and dealt with the local rulers about rights for grazing, water, and travel, a way of life known from Mari documents of the eighteenth to seventeenth centuries BC.

None of these examples proves the dating of the Genesis stories, since many of these customs were also practiced at later dates. Indeed, the more archaeologists unearth artifacts and documents, the more difficult it is to date any particular custom or practice to a single period. Many particulars of the story do generally fit the conditions that prevailed in the Near East before the rise of strong Egyptian control after 1500 BC. Thus, for example, the apparent weakness of local rulers over the hill country of central Palestine in Abraham's time is supported by archaeology's failure to find any major settlement there from 2000 to 1500 BC, except possibly Shechem. On the other hand, camel caravans and mention of the Philistine states and other details support a time of writing that is much later than the period in which they have set the events.

Genesis 12–25: The Story of Abraham and Sarah

There are several keys to getting more out of the Abraham narratives. One way is to read the story as Abraham's journey from being a landless alien in chapter 12 to its completion in chapters 23 and 25 when Sarah and then Abraham are buried in a tomb they own and in land they possess. Another way is to follow the series of promises to Abraham and Sarah as they are slowly but surely fulfilled. There are two major series in parallel: (1) the promise of land, and (2) the promise of a son to carry on the family name and to become a great people (see below).

Promise of a Son	
Gn 12:2	I make you a great nation
Gn 15:5	at the night covenant
Gn 17:4	the P covenant
Gn 17:16	the promise of Isaac
Gn 18:10	the three angels
Gn 18:18	recap of 12:2f
Gn 21:12	a promise to Isaac
Gn 22:17	at the sacrifice of Isaac
Gn 26:4	promise repeated to Isaac

Promise of Land	
Gn 12:1	"go to a land I that I will show you"
Gn 12:7	at the terebinth of Moreh
Gn 13:14	at the departure of Lot
Gn 15:18	at the night covenant
Gn 17:8	the P covenant
Gn 24:7	the messenger for Isaac
Gn 26:4	repeated promise to Isaac

	Trusting Response		Obstacle
Gn 12:1–9	Abraham leaves home	Gn 12:10–20	Abraham in Egypt
Gn 14:1–24	War and blessing of Melchizedek	Gn 13:1–18	Lot allowed to choose the land
Gn 15:1–21	The covenant with God	Gn 16:1–14	Abraham has a son by his slave wife
Gn 17:1–27	Abraham's covenant renewed	Gn 18:1–15	Sarah doubts the promise of a son
Gn 18:16–33	Abraham intercedes for Sodom	Gn 20:1–18	Abraham nearly repeats his denial of Sarah
Gn 21:1–20	The birth of Isaac	Gn 22:1–14	Will Abraham pass the test of sacrificing Isaac?
Gn 21:21–33	Abraham establishes rights to water		
Gn 23:1–20	Abraham buys land		

Genesis 12–25 can also be viewed as the story of a struggle to have trust and faith in God. Abraham and Sarah create as many obstacles to God's plan as they do helpful responses built on faith (see table above).

Still another structure can be found in the drama that leads up to the birth of the promised son, Isaac, from chapters 12 to 21. Here the series of major events are balanced in two blocs that each focus their climax on the birth of a son. See diagram on RG 112.

According to this diagram, the story moves dynamically forward through two series of parallel actions. Abraham wrestles with his call in betraying his wife and dealing with Lot but finally trusts fully in God's covenant by chapter 15, which leads to receiving a son, Ishmael. This is immediately followed by the expanded divine covenant of chapter 17, followed by further uncertain dealings with Lot and a new betrayal of his wife. But then God relents with a son Isaac, from Sarah, as fulfillment of the Promise found in chapter 12:1–3. This entire series moves toward the great test of sacrificing his son in chapter 22. When Abraham proves himself competely obedient to God's will at that awful moment, the story comes to a rapid conclusion. Once the promise of a son is secured, purchase of a tomb in chapter 23 guarantees a claim on the land, and so Abraham's role is now ready to pass on to Isaac. And then both Sarah and Abraham pass from the scene.

Genesis 24–27: The Story of Isaac and Rebekah

Isaac plays an important role in the life of Abraham as the promised son, but it is a passive role, even in the great scene where he is about to lose his life in chapter 22. He briefly comes to the fore in chapters 24 to 27 but they mostly duplicate scenes from the life of Abraham. The long account of arranging his marriage in chapter 24 links Isaac back to the family roots in northern Mesopotamia reported in chapter 12. His encounter with Abimelech and the surrender of his wife, as well as the concern with water rights in chapter 26, reflects two similar scenes in chapters 20 and 21; and in 26, 4 Isaac receives the renewal of the promises of land and descendants given to Abraham in chapters 12, 17, 18, 21, and 22.

Isaac's role might be best understood as permitting the transition from the role played by Abraham before him to the role played by Jacob after him, except for one thing: the remarkable person of Rebekah! The scene in chapter 24 of the messenger persuading Rebekah and her brother Laban to let her marry Isaac, and the journey home to Palestine, is a masterpiece of ancient writing art. Pay attention to how much emphasis is given to this one event—a total of sixty-seven verses. Rebekah will also become the key player in the next step of God's plan, the selection of the child Jacob over his older brother, Esau. In chapter 25, the birth of twins

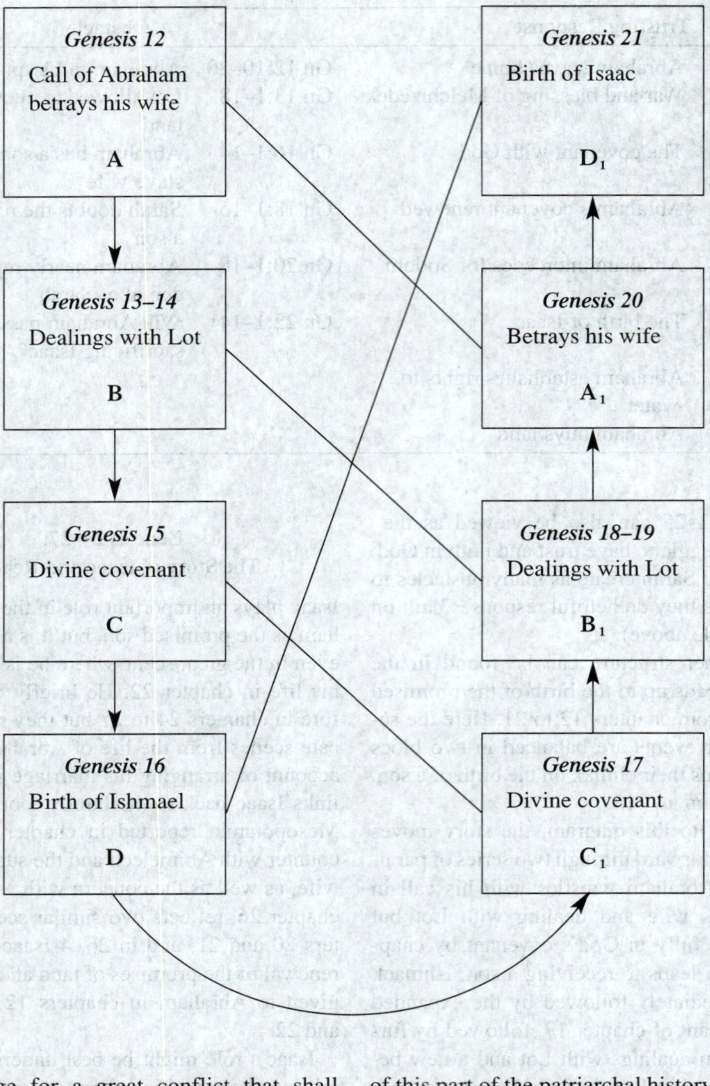

sets the stage for a great conflict that shall shadow the promise for many years ahead, the hatred of two brothers for one another, trickery on the part of Jacob, and the triumph of the younger brother over the older. And through it all, Rebekah steers a clear course that will end up winning the day.

Genesis 27–36: The Story of Jacob

In reading the story of Jacob, modern Christians are often horrified by the trickery and dishonesty involved in the way his career is presented in the text. In order to appreciate the religious message of this part of the patriarchal history, we must be willing to read with our eyes wide open to all the possible levels that can be discovered in this very powerful piece of literature.

The following are a few initial observations and guidelines to help a better reading of these chapters: (1) Remember the overall purpose of Genesis 12–50 is to carry forward God's promise *despite all obstacles*. Thus we can expect that Jacob, like Abraham, will himself be one of those obstacles. (2) These chapters really are made up of many old sagas or folk hero stories. Although they have been gathered and polished and finally given a very religious edge, they still retain some of the early and less edifying characteristics of such traditions. (3) You as *reader* live in the twenty-first century with a modern ethical sense that is far more refined than the more basic code of conduct centered on maintaining honor, avoiding shame, demanding fair play, and upholding honesty of the ancient world. It is possible to understand the text without necessarily agreeing with everything in it. (4) This is intended as an exciting action narrative where the outcome hangs in doubt, and so we should not expect it to be a gentle, pious biography of a saint.

With these cautions in mind, we can look at all the elements that have been collected to make up the narrative as a whole:

Original Sources

The materials from which the narrative develops can be grouped into four types:

1. The conflict between the two brothers, Jacob and Esau, 25:19–34; 27:1–45; 32:3–21; 33:1–17

2. The conflict between Jacob and Laban, and the founding of a family, 27:46–28:9; 29:1–32:2

3. Divine appearance by God to Jacob to guide him, 28:10–22; 32:22–32; 33:18–20; 35:1–15

4. Special sources on the homelands of Jacob and Esau, 34:1–31; 36:1–43

In looking at these groupings, it immediately becomes clear that the cycles of stories about Jacob and Esau, and Jacob and Laban, are really about the struggles for identity and status of the Israelite tribes against the Edomites (Esau's people) in the first, and against the Mesopotamian peoples who are Israel's ancestors (Laban's claim over the family)in the second. These are older tales that were once recited orally to glorify Israel's past. To a modern sensitivity, Jacob may appear to be a deceiver and dishonest, but to an ancient his antics were clever, wily, and proved to be far wiser and more skillful than those of either the Edomites or Aramaeans.

Note, for example, that there are four separate conflicts between Jacob and Esau:

1. There is a struggle in the womb between them, with a prophetic word that Jacob shall triumph over Esau, his older brother (25:21–28).

2. There is a struggle over the birthright (25:29–34), which Jacob wins.

3. There is another struggle over the family blessing (27:1–45) and Jacob wins again.

4. Finally, there is a great confrontation years later (32:3–33:17), which ends in a reconciliation between the brothers.

These incidents probably originated in bragging stories around the campfires of Israel's ancestors about how their founder Jacob outsmarted the Edomites. But they now form a series of obstacles that Jacob must overcome to carry on the divine plan, but they end in a finale of reconciliation that proves how everything works for the good in God's plan.

The same patterns can be detected in the Laban stories over the question of which wife is truly Jacob's primary spouse (and naturally therefore which sons are more important!), whose are the family gods, and whose are the possessions; in each of these conflicts, Jacob emerges the winner.

Major Themes of the Jacob Story

The Jacob stories are not intended to be a chronicle of historical events narrated in the actual order that they happened. Different factors all play a role in the development of the tradition: (1) In several cases ancient folk themes, such as the competition between the hunter and the sheepherder, or the struggle of a young shepherd against an established older one, are the source of an incident. (2) In other passages there are elements of a nationalistic boast that our clan is better than your clan. (3) Like true sagas, the personal battles stand for the tensions between actual nations. Thus, each of Jacob's twelve sons has the name of a real tribe; Esau is called "red and hairy," which in Hebrew makes a pun on the names of Edom and Seir, because he does represent Edom. (4) It is also about roots—to whom is Israel related? Certainly to the Arameans in Mesopotamia, and to the Edomites. (5) And, of course, another theme is that God writes straight with crooked lines. Examples include the choice of a younger son over the rightful older son as heir, and the triumph of the advice of a mother rather than the judgment of the father of the promise, Isaac himself.

The Appearances of God

Most importantly, the authors have added into the older folktales their strictly religious accounts of how God spoke to Jacob at various times in his life. These are also likely to be based on old stories that were cherished and retold at various shrines that grew up at the spots where God was known to have appeared, such as Bethel, Shechem, Paddan-Aram, and Penuel. But it is precisely through these scenes that the authors reveal the real purpose of the story. In the first vision at Bethel in chapter 28, Jacob receives the promise made to Abraham and Isaac; at Penuel he is designated the father of Israel as a nation, and his name is changed to match. In Shechem he acknowledges that God is the only god of Israel; and at Paddan-Aram in the final scene (chapter 35), God reconfirms that Jacob is to be the people Israel and that the promise of a great nation of descendants is on the verge of fulfillment.

The Result

When we combine all the elements that we have looked at, it presents us with a complex picture of Jacob as the model of Israel as well as its founding father. God is now about to forge these twelve sons into the future great nation, but it won't be done without problems of human blindness and often very disobedient or shortsighted or even slightly unscrupulous individuals. Jacob was all of these—but used his human talents to pursue faithfully the course that God had shown him; and lo and behold, God's plan came about! The Joseph story will illustrate the first step of building the brothers into a nation.

Genesis 37–50: The Story of Joseph

As in the preceding stories, the drama of Joseph's story can be read on two levels. The first is the search for the interesting traditions and themes that reach far back into Israel's history. The second is the overall theological purpose that the story now plays as part of the larger religious message of Genesis. On the first level, many scholars have traced the combination of the Yahwist and Elohist sources woven together to form a unified series of adventures. Perhaps even a modern reader might notice what appears to be slight differences and inconsistencies, which give away the fact that there were originally two accounts. One of the easiest places to see this is in the opening of the story in chapter 37, where J can be found in verses 3–4, 12–17, 23, 25–28, 31–34, and E in verses 1–2, 5–11, 18–22, 24, 28–30, and 36. Note, for example, such disagreements as shown in table on RG 115.

Scholars also point to two separate journeys of the brothers back and forth to Egypt: the first one, in chapter 42, is seen as E; the second, in chapter 43, is usually understood as J's parallel account.

Also still on the first level, research has pointed to the great number of parallels in the Joseph story to ancient Egyptian literary masterpieces that have been discovered. One such story tells of seven fat years followed by seven lean years of harvest (compare this to chapter 41: 1–32), while another tells the story of a young man who resists the attempts of his older brother's wife to seduce him, with the result that she screams and falsely accuses him of trying to rape her (see chapter 39:6–20). Another famous Egyptian tale of one Sinuhe recounts how he fell out of favor with the pharaoh but was restored to favor when he proved to be a truly faithful servant of the king's interest (Joseph's imprisonment and rise to power shares some of this theme). There is yet another interesting parallel in an account found on a statue of King Idri-mi of Alalakh, a city in Syria, to be dated about the fifteenth century BC. It tells how Idri-mi's father was dethroned and the family forced to flee into exile and how Idri-mi could not get his brothers to help win back the father's kingdom; but when he managed it alone, he forgave them and took them back into his confidence.

All of these examples share some theme or another with the Joseph story, but none is more than a passing element of the whole. They do, however, confirm that the basic motifs and descriptions of chapters 37–50 are borrowed from, or echo ideas about, the world of Egypt in the second millenium BC, even if they are really the product of later imaginative creation without any basis in hard facts. Indeed, the whole way in which the Joseph story is presented connects well to the quite vague memories of the Hyksos period in Egypt (1750–1550 BC), a highly romanticized period when Semitic conquerors ruled much of the northern part of the country.

A third series of motifs on the first level of tradition is derived from the wisdom schools, perhaps as they flourished in the days of David and

J	E
The father is named Israel	The father is named Jacob
The brother Judah intercedes	The brother Reuben intercedes
The merchants are Ishmaelites	The merchants are Midianites
The long coat causes the brothers' jealousy	Joseph's dreams cause the brothers' jealousy

Solomon, but possibly, or even probably, at an even later stage of editing. Wisdom themes abound in the person of Joseph, who fits the ideal of both Egyptian wisdom sayings and those of the book of Proverbs in the Bible. He speaks only what is appropriate, keeps his own counsel, accepts misunderstanding, shows great skills as an administrator of public affairs, is adept at translating dreams, is skillful in political intrigue games, and avoids entanglement with foreign women. Above all, Joseph is attentive to God's plan, which works differently from the course of human planners (note especially the remarks of Joseph in 45:5–8 and 50:20, and compare these to Proverbs 16:9 and 19:21).

So far we have uncovered a variety of separate traditions that have gone into these chapters. What is remarkable about this particular narrative of Joseph, however, is precisely its dramatic integrity. Each step of the plot lays the groundwork for the next event. If you took away one of them, such as Joseph's imprisonment, there would be no way to get him into the king's favor in Egypt. If he didn't trick his brothers into bringing their father, Jacob, to Egypt, the master plan of God to rescue them at a later date would never have been put into place. Some scholars liken Joseph, not to the string of sagalike stories that make up the Abraham, Isaac, and Jacob cycles, but to a modern short story of fiction with a very carefully constructed plot. Some genius, perhaps the J source itself, or one of its later editors, has taken all the old themes and separate traditions and created a literary work of art, the earliest such masterwork that we know anywhere.

Once we recognize its dramatic unity, we can begin to understand its theological message on the second level of the book of Genesis itself. Certainly, Joseph must first be understood as one of Jacob's twelve sons. Through him, one of the youngest, God will work his plan, despite the ambitions or hopes of the older and supposedly more deserving brothers. What Joseph does is entirely done through divine guidance. Joseph's vanity causes his initial problems with his brothers, and only the divine gift of dream interpretation eventually gets him out of a hopeless prison situation. By ironic twists of fate and the reversal of roles, God brings about the totally unexpected end in which a lowly Palestinian shepherd becomes the second most powerful official in Egypt. In what looks like the final triumph of the blessing of success and power and progeny promised to Abraham and Isaac, Jacob moves into Egypt. Genesis now closes with a question for all readers: what has happened to the hopes and promise to Israel that it would be a great people in possession of Canaan? Is there something yet to happen? Genesis ends with a clear message that God's work, as great as it has been, is not yet finished.

EXODUS

[see pages 81–133 of the Old Testament]

General Structure of the Book of Exodus

Exodus begins where Genesis leaves off. With Egypt now prosperous because of the efforts of Joseph, while Jacob and his sons enjoy great blessings there themselves, one might think that all the promises to Abraham in Genesis 12:1–3 have been fulfilled as Exodus opens. Exodus 1:1–7 hints as much. But the drama is to continue with a cruel twist of fate in which blessing turns to desperation, and then in a surprising rebound, a new blessing unfolds that reveals Israel's destiny is not to be in the land of Egypt but in Palestine. Like Genesis, Exodus is a tension-filled dramatic play in which we discover God's mysterious purposes at work. Scholars see parallels between this book and a variety of well-known literary types, such as the classic "hero as rescuer" story, or the mythical pattern of God the mighty warrior establishing his rule over enemy powers, or the rite of passage (and purification) in which Israel goes from a slave childhood to responsible covenant adulthood. It perhaps shares elements of all of these, but stands in the end as a unique literary creation.

A Literary Overview of the Book as a Whole

We must therefore expect that this book, too, like Genesis, will be structured quite artistically and purposefully. It has two major halves: chapters 1 through 18 and 19 through 40. The first half carries the story line from success and security in the land of Egypt down through enslavement, and up again in deliverance and escape into a desolate wilderness to a meeting with God at Mount Sinai. These chapters create an exciting action story that keeps the reader wondering whether the people will really reach their goal of freedom and a new security. This is achieved by returning to each theme again and again so that they are never quite resolved; a certain tension remains whether God will be completely successful and whether the people will continue to follow where Moses is taking them—right up to the moment that they arrive at the mountain of God. Questions abound and add to the drama: Is God's promise in doubt? It seems so; yet at this same moment, God is already setting a new plan in motion with the birth of Moses. Will Moses respond to God's plan as Joseph did? Can God overcome the magic power of Pharaoh? Will the people follow Moses? When God delivers, will they believe enough to leave Egypt? In the trials of the desert, will they remain faithful? Each question receives its answer. Each stage prepares for the next. So we can diagram the book as an interlocking puzzle (see RG 117).

The second half, in chapters 19 through 40, dwells at length on two key activities that take place at the mountain. The first is the making of a covenant between God and the people, and the second is the description of two key elements of divine worship: the building of a sanctuary tent and an ark to serve as God's throne, and the establishment of priestly ministers. Dramatic tension is maintained here also, as observed in the people's idolatry in chapter 32; but much more so than in the first half, it establishes an orderly balance and state of security by the proclamation of the law by God and the people's oath to keep the covenant, followed by the orderly and well-planned description of the sanctuary and its auxiliary elements. This effect of balance is also achieved by interlocking the legal and liturgical descriptions. The descent of the glory of God into the sanctuary in chapter 40:34–38 concludes the book, with the people united to the divine presence in harmony much as they were at the beginning of the book in chapter 1, but now with a far different destiny.

So the book is really an intricate mixture of narratives and legal regulations for the community. This did not happen by accident. The story of God's act of merciful liberation from slavery lays the foundation for his merciful guarantee to be with the people for all times that is reflected in the laws and institutions for public worship.

A Second Way of Dividing the Book

Besides the larger and more complicated plan of the book, we might better divide it for ease of study into the three geographical regions in which God meets Israel:

1. **Exodus 1–12** In the land of Egypt God works wonders to free the people from slavery;
2. **Exodus 13–18** In the wilderness God guides the people to safety and a personal encounter;
3. **Exodus 19–40** At Mount Sinai God establishes a community in covenant, law, and worship.

In each of these sections, Moses plays a leading role as God's agent, but there is never any doubt who controls the action. This is a story where God acts in each and every place with power and authority—no land or king is outside of the divine lordship. In tracing the thread of divine action through the long series of events described in the book, we need to be alert to the sudden and unexpected. What appears to be a hopeless situation where everything may be lost is suddenly changed. God turns near-defeat into victory, near-despair to triumph. In a certain way, the story is constructed like the traditional

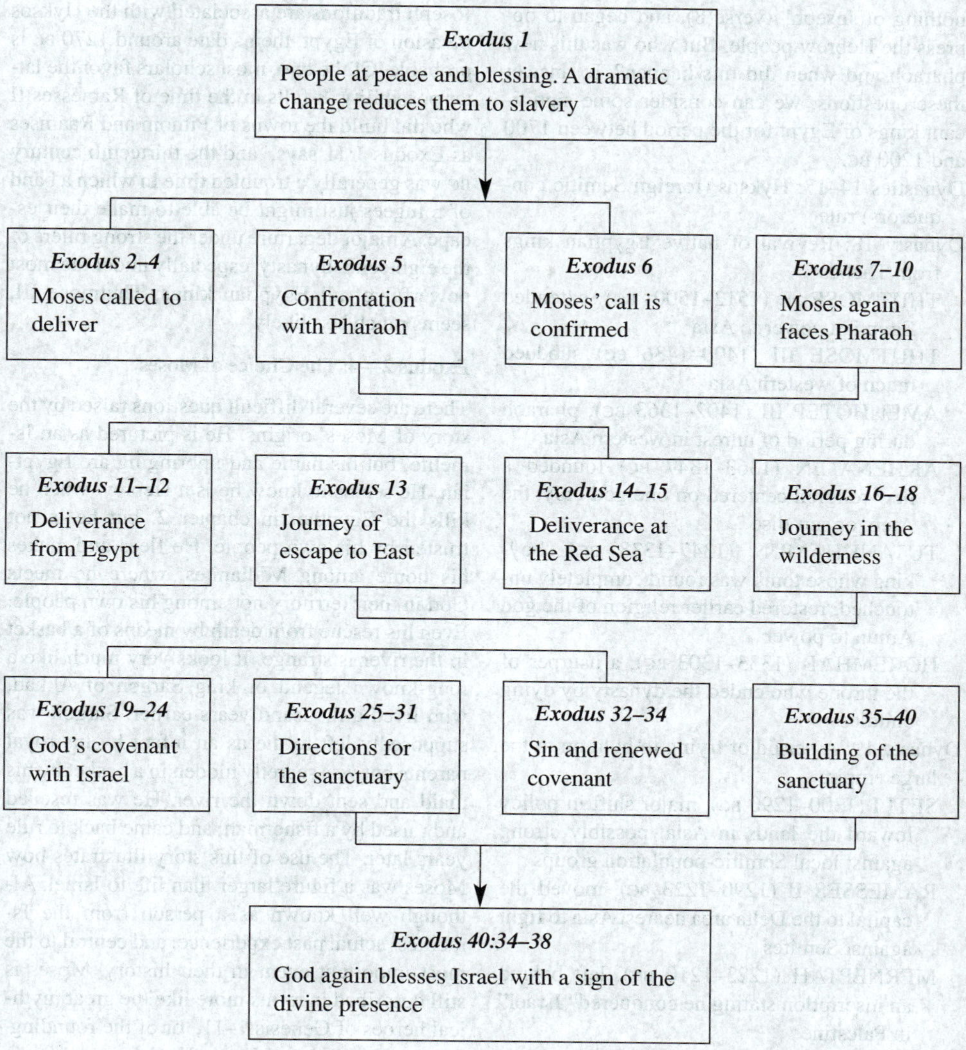
Exodus 1
People at peace and blessing. A dramatic change reduces them to slavery
Exodus 2–4
Moses called to deliver
Exodus 5
Confrontation with Pharaoh
Exodus 6
Moses' call is confirmed
Exodus 7–10
Moses again faces Pharaoh
Exodus 11–12
Deliverance from Egypt
Exodus 13
Journey of escape to East
Exodus 14–15
Deliverance at the Red Sea
Exodus 16–18
Journey in the wilderness
Exodus 19–24
God's covenant with Israel
Exodus 25–31
Directions for the sanctuary
Exodus 32–34
Sin and renewed covenant
Exodus 35–40
Building of the sanctuary
Exodus 40:34–38
God again blesses Israel with a sign of the divine presence

psalms of lamentation that we find so often in the Psalter. A situation of desperate need calls forth a cry for help to God; God hears and answers their prayers with aid; and the people sing the divine praises (compare Psalms 7, 10, and 53).

Helps for Individual Sections of Exodus

In studying Exodus 1–18, there will be very little problem following the story line or plot of the drama. We must recall that there will be a number of inconsistencies and duplications because of the combination of the three major sources which all reported the Exodus event. But these have been worked together smoothly for the most part, and only a careful examination will show how they are present. For many passages in these chapters, however, selected pieces of historical information or examples from other ancient peoples' literatures may help us to understand them more deeply.

Exodus 1: The Egyptian Setting

The narrative begins with a time of success in Egypt, but soon moves to a pharaoh "who knew nothing of Joseph" (verse 8), and began to oppress the Hebrew people. But who was this new pharaoh and when did this happen? To answer these questions, we can consider some significant kings of Egypt for the period between 1700 and 1200 BC.

Dynasties 14–17: Hyksos (foreign Semitic conquerors) rule

Dynasty 18: Revival of native Egyptian kings from Thebes

- THUTMOSE I (1512–1500 BC) extended Egyptian power to Asia
- THUTMOSE III (1490–1436 BC) subdued much of western Asia
- AMENHOTEP III (1402–1363 BC), pharaoh during period of unrest in western Asia
- AKHENATEN (1363–1347 BC) founded a new religion centered on one god only, the Aten, or sun-disc
- TUTANKHAMUN (1347–1338 BC), boy-king whose tomb was found completely untouched; restored earlier religion of the god Amun to power
- HOREMHAB (1333–1303 BC), a usurper of the throne who ended the dynasty by dying childless

Dynasty 19: A period of trying to hold on to the large empire

- SETI I (1300–1290 BC), major shift in policy toward the lands in Asia, possibly strong against local Semitic-population groups
- RAMESSES II (1290–1223 BC), moved the capital to the Delta area nearest Asia to fight against Semites
- MERNEPTAH (1223–1210 BC), left behind an inscription stating he conquered "Israel" in Palestine

Dynasty 20: Period of loss of empire

- RAMESSES III (1198–1166 BC) had to fight off the Philistines

The Bible itself gives suggested dates for the time of the Exodus. 1 Kings 6, 1 says the Temple of Solomon was built 480 years after Israel left Egypt; Exodus 12:40 states that the Israelites had been in Egypt 430 years when they departed with Moses. If such dates are exact—and probably they are not, because they appear to be rounded out or even symbolic (12 times 40 years suggests twelve generations)—two different centuries are at stake. If the Temple was built around 960 BC, it would place the Exodus in 1440 BC; and if the Joseph traditions are associated with the Hyksos invasion of Egypt, then a date around 1270 BC is probable. Of the two, most scholars favor the latter possibility. It falls in the time of Ramesses II who did build the towns of Pithom and Raamses as Exodus 1:11 says, and the thirteenth century BC was generally a troubled time in which a band of refugees just might be able to make their escape. A major departure under the strong rulers of the eighteenth dynasty, especially under the most powerful of all Egyptian kings, Thutmose III, seems much less likely.

Exodus 2—4: The Choice of Moses

There are several difficult questions raised by the story of Moses' origins. He is pictured as an Israelite, but his name and upbringing are Egyptian. He seems to know he is a Hebrew when he kills the Egyptian in chapter 2, but he is not trusted by his own people. He flees and makes his home among Midianites, where he meets God in their territory not among his own people. Even his rescue from death by means of a basket in the river is strange. It looks very much like a long-known legend of king Sargon of Akkad, who lived a thousand years earlier. Sargon was supposedly left to die as an infant by his royal parents but was secretly hidden in a basket by his maid and sent down the river. He was rescued and raised by a fisherman, and came back to rule years later. The use of this story illustrates how Moses was a figure larger than life to Israel. Although well known as a person from the Israelites' actual past experience, and central to the most important event in their history, Moses is still described in terms more like the great mythical heroes of Genesis 1–11, or of the founding fathers Abraham and Jacob. He dominates every book of the Pentateuch except Genesis and, when his death is finally recorded in Deuteronomy 34, 1–8, he leaves the earth at 120 years old in the full vigor of youth and to a grave unknown. Thus, we must expect the initial encounter with such a person will be spectacular.

Note that chapters 2 through 4 form a series of scenes in a play: (1) The birth of the hero in a nearly miraculous fashion forces us to wonder what his mission in life will be; (2) The situation begins to look desperate—he is neither respected nor successful and ends up fleeing to barbarians for his safety; (3) There he is called to a nearly impossible task by God and accepts reluctantly (Ex 3:1–12); (4) God gives him a special revelation of the divine name and an intimacy in communication not offered to others (Ex 3:12–22); (5) God is forced to confirm the promise, reassure Moses about his mission, and give him his brother Aaron as a helper to speak on his behalf (Ex 4:1–22); (6) Finally, the people accept him and his mission (Ex 4:28–31).

Two notes might be added to help understand this section better:

The call of Moses has a certain pattern to it that is used throughout the Bible as the model of a call of the great prophets and leaders. Note that it is made up of the following stages:

1. God appears or speaks to Moses (Ex 3:1–4)
2. He explains the reason for his coming (Ex 3: 4–9)
3. He commissions Moses to his task (Ex 3: 10)
4. Moses objects (Ex 3:11)
5. God reassures him and insists (Ex 3:12)
6. God follows with a sign or prediction (Ex 3: 12; 4, 1–5)

Note similar patterns for the call of the prophets and others. See table on RG 120.

The revelation of the divine name to Moses is a very special moment in the story. Note how it may be the combination of both the J and E sources because of the way it starts in Exodus 3: 1 with "the LORD" (J), and continues with "God" (E). To prepare Moses to understand the meaning of the name, God first reveals that this is the same God known to his ancestors Abraham, Isaac, and Jacob (a statement repeated three times in this chapter for emphasis!), and that God is showing love and compassion as he had done in the past when giving the promises to those earlier generations. It then comes to the moment in verse 13 when Moses asks for God's identity more clearly. The text gives several versions of the divine name: "I am who am," "I am," and "He who is" (or better, "He who causes to be"). The one certain thing is that all of these come from the same verb in Hebrew, *hayah,* the verb "to be." It is not usual to use the verb in this way. So, on the one hand, God refuses to give a regular name, but hides his real identity behind claims that He simply exists. And, on the other hand, the name suggests that God exists for something specific; in this case for the salvation of Israel. Since the unique first person form, "I am who am," is found only here in Exodus 3:14, the third-person form, *yhwh,* must mean either "He who makes this happen" (that is, the great act of salvation about to be performed), or, just possibly, it identifies God as the creator that causes all things to be. At least in this one event, the addition of the first person "I am" strongly suggests that God is, above all, assuring Israel that "I am always with you."

The word *Yahweh* occurs 6,823 times in the Old Testament and, following a very ancient Jewish custom, we traditionally do not use this name in prayer but replace it out of reverence for the divine greatness with the more formal "LORD." This is the practice throughout the NAB translation. Whenever the word appears in that way, printed in capitals and small capitals, it means that the underlying Hebrew word is Yahweh.

Exodus 5–12: Confrontation with the Pharaoh

The structure of these chapters also follows the pattern of a drama. There is Moses' initial attempts to show God's power to Pharaoh, and his subsequent frustration when the powers of Egyptian magicians seem as strong as God's (5: 1–13). Then the people themselves grumble that Moses is making things worse (5:14–21). Chapter 6 opens with what seems to repeat the call of Moses from chapters 3 and 4, but scholars believe it was a separate account of the call of Moses from the P source. The editors added it to reinforce God's promise not to abandon Moses or the people, but to bring about their liberation.

The battle heats up when God begins to send plagues upon the land. There are a few inconsistencies in their presentation that suggest originally several sources were combined. Note, for example, that sometimes Moses stretches out his staff (9, 22f) and sometimes Aaron does instead (8:1–3). The first usage is E, the second J. So, too, sometimes Pharaoh hardens his own heart, (9:34), and sometimes God hardens his heart (10:20). The first is J, the second is E.

The NAB notes (at 7:14) that they are typical natural disasters that regularly trouble Egypt. The miracle is not in the actual plague, such as hail or gnats or flies, but in the timing of the contest between God and the pharaoh who has placed himself higher than the Lord. Can God

1. God appears	Jgs 6:11f	Is 6:lf	Jer 1:4	Ez 1:1–28a
2. The reason	Jgs 6:12f	Is 6:3–7	Jer 1:5	Ez 1:28b–2:2
3. Commission	Jgs 6:14	Is 6:8–10	Jer 1:5	Ez 2:3–5
4. Objection	Jgs 6:15	Is 6:11	Jer 1:6	Ez 2:6–8
5. Reassurance	Jgs 6:16	Is 6:11f	Jer 1:7f	Ez 2:6f
6. The sign	Jgs 6:17	-------	Jer l:9f	Ez 2:8–3:11

actually overcome the hardheartedness of the pharaoh? Each time, a plague seems to work; then it fails as the pharaoh changes his mind. The train of events struggles forward toward the climactic moment when God finally sends the tenth plague in chapter 12:29–36. This last plague will be an act of terror and of death: by slaying Egypt's firstborn, God symbolically ends the universal leadership of Egypt and transfers divine favor to Israel's firstborn, who were spared.

It is not an accident, therefore, that this event is prefaced with an elaborate description, not of a meal as it might have been actually eaten in fear and haste, but of the full liturgical ritual of the annual feast of Passover. This feast was developed as a liturgy to recall and relive the miracle of the Exodus, the "passing over" of the angel of death and the liberation of Israel from slavery. Part of the significant theology of the book of Exodus is the unity between later rituals and the original events. What our ancestors experienced in the land of Egypt, we relive and celebrate anew in our feasts. Christianity has at least one excellent parallel to this way of thinking in that the synoptic gospel accounts of the Last Supper recount Jesus' words over the bread and wine, just as they were recited in home eucharists of the first century. To see this for yourself, compare Paul's description in 1 Corinthians 11:23–26 with Luke 22:14–20.

Exodus 13–15: The Escape through the Sea

These chapters can be divided into three parts. The first, in Exodus 13:1–16, lists two further practices that the Israelites must do in order to remember how God saved them from the angel of death: (1) avoidance of leavened bread on the feast of the departure itself, and (2) the consecration of all firstborn males to God. No doubt both the avoidance of leaven and ceremonies of special dedication of a firstborn to God were practiced by Israel as well as its pagan neighbors long before the time of the Exodus. But now they are given new meaning as a reminder that the real source of Israel's life is a God who delivered them from death. They mark the moment when God confirmed that divine favor has been transferred from Egypt's firstborn to Israel's firstborn.

The second part, in Exodus 13:17–14:31, gives a detailed account of how the Israelites once more escaped from the hands of the Egyptians, this time through the sea when it seemed impossible. And the third part, in Exodus 15: 1–21, recites a song of victory that celebrates the escape through the sea and may have been a hymn for a feast day. In structure this account of the great act of rescue in chapters 13 and 14 is preceded and followed by materials that come from the religious practices of later Israelite times. This is in line with the attitude expressed in chapter 12 that saw no problem relating the Passover escape side by side with a description of the much later rituals that celebrated those events.

The form of the third part, the Song of the Sea in Exodus 15, is quite old. Some scholars consider the basic text under the present enlarged form to be the oldest written text in the Bible. It uses extensive poetic parallelism for effect, and it breathes the spirit of God as a warrior chieftain in battle who comes to the rescue of his besieged people. The older part occurs in the first half, verses 1–12. It tells of the actual battle that God wages; the second part in verses 13–18 recounts how God then led victorious Israel through the desert to the Promised Land. The events that are told in verses 13–18 culminate in the establishment of a shrine (or home) of God in Palestine and could not have been written before the period of Settlement, perhaps as much as two centuries after the Exodus. Nevertheless, the hymn as a whole preserves an idea of God that belongs to the time before Israel settled in Palestine and developed a monarchy. Thus, the original poem may well have been composed sometime not long after the Exodus, during the age of the judges, with further developments added to it.

Several Egyptian documents help us to understand better the cultural background of Israel's flight from Egypt. One from shortly after the time of Moses is a report of a frontier official in the Sinai, which he sent back to headquarters in Egypt, and it reveals that Egypt regularly allowed groups of tribes to pass in and out of Egypt in times of drought or famine to save their lives:

> We have finished letting the Bedouin tribes of Edom pass the fortress of Mer-ne-Ptah Hotep-hir-Maat which is in [the eastern Delta area] to go to the pools of Per–Atum . . . to keep them alive and to keep their cattle alive.

The second document is from the same period (about 1200 BC) and describes Egyptian military searches for runaway slaves:

> I was sent forth from the broad halls of the palace . . . after two slaves. . . . Now when I reached the fortress, they told me that the scout had come from the desert saying that they had passed the walled place north of the fortress of Seti-Mer-ne-Ptah. . . . Which watch found their tracks? What people are after them? Write to me about all that has happened to them and how many people you sent out after them.

Two points can be made here: movement of groups was common across the Sinai borders, and the problems associated with slaves, slave escapes, and slave rebellions were of some concern to Egypt, as they were to later slave-owning societies such as Rome or the American South.

Exodus 16–18: The Hardships in the Desert of Sinai

The next stage of the journey takes the Israelites from the location of the sea to the foot of the mountain of Sinai in two months. The journey follows an itinerary which is listed for us, but unfortunately few of the places can be identified with any certainty. Even the location of Mount Sinai is open to discussion. But we can at least note some aspects with the aid of a map of the Sinai peninsula (see map 2 at the back of this book).

If we back up to the first part of the journey in chapters 13 and 14, we discover that Israel did not travel directly toward Palestine on the main highway along the coast. Egyptian forts guarded this way, and so they avoided it (13:1–7f). Instead, they moved along the edge of the fertile Delta area just where it met the Sinai desert. The place-names in 14:1–3 might be located either very close to the Mediterranean coast or perhaps near a swampy lake that lay along the depression line now followed by the Suez canal.

The name *Red Sea* is not certain. The Hebrew name can also mean either the "reed sea" or the "sea of chaos" or "sea of the end," which would signify doom or the final confrontation with the power of chaos in an echo of the great myths. Possibly today's Red Sea was called the "Sea of Reeds," but it is just as possible that it designated another body of water, perhaps one of several swampy lakes; on the other hand, if "sea of chaos" was intended, it could be anywhere, since the name is to be taken in a symbolic sense for the place where the Lord would finally defeat Pharaoh's army as the servants of chaotic evil.

Thus, scholars who try to identify the place-names in 15:22 and following chapters have trouble knowing where to start. *Marah, Elim,* the desert of Sin, and *Rephidim* all remain mysteriously difficult to pinpoint. There are quite a number of oases throughout the Sinai, north and south, but none can be identified for certain with these names.

Usually three possible options for the route of the journey are given. The most northern route is the so-called Way of the Philistines and was, of necessity, avoided. The second route also went across the north somewhere and was a major caravan route to both Beersheba in Palestine and to Petra in Edom. It would also have two other strong claims: it passes very near Kadesh Barnea, Israel's main camping place where, according to Deuteronomy 2:14, they spent thirty-eight years; and it was territory known to support nomadic groups such as the Midianites with whom Moses had spent time. It is listed on the chart as "The Way of Shur." A third possibility, and the one favored since Byzantine monks arrived at the very impressive mountain Jebel Musa in the sixth century AD, is the circular route along around the southern part of the Sinai peninsula. It has in its favor that Jebel Musa and its neighboring peaks are by far the most impressive mountains in Sinai. Moreover, there is strong evidence that Egypt itself mined the Sinai for gems and minerals in this area, using Semitic slaves. Such a mine has been found at Serabit el Khadim, and it is just possible that Moses knew the place. Finally, this longer route would permit the large number of moves that the books of Exodus and Numbers say the Israelites made. This is all we can say with our present knowledge.

Identifying the geography does not really explain the meaning of these chapters in reciting the lengthy journey of Israel away from Egypt. The events of Exodus 15:22–18:27 are not related to tracing the physical steps of the people as much as showing the tension between them and Moses. This is, above all, a tension between their frustrations with hardship and their duty to show gratitude to God for their freedom. At Marah, their grumbling leads to the lesson that God is a healer (15:25f). At Sin, the dispute over food leads God to reaffirm his goodness as provider and to reinforce his demand that the Sabbath be observed (16:16–36). At Rephidim, the people's anger over the lack of water leads to God's gift of water from the rock as a reminder of the miracle at the Red Sea (17:1–7). The final two events, both in chapter 18, show first, a divine rejection of the Amalekites, and second, a positive relationship between Israel and the Midianites, who help organize judges and leaders to assist Moses. This is done with the assistance of Moses' father-in-law, Jethro. But it is a preparation for the greater organization around the divine commands, which are about to be given on Mount Sinai.

Exodus 19–24: The Covenant with God

These chapters describe the high point of the Pentateuch. If we wanted to draw a diagram to show this, we might draw a highway between point A, the moment of creation, to the final point, Z, which would be the border of the promised land. This would cover the Pentateuch as a journey from Genesis 1 to Deuteronomy 34. The highway would climb steadily through Genesis and Exodus 1–15 to the top of Mount Sinai, go along its crest from Exodus 19 to the end of Numbers 10, and then descend forcefully to the shores of the Jordan River from Numbers 11 to the end of Deuteronomy. See diagram below.

On the crest of the mountain there is a long pause while God teaches Moses the laws by which Israel is to live. But these laws themselves are the fulfillment of the covenant that is established between God and the people in Exodus 19–24. So, ultimately, they are one. To understand these chapters, we should first note how they are organized into four scenes. See diagram at top of next page.

In scene one, Moses goes up and down the mountain several times, which may be a sign of more than one source combined, but it all serves to create an aura of holiness and reverence. Indeed, it so resembles the awesome experience of the Temple that many scholars have understood this to be a very late introduction built around the beautiful theological definition of Israel, found in verses 4–6: Israel is to be God's special possession.

Scene two records God's first words as a kind of summary of all that will follow. These are the key demands of any relationship with God; they cover duties toward God and toward one another and are limited to ten for easy teaching to children, who can count them on their fingers. Many of the commandments also have a special covenant motive for why they should be kept.

This is continued in scene three with an en-

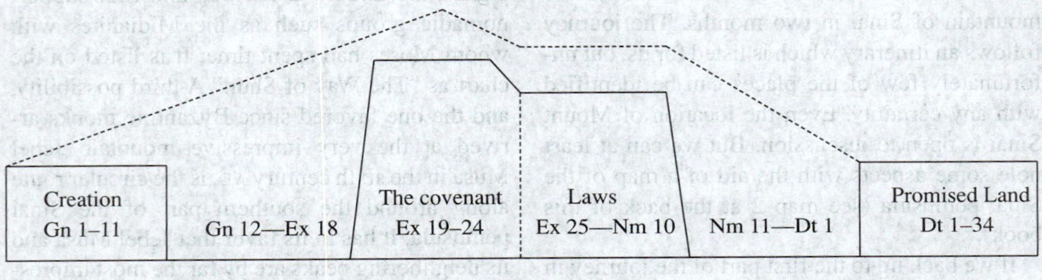

19:1–25 A	20:1–21 B	21:22–3:33 C	24:1–18 D
The purification of the people to meet God	The ten commandments as a summary of the covenant	The individual laws by which the people are to live	The solemn acceptance of the covenant

tirely different type of requirement. Unlike the Ten Commandments, which simply demand response with no answer to what will happen if you don't obey them, these requirements give a practical situation and the proper settlement of each case. The laws of chapters 21 through 23 are usually called "The Covenant Code," and are similar to civil laws throughout the ancient Near East. It is a minisample of how to act justly under the covenant.

Finally, in scene four, the people give their full assent to the divine offer of a covenant, and it is sealed by two rituals, again, perhaps, once separate from each other: a sprinkling with blood (24:3–8), and a covenant meal in which Moses, Aaron, and the seventy elders banquet with God (24:1, 9–11).

The entire series thus combines lawgiving and ritual in an awesome setting of divine holiness and human sanctification to impress on the reader that *this* is the foundation stone of Israel's relationship to God and the source of all its religious obligations.

Exodus 25–40: Establishing God's Home in Israel

Once the Lord and Israel have been solemnly joined together, the dramatic action turns toward establishing a permanent dwelling for God in the midst of the people. Chapters 25–31 and 35–40 largely repeat each other as command and fulfillment: (1) a series of directions for building and appointing, and (2) the carrying out of those directions described in detail. The perspective on the themes of building God's house, and establishing a special office of priests who will be consecrated and set aside for divine service, seem to stem largely from the later P source, which was concerned with showing that the Lord's Temple in Jerusalem had its original mandate at Mount Sinai. The desert tent and ark are described in terms of what a nomadic people of the wilderness might use; thus they are constructed to be portable. But all the major vessels and objects of the later Temple are already given a place during this desert period. In this manner, the text shows the unbroken continuity between God's earliest covenant bond and all later expressions of it. At the same time, these stories emphasize that the covenant cannot be observed unless worship is at its heart.

With this purpose in mind, the authors have taken the stories of Israel's first failure to keep the covenant, its idolatry with the golden calf, Moses' breaking the tablets of stone, and the regiving of the covenant words (32–34) and inserted them between the two halves of the sanctuary narratives. Worship and covenant are thus inseparably interlocked. See diagram below.

The Theology of the Covenant

Before moving on to the book of Leviticus, it will be worth a short reflection on the meaning of the term *covenant* for the faith of Israel as presented in the Pentateuch. There are several points to keep in mind:

• A covenant is a solemn agreement made with a religious ritual. In the early days it may

Exodus 19–24	*Exodus 25–31*	*Exodus 32–34*	*Exodus 35–40*
covenant given	sanctuary directions	covenant renewed	sanctuary built
A	B	A	B

have been mostly oral and put to memory, but in later biblical times it was always written in a formal document. It serves the same purpose as a contract—it is legally binding on both parties.

• Covenants can be made between individuals or between nations. Examples of individual covenants in the Pentateuch can be found in Genesis 26:26–28; 31:44–46. National covenants are mentioned often in the historical books: Joshua 9:3–15; 1 Kings 5:2–12; and 1 Kings 15: 19. It can also be made between a god and a people. For example, at the time of the flood, God promises Noah a covenant in Genesis 9:4–12; and Abraham receives a covenant in Genesis 15: 10–21.

• These covenants between nations or with gods are modeled after typical treaties known throughout the ancient Near East. The particular type found at Mount Sinai is called a *vassal treaty* because it is made between a great king or ruler and a lesser subject state. A vassal treaty is not an equal deal. The great king promises kindness and favor; the vassal promises a long list of particular obligations that will be performed faithfully.

• These treaties were considered to be valid for all time. They could not be taken back or rejected once solemnly made.

• There are examples of covenant treaties from both seventh-century Assyria and the thirteenth-century Hittites. Biblical wording shows similarities to aspects of both forms. But the clearest model of a typical vassal treaty is known from the Hittite examples. It has six parts:

1. A preamble stating the name of the parties.
2. A historical listing of all the good things the great king has done for the vassal.
3. The laws and obligations that the vassal must perform.
4. A directive that the document be saved and read publicly.
5. A list of gods who witness the treaty.
6. Lists of curses the gods will bring on those who break the treaty, and the blessings given to the parties if they keep it.

• If we take these six steps, we can see them present in Exodus 19–24 in a general way:

1. Ex 20:2 the preamble
2. Ex 20:2 (19:4) the historical list of favors
3. Ex 20:3–17; 20:23–23:17 the obligations of the vassal
4. Ex 24:3–8; 24:12 oath ceremony and saving the tablets
5. — no divine witnesses
6. Ex 20:5f; 23:25 blessings and curses

No gods witness the treaty because in Israelite belief there are no other gods who can testify to what the Lord does. However, we must not push these similarities too far. Exodus describes, first of all, a momentous event of encountering, and then promising exclusive worship to, the Lord who has saved and shown himself a benefactor to this small refugee people.

Only later did the full legal treaty language become fixed in the tradition, such as in the covenant summary statement often found in the prophets, "You shall be my people and I will be your God" (Jer 7:23; 11:4; 24:7; Ez 11:20; 14: 11; Hos 2:25, etc.). Perhaps closer to the original formula of the covenant relationship is the moving proclamation put first on God's own lips in Exodus 20:5f and then again in the renewal of the covenant in 34:6f: "The LORD, the LORD, a merciful and gracious God, slow to anger and rich in kindness and fidelity, continuing his kindness for a thousand generations, and forgiving wickedness and crime and sin; yet not declaring the guilty guiltless . . ." This same text, as indicated by John Paul II in *Dives in Misericordia,* is the basis of Israel's hope, and therefore the hope of the modern world (#4).

We can appreciate the power of the idea of a covenant because it confirms the special relationship that Israel claimed with the Lord, based on a unique and moving personal experience of the favor of that God for them. At first the covenant was mostly celebrated in worship with a national sense of destiny. Only with time do we find that later prophets like Jeremiah and Ezekiel express a growing concern to stress the legal relationship that cannot be broken even by disasters, but can require punishment and legal penalties if the covenant terms are broken.

LEVITICUS

[see pages 133–172 of the Old Testament]

Reading the Book of Leviticus Today

Jewish tradition has given a very honored place to the book of Leviticus because it contains a significant number of the laws and commandments by which Judaism defines its life and practice. Six hundred and thirteen commandments have been identified in the Pentateuch that are binding on Israel, and of these some 247 occur in Leviticus. The early rabbinic commentators of the Talmud spent many volumes examining the meaning of the statements in Leviticus and establishing practical ways in which they could still be observed many centuries after they were written down. The learned teachers of the law in the first centuries after Christ (from about AD 70 to 500) never tired of debating the myriad ways of understanding the legal materials in Leviticus and elsewhere. This may seem particularly surprising since nearly all of the laws of sacrifice that fill the first quarter of the book of Leviticus had been rendered impossible to perform by the Roman conquest of Jerusalem and after the destruction of its Temple in AD 70. It indicates, however, how richly diverse are the contents of the book, that even with the inability to perform so many of its commands, it still remains the most important statement of Torah for Judaism.

It is therefore important to recall that in Judaism *Torah* does not have the narrow and constricting meaning of "Law" so common among modern people. Torah means "teaching" or "way" and it can be best understood as a means of expressing ourselves before God as a faithful and obedient and beloved son or daughter. Jews always link Torah commands with simultaneous joy. Note the extremely upbeat and positive nature of the Bible's most famous hymn in praise of the Law, Psalm 119. The opening verses read,

> Happy those whose way is blameless,
> who walk by the teaching of the LORD.
> Happy those who observe God's decrees,
> who seek the LORD with all their heart,
> They do no wrong;
> they walk in God's ways.

and it continues in this manner for another 173 verses, more than three times the length of any other psalm in the Psalter!

How opposite has been the reaction of the Christian church as it reads Leviticus. Most Christians are horrified by the idea of animal sacrifices, and they consider the questions of what should be eaten or not eaten far too restrictive; many even experience a mild case of disgust at the topics of the purity and impurity of bodily functions. Since many of the actions described in the first half of Leviticus are tied to priestly roles in the Temple, the book has become a negative symbol for Christians who emphasize the so-called freedom from the Law that Paul speaks of in his letters in the New Testament. Even the current name of the book means basically "That which pertains to the levitical priests," although in Hebrew it is called simply by its opening word, *wayyiqra'* ("And he called"). Thus it is very likely that a Christian reader will come to this book with a certain prejudice that it will be boring, irrelevant, and largely supplanted by a newer theology of the freedom of the spirit. This is not a good starting point to discover any treasure in the book, nor to realize, even in regulations that a Christian no longer observes, how profound insights into the mystery of God shine through regularly.

To gain as much appreciation for the book as we can, we need to reflect on its message on two levels. First, we can explore what religious insight and meaning the various laws and practices had for an ancient Israelite. Second, we can look at the major themes it treats in terms of how they reveal the enduring character of God's revelation and divine purpose, which gave direction and vitality to Israel's fidelity and witness through the centuries, and that have become central to Christianity's own teaching. An example of the two levels would be the understanding of sacrifice. Unless we learn the central role that sacrifice played in Leviticus as a primary means of both acknowledging God's saving blessing and also asking for forgiveness, our interpretation of Jesus' own death and the Church's explanation of the Eucharist will be seriously weakened and perhaps even incomprehensible.

The Overall Structure of the Book

Leviticus can be identified entirely with the style and theology of the Priestly source found throughout the Pentateuch. Leviticus is very interested in classifying and listing all things in their proper place, just as the P story of creation does in Genesis 1 or the list of nations does in Genesis 11, 10–32. It is also very concerned with distinguishing the realm of the sacred from that of everyday life. Most of the topics it treats deal directly with this question of what is appropriate or inappropriate in matters of approaching the divine.

The book has really two major divisions that are quite different in spirit. Chapters 1 through 16 give regulations for matters that are handled directly by the priests; chapters 17 through 27 treat the larger social areas of community behavior and public worship that express the spiritual heart of living within the covenant. In a diagram it might look like the table on RG 127.

Explanation of the Outline

Chapters 1–16. The initial collection of various regulations on sacrifice in chapters 1 through 7 is followed by a narrative explanation in chapters 8 through 10 of the proper role and status of the priestly officials, illustrated by Aaron's first major sacrifice under the covenant. Then chapters 11 through 15 contain a collection of rules and distinctions that govern the proper respect for food and bodily functions; chapter 16 follows with an elaborate description of the annual ritual that atoned for and cleansed the people of all guilt from their sins. In both parallel patterns, laws are followed by actions. Neither set is intended to comprise all the laws that must be observed, nor do the rituals described exhaust all ways of celebrating or performing sacred liturgical actions. What they do above all is establish a close connection between the ways we define our lives and the ways we celebrate in worship.

For the authors of Leviticus, this structure emphasizes that holiness is central to Israel's relationship with God, and that holiness may be defined as respect for the sacred mystery of life and for the divine presence that is found everywhere, even in ordinary day-to-day life.

Chapters 17–26. The same spirit of a holiness that sets apart areas of special divine reverence from ordinary ways of acting also governs this second part of Leviticus, which is often called simply "The Law of Holiness." It has special characteristics that mark it off as a separate set of laws from chapters 1 through 16. This set can be divided roughly into two parts: chapters 17 through 20 stress the ethical areas of life that bind us socially in communal life; chapters 21 through 25 concentrate on the sacred areas of priestly ministry and worship. They roughly correspond to the same dynamics that we find in chapters 1–16 between commands on ways of life and commands on more directly priestly ritualizing. Chapter 26 concludes this body of law, but it is so impressive in scope that it really serves as the conclusion of the whole book. It reflects much of the specific language associated with covenants. Chapter 27 was added later as an appendix.

The Literary Unity and Diversity of the Book

All scholars today recognize the basic unified viewpoint that the book takes. It is priestly. This means that it gathers together laws and directions that govern activities that should be monitored by the priests in the community. Some of these, as in the chapters on sacrifices and major feasts, have to do with public worship. Others have to do with personal behavior and conditions that affect our proper place before God. These may involve laws on food, clothing, skin diseases, sexual activity, as well as truly ethical decisions about justice, love, and right behavior between members of the covenant community.

All these laws, however, are seen to be part of what separates the sacred from the ordinary. God is holy and not to be treated in just any old way. Judaism and Christianity have always made the transcendence of God a first priority; that is, they have recognized the gulf that divides us as creatures from the one who creates. Certain moments of our lives and certain activities highlight this profound difference. Humans enter into the realm of the sacred that is set apart on a holy day or at a holy place or by the rituals performed by a consecrated (thus "holy") person. Certain features of our being, too, are holy, such as sexual-

Outline of the Book of Leviticus

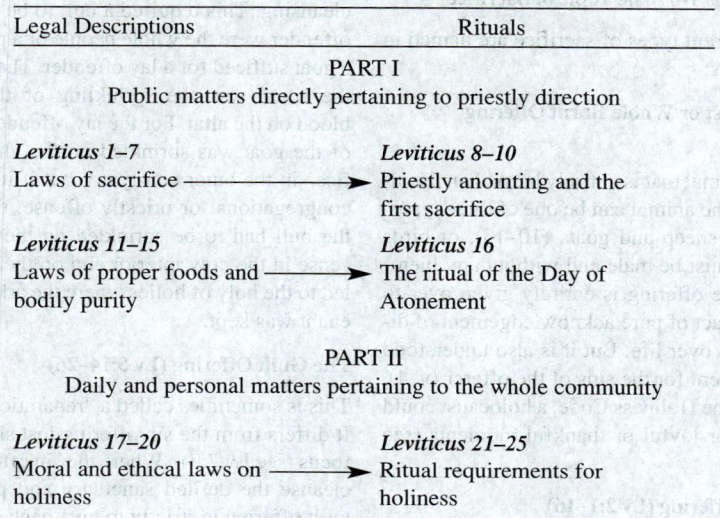

Legal Descriptions		Rituals
	PART I Public matters directly pertaining to priestly direction	
Leviticus 1–7 Laws of sacrifice	→	***Leviticus 8–10*** Priestly anointing and the first sacrifice
Leviticus 11–15 Laws of proper foods and bodily purity	→	***Leviticus 16*** The ritual of the Day of Atonement
	PART II Daily and personal matters pertaining to the whole community	
Leviticus 17–20 Moral and ethical laws on holiness	→	***Leviticus 21–25*** Ritual requirements for holiness
	PART III ***Leviticus 26*** Covenantal conclusion to both chapters 17–25 and to the entire book ***Leviticus 27*** [Appendix of laws on vows]	

ity, birth, and death, because they are at the heart of the mystery of divine creation and divine control over our existence. They are to be treated with special reverence. Exodus covered the *making* of all necessary sacred objects and some ordination rites; Leviticus concentrates on *how* Israel is to act according to holy principles.

Although this theme controls every topic treated in Leviticus, the book was not written all at once. The signs of different groups of laws that at various times were joined into larger and larger collections can be seen when we look closely at the text. As an example, if we read the sacrifice rules in chapters 1–7 quickly, they may appear to be all in the same style. But we could then go back and look at particular expressions. In chapters 1–3 the sacrifices are regularly "brought *before* the Lord," so that there will be a "sweet-smelling oblation" to the Lord. These expressions are rare in chapters 4–5. Instead, these chapters deal with a special type of offering for sin and use the label, "The Lord said to Moses . . ." more frequently. They also stress that the priest will make atonement for others. Chapters 6–7 are arranged according to a still different formula, "This is the ritual of . . ."

Probably, then, there are three slightly different sets of sacrifice laws that have been combined to make up these seven chapters. Again, the style of listing laws in chapters 1–16 is so different from the more preachy style of chapters 17–26 that all commentators have been convinced that we have separate origins for these two halves. Nevertheless, the editors have made this into one of the most unified books that we have in the Pentateuch, second only to Deuteronomy.

The Major Themes of the Individual Sections

Since much in Leviticus is foreign to modern Christian religious observances, it will be worth looking at each division with a few charts and background aids to understanding.

Leviticus 1–7: The Topic of Sacrifice

Several different types of sacrifice are named in these chapters:

The Holocaust or Whole Burnt Offering (Lv 1:1–17)

This is an animal that is entirely burned on the altar to God. The animal can be one of three types: cattle (3–9), sheep and goats (10–13), or birds (14–17). It must be male and without any blemish. Since the offering is entirely given over to God, it is an act of pure acknowledgement of divine lordship over life. But it is also understood as an atonement for the sins of the offerer (v. 4). Yet, later in the Holiness Code, a holocaust could be offered for joyful or thankful moments (see 22:17).

The Grain Offering (Lv 2:1–16)

The NAB calls this the "cereal offering," but in Hebrew the word is simply "the gift offering" *(minhah)*. This may be understood in part as a substitute for expensive animals so that the poor could afford a holocaust. But more usually it was a thanksgiving to God for good crops and to celebrate joyful times. Since only the symbolic bits of grain, oil, and frankincense on the top were actually burned up, the rest went for the support of the priest.

The Peace Offering (Lv 3:1–17)

This might better be called a "well-being sacrifice," for its main difference from the holocaust was that it was not completely burned up but largely saved and eaten by the offerers and their families. It could be taken from either cattle or sheep and goats, but not from birds. Since this offering was for a group, a bird would have been too small. Like the holocaust it had to be without blemish, but unlike the holocaust it could be either a male or a female animal. Only the fat parts (tail, inner organs and their fat, the two kidneys) were burned to God.

The Sin Offering or "Purgation Offering" (Lv 4:1–5:13)

This sacrifice specifically deals with those times when a sacred thing had been violated, often by accident or without knowing it. The sacrifice was necessary in order to atone for the loss of holiness and proper purity of holy things by an act of cleansing. This required a bull to be killed if the offender were the whole people or a priest; while a goat sufficed for a lay offender. The key part of the ritual was the sprinkling of the animal's blood on the altar. For the lay offender, the blood of the goat was sprinkled on the altar of sacrifices in the outer courtyard; but if it had been a congregational or priestly offense, the blood of the bull had to be sprinkled on the altar of incense in the holy interior and on the curtain that led to the holy of holies where the ark of the covenant was kept.

The Guilt Offering (Lv 5:14–26)

This is sometimes called a "reparation offering." It differs from the sin offering just slightly in its focus (see Lv 7:7). Where the sin offering was to cleanse the defiled sanctuary and persons, the guilt offering is strictly to give back a reparation or "payment" to God for failure in something we ought to have given or done. That is, we have cheated God or a member of the covenant community, and so not only does the wrong itself have to be fixed up, but God must be given a reparation offering over and above the actual amount that was neglected. For this offering a ram is specified, and the blood is sprinkled on the altar itself. It is clearly a ritual of atonement for sin to heal the sinner of guilt.

Instructions for the Performance of the Different Sacrifices (Lv 6:1–7:36)

The specific actions of the priests for each of the above types of sacrifice are now spelled out in more detail in 6:1–7:10. Special instructions for the lay participants in the peace offerings are added on in 7:11–36. This was necessary because, in these particular sacrifices, the offerer and his party ritually ate most of the sacrificed animal and thus needed instructions similar to those given to the priests. It did not hurt, of course, from the priestly point of view, to reemphasize to those who brought sacrifices their obligation to supply a portion to the priests for their livelihood.

Conclusion (Lv 7:37–38)

The last two verses of chapter 7 are an especially solemn closing that underscores for the reader how seriously sacrificial regulations and the importance of this practice for the faith was to be understood.

The Anointing and Service of Aaron and His Sons (Lv 8:1–10:20)

Once the instructions on how sacrifice is to be done have been thoroughly learned in chapters 1–7, the action can begin. These next chapters deal with the installation of the proper priesthood, that is, Aaron and those descended from him (chapter 8); the model performance of the first sacrifices (chapter 9); and several crucial problems that need a solution (chapter 10). Thus, the section is very well organized even though there are several signs it may have originated from a variety of sources. The description of the first sacrifice in 8:14–30 seems almost to be duplicated in the octave-day sacrifices of 9:1–21. The story difference is that in the first, Moses actually leads Aaron; in the second, Aaron does it on his own authority.

The details of chapter 8 fulfill the requirements for proper priestly performance of the sacrifices. Verses 1–13 carry out the commands on the appointment of priests found in Exodus 29; verses 14–30 correspond to the sacrifice laws in Lv 1:1–5:13.

In chapter 9 three events are recorded: the first sacrifice of atonement for Aaron and the priests (9:8–14), the first sacrifice to atone for the whole people (9:15–21), and finally, the blessing over the people (9:22–24). This text reinforces the lesson that sacrifices must be done correctly and with a special awareness of their sacred character. Only if they are done with such careful reverence will the glory of the Lord be present in their midst (9:6, 22–24).

In chapter 10, the lesson about God's holiness is driven home with still greater force. In the first case, verses 1–5, even the sons of Aaron will be stuck down if they fail to observe the proper awe and correct manner of approaching the divine presence. In the second case, verses 6–11, the priests must refrain from a number of behaviors that would profane the sense of holiness in the performance of their duties. These include improper dress, stepping beyond the boundary of the Tent of Meeting, and using alcoholic beverages. But they are also given the positive duty of teaching the law in its entirety to the people (v. 11). And in the third case, verses 12–20, the correct manner of eating the sacrifices is dealt with. It is illustrated by an unusual exception that tests the rule: Eleazar and Ithamar don't eat the sacrifice as they should but give it all up as a burnt offering to God. Their excess zeal is permitted because it offered to God what they were entitled to have for themselves. If they had instead done the opposite, and taken part of God's share for themselves, one is left to imagine the death they would incur as punishment.

So then, chapters 8–10 serve two functions. They show how the laws in chapters 1–7 are performed by the true priests (see the diagram RG 127) and they fulfill the instructions given in Exodus 25–31. Those chapters gave the Lord's commands both for building a tent and ark, and for consecrating priests. But only the building program was completed by the end of Exodus. Only now does the priestly consecration finally take place. We could show the development by another diagram, on RG 130.

In this schema the Levitical editors have inserted Exodus 32–34 from the older J story of the covenant between the commands to prepare the sanctuary and priesthood and their fulfillment, both from P. This links the covenant to the regulations on worship by interlocking sections of one with the other; at the same time it integrates the two traditions of J and P. Note that it also reinforces the notion that the people easily fall into idolatry and transgress the holiness of God and so need the careful priestly performance of the cult to preserve their proper relationship to God.

The Laws of Purity (Lv 11:1–15:33)

These chapters take up four separate types of uncleanness associated with living beings:

1. Lv 11:1–47 Animals
2. Lv 12:1–8 Childbirth
3. Lv 13:1–14:57 Contagious diseases
4. Lv 15:1–33 Genital discharges

The Levitical editors have made a number of important distinctions within these categories. In chapter 11, for example, some animals are considered clean, that is, fit for eating, while others are not. In general, those same animals that are unclean for eating also contaminate anyone who touches their dead bodies. In the third category, contagious diseases, special procedures are required for each different case: if it is a human

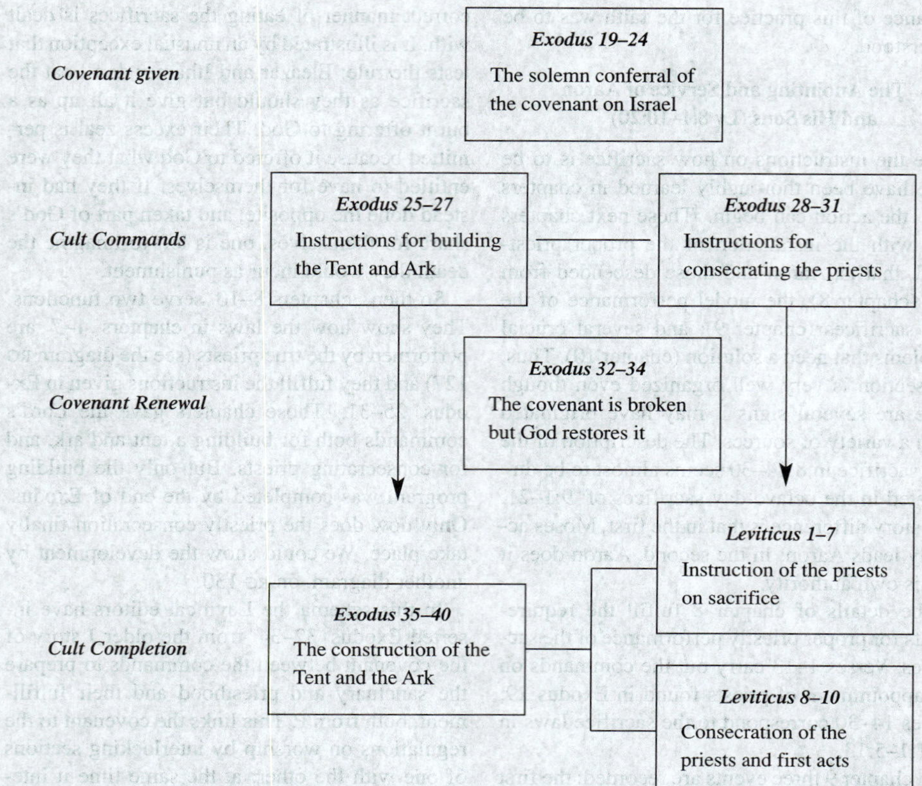
Covenant given
Exodus 19–24
The solemn conferral of the covenant on Israel
Cult Commands
Exodus 25–27
Instructions for building the Tent and Ark
Exodus 28–31
Instructions for consecrating the priests
Covenant Renewal
Exodus 32–34
The covenant is broken but God restores it
Leviticus 1–7
Instruction of the priests on sacrifice
Cult Completion
Exodus 35–40
The construction of the Tent and the Ark
Leviticus 8–10
Consecration of the priests and first acts

skin disease, the person must be quarantined; if it is a fungus on a house wall, the building is quarantined; if it is a matter of sexual emissions, different rituals are prescribed for men and women.

These purity laws are based on a simple consideration, namely that many areas of human life touch the mystery of the divine, and in those areas there can be nothing that is impure or unworthy. This does not just apply to sacred spaces such as temples, or sacred moments such as birth, marriage, and high holy days; it also includes those areas of everyday experience that touch issues of life and death, including the mysterious power of sexual activity and the sometimes dangerous loss of blood and other bodily fluids.

Uncleanness refers specifically to those situations that prevent us from approaching the divine in a worthy manner. They cannot be taken lightly. The final word on the question of those who defile God's house by appearing in it in a state of uncleanness is a warning that it will cause their death (Lv 15:31). At one point, also, the command to avoid swarming insects as unclean is identified with loyalty to God himself, and its violation defiles God's own holiness (Lv 11:44f). Moreover, the laws can have devastating effects on the individuals involved. For example, if the skin disease does not go away, the person can be permanently exiled from the community.

Many scholars have debated the reasons why some animals are considered clean and therefore edible, while others are forbidden. Frequently they argue for a primitive science of hygiene that recognized that the unclean animals were possible carriers of disease. An example would be the pig, long known to be a possible bearer of trichinosis. Others argue that the real basis is a religious reflection on the proper order of creation as told in the Genesis creation stories. Only fish that swim, birds that fly, and animals that graze fulfill the normal pattern of God's plan; all others seem to be not quite perfect—flightless birds such as ostriches, sea creatures that walk like animals, animals that crawl close to the ground like insects, etc. A little of both views may well have influenced the theologians who made up the lists. We just do not know.

The categories covered in Leviticus 11–15 do not exhaust the realm of the clean and unclean. The Passover regulations of Exodus 12–13 deal with old leaven, which was unclean; Deuteronomy 20 demands purity conditions for waging war in God's name. But the four areas found in Leviticus usually touch those matters that come under the supervision of the priests, often require one or more sacrifices for the purification of the individuals affected, and might involve situations where the unclean person joins those who come into the Temple and would thereby consciously or unconsciously defile God's dwelling place.

The Day of Atonement (Lv 16:1–34)

In one sense, chapter 16 takes up where the story left off in chapter 10 with the death of Aaron's sons and the need for atonement. In another sense, the ritual of a Day of Atonement described in this chapter heals all the cases of uncleanness and impurity that have defiled the land during the year. It thus sums up the proper response of the people to the dangers of impurity named in chapters 11–15. In a still larger sense, it is the climax of all the laws on sacrifice, priestly service, and purity from chapter 1 on, since they all involve the need for atonement at one level or another. The sacrifices always include some atoning function; priestly service risks constant danger of some fault in its performance that may demand atonement; and, of course, all daily cases of impurity need atoning. Going further, verse 21 tells us that the Day of Atonement ritual was to purify the people and the land of *both* unintentional *and* intentional sins and transgressions.

The actual rite is probably pre-Israelite. Similar ceremonies of transferring the sins of the people onto animals and then slaughtering them were known in many ancient cultures, including those of both Babylon and Rome. Similarly, smearing the blood of a sacrificial animal on the walls of a temple to purify it was done at Babylon. The reference to Azazel in verses 8, 10, and 26 remains uncertain. It probably refers to an ancient belief that there was a desert demon by this name that claimed the goat sent out to it. But there is no evidence for belief in any such demon here—it is a poetic way of casting out sin into the realm ruled by evil powers, the desert. It is as though the people said to the goat, "Go to hell!"

Chapter 16 carefully describes each step. It lists first the proper procedures and clothing for Aaron and any future high priest to enter the presence of God in the holy of holies; then it outlines each step of the ritual, including the prayer and hand gestures over the goat; and finally it closes with a command to do this forever. Yom Kippur, with its themes of atonement and repentance of the whole community, still occurs on the ninth day after Rosh Hashanah (the New Year) each fall. For the mixing of past and present, this passage should be compared to the parallel directions for Passover in Exodus 12.

The Holiness Code (Lv 17:1–25:55)

In chapters 1–16 all the topics dealt with things that needed to be observed or performed to overcome the barrier between God and human beings. Thus even the sacrifices can be included under the rubric of concern for being clean before God. Chapters 17–25 take up the opposite and just as necessary qualification of holiness: what we do *positively* to relate to God. The first sixteen chapters center on removing the blocks to our relationship; chapters 17–25 propose building new blocks in communal action in imitation of God. Actually, both areas overlap considerably with one another, and there is an excellent harmony between chapters 1 through 16 and 17 through 25.

There are nevertheless some differences. The style of 1–16 was largely listing what had to be done, but 17–25 is more like a sermon exhorting people to fidelity. Almost all of the first sixteen chapters were ritual requirements; most of 17–25 deals with ethical and social obligations. In 1–16 the accent fell on what we as mere creatures need to do to bridge the gap to the divine; in 17–25 the accent falls on how a holy people live in the image and likeness of God. In many ways the Holiness Code of 17–25 resembles the homiletic style of the book of Deuteronomy and the impassioned warnings of the prophet Ezekiel (see Ezekiel 22 for a good comparison with

Leviticus 18–20). It probably originated in the same period as Deuteronomy and Ezekiel, near the time of the Exile of 587 BC, or a little earlier. It is also a moving call to holiness and integration of all aspects of our lives around God as our central concern.

In structure, 17–25 can be divided into two parts: (a) chapters 17–20, which cover ethical demands on the whole community, and (b) chapters 21–25, which deal primarily with priestly matters of public worship. Each part has a well-ordered progression:

Part 1 (17–20)

17:1–16 All sacrifices must be done at the central sanctuary; there must be great reverence for life by respect for the blood—it is not for human consumption but to be given back to God.

18:1–30 Sexual behavior must be regulated by careful respect for appropriate human relationships, so that lust and orgiastic urges are controlled and that Israel does not become as carnally bankrupt as its pagan neighbors.

19:1–37 Contains a wide variety of norms for dealing with one another as members of the covenant with God; and as verses 19–36 make clear, far differently from the way the Canaanites behave. The laws are especially concerned with protecting the rights of the weak so that there will not be a degraded serf class as was found among the Canaanite city states.

20:1–27 Repeats many of the commands already given but adds penalties to each, often severe in respect to idolatry and incest. Once again it ends with a warning to avoid the practices of the Canaanites.

Part 2 (21–25)

21:1–24 The role of priest demands wholeness and particular witness, so special rules governing marriage, deformities, and uncleanness are spelled out.

22:1–33 Regulations for the wholeness and fitting perfection of the animals sacrificed are made parallel to those governing the priests.

23:1–44 The annual feast days must be regulated with the same care as the priests and sacrifices. This section treats the weekly Sabbath as the model feast (23:2f); and then seven annual feast days: Passover, First Fruits, Weeks, New Year, the Day of Atonement, Booths, and the eighth day after Booths.

24:1–23 Still further regulations of worship follow. These explain how the lamps and the showbread in the sanctuary are handled; also the death penalty for blasphemy is explained by a concrete case.

25:1–5 A special concluding description of the *sabbatical year* every seventh year when no planting may be done; and of the *jubilee year,* every fifty years, when all property and debts return to their original owners. Both probably originated as acts of acknowledgment that God owned the land. Now they are explained as acts of social justice to restore help to the poor and landless.

These laws are an ideal code and it is not absolutely certain that some of the most idealistic among them, such as the very unlikely jubilee year, were ever put into actual practice. They stand together, however, as a vision of Israel living completely under the dominion of God and in obedience to the divine will—they are holy as God is holy, and all Israel's actions respect the integrity and purpose of God's creation. This is made clear over and over again in these nine chapters by repeating the formulas "I the Lord am your God," "I am the Lord," or "I the Lord am holy." To these is often added the reminder "I the Lord led you out of Egypt." Israel, who received such divine compassion, must always act in turn out of a like compassion for others!

The Conclusion to the Holiness Code (Lv 26:1–46)

This is the true conclusion to the Holiness Code, but it stands apart by its form as a series of blessings on all who keep, and curses on all who violate, the covenant. In this way, it now stands as the general conclusion to chapters 1–16 and 17–25. The regulations on approaching God in worship and obeying him in society have been spelled out, and now Israel must choose. Its covenant structure resembles very closely the vassal-treaty form discussed previously in Exodus 19–24, and it has strong similarities to a closing list of blessings and curses in Deuteronomy 27.

It also reflects the thinking of the priestly editors at the end of the Exile. Not only does it foresee both blessing and eventual curse for disobedience, but it adds a short concluding word on a renewed blessing and a promise that God will not forget his covenant with Israel completely (vv. 40–46). It is imbued with the spirit of the exilic prophets Jeremiah and Ezekiel that God was about to instill a new covenant, written on the hearts of Israel, so that no longer would obedience come in response to an external law but would rise from an interior consent born of the knowledge and love of the Lord. It is at this point that the original book of Leviticus ended on a note of great hope for the future.

The Appendix on Gifts Vowed to the Sanctuary (Lv 27:1–34)

This section was added sometime after Leviticus was completed to take care of an important problem that touched on holiness: how to handle various offerings that were vowed to the Lord but were not always appropriate for sacred use. These include such diverse subjects as persons, animals, houses, land, firstborn animals, objects vowed, and tithes. If something is not fitting to be consecrated to God, it should be sold for money for the sanctuary or be exchanged by the offerer. But once even impure offerings have touched the sanctuary, they are not to be simply returned to ordinary life again.

While these are important areas, they can be subject to rash vows by people. Note Jesus in Matthew 5:3–9 condemns those who vow to God what belongs to the support of their parents.

NUMBERS

[see pages 172–222 of the Old Testament]

The Nature of the Book of Numbers

The name "Numbers" is taken directly from the title of the book in the Septuagint Greek translation: *Arithmoi*. It refers to the importance of taking the census of Israelites in both chapters 1 and 26. This probably reflects the early Hebrew title for the book as well, although later Jewish tradition has identified it by the name *bemidbar* ("In the desert"), the first words of the book. Generally, commentators have had trouble agreeing on the organization and purpose of the book of Numbers. They identify a rough outline of three divisions, but judge that the materials in each section are not well ordered and seem to be loose collections of topics and events that do not belong anywhere else. This approach, however, does not help us to study the book easily, and it probably reflects the difficulties that modern minds have with ancient ways of thinking, rather than being an accurate assessment of what the authors and editors of the book of Numbers thought they were doing. Several considerations might help us find more purpose and order in the book than would appear in a hasty reading.

1. Numbers Links the Mountain of Sinai and the Promised Land. It stands between the events described in Exodus and Leviticus and the situation found in Deuteronomy. It is about a journey that moves the people from Mount Sinai (Exodus and Leviticus) to the border of the Promised Land (Deuteronomy). The focus of all the stories and legal lists is either on preparations for the journey, or on problems encountered on the journey, or on attitudes that threaten the journey.

2. It Is Paired Thematically with the Book of Exodus. In the overall drama of the Pentateuch, Genesis matches Deuteronomy as first and last book because both focus on life in the land itself; Exodus matches Numbers in the second and fourth positions on both sides of Leviticus in the middle: Exodus leads up to Sinai, and Numbers away from it. Many incidents are repeated in both, such as the manna scene and Moses bringing water from a rock, but Numbers judges Israel's response differently and more judgmentally because in Numbers the Israelites have accepted the covenant and Torah and must live obediently.

3. Its Themes Build on the Laws of Leviticus. Numbers naturally flows from the materials treated in Leviticus. The central theme of Leviticus is holiness in the ordinary areas of life, such as food, clothing, sickness, moral ethics of society, and regular worship. Numbers intensifies the expectations of holiness by stressing the need for dedication and total commitment to God, in order for Israel to succeed as a nation if its goal is to live prosperously in the Holy Land. To do so, it must be obedient to divine commands and so Numbers treats rebellion and hard-heartedness as worthy of punishment.

4. Like Exodus and Leviticus, It Combines Narratives and Laws. The book contains a combination of narratives and laws just as do Exodus and Leviticus. Each collection of laws relates to the experiences and lessons learned from the past. Israel enjoyed reading these living connections that remembered the deeds of their ancestors in light of the laws they still lived by today.

5. This Is No Ordinary Journey but a Solemn March. It is a military campaign of Israel as an army advancing against the enemy. It is a journey of conquest, and it will not be completed until the end of the book of Joshua when the people have rest in the Promised Land. Most of the laws, as well as the elaborate preparations for leaving Sinai and the detailed descriptions of battles on the eastern side of the Jordan River, are framed around proper "military" behavior. This is a metaphor for obedient religious observance: a soldier in God's army must be holy and single-minded. Special aspects of this emphasized in Numbers include loyalty to Moses, rejection of paganism and pagan nations, and willingness to sacrifice for God.

6. Numbers Prepares for Deuteronomy by Centering on the Promise of the Land. The people are on the move as a great and fearsome force; they no longer need worry about the promise of a son that was the central concern in the stories of Genesis. Now the *land* dominates their thinking. It dominates as a hope for prosperity that will be in stark contrast to the deprivation and suffering of their time in the desert. And it dominates in the reflections and legal directives on how to live faithfully and loyally in the land as a people of the covenant.

The Outline of the Book of Numbers

The most common division of the book is into three large blocs that correspond to major stages of the journey narrative:

Nm 1:1–10:10 The proper preparation of a military expedition in a holy war.

Nm 10:11–20:13 The journey through the desert and the trials of the people's faith in God.

Nm 20:14–36:13 Final directions and campaigns to prepare for assault on the Promised Land.

This breakdown of the book's order highlights that it remains controlled by the overall sense of movement toward the divinely promised goal of the land first stated at Genesis 12:1–3. The first bloc is a flurry of activity in getting ready to depart; the second is an actual journey from Sinai to the oasis of Kadesh Barnea; and the third division has the people move on through the Transjordan area of Edom, Moab, and the Amorites to arrive in battle array across the river from the major Canaanite stronghold of Jericho. Numbers 33 summarizes the movements of the Israelites from Egypt until they reach the edge of the Jordan by listing the stopping places where they camped. Such a record of the stages by which they traveled calls attention to the fact that, at each one, God gave special guidance and assistance, and that no movement took place without the divine initiative. But each major division of this journey contains those ritual and legal concerns that seem to fit best at that spot (see chart on RG 135).

The Development of the Major Themes in Numbers

To help us appreciate a little more the dramatic flow of the book, it might be useful to describe it narratively:

Numbers 1:1–10:10

The book opens with the census of all males able to go to war (1:45). Levites, who serve in the sanctuary, are exempted. In chapter 2 these newly commissioned soldiers are then organized into a military camp prepared for defense as well as for a quick march in time of danger. The book then turns to the special role of the Levites who are to dwell around the tent and ark at the center of

The Divisions of the Book of Numbers with a Summary of the Contents of Each Chapter

Nm 1:1–10:10	*Nm 10:11–20:13*	*Nm 20:14–36:13*
The camp is prepared for a holy war battle march	The journey to Kadesh with challenges to Moses' rule	Events and rules stemming from the arrival at Jordan

Chapter		*Chapter*		*Chapter*	
1	Census of males for armed service	10	The battle order: the Ark is first	20	Move through Edom; death of Aaron
2	Order of the camp	11	Two occasions of rebellion	21	More victories and more murmuring
3	Special role for Levites	12	Miriam and Aaron oppose Moses	22–24	Balaam tries to stop Israel
4	Levitcal roles in bearing the Ark	13	The spies scout the Promised Land	25	The people abandon God at Baal of Peor
5	Laws of purification for battle	14	People resist taking the land	26	The census repeated and land promised
6	Vows of Nazirite dedication	15	Laws relating to possessing land	27–30	Laws on inheritence, vows, and worship
7	Sacrifices and gifts for leaving	16	Levite rebellion against Aaron	31	The Midianites are defeated
8	Levites anointed for service	17	Aaron's authority restored	32	Transjordan conquests of two and a half tribes
9	Passover celebration; camp is broken	18	Proper portions for priests and Levites	33–34	Stages of the march and boundaries
10	The trumpets sound the departure	19	Atonement for any uncleanness	35	Special Levitical cities and laws
		20	Murmuring over water	36	Inheritance laws and conclusion

camp; they represent God's ransom of all firstborn males (3:5–12). In this way, all the fighting force becomes a consecrated army linked to holy service of the Lord through the Levitical substitutes. Then follow the duties of the Levites for moving the sanctified objects of the sanctuary when on the march (4), and a set of laws on uncleanness, theft, adultery, and other sins that would defile the army's holy status to fight for God (5). Chapter 6 completes this preparation of the camp by giving rules for those (the Nazirites) who take extra vows of rigor. Chapters 1–6 end with the blessing of Aaron over the camp (6:22–27).

Chapters 7 through 10 then move on to the questions of proper ritual actions for the sanctuary itself, including the giving of gifts (7); the care of the lampstands, the purification of the Levites for service in the tent, and time limits for their years of duty (8); and finally the solemn celebration of the first Passover since leaving Egypt, which is to take place on the first anniversary of the miracle itself (9:1–14). This larger division then concludes with a notice that the divine pillars of cloud and fire would move with the people, and they are to be summoned to departure by the silver trumpets (9:15–10:10).

Numbers 10:11–20:13

This traces the actual journey from Sinai toward the land of Canaan. The cloud moves, the tribes set out in marching order, all appears to be proper. But trouble immediately looms with the repetition of the grumbling of the people that had so characterized the period between their deliverance in Egypt and their arrival at Sinai in Exodus 13–18. Many of the chapters in Numbers repeat and duplicate the same grumblings recorded in the Exodus narratives. First, people complain about the lack of meat (11) and are punished by fire; but Moses intercedes and saves them. At this point, too, some of Moses' authority is shared with the elders (11:24–30). In the next chapter, even Miriam and Aaron challenge Moses' authority and are struck with leprosy, but again Moses intercedes successfully. Next they arrive near the southern boundaries of the Promised Land and are able to advance straight into it. The scouts return with glowing reports of its bounty, but only Joshua and Caleb are fearless enough to want to attack the inhabitants. The people cringe in fear and reject Moses' leadership. God wishes to destroy them all, but Moses once again intercedes and God once again relents. But he does decree that not one shall enter the Promised Land from this generation except Caleb and Joshua, who were loyal (13–14).

Here the editors insert laws that will be required when Israel gains possession of the land (15). But again, rebellion flares up as several Levites now refuse to follow Moses. They receive death as their punishment (16), and Aaron then assumes the priestly role of reconciling and purifying the people in their relationship to God (17). This in turn is followed by a number of laws that regulate the proper payment due to priests and Levites for their services to the sanctuary, and which, to the minds of the ancient editors, fitted perfectly here after the discussion of Aaron's role.

Since uncleanness has been a major theme of these narratives, especially in the case of those who go near God's sanctuary unworthily, chapter 19 follows with a ritual that uses the ashes of a red heifer for preparing a permanent holy water to sanctify those found in an unclean state. This whole division now ends with a final case of grumbling over the lack of water in which even Moses and Aaron fail in their trust in God, and they are told that they, too, cannot enter the Promised Land.

The materials from chapters 10 to 20 have thus emphasized the fragility of the people's loyalty to the Lord, even in their state of military awareness. They also underline the need for constant purification of action and loyalty to God, if Israel is to succeed in possessing the land. Above all, they emphasize the central role of the priests and Levites in that process of purification, and their role in developing complete fidelity through proper ritual and holiness.

Numbers 20:14–36:13

The action now turns to the actual conquest of the land. Their march takes them around the land of Edom and up the desert highway along the east side of the Transjordan plateau. They bypass the land of Moab and attack the Amorites farther north. This victory in chapter 21 leads the king of Moab to try to stop them. He hires a famous prophet, Balaam, to curse them. Chapters 22 through 24 consist of a very old series of stories about Balaam's efforts and his failure. They do provide a climactic statement to the patriarch's promise, as Balaam foresees the greatness of Israel in the centuries ahead.

In sharp contrast to this future greatness, however, the very next chapter records how Israel betrayed even the first commandment and fell into idolatry and the orgiastic practices of the Canaanites. All who participated are executed (25). This sets the stage for a renewed military dedication to the cause of the Lord, symbolized by taking a second census in chapter 26 to summon forth the fighting men for the war ahead.

But before any battles are fought, there is an interlude of four chapters (27–30) in which another series of regulations and laws are set forth that pertain to the organization of Israelite society when it is settled in an agricultural and urban type of life. These laws are triggered by the problem of relations between families and their obligations to one another, which the taking of the census leaves unanswered. They cover inheritance laws for the widows and daughters of men who might be slain in battle or who die prematurely. They also involve the proper rules for celebration of the feast days in a new land, and the rules governing different types of vows made by different classes of people.

Finally, fighting resumes with a major victory over Midian, which is interpreted as revenge for the Midianites' part in the idolatrous acts at Baal of Peor (31). Shortly thereafter, the tribes of Reuben, Gad, and Manasseh conquer territory on the eastern side of the Jordan River (32). This is permitted only with deep reservations since it may mean accepting less than the Promised Land itself. But those tribes promise to do their part in the conquest of Palestine when the moment comes.

The final chapters of Numbers sum up. Chapter 33 lists all the camps through which Israel had journeyed, ending with the final stopping place on the river across from Jericho. They are given a solemn command to take the land, drive out its inhabitants (33:53–56), and divide the land among the tribes so that they fill the generous boundaries that Moses describes (34:1–15). The book closes with a series of laws that reflect the tricky problems of legal boundaries and multiple jurisdictions. These include laws on special cities for the Levites, towns set aside as asylums for accused persons, murders in open territory between tribes, and property rights for women and the defenseless. Once again the laws illustrate the nature of the narrative that had immediately preceded them.

Conclusion

The developmental pattern of Numbers not only tells a story of adventure and difficulty, it ties this story to lessons that must be applied when the people live a totally different type of life in the Promised Land. Laws and regulations that would never apply in nomadic or seminomadic situations will become crucial when the circumstances change dramatically and the people become a settled population. The book, however, manages to unite the dramatic history of the Israelites' time in the wilderness as a people on the move—without home or power—with the later needs and practices that characterized their life in Canaan in the years following.

There are few parallels to this type of writing in modern literature, but we can learn to value and even enjoy this intense combining of (boring) laws with historical adventures, if we think of it as the answer to a profound question: How does a people preserve the lessons of the great days of salvation and guidance in the desert without losing them in later ages? They remember both the stories of the desert and the laws that came from them . . . and then observe the laws!

The Literary Unity of Numbers

Like Leviticus, Numbers reflects throughout the hand of the Priestly source guiding its order and structure. In only a few sections can we find the J and E sources from the older tradition still present: (1) in the narrative stories of chapters 11:13–14:16; 21, 25, and 32; and (2) in the Balaam cycle in chapters 22–24. The major themes of J and E focus on challenges to Moses' authority and punishment for rebels who don't trust in God, as well as preparing Israel for occupation of the Promised Land. P, however, adds numerous laws that extend the reach of those already seen in Leviticus and also to make the J and E warnings even more definitive. P sections also emphasize the proper ordering of Israel's tribes, and the roles of Priests and Levites, by adding many ritual lists. Many commentators think that P is developing a response not only to J and E but also to the laws of Deuteronomy, thus placing the P sections after the Exile in the last stages of Pentateuch development. For example, the description of major feast days in Numbers 28–29 would reflect the latest development level of the many levels in the Pentateuch.

Major Priestly Religious Concerns in Numbers

These Priestly editors have emphasized certain themes above others while keeping the journey narrative moving ahead. Certainly ritual matters were important to them, for scattered references to various states of uncleanness and the rites to overcome them occur frequently in chapters 13–20. So also, numerous passages distinguish particular duties of Priests and Levites in chapters 26–36. Legal regulations for various social areas of conflict, which would arise when land is involved, are also interspersed at fitting places in the text.

And finally, the theological themes that center on God's power to bring about the promise are continued from the books of Genesis and Exodus. These include: (1) questions about the authority of leaders, namely Moses, Aaron, and the elders; (2) murmuring and lack of trust on the part of the people; (3) in the Balaam stories, the power of the prophetic word to bring about God's will; (4) the role of Joshua as sole leader to succeed Moses; and (5) the decisive victories God bestows in battle.

In order to better grasp the main religious message of these various topics scattered throughout the book, it is worth listing some of the groupings in more detail:

Priests and Levites. Genesis 34:24–31 and 49: 5–7 both view Levi as a violent and renegade tribe; the book of Exodus, however, not only notes that Moses and Aaron are from the tribe of Levi but also praises the Levites in 32:25–29 as the only tribe that remained faithful to the Lord during the golden calf incident. The tribe of Levi is therefore worthy of priestly service to the Lord. Deuteronomy 33:8–11 adds that the Levites alone were faithful at Massah and Meribah when Moses struck water from the rock, although the two accounts (Ex 17:1–7; Nm 20: 2–13) never mention any Levitical role. There may have been two separate traditions about the Levites, one positive and one negative. Certainly there is some reason to wonder, since in several places such as Deuteronomy, Joshua, and a few prophetic texts (Ez 43:19–44:15; Mal 2:4), the Levites are referred to as priests; while in the majority of other references they are an auxiliary group to help in the Temple but are distinct from the priests, who can come only from the house of Aaron. Perhaps these conflicting reports stem from the historical reality that originally Levites were priestly in character but became subordinated to a particular branch of the family of Aaron after the Exile in 586 BC.

In Numbers, however, the Levites receive very high honor, even though the book takes the position that they are not the same as the priests and must not seek to perform priestly offices. Four sets of regulations pertain to the Levites:

- They alone have the privilege of carrying the ark of the covenant (1:49–53), and they are also responsible for the other sacred objects in the sanctuary and for its transport during the desert years (4:1–49).
- They are honored to be set aside as a ransom for each firstborn male among the people as a whole. Thus they are consecrated to God and may not have military roles or possess land (3: 5–20; 3:40–51; 8:3–24; see Dt 18:1–5).
- In Numbers 16–17, some Levites under Korah rebel against Aaron and Moses, and demand equal priestly rights. God punishes them severely, and the story serves as a motive for why Levites are not allowed to do priestly ministry.
- Certain cities are set aside by Moses in Numbers 35:2–8 as refuge centers for people suspected of crimes. This contradicts claims in other books that Levites had no title to land. It also provides a basis for seeing an important role for the Levites in the local administration of justice in Israel; probably they also serve as local religious leaders who functioned as priests in the small communities far from Jerusalem.

The Holy War. There is always a great amount of uneasiness when modern readers hear the stories of sacred campaigns in which the enemy—men, women, and children—are doomed and executed if Israel is victorious. Such a campaign takes place in Numbers 21:1–3 when Israel fights Arad, and again in Numbers 31:1–54, in the battle against the Midianites. Similar military campaigns are described in Joshua, Judges, and the books of Samuel. It is worth noting about these, however, that to the Israelite reader of the Bible who lived many years after the days of Moses, Joshua, and the judges, these accounts then belonged back in the founding days. They had a special character because it had been a life-and-death struggle between the Lord and the Canaanite gods that demanded drastic action. They knew that in their earliest traditions, God was a warrior who fought on their behalf against overwhelming odds; note in particular the description of God as a warrior in the oldest poem in the Pentateuch, Exodus 15.

Numbers gives one of the fullest explanations of Holy War theory in the passage on the Midianites in chapter 31. It is quite fierce. But in another account from about the same time as Numbers or a little earlier, Deuteronomy 20, a number of restrictions are put on such a war so that it is less than a total massacre. So, too, the first chapters of Numbers try to expand the concept of the Holy War to include the whole people as an army of the Lord on the move to Palestine. Purity and obedience are the keynotes of this army, not vengeance, and we might safely assume that already the editors of Numbers wanted to soften the stories of the old total war. They suggested, instead, that now this concept could be lived out by a total commitment of life to the way of the Lord. The battles against Arad, Midian, and finally Canaan, were still stirring episodes from the past, but they were not the way of the present! This would fit the picture painted by several prophets that war was not the way to do God's will; peace and faith were (see Is 7:1–14; Hos 10:13f; Jer 21:3–10; 34:1–5). There was a development in theology and attitude over the centuries, and Numbers at least shows some of both viewpoints mixed together.

The Murmuring Tradition. One striking aspect of the stories in Numbers 10:11–20:13 is the recurrence of so many incidents of grumbling and rebellion against God by the people in the desert that resemble accounts in Exodus 14–18. Note the following:

Nm 11:1 People grumble against Moses at Taberah; fire comes down.

Nm 11:4f People grumble about the lack of meat at Kibroth-hattaavah; God sends a plague, but then a gift of quail for food.

Nm 12:1–16 Miriam and Aaron rebel against the sole authority of Moses; Miriam becomes a leper, but God later heals her.

Nm 14:1–38 The people refuse to attack Canaan; God will make them die in the desert and their children wander for forty years.

Nm 16:1–36 Korah, Dathan, and Abiram all rebel against Aaron's authority; they are consumed by fire from heaven.

Nm 17:6–15 The people again grumble against Moses and Aaron; the scourge of punishment is lifted by Aaron's actions.

Nm 20:2–13 The people complain about lack of water; God has Moses strike the rock for water but keeps him from entering the Promised Land.

Nm 21, 4–9 The people again grumble about food, and God sends fiery serpents to bite them; they are saved by a bronze serpent made by Moses.

These incidents may be compared to similar examples from the book of Exodus: Exodus 14: 10; 15:23; 16:13; and 17:5–7. The last case is a duplicate of Numbers 20:1–13 in which Moses strikes the rock for water. Numbers 11, 31 seems to be the same as Exodus 16, 13, in which God sends the people quail to eat. These two cases may actually borrow material from J or E sources. The other examples in Numbers, however, all seem to have a similar interest in how God punished the people and then allowed Moses or Aaron to intercede and restore them.

Numbers, true to its priestly concern, wishes to emphasize the need of the community to atone for its sin and rebellion, and turn back to God through liturgy and purification. Even the bronze serpent in Numbers 21 implies healing through some ritual action. According to 2 Kings 18:4 this object was receiving special veneration right up to the time that King Hezekiah reformed the religion in 715 BC and smashed the bronze serpent. Numbers tells the story—despite the obvious danger that it might be considered magically powerful—to illustrate the need to turn to God for healing.

The Roles of the Twelve Tribes in the Conquest Plan. The end of Numbers records the controversies among the tribes over whether they all must enter the land, or whether Reuben, Gad, and half of Manasseh may live on the Transjordan side of the river. A similar suggestion that harmony did not always prevail among the tribes stands out in the conflict between Joshua, Caleb, and the other scouts in Numbers 13–14. In fact, such divisions within the twelve tribes appear frequently in the books of Joshua and Judges as well. There are also numerous differences within the lists of the tribes themselves that suggest the tradition was not always uniform about which tribes made up the original people of Israel. There are seven separate listings of the tribes in the book of Numbers, and they do not always agree (see table on RG 140).

In Numbers 34, the two tribes that stayed across the Jordan, Reuben and Gad, are omitted; otherwise every list includes twelve tribes. None of these, however, mentions Levi, although he is included in all lists in Genesis and Exodus (Gn 29:31–30:22 plus 35:16–20; 35:22–26, 46:8–25; 49:2–27; Ex 1:1–5). In his place, the lists in Numbers always give Joseph's two sons, Ephraim and Manasseh, as two tribes that replace those of their father, Joseph, and Levi. Several lists begin with Reuben, the firstborn son of Jacob; others begin with Judah, the chief tribe in the Priestly view. Moreover, the tribes occur in varied orders throughout the seven lists, as well as in lists in other books.

Each list came down with its own purposes in mind, of course. Numbers 2:3–29, for example, reordered tribes to fit in a neat square around the tent and ark. We will not be too confused if we pay attention to the divergent materials and viewpoints that have been collected in Numbers and in other texts that deal with how the conquest of Palestine took place. They had no modern historians on the scene, so that much of the traditional narration of these events was in the form

The Tribal Lists in the Book of Numbers

Nm 1 5–15	Nm 1 20–43	Nm 2 3–29	Nm 7 12–83	Nm 13 4–15	Nm 26 5–50	Nm 34 19–28
Reuben	Reuben	Judah	Judah	Reuben	Reuben	Judah
Simeon	Simeon	Issachar	Issachar	Simeon	Simeon	Simeon
Judah	Gad	Zebulun	Zebulun	Judah	Gad	Benjamin
Issachar	Judah	Reuben	Reuben	Issachar	Judah	Dan
Zebulun	Issachar	Simeon	Simeon	Ephraim	Issachar	Manasseh
Ephraim	Zebulun	Gad	Gad	Benjamin	Zebulun	Ephraim
Manasseh	Ephraim	Ephraim	Ephraim	Zebulun	Manasseh	Zebulun
Benjamin	Manasseh	Manasseh	Manasseh	Manasseh	Ephraim	Issachar
Dan	Benjamin	Benjamin	Benjamin	Dan	Benjamin	Asher
Asher	Dan	Dan	Dan	Asher	Dan	Naphtali
Gad	Asher	Asher	Asher	Naphtali	Asher	
Naphtali	Naphtali	Naphtali	Naphtali	Gad	Naphtali	

of hero stories, great legendary actions of the tribes, and local memories preserved by one tribe or another. They have been organized with more neatness and more attention to continuity than may have actually been the way the events themselves happened.

No doubt some tribal groups entered Palestine separately from the main body of attackers under Joshua, while some tribes may have had large numbers of their members already in the land. Finally, the constant substitution of Ephraim and Manassah for Joseph may indicate that it was these two tribes in particular that did most of the fighting and conquering with Joshua. Indeed, to support this view, we can note that the book of Joshua indicates the action against the Canaanites largely took place in the territory of those two tribes. And the controversy with the two and a half tribes that did not want to go with the rest may only be the tip of a very large iceberg, in which the much larger hidden part is the reality of how few actually joined the invasion with Joshua.

The Balaam Oracles. The story of Balaam, the mysterious prophet summoned from the East to curse Israel, is perhaps the most fascinating part of the book of Numbers. It contains some of the older materials derived from the J and E sources that have been incorporated into the Priestly view of the conquest. In studying this part of the book, several points should be noted:

There are mixed views of Balaam in the Bible. Numbers 22:1–24:25 presents Balaam as a prophet from Mesopotamia who is hired to curse Israel and then forced by God to bless them. Indeed, the folk story about Balaam and his ass in chapter 22 presents him as willing to do whatever the Lord wants. Thus one might conclude that he is presented sympathetically and perhaps even as an instrument of God. But later on in Numbers 31:8 and 16, Balaam is slaughtered by the Israelites as a Midianite king because he led people astray at Baal of Peor. This must stem from a separate tradition than that of Numbers 22–24. This double view reappears in the book of Joshua where Balaam is the seer who curses Israel in 24:9–10, but who was among the Midianites in 13:22. Deuteronomy 23:4f; Micah 6:5, and Nehemiah 13:2 all view Balaam as the seer. On the other side, Genesis 36:32 describes him, under the name of Bela, as a king of Midian (also known as Edom).

Interestingly enough, the New Testament picks up a still later tradition that Balaam was greedy for money. 2 Peter 2:16; Jude 11; Revelation 2:14 all see him as a false teacher motivated by greed. The real Balaam may never be known, but he seems to have been famous as a prophet in other nations than Israel. A sixth-century BC Aramaic text speaks of him in this vein. So at least the basic point of Numbers 22–24 seems to be based on very old tradition.

There are four oracles in chapters 23 and 24. Most scholars hold that the two oracles in chapter 23 are from the Elohist (E) source, and the two in chapter 24 are from the Yahwist (J). Look at them closely and note the elaborate formulas of introduction in 24:3f and 24:15f that imply a very formal manner in which prophets in Judah may have normally spoken. These also stress the glory of the king (24:7, 17), a viewpoint typical of the Davidic monarchy. On the other hand, the oracles from the E tradition lack such elaborate formulas and stress the blessing on the whole people given by God.

Some scholars believe the words of Balaam formed the endings to both the J and the E narrative sources. In this view, the prophet looks ahead to the fulfillment of the promise in the days of the monarchy many years hence. If chapter 23 does end the E story, and chapter 24 the J story, then further stories of the conquest in Numbers 32 and in the book of Joshua that have concerns similar to those of J and E would have to be explained. We could at least say this much—that the final form of the book of Numbers sees the Balaam prophecies as important. They confirm with a divine word the coming victory of Israel's battle for the lands on both sides of the Jordan.

The Theology of the Priestly Writers

The P source probably had many earlier written pieces to draw on in putting together its descriptions in Numbers. Such might have been lists of tribal leaders (Nm 1:5–15; 2:3–31; 7:12–88; 10: 14–28); the descriptions of the battle camp in chapters 2 and 10; census lists of some kind for chapters 1 and 26; Sinai place-names in Numbers 33; and, of course, J and E for such passages as Numbers 13–14, 22–24, and 32.

The P school has already stated its primary emphasis for Israel's life in Exodus 25–40: the divine presence will be known in Israel in the sanctuary (a tent in the desert years, a temple later) and will manifest its glory there. The proper response of Israel will be observance of sacrifice and the laws of holiness. This "holy" community is given its final climactic description at the end of Leviticus in chapter 26, in the form of a warning speech.

To this, the P authors have added in Numbers some important specifications about how this holiness can be carried out through national institutions and in the relations among the tribes with respect to their possession of the land. Moreover, the cultic organization of Israel's life must be observed even in a state of exile (the idea of the battle camp in the wilderness), and even when the proper order is threatened and broken down by disobedience (the meaning of the numerous rebellions against Moses in chapters 11–21). God will certainly punish this disobedience, but the mediation of priests and leaders (Aaron and Moses) can turn away God's wrath and restore blessing. Most of all, nothing will deter the divine fulfillment; yet at the same time, God does not depend on any one leader no matter how great (even Moses can be denied entry to the Promised Land!). Although the people have no land or home now, they have all the necessary means of worship and obedience to hold on until the divine promise is fulfilled just a short time ahead.

Seen in this light, Numbers is the final statement of the Priestly theology in the Pentateuch. Now Moses can depart (note how his death should follow at the end of Numbers 36, but it is delayed until Deuteronomy 34 for editorial reasons), and the conquest begin. But first, an interlude with the book of Deuteronomy.

DEUTERONOMY

[see pages 222–266 of the Old Testament]

The *New American Bible* and the Book of Deuteronomy

The introduction to the book of Deuteronomy in the NAB points to a number of significant aspects for any deep study of the book. First, its style is distinctive and not like any seen up to this point in the Pentateuch. It is more like a sermon with its urgent appeals to obedience and loyalty to God, and its thundering warnings of the dire consequences that will occur if the people do not follow the deuteronomic teachings. Second, the NAB notes that scholars believe it was written near the end of Israel's time as an independent kingdom, that is to say, about the seventh century BC, and comes not at all from the time of Moses. It actually looks back on Israel's history although written as if it looked ahead to their possession of the land. Third, the NAB notes how significant Deuteronomic theology is for understanding the New Testament world of Jesus. Fourth, the NAB gives us a simple outline of how to approach Deuteronomy.

We can expand on all of these to assist us in the study of the book, as well as add some reflections on three other points: (1) The particular theological and historical perspective the book offers on Israel's earlier traditions; (2) the theology of the covenant that permeates the book; (3) its connections to the wider grouping of the historical books of Joshua, Judges, Samuel, and Kings, all of which seem to receive their inspiration from Deuteronomy. We will order these seven areas according to their logical development.

The Outline of the Book

The following detailed breakdown of the contents of Deuteronomy expands the NAB's outline and reorders it slightly to combine its parts I and II, and divide its part IV into two sections:

- I. Introduction to the Deuteronomic Law Code (1:1–11:32)
  - A. General Historical Introduction (1:1–4:43)
    - 1. Historical survey (1:1–3:29)
    - 2. Summary about the Law's goodness (4:1–43)
  - B. Particular Introduction to the Law (4:44–11:32)
    - 1. Introductory context (4:44–49)
    - 2. Moses and the Ten Commandments (5:1–33)
    - 3. Instruction on obeying the Law (6:1–25)
    - 4. Attitudes toward foreign gods (7:1–16)
    - 5. The desert lesson: depend on God! (8:1–20)
    - 6. The golden calf lesson: idolatry (9:1–10:22)
    - 7. General urging to love covenant (11:1–32)
- II. The Deuteronomic Law Code (12:1–26:19)
  - A. The Introductory Law: one sanctuary (12:1–31)
  - B. The Individual Laws (13:1–26:15)
    - 1. Laws on idolatry (13:1–19)
    - 2. Ritual food laws and tithes (14:1–29)
    - 3. Sabbatical release for the poor (15:1–18)
    - 4. Sacrifice of the firstborn (15:19–23)
    - 5. Pilgrim feast days binding on all (16:1–17)
    - 6. Officials: kings, priests, prophets (16:18–18:22)
    - 7. Cities of refuge (19:1–21)
    - 8. Rules for the Holy War (20:1–20; 21:10–14; 23:9–14)
    - 9. Unknown murders (21:1–9)
    - 10. Laws on social problems (21:15–22:12)
    - 11. Sexual and marriage laws (22:13–23:1)
    - 12. Divorce, marriage, and charity (23:1–25:19)
    - 13. Tithes on first fruits (26:1–15)
  - C. Conclusion: Summary of the Covenant (26:16–19)
- III. Solemn Acceptance of Covenant Law Code (27:1–30:20)
  - A. The Covenant Ceremony (27:1–28:68)
    - 1. Curses and blessings (27:1–26)
    - 2. Added curses and blessings (28:1–46)
    - 3. An exilic expansion (28:47–68)
  - B. Moses' Final Exhortation on Covenant (29:1–30:20)
    - 1. Covenant warning to exiles (29:1–27)
    - 2. Promise of mercy in exile (30:1–20)
- IV. The Final Conclusion of the Pentateuch as a Whole (31:1–34:12)
  - A. The Choice of a Successor (31:1–13, 23–29)
    - 1. Joshua selected (31:1–13)
    - 2. Law placed in the Ark (31:23–29)

B. The Song of Moses (32:1–44)
  1. Moses commanded to sing (31: 14–22)
  2. The song of Moses (31:30–32: 44)
C. The Blessing of Moses (32:45–33: 29)
  1. Moses' last view of the Land (32: 45–52)
  2. Moses' final blessing (33:1–29)
D. The Death of Moses (34:1–12)

The outline shows that the basic structure is built around a new presentation of the Law that restates many of the earlier laws of Exodus through Numbers. There is further internal evidence from the original Hebrew text of the book that it was not all written at the same time. Some of the speeches in chapters 1 through 11 and 26 through 30 are addressed to the individual Israelites, "you," while others are addressed to the plural "ye" or "you all." Certain sections, such as chapters 1 through 3 are almost entirely in this plural form, while other sections, such as chapters 4 through 11, are almost completely in the singular. This has led scholars to detect separate stages of development in the book.

It might be noted, especially, that the materials gathered in chapters 31 through 34 are not quite as tied to the laws as are those of chapters 1 through 30. These last four chapters gather together all of the diverse traditions and long-established works belonging to the memory of Moses that have not found any other place in the Pentateuch. These final chapters in some way form an appendix to the first thirty chapters.

The Covenant Structure of the Book

In looking at Exodus 1:9–24, some general similarities stood out between the description of how Israel received its covenant and the general shape of ancient secular covenants between kings. There were six typical parts to a covenant treaty, which are reflected in a vague way in the structure of the dramatic account of those chapters. These six parts were: (1) a preamble that identified the great king giving the treaty; (2) a historical prologue listing his gracious deeds to the lesser king; (3) the legal stipulations binding on the lesser king (the vassal); (4) the provisions for public reading of the document; (5) the list of gods who witnessed the treaty; and (6) the curses and blessings on those who break or keep the treaty.

The same pattern can be found in the book of Deuteronomy 1–30:

- the great king's self-identification (Dt 1:1)
- the historical prologue (Dt 1:2–4:43)
- the laws binding on the vassal
  1. exhortatory introduction (Dt 4:44–11: 32)
  2. the law code in detail (Dt 12:1–26:19)
- provisions for reading the law aloud (Dt 27:8)
- witness of the gods none
- curses and blessings (Dt 27:1–28:68)

In examining this structure, it becomes certain that the final form of Deuteronomy is made to be in the general shape of an actual treaty document. As in the Exodus narrative, there is no suggestion of divine witnesses, since there can be no other gods beside the Lord to perform that role. But, in distinction to the Exodus story, this covenant account ends with a very long series of curses and blessings that fill chapters 27 and 28. In this way it resembles the types of treaty covenants we know from the Assyrian period, especially in the seventh century BC, rather than the earlier Hittite models that perhaps influenced the Exodus accounts of the original covenant.

It is important to note at this stage, however, that the book as a whole—beginning with the first sentence and concluding with the notice of the great leader's death—combines a second format. It is framed as a farewell speech of Moses to the people. It might also be compared to an aging father's advice to his son so that the son might gain wisdom. Both forms are well known in ancient literature. Joshua 23–24 has been structured as a deathbed speech to the people, and 1 Samuel 12 serves as the prophet Samuel's farewell speech. In the New Testament, John's Gospel has gathered many of Jesus' words into a long farewell speech at the Last Supper (John 13–17). On the other hand, the form of both Proverbs 1–9 and the book of Ecclesiastes is that of a speech from an aged father who passes on the wisdom he has learned to his sons and disciples. Many Egyptian wisdom works also use this technique. Quite possibly Deuteronomy combines elements of both the deathbed legacy of the great leader and the wisdom of a father that is handed on to his sons.

The nature of the book as a covenant structure given by Moses himself, as well as its impassioned language of urgency, suggest that the authors saw it as a program for renewing the covenant by the people. Indeed, this will prove to be an important factor in trying to date the document to the seventh century BC.

The Unique Style of the Book

Deuteronomy has long been recognized as an independent source within the Pentateuch, which has no direct connection with any of the other three sources, J, E, or P. Not only is it entirely self-contained, as a speech from beginning to end, but its vocabulary and phraseology are generally unmatched anywhere among those sources. A good flavor can be found by reading chapters 4 through 11, where expressions such as the following occur repeatedly:

1. These are the ordinances, statutes, and decrees which the LORD, your God, has enjoined on you (cf. 4:45; 5:1; 6:1; 6:20; etc.).
2. Take care to observe them (4:5; 5:1; 6:3; 7:12; 8:1; etc.).
3. You must learn them, or teach them in the land (5:1; 5:31; 11:19; etc.); and teach them to your children (4:9; 4:10; 11:19; etc.).
4. In the land you are about to enter to possess (5:31; 6:1; 6:10; 6:18; 9:5; etc.).
5. So that you might live long and prosper (4:40; 5:33; 6:2f; 6:24; 11:9; etc.).
6. You will love the LORD, your God (6:5; 10:12; 11:13; etc.).
7. With all your heart and soul (4:29; 6:5; 10:12; 11:13; etc.).
8. Take to heart these words (6:6; 11:18).
9. Walk in his ways and fear the LORD (8:6; 10:20; 11:22).
10. Do not turn aside after other gods to serve them (6:14; 7:4; 8:19; 11:16; etc.).
11. Lest God's anger flare up against you (6:15; 7:4; 11:17; etc.).
12. Do not forget the LORD (8:11; 6:12; etc.).
13. I set before you today a blessing and a curse (11:26; cf. 30:19).
14. The land which the LORD swore to our fathers (6:10; 6:18; 6:23; 7:13; 10:11; etc.); a land flowing with milk and honey (6:3; 11:9; etc.).
15. Do what is right and good (6:18; cf. 12:28; 13:19; etc.).

Deuteronomy has a repetitive style, which serves well the preacher's need to get a message across. The type of language, with its intense use of imperatives and rhetorical piling up of several synonyms in a row for the same idea, hardly qualifies as plain narrative. It is persuasive language, calculated to move an audience to decision or change. Similarly, it uses several rhetorical devices to emphasize its major theme of obedience *in the land*. On one hand, it rarely speaks of the land simply, but names it as the land flowing with milk and honey, a good land, a land that God swore to your ancestors, and other phrases of appealing description; and on the other hand, it constantly recalls all the good deeds of the Lord toward Israel that involve divine care and help in the land, especially against foreign opposition. The authors have a perspective that seems extraordinarily concerned with warning about misuse of the land through serving other gods and at the same time disobeying all of God's commands.

The Historical Development of the Book

Arguments for dating Deuteronomy sometime in the later part of the monarchy of Judah, rather than in the time of Moses, can be given briefly. These points will focus some of the background problems and crises facing those who put it together, so that the religious message can stand out more sharply for modern readers.

Second Kings 22:1–23:30 narrates the events of the reign of King Josiah (640–609 BC). In the eyes of the authors of Kings, by far the most important single action of the king was his decision to reform the religious practice of the people and thus renew the covenant commitment of the nation, as a result of finding a "Book of the Law" in the Temple during its rebuilding. The king immediately consults a well-known prophetess, Huldah, who delivers a divine oracle (2 Kgs 22:16f) that can be compared to the list of Deuteronomic phrases in the previous section. Almost all of Huldah's words are duplicated in typical Deuteronomic passages. 2 Kings 23 then records the effects of Josiah's conversion and his decision to institute a major reform. What he did conforms almost exactly to the program laid down by the law code of Deuteronomy. Note the following parallels in the table on RG 145.

2 Kings 23		Deuteronomy
23:4, 6, 7, 14	abolition of the asherim	7:5; 12:3; 16:21
23:4f	destroy the host of heaven	17:3
23:5, 11	end worship of sun and moon	17:3
23:7	stop sacred prostitution	23:18
23:10	end the cult of Molech	12:31; 18:10
23:13	tear down heathen high places	7:5; 12:2f
23:13	remove the foreign gods	12:1–32
23:14	destroy the "pillars"	7:5; 12:3
23:21f	Passover to be observed only in Jerusalem	16:1–8
23:24	forbid necromancy	18:11

According to the text of 2 Kings, the lawbook was found in Josiah's eighteenth year (622 BC) just as he became interested in reform. In a second version, told in 2 Chronicles 34, he became interested in reform in his twelfth year (628 BC), and the book was discovered after the changes were well under way. In either case, the similarities between this lawbook, which was found in the Temple during Josiah's reign (and which led to or supported a massive reform), and the urgent preaching of Deuteronomy are too close not to refer to the same book. Scholars conclude from this that at least the core of our present book of Deuteronomy was known by 622 BC.

Close examination of the contents of Deuteronomy, however, reveals that it has strong similarities with many ideas and books, which came down from the Northern Kingdom of Israel when it was destroyed in 722 BC by the Assyrians—almost exactly one hundred years earlier. It shares a strong interest in the love of God, the covenant as relationship, and the imagery of a father leading a son, all of which made the northern prophet Hosea so unique. It has a strong polemic against Baal and the gods of Canaan, a major temptation for Israelites who lived in the northern area nearest Tyre and Sidon; it has a fierce, warlike campaign strategy against Canaanite religion typical of some of the stories told of the northern prophets Elijah and Elisha in 1 Kings 17 to 2 Kings 10. Moreover, its attitude of doubt about the king's faithfulness in chapter 17 is more typical of a northern viewpoint than of the kingdom of Judah where the house of David ruled. It also strongly supports the role of Moses as a charismatic leader, much in the style of the northern E source in the Pentateuchal traditions of Exodus and Numbers. One could also point to the location of the covenant ceremony of curses and blessings in Deuteronomy 27–28 at Mounts Ebal and Gerizim, the traditional centers of the Northern Kingdom.

Could there be a northern origin to the earliest level of Deuteronomic traditions? The answer is a possible yes if we look to a passage in 2 Kings 18:3–7, in which the authors state that King Hezekiah of Judah began a similar reform to that of Josiah around the time he became king, perhaps 715 BC. But did Hezekiah already know of the teachings of Deuteronomy back then? Again, it is possible that the refugees from the north brought down the fundamental Deuteronomic laws and traditions with them as they fled the Assyrians a mere seven years earlier, and it was these that Hezekiah decided to put into practice even in Judah.

What happened to the book of Deuteronomy between Hezekiah and Josiah is unknown. According to the book of Kings, King Manasseh, who ruled for most of the intervening years, violently opposed all reform (2 Kgs 21:1–15; 23:26f) and probably persecuted its leaders. They in turn either hid the already-written book, or kept their teachings to themselves until a more favorable king came to the throne in Judah; then they had them written down.

The Development of the Religious Perspective of the Book

With such a long and complicated history behind Deuteronomy, we must be cautious in trying to answer what particular point of view it represents. Possibly it developed in the following manner:

1. When the Northern Kingdom went its own way after the death of Solomon about 930 BC, this kingdom claimed that it was more faithful to the older covenant of Moses and was opposed to the claims of the house of David in Jerusalem—through which royal promise to David God redirected the covenant in 2 Samuel 7. The new northern kings, however, quickly adopted all sorts of Canaanite practices and allowed devotion to Baal, Asherah, and other deities to exist alongside the worship of the Lord. This violated the fundamental law of the covenant that there must be no god beside the Lord. The most likely source for sustained opposition to these policies came from the circles of prophets around Elijah and Elisha who violently opposed any compromise with the cult of Baal, and from among the Levitical priests charged with teaching and maintaining the covenant demands. They began to put together a new statement of the law centered on the warning that if Israel did not do better and keep its covenant, it would lose its land.

2. The defeat of the north by Assyria in 722 BC proved these reformers right, but it also left them homeless. Many fled to Judah, and there the terrible lesson that disobedience led to disaster impressed Hezekiah and his Judean priests. They tried to implement the Deuteronomic reform ideas in Judah, which did not really take hold at that time because Judah felt little need to reform after the miraculous escape from an Assyrian invasion in 701 BC, during the later years of Hezekiah. The people of Judah credited this to God's promise to David to never abandon his dynasty nor his city, Jerusalem. The Southern Kingdom became convinced God would protect them no matter what they did.

3. In the days of Josiah, Judah began to expand and retake the old Northern Kingdom of Israel because the Assyrian empire was falling apart. To win over the half-believing northerners to his side, Josiah wanted something to unite the country in faith. Once he became aware of Deuteronomy's program, from the discovery of the book in the Temple, he decided to use it. It was at this stage that the book was enlarged to its present size, except for a few chapters at the beginning and end.

4. This new setting in the kingdom of Judah led to the particular southern emphases in the book on (a) a single place of worship where God's name would dwell (12:1–14), and (b) the frequent use throughout of the verb "choose" to describe the place God has chosen to set the divine name. The Hebrew verb is used to describe God's choosing David and is thus a kind of sacred term for the royal dynasty in Jerusalem—that God chose them—stressing God's special choice of both the house of David and the Temple of Jerusalem.

Important Themes of Deuteronomy

The development of its historical and religious perspective led Deuteronomy to give great stress to certain areas of faith over others. In reading the long introduction in chapters 1–11 and looking at the particular points that the body of laws covers in chapters 12 through 26, note these frequent themes:

The Importance of the Covenant

Deuteronomy is edited in the form of a covenant treaty between God and the people, but it is also a speech of Moses, which recalls all the covenant benefits that God has done for Israel in the desert. There is also an emphasis throughout the book on the love of father and son as a way of speaking about God and Israel. The Deuteronomic authors borrowed this from standard covenant treaties of the times, which used the motivation of love to encourage loyalty between the parties. It can be said that for Deuteronomy, covenant love and fidelity are everything!

The Law Is Not Simply Laws, but Total Commitment

Another way of approaching Deuteronomy's message is to say it demands a full commitment of heart and mind and strength to God. It is no accident that the most important statement in Deuteronomy (6:4f) has become the daily prayer and faith confession of Jews everywhere; it was cited by Jesus himself as the greatest commandment for Christians: "Hear, O Israel! The LORD is our God, the LORD alone! Therefore, you shall love the LORD, your God, with all your heart, and with all your soul, and with all your strength."

Even the piling up of words for law, "the commandments, the statutes and decrees" (6:1), or "ordinances, statutes and decrees" (6:20), and similar phrases, emphasize that the great multitude of laws really points to a deeper and more permanent commitment to the Lord that lies beneath.

There Is Consistency to God's Dealings with Israel

One of the significant elements in Deuteronomy's presentation is the recital of Israel's history and the looking forward to still more problems that the people will face in the years ahead. The book sees a design in how God works in history. The pattern can be summarized briefly in this challenge: There are two choices before you—the first is to obey God, follow his ways, and be loyal with all your heart, then you shall receive the blessing of prosperity and long existence on the land. The second is to abandon God, follow the ways of the pagan gods such as Baal, and receive divine punishment and God's curse by which you will be thrown off the land and subjugated to your enemies. This pattern is given very concrete form in chapters 7 and 8, and again in 30:15–20. A corollary of this choice is that God's wrath blazes out against any idolatry on the part of Israel.

God's Blessing Is Conditional on Israel's Response

One of the themes that sets Deuteronomy apart from earlier thinking in Israel is that God's promises either to Moses or to David are not simply guarantees that God will stand by this people with protection and help, no matter what they do. Earlier theologies of God as a divine warrior who always fights for his people is now transformed into a new view of a God who will uphold the covenant and all of its terms, including blessing and curse, according to how Israel keeps its part of the treaty. The stress falls on both faithful worship and social justice as ideals for Israel. Repentance and change of heart are often required if Israel is to return to covenant loyalty. In this way, Deuteronomy represents its call for fidelity to be a turning point that can reverse the judgment against the nation.

The Land Itself Is Conditional

Deuteronomy stresses that the covenant is tied to life in the land; misuse of the land, failure to create a just society, and dishonest policies of rulers will cost Israel its right to the land. One reason why the authors put the book into the form of a farewell speech from Moses in the desert is that it makes the warning come from a time when they had no land yet, and it hints that this may happen again if the people do not heed his words. Perhaps the book became most influential once the exile began (598–587 BC), since the readers could then recognize that they were now indeed in their sorry state because they had not obeyed the Lord as Moses had warned. It spoke to their misery and to their repentant hearts!

There Is To Be One Sanctuary

An important part of the program of Deuteronomy was to center the people's attention on Jerusalem and away from the local shrines and cultic centers, which too often had connections to pagan beliefs and practices. It was an attempt to make the people think as a single mind about unified obedience to the Lord, a unified commitment to each other as a people, and a unified source of all blessing. The kingship of the Lord over the land will then be recognized by all, so that the land, the law, and the people will finally be united as one.

Deuteronomy Updates the Covenant Law

A final point worth noting is how often the laws listed in the outline of Deuteronomy match those of the earliest law code in Israel, the "Covenant Code" found in Exodus 20:22–23:33. In each case, however, the older laws are stated in a way that makes them more adapted to life in the towns and cities of a kingdom in the eighth to sixth centuries BC. They accent the obligations of citizens and members of the covenant to one another and to the weak and dispossessed so that justice can be done.

In your own study, compare the two sets of laws listed here to see if you can tell the differences:

Exodus 21–23	Deuteronomy 14–19
Ex 21:1–11	Dt 15:12–18
Ex 21:12–14	Dt 19:1–13
Ex 22:29f	Dt 15:19–23
Ex 22:31	Dt 14:3–21
Ex 23:1	Dt 19:16–21
Ex 23:10f	Dt 15:1–11
Ex 23:14–17	Dt 16:1–17

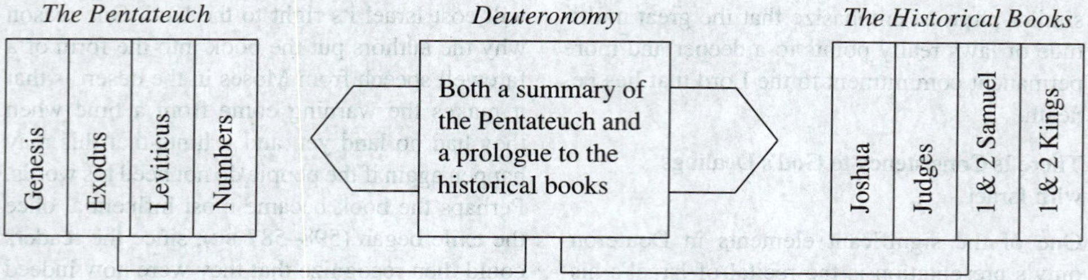

Connections of Deuteronomy and the Historical Books

Scholars in this century have stressed the strong connection between the theology of Deuteronomy listed above and the viewpoint that can be found throughout the books of Joshua, Judges, Samuel, and Kings. The same emphasis on having a choice to obey or disobey, with the resulting blessing or curse, seems to underlie how these books evaluate each major historical period and each individual leader. In comparing the book of Deuteronomy to the historical books, read together the beautiful passage in Deuteronomy 6:3f about loving the Lord with all your heart and soul and strength, and the statement made at the end of the books of Kings about King Josiah: "Before him there had been no king who turned to the LORD as he did, with his whole heart, his whole soul, and his whole strength, in accord with the entire law of Moses" (2 Kgs 23:25). Note also the echoes of Deuteronomy in the praise given to King Hezekiah in 2 Kings 18:5f. These are enough to give a flavor of how Deuteronomy's thought pervades the historical accounts. For further study, look also at these key passages in the histories that reflect Deuteronomy most strongly:

- **Jos 1:11–15** The promise
- **Jos 23–24** The covenant renewal at Shechem
- **Jgs 2:11–23** The pattern of sin and curse
- **1 Sm 12** Samuel's final warning on fidelity
- **2 Sm 7** The promise to David
- **1 Kgs 8–9** The conditional promise to Solomon
- **2 Kgs 17** The reason for the fall of the North
- **2 Kgs 23:25–27** The final evaluation of Judah's kings

Deuteronomy and the New Testament

The NAB lists two important citations of Deuteronomy used in Matthew's Gospel to explain the temptation in the desert and to answer the question of which was the greatest commandment. We can, however, see a much greater influence of Deuteronomy than merely these two direct quotations from the book itself. It is in the overall attitude. The heart of Deuteronomy is covenant loyalty, and Deuteronomy stresses the idea of God's fatherhood and love for the people as his children. Deuteronomy also focuses on wholehearted obedience that does more than the minimum required. It sees all of life as a walking in the ways of the Lord. And finally, of course, it understands life to be full of choices made by faith; to obey or disobey. These are all the themes of Jesus' own life. Some scholars have called Luke's Gospel a new Deuteronomy, but this could be truly said of any of the Gospels. If we understand the demand of Deuteronomy for single-mindedness, together with its vast vision that all of life must be an integrated whole, we will be prepared for a deeper reading of the New Testament.

Conclusion

Deuteronomy sits last in the Pentateuch, and so sums up in a "Second Law" (from the Greek *deutero-nomos*) the essential message of the earlier Pentateuchal stories for Israel's existence as a kingdom rather than as a tribal alliance in the desert. It also looks ahead from the time of Israel's beginnings to that later life as a kingdom, which is told in the historical books. Thus, it serves as both a conclusion to the desert period and a preface to the possession of the land. It links the Pentateuch traditions with the works of the historians of its own school that put together Joshua through 2 Kings. A diagram brings this out, and so prepares us to take up the study of the historical books themselves. See diagram above.

THE DEUTERONOMISTIC HISTORY

LESLIE J. HOPPE

JOSHUA

[see pages 268–296 of the Old Testament]

Before Beginning . . .

The book of Joshua is the sixth book of the Bible and carries on the story that begins in Genesis and continues through Deuteronomy. Abraham's descendants, who had been slaves in Egypt, are ready to take possession of the land promised to their ancestors. The land was not simply a gift of God to Israel—it was the gift that made God's power and presence in Israel's life something real and tangible. It was an act of grace like no other, for the gift of the land made it possible for the people of Israel to survive. The land provided Israel with its food, clothing, and shelter. Without it, Israel could not be a people. The land as God's gift to Israel was a theme that was central to its faith. It was a motif that was at the core of ancient Israel's stories, poetry, and prophecy. The book of Joshua is one product of the storyteller's art, while the theme of the gift of the land is found in several psalms such as Psalms 105, 106, 135, and 136. The prophets based their indictment of Israel's infidelity on the gift of the land that should have led Israel to the loyal and exclusive service of its God, e.g., Jeremiah 2: 6–7; 32:20–23.

Joshua is both the conclusion of one story and the beginning of another. It concludes the story of the liberation of the Hebrew slaves and their guidance in the wilderness to the Promised Land. It is also the first part of another story: the story of Israel in that Promised Land. The books of Judges, Samuel, and Kings are the other components of this story. It begins with Joshua and the Israelite tribes taking control of the land, continues with stories about the judges who lead Israel in maintaining their presence in the land, and concludes with the stories of Israel's kings, who eventually lose control of that land. The story ends the same way it begins—with the Israelites outside the land. At the beginning they are ready to cross the Jordan and take control of the land; at the end they are in exile from the land, wondering about their future. It is a sad story, a tragic story. It is a story that begins with much promise and ends with great disappointment.

The ancient rabbis called the books that made up the story of Israel in its land "the Former Prophets" because they ascribed these books to prophetic authorship. Scholars have called these books "the Deuteronomistic History of Israel." But that name can be misleading since these books are not histories—at least not in the modern sense. In the form we now have, the books date to about the middle of the sixth century while Israel was in exile. The story of Israel in the Promised Land turns Israel's past into a sermon in order to provide the exiles some basis for hope by affirming that Israel can have a future, despite the terrible losses it experienced when Jerusalem fell. The book of Deuteronomy provided the theological principles that guided the telling of the story of Israel in its land. Among these principles was the importance of serving the Lord alone by shaping one's conduct according to the norms of traditional Israelite morality, as found in the Torah that God revealed to Moses. The books of Joshua to 2 Kings show what happens when Israel is obedient and what happens when it is not. The story of Israel in its land, then, asserts that Israel can have a future if it chooses—because God has set before Israel the choice of life and death (Dt 30:15).

The book of Joshua answers two questions that were on the minds of its first readers. Is God able to restore Israel? Is God willing to do so? The answer that the book gives to the first question is a resounding yes. The book will tell the story of how Israel acquired its land ostensibly under Joshua's leadership. But as the story unfolds, it will become clear that it was God who was leading Israel all the while. The answer to the second question is a qualified yes. God has promised blessings to those who obey the Torah: if Israel chooses the path of obedience, it can expect to have a future in the land promised to its ancestors. If, however, Israel chooses the way of disobedience, there can be no hope.

Reading through the Book of Joshua

The homiletical character of the book of Joshua is evident from the very beginning. About twenty percent of the book's text describes the elaborate preparations for the entrance of the Israelite tribes into Canaan. Before the crossing of the Jordan begins, the book makes it clear the land is a gift that God is giving Israel (1:1–5). The way to insure that Israel will be in a position to receive that gift is obedience to the Torah (1:6–9). The rest of the book simply illustrates these two assertions. First, under Joshua's leadership, the tribes will take the land with relative ease because God is handing it to them. Second, because Israel is obedient, it takes possession of the land, which is then distributed equitably among the tribes.

Israel Enters the Promised Land (Jos 1:1–5:12)

The book's first chapter consists of four speeches: the Lord to Joshua (1:1–9); Joshua to the Israelite leadership (1:10–11); Joshua to the tribes from east of the Jordan (1:12–1 5); and the eastern tribes to Joshua (1:16–18). These speeches are the means of conveying the central religious affirmations of the book: the presence of God with Joshua and the Israelites, the importance of obedience to the Torah, the land as a gift from God, and Joshua as the successor of Moses. These affirmations provide a framework for understanding the stories that will follow. As the stories unfold it will become clear that Israel receives the land as a gift from God given to those who obey the Torah under the guidance of Joshua. No military preparations are mentioned and none are necessary as long as Israel observes the Torah.

The episode with the two Israelite spies and Rahab, the prostitute from Jericho (2:1–21), also betrays the book's purpose. Rahab's conversation with the two spies makes it seem as if she had been reading the book of Deuteronomy. Because she helps the Israelite spies, she is fulfilling the divine will and will escape the fate that the rest of Jericho's citizens will suffer (6:22–25). If Israel had followed her example, the fate of Jerusalem and its exiles would have been much different. If, like Rahab, Israel now chooses the way of obedience, it will return to its land to live in peace.

The scene depicting the crossing of the Jordan (3:1–4:24) underscores the book's intent to present the taking of the Promised Land as a wonder performed by God to fulfill the commitment made to Israel's ancestors. The book purposely describes the crossing of the Jordan River as a miracle like the crossing of the Red Sea (4:23), even though the Jordan is, in fact, easily fordable at several places. The miraculous crossing of the Jordan demoralizes the people of Canaan, robbing them of the will to resist (5:1). Again, it is clear that Israel's possession of the land was God's doing.

In 5:2–12, perspective then shifts to Israel. At God's instructions, the preparations to enter the land and face its inhabitants involve nothing of a military nature. In fact, these preparations actually render Israel's army quite vulnerable to attack because all the males had to be circumcised, making them temporarily unable to be an effective fighting force. But the mass circumcision does, however, make the community fit to celebrate the Passover (5:2–12). Both these observances became important markers of Jewish identity during and after the exile. Certainly the book of Joshua intends to promote these practices.

The Battle for the Promised Land (Jos 5:13–11:23)

Although the book of Joshua is often thought of as a chronicle of a massive invasion of Canaan by a united Israelite army under the leadership of Joshua, only one quarter of the book actually deals with the battles for the Promised Land. At the end of this section, the author comments that "Joshua captured the whole country" (11:23). But the account of the battles fought by the Israelite tribes focuses almost entirely on the central region of Canaan (6:1–10, 27). Battles in the south (10:28–43) and the north (11:1–14) are treated in summary fashion. The two places that receive the most attention are Jericho (6:1–27) and Ai (7:2–8:29). But before Joshua begins the attack on Jericho, the mysterious "captain of the host of the LORD" arrives (5:14). When this person tells Joshua that he must take off his sandals because he is standing on holy ground, the attentive reader recognizes the similarity to the story of Moses' encounter with God at the burning bush (Ex 3:1–6) and knows that the leader of Israel as he moves out to take the land is someone other than Joshua.

Jericho was a town that had been abandoned for centuries before the time of Joshua, probably because its water source had become severely polluted, making its waters no longer drinkable. Ai was a town that flourished in the Early Bronze Age—more than a thousand years before the Israelite tribes emerged in Canaan. It too had been abandoned for centuries before the Israelite tribes made their appearance. The stories of the capture of Jericho and Ai in Joshua (6–8), then, are not historical records. But apparently, the people of Israel celebrated the gift of the land that they received from God at shrines near Jericho. Certainly, the story of Jericho's fall reads more like an account of a liturgical ceremony than that of a military adventure.

The book tells the tale of Jericho and Ai as object lessons for its readers. Neither Joshua's military leadership nor the bravery of the Israelite army was responsible for the fall of Jericho. The town was taken because Israel followed God's directions. The city's walls collapsed after an elaborate procession with the ark—not because of any military operation. This led to a complete victory, but Israel was told not to enjoy the fruits of the victory: no one was to loot the city nor was there to be any Israelite settlement there. While Israel had no difficulty taking Jericho, Ai was another story (7:1–8:30). Because Joshua's spies misjudged the enemy's strength, Israel attacked Ai without sufficient force and suffered a grave defeat. The book accounts for this stunning setback by describing how Achan kept some of the booty from Jericho for himself, contrary to Joshua's instructions (6:17–21). After Joshua prayed and Achan was punished, God provided Joshua with tactical instructions for the defeat of Ai's army.

To keep the significance of the Torah before the reader, the book tells of a detour to the north that Joshua took in order to build an altar on Mount Ebal, which flanks the valley in which Shechem is located (8:30–35). On the stones used to make the altar, Joshua wrote the Torah. He then read the Torah—complete with the blessings and curses contained in it—to the people, reminding them that they will shape their future by the choices they make.

When the book returns to the story of the battle for Canaan, Joshua and his army are at Gilgal. Their victories led kings of the city-states in Canaan to form an alliance to stop the Israelite advance. The people of Gibeon tried a different approach. They sought an alliance with the Israelites by claiming to be, like the Israelites, newly arrived in Canaan (9:1–27). When the Israelites discovered that they were tricked by the Gibeonites, they suggested that the Gibeonites accept a low social status in the Israelite community as laborers in the Temple.

Like Jericho and Ai, Gibeon was not inhabited in the thirteenth century BC. This story is not based on any memory of an event in Israel's past; it is another homily on obedience. Like Rahab, the Gibeonites seem to know their Bible and are familiar with the Exodus tradition and the laws of Deuteronomy regarding relations with nearby and distant towns (Dt 20). But the story also serves as a warning to consult with the Lord in difficult circumstances, which the Israelites did not do in this situation—much to their regret (Jos 9:14). Without consulting God, Israel found itself regretting its actions. There will be several occasions in the monarchic period when Israel and Judah get into great difficulties because of the treaties they made with other nations, for example, Ahaz's alliance with Assyria (2 Kgs 16: 7–9).

One reason for Israel's regret in this case was that it had to face a coalition of Gibeon's neighbors to the south who were not happy because of its alliance with Israel. Of course, Israel was victorious, not because of its military prowess but because God enlisted the sun and moon to seal Israel's victory (10:1–14). In the ancient Near East, the sun and the moon were gods in their own right, but here they are simply weapons in the Lord's arsenal. Verse 13 notes that the couplet celebrating this miracle came from a now lost text: the book of Jashar (see also 2 Sm 1:18). Ancient Israel produced more literature than the Bible preserves, and occasionally the Bible will cite these texts. The book of Jashar is one example.

Following Joshua's defeat and execution of the kings allied against him, he moved against the south and brought that region under Israelite control (10:25–43). The story of Joshua's victory over a coalition led by Jabin of Hazor (11: 1–23) is meant to account for the taking of the entire northern third of Canaan: the Jezreel Valley and the Galilee. Once the author tells of the capture of Hazor, the story of the land-taking ends. The second section of Joshua ends with summary statements (11:15–23), the most important of which is that Joshua carried out the orders that God gave to Moses. The story of the battle for the Promised Land, then, is a story of the success that obedience brings.

The gift of the land is a motif that is woven throughout the Old Testament, but the references to how that land was acquired by Israel are not very specific. For example, though the story of Jericho's miraculous fall is an important part of Joshua, it is not mentioned elsewhere in the Old Testament. What precisely were the experiences that generated the first stories about Israel's acquisition of its land are unknown. But before they came to have their present form, they were shaped and reshaped by almost six hundred years of life in that land. Ancient Israel's storytellers witnessed the rise and fall of the two Israelite national states. These experiences certainly left their mark on the story of Joshua and the emergence of the Israelite tribes in Canaan.

The story of the battle for the Promised Land effectively turned the past into a sermon whose purpose was to stimulate the faith and hope of those who first heard or read it. They learned that there could be a future for the people of Israel if they, like Joshua's generation, were obedient to the Torah. The homiletical character of this story makes its use in reconstructing the early history of Israel problematic. Archaeological excavation supports the conclusion that the stories of conquest found in Joshua were not based on memories of actual battles that took place at Jericho, Ai, or in the environs of Gibeon. But archaeology has shown that people living in Canaan in the thirteenth century BC experienced serious disruptions. Towns and villages were destroyed and abandoned. The Israelite tribes emerged in the central highlands of Canaan precisely during this difficult period, so it is likely that Israel acquired the land that was to be the scene of its subsequent history, in part, by violence. It is difficult, from the evidence offered by the book of Joshua, to say much more. What the book does affirm unequivocally is that Israel came to possess the land because of God's power, and Israel was able to receive that land as God's gift because of its obedience. These affirmations, however, were meant to give Israel a vision of the future rather than information about the past. To those who wondered if God were capable of restoring Israel, the book of Joshua answers with a resounding yes.

Israel's Inheritance (Jos 12:1–19:51)

After listing the territories brought under Israelite control during the battle for the Promised Land (13:1–7), the book of Joshua has an extensive section dealing with the distribution of the land among the Israelite tribes (13:8–19:51). Working through this section is difficult for modern readers since it is full of geographical detail that is meaningless to many. While the precise borders of the various tribal allotments may have been very important to the people of ancient Israel, their significance today is exclusively historical. Still, there are some details in this part of the story that even contemporary readers should attend to.

It is important to remember that ancient Israel's economy was based on agriculture. Ownership of land was crucial to survival in such an economy. Possession of a plot of land enabled the Israelite to produce enough food for his family and livestock with a surplus to be used for replanting and for sacrificial offerings. Without land, a person had no access to the means of production. Such a person was dependent for survival on the charity of his fellow Israelites. Of course, there were some people who supported themselves as merchants and artisans, but they too ultimately depended on Israel's peasant farmers for their prosperity.

The account of the land distribution among the tribes begins with a reminder of the areas of Canaan that the Israelites did not control (13:1–6). This was a necessary corrective to the exaggerations in the previous section of the book, which claimed that Joshua and the Israelite subdued "the entire land," "the whole country" (Jos 9:24; 11:23). Then follows a review of the territories previously allotted by Moses to those Israelites who were going to live east of the Jordan River (13:7–33). Israel's control over this region was neither firm nor constant, but its inclusion among the tribal allotments expresses Israel's claim on that territory, even though Israel was not always able to support that claim. When Ezekiel described his vision of an Israel restored after the exile, he did not have any of the tribes living east of the Jordan (Ez 48:1–29).

When the account of the distribution of the land west of the Jordan begins in chapter 14, both Eleazar the priest and Joshua preside over the distribution (14:1; see also Nm 34:17). The preceding sections of the book did not emphasize the role of the priest except for the liturgical actions (e.g., 3:6; 6:1–9). The priority given to Eleazar here may reflect the more significant role that the priests played in the leadership of the community after the state collapsed and the dynasty ended, as is evident from Haggai, Zechariah, and Ezra. Eleazar's presence may also be a consequence of having the land distributed by lot (14:2). Although Deuteronomy explicitly forbids attempts to determine the divine will through the techniques of divination (Dt 18:9–12), the casting of lots seems to have been widely practiced and accepted as legitimate. The lot oracle was committed to the priests (Ex 28:30; Lv 8:5–9). To show that the distribution of the land was done according to God's will, it was accomplished by the use of lots in a procedure presided over by a priest. The New Testament gives evidence of the continuing popularity and acceptance of using lots to determine the divine will (Acts 1:26).

The report of the land's distribution among the Israelites pays most attention to the region in the very center of what became the territory of the two Israelite kingdoms (14:6–17:17). This is the territory that will be given to Judah, Ephraim, and Manasseh. While the territory of Benjamin (18:11–20) also merits special regard because it was coveted by both Israelite kingdoms, the allotments of the other tribes get comparatively meager attention. Judah is considered first. Its territory comprised most of what would be the Southern Kingdom. Since the Old Testament reflects a southern perspective, the priority given to Judah is understandable. The territory of Ephraim and Manasseh became the heartland of the Northern Kingdom and could not be ignored. The entry about the allotment of Dan is unusual (19:40–48). It notes that the territory given to Dan was located along the coastal plain. This will be the setting of the story of Samson, a Danite hero (Jgs 13–16). But the entry goes on to note that Dan was unable to take control of that territory from the indigenous population, and so the tribe relocated to the far north. The story of this relocation is told in Judges 17–18. The story of the land's distribution concludes in 19:49–51 with the note that Joshua received the town in Ephraim that he requested for himself.

Special Towns (Jos 20:1–21:45)

Two of ancient Israel's social institutions are the subject of the fourth section of the book of Joshua. The first is the city of refuge. There were six of these cities—three on each side of the Jordan. According to Numbers 35:9–34, it was Moses who announced God's plan to have such cities where a person who accidentally caused another's death could be safe from the victim's relatives, who might seek vengeance. Moses had already named the three cities east of the Jordan, and now Joshua designated three more west of the Jordan. The books of Samuel, Kings, and Chronicles never mention this institution since they were not needed following the centralization of authority by the monarchy. The book of Judges mentions two examples of private vengeance: 8:13–21 and 20:1–11. It is clear from these examples that the biblical tradition does not approve of such acts. A second set of forty-eight towns is set aside for the Levites. The tribe of Levi received no territory of its own because the men of that tribe served as priests, who were to teach the Torah to Israel and offer sacrifice to the Lord (see Dt 33:8–11). To fulfill these functions the priests need to be available to the people; therefore the cities where the Levites have residential and grazing rights are scattered throughout the country.

This section on special towns has been inserted in the account of the tribal allotments, as is evident from Joshua 21:43–45. This text makes no mention of the special towns but has been detached from 19:51 to allow for the insertion.

A Threat of Civil War (Jos 22:1–34)

The Israelites whose territory was east of the Jordan River had joined in the battle to take control of the area west of the river. Since that battle was completed successfully, Joshua allowed them to return to their homes (vv. 1–8). This is a prelude to a conflict between the Israelites east of the river and those on the west (vv. 9–34). The tribes from the east side of the river built an altar near the Jordan, and this offended the Israelites from the west. War was averted because Phineas, Eleazar's son, succeeded in negotiating peace between the two groups. The precise nature of the offense is not obvious, though it may reflect the Deuteronomic belief that there was to be only one place where sacrifices were to be offered. Apparently, the book of Joshua assumed that this place was Shiloh. When the easterners explained that they did not intend to offer sacrifices on the altar they built (v. 26), this defused the problem. The tribes from the west of the Jordan were satisfied that those from the east side meant no offense and were not repudiating the Lord. Joshua had no role in this story; it was a priest who brought about a happy ending to what could have been a great disaster. Again, this presages the leadership role that priests assumed in Israel's life following the end of the monarchy.

An Era Ends (Jos 23:1–24:33)

The final testament of such an important person as Joshua was highly significant. The storyteller creates a speech for his hero that could have come right out of the book of Deuteronomy. Israel's continued presence in the land depends on its adherence to "all that is written in the book of the law of Moses . . ." (23:6). Joshua reminds Israel to love God (23:11), the Torah's greatest command. But then Joshua issues a warning that any failure on Israel's part to remain completely and exclusively loyal to God will have the gravest of consequences (23:15–16). While the land is a gift from God to Israel, the gift can be revoked. Of course, this is a theological conclusion that came from Israel's experience. By the time the book of Joshua took the form that it now has, Israel did "perish from the good land" that it had received from God (23:16). Israel's faith in God's fidelity, however, led to the hope that a new dedication to the Torah and a renewed commitment to the covenant will bring a reversal of the misfortune that Israel brought on itself. The book then describes an elaborate ceremony in which Israel of Joshua's day renews its commitment to God and the Torah (24:1–28). Clearly this final chapter is a model for Israel of the sixth century BC, which has experienced the full consequences of its infidelity. But a renewal is possible if the people and their leaders remember how God has been faithful to fulfill the promises made to Abraham, Isaac, and Jacob. Like the ancestors in the days of Joshua, Israel must again commit itself to serve and obey God alone.

The burial notices with which the book ends (24:29–30, 32–33) are significant because of the prominence given to Eleazar, the priest. This is very likely another indication of the leadership role assumed by priests after the fall of the Israelite monarchy. Verse 31 is the verdict on the era of Joshua: it was an era marked by obedience and loyalty. That is the reason Israel came to possess the land: obedience brings God's blessing.

The Continuing Significance of the Book of Joshua

Most Christians who read the book of Joshua have a difficult time with the image of God that the book appears to have. It is a God who orders an invasion of Canaan and the annihilation of the armies sent to oppose the Israelites, and even of the civilian population of towns under attack by Israel. The conflicts depicted in the book of Joshua have been described as examples of "holy war," but this expression never appears in Joshua or anywhere else in the Bible. Still, it is true that ancient Israel did acquire control over Canaan, in some measure, by violent means. But it is difficult to be more specific than this when trying to reconstruct the process of Israel's emergence in Canaan. It is clear, however, that the image of a large Israelite armed force, organized under Joshua's leadership, invading Canaan from the east and quickly gaining control over the whole land has its roots in the religious imagination of ancient Israel rather than in the experience of the Israelite tribes.

There were serious and widespread conflicts in Canaan of the thirteenth century BC. Archaeology has shown that. But the conflicts were probably not initiated by an invading military force. They began as the centralized political and military authority over the region exercised by Egypt began to deteriorate in the fourteenth century. Canaanite city-states began fighting one another for dominance in the region. Some peasant farmers of Canaan, who bore the burden of these conflicts, withdrew their allegiance from these city-states and began to develop an alternate polity. In the central highlands, groups united by kinship and the worship of the Lord emerged as a significant force. It is possible that a group of people who worshipped the Lord, and who had escaped from slavery in Egypt, energized the people of the central highlands to resist their oppressors by telling their stories of a miraculous escape made possible by their God. In any case, the people of Israel rejected the hegemony of the city-states and ruled themselves according to traditional norms of behavior as interpreted by their elders. Over time the power of the city-states waned, and the Israelite tribes were able to strengthen their hold on the central highlands and enjoy a measure of peace and prosperity with the Lord, rather than with a human being as their sovereign. Instead of paying taxes to a human overlord, they offered tithes of their agricultural produce to the Lord at the shrines where they thanked God for the gift of the land. The Israelites believed that it was the God of their ancestors who made it possible for them to take control over their lives and destinies. This reconstruction of the emergence of the Israelite tribes in Canaan is based on the results of archaeological excavations, combined with what is known from the Bible and other ancient Near Eastern texts using models derived from anthropology and sociology.

This, however, is not the story related in the book of Joshua. That story was not written to describe the process by which the Israelite tribes came to dominate parts of Canaan. The book of Joshua was composed to encourage the exiles of Judah and Jerusalem to believe in the power of their ancestral deity to lead them from exile in Babylon back to the land promised to Abraham's descendants. The fall of Jerusalem, the destruction of its Temple, and the end of the dynasty and national state led the people of Judah to wonder about the power and the willingness of their God to save. The book of Lamentations gives voice to the questions that the exile raised in the hearts of believers. It begs God to remember what has happened to Israel and to start acting like God (Lam 5:1, 19), but Lamentations ends with what is best translated as a plaintive question: "Have you utterly rejected us?" (Lam 5:22). The book of Joshua, then, is best understood as a response to questions such as this one—not to questions about how ancient Israel acquired its land.

The great irony of the book of Joshua was that its stories about the Israelite army conquering great cities and annihilating their populace were written at a time when ancient Israel was at its lowest ebb politically and militarily. The two Israelite national states no longer existed. Their territory was absorbed into the Babylonian provincial system. The leading citizens of Judah were taken to Babylon to prevent them from fomenting any resistance to the new order in the region. Those Judahites who remained in the land were subsistence farmers and not in a position to challenge Babylonian rule. Certainly the stories about the mighty Israelite army winning victory after victory under Joshua was a parody of the military and political impotence of Judah in the sixth century BC.

Unfortunately, the stories of the book of Joshua have served to provide support for the wars of conquest waged by Christians over the centuries. The Crusades, the wars against the Native Americans, and the Boer conquest of South Africa are just three examples of the lethal mixture of war and religion. The book of Joshua was written not to inculcate a martial spirit in its readers but instead a spirit of obedience and commitment to the Torah. The book assumes that the exile of Israel from the land that God gave it was not due to any military misadventures. Israel lost its land because of its failure to keep the Torah that God revealed to Moses. The only hope for restoration was for Judah to join their ancestors in recommitting themselves to their God: "Far be it from us to forsake the LORD for the service of other gods. For it was the LORD, our God, who brought us and our fathers up out of the land of Egypt, out of a state of slavery. He performed those great miracles before our very eyes and protected us along our entire journey and among all the peoples through whom we passed. At our approach the LORD drove out [all the peoples, including] the Amorites who dwelt in the land. Therefore we also will serve the LORD, for he is our God" (Jos 24:16–18).

FURTHER READING

Boling, Robert G., and G. Ernest Wright. *Joshua.* Anchor Bible 6. Garden City: Doubleday, 1982.

Butler, Trent C. *Joshua.* Word Biblical Commentary 7. Waco, TX: Word, 1983.

Coote, Robert B. *Early Israel: A New Horizon.* Minneapolis: Fortress, 1990.

Gottwald, Norman K. *The Tribes of Yahweh.* Maryknoll, NY: Orbis, 1979.

Hamlin, E. John. *Inheriting the Land: A Commentary on the Book of Joshua.* International Theological Commentary. Grand Rapids, MI: Eerdmans, 1983.

Hoppe, Leslie J. *Joshua and Judges with an Excursus on Charismatic Leadership in Israel.* Old Testament Message 5. Wilmington, DE: Michael Glazier, 1982.

Lind, Millard C. *Yahweh is a Warrior.* Scottsdale, PA: Herald Press, 1980.

Mitchell, Gordon. "Together in the Land: A Reading of the Book of Joshua." *Journal for the Study of the Old Testament (JSOT),* no. 134. Sheffield: Sheffield Academic Press, 1993.

Polzin, Robert. *Moses and the Deuteronomist: A Literary Study of the Deuteronomic History, Part I, Deuteronomy, Joshua, Judges.* New York: Seabury Press, 1980.

Rowlett, Lori L. "Joshua and the Rhetoric of Violence: A New Historicist Analysis." *JSOT,* no. 226. Sheffield: Sheffield Academic Press, 1996.

JUDGES

[see pages 296–326 of the Old Testament]

Before Beginning . . .

The book of Judges is the second book in the collection the early rabbis called the "Former Prophets" and modern interpreters the "Deuteronomistic History of Israel." It is a collection of stories about several Israelite heroes set in the time between the settlement in Canaan under Joshua and the establishment of the Israelite monarchy. The title of the book comes from the designation of its principal characters. The "judges" were charismatic leaders of the Israelite community, especially in times of fierce competition over the land of Canaan. Their authority came from the Lord, and their duty was to enable Israel to live in faithful obedience. The judges had to deal with two problems: the failure of Israel to serve the Lord alone, and the competition for control of the land from other peoples. The book presents these two problems as interrelated. When Israel failed to maintain its commitment to serve the Lord exclusively, then God allowed Israel's neighbors to make its life very difficult.

The competition for control over the land of Canaan in the thirteenth century BC was very high. In the course of that competition, individuals emerged who proved very capable of managing that competition to the benefit of the Israelite tribes. Stories about these individuals and their feats circulated among the Israelites and eventually found their way into the collection we know as the book of Judges. This collection, however, served a purpose beyond simply preserving the memory of ancient heroes. Its purpose was to illustrate the consequences of Israel's failure to live in faithful obedience to the Lord. It deals with a practical and theological problem: the absence of the kind of leadership provided by Moses and Joshua. How should Israel be governed? Who would insure that Israel will live according to the Torah in the land it had received from the Lord?

The book of Judges has three parts. The first (1:1–3:6) provides readers with a framework for understanding the significance of the stories about these ancient heroes. The second part (3:7–15:20) rehearses the exploits of the judges. The book concludes with a few supplementary stories (16:1–21:25) that show how the Israelite tribes were on a path of self-destruction. Originally the stories about the individual judges served to excite a certain measure of pride in the achievements of the tribes in maintaining control over the land of Canaan. But once these stories were put into their present context in the book of Judges, the effect was to show that there was something terribly wrong about the way the Israelite tribes were living their lives in the land that God had given them. Readers are led to conclude that matters could not go on like this—something had to be done, for the life of the Israelite tribes was degenerating into anarchy.

Reading through the Book of Judges

Understanding the Time of the Judges (Jgs 1:1–3:6)

The book begins by raising the question of leadership: "Who shall be first among us to attack the Canaanites and to do battle with them?" (1:1). The initial answer is Judah, the tribe that eventually became the nucleus of the Southern Kingdom. After some initial success, the tribes' progress bogged down, and the first chapter concludes with a list of areas over which the Israelites were not able to assert their control (1:27–35). The picture here is just the opposite of that given in the book of Joshua according to which Joshua "captured the whole country, just as the LORD had foretold to Moses. Joshua gave it to Israel as their heritage, apportioning it among the tribes" (Jos 11:23). The process by which the Israelites achieved control over Canaan was clearly long and complicated. Once the Egyptians no longer dominated the region, the political and military reins they held were gone. The indigenous population of Canaan had to face raiders from the fringes of the settled areas, various kinship groups, refugees from economically and politically volatile regions, and invaders looking for new settlement possibilities—all of whom converged on the area between the Mediterranean Sea on the west and the desert on the east, the mountains of Lebanon on the north and the Sinai peninsula on the south. Eventually the national states of Edom, Moab, and Ammon arose east of the Jordan River. The Israelite kingdoms were established west of the Jordan about two hundred years later because, apparently, the Israelite tribes seemed to prefer a more decentralized polity supported by a religious ideology that held that Israel's king was not a human being but the Lord. Until the rise of their national states, the Israelites had to make do with local and temporary leadership.

The second chapter describes the price Israel had to pay for its preferred pattern of leadership: the Israelite tribes found themselves in danger of being overcome by the other groups competing for the limited territory of Canaan. The explanation for this potential disaster is the failure of the Israelites to keep their covenant with the Lord. Israel will have to deal with other contenders for the land by themselves. God's help will not be forthcoming. The contrast between the period of Joshua and that of the Judges could not be more absolute. Under Joshua's leadership, "Israel served the LORD" (Jos 24:31) and it had experienced victory after victory and came to possess "all the land." Without the type of leadership Joshua provided, the Israelite tribes were on the verge of annihilation because of their failure to obey the Lord. The Israelite response was lamentation at a place named *Bochim,* (weepers) (Jgs 2:5).

The next section (2:6–3:6) elaborates on the religious interpretation of the problems the Israelite tribes had in maintaining a foothold in the land promised to their ancestors. The reason for Israel's difficulties is simple enough: "the Israelites offended the LORD by serving the Baals" (2:11). The threat to Israel's continued presence in Canaan was a direct by-product of the Israelite worship of Baal, which presented a most serious threat to the exclusive service that Israel owed to its God. Baal is the title ("Lord" or "Owner") by which Hadad, the Canaanite god of the storm and fertility, was known.

One of the principal sources of anxiety in the Bronze and Iron Ages in Canaan and Israel was having enough food to eat. The problem was not the soil—it was fertile enough. The problem was water. The region was not blessed with a river system as were Egypt and Mesopotamia, whose river systems made large-scale irrigation possible. In Israel, whatever moisture there was to water the land had to come as rain. The Israelites, following the lead of the Canaanites, relieved their anxiety about having enough rain to make the land provide enough food by worshipping Baal and his consort Ashtaroth (2:13) because rain and fertility were their specialties. Israel's ancestral deity, by way of contrast, came from southern, arid regions (see Hb 3:3). It is likely that most Israelites did not consider the worship they offered to Baal and Ashtaroth as incompatible with loyalty to the Lord, but certainly the author of Judges did. It took centuries for the people of Israel to be convinced of how critically important it was for them to serve the Lord alone. The book of Judges was an important contribution to this process.

The pattern for the way the stories of the judges will be told is set in 2:11–23. The book introduces the narrative of each of the judges with the formula found first in 2:11: "Israelites offended the LORD . . ." The consequence of this infidelity was domination over the Israelite tribes by their rivals for hegemony in Canaan. But the period of the judges was marked not only by divine judgment but by divine mercy. The Lord always heard the sounds of Israel's pleading and responded by raising up a leader who rescued Israel from the oppression they were experiencing. Unfortunately, at the death of the judge who rescued them, the Israelites returned to their evil ways. God determined, then, that Israel would have to continue facing the threat of extinction as long as it continued to serve the Baals (2:16–23). The introduction to the book ends with 3:1–6, which explains that Israel's competitors will remain in the land to test the loyalty of future generations. But one consequence of this intermingling will be that some Israelites will marry Canaanite spouses, which will often mean that the Israelite partners in such unions will abandon their ancestral religion.

Two final observations need to be made about the introduction. In the stories that follow, the threat and resistance are usually local. But Judges transforms the stories of local heroes into stories that have a significance for all Israel. Second, as readers work their way though the stories of the judges, the question arises about how long God will continue to abide Israel's infidelity. Is there some limit to God's forbearance?

The Stories of the Judges (Jgs 3:7–15:20)

Othniel (Jgs 3:7–11)

The book of Judges begins with a divine oracle that names the tribe of Judah as the leader of the Israelites in the attempt to take control over Canaan (1:1–2), and the first of the judges, Othniel, is from Judah. He has already made an appearance in the book as the conqueror of Debir, a city in the southern hill country of Judah (1:11–13). Here Othniel's story is told with a minimum of detail, but its basic pattern will be repeated throughout this section of Judges: The Israelites served Baal instead of the Lord. God allowed an enemy to oppress them—in this case for eight years. They cried out for deliverance, and God sent a judge to rescue them. God endowed the judge with the spirit of the Lord, which empowered him to accomplish extraordinary deeds. Israel then served the Lord for the lifetime of the judge—in this case forty years.

The NAB accepts the reading of the Hebrew Bible for the name of Cushan's base: *Aram Naharaim,* a city on the Euphrates River in northern Syria. This reading cannot be correct since the judges all deal with threats from within Canaan. One suggestion is that the text should read *Armon-harim* ("fortress in the hills").

Ehud (Jgs 3:12–30)

Ehud came from the tribe of Benjamin, whose territory is immediately north of Judah. The first detail given about Ehud is that he was left-handed. While the people of the ancient world considered left-handedness abnormal, it was a distinct advantage in hand-to-hand combat. Although the name Benjamin means "the son of my right hand," the tradition behind the book associates this tribe with a high incidence of left-handedness. Judges 20:16 asserts that Benjamin could boast of seven hundred highly skilled left-handers.

Israel's sin was responsible for the oppression, which took the form of raids by Eglon, the king of Moab. Moab was a kingdom located in the central part of the Transjordan directly across the river from Benjaminite territory. While engaged in these raids, Eglon made "the City of Palms" (probably Jericho) his headquarters. These raids continued over an eighteen-year period. Ehud, who was supposed to bring Benjamin's tribute to Eglon, instead assassinated him. After making his escape, Ehud was able to convince men from the tribe of Ephraim to join him in expelling the Moabites from Israelite territory. So total was

Ehud's victory that Israel had peace for eighty years.

The story of Ehud's assassination of Eglon ridicules the Moabites for their carelessness, naïveté, and stupidity. Of course, the story must have been highly entertaining because it was retold countless times. Certainly one can picture the Israelite audience having a good laugh at the expense of the Moabites. The book takes this entertaining story about a Benjaminite hero and makes it part of a comprehensive theological presentation about the importance of serving the Lord alone.

Shamgar (Jgs 3:31)

There is some doubt whether Shamgar ought to be understood as a judge like the others in the book. His name is not Semitic nor does the text claim that God raised him up in response to Israel's cries. The Song of Deborah (Jgs 5) notes that the caravan trade was interrupted "in the days of Shamgar" (v. 6). Perhaps he was responsible for this disruption. In any case, Shamgar single-handedly defeated an entire Philistine force. While his service on Israel's behalf may have been indirect, he did make life easier for some Israelites by defeating the Philistines. The book mentions him after Ehud—someone else who single-handedly delivered Israel.

Deborah and Barak (Jgs 4:1–5:31)

With the story of Deborah and Barak, the scene shifts northward—to the vitally important Jezreel Valley. The valley, which extended southeast from the Plain of Acco on the Mediterranean coast to the Jordan Valley, separated Galilee from the central highlands. Once under Israelite control, communication between the tribes in the Galilee and the those in the highlands to the south became possible. Also significant was the agricultural and trade potential of the Jezreel Valley. Israel had to control this important piece of real estate. But standing in its way was Jabin, the king of Hazor, who wanted to keep the Jezreel for himself. He dispatched his general Sisera with a force that included nine hundred chariots to keep Israel out of the valley. The story and poem about Deborah and Barak testify to the significance that the Jezreel Valley held. It is the celebration of a great and unexpected victory: that of an army of peasants over professional soldiers with the best of equipment.

The book of Judges presents Deborah as the hero of the conflict with Sisera's army. Barak made his contributions with great reluctance. The story labels Deborah as a prophetess and a judge (4:4) without further explanation. Because judges and prophets were charismatic leaders, these roles were open to women. The patriarchal structures of ancient Israelite society did not obstruct the "spirit of the LORD," and clearly people understood this. Deborah shamed Barak into raising a force from Naphtali and Zebulun to oppose Sisera and his chariots. Naphtali and Zebulun were Galilean tribes, and their territory was located just to the north of the Jezreel Valley. As the reader expects, God gave victory to the Israelites. Sisera escaped the rout only to be killed by the Kenite Jael while assuming she was protecting him from the pursuing Israelites. This event fulfilled, in an unforeseen way, Deborah's prophecy, which was intended to goad Barak into action (4:9).

The book of Judges preserves what many consider to be one of the oldest texts found in the Bible: the song of Deborah (5). This is a hymn celebrating the victory of Israel over Sisera's army. Here readers find out how the victory was achieved. A sudden rain causing a flash flood in the valley rendered the chariot force immobile and eliminated Sisera's advantage. Also, the poem asserts that the Israelite force included not only Zebulun and Naphtali but also Ephraim, Benjamin, Issachar, and Machir, which may be that portion of Manasseh west of the Jordan. Other tribes are criticized for not responding to the threat posed by Sisera: Asher, Dan, Reuben, and Gilead, which may be that portion of Manasseh east of the Jordan. The poem does not mention Judah, Gad, or Levi.

The poem contrasts two mothers: Deborah, mother of Israel, and Sisera's unnamed mother. Deborah was responsible for a great victory, while Sisera's mother came to realize that Sisera's failure to return promptly from the battle means that she would never see her son again.

Gideon (Jgs 6:1–8:35)

No judge receives more attention from the book of Judges than Gideon. His story begins with Israel being harassed by the Midianites, who enjoyed a great advantage over Israel. The Midianites were mounted on camels when they raided Israelite territory at harvest time. These mounted attacks made the Midianites unstoppable. They simply confiscated the harvest that the Israelites produced, making life impossible for the Israelite peasants (6:1–6). An unnamed prophet announces the religious cause of the Midianite oppression (6:7–10). To the angel sent to recruit Gideon to deliver Israel, the reluctant general points out his lack of suitability—a motif also found in the call of Moses (Ex 3:10) Isaiah (Is 6: 5) and Jeremiah (Jer 1:6).

There is a great anomaly in Gideon's story: he is frequently called *Jerubbaal,* a name that seemingly honored Baal, the Lord's rival for Israel's loyalty. The meaning of that name (let Baal sue or take action) helps explain the anomaly. Gideon's dismantling of an altar for sacrifices to Baal aroused the anger of the local populace, and they were ready to kill Gideon for his sacrilege. Gideon's father suggests that they should leave the matter up to Baal—let Baal sue—"since he destroyed his altar" (Jgs 6:25–32).

The rest of Gideon's story describes his efforts to deal with the Midianites and others that were threatening the Israelite tribes in the central highlands. He rallied to his side not only members of his own tribe (Manasseh) but the militia of three others (Asher, Zebulun, and Naphtali). But Gideon refused to proceed without receiving another sign that his mission was from God (6: 36–40). Next came a test of Gideon's militia administered by God, who had Gideon dismiss those who lapped up drinking water and thus reduced their vigilance. Gideon received additional orders from God, requiring him to keep only three hundred fighters to insure that the militia could not ascribe the coming victory to their military skills but to God (7:1–8). The three hundred vanquished the Midianites by a surprise nighttime attack without doing any actual fighting—again underscoring the divine origin of Israel's victory. The Ephraimite militia joined in the pursuit of the Midianites. They captured and executed two Midianite kings, Oreb and Zeeb. The story concludes with Gideon pursuing the fleeing Midianites into the Transjordan where he took two more Midianite kings, Zebah and Zalmunna. Gideon also engaged in an act of private vengeance against the town of Penuel that refused to help his men during their campaign.

Gideon's story then takes a new twist as the Israelites ask Gideon to rule as king and thus establish a dynasty to provide ongoing protection from groups like the Midianites. Gideon refused, citing the Israelite notion that the Lord is king of Israel. Gideon then uses part of the valuables confiscated from the Midianites to construct an ephod, a priestly vestment probably used for divination. The book does not consider this a positive development but notes that, nonetheless, Israel enjoyed peace for forty years (8:22–28).

Gideon's story ends with a transition to what follows by introducing his many wives who bore him seventy children. The one child mentioned by name is Abimelech, who will be the principal character in the next story. After Gideon died, the people of Israel reverted to the worship of Baal and forgot both the Lord and Gideon's achievements (8:29–35).

Abimelech (Jgs 9:1–36)

Although it is in the middle of the book of Judges, the story of Abimelech is an oddity because Abimelech is not a judge. He did not free Israel from any oppression. Abimelech convinced the people of Shechem to accept him as the sole ruler of their city and its environs, replacing the more diffuse pattern of leadership as exercised by Jerubbaal's seventy sons. To solidify his one-man rule Abimelech murdered all his brothers except Jotham, who survived, cursed his brother and then fled the Shechem area—never to be heard from again.

The book places on Jotham's lips a bitter diatribe against his brother (9:7–15). Jotham addresses Shechem's leadership in a fable about trees who were looking for a king but could persuade only a worthless thornbush to accept the position. Is this a criticism of the monarchy as an institution or merely a criticism of Abimelech? The book can barely hide its animosity toward Abimelech. It is important to remember that the book of Judges—in the form in which it now exists—was the product of someone who witnessed the fall of the Davidic dynasty and the end of the Judahite national state. Certainly the failure of the monarchy to prevent the disaster that came upon Jerusalem had to weigh heavily on the writer's mind. The role of the monarchy in Israelite life, then, was not simply a theoretical question. It is important to note that the setting of this story is Shechem, where earlier Israel had reaffirmed its covenant with the Lord (Jos 24). In

Abimelech, Shechem accepts a human being as its lord. Such a choice will be disastrous.

Abimelech's rule in Shechem was indeed a disaster for him and for the city. Although Abimelech claimed to be a Shechemite "flesh and bone" (9:2), a revolt was fomented by Gaal, who implied that Abimelech was only a half-Shechemite. The trouble started by Gaal was serious enough that Abimelech had to be ferocious in his response (9:42–49). Abimelech died as he was putting down the revolt. The book implies that his ignominious death was a fitting conclusion to a bad episode. In 2 Samuel, Joab and David will recall the story of Abimelech's death as they scheme to have Uriah die during the siege of Rabbath-Ammon as part of the cover-up of David's adultery with Bathsheba (2 Sm 11:18–24). After Abimelech's death, the Israelite militia, which Abimelech also led, dispersed (Jgs 9:22, 55).

Tola and Jair (Jgs 10:1–5)

There were several judges about whom the book provides almost no information, but they are mentioned to leave the reader with the impression that judges were part of the experience of people in every region of Israel. Tola judged in Ephraim, the western portion of the central highlands, and Jair in Gilead, the northern part of the Transjordan controlled by Israel. References to their service provide the outer frame for the much more developed story of Jephthah.

Jephthah (Jgs 10:6–11:40)

Because Jephthah, as the son of a prostitute, had an even lower social standing than Gideon or Deborah, he too was at first an unlikely candidate for the leadership of the Israelite militia. He did, however, possess one advantage. As the leader of a group of raiders, Jephthah had military experience and was just the kind of man that the elders of Gilead were looking for when the Ammonites were trying to push their border northward into Gilead's territory. Gilead was an Israelite territory east of the Jordan; Ammon was a kingdom to the south of Gilead.

There are several unique features to Jephthah's story. First, before resorting to armed conflict, Jephthah tried to negotiate a settlement with the Ammonites (11:12–28). When the negotiations failed to convince the Ammonites to stop their incursions, the spirit of the Lord came upon Jephthah, empowering him for the extraordinary efforts necessary to neutralize the Ammonites. But then there is a second unusual detail in the story. Jephthah makes a hasty and carelessly worded vow before the battle. The reader wonders if this indicates that the judge was less than confident in the outcome of the approaching battle. When Jephthah handily defeated the Ammonites, it was time to act on the vow he made. The NAB translation of 11:31 suggests that the victim was to be a human being, but that is misleading. A better translation is "the first thing to come out . . ." But Jephthah thought that he was trapped by the imprecise wording of his vow, and so he believed that he had to sacrifice the daughter who ran out to meet him on his return from the battle with the Ammonites (11:34–35). The religious and cultural significance of the practice of lamenting for Jephthah's daughter (11:37–40) is not clear.

The third unique episode in Jephthah's star-crossed career is a brief war between the Israelites from Gilead and those from Ephraim. The latter were jealous of Jephthah's victories and angry that they were not invited to join his expedition against the Ammonites. The conflict between Ephraim and Gilead may reflect an attempt by the former to dominate the latter. Jephthah tried negotiations a second time and failed again. In the ensuing conflict, the Ephraimites suffered severe casualties. Those who tried to escape were caught because they did not pronounce the *sh* sound in the Hebrew word *shibboleth* (current) because of their Ephraimite dialect.

Though Jephthah did neutralize the Ammonite threat and judged Israel for six years, the impression left by the book is that Jephthah's career was marked by failure and tragedy. He was not able to successfully negotiate with either the Ammonites or the Ephraimites. He lost his daughter because of a carelessly worded vow, and his victories ignited an intertribal war. The picture of Israel during the time of the judges is getting darker.

Ibzan, Elon, and Abdon (Jgs 12:8–15)

The second part of the frame surrounding the story of Jephthah is a brief notice about three more judges, each of whom judged Israel in the region west of the Jordan River. Since Elon and Abdon were from the north, it is likely that Ibzan was too. The village of Bethlehem that was Ibzan's home was located in Zebulun (Jos 19: 15)—not in Judah. There are no warfare stories connected with any of the three.

Samson (Jgs 13:1–15:20)

Although Judges 15:20 states that Samson was a judge in Israel for twenty years, his career was different from that of the judges whose stories the book has told so far. Samson never led the Israelite tribal militia. His was more of a solo act. The setting of Samson's story is the long conflict between the Israelites and the Philistines for control of Canaan. When the Egyptians and Hittites exhausted themselves vying for control of the trade routes that ran through Canaan, this left a vacuum of power waiting to be filled. The first to try to take advantage of Egypt's weakness were the Philistines. Who these people were and where they came from are not clear. Perhaps they were Mycenaeans who crossed the Mediterranean from Greece following the collapse of their empire in the thirteenth century BC. Mycenaeans served as mercenaries in the Egyptian army and knew the strengths and weaknesses of Egyptian defenses, but their invasion of Egypt still failed. The would-be conquerors of Egypt retreated to the southern part of Canaan's coastal plain, which in Hebrew was known as *peleshet*. The Bible calls these people *pelishtim* (Philistines), i.e., the people who live in the *peleshet*. The Philistines organized themselves politically into a confederation of five city-states: Gaza, Ashkelon, Ashdod, Ekron, and Gath. As the Philistines expanded to the north, they threatened the tribe of Dan, which was located on the central part of the coastal plain. Samson was a Danite.

Another unique feature of Samson's story is the narrative about the events surrounding his conception and birth that took place after Israel suffered forty years of Philistine oppression (13: 2–25). Samson's mother is told that the son she will conceive is to be a Nazirite. The word *Nazirite* comes from a Hebrew root that means "to separate, consecrate, abstain." Numbers 6 describes the lifestyle of the Nazirite. They were not to drink fermented beverages, wine, or vinegar. They were not even to drink grape juice or eat grapes or raisins. This prohibition probably was meant to insure that Nazirites would not lose the spirit of the Lord because of intoxication. Second, Nazirites were not to cut their hair. This prohibition likely reflects a belief that a person's hair was especially significant as a place where spirits dwelt. Finally, Nazirites were not to touch any corpse because they were to remain ritually pure, and contact with a corpse rendered a person impure. A person could take the vows of a Nazirite for a set time, or a person could become a permanent Nazirite.

Samson's conflicts with the Philistines appear to be private in nature. The first comes as a result of a lost wager that Samson made with the Philistines during the celebration of his marriage to a Philistine woman (14:1–20). The second is a reaction to his wife being given to another man (15:1–7). The third involves an attempt by some Judahites to turn Samson over to the Philistines (15:8–20). The story affirms three separate times that the spirit of the Lord came upon Samson. Each time the spirit gave Samson strength in situations when his life was in danger. The book implies that while Samson's struggles with the Philistines were personal, he caused the Philistines the type of setbacks that eased pressure on Dan for twenty years.

Israel's Self-Destruction (Jgs 16:1–21:25)

As readers make their way through the stories of the judges, the question arises, How long will God allow this pattern of apostasy and repentance to repeat itself? Will Israel ever learn to serve the Lord alone? The book of Judges answers those questions by concluding with a series of stories that show Israel clearly on the path of self-destruction. What God would not allow the Moabites, the Midianites, the Ammonites, or the Philistines to do, Israel seems bent on doing to itself. The final chapters make it appear that the Israelites become addicted to chaos—chaos that threatens their continued existence as a people.

As the previous section ends with the stories of Samson's private vendettas easing the pressure that the Philistines were bringing to bear on Israel, so this final section begins with Samson's descent into self-destruction. What is even worse is that Samson nearly took Israel with him. In Judges 16:1–3, Samson's visit to a prostitute nearly cost him his life. Apparently, he learned nothing from that brush with death, and his affair with Delilah did end with his death. Delilah was from the Valley of Sorek, located about thirteen miles west of Jerusalem. The land there was much more agriculturally valuable than the land the Israelite tribes had in the central highlands. Its one disadvantage was that it abutted Philistine territory; there was a constant threat of harassment hanging over the Israelite farmers in the Sorek because the Philistines too had moved into that valley. The book of Judges suggests that the Philistines soon dominated the region (Jgs 13:1). Delilah is never actually called a Philistine, but the implication is there. The cutting of a Nazirite's hair was a public statement that he was released from his vows (see Acts 18:18). In Samson's case, it meant that he was no longer equipped to defend Israel from the Philistine threat. His hair grew back, and Samson had one more opportunity to avenge himself, but at the cost of his life (Jgs 16:23–30). Samson's flaws proved fatal. His death presaged that of the Israelite kingdoms whose story is introduced by that of the judges.

Micah (Jgs 17:1–13)

The scene shifts from the fate of Samson to that of Israel as a whole. The story about Micah is a symptom of the disease that afflicts Israel—the failure to serve the Lord alone. Micah built himself a shrine and, with his mother's help, outfitted it with images and an ephod, the latter probably used in divination. Micah had one of his sons serve as the priest of the shrine until a Levite happened to come by. What follows reflects the preference that Israelites had for priests from the tribe of Levi, who were likely seen as authentic representatives of the Yahwistic tradition. Indeed, Micah himself believes that as a result of his installing a Levite as a priest of his domestic shrine, he will enjoy blessings from the Lord (Jgs 17:13). The only comment that the author of Judges makes on what he considers to be a warped notion of Israelite religious traditions is found in Judges 17:6: "In those days there was no king in Israel; everyone did what he thought best." Without some central authority, religious anarchy reigned in Israel.

Chapter 18 describes the migration of the tribe of Dan from the central part of the coastal plain to the far north of Galilee. The story begins by repeating the refrain "At that time there was no king in Israel" (Jgs 18:1). The story continues to describe the religious anarchy among the tribes. The Danites steal the liturgical appurtenances from Micah's shrine and abduct his priest. After they take the city of Laish, they install the Levite and the shrine in their new home, which they rename Dan. Finally, the identity of the Levite is revealed. His name is Jonathan, and he is a grandson of Moses. The book of Judges regards this shrine as illegitimate because the "house of God" was located at Shiloh (Jgs 18:31). That Moses' grandson was associated with an illegal shrine so scandalized later scribes that they introduced another letter into the name of Moses in 18:30, changing it to Manasseh, which was also the name of the most notorious apostate of all Judah's kings (see 2 Kgs 21).

The story of the corrupting of a young Levite from Bethlehem (Jgs 19) is followed by the story of a well-established Levite from Ephraim. This story, too, begins with the refrain: "At that time . . . there was no king in Israel" (v. 1)—a warning that what follows is another example of the religious anarchy that plagued Israel in the time of the judges. On his way home from reclaiming his secondary wife (concubine), who had returned to her father in a fit of anger, the Levite and his concubine spend the night in Gibeah, a town in the territory of Benjamin. In what has been aptly characterized as a "text of terror," the Levite's wife is gang-raped and murdered (vv. 11–30). Evidently, the hospitality and protection due a stranger in Benjamin did not extend to a secondary wife who may accompany him. Despite his own implication in facilitating this crime, the Levite summons the Israelite militia for vengeance. The tribal militia is not engaged in a defensive war against oppression but now fights in civil war. After two terrible losses, the Israelite militia finally defeats the Benjaminites, leaving only six hundred surviving males.

While the militia reassembles at Bethel, the people realize what they have done. When they seek an oracle from God to determine why one tribe has been virtually wiped out, none is forthcoming. The answer should be obvious: the Israelites try to undo what they have just done, and their solution involves them in another civil war against the people of Jabesh-gilead, who did not join in the muster against Benjamin and, thus, were likely candidates to supply wives for the six hundred remaining Benjaminites. When the war did not provide enough women, the supposedly wise elders suggested that the Benjaminites kidnap as many as they needed from Shiloh. With that, the militia disbands.

The author of Judges has painted a very bleak picture of the Israelite tribes. He leaves his readers with the by-now-familiar comment on the religious and civil anarchy that gripped the life of Israel in its land: "In those days there was no king in Israel; everyone did what he thought best" (Jgs 21:25). What follows is the story of Israel's experience with the monarchy, which ultimately proved just as incapable of forestalling disaster for the people of Israel.

While the book of Joshua is a highly stylized portrait of Israelite beginnings, the book of Judges reflects the disordered state of life in Canaan at the end of the Late Bronze Age in Canaan. It was a very unsettled time in the region, and certainly the book of Judges gives some idea of the chaos that affected the Israelite tribes who were trying to gain a foothold in the region. This is not to suggest that the book of Judges is a historical account of events as they happened. To some extent the narratives in Judges present an idealization of the early years of Israel's existence in Canaan: the stories of local heroes are arranged in what appears to be chronological order. What these stories show is that loyalty and commitment to the Lord are what stand between Israel's well-being and its destruction.

Continuing Significance of the Book of Judges

If the modern religious reader of Judges is repulsed by its narratives, the ancient author has been successful. The picture of Israel—especially at the end of the book—is far from attractive or edifying. But it does show what happens to a nation that ignores traditional ethical and moral values. Disaster inevitably follows. If the people of Judah would restore their community's life in the land promised to their ancestors, they need to remember the centrality of the covenant that God made with those ancestors. The stipulations of that covenant require fidelity, commitment, and absolute loyalty to the Lord. The book of Judges is an object lesson about what happens to a people when they ignore the Lord in their national life. The pattern of recurring apostasy has to be replaced by a consistent loyalty. But how does a nation evaluate its level of commitment to the moral values to which it is an heir? This will be the subject of much of the story of Israel's kings that begin in the books of Samuel and continue in the books of Kings.

FURTHER READING

Alter, Robert. *Language as Theme in the Book of Judges*. Cincinnati: University of Cincinnati Press, 1988.

Bal, M. *Death and Dissymmetry: The Politics of Coherence in the Book of Judges*. Chicago: University of Chicago Press, 1988.

Boling, Robert. *Judges*. Anchor Bible 6A. Garden City, NY: Doubleday, 1975.

Brenner, Athalya. "A Feminist Companion to Judges." *Journal for the Study of the Old Testament*. Sheffield: Sheffield Academic Press, 1993.

Finkelstein, Israel. *The Archaeology of the Israelite Settlement*. Leiden: Brill, 1988.

Hamlin, E. John. *At Risk in the Promised Land: A Commentary on the Book of Judges*. Grand Rapids, MI: Eerdmans, 1990.

Klein, Lillian R. *The Triumph of Irony in the Book of Judges*. Sheffield: Almond Press, 1988.

Mayes, A. D. H. *Israel in the Period of the Judges*. London: SMC Press, 1974.

Pannick, David. *Judges*. New York: Oxford University Press, 1987.

Soggin, J. Alberto. *Judges*. Old Testament Library. Philadelphia: Westminster, 1981.

Yee, Gale A., ed. *Judges and Method: New Approaches in Biblical Studies*. Minneapolis: Augsburg Fortress, 1995.

RUTH

[see pages 326–331 of the Old Testament]

Before Beginning . . .

The book of Ruth contains a rare and delightful story that continues to captivate its audience no matter how often it is read. Few can forget the loyalty of Ruth, the bitterness of Naomi, the forthright Boaz. The story has been of special interest to Christians since Matthew lists Ruth among the ancestors of Jesus (Mt 1:5).

Ruth as Story

The book of Ruth is a short story, similar to the Joseph story in Gn 37–50. It is an artistically told tale with a simple plot. While the story of Joseph is set with the court of Pharaoh and deals with important personages and events, Ruth's characters are ordinary people; its events, mundane. Its closeness to life enables us to identify with its characters, to sympathize with their situation, and to rejoice when their problems are solved. The plot of the book is controlled by the problems that Ruth and Naomi have as they adjust to their new status as widows. These problems are resolved through the interaction of the book's main characters: Ruth, Naomi, and Boaz, relieving the tension created by the uncertain future that the two women faced. The principal characters are exemplary persons whose goodness is rewarded in the end, reinforcing the belief that human events are in some sense under the control of a power which insures that good triumphs. As story, its purpose is to entertain and delight, and this it does, but at the same time it also instructs. Though God never directly speaks or acts in the story, nevertheless it is clear that the story has something to teach us of the way that God is present in life.

An important element in the story is Ruth's Moabite ancestry. It is especially significant since the book presents her as the great-grandmother of David. Though Deuteronomy 22:4 forbids a Moabite from becoming part of the Israelite community, Ruth not only does so but is a forebear of the great King David. Perhaps the author of the book made a connection between David and the Moabites because the story of David's rise to kingship has him place his parents in the safekeeping of the king of Moab, while David is trying to elude capture by Saul (1 Sm 22:3). There is, of course, no possibility of verifying the details of Ruth's story.

Dating the Book of Ruth

It is difficult to date the book of Ruth with any certainty, for though it has been argued that it is postexilic in origin, more and more frequently arguments for a preexilic date are being advanced. Those who postulate a postexilic date see the book of Ruth as a polemical work challenging the policies of Ezra. In his reform of the postexilic community, Ezra implemented a policy forbidding intermarriage with foreign women. The book of Ruth questions such a policy by showing that Ruth, although a foreign woman, is pious and faithful. Moreover, the kinship between Ruth and David indicates that David, the greatest of Israel's kings, was himself of mixed blood. Such a challenge to Ezra's policies would emerge close to the time of Ezra's activity, ca. 450 BC. The evidence for a preexilic date comes from an analysis of style and theology. There is nothing in the style of the book that would force one to assume a late date. Its theology is similar to that of the Joseph story (Gn 37–50) and the court history of David (2 Sm 9–20; 1 Kgs 1–2), both thought to be preexilic in origin. We cannot resolve here the complex issues surrounding the date of the book of Ruth, but the diversity of opinion cautions us against easy answers. Recent linguistic analysis of the Hebrew of Ruth suggests that a date in the early postexilic period is likely (late sixth century BC).

Ruth's Place in the Canon

While there is universal agreement about Ruth's canonical status, there is some disagreement about the book's place within the canon. Christian Bibles, including the *New American Bible*, place the book of Ruth after Judges and before 1 Samuel, following the order of books in the Septuagint, which was the version of the Old Testament read in the early church. No doubt the Septuagint placed Ruth *after* Judges because the story is set "in the time of the judges" (Ru 1:1). It is important to note that despite its placement, the book of Ruth is not a part of the Deuteronomistic History—the story of Israel from conquest to exile found in the books of Joshua, Judges, 1 and 2 Samuel, and 1 and 2 Kings. It does not reflect the thought or style of the Deuteronomistic History; it does not have Deuteronomistic theological overtones. In Jewish Bibles, the book of Ruth is placed in the third division of the Jewish Canon—the Writings, a collection of miscellaneous works. Jewish liturgical practice includes Ruth among the five *Megilloth*, i.e., the scrolls that are read on major Jewish festivals. The book of Ruth is read on the Feast of *Shavuot* (Weeks), which Christians know as Pentecost.

Theology in the Book of Ruth

In an age when the Torah was on the way to becoming the central religious symbol of early Judaism, the book of Ruth presents three characters, Ruth, Boaz, and Naomi, whose actions go beyond what is required of them. Ruth makes a commitment to her mother-in-law, Naomi, that ignores the claims of religious traditions and national origins. Naomi shows her loving concern for Ruth by devising a scheme to induce Boaz to marry Ruth, even though that scheme could have backfired on her. Boaz ignores his self-interest to marry Ruth and thus redeem the property of Naomi's husband. The story shows how people who think of others' needs before their own find their truest happiness. God approves the conduct of these people by giving a son to Ruth and Boaz—a son who removes the emptiness and uncertainty that faced the widow Naomi. The author of Ruth is certainly saying to the book's readers: "Go you and do likewise."

How to Proceed

The book is short, and it can be read easily in one sitting. Because a story conveys its meaning in terms of what is said of its actors and their actions, it is important to pay close attention to the characterization of Ruth, Naomi, and Boaz, and what they do. Pay particular attention to the subtle presence of God in the story. Notice, too, recurring motifs and patterns that will function as clues to meaning.

The Book of Ruth in Outline

The story is worked out in scenes set between an introduction that presents the problem, and an epilogue that follows the resolution of the problem.

1:1–5 Prologue: A Family Dies

1:6–22 Naomi and Ruth in Bethlehem: Emptiness and Uncertainty

2:1–23 Naomi, Ruth, and Boaz (I): A Meeting with Possibilities

3:1–18 Naomi, Ruth, and Boaz (II): A Husband for Ruth

4:1–12 The Climax: Boaz Acts

4:13–17 A Son for Naomi

4:18–22 Epilogue: A Family's Genealogy

Reading through the Book of Ruth

The Prologue: A Family Dies (Ru 1:1–5)

A family from Bethlehem, which had been driven by hunger to Moab, is now left without any hope of progeny since the men of the family have recently died. This is a principal problem of the story: Naomi is left without husband or sons (1:5). The author makes a special note of identifying the family's origin in Bethlehem of Judah (1:1), noting more specifically that they were "Ephrathites from Bethlehem of Judah" (1:2). This detail, emphasized as it was, certainly led those who first read the story of Ruth to think of the most famous of all Ephrathites: David, the son of Jesse (see 1 Sm 17:12). Thus, the opening verses of the story hint at its eventual resolution.

The Geographical and Cultural Setting

The events recounted in these opening verses reflect conditions typical of life in Canaan. Because the region did not have a river system that made large-scale irrigation possible, agriculture was completely dependent on rain. When the rainfall was inadequate, famine was the inevitable result. One way to cope was to move to areas unaffected by the famine—usually this meant Egypt (see Gn 12:10; 26:1). Moab was an unusual choice. It was located east of the Dead Sea and, like the lands to the west, it too was entirely dependent on rain for agricultural productivity. Presumably a drought that affected Bethlehem would have affected Moab as well. Also unusual is that no negative comments are made regarding the marriage of Naomi's sons to Moabite women. But these details also serve to prepare the reader for an even greater anomaly coming at the end of the story.

Childless widows were particularly vulnerable in the social and economic system of the societies of the ancient Near East. A husband and sons provided a woman with security. Naomi found herself without such protection in a foreign land. She bitterly lamented her fate (Ru 1: 13), but in an unusual move one of her daughters-in-law chose to ignore her own welfare and care for Naomi. Instead of attaching herself to a man to provide for her welfare, Ruth attaches herself to Naomi, who can offer her nothing.

The Motif of Emptiness

Naomi's "emptiness" is the principal problem of the story. With great artistry the author of Ruth weaves into the story a motif of emptiness, which sets the action of the story in motion and will be reversed by the end of the story. The emptiness of the land (famine) causes Naomi's family to leave the land. The emptiness of the land gives way to the emptiness of Naomi as she loses her husband and her sons. Naomi dismisses her daughters-in-law because her "emptiness" cannot be cured. She is too old to give birth again. Naomi's emptiness is accentuated when she contrasts her previous abundance with her present destitution (1:21). The story ends with Naomi no longer empty. She takes Ruth's child to her breast and cares for him. The women of the neighborhood congratulate her: "A son has been born to Naomi" (Ru 4:17, literal translation).

Naomi and Ruth in Bethlehem: Emptiness and Uncertainty (Ru 1:6–22)

The length of this scene indicates its importance for the author of Ruth. Naomi decides to return home because the famine is over in the land of Israel. Also motivating her decision must be the realization that she will have a better chance of survival among her own people than as an Israelite widow living among Moabites. Naomi's words to her daughters-in-law accentuate the tragedy of her situation. She is too old to marry and can no longer bear children. She can hope for nothing. Her daughters-in-law share Naomi's desperate situation, but she advises them to return to their people. Among their own people they may be able to find husbands and thus secure their future. With Naomi there can be no future. Ruth's loyalty is shown in her refusal to abandon her mother-in-law in spite of the hopelessness of Naomi's future; she will stay with Naomi despite the prospect of poverty.

The Character of Ruth

By drawing out the hopelessness of Naomi's situation coupled with Ruth's refusal to leave her mother-in-law, the author highlights Ruth's character: she is faithful. While there is nothing wrong with Orpah's returning home, Ruth's virtue is shown in sharp relief by the contrasting actions of these two women. Ruth is willing to share the plight of Naomi. Ruth's character is spotlighted even more in its biblical context. She is not called by God. She receives no promises. No reward awaits her. She acts solely for the good of Naomi. Her loyalty will draw the attention of Boaz, which eventually will lead to the resolution of the problem facing Ruth and Naomi, and thus everything in the story depends on this young widow.

God's Presence in the Story

It is important to note that, in the story of Ruth, most often God is referred to in the blessings and oaths that are spoken by the main characters. Naomi blesses her two daughters-in-law (1: 8f); Boaz blesses Ruth for her loyalty to Naomi (2:12) and her good character (3:10); Naomi blesses Boaz for his kindness to Ruth (2:20); the blessing of fertility is bestowed upon Ruth by the citizens at the city gate (3:10). All of these blessings are issued in God's name, but it is through the actions of the main characters that the blessings are fulfilled. God stands behind all as cause (4:14), but God's activity is mediated by those who live faithful lives.

Other references to God in the story imply that God is the cause of all that happens. God is the one who has ended the famine in the land of Israel and filled it with food (1:6). God is blamed for Naomi's destitution (1:20f); God is also responsible for Naomi's abundance at the end of the story (4:14) by enabling Ruth to conceive and bear a child (4:13). The hand of God is to be found in all that happens in the lives of Naomi, Ruth, and Boaz. But there are no miracles, no theophanies, no signs and wonders to illuminate Ruth's way. It is through the ordinary lives of ordinary people, who demonstrate extraordinary care for each other, that the divine is manifest.

Ruth, Boaz, and Naomi (I): A Meeting with Possibilities (Ru 2:1–23)

Ruth takes the initiative in this scene, requesting permission from her mother-in-law to glean in the fields. Picking the few stalks of grain left by the harvesters was one way that people without land were able to feed themselves. Both Leviticus and Deuteronomy require that harvesters not be so thorough as to leave nothing for the poor (Lv 19:9f; 23:22; Dt 24:9). Ruth, seemingly by chance, enters the fields of Boaz, a prominent relative of Naomi. Boaz has heard of Ruth's kindness to her mother-in-law, and sees to it that she is protected and allowed to gather a considerable amount of barley.

The Character of Boaz

The story depicts Boaz as generous and noble. He insists that Ruth glean only in his fields, he extends his protection to her, he provides her with food and water, and he sees to it that she will prosper in her gleaning. The motive for his behavior toward Ruth is her kindness and loyalty to Naomi. We see in his gracious response to Ruth's faithfulness that Boaz is a person of integrity and honor.

Naomi, Ruth, and Boaz (II): A Husband for Ruth (Ru 3:1–18)

Naomi does not want Ruth to remain a widow, so she decides to take advantage of the positive encounter between Ruth and Boaz. She suggests a plan to Ruth that could lead to marriage with Boaz. Although the writer uses euphemisms that reflect his culture's reticence about private matters, the sexual overtones of Ruth's actions are clear. Her encounter with Boaz on the threshing floor could have turned out differently, but Boaz's integrity and generosity led in the direction Naomi hoped: Ruth will have a husband.

The Climax: Boaz Acts (Ru 4:1–12)

The storyteller introduces a new wrinkle into his tale to complicate matters just before the denouement. For the first time in the story, Elimelech's land becomes an issue. Probably the story's first readers would have wondered when the storyteller was going to get around to dealing with this most important matter. Boaz assembles ten of the town's elders to witness how the matter of the land was going to be settled among Elimelech's relatives. The presence of the elders insured that the details of settlement became "public record." An unnamed relative who had a prior claim on the land was willing to buy it back, thus making sure that Elimelech's land would stay "in the family." Of course, doing so will benefit that man economically. But then Boaz adds that with the land came Ruth, Mahlon's widow. The land in question would pass to any child born of Ruth and the relative in question. It is at this point that he demurs and cedes his rights to Boaz. The storyteller implies that the unnamed relative was concerned solely about his interests, unlike Naomi, Ruth, and Boaz, who, throughout the story, are concerned less about themselves and more about the welfare of others. With the tension brought on by this last complication, the storyteller can proceed to the "happy ending," which has Ruth acquire a husband, Boaz acquire both a wife and Elimelech's land, and Naomi acquire a son who will fill her emptiness.

Levirate Marriage and Land Redemption

Some interpreters suggest that the marriage of Boaz and Ruth represents a variation of the levirate marriage. A levirate marriage was the marriage of a woman with the brother of her deceased husband (*levir* is the Latin word for "brother-in-law"). Such a union was mandated if the marriage was childless (Dt 25:5–10). The practice developed to insure that the line of the deceased man would continue, in spite of the fact that he died before his wife bore him a child. Though Boaz claims Ruth as wife to raise up a family for her late husband, he is not her brother-in-law and thus the law of levirate marriage did not apply. The storyteller presents Boaz as going beyond his obligations in order to help two widows in need.

Land redemption was a strategy that developed to make sure that circumstances that forced a man to sell his land would not lead his family into a permanent state of poverty. According to Lv 25:23–38, it was the responsibility of a relative to buy the land before it was sold outside the family or to buy it back if it had already been sold. The land remained the property of the relative who bought it back until the Year of Jubilee, when its ownership reverted to the descendants of the man who was forced to sell it.

A Son for Naomi (Ru 4:13–17)

Ruth's marriage to Boaz is blessed with a child. Naomi's loss is replaced by Ruth's gain; the tragedy of death, with which the story opened, is balanced by the joy of new life. Notice the women of the village congratulate Naomi as if she were the mother: "A son had been born to Naomi" (Ru 4:17, literal translation). The storyteller thus solves the problem of Naomi's emptiness. The NAB translation obscures this point by calling the child Naomi's "grandson." While the child indeed was Naomi's grandson, the text nonetheless shows Naomi acting as if she were the mother (Ru 4:16) and being recognized as such by the women of her village (Ru 4:17).

The Epilogue: A Family's Genealogy (Ru 4:18–22)

The story's epilogue takes the reader back to the prologue, which identified Naomi's family as "Ephrathites from Bethlehem" (Ru 1:2) and thus informs the reader of the wider significance of this charming story of one family's problems. The most famous Ephrathite from Bethlehem was David, who, it turns out, was a descendant of Boaz and Ruth. Usually a genealogy serves to legitimate the status of the last person named. Here David, the last person named, serves to show the significance of what happened to three people from the village of Bethlehem for all Israel.

Continuing Significance of the Story of Ruth

While early Judaism came to regard careful observance of the Torah as the key to its future, the book of Ruth shows three people whose relationships with each other are based not on obligations but on love and concern for another in need. Such relationships have significance far beyond the lives of the three people involved directly. Jesus develops these insights in his Sermon on the Mount in which he calls his followers to go beyond the commandments—as irreplaceable as they are. The charming story of Naomi, Ruth, and Boaz shows that an ethical system fulfills its purpose if those who accept it learn to go beyond its requirements. The Torah asserts that no Moabite is to be admitted into the Israelite community (Dt 23:4). But the book of Ruth presents a Moabite woman whose actions on behalf of her Israelite mother-in-law proceeded from love that ignored religious and ethnic boundaries, which serve to keep people from responding to each other in love. The book of Ruth, then, presents this young Moabite woman to its readers and suggests that they follow her example. The ending of the book wishes readers to recognize that, when people give of themselves for the sake of others, they find their truest happiness. This paradox lies at the heart of the book of Ruth and makes it the charming and admirable story that it is.

FURTHER READING

Bush, Frederic W. *Ruth; Esther.* Word Biblical Commentary 9. Waco, TX: Word, 1996.

Campbell, Edward F., Jr. *Ruth.* Anchor Bible 7. Garden City, NY: Doubleday, 1975.

Fewell, Danna Nolan, and David Miller Gunn. *Compromising Redemption: Relating Characters in the Book of Ruth.* Literary Currents in Biblical Interpretation. Philadelphia: Westminster John Knox, 1990.

Hals, Ronald. *The Theology of the Book of Ruth.* Biblical Series, no. 23. Facet Books. Philadelphia: Fortress, 1969.

Larkin, Katrina J. A. *Ruth and Esther.* Old Testament Guides. Sheffield: Sheffield Academic, 1996.

Trible, P. "A Human Comedy." In *God and the Rhetoric of Sexuality.* Philadelphia: Fortress, 1978.

1 AND 2 SAMUEL

[see pages 332–399 of the Old Testament]

Before Beginning . . .

The books that we call 1 and 2 Samuel were originally one book. The division into two was the work of those responsible for the Septuagint, the third-century BC Greek translation of the Hebrew Bible. Perhaps the translators thought it was necessary to make two shorter books out of one long one. The division was introduced into the Hebrew Bible in the sixteenth century AD and has become standard ever since. Ending 1 Samuel with the death of Saul seems to make sense until the reader realizes that this division breaks up the story of David's rise to the throne. The story of the succession to David, which begins in 2 Samuel 9 is interrupted by extraneous material in 2 Samuel 21–24 and is not completed until 1 Kings 1–2.

The books of Samuel are so named because the early rabbis believed the prophet wrote 1 Samuel 1–25. They held that the rest of 1 Samuel and the whole of 2 Samuel were the work of the prophets Nathan and Gad on the basis of 1 Chronicles 29:29. Modern scholarship ascribes the books of Samuel in their present form to the anonymous author of the Deuteronomistic History of Israel, which begins with the book of Joshua and continues through 2 Kings. Its purpose is not historiographic but homiletical. The story of Israel in its land is told to provide the people of Judah with hope for their future and a pattern for renewing their life in the land promised to their ancestors.

Reading through the Books of Samuel

The stories in the books of Samuel revolve around three characters: Samuel (1 Sm 1–25), Saul (1 Sm 9—2 Sam 2), and David (1 Sm 10—2 Sm 24). The stories of these three figures overlap and are supplemented with stories about the ark, Jerusalem, and other members of the royal family. Through most of 1 Samuel, the story moves toward the eventual accession of David to the throne of Israel. In 2 Samuel, the story describes the clear move toward religious and political centralization in Jerusalem. The books also reveal the political and religious opposition to the attempt to center all power in the Davidic dynasty and in Jerusalem. Of course, the move to establish a dynasty and concentrate all political power in the royal house had serious economic repercussions, and these too unfold in the book. The story of Israel as it establishes a monarchy is a fascinating tale of a social, political, and economic innovation, which could advance only by overcoming the religious restraints that flowed from the belief that the only king of Israel was the Lord. Finally, though the stories seem to focus on three great figures in Samuel, Saul, and David, there is an impressive list of characters—from David's wives to Saul's crippled grandson—who have critical roles in the story of Israel as it unfolds. In fact, the apparent "little people" affect the lives of the great personages of the books of Samuel in most critical ways. But it is important to remember that for the author of the Deuteronomistic History, Israel's life in its land is shaped not by human beings nor by political or economic forces. Israel, whether it is aware of it or not, is bound to fulfill God's purposes. Israel's God is *the* principal character in the story, even though God's action is sometimes subtle and unnoticed.

Samuel (1 Sm 1:1–8:22)

Samuel's Birth (1 Sm 1:1–2:10)

In one sense, the books of Samuel try to answer the question "Who is a legitimate leader in Israel?" At first, Samuel provides leadership for the tribes in an unprecedented way. He is a priest, prophet, and judge, and uniquely able to inform Israel of the Lord's will. He represents the perspective that sees God's presence in Israel as mediated by charismatic and prophetic individuals. The story of Samuel's conception and birth (1: 1–28) marks him as one whom God has chosen as an instrument. The book follows a familiar pattern to indicate Samuel's significance: he is born to a woman who had been thought of as infertile. The same motif was used to indicate the special role of Isaac (Gn 17:15–22), Jacob (Gn 25:19–28), Joseph (Gn 30:22–24), and Samson (Jgs 13:2–7). Like Samson, Samuel, it appears, was destined from birth to be a Nazirite (1 Sm 1: 11). The story of Hannah (1 Sm 1:1–2:11) is one of those brief episodes in which a supporting character plays a crucial role in the narrative. Samuel was born because God rewarded Hannah's persistence in praying for a child. Samuel entered God's service because of her gratitude. To conclude Hannah's story, the author of 1 Samuel inserted a poem whose theme is the reversal of fortunes brought about by the Lord in the lives of the faithful (2:1–10). Certainly, the poem's theme reflects Hannah's experience.

Samuel and the Sons of Eli (1 Sm 2:11–36)

The story of Samuel's career is introduced by contrasting him with the sons of Eli, the priest of Shiloh. That Samuel, rather than Eli's sons, succeeded the old priest required some explanation since the priesthood was a hereditary occupation. The answer is simple enough: Eli's sons were corrupt and abused their office to enrich themselves. The author of 1 Samuel skillfully weaves the indictment of Eli's sons (2:12–17, 22–25) with the reports about Samuel's growth to adulthood (2:1, 18–21, 26). The indictment of Eli's sons prepares the reader for the judgment on the house of Eli given by the unnamed "man of God." The oracle begins with a series of questions (2:27–29) that provide the basis for the judgment that is to follow. The man of God, then, announces God's judgment (2:30–34). The oracle concludes with the promise that God will raise a new priestly house, and Eli's descendants will be reduced to poverty (2:35–36). The fulfillment of this prophecy comes in two places. The immediate fulfillment comes in 1 Samuel 4:11 with the death of Eli's sons, and its final fulfillment is noted by 1 Kings 2:26–27 when Solomon exiles Abiathar and deprives him of the priesthood. The fulfillment of prophecy is another important motif in the story of Israel in its land.

The announcement of judgment against the house of Eli sets a pattern for understanding the story of Israel as a whole. The rehearsal of God's goodness toward Israel is followed by a listing of infidelities. The judgment makes clear the terrible consequences of infidelity—consequences that cannot be avoided. But judgment is not God's final word to Israel. Just as God raised up a new priestly dynasty to replace Eli's discredited family, so there is hope for Israel as a whole. The book offers a reason to expect God to restore Israel to the land that it lost because of its infidelity.

Samuel and Eli (1 Sm 3:1–4:1)

Samuel is no longer a child. It is time for him to begin his ministry on Israel's behalf. The book, however, first offers a final contrast between Samuel and the house of Eli in order to show that the role Samuel will play in the narratives to follow was sanctioned by God. Samuel's career began with an initial experience of the word of God while Samuel was in Shiloh at the shrine where the ark was kept. The book notes that such experiences were rare at the time. Though Samuel appeared unsure of himself, he did show himself to be receptive as he referred to himself as God's "servant" and asserted his willingness to obey. The message that Samuel receives is one that rehearses the condemnation of Eli's priestly dynasty in harsh and uncompromising terms. Eli accepted the verdict on his house, realizing that a new era in Israel's life was beginning. God's chosen means of communicating with Israel will be a prophet—the prophet Samuel. The book concludes the story of Samuel's call by noting that all Israel recognized Samuel's role in communicating God's word. It also affirms that God continued to speak to Samuel at Shiloh and that every word that Samuel announced came true.

In the chapters to follow, the focus will be on the fate of the ark. Samuel will not appear in the story until chapter 7. This is probably to dissociate him entirely from the reverses Israel will experience—especially the loss of the ark to the Philistines.

The Story of the Ark (1 Sm 4:2–7:1)

The ark was a unique element of ancient Israelite religious tradition. It served to represent the presence of God in a religion that did not allow an image of its deity to serve that purpose. But the tradition understands the immediate function of the ark differently. In some texts, it is simply a box that contained the two tablets of the Ten Commandments (Ex 25:22; Dt 10:3), but other traditions spoke of it as God's footstool or throne (1 Sm 4:4; Ps 99:5; 137:2; 1 Chr 28:2). In this section of 1 Samuel, however, the ark is a type of battle palladium accompanying the army of Israel as it fought against those who threatened its existence. It obviously symbolized the presence of God with the army. The first part of the ark's story describes its capture and return. The story will be taken up again when David brings the ark to Jerusalem (2 Sm 6).

The Philistines, who became the principal threat to Israel's existence, were intent on enlarging their holdings in Canaan. They controlled the area along the southern coast and were determined to expand their territory to the north and east. This move brought them into direct contact with Israel. The Philistine encampment at Aphek signaled their determination to act. After an initial defeat, the elders of Israel wondered about the cause and, thinking the ark could make a difference, they bring it to the battlefield from its shrine at Shiloh. The presence of the ark, however, did not prevent a second loss and the capture of the ark.

It is important to be aware that the numerical losses of the Israelites were not as staggering as the English text implies. In the first battle, Israel lost "four thousand men" and in the second, thirty thousand. The Hebrew word that is translated as "thousand" also represents a military unit that was relatively small—probably between five and twenty men. The book asserts that in the first battle, the Israelites lost the equivalent of four such units. In the second, they lost the equivalent of thirty such units. But, as the text makes clear, this loss was devastating nonetheless.

It is also important to note that the text does not blame the defeat of Israel on the sons of Eli, who accompanied the ark from Shiloh. The story of the ark contains no negative comments about Hophni, Phinehas, or their father, Eli, who died upon hearing the news of the disaster at Ebenezer. The first part of the ark's story ends with the naming of Phinehas's newborn child to memorialize the loss of the ark (4:19–22).

Both the Israelites and the Philistines expected Israel to be victorious at the battle of Ebenezer (4:4–9), but Israel suffered two crushing defeats plus the loss of the ark. To insure that readers would not draw the wrong theological conclusion from Israel's defeat, the book describes two great victories of the Lord over Dagon, the Philistine god. These two victories were mirror images of Israel's defeats, i.e., Dagon's second loss was more severe than the first. Dagon was a Mesopotamian deity imported into Canaan and honored as Baal's father. Dagon's attributes are unknown, but he is likely a fertility god since the Semitic root from which his name derives means "grain." This text asserts that there was a temple of Dagon at Ashdod, but excavations have not located one even though 1 Maccabees 10:83–84 provides evidence that Dagon was worshipped there into the second century BC. The Lord's victory over Dagon spread panic through the Philistine cities (1 Sm 4:3, 6, 11). No Philistine city wanted the ark because of all the devastation that it caused so the decision was made to return the ark to Israel.

The victory of the Lord is made all the more indisputable by the method the Philistines choose to return the ark. First, they return the ark with gifts (6:1–5). The golden hemorrhoids and mice were given as offerings to fend off additional plagues. But to be certain about the true origin of their troubles, the Philistines set up a test (6:7–9). Getting milk (milch) cows to overcome their maternal instincts, their lack of experience with pulling a cart, and having them arrive at a precise place would certainly indicate divine power. Of course, Israel's God passed the test, and the ark arrived back at Beth-shemesh, a town on the border of Philistine and Israelite territory. There was a sizable crowd to greet the ark on its return because the people were in the fields harvesting the wheat crop (6:10–13). A large stone in the field served as a substitute altar on which the milk cows were sacrificed (6:14) though normally only the males of the species were to be sacrificed (Lv 1:3; 22:19). The Philistine lords witnessed all this. The victory of Israel's God was complete.

The people of Beth-shemesh, however, did not want to keep the ark in their village, perhaps to avoid provoking the Philistines across the border. The village of Kiriath-jearim, which was a few miles farther east, accepted the ark, designating a certain Eleazar to care for it. The ark remained in that village until David brought it to Jerusalem (2 Sam 6).

Samuel and the Israelite Monarchy (1 Sm 7:2–8:22)

Samuel reenters the story as an adult who will have a special role in the establishment of the Israelite monarchy. While the book's attitude toward the monarchy is a bit ambiguous, it is clear from the story of Samuel's victory over the Philistines (7:2–17) that from a military point of view, the monarchy was unnecessary. If Israel would be absolutely loyal to the Lord, no enemy could do it much harm. The story begins with Israel's return to the exclusive service of the Lord after twenty years of Philistine domination, despite the ark's presence in Israel. The book makes it clear that the ark was no guarantee that Israel would live undisturbed in its land—only the exclusive service of the Lord will bring Israel peace.

Samuel assembled the Israelite militia at Mizpah in response to the people's desire to return to the Lord. The Philistine response to this provocation was an utter failure, and Israel's victory removed the stigma of the two defeats at this very battlefield (1 Sm 4:2–11) so Samuel renamed the place *Ebenezer,* i.e., "the stone of (God's) help." Israel remained free of Philistine domination under Samuel's leadership, making it appear unnecessary for Israel to choose a king as it would at Mizpah (1 Sm 10:17), the scene of the great victory inspired by Samuel. The book, then, emphasizes that it was Israel's repentance—not the presence of the ark or the leadership of a king—that would secure Israel's future. Of course, when the books of Samuel were written, Israel no longer had the ark nor a king. Its only course was to return to its ancestral deity.

The effort to establish a monarchy accelerated because of the corruption of Samuel's sons (8: 1–9). The people's request, however, angered Samuel who claimed that a king would not be an instrument of justice but of oppression (8: 10–18). The people adamantly insisted on having a king "like other nations" to fight their wars, so God told Samuel to honor their request. But for Samuel, the request for a king was tantamount to apostasy. After all, God had always defended a loyal Israel. Why would Israel want a king? Samuel warned the Israelites that their rejection of God would lead to God's refusal to answer them in time of need (8:18). They will have to depend on their king. This story, of course, reflects Israel's experience of the monarchy. It proved ineffective in preventing the disasters that eventually befell the two Israelite kingdoms. The book suggests that this outcome was, in some sense, determined by the people's sinful request for a king.

Saul (1 Sm 9:1–15:35)

Samuel and Saul Meet (1 Sm 9:1–10:16)

The story of Samuel's initial encounter with Saul, whom he eventually anointed king, knows nothing of the people's sinful request for a king. On the contrary, it presents Saul's rise to kingship very positively. Saul is a handsome man from a wealthy family, a good choice for a king. The book preserves this charming tale of a man who went looking for donkeys but found a kingdom in order to show that Saul was God's choice to be king and how he could have remained in God's good graces. But as Saul's story continues, the reader learns that the young man, endowed with so many gifts and blessed by the spirit of the Lord, squandered everything. This is the story of Israel in microcosm. Like Saul, Israel was blessed with many gifts but, in the end, it too squandered them all and found itself in exile. But will Israel's end be different from that of Saul?

The futile search for his family's donkeys led Saul to seek out a "man of God," who turned out to be Samuel. The revelation to Samuel about a "man of Benjamin" whom he would meet indicates that Saul was God's choice to be king, even though Samuel's message surprised Saul (9: 14–21). Another indication of the divine choice of Saul was the fulfillment of the signs that Samuel gave to Saul to confirm his new status. The third sign is the most significant because it promised that "the spirit of the LORD" was going to descend on Saul. This gift, of course, will enable him to do extraordinary deeds in saving Israel from its enemies (10:1, 6). Upon returning home with his family's donkeys, Saul said nothing about his peculiar encounter with Samuel. This detail is necessary to make a smooth connection with the following story that describes Saul's public acclamation as king.

A positive attitude toward Saul as king continues in the story of his public acclamation (10: 17–27). Still, there are features in the story that reflect the book's overall discomfort with the monarchy as an institution. First, Samuel assembled the people at Mizpah—the very place where he had shown that a king was unnecessary since God will always protect a repentant and loyal people (10:17; see 1 Sm 7:2–12). Second, Samuel, speaking in the name of God, asserted that the request for a king was another of Israel's actions rejecting their God, who had proved in the Exodus and in other situations to be a savior beyond compare (10:18–19). Still, by using lots to select the king, Samuel demonstrates the choice of Saul was God's. The people, impressed by Saul's bearing, acclaim him as their king. Samuel then committed the laws governing the new institution to writing and dismissed the people. There were a few people, whom the text characterizes as "worthless" (10:27), who did not support the choice of Saul. To do so, however, involved questioning the choice that God had made.

The story of Saul's public acclamation is another instance of the book's ambiguity about the establishment of the monarchy in Israel. While the story presents Saul as God's choice to be king, it also presents Israel's choice to have a king as sinful. This ambivalence is not only a theological issue; it is also a literary technique that builds up suspense in the story. Can this paradox be resolved? Can the monarchy be something that contributes positively to maintaining Israel's relationship with God? Or is it only a matter of time before the monarchy's doom becomes apparent? How can Israel reject God as its savior and still expect to survive?

The "worthless men" who did not support Saul are the only connection between the story of Saul's choice by lots (10:17–27) and the story that follows (11:1–15). The story of Saul's victory over the Ammonites is the high point of the Saul cycle. Here his kingship differs little from the pattern of leadership represented by the judges. He rallies all Israel to follow him in lifting the oppression brought to bear on Jabesh-gilead, a town east of the Jordan that was threatened by Ammonites, who were expanding their holdings to the north. The victory of the Israelite militia led by Saul was total. Saul proved to be magnanimous in victory as he spared the lives of the "worthless men" who opposed his accession (11:14). Saul was then proclaimed king at the old tribal shrine at Gilgal. Saul shows what the kings of Israel should have been: the saviors of the oppressed. Unfortunately, Saul and most of his successors proved to be more obsessed with their power than with the good of the people.

The book's final reflections on the rise of the Israelite monarchy appear in chapter 12. In chapter 7 the book already showed that Israel could have gotten along very well with the Lord as its only king. Still, God acceded to the people's wishes, so having a king should have been compatible with Israel's commitment to its God. Indeed, the book does treat Saul favorably (9:1–11:15). That God chose Saul to be king of Israel was underscored in several ways: through the anointing, the empowerment by the spirit of the Lord, the lot oracle, the prophetic designation, the popular acclamation, the victory over the Ammonites—even by Saul's pardoning of those who opposed his accession. Samuel's presence lent credibility to the establishment of the Israelite monarchy. At the same time, the book showed less than complete support for kingship by noting that Samuel was able to keep the Philistines in check for twenty years, implying that no king was needed to defend Israel. Samuel also points out the negative social and economic impact the monarchic system will have on Israel. Finally, Samuel twice characterizes the request for a king as apostasy. But despite all this, God commanded Samuel to give in to Israel's request.

The book goes over this ground one more time in chapter 12. Samuel's address to Israel begins with a legal argument showing that both God and Samuel were blameless in the process that led up to Saul becoming king. Israel's future under its kings depends on its commitment to observe the Lord's commands (12:14). When it rains during the dry season, the people see in this unusual occurrence additional proof that God and Samuel bear no responsibility for what will happen to Israel under its kings. The people also admit that their request for a king was sinful. But God has chosen not to abandon Israel. Samuel will be with the people to pray for them and to teach them. The implication is that as long as the people obey the prophets sent to them, God will bless them. The quality of Israel's life under its kings depends on Israel's obedience. Those who first read 1 Samuel knew that Israel and its kings failed, so the judgment that came upon the people was the fulfillment of the words spoken to Israel by Samuel as it began its life under a king.

Saul Defeats the Philistines
(1 Sm 13:1–14:52)

Saul's reign began well enough, at least from a military point of view. Saul maintained a small army, while allowing the bulk of the Israelite militia to return to their homes. After either Saul (13:4) or his son Jonathan (13:3) attacked a Philistine outpost not far from Saul's own town, both sides prepared for war. 1 Samuel 14:1–21 describes the Israelite success in that war. That success came despite the Philistines' numerical (13:5) and technological superiority (13:19–22). The reason for the latter was the ability of the Philistines to forge iron. The Israelites had to make do with the less-effective bronze for their tools and weapons. The average Israelite farmer could not pay the price that the Philistine charged for iron agricultural implements—much less for iron weapons. Of the Israelite forces only Saul and Jonathan had iron swords and spears. The book, of course, implies that only a miracle could have enabled Israel to defeat the Philistines.

In the midst of the story about Saul's successful war against the Philistines, the book relates an ominous incident that took place at the tribal sanctuary at Gilgal (13:7b–15). Because Samuel was late in arriving at Gilgal, Saul offered a sacrifice there as a prelude to the attack on the Philistines. Samuel regarded this as an offense that led God to reject Saul in favor of "a man after [God's] own heart" (13:14), whom the reader knows to be David. The book does not specify the precise nature of Saul's offense, but Samuel regarded it as some sort of an unlawful usurpation on Saul's part. It was so serious that it ended all prospects of a Saulide dynasty.

The Philistines decided to fight the battle at Michmash, a town just nine miles northeast of Jerusalem and just over a mile east of Geba, Saul's village. Michmash was located in a canyon that was impassable on the east, so it was a good place for the Philistines to mass their troops in anticipation of an Israelite attack. That attack was led by Jonathan (14:1–14), who did not inform Saul of his plans. When Saul heard the sound of battle, his reaction was strangely indecisive. First, he sought an oracle to determine if the Israelite army should attack, but then he stopped the process before it was completed and attacked. When the Philistines began their retreat, Saul let piety overcome his military sense. He ordered his men to fast until the victory over the Philistines was consolidated. The hungry troops not only disobeyed but ate meat that had not been properly drained of its blood (see Dt 12:23). Jonathan, too, ate, but he ate some honey without knowing that his father had pronounced a curse on anyone who ate before the victory was complete.

When Saul heard about his soldiers' disregard of his orders, he had a ritual performed to deflect the curse on those who had eaten the meat. Then Saul sought another oracle to determine if he should continue pursuing the Philistines. When no answer was forthcoming, Saul concluded that someone had sinned, and he was determined to execute that person even if it were his son. To determine the guilty party Saul uses the lot oracle (the *urim* and *thummim;* see Dt 33:8). Though Jonathan's guilt is discovered, the army prevented Saul from taking Jonathan's life. Saul did not continue his pursuit of the retreating Philistines. The book then appends a short notice (14: 47–52) that summarizes Saul's many battles to make it clear that God was faithful to the promise made to Samuel as reported in 1 Samuel 9:16.

Saul and the Amalekites (1 Sm 15:1–34)

Here is the book's final word on Saul's kingship. It simply comments that God "regretted" having made Saul king (vv. 10–35). This verdict on Saul comes after another act that Samuel regards as disobedient. Saul and his army were to take no booty from the Amalekites, whom the tradition remembered as violently opposing the entrance of the Israelite tribes into Canaan (Ex 17:8–13; Dt 25:17–18). When confronted by his disobedience, Saul did confess and ask for pardon, but it was too late. The prophet and the king never saw each other again alive. Samuel mourned for Saul, but God was determined to give the kingdom to another. The story of Saul describes the power of human choice. Though God selected Saul to be king, Saul was able to annul that choice by his failures. Again, this is precisely what Israel did by its disobedience.

David (1 Sm 16:1–31:13)

Saul and David Meet (1 Sm 16:1–23)

The book does not hesitate to enumerate the schemes that David contrived to become king: his political moves, his marriages, and his career as a guerrilla and as a Philistine mercenary. None of this is particularly flattering to David. Despite this, the book affirms that David was God's chosen. Samuel would have anointed another of Jesse's sons, but David was God's sovereign choice, and the anointing served to commit God to David. This commitment was confirmed by the spirit of the Lord that seized David and never departed from him. But Saul, deserted by the spirit of the Lord, is a broken man, afflicted by melancholy. In a supreme irony, the old king had to look for relief from his rival for the throne. Saul's servants brought David to the court to deal with their master's moods, but the reader recognizes that their description of David makes him overqualified to be simply a musician.

David and Goliath (1 Sm 17:1–18:5)

The story of David and Goliath stands as a paradigm of what a person of faith can accomplish. Clearly the book wants the Jewish exiles to identify with the young David, whose words and deeds testify that it was God who brought down the Philistine giant. The story also underscores David's credentials for leadership, which even Saul recognized since he appointed David to a permanent military command, not realizing that he was paving the way for his successor. Jonathan's gift of his own clothes and weapons to David makes it appear that Saul's son is divesting himself of the right of succession in favor of his new friend, the son of Jesse. The book's rush of enthusiasm in narrating this great story led to an obvious anachronism. According to verse 35, David brought Goliath's head to Jerusalem, but that city was still in Canaanite hands and remained so until David captured it and made it his capital (see 2 Sm 5:6–10).

Saul's Jealousy (1 Sm 18:6–30)

Saul had good reason to be jealous of David. Not only did the people love him but so did Jonathan and Michal, Saul's children. But no matter how Saul tried to eliminate his rival, David's popularity continued to grow. Saul tried to kill David twice (v. 11), but eventually realized that David's success was divinely ordered (vv. 14–15). Saul suggested that David marry his eldest daughter. David was thrilled at the prospect of marrying into Saul's family, but Saul married her off to someone else. Recognizing David's eagerness, Saul offered David another daughter if he was willing to pay a bride-price that exposed him to great danger. But David accomplished the task, outperforming Saul's servants. When he saw how the people held David in high regard, Saul's reaction was fear and hatred.

David the Fugitive (1 Sm 19:1–28:2)

Saul became so obsessed with David's success that he tried to kill him. David had to flee Saul's court and take up the life of a fugitive. Coming to David's aid is an unlikely group of supporters that range from Saul's own children to the Philistines, Israel's rival for control of Canaan. In telling the story of David's life on the run, the book sees God's hand protecting David from Saul and leading the young shepherd boy inexorably to the throne of Israel.

David's successes and popular acclaim triggered Saul's first attempts on David's life, but these were unsuccessful (1 Sm 19:1–24). First, Jonathan talked Saul out of killing David (vv. 1–7). After another one of David's military victories over the Philistines, Saul could not control his hatred and made another attempt on David's life, but the latter's dexterity saved him (vv. 8–10). Michal, Saul's daughter and David's wife, prevented a third attempt from being successful (vv. 11–17). Finally, David fled to Samuel. Saul found him but a prophetic ecstasy, which once confirmed Saul's kingship (1 Sm 10:5–12), now made possible David's escape (1 Sm 19:24). The reader is meant to recognize the hand of God in David's escapes.

Though Jonathan was loyal to his father, he nonetheless recognized the injustice of Saul's intentions toward David (1 Sm 20:1–21:1). The story of Jonathan is a story marked by conflicting emotions as Jonathan has to stand up to Saul in order to protect David. Saul's anger led him to hurl a demeaning insult at Jonathan and his mother (v. 30). The book underscores David's innocence in all this by having different characters affirm it three times (vv. 1, 8–9, 32). The irony surrounding David's rise to kingship continues as he depends on Jonathan, the presumptive heir to Saul's throne, to insure his safety. But by saving David, Jonathan is, in effect, denying himself the throne and his father a dynasty. Although the book does not say so explicitly, the reader knows that God is guiding the events that will eventually bring David to the throne.

Jonathan, Samuel, and Michal were not the only members of Saul's entourage to help David escape from Saul. While Jonathan and Michal consciously decided to help David, Ahimelech, a priest from a sanctuary near Saul's town, was duped by David into providing him with food and a weapon (1 Sm 21:2–10). Unfortunately for Ahimelech, Doeg, an Edomite in Saul's service, witnessed the exchange between David and Ahimelech, but the consequences of that will be clear only in 1 Samuel 22:6–23. But the book shows the ever-widening circle of those who assisted David. In his desperation David even sought refuge in Gath, a Philistine city that was home to Goliath. But David was unable to remain incognito. He feigned lunacy, and the Philistine king fell for David's act (1 Sm 21: 11–16). David will eventually join the Philistine army (27), but the book makes it clear here that David's actions were not treasonous but were motivated by his need to escape Saul's murderous intentions.

To survive on the run David sought safety in numbers. His family joined him as he assembled a force of 400 men. Evidently, even the king of Moab was among David's supporters since the king agreed to protect members of David's family. Other help came from the prophet Gad, who advised David to seek a haven in the territory of Judah. Saul, on the other hand, massacred a group of priests that had supported his rival. Saul was now almost completely isolated. His son, daughter, the priests of Nob, and even his fellow Benjaminites were giving passive and often active support to David. In addition to all these people, Saul's atrocity at Nob drove Abiathar, the sole surviving priest, into David's camp (1 Sm 22:1–23).

What the book implied in its accounts of David's flight from Saul, it now states explicitly in verse 14: God did not surrender David into Saul's hands. To illustrate this the book relates two of David's narrow escapes. One of these follows David's defeat of the Philistines who were raiding the Judahite town of Keilah. When Saul heard that David came to the town's defense, he saw that this afforded him the opportunity to finally capture his rival. In reversal of the usual pattern, Saul found people who were willing to betray David. But David, through divination, learned of Saul's intention and escaped. David was betrayed by the Ziphites, who also belonged to the tribe of Judah, but before Saul could act on the intelligence they provided, he had to deal with a new Philistine threat. Sandwiched between these two stories of treachery by David's fellow Judahites is another account of a Benjaminite—indeed Saul's own son and heir—declaring support for David. Jonathan had more to lose than anyone as a result of David's rise to power, but he acted in accordance with what the book presents as the will of God (1 Sm 23:1–28).

The tables turn and David has an opportunity to kill Saul, his antagonist, but he refuses to raise his hand against the old king (1 Sm 24:1–23). This story of David's refusal to kill Saul when he had the opportunity is a fine piece of political propaganda. The story puts David in an extremely good light and serves to legitimate his eventual ascent to Israel's throne. Indeed, even Saul recognized that David should be king. The story also serves to put a positive spin on actions that David will take to neutralize any claims to the throne that Saul's descendants might make. The implication here is clear: David was entirely blameless in the matter of the succession. The book, however, uses this story to underscore the role that God had in David's rise to kingship.

Between two accounts that make David appear reluctant to take the throne forcibly, there is one that shows him to be taking steps that make him Saul's successor nonetheless. One of these steps involves marrying a woman from an influential Judahite family (1 Sm 25:1–41). But before the story of David and Abigail begins, the book notes the passing of Samuel, who has had no significant role in the narratives for a while. Before the book can have Saul conjure up the spirit of Samuel (28), it is necessary that Samuel die.

One of the anomalies of the story of David's rise is the treachery of people from David's own tribe. Nabal is another Judahite who was simply not impressed with David and refused to help him. Abigail, Nabal's wife, persuaded David not to take any reprisals on her husband. When Nabal died, David immediately proposed marriage to Abigail. It will not be the first time that David will marry a woman from an influential family, who had previously been married to another. David clearly saw such marriages as helping to solve the problems he had been having with certain elements from Judah. The marriage to Abigail gave David new status in Judah.

For a second time, it was possible for David to kill Saul, and again he refused to do so (1 Sm 26:1–25). The Lord would choose the time and circumstances of Saul's death. David upbraided Abner, Saul's general, for the lax security that gave David the opportunity to assassinate Saul. Although Saul was grateful to David, there was no reconciliation between the two, and this was the last time the two would meet. Saul's final words to David are a blessing and a prediction of David's ultimate success.

Saul's pursuit of David was relentless despite what appeared to be reconciliation between the two in chapters 24 and 26. Ironically, the only place David was safe from Saul was with Israel's implacable enemies, the Philistines (1 Sm 27:1–28:2). David lied his way into the trust of Achish, who once thought him mad. David claimed to have been raiding Judahite settlements while all the time raiding those of other peoples. David was put in a very awkward position when Achish announced that a raid on Israel was in the offing. He had to assure Achish of his loyalty.

Saul's Tragic Death (1 Sm 28:3–2 Sm 1:27)

Saul went out to meet the Philistines one last time. The place of this final confrontation was a town near Mount Gilboa, which overlooks the Jezreel Valley. The king was terrified at the prospect of having to face the Philistines again. He consulted the Lord but received no answer. He thought to consult Samuel, who had died earlier. To do so he had to engage a specialist in conjuring the spirit of the deceased—something forbidden to Israel (see Dt 18:11). The prophet's spirit did not give the king good news: the Israelite army would be defeated. Saul's fate is sealed.

David was saved from having to fight against Saul and the Israelites because not all the Philistines trusted him. Achish allowed David to engage in raiding the Amalekites, another of Israel's traditional enemies (1 Sm 29:1–30:31). The story of David's conduct during these raids stands in contrast to Saul's impotence before the Philistines: David was courageous in battle; he was fair and even generous with his soldiers; he defended the Israelites who fell victim to Amalekite power; above all, he was victorious. David's victories over the Amalekites coupled with Saul's impending loss to the Philistines showed that God was behind David's rise to power.

The book relates the end of Saul with dignity and sympathy (1 Sm 31:1–13). Saul died doing his duty as king. Though he knew that defeat was inevitable, Saul fought bravely and died by his own hand to insure that the Philistines would be deprived of making sport of him. They did, however, hang his corpse and that of Jonathan from the walls of Beth-shan, a city near Mount Gilboa. This afforded the people of Jabesh-gilead an opportunity to repay the favor that Saul did for them in better times. They took the bodies off the city wall, transported them to Jabesh, buried them, and then began a period of mourning for their one-time benefactor.

Transitions of power in the ancient Near East were rarely smooth. Palace revolts and assassinations occurred with some frequency. The book wishes to end any rumors about David's role in Saul's death, so it portrays David as deeply affected by the deaths of Saul and Jonathan (2 Sm 1:1–27). The Amalekite confessed to Saul's murder though the reader knows that the Amalekite is lying—perhaps to ingratiate himself with David. Still, David acted on the only information he had and ordered the confessed regicide to be executed. While David came into possession of the royal insignia (v. 10), he did so without any foul play on his part. The poem lamenting the tragic deaths of Saul and Jonathan, which the book places on David's lips, came from a now-lost collection called the "Book of the Just" (see also Jos 10:13). It shows that in some quarters, the memory of Saul and Jonathan was cherished. The book has David recite these poignantly beautiful lines to demonstrate David's innocence in Saul's death.

David Becomes King (2 Sm 2:1–5:25)

Saul's end was sad and tragic, but the reader has a sense of relief that David has survived both Saul and the Philistines. He is now in a position to claim the kingship for which he was anointed by Samuel. Still, it will be several years before David's position over all Israel will become secure. While David had no trouble being recognized as king in Judah (2 Sm 2:4), his position with regard to the other tribes was a different matter. Though Abner, Saul's general, placed Ishbaal, Saul's surviving son, on the throne, Ishbaal proved incompetent. This paved the way for David's rule over all the tribes. David consolidated his rule by taking Jerusalem and making it his political capital as well as Israel's religious center.

Although the book implies that a united Israel under one king was the ideal, it is clear from the story of the war between Israel and Judah in 2 Samuel 2:12–3:1 and subsequent stories that there were strong political differences and intense rivalry between Israel and Judah. Even a common language, religion, and culture could not overcome these differences. For most of their history, Israel and Judah were political opponents, each establishing its own national state. The story of this rivalry is told from a southern perspective. Also, the story of the civil war between the supporters of Ishbaal and David is a necessary prelude to the actions that Solomon will take in assuring his succession to David (see 1 Kgs 2:23–33).

The list of David's children (2 Sm 3:2–5) inserted in the account of David's struggle over the succession to Saul is important because it introduces characters who will have significant roles in the story of Solomon's succession. Amnon, Absalom, and Adonijah each had a better claim on the succession than Solomon. But it is Solomon who would follow David on the throne.

The book describes in some detail the political maneuvers that were necessary to secure the kingship for David (2 Sm 3:6–4:12). A rival king and his military supporters have to be eliminated, so both Abner and Ishbaal are killed. The story absolves David from any complicity in these acts, but the waters are becoming murkier. David is no longer the simple shepherd boy who saved Israel with his slingshot. The book makes it obvious that with the monarchy come intrigues, double-dealing, even murders, which are inevitable consequences of the quest for power. While the story of David's rise to kingship is not an antimonarchic tract, the book lays bare more of the consequences of Israel's decision to have a human lord in place of its Divine Lord.

Once Ishbaal was assassinated, the elders of Israel bowed to the inevitable and accepted David as king. The newly acclaimed king then moved to eliminate the one tract of land that still separated Judah from the Israelite tribes in the north. David captured Jerusalem and made it his capital. The book pauses in its story to assert that all this happened because God was with David (5:1–12), but then it returns to the actions that David took to solidify his hold on the throne. One of these was to marry women from Jerusalem and thereby gain sympathy from its citizens (5:13–16).

Another practical step in David's solidifying his rule over Israel is his ending the Philistine domination of Canaan (5:17–25). David freed Israel from the Philistine threat while Saul failed to do so (see 1 Sm 9:16; 2 Sm 3:18). Of course, the victory over the Philistines really belonged to God who gave David the victory (2 Sm 5: 19,24)—another indication that David was God's choice to be king. The book suggests that David's victory was so overwhelming that the battlefield was named Baal-perazim, which can be translated "the Lord of the raging flood" (2 Sm 5:20; see Is 28:21).

The Ark in Jerusalem (2 Sm 6:1–23)

The final step in marking the legitimacy of David's accession to kingship was the transfer of the ark. Michal's negative reaction to David's dancing before the ark suggests the displacement of Saul's family by that of David. The housing of the ark in David's city underscores the centralizing tendencies of the monarchy, which appropriates all political, military, and religious authority to itself. This attempt to make human authority absolute will ultimately lead to the undoing of the monarchy and the national state.

Temple and Dynasty (2 Sm 7:1–29)

In the ancient Near East, the building of a temple for a nation's patron deity was a royal prerogative. Another way that David sought to legitimate his accession to Israel's throne was to build a temple for Israel's God. The book shapes its account to make two important points. The first is that a temple was not an absolute necessity in ancient Israel's religion (2 Sm 7:5–7). The second was that God was going to establish a "house" (a dynasty) for David that would endure forever (2 Sm 7:16). That a prophet makes this promise in God's name marks it as authoritative (vv. 4–5). It is important to note that the promise places limits on royal authority. There are obligations that the king must fulfill (v. 14; see also Ps 89: 30–32). But failure on the king's part will not nullify the promises (vv. 15–16). While a temple was built and David's dynasty did rule for four hundred years, both came to inglorious ends in the sixth century. Eventually the Temple was rebuilt but under the patronage of a foreign dynasty (see Ezr 1:1–4, 5–6). The Davidic dynasty was never restored to rule.

A member of the Davidic family ruled over the Kingdom of Judah throughout its history, except for the six years of Athaliah's reign (2 Kgs 11), and the books of Kings allude to 2 Samuel 7 and its promises several times (1 Kgs 2:4; 8:20, 25; 9:4–5; 11:5, 13, 32, 36; 15:4; 2 Kgs 8:19; 19:34; 20:6). But the storied stability of the Davidic dynasty is an illusion. Of the twenty-one kings that succeeded to David's throne, five were assassinated, three were taken into exile, three died during sieges, and one died in battle. Five kings ruled for periods of less than three years. Most ruled by the favor of imperial powers, and at least two were placed on the throne by such powers. The kings of the Davidic dynasty were unable to stave off the disaster that came to all of the small national states in the Levant once the revived Mesopotamian empires implemented their expansionist policies. The books of Kings, however, suggest that the fall of both Israelite kingdoms was due to the religious failures of the kings who ruled over them. While finding some fault with most of Judah's kings, the books of Kings lay the principal blame on Manasseh (2 Kgs 21:8–9; 2 Kgs 23:26–27). The collective failure of the Davidic dynasty makes the promises made to David in 2 Samuel 7 a poignant reminder of what should have been. The story of Judah's kings is the story of Israel. What began with so much promise ends tragically.

The Babylonians deposed Zedekiah, the last king of David's line, in 587 BC, and David's house was destined never to rise again. Still, there were some who believed that Israel's future was, in some way, tied to the destiny of the Davidic dynasty. The prayer of David (2 Sm 7:18–29) and Psalms 2; 89; and 132 reflect their views. In fact, Psalm 89:4 and 2 Samuel 23:5 likely have 2 Samuel 7 in mind when they speak of a "covenant" that God made with David. The Davidic covenant is similar to "covenants of royal grant" in which ancient Near Eastern kings rewarded individuals who served them loyally. It is also similar to the covenant made with Abraham (Gn 15:7–20; 17:1–8) in which God promises Abraham a land and descendants. But the Davidic stands in some tension with the Mosaic covenant, which depends upon Israel's obedience for its durability. There are texts, however, which attempt to make the promises to David conditional, e.g., 1 Kgs 2:4; 8:25; 9:4–5; Ps 132:12. The Scriptures preserve both the Mosaic and Davidic covenants, and the two should be seen as complementary. The former emphasizes human responsibility and the latter divine constancy.

The fall of Jerusalem, the end of the Judahite state, and the deposition of the Davidic dynasty led to a reinterpretation of the promise that there would always be a descendant of David ruling from his throne (v. 16; see Is 55:3–5), but Zerubbabel's connection with the Davidic family (1 Chr 3:16–19) led some Jews to look for an imminent restoration of the native dynasty (see Hg 2:2–23; Zec 3:8; 4:7) following the return from Babylon. The Persians did not permit this to happen, yet there remained some Jews who did expect an eventual restoration of the dynasty (see Jer 33:14–26; Ez 37:24–25). Such hopes could not be sustained for too long, and the restoration of the Davidic dynasty became a feature of Jewish eschatological hopes. Clearly, the promises made to David were not fulfilled in a satisfactory way following the exile. Since these promises had to find fulfillment, that fulfillment would come in the future. These developed into early Jewish hopes for a "messiah." While such hopes were not prominent in early Jewish literature, renewed interest in the promises made to David did reemerge in the first century BC. The Davidic messiah is an important figure in the Dead Sea Scrolls. The New Testament exploits this expectation as it presents Jesus as the one who will inherit the throne of "David his father" (Lk 1:32). Indeed, the Gospels refer to Jesus as "the son of David" almost twenty times.

David's Kingdom and Its Administration (2 Sm 8:1–18)

The book notes that David did not limit his rule to the territories given to the Israelite tribes. David mounted expeditions to extend the borders of his kingdom. Not content with limiting his role to protecting the people of Israel from external threats, David engaged in the type of expansionist militarism to which Israel and Judah would eventually fall victim. But because David was God's chosen, he was victorious (2 Sm 8:14b). David needed people to assist him in the administration of his kingdom. The list in 2 Samuel 8:15–18 names those who assisted David in the military and religious spheres. Though David's sons take the role of priests, eventually Levites were recognized as the sole legitimate priests; when the Chronicler gives his list of David's administrators, he calls David's sons his "chief assistants" rather than "priests" (see 1 Chr 18:17).

David's Family and the Succession (2 Sm 9:1–20:26)

The rise of David to kingship appeared to be unstoppable, but the book notes that holding on to the throne and selecting a successor were entirely different matters. Scattered throughout the story of David's rise were assurances that all happened because of God's actions. In the story of the succession to David, God is mentioned infrequently. The book shows what kind of an institution the monarchy really was, making it clear why, in the end, the monarchy failed Israel.

The story of the succession begins with David

inquiring if any of Saul's family were still alive. While David feigned concern to fulfill his commitment to Jonathan, he effectively placed a claimant to the throne and his family under house arrest (2 Sm 9:1–13). David thus blunted any opposition that might have sought to use the disabled Meribbaal to rally against him. The war with the Ammonites and Arameans provided the framework for another of David's attempts to secure his throne more firmly. His strategy was to marry a woman who belonged to an influential family. This is the third such marriage of David (see 1 Sm 18:20–27; 1 Sm 25). The story seemingly makes it appear as if David's encounter with Bathsheba was fortuitous, but the attentive reader recognizes a pattern in David's marriages. David married women who could help him gain and hold onto power. Bathsheba's grandfather Ahithophel was one of David's key advisers (2 Sm 16:23), and her father, Eliam, was an important military commander (2 Sm 23:34). The book implies that David knew exactly who Bathsheba was. He did not hesitate to use his royal power to have Bathsheba's husband eliminated so that he, David, could marry her (2 Sm 11: 2–27).

The book then transforms a tale of adultery and murder into a homily on repentance (2 Sm 12: 1–15). The prophet Nathan appeared before the king without being summoned to announce God's verdict on David's actions. The confrontation led to David's repentance so that the sentence of death was not imposed on him. The book wants to lead its readers to conclude that if they too listened to the prophets sent to them, their lives will be spared as well. David here becomes a model of repentance. Still, the power of evil that David unleashed by his sins led to the death of Bathsheba's newborn (12:16–23). In time, Bathsheba bore David a son, who eventually would succeed his father as king. Bathsheba named her son Solomon, while Nathan named him Jedidiah (2 Sam 12:24–25). The reason for the prophet's action is unclear since parents were responsible for naming their child. Jedidiah means "beloved of the LORD" and may signal God's choice of Solomon as David's successor. With the story of David and Bathsheba concluded for the present, the book remarks that the war against Ammon was successful (2 Sm 12: 26–31).

David's adultery with Bathsheba and his murder of Uriah meant that David and his family would have the specter of sexual excess and murder hanging over their lives for a long time to come. The first to fall victim were David's eldest son, Amnon, and Tamar, his half-sister. Amnon's attraction to his sister led him to rape her (2 Sm 13:1–21). While appalled at his son's crime, David did not punish Amnon. The disconsolate Tamar moved in with Absalom, her full-brother. Nothing more is heard of her. Absalom, however, brooded over his sister's fate for two years. When the opportunity presented itself, Absalom had Amnon murdered. Absalom then found sanctuary in Geshur, which was located in the southern part of the area now known as the Golan Heights. His maternal grandfather was king there (2 Sm 13:23–37; see 2 Sm 3:3).

Eventually Joab, David's nephew and general, was able to effect a reconciliation between David and Absalom, enabling Absalom to return from exile (2 Sm 14:1–33). Absalom was impatient with the pace of his rehabilitation, and it is clear that no genuine reconciliation between father and son took place. Absalom was still harboring grudges. This led the son to take advantage of those who expressed dissatisfaction with David's rule (2 Sm 15:1–6). Absalom's intrigues led to a full-blown revolution, which almost succeeded (2 Sm 15:7–12). David had to flee for his life, but he had the presence of mind to instruct his priests to remain in Jerusalem to bring him news of how the rebellion was progressing and to have his friend Hushai infiltrate Absalom's retinue. Another supporter was Ziba, one of Meribbaal's servants, who provided David with supplies and informed him that Meribbaal had designs on the throne (2 Sm 16:1–4). During this retreat from Jerusalem, David met Shimei, one of Saul's supporters, who assured him that the rebellion was just what David deserved for usurping Saul's throne (2 Sm 16:5–14).

Upon entering Jerusalem, Absalom dramatized his break with his father in a most decisive way. He had sexual intercourse with David's concubines in full view of the people, fulfilling the curse on David pronounced by Nathan in God's name (2 Sm 12:11–12). Ahithophel, one of David's counselors who went over to Absalom, advised quick action against the retreating David. Hushai, David's spy in Absalom's retinue, bought David time by suggesting that Absalom assemble a large force from all the tribes to deal with David. Absalom took Hushai's advice. Here is one instance where the book calls the reader's attention to the divine hand ordering events. It asserts that God prevented Absalom from taking Ahithophel's advice (2 Sm 17:14b). David used the time bought by Hushai to prepare a successful counterattack. Absalom fled but was caught by David's troops and killed by his cousin Joab, who countermanded David's express orders that Absalom be spared. David's obvious grief over Absalom disconcerted his soldiers who risked their lives in putting down Absalom's rebellion. David regained his composure and met with his army (2 Sm 16:20–19:9).

The book, however, does not have David's difficulties end with the collapse of Absalom's rebellion. David had to encourage members of Judah, his own tribe, to welcome him back as king. He had to deal with Shimei who cursed him and Meribbaal who sought to take advantage of the rebellion. He spared both. David wanted to reward Barzillai's kindness, but the latter demurred. As a result of having to face an uprising led by his own son, David realized that he owed this throne to the people and their support (2 Sm 19:23b).

Tensions among the tribes continued, presaging a split that would occur following the death of Solomon (1 Kgs 12). A more immediate consequence of this tension is a second revolt against David. Amasa, who had been a leader of the revolt that Absalom fomented, was rehabilitated by David, who charged him with putting down a second revolt led by Sheba of Benjamin, Saul's tribe. When Amasa dawdled, Joab quickly moved in, killing Amasa and leading David's forces against Sheba, who took refuge in Abel Beth-maacah, a city in the north. The revolution ended when a woman of Abel Beth-maacah persuaded the people of the town to hand over the revolutionary (2 Sm 19:41–20:22).

A list of David's principal officials concludes the story of David's problems in maintaining his position as king. There were two military officials: Joab, who commanded the Israelite army, and Banaiah, who led the mercenary forces. There were two civil magistrates, Shawsha and Jehoshaphat, and two priests, Zadok and Abiathar. Adoram oversaw the prisoners of war who had to do forced labor. The duties of Ira as David's priest are unknown (2 Sm 20:23–26).

Miscellaneous Material (2 Sm 21:1–24:25)

The story of David's reign is interrupted by six appendices arranged in a chiasm:

A . A famine (21:1–14)
B . Military Exploits (21:5–22)
C . David's hymn of victory (22:1–51)
C'. David's final hymn (23:1–7)
B'. Military Exploits (23:8–39)
A'. A plague (24:1–25)

The lack of a river system to provide for irrigation made ancient Israel particularly vulnerable to famine when rainfall was not sufficient. The book describes one such famine, which was ascribed to the failure by members of Saul's family to honor the covenant between Israel and Gibeon (see Jos 9). David allowed the Gibeonites to take their revenge on Saul's family (2 Sm 21:1–11). The famine ended when David provided an honorable burial for Saul and Jonathan (2 Sm 21:12–14).

The second component of the supplementary material is difficult to square with 1 Samuel 17, which describes the young David's defeat of Goliath. 2 Samuel 21:15–19 asserts that Goliath was killed by one of David's soldiers—a certain Elhanan—while one of David's brothers is credited with killing another formidable Philistine warrior (2 Sm 21:20–22). One attempt at harmonizing 1 Samuel 17 and 2 Samuel 21 suggests that David and Elhanan were the same person. Elhanan supposedly took the name "David" upon taking the throne of Israel. A second alternative assumes that David killed a Philistine whose name was not preserved. David's anonymous foe was then confused with Goliath whom Elhanan killed. While both solve the problem, neither has any support in the biblical text. Following the account of Israel's victories over the Philistines, the book inserts a hymn of victory that David composed. It is virtually identical to Psalm 18. Verses 21–25 assert that it was David's obedience that led to his victories—a perspective that resonated with the views of 2 Samuel.

The poetic "last words of David" (2 Sm 23:1–7) are really a theological commentary on David and his dynasty that emphasize the importance of justice and devotion to God (v. 3). These will lead to God's blessings on the dynasty. Those who ignore the demands of justice are doomed (vv. 6–7). David's rule as king did not depend on his virtue alone but on the support of many people. Some of these are mentioned by name in 2 Samuel 23:8–39. Ironically, the last person on the list is Uriah. His loyalty was not reciprocated by David—something that the reader knows without being told.

The last episode in 2 Samuel describes another natural disaster: a plague (2 Sm 24). David is blamed for bringing it about by taking a census of the people. The census provided the data necessary for taxation and conscription of the population. David showed that he was not content to protect the people from their enemies; he wanted to reduce them all to the status of the king's servants. The plague destroyed the value of the data. David relented, and God delivered the country from the plague.

The books of Samuel describe the transition in leadership from that of the judges to Samuel, from Samuel to Saul, and from Saul to David. The question that arises for the reader is who will succeed David as king. One son was a rapist and was murdered to avenge his crime. Another was guilty of fratricide and attempted patricide, and died in the course of a revolution against his father. The prospects for the house of David look bleak. The opening chapter of Kings will describe the solution to the problem of succession.

Continuing Significance of the Books of Samuel

As one reads the books of Samuel and its tales of jealousy, rape, murder, and revolution, one can almost hear the author of the books of Samuel saying: "If you want a monarchy, this is what you get." The contemporary reader ought to recognize the folly of making any human institution absolute. The story of David's family shows what can happen when one is unable to keep in check the tendency to make absolute the institution of the monarchy. The ability of any society to criticize its social structure, its economic policies, its political system is necessary to keep that society from consuming itself. Second Samuel describes how Judah's royal family began to consume itself. Though monarchies are, for the most part, relics of another age, nations still succumb to the temptation of making their political, social, and economic institutions into absolutes. The story of Israel in its land shows what happens when a nation and its leader ignore the fundamental moral values.

FURTHER READING

Anderson, Arnold A. *2 Samuel.* Word Biblical Commentary 11. Waco, TX: Word, 1989.

Brueggemann, Walter. *First and Second Samuel.* Louisville: Westminister John Knox, 1990.

Halpern, Baruch. *The Constitution of the Monarchy in Israel.* Harvard Monograph Series, no. 25. Chico, CA: Scholars Press, 1981.

Frick, F. S. "The Formation of the State in Ancient Israel: A Survey of Models and Theories." *Journal for the Study of the Old Testament (JSOT).* Sheffield:, Sheffield Academic Press 1985.

Gunn, David. "The Fate of King Saul." *JSOT.* Sheffield: Sheffield Academic Press, 1980.

—. "The Story of David." *JSOT.* Sheffield: Sheffield Academic Press, 1982.

Hertzberg, Hans W. *1 & 2 Samuel.* Old Testament Library. Philadelphia: Westminster, 1964.

Ishida, T. *Studies in the Period of David and Solomon.* Winona Lake, IN: Eisenbrauns, 1983.

Klein, Ralph W. *1 Samuel.* Word Biblical Commentary 10. Waco, TX: Word, 1983.

McCarter, P. Kyle. *1 Samuel.* Anchor Bible 8. Garden City, NY: Doubleday, 1980

—. *2 Samuel.* Anchor Bible 9. Garden City, NY: Doubleday, 1984.

Miscall, Peter D. *1 Samuel: A Literary Reading.* Bloomington, IN: Indiana University Press, 1986.

1 AND 2 KINGS

[see pages 401–474 of the Old Testament]

Before Beginning . . .

First and Second Kings continue the story of Israel in its land. They are the final two components of the Deuteronomistic History of Israel, which turns that story into a sermon that takes its theological principles from the book of Deuteronomy. First Kings takes up where 2 Samuel 20 ended. It describes how the problem of the succession to David was resolved. The book then goes on to tell the story of the two Israelite kingdoms that arose following Solomon's death. The division between 1 and 2 Kings is artificial since it is made in the middle of telling the story of King Ahaziah of Israel. Second Kings ends rather abruptly after telling of the parole of King Jehoiachin of Judah from prison in Babylon. The book allows readers to draw their own conclusions regarding the significance of this event. There is, then, no happy ending to the story of Israel in its land. What began with so much promise ends with great tragedy.

Reading through 1 and 2 Kings

Certainly, the author of Kings used a variety of sources—from royal archives to prophetic legends—in composing his story. But in the form in which we read the book of Kings, it is probably the work of a single individual, writing during or shortly after the exile when the shape of Judah's future was unclear. The institutions that gave meaning to Israel's national and religious life were dead. The Temple of Jerusalem was in ruins and its priesthood scattered. The likelihood of a restoration of the Davidic dynasty seemed remote. The Israelite national states no longer existed. Their territory was simply incorporated into the conquering Mesopotamian empires. Imbued with the religious perspectives of the book of Deuteronomy, Kings clearly states that the downfall of Israel and Judah was a consequence of their disobedience, but it implies that Judah may still have a future if it learns obedience.

The books of Kings are anything but objective. First, they reflect a clear bias in favor of Judah and so they write off the Northern Kingdom as a complete loss. Not a single monarch from the Northern Kingdom receives a positive evaluation. Second, Kings does praise a few kings of Judah, but most are condemned. In the author's eyes, most kings promoted or at least allowed worship that did not reflect the uniqueness of Israel's God and the absolute loyalty that Israel owed to its divine patron. Third, the author is completely convinced of the centrality of the Torah in Israel's life with God. Every other religious institution is secondary to it. To make its theological points, the book uses speeches, prayers, and sometimes editorial comments. Attention to these forms will help the reader become acquainted with the spin the book puts on the events it narrates.

Finally, the books of Kings are part of a larger work that begins with Joshua and is sometimes called the "Deuteronomistic History." It is important to remember that while the adjective Deuteronomistic is appropriate, the term history is not. The book is an exponent of Deuteronomy's theology, but the author is not a historian—at least not in the modern sense. The author is more of a preacher or moralist as he turns Israel's past into a sermon. The author of Kings directs those who want "historical" information to sources like the Chronicles of Solomon (1 Kgs 11:41), the Chronicles of the Kings of Judah (1 Kgs 14:29 and fourteen more times) and the Chronicles of the Kings of Israel (1 Kgs 14:19 and sixteen more times)—sources that are, unfortunately, lost. Also, the relative chronologies of the kings of Judah and Israel do not mesh, and contemporary historians have not been able to reconcile these differences. The book passes over kings of great historical import with a few lines, while it devotes chapters to kings that the book considers models of religious commitment. One can use the books of Kings to help reconstruct the history of the Israelite kingdoms, but these books were not written for that purpose. It is important to relate the contents of the books of Kings to other ancient Near Eastern written sources and to the results of archaeological excavations. But none of this diminishes the book's theological achievements. This massive work enabled the exiles to make sense of events that challenged their most deeply held religious beliefs. The book's passion to keep Judah's faith in its ancestral deity alive despite terrible odds offers a model to all those who hand on the faith today, so reading the books of Kings can be as important today as it was millennia ago.

Solomon's Accession (1 Kgs 1:1–2:46)

With David a very old man, unable even to keep himself warm, the question of succession became acute. There were two competing candidates: Adonijah and Solomon. Neither was designated by a divine word given through a prophet as were Saul and David. The throne would go to the better practitioner of power politics. Adonijah was born in Hebron and was favored by David's oldest supporters: Joab and

Abiathar. Solomon was born in Jerusalem and was favored by his mother Bathsheba and those who supported David after he established himself in that city. That Adonijah was Absalom's full brother (1 Kgs 1:6) presaged the outcome of the contest.

Adonijah and Solomon took different approaches toward the succession. Adonijah acted in his own person, claiming the throne for himself. Solomon was content to let his supporters manipulate his father into designating him as the successor to the throne. The book describes two simultaneous ceremonies—each of which was to inaugurate David's successor. The ceremonies took place near Jerusalem at two sites in shouting distance of each other. Adonijah chose Enrogel, a spring located at the juncture of the Hinnom and Kidron Valleys just south of Jerusalem; Solomon had his ceremony at the Gihon Spring, Jerusalem's main water source, at the base of the eastern slope of David's city. Solomon was able to bring more people to his ceremony; after all, he was the candidate of the Jerusalem party. When Adonijah and his supporters heard the crowd acclaim Solomon as their king, they lost heart and fled. Adonijah submitted to Solomon's authority and begged for his life, which Solomon chose to spare.

With the succession settled, the book had David make his exit. Of course, a person as important as David must have some significant last words to say. The book provides David with a schizophrenic-like testament (1 Kgs 2:1–9). The first to speak is the "pious David" who charges his successor to be obedient to the written authoritative Torah, i.e., the book of Deuteronomy. It will be through his obedience that Solomon will secure the throne for himself and his successors (vv. 2–4). Then it is the turn of the "practical David." He knew from experience that gaining the throne and keeping the throne are two different things. The last words of David recorded in 1 Kings identify those who have shown themselves a threat to the dynasty. David was certain that Solomon would know what needed to be done (vv. 5–9).

The reader does not have to wait long to learn how Solomon dealt with potential troublemakers (1 Kgs 2:12–46). First, he had Adonijah killed. The imprudent Adonijah gave Solomon a pretext when he asked to marry Abishag, one of David's secondary wives. Solomon chose to interpret Adonijah's foolish request as treason. The new king then dealt with Adonijah's principal supporters. He had Joab killed and sent Abiathar to internal exile. For good measure, Solomon had Shimei, David's tormentor, executed as well (see 2 Sm 16:6–14; 19:16–24). The book allows its readers to draw their own conclusions regarding the path Solomon took to the throne. Notably absent from these first two chapters is any statement or even a hint that God had any role in Solomon's succession.

It is important to note the role that Bathsheba, Solomon's mother, played in his rise to the throne. After he became king, she enjoyed access to him and was seated near his throne at official functions (1 Kgs 2:19–20). The books of Kings name the mothers of seventeen other kings—all but two kings of Judah (Jehoram and Ahaz) and two kings of Israel. This had led to the conclusion that the "queen mother" has an official position and exercised political and religious power. Unfortunately, the book does not provide the type of information that would permit firm conclusions to be drawn. That the author made it a point to mention the mother of eighteen kings by name, however, makes it obvious that the "queen mother" enjoyed a specific rank and exercised some power—especially over domestic matters.

Solomon's Reign (1 Kgs 3:1–11:43)

The account of Solomon's reign begins with an introductory statement that encapsulates the book's ambivalence toward David's son (1 Kgs 3:1–3). On the one hand, the reader is told that Solomon "loved the LORD" (v. 3), fulfilling the great commandment of Deuteronomy (see Dt 6: 5). But, on the other hand, he married a foreign princess and worshipped on the "high places." The Deuteronomic tradition takes a dim view of both patterns of behavior (see Dt 7:1–4; 1 Kgs 3: 2–3 and twenty-eight more times). Like Israel's life in the land, Solomon's reign will begin well enough, but it will soon founder because of an unwillingness to be faithful to the most basic of the Torah's commands: absolute fidelity to Israel's God.

The book finally gets around to providing divine legitimation for Solomon's accession (1 Kgs 3:4–15). It does so by having God approve of Solomon's status as king through an appearance in a dream, which the Bible considers as one way that God communicates with human beings. The story reflects an ancient Near Eastern practice (called "incubation") of seeking an oracle by sleeping in a sanctuary after offering the prescribed sacrifices. Any dream experienced during this sleep was considered a revelation from the god honored at the sanctuary. The dream concerned Solomon's request for God's help in ruling Israel wisely. The request was granted. The book follows up the account of the dream with a tale illustrating Solomon's wisdom (1 Kgs 3:16–28). Solomon was able to settle a dispute between two women over an infant, which each claimed as her own, because he knew that the true mother would sacrifice anything to insure the welfare of her child.

The book pauses in its narrative about Solomon's reign to include information about Solomon's administration, wealth, and wisdom (1 Kgs 4:1–5:14). The editors of the NAB rearrange the versification of this section as follows: 4:1–6 (Solomon's administrators); 4: 7–19; 5:7–8 (districts for taxation); 4:20 (the kingdom's prosperity); 5:2–6 (Solomon's wealth); 5:9–14 (Solomon's wisdom). First Samuel mentioned almost nothing about Saul's administration. Second Samuel named nine administrators during David's reign (see 2 Sm 8: 16–18; 20:23–26). It is clear from the list of Solomon's administrators (1 Kgs 4:1–19) that the centralization of all authority in the monarchy became a priority under Solomon. He developed an efficient apparatus to do what Samuel warned them that their king would do: tax them (see 1 Sm 8:10–18). The book also makes a point of noting that Solomon set up his sons-in-law over two of the districts (1 Kgs 4: 11,15) and that Judah, Solomon's tribe, was not included among the taxation districts. The people had asked Samuel for a king to rule over them "like other nations" (1 Sm 8). The book implies that the taxation, nepotism, and cronyism assure them that they have such a king. Deuteronomy requires that the king study the Torah so that he not "become estranged from his countrymen" (Dt 17:20). The list of the king's daily provisions (1 Kgs 5:1–5) certainly sounded more than extravagant to Judah's subsistence farmers. The divide between the royal establishment and the general population was becoming more pronounced. Still, 1 Kings 4:20 (note: this verse has been moved to ch. 5) and 5: 5 describe Solomon's reign as a time of peace and prosperity.

Just as Moses was associated with Torah and David with the psalms, Solomon was remembered as a sage (see Prv 1:1; Sir 47:12). To conclude its initial portrait of Solomon, the book asserts that Solomon's wisdom was unsurpassed. His wisdom attracted admirers from all over the world (5:9–14). The reader recognizes that Solomon's court is far different from that of Saul—and even David.

Next, the book describes a project with which Solomon's name is always associated: the building of the Temple (1 Kgs 5:15–32). While the account implies that the project was ordained by God, temple building was a royal prerogative in the ancient Near East. By initiating the project of erecting a temple to Israel's patron deity in Jerusalem, his capital, Solomon was asserting, in most dramatic form, his claim to Israel's throne. The book has Solomon explain that David did not build a temple because he was almost continuously at war (1 Kgs 5:17). Solomon also used good Deuteronomic language as he said that he was going to build a temple "for the name of God" (v. 19, literal translation). The Deuteronomic tradition usually avoided describing the Temple as God's dwelling place, preferring to speak of the Temple as the place for God's name (see Dt 12:11). To be consistent with its portrait of Solomon as an Israelite king with an international reputation, the book has the king using his contacts to assemble the best material and artisans from surrounding countries for his project, while ordinary Israelites contributed their labor to the project.

The book goes into some detail in describing the building of the Temple. It gives the date for both the beginning and the completion of the project (1 Kgs 6:1–37) and describes the dimensions of the building and its tripartite structure. The Temple was to have a porch, a nave, and a "holy of holies." The latter was a windowless room that was to contain the ark of the covenant, the symbol of the divine presence. In the holy of holies, there were to be two cherubim (1 Kgs 6: 23–28). A cherub was a mythical creature that had the face of a human being, the forequarters of a lion, the hindquarters of an ox, and wings of an eagle. The ark of the covenant would be placed between the two cherubim.

The book clearly wants readers to think of the Temple as a most impressive building. Solomon spared no expense in its construction and ornamentation. He overlaid the entire structure with gold (1 Kgs 6:22). At the same time, however, the book offers an explanation for the eventual destruction of this singular structure. It presents God as warning Solomon that God will never forsake Israel, the dynasty, or the Temple if he keeps the commandments (1 Kgs 6:12). Kings will describe how Solomon and most of Israel's kings failed, leaving God to abandon the Temple that Solomon built.

The book inserts a short description of five other structures that it credits to Solomon's building activity (1 Kgs 7:1–12), implying that as much as the Temple was designed to show that the Lord was a great God, it and the other buildings Solomon had built were designed to show that Solomon was a great king. These five structures were the "Forest of Lebanon," which was larger than the Temple, the "Columned Hall," the "Throne Hall" (or "Hall of Justice"), and palaces for himself and for the pharaoh's daughter. Completing these projects took almost double the time it took to build the Temple (1 Kgs 6: 38; 7:1). The text provides little information about the structures themselves, and archaeological excavation has not uncovered any such buildings.

After mentioning Solomon's other projects, the book returns to the Temple and describes some of its furnishings (1 Kgs 7:13–51). The artisan responsible for crafting these furnishings was named Hiram though v. 40 (in the Hebrew) calls him Hirom. The Chronicler remembers him as Huram (2 Chr 4:11) and Huram-abi (2 Chr 2: 13; 4:16). Of particular interest are the two bronze pillars (1 Kgs 7:15–22). Their appearance and function are difficult to reconstruct given the information in the text. They were probably symbolic because they did not support any part of the structure and because they were given names. The bronze sea (vv. 23–26), the wheeled stands (vv. 27–37), and the basins (vv. 38–39) testify to the need for large volumes of water that had to be kept in the Temple area to cleanse it from the contamination caused by the blood of the sacrifices offered there.

With the Temple and its furnishings completed, all is ready for the building's dedication. The book provides a narrative framework (1 Kgs 8:1–9; 62–66) for a lengthy prayer that Solomon offered at the dedication. The framework describes the transfer of the ark to the newly built Temple and the sacrifices offered there for the first time. The prayer, however, seems to prepare the reader for a world without a Temple. The words of the prayer are, at times, in conflict with each other. Verses 10–13 speak about God's presence in the Temple while v. 27 asserts that God cannot be contained in the building that Solomon had just built. The prayer also appears to transform the Temple from a place of sacrificial offerings (vv. 5 and 66) into a place of prayer where Israelite and non-Israelite alike can ask for forgiveness (vv. 42–43). Indeed, one does not even need to be present in the Temple to be heard by God. All that is necessary is that one pray in the direction of Jerusalem and its Temple (vv. 38, 48; see Dn 6:11). The author of Kings composed this prayer to help his readers cope with the loss of the Temple.

The book uses another speech to reiterate its explanation for the disastrous end of the Davidic dynasty and the destruction of the Temple (1 Kgs 9:1–9). After all, the prayer of Solomon had just praised God for fulfilling the promise to David (1 Kgs 8:14–29) and celebrated the dedication of the Temple. God appeared to Solomon and warned him that the future of the dynasty and the Temple depended on the fidelity of Israel's kings to the commandments and on Israel's exclusive loyalty to its ancestral deity. The conclusion is obvious: the destruction of the Temple and the end of the dynasty did not occur because of any lack of fidelity on God's part. The people of Israel and their kings bear full responsibility for the fall of the two Israelite states and the exile of their people. Of course, the book wants its readers to recognize that the converse is true as well: obedience will bring God's blessing to the people and their land.

The book brings its treatment of the temple to a close by mentioning some economic and personnel issues (1 Kgs 9:10–25). The assistance that Hiram, the king of Tyre, gave to Solomon in completing his building projects came at a price. Solomon ceded twenty cities along the Galilean border with Tyre to Hiram. Also, the labor for the projects was supplied not by Israelites but by prisoners of war. The issue of forced labor proved to be one that undermined the relations between the king and people. Even though 1 Kings 5:27 suggests that Solomon got skilled workers for the Temple project from Israel, 1 Kings 9:20 asserts that the laborers came from non-Israelite prisoners of war. The Millo mentioned in 1 Kings 9:24 was probably a structure that supported the terrace work that allowed building on the steep grades of the Ophel hill on which monarchic period Jerusalem was built.

Next, the book describes the splendor of Solomon's reign by focusing on his wealth, wisdom, and chariot forces (1 Kgs 9:26–10:29). Eleven times the text mentions the gold that the king amassed. It also notes that the queen of Sheba came to Jerusalem because of Solomon's renown as a sage. Sheba was located at the southwestern corner of the Arabian peninsula and was likely one of Judah's trading partners. Goods passed between these two countries through the Red Sea port at Ezion-geber. According to an Ethiopian tradition, their country was Sheba, and the results of the queen's visit to Solomon included her conversion to his religion and a son fathered by Solomon. This son visited his father and returned to Ethiopia with the ark of the covenant. While there is no biblical support for this tradition, it does explain the reason some people claim that the ark of the covenant is in Ethiopia.

From the book's perspective, the luster of all Solomon's achievements was tarnished by his failure to support the worship of the Lord alone. The reason offered for Solomon's infidelity was his marriage to non-Israelite women. Of course, the book is trying to promote marriage within the Judahite community as one way to maintain Judahite identity. To show the seriousness of Solomon's failure, the text has God speak to Solomon for a third and final time, announcing the end of the Davidic-Solomonic kingdom and the rise of another Israelite national state, which will occur after Solomon's death (1 Kgs 11:1–13).

First Kings concludes its story of Solomon's reign by mentioning three of Solomon's rivals (1 Kgs 11:14–40). The first is Hadad, king of Edom. Judah and Edom were perennial rivals for control of the southern part of the Levant. The second was Rezon who was "king of Damascus," the capital of Aram. Israel and Aram struggled for many years for hegemony in the northern part of the Levant. The most serious threat, however, was an internal one. Jeroboam, one of Solomon's administrators, was supported in a bid for kingship by Egypt and with prophetic designation, threatening the rule of the Davidic dynasty. Although the rebellion was not successful at first, the book explains the origins of the two Israelite national states, Israel and Judah, as a consequence of Jeroboam's attempt to replace Solomon, who simply failed to observe the commandments and to worship the Lord alone. It is important to note that the book asserts that, despite Jeroboam, the Davidic dynasty continued in existence not only for the sake of David but also for the sake of Jerusalem. That city was destined to take on paramount importance for Judaism. The Temple, however, is not mentioned specifically. Also significant is the role played by the prophet Ahijah, who like Samuel, pronounced words of judgment on the king. The book again was suggesting that Israel listen to the prophets sent to it.

Like the reigns of his predecessors Saul and David, Solomon's began with great promise but ended with an unfavorable picture of the king, thus presaging the story of the people of Israel in their land. The book notes that Solomon was buried in the City of David after a reign of forty years and was succeeded by his son Rehoboam.

The Two Kingdoms
(1 Kgs 12:1—2 Kgs 17:41)

The two Israelite national states arose in the Levant sometime in the ninth century BC. Historians still have not arrived at a consensus as to the developments that led to their establishment. First Kings, however, describes the origins of the two Israelite states as the result of divine judgment on Solomon's rule, communicated by the prophet Ahijah. What Ahijah foretold was fulfilled almost immediately after Solomon's death and the accession of his son Rehoboam. But as it did with the origins of the monarchy, the book will describe the origins of the two Israelite national states in economic as well as religious terms (1 Kgs 12:1–25). Rehoboam refused to lighten the economic burdens that Solomon imposed on his subjects, and before Rehoboam was able to consolidate his hold on his father's realm, there was a revolution that led to the establishment of the Kingdom of Israel separate from the Kingdom of Judah. When Rehoboam attempted to use military force against the rebellion, he was dissuaded by another prophetic word given through Shemaiah.

While Kings implies that the Israelites had legitimate grievances, it does not approve of religious practices, which it characterizes as obscuring the unity of Israel's ancestral deity, as violating the prohibition of images, and as ignoring the place that God chose. The book presents Jeroboam as fearing that the Jerusalem Temple will be a magnet, drawing the people to Jerusalem and to the Davidic dynasty. To counter this Jeroboam built cultic centers at Dan at the extreme north of his kingdom and at Bethel in the extreme south (1 Kgs 12:26–33). The book makes its attitude toward these cultic centers absolutely clear when it depicts an unnamed "man of God" from Judah condemning the shrine at Bethel (1 Kgs 13:1–10). As the story of the Northern Kingdom unfolds, every king of Israel will be condemned for maintaining these shrines and continuing "the sin of Jeroboam."

This man of God left Bethel because God had told him to eat or drink nothing there but to return to Judah. On his way home, he met an unnamed prophet, who convinced him to return to Bethel and enjoy his hospitality. Because he disobeyed God's instructions, the man of God from Judah died a violent death. But the prophet from Bethel lied to the man of God in convincing him to accept hospitality (1 Kgs 13:11–32). Here the book exposes a practical problem connected with prophecy: how does one know whether a prophet is actually speaking in the name of God? Of course, the book wants its readers to recognize that the written authoritative Torah (the book of Deuteronomy) is the authentic, reliable, and unambiguous statement of God's will for Israel.

First Kings concludes its treatment of Jeroboam by revisiting the theme of succession (1 Kgs 14:1–20). Abijah, Jeroboam's heir, fell ill and Jeroboam had his wife visit the prophet Ahijah in order to elicit a favorable oracle on behalf of the child. The prophet, however, predicted not only that the child was to die but also that Jeroboam's dynasty would end violently. Ahijah's speech is an intense and sometimes vulgar invective. While the prophet was not specific about Jeroboam's failures, he was quite specific about the king's future and that of the nation. He even blamed the exile on Jeroboam (v. 16).

The book intertwines narratives about the kings of the two Israelite national states until it tells of the fall of the Northern Kingdom to the Assyrians in 2 Kings 17. The two Israelite kingdoms were rivals at first. Disputes over the border that they shared were almost continuous. The book notes that Israel and Judah fought continuously during the reigns of Jeroboam and Rehoboam (1 Kgs 14:30). Rehoboam also had to deal with a raid by Pharaoh Shishak, who had given asylum to Jeroboam during the reign of Solomon (1 Kgs 11:40). While the Egyptians were not in a position to reestablish the hegemony over the region, they raided 154 towns in the two kingdoms. Jerusalem was spared only because Rehoboam paid a large indemnity to Shishak (1 Kgs 14:26). The book characterizes Rehoboam's reign as a time of apostasy (1 Kgs 14:21–24).

The border wars between the two Israelite kingdoms continued during the reign of Abijam in Judah (1 Kgs 15:7). The book provides no other information about Abijam's short reign except to note that he that he was nothing like David, whom the book begins to idealize even though it mentions David's lapse "in the case of Uriah" (1 Kgs 15:5; see 2 Sm 11). The book devotes more attention to Asa, Abijam's son. He is one of the few kings of Judah whom the book commends because of his actions to rid Judah of non-Yahwistic worship. Asa also induced the Arameans to invade the Northern Kingdom. With the army of Israel occupied with the Arameans, Asa had a free hand to extend the border to Mizpeh, a town about five miles north of Jerusalem, where it remained until the fall of the Northern Kingdom in 721 BC.

The book next turns its attention to the Northern Kingdom for almost the rest of 1 Kings (15:25–22:40). After Jeroboam's twenty-two-year reign, the political situation in the north became very unstable. Nadab, Jeroboam's son and successor, was assassinated in the course of a war with the Philistines. The coup was led by Baasha, who purged Jeroboam's entire family in order to secure his own accession to the throne. Of course, the book sees this as a fulfillment of Ahijah's prophecy (1 Kgs 14:10) and a consequence of Nadab's infidelity. Baasha proved to be no improvement over Nadab although he did manage to hold the throne for twenty-four years (15:33–16:7). Kings notes that a prophet named Jehu announced the end of Baasha's dynasty (16:1–5, 7) just as Ahijah announced the end of Jeroboam's dynasty. Jehu's words were fulfilled as Baasha's son and successor Elah was assassinated during a military coup after just two years on the throne. Zimri, the leader of the coup, purged all the descendants of Baasha to solidify his claim to the throne (16:8–14). Omri, another Israelite general, decided to lead a coup of his own. His success led Zimri to take his life after a reign of just seven days. Of course, the book suggests Zimri's fate was the consequence of his religious infidelity. After a short civil war (1 Kgs 16:21–22), Omri became king of Israel.

Even though Kings almost completely ignores Omri (1 Kgs 17:23–28), he was arguably the most able ruler of the Northern Kingdom. His reign reversed Israel's fortunes. He ended the Aramean threat. He revived Israel's commercial fortunes by aligning himself with Phoenicia, sealing the alliance with the marriage of his son Ahab with Jezebel, the daughter of Ethbaal, king of Sidon. Omri ended the fifty years of fruitless conflict with Judah. He subjugated Moab and this brought the King's Highway, a major commercial highway east of the Jordan, under his control. The dynasty he established lasted four generations, providing a measure of stability to Israel. All this brought a new era of peace and prosperity to the Northern Kingdom. While Kings ignores these achievements because they do not correspond with its theological purpose, it does note that Omri established his capital at Samaria where Omri was buried.

Ahab succeeded his father Omri. It was the first successful dynastic succession in the Kingdom of Israel. From a military, economic, and political perspective, Ahab's reign was remarkably successful. His only defeat was the loss of Moab toward the end of his twenty-two-year reign. Excavations at several cities in the north show that Ahab's reign was one of economic growth and military strength. His greatest military achievement took place at the battle of Qarqar, which the book ignores. Ahab led a coalition of small states that successfully engaged the Assyrians and prevented them from taking control of the region. Ahab led the largest force in the coalition. The book chooses to focus on Ahab's serious internal problems by introducing several stories about the prophets Elijah and Elisha. Both prophets were highly critical of the religious and social policies of Ahab and his successors.

Kings implies that Ahab's problems were caused by his Phoenician wife Jezebel, who promoted the worship of Baal. The prophet Elijah forcefully opposed her. The conflict between Elijah and Ahab over Jezebel's activity dominates the portrait of Ahab in the Bible and makes it appear as if he were a weak and ineffective ruler when the opposite was true. The worship of Baal was attractive because this god was thought to provide the rain that made Israel's survival on its land possible. To show that Baal was unable to provide rain, Elijah announced a drought (1 Kgs 17:1). God's power to provide was obvious when a dry river bed yielded water for the prophet, and ravens brought him food. When the stream dried up again, the prophet went to beg in a Sidonian town. A poor widow from that town, who took pity on the prophet, never ran out of food despite the famine induced by the drought (1 Kgs 17:2–16). An even more remarkable demonstration of God's power occurred when the prophet brought the widow's deceased son back to life (1 Kgs 17:17–24).

Elijah finally met Ahab, who blamed the prophet for the drought. Of course, the reader knows that the fault lies with Ahab. While the confrontation with the prophets of Baal on Mount Carmel was another indication of the power of Israel's God (1 Kgs 18:20–40), it was the prophet's prayer for rain that brought relief to the suffering people (1 Kgs 18:41–46). The rain that comes on the land does not end the tension in the story because Jezebel was determined to avenge Elijah's victory at Mount Carmel. The prophet fled to the south, stopping at Beersheba, a town that abuts the Negev desert. After a brief pause, Elijah continued his journey until he reached Horeb, which is the name by which the Deuteronomic tradition knows Mount Sinai. At the place where the Israelites experienced God's presence in a most dramatic way, the prophet experienced only God's absence until he realized God was present in a "whispering sound" (1 Kgs 19:12). God then commissioned the prophet to take specific steps to deal with the apostasy fomented by Israel's royal family. One of these steps is the anointing of a prophet to succeed him. Elijah found Elisha, whom the Lord had designated, and called him to his prophetic ministry (1 Kgs 19:13–21).

The book sets aside its narrative about Elijah and Elisha and interjects a story about an unnamed prophet who confronts Ahab during a war between Aram and Israel (1 Kgs 20:1–43). Aram, southern Syria with its capital Damascus, was probably the most powerful kingdom in the Levant between the eleventh and eighth centuries BC. However, historians have had problems with the stories of a war between Aram and Israel during Ahab's reign. Both Ahab and Omri were powerful kings and were not dominated by the Arameans as suggested in this story (1 Kgs 20:1–9, 34). The details of the story reflect the relations between Aram and Israel, which were characteristic of the reigns of Jehoahaz and Jehoash fifty years later when Israel was much weaker politically and militarily. Although the book may have provided this story with an incorrect setting, its theological point is clear enough as it tells a tale similar to that of Saul and the Amalekite war in 1 Samuel 15. Both Saul and Ahab fail to heed the instructions given by a prophet and stand under divine judgment. The lesson is obvious: Israel must listen to the prophets sent to it if it is to have any future.

The book returns to the conflict between king and prophet as it tells the tale of Naboth's vineyard (1 Kgs 21:1–29). Again, it is Jezebel, Ahab's non-Israelite wife, who is responsible for the trouble. Ahab recognized that Naboth was within his rights in refusing to sell the king his vineyard. Jezebel, however, co-opted the elders of Naboth's city into convicting him on trumped-up charges of blasphemy and treason. Naboth was executed and his property forfeited to the crown, so Jezebel was able to present her husband with Naboth's vineyard. Of course, Elijah condemned this blatant injustice in God's name. Surprisingly, Ahab repented upon hearing the prophet's words of judgment, and God spared his life. Again, the book's message is obvious: if Israel listens to the prophets God sends to it, Israel's life will be spared as well.

But just as the book finished commending the prophetic word to Israel, it shows that discerning that word is not a simple matter. To do so the book describes preparations for a second war between Israel and Aram during the waning years of Ahab's reign (1 Kgs 22:1–28). This time Ahab sought help from Jehoshaphat, the king of Judah. Relations between the two Israelite states had steadily improved since the time of Ahab's father, Omri. Indeed, Ahab offered his daughter in marriage to Jehoram, Jehoshaphat's son (2 Kgs 8:8). The king of Judah, however, suggested seeking a word from God before embarking on any campaign against the powerful Arameans. Ahab assembled four hundred prophets to impress Jehoshaphat. After the four hundred encourage an attack, Jehoshaphat, apparently reluctant to fight the Arameans, asked if there were any more prophets who might be consulted. Ahab summoned Micaiah ben Imlah, who predicted an Aramean victory. Micaiah asserted that God put a "lying spirit" in the four hundred prophets to insure that Ahab would be defeated. How then could prophecy be a reliable guide if God can inspire prophets to lie? The book assumes that the one reliable and unimpeachable guide to Israel's life is the written, authoritative Torah, the book of Deuteronomy. The attitude of Kings toward Ahab is evident from the description of what happened when Ahab's chariot was cleansed of the fallen king's blood (1 Kgs 22:38).

The book returns briefly to the Judahite monarchy and gives a qualified commendation to Jehoshaphat, who followed the good example of his father, Asa. The book also notes that Jehoshaphat was "at peace" with Israel, though it also claims that the king led Judah bravely in some wars but gives no details (1 Kgs 15:45–46).

The story of Ahaziah of Israel straddles 1 and 2 Kings. Since he reigned for a little more than one year, the book gives just a brief and disapproving summary of his rule, emphasizing his promotion of Baal worship (1 Kgs 22:52–54). The first chapter of 2 Kings offers an illustration of Ahaziah's apostasy (2 Kgs 1:2–6). The king sought an oracle from the Baal worshipped at Ekron.

When Elijah intercepted the king's messengers and proclaimed an oracle from the God of Israel, Ahaziah sought to arrest him. But the conflict between king and prophet was no real match (2 Kgs 1:7–16). The book is building up its case showing the failure of the monarchy. It wants to show that the political disasters that befell both Israelite kingdoms were a direct result of the apostasy of their kings (see Dt 4:25–28).

The book presents the prophets as the foils of Israel's apostate kings, so after describing the failures of Ahab and his son Ahaziah, it turns its attention back to Elijah and Elisha and the transition from the prophetic ministry of the former to that of the latter (2 Kgs 2:1–18). The narrative is purposely reminiscent of the traditions regarding the transition in the leadership of the Israelite community from Moses to Joshua. The book sees the succession of Elisha to the prophetic ministry as a genuine act of God. Perhaps a story with such spectacular details served to show that Elisha was a true witness to the God of Israel as was Elijah in contrast to the prophets that supported the house of Ahab (see 2 Kgs 3:13). Fifty "guild prophets" witness the passing of the prophetic mantle to Elisha (2 Kgs 2:15). Except for 1 Kings 20:35, these guild prophets are always mentioned in connection with Elisha and may have been his supporters against the king and his prophets. The book concludes its introduction to the cycle of stories about Elisha with two tales that encourage Israel to obey the prophets sent to it (2 Kgs 2:19–25).

The book shifts attention to the house of Ahab again. After the short reign of the childless Ahaziah, his brother Jehoram (Joram) became king of Israel (2 Kgs 3:1–3). While Kings asserts that Moab's revolt took place during Jehoram's reign, it was more likely during Ahab's final years. Jehoram was simply unsuccessful in regaining control over Moab. Moab was a kingdom located east of the Dead Sea and west of the Arabian desert. It had been a vassal to Israel since the time of Omri. The Mesha stele, a monument celebrating Moab's victory over Israel, gives an account of this revolt from the Moabite perspective. Although both the biblical and Moabite accounts agree that Mesha, the king of Moab, was successful in regaining his country's independence, the book provides little historical information but a clear theological interpretation. It insists that apostasy always brings defeat. The extent of the territory under Israelite control was a tangible indication of God's blessings according to the book, and the success of Mesha's revolt and the consequent loss of Moab show that Israel was on a downward spiral because of its infidelity (2 Kgs 3:4–27).

The book transfers the focus of its story away from kings and international political conflicts to ordinary folk in need—people whose names are never given (2 Kgs 4:1–44). Elisha, whom this chapter refers to as a "man of God," responds to those needs with compassion. While the effect on the reader is to wonder at the miracle-working power of Elisha, the stories do not even hint that the man of God worked these miracles to establish his reputation. The book implies that Elisha did what the kings were supposed to do: respond to the needs of the lowly and poor. In fact, the reason ordinary people were in need was the economic and political policies of the monarchy. God redresses this injustice through Elisha. The prophetic task is not simply to speak words of judgment on injustice but to undo the effects of the greed that creates poverty.

With the story of Naaman, Elisha moves back into the arena of international politics (2 Kgs 5: 1–19). This is the second time the book has told a tale of someone searching for healing in a foreign country. In 2 Kings 1, it was King Ahaziah of Israel looking for healing in Ekron from Baalzebub. In 2 Kings 5, it is Naaman from Aram who looks for healing in Israel. Whereas the healings in 2 Kings 4 took place because of Elisha's compassion for those in need, here there is an overt apologetic purpose: Naaman is to learn that there was a prophet in Israel who could heal in the name of Israel's God. The Aramean general learned this lesson. There is also a homiletic character to the story. Naaman is a model for Israel. Although reluctant at first, the Aramean general obeyed the prophet and was healed. Israel surely should obey the prophets sent to it. Two more stories with a clear homiletic thrust follow (2 Kgs 5:20–6:7). Both stories concern the prophet's followers. In the first, Gehazi seeks to reap a monetary profit from his association with Elisha and is duly punished for his avarice. In the second, Elisha's supporters find themselves in an embarrassing situation, which the prophet resolves. The book warns against venality. Though the story of Naaman presupposes that there was peace between Aram and Israel, the book asserts that the situation changed as it describes two incidents between Israel and its neighbor to the north. The first shows that of itself Aram posed no danger to Israel (2 Kgs 6: 8–23). The prophet made the Arameans look foolish as he led them into Samaria. Fortunately for them, the prophet told the king to spare the lives of his prisoners.

The circumstances change abruptly in the story of Ben-hadad's siege of Samaria (2 Kgs 6: 24–33). A siege sought to force surrender by cutting off the supply of food. Ben-hadad's siege of the Israelite capital was working as is evident from the horrific details that the book gives (vv. 28–29). The apostasy of Omri and his successors is having its full effect as Aram jeopardized Israel's very existence. The king, of course, did not accept responsibility for Samaria's troubles; he blamed the prophet whom the book describes as cowering behind a closed door in fear of the king's anger. The Aramean threat was a harbinger of things to come. Aram here is an instrument of divine judgment on Israel's apostasy—apostasy that continued without abatement. But Israel's time had not yet come, so 2 Kings 7: 1–20 tells of the lifting of the Aramean siege of Samaria. The book makes it clear that the lifting of the siege and the relief of Samaria were not the work of Israel's military. God's power lifted the siege, and four lepers—by sheer happenstance—open the way to the city's relief from the famine. The book shows readers that Israel's God shapes human events through the prophetic word. Just as easily as God made Aram a threat to Israel, God removed that threat. This is another hint to the book's first readers that God can end their exile.

The epilogue to the story of Elisha and the woman of Shunem (2 Kgs 8:1–6; see 2 Kgs 5: 8–37) is unusual on two counts. First, the prophet does not directly solve her problem. In fact, she is suffering economic privation precisely because she followed the prophet's instructions to relocate from Israel. Upon returning, she found her property had been confiscated. Still, just the power of the prophet's fame was enough to solve her problem. Second, it was the king who restored the woman's property. For once, an Israelite king did act for the benefit of those in need. The book illustrates the power of God to extricate people from difficult situations. That power is such that it can lead people to act contrary to their normal patterns to bring about the fulfillment of the divine will. In a sense, the woman of Shunem is Israel in microcosm. She experienced exile, loss, and eventually restoration. What happened to her, the book implies, can happen to Israel as well. It too can experience restoration after exile.

The book introduces a new character into its story of the Northern Kingdom and its kings: Hazael, who was to become king of Aram and a very serious problem for both Israel and Judah (2 Kgs 8:7–15). Hazael was an emissary sent to seek a positive oracle for Ben-hadad, the king of Aram, who was dying. In the course of giving this oracle, the prophet became aware of the great problems Hazael would cause the Israelite kingdoms. Hazael appears to be surprised by the prophet's words. Hazael's succession was indeed irregular. He did not belong to the royal family but usurped the throne of Aram following Ben-hadad's death.

For the first time in 2 Kings, the book turns its attention to Judah as it offers judgment on the reign of Jehoram (2 Kgs 8:16–25). The relations between Judah and Israel were peaceful, sealed by the marriage of Jehoram to Athaliah, a daughter of Ahab. Certainly in any alliance between the two kingdoms, Judah was the junior partner. The book notes that Jehoram replicated the behavior of the kings of Israel. This brought serious consequences for Judah. As Israel lost control over Moab (2 Kgs 3), so Judah's domination of Edom came to an end. The power of the Israelite kingdoms was steadily diminishing. For the book this was an obvious sign of God's displeasure with Israel, Judah, and their kings. Jehoram of Judah died after only eight years as king, leaving his twenty-one-year-old son Ahaziah to ascend David's throne. Ahaziah was a brother-in-law to Jehoram of Israel. The two kings decided to strike the Arameans under Hazael because of the threat that the Arameans posed. But Jehoram was severely wounded in battle and went to Jezreel to recover. Ahaziah went there to visit him (2 Kgs 8:25–29). In providing these details, the book is setting the scene for the violent end that will come to the dynasty established by Omri.

To illustrate the disintegration of the Kingdom of Israel, the book describes a revolution that brought an end to the House of Omri (2 Kgs 9: 1–10:22)—a revolution so bloody that it was still remembered with horror a century later (see Hos 1:4–5). According to Kings, Jehu's revolution was set in motion by the apostasy and injustice practiced by Israel's kings, and the terrible end of these kings reflects the prophetic judgment on their actions (1 Kgs 14:11; 16:4; 21: 19–24). The book then presents Jehu's revolution not in political but theological terms; it begins with the prophet Elisha's naming of Jehu, an officer in Jehoram's army, as the one to replace the king. After Jehu assassinated Jehoram of Israel and Ahaziah of Judah, he turned to Jezebel, who taunted him as no better than Zimri, the assassin who was king of Israel for just seven days (see 1 Kgs 16:15–19). Jezebel shared the fate of her son Jehoram at Jehu's hand (1 Kgs 9:1–27).

As a usurper, Jehu had to eliminate claimants to the throne with better credentials. His revolutionary goals were to take Jehoram's place on the throne and end the Phoenician influence over the Kingdom of Israel. To secure his throne, Jehu purged the entire royal family (2 Kgs 10: 1–11,15–17) and to eliminate Phoenician influence, he killed the prophets of Baal and destroyed their temple (10:18–27). Because he also killed Ahaziah of Judah, Jehu had to deal with a force from the Southern Kingdom seeking to avenge Ahaziah. But the book does not tell the story of Jehu's action to give an accurate picture of the progress of his revolution. The book wishes to describe the religious significance of that revolution. From this perspective, for all his brutal thoroughness, Jehu was a failure. He did not follow the Lord when he was king but followed instead the pattern of apostasy as set by Jeroboam. Because of this sin, Jehu did not stop Israel's slide to oblivion. Like his predecessors, Jehu witnessed Israel's power diminishing. More territory was lost—probably to Aram. Israel's doom was just a matter of time (2 Kgs 10: 28–36).

The book next shows that the baleful influence of the House of Ahab was not limited to the Northern Kingdom. The queen mother in Judah was Athaliah, a princess of the House of Ahab, who was given in marriage to Jehoram, the crown prince of Judah, thus ending the tensions between the two Israelite kingdoms. When Athaliah's son, Ahaziah, was assassinated in the course of Jehu's revolt, she decided to seize absolute power in Jerusalem. Because she, like Jehu, was a usurper, she had to eliminate all potential rivals for power so she had all the males from the House of David killed (2 Kgs 11:1). Ahaziah's son Joash was saved by his aunt Jehosheba and escaped the massacre orchestrated by his grandmother Athaliah. During her seventh year on the throne, Athaliah was assassinated in the course of a revolution led by Jehoiada, a priest. The temple of Baal that Athaliah built in Jerusalem was torn down, and the unprecedented rule of a woman as sovereign ended. Joash was enthroned in place of his assassinated grandmother. The book notes that support for Joash came from the people in rural areas. Jerusalem's population had evidently been co-opted by Athaliah and made no effort to support the new king (2 Kgs 11:20).

Since Joash was placed on the throne by a priest, it is not surprising that he concerns himself with restoration of the Temple of the Lord, which probably suffered from neglect during Athaliah's reign. Still, it is important to note that the "king's secretary" oversaw the financing of the project (2 Kgs 12:11). This is the first attempt to put more control of the Temple and its affairs in the hand of the king. Hezekiah and Josiah will continue the policy. Even though Joash developed an efficient way to finance the maintenance of the Temple, his efforts were wasted since he had to pay a heavy indemnity to Hazael, who threatened Jerusalem. Nothing else is told of this king's forty-year reign except that he was assassinated by his own courtiers. With three successive rulers assassinated, the stability of the Judahite state was seriously undermined. The book implies that the future of the Judahite state was in question.

The downward spiral of the Kingdom of Israel continued during the seventeen-year reign of Jehoahaz (2 Kgs 13:1–9). Almost constant warfare between Israel and Aram led to the severe depletion of Israel's army (v. 7). Total disaster was averted by an unidentified "savior" (v. 5). It is likely that this savior came in the form of the Assyrian army that invaded Aram at the end of the ninth century, easing the pressure on Israel. With this account of Israel's deteriorating military power, the book begins its description of the fall of the house of Jehu. The end of Jehu's dynasty is inevitable because of the continuing apostasy of Israel's kings (v. 2).

Israel enjoyed a temporary respite from military reverses at the hand of the Arameans during the reign of Jehoash (Joash) (2 Kgs 13:10–25). Before Elisha died, he predicted a revival of Israel's military fortunes. The short note about the revival of a corpse that touched the bones of the dead prophet illustrates how the prophetic word can bring life to the sick body of Israel, because God's saving will did not wish to bring the full force of judgment upon God's people. Tangible proofs of that were the victories of Jehoash and his recovery of Israelite territory lost to Aram.

The book's attention refocuses on Judah, which fared poorly during the reign of Amaziah (2 Kgs 14:1–22). The king did merit qualified praise for his loyalty to God, though worship at the high places, which the book regarded as improper, continued during his rule. While the king was good, he was not good enough to insure Judah's success in the political and military sphere, which the book uses as a benchmark indicating the nation's standing before God. Amaziah was successful in bringing Edom back under Judahite domination, but when he turned his attention to the north, he was unsuccessful. He was defeated by Israel and made a prisoner of war. He witnessed the Israelite forces partially destroy Jerusalem's walls and sack the Temple. His folly in starting a war with the more powerful Northern Kingdom led finally to Amaziah's assassination. The Southern Kingdom's disintegration continues.

The book dismisses the forty-year reign of Jeroboam II in a few verses, but it cannot ignore it completely (2 Kgs 14:23–29). Jeroboam has notable success in expanding the boundaries of his kingdom, which the book usually considers a sign of God's blessing. Here it asserts that Jeroboam's success was the fulfillment of a prophetic word given by Jonah. Although there is a book ascribed to Jonah in the collection of the prophets, the oracle given to Jeroboam is not preserved in that book or anywhere in the Bible. Kings goes on to explain the anomalous success of Jeroboam by claiming that it was the result of God's compassion on Israel (vv. 26–27). Jeroboam's reign is often described as a time of peace and prosperity; in fact it was not. The expansion of Israel's territory had to come by way of war. His building projects put a strain on the country's resources, which eventually led to the severe economic problems that Israel faced following Jeroboam's death. The chasm between rich and poor grew during Jeroboam's time.

Like Jeroboam II, Azariah of Judah enjoyed a very long reign; it was, however, marred by a skin disease that rendered him unable to perform rituals that were reserved to the king (2 Kgs 15:1–7). His son Jotham assumed many of Azariah's duties. Even though the book praises Azariah, this praise is tempered by the comment that he did nothing about the high places that the book considered as illegitimate. Under Azariah, the Kingdom of Judah enjoyed a resurgence, which the book chooses to ignore since it does not reflect its notion of the direction Judah is heading.

Following the long reign of Jeroboam II, the Northern Kingdom began a rush to its total collapse. The text gives little more than the basic outline of a nation devolving into political chaos in the final years of its existence. Zechariah, Jeroboam's son and successor, is barely able to hold the throne for six months before he is assassinated (2 Kgs 15:8–12). Shallum, Zechariah's assassin, managed to hold on to the throne for only one month before his assassination by Menahem, whose ruthlessness kept him on the throne for ten years (2 Kgs 15:13–16). During Menahem's reign, Tiglath-pileser III of Assyria, which the text sometimes calls Pul, began Assyria's expansion at Israel's expense (2 Kgs 15:17–22). Pekahiah, Menahem's son, was able to hold the throne for only two years before his assassination by Pekah (2 Kgs 15:23–26). It was during his reign that the Assyrians began dismantling the Northern Kingdom. Pekah, too, was assassinated after a twenty-year reign by Hoshea, who was destined to be the last in the line that began with Jeroboam I. The book provides few details about the reigns of these five kings because it is more interested in the fate of Israel as a nation whose doom it is describing. The five kings each receive the usual condemnation that is given to all the kings of the north, and their individual fates presage the disaster that Northern Kingdom will experience.

The book has to break off its account of Israel's final years to tell the story of the last conflict between Israel and Judah. Pekah formed a coalition with Aram, Israel's chief rival in the Levant, to deal with a common threat: Assyria, whose expansionism and militarism imperiled them both. Pekah tried to enlist Judah in the coalition but Jotham resisted, while Kings insists that it was God who led Aram and Israel against Judah. Before the issue was decided, Jotham died (2 Kgs 15:32–38). Jotham's son Ahaz is left to deal with the crisis.

The book has no regard for Ahaz, condemning him without reservation (2 Kgs 16:1–20). Ahaz's desperation in the face of the invasion by the combined forces of Aram and Israel is evident from his resorting to child sacrifice as a way to gain divine favor. Ahaz's situation was grievous because he had to face hostilities on two fronts—the Edomites were moving in the south (v. 6), and Aram and Israel were coming from the north. This military pressure led Ahaz to align himself with Tiglath-pileser to whom he paid a large indemnity. The Assyrian king quickly put an end to the coalition seeking to depose Ahaz. Kings then describes in great detail changes that Ahaz made to the Temple and its altar. These are regarded as acts of apostasy (vv. 10–20).

With the account of Ahaz's reign completed, the book returns to Israel, which was on the brink of total collapse. After narrating the events that led to the end of Israel's political existence (2 Kgs 17:1–6), the book launches into a long editorial comment to explain the fall of the Northern Kingdom as a consequence of its failure to shape its national life on the basis of the Torah (2 Kgs 17:7–23). The Assyrians annexed the territory of the former Northern Kingdom into their provincial system. To pacify the region, they led the prominent citizens of Israel into exile and brought in people from other regions of their empire to settle in what had been the Kingdom of Israel. The author of Kings maintains that the Samaritans of his day were the descendants of these foreign settlers and describes their patterns of worship as a hybrid of Yahwism and the worship of foreign deities (2 Kgs 17:24–41).

The Final Years of the Kingdom of Judah (2 Kgs 18:1–25:30)

After describing the fall of the Northern Kingdom, the book details the last years of the Southern Kingdom. Kings begins with the story of Hezekiah, a king greatly admired because of his obedience to the Torah and his destruction of the high places. Hezekiah was able to augment Judah's territories at the expense of the Philistines. In contrast to Israel, Judah and its king appeared to be prospering (2 Kgs 18:1–12). However, the Assyrians ended Hezekiah's peace by invading Judah and besieging Jerusalem; and although Hezekiah offered an indemnity to Sennacherib, the Assyrian king, the siege continued. Sennacherib demanded the surrender of Jerusalem, claiming that Judah's own patron deity had ordered him to conquer the country (2 Kgs 18:1–37, esp. v. 25).

In his despair, Hezekiah turned to the prophet Isaiah, who assured him that Sennacherib would lift the siege and return to his country (v. 7). For reasons that are not clear to historians, the Assyrian army retreated and Sennacherib was assassinated later—just as the prophet predicted (2 Kgs 19:1–37). Of course, Kings sees the lifting of the siege as an act of God. The final episode in Hezekiah's story puts the king's reputation under a cloud. Though God healed him and promised him a longer reign, Hezekiah wanted proof that the promises made to him by Isaiah would be fulfilled. The arrival of an ambassador from Babylon gave Isaiah the opportunity to announce Judah's approaching defeat and exile. Instead of this announcement moving Hezekiah to repentance, the king expresses relief that the disaster will come after he is gone. It is as if Hezekiah learned nothing from the near disaster brought about by the Assyrians (2 Kgs 20:1–21).

Hezekiah was succeeded by his son Manasseh. From Kings' point of view, Judah never fell so low as it did during the fifty-five-year reign of this king. It accuses Manasseh of apostasy, idolatry, and murder, and explicitly identifies him as the Judahite Ahab, leading the Southern Kingdom to disaster as Ahab had in the Northern Kingdom. Unnamed prophets pronounced divine judgment on Manasseh's actions. There is no doubt that Manasseh kept his throne by demonstrating his loyalty to the Assyrians, in part by introducing Assyrian religious rituals to the Jerusalem Temple. He also had to be ruthless in preventing a nationalistic spirit to express itself in open revolt against the Assyrians. The book offers no reason for Manasseh's great apostasy, letting the king's actions speak for themselves. The consequences of his actions could not be set aside with an appeal to God's promises to the patriarchs or to David. Judah's fall is only a matter of time (2 Kgs 21:1–18).

Manasseh was succeeded by his son Amon, who continued his father's policies. This led to his assassination by his own courtiers. Evidently the assassination of yet another king provoked the ordinary folk, who supported the Davidic dynasty. They likely believed that another round of assassinations would be the end of Judah, so they killed the conspirators and installed Amon's young son, Josiah, as king (2 Kgs 21:19–26). It is during Josiah's reign that Judah made one last attempt at reform; it proved to be too late to avert divine judgment.

Josiah's reign was a short pause as Judah moved to the inevitable (2 Kgs 22:1–23:30). Kings describes Josiah as a monarch who "pleased the LORD" (2 Kgs 22:2). A critical event in Josiah's reign was the discovery of a book in the course of renovations that were being made on the Temple. Kings wishes its readers to assume that the "book of the law" was what we know as the book of Deuteronomy. Josiah responded to hearing the words of the book with a gesture of repentance. He had the book authenticated by a prophet. Although Jeremiah was active at this time, the prophet consulted was an otherwise unknown woman named Huldah. She authenticated the book but announced that the curses on the unfaithful found in the book would fall on Judah and Jerusalem but not in Josiah's time.

Fortunately for Josiah, he came into power about the time Assyria's control over the Levant was waning; he moved quickly to reclaim Judah's sovereignty in matters of religion and politics. The book concentrates on Josiah's actions in the sphere of religious practice. The king took action against all types of non-Yahwistic religious activity and promoted such traditional practices as the Passover. His move into the north was likely prompted by a determination to take advantage of Assyria's weakness to extend the territory under his control. Josiah's attempts to reassert and expand Judahite sovereignty ended when he died during an ill-advised attempt to involve himself in international politics. He endeavored to stop the Egyptian army as it was advancing into Mesopotamia and was killed in battle. Josiah's "reform" died with him because Judah once again came under foreign domination. The Egyptians asserted their control over Judah by deposing Josiah's successor Jehoahaz and exiling him to Egypt. They placed another of Josiah's sons, Eliakim, on the throne, changing his name to Jehoiakim (2 Kgs 23:31–35). Judah had to pay an indemnity to the Egyptians. This, of course, burdened Judah's economy, which had been already made fragile by Josiah's military adventures.

With no other choice, Jehoiakim remained a loyal Egyptian vassal until Nebuchadnezzar defeated the Egyptians in two decisive battles, ending Egyptian domination of the Levant. Judah then was forced to submit to Babylon. When Babylon's fortunes changed, Jehoiakim came under Egyptian control again. But Babylon's setback was only temporary, and Judah was forced to submit to Nebuchadnezzar a second time after a siege of Jerusalem, during which Jehoiakim died. Of course, the book sees all this political and military activity as an act of divine judgment on Judah (2 Kgs 23:36–24:7).

Jehoiachin succeeded his father just as the Babylonian siege of Jerusalem was about to end with the city's surrender and the sacking of the Temple. While Judah was able to maintain the appearance of sovereignty, it was more firmly under Babylon's control than ever. Jehoiachin was deposed and exiled along with many of Judah's leading citizens. The Babylonians placed Mattaniah, another of Josiah's brothers on the throne, changing his name to Zedekiah. The book lets the events speak for themselves as Judah's final collapse appears to be imminent. Zedekiah was to be the last king of the Davidic line. He managed to keep his throne for eleven years. No longer able to resist calls to rebel against Babylonian domination, Zedekiah sealed the fate of the dynasty and the kingdom. The Babylonians responded to his rebellion by taking Jerusalem a second time, killing Zedekiah's sons, blinding the king, and leading him into exile. Zedekiah was never heard from again (2 Kgs 24:18–25:7).

Jerusalem too paid for Zedekiah's folly in revolting against Nebuchadnezzar. The city was put to the torch and its Temple was left in ruins. Many of Jerusalem's leading citizens were executed, and the rest were deported to Babylon. Nebuchadnezzar completely reorganized the government of Judah. The Babylonians appointed Gedaliah, who did not belong to the royal family, to administer what would become a new province of the Babylonian empire. They also moved Judah's administrative center from Jerusalem to Mizpah.

Assassins led by a survivor of Judah's royal family killed Gedaliah along with his Judahite and Babylonian retainers. This led many Judahites to seek refuge in Egypt, and those that remained were subject to a third deportation (see Jer 52:30; 2 Kgs 25:8–26). And so ends the story of Israel in its land.

As an epilogue, Kings mentions the parole of Jehoiachin from prison in Babylon (2 Kgs 25: 27–30). Unfortunately, the book does not reflect on the significance of the exiled king's new status for Judah's future. At the most critical moment in his story, the author of Kings is inexplicably reticent, leaving the reader to wonder what will become of Judah and Jerusalem. Is the divine judgment brought on by Judah's failure to be loyal to the Lord and shape its life according to Torah final? Perhaps Jehoiachin's parole is a harbinger of Judah's rehabilitation. The book does not give an explicit answer to these questions. The books of Kings end on a most ambiguous note, requiring its readers to make sense out of a tragic tale.

Continuing Significance of the Books of Kings

Like the other books that make up the Deuteronomistic History of Israel, the books of Kings put in sharp focus the consequences of failing to remain absolutely committed to the Lord and to the pattern of life given to Israel in the book of Deuteronomy. What the books illustrate is a continuing pattern of failure to live responsibly. Although Kings focuses almost exclusively on the actions of the ruling class, it certainly intended its message for a wider audience. These books remind believers today that they bear a responsibility to act on the Word. Election offers no guarantees; rather, it calls believers to greater commitment. The books of Joshua to 2 Kings tell a sad and tragic story. What began with so much hope ends in disaster. It is not a pleasant story—especially in 2 Kings, when it becomes clear that the two Israelite kingdoms are headed toward self-destruction. But the reader today knows that Jerusalem's fall, the end of the national state, and the collapse of all Judahite religious and political institutions were not the end of the story. God's mercy triumphed over God's justice, and a renewed Judah emerged from the exile. The story of Israel in its land makes it absolutely clear that God's moral demands must be taken seriously. Failing to do so brings disaster. But despite this, believers recognize that God is still love.

FURTHER READING

Cogan, Mordechai. *1 Kings*. Anchor Bible 10. Garden City, NY: Doubleday, 2001.

Cogan, Mordechai, and Hayim Tadmor. *2 Kings*. Anchor Bible 11. Garden City, NY: Doubleday, 1988.

DeVries, Simon J. *1 Kings*. Word Biblical Commentary 12. Waco, TX: Word, 1985.

Gray, John. *1 and 2 Kings, a Commentary*. Old Testament Library. 2nd rev. ed. Philadelphia: Westminster, 1976.

Hobbs, T.R. *2 Kings*. Word Bible Commentary 13. Waco, TX: Word, 1985.

Jones, Gwilym H. *1 and 2 Kings*. 2 vols. Grand Rapids, MI: Eerdmans, 1984.

Long, Burke O. *1 Kings: With an Introduction to Old Testament Historical Literature*. Forms of Old Testament Literature 9. Grand Rapids, MI: Eerdmans, 1984.

———. *2 Kings*. Forms of Old Testament Literature 10. Grand Rapids, MI: Eerdmans, 1991.

Nelson, Richard. *First and Second Kings*. Louisville, KY: John Knox, 1987.

Rice, Gene. *Nations Under God: A Commentary on the Book of 1 Kings*. International Theological Commentary. Grand Rapids, MI: Eerdmans, 1990.

Rofé, Alexander. *The Prophetical Stories: The Narratives about the Prophets in the Hebrew Bible, Their Literary Types and History*. Jerusalem: The Magnes Press, 1988.

THE CHRONICLER'S HISTORY AND THE LATER HISTORIES

LESLIE J. HOPPE

1 CHRONICLES

[see pages 474–508 of the Old Testament]

The Chronicler's Work

As the introduction to this book notes (OT, p. 474), the first book of Chronicles is part of a larger work that includes the second book of Chronicles, Ezra, and Nehemiah. This larger work begins with Adam (1 Chr 1:1) and concludes with the writer's own day: the fifth century following the restoration of the Jerusalem Temple after the Babylonian Exile that lasted from 587 to 539 BC. Originally 1 and 2 Chronicles formed one book. The division into two came with the printed Bible. Similarly, the books of Ezra and Nehemiah were a single work that was divided into two.

Although Chronicles begins with Adam, it repeats none of the familiar stories found in Genesis. The first nine chapters of 1 Chronicles are almost completely without narrative material. The text is little more than genealogical lists that the author gleaned from biblical texts and other sources available to him. The narrative proper begins with the story of Saul's death and burial (10:1–14). Perhaps this is the Chronicler's way of stating that it is with David that Israel's story really begins (see note to 1:1–9:34, OT, p. 475).

About half of the material found in Chronicles comes from the books of Samuel and Kings. While Samuel and Kings describe and explain the rise and fall of the Israelite kingdoms, the Chronicler appears to be more interested in the future of the Israelite people. Examining how the Chronicler uses material from Samuel and Kings, and analysis of the material unique to Chronicles, reveals the Chronicler's religious message: Judah's religious institutions and their continuity with the past are critical for its future. One aim of the work is to defend the legitimacy of the Temple of Jerusalem and the significance of its worship for Israel's life. The Chronicler believed that Israel could secure its future only by worshipping its God according to the pattern set by David at God's direction. Israel's hope, then, did not reside in the restoration of its political institutions but in the renewal of legitimate worship in the Temple of Jerusalem under the direction of its priests and Levites.

Position in the Canon

The Septuagint (the ancient Greek translation of the Hebrew Bible) titled the books of Chronicles *Paraleipomena* ("things that were left out"). This was also the name for Chronicles used in the Douay-Rheims version and some other Roman Catholic versions. Evidently those responsible for the Septuagint considered Chronicles a kind of supplement to the books of Samuel and Kings. Perhaps that is why the Septuagint places Chronicles immediately following the books of Kings. Jerome followed this order in the Vulgate (his Latin translation of the Bible). English

Bibles used by both Protestant and Catholic Christians also follow this order.

The books of Chronicles are the last books in the Jewish Bible. Christian Bibles follow an arrangement that has the Old Testament end with the Prophets. The final passage is Malachi's prophecy of the return of Elijah, who will announce the "day of the Lord" (Mal 3:23f). The Church reads a messianic meaning in this text and, following the lead of the New Testament, identifies John the Baptist, the precursor of Jesus, as the returning Elijah (Mt 11:11–14; 17: 11–13). A prophecy regarding the precursor of the Messiah is the perfect way to lead into the story of Jesus' birth with which the New Testament begins.

In the Hebrew Bible as arranged by the rabbis, the prophetic books follow the books of Moses (the Torah or the Pentateuch), since the early rabbis viewed the prophets as expositors of the Torah. The rabbinic Bible has a third division, called the Writings, which is a miscellaneous collection of books that belong to neither the Torah nor the Prophets. The last books of this collection are 1 and 2 Chronicles. Thus the Hebrew Bible ends with the decree of Cyrus (2 Chr 36:23) that calls for the people of Judah to return to Jerusalem and rebuild the Temple in Jerusalem. For two millennia, then, religious Jews scattered throughout the world have found that the last words of their Bible were a call to return to Jerusalem (see also the note to 2 Chr 36:22f, OT, p. 508).

Reading the Book

The first book of Chronicles has a very simple arrangement. The first nine chapters (1:1–9: 34) contain genealogical lists. The rest of the book narrates the story of David (9:35–29:30). The Chronicler's story of David idealizes the king and transforms him into the founder and sponsor of Jerusalem's Temple.

Genealogical Lists (1 Chr 1:1–9:34)

The genealogies of Chronicles represent an extraordinary achievement by the author. The genealogical lists extend from Adam (1:1) to the returnees from the Babylonian Exile (9:2–34).

The author uses the genealogies from the book of Genesis in his own tables that begin with the descent from Adam to Abraham and his sons (1:1–27; see Gn 5; 10; 11). From there the focus is on the twelve sons of Jacob (1:28–2:2). Once the genealogy reaches Judah, one of Jacob's twelve sons, the Chronicler arrives at the centerpiece of his presentation: David (see note to 2:3–4:23, p. 476). There is a genealogy of Judah down to David and his relatives (2:3–17) along with lateral branches of the descendants of Judah (2:18–55; 4:1–23). Chapter 3 lists David's descendants, all the Davidic kings, and their descendants into the postexilic period.

The genealogies of the other tribes follow (4: 23–8:40). These lists are not as extensive as the one for Judah except for the genealogy of the tribe of Levi (5:27–6:6; see note to 5:27—6: 66, p. 481). Another interest of the Chronicler was the priestly tribe of Levi and the cult in which they ministered. Genealogies of Saul's descendants (8:33–40; 9:35–44) frame a list of those who returned from the Babylonian Exile (9:1–34).

The impression left from reading these genealogies is that the true beginning of Israel was not at Sinai with the giving of the Torah, as the Priestly document would have it, but with the rise of David. The Chronicler's unique appreciation for David and his achievements becomes clear in the next section of the book.

The History of David's Reign: (1 Chr 10–29:30)

This section begins with a report on Saul's death and burial (10:1–12), together with a short editorial comment on the dangers Saul's reign posed for Israel because Saul was not faithful to God (see note to 10:13f, p. 449). For the Chronicler, Saul is little more than a foil for David, whose portrait the Chronicler painted with the strokes of piety and fidelity.

The Chronicler includes nothing from the books of Samuel that compromise his idealized portrait of David. For example, he omits David's conflicts with Saul, his service with the Philistines, David's career-advancing marriages, and the political maneuvers that led to his acclamation as king of Israel. For example, 2 Samuel 2: 4 states that "the men of Judah" anointed David as the king of their tribe following Saul's death. David ruled over Judah for seven years before the elders of Israel chose him as king over the rest of the tribes (2 Sm 5:1–5). The Chronicler, however, states that "all Israel" made David king immediately following Saul's death (1 Chr 11: 1–3). Among the notable additions to David's story as told in 2 Samuel is the story of the ark. While 2 Samuel portrays David's decision to bring the ark into Jerusalem as a decision made by David alone (2 Sm 6:1f), the Chronicler describes the same event as an act sanctioned by all the people (1 Chr 13:1–5). The Chronicler's account of the ark's entrance into Jerusalem highlights the role of the Levites. David appoints them to carry the ark into the city (1 Chr 15: 11–15). Since David also commissioned them to be singers in the Temple (1 Chr 15:16–22), they sing a psalm (1 Chr 16:7–36).

For the Chronicler, David's significance for Israel does not lie in the political sphere but in the religious. This spin on the story of David leads the Chronicler to suppress anything that sullies David's reputation. For example, the Chronicler omits the entire story of how Solomon succeeded David as king (2 Sm 9–20; 1 Kgs 1–2) from his narrative. The Chronicler says nothing about David's adultery with Bathsheba and the events that followed it, including Nathan's condemnation of David (2 Sm 12:1–12). Similarly the Chronicler makes no mention of the two revolts against David (see 2 Sm 15–18; 20:1–22).

The Chronicler devotes the bulk his story of David (17–29) to the plans for building the Temple, which Solomon will carry out. This, of course, makes Solomon a central figure in the Chronicler's story (see note to 22:2ff, OT, p. 461) so the Chronicler also idealizes David's son, eliminating the stories from 1 Kings that highlight Solomon's religious and moral failings. The Chronicler's story of Solomon's succession to David appears to be a deliberate effort to imitate the account of the transition from Moses to Joshua in Deuteronomy 21 and Joshua 1. The Chronicler considered Solomon's succession to David's throne as important as Joshua's succession to the Mosaic office.

The Establishment of the Temple

The Chronicler paints the portraits of David and Solomon in order to underscore their respective roles in the establishment of the Temple and its liturgy. Worship, then, is one of the Chronicler's principal concerns. The God who is present in Judah's experience evokes a response in worship from the people whose destiny this God guides. The Chronicler tries to show that Judah's future is dependent upon its fidelity to the proper forms of worship that God has revealed through David. There is a reciprocal relationship between God and Judah. God blesses Judah, and Judah worships God.

For the Chronicler, the Temple and its liturgy were symbols of God's continuing presence among the people of Judah. As long as the priests offered the correct sacrifices at the appropriate times in the presence of a grateful people, the Lord will dwell in Judah's midst. For the Chronicler, the history of Israel was not a series of unrelated actions by kings and prophets. Its nucleus was the worship led by the priests appointed by Moses and David. The Chronicler recognized that there were times when Judah's sin led to serious failures to offer proper worship, but Judah's sin was never fatal. Judah was always able to recover, resume proper liturgical services, and thus be certain of God's abiding presence. The fall of Jerusalem and the exile to Babylon formed an unfortunate interruption in an otherwise unbroken history of Judah as a community that offered legitimate worship to its ancestral deity. The only way to avoid a similar disaster in the future was to worship God in Jerusalem's Temple according to rituals that go back to those developed by David.

The Importance of the Temple

For proper worship of the Lord, a Temple is indispensable. Like the books of Kings, Chronicles recognizes the legitimacy of only one temple—the Temple at Jerusalem. At the time of the composition of the Chronicler's history, the worshippers of Israel's ancestral deity were not unanimous in recognizing Jerusalem's Temple as the only legitimate place of worship. There was a temple dedicated to the Lord in Samaria, and at Elephantine (a Jewish military colony located on an island near the modern city of Aswan in Egypt). In telling the story of the Northern Kingdom, the Chronicler does not even choose to mention the sanctuaries at Dan or Bethel that Jeroboam I built (see 1 Kgs 12:26–29). For the Chronicler there could be only one Temple. David built this Temple under the same kind of divine guidance that led Moses to build the tabernacle in the wilderness. The Lord gave David the plans for the Temple in Jerusalem (1 Chr 28: 19). No other sanctuary could be a legitimate place to worship the God of Israel.

The Temple Personnel

Chapters 23 through 27 appear to be intrusive in the Chronicler's story about David and Solomon, but they are central to the Chronicler's concern to describe the contours of the proper worship of God. Chapter 23 deals with Levitical class; 24 with priestly classes; 25 with Levitical singers; 26 with the gatekeepers of the Temple, and 27 with army commanders, tribal leaders, and royal advisers. The passages that deal with the priests and Levites are important for the Chronicler's general purpose. Not only is the proper place for worshipping God crucial but so is having the proper personnel to officiate at the rites (see also 2 Chr 13:9–11). The Chronicler provides quite a lot of detail about the people whom God chose to officiate at the liturgy in Jerusalem. At one time, any male Israelite could offer sacrificial worship. Gradually, however, members of the tribe of Levi became the preferred ministers of the ritual. Chronicles reflects a further development. Some members of the tribe of Levi were priests, who offered sacrifices, while the rest were temple singers and assistants to the priests.

The Priests

Although the Chronicler recognized the priests as the chief religious officials, there are clear indications that he did not regard them too highly (2 Chr 29:34; 30:3). Among the duties of the priests, there was the responsibility to blow the trumpets (1 Chr 16:6), to minister in the inner sanctuary (2 Chr 5:14), to offer sacrifice on the altar (2 Chr 29:21), and to burn incense (2 Chr 26:18). Though the Deuteronomist recognized that others besides the tribe of Levi could serve as priests, the Chronicler makes no exception other than David himself. For example, the Deuteronomist relates that David's sons were priests (2 Sm 8:18), but in a parallel passage (1 Chr 18:17), the Chronicler calls them "chief assistants to the king" (see the note to 18:17, OT, p. 497). The Chronicler does depict David as exercising priestly prerogatives: he wore priestly vestments (1 Chr 15:27), he blessed the people (16:2), and he offered sacrifice (16:26). David, however, was the only exception.

The Levites

The Chronicler asserts that the Levites did more than a few menial chores connected with the liturgy of the Temple. They carried the ark (1 Chr 15:15). They were singers (15:16–22) and gatekeepers (15:23). The Levites fulfilled all their responsibilities under the direction of priests (1 Chr 23:27–32). The Levites were a type of "lower clergy." They also had roles that were not directly related to worship. The Levites were judges (2 Chr 19:8, 11), prophets (2 Chr 20:14f), and fund raisers (2 Chr 24:5; 34:9).

Temple Slaves

The Chronicler also describes a third group of religious personnel: the "temple slaves" (Ezr 8: 20). The Chronicler mentions them only a few times in his history. They were the lowest class of liturgical functionaries (Neh 7:72), and their task was to help the Levites (Ezr 8:20).

Roman Catholic Priesthood

The sacrament of Orders in the Roman Catholic Church is largely a part of our heritage from ancient Israel. The rituals of ordination recognize this heritage. The division of orders in the Roman Catholic Church into the episcopacy, presbyterate, and diaconate mirrors to some extent the Chronicler's division of temple personnel into priests, Levites, and temple slaves. Of course the status, role, and interrelationships of the orders in the Church are different from those of the Old Testament's cultic personnel, yet the concern in the Church for a hierarchy among the people directly concerned with worship is similar to that of the Chronicler.

There is not a single instance in the New Testament of anyone called a "priest" presiding at Christian worship. It is the Chronicler (and even more the Priestly strand of the Pentateuch, especially Leviticus and Numbers) who tries to make the reader sensitive to the presence of God in the act of sacrificial worship led by "official" ministers. For the Chronicler the priests and Levites were those through whom God's abiding presence among the people was evident. The rituals that they conducted were a source of blessing for the people and an act of devotion to their God. The Chronicler's God was not a hidden God. The people experienced God in worship more than anywhere else. It should be clear that the value that the Church places on the liturgy and priesthood finds a strong support in the Chronicler's history.

FURTHER READING

Ackroyd, Peter R. "The Chronicler in his Age." *Journal for the Study of the Old Testament Supplement Series,* no. 101. Sheffield: Sheffield Academic Press, 1991.

Berquist, Jon L. *Judaism in Persia's Shadow: A Social and Historical Approach.* Minneapolis: Augsburg Fortress, 1996.

Graham, M. P., ed. "The Chronicler as Historian." *JSOT Supplement Series,* no. 238. Sheffield: Sheffield Academic Press, 1997.

Mangan, Celine, O.P. *1–2 Chronicles; Ezra; Nehemiah.* Old Testament Message Series 13. Wilmington, DE: Michael Glazier.

Myers, Jacob M. *1 and 2 Chronicles.* Anchor Bible 12 and 13; Garden City, NY: Doubleday, 1965.

——. "The Kerygma of the Chronicler." In *Interpretation 20* (1966): 259–73.

Williamson, H. G. M. *1 and 2 Chronicles.* New Century Bible Commentary. Grand Rapids: Eerdmans, 1982.

2 CHRONICLES

[see pages 508–547 of the Old Testament]

Chronicles and the Israelite Kingdoms

The second book of Chronicles continues the story of Israel with the accession of Solomon to the throne of David. Comparing the way Chronicles tells this story with the narratives in the books of Kings helps to see the purpose of the Chronicler. For example, after Solomon's death and the breakup of the Davidic-Solomonic empire into the two national states of Israel and Judah, the Chronicler all but ignores the Northern Kingdom (Israel) and its kings. He focuses his attention on the Southern Kingdom (Judah). The Chronicler mentions Israel only when the story of Judah makes it necessary to do so. By contrast, throughout the books of Kings, the author synchronizes the reigns of the kings in the south with those in the north (for example, 1 Kgs 15:1,9,25,33). In 2 Chronicles there is only one such synchronization: 2 Chronicles 13:1. The Chronicler wishes to focus on the Davidic dynasty and what was, in his opinion, its finest achievement—the Temple in Jerusalem. Also, the Chronicler's treatment of Judah's kings focuses almost entirely on the promotion of legitimate worship and the performance of the proper ritual.

Reading the Book

Solomon

The story of Solomon (2 Chr 1–9) deals exclusively with the building of the Temple as envisioned by David. Again the Chronicler does not repeat the negative aspects of Solomon's story that 1 Kings recounts. For example, the Chronicler omits the details about how Solomon secured his throne through the execution of potential opponents, including his half brother Adonijah (1 Kgs 2). Also unmentioned is Solomon's marriage to the daughter of Pharaoh (1 Kgs 3:1) and other non-Israelite women (1 Kgs 11:1–13) that the book of Kings presents as a compromise of the exclusive loyalty that Solomon owed to the God of Israel. In his description of the wealth and glory of the Temple, the Chronicler goes beyond the words of Kings (compare 2 Chr 3–4 with 1 Kgs 6–8). After Solomon's prayer of dedication, fire falls from heaven and consumes the sacrifice. God's glory fills the Temple (2 Chr 7:1f). Here the Chronicler models the story of the Temple's dedication on that of the tabernacle in the wilderness (Ex 40:34f). Throughout the description of Solomon's achievement in building and dedicating the Temple, the Chronicler reminds his readers of David's preparations (2:6, 13, 16; 3:1; 5:1; 6:3–11). In the eyes of the Chronicler, the Temple was the combined enterprise of David and Solomon, who each made his own contribution to the completion of this great work.

The Kingdom of Judah

The remaining chapters of the book (10 through 36) rehearse the history of Judah to the Babylonian Exile from the singular perspective of the Chronicler. 2 Chronicles passes over much detail important in 1 and 2 Kings without a mention because of its focus on the liturgy of the Temple. On the other hand, the Chronicler mentions various building activities, military, and administrative matters that the Deuteronomist ignores. Most of these reports occur in passages about kings that the Chronicler evaluates positively because they promoted what the Chronicler regarded as the proper worship of Israel's God.

Rehoboam, Solomon's son and successor, builds fortifications (11:5–12) at the beginning of his career. His failure to remain completely faithful to the Law of God results in the partial conquest of his realm by the pharaoh Shishak (12:1–5). The Chronicler is favorable to Abijah, Rehoboam's successor, in contrast to 1 Kings, which calls him Abijam (1 Kgs 15:1–8). At the outset of a war he wages against the Northern Kingdom, Abijah addresses a long theological speech to his opponents. In it he states that the legitimate cult of Judah guarantees its victory over Israel because Israel has forsaken the true worship of the Lord (2 Chr 13:4–12). This speech is a good indicator of the Chronicler's principal concerns. Both Asa and Jehosophat, Judah's next two kings, receive a positive evaluation from the Chronicler, who recounts their building, military, and cultic projects (14:5–15:15; 17:6–9; 19:4–20:30). Second Chronicles, then, depicts the first four kings that ruled Judah following the breakup of the Davidic-Solomonic empire as conscientious, qualified, and loyal to the Lord.

Following the lead of 2 Kings, the Chronicler rates positively several other kings from the Davidic dynasty: Uzziah (2 Chr 26:4; see 2 Kgs 15:3, which calls him Azariah; see also the note to 2 Kgs 14:21, OT, p. 458), Jotham (2 Chr 27:2; see 2 Kgs 15:34), Hezekiah (2 Chr 29:2; see 2 Kgs 18:3), and Josiah (2 Chr 34:2; see 2 Kgs 22:2).

Chapters 29 through 31 describe a thoroughgoing reform of Judah's liturgy under Hezekiah. This reform included a confession of past neglect of proper worship (2 Chr 29:5–11), the cleansing of the Temple (29:16f), and the celebration of the Passover. Hezekiah invited the northerners who survived the Assyrian conquest to join the people of Judah in the renewal of the covenant (30:1–9). The account of Hezekiah's reign in 2 Kings 18–20 says little about Hezekiah's reform because 2 Kings wished to portray Josiah as a second David who restored the covenant (2 Kgs 22–23). Another striking contrast to 2 Kings is the Chronicler's portrait of Manasseh, whom 2 Kings presents as the most evil of all Judah's kings. His sins were responsible for the fall of the Southern Kingdom (2 Kgs 21:1–18). The Chronicler rehabilitates Manasseh by describing his conversion, which leads to a reform of Judah's worship (2 Chr 33:11–17). It is likely that the Chronicler wanted his readers to identify with Manasseh by confessing their sins and renewing their commitment to the proper worship of Israel's God. The Chronicler's portrait of Manasseh inspired the apocryphal work known as the *Prayer of Manasseh,* a second-century BC text that is a classic of penitential devotion. (Although Jerome included a translation of this work in the Vulgate, the Council of Trent decided not to include the *Prayer of Manasseh* in the canon of the Old Testament.)

The Chronicler's version of Josiah's reform (2 Chr 34–35) distinguishes several stages. This probably reflects the actual event more accurately than the account in 2 Kings 22–23 that telescopes all the activities of the reform into a single year (see the note to 34:3, OT, p. 543).

The Chronicler evaluates the last three kings of Judah (Jehoiachin, Jehoiakim, and Zedekiah) negatively (2 Chr 36:5–14). After an editorial comment explaining the cause of the exile (36:15–21), the book ends with the decree of Cyrus that calls for the restoration of Jerusalem and the rebuilding of its Temple (36:22–23).

The Purpose of the Chronicler

Why did the Chronicler bother to retell the story of Judah's monarchy? After all, 2 Samuel through 2 Kings already told that story. Indeed, the Chronicler derived much of his story from these books. Still, when we look more closely at the Chronicler's treatment of the Judahite national state and its kings, we can see that the basic purpose of this new version of the story of David and his dynasty was to guide the Jerusalem community as it was reestablishing itself following the exile. In the eyes of the Chronicler, the one lasting contribution of the Davidic monarchy was the Temple, its rituals, and its priesthood. The Jewish community as a whole functioned as the successor of that dynasty. Once the people rebuilt the Temple and restored the proper form of its liturgy, the essential elements of Jewish life were in place. According to the Chronicler, David and Solomon combined forces to establish a divinely ordained liturgy in Jerusalem. The people, led by Ezra and Nehemiah, have resumed the service of God according to the pattern set by David. In the Chronicler's scheme, the restoration of the national state and the Davidic dynasty was not as crucial as the reestablishment of the proper worship of the Lord in Jerusalem. The people who supported the Temple and resumed the authentic worship there have fulfilled all the really important tasks of monarchy.

The Theology of the Chronicler

The Chronicler's account of the ancient Israelite monarchy differs markedly from that found in the books of Samuel and Kings. Although the Chronicler used these books as sources for his own work, he reinterpreted the material in them in order to provide his readers with a new understanding of the Davidic dynasty. While the books of Kings underscore the failure of the dynasty, the Chronicler presents the dynasty in the best possible light. The Chronicler wants to assure his readers that Judah's future depends upon the resumption of Temple service as established by David and as maintained by most of his successors. But there may have been political considerations at work in the Chronicler's telling of the story of Judah's monarchy as well. Determining this depends upon the question of dating the books of Chronicles. The introduction to 1 Chronicles dates these books to "the end of the fifth century BC" [OT, p. 475]. At this time, relations between the people of Judah and the people of the former Northern Kingdom were strained. Apparently the northerners were attempting to exert political control over Judah. This caused the animosity that grew over the years and continued into the New Testament period. The people of Judah came to regard the northerners, whom they called "Samaritans" after their ancient capital Samaria, as apostates. Both theological and political considerations combined to lead the Chronicler to reinterpret the history of Israel's monarchy in the way he did. He believed that the future of Judah depended on its absolute commitment to the authentic worship of the Lord in the Jerusalem Temple, which the Northern Kingdom rejected.

Jews and Samaritans

The books of Chronicles reflect one stage in the division that arose between the Jews and the Samaritans. Historical reconstruction has not been able to identify any sudden and dramatic act that divided the two groups irrevocably. According to Samaritan sources, the division took place at the end of the period of the judges (eleventh century BC) when Eli left Shechem and established a high-priestly line at Shiloh. According to the biblical tradition (2 Kgs 17), the separation took place in the eighth century BC, when the people of the former Northern Kingdom intermarried with foreign peoples whom the Assyrians introduced into their territory. Although it is not possible to treat either of these two accounts as straight history, they do point to important concerns. In the Chronicler's perspective, the Samaritans did not have the true priesthood (2 Chr 13:9), and therefore their sacrificial worship was worthless.

Aside from the polemics of Jewish and Samaritan sources, the Samaritans were one example of the rich diversity in early Judaism. Their religious traditions developed independently of the leadership of the community that arose around the priests of Jerusalem. Other examples of the variety of religious perspectives in early Judaism include the Hasidim, the Essenes, and the Pharisees. An important moment in this development was the building of the Samaritan temple on Mount Gerizim (near Shechem) sometime in the early Hellenistic period (late fourth century BC). It was the building of this temple by the Samaritans and its later destruction by the Jewish king John Hyrcanus in 128 BC that led to the definitive break between the Jews and the Samaritans.

It is within this context that one should read John 4 in which Jesus meets the Samaritan woman at the well in Shechem. Her comments reflect the religious and historical conflicts between her people and the Jews. Jesus, of course, says that there will come a day when true worship of God will transcend the conflict between Jew and Samaritan (Jn 4:21). T he Chronicler's attitude toward those outside the community who worshipped the Lord centered in Jerusalem offers a striking example of an unwillingness to accept too great a diversity among those who considered themselves to be worshippers of the Lord. The reasons for the Chronicler's attitude are complex. In part they were political and economic. Apparently the province of Samaria wanted to control Jerusalem, while the leadership of the Jerusalem community wished to remain independent of such control. In part the reasons were religious and liturgical. Although the people in the north wished to help with the rebuilding of the Jerusalem Temple (Ezr 4:2), the Judahites refused their help. Perhaps they did not believe that the northerners were sincere because of their continued use of the sanctuaries at Dan and Bethel. The Judahites considered the cult at these sanctuaries to be illegitimate. In part the reasons for the rift were historical. The Israelite tribes in the north and the south developed somewhat independently of one another, and the northerners cherished this independence fiercely. Whatever the reasons for the Chronicler's attitude toward the northerners who considered themselves to be authentic worshippers of the Lord, it was decidedly negative. It contributed to the tension between Jews and Samaritans that has lasted into the present.

The Chronicler's approach to the problem of religious diversity was understandable given the political and religious realities of the fourth century BC. The rigid application of the directives of Ezra and Nehemiah and the intensity of the Chronicler's rhetoric (see 2 Chr 13:4–12) made it difficult for succeeding generations to overcome the division between Jew and Samaritan. Indeed, further divisions occurred within the Jewish community. The Essenes opposed the Hasmoneans. The Pharisees disputed with the Sadducees. The Herodians fought with the Zealots. In the middle of all this, Christianity emerged. Eventually, because of historical circumstances, the Pharisaic party survived the fall of Jerusalem in AD 70 and was the precursor of rabbinic Judaism. The Kairites of Babylon refused to accept the authority of the rabbis. Even within Judaism today, some Orthodox rabbis do not accept the legitimacy of Conservative and Reform Judaism. The Chronicler did not succeed in eliminating religious diversity among those who considered themselves worshippers of the Lord.

Relationships among Christian Churches

Until the Second Vatican Council, the attitude of Catholics toward other Christians was similar to the lack of tolerance that the Chronicler showed toward religious diversity. One of the principal concerns of the Council was promoting the restoration of unity among all Christians (*Decree on Ecumenism,* 1). Like the Chronicler, who is in part responsible for the rift between Jew and Samaritan, the Catholic Church, according to the Council, shares in responsibility for the divisions among Christian churches (*Decree on Ecumenism,* 3). One way to overcome these divisions is through dialogue that leads to a knowledge and appreciation of the doctrine and religious life of the many Christian churches.

Of the two main kinds of division within the Christian community, that which separates the East from the West resembles the separation between Jew and Samaritan that developed in the last four centuries before Christ. Although there were tensions between East and West for a long time, they came to a head in AD 1054 with the excommunication of the Patriarch of Constantinople by the papal legate and the patriarch's consequent excommunication of the pope's delegate. Four centuries later, other divisions arose in western Christianity as a result of the Reformation. The differences between Christian churches are not simply theological but are also historical, political, sociological, cultural, and even psychological.

To help overcome these divisions within Christianity, the Council suggested that dialogue among Christian churches focus first on those elements that the various Christian churches share: the Scriptures, belief in Christ, baptism, and the Eucharist. The diversity of customs and doctrines will not then necessarily be obstacles to unity. We will recognize them as contributing to the Church's beauty, helpful adaptations to differences of culture, necessary for the good of the faithful.

To the Christian churches that today are struggling with the project of restoring the Church's unity, the Chronicler presents an object lesson regarding what can happen when concern for the survival of one religious community leads to a type of narrow exclusivism that ignores the values of other people's approach to God. The tasks of Ezra and Nehemiah and the duty of the Chronicler were clear: to ensure the survival of the small community of the Lord surrounding Jerusalem whose continued existence was in doubt. They fulfilled their responsibilities. The responsibility of Christian churches is somewhat different today: to restore Christian unity. To make unity a possibility, Christians will need to be more willing to live with religious diversity than they have been. The Chronicler's hesitancy regarding religious diversity is understandable. Judaism was struggling for its very survival. Christianity today is not as beleaguered as was Judaism in the Chronicler's day. Achieving unity while respecting diversity should be easier for us.

FURTHER READING

Coggins, R. J. *Samaritans and Jews: The Origins of Samaritism Reconsidered.* Atlanta: John Knox, 1975.

Crown, A. D. and others, ed. *A Companion to Samaritan Studies.* Tübingen: J. C. B. Mohr, 1993.

Dexinger, F. "Limits of Tolerance in Judaism: The Samaritan Example." In *Jewish and Christian Self-Definition.* Vol. 2, *Aspects of Judaism in the Graeco-Roman Period,* edited by E. P. Sanders and others, 88–114. Philadelphia: Fortress Press, 1981.

See also 1 Chronicles.

EZRA

[See pages 548–560 of the Old Testament]

The Book of Ezra

This book and the book of Nehemiah are the only narrative accounts of the postexilic period to have survived in the Hebrew Bible. Originally the books of Ezra and Nehemiah were components of a single work. The book of Nehemiah does not even have its own title in Jewish Bibles. There is simply a marginal notation alongside Nehemiah 1:1 that reads "The Book of Nehemiah." In most editions of the Septuagint (the second-century BC Greek version of the Hebrew Bible), the two books form a unit.

The Vulgate (St. Jerome's translation of the Bible) separated the two books, and this is how the separation came into our English Bibles. It was only during the sixteenth century AD that what was one book became two in Jewish Bibles (see the introduction to the book of Ezra, OT, p. 548).

There is some internal evidence that these books form a coherent unit. The whole period of the restoration as covered by the books of Ezra and Nehemiah is one great era of return and rebuilding framed by two celebrations of the Feast of Booths. (Booths is the fall harvest festival, also known as Tabernacles and as Sukkoth, its Hebrew name.) The first celebration takes place after the return (Ezr 3:4) and the second after the rebuilding is complete (Neh 8:13–18). Both celebrations are in accord with what is "written" in Torah (Ezr 3:4; Neh 8:14, 18).

The Restoration

The books of Ezra and Nehemiah deal with the restoration of Judah following the years of exile in Babylon (587–539 BC). These books deal with two phases of the restoration. The first is the rebuilding of the Temple in Jerusalem, and the second is the reordering of Jewish life. The Temple was rebuilt in 515 BC. Determining the dates for the work of Ezra and Nehemiah, who were responsible for the reordering of Jewish life in Jerusalem, is one of the more perplexing problems for the historian of early Judaism. The problem centers on Ezra 7:7f and Nehemiah 2:1. The former asserts that Ezra's ministry began in the seventh year of Artaxerxes' reign, while the latter states that Nehemiah's projects began in "the twentieth year of King Artaxerxes." There were, however, three Persian monarchs who had this name and who are potential candidates for the Artaxerxes mentioned in these texts.

The biblical text appears to assume that Ezra's ministry preceded that of Nehemiah. The chronological priority is due less to historical memory than to the Bible's view that Ezra was the real restorer of Jewish life following the exile. Although there is no real consensus on this issue, it is probable that Nehemiah's ministry preceded that of Ezra. Ezra's work appears to presuppose that the reconstruction and repopulation of Jerusalem had taken place, but it was Nehemiah who was responsible for restoring the city. Then, too, the high priest during Nehemiah's time was Eliashib (Neh 3:1, 20; 13:4) while the high priest during Ezra's time was the son of Eliashib, Johanan (Ezr 10:6; see note on this verse, OT, p. 559). The order and names of the postexilic high priests are additional problems for historians; still it seems likely that Nehemiah preceded Ezra. It is more likely that the restoration of communal life in Jerusalem preceded the restoration of religious life. Nehemiah, then, worked during the reign of Artaxerxes I and arrived in Jerusalem in 445 BC, while Ezra worked during the reign of Artaxerxes II and arrived in Jerusalem in 398 BC.

The chronology of the Judean restoration given in the books of Ezra and Nehemiah is ambiguous. Reconstructing this chronology is not very easy. The books of Ezra and Nehemiah are more interested in presenting the religious dimension to the activities of the two men whose names they bear. Despite the many problems in reconciling the details of this narrative, the author of Ezra and Nehemiah achieved his principal goal: to describe the beginning of renewal in the life of Judah.

There are important political reasons that explain why Persian rulers expressed concern about conditions in Judah. By supporting the rebuilding of the Temple in Jerusalem, the Persian emperors were staking their claim to be the legitimate rulers of Judah. In the ancient Near East, temple building was a royal prerogative. Since the beginning of both Nehemiah's and Ezra's missions coincided with Egyptian revolts against Persian hegemony, it was important for the Persians to have a sympathetic and supportive Judah in their rear as they moved against the rebellious Egyptians.

Reading the Book of Ezra

The book of Ezra falls into two parts covering the two periods of postexilic history. Chapters 1 through 6 cover the themes of the return from exile and the rebuilding the Temple. Chapters 7 through 10 describe the mission of Ezra to reconstitute Judah as a community living in accord with the Torah.

The Return from Exile and Rebuilding of the Temple (Ezr 1:1–6:22)

Aramaic

The most striking feature of this section is not apparent to those who read it in translation. While the rest of the book of Ezra is in Hebrew, 4:7–6:18 is in Aramaic. The author cites a few official Persian documents relating to the restoration of Judah. These documents were written in Aramaic, the common language of the diverse peoples that made up the empire and the official language of the imperial administration. The alternation between Hebrew and Aramaic shows that the people for whom the author wrote were bilingual.

Originally Aramaic was the language of the Arameans. It is a Semitic language that is akin to Hebrew. Because the Arameans were active in commercial affairs in the ancient Near East, the language became widely known. Aramaic came to be the language of diplomacy. According to 2 Kings 18:26, both the Assyrian and Judahite officers understood the language, while the common people did not. By the sixth century BC, however, it became the most commonly used Semitic language. It was in general use in Palestine until Greek became the language of commerce, government, and literary culture after the conquests of Alexander in the fourth century BC. Aramaic, however, remained the language of the common people until the seventh century AD when Arabic replaced it. Aramaic was the language in which Jesus conversed, although he may have known Greek as well. Hebrew was not a language of everyday conversation. Rabbinic traditions, however, continued to be transmitted in Hebrew. The *Mishnah,* a collection of legal traditions, and the *Midrashim,* homiletic texts, were composed and transmitted in Hebrew. Because people did not regularly converse in Hebrew, however, it became necessary for Jews to make Aramaic versions *(Targums)* of the Old Testament. Aramaic is also the language of the Talmud (the compendium of Jewish law dating from the sixth century AD). It was not until the twentieth century that the Hebrew language was reborn and once again became a language of ordinary discourse in the modern state of Israel.

The Return of the Exiles

Chapters 1 through 3 cover the return from exile. First there is a proclamation made by Cyrus, king of Persia, that every exile from Judah who was ready to return to Jerusalem to rebuild its Temple should do so (1:1–4). Then the following verses describe the return itself (1:5–11). Chapter 2 gives a list of the returnees. At the top of the list is Zerubbabel, a member of the Davidic family, and Jeshua, a member of a prominent priestly family. In chapter 3, these two play important roles in the revival of worship in Jerusalem. Sacrifices begin on a provisional altar (3:1–3). The people observe the Feast of Booths (3:4) and they initiate the regular sacrifices (3:5). Most important of all, they prepare for the rebuilding of the Temple (3:6–13).

There were problems with the rebuilding. The author lists these in 4:1–6:13. Opposition to the project came from "the enemies of Judah and Benjamin" (4:1) and "the people of the land" (4: 4). Both groups tried to convince the Persians that the restoration of Jerusalem was an act of political disloyalty. In 4:7–23 there is opposition to rebuilding the walls of the city. In the end all opposition failed, and the people of Judah successfully completed their project with the full support of the Persian imperial authorities (6: 14, 22).

Ezra's Mission (Ezr 7:1–10:44)

Ezra's Commission from the Persian Emperor

The account of Ezra's activity begins with chapter 7 and concludes with chapter 10 although Nehemiah 8 also mentions Ezra. Ezra 7–8 provide an account of Ezra's journey from Babylon to Jerusalem. The genealogy in 7:1–5 shows that Ezra was a Zadokite priest. (The Zadokite priests were those associated with the Jerusalem Temple in the preexilic period. Zadok was the priest who served David and Solomon.) Ezra was an expert in the Torah (7:6) which the priests who were in exile developed while in Babylon. Another Aramaic document (the credentials that Artaxerxes gave to Ezra) takes up 7:12–26. This imperial commission includes information about contributions to the Temple in Jerusalem (vv. 13–25) and the order to reestablish Judahite society based on the "law of God" (vv. 13–15,25). It was Persian policy to restore and support the worship of national deities throughout their empire. Additionally, the Persians usually charged the priests of temple cities with codifying local customs into a legal corpus to maintain the ethnic identity and local traditions. By their acceptance or rejection of the Torah, the Judahites defined themselves as belonging to or rejecting membership in the Jewish community. The emperor granted Ezra power to establish an executive structure for the governance of the Jewish community. This means that in the view of the Persian government the priestly version of ancient Israel's ancestral faith was the "official" religion of Judah.

The account of Ezra's journey to Jerusalem begins with a list of those returning with him (8: 1–14) and Ezra's persuading of the Levites who had been unwilling to make the journey (vv. 15–20). The author seems to have modeled the rest of the chapter on the description of the Exodus from Egypt (Ex 14) and the crossing of the Jordan and the occupation of the land (Jos 3–4).

The Problem of Mixed Marriages

The remaining two chapters deal with Jews who have married outside their religious community (9:1). Ezra finds their behavior unacceptable and recites a long penitential prayer on their behalf (9:5–15). The people decide to set matters straight (10:1–3), and they ask Ezra for help (10: 4–6). After a public assembly takes place, a special commission begins work (10:7–17). It produces a list of those who married Gentiles (10: 18–44). The text of 10:44 does not make sense in Hebrew ("and there were from them wives and they put sons"). The translators based their rendering of this text on the Septuagint, the ancient Greek version of the Old Testament. The Hebrew text is unclear about the action taken in this matter, but some Jewish men probably divorced their non-Jewish wives in response to Ezra's urging.

Exclusivism in Ezra

In denouncing mixed marriages, Ezra speaks of the Jews as a "holy race" (Ezr 9:2). He accuses the people of Judah of desecrating themselves with "the peoples of the land." The Jewish community of the fifth century BC faced the same types of threats to its existence as did the Israelite tribes centuries before the establishment of the Israelite national state (thirteenth to the eleventh centuries BC). At that time the Israelites faced hostile neighbors. They were unable to defend themselves adequately. There was little unity or even cooperation among the tribes. In the eleventh century BC, the prophet Samuel, responding to these problems, complied with popular sentiment and established the monarchy. The king provided order and stability to the foundering Israelite tribes. The Davidic dynasty, which that lasted from the eleventh to the sixth centuries BC, furnished a sense of continuity. In the fifth century BC, Persian hegemony made the reestablishment of Judah's native dynasty impossible. Ezra provided the community with another source of stability and continuity.

Ezra offered the Jewish community the Torah, which the Jews came to see as encompassing an eternal order given by God to Israel alone. This notion of Torah had some profound effects in the social order. It made the Jewish community exclusive. It led to the idea of a "holy race" (Ezr 9:2), which was to remain unsullied by contact with the nations. Ezra believed that the Jews were in danger of being absorbed by the non-Jewish culture that surrounded them and therefore becoming extinct. In response to this threat, he taught that there was a very specific criterion for membership in the Jewish community. A principle of heredity supplied the Jewish self-definition. It was a definition that was clear to every member of the community. Earlier traditions also attempted to deal with the loss of identity through assimilation by intermarriage with Gentiles (Ex 34:16; Dt 7:3; 23:3–5). Such marriages were acceptable in some traditions (Gn 41:45; Ru 1). Even Moses himself married a non-Israelite (Nm 12:1). With Ezra this all changed, and mixed marriages were no longer permissible. Under Ezra, the Jewish community was not open to outsiders.

The elevation of heredity to the position of defining the people of God is understandable, yet it compromised Israel's role as a source of blessing for the nations (Gn 12:2f) and as God's servant bringing the Torah and its peace to the nations (Is 49:1–7). The Samaritans whom Ezra's decrees excluded from the people of God considered him their archenemy. Samaritan writings are full of derogatory comments about Ezra. In contrast, the Talmud considers Ezra to be a second Moses (Sanhedrin 2 ib) because he restored observance of the Torah when the people had forgotten about it (Sukkah 20a). Early Christianity also had to deal with Ezra's legacy as it faced the consequences of its highly successful mission to the Gentiles (Acts 10:1–15:35). The early Church abandoned the views of Ezra on membership in the people of God.

The Achievement of Ezra

Without the efforts of Ezra, though, the Jewish community may very well not have survived the threats to its identity that were so serious in the Persian period. It is also important to remember that, along with Ezra, the Bible has included the stories of Jonah and Ruth, both of which offer voices of dissent against the exclusivism of this book.

We need to see Ezra's notion of a holy race against the backdrop of the cultural assumptions of ancient Near Eastern people. The key word here is *holy.* The solution to Judah's problems according to Ezra was the determination of the Jews to observe the Torah. Part of this observance revolved around the notion of separation from all that was not *ritually* pure. "Holy" here is a cultic term rather than a moral one. Ezra did not imply that the Jews were morally superior to the other nations. He did believe that they were in a unique position to offer the God of their ancestors the type of worship that this God required. Unfortunately, the more the Jews associated with Gentiles the more difficult it was for them to remain ritually pure. Both Ezra and Nehemiah demanded that the Jews remove this danger to their religious observance. Books such as Jonah and Ruth reminded their readers that the Jews could not claim moral superiority. The Gentiles too could please God.

The Call to Inclusion

The book of Ezra speaks to a beleaguered religious community on the brink of extinction. It sees assimilation as one of the main threats to that existence. It fosters an attitude of separation and exclusion. Today the threat to human existence comes precisely from the ignorance, prejudice, and hatred that keep the peoples of the world apart. The Second Vatican Council recognized this when it decided to issue a separate document dealing with non-Christian religions. Originally *Nostra Aetate* (1965) was to be just a chapter in the schema on ecumenism. The bishops of the Council became aware of the importance of this topic and developed this full-scale document.

The basic assumption of *Nostra Aetate* is that

all peoples comprise a single human community. All members of this community have the same final goal: God. The religions of the world result from the universal human attempt to probe the mystery of the divine. The Council encouraged Catholics to speak and work with followers of other religions. They are to acknowledge, preserve, and promote the spiritual and moral values found in non-Christian religions.

Singled out for special attention in the Council's declaration are the two other monotheistic faiths: Judaism and Islam. In particular, the Council repudiated any form of persecution and hatred that existed between the Christians and Jews at any time and from any source (*Declaration on the Relationship of the Church to Non-Christian Religions,* 4). The Church also rejected any type of discrimination directed at people because of their religion. The bishops called upon all Catholics to maintain "good fellowship" with all peoples by living with them in peace.

The circumstances faced by the Christian communities of the Holy Land today are similar to those faced by the Jews in Ezra's day. The adverse political, social, and economic situation faced by Christians in the Holy Land makes their continued presence in the land Jesus called home very difficult. Many have chosen to leave. There is the very real danger that the Christian presence in the Holy Land will be reduced those who care for its shrines. The very place where the Church began may be left without a living, local church. The book of Ezra stands as an object lesson in the kind of decisive action that is necessary to respond to critical circumstances. Christians cannot make use of the specific way that Ezra responded to the problems faced by the Jewish community of his day, but they can emulate his passionate commitment to the survival of his people. Christians certainly ought to commit themselves to the survival of the Christian community in the Holy Land.

FURTHER READING

Blenkinsopp, Joseph. *Ezra–Nehemiah. A Commentary.* Old Testament Library. Philadelphia: Westminster, 1988.

Fensham, F. C. *The Books of Ezra and Nehemiah.* The New International Commentary on the Old Testament. Grand Rapids, MI: Eerdmans, 1982.

Grabbe, Lester L. *Ezra–Nehemiah.* London and New York: Routledge, 1998.

Myers, Jacob M., *Ezra–Nehemiah.* Anchor Bible 14. Garden City, NY: Doubleday, 1965.

Throntveit, M. A. *Ezra–Nehemiah.* Interpretation: A Commentary for Teaching and Preaching. Louisville: John Knox, 1992.

Williamson, H. G. M. *Ezra and Nehemiah.* Old Testament Guides. Sheffield: JSOT Press, 1987.

See also 1 Chronicles.

NEHEMIAH

[see pages 561–577 of the Old Testament]

The Relation between the Books of Ezra and Nehemiah

The introduction to this book (OT, p. 561) assumes that Ezra and Nehemiah are components of what was originally a single work. The book of Nehemiah deals with the political and administrative side of the restoration, while the book of Ezra focuses on the establishment of Torah as the "constitution of the returned community."

Besides these different concerns, there is one striking difference between the two books based on literary form. According to Nehemiah 1:1 ("The words of Nehemiah . . ."), the book is an account for which Nehemiah himself is responsible. A significant portion of the book is written in the first person (1:1–7:5; 12:31–13:31). These are the so-called "Memoirs of Nehemiah" (see introduction, OT, p. 561).

It is important to see the work of both Nehemiah and Ezra against the deplorable conditions that the prophet Malachi depicts (see Mal 1–2). Without the type of concrete communal structures that Ezra and Nehemiah were to provide, the people found it impossible to live according to the high ideals of their ancestral religion since they lacked a healthy social and religious life.

Reading the Book

This book describes the work of Nehemiah (1:1–7:72) and the place of Torah in the restored community of Jerusalem (8:1–13:31).

The Rebuilding of Jerusalem (Neh 1:1–6:19)

Because of the bad reports that came to the Persian imperial court from Jerusalem, the emperor Artaxerxes agreed to send Nehemiah, his cupbearer, to rebuild the city (1:1–2:8). There was opposition from both within and without the Judahite community to this project. Though Sanballat, the governor of Samaria, was Nehemiah's principal antagonist, opposition came from governors of other neighboring provinces as well (4: 1). They mocked Nehemiah's plans (2:19f; 3: 33–37) and even proposed military action against Jerusalem (4:1–5). When their criticism and plots failed to dissuade Nehemiah from his mission, they began plotting against his life (6: 1–14). There were also some elements within Judahite society that associated themselves with these plots against Nehemiah (6:17–19). This internal opposition came from the upper classes who had a stake in maintaining the status quo. Their unjust behavior led to disturbances that hindered the task of rebuilding the city (5:1–5). Nehemiah realized that rebuilding the city's walls was not enough to insure stability. He ordered the people of means to stop their economic abuse of the poor (5:6–13). Despite all the opposition, Nehemiah completed the project of rebuilding the walls of Jerusalem in just fifty-two days (3:1–32; 4:9–17; 6:15–19).

Jerusalem had been the capital of the Judahite national state. It was the location of the temple dedicated to the patron deity of that state. But the Babylonians leveled the city and its temple in 587 BC (2 Kgs 25:10). Although the temple was rebuilt and Nehemiah refortified the city, the second temple was far less ornate than the one built by Solomon (Ezr 3:12), and Nehemiah's walls enclosed only a fraction of the preexilic city. Jerusalem was no longer the capital of a Judahite national state. Still, it was the leading city of the Persian subprovince of Yehud. It was the center for preserving the particular worship of the Jewish community, and Persian imperial policy supported the preservation of this worship. Nehemiah's project was opposed by neighboring rulers because they saw this leading to a new economic and possibly political status for Jerusalem, which they saw as threatening their interests.

The Population of Jerusalem

Chapter 7 provides a transition from the description of Nehemiah's successful rebuilding project to the promulgation of Torah. Following the comment about the meager population of Jerusalem (7:4), there is a repetition of the list of those who returned from Babylon (7:6–72). This list duplicates the one found in Ezra 2:1–67.

The Promulgation of Torah (Neh 8:1–13:31)

At this point the Nehemiah memoirs break off. Chapters 8 through 10 describe a ritual that Ezra conducts. This ceremony brings to closure both the rebuilding of the city and the reconstitution of its religious life. The community of Jerusalem heard the words of Torah (8:1–12). It responded by celebrating the Feasts of Booths according to the prescriptions of the Torah (8:13–18). Two weeks later the community began a fast (9:1–3), and then Ezra made a great confession of sin in the name of the people (9:6–37).

Torah

An important theme in both Ezra and Nehemiah is the Torah as a *written* authoritative guide for the life of the Jewish community. In Nehemiah 8, Ezra reads the law. In Nehemiah 9, the people of Jerusalem confess their failure to observe the law. In Nehemiah 10, the people agree to live according to its precepts. Unfortunately for our understanding of these passages, too many Christians have a very distorted notion of the Torah. These distortions have arisen because of the polemical atmosphere in the Gospels that recount Jesus' debates with the Pharisees regarding the interpretation of Torah (Mt 5:21–48; 23:13–36), and the bitter exchanges between Paul and some early Christians who considered the observance of the Torah essential for all (Gal 3:10–14).

Despite their disputes with those who opposed their teaching on the law, both Jesus and Paul could be effusive in their praise of the Torah: "Do not think that I have come to abolish the law or the prophets . . . Whoever breaks one of the least of these commandments and teaches others to do so will be called least in the kingdom of heaven" (Mt 5:17–19) and "So then the law is holy, and the commandment is holy and righteous and good" (Rom 7:12). Still, the word "law" has a pejorative ring to it in the ears of most Christians.

The key to understanding and appreciating the Torah is to begin with the biblical context from which it emerged. But like most theologically important words in the Hebrew Bible, the text uses the term *Torah* in several different ways within the Bible. There is even some dispute over the etymology of the word. Some hold that the word *Torah* derives from the Hebrew word *yarah,* which means to throw or to cast lots. Thus, the original meaning of Torah may have referred to the determination of the divine will with some sort of a lot-oracle. In another linguistic form, *yarah* means to point the way, to instruct. Thus Torah may have originally derived from the instructions priests gave to the people.

In the Bible, Torah usually refers to God's instructions to Moses at Sinai that he handed on to ancient Israel. Sometimes these instructions deal with specific sacrificial laws, ethical norms, regulations dealing with purity and impurity (Lv 4: 1–7:38; 10:10; 11:1–13:59; 14:57; 23:44). In the book of Deuteronomy, Torah takes on a more comprehensive sense and becomes that which determines Israel's cultural, religious, and national identity. Torah is the written authoritative law, which is Israel's "constitution" for life in the land that was its inheritance from God (Dt 28:61; 29:20; 30:10; 31:26).

The books of Joshua to 2 Kings follow the lead of Deuteronomy and speak of Torah in the comprehensive sense as "the book of the Torah" (Jos 1:7f; 1 Kgs 2:3; 2 Kgs 23:5). The prophets use the term *Torah* in a variety of senses. Sometimes the term refers to cultic regulations (Hos 4:6); sometimes it includes God's moral commands (Is 5:24; 30:9), and ethical norms (Hb 1:4). It is also divine teaching given through the prophets (Is 1: 10; 8:16). Sometimes the prophets use *Torah* in the comprehensive sense (Jer 6:19; 9:12; Is 42: 21, 24; Mal 3:22).

The Psalms praise both the Torah and those who live by it (Ps 1:2; 19:8; 37:31; 40:9; 94: 12; 112:1; 119:97). Psalms 19 and 119 reflect the joy of ancient Israel in the Torah. Proverbs speaks of Torah as the advice of parents or a sage (1:8; 3:1; 13:14). Later Jewish sages identify wisdom and the Torah (Sir 24:1–31; 39:1–11). Ezra (3:2; 7:6, 10) and Nehemiah (8,:1; 9:3; 10: 30; 13:1) assume a fixed written Torah.

The early rabbis believed that they were responsible for transmitting not only the written Torah but also an oral Torah, which contained the teachings of revered sages who advanced the obligations of the law beyond the words of the written Torah, and thus made violations of the written Torah more difficult. These rabbis traced the origins of this oral Torah back to Moses *(Pirke Avot, 1,1).* Around AD 200, Rabbi Judah the Prince committed this oral law to writing in a work called the *Mishnah.* This was the beginning of the Talmud (the code of rabbinical teaching on the manner of observing the law.) Thus, in contemporary Judaism Torah refers not only to the books of Moses but to the Talmud and the entire Jewish ethical tradition.

Proverbs 1:8 and 3:1 may provide the key to appreciating Torah. These texts speak of Torah as parental guidance for a child. The Bible often speaks of Israel as God's children (Ex 4:22; Dt 14:1; 32:10–12; Hos 11:1; Jer 31:9, 20; Is 66: 13). Some people then understood Torah as the teaching imparted by the parent God to the child Israel. In this light, the giving of the Torah is an act of the highest love.

Another key to appreciating the Torah is the recognition that it refers not only to the vehicle of revelation but also its entire content. Torah contains both the story of Israel's election and salvation, and the stipulations of its covenantal relationship with God. Torah then includes the story of the free acts of God that presented ancient Israel with the model of righteousness. It also includes specifications of how Israel should live in obedient response to those free acts of God. The people of ancient Israel did not experience the Torah as a burden that they had to bear with patient endurance but as the way to life and a source of joy.

In the perspective of the books of Ezra and Nehemiah, obedience to the written, authoritative Torah is a condition for survival. Without careful observance Judaism is in danger of being lost in the sea of assimilation. It is assimilation that will do to the Jewish community what the exile failed to do. Thus, the Torah is Israel's life. The devotion to ethical principles, the enduring attitude of self-examination and self-correction that observance implies, the maintenance of identity by adherence to a moral code—all these are values that Christians could learn from Judaism, ancient and modern.

The word *Torah* has many meanings and reflects many different values. Perhaps only those who observe the law as an act of obedient love for God can experience its fundamental meaning. For the observant Jew it is the truth revealing God's election and salvation of Israel. It is also the way to respond to God's graciousness. It is finally the way to life. For Ezra and Nehemiah the Torah was Judah's way to the future.

The Promulgation of the Torah

The elements of the ritual found in Nehemiah 8 may have served as the model for the synagogue service that developed somewhat later in Judaism. There is the bringing of the Torah scroll (8:2), the mounting of the platform that contains the desk for reading (8:4), the opening of the scroll (8:5), the blessing (v. 6a), the communal *Amen* (8:6b). The "interpretation" that 8:8 refers to may be an Aramaic translation of the Torah, which Ezra read in Hebrew. Some people may have needed an Aramaic translation of the Torah since they no longer understood Hebrew very well. Aramaic was the language common to all the peoples of the Persian empire and, since the sixth century BC, Aramaic was replacing Hebrew as the language of everyday speech in Judah.

The Confession

Nehemiah 9:6–37 is one of the important creedal statements in the Old Testament. It recounts Israel's communal experience of God from the time of Abraham (9:7) to the period of restoration (9:33). The purpose of this confession of faith is to acknowledge Israel's failure to keep the commandments despite God's goodness and fidelity. It is also a remarkable act of faith in divine forbearance. There is a similar prayer of confession in Ezra 9:7–15. The note to Ezra 9:7 (OT, p. 519) suggests that these two confessions were originally parts of the same prayer.

The Agreement of the People

Chapter 10 contains a written pledge made by those listed in verses 1b–29 to observe the Torah of Moses. As the note to 10:1–39 (OT, p. 572) suggests, this text should come after Nehemiah 13, which lists reforms of Nehemiah. The pledge made by the people could hardly be made before Nehemiah initiated the reforms. Among the specific points made in the pledge is the prohibition of marriage with Gentiles (10:31; see 13:20–23a) and observance of the Sabbath (10:32; see 13:15–22). Those who made the pledge also promise to provide firewood for the altar (10:35; see 13:31), first fruits for sacrifice (10:36f; see 13:31), and tithes for the support of the Levites (10:38–40; see 13:10–14).

The Resettlement of Jerusalem

Nehemiah 11 begins with a lottery used to resettle Jerusalem (11:1–3). Then follow lists of the inhabitants of Jerusalem (11:3–24) and of the rural areas of Judah (11:20–30), and of the Benjaminites (11:31–36). Nehemiah 12 begins with lists of priests and Levites (12:1–26). Then follows a description of the dedication of the walls (12:27–43). The book concludes with a listing of the various reform measures begun by Nehemiah (12:44–13:31), to the observance of which the people pledged themselves in Nehemiah 10.

Ritual Purity

Like the book of Ezra (9:1f), Nehemiah condemns mixed marriages (Neh 13:23–29). These books reflect the belief that if the Jews were to survive as a people, they had to keep themselves separate from other ethnic and religious groups. An important emphasis in both books, then, is the purity of the reconstituted community. On a surface level this concern appears to be a type of ethnic discrimination. There could have been some of that at work here; however, it is important to note that this emphasis on purity concerns cult and ritual. The call of Ezra and Nehemiah for purity is a call for ritual, not ethnic, purity. Ritual purity was in some sense dependent upon ancient Near Eastern ideas of order. Mixing two peoples through marriage or in worship offends this notion of order. Exclusion of Gentiles from the cult does not come from a belief in *ethnic* superiority. The call for separation from others is pervasive in Ezra and Nehemiah (Ezr 4:1–3; 6:21; 9–10; Neh 2:20; 3:3; 9:2; 10:29; 13:23–29). It is a component of the directives associated with rebuilding the Temple and in the rest of the restoration program led by both Ezra and Nehemiah.

The New Testament affirms that the Christian worship transcends these patterns. According to John, Christians worship in "Spirit and truth" (Jn 4:23). Classifications based on "flesh" are no longer relevant. Paul makes it clear that in Jesus there is "neither Jew nor Greek" (Gal 3:28). Matthew writes that Jesus' final command was to "make disciples of all nations" (Mt 28:19). This insight did not occur to the first Christians automatically. The Acts of the Apostles shows that the inclusion of the Gentiles into the Christian community was a matter of spirited debate among the Jewish Christians (Acts 15:1–35).

The synagogue also struggled with the question of the exclusion/inclusion of the Gentiles. Some rabbis favored the more exclusive strain found in books such as Deuteronomy (Dt 23), Ezra, and Nehemiah. Others endorsed the more inclusive tendencies in texts such as Isaiah 56, which stated that the Temple was to be "a house of prayer for all peoples" (Is 56:7).

The Conclusion

The last sentence of the book ("Remember this in my favor, O my God!" Neh 13:31) may give an insight into the purpose of the book. This formula is similar to those attached to texts inscribed on walls of ancient Near Eastern temples. From the location of these texts *within* the temple, clearly those who made them were addressing the deity since only priests entered the temples themselves. This same formula, petitioning for divine remembrance, is typical of memorial inscriptions found in Jewish monumental buildings such as synagogues from a much later period. Besides being an act of piety, inclusion of this formula was probably an attempt to commend this work to its readers.

FURTHER READING

See 1 Chronicles and Ezra.

TOBIT

[see pages 578–595 of the Old Testament]

The Moral of the Story

The book of Tobit is a complex literary work with a very uncomplicated moral. The book narrates important incidents in the lives of Tobit, Sarah, and Tobiah. It tells the story of their tragedies and triumphs. The author weaves the stories of these three people together very skillfully so that the book results from the intersection of three different but related plots. This rhetorical feat of weaving the stories of these three people so tightly has a theological purpose: to show how God can manage the circumstances of people's lives in order to bring God's plans to fulfillment. Its primary religious message is simple: God rewards those who are faithful.

Approaching the Book: The Literary Form of Tobit

The introduction to this book describes Tobit as a "religious novel" (OT, p. 579). The historical and geographical details given in the book are there simply to provide a plausible setting for the story. Tobit is not a work of history-writing. Its author confuses the kings of Assyria, shows an ignorance of the topography of Mesopotamia, and dates Tobit's exile earlier than it could have been (see notes to 1:2, 15; 5:6; and 14:15). Though calling Tobit a novel may not be entirely satisfactory, the book is the work of a single author and not a product of oral or literary tradition despite the author's attempt to associate his principal character with Ahiqar, a very popular figure of ancient Near Eastern wisdom tradition (see note on 1:21; OT, p. 581). As a novel, the book of Tobit presents three characters in an intricately developed plot that the introduction summarizes on p. 579.

What is especially important to notice is how the author of Tobit tells the stories of Tobit and his relative Sarah. Both suffer undeservedly. Tobit became blind while doing an act of charity by burying the dead. In his despondency he prays for death. Sarah believes that she will remain a childless widow. A demon has killed each of her seven husbands on their respective wedding nights. Sarah too prays for death. God answers their prayers by enabling Tobiah, Tobit's son, to cure Tobit's blindness and break the power of the demon that was killing Sarah's husbands. Tobiah is able to accomplish this with the help of the angel Raphael. The action of Tobiah solves the problems of both Tobit and Sarah.

Since Tobit is such a cleverly told story, it is important that one read the story through in order to appreciate the author's message. Tobit is short enough to read in a single sitting. One key to understanding the author's purpose is the unfolding of the story and how God answers the prayers of the innocent Tobit and Sarah in a way they hardly expected.

The Religious Horizons of the Book

The basic concern of this book becomes clear as God acts through Raphael to solve the problems of Tobit, Sarah, and Tobiah. Each problem contains the germ of a solution for the others. Tobit is going to die, so he sends his son Tobiah to collect an outstanding debt. This brings Tobiah in contact with Raphael, who gives him a way to cure his father *and* to eliminate Sarah's problem. In the process of traveling to collect the debt, Tobiah meets Sarah and falls in love with her. Tobiah is able to break the power of the demon that tormented Sarah. In the end, the medicine Raphael gives Tobiah cures Tobit's blindness, Tobiah recovers the money owed to his father, Tobiah marries Sarah, and together they raise a family.

The purpose of this engaging tale is to show that God controls events and manages the circumstances in order to ensure that God's own purposes come to fruition. The story assumes God's sovereignty in people's lives and God's determination to reward the just. When the just suffer, there is a limit to that suffering. Once that limit occurs God will intervene, and sometimes that intervention is miraculous.

Tobit's reaction to his suffering and its alleviation underscores the religious views of the book. At first Tobit's response is one of despair, since he sees death as the only way of deliverance. Once he experiences God's deliverance, Tobit is eloquent in his praise of God's mercy. The book's answer to the problem of suffering is in 11:15: ". . . it was he who scourged me, and it is he who has had mercy on me."

The Judaism of the Book

The introduction (OT, p. 578) states that the book of Tobit appeared fewer than two hundred years before Christ. It reveals a form of Judaism that accepted magic and had a strong belief in angels and demons. Raphael, an angel of God, suggests the means for negating the power of the demon (6:7–9), and so the magical means of dealing with demonic powers must be legitimate for any Jew. Mysterious powers in the entrails of a fish serve not only to cure illnesses but also to bind the demonic powers that harm people.

Tobit, then, represents a Judaism that sees angels and demons as having important roles to play in the drama between God and human beings. This contrasts sharply with books such as Judith and Esther where human beings are in control of their own destiny without any intervention of angelic and demonic powers. The author of Tobit considers angels to be more than simply God's messengers: they mediate prayers in God's throne room (3:16; 12:12–15); they oppose demons (8:2f); they commission the writing of books (12:11f). Belief in demons accompanies a belief in angels. While angels make their interventions for the good of people, demons are hostile powers.

The book also reflects the importance that the book of Deuteronomy came to have in early Judaism. This is especially clear in Tobit 14: 4–7, which asserts that the exile happened because of Israel's infidelity (see Dt 28:15–68), that the exile is not God's final judgment on Israel but that there is hope for mercy (see Dt 30: 1–4), and that the Temple of Jerusalem is the only legitimate place for worship (see Dt 12: 1–14). The Judaism that Tobit depicts is a Judaism that measures fidelity to God in terms of fulfillment of the Torah, which is just what Deuteronomy preaches.

Finally Tobit seems to reflect the circumstances of Jews in the Diaspora (Jewish settlements outside of Palestine). The book portrays Gentiles as unsympathetic to Tobit's activities (2:8) and as those responsible for persecuting him (1:16–20). The book presents marriage within Judaism as a duty. It teaches that God is sovereign over all people and that God is present to those in exile, even in the midst of their suffering. It underscores the need to maintain Jewish identity in the Diaspora. The means to accomplish this is the family. The book's emphasis on the family is one reason that Tobit remained popular in the Church, even though the book did not become part of the Jewish canon of the Old Testament.

Reading the Book

The only way to savor the book's literary artistry and to appreciate its religious perspectives is to follow the way the author unfolds the events related to Tobit's life. Notice the suffering of Tobit, Sarah, and their families in the first part of the book. In despair they pray for death since they do not experience God's presence in this life. Notice how the stories of Tobit and Sarah parallel one another. See table below.

God hears these prayers but responds to them in a totally unexpected manner. Raphael stands as a symbol of God's presence with both Tobit and Sarah. Even though they felt abandoned by God, God was with them in the midst of their suffering. When Tobiah finishes his journey and Tobit realizes the presence of God in his own life and in the lives of his son and new daughter-in-law, he breaks into enthusiastic and joyful praise of God. The reader should notice the movement in the book from despair to thanksgiving and praise.

Angels and Demons

There are two important nonhuman characters in the book: Asmodeus, the demon who torments Sarah (3:8) and Raphael, who reveals himself as one of the seven angels who "serve before the Glory of the Lord" (12:15). The book of Tobit, then, reflects the belief of early Judaism in angels and demons as supernatural beings. The first form of this belief seems to be "the messenger of the Lord," which belongs to the earliest narratives in the Hebrew Bible. In some of these stories, clearly the messenger of the Lord is not different from the Lord (see Gn 16:13; 21:18; 31:13). Since God confronts people directly in many of the early stories, the appearance of angels is somewhat irregular. As people begin to think of God as transcendent, far beyond the human sphere, angels become a more regular feature of the narratives. Ideas develop about good angels and bad angels (the demons), a hierarchy of angels, and the various duties of angels. In Tobit, Raphael is one of the seven holy angels who offer up the prayers of the pious (Tb 12:15).

Angels and demons play a prominent role in the noncanonical literature of early Judaism. For example, in the book of Enoch, Raphael is an archangel (1 Enoch 20:3). He heals the illnesses and injuries of human beings (1 Enoch 40:9). By the time of the New Testament, angels were thought of as spiritual beings who were God's allies in opposition to Satan and his "angels," the demons.

It is possible to see popular imagination at work in the description of angels. They wear white garments (Dn 10:5f; 1 Enoch 87:2). The angels have wings (Dn 9:21 [note that the NAB follows the Septuagint and translates the Hebrew phrase "borne in winged flight" as "came in rapid flight"]; 1 Enoch 61:1). Finally, around the turn of the era, there appears in a few Jewish texts what seems to be the belief that it was permissible to portray figures from Israel's past, especially Adam and Jacob, as angels. Evidently some Jews held that it was possible for a select few to transcend humanity and become angels.

Belief in angels was not universal in early Judaism. Acts 23:8 asserts that the Pharisees representing more liberal and popular beliefs acknowledged the existence of angels, while the more conservative and aristocratic Sadducees rejected the existence of angels along with belief in spirits and the resurrection.

The Purpose of the Book

Why did the author tell the story of Tobit? Was it simply to entertain? Even though the book is highly entertaining as a short novel, its purpose goes far beyond the enjoyment of its readers. The author tells his story to teach while entertaining. The book calls for prayer, fasting, and especially almsgiving (4:7–11; 12:8). It presents the Jew-

Tobit's piety (2:1–7)	Sarah's innocence (3:14)
Tobit's blindness (2:9–10)	Sarah's demon (3:8)
Tobit's reproach (2:14)	Sarah's reproach (3:7–10)
Tobit's prayer (3:1–6)	Sarah's prayer (3:10–15)

ish family as the means of maintaining fidelity to the ancestral religion of the Jews (4:12f). It affirms that it is possible to remain faithful to God and the Law—even in the difficult circumstances of the Diaspora. Finally, it presents repentance as the key to the future of Judaism (13:6).

The author addresses his message to people who easily identify with the principal characters of the book. They wonder about the value of fidelity to their God since it sometimes brings them undeserved difficulties. Tobit reaffirms the value of fidelity. While there may be difficult times, God will never desert those who remain faithful, and the God who controls human events will ensure that the faithful will find their reward.

The author wishes to affirm the importance of the community. One's commitment to the community is the measure of one's commitment to God. It is important to support the poor, bury the dead, honor one's parents, marry within the community. The Jewish community will have a future as long as there are Tobits who pledge themselves to its preservation.

The purpose of the book is to move its readers from despair to prayer. The figure of Tobit is a paradigm for the pious Jews who experience not God's presence but his absence in their suffering. The central affirmation of the book is that God is with Tobit even when Tobit does not experience the divine presence. Once Raphael makes Tobit aware that God has always been with him, Tobit launches into a song of praise (13:1–18).

FURTHER READING

Craghan, John F. *Esther; Judith; Tobit; Jonah; Ruth.* Old Testament Message 16. Wilmington, DE: Michael Glazier, 1982.

Fitzmyer, Joseph A. *Tobit.* Berlin and New York: de Gruyter, 2003.

Levine, Amy-Jill. "Diaspora as Metaphor: Bodies and Boundaries in the Book of Tobit." In *Diaspora Jews and Judaism,* edited by J. Andrew Overman and Robert S. MacLennan. Atlanta: Scholars Press, 1992.

McCarthy, Carmel, and William Riley. "The Book of Tobit: The Pattern of Mercy." In *The Old Testament Short Story: Explorations into Narrative Spirituality,* edited by Carmel McCarthy and William Riley. Message of Biblical Spirituality 6. Wilmington, DE: Michael Glazier, 1986.

Moore, Carey A. *Tobit.* Anchor Bible 40A. NY: Doubleday, 1996.

Soll, Will. "The Book of Tobit as a Window on the Hellenistic Jewish Family." In *Passion, Vitality, and Foment: The Dynamics of Second Temple Judaism,* edited by M. Lamonette Luker. Harrisburg: Trinity, 2001.

JUDITH

[see pages 595–614 of the Old Testament]

The Book's Literary Form

There have been several attempts at classifying the book of Judith according to its literary type. The book is certainly not a historical account. The introduction points out the uselessness of trying to read this book against the backdrop of Jewish history in relation to the empires of the ancient world (OT, p. 595). There are just too many historical errors and anachronisms in the book. For example, the book describes Nebuchadnezzar as the king of the Assyrians (1:1) when he was king of Babylon. His attack against Judah supposedly took place after the return from exile (4:1–3)! The historical errors are so egregious that it is likely that the author meant readers to recognize them as such. Is the book of Judith a historical novel, midrash (the expansion, probing, and exposition of biblical texts to find new meaning in them), or a fictional drama? None of these classifications is completely satisfactory. This book is the result of a conscious, systematic, and faith-filled meditation on God's providential care for Israel. The book attempts to show how the invisible hand of God rescues Israel through the hand of Judith.

Reading the Book

As the introduction notes (OT, p. 595), the tale of Judith is well known. Over the centuries her story has attracted a remarkable amount of attention from writers, artists, and composers.

Chiasm I	
1. **2:14–3:10**	Holofernes begins campaign; nations surrender
2. **4:1–15**	Israel prepares for war
3. **5:1–6:11**	Holofernes talks with Achior
3'. **6:12–21**	Achior talks with Israel
2'. **7:1–15**	Holofernes prepares for war
1'. **7:6–32**	Holofernes begins campaign; the people wish to surrender

Chiasm II	
A. **8:1–8**	Introduction to Judith
B. **8:9f**	Judith plans to save Israel
C. **10:9f**	Judith leaves Bethulia
D. **10:11–13:10a**	Judith overcomes Holofernes
C'. **13:10b–11**	Judith returns to Bethulia
B'. **13:12–16:20**	Judith plans to destroy Israel's enemies
A'. **16:21–25**	Conclusion about Judith

Many composers, such as Thomas Arne, Antonio Vivaldi, and Arthur Honegger, chose Judith as the subject of their oratorios and operas. Painters have represented her story on canvas, and the sculptors of the facade of the cathedral at Chartres depicted her story in stone. One reason for all this attention is that Judith's story is such a good one. It is a heroic tale in which an unlikely character overcomes the cowardice of her own people in the face of the enemy. She defeats an arrogant general who thought that he was invincible in love and war. The plot begins in part I (1:1–7:32) with the introduction of the antagonists: Nebuchadnezzar and his general Holofernes.

• **1:1–16:** Nebuchadnezzar declares war on the Medes and demands that his vassals aid him in his campaign. His vassals, Judah among them, ignore his call. Despite this, Nebuchadnezzar is victorious.

• **2:1–13:** Nebuchadnezzar commissions Holofernes to punish the disloyal vassals.

The story then focuses on the fate of Judah, whose king and people ignored Nebuchadnezzar and now await his retribution. In telling the rest of the story, the book of Judith arranges the plot in two chiasms. (A chiasm is a type of inverted parallelism.) This is a frequent rhetorical device in biblical literature. Each incident leading up to a central event is balanced in reverse order with a similar incident following the central event.

Chiasm I (2:14–3:10) delineates the struggle. That it is both a religious and political conflict is clear from the words of Holofernes deriding the Israelite hope for victory when be boasts: "Who are you, Achior . . . to tell us not to fight against the Israelites because their God protects them? What god is there beside Nebuchadnezzar?" (6: 2). Achior was an Ammonite whom Holofernes, Nebuchadnezzar's general, summoned to provide him with intelligence about the Israelites. Achior eventually converted to Judaism.

Chiasm II (8:1–16:25) introduces Judith, the heroine who relieves the tension created in Chiasm I. She defeats Holofernes and proves that the Lord alone is God. Chiasm II portrays Judith as a model of faith. She not only crushes the arrogance and pride of Nebuchadnezzar and Holofernes but overcomes the cowardice and timidity of her fellow Jews who are ready to surrender. She takes her action without any guarantee from God that she will be successful. Her only guarantee is her faith.

The Image of Judith

The heroine's name is not a proper name. It means simply "Jewish woman." Judith, then, is more than an individual; she is a composite of all the women who have saved Israel in the past by their piety, wisdom, and action. On one level, the book of Judith is a tribute to those women whose achievements and memory ancient Israel cherished. Like Miriam (Ex 15:20f) she led Israel in a song of thanksgiving following God's deliverance of the people (Ex 15:14–16, 17). Like Deborah (Jgs 4:4–9) she aroused the flagging faith of Israel, besieged by its enemies (Jgs 8:9–27). Like Jael (Jgs 4:17–21) she assassinated her people's adversary. Like the wise woman from Abel Beth-maacah (2 Sm 20:15–22) Judith challenged the strategy of Israel's leaders and substituted her own (8:16; 9:2). By telling the tale of Judith, the storyteller was in effect honoring all the women whose memory ancient Israel revered. These women saved the people of ancient Israel at times when the more usual channels of leadership were not able to meet the challenges to their faith.

The first people to hear the story of Judith lived in a traditional society in which the roles assigned to men and women were distinct. The book of Judith offers a surprising dissent from the assumptions of its culture about the role and status of women. In this story, the men proved to be utter failures in the face of the threats of Nebuchadnezzar and Holofernes. As happened several times in Israel's past, God chose a woman to be the instrument of salvation. Judith, like her predecessors, is a most impressive channel of God's deliverance. The usual channels (the king, priests, and other notables) failed. The impact that this story made on a traditional society like that of early Judaism is difficult for us to appreciate because we live in a society where change occurs with greater frequency and rapidity.

Despite its countercultural veneer, the book of Judith is otherwise conservative in its outlook on the role of women in Jewish society. By rescuing her people from destruction at the hands of Gentiles, Judith is a model for the Jewish woman as the conservator of tradition. Her socially assigned role is to preserve tradition and keep her family protected from the pressures to assimilate to the dominant non-Jewish culture that threatens to envelop it. Judith is a paradigm for the Jewish woman who shields her family against incursions from the outside that threaten to dilute their loyalty to their ancestral religion. The heroine of the book carries out the role assigned to her by her culture, but she also transcends that role.

The Irony in the Book

The story of Judith is full of unexpected turns. The first and most obvious, especially to those who first heard or read Judith's story, was that a woman—not a man—saved Judah in its time of severe distress. Judith is more faithful and resourceful than any of the men of Bethulia. She is more eloquent than the king and more courageous than any of the leading citizens of the city, yet Judith is a very unlikely heroine. She is a childless widow; as such she occupied a very low place in the social hierarchy. While the king, the priests, and other leaders of Judahite society show themselves incapable of dealing with the crisis, lowly Judith stands up to the threat posed by Holofernes and takes decisive action to end it.

The means that Judith used to accomplish her end may offend some. She used her beauty to gain access to the enemy camp and to beguile Holofernes. Judith, though, was using the one weapon that she had available to her, and it happened to be a weapon that exploited the weakness of Judah's enemy. This leads to the second irony. Judith destroys Judah's enemies not with military might but with her beguiling charm and disarming beauty. The Bible sometimes portrays a woman's beauty negatively as a snare (2 Sm 11:2–5; Prv 6:26; Sir 9:2f), but here it is the means of deliverance.

Finally, Judith is a childless widow, yet the book portrays her as the mother of faith. It was her faith that gave new life to Israel. That is why the high priests and elders praise her so highly (15:9). The Latin hymn *Tota pulchra es* applies these words of praise to Mary. The liturgy finds the story of Judith as an appropriate image to speak of the Virgin Mary, who is the Mother of the Church.

The Judaism of the Book

The book of Judith asserts that the deliverance of the Jews in Bethulia depends not on power and might but on fidelity to the law. This is the point that Achior makes to Holofernes (5:5–21) and that Judith makes to the elders of Bethulia (8:17–21). The author portrays Judith as living according to the law as Jews interpreted it at that time. As a widow, she lived in a state of mourning marked by fasting (8:4–6). She prayed daily at the hour of the incense offering in the Temple (9:1). She observes the Jewish dietary laws (10:5 and 12:2, 19). She purifies herself by bathing in running water at the appropriate time (12:7–9). Judith criticizes the people of Bethulia for violating the law of first fruits and tithes (11:11–14).

The book departs significantly from earlier tradition as it describes the conversion of Achior the Ammonite (14:10). According to Deuteronomy, the Israelites were never to admit an Ammonite into their community (Dt 23:4). Presumably the author was able to justify this by the example of Ruth, who (as a Moabite woman) belonged to the other nation that Deuteronomy excludes from ever becoming part of the Israelite community. While the book of Judith presents obedience to the Torah as the key to Israel's deliverance, it shows a type of flexibility that is able to respond to a person such as Achior, who wishes to join the Israelites in the service of God. The issue of inclusion and exclusion was a perplexing one for Judaism, as it was for the first Christians (Acts 10:1–49; 11:1–18; 15:1–12).

Though the story of Judith remained a popular one among Jews for two thousand years, there is no evidence that the book was ever regarded as canonical in Palestine. It was, however, included in the Greek translation of the Old Testament made for Diaspora Jews, many of whom could no longer read Hebrew. There were continuing debates among Christians about its canonical character. The Council of Trent (1546) included Judith in its list of canonical writings, while Protestants, following Luther, did not.

The Religious Horizons of the Book

The book of Judith may date from as late as the first century (see the introduction, OT, p. 595), but in some respects it reflects the circumstances of the Maccabean revolt in the second century. For example, there are strong parallels with the defeat of Nicanor, Antiochus's general, as narrated in 1 Maccabees 7:43–50. In some ways, Judith is the feminine counterpart of the Maccabees. The book is an eloquent statement of traditional worship of the Lord. It affirms belief in the one God (6:2; 8:16f; 14:18; 16:13). It asserts that this one God guides all human events toward their intended goal (9:5f). Finally it describes this God as One who is present with the weak and oppressed (9:11).

The storyteller paints a portrait of Judith much like the Israelite storytellers who told of the exploits of Ehud (Jgs 3:12–30), Jephthah (Jgs 11:1–40), Samson (Jgs 13–16), and David (1 Sm 16:1—1 Kgs 2:10). Their personal character and the means they used to save Israel did not come under careful moral scrutiny. Judith uses seduction and assassination to achieve her ends, although the text is careful to state that Judith did not have to complete her seduction of Holofernes before she could kill him (13:16). Like these earlier stories, the book of Judith shows that God brings deliverance out of the evil that people create for themselves. Even though the book is ostensibly about Judith, its pivotal affirmation is about the God of Israel:

> Your strength is not in numbers, nor does your power depend upon stalwart men; but you are the God of the lowly, the helper of the oppressed, the supporter of the weak, the protector of the forsaken, the savior of those without hope (9:11).

The book of Judith then is a profession of faith in the God of Israel who saves the lowly. The story of Judith is simply an illustration of this article of ancient Israelite faith.

The book also asserts very forcefully that God's deliverance does not come except through the faithful action of people such as Judith. Unlike the king, the priests, and the elders of Bethulia who were content to pray and then surrender to Holofernes, Judith's prayer leads her to take action to save Bethulia. Though she receives no revelations or guarantees from God, her faith supplies the support she needs to begin and complete the perilous adventure that saved Israel. God saves the lowly, and prayer puts people in contact with that God, yet God's presence among the people does not absolve them from the duty to act on their beliefs. Judith is a mother of faith not only because she believed and prayed but especially because she acted on her beliefs—another perspective this book shares with 1 Maccabees.

The Image of Women in the Church

The book of Judith offers a model for the process of contemporary theological reflection on the role and status of women in the Church. It is itself one product of early Judaism's reflection on the role of women in its own social and religious system. At the very least, the book sees women as at times better fit to be instruments of salvation than men—a conclusion that was an unexpected one, given the cultural milieu in which it arose. Like Judith, Catholic women throughout the centuries have made enormous contributions to the life of the Church and are invited to see themselves as conservators of what is best in our religious heritage.

FURTHER READING

Brenner, Athalya, ed. *A Feminist Companion to Esther, Judith and Susanna*. Feminist Companion to the Bible 7. Sheffield: Sheffield Academic Press, 1995.

Craghan, John F. *Esther; Judith; Tobit; Jonah; Ruth.* Old Testament Message 16. Wilmington, DE: Michael Glazier, 1982.

Craven, Toni. *Artistry and Faith in the Book of Judith.* Chico, CA: Scholars Press, 1983.

Moore, Carey A. *Judith.* Anchor Bible 40B. Garden City, NY: Doubleday, 1985.

VanderKam, James C., ed. *No One Spoke Ill of Her: Essays on Judith.* Atlanta: Scholars Press, 1992.

ESTHER

[see pages 614–628 of the Old Testament]

Esther and Judith

The central character in both Esther and Judith is a beautiful Jewish woman whose bravery and wiles save her people from certain destruction. The Hebrew text of Esther mentions neither God nor any religious institutions or practices except fasting, while the book of Judith is filled with allusions to God and numerous religious beliefs and practices. But it was the book of Esther that came to be included in the Jewish canon. Though rabbis recognized Esther's canonicity after a long debate, there is no evidence that Judith was ever considered canonical in Palestine.

A Threat to the Jewish Community

Like the book of Judith, the central concern of the book of Esther is the survival of the Jewish minority in the midst of a world that is growing more hostile to it. This book tells the story of one threat to that survival and the removal of that threat by relating the tale of Mordecai, a Jewish courtier in the service of the Persian emperor. The book of Esther makes it clear that God will act in order to preserve the Jewish community. God does not intervene directly to resolve the problem but, though this divine action may be hidden, it is nonetheless real.

The Additions to the Book

An Element of Confusion

A perplexing aspect of the shape of this book in the *New American Bible* is the order and numbering of its chapters and verses. There are six chapters that have alphabetic identification scattered in the midst of ten chapters that have the more familiar numerical identification. This is a result of the way the book of Esther has come down to us. The introduction (OT, pp. 614–15) notes that the book of Esther has survived in two forms: a shorter Hebrew text and a longer Greek one. The Greek text has about 107 verses more than the Hebrew. Jerome did not believe that the additional verses of the Greek Esther were inspired, so when he produced his Latin translation, he took the additional verses in the Greek Esther out of their proper context and put them in an appendix to the book. When chapter and verse numbers were given to biblical texts during the Middle Ages, these additions received their numbers according to the position they had in Jerome's Vulgate rather than according to their proper position in the Greek version of the book.

The canonical status of the Greek additions was not settled for Catholics until the Council of Trent decided in their favor. (The Protestant churches do not accept the additions to Esther as canonical.) The arrangement of the text of Esther in the NAB reflects the attempts to follow the order of the Greek version of Esther while preserving the traditional numbering of chapters and verses following Jerome's arrangement. This seems to be the best solution possible in the circumstances. It allows the reader to find the additions in their proper contexts, and it preserves the numeration of chapters and verses that is universally followed.

The Purpose of the Greek Additions

The function of the Greek additions to the Hebrew version of Esther is clear. First, the additions introduce explicit religious elements (for example, the prayers of Mordecai and Esther in addition C:1–30). The Hebrew version lacks a single reference to God except for the possible allusion in 4:14. Hebrew Esther is not overtly religious. It is a tale about how Jews used their wits to outsmart their enemies. Second, by introducing "documents" (B:1–7; E: 1–24), the additions lend an air of authority and authenticity to the book. The additions make the book read as if it were a historical work. This probably was done to encourage the celebration of the Feast of Purim with which the story of Esther became associated.

The Story

At first the story sounds like a typical tale of palace intrigue. Two royal officials, Mordecai the Jew and Haman the Agagite, vie for power and position in the court of the Persian emperor. They do not hesitate to hatch plots against each other in order to secure a more important status for themselves. But in chapter 3 the story takes an ominous turn. It is no longer a tale about personal enmity between rival courtiers. Haman's plots threaten not only Mordecai but also the entire Jewish community of the Persian empire. Additions A and F (Mordecai's dream and its interpretation) with their imagery of the two dragons and the phenomena in heaven and earth (A: 4–10) transport the conflict to a cosmic level. Addition F makes it clear that it was God who saved Israel (F:5–9).

The story that the introduction summarizes (OT, p. 614) takes place in the Diaspora (the Jewish settlements outside of the land of Israel), and it contains no references at all to the homeland of the Jews. The tension in the story revolves around the rivalry of Haman and Mordecai, but soon all the Jews find themselves swept up in the conflict because of the specifically Jewish patterns of behavior (3:8). When Esther joins Mordecai in a plan to frustrate Haman's murderous plots, the tension is resolved. What was to be a pogrom, an officially organized massacre, against the Jews becomes a celebration of the Jews because Haman and his conspiracy fail.

The Personalities in the Story

Haman and Mordecai

The story refers to Haman as an Agagite (3:1), i.e., a descendant of Agag, who was the king of the Amalekites whom earlier traditions remembered as the most dangerous of ancient Israel's opponents (Ex 17:14; Dt 25:17–19). Mordecai's genealogy (1:1) makes him a descendant of Kish, the father of Saul (see 1 Sm 9:1). At the conclusion of his conflict with Agag, Saul wanted to spare the life of this enemy of Israel and is criticized for it (1 Sm 15:8f). Mordecai makes no such mistake regarding Haman (Est 7:9f).

Vashti and Esther

The story of Esther begins with the deposition of Vashti, the queen of Persia. Vashti lost her position as queen because she refused to obey the command of her husband, Ahasuerus, the king of Persia. During a banquet he gave, the king became drunk and ordered his wife to "display her beauty" before his male courtiers (1:11). Because she declined to submit to this indignity, the king's officials advised the king to remove her as queen. They feared that their wives might imitate her example and refuse to be submissive and obedient (1:16–18). The king then issued "an irrevocable royal decree" deposing Vashti and insisting that "every man should be lord in his own home" (1:19–22). Esther, an orphaned Jewish girl who was the ward and cousin of Mordecai, won the beauty contest that determined Vashti's replacement (2:1–10). The name Esther was a Mesopotamian name; her Jewish name was Hadassah (see note to 2:7; OT, p. 618). Unlike Judith, Esther is hardly a model for feminists. She participates in the process to replace Vashti, who is the real heroine in this story according to a feminist reading of the text. Vashti refuses to become an "object" and insists on her dignity as a person, even though this means that she loses her position as queen. In a sense, Esther betrays Vashti by seeking to replace her.

The Historical Character of the Book

The author of Esther shows a familiarity with the royal court and administrative system of Persia. That is why interpreters favor a date toward the end of the Persian period for the bulk of the text (see the introduction, OT, p. 614). While the author describes the Persian court accurately, still the story of Esther is fictional. It is a novella on the theme of the persecuted righteous and their deliverance. The story does have a historical flavor, but it does not intend to report an actual event. (See notes to A:1, OT, p. 616, and 1:9, OT, p. 617, for two historical problems with the story of Esther.)

The Book of Esther and the Feast of Purim

According to F:10, God wished the Jews to celebrate a feast on the fourteenth and fifteenth of

Adar (February/March) to celebrate their deliverance. This is the Feast of Purim. The name of the feast (Purim) means "lots" and is a reference to 3:7 and 9:24, 26. The Bible mentions this feast nowhere else except in a possible allusion in 2 Mc 15:36 that mentions "Mordecai's Day." The relationship between Purim and the book of Esther is not absolutely clear. Did the feast come first and the story later, or did the feast come from the book?

It may be that the Jews in the Persian diaspora adopted a local spring festival and attached a story of deliverance to it. Passover, the principal Jewish spring festival, shows a similar origin since Passover was a festival celebrated by nomads as they changed grazing areas in the spring. The Israelites attached the story of the deliverance from Egypt to this celebration. Since the Torah did not mandate the observance of Purim, the story of Esther served to promote its observance. In time, the Jews of Palestine came to observe this feast, as Josephus (a first-century AD Jewish historian and apologist) reports.

It is a mistake, however, to regard Esther 9:20–32 as nothing more than an addition to the book that justifies the celebration of Purim. It is true that this portion of the book does make an institution of the feast and requires that future generations of Jews celebrate the festival. The text fixes the exact time and manner of its celebration. The effect of these verses is to transform the story of a frustrated pogrom and the victory of the Jews over their enemies into a religious observance.

The Jews are to observe the Feast of Purim by mourning and fasting, by the giving of gifts—especially to the poor—and by remembering the story of Esther (9:22). These prescriptions give a religious dimension to a purely secular story. For succeeding generations the observance of Purim is to be a religious experience. The Jews are to understand their survival not just in nationalistic terms but as a religious obligation. Thus, 9:20–32 reinterprets the book of Esther for its readers. Even though the Hebrew version of the book makes no reference to God, celebration of Mordecai's victory as a religious feast makes it clear that the victory came from God.

The Theological Horizons of the Book

Like the Joseph story (Gn 37–50) and the Succession Narrative (1 Sm 9–20; 1 Kgs 1–2), God remains in the background in the book of Esther. The Hebrew version of the story never mentions God except for what may be an oblique reference in 4:14 (see note to 4:14, OT, p. 576). The rise of Esther to the position of queen of Persia allowed her to defend the Jews, just as Joseph's rise to the position as second only to the pharaoh in Egypt (Gn 41:37–43) placed him where he could save his family (Gn 50:20f). Similarly the succession of Solomon to David's throne was according to the divine will (2 Sm 12:24f), but it occurred without direct divine intervention. Solomon ascended the throne of David following the successful machinations of his mother, Bathsheba, and courtiers who supported his accession (1 Kgs 1).

The story of Esther describes the Byzantine-like intrigue and plots by the antagonists and counterplots by the protagonists. The biblical text does not approve the actions of either Esther or Mordecai but only their result. What God intended was the survival of the Jewish community. God did not dictate the means to insure that survival; the human personalities involved determined these. The absence of any explicit references to God in the story may have been a deliberate attempt to emphasize the importance of the Jews taking the matter of their survival into their own hands. The additions to the Hebrew version show that some people saw this reticence as something that needed correction. These additions make the religious dimensions of the story more explicit:

Additions A and F. The story of Mordecai's dream and its interpretation make it clear that God controls the final destiny of Israel. Esther is the deliverer that God chose in answer to the prayers of the Jews.

Addition B. The decree of the Persian monarch against the Jews shows how some Gentiles regarded specifically Jewish observances as evidence of their disloyalty to the king (especially 4–7).

Addition C. This addition contains the prayers of Mordecai and Esther. The text makes it clear that the deliverance of the Jews is in response to those prayers. C:26–29 answers any objections that readers might raise about the propriety of Esther's marriage to a non-Jew. The reference in C:20 to the Temple is an anomaly, given the setting of the story in the Diaspora.

Addition D. Verses 2 and 8 assert that the king's change of opinion regarding the Jews resulted from God's response to the prayer of Esther.

Addition E. God condemns the enemy of Israel (vv. 2–6). The king finds the Jews innocent of all the accusations that Haman brought against them (vv. 15–16). The king acclaims the God of the Jews as sovereign over all (v. 21).

A Christian Reading of the Book

The presence of this book in the *Christian* Old Testament is a problem for some readers because of its supposed Jewish nationalism. One way to deal with this problem is to "excuse" the book's story of revenge on the enemies of the Jews by observing that the command to love one's enemies had not yet been taught by Christ (see introduction, OT, p. 614). In effect, people will dismiss the book's message because it is supposedly "sub-Christian."

The message of the book of Esther, however, has an important and positive role in the *Christian* canon. It offers an opportunity to check the tendency to spiritualize the people of ancient Israel and their contemporary descendants. The biblical text moves Christians beyond the statements made about the Jews in the Second Vatican Council's *Declaration on the Relationship of the Church to Non-Christian Religions (Nostra Aetate),* article 4. The Council affirmed that there is a spiritual bond between Jews and Christians, that the Church received the revelation of the Old Testament from the Jews, and, above all, that the Jews are not responsible for the death of Jesus. The book of Esther asserts that the preservation of the Jewish people is a *religious obligation.* The presence of this book in the Christian canon is a statement of the religious significance of the Jewish people as an ethnic group, and it implies the abiding validity of Judaism. It makes the sin of anti-Semitism even more reprehensible than the irrational injustice that most Christians understand it to be today, and it undercuts the claim made by some Christians that God's covenant with the Jews has been replaced or superseded by Christianity.

Tales from the Diaspora and Today's Migrants

Stories about life in the Diaspora (Est, Tb, Dn 1–6) suggest that fidelity to Jewish religious traditions is not easy for Jews living outside Palestine. The special circumstances that come from living outside the Promised Land and apart from the community of faith contribute to a special feeling of vulnerability. They experience their new surroundings as hostile to the maintenance of their very identity as Jews. They see political authorities as potential or real threats to their religion and very existence. These stories show how people cut off from their roots can feel lost and menaced.

With the greater mobility that is characteristic of our age, there are more and more people who can identify with the Jewish characters in these tales from the Diaspora. Immigrants sometimes feel that they must choose between economic and political security and their own cultural and religious identities. Aware of those needs, Pope Paul VI issued his *Instruction on the Pastoral Care of People Who Migrate* (1969). Responding to the pope's initiative, the bishops of the United States issued *The Church and the Immigrant* (1976) and established the Bishops' Committee on Migration to respond to the needs of immigrants to this country. One of the main duties of this committee is to help today's immigrants adjust to their new life in a new and sometimes threatening cultural milieu. Specifically, the committee concerns itself with immigration laws, the problems of undocumented immigrants, economic and social discrimination experienced by people on the move, and pastoral initiatives to help people who feel the dislocation that comes with being an immigrant. One of the achievements of this committee was the preparation of *Together, a New People,* a pastoral statement on migrants and refugees published by the National Conference of Catholic Bishops in 1986.

FURTHER READING

Clines, David J. A. "The Esther Scroll: The Story of the Story." *Journal for the Study of the Old Testament Supplement Series,* no. 30. Sheffield: Sheffield Academic Press, 1984.

Craghan, John F. *Esther; Judith; Tobit; Jonah; Ruth.* Old Testament Message 16. Wilmington, DE: Michael Glazier, 1982.

Craig, K. *Reading Esther: A Case for the Literary Carnivalesque.* Literary Currents in Biblical Interpretation. Louisville: Westminster John Knox, 1995.

Fox, Michael. *Character and Ideology in the Book of Esther.* Columbia: University of South Carolina, 1991.

Larkin, Katrina J. A. *Ruth and Esther.* Old Testament Guides. Sheffield: Sheffield Academic Press, 1996.

Levenson, Jon D. *Esther: A Commentary.* Old Testament Library. Louisville: Westminster John Knox, 1997.

Moore, Carey A. *Esther.* Anchor Bible 7B. Garden City, NY: Doubleday, 1971.

—. *Daniel, Esther and Jeremiah: The Additions.* Anchor Bible 44. Garden City, NY: Doubleday, 1977.

1 MACCABEES

[see pages 628–664 of the Old Testament]

The Maccabees

The word *Maccabee* derives from the Hebrew word for hammer and was a nickname for Judas, a leader in the Jewish revolt against the Seleucid ruler, Antiochus Epiphanes (175–164 BC). (Seleucid is the name of the Greek dynasty that ruled in Syria following the death of Alexander the Great. It is derived from the name of Seleucus, one of Alexander's generals.) The nickname *Maccabee* later became a designation for other members of Judas's family who succeeded him as leaders in the revolt. Thus, Judas and his brothers came to be known as "the Maccabees." The term *Maccabean* came to designate the period of Jewish history that witnessed the successful revolt against the Seleucid empire.

After the revolt, the descendants of the Maccabees assumed religious and later political leadership of the Jewish community in Palestine. They ruled an independent Judah from 135 BC until Pompey conquered Palestine for Rome in 63 BC. The name given to this dynasty, the post-Maccabean generation of high priests and kings, was the "Hasmonean" dynasty. That name derives from the ancestor Asamonaeus whom Josephus (a first-century AD Jewish historian and apologist) identifies as the father of Mattathias, who was himself the father of Judas and his brothers. It was Mattathias who started the revolt against Antiochus (1 Mc 2:15–30).

The Maccabean Literature

There are four books "of the Maccabees" that have survived from early Judaism. None of the four are in the Hebrew Bible and therefore are not in Jewish or Protestant Bibles. Jerome included the first two books of the Maccabees in the Vulgate (his translation of the Bible into Latin), so those two books became part of the Roman Catholic canon. Third Maccabees has canonical status in Eastern Christianity. No Christian tradition accepts the fourth book of Maccabees as divinely inspired, though some Eastern churches include it as an appendix to their Bibles. Because of its focus on martyrdom, Fourth Maccabees has influenced Eastern spirituality.

The four books of the Maccabees do not form a continuous narrative like the story of Israel in its land as found in the books of Joshua to 2 Kings. First Maccabees is a historical narrative of events in the life of the Jewish community in and around Jerusalem from the reign of the Greek Seleucus IV (175–164 BC) to the accession of the Jewish ruler, John Hyrcanus (134–104 BC). Second Maccabees is an abridgement of a five-volume history of the Maccabees that no longer exists. It covers the period of Jewish history in Palestine from the time of the high priest Onias III (180 BC) to the victory of Judas Maccabee over the Greeks in 161 BC. Third Maccabees is a misnomer. It has nothing to do with the exploits of the Maccabees. The book is a first-century BC work that describes the persecution of the Jews in Egypt under Ptolemy IV (221–203 BC). Fourth Maccabees is a first-century AD discourse on religious reason as exemplified by Jewish martyrs during the Maccabean revolt.

History and Theology in 1 Maccabees

Unlike the books of Tobit, Judith, and Esther that use historical events and persons as a backdrop for what are fictional tales, 1 Maccabees is a historical narrative that is one of the main sources for reconstructing the history of the Jews in Palestine during the middle of the second century BC. This book, however, is more than a catalogue of events. Its author tries to show the significance of those events. The purpose of the work was to assert the legitimacy of the Hasmonean high-priestly dynasty. The book implies that the right of the Hasmoneans to rule is clear from the achievements of their ancestors: (1) the Maccabees saved the Jews from persecution; (2) they restored observance of the Torah; and (3) they inaugurated an era of peace and prosperity. The author of this book believed that God willed that the Hasmoneans assume the mantle of leadership over the Jews of Palestine.

Reading the Book

Setting the Scene

The story told in this book is a small part of a much larger story: *hellenization,* which was the shifting of cultural orientation from East to West, in the eastern Mediterranean region. Alexander conquered this area in the fourth century BC. It was his dream to take the culture of Greece and wed it to the cultures of the ancient Near East so that people could benefit from the best of each.

Alexander's premature death in 323 BC prevented him from fulfilling that dream. Alexander's generals divided his empire among themselves. The area of the former Israelite kingdoms came under the control of Ptolemy, who ruled from Egypt. Ptolemy permitted the Jews to practice their ancestral religion without much interference. The process of hellenization proceeded in the cultural, political, and economic spheres. The response of the Jewish community to Hellenism was equivocal: some Jews resisted hellenization; others eagerly accepted the new wave that was sweeping the world.

The region of the ancient Mesopotamian empires fell to another of Alexander's generals: Seleucus. He thought that the territory of the old Judahite and Israelite kingdoms rightfully belonged to him. The Ptolemies and Seleucids fought over this region until it passed into the hands of the Seleucids in 200 BC. At first they allowed the Jews to practice their ancestral religion without interference. But circumstances changed in 168 BC when the Seleucid king Antiochus IV Epiphanes seized upon the opportunity provided by divisions within the Jewish community. Antiochus obviously favored the hellenizers in that community because they gave him financial support. To insure the victory of the Jewish hellenizers, Antiochus forbade the practice of the Jewish religion.

Mattathias (1 Mc 1:1–2:70)

The first chapter sets the scene for the bloody confrontation between the Jews and the Seleucids. It describes the hellenization of Jerusalem (1 Mc 1:11–15), the military attacks on the city by two Seleucid armies (1 Mc 1:16–40), and the prohibition of Jewish religious practices (1 Mc 1: 41–61). Antiochus's efforts at obliterating the Jewish religion culminated with the construction of an altar dedicated to Zeus Olympus upon the altar of holocausts, the holy place in the Temple where burnt offerings were made. This effectively transformed the Temple of Jerusalem into a shrine to Zeus (1 Mc 1:54). Tradition remembered this act as the "horrible abomination" (Dn 11:31; 12:11). But the book asserts that there was opposition to the royal decrees (1 Mc 1:62f).

The second chapter is important because it describes the specific type of opposition that the Maccabees and their followers were mounting against the hellenization of Antiochus and his Jewish collaborators. Though there were many Jews who opposed Antiochus, their responses were not always the same. For example, the book of Daniel inculcates a type of passive resistance to the Seleucid program of forced hellenization. The response of the Maccabees in the person of Mattathias is militant opposition. A key text is 2: 23–46, which describes Mattathias's fury at the prospect of Jewish apostasy. The author editorializes as he compares Mattathias's response with that of Phinehas (see Nm 25:6–14). With this comparison, the author implies that Mattathias's action prevented God's anger from consuming the Jews because of the apostasy of some, and that this zealous action merited the high-priestly office for the Hasmoneans as the high priesthood was the reward for Phinehas's zeal against idolatry (Nm 25:13). Besides Numbers 25, other examples of zealous action leading to priestly credentials include Exodus 32:25–29. Mattathias became the leader of a large guerrilla force whose aim was to end Seleucid military domination of the Jews and the proscription of their religion.

The Militancy of 1 Maccabees

The response of Mattathias to the proscription of his ancestral religion was militant: he and his followers took up arms against the Seleucids and their Jewish collaborators. The United States Bishops' Pastoral, *The Challenge of Peace,* asserts the "the sacred scriptures provide the foundation for confronting war and peace today" (#27). In trying to formulate a Christian response to these issues, one has to face the militancy of 1 Maccabees. Mattathias and his sons responded to the Seleucid persecution with armed resistance. Their theological support for such a response was taken from the religious traditions of ancient Israel (see Dt 20).

It is also important to remember that the response of 1 Maccabees to the threat posed by Antiochus was not the only one among religious Jews in Palestine. Though there was agreement among religious Jews that they ought to resist Antiochus, there was a variety of viewpoints on how resistance ought to proceed. First Maccabees reflects the view of those who insisted on armed resistance. There were others who opted for martyrdom, nonviolent resistance, and even pacifism in the face of the threat posed by Antiochus's anti-Jewish laws.

While 2 Maccabees shares the militancy of 1 Maccabees, it looks at the revolution against the Seleucids from a somewhat different perspective. While it recognized the traditions associated with the wars of the Lord (see Dt 20), it also saw martyrdom as a way the faithful might contribute to the final victory over their enemies. Military prowess is not the only way. The blood of martyrs who died rather than violate the Torah cries out to God for vengeance and thereby seals the victory for the Jews.

The book of Daniel likewise describes a war between the forces of good and evil, but it believes that the real conflict takes place not on earth but in heaven, where God will be victorious over the powers of evil. Antiochus will fall, but not by human hands (Dn 8:25). The book of Daniel holds that resistance is necessary but is nonviolent. It expresses itself in willingness to undergo suffering and even death for the sake of the Torah. Daniel can offer nonviolent resistance as an option because of its confidence in the resurrection of the faithful (Dn 12:2f). The warfare against the forces of evil is left to God and Michael (Dn 12:1) so the faithful do not need to fight against Antiochus since God has sealed his fate already (Dn 7:26f). All the faithful need do is to stand up to the king by not complying with his orders to abandon their ancestral religion. The book of Daniel gives the whole credit for the inevitable victory over Antiochus to God's initiative. Daniel gives no credit to the contributions of the Maccabees at all.

Some Jews chose pacifism as a response to Antiochus's policies. This is evident from reading the *Testament of Moses,* a noncanonical work, portions of which were written about the same time as 1 Maccabees. The *Testament of Moses* has no room for the militancy of 1 Maccabees. It expected deliverance to come by direct divine intervention. The catalyst for the deliverance of the Jews is the death of those who have remained faithful to God and the Torah. The result of this deliverance will not be a Jewish state but Israel's separation from the nations and its exaltation in the heavens.

The militancy of 1 Maccabees represents just one response to the problems that the Jewish community in Palestine had because of Antiochus's persecution. The Bible and noncanonical Jewish literature offer others. In their pastoral letter, the bishops recognize that the Scriptures reflect many varied historical situations (#28). They could also have noted that the Scriptures reflect varied responses to the same historical circumstances. While we can understand the militancy of the Maccabees, such a response makes little sense in a nuclear age. There is no comparison between warfare of the second century BC and warfare today. That is precisely why the bishops of the United States spent so much time dealing with this issue and why they join recent popes in calling for nuclear disarmament.

Mattathias's Farewell

Chapter 2 concludes with Mattathias's testament (vv. 49–62) in which he consigns his military authority to his sons (vv. 65–66). Before doing that, he commends the example of Israelite heroes of the past (vv. 51–60) to his sons in order to support his militant ideology (vv. 50,66–68). He is certain that Antiochus will fall, and the suppression of Jewish religion will end with him (vv. 61–63).

Judas (1 Mc 3:1–9:22)

About 40 percent of the story in 1 Maccabees centers on the exploits of Judas, who succeeded his father as leader of the Jewish guerilla forces. Though the text acclaims Judas's exploits and applauds his bravery (3:3–9; 9:22), the author is very careful to imply that Judas's victories came about because of divine help. Judas prays before he begins any battle (3:46; 4:30–33; 5:33; 7:40–42). He boosts the morale of his army by reminding his men of how God has helped their ancestors in the face of overwhelming odds (4:8f; 7:41). Judas's preparations for battle (3:47–49), his dismissal of those whom Deuteronomy exempts from war (3:56, see Dt 20:5–8), and the way he deals with the defeated enemy and the spoils of war (5:28,35,51) all exemplify the beliefs of a man who is certain that he is fighting in accord with a divine command. Finally Judas praises God when he celebrates his victories (4:24, 33, 55).

Hanukkah, or the Feast of the Dedication

Hanukkah is a Jewish feast celebrating the rededication of the Second Temple during the Maccabean revolt (the Hebrew word *hanukkah* means "dedication"). It was Judas Maccabee who mandated the observance of this festival (1 Mc 4:59). Antiochus polluted the altar of the Temple (1 Mc 1:54). This was probably the "horrible abomination" of Daniel 9:27. When the Maccabees gained control of the area of the Temple, they purified the Temple and rebuilt the altar three years to the day of Antiochus's desecration (1 Mc 4:36–58).

Josephus calls this festival "the feast of lights" (*Antiquities* 12:7:7) because the rededication of the Temple also involved rekindling the Temple's menorah (a lampstand with seven branches). Jews observe this festival at home by lighting one candle on a special Hanukkah menorah each night. The Talmud relates the story of how one day's supply of holy oil lasted for the full eight days of the original festival until the priests could obtain more oil for the menorah in the Temple. The significance of Hanukkah lies in its glorification of the deeds of those who refused to acquiesce in the proscription of their ancestral religion. They took up arms and won their freedom. The victory of the Maccabees over Antiochus undoubtedly enabled Judaism to survive.

Jonathan (1 Mc 9:23–12:54)

Judas died in battle, and his brother Jonathan succeeded him. While the text hails Jonathan's military exploits, of particular importance is his acceptance of the appointment as high priest from the Seleucid king Alexander who succeeded Antiochus (10:20f).

Simon (1 Mc 13:1–16:24)

After the followers of Trypho, a pretender to the Seleucid throne, assassinated Jonathan, the leadership of the Jewish community passed to his brother Simon. Simon's stirring speech (13:3–6) moved the people to acclaim him as their ruler (13:8f). Later, a formal assembly composed of priests, elders, and leaders of the people ratified this popular action (1 Mc 14:41). First Maccabees reaches its climax with the accession of Simon as leader and high priest. The purpose of the book is to present the establishment of the Hasmonean house as the legitimate political and religious dynasty for the Jews of Palestine.

The poem in 14:4–15 is an amalgam of biblical motifs suggesting that with Simon a state of peace and prosperity has come to the Jews, the likes of which had not been seen since the days of David and Solomon. With Simon a new "golden age" has dawned. The change effected by the rule of the Hasmoneans over the thirty years since Mattathias's revolt began is dramatic. For the sake of its religion, a beleaguered minority within the Jewish community stood up to a powerful empire and prevailed. The author of 1 Maccabees considered the defeat of the Seleucids to be clear evidence that God was working through the Hasmoneans to save the Jewish community and religion.

The book, however, closes on a tragic note. After an aged Simon appointed his two eldest sons, Judas and John, as his successors, a political rival murdered Simon along with Judas and another one of his sons, Mattathias. John captured the assassin and had him executed. The succession was safe and another Hasmonean, John Hyrcanus continued the line of those "men to whom it was granted to achieve Israel's salvation" (5:62). John ruled the Jewish community in Palestine as high priest and *ethnarch,* a title whose Greek etymology means "ruler of a people."

The Legitimacy of the Hasmoneans

The purpose of 1 Maccabees is clear: it defends the legitimacy of the Hasmonean dynasty, which ruled over the Jews in Palestine for about one hundred years until Herod the Great ended their rule. The members of this dynasty, who assumed both religious and political leadership in the Jewish community, were not without their opponents. After all, they ruled as kings when many Jews believed that the only legitimate political leaders ought to be descendants of David. As a priestly family the Hasmoneans were not members of David's tribe (Judah) let alone his family. The Hasmoneans functioned as high priests even though they were not descendants of Aaron as required by tradition. The principal opponents of the Hasmoneans were the *Hasidim* (the Pious Ones) who were the spiritual ancestors of the Essenes and the Pharisees.

The Hasidim saw themselves as careful observers of the law but held the Hasmoneans to be illegitimate interlopers as religious and political leaders. First Maccabees tried to show that the Hasmonean dynasty owed its origin to a revolutionary movement that had zeal for the Torah at its heart. According to 1 Maccabees, the Hasidim were not always very prudent in their self-styled devotion to the Torah. In their concern to have a high priest from the family of Aaron, they accepted a collaborator who betrayed them (7: 8–18). The author of 1 Maccabees considered the victories that God granted the Maccabees to be a sign from God pointing to the legitimacy of the Hasmonean dynasty. The book asserts that the most prudent approach was for the Jews to accept the dynasty until a "true prophet" will arise to say that God wishes otherwise (14:41). This is precisely what most of the Jewish people and their leaders did (14:28).

First Maccabees reflects a type of pragmatism that was incompatible with the religious zealotry of the Hasidim. For example, 1 Maccabees 8 is lavish in its praise of the Romans. This shows that the Hasmoneans were willing to compromise with foreigners when circumstances made it necessary. In Jesus' day, the Sadducees adopted this same position and later so did the early church (see Rm 13:1–7 and 1 Pt 2:13–17).

First Maccabees was not content with establishing the legitimacy of the Hasmonean dynasty on purely religious grounds. It shows that the major political powers of the day recognized the Hasmoneans as the political leaders of the Jewish people. It cites several Seleucid documents to the effect (10:18–20; 10:25–45; 11:30–37; 13: 31–40; 15:2–9). Both the Spartans (12:5–23 and 14:16–23) and the Romans (8:1–32; 12:1–4; 14:16–19) also acknowledged the Hasmoneans as the leaders of the Jewish people.

First Maccabees in Catholic Tradition

This book is not part of the Hebrew Bible. There is no evidence that it formed part of the Qumran library, and Josephus did not include it on his list of sacred books. The book fared better among Christians. Reverence for the book by the Church's early theologians was perhaps one reason that the Councils of Florence and Trent both affirmed its canonicity. This book, however, has had no real impact on Christian theology. Its use in the liturgy is minimal. The liturgy does not make use of 1 Maccabees during the cycle of Sunday readings but reads portions of chapters 1 through 6 on four successive weekdays in Year II (nos. 497–502). Appropriately enough, the text from chapter 4 about the rededication of the altar in the Temple is a suggested reading for the Mass on the occasion of the dedication of an altar and 2:49–52; 57–64 is the reading for the votive Mass for Persecuted Christians.

It is important to remember that 1 Maccabees was written to convince Jews that the armed revolution led by the Maccabees and their quest to expand the territory under their control to all of Palestine was ordained of God. This, of course, means that the Jewish community needed some convincing. Wars that seemingly have their basis in religion have caused so much harm that the argument of 1 Maccabees is not at all convincing to most readers today. The author of this book was able to make his argument because the Maccabean revolution succeeded. In contemporary armed conflicts, there are rarely any winners.

FURTHER READING

Bartlett, John R. *1 Maccabees*. Sheffield: Sheffield Academic Press, 1998.

Bickermann, Elias. *From Ezra to the Last of the Mac-*

cabees: The Historical Foundations of Post Biblical Judaism. New York: Schocken, 1962.
Collins, John. *Daniel, 1–2 Maccabees*. Old Testament Message 15. Wilmington, DE: Michael Glazier, 1981.
Goldstein, Jonathan A. *1 Maccabees*. Anchor Bible 41. Garden City, NY: Doubleday, 1976.
——. *2 Maccabees*. Anchor Bible 41a. New York: Doubleday, 1983.
Harrington, Daniel J. *The Maccabean Revolt: Anatomy of a Biblical Revolution*. Wilmington, DE: Michael Glazier, 1988.
Sievers, Joseph. *The Hasmoneans and Their Supporters: From Mattathias to the Death of John Hyrcanus I*. Atlanta: Scholars Press, 1990.
Williams, David S. *The Structure of 1 Maccabees*. Washington, DC: Catholic Biblical Association, 1999.

2 MACCABEES

[see pages 664–689 of the Old Testament]

The Relationship between 1 and 2 Maccabees

Second Maccabees does not continue the history of the Jewish revolt against the Seleucid empire and its aftermath, which is the subject of 1 Maccabees. The second book is an abridgement of a five-volume work on the Maccabees by one Jason of Cyrene (2:23). This longer work has not come down to us. The unknown editor who is responsible for the present form of 2 Maccabees wished to simplify Jason's work so that readers could remember its most important features (2:25).

Second Maccabees begins its story of the Jews in Palestine with the reign of Seleucus IV when Onias III was the high priest and ends with the defeat of the Seleucid army by Judas Maccabee. The period extends from approximately 180 to 161 BC. Thus, the story of 2 Maccabees overlaps with that in 1 Mc 1:10–7:5. In particular, there is quite a lot of similarity between 2 Mc 8–15 and 1 Mc 3–7.

While 2 Maccabees does not cover as much of the history of the Maccabees as does 1 Maccabees, it is a more polished literary work. Also, 2 Maccabees is less of an apology for the Hasmonean dynasty and more of an attempt to illustrate an important theological theme: God's justice in rewarding the faithful and punishing the impious. The book provides an inventory of how God dealt with both Jews and Greeks who disregarded the divine will. Its focus, however, is on those Jews who accepted death rather than be guilty of an act of disobedience. Second Maccabees highlights the death of Jewish martyrs to affect the emotions of its readers so that they may recommit themselves to faithful observance.

Reading the Book

Letters to the Jews in Egypt (2 Mc 1:2–2:18)

The book begins with two letters directed at the Jewish community in Egypt. Both call upon that community to celebrate a festival in honor of the rededication of the Temple following the victory of the Maccabees over the Seleucids. The feast in question is Hanukkah. Since the Torah did not mandate the celebration of this feast, the leadership of the Jewish community had to take this special step to encourage its observance.

The Jewish community in Egypt built its own temple under the direction of Onias IV, the son of the last legitimate high priest. Perhaps one purpose of these letters was to redirect these peoples' loyalty to the community in Jerusalem. Encouraging the Jews in Egypt to celebrate a festival in honor of the rededication of the Temple in Jerusalem may have been an attempt to keep them from forgetting their ties with Palestine. Also it may be that the person responsible for the present form of 2 Maccabees added these letters to the story of the triumph of the Maccabees in order to make the book into a festal scroll for Hanukkah as is the book of Esther for the Feast of Purim.

The Author's Preface (2 Mc 2:19–32)

The person responsible for this preface is the individual who has decided to abridge the work of Jason of Cyrene. He states that he wishes to simplify Jason's work to make it helpful to more people (2:24–26). He also advises his readers that he will add his own touches to Jason's work

(2:29). Second Maccabees, as it stands today, is not simply a digest of a much longer work. There are portions of the book that do not come from Jason but were the product of the same person who made the abridgement.

Hellenization

Second Maccabees, like 1 Maccabees, reflects those circles in second-century BC Judaism that rejected the program of enforced hellenization imposed by Antiochus. It offers the example of martyrs who died rather than abandon their ancestral religion (see 2 Mc 6:18–7:42). Despite this strong objection to Hellenism, even the most pious Jews could not avoid its influence completely.

Hellenism is a term that describes the culture, ideals, and institutions that reached their apex in fifth-century BC Athens and that came to have a momentous influence throughout the eastern Mediterranean region. Until the time of Alexander the Great, this region was oriented culturally to the East. The two Israelite kingdoms were subject to the political, economic, and cultural sway of the eastern empires: Assyria, Babylon, and Persia. Alexander did more than bring Palestine into Greece's political orbit; he effected a genuine cultural reorientation. Until the Moslem conquest in the seventh century AD, the entire eastern Mediterranean region, including the territories of the former Israelite kingdoms, came under the cultural influence of the West.

The city or *polis* with its marketplace *(agora)*, colonnaded streets, temples, theater, and gymnasium was the instrument of economic prosperity in the Near East and of the diffusion of Hellenism as well. Throughout Palestine the Greeks remade ancient cities. There was Ptolemais (Acco) along the Mediterranean in the north, Gaza along the Mediterranean in the south, Scythopolis (Beth-shan) in the Jordan Valley, Marisa (Mareshah) in the south. Even Jerusalem was made over (1 Mc 1:11–14).

It is not surprising that there was resistance among some Jews to hellenization. After all, the Jews had a very ancient culture and one that did not accept change very readily. There were, however, people—especially among the aristocratic stratum of Jewish society—that embraced the new cultural wave. At first, the Hellenism that the Jews faced was mild. From the time of Alexander's death in 332 BC to about 200 BC, the Ptolemies ruled Judah from Egypt. The Ptolemies were the least culturally aggressive of all the Hellenistic dynasties. Matters changed dramatically under the Seleucid king Antiochus IV, who imposed Hellenism upon the Jews. Antiochus's policies sparked the Maccabean revolt.

Like 1 Maccabees, this work is also opposed to the forced hellenization program of Antiochus. Second Maccabees is intensely devoted to the Torah. Death, even suicide (2 Mc 14:37–46), is preferable to violating the Torah. The reward for such loyalty for the individual is resurrection, and for the community it is the possession of Jerusalem. Despite this opposition to hellenization, it is impossible to escape the influence of Hellenistic culture. Second Maccabees itself uses rhetorical forms that come from Greek literature. For example, 2 Maccabees appeals to the emotions of its readers. The work does not hesitate to describe the death of Jewish martyrs in vivid detail. This approach is typical of Hellenistic history writing. The same is true of appeals to the supernatural (for example, 2 Mc 3:22–30). The miraculous episodes in 2 Maccabees are comparable to episodes in Greek histories. The author does not hesitate to employ these Greek rhetorical patterns because they help the book achieve its purpose: to move its readers to renewed commitment to their ancestral religious traditions.

As opposed as 2 Maccabees is to the growing influence of Greek culture over the Jews of Palestine, the book recognizes that some Greeks are sympathetic to the Jews and their religious traditions. It even has Antiochus convert to Judaism as he is dying (9:11–18). The book implies that the Jews do not object to the rule of the Greeks as such and that Jews can be good citizens of the empire. What they *do* object to are the excesses that came with Antiochus.

There comes a point when the pious must choose. Antiochus made the choice unavoidable. With Hellenism there came a whole bevy of gods and goddesses. There were even deified kings. More subtle were the novelties in philosophy and ethics. For the pious Jew, Hellenism represented a religious ideology and practice that was quite unfamiliar. Jewish literature of the period shows an extreme distaste for non-Israelite religion (Dn 3:6; 1 Mc 1:43; Wis 13:10–19; 14:12–21). But there was no escaping the influence of Greek culture at this time and on into the future. For example, almost seven hundred years later during the Byzantine Period (fourth to sixth centuries AD), there were a few synagogues in Palestine that had decorative motifs that included a zodiac complete with the god Helios in the center of a mosaic floor.

Second Maccabees represents the earlier view that rejected any compromise with Hellenism. There are absolute values that do not allow for any compromise. Even in the face of death, the righteous will chose fidelity to the Torah. Second Maccabees can be confident that such a choice is not in vain because of its belief in the resurrection.

The Story of the Maccabees (2 Mc 3:1–15:36)

A theological purpose dominates the way 2 Maccabees tells its story: to show how the events of Jewish history—from the time of Onias the high priest to the time of Judas Maccabee—disclose a God who cares for the Jewish people by rewarding the faithful and punishing evildoers. In telling his story, the author uses a scheme first devised by the author of the story of Israel in its land as found in the books of Joshua to 2 Kings. This story, infused by Deuteronomic theology, told how Israel came to possess the land of Canaan under Joshua and then how it lost the land because of the infidelities of its kings. The story of Israel in its land (Jos through 2 Kgs) is a story of how Israel's infidelity transformed the blessing into a curse.

The story told in 2 Maccabees begins with a period of blessing (3:1–40) during the time of Onias III when people observed the Torah (3: 1–3). During the time of the high priests Jason and Menelaus, the people and their leaders sin by violating the Torah and following the customs of the Greeks (4:1–5:10). This inevitably leads to punishment (5:11–6:17). Antiochus was the agent of God's judgment just as the Assyrians and Babylonians were agents of divine judgment in 2 Kings.

In the midst of Antiochus's persecution of the Jews, the prayers of the people, and especially the heroic death of the Jewish martyrs, led to a turning point (6:18–8:4). The refusal of the martyrs to sin, their obedience to the Torah, and their innocent death bring a change in circumstances. God extended mercy to the Jews and brought an end to their persecution. Although the book was aware that it was the military victories of Judas Maccabee that ended the domination of Antiochus, it assumed that it was the death of the martyrs that turned God's anger to mercy and made the Maccabean victories possible.

This section of the book has influenced the development of the Christian notion of suffering as a positive value. Suffering can be a form of divine education (6:18–7:42). God did not design the suffering of the Jewish people under Antiochus to destroy the people but to discipline them. God may discipline the people but does not abandon them (6:12–16).

The suffering of the innocent led the author to affirm his belief in the resurrection of the dead (7:9, 11, 14, 23; 14:46). This belief enabled the Jewish martyrs to accept their suffering because God will deliver the pious despite their death at the hands of the impious. (See the Reading Guide on Daniel, RG 337). The history of the Maccabean wars ends with a summary of Judas's victories (8:5–15:36) that brings salvation to the beleaguered Jewish community. The cycle is complete: blessing has returned to the Jewish people.

Parallel to this story of salvation is another story of retribution. The enemies of the Jews came to a terrible end: Antiochus died in agony (9:8), the Greek who murdered the good high priest Onias was himself killed (4:38), and the general who commanded the siege against Jerusalem died in battle and his head was hung from the citadel of the city (15:35). The wicked among the Jews also suffered under divine judgment. The evil high priests Jason and Menelaus both came to miserable ends (5:1–10 and 13:7f).

Prayers for the Living and Dead

One of the most significant texts in this book for Roman Catholic theology is 12:42–46. Here the author wished to show that Judas Maccabee believed in the resurrection of the dead since he ordered prayers and sacrifices for those who had fallen in battle. The author concludes that such prayers would be futile unless Judas believed that they would rise again (12:44). Sometimes this text is used as support for the Roman Catholic belief in purgatory and the efficacy of the prayers of the living for the dead.

Another significant text for Roman Catholics is 2 Maccabees 15:12–16. Here Judas Maccabee has a dream in which he sees the prophet Jeremiah praying for the Jews and Jerusalem. Catholic tradition accepts this text as one support for the belief in the efficacy of the intercession of the saints.

The Epilogue (2 Mc 15:37–39)

The author ends his work rather abruptly with a hope that readers will find his work pleasant reading.

FURTHER READING

Doran, Robert. *Temple Propaganda: The Purpose and Character of 2 Maccabees.* Washington: Catholic Biblical Association, 1981.

van Henten, J. W. *The Maccabean Martyrs as Saviors of the Jewish People: A Study of 2 and 4 Maccabees.* Leiden: Brill, 1992.

See also 1 Maccabees.

THE WISDOM BOOKS

DIANNE BERGANT

Introduction

The corpus of books that we know as wisdom literature (Proverbs, Job, Ecclesiastes, Sirach or Ecclesiasticus, Wisdom of Solomon) stands apart from the other literature of the Old Testament. It asks the question, what kind of role does God play in everyday life? The answers to that question did not contribute to the national story that we have come to know as "salvation history." Instead, these books form a kind of guide for successful living. Since every person in every culture must struggle with the questions of life, there is a universal character to this literature. This might explain why, even today, people of other religious cultures often can more readily identify with the teaching of the wisdom books than with the uniquely Israelite or Christian theology found in other sections of the Bible.

The Israelites came to believe that their God was the great Creator-God, the one responsible for the world and everything in it. Observing the regularity in creation, they concluded that there was some kind of order inherent in nature itself. They believed that, if they could discern how this order operated and then harmonize their lives with it, they would be successful and at peace. The ability to perceive this order and to live in accord with it was known as wisdom.

The primary interest of the wisdom tradition is instruction in the proper ways of living. The writers made use of various teaching techniques such as storytelling, exhortation, warning, and questioning. In addition to the standard proverb, they used riddles, parables, and metaphors to instruct, advise, and persuade. There are usually very definite lessons that they wanted to teach, and so we should not be surprised when we come across what appears to be "the moral of the story."

The sages were humanists; they were concerned with the study of human beings and attentive to human welfare, values, and dignity. They taught that whatever benefited humanity was a good to be pursued, and whatever was harmful should be avoided and condemned. Training of any kind, whether within the family, the court, or in preparation for a profession, ought to impart the skills needed to succeed in the relevant setting. The criterion for judging the value of any venture was the degree of success or happiness that it brought. The sages regarded well-being and happiness as evidence that life was in accord with the order of creation. They did not advocate the pursuit of happiness for its own sake, but as a by-product of the right kind of life. Success and happiness were also considered concrete evidence of the wisdom of the successful person. The judgment of right or wrong, and the laws that supported this judgment, grew out of just such a critical reflection on the experience of life.

Although Israel's wise women and men believed that there was a right way of behaving, they did not insist on a rigid standard that would fit every circumstance. Each case was different. The wise person was the one who had a store of wisdom gained from experience and who knew which way of behaving was appropriate to each situation. There is a great deal of pragmatism in such a way of viewing life. If an approach did not accomplish the desired goal, it was discarded for one that would. This is not a case of the end justifying the means. Rather, the Israelites believed that goodness was a force that determined life. They were convinced that goodness became evident in whatever built up, sustained, or enriched life. From this point of view, the consequences of an action or the quality of the end were seen as evidence of the goodness of the means. Such an understanding of life presumed that conformity to the inherent governing principles of the world would result in a life filled with success and prosperity. On the other hand, adversity was attributed to failure to observe these authoritative directives. On occasion, this tradition does acknowledge the limitations of this point of view (Job and Ecclesiastes are prime examples). Nonetheless, the theory of retribution (the good shall be rewarded; the evil shall be punished) undergirds most of the wisdom literature.

Israel's wisdom tradition did not develop in a vacuum. It was part of a much broader movement within the ancient Near Eastern world. Reference to the sages of foreign nations can be found throughout the biblical text itself, usually within passages that depict an Israelite outstripping a non-Israelite in wisdom. For example, Joseph succeeded in interpreting Pharaoh's dream when the magicians and sages of Egypt failed (see Gn 41), and Job had a reputation that surpassed those of all the sages of the East (Jb 1:3).

There is remarkable similarity between the biblical wisdom material and some Egyptian, Mesopotamian, and Canaanite texts. There is common subject matter, the literary forms are similar, and the worldview corresponds. Critical examination shows that the non-Israelite texts are significantly older than comparable biblical material. Israel probably borrowed from a common pool of traditions and then adapted and reinterpreted material when necessary. Despite these similarities, Israel's wisdom tradition is clearly in accord with its Yahwistic faith. It may not focus on specifics of religion, but it is highly ethical and fundamentally monotheistic, and, at times it equates wisdom with fidelity to the law of Israel.

FURTHER READING

General Introductions to Wisdom Literature:

Bergant, Dianne. *Israel's Wisdom Literature: A Liberation-Critical Reading*. Minneapolis: Fortress, 1997.

Crenshaw, James L. *Old Testament Wisdom: An Introduction.* Rev. ed. Louisville: Westminster John Knox, 1998.

Davis, Ellen F. *Proverbs, Ecclesiastes, and the Song of Songs*. Westminster Bible Companion. Louisville: Westminster John Knox, 2000.

Murphy, Roland. *The Tree of Life. An Exploration of the Biblical Wisdom Literature*. New York: Doubleday, 1990.

JOB

[see pages 691–727 of the Old Testament]

About the Book

Certain aspects of the book of Job have evoked as many interpretations as there are interpreters. Since the way we explain these points may influence our understanding of the message of the book, it might be helpful to consider some of them before proceeding. There is no agreement regarding the book's date, its place of origin, or the source of some of its parts. There is not even total agreement as to its principal theme. In fact, the richness of the book and its universal appeal prevent us from easily categorizing it. Evidence from the book itself is often given in support of a preexilic dating (seventh century BC). Job's complaints are reminiscent of the laments of Jeremiah, and some consider the book an outcry against the destruction of Jerusalem and deportation into exile. However, similarities with the theology and style of Deutero-Isaiah (the portion of Isaiah beginning with chapter 40) seem to carry more weight, tipping the scale in favor of a postexilic dating (sixth to fifth century BC). It is in the postexilic period (or around 400 BC) that Satan appears as the proper name of the "evil one" (1 Chr 21:1). The book of Job must have originated sometime before Chronicles, for within its pages "the satan" is still a common term that refers to an adversary in a court of justice.

Job's struggle with suffering is a universal and perennial problem, and there is much in the book that has international flavor and appeal. There were older ancient Near Eastern accounts of innocent sufferers that may have been known to the author of Job. Several characteristics of the book, such as the names and places of origin of the three visitors, suggest foreign influence and perhaps even borrowing from other sources. Still, whatever may have originated elsewhere now clearly bears the mark of Israelite theology.

Like most pieces of ancient literature, Job is a composite rather than the work of a single author. It appears to be a prose folktale (1:1–2:13; 42:7–17) within which extensive poetic speeches (3:1–42:6) have been inserted. In the book's present form, the two parts of the folktale serve as prologue and epilogue to the speeches. Even within these speeches, we can detect units believed to have originated from someone other than the principal author: for example, the Wisdom Poem (28), the Elihu Speeches (32–37), the second Speech of the Lord (41). Regardless of when or from whom these different sections originated, they all belong to the final form, and it is this final form that has been handed down to us as sacred Scripture. Therefore we should read the book as a unified literary work.

Finally, the universal appeal of the book stems from the nature of the questions posed by the tormented Job. Who has not struggled with the dilemma of incomprehensible suffering? Who has not cried out to God: "Why?" The principal theme of the book has been variously identified as human integrity; innocent suffering; disinterested piety; human limitations and the incomprehensibility of God; ultimate trust. Actually, these interpretations are not mutually exclusive; they are interrelated. They each express a different nuance of the all-encompassing mystery of the manner in which God is present in the world and they suggest the manner in which we should respond to that presence.

The Literary Style

Most people know the story of the innocent man who was mysteriously stricken yet remained steadfast in his loyalty and was rewarded in the end for his faithfulness. This simple understanding does not accurately represent the story; it is merely the plot of the framing folktale. The principal part of the book is the poetic dialogues. The prologue and epilogue merely set the stage and bring to conclusion the real drama. The more we understand the function of the form of the book, the better we will discover the message within it.

The dialogues consist of speeches in Hebrew poetic form. Each time Job cries out against his sorry state, Eliphaz, Bildad, or Zophar offer him counsel or attempt to convince him of his error. The orderly manner in which this exchange takes place constitutes the cycles of speeches. The third set of speeches is somewhat fragmented. Bildad's remarks are abbreviated, Zophar's are missing altogether, and Job's replies are inordinately long, often containing material that seems to contradict his basic point of view. Some scholars believe the dislocation of material that really belongs to either Bildad or Zophar explains such discrepancies, and they reconstruct the speeches in order to remedy this. Such reconstruction explains why the verses are sometimes out of numerical order in some translations.

The speeches of Elihu do not fit into any of the three cycles. While there are some differences between this Elihu section and what precedes it, the theological point of view expressed by this speaker neither fundamentally departs from nor significantly adds to that of the first three visitors. This fact has led some commentators to conclude that either the speeches are a later literary and theological addition of the original author or they are the work of another writer. This section is now part of the book, however, and cannot be discounted.

The literary form and the content of the Lord's speeches are reminiscent of an ancient Near Eastern pattern known as *onomasticon* (a Greek word meaning "list of names"). This was a constructed listing of names of things that had similar characteristics. This could include cosmological, meteorological, or other natural phenomena. These listings were probably prescientific attempts at classifying natural phenomena. They demonstrate the universal human search for understanding the universe. In the book of Job we find a creative use of this form. The author casts God in the role of wisdom teacher who poses challenging questions—a teaching technique typical of the wisdom tradition—that test Job's comprehension of the wonders of the universe. The content and the form of these questions are similar to the onomasticon. The use of nature as a means of instruction is characteristic of the wisdom tradition. While this technique occurs throughout the entire book, nowhere else does it have the effect that it does in these speeches. Because God does not directly address Job's demands, some commentators have concluded that God ignores Job's concerns. In saying this, they have not adequately considered the way the author makes use of this literary form.

The poetry found within the book is unlike most classical or contemporary poetry. There is virtually no rhyme, and the rhythm follows tonal patterns that are usually lost when the original Hebrew is translated. One characteristic that is identifiable even in translation is the correspondence of thought in successive half lines. This feature is known as parallelism. The thought in the first line can be repeated:

> Does God pervert judgment,
> and does the Almighty distort justice?
> (Jb 8:3)

or contrasted (there are no clear examples of this in Job):

> Hatred stirs up disputes,
> but love covers all offenses (Prv 10:12)

or advanced:

> Pity me, pity me, O you my friends,
> for the hand of God has struck me!
> (Jb 19:21).

Parallelism is used effectively in Job as an aid in furthering the arguments of the various speakers.

There are two other literary forms that should be mentioned. They are the lawsuit and the lament. Elements of these forms are found throughout the speeches of Job. Again and again he demands that God meet him in court where his (Job's) case will be tried and he will be found innocent (for example, 23:2–4). Even more frequently, Job cries out to God in complaint. He laments the day of his birth (3:1–10), and life itself (10:1–7), and he pleads for help (13:20–27). In all of these ways, the literary style of the author contributes to the development of the book's message.

The Drama

Each section of the book has its own dynamic and carries the story forward to its conclusion. The prose prologue plays a very important role in the unfolding of the theological message of the book. It is there that Job's innocence is established beyond any doubt, and it is there that we see who is really responsible for Job's misfortune. It is God who permits this righteous man to suffer in order to test the quality of his integrity. Job never knows this, nor do his visitors. Only the reader is witness to what took place in heaven. It is important that we know this as we listen to the theological debate that follows. The arguments in the poetic speeches are repetitious and appear to be quite monotonous, but this is an essential part of the author's treatment of the problem. By adding layer upon layer of the same accusation and rebuttal, the author brings us into the very midst of the impasse. It does not take long for us to recognize the pointlessness of the debate. Job makes his claims, and his counselors make theirs. Neither side is convinced by the other. Only some manifestation from God can resolve the deadlock.

Job demands a hearing, and God does finally confront him—but in a manner that far surpasses Job's imagining. God breaks the cosmic silence and thunders through the heavens. Job had made his appeal to the justice of God. God answers Job from the midst of creative power. Even though his questions are not answered, the opposing tensions with which Job had struggled are clearly reconciled. But why? and how?

The epilogue and its last verses of prose complete the reworked folktale. Job is vindicated and, as was the rule in this ancient society when someone had been unjustly dispossessed, he is compensated for his losses by double payment. However, his question "Why" is never answered. As the book ends, all Job knows is that the innocent can indeed be afflicted for no apparent reason and with no guarantee that the reason will ever be disclosed.

The Message

While the book of Job is a poetic narrative, it is also a theological statement made up of several themes intricately interwoven. The way we understand this theology will influence the way we perceive the arguments in the book. The themes are treated here not in order of importance but as they appear in the book itself.

Reward and Punishment

As mentioned in the introduction, the theory of retribution undergirds most of the wisdom literature. It is, after all, the basis of any notion of justice. Goodness should be rewarded and evil should be punished. This theory probably originated from the experience of life itself. Actions frequently generate their own consequences. When it appears that this will not happen in the natural course of events, someone in authority steps in to see that justice is indeed done. We not only expect this to happen, we need it in order to live with a certain degree of security. The theory clearly plays an important role in the book of Job. Although Job endures insufferable loss and physical distress, his real agony seems to lie in the incomprehensibility of his situation. He has been a righteous man, and righteous people are not supposed to be so afflicted. Job's claim of righteousness is not an empty one. The author has taken great pains in the prologue to show us that Job is indeed a man of unsurpassed integrity. Then why should he have to bear the burden that, according to this theory, is the consequence of wickedness? Has God forgotten Job's faithfulness? Or, even worse, is God indifferent toward it? These are the kinds of questions at the heart of Job's dilemma.

It is quite clear that those who visit Job consider the theory of retribution a valid way of interpreting life. Since Job is suffering, he must be guilty of wrong. Since his suffering is so comprehensive and so intense, his sin must be serious. His visitors use every argument they can devise to convince Job of his error and persuade him to repent. They draw their conclusions about the morality of his behavior from the nature of his present situation. They do not question Job's suffering, and so they assume that he is guilty. (This same kind of thinking prompted the apostles to ask Jesus whether it was the sin of the blind man or of his parents that resulted in the man's blindness [see Jn 9:21].) Job himself adheres to the same theory, but he makes his claims from a different point of view. He knows that he has done nothing to deserve such misfortune. Still, a strict understanding of retribution offers no other explanation for his troubles and, therefore, Job blames God. Being a man of faith, he believes that God is the architect of the order in the universe. God is the one who has made things to work as they do. Ultimately, God is the one who decides who will be rewarded and who will be punished. God usually accomplishes this through the laws that were set at creation. When they seem to fail, God can and, as the traditions of Israel claim, God does intervene to enforce justice. From Job's point of view, God has failed to do this in his case.

Since the bulk of the speeches consist of arguments in defense of or in opposition to Job's righteousness, one would think that when the Lord spoke the matter would be clarified, and we would know who was correct. When God finally does thunder from the whirlwind, the question of justice is not addressed. Instead, the focus of the divine speeches is the creative wisdom and power of God. Still, this should not be seen as avoidance of the question. Remember, in this book God is cast in the role of wisdom teacher. It is characteristic of such a teacher to ask rhetorical questions and to make reference to the natural world in order to make a point. By means of such questioning, God leads Job to see that, as there is much in nature that Job cannot understand, so there is much in human experience that is beyond him. Indirectly, God reveals the inadequacy of the theory of retribution. God shows Job that happiness and success are not demonstrable rewards for righteous living, nor are grief and failure punishment for unfaithfulness. In other words, suffering is not the sure sign of alienation from God.

The theory of retribution continues to be operative in our thinking today. When we fall upon hard times or are victims of some tragedy, we frequently ask: What have I done to deserve this? Why is God punishing me? We too have a sense of how things are supposed to work and when they don't unfold as we expect, like Job, we demand an explanation from God. Perhaps, again like Job, we will have to learn that not everything can be explained according to the theory of retribution. We will have to admit that life is too complex to be forced into one pattern.

Theodicy

Once we are convinced that certain suffering is undeserved, we are faced with a very troubling question: Why does God seem to allow injustice to occur? Theodicy (from the Greek meaning "justifying God") is the name given to our attempt to explain the problem of evil, while at the same time maintaining belief that God is a moral creator who is in control of all things and who loves those who suffer. If Job did not believe that

God is moral, the question of evil would take a totally different turn. If God is not just, then Job's suffering might be equally difficult for him to bear, but it would not be the puzzle that it is. He would know that he could not depend upon God for justice. Instead, his happiness and unhappiness would hinge on the whims of a capricious God. It is clear that such a view was foreign to Israel's faith. Job's counselors never question God's integrity, and Job does so only reluctantly and at the risk of falsely accusing God.

According to another view, God could be moral but not able to control evil completely. This is the theory advanced by several post-Holocaust Jewish thinkers who cannot explain why God allowed so many millions of innocent people to be exterminated during World War II. It is also a view expressed in the popular book by Harold S. Kushner, *When Bad Things Happen to Good People*. Although a number of recent thinkers have held this view, it is not found in the Bible. Israel believed that its God was the undisputed almighty creator (see Is 45:7; Am 3:6). None of the characters in the book of Job doubt God's control. In fact, if Job could believe that God was not somehow responsible, his torment might even be lessened.

A final perspective suggests that perhaps God is both moral and omnipotent, but unconcerned about simple people. Surely the almighty God has more important things to do than to worry about the fortunes or misfortunes of one man. The traditions of Israel contradict this notion as well. From the earliest stories of the ancestors (Abraham and Sarah, Isaac and Rebekah, Jacob and Rachel and Leah), we see God portrayed as attentive to the most personal needs of the individual. This is the memory of God that Job recalls as he laments his present predicament (29:1–6). How could a gracious God who cared for him in earlier years turn against him now?

Theodicy is not an issue for the visitors, since Job's misery is not a puzzle for them. Job himself is intent on defending his own integrity rather than God's, and so theodicy is not a concern of his either. It is, however, of major importance to the author of the book, who depicts God as all-powerful and provident, and a God of unchallenged goodness. At the end of the book, the question of suffering may be left unanswered, but the integrity of God is no longer questioned.

Disinterested Piety

In a very real sense, the drama of the book stems from the satan's challenge found in 1:9: "Is it for nothing that Job is God-fearing?" The satan insinuates that Job is righteous because of the rewards that he now enjoys and will continue to enjoy as long as he remains faithful. He claims that it is easy for Job to be loyal to God when things are going right and he is happy with life. Take away his prosperity and the good things of life, and he will not only give up his way of integrity but will actually curse God. The reader should note that God takes the dare. Twice Job is assaulted. His initial response to the tragedy that has fallen upon him proves that the satan's accusation is groundless. Job neither curses God nor veers from his attachment to God. Despite his complete reversal of fortune, Job's confidence is not shaken, and he actually praises God (see 1:21 and 2:10).

It is clear that Job is not God-fearing simply for the sake of blessing, for his afflictions do not diminish his devotion. Even in adversity he maintains that all things are in God's hands, and God will render whatever God deems fit. Still, Job probably did expect to be blessed for being faithful. The admonitions of his visitors as well as his own later assertions mark an expectation common to all of them (see 4:7; 8:20; 11:15; 13:16). All seem to believe that goodness will not go unrewarded nor will wickedness fail to be punished—a conviction that is fundamental to the notion of justice. Therefore, in the face of such expectation, to what extent is his piety really disinterested? The content of Job's laments and pleading show that Job does not look for recompense; he wants vindication. He is not concerned about possessions; he insists that his integrity be acknowledged. When he finally understands the lesson that God set out to teach him, he is silent and seems content with his new insights. It is apparent that the depth of Job's piety is based on his relationship with God, not on some promise of reward.

We must remember that at this time Israelites did not have a clear idea of reward or punishment in an afterlife, as Christian theology teaches. If justice was not meted out in this life, they had no hope at all for retribution. This makes Job's disinterested piety even more admirable. It also serves to challenge the quality of our own fidelity. Job's faithfulness can also be an encouragement to us. Here is a man who is not willing to accept unquestioningly what he considers a grave injustice. He rejects the instruction and counsel of those regarded as teachers of the religious tradition. Job is not blindly docile in his suffering, nor is he afraid to complain to God in his frustration. At this point we must be careful to understand Job's anger correctly. He does not argue with God because he is suffering, but because he perceives a conflict between what he considers his unwarranted suffering and his faith in the justice of God. The Job who accuses God is no less pious that the man who acknowledged, "The LORD gave and the LORD has taken away" (1:21). Devout people certainly do have their differences with God. We are reminded of the great Teresa of Avila, who in frustration also complained to God, "No wonder you have so few friends."

Suffering

Although the customary way of understanding suffering was as punishment for sin, the book of Job does provide other explanations for it. The prologue itself tells us that God allowed Job's misfortunes to befall him so that Job's integrity might be tested (1:11; 2:3, 5). A similar incident in the cycle of stories about Abraham comes to mind. There, "God put Abraham to the test" (Gn 22:1) and told him to sacrifice his son Isaac. There is a significant difference here, however. In the end, Abraham was told that he had been tested (Gn 22:16), while Job never knows about God's dealings with the satan. Job himself never regards his misfortune as a test.

Suffering is also seen as a source of moral discipline. Elihu claims that pain and sickness sometimes act as warnings against sin and as a defense against pride and complacency (33:15–24). Other interpretations of suffering include: vicariously enduring the punishment of others (the Suffering Servant: Is 52:13–53:12); personal purification (Ps 66:10); a necessary way of accomplishing the will of God (Joseph in Egypt: Gn 50:20). Only the first two explanations are found in the book of Job.

Yet another way of understanding suffering was as the "curse of the evil deed." According to this view, those who engage in evil infect themselves in the process. This notion is behind the saying: "He who digs a pit falls into it" (Prv 26:27). Just as the Israelites had a sense that goodness was a force that determined life, so they believed that evil carried its own consequences. This view differs from that of retribution since it does not believe that God intervenes to punish. In fact, it tends to exclude divine activity. This may explain why, in Israel, the idea of retribution seldom appeared by itself. It is always tempered by belief in God's ultimate control of good and evil.

The biblical writers seem to have been more interested in the reason and purpose of suffering than in its origin. They addressed the fact of suffering and tried to give meaning to this reality, which no one can escape. They offered provisional explanations intended to strengthen people in their struggle. These explanations were not meant to be conclusive answers, because circumstances change and they might cease to be appropriate. This is precisely the case with Job. The instruction and advice offered by his visitors may very well have been fitting in other circumstances, but in Job's situation they are empty of meaning. No one seems able to offer him an adequate explanation for his suffering. Most likely, this is precisely the reason that the book of Job has always enjoyed a place of prominence in the literature of the world and in the hearts of countless people. It demonstrates that no one is protected from undeserved personal misfortunes such as the sudden and tragic death of loved ones, human exploitation or betrayal, the unexpected collapse of a business or career, or from disasters such as flooding or fire or other ravages of nature. The horrors of war, of ethnic, racial, sexual, or other social discrimination or brutality victimize untold children, women, and men, and thus defy all standards of justice. Over the centuries this pitiable man has stood as proof that suffering is not a sure sign of infidelity. Job continues to be a source of consolation for many today who suffer innocently.

Experience and Tradition

One might conclude from this that a fundamental principle, which underlies wisdom thinking and which plays an important role in the book of Job, is the relationship between experience and tradition in the formation of new theological understanding. We have all been taught the importance of conforming our lives to the teachings of our religious tradition. A new and sometimes conflicting attitude is developing today, namely, that it is the *tradition* that must give serious consideration to contemporary life. In fact, a more complete understanding shows that there should be a dynamic correlative interaction between experience and tradition, with each influencing and refashioning the other. In the book of Job we see that neither Job nor the men who came to advise him took note of this dynamic. In the final summary of his cause, Job insists that he has always complied with the prescriptions of the law (see chapter 31). In fact, he went far beyond the demands of the law. It was precisely because of the faithfulness of his behavior that he expected a life of peace and prosperity. From where he stood, there is something seriously wrong with the order of things. Job was not willing to question his own integrity, and he was not ready to challenge the tradition. That is why, as stated earlier, he found fault with God. The others also evaluated Job's life according to the tradition. Adhering to the conventional way of interpreting suffering, they insisted that his present state of misery was the direct consequence of some sin. From where they stood, God was justified in afflicting Job, and the tradition was adequate in explaining the situation. They discounted the authenticity of Job's experience of innocent suffering.

We might miss this important theme were it not for something that God said to Eliphaz in the epilogue: ". . . you have not spoken rightly concerning me, as has my servant Job" (42:7). Where were these men wrong and Job right? What did they say that was not part of the traditional teaching? The only issue over which there was serious disagreement was that of Job's innocence. Job insisted that God had afflicted him without cause. Upholding an inflexible interpretation of the tradition, the visitors maintained that God would never act in such a manner. We know that they are the ones who were wrong.

Job's experience of innocent suffering calls for a new and more critical look at the tradition. It is strange that neither Job nor his counselors challenged this unbending interpretation of theology, because it is precisely the ability to be faithful yet flexible in new situations that constitutes wisdom. Perhaps the author of the book wanted to demonstrate what could happen when theology is rigidly applied.

The Catholic bishops of the United States have consciously included reflection on contemporary experience in the process of writing their most recent pastoral letters. They are keenly aware of the need to be faithful to official teaching while at the same time realistic about changes in the world. They have frequently held open hearings in order to gain insights from the experience of the broader church and society before writing their documents. This practice can both endorse new wisdom and contest the old. For that reason it has been applauded by some and criticized by others.

The God of Mystery

Most of the themes considered in this reflection have focused attention on Job. Now we turn our gaze toward the depiction of God. How is God portrayed? In his complaints, Job characterizes God as powerful and oppressive when near and unconcerned when at a distance. Job's companions describe God as a prosecuting judge. However, the image revealed in the speeches of the Lord is quite different. There we see that God is indeed powerful, but it is a wondrous, awe-inspiring power (see 40:3–5). It is also true that God is transcendent, but this does not prevent God from being solicitous for even the mountain goat about to kid (see 39:1). Finally, God does not assume the role of judge, summoning Job before the divine tribunal, there to find him guilty and to sentence him. Instead, Job is questioned by the divine teacher and led to new horizons of insight. He is brought to understand that he has been treading on mystery—"things too wonderful for me" (42:3). In the book of Job, God is the provident but nonetheless mysterious God of creation. It is the same God who works in the lives of each of us, yet who remains a mystery.

The Dramatic Effect of the Story

While it is true that we can dip into any section of the book of Job and draw out bits of profound teaching, the best way to read it is as a drama from beginning to end. Only in that way can we feel the frustration of the counselors mount and the desperation of Job deepen. As is the case in every good story, there is a dramatic movement here that sweeps us up into itself. We might best appreciate the richness of its message and the true-to-life description of its complexity by identifying first with Job and then with one of the visitors. Our own experience of suffering should help us to understand Job's plight. It is revealing, however, to realize how easy it is to offer empty words in our sincere attempts to console others, and to see how quickly we can become indignant when our advice is ignored.

The final effect of reading the book in this way includes an admission of the incomprehensibility of much of life. Whether we have identified with Job or with one of the others, we come to the speeches of the Lord and we realize that *no one* can answer the questions put to Job. Everyone, whether Job, Eliphaz, Bildad, Zophar, Elihu, or the reader, when confronted with the incongruity and incomprehensibility of human life, stands silent before this transcendent God.

FURTHER READING

Habel, Norman C. *The Book of Job.* Old Testament Library. Philadelphia: Westminster, 1985.

Janzen, Gerald J. *Job.* Interpretation. Atlanta: John Knox, 1985.

Newsom, Carol A. *The Book of Job.* New Interpreter's Bible 4, 319–637. Nashville: Abingdon Press, 1996.

Perdue, Leo G. *Wisdom in Revolt: Metaphorical Theology in the Book of Job.* Sheffield: JSOT Press, 1991.

Pope, Marvin H. *Job.* Anchor Bible 15. New York: Doubleday, 1979.

Wharton, James A. *Job.* Westminster Bible Companion. Louisville: Westminster John Knox, 1999.

PSALMS

[see pages 727–834 of the Old Testament]

About the Book

The book of Psalms, also known as the Psalter, is really a collection of books each of which ends with a short doxology or hymn of praise. This is very clear to anyone who looks closely at the arrangement of the psalms. The editors of the *New American Bible* have indicated this order by adding subdivisions within the text itself. "The First Book—Psalms 1–41" ends with a doxology in 41:14; "The Second Book—Psalms 42–72" ends with 72:18–20; "The Third Book—Psalms 73–89" ends with 89:53; "The Fourth Book—Psalms 90–106" ends with 106:48; "The Fifth Book—Psalms 107–150" ends with an entire psalm of praise, Psalm 150.

There is evidence within the book of Psalms itself that our present anthology was composed of even earlier collections. Several psalms, found principally in the first book, are attributed to David. This may account for the popular, but probably not historically accurate, tradition that David himself wrote most of the psalms. Several psalms in the second and third books are ascribed to Korah and Asaph, the two great guilds of temple singers during the period of the Second Temple (confer 1 Chr 6:33ff; 25:1f). These groupings may have been the original collections around which other psalms clustered. Finally, the fifth book is made up of a number of Songs of Ascent and psalms of praise known as Hallel or the Hallelujah collection.

These collections have another distinguishing characteristic. They vary in the preferred name for God. *Yahweh* (translated LORD) is generally used in the first, the fourth, and the fifth collections. This has led some to refer to them together as the "Yahwist Psalter." The name *Elohim* (translated "God") is preferred in the second and third books. Together they are sometimes called the "Elohist Psalter." Many scholars believe that Elohim is a substitution made by a postexilic editor who wished to show reverence for the divine name (Yahweh) by avoiding its use.

All of these various collections overlap, and so it is difficult to identify precisely the original groupings. It is enough to know that the final compilers had an array of psalms from which to choose. The presence of psalmody in places other than the Psalter (for example, the Song of Moses in Ex 15 and the Song of Deborah in Jgs 5) indicates that there were many more psalms current in ancient Israel than have been included in the Psalter.

Types of Psalms

Commentators classify the psalms in slightly different ways. (The categories here are quite general.) There is widespread agreement, however, that the major headings are three: lament, hymn, and thanksgiving. In addition to these major groups, there are royal psalms, wisdom poems, and some psalms that might fit into more than one category. Since psalms are the prayerful responses to life experiences, a study of their forms as well as their content will throw light on the life situation of the community from which they sprang.

Laments

The type of psalm that occurs most frequently in the Psalter is the lament. Nearly a third of all the psalms belong to this category. Depending on the identity of the speaker, laments are further classified as community laments or laments of the individual. The structure of the lament is not exactly the same in every case. Not all laments appear to be complete, and even when the most common elements are present, they do not seem to have any fixed order. Still, laments are usually comprised of an invocation directed toward God; the actual lament or complaint that describes the suffering endured by the one(s) praying; a plea for deliverance from this misfortune; some kind of praise of God, often an expression of confidence that God will come to the rescue of the community or the individual; a vow to perform an act of worship in gratitude for God's intervention. Some laments also include an acknowledgment of guilt or an assertion of innocence. Finally, there is frequently a curse hurled against those believed to be responsible for the intolerable situation that precipitates the lament. This last feature has caused considerable difficulty for those who wish to use the psalms in their own prayer.

It is quite clear that the community laments (Pss 12; 14; 44; 53; 58; 60; 74; 79; 80; 83; 85; 89; 90; 94; 106; 123; 126; 137) were somehow associated with the official cultic worship of Israel. Most probably they were used when the people gathered to fast and pray on special occasions arising from national humiliation or distress. The enemies referred to are usually national enemies who, by being opponents of Israel, were viewed as opposed to the Lord. These psalms often contain a recital of the former marvelous deeds that God had accomplished in the history of the nation. This was meant to remind God of past favors and thus encourage God to grant new ones, as well as to remind the people of God's earlier blessings in order to instill confidence in their hearts.

The laments of the individual (Pss 3–7; 13; 17; 22; 25–28; 31; 35; 36; 38–40; 42/43 [considered a single psalm, as explained in the NAB footnote]; 51; 52; 54–57; 59; 61; 63; 64; 69–71; 77; 86; 88; 102; 109; 120; 130; 140–143) were most likely prayerful responses to personal misfortunes such as illness or persecution. Commentators believe that they were an integral part of personal liturgical devotion. Frequently, people who were suffering went to the Temple or to some shrine for the purpose of making a formal request to God for deliverance. Laments, with their declaration of trust in God, were simultaneously prayers to God and testimonies of hope for the benefit of the community gathered around the one suffering.

Hymns

The hymn is a song in praise of God. While many hymns appear to be the prayers of individuals, most of them seem to have been composed for use in the liturgies of Israel's major festivals. The reason for praising God, as expressed in the psalm itself, enables us to further classify certain hymns as psalms of the kingship of the Lord or as songs of Zion.

The structure of the hymn (Pss 8; 19; 29; 33; 100; 103–104; 111; 113; 114; 117; 135; 136; 145–150) is quite simple. It begins with a call to praise, which suggests that this type of psalm originated within a community setting and, at this point, some kind of liturgical leader is calling the others to prayer. This introductory exhortation is followed by an account of the wondrous acts of God, deeds that cause us to stand in awe. Depending upon the psalm, God is praised for the glories of creation (for example, Ps 8) or for the marvelous feats performed specifically for the people of Israel (among others, Ps 114). Having proclaimed God's glorious deeds, the psalm ends with a repetition of the initial call to praise, some expression of exaltation of God, and a plea for God's blessing. (This is a general description. Not all of the elements are present in every psalm.)

Hymns of the Lord's kingship (Pss 47; 93; 96–99) are a distinct group among the psalms. Their focus is the Lord, the universal king, and they have many images and motifs in common. Some scholars claim that these psalms were composed for the annual celebration of the feast of the Enthronement of the Lord. Therefore, they refer to this group as "enthronement psalms," and they place them in a category of their own. No account of such a festival can be found in the Bible itself, however. For that reason, and also because this group of psalms fits the general hymnic pattern perfectly, they are here simply classified as hymns.

The songs of Zion (Pss 46; 48; 76; 84; 87; 122) extol Mount Zion as God's holy mountain and Jerusalem as the city that God chose to inhabit. There is a variation in the structure of these psalms. Both the introductory and concluding call to praise, which are typical of hymns, are missing. Still, the body of this type of psalm celebrates the mighty God of Israel, who held back every kind of primeval attack on the city and who now dwells on its sacred mountain. As with the psalms in praise of the Lord's kingship, we are not certain about the cultic setting at which the songs of Zion were sung. We may be heirs to Israel's songs, but we do not know more than a few general facts about its cultic calendar, and we cannot reconstruct its system of worship.

Confidence and Thanksgiving

It is rather difficult to classify psalms of thanksgiving, because expressions of confidence and gratitude are often found within laments. This has led many interpreters to list these psalms with either community or individual laments. There are some psalms, however, that might be considered explicit psalms of confidence, either communal (Pss 115; 125; 129) or individual (Pss 11; 16; 23; 62; 91; 121; 131). Psalms of thanksgiving, again either communal (Pss 65–68; 75; 107; 118; 124) or individual (Pss 9/10; 30; 32; 34; 41; 92; 116; 138), also comprise a distinct category. It is the subject matter rather than the form that characterizes these psalms. Like the laments, they were probably part of the communal and personal liturgical life of the people and were used in cult and devotion when the religious sentiments that they express were in order (perhaps at a time of great peril, in the case of the psalm of confidence, or during a harvest festival or after a threat had been successfully resisted, in the case of the psalm of thanksgiving.

Royal Psalms

There are several psalms that direct our attention specifically and exclusively to the king. Some scholars believe that they point to a prominent royal role in the cult. Others contend that the king did not have to be a cultic leader to enjoy a significant place in the ritual. His political and religious importance was enough to assure him of a cultic function. We must remember that Israel was a nation that perceived its king as the representative of the whole people before God and as God's special envoy for the people. This shared perception entitled the king to the prominence he enjoyed.

Various occasions in the life of the king constitute the setting of these psalms. There are coronation hymns (Pss 2; 72; 101; 110), an anniversary hymn (Ps 132), a royal wedding song (Ps 45), petitions in behalf of the warrior-king (Pss 20; 144), and prayers of thanksgiving for his successes (Pss 18; 21). These royal psalms are often referred to as "messianic psalms." "Messiah" means "anointed one," and the king is called "messiah" or "anointed" in Psalm 2. To read them as messianic psalms implies that they refer to an ideal king who is to come in the future. These psalms take on new meaning in the Christian tradition when they are applied to Jesus, the king par excellence and the one "anointed" by God.

Wisdom Poems

These poems (Pss 1; 37; 49; 73; 112; 119; 127; 128) are clearly different from those psalms that probably originated in, and were used during, liturgical celebrations. They differ in both content and style. The wisdom tradition in general is concerned with the problem of evil, the suffering of the righteous, and the justice of God. These same themes, along with language and imagery characteristic of that tradition, are found in the wisdom psalms. Finally, the manner of address here is intended to instruct rather than evoke a response. The wisdom psalms call people to listen and learn, not to pray.

Although wisdom psalms do not follow a uniform style, they do have some distinctive literary characteristics. The sages of ancient Israel made use of several techniques that were judged helpful for learning. Some of these techniques appear in the wisdom psalms. One of the most popular ones is the acrostic arrangement. This is a poetic form in which the alphabet determines the initial letter of the first word of each successive line. Several wisdom poems follow this arrangement (for example, Pss 37; 112 along with the hymns 111; 119). Because they conform to this pattern, some commentators include as wisdom poems some of the psalms listed here under other categories (hymn—Ps 145; lament—Ps 25; thanksgiving—Pss 9/10; 34).

It may be difficult to understand how and why this type of psalm originated and was included in the various collections. What may be even more puzzling is the fact that the Psalter begins with a wisdom poem (Ps 1). Most likely a postexilic compiler placed this psalm first at a time when there was neither Temple nor temple worship, and those responsible for the religious life of the community wanted to keep the psalms alive in Israelite devotion. At this particularly critical time the psalms might have been seen as a treasury for much-needed instruction as well as for prayer. The organization into five books might well have been patterned after the Torah or five books of Moses, wherein the major teachings of the faith were found.

Various Psalms

There are other psalms that quite obviously were used during a pilgrimage to or procession around Jerusalem and the Temple. The Songs of Ascent, one of the early collections alluded to above, preserves the memory of such psalms. In addition to this group, there are other psalms that were sung during processions (Pss 15; 24; 95). A few psalms appear to have been composed after the style of prophetic speech (Pss 50; 81; 82). Since people frequently came to the Temple or to a shrine in search of some word from the Lord, it is understandable that traces of this form would remain in some psalms. Finally, a small number of psalms seem to defy classification. They are either historical recitals of the salvific feats of the Lord (Pss 78; 105), composites of other psalm forms (Pss 108; 133; 139), or general liturgical songs (Ps 134).

The Piety of the Psalmist

The psalms generally speak *to* God rather than *about* God. Although most of the important historical events of the nation, as well as the universal needs of women and men, are described or addressed somewhere in these prayers, the psalms are just that—prayers to God. If we look carefully at the sentiments expressed in these songs, we will be able to detect the major outlines of the piety of ancient Israel, a piety to which we are heirs. We have already seen that it is possible to classify the psalms according to literary form (lament, hymn, thanksgiving, etc.). A further look at these forms will show us that different types of psalms express different sentiments of devotion. Therefore it will be helpful to return to these classifications as we explore the piety of Israel contained in the psalms. (The reader is advised to consult the listings of the psalms belonging to each category. These listings are found under the heading Types of Psalms.)

Grief, Fear, Repentance, and Confidence

We all have a certain sense about how life is supposed to unfold. We learn this as we are fashioned in and by the various social groups of which we are a part. While societies may differ over values and lifestyles, all agree that basic to our nature as human beings is the desire to be happy. Our social groups train us in the acceptable ways of achieving and maintaining the happiness we seek. When we have not attained what we believe is our right, or when having once attained it, we lose it, we cry out in protest. We tend to balk at the unfairness of adversity regardless of whether we are in any way responsible for the loss. We do expect that life will be good to us. This natural human instinct, coupled with the conviction of God's special love and care, led Israel to expect security in a hostile world, success in its undertakings, and a life of serenity and prosperity for the nation as a whole and for each individual within that nation. Such a state of affairs is what the Bible refers to as *shalom* or peace. Psalms of lament grew out of the absence of just such peace.

The references in communal laments usually

apply to some national disaster that has already taken place. Depending upon the dating of the particular psalm, this calamity could have been the fall of the Northern Kingdom of Israel (about 722 BC), the Babylonian exile (about 586 BC), or the Maccabean conflict (about 167 BC). Allusions to the vulnerability of the nation would fit any one of these three emergencies. Any description of the destruction of the Temple, however, must be dated after the time of the exile and before the rebuilding of the Temple (515 BC; see Reading Guide to Ezra and to Nehemiah).

The fact that the psalmist cries out to God demonstrates Israel's belief that God has both the power and the will to intervene and deliver the nation from its present distress. Several psalms themselves indicate that this belief is based on former saving-events in the history of the people (for example, Pss 44:2–4; 74:2; 83:10). Israel believed that God's might was in no way exhausted by earlier feats. On the contrary, Israel held that the all-powerful God was always ready to defend the nation whenever it was threatened with extinction. Even as the people cried out in complaint, they were proclaiming God's all-encompassing power and declaring their trust in God's continued concern for them, a concern based on divine covenantal promises. An expression of confidence, then, is an important characteristic of the lament.

As there were times when Israel felt that it was the innocent victim of the aggression of another nation, there were also instances when it admitted that the straits in which it found itself were directly related to its own sinfulness. Suffering at the hand of another was seen as punishment from God for violation of the covenant. In some of the laments, Israel admits its guilt, pleads for forgiveness and for an end to its suffering, and promises to amend its ways. One of the communal laments recounts the nation's history as if it were no more than a series of offenses against a loving God (Ps 106). Others plead that God forgive the people for their sins and restore them to divine favor (Pss 80; 5–8; 90:7–17). In these psalms, suffering is understood as recompense from a God who is just but also forgiving.

Many of the sentiments found in the communal laments are present in individual complaints as well. The authors of these prayers claim that they are physically or spiritually afflicted or that others are wrongfully oppressing them. In their distress they turn to God for release. They do not doubt God's ultimate control over the workings of nature or the social order. Nonetheless, they might, on occasion, question why God allowed them to be besieged in the first place. Their confidence in God rests on both the recollections of past blessing and reliance on God's own faithfulness to covenant promises.

Praise

Praise is that sentiment that wells up within us as we are overwhelmed by the wonders around us or by the provident concern afforded us by the events of life and by life itself. It is not so much something that we are taught as it is something that we experience. Praise of some sort is natural to human beings. Who has not been swept away by the extravagance of a sunset, by the delicacy of spring's reawakening, by the refreshment of a gentle summer breeze, by the magnitude of the ocean's horizon or the night sky's depth? We stand in awe before the splendor of creation—and we are drawn out of ourselves. If we are attentive to the religious tendencies within ourselves, we will be moved to praise. We discover this same sentiment in the hymns. The psalmist does not seem able to find words adequate to describe the grandeur of creation (Pss 8; 29; 104; 148), and so all the forces of nature are called upon to join the psalmist in glorifying God. Underlying such sentiments of praise is the belief that God is the creator of all things and that all that God has created is beautiful, deserving of our respect, and a reminder of the majestic creator.

Other hymns applaud God for the marvelous feats performed on behalf of the Israelites (Pss 105; 114; 135). Again and again the miraculous power of God intervened for them, thus saving them from certain extinction. Since the initial and preeminent experience of deliverance was liberation from the oppression of Egypt, the Exodus became for them the symbol of all liberation. In these psalms God is perceived as tireless savior, and the psalmist's praise is an acknowledgement of the nation's total dependence on God for its continued survival.

These hymns presume that nature is benign and that God is committed to the well-being of the people. Such a view of life does not usually emerge spontaneously. It arises either from an experience of life that is basically untroubled or from a religious belief that God is indeed on our side and life should really favor us. Still, the biblical hymns are not the flights of fancy of people who have been protected from the hard realities of life or from the indifference of nature. They are also songs of praise of people who, despite misfortune, persist in their reliance on an all-powerful yet attentive God.

The Lord is further acclaimed as the sole and eternal king over all nations. The God of Israel earned this title of Champion in the primordial struggle with chaos (Pss 96, 4f; 98, 1) by undermining the influence of the other gods and ascending the heavenly throne to reign with universal and undisputed authority. The concept of God as victor in the cosmic conflict embraces the notion of creator, for the initial understanding of primordial creation is the establishment of order out of chaos (see the creation narrative in Genesis 1). Unlike the hymns discussed above, the psalms lauding the kingship of the Lord acknowledge the threatening powers present in the universe. Chaos was conquered by the Lord, but not totally destroyed. Admission of this in no way detracts from the universal reign of God proclaimed in the psalms. Instead, it was a way that Israel dealt with the fact that creation is not always friendly and life does not always appear to be favoring us. In the face of this fact, Israel believed that the Lord was truly in charge, involved in creation while ruling from the divine throne in the heavens, controlling all of the forces of the universe and, therefore, deserving of our undivided allegiance.

The songs of Zion contain some of the same imagery found in the psalms in honor of the Lord-King. Ancient Canaanite mythology, from which much of the Israelite imagery originated, recounts the cosmic battle described above. After the forces of evil were quelled, a palace was built for the victor on the summit of the highest mountain. From this vantage point the conquering hero holds sway over the entire universe. Israel revered Mount Zion as this sacred mountain and revered the Temple as the palace of the victorious creator-God. A significant shift can be detected in these psalms. Zion and the Jerusalem Temple move the drama from the cosmic scene of primordial creation to the political and cultural world of Israel. The reality of God's divine creative power is now associated with one nation and, because of the close connection between Zion and David, specifically with the Davidic monarchy. These psalms depict God as unabashedly committed to the welfare of Israel over all other nations. The creator-God who is praised in these psalms is not distant from this people but lives in their very midst, allowing them to approach the divine presence that somehow mysteriously dwells in the Temple. (There was an attempt to balance this apparent exclusivity by inviting all other nations to worship the Lord on Zion [see Is 2:2f; Mi 4:1f].) Thus God is perceived as near and accessible, and Zion and the Temple command veneration.

The hymns provide us with several perceptions of God: the creator of the universe, national liberator, cosmic champion. At times these perceptions overlap, producing a collage of images intended to call forth praise. The psalmist extols God for the wonders of creation, for continued deliverance from destruction, for God's victory over the forces of evil, and for the fact of God's presence in the midst of the people. These are some of the sentiments voiced in the biblical hymns.

Gratitude

Little need be said about the expression of gratitude found in the psalms. Prayers of thanksgiving are similar to those of confidence in that the latter expect blessing and the former thank God for it. At times this gratitude flows from favors already received. At other times it anticipates the blessing that the psalmist is confident will come. The structure and content of the thanksgiving psalm resembles those of the hymn. There can be no thanksgiving until God has first been praised for the goodness that God has accomplished.

National Loyalty

The royal psalms emanated from national pride and spirit. Allegiance to the king was regarded as loyalty to the nation. Since the king was considered the representative of the whole people before God and as God's special envoy for the people, loyalty to the king and to the nation were seen as acts of devotion to God. These psalms originated out of various royal settings and they express sentiments appropriate to the respective occasion (for example, coronations, weddings, danger to the king during warfare, etc.). Despite their diversity, the sentiments of all of these songs flow from what today would be considered a type of patriotism.

An Understanding Heart

The wisdom poems generally do not address God. They are usually directed toward the community. The piety of the psalmist is not as explicit here as it is in the prayers we have already examined. Still, it can be discerned by looking carefully at the way the poet treats the themes that appear to be prominent. The problem of evil, the suffering of the righteous, and the justice of God are principal concerns of the wisdom tradition and are all facets of the same issue, namely, right order in the universe. It is clear that the wisdom psalmist presumes that there is an order to the world, and that there is a way in which we can live in this ordered world so as to be secure and prosperous. It is also evident that the psalmist sees God as the source and guarantor of this order. On the other hand, evil that clearly is not punishment can challenge the sovereignty of God. When this evil raises its head, God is expected to step in, subdue it, and restore the world to its former and appropriate state. When this does not happen, the power of God or the uprightness of God may be questioned. This might happen because either God cannot repress the evil or is unwilling to do so. While Job and Ecclesiastes live with the unanswered question of innocent suffering, and Job even demands that God take responsibility for it, the wisdom psalms do not challenge the prevailing situation. They seem to presume that the suffering of the righteous is for some legitimate purpose, which God will reveal at the appropriate time and will then correct.

The themes, language, and imagery of the wisdom poems depict God as creator of all. In this they resemble the hymns and the psalms of thanksgiving. In their insistence on justice, they are like the laments. These similarities explain why commentators classify the wisdom poems in different ways. These psalms may not be explicit expressions of Israelite piety, but they do reveal a trait that is characteristic of religious sentiment, that is, an understanding heart (see 1 Kgs 3:9, 12).

Enthusiasm, Humility, and Faithfulness

The processional psalms are charged with excitement and anticipation. They invite the observant Israelite to participate with heart and soul in various liturgical celebrations. The major festivals of ancient Israel (Passover or Unleavened Bread, Pentecost or the Feast of Weeks, Sukkoth or the Feast of Tabernacles) were all commemorated with pilgrimages to Jerusalem. Psalms were sung as the people approached the city. There were shouts of profound joy as well as humble acknowledgements of the need for pure hearts when approaching the holy city and the Temple of the Lord.

Prophetic psalms were also linked closely to the Temple. They embrace sentiments of humility and religious devotion and they summon the people to be faithful to their covenant commitment.

The wide range of religious sentiment found in the Psalter reveals the extent of Israel's piety. Every human emotion is tapped because Israel believed that God is involved in every aspect of life. It is no wonder that the psalms have touched the lives of women and men throughout the ages and that they continue to inspire the human spirit even to our own day.

The Theology in the Psalms

The expressions of piety found within the book of Psalms give us insight into the theology of ancient Israel. Although much of this theology has already been noted, it will be helpful to look at it in a more systematic fashion.

The God of Israel

The portrait of God that is sketched in the psalms draws together all of the divine faces found in the rest of the Israelite tradition. This God is the creator of the universe (Ps 8:4) and the source of all life (Ps 36:10), enthroned in heaven (Ps 47:6) yet dwelling in Jerusalem (Ps 76:3). Initially the Lord may have been perceived as Israel's exclusive liberator (Ps 66:6), but the universal scope of God's power and protection came into view as the nation moved closer and closer to a monotheistic faith. Although uniquely committed to Israel by means of the Mosaic covenant (Ps 114: 2), and to the monarchy through the royal covenant with David (Ps 132), God is envisioned as concerned about the well-being of all people (Ps 117).

This majestic God inspires both fear (Ps 89:8) and confidence (Ps 23), is both demanding (Ps 75:8) and forgiving (Ps 85:3). Above all else, the God of Israel is "merciful and gracious . . . slow to anger, abounding in kindness" (Ps 103: 8; see Ps 86:5). The key characterization is that God is Israel's covenant partner. Everything that is important to Israel flows from this perception of God.

The Image of God

The human person is held in high regard in the psalms. (It must be noted that the psalms come from a society where the male person was the norm for what is human. The language and imagery that issued from this fact have caused great distress for many. Without perpetuating this male-preferred situation and by making appropriate substitutions while reading or meditating, we can still value the psalms for their religious insight and sentiment.) Honored as a unique manifestation of God's creative ingenuity, humanity is given responsibility for the other living creatures of the earth (Ps 8; see Gn 1). Again and again the psalmist marvels at this singular work of divine artistry. Why should God be personally committed to such an insignificant being (Pss 8: 5; 144:3f)? As extraordinary as they are, humans live a fleeting life (Ps 39:5f) and then perish like the flowers of the field (Ps 103:15f). Realization of the impermanence of life becomes even starker when we remember that the psalmist did not have any clear notion of life after death. Human dignity was related to life in this world.

There is no doubt in the mind of the psalmist that human beings are thoroughly understood by and totally dependent upon God (Ps 139). God provides for their basic physical needs (Ps 65:10–14) and protects them from harm (Ps 121). In a special way, God is the guardian of the poor and afflicted (Ps 40:18), the defenseless widows and orphans (Ps 68:6), and the *anawim* or lowly ones (Ps 147:6). The psalmist goes to great lengths to show that what appears to be the insignificance of the human creature is, in fact, the occasion for the solicitude and tender care of God.

Natural Creation

The psalms reveal a special regard for natural creation as the handiwork of God (Ps 104). This may well have originated from a polytheistic belief that the mysterious powers in nature are really manifestations of various deities. As Israel's understanding of God developed, expanded, and incorporated within itself reverence for these extraordinary manifestations, these powers came to be seen as expressions of the Lord. God is revealed in the thunderstorm (Ps 29) and in the design of the natural world (Ps 65: 7). Creation was thus no longer seen as a rival for the homage of the people. Instead, it became a partner in the praise of God (Ps 148).

The Future

Ancient Israel was interested in both the future of the nation and the fate of the individual. The positive view that it takes on this issue, which is called eschatology, stems from its faith in the goodness of God toward all creation. Despite the struggles that the nation faced in its attempts to survive and to flourish in a contentious world, Israel believed that the final victory would be the Lord's and that through God's triumph it too would prosper. Individuals also looked to God to remedy the injustices of a burdensome life. They clung to the conviction that God would eventually right all wrongs, and they would then enjoy the happiness that was their due.

The psalms that praise the kingship of the Lord and describe God's defeat of the forces of evil, also promise the restoration of the nation (Ps 14:7). When this happens, the gods of the other nations will be recognized as the empty idols they are (Ps 96:5), and all the peoples will join in praising the Lord (96:7–10). According to some of the royal psalms, this decisive turning point in history will be brought about through the agency of a "messiah" (Ps 2:7–9).

Great attention is paid in the psalms to the fate of the individual. Although earlier theology taught that reward and punishment would be worked out within the community or down through the generations (see Ex 20:5), the post-exilic prophets maintained that retribution would be meted out according to one's own deeds (see Ez 18). In the face of this new perspective, the prosperity of the wicked challenged the theory of retribution. In response, the psalmist claimed that such prosperity would not last and so the upright should not envy sinners (Ps 37:1). Still, the apparently peaceful death of those who were wicked and prosperous, and the unmerited suffering or adversity of the righteous, remained an unresolved problem.

The psalms say very little about life beyond the grave, but they frequently mention the shadowy existence known as *Sheol* (Ps 49:15). This was not a place of retribution; it included neither reward nor punishment. It was simply a place of darkness and dust. It probably referred to nothing more than the grave, the abode of the dead. Still, it suggests that while Israel did not have a clear idea of life after death, it entertained the possibility that the dead did not cease to exist.

The Psalms and the New Testament

We may not always appreciate the specific theological importance of the psalms because today we tend to distinguish between explicit theological statements on the one hand and prayer on the other. In many ways, this is a false distinction. Statements of faith may well be the reflection on or development of theological thought, but prayer is theology as it is experienced. It is quite clear that the early Christians seldom made such distinctions. For them, the psalms were not only vehicles of prayer but they also contained important statements of faith, statements that found their fulfillment in the person and mission of Jesus (see Lk 24:44).

The New Testament both alludes to and specifically cites various psalms. Five of them seem to be referred to more than the rest. They are the messianic psalms 2 and 110; the individual laments 22 and 69; and the communal psalm of thanksgiving 118. The first two are cited in discussions of Jesus' messianic preeminence (see Acts 13:33; Heb 1:5). Motifs from the two laments are used in accounts of his passion and death, interpreted by some as evidence that the psalmist was really foretelling Jesus' suffering. Psalm 118 speaks of the rejected stone that becomes the cornerstone (v. 22; see Mt 21:42) and the blessedness of the one who comes in the name of the Lord (v. 26; see Mk 11:9), themes that the New Testament writers see fulfilled in Jesus. Thus the early Christian theologians developed the theology of the psalms in ways that would enhance their own understanding of Jesus the Christ.

The Psalms Today

Most people are acquainted with the psalms because they are incorporated into the regular prayer of the church. Others may be more familiar with some of them through their own personal use in private devotion. Everyone interested in the psalms will also want to know more about how they function as means of prayer. Moreover, a study of the psalms would be incomplete if we did not address the role that they have played and continue to play in shaping the minds and hearts of believers. We cannot arrive at this insight by limiting our examination exclusively to historical or literary analyses. While the psalms are certainly religious literature they are at the same time means to spiritual transformation.

Poetic Imagery

The psalms are poetry. They are, in fact, some of the most beautiful poetry that the human spirit has created. The imagery is vivid, the verbs are energetic, and all can share the sentiments expressed. One need not be familiar with the historical situations from which the psalms sprang in order to appreciate their enduring worth. Like all classic literature, they express fundamental human values that speak to every culture and every age. By merely reading the psalms thoughtfully and respecting their integrity, we can be touched by their lyrical artistry and drawn into the dynamic world that they envision.

This reflective, even contemplative, reading can plunge us into the religious dispositions of the psalmist, for the words and the images that grew from these dispositions can now readily serve as vehicles carrying us back into them. We may not come to the psalms with hearts filled with praise or thanksgiving or grief, but the world mirrored there, a world that is real though perhaps not identical with ours, often resonates deep within us. It is as if we know that world, or at least we sense that we should know it and, recognizing it, we cry out in praise or thanksgiving or grief. In this way the poetic imagery can be the starting point of our meditation on the psalms.

Genuine Prayer

For Jews and Christians, the psalms are much more than profoundly moving poetry. They are the voice of our respective religious faiths. First heard centuries ago in a land far removed from ours, they have been on the lips of believers in every historical period since that time. It is not merely that we use the psalms to express our devotion; they in fact profoundly shape our religious consciousness. The psalms have served as a prism that spreads before us the many facets of our relationship with God. Gilead, Manasseh, and Ephraim (see Ps 60:9) may be unfamiliar names to many, but they were beneficiaries of God's promise of protection of which we are heirs, and so we identify with them. We "join in procession with leafy branches up to the horns of the altar" (Ps 118:27), convinced that our prayers too will be answered.

Liturgy is not merely a celebration of some past event. It is an enactment in which and through which promises and claims that were made in the past become present realities. The Exodus was certainly a concrete historical event. Whenever Israel reenacted this event, however (see Jos 24), the reality of the Exodus became present with all of its power and possibility. The participants of the liturgical celebration were not participants of the original escape. "When the Egyptians maltreated and oppressed us, imposing hard labor upon us, we cried to the LORD, the God of our fathers, and he heard our cry and saw our affliction, our toil and our oppression. He brought us out of Egypt" (Dt 26:6–8a). The psalms have a role to play in this creative reenactment. Not only do they address God in sentiments appropriate to what has been described, but they also fashion a world wherein *we* interact with God by means of these very sentiments. When we really enter the world sketched in the laments, *we* are plunged into fear and distress and *we* cry out to the Lord. Now this is *our* world; these are *our* sentiments; this is *our* prayer.

When we pray the psalms in this way, we are not simply using their religious imagery to express our own personal devotion. Nor are we merely calling to memory events of the past in order to be inspired by the saving acts of God in our history. We are entering into and carrying forward our creative, dynamic religious heritage. In this way the heritage becomes the inspiration of our personal devotion, and our devotion is shaped by this biblical heritage.

The World beyond the Psalms

The psalms not only invite us into the world created by their imagery and sentiments, they also prompt us to move beyond this world, back into our own world and circumstances, there to reengage in the transformation we ourselves have already undergone. The implications of this transformation of our world and the forms it may take will vary according to the sentiments found within the psalm. (Once again it will be helpful to return to the classification of psalms outlined above under the heading Types of Psalms.)

Laments

The laments, the largest category of psalms found in the Bible, continues to cause considerable difficulty for many contemporary believers. Some people think that prayer should be primarily praise, petition, or thanksgiving. The fact that many of the sections of the laments, which contain accusations against God or the cursing of antagonists, have been deleted from liturgical texts seems to support this misconception. We have become so accustomed to seeing ourselves as "Alleluia People" that we relegate any mention of suffering and pain to the prayers of petition. This is unfortunate because it prevents us from dealing honestly and straightforwardly in worship with the grief and frustration we experience in the face of national crisis or personal misfortune. It is natural to complain, even to complain to God. Laments are often admissions of guilt, pleas for forgiveness, and promises of amendment. When we pray the laments in this spirit we confess that God is a just yet forgiving judge, and we pledge ourselves to lives of faithfulness to our own covenant responsibilities.

The laments are not only protests of our grief or fear or anger, but they are also testimonies of our trust in God's faithfulness to covenant promises. They do not originate in the hearts of nonbelievers. Rather, they spring from the conviction that God is on our side, willing and able to provide for us in our distress. Remembrance of past protection is at the heart of this conviction. If God was compassionate in the past, surely

God will show us the same compassion in the future.

Finally, there is another way to enter the world of the laments. It is through solidarity with those who suffer and are oppressed. While laments may not come easily to the lips of the comfortable, they are integral to the prayer of those who are in distress. As we share or stand by them in their suffering, their prayer becomes our own; as we enter into the sentiments of the laments, we begin to understand and identify with their suffering. Laments can strengthen us in our commitment to justice and peace.

Hymns

As we praise God for the splendor of creation and acknowledge that the universe belongs to this divine architect and not to us, we should also be moved to profound respect for the world of which we are a part. We may exercise a kind of dominion over the animals with whom we share the earth, but we exercise this rule in God's stead. Hymns of praise can instill in us the dispositions necessary to become responsible stewards of the treasures of creation.

The hymns extolling the Lord for having delivered Israel from the threats of extinction depict God as an ever-present savior. This nation has been rescued from oppressive policies that threaten its well-being and prevent its self-determination. In praising God as a faithful liberator, Israel is also acknowledging God's enduring commitment to justice. God's people—and that includes all people—must be free to follow the inspiration of God as they receive it. As we pray these hymns, we too should find ourselves committed to justice toward and respect for the autonomy of all nations.

The Lord is also acclaimed as champion in the cosmic struggle with the threatening forces of chaos. Acknowledging that these forces were never completely destroyed, psalms that acclaim the kingship of the Lord declare that God is still in charge and, thus, deserving of our undivided devotion. If we praise the Lord in this fashion, we can hardly allow anything—whether wealth, power, or national loyalty—to rival the allegiance we have pledged to God.

The final division of hymns consists of the songs of Zion, which honor the mountain on which the Lord dwells, from which the Lord reigns, and to which all the nations are invited. We have seen that in these psalms the drama has moved from the cosmic plane to the world of history. The Lord is not in some distant remote place, inaccessible to the people. On the contrary, God is in the midst of the people, approachable, even inviting. We may have no allegiance to Zion itself, but with these psalms we are really acknowledging God's commitment to our well-being and God's faithful presence in our midst. A word of caution is in order here lest we fall into the trap of national chauvinism. Zion has significance because the Lord chose it, not because it chose the Lord. Whenever Israel confused being *elect* with being *elite,* it faced prophetic condemnation (see the prophet's reprimand of Jerusalem and the Temple in Jer 7; 26). We today are not preserved from this same temptation. The songs honoring Zion must be understood for what they are—hymns in praise of God, not simply songs of national pride. In fact, long-standing Christian tradition saw in the imagery of Zion, with its connection to Jerusalem and the Temple, a foretaste of the Church itself where God would dwell in the midst of his people.

Psalms of Thanksgiving

It is very difficult to be sincerely grateful when we think we deserve the good fortune that is ours. Psalms of thanksgiving help us to remember that whatever we enjoy has come to us from the hand of a gracious God. When these psalms are associated with laments, they serve as expressions of gratitude for deliverance. This suggests that Israel recognized that its own security and prosperity were blessings from God. Psalms of thanksgiving will be genuine prayer only when they spring from the conviction that our blessings also are gratuitous gifts from God. We cannot claim them by right, and so we would do well to be as generous with them with others as God has been with them with us.

Other Psalms

As with the songs of Zion, we must be on guard against national chauvinism when praying the royal psalms. Israel may have believed that loyalty to the king was an act of devotion to God, but the king was accountable to the same covenantal responsibilities as were the rest of the people. The law of the nation was an early attempt to guarantee protection and prosperity to each member of the community. (Since this was a patriarchal society, full membership was restricted to adult men.) Rather than exempting the monarchy from covenantal obligations, the royal psalms proclaim that the king was an agent through whom the blessings of fidelity were bestowed upon the people. These psalms provide us with language and imagery to celebrate the benefits we receive from God as citizens of our own country.

One of the characteristics of the wisdom poetry is its lavish use of nature imagery. The balance and regularity of the natural world are held up as examples after which society and human relationships should be patterned. This may help us understand why several "New Age" or "Creation-Centered Spirituality" movements turn to the wisdom tradition of the Bible for inspiration. We can all benefit from the insights of these groups, for this dimension of our tradition has for too long been overlooked and reclaiming it can only enrich us. Still, we cannot allow reflection on the harmony in nature to hinder us from addressing the more challenging social issues of the wisdom psalms. These poems confront us with their interest in the problem of evil, the suffering of the righteous, and the justice of God. As these hymns become our own, their interests will become our commitments.

The excitement and enthusiasm that permeate the processional psalms reveal a nation that takes its liturgical celebrations seriously. There is unfeigned joy at the thought of approaching the throne of God, but there is also humble realization that only the pure of heart will be granted access. In many ways, our own access to the divine enjoys a kind of familiarity. In a society such as ours, which is so focused on human progress and accomplishment together with technological advances and secularization, many people have lost an appreciation of the transcendent. Processional psalms remind us that, while God is indeed in our midst and accessible to us, God is still God, holy and transcendent.

It should be clear from this consideration of the psalms that their real importance is not primarily in their literary meaning but in their religious nature. As believers, we cannot be uninterested in our study of the primary prayers of our tradition, for we come to the psalms not only with open minds but also with open hearts.

FURTHER READING

Brueggemann, W. *The Psalms and the Life of Faith.* Minneapolis: Fortress, 1995.

Limburg, James. *Psalms.* Westminster Bible Commentary. Louisville: Westminster John Knox, 2000.

Mays, James L. *Psalms.* Interpretation. Louisville: John Knox, 1994.

McCann, J. C. *A Theological Introduction to the Psalms: The Psalms as Torah.* Nashville: Abingdon, 1993.

——. *The Book of Psalms.* New Interpreter's Bible 4, 641–1280. Nashville: Abingdon Press, 1996.

Miller, P. D. *Interpreting the Psalms.* Philadelphia: Fortress, 1986.

——. *They Cried to the Lord. The Form and Theology of Israelite Prayer.* Minneapolis: Fortress, 1994.

PROVERBS

[see pages 834–878 of the Old Testament]

About the Book

Proverbs is probably the biblical book that best characterizes the wisdom tradition. It appears to be the "guide for successful living" referred to in the introduction. Its primary purpose is to teach wisdom. It makes its appeal to various groups of people in different walks of life. It exhorts children (not necessarily or only young children) to heed the teaching of their parents (1:8), and it directs citizens to act with respect toward the king (16:10–15). It warns young men of the dangers of undisciplined living (5:1–14; 23:29–35), and it offers a portrait of the model wife for women to emulate (31:10–31).

The book is composed of eight discernible collections of didactic teaching. These are quite distinct sections. Several of them are identified within the biblical text itself. Others can be distinguishable by means of their particular literary forms.

The first section consists of a general introduction to the entire book (1:1–7) and a collection of instructions (1:8f, 18). It is in this section that we find the student addressed again and again as "my son" and exhorted to listen to the teaching that is advanced. Fifteen of the twenty-three instances of this address appear in the first seven chapters of the book. The form clearly marks this section as instruction. The second section (10:1–22:16) is explicitly identified as "The Proverbs of Solomon" (10:1). Each verse in this section is a saying in its own right whose meaning does not depend on what precedes it or on what follows it. Some scholars classify this as sentence literature. A second characteristic of this section is the antithetical nature of each proverb. (This poetic feature will be discussed below.) These characteristics clearly delineate the section as a distinctive collection.

It is possible that the third section of the book (22:17–24:22), instructions titled "The sayings of the wise" (22:17), is patterned after a collection of an Egyptian scribe, Amen-em-Ope (22:19). If this is the case, it is probably the most obvious example in the wisdom tradition of Israel's literary borrowing (see RG 236). The fourth section (24:23–34), a group of sentences designated "also . . . sayings of the wise" (24:23), is quite short. It is followed by a much longer collection of sentence literature (25:1–29:27) titled "the proverbs of Solomon" (25:1). This collection is further linked with the sages of the court of Hezekiah, the Judean king who ruled around the turn of the seventh century BC. It seems that he inaugurated a period of religious reform and literary activity. The mention of his name in a collection of proverbs may be evidence of this movement.

The sixth section, called "The words of Agur" (30:1), is the shortest (30:1–6). It is followed by a collection of proverbs that are distinguished by their literary form (30:7–33). These numerical proverbs, so named because of their use of numbers (x, x + 1), have much in common with the riddle. The latter is a form mentioned in one of the introductory verses (1:6) and in other places of the Bible (see the riddle of Samson, Jgs 14:12, and the test of the queen of Sheba, 1 Kgs 10:1), but are found nowhere in the book of Proverbs itself. The eighth and last section can be divided into two parts: instruction (31:1–9), titled "The words of Lemuel" (31:1); and a poem describing the ideal wife (31:10–31).

The first verse of the book states that Solomon is the author of the proverbs. There was a tradition that this king was not only versed in human wisdom (see 1 Kgs 3:16–18) but had encyclopedic knowledge as well (see 1 Kgs 3:4–14). Ancient people believed that wisdom belonged by right to the god and, since the king was the human representative of the god, it was the special possession of the king. Since Solomon ruled during a time of splendor and enlightenment, he became known in popular devotion as the wise man par excellence. His reputation gave credibility to wisdom writing and, as more wisdom writing was attributed to him, his reputation grew. Ascribing Solomonic authorship to Proverbs gives the book the status of official teaching and credits the king with comprehensive wisdom. There is a possibility that the real royal authority behind the Proverbs is Hezekiah. Collections of proverbs could well have been compiled during the time of his religious reform, and he himself could have ascribed them to Solomon. We do not have enough information to reconstruct accurately this historical period. The book of Proverbs itself, however, attests to both Hezekiah's influence (25:1) and Solomon's reputation (1:1; 10:1; 25:1).

The Proverb

There is no English word that adequately translates the Hebrew *mashal* (translated "proverb"). It embraces a broad category of literary forms: oracle (Nm 23:7); discourse (Jb 29:1); parable (Ps 78:2); taunt-song (Is 14:4). In each case there is a lesson to be learned, and for this reason the *mashal* might best be understood as "an example from life" intended to instruct. (Although some scholars understand *mashal* in the limited sense of a specific form, it will be used here as a general category unless otherwise indicated.) This is the word that identifies two major collections as "The Proverbs of Solomon" (10:1; 25:1) and from which the book itself receives its name. The root meaning of *mashal* is "likeness" or "comparison" as in "Like mother like daughter," or in the contrast "Better safe than sorry." As a comparison, it usually consists of two parts in some kind of poetic construction. The *sentence* (10:2ff), the purest form of the proverb, is distinct from the *instruction* (22:17ff), which is a much longer unit, sometimes almost a short essay. Sentence and instruction alike, however, are expressed in poetic form, the two parts being either compared or contrasted in parallel balance of "thought rhyme." This *parallelism* is an easily recognizable feature of Hebrew poetry (see RG 238).

While there are various types of parallelism, it is usually some form of balanced equivalence or opposition. An example of the first is:

On the way of wisdom I direct you,
I lead you on straightforward paths (4:11).

An example of the latter is:

The memory of the just will be blessed,
but the name of the wicked will rot (10:7).

It is clear that the first type does not demand exact equivalence, nor does the second require precise contrast. Thus the second part of each of these poetic lines can be drawn from a wide variety of possibilities. The result is a collection of sayings, which are remarkable for their accuracy of insight and fluidity of expression. It is precisely this openness to interpretation and application that distinguishes a proverb in the strictest sense from a simple simile or metaphor whose interpretation is indicated and whose use is thereby limited.

It is important to appreciate the prominence of poetry in the Bible. Israel did not casually choose to express itself in poetic form. Its very perception of reality was poetic. The modern world of science and technology does not always grasp, much less appreciate, the aesthetic perspective of the ancient world. It insists on the language of exact sciences because it tends to perceive reality scientifically. Ancient Israel did not. Its encounter with reality was aesthetic and, therefore, it expressed itself in artistic thought patterns and literary forms. This does not minimize the validity of its perception and the truthfulness of its expression, or ours for that matter. They are two very different ways of looking at reality and talking about it.

The proverb itself serves two important functions. It depicts a situation from the past, and from this depiction it suggests a way of acting in the future. Understanding how this literary form works should help us to grasp the dynamics of the wisdom tradition. Wisdom is not a collection of quaint catchy phrases, which in some simplistic fashion suggest that life will unfold according to plan if we just follow the directions. Proverbs are artistically honed images of specific facets of life, and from these we can learn something about our own living. They direct our attention to the commonplace and there, usually by some type of comparison or contrast, provide us with an opportunity to gain insight into the complexities of life. Different proverbs do this in different ways. The wise person is the one who understands life from more than one proverbial point of view and can discern the appropriate way of responding to it.

Our comprehension of proverbs depends upon our ability to recognize what very different things might have in common:

The way of an eagle in the air,
the way of a serpent upon a rock,
the way of a ship on the high seas,
and the way of a man with a maiden (30:19).

What do these dissimilar realities have in common? It is apparent that none of these "ways" is a distinctly defined route. The kind of analogy present in a proverb operates according to the same principles, as do the riddles, which people might use to challenge each other's wit. Different realities have something in common; what is it?

Proverbs do not command, they persuade. They do not dictate what must be done. Rather, they describe how things work. Their purpose is not to indoctrinate, but to educate. They are not precepts that call for obedience, but adages that invite prudent response. The book of Proverbs clearly insists on the importance of living an ethical life. The ethics it promotes, however, issued from reflection on life rather than from conformity to law.

The Teacher and the Student

Scholars hold various opinions regarding the identity of the wisdom teachers and the settings within which they taught. Some believe that there was a professional class of teachers attached to the court and appointed to train young men in the arts of diplomacy. They claim that much of the wisdom that we find in Proverbs is specialized knowledge imparted in well-defined schools. Others maintain that the elders of the family were the recognized teachers of wisdom who handed down the tradition to the next generation. These others believe that wisdom was part of the common cultural heritage of the people, and all members of the society were fashioned in its teaching.

All scholars agree that the primary education of ancient Israelite youth took place in the home and was the responsibility of the father and, as Proverbs 1:8 tells us, the mother. (Some commentators do not believe that women played a role in the education of sons. They contend that the inclusion of "mother" is merely for the sake of poetic balance of thought [see *parallelism* above]. While that may be the case in this instance, such a poetic construction probably would not have been envisioned without some grounding in experience.) The pertinent information and operating principles of hereditary occupations were also handed down within the confines of the family, perhaps within an extended family. Such hereditary professions included the monarchy, the priesthood, and the scribal class. Education in these professions might well have been an extension of family training.

The biblical texts show that Israelite kings modeled their courts after the pattern of other ancient Near Eastern nations. They appointed men to advise them, to administer royal policies, and to keep official records. It is obvious that these men had to be trained. We should not, however, automatically conclude that such centers were the exclusive or even the principal settings for the teaching of wisdom. Some insist that since the relationship between teacher and student was analogous to that between father and son, (in patriarchal societies women seldom benefit from the educational system) the address "My son," should not be viewed exclusively as familial. While this may be true, the inclusion of "your mother's teaching" (1:8) argues for a family setting.

If wisdom is basically the way a culture addresses the fundamental questions of life, then all members of the society are trained in it and all possess this wisdom in varying degrees and live it out in their lives in diverse ways. The "way of wisdom" may have been very general and indistinguishable, or specialized and distinctive. Intelligence may be an innate quality, but wisdom is acquired by learning from others and from life experience. Such wisdom is neither static nor the exclusive domain of an official class. It grew up within the people, and it was their public property.

The Way of Wisdom

Wisdom came to be understood in several ways. Consequently, "the way of wisdom," a phrase that scholars use, refers to the proper way of doing things, whether in human society, in the world of nature, or on the cosmic plane. The first of these is the kind of wisdom that has been described thus far. Often called practical or folk wisdom, it is primarily concerned with the consequences of social interaction. Since peace and harmony can exist only where some kind of social order is maintained, whatever guaranteed such order was pursued, and whatever threatened it was avoided. This, in fact, is the dimension of wisdom thinking that gave rise to the theory of retribution—the wise will enjoy peace and security; the fool will suffer the consequences of foolishness:

> The virtue of the upright saves them,
> but the faithless are caught in their own
> intrigue (11:6).

Proverbs declare that there are only two ways open to women and men: the way of the wise (those who learn from experience), and the way of the foolish (those who do not learn). Since successful living demands an ongoing search for meaning, one can never settle for the solutions of the past. New situations constantly present themselves; new choices must be made. The ever-developing tradition of wisdom provides various examples of behavior that resulted in success as well as behavior that ended in disaster. The wise, enriched by this store of practical knowledge, will take to heart these lessons. They are the ones who have developed a certain facility in drawing from the accumulated wisdom of the past and, in an imaginative way, successfully bring it to bear on new situations. Thus they follow "the way of wisdom."

A second kind of wisdom deals with our need to survive and prosper in the natural world. Reflective observation of nature and the movements within it led people to recognize a certain amount of regularity in its operations and similarity in its various manifestations. This regularity was charted, the similarities noted, and a kind of nature wisdom developed that was a precursor of the physical sciences. People learned how to live in harmony with nature and, through comparison and contrast, they drew lessons from nature for their daily lives:

> Like snow in summer, or rain in harvest,
> honor for a fool is out of place (26:1).

This too was "the way of wisdom."

Some have questioned the religious value of folk wisdom, because there is no mention of God. The proverbs appear to be anthropocentric (human-centered) rather than theocentric (God-centered). We must be careful not to compare an ancient Near Eastern humanistic point of view with a kind of modern humanism that is faithless. Biblical Israel was not a secular society. It never questioned the divine power working to hold the world in proper balance. It might not understand God's actions, but it did not doubt God's power. The wisdom tradition was built on the conviction that God expected people to use their human abilities to the fullest. Whether or not there is explicit mention of God, Israelite wisdom was religious teaching, and the ethical orientation of the proverbs should be seen as evidence of their religious character.

Finally, people in the ancient Near East believed that there was a kind of wisdom that was beyond their grasp and their comprehension. Their belief rested on the conviction that there was some kind of cosmic order within which they lived, an order that was reliable though mysterious, an order that revealed the wisdom of the creator-god. They maintained that this cosmic order not only predated the natural world but also was actually somehow responsible for its existence. The primordial wisdom associated with this cosmic order fashioned the world and keeps it functioning properly. Of all the kinds of wisdom, it alone contains the secrets of the universe and the complete answers to all questions. The sages knew that this was the only wisdom that would satisfy the human search for meaning. Since it was clearly beyond human reach, it was considered a cosmic reality and it was described as such:

> From of old I was poured forth,
> at the first, before the earth (8:23).

Creation is "the way of wisdom" on this cosmic plane. Israel believed that God was creator of all things, and thus it spoke of a theological dimension to each of these three manifestations of wisdom. Although theological expression is more explicit in later writings, it was never absent from Israel's worldview. The optimistic view of life that permeates the book of Proverbs flows from the conviction that there is an order to the universe and, with God's help, we can discover it, live in harmony with it, and thus enjoy peace and prosperity. This, above all, is "the way of wisdom."

The Teachings of the Wise

Before we look at some of the specifics of the wisdom teaching, it is important for us to remember a few fundamentals of the movement. Here, emphasis is on the human person in general rather than on the nation as a collective group. Its scope is universal, not exclusively Israelite. The counsel offered addresses issues from everyday life rather than cultic experience. It is concerned with pragmatic ends, not transcendent values. If we expect this teaching to address questions not found within its range, not only will we find it wanting but also we might even fail to appreciate the riches that are to be found there.

Fear of the Lord

"The fear of the LORD is the beginning of wisdom." Several variations of this familiar saying appear in the book of Proverbs (1:7; 9:10; 15:33). This notion of fear is based on the recognition of the holiness of God. There may very well be a certain dimension of terror in those who behold the awesomeness of God and realize their own deficiency in the face of it, but this is not the primary meaning that "fear of the LORD" intends to convey. This fear is better characterized as awe and reverence than as terror and dread. Awe, not dread, is awakened when one realizes the transcendence of a God who is protective, not threatening.

Israel did not view this reverential fear as merely an attitude of mind. It was the foundation of its moral conduct. It included respect, loyalty, obedience, and covenant love. Owing to the special character of Yahweh, "fear of the LORD" (the Hebrew word that we translate as LORD is *Yahweh,* the name of Israel's God) becomes a uniquely Israelite expression. Eventually, this phrase became the summation of Israelite religion and piety. In Proverbs this "fear of the LORD" is linked with wisdom, which is practical knowledge that comes from reflection on experience. These are two quite distinct ideas that, when brought together, significantly reinterpret the meaning of wisdom. Comparing two proverbs can see this:

> The beginning of wisdom is: get wisdom . . . (4:7)
>
> The beginning of wisdom is the fear of the LORD . . . (9:10).

In the first proverb, ordinary life is the source of wisdom. In the second, wisdom flows from religious faith. This change in perspective may be the result of sages trying to bridge the gap between the wisdom teaching that they held in common with other Near Eastern nations and that which was distinctively Israelite.

"Fear of the LORD" might be understood in another way. The Israelites believed that behind the breathtaking order of the universe was an all-wise and all-powerful God. They believed that the more they knew about their world, the more they would discover about God. The reverse was also held. Knowledge about God was the beginning of true knowledge about the world. The more one was committed to God, the more one was in harmony with the order placed in the world by this same God. Thus, the proper religious attitude toward God was the source of wisdom.

Training in Virtue

As stated above, the emphasis in the wisdom tradition is on the individual person rather than on the nation. This should not be understood as a kind of privatized individualism as we know today. It was precisely as a member of the covenant community that an Israelite searched for meaning in the events of life. The social ramifications of one's personal life were seldom far from the minds of the people. (It is merely for the sake of this investigation that we separate personal virtues from social virtues. The former characterize behavior in every kind of situation. The latter suggest specific social settings implied in the proverbs themselves.)

The connection between wisdom and personal virtue is clear and frequently stated. The way of wisdom is the way of virtue. It is also the only way to happiness (see Prv 10–13). Many proverbs praise self-control, especially restraint in speech (21:23). They direct one to speak with words that are pleasing (16:24), not foolish (14:23). They admonish discipline in other areas of life as well. For instance, the student is counseled: "With closest custody, guard your heart" (4:23). Honesty (13:5), diligence (6:6–11), docility (13:10), and humility (22:4) are but a few of the virtues that are recommended to the young who, if they live their lives according to this counsel, are promised a good reputation (22:1) and long life (10:27). Once again we see that the people are advised to put their trust in the Lord and not be overconfident of their own ability (3:5).

There are numerous warnings against the seduction of adulterous women. In a strict patriarchal society, the virtue of men is of primary concern; women are frequently regarded as property and are confined in restrictive seclusion in order to guarantee their fidelity and thus assure the legitimacy of the male's offspring. Only women of questionable virtue move freely in such societies, and these are precisely the women against whom the young men are cautioned (see 2:16–19; 6:20–35).

A significant amount of instruction is unmistakably social in its focus. It is bent on developing relationships necessary for societal tranquility. The proverbs themselves provide glimpses into the social settings within which they might be effective. It is obvious that the family plays a prominent role as the initial setting for education. Several proverbs admonish young people to heed the teaching of their parents (1:8; 6:20). The sages realized that the family is the foundation of society, and social virtues are cultivated there. They understood that the lessons of respect and obedience learned within the family go a long way in other less personal social situations. A fair amount of counsel about training and chastisement can also be found (22:6; 13:1; 24; 19:18). This advice might be directed either to training within the family or to occupational education (see The Teacher and the Student).

The distinct influence of Yahwism may not be easily detected in some proverbial instruction, but the call to justice in Proverbs is similar to what we find in the covenant. It manifests itself in concern for the relationship between the rich and the poor. Despite the fact that riches were viewed as fitting reward for righteous living, the inherent dangers of possessing wealth were still acknowledged (28:3, 8; 11:28; 21:13). The poor were to be respected, for they too came from the hand of God (14:31; 22:2) and were sometimes more virtuous than the rich (28:6).

Advice is given to both the ruled and the ruler. Subjects are told to esteem the king, because he exercises considerable power over them (16: 14f). Kings, on the other hand, are bound to be fair and upright (16:10–12). The demand that kings observe justice is part of the ideology of kingship throughout the ancient Near East.

Moral teaching such as this might presuppose an almost mechanical view of retribution. It suggests that the universal order upon which the world depends is neat and reliable. The rewards and punishments, considered the consequences of particular styles of living, seem almost to issue from impersonal laws inherent in the actions themselves, or they are deemed the direct intervention of a God who is executing justice. The book of Proverbs may appear to oversimplify the complexities of human life. It does not question the status quo. One will have to look elsewhere for a critique of social structures or of the prevailing philosophy of life. The applicability of the theory of retribution is not challenged in this book as it is in Job and in Ecclesiastes.

The Figure of Wisdom

An interesting feature of this book is the figure of Wisdom personified. In the very first chapter (1: 20–33), wisdom is depicted as a woman who goes through the city looking for disciples. Many of the traits that characterize her are found throughout the book in proverbs that describe either the wise teacher or the wisdom teaching itself. This woman is frequently contrasted with a second woman, Folly (9:13), who attempts to seduce the simple into her ways. It is not unusual to find personification itself in Hebrew poetry. The prophets used it:

Break out together in song,
  O ruins of Jerusalem! (Is 52:9)

as did the psalmists:

Let the rivers clap their hands,
  the mountains shout with them for joy
    (Ps 98:8).

What is unusual here is that wisdom is characterized as a woman. Several explanations for this have been advanced. Some believe that this is a remnant of ancient Near Eastern (even Israelite) worship of a goddess of wisdom. Others see it as merely a development from the feminine form of the word *hokmah*, "wisdom." A widely accepted explanation for this might be found in the nature of the society itself. Wisdom was regarded as the most desirable possession. In this patriarchal male-preferred society, it is understandable that what is desired would be personified as a woman. The same is true for folly. Women are no more inherently seductive than are men. However, they are a better representation of what men find enticing.

This might explain certain features of the figure of the woman in the market place (8:1–21), but the real mystery lies in the identity of the figure that was present at creation (8:22–31). Over the centuries this figure has been interpreted in various ways.

The Bible quite explicitly states again and again that God alone is the creator. However, there we also find Wisdom claiming to have exercised some role in creation (8:30). This claim must be reconciled with the traditional Israelite faith. One way to do this has been to understand the figure of Wisdom as the personification of a divine attribute. According to this view, the personification is merely a stylistic feature of the author. Such an imaginative technique is not foreign to the Bible. The kindness, truth, and justice of God have also been personified (see Ps 85: 10–14).

As helpful as this explanation may be, it does not take into account the fact that Wisdom is identified as an entity separate from the creator (8:22). Such a characterization is more than personification. It is closer to *hypostasization* (taking what is normally a personal trait and transforming it into a person with its own existence). It is apparent that once Wisdom is created, she has a life of her own. It is also clear that she is a creature with cosmic dimensions. She existed before the rest of creation, and she appears to be active beyond the confines of space and time. According to some commentators, this suggests a mythological origin. Such an interpretation would not be against biblical religion, for there are several other sections of the Bible that contain mythological elements (for example, the garden with the talking serpent [Gn 2–3]; the sea dragon [Is 27:1]).

A third interpretation of this mysterious figure is gaining more prominence today. It claims that Wisdom was originally a goddess. Some say that she was a Canaanite deity; others argue that she was actually early Israelite. Scholars have long maintained that Israel moved from believing in many gods (polytheism), to acknowledging that other nations might have their gods but Israel would worship only one (monolatry), to insisting that there is only one God (monotheism). It is possible that the ancestors of Israel once believed in a goddess of wisdom from whom Woman Wisdom originated.

Whatever the origin of this enigmatic figure, she is no longer perceived as a goddess. She probably represents that inaccessible dimension of wisdom that all people desire but which resides with God alone, the kind of wisdom that is within creation but beyond us. This is the wisdom that explains the universe but which we cannot attain. The mysterious figure, whatever her origin, reminds us that the fullness of wisdom cannot be gained through human experience. It belongs to God.

The Role of Wisdom Today

There are several reasons why Proverbs may not be popular reading. It seems to describe a world that does not exist, a world where life has a proper order and events follow a cause-and-effect sequence. We know to the contrary that life is very unpredictable. We may be able to discern some of the order in nature, but the events of life itself cannot be charted or foreseen. Consequently, Proverbs appears to be very naive and somewhat static.

Furthermore, the world of Proverbs seems to be the world of the comfortable, not the world of those who struggle. Even directions about justice are given from the point of view of those who are in charge, and the advice does not question the way things are. Since people supported by the status quo seldom challenge it, Proverbs might well be perceived as a guide to "Win Friends, Influence People, and Get Ahead in the World as It Is." Advocates of justice and peace usually turn to the prophets for inspiration, not to the proverbs.

Such an evaluation of the wisdom tradition misses a few very important points. First, proverbs do not claim to describe everything, but they do depict a bit of the world. Each proverb reflects a snippet of life. Together they offer a collage, not a blueprint. Second, the process that produces proverbs may be more significant than the content of the proverbs themselves. It teaches us the importance of serious reflection on experience and the need to adjust both our understanding and our behavior as circumstances change. The wise person is the one who can adequately assess the demands of a situation and who is experienced and flexible enough to behave in a way that is appropriate to that particular situation. If we read proverbs as directions that we must follow rather than as examples from which we can learn, we will misunderstand the force of their teaching. However, if we read them rightly, we will discover that the way of wisdom is neither naive nor static.

Although people do not turn to the proverbs for prophetic inspiration, the wisdom method of reflection on life experience found there has gained prominence in recent years. Frequently, experience is the starting point from which contemporary theologians develop their insights. This approach has spread from the base Christian communities to Bible discussion groups around the world. People are beginning again to realize that they encounter God *through* human experience, not *despite* it.

The charge that Proverbs is a book of upper-class ethics can be debated. It is true that several proverbs seem suited to the court or to some other diplomatic setting. However, most of them could easily have been used in the normal everyday training of youth. They do presume an underlying order that is stable and reliable, but that is common in most initial training programs. Proverbs is the kind of teaching that socializes members into the group. It does not question the credibility of the group and so it lacks a prophetic edge. However, Proverbs does offer an appreciation of life and an encouragement to live it to the fullest.

FURTHER READING

Clifford, R. J. *Proverbs*. Old Testament Library. Louisville: Westminster, 1999.

Fox, M. V. *Proverbs 1–9*. Anchor Bible 18A. New York: Doubleday, 2000.

Perdue, Leo G. *Proverbs*. Interpretation. Louisville: John Knox, 2000.

Murphy, Roland E. *Proverbs*. Word Bible Commentary. Waco, TX: Word, 1998.

ECCLESIASTES

[see pages 879–890 of the Old Testament]

Ecclesiastes does not enjoy the renown that belongs to other writings of the wisdom tradition, specifically Job or Psalms. However, even people who are unfamiliar with the book often use expressions that arise from its provocative view of life. Sayings such as "You can't take it with you!" or "There's nothing new under the sun!" show that the thinking of Ecclesiastes is not foreign to our own contemporary worldview.

About the Book

Ecclesiastes manifests some of the literary characteristics of a *Royal Testament,* a common type of literature of the ancient Near East intended for the instruction of the king's successor. The Royal Testament was written in the first person and claimed to be advice gleaned from the experience of life. Although the book begins with a kind of third-person descriptive prologue (1: 1–11) and ends with an epilogue also in the third person (12:9–14), everything else within it suggests but one speaker and, despite some conflicting statements, one point of view. There are also several unresolved literary questions regarding the book's authorship, dating, place of origin, composition, and structure.

The very first verse of the book describes rather than identifies the speaker as "David's son, Qoheleth, king in Jerusalem." (See the Solomonic attribution of the book of Proverbs, early in the Reading Guide to that book.) Since there is no biblical mention of a Davidic son by the name of Qoheleth, some other connotation must be intended. The exact meaning of the name Qoheleth is debated. It probably comes from the Hebrew word *qahal,* meaning assembly. The form of the word suggests that it is not a name but a participle that designates someone who does something. This explains why most commentators maintain that the word refers to someone who calls forth or presides over a meeting, perhaps for the purpose of teaching. The Greek word used to translate *qahal* is *ekklesia,* meaning a citizens' assembly in Greece. In this biblical book, the one who presides over the assembly is called Ecclesiastes or Preacher.

The man is further designated as the son of David, king of Israel. The reference is obviously to Solomon, the one revered in popular devotion as the wise king par excellence. The author seems to be claiming that Solomon is the speaker, and therefore the teaching in the book has the authority of Solomon's wisdom. Although this claim appears only in the first two chapters, it sets the tone for the rest of the instruction. From the outset the teaching has authority even though it may prove to be unorthodox.

The language of the book resembles the kind of Hebrew that appeared during a very late biblical period and was used almost exclusively for literary purposes. The inclusion of several Aramaic words has led scholars to date the book around the third century BC. The place of origin is more difficult to determine. Some say it was Phoenicia, others suggest Egypt. The international character of the wisdom tradition adds to the complexity of precise identification (see introduction to the Wisdom Books, RG 236).

There are also different opinions regarding the structure of the book. Some believe that it is simply a collection of wisdom pieces lacking organization. Others divide the book into two major parts: Qoheleth's observations of life, and the conclusions that he draws. (The *New American Bible* belongs to this latter group.) Since there is only one speaker, a structure based on alternate speeches is ruled out.

Besides instruction, the author makes use of several other teaching techniques. These include proverbial quotations, contrasting proverbs, and rhetorical questions. Several of these forms are mentioned in the prologue to Proverbs, ". . . proverb and parable, the words of the wise and their riddles" (Prv 1:6). All of this fosters the characterization of Qoheleth as a respected teacher of wisdom.

Ecclesiastes is one of the five books that make up the *Megilloth,* or "Scrolls," a special collection that includes Song of Songs, Ruth, Lamentations, and Esther. These books were read during various liturgical festivals and were gathered together for the sake of convenience. Ecclesiastes was read during the harvest celebration of Sukkoth, also known as Tabernacles or Booths. This major pilgrim feast was so called because the harvesters lived in booths as they gathered in their crops. It is not clear how this practice of reading began or why Ecclesiastes was chosen for this festival. Perhaps the somber tone of the book, the seasoned reflections of an aging sage, fit the maturity of harvest. Although reading the book was not always a consistent synagogue practice, Ecclesiastes continues to be considered part of the Megilloth.

The book clearly begins with the distinctive "Vanity of vanities, says Qoheleth, vanity of vanities! All things are vanity!" (1:2) and ends on the same tone "Vanity of vanities, says Qoheleth, all things are vanity!" (12:8). What some consider a kind of prologue (1:1–11) might well come from the original author. The epilogue (12: 9–14) is different: at least one, possibly two people besides the primary have added something. Verses 9–11 praise Qoheleth as a wise teacher and compiler of wisdom sayings. Whoever added these verses plainly agreed with Qoheleth's conclusions despite their critical and sometimes unconventional viewpoint. The tone changes, though, with verse 12, which begins with the same Hebrew word as does verse 9. Some hold that this is textual evidence of a second epilogue. This is the only place in the book where the student is identified in a manner found frequently in Proverbs. However, the student is warned against too much speculation and is advised to trust in the retributive justice of God, a theme that Qoheleth consistently challenges.

It would appear from all this, that the author created a literary character, Qoheleth, and ascribed Solomonic authority to him in order to give his own instruction credibility. A later editor further authenticated this teaching by explicitly assuring the reader of Qoheleth's wisdom. However, with two short verses a second editor tried to temper some of Qoheleth's statements.

There are two possible explanations for this inconsistent ending: (1) The book was already well enough accepted so that its critics could not dismiss it. Still, someone was in a position to append a caution to what might be considered questionable teaching. (2) If there was only one editor who agreed with Qoheleth's teaching, that person realized that without some kind of tempering it would not be preserved. In order to assure acceptance, the last verses restate the traditional view of retribution and seem to return the entire teaching to the circle of orthodoxy.

A Critical Point of View

There is a wide range of scholarly opinion regarding the meaning of the book. Qoheleth has been described as a skeptic, a cynic, or, more positively, a pragmatist. His view of life has been called everything from pessimistic and fatalistic to realistic. Some judge his religious outlook hedonistic or pleasure-seeking, while others think it is faithful to Israelite values. It is clear that he is disillusioned with certain facets of his society, yet he lacks the enthusiasm of a reformer and the vision of a mystic. This has led some critics to label him a frustrated man who is resigned to the injustice and meaninglessness of life and who is intent on making the most of any fleeting pleasures, in the spirit of Epicureanism. It is difficult to make a distinction between a challenge to the way life is understood and dissatisfaction with life itself. Perhaps in the actual living of life, it is impossible to separate the two. A careful reading of Qoheleth, however, will show that he does not really despair of life but only of unrealistic expectations regarding it. Qoheleth's real struggle is with the meaning of life, especially life viewed from the perspective of the theory of retribution (see introduction).

A Chase after Wind

Qoheleth sets out to discover everything of value within human experience (1:13). Since he is identified as a king, he has both the wealth and the leisure to embark on this quest. As possessor of extraordinary wisdom (1:16), he of all people is equipped to experience life to the full. The text states that he has acquired wisdom, but satisfaction in what he sought was always beyond his grasp, "a chase after wind" (1:17). It is clear that in his search for wisdom, he was looking for something else as well. Qoheleth next turned to the pursuit of self-gratification, and in many different ways he was successful in this pursuit, but still he was not satisfied (2:1–11). It seems that he accomplished everything to which he had set his mind in his search to answer the fundamental question: "What profit has man from all the labor which he toils at under the sun?" (1:3). He consistently arrived at the same conclusion, however. There is no lasting gain, no tangible dividend, "with nothing gained under the sun" (2:11).

The theory of retribution claims that there is a direct relation between the uprightness of one's behavior and the good or ill fortune that one enjoys or endures. According to this theory, Qoheleth's wisdom and wealth would be perceived as concrete proof of his goodness and a guarantee of future prosperity. But Qoheleth does not really enjoy his good fortune, and so he questions its value. Since death comes to all, he wonders, "why then should I be wise? Where is the profit for me?" (2:15). It is not life as such, nor the search for fulfillment in life, that frustrates him. What he loathes (2:17) is the profitlessness of human striving. It is not fulfilling. Since Qoheleth did attain the wisdom and wealth and pleasure that he sought, his frustration must stem from his failure to attain something in addition to these goals. Qoheleth is asking more of life than merely success and prosperity.

He is also troubled about the inevitability of death and the sense of futility it often imparts. Regardless of how one lives, death is the ultimate fate of all. Any advantage that one might have because of righteousness, wisdom, or wealth is only temporary and, therefore, questionable. In fact, the fool who disregards societal rules may actually have an edge over the one who conforms to them at the cost of enjoyment. Death and the total relinquishment that it demands force Qoheleth to question the value of any human accomplishment and to wonder if perhaps life itself is "a chase after wind."

Nothing Is New under the Sun

We have already seen how the wisdom teachers appealed to the obvious order within the natural world as they urged people to live in compliance with acceptable social custom (see Proverbs: The Way of Wisdom, RG 257f). The author of Job used the same technique with a slightly different twist. There we see that Job was overwhelmed by the wonders of nature and led to acknowledge the incomprehensible dimension of life (see Job: Reward and Punishment, RG 238f). The author of Ecclesiastes also directs our attention to the regularity in nature (1:2–11), but he does so in order to highlight its monotony. The activity of the earth does not change; it seems constant. The sun rises and sets and rises again and sets again in the same mode day after day. Although the wind appears at times to be irregular, it follows certain paths that, upon observation, can be predicted. Even the sea, though constantly fed, is never full. The regularity detected in nature appears to be devoid of any progress. There is nothing new under the sun.

What advantage does the earth have in being constant? What does the sun accomplish by rising and setting if it must repeat the cycle again and again with no variation and no advance? What profit comes from the wind's endless movement if it never arrives at any destination? To what avail do the streams nourish an insatiable sea? Qoheleth urges us to learn yet another lesson from nature. Human striving for gain is nothing but wearisome labor that must be repeated and repeated with no promise of conclusion and no assurance of gratification. Human life is basically the same regardless of the society or the generation into which one is born. Life itself follows the same cycles, and experiences are quite similar. Momentous events do occur, but they seldom interfere with the fundamental rhythms of existence. Nature repeats itself and so does human history. Nothing seems to have lasting significance.

In what may be the most familiar section of the entire book (3:1–9), Qoheleth declares that each event of human life has its own appointed time. Here, each event is linked in poetic construction with its opposite. There are two ways of understanding this pattern. First, juxtaposing opposites is a poetic way of expressing totality. It creates an inclusion that encompasses both poles and everything in between. Examples of this include: "knowledge of good and bad" (see Gn 2:9, 17) meaning comprehensive knowledge; "bone and flesh" (see Gn 2:23) referring to the entire body. The contemporary phrase "flesh and blood" has the same meaning.

The second way of understanding this poetic form is as an expression of relativity. There is an inevitability to human events that is nonetheless relative. The circumstances of life determine what is fitting and what is not. What is appropriate at one time or in one situation can be out of place when the circumstances change. This may be the author's way of insisting that there are no absolutes; that is, everything is always relative to all else. There is a time to die as well as a time to be born. Neither seems to have an advantage over the other. However, we do not know the rules that govern these appointed times, and so we are helpless to control them and may feel that we are at their mercy.

The task of living is not easy. Qoheleth explains why in 3:11. This verse may be the most difficult one of the book because of the questions surrounding the translation and interpretation of the Hebrew *olam*. Although some versions translate this word as "world," or "future," or even "ignorance," the NAB renders it as "the timeless." God has put *olam* in the human heart, and we want to know, to understand, and even to control everything in the world. It seems that while human beings are finite, their desires transcend the limits of time. Qoheleth has described the world as fixed and closed. There is, nonetheless, urgency within the human heart that seeks to burst the confines of restrictive determinism in order to delight in the wonders of freedom and mystery. We are reminded of St. Augustine's famous saying: "You have made us for yourself, O Lord, and our hearts are restless until they rest in you."

All Is Vanity!

"All is vanity" is the expression that has come to characterize the entire book. The Hebrew word *hebel,* which is here translated as "vanity," can also be rendered as "vapor" or "thin air." It means pointlessness or futility, and it refers to something that may be real but that has little or no lasting substance. We have seen that Qoheleth has accomplished everything he set out to do. He has acquired wisdom and wealth; he has enjoyed pleasure and prosperity; he has achieved all of his goals. And yet he declares "All is vanity!" All of the energy he put into his projects was pointless; all of his toil was futile. One might expect him to advise against ever trying to be happy, but he does not. Quite the contrary! We will see that he urges people to enjoy what they have. Then what about life does he regard as vanity?

Qoheleth observed in the lives of others what Job experienced in his own life: The righteous do not always enjoy the good things of life, nor are the wicked always deprived of them (4:1; 8:l0f). Life itself has shown both Job and Qoheleth the inadequacy of the theory of retribution. This theory may be helpful in explaining some things and in encouraging a certain kind of behavior, but it falls short in many areas. While both men seem to have arrived at this insight, Qoheleth's dissatisfaction in the face of his own prosperity and success has led him a step further in challenging the theory. It is not only that a righteous person sometimes does not prosper; it is also that, even when one does realize some desired goal, there is no guarantee of fulfillment. To suppose that the attainment of goals, even noble goals, can fulfill human longings is, according to Qoheleth, vanity!

The Wisdom of the Sage

The wisdom of Qoheleth consists not only in a critical examination of everything that is supposed to bring happiness but also in providing positive counsel. Although he finds fault with some aspects of human striving, he advises something that is often overlooked in times of feverish activity, something that is always within reach and may well be the key to true happiness and contentment. He exhorts his hearers to relish the simple pleasures that are at hand (2:24; 3:13, 22; 5:19; 8:15; 9:9). These pleasures can be experienced in the very act of living: in eating, in drinking, in labor itself rather than in the wealth that one may hope to produce by it. According to Qoheleth, this pleasure, like everything else in life, has come from the hand of God and should be enjoyed.

One cannot calculate this enjoyment or manipulate it as might be possible in a purely business transaction. Life is not a business transaction and to expect a strict quid pro quo (this for that) return, as one might expect in a rigid interpretation of retribution, will only end in disappointment. Qoheleth believes the enjoyment should be sought in the doing rather than in the outcome. To wait in anticipation of something more than the natural satisfaction that accompanies human activity is foolish, because the future is uncertain.

Qoheleth does not spurn the search for wisdom or the normal human striving for success and prosperity. He objects to making human accomplishment the primary or exclusive goal in life. He calls upon all to find pleasure in what they are doing and, if they are fortunate enough to become successful in the process, to see this as a gift from God as well.

A Challenge for Today

Ecclesiastes is not an account of Qoheleth's journey in faith. It is more like jottings or a report of his experiments in living. He did not share Job's struggle with theodicy (a defense of God against the accusation of injustice). Rather, Qoheleth addressed human misconceptions about divine activity, not the incomprehensible itself. He seems to have gone right to the core of things. He scrutinized some of the primary undertakings and fundamental goals of people.

Qoheleth would probably be unrelenting in his criticism of many of the attitudes found within our contemporary society. He knew that prosperity is often fleeting and cannot ensure happiness, even when it is at one's disposal. The complexity of modern society and the instability of the world's economy make it more difficult to amass wealth today than may have been the case in the past. For this reason, the strain and conflict that often accompany the struggle for "upward mobility" have been heightened. This is true for nations as well as for individuals. Much of the injustice in present society stems from greed and an avaricious devouring of the wealth of the world. Too many people believe that having more will make them happy.

Qoheleth never disparaged ingenuity or hard work. Rather, he criticized those who judged the worth of human endeavor by the amount of output rather than the quality of input. There is a very thin line between directing all of one's energies toward accomplishing a noble goal and sacrificing everything for the sake of success. Qoheleth wholeheartedly endorsed the former while he condemned the latter. He would most likely criticize any attitude or system that places more value on the product than on the person producing it. Today's business practices, whether local, national, or international, would come under his scrutiny in this regard.

The struggle for upward mobility is not the only dimension of contemporary society that Qoheleth would most likely challenge. Many people spend a lifetime climbing the ladder of prominence and power. Others will do almost anything to gain acceptability in prestigious social, professional, or political circles. And who does not aspire to a reputation for wisdom or exceptional intelligence? Qoheleth would challenge us to put all such ambition in the right perspective.

This sage teacher was not blind to the many disappointments and tragedies of life, but neither was he an advocate of radical social change. He cautions against wishing for what cannot be, and he urges his hearers to make the most of what they have. This may not be an encouraging message for those who are deprived of the necessities of life, but most likely it was not intended for them. He is not contesting the justice of the social order. He is questioning the value of the motivation behind obsessive striving for success.

Finally, Qoheleth was convinced that the future is not totally under our control. It cannot be manipulated by human decision nor determined by human behavior. A strict interpretation of retribution frequently includes the notion that God is bound to respond to our actions with appropriate reward or punishment, whichever the case may be. This normally unconscious attitude surfaces when we are faced with unexplained reverses of fortune. We wonder what we have done to bring adversity upon ourselves, or we accuse God of behaving unfairly toward us. Qoheleth would remind us that God is not bound by our interpretive theories. We can accurately predict neither success nor failure.

Qoheleth would insist that the primary goal of life is living. All work, all progress has one principal purpose and that is the enhancement and promotion of life. Every other end is at best secondary or otherwise "a chase after the wind." This is a profoundly religious teaching, for Qoheleth believed that it was the creator who placed the desire for happiness within each human heart, made living an exciting adventure, and willed that every person be given the chance to find pleasure in life. He would strongly object to any materialistic point of view that might minimize or deny this basic conviction. Qoheleth was a champion of the greatest of God's gifts—life itself.

FURTHER READING

Brown, William P. *Ecclesiastes*. Interpretation. Louisville: Westminster John Knox, 2000.

Crenshaw, James L. *Ecclesiastes*. Old Testament Library. Philadelphia: Westminster, 1987.

Murphy, Roland E. *Ecclesiastes*. Word Bible Commentary 23A. Waco, TX: Word, 1992.

Seow, C. L. *Ecclesiastes*. Anchor Bible 18C. New York: Doubleday, 1997.

Towner, W. Sibley. *The Book of Ecclesiastes*. New Interpreter's Bible 5. Nashville, TN: Abingdon Press, 1997.

THE SONG OF SONGS

[see pages 890–898 of the Old Testament]

No book of the Old Testament is more difficult to interpret than the Song of Songs. It is clearly a collection of love poems full of sensuous imagery. It promotes no apparent theological or moral values, and it never even mentions God. It is no wonder that its acceptance into the canon of inspired writings was seriously questioned. The very character of the book has led to many quite distinct interpretations.

About the Book

Scholars vary in their explanation of the book, but they agree that it did not originate as a single composition. They concur that it is a collection of poems of various lengths, but they propose different ways of grouping these poems. Some have suggested a movement from longing to union and then to separation. This pattern is repeated through the eight short chapters. Others maintain that, while the lyrics do express such sentiments, the arrangement of the poems lacks any definite pattern. The book may have no clearly defined structure, but it is marked by frequent repetitions (for example, 2:7; 3:5; 8:4). Since there is no narrative plot and the speakers are neither identified nor introduced, one can only speculate about the compiler's original intention.

This relatively short book has an unusually large number of uncommon words. Its 117 verses contain forty-nine words that appear nowhere else in the Old Testament. This adds to the difficulty of comprehension, for we are prevented from comparing the meaning of the word found in one context with its meaning in another. This obscure vocabulary also opens the poem to a multiplicity of interpretations, thus making it somewhat cryptic but also allowing for a rich diversity of meanings.

Like Proverbs and Ecclesiastes, the Song is associated with Solomon. This ascription to the famous king is found only in the editorial introduction (1:1) and is preceded by a preposition that can be translated in various ways: "by" Solomon; "to" Solomon; "for" Solomon; "of" Solomon; "concerning" Solomon. The attribution need not imply authorship. Still, ascribing the book to Solomon probably gave it credibility, linked it with the other wisdom traditions, and contributed to one of its best-known allegorical interpretations. The book does include other references to Solomon (3:7, 9, 11; 8:11f), and this has convinced some interpreters of the Solomonic identity of the amorous shepherd. However, in none of these passages does Solomon speak, and the references could actually be merely figurative allusions to fabulous wealth.

The geographic references within the Song are quite wide reaching. Northern locations are mentioned (2:1; 3:9; 4:8; 6:4; 7:5–6), as are places in Transjordan (4:1) and Judah (1:14; 3:5). This variety may reflect the early northern Israelite source of some of the original poems and a later southern, perhaps Jerusalem, setting for the final edition. The appearance of the Persian word for orchard or park (4:13) suggests a postexilic date (after 539 BC).

The Song of Songs is also found in the *Megilloth* scroll (see Reading Guide to Ecclesiastes, RG 262). It is read on the last day of the celebration of Passover. Perhaps the announcement of the end of winter (2:11) made the poem suitable for use during a spring festival. Many consider the reference to the horses and chariots of Pharaoh (1:9) a clear allusion to the Exodus, the event commemorated at Passover.

Voices in the Song

There are letters in the left-hand margins of the NAB that identify the speaker of the verses. These letters are in fact an interpretation. The references to the "Daughters of Jerusalem" (see 1:5; 2:7; 3:5; 5:8,16) do not present any problem, but the meaning of "bride" (see 4:8–12; 5:1) is not clear. The Hebrew text clearly refers to the young woman in this way, but the word itself designates a woman who is betrothed but not yet married to a man. While the text does allude to the sexual union of the lovers, it never describes a marriage and so the male partner is not necessarily a "groom." (The reference in 3:11 is to the splendor of Solomon, not to the marriage of the lovers in the Song.) Furthermore, there seem to be two distinct portraits of this elusive lover. One of them is a royal figure from Jerusalem (see 1:12–17; 3:6–11), and the other is a rustic youth from the north (see 1:7f; 2:8–17). Nowhere in the book do we find an explicit combination of the two.

Who are these mysterious lovers? The way one understands the meaning and function of the book will influence the way one identifies the characters within it. If these are ancient wedding songs, then, of course, the lovers are a bride and a groom. If this is love poetry of the type we know existed in ancient Egypt, then "bride" can be understood in the figurative sense of a lover, and her partner is the man with whom she is intimately involved. He is called "lover" or "beloved" (see 1:13; 2:16; 5:8; etc.), not husband. It is only as the result of some interpretive approach that one might identify the young man as Solomon and thus understand the Song as a poem composed on the occasion of one of his marriages to some foreign princess.

Form and Meaning

For more than two thousand years, the Song of Songs has been not only a fascination but also something of a riddle. It is its very uniqueness that has made it a challenge to understand. There are basically four ways of interpreting it: allegorical, cultic, dramatic, and literal. Each of these interpretive approaches reveals different facets of the literary quality of the book and opens up possibilities for our religious enrichment. All of them have gained acceptance within Roman Catholic tradition. The book itself contains characteristics that support each of these methods, thus lending it to any one of the approaches. It is interesting to note that while currently the first and preferred method of interpretation of most of the Bible has been the literal approach, the opposite has been true with this book. Perhaps much of the sexual imagery has been so explicit or suggestive as to offend the sensitivities of many of the faithful. Thus, commentators have presumed that the poems were not meant to be understood literally, and therefore they must have some concealed religious meaning.

When we talk about interpretation, it is important to distinguish between what the book *meant* in the past and what it might *mean* for the present. Those interpreters who employ a strict historical-critical approach (cf. Harrington) insist that the original sense must be the focus of our explanation. For them, discovering the earliest form and meaning of the book is crucial. They believe that it is this original meaning that continues to be revelatory for us today. Other commentators believe that the book can be interpreted in various ways. These latter interpreters do not categorize approaches as right or wrong but as helpful or not helpful. They would be more open than the former group to various interpretations of the Song of Songs.

Allegorical Interpretation

An allegory is an analogy or a comparison of two areas of human experience, usually a more concrete or everyday area and one that is more abstract or farther removed from ordinary experience. Our understanding of the more abstract area is helped by the analogy with our everyday experience. For example, in our courts Justice is often represented as a beautiful woman wearing a blindfold and holding balancing scales. The woman's beauty symbolizes the attractions of Justice: as we are drawn to beauty, so should we be drawn to Justice. Her blindfold symbolizes the impartiality of Justice: no matter how important or unimportant the person who appears before her, she is concerned only with the merits of the case presented. The balancing scales symbolize the objective nature of Justice: decisions are made according to public standards, and anyone can observe how they are made. Thus by using concrete images, the allegorical figure helps us understand our ideals of Justice.

An allegorical method of interpretation presumes that the real significance of the material under consideration is more than just its factual or historical content. In this view, the surface meaning is a figure of speech that signifies some deeper spiritual truth. This interpretive approach was quite prevalent in ancient Jewish circles (Philo, 20 BC–AD 54) as well as among early Christian writers (Origen, AD 185–254). Jewish commentators who allegorized the Song interpreted it as symbolizing God's dealings with Israel. They claimed that the book narrates this relationship, tracing it from the time of the Exodus to the coming of the messiah. They believed that it extols the steadfast love that God bestowed on Israel and describes the fickleness that characterized Israel's attitude toward its divine lover.

As the Christians began to read the Hebrew traditions in light of their faith in Christ, this allegorical method produced new meanings. One of their interpretations identified the lovers in the Song as Christ and the Church. Another read it as a description of the mystical union of God and the individual soul. Some of the most profound theology in the Christian mystical tradition is grounded in this kind of allegorical interpretation of the Song. The works of saints Bernard of Clairvaux and John of the Cross are the chief examples of this kind of writing. The bride has even been identified as the Virgin Mary. Although this interpretation is not easily accommodated to the poems, it has become quite prominent within Roman Catholic tradition. One reason for this is the belief that Mary is the exemplar of the individual soul in union with God. A second and probably stronger reason for the acceptance of this representation is the fact that sections from the Song are read during the liturgy on several Marian feasts. Thus by association this particular allegorical interpretation has been introduced into popular devotion.

Cultic Interpretation

A second way of understanding the Song of Songs assumes that it was originally a liturgical reenactment of a drama that takes place in nature each spring. This drama is reflected in a well-known fertility myth of the ancient Near Eastern world. The great god (the Canaanite Baal or the Babylonian Tammuz) dies after the harvest and is mourned by the fertility goddess (Anath or Ishtar respectively). She frantically searches for him during the barren winter. Her efforts are finally successful, and they are eventually united. Nature is revived with the coming of spring, and the cycle of life is repeated. The fact that this book was read during the spring festival of Passover seems to support the theory that Israel was indeed influenced by the agricultural celebrations of the time.

There is ample evidence in the Bible of Israel's appropriation and subsequent reinterpretation of Canaanite cultic practices. Passover itself is probably a combination of two festivals: an early nomadic celebration meant to ensure the fertility of the flock, and an agricultural one, the Feast of Unleavened Bread, meant to ensure the growth of the crop. The nomadic festival took on historical significance as it was used to commemorate God's deliverance of the people from Egyptian bondage, and it was associated with the Feast of Unleavened Bread after the people had settled in Canaan and had moved from a nomadic to an agricultural form of life. These two very different festivals merged into one celebration, and elements of both became details of the standard story of the first Passover celebration (see Ex 12).

The Song itself includes several features that are characteristic of fertility liturgies. Women always play a prominent role in these cultic reenactments. There is frequently a chorus of women, and the chief character is a goddess who is separated from her lover. The speakers are seldom named, and their speeches are more monologues than dialogues. The goddess is sometimes a bride, sometimes a sister, sometimes a mother; the beloved is depicted as a king, but more frequently as a shepherd. It is quite possible that, while this ritual drama was never incorporated into the official liturgy of Israel, it enjoyed widespread acceptance in the isolated rural communities (see Ez 8:14). Those who endorse this theory of interpretation contend that the book was included in the canon precisely because of this popular use. Commentators who reject the cultic theory do so because there is no explicit evidence that Israel included the rite of the dying/rising god in its own ritual. They do not deny the possibility of popular acceptance, but they insist that any association with fertility religion would work against the book's inclusion in the canon. They regard the cultic interpretation as merely a sophisticated form of the allegorical approach.

Dramatic Interpretation

The third approach has a long history in the church's tradition. As early as the second century of the Christian era, Origen claimed that the Song was a wedding poem written in dramatic form by Solomon himself. Some interpreters today divide the book into a drama of five movements: the anticipation and tryst (1:1–2:17); the separation (3:1–11); reunion (4:1–5:1) a second separation (5:2–6:3); and final union (6:4–8:14). Such a division attempts to show how the Song includes the dramatic elements of conflict and resolution. The fact that there are only speeches and no narrative sections lends support to this theory of interpretation. However, it is the commentators not the author(s) who assign the speeches to the characters, as is done in the left-hand margins of the NAB, and who identify the various scenes by means of subtitles within the text.

The two major characters of the drama are the royal shepherd and the Shulammite maiden. A two-character interpretation has serious deficiencies, however. There is no dramatic development, and the book lacks ethical purpose. A three-character approach was developed to address these weaknesses. It distinguishes two male individuals, the king and the shepherd. The former tries to win the love of the beautiful maiden, but she remains faithful to her shepherd lover. The difference between these two interpretations is obvious. In the first one, the royal shepherd is noble and worthy of the faithful love of the Shulammite. This royal personage might well represent Solomon. In the second interpretation, the king is a villain who tries to seduce the maiden with the promise of luxury and comfort. One wonders how such a disapproving portrait of Solomon could survive as part of the wisdom tradition, a tradition ascribed to the wisdom of the very king who is maligned by this depiction. The weaknesses of this approach are obvious. Since the biblical text does not supply speech designations, the decisions about their identification are influenced by the biases of the interpreter. Stage directions are also imposed from without rather than discovered within the poems themselves. Finally, there is neither story line nor character development, essential traits of good drama.

Literal Interpretation

It may be that the original meaning of the Song is found in its literal interpretation. Most likely, the Song of Songs is simply a collection of love poems that neither symbolized divine love nor developed from fertility rites. The poems teach no lessons, tell no story. They simply celebrate the passion of human love. Some believe that these are secular poems. Others doubt that purely secular love songs would ever have been admitted into the canon. These latter commentators believe that the poems are examples of Judean wedding songs. They also discover in them traces of a poetic form called the *wasf,* an Arabic word meaning description. These are poems that use images from nature to describe parts of the male or female body. This literary form might explain some of the strange imagery found in the Song (see 4:1–5; 7:2–6).

If this literary reading is really the meaning of the Song of Songs, a fundamental question surfaces: Why was the book considered inspired and thus included in the Bible? One can only offer a hypothetical answer. Israel may have followed the same wedding customs, as did its Syrian neighbor, celebrating the event for seven days. During the festivities the bride was characterized as "maiden" and the groom as "king." On the eve of the wedding itself the girl would dance for her lover and recite *wasf* for his enjoyment. The representation of the man as "king" and the extravagance of the celebration could blend quite easily with the tradition about Solomon's erotic exploits (see 1 Kgs 11:1). Some believe that one of the poems was actually composed on the occasion of one of his marriages (3:6–11). Thus, what was initially a collection of wedding songs was now regarded as a description of the king's sexual adventures and was joined with two other writings that claim divine inspiration and Solomonic authorship, namely, Proverbs and Ecclesiastes. Each of these three books explicitly attributed to Solomon addresses some of the central issues of life, issues that are basic to the wisdom thinking of the ancient Near East, Israel included. Proverbs provides directions on how to achieve peace and prosperity. Qoheleth addresses the search for meaning in life. The Song of Songs celebrates a fundamental human emotion, namely, erotic love. None of these books fits into the category of salvation history, but each one is an example of the way of wisdom.

Once writings were associated with Solomon and the wisdom attributed to him, it was not long before they possessed their own authoritative significance. This seems to have been enough to ensure inclusion in the canon. These three books may be quite distinct from each other, but they have come to represent different moments in the life of the same man. The Song of Songs reveals a young, passionate, unguarded Solomon; Proverbs shows a moderate but optimistic man who has learned from his experience of life; the musings of Qoheleth come from someone who approaches the end of life challenging the enduring value of human accomplishment. The quality of these anthropological, but nonetheless theological, concerns is evidence of their religious value. Solomonic ascription provided the books with canonical status.

Wisdom Teaching

Each of the interpretive approaches described above leads us to the central question: What is the book's theological value? Since it belongs to the wisdom tradition, we might also ask: What does it teach us? We have considered four different methods of interpretation, and we should not be surprised if we discover four quite distinct answers to these questions.

The allegorical approach provides us with a figurative way of understanding the nature of our relationship with God. It portrays the relationship as dynamic, energizing, mutually loving, and intensely intimate. This depiction of God runs counter to the images of an impassive creator or an avenging judge, characterizations that may be the prominent images of God held by many people. We may be familiar with the notion of God as a loving parent or of Jesus as a faithful friend, but the Song of Songs offers us a portrait of a passionate lover, one who desires union with us. Some might find this notion scandalous, but the wisdom tradition (specifically Job and Ecclesiastes) repeatedly teaches something about God or human nature that is unconventional.

At the heart of the dying/rising ritual is the conviction that death does not have the final victory. The love of the grieving goddess is strong enough to bring her lover back to her and to revitalize the lifeless earth. To the proverb: "For love is strong as death" (8:6; *Revised Standard Version* translation), one might add: "In Spring a young woman's fancy turns to thoughts of love."

The dramatic interpretation depicts an example of faithful love. Whether one favors the two- or the three-character account, the fidelity of the bride is held up for all to admire and imitate. She is unrelenting in her search and steadfast in her commitment. This image of a faithful woman conforms to the one found in other places of the wisdom tradition (see Prv 31:10–31).

The literal understanding of the Song skirts all symbolic interpretation and makes no apology for its erotic imagery. It affirms that sexuality is one of the gifts that God gave for our enjoyment (see Prv 5:15–21; Eccl 9:9). Still, sexual pleasure is not sought promiscuously. It is pursued only within the context of faithful and exclusive commitment.

Finally, the portrait of the maiden in the Song of Songs is exceptional for literature that originated in a patriarchal culture. The woman is not portrayed as naïve or passive, solely dependent upon a man for protection and sustenance. She takes the initiative in the romantic exchange of the poem, uttering twice as much of the erotic poetry as does the man. The maiden is portrayed as an independent and mature person in her own right. She has her own vineyard (1:6) and is encouraged to pasture her flocks (1:8), occupations normally assigned to men. Through its use of the metaphor of human love, the Song of Songs proclaims a biblical conviction that will also be amplified in sound Christian tradition: human sexuality—male and female—is a creation of God and, expressed in accord with God's law, is both noble and enobling.

FURTHER READING

Fox, Michael V. *The Song of Songs and the Ancient Egyptian Love Songs*. Madison, WI: University of Wisconsin, 1985.

Murphy, Roland E. *The Song of Songs*. Hermeneia. Minneapolis: Fortress, 1990.

WISDOM

[see pages 899–924 of the Old Testament]

The Hellenization of the World

The last half of the fourth century BC saw rapid and sweeping changes in the ancient world. The conquests of Alexander the Great had brought the entire eastern world under the influence of Greek culture. This served to unify an otherwise diverse and disorganized world. It also threatened the integrity of other cultures and religious perspectives. With Alexander's death in 323 BC, the empire was divided among his followers, and three independent and mutually hostile kingdoms were formed. Two of these kingdoms played significant roles in the affairs of the Jewish nation. Ptolemy gained control of Egypt and established himself in Alexandria; Seleucus triumphed over Babylon and made Antioch his center. In its own way, each kingdom contributed to the shaping of biblical tradition.

The hellenization that was forced upon the Jewish community by the Seleucid ruler Antiochus Epiphanes was the background for the Jewish war of independence known as the Maccabean revolt (167–142 BC). This struggle is narrated in 1 and 2 Maccabees (see Reading Guides on Maccabees) and is the real context for the story found in the book of Daniel. The military and religious victory the Jewish people gained at this time is celebrated each year at the feast of Hanukkah.

The influence of the Ptolemies is more relevant to an understanding of the wisdom literature. It occurred earlier than that of the Seleucids and appears to have been quite well received. A large colony of Jews lived in Alexandria and accommodated itself to Greek language and culture. This was the group that translated its religious traditions from Hebrew into Greek, thus producing the basis of what has come to be known as the Septuagint (Latin for seventy, frequently designated LXX). A tradition grew up claiming that seventy scribes, working independent of each other, labored over the translation for seventy days in seventy different locations and produced identical versions. This marvel was seen as evidence of the inspired nature of the translation. Most likely the task took decades, but this fact did not detract from the reverence accorded the Septuagint over the years.

The Alexandrian or Greek version of the Scriptures was probably the one in popular use during the first century of the Christian era. During this same period, however, the Jewish community adopted the older Palestinian or Hebrew version as its official text. The Christian practice of adding its own writings to the collection may have contributed to this decision.

Christians continued to revere the Alexandrian tradition. In fact, by comparing the Old Testament citations used by New Testament writers, scholars conclude that a good number, if not most of them, come from the Alexandrian rather than from the earlier Palestinian version. At the time of the Reformation, the official version of the Old Testament became a point of disagreement among Christian denominations. Protestant churches retained the shorter Hebrew canon and thus preserve the more ancient Jewish version of the tradition. The Roman church accepted the wider Greek canon and thereby preserves an authentic early church tradition. The collection of those books not found within the Hebrew canon are called *deuterocanonical* (second-listing) by Roman Catholics and *apocryphal* (originally meaning "hidden," now understood as inspirational but not canonical) by Protestants. This explains why some Bibles include such books as Wisdom and Sirach, while others do not.

About the Book

Over the centuries this book has been called "The Book of Wisdom" (from the Latin translations), "The Wisdom of Solomon" (from the Septuagint), or variations of either title. Although the author does not explicitly identify himself as Solomon, the identification is implied in several first person references (7:5; 8:21; 9:7f; see 1 Kgs 3:5–15). This might be due to the author's presumption that the somewhat unconventional character of the book's ideas might require Solomonic authority to be accepted as orthodox teaching. (For an explanation of Solomonic authorship see Proverbs, RG 254; Ecclesiastes, RG 262; Song, RG 267, 270.)

The book itself suggests an origin from within the Jewish community of Alexandria. It is clear that the author was steeped in the history of the Exodus (11:2–16; 12:23–27; 16:2–19, 22), was acquainted with the religious practices of Egypt (15:14–16:1), and was well versed in Hellenistic philosophy and science (6:22–11:1). The author reinterpreted his own religious heritage and critiqued the traditions, practices, and insights of the other two cultures. He did this in an attempt to support those Jews who were questioning the relevance of their ancient faith in the face of the radical cultural changes they were undergoing.

Most scholars date this book somewhere around the turn of the era, during the first century BC. At this period of history, the primary threat did not arise from the hellenizing Greeks but from the hellenized Jews themselves. The oppression from outside the community that had led to the Maccabean revolt had given way to a subtle undermining of traditional teaching and values. Even the religious leaders were not immune to this kind of worldliness. The author appears to have been concerned that the pious not be led astray, that those enthralled by Greek culture be convinced of the excellence of the biblical heritage, and that those already carried away by the currents of change be rescued.

Literary features of the book confirm that it originated in Greek. The form of the language is natural and free-flowing, not awkward, as might be the case if this were a translation from Hebrew. The extensive scientific vocabulary reveals an author who possessed an exceptional comprehension of Hellenistic learning. References to earlier religious tradition correspond to the style of the Alexandrian rather than to that of the Palestinian version. The thought is similar to what is found in Jewish-Alexandrian works of this period. The author frequently employed a form of expression that resembles the diatribe, a method of argument developed by the Cynic and Stoic philosophers of Greece that creates imaginary opponents who raise questions that the philosopher refutes.

Despite these Greek characteristics, this is basically a Jewish work. It is not difficult to detect the influence of Hebrew parallelism in the poetry. (For an explanation of parallelism see Job, RG 238.) The description of God's care during the Exodus is a kind of homiletic *midrash* (a method of interpretation that the Jewish community devised in order to apply the Bible to new situations). Thus a law was restated as *halakah,* and a narrative is retold as *haggadah* in such a way as to give direction to a new generation. On the other hand, the Greeks, particularly Philo, developed allegory as a principal method of interpreting traditions. It is significant that the author of Wisdom employed midrash rather than allegory. This characteristic of the book further substantiates its Jewish, rather than Greek, origin.

The structure of Wisdom is a matter of dispute. There are not obvious divisions as can be found in some books of the wisdom tradition. The editors of the NAB have adopted a fairly general thematic division: (1) The Reward of Justice; (2) Praise of Wisdom by Solomon; (3) Special Providence of God during the Exodus.

Wisdom Teaching

The unifying theme of this biblical book is "the praise of wisdom." Each of the three major sections addresses this theme from its own distinctive point of view. A cursory examination of each section will highlight significant theological elements found there.

The Reward of Justice (1:1–6:21)

The first section is often called "The Book of Eschatology." (Traditionally, eschatology refers to the last or final things: the end of the age, death, judgment, reward, and punishment.) In it we find the destinies of the righteous and of the wicked described in vivid contrast. The former, regardless of their obvious suffering, "are in the hand of God" (3:1), while the latter "shall receive a punishment to match their thoughts" (3: 10). This entire section serves as a summons to fidelity to the religious traditions of Israel, a fidelity that will guarantee the rewards of wisdom.

At first glance this teaching might seem to be merely a restatement of the doctrine of retribution. A closer look will show that it is instead a radical departure from the traditional understanding. The author not only challenged some traditional views but also introduced several radically new ideas. First, he insisted that childlessness, a condition that by itself brought reproach in ancient society (see Gn 16:4; 1 Sm 1:7) is not a mark of divine displeasure (3:13f; 4:1). Regardless of the importance of offspring for the survival of the race, moral not physical fruitfulness is emphasized here.

The author further denied that suffering itself presupposes sin. In fact, an untimely death may be a righteous person's rescue from the wickedness of life (4:14). We are reminded of the adage: The good die young. This author agreed with both Job and Qoheleth that virtue is not always rewarded in this life, nor is evil always punished. He went on to suggest, however, that whoever thinks that the death of the righteous is affliction or destruction is foolish (3:2f). Such death is, rather, a trial that they must endure in order to be with God (3:5f).

It is in this book that the reader of the Old Testament is first introduced to the Greek concept *psyche* (soul, 1:11; 3:1). Although in some passages the word is used with the same meaning as the Hebrew *nephesh* (being or life, 12:6; 14:5; 16:9), in other places it clearly marks the adoption of the body-soul dualism, which was part of the Greek understanding of human nature. The Greeks held that human nature was a combination of an impermanent material body and an eternal spiritual soul. This combination was dissolved at death. Caution is in order here. We must be careful not to take accommodation to Greek thought farther than the author did. Nowhere does this book speak of an immortal soul.

A second and related idea is that of life after death. This notion is quite different from the earlier perceptions of Sheol, the abode of the dead (see Psalms, RG 250). There is just enough ambiguity in the use of the words "immortality" (3:4; 4:1; 8:13, 17; 15:3) and "incorruptibility" (2:23; 6:18f) to prevent us from making too many definite statements about the author's view. One thing does seem clear, however. Immortality is not an inherent quality of human nature; it is the fruit of union with wisdom (8:13, 17; 15:3). Although 2:23 claims that God made humans to be incorruptible (imperishable), 6:18 suggests that incorruptibility is contingent upon fidelity to wisdom. We are not sure whether the author was speaking merely of physical death, or of physical death followed by spiritual death, or of spiritual death alone. The thought does seem to pass over physical death, and attention is directed toward spiritual death. Later in history, Saint Paul will have to face this same question when dealing with the unexpected deaths of Christians (1 Thes 4:13–18). Unlike the author of Wisdom, his answer will be quite specific.

Finally, the author of the book of Wisdom brought the two earlier creation narratives together and reinterpreted them. The statement about being made in God's image (2:23), an allusion to Genesis 1:16, 28, is followed by the claim that the devil's envy brought death into the world (2:24), a reinterpretation of Genesis 3. (A few commentators believe that the latter reference is to the envy of Cain, which resulted in the death of Abel [Gn 4:1–8]. However, in a non-biblical Jewish text, another writer of this time stated that Gadreel, a fallen angel, led Eve astray [1 Enoch 69:6]. This latter citation supports the interpretation offered here.) The author of Wisdom was the first biblical writer to identify the serpent of the Genesis account with the devil.

Praise of Wisdom by Solomon (6:22–11:1)

The second major section of the book is an address acclaiming the glories of wisdom. It is from this section that the book receives its name, and it is here that we find a representation of personified Wisdom (see Proverbs, RG 260). This characterization of Wisdom is quite different from that found in the earlier tradition. The author may have realized the unconventional nature of his depiction and felt that claiming Solomonic authority would be necessary in order to gain acceptance for this reinterpretation. At any rate, this section begins with an account of his own humble origin, his prayer for wisdom, and God's bestowal of this immeasurable gift in answer to his pleading (7:1–7; also see 9:1–18). This is unquestionably an allusion to the prayer of Solomon (1 Kgs 3:5–15), and it characterizes the author as the wise king.

The actual description of Wisdom is composed of elements from various sources: Israelite tradition (7:22a; see Prv 8:30); from the cult of the Egyptian deity Isis, goddess of wisdom and patron of culture, whose praises were extolled in the form of listings similar to that found in 7:22–8:1; and from Hellenistic philosophy and science (see 8:7 for mention of the cardinal virtues of Plato). This section may well be the heart of the author's argument in favor of the superiority of the religion of Israel.

Earlier traditions spoke of "a spirit of wisdom" (Is 11:2), but here Wisdom itself is called a spirit (1:6; 7:22). The author has brought two quite distinct and dissimilar concepts together by merging the notion of intelligence, the basic meaning of wisdom, with that of energy or power, the central idea in spirit. Having done this, he could then speak of the wisdom-spirit as "an aura of the might of God" (Wis 7:25). It is in this book that Wisdom is referred to as "the spirit of the LORD" (1:7). (The theology in this verse functions significantly in the liturgy of Pentecost.) Although spirit played a major role in Stoic philosophy, it was clearly a prominent theme in Jewish tradition as well. In his description of the nature and dignity of Wisdom (7:22–24), the author may well have employed the attributes of the world spirit, a concept found in Stoic philosophy. However, when he recounted the early history of Israel he equated Wisdom with the spirit of the Lord. He did this by ascribing to Wisdom what earlier Israelite writers attributed to the spirit of the Lord: the creative power in the world (7:22a; see Jdt 16: 14); the source of Joseph's honor in Egypt (10:13; see Gn 41:38); the inspiration that prepared Moses for the Exodus and led the people through the wilderness (10:16f; see Is 63:11, 14).

There has been a significant amount of discussion regarding the influence of this figure of Wisdom on New Testament writings. Some scholars believe that the influence was direct. Others hold that the obvious similarities suggest that there was a general treasury of thought, imagery, and language that served as a common source. Whichever position is more accurate, early Christian theologians reinterpreted the figure of personified Wisdom as they struggled to understand Jesus the Christ. Paul explicitly referred to Christ as the wisdom of God (1 Cor 1: 24,30). The most obvious example of this reinterpretation, however, is found in the Gospel according to John. There we find Jesus described in ways that Wisdom had been depicted earlier: as being with God in the beginning before the world existed (Jn 1:1; 17:5; see Wis 2:22); as sent from heaven to accomplish the will of God (Jn 6: 38; see Wis 9:10). Current scholarship is only beginning to pursue the implications of Wisdom imagery for Christology.

This section of the book ends with a summary of the way that Wisdom guided the ancestors of Israel, brought them out of Egypt, and, through the agency of Moses (see Hos 12:14), enabled them to prosper (10:1–11:1). It is clear that this Wisdom, once thought to be the possession of the king, was now considered the constant companion of true Israelites, those faithful ones of the past as well as the committed Jews of the present.

Special Providence of God during the Exodus (11:2–19:22)

Here the book shows an observable shift in focus. The poem in praise of Wisdom gives way to midrash that extols the ancestral God of Israel. This version of the experience of the Exodus and the time in the wilderness illustrates two points: (1) the sufferings that befell the Egyptians were the direct result of their sinfulness (11:16); and (2) the very elements that afflicted the Egyptians benefited the Israelites (11:5). This rereading of the past is done through a creative selection of biblical data as well as the addition of material not found elsewhere. The author did not set out to recount historical facts or to repeat traditional testimonies. He seemed intent on addressing the challenge raised by Hellenism. His goal was to remind Alexandrian Jews that once before they had suffered at the hands of the Egyptians and, in the face of impossible odds, had been rescued. This midrash provides "historical" basis for continued trust in the God of Israel.

There are two digressions within this third division of the book. Both of them are found in the second example of God's providence. The first is a testimony to God's mercy (11:17–12:22). Although it breaks the midrashic line of thought, it may have been prompted by the mention of punishment in the preceding line (11:16). The second digression is a condemnation of idolatry (13: 1–15:17). It follows the claim that the Egyptians "saw and recognized the true God whom before they had refused to know" (12:27), yet they continued in their idolatry. It should be noted that the language used in the condemnation of nature worship (13:1–9) might be the best example of the author's broad grasp of scientific knowledge.

Theology in a New Context

The author of Wisdom did not set out in search of new theological insights. Since he was committed to prove the enduring value of the religion of

Israel, he explained traditions and themes that were familiar to the Jews of his day. What made his contribution unique was the method that he employed as he went about his task. He incorporated elements of other cultures into this theological thinking.

Throughout its history, Israel had been forced by circumstances to deal with the religious and cultural traditions of other societies. The Bible itself shows that these encounters were sometimes peaceful and beneficial, and at other times violent and destructive. Whatever the situation may have been, elements from those cultures found their way into the traditions of Israel. The religion of Israel reinterpreted features of the other cultures and then assimilated these new ideas into its own perspective. Israel seldom assumed the fundamental religious worldview of the other culture. This changed with the hellenization of the world. It was precisely the attraction of Greek civilization that threatened Jewish faith. Now the community wrestled with an agonizing dilemma: Could one accept the prevailing culture and remain faithful to the traditions of the ancestors? The author of Wisdom undertook the task of answering this question in the affirmative. In doing so, he did not try to reconcile Judaism with Hellenism. Instead, he used the ideas, the language, and the literary style of Greek culture to demonstrate the excellence of the Jewish faith.

In taking Greek culture seriously, this theologian did what theologians after him would have to do whenever cultural lines were crossed. The challenge of interpretation facing him was not so different from the one facing us today; that is, to render a religious heritage that originated in one cultural context into another very different one. The purpose of the author of the book of Wisdom was apologetic. He sought to defend his ancestral faith. Our purpose in reinterpretation is usually evangelical. We seek to proclaim the word of God in a variety of contexts. In this we have much to learn from both the message of this wisdom teacher and from his method of theological reinterpretation.

FURTHER READING

Collins, John J. *Jewish Wisdom in the Hellenistic Age.* Louisville: Westminster John Knox, 1997.

Kolarcik, Michael. *The Book of Wisdom.* New Interpreter's Bible 5, 435–600. Nashville: Abingdon Press, 1997. Fine literary and theological commentary.

Winston, David. *The Wisdom of Solomon.* Anchor Bible 43. New York: Doubleday, 1979.

SIRACH (ECCLESIASTICUS)

[see pages 924–986 of the Old Testament]

About the Book

Over the years the book of Sirach has been known by different names: "The Wisdom of Jesus Ben Sira"; "The Book of Sirach" (Sirach is a shortened form of the Greek *Sirachides,* grandson of Sira); "Ecclesiasticus" (from the Latin for book of the church, a designation that probably stems from its frequent use as a catechetical aid in the early centuries of the Western Church).

Sirach is the only biblical book that identifies its author (50:27), refers to its translator (a grandson of the Ben Sira), and dates its translation ("the thirty-eighth year of the reign of King Euergetes," sometime after 132 BC—information found in the foreword). Although the prophetic books claim not only to have originated from specific prophets and to locate the ministry of those prophets during the reigns of specific kings (for example, Hos 1:1; Is 1:1; Jer 1:2f; etc.), the references there are to prophetic activity and not to the books that bear the names of the prophets. Here we have a clear reference to literary activity.

The foreword also provides us with some interesting information about the composition of the biblical canon (the official list of inspired books). Three times the grandson of Ben Sira speaks of "the law, the prophets, and the later authors" (or "the rest of the books"). This reference tells us that by the second century BC the Jewish community already had what has come to be known as a tripartite (three-part) Bible. Scholars believe that the first two parts (the Law and the Prophets) most likely included the books as we have them today. The third part (the Writings) was probably quite fluid until well into the Christian era.

Like the book of Wisdom, Sirach belongs to the collection called *deuterocanonical* by Roman Catholics or *apocryphal* by Protestants (see Wisdom, RG 272). The foreword, which is considered historical introduction and not inspired instruction, recounts the translator's arrival in Egypt, where he discovered that the Jews' "valuable teaching" had been translated from Hebrew into Greek, the language of the day. This inspired him to undertake the translation of his own grandfather's teachings. The Hebrew version from which he worked seems to have dropped out of sight until copies of it were found in 1896.

It is not clear why the Jews did not accept Sirach as canonical. Some commentators offer a twofold reason: (1) Ben Sira was interested in the Temple and the cult (concerns of a first-century AD group called Sadducees); and (2) he did not seem to believe in the resurrection of the body (a position held by a rival religious group of the first century called the Pharisees). Therefore the Pharisaic rabbis who decided on the canon rejected Sirach. Whatever the case may have been, its absence from the Jewish list explains its exclusion from the Protestant canon.

The manner in which the high priest Simon is described (50:1–21) leads one to conclude that he had only recently died. This would locate the writing of the original Hebrew version of Sirach sometime during the first quarter of the second century (200–175 BC). The description of Simon's priestly performance suggests that the author was quite familiar with the Jerusalem ritual. Perhaps he was even a resident of the city. Many commentators believe that Jerusalem was in fact the place of the book's composition.

The book appears to be a collection of proverbs organized in such a way as to resemble short essays. While there is no explicit arrangement in the book itself, one can divide the material both thematically and according to literary form. Chapters 1 through 43 principally deal with moral instruction, a characteristic that Sirach has in common with the rest of the wisdom literature. This first section can be further subdivided into two parts, each of which is introduced by a poem praising wisdom (see 1:1–29 and 24:1–31). The entire first section ends with a poem extolling God's activity in nature (42:15–43:35). The poems that acclaim time-honored heroes of Israel (44:1–49:16) and the high priest Simon (50:1–24) are followed by a kind of epilogue, which contains a denunciation of some of the traditional enemies of Israel and a subscription identifying the author (50:25–29). The book closes with two appendices: a psalm of thanksgiving for deliverance from danger (51:1–12); and a personal testimony in the form of an acrostic poem (51:13–30; see Psalms, RG 245).

The Reason for Writing

The hellenization of the Near East had already taken hold among the educated upper classes by the time Ben Sira put his teachings into writing (see Wisdom, RG 272). Many Jews must have wondered whether their ancient traditions could match the comprehension and depth of Greek thought. Being a well-traveled man (34:11), Ben Sira would have witnessed the decline in fervor that overtook his coreligionists. Being an observant Jew, he would have been greatly troubled by this. It seems clear that his object in writing was to show the Jews of his day that real wisdom was to be found in the traditions of Israel and not in the godless Greek philosophy of the day. He intended his work to be a comprehensive authoritative reference wherein could be found guidance and instruction for every circumstance of life.

Ben Sira exhorted his readers to study the ancient traditions to find there the kind of direction needed to cope with their new and challenging situation (2:10). He warned against trying to live according to the standards of both Judaism and Hellenism (2:12), and he condemned those who chose the latter over the former (2:13f). Using a traditional wisdom figure of speech (those who fear the Lord), he identified the wise as those who were faithful to the religion of Israel (2:15–17). While the content of most of his wisdom teaching is quite conventional, the way Ben Sira blended it with Israel's history, and its legal and cultic traditions is distinctive. Earlier wisdom writing showed little interest in specifically Israelite matters. Ben Sira claimed that true wisdom resides in Israel (24:1–21), and later he used history to support this claim (44:1–49:16). He identified Wisdom with the Law of

Moses (24:22), and in that way he accorded the Law of Moses a place of honor above the traditions of other cultures. Unlike other wisdom teachers, he demonstrated a profound concern for the cult and the role of the priesthood (46: 6–20; 47:12f; 50:1–21). All of this was, no doubt, Ben Sira's way of arguing in favor of fidelity to Judaism.

If we are correct in determining the date of the translation, the final form of this book probably appeared after the Maccabean revolt but before the writing of the Wisdom of Solomon. Such historical reconstruction will help us to see how Israel's response to Hellenism varied with time. Ben Sira did not make accommodations to the process of hellenization to the extent that the author of Wisdom did. If "traditionalist" means maintaining unchanged the answers of the past because they alone are adequate to meet the problems of the present, then Ben Sira can be called "traditionalist" in his response to Hellenism.

Wisdom Teaching

In many ways the teaching of Ben Sira resembles that of the book of Proverbs. Its primary focus is moral guidance. The book lends itself to being an instructional manual containing maxims, many of which are grouped according to topic. The result is a series of short essays addressing topics such as duties toward God, toward one's parents, and toward rulers. There are instructions on how to train children, how to choose friends, and how to guard one's speech. There are warnings against excess, sloth, and foolishness. Whatever one needs to succeed in life, while at the same time remaining faithful to the traditions of the elders, is addressed in the instructional section of this book.

Sirach is also like Proverbs in its celebration of the glories of personified Wisdom (chapters 1 and 24). It is distinctive, however, in the way it takes this characterization a step further than did the earlier work. Here we see Wisdom searching for a place to dwell and finally pitching her tent in Jerusalem. Allusions to this poetic characterization can be found in the prologue to the Gospel of John where the Word, present with God from the beginning and involved in the creation of all things, "pitched his tent among us" (Jn 1:1–14).

Ben Sira's poems describing the role of divine wisdom in creation (16:22–17:18; 39:12–35; 42:15–43:35) are really commentaries on the opening chapters of Genesis. The rather technical way he developed his thought shows us the extent to which Ben Sira was influenced by the scientific knowledge of his day.

This book contains some of the harshest statements about women found anywhere in the Bible. Proverbs may have warned the naive youth to beware of wily and seductive women, but this author seems to speak disparagingly against women in general. Ben Sira is the one who blames woman for sin and death (25:23). It is further apparent that he expected wives to be subservient to their husbands, for he seems to advocate punishment, even including divorce, if they refuse to obey (25:24f). Perhaps the worst example of this misogyny is found in the description of the unwed daughter (42:9–14). The author clearly considers her a liability, and his concern is exclusively with the reputation of the father.

The author holds a thoroughly traditional view of retribution (4:11–19; 7:1–3; 16:1–21; 21:1–10). The possibility of rewards or punishments after death does not seem to have been considered by this wisdom teacher (14:15–19). He counsels mourning at the death of another, but he admonishes his reader to moderation even in the acceptable expression of grief. The reason why the display should be temperate is that the dead are dead, and nothing can be changed by uncontrolled sorrow (38:1–23).

While this view of life and death may have been in agreement with earlier notions of retribution, it was clearly not universally held in Israel at this time. Hope of reward after death for fidelity during persecution is found in other writings of this period (for example, Dn 12:1–3; 2 Mc 7:9,23,29). Although Ben Sira probably lived before the Maccabean revolt (events surrounding this period are recorded in the other books mentioned above), his grandson-translator certainly lived after the rebellion, and he upheld Ben Sira's traditional view.

Ben Sira's adherence to the traditional notion of retribution and its consequent rejection of any notion of life after death, coupled with his support of the priesthood and interest in the cult, have prompted many interpreters to regard him as a Proto-Sadducee. Although Sadducees as a group probably did not yet exist until after the Maccabean revolt, many of the theological views found in this book were eventually adopted by this aristocratic priestly party.

The Influence of Sirach

Since the New Testament writers seem to have preferred the Alexandrian Bible, it is not surprising that the influence of Sirach can be detected in some of their writings. The Letter of James is a clear example of this. Both books address questions of pride (Sir 10:7; Jas 4:6) and humility (Sir 3:18; Jas 1:9), of rich and poor (Sir 10:19–24; Jas 2:1–6), and of true wisdom (Sir 19:17–21; Jas 3:13–17), to name but a few examples. There are also obvious parallels between directives found in Sirach and those found in the Gospels. This includes teaching on magnanimity (Sir 29:12; Mt 6:19) and forgiveness (Sir 28:2; Mk 11:25) and against placing false hopes in possessions (Sir 11:18f; Lk 12:16–21).

While the canonical status of Sirach was and remains a question for debate, from the time of its appearance it has exerted significant influence in both the Jewish and the Christian communities. Over the years it has served as a kind of handbook of practical ethics, and its teachings can be found in the liturgical texts of both religious groups. The discovery at Qumran of a scroll of Ben Sira is evidence that the book was widely known before the turn of the era. It also appears in copies of liturgical scrolls that were read in synagogues around the tenth century AD. Finally, the book is also quoted at least once in the Talmud. The early church theologians Cyprian (third century AD) and Jerome (fourth century AD) attest to Christian use of the book. Clement of Alexandria (second century AD) quotes it so often that his citations have come to be considered an authoritative version of the text. This controversial book continues to exercise its influence even today. Passages from Sirach are used as lectionary readings. For many, perhaps most, Catholics, the liturgical celebration is their primary exposure to the Bible. Within this context the teachings of Ben Sira continue to exhort hearers to fidelity to the tradition and to upright moral living.

It is interesting to note that in response to the Vatican document *Decree on the Training of Priests* (16), moral theologians are reexamining the moral instructions found in Scripture. They do not turn there in search of ageless answers to contemporary questions but in an attempt to discover how moral decisions were made in the past. Biblical specialists provide them with insights into the manner in which writers, especially the teachers of wisdom, brought the time-honored religious tradition to bear on new situations. The book of Sirach, with its essaylike instruction, remains a source of information in this area. It opens a window into a community struggling with its identity as it finds itself at the crossroads of traditional religion and contemporary culture. Sirach and Wisdom provide us with two ways of responding to this challenge. While we may not be able to follow their specific advice, we can learn from their example ways of reinterpreting the tradition creatively, while at the same time remaining loyal to its revelatory message.

FURTHER READING

Collins, John J. *Jewish Wisdom in the Hellenistic Age*, 21–111. Louisville: Westminster, 1997.

———. *The Wisdom of Jesus Son of Sirach*. The Oxford Bible Commentary, 667–98. Edited by J. Barton and J. Muddiman. Oxford: Oxford University Press, 2001.

Crenshaw, James L. *The Book of Sirach*. New Interpreter's Bible 5, 603–867. Nashville: Abingdon Press, 1997. Excellent theological commentary.

Skehan, P. W., and A. A. DiLella. *The Wisdom of Ben Sira*. Anchor Bible 39. New York: Doubleday, 1987.

THE MAJOR PROPHETS, BARUCH, AND LAMENTATIONS

RICHARD J. CLIFFORD

ISAIAH

[see pages 929–1071 of the Old Testament]

In the Jewish Bible (Tanakh), Isaiah, Jeremiah, Ezekiel, and "the Twelve" (the Minor Prophets) are in the second section, which is called "The Latter Prophets." Together with "The Former Prophets" (Joshua to Kings), they come after the Pentateuch (Torah), and before the Writings. Jews regard the Latter Prophets primarily as expositors of the instructions and laws contained in the Torah. The Christian Bible, in contrast, places the Prophets in the third and concluding section of the Old Testament (after the historical and wisdom books), a position that links the prophetic books directly to the New Testament and emphasizes the prophets as heralds of the last days, the time of Jesus Christ. Both Jewish and Christian understandings of prophecy prize the book of Isaiah, for it insists equally on exclusive faith in God (e.g., 7:1–9; 28:14–22) and social justice (e.g., 5:1–24), and it instills hope for a renewed Zion and Davidic king (8:23–9:6; 11:1–9).

The book of Isaiah contains a wide variety of styles and material. Chapters 1 through 39 blend denunciations of Zion and Judah, promises of blessings, announcements of interventions ("judgments") of God, oracles about foreign nations, and narratives about the prophet. The dominant foreign nation threatening Israel is Assyria. Chapters 40 through 55 are quite different. They contain no narratives, denunciations, or prophetic biography, but they have carefully crafted speeches announcing forgiveness of sins to the exiles in Babylonia and inviting them to return to Zion. The dominant foreign nations in these chapters are Babylon and Persia (Cyrus in 44:28; 45:1,13 is the king of Persia). Chapters 56 through 66 are also distinctive. They presume an audience that is back in Zion and intent on rebuilding itself; criticisms and promises center on Zion, and some sections (e.g., 56:1–6; 60–62; 65–66) deliberately refer back to chapters 1 through 39. This section contains no prophetic biography nor does it mention any dominant foreign power. Like chapters 40 through 55, no author is mentioned. From these and other data, biblical scholarship from the late eighteenth century forward has come to agree there are "three Isaiahs" in the sense of three distinct sections: Chapters 1 through 39 preserve the preaching and deeds of Isaiah of Jerusalem of the late eighth century (though the editing of these chapters is later); chapters 40 through 55 interpret the Isaian legacy for exiles in the mid-sixth century; and chapters 56 through 66 interpret the same legacy for the rebuilding of Zion. Scholars conventionally refer to the three sections as First, Second, and Third Isaiah, though it is possible there were actually only two prophets. It is possible that "Second Isaiah" was the author of chapters 56 through 66 as well as of chapters 40 through 55. Over the last four decades, study of the book of Isaiah has taken a new turn. Without abandoning the views sketched above, scholars have turned their interest to the book of Isaiah as a unified literary work and are concerned with the way that its three sections relate to each other.

The following pages will discuss the historical background, literary structure, and message of the three sections, and then will give an overall view of the book.

Isaiah of Jerusalem (First Isaiah)

Historical Background of First Isaiah

Why did the writing prophets, Hosea, Amos, and Isaiah, appear in the mid-eighth century? Although a complete explanation is not possible, two significant ones are the emergence of Assyria as a superpower, and gross inequalities in the society of the time, especially concerning land tenure. Israel's enemies in the previous century, the ninth-century Aramean city-states to the north such as Damascus and Hamath, were more or less on a par with Israel; it was possible to mount a defense against them and go to war with some hope of victory. In the first half of the eighth century, the Arameans were in decline, which enabled the two halves of the divided kingdom, Israel in the north and Judah in the south, to flourish. The Neo-Assyrian Empire revived in the mid-eighth century, however, and turned its gaze to the eastern coastlands of the Mediterranean (the Levant). For the next two hundred years Assyria dominated the Levant, though the quality of its presence varied according to the strength of individual kings. Assyrian pressure destabilized the Northern Kingdom of Israel (a process recorded by Hosea). In 722 Shalmaneser V (728–722) conquered Samaria, the capital of the Northern Kingdom (Israel), though Sargon falsely claimed credit; and the Northern Kingdom was divided into Assyrian provinces (2 Kgs 17; 18:1–12). Judah had to play thereafter the role of loyal vassal, although it did on occasion join with neighboring states and with Egypt against Assyria, most notably against Sennacherib in 701. Despite these occasional forays, the Southern Kingdom managed to retain its vassal status, chiefly by paying large tribute to the Assyrians.

For the prophet Isaiah, the Assyrian presence in the holy land of Israel provoked a major crisis. Unlike Egyptian and Aramean forays in Palestine in previous centuries, Assyria was a superpower against which no state in the Levant could possibly defend itself. So invincible was Assyria that its presence in the holy land called into question the sacred story that Israel lived by. In one version of that story, Israel had been rescued from Pharaoh's dominion in Egypt and led through the wilderness to the Lord's own land there to enjoy his protection and nurture (e.g., Pss 44; 78; 105; 136). Another version, used by Isaiah, focused on Zion (another name for Jerusalem), which was regarded as unconquerable as befitted the dwelling of the Lord. In Zion reigned the Lord's lieutenant on earth, the Davidic king, dispensing divine blessings and protection upon the land. Mighty Assyria bestriding the land seemed to invalidate the symbols of Zion and the king and the story told about them. In response to this crisis of meaning, Isaiah offered an interpretation of the tradition: far from being a violator of a holy place, he asserted, the Assyrian king had been invited by the Lord to punish Israel for its unjust behavior (10:5–19). In due course, Assyria would be punished for its excesses, but now Judah must regard the Assyrian king as carrying out the judgment of the Lord. In putting forth this viewpoint to his contemporaries, Isaiah met strong resistance. To publicize his view and make it available to the next generation, Isaiah wrote his message down: "The record is to be folded and the sealed instruction kept among my disciples. For I will trust in the LORD, who is hiding his face from the house of Jacob; yes, I will wait for him. . . . And when they say to you, 'Inquire of mediums and fortune-tellers (who chirp and mutter!); should not a people inquire of their gods, apply to the dead on behalf of the living?'—then this document will furnish its instruction" (Is 8:16–20).

The second historical factor in the rise of writing prophets was the increase of cruel and violent behavior among the people, which was especially directed against the poor. Though direct evidence of the condition of Israelite society is scarce, the prophets speak with such a unified voice about the inequality and social abuses that one must conclude such behavior was rampant. Isaiah goes so far as to speak in God's name to reject sacrifice until justice is done for the poor (1:12–16). He is scathing against those who form estates from land seized from the poor (5: 8–10) and against those whose wealth made them arrogant (5:11–12). The people's unequal access to the land provoked a crisis in the ancient traditions no less troubling to faithful Israelites than that caused by the Assyrian threat. In both cases, the people were unable to enjoy the fruits of the land that, according to their sacred traditions, the Lord owned and had given them for their use. Leviticus 25:23 stated the ideal with unmistakable clarity: "The land shall not be sold in perpetuity; for the land is mine, and you are but aliens who have become my tenants." Isaiah's interpretation is that Zion (which in his thinking seems to stand for the holy land) would have to be purged to restore its original purity (e.g., 1:21–28; 28:1–8) and that Assyria was to be the instrument of purgation.

Several major interactions between Israel/Judah and the Assyrian Empire are reflected in the book of Isaiah. In his first western campaign, 743–738, the Assyrian king Tiglath-pileser III (745–728) crushed a coalition of Hamath and northern coastal cities led by King Uzziah of Judah. Subsequently, there were three important periods of conflict between the two states, the first being the Syro-Ephraimite War (735–732) in which Damascus ("Syro-") and Israel ("Ephraimite") attempted to force King Ahaz of Judah to join their coalition against Assyria. Ahaz refused (chapter 7), called in Assyria to defend Judah, being happy, it seems, to enjoy some of the privileges of being a vassal of a great empire. Damascus and Israel failed in their war against Assyria, and the Northern Kingdom regions of Megiddo, Dor, and Gilead became Assyrian provinces (8:23–9:6).

A second period of conflict between Assyria and Judah came in 715–705 when King Hezekiah of Judah made several attempts to join anti-Assyrian alliances, notably a rebellion in the Philistine city of Ashdod in 713–711 (Is 20:1–6; 18:1–19:15; 14:28–32). The third period was in 701 when Hezekiah revolted against Sennacherib, assuming leadership of an alliance consisting of Phoenicia, Philistia, and Egypt. Sennacherib of Assyria marched west, pacified Phoenicia and Philistia without difficulty, and defeated Egyptian troops of Shabaka at Elteqeh. Hezekiah sued for peace (22:9–11). Isaiah 36 through 38 refers to the same events, although it contains a legendary section that complicates interpretation. Most probably 2 Kings 18:13–16 is a factual chronicle, to which a legendary account (2 Kgs 18:17–19:37) was appended.

Literary Structure

Most scholars regard chapter 1 as an introduction of the main themes of the whole book: imminent divine judgment, the necessity of social justice, and the painful process that transforms Zion into a holy and righteous city. Chapter 39, at the other end, seems to be an editorial transition to chapters 40 through 55, hinting at Judean arrogance that will eventually lead to the Babylonian captivity. Chapters 2 through 12, mainly concerned with the Syro-Ephraimite War (735–732), clearly form a unit. Built around a core, chapters 6 through 9 narrate the commission of Isaiah, King Ahaz's refusal to believe, and further threats and promises. This unit ends with a thanksgiving (chapter 12) that anticipates the salvation of Zion. Chapters 13 through 23, containing oracles concerning foreign nations, conclude with the upholding of Zion and punishing of the city that is counter to Zion (24–27). Chapters 28 through 33 blend denunciations and promises concerning Zion; chapters 34–35 describe the Day of the Lord and healing of nature in the style of Second Isaiah; and chapters 36–38 are a third-person narrative about the prophet and King Hezekiah in the Assyrian crisis of 701.

Lawrence Boadt has suggested that the editors arranged the three blocks, 2 to 12, 13 to 33, and 34 to 38, into three stages in order to make Isaiah's preaching applicable to later audiences. Each of the three stages displays a tripartite or ABC pattern: the Day of the Lord (appearance of the Lord as a warrior), human response, and divine act. The appearance of the Lord (A) invites a response by the people or the king (B), which is followed by (C) a divine intervention implementing justice. The pattern makes it possible for any reader of the Isaiah scroll to experience the powerful coming of the Lord and to respond accordingly. Thanks to the ABC structure, later readers of Isaiah are at no disadvantage compared to the original listeners or readers. The following four paragraphs suggest how the ABC pattern operates in chapters 2 through 38.

The pattern is clearest in Stage 1 (2–12). It should be noted that the opening scene (2:1–5)—Jerusalem as the preeminent place of instruction and the goal of the nations' pilgrimage—falls outside the pattern. Its function in the book is to introduce the pilgrimage to Zion that is such an important motif in the book. The procession to Zion comes to a preliminary conclusion in chapter 12 and to a final conclusion in chapters 60 to 62 and 56 to 66.

The tripartite pattern of 2:6–22 actually begins with the Day of the Lord "against all that is proud and arrogant, all that is high" in v. 12. The Day of the Lord section ends positively with a promise of glory for Zion (4:2–6). The B section of the pattern (5:1–9:6) can be subtitled "rebelliousness and its royal example." It indicts the people for unjust conduct, shows the commissioning of Isaiah and his condemnation of King Ahaz for refusing to trust in God's promises to defend Zion and thus protect the king. The chapters go on to promise a better king (8:23–9:6). Salvation is impeded, but not ended, by the king's disbelief. The C section (9:7–12:6) can be titled "sin, judgment, and restoration of Zion." It begins with a condemnation of the people (9:7–10:4), tells of the choosing of Assyria as the punisher who will be punished later on (10:5–34), gives a promise of a better king (11), and concludes with an anticipatory thanksgiving (12).

Stage 2 (13 through 33) also displays the tripartite pattern. It begins with the dramatic depiction of the Day of the Lord (against Babylon) in chapter 13. Denunciations of other foreign nations follow; Assyria, Egypt, Moab, Damascus (and Jerusalem) are severely chastised for not accepting the sovereign design of the Lord. The mention of "Babylon" in chapter 13 raises difficulties to First Isaian authorship, for Babylon was Israel's enemy in the late seventh and sixth centuries, not the eighth century. The occurrences of "Babylon" elsewhere in the section (14:2 and 22, and 21:9) are not problematic, for 14:2 and 22 are in the frame of the poem (where they could have been added later), not in the body of the poem; Isaiah 21:9 ("fallen is Babylon, and all the images of her gods") can refer to Assyria's documented destruction of Babylonian images in 689. To explain the occurrence of "Babylon" in chapter 13, several solutions have been proposed: (1) Chapter 13 was written in the seventh or sixth century when Babylon was the world power and inserted when the entire scroll was edited in the sixth or fifth century (the majority view); (2) Babylon referred to in chapter 13 is turn-of-the-eighth-century Babylon under Merodach-baladan, which rebelled against Assyria, and had to be recaptured at least four times (in 708, 703, 700, and 689); and (3) Isaiah 13:1–14:27 was originally written against Assyria by First Isaiah and later editors inserted Babylon in the sixth century. The last solution is the most probable since Assyria and Babylon, both great empires, became symbols of organized hostility to God; their names became virtually interchangeable as proverbial enemies of God.

Chapters 24 through 27 seem to stand apart from the rest of First Isaiah. Scholars sometimes entitle them "The Isaiah Apocalypse," but the name is unsatisfactory. The chapters speak of universal destruction and then speak of two cities: one the city of God, and the other a city opposed to God. Lack of specific references make interpretation of these chapters tentative. The chapters are perhaps best understood as the conclusion to chapters 13 through 23, generalizing the particular descriptions in the earlier chapters. Evidently, chapters 24 through 27 conclude the oracles against the foreign nations by showing the universal and timeless outreach of the Lord. The sovereignty of God encompasses the nations of the world. At any rate, in the tripartite editing, the chapters vividly portray the Day of the Lord.

The B section in Stage 2 appears in chapters 28 through 31, which contain examples of sinful alliances (especially on the part of the Northern Kingdom, called Ephraim). Judah is no better than her northern sister, the text asserts, yet the promises concerning Zion invite the people to repent. Section C (32–33) gives assurances that Assyria will be destroyed in the end and that an obedient king will be part of the new order for Israel.

Stage 3 (34 through 38), like the other two stages, begins with the Day of the Lord that punishes the wicked (in this case Edom as the representative of Israel's enemies) and upholds the faithful who return to Zion (34 through 35). The latter chapters employ components familiar from the pattern: the inevitable defeat of Assyrian arrogance, the king who responds for the people (unlike Ahaz, Hezekiah trusts), and Zion's salvation. This time, however, salvation is immediate and not postponed to the future. Hezekiah turns to the Lord fully, and his trust makes him a model for all the people.

The Theology of First Isaiah: the Plan of the Lord

Of the many possible ways of approaching the theology of Isaiah of Jerusalem, one of the most fruitful is to examine his understanding of the Lord's "plan" or "work." There are many synonyms for the divine plan or work in Isaiah and in Second Isaiah: "work, deeds" (5:12; 41:4; 45:11) "thoughts (plans)" (55:8–9), the phrase "the Lord was pleased to . . ." (42:21; 53:10), "deed" (5:19; 28:21), "word" (e.g., 2:3; 5:24; 30:12; 44:26). The most illuminating Isaian word, however, is "plan," which the prophet uses both as a noun and a verb. The best illustration of "plan" is 5:19, which attacks those who deny the Lord is acting in the present crisis, "those who say, 'Let [the Lord] make haste and speed his *work,* that we may see it; on with the *plan* of the Holy One of Israel! let it come to pass, that we may know it!' " In Isaiah, words for "plan" or "work" are used in two different contexts: (1) for God's plan that will inevitably be realized and (2) for human plans or works that will inevitably fail. An example of the second usage is 8:10, addressed to the hostile nations: "Form a plan, and it shall be thwarted; make a resolve, and it shall not be carried out, for 'With us is God!' " (cf. 19:3, 11). The passage shows that the prophet believes, contrary to the people, that the Lord has a plan for Israel and the nations, and he, Isaiah, is to announce it and help the people respond positively to it. The divine plan is clear in Isaiah: Israel's social injustice has necessitated divine judgment with the goal of renewal, and it will be carried out by Assyria. Later, Assyria will be punished for its excesses and arrogance. Judah and Zion must respond with openness and trust in the Lord's promises concerning Zion and the Davidic king. The plan concerns divine judgment. "Judgment" is not a negative concept in the Bible; it is an intervention by which justice is brought about by punishing evildoers and upholding the righteous. In First Isaiah, the attack of Assyria is part of a process of restorative justice that will end with the renewal of Israel. Though "plan" in First Isaiah describes the punishment of Jerusalem and eventual destruction of Assyria (e.g., 14:26), in Second Isaiah "plan" always has a positive sense, as in 44:26, where "I carry out the *plan* announced by my messengers; I say to Jerusalem: Be inhabited; to the cities of Judah: Be rebuilt; I will raise up their ruins" (cf. 46:10–11). First Isaiah establishes clearly that God has a plan, a judgment that involves the Assyrians as a temporary agent. The plan requires a response from the people, and it will ultimately lead to the renewal of Israel. It will fall to Second Isaiah to elaborate the plan of Isaiah of Jerusalem.

The Traditions Isaiah Used

One cannot appreciate the First Isaian "plan of the Lord," or indeed his entire message, without some idea of his use of traditions. Of the traditions he used, the most important were those celebrating the Lord as the king of heaven and earth (e.g., 6:5; 33:22) who chose Mount Zion as his dwelling (e.g., 1:21–28; 2:1–4; 4:2–6; 28:14–22; 31:4–9; 33; 37:22–29) and David as his client king (e.g., 7:1–17; 32:1–8; 17–24; 36–38). His favored title "Lord of Hosts" (sixty-two times) implies kingship over heavenly beings, typically won by a victory that no other heavenly being could achieve. Behind the title and these traditions lies a worldview that generated the stories through which people explained reality, making it possible for them to answer basic questions concerning human existence. The stories and the answers found expression in cultural symbols, and they also inculcated a way of living. Zion and the Davidic king were cultural symbols in this profound sense.

From what story do the Isaian symbols of Zion (the divine dwelling) and Davidic kingship derive their meaning? The story is called the combat myth by modern scholars. Of the versions of the myth in the ancient Near East, the following version was the most widely known: a monstrous force (often Sea) threatens cosmic order, and the gods are at a loss how to respond. The gods finally commission a young god who defeats the monstrous threat and restores (or creates) order and fertility. The gods acclaim him king, and he constructs a palace to symbolize his kingship. The myth is also attested in the Bible. A good example of the Israelite adaptation of the myth is Ps 93.

The LORD is king, robed with majesty;
the LORD is robed, girded with might.
The world will surely stand in place,
never to be moved.
Your throne stands firm from of old;
you are from everlasting, LORD.
The flood has raised up, LORD;
the flood has raised up its roar;
the flood has raised its pounding waves.
More powerful than the roar of many waters,
more powerful than the breakers of the sea,
powerful in the heavens is the LORD.
Your decrees are firmly established;
holiness belongs to your house, LORD,
for all the length of days. (Ps 93:1–5)

The psalm acclaims the Lord as king, robed with the glorious garments of a victorious warrior (v. 1a), ruling over a world that is now stable and safe from the cosmic threat personified by Sea (vv. 1b–2). Verses 3 and 4 tell of the great battle and the Lord's victory, and verse 5 describes the decrees the Lord speaks and the palace the Lord builds.

Such is the mythological background of Mount Zion, where the Lord rules as the incomparable Holy One and king of the universe. No wonder that the poets call Zion the highest mountain in the world (Ps 2:2) and the dwelling of the Holy One (e.g., Pss 4:3–5; 8:18; 12:6). The Davidic king was part of the same story. In some psalms, his commission as king was linked to the creation of the world. In Psalm 89, David is appointed as the "Most High over the kings of the earth" (89:28), just as the Lord is superior to all the gods (89:6–15).

Isaiah employed the traditions of the Lord as the king of the universe, Mount Zion as the dwelling of the incomparable Holy One, and the Davidic king as the delegate of the Lord. Jeremiah preferred to work with the Exodus, and Ezekiel worked with the full range of traditions, those of the holy Temple and land, Exodus, and divine king. Though it is probable that these prophets were aware of the full range of Israel's traditions, they selected those traditions that best suited their own temperament and pastoral aims.

Messianic Passages in Isaiah

The English word *messiah* comes from a Hebrew word meaning "anointed one." The Greek translation, *christos* (English "Christ"), appears in the New Testament. The Old Testament uses messiah of certain officials who were anointed with oil for their office—priests (e.g., Ex 40:15) and especially the Davidic kings (e.g., 1 Sm 9:10). Although the Davidic dynasty was regarded as everlasting in the sense that there would always be a son of David on the throne, the Old Testament never uses messiah of future kings. Only in the first century BC is a future son of David called a messiah, in the Dead Sea Scrolls and in the noncanonical Psalms of Solomon. The earliest New Testament books use "Christ" (Messiah) as the second name of Jesus (e.g., 1 Thes 1:11). Paul inverts the order of words to "Christ Jesus" and announces that Jesus has fulfilled the expectations of the messiah, which are rooted in the Old Testament.

Popular usage is less exact, however. It often uses the term *messianic* of any Old Testament passage that speaks of a future son of David as in the above title, "Messianic Passages in Isaiah." In this broad sense, there are several messianic passages in Isaiah, notably in chapters 7 through 9, and 11, which have played an enormously important role in Christian reflection on Jesus. Isaiah 7:1–17 is the most famous messianic passage in the entire Old Testament. The historical context is the attempt by the Northern Kingdom (Israel) and Damascus to force Ahab, king of Judah, to fight with them against Assyria. Isaiah, who opposed this alliance, challenges Ahab to place his trust in the promise of divine protection made to his ancestor David and not to fear "these two stumps of smoldering brands." When Ahab refuses to ask for a sign confirming the promise, Isaiah gives him one: "Therefore the Lord himself will give you this sign: the virgin shall be with child, and bear a son, and shall name him Immanuel" (Is 7:14). Most probably, Isaiah says to the king that the sign is the pregnancy of your wife whose son (and not you) will one day bear the happy name Immanuel ("God is with us") and embody the divine protection of Jerusalem. A sign is a hint or foretaste of the divine power that will later appear in full. Such protection of Jerusalem is mentioned in such psalms as 46; 48; and 76. The son mentioned in the Isaian oracle was evidently Hezekiah (king from 715–687/6 BC), who in fact turned out to be a faithful son of David. How can a word uttered in the eighth century have significance for later generations? The answer is that Isaiah's sign, being a word of God, was not fully realized in eighth-century events to which it was originally addressed. Rather, the word retained its power so that, Christians believe, it was fulfilled completely only in the birth of Jesus. In Mt 1:23, Joseph is told that Mary's child is from the Holy Spirit. The assurance is explained by quoting Is 7:14, "Look, the *virgin* shall conceive and bear a son." Expansions to the promise in Is 7:18–25 show that even in the very earliest times interpreters regarded the promise to the son of David as enormously significant.

Another important messianic oracle is Isaiah 8: 23–9:6 (9:1–7 in some versions): "First he degraded the land of Zebulun and the land of Naphtali; but in the end he has glorified the seaward road, the land west of the Jordan, the District of the Gentiles. Anguish has taken wing, dispelled is darkness: for there is no gloom where until now there was distress. The people who walked in darkness have seen a great light; upon those who dwelt in the land of gloom a light has shone. . . . For a child is born to us, a son is given us; upon his shoulder dominion rests. They name him Wonder-Counselor, God-Hero, Father-Forever, Prince of Peace. His dominion is vast and forever peaceful, from David's throne, and over his kingdom, which he confirms and sustains by judgment and justice, both now and forever. The zeal of the LORD of hosts will do this!" Like Isaiah 7:14, this oracle arose in a specific historical circumstance—the coronation of a Davidic king of Judah, possibly Hezekiah. Whenever a new Davidic king was installed, people remembered the ancient Davidic promises (cf. 2 Sm 7) and hoped the promises of prosperity and protection would be realized under the new king. The old tribal areas (Zebulun and Naphtali) had become, in the Assyrian conquest of 722 BC, three Assyrian provinces: Galilee, Dor, and Gilead. For the unfortunate Israelites living in the conquered territories, light has dawned because the newly installed Davidic king will, the prophet hopes, replace Assyrian rule with the Lord's. Like Isaiah 7:14, an oracle uttered at a particular time and place (late eighth century, Jerusalem) retained its force after the eighth century to take further effect at a later day. In Luke 1:32, the angel alludes to the passage when he tells Mary that her son "will be great and will be called Son of the Most High, and the Lord God will give him the throne of David his father, and he will rule over the house of Jacob forever, and of his kingdom there will be no end."

The last of the famous Isaian messianic prophecies is 11:1–9, "But a shoot shall sprout from the stump of Jesse, and from his roots a bud shall blossom. The spirit of the LORD shall rest upon him: a spirit of wisdom and of understanding, a spirit of counsel and of strength, a spirit of knowledge and of fear of the LORD, and his delight shall be the fear of the LORD. Not by appearance shall he judge, nor by hearsay shall he decide, but he shall judge the poor with justice, and decide aright for the land's afflicted. He shall strike the ruthless with the rod of his mouth, and with the breath of his lips he shall slay the wicked. Justice shall be the band around his waist, and faithfulness a belt upon his hips. Then the wolf shall be a guest of the lamb, and the leopard shall lie down with the kid; the calf and the young lion shall browse together, with a little child to guide them. The cow and the bear shall be neighbors, together their young shall rest; the lion shall eat hay like the ox. The baby shall play by the cobra's den, and the child lay his hand on the adder's lair. There shall be no harm or ruin on all my holy mountain; for the earth shall be filled with knowledge of the LORD, as water covers the sea."

Like the previous oracles, Isaiah 11:1–9 has a very specific origin. It seems to have been the installation or the anniversary of the installation of the king. The "shoot" that shall sprout (verse 1) is a reference to the Davidic dynasty, which had seemed a mere stump to its enemies (Is 10: 33–34). As the agent of the Lord's justice, the king would surely be endowed with power and wisdom (verses 2–3a). Divine justice is not necessarily the same as human justice, so that the king will not judge by human standards (verses 3b–5). The result of the king's rule will usher in an idyllic age, free of violence, when all will be taught by God. The language of the oracle is influenced by "court style"—poems about the king used embellished and exaggerated speech. The king is the agent through whom the Lord will bring about the peaceable kingdom. The Septuagint translation adds another gift to the six mentioned in the Hebrew text—"piety"—providing the biblical basis for the traditional Christian seven gifts of the Holy Spirit. For Christians, this passage predicts the outpouring of the Spirit in the New Testament.

The Message of Isaiah of Jerusalem

Only when one knows Isaiah's traditions can one appreciate the originality of his interpretation and the pastoral program that he proposed. The traditions of Zion and David were pure reassurance. Knowing that the time of judgment had come, Isaiah had to alter the triumphant ideology of king and temple. He believed that the coming judgment would not end in destruction but in salvation if the people trusted the Lord's plan. Astonishingly, he teaches that the historical means of judgment is Assyria ("Woe to Assyria! My rod in anger, my staff in wrath" (10:5). The people must allow the Assyrian king free reign as the agent of judgment. If Judah rebels by entering into alliances with Egypt and neighboring city-states, Zion will be destroyed and the king cast aside, and salvation, if it comes at all, will be deferred to the far future. In Isaiah's radical thinking, Israel's refusal to believe in the Lord's "plan" is tantamount to political rebellion and idolatry (28:14–22). With a kind of "political trust," the people must believe in the Lord's plan and cooperate with it.

Isaiah interprets the sacred (and reassuring) traditions for a new historical context: social injustice had become rampant, and an unstoppable superpower (Assyria) loomed over the defenseless nation. For Isaiah, the triumphal traditions of Zion's inviolability and the Davidic king's universal rule can have no validity as long as injustice and idolatry are triumphant (chapters 2; 5; and 28) and the leaders refuse to accept Assyria as the divine instrument. Isaiah's pastoral strategy flows directly from his analysis of the situation. He exhorts the people to rely solely on the Lord, to accept his plan that Assyria will be his instrument of justice, and to give up trying to stop Assyria. He urges them to favor the poor and the dispossessed (the king has a special role here). Only then will their Temple offerings be accepted and God bless them. In Isaiah, interpretation and ethics are intrinsically linked: his theology is preaching and his preaching is theology.

In summary, Isaiah recognized that the relationship of the Lord and Israel had reached a critical point in the late eighth century. With a prophet's radical eye, he saw on the one hand the people's failure to live in accord with the dictates of the Holy One in their midst and, on the other, the presence of a new kind of enemy on their borders, the superpower Assyria. He recognized a connection between the two facts: Assyria was God's instrument to "judge" Israel, that is, to force Israel to go through a process of purgation. If they accepted in faith God's ruling in this difficult time, the people would emerge purified and pleasing to the Lord. There was no easy path to renewal; it involved judgment. Isaiah reminded the people that the institutions through which the Lord had met and governed them, the temple and the king, did not operate automatically but only if the people approached them in faith and trust. The king played an important role as the one chosen by the Lord and in some sense as a representative of the people. But the king had to trust in the Lord and would be reckoned as good or bad to the extent that he trusted in the promises about Zion and his kingship.

Isaiah's message remains powerful today, largely because his message has been written down in the threefold pattern described above under "Literary Structure": (A) the appearance of the Lord in power (B) requiring a response by the people or their representative (C) followed by a divine intervention that implements justice. When one reads Isaiah today, one confronts the Lord who demands justice of human hearers and yet will inevitably bring about a just world. Isaiah never doubts that the Lord will remain faithful to the people and eventually bring about a renewed Israel ("I will restore your judges as at first, and your counselors as in the beginning; after that you shall be called city of justice, faithful city" 1:26). Christians will revere Isaiah for his teaching about the Davidic king's major role in a renewed Israel, his insistence on embracing divine judgment for a renewed Israel, and his portrayal of all holy God who delights in living in the midst of Israel.

Second Isaiah

Scholarly analysis of Second Isaiah has been hindered because of a lack of consensus on the length of the poems. Scholars have given an exceptionally wide range of answers to the question of how many poems should be distinguished. They range from fifteen to seventy distinct poems. Judgment of poetic length is crucial for the interpretation of the prophet's message. If one assumes chapters 40 through 55 to be a collection of very short pieces, one will be inclined to view the prophet as a lyric poet given to short outbursts. But if one judges these same chapters to consist of lengthy poems, then one will be inclined to regard the author as a thinker who develops ideas in a complex way.

Why has there been such a wide range of assessments? In the early decades of the twentieth century, many scholars were influenced by the assumption of form criticism that the prophets borrowed literary forms from daily life, such as accusations from the law court, hymns and laments from temple worship, and love songs. That assumption is in fact largely correct, for the prophets communicated in language and genres that were familiar to their audience. Yet the prophets, especially Second Isaiah, were also theologians who developed their ideas in new ways in order to persuade people to certain modes of action. Thus they went far beyond popular speech and the familiar genres of everyday life. This essay takes the view that Second Isaiah was a thinker and theologian who composed lengthy poems to develop his ideas. The list below proposes the following poems in Second Isaiah and for each gives a title expressing in very brief form the content and point of the poems.

1. The Lord speaks good news to Israel (40:1–11)
2. Strength for an exhausted people (40:12–31)
3. Judgment in favor of Israel (41:1–42:9)
4. The divine warrior removes the obstacles to his people's return (42:10–43:8)
5. Israel raised to be a witness to the Lord (43:9–44:5)
6. Witness to their Maker (44:6–23)
7. The Lord appoints Cyrus king (44:24–45:13)
8. The Lord will not leave the holy city in ruins (45:14–25)
9. The Lord carries his people to his city (46)
10. The destruction of Dame Babylon (47)
11. Openness to the interpreting word (48)
12. The servant performs his task in the sight of the nations (49)
13. The light that follows punishing darkness (50:1–51:8)
14. A prayer that the Lord destroy the foe and bring his people to Zion (51:9–52:12)
15. The many confess that the Lord upholds his servant (52:13–53:12)
16. Zion, the secure city of the Lord (54)
17. Come into the life-giving presence of the Lord! (55)

Second Isaiah wrote in the mid-sixth century, about a century and a half after First Isaiah (in modern terms the span of time between the American Civil War and the present). The prophet's audience was in Babylon, not Palestine as in chapters 2 through 38 and 56 through 66. The traditions he employed differed strikingly from First Isaiah's. Instead of traditions concerning Mount Zion and the Davidic king, Second Isaiah preferred to work with those concerning the Creation and the Exodus. He employed different genres: chiefly, trial scenes and oracles of salvation rather than the biographical narratives and warnings about social justice favored by First Isaiah. His message, too, was distinctive: not warnings to prepare for the judgment, but calls to return to Zion. How then can Second Isaiah be said to continue the preaching of First Isaiah?

The reason that Second Isaiah can be called his legitimate successor, despite his differences from First Isaiah, is that he had the same view of the judgment process as First Isaiah and regarded his commission as continuing the commission given earlier to First Isaiah. The judgment was an ongoing process, in his view, continuing into his own day. Second Isaiah, too, felt called to monitor its progress and to invite the people to play their part as it unfolded. The difference in Second Isaiah was that a new stage had been reached: the earlier phase of punishment and destruction was over and a new phase was about to begin—rebuilding. Second Isaiah received the commission to preach consolation (40:1–11) in the very same divine assembly where First Isaiah earlier had received the commission to announce devastation (6:1–11). These passages calls are portrayed as parallel commissions. As Isaiah of Jerusalem had lamented his people's suffering, "Woe is me, I am doomed! For I am a man of unclean lips, living among a people of unclean lips" (6:5), so Second Isaiah likewise felt obliged to express the vast suffering the people have already undergone, "The grass withers, the flower wilts, when the breath of the LORD blows upon it.

[So then, the people is the grass]" (40:7). At first sight, Second Isaiah's commission seems to be the opposite of the first: "Comfort, give comfort to my people, says your God" (40:1) versus First Isaiah's commission, "You are to make the heart of this people sluggish, to dull their ears and close their eyes; else their eyes will see, their ears hear, their heart understand, and they will turn and be healed" (6:10). In fact, the commissions are complementary, for the second reveals the next stage in a seamless plan of destruction and rebuilding. The pastoral task now consists in summoning the people back to Zion rather than in calling them to social justice.

There is a second striking progression in the judgment process. The pagan royal instrument of God is Cyrus of Persia rather than the king of Assyria. Instead of "Woe to Assyria! My rod in anger . . . Against an impious nation I send him!" (10:5–6), Second Isaiah announces "Thus says the LORD to his anointed, Cyrus, whose right hand I grasp, subduing nations before him, and making kings run in his service, opening doors before him and leaving the gates unbarred" (45:1). Both kings are unaware of the divine choice (10:7; 45:4).

The commission to announce the divine plan provides the basis for the continuity between First and Second Isaiah. The divine plan in chapters 40 through 55 is a mirror image of the plan in chapters 1 through 39, which accounts for the correspondences between the two prophets. It is the mirror imaging of the main points of the message of one prophet in the other that one most readily senses the continuity between them.

As with First Isaiah, the revelation to Second Isaiah demanded a response on the part of the people. Theory and practice were not sharply distinct in the prophets. Second Isaiah heard a member of the heavenly council give the orders, "In the desert prepare the way of the LORD! Make straight in the wasteland a highway for our God!" (40:3), that is, build a road through the desert from Babylon to Zion so the exiles can return home. Convinced that his task was to persuade people to embark on the journey, he announced: "Go forth from Babylon, flee from Chaldea!" (48:20). The exiles were to return to their native city and begin anew. It would, however, be a mistake to view Second Isaiah solely as a pragmatist whose only task was to make certain that the people returned home as quickly as possible. In the prophet's dramatic view of national vocation, the people had ceased to be Israel when they were removed from the land that gave them their identity. To become Israel fully, they must do what Israel had originally done to become a people—participate in an exodus from the land of bondage to the land of promise. Israel was far from their homeland like the Hebrews in Egypt; the wilderness was like the Red Sea, and the servant who will lead them was like Moses (49:1–6). The new exodus advertised to the nations that the Lord, the God of Israel, still acted in the world.

As was common in Hebrew rhetoric, the new exodus was depicted with mythic as well as historical qualities. The mythic dimension gives the event a universal scope. A good example of the mixing of historical and mythic levels is 51: 9–11, where the prophet prays that the Lord act, invoking his powerful arm:

> Awake, awake, put on strength,
> O arm of the LORD!
> Awake as in the days of old,
> in ages long ago!
> Was it not you who crushed Rahab,
> you who pierced the dragon?
> Was it not you who dried up the sea,
> the waters of the great deep,
> Who made the depths of the sea into a way
> for the redeemed to pass over?" (Is 51: 10–11).

Blending even more obviously mythic and historical elements is 43:16–21:

> Thus says the LORD,
> who opens a way in the sea
> and a path in the mighty waters,
> Who leads out chariots and horsemen,
> a powerful army,
> Till they lie prostrate together, never to rise,
> snuffed out and quenched like a wick.
> Remember not the events of the past,
> the things of long ago consider not;
> See, I am doing something new!
> Now it springs forth, do you not perceive it?
> In the desert I make a way,
> in the wasteland, rivers.
> Wild beasts honor me,
> jackals and ostriches,
> For I put water in the desert
> and rivers in the wasteland
> for my chosen people to drink,

The people whom I formed for myself,
 that they might announce my praise.

The old exodus is depicted both as the conquest of Sea and the military defeat of Pharaoh, and the new exodus is depicted both as the conquest of desert and a journey through the wilderness to Palestine.

Though the above paragraphs have stressed continuity between the programs of First and Second Isaiah, there were discontinuities as well. One of the most striking was the role of the Davidic king who was the delegate of the divine king (6:5). In the time of Second Isaiah, there was no reigning Davidic king. What did Second Isaiah do with this central tradition that no longer had meaning? He mentioned the Davidic king in only one verse, and that verse transferred the representative role of the king to the people.

Come to me heedfully,
 listen, that you may have life.
I will renew with you (plural) the everlasting
  covenant,
 the benefits assured to David.
As I made him a witness to the peoples,
 a leader and commander of nations,
So shall you summon a nation you knew not,
 and nations that knew you not shall run to
  you,
Because of the LORD, your God,
 the Holy One of Israel, who has glorified
  you" (Is 55:3–5).

The verses have sometimes been interpreted as a wholesale democratizing of kingship, a transfer from individual kingship to a kind of corporate kingship; they are, however, much more limited in scope. They transfer only the Davidic king's witnessing of his patron deity's glory to the nations as in Ps 18:44–45, "You rescued me from the strife of peoples; you made me head over nations. A people I had not known became my slaves; as soon as they heard of me they obeyed. Foreigners cringed before me." The people's embarking on a new exodus made them witnesses of their patron deity's power to determine the course of world history.

In summary, Second Isaiah freely selected omitted, or developed earlier, Isaian traditions because he saw himself as an inspired proclaimer continuing the divine plan first discerned by his predecessor. The plan has its times and seasons, and God propels it through different situations as a farmer nurtures and processes different crops with different means (cf. 28:23–29). Second Isaiah focused on the Exodus traditions, rather than on the Zion and David traditions, because this tradition best served his strategy of moving the people from Babylon to Zion in a new exodus—land taking. Using historical and mythical language, he showed the urgency and significance of the great project. Engaging in the new exodus will bring Israel back into existence and show the nations that the Lord is supreme by reason of this act.

The Servant of the Lord in Second Isaiah

Among the most important and much discussed features of Second Isaiah is the servant of the Lord. The word *servant* occurs twenty-one times in chapters 40 through 55. In all but eight instances, *servant* refers to the people Israel. At the end of the eighteenth century, with the advent of modern biblical scholarship, many scholars singled out four passages about the servant (42:1–9; 49:1–7; 50:4–11; 52:13–53:12) and claimed that these passages refer, not to the nation, but to an individual. (Many scholars still identify the servant as Israel in ideal form.) They differ on the identity of this individual; among the proposals are Moses as an ideal figure, Cyrus the Persian king (cf. 44:28; 45:1, 13), and the prophet himself. The first two suggestions are unlikely. It is hard to imagine what meaning an abstract figure would have for an exiled population undergoing suffering and deprivation. Cyrus is virtually excluded because his role in the book is as antitype to the Assyrian king, not as servant, as explained in the section above. A substantial minority of scholars have always believed that the servant in these passages is the people Israel, but personified with traits of Moses and the prophets. A mediating position is suggested here: the servant is the prophet in a dialectic relationship to the people, like that of Moses or the prophets to Israel. Moses and the prophets stood between the Lord and the people. They were "out front," often undergoing in advance those events that would later happen to the people. In Exodus, Moses fled Egypt pursued by Pharaoh and met the Lord at Sinai; later, the people fled Egypt and met the Lord at Sinai. Moses' example showed them how to do it. Isaiah and Jeremiah also offered examples of obedience and patient suffering to the people, for they too underwent in advance what the people would later undergo. One can interpret the four servant songs in a similar fashion. The prophet is fulfilling the vocation of the people Israel, offering them an example and a warning. His songs evoke the great servant of the Lord, Moses, as well as Jeremiah and, of course, his great predecessor, Isaiah of Jerusalem.

Though scholars continue to discuss the identity of the servant, there is no doubt about the purpose of the servant songs. They proclaim to the nations that Israel's exile and great sufferings do not mean that the Lord is ineffectual, but that he is just and compassionate in a new way. He continues to reign. Israel's sufferings show God's justice and compassion.

The servant songs were influential on later biblical literature. Several verses from the fourth servant song were particularly influential: "See, my servant shall prosper (Hebrew *yaskil*), he shall be raised high and greatly exalted" (52:13); "If he gives his life as an offering for sin, he shall see his descendants in a long life, and the will of the LORD shall be accomplished through him"; "Because of his affliction he shall see the light in fullness of days; through his suffering, my servant shall justify many, and their guilt he shall bear" (53:10–11). The influence of these verses can be seen in Dn 11:33–35 (italics show the borrowing from Is 52–53: "The nation's *wise men (maskilim) shall instruct the many;* though for a time they will become victims of the sword, of flames, exile, and plunder. . . . *Of the wise men,* some shall fall, so that the rest may be tested, refined, and purified, until the end time which is still appointed to come." The group who sponsored the book of Daniel saw themselves as "the wise" who instructed "the many" in Israel, even to the point of dying for them.

The fourth servant song influenced the portrayal of Jesus in the New Testament. When Jesus rebukes the apostles' unseemly striving for honor in Mark 10:35–45, he concludes his criticism with a borrowing from Isaiah 52:13–53:12: "For the Son of Man did not come to be served but to serve and to give his life as a ransom for many." The most explicit New Testament text on the suffering servant is Acts 8:26–40, the encounter of Philip, the deacon, with the Ethiopian eunuch. The eunuch, an official in the kingdom of Meroe, was reading Isaiah 53:7–8. He asked Philip, " 'I beg you, about whom is the prophet saying this? About himself, or about someone else?' Then Philip opened his mouth and, beginning with this scripture passage, he proclaimed Jesus to him." Philip's response is not preserved, but one can infer from the eunuch's request for baptism that the text was very important in early Christian instruction, providing a way of understanding the death and resurrection of Jesus.

An important question is whether Jesus historically saw himself as the servant whose sufferings redeemed Israel. Scholars are divided on the issue. Some believe that the early church interpreted Jesus as the suffering servant subsequently, in the light of further reflection on the Scriptures. Even though the question cannot be definitively answered, it would be exceedingly strange if Jesus, so in tune with the Hebrew Scriptures, had not profoundly reflected on such a key Old Testament text and applied it to himself as he faced his death.

Third Isaiah

Chapters 56 through 66 were written several decades later in Palestine rather than in Babylon. It is possible that the author, now older and facing different issues, was also the author of chapters 40 through 55. It is equally possible that he was another person who felt authorized to continue and complete Second Isaiah's work. It is impossible to decide. Chapters 56 through 66 presume that many exiles have returned to Zion, and that they, along with those who remained in Palestine, are busy rebuilding the community. Second Isaiah's task had been to announce to the people that a new stage in the unfolding of the divine plan had been decreed—restoration rather than destruction—and to persuade them to respond by returning to Zion. Yet how were the people to rebuild once they were in Zion? What must they do to become a new people? It is precisely these questions that Third Isaiah addresses. His theme is rebuilding the community in its twofold sense of building a city and forming a people (60–62; 66).

The various speeches of Third Isaiah have been edited into a coherent whole. Chapters 60 through 62, concerning the glorification of Zion, is the centerpiece, for five poems precede (56:1–8; 56:9–57:13; 57:14–21; 58; 59) and five follow (63:1–6; 63:7–64:12; 65; 66:1–16, 17–24). The centerpiece is framed on one side by a lament plus a brief description of the coming of the Lord to Zion (59:1–20, 21) and, on the other, by a brief description of the coming of the Lord to Zion plus a lament (63:1–6; 63:7–64:1). It is helpful to give a schematic presentation of chapters 56 through 66, and to give to each poem a title that summarizes its essence.

1. The Lord will gather yet more worshippers (56:1–8)
2. Punishment for the idolatrous oppressors of the faithful (56:9–57:13)
3. God will lead the humble faithful (57:14–21)
4. The fast that the Lord wants (58)
5. Those who repent in Zion will be saved (59)
6. Zion's glory (60)
7. The prophet is sent to the poor (61)
8. Prayer for the city's restoration (62)
9. Day of punishment for the nations (63:1–6)
10. Communal lament (63:7–64:12)
11. The righteous are upheld in judgment: they shall inherit the land (65)
12. Judgment in Jerusalem in favor of the righteous (66:1–16)
13. Jerusalem as the goal of the nations' pilgrimage (66:17–24)

With regard to inherited traditions, Third Isaiah shows the same freedom as does Second Isaiah. Third Isaiah does not use, for example, the royal traditions so dear to First Isaiah, and the Exodus traditions dear to Second Isaiah appear only once or twice. Third Isaiah's favored traditions are the mountain of the Holy One, and Zion as the goal of pilgrimage (chapters 60; 62) and place of divine judgment (65:1–6; 65; 66:17–24). How then can Third Isaiah be said to continue the preaching of the two previous prophets? How is this section linked to the preceding two? The answer is the same as for Second Isaiah—the prophet is concerned with the same divine plan as his predecessors. Third Isaiah believes the divine plan continues to operate, and that he has been authorized by God to monitor the judgment-process as it appears in his own day, helping the audience respond to its ethical demands.

Here, then, is the program of Third Isaiah. To the returnees, uncertain about their claim on the land and their identity as Israel in a still devastated city, the prophet announces that the Lord will rebuild the community in Zion so as to reveal the divine glory. To be Israel in an authentic and meaningful way means to adhere to God's commandments, especially those concerning right worship and social justice (57–58), and to await in faith the visitation of God that will transform the city (e.g., 59:15–21; 65; 66). The visitation will separate *true* Israel from the *counterfeit* Israel that oppresses its neighbors and closes itself off from the coming renewal. Third Isaiah declares that living in the city of Zion is not enough; one must live in accord with the commands of the Holy God dwelling there, and one must await in lively faith the Lord's initiatives. This point is made at the very beginning of the prophet's message. To emphasize the holiness expected of inhabitants in Zion, Third Isaiah invites to "my holy mountain" two hitherto excluded categories, eunuchs and foreigners, solely on the basis of their sincere commitment to the covenant (56:1–8). The nations and Israel are given one and the same criterion for admission to Mount Zion: "Observe what is right, do what is just; for my salvation is about to come, my justice, about to be revealed" (56:1).

The Unity of the Book of Isaiah

One might not expect a book recording the prophetic deeds and utterances of three prophets and editors over two and half centuries to have much unity. The book begins when Israel and Judah were independent kingdoms; it records Assyria's destruction or partition of Israel and subjugation of Judah in the late eighth century, the effects of the destruction of Jerusalem and exile of Judahites a century later, and finally the return and initial efforts at rebuilding Zion in the sixth century. As has been shown above, despite the upheavals and discontinuities of the history, all the Isaian writers discerned a single ongoing judgment-process aimed at renewing Zion. Zion was a symbol of the people and their sacred land. All the prophets in this tradition announced the progress of divine action and invited the people to suitable response, whether repentance, hope, return, or rebuilding.

Editorially, the unity of the book is reinforced and signaled by a number of literary devices. It is not certain who the final editors were. Were they scribes who edited and published the literary legacy of preexilic Israel for the postexilic generations? Or did the author of Second and Third Isaiah gather and edit the whole? A few scholars have suggested that Second Isaiah wrote chapters 40 through 55 and 56 through 66, and then arranged 1 through 39 so the entire scroll would form a coherent message. At any rate, it is clear that the last half of Third Isaiah (60–62; 63:7–66:24) is particularly important in the structure of the book. A good example of editing is the placement of the scenes of the pilgrimage of the nations to Zion. First Isaiah begins with a preface (1:2–4) depicting a pilgrimage of the nations to Zion to listen to the instruction of the Lord. Chapters 60 through 66 is the other end of the great arc begun in chapter 2. In chapter 60, the nations stream toward a brilliantly lit Zion, and in 66:15–24 the nations come to Zion with gifts, bringing the book to a conclusion.

Another indication of unity is the theme of the judgment and rebuilding of Zion. Chapter 1 indicted an obtuse people for not realizing that their present misery was the result of their infidelity and injustice (1:2–20). The important poem in 1:21–30 describes an attack on the city of Zion by the Lord himself in order to purify it from the injustice that has taken over the city. The divine attack is an act of judgment that puts down wickedness and upholds justice. The promise of such a judgment is repeated in Isaiah 4:2–6; 28:14–22; 33:17–24. The elaborate community lament in 63:7–64:11 is a long and urgent appeal for a transformative visitation: "Zion is a desert, Jerusalem a waste. Our holy and glorious temple in which our fathers praised you has been burned with fire; all that was dear to us is laid waste. Can you hold back, O LORD, after all this? Can you remain silent, and afflict us so severely?" Responding to that lament, Isaiah 65 describes the longed-for judgment that transforms Jerusalem into the righteous city promised by First Isaiah. Isaiah 65:17–19 declares, "Lo, I am about to create new heavens and a new earth. . . . Instead, there shall always be rejoicing and happiness in what I create; for I create Jerusalem to be a joy and its people to be a delight; I will rejoice in Jerusalem and exult in my people." Chapter 65 seems to reverse the threat of 1:24–27, "Now, therefore, says the Lord, the LORD of hosts, the Mighty One of Israel: Ah! I will take vengeance on my foes and fully repay my enemies! . . . I will restore your judges as at first, and your counselors as in the beginning; after that you shall be called city of justice, faithful city. Zion shall be redeemed by judgment, and her repentant ones by justice."

Two word pairs occur throughout the scroll and play an important role in elucidating its message. The first word pair is *mishpat* and *sedaqah* in Hebrew, which are usually translated as "justice and righteousness" or, as in the NAB, "judgment and justice." The two words convey one idea, the social and personal justice that should inform human actions. The word pair occurs only in First and Third Isaiah. Using the word pair, First Isaiah indicts Israel for its lack of judgment and justice, as in 5:7: "The vineyard of the LORD of hosts is the house of Israel, and the men of Judah are his cherished plant; he looked for judgment, but see, bloodshed! for justice, but hark, the outcry!" Even the holy city Zion lacks these qualities, requiring God to restore them in the future, "Zion shall be redeemed by judgment, and her repentant ones by justice" (1:27). The rebuilding of Zion (in the sense of city and people) must include judgment and justice, for it was the lack of these qualities that led to the destruction of Zion. It is no surprise, therefore, that when Third Isaiah speaks about the rebuilding of Zion, he insists on precisely these two qualities, for without them all rebuilding is in vain (56:1; 58:2bc; 59:4; 59:9, 14).

The second important word pair in Isaiah is "salvation and justice" (*yeshua*ʿ and *sedaqah,* with variation in the order of words). This pair occurs only in Second and Third Isaiah, as in 45:8: "Let the earth open and salvation bud forth; let justice also spring up! I, the LORD, have created this," and in 56:1, "my salvation is about to come, my justice, about to be revealed." As the first pair expresses *human* response to God's initiatives, so the second word pair expresses *divine* action that is saving and righteous. Only the two latter prophets had the good fortune to see God's restoration and rebuilding, which they describe as "salvation." Significantly, Third Isaiah's opening line (56:1) brings both word pairs together in a synthesis, implying that the long-sought justice of Isaiah of Jerusalem can at last be realized because of the turning point in history signaled by the return from exile: "Thus says the LORD: Observe judgment, do justice, for my salvation is about to come, my justice, about to be revealed" (Author's translation). The first colon expresses a moral demand of humans, and the second line, the coming divine order. Now is the time for both to be realized! Renewed Zion demands conduct befitting its holiness. The use of the word pairs suggests a careful editor, who attempted to show that the indictment of First Isaiah can be overcome in the renewal of Zion, and the promises of return and renewal in Second Isaiah can be realized in Third Isaiah's day.

Zion is made holy by divine judgment (65). Being righteous, it becomes a magnet to the nations (66:15–24), a role that fulfills the promise of 2: 1–5. Third Isaiah redefines Zion: it is no longer simply a place of assured blessings and safety, but the goal of pilgrimage for the nations and site of a teaching that is authoritative for the nations.

Conclusions

The unity of Isaiah does not come from the traditions used by the three prophets, for each used different ones. Still less does its unity come from an ongoing "school of Isaiah" postulated by an earlier generation of scholars; there is no evidence for such a school. Isaian unity comes from the unified plan or work of the Lord, which all three sections of the book announce and promote. It had been revealed to Isaiah of Jerusalem that the Lord had begun a process (judgment) to rectify the pervasive injustice marring Zion, and that the process would ultimately bring about a renewed people and land. Second and Third Isaiah were convinced that God had revealed to them a new stage in the divinely led process or judgment initially revealed to First Isaiah. The progress of the judgment was not determined in advance, but, like other important divine responses, changed according to the behavior of Israel and circumstances of history. Second Isaiah discerned a turn in world history that permitted the exiles to return to Zion and gave them the opportunity to be witnesses to the nations that the Lord is supreme. Following in his footsteps, Third Isaiah discerned a further stage, the rebuilding of Zion in accord with divine righteousness. All three prophets entrusted the completion of the plan to God and thus left the future open.

A special contribution of First Isaiah is his view that divine judgment is realized in human history. God uses human agencies, even the enemies of Israel, and guides them to bring about a righteous world. The judgment can involve destruction as well as salvation. What is rebellious will be destroyed; what is righteous will be upheld. In every one of its phases, the Lord's plan calls for human response and participation. Isaiah's view of history proved to be invaluable for Israelite thinkers of the exilic period trying to make sense of Israel when the monarchy collapsed and the Temple and the city were destroyed. The old traditions celebrating the Lord in the midst of a people living happily and safely in the land had lost all credibility. One cannot help wondering what exilic thinkers would have done if Isaiah had not earlier taught that the most sacred institutions do not offer protection on their own, but only because the Holy One is graciously present in them. Times change, and God is present to his people in new ways.

The Influence of Isaiah on Biblical Books

Isaiah's view of history—that the great empire was the Lord's means of "judging" or making Zion just—deeply influenced the prophet Jeremiah a century and a half later. Though for Jeremiah the great empire was not Assyria but Babylon, he taught that it was the Lord who brought "the enemy from the north" (i.e., Babylon; Jer 4–10) as an instrument of judgment. Judeans should submit to this chosen instrument with the hope that the Lord would renew them and ultimately bring them home (e.g., Jer 20:4–6; 25: 9–12; 29:1–24). Isaiah's view of history also influenced the author of Daniel in the second century. According to chapters 2 and 7, the Lord controlled the succession of four world empires, the last of which would be punished as Israel rose to supremacy.

In the second and first centuries BC, Jewish sectarians at Qumran on the Dead Sea believed that Isaiah 40:1–11 was about to come true: "In the desert prepare the way of the LORD! Make straight in the wasteland a highway for our God! . . . Then the glory of the LORD shall be revealed, and all mankind shall see it together; for the mouth of the LORD has spoken" (Is 40:3, 5). Therefore, they waited on the edge of the desert for the Lord to enter the land and inaugurate a new age. Jesus shared some of this lively expectation of the return of the Lord to Zion and an outpouring of the holy Spirit, as is evidenced by the preachment "Repent, for the Kingdom (rule) of God is at hand!" and the outpouring of the Spirit (Mk 1:12–13; Lk 4: 16–30; Rom 8). The Gospel of Mark interprets Isaiah 40:1–5: "Behold, I am sending my messenger ahead of you; he will prepare your way. A voice of one crying out in the desert: 'Prepare the way of the Lord, make straight his paths.' John (the) Baptist appeared in the desert proclaiming a baptism of repentance for the forgiveness of sins." The exegesis of the time referred these verses to the return of the exiles at the end of days, accompanied by spiritual renewal and indeed renewal of the cosmos itself. Isaiah's proclamation of the birth of a son of David in Isaiah 7:14 ("Therefore the Lord himself will give you this sign: the virgin shall be with child, and bear a son, and shall name him Immanuel") was of enormous significance in the gospels (Mt 1:22–23; Lk 1:31). Matthew 1:22–23 is explicit: "All this took place to fulfill what the Lord had said through the prophet: 'Behold, the virgin shall be with child and bear a son, and they shall name him Emmanuel,' which means 'God is with us.' " The spiritual endowments of the king in Isaiah 11:1–9 provided images for Christian writers in Matthew 2:23; 1 Peter 4:14; Revelation 1:4; and Ephesians 6:14. Isaian words and images were taken up by Christian writers. The Christian liturgical season of Advent draws heavily on the texts of Isaiah. The intellectual and spiritual achievement of Isaiah of Jerusalem turned out to be exceptionally long-lived and productive.

FURTHER READING

First Isaiah

Barton, John. *Isaiah 1–39*. Old Testament Reading Guide. Sheffield: Sheffield Academic Press, 1995. Well balanced, clearly written introduction; it is not a commentary.

Blenkinsopp, Joseph. *Isaiah 1–39; Isaiah 40–55; Isaiah 56–66*. Anchor Bible 19; 19A; 19B. New York: Doubleday, 2000, 2001, 2002. It is an advantage to have a major commentary on all sixty-six chapters from one scholar. The book is up to date and very well done. For advanced students.

Boadt, Lawrence. "Re-examining a Pre-exilic Redaction of Isaiah." In *Imagery and Imagination in Biblical Literature: Essays in Honor of Aloysius Fitzgerald*. Catholic Biblical Quarterly Monograph Series 32: 169–70. Washington, DC: Catholic Biblical Association, 2001. Argues for editorial unity in chapters 1 through 39.

Brueggemann, Walter. *Isaiah 1–39*. Westminster Bible Companion. Louisville: Westminster John Knox, 1998. Canonical approach, written with lay Christians in mind.

Childs, Brevard S. *Isaiah*. Old Testament Library. Louisville: Westminster John Knox, 2001. Written from a canonical perspective that stresses the book as Scripture.

Clements, R. E. *Isaiah 1–39*. New Century Bible Commentary. Grand Rapids: Eerdmans, 1980. Clear and balanced commentary.

Collins, John J. *Isaiah*. Collegeville Bible Commentary 13. Collegeville, MN: Liturgical Press, 1986. Succinct, competent, a popular explanation.

Goldingay, John. *Isaiah*. New International Biblical Commentary. Peabody, MA: Hendrickson, 2001. Concerned with showing the coherence of Isaiah for a wide readership. Suitable for pastors and students.

Jensen, Joseph, O.S.B. *Isaiah 1–39*. Old Testament Message 9. Wilmington, DE: Michael Glazier, 1984. Excellent commentary, combining exact scholarship and theological analysis.

Schmitt, John J. *Isaiah and His Interpreters*. New York: Paulist Press, 1986. A helpful and readable survey of the scholarship on Isaiah.

Seitz, Christopher R. *Isaiah 1–39*. Interpretation. Louisville: John Knox, 1993. Largely concerned with the coherence and structure of the book.

———. *The Book of Isaiah 40–66*. The New Interpreter's Bible 1, 307–552. Nashville: Abingdon Press, 2001. Concerned with theological themes and biblical theology.

Tucker, Gene M. *The Book of Isaiah 1–39*. New Interpreter's Bible 1, 25–305. Nashville: Abingdon Press, 2001. Thorough and well balanced, with a strong interest in pastoral application.

Wildberger, Hans. *Isaiah 1–12; Isaiah 13–27; Isaiah 28–39*. Continental Commentary. Minneapolis: Fortress, 1991, 1997, 2002. The most detailed commentary on First Isaiah. Recommended for advanced students and scholars.

Second and Third Isaiah

Baltzer, Klaus. *Deutero-Isaiah*. Hermeneia. Minneapolis: Fortress, 2001. Baltzer assumes throughout that the book reflects a drama, an assumption that limits the usefulness of the volume.

Blenkinsopp, Joseph. *Isaiah 40–55; Isaiah 56–66*; Anchor Bible 19A; 19B. See comments above.

Clifford, Richard J. *Fair Spoken and Persuading*. New York: Paulist Press, 1984. Studies the literary and theological side of the chapters.

Scullion, John. *Isaiah 40–66*. Old Testament Message 12. Wilmington, DE: Michael Glazier, 1982.

JEREMIAH

[see pages 1071–1142 of the Old Testament]

Jeremiah began his prophetic ministry in 627 BC, during the reform initiated by King Josiah (640–609) and is last heard from as an unwilling exile in Egypt in the period between 582 and 570. Though his ministry began in a period of bright promise and reform, his recorded preaching focused on the disintegration of Judah from 609 forward, after King Josiah was killed and Babylon's assaults began. Especially noteworthy is his preaching during the grim period leading up to the destruction of Jerusalem and the Temple in 586 and its aftermath. The Hebrew version of Jeremiah falls into three main parts: (1) chapters 1 through 25, poetic oracles of judgment against Judah and Jerusalem, including sermons, reports of prophetic actions, and laments; (2) chapters 26 through 45, chiefly narratives about the prophet with some sermons; (3) chapters 46 through 51, oracles concerning foreign nations. Chapter 52, a historical appendix, provides further information about Zedekiah, the fall of Jerusalem and the exile.

Historical Background

To understand Jeremiah's ministry, one must have some grasp of events in Israel and Judah (the southern and northern kingdoms) from the time of Isaiah in the late eighth century to the Babylonian Exile (conventionally 586 to 539). Isaiah of Jerusalem, whose words and deeds are recorded in Isaiah 1–39, exercised his prophetic ministry from ca. 738 to the rebellion of 701 and possibly to the death of King Hezekiah in 687. His successor, Manasseh (687–642), was weak, choosing submission rather than resistance to Assyrian rule. He is remembered in the Bible as a faithless and false leader (2 Kgs 21:9–17; Jer 15:4). During the first three quarters of the seventh century, the Assyrian Empire flourished in the eastern Mediterranean. It even conquered Egypt and, for a time, occupied it. Assurbanipal (669–ca. 627) was the last great Assyrian king. After him, the empire, already overextended, collapsed with exceptional speed. In 612 a coalition of King Cyaxares of Media and King Nabopolassar of Babylon brought it down, and the entire Near East celebrated.

The long dominance and sudden collapse of the Assyrian empire are sensitively reflected in Judean politics. In 640, at the age of eight, Josiah came to the throne aided by people eager for reform, but Assyrian power kept him quiet in his early years. Beginning in 627, the year of the death of Assurbanipal that precipitated the rapid slide of Assyria, Josiah led a resurgence of national and religious rebuilding. He restored the old boundaries of the kingdom of David, annexing the former Assyrian provinces of Samaria, Gilead, and Galilee (2 Kgs 23:19). Further impetus was given to his reform when, in 622, workers restoring the Temple found an ancient law book. The book was the nucleus of Deuteronomy and became the basis of religious reform (2 Kgs 22:1–23:27). Unfortunately, the promising reform was cut short by Josiah's unexpected death at the hands of the pharaoh Neco in 609 (2 Kgs 23:28–30; 2 Chr 35:20–24). At about the same time, Babylon began its rise to power in the west. First Egypt and then (after 605) Babylon became the dominant power in Palestine.

Where was Jeremiah during these extraordinary events? Even though he was commissioned a prophet in 627 and thus lived through Josiah's reform (Jer 1:2; cf. also 3:6; 36:2), he is, surprisingly, not recorded as supporting it with his preaching. Some scholars suggest he rejected Josiah's reform efforts as too little too late, although it is more likely that his oracles in support of it have been reused and applied to the new situation following Josiah's death. A good example is the famous "Book of Consolation" in chapters 30 and 31, which seems to have been addressed originally to "Israel," that is, the Northern Kingdom, the inhabitants of Samaria, Gilead, and Galilee, whom King Josiah invited into his Davidic empire. In several passages (e.g., Jer 30:3, 4), the phrase "and Judah" seems tacked on to "Israel" (Northern Kingdom), the group originally addressed.

After the tragedy of 609, Josiah's son Jehoahaz (also called Shallum) succeeded him as king, but within three months the Egyptians replaced him with Jehoiakim, another son of Josiah. Judah paid tribute to Egypt. Jehoiakim was denounced by Jeremiah for using forced labor to build himself a fine palace (22:13–19). When the Babylonians defeated the Egyptians at the decisive battle of Carchemish (605), Babylon became the major political power in the Levant (the eastern Mediterranean coast), and Jehoiakim duly transferred his loyalties to the victorious power. In the same year occurred the famous incident of Jehoiakim burning column by column the scroll containing Jeremiah's preaching (36:1, 23). He was offended by Jeremiah's prediction that Babylon would destroy Israel. Harboring hopes of independence, Jehoiakim revolted after three years. Nebuchadnezzar responded with troops from Moab, Ammon, and Aram, though Judah limped on for a few more years (2 Kgs 24:2; Jer 25:11). Jehoiakim died in 598, either by natural causes (implied by 2 Kgs 24:6) or after being captured by Nebuchadnezzar and taken to Babylon (2 Chr 36:5–8). His son Jehoiachin succeeded him, reigning only three months before he too was taken to Babylon in 597 with other leaders. The prophet Ezekiel was in this deportation. Nebuchadnezzar installed yet another son of Josiah, Zedekiah, as vassal king. Jeremiah wrote down his vision of the good and bad figs (24:1–10) to tell the exiles that God would make them the basis of a remnant in preference to those who stayed behind in Jerusalem. Rumors of revolt were rife in Jerusalem. Such rumors provoked Jeremiah's symbolic action of carrying the ox-yoke (27:1–22), his confrontation with the prophet Hananiah (28:1–17), and his letter to the exiles (29:1–32).

Finally, in July 586, the unthinkable happened: the walls of Jerusalem were breached, the city was set afire, and the Temple was looted and destroyed. The rebellious King Zedekiah was captured and forced to look on as his two sons were murdered; then his own eyes were put out, and he was taken in chains to Babylon (2 Kgs 25; Jer 39:7). After Jerusalem fell, the Babylonians, grateful for Jeremiah's exhortations to his countrymen to submit to them, freed him from the prison where he had been consigned (Jer 39: 11–14; 40:1–6).

Nebuchadnezzar established his seat of government at Mizpeh and appointed Gedaliah, a member of an important Judean family, as governor (2 Kgs 25:22–26). Gedaliah, however, was assassinated by Ishmael and other fanatical nationalists ca. 582 (Jer 40:7–43:7). Fearful of another Babylonian deportation, a group of prominent Judeans fled to Egypt and took a reluctant Jeremiah with them (Jer 43:8–44:30). Active for a while in Egypt, he finally disappears from the historical record.

Dateable Utterances and Events in the Book of Jeremiah

The previous section sketched the history and politics of the period from Isaiah of Jerusalem to Jeremiah, and made a few passing references to passages in Jeremiah. This section focuses on the passages in the book that carry a date or can be dated from the context. Although the book was not edited according to a strict chronology, datable passages provide a good way to understand the prophet's response to the events of his time. For many of the oracles and sermons, an editor took great care to provide information on their time and place. The dates provide valuable clues to understanding a complex and dense book. Although the events described in the passages below are dated to chronological periods, one must always recognize that the passages themselves may in some cases have been edited at a later time in view of the whole message of Jeremiah.

The first passage is 1:4–19, the prophet's call, which dates to the thirteenth year of Josiah's reign (1:2) in 627. A few scholars believe 627 was the year of Jeremiah's birth and the call came much later, but few scholars have been persuaded by the arguments in support of it. The year is important, for it shows Jeremiah began his ministry during the early years of the Josianic reform, which was inspired in part by the "book of the law [or instruction]" found in the Temple (2 Kgs 22), the nucleus of the present book of Deuteronomy. In Deuteronomy, Moses proclaims the law to the people about to cross over into the promised land so that they will know how to live in the land so as to enjoy God's blessing. Significantly, Jeremiah's call is modeled on that of Moses (Ex 3–4); like Moses, he first resists until the divine word is placed in his mouth. Deuteronomic themes are important in the book: avoidance of idols, insistence on wholehearted observance of Moses' words, association of heart and covenant, inevitability of divine punishment for breach of covenant yet possibility of renewal and return. Another passage that seems to reflect the early ministry of Jeremiah in the time of Josiah is Jer 16:1–13, where the Lord commands the prophet not to take a wife. Such a command, contrary to the culture of the time, must have been given when Jeremiah was at an age to choose a wife, that is, when he was a young man. Many scholars believe that chapters 30 and 31 were originally addressed to Israel, the Northern Kingdom. Evidently, Jeremiah supported Josiah's invitation to the former Assyrian provinces in the north to join their kinfolk in the south and become again one people as in the great days of the united monarchy under David and Solomon. Chapters 30 and 31 were later reinterpreted as applying not to the exiles of the former Assyrian provinces but to the sixth-century exiles scattered in Babylon and Egypt. There is no reason why Jeremiah himself could not have redirected his own oracles.

With Josiah's death in 609, his reform collapsed. Any lingering hopes attaching to Josiah's son Jehoahaz were shattered when the Egyptians replaced him with another son of Josiah, Jehoiakim. Among the passages interpreting this frustrating turn of events is 22:10–19, which evaluates the three kings of the period, Josiah, Jehoahaz, and Jehoiakim. Jeremiah's bold sermon attacking mindless confidence in the Temple (7:1–15; abbreviated in 26:1–24) was given in 609 according to 26:1. It would have been natural for Jeremiah to support Josiah's son as he supported his father, but by this time the prophet appears to have reached the conclusion that Josiah's reform was dead and that the Babylonians were the instrument of divine judgment. Isaiah's earlier interpretation of Assyria as the instrument of Israel's punishment provided a precedent for a similar interpretation of Babylon. The lackluster performance of the sons of Josiah only reinforced his gloomy conclusion.

In the fourth year of Jehoiakim (605), Jeremiah dictated to his secretary Baruch his oracles up to the present (Jer 36). When the scroll was read to the king, he was outraged and personally burned the scroll, making it necessary for Jeremiah to dictate the scroll again. The scroll that Jeremiah dictated to replace the burned scroll is presumably the basis of the present text of Jeremiah, and scholars have speculated endlessly about its contents. From Jehoiakim's reaction, one can assume that the scroll contained predominantly prophecies of woe and vigorous criticism of the king and the establishment. These are the chief themes of chapters 1 through 25. After the stressful conflict with the king, Jeremiah spoke reassuring words to his secretary Baruch, who was caught in a situation that was not of his own making. Those words were reinterpreted as applying to the greater distress of the exile (Jer 45). Jeremiah's praise of the austere lifestyle of the Rechabites is editorially linked to chapter 36, so is likely to have taken place at the same time as the encounter with Jehoiakim. In the same year, Jeremiah predicted the Babylonian captivity and specifically identified "the enemy from the north" as Babylon (25:1–14). Perhaps three or four years later, Jeremiah smashed the clay jug, a prophetic gesture symbolizing the Lord's smashing of the people (19:1–15). The gesture provoked the priest Pashhur's punishment (20:1–6).

Two passages are concerned with Jehoiachin's three-month reign in 597: Jeremiah 22:24–30 regards the king as having no hope of success; 24:1–10 with its vision of the basket of good figs and the basket of bad figs, teaches that the deportees, not those left behind, will form the basis of a new community.

Another important date is 594, when emissaries from Edom, Moab, Ammon, Tyre, and Sidon came to Jerusalem to persuade King Zedekiah (597–587) to rebel against the Babylonians. Egypt would also join them, some hoped. Jeremiah vigorously opposed the plan with the shocking assertion that the Lord intends that all those nations submit to Babylon (27:1–22). Such assertions did not go unchallenged. The prophet Hananiah vehemently opposed Jeremiah (though ultimately to his own cost, 28:1–17) in that same year. It was then that Jeremiah wrote a letter to the exiles telling them to resist such prophets of weal and prepare for an exile of seventy years (29:1–32; 51:59–64). The above chronology is based on the Septuagint (Greek) rendering of Jeremiah 28:1.

The largest number of dated passages occur in the period leading up to the destruction of Jerusalem and the Temple in 589–587. Zedekiah asked Jeremiah to inquire of the Lord as Babylon closed in (21:1–10), but, according to 34:1–7, the prophet predicted that Babylon would burn down Jerusalem and capture the king. When King Zedekiah freed Hebrew slaves in an attempt to gain divine favor in the crisis and then reneged, Jeremiah excoriated him: "But then you changed your mind and profaned my name by taking back your male and female slaves to whom you had given their freedom; you forced them once more into slavery. Therefore, thus says the LORD: You did not obey me by proclaiming your neighbors and kinsmen free. I now proclaim you free, says the LORD, for the sword, famine, and pestilence. I will make you an object of horror to all the kingdoms of the earth" (34: 16–17). In contrast to such waffling, Jeremiah during the crisis redeemed a relative's field to demonstrate his trust that the exiles would eventually come back to Judah. Chapters 37 and 38 narrate how during that tumultuous time Jeremiah was imprisoned.

In 586 Jerusalem was destroyed (Jer 39). Jeremiah was freed from prison and given the opportunity of going to Babylon (40:1–6), but he declined. The final dated passages narrate events of 586–582, when civil order was collapsing and groups were making plans to leave the ruined city (40:7–43:7). After receiving the word of the Lord, Jeremiah counseled people to remain in Jerusalem (42:7–17). The prophet, however, ended up in Egypt, having been forced to accompany a group trying to escape further Babylonian violence (43:8–13).

The Biography of Jeremiah

More than any other prophet, Jeremiah made himself the message. His own life, especially his anguish over the ruin of Israel, was the palette supplying the colors of his preaching. His inner life is revealed in the very first chapter, where he wrestles with his call to be a prophet. His laments in chapters 11 to 20 are the most famous examples of his highly personal understanding of the prophetic task of proclaiming the divine word as it guides history. One can say that the events that would later happen to the people first played themselves out in Jeremiah's life, so that he could reflect on them and prepare the people for what was coming.

Jeremiah's ancestry can be traced back to Eli, the priest in charge of the sanctuary at Shiloh (1 Sm 1–4; 14:3). King Solomon exiled Eli's great-great-grandson, Abiathar, to Anathoth, a town three and a half miles northeast of Jerusalem (1 Kgs 2:26). Jeremiah hailed from this town (1:1). Jeremiah's name, like most names of the time, is a sentence name, derived from the Hebrew verbal root *rûm,* "be high, exalted, rise." It means "May Yahweh (*-iah*) exalt/raise him up" (*Jerem-*), expressing the hope that the Lord would give him honor during his life.

Politics helped forge the message of Jeremiah. As Assurbanipal, the last great Assyrian king, grew old, the empire began to disintegrate. In Jerusalem, King Josiah repudiated the Assyrian gods. To have done so earlier would have been considered treason by Assyria and would have cost him his throne. In the year that Assurbanipal died (627), civil war wracked the empire and Babylon, Assyria's ancient rival to the south, secured its independence. That same year Jeremiah received a call to prophesy (Jer 1:1–14), and in 621 King Josiah inaugurated his great "Deuteronomic reform" (2 Kgs 22–23). The collapse of the Assyrian empire enabled him to invite the northern tribes, formed into Assyrian provinces a hundred years earlier (2 Kgs 17), to join to the kingdom of Judah. Jeremiah 30 and 31 preserve some of his preaching of this time. Jeremiah also condemned idolatry at Jerusalem (Jer 2–6). Tragically, Josiah was killed by the Egyptians in 609 (2 Kgs 23:29f) and was eventually succeeded by his son Jehoiakim whom Jeremiah severely criticized (Jer 22:13–19). Babylon, under Nebuchadnezzar, had become the world power in place of Assyria. When Jehoiakim revolted, the Babylonians recaptured the city, plundered it, and took many prominent Israelites into exile. Jeremiah urged the next king, Zedekiah, to refrain from joining the Egyptian party in another revolt. Weak and easily swayed, Zedekiah secretly consulted Jeremiah but took public positions against him (Jer 38). In July 586 the Babylonians stormed the city and a month later burned Jerusalem and its Temple to the ground. After the king witnessed the slaughter of his sons, the Babylonians blinded him and carted him off into oblivion (2 Kgs 25; Jer 52).

Jeremiah was treated well by the Babylonians, probably because he persistently urged Judah to submit to them. The Babylonians gave him the choice of either enjoying a palace in Babylon or remaining behind in the land. He chose the latter

(40:1–6). When the remnant in Jerusalem rejected his advice and fled into Egypt, they dragged the prophet with them (Jer 42:1–43:7). There Jeremiah died, to become a tradition and a book.

The character of Jeremiah shines from every page of this extraordinary book: joyful optimism (31); honest, painful struggling with God (12: 1–5; 15:10–21; 20:7–18); courage in confronting kings (37); anguish over the tragic fate of Jerusalem (8:18–9:10); perseverance amid continuous rejection (20:9). At times he is petulant and revengeful as his confessions show (12: 1–5; 15:10–21; 17:12–18; 18:18–23; 20:7–18).

Jeremiah responded sensitively to life and beauty, to the growth and blossoming of nature: the almond tree's first flowering in spring (1:11); the silence of the air when the last bird has flown away (4:25); the gurgling freshness of spring water (2:13). Celibacy was not an easy decision, and he felt its loneliness severely (16:1–4). Paradoxically, it bonded Jeremiah with the people in their most difficult moments of loss and so led the way to peace with God.

Stylistically, Jeremiah extended the vocabulary of prayer in Israel, contributing especially to the individual lament (more precisely, petition with extended complaint) and the argumentative questioning of God. Moses argued with God (Ex 32:11–14). So did Jeremiah's contemporary, Habakkuk, who devoted two chapters of his prophecy to such challenges. Jeremiah's confessions, however, pushed this moment of defiance to its extreme. Job further developed the genre, demanding an audience with God to press his case (Job 13:14; 19:26; 31:35–37).

Jeremiah's life spanned a tumultuous age in religion, politics, and war. It began with national independence and religious revival, and it saw the downfall of the Assyrian empire and its replacement by the Babylonian empire. The period witnessed the defeat and violent death of Josiah, the collapse of his reform, ineffective Judean kings, and the Temple's disintegration in fire and smoke. From this vantage point, one can understand Jeremiah's emotional highs and lows, admire his passion and courage, and appreciate his ability to find grounds of hope.

The Traditions That Jeremiah Used

Rather than writing a theological treatise as a modern preacher might, the prophets of Israel interpreted the traditions of their people. The people evidently knew their traditions well and could appreciate the variations and the new slants the prophets introduced. The national traditions were usually in the form of *narratives* that dealt with serious issues of national identity, found expression in *symbols* (institutions like the Temple or events like the Exodus), and included a way of living, *action*. Each prophet focused on different aspects of the national traditions. Isaiah of Jerusalem, for example, employed the traditions about Mount Zion (the site of the Temple) and about the Davidic king as the legate of the Holy One whose task was helping the people serve their Lord. In contrast, Jeremiah concentrated on the Exodus, which for him was the Lord's great act of love for Israel, which demanded a sincere response of exclusive fidelity. The Exodus was the time when Israel was faithful to the relationship (e.g., Jer 2:1–13; cf. 31:2–6). The Exodus also included symbols, such as the law given on Mount Sinai (9:12; 16: 11; 31:33) and the teaching office of Moses. The Exodus entailed action, for the people were expected to respond in faithful love to the Lord who had loved and chosen them, and they were expected as well to obey the commandments given on Sinai. A sign of how powerful the Exodus was for Jeremiah is his call, for 1:4–10 is modeled on the call of Moses (Ex 4:10–12). Like Moses, he resists the call of God and must have his resistance overcome by divine reassurances. There are differences, however. One is that, unlike Moses (15:1), Jeremiah is expressly forbidden to exercise the traditional prophetic role of interceding for the people (Jer 7:16; 11: 14) in contrast to Moses' magnificent intercession in Ex 32–34; Dt 9:20. Another tradition important for the prophet is that of the Davidic king, which is most clearly set out in 2 Samuel 7: and widely celebrated thereafter, especially in the psalms (e.g., 2; 72; 89, etc.). As noted, Jeremiah once promoted King Josiah's reform. Even when he excoriated Josiah's royal successors, he did so with a keen sense of their dignity and responsibility as legates of the Lord. Jerusalem was rich with traditions about the grandeur of Zion as the city of the Lord and the site of the divine dwelling (e.g., Pss 46; 48; 76; 87; Is 2:1–4; 60–62). Although Jeremiah did not employ the exalted language about Zion and the Temple that was in the tradition, he regarded Zion with awe, for it was the Lord's beloved city. But he expressly rejected blind trust in the Temple (Jer 7: 1–15; 8:19). Though Zion was devastated and forlorn (4:31; 26:18; 30:17), he promised that the people would one day return there in peace (3:14; 31:2–6). Such were the major traditions and symbols that Jeremiah interprets. It is obvious that in the book they were not mere items in a list of national lore, but powerful stories and symbols feeding people's imagination and stirring them to action.

How did Jeremiah interpret these venerable traditions and symbols for the sake of the people in their hour of crisis? As regards the Exodus, his early preaching gives the clearest indication: it was a time when Israel's identity was formed and they were faithful to the Lord.

I remember the devotion of your youth,
how you loved me as a bride,
Following me in the desert,
in a land unsown.
Sacred to the LORD was Israel,
the first fruits of his harvest (2:2–3)

Jeremiah believed that the people became corrupted when they entered the land and worshipped the local deities: "When I brought you into the garden land to eat its goodly fruits, you entered and defiled my land, you made my heritage loathsome. The priests asked not, 'Where is the LORD?' Those who dealt with the law knew me not: the shepherds rebelled against me. The prophets prophesied by Baal, and went after useless idols" (2:7–8). Amos might indict the people for not observing specific precepts of the Mosaic law (Am 2:4–3:2), but Jeremiah was concerned with the quality of the relationship itself. The people's fault, he never tired of repeating, was that they corrupted the relationship and pursued other gods (2–6). His concern with the sincerity of the people's commitment to the Sinai covenant prompted him to mention again and again the inclination of the human heart to rebel against the commands of the Lord (e.g., 5:23; 7: 24; 9:13; 11:8). He used the striking metaphor of the uncircumcised heart (4:4; 9:25). In short, Jeremiah proclaimed that the people violated the Sinai covenant. His task was not completed with this announcement, however. A pastor as well as theologian, he had the task of moving them to respond with appropriate *action,* in this case to accept the divine punishment—the Babylonian invasion—and to wait in hope for restoration in the form of a new exodus (16:14–15; 23:7–8; 31:8).

He also interpreted the traditions about the Davidic king. Though critical of the kings of his time (with the exception of Josiah in 22:15–16), Jeremiah and the Jeremiah tradition envisioned a blessed future with the Davidic king playing a positive role: "Behold, the days are coming, says the LORD, when I will raise up a righteous shoot to David; as king he shall reign and govern wisely, he shall do what is just and right in the land" (23:5; cf. 33:14–26). The most explicit vision of the future is the Book of Consolation in chapters 30 and 31. These chapters (apart from 30:9) do not, however, assign a major role to the king.

Some of the traditions Jeremiah used are associated with those that had evolved in the Northern Kingdom. Among these traditions are the sermons collected in the book of Deuteronomy and the stories in the Deuteronomistic books of Joshua, Judges, 1 and 2 Samuel, and 1 and 2 Kings. By contrast, Isaiah of Jerusalem was a "southerner," attached to Jerusalem and its Temple, to the covenant with the Davidic dynasty, and to the promises granted to each of these institutions.

The Contents of the Book

On a first reading, the arrangement of material in the book of Jeremiah is like that of Isaiah and Ezekiel: oracles of doom against Israel, oracles concerning foreign nations, oracles of salvation, and historical narratives. Although the Hebrew text of Jeremiah (the basis of all modern translations) breaks this pattern by placing the oracles concerning foreign nations at the end (46–51), the more original Greek version placed the oracles concerning foreign nations after the oracles of doom against Israel (beginning in 25:13), so that the original book followed the traditional order.

The oracles of doom against Israel are concentrated in chapters 1 through 25, though the chapters do not form a coherent whole. There is a common viewpoint in the chapters, but the individual units are quite diverse in content and style. Prose alternates with poetry. Such variety suggests that multiple authors contributed to the section, though one should not conclude simplistically that the poetry comes from Jeremiah and the prose comes from disciples or editors. For one thing, Hebrew poetry is not always sharply distinguishable from rhythmic prose, and, for another, modern translations sometimes do not print poetry in sense lines.

Chapters 26 through 34 are concerned with future salvation: 26 through 29 deal with true and false prophets, and 30 through 34 with future salvation. Chapters 35 through 45, all in prose, narrate the sufferings of Jeremiah in the final period of his ministry. The oracles concerning the foreign nations, 46 through 51, are mostly in poetic form. Chapter 52, drawn from 2 Kings 24: 18–25, concludes the book. The following paragraphs examine the sections in more detail.

The commission narrative in 1:4–10, is supplemented by two visions followed by a summary of Jeremiah's main themes (1:14–19). Chapters 2 through 6 contain separate oracles largely concerned with the Northern Kingdom and the threat of "the enemy from the north" (1: 13–15; 4:6; 6:1, 22), the prophet's designation for an invader that was later identified explicitly with Babylon. Chapter 2 is a covenant lawsuit indicting Israel for its lack of love and loyalty to its Lord, and chapter 3 follows with insistent demands for conversion (Hebrew *shub,* literally "turn," occurs ten times). Chapters 4 through 6 are a good sample of Jeremiah's preaching. Though some destruction has already taken place, the prophet does not dwell on it as if there is no future. The invasion of Babylon is regarded both as an inevitable historical event *and* a divine judgment on sin. Chapters 2 and 3 specify Israel's sin as apostasy and idolatry, whereas chapters 4 through 6 specify the sin as social injustice and the corruption of leadership.

These threats and anticipatory laments are interrupted by 7:1–8:3, the Temple sermon and related oracles, but reappear in 8:4–10:25 with an even greater emphasis on lament. Though several voices interact in the chapters—God, the prophet, the people mourning or praising—a recurring process is discernible, which proceeds from sin to judgment to lament. The people's sin is uncovered; divine judgment will punish it; lament (prayer emphasizing distress) attempts to assuage God's anger, and bring respite and salvation. Chapter 10 attacks other gods and their images. Though using new images and different perspectives, these chapters continue the themes of chapters 2 through 6: the enemy from the north, the insistence on repentance ("turning"), the people's malicious hearts, the failure of the leaders, and the prophets who speak falsely in God's name.

The long section, Jer 11:1–20:18 is a collection of diverse material: laments, oracles, and prophetic actions. Dominating the section are Jeremiah's seven "confessions" (actually petitions making special use of complaints and laments): 11:18–23; 12:1–6; 15:10–21; 17:14–18; 18:18–23; and 20:7–13; 20:14–18. The usual structure has two parts, the prophet's complaint and the Lord's response. How these laments are to be understood is debated. They are certainly related to the public presentation of the prophet, elaborating the original commission (1) and vindicating the divine judgments in 2 through 10 by portraying Jeremiah as an example of one who has suffered *and* been upheld by God's mercy. Judgment in the Bible, it must be noted, is a process involving punishment of the wicked and upholding of the righteous. It is a synonym for punishment. Also found within the section are divine oracles (including divine lament, 12:7–13), prophetic speeches, and prophetic actions. These prophetic actions (13:1–14; 16:1–13; 17:19–27; 18:1–12; 19:1–20:6) are interspersed like the "confessions" throughout the section. In this section the earlier emphasis on repentance lessens, and more attention is paid to the negative side of judgment. The section ends with the most despairing of Jeremiah's laments (20:14–18), which demonstrates the prophet's sincerity and also provides a model of the national suffering and vindication awaiting the whole nation.

The next section, Jeremiah 21:1–25:38 is concerned with the leadership of Judah at the time of the fall of the Kingdom of Judah. The prophet inveighs against King Jehoiakim for extravagant building projects at the expense of the poor (22:13–19) and later dashes royal hopes by declaring that King Zedekiah will fall into the hands of the Babylonians (21:1–10). False prophets, a particular problem for Jeremiah, come in for severe attack (23:9–40). Chapter 25 has a dual role in the book, concluding the first part of the book by the summary in 25:1–14, and pointing forward in verse 13 to the scroll Jeremiah dictated to Baruch in chapter 36, "Against that land I will fulfill all the words I have spoken against it (all that is written in this scroll [NAB "book"], which Jeremiah prophesied against all the nations" (25:13).

Jeremiah 26:1–36:32 consist of blocks of material (all are in prose except 30 and 31) describing scenes of conflict or comfort. Chapter 26 is a version of the Temple sermon in chapter 7, reiterating the Jeremianic theme that the only way forward is to allow full freedom to the Lord's work of judgment. It serves as prologue both to Jeremiah's attacks on the foolish utopian schemes detailed in 27 through 29 and to his invitation to genuine hope beyond judgment in 30 through 33. Like chapter 36, chapter 26 is set in the opening years of Jehoiakim's reign (609); it is probable that these two chapters form a frame around the section in between. Chapter 34, on the conditional freeing of slaves, provides a negative contrast to the full hearted following of the Lord by the austere Rechabites in chapter 35. Chapter 36 brings the section to a close, for King Jehoiakim, attempting to destroy the scroll of Jeremiah (probably much of chapters 2 through 25), unwittingly insures that the words of the scroll will continue to guide the people even after Jeremiah himself leaves the scene.

A good title for chapters 37 through 45 is "The last days of Judah and the last days of the prophet." The chaos just before and during the final catastrophe is narrated in 37 through 39. The desperation of the people and King Zedekiah is reflected in his alternately consulting and imprisoning Jeremiah, who nonetheless insists on only one counsel: do not resist, for it is by divine will that the Babylonians will triumph. Chapters 40 and 41 tell of the political changes as Babylon takes over the governance of the land. Jeremiah's counsel to people fearful of further Babylonian assaults that they should remain in the land is ignored. A frightened group of Judeans takes him to Egypt, where his words fall on deaf ears (42–43). The final chapter (45) in the section promises that Baruch will survive, a pointer to the preservation of Jeremiah's words for future generations.

Oracles concerning the nations close the book in the Hebrew version (46–51). Such words are expected, for Jeremiah had been appointed as a prophet to the nations (1:5). Various countries are named and come under critique: Egypt, Philistia, Moab, Ammon, Edom, Damascus, Arabian tribes, Elam, and, most extensively, Babylon. Some are long, others are short; some are bitter, others are not; and a few even promise restoration after the judgment. Reasons for the punishment are given for some but not for all. One can surmise that at least some of these nations violated treaties with Israel and Judah, or inflicted grave injuries upon them. Or perhaps Jeremiah simply assumed that the great judgment operative in Judah and Jerusalem must inevitably affect its near neighbors as well.

Chapter 52, a slightly adapted version of 2 Kings 24:18–25:30, summarizes the Babylonian destruction of the Temple and of Jerusalem, concluding importantly with the release from prison of King Jehoiachin, the Davidic scion. Jeremiah 23:5–8, had spoken about raising up a righteous branch for the house of David, and the editor wants the book to end on a hopeful note.

The Composition of the Book

The book of Jeremiah poses severe difficulties for modern readers. A brief, passionate poetic oracle may be followed by a prose sermon in the style of Deuteronomy, and then by a biographical account in the style of the book of Kings. Some passages are pure doom, whereas others speak confidently of restoration and rebuilding. What kind of editorial process produced a book of such diversity? Scholars have given much thought to the question, and their answers show a considerable range. For example, William L. Holladay's detailed two-volume commentary (1986, 1989) believes that much of the material can be dated to specific moments in Jeremiah's life, whereas Robert P. Carroll (1986) regards the book not as a collection of Jeremiah's words and deeds but as a stream of tradition to which a variety of authors contributed, including postexilic authors wishing to legitimate the rebuilding of Jerusalem and Judah. Because the evidence is sparse, scholarly unanimity on the composition of the book is unlikely. Nonetheless, it is possible to give some account of the problem of the sources and their use in the book.

Scholars generally single out three categories of material in the book. The first category is the "authentic words" *by* Jeremiah, which are found largely in the poetic traditions preserved in chapters 1 through 25. The second is the historical narratives *about* Jeremiah, for example, 19:1–20:6; 26; 28; 36; 37–38; 40:7–43:12. These sections are usually attributed to Jeremiah's secretary, Baruch, who, according to chapter 36, wrote down the preaching of the prophet. The third category is the "Deuteronomic" sections, sections that resemble the sermons found in the book of Deuteronomy, for example, 7:1–8:3; 11:1–14; 18:1–12; and most of chapters 32 through 35. Scholars disagree whether the sermons and other prose pieces are based directly on Jeremiah's oral preaching (perhaps even written down by the prophet) or whether they are free compositions written long afterwards by others.

The first and the third category deserve comment. Regarding the first category, Jeremiah's alleged authentic words, it is very difficult, if not impossible, to get at the very words of *any* ancient teacher, especially in the ancient Near East. Teachers stood within a circle of disciples who carefully pondered and then repeated, sometimes with variants and illustrations, their master's teachings. "Authentic" and "inauthentic" mean something entirely different in that world than in ours. Poetic form as such is no guarantee that Jeremiah is the author, nor does prose form prove he is not. It is likely that most of the poetic oracles in chapters 1 through 25 are from Jeremiah; their reiterated themes and consistent viewpoint expressed in ever fresh images and new angles suggest as much. It must be admitted, however, that followers of Jeremiah might have learned the style, and that some of their work, "elaborations of the work of the master" they would have called it, made it into the final collection. The third category, the "Deuteronomic sermon," requires more precision. "Deuteronomic" is used of both the book of Deuteronomy (especially of its law-based sermons in 5–26) and also of the Deuteronomic History (Deuteronomy–Kings). Both works contain preaching typical of the period prior to and during the exile (late seventh to sixth centuries BC). It is not surprising that the sermons in Jeremiah resemble other sermons written at the same period. The inconsistencies in the oracles and the sermons can be explained by the different demands of the genre and the different periods in which they were written. That some sections offer hope and others speak unrelievedly of doom is not necessarily a sign of multiple authorship. Jeremiah, like other prophets, regarded divine judgment as a *process* that established justice on earth. Destruction was not its goal but the means to a just and peaceful world. For Jeremiah, doom was not the last word of God. Though he saw the Babylonian invasion with all of its horrors as inevitable, it was not for him ultimate. For this reason, oracles of salvation in the book should not too quickly be judged "late" or "secondary."

There are three sources that do not fit into the categories mentioned above and deserve special treatment: the laments in chapters 11 through 20, the Book of Consolation in 30 and 31, and the oracles concerning foreign nations in 46 through 51.

1. The personal laments (confessions) of Jeremiah with their divine responses are found in 11:18–23; 12:1–6; 15:10–21; 17:14–18; 18:18–23; 20:7–13; and 20:14–18. Some scholars have regarded them primarily as autobiographical, that is, the record of the inner anguish of a gifted and sensitive soul. Such a judgment does not explain, however, why the record of purely private grief would end up in a book dealing with national issues. The confessions are rather petitions of a beleaguered prophet employing the lament style of the Psalter and Job. Suffering under the burden of a prophetic commission he cannot renounce, Jeremiah confronts evil embodied in enemies who seek to silence, imprison, and even kill him. He struggles to understand how God could have left him alone to face enemies of the prophetic word. What is especially striking is not that Jeremiah composed and used these laments (every human being at some point probably uses such prayers), but that he made them public. They are part of his preaching and have a dual purpose. First, Jeremiah wants to differentiate himself from false prophets by showing that his word does not come from himself but from God. Why would he ever put himself in such danger and anguish by speaking an unpopular message? Second, he himself is an example of one who is suffering divine judgment. His anguish will later be every Israelite's, and he wants to show the people how to suffer faithfully and not lose hope that the destruction is only the first stage in the process of divine judgment that will end in redemption. His laments are interspersed throughout the section chapters 11 through 20

and are perhaps meant to complement the similarly interspersed prophetic actions described in 13:1–14; 16:1–13; 17:19–27; 18:1–12; 19:1–20:6. Both lament and prophetic gesture illustrate the process of divine judgment.

2. Chapters 30 and 31 are known as the Book of Consolation, and the same theme of restoration is continued in chapter 32 (Jeremiah's purchase of a field in view of eventual return) and chapter 33 (promises of restoration). As already suggested, 30 and 31 were originally addressed to the Northern Kingdom of Israel during the reign of Josiah, which in 722 had come under Assyrian rule, to assure her that she still had a future as part of the chosen people. References assuring Judah that she too could look forward to a similar bright future have been added (e.g., "Israel *and Judah*" in 30:1, 4). Though some scholars deny chapters to Jeremiah because of their alleged Deuteronomic phraseology and theology, it is hard to understand it as a purely sixth-century exilic piece. Why, for example, would an exilic author use chiefly Ephraimite (northern) traditions and appeal to the old Northern Kingdom rather than to *all* Israel, north and south? The adjective "Deuteronomic" does not necessarily imply a sixth century date. The most satisfying explanation is that the core (31:2–22, 31–34) was written by the young Jeremiah to support Josiah's restoration of the old Davidic empire by inviting people of the former Assyrian provinces in the north (2 Kgs 23:19; 2 Chr 35:17). Jeremiah 31:31–33 is the famous reference to the new covenant: "I will make a new covenant with the house of Israel and the house of Judah . . . not be like the covenant I made with their fathers the day I took them by the hand to lead them forth from the land of Egypt. . . . I will place my law within them, and write it upon their hearts; I will be their God, and they shall be my people." It appears to be related to the discovery of the ancient law book in the Temple in 622. With the death of Josiah and collapse of his reform, Jeremiah applied the promises to the far greater dispersion of the sixth-century exile in the belief that God's words must ultimately prove true.

3. Oracles concerning or "against" (the Hebrew preposition has both meanings) foreign nations occur also in Isaiah, Ezekiel, and Amos. In the Greek version of Jeremiah, these oracles appear in the middle of the book (as they do in Isaiah and Ezekiel), following immediately after 25:13. Some scholars believe collections of oracles against foreign nations were in general circulation, and that editors of Jeremiah simply selected preexisting material to insert into the book. The oracles in chapters 46 through 51, however, are compatible with Jeremiah's views, for example, the oracles concerning Egypt in chapter 46. Although the hostile pronouncements against Babylon in chapters 50 and 51 differ sharply from the more positive view of Babylon elsewhere in the book, it is possible that Jeremiah regarded Babylon in the same way as Isaiah regarded Assyria: as the Lord's instrument of judgment that would itself fall under judgment because of its excesses. There is, however, material found also in other prophets, for example, passages about Moab in 48:1–47 has strong similarities to Isaiah 15–16, and the passage about Edom in Jeremiah 49:7–22 is similar to Obadiah 1–10. Collections of poems against Israel's enemies might have been drawn upon to complete the book.

The Message of Jeremiah

Jeremiah's outlook is far reaching, extending even to the nations as one might expect from his commission, "before you were born I dedicated you, a prophet to the nations I appointed you" (1: 5). He is concerned with a world view that finds expression in story, symbol, and action. The worldview is not static or fixed, however, for it is profoundly shaped by events, the movement of history, which the prophets believe is directed by the Lord. To the prophets is revealed the significance of that history for Israel. To Jeremiah in particular was revealed the significance for Israel of the decline of the Assyrian Empire and the rise of the Babylonian, as well as the significance of the inability of the people and their leaders to reform their lives and respond to the Lord. Many prophets, like Hananiah (28), assured the people that the hostile empires were a passing phase, and that God would rescue them or bring them back from Babylon after a very short stay. No change in the attitude of the people was called for. Jeremiah knew better. Rejecting such false comfort, he was convinced that the people had to go through a terrible process of judgment before there could be any restoration. He believed the false prophets had dreamed up their soothing message. He asked them the crucial question:

"Who has stood in the council of the LORD, to see him and to hear his word? Who has heeded his word, so as to announce it?" (23:18). The answer: only Jeremiah. Why would he invent a message that cost him such suffering?

Jeremiah's message cannot be separated from the traditions that he chooses to retell and interpret. The Exodus in all its breadth was the tradition that most captivated the prophet's imagination and shaped his message. He viewed it not as a wonder of the past but as a divine deed that was still powerful. He had a tremendous trust in the Exodus as the founding event of Israel. In the Exodus, God established the community by freeing them from Egyptian tyranny and forming them into a new people. This dual action, liberation and formation, showed the Lord's love and invited in turn an affectionate and exclusive response from the people. Once upon a time, in the early days of Josiah, Jeremiah expected the king's reform to purify hearts and engender the love and devotion of the original Exodus. Events taught Jeremiah something else: first there must be divine judgment, a process that will punish and, he hoped, purify the people so that God and people could enter into that relationship afresh. Judgment would be accomplished within history, by Babylon (here he was taught by Isaiah's view of Assyria), and only after purgation could restoration take place. Meanwhile, the prophet must make the people understand that the enemy from the north is inevitable; it is the Lord's instrument. The people must accept the Babylonian incursion from the Lord's hand, and not deceive themselves by entering into anti-Babylonian alliances or by credulous acceptance of prophets who proclaimed "Peace! Peace!" Jeremiah's own struggle with this hard divine decision could serve as a model for the people as they face this bitter process.

Characteristic of Jeremiah is his fidelity to the Exodus of which the covenant is an essential component. Despite the bitterness of his message about the immediate prospects of the people, his view of the future is positive because it is based upon the Exodus as an enduring event done by the Lord.

The New Covenant

Though a few modern scholars separate the Exodus from Egypt from the giving of the law at Sinai, Jeremiah regarded them as constituting one great event. When he spoke about the covenant, he implied that God had first initiated the relationship in the liberation from Egyptian bondage. The new covenant spoken of in the Book of Consolation (chapters 30 and 31) is shorthand for the entire Exodus. As already suggested, the chapters seem to have been originally addressed to people of the former Northern Kingdom of Israel and was adapted to the inhabitants of Jerusalem within the Southern Kingdom of Judah. The covenant had been annulled by the people's apostasy (11:1–17; cf. 2 Kgs 17:1–24; 22:10–15). Jeremiah knew, however, that the Mosaic covenant, immediately after being mediated by Moses at Mount Sinai, had been broken when the people worshipped the golden calf (Ex 32). Yet God forgave even that apostasy after Moses' strenuous intercession: "If I find favor with you, O LORD, do come along in our company. . . . 'Here, then,' said the LORD 'is the covenant I will make. Before the eyes of all your people I will work such marvels as have never been wrought in any nation anywhere on earth, so that this people among whom you live may see how awe-inspiring are the deeds which I, the LORD, will do at your side' " (Ex 34:9–10).

This forgiveness of the people in the Sinai wilderness can be considered a renewed or "new" covenant, and it served as a precedent for Jeremiah's new covenant. Aware that in his own day the people had again rejected the covenant, Jeremiah proclaimed that the people could keep it only if God changed their hearts. In the Bible, the heart is the organ of memory and decision rather than the organ of affections. The new heart is a metaphor for a fresh initiative by God to strengthen the will of the people. In mentioning the heart, Jeremiah was not eliminating teachers and preachers; otherwise, he himself would have no right to preach! But he was emphasizing God's role in helping human beings to respond to the divine word.

It is important to remember two things about the new covenant. First, the new covenant does not replace the old. Old does not mean worn out and ready to be discarded; it means venerable yet capable of being renewed, like the Sinai covenant after the apostasy of the golden calf (Ex 32–34). Second, the exiled people of Judah were included in Jeremiah's new covenant, for they returned to the land and observed once again their ancient covenant with the Lord. One need not hold that the new covenant of the New Testament invalidates the old covenant in the Old Testament. In his first epistle John paradoxically plays with the idea of the old and the new:

> Beloved, I am writing no new commandment to you but an old commandment that you had from the beginning. The old commandment is the word that you have heard. And yet I do write a new commandment to you, which holds true in him and among you, for the darkness is passing away, and the true light is already shining. (1 Jn 2:7–8)

The old became new in a distinctive way within the "coming days" through the death and resurrection of Jesus (Rom 1:1–4; 1 Cor 15:12–28). This new covenant is commemorated in each Eucharist (Lk 22:20; 1 Cor 11:25). The "newness" of the new covenant appears ever more clearly in one of the final New Testament compositions, Hebrews 11:7–13. Finally, Vatican II's document on the Church turned to this passage as a biblical foundation for rediscovering a communitarian model of the Church as the "people of God" (*Lumen Gentium*, n. 9).

Sin and Atonement

The prophet declares realistically that sin inevitably brings its own punishment. If the people "went after empty idols, [then they] became empty themselves" (Jer 2:5), and again in the same chapter: "Your own wickedness chastises you" (2:19). One is transformed for good or bad into that which one desires.

Another aspect of Jeremiah's theology of sin and atonement becomes clear through the Hebrew verb for "chastise": *yasar.* It stresses the purifying and strengthening results of punishment as well as God's compassion:

> I hear, I hear Ephraim pleading:
> You chastised me, and I am chastened; . . .
> If you allow me, I will return,
> . . .
> Is Ephraim not . . .
> the child in whom I delight? . .
> My heart stirs for him,
> I must show him mercy, says the LORD (31: 18, 20).

This sequence of sin-suffering-repentance-forgiveness-new life is also found in the Deuteronomistic History (Deuteronomy to 2 Kings); Judges 2:10–23 is a particularly good example. Jeremiah develops the tradition. In the movement from sin to suffering, Jeremiah was never far removed from the agony of the people Israel (3:19–25). In this way he understood his call to celibacy (16:1–4). Yet, as another passage points out, hope is always stirring within the barren earth (17:5–8).

Faith and Prayer

Jeremiah is continually laying bare the anguish of his heart. Nowhere, however, does he wrestle with God so fiercely as in his confessions: 12: 1–5; 15:10–21; 17:12–18; 18:18–23; 20:7–18. Here Jeremiah confronts God with defiant questions, yet stands on the solid rock of faith in God's fidelity and concern. In 12:1 Jeremiah begins with faith but immediately proceeds to question that faith. Translated literally, verse 1 sternly speaks its message:

> You [are] just, LORD! Yet I must argue my case publicly against you. Why does the way of the godless prosper?

God never answers Jeremiah's question but rather expects his faith to become even sturdier. A literal translation of 12:5 reads:

> If running against human beings wearies you,
> how will you race against horses?
> If you are secure only in a land of peace,
> what will you do in the thickets of the Jordan?

Symbolically Jeremiah is admitting that things must get worse before they can get better. He will in any case plunge ahead.

True and False Prophecy

Jeremiah defies the conventional expectations of an authentic prophet. First of all, he seldom if ever claims this title; editors or biographers bestow it upon him. Another proof for an authentic prophet's mission from the Lord was to be found in the fulfillment of prophecy (Dt 18:21–22; Jer 28). Jeremiah's prediction about the return of the northern tribes in 31:1–20 seems never to have come true in the literal sense initially intended by the prophet, but only in its extended form as applied to all the Babylonian exiles. Another kind of fulfillment of the same passage was Matthew 2:16–23, which applies Jeremiah's words to the return of Jesus to Palestine after the tyrant no longer threatens the child.

In chapter 23, Jeremiah stressed moral integrity as a sign of true prophecy. He lashed out angrily:

> Concerning the prophets:
> My heart within me is broken,
> my bones all tremble . . .
> Because of the LORD,
> because of his holy words.
> With adulterers the land is filled . . .
> Both prophet and priest are godless!
> In my very house I find their wickedness,
> says the LORD. (23:9–11)

In calling the priests and temple prophets adulterers, Jeremiah is speaking metaphorically; in their ministry they have betrayed the supreme and intimate love of God. To justify their own halfhearted and wicked ways, they failed to warn the people, who were guilty of injustices and sensuality.

Yet personal faultlessness is a difficult criterion of true prophecy. Few if any prophets were without faults. For instance, someone might use against Jeremiah and Amos their own bitter, revengeful language (Am 4:1; Jer 18:19–23; 22:18f).

Some may think that prophets are genuine if they carry within themselves a strong conviction of their divine call. Against this credential is Jeremiah's own indecisiveness, waiting "some time" (28:12) or "ten days" (42:7) before replying. His confessions reveal still more trepidation and uncertainty. Still another credential, advanced for true prophecy, comes from community acceptance. Against this condition we think at once of Jesus' remark: "no prophet is accepted in his own native place" (Lk 4:24). Jeremiah is the classic example of the rejected prophet.

Judgment and Restoration

One of the enduring contributions of Jeremiah is his conviction that Israel must undergo a kind of death before it can be given new life by God. Evidently he once thought that royal reforms could remake the people, but after viewing the warlike Babylonians, the cowardly kings after Josiah, and the moral failings of his people, he came to the conclusion that destruction was inevitable. Believing in the Lord's control of God of history, his justice, and his love for Israel, Jeremiah concluded that the divine judgment about to fall, however horrible, would in fact bring about divine justice. The people Israel had nothing ultimately to fear from their Lord who even in judgment was liberating and forming them, as in the Exodus of old. Their "death," accepted with trust, would lead to their "resurrection." Just as Jeremiah continued to believe in the Lord who plunged him into a furnace of suffering in the hope he would rescue him from it, so the people must trust in their just and loving Lord. Judgment was a process that involved more than punishment; it brought restoration of a purified people and made possible a new covenant.

The Text of Jeremiah and Its Transmission

There are two versions of the book of Jeremiah. The Masoretic Text (in Hebrew), used by Jews and Christians today and the basis of all modern translations, is one-eighth longer and has a different organization (after Jer 25:13a) than the Greek (Septuagint) version. The oracles concerning the nations appear at the end of the Hebrew text in chapters 46 through 51, and in the Greek in the middle in chapters 26 through 31. Prior to the discovery of the Dead Sea Scrolls, it was generally thought that the Hebrew text was original and that the Greek text was an abbreviation. Study of the Dead Sea Scrolls caused a change in that judgment, for among the many biblical manuscripts (dating from the third century BC to the first century AD) were four Hebrew fragments of Jeremiah matching the Greek textual tradition rather than the Hebrew. As a result, scholars now regard the Greek text as a translation of a Hebrew text current in Egypt; the translation was made sometime between 250 and 150 BC. The Greek version seems to preserve the first edition of the book, whereas the Masoretic Text preserves the second edition. Changes in the second edition include duplications (e.g., 8:10b–13 duplicates 6:13–15), additions (e.g., 33:14–26 and 51:44b–49a), and expansions of proper names and formulas. These facts suggest many stages in the composition of the book. Evidently not only Jeremiah the man but also Jeremiah the book underwent a long and difficult journey before arriving at the present authoritative Scripture.

The Influence of Jeremiah on Other Biblical Literature and the New Testament

In the second century BC, Daniel 9:22–27 reinterpreted Jeremiah's famous prediction that the exile would last seventy years (Jer 25:11–12; 29:10); it would last seventy weeks of years, that is, seven times seventy. The apocryphal Letter of Jeremiah of the second century BC ridicules divine images, developing biblical attacks (cf. Dt 4:27–28; Is 40:18–20, and Jer 10:2–16). Rabbinic literature remembers Jeremiah as the great prophet of doom. The Talmud evidently places Jeremiah at the beginning of the Latter Prophets.

Christian tradition regards Jeremiah as a type and model of Jesus Christ. Isaiah announces the promised Messiah by words, so to speak, and Jeremiah by his life. So many details parallel the life and ministry of Jesus that one is not surprised to hear the answer to Jesus' question, "Who do people say that the Son of Man is?" as, "Some say John the Baptist, others Elijah, still others Jeremiah or one of the prophets" (Mt 16:14). With Jeremiah it was more a matter of works than words. God was offering in Jeremiah a model for imitation rather than a message for study. The same event in Jeremiah's career—for instance, called from the mother's womb—applies to others besides Jesus, in this case the suffering servant of Isaiah (Is 49:1) and John the Baptist (Lk 1:39–45). Rather, both Jesus and especially the evangelists turned continually to Jeremiah to contemplate and illuminate the mystery of where God was directing their life and ministry. Jeremiah's prophecy is a rich source for appreciating Jesus' words and actions.

The following points of resemblance, by no means exhaustive, show up between Jesus and Jeremiah: (a) confirmed in grace from the mother's womb (Jer 1:5; Lk 1:26–38); (b) unmarried (Jer 16:l–3); (c) hounded by hometown citizens and family (Jer 12:6; Lk 4:24, 29); (d) weeping over Jerusalem (Jer 8:23; Lk 19:41); (e) speaking of the Temple as "a den of thieves" (Jer 7:11; Mt 21:13); (f) consulted secretly and fearfully by those who believe (Jer 37:17; Jn 3:1–21); (g) foreseeing a new covenant (Jer 31:31–34; Lk 22:20).

FURTHER READING

Basic Commentaries

Achtemeier, Elizabeth. *Jeremiah.* Knox Preaching Guides. Atlanta: John Knox Press, 1987. Background and summaries lead up to solid application.

Boadt, Lawrence, C.S.P. *Jeremiah 1–25; Jeremiah 26–52; Habakkuk; Zephaniah; Nahum.* Old Testament Message. 2 vols. Wilmington, DE: Michael Glazier Inc., 1982. Well-balanced treatment and does not neglect the religious value of Jeremiah.

Brueggemann, Walter. *A Commentary on Jeremiah: Exile and Homecoming.* 2 vols. Grand Rapids: Eerdmans, 1998. A fine commentary, accessible, with theological reflection and preaching application.

Clements, Ronald. *Jeremiah.* Interpretation. Atlanta: John Knox, 1988. Emphasis on the theological and homiletic use of Jeremiah.

Couturier, Guy, C.S.C. *Jeremiah.* New Jerome Biblical Commentary, 265–304. Englewood Cliffs, NJ: Prentice Hall, 1990. Well-balanced treatment.

Miller, Patrick D. *The Book of Jeremiah.* New Interpreter's Bible 1, 555–926. Nashville: Abingdon Press, 2001. Up to date. A fine blend of historical, literary, and theological approaches.

Nicholson, E. W. *Jeremiah 1–25; Jeremiah 26–52.* 2 vols. Cambridge Bible Commentary on the New English Bible. New York: Cambridge University Press, 1973, 1975. Clear, short explanations, especially of historical, geographical details.

O'Connor, Kathleen. *Jeremiah.* Oxford Bible Dictionary, 487–528. New York: Oxford University Press, 2001. Detailed, yet accessible.

Overholt, Thomas. *Jeremiah.* HarperCollins Bible Commentary, 538–76. San Francisco: Harper, 2000. Brief, scholarly, yet accessible.

Advanced commentaries

Carroll, Robert P. *Jeremiah.* Old Testament Library. Philadelphia: Westminster, 1986. Skeptical that this book contains the words and deeds of Jeremiah; rather it was an ever-growing "stream of tradition."

Holladay, William L. *Jeremiah 1; Jeremiah 2.* Hermeneia. Philadelphia: Fortress, 1989. Detailed and technical, interested in locating the prophecy in the life of the prophet.

Keown, Gerald L., Pamela J. Scalise, and Thomas J. Smothers. *Jeremiah 26–52.* Word Bible Commentary 27. Dallas: Word, 1995. Judicious and thorough.

Lundbom, Jack R. *Jeremiah 1–20.* Anchor Bible 21A. New York: Doubleday, 1999. Technical treatment, with a special interest in literary and rhetoric matters.

McKane, William L. *A Critical and Exegetical Commentary on Jeremiah.* 2 vols. International Critical Commentary. Edinburgh: T & T Clark, 1986. Technical, strong on textual and philological matters.

LAMENTATIONS

[see pages 1142–1151 of the Old Testament]

The book of Lamentations consists of five prayers of complaint, mourning before God the destruction of Jerusalem and the Temple. Since Jerusalem and the Temple were destroyed by the Babylonians in 586 and a new one constructed in 520, the prayers must have been composed in the sixty-six-year period when the Temple lay in ruins. The confusion and anguish of the prayers suggest they were composed shortly after the destruction in 586. In form, the poems are acrostic, that is, the initial word of each verse or each stanza begins with a successive letter of the twenty-two-letter Hebrew alphabet. Each poem, therefore, has either twenty-two stanzas or twenty-two verses. Although the fifth poem does not use initial letters of the alphabet, it also has twenty-two verses and so, in a broad sense, is acrostic. In the Hebrew Bible, the poems are called by the opening word of the first line of the first poem, *ʾekah, "How* lonely she is now, the once crowded city!" In antiquity, literary works were often known by their opening words. Jewish tradition follows this ancient usage. In the Christian Bible, "Lamentations" is the title of the work; it is the English translation of the Septuagint (Greek) title *threnoi,* "lamentations."

First-time readers may find the five poems dreary, repetitive, and far too comfortable with the role of victim. Closer study reveals subtle dramatic movement within each poem and between the poems; a range of emotions is skillfully explored and expressed—grief, anger, something near despair, acceptance, glimmers of hope and joy, and an indomitable will to carry on. Though many people today tend to exclude such "negative" feelings from their prayers and thoughts, Lamentations considers such feelings an inescapable part of life and makes them the stuff of prayer.

Historical Background

In the two centuries before the Lamentations were composed, Israel was in political decline, and its religious and national traditions in crisis. For those two centuries (from ca. 738 to 539 BC), with the exception of a brief resurgence under King Josiah during 627–609, the people lived under the control of two great empires, Assyria and then Babylon. The early sixth century, when Lamentations was written, was particularly difficult. That period witnessed Babylonian pressure, uncertain Judean leadership, and ultimately the destruction of Jerusalem and the Temple and large deportations to Babylonia. The countryside was devastated, and the economy destroyed. Such dismal conditions called into question the national traditions that had provided earlier generations with meaning and helped them make sense of everyday life. The traditions proclaimed that Israel's God was supreme over all gods and nations and had liberated Israel from the Egyptians and given them the land of Canaan; the Lord made the land fertile and protected the people from their enemies. For most of the two centuries prior to Lamentations, the nation's experience had been otherwise. The nation's brilliant traditions seemed to mock the nation's bitter experience. The people were not liberated; their land belonged to others; many of them had been shipped off to servitude in Babylon. Where was the Lord in all this? What could the people hope for? Though the immediate cause of the composition of Lamentations was the destruction of the city and Temple in 586, the poems actually mourn a much longer period of divine absence and national humiliation.

Destruction of the Temple dealt a terrible blow to the ordinary way in which public prayer was carried out. Public prayer texts such as the psalms presupposed that the Lord chose to dwell on Zion (Jerusalem) and there receive the praise and petitions of Israel. Zion was the privileged place of encounter between Yahweh and the holy people. Through its elaborate ceremonies the Lord received the honor due the sovereign of the entire universe. The reform measures of King Josiah (622–609; see 2 Kgs 22–23 and 2 Chr 34–35) served to reinforce the position of Jerusalem as the center of Israelite worship. Among the hopes connected to Zion was that the nations would make pilgrimages to Zion to hear the Lord's word and offer their gifts to the supreme God (Is 2:1–4; 60–61; 66:18–21). The Temple deeply influenced the prayer of Israelites no matter where they lived. Even exiles customarily prayed in the direction of the Temple (1 Kgs 8: 35; Dn 6:10; 1 Esd 4:58) in order to enter into its prayer rhythms. Texts such as the psalms allowed individual Israelites to align their own prayer to the worship conducted in the Temple.

Moderns might assume that the Lord can appear equally at any time and any place, but ancients thought otherwise. Though Yahweh, the God of Israel, might appear and act in other places, Zion was his preeminent place of disclosure and encounter with Israel; only here was Israel fully "before the Lord." Here the Lord was enthroned upon the cherubim (Pss 80:1; 99:1) and "judged," that is, governed Israel and the nations. Zion was the goal of the three annual feasts of pilgrimage. Though the universe might totter, Zion, it was believed, would remain unshaken and secure (Pss 46:2–3; 48:4–8; 76:3). The "Songs of Zion" (Pss 46; 48; 76; 84; 87; 121; 122) celebrated the city as the site of the victory over primordial enemies and the residence of Yahweh, patron of the Davidic dynasty. But with the Temple lying in ruins, Israelite worship changed profoundly. Lamentations attempted to find new modes of prayer—prayer in time of destruction.

Genre of the Book

Two traditional genres (or types) of prayer influenced the book of Lamentations. One was the communal lament found in the Psalter, and the other was the city lament, common in Mesopotamian religious literature and found here and there in the Bible. It is instructive to compare Lamentations to the community laments that also mourn a national loss. For example, Psalm 89 laments the defeat of the Davidic king, Psalms 44; 77; and 80 the loss of sacred territory, and Psalm 74 the destruction of the Temple. A major difference between the Psalms and Lamentations is that the lament psalms *remember,* that is, narrate in words (and perhaps in ritual actions) the divine act that installed the king, gave the land, or built the Temple in order that the Lord will renew the original act. With confidence in God's great acts of the past, they pray for God to renew those powerful acts now. Lamentations, on the other hand, does not *remember* in that sense; the poems do not work from the same confidence in the national traditions. Lamentations rather chooses the lyrical option; the poems explore the human emotions evoked by the catastrophe—the sorrow, guilt, anger, and hope—and bring them before the Lord. Just as the Psalms made it possible for every Israelite, even those far from Jerusalem, to participate in the worship carried out in the Temple, so Lamentations made it possible for all Israelites during the exile to explore and express their grief, anger, and hope concerning the Temple and the God who once dwelt there. Today, the book makes it possible for all Christians and Jews to explore and express their own sorrows and forms of exile.

It is important to underline that Lamentations are prayers asking God to do something for Israel. They are not merely expressions of personal and communal misery. Even though their tone is disappointed and often bitter, they believe that the Lord is behind the present distress of the community and has the power to turn and bring healing and prosperity. The strategy of the prayers is to remind God of his failure to carry out his promises to protect the people and make them prosperous. The people's wretched state advertises the ineffectiveness and callousness of their deity. Thus, they proclaim that they are miserable and abandoned in the hope (however dim) that God will finally "get it" and come to their rescue. The prayers equivalently ask the Lord to turn from his callous ways.

Though it shares features with the communal lament found in the Psalter, Lamentations has the strongest affinity with the city lament, a literary genre found in ancient Mesopotamia (modern Iraq). Temples were composed of mudbrick and other nondurable materials and had frequently to be restored and rebuilt. In order to placate the gods of the city temples for the destruction that preceded the rebuilding, city laments were recited. They described the destruction of the city and its chief shrines, acknowledged the god's "abandonment" of his or her sanctuary, and prayed for the eventual return of the god to the temple. They described the enemies' attack and the laments of the city's chief goddess. Obviously, these city laments did not envision an unhappy future. The temple would be rebuilt and the god would return. Lamentations seems to draw on this genre. The biblical book is not, however, slavishly dependent on Mesopotamian models. It appears that the city lament was at home in Israel long before Lamentations. Isaiah 1:21–28 is an example: "How has she turned adulteress, the faithful city, so upright! Justice used to lodge within her, but now, murderers. Your silver is turned to dross, your wine is mixed with water" (Is 1:21–22). The major difference between the Mesopotamian and biblical city laments is that the biblical laments cannot count on the return of the deity to the temple. They are not "playacting." Lamentations ends bitterly, without any assurances that the Lord will return to the Temple.

Poetic Analysis of the Book

The literary structure of Lamentations blends the fixed forms of Hebrew poetry with exceptionally free movement. The first four poems follow the alphabetic or acrostic arrangement: the first letters of the stanzas in Hebrew are the letters of the alphabet, in order. In the third Lamentation all three lines of a stanza start with the same letter. The first four songs follow the *qinah* meter of lament, one of the clearest metric styles in Hebrew poetry. The common Hebrew poetic line has two parts with equal number of accents in each part. The *qinah* meter has five beats, 3 + 2, so that a beat is missing in the second part. The final moment remains suspended and unfinished. It is associated with the topics of lament and loss.

An exceptional variety of attitudes follow one another: national and individual laments of misery (1:12–16; 3:43–45); prayer for help (1:9c); confidence (3:22–25); faith in the wisdom of God to assure that all receive what they deserve (3:26–42); hymn of praise (5:19). Jerusalem is addressed by the congregation (1:1) and also speaks in her own name (1:12–16).

While lamenting how chaos erupts everywhere (even cannibalism in 2:20 and 4:10), the author surrounds the entire exposition with the strict rules of alphabetic poetry and *qinah* meter. The poetry implies that God is still in control; all is not lost. Good order must return, and Israel's theology must absorb and teach the lessons of Jerusalem's destruction and exile. Lamentations asks that this process not be hurried. Israel needs space for mourning, time for disorder. Theology too cannot be hurried in unraveling an explanation of redemptive suffering.

Authorship and Place in the Bible

The irregularity of the book shows up in still other ways. Despite later tradition, quite a few signs point to someone other than Jeremiah as the author. Lamentations speaks favorably of the Davidic kings (4:20, "The anointed one of the LORD, our breath of life, was caught in their snares, he in whose shadow we thought we could live on among the nations"), whereas Jeremiah suffered severely from them (Jer 22:13–19; 37) and did not center his hopes for the future on them. The vocabulary and religious perspective of the two books are quite different. The most ancient manuscripts of Lamentations do not mention Jeremiah as the author. Moreover, the two books are found in different parts of the Hebrew Bible, Jeremiah among the Prophets, and Lamentations among the Writings. The ascription of the book to Jeremiah came much later, an instance of the ancient practice of ascribing originally anonymous works to a famous hero. The statement in 2 Chronicles 35:25 that Jeremiah composed a lamentation over King Josiah, "which can be found written in the Lamentations," does not refer to the present book of Lamentations. In the Septuagint, the second-century BC Greek translation, this book and that of Baruch (see Jer 36) are found immediately after the prophecy of Jeremiah. A Christian tradition points to a hillside cave north of the walled city of Jerusalem as the place where Jeremiah wept over the city and composed these laments. So common was the ascription to Jeremiah that the Council of Trent's enumeration of the inspired books of the Old Testament does not name Lamentations, but only "Jeremiah with Baruch" (Session IV, April 8, 1546). Lamentations became a part of the tradition of Jeremiah in reflecting upon suffering as a way of expiating sin.

Lamentations has a special affinity with the prophecies in the second and third parts of Isaiah (Is 40–55 and 56–66). Each deals with the horrendous problem of the destruction of Jerusalem, the Babylonian exile, and the return to a miserable postexilic Jerusalem. Both books have common images: the tongue parched with thirst (Lam 4:4; Is 41:17); the pouring out of wrath (Lam 2:4; 4:11; Is 42:25); the call to the mind or heart (Lam 3:21; Is 44:19). The almost hopeless agony and strong pleading of Lamentations still resound for us today:

> Our holy and glorious temple
> in which our fathers praised you
> Has been burned with fire;
> all that was dear to us is laid waste.

Can you hold back, O LORD, after all this?
Can you remain silent, and afflict us so
severely? (Is 64:10f)

Prayer linked the disciples of Isaiah in exile with those of Jeremiah among the ruins of Jerusalem. In addition to these shared traditions, Lamentations seems to receive and develop traditions found in Deuteronomy and Hosea. These books, with their stress on sensitivity, compassion, and fidelity, nourished the authors of Lamentations as they lamented their national catastrophe before God.

Was there a single author of Lamentations? Even though the five poems of Lamentations have much in common, it is difficult to decide upon a single author. They are better explained by traditions of prayer amid Israelites struggling to survive in the rubble of Jerusalem.

Praying with the Book

The five chapters are not intended to solve the problem of suffering; rather, they let us remain, sorrowing in God's presence. Prayer, like friendship, is not meant to accomplish something, only to be aware of the one we love. Nonetheless, we may find help in a few markers along the way.

The first lamentation begins with the sorrow of the author at the sight of the ruined city (vv. 1–11). Then Jerusalem herself confesses her sins, her hopes and her anger against the enemy (vv. 12–22).

The second lamentation lays the devastated city before God (vv. 1–10). Technically this is the style of a lament: simply to present the situation as it is in its pain and horror. After revealing personal sorrow (vv. 11f), the poet addresses the city from the depths of compassion (vv. 13–22), beginning: "To what can I liken or compare you, O daughter Jerusalem?"

The third lamentation turns into an *individual* cry of sorrow. It begins with an assertiveness that startles us at a time when people's spirits, like their homes, are broken apart:

I am a man who knows affliction
from the rod of his [God's] anger.
One whom he has led and forced to walk
in darkness, not in the light.

While the poet speaks in his or her own name during most of the poem, in verses 25–47 other voices speak from a group of sages or wise persons and other friends, baffled by the tragedy (vv. 40–47). This poem is the most complex of all.

The fourth lamentation returns to the style and mood of the first two. The opening verses tell the end of nobles and children (vv. 1–10), followed by a meditation on Jerusalem (vv. 11f). After the responsibility is placed upon the religious leaders (vv. 13–20), the poem ends with a curse upon the enemy (vv. 21f).

The fifth and last lamentation was titled by the Latin Vulgate "The Prayer of Jeremiah." This liturgical prayer sustains its beauty and serenity despite its topic of rejection and tragedy. It asks very little, only that the Lord remember.

Prayer beyond Theology

Lamentations allows us to remain with grief and tragedy long enough to mourn beauty and goodness as they deserve. If we do not mourn adequately, we may assume that nothing too precious was lost. We remain with God, even if events seemingly destroyed God's promises and, in the case of Lamentations, God's presence with us in the Temple. If our sorrow extends beyond the limits of our reasoning, then we plunge into a moment of time not for arguing theology but for allowing emotions to rush forward. Lamentations gushes from the dark, subterranean wellsprings of faith and sears the highest heavens in an outcry of anguish.

Without ever giving a reason, the book of Lamentations allows us to absorb a good purpose even in meaningless suffering. God, compassionate enough to bear our human outrage, walks us through dark gullies to a plateau of peace. This book is a triumph of faith over theology, at least theology in the days of the prophet Jeremiah. Because the Davidic dynasty and the holy city of Jerusalem received promises of God's eternal protection (Pss 46; 89; 132), priests and other prophets wanted Jeremiah killed for threatening the city with destruction (Jer 26). National laments, other than Lamentations, had already plunged beyond the limits of theology. In its second part of lament and reflection (vv. 10–23), Psalm 44 reverses the theological statements of the introduction (vv. 2–9) and introduces its final section almost blasphemously: "Awake! Why do you sleep, O Lord?" Blasphemous, because Psalm 121 declares: "The LORD, the maker of heaven and earth . . . never slumbers nor sleeps.

The LORD is your guardian" (vv. 2 and 4). It is not that theology is false, only that it has its limits. At such times contemplative prayer does what nothing else can do for us; it sustains us in God's presence with our agony and outrage.

Israelites prayed to God in the place which God had abandoned (Ez 10:18–23). They gathered in the Temple ruins (Jer 41:4–7), a dead place that paradoxically comes alive to address the assembly:

Come, all you who pass by the way,
 look and see
Whether there is any suffering like my
  suffering . . .
When the LORD afflicted me
 on the day of his blazing wrath (Lam 1:12).

Other prayers besides Lamentations were being composed: for instance, Isaiah 63:7–64:11; Pss 79 and 80. Israel seemed to survive less by theological tradition, more within a community at prayer before a compassionate God. This same God admits publicly in Second Isaiah that Israel has received double for all her sins (Is 40:2), that is, too much. There are instances, again beyond the limits of theology, where God regrets divine anger and punishment (Ex 32:14; 2 Sm 24:16; Jer 42:10).

Influence of Lamentations in Judaism and Christianity

Later Jewish tradition counted Lamentations as one of the five festival scrolls (the Megilloth), with Song of Songs, Ruth, Ecclesiastes, and Esther. Lamentations was read in the liturgy on the "ninth of Ab," sorrowfully remembering the two destructions of Jerusalem, by the Babylonians in 587 BC and by the Romans in AD 70.

The Christian church has used Lamentations in reference to Christ's Passion. In the Latin church, Lamentations played an important and memorable role in the Holy Week services prior the reforms of Vatican II. They were sung during the ceremony of Tenebrae ("darkness"), probably named from the custom of extinguishing one candle after each psalm until the church was left in darkness. Several of the Tenebrae texts (though not Lamentations) have survived in the revised morning offices for Good Friday and Holy Saturday. In general, the Lamentations are used sparingly in the Roman Catholic lectionary; there are only three selections among the many Old Testament selections for masses for the dead and only one in the readings for masses "for any need." It remains a challenge for the church to learn how to incorporate laments into its public prayer so that the pains and difficulties of Christian discipleship are represented as fully as the peace and joy of faith.

FURTHER READING

Basic Commentaries

Dobbs-Allsopp, F. W. *Lamentations.* Interpretation. Louisville: John Knox Press, 2000. Excellent; scholarly, yet accessible to first-time readers.

Fischer, James A., G.M. *Song of Songs; Ruth; Lamentations; Ecclesiastes; Esther.* Collegeville Bible Commentary 24. Collegeville, MN: Liturgical Press, 1986. Very brief and good treatment.

Gottwald, Norman K. *Lamentations.* HarperCollins Bible Commentary, 577–82. San Francisco: Harper, 2000. Gottwald has long worked on Lamentations; this short commentary is the fruit of his labors.

Guinan, Michael D. *Lamentations.* New Jerome Biblical Commentary, 558–62. Englewood Cliffs, NJ: Prentice Hall, 1990. Balanced and concise.

Kodell, Jerome. O.S.B., *Lamentations . . . Baruch.* Old Testament Message. Wilmington, DE: Michael Glazier Inc., 1982. A good, though brief, exposition.

O'Connor, Kathleen M. *Lamentations.* New Interpreter's Bible 6. 1011–73. Nashville, TN: Abingdon Press, 2001. A fine analysis.

———. *Lamentations and the Tears of the World.* Maryknoll, NY: Orbis Books, 2002. A perceptive commentary with reflections on the meaning of the book for today.

Advanced Commentary

Hillers, Delbert R. *Lamentations.* Anchor Bible 7A. Garden City, NY: Doubleday, 1992. Interested in the linguistic questions and in comparable laments in the ancient world.

BARUCH

[see pages 1151–1160 of the Old Testament]

Baruch, son of Neriah, was the secretary of the great prophet Jeremiah. He wrote down the prophet's preaching to preserve it for later generations, and on occasion he read that preaching to audiences when Jeremiah was not able to do so (Jer 32; 36; 45). Much more than a simple record keeper, he was from an important Jerusalem family and scribe in the employ of the palace. Sharing Jeremiah's fate as an exile in Egypt, he is last heard from in that country around 582 BC (Jer 43:5–7). The book bearing his name is a collection of four sections, probably of separate origin, which were written long after Baruch, probably in the second or early first centuries. In the Second Temple period (520 BC to AD 70), it was not unusual to use the name of a well-known ancient personage as the title of a contemporary work in order to link the work to earlier traditions and enhance its authority.

The book of Baruch has four sections: an introduction (1:1–14), a long confession of sin (1:15–3:8), a poem on wisdom (3:9–4:4), and a consoling poem (4:5–5:9). In Roman Catholic Bibles, the so-called Letter of Jeremiah is often printed as the sixth chapter of Baruch. When included in the book of Baruch, as it sometimes is, it makes a fifth section. Though the sections may have had separate origins, they are linked to one another, giving the book a clear unity. It is generally agreed that Baruch was written in Hebrew. No Hebrew manuscript survives, however. The Greek version serves as the basis of modern translations. Other ancient versions are in Syriac, Latin, Coptic, Ethiopic, Arabic, and Armenian.

Baruch is in the Orthodox and Roman Catholic canon of sacred Scripture. In the Protestant canon it is classed among the Apocrypha. Catholic Bibles such as the *New American Bible* add the Epistle of Jeremiah to Baruch as its sixth chapter.

The Historical Background of the Book

When was the book of Baruch written? Evidence must be indirect, for there are no references to contemporary events in the book. Historical inconsistencies and inaccuracies in the introduction (e.g., that Baruch lived in Babylon rather than Egypt, contrary to Jer 43:6, and the strange "fifth year" in 1:2) indicate the book was written long after the early sixth century when the historical Baruch lived. Since the prayer in chapters 1 and 2 (especially 1:15–2:5) depends on Daniel 9 (ca. 164) and the wisdom poem (3:9–4:4) depends on Sirach 24 (ca. 180), Baruch must have been written after the completion of these works, unless the two sources were in existence before the composition of the books in which they now appear. Many scholars therefore suggest that the date of composition was sometime in the late second or early first centuries.

What had happened in the history of Israel from the sixth to the second centuries to make the book of Baruch possible? The Babylonian exile is conventionally dated 586 to 539. Babylonian deportations in the early sixth century impoverished Jerusalem and Judah. The Temple ceased operation, and the economy was devastated. In 539 the Persians entered Babylon and effectively ended the empire. The period from 539 to 333 is known as the Persian period and the period from 333 to 63 as the Hellenistic (Greek) period. The defeat of Babylon by Cyrus the Persian greatly benefited people in Judah and in the exiled community. Cyrus authorized the rebuilding of the Temple and the return of the sacred vessels, and permitted the return of the exiles (Ezr 1:1–4; 6:1–5). Most exiles stayed where they were, however, and the Diaspora (dispersion) communities in Babylon and elsewhere grew and flourished in the centuries that followed. Only in 520 was the Temple rebuilt (on a very modest scale), a sign of the practical difficulties in returning to normal and a sign too of the animosity of neighboring peoples. The rebuilt Temple became the center of the restored community, even though, as Isaiah 56 through 66 clearly shows, the people struggled with different visions of restoration.

The postexilic period was a time of literary creativity. Most Old Testament books underwent final editing at this time, including the Pentateuch, the Deuteronomistic History, and the prophetic books. Other books were composed later in this period, among them Chronicles and Ezra-Nehemiah. Some of the late books looked back at the preexilic period with awe and reverence, regarding its literature as timeless standards. Their authors paid homage to the golden-age works by allusions and borrowings. The attribution of the book of Baruch to the sixth-century secretary of Jeremiah is an example of such reverence. Another indication is Baruch's multiple allusions to Deuteronomy (especially Dt 28 and 30), Jeremiah (e.g., Jer 8:1; 11:17; 24:7, 9; 31:33), Deutero-Isaiah (Is 40–55), and Daniel (especially Dn 9). Among the abiding concerns of exilic literature were the Jerusalem Temple, the meaning of exile, and the problem of authority in a changed society. With the disappearance of the old institutions of religion and government in Judea, where was the divine presence to be found and who had religious authority? Related questions were where wisdom was to be found and the location of authoritative teaching or *torah*. These concerns are addressed in the book of Baruch.

In the course of time, the Persian Empire expanded westward and came into conflict with Greece, which eventually led to the defeat of the Persians. In 333 Alexander the Great swept down the coast of the western Mediterranean and conquered the Phoenician coast. Jerusalem surrendered and became a province in yet another empire, the Ptolemaic empire (capital in Egypt) and then the Seleucid (capital in Antioch). More important, it came under the influence of Greek culture. The new culture raised several points relevant to the book of Baruch. One was the question of Jewish identity. New centers of Judaism rivaled Jerusalem: Alexandria in Egypt and Babylon in Mesopotamia. As most Jews now lived outside the boundaries of Palestine and did not speak Hebrew, the question of what made a Jew became pressing. What was the relation of the diaspora communities to the Jerusalem and the Judean community? When would the exile completely end so that Judah might be independent and have its own king? Was the period of divine wrath ongoing? These questions concerning the identity of Judah among the nations appear in the book of Baruch.

Analysis of the Book

1. **Introduction (1:1–14).** According to the opening lines of Baruch, on the fifth anniversary of the destruction of the Temple in Jerusalem, Baruch read the book to Jehoiachin (Jeconiah) and to all who could come—nobles, princes, elders, everyone high and low. Jehoiachin was the Davidic king who had been exiled to Babylon in 598/597 and represented hopes for a restored monarchy (2 Kgs 25:27–30; Jer 52:31–34). When they heard it, they wept, fasted, and prayed, and then took up a collection for the high priest and the people in Jerusalem. Baruch arranged for the return of the silver vessels that Nebuchadnezzar robbed from the Temple. The verses evoke golden-age scenes of leaders gathering the people and speaking authoritative words to them, for example, Moses in Deuteronomy, King Josiah in 2 Kings 22–23, and (in a reverse of the present scene) Baruch reading the book to the unreceptive King Jehoiakim in Jeremiah 36. Baruch here speaks with scriptural authoritativeness; such is the sense of verse 3, literally "Baruch read the words . . . in the ears of all the people who came to hear the book." Not only do Baruch and the people send vessels to Jerusalem; they also send money for offerings, suggest what the Jerusalemites should pray for (the welfare of the king and the forgiveness of the sins of the exiles), and even write a prayer for Temple worship (1:10–14). The latter is not a private prayer; it is to be read on feast days in the Temple. The text of the prayer follows in 1:15–3:8, which links the first and second parts of the book.

The key to the opening scene is that Baruch, the secretary of the great Jeremiah and his sometime spokesman, is the speaker. Baruch's interpretation of the prophet's famous letter to the exiles in Babylon in Jeremiah 29 is accepted as authoritative by the leaders in Babylon: "Promote the welfare of the city to which I have exiled you; pray for it to the LORD, for upon its welfare depends your own. Thus says the LORD: Only after seventy years have elapsed for Babylon will I visit you and fulfill for you my promise to bring you back to this place. . . . Yes, when you seek me with all your heart, you will find me with you, says the LORD, and I will change your lot; I will gather you together from all the nations and all the places to which I have banished you, says the LORD, and bring you back to the place from which I have exiled you" (Jer 29:7–15). Baruch apparently reinterprets "seventy years" to mean an indefinite period of time. Daniel 9: 20–27 had famously reinterpreted the seventy years to seventy weeks of years, that is, seven times seventy (= 490 years), but Baruch's interpretation is even more open-ended. According to him, the exiles must serve the king of Babylon for "many days" (Bar 1:12). The wrath of God has not yet turned away from the exiles (1:13). In the meantime, Baruch advises fervent prayer (1:15–3:8) and, in the following passages, teaches the exiles how to seek life-giving wisdom in this less than perfect situation.

2. **A prayer that the Lord might relent and once again be gracious (1:15–3:8).** It is assumed that prayer offered in the Jerusalem Temple is more efficacious than private prayer. The confession acknowledges that the people have sinned and that the covenant curses listed in Deuteronomy 28 have been unleashed. All the ills that have come upon the people are deserved; no excuses are offered. The first part of the poem (1: 15–2:5) is to be said by the people of Jerusalem, and the second part by the exiles (2:6–16). 1:15 ("Justice is with the LORD, our God; and we today are flushed with shame, we men of Judah and citizens of Jerusalem") matches 2:6 ("Justice is with the LORD, our God; and we, like our fathers, are flushed with shame even today"), suggesting that both verses begin parallel sections. Furthermore, 2:13–14 indicates that the exiles are speaking, so it is natural to regard 2:6 as the point where the exiles' prayer begins. The prayer draws heavily on Daniel 9:7–8, 10–14; almost every word in Daniel finds an echo in Baruch. Jeremiah and Deuteronomy are also quarried. In the prayer, the people give up all claims of righteousness and place all hopes of rescue in the character of God, the Lord's care for his good name.

3. **Wisdom is to be found in Israel's law (3:9–4:5).** Where can wisdom be found? Always elusive (Job 28), life-giving wisdom is especially hard to find in the exilic crisis. After the prayer, which gives up all human sources of salvation (1: 15:3–8), the book begins a new section with the authoritative command, "Hear, O Israel, the commandments of life" (3:9). It is an apt summons, for the people live in a foreign land, virtually among the dead (3:11). The charge that they "have forsaken the fountain of wisdom" (3:12) is probably an allusion to Jeremiah 2:13, "Two evils have my people done: they have forsaken me, the source of living waters; they have dug themselves cisterns, broken cisterns, that hold no water." Borrowing from the wisdom poem in Job 28 (among other biblical texts), the poem insists that human beings cannot lay hold of wisdom by their own efforts; it must be given by God. God has in fact given wisdom to Israel—in the form of their *torah* or law: "[Wisdom] is the book of the precepts of God, the law that endures forever; all who cling to her will live, but those will die who forsake her. Turn, O Jacob, and receive her: walk by her light toward splendor" (4:1–2). Baruch here draws on Sirach 24 (ca. 180), which also teaches that divine wisdom is to be found in the law given to Israel, "All this [wisdom] is true of the book of the Most High's covenant, the law which Moses commanded us as an inheritance for the community of Jacob" (Sir 24:22).

Three points about this wisdom poem should be noted. First, it comes immediately after the community confession of helplessness and blindedness, suggesting that wisdom is God's answer to the people's quandary. The hymn sings of the inaccessibility of wisdom and nonetheless asserts it can be found. This is just what the community, adrift, needed to hear. Second, the focus on *torah* was an important religious development in early Judaism. The old markers of community identity no longer played the role that they once did—the Temple, a common land, a king and independent government. New boundary markers were necessary so that the community might define itself among the nations. Among the new markers were the law or *torah* and the Scriptures. What was written could be read by people of different lands, cultures, and languages. Eventually, the word *torah* came to be applied to the Pentateuch, the great authoritative narrative. Third, the wisdom hymn associates wisdom preeminently with one nation, Israel. Previously, wisdom was more "international"; to pursue it was the duty of every human being. The "nationalizing" of wisdom can be seen as early as Deuteronomy 4:6, probably from the sixth century: "Observe [the statutes] carefully, for thus will you give evidence of your wisdom and intelligence to the nations, who will hear of all these statutes and say, 'This great nation is truly a wise and intelligent people.' " In a memorable phrase, Baruch says that to live according to the wisdom of the *torah* is to "walk by her light toward splendor" (4:2). Israel has the great privilege of knowing what is pleasing to God (4:3).

4. **A poem of encouragement (4:5–5:9).** Like the two preceding sections, this section alludes to the writings of the golden age, especially Isaiah 40 through 55. Isaiah personified Babylon (Is 37) and Zion (Is 49:14–26; 54) as queens, imagining them as wives of the national god and mothers of their citizens (cf. Ps 87). With the destruction of the city and the exile of its citizens, each personified city lost her husband and her children. In Isaiah 40 through 55, Woman Zion is assured by her Lord that her children will return. Isaiah 60 and 62 envision the return of Zion's exiled children and her husband: "Raise your eyes and look about; they all gather and come to you: Your sons come from afar, and your daughters in the arms of their nurses" (Is 60:4), and "No more shall men call you 'Forsaken,' or your land 'Desolate,' but you shall be called 'My Delight,' and your land 'Espoused.' For the LORD delights in you, and makes your land his spouse" (Is 62:4). In Baruch, personified Zion is not yet fully restored. Despite her great suffering, however, she thinks only of the suffering of her children. With great compassion, she explains their real situation to them: their sins angered the just God who punished them by bringing a distant nation against them (4:15). Zion intercedes with God on their behalf (4:17–20), setting an example of hope (4:21–26) and faithfulness (4:27–29). Though bereft of her children, Zion continues to act as a true mother of her children.

The second section of the poem of consolation (4:30–5:9) is addressed to Zion. Reprising a key verb from Zion's speech, "*Fear not,* my children; call out to God! He who brought this upon you will remember you" (4:27), the new poem begins by responding to her, "*Fear not,* Jerusalem! He who gave you your name is your encouragement." The second part of the poem is the divine answer to the words of Woman Zion in 4:5–29. She had told her children she was interceding for them with sackcloth and prayer (4:20) and expressed her steadfast hope they would return to her. The second section (4:30–5:9) assures Zion that her hope will come true. Three verbs in the imperative mood introduce the three sections of the speech: (1) "Fear not, Jerusalem" in 4:30; (2) "Look to the east, Jerusalem! behold the joy that comes to you from God" in 4:36; and (3) "Up, Jerusalem! stand upon the heights; look to the east and see your children" in 5:5. Section 1 asserts that Zion's enemies will be punished; section 2 that her children will return and that she can take off her widow's garments; and section 3 that the hills and valleys have been leveled to make a beautiful highway for the exiles to walk as they return home to Zion. Baruch here draws on Isaiah 40 through 55.

5. **The Letter of Jeremiah.** In Roman Catholic Bibles, the Letter of Jeremiah is often printed as chapter 6 of Baruch. Protestant editions of the Bible place both Baruch and the Letter of Jeremiah among the Apocrypha, and print the Letter of Jeremiah as a separate work immediately after Baruch. Addressed to the exiles in Babylon like Baruch, the Letter of Jeremiah develops themes of Jeremiah's famous letter to the exiles (Jer 29). The Letter of Jeremiah interprets Jeremiah's "seventy years" (Jer 25:11–12; 29:10) as seven generations (Bar 6:3). Its chief concern, however, is in launching a satiric attack on idols (Jer 10:2–16): avoid divine images and worship Israel's God exclusively. In the exilic and postexilic periods Israelite thinkers became more reflective about their monotheistic faith. Part of that reflection was expressed in satirical attacks on divine images, which were, in the ancient Near East, the normal means of encountering the deity. Jeremiah 10 and Baruch 6 are not the only satires on divine images in the Bible. Others are found in Deuteronomy 4:27–28; Psalms 115:4–8; 135:15–18; Isaiah 40:18–20; 44:9–10; 46:1–7. The Letter of Jeremiah consists of ten warnings, all but the last ending in a refrain that the statues are not divine and that people should not "fear" them, that is, accord them divine honor.

The work is attributed to Jeremiah because it furthers his work of preaching to the exiles. It was known to the author of 2 Maccabees 2:1–3, and must therefore have been written toward the end of the second century. The original language seems to have Hebrew or Aramaic, for the extant Greek occasionally reflects Semitic syntax.

The Message of the Book of Baruch

Baruch, the secretary of Jeremiah, preserved and interpreted the words of his master for a new time and situation. By the time Baruch was written (probably the late second or early first century BC), the exile had gone on far longer than what Jeremiah predicted. Jeremiah's "seventy years" had come and gone and the exile continued. "Exile" had come to mean something more complex than absence from one's homeland. It meant also subjugation to a foreign government, high rates of taxation, harassment, and arbitrary treatment by an occupying power. The author of the book believes in the authority of the Jeremiah tradition but realizes it has to be interpreted for a new situation. Jeremiah's seventy years of exile (Jer 25:1–12; 29:10) become in Baruch "many days" (Bar 1:12; 4:35, literal translation; NAB "long" and "long time"). In the Letter of Jeremiah, it becomes "many years, a period seven generations long" (Bar 6:2). Jeremiah advised the exiles to settle down and pray for the welfare of Babylon (Jer 29:5–7) and promised that the Lord had a plan to bring the exiles back provided they were constant in prayer (Jer 29:10–14), "When you call me, when you go to pray to me, I will listen to you" (Jer 29:12). Baruch provides a model of such prayer (Bar 1:15–3:8): the nation abases itself and places all its hopes in the Lord. Baruch also shows the people that there are other ways to gain life during exile, especially the pursuit of wisdom, which is to be found in the law of the Lord (3:9–4:5). Mother Zion instructs the people how they are to live so that the Lord will bring them back: maintain a lively hope that the Lord will bring them back to Zion (4:5–5:9).

Baruch shows that many Jews, at least in Judea, considered the exile to be still continuing. It had not ended when the first exiles returned in the latter part of the sixth century. Rather, it continues as long as Israel is not free and another empire rules their land, as long as their Temple is subject to foreign supervision, and their rulers govern under the direction of others. Such subordination is an insult to the Lord of heaven and earth who is Israel's God.

For modern readers, Baruch shows how ancient Scripture can be interpreted to give life and meaning to people in new situations. The book's insistence that one must place all one's hope in the Lord, that one can find the Lord in the inspired Scriptures, and that one must hear words of hope make it perennially valuable for all ages.

Influence in Judaism and Christianity

The Hebrew text was not preserved in Judaism. According to Jerome, in the late fourth century AD, the Jews did not even possess a Hebrew text. In early Christianity, however, Baruch was widely quoted and cited as sacred Scripture. Baruch 3:36–37, concerning the appearance on earth of the wisdom of God, was a particular favorite because it was given a Christological reference. Fathers of the Church often quoted it, though they sometimes cite it as "Jeremiah," because in the Septuagint (Greek) translation Baruch was an appendix to Jeremiah. The work appears in several canonical lists of Greek fathers but never in lists compiled by Latin fathers. The book was included in the canonical list of the Council of Trent in 1546 and was ratified by Vatican I in 1870. Luther and other reformers followed Jerome's example and excluded Baruch from the canon. Protestants place it among the Apocrypha.

FURTHER READING

Fitzgerald, Aloysius, F.S.C. *Baruch.* The New Jerome Biblical Commentary, 563–67. Englewood Cliffs, NJ: Prentice Hall, 1990. Fine short commentary.

Harrington, Daniel J., S.J. *Baruch. Letter of Jeremiah.* HarperCollins Bible Commentary, 781–88. San Francisco: Harper, 2000. Concise, competent, the best short commentary.

Kodell, Jerome, O.S.B. *Lamentations; Baruch.* Old Testament Message 14. Wilmington, DE: Michael Glazier, 1982. Good basic commentary.

Nickelsburg, George D. "Baruch and the Epistle of Jeremiah." In *Jewish Writings in the Second Temple Period,* edited by M. E. Stone, 140–48. Assen: Van Gorcum, 1984. Authoritative essay.

Saldarini, Anthony J. *The Book of Baruch. The Letter of Jeremiah.* New Interpreter's Bible 6. 927–1010. Nashville, TN: Abingdon Press, 2001. The most recent, thorough, and judicious commentary.

EZEKIEL

[see pages 1161–1220 of the Old Testament]

The book of Ezekiel is a unique blend of divine utterance (rather than prophetic utterance), strange imagery, and careful arrangement. It is the only prophetic book displaying a chronological order. There are four major blocks of material, which are in the same sequence as in the books of Isaiah and Jeremiah. Chapters 1 through 24 are oracles concerning Judah and Jerusalem; chapters 25 through 32 are oracles concerning the nations; chapters 33 through 37 announce restoration; and chapters 38 through 48 describe the final battle and the vision of the new Temple and city. This essay discusses the historical background, the dated oracles and life of the prophet, the traditions Ezekiel used, the literary structure of the book, some key passages, the theology of the book, the Hebrew and Greek text, and the influence of Ezekiel on early Judaism and on the New Testament.

Historical Background

To understand Ezekiel's message, one must go back a century and a half before Ezekiel, to the earliest writing prophets—Amos, Hosea, Micah, and Isaiah of Jerusalem. What provoked these individuals to initiate a new religious movement and write down their prophecies and publicize them for the widest possible audience? Though we will probably never understand the reasons fully, two factors played a major role: (1) the prophets' conviction that the Lord's relationship to Israel had reached a crisis point; and (2) the fact that Israel faced a new kind of enemy, a superpower (Assyria) against which it could not defend itself. The earliest prophet, Amos, it is true, did not mention Assyria, but stated decisively that Israel's special relationship to the Lord had ended (8:1–3) and that Judah and Israel, like the nations, now stood under the severe judgment of God (2:4–3:2). Before the rise of the writing prophets, prophets fought for the Lord and the cause of righteousness in Israel, but never called into question the relationship itself. Reform measures would bring the people back into right relationship with the Lord, they thought. Indeed, it was possible to mount defenses against the modestly scaled armies that attacked Israel in those days. In the last third of the eighth century BC, however, Assyria moved into the area. Massive, relentless, and superior in war, it could not be defeated in any meaningful sense. The best one could do was to pay tribute.

How did these two new factors—the military situation and the prophets' conviction that the relationship had ended—affect Israel's traditions? These two factors severely damaged the credibility of the traditions, for the usual version of the national story, preserved in such psalms as 105, 114, and 136, proclaimed that the Lord set Israel apart for himself, freed them from Egyptian bondage, and gave them the Promised Land. The political changes of the mid-eighth century made the people's possession of their land precarious and uncertain. Israel's identity as a special people was called into question when the Lord remained silent before this new threat. Prophets were needed to reinterpret the ancient traditions for a radically new turn of events and to make it possible for the people to respond in a new situation. Each prophet emphasized in his own way the centrality of the relationship to the Lord and guided the people to appropriate actions. Hosea, for example, used the metaphor of marriage and the prospect of a new exodus to exhort Israel to remain faithful to the relationship. Amos mercilessly exposed the social injustice of the people and revised the traditional notion of the Day of the Lord to mean that the Lord might attack *Israel* rather than its enemies. Isaiah uncovered forgotten aspects of the Zion and David traditions to show that the promises were demands for fidelity as well as assurances of divine help. Jeremiah used the Exodus tradition and attempted to show that the divine judgment the people were experiencing could have a positive outcome if the people were obedient. Ezekiel, it will be shown below, interpreted the same historical events as Jeremiah, but saw them from a quite different perspective—that of a priest. The writing prophets, therefore, had a twofold task: to interpret the national traditions in the light of the ever-changing course of history, and to persuade people to act in accord with the required changes. Theory and practice, interpretation and praxis, were inseparable for the prophets.

Shortly before Ezekiel appears on the scene, in the last quarter of the seventh century, the hitherto dominant Assyrian empire collapsed with astonishing speed, enabling small states in the Levant such as Judah to regain their freedom and rebuild. (The Levant is the land area bordering the eastern Mediterranean.) Under Assyrian rule, the Northern Kingdom of Israel had become an Assyrian province, and Judah, with territory reduced, was a vassal state. These were the times of the prophets Hosea, Micah, and Isaiah, who had the task of explaining to the people that what was happening, however horrific, was the work of the Lord, that the events did not necessarily mean the end of Israel, and that the divine work demanded a faithful response.

In 640 BC, Josiah came to the throne in Judah. A child just eight years old, Josiah was assisted by a group of people loyal to the Lord and the authentic traditions of Israel. The death of the Assyrian king Assurbanipal, in 627 BC, freed him to launch a reform and reclaim the people's national and religious identity. Josiah sought to restore the old boundaries of the kingdom of David, annexing the former Assyrian provinces of Samaria, Gilead, and Galilee (2 Kgs 23:19). In 622 BC, an ancient law book, the nucleus of the present book of Deuteronomy, was found in the Temple in the course of restoration work. It became the basis of a wide-ranging religious reform (2 Kgs 22:1–23:27). Unfortunately, the promising reform collapsed with Josiah's unexpected death in 609 BC (2 Kgs 23:28–30). Judah was again reduced to a vassal state, first under Egypt and then, after Nebuchadnezzar defeated Egypt at the battle of Carchemish (in northern Syria) in 605 BC, under Babylon. Descendants of Josiah came to the throne in succession, all at the command of foreign powers: Jehoahaz (609, three months), Jehoiakim (609–598) and his son, Jehoiachin (598/7, three months), and Jehoiachin's uncle, Zedekiah (597–587/6). Though it had to yield control of Palestine to Babylon, Egypt remained a formidable state, never letting an opportunity pass to encourage Judah to rebel against Babylon. Jehoiakim and Zedekiah, for their part, played one great power against the other, but found, to their cost, that Egypt was weak and unreliable. Jeremiah vigorously opposed such attempts to fend off Babylon, which he regarded as God's instrument to punish and purge Judah. Jeremiah was right. Judean political juggling roused the Babylonians, and in 598 its army sacked the city and deported many of its leaders to Babylonia (2 Kgs 24:8–17). Jehoiakim died during the siege, and the Babylonians took his eighteen-year-old son Jehoiachin to Babylon as a hostage to prevent further rebellion. Many people placed their hopes for eventual restoration in Jehoiachin, a king in the line of David; to them, his release from prison was a good omen (2 Kgs 25:19; Jer 52:31–33). Jehoiachin's uncle Zedekiah was named regent (2 Kgs 24:18–20), and he continued his predecessors' rebellious policies. Nebuchadnezzar responded with force. After a campaign lasting three years (588–586 BC), he destroyed the cities of Judah and looted and burned Jerusalem and its Temple (2 Kgs 25; Jer 52). Babylon had done what Assyria had not done—destroy Jerusalem and the Temple.

King Zedekiah had to face the awful consequences. Captured, he was forced to look on as his two sons were murdered, then his own eyes were put out (2 Kgs 25). Among the eight or ten thousand deportees of 597 (2 Kgs 24:14–16 give both figures) was Ezekiel (Ez 1:1), evidently a Zadokite priest. With other exiles, he settled in Nippur and seems to have occupied a prominent place in the transplanted community and was often consulted by them (Ez 8:1; 14:1; 20:1). To judge by his commission to stand in opposition to the community and by his vigorous criticism of their opinions, he had a very different understanding of the exile than they did. He saw the exile as a long process of judgment that required faith. The people, on the other hand, saw themselves as helpless victims and hoped for a speedy and trouble-free return. No wonder that the Lord said to the prophet: "Hard of face and obstinate of heart are they to whom I am sending you. But you shall say to them: Thus says the Lord GOD!" (2:4).

Dated Oracles in the Book of Ezekiel

The book contains two series of seven dates that introduce selected oracles throughout the book.

(The first date [1:1] is outside of the sequence.) One series of seven dates introduces foreign oracles in chapters 25 through 32 (26:1; 29:1, 17; 30:20; 31:1; 32:1, 17), and range from 587/586 to 571; all but one, 29:1, 17, are in chronological order. The sections describe specific actions of enemy nations. The other series of seven dates (1:2; 3:16; 8:1; 20:1; 24:1; 33:21; 40:1) introduces important moments in the prophet's ministry. Ezekiel 1:2 and 3:16 mark his call and commission. The crucial vision of the departure of the divine glory from the Temple in chapters 8 through 11 is signaled by the date heading in 8:1. The fourth date, 20:1, is less certain; it may allude to the beginning of Zedekiah's rebellion, which was so fraught with consequences for the nation. The fifth date, 24:1, marks the beginning of the siege of Jerusalem in January 588. The last two dates are concerned with restoration: 33:21 is the date of the arrival of the news that Jerusalem has fallen, indicating that the prophet can now devote his attention to the revival of the nation; 40:1 begins the final vision of the new city and its Temple in 573. Carefully arranged in chronological order, these dates show how Ezekiel's preaching corresponded with God's judgment that unfolded over time. The number seven, which often expresses fullness and completion in the Bible, underlines the comprehensive nature of the divine plan. The dates suggest that the plan will come to completion even if human beings resist it.

Two dates require special comment. Ezekiel 1:1 gives the date of his call, "In the thirtieth year, on the fifth day of the fourth month, while I was among the exiles by the river Chebar, the heavens opened, and I saw divine visions," whereas the immediately following date (1:2) gives the date as July 593, "On the fifth day of the month, the fifth year, that is, of King Jehoiachin's exile, the word of the LORD came to the priest Ezekiel." To what does "the thirtieth year" refer? It could mean several things: Ezekiel's age at the time of his call (a priest could begin work in the Temple at thirty, according to Nm 4:3); the year when the book was finally edited; or thirty years after an event known to Ezekiel's original readers but not to us. The first suggestion makes the most sense: though Ezekiel was at the proper age for ordination, he could not be ordained in Babylonia because he could not go to the Temple; he would therefore serve at the Temple through visions (see 8–11 and 40–48). The other date, March/April 571 (19:17) is not in the proper chronological sequence; it may update an oracle originally given earlier.

The dates link Ezekiel's preaching to specific events in human history. Since Ezekiel employed divine speech and visionary experiences more than any other prophet, the date formulas remind readers that he was interpreting real events and urging hearers to practical action.

The Biography of Ezekiel

According to the date formula in 1:2, Ezekiel's prophetic ministry began with his call in July 593 near a canal ("River Chebar" in NAB) near Nippur, a few miles south of the city of Babylon. He was among the eight or ten thousand able men exiled to Babylonia after the siege of Jerusalem in 597 BC (2 Kgs 24:14, 16). (Evidently other family members were not counted in the census.) The last dated formula in the book is March/April 571 (29:17), which introduces a promise that Babylonia will plunder Egypt. The time span between the first and the last oracle is twenty-two years. To judge from the contents of the oracles, most of his ministry took place from 593 to 585. Ezekiel, however, may well have continued teaching and writing after 571 about matters that did not require a date, for example, the future events depicted in chapters 33 through 48. His public career was spent completely in dismal circumstances. The period from 593 to 571 was one of unrelieved doom—unhindered Babylonian domination, inept and cowardly Judean leadership, the fiery destruction of Jerusalem and the Temple, and exile in humiliation and poverty. These were the events that required Ezekiel's attention and comment. No wonder that the scroll in his inaugural vision "was covered with writing front and back, and written on it was: Lamentation and wailing and woe!" (2:10). It is a tribute to his faith and imagination that the prophet's message is ultimately about the bright future God has in store for his people.

The fact that Ezekiel is called a priest is of enormous significance: "The word of the LORD came to the priest Ezekiel, the son of Buzi, in the land of the Chaldeans by the river Chebar. There the hand of the LORD came upon me" (1:3). It has already been noted that his call "in the thirtieth year" most probably refers to the age of ordination. Priestly ordination was complex, however, requiring animal sacrifice (Ex 29 and Lv 8), which could only be carried out in Temple precincts. Ezekiel seems to be saying that normal ordination and priestly service was impossible for him, for he had no access to the Temple. He would be present in Jerusalem and exercise his priestly service in a new way, through *visionary experience*. Like that of Isaiah (Is 6), Ezekiel's inaugural vision is one of the throne of the Lord (1:26). In chapters 8 through 11, he will tour the Temple in a vision and will show how profoundly it has been corrupted by unholy conduct. In chapters 40 through 48, he will go on a visionary tour of the new city and the new Temple. As a priest, his categories are purity and impurity, and the boundaries between profane and sacred. As a prophet his purview included social justice and the fidelity required by the covenant. Holiness implied social justice (cf. Lv 19) and social justice implied right worship (cf. Is 1: 2–20). Ezekiel demands both exactness in rituals and compassion toward one's neighbor. An example is 18:5, "If a man is virtuous—if he does what is right and just, if he does not eat on the mountains, nor raise his eyes to the idols of the house of Israel; if he does not defile his neighbor's wife, nor have relations with a woman in her menstrual period . . . ," 18:5–6). The fact that he is a priest, even if not actually ordained in the Temple, does not take away in the least from his calling as a prophet. He often prophesies about Israel's problems and possibilities in priestly terms: how God will dwell in the midst of a sinful people, rebuild the Temple to protect its holiness, and arrange the people in the zones of holiness around the Temple. (See "The Traditions That Ezekiel Used.")

Ezekiel does not tell us very much about his personal life, for evidently he did not consider it significant for his public task. We know that his wife died in 588 only because it was important to his preaching (24:15–27). To dramatize how devastating would be the loss of "the delight of your eyes" (referring to the Temple), Ezekiel was forbidden by God to perform the customary mourning rites for his wife ("the delight of your eyes") when she died. The examples show that the book is not a biography but a record of preaching.

Several verses show Ezekiel's style of communicating to the elders of the people (8:1; 14: 1; 20:1). The elders gathered around him to consult the Lord. The verb "to consult the Lord" was a technical term for seeking an oracle from the Lord. That the elders would come to Ezekiel shows that they recognized him as an authentic prophet. Like a true prophet, he had no hesitation in criticizing them vigorously (14:1). Though his frequent use of divine speech might suggest that he did not converse with his hearers, several oracles directly respond to sayings current among the people. An example: "What is the meaning of this proverb that you recite in the land of Israel: 'Fathers have eaten green grapes, thus their children's teeth are on edge'?" (18:2). Ezekiel proceeded to a detailed refutation of this popular saying. Other popular sayings provoked a similar critique (12:22, 23, 27; 22:28; 37:11). Some exiles dismissed him as no more than an entertaining figure, as the Lord informed the prophet: "Your countrymen are talking about you along the walls and in the doorways of houses. They say to one another, 'Come and hear the latest word that comes from the LORD.' My people come to you as people always do; they sit down before you and hear your words, but they will not obey them, for lies are on their lips and their desires are fixed on dishonest gain. For them you are only a ballad singer, with a pleasant voice and a clever touch. They listen to your words, but they will not obey them" (33:30–32).

Ezekiel's style has caused some modern commentators to question his balance and even his sanity. Chapters 1; 8; 10; 37, and 40 describe ecstatic visions seizing the prophet's whole person. Among his prophetic gestures are clapping his hands and stamping his feet (6:11), digging through the wall of his house at night with a pack on his back to illustrate the exile (12:5), lying on his side for 390 days, and arranging his cut hair in three piles (5:1–17). Though some scholars of the previous generation argued that such behavior indicated mental instability, most today recognize that the actions are prophetic gestures, like Isaiah walking naked in Jerusalem for three years to dramatize the Assyrian conquest of Egypt (Is 20). They are a kind of living parable, designed to shock and provoke reflection. They do not provide a glimpse of "the real Ezekiel," whose personality (in the modern sense of personality) is largely hidden from our eyes.

The Traditions That Ezekiel Used

Every prophet favors certain traditions out of the many in Israel's lore. Isaiah made great use of the traditions about Zion and the Davidic king. Though Jeremiah cited the royal traditions, they were less important to him than the Exodus, which was the event that established the relationship between the Lord and the people. The traditions, it should be noted, do not exist as separate entities; they are related to one another as parts of a whole.

Ezekiel employed several traditions: the Exodus (especially the building of the tabernacle with its *kabod,* "glory") and the wilderness journey; Israelite and ancient Near Eastern traditions about the Temple and temple-city; and mythological traditions about the creation and maintenance of the world. The Exodus figures especially in one passage, chapter 20, where it is given an extraordinary reinterpretation. Unlike Amos and Jeremiah who regarded the Exodus as the golden moment of Israel's fidelity before the corrupting influence of the land, Ezekiel saw Israel's infidelity as beginning in the founding moment itself. Even before they left Egypt, the people had compromised themselves. To the elders consulting him, Ezekiel received the oracle: "Make known to them the abominations of their ancestors in these words . . . ; in the land of Egypt I revealed myself to them and swore: I am the LORD, your God. That day I swore to bring them out of the land of Egypt to the land I had scouted for them, a land flowing with milk and honey, a jewel among all lands. Then I said to them: Throw away, each of you, the detestable things that have held your eyes; do not defile yourselves with the idols of Egypt: I am the LORD, your God. But they rebelled against me and refused to listen to me; none of them threw away the detestable things that had held their eyes, they did not abandon the idols of Egypt" (20:4–8). Only zeal for the divine name held back the Lord from pouring out his anger against them then and again during rebellions at the giving of the law and at the rise of the next generation.

Why did Ezekiel radically devalue the revered traditions of the Exodus? The elders consulted him in 591 (20:1); in four years the siege would begin that will bring down Jerusalem and the Temple. Ezekiel had to prepare the people to believe that the destruction would be the Lord's doing. The prophet must unmask the false hopes that have deluded the people up to this point. He could not allow even the Exodus, the sacred moment of foundation, to be a source of pride. Israel was unfaithful even then. The people's only hope was the Lord, and in the last part of chapter 20 (vv. 33–44) Ezekiel outlined in glowing terms how the Lord, with a dazzling display of power, would enter into judgment with the people and lead them in a new exodus.

Another instance of the centrality of the Exodus is found in the account of the new temple-city and worship in chapters 40 through 48. Ezekiel 45:7–17, 21–25 and 46:1–18 speak of the prince (Hebrew *nasi*) instead of the king. Why? Because, it seems, the prophet wants to return to the ideals of the Exodus period, before there was a king. In ancient tradition, the *nasi* was the leader of each tribe in the march in the desert (Nm 2 and 7). Another indication of the importance of the Exodus is Ezekiel's demotion of the Levitical priests and promotion of the Zadokites (44:6–16; 48:11). The warrant for demoting one group and promoting another was apparently inspired by the people's apostasy and punishment in Numbers 25. Phineas, of the line of Aaron, killed the apostates and it was reckoned "for him and for his descendants after him the pledge of an everlasting priesthood, because he was zealous on behalf of his God and thus made amends for the Israelites" (Nm 25:13). A true priest rejects all foreigners in worship. The Levitical priests had been lax in excluding them from preexilic worship (Ez 8–11; 44:10–14). In contrast, the ancestor of Zadok, Phineas, had shown himself a zealous defender of orthodox worship, and so it is only fitting that his descendants, the Zadokites, are made priests in the renewed liturgy. One may also note that the mountain in chapters 40 through 48 is associated with Mount Sinai; chapters 40 through 48 is the only body of law not uttered by Moses; and Ezekiel plays the role of Moses providing the plans for a Temple and arranging for the encampment of the tribes. To Ezekiel is revealed the blueprint of the divine dwelling, as it was to Moses in Exodus 25:9. The purpose of the revelation on the mountain in Ezekiel is right worship and the proper ordering of the community, the same purpose as the legal material in Exodus, Leviticus, and Numbers.

The most important traditions for Ezekiel are

priestly, although it is difficult to trace exactly all the antecedents of his vision in the existing priestly traditions in Exodus 25–31 and 35–40 (the tabernacle with its equipment and rituals), Leviticus, and Numbers 1 through 10. There are similarities in Ezekiel to the so-called Holiness Code (Lv 17–26), a collection of laws concerned with the holiness of the people and the land they are entering. Examples of such similarities are the phrase, "for I, the LORD, am your God" (Lv 26:2; in Ezekiel, "I am the Lord") as a motive to act rightly, and the mixing of "ritual" and "moral" laws (e.g., Lv 19). Some scholars distinguish two traditions in Leviticus, a "priestly code" in chapters 1 through 16 (abbreviated P) and a "holiness code" in chapters 17 through 26 (abbreviated H). Each tradition has distinctive ideas about sin and holiness. In P, the Temple is the primary locale of holiness, and in H, it is the land. Ezekiel seems to straddle the two viewpoints: Chapters 8 through 11 focus on the holiness in the Temple, and chapters 40 through 48 focus on the holiness in the land in its concern to arrange the tribal allotments around the Temple in the center. His priestly outlook is consistent. For him, Israel's sin consisted in defiling the sanctuary (5:11), in committing "abominations" (a term used in worship, e.g., 5:9; 7:4; chapters 8 and 11), and in worshipping images (14:3–5). An important metaphor for him is the priestly one of uncleanness (e.g., 20:30–31; 22:26; 36:18). Uncleanness plays an important role in the long allegory of the two sisters in chapters 16 and 23, and in his attack on against the mountains, corrupted by the people's abominations. In chapter 18, Ezekiel gives a priestly torah, or teaching, on the question whether the guilt of one generation is passed on to the next.

Ezekiel also draws on mythological traditions. According to one definition, a myth is a traditional story set in the primordial past and involving supernatural elements. Myth and history are not necessarily opposed; mythological concepts and language were employed by biblical authors to show the transcendent significance of the historical laws and events they interpreted. Ezekiel, for example, used mythological language to describe his vision at the Chebar canal: the Lord appears to him in a storm cloud, luminous yet dark with water, borne by four composite figures having traits of animals and humans. The Lord is here portrayed as the divine warrior, a familiar portrayal in ancient Near Eastern religion and art (and in the Bible as well, for example, in Ex 15; 1 Kgs 18:41–46; 19:1–18). How much more effective and "true" is Ezekiel's mythic-historical report of his experience in 1:3–3:15 than a bare and unadorned statement that the Lord had appeared to him! Ezekiel's language conveys a sense of the transcendent. The mythic motifs are not mere decoration, however. They occur within a story, called by modern scholars "the combat myth," which was widely known in the ancient Near East from the third millennium BC to well into the common era. Ezekiel assumes that his hearers and readers know the story.

Though every version of the combat myth was unique, there was a basic plot: a power (often depicted as a monster) threatens the cosmic and political order of the universe. The assembly of the gods cannot find a senior god to repel the monster; the assembly appoints a young god, promising him kingship if he succeeds. Defeating the monster, the god restores the prethreat order (in some versions creates the world), builds a palace, and is acclaimed king by the gods. In biblical adaptations of the combat myth, the victory of the warrior God is normally the creation of the world or the creation of Israel. Ezekiel's adaptation of the combat myth is clearest in chapters 38 through 48. Before the Lord can build his palace and city, an enemy, greater and more resistant than the historical nations mentioned in chapters 25 through 32, must be faced and defeated. That enemy is Gog of the land of Magog. Only when he and his armies are defeated (38–39) can the Temple be built. With Gog of the land of Magog eliminated, the Lord can build his city and decree new ordinances. When one appreciates the mythic nature of these chapters, one realizes that Ezekiel is speaking of the *far future* in these chapters. Before the new world can come in definitively, evil itself, which is more than the evil of any one nation, has to be defeated. One can see how a mythological perspective enables the prophet to speak of matters that transcend history as such, yet without cutting loose from history, for he is speaking of history's goal.

The Literary Structure of the Book

Of all the prophetic books, Ezekiel is arranged with the most skill and purpose. To some extent, the structure is the message. Chapters 1 through

24 are oracles against Judah; 25 through 32 are oracles against foreign nations; and 33 through 48 are oracles of restoration for Judah and Jerusalem. Since the oracles *against* the foreign nations are by that fact *for* Judah, they can be viewed under restoration. The whole book falls into two equal parts, doom (1–24) and restoration (25–48). Like a good sentinel (3:16–21; 33:1–6), Ezekiel preached doom and warning right up to the fall of Jerusalem in 586 BC. After that great event, his task was to preach restoration. The two halves of the book are closely connected. The first part announced the fall of the city and urged Israel to give up its delusions and false hopes of speedy relief. Divine judgment had to come, for only a divine action makes possible the reign of God. The reign of God means, first, the overturning of the false rule of the pagan nations (25–32) and, second, the implementation of the justice of God in the land (33–48). The implementation has three aspects: (1) a new exodus and conquest of the land (33–37); (2) the vanquishing of primordial evil greater than that in any one nation (38–39); and (3) the new temple-city, the return of the Lord who departed in chapter 11, the regulations of the new worship, the river coming from the Temple, and the new encampment of the tribes around the temple-city (40–48). A detailed outline illuminates the significance of the structure. See outline, RG 327.

Three visions provide a complementary structure: chapters 1 to 3, 8 to 11, and 40 to 48. The first depicts the prophet's call, the second is the judgment against Jerusalem and the Temple, and the third is the restoration of the Temple and the arrangement of the holy land. Ezekiel 43:3 expressly relates the three visions: "The vision was like that which I had seen when he came to destroy the city, and like that which I had seen by the river Chebar." Although there are visions in other prophetic books (Zec 1–6), only in Ezekiel are they woven into the architecture of the book. In the first vision, Ezekiel sees the glory (Hebrew *kabod*) of God that dwelt in the tabernacle in the wilderness and in the Temple in Jerusalem. Phrasing carefully in order to safeguard the sacrality and otherness of the glory, the prophet describes only the wheels of the divine throne. The throne is mobile; it is in Babylon rather than Jerusalem. This opening scene foreshadows the departure of the glory from Jerusalem in 10:1–11:25 and the return in 43:1–12. A deity able to move, unlike the traditional picture of the deity dwelling in the Temple in Jerusalem, is an ominous beginning to the book. Ezekiel's unpopular message has evidently isolated him from the other exiles as he sits alone at the banks of the canal. God finds him by a canal outside the city. The next vision (8–11) is pivotal in the book: an angelic figure transports Ezekiel from Babylon to Jerusalem, gives him a tour of the Temple, and points out men committing cultic abominations and injustice against others. Angelic servants kill all those within who have not been marked as contrite, a harbinger of the slaughter that will take place when the Temple is destroyed. In the ancient Near East no temple is destroyed unless its god has already abandoned it. The glory abandons the city, lifted up by the wings of the cherubim. Ezekiel describes the vision to his fellow exiles and attempts to show them its significance. In the last vision (40–48) the Lord returns to the temple-city, rebuilt on a heavenly model and protected from all corrupting foreign influence. A new torah or authoritative teaching is given and all is made ready for a new people.

Within the structure, there are some correspondences between chapters 1 through 24 and 25 through 48. The news of the destruction of Jerusalem plays a key role in the book. Shortly before the city fell in July 586, Ezekiel's wife died, and the prophet was forbidden to perform the mourning rites for her as a symbol of the loss of the city (24:15–27). He was also struck dumb (3:26–27; 24:27). When the news comes, he was able to speak (34:21–22) and proclaimed the Lord's restoration. In 3:16–21, Ezekiel was made a sentinel charged with telling his people of their impending destruction. When the destruction took place, his sentinel task was reaffirmed (33:1–9) for the new phase in God's plan for the people. In 36:1–5, the prophet blessed the mountains of Israel, reversing his earlier denunciations in 6:1–10; the mountains evidently stand for the entire land.

Some Key Chapters in the Book

In the vision of the throne chariot and the commission (1:2–3:15), the prophet stood alone beside the Chebar canal and saw a large lumi-

Outline of the Book of Ezekiel

- I. Impending Doom (1–24)
  - A. Title and introduction (1:1–3)
  - B. Vision of the Enthroned One and Commission of Ezekiel
    - 1. Vision of the divine throne (1:1–28)
    - 2. Commissioning of the prophet (2:1–3:27)
  - C. Symbolic Acts and Oracles
    - 1. Three symbolic actions (4:1–5:4)
    - 2. Three matching oracles (5:5–7:27)
  - D. Vision of Divine Judgment on the Temple
    - 1. The abominations committed in the Temple (8:1–9:11)
    - 2. God departs from the city (10:1–11:25)
  - E. Condemnation of Leaders and People
    - 1. Symbolic gesture foreshadowing the exile (12:1–28)
    - 2. Condemnation of false prophets (13:1–23)
    - 3. Idolatry *versus* right behavior (14:1–23)
  - F. Allegories and Metaphors of Judgment
    - 1. Allegory of the vine wood (15:1–8)
    - 2. Allegory of Jerusalem as God's faithless wife (16:1–63)
    - 3. Allegory of the two eagles (17:1–24)
    - 4. Priestly decisions on intergenerational responsibility (18:1–32)
    - 5. Two allegories on the king (19:1–14)
  - G. Final Indictment and Condemnation
    - 1. Review of the Exodus (20:1–44)
    - 2. The sword oracles (20:1–21:32)
    - 3. The guilt of Jerusalem (22:1–31)
    - 4. The allegory of the two sisters (23:1–49)
    - 5. Two signs of the end (24:1–27)
- II. Restoration (33–48)
  - A. Oracles against Foreign Nations
    - 1. Against neighboring states (25:1–17)
    - 2. Against Tyre (26:1–28:19)
    - 3. Against Sidon (28:20–26)
    - 4. Against Egypt (29:1–32:32)
  - B. Justice in the Land
    - 1. The second commission of the prophet (33:1–33)
    - 2. The good Shepherd replaces false shepherds (34:1–31)
    - 3. Oracles against the mountains of Edom (35:1–15)
    - 4. Blessings on the mountains of Israel (36:1–15)
    - 5. Renewal of Israel (36:16–38)
    - 6. The people are brought back to life
      - a. Vision of dry bones (37:1–14)
      - b. The two sticks rejoined (37:15–28)
  - C. The conquest of Gog of Magog
    - 1. Gog's attack on the people of God (38:1–23)
    - 2. God's victory (39:1–29)
  - D. The New Temple and the New Worship
    - 1. Description of the new Temple
      - a. The Temple court (40:1–47)
      - b. Inside of the Temple (40:48–42:20)

Outline *continued*

- c. The return of the Lord (43:1–12)
2. Prescriptions for worship
   - a. Altar of sacrifice (43:13–27)
   - b. Priestly ministers (44:1–31)
   - c. Division of the land (45:1–17)
   - d. Regulation of the feasts (45:18–46:24)
3. The river issuing from the door of the Temple (47:1–12)
4. Boundaries of the new land
   - a. National boundaries (47:13–23)
   - b. Land allotments for each tribe (48:1–29)
   - c. The new city (48:30–35)

---

nous cloud moving in his direction. It was radiant (1:4), like the luminous clouds that accompanied appearances of the Lord in such ancient traditions as Exodus 19:9; 24:16; 33:9; and 34:5. As it came near, he discerned four creatures, all radiant, in its lower part; they had human feet and hands but with four wings and four faces. They moved as one; below and alongside each there was a wheel rimmed with eyes, and above them was a shining expanse. As the creatures' wings slackened and the apparition came to a halt, the prophet looked up and saw a sapphire throne upon which a human figure sat, glowing, ringed by a rainbow. It was the throne of God. The order of the narrative is the order of the prophet's perception: sights, then sounds; the lower part of the vision, then the upper; the movement of the apparition, then the halting. (These remarks do not apply to 1:8b–12, which are dislocated.) Though unparalleled in its bold portrayal of divinity, the vision is also traditional; Psalms 18:8–14 (parallel in 2 Sm 22) is a similar storm appearance; the composite creatures are found in Isaiah 6 and attested in Mesopotamian and Syrian religious symbolism. To perceive the full significance of the divine manifestation, one must take into consideration the commission in 1:28–3:15. As Moshe Greenberg points out, one can assume from the commission to preach to a hardhearted people that Ezekiel was already an outcast from his community. Instead of facing the impending disaster, the people put their faith in prophets who said the whole thing would soon be over. The majestic vision vindicated the prophet's minority view; the Lord told him his community would not believe his message and yet he must speak, saying, "Thus says the LORD God." Further, in 3:1–3 the Lord commanded him to eat the scroll like Jeremiah, "When I found your words, I devoured them; they became my joy and the happiness of my heart" (Jer 15:16; cf. Pss 119:103). Though the gesture of eating the scroll seems bizarre, it was typical of Ezekiel to use traditional material with unusual concretization and dramatization. In any event, Ezekiel's *writings* seem to have been arranged with exceptional artistry and confidence in the power of the written word to instruct and teach. One last point: the mobile throne shows the Lord able to leave the Jerusalem Temple and meet the exiles in their new residence; such mobility will be demonstrated negatively by the departure in chapter 11 and positively by the return in chapter 43.

More than any other prophet, Ezekiel uses gestures to provoke his audience to question him (e.g., 4:1–3, 4–8, 9–17; 5:1–4; 12:1–11; 37:15–24). The gestures are a kind of street theater to capture the attention of an unreceptive audience. On one occasion, Ezekiel was told to take a brick, sketch a city on it, build miniature siege works against it, and put a metal plate between himself and the city; he then was told to lie on his left side for 390 days, then on his right side for forty days. He had also to eat bread made of different grains (as one might in a siege) and ration his water. This action was an anticipation of the disasters lying ahead for the people when Jerusalem would be destroyed (chapter 4). The prophet was evidently acting out the disaster that the people were refusing to face as they clung to hopes of a speedy return to their normal lives in Judah. The people will lie helpless as they "bear their punishment." The prophet's sign of not mourning one's wife in 24:15–27 is an example of a sign provoking a reaction: "Then the people asked me, 'Will you not tell us what all these things that you are doing mean for us?' " (24:19).

The vision of the corruption of the Temple and the departure of the glory (8:1–11:25) can be confusing. Chapters 8 through 11 are linked to the opening vision in chapters 1 through 3 in reverse order: the luminous figure in 8:2 is linked to 1:27; the throne in 10:1, to the throne in 1:26; the sounds of wings in 10:5, to the sounds of wings in 1:24; the wheels in 10:9–13, to the wheels in 1:15–18, and the faces in 10:14, to the faces in 1:10. The "cherubim" in chapter 10 are the same as the "living creatures" in chapter 1. According to Greenberg, a chiasm, or sandwich structure, shapes chapters 8 through 11:

A. Ezekiel converses with the elders (8:1a)
    B. The hand of the Lord fell upon him (8:1b)
        C. A luminous figure (8:2–3)
        C'. The glory of the Lord (11:22–23)
    B'. The spirit lifted him up (11:24b)
A'. Ezekiel tells the exiles what the Lord has revealed to him (11:25)

In the section framed by this chiasm (8:4–11:21), the angelic guide gives Ezekiel a tour of the corrupt practices that have polluted the Temple and the social wrongs that have ruined the people (8:5–18). Punishment is imposed (9:10–11). Meanwhile, the glory of the Lord begins to move, on its way to leave the Temple (10:4–5); the cherubim stop at the entrance of the east gate (10:8–22). Next, in a passage that balances the description of the first group of men in Chapter 8, the spirit brings Ezekiel to the east gate to view more evidence of wicked behavior (11:1–13). In 11:14–21, a reassuring word comes to Ezekiel that the exiles will not lose their property back in Judah. Though the Lord removed them far away among the nations, yet he has been a sanctuary to them for a little while in the countries where they have gone (11:16, different translation from NAB). The Lord abandons his Temple. At the time of this vision, perhaps not too long after the prophet's commission in 593, the exiles were unprepared for the possibility that the Temple might be destroyed.

Chapter 18, one of the most famous chapters in Ezekiel, gives priestly decisions (torah) on questions that had become especially pressing because of the people's situation. Though sometimes misinterpreted as a charter of religious individualism, chapter 18 makes two distinct points: (1) 18:1–20 teaches that one generation will not have to suffer for the sins of a previous generation, contrary to an older view preserved in Exodus 20:5, "For I, the LORD, your God, am a jealous God, inflicting punishment for their fathers' wickedness on the children of those who hate me, down to the third and fourth generation"; (2) 18:21–28 teaches that past sins do not encumber a person currently leading a good life. These teachings were provoked by a fashionable proverb of the time, "Fathers have eaten green grapes, thus their children's teeth are on edge." The proverb implicitly accused God of punishing the innocent descendants of wicked forbears. The prophet denies any "vertical" guilt (between generations) but insists on "horizontal" guilt, that is, the present generation must bear its own guilt. The people are not simply victims of someone else's sin.

Other chapters of the book are long essays detailing the history of the Lord's relationship with the people—chapters 16 (the Lord's relationship with personified Jerusalem), 20 (the retelling of the Exodus), and 23 (the story of the two sisters, Oholah and Oholibah, respectively Samaria and Jerusalem). In the two allegories (16 and 23), the Lord came upon helpless women and made them noble, yet they fought him every step of the way. What is the purpose of these exceedingly negative retellings of Israel's history? One must be aware that Israel found its identity by telling its national story. A comparison may be helpful. A modern person's identity arises largely from his or her own story: who one's parents were and of what social class; where one grew up, went to school, where one worked, and whom one married. If one becomes unhappy or dysfunctional, one examines one's story and seeks to find a new and more productive way of telling that story. Similarly, Ezekiel felt the people misunderstood their national story; they had to be shown that their version no longer made sense; it was not uniformly glorious as the people commonly believed. So Ezekiel retold the story in new and perverse ways. He said that the people were unfaithful from the beginning; their history gave them no reason for pride.

Ezekiel's retellings of the story in chapters 16 and 23 can offend modern readers. Two things must be noted. First, Ezekiel has a peculiar strategy of dramatizing a reality and, to modern tastes, exaggerating it. His use of the marital metaphor for the relationship of the Lord and Israel is an example. The metaphor was at least as old as Hosea 1–3; Ezekiel makes it concrete far beyond any usage in Hosea, drawing out the personification and dwelling on its sexual aspects. Second, Ezekiel describes the infidelity of Israel as flagrant sexual misconduct: she is a prostitute and deserves to be humiliated and punished. The prophet is a child of his time, portraying the broken relationship as a woman's betrayal of a man, and the deity's act of justice as satisfying his male rage and jealousy (e.g., 16:23–24). Furthermore, either Ezekiel or an editor in 23:46–49 goes on to make the story a warning against all women's lewd behavior. The warning, of course, makes a legitimate point: lewd conduct is wrong in women (as well as in men). One must be careful, however, not to imply that women are usually unfaithful. In speaking about such biblical passages, it is pastorally advisable to speak of the marriage metaphor as a favored metaphor for the relationship of the Lord and Israel. The metaphor expresses a relationship that is mutual, passionate, self-giving, nurturing, and faithful.

Unlike chapters 16 and 23, chapter 20 speaks without allegory about the people's past and future. The occasion for this essay is an inquiry to Ezekiel by some of the elders for an oracular response. Instead, the Lord tells the prophet to indict them, to make known to them the abominations of their ancestors (v. 5). To indict them, he tells the history of the people in four stages: Egypt (vv. 5–10), the first wilderness generation (vv. 11–17), the second wilderness generation (vv. 18–26), and in the land (vv. 27–29). Verses 30–44 are the application and consequences: God refuses again to respond to an inquiry (vv. 30–31) and then reveals a new exodus (vv. 32–44): "I will lead you to the desert of the peoples, where I will enter into judgment with you face to face" (v. 35), and the people will finally come into the land and serve the Lord on the holy mountain (v. 40). The prophet retells the history in such a way as to take away all cause for pride. The people's task is to allow the Lord in the future to redo the Exodus so that the result will be a faithful people.

The oracles against the foreign nations are in chapters 25 through 32, the center of the book, the same placement as Isaiah (chapters 13–27) and the Greek text of Jeremiah (25:13; 31). Ezekiel's arrangement is careful: chapters 25–28 are oracles against six nations (Ammon, Moab, Edom, Philistia, Tyre, and Sidon), beginning with the nation directly east (Ammon) and then proceeding clockwise ending in the direction of northwest (Sidon). Geographically, one would expect the list to end with the north, the direction from which the enemy of Israel at this time, Babylon, would invade. Jeremiah 25:9 even calls Babylon the "the enemy from the north." For Ezekiel, however, Babylon is not the enemy but the instrument of the Lord's judgment, even exercising judgment against the seven nations (e.g., Ez 26:7; 19:18; 30:10). Instead, the book places Egypt in the seventh and climactic arrangement. Moreover, there are seven oracles against Egypt (29–32). One is prepared for the concentration on Egypt by the lengthy oracles against Tyre (26–28). The placement of the oracles in this part of the book contributes to the meaning of the prophet's message in at least three ways: (1) since the Lord of all the world has judged Judah and Jerusalem, surrounding nations are affected by that judgment; (2) the punishment of the nations that persecuted Judah is the first step in the restoration of Judah, which will be announced in more positive form in chapters 33–37; (3) chapters 25 through 32 prepare for chapters 38 and 39: just as the defeat of the nations makes possible the restoration of Judah upon its land, so the defeat of all human and cosmic evil in chapters 38 and 39 makes possible the definitive kingdom in chapters 40 through 48.

Chapters 33 through 37 contain a message of restoration. The opening chapter recalls earlier passages and moves one into a new age for Israel. The prophet as watchman (33:1–9) harks back to 3:16–21 and Ezekiel's initial call; the passage on individual retribution (33:10–20) has relevance for chapter 18, which treats sin, guilt, and punishment; the arrival of the fugitive from Jerusalem and the end of Ezekiel's muteness (32:22) alludes to 3:22–27 and 24:25–27. Ezekiel 33:23–33 insist that salvation is reserved for those in exile who have been transformed. It anticipates 36:16–38. Chapter 34, the divine king as shepherd, stands in the tradition of referring to kings as shepherds: 2 Sm 5:2; Mi 5:4; Jer 2:8;

3:15; 23:1–6. Ezekiel's passage in turn influenced Zec 11:4–17, and together they helped to form New Testament passages on the divine shepherd like Mark 6:34 and John 10.

Ezekiel 36:16–38 makes points similar to those in Jeremiah 31:31–37. Both passages speak of an interior renewal. As a priest, Ezekiel introduces a number of ritual details to accompany the interior transformation: cease to profane my holy name; witness to my holiness; sprinkle with clean (or holy) water; be cleansed of idols; observe my decrees. Chapter 37 uses two different images to recount Israel's revival: dry bones scattered across a field are fitted together, covered with sinews and flesh, and brought to life by the breathing of the spirit and the two sticks brought together.

The final part of the book begins with chapter 38, not chapter 40, for the battle of Gog of the land of Magog against the Lord is the necessary prelude to the construction of a new temple-city, its regulations, and the positioning of the holy people around it. Chapters 38 and 39 presume that Israel has returned from exile and dwells peacefully on its own land (38:12). In a grand finale, God, the divine warrior, musters the armies of the world and lures them into a massive battle that results in their annihilation and his glory. Such a divine initiative was, according to 38:17, predicted in such earlier prophetic passages as Isaiah 29:7; Micah 8:11–13; Jeremiah 1:14. Isaiah 14:24–27 predicted that the great empire Assyria would be destroyed in the midst of the holy land. Furthermore, Exodus texts said that the Lord was glorified by the defeat of the Egyptians: "Thus will I make Pharaoh so obstinate that he will pursue them. Then I will receive glory through Pharaoh and all his army, and the Egyptians will know that I am the LORD" (Ex 14: 4). Such a statement sounds very much like Ezekiel 39:13, which describes the victory as the day the Lord reveals his glory. To a first-time reader, the text of chapters 38 and 39 seems confused, and indeed there may have been revisions or additions to underline the meaning. Its structure, however, seems clear: 38:1–16, Gog's attack on Israel; 38:17–23, God's war against Gog; 39:1–16, God's victory (39:1–3 is parallel to 38:1–6); 39:17–29, God's glory is revealed to all. Although based vaguely on historical characters (Gog seems based on the Lydian ruler Gyges; Magog, his homeland, was probably created to rhyme with Gog; Gomer is from the Cimmerians), the scene is *transhistorical;* it is an event that will happen at an unspecified future time. Divine initiative is stressed repeatedly, just as it is in the Exodus accounts. Gog does not attack on his own initiative; the Lord brings the army into the holy land so that he can destroy it on the mountains of Israel. The text seems to presume that there is some primordial evil, greater than any one empire that must be identified and destroyed before Israel can live in complete peace. In a sense, the composite battle and victory is a theological reflection on evil and a statement of the hope that God will someday eradicate every vestige of that evil.

According to the combat myth, after winning the cosmic battle, the victorious deity is recognized as the supreme god and builds his palace (temple), announcing his decrees for the ruling of the world. In chapter 40:1–4, the hand of the Lord brought Ezekiel in a vision to the land of Israel and set him down on a very high mountain on which there was a city and a temple. An angelic figure shows him the ground plan (there are no elevations in the plan) of the Temple area; the tour is a counterpart to the tour of chapters 8–11. The order of topics in 40 through 48 follows generally those of the priestly writings of the Pentateuch (Ex 25–31; 33–40; Lv; Nm 1–10; 32; 34–35). The temple plan follows generally the latest form of the Solomonic Temple but with an emphasis on safeguarding the sanctity of the temple from profane contact. For example, the eastern gate ("the gate which faced the east," 40: 5) is a military gate, like gates found in Gezer, Hazor, and Megiddo, which contain four successive recesses so that guards can interrupt chariots rushing the gate. The nearness of the king's palace to the temple in the old system is vigorously criticized (43:6–12). The Lord returns to the temple (43:1–5), and Ezekiel sees "that the temple was filled with the glory of the LORD" (v. 5).

The next section of the vision (43:13–46:24) is concerned with the altar, the reorganization of the clergy making the Zadokites alone full priests (45:15–31), the territory set apart for them (45: 1–9), and the prince's responsibilities for supporting the temple (46) and overseeing justice (45:9). "Prince" is an ancient premonarchic title that Ezekiel revives in place of "king," which for him had become a symbol of failed leadership. The third section is introduced by 47:1–11, the water flowing from the temple throughout the land, which serves as a transition from temple to land. Water in Ezekiel is associated with the deity (1:24 and 43:2). The sacred mountain is the garden of God, the source of all fertilizing waters (Gn 2:10–14; cf. Ez 28:13; 31:8–9; 36:35). Mount Zion is also associated with that tradition (e.g., Ps 46:4 and Is 12:3; 33:20–24). One of the four great rivers arising in the garden of Eden was the Gihon, which is, according to 1 Kings 1:33, the river of Jerusalem. The remaining chapters speak of the boundaries of the future land of Israel (essentially the same as Nm 34:1–12), the redistricting of the tribes in equal east-west strips, each with coastal land, uplands, and territory in the Jordan-Dead Sea depression. The new name given to Jerusalem, "The Lord is there," is the last verse in the book.

The Theology of the Book

Ezekiel's theology originated in his prophetic interpretation of the situation of his community—the Judeans living as exiles in Babylonia—and his counsels on how they should live in their new circumstances. His theology includes praxis, or observance. Although Ezekiel is concerned with the actions of the Lord and the course of Israelite history, he must also deal with the people's immediate anxieties and concerns, among which are concerns about whether they have title to their land and whether they have a future as a people. In other words, should they give up their dreams of being the Lord's special people and, instead, acculturate themselves into the Babylonian empire? As many exiles saw things, their ancestors' sins definitively severed the relationship of the Lord to Israel. This bitter truth was especially visible among the landless and unhappy exiles. Ezekiel thus had to explain concrete issues without losing sight of the overall purposes of the Lord whose spokesman he was.

At the basis of his theology was the great founding moment of Israel—the Exodus from Egypt and entry into Canaan *as seen through priestly eyes*. It has already been pointed out that the Priestly source deeply influenced the prophet. An example of its influence is the dominant structuring device of the glorious Lord on the throne of wheels: the glory appeared to the exiled prophet (1:28; 3:23), departed from the Jerusalem Temple (10:18; 11:23), and will return to the temple-city (43:2–5), to fill the Temple (44:4) as the glory once filled the tabernacle in the wilderness in Exodus 40:34. The mobility expressed by the throne with wheels is very important: the Lord is not tied down to one place or to a particular way. Like Micah's prediction, affirmed by Jeremiah, that the Temple was not sacrosanct and could be destroyed (Mi 3:12; Jer 7:4), and like Isaiah's prediction that the Lord was doing a new thing (Is 43: 19; 48:6), Ezekiel strikes a blow for the freedom of God. It is important to note, however, that the Lord does not leave the Jerusalem Temple to become a spiritual presence available in every time and place. Rather, the Lord will come back to a specific place, there to meet the people in a purified and sacred place. The great empires, Assyria and then Babylonia, and the writing prophets' assessment that Israel had failed to live up to its covenantal responsibilities, changed forever the situation of Israel, in a sense "requiring" the Lord to do a new thing. What is the "new thing"? Those empires will be the instruments of Israel's purification ("judgment") and eventual return to the Lord. Hence, exile and destruction are not the end of the relationship; rather they constitute the judgment process that will establish justice, that is, uphold the righteous and put down the wicked. God is not absent from the process. Ezekiel does not hesitate to affirm that the Lord is present among the exiled population and that if people give up their delusions and their sinful ways, the Lord will raise them from the death of exile and give them a new city and temple. In the general picture of exile and restoration just presented, Ezekiel did not differ significantly from his prophetic predecessors. What then was his peculiar contribution to the Bible and to the contemporary church?

Though not cited as often by Christians as other prophetic books, Ezekiel says much to modern Christians. It insists on the Lord's transcendence and freedom; one can be overwhelmed and transformed by the presence of the Lord whom one cannot see. The Lord moves easily from the Temple to the exile and back to a restored Temple. Yet this utterly free and sovereign Lord has fallen in love with Israel and cannot leave or abandon her. Ezekiel insists more than any other prophet that the Lord acts because of the Lord's own reasons, not because of Israel's virtues or miseries. In fact, the prophet insists on this point with such vehemence that some modern readers are offended. The text locates the authority of the prophetic oracle in the Lord: the prophet is constantly referred to as "son of man," that is, mere human in comparison with God. The phrase "oracle of the Lord" occurs eighty-five times; the so-called recognition formula "that they may know that I am the Lord" occurs fifty-four times; and the assertion that the Lord acts so his name will not be profaned among the nations is constant. Although at first reading they might suggest a self-centered deity, they actually make a positive statement, for they locate the reason for God acting *in God's very self* in the divine character. How dangerous it would be if God acted because of human righteousness! God acts because of who he is, not because of who Israel is. That is the basis of true hope, and it is why Ezekiel is so intent on destroying all human grounds for hope. True hope is based in God, not in human beings.

Another important contribution of the book is its careful literary structure. Ezekiel is a writer as well as a speaker. The structure in a sense frees Ezekiel from his immediate context to address a wider audience. In the book, one sees the glorious Lord, obligated to no human institution, choosing an individual to announce a painful judgment on beloved Israel that will eventuate in the renewal of that people. The metaphors for this process are dominantly those of love (marriage and betrothal) and personal presence (departing and returning), even though Ezekiel employs the metaphors in his peculiarly concrete and dramatic way. The judgment process extends to other nations as well and has as its ultimate aim restoration rather than destruction. When the final blow comes (the destruction of the Temple), the judgment process enters a new phase, that of restoration. Again, this phase uses relational metaphors—a loving shepherd, the mountain lands of Israel, dry bones, and a stick rejoined. The restoration phase addresses the problem of permanent and residual evil in the universe in the great victory over Gog of Magog. Only after that evil is destroyed (in some future time) is it possible for the Lord's own palace and city to be constructed. Chapters 33 through 37 speak of the *immediate* future and chapters 38 through 48 of the *indefinite* future. It is his vision of the process of judgment that Ezekiel makes his greatest contribution to the Christian Bible.

In the confusing and destructive events of the early sixth century, Ezekiel recognized the judgment of the Lord. He allowed the Lord to act in justice and compassion and do a new thing—bring about a restored people living peacefully and happily with God at the center. Without panic, steadily and insistently, he instructed the people how to live in the judgment process. He showed them its immediate goal (33–37) and its ultimate goal (40–48). They thus could endure, trust in God alone, and hope in the world that God would bring in. Ezekiel illuminates the New Testament, in which judgment leading to life plays a significant role. The book illuminates as well the life of Jesus, who underwent his own process of judgment: a righteous poor person, killed by sinners, but raised up to life.

Another important contribution of the book is its insistence that the Lord has a dwelling among human beings and among the people of Israel. God is not abstract and universal. Rather, God provides a place where people can hear and encounter him, and where fertilizing waters can flow over the earth from that precious center.

The Text of Ezekiel

The Hebrew text at times seems repetitive and overloaded. In the view of many scholars, it contains doublets (repeated verses) and expansions by disciples or scribes. The problem is particularly acute in the vision of the divine chariot in chapters 1 and 10. The Septuagint, the Greek translation made in the second century BC, is about 4 or 5 percent shorter than the Hebrew text and seems to be an earlier edition of the book. The Hebrew text is a later form of that text, which has been supplemented by systematic additions, some of which resemble language and concepts in Deuteronomy. The additions are mostly minor: additions of parallel words or phrases, explanations, filling out of the context, harmonizing additions, and Deuteronomistic formulations. The textual situation is much like that in Jeremiah, where the Greek text is 15 percent shorter than the Hebrew, and is an earlier version of the text. Scholars are divided on how to explain the longer Hebrew text and the apparent doublets, repetitions, and expansions, many of which are in the Greek text as well as the Hebrew. A few scholars defend the position that Ezekiel is the author of virtually the entire book and so attribute the repetitions and expansions to the prophet's rhetorical style. The older position, which is still the majority position today, believes that that additions and expansions were added to the text in course of copying it. Many expansions could have been made by Ezekiel himself, who apparently realized early on that the prophetic book itself could carry on his God-given task of instructing Israel. Walther Zimmerli, a respected recent interpreter, suggests, for example, that 16:1–43 is the original core of this long chapter, and that verses 44–58 and 59–63 are expansions.

Oral proclamation can change greatly when written down, because the writer or disciple now has a new and quite different audience in mind. The arrangement of the entire book can take on a entirely new significance, for it helps *readers* to interpret the prophet's proclamation for a different situation. The editing and arranging of Ezekiel was done with such care and intelligence that it is a further step in the prophetic task of interpretation and exhortation. Thus, the additions to the book of Ezekiel do not obscure his purpose but make it available to readers. Israel never regarded the prophetic books primarily as biographies or histories. Rather, the books were and are still regarded as preaching the divine word to every generation.

Ezekiel in Jewish and Christian Tradition

In rabbinic literature, Ezekiel became a favorite of unorthodox forms of Judaism and thus was regarded with some caution by the rabbis. Four aspects of Ezekiel's prophecy were singled out. First, the divine chariot revelation in chapter 1 became the basis of Jewish mysticism and also of heretical speculation of various kinds. The mysticism is sometimes referred to as "merkabah (chariot) mysticism." Second, the rabbis feared that Ezekiel's severe denunciations of Israel in the first part of the book could be used by Christians in an anti-Jewish way and so were unacceptable. Third, the resurrection of the dry bones in 37:1–14 was a favorite of sectarian groups and hence was played down by the rabbis. Fourth, Ezekiel's vision of the future temple and his laws seemed to contradict the Pentateuchal instructions and nearly led to the exclusion of the book from the canon.

In the New Testament, the Gospels do not quote any text from Ezekiel. Matthew 13:32 refers to Ezekiel 17:23; Matthew 25:35 to Ezekiel 18:17, and there are a few more allusions. The most obvious debt is the portrayal of Jesus as the Good Shepherd (Mt 18:12–14; Jn 10:1–18), which comes from Ezekiel 34. First Peter 3:9 harks back to Ezekiel 18:23 and 33:11. The New Testament book that makes constant reference to Ezekiel is Revelation (Apocalypse), usually in brief snatches and allusions. A few examples: Revelation 4:1–8 develops the throne vision of Ezekiel 1; and Revelation 5:1; 10:1–4, 8–11 pick up the image of the eating of the scroll from Ezekiel 2:8–9; Revelation 17:1–6,15–18 use the figure of the prostitute (Ez 16 and 23) to condemn Babylon; Revelation 19 and 20 derive the image of God from Ezekiel 38:19; and Revelation 11:21–22 are built on the vision of the new temple-city in Ezekiel 40–48. Revelation 7:1–4 is linked to Ezekiel 7:2 and 9:4–6; Revelation 21:15–16 uses Ezekiel 40:3–5. Among the Apostolic Fathers, Ezekiel is the least cited of the prophets; in one count he is cited nine times in contrast to Isaiah, who is cited fifty-four times.

FURTHER READING

Basic Commentaries

Blenkinsopp, Joseph. *Ezekiel*. Interpretation. Louisville: Westminster John Knox, 1990. Readable, geared to pastors.

Boadt, L. *Ezekiel*. New Jerome Commentary, 305–28. Englewood Cliffs, NJ: Prentice Hall, 1990. Though relatively brief, extremely fine commentary.

Cody, Aelred. O.S.B. *Ezekiel*. Old Testament Message. Wilmington, DE: Michael Glazier, 1984. Theological focus with a particular interest in priestly matters, yet popular in style.

Craven, Toni. *Ezekiel. Daniel*. Collegeville Bible Commentary. Collegeville, MN: Liturgical Press, 1986. Good basic commentary.

Darr, Katheryn Pfisterer. *The Book of Ezekiel*. New Interpreter's Bible 6, 1075–1607. Nashville: Abingdon Press, 2001. Detailed, yet accessible. Reader-oriented method.

Galambush, Julie. *Ezekiel*. The Oxford Bible Commentary, 533–62. Oxford: Oxford University Press, 2001. Up to date, well informed.

Gowan, Donald E. *Ezekiel*. Knox Preaching Guides. Atlanta: John Knox Press, 1985. Pastoral application.

Wilson, Robert R. *Ezekiel*. HarperCollins Bible Commentary, 583–622. San Francisco: HarperCollins, 2000. Critical and concise.

Advanced Commentaries

Block, Daniel I. *The Book of Ezekiel: Chapters 1–24; The Book of Ezekiel: Chapters 25–48*. New International Commentary on the Old Testament. Grand Rapids, MI: Eerdmans, 1997, 1998. Massive, detailed, judicious, with large bibliography on each section, written from an evangelical viewpoint.

Eichrodt, Walther. *Ezekiel*. Old Testament Library. Translated by C. Quin. Philadelphia: Westminster, 1970. Classic commentary in the German Protestant tradition, focus on theological interpretation.

Greenberg, Moshe. *Ezekiel 1–20*. Anchor Bible. Garden City, NY: 1983. Helpful for the religious challenges in Ezekiel's world and for postbiblical Jewish writers.

Levenson, Jon D. *Theology of the Program of Restoration of Ezekiel 40–48*. Harvard Semitic Monographs 10. Cambridge, MA: Scholars Press, 1976. Important study that shows chapters 40 through 48 are a carefully articulated program of restoration.

Zimmerli, Walther. *Ezekiel 1; Ezekiel 2*. Hermeneia. Philadelphia: Fortress Press, 1979, 1983. A much admired and influential commentary, successfully demonstrating Ezekiel was a serious and consistent theologian.

DANIEL AND THE MINOR PROPHETS

JOHN J. COLLINS

DANIEL

[see pages 1220–1245 of the Old Testament]

The book of Daniel falls into three sections. The first (chapters 1–6) consists of stories in which Daniel and his three companions are the heroes. The second (7 12) is made up of revelations told by Daniel in the first person. The third (13–14) contains short stories that are not found in the Hebrew/Aramaic text of Daniel but only in the Greek and Latin versions. Jews and Protestant Christians do not accept these stories as canonical, but Protestants include them in the Apocrypha, a collection of ancient Jewish writings, which they consider edifying even if not inspired. The different kinds of material in the three divisions of Daniel reflect the gradual growth of the book. The stories in chapters 1 through 6 are the oldest part and may originally have been independent stories. We know that the revelations were composed during the persecution of the Jews by Antiochus IV Epiphanes of Syria in 168–164 BC. The "Additions" were added some time later, probably before the beginning of the Christian era.

The Tales

The stories in the first six chapters are similar in kind to historical novels—they mention historical names and places but are, nevertheless, fictional. At several points they contradict what we know from other sources about the history of the times. For instance, Belshazzar is presented as a king of Babylon and son of Nebuchadnezzar. Ancient Babylonian inscriptions show that he was son of Nabonidus (a slightly later king), and that he served as deputy ruler in Babylon but was never king. Darius the Mede is not attested independently of the book of Daniel, but Darius was the name of an early Persian king.

In each of these cases the book of Daniel has a smattering of history, but it is not ultimately concerned with historical accuracy. The stories are means of conveying a religious message, like the parables of Jesus, and so the occasional historical characters and places are not the main point. Daniel, like Noah and Job (with whom he is mentioned in Ez 14:14), may never have existed, but the religious value of the stories is none the less for that.

The stories paint a picture of the life of Jewish exiles in Babylon. It is an ideal rather than a realistic picture, but it expresses hopes and defines acceptable behavior. There is a certain analogy between the situation of the Jews in a pagan world and the modern situation of Christians in a secular world, which makes the message of the tales still relevant today. This message has two facets: it affirms the possibility of life in a Gentile environment, and insists on the importance of fidelity to the essentials of the Jewish tradition.

Affirmation of the Gentile Environment

Daniel and his companions are taken into the service of the Babylonian king and are trained in "the language and literature of the Chaldeans." They express no reservations about this training. Indeed they outshine the Babylonians at their own skills (1:20). The point of chapter 2 is that Daniel can interpret the king's dream when the Babylonian wise men fail, because of the assistance of his God. His superior ability to interpret mysteries is again in evidence in chapters 4 and 5.

King Nebuchadnezzar's dream in chapter 2 provides an interesting case study in Daniel's attitude to Gentile kingship. The dream concerns the famous statue of four metals symbolizing four kingdoms, which will all be destroyed by a stone and which symbolizes the kingdom of God. This dream foretells that ultimately *all* Gentile kingdoms will be destroyed. There is no urgency about this prophecy, however. God has allotted a lengthy period of time for Gentile rule, and during that period Jews can find fulfillment in the service of a pagan king. The spirit of the passage is similar to that of Jeremiah 27:6–8, which affirms that all nations must serve Babylon until its time too shall come.

Chapters 4 and 5 present two case studies of pagan rule in action. In chapter 4, Nebuchadnezzar becomes proud because of his great kingdom. For this he is punished by being reduced to the condition of a beast. After a time his reason is restored, and he gives praise to God. He is then restored to his kingdom. In chapter 5, Belshazzar behaves arrogantly at a feast and profanes the sacred vessels of the Jews. Mysterious writing appears on the wall, which only Daniel can read. It pronounces judgment on the king. Because Belshazzar did not learn from the experience of Nebuchadnezzar, he is weighed in the balance and found wanting, and his kingdom is given to the Medes and the Persians. In short, Gentile kings must be subject to God in the fundamental sense that they must temper their arrogance and behave with restraint. If they do this, Daniel has no objection to their rule, and indeed he shows sympathetic concern for Nebuchadnezzar. Only when the kings exceed their limits do they incur the judgment of God.

The Importance of Fidelity

Despite their success at the pagan court, Daniel and his companions remain faithful to their Jewish religion. In chapter 1, they refuse to eat the king's food, because it is not *kosher.* (See the laws concerning clean and unclean food in chapter 11 of the book of Leviticus.) In chapter 3 the three youths refuse to worship the king's statue at the risk of death, and in chapter 6 Daniel likewise refuses to depart from his custom of daily prayer even at the cost of being thrown into the lions' den. In each case the Jews ultimately win the respect of their rulers and emerge more successful than before. The stories of the fiery furnace and the lions' den, like all miracle stories, are meant to arouse a sense of wonder. They are not realistic stories. The long history of Christian martyrdoms and of the persecution of Jews (down to the lethal furnaces of Auschwitz) shows that God does not usually intervene to rescue the innocent. Christian tradition appropriately understood the stories of the furnace and lions' den as representing resurrection from the dead. The essential point in Daniel's stories, however, is that God has the power to save, or to do whatever is for the best. Daniel and his companions have trust in God, and this liberates them to do whatever they ought to do regardless of the immediate consequences. The attitude of the tales is well expressed in the words of the three youths (3:17f): "If our God, whom we serve, can save us from the white-hot furnace and from your hands, O king, may he save us! But even if he will not, know, O king, that we will not serve your god or worship the golden statue which you set up." Their fidelity is not conditional. It is a matter of integrity, and this integrity is the key to their success.

The tales in Daniel 1 through 6 have a very optimistic view of the Gentile world. The Jews have enemies at the royal court, largely for reasons of envy, but the kings are well disposed and repeatedly praise and acknowledge the God of Daniel. In chapter 6, King Darius is dismayed when he is tricked into throwing Daniel to the lions. He is delighted when Daniel survives and readily confesses "the living God, enduring forever." The stories stop short of having the king convert to Judaism. In a sense it is even more gratifying to have a pagan king acknowledge the power of the God of the Jews. These tales express confidence that the truth of Jewish religion is powerful enough to impress any person of goodwill. Judaism has nothing to fear from the Gentile or secular world.

Daniel 1 through 6 conveys a sense that God is in control and that all will work out for the best. The kingdom of God can be exercised through the rule of pagan kings. True religion does not require any particular political system. This optimistic view of the world arose from the experience of Jews in foreign lands in much of the ancient world. It is similar to the liberal theology that has flourished in modern times wherever Christians or Jews have lived under tolerant political regimes. It is an attractive view of the world, which emphasizes the good in human nature, and is a viable theology in normal times. Unfortunately, times are not always normal, and there are occasions when we have to give more recognition to the forces of evil in the world. One such occasion in antiquity was the persecution of the Jews in the Maccabean period (see "Bible History and Archaeology," RG 52), and it was in this situation that the apocalyptic visions of Daniel (7–12) were written.

The Revelations

The Apocalyptic Genre

Daniel's visions belong to the genre of apocalyptic literature, which takes its name from the book of Revelation in the New Testament. "Apocalypse" *(apokalypsis)* is simply the Greek word for revelation, but the word has come to be associated with a particular kind of revelation, with certain recurring characteristics.

One trademark of the Jewish apocalypses (though not of the book of Revelation) is pseudonymity—that is, the real authors (whose names are not known) wrote under the names of famous people who had lived long before. Enoch, the most popular visionary, was supposed to have lived before Noah and the flood. (Enoch appears in Gn 5:18–24.) Surprisingly, the people of the second century BC do not appear to have been skeptical about his authorship. Rather, his great antiquity added to the prestige of his writings.

Another trademark of an apocalypse is the presence of a mediating angel. An angel explains the visions to Daniel. In other apocalypses, which are not included in the canon, a visionary such as Enoch is taken on a tour of the heavens, accompanied by an angel as tour guide. The presence of the angel emphasizes the supernatural character of the experience and adds to the sense of mystery. (The interpreting angel first appears in biblical literature in the book of Zechariah.)

Apocalypses also have a typical subject matter. This deals on the one hand with the heavenly world of the angels, and on the other with predictions of the future, especially of a final judgment. This kind of writing was developed in Judaism from the third century BC on and was very popular in early Christianity. The most important Jewish apocalypses are 1 Enoch, 2 Enoch, 2 Esdras, 2 Baruch, 3 Baruch.

No genre of biblical literature is more difficult for the modern reader than the apocalypses. This literature is exceptional even within the Bible. In the modern world liberal Christians tend to avoid it, while fundamentalists too easily adapt it to their own ends. Several factors contribute to the difficulty.

The Heavy Use of Symbolism

Apocalypses do not speak directly but veil their meaning in symbolic language, which is closely related to the language of dreams. All scholars agree that King Antiochus Epiphanes is a major figure in Daniel 7–12 (see note on 7:7). Yet the king is never mentioned by name. Instead we read of a beast with ten horns, which sprouts an eleventh, and we can infer from other historical information that the eleventh is Antiochus. The text gives us a clue. It tells us that the four beasts, of which the horned beast is the last, are four kingdoms, but it never identifies them explicitly. The lack of specificity is typical of oracles in the ancient world. It adds a sense of mystery, and strengthens the impression that the prophecy is of supernatural origin. It also has an effect on the long-term interpretation of the apocalypse. Two hundred years after Daniel was written, people could interpret the fourth kingdom as Rome, and the eleventh horn as a Roman emperor. Down through the centuries the beast could be interpreted as the villain of the day. This kind of reinterpretation is helpful if it is done with proper understanding. The apocalyptic vision describes types of characters who reappear in history. Antiochus Epiphanes was not the only tyrant worthy of being described as a beast. One of the uses of an apocalyptic vision is that it gives us language to describe new situations: the scene of beasts rising from the sea could be applied appropriately to the outbreak of World War II. It is important to realize, however, that Daniel was not predicting this war. He was speaking of a persecution in the second century BC, and his vision can be applied to other situations only by analogy. Fundamentalists often read Daniel or the New Testament Apocalypse as if they were written to predict our modern situation. In fact, they were written for their own time and place, but they can help us understand our modern situation because they describe patterns that recur throughout history.

Angels and Demons

Some modern Christians find the prominence of angels and demons in apocalyptic literature to be a problem. For Daniel, the battles between Jews and Greeks are only a reflection of a battle in heaven. Moreover, it is not God who fights for the Jews but the archangel Michael, who is mentioned here by name for the first time. Most people in the ancient world believed that the heavens were peopled with supernatural beings. Usually these were called "gods," but Jewish and Christian tradition makes a sharp distinction between the supreme deity and the lesser heavenly beings, called angels. The modern secular world, with its scientific approach to the heavens, has little room for such beings. An apocalypse, however, is not a scientific treatise but a work of imagination. To say that there is a battle in heaven between the patron angels of Greece and Judah is to say that earthly war is not entirely subject to human control. Angels provide a vivid way of dramatizing providence or divine control. To understand an apocalypse, we should not ask, "Do these angels exist?" but "What do they stand for?" and especially, "If we imagine a world with angels, what effect does this have on the way we view human life?"

Pseudonymity

We have noted above that all Jewish apocalypses are pseudonymous. This device added to the authority of a book. In an apocalypse it had another advantage: it enabled Daniel to "predict" four hundred years of history, which were already past when the book was written. Since the prediction was demonstrably accurate over these four hundred years, people were more likely to believe the real prediction of what was still to come. From a modern viewpoint this practice seems deceptive and therefore unethical. We consider pseudonymous writing a forgery. The practice was widely accepted, however, in the Greek and Roman world as well as in Judaism. While the common people presumably believed that the revelations were genuinely old, the real authors must have been known to an inner circle. It is difficult for us to reconstruct the mindset of people who wrote pseudonymous books, but it is certain that they did not regard their work as deceptive. It is possible that the authors put themselves in the place of Enoch and Daniel, and imagined that they were actually describing the visions of these ancient worthies. In any case, the enduring value of the apocalypses does not lie in the accuracy of their predictions but in the kind of conduct they inspired and supported. In the case of Daniel, the question is not whether Daniel really predicted all these things in advance, but whether his stance in the face of religious persecution is a good one.

Determinism

Apocalyptic literature typically assumes that history has a fixed duration and can be divided into a set number of periods (for example, four kingdoms or seventy weeks of years). The course of events can be predicted centuries in advance. Consequently, history appears to be predetermined. It is important to realize that this does not mean that human decisions are predetermined. On the contrary, the book of Daniel is basically a call for decision in a time of crisis. The course of history is set, and the fate of the righteous and the wicked is predetermined. The fate of any individuals, however, remains to be decided and will be determined by the kinds of decisions they make.

Predictions of the End

Perhaps the aspect of apocalyptic literature that most offends modern sensibilities is the attempt to predict exactly the time of the end. (In Daniel, the end in question is the end of the persecution. In later apocalypticism it is often the end of the world.) Down through the centuries, apocalyptic groups have often set a date for the end of the world, only to see it come and go. Naturally such predictions have been discredited by their frequent failure. The book of Daniel actually gives three very precise dates for the end of the persecution. In 8:14, an angel says that the Temple will be desolate for 2,300 evenings and mornings, or 1,150 days. At the end of chapter 12, however, we are given two different figures: 1,290 days and 1,335 days.

Presumably the number was increased when the end was delayed. We can understand the function of these numbers in the time of persecution: it was easier to keep going if one believed that relief would come on a specific day. Remarkably enough, however, the failure of these exact predictions did not discredit the book of Daniel. Later interpreters assumed that the figures must have some symbolic meaning and were not to be taken literally. In fact, the attempt to predict the end is only a very minor element in apocalyptic literature, and its importance should not be blown out of proportion. It served a limited purpose in its historical setting, but it must be admitted that such attempts were ultimately counterproductive. This is not an aspect of apocalyptic literature that anyone should try to imitate in a modern setting.

Information or Exhortation?

The problems of interpreting apocalyptic literature in the modern world can be summarized by asking whether we should read these books for information or for exhortation. It is a fact that any apocalypse combines the two aspects. It tries to teach us a view of the world, and if we accept that view we will be disposed to act in a certain way. The problem is that the apocalyptic view of the world is no longer acceptable. Angels and demons are not part of our universe, and we can no longer believe that the duration of history is coming to an end. Much of the "information" provided by an apocalypse is now incredible if taken literally. It still has value, however, if we regard it as symbolism and focus on the attitudes and actions it was designed to support. Such an ethical focus is fundamentally important for understanding the book of Daniel and its relevance to modern times.

A Symbolic Vision

Chapter 7 is one of the most famous and influential of all apocalyptic visions. In part it resembles Nebuchadnezzar's dream in chapter 2: it describes four human kingdoms, which will be followed by a kingdom set up by God. The imagery, however, is very different. Instead of four metals, Daniel 7 describes four beasts that rise out of the sea. In biblical poetry the sea is often a symbol of chaos, of all that is opposed to God, and it is sometimes said to be inhabited by monsters (for instance, Is 27:1: God "will slay the dragon that is in the sea"; compare Is 51:9f). When chapter 7 in Daniel represents the pagan kingdoms as beasts from the sea, then the point is that they are rebellious and opposed to God. This represents a view of the pagan kingdoms, which is much more negative than anything in Daniel 1–6.

After the vision of the four beasts, Daniel sees a judgment scene in which an "Ancient One" sits on a throne, surrounded by thousands of angels, and the fourth beast is condemned to the fire. Then "one like a son of man" appears on the clouds of heaven. Christian tradition, beginning with the Gospels, identified this figure as Jesus Christ, but the passage could not have been understood in that way by Jews in the second century BC. Jewish tradition identified the "son of man" as the messiah. Modern scholarship is divided between two interpretations: some see the figure as a collective symbol for Israel, others as the archangel Michael. It is quite clear that he represents the triumph of the Jewish people over their persecutors. The issue in dispute is how that triumph was understood. The view that the son of man figure is Michael relies on the analogy with Daniel 10–12, where Michael represents Israel in a heavenly battle with the angelic prince of Greece. The triumph of the Jews, then, is imagined in the apocalypse as a victory by their heavenly patron. The son of man is always understood as a heavenly individual in other Jewish apocalypses (1 Enoch, 2 Esdras).

Daniel 7 was written during the persecution of the Jews by Antiochus Epiphanes of Syria, which is described in 1 and 2 Maccabees. The experience of persecution colored the author's perception of all Gentile kingdoms. The message of the vision is that pagan rulers are evil and in rebellion against God, but that they will be defeated by the power of God. The symbolism of the vision, however, with its beasts and fire and figure riding on the clouds, expresses this idea with exceptional power and vividness. Consequently, the imagery has been used over and over again in new situations. It provides language that can express the evil, which erupts from time to time in human affairs (think of the Holocaust as a modern example) and which can also express a hope that does not depend on human power. The message of the vision is one of hope. Although the forces against us may be demonic, the power of God and the angels will ultimately prevail. The imagery of this vision is used repeatedly in the Gospels and most elaborately in the book of Revelation.

Daniel 8 is a symbolic vision very similar to chapter 7. Even some of its imagery (the little horn) is taken from the earlier chapter. In this case the central episode of the imagery concerns the revolt of the little horn against the host of heaven. There is a reminiscence here of the morning star, son of the dawn in Isaiah 14, which rises above the stars of God but is then cast down to the depths. Antiochus Epiphanes is identified as an example of the general pattern represented by the Isaianic passage. Again, the prophecy is one of hope since the pattern guaranteed the fall of the rebel.

A Prophecy Reinterpreted

A different kind of revelation is found in chapter 9. In this case, a biblical prophecy provides the point of departure. Jeremiah had prophesied that the land would be subject to Babylon for seventy years. According to 2 Chronicles 36:20f, this prophecy was fulfilled by the restoration under Cyrus of Persia (although only fifty years had elapsed). Zechariah 1:12 related it to the rebuilding of the Temple (about sixty-six years after its destruction). The author of Daniel evidently did not think that the restoration of the Persian period satisfied the prophecy. Rather than discard the prophecy as a failure, however, he reinterpreted it. Seventy years really means seventy weeks of years, or 490 years. The way of interpreting Scripture here is basically the same as the way of interpreting dreams and visions in the previous chapters. (It is also typical of the Pesharim, or biblical commentaries, found among the Dead Sea Scrolls.) The numbers in Jeremiah's prophecy are taken as symbolic. The implications of this procedure are far-reaching. When the visionary says that only three and a half years are left before the end, we cannot be sure that this will not turn out to mean three and a half weeks of years. In short, the impression of precise prediction, which we get from the use of numbers, is misleading. What Daniel ultimately affirms is not the particular timetable but the reliability of the promises of God, however mysterious their timing may be.

Chapter 9 also includes a remarkable prayer on the lips of Daniel. The prayer is of a type common in the postexilic period. (See for example Neh 9.) Its theology is typical of the tradition influenced by the book of Deuteronomy. Israel is punished for its own sin and can only appeal for the mercy of God. This theology is rather different from the usual theology of Daniel. The primary cause of Israel's suffering in apocalyptic theology lies in the wickedness of the nations that rebel against God, and indeed in the predetermined plan of history. In response to the prayer, Daniel receives a revelation, but there is no question of forgiveness, or of shortening the time of trial because of repentance. From the viewpoint of the book of Daniel, it is appropriate to express repentance, as Daniel does, but we should not expect our prayers to alter the course of events.

Another Dimension of History

Daniel's apocalyptic view of history is most fully laid out in chapters 10 through 12, which make up one long vision. There, an angel explains to Daniel that there is an ongoing battle in heaven between the archangels Michael and Gabriel on the one hand and the angelic "princes" of Persia and Greece on the other (10:13, 20f). This battle is reflected on earth in the wars of the Hellenistic age, which are described at length in chapter 11, and especially in the career of Antiochus Epiphanes who takes up approximately half the chapter (11:21–45). At the end Michael will arise in victory (12:1), and the resurrection will follow.

This long passage makes several claims about history, which would not be apparent to the typical observer:

First, what is involved is not just warfare between human kingdoms, but a battle between angelic powers, and the outcome of this cannot be decided by human power.

Second, the course of history is fixed in advance. The battles of the Hellenistic age can be revealed to Daniel in the Babylonian exile. In fact, the passage was written during the persecution under Antiochus Epiphanes. It gives an accurate account of history down to that time (11:39). Such "prophecy after the fact" implies that the course of history is predetermined, and it inspires confidence in the actual prediction with which the passage concludes (in this case, the imminent death of the king 11: 40–45, and the resurrection, 12:1–3).

Third, history culminates with the resurrection of the dead. Daniel is the only book in the Hebrew Bible that clearly affirms the resurrection of individuals. Earlier prophecy sometimes uses the language of resurrection for the restoration of the Jewish nation, as in Isaiah 26:19 and Ezekiel 37. The book of Wisdom, which was composed in Greek about the time of Christ, also has a clear doctrine of immortality. The idea of resurrection had probably been introduced into Judaism before the time of the Maccabees. The noncanonical 1 Enoch, chapter 22, which describes the abodes of the dead as they wait for resurrection, is probably older than Daniel. There is no doubt, however, that the experience of martyrdom in the time of persecution made the Jews more receptive to belief in resurrection than they had been before. The importance of resurrection in that setting can be seen from the story of the seven brothers in 2 Maccabees 7.

Belief in resurrection made an enormous difference to Judaism, and was essential to the origin of Christianity. Traditional Jewish religion had taught that the reward for a just life was to see one's children's children, to the fourth generation, and the welfare of the nation as a whole. In the time of the Maccabees, however, pious Jews were put to death precisely for obeying the Law and so were cut off from the traditional reward for a just life. Belief in life beyond the grave, in the company of the angels, provided an entirely new perspective. Martyrdom was no longer an absurdity, but the means to a greater end. So Daniel announced that the wise would take their stand in the time of persecution, even though some of them would fall (11:33–35). These "wise" do not, apparently, join the Maccabees to fight for national independence. Rather, they put their trust in Michael and the heavenly world and choose the way of passive resistance. The stand of these wise teachers exemplifies the ethical stance of the book of Daniel, which is the most enduring message of the book.

There is clear continuity between the apocalyptic message of Daniel 10–12 and the older stories of the fiery furnace and the lions' den. On the one hand there is the belief that God rules all kingdoms and has the power to save. On the other is the conviction that one must act with integrity even at the cost of life itself. The belief in resurrection makes this conviction easier to maintain.

The apocalyptic visions offer a much less optimistic view of the Gentile world than the tales of chapters 1 through 6. This again is not a view for all seasons but for situations of crisis, which we should hope are exceptional. Pagan powers are not always "beasts from the sea," although they may be so on occasion. The ethical stance advocated by the "wise" in Daniel 11, that of passive resistance, is not necessarily normative for all situations either. The militant revolution of the Maccabees is also canonized in the Old Testament. The book of Daniel exemplifies one possible way in which a faithful Jew or Christian may respond to a situation of oppression and persecution. Whether it is the right way can only be decided in light of the specific circumstances of each situation, but it always demands serious consideration.

The Additions

Daniel 13 and 14 are rightly labeled as an Appendix in the *New American Bible,* as they are independent stories in which Daniel happens to play a part. Susanna is placed before Daniel 1 in one Greek translation (that attributed to Theodotion), since Daniel appears there as a young boy, but there is no doubt that the story was originally independent.

Susanna

In the story of Susanna, Daniel appears as the wise judge. This role is suggested by his name (*Dan* comes from the Hebrew verb, to judge) but not by anything in Daniel 1–12. His judgment recalls that of Solomon in 1 Kings 3. The story as a whole may be described as a parable, insofar as it is a short story that reverses our expectations in some important respect. (Compare Nathan's parable in 2 Sm 11 and several of Jesus' parables.) Normally elders who have been appointed judges are the righteous ones, and the word of a young woman would carry little weight against theirs. Yet it is characteristic of biblical narrative that the underdog prevails or is justified. (A comparable story involving a woman, Tamar, can be found in Gn 38.) The story of Susanna loses some of its dramatic effect by telling us at the outset that the judges are wicked. Nonetheless the story provides a nice illustration of the unreliability of conventional expectations.

In one respect, at least, the story of Susanna has the same viewpoint as the rest of the book of Daniel: In verse 23, when Susanna is trapped, she declares: "Yet it is better for me to fall into your power without guilt than to sin before the Lord" (Dn 13:23). This is the same lesson that we learned from the three young men, from Daniel in the lions' den, and again from the martyrs of the Maccabean period. The story is closer to Daniel 1–6 than to 10–12, since it envisages salvation in this life, and, appropriately, the execution of Susanna's accusers.

Bel and the Dragon

Daniel 14 contains two stories that make fun of pagan idolatry. These stories are caricatures. They should not be taken as accurate descriptions of Babylonian religion, any more than anti-Catholic caricatures should be taken as fair representations of the Catholic veneration of statues.

The Babylonians in the stories are excessively stupid, and their devices are too easily exposed. The story of the dragon shares with Daniel 6 the motif of the lions' den but does not necessarily depend on the earlier chapter. All we can say is that Daniel was associated with the lions' den in oral tradition, and that both these stories made use of the motif. Bel and the Dragon is more fantastic than Daniel 6: he remains in the den for six days and the prophet Habakkuk is transported from Judea by an angel to feed him. These fantastic elements give the tale a lighthearted quality, but the background here is more tense than in Daniel 1–6. Daniel confronts the Babylonian religion in a way that he never does in the earlier chapters. The Babylonians threaten him because of his religious zeal, not because of professional envy as in chapter 6.

There is a sense here that Judaism and paganism are fundamentally incompatible. The king is still benevolent, but the Babylonians suspect that he has become a Jew. There is, of course, ample precedent for demanding a clear-cut choice between the Lord and other deities (compare Elijah in 1 Kgs 18). Daniel 1 through 6 also presupposed such a choice, but did not present it as starkly as chapter 14. There are times when confrontation can be avoided and fruitful interaction is possible. Bel and the Dragon, on the other hand, does not allow for any ecumenical relations with pagan religion. Presumably this attitude reflects the situation in which the story was written. Here again we see that the biblical stories are not timeless in character but are shaped by historical circumstances. Their modern relevance, likewise, depends on the circumstances in which we read them.

FURTHER READING

Collins, John J. *Daniel; 1–2 Maccabees*. Old Testament Message, 15. Wilmington, DE: Glazier, 1981. Introductory commentary, along the lines of this Reading Guide.

Seow, C. L.. *Daniel*. Westminster Bible Companion; Louisville: Westminster John Knox, 2003. Clear, introductory commentary intended for lay readers.

Smith-Christopher, D. L. *The Book of Daniel*. New Interpreter's Bible 7, 19–152. Nashville: Abingdon, 1996. Commentary designed for preachers. Liberationist, postcolonial perspective.

For more detailed, scholarly commentary see:

Collins, John J. *Daniel. A Commentary on the Book of Daniel, with an essay, "The Influence of Daniel on the New Testament," by Adela Yarbro Collins*. Hermeneia. Minneapolis: Fortress, 1993. Detailed commentary on the full book, including the additions.

Montgomery, James A. *The Book of Daniel*. International Critical Commentary. Edinburgh: Clark, 1927. Reprint, 1979. Classic scholarly commentary, although out of date in some respects.

For the Additions to Daniel see:

Moore, C. A. *Daniel, Esther and Jeremiah: The Additions*. Anchor Bible 44. Garden City, NY: Doubleday, 1977.

The noncanonical apocalyptic literature can be found in:

Charlesworth, J. H., ed. *The Old Testament Pseudepigrapha*. Vol. 1. Garden City, NY: Doubleday, 1983.

Sparks, H. F. D., ed. *The Apocryphal Old Testament*. Oxford: Oxford University Press, 1984.

For a study of this material see:

Collins, J. J. *The Apocalyptic Imagination*. 2nd ed. Grand Rapids, MI: Eerdmans, 1998.

THE TWELVE MINOR PROPHETS

The Book of the Twelve is a collection of prophetic oracles that were composed over a period of about 300 years. The number *twelve* is probably chosen because of the twelve tribes of Israel. At least in some cases the books are artificial—for example, it is quite clear that Zechariah 9–14 do not come from the same prophet as Zechariah 1–8. While we will review the books in their canonical order, it may be helpful at the outset to group them according to their origin.

1. Three prophets, Amos, Hosea, and Micah, were active in the eighth century BC, and were contemporary with the earlier part of Isaiah's career. Hosea was a northern prophet and Micah a southern, while Amos was a native of the Southern Kingdom who prophesied in the north. (On the two kingdoms, see the historical sketch, RG 45–50.)

2. Another cluster of three prophets can be dated in the Babylonian period, toward the end of the seventh century BC. Zephaniah is dated to the time of King Josiah (640–609 BC), Nahum proclaimed the fall of Nineveh in 612 BC, and Habakkuk prophesied when the Babylonians were already advancing westward (605–597 BC).

3. Two prophets, Haggai and Zechariah are known to have been active in the rebuilding of the Jerusalem Temple in 520–518 BC. Again, only chapters 1 through 8 of the book of Zechariah can be attributed to this prophet.

4. The remaining four books, Joel, Jonah, Obadiah, and Malachi, and the latter part of Zechariah, come from the postexilic period, but their dates cannot be determined precisely. Malachi may be roughly contemporary with Ezra in the fifth century BC. The book of Jonah and the second part of Zechariah could be as early as the fifth century or as late as the Hellenistic period (after 330 BC).

Most of these books are made up of short poetic oracles. (The book of Jonah, which is a short story, is an exception.) The nature of prophecy is that it addresses specific situations, and so it is important to know something of the time and place of the different prophets, when this is possible. At the same time, these oracles were preserved because they had enduring relevance and could be applied to new situations by analogy. All of this material was handed down orally for some time before it was put in written form. Consequently, there is often reason to doubt whether a particular prophecy was actually uttered by the prophet to whom it is ascribed. So, for example, Micah 4:1–3 contains a passage that is also found in Isaiah 2:1–4. We cannot now be sure which, if either, of these prophets originally spoke these lines. Moreover, these books were edited in the postexilic period, and the editors also added some passages. While it is always helpful to know the situation in which an oracle was originally given, it is not possible to be sure of the original setting of each passage.

As we might expect, there is considerable diversity in this collection, but there are also some dominant themes:

1. Most of these prophets focus their attention on the sins of their own people. There are exceptions. The oracles of Obadiah and Nahum consist entirely of condemnations of foreign nations. Haggai and Zechariah, in the period immediately after the Babylonian exile, are exceptionally supportive of their leaders and institutions. Nonetheless, most of these prophets were characterized by their critical spirit.

2. The sins they denounced were both social and cultic. The social agenda of prophecy was set by the great eighth-century BC prophets, especially Amos and Micah, but concern for the weak and unprotected persists throughout the corpus, down to the oracles of Malachi. Hosea engages in extensive polemic against the worship of gods other than the Lord, and this concern reappears from time to time in the other prophets. The prophets were even more concerned, however, with abuses in the worship of the Lord, even when there were no pagan elements involved. Amos and Micah denounced the cult of their day because it made the people complacent and distracted them from the injustice of their society. At the end of the collection, we still find Malachi criticizing the priests for failing to live up to the ideals of their office. People who performed the prescribed rituals were not necessarily pleasing to God for that reason. The prophetic critiques do not mean that ritual is not

important. On the contrary, it is precisely because it is vitally important to the religious life of a community that they devote so much attention to it.

3. It is common in biblical theology to say that God acts in history. The prophets say more than this: they teach that whatever actually happens is the work of God. So they understood the great calamities, which befell the Northern Kingdom of Israel in 721 BC and the Southern Kingdom of Judah in 587/6 BC, as acts of divine judgment. Indeed these catastrophes added to the authority of the prophets, since they were seen as the fulfillment of their oracles. The constant reference to historical events ensures an element of realism in the preaching of the prophets. They are not only concerned with moral ideals, but also with what works in practice.

4. The theme of judgment undergoes some development in the later prophets. This can be seen by following the motif of the Day of the Lord. This motif first appears in Amos. In the context it seems clear that the Israelites expected the Day of the Lord to vindicate them against their immediate enemies. For Amos, however, the Day of the Lord would be the occasion of judgment on Israel. In the postexilic period, Joel anticipates a day of judgment for all nations in the valley of Jehoshaphat. In Zechariah 14 it is the day when all the nations assemble for battle against Jerusalem, to be defeated by the Lord. The Book of the Twelve ends with a forward look to "the day of the Lord, the great and terrible day." Increasingly, it is a day of definitive universal judgment.

5. The theme of the salvation of Israel is also more prominent in the postexilic period. Already in the eighth century BC, Hosea looked beyond the impending destruction by the Assyrians and spoke of a new beginning like the Exodus of old. After the exile it made little sense to speak of further destruction of Israel. Very often the prophets imagine a situation that is different from the present. When Jerusalem was in ruins, or restored in only modest circumstances, they revived the dream of Zion, the holy mountain, and divine abode (so Joel, Zephaniah, and a postexilic passage in Micah 4). Similarly, the hope for a restored Davidic monarchy is at home in the period after the exile (Mi 5; Zec 9). The phrase "on that day" frequently introduces prophecies of the great transformation that is to come (for example, Zec 14:6,8,13,20). It is likely that at least some of these oracles were inserted by those who put this collection together, gathering and arranging the scattered materials. These editors wanted to insure that the recollection of the past did not outweigh the hope for the future. The tendency of the editors to put the words of judgment in perspective is most strikingly evident at the end of the book of Amos. After the prophet's threat that God would wipe Israel off the face of the earth, the editor adds, "but I will not destroy the house of Jacob completely" (9:8) and goes on to prophesy the restoration of the Davidic dynasty.

Taken as a whole, the Book of the Twelve is both a reflection on the past and a lesson for the future. The order of the oracles is not easily apparent, and this makes reading through the collection difficult. They are certainly not arranged in chronological order, and even the thematic order is only occasional. We can, however, find a pattern, in which sin is followed by judgment and judgment by salvation. Not all the individual prophets saw this full pattern. Some, like Amos, simply announced the imminent judgment. Others, like Haggai and Zechariah, focused on the moment of restoration. The editors of the prophetic books were heavily influenced by the theology of Deuteronomy. According to that theology, sin does not go unpunished, but God is ultimately merciful and wants only the repentance and restoration of Israel. The collected prophets, then, can be read as a call for repentance, to be sustained until the final Day of the Lord. The first book in the collection, Hosea, ends with the invitation, "Return, O Israel, to the LORD, your God" (Hos 14:2). The final book, Malachi, ends with a reminder to keep the law of Moses, and a promise that Elijah will come to reconcile parents and children. In this way, the lesson of the prophets is tied in nicely with that of the Pentateuch.

FURTHER READING

Blenkinsopp, J. *A History of Prophecy in Israel.* 2nd ed. Louisville: Westminster John Knox, 1996. Comprehensive, reliable introduction to the prophetic books.

Petersen, D. L. *The Prophetic Literature. An Introduc-*

tion, 169–214. Louisville: Westminster John Knox, 2002. Focuses on the literary character of the collection.

Sweeney, M. *The Twelve Prophets*. Collegeville: Liturgical Press, 2000. A commentary on the twelve minor prophets.

von Rad, G. *Old Testament Theology.* Vol. 2. Louisville: Westminster John Knox, 2001. Reprint of 1965 edition. Still very useful theological introduction.

HOSEA

[see pages 1245–1259 of the Old Testament]

Hosea is not the first of the prophets chronologically, but he provides a good introduction to the prophetic corpus, as he is unrivaled for the beauty of his poetry and the emotional power of his oracles. He lived at a time of great crisis for the Northern Kingdom of Israel. He began his career in the middle of the eighth century (about 750 BC). Little more than a decade later Israel came under threat from the mighty Assyrian empire, which was expanding westward. The king of Israel became a vassal, or subject, of Assyria in 732 BC, the kingdom was brought to an end, and its capital Samaria destroyed, in 722 BC. In the period between the death of King Jeroboam II (who is mentioned in Hos 1:1) in 746 BC and the first submission of Israel in 732 BC, no fewer than five kings sat on the throne (and a sixth succeeded in 732 BC). It was, then, a period of great instability. While we cannot specify the occasions of Hosea's individual prophecies, it is important to be aware of this general background.

As noted in the *New American Bible,* the first three chapters stand apart from the rest of the book because of the theme of the prophet's marriage. It is difficult to discern any pattern in chapters 4 through 14. Most of the oracles proclaim the destruction of Israel, but the book ends with an invitation to repentance (14:2–9). There is also an important prophecy of restoration at 11: 8–11.

The Metaphor of Marriage

The attractiveness of Hosea's prophecy springs from his use of metaphor and symbol, especially imagery drawn from human relationships. His most fundamental metaphor is that of marriage. The book opens with one of the most bizarre commands in all the Bible, "Go, take a harlot wife. . . ." It may be that the woman, Gomer, was not a harlot when she married, and that the command anticipates her later behavior. There is an alternative view, however, held by many scholars, which sees the choice of a harlot wife as a deliberate symbolic act on the part of the prophet (compare the bizarre symbolic acts in Isaiah 20 and Ezekiel 4). Some scholars think that Gomer was not only a prostitute but a cult prostitute, devoted to the worship of the pagan god Baal. By marrying such a person, Hosea would have attracted considerable attention, and dramatized his message that "the land gives itself to harlotry" (1:2). In any case, the prophet uses the experience of infidelity in marriage, all too familiar to his audience, to convey an understanding of Israel's behavior toward the Lord, the God of Israel. The metaphor was appropriate for several reasons:

1. It is a fundamental presupposition of Hosea that Israel is bound to God by the covenant given to Moses. A covenant is a contractual arrangement, like a marriage. The relationship can be expressed in the declarations "You are my people" and "My God" (2:25) on the analogy of the standard marriage formula "she is my wife, he is my husband."

2. One of the major problems addressed by Hosea was idolatry, specifically the cult of the Canaanite god Baal. The word *baal* was used in Hebrew as the common word for husband. Moreover, Baal was attractive to the people because he was a fertility god who was supposed to guarantee the productivity of land, animals, and people. Some scholars have supposed that the worship of Baal involved sexual acts with sacred prostitutes. This is now viewed as unlikely, but the imagery of prostitution and fornication is often used to symbolize idolatry. Hosea was contrasting the covenant with the Lord, understood

as a marriage, with the cult of Baal, understood as prostitution. The prophet's wife exemplified the behavior of Israel, by straying from the marital relationship.

3. Hosea's whole understanding of God is based on the assumption that God is like the best in human nature, only more so. Since marriage is the culmination of love between man and woman, it is appropriate that it should also provide the analogy for understanding the love between the Lord and Israel.

The fact that the prophet uses the most intimate aspect of his own life to convey his message is indicative of his total involvement in his prophecy. The involvement extends to his children, who are given such symbolic names as "not pitied" (Lo-ruhama, 1:6) and "not my people" (Lo-ammi, 1:8). There is no concern for private, personal life. The prophet and his family are at the disposal of God for the welfare of the people.

The Lord and Baal

In the great poem in chapter 2, Hosea argues that the people are mistaken when they credit Baal with providing the grain, the wine, and the oil. It is the Lord who really controls fertility. What is involved here is not simply a matter of knowing the most appropriate name for the God of nature. To acknowledge the Lord as lord is to accept the Sinai covenant, with its code of ethics for society. Israel's infidelity in worshipping Baal is the symptom of a pervasive disease. Hosea's grievance against the people is summed up in 4:1–3:

> There is no fidelity, no mercy,
> no knowledge of God in the land.
> False swearing, lying, murder, stealing and adultery!
> in their lawlessness, bloodshed follows bloodshed.
> Therefore the land mourns. . . .

The list of offenses closely follows the Ten Commandments, but the point is not just that specific laws are broken. It is a question of fundamental attitude. Infidelity manifests itself in sexual behavior, in idolatry, in the repeated assassination of rulers, in wavering political alliances. This lack of constancy certainly had an effect on the political fortunes of the nation. Hosea believed that it also had an effect on the land itself. He may have been right insofar as the rulers neglected the proper care of the land because of intrigue and opportunism.

Land and Desert

In the poem in Hosea 2, the prophet plays on the rich associations of the promised land. The foundation of Israel's identity was the story of the Exodus. The escape from Egypt had been followed by forty years of wandering in the desert. After that experience, Israel had indeed looked like "a land flowing with milk and honey." Now the prophet threatened to take all that away: "I will make her like the desert, reduce her to an arid land." To appreciate the full force of this threat we must remember that for ancient Israel the gift of the land was the primary expression of salvation. There was no belief among Israelites of that time in a blessed hereafter. To reduce the land to a desert would be, in effect, to undo the Exodus. In fact, the devastation of the Assyrian invasion might well be said to do that, some years after Hosea spoke.

The desert, however, was not only a place of death. It was also a place of hope. Israel wandered in the desert in "the days of her youth." Hosea changes his metaphor in 2:16 and plays on the positive connotations of the desert, as a place where a man might take a young woman in privacy, away from the town, to court her. What he is suggesting is that the destruction at the hands of Assyria is not the end. It is rather a transitional stage, necessary to clear away the cult of Baal and the other abuses in Israel. When Israel has been stripped down, so to speak, by the Assyrians, a new beginning will be possible, in effect a new Exodus.

The motif of a new Exodus, introduced here for the first time, would later be important for Second Isaiah (Is 40–55) after the Babylonian exile. It would be taken up again by the people who wrote the Dead Sea Scrolls, shortly before the time of Christ, and it is implied in the career of John the Baptist (Mk 1:2f).

Criticism of the Cult

The cult of Baal was attractive in part because it was a matter of ritual rather than of ethical conduct. The Israelites were also willing to perform rituals for the Lord. Hosea complains at the facile way in which they professed repentance, only to have the sentiment vanish as soon as they left the Temple (6:1–4). In the course of this passage the Israelites say: "He will revive us after two days; on the third day he will raise us up." This reference to raising up on the third day has often been related to the resurrection of Christ. In its context, however, it simply expresses the hope that God would restore the fortunes of the people after a short time.

Hosea goes on to enunciate one of the classic formulations of biblical religion in 6:6: "It is love that I desire, not sacrifice, and knowledge of God rather than holocausts." Sacrifice was not bad in itself, but it was only as good as the attitude it represented. Without the love that expressed itself in ethical conduct, sacrifice was meaningless, no matter what it cost. The inadequacy of sacrifice without the practice of justice is one of the major themes that runs through the prophetic corpus.

The Importance of Metaphors

The power of Hosea's prophecy comes in large part from his stock of striking metaphors. Israel is compared to a "cake unturned" (7:8), a "wild ass" (8:9), or a "luxuriant vine" (10:1). These metaphors have an emotional effect because of the associations they carry with them, and this enhances their power of communication. Nowhere is this more evident than in chapter 11, which begins "When Israel was a child I loved him." The reference is to the Exodus, but the effect is very different from the rather violent accounts in the Pentateuch. By comparing Israel to a child, Hosea paints a vivid picture of God as the loving parent, teaching the infant to walk and lifting it up. By implication, Israel should have the same kind of elemental bond with the Lord that a toddler has with its parents.

Development of this metaphor leads Hosea to one of the most remarkable passages in the Old Testament. The thought of destroying his or her own child is repugnant to any normal parent. The Lord, too, asks "how could I give you up, O Ephraim?" (11:8). Following the thrust of the metaphor the answer is inevitable: "I will not give vent to my blazing anger, I will not destroy Ephraim again." The rationale may surprise us, however—"for I am God and not man." Human parents are fallible and may be overcome by anger; God is not subject to weakness. The difference between God and humanity is that we fall short of what we know to be best, while God has no such limitation.

Hosea, like all the great prophets, was a realist. He recognized that Israel would be destroyed, and whatever actually happened was the work of God (a point which will be made again by Amos). The same God whose heart is stirred to pity in chapter 11 declares that "My eyes are closed to compassion" in 13:14. There is an apparent contradiction here. The mood of the prophet might naturally swing with changing circumstances, but if the Lord is "God and not man," we expect consistency. Hosea was not a systematic theologian, however, and all his insights do not fit neatly together. He was a shrewd enough observer to realize what would befall Samaria at the hands of the Assyrians—little ones dashed to pieces, expectant mothers ripped open (14:1). Yet he affirmed that God still loved Israel like a child, or, in the imagery of chapter 2, that after God had divorced Israel he would start over again with a new courtship. In this his faith is like that of a modern Jew who still believes in the love of God after the Holocaust. The conviction that God is love, despite all the evidence for random brutality and hatred in the world, is also an integral part of Christian faith.

One of Hosea's harshest words of judgment is given an ironic twist in the New Testament. In 13:14 the Lord asks, through the prophet, "Where are your plagues, O death! where is your sting, O nether world!" The point of the passage is that God is about to use the sting of death against Israel. In 1 Corinthians 15:54f, Saint Paul quotes this passage. In this case, however, the question is a mocking one—the sting of death has been broken by the resurrection of Christ. While Paul changes the meaning of the passage he quotes, the new meaning is not altogether alien to Hosea, since he too looked beyond the death of the nation Israel and hoped for its "resurrection."

The Relevance of Hosea

Hosea's message of divine love and the need for fidelity has lost none of its relevance in the modern world. The most important lesson to be learned from Hosea, however, may well be a matter of theological method. The way to the knowledge of God is through the observation of human experience. We know that it is better to pity than to destroy because of our experience in raising children. We know that infidelity is destructive because of the experience of our relationships, or because we have seen it in the relationships of others. Our knowledge of God is inferred from those basic human values which we know intuitively. Essentially the same theological method can be found in the parables of Jesus (for example, the Prodigal Son and the Good Samaritan) which are based to a great degree on the observation of human relationships.

FURTHER READING

King, P. J. *Amos, Hosea, Micah—An Archaeological Commentary.* Philadelphia: Westminster, 1988. Good use of archaeology to illustrate the prophetic texts.

Mays, J. L. *Hosea, A Commentary.* Philadelphia: Westminster, 1969. Balanced exegetical commentary.

Wolff, H. W. *Hosea.* Hermeneia. Philadelphia: Fortress, 1974. The best detailed commentary.

Yee, G. A. *The Book of Hosea.* New Interpreter's Bible 7, 197–297. Nashville: Abingdon Press, 1996. Homiletical commentary with feminist sensitivity.

JOEL

[see pages 1259–1265 of the Old Testament]

In sharp contrast to Hosea, the book of Joel makes no reference to known historical events, which would enable us to establish when it was written. It is safe to say, however, that it is one of the later prophetic books, and the date 400 BC (OT, p. 1259) is a reasonable guess. Two considerations favor a relatively late date. First, according to 4:6 some people of Judah were sold as slaves to the Greeks. This reference suggests a date after the Babylonian exile, when Judah was weak and contacts between the Greeks and the Near East were increasing. Second, the imagery of the Day of the Lord and the judgment of the nations has a strongly apocalyptic character. Such imagery is characteristic of the postexilic period.

The reference to Jews sold into slavery is indicative of the circumstances in which the book was written. It was a time of deprivation and exploitation. The first two chapters refer to a plague of locusts that had ravaged the harvests of Judah, thereby aggravating the problems of the poor. These circumstances are significant for understanding why the prophet predicts cosmic upheaval and radical change.

The book is characterized by movement from specific concern with the plague of locusts to a more general prophecy of universal judgment. Joel 1:1–2:17 combines description of the plague with exhortations and prayers for deliverance. Chapter 2, verses 18 to 27 give a reply and reassurance from God. All of this may reflect an actual Temple liturgy for relief from the disaster. Chapter 3 is concerned with a future time, when God will intervene to pour out the spirit and save a remnant of the people. Chapter 4 proclaims the final judgment of the nations and salvation of God's elect.

The Day of the Lord

The theme of the Day of the Lord runs through the book as a unifying thread. The earliest mention of the Day of the Lord is in Amos 5:18. It is apparent from that passage that this was originally a festive day, to which people looked forward in joyful anticipation. Amos, however, declared that it would be a day of darkness and not light. By the time the book of Joel was written, any great disaster could be dubbed a "Day of the Lord." In Joel 1–2 the reference is quite specifically to a plague of locusts, which transforms the land from being like "the garden of Eden" to a "desert waste" (2:3). Joel speaks of the locusts as an invading army, with the Lord at their head (2:11)—whatever actually happens is the work of God. The people respond to the emergency in ways typical of the ancient world, by bringing offerings and libations. It is characteristic of the Hebrew prophets, however, that a crisis such as this is made into an occasion for reform and repentance. The exhortation in 2:13 is a classic expression of the prophetic view of proper ritual: "Rend your hearts, not your garments."

In the modern secular world we do not usually regard natural disasters such as locusts or tornadoes as visitations from God, nor do we rely on rituals for relief. It would indeed be unfortunate if recourse to ritual kept people from taking whatever practical measures were possible to resolve their problems. The situation in Joel, however, was beyond human control, at least in that time and place. The ritual, then, was all that people could do. It was their way of expressing their desperate concern and their hope that God would give them relief. In urging them to use the crisis as an occasion for reform, the prophet is bringing some good out of a bad situation. He is also recognizing that all of life has religious significance. The prophetic idea of salvation is primarily concerned with the welfare of the people on earth. Anything that threatens that welfare is worthy of the prophet's attention, even if it is not the result of human activity in any evident sense.

The plague of locusts was undoubtedly traumatic for those who experienced it, but it was not an event of great historical moment. We do not even know when it took place. In the context of the book of Joel it takes on a broader significance. It is a prefiguration of a greater Day of the Lord, when God will come to judge the nations. The destruction of the land by the locusts is a small-scale rehearsal for the final judgment. In chapter 3, then, the Day of the Lord takes on a different meaning from what it had in the first two chapters. It now refers to the Day of Judgment. The description in 3:1–5 has become a classic passage because it is quoted in Acts 2: 17–21. The imagery suggests the end of the world—the sun will be turned to darkness and the moon to blood. Such imagery is increasingly common in prophecy of the postexilic period (compare Is 13:9–11; 34:1–4).

Despite the vividness of the imagery, Joel does not envisage the end of the world, in the sense familiar from the book of Revelation. The language here is metaphorical. The darkening of sun and moon is a way of expressing that there will be a time of great tumult and confusion. The world order as we know it will be turned upside down and, most importantly, the foreign nations who have oppressed the Jews will be overthrown. The magnitude of this upheaval is expressed through the imagery of the physical universe. This kind of imagery is very common in the apocalyptic literature from the second century BC on, (see the Reading Guide to Daniel). The later apocalyptic writers, however, took the imagery more literally and came to believe in an actual end of the world. This is not yet the case in Daniel, but it is commonplace by New Testament times. In 2 Esdras 7:30 (a Jewish writing from the end of the first century AD), the earth is turned back to primeval silence for seven days before the resurrection, so that the new creation is clearly separated from the old. Joel, in contrast, has no resurrection, and looks for a transformation of this world rather than a new creation.

A Vision of Plenty

There are two aspects of Joel's hope for the transformation of the earth. First is the universal human hope for freedom from hunger. This is a natural reaction to the locust plague. In a time of scarcity Joel comforts his people with the promise that they will eat and be filled (2:26) and even rhapsodizes that "the mountains shall drip new wine, and the hills shall flow with milk" (4: 18). This kind of prediction is very common in the Prophets (see, for example, Is 11). It evidently involves a strong element of wish fulfillment. More than two thousand years later, the world is still a long way from being rid of hunger. The optimistic prophecy has two functions. It gives hope to the poor, not certainty indeed but a hope that is within the bounds of possibility, and it reminds us all of a goal toward which we should work. The role of the prophecy is to sustain energy and morale in depressing times. In itself, the prophecy did not feed the hungry, but then humanity does not live by bread alone, and the prophet supplied strength in other ways.

Vengeance on the Nations

The second aspect of the Day of the Lord is one that Christians sometimes find distasteful, although Christians have certainly indulged it in the course of history. This is the desire for vengeance. It is not enough that Judah flow with wine and milk, the hated neighbor Edom must be a desert waste (4:19). If the Philistines have sold Jews as slaves, their own children must be sold in turn (4:4–8). Where other prophets called on people to beat their swords into plowshares (Is 2: 4; Mi 4:3), Joel reverses the call and looks forward to a showdown in the valley of Jehoshaphat. Vengeance is not one of the nobler human emotions, but it is certainly understandable and sometimes irresistible. Distaste for vengeance should not distract us from the more fundamental problems that give rise to it. The prophets' call for vengeance is usually a call for justice. In the case of Joel it is a protest of the powerless who had seen their children sold into slavery. Slavery was a far more fundamental sin against humanity than vengeance, real or imagined.

In the modern world, the vengefulness of the prophet often finds its counterpart in the feelings of Third World countries toward the more developed West. Vengeance is all the more distasteful when it is directed against ourselves, for reasons we seldom understand. Since the Hebrew prophets are part of our own tradition, they may help us reach some understanding of the mentality of those who see themselves as oppressed and want to see the tables turned on their more powerful neighbors. This is not to approve of vengefulness, but to affirm that we can learn something even from a somewhat distasteful text.

FURTHER READING

Achtemeier, E. *The Book of Joel.* New Interpreter's Bible 7, 301–36. Nashville: Abingdon Press, 1996. Brief homiletical commentary.

Crenshaw, J. L. *Joel.* Anchor Bible 24C. New York: Doubleday, 1995. Excellent, up-to-date commentary.

Wolff, H. W. *Joel and Amos.* Hermeneia. Philadelphia: Fortress, 1977. Classic detailed commentary.

AMOS

[see pages 1265–1276 of the Old Testament]

Amos is the earliest of the prophets who have books in their names. In fact, his oracles were transmitted orally and were only collected in book form much later. The opening verse mentions the kings Uzziah of Judah and Jeroboam II of Israel, who are the earliest kings mentioned in Hosea 1:1. The later kings listed in connection with Hosea are not mentioned in Amos. The historical background of the two prophets is very much the same. The dominant factor is the threat of destruction by Assyria. Nonetheless, the problems on which the two prophets focus are quite different. Hosea paid great attention to idolatry and cultic behavior, which symbolized the deeper problems of the society. Amos also comments on the cult but scarcely hints that idolatry is a problem. Instead he speaks directly to the issue of social justice, with a vigor unparalleled anywhere in the Bible.

The Career of Amos

We know very little about the career of Amos. He came from the village of Tekoa in the Southern Kingdom of Judah, but he delivered his oracles in the Northern Kingdom, especially around the temple of Bethel, just north of the border. He did not, in any case, attach great importance to political boundaries. It is a theme of his prophecy that all peoples are equal in the sight of God.

Only one episode from his career is recounted in the book. In 7:10–17 we hear of an encounter between Amos and the priest of Bethel. The priest was worried because Amos was prophesying against the king in the Temple precincts. The priest could not afford to offend the king, and so he told Amos to go back to Judah. Amos's reply has given rise to much debate. Literally the Hebrew says "No prophet I, nor the son of a prophet." The NAB opts for one possible interpretation of this utterance: "I was no prophet" (until the Lord called me). An alternative view is that he rejected the very name "prophet." In either case, the point at issue is that Amos is not a member of a guild of professional prophets, such as we see in action in 1 Kings 22, the story of Micaiah, son of Imlah. He was an independent agent. He was a shepherd and a dresser of sycamores (the fruit, resembling a fig, had to be tended in order to prevent insects from destroying it), and so had his own means. He did not depend on king or priest for support and was not beholden to them, and thus did not require their permission to prophesy. This independence left him free to speak the truth as he saw it, without political constraint.

The style of Amos is blunt, even offensive. He calls the women of Samaria "cows of Bashan" (4:1) and tells the priest Amaziah that his wife will be a harlot in the city (7:17). This is not the way to make friends and influence people, and it is not a style recommended by professors of homiletics. Amos makes no attempt to win the sympathy of his audience, as Nathan did with David (2 Sm 12) or as Jesus does in the parables. He is a prophet in the mold of Elijah, whose denunciations come close to cursing. This crude style of preaching must be seen in its social context. Nathan was a trusted adviser to David and could expect to have an effect on him. Amos, like Elijah, was an outsider. He did not have the ear of the king and saw no likelihood that the upper classes would change their ways. Consequently, he does not appeal for repentance. He simply proclaims the doom that is coming. He testifies to the conditions of his time and puts them on record, but he does not suggest that the catastrophe could be avoided.

The oracles of Amos are grouped in distinct blocks. The first two chapters contain a series of oracles against various nations, culminating in a denunciation of Israel. Amos 3:1–5:9 contains three long oracles (or strings of short utterances), which are introduced as "words." These are followed in 5:7–6:14 by three "woes" against Israel and Judah. (The verses in 5:7–9 are out of order and must be rearranged. See OT, p. 1270.) Chapters 7:1 through 9:8b contain a series of visions of destruction. Chapter 9:8c–15 is an epilogue, probably added by a later editor.

The Oracles against the Nations

The book begins with oracles of judgment against Israel's immediate neighbors, in the area now occupied by Lebanon, Syria, Jordan, and part of the occupied territory of Palestine. The oracle against Judah may have been added by the editor of the book to bring it up to date, after Israel had been destroyed. It was not unusual in the ancient world for a prophet from one country to denounce or curse other nations: see Numbers 22–24, where Balaam is called to curse Israel. What is unusual here is that Amos doesn't stop after he has denounced the other nations, but goes on to pronounce a similar judgment on Israel. His listeners would surely have expected to hear that Israel would be glorified when Edom was humiliated (as we saw in Joel 4). Amos, however, insists that Israel is no different from other nations in the eyes of God. Any nation that sins deserves punishment. The sins of the other nations are not all offenses against Israel. Moab is condemned for burning to lime the bones of the king of Edom (2:1), which is an outrage against humanity as such, or against natural law. The sins of Israel, too, are sins against humanity: they sell the just man for silver and the poor man for a pair of sandals (2:6).

The oracle against Israel in Amos 2:6–16 can be read as a "covenant lawsuit," that is, a speech in which the prophet indicts Israel for failing to keep the Sinai covenant. The covenant had three essential elements: (1) the recollection of salvation history, culminating in the Exodus; (2) the commandments, and (3) blessings for keeping the commandments and curses for breaking them. The history as well as the curses and blessings both provided motivation to keep the commandments. The typical argument of a "covenant lawsuit" is that (1) God earned the loyalty of Israel by bringing it out of Egypt but, (2) Israel proved disloyal by breaking the commandments. In Amos 2, the sins of Israel are listed first (vv. 6–8). Then the prophet recalls the Exodus and the obligation it entailed. He concludes with a threat, which is in effect a curse: "Beware, I will crush you into the ground" (2:13). Many scholars think, however, that the recollection of the Exodus here was added by an editor, who wanted to put the prophetic preaching in the context of the theology of Deuteronomy (which is also exemplified in the books of Joshua, Judges, Samuel, and Kings). Amos himself had a wider frame of reference. The practices he condemns are, to be sure, forbidden by the law of Moses, but that is not the point in Amos. People of any nation should recognize that it is criminal to sell a just man for silver. So it makes no difference to Amos whether or not a particular nation knows the law of Moses. The basic requirements of justice should be obvious to all. In short, Amos appeals to natural law, as it was understood in the ancient Near East. The law of Moses coincided with that law to a great extent, but the essentials of ethical behavior should be known even to pagans. In the New Testament, Saint Paul makes the same point in Romans 1, where he says that pagan idolaters have no excuse, "for what can be known about God is evident to them."

Amos and the Covenant

The equivalence of Israel and other nations in the sight of God is a theme that runs through the book of Amos. It raises a question as to whether the prophet regarded Israel as a chosen nation in any sense. He was certainly familiar with the story of the Exodus and the recitation of salvation history. For Amos, however, the Exodus guarantees Israel no privilege, but only adds to its responsibility. Two other passages in the book address this question very directly.

1. In 3:2 we read "You alone have I favored, more than all the families of the earth." We expect this statement to be followed by a reassurance, such as "therefore I will protect you like the apple of my eye" or the like. Instead we read "Therefore I will punish you for all your crimes." Here, as in the oracles against the nations, Amos deliberately shocks his audience by telling them what they neither expect nor want to hear. (Jesus uses a similar technique in the parable of the good Samaritan.) In a sense he is only spelling out the implications of the covenant, which always carried the threat of the curses for breaking the laws as well as the promise of the blessings for obedience. This is not how most people in Israel understood the covenant, however. They thought, naturally enough, that the Exodus guaranteed them divine protection, that they were already "saved." According to Amos, the only way Israel differs from the other nations is that it should know better and therefore is all the more blameworthy for its crimes.

2. Amos puts the Exodus in perspective even more bluntly in 9:7: "Are you not like the Ethiopians to me? . . . Did I not bring the Israelites from the land of Egypt as I brought the Philistines from Caphtor and the Arameans from Kir?" Israel is special in the eyes of God . . . but so is every other people. The Philistines and Syrians had their salvation history too. None of this means that the Exodus was not important. It was absolutely fundamental to the identity of Israel. It did not, however, mean that Israel would be favored in any way, except that it should know more clearly than others what was demanded of it.

Amos's sustained denial that Israel was any different from other peoples has its best parallel in the Wisdom literature (especially Proverbs), which ignores the special revelation to Israel and focuses on the universal moral law. Amos seems to have been an educated man. He displays an impressive knowledge of international affairs, and he was certainly no ignorant peasant. We do not know how he acquired his learning. He was probably well versed in traditional wisdom, whether he was formally educated in a school setting or not.

The Words and Woes

The three "words" of Amos are really a string of shorter oracles, mainly concerned with the sins of the Israelites. In 3:3–8, however, he lays out some of his theological presuppositions. He assumes that there is an order in nature and things do not happen by chance ("Does a lion roar . . . when it has no prey?"). This order is the work of God. Amos is a radical monotheist, not only in the sense that he ignores other gods but that he regards everything that happens as the work of the Lord. Religious people always credit God with the good things that happen. Amos goes further: "If evil befalls a city, has not the Lord caused it?" God is responsible for the bad as well as the good. (Remember the Israelite religion at this time had no devil on whom evil could be blamed.) The acts of God in history, then, are not confined to special events like the Exodus, but embrace everything that actually happens. This conviction lays the foundation for a thoroughgoing realism in his view of international politics. If Assyria is more powerful than Israel, this is not by chance but is the will of God. Jeremiah took a similar view of the power of Babylon when it destroyed Jerusalem.

Amos directs many of his oracles against the cult at Bethel. When people go to make offerings to atone for sin at Bethel, Amos says that they "come to Bethel and sin" (4:4). There is a pun in the Hebrew because of the similarity of the terms for "sin-offering" and "sin," and Amos uses the word play to equate the two. His sharpest critique of the cult, however, is delivered in the famous "Woe" against those who yearn for the Day of the Lord (5:18–25). The Day of the Lord was a major festival day, most probably the Feast of Tabernacles or Sukkoth, a harvest festival in the fall. It was an occasion for celebrating the victory of the God of Israel and the defeat of his enemies. Amos, characteristically, tells the people that it will be the opposite of what they expect. The real Day of the Lord, when God appears before the people, will be a day of judgment. Amos was the first prophet to speak of the Day of the Lord as a day of judgment on Israel, and thereby he introduced one of the major themes of the prophetic literature.

Amos goes on to issue a broadside against all the festivals of Israel. He implies that Israel survived for the forty years in the desert without offering sacrifices (5:25). His point is not that all ritual is necessarily bad, but that it is not of the essence of religion. For Amos, the essence of religion is social justice. If ritual furthers justice, well and good, but too often it does not. In the prophet's view, the Israelite cult only made the upper classes complacent. They identified themselves as "Israel" and felt that they were God's chosen people. Their cultic celebrations reminded them of the Exodus and the great things God had done for them, and reassured them that God would deliver them from danger again. They need not, then, be too concerned about the plight of the poor. When the festival was over, they could go back to cheating in the marketplace (8:5). Amos insisted that all this was self-delusion. God would not overlook the injustice of the society because of the sound of the harps, and the Assyrians would rudely shatter the naive belief that God would protect Israel no matter what.

The final "Woe" in chapter 6 paints a vivid picture of "the complacent in Zion [and] the overconfident on the mount of Samaria," the upper classes of both kingdoms of Israel. These were the people who sold the poor into slavery while they lived in luxury themselves. Amos announces with evident anticipation that these would be the first to go into exile. This was not mere wish fulfillment on the prophet's part. He knew the practice of the Assyrians, which was to take the upper classes into exile so that there would be no one left to lead a revolt. In his view, it was a fate that they richly deserved.

The Visions

Chapters 7 through 9 are primarily visions of the destruction of Israel. At first the prophet is moved by the enormity of the destruction and intercedes with God on behalf of Israel. After the vision of the locusts and of the fire, God relents, but the time for forgiveness runs out. The message is summed up in the vision of a basket of ripe fruit. The Hebrew here involves another pun. The word for "ripe fruit" is very similar to the word for "end." Amos 8:2 "the time is ripe" can also be translated "the end has come." This was the first time the idea of an "end" was proclaimed in ancient Israel. The end in question was the end of Israel as an independent nation. Later biblical writers would extend the idea and envisage an end of history or of the world. (The technical theological term "eschatology," which refers to the doctrine of the last things, is derived from the Greek word for "end.") Amos, however, was not speaking of the end of the world. The end of Israel in the eighth century BC, which he predicted, was final, in the sense that the political entity that had existed for two hundred years was wiped off the map and never restored. The influence of Amos on later tradition was undoubtedly increased by the fact that his prophecy was so completely fulfilled.

The Israel whose end Amos announced was primarily the Israel of the upper classes, who held political power. They were the ones who identified themselves as Israel in the cult and in international political relations. The peasants would undoubtedly suffer during the Assyrian invasion, but ultimately it may not have made much difference whether one paid taxes to a foreign power or to predatory Israelite landlords. From the viewpoint of the peasants, and of Amos, the survival of Israel as a nation was not of great importance. What mattered was not political identity but the living conditions of the poor within the society.

The Epilogue

Much of the force of Amos's prophecy derived from its finality. When he said that God would destroy the kingdom of Israel off the face of the earth (9:8), that was his last word. A later editor felt that this stark conclusion did not do justice to history. Israel in the broader sense of the people of the Lord, north and south, was not terminated. The message of the prophetic corpus as a whole is ultimately not one of destruction but of hope. What the epilogue does, then, is put the prophecy of Amos in a broader perspective. Death and destruction have their time and place, but there remains the hope for an ideal future, as we have seen in the prophecy of Joel. This ultimate optimism is an essential ingredient of biblical faith.

Three points in the epilogue deserve special attention.

1. Amos 9:9f suggests that God's judgment on Israel will be selective, so that only the sinners will die. Obviously the Assyrians were not so selective, nor were the Babylonians after them. The preexilic prophets spoke of the fate of the whole nation, not of individuals, and this was realistic if divine judgment was executed through warfare. In the postexilic period, however, there is increasing sensitivity to individual responsibility. (See the great reflection on this subject in Ez 18.) In the apocalyptic literature (for example, Daniel) the problem is resolved by the belief that just and wicked receive their appropriate retribution after death.

2. The hope for the future is focused on "the fallen hut of David." This oracle probably comes from the period after the exile when there was no longer a Davidic king on the throne in Jerusalem. The hope expressed here is messianic, but should not be confused with the later Christian understanding of the Messiah. The hope here is that the native Jewish kingship will be restored.

3. Finally, the ideal state of the end-time is decidedly earthly in character. The hope is for peace and prosperity, with an abundance of wine and fruit. One of the major points that the Hebrew Bible can contribute to Christian spirituality is a healthy appreciation of the good things of this world.

The Relevance of Amos

No prophet is more easily related to the modern world than Amos, for the social inequities that he denounced in eighth-century BC Israel are still very much with us. The American bishops adopt a much milder tone than Amos in their pastoral letter on the economy, but their concerns are very much in line with his. The bishops insist that "government has a moral function: protecting human rights and securing justice for all members of the commonwealth" (*Economic Justice for All*, p. 35), and that "the fulfillment of the basic needs of the poor is of the highest priority" (p. 27). In the ancient world it was the role of the prophet to be the conscience of the nation and speak up for the powerless. In the modern world, that role falls to religious leaders, who are not themselves involved in the business of government and so can view it with some perspective.

The first lesson to be learned from Amos is that social justice is the business of religion. The test of piety is what happens in the marketplace rather than what happens in the church or temple.

A second lesson is less obvious at first, but bears some thought. Amos was convinced that there is an intrinsic connection between the justice of a society and its long-term prosperity. This conviction arose from his radical monotheism. The God who gives prosperity is also the God of justice. In the modern world we are hesitant to see such an immediate connection between morality and success. Nonetheless it is probably true that the greed of the Israelite upper classes contributed to their own downfall. On the one hand their aspiration to power and independence brought them into conflict with Assyria. On the other hand the exploitation of the poor, and the individualism of the rich, weakened the society internally. The Assyrians might have rolled over Israel whether it was a just society or not, but the blow might not have been so severe if its leaders had been less concerned with political power and more concerned with equality and justice.

FURTHER READING

Coote, R. B. *Amos Among the Prophets: Composition and Theology.* Philadelphia: Fortress, 1981. Lively presentation of the message of Amos.

Gowan, D. E. *The Book of Amos.* New Interpreter's Bible 7, 339–431. Nashville: Abingdon Press, 1996. Homiletical commentary.

Jeremias, J. *The Book of Amos.* Louisville: Westminster John Knox, 1998. Exegetical commentary with emphasis on the composition of the book.

King, P. J. *Amos, Hosea, Micah—An Archaeological Commentary.* Philadelphia: Westminster, 1988. Uses archaeology to illustrate the teaching of the prophet.

Mays, J. L. *Amos, A Commentary.* Philadelphia: Westminster, 1969. Balanced exegetical commentary.

Wolff, H. W. *Amos the Prophet, The Man and His Background.* Philadelphia: Fortress, 1973. Summary of the findings of the author's commentary.

The best detailed scholarly commentary is that of H. W. Wolff, *Joel and Amos* (Hermeneia. Philadelphia: Fortress, 1977).

OBADIAH

[see pages 1276–1278 of the Old Testament]

With only twenty-one verses, the book of Obadiah is the shortest of the prophetic books. It consists of a series of short oracles against Edom (vv. 1–14), then an oracle against all the nations (15f), followed by a prediction of the restoration of Judah. Edom was a small state to the south of Judah. (It was later called Idumaea.) The Edomites incurred the lasting hatred of the Jews in the sixth century BC by exploiting the weaknesses of Judah and pillaging its territory after the Babylonian invasion. Relations remained very bitter when the Jews returned from the exile and restored the city of Jerusalem. The prophecy of Obadiah belongs to this general period (sixth or early fifth century BC) but contains no indication of its specific date. The hatred between Judah and Edom was intense and lasting. Long after Edom had ceased to be a threat to the Jews, the name Edom was used in rabbinic literature as a code name for Rome, the hated enemy of the day.

Oracles against Edom

Oracles of vengeance against Edom were common in the postexilic period. Compare the related utterances in Jeremiah 49:7–22. For the modern reader, these oracles pose the usual problem of how to deal with vengeance. In fairness, it should be noted that the logic of Obadiah is quite similar to that of Amos. There is a natural moral law that applies to the actions of all peoples. That law forbids violence against one's neighbors and then gloating over their distress. One who violates that law, however, loses its protection. The underlying principle is succinctly stated in verse 15: "As you have done, so shall it be done to you." The natural law requires that the punishment fit the crime. Obadiah indicts Edom for behavior similar to that for which Amos indicted Israel. While it may seem more noble to direct criticism against one's own people, the moral principle is the same. Edom deserved the prophetic denunciation.

Judgment upon the Nations

In broadening his attack to all the foreign nations, Obadiah uses the now familiar motif of the Day of the Lord (see the guide to Amos). Here the judgment is directed only against the foreign nations. Israel did not need a word of judgment at this time. The Day of the Lord here is simply the day of judgment. It implies a decisive change in the course of events, but nothing like the end of history or of the world. The judgment will be governed by the law of retribution: as you have done to others, so shall it be done to you. Obadiah applies this principle to whole nations rather than to individuals.

The Restoration of Judah

The idea that a remnant will be saved on Mount Zion was developed especially by Isaiah. In the present context one is struck by the modesty of the hope. The kingship of God does not imply that Judah will rule all the nations, only its immediate neighbors who have most recently afflicted it. While a note of vengeance is present it should not be exaggerated. The oracle is really a testimony to the indomitable hope of a people who had been reduced to poverty and insignificance, and were at the mercy of their neighbors. Belief in the kingship of God on Mount Zion was a deep-rooted part of the Jerusalem cult under the monarchy (see for example, Pss 93; 97–99). In the aftermath of the exile it became a source of hope for deliverance.

FURTHER READING

Pagán, S. *The Book of Obadiah*. New Interpreter's Bible 7, 435–59. Nashville: Abingdon Press, 1996. Brief homiletical commentary.

Raabe, P. R. *Obadiah*. Anchor Bible 24D. New York: Doubleday, 1996. Thorough philological commentary.

Wolff, H. W. *Obadiah and Jonah: A Commentary*. Minneapolis: Augsburg, 1986. Classic scholarly commentary.

JONAH

[see pages 1278–1281 of the Old Testament]

The book of Jonah is unique among the Prophets for two reasons. First, it is not a collection of oracles but a narrative, and second, Jonah is in many ways an antiprophet, whose behavior is approximately the opposite of what we expect from a prophet. The story may be termed a fable, because of the role of the fish (compare the role of animals in Aesop's fables). It can also be considered as a parable, in the sense that it is a short story that goes against our expectations, like many of the parables of Jesus. The story is set in the Assyrian period (like the prophecies of Hosea and Amos), but there is general agreement that it comes from a much later time. While we cannot pinpoint the time of composition, it was certainly sometime in the postexilic period. The actual setting, then, was close to the time of Joel and Obadiah, but Jonah has a very different perspective on the problems of the period.

The division of the book is adequately represented by the chapters. The long psalm in chapter 2 stands out from its context. It may have been added by a later editor who was more interested in the miracle of Jonah's survival than was the original author.

Three considerations are especially important for appreciating the book of Jonah:

1. The story is quite deliberately humorous,

2. Its primary subject matter is the proper attitude to foreign nations, not Jonah's miraculous escape from drowning,

3. The story gives a mildly critical perspective on the religious zeal that is a trademark of prophecy.

The Humor of the Story

The humorous quality should be apparent from the opening verses. Where else do we ever hear of a prophet who so flagrantly disobeys a divine command? The idea that one could get away from the Lord by sailing to a remote place is not only naive but deliberately ridiculous. The pagan sailors exhibit more "fear of the Lord" than does Jonah. When he finally goes to Nineveh, the Assyrians respond with a fervor unparalleled in Israel. Even the animals join in the repentance. The author of this passage is not concerned with historical plausibility—everyone knew that Assyria had never turned from its "evil way." The fantastic repentance of the Assyrians simply adds to the enjoyment of the tale.

The centerpiece of the humor of the story is even more fantastic than the repentance of the Assyrians. A great fish arrives just in time to catch Jonah when he is thrown overboard and vomits him up on the shore. Nothing could be more remote from the spirit of this story than to believe that this actually happened. The episode of Jonah and the fish has rich theological implications, especially for Christians, but there is no theological virtue in mistaking a fantastic joke for literal fact.

The humor of the story has an ironic quality. It refuses to give the prophet the dignity associated with the office, or to take his convictions seriously. It invites us to reconsider our stereotypes of both pagans and prophets. Unlike the oracles of Amos, it assumes the goodwill of its readers and tries to lead them to new insight.

The Attitude to Foreign Nations

The primary subject matter of the book is indicated at the outset when the prophet is sent to preach to the Assyrians rather than to his own people. The wickedness of Assyria is not in doubt; it is the premise of the story. Jonah, naturally enough, wants to see justice done and is upset at God's excessive mercy. The incredible repentance of the Assyrians forces the issue: does Assyria, the most destructive tyrant of its day, deserve divine forgiveness? It is as if the Nazi leaders made a show of repentance after World War II and were pardoned. Jonah is not exceptionally narrow-minded here. His demand for justice is just as reasonable as that at the Nuremberg trials. It is not accepted, however. God speaks here as creator, to whom the Assyrians are as important as the Israelites (or, in modern terms, Nazis are as important as Jews or Christians). The concluding verse of the book recognizes that "the Assyrian in the street" is no more guilty of the crimes of his nation than are the cattle, but guilt or innocence is not the point. The book of Jonah sees God in the same terms as the much later book of Wisdom 11:24: "For you love all things that are and loathe nothing that you have made; for what you hated, you would not have fashioned." The magnanimity of this sentiment is astonishing, especially when we consider the situation of the Jews in the postexilic period, when they had every reason to resent foreign powers. We may compare this story to Jesus' parable of the good Samaritan. The parable presupposes that most Jews would have regarded "good Samaritan" as a contradiction in terms. The penitent Assyrian is at least as great a contradiction, and as hard to accept. Admittedly, when the book of Jonah was written the Assyrian invasion was already ancient history, and it did not arouse emotions to the same degree as the Holocaust in our time. Nevertheless, it is not that Jonah was exceptionally narrow-minded here, but rather that God is exceptionally tolerant.

The Perspective on Prophetic Zeal

Jonah reacts to God's mercy by sulking and praying for death (4:8). He is not the first prophet to do so. The great Elijah also sat under a tree and asked God to take his life (1 Kgs 19:4f). Elijah, more than any prophet, was known for his zeal in destroying sinners (witness his treatment of the prophets of Baal in 1 Kgs 18:40). Jonah is a prophet in the same mold. In this case, however, the zeal of the prophet does not meet with approval. The book of Jonah sees the limitations of prophetic zeal. God's rebuke is mild. Jonah is well intentioned and is acting in accordance with a long tradition. Conformity with tradition is not enough, however. Hosea had marked a breakthrough in the Israelite tradition by the recognition that it is more fitting for God to have mercy than to punish. The book of Jonah extends that insight to the treatment of foreign nations. Even the prophet must learn that reconciliation holds a higher value than strict retribution. Not all the prophetic books reflect this insight, but it is certainly the view affirmed for Christianity in the Gospels.

The Sign of Jonah

The episode in the belly of the fish is a minor humorous motif in the original story, but it acquires greater significance in later tradition. In Matthew 12:39f, Jonah's stay in the belly of the fish is taken to prefigure Jesus' time in the tomb, and Jonah is often used as a symbol of resurrection in early Christian art. The symbolic significance of this episode appears already in the psalm in chapter 2. There the belly of the fish is equated with the netherworld, and Jonah's rescue is equivalent to resurrection from the dead. In the context of the Old Testament, the resurrection is metaphorical and means simply that the psalmist is delivered from desperate circumstances. It is a confession of the power of God to give life and take it away. We should note that what Jonah regrets about the netherworld is that he is separated from the presence of God. What he asks is not just continued survival but restoration to that presence. Fullness of life, for most Old Testament writers, is not life without end but the experience of God's grace, which is so satisfying that it is better to have "one day in your courts than a thousand elsewhere" (Ps 84:11).

The Relevance of Jonah

Jonah's message of tolerance and forgiveness is as urgent in the modern world as it was in the fifth century BC. It is a hard word and should not be sentimentalized. It demands not only tolerance and understanding for those who are different from us, but forgiveness for those who have truly behaved wickedly, if they are willing to accept it. It is not yet a demand for unconditional forgiveness, since it has the precondition of repentance, but it is not an easy demand for all that.

The sign of Jonah caught the imagination of later generations as a sign of hope. That hope nicely undergirds the message of tolerance and forgiveness, since the wicked deeds of the oppressor are not as final as they seem. Those who hope for deliverance from the belly of death can afford to forgive the injustices of life. Belief in resurrection is often associated with the hope that the wicked will be damned. The book of Jonah, read in the light of the New Testament and Christian tradition, suggests that resurrection can also give a larger perspective on life, which has room for tolerance and forgiveness.

FURTHER READING

Limburg, J. *Jonah.* Louisville: Westminster John Knox, 1993. Commentary, with interest in later interpretations of Jonah in literature and art.

Sasson, J. *Jonah*. Anchor Bible 24B. New York: Doubleday, 1990. Full commentary, with interest in folkloric motifs.

Trible, P. *Jonah*. New Interpreter's Bible 7, 463–529. Nashville: Abingdon Press, 1996. Excellent literary commentary.

Wolff, H. W. *Obadiah and Jonah: A Commentary.* Minneapolis: Augsburg, 1986. Classic scholarly commentary.

MICAH

[see pages 1281–1289 of the Old Testament]

Micah was a prophet of the eighth century BC, contemporary with Amos, Hosea, and Isaiah. As a prophet of the Southern Kingdom of Judah, he most closely resembles Isaiah. The book that bears his name does not all come from his hand. There is general agreement that his words are preserved in chapters 1 through 3, probably also in chapter 6, and in parts of chapter 7. Chapters 4 and 5, however, were probably added after the Babylonian exile. The original words of Micah, like those of Amos, are largely preoccupied with issues of social justice and the coming Assyrian invasion.

The Impending Judgment

The first oracle begins with a classic description of a *theophany,* or apparition of God. Traditionally such a theophany was associated with divine deliverance, as in Deuteronomy 33 and Judges 5 (compare also the theophany on Sinai). Micah's theophany, however, is like Amos's Day of the Lord. God is not coming to save but to judge. The immediate presence of God is destructive for a sinful people. In eighth-century BC Israel, the presence of God was not experienced as fire and earthquake but as the invasion of the Assyrian army. The destruction would fall most heavily on Samaria and Jerusalem, the major cities, homes of the royal houses and ruling classes.

The reasons for the coming destruction are spelled out most clearly in chapter 2. The problem is that the rich devise ways to force the smaller landowners into debt and then seize their property. Isaiah 5:8 complains about the same problem ("Woe to you who join house to house, who connect field with field, till no room remains, and you are left to dwell alone in the midst of the land"). From the prophet's viewpoint, it was only fitting that this land would be seized again by the Assyrians, so that the greed of the big landowners would be in vain.

Micah also discusses another fact of life in ancient Israel, which was only hinted at by Amos but was later a major theme in the prophecy of Jeremiah. The professional prophets were leading the people astray (3:5). This is why Amos made his protest "No prophet I." The phenomenon is natural enough. Prophets found that people liked to be reassured and told that all was well, and they tailored their message to their market. They were concerned with their own well-being more than that of the nation. A classic illustration of the professional prophets in action can be found in 1 Kings 22. In contrast, Micah saw the task of the true prophet as "to declare to Jacob his crimes and to Israel his sins" (3:8). Compare the assertion of Jeremiah that "From of old, the prophets who were before you and me prophesied war, woe, and pestilence" (Jer 28:8). Such a prophet would never be popular, but at least there could be no doubt about his sincerity.

The true prophet here, as so often in the history of Israel, finds himself in opposition to the religious leaders, the priests, and the official prophets (3:11). On the surface of things, the priests appear to have great faith: no evil can come upon Israel because the Lord is in its midst. Such faith is no virtue for Micah. Rather virtue lies in the practice of justice and in facing reality honestly. He regarded the Temple on Mount Zion, often the focal point of Jewish religion in antiquity, as a negative force. According to the psalmist, Mount Zion was "the holy dwelling of the Most High. God is in its midst; it shall not be shaken" (Ps 46:6). If kings came to attack it, they would be seized with terror and put to flight (Ps 48:5f). Micah realized that the Assyrians would not panic at the sight of Jerusalem. The belief that Zion could not be destroyed was a source of complacency and illusion. So Micah uttered his radical prophecy that Zion would be plowed like a field. This prophecy is quoted in Jeremiah 26:18 as a precedent for the equally radical prophecy of Jeremiah. It was not fulfilled in Micah's time, but it was not forgotten either, and it was justified in time. Faith cannot be based on any religious institution, no matter how sacred. No temple is permanent, and no one is guaranteed the unconditional protection of God.

The Indictment of Israel

Chapter 6 presents an example of the "covenant lawsuit," which we have discussed above in connection with Amos. According to the logic of the Sinai covenant, Israel was bound to keep the commandments because God had brought it out of the land of Egypt. If the people kept the commandments they would be blessed, if not they would be cursed. In Micah 6:1–5 God indicts Israel by recalling that the divine part of the obligation had been satisfied in the Exodus. It is not necessary to spell out how Israel has failed to keep its part, or what the consequences will be.

Micah does not suggest that the Israelites were indifferent to religion. On the contrary, they were willing to perform any ritual that might further their interests, even human sacrifice (6:7). According to 2 Kings 21:6, a king of Judah, Manasseh, immolated his son by fire in the seventh century BC. The prophet cuts through the pretenses of such superstition with a succinct formulation of the essence of religion: "to do the right and to love goodness, and to walk humbly with your God" (6:8). No special beliefs or cultic observances are required. There was general agreement on what it meant to do the right. The anguished quest for the right sacrifice, then, is shown to be mere hypocrisy. The business of religion is quite straightforward. It only requires the will to do what we know we ought. It is significant that the American bishops used Micah 6, 8 as a summary of the heritage of the biblical prophets in setting the tone for the entire letter *Economic Justice for All* (n. 4). We might compare this passage with the Judgment scene in Matthew 25:31–46. There the Son of Man does not ask about beliefs or ritual practices, but whether one fed the hungry and clothed the naked.

The Faith of the Prophet

The prophets only rarely provide glimpses of their personal faith, such as we find in the "confessions" of Jeremiah. One such glimpse is provided in Micah 7:7–10. Micah appears as a lonely figure, as we might expect in view of his relationship to the other prophets. His attempt to reach his public appears to have failed, but he is sustained by the conviction that God will vindicate him. In all of this he resembles Jeremiah, whose trials are described at greater length. The experience of prophets such as these contributed to the ideal of the Suffering Servant (Is 53), which has played such an important part in Christian theology.

The Prophecies of Restoration

The oracles inserted in Micah 4–5 in the postexilic period include two that are especially memorable. The prophecy of the restoration of the house of the Lord in Micah 4:1–3 is also found in Isaiah 2:2–4. The author of this oracle is unknown. The idea that all nations would find a spiritual center in Jerusalem may be quite old, but it flourished especially in the postexilic period when Jews who lived in other lands went to Jerusalem on pilgrimage. The prophecy is artfully placed here, immediately after the prediction that Zion would become a plowed field. The editors of the prophetic books typically placed an oracle of hope after one of judgment. In Micah's day the influence of the Temple was such that he needed to remind people that it would not last forever. By the time the book was edited the need for judgment had passed, and it was appropriate to remember the potential of the Temple for good.

Micah 5:1–4 speaks of a ruler who will come from Bethlehem. This prophecy has been treasured by Christians for obvious reasons. In the Jewish context, the significance of Bethlehem lies in the fact that it was the birthplace of David. The prophecy, then, is that the Davidic line will be restored. In mentioning Bethlehem rather than Jerusalem, however, the prophet is making a further point. He is recalling the humble origins of the monarchy, when it was associated with a village rather than with a city, and was not yet tainted with the corruption of Solomon's empire. The hope for restoration of the native kingship, which would bring peace to the land, is similar to what is described in more rhapsodic language in Isaiah 11.

FURTHER READING

Hillers, D. R. *Micah.* Hermeneia. Philadelphia: Fortress, 1984. Interprets Micah as a prophet of a revitalization movement.

King, P. J. *Amos, Hosea, Micah—An Archaeological Commentary.* Philadelphia: Westminster, 1988. Uses archaeology to illustrate the prophetic book.

Mays, J. L. *Micah, A Commentary.* Philadelphia: Westminster, 1976. Balanced exegetical commentary.

Simundson, D. J. *The Book of Micah.* New Interpreter's Bible 7, 531–89. Nashville: Abingdon Press, 1996. Helpful homiletical commentary.

Wolff, H. W. *Micah, A Commentary.* Minneapolis: Augsburg, 1990. Classic scholarly commentary.

——. *Micah the Prophet.* Philadelphia: Fortress, 1981. Summarizes findings of the author's commentary.

NAHUM

[see pages 1289–1293 of the Old Testament]

The oracles of Nahum are concerned with a single event, the fall of Nineveh in 612 BC. The euphoria of the prophet is understandable. Never again would Judah be invaded by Assyria. Some centuries later the author of Jonah might pity Nineveh, but that was more than could be expected at the time of its downfall. It is characteristic of biblical prophecy that the fall of one Gentile nation at the hands of another is assumed to be the work of the Lord.

A Jealous God

The opening verse of Nahum's prophecy is somewhat shocking to modern ears: "A jealous and avenging God is the LORD." Such a characterization of God was not new. One of the oldest descriptions of the biblical God is found in Exodus 15:3: "The LORD is a warrior" and on Sinai the Lord declares that he is a jealous God (Ex 20:5). This aspect of the divinity was never thought to be incompatible with mercy and love. It is simply the expression of justice: "the LORD never leaves the guilty unpunished." The wrath of God is only the manifestation of the moral order in the universe. Events like the fall of Nineveh were precious, because they showed that justice eventually prevailed. Nahum also says that the Lord is slow to anger (1:3) and emphasizes his goodness to the righteous (1:7). The immediate demonstration of that goodness was that God gave the smaller peoples of the Near East the satisfaction of seeing the fall of Assyria.

A Shortsighted Prophecy

The most striking thing about Nahum's prophecy, however, is how shortsighted it was. While Judah was freed from one oppressor it would soon be subjected to another, no less destructive. A mere fifteen years after Nahum proclaimed security, Jerusalem would again be under siege.

The lesson to be learned from Nahum is a two-edged one. The fall of Assyria is a reminder that all tyrants fall sooner or later and therefore is a cause of hope. The hope is tempered by the realization that the fall of a particular tyrant is not the end of all tyranny. History is full of surprises, not all of them pleasant. Nahum's exultation over the fall of Nineveh is echoed in the New Testament in John of Patmos's anticipation of the fall of Rome (Revelation 17–18). John uses the image of the harlot, which is found in Nahum 3:4. Rome, too, fell eventually, but other tyrants took its place. Yet there is consolation in the knowledge that no power lasts forever.

FURTHER READING

Boadt, L. *Jeremiah 26–52; Habakkuk; Zephaniah; Nahum.* Old Testament Message 10. Wilmington, DE: Glazier, 1981. Helpful brief commentary.

Roberts, J. J. M. *Nahum, Habakkuk and Zephaniah.* Louisville: Westminster, 1991. Concise scholarly commentary.

HABAKKUK

[see pages 1293–1297 of the Old Testament]

The prophecy of Habakkuk is considerably more reflective than that of Nahum. He prophesied a few years later, when the Babylonian threat had become obvious. Habakkuk, however, not only reacts to the immediate danger but ponders the underlying problem. Why do the wicked circumvent the just? Why do the wicked devour those more righteous than themselves? Granted that the blame falls on humanity, why does God allow such a situation to prevail? The question, in short, is one of *theodicy,* or the justice of God and is more typical of wisdom literature than of prophecy. The classic treatment is found in the book of Job. The question of theodicy arises later in the apocalyptic literature especially in the great apocalypse of 2 Esdras, which is printed with the Apocrypha in Protestant editions of the Bible.

Habakkuk was concerned first of all with the injustice within Jewish society. It is illuminating to compare the "woes" in chapter 2 with Jeremiah's critique of King Jehoiakim (609–598 BC), which accuses the king of oppression and exploitation, especially in building a cedar palace by forced labor (Jer 22:13–19). Jehoiakim might well be accused of storing up what is not his (Hb 2:6) and of setting his nest on high (2:9), and even the violence done to Lebanon (2:17) may refer to his use of cedar. The critique, however, is couched in general terms and can apply to any wealthy and arrogant man.

Habakkuk's answer to the question of theodicy anticipates the kind of response that the apocalyptic writers would later offer. He does not provide an explanation but a promise that the situation will be rectified in time. At first the solution seems worse than the problem: God will raise up the Babylonians (1:6–11). Isaiah (chapter 10) had spoken of Assyria as the rod of the Lord's anger. Babylon apparently fills this role in Habakkuk, by bringing about the downfall of King Jehoiakim. In Isaiah the rod itself would eventually be broken. The eventual destruction of Babylon is implied in Habakkuk too. The prophet cannot have been unaware that Babylon was a prime example of the wicked who devours one more just than himself and whose throat was insatiable as death (2:5). Because of the similarity between the behavior of Babylon and that of the wicked in Judah, it is sometimes unclear to which Habakkuk is referring. The lesson, however, is clear. Even though justice is not apparent in the world, one should trust in the Lord and be patient.

Righteousness and Faith

The most famous utterance of Habakkuk is undoubtedly 2:4, "the just man, because of his faith, shall live," which acquired pivotal importance in the theology of Paul (Rom 1:17; Gal 3: 11). In its original context, "faith" does not have the pregnant sense that it has in Paul. It is simply the trust in God that enables one to wait for the future, closer perhaps to hope than to faith in the traditional Christian sense. The contrast here is between the rash man (the fool, in the terminology of Proverbs) and the one who is able to take a longer view. The person who judges only in light of the immediate present sees no justice in the world and may be tempted to conclude that there is no divine control. The righteous, or wise, person, in contrast, trusts that justice will prevail and is content to wait for it.

The faith of Habakkuk finds its most poetic expression in chapter 3. The description of the theophany, which has God come in triumph as a warrior, stands in a long tradition of such hymns (compare Dt 33; Jgs 5; Mi 1). The early hymns of this kind referred to God's past activity on behalf of Israel. Habakkuk expects such a manifestation in the future. It will be directed against "the people who attack us" (3:16), presumably the Babylonians, although Jewish oppressors may also be included. What the prophet envisages is a decisive intervention of God, to wipe out all wickedness and oppression. In this he is close to the kind of future hope that we find later in the apocalyptic literature, except that he does not envisage any judgment of the dead. It is not surprising then that Habakkuk was popular in apocalyptic circles. The Dead Sea Scrolls include a commentary (called a *pesher*) on Habakkuk, which interpreted the prophecy with reference to the history of the Qumran sect (taking the Chaldeans as the Romans). The notion that "the vision still has its time" (Hb 2:3) is echoed in Daniel 8:17, in a context where people were again asking "how long, O LORD?"

The faith of Habakkuk is a faith against appearances: "Though the fig tree blossom not nor fruit be on the vines . . . Yet will I rejoice in the LORD" (3:17f). It is based on the conviction that God is just, and so justice must ultimately prevail. The only question is "how long?" It is a question that has been repeated in every generation and has yet to receive a final answer. In the meantime, those who share the faith of Habakkuk find strength to go on. The value of such faith does not depend on the fulfillment of its expectations but on its power to transform the lives of the faithful.

FURTHER READING

Boadt, L. *Jeremiah 26–52; Habakkuk; Zephaniah; Nahum.* Old Testament Message 10. Wilmington, DE: Glazier, 1981.

Gowan, D. E. *The Triumph of Faith in Habakkuk.* Atlanta: John Knox, 1976.

Hiebert, T. *The Book of Habakkuk.* New Interpreter's Bible 7, 623–55. Nashville: Abingdon Press, 1996. Brief homiletical commentary.

Roberts, J. J. M. *Nahum, Habakkuk and Zephaniah.* Louisville: Westminster, 1991. Concise scholarly commentary.

ZEPHANIAH

[see pages 1297–1301 of the Old Testament]

Zephaniah prophesied a little earlier than Nahum and Habakkuk in the reign of Josiah, the king who instituted the Deuteronomic reform (2 Kgs 22–23). One of his themes concerns idolatry (1:4–6). He may have been active before the reform, but Josiah was not very successful in his attempt to stamp out foreign cults in any case. Indeed, the prophet inveighs against the king's sons for adopting foreign customs (1:8). Zephaniah was contemporary with the early career of Jeremiah. The surviving oracles are almost entirely taken up with the proclamation of the Day of the Lord.

A Day of Judgment for Judah

The first oracle on the Day of the Lord is directed against Judah. The main offenses, which he denounces, are idolatry and lack of faith in the Lord (1:12). In the context of Josiah's time, rejection of the Lord was rejection of the Deuteronomic law. The emphasis of Zephaniah is not on the sins of Judah but on the destructiveness of the Day of the Lord. It is portrayed in cosmic terms: God will make an end of all who live on earth. The day of judgment is seen as the vindication of the majesty of God against the unworthiness of the people. Compare the destructive effect of the holiness of God in Isaiah 6.

A Day of Judgment on the Nations

The wrath of the Lord is not only directed against Judah. Chapter 2 catalogues the surrounding peoples, most of whom have been guilty of offending Judah in some way. The list extends to Assyria, the most arrogant of all. The boast of Nineveh ("There is no other than I") is the same as that of Babylon in Isaiah 47:10. The most fundamental human sin is self-divinization. This was already the temptation of Adam and Eve, and it is a charge often made by the prophets (see, for example, Is 14 and Dn 4). Zephaniah's prophecies of the Day of the Lord dramatize the gulf between God and humanity and are basically a put-down of all human pride.

Reproach and Promise for Jerusalem

The final chapter does not use the catchword "Day of the Lord" but deals with related themes. The phrase "on that day" (3:11) refers to the Day of the Lord and is often used to introduce additions to the prophetic books in the postexilic period.

In the opening oracle of the chapter (3:1–8), Jerusalem is denounced as the tyrannical city that accepts no correction. The reference may be to the failure of the Deuteronomic reform or simply to the rejection of the prophet himself. The concluding oracle, however (3:11–20), prophesies restoration for Jerusalem, when God "will leave as a remnant in your midst a people humble and lowly." The motif of the remnant is familiar from the preaching of Isaiah, a century before Zephaniah, and there is no doubt that Isaiah had considerable influence on the later prophet. It is possible, then, that Zephaniah uttered this oracle, but it is more likely that here we have another example of an optimistic oracle added on to the end of a prophetic book by an editor.

While the concluding oracle may not have come from Zephaniah, it has its own validity. The judgments of the Assyrian and Babylonian eras were not God's last word to Israel. Even after the destructive Day of the Lord, hope was still possible.

FURTHER READING

Berlin, A. *Zephaniah.* Anchor Bible 25A. New York: Doubleday, 1994. Careful technical commentary.

Boadt, L. *Jeremiah 26–52; Habakkuk; Zephaniah; Nahum.* Old Testament Message 10. Wilmington, DE: Glazier, 1981. Helpful brief commentary.

Roberts, J. J. M. *Nahum, Habakkuk and Zephaniah.* Louisville: Westminster, 1991. Brief scholarly commentary.

HAGGAI

[see pages 1301–1304 of the Old Testament]

The activity of Haggai can be dated quite precisely to the year 520 BC, almost two decades after the return of the Jews from the Babylonian exile. During that time various problems had beset the returned exiles, and they had not succeeded in rebuilding the Temple. We know from Ezra 5, 1f that it was at the urging of Haggai and Zechariah that the task was finally brought to completion. The book of Haggai preserves both the words Haggai used to exhort the Jews to finish the building and his attempt to cope with their disappointment after it was finished.

The Exhortation to Rebuild

The first chapter of Haggai paints a vivid picture of the impoverished state of the Jewish community after the return. The difficulty of their situation was compounded by drought and crop failure. Haggai offered a daring interpretation of this situation: their difficulties were due to the fact that they had not rebuilt the Temple but had concentrated instead on rebuilding their own houses. We find here a classical case study in religious priorities. Socially minded critics tend to see Haggai as merely superstitious. The people needed the shelter of their own houses. God did not need a temple. This criticism is congenial to modern thought, but we also find it in antiquity. The anonymous prophet in Isaiah 66:1–2 asks: "The heavens are my throne, the earth is my footstool. What kind of house can you build for me?" That passage very probably comes from Haggai's time and suggests that there were other prophets who opposed the rebuilding. Yet there was social wisdom in Haggai's position. The morale of the community was at a low ebb. One way of raising that morale was to engage in a community project, which would encourage people to think of the good of the community as a whole rather than dwell on their own misfortune. This is not to suggest that Haggai thought consciously in such sociological terms but, in fact, by urging the people to think of God rather than of themselves he was directing their attention to the greater good of the community. A comparable situation occurred in the United States in the late nineteenth and early twentieth centuries. The immigrant communities from Europe were made up of poor working-class people. Nonetheless they took pride in erecting great churches and schools in cities like New York and Boston. These edifices were put up at no small sacrifice, but their value to the communities was enormous. While success was difficult for individuals, it was possible for communities that banded together. The buildings were simultaneously an offering to their God and an expression of their own self-worth.

The Reaction to the Finished Temple

We are told in the book of Ezra that when the foundation of the new Temple was laid, the old men who remembered Solomon's Temple cried out in sorrow, and their laments could not be distinguished from the shouts of joy. This was because the new Temple was puny in comparison with the old (Ezr 3:12f). Haggai 2:3 records this reaction. Besides, the completion of the Temple did not bring about the dramatic reversal of fortunes that Haggai had predicted. Haggai's reaction to this situation is typical of prophets through the ages whose predictions have not come to pass. First, he tells the people to wait "a little while." The prediction is not wrong, only the time is delayed. Second, he diagnoses a reason for the delay. The people are not observing purity laws and their offerings are unclean. He ends by reaffirming that God will shake the heavens and the earth when conditions are right.

It must be admitted that this reaction shows some embarrassment on the part of the prophet, which can only have increased with the passage of time when his predictions remained unfulfilled. The case of Haggai points out the Achilles heel of predictive prophecy. The hopes raised by the prophet were good for the morale of the community, but only for a time. When they were not fulfilled, they led to disillusionment. The same problem would beset the apocalyptic and messianic expectations of later generations, and eventually tend to discredit them.

The Lesson of Haggai

There are, then, two lessons to be learned from Haggai. One is that hope should not be focused on specific predictions. The faith of Habakkuk was secure because it was a faith in ultimate justice and did not depend on specific events coming to pass within a short space of time. Haggai's more specific prediction gives rise to problems. The other is that he has a positive lesson to offer on the value of religious symbols and ritual as a means of bringing the community together. It was largely through his efforts that the Temple was rebuilt. While the Temple may not have satisfied immediate expectations, its contribution to Jewish life over the next five hundred years was enormous, and would far outweigh the initial disappointment which many felt when it was completed.

FURTHER READING

Hanson, P. D. *The Dawn of Apocalyptic*, 240–62. Philadelphia: Fortress, 1975. Groundbreaking study of postexilic Judah.

March, W. E. *The Book of Haggai*. New Interpreter's Bible 7, 707–32. Nashville: Abingdon Press, 1996. Brief homiletical commentary.

Meyers, C. L., and E. M. Meyers. *Haggai, Zechariah 1–8*. Anchor Bible 25B. Garden City, NY: Doubleday, 1987. Thorough scholarly commentary.

Petersen, D. L. *Haggai and Zechariah 1–8*, 17–106. Philadelphia: Westminster, 1984. Concise but excellent scholarly commentary.

Wolff, H. W. *Haggai*. Minneapolis: Augsburg, 1988. Classic scholarly commentary.

ZECHARIAH

[see pages 1304–1317 of the Old Testament]

The book of Zechariah contains the work of more than one prophet. It takes its name from the contemporary of Haggai who was also instrumental in the completion of the Temple. "Deutero-Zechariah" (Zec 9–14) comes from a much later time. Some scholars even distinguish a "Trito-Zechariah" in chapters 12 through 14.

The Original Zechariah

The original oracles of Zechariah are characterized by a series of visions that are explained to the prophet by an angel. The interpreting angel appears here for the first time in biblical literature. It becomes a standard feature of apocalyptic literature, beginning with Daniel 7–12. These symbolic visions disclose the prophet's view of what is really going on in the postexilic period by revealing a dimension of these events, which is hidden from the ordinary observer. So the first vision shows four (presumably angelic) horsemen whom the Lord had sent to patrol the earth. The implication is that God is indeed in control, although the divine activity may not be obvious. The visions in chapter 2 show four heavenly blacksmiths coming to beat down the horns of the nations and an angelic "man" making preparations for the restoration of Jerusalem. In all of these visions the hidden, heavenly activity is reassuring and a source of confidence for the fledgling Jewish community.

High Priest and King

Down to the time of the Babylonian exile, the prophets had been sharply critical of the monarchy and usually also of the priesthood. When Zechariah prophesied, the monarchy was no more, but Zerubbabel, a descendant of the Davidic line, held the position of governor under the rule of the Persians. In the absence of a king, the high priest enjoyed new power and authority. Both Zerubbabel and the high priest of the day, Joshua, had their critics. Zechariah, in sharp contrast to earlier prophets, came to the defense of the community's leaders. The vision in chapter 3 is a remarkable defense of Joshua. In the vision, Joshua stands before the angel of the Lord and is accused by Satan. This is one of the earliest appearances of Satan in the Old Testament. (He also appears in Job 1–2 and 1 Chr 21:1.) He has not yet taken on the character of the Devil of later mythology. Rather he is an angel in the service of God, whose mission is to detect and prosecute wrongdoers in the manner of a federal attorney. The fact that Satan is said to bring accusations against Joshua is the prophet's way of dramatizing the opposition to the high priest in the Jewish community. Satan symbolizes Joshua's critics. He receives a stinging rebuke from the angel of the Lord. The point is not that Joshua is faultless, but that criticism is not appropriate when the community is struggling. Joshua is "a brand snatched from the fire" (Zec 3:2)—that is, most of the leadership and institutions of Judaism had been destroyed, and what was left should be supported not criticized. So Joshua's faults are cast aside like dirty clothes, and he is affirmed in the sight of the Lord. Zechariah does not give Joshua a blank check. He is charged to walk in the ways of the Lord (3:7). Nonetheless, the contrast with earlier prophetic attitudes to the priesthood is striking. In earlier times, religious institutions were often problematic insofar as they bred complacency in the people, and so a prophet like Amos spoke as if the sacrificial cult could be abolished. After the experience of the exile, however, Zechariah recognized the importance of institutions. While they are not an end in themselves, no society can live without them.

The prophet is equally positive about Zerubbabel, who is extolled for laying the foundation of the Temple. The two leaders are pictured as olive trees in chapter 4, because both priest and king were anointed with oil—hence the title "messiah" or "anointed one." The people of the Dead Sea Scrolls followed the lead of Zechariah and expected two messiahs, a priestly messiah of Aaron and a royal messiah of Israel. In chapter 6, the prophet is told to make a crown and to put it on the head of the high priest Joshua. Most scholars have recognized that the text has been altered here. (See the note on p. 1309, OT.) Originally, it would have provided crowns for *both* Joshua and Zerubbabel. The coronation of a Davidic prince would have been a highly dangerous undertaking, because the Persian overlords would surely have taken it as a gesture of rebellion. We do not know whether Zechariah ever carried it out. At some point the text was changed to eliminate the crown for Zerubbabel and thus avoid the suggestion of rebellion.

The understanding of the monarchy became increasingly idealized in the period after the exile, when the shortcomings of the actual kings were forgotten. The future king would be the messiah, the anointed one who would make Jerusalem again a holy city (8:3). Zerubbabel could hardly have lived up to those expectations if he had been crowned, but his career, and that of Zechariah, helped keep alive the dream of independence for Judah.

The Appreciation of Ritual

Just as Zechariah shows a renewed appreciation for the institutions of priesthood and monarchy, he also has a more positive view of ritual than some earlier prophets. In 5:5–11 he sees wickedness in the form of a woman, who is put in a bushel container and carried off to Babylon. The vision suggests that wickedness can be gotten rid of by a symbolic physical action. This idea is very similar to the scapegoat ritual in Leviticus 16 and shows that the prophet appreciated the power of ritual. While wickedness cannot be put in a container and disposed of, the ritual action expresses the human desire—and strengthens the resolve—to rid the society of evil. It has its effect on the emotions and motivations of the people who perform it.

Zechariah also appreciated the limits of ritual. In chapter 7 he is asked about the proper number of fast days. He answers that motivation is more important than keeping the exact number. What is most important is to "render true judgment, and show kindness and compassion toward each other" (7:9). Here Zechariah echoes the sentiment of Hosea 6:6: "it is love that I desire, not sacrifice." After the experience of the exile and the destruction of the Temple, Zechariah knew that sacrifice was important too, but his priorities are still the same as those of Hosea.

Zechariah 9–11

Two passages in chapters 9 through 11 merit special attention: the messianic oracle in chapter 9, and the allegory of the shepherds in chapter 11.

The Messianic Oracle

The messianic oracle in 9:9f is famous because of its association with Palm Sunday in Matthew 21:5 and John 12:15. The ass was not as humble an animal in the ancient world as in modern times and was the vehicle of nobility in Genesis and Judges, but in the postexilic context it was a throwback to an earlier, simpler time. The hope is for a ruler who will restore Solomon's empire ("from the river to the ends of the earth") but will avoid the arrogance of the monarchy (symbolized by horses and chariots) and will be closer in style to the Judges.

As in Micah 4 and Isaiah 2, the messianic age will be a time of universal disarmament. One could scarcely describe Zechariah 9 as pacifistic, however. The logic of the passage is that the Lord will fight for Judah so that "they shall drink blood like wine" (9:15). The mentality of this passage is close to what we find later in the apocalyptic books. In Daniel, it is Michael the archangel who fights the battles of Israel. The human role is to maintain purity and be obedient to the law. For Deutero-Zechariah, the Lord assumes the role of warrior directly, in accordance with much of Israelite tradition (for example, Ex 15:3). The Jewish people will not need the warrior's bow because God will kill their enemies for them.

This oracle could have been written at almost any time in the postexilic period when the monarchy was no more, and the Jewish people, in any case, were not equipped with horses and chariots. If the reference to Yavan (Greece) in verse 13 is original, the setting may be about the time of Alexander's conquests. The modest messiah, riding on an ass, provides an attractive contrast to the mighty Macedonian conqueror.

The Allegory of the Shepherds

The allegory of sheep and shepherds is very widespread in the ancient Near East, with the shepherds representing kings and rulers. The allegory of Zechariah 11 must be understood against the background of two passages in Ezekiel. Ezekiel 34 has an extended prophecy against the shepherds of Israel who exploited their flock. The movement of the prophecy, however, is from judgment to salvation, as the Lord takes over the job of shepherd. In Ezekiel 37:15–22, the prophet takes two sticks, representing Israel and Judah, and joins them together, signifying that they would henceforth be one nation under David their king. In Zechariah 11 we also find exploitative shepherds (compare Zec 10:2f), but there is no movement to salvation. The flock is designated for slaughter from the outset. The prophet is assigned to shepherd it for a while, but even he gives up on it and in the end they are given over to a foolish shepherd who takes no care of them. The wage of the prophet is the price of a slave, which is the value that the sheep merchants (foreign powers) attach to the God of Israel. It is also the wage of Judas in Matthew 26:15. The two staffs of Zechariah 11 symbolize two covenants, one with the nations, and the other between Judah and Israel. Both are broken in the course of the prophecy. In all, then, Deutero-Zechariah reverses Ezekiel's predictions of salvation.

There is no agreement among scholars as to just when this prophecy was written or what context it addressed. All we can say is that it is an expression of extreme dissatisfaction and disillusionment from the postexilic period. The author of this passage is very far from the trust in the institutional leaders that characterized the original Zechariah in chapters 1 through 8. There is no confidence here either in the Jewish leaders or in their foreign masters. All the prophet can do is protest, in the traditional language of prophecy: "woe to my foolish shepherd . . ." Like every great prophet from the time of Elijah, the anonymous speaker of these lines uses the power of the word to proclaim judgment and even to curse. Even if there is little hope of changing the situation, it is the duty of the prophet to testify and to ensure that people see reality for what it is.

Zechariah 12–14

The last three chapters of Zechariah are even more confusing than the previous three. There is persistent criticism of the rulers. Chapter 13 includes a "song of the sword" (compare Ez 21) against the "shepherd" and predicts that only one-third of the people will be spared. More surprising than this is the prediction of the end of prophecy (13:1–6).

The Decline of Prophecy

Prophecy had been discredited for various reasons. One was the failure of predictions, especially the prophecies of glorious restoration after the exile. Another was the conflict between prophets themselves and the willingness of some to mislead the people for their personal gain. This had been a problem already in the time of Micaiah, son of Imlah (1 Kgs 22) and was severe in the time of Jeremiah. It was only natural then that prophets would come to be viewed with suspicion. In Zechariah 13:3 even a prophet's parents assume that an oracle spoken in the name of the Lord is a lie.

After Haggai and Zechariah, prophets seem to have lost status. We do not even know the real names of the prophets whom we call Third Isaiah, Deutero-Zechariah, and Malachi. The visionaries of the Maccabean period attributed their visions to ancient heroes such as Daniel and Enoch. Undoubtedly there were prophets in Judaism in the Hellenistic period (John the Baptist is a late example), but they did not command the same respect as those of the Assyrian and Babylonian eras.

The Final Battle

The motif that runs through these chapters is that of a final battle in Jerusalem. The traditional motif was that in the last days all the nations would assemble to fight against Mount Zion (for example Ps 2; Ez 38–39). This motif is elaborated here in chapters 12 and 14. Chapter 12 suggests that there has been some tension between Judah and Jerusalem. Judah must be saved first so that Jerusalem will not gloat over it. Rivalry between city and countryside is natural enough and does not help us identify the situation in which the oracle was composed. In Zechariah 12 the emphasis falls on reconciliation. Jerusalem and the Davidic house will be compassionate and will "look on him whom they have thrust through" (12:10). This enigmatic allusion has given rise to endless speculation. Some scholars have thought that the reference was to King Josiah, who was killed in battle at Megiddo in 609 BC, but this oracle is certainly from a much later time. Others have thought the figure is deliberately mysterious like the Suffering Servant in Isaiah. John 19:37 saw the fulfillment of this prophecy in the piercing of the side of Christ on the cross. We cannot now be sure whether the passage referred to a specific individual in its Jewish context. What is clear is that the prophet looked for a time when the leaders in Jerusalem would show compassion for the people they had oppressed and be reconciled with them.

The final oracle, in chapter 14, also envisages reconciliation between Judah and the nations, so that even the Egyptians will celebrate the Feast of Tabernacles. There is a threat of coercion, which betrays the prophet's awareness that such a conversion of the Gentiles was implausible. Nonetheless, the future hope of Zechariah 14 is remarkable for its broadminded universalism, insofar as it wants to include the Egyptians in the worship of the true God.

FURTHER READING

Hanson, P. D. *The Dawn of Apocalyptic,* 280–380. Philadelphia: Fortress, 1975.

Meyers, C. L., and E. M. Meyers. *Haggai; Zechariah 1—8.* Anchor Bible 25B. Garden City, NY: Doubleday, 1987.

——. *Zechariah 9—14.* Anchor Bible 25C. New York: Doubleday, 1993.

Ollenburger, B. C. *The Book of Zechariah.* New Interpreter's Bible 7, 735–840. Nashville: Abingdon Press, 1996. Useful commentary with homiletical reflections.

Petersen, D. L. *Haggai and Zechariah 1—8,* 109–320. Philadelphia: Westminster, 1984.

MALACHI

[see pages 1317–1322 of the Old Testament]

The three chapters that make up the last book of the prophetic corpus are, like Deutero-Zechariah, anonymous—we do not know who wrote them. Malachi is not a proper name but means "my messenger." The word is taken from 3:1 ("Lo, I am sending my messenger") to designate the one through whom this word of the Lord was given. The book is made up of 6 oracles: 1:2–5; 1:6–2, 9; 2:10–16; 2:17–3:5; 3:6–12; and 3:13–21. There are two short appendixes in 3:22–24.

The first oracle, 1:2–5, is a standard polemical oracle against Edom, Judah's neighbor and bitter enemy in the postexilic period. This oracle is rather atypical of Malachi, however, as the others are all critical of Judah itself. He is especially critical of the priesthood and of breaches of faith by the people.

The Priesthood (1:6–2:9)

Malachi stands in a long line of prophets, beginning with Amos, who were critical of the priesthood. In this case, the charge is that the priests have been offering cheap sacrifices, disposing of sick and lame animals instead of offering the best ones. The logic of Malachi's argument deserves notice. No one would offer a sick animal to the governor, yet the priests make such offerings to God. An offering has symbolic significance and reflects the attitude of the one who brings it. Malachi is not opposed to the priesthood as such. Far from it. He speaks of a covenant with Levi (2:4), which is never mentioned in the Pentateuch or historical books. (Levi is, however, set apart for a special role in Dt 10:8f and 33:9f.) He has the greatest respect for the ideal of the priesthood. Because so much is expected of the priests they are all the more guilty.

The most striking statement in this passage, however, is the declaration that "from the rising of the sun, even to its setting, my name is great among the nations" (1:11). The Gentile nations certainly did not worship the Lord explicitly, so it is not certain what the prophet had in mind. One theory holds that the reference is to the Jewish Diaspora, the scattering of Jewish exiles among the nations, but Jews were not supposed to offer sacrifices outside of Jerusalem, although they sometimes did. Two considerations may throw light on this problem. First, the Persian kings were generous in providing funds for the support of the Jewish Temple, and Malachi may have recognized this support as an offering to the Lord. Second, in the official correspondence in the books of Ezra and Nehemiah, the Lord is called the God of heaven (for example, Ezr 6: 10). The high god of the Persians, and other sovereign deities could also be acknowledged as "the God of Heaven," and so the Gentiles could be understood to worship the same God as the Jews. This view of pagan religion would be decidedly broad-minded and liberal.

Breaches of Faith

The most controversial passage in the book of Malachi is found in the third oracle, 2:10–16. The prophet begins with the rhetorical question: "Have we not all the one Father?" He goes on to denounce two breaches of faith. First, Judah "has married an idolatrous woman" (literally, "the daughter of a foreign god," 2:11). The second problem is the divorce of "the wife of your youth," (2:14).

It is reasonable to assume that the background of this oracle is related to the situation described in Ezra 9, where the leaders of the people inform Ezra that "neither the Israelite laymen nor the priests nor the Levites have kept themselves aloof from the peoples of the land . . . for they have taken some of their daughters as wives . . ." The usual explanation of the passage in Malachi is that Jewish men were divorcing the Jewish wives of their youth and marrying Gentile women, possibly for social reasons. Inevitably, they then became implicated in the cult of pagan deities. On this interpretation, the question, "have we not all one Father?" is addressed *only* to Jews and is not as universalistic as it initially seems.

This interpretation is certainly possible. There is no doubt that Malachi disapproved of mixed marriages. There is no other evidence, however, that Jews in the postexilic period divorced their Jewish wives. In fact, the only instance of divorce for which we have evidence is found in

Ezra 10, where the Jewish men who had taken foreign wives send them away at Ezra's command. Malachi's categorical statement, "for I hate divorce, says the LORD" (2:16), is hard to reconcile with Ezra's policy. It is possible, then, that Malachi is quite universalistic, despite his disapproval of mixed marriages. Once a marriage had been entered into, it was sacred. The Jewish men should have taken care that their offspring were "godly" (2:15) rather than try to undo the marriage. Conversion of the spouses, rather than divorce, was the solution. On this interpretation, the "one Father" is the creator of all, Jews and Gentiles. Ethnic distinctions do not matter if one is willing to recognize the one God. The "daughter of a foreign god" only becomes so by her choice of which God to worship. If this interpretation is correct, Malachi exhibits some of the spirit of Saint Paul in his openness to the Gentiles. He would have been in direct conflict with Ezra, had they been contemporaries. We know that there was some diversity of opinion in Judaism at this period. Ezekiel 44:7 insisted that no "foreigners, uncircumcised both in heart and flesh" be admitted to the Temple. In contrast, an oracle preserved in Isaiah 56 shows a very open attitude to "the foreigners who join themselves to the LORD," and assures them of a place on the holy mountain. Malachi may be seen as part of this "liberal" tradition, which welcomed foreigners if they were willing to convert to Judaism.

The Day of the Lord

The final chapter of the book is dominated by the expectation that God will come in judgment. The image of the refiner's fire is embedded in our memory by Handel's *Messiah*. The idea of a day of destructive judgment is, of course, an adaptation of the traditional Day of the Lord. The most distinctive aspect of Malachi's use of the theme is the motif of the messenger who prepares the way. In the final appendix, this messenger is identified as Elijah the prophet. Since Elijah had not died but was taken up alive to heaven (2 Kgs 2:11), there was speculation that he would return to complete his earthly course. In the New Testament, John the Baptist is cast in this role (Mt 11: 14; 17:12f). Elijah's task is to warn the people and give them a last chance at repentance. It is likely that the prophet we call Malachi saw himself as performing this task.

The final oracle of Malachi is also the conclusion of the prophetic corpus. The editors of the prophetic books specifically wanted the collection to reinforce the laws of the Pentateuch: "Remember the law of Moses. . ." (3:22). They also underlined the theme of the coming judgment, which runs throughout the collection. The purpose of the collected prophetic books is not only to remind us of the past but especially to motivate us in the present by making us look to the future.

FURTHER READING

Hill, A. D. *Malachi.* Anchor Bible 25D. New York: Doubleday, 1998. Thorough scholarly commentary.

Petersen, D. L. *Zechariah 9–14 and Malachi.* Louisville: Westminster John Knox, 1995. Concise but excellent commentary.

Schuller, E. M. *The Book of Malachi.* New Interpreter's Bible 7, 843–77. Nashville: Abingdon Press, 1996. Helpful commentary with homiletical reflections.

THE GOSPELS AND ACTS

DONALD SENIOR AND PHEME PERKINS

INTRODUCTION TO THE SYNOPTIC GOSPELS

The Similarities and Differences among the Synoptic Gospels

Because of their striking similarities, the three Gospels of Matthew, Mark, and Luke have traditionally been called *synoptic,* from the Greek meaning to "view together." The observer of these three Gospels would, in fact, notice many parallels among these stories of Jesus if they were laid side by side.

At the same time, the general structure and style of the Synoptic Gospels are distinctively different from John's Gospel. For example, in each of the Synoptic Gospels, Jesus begins his public ministry of teaching and healing in Galilee, travels with his disciples on a single purposeful journey to Jerusalem, and there experiences final rejection, death and, ultimately, resurrection. Jesus' sayings in these Gospels are generally either succinct and pointed or in the story form of the parable; his actions are characterized by marvelous healings and exorcisms; a major theme of his preaching is the advent of the "Rule of God." In John, on the other hand, Jesus moves back and forth between Galilee and Judea, and his teaching is often expressed in long, meditative discourses. There are no parables in John, no exorcisms, and fewer healing stories; the Rule of God motif plays a very minor role.

But it would be a mistake to consider Matthew, Mark, and Luke as carbon copies of each other. As the Reading Guides and *New American Bible* introductions make clear, modern biblical scholarship has emphasized the unique style and theological perspective of each of the Gospels. While obviously related to each other in form and content, the three Synoptic Gospels develop their own distinct view of Jesus and his mission. Mark, for instance, begins his story of Jesus with his baptism at the Jordan, whereas Matthew, by means of the infancy narrative at the beginning of the Gospel, traces Jesus' origin back into the history of Israel. Luke, too, begins with an infancy narrative but gives much more positive emphasis to Jerusalem than either Mark or Matthew. In Luke's Gospel the young Jesus goes to Jerusalem to listen to the teachers in the Temple courtyard, and the disciples of Jesus will gather to pray in the Jerusalem Temple after his resurrection. Luke also adds a second volume to his Gospel; the Acts of the Apostles picks up the story of Jesus and his apostles where the Gospel left off, and shows its continuing force as the community of the Risen Christ moves out into the world.

The "Synoptic Problem"

Both the similarities and the distinctive differences among the Synoptic Gospels have led to ongoing debate about their interrelationship, or the "synoptic problem" as it is called. The canonical order of the Gospels—Matthew, Mark, Luke—influenced scholars in the early church, such as Augustine, to assume that Matthew was the first Gospel written, with Mark and Luke dependent on it.

In the late nineteenth and early twentieth centuries, however, this general consensus was challenged. Analyses of the style and content of Mark led scholars to conclude that Mark was the first Gospel written, with Matthew and Luke directly dependent on Mark. The presence of other material in Matthew and Luke that was not found in Mark, such as the sayings of Jesus in the Sermon on the Mount, led to the hypothesis of an additional source for Matthew and Luke. This hypothetical source of material—which scholars call "Q" (from the German word *Quelle* or "source")—was probably a collection of sayings and parables of Jesus that circulated in the earliest Christian community. Independently of each other, if this hypothesis is correct, Matthew and Luke blended this source with their new renditions of Mark and perhaps with some other materials or traditions specific to their own communities.

This hypothesis about the interrelationship of the Synoptic Gospels is called the "two-source hypothesis" because it postulates two literary sources for the Gospels of Matthew and Luke, namely the Gospel of Mark and Q. It presumes that Mark was the first Gospel to be written and that Mark, in fact, set the basic format for the story of Jesus, a format that both Matthew and Luke used as the starting point for their own narratives. This relationship would account for the similarities among the Gospels. Each Gospel writer's particular interpretation of Mark, the use of other sources, and the unique pastoral and theological perspectives of the writers and their local churches, would lead to the distinctiveness of each of the Synoptics.

Most New Testament scholars today, including Roman Catholics, accept the two-source hypothesis as the most plausible explanation of the interrelationship among the Synoptics. But even though a majority of scholars accept it, it is still a theory and therefore vigorous debate continues about other solutions to the synoptic problem. There are those who are convinced that Matthew or even Luke should be considered the first Gospel to be written, or others who are not persuaded that there was any literary contact among the Synoptic Gospels, but rather that each developed independently from a common gospel tradition.

The issue of the relationship of John's Gospel to the Synoptics is even more problematic. Until the midpoint of this century, most modern biblical scholars assumed that John knew of the Synoptic Gospels and that his own Gospel was a very distinctive variation on the synoptic tradition. But more recently, a significant number of scholars speculate that John may represent an independent stream of tradition that had little, if any, contact with the Synoptic Gospels.

The Synoptic Gospels and Their Portrayal of Jesus

Whatever may be the ultimate solution to the synoptic problem, it is clear that the Gospels of Matthew, Mark, and Luke have made an essential contribution to our understanding of Jesus and his ministry. The strongly transcendent Jesus of John's Gospel, with its emphasis on the preexistent Word and the incarnation of that Word in human flesh, has had a profound influence on Catholic Christology. But in the twenty-first century, Catholic theology has turned with renewed energy to the portrayals of Jesus in the Synoptic Gospels. The overarching symbol of the Rule of God proclaimed by Jesus in the Synoptics has provided an important framework for understanding the social and liberating implications of Jesus' message. Modern Christology's deep interest in the humanity of Jesus also turns to the portrayals found in Mark, Matthew, and Luke. The trauma of the Holocaust and the Christian-Jewish dialogue have led to a new appreciation of the Jewishness of Jesus, and here, too, the Synoptics' portrayal of Jesus and his milieu has provided an important backdrop. Interest in the literary quality of the Gospels has also focused attention on the Synoptic Gospels with their rich variety of sayings, parables, healing stories, conflicts, and other types of literary forms.

In short, the Synoptic Gospels are a major and essential source for a genuine understanding of Jesus and his message. That richness is described in detail in the Reading Guides that follow.

D.S.

MATTHEW

[see pages 1332–1399 of the New Testament]

Before Beginning . . .

As pointed out in the introduction (NT pp. 1332–36), Matthew's Gospel has long held a special place in the life and teaching of the church. The special character of this Gospel alerts us to some things to keep in mind as we set out to study it more closely.

A Story

Like each of the Gospels, Matthew's work is a story or a narrative. It begins with the roots of Jesus' family tree, describes the circumstances of his birth, and then turns to the events of his ministry, culminating in his death, resurrection, and final appearances to his disciples.

Even though Matthew's way of telling a story is influenced by his time and culture, his narrative has many of the same characteristics as storytelling today. There is an unfolding plot that carries the story from the beginning of Jesus' life, with its mixture of success and opposition, through to the death and triumph of its conclusion. There are characters (Jesus, the disciples, the opponents, etc.): some of them are quite developed (for example, Jesus and Peter), some seem one-dimensional (for example, the Pharisee opponents), others have only minor roles (the mother of James and John). All of these elements play a part as one reads or studies the Gospel of Matthew.

In describing Matthew's Gospel as a story we are not implying that it has no historical basis. There is no doubt that Matthew uses materials rooted in history (most of which he draws from the Gospel of Mark, one of his principal sources). But the evangelist, or Gospel writer, casts these traditions about Jesus into the form of a running story. A story or narrative helps catch up the reader into the dynamism and feeling of the events being recounted. This feature of the Gospel can engage us when we come to study or read it in more depth.

A Fund of Teaching

While Matthew's Gospel remains a dynamic story, it is also enriched—more than any of the other Gospels—with the sayings of Jesus. This feature has led commentators over the centuries to consider Matthew a kind of "catechism" or teacher's manual. In addition to the basic story of Jesus' life and ministry, which Matthew drew mainly from the Gospel of Mark, he also had a fund of the important sayings of Jesus (many of which he shares in common with the Gospel of Luke). The evangelist has organized many of these sayings into discourses or speeches of Jesus (see introduction pp. 1333–35). These are not transcripts of actual talks given by Jesus because there is little logical progression found in the discourses as a whole. Rather, the evangelist has clustered the sayings of Jesus around basic motifs. Explanations of many of the sayings are found in the notes to the biblical text; later in the study guide we will discuss some of the major themes of the discourses. These discourses bring the reader of Matthew's Gospel into vital contact with the power of Jesus' teaching.

The Jewish Heritage of Jesus and the Early Church

While all of the New Testament writings illustrate the essential dependence of Jesus and the early church on Judaism, none does it more forcefully than Matthew's Gospel. In fact, one of the primary purposes of this Gospel may have been the attempt to link the story of Jesus with the history of Israel. Any reader of Matthew who wants to go deeply into this Gospel must be alert to its Jewish background.

This feature of Matthew springs to our attention from the opening lines of the Gospel, which begin with a genealogy or family tree, tying Jesus into the history of Israel. The frequent use of Old Testament quotations, the concern with the Jewish law and customs of purity and prayer, the sharp critique of the Jewish leaders for their rejection of Jesus and for their failure to lead a life of holiness—all of these show that Matthew was absorbed with Jesus' Jewish heritage.

But it is also apparent that Matthew is concerned with how this Jewish Jesus is Messiah for the whole world. As we will indicate below, the universal mission of the church is also a prime motif of this Gospel. In fact, Matthew seems to be telling the story of Jesus so that it can help both the Jewish Christians and the Gentile converts of his community. After reading the Gospel they would be able to understand that Jesus fulfills the hopes and dreams God planted in the people of Israel, and now extends the offer of God's salvation to all the world.

Strange as it may seem, Matthew's Jewish roots may also explain another difficult feature of his Gospel: his strong critique of the Jewish leaders. The Jesus of Matthew's Gospel blisters his opponents for their hypocrisy and lack of faith. They are held up to the reader of the Gospel as negative examples of what an authentic disciple should avoid becoming. The sharp edge to Matthew's critique may stem from the tragic division and hostility that grew between Judaism and Jewish Christianity in the early decades of the church. For Matthew, the fact that most of Israel did not accept Jesus or the Gospel—while many Gentiles did accept it—was a baffling and unexpected turn in salvation history, and his telling of the story of Jesus reflects this. Unfortunately, Matthew's characterization of the Jewish leaders also provided an opportunity for later anti-Semitism to develop (itself a violation of the Gospel's teaching).

How to Proceed

Since Matthew's Gospel is a story, it would be best to begin at the beginning! Although one could approach the Gospel thematically, that is, taking a certain topic (for instance, discipleship) and tracking passages throughout the Gospel that relate to this theme or motif, the best method might be to let the story line of the Gospel be your guide. Begin where Matthew begins (chapter one, verse one) and let overarching ideas or themes emerge as the story of Jesus unfolds. This will be the method of the study guide: for each major section of the Gospel, we will discuss some key themes. You will find more detailed commentary on each section in the ample notes that accompany the Gospel text itself.

Working through Matthew's Gospel

The outline or major segments of Matthew's Gospel can be determined only by paying attention to the contours of his story. In harmony with the discussion found in the introduction (see NT, pp. 1332–36), we propose the following division:

- *The Origin of Jesus* (1:1–2:23). Here Matthew presents the events surrounding Jesus' birth and infancy.
- *Preparation for the Ministry of Jesus* (3:1–4:7). The test in the desert and the ministry of John the Baptist help prepare for the formal beginning of Jesus' mission.
- *The Galilean Ministry of Jesus* (4:7–16:12). This major section spans the ministry of Jesus from his entrance into Galilee until his announcement of the Passion and his intent to go to Jerusalem. It can be subdivided into other important segments:

1. The Sermon on the Mount (4:17–7:29)
2. Jesus the Healer (8:1–9:35)
3. The Mission Discourse (9:36–11:1)
4. Mounting Hostility to Jesus (11:2–12:50)
5. The Parable Discourse (13:1–53)
6. The Kingdom and the Disciples (13:54–16:12). This section includes the ongoing activity of Jesus and reactions to it, but with special emphasis on Jesus' relationship with Peter and the rest of the disciples.

- *The Way to Jerusalem* (16:13–20:34). Jesus' fateful journey to Jerusalem with his disciples dominates this section. Three times during this journey Jesus predicts his Passion and Resurrection (16:21; 17:22f; 20:17–19) and instructs his disciples on the cost of following him. There is also the important discourse on community life (18:1–35).
- *Final Teaching in Jerusalem* (21:1–25:46). This section of the Gospel takes place in Jerusalem. It concentrates on Jesus' final exchanges with his opponents (esp. 21:12–22:46), his condemnation of the scribes and Pharisees (23:1–39), and the long discourse on the final age and judgment (24:1–25:46).
- *Death and Resurrection* (26:1–28:20). The concluding segment of the narrative contains the Passion narrative and the account of Jesus' burial (26:1–27:66), the events surrounding the discovery of the empty tomb (28:1–15), and Jesus' final appearance to the eleven disciples on a Galilean mountaintop (28:16–20).

Reading through Matthew's Gospel

This section traces major themes and characteristics in each segment of Matthew's Gospel. It supplements the introduction and notes that accompany the Gospel text itself.

The Origin of Jesus (Mt 1:1–2:23)

The first two chapters of Matthew's Gospel are like a prologue to a great drama, sounding major themes that will be played out in the rest of the story. In this way the evangelist or Gospel writer alerts the reader to the particular tones he will give his portrayal of Jesus.

A Messiah Rooted in the Hopes of Israel

The Jewish heritage of Jesus is stressed in the very first lines of this Gospel. He is the "son of David, the son of Abraham" (1:1) and his messianic lineage is traced through Jewish history from Abraham to Joseph, the husband of Mary (1:2–18). Explicit quotations from the Old Testament (for example, 1:23; 2:6; 2:15; 2:18; 2:23) are augmented by numerous allusions to Old Testament figures and events (for instance, the hostility of Herod recalls the rage of Pharaoh against the Israelites; the reference to a star recalls the prophecy of Balaam about a future deliverer for Israel in Nm 24:17; Joseph, who is guided to protect the holy family through dreams and goes into Egypt, is reminiscent of another Joseph who was also a dreamer and one who rescued Israel in Egypt during a time of famine and distress). In all these ways Matthew proclaims something that echoes throughout the Gospel: Jesus is the promised *Messiah,* the one through whom God's longed-for salvation would be achieved. Thus continuity with the Old Testament is stressed (compare Mt 5:17).

A Messiah Close to His People

The experiences of Jesus and his family evoke another theme important to this Gospel, namely Jesus' identification with the "least." The Matthean Christmas story has a sober mood to it. Right from the beginning, Jesus and his family are threatened with death by a tyrant. Innocent people are killed because they are identified with Jesus. The holy family is forced into exile (just as Israel had been in its tortured history). Even when they return from Egypt (a new exodus?) they are unable to go home to Bethlehem but must become displaced persons, living in Nazareth (2:22f).

This identification with the great events of Israel's struggle to be free may help explain one of the names given Jesus in Matthew's story. He is to be called *Emmanuel,* that is, "God is with us" (1:23). As subsequent events of the Gospel will show, the Matthean Jesus has extraordinary compassion for the suffering (see, for example, the healings in chapters 8 and 9), explicitly identifies himself with the "least" (see Mt 25:31–46; 10:42), and promises to remain with his church as it continues its mission in the world (28:20; 18:20).

Jesus as Messiah of Israel and Savior of the World

While Matthew stresses the Jewish roots of Jesus and his messianic mission, he also signals the ultimate worldwide scope of that mission. As Herod and the leaders of Jerusalem plot to destroy Jesus, the magi, Gentile wise men, come seeking to pay homage to him (2:1–12). Even in the family tree of Jesus, Matthew may be hinting at the wider horizons of Jesus' mission. While most of the genealogy traces the male line of Jesus' ancestry, there are several women mentioned—Tamar, Rahab, Ruth, Bathsheba—all of whom were foreigners whose entry into Jewish history was under unusual, sometimes even scandalous, circumstances. Even Mary, the mother of Jesus, seems to be put in this category since her association with the royal Davidic line is not by natural means but only through the initiative of the Spirit—something that causes consternation to Joseph (1:18–19).

Thus from the beginning outsiders had been part of Jesus' history. This is a major theme of Matthew's Gospel. He will emphasize the rejection Jesus experiences from the Jewish leaders and at the same time provide scattered examples of Gentiles groping toward faith (for example, the centurion in 8:5–13; the Gadarene demoniacs in 8:28–34; the Canaanite woman in 15:21–28). Matthew carefully notes that Jesus' historical ministry focused on Israel (10:5) but with the new age of resurrection, that mission of salvation would now extend to all nations (28:19).

The infancy narrative also hints at the kind of salvation Jesus will bring. Of all the Gospels, Matthew alone stresses the significance of the name *Jesus.* The angel gives the divine instruction that the child is to be named Jesus "because he will save his people from their sins" (see the explanatory note at 1:21). Jesus is depicted as *savior* throughout the Gospel as he delivers people from their burdens of sickness, oppression, and sin. This is a Jesus who thirsts for justice or righteousness (3:15) and blesses those who, like the prophets before them, suffer in the pursuit of justice (5:10). Jesus exercises divine power in forgiving sins (see 9:1–8) and urges his disciples to reflect this same sense of reconciliation in dealing with each other (see especially 5:43–48; 18:21–35).

The overall mood of Matthew's Christmas story is quite different from that of Luke's. There are no triumphant angels, no picturesque gathering of shepherds, little focus on a tender vision of mother and child. Instead there are ominous plots against the child, outbreaks of violence, displacement, and exile. But throughout there is also the promise of God's abiding presence, bringing salvation in spite of sin and rejection. Perhaps we can think of Matthew's infancy Gospel as an "adult" Christmas story, one that has a special truth for the many people experiencing violence and persecution today. It tells a story that begins in the strength and beauty of a particular history and culture but will ultimately reach across boundaries to touch all peoples. In any case, these two chapters prepare us for the story that will follow, a story that will trace Jesus' mission of salvation through bitter rejection to ultimate triumph.

Preparation for the Ministry of Jesus (3:1–4:17)

This transition section brings the reader from the infancy narrative into the beginning of Jesus' ministry in Galilee. It opens with the preaching of John in the desert and closes with the first footstep of Jesus into Galilee, the northern region of Israel where he proclaims the advent of the Kingdom.

Two characteristic Matthean themes dominate this segment of Matthew's narrative.

The Dawn of a New Age

Throughout his Gospel, Matthew is conscious that the coming of Jesus was the decisive turning point in the history of salvation. In Jesus, God was offering the world salvation; the final age longed for by Israel was now beginning. This conviction is expressed through the figure of John the Baptist, whose appearance is reminiscent of Elijah, the great prophet expected to return at the end of the world (see note to 3:4) and whose message heralds the imminent approach of God's Kingdom (3:2). That message will be driven home by Jesus himself. He, too, preaches the nearness of the Kingdom (4:17). Whereas John is clearly a prophet preparing the way, Jesus is the one who brings the Kingdom to reality. Jesus is clearly superior to John: the Spirit of God descends on Jesus (3:16) and a "voice from heaven" (a Jewish way of speaking obliquely about God) declares that Jesus "is my beloved Son" (3:17). Jesus' entry into the region of Galilee and the start of his mission there will be light and hope to people who languish in darkness and the fear of death, (see 4:13–16). Even at this early stage of his Gospel, the evangelist hints at the universal scope of Jesus' message (see note to 4:12–17).

Repentance and Good Deeds

Both John and Jesus call people to repentance. The reality of God's kingdom and the consciousness of living in a new and decisive age of salvation should move Israel to change its way of thinking and its way of acting. Throughout his Gospel, Matthew will insist that the touchstone of authentic repentance is good deeds. So here John the Baptist challenges the Jewish leaders: "Produce good fruit as evidence of your repentance" (3:8). It is not sufficient for them to claim to be children of Abraham (3:9); status within God's reign is not dependent on blood lines or rank but on one's response to God's love embodied in Jesus.

The testing of Jesus in the desert also illustrates this point (see notes to 4:1–11). As was the case in the infancy narrative, Jesus recapitulates the experience of Israel. In their wandering through the desert, Israel and its leaders had often failed God's covenant, but Jesus, faithful Jew and faithful Son of God, will not fail, despite the efforts of Satan to draw him away from his messianic mission. The Jesus of Matthew's Gospel shows a fierce and loving loyalty to God. As he tells John, he must "fulfill all righteousness" (3: 15). Jesus is not content merely to preach fidelity to God; he demonstrates it here in the mysterious realm of the desert test and in his commitment to his mission even to the point of death on the cross.

The Galilean Ministry of Jesus (4:17–16:12)

A major section of the Gospel begins with Jesus' entry into Galilee and the inauguration of his ministry of teaching and healing. We will consider the material in six segments, following the flow of Matthew's narrative.

The Sermon on the Mount (4:17–7:29)

The Sermon on the Mount, the first of Jesus' five great discourses in this Gospel, is perhaps the best-known passage of Matthew's Gospel.

The Sermon itself spans chapters 5 through 7, but preparation for this great discourse begins in chapter 4. After sounding the theme of the Kingdom of God (4:17), Jesus calls his first disciples to follow him and to share in his mission (4:18–22). Jesus is committed to teaching, proclaiming the Kingdom of God, and healing (4:23). That liberating mission draws a response from every point of the compass as throngs of broken and needy people surge toward Jesus and his message of God's mercy (4:24f). Jesus' teaching, Matthew implies, is not mere abstract truth. Jesus' words and his healing touch have the power to transform lives.

The Sermon on the Mount does not have a neat progressive structure; rather, sayings of Jesus are clustered around basic motifs. We will note some of them here:

A New Teaching for a New Age. Matthew's conviction that Jesus is the Messiah, and therefore the authoritative teacher of God's will, runs throughout the Sermon. With Jesus the final age of salvation dawns and, with it, new insight into God's will. Matthew's Jesus sees that will of God as being in continuity with the revelation that came through the Law of Moses in the Old Testament, but now bringing that law to its fullest and most compelling expression. In the opening verses of the Sermon Jesus states: "Do not think that I have come to abolish the law or the prophets. I have come not to abolish but to fulfill" (5:17; see the comments in the notes to this text).

The conviction that the end of the world will be a triumph of God's grace—a conviction based on belief in the life, death, and resurrection of Jesus—runs throughout the Sermon and gives it special force. The false values assumed by the world are crumbling. This is the message of the beatitudes (5:3–12): those who are "poor in spirit" or who "hunger and thirst for righteousness" or are "peacemakers" are blessed because God will vindicate their hopes. Similarly, because it is a new age with new possibilities, the old wisdom is no longer adequate. A series of six antitheses or contrast statements mark off the difference between former interpretation of the Jewish law and Jesus' own radical teaching (see 5:21–48).

The Supreme Law of Love Expressed in Committed Action. Matthew's emphasis on good deeds, cited above (see comments on Preparation for the Ministry of Jesus [3:1–4:17]), is clearly in evidence here. The words of Jesus at the conclusion of the Sermon are unequivocal: "Not everyone who says to me, 'Lord, Lord,' will enter the kingdom of heaven, but only the one who does the will of my Father in heaven" (7:21). But the Sermon demonstrates that Matthew's Jesus is not simply talking about frenetic action. The heart and soul of Jesus' teaching is the command to love. That comes to its fullest expression in the last of the contrast statements where Jesus tells his disciples they are to love even the enemy (5:44) because God's own love is lavish and indiscriminate, bathing both just and unjust in its light and refreshment (5:45). Matthew is consistent on this point throughout the Gospel (see 7:12; 22:34–40). Asking his disciples to strive for love of enemies—the most challenging demand that can be made on the human heart—expresses the ultimate spirit of all of Jesus' teaching on human relationships. For this reason, the disciple is to strive for complete honesty (5:33–37), avoid retaliation for injury (5:38–39), and is not to violate another through lust or manipulation (5:27–30).

Jesus' teaching roots all of this in God's relationship to us. The teaching on love of enemy and nonretaliation is, therefore, not a peripheral part of the Gospel nor is it an abstract ideal. This fundamental teaching of Jesus remains a challenge for Christians who wrestle with what this Gospel teaching demands of us who live in a violent world where the use of force is commonplace.

Revelation of a Close and Compassionate God. Jesus' teaching in this part of the Gospel also gives a profound insight into the Gospel's image of God. God's boundary-breaking love is not based on merit but reaches out even to the unjust and the "enemy" (5:45–48). God cares for us more than for birds of the air or the wild flowers, whose freedom and beauty are signs of God's provident love (6:25–32). Therefore, the disciple is to have complete trust in God and to pray with confidence and without pretense (7:7–11). Jesus' model prayer (6:9–15) catches up much of the spirit of the entire Sermon. There is a wonderful simplicity and honesty about the instructions on piety in the Sermon (6:1–18); God's relationship to us is direct and close. There is no place for posturing before such a loving God.

The Authority of the Sermon. How to live with the Sermon on the Mount has been a constant point of discussion in the church. Are these demanding words to be taken as impossible ideals, meant only for a perfect world or for perfect people? Or do they make sense only in the setting of Jesus' own times, when people thought the end of the world was near and so might be capable of responding heroically in such an emergency situation?

None of these solutions are adequate. The instructions of Jesus are not a system of clear-cut laws spelling out exactly how we are to act in every circumstance, nor are they abstract or impossible ideals. These teachings give us practical guidance as we seek to live a life faithful to the Gospel. They illustrate the core spirit of Jesus' teaching, a spirit we must embody in our own circumstances. The possibility of living in accord with the teaching of Jesus is based on God's grace; the Sermon illustrates the difference grace can make in a person's life and relationships. Within the array of moral choices that confront us, the examples Jesus gives in the Sermon such as the call for integrity in our relationships, for nonretaliation, and for a commitment to reconciliation help direct us in the right way.

Jesus the Healer (8:1–9:34)

Introduction: This is a powerful section of the Gospel in which Matthew displays another dimension of Jesus: he teaches, he also heals. As the notes to the text state (see comments under 8:1), Matthew draws most of these stories from his source, Mark's Gospel, but the evangelist significantly reedits this material. He abbreviates many of Mark's stories, omitting some of the colorful details in order to concentrate on Jesus' essential actions and accompanying words. Matthew also clusters the nine major stories of these chapters into three segments (a tenth miracle is reported but barely narrated in 9:32; it serves to contrast the reactions of the Pharisees with that of the crowds): 8:1–17; 8:18–9:17; 9:18–34.

Each of these clusters of stories seems to have a dominant motif. In 8:1–17 the emphasis falls on Jesus' power to heal. The second section, 8:18–9:17, concentrates on the demands of discipleship. And the final section, 9:18–34, illustrates the essential role of faith in the healing narratives. These motifs are by no means exclusive, however; the richness of the healing stories allows the Gospel to proclaim many levels of meaning at the same time. We will examine more closely each of these dominant themes.

Christology. By narrowing the spotlight on Jesus in the first three stories, Matthew emphasizes the divine power that works through the Messiah. Jesus cleanses the leper, heals the servant of a Gentile soldier, and dispels the fever of Simon's mother-in-law. Except in the case of the centurion, there is little attention to the plight or disposition of the sick person in these stories. The concluding verse of the section (8:17) makes Matthew's intended point; by his healing touch Jesus fulfills the prophetic promise of Isaiah 53:4: "He took away our infirmities and bore our diseases."

By their very nature the healing stories serve Matthew's purpose. All of us experience sickness or disability at one time or another in our life. We all experience our limitations and realize too well that death looms before us. Jesus is moved with compassion (9:3, 36) and does not hesitate to stand in solidarity with those whose condition makes them "outsiders" (see his association with the leper, the Gentile, the tax collectors).

The Conditions of Discipleship. In the second set of stories Matthew illustrates some of the demands of discipleship. Only those fully committed to proclaiming the Kingdom of God and following Jesus are able to go with him across the sea (see 8:8–23). But even for those who remain, following Jesus can mean the threatening experience of the storm at sea (8:24–27) and strange encounters with the power of evil (8:28–34). The true disciple is one who learns that mercy and compassion drive Jesus, a lesson the

Pharisees (whom Matthew consistently portrays in negative tones) seem unable to grasp (9:9–13).

Faith. The healing stories often serve to illustrate the meaning of faith. Faith is, first of all, trust in Jesus' power to heal and transform us. That faith is evident in the leper who approaches Jesus (even though the law forbade him to do so), in the centurion who pleads on behalf of his servant (see 8:10), in the friends who bring the paralytic to Jesus (9:2), in the woman with the hemorrhage who touches the tassel of his cloak (9:22), and in the two blind men who trust that Jesus can do what no one else can (9:28f).

Note, too, the faith illustrated in these stories often takes a very active form. The leper boldly comes up to Jesus; the woman dares to touch him; the Gentile swallows his pride and pleads with a Jewish healer; the friends of the paralytic gain him access to Jesus. The sick and disabled can teach us this lesson: trusting in God does not mean mere passivity, waiting for a bolt from heaven. Transformation comes when we exercise our trust in God, and commit our own resources to seeking a new life.

The Mission Discourse (9:35–11:1)

Now that Matthew has completed his portrait of Jesus as teacher and healer, he moves to a new segment of the Gospel. Using his own mission as a model, Jesus gathers his twelve apostles and commissions them to proclaim the Kingdom of God, and to heal. The motivation for their mission is the same that animated Jesus' own energetic healing in the previous two chapters: the crowds are "troubled and abandoned, like sheep without a shepherd" (see Mt 9:36–38).

This forms the second of the five great discourses of Matthew's Gospel. The evangelist draws some of the material in this discourse from chapter 13 of Mark's Gospel (see especially the material in Mt 10:16–23); the rest comes from Q, the sayings source he holds in common with Luke (see introduction), or from Matthew's own sources.

Note that the discourse can be read from two different perspectives: (1) as part of the unfolding story of Jesus' ministry and his relationship with his disciples; (2) and an instruction for the post-Easter church. In the former time frame, Jesus tells his apostles to restrict their mission to Israel, the chosen people of God (10:5f); but in the new age, when the gospel must be proclaimed to all the world (see 28:16–20), Jesus' words apply to the universal mission of the church.

Typical Matthean themes run through the discourse. The Twelve (including Matthew the tax collector, 10:3) share in Jesus' own mission of proclaiming the Kingdom and healing those in need (10:7f). Note that the apostles are not yet commissioned to "teach"—that comes only after the Resurrection (see 28:20) when they have a deeper grasp of Jesus' mission. Any disciple who follows Jesus can expect to meet indifference, hostility, or rejection (see, for example, 10:16–25,34–39). The discourse is not naive but clearly warns the apostles about the cost of proclaiming the gospel in an authentic way.

But there is also strong affirmation of the power of the gospel and of the sense of confidence that should go with those on mission. They are not to be afraid of those who threaten their lives (10:26–28) or flinch before the divisions that may come. The loving God who has an eye for the sparrows and counts the hairs on our heads will not abandon those who follow the way of Jesus. Christians who live in circumstances of persecution and violence understand well these words of Jesus. Those who live in more comfortable circumstances need to ask themselves if the gospel values they reverence are not sometimes co-opted by the seductions of the dominant culture.

Matthew's concern with the mission of the church will reemerge in the final scene of the Gospel when the mission of Jesus, confined to Israel during his lifetime, bursts out into the world through the mission of the church (28:16–20).

Mounting Hostility to Jesus and His Mission (11:2–12:50)

In the mission discourse Jesus warned his disciples to expect opposition when they preached the gospel. Now Jesus himself becomes embroiled in conflict because of his mission. For the next two chapters Matthew traces the opposition that swirls around John the Baptist and Jesus.

The motif of conflict is apparent from the first words of chapter 11—John the Baptist is in prison and soon to die. He sends his disciples to Jesus with the key question: "Are you the one who is to come, or should we look for another?" (11:3). That question leads to a summary of Jesus' great deeds, and to Jesus' reflection on John's ministry and his own.

The opposition to Jesus is crystallized in "this generation" (11:16), which understood neither the ascetical John nor the gentle and compassionate Jesus (11:18f). "Wisdom," that is, God's message to Israel embodied in Jesus himself, will be proven present in the liberating works that Jesus performs in his ministry (11:19).

Matthew weaves together in this section profound insight into the bond between Jesus and his Father (11:25–27)—one of the most beautiful passages of the Gospel—with tumultuous scenes of conflict, as the enemies of Jesus fail to perceive that he is the Messiah and attack him for healing on the Sabbath (see the series of stories in chapter 12). Judgment, another typical Matthean motif emerges from all this. The Jewish towns that refuse to transform their lives in the light of the gospel bear the responsibility for their failure. Matthew's emphasis on judgment goes hand in hand with his emphasis on the necessity of good deeds. Living out the gospel should not be confused with mere noble aspirations and religious rhetoric. A tree is known by the fruit it produces (12:33).

The section closes with this insistence: the true family of Jesus are not those who merely claim kinship with him but those who do the will of God (12:50).

The Parable Discourse (13:1–50)

Parables were the trademarks of Jesus' teaching style. As the notes to the text explain (see 13:11), these pointed stories both reveal and veil the mystery of the Kingdom. Unless the listeners are willing to probe beneath the surface of the parables, the true meaning of Jesus' words will escape them (13:14f).

Typical themes of Matthew's Gospel emerge again in this discourse. The certain triumph of the Kingdom, which was a strong theme of the Sermon on the Mount, dominates the parable of the sower (13:1–9) as well as the parables of the mustard seed (13:31f) and the yeast (13:33f). Discipleship motifs stand out in the parables of the treasure and the pearl (13:44–46): true followers of Jesus are to put aside everything and be fully committed to the compelling beauty of God's reign.

Many of the parables in Matthew's Gospel have obvious moral messages (see also the stories in chapters 24 and 25). The parable of the weeds sown among wheat (13:24–30; explanation, 13:36–43) makes the point that the church, like the world itself, is a mix of good and evil. The disciples should not be discouraged by this but be confident that God's grace will triumph at the end of time, and evil will be punished. The theme of judgment present in the previous section of the Gospel reemerges here.

The conclusion of the parable discourse seems almost to be a signature of the Gospel writer (13: 52). The scribe who is instructed (literally: "discipled") in the kingdom of heaven is like the householder who can bring from the storehouse "both the new and the old." Preserving the best of the past and yet making it come alive for a new generation seems to be one of the main purposes of Matthew's Gospel (see introduction p. 1249). Matthew was convinced that Jesus did not destroy the beautiful traditions of Judaism but gave them new meaning. Bridging past and present in an open and respectful manner is one of the greatest challenges of religious leadership in any age.

The Kingdom and the Disciples (13:51–16:12)

It is difficult to characterize this long section of Matthew's story under any single heading. Jesus' ministry of teaching and healing continues but now begins to burst beyond the confines of Galilee into Gentile territory. Clashes with his opponents, mainly the Pharisees, also continue to erupt. But the haunting story of Jesus' walking on the water and Peter's awkward attempts to trust his master (14:22–33) may give us a clue to the special character of this section. With new intensity Jesus begins to instruct his disciples on the mystery of the Kingdom, and they begin to realize the awesome identity of the Messiah. Several motifs run through these chapters:

The Inclusive Mission of Jesus. Following the lead of Mark's Gospel, Matthew begins to trace the boundary-breaking nature of Jesus' ministry (see Reading Guide to Mark's Gospel, RG 391–92). After another conflict with the Pharisees (15:1–20), Jesus ventures near the Gentile region of Tyre and Sidon and there encounters a “Canaanite” woman (15:21–28). This is one of the most intriguing stories in the Gospel. At first Jesus resists the woman’s entreaties on behalf of her daughter. The Matthean Jesus remains committed *only* to the people of Israel (see 10:5f). But the woman’s insistence, an expression of her active faith, breaks down Jesus’ resistance and seems to open the horizons of his own vision. Matthew uses this story to instruct his own church: they, too, may have had too narrow a concept of their mission, thinking that only Jews could become Christians. But the needs and genuine faith of the Gentiles showed the early church that God intended to extend the boundaries of the Kingdom to include all people.

The two stories of the miraculous feedings (14:13–21; 15:32–39) give a similar impression of expansiveness. Jesus will not let the vast crowds go hungry and uses the occasion to instruct his disciples. Another epic scene takes place on the mountaintop, a favorite place of revelation in Matthew’s Gospel (15:29–31). Similar to the vista at the beginning of the Sermon on the Mount (see 4:23–25), vast crowds of the sick and disabled surge toward Jesus and he cures them. Once again the disciples can observe the boundless compassion that drives Jesus.

Opposition and Rejection. Despite the mercy of Jesus, his opponents continue to resist and misunderstand his message. The parable discourse had warned that some would prefer not to “see” and not to “hear” what Jesus preached. That prediction comes true in Nazareth (13:54–58) where Jesus’ own people rebuff him and take offense at his “wisdom and mighty deeds.” The story of Herod and the death of John the Baptist (14:1–12) are early warning signs about Jesus’ own fate. His enemies were so immersed in their opposition that they would carry it to the point of trying to destroy Jesus.

In this conflict about the tradition of washing hands before eating (15:1–20), the Gospel offers one explanation of the intransigence of Jesus’ opponents. They have allowed their own traditions to “nullify the word of God” (15:6). In other words, they had lost a sense of priority, placing good but not essential values ahead of those that were most fundamental. Matthew continues to stress that Jesus was not opposed or indifferent to the Law, but he wanted to inject new life into its observance by insisting that the love command was the basis of all fidelity (see discussion at 5:17).

The Disciples. The story of Peter walking on the water contains material unique to Matthew’s Gospel and illustrates both the importance of Petrine traditions in this Gospel and the evangelist’s view of discipleship. Peter begins to sink in the waves because he “doubted” or “hesitated” and because he has “little faith” (14:31). The latter phrase is particularly characteristic of Matthew’s Gospel (see p. 1334). Matthew’s portrayal is sympathetic and realistic: the disciples believe but their faith is weak. Deeper trust in Jesus is needed.

At the same time, the disciples are quite different from the opponents of Jesus. While the opponents reject Jesus and align him with Satan (12:24), the disciples acclaim Jesus as “the Son of God” (14:33). The enemies of Jesus cannot understand his teaching, but the disciples, albeit hesitantly, do “understand” (16:12; see also 13:16, 51).

The Way to Jerusalem (16:13–20:34)

A dramatic shift in the setting of the Gospel story is about to take place. Jesus goes with his disciples to the northernmost reaches of Israel, Caesarea Philippi (16:13). There he will ask the fundamental question of the Gospel: “Who do you say that I am?” (16:15). Jesus’ question and Peter’s response represent a turning point in the narrative. “From that time” (16:21) Jesus will begin to speak openly about his approaching death, and the action of the Gospel will point toward Jerusalem and the events of the Passion and Resurrection.

The announcement of Jesus’ journey to Jerusalem (16:21) thus introduces the motif of a “journey,” a theme already present in Mark’s Gospel (see comments on Mark 8–10) and one greatly expanded in the Gospel of Luke (see comments on journey narrative in Luke RG 406–8). The threefold prediction of the Passion (in Matthew, see 16:21; 17:22f; 20:17–19) punctuates the journey and keeps the reader’s attention directed to Jerusalem and Jesus’ death and resurrection. That great climax to the Gospel, already alluded to as early as the infancy gospel (see comments in RG 375), dominates the entire narrative and gives urgency to Jesus' teaching. The transfiguration reflects this: immediately after Jesus predicts his death for the first time, the light of resurrection glory seems to emanate from his person in a mountaintop scene reminiscent of the revelation given to Moses on Sinai (see the notes to 17:1).

During the journey narrative, the spotlight seems to fall with new intensity on Jesus' relationship with his disciples. Although some conflicts with the Pharisees take place (see, for example, the dispute about divorce, 19:1–12), most of Jesus' words are directed to his disciples, revealing to them what it means to follow a Crucified Messiah. Special Petrine traditions are present in this section, too, including Peter's confession at Caesarea Philippi and Jesus' blessing upon him, his mediating role in paying the Temple tax on behalf of Jesus and himself (17: 24–27), and his lead question about forgiveness in the discourse on community life (18:21).

The Ministry of Leadership

Matthew gives special attention to Peter in his Gospel (see comments on 14:22–33).

Although the disciples had already confessed Jesus as "the Son of God" (14:33), Peter himself has an opportunity to confess his own belief that Jesus is "the Messiah, the Son of the Living God" (16:16). Thus the focus in the Caesarea Philippi scene is not on the disciples in general but on Peter and his faith in Jesus. Peter's firm belief in Jesus is rewarded by a special blessing. He receives a new name, "Peter" or "Rock" (see comments in notes to 16:18, p. 1366) because he will be the foundation upon which Jesus' church will be built. Peter is given the "keys of the kingdom of heaven" and empowered to "bind" and "loose." Both of these images, as the notes to the text indicate, refer to the responsibilities of leadership entrusted to Peter. He becomes, in effect, the prime minister of the community.

Matthew will balance out this focus on Peter by also asserting the authority of the community in chapter 18, but at this point in the Gospel he is showing the important role entrusted to the leader of the community. Undoubtedly this reflects a ministry of leadership already present in Matthew's church. The Gospel uses Peter as a model for leadership. Historically, Peter had been an important leader in the church. In Acts we are told that he helped mediate between the Jewish Christian church of Jerusalem and the emerging Gentile churches (see Acts 10–15). Paul, too, acknowledges the importance of "Cephas" (see, for example Gal 1:18; 2:11–14). And the Letters of Peter, even if not written directly by the Apostle, testify to the importance of his memory in the early church (see Reading Guides to 1 and 2 Peter).

While it would be going too far to impose on this Gospel scene the full-blown institution of the papal office, Roman Catholic tradition can legitimately see in the figure of Peter the founding model for the later emergence of this office in the church. Peter is blessed because of his strong faith in Jesus and because he served a key role in maintaining the unity of the church. Equally important to remember, however, is that the gospel refuses to idealize Peter or to place him above the demands of the gospel. The same Peter that Jesus blesses lavishly here is also called "Satan" and "obstacle" (16:23), will underestimate the need for reconciliation (18:21), and will deny his discipleship in the face of the Passion (26: 69–75). Leaders within the community must remain disciples (see 23:10).

Life in the Community

The fourth discourse of Matthew's Gospel, the discourse on community, occurs in this section of the Gospel (18:1–35). The notes supply detailed commentary on this powerful example of Jesus' teaching. Matthew gathers here two parables of Jesus (the lost sheep, and the unforgiving servant) and several sayings, and he molds them into a discourse.

Two key sayings divide the chapter and strike its major themes. At the end of the first major section, Jesus tells the disciples: "In just the same way, it is not the will of your heavenly Father that one of these little ones be lost" (18:14). The call to urgently seek out and care for the "little ones," that is, the weak or alienated members of the community, dominates the first half of the discourse. The members of the community are not to seek their own aggrandizement (18:1–5) and are never to "scandalize" or despise those on the margins of the church (18:6–10). Matthew's version of the lost sheep parable drives that lesson home: the leaders of the community are to seek out the stray, not to condemn them.

The second half of the discourse concludes with another key saying: "So will my heavenly Father do to you, unless each of you forgives his brother (or sister) from the heart" (18:35). The need for reconciliation dominates the latter half of the discourse. Disputes are to be settled in a fair and practical manner (18:15–17), and even if strong discipline must be taken toward a recalcitrant member, he or she is to be treated "like a Gentile or a tax collector"—a poignant note in a Gospel where Jesus seeks out just such people (see, for example, 9:9–13)! Those who have experienced limitless forgiveness from God should not put limits on reconciliation within the community. That is the radical message of Jesus' reply to Peter, and the concluding parable of the story. Its message is similar in content to Jesus' teaching on love of enemies in the Sermon on the Mount (see 5:43–48). We are to strive to love even the enemy because God's own love is lavish and indiscriminate.

This entire chapter offers a remarkable model for the church. There is little concern here for structures and budgets (important as they are for us and may have been for Matthew's community, too); emphasis falls rather on the care we need to have for each other if we are to be followers of Jesus.

Final Teaching in Jerusalem (21:1–25:46)

The Gospel drama now enters Jerusalem, the capital city, where Jesus will experience death and resurrection. The great temple of Herod dominated this city in the time of Jesus, and its shadow falls across the scenes Matthew narrates in these chapters.

Jesus the Messiah enters his city in triumph, but he is seated on a donkey's colt, which Matthew interprets as a sign of Jesus' humility (see comment on 21:5). As a fearless prophet, Jesus cleanses the house of God, another sign of his God-given mission to call Israel to repentance. The next day Jesus returns to the Temple compound and begins to teach the crowds (21:13). There follows a number of key texts that reveal the heart of Jesus' message. But the Jewish authorities (the Pharisees now joined by the "chief priests and elders of the people," all members of the Sanhedrin, an informal ruling body whose base would, in fact, have been Jerusalem) remain hostile to Jesus and his message. This section of the Gospel is filled with sharp clashes between Jesus and his opponents.

Two important clusters of sayings and parables are found here. In the first, 23:1–39, Jesus excoriates the scribes and the Pharisees, portraying them in purely negative tones for their hypocrisy and lack of fidelity. As we will discuss below, this is Matthew's most intense assault on the Jewish leaders. The second collection of sayings and parables forms the fifth and final discourse of the Gospel, the so-called eschatological discourse or discourse on the end of the world (see the note to 24:1). While gazing at the stunning Temple from the Mount of Olives, Jesus reflects on the fate of the Temple and the end of human history. This leads to a series of parables, some of them unique to Matthew, urging the disciples to remain faithful and to exemplify that fidelity through good deeds (see 24: 36–25:46).

The Authority of Jesus

Matthew portrays Jesus in strong, authoritative tones in this section. The Messiah enters the royal city in triumph with the acclamations of the crowds filling the air (21:1–11). "The Lord of the sabbath" (12:8) asserts his authority over the Temple by driving out the merchants and money changers, reclaiming God's house (21: 12–17). He meets head-on the challenges of each of the major religious authorities of Israel: the scribes, the Pharisees, the chief priests, the elders of the people, the Sadducees. Even though Jesus will soon be a prisoner, Matthew wants to leave no doubt in the mind of the reader: Jesus is the Messiah, the true Teacher of Israel.

The foundation of that authority is Jesus' identity as God's Son. The parable of the tenants reaffirms that (21:33–46); Jesus describes himself in this allegory (see note in text, p. 1379) as the son of the vineyard owner, the "heir," whose maltreatment will bring judgment on the tenants. He is more than David's Son—even David the King had to call the future Messiah "Lord" (22:41–46).

Matthew also presents Jesus dealing with questions of the law in characteristic fashion. The law is not rejected out of hand but reinterpreted. The dispute about the greatest commandment of the law (22:34–40) is most revealing: "the whole law and the prophets" depend on the love command. The core of Jesus' teaching and the basis for all interpretation of tradition are the values of love and compassion (see 5:43–48, and comments on chapter 18).

Jesus and His Opponents

In chapter 23 Matthew presents Jesus as launching into a fierce assault on the hypocrisy and infidelity of the scribes and Pharisees. As the notes observe (see comments on 23:1–39), they become, in effect, negative examples—the reverse side of the portrayal of the faithful disciple found in the Sermon on the Mount. Reading this discourse tells us what values Matthew's Jesus holds most dear: practicing what one preaches (23:3), being compassionate rather than laying heavy burdens on others (23:4), not using religion as a means of self-aggrandizement (23:5f), having a proper sense of values and therefore understanding that mercy and justice are always the highest priority in interpreting the law (23: 23–28). Jesus urges his disciples to be leaders who have a sense of solidarity with the community rather than viewing others as inferior and subordinate (23:8–12).

This strong indictment of the failings of the leaders is not intended solely to pummel the opponents of Jesus. Rather it is meant as a sober instruction for the Christian readers of the Gospel. Nevertheless, the negative stereotyping of the Jewish leaders, especially when it is read apart from its historical context in the Gospel, can have destructive effects. We who live in the horrible shadow of the Holocaust must be responsible readers of this Gospel and, while taking to heart the important lessons of this discourse, must not allow its negative image of the Jewish leaders to influence our attitude to Jews today. Every modern pope and the teaching of the Second Vatican Council has attacked anti-Semitism and reminded Catholics of their spiritual and historical roots in the living faith of Judaism (see particularly, the 2002 statement of the Pontifical Biblical Commission, *The Jewish People and Their Sacred Scriptures in the Christian Bible*).

Judgment

The parables that make up the eschatological discourse have a familiar Matthean ring to them (see 24:36–25:46). Once again the evangelist dwells on the importance of doing good deeds as the authenticating expression of one's discipleship. The "faithful and prudent servant" is the one who is found taking care of the household and distributing food to those in need (24:45f); the wise virgins have their lamps filled with oil and are ready to respond at the proper moment (25:1–13); the servant who employs his or her talents is the one blessed on the master's return from a long journey (25:14–30); those who will be invited to inherit the Kingdom are those who carried out the love command—feeding the hungry, clothing the naked, visiting the prisoner, and welcoming the stranger (25:31–46).

The climactic parable of the sheep and the goats illustrates how far Matthew is prepared to press his insistence on good deeds. The "sheep" had not even recognized the Risen Lord present in the needy but yet acted out of compassion. They are blessed by the Son of Man in his glory because they have proven to be faithful servants. More than once in his Gospel Matthew has stated that doing the good deeds of compassion and justice weigh far more than knowing the right words and wearing the right vestments (see a similar message in the parable of the two sons, 21: 28–32). There is little tolerance for religious hypocrisy in this Gospel.

The Death and Resurrection of God's Son (26:1–28:20)

The Passion (26:1–27:66)

The Passion story moves quickly from Jesus' prediction of the plot against him (26:1–5), through the last supper with his disciples (26: 20–30), his anguished prayer and arrest in Gethsemane (26:36–56), the interrogation and trial before the Sanhedrin or Jewish Council (26: 57–75), the Roman trial before Pilate (27:1–31), and the final scene of crucifixion, mockery, and death (27:32–56). The burial in Joseph of Arimathea's tomb and the Pharisees' demand that Pilate post a guard (27:57–66) prepare the reader for the explosive events of the Resurrection.

The peculiar emphases Matthew gives the Passion story can be summarized under three major themes:

The Majesty of Jesus. Even in the Passion story, Jesus remains the majestic Messiah of Israel. This is already true in Mark's account but it is given particular emphasis by Matthew. Jesus is imbued with prophetic knowledge of the events about to take place: he predicts the plot of the leaders (26:1f), is fully aware of his impending death (26:12, 18), knows the identity of his betrayer (26:25), and the certainty of Peter's denials (26:34). His captors cannot seize him until Jesus confronts Judas with his treachery (26:50). And when the high priest commands with an oath that Jesus reveal his identity, Jesus predicts with calm majesty his eventual triumph as the Son of Man who will be exalted at the right hand of God (26:64). Death cannot destroy or defeat God's Son—that is the heart of Matthew's message in the Passion story. The parade of mockers who file past the cross jeer Jesus and ridicule his claim to be God's Son (27:39–44). But as death comes, Jesus is acclaimed as the true Son of God, and nature itself erupts in testimony to Jesus' victory (see comments on 27:51–54).

The Dawn of the New Age. The death of Jesus is the center point of sacred history in Matthew's perspective. As discussed above (see comments on RG 381), Matthew, along with all of the New Testament, considered Jesus as the advent of the final and decisive age of salvation promised by God to Israel. The death of Jesus was the climactic act of his entire mission: here all of his love and commitment were compressed into one intense act of fidelity to the will of his Father. Thus the death of Jesus becomes in a special way the turning point between the old and the new age. With the death (and resurrection) of Jesus the final age of human history had begun and, therefore, humanity must respond to God's grace in a new way.

Several features of Matthew's Passion story proclaim this theology of history. At the moment of death (27:51–57) signs of the new age break out: nature convulses, the tombs are split open, and the dead are liberated—just as the dream of the prophet Ezekiel had envisioned, with the dead bones of Israel's hopes taking flesh and escaping the tomb (see Ez 37). The age of death is over; the age of resurrection begins.

The attention Matthew gives to the response of the leaders and people of Israel to Jesus is another part of his theology of history (see, for example, 27:24f). Paradoxically, because Israel rejects Jesus, the way will now be open for the gospel to be proclaimed to the Gentiles. This does not mean that Matthew despairs of having the Jews accept the message of Jesus (he seems to offer some hope of this in 23:39), but he does believe that the mission to the Gentiles is now possible in the new and final age of salvation, and one of the catalysts for that mission was the fact that the mission to Israel had failed. Paul, too, has a similar theology in Romans 9–11, where he reminds his readers that in the mystery of God's providence the failure of Israel becomes a moment of grace for the Gentiles. For Paul, Israel remains special because God is faithful and will never forget the promises made to the chosen people. This biblical teaching is reaffirmed in the theology of the Second Vatican Council where in the document on relationships with non-Christian religions *(Nostra Aetate)* the Council explicitly refers to Romans 9–11 to state that the Jewish people have a special and enduring place in the history of salvation. Pope John Paul II in his historic visit to the synagogue of Rome affirmed that Catholicism has a relationship with Judaism "which we do not have with any other religion." For these reasons the Pontifical Biblical Commission declared that "an attitude of respect, esteem and love for the Jewish people is the only truly Christian attitude in a situation which is mysteriously part of the beneficent and positive plan of God" (*The Jewish People and Their Sacred Scriptures in the Christian Bible*, par. 87).

Examples and Counterexamples. The Passion story also serves Matthew's teaching about discipleship. In the crucible of suffering and death, one's true character is revealed. The Passion is filled with examples, both positive and negative, of how people respond to the gospel in crisis. The leaders remain implacably hostile to Jesus and demand his death. Peter and the rest of the disciples prove their "little faith," with Peter denying he knows Jesus and the others fleeing in panic. Judas betrays his master and gives in to despair rather than seeking repentance (27:3f).

There are also bright moments: the woman of Bethany who performs a last kindness for Jesus, anointing him for burial despite the protests of the disciples (26:6–13); Pilate's wife who pleads on behalf of "that righteous man" (27:19); the centurion and his companions who acclaim the crucified Jesus as the "Son of God" (27:54);

the women who stand by Jesus at the cross and see to his burial (27:56); Joseph of Arimathea, the rich disciple who risks his reputation by burying a publicly executed man in his own new tomb (27:57–61). And, of course, Jesus himself is the prime exemplar of fidelity—seeking God's will despite the threat of death, refusing violence at the moment of his arrest, and trusting in God even as his life's breath is taken from him.

There is no doubt that Matthew intended the readers of the Passion to place themselves in the story and to ask the troubled question posed by the disciples: "Is it I, Lord?" (26:22).

The Resurrection (28:1–20)

The Gospel concludes with the events surrounding the empty tomb and Jesus' appearances to his disciples. None of the Gospels attempts to narrate the resurrection itself, but Matthew comes closest to that in mentioning an "earthquake" and an "angel of the Lord" who comes from heaven to roll back the stone from the tomb (28:2). Marvelous events such as these and the opening of the tombs at the moment of Jesus' death (see 27:51–53) continue to signal the final and glorious age when God's presence would be felt in a vivid way.

Mark's original ending does not include the report of any appearances of the Risen Christ; the discovery of the empty tomb, and the words of the heavenly messenger about Jesus' triumph over death are enough to proclaim the message (see Mk 16:1–8). But in Matthew's Gospel, Jesus appears first to the women as they leave the empty tomb (28:9f), and then to the eleven disciples (here Matthew does not forget Judas's tragic fate) in Galilee (28:16–20). Matthew's denunciation of the Jewish leaders continues right to the end of the Gospel: when the chief priests and elders learn from the soldiers about the astounding events at the tomb, instead of believing in Christ's triumph, they concoct a false story about the disciples stealing the body of Jesus (28: 11–15).

The final scene of the Gospel (28:16–20) is on a mountaintop, the favored site of special revelation throughout the Gospel (see, for example, the temptation, the Sermon on the Mount, the transfiguration, the healing of the crowds, 15:29–31). The Risen Christ comes in triumph, as he had predicted during his Passion, and commissions his disciples to go to "all nations," making disciples, baptizing them into the community, and teaching them to observe all that Jesus had commanded.

Major themes of the Gospel are compressed into this scene: Matthew's concern with the universal mission of the church; his emphasis on Jesus as teacher; his realistic portrayal of the disciples (who even now "hesitate" as they encounter the Risen Christ, see 28:17!); his interest in the church. This scene has inspired countless Christian missionaries throughout the centuries to leave their homeland to bring the gospel to others. Above all, the Gospel's majestic portrayal of Jesus as the church's firm foundation and abiding hope is reaffirmed. No matter how turbulent will be the church's future, the Risen Jesus will not abandon it. Matthew concludes his Gospel with the final promise of one who was named *Emmanuel*, "God is with us" (see 1:23): "I am with you always, until the end of the age" (28:20).

D.S.

FURTHER READING

Carter, Warren. *Matthew: Storyteller, Interpreter, Evangelist.* Peabody, MA: Hendrickson, 1996.

Davies, W. D., and Dale C. Allison. *Matthew.* International Critical Commentary. Vols. 1–3. Edinburgh: T & T Clark, 1988, 1997.

Harrington, Daniel J., S.J. *The Gospel of Matthew.* Sacra Pagina. Collegeville, MN: Liturgical Press, 1991.

Senior, Donald. *The Death of Jesus in the Gospel of Matthew.* Passion Series 1. Wilmington, DE: Michael Glazier, 1985.

—. *What Are They Saying About Matthew?* Rev. ed. Mahweh, NJ: Paulist Press, 1996.

—. *Matthew.* Abingdon New Testament Commentaries; Nashville: Abingdon Press, 1998.

MARK

[see pages 1400–1432 of the New Testament]

Before Beginning . . .

As the introduction in the text suggests (see p. 1400), Mark's Gospel was probably the first Gospel to be written. Mark can take credit for shaping the Christian message into its most effective and moving form, that of a story about Jesus. The evangelist knitted together sayings of Jesus and stories about his ministry into a single dynamic narrative, tracing the life of Jesus from his first encounter with John the Baptist at the Jordan to his dynamic mission in Galilee, and on to his death and resurrection in Jerusalem. Mark's purpose was not simply to preserve the church's memory about Jesus but to make that memory take on new force in the lives of his readers.

Although we cannot be sure of the date, Mark probably wrote for Roman Christians, shortly after the persecutions of Nero (AD 64), when the community was still reeling from that tyrant's cruelty. Some Christians had reacted to Nero's attacks with heroic martyrdom, but others had betrayed the community or slipped away in fear. Mark's story of the crucified Jesus and his disciples who struggled to remain faithful would have been a powerful lesson for this early Christian church.

Characteristics of Mark's Gospel

There are some typical features and motifs, or themes, of Mark's Gospel that the reader should be alert to.

A Theology in Narrative

One of the most obvious features of Mark's Gospel, but one that should not be overlooked, is the fact that it is a narrative, a "story," about Jesus. Mark proclaims to his readers the good news of salvation (the literal meaning of the term *gospel*), but he does it not by a series of abstract statements or propositions but through a dynamic story that grips the reader with its force and emotion.

Some of the characteristics of Mark's narrative style reveal his theological message. The pace of the story is urgent. Jesus moves rapidly from place to place; there is little wasted motion and a minimum of verbiage. The dynamism and urgency of the Gospel coincide with Mark's conviction that the mission of Jesus is compelling and one must respond to it without hesitation. The Gospel is also filled with conflicts between Jesus and his opponents and between Jesus and the demons; the climactic passion story dominates the whole Gospel. Here, too, Mark's theological perspective is at work: because the message of Jesus calls for radical change and challenges the powers of this world, it is not surprising that conflict and suffering have such a major role to play in Mark's story.

Christology

The central and guiding question of Mark's Gospel is posed in 8:29: "Who do you say that I am?" Understanding the mystery of Jesus' identity and responding to it with faith are the major concerns of the Gospel. Mark proclaims that Jesus is the Son of God and the Messiah, typical convictions of the entire New Testament, but the evangelist proclaims this fundamental faith by means of his story. Jesus' healings, his parables, his instruction of the disciples, his encounters with demons, his conflicts with opponents, and, above all, his death and resurrection reveal the profound mystery of Christ. Jesus' dynamic ministry of healing and exorcisms demonstrates that, through him, God's liberating rule was now breaking into history and freeing people from the grip of death.

For Mark, however, the most important means of revealing Jesus' identity was the cross. The cross becomes the touchstone of all authentic faith in Jesus; in his death for others Jesus reveals the heart of his mission. All of the other titles and images applied to Jesus such as "Messiah" *(Christ)*, or "Son of Man," or healer, take on their true meaning when seen in the context of Jesus' redemptive death. Throughout Mark's narrative we will see this focus on Jesus at work.

Discipleship

Mark's Gospel is also concerned with what it means to follow Jesus; the disciples of Jesus play an important role in Mark's story. Jesus commissions them to follow him early in his ministry (1: 16–20), and they are present for almost every scene. One of the intriguing features of Mark's portrayal is that the disciples have a hard time understanding Jesus. As the Gospel drama unfolds and as the Passion of Jesus approaches, the disciples begin openly to misunderstand Jesus and eventually fail him. The Gospel will end, however, on a note of reconciliation and renewal: the heavenly messenger at the tomb tells the women to instruct the "disciples and Peter"—all of whom were absent at the crucifixion—to go to Galilee where they will once again encounter Jesus (16:7).

There is little doubt that Mark sees the disciples not simply as historical figures from the past but as representative of the Christians of his own time. The instruction Jesus gives his followers, the difficulty they encounter in understanding who Jesus truly was, and Jesus' unbreakable bonds with them despite their failures are all meant as a challenge and consolation to the Christians who read the Gospel.

How to Proceed

The best way to study Mark's Gospel is to follow his story of Jesus from beginning to end. Mark's brief narrative is taut and compelling; it can be read in one sitting, and, in fact, that is a good thing to do before concentrating on a particular passage of the Gospel. To prepare the reader, we will trace the main segments of the story line and then discuss in more detail some of the major themes of each section.

The evangelist uses geography to organize the main lines of his story: the Gospel drama opens in the Judean desert with John baptizing at the Jordan River, then moves to Galilee where most of Jesus' public ministry takes place, and finally to Jerusalem for the climactic events of the Passion and Resurrection. (See map #13.)

Working through Mark's Gospel

Overture in the Desert (Mk 1:1–13)

The Gospel drama begins in the Judean desert where the prophet John preaches a baptism of repentance. Jesus, the Galilean, makes his way south to the desert to proclaim his dedication to God. At the moment of baptism Jesus' true identity as the Son of God is revealed, and he is endowed with an abundance of God's Spirit. A haunting scene in the desert follows where Jesus struggles with Satan.

The Galilean Ministry of Jesus (1:14–8:21)

This major section covers most of Jesus' public ministry. It takes place in Galilee, the northern region of Israel (see map #13).

• 1:14f. The keynote of Jesus' ministry: "The Kingdom of God is at hand."

• 1:16–45. The call of the first disciples and the first day of Jesus' healing ministry.

• 2:1–3:6. A series of conflicts with the religious leaders that ends with their determination to destroy Jesus.

• 3:7–4:34. The ministry of Jesus continues and so, too, does opposition to him. The misunderstanding of his family and the accusations of the Pharisees are reflected in the parable discourse of chapter 4 where Jesus states that the mystery of the Kingdom is revealed only to the disciples, not to those who oppose the Gospel.

• 4:35–8:26. The mission of Jesus widens in scope as he moves across the lake to Gentile territory and travels beyond the borders of Israel to Tyre and Sidon.

The Journey from Galilee to Jerusalem (8:27–10:52)

This major section begins in the northernmost reaches of Israel, the town of Caesarea Philippi, where Peter confesses that Jesus is the Christ. The attention of the Gospel now begins to fix on the upcoming Passion (8:31; 9:31; 10:32–34), as Jesus and his disciples move south to Jerusalem. The section is also filled with Jesus' teaching on the meaning of discipleship. Two stories of Jesus healing blind men frame the entire passage (8:22–26; 10:46–52), stories that symbolize the difficulty the disciples have in grasping Jesus' teaching.

Death and Resurrection in Jerusalem (11:1–16:8)

The rest of Mark's story takes place in Jerusalem, the Temple city.

• 11:1–12:44. Jesus' prophetic sign condemning the Temple introduces a series of controversies with the Jewish leaders.

• 13:1–37. In the shadow of the Temple, Jesus predicts its destruction and counsels his disciples on the struggles of the community as it awaits the consummation of human history.

• 14:1–15:47. The climactic Passion account.

• 16:1–8. The Gospel closes with the discovery of the empty tomb and the heavenly messenger's announcement of Jesus' victory over death.

As the notes explain (see comments on 16:9–20) there are additional endings appended to Mark's Gospel, but these were added later by someone other than the evangelist. In our comments on the Gospel we will assume that the original ending to Mark's Gospel was 16:1–8.

Reading through Mark's Gospel

The goal of this section is to trace major themes and characteristics of each segment of Mark's Gospel. What is said here complements the more detailed commentary found in the introduction and in the notes to the biblical text.

Overture (Mk 1:1–13)

Like an overture to a musical piece, these verses sound major themes that will echo throughout Mark's Gospel. The setting for these opening scenes is the Judean desert, that haunting place so full of symbolism in the Bible. It was in the desert that Israel was first forged into a people, as God led them from slavery to freedom and sealed a covenant with them at Sinai. The desert was a place of new beginnings, and Jesus, like John, comes here to start his mission. But the desert is also a place of testing, the parched arena where the children of Israel rebelled against God and where the forbidding terrain revealed the true character of those who dared its stretches. Here, too, Jesus would be tested by Satan before the beginning of his mission in Galilee.

Mark signals several major themes in these brief opening scenes:

• John comes dressed like Elijah (see note to 1:6, p. 1402), the great prophet who was expected to return at the end of the world. By presenting John in this fashion, Mark indicates that the old age is coming to an end and a new age is beginning. That is the reason for the urgent message of repentance John preaches. This sense of a new age dawning with Jesus moves throughout the Gospel.

• Mark also clearly identifies Jesus as the Son of God. The divine voice from heaven leaves no doubt about Jesus' awesome identity (1:11). The Spirit of God descends on Jesus and imbues him with the power to carry out his mission as the Messiah, God's anointed one who would liberate the world from death (1:10). As we noted in the introduction, Christology is a major concern of the Gospel.

• The desert test (1:12f) where Jesus wrestles with the demon is also a preview of the ministry of Jesus. In his mission of healing, Jesus casts out demons and liberates the sick and disabled from the shackles of pain. To carry out his mission, Jesus must often struggle with opponents; from the opening scene of the Gospel, Mark tells us that the process of saving human life can be filled with conflict. Experience bears this out: very often true liberation from sin and false values comes only through great struggle.

The Galilean Ministry of Jesus (1:14–8:21)

This major section spans almost one half of the Gospel, and covers Jesus' ministry of teaching and healing in the northern region of Galilee. We can divide it into five segments, each with distinctive tones.

The Keynote of Jesus' Mission (1:14f)

These two verses condense much of the Gospel message. As he enters into his home region of Galilee, Jesus sounds the major theme of his ministry: "the kingdom of God is at hand" (1:15). Each phrase evokes a major Markan theme:

"This is the time of fulfillment" (1:15). The new and final age of salvation—longed for by Israel over centuries—now dawns with the advent of Jesus. That new age will call for new responses by those graced to experience it (see Jesus' teaching on catching the mood of the times and the need to pour new wine into new wineskins, 2:18–22).

"The kingdom of God is at hand" (1:15). This biblical symbol expresses Israel's hope for salvation, for the time when God would come once and for all to rule Israel with justice and peace, not in the manner of the Jewish kings who so many times had failed the people and been themselves agents of oppression. The Gospel portrays Jesus not only as the messenger of that coming Kingdom but as actually inaugurating God's rule through his healing touch, his commitment to justice, and the liberating act of giving his life for others.

"Repent, and believe in the gospel" (l:lf). God's offer of salvation through Jesus calls for a response. Those who hear the good news should "repent." The literal meaning of the Greek word *metanoiein* means to change one's mind or perspective. Throughout his Gospel Mark uses images of perception—hearing, seeing, understanding—to describe faith. The disciples of Jesus are asked to see reality—God's reality—with the new eyes of faith and to transform their lives accordingly.

The Call of the Disciples and Jesus' First Day of Ministry (1:16–45)

The remaining verses of chapter 1 present the first day of Jesus' dynamic mission. This section is most characteristic of Mark's portrayal of Jesus: After choosing his first disciples, Jesus plunges into the sickness and pain of his world, healing and casting out demons. The action takes place around Capernaum, the small fishing village on the northwest corner of the Sea of Galilee, the arena for most of Jesus' ministry in Mark's account.

The Call of the Disciples (1:16–20). The meaning of discipleship is a major theme of the Gospel. Right at the beginning of his mission, therefore, Jesus calls disciples to follow him and to share in his own ministry of fishing for people. This rapid-fire story condenses the early church's theology of discipleship: (a) discipleship is a gift; all of the initiative comes from Jesus, not from the disciples themselves; (b) the essence of discipleship is following Jesus, an allegiance that takes precedence over every other value; (c) the disciple is privileged to share in the mission of Jesus, here expressed in terms of "fishing" for people. In the Bible (see, for example, Jer 16:16; Hb 1:14f), that image of fishing is used to describe the gathering of people for the final day of judgment. Jesus' own ministry has similar strong tones.

Exorcism and Healing (1:20–45). This whole section is filled with reports of exorcisms and healings. The first action of Jesus is typical of his entire ministry. He enters the synagogue at Capernaum on a Sabbath and liberates a man whose life was tormented by an "unclean spirit" (1:23). Exorcism, or the expulsion of evil spirits who hold human beings in their tormenting grip, is frequently mentioned in Mark's Gospel. Here the demons recognize that they are struggling with "the Holy One of God" and know that Jesus has come to destroy them. The people who witness the liberation of the man respond: "A new teaching with authority!" For Mark, such liberating acts are precisely the "new teaching" of Jesus, and that is why the evangelist highlights the exorcisms. They present in dramatic form the ultimate meaning of Jesus' ministry: he has come to destroy the power of death in all its forms and to free humanity from its grip.

The ancient world attributed many psychic and physical ailments to the power of evil spirits, a recognition that their lives were ruled by powers they could not control. While our own modern world view may be less inclined to attribute illness to evil powers, the message of the Gospel is still relevant. We can still learn from Jesus' fierce commitment to alleviating pain and to freeing people from situations and powers that oppress them. And there are many situations where human beings are caught in the grip of overpowering evil, whether it be economic oppression, systemic violence, obsessive or addictive behaviors, or racism—situations often beyond the control of any individual. The Gospel tells us that God's will and the goal of all authentic Christian mission is to liberate humans from such tyrannies of evil.

Conflict (2:1–3:6)

The reader will notice a significant change of tone in this section of the Gospel. As Jesus continues his ministry of healing, he meets with strong oppression from the Jewish leaders. The five conflict stories in this section reach their climax in 3:6 where the leaders begin to plot Jesus' death. Right from the beginning of his story Mark draws our attention to the Passion. Like some distant tolling of a bell, warnings had already been given in 1:14 where Mark, almost offhandedly, mentions that Jesus begins his ministry in Galilee "after John had been arrested." And the fierce struggle with the demon in the synagogue of Capernaum (1:21–28) was a preview of more deadly conflicts to come.

An important point to notice in these stories

is that the conflicts revolve around the central values of Jesus' ministry. The scribes object because Jesus claims the power to forgive sins and to heal (2:1–12). Pharisees take offense at his association with sinners and outcasts (2:16f) and at his compassionate interpretation of the law (2:23–28). His healing of a man's withered arm on a Sabbath is the final affront (3:1–6). Thus Mark implies that fidelity to the good news of mercy and compassion can, paradoxically, lead to conflict with those who have other values and other priorities.

The discussion about fasting that stands in the middle of this section (2:18–22) gives the reader another clue about Mark's message. A series of sayings emphasize that, with Jesus, a new age has dawned. It is the time of the "bridegroom"; a time for replacing the whole cloth, not just a patch; a time for new wine and new wineskins. Each of these images stresses that the new age of salvation is present in Jesus and, therefore, new things are possible. The Pharisees and scribes miss this reality and blindly oppose Jesus. As we mentioned above, Mark employs perception metaphors—seeing, hearing, understanding—to describe the experience of faith (see comments, RG 389).

Finally, in this section, we should not overlook Mark's continuing concern about discipleship. Another call story similar to that in 1:16–20 takes place when Jesus encounters the toll collector Levi, sitting at his customs or toll post (Capernaum was a border town between the territories ruled by the vassal kings Herod Agrippa and Phillip). Once again, the call story emphasizes that faith and discipleship are a gift to which we must respond. This story also reminds us that the community is open to everyone: the just and the sinner. The opponents of Jesus are blind to this fact, too, and take offense at his sharing a meal with "tax collectors and sinners" (2:16). But Jesus responds that being a "physician" to the sinners was precisely his mission (2:17).

This entire section has strong lessons for Christian life. It reminds us that true fidelity to the gospel has a price and that we should not be surprised to encounter opposition and conflict, even deadly hostility, from those whose values are challenged by the justice and compassion of the gospel. Jesus' compassion and his strong commitment to include the disabled, the sick, and other social outcasts in the community can also instruct us on the nature of the church and its mission.

The Mystery of the Kingdom (3:7–4:34)

By means of a summary, Mark continues his reporting of Jesus' dynamic ministry of healing and exorcisms (3:7–12). The disciples' stake in all this is made clear in 3:13–19: Jesus climbs to the top of a mountain (a typical place of revelation in the Bible) and solemnly commissions the Twelve "to be with him," "to preach," and "to have authority to drive out demons." The disciples share fully in the ministry of Jesus.

But the note of conflict and misunderstanding sounded in the previous section continues to dominate here. All of the people close to Jesus seem to be out of sympathy with him. His own relatives want to take him back home because they think "he is out of his mind" (3:21). Mark follows through with this incident in a later scene where Jesus' "mother and his brothers" arrive to take him back home (3:31–35). But Jesus puts distance between himself and his uncomprehending family when he looks at the circle of disciples who are inside the house with him and says: "Here are my mother and my brothers . . . whoever does the will of God is my brother and sister and mother" (3:35).

The parable discourse (4:1–34) attempts to give a reason for all this misunderstanding. The parables, like Jesus himself, are a mysterious revelation of the Kingdom of God. Those not in sympathy with Jesus cannot understand his words. But those called to be disciples are "granted the mystery of the Kingdom of God" (see note to 4:11–12, p. 1407). While honoring human freedom, Mark wants to affirm that God's providence guides all of human life, even in the darkest moments such as the rejection of Jesus.

Mark's reflection on the parables also reaffirms that faith in Jesus is a gift; it is not something we control or achieve solely through our own efforts. The disciples are "given" the mystery of the Kingdom of God.

Other important themes of Mark's Gospel are communicated in the parables. The stories of the sower casting small, vulnerable seeds on rough ground (4:3–9), the tiny mustard seed (4:

30–32), and that of the seed growing without the farmer's knowledge (4:26–29) affirm, on the one hand, that the reality of God's Kingdom seeps into our lives in a hidden and often unnoticed fashion. Such is often the case in Mark's Gospel when people fail to recognize *who* Jesus is because they are looking for another type of Messiah. On the other hand the parables proclaim that God's kingdom will be wonderfully triumphant despite opposition: the harvest of new life and peace will be abundant, "thirty, sixty, and a hundredfold" (4:8).

Throughout this section Mark's portrayal of the disciples remains constant. Even though they are privileged to be chosen as followers of Jesus, they still have a hard time understanding his message (4:13).

The Universal Mission of Jesus (4:35–8:21)

This concluding section of Jesus' Galilean ministry embraces a large amount of material that can be loosely gathered under the theme of the universal scope of Jesus' mission. The Sea of Galilee begins to be an important factor, not simply as a geographical phenomenon in the center of Galilee, but as an important symbolic boundary between Jew and Gentile (consult the map of Galilee, map #13; the region to the west of the Sea was mainly Jewish in population, while on the eastern shore the population was mainly Gentile).

Jesus and his disciples cross the sea several times in this section, occasionally having to endure its turbulent storms. The first time is in 4:35 when they cross through the storm and arrive in the Gentile territory of the Gerasenes (5:1). There Jesus will liberate a Gentile man from a terrible demon. Another missionary journey begins in 7:24, after Jesus' dispute with the Pharisees. This begins to the northwest where Jesus encounters the Syrophoenician woman (7:24–30) and extends around once more to the Decapolis on the eastern side of the lake (7:31). The entire section ends with Jesus and his disciples again in the boat together heading for the Gentile shore (8:13).

Other important blocks of material give a mission flavor to this section, such as the commissioning of the Twelve and sending them out (6:7–13:30f). The flashback to the death of John the Baptist at the hands of Herod is a reminder about the true cost of discipleship (6:14–29). So, too, are Jesus' continuing disputes with his opponents (see, for example, 7:1–23 and 8:11–13). Two of Jesus' greatest signs also tell us something about the nature of Jesus' mission; once on the Jewish side and once on the Gentile side of the lake, Jesus miraculously feeds massive crowds of hungry people (6:34–44; 8:1–10).

The following are some of the major themes of this section:

The Universality of the Gospel. Even though Jesus' ministry was confined mainly to Israel, Mark's Gospel shows the universal character of Jesus' words and actions. God's saving love was not meant exclusively for one group or one region. The stories of Jesus' healing Gentiles such as the Gerasene man (5:1–20), the Greek woman's daughter (7:24–30), and the deaf-mute from the Decapolis (7:31–37) illustrate this. So, too, does the fact that Jesus feeds Gentiles as well as Jews.

But crossing religious and cultural boundaries, and being open to people who are different from us, does not come easily for the human spirit, as history has repeatedly demonstrated. The early church, too, struggled with the need to reach out beyond its own boundaries (see, for example, the story of Cornelius's conversion in Acts 10–11). Mark hints at this in his Gospel, too. To cross to the Gentile side of the lake, Jesus and the disciples must brave the terror of the storm (4:35–41). Jesus himself seems hesitant before the request of the Syrophoenician woman (7:27), and the disciples want the crowds to be sent home rather than take the responsibility to feed them (8:4).

The universal character of the church has become more apparent to Christianity in modern times as the church has become less dominated by its European and Western traditions, but we still struggle to be a truly global church and thus open to people of different races, nationalities, and economic status. There are deep tensions between peoples of different religious traditions, and racism is still strong. This section of Mark's Gospel reminds us that the message of Jesus was inclusive from the beginning.

Nourishing God's People. The two feeding stories are eloquent statements of Jesus' mission. As God did during the Exodus from Egypt with manna, so Jesus, too, feeds God's hungry people. These feeding stories illustrate the justice dimension of the Gospel; the hungry are not to be sent away on their own thin resources (as the disciples suggest to Jesus!). Jesus came to feed them—a clear instruction for the mission of the church. At the same time, the feeding stories also evoke the Eucharist (Jesus' gestures of blessing and distributing the bread are identical to the Last Supper, 14:22); Jesus' mission was to reach across boundaries and to gather God's people into one body.

The Struggle of the Disciples. As the Galilean ministry of Jesus comes to a close, the disciples' difficulty in understanding Jesus seems only to increase. They are completely baffled at his mysterious power in calming the storm (4:38–41), and walking on the sea (6:45–51)—two haunting stories that reveal the divine power of Jesus. They are out of sympathy with Jesus' compassion for the crowds (6:35f; 8:4). And the section ends with their complete confusion about the meaning of Jesus' words and deeds (8:14–21). Jesus had come to break one loaf for the many, but there was still a long journey ahead before the disciples would grasp the meaning of that mission.

The Journey from Galilee to Jerusalem (8:22–10:52)

Mark's story now comes to a major turning point. Jesus and his disciples travel to the northern boundary of Israel, to the town of Caesarea Philippi. Along the way, Jesus poses the key question of the Gospel: "Who do you say that I am?" (8:29).

The Gospel has been answering that question for the reader all throughout the preceding chapters as it revealed—through Jesus' eloquent words and powerful ministry of healing and exorcism—his identity as God's Messiah and savior. But Jesus' opponents proved blind to that revelation, and even the disciples have been unable to grasp it. In this section Jesus provides more urgent instruction on his mission and the demands of discipleship. For the first time in the Gospel he begins to speak openly of his death and resurrection. Three Passion predictions punctuate these chapters (8:31; 9:31; 10:33–34). The cross, as a sign of Jesus' total commitment to his Father's will and his compassionate and selfless love for others, becomes the touchstone for understanding who Jesus is and what discipleship means.

Geography and the symbol of a journey also give a special character to these key chapters of the Gospel. Jesus and his disciples will travel from Caesarea Philippi in the north to Judea and its capital city of Jerusalem in the south (see map 13). But this is no routine journey in Mark's perspective. This purposeful journey toward Jerusalem is also Jesus' journey toward the cross where he will experience death and victory. The disciples must follow this same path if they are to be faithful to Jesus and his message. Thus this journey evokes other biblical journeys, especially the journey of the Israelites from Egypt to the promised land; that, too, was a journey from death to life. As we will see in the next section of the Gospel (11:1–13:37), Jerusalem, with its great Temple and the priests who attend it, becomes a negative symbol in Mark's theology. There Jesus will suffer his final rejection. Because of that, the Jerusalem Temple will give way to a new temple, Jesus himself.

The disciples are also an important focal point in this section. While disputes with opponents and other incidents take place, most of the action revolves around Jesus and his followers. After each of the Passion predictions, the disciples display their extraordinary lack of understanding of Jesus and his message. Peter attempts to silence Jesus (8:32); all of the disciples argue about which of them is the greatest (9:33f); the sons of Zebedee ask for special places of influence and power with Jesus, triggering the jealousy of the rest of the disciples (10:35–37, 41). The disciples also try to discourage the children from coming to Jesus (10:13); they are unable to perform an exorcism on a sick boy (9:18) despite being given the power to do so (see 6:7), and they continue to be baffled by Jesus' teaching (see, for example, 10:24–26).

In response to their lack of understanding Jesus gives even more intense instruction on the meaning of discipleship after each of the Passion predictions. The disciples must be willing to "take up the cross" and follow Jesus; to "lose" their lives for the sake of Jesus and the gospel (8: 34–38). Instead of being absorbed with self-aggrandizement, the disciples should imitate the child and seek to be the "servant of all" (10:35f). To follow Jesus means putting aside whatever holds us back from being free to serve others, such as excessive possessions (10:17–31). True greatness is not defined by "lording it over" others but by giving our lives for them (10:42–45).

In all of these instructions, the image of the cross is key. Jesus, the Son of Man (see the note to 8:31 for this important title in Mark), came not to be served but to serve, "to give his life as a ransom for many" (10:45). The death of Jesus on the cross is seen not as a tragic failure but as the ultimate expression of Jesus' entire mission. His death—like his life—was an act of love for others. Therefore the disciple, too, must "take up the cross" and make giving of life for others the animating principle of every action.

Because the disciples were absorbed in their own interests and fears, they understood Jesus' message dimly at best. Mark frames this entire section of the Gospel with two stories about Jesus' healing blind men. In 8:22–26 it is a case of deep-seated blindness. Jesus must lay hands on the man's eyes twice before he can see clearly. In the beautiful story of Bartimaeus (10:46–52), the focus shifts to the blind person's own determination to reach Jesus. Even though the bystanders attempt to stifle his cries for mercy, Bartimaeus's pleas reach Jesus' ears. Jesus poses a profound question: "What do you want me to do for you?" Bartimaeus replies: "Master, I want to see." That humble trust and honest expression of need save Bartimaeus. He receives his sight and begins to follow Jesus on the journey of discipleship (10:52). Mark has clearly interpreted this healing story as a discipleship story.

These two stories are penetrating commentary on the plight of the disciples. The disciples are blind in a sense far more disabling than that of physical blindness; they have a deep-seated block to understanding Jesus and his message. Bartimaeus, by contrast, reaches out to Jesus in his need and asks for the light of faith; that is the solution the disciples have yet to discover.

Death and Resurrection in Jerusalem (11:1–16:8)

Beginning with chapter 11, Mark's story enters its final phase. Jesus and his disciples have completed their journey from Galilee to Jerusalem. As the triumphant Messiah, Jesus enters the city of David where he will face determined opposition, death itself, and then final victory.

The material in these chapters can be subdivided into four major sections: the first two focusing on the Temple; the latter two comprising the Passion narrative and the discovery of the empty tomb.

Jesus and the Temple (11:1–12:44)

Jesus enters Jerusalem in seeming triumph; there are admiring crowds and acclamations of hosanna. For this brief moment, at least, the true identity of Jesus—so prone to be misunderstood by the characters in the Gospel—shines out clearly. But the mood of this section soon turns somber. Mark surrounds the story of Jesus' cleansing of the Temple (11:15–19) with the curious incident about the fig tree (11:12–14: 20f). The fig tree is cursed and withers because its fruits are not ready at the proper time for Jesus to harvest them. The fruitless tree becomes a sign of the Temple's own failure. Jesus' stern prophetic actions in the Temple area take on added meaning in Mark's text—the Temple is not only cleansed of abuses, it is declared no longer valid. Mark's Gospel foresees a new temple and a new worshipping community emerging in Jesus and his future community of disciples. This will be reaffirmed in the Passion story when Jesus is accused of predicting a temple "not made by hands" (14:58) and when the Temple veil is torn asunder at the moment of Jesus' death (15:38). This same motif is alluded to at the end of the parable of the tenants: the rejected Son who is killed by the tenants will become the "cornerstone" of a new edifice.

Thus Mark takes a dim view of the Jerusalem Temple because he sees it as symbolic of religious practice that has become hollow. This also emerges in the conflict stories that abound in this section. Like a great champion, Jesus seems to wrestle with each faction of the leaders: the chief priests, the elders, the scribes, the Herodians, the Pharisees, the Sadducees. They challenge the authority of Jesus but are reduced to silence by his penetrating answers.

These scenes underscore the power and majesty of Jesus, even as death approaches. He is indeed one greater than David (see 12:35–37), one who is Lord of the Temple. But the encounters with the Jewish leaders also help reaffirm important facets of Jesus' teaching. A scribe (who, in fact, seems in sympathy with Jesus and is representative of all those who seek God with a sincere heart) is led to an insight that goes to the heart of Jesus' message: "to love God with all your heart, with all your understanding, with all your strength, and to love your neighbor as yourself is worth more than all burnt offerings and sacrifice" (12:33).

The entire section ends with sharply contrasting images that also ram home the message Mark emphasizes in this section of the Gospel: Jesus excoriates the leaders who love the trappings of religion while "devouring the houses of widows," but he blesses the poor widow who gives everything she has to God (12:38–44).

Toward the End-Time (13:1–37)

This final discourse of Jesus to his disciples is one of the most enigmatic yet important passages in Mark's Gospel. It provides us with a powerful reflection on the ultimate meaning of history. The setting for the discourse is Jesus' prediction that the majestic Temple of Herod would one day be destroyed (as it was in AD 70), thus continuing the negative view of the Temple from the previous section.

The real focus of the chapter is on the future of the Christian community as it will carry out its mission in history, after the death and resurrection of Jesus. This discourse is not a transcript of a single speech by Jesus. The evangelist weaves together in this chapter sayings of Jesus with numerous quotations from the Old Testament, especially the apocalyptic literature that dwells on crisis. The chapter's main themes represent a profound reflection on the community's future:

Warnings about Persecutions and Divisions as the Community Carries Out Its Mission. Mark clearly asserts that before the end of the world can come, the church must complete its mission of proclaiming the gospel to all the world (13:10). In the course of that mission, however, will come persecution from both Jews and Gentiles (13:9–11) and internal divisions (13:12f). Mark's story has already illustrated how Jesus himself experienced opposition from his opponents and misunderstanding by his family and disciples.

The Christian Is to "Stay Awake." As the community moves out into history, it must be alert and sober, ready to catch glimpses of God's presence breaking into history (13:33–37). Mark makes it clear that this does not mean that the community is to be anxiously scanning the calendar and speculating about the end of the world. In fact, such doomsday predictions are branded as the words of "false Christs" and "false prophets" (13:5f, 21f). Rather, the Christian is to be committed to proclaiming the gospel and to living with the realization of God's imminent presence in history.

God's Triumph in History. The most important message of the chapter is to affirm that the final moment of human history will not be chaos or the defeat of goodness but the triumph of grace. Jesus, the Son of Man, will return to gather his disciples from the four corners of the earth and lead them to God (13:24–27). While acknowledging the reality of human suffering and the crises that the Christian community will have to face, Mark's view of history is ultimately full of hope.

The Passion (14:1–15:47)

These two chapters form the longest single narrative in the whole Gospel, reaffirming the importance the Passion holds for Mark's perspective. Jesus' death for others sums up his entire mission and is the ultimate revelation of his identity as the Son of God.

The Passion story moves rapidly to its climax at the cross. The opening scenes (14:1–11) set the mood as the leaders and Judas plot Jesus' death, while a faithful woman anoints his body for death. The Last Supper with the disciples dominates the next section (14:12–31); the breaking of the bread and the sharing of the cup are living signs of Jesus' impending death for others. The mood darkens when Jesus and his disciples go to Gethsemane (14:32–52). While Jesus earnestly prays for the strength to follow God's will, the disciples sleep. Then Judas leads an armed band into the garden to arrest Jesus. In the face of that threat, the disciples all flee in panic. The trials before the Sanhedrin (14:53–72) and before Pilate (15:1–20) dominate the rest of the Passion narrative. The crucifixion, death, and burial of Jesus bring the great drama to its conclusion (15:21–47).

Two major motifs move throughout the Passion story:

The Crisis of Discipleship. The disciples' inability to understand Jesus, so apparent throughout the Gospel, leads ultimately to their failure in the crisis of the Passion. Despite their bravado at the Last Supper (14:31), all of the disciples abandon Jesus at the moment of his arrest (14: 50–52), and Peter publicly denies he even knows Jesus (14:66–72). Mark gives his reader a sober lesson: suffering and persecution can prompt heroism, but it can also expose weak faith and superficial commitment (see 4:17).

The disciples' failure is in sharp contrast to the courageous loyalty and faith of other characters in the drama, such as the anonymous woman who anoints Jesus (over the protests of some of his followers, 14:3–9), the Roman centurion who acclaims Jesus at the moment of his death (15:39), the faithful women who stand by the cross (15:40f), and Joseph of Arimathea, a member of the Sanhedrin, who takes courage and asks to bury the crucified Jesus (15:42–47). These "unexpected" people—women, a Gentile soldier, a member of the opposition—illustrate the true meaning of faithful discipleship, an obvious lesson for the church.

The Revelation of Jesus as the Christ, the Son of God. The Passion story provides the final answer to the question that underlies all of Mark's Gospel: Who is Jesus? As Jesus courageously proclaims to the Sanhedrin: he is the Christ, the Son of God (14:61ff). But coming in the midst of the Passion narrative, with Jesus standing as a prisoner about to be condemned and executed, the use of these titles takes on new meaning. Jesus is the Christ or Messiah, God's royal son who comes to liberate Israel; but he is not a liberator or monarch in the usual triumphant mode one might expect. Jesus liberates not through dominating power but by giving his life for others (see the key text of 10:45, p. 1421). Jesus truly is the Son of God, but the God he reveals is not an exalted potentate but a God revealed in the apparent "weakness" of a life totally committed to others.

In the perspective of Mark's Gospel, the Passion provides the right context for understanding who Jesus is. (See a similar conviction in Paul's 1 Cor 1: 18–31.)

The Empty Tomb (16:1–8)

Although brief, this concluding scene of the Gospel proclaims a substantial message. An author later than Mark added a longer ending, but this story of the empty tomb was probably the original conclusion to Mark's story (see the discussion in the notes to 16:1–8).

Jesus' Victory over Death. The fundamental message of the passage is that the crucified Jesus is triumphant over death. That is the powerful symbolism of an empty tomb and the explicit message of the mysterious "young man" the women discover there: "You seek Jesus of Nazareth, the crucified. He has been raised; he is not here" (16:6). Without this assurance Mark's story would not be "gospel"—good news.

Reconciliation with the Disciples. This scene also picks up the story of the absent disciples. The women are instructed: "But go and tell his disciples and Peter, 'He is going before you to Galilee; there you will see him, as he told you' " (16:7). Even though the disciples had deserted and denied Jesus, the Risen Christ does not abandon them. He had promised that at the Last Supper: "after I am raised up I shall go before you to Galilee" (14:28). Now, that promised reconciliation is about to take place. In a very true sense, the disciples had "died" during the Passion; they, too, would experience resurrection to a new life of discipleship.

Back to Galilee: The Mission Begins. The disciples will "see" Jesus in Galilee, the place where Jesus had carried out his universal mission of healing and teaching, and the place where he had first called his followers to be with him and to share in his ministry. What precise meeting with Jesus does Mark have in mind—resurrection appearances? Or the final meeting with the Risen Christ at the end of the world? Or does he mean that the Risen Jesus would be with his disciples as they take up their mission? Mark leaves the question unanswered and perhaps has all of these encounters in mind.

The Gospel ends on a note of awe; the women leave the tomb, trembling and bewildered, struck silent by the awesome message entrusted to them (16:8). Some interpreters understand their silence as another instance of discipleship failure; the message given them is never delivered because of paralyzing fear. But it is unlikely Mark wants to suggest that the women never told the disciples about the empty tomb. The notes of awe and silence and fear are Mark's way of expressing profound reverence for the events he narrates. In Jesus' victory over death, God's power has transformed the world forever.

D.S.

FURTHER READING

Donahue, John, S.J., and Daniel J. Harrington, S.J. *The Gospel of Mark.* Sacra Pagina. Collegeville, MN: Liturgical Press, 2002.

Moloney, Francis J. *The Gospel of Mark: A Commentary.* Peabody: Hendrickson, 2002.

Reiser, William. *Jesus in Solidarity With His People: A Theologian Looks at Mark.* Collegeville, MN: Liturgical Press, 2000.

Senior, Donald. *The Death of Jesus in the Gospel of Mark.* Passion Series 2. Wilmington, DE: Michael Glazier, 1984.

LUKE

[see pages 1433–1485 of the New Testament]

Before Beginning . . .

Luke tells us that he was not an eyewitness to the events of Jesus' ministry. He is dependent upon others who have already put the testimony of such witnesses in narrative form (1:2). Scholars have identified three of the sources that Luke used: Mark's Gospel; a collection of Jesus' sayings that was also used by Matthew, called *Q;* and a source for additional material about Jesus, which scholars designate *L* (see *New American Bible,* introduction, p. 1434). Luke seems to preserve the order of sayings in his written source rather than shifting them to new discourse units as in Matthew. The introduction suggests that Luke is a second- or third-generation Christian looking back on the founding years of the movement. Luke's ability to write in different styles—including that of the Septuagint, the Greek translation of the Hebrew Scriptures, which was the Bible for most of the early Christian communities—and to use conventions of Hellenistic literature, such as the opening dedication to a prominent patron, suggest a well-educated author. To have received a literary education of this sort, Luke probably came from a prosperous urban family. Unlike the other Gospel writers, Luke's account did not end with the Gospel. He wrote a second volume, Acts, which showed that God's salvation, begun in Jesus, moved beyond Jerusalem and the pious of Israel into the whole world.

Luke's Gospel provides an account of Jesus' life and teaching for that universal mission. Today, people sometimes think that Christianity and its Gospels belong to North American and European culture. They wonder whether Christians can spread the message to people in other cultures without destroying those cultures. We need to remember that the story of Jesus originated in a Semitic culture. Luke and other early Christians were already engaged in intercultural dialogue when they retold the story of Jesus for the Greek-speaking, non-Jewish converts who inhabited cities in the eastern part of the Roman empire. Their example shows that the gospel message is not limited to any one culture. The story of Jesus belongs to all peoples.

An Assured Teaching

Luke's desire to establish Christianity within the larger world of the Roman empire is evident in references to Roman emperors and events. For example, he links the birth of Jesus to Caesar Augustus (2:1). People have sometimes thought that Luke was attempting to write what we would call a history of Jesus and the earliest disciples. Most of the "historical" references, however, are not accurate even by ancient standards. Luke calls his work a *diegesis,* meaning a "narrative account," not a history. He claims that it is thorough, accurate, and orderly. He has traced the events that have occurred among "us" (that is, the Christian community) from the beginning (1:1–4). The purpose of his writing is to provide *asphaleia,* "assurance" for the instruction that Christians give. In other words, Luke's book will show that what the church preaches is rooted in the ministry of Jesus and the preaching of the first apostles.

Luke takes patterns for his story from biblical history. This literary device is especially evident in the infancy narratives, which show God's promises of salvation being fulfilled in Jesus. When Luke claims that his narrative is "orderly," he refers to the literary order, which sets out the periods of salvation. Luke also provides assurance for the Christian preaching by showing that the Spirit of God has guided the whole process from the earliest days of Israel through the ministry of Jesus. In the second volume, Acts, he shows the same Spirit at work in the developments in the early community. Civic authorities were suspicious of new religious movements. Luke's work addresses those fears by highlighting the high moral standards and social value of Christianity.

An Ordered Narrative

Luke has told us that he is dependent upon earlier accounts but that he has reworked his material to provide a more accurate and orderly account. We have seen that accuracy and order do not refer to historical inquiry but to Luke's desire to set forth the way in which God's plan of salvation is fulfilled in the Christian movement. Scholars have made detailed studies of additions, deletions, and changes that Luke has made in the order of material taken over from Mark. There are three major additions that even the beginning Gospel reader can spot. Mark begins abruptly with the appearance of John the Baptist. Luke (as does Matthew) begins with an account of Jesus' birth (1: 5–2:40). He adds a tale about the child Jesus (2:41–52). Then, between the baptism and temptation stories, Luke reintroduces Jesus by giving his genealogy (3:23–38). A long section in which Jesus is journeying toward Jerusalem with the disciples (9:51–19:27) contains much of the teaching of Jesus. It includes parables that Luke has taken from Q (and from his special tradition) and retold in a way that serves as instruction for the church. By contrast, Mark's Gospel has only a short section of instruction to the disciples on the trip to Jerusalem.

Finally, you will notice several differences in the Passion and the Resurrection materials. Mark ends with the women running from the empty tomb. Luke 24, on the other hand, has accounts of appearances by the Risen Lord as well as instructions to the disciples. Luke's Passion narrative differs from Mark (and Matthew) as well. Jesus is never formally tried by the Jewish court. There is an unusual episode in which Pilate sends Jesus to be investigated by Herod (23:6–12). Pilate persists in declaring that Jesus is innocent of the charges against him (23:4,14f, 22). The dying Jesus prays for forgiveness for his enemies (23:34) and enacts the message of the gospel by promising salvation to a repentant criminal who dies with him (23:39–43).

Each of these sections contributes to our sense that God's plan of salvation is being carried out. The infancy narratives recapitulate the hopes of the faithful people of Israel. As Jesus begins the journey to Jerusalem, he knows that he is to be taken up from there in death (9:51). This journey is a time to prepare the disciples both for the events in Jerusalem and for their future role as witnesses to Jesus' teaching. In the narrative of Jesus' death and resurrection, Luke emphasizes the fact that it "was necessary"—that is, part of God's plan already set out in the Prophets—for the Messiah to suffer and die in Jerusalem (see 22:22; 24:26f). The episode with the repentant criminal shows that the death of Jesus extends salvation and forgiveness to others.

The Tragedy of Israel

Luke's strong narrative sense of a divine plan moving toward its fulfillment often dominates our imagination as we read Luke-Acts. If we allow this sense of divine purpose to lull us into accepting as good or necessary all the events through which God's plan is achieved, then we will miss another component in Luke's story—the tragedy of Israel. The infancy stories awaken the joyful expectation that Israel's messianic king has arrived to bring salvation. Through him, God's peace and blessings will come to both Jews and Gentiles (2:29–32). Yet, as the story unfolds, this promise will not be fulfilled.

Persistent rejection, first of Jesus and then of the disciples' mission, leaves Israel excluded. Luke points out the tragedy of this situation in a series of prophetic laments that Jesus utters over Jerusalem and her inhabitants. The first is a Q tradition (13:34f; Mt 23:37–39), which Luke has attached to an episode from his special tradition (13:31–33). The episode contained a warning that Herod was seeking Jesus' life. Jesus connects the divine necessity that he die in Jerusalem (13:33) with a lament for the city. The second, from Luke's special tradition, occurs as Jesus is looking out over the city where he is to die (19:41–44). Jesus weeps at the thought of the peace that will elude the city and the terrible devastations of war that she is to suffer. The final lament, also from L, occurs as Jesus is on the way to his death. He looks out at the weeping women of Jerusalem and warns them to weep for themselves instead (23:27–31).

The church has constantly reminded Catholics that, even though the ancestors of today's Jews chose not to accept Jesus as Messiah, Christians cannot reject or persecute Jews. She has also insisted that Christians share a common heritage with the Jewish people that is rooted in the Hebrew Scriptures. Luke's narrative insists that the heritage of the Christian movement lies in the faithful and just persons of Israel. Jesus' own family are among the righteous ones who trust in God for salvation. Though Luke's Passion narrative holds certain Jewish leaders responsible for some of the events, Jesus does not condemn them but asks God's forgiveness. Luke also presents us with a Jesus who is able to weep as he foresees the terrible fate of Jerusalem. The prosperous and beautiful city of his day will be reduced to the rubble of war. She will not enjoy the peace that God so longs to give the people.

Reading through Luke

Before you sit down to study Luke, read through the whole Gospel. Many of the stories will be familiar to you, since Luke contains some of the best-loved stories in the Gospels. You will notice that Luke is a gifted storyteller. Even in the parables of Jesus, he creates short episodes and switches from the third-person report into dialogue between the characters. Young children often enjoy the stories in Luke more than those in the other Gospels. As you are reading, you might note passages that particularly appeal to you. Do you find any common themes in those stories? Here are some of the themes that you will find running through the Gospel.

Salvation Is a Joyous Surprise

You will soon notice that Luke has many images of celebration and rejoicing. From the very beginning of the story to the very last verse, people are praising and thanking God for the salvation that they experience in Jesus. Salvation is a "surprise" or gift because those who receive it could never have anticipated that it would come. Mary's *Magnificat* (1:46–55) sets the tone. God has come and rescued the humble, poor, oppressed, and lowly people of the land. Jesus begins his ministry (4:18) by quoting a promise from Isaiah: a threefold release from poverty, from sickness, and from sin. Luke drives home this point about salvation by showing that Jesus has the power to forgive sins and to heal people (see 5:17–26). Even the rich tax collector Zacchaeus hears the message, demonstrates his repentance by making restitution to those he had cheated, and expresses his joy by throwing a banquet (19:1–10).

God's mercy is the source of this salvation. Christians are to show mercy in the same way that God is merciful (6:36). When Jesus gives examples of what God's mercy and forgiveness are like, he uses very active images. God is not waiting for people to come crawling back, begging forgiveness. God is out looking for people to help like the shepherd and the lost sheep, the woman and the lost coin, or the wayward son's father, who goes running out of the house and immediately orders a large celebration (see 15:3–32). The elder brother in the story of the Prodigal Son shows us the other side of the coin. Jesus recognizes that some people find it difficult to accept this open-handed offer of forgiveness to sinners, when they themselves have struggled all their lives to do everything that they are required to do and have never even had a banquet to celebrate.

Salvation Includes Everyone

In Acts, Luke will show us that God directed the disciples to take the gospel to all the peoples of the earth. The Gospel demonstrates the universality of God's love and salvation in a different way. It stresses the fact that Jesus reached out to all sorts of people, even to those who seemed to have no chance at salvation. Zacchaeus, the tax collector, was a sinner who had defrauded people to enrich himself (19:1–10). The Samaritans, traditional enemies of the Jews, turn out to be examples of Jesus' teaching. The mercy shown by the Good Samaritan (10:37) is so well known that we can speak of anyone who shows mercy or unmerited assistance to another as a "Samaritan." Less well known is the Samaritan leper (17:12–19) who is the only one of the group healed by Jesus to return and give him thanks. Women—often excluded from higher education, public leadership, and cultural events in antiquity—are constantly included in Jesus' ministry. A sinful woman provides a better demonstration of love and hospitality than the Pharisee. Her sins are forgiven (7:31–50). Mary is permitted to sit and listen to Jesus as a disciple. She does not have to busy herself with the traditional woman's business of serving the male guests that has her sister so distracted (10:38–42).

Today, many women experience the tension between Martha and Mary in their own lives. On the one hand, they are anxious to participate in opportunities for education, careers, and involvement with the community outside the home. On the other hand, they are still responsible for most of the work and caregiving that goes on within the home. Some women who are financially able to devote themselves to homemaking and volunteer community activities on a full-time basis report that they feel "looked down on" because they do not have a paying job. When Jesus defended Mary's place as listening to his teaching, he was not condemning Martha's devotion to serving her guests or the traditional tasks of women in the home. Jesus was really issuing an invitation to her to join her sister. Martha was so busy that she was missing the one necessary thing, to hear Jesus' message about the Kingdom (10:41f). As our lives continue to fill up with activities at home, work, and in the community, we need to ask whether we are shoving out the time we need for the one necessary thing, hearing the word of the Lord.

Special Concern for Those in Need

We have already seen that salvation has very concrete aspects in Luke. Those who are poor, helpless, in prison, sick, and the like are promised release. Jesus and the apostles are able to relieve the suffering of the sick by healing. Acts contains many stories in which God intervenes to free the apostles from prison. To achieve this goal, however, miraculous events are not required. The story of the Good Samaritan (10:25–37) shows how this salvation can come about through concrete actions. The Samaritan uses his own resources to see that the man beaten up by robbers is restored to health, even though, as a Jew, the victim is his enemy. The parable of the Great Supper, in which the host replaces with the poor the friends who refused to come, and the sayings about showing aid to those who cannot repay (14:12–24) are other examples of how salvation can come to those in need.

You may have noticed in reading through Luke how often it returns to the theme of rich and poor. The rich often fail to receive salvation because they are trapped by their own desires for money or pleasure (see 12:13–21; 16:19–30). Even those who are good people like the Rich Ruler (18:18–24) are so locked in by possessions that they cannot achieve the eternal life they desire. That does not mean that Luke thinks all rich people are excluded from the Kingdom. The Samaritan, Zacchaeus, and anyone else who is willing to share his or her wealth generously with those who are in need can become a disciple of Jesus. Acts will return to this theme in its picture of sharing possessions in the early community. Luke also retains the sayings of Jesus that call upon followers to renounce material goods in order to become disciples (6:35; 9:3; 10:4; 12:33; 14:33; 16:13). By doing so, Jesus, and later the apostles, demonstrate that they are completely dedicated to God. But Luke knows that such discipleship is possible only if the basic needs of the group are met through the generosity of others. He reports that a group of women followers provided the necessary support (8:1–3). In Acts, he reports that Paul achieved the same end by laboring at his trade (Acts 20:33–35).

Mary Is the First Disciple

Catholic Christians have always paid special honor to Mary, the mother of Jesus. Since much of the elaborate Marian piety of the church did not develop until medieval times, people sometimes feel that Mary has been left out in the biblical renewal. Luke's Gospel provides the basis for the devotion that we show to Mary. Her assent to God's work of salvation initiates the whole story. Her *Magnificat* is a strong affirmation of God's faithfulness and mercy. Sometimes people think that we honor Mary simply because she experienced a miracle in Jesus' birth. That is not Luke's picture. For Luke she is both the epitome of the faithful people of Israel who wait confidently for God's salvation, and the beginning of the new life of those who will be disciples of Jesus. Jesus defines her role in 8:21. She is one who hears and does the word of God. He repeats this affirmation in 11:27f. The crowd praises Jesus' biological mother. Jesus corrects them by insisting that hearing and keeping the word of God constitutes the true source of blessing.

The infancy narrative demonstrates that Mary has this quality of true discipleship. She has accepted God's will in the Annunciation scene. Later she keeps in her heart words spoken to her about Jesus, as well as the extraordinary events that she witnesses (2:19, 51). Simeon includes her in his oracle about the impact of Jesus' ministry in Israel (2:34f). She too will be caught in the divisions to come. But Mary remains among the faithful disciples of Jesus. She was present among those disciples gathered in Jerusalem after the Resurrection (Acts 1:14).

An Outline of Luke

Luke's Gospel falls into a neat pattern that moves from the infancy narrative, in which we are among the righteous of Israel in Jerusalem, through the ministry in Galilee, back to the Jerusalem Temple, and finally to Jesus' death and resurrection. The Gospel leaves us with the disciples in Jerusalem awaiting the coming of the Spirit. Acts will take the Gospel from Jerusalem out into the world. Jerusalem forms a symbolic center to the Gospel, as much of the narrative takes place either in or on the way to the holy city. The major divisions in the story are clearly marked transitions in the unfolding of the plot:

- Prologue (1:1–4)
- Infancy Narrative (1:5–2:52)
- Preparation for the Public Ministry (3:1–4:13)
- The Ministry in Galilee (4:14–9:50)
- The Journey to Jerusalem (9:51–19:27)
- Teaching Ministry in Jerusalem (19:28–21:38)
- The Passion Narrative (22:1–23:56)
- The Resurrection Narrative (24:1–53)

Now it is time to read through Luke in detail. We will be looking to see how Luke develops a picture of Jesus, salvation, and Christian discipleship. Since Luke preserves important blocks of the teaching of Jesus, we will also be interested in how Luke presents the teaching of Jesus for Christians in his time. Discipleship requires doing the word as well as hearing it.

Prologue (1:1–4)

Luke introduces his Gospel with a prologue, because he considers that his work belongs alongside other Hellenistic literature. The prologue consists of a single complex Greek sentence that ends with the word *asphaleia,* "assurance." Luke intends the orderly account of the events that constitute the Christian story of salvation to demonstrate the integrity of the Christian message that the church in his day proclaims. (A close parallel for this use of *kathexes,* "orderly," appears in Acts 11:4. Peter is going to narrate the events that led him to baptize the Gentile Cornelius and his household and to share table fellowship with them. This account will persuade the leaders of the church in Jerusalem that God was operating behind those events.)

The Infancy Narrative (1:5–2:52)

Structure of the Lucan Infancy Narrative

This section is built on an elaborate parallelism between Jesus and John the Baptist. In each case, Jesus is greater than the Baptist, who is only the forerunner of the Messiah. The most detailed parallels occur between the two angelic birth announcements (John, 1:5–25; Jesus, 1:26–38): (a) neither parent is expecting a child; (b) an angel appears, the parent is troubled and told not to fear; (c) the child is announced, his name given, and a statement is made about his future greatness; (d) the parent raises a question about how this can happen; (e) the angel gives an assertion that it will happen, and a sign; (f) Zechariah is forced to be silent; Mary's spontaneous answer affirms God's will. The birth announcements are followed by an episode that brings the two together and confirms the angel's statement to Mary, the Visitation (1:39–56). In this episode the Baptist testifies to the presence of Jesus as savior by moving in the womb.

The next cycle recounts the births (John, 1:57f; Jesus, 2:1–20) and circumcision/naming of the two children (John, 1:57–80; Jesus, 2:21–40). Each birth section includes an affirmation of the joy attending the birth. Each naming section concludes with an affirmation that the child grew. This cycle is followed by an episode that prefigures Jesus' last days, the Finding in the Temple (2:41–52). Jesus will return to the Temple to teach before his death (see the outline of the Gospel). The narratives make it clear that God is responsible for the origins of both children. For the Baptist, God has overcome the barrenness of his parents, just as other barren women in the Hebrew Bible, like Sarah and Hannah, had been given children. For Jesus, God has done something even greater by bringing the child into existence in the womb of his virgin mother.

Songs of Salvation: The Canticles

These episodes contain several canticles, which have become a treasured part of Christian worship: Mary's *Magnificat* (1:46–55); Zechariah's *Benedictus* (1:68–79); the canticle of the angels (2:13f); Simeon's *Nunc Dimittis* (2:29–32). Many scholars think that Luke has taken the *Magnificat,* the *Benedictus,* and perhaps the *Nunc Dimittis* from a Jewish Christian source. They employ a mosaic of expressions taken from the Hebrew Bible and other Jewish psalms and hymns from the time of Jesus. Mary's *Magnificat* is an individual song of praise, which seems to be modeled on the Song of Hannah (1 Sm 2: 1–10). After celebrating God's greatness toward the lowly handmaid, the second strophe (vv. 51–53), in a series of strong, active verbs, alludes to God's past deeds of salvation. The final verses (54f) relate the career of Jesus to the covenant God had made with Abraham. Scholars think that this hymn originated among Jewish Christians who identified themselves with the "poor ones," the *anawim,* of Israel. The term designated those who were unfortunate, lowly, sick, downtrodden. The rich and powerful, those who feel no need of God, are opposed to the *anawim* (see Ps 149:4; Is 49:13; 66:2). The poor ones are the righteous remnant in Israel who know that they must look to God for salvation.

The *Benedictus* begins as a song of thanksgiving (vv. 71–75) recalling the dynastic oracle concerning the house of David (see 2 Sm 7:12f). The hymn affirms that Jesus will fulfill this messianic role. It then shifts to the form of an oracle concerning the destiny of the newborn child (vv. 76–79). The Baptist will prepare God's people for the coming Messiah. We are reminded that God comes to save the people out of merciful compassion. Luke will make the theme of mercy a central motif in the ministry of Jesus.

The *Nunc Dimittis* draws upon two passages of Isaiah (Is 40:5; 49:6). Simeon has now seen the salvation which they promised. The image of an aged patriarch blessed with a glimpse of God's promise is rooted in the Hebrew Bible (see Joseph, Gn 46:30; Moses, Dt 32:49–50; 34:1–5; Anna and Tobit, Tb 11:9, 14). Verses 31–32 point to another important theme in Luke: God's salvation is given for all peoples. Endowed with the prophetic spirit, the aged Simeon not only recognizes the dawning of salvation, he also warns that Jesus' coming will bring about divisions. God's plan includes the rejection of the Messiah by his own people (see 4:29; 13:33–35; 19: 44, 47f; 20:14, 17).

Virgin Birth and Christology in the Infancy Narrative

We have already seen that the canticles celebrate Jesus' coming as the fulfillment of all God's promises to the faithful people of Israel. The *Benedictus* pointed to Jesus as the anticipated Messiah of the Davidic house. The most striking Christological statements in the infancy narrative occur in the angelic birth announcement (1: 28–37). The announcement proceeds in two stages. Verses 32f parallel 2 Sm 7:9,13,14,16. Jesus will inherit the Davidic throne and rule over Jacob's house forever as "son" of God. The second stage in the announcement moves beyond these messianic promises to the special sense in which Jesus is Son of God: Jesus is begotten through God's intervention. Some scholars suggest that Luke has created this two-step process from older Christological affirmations like Romans 1:3f. There, Jesus is "Son of David" during his earthly life and is designated "Son of God" through the power of the Holy Spirit when he is exalted to God's right hand at the Resurrection. The announcement to Mary speaks of God's Spirit overshadowing her and bringing into being a child who is Son of God from the time he is conceived. For Luke, Jesus is fully human but is never just another ordinary human being.

Mary's virginity serves to sharpen the Christological focus: the child to be born is God's Son. The step-parallelism between the Baptist and Jesus provides additional literary evidence that Luke considers the birth of Jesus to be an even greater example of divine power than that of the

Baptist. Mary is not like the barren woman, someone whose womb could unexpectedly open and produce a child. As a virgin, there is no human way for her to have a child without God's unique presence in that process. Ancient Greek biology taught that the spirit in a father's sperm gave shape to the material in a mother's womb. The more active the spirit, the more closely a child resembled its father. Thus Mary's virginity indicates a relationship between Jesus and God unlike that of any other human being. The honor that Mary enjoys is not due to the fact of her virginity but to her willingness to accept a role in God's plan for the salvation of humanity.

A second angelic announcement, that of the angels to the shepherds, accompanies the story of Jesus' birth (2:1–20). Luke introduces this section with a reference to Caesar Augustus and the expansion of Roman rule indicated by the census. Historically, there was no worldwide census under Quirinius. When the Romans took over administration of Judea in AD 6, they took a census of that province. Residents of Galilee, which was still ruled by one of Herod's sons, would not have been obligated to return to an ancestral village in Judea. Matthean tradition claims that Jesus was born toward the end of the rule of Herod, the Great, who died in 4 BC. Though Luke lacks precise historical information in this scene, its Roman associations permit a symbolic contrast. Augustus emphasized the fact that his rule had brought peace in the world. The doors to the temple of war, pictured on coins, were shown closed. Luke uses the angelic announcement (2:10–14) to show that the true source of peace lies elsewhere: in the Savior, Messiah, the Lord who has been born in the Davidic town, Bethlehem.

Preparation for the Public Ministry (3:1–4:13)

Many of the themes in the ministry of Jesus have been anticipated in the infancy narratives. We have seen that Jesus fulfills God's promises of salvation, and we have heard some of the major Christological titles: Son of David, Messiah, Savior, Lord, and Son of God. The Spirit, which overshadowed Mary at his conception, will remain with Jesus throughout the ministry. Mary's *Magnificat* introduced the images for salvation as "reversal," a lifting up of the poor ones, those who have no one but God to turn to in their need. We have seen the importance of thanksgiving, rejoicing, and prayer as well as the posture of the faithful disciple who hears the word of God. But we have also heard the warning that all of Israel will not rush to greet its Messiah with the same joy found in these stories. Before Luke begins to recount the public ministry, he introduces three additional blocks of material: (a) the Baptist's mission in preparing the way for Jesus and Jesus' baptism; (b) a genealogy, and (c) the temptation of Jesus.

The Baptist's Ministry (3:1–22)

Luke has gathered together traditions about John the Baptist from different sources. John is fulfilling the mission given him to serve as forerunner for God's Messiah. Luke has arranged his account so that the fiery preacher of repentance also serves as precursor to Jesus in the content of his message: (a) repentance and forgiveness, two of the effects of salvation in Luke, and (b) the requirements for dealing with material possessions: share with those who have nothing, avoid greed and injury to others, act fairly. The ethical section of John's preaching (vv. 10–14) illustrates the "good fruit," which must come from repentance (v. 9). When we bear in mind the whole sweep of salvation history in Luke, the warning that God can raise up children of Abraham from the stones takes on a more ominous note. As the episode comes to a conclusion, the Baptist responds to speculation about his own status by separating himself clearly from the Messiah who is about to come with the Spirit and fire. John belongs to the age of prophetic figures. Jesus will inaugurate the messianic age. Luke then completes the story of the Baptist by reporting the fact that John was imprisoned by Herod Antipas before Jesus appears on the scene. This order creates some chaos in the account of Jesus' baptism, which follows it (vv. 21f). For Luke, the baptism of Jesus can never suggest that Jesus was dependent upon the Baptist. Rather, the episode permits a divine affirmation that Jesus is son of God and provides the occasion for the Spirit to descend on Jesus and inaugurate his ministry.

Genealogy of Jesus (3:23–38)

This unusual genealogy corrects a misapprehension about Jesus. People may think he is the son of Joseph. The Christian community knows better. It traces Jesus' ancestry back to the first "son of God," Adam, and thus links Jesus to the entire human race, not just to the house of David.

Temptation of Jesus (4:1–13)

Jesus goes to the desert under the impulse of the Spirit. The temptations Satan poses are challenges to Jesus' identity as "Son of God," which has been the central title in Luke's narrative to this point. Temptation, in this sense, is not an impulse toward some sinful act. Rather, as in the testing of Abraham by the demand that he sacrifice Isaac, temptation puts the person before a crisis that will demonstrate whether the individual's faith in God can be destroyed. Jesus refuses to use his status as Son for personal gain. Though Satan is silenced, the story ends on an ominous note; though Jesus' ministry will undermine demonic power (10:18; 13:16), Satan may yet return. In Luke 22:31f Jesus speaks of a confrontation with Satan on behalf of his disciples; though they will be seriously tested by the events of the Passion, Jesus has prayed that their faith will not fail. When the temptations are finished, Jesus has demonstrated that he is the obedient Son of God who will carry out God's plan of salvation—whatever the cost.

The Ministry in Galilee (4:14–9:50)

The introduction to this section (4:14f) highlights the power of the Spirit active in the ministry of Jesus (1:35; 3:22; 4:1, 14, 18).

In Nazareth and Capernaum (4:16–44)

Luke's sources had Jesus' ministry begin in Capernaum (see Mk 1:21–35). Luke has reordered events (v. 23 refers to the Capernaum tradition) to open with a sermon in Nazareth that depicts Jesus as the one who fulfills what the Hebrew prophets foretold (vv. 17–21). Throughout Luke-Acts, programmatic announcements occur in synagogues and at the Temple. Jesus announces the joyous freedom of the Year of Jubilee (combining Is 61:1–11 and Is 58:6). Luke's genealogy has prepared readers for the skepticism attributed to those who think that Jesus cannot possibly be the messiah, since he was considered to be Joseph's son (3:23; 4:22). Once again, Luke previews the story yet to come. Jesus points to Hebrew prophets Elijah and Elisha, who were directed to assist persons who were not Israelites. These words provoke a deadly hostility in the hearers (vv. 25–30).

The rest of the chapter consists of healing stories that illustrate the liberation Jesus has just announced. The demons acknowledge that Jesus is "from God." However, the popular acclaim, which results from the miracles, makes it so difficult for Jesus even to move about that he leaves for synagogues in Judea (vv. 42–44).

Jesus Gathers Disciples (5:1–39)

Jesus' activities in Nazareth and Capernaum come before he has any disciples. This arrangement provides those who are called with some reason for following Jesus. By the time he gathers his first disciples, Jesus already has a reputation as healer and teacher. Simon Peter's call to follow Jesus is linked with a tale of a miraculous catch of fish. Peter's acknowledgment that he is a "sinner" would make the ancient reader think of stories like those in Homer that he or she heard at school. Mortals cannot see the gods, but certain events make their presence evident. So Peter, viewing the catch, announces that he is unworthy to be in the presence of the divine (v. 8). Peter's reaction to the catch is also similar to the "fear" exhibited at the appearance of the angels in the birth announcement stories. Like the angel, Jesus first tells Peter not to be afraid. Then he states what Peter's future destiny is to be: "from now on you will be catching men" (v. 10). The Christian reader knows of Peter's role as missionary apostle in Acts. Peter and the sons of Zebedee, James and John, respond as exemplary disciples. They will leave everything to follow Jesus.

Jesus continues to establish his authority through healings, first of a leper (vv. 12–16), then of a paralyzed man (vv. 17–26). When Luke took over the account of the healing of the paralyzed man, it was already a controversy story over Jesus' authority to forgive sins (see Mk 2:1–12). The reader already knows that Jesus has the power to heal anyone he wishes. In this case, the miracle becomes both an occasion to free the man from sin through forgiveness *and* a demonstration of the authority by which Jesus can claim that the man's sins have been forgiven. Its introduction (v. 17) recalls the boy Jesus in the Temple (2:46–47): there are Pharisees and scribes gathered from the villages of Galilee and Judea as well as Jerusalem. The crowd goes home praising God, but the Pharisees and scribes have become suspicious of Jesus. His offer of forgiveness appears to be a blasphemous attempt by a human being to seize a power that belongs to God (v. 21). Luke's reader knows that Jesus is not just any human being but the obedient Son of God. Jesus would never seize any power that rightly belongs to God (see 4:5–8).

As Jesus calls his next disciple, the toll collector Levi, he incurs further complaints from the Pharisees and scribes. They go to Jesus' disciples to ask why he eats with persons who are considered sinners. Jesus first cites a proverb in defense of his actions and then insists that the goal of his mission is to call sinners. He is not out to preach to the righteous.

Jesus is accused of not instructing his disciples in piety as a true teacher would do. The disciples of both the Baptist and the Pharisees fast. Jesus' disciples do not. Jesus' defense consists of a brief parable and a string of proverbs (5:33–39). The first employs a human analogy: it is impossible to fast at a wedding. The abundance of the wedding feast was also a common metaphor for the time of salvation. When Jesus is no longer present, Christians will fast (v. 35). The proverbs demonstrate the absurdity of trying to mix the old ways of life with the new time of salvation. Persons accustomed to the old may find it difficult to accept the new (v. 39).

Jesus then defends his disciples against charges of breaking the Sabbath (6:1–5), first by appeal to Scripture (1 Sm 21:1–6), then by insistence upon his authority as Son of Man (compare 5:24), and finally on humanitarian grounds: it is always right to preserve rather than destroy life (vv. 6–11). The section concludes with the choice of the Twelve from the larger group of disciples who will share Jesus' mission and serve as witnesses to what Jesus has done and said.

Sermon on the Plain (6:17–49)

Jesus' first major sermon sounds familiar notes of reversal from the *Magnificat* as well as the opening of his ministry (4:18). The Kingdom is good news for the poor and oppressed, and divine judgment against the wealthy and prosperous. As the stories of Christian missionaries in Acts will demonstrate, Christians must expect rejection and persecution for preaching about Jesus (see Acts 7:52). Juxtaposing the command to love enemies with sayings on persecution provides a concrete context in which that love is to be practiced (vv. 27–30). The love command covers all forms of mercy since it is to be modeled on the mercy of God. Examples point to general ethical precepts: give to one who asks; lend to those who cannot repay; treat others as you would be treated. Judgment sayings strengthen this ethical teaching. We are judged by the judgments we make about others (vv. 37–42).

Jesus Is the Promised Savior (7:1–9:18)

Jesus' ministry in Galilee continues with a series of traditional miracle stories told so that they testify to Jesus' identity: (a) cure of the centurion's slave indicates that there is greater faith among the Gentiles than in Israel (7:9); (b) the widow's son evokes the allusions to Elijah and Elisha in the opening sermon (4:25f); awestruck, the people acknowledge that a great prophet has arisen (7:16). Further miracles demonstrate the truth of Jesus' reply to the Baptist's disciples, that he is indeed the one to come (vv. 18–23). Luke edits his sources to draw a distinction between those who received John's baptism and also receive Jesus with praise, and those who reject the plan of God—the lawyers and Pharisees (vv. 28–30). The call of Levi (5:27–32) illustrated the conversion of tax collectors. This contrast prepares the reader for the sharp contrast between the Pharisee Simon, who failed to show Jesus the hospitality due an honored guest, and the sinful woman, who anoints Jesus and whose sins are forgiven (7, 36–50). The parable of the Pharisee and the tax collector makes a similar point (18:9–14).

Examples of women who followed Jesus (8:1–3) and Jesus' mother as model disciple, one who hears and keeps the word of God (8:19–21), frame the instruction about discipleship provided by the parable of the sower (8:4–15), the lamp (8:16–17), and a general warning to be careful how one hears the word (v. 18). The interpretation of the sower parable indicates the threats to discipleship: (a) some will not believe the initial preaching; (b) some will be turned from discipleship by temptation, cares, riches, and pleasure; and (c) still others will lack the patient endurance necessary to bring forth the harvest.

Another series of miracles emphasizes Jesus' power to save. The disciples are rescued from the storm (8:22–25); the Gerasene saved from the multitude of demons that made it impossible for any human bonds to restrain him (vv. 26–37). The concluding instructions are pointed toward Christians as well: go and declare what God has done for you (vv. 38f). The healing of Jairus's daughter and the woman with the hemorrhage focus on the faith of the recipients (vv. 40–56). Jesus expands his mission of preaching and healing by sending out the Twelve (9:1–6). The brief notice about Herod's perplexity raises expectations about Jesus' true identity. If he is not the Baptist returned, then he must be like one of the great prophets of old such as Elijah (9:7–9). This section concludes with the feeding of the five thousand (9:13–17). As Luke shapes the story, this miracle represents food for the hungry (6:21) as well as a response to Satan's challenge to turn stones into bread (4:3f). Jesus does live by the word of God alone.

The Messiah Who Must Suffer (9:18–50)

None of the external opinions about Jesus' identity capture the truth that Jesus is the Messiah who must suffer. Luke applies this insight to the followers of Jesus by insisting that the disciple must be ready to take up the cross "daily" (9:23). Not only does God affirm Jesus' sonship at the Transfiguration (as in Mark 9:7), but Moses and Elijah also converse with Jesus about his coming departure from the world at Jerusalem (9:30f). Luke has omitted Markan material critical of the disciples from the Passion prediction (Mk 8:33), the Transfiguration (Mk 9:6), and the healing of an epileptic boy (Mk 9:28–29). In doing so, Luke brings the dramatic theophany of the Transfiguration into closer proximity with the predictions of the Passion. God prevents the disciples from understanding what Jesus has said to them. Their arguments over greatness and jealousy of a outsider who uses Jesus' name (9:46–50) show that they are not yet ready to follow Jesus in suffering.

The Journey to Jerusalem (9:51–19:27)

The journey to Jerusalem is the time of preparation for the disciples. Teachings of Jesus, especially extended narrative parables, dominate this section of the Gospel. Miracles underline Jesus' conflict with the Pharisee teachers over the merciful application of the Law (13:10–17; 14:1–6); they point to the virtues of faith and gratitude (shown by a Samaritan, 17:11–19), and they anticipate Jesus' triumphal entry into Jerusalem (18:35–43). We will pick out some of the key themes in this section.

Criticism of the Pharisee Opponents of Jesus

The shape of this criticism was anticipated by the story of the sinful woman in the house of a Pharisee (7:36–50). Luke sharpens the charges and also generalizes them to apply to Christians as well: (a) it is hypocritical to use the Law to condemn in one case what one's actions in another approve; applications of purity regulations demonstrate this principle (11:37–44); (b) lack of love of God leads to self-aggrandizement and even persecution of those sent by God (11:45–52). The Pharisees are persistently pictured as driven by love of money, desire for honor among others, and self-justification that stems from their application of the Law. The first two characteristics (16:14f) reappear in Acts as typical of magicians and false prophets in paganism (see Acts 8:9–25).

Luke is using the Pharisees as characters to warn Christians about dangers that they face. We should not take a superior attitude as though such failings only happen to persons who reject Jesus' teaching. Legalistic condemnation of one group for actions that our own practices tolerate in another context, such as racism or other forms of discrimination, cannot be acceptable Christian behavior. Nor can we claim to be Christians and yet spend our lives pursuing money, social status, and other forms of power over others.

Warnings about Judgment

Luke does not anticipate the return of Jesus in judgment in the immediate future. Consequently, warnings to be watchful apply to both Jesus' opponents and Luke's Christian readers. Jesus speaks prophetic woes against unrepentant cities (10:13–15). Demands for a sign only prove that there was more wisdom among Gentiles in the past than among God's people in the present (11:29–32). Hypocrisy can never be hidden from God's judgment (12:1–3). The stories of faithful and unfaithful servants warn against presuming that the delay in Jesus' return means that all restraints are removed (12:35–48). Although they can read the signs of the weather, Jesus' contemporaries are unable to see what is before them in Jesus (12:54–56). People must not fall into the false confidence born of the tragedies that happen to others. The fact that we have not suffered the disasters that happen to others does not mean that those who suffer are worse that we are, or that God is more pleased with us (13:1–5). The parable of the barren fig tree provides an alternate reading of the situation. It could be that we are like the tree being given its one last chance (13:6–9). The narrow door and shut door warn that Jesus' audience could be excluded and replaced with foreigners in the Kingdom (13: 22–30). Framing the parable of the servants entrusted with the master's wealth with the parable of the ruler who had gone into a distant country emphasizes the problem of discipleship in a time of delay (19:11–27). Delay need not mean the absence of the Kingdom. Luke preserves sayings that point out the presence of the Kingdom for Jesus' disciples as well as its sudden arrival (17:20–37). Luke expands the traditional saying about the coming of the Son of Man in judgment with another affirmation that the Son of Man must first suffer and be rejected by his own generation (17:25).

Discipleship: Renunciation, Devotion, and Suffering

The journey opens with sayings that warn would-be disciples that they must be completely devoted to the Kingdom (9:57–62). Such disciples renounce normal human ties to family. They are the ones sent to heal and to preach the approach of the Kingdom (10:9). Their words are equivalent to the words of Jesus (10:16). Luke 10:17–20 acknowledges the potential dangers that the disciples face. However, Satan's fall from heaven indicates that the mission is weakening evil's power over humanity. Stories of the apostles in Acts will illustrate the certainty of divine protection. Sayings against anxiety require the disciple to have confidence in the generosity of others (12:22–34). Luke's addition to the traditional saying—sell possessions, give alms, and so provide yourself with heavenly treasure (v. 22)—points to one way in which the material needs were met.

The church's economic teaching reminds Catholics that they have a moral obligation to work for a society that provides for the needs of its weakest members. The good news for the poor depends upon consistent efforts by all Christians to help those who are disadvantaged. Our social programs should not make such people feel despised or rejected. Jesus and the early church welcomed such people into the community in addition to providing food and clothing for them.

The Martha and Mary story (10:38–42) also illustrates a discipleship that abandons the cares of this world, even the obligations of hospitality, for the one thing necessary to salvation—hearing and keeping the word of Jesus (also see 11: 27–38).

Disciples must also expect division. Jesus' ministry brings division even within families (12:49–53; see also 2:34f). Jesus challenges disciples to recognize the full cost of being a disciple: both suffering and patient endurance to follow Jesus to the end are required (14:25–33). The slave can never tell the master, "I quit" (17: 7–10).

Discipleship and Material Possessions

Riches can be a major hurdle to becoming or remaining a disciple of Jesus (8:14; 18:18–25). Disciples have left everything to follow Jesus (18:26–30). Lucan parables demonstrate the folly of being possessed by wealth: the rich farmer dies before he can build his barns (12: 13–21), and the rich man who cannot see the poor Lazarus at his door is so blind to his sinful behavior that he thinks he can bargain even with Abraham from hell (16:19–31). Alongside the call for renouncing everything, Luke presents another way in which Christians can use material possessions: they can share them with the unfortunate as the Good Samaritan does (10:30–36). Instead of feasting with friends, they can provide for the poor, lame, homeless persons who have no resources (14:12–24). Luke presents the parable of the dishonest steward as a warning to Christians that they cannot mix service to God with the pursuit of wealth (16:1–13). The final episode in the travel narrative, the parable of the pounds (19:11–27) draws on a common experience in a world without instant communications, uncertainty about the fate or return of those on a journey. Luke recognizes that Jesus may not return in judgment for a long time. Disciples must remain faithful stewards of what God has given them.

Prayer in the Life of Disciples

The infancy narrative showed the exemplary piety of those righteous persons for whom the Messiah came. Jesus frequently turns to prayer (3:21; 6:12; 9:18, 28; 11:2; 22:32, 41; 23:46), and he instructs the disciples about prayer as a response to their request to be taught as the Baptist had taught his disciples (11:1; see also 5:33). Luke follows the Lord's Prayer (11:2–4) with the parable of the persistent friend (vv. 5–8) and instruction on the efficacy of prayer (vv. 9–13). The issue of efficacy returns in the parable of the importunate widow (18:1–6). If an unjust judge with no moral conscience can be badgered into hearing the widow, how much the more quickly will God respond to the pleas of the suffering lowly ones? After all, God is not withdrawn, waiting for humans to come begging, but is actively seeking those who are lost (see chapter 15).

Jesus' Teaching Ministry in Jerusalem (19:28–21:38)

Jesus' arrival in Jerusalem brings the narrative back to its beginning.

The Messiah Comes to City and Temple (19:28–48)

The Messiah who should have brought peace to Jerusalem will not be able to do so (19:41–44). Luke has revised the story of Jesus' entry (Mk 11:1–10) so that the crowd consists of followers testifying to the works Jesus has done in Galilee (v. 37). Jesus proceeds directly to the Temple so that the entry reflects the Greek version of Mal 3:1, "the Lord whom you seek shall suddenly come to his own temple." But Jesus has not come to set up the kingdom of David (19:11; Acts 1:4). The conclusion of the acclamation resembles the angelic announcement that peace is coming to God's faithful (2:14). Here, the city is the object of a prophetic lament—peace comes in the heavens, not on earth (v. 38). Allusion to Hb 2:11, the stones crying out from the walls against a nation that plunders the people (19:39f), heightens the narrative sense of a city about to meet its divine destiny. Jesus purges the Temple so that it can be a place of prayer as well as the location for Jesus' teaching in Jerusalem (19:45–48).

Jesus Teaches Daily in the Temple (20:1–21:4)

A traditional series of pronouncement stories (Mk 11:27–12:44) provides the content of Jesus' teaching now that he has returned to "his Father's house" (2:49).

The Authority For Jesus' Actions. Jesus responds with a counterquestion hinting that those who reject him do not believe the Baptist either. Compare Jesus' answer (20:8) with his response to the Council when they demand to know whether Jesus is Messiah (22:67). If Jesus speaks they do not believe; if Jesus asks a question they do not answer.

Wicked Tenants. Christians have traditionally read this parable as an allegory for the replacement of Israel as God's covenant people. Today we recognize that neither Jesus nor Luke think that a faithful God would give up on the Jewish people. Jesus directs this tale at his opponents. Luke has expanded the narrative with the owner's soliloquy and increasing violence against servants. Luke also adds an image of persons being crushed by the rejected stone (compare 2:34), which intensifies the judgmental overtones of the saying.

Tribute Due God and Caesar. Luke's addition of verse 20 intensifies the hostility implied in the question. Jesus' opponents are seeking evidence for charges of stirring up political rebellion to bring against Jesus at trial (see 23:2–5). The spies pose their malicious question under the guise of pious flattery. Jesus, they say, teaches the truth and exhibits a godlike impartiality toward persons. Again, Jesus responds with a counterquestion. He forces the opponents to acknowledge that they are carrying coins with Caesar's image and they utter Caesar's name. Jesus' reply serves as a judgment against their failure to pay God the honor due God. Readers know that Jesus' disciples have left coins and human positions of honor behind. They recognize that only God claims our loyalty. Thus, this passage does not teach the doctrine of separate powers of church and state that has traditionally been attached to it.

Resurrection of the Dead. The final challenge receives a double answer. The absurd case based on a hypothetical reading of levirate marriage (that is, that a man must marry his dead brother's wife if she had not yet borne children [see Dt 25: 5; Gn 38:8]) probably came from the debates between Sadducees and Pharisees over resurrection. Jesus' first answer affirms that the "children of God" (note the contrast with the woman who dies childless) are resurrected to an angelic existence. His second answer (20:37f) points to the revelation of God to Moses. If God is God of the patriarchs, they must be living.

Jesus Challenges the Opposition. Having silenced those who came to question him, Jesus poses challenges of his own. The question about how David's Son can be greater than his ancestor draws upon Psalm 110:1, a text frequently used in early Christianity to speak of Jesus' exaltation. The warning about the scribes (20:45–47) invokes the Lucan contrast between the wealthy and the oppressed poor. Jesus emerges as advocate for the poor. Finally, the comment on the widow's offering (21:1–4) repeats the contrast between a poor person and the wealthy. The radical gift of the widow condemns the abundance that stands behind the gifts of the rich. Jesus is not approving the poverty in which the widow lives, but he is asserting that her acts demonstrate a piety greater than that of the rich.

Fate of the Temple and the Coming End-Time (21:5–38)

The Jerusalem teaching ends with Luke's version of the apocalyptic sayings in Mark 13. He has recast the traditional material to support the view that the end-time is not about to come by separating the destruction of the Temple (21: 5–7) from events which signal the end-time.

Even traditional signs of the end, false messiahs and rebellions, do not point to an immediate second coming (vv. 8–11). They are part of a time of persecution. God protects the Christian who must face hostility or even death from Jews, Gentiles, and even family (21:12–19). The fall of Jerusalem does not lead to the end-time. Instead, it inaugurates a new stage in salvation history. Jerusalem will be overrun until the age of the pagans reaches its conclusion (21:20–24). After all these events the Son of Man will return in glory (21:25–28). The Christian who lives in the world between Jesus' ascent to heaven and the second coming can remain confident that Jesus' words will never pass away (21:29–33). Christians remain watchful and pray for strength to endure and appear before the Son of Man (21: 24–36).

The Passion Narrative (22:1–23:56a)

The Passion narrative is not a court record of what happened but a narrative shaped by the conviction that Jesus is the suffering Messiah, the obedient Son who has been raised by God. Apologetic motifs dominate Luke's version of the Passion. Political charges (23:2, 5, 18f) are false and recognized as such by Pilate, who declares Jesus innocent three times (vv. 4, 14f, 22). Pilate yields to pressure from Jewish leaders, to whom he hands over Jesus for crucifixion (23: 23–26).

Conspiracy to Kill Jesus (22:1–6)

Luke blames only certain Jewish leaders for the plot that costs Jesus his life (22:1–2). Acts 1: 16–20 reports a legend that divine retribution took the life of Jesus' betrayer, Judas.

The Last Supper (22:7–38)

Jesus is aware of the suffering he is about to undergo. It provides a symbolic interpretation of the cups of wine and bread at the Passover meal. A new covenant will be made in the death of Jesus. As the Jews had been told to remember the Exodus during Passover, Jesus tells his disciples to remember his death as the new focal point of salvation history.

The second element in the Last Supper scene is the farewell speech. Such speeches were delivered by dying patriarchs to their children, encouraging them to remember the ancestor's example by remaining faithful to the Law and then predicting their failures to do so. Luke creates Jesus' speech out of four independent sayings: (a) oracle against the betrayer (22:21–23); (b) the disciples' place in the Kingdom (vv. 24–30); (c) prophecy of Peter's denial and eventual restoration (vv. 31–34), and (d) a saying about two swords (vv. 35–38). Jesus sets the disciples an example in his death. The worst sin committed by a disciple is Judas's betrayal, which is rendered even more heinous by the echoes of covenant sacrifice associated with the meal.

Division and backsliding are set themes in betrayal stories. Luke relocates the dispute about greatness (see Mk 10:42–45) to the Supper, where it forms a contrast with Jesus' example as "one who serves" (22:27). The sayings critique cultural patterns of benefactor and client obligations that dominated social relationships in ancient society (vv. 22–25). Jesus' earlier instructions to invite persons to your banquet who cannot repay you rather than invite those, like you, who can afford to give banquets, and Jesus' own appearance as slave rather than master, provide additional illustrations of the Lucan theme of reversal in the Kingdom.

Beyond the ominous events of Jesus' death, Judas's betrayal, and Peter's denial, the discourse presents images of fulfillment. The Twelve who stand by Jesus will occupy the twelve thrones of the tribes of Israel. (Judas will be replaced; see Acts 1:15–26). The meal anticipates a future celebration with Jesus in glory—a communal celebration with Jesus, not the ranked banquets of those whose idea of greatness Jesus rejects. Before this banquet can occur, Jesus must suffer to enter glory. Satan makes the threatened return (4: 13) in Judas (22:3) and in testing Peter. Jesus' prayer prevents the sifting of the disciples from being more severe (22:31f; for sifting as an act of judgment see Amos 9:9). This perception that the future will be more difficult than during Jesus' life appears in the saying about the swords. Jesus cancels the earlier rules against taking provisions (22: 35–36; see also 10:1–12), meaning that missionaries may now provide themselves with purse, knapsack, and sandals.

Arrest of Jesus (22:39–53)

Jesus demonstrates his fidelity to God as obedient Son in prayer before his Passion. Luke deflects criticism of the disciples for failing to stay awake by alluding to their grief. They are warned that they must pray to avoid being tested. Jesus exhibits his freedom from fear over his fate in his words to those who come to seize him. He is no robber in hiding. They could have taken him publicly in the Temple, but the present hour of darkness is permitted by God's plan (v. 53).

Trial of Jesus (22:54–23:25)

Fulfillment of Jesus' predictions provides further evidence that God's will, not the plan of his enemies, controls the events around Jesus' death. Luke puts the story of Peter's denial before the trial of Jesus begins. Jesus reminds Peter of the earlier prediction by looking at him; Peter breaks down in tears. When Jesus' captors challenge him to prophesy as a form of mockery (22:64), readers have evidence from the Peter episode to show that Jesus is a true prophet. Luke does not report a legal trial by Jewish authorities. The false accusations and the verdict have been fixed before the Passion even begins. Jesus responds to the question about his messiahship with a judgment saying about the Son of Man. The Sanhedrin concludes that Jesus claims to be "Son of God" (22:66–71). Readers know (22:42) that Jesus will suffer death as the obedient Son of the Father.

Luke's version of the trial before Pilate insists that Jesus was innocent of the charges of stirring up political rebellion used to secure his death. Luke adds the geographical note, "from Galilee where he began even to here" (23:5), and then clears Jesus from guilt in Galilee by having him appear before Herod (vv. 6–12). That scene represents the climax of the earlier accounts of Herod's reaction to Jesus, which shifted from fascination to opposition (9:9; 13:31–33). Herod desires a miracle, but all he sees is the silent prisoner who is the object of violent accusations and mockery. Ironically, the incident creates peace between the old enemies, Herod and Pilate (v. 12). Even though Pilate persists in affirming Jesus' innocence, he is manipulated by the angry crowd into handing Jesus over for crucifixion. The leaders who orchestrated Jesus' death are really the ones fostering rebellion. They ask for the release of a known murderer and rebel (23:25).

Crucifixion and Burial of Jesus (23:26–56a)

As he is led to his death, Jesus prophesies the terrible fate awaiting Jerusalem once more (23: 26–32; 19:41–44). Scorned and considered a criminal, Jesus is able to offer salvation to the repentant sinner (23:39–43). The crowd challenges Jesus to save himself from his fate, which, as it turns out, is the entry into paradise for both himself and those who repent and are forgiven (see 22:28–30; the disciples who feast with Jesus in the Kingdom are those who have endured with him in his trials). This episode shows the reader that God's mercy can be experienced even in the midst of brutal hostility. Apocalyptic signs accompany Jesus' death, which is witnessed by the women and other followers from

Galilee. The centurion proclaims Jesus' innocence while the crowd laments (23:44–48).

Joseph, a member of the Council, buries Jesus as an act of piety. He represents the righteous of Israel who sought the Kingdom of God (v. 51). The women prepare to anoint the body, but they are interrupted by the Sabbath. The burial scene shows that Jesus was buried with honor, not like a criminal, and that the place was known to his followers. Luke is telling us that when the women return to complete the anointing, there can be no possibility that they have mistaken the place of burial.

Resurrection of Jesus (23:56b–24:53)

Jesus' departure takes place in Jerusalem on the third day (24:21, 51). Luke has rewritten traditional stories about the empty tomb and about mealtime appearances of the Risen Lord in order to create a sequence of three scenes. Luke arranges these scenes so that the Resurrection faith is more and more explicitly spelled out. The Gospel concludes with the disciples offering prayer and praise in Jerusalem while waiting for the Holy Spirit to initiate the next stage in the drama of salvation, the spread of the gospel from Jerusalem to the whole world.

The Women at the Tomb (23:56b–24:12)

The first of the three scenes opens when the women return to the tomb. Angels chide them for seeking the living among the dead (compare 20:38). Instead of a simple proclamation of the Easter faith as one finds in Mark 16:6b, Luke's angels remind the women of Jesus' predictions of the Passion and Resurrection. The women report that the angels said Jesus was alive (24:22f). When Luke repeats variants of a scene, we can expect the subsequent accounts to expand on hints in the first version.

Jesus Appears on the Road to Emmaus (24:13–35)

Confirmation of the women's report about the tomb had not yet led to disciples seeing the Risen Lord. In the second scene, Luke uses a folktale motif: the appearance of a divine being disguised as a stranger who must be shown hospitality. Jesus expands on what the angels at the tomb said, and he interprets Moses and the Prophets in order to demonstrate that the suffering of the Messiah was God's plan. Then a new theme comes in: the manifestation of Jesus in the breaking of bread. (John 21:1–14 contains a variant of the manifestation of Jesus in the guise of a stranger at a meal.) The Messiah has suffered, entered into glory, and now renews his presence to the disciples in the meal.

Jesus Appears to the Disciples in Jerusalem (24:36–43)

Luke knows the tradition that Jesus had appeared to Peter (24:34; see 1 Cor 15:5) but recounts only the appearance to the disciples at a meal. The third appearance confirms the fact that the Jesus who appears is the crucified one, raised up by God, not some ghost or other psychic phenomenon. The body that was missing from the tomb has been taken up by the risen Jesus.

That bodily transformation distinguishes Christian belief in resurrection from theories about the immortality of the soul or reincarnation. Neither near-death experiences nor so-called psychic phenomena provide support for our Christian faith in resurrection.

Jesus Commissions the Disciples (24:44–49)

In the third scene, as in the previous two episodes, Luke reminds us that the Messiah had to suffer and die in order to fulfill Scripture (vv. 44–46). The story then takes up the central element in all resurrection appearance stories: commissioning the recipients. These stories all point to the future mission of the disciples and founding of Christian communities in which Jesus continues to be present. The commission in verses 47–49 is a prelude to the story of the first apostles, which Luke will tell in Acts. The disciples' mission to preach repentance and baptism to all nations in Jesus' name, beginning from Jerusalem, continues the preaching that occurred during Jesus' ministry and reflects a new stage in salvation history. (Matthew 28:19f reports a variant tradition in which the disciples are to make disciples of the nations, baptizing them, and teaching them to observe Jesus' teaching.)

Jesus Departs (24:50–53)

The ending of the Gospel reflects the departure that Jesus discussed with Moses and Elijah (9:31), as well as showing the Son of Man in glory at the right hand of God (22:69). Jesus' resurrection appearances are understood to be from his place of glory with God (24:26). The stories have introduced ways in which Jesus will now be present to the church, through the Spirit promised by the Father (verse 49), and in the breaking of the bread (verse 35). The church's mission will be to take Jesus' teaching throughout the world.

Things We Have Learned from Luke

Jesus Is Savior for All Peoples

From the very beginning, Luke shows that the hopes that poor, weak, suffering, righteous persons have are fulfilled in the coming of Jesus. The Gospel shows that women as well as men; foreigners and Gentiles as well as Israelites; sick, weak, sinful, and despised persons as well as the well-off and respected people can come to Jesus. God seeks to reverse the situation of the poor and suffering. Consequently, Jesus comes as a suffering, servant Messiah, not as a liberator or king, who will take his place with the powerful of this world. Jesus' parables reveal that the love and mercy of God prompts this gift of salvation.

Disciples Participate in the Mission of Jesus

The disciples do not simply preach about Jesus or the Kingdom of God, they also participate in the reversal of roles, status, and concerns that the coming of salvation brings. Some disciples renounce everything that ties them to the social structures of the world. Others use their material resources in ways quite different from those around them. They do not seek exchanges between friends, which would create obligations to reciprocate. They do not try to pile up wealth or to indulge themselves and their friends in consuming luxurious goods. Their lives are not dominated by concern for acquiring and preserving material things. Instead, they aid people who will never be able to repay them. They give away wealth to meet the needs of other people.

Their only "anxiety" is acquiring heavenly treasure. All disciples are willing to follow Jesus' example of suffering service rather than demanding that others honor and serve them.

Prayer and Worship Are the Center of Christian Life

Even acts of mercy and compassion would not establish a relationship with God if people did not praise God in worship and ask God's assistance in meeting the challenges that the life of discipleship poses. Throughout the Gospel, Jesus sets the example. He worships with others in the synagogue and withdraws for prayer at critical moments. The disciples turn to prayer and praise after the Resurrection. Luke also contains examples of prayer in the Lord's Prayer and the canticles of the infancy narrative. Jesus warned disciples in the garden that they would have to pray to be spared testing, a reminder of the last petition of the Lord's Prayer. In Acts, the early community will continue to follow the example set by Jesus.

P.P.

FURTHER READING

Bovon, F. *Luke 1: A Commentary on the Gospel of Luke 1:1–9:50.* Hermeneia. Minneapolis: Fortress Press, 2002.

Fitzmyer, J. A. *The Gospel According to Luke 1–9 and 10–24.* Anchor Bible 28; 28A. Garden City, NY: Doubleday, 1981, 1985.

Johnson, L. T. *The Gospel of Luke.* Sacra Pagina 3. Collegeville, MN: Liturgical Press/Michael Glazier, 1991.

JOHN

[see pages 1486–1525 of the New Testament]

Before Beginning . . .

The Fourth Gospel has a double conclusion. After the Resurrection stories in Jerusalem, we are told that Jesus did many other signs but that those in the book seek to lead to belief in Jesus as Son of God (20:30f). After the Resurrection stories in Galilee, we learn that the Beloved Disciple was the source of the Johannine tradition and that all the things Jesus did could not be written down (21:24f). Expanded or revised editions of a book were not uncommon in antiquity. Both conclusions remind readers that the Gospel has been written to inspire and confirm their faith in Jesus.

Composition of the Fourth Gospel

The double ending indicates that John's Gospel has revised an earlier version. Other additions to the narrative and awkward transitions between sections also lead to this conclusion (see introduction to John, *New American Bible)*. For example, John 14:31 brings the discourse to an end. Yet the Gospel as we have it contains three more chapters of discourse material. John 12:44–50 appears to be tacked on at the end of chapter 12. Some of the additional material may have been added to the Gospel by later disciples of the author. As you read the Gospel, you will also see that Jesus often identifies with great religious symbols like light, life, water, bread, shepherd, and vine. The author of the Gospel assumes that its readers will recognize that these symbols have roots in the Hebrew Scriptures. This symbolic way of speaking about Jesus was probably developed within a community of Christians, which included the Beloved Disciple, followers who compiled the final edition of the Gospel, and another teacher who wrote the Johannine letters.

The Fourth Gospel and the Other Gospels

John is very different from the other Gospels. You will immediately notice that Jesus speaks in long symbolic discourses, not in short sayings and episodes that end in sayings. The only piece of ethical teaching in the Fourth Gospel is the love command. There are also major differences in the order of events. John pictures Jesus' ministry extending over three Passovers. The cleansing of the Temple comes at the beginning (2:13–22), not at the end of Jesus' ministry. Jesus' death is attributed to the following that he gained when he restored Lazarus to life. John attaches symbolic discourses to many of the miracles so that the miracle becomes a claim about Jesus' relationship to God. Most scholars think that John draws on traditions about Jesus that were independent of those preserved in the Synoptic (Matthew, Mark, Luke) Gospels.

Symbols, Irony, and Misunderstanding

The Fourth Gospel uses symbols to present its message that Jesus is the unique Son of God. No one who persists in taking Jesus' words literally can understand the truth that Jesus reveals (see the rejection of literal understandings of Jesus' words and deeds in 3:4–10; 4:10–15; 6:26–33). The reader knows the true meaning of Jesus' words when the characters in the story do not.

The Fourth Gospel and the Jews

Though some Jews, like Nicodemus, are sympathetic to Jesus (3:1–11; 7:50–52; 12:42), the Gospel often uses the expression "the Jews" as a symbol for all those who oppose Jesus. They display a murderous desire to kill God's envoy and will be condemned by the founders of their own tradition, who testify to Jesus (Moses, 5:41–47; Abraham, 8:48–59). The hostility in the Johannine account may have had its roots in the expulsion of Christian Jews from the synagogues, referred to in John 9:27 and 16:1–4a (see introduction).

If you read carefully, you will notice that John often does not bother to distinguish the various groups within Judaism of Jesus' day, such as Sadducees, Herodians, scribes, lawyers, and Pharisees. He often speaks of "the Jews" as though summarizing a story in which Jesus is facing "the bad guys." This habit creates a tension between the fact that Jesus and his followers were also Jews and the way in which the Gospel is using "Jews" as a term for a role in the story. John 18:35f illustrates this tension. Pilate treats Jesus with scorn because Jesus is a Jew, handed over by fellow Jews. Jesus' answer distinguishes himself and his followers from "the Jews," that is, the group opposed to him. John is not making a statement about the Jewish people when he uses "the Jews" to fill the role of "bad guys." The Vatican has reminded Catholics that anti-Semitism is one of the worst forms of racism. We must acknowledge that in the past people have not distinguished between John's use of "the Jews" as characters and the Jewish people. Today, we must be very careful not to continue that misreading. In some contexts, it might be appropriate to substitute another phrase like "Jesus' enemies" or a more literal rendering of the term used for "the Jews," "the Judeans," when retelling the Johannine story in order to avoid confusion. Such substitutions are particularly important when working with young children who cannot make the distinction easily between "the Jews" as characters in a story and their Jewish classmates and neighbors.

Reading through John

In reading John, we must be sensitive to the use of symbols, irony, and misunderstanding. The characters who interact with Jesus in the story are at different levels of understanding as to who Jesus is. The disciples begin with faith that Jesus fulfills the messianic promises to Israel, but this faith is not yet knowledge of Jesus as the revelation of God. Their faith must be completed by the post-Resurrection process of coming to understand Jesus, the perspective which the evangelist shares with the readers (16:25). Jewish sympathizers and the crowds have a vague idea that Jesus might be "from God" or even be the Messiah. John often divides the opinions of the crowd in two. One opinion is wrong or literal-minded; the other is partially correct (12:27–29). Unlike the Jewish crowds, who sometimes accept Jesus, John also uses the expression "the Jews" to represent religious authorities hostile to Jesus. They reject all testimony to the truth that Jesus comes from God, and they are the ones responsible for his death.

Signs and Faith in the Fourth Gospel

The symbolic perspective influences John's account of miracles (see introduction). Taken literally, they cannot lead a person to faith (2: 23–25), but seen as "signs" pointing to Jesus' identity with God, his "glory" (2:11), they may serve as the beginning point for faith. John embeds four of the miracles in discourses, which interpret their symbolic meaning. The symbols of life, light, and bread point to Jesus as the source of eternal life for all who believe.

Today, people continue to wonder whether they should "believe in miracles." There is no doubt that Jesus was well known for his ability to heal. The Gospels insist that Jesus used his healing power to bring people closer to God. He never used miracles to enrich himself or to gain popularity. Even though miracles can be a sign that God is working through Jesus, they can also be a trap. Sometimes people think they can bargain with God. If God will just heal them of disease or help them out of a jam, then they will become faithful Christians. John reminds us that our faith is not based on miracles. Our relationship with God is based on what Jesus has shown us about God's love for the world. It is not wrong to seek healing through prayer. Sometimes God will express love by a miraculous healing, but we should not think that miracles are anything more than a small sign of God's greatness.

Dualism in the Fourth Gospel

The Gospel uses a number of dualistic expressions, such as light/dark, life/death, from above (heavenly)/from below (earthly), not judged/condemned. They illuminate a process of division that occurs within the story. Persons confronted with Jesus' word either believe and become children of God who will inherit eternal life, or they reject Jesus and are condemned by God. This dualism gives John a certain harshness. There is no middle ground between belief and unbelief (12:44–50). Believers are united with Jesus and the Father. They may even experience the larger world as hostile (15:1–27). Dualistic imagery and a negative picture of the nonbelieving world often appears in sectarian groups. The notes in the NAB point out significant parallels between Johannine symbols and those used by the sectarian Jewish community at Qumran.

Belief and Eternal Life

Christians usually think of salvation or eternal life as a reward that comes in the future when they join Jesus in heaven (14:2f; 17:24) or when Jesus returns to judge the world (5:27–29). John retains this traditional language but introduces a new perspective on salvation. Belief brings persons into unity with Jesus. Therefore, they can be spoken of as already having passed through death to life (5:24–26; 3:16–21).: Those who reject Jesus are already condemned. Judgment really occurs when Jesus, who has come into the world as light, is accepted or rejected. Though various witnesses provide testimony—the Baptist, Scripture, and the deeds which Jesus does—the believer must accept Jesus' word about God. Only Jesus comes from heaven to reveal God (3: 31–36).

Jesus as God in the Fourth Gospel

The Gospel presents Jesus "from above" by identifying him with the Word, which is always present to God and through which God created the world (1:1–5). John defends the claim that Jesus is equal to God in functional terms: (1) Jesus makes God known; (2) Jesus exercises functions attributed to God, giving life and judging; (3) humans ought to respond to Jesus with the honor appropriate to God. John also emphasizes the special Father/Son relationship between Jesus and God. Jesus is obedient to the mission the Father has given him. Jesus' death will be a sign of God's love for humanity. The disputes between Jesus and "the Jews" (chapters 5–12) turn on the issue of Jesus' relationship to God. This section ends with the ironic fact that Jesus' opponents seek to kill the source of life.

An Outline of John

The plot of the Fourth Gospel follows a pattern of descent and ascent. Jesus comes into the world from the Father seeking "his own," those who will believe. Then, Jesus confronts the world. His ministry divides believers from unbelievers. The hostility of unbelief leads to the "hour" of his crucifixion, which John treats as an exaltation. Jesus returns to the glory that he had enjoyed with the Father from the beginning. The Gospel is clearly divided into two parts: first, the account of Jesus' confrontation with the world, which many scholars refer to as the "book of signs" (chapters 1 through 12); and second, the account of Jesus' return to the Father when the destined hour arrives, referred to as the "book of glory" (chapters 13 through 20).

• *Prologue* (1:1–18). A hymnic section introduces us to Jesus as God's Word, which has come into the world.

• *The Book of Signs* (1:19–12:50). Jesus' confrontation with the world represents God's judgment against unbelief. This section falls into two parts:

Gathering Witnesses to Jesus (1:19–4:54). Jesus demonstrates his glory to disciples and others who will believe in him before the confrontation with unbelief begins.

Confrontation with the World (5:1–12:50). The light has come into the world for judgment. Jesus confronts those who refuse to believe with testimony to his divine origin.

• *The Book of Glory* (13:1–20:31). Jesus' whole life has been moving toward the hour of his glorification and return to the Father. This section falls into two parts:

Preparing the Disciples for the Hour (13:1–17:26). At the Last Supper, Jesus delivers lengthy discourses about his return to the Father and its meaning for the disciples.

Jesus' Arrest, Crucifixion, and Resurrection (18:1–20:31). John understands the crucifixion as the moment of Jesus' life-giving exaltation and return to the Father.

• *Epilogue: Resurrection Appearance in Galilee* (21:1–25). Second conclusion reports further appearances of Jesus and points toward the destiny of two leading disciples, Peter and the Beloved Disciple.

Now it is time to read through the Gospel. You will find it easy to pick out the symbols and the sharp divisions between characters in the story. Remember that John wrote to encourage faith in Jesus as Son of God, because that faith is the source of eternal life. What happens to faith in each episode? Why do some characters move toward a more complete faith in Jesus while others pull away and become hostile?

The Prologue (1:1–18)

A Hymn to the Divine Word

The introduction to John is different from all of the other Gospels. It begins even before creation. John might even be following the opening words of Genesis 1 in which God creates the world out of formless chaos by speaking. Because of Jesus, John has a new insight about the divine Word. The Word is not simply speech or some abstract power that God can use to create. The Word actually became known to us in a person, Jesus. We speak of the Incarnation, of God becoming human. This idea of God is the special revelation of Christianity. It differs from the monotheism of Judaism and Islam, which insists that the unity of God cannot be shared. The Christian claim that Jesus can be spoken of as God is at the core of the controversies in the Fourth Gospel. John makes it clear right at the beginning that we can speak about God under two distinct aspects, God as the ultimate source of all things (that is, the Father) and the Word, through whom God creates and sustains the world and guides humans (that is, the Son). Later in the Gospel we will also learn that the Spirit comes from God to those who believe. Christians believe that the Father, Son, and Spirit are three distinct persons that make up the one God.

You will notice that many of the verses in this

section have a poetic quality made up of short parallel lines that employ the symbols of life, light, darkness, and glory. You will also notice that other verses speak of the role of John the Baptist as witness to the light (1:6–8, 15). Still other verses speak in the first person plural of what "we" have received from the coming of the light (vv.12, 14b, 16). "We" clearly means the Christian community that believes in Jesus. They have received the power to become children of God thanks to Jesus (v. 12). Many scholars think that the poetic verses belonged to an early hymn, which John has used for the introduction. The NAB prints these verses in a poetic form so that you can distinguish them from the prose comments that the author inserted to create the introduction.

Salvation, a Gift from the Word

This section makes it clear that only those people who receive Jesus as the incarnate Word can attain salvation. The Word actually existed before anything was created, but people may still fail to receive the Word when it comes to them. The Prologue contains several hints about the fate of the light when it comes into our world. People who should have received Jesus, do not. But those who do, receive the grace of becoming children of God and coming to know God as revealed by Jesus. The contrast between the Law that came through Moses and the "grace and truth," probably a rendering of the Hebrew expression for God's love and fidelity to the covenant (see note to 1:14), anticipates the conflict between Jesus and the Jewish leaders. Jesus will establish a new covenant between God and those people who come to believe in him.

The Book of Signs (1:19–12:50)

John uses the word "signs" to emphasize the symbolic role of Jesus' miracles in pointing to Jesus' true, divine origin. In order to understand the truth revealed by the signs, a person must think of their symbolic reality, not of the literal words or events. The "Jews" will be portrayed as persons who are unable to see the symbolic truth of Jesus' words.

Gathering Witnesses to Jesus (1:19–4:54)

The Prologue told us that the Baptist was sent to testify to Jesus. He opens this section with that testimony (1:19–34). Although there are hints of hostility to come, the first four chapters are generally positive. Jesus gathers followers who believe in his divine mission.

John Testifies to Jesus (1:19–34)

The Baptist testifies on different occasions to two different groups of officials that he is not the Messiah. He is simply preparing the way for the one who is coming (1:19–28). The Synoptic Gospels contain a scene in which Jesus is baptized and hears God announce that he is God's beloved Son (see Mk 1:9–11). Jesus has no need of such a revelation in the Fourth Gospel. The evangelist transforms the traditional scene into another example of testimony about Jesus. The Baptist sees the Spirit descend from heaven like a dove and remain on Jesus. God has given him that sign to identify the Messiah, who will baptize with the Spirit and will take away the sin of the world (1:29–34).

Jesus Gathers Disciples (1:35–51)

A series of brief scenes shows us how Jesus gathered the rest of his disciples. They follow a set pattern. Persons who come to Jesus through the testimony of others have their own experience with Jesus, which makes them true disciples. The Baptist sends Jesus the first disciples (vv. 35–37). Notice that this chapter is collecting all of the titles that early Christians used to speak of Jesus: Lamb of God (v. 36); Messiah (v. 41); the one predicted by Moses and the prophets (v. 45); Son of God (v. 49); King of Israel (v. 49); and Son of Man (v. 51). The final verse is very enigmatic. It hints at the story of the ladder, which Jacob saw in a dream vision (Gn 28:12). But Jesus as the heavenly figure, the Son of Man, has replaced the ladder. According to John, no one sees God except through Jesus (see 1:18).

Cana Miracle Manifests His Glory (2:1–12)

Now that he has gathered the disciples, Jesus' first miracle reveals his divine glory to them. The real revelation of Jesus' glory, however, cannot come until the Crucifixion. Therefore, Jesus first appears to reject his mother's request (vv. 4f). A wedding feast was often used as a symbol for the time of rejoicing that would follow God's judgment. Jesus has provided the wine for such a feast. We will see that Jesus replaces some of the most important Jewish feasts and customs. Christians no longer follow traditional patterns of worship. Here, Jesus replaces the water, which was to be used for ritual purification.

Cleansing of the Temple (2:13–25)

Unlike the Synoptic Gospels, which include only one visit to Jerusalem in Jesus' ministry, John has three different Passover visits as well as episodes during other feasts. The other Gospels link the cleansing of the Temple with the Passover of Jesus' death. John puts that episode much earlier. It enables him to tell the Christian reader that Jesus will also replace the Temple. The evangelist reminds readers that Jesus' disciples could not have understood the saying until after the Resurrection (2:22). The end of the chapter warns against faith that is based simply on miracles (vv. 23–25). Many attracted by Jesus' miracles will not remain faithful.

Dialogue with Nicodemus (3:1–21)

The next two dialogues, with Nicodemus and with the Samaritan woman, employ the technique of misunderstanding in which the person to whom Jesus speaks takes Jesus' words literally and thus provokes further comment. You will notice that Jesus always responds with an even more difficult statement than the one that provoked the original misunderstanding. In this case, Jesus' words appear to leave Nicodemus behind, but he will reappear as someone sympathetic to Jesus (7:50–52). Since Jewish writings of the period also speak of a cleansing of the righteous by the Holy Spirit, Nicodemus might have been expected to understand that Jesus was speaking about a rebirth "from above," that is, through the Spirit rather than "again" (see note to 3:3). John's Christian readers probably saw an allusion to baptism in the insistence that people had to be reborn to enter the Kingdom. The episode marks a clear distinction between the teacher of Israel who cannot even understand the idea of spiritual rebirth, and Jesus who is, in fact, the very source of life.

A sudden shift to the plural "we" and "you people" echoes the confrontation between Christians and their synagogue opponents in the evangelist's time (v. 11). Verses 12–15 follow a pattern similar to 1:50f. Belief on the grounds of some "earthly" sign is challenged by the heavenly reality, which is to be revealed in Jesus. In both cases a saying about the Son of Man represents the higher truth. Drawing upon the story of Moses lifting up a bronze serpent in the wilderness (Nm 21:9), the evangelist asserts that Jesus will have to be lifted up (on the cross) to become a source of eternal life for all believers. Verses 16–21 speak to the Christian reader about the coming of Jesus. Elsewhere in the Gospel "world" is a negative symbol for those who are hostile to the Word. Here the world refers to all humans as the object of God's love. Though darkness did not overcome the light (1:5), humanity can still reject the light. The passage offers one explanation for the tragic fact that people will prefer darkness to light; they would rather hide their evil ways than "live the truth," a Semitic expression for following the will of God revealed in the Law.

We should remember this human tendency to "prefer darkness to light" when we confront issues of moral or personal reform today. When we are faced with situations in which people are addicted to drugs or alcohol, we find that the most difficult step is overcoming the denial of the problem. We may become frustrated in our efforts to help such people because it seems that they would rather destroy their lives and those of others than accept available help. Certainly, we should not write off people who need our help, but this passage shows us that we cannot always expect easy results.

Jesus and John the Baptist (3:22–4:3)

John once again testifies to Jesus as the one to come. The saying about the Bridegroom appears in the Synoptic Gospels as part of an exchange over fasting. John's disciples fast while Jesus' do not (see Mk 2:18–19). In John's Gospel the emphasis lies on the identity of the two men. The Baptist's role ends once he has given witness to Jesus. Verse 27 points to the importance of grace in the Gospel: no one can have anything that God has not given to that person. Verses 3:31–36 seem to be the evangelist's summary of the entire chapter. The Son is the one who has been given "everything" by the Father (v. 35). His mission is to give the Spirit—or eternal life—to those who believe (vv. 33f,36). The contrast between the "one from heaven," who testifies to the truth and speaks the words of God, and those who belong to earth, who reject the Son, once again demonstrates that the coming of the Son also brings judgment (v. 36b).

The Samaritan Woman (4:4–42)

John has divided this story into a series of scenes that progressively reveal the truth about Jesus and his mission. Jesus comes to be known as greater than the patriarch Jacob, who met his future wife at a well. Legend had it that in the new age, the water would bubble to the top of Jacob's well so that people did not have to labor at drawing water. Jesus is more than a messiah figure who would vindicate the Jews by exalting Jerusalem. Jesus is more than the prophet like Moses whom the Samaritans expected to establish their version of the Law and place of worship against the claims of their Judean neighbors. Readers know that when Jesus speaks of a gift of living (that is, flowing) water, he speaks symbolically of the gift of the Spirit (3:8). The woman persists in treating Jesus' words literally until the enigmatic reference to her marital status persuades her that Jesus is a prophet. When Jesus responds to her challenge to settle the old dispute between Jews and Samaritans over *where* to worship God by speaking of worship in "Spirit and truth," Jesus is alluding to himself as the replacement of the Temple (see 2:13–22). The woman finally accepts Jesus as Messiah. Like the disciples in chapter 1, she puts that insight into action by bringing others to Jesus (v. 29).

Jesus' dialogue with his disciples about mission and harvest (4:31–38) indicates that, like the woman, they too are sent to preach to others. Along with the previous episode, in which Jesus was said to be baptizing more people than the Baptist, this story makes it clear that Jesus was able to convert people with his preaching. The hostile controversies of the next section might otherwise give the impression that Jesus' mission was largely a failure. The large numbers of Samaritans who come to Jesus indicate the truth of Jesus' words to the disciples about the rich harvest. The story concludes with the ringing affirmation that Jesus is "Savior of the world."

Healing the Royal Official's Son (4:43–54)

The section on gathering followers concludes with a second miracle in Cana. Jesus' word spoken at a distance is enough to heal the official's son (4:53). Now that Jesus' identity as the Son sent from God to save the world has been established, we are ready for the confrontation between Jesus and those who do not believe.

Confrontation with the World (5:1–12:50)

The sharp confrontation with unbelief that makes up this section of the Gospel does not represent failure, since it leads to the hour of Jesus' exaltation and return to the Father. Jesus succeeds in gathering as children of God those persons who believe his words despite all the obstacles that others put in their way.

Healing on the Sabbath:
Jesus Gives Life and Judges (5:1–47)

The tradition that Jesus provoked hostility among religious leaders by healing a paralyzed man on the Sabbath and associating that healing with the forgiveness of sins is well established in the tradition (see Mk 2:1–12). John uses the discourse that follows the miracle story to draw out what the real issue is: Jesus' claim to equality with God (5:16–18). Opposing teachers could appeal to the Law of Moses to argue that no human being can claim to do things which are God's alone, to give life to the dead and to judge (see notes to 5:21, 22). We have already seen that in John's view the decisive encounter with Jesus is the moment of judgment (see vv. 24–26). Jesus defends his claim to give life and judge by appealing to the special relationship he enjoys with God. As "Son," Jesus does what the Father has given him to do. He does not act on his own authority (v. 30). Furthermore, those who question his behavior should look to the witnesses he can bring forward: the Baptist (vv. 31–35), the deeds which God has enabled him to do (v. 36), and the witness that God has given through Scripture (vv. 37–39). Jesus accuses his opponents of failing to recognize that he is from God because they are not really concerned with the glory that belongs to God. They are only interested in the human glory they receive from other people. He warns them that their confidence in Moses is misplaced. Moses witnesses to Jesus and will condemn anyone who rejects that testimony (vv. 40–47).

Jesus Is the Bread from Heaven (6:1–71)

Chapter 6 is based upon a traditional cycle of material that included the feeding of the multitude, calming the storm at sea, a demand that

Jesus give people a sign, a challenge to Jesus based on his human origins, and Peter's confession of faith in Jesus as Messiah. John reshapes this material by including a lengthy discourse on Jesus as the bread of life, which has come down from heaven (vv. 22–59). Those who fail to see the symbolism of the feeding miracle or who focus on earthly facts about Jesus will not receive Jesus as the bread of life. Just as Jesus had promised the Samaritan woman a gift of water that would lead to eternal life, he promises bread that will give life to the believer. But the "Jews" are going to copy the behavior of their ancestors, who murmured against Moses. John explains that those who do come to believe in Jesus have been brought to him by God (vv. 37–39,44f). The comment that Jesus will not cast out those who come to him (v. 37) probably refers to the members of John's church who had been expelled from the Jewish community by officials. That experience is prefigured in the story of the blind man (9:22).

Jesus' words are the source of eternal life in the first part of the discourse. Christian tradition associates the manna and the "bread of life" with the Eucharist. This tradition appears in 6:51–59. It is necessary to eat the life-giving bread and wine, the flesh and blood of Jesus. This meal establishes a special relationship between Jesus and the believer: they "abide in" one another. Just as the Father is the source of Jesus' life, so Jesus becomes the source of life for the Christian. In this episode we learn that receiving eternal life is not the result simply of *thinking* that Jesus is God's Son. It really involves an entirely new relationship with God that is possible in Jesus. John 6:51–58 places the Eucharist at the center of that relationship. If Jesus' words about eating his flesh and blood were taken literally, they would be a blasphemous participation in a human sacrifice. Even if Jesus' audience understood that Jesus was speaking symbolically, they might be horrified at the idea that Jesus could identify himself with God so closely.

The chapter concludes with a reaction among Jesus' followers, which shows that these words were too difficult for many to accept. Faced with the possibility of abandoning Jesus, Peter confesses that there is no one else to whom they could turn. Only Jesus has the words of eternal life.

Conflict and Division at the Feast of Tabernacles (7:1–8:59)

The episodes in this section occur at the Feast of Tabernacles and at an unnamed feast that follows it. The symbolism of light and water were part of the Tabernacles ritual, and Jesus uses them to express his identity (7:37–39; 8:12). Throughout the section we are reminded that officials are seeking Jesus' death even when they deny that fact (7:1,19f, 25; 8:39f). Jesus is accused of "leading the people astray." He is also accused of being possessed by a demon. Since it is not yet Jesus' hour, however, attempts to arrest (7:32, 44), legally condemn (7:45–52), and stone (8:59) Jesus fail. Several scenes picture the divided opinion among the crowd. These scenes may also provide answers to Jewish objections against Jesus: (a) Jesus did not keep the Law in healing on the Sabbath, but the Law permits activities like circumcision on the Sabbath (7:19–24); (b) Jesus' origins make it impossible for him to be the Messiah, yet Jesus' real origins are "from heaven," and the signs he has done testify to that fact (7:25–31, 40–44); (c) Jesus is not an established teacher of the Law, yet Jesus has received his words and teaching from God so that he does not seek personal glory as human teachers do (7:15–18).

Jesus begins to prepare the reader for his departure. He speaks of it in a symbolic way, which the crowd cannot fully understand. Jesus will go to a place where they cannot follow him (7:32–36). The crowd thinks that Jesus will go to the Jewish communities outside Palestine. There is a symbolic truth in that statement: Christianity will spread in those communities. Or, perhaps, Jesus intends to commit the blasphemous act of killing himself (8:21f). The ironic truth of that statement is that Jesus will give up his life on behalf of others. He predicts that when his enemies have executed him, they will find that Jesus is the one who comes from the Father. Jesus even bears the divine name "I AM" (8:28). The bitter conflict between Jesus and the Jewish leaders in chapter 8 repeats this identification of Jesus with God's I AM in a dispute over descent from Abraham. Those who seek to kill Jesus cannot be descendants of Abraham, since what Abraham saw and rejoiced in was Jesus. Therefore, they are branded children of Satan (8:39–59). The story acknowledges the difficulty of Jesus' words. He is asking us to identify a human being with the God revealed to Abraham and to Moses.

The Blind Man Believes in Jesus (9:1–41)

This story shows that it was possible for the blind man to move *from* the miracle by which Jesus restored his sight *to* true faith in Jesus. He does so as the religious authorities pressure him to condemn Jesus. He comes to recognize more and more clearly that Jesus cannot be a sinner, and therefore Jesus must have come from God. The fear that "Jews" (= authorities) will drive them out of the synagogue keeps the man's parents from testifying (9:22f). This story may represent the experience of members of the Johannine community. Jesus returns at the end of the story to show the man his identity and condemn the blindness of the Jewish leaders (vv. 39–41).

True Shepherd Gives His Life (10:1–42)

We already know that Jesus' death is an expression of God's love for the world (3:16). Religious authorities have said that Jesus deserves death for leading people astray (7:45–52). Here, parables of the shepherd and his sheep demonstrate that Jesus is the true leader of the people—at least for those whom God has enabled to respond to his call (10:1–30). Jesus will even give his life for the sheep, something that none of the hired hands who claim to lead the people will do. Offended by his claim to identity with the Father (vv. 30–39), the crowd again tries to stone Jesus. We are reminded that Jesus' death is a free offering on his part, not a victory for those allied against him (vv. 17f).

Raising Lazarus: Gift of Life Means Death (11:1–57)

John has used the raising of Lazarus to bring out the irony of what the religious leaders are seeking to do. Jesus is the source of life (vv. 24–26), yet they think that they can silence Jesus by killing him. The Lazarus episode also serves to remind Christians that if they truly believe that Jesus is resurrection and life, then they should not mourn physical death as others do. Jesus often seems remote from others, but here Jesus displays his love for Lazarus and his sisters. Ironically, the following that Jesus gained from his greatest sign led to the formal decision of the Jewish Council to arrange his death (11:45–57). Although the high priest does not know the truth of his words, it will turn out to be a good thing that one person dies for the people, and, as the evangelist points out, for all the peoples of the world (vv. 50–52).

The Light Is Departing (12:1–50)

John locates the traditional story of Jesus' anointing at Bethany (Mk 14:3–9) in the home of Lazarus and identifies the anonymous woman as his sister Mary. She recognizes the approach of Jesus' death. Ironically, the traitor, Judas, is the one who protests (vv. 1–8). Hints of the future Christian mission are evident in the Pharisees' response to the entry, "the whole world has gone after him," (v. 19) and the coming of some Greeks to seek Jesus. Their arrival marks the hour of Jesus' death. He prophesies that when he is lifted up on the cross, he will draw all people to himself (vv. 20–32). The "Book of Signs" concludes with reflections on the tragedy of disbelief (vv. 39–43 and 44–50).

The Book of Glory (13:1–20:31)

We already know that Jesus offers his life out of love; that Jesus' crucifixion is the moment of his exaltation and return to the Father; that this death is the source of eternal life for all who believe and the manifestation of a new relationship between believers and God. The truth about Jesus' death lies in the revelation that occurs on the cross, not in the plots of Jesus' enemies.

The Supper Discourses (13:1–17:26)

Jesus prepares the disciples for the events to come, as well as their future life as a community of believers. The foot-washing not only reflects the service Jesus is about to perform in his death, it also sets a pattern for relationships among disciples. They are going to be the ones sent to represent Jesus and must follow the model given by their teacher (13:1–20). John has never let us forget that one of Jesus' disciples, Judas, does not really belong to Jesus. He is the agent of God's purpose even though he is in the grip of Satan (6:70f; 12:4–6; 13:2, 11, 21–30; 17:12). Throughout this section, the evangelist reminds us that the disciples understood the significance of what Jesus said and did only after he had been glorified (13:7; 14:29; 16:4, 25). As Judas is about to depart, a new character, the Beloved

Disciple, appears in the narrative. He is closer to Jesus than any other disciple (13:23) and will show special insight into events of the Passion and Resurrection. The Johannine community revered the Beloved Disciple as the source of its tradition.

The discourses in 13:31–17:26 may have been composed as independent units. John 13:36–14:31 treats the disciples' grief, Jesus' departure and return, and the coming of the Advocate. Jesus also returns to the disciples as an indwelling presence along with the Father. John 16, 4b–33 also deals with the disciples' grief, Jesus' departure and return, and the coming of the Advocate. It lacks the development of the return theme, however, as the mutual indwelling of Father and Son. John 15:1–16:4a encourages the disciples to remain united with Jesus the true vine and to love one another. This unity may be severely tested, since the disciples must also expect hatred, persecution, and even death from the world (15:18–16:4a). Finally, John 17:1–26 contains a prayer in which Jesus speaks to the Father about the disciples he is leaving behind. They are the evidence that Jesus has completed the task he was sent into the world to accomplish (17:6–11a). Left in the world, the disciples are no more "of the world" than Jesus, but without Jesus they require God's protection (17:13–19). As the Father sent him, so Jesus is sending the disciples into the world. The prayer looks beyond the immediate community of disciples to the community that will be the result of their preaching. Jesus expresses a vision of Christian community that runs throughout these discourses. The community is to express the love and unity, which has its source in the love and unity that exists between the Father and the Son (17:20–26).

Mutual love and unity grounded in their vision of God are the focal points of the discourses. You may have noticed that the only explicit commandment given in the Fourth Gospel is the command to love one another (13:34f). This love expresses the love of God (14:21, 23f; 17:23) and of Jesus for "his own," which is about to be demonstrated on the cross (13:1; 14:21b; 15:11–15). These discourses also suggest that mutual love and unity will be severely tested. The disciples do not yet fully understand what Jesus has revealed to them. The Advocate, who comes from God, must continue the process of bringing understanding to the community (14:25f; 16:13–15). Hatred and persecution from outsiders may also take their toll, as the synagogue exclusion apparently did. The Advocate will help the disciples who have to stand trial (15:26f) and convict the world of its unrighteousness and sin (16:8–11). The community may not remain in the "name of God," which Jesus has revealed (17:11). If you read 1 John, you will see that the Johannine churches suffered serious internal divisions. These discourses remind us that Jesus' revelation of God's love is the foundation of Christian unity. Christians who follow this ideal face a hostile world in which their faithfulness to it survives only if they remember its source and persist in praying for the guidance of the Spirit necessary to achieve mutual love and unity.

Jesus' Arrest, Crucifixion, and Resurrection (18:1–20:31)

Throughout his Passion, Jesus remains in complete control of his destiny. Jesus lays down his life; others do not take it from him. When Jesus identifies himself with the name I AM, used of God in the Old Testament, all those who came to seize him fall to the ground (18:1–14). Jesus confronts his accusers with the evidence of his public teaching. He demands that they bring evidence against him, which they are unable to do (18:19–24). Jewish officials try to hand Jesus over to Pilate without a formal charge (18:28–32). Consequently, the inquiry that Pilate conducts picks up the theme of kingship. John's use of double meanings throughout the Gospel has prepared us for the dialogue that follows. Jesus both denies any earthly kingship and assents to the title "King of the Jews" (18:33–38). Nor are we surprised to find the soldiers' mockery turn Jesus into a king symbolically and then to see Pilate present the "king" to the Jewish people (19:1–5).

When Jesus is presented as "king," the trial scene breaks out into vicious hostility. Pilate knows Jesus is innocent but can only speak to the Jewish officials and to Jesus with bitterness and sarcasm. He knows nothing about truth (18:38). Jesus does not accept Pilate's claim to authority (19:10f). Pilate is the one who fears the political power of others. He will give in to threats of being denounced to Caesar and execute an innocent man. At the same time, he retaliates against those responsible by insisting that the charge read "King of the Jews." The chief priests demonstrate how far away from God they are by proclaiming that they have no king but Caesar (19: 12–22). The violent cruelty and bitterness of this scene show us what brute force and political power are like when those in power have no awareness of their responsibilities toward God. Pilate is interested only in asserting Roman control over the conquered Jews. The death of an obscure Galilean is of no concern to him. When we meditate on this passage, we should recognize that we have a responsibility to protest such abuses of power in our own world. We cannot stand by and permit innocent people to be brutalized and even killed to support tyrannical power.

Details in the crucifixion scene, which fulfill passages of Scripture, demonstrate that everything is happening according to God's plan (19: 23f,28,33–37). Jesus provides for those faithful to him by entrusting his mother to the Beloved Disciple as "son" (19:25–27). Unlike the others crucified, whose legs were broken to hasten their death (19:31–33), Jesus departs to the Father as soon as his mission is accomplished (19:30).

Jesus' crucifixion and death are witnessed by friends and enemies alike. When Pilate releases the body to Joseph of Arimathea and Nicodemus for burial, we know that Jesus has really died and been buried according to accepted customs (19: 38–42). Consequently, Mary's reaction to discovering the tomb open is to conclude that "they" (possibly hostile authorities) have taken the body (20:1f). Though the Beloved Disciple arrives at the tomb first and is said to believe, all he and Peter discover is the grave wrappings in one pile and the face cloth rolled up in another place. The evangelist comments that they could not understand what had happened because they did not know the Scripture about Jesus' Resurrection (20:9).

Mary of Magdala's encounter with the Risen Lord combines the old tradition of an angelic appearance to the women at the tomb, announcing the Resurrection, with the tradition that Jesus himself appeared to the women in the vicinity of the tomb (20:11–18; see Mt 28:1–10). As in the other tomb stories, Mary receives a message for the disciples. She is not to cling to the Lord but to announce Jesus' return to God. John's account puts the occurrence of all the events—Resurrection, ascent to the Father, and bestowing the Spirit on the disciples—on Easter. When Jesus appears among the disciples, the marks on his body prove that the Risen Lord is the one who had been crucified. The disciples are now officially sent to the world as Jesus had been, and they receive the promised gift of the Spirit, a sign that Jesus' mission has been completed (7:39; 3: 34). Forgiveness of sins as an activity of the Spirit within the Christian community (21:23) appears only here in John's Gospel, but it is familiar from the Synoptics (see Lk 24:47; Mt 18: 18). First John presupposes some form of "forgiveness" available within the community (see 1 Jn 1:8–2:2; 5:16f).

John creates a second episode from the tradition of Thomas's doubt. The demand for physical evidence is a sign of unbelief. Christians who have not seen and yet believed are the ones who are really blessed (20:28f).

Epilogue (21:1–25)

This chapter seems to have been added to the Gospel by another hand sometime after its completion (see introduction, p. 1486). It elaborates on a tradition of Resurrection appearances in Galilee. The miraculous catch of fish has a parallel in the miracle associated with the calling of Peter in Luke 5:1–11. This chapter focuses upon the two heroes from the apostolic age: Peter, who inherited Jesus' role as shepherd, and the Beloved Disciple, who established the Johannine tradition. Peter had died a martyr's death. The Beloved Disciple lived a long time but has also died. Johannine Christians can look back upon that generation of disciples as faithful witnesses to Jesus.

Things We Have Learned from John

John has presented us with a unique story of Jesus. Instead of collecting sayings and parables in which Jesus spoke about the Kingdom of God, the evangelist focuses our attention on the special relationship between Jesus and God. We need to remember this special relationship between Jesus and God, because we often slip into thinking of Jesus as though he were just another human religious leader. If we think that way, then Jesus becomes something of a hero, someone who could just as easily be replaced by another person whose life and message seemed more inspiring at another time in our lives. We need to remember that Jesus is more than a great human being. Jesus is our revelation of God.

Jesus Is the Unique Son of God

No one can come away from the Fourth Gospel without recognizing that Jesus is identified with God. The Prologue described that relationship as the Word, which is always with God and through which God acts in the world. In the narrative, Jesus appears as the unique Son of the Father. The Son is the only one who can reveal the Father. Father and Son are united by a common love and the Son's obedience to everything the Father requires.

Salvation Comes through Belief in the Son

Salvation, which John usually describes as eternal life, requires belief in Jesus as God's Son. It cannot be delivered by human institutions such as those the Jewish leaders think will provide security. Salvation consists in a new relationship to God through Jesus. This relationship is open to anyone to whom God has given the grace to believe in Jesus. Sometimes we meet evangelical Christians who tell us that unless we accept Jesus Christ as our personal Lord and savior, we cannot be saved. They try to suggest that there is something wrong with the belief in Jesus that we have unless we go through the type of conversion experience typical of members of that church. Reading the Gospel of John makes it clear that anyone who believes that his or her salvation has come through the revelation that Jesus brought has already accepted Jesus as Lord and Savior. That special relationship is what we mean when we talk about faith.

Jesus' Death Expresses God's Love for Humanity

Jesus is not the victim of human injustice even though those who killed him were evil people. Jesus chose to offer his life for others so that they could see God's love revealed on the cross. When we see God's love on the cross, we are reminded that God identifies with the lowly, suffering people of the world by joining with them. God does not approve of the injustice that creates such suffering. Jesus reminded Pilate that his own death was an "offering," not the triumph of Pilate's power. Christians must look for ways of identifying with and helping the suffering, rather than expecting God to act through the powers of the world.

Mutual Love and Unity in the Church Express the Love of God

The love shown by Christians is not simply an expression of a moral virtue. Christians always have the example of Jesus' love to follow. They also have the experience of the Father and Son dwelling in the community to inspire their efforts to achieve unity.

P.P.

FURTHER READING

Brown, R. E. *The Gospel According to John 1–12 and 13–21*. Anchor Bible 29; 29A. Garden City, NY: Doubleday, 1966, 1971.

Moloney, F. J. *The Gospel of John*. Sacra Pagina 4. Collegeville, MN: Liturgical Press/Michael Glazier, 1998.

Smith, D. Moody, Jr. *John*. Abingdon New Testament Commentaries. Nashville: Abingdon Press, 1999.

ACTS

[see pages 1526–1575 of the New Testament]

Before Beginning . . .

Acts continues the story that began with Luke's Gospel. What began with Jesus' life did not end on Easter. God's plan requires another act: the gospel must spread beyond Jerusalem to all the peoples of the earth (Lk 24:47; Acts 1:8). Luke recounts the deeds of the first generation of apostles by which God took the movement out of the Galilean and Judean environment of its birth. He has not provided a detailed chronicle of everything that occurred during the period between the resurrection of Jesus and Paul's arrival in Rome (ca. AD 30–62). Peter disappears from the story once Paul's mission to the Gentiles is established as God's plan. Acts ends with Paul under benign house arrest in Rome, able to preach to visitors (28:17–31). We hear nothing of the martyrdom of Peter and Paul there under Nero, although allusions show that Luke's readers are expected to know of Paul's death (20:25; 21:13).

A Story of God's Salvation

Acts has an unusual ending. One of its heroes is under arrest in Rome, and we never find out what happens to him. As soon as you read Paul's letter to the Romans, you find out that he was not the first missionary to reach Rome. There was an established Christian community before he arrived (1:8–15). Paul mentions a number of people associated with that church at the end of the letter (16:1–16).

Luke did know about these people. He mentions the fact that two famous missionaries, Aquila and Priscilla (Acts 18:2; see Rom 16:3f), had had to leave Italy when the Emperor Claudius expelled Jews from Rome. Roman sources tell us that riots over the name of "Chrestus" was the cause (Suetonius, *Life of Claudius* 25). This event may have taken place as early as AD 40 (see note to Acts 18:2). While Luke has not included all of the events in early Christian history that were known to his readers, he has adopted a literary genre close to what the ancients would consider an "historical monograph." Unlike secular histories of great wars, lives of emperors, the founding of states, and the like, Luke has models for history writing in the Jewish Scriptures. Biblical history wants to show how God's plan of salvation worked out through special people and events. We use the expression "salvation history" for this type of writing.

Understanding Salvation History

How do we even know what God's plan is? You will see as you read the stories in Acts that even the disciples did not know what God intended. They had certain guideposts. The most important was what they knew about Jesus. Jesus had also told them in very general terms that a new stage in God's plan was about to unfold and that they would be an essential part of carrying it out. They also knew passages from the Old Testament that had helped them understand how Jesus' life and death fitted into God's plan. Luke makes it very clear, however, that even with these resources the disciples would not have been able to figure out God's plan in advance. God intervenes through the Holy Spirit at the critical turning points in the story.

Though God's intervention is crucial to salvation history, human beings are not manipulated like puppets. You will notice that the disciples in the story have to figure out the significance of the unusual experiences that happen to them during their mission. They ask for further assistance from God in prayer. They also discuss the events that have occurred as they prepare to take new steps in preaching the gospel. Their ability to look back on past examples of God's action helps them understand what God is doing in the present. Sometimes they might even have taken the wrong step if God had not intervened. Acts 16:6–10 reports that the Spirit of Jesus actually caused Paul to change his travel plans in Asia Minor and then to go over to Greece. It was time for Paul to spread the word farther to the west.

The Plan of Salvation History in Acts

Perhaps you have figured out a way of understanding the end of Acts from this passage. The book employs a geographical plan for the spread of the gospel. We begin where the ministry of Jesus had ended, in Jerusalem. We move west until we come to the center of the empire that embraced the whole circle of the Mediterranean: Rome. By the end of the book, you will see that Christianity is no longer confined to the band of followers in Jerusalem. Christian churches dot the empire. Take a look at the map of Paul's missionary journeys in Acts. (See map #14.) You will notice that Paul touches the major cities along the roads and sea routes of his time.

As you read through Acts, you will also notice another feature of the early mission. The disciples preach first to Jews and then to Gentiles. Apollos is active in the synagogues (Acts 18:26–28). Some of Luke's summaries refer to converts from both Jews and "Greeks," an expression used for non-Jews, or Gentiles, rather than for persons of Greek descent (see Acts 18:10). But often the mission to non-Jews begins only when influential people in the synagogue turn the audience against the missionaries (see Acts 13:44–52). Israel has first place in the plan of salvation. She receives another chance after the rejection of Jesus when the disciples begin to preach the gospel (see 3:11–26). The pattern of rejection by Jews followed by enthusiastic reception on the part of Gentiles, makes us aware of a turning point in the story of salvation. The Hebrew Scriptures and the public ministry of Jesus told of God's dealings with Israel. From now on, the story of salvation would involve all the peoples of the world. Luke's pattern of Jews first, then Gentiles, also reminds us that Christianity is indebted to Judaism. That link is not a trivial cultural accident but part of the divine plan of salvation. The Catholic church has called upon Christians to acknowledge this common heritage by rejecting all forms of anti-Semitism. Through interreligious discussions with Jewish believers, Catholics can come to appreciate the contribution that Jewish traditions have made to their own faith in God.

Reading through Acts

Before you sit down to study Acts, read through the whole book. You will notice that there are some types of stories that occur again and again. The apostles are put in jail. They must make speeches before various courts and officials. Sometimes God rescues them from jail or some other hostile action. Besides the legal speeches, Luke adds the drama of speeches that announce the gospel. The apostles frequently gain attention through miracles, which they are able to work in Jesus' name. In other stories, the apostles challenge the religious beliefs, superstitions, and magical practices of the Gentiles. As the gospel moves out from Jerusalem, these dramatic episodes are fitted into a pattern of journeys.

Acts as Entertainment

We have already seen that Acts has been structured to make a religious point about God's plan of salvation. As Luke tells the story, he provides the reader with a number of entertaining incidents (confusing Paul and Barnabas with pagan gods in Acts 14:8–18, for example). Persecutions, trials, imprisonments, journeys, and dramatic shipwrecks all had their counterparts in novels that were popular during this period. The novels usually had a romantic theme rather than a religious one, but the use of comparable tales reminds us that Acts provided readers with pleasure as well as instruction.

Acts and the Early Community

You will also notice as you read through Acts that there appears to be great harmony among Christians in the early communities. We know from Paul's letters that the early churches were sometimes torn by dissent and often had to be encouraged by the apostle to demonstrate in their actions the love that Christians were to show one another.

Luke knows that the early communities were not always perfect. Acts shows us how the churches ought to live together. It even shows us how Christians should work out difficulties that they face. They are never to forget that their purpose is to thank God for the salvation they have received and to preach the same message to others. There is no place for the love of money, for the jealousy, maliciousness, and deceitful behavior that those who persecute the apostles demonstrate.

An Outline of Acts

• *Preparation for the Christian Mission* (1:1–2:13). This section includes all of the events between Easter and the first missionary sermon that Peter preaches on Pentecost.

Waiting in Jerusalem (1:1–14)
Replacing Judas (1:15–26)
Pentecost, the Coming of the Spirit (2:1–13)

• *The Mission in Jerusalem* (2:14–8:3)

Two Sermons by Peter (2:14–3:26)
Peter and John before the Sanhedrin (4:1–31)
Sharing Possessions in the Community (4:31–5:16)
Trial before the Sanhedrin (5:17–42)
Deacons for the Hellenists (6:1–7)
Trial and Death of Stephen (6:8—8:3)

• *Mission in Judea and Samaria* (8:4–9:43). The gospel begins to spread into areas around Jerusalem.

Philip Preaches Outside Jerusalem (8:4–40)
Conversion of Paul (9:1–30)
The Church Continues to Grow (9:31–43)

• *Inauguration of the Gentile Mission* (10:1–15:35). These chapters set the stage for the mission of Paul by showing that the Gentile mission began from Jerusalem itself.

Conversion of Cornelius (10:1–11:26)
Paul's First Missionary Journey (11:27–14:28)
Gentile Mission Confirmed in Jerusalem (15:1–35)

• *Paul's Mission to the Ends of the Earth* (15:36–28:31). Paul now fulfills the mission that God gave him by carrying the gospel throughout the Roman empire from Jerusalem to Rome itself.

Second Missionary Journey (15:36–18:23)
Third Missionary Journey (18:24–21:14)
Paul's Arrest and Imprisonment at Jerusalem (21:17–26:32)
Paul's Journey to Rome (27:1–28:31)

Now it is time to read through each section of Acts in detail. We will be looking to see how Luke describes the development of the early church. Even though the apostles do not always know where God is leading, they remain open to the Spirit. Even though the apostles experience hostility and some deaths, they never cease to tell people about Jesus. God has shown them that Jesus came to be the savior for all the nations of the world.

The Preparation for the Christian Mission (1:1–2:13)

Waiting in Jerusalem (1:1–14)

Acts continues the story that Luke's Gospel had ended with Easter (Lk 24:50–53). The New Testament refers to a number of different appearances by the Risen Lord (see 1 Cor 15:3–7).

Jesus did not continue to appear to his disciples indefinitely. Nor did he remain with them continuously as he had during his lifetime (see Jn 20:19–29). Luke has used the biblical number of forty to set a time frame for the appearance of the Lord (see note to Acts 1:3). He insists that the risen Jesus is identical with the person who had died on the cross (v. 3a). Jesus' teaching during this interim period repeats the Kingdom theme of the Gospel. The disciples must wait in Jerusalem until the Holy Spirit comes on them as it had come on Jesus at the beginning of his mission (see Lk 3:22). This event will mark the transition to a new phase of the salvation story—the age of the church. The Ascension (vv. 6–12) also marks a change in the idea of how God will bring salvation. Jesus has not gone to heaven so that he can return with divine power and set up God's kingdom in Jerusalem as some people thought (1:6–7). After receiving the Holy Spirit, Jesus' disciples will become witnesses to Jesus throughout the world.

The apostles and other followers of Jesus, including his mother, Mary, and some other women, form the first community. Luke emphasizes the importance of prayer in the life of the church. Gathering for prayer and celebration of the meal together is one pillar of the church. We will see that the other is charity toward the poor.

Replacing Judas (1:15–26)

The number of apostles has to be restored to Twelve. The Twelve represented the twelve tribes of Israel (see Lk 22:30). This group, however, did not become a permanent office or council in the early church. The church was to become the new Israel (see note to 1:26). By using lots to determine which of two candidates would take Judas's place, the early Christians are permitting God to have the final say in this decision. The qualifications for the candidates—that they followed Jesus from the beginning to the end of his ministry—reflect Luke's understanding of the apostles as the "witnesses" who guarantee the validity of the gospel that is being preached in the churches (see Lk 24:48; Acts 1:8). Luke also takes this occasion to repeat a legend about the death of Judas (vv. 17–20). Peter uses Scripture to show that Judas's betrayal did not destroy God's plan. Judas's death reflects divine punishment for a person who has committed a blasphemous act against God. (A different legend about Judas's death appears in Mt 27:3–10.)

Pentecost, the Coming of the Spirit (2:1–13)

Fire and strong winds are typical elements in appearances of God (see notes to 2:2f). The Greek translation of Isaiah 66:15, 18 says of God's coming: "For behold the Lord will come as a fire, with a flame of fire . . . I am coming to gather all the nations and tongues." The new turn in salvation history, represented by Acts, shows us that God is gathering the "nations and tongues" into one church through the Christian mission. Luke makes Pentecost a double miracle. Not only does the Spirit inspire the disciples' speech, but persons from different nations are able to understand their message. Pentecost anticipates the goal of the missionary effort which the Spirit will inspire in the Church.

The Mission in Jerusalem (2:14–8:3)

Two Sermons by Peter (2:14–3:26)

Luke follows a similar pattern in all of Peter's sermons. His Pentecost sermon is the most famous (2:14–36). It begins with the theme of prophetic fulfillment. The prophets anticipated a powerful outpouring of God's Spirit in the last days. Though the world is *not* ending, God has given that Spirit to the disciples. Peter uses several Old Testament quotations to demonstrate that the risen Jesus is the Messiah whom God had promised. God has established the crucified Jesus as Lord and Christ in heaven (v. 36).

Peter's speech has a profound impact on the crowd. The universality of the Christian mission is represented by these converts from the distant corners of the earth. Baptism is the rite though which the new converts receive forgiveness of sins and the gift of the Holy Spirit (2:37–41). Acts 2:42–47 describe the unity of the growing community. The fundamental elements of Christian community are presented: teaching, fellowship, breaking bread, and prayer.

Christians demonstrate their care for one another by giving to the poor. The early church did not force members to renounce everything, as Peter and the others had done. Many would continue to own property and practice their trade. In this the church was different from groups like the Jewish sect called the Essenes. It expected members to turn over property to the sect as a condition of joining monastic-like groups. Essenes who lived in villages were required to turn over a set number of days wages to the group's overseer. Ancient philosophers described the ideal relationship between friends as sharing all things in common. Acts depicts a Christian community that spontaneously fulfills such ideals.

Luke frequently uses miracles to provide evidence for the faith that people should have in Jesus. The healing of a crippled man (3:1–10) provides the occasion for Peter's second speech (3:11–26). Once again the speech is a brief recitation of the salvation history, which has been fulfilled in Jesus. God's promise to Abraham has been realized in Jesus (3:25f).

Peter and John before the Sanhedrin (4:1–31)

This scene is the first of a number of trial scenes in Acts. A pattern is developed: (a) the miracle attracts attention; (b) the apostles teach those who have been attracted by the miracle; (c) arrest of the missionary by jealous (Jewish) officials; (d) trial of the missionary; (e) miraculous escape or vindication of the mission. At first, the trials are orderly. The judges take a moderate approach and only warn the disciples, but opposition to the Christian mission will increase until Stephen is murdered by an enraged mob. You will notice that the apostles never claim any miraculous powers for themselves. Miracles are done in the name of Jesus (v. 10). All of the miracles have some connection with the mission to spread the gospel. Acts 4:12 expresses the belief that motivates preaching the gospel throughout the world: "There is no salvation through anyone else, nor is there any other name under heaven given to the human race by which we are to be saved."

The communal prayer that follows the apostles' release (4:23–31) shows that Christians never lost their confidence in God's power to rescue them from danger. What happened to Jesus, and will shortly happen to martyrs like Stephen, is not a defeat for Christians. God's plan for salvation can make use of such events. God responds to this prayer with a second Pentecost: the Holy Spirit comes to all who are present.

Sharing Possessions in the Community (4:32–5:16)

Luke elaborates on the theme of shared property. He first presents striking examples of generosity by persons who were willing to follow the sayings of Jesus that encouraged people to sell all and become disciples (see Lk 12:33; 16: 9,11,13). The story of Ananias and Sapphira provides a somewhat comic illustration of what might happen to persons who attempt to pretend that they have the generosity of disciples while secreting money for their own use (compare the Rich Fool, Lk 12:16–21). Once again, death is viewed as God's judgment against persons who have done something blasphemous. They were not required to sell the property in order to be part of the community. Their sin was in the attempt to deceive the Holy Spirit. Human beings can be taken in by fraud, but God will always know what is in a person's heart. No one can cheat God. We may refuse to follow these examples of Christians helping those in need. We may even devise a scheme to appear to help the poor while keeping more for ourselves, but if we do, we will have to answer to God.

Trial before the Sanhedrin (5:17–42)

The miracles of the previous passage lead to jealousy and another imprisonment. This time we learn that no one could keep the apostles in jail if God wished them to continue preaching elsewhere. An angel takes them from prison to preach in the Temple area. This miraculous sign further enrages the opposition. The apostles are released thanks to the judicial prudence of Gamaliel, a Pharisee who demonstrates respect for God's plan (v. 39), but some people are now angry enough to kill the apostles (v. 33).

Deacons for the Hellenists (6:1–7)

This passage presents several difficulties, since it does not fit with what follows. The distinction between Hebrews and Hellenists seems to be based on an individual's mother tongue. The Hellenists would be Jewish converts to Christianity who spoke Greek. The description of the Seven as persons who would take care of the distribution of food, so that the apostles could devote themselves to prayer and preaching, suggests that the Seven were to be like deacons in the church at a later date. They must oversee the material arrangements and aid to the poor. Verse 6 describes the process, prayer, and laying on of hands by which persons were installed in offices in the church during Luke's time. In the next episode (v. 8) we learn that the most famous of the persons chosen engages in ministry of preaching like Peter and the other apostles.

Trial and Death of Stephen (6:8–8:3)

This trial scene is the longest in Acts. Stephen emphasizes Israel's past failures. His speech prepares for the mission to the Gentiles as it develops in the plot of Acts. Luke creates a link between Stephen and the hero of that mission, Paul, by picturing Paul—who tells us that he had persecuted the church out of zeal for ancestral tradition (see Gal 1:13; 1 Cor 15:9b; Phil 3:6)—as a witness to Stephen's death (8:1). Luke's Paul later refers to this event as evidence of his initial hostility to Christianity (22:20). Luke also uses the Stephen episode to tie the emergence of a non-Jewish Christianity to the ministry of Jesus. The charges against Stephen (6:13f) are similar to those brought against Jesus. False witnesses testify that Stephen attacks the Temple and the Law, and they predict that Jesus will destroy the Temple. The tradition that Jesus' predictions about the destruction of the Temple were brought into his Jewish trial is well established in the Synoptic Gospels (see Mk 14:58; Mt 26:61; Mk 15:29; Mt 27:40). Luke omits this detail from the appearance of Jesus before the Council in his Gospel and places it here.

Predictions that God will destroy a corrupt Temple to establish one that is a holy place appear in the Prophets (see Jer 7:11; Zec 14:21; Mal 3:1; Is 56:7). The Jewish sect (known as the Essenes) was severely critical of the corrupt priesthood and calendar used in the Temple. Their criticism stems from a concern for more exact observance of the Law. By contrast, the Stephen episode ties criticism of the Temple to an attack on the Law.

Later in Acts, similar suspicions will be voiced against Paul (see 22:20f). Like Stephen, he will be seized on the grounds that he is attacking the Temple (= "this place") and the Law. Two further charges are made against Paul. He speaks against the Jewish people, and he has committed a sacrilegious act by bringing a Gentile into the area reserved for Jews (22:28). Luke's narrative shows that Stephen and Paul were not attacking the Law. Luke has shown that the Jerusalem Christians were constantly in the Temple praying. There is no basis for the accusations brought against either Stephen or Paul, just as there had been no basis for the charges against Jesus (see Lk 23:4f, 13–15, 22).

Many interpreters have suggested that Luke is using the trial scenes in Acts to defend Christianity against the suspicions of outsiders (see introduction to Acts, p. 1526). Political insurrection, disregard for ancestral traditions, and acts of impiety like defiling a temple were terrible deeds, all of which could stir local as well as Roman officials to punish the perpetrators. The Roman authorities were particularly suspicious of groups that they thought might lead to rebellion among the peoples of the empire. At the same time, the Romans protected sacred places and traditional religious practices. Special edicts from the emperor prohibited local officials from taking advantage of their Jewish populace by seizing money collected for the Temple in Jerusalem, forcing Jews to appear in court on the Sabbath, and the like. Christians were particularly suspect, since their religious practices were not the traditions of an ancient people. Luke may be attempting to answer this objection by demonstrating that Christianity is the true heir of the Jewish tradition.

Stephen's speech (7:2–53) recites salvation history to indict Israel for failure to obey God's commands. Such a speech would not be out of place in a Jewish context. One of the rule books of the Essene sect, *The Damascus Document,* begins in a similar way. It concludes that because Israel had been unfaithful, even though she had suffered punishment for various misdeeds, God had taken the promises away from the nation as a whole. Only the small remnant of righteous Jews who made up the Essene sect will experience the blessings of salvation when the Messiah comes.

By implying that the audience shares an ancestral hostility to God's prophets (vv. 51–53), Stephen fuels a rage that not only kills him but also spawns persecution against other Christians. Since it scatters Christians outside Jerusalem (8:1), this hostility indirectly furthers God's plan. Stephen's vision of the risen Lord exalted in heaven recalls a saying that Mark reports Jesus using before the high priest (Mk 14:62). Visions of the heavenly Son of Man usually carry overtones of divine judgment in the New Testament (compare Rv 1:7–18). As readers, we know that God will vindicate the faithful witness. You may have picked up another similarity between the death of Stephen and that of Jesus. Stephen dies peacefully with words of forgiveness on his lips (compare Lk 23:34, 46). There is one important difference. Jesus had prayed to God, the Father; Stephen addresses his prayer to Jesus whom he has seen standing at God's right hand.

Mission in Judea and Samaria (8:4–9:43)

Philip Preaches outside Jerusalem (8:4–40)

The gospel begins to be spread outside Jerusalem to those who have some contact with Judaism: the Samaritans, who had their own version of the Law of Moses, and an Ethiopian, who was already interested in the traditions of the Jewish people. Several Lucan themes appear in this section. Philip's instruction about Isaiah (8:30–35) shows that Jesus is the fulfillment of what is written in the Prophets. Unlike the Jerusalem crowd who had turned a deaf ear to such arguments, the Ethiopian demonstrates the proper response: he becomes a disciple of Jesus by being baptized. This story also introduces a minor theme, which some scholars consider part of Luke's apologetic task. Prominent people either become Christians, listen to the apostles' preaching with sympathy and often ask them to return, or provide some other form of assistance.

The conversion of the Samaritans and the conflict with Simon the magician introduce two more themes: the continuity of the new Christian mission with the Jerusalem apostolate and the superiority of Christianity to all forms of pagan superstition and religion. We have already seen that the gift of the Holy Spirit defines Christian baptism for Luke (Acts 2:38; 10:48), who contrasts it with the water baptism of John the Baptist (Lk 3:16; Acts 1:5; 11:16; 18:25; 19:3f). Christians are baptized in the name of Jesus. Baptism involves forgiveness of the past sins of a life without God, as well as receiving the Spirit. Acts 8:16 departs from the normal pattern, since Philip has baptized in the name of the Lord, but his converts did not receive the Spirit until Peter and John came from Jerusalem to lay hands on them (8:14–17).

In Catholic tradition this text has been cited as one of the biblical foundations for the sacrament of confirmation in which the Spirit is conferred subsequent to baptism (see, for example, *The Catholic Catechism,* No. 1288). Pentecostal Christians affirm that persons who have not experienced the Spirit coming over them are not yet fully Christian. As presented in the Acts of the Apostles, episodes in which the Spirit is separated from water baptism reflect exceptional occurrences. In the conversion of Cornelius, for example, the Spirit will indicate that God has accepted the new converts even before water baptism. Here, the separation between water baptism and receiving the Spirit allows Luke to show that the new mission takes place under the sponsorship of Jerusalem. Luke indicates that the Spirit always operates in and through the church.

The encounter with Simon the magician allows Luke to address another possible objection to Christianity. We have seen that Luke frequently uses miracle stories or references to miracle working to initiate interest in the Christian preaching. In antiquity, healings and other extraordinary events that occurred through assistance from a god or goddess might be called miracles, but a hostile bystander might accuse the miracle worker of being nothing more than a magician. The contest between Moses and the magicians at Pharaoh's court (Ex 7:8f, 12) provides a biblical pattern for evaluating magic. Even though they may duplicate some of Moses' miracles, no magician can duplicate or withstand the power that comes from the Lord. The Simon incident demonstrates the power of Christianity to destroy such superstitions. Luke mentions another common charge against religious charlatans: greed. The Christian mission is not driven by desire for money (3:1–10). Christians sell property and share their possessions.

Conversion of Paul (9:1–30)

Paul's conversion demonstrates God's power to use everything, even the hostile persecutor, to achieve the divine purpose. Paul himself tells us little about the call from God that transformed him from being an enemy of the Jesus movement to being its advocate (see Gal 1:11–24). Luke then presents three versions of Paul's conversion (Acts 9:1–19; 22, 4–16, 17–21; 26:12–18), which differ from each other. Each of the four accounts serves an apologetic purpose. Paul's own account in Galatians 1 belongs to an impassioned defense of his preaching to the Gentiles. He must show that, in telling them they could be saved through belief in Jesus without also taking on obligations of the Jewish Law, he is not distorting the gospel or breaking agreements made with Jerusalem. Acts 9 must vindicate Paul as the representative of God's offer of salvation to the Gentiles. The next two accounts (Acts 22 and 26) of Paul's conversion occur in speeches that Paul gives while imprisoned in Jerusalem.

Luke's accounts share a core of details: (a) letters from the high priest; (b) Paul is approaching Damascus; (c) light from heaven shines around Paul [and in #3, Acts 26, around those with him]; (d) he [#3: we] falls to the ground; (e) hears a voice speaking to him (#3: in Hebrew); (f) "Saul, Saul, why are you persecuting me?" [#3: "hard for you to kick against the goad"); (f) asks identity of speaker; and (g) "Jesus, whom you are persecuting." This core suggests a common story about Paul's conversion. After this point the three accounts diverge. Acts 9:12–16 expands on the theme of Paul's blindness. Ananias comes to Paul as "healer" (note the emphasis on the cure in v. 18). Acts 22:11a, 12f gives a more abbreviated account, and Acts 26 omits these details altogether as it does the details about the actions of Paul's companions after the appearance, the visit of Ananias, and Paul's baptism. In Acts 9:16, the Lord tells Ananias of Paul's commission. In Acts 22:14f, Ananias gives the commission to Paul, but in 26:16b–18, Paul receives the commission directly from the Lord.

The blinding/healing sequence in Acts 9:12–19 suggests that the blinding of Paul is an act of God's displeasure similar to the temporary blindness God inflicts on the magician Elymas (Acts 13:9–11; see also the threat of divine punishment in Acts 8:22–24). Paul's own version and the later stories in Acts emphasize Paul's commission, but this plays no role in the narrative about Paul. God uses it as an argument to persuade Ananias to go to Paul. Acts 9:15 has been phrased so that it reflects the commission given the disciples in 1:8. The ensuing versions of the story will relate the commission to Paul's vision of Christ and to the details of his specific role in the Gentile mission as it has unfolded in Acts. Here, Luke uses the story of the miraculous conversion of the persecutor of Christianity to initiate the preparation for that global mission, which is the subject of this section of the book.

The Church Continues to Grow (9:32–43)

Luke concludes the section with two stories from Peter's mission. The healing of Tabitha follows the same pattern as Jesus' own healing of Talitha, (see Mk 5:41; Lk 7:15). Tabitha indicates the important roles that women believers play in the growth of Christianity. Not only is she an example of piety and charity, but she also has a group of poor widows who assemble in her home. This period of peace and growth shows that the community has successfully weathered the storm of persecution that began with Stephen's martyrdom.

Inauguration of the Gentile Mission (10:1–15:35)

Conversion of Cornelius (10:1–11:26)

Before Paul can fulfill his role as one who carries the gospel from Jerusalem to Rome, the leaders of the church must formally accept Gentiles into the Christian fellowship. The common meal was the basic expression of Christian unity. Paul reports an episode in which Jewish Christians from Jerusalem were unwilling to eat with the Gentile members of the Antioch church, presumably because they felt that such behavior would have violated the food laws that set Jews apart from other peoples. Paul says that before these people came, Peter himself was willing to share the meal with Gentile Christians, but that when the stricter Jewish Christians arrived, Peter, Barnabas, and other Jewish Christians began to celebrate a separate meal (see Gal 2:11–14). Peter may have been attempting to preserve harmony in the church by not offending Jewish Christians who could not bring themselves to change a whole lifetime of kosher food laws. The story of how Peter came to accept Gentile converts, which Luke repeats here, bears traces of that old dispute. God must direct Peter, in a vision, to renounce his former understanding of what represented clean and unclean food.

Peter takes others with him to Cornelius's house so that he has witnesses to what has happened. His sermon acknowledges the fact that God is impartial. Anyone can receive salvation through Jesus if that person honors God and acts justly. The Spirit even demonstrates to Peter and the others that Gentiles are to be accepted into the church by granting Cornelius and his household a mini-Pentecost before they are baptized (10:44–48). Upon his return to Jerusalem, Peter gains official approval for his actions from the other leaders there. He reports everything that had happened in connection with the Cornelius episode so that those in Jerusalem agree that "God has then granted life-giving repentance to the Gentiles too" (11:18).

The first church to include Jews and Gentiles in a single fellowship is founded by anonymous Christians in Antioch. Quickly, however, they obtain the services of two famous apostles, Barnabas and Paul. Barnabas is sent by the authorities in Jerusalem. He provides the link between Antioch and the church in Jerusalem (11:19–26). Acts 11:26 notes that the name "Christians" originated in Antioch. It appears that this name was first given to followers of Jesus by outsiders. It may have implied some scorn for the leader whom Christians worshipped, as appears to be the case when Agrippa uses it in Acts 26:28.

Paul's First Missionary Journey (11:27–14:28)

The missionary efforts of Barnabas and Paul illustrate one of the principles of Luke's account of salvation history. Jewish rejection of the gospel leads the apostles to turn to the Gentiles, who receive God's salvation with joy. Paul's letters contain a number of references to an offering from his Gentile churches, which he took to Christians in Jerusalem (see Gal 2:10; 1 Cor 16:1–4; 2 Cor 8f). He does not deliver that collection until the final visit to Jerusalem (Rom 15:30–32). Many scholars think that Luke has confused that episode with another tradition about some form of famine relief that had been associated with the predictions of a Christian prophet (Acts 11:27–30).

The Jerusalem church suffers yet another round of persecution. We are told that James, the son of Zebedee, was martyred by the Jewish king and that Peter was imprisoned. He would have been executed if God had not intervened to rescue him from jail (Acts 12:1–19). Herod Agrippa suffers a tortured death as divine punishment for his impiety (12:20–24). In ancient stories, being eaten by worms was a typical punishment for tyrants who scorned the gods. A Jewish account of Herod's death has been preserved by the historian Josephus. His version agrees with Luke that Herod had accepted divine honors from his subjects and so been struck down. Josephus says, however, that the occasion was the celebration of athletic games at Caesarea.

Paul's first missionary journey establishes the pattern of first preaching in Jewish synagogues and then turning to the Gentiles. Paul makes this principle explicit in his sermon at Pisidian Antioch (13:44–47). We have already seen that Luke wishes to show that Christianity is superior to pagan superstition. Paul overcomes a Jewish magician who had had influence with the Roman proconsul on Cyprus (13:4–12), and in keeping with Luke's interest in the conversion of prominent persons, the proconsul becomes a believer. At Lystra, Paul and Barnabas must actually prevent the people from offering sacrifices to them as if they were pagan gods in human form (14: 8–18). Throughout this journey the apostles are plagued by hostility from Jews at the same time that they receive warm receptions from the Gentiles.

Gentile Mission Confirmed in Jerusalem (15:1–35)

All of these events prove to the leaders of the church that God does want them to accept Gentiles into the church. They must face the objections of Jewish Christians, however, who feel that to admit Gentiles without requiring them to observe the Law contradicts the whole story of God's covenant with Israel. They insisted that Jesus was the Messiah for those who sought to be faithful children of Abraham and followers of Moses. In addition to Acts, we have Paul's report of the council in Jerusalem (Gal 2:1–10). The two versions of the meeting in Jerusalem do not agree in many of their details. Some scholars think that Paul is referring to an earlier meeting. When the agreement to divide missionary efforts, with Peter going to Jews and Paul to Gentiles, failed to resolve the difficulties that arose in mixed churches like Antioch, another meeting was held. At that meeting some restrictions were laid on the Gentiles. They had to avoid idolatry, avoid meat that Jewish law would have considered impure, and not enter into marriages that Jewish law considered incestuous. The decree is mentioned again in Acts 21:25. The list of prohibitions is based on rules in Leviticus 17–18 that regulate the behavior of non-Jews who live among Jews. Adopting these rules would make it possible for Jewish and Gentile Christians to enjoy table fellowship.

Luke knew of a letter sent by James to Antioch that stated these rules. He presumed that they came from the same meeting at which Paul and Barnabas received authorization for a mission to the Gentiles that would not require the Gentiles to observe Jewish practices. Paul insists that there were no rules imposed on the Gentiles (Gal 2:6). By Luke's time, the problem of table fellowship had disappeared, as most churches were predominantly Gentile. The significance of the Jerusalem Council lies in the way in which church leaders were able to recognize and officially affirm the new direction in salvation history that would permit expansion of the gospel beyond the nation and culture in which it was born to all peoples of the earth.

The Mission of Paul to the Ends of the Earth (15:36–28:31)

Second Missionary Journey (15:36–18:23)

Paul now begins the journeys that will take the gospel throughout the rest of the empire. On this journey, he will take the decisive step of crossing from Asia Minor into Greece, where some of the most important Pauline churches would be founded. The New Testament contains Paul's own letters to churches in Thessalonica, Philippi, and Corinth. When Paul arrives in Europe, the narrative style suddenly changes from the third person to the first person "we." Sections of journey narrative in the "we" style appear throughout the rest of Acts (16:6–12 [beginning of the European mission]; 20:1–7, 13–16; 21: 1–9, 15–17 [last journey to Jerusalem]; 27:1–28:16 [voyage to Rome]). Some scholars attribute the "we" sections to a travel diary kept by a companion of Paul. The content of these sections matches that of the journeys that Luke has already used to describe the Pauline mission. A shift into the first-person plural was often used by ancient authors for its literary effect. The change in style may represent Luke's way of telling us that *we* have now arrived at the mission for which the rest of the narrative has prepared us. The gospel is to be taken completely beyond Judaism. In time these Gentile Christians will be the sole custodians of a tradition, which God has been preparing since Abraham. It will be their responsibility to see to it that the gospel continues to be preached in all the nations of the earth.

A dream vision takes Paul into Macedonia (16:6–16). Dream visions were frequently cited as the source of divine guidance in the ancient world. Paul's first major foundation is at Philippi, a Roman colony that enjoyed the rights of an Italian city. Paul's letter to the Philippians indicates that he enjoyed close relationships with this church. They sent assistance to Paul when he was imprisoned or working in other areas, and both men and women from the Philippian church worked as missionaries preaching the gospel to others (see Phil 1:14; 4:2f). Acts does not contain much information about the extensive periods of time that Paul lived in communities like Philippi, Thessalonica, and Corinth, nor does Luke refer to persons and issues mentioned in Paul's letters to those churches. There is no evidence in Acts that Luke was familiar with any of Paul's letters. If he had accompanied Paul on some part of his missionary work (see Phlm 24; Col 4:14), Luke cannot have been involved in the major events of Paul's mission in the way that Timothy, Titus, and Silvanus were.

Luke appears to have drawn upon anecdotal material for the major events in each of the cities. He then shapes that material to illustrate his understanding of the growth of the early church. The Philippi episode repeats themes that we have already encountered. Christian preaching is well received by wealthy, respectable citizens, in this case Lydia, a woman who trades in purple cloth (16:12–15). Christianity triumphs over pagan superstition and exploitation of the supernatural for personal gain when Paul exorcises the demon from a slave girl (16:16–18). Like the demons in the Gospel stories (see Lk 4:31–37), this demon recognizes the purpose for which the apostles have come.

Jealousy and lost profits once again fuel false charges against the apostles as persons who incite disorder and destroy ancestral customs. The real opponents of Roman order are the accusers, who stir up the mob with the charges, and the magistrates, who violate Roman law by flogging a Roman citizen. In this case, another miraculous deliverance from prison permits a dramatic conclusion in which the apostle confronts the magistrates with the illegality of their own behavior (16:19–39). It also provides an opportunity for the gospel to be heard by the jailer and his household. We have evidence from Paul's own letters that his preaching in prison resulted in converts (see Philemon).

The episodes at Thessalonica (17:1–9) and Beroea (17:10–15) repeat the patterns of the Philippi episode. Initial success, including prominent converts, leads to jealousy and charges that the apostles are destroying public order and encouraging revolt against Rome. Luke's readers already know that such accusations are false and that hostility will not impede the apostles' mission.

Paul tells us nothing of his stay in Athens except that he remained there alone after sending Timothy to strengthen the faith of the recent converts in Thessalonica (1 Thes 3:1f). Paul may not have succeeded in establishing a church there. Luke, however, uses the occasion to advance his case for the religious superiority of Christianity by showing it to be equal to the philosophical understanding of the divine principle governing the universe, and not simply another form of religious cult, magic, or superstition that sought to sway the masses for the financial gain of its preachers. Its reputation was built on its philosophic schools. Luke refers to the two most popular types of philosophy among the Romans, Epicurean and Stoic (17:18–21). The speech which Paul delivers at their request (17:22–34) touches on common themes in the philosophical account of religion, which was opposed to the superstitious beliefs about the gods found among the masses. God, the invisible, omnipresent creator and sustainer of the universe, is not swayed by rituals nor partial to one group of people over another. Hellenistic Jews had also taken over the language of philosophical monotheism to advocate the superiority of their religious tradition.

Athenians were well known for their piety and their curiosity. Following the practice of ancient rhetoric, the speech opens by seeking to render the audience friendly to the speaker. Paul praises them for these traits. In composing the speech, Luke has apparently modified a common type of altar inscription, ". . . altars of the gods, named unknown, and heroes. . ." to the singular (v. 23). Paul then develops three claims about God that were philosophic commonplaces among both pagan and Jewish authors: (a) God is the creator of the entire universe and consequently has no need of human service or temples (vv. 24f); (b) God has allotted certain zones of the earth for the nations of human beings, who should be grateful for God's ordering of the universe and seek to serve God, who sustains and is present to all created things (vv. 26–28); (c) true worship of God will reject all superstitious practices, such as identifying the creator with the products of human artistry and imagination (v. 29).

The conclusion shifts from the common ground between the Christian preacher and philosophical enlightenment to an appeal for conversion (vv. 30f). It recalls the "unknown" taken from the altar inscriptions, which had served as an example of Athenian piety in verse 24. Inscriptions to unknown deities are a feature of polytheism, since they point to an anxiety to honor deities who might influence events but who are not "named" in the local traditions. Now is the time for a true monotheism. God is not an abstract, creative, sustaining principle, called by many names in the different nations. God is the one who calls on Paul's listeners to repent (= abandon even their philosophical paganism) and accept the message about Jesus as the one in whom all the nations of the earth are to receive salvation. As was the case in earlier missionary speeches, the Resurrection appears as God's evidence for the status of Jesus as judge of all. This departure from the common ground with philosophical theism, however, only draws skepticism or, at best, a puzzled willingness to hear more. The church-founding conversions of other missionary episodes do not occur.

Luke's account of Paul's extensive work in Corinth (18:1–17) refers to the fact that Paul worked at his trade while preaching there, as he did in all of his churches (see 1 Thes 2:9; 1 Cor 4:12; 9). Luke supplies the additional information that Paul's trade was that of tentmaker, probably someone making tents of leather and rough cloth, as well as other items, such as harnesses. He mentions two of Paul's close associates from that mission, Priscilla and Aquila (1 Cor 16:19; Rom 16:3). Luke also tells the story of their instruction of Apollos (18:24–28), whose apostolic work in Corinth Paul mentions in 1 Corinthians 1–4. Luke's brief account of the founding follows the line he has already established: after success in attracting influential persons, hostility from the Jews forces the apostle to turn to the Gentiles. They bring Paul before the Roman proconsul Gallio, who refuses to hear a charge involving Jewish religious law. Gallio's response (v. 14f) reflects what Luke considers to be the ideal response when Christians accused of disturbances, which are internal Jewish affairs, are brought before officials. His reference to Priscilla and Aquila's suffering exile from Rome (18:2) indicates that he knows that Romans often responded differently to disputes that Christian preaching generated within the Jewish community. Gallio's indifference is demonstrated in "burlesque" fashion—that is, by exaggerated and stereotyped actions—in verse 17. He remains indifferent when they beat Sosthenes, the ruler of the synagogue, before his tribunal.

Third Missionary Journey (18:24–21:14)

This section of Acts builds on episodes about the mission in Ephesus, which was the residence of the governor of the province of Asia and the fourth largest city in the empire. Ephesus was also the location of a famous temple of the goddess Artemis, which was one of the wonders of the Hellenistic world. Silver coins from the city depict the temple with the statue of the goddess inside. Paul's confrontation with that cult occupies most of the account of his mission there (19:8–41). Later Paul delivers his farewell speech to leaders of the church in Ephesus (20:17–38). Luke's emphasis on Ephesus may have led him to locate two episodes there that seem to come from separate traditions: (a) the instruction of Apollos, who had received only the baptism of John (18:24–28) and (b) the conferring of the Spirit on persons who had received only the baptism of John (19:1–7). Luke's account assumes that Priscilla and Aquila have moved to Ephesus from Corinth and that Ephesian Christians urged Apollos to go to Corinth. Luke seems to assume that Apollos and Paul had not met (19:1), although Paul writes 1 Corinthians from Ephesus or its environs and says that Apollos was unwilling to return to Corinth (1 Cor 16:8, 12). And although Apollos had only received John's baptism, he is not rebaptized. Priscilla and Aquila are able to bring persons into full Christian discipleship. Yet, the disciples of 19:1–7 have not even heard of the Holy Spirit! Scholars have suggested that this episode would be more appropriate in the area of Syro-Palestine where Jewish baptismal sects would continue to exist well into the third century.

The episode is similar to one in which Peter and John confer the Spirit on Samaritan converts (8:14–25). It serves two functions in Luke's schema for the expanding mission: (a) it shows that Paul is able to win over Jewish sectarians, and (b) it demonstrates the continuity between the Pauline mission and the activity of the Jerusalem church. He brings persons into the community that the Holy Spirit has been creating through the apostles since Pentecost.

Paul's mission in Ephesus is the last story of Paul's activity that is not shadowed by his impending arrest at Jerusalem. Luke's summary continues the pattern of synagogue preaching followed by withdrawal to a Gentile environment. Miracles draw attention to the new movement. They also demonstrate the power of Christianity to destroy superstition and magical practices among the people (19:8–20). The success of Christian preaching, however, awakens hostility from persons who exploit the presence of the temple of Artemis. Demetrius's speech (see v. 26) to his fellow silversmiths alludes to the speech of Acts 17:24f. Christian preaching teaches people that human temples and artifacts do not represent God. As had been the case in earlier conflicts with magicians, fears for the economic loss that would result from accepting the Christian gospel spark the hostility. As in the Gallio case, the local town clerk refuses to become involved. The Christians have not committed any impious acts such as robbing the temple or dishonoring the goddess. Demetrius is the one who is endangering public order by inciting the crowds.

This conclusion seems to represent an ideal rather than reality. As Luke fills out the rest of the journey with brief notices of stops and miracles performed by the apostle (20:1–16), he makes it appear that Paul left Ephesus of his own volition and that he avoided returning there in order to save time needed to reach Jerusalem by Pentecost (20:16). Yet the summons to the officials of the church in Ephesus for a farewell meeting at Miletus (20:17f) suggests that in fact Paul may have been banished from Ephesus. Paul's obscure reference to conflict in Ephesus (see 1 Cor 15:32a) implies that at one time he suffered imprisonment or punishment there.

Paul's farewell to the Ephesians (20:17–35) provides the occasion for Luke to reflect on the transition from the generation of the apostles to the church of his own day. The farewell speech of the dying patriarch was an established genre in Hellenistic Jewish writing. The Old Testament contains a farewell speech from Moses to Israel (Dt 29–32). In such speeches, the dying patriarch exhorts his offspring to follow the Law, anticipates their future disobedience (in most cases), and sets before them the example of his own life. Moses also provides for the future leadership of the people by appointing Joshua as his successor. You can see that Luke has incorporated many of these elements in this speech. The Spirit has been warning Paul that he faces imprisonment and hardship in Jerusalem. He holds up his own life as an exemplary model of complete devotion to bearing witness to the gospel no matter what the circumstances. Unlike the pagans, who sought to enrich themselves from the superstitions of the people, Paul has never sought money from his converts. He commends his own example of working at a trade, not only because it frees the apostle and his associates from suspicion of greed but also provides the opportunity to give aid to the weak (v. 35). Thus we find Paul's final word of admonition returning to the example that the earliest Jerusalem community had set. Christians donate their property for support of the poor.

The farewell speech is also the time to look from the ideal of the past into the dangers of the future. Paul warns of divisions even within the ranks of the community's leaders. He admonishes the presbyters and "overseers" (v. 28; see Phil 1:1), who have charge of the community left behind by the apostles, to watch over themselves as well as the church. They must continue proclaiming the gospel and exhorting others to faith and repentance. In Luke's narrative we have now seen the completion of the apostolic period. Officials from local churches, who are called "elders" or "overseers," must take over the community. These persons have been appointed by apostles and commissioned by imposition of hands (14:23). In that sense, they appear as successors to the apostles. But just as Joshua could not be another Moses, so they are not replacement apostles. The Spirit that has guided the church throughout the developments of the apostolic period must continue to direct her course.

Paul's dedication to his mission, even in the face of sure suffering, leads him to continue the journey (21:4). Even the Christian prophet Agabus, whom we know to be reliable because he predicted the famine under Claudius (see 11: 28), warns Paul that in Jerusalem the Jews will bind him and hand him over to the Romans. See what Paul himself wrote to the Romans just before he left for Jerusalem (Rom 15:31). He was concerned about what he might suffer from unbelievers as well as the fact that the Jewish Christian church might reject the offering that he brings.

Paul's Arrest and Imprisonment at Jerusalem (21:15–26:32)

As soon as Paul arrives in Jerusalem, James warns him that devout Jewish Christians suspect Paul of leading Christians who are Jewish away from their ancestral traditions. James proposes that Paul demonstrate his own piety by paying the expenses for some persons who had taken a private vow. Ironically, Paul's participation in these rites leads to his arrest. We have already seen that the charges against him for turning people against the Law and the Temple were anticipated in the story of Stephen's martyrdom. Luke uses the situation of Paul's imprisonment in Jerusalem to provide speeches in which Paul defends and explains his mission. His first speech to the Jerusalem crowd (22:1–21) points to the extreme piety of his early life. Only the direct intervention of God could change Paul's behavior. Paul refers to his conversion as evidence for God's direction of his life and ministry. This theme is underlined by a second vision of Christ as Paul is praying in the Temple (22:17–21).

During his imprisonment at Philippi, Paul said nothing about his Roman citizenship until after he had been flogged (16:37). Here he stops the Roman commander as he is about to interrogate Paul under torture (22:25–29). Though Paul is able to stall the Sanhedrin by pitting the Pharisees against the Sadducees, the Romans must intervene by moving Paul to Caesarea under heavy guard (Acts 23). With the transfer to Caesarea, Paul is now in Roman hands. However sympathetically they listen to Paul's preaching, the Roman authorities take no steps to gain his release. Paul's first speech before Felix, the Roman procurator of Judea, defends the Jewish character of his own personal conduct (24: 10–21). He remains in prison through a change in the Roman administration of the province. The Jews hope that the new procurator will turn Paul over to them. Faced with the possibility that he might be tried in Jerusalem, Paul invokes the ultimate privilege of a Roman citizen, the right to be heard by a court in Rome itself (25:1–12). The Roman procurator repeats the details of Paul's situation to the visiting Jewish king, Herod Agrippa II. Festus, Felix's successor as procurator, clearly understands that Paul has not been charged with any crime under Roman law. At best, the squabble concerns points of Jewish law. Since Agrippa is curious about Paul, Felix arranges for a final speech by the apostle (26: 1–23). Paul defends himself by repeating the circumstances of his life as a devout Jew who was converted by a divine vision which no one could ignore. In this account of Paul's conversion, Luke focuses upon the divine commission to be a missionary to the Gentiles (26:16–18). After the hearing, both Festus and Agrippa agree that Paul is innocent. Luke may be following the pattern set out in Jesus' trial. Pilate and Herod both agree that Jesus is innocent. But Paul cannot be released, since he has demanded a hearing in the imperial court (26:30–32).

Paul's Journey to Rome (27:1–28:31)

We have already seen that the conclusion of Acts, in which Paul is preaching the gospel at Rome, though under house arrest (28:17–31), brings Luke's plot to a climax. The gospel has reached the capital of the civilized world. Luke's account of how Paul came to Rome makes use of another type of ancient adventure story, the sea voyage. Such voyages frequently included descriptions of how the hero escaped from shipwreck, pirates, and other such dangers. The story of Paul's journey is told with all the high drama of such tales. During the vicious storm that destroys the ship and has the survivors washed up on the beach at Malta, Paul demonstrates his own confidence in God and superiority to the fears of the ship's crew. Paul is even able to celebrate a meal of bread, which he has blessed (27:35f). The wording reminds Christians of the Eucharist (note to 27:35). It is impossible to sail across the Mediterranean in winter, so the group is forced to stay on Malta. The episode associated with that stay includes the drama of native peoples watching the shipwrecked party. When Paul is unharmed by a poisonous snake, they conclude that he must be a god (28:3–6). Paul wins more friends on the island by healing the sick, and they are provided with everything needed to continue the journey (vv. 7–10). Although clearly narrated with an eye toward entertaining the reader, the Malta story also points out that God will provide whatever is necessary for the apostle to fulfill his mission. The superstitious pagans had ignored Paul's prophetic warning that attempting to sail so close to winter would destroy both ship and cargo. The island natives thought that the snake was divine punishment for some evil Paul had committed until they saw that he escaped unharmed. In each case, the apostle comes through the threat to his life because he places all of his trust in the Lord.

Things We Have Learned from Acts

Now that we have finished reading through Acts, we should take some time to reflect on the impact of the narrative as a whole. Luke has made striking use of traditions he inherited about the apostles—a plan of salvation history and the art of storytelling to instruct us about the development of God's plan of salvation in the apostolic age.

Judaism Is the Inherited Tradition of the Church

The church developed according to a divine plan of salvation, which remains rooted in the experiences of Israel. When God led the church to turn toward the Gentiles, this heritage was not forgotten although it was no longer necessary for a person to be culturally and legally a Jew in order to experience salvation.

God Seeks the Salvation of All the Peoples on Earth

Acts shows us that the apostles had to venture beyond their own Jewish culture in order to take the gospel to the ends of the earth. Though they found this task difficult, since it often resulted in hostility from fellow Jews, all the apostles accepted this growth toward becoming a truly universal church as an expression of God's will. The task is not over. The church still must venture into other lands and cultures to fulfill the mission that is hers until the end of time: to bear witness to the gospel everywhere.

The Church Is a Spirit-Guided Institution

You will notice that in Acts the Spirit works in and through the official leaders and structures of the community. Developments like the admission of Gentiles were clearly difficult adjustments, but we see that the leaders of the community in Jerusalem eventually come to express what is the will of God. Furthermore, as the apostle Paul leaves the scene, he has established "elders" or "overseers" in his churches. It is necessary that persons be designated as leaders now that the apostolic age has passed. Although many people think that an institution can never be the vehicle for the Spirit, Acts insists that the church is such a vehicle.

Christians Must Be Willing to Suffer for the Gospel

Since the apostles overcome the sufferings and imprisonments they face, we may forget how relentless the onset of hostility is. No form of suffering causes any of the apostles to stray from the mission given by God and cease to proclaim the gospel. There is no instance in which preaching the gospel does not awaken some form of resistance.

The Christian Fellowship Has Special Marks of Its Identity

Luke has presented us with ideal pictures of what the church should be. We see the harmonious gathering of diverse peoples for prayer, preaching by the apostles, and community meals. We also see a community in which concern for the weak and needy is one of the most important parts of its communal life.

The Church Calls People to Religious Conversion

Because the church preaches religious conversion, it comes into conflict with all forms of pseudo-religion and superstition. Magical practices have no place in Christian life, nor do movements that use the religious sentiments of the masses to collect money from those who are taken in by the propaganda of such false cults. Christians give their resources to help those in need. They speak out against any false idea of God that would require buildings and other material goods for God or God's servants. Christians remain loyal to the basic institutions of their society, even when those institutions seem to be used against them by persons who do not like the criticism of false beliefs and behavior that comes from the gospel.

P.P.

FURTHER READING

Barrett, C. K. *The Acts of the Apostles*. Vol. 1: *Preliminary Introduction and Commentary on Acts 1–14;* Vol. 2: *Introduction and Commentary on Acts 15–28*. International Critical Commentary. Edinburgh: T. & T. Clark, 1994, 1998.

Fitzmyer, J. A. *The Acts of the Apostles*. Anchor Bible 31. New York: Doubleday, 1998.

Johnson, L. T. *The Acts of the Apostles*. Sacra Pagina 5. Collegeville, MN: Liturgical Press/Michael Glazier, 1992.

Klauck, Hans-Josef. *Magic and Paganism in Early Christianity: The World of the Acts of the Apostles*. Minneapolis: Fortress, 2003.

PAUL AND HIS WRITINGS

MARY ANN GETTY AND CAROLYN OSIEK

According to Acts, Paul was born in Tarsus, a city on the eastern end of the Mediterranean Sea, in what is now Turkey, around AD 10. He was a Roman citizen from birth, a status that carried certain privileges. He was also, according to Acts, a student of Gamaliel, a renowned rabbi, and a Pharisee, that is, a member of a strictly observant Jewish party. His own writings indicate that he was well educated in the Greek language and in Pharisaic methods of biblical interpretation. Both Paul and Acts say that he was so zealous for the Jewish Law before his conversion that he persecuted those who, he believed, had strayed from the Law by believing that Jesus was the Christ. During this earlier part of the sketch of Paul's life in Acts, he is called by his Jewish name, Saul. When in the narrative he begins to encounter the Roman world (13:9), Luke calls him by his Roman name, Paul.

After experiencing a revelation of the Risen Christ from God, however, Paul himself joined these followers of "the Way" as a young adult, about AD 34. He firmly believed that his conversion included a call to preach the Christian message of salvation to all people, including the Gentiles. Paul spent the rest of his life, about thirty years, in pursuit of this mission. After three years in Arabia and a brief visit to Jerusalem, he embarked on his missionary career. After some years working in the Eastern Mediterranean area as far west as Greece, he visited Jerusalem to deliver relief funds collected in Asia Minor and Greece. He then intended to visit Rome and Spain, but in Jerusalem he met with increasing opposition from some Jewish leaders and was arrested and brought to Rome around AD 60. Between AD 48 and his death around AD 62, Paul wrote letters to communities with which he had worked, answering their questions and preaching the gospel as he understood it to have been revealed to him.

Sources

We learn about Paul's life from his own letters and from Luke's account in the Acts of the Apostles (cf. Acts 9:1–30; 11:1–28:31). There are some discrepancies between what Paul says and what Luke records about certain incidents of Paul's career: for example, Luke and Paul do not agree about whether the Council of Jerusalem, around AD 50, stipulated that the Gentiles should keep some aspects of the Jewish Law (see Acts 15 and Galatians 2:1–10). We must remember that when Luke writes about Paul's life, his account is a secondary source: it was written more than a generation after Paul (about AD 85), at a time when the major issue of non-Jewish converts was no longer as pressing. Luke minimizes the tensions involved in integrating the Gentiles into the church.

The Epistles of Paul

There are thirteen letters or epistles ascribed to Paul, but most commentators recognize only seven of these as definitely written by the apostle; the others are attributed to disciples of Paul. The seven letters certainly written by Paul himself are Romans, 1 and 2 Corinthians, Galatians, Philippians, 1 Thessalonians, and Philemon. The remaining six letters (that is, Ephesians, Colossians, 2 Thessalonians, 1 and 2 Timothy, and Titus) are often called "Deutero-Pauline." Among the latter group, the Pauline authorship of 2 Thessalonians and Colossians is most disputed. For various reasons commentators believe that these six letters were not actually written by Paul but instead were written by later Christians familiar with his teachings. Disciples could have claimed to be writing in Paul's name in order to gain authority for their own adaptations of his teaching, an accepted practice among the ancients. In the New Testament, the Pauline writings are arranged in two groups: first, letters to communities; second, letters to individuals. Within each group they run roughly from the longest to the shortest. The letters are not arranged in the order in which they were written.

Letters and Epistles

Paul's letters follow the fairly simple structure of a letter in Greek or Roman culture. Such letters were not placed in envelopes, so the address is given right at the start. Then follows the body of the letter; finally, the conclusion contains personal greetings and instructions. Some scholars have suggested a distinction between more formal, systematic "epistles" and informal "letters." In this way of thinking, Romans would be an example of a formal epistle, whereas Philemon or Titus would be examples of an informal letter. Even some of those letters supposedly written to individuals may really be formal "epistles" intended for wider circulation. Many interpreters have also noted a fundamental structure discernible in many of Paul's writings, but most clearly in Romans. Paul first outlines his most basic teachings in a section sometimes called the doctrinal or "indicative" part. This is followed by an application of these teachings in Paul's exhortations to the community, a section called the "imperative" or "parenetical" (that is, exhortatory) part of the body of the letter.

The Apostle and His Gospel

Much of the Christian vocabulary we have become so familiar with and associate with the ministry of Jesus actually originated with Paul. For example, Paul was, as far as we know, the first to coin a Christian meaning for the words *apostle, gospel, charism, ministry,* and many doctrinal phrases such as "justification by faith." As the first Christian writer, Paul began to develop specifically Christian terminology, even though many of the terms he uses will have roots in Judaism, or other meanings in secular Greek.

Paul's writings predate any of our written Gospels. Paul is the first to speak about preaching the gospel, although he does not conceive this as a story about the life and ministry of Jesus. The idea of the gospel, which appears even in the Old Testament (see, for example, Is 61:1–2, "glad tidings") means the "good news." For Paul this is the message of salvation now accessible to all through faith in Jesus Christ. In Romans, Paul describes the gospel as the "power of God" to save all who believe (Rom 1:16). Thus, Paul does not think of the gospel as a story of the events in Jesus' life, nor even as a set of beliefs about Jesus. Rather, the gospel is the "good news" that all who believe in Jesus are already saved.

Paul rarely speaks of any actions or words of Jesus during his lifetime. Rather, he focuses on God's power, working through the death and resurrection of Jesus, to save Jews and Greeks (that is, all people) alike. While reading Paul it is well to remember that, for him, the term *gospel* means the proclamation of faith in God's forgiveness or the realization in human life of the "good news" that Jesus Christ has come to bring salvation to all people.

In his writings, Paul usually identifies himself as an apostle (Rom 1:1; 11:13; 1 Cor 1:1; 4:9; 9:lf, 5; 15:9; 2 Cor 1:1; 11:5, 13; 12:11, 12; and so on). The term *apostle* literally means "one sent," who represents the sender and is entrusted with the sender's authority and message. God is the source of Paul's apostleship.

The Letters in Circulation

The apostle's authority was in his words and example. It became real when the community as a whole discerned Paul's meaning and decided on the actions, which they as believers should derive from Paul's words. In his letters, Paul teaches, exhorts, encourages, and corrects. The communities reverenced his instructions, reading and preserving them. They circulated these letters, sharing them with other communities. In this way the letters eventually gained the authority of Christian Scriptures as the communities were increasingly strengthened, formed, and informed by a common tradition. Most people in Pauline communities probably could not read, so a reader would read Paul's letter aloud to the assembly of believers. There they reflected together on its contents. From Paul's writings we can get a picture of how the early church operated, how it worshipped and governed itself, and how it grew.

ROMANS

[see pages 1577–1599 of the New Testament]

Before Beginning . . .

The placement of Romans at the beginning of the New Testament letters is appropriate not only because it is the longest of Paul's letters but also because it may very well be his most important work. Romans has always held a special place among Paul's writings. Especially since the time of the Protestant Reformation in the sixteenth century, the importance of the doctrine of "justification by faith," which Paul develops in Romans (and, in a more succinct version, in Galatians) has been recognized by Catholics and Protestants alike as one of the most significant teachings of Paul and, in fact, of Christianity.

Paul and the Roman Christians

The Roman Christian community must have been fairly large by the time of Paul's arrival there. It is estimated that the Jewish community of Rome in the early first century numbered 50,000. Among Christians, it seems from Paul's letter that there were both Jews and Gentiles. Some of the information given in chapter 16 indicates quite a few house churches. Of course, Paul did not intend to arrive in Rome as a prisoner but as a free missionary. Yet according to the account in Acts, he arrived not the way he intended, but rather under arrest.

Several unique characteristics of Romans distinguish this letter from the other writings of Paul. In this letter, Paul addresses a church he has not founded. He writes to introduce himself and his gospel and to seek the Roman community's acceptance and help. Before fulfilling his desire to come to Rome on the way to Spain (cf. Rom 15:22–33), Paul must first deliver the collection of money from the Gentile churches for the "poor among the holy ones in Jerusalem" (15: 26), who have been suffering from a famine. When these funds are delivered, his sights will be set for Rome.

So it is that both the Jewish mission field represented by the church in Jerusalem and the open-ended Gentile mission represented by Rome and Spain are on Paul's mind as he writes this letter. Paul is concerned about unity among Christians. Although he has not founded the Roman church, he refers to the common faith he shares with believers there. He stresses the common fund of teaching from which both he and they draw. The issues of community in faith and of reconciliation permeate all of Romans and contribute to its perennial appeal to believers of every age.

Except for chapter 16, which may have been added later (cf. below, our commentary on this chapter, and the notes of the NAB), Romans lacks the personal tone characteristic of most of Paul's letters. Some manuscripts omit the words "in Rome" in 1:7 and 15. Without this designation and the greetings of chapter 16, Romans might be considered as a circular letter, a general development of Paul's most basic theological ideas. In Romans, Paul expounds upon universal salvation, upon the notion of justification by faith, and on the relationship between Israel and the church as transformed by Christ. These are some of the most important and generally applicable aspects of all of Paul's theology. The general nature and universal applicability of Romans contribute to its wide appeal as an introduction to Paul.

Romans as "Diatribe"

More than any other Pauline writing, Romans is like a formal treatise, a summary of Paul's theology that serves both as a self-introduction to a community not yet personally acquainted with Paul and as a summary for the message Paul preaches. Even though Romans has the formal features of an epistle, it can also be understood as a philosophical diatribe, a written exposé that tries to anticipate real or supposed objections or rebuttal. The diatribe, used by some ancient philosophers in teaching and writing, often interjected traces of dialogue in order to answer questions expected of opponents. For example, Paul brings his arguments forward by interspersing throughout Romans such rhetorical questions as "What advantage is there then in being a Jew?" (3:1) or "Well, then, are we better off?" (3:9) or "What then can we say that Abraham found, our ancestor according to the flesh?" (4:1). Thus, in comparison to Paul's other works, Romans is structured more as a philosophical treatise. Most of the other letters reflect more the give and take of real dialogue among people actually working and interacting together.

Working through Romans

The typical Greco-Roman letter form applied to Romans yields the following divisions: the *address,* consisting of a greeting and a thanksgiving, is contained in Rom 1:1–15; the *body* of the letter comprises 1:16–15:13. It contains the essential message of Paul, basically following what has helpfully been called the "indicative-imperative" structure (see "Letters and Epistles," RG 440). The *conclusion* in 15:14–16:27 contains Paul's travelogue, his personal greetings, and a final doxology.

A working outline of Romans follows:

I. The Address (Rom 1:1–15)
II. The Body of the Letter (1:16–15:13)
 A. The Theme; the "Indicative" (1:16–17)
 B. The Common Predicament of Gentiles and Jews (1:18–3:20)
 C. Central Declaration of Justification by Faith (3:21–31)
 D. Abraham, Model of Faith (4:1–25)
 E. The Two Adams (5:1–21)
 F. A Preliminary "Imperative" (6:1–23)
 G. Life without the Spirit (7:1–25)
 H. Life in the Spirit (8:1–39)
 I. But What of Israel? (9:1–11:36)
 J. The Final "Imperative" (12:1–15:13)
III. Conclusion (15:14–16:27)

Reading through Romans

The Address (1:1–15)

The address typically includes greetings and a thanksgiving. The greeting of Romans, identifying the sender, Paul, and his addressees, is an elaboration of the standard form of Greco-Roman letter s (see note 1:1–7, p. 1578, and "Letters and Epistles," RG 440). Here and in some other letters, notably Philippians, Paul has woven this brief feature into an extended prayer. In no other authentic Pauline letter besides Romans does Paul write in his name alone. He usually has with him some co-worker known to the recipients. In chapter 16, this is certainly the case. But even in Romans, Paul is not entirely independent. He needs the Romans' acceptance. He is grateful for their perseverance, and he looks forward to being strengthened by them through their common faith (1:11). Paul says that although he is personally unknown to the Romans, the gospel or Christian message he preaches is the same as that which they have received from other Christian missionaries.

Although Paul usually refers to his addressees as "the church in ___________," he does not use the term "church" in the address of Romans. But he does remind the Roman Christians of their vocation to holiness. In developing a Christian terminology in the Greek language, Paul will consistently draw upon images and phrases that appear in the Hebrew Scriptures. An example is Paul's description of the believing community as holy, as saints, called and sanctified by God (for instance, 1 Cor 1:2). Israel is a "kingdom of priests, a holy nation," according to Exodus 19:6. The Law sets Israel apart, making it distinct from its neighbors because it has a covenant relationship with God. This holiness has nothing to do with the virtue of the members but arises from the fact of God's call. Their personal holiness is then a response to that call.

The Body of the Letter (l:16–15:13)

The Theme (1:16–17)

Romans 1:16–17 states the theme. In the chapters that follow, the gospel is described as the power of God for universal salvation. This theme is developed in both its positive and negative implications. Positively, Paul insists that faith is accessible to all through Christ. But Paul also realizes some negative implications, even of his belief that all are saved in Christ. For example, it is clear that all have sinned and are in need of salvation. The emphasis on universal sinfulness deserving of God's wrath is the negative pole of the theme of Romans. There is no human means of achieving salvation for ourselves; it must be given.

Note that for Paul the starting point is not that all have sinned but rather that all have been saved. This is the conviction of faith. Paul considers sin to be an illustration of the universal need for salvation. This explains why Paul's hope, eloquently expressed especially in chapters 5, 8, and 15, is so deep and certain. No human sin is sufficient to separate us from the love of God that saves us.

Paul's Fundamental Conviction

The Greek words that we translate "just," "justice," "justify," and "righteousness" are all derived from the same root word, *dikaios* (just), *dikaiosyn* (justice, righteousness, or justification). Even more important, for Paul the concepts are closely linked. He connects the justice of God with God's power and will to "justify" all people, that is, to regard them as just.

The Scriptures show that God's justice is revealed, that is, it cannot be completely attained through human effort or study. Isaiah reminds us that God's thoughts are not human thoughts, and God's ways not our ways (see Is 55:7–8). Yet the Scriptures also tell us that we are to be just, that we must act in imitation of God, that we are to walk blamelessly before God and be perfect (see Gn 17:1; Hos 6:6). Thus, justice is not completely foreign to us. The God-fearing Israelite seeks to act justly, that is, in ways that are acceptable to God and in accord with God's covenant. These ways are also revealed through the Jewish Torah ("instruction") or Law. The Torah was handed down from Moses and interpreted throughout the history of the Jewish people, who reverenced it as the revealed will of God. So, for example, Abraham in Genesis (Gn 15:6) and Joseph in the infancy narrative (Mt 1:19) are described as "righteous" *(dikaios)* men.

It is not that acting justly or keeping the Law earns salvation or God's approval, but rather the opposite. The covenant is God's gift to Israel. Israel's response is to keep the Law. The Jewish person seeking justice is enjoined to study and to follow the Torah or the instruction of God. In the covenant is the hope of being justified, that is, "made just" in God's sight. Thus, for the Old Testament as for Paul, the related terms "justice," "just," and "justified" all originate in God, who reveals how we are to act and judges us accordingly. Although all people are sinners, Jewish theology teaches that we may expect to learn the way of justice through a faithful following of the Law in all things. This is the background for Paul's understanding of justification through Jesus Christ.

There are two main ideas that we must understand if we are to grasp the argument about justification that Paul puts forth in Romans and in some of his other writings. The first is the meaning for him of trying to attain justification or salvation by obeying the Law. (This is dealt with particularly in chapter 3 of his Letter to the Galatians; see the Reading Guide to Galatians.) The second main idea pertains to Paul's explanation of how the Gentiles, or those who do not have the Law, are justified.

First, for Paul, justification through the works of the Law is a false hope for several reasons. The idea that the Law held the key to justification was the position of the Jews who did not become Christians as well as of the Christian-Jewish group, led by Peter and James, who constituted the majority of the church when Paul began his mission. The theological challenge Paul faces is that his experience of the Risen Christ and his mission to preach that justification is available to all, both Jews who have the Law and the Gentiles who do not, convinced Paul that justification is an act of God, given freely to all who believe. Like his Jewish contemporaries, Paul himself was zealous for the Law (cf. Rom 10:1–3; Phil 3:3–7; Gal 1:11–14), but now his experience has taught him that this is not the way to go. Now in his zeal to win people over to the way he is convinced is right, Paul argues that the Law is impossible to keep and can only lead to frustration and self-righteousness. This caricature of the Law must be understood as rhetorical attempts to persuade Gentiles attracted by Law observance to his point of view.

Second, justification through the Law is insufficient because it excludes the Gentiles, who, as Paul has described the situation in Romans 1:18–3:31, are in the same sinful predicament as the Jews. But both Abraham and Christ show that the Gentiles, no less than the Jews, are now justified through faith. According to the Law, Jesus was condemned to death. But God overturned the Law's verdict in raising Jesus to life (see Gal 3:10–14). Thus, for Paul, the Law has been superseded by the death and resurrection of Jesus.

As a consequence of this, the Gentiles are now included among the justified. By accepting Jesus' gift of justification, and consequently living in accord with God's will, Jews and Gentiles both are saved. Following the just requirements of the Law or the precepts of the church is not a *prerequisite* for but a *result of being justified*.

Paul understands justification as already having taken place through the death and resurrection of Christ. Salvation is in the future, promised to those who believe in Christ and live according to this belief. As Paul himself says it, "Indeed, if, while we were enemies, we were reconciled to God through the death of his Son, how much more, once reconciled, will we be saved by his life" (Rom 5:10).

We must also comprehend Paul's idea of faith in order to understand the argument of Romans. It may seem that he is simply replacing one human action, obedience to the Law, with another human action, faith in Jesus Christ. But for Paul faith is trust: the belief that it is God's power, not our own, and our reliance on God, not on our own abilities, that saves us. Paul saw the obvious danger for sinful people: the danger that they would continue in their wrong behavior and so close themselves off from God forever. But Paul also saw the danger for those people who seemed moral and upright: the danger that they would believe God was forced to save them because they had earned their way into God's love.

For Paul, this thinking is a fatal mistake. It assumes that we can manipulate God by our actions. Paul breaks through this misunderstanding by his assertion of the necessity of faith. Faith is our acknowledgment that it is God's power that saves us, not our own efforts; that we are helpless, in that we are all sinners; and that we can trust in God.

We should note that Paul begins with the affirmation of faith in God's work of salvation to which all have access in Christ. He does not start with the premise of defeat nor emphasize that each person must individually become convicted of sin. Rather, Paul stresses first the goodness and power of God to save, and then tries to demonstrate the universal need for salvation to be given.

Paul uses terms such as "redeem" and "justify" and "reconcile" in relationship to one another and sometimes almost interchangeably (see Rom 5:9–11 and discussion on that passage below). These terms originally belonged to the world of finance; for Paul they appropriately illustrate the economy of salvation. The "debit" columns of sin and guilt and punishment are converted by God into the "credit" columns of forgiveness, redemption, and reconciliation. Through faith we are reconciled to God and to one another. We are redeemed by the blood of Christ, and our sins are forgiven.

Paul came to believe that the revelation of the Law was fulfilled and superseded by the death-resurrection of Christ. In Romans, Paul will develop a dichotomy between what was "formerly" and what is "now." For Paul, God's justice is only fully revealed in Jesus. The emphasis on "now" also implies an emphasis on the accessibility of God's justice to all through faith. The Law (or Torah) formerly divided humanity into "Jews and Gentiles," the latter not sharing in the promise represented by the Law. This division is overcome, and all now have equal access to God's revelation of justice expressed in Christ.

The Common Predicament of Gentiles and Jews (1:18–3:20)

Having stated his conviction that the gospel is God's power to save all people through faith (1:1–16f), Paul proceeds to demonstrate the need of all for salvation. Universal sin illustrates this need. Paul shows that "all," both Gentiles and Jews, have sinned and incurred the wrath of God. The "wrath of God" is being revealed in that the Gentiles are experiencing disastrous consequences of their own behavior (Rom 1:18–32). The wrath of God is an image borrowed from the Old Testament prophets (see Is 9:8–12; 10:5; Jer 50:11–17; Ez 5:13; 36:5–6). It depicts God's rejection or "abandonment" (Rom 1:24,26,28) of people to their own sin. The story of Saul's disobedience to God in 1 Samuel 15 dramatizes this dynamic: from the moment when God no longer accepts Saul's kingship, Saul's downfall is certain.

Although the Gentiles *could* know God through creation, the evidence of their godless lives means that they have rejected knowledge of God. Belief in God is no mere intellectual affair but involves a conversion to "the living and true God" (see 1 Thes 1:9) expressed in a virtuous life. Paul adopts the Old Testament notion of the relationship between idolatry and immorality evident among the pagans. (But see the NAB note on 1:18–32 that cautions that the lives of many in the Greco-Roman culture could serve as models for Christians today.) Paul speaks in generalities here, trying first to indict the Gentiles (1:18–31) and later (in 2:1–3:9) the Jews, in an effort to show the effects of universal sin and the need of all humanity for God's salvation.

Central Declaration of Justification by Faith (3:21–31)

Paul summarizes his previous demonstration of universal sinfulness (3:23) but prefaces it with the way out, accomplished by God through Christ, then makes the central assertion: we are justified by faith apart from the works of the Law (3:28). He emphasizes that God's just judgment comes upon all people, for God shows no partiality (2:11; see also Dt 10:17; 2 Chr 19:7; Sir 35:12f; Acts 10:34; Gal 2:6; Eph 6:9; Col 3:2, 5; 1 Pt 1:17). Having indicated that the Gentiles are sinners, Paul turns to concentrate throughout Rom 2:1–3:20 on the Jews. Here Paul adopts the language of the prophets, who not only charged sinfulness to the pagans but also accused the Jews of having "a stubborn and impenitent heart."

Abraham, Model of Faith (4:1–25)

For Paul, Abraham is a type of Christ; that is, Abraham follows the pattern of Christ. Adam and Moses, on the other hand, are antitypes—reverse patterns. For Jews, circumcision, the ritual removal of the foreskin of the penis of infant boys, symbolizes the individual's membership in the people of God, and therefore the individual's acceptance of God's law and teaching. Since Abraham was justified before his circumcision, he was justified independently of the Law. Therefore Abraham is the ancestor of both Jews and Gentiles. Abraham's example illustrates the theme of Romans: all have access now to salvation through faith. (For further discussion of the image of Abraham for Paul, see the Reading Guide to Galatians.)

The Two Adams (5:1–21)

In chapter 5 Paul contrasts Christ's saving actions (that is, his death and resurrection) with the devastating consequences of the sin of the first Adam. By the time of Paul, it was generally understood that the first human beings were created immortal (Wis 2:23f) but that their sin brought death into the world. Subsequent generations continue the sentence of death by continuing to sin (Rom 5:12). Adam represents all people under sin with its curse of death. But Adam is also a figure drawing out God's promise of redemption. The writer of Genesis portrays the situation of Adam as obviously in need of some divine action: even before the curse for sin is pronounced in Genesis 3:16–19, God promises to save the human family in the end (Gn 3:15). The early church Fathers, above all Augustine, used these passages, especially Romans 5:12, as a basis for description of the devastating effects of original sin, although Paul does not use this terminology. Rather, he argues that if the first sin had such widespread effects that since Adam all people have been under its influence, how much more effective and powerful is the gift of salvation won through Jesus Christ. That gift is called grace, which brings eternal life (5:21). The mode of argument here is a familiar rhetorical construction: from lesser to greater. If so much damage was caused by the first human being, Adam, how much greater is the grace and redemption won by the ultimate human being, Christ.

Paul insists that Christ's death and resurrection have affected all of human history. His argument is basically this: if the sin of Adam was so far reaching, how much more encompassing is the gift of God in Christ for all. Paul's thinking is at the basis of the church's ecstatic thanksgiving, "O happy fault that has merited so great a redeemer!" The Roman liturgy recalls this prayer during the Easter Vigil each year in the recitation of the *Exsultet*.

Salvation is a reality that Paul describes here and elsewhere (see 1 Cor 6:11; 2 Cor 5:10–15; 10:5–10), using multiple terms like reconciliation, redemption, justification, and sanctification. The verb "to save" refers to God's intervening action when human beings are in need. It connotes actual, sometimes physical, rescue as well as deliverance in spiritual distress. The Old Testament often refers to God as "Savior." Reference to God's saving action is one of the Bible's most frequent ways of referring to God, appearing literally hundreds of times. In the New

Testament this term is often used in connection with Jesus. The disciples, for example, prayed "Lord, save us" (for example, Mt 8:25). Paul assumes we are familiar with the long Old Testament tradition of God's saving actions on behalf of people. But Paul, in relating God's action to the death and resurrection of Christ, gives a new emphasis in the theology of salvation or "soteriology." Many scholars point out that all of Paul's Christology or thinking about Christ is really a soteriology or doctrine of how God saves through Christ.

A Preliminary "Imperative" (6:1–23)

Paul's view of humankind, that is, his theological anthropology, is evident in this chapter. He considers all people to be under some dominant influence, living either for God under grace or living for sin. This is a different perspective from our contemporary one that considers human freedom as an autonomous, absolute ideal. For Paul, freedom is related to life for God (6:10) in contrast with slavery to sin (6:6). By means of the opposites of death and life, Paul contrasts the former condition of sin and death to the new life of freedom won by Christ and obtained by the believer through baptism.

The term *baptism* means "immersion," and Paul plays on this original sense even as he has the initiatory rite in view. He coins several expressions in chapter 6, compounding verbs with the prefix *syn*—(meaning "with") that signify believers' solidarity with Christ. We have "died with" him and are "buried with" him; therefore we will be "raised with" him and now "live with" him. This incorporation into the death-resurrection of Christ by means of baptism necessarily has implications for the moral life. As a result of this incorporation, we "walk" (a term designating moral living) in the newness of life (6:4). Paul will postpone a fuller discussion of the implications of this "newness of life" until chapters 12 through 15.

Life without the Spirit (7:1–25)

The major part of chapter 7 follows the style of a diatribe (see the NAB notes on chapter 7 and RG 441). Paul anticipates the objections of real or imaginary opponents in a kind of dialogue designed to present his own ideas in an orderly fashion. The most important aspects of Paul's argument are three. First, the Christian views the Law differently now, having been freed from its service (Paul says "bondage") by participation in the death of Christ. Second, the function of the Law is to specify what is sinful. Thus the Law did not encourage grace or freedom but only identified sin. Third, anticipating an objection that the Law is therefore sin, Paul responds emphatically, "No!" Yet knowledge of what is good does not enable us to do what is good. The Law is one more factor, then, in the judgment against humanity, convicting all of sin. The Law concurs with human conscience, judging us as sinners. This is the meaning of the expression, "the good that I want to do I avoid and the evil I wish to avoid I do" (see 7:19–21). But it is important to realize that his statements about this unhappy predicament are rhetorical, not autobiographical. They are not expressions of his personal conscience but of the situation of humanity without God.

Life in the Spirit (8:1–39)

Chapter 8 celebrates the message of salvation. "There is no condemnation for those who are in Christ Jesus" (8:1). "[Nothing can] separate us from the love of God in Christ Jesus our Lord" (8: 38f). Nowhere is Paul's understanding of the role of the Spirit more eloquently expressed than here. Paul begins chapter 8 with a consideration of the opposition between the flesh and the spirit. He often tries to illustrate his meaning by opposing two poles of thought. This is a way of showing the mutually exclusive categories of sin and death versus grace and life. Paul adapts the Greek notion of the *flesh* in order to express the sinful condition of humanity before grace. In the Greek philosophical tradition, flesh, like spirit, had several connotations. The flesh means, of course, that which pertains to the body. But it can also mean the inferior aspect of human existence, whatever in human life is weak or limited. For the Greeks, the flesh referred to what they regarded as baser desires, which for them included sensual and sexual instincts. The flesh is mortal and must be controlled by the spirit (that is, the mind and will), which in Greek thought is immortal. Paul adapts this notion to sometimes speak of the flesh as the moral equivalent of sin. For Paul, however, sins of the flesh include not just bodily sins, such as gluttony, but also spiritual sins, such as pride. Drawing on the same tradition, Paul uses the term *spirit* to refer to the new life accessible to all through Christ. In stressing the life of the spirit, Paul contrasts the present salvation with the past that was characterized by sin, death, and slavery to the dictates of the flesh.

The Holy Spirit is an advocate, coming to our aid and strengthening us. Like the Israelites in Egypt, we formerly could only groan in the suffering and weakness caused by sin. The Spirit converts our incoherent cries into a prayer that recognizes God as Father and ourselves as children of God. Thus through the Spirit we are liberated from slavery to sin and enabled to pray as the children of God, saying *Abba* (8:15). From Paul's use of this prayer, we can assume that he is indirectly referring to the Gospel tradition that tells us that Jesus himself addressed God as "*Abba,* Father" (Mk 14:36). We are confident, too, that the suffering we experience and witness is as nothing compared to the glory that is to come. All creation shared in the sin of Adam and groans with humanity in its suffering. Now all creation awaits the revelation of the children of God (8:20–25).

At the end of chapter 8, Paul exclaims that nothing can separate us from the love of God. But he goes on to acknowledge in chapters 9 through 11 that the Jewish rejection of the Christian message is a challenge to this belief. Some may say that now God has run out of patience with Israel. But if Israel's rejection of Christ limits God's fidelity to the covenant and God's justice, what does that mean not only for Israel but for the Christian church, which is adopting the prerogatives of Israel? Has God had a change of mind? These are some of the questions Paul puzzles out in these chapters in a remarkable review of the history of salvation.

But What of Israel? (9:1–11:36)

The form of this three-chapter unit is a philosophical diatribe. Paul responds to anticipated questions or challenges in the form of an artificial dialogue. In the course of developing his views, he makes abundant use of the Old Testament. Before dealing with some ethical conclusions to the doctrines in chapters 12 through 15, Paul senses the necessity of taking up this personally painful question about God's fidelity to the Jews. Israel's rejection of Christ was clearly a problem not only for Paul but also for the early church. Paul's consideration of this question properly belongs with the doctrinal development of Romans.

Paul's summary of the privileges of Israel in Romans 9:1–5 prompts him to redefine the term *Israel* in chapters 9 through 11. Israel is not a mere ethnic or historical reality, but one that always had theological connotations. The Jewish Scriptures show, Paul argued, that "not all who are of Israel are Israel" (9:6). The element of divine choice was operating throughout Jewish history, illustrating that God is free to show mercy as God wishes. Not all are children of Abraham simply because they descended from him, as the preference for Isaac over Ishmael shows (see 9:7–9; Gal 4:22–31). God chose Jacob over Esau (Rom 9:10–13). God hardens some, as in the case of Pharaoh; but divine mercy is shown to Moses and the Hebrews in Egypt (9:15–17). Paul also cites examples from the prophets, especially Jeremiah, Hosea, and Isaiah to support God's freedom to choose. For Paul, God's mercy is God's justice. Paul carefully builds his arguments to show how God is now including the Gentiles among the new "Israel of God" (Gal 6:16).

Paul begins chapter 10, as he had chapter 9, with a defense of his kinspeople. He testifies to Jewish zeal in pursuit of the Law as he himself was zealous for the Law prior to his faith in Christ (see Gal 1:14). But as "end of the law" (Rom 10:4), Christ brings justification for all who believe. Thus Christ renders the Law useless and eliminates the differences between Jew and Gentile. To support his assertion that Christ is the end of the Law, Paul develops an explanation of Scripture in the style of a Jewish *midrash* or "running commentary." Paul applies the Old Testament to Christ and so gives an example of how the "law and the prophets testify" to the righteousness given by God in Christ (cf. Rom 3:2ff). Paul argued that there is only one God of Jews and Gentiles in Romans 3:21–31. Similarly, here in chapter 10, Paul says that there is only one Lord over all and accessible to all who call upon him. That Lord is Christ. Near the end of the chapter, in 10:14–21, Paul echoes the traditional prophetic denunciation of Israel who alone is responsible for her infidelity. But God continues to reach out to a "disobedient people" (10:21).

God's fidelity, proven in the past and present

(chapters 9 and 10) will ultimately be for the salvation of "all Israel" in the future (Rom 11). God has not finally abandoned Israel since a remnant remains faithful to God as a sign of the ultimate salvation of "all Israel" (Rom 11:26). Paul cautions the Gentiles, included by the action of Christ into "all Israel," to remember that it is only by grace that they are saved. This is a mystery revealing God's infinite mercy. The power of God is the divine compassion by which all are enfolded into the salvation of "all Israel."

The Final "Imperative" (12:1–15:13)

Paul's ethical conclusions apply his teaching, and form the "imperative" or "parenetic," exhortatory part of the letter. This can be subdivided into consideration of the church and the world (12:1–13:14) and a call for reconciliation and unity (14:1–15:13). Romans 12:1–2 has been called the heart of Pauline ethics. Here Christians, who do not yet have a sacrificial ritual like most of their neighbors in their temples and like the Jews in Jerusalem, learn that their lives are their living sacrifice, purifying them to be able to live not in conformity to the world (seen as being in opposition to God), but with transformed understanding. In describing the Christian community, Paul adapts the image of the "body" (12: 4–8), a popular image used by Stoic philosophers to illustrate the interdependence of members in a state. Older Catholics may be familiar with this image for the church and probably relate it to ideas developed by Pope Pius XII in an encyclical titled "The Mystical Body" *(Mystici Corporis)*. This encyclical stressed the various ways members of the Christian community, both now and in past ages, are related to one another. We can also note that Paul develops the image to stress the very real mutual dependency of Christians who should not think of themselves "more highly than one ought to think" (12:3) but as "one body" (12:4) having many parts. The image of the body provides the transition between the liturgical language that describes Christians' behavior as "spiritual worship" (12:1), and the obligations of the mutual love that is to be characteristic of Christians.

Romans 13:1–7 takes up the question of the Christian community's relation to civil government. We must remember that Paul is speaking to a minority community within an alien state. At first glance his advice appears simplistic. Paul says that all authority is ordained by God and has its origin in God. Christians in Paul's time were trying simply to survive. Society expected citizens to follow the religion of the state. Paul instructs Christians to be good citizens while not being conformed to the standards of the world around them. Then, having spoken about giving society its due, Paul considers the question of the debt believers owe one another: love is the fulfillment of the law. Apparently Paul is acquainted with the love command of Jesus (see Rom 13:8–10). He reviews the commandments from adultery to covetousness, repeating finally in verse 10 what he stated in verse 8: "Love is the fulfillment of the law."

Divisions over Observances and the Call to Unity (14:1–15:13)

Paul frequently enjoins his addressees to be of one and the same mind (for example, Phil 2: 1–4). Yet disputes over ethical issues threaten the unity that should characterize the Christian church. The Roman Christians disagree over dietary matters and the observance of certain feast days. In a mixed community of Jewish and Gentile Christians, such questions could not help but arise.

Referring to the different sides of this debate, Paul speaks of those with "weak" and those with "strong" faith. His emphasis is not so much on the opinions or positions of individual believers but on the common attitudes to be cultivated among believers. He refers to the faith of the community and of members' responsibility to be united with the faith of the whole body.

Paul exhorts the Christians to a fundamental harmony that is expressed in mutual respect and concern for one another. Paul reminds the Roman Christians, many of whom are Jewish, that the Scriptures are written for our instruction and encouragement. The term *encouragement* is linked to the hope that abounds in the community "by the power of the holy Spirit" (15:13). Hope, joy, and peace are linked to belief. Faith is a confession about the meaning of Jesus' death and resurrection (see Rom 10:9). But it is also, according to 15:7–13, acceptance of other members of the Christian community.

Conclusion (15:14–16:27)

Paul reminds the Romans again, as he did at the beginning of his letter, about their common faith and his confidence in them. In 15:14–33 the apostle speaks of his need for their hospitality soon; he requests prayers as he embarks on his mission to Jerusalem to take the collection there. Although Paul is personally unacquainted with the Romans, he has written "boldly" because he is a "minister" of Jesus Christ. He describes his ministry in liturgical language, as a "priestly" *(leitourgos)* duty (15:16). Paul is of course not referring to a sacramental priesthood, since Christians have not yet developed a theology of sacrificial cult, but to his mission to preach the Christian message to the Gentiles. He uses language common to the Jerusalem Temple priesthood and to other religious worship of the day.

Paul reports that his immediate plans include a visit to Rome in passing on the way to Spain, after taking the collection to Jerusalem. He understands the collection as a symbol linking Jews and Gentiles, the fulfillment of a responsibility he accepted at the Jerusalem council (Gal 2:10). There is yet only the unfinished matter of taking the offering from the Gentiles to Jerusalem. This material gift represents a debt owed the Jews whose spiritual heritage is now shared by the Gentiles. The term *debt* occurred in Romans 13: 8–10 where Paul described love as the only legitimate debt a believer can incur. Since spiritual blessings are much greater than material things, the Gentiles owe these lesser goods to the Jews as a consequence of their inheriting Israel's spiritual blessings now through Jesus Christ. Common faith makes kin of Jews and Gentiles and links both in mutual responsibility. Paul's strategy, then, is twofold: to ensure that the offering is sizable and that it is accepted as symbolic of the true faith and equal status of the Gentile Christians. If the Jewish Christians accept the gift, they are thereby accepting the mission to the Gentiles.

Chapter 16 consists mostly of greetings to and from various people known to Paul. It is possible that it was originally part of a letter intended for Ephesus, and was for some reason later added to the preceding fifteen chapters of Romans. This chapter seems almost like an afterthought, and further examination suggests it even contains some discrepancies to material stated or implied in the first fifteen chapters. Paul commends Phoebe, bearer of the letter to the Romans, speaking of her as *diakonos* (the only named person in the New Testament who is a "deacon" of a particular church) and *prostatis,* that is, his patron and benefactor. Then he greets numerous people as if he is well known to them and as if he and the Romans have a number of mutual acquaintances. Until now the apostle has maintained a certain distance from the Roman Christians, insinuating that his introduction to himself and to his gospel could serve in lieu of the personal contact he usually has with communities he has founded. But if Paul knows as many Romans as this chapter indicates, the uncharacteristically general and impersonal tone of chapters 1 through 15 of the letter is strange. The note on 16:1–23 draws attention to the mixture of Jewish and Gentile names, representative of the mixed background of the Roman community. Much valuable social information about acquaintances and collaborators of Paul, both male and female, whether in Ephesus or Rome, is contained in these verses.

The placement and originality of the final doxology or blessing is debated (see note). But its appropriateness at the end of this epistle is undisputed. The doxology echoes several themes developed in the course of the letter. Paul speaks of "my gospel" (see 1:16–17), the mystery kept secret for long ages (11:25–32), manifested through prophetic writings (numerous allusions to the Old Testament throughout this epistle), and to the obedience of faith (see 1:5; 15:28). Paul has pronounced a blessing at various points throughout his development (7:24; 8:35–39; 11: 33–36), as if carried away by the abundance of God's wisdom and mercy. This reflects the Jewish custom of celebrating the wonders of God with praise. Nowhere is the doxology more fitting than after Paul has reviewed the fundamentals of his gospel, with emphasis on the universality of redemption and the imminence of God's victory over all evil in the triumph of Jesus Christ.

Concluding Remarks

Throughout our commentary on Romans we have tried to show the relevance of the major themes developed here: justification by faith, the emphasis on the present reality of justification contrasted with the former life of sin, and most importantly, the inclusion of all—Jews and Gentiles—in a new Israel of God, the church. The ethical section of Romans may be seen as a description of the church living in but not of the world. It would be hard to overestimate the influence of Romans in the development of Christian doctrine and morality throughout history.

THE LETTERS TO THE CORINTHIANS

Introduction

The letters to the Corinthians reveal Paul the pastoral theologian in ways that his other surviving letters do not. The sheer number of pastoral problems posed and answered, especially in 1 Corinthians, leads us to think that here Paul was most challenged to apply the principles he knew to real, new circumstances in the lives of his community. The Corinthians could never be accused of lack of initiative. Rather, they seem to have taken seriously (perhaps more so than Paul would have liked) his encouragement to find new freedom in Christ, so that his relationship with them was complex and tumultuous.

Corinth was the capital and central city of the Roman province of Achaia, which comprised southern Greece. Its location near the isthmus dividing the Peloponnesus from mainland Greece made it a major seaport and trading center. It was also a Roman freedmen's colony and therefore its population was made up of various peoples, but with a heavy concentration of Roman citizens and Roman interests. With its mixture of national and religious groups, rich and poor, Jews, pagans, and Christians, and moral and immoral people, it was an exciting but difficult environment for the small Christian community, which was predominantly Gentile but probably had a small Jewish minority.

The letters we call 1 and 2 Corinthians formed part of a larger collection that originally consisted of several letters Paul wrote to the community. He speaks in 1 Corinthians 5:9 of a previous letter written to the Corinthians instructing them to avoid immoral people. Such a letter no longer exists and nowhere do we have this instruction from Paul, unless, as has been suggested, a piece of it survives as 2 Corinthians 6:14–7:1. Similarly, the reference to a letter written in "much affliction and anguish of heart" (2 Cor 2:4) hardly fits the tone of 1 Corinthians. Furthermore, 2 Corinthians is characterized by discontinuity, suggesting that it is actually a composite of several letters (see *New American Bible,* introduction to 2 Corinthians).

We learn that the Corinthians also wrote to Paul (see 1 Cor 7:1), and that the Corinthian church, difficult as it was for Paul, preserved and honored his advice, undoubtedly reading his letters at liturgical gatherings as Paul had instructed them to do. We are left with the impression that the extant letters reflect an editing and combining of writings, compiled as the community processed and integrated the words of the apostle.

1 CORINTHIANS

[see pages 1600–1624 of the New Testament]

Before Beginning . . .

In writing 1 Corinthians around AD 56, Paul was responding to some disquieting reports he had received about the community. First Corinthians addresses real, not theoretical, situations. Paul's knowledge of what was going on was based on verbal accounts from reliable sources, letters from members of the community, and Paul's own eighteen-month experience of living amidst this community (Acts 18:11).

First Corinthians is a particularly fruitful source of reflection for our contemporary church because it raises so many issues that are still relevant: divisions based on ideologies or different world views, incest, lawsuits among Christians, scandal, marriage and celibacy, theology of woman and the participation of women in the church, the proper way to celebrate Eucharist, charismatic gifts, and belief in the Resurrection. We, like the Corinthians, are challenged to find the right role and qualifications of leadership in a pluralistic society. Like the Corinthians we need to recognize that behavior is an indicator of what we believe.

In a sense, the singular "community" might misrepresent the Corinthians. We may tend to think of the community as a specific group that met at the house of a particular individual in a city. But the Corinthians were not a single large community. It is probable that in that particular city there were several Christian communities that congregated at different houses. Apparently these communities represented different competitive factions. Each community was developing divergent expressions of Christian life and worship. Some groups were homogeneous, preferring to worship with like-minded people from similar social and religious backgrounds, who followed certain diets and enjoyed certain prestigious spiritual gifts.

A variety of liturgical celebrations developed. The Corinthians disagreed about whether Christians ought to marry or, if married, should remain married after baptism. Paul responds to these issues among the Christians at Corinth. Although our problems and divisions may be expressed somewhat differently, Paul's admonitions to the Corinthians on the importance of unity, charity, and mutual respect based on a common faith provide us with a model for approaching our own problems. First Corinthians discloses to us the pastor Paul, who encourages the Corinthians to imitate him as he imitates Christ (11:1).

Working through 1 Corinthians

Our comments on the major themes and relevance of this epistle will follow the structure suggested in the NAB introduction (p. 1601), with some rather minor adjustments. First Corinthians contains the usual letter format: an *address* in 1:1–9, the *body of the letter* in 1:10–15:58, and a *conclusion* in 16:1–24.

Since this letter is a response to the concerns of the Corinthians, there is not the same kind of objective, formal structure we saw in Romans. Yet we can detect in 1 Corinthians a structural pattern that helps shed some light on the emphasis and meaning of Paul's message. Paul's general approach to issues follows an A-B-A' pattern by which Paul introduces and begins to develop a topic (A), disrupts his reflections by bringing up a second issue (B), and then returns to the original topic (A'). Often he uses this pattern to emphasize the middle, or B, statement. One illustration is Paul's discussion of abuses in the celebration of the Eucharist. He describes the abuses in 1 Corinthians 11:17–22 (A) and in verses 26–34 (A'). Paul interjects into the middle of this description his account of Jesus' Last Supper the night before he died (see 11:23–25, [B]). In this way Paul tries to remedy the abuses at Corinth by recalling what Jesus did and reminding the Corinthians that they are to act "in memory of" Jesus. Further examples of Paul's use of the A-B-A' pattern will be discussed as they appear in this letter. For the moment simply note that the pattern has the effect of emphasizing the B section as a corrective for the situations described in A and A'.

A working outline of 1 Corinthians is the following:

- I. Address (1:1–9)
- II. The Body of the Letter (1:10–15:58)
  - A. Reported Divisions and Abuses (1:10–6:20)
    - 1. Factions (1:10–4:21)
    - 2. Immoral Behavior (5:1–6:20)
  - B. Answers to the Corinthians' Questions (7:1–11:1)
    - 1. Marriage and Virginity (7:1–40)
    - 2. Food Offered to Idols (8:1–11:1)
      - a. Exercising knowledge and love (8:1–13; 10:1–11:1)
      - b. The example of Paul (9:1–27)
  - C. Problems in Liturgical Assemblies (11:2–14:40)
    - 1. Dress and Decorum in the Assembly (11:2–16)
    - 2. Celebration of the Eucharist (11:17–34)
    - 3. The Spiritual Gifts (12:1–14:40)
  - D. The Resurrection (15:1–58)
- III. Conclusion (16:1–24)

Reading through 1 Corinthians

The Address (1:1–9)

The address contains a greeting (1:1–3) and thanksgiving (1:4–9). In the greeting, Paul refers to himself as an "apostle of Jesus Christ" and identifies a "brother," Sosthenes, as co-author who, however, does not reappear in the letter. He is perhaps to be identified with the synagogue official of the same name in Acts 18:17. Paul addresses the community as a "church" *(ekklesia),* which has been "sanctified in Christ Jesus" and "called to be holy." Paul thus reminds the Corinthians that they have a common vocation (*ekklesia* literally means "called out of"). This is Paul's usual word for the assembly of believers, taken from the civic word for the assembly of citizens in a free city-state. It may also be a conscious translation of the Hebrew *qahal,* the biblical assembly of Israel. The Corinthians have a new identity, rooted in God, that distinguishes them from the world around them.

Paul's adaptation of the thanksgiving usually found in Hellenistic letters focuses on the blessings received by his addressees. Moreover, the thanksgiving announces themes Paul will develop in the letter. The Corinthians lack no spiritual gift whatsoever (1:7). The factions among them that so concerned Paul are rooted precisely in their envy of and competition for extraordinary gifts.

The Body of the Letter (1:10–15:58)

The whole of 1 Corinthians addresses specific issues that caused dissension and strained the fabric of the Corinthian community. In the first section of the body or main part of the letter, Paul discusses the divisions he has heard about among the Corinthians (1:10–6:20). He then turns to address matters that the Corinthians had themselves directed to him (see 7:1–11:1). Finally, Paul will consider other issues relevant to the Corinthian community; namely appropriate ways of celebrating the Eucharist (11:2–14 40), and the meaning of the Resurrection (15:1–58). Following this general outline, we can now comment on the main message of 1 Corinthians.

Reported Divisions and Abuses (1:10–6:20)

Reports from Chloe's people (see 1:11) identified some problems at Corinth stemming from two matters: (1) factions (1:10–4:21) and (2) immoral behavior (5:1–6:20).

Factions in Corinth (1:10–4:21). The variety of backgrounds of its members caused many problems in the community of Corinth. Various members of the community turned to different leaders, and groups began to vie with one another for superiority and recognition. Paul first takes up the slogans adopted by groups who profess allegiance to the various leaders. He names group leaders, specifically Cephas (that is, Peter), Apollos, and himself. He shows the absurdity of divisions based on leadership, which is superficial compared to the common baptism by which all Christians are sanctified and saved.

The Corinthians disagreed among themselves about which leaders were the most important and which group of Christians was the most prestigious. They may have taken their lead from disagreements among the great figures themselves. James disagreed with Paul, for example, about whether any aspects of the Jewish Law were required of Gentile Christians (Gal 2). Peter favored at least minimal requirements, while Paul advocated complete freedom from the Jewish Law for Gentile converts. First Corinthians suggests that the leaders' disagreement affected the Corinthians and caused many to side with one leader against another. But the Corinthians also had their own divisions.

Another leader was Apollos who, for very different reasons, had a following that competed for the Corinthians' loyalty. Apollos attracted many Corinthians because of his eloquence in speaking (see Acts 18:24–28). Meanwhile, some of the Corinthians cited Paul's unimpressive physical presence and speaking abilities as reason to reject him (1 Cor 2:1–5; 2 Cor 1:10). Paul chided the Corinthians for judging by human standards, not by God's as revealed in the cross of Christ. Paul reminded them that neither he nor Peter nor Apollos were crucified for them. The Corinthians were baptized in Christ's name and belonged to Christ. The formation of competitive groups within the Christian community is absurd. Paul admonishes the Corinthians to remember who they are—that by worldly standards few among them have any reason to boast (1:26–31)—but that "in the Lord" they can boast that they are saved and form a "new creation" (2 Cor 5:17). They do not have wealth or nobility or education, but they are rich in the blessings of the Spirit of God. The "not many of you" in verse 26 has been read both ways: Paul is stressing the humble origins and status of most, but in saying this he suggests that some really were of higher social status and wealth.

The first part of this letter (1:10–4:21) may be summarized as the gospel paradox, the teaching that God's wisdom is greater than human wisdom, that the power of the cross outweighs all human power. The Corinthians portrayed themselves as sophisticated, mature, and truly wise. Paul describes them as rather immature, of the "flesh" rather than spiritual (3:1), deceiving themselves and therefore lacking in the most fundamental knowledge. They erroneously judged according to standards that are transitory rather than eternal. The riches and wisdom of God surpass all understanding and may be perceived only through wisdom that is revealed by the Spirit (2:10).

Immoral Behavior (5:1–6:20). In chapters 5 and 6, Paul gives instances when judgments on the appropriate behavior for believers would be necessary. The Christian message of salvation has many implications—doctrinal, liturgical, ethical. Certain behavior is inconsistent with belonging to the Christian community. Chapters 5 and 6 specifically mention incest, bringing lawsuits against other members of the community, and sexual promiscuity, as liable to the community's judgment.

The Corinthians were complacent about keeping in their community someone who violated Jewish incest laws by living with his stepmother. Paul uses a traditional image of "yeast" to help describe the impact of the presence of such a one in their midst. The proverb "a little yeast leavens all the dough" illustrates the extent to which the sinner's action corrupts the whole community. Jesus uses this same image to warn about the influence of the Pharisees on the disciples (Mt 16:6; Mk 8:15; Lk 12:1). Paul was concerned about the impact of the sinner on the community and the "contagion" of sinful actions. Throughout this letter, a fundamental point of Christian theology is emphasized: namely, as Christians we cannot act alone without regard for one another. Our actions affect others, for good or evil. Paul sees conversion as turning "from idols to serve the living and true God" (1 Thes 1:9). This conversion requires a readiness to change not only our hearts but also our actions so that we may live in accordance with our baptism. Continuing the yeast image, Paul cites the formula of the paschal lamb and unleavened bread, pure and free from yeast. Yeast, as it is here, is usually a negative symbol. The connection is especially relevant at the time of the year in which Paul writes, the season of Passover (16:8).

It troubles Paul to hear that some in the community are bringing lawsuits against one another, when what they should be doing is suffering wrongs in imitation of Christ. At best, they should settle such disputes among themselves. He reminds them of the eschatological scenario in which God's holy ones will judge the earth. They therefore have no business submitting their grievances to unbelieving judges now. Nor do they know what they are doing by participation in prostitution. "Everything is lawful" to the one who is free in Christ, but this does not mean everything is acceptable. The body of every believer is a temple of the Holy Spirit that cannot be profaned.

Answers to the Corinthians' Questions (7:1–11:1)

Paul then takes up the Corinthians' own questions about how daily life is an expression of their faith. The Corinthians themselves identified certain issues within their community that were disturbing their unity. They wrote to Paul about these two types of questions: those about marriage and virginity (see 7:1–40), and those pertaining to the eating of idol meats and participation at pagan meals (8:1–11:1).

Marriage and Virginity (7:1–40). In chapter 7 Paul specifically discusses three life choices that many Christians believed were affected by baptism with an advantage on one side: marriage or virginity (7:1–7, 16), fidelity to Judaism signified by circumcision versus uncircumcision (vv. 18–20), and slavery versus manumission or freedom (vv. 21–24). According to 1 Corinthians 7, a specific question arose concerning whether married Christians ought to remain married. An understanding of baptism as initiation into the eschatological community seemed to imply that the baptized should renounce the constraints and responsibilities of marriage. Jesus' opposition to divorce is first attested here (7:10, 11). Some asked whether a Christian married to an unbeliever could or should remain in the marriage. Some men wondered if there was an advantage to circumcision. Some slaves thought, and perhaps expected, that they would be better off freed.

Paul's general advice is to "remain in the state in which you were called" (see 7:17,20,24). His reasoning is that the time is short (7:29, 31), too short for unnecessary social entanglements. It is debatable whether Paul believed literally that the eschatological end was imminent or whether this was his way to see all of life as contingent on the absolute power and will of God. Although Christians are "in" the world, they are not "of" it as John says (Jn 17:14–16). The particular circumstances of believers do not interfere with or lessen the effect of the new status of their identity in Christ. Christians have always sensed the need to express the implications of their new identity as baptized persons with an appropriate way of life.

Paul agreed with a position held by some in Corinth, that "it is a good thing . . . not to touch a woman" (1 Cor 7:1). Paul acknowledged his own preference for celibacy that leaves one "free of anxieties" (7:32). The Gospels record Jesus' saying that "in heaven there is neither giving nor taking in marriage" (see Mk 12:25 and parallel passages). Sexuality, circumcision, even slavery do not have significance in the new age. Indeed, the hope for a new society of equals was one of the reasons Christianity was so appealing to many "minority" groups, including women, slaves, and others who lacked status in the Greco-Roman world.

Paul's response is to advocate no change in social status since it is unimportant in the Christian context. Responding to those who challenge the right of Christians to marry, Paul drew on the word of Jesus regarding the indissolubility of marriage (7:10–11). Yet Paul added an exception that considerably weakens the effect of Jesus' statement. In the case of unwillingness of the unbelieving spouse to remain married to a baptized person, they may separate. Furthermore, Paul applied the exception to both men and women, giving women the same rights as men.

We should note Paul's remarkable freedom in relating Jesus' words to the pastoral situation of Corinth. In all of the questions with which he has to deal, Paul demonstrates a surprising creativity and flexibility.

Food Offered to Idols (8:1–11:1). Here Paul responds to three very practical situations about which the Corinthians must make everyday decisions: whether they should (1) eat meat bought in the marketplace that was probably originally offered in sacrifice at a pagan temple; (2) accept dinner invitations in rented banquet rooms in pagan temples, during which there was a sacrificial libation to the god in whose temple they were; (3) accept dinner invitations to the homes of unbelievers. He asserts a basic theological position that these gods are not really gods at all, supporting it with reference to Israel's history as recorded in the Scriptures (10:1–13) and with the example of his own experience. But the bottom line is the unity of the community. If anyone of weaker conscience will be scandalized, then it is not to be done.

Exercising Knowledge and Love (8:1–7 and 10:23–11:1). Paul quotes a Corinthian slogan, acknowledging the truth that "all of us have knowledge" (8:1). The Corinthians apparently assumed that such knowledge made some of them superior to others. So, for example, it was their "knowledge" that allowed them to overlook incest in one of their members (see chapter 5). It was the competition for the gifts considered superior that was disrupting their assemblies (14:20–33) and even the Lord's Supper (11:17–18). Paul proposes charity as a remedy for the rivalry of the various kinds of "knowledge" that inflate the ego and that were causing factions in the Corinthian church. Whereas knowledge divides, love unites, enabling the Corinthians' many gifts to supply various needs in the community, helping them to "build up" (see the description of the role of prophecy in 1 Cor 14:3), rather than destroy (1 Cor 11:17–34).

In discussing the factions between the "weak and the strong," Paul speaks of "conscience," a term that appears almost exclusively in Pauline writings with little impact on other New Testament authors (for instance, Rom 2:15; 9:1; 13:5; 1 Cor 8:7, 10, 12; 10:25, 27, 28, 29; 2 Cor 1:12;

1 Tm 1:5; 2 Tm 1:3; Ti 1:15; see also Acts 23:1; Heb 9:9, 14; 1 Pt 2:19; 3:16, 21). In biblical thinking, conscience is never an individualist function. It always has to do with how one sees oneself in relation to one's community. Paul gives a communal meaning to conscience and places it in a new Christian context. In this context, the personal consciences of both the "weak" and the "strong" are subordinate to the obligations of mutual charity. The weak must not judge the strong and the strong not scandalize the weak. For Paul, conscience is not autonomous. It cannot be the last court of appeal among Christians. It is subject to charity and concern for one "for whom Christ has died" (8:11).

In 1 Corinthians 10:23–11:1, Paul summarizes his discussion of knowledge of the specific issues regarding pagan meals and customs, and of imitation of his own example. Quoting another Corinthian slogan (as he did in 8:1 where he said "all of us have knowledge"), Paul agrees "Everything is lawful" (10:23). Yet, he continues, not everything is beneficial. The merit of an action is related to its effects on the community. Concrete questions about whether to eat or not should be resolved in view of their effect on the other members of the community. For Paul, the morality of a decision depends upon its impact on the conscience of other brothers and sisters. Paul's attempt to win others over rather than to alienate them keeps their salvation in view. Thus he concludes that Corinthian Christians ought to imitate him as he does Christ (11:1).

The Example of Paul (9:1–27). To support his argument about mutual love and avoidance of scandal, Paul inserts between the two parts of the argument the example of his own conduct. (Chapter 9 represents B in the A-B-A' pattern discussed in the introduction.) Though he could demand material support, though he could exercise a great deal more freedom and authority, he instead tries to become all things to everyone by being as much like them as possible. The hint is clear: you too do not need to exercise all the freedom to which you have a right, but you can subordinate some of it sometimes for the good of the whole. The Corinthians' problems reflect their mixed makeup of predominantly Gentile but also partly Jewish members, as well as a certain level of education and intellectual refinement. Greek intellectual life valued gifts of mind and spirit, such as knowledge and eloquent reasoning. Such gifts contributed to the status of the individuals who possessed them, sometimes to the detriment of charity.

In many of his letters Paul refers to the fact that he works with his hands and thus gives an example for his addressees to follow (1 Thes 2: 9; 2 Thes 3:7–10). Paul freely forfeited the apostolic privilege of support in order "not to place an obstacle to the gospel of Christ" (1 Cor 9:12). He served all—Jews, Gentiles, the "strong and the weak"—so that through this service the gospel message would be available to them. No one should be denied the gospel because of inability to pay. This forfeiting of privilege makes Paul freer to serve. Yet, as he will argue in 2 Corinthians 8:1–9:15, after receiving the gospel message Christians have a responsibility to contribute to the support of other Christians in need. Here he ends this digression about his own example with an athletic image. Just like a professional athlete, he disciplines himself, training not for a perishable crown of laurel or celery, as did the athletes of the day, but for an imperishable one.

Asceticism has played an important role in Christian spirituality throughout the history of the church. Paul legitimizes asceticism or self-denial for apostolic reasons. Today we live in a world that encourages individual freedom without constraints and the pursuit of happiness almost to any length. Such a mentality is not so distant from the sophisticated world of the Corinthians. Paul's corrective view suggests another approach altogether. The community's pursuit of charity should be the focus of the individual's energies and form the individual's conscience. Freedom is for the service of the gospel message. A person's rights are subject to God's call to preach the gospel. The charity of God compels us, training us in the school of self-denial and the pursuit of God's will in our lives.

Problems in Liturgical Assemblies (11:2–14:40)

Paul now turns to issues affecting the ways that the Corinthians are worshipping together. They fall into three categories: decorum at assemblies (11:2–16), celebration of the Lord's Supper (11: 17–34), and the unity and variety of spiritual gifts (12:1–14:40).

Dress and Decorum in the Assembly (11:2–16). This is a problematic passage that has received much attention. Throughout the ancient Mediterranean world, among Jews, Greeks, and Romans alike, the subordination of women to men was a common part of the thinking, even though by this time women of sufficient wealth and status exercised a great deal of social and economic autonomy. It was common custom that respectable adult women veiled themselves in public, even though that custom was changing in social circles that were more sensitive to Roman customs. In more traditional circles, as is still the case in some cultures, the unveiled female head was a sign of sexual availability. It appears that some female members of the Corinthian church, however, were combining their knowledge of newer social customs with Paul's own preaching about freedom in the Spirit, and concluded that the veil was no longer necessary in some circumstances, particularly the church assembly, where others, including Paul, judged that it was. While never questioning women's right to pray and prophesy publicly (11:5), he simply judged that it must be done with traditional dress. In his attempt to provide a theological explanation, Paul draws on traditional images of headship and subordination, using as illustration three parallel examples: Christ and man, man and woman, God and Christ. He then goes on to appeal to "nature," which really means "common sense," that is, what people were used to. Finally, he realizes that he has not proved his case and simply withdraws to the position of authority: we just don't do it that way (11:16)! While affirming women's full position in the church, he capitulates on the question of dress in favor of something that will not cause scandal among conservative outsiders (and perhaps some insiders, too) who are undoubtedly watching this new movement.

Celebration of the Eucharist (11:17–34). There were divisions among the Corinthians on social and economic grounds. Wealthy Christians apparently boasted great meals at which the poor were either not welcomed or treated badly. Some became drunk while others went away hungry (11:20–22, 33–34). Paul says that this is not the Lord's Supper and that the Corinthians are eating and drinking their own condemnation (see 11:27–29). Within the context of the discussion of abuses in the community's liturgical celebrations, Paul inserts his account of the institution of the Last Supper in order to put the troubles in the proper context. This is the earliest written account of the institution of the Lord's Supper in the New Testament (see the note on 11:23–25). Paul's version, also reflected in Luke 22:14–20, contains at least three significant differences from the version given in Mk 14:22–25; Mt 26:26–29. These variants are in the additions of the words "for you," the command "Do this in remembrance of me" (v. 24), and the qualifier "new" before "covenant" in 11:25. These variants witness to several early versions of the eucharistic sayings.

By emphasizing that Jesus' body was given "for you," Paul reminds the Corinthians of Jesus' self-giving act in which they participate by receiving the bread and the cup. They are then warned that an "unworthy" reception would not bring salvation but rather condemnation. The command to do this in memory of Jesus calls the Christians to offer a fitting memorial, including calling to mind Jesus' self-offering and imitating him in this. The insertion of "new" before "covenant" reminds the Corinthians that Jeremiah's prophecy of a "new covenant" is fulfilled in Christ (see Jer 31:31; 2 Cor 3:3, 6). This is an inclusive covenant, one that is already proclaimed in ancient Israel and that will be extended to all, one that provides the basis for a new society and a new relationship with God. It is important to realize that Paul's critique of the Corinthian Eucharist is not proper reverence toward the sacrament, but proper reverence toward the poor and all members who participate in it.

The Spiritual Gifts (12:1–14:40). The divisions among the Corinthians based on competition for the higher gifts continues to occupy Paul. He reminds the Corinthians that when they were pagans they were "attracted and led away" by idols (12:2). Idolatry attributes the honor and devotion that belongs to God to false gods. Paul advises the Corinthians that in true conversion to Jesus Christ there is unity with others who also worship the same God.

The hymn of love in 1 Corinthians 13, inserted within the context of chapters 12 and 14 on the variety of gifts, may not be a Pauline composition but something borrowed from Stoic sources, which he found helpful to illustrate the unity that should characterize the Corinthians (see note on 13:1–13). In chapter 11, Paul alluded to the divisions between the wealthy and the poor at the common table. In chapters 12 and 14, it is not so much the social distinctions as striving for spiritual gifts that threatens the Corinthians' unity. As remedy, Paul offers reflections on the community as the body of Christ (12:12–27), a new adaptation of an old image of social unity. A very high estimation is placed on prophecy, the action of the Spirit through members of the community. But the new context Paul provides emphasizes that love is the highest spiritual gift, one to which all believers must aspire to achieve (13:13). Love remains the most important of all the spiritual gifts in the church. This is not to diminish faith and hope and the other spiritual gifts such as teaching and administration. Love is an expression of God's own love, enabling us to act mercifully and kindly toward one another. Love in action, at the service of others, is the essential message of the gospel.

The Resurrection (15:1–58)

For Paul, the death, burial, and resurrection of Christ are the central mystery of the Christian life—but not in isolation. If we are to experience death and burial, we are also to experience resurrection. Paul claims to have met the Risen Christ directly, and we can assume that some of his assertions about the Resurrection are derived from that experience (Gal 1:12, 15–16). Others perhaps came from his meeting with Cephas (Gal 1:18), who had participated in the post-Easter appearances, and from his own apocalyptic theology in Pharisaic context. Paul implies that if the Corinthians really grasped and accepted the Resurrection and its implications, many of the problems he has addressed throughout the letter would have been resolved. In the first part of this chapter (15:1–11), he states the fundamental teaching on the resurrection of Christ and recites the earliest surviving creed and list of appearances. He stresses the appearances of the Risen Christ that were the foundational experiences, beginning with Peter's and ending with his own.

A second section (15:12–28) states emphatically, "If Christ has not been raised, your faith is in vain" (15:14, 17). The resurrection of Christ forms the basis of faith and causes believers to reassess all of life and death. By his resurrection, Christ is revealed as the "firstfruits of those who have fallen asleep" (15:20). Christ is our hope, our assurance that we too will have the same experience. Without it, perseverance in faith, including the sacrifices involved in suffering persecution, is pointless.

In a third section (15:29–34), Paul is trying to shame the Corinthians by showing them the absurdities of some Christian practices and beliefs without faith in the Resurrection as the fate of all the faithful. The slogan quoted by Paul, "Let us eat and drink, for tomorrow we die" (15:32) is the wisdom of those without hope in the life to come.

In the next section (15:35–50), he takes up those who speculate on the nature of resurrection and the risen body. He uses the example of dissimilar creatures such as birds and fish, the sun and the moon, to show the qualitative difference between bodies, as a way of stressing, without going into detail, the differences in our bodies before and after the resurrection. The seed sown in the ground is not the same as the green shoot that springs from it, yet the shoot is continuous with the life of the seed that must die in order to produce it. Paul draws a contrast between the first Adam, the earthly, corruptible one whose image we now bear, and the last Adam, Christ, the incorruptible and eternal one, whose image we will bear in the resurrection.

The last section of 1 Corinthians 15 (vv. 51–58) incorporates a hymnic celebration of God's victory through Christ over sin and death, compiled from verses of Isaiah and Hosea. Conquered by Christ, sin and death have lost their sting. By the resurrection of Christ, God has shown us that sin and death are not the last word, but only lead to life. Therefore Paul sings God's praises for the hope that the Resurrection gives. He reminds the Corinthians that their "labor is not in vain in the Lord" (1 Cor 15:58). The rousing message of the chapter is: hang on! The best is yet to come!

Conclusion (16:1–24)

Finally, Paul speaks of the collection and how it is to be taken to alleviate the suffering of the saints (16:1–4). Paul then reports his travel plans, sends greetings to his friends, and concludes with a blessing. Comparison of the persons named with those mentioned in 1 Corinthians 1 and Acts 18 renders an interesting profile of the Corinthian community with its mixture of notable men and women, rich and poor, powerful and ordinary citizens. Paul greets representatives of all categories, personally demonstrating the acceptance and unity he has been advocating.

Concluding Remarks

Some readers may find it surprising to realize that Paul deals in 1 Corinthians with some of the same questions that continue to challenge the church today. Christians still struggle with whether there are more limits on the freedom allowed to women than to men. The rights and responsibilities of ministers in the church are at the heart of the renewal of the priesthood initiated by Vatican II and continued in various important pastoral and ecclesial efforts locally and in the universal church. Issues such as the requirements for a sacramental marriage and qualifications for the ordained ministry, the possibilities for lay ministries, or the role of the sacraments (especially baptism and the Eucharist) in Christian life were not answered by Paul, or even by Vatican II, once and for all. But the church continues to use Paul's pastoral approach to guide and to respond to the needs of its members.

The Corinthians were a church like ours—real people with real problems. They struggled for charity in the midst of disagreements, for respect for leaders without exaggerating these leaders' roles. Paul stressed the role of ministers as servants of God and Jesus Christ. Paul recognizes the authority of the church to discipline its members, including the immoral, those in dispute, the strong as well as the weak. Paul tried to help remedy their problems by advising them to seek spiritual gifts, especially charity. Paul advocated a healthy respect for the body without failing to see the value of asceticism. Paul recognized roles for both women and men in the liturgy. He gave some concrete examples of practical implications of living the gospel message as a community of equals. He protests discrimination against the poor or those considered inferior because they possess lesser gifts. Further, Paul stresses already in 1 Corinthians, and more so in 2 Corinthians, the necessity of aiding the less fortunate. The first epistle to the Corinthians is truly an interpretation of the gospel message that continues to challenge us with its many implications.

2 CORINTHIANS

[see pages 1624–1643 of the New Testament]

Before Beginning . . .

Second Corinthians features some of the most profound moments of Paul's theology, but in a puzzling arrangement. If 1 Corinthians has a structure that is clear and easy to follow, his second letter to the same church is characterized by disorderly sequence, to such a degree that many scholars think it is actually a composite of several letters Paul sent to the same church. The tone tends to be more defensive than most of his letters, and the flow of thought choppy. Some fragments (for example, 6:14–7:1) appear completely out of context. The transition from 2:13 to 2:14 is very rough, while 7:5 seems to pick up exactly where 2:13 left off. Further, chapters 8 and 9 seem to have been originally two separate letters, each dealing with the collection, but neither assuming the other nor conditioned by the whole context of chapters 1 through 7 and 10 through 13. Finally, chapters 10 through 13 could stand alone as an "apologia," an explanation in defense of Paul's own spiritual experience, his vocation, and apostolic credentials. Certainly 2 Corinthians exhibits traces of an ongoing conversation.

Yet the lack of cohesion in Paul's thought may be only apparent. It is also possible that there is an order to the letter that demonstrates Paul's typical A-B-A' pattern, which also influenced 1 Corinthians. So, for example, Paul begins and ends 2 Corinthians with personal testimony about the painful difficulties both he and the Corinthians have experienced in the course of their relationship (see 1:12–7:16 as A, and 10:1–13:10 as A'). Within this frame, the two middle chapters, 8 and 9, dealing with the collection for the poor in Jerusalem (B section) illustrate that for Paul, the generosity of the Corinthians symbolizes the success of the Gentile mission. The older scholarship, with its emphasis on literary sources and redactions, is more prone to see the letter as composed of several fragments. In this case, a later editor combined the pieces into the whole that we now have, but the parts sometimes do not fit together well. If this is the case, an explanation is needed as to why the editor did such a poor job. Newer scholarship, with its emphasis on literary analysis, tends to try to look at the letter as a unified whole. In this case, the disruptions in the flow of the text are due to Paul's deliberate digressions for rhetorical effect.

Whichever may be the true situation, we need to work through 2 Corinthians in its final, canonical form, even if it also represents originally separate letters or letter fragments. We approach 2 Corinthians as part of the New Testament canon, a letter preserved by the early church and read at liturgical gatherings in spite of its criticisms of the Corinthians and the many challenges it raised for the church there. Despite the many troubles and misunderstandings between them, the Corinthians seem to have respected Paul's authority enough to preserve his words, reflect on them, and circulate them to other churches. Lest we think that ours is the only age in which deep divisions appear in the church, this letter reveals that Christian community in the first years was no idyllic experience. The Corinthian letters will serve as a corrective to such mistaken idealism.

Working through 2 Corinthians

Some initial observations about the connection of parts of the text will help us read 2 Corinthians with better understanding. As already indicated, 2 Corinthians follows a rather disrupted and choppy sequence. Following the usual Greco-Roman letter structure, 2 Corinthians has the three main parts of the *address* in 1:1–7, the *body* of the letter in 1:8–13:10, and the *conclusion* in 13:11–13. Our comments will consider each of these parts. A working outline of 2 Corinthians is as follows:

I. The Address (1:1–7)
II. The Body of the Letter (1:8–13:10)
  A. Crisis Between Paul and the Corinthians (1:8–7:16)
    1. Past Difficulties and Relationships (1:9–2:13)
    2. Paul's Ministry (2:14–7:4)
    3. Resolution of the Crisis (7:5–16)
  B. The Collection for Jerusalem (8:1–9:15)
  C. Paul's Defense of His Ministry (10:1–13:10)
III. Conclusion (13:11–13)

Reading through 2 Corinthians

The Address (1:1–7)

In the *address* Paul names Timothy as co-author. Timothy and Titus (2:13; 7:6; 8:16, 23; see also Gal 2:1) were apparently more trusted by the Corinthians than Paul himself. Timothy is not named again in 2 Corinthians although some suppose he is the unnamed "brother" who accompanies Titus with the collection. Luke tells us that Timothy was a faithful companion of Paul, especially on the second and third missionary journeys (see "The Pastoral Letters," RG 486–7).

The greeting includes a doxology or prayer glorifying and praising God whose "encouragement" is strength in affliction (see 2 Cor 1:3–4). This encouragement *(paraklesis)* in noun or verbal form occurs ten times in five verses, 3 through 7. This addition gives us a hint as to the overriding mood of 2 Corinthians. Paul and the Corinthians have experienced much misunderstanding, but Paul wants to move on to great consolation. Transcending all the pain is the certainty of God's presence with them and Paul's confidence that God is at work in their lives.

The Body of the Letter (1:8–13:10)

The message of 2 Corinthians is developed in three main parts: (A) In the first part (1:8–7:16), Paul reviews his past relationship with the Corinthians; (B) Chapters 8 and 9 form a second part in which Paul develops a theology of giving, speaking of the collection among the Gentiles and specifically of the generosity of the Corinthians as a symbol of the fruitfulness of the Gentile mission; (A') In the third part, 10:1–13:10, Paul revisits topics he raised in the first part and returns to the theme of his credentials as an apostle, accenting his own weakness and the call of God. It is here that Paul develops a theology of suffering, speaking candidly and with great feeling about his own experience of the grace of God. Many in the history of Christianity have seen in these chapters a spiritual reality by which they are helped to interpret their own personal experience of God: "My grace is sufficient for you, for power is made perfect in weakness" (12:9). We can read through these three parts of the body of 2 Corinthians, reflecting on the relevance of this composite letter for our own experience as Christians.

The Crisis between Paul and the Corinthians (1:8–7:16)

The relationship between Paul and the Corinthians seems to have been marked by crisis. This is evident in both 1 and 2 Corinthians. We shall focus now on the problems Paul mentions in the first part of 2 Corinthians. The apostle first reviews his past relationship with the Corinthians and then his ministry with them. Paul mentions several instances of mistrust and tension between himself and the Corinthians in his review of their past relationship.

Past Difficulties and Relationships (1:8–2:13)

First, Paul reviews the difficulties he had in "Asia," meaning the Roman province that covered the western part of Asia Minor. He probably alludes to Ephesus, where because of this and 1 Corinthians 15:32 many scholars think he endured an imprisonment not recorded in Acts. Paul then focuses on several areas—a change of plans and the Corinthians' subsequent accusation of inconstancy and lack of sincerity; his confrontation with an offending member of the community and his plea for leniency in the punishment of this person whom he has forgiven; and Paul's anxiety about the lack of information about the Corinthians from Titus. Paul appears frustrated at the apparent lack of communication, sympathy, and confidence. The factions that were mentioned in 1 Corinthians could have made a simple change of mind such as this a source of strife. Paul's detractors accused him of being unreliable.

Paul appeals to God's own fidelity as part of his response (1:18), showing that his word is sincere and his care constant. Yet he decided to change his plans in view of the recent painful letter (2:4) that he had found it necessary to write to the Corinthians. He postponed a promised visit only to give time for healing (2:1–4). With sufficient reflection Paul is confident that the Corinthians would realize the abundant love he has for them (2:4).

Apparently someone in the community publicly offended Paul (2:5–11), though the nature of the offense remains obscure. As in 1 Corinthians 5, Paul advocates a judgment not by outsiders but within the church. The action by the majority was acceptable and judged sufficient by Paul. In the case of the incestuous man of 1 Corinthians, he recommended expulsion from the church (see 1 Cor 5:2, 4–5). But in 2 Corinthians 2:5–11 Paul says that the time has come for forgiveness and reintegration lest Satan be granted a victory in the offender. Like many other biblical writers Paul sees the world as an arena where the conflict between good and evil forces is ongoing, each vying for human allegiance. The church is entrusted with the "ministry of reconciliation" as Paul describes it in 2 Corinthians 5:11–16. The forgiveness of the one who offended Paul is a specific example of that ministry in practice.

In 2:12–13 Paul mentions the anguish he felt at his inability to find Titus and receive news about the Corinthians. This anxiety is a further indication of Paul's sincere affection for the Corinthians. In 1:12–24 he defends his change of plans and insists on his anxious concern for the Corinthians. It would seem that this was written before Paul received the happy news from Titus described in 7:5–16.

Paul's Ministry (2:14–7:4)

Paul interrupts his review of the events that troubled his relationship to the Corinthians in order to describe in more general theological terms his apostolic ministry. Within the overall A-B-A' structure of 2 Corinthians we see subsections like 1:12–7:16 also exhibiting this same pattern. In this instance, 2:14–7:4 (B), describing

Paul's ministry, is framed by, and grounds theologically, the practical and painful experience of Paul's relationship with the community described in 1:12–2:13 (A) and 7:5–16 (A'). Paul's description of his ministry develops several important themes:

the new covenant enacted by Christ (3:1–18);

the paradox of the ministry: strength in weakness (4:1–18);

the ministry of reconciliation entrusted to them (5:1–21).

This description begins (2:14–17) and ends (7:2–4) with expressions of confidence in God and in the Corinthians. We will briefly discuss each of the three Pauline themes.

The New Covenant Enacted by Christ (3:1–18). Here, Paul's reasoning is based on the Old Testament passages and on one of his favorite contrasts, between spirit and flesh (see Rom 8:1–10; Gal 2:3; 5:17–23). It exemplifies the method taught him in his biblical training, taking several passages from different sources and combining them to produce a new conclusion. Jeremiah's promise of a "new covenant" (31:31–34) is combined with Ezekiel's prophecy of God's promise to replace human hearts of stone with hearts of flesh and to give a covenant in the spirit (Ez 36:26–36). Exodus 34 described the relationship between God and Moses as so glorious that Moses had to come down from Mount Sinai with a veil covering his head lest the Israelites die at the sight of his glowing face (Ex 34:33–35). These passages from the Prophets and the Law provide the scriptural basis for Paul's argument that the ministry *(diakonia)* of the new covenant, to which Paul is devoted, is superior to that of Moses. Using the familiar rhetorical method from lesser to greater, Paul argues that if Moses' covenant was so spectacular yet was still written on stone and in hearts of flesh, how much greater is Christ's covenant, which is the fulfillment of the prophetic promise of the Spirit!

Paul contrasts the Mosaic covenant written "in ink" or "on stone" with the "new covenant" written by the "Spirit" on "hearts of flesh." In the process he uses the phrase "old covenant" (2 Cor 3:14), the only instance of this expression in the Scriptures. This "old" covenant was that enacted by God with Moses. Jeremiah and Ezekiel had spoken of a new enactment of the covenant reality, in which intimate access to God would be realized. Paul picks up this theme to write that this promise of a "new covenant" is realized in the work of Jesus. The difference between the covenants illustrates the contrast between Moses and Christ, and indicates the superiority of the covenant in Christ. Paul and the Corinthians are ministers or agents *(diakonoi)* of the new covenant that brings life and the Spirit. In the last part of the passage, he switches the image of the veil to apply it not as a protection on Moses' face to prevent injury to the people but as an obstacle to clear vision, now upon the faces of those who are unable to see the glory of the new covenant in Jesus (3:14–18). Christian readers today should remember that Paul was working within the Jewish context of biblical interpretation to work in a new way with familiar texts and images. While his message was definitely that a new thing had been done in Christ that would fully include the Gentiles, he was not drawing a contrast between an old Jewish covenant, now obsolete, and a new Christian covenant that would replace it. Rather, he wanted new Gentile members of the church to realize their debt to our Jewish brothers and sisters for the spiritual heritage they preserved and which we share with them. The Old Testament Scriptures continue to provide a fertile field for mutual reflection and understanding among Christians and Jews.

The Paradox of the Ministry: Strength in Weakness (4:1–18). Even though Paul is a minister of this great new covenant, he knows that the glory is God's, not his, and that the mystery of reception in faith is not within his control. He expresses the weakness and fragility of this ministry by the familiar image: "We hold this treasure in earthen vessels" (4:7), a poetic translation of meaning that could be said more prosaically: "We hold these treasures in clay pots," as a reminder that the power is from God, not from human agents. Paul recalls the price to be paid: "We are afflicted in every way . . . perplexed . . . persecuted . . . constantly being given up to death for the sake of Jesus" (4:8–11). But Paul continuously alludes to God as the source of his own hope, confidence, and power.

Grace is given in greater and greater abundance through the mystery of Christ for the glory of God. Even while they experience diminishment of their "outer self," the "inner self" grows stronger. The afflictions they experience are passing, but the invisible power of God is what lasts forever.

The Ministry of Reconciliation (5:1–21). Throughout 2 Corinthians 2:14–7:4 Paul wrestles with the redemptive aspects of suffering for the sake of the Christian message. This aspect has several implications: first, the negative is not overwhelming; rather, there is always some experience of rescue or salvation. Second, the experience of suffering ends not with the apostle but redounds to the good of the community and, beyond the community, relates to the will of God. Third, for Paul, redemption effects a radical change in believers, taking them out of a particular sinful mode of existence and introducing them into another mode of reality that is in Christ. Fourth and finally, Paul and the Corinthians, like all ministers of the gospel, are involved in the ministry of reconciliation of the whole world to God.

Earthly existence is fraught with difficulties. In Paul's words, we "groan and are weighed down" (5:4) by the difficulties of human existence and of fidelity to the work entrusted to us. We are longing to be covered not with a "tent" but with a heavenly dwelling not made with human hands. We walk by faith (5:7), trying to please the Lord by whom, in the end, we will be judged (5:10) not only on our own deeds but also on the effect of those deeds on others' actions. Catholic interpretation has always emphasized the communal responsibility or the obligations believers have toward others. Paul goes on to explain in the remainder of chapter 5 (vv. 11–21) that Christ's work is a ministry of reconciling the world to God. But that work is not finished once and for all. Through Christ we have been given the astounding mission and responsibility of carrying on that work of reconciliation (5:17–20). In this context, Paul pleads with the Corinthians to be reconciled with God and thus, implicitly, with him.

Resolution of the Crisis (7:5–16)

Paul returns to the concrete situation in Corinth, alluding to his anguished wait until he encountered Titus. Paul's representative, Titus, had now furnished good news about the Corinthians' reception of Paul's difficult letter (2:4 and 7:8), which some argue is actually chapters 10 through 12 of the present letter. Now the conflict between Paul and the Corinthians was apparently resolved. Paul's exuberant gratitude overshadows all of the former sadness and anxiety. It appears as though all is completely restored, and there is no more reason for concern.

If we have been reading along with Paul, we have noted that some of the problems that afflict our church were present in the experience of the earliest Christians. Paul was an itinerant preacher who normally traveled from community to community preaching the gospel. But Paul lived among the Corinthians longer than with any other community (eighteen months [Acts 18:11]). He invested enormous energy in this community and could not be indifferent to their problems and questions and mistakes. No one can doubt that this is a problematic relationship, yet it was not severed. The deliberate rhetorical contrast in this letter is between the apparently conflicting data of 2 Corinthians 1:12–7:16: the lofty statements about the ministry of the new covenant as well as the insinuations of distrust, discouragement, and anxiety between apostle and community. Paul describes the Christian ministry as a ministry of reconciliation, but he also reminds us of the fragility of the human agents, as earthen vessels holding the treasure. All the hardships are apparently forgotten in Paul's exuberant conclusion: "I rejoice, because I have confidence in you in every respect" (7:16).

The Collection for Jerusalem (8:1–9:15)

Chapters 8 and 9 appear originally to have been two independent "fund-raising letters" on the importance of a generous and substantial offering to the Jerusalem church. This collection for Jerusalem presumably was the condition for acceptance there of Paul's mission to the Gentiles in Gal 2:10. Jerusalem may have been a collection center for distribution of relief to other churches of Palestine and Syria. This collection is important because it represents the full participation of the Gentile Christians in the community of the new Israel, the Church. On the one hand Paul encourages the Corinthians to give generously, seeing this request as a "test [of] the genuineness of your love by your concern for others" (8:8). On the other hand Paul will see the acceptance of the Gentiles' offering as evidence of the Jewish Christians', and specifically of the Jerusalem church's, willingness to accept the Gentile mission (Rom 15:22–33).

Paul uses the tactic of creating competition among the Gentile churches. He encourages the Corinthians to give as generously as the Macedonians (Philippi and Thessalonica), who were generous even when they themselves were "tested by affliction" (8:2). But in 9:2 Paul claims that he has boasted of the Corinthians' generosity to the Macedonians. In Romans he says that both the Achaians (the Corinthians) and the Macedonians were only too happy to contribute because they understood it as their obligation (Rom 15:27). The Gentiles were "indebted" to the mother church in Jerusalem and to the other Jewish Christian churches whose spiritual heritage they shared. The language of wealth and poverty in these passages is rhetorical and should not be taken as economic indicators. At the end of the chapter Paul speaks of envoys or messengers from and to the churches, among whom is Titus. The others are unnamed but probably known to the recipients of the letter. They are in fact called "apostles" of the churches (8:23). Along with this title applied to Epaphroditus in Philippians 2:25 and to Andronicus and Junia in Romans 16:7, it indicates that the title of apostle was held by many in the Pauline churches.

Paul begins chapter 9 as if he has not written chapter 8. Although he has just encouraged generosity in the collection, he says in 9:1, "It is superfluous for me to write to you" about the collection. There are many other ideas repeated in chapter 9 that were raised in chapter 8. It would be very strange for Paul to say the difficult things he says to the Corinthians before and after these chapters and even deal with their accusations against him (chapter 10), while here in the middle asking them for money! These arguments, and the apparent independence of these chapters not only from each other but also from the context of the rest of the letter, prompt many interpreters to consider them as originally separate letters or letter fragments. For us, however, they represent a crucial example of the importance of Paul's role as apostle to the Corinthians. This is the role he reviewed in chapters 1 through 7 and ardently defends in chapters 10 through 13, to which we now turn.

Paul's Defense of His Ministry (10:1–13:10)

In the course of defending his ministry again, Paul can be seen following the A-B-A' pattern, by which he introduced arguments in 10:1–18 (A), which he will continue in a concluding section in 12:19–13:10 (A'). Between these he interjects 11:1–12:18 (B), his own experience with the Corinthians and his sufferings as an apostle. Thus Paul's development includes responses to accusations that continue among the Corinthians: he is weak (10:1–2), not an eloquent speaker (10:10), not supported by the community (11:7–10). Paul reminds the Corinthians at the beginning (10:2, 11) and end (12:20–13:2, 10) that he intends to visit them soon and deal with such issues in person. In the midst of his responses to charges, Paul develops in a famous and memorable passage (11:1–12:18) his own lived theology of the cross.

Paul's Response (10:1–18; 12:19–13:10)

Paul's impatient tone in chapters 10 through 13 suggests that he has already dealt with their accusations against him, and they ought to have been laid to rest. The Corinthians appear to be elitists, perceiving themselves to be superior in knowledge and gravitating toward those they suppose possess superior gifts. These include eloquence and an impressive appearance. Some of the Corinthians apparently favored Apollos' eloquence over the "contemptible speech" of Paul (see 1 Cor 3:4–5; 4:6–7). They noted Peter's freedom, his authority, the fact that he accepts support from the community (see 1 Cor 9:6), and challenged Paul's reasons for refusing community support. Apparently the Corinthians are affronted by Paul's refusal to accept their patronage and continue to see Paul's forfeiture of this "apostolic right" to support as an admission that Paul is not of the same stature as Peter.

The Corinthians' complaint that Paul is an impressive writer but that his presence is disappointing (10:1, 10) is arrogant but perhaps speaks a truth that led him to rely so strongly on the written word. Oratory was highly prized; perhaps Paul did not measure up to expectations in that regard. In response, Paul warned that he was empowered by Christ to "act boldly." He would use spiritual weapons to subdue in the end every enemy and disobedient thought in all to make all things subject to Christ (10:2–6). Paul warned the Corinthians against false pride and conceits and jealousies. He had earlier told the Corinthians to decide whether he came peacefully or "with a rod" (1 Cor 4:21). Now he promises to visit again soon and warns that he shall not be lenient with them (13:1–10). The Corinthians should examine themselves and see whether Christ is in them. For his part Paul is confident that Christ is with him. This warning tone is difficult to imagine in the same letter with and following the reconciling tone of 7:5–10.

Paul Boasts of His Labors and His Weakness (11:1–12:18)

Since the Corinthians are attracted by knowledge, Paul proposes to speak of "foolishness," and asks their indulgence. Remember that in 1 Corinthians 1–3 Paul described the wisdom of God as folly for humans and added that God confounds the wise with the wisdom of the cross. In this section of 2 Corinthians, Paul talks about the role of the cross in his own life.

Again, it is Paul's opponents who draw out this vehement testimony about the source of his authority. There are those Paul sarcastically calls the "superapostles" (11:5), with the same tone with which one might say "supermouse" or "superrabbit"; a few verses later, they are labeled for what Paul really thinks of them, as "false apostles" (11:13; see the "false brothers" of Gal 2:4). In any case, others are leading the Corinthians astray; Paul fears that the Corinthians are like Eve (11:3), deceived by the serpent's cunning. This little aside indicated Paul's acceptance of the prevailing male wisdom of his time, since Sirach 25:23, that Eve represented the more easily seduced segment of humankind. The comparison with Eve, so regarded, would be insulting to the lofty Corinthians, a strategy Paul uses to bring them back to humility.

Continuing his paradoxical development of knowledge and foolishness, Paul describes the wisdom he has learned through suffering. His beautiful testimony can hardly be adequately paraphrased. It must be read and reflected upon. The experiences which the Corinthians construe as "failures"—the beatings, humiliations, imprisonments, dangers—are Paul's apostolic credentials. He has experienced visions and revelations and ecstasies. He might have been tempted to pride in these (as he suggests the Corinthians would be). But Paul also experienced a "thorn in the flesh . . . an angel of Satan, to beat me" (2 Cor 12:7). The wisdom Paul learned from this suffering, so beautifully expressed, is that God's power is made perfect in his human weakness. In the end we can understand why Paul says, "I boast most gladly of my weaknesses, in order that the power of Christ may dwell with me" (12:9).

Conclusion (13:11–13)

The conclusion is brief and encouraging, and could be the conclusion to any Pauline letter. It does not reveal the depth of pain involved in some of its earlier content. By following Paul's apparently circuitous arguments, we are enriched far beyond the effort of understanding the specific situation Paul addressed in Corinth centuries ago. An outcome of studying 2 Corinthians is the realization that all the suffering involved in creating the church among limited human beings bears fruit in fidelity and hope. From 2 Corinthians we are brought to a whole new appreciation of the role of the cross in the Christian vocation to holiness.

GALATIANS

[see pages 1643–1654 of the New Testament]

Before Beginning . . .

Galatians is the only Pauline letter written as a circular letter to various churches of a geographical region rather than an urban center. The old territory of Galatia comprised a large central and northern area of Asia Minor. The Roman province of Galatia, to which Paul probably refers, included some of the cities, such as Iconium, Lystra, and Derbe, in which Paul worked, according to Acts.

Paul's tone in the opening lines of Galatians is defensive and emotional, shown by the absence of the usual prayer of thanksgiving following the address, which is a common characteristic of Paul's letters. Paul sees the problem in the Galatian communities as a great threat not only to his own reputation and mission but to the gospel itself. Other missionaries, whom scholars commonly call "Judaizers," came into Galatia after Paul and claimed that Gentiles must follow some aspects of the Jewish law, including circumcision, in order to be fully Christian. Perhaps they said that Paul taught the fundamentals, and they would now give the Galatians the full Christian message. They were undermining Paul's authority and the sufficiency of faith in Christ that Paul preached. Consequently, he writes heatedly to convince the recipients that he has the full truth. From the emotional tone of chapters 1 and 2, he passes to the complex biblical demonstrations of chapters 3 and 4, finally into the ethical teaching of chapters 5 and 6.

The issues of freedom and faith, diversity of teaching and different understandings of the gospel message, and the relationship of Christianity to Judaism are as important to us as they were to Paul's addressees in Galatia. Yet today's reader of Galatians must see past the combative tone of this letter, the circumstances of its writing, and the historical context in which Paul first developed his dichotomy between faith and works. These tasks are well worth the effort if we are to understand this important epistle of Paul. It is also essential to realize that this letter in which Paul talks the most about freedom is also the letter in which he most identifies with the cross of Christ. Freedom is for the sake of service.

Jews and Gentiles in the Pauline Churches

We cannot adequately comprehend Galatians without recognition of an important historical issue that was at the basis of Paul's missionary perspective. That issue involves the relationship between Judaism and the infant church that struggled to integrate the non-Jews or Gentiles into a new "Israel of God" (Gal 6:16), and between Jews and Gentiles in that church. Although this may seem like a remote issue unrelated to the problems the church faces today, it is actually quite relevant for us with our increasing ethnic diversity and ecumenical concerns. The question of "Who shall belong?" had to be resolved differently than it was in Judaism, where circumcision was the sign of initiation, and obedience to the Mosaic Law signified membership.

Those Christians who were already ethnically and religiously Jewish saw the message of Jesus largely within the context of Judaism. Indeed, Christianity might have remained as a sect within Judaism had it revolved only around belief that Jesus was the Messiah. Early Christianity, however, was almost immediately open to the conversion of the Gentiles (sometimes called the "nations" or the "pagans" in translations). We must also remember that before his conversion to Christ, Paul the Pharisee was so zealous for the observance of the Law that he persecuted the church (Gal 1:13). According to Acts, Paul obtained authorization to hunt down and bring to trial in Jerusalem those fellow Jews who had become convinced that Jesus was the Messiah (Acts 9:1–2). As a strict Jew, Paul had perceived along with many others that the message of Christ was a threat to Jewish claims to a unique access to the one true God through the covenant. The Pharisaism to which Paul belonged already was open to Gentile membership, based on the universal vision of the later prophets, especially Second and Third Isaiah, but with the requirement that they convert to Judaism. After Paul had accepted the messianic identity of Jesus through revelation and had begun to proclaim it as a missionary (1:15–16), he held the conviction that this new movement must be able to absorb both Jews and Gentiles, but in a new way. His own special attraction, based on a personal revelation, was to preach the gospel to Gentiles, an attraction that he says the leaders in Jerusalem accepted (2:7–9). Through his pastoral experience, he had come to the conclusion that the only way to integrate Jews and Gentiles fully into the churches was to eliminate the need for conversion to Judaism on the part of the Gentiles.

In other words, Paul reassessed, as a result of his vocation, the role of the Jewish Law to which he had always been devoted. In light of his God-given vocation to preach the message of Christ to non-Jews, Paul began to see the Law as superseded. According to the Law as it was then understood, the Gentiles had been excluded from salvation. Through Christ, Paul taught, they are included—and on their own terms, not as converts to Judaism. As a result of a revelation from

God, Paul identified himself as an apostle to the Gentiles. Consequently Paul felt as committed to the Gentile mission as he ever had felt formerly with regard to the Jewish Law.

The Gentile mission, however, did not begin with Paul. Stephen (see Acts 6) and others, including Peter (Acts 10), had preached to Gentiles and baptized them before Paul. Nevertheless, not all of the early Christian leaders felt the same degree of freedom from the Jewish Law as Paul did. Nor did everyone agree that Gentiles who were becoming part of the church should neglect the prescriptions of the Jewish Law. Peter and James, for example, who were recognized Christian leaders, both felt that some observance of Jewish Law should be required of the Gentiles. James was a very significant figure in the Jerusalem mother church. Peter, of course, was one of the Twelve and a leader of the Jerusalem community as well as a known authority in the predominantly Jewish Christian community at Antioch. Representatives from James apparently were preaching at least a minimal observance of Jewish Law and gaining a significant hearing among the Gentile converts (see Acts 11:1–26; Gal 2:1–10).

The matter was confusing for several reasons. Christianity incorporated the monotheism and the high ethical principles of Judaism, which were very attractive to many Gentiles. The appeal of these basics of Judaism made more reasonable the position of those who "Judaized" (a verb Paul uses only in Gal 2:14, where it is translated "live like Jews"). The "Judaizers" claimed that Gentiles should fulfill some basic requirements of the Jewish Law, particularly circumcision and some dietary restrictions, in order to demonstrate that they had actually converted from pagan ways. But from the beginning of the Christian preaching, faith in Jesus crucified and raised from death by God had been the only requirement for baptism. Even Peter testified that the Gentiles, like the Jews, were saved through faith and that "God shows no partiality" (Acts 15:9; Gal 2:6). Paul vehemently opposed any additional requirements for the Gentiles. He believed that these additions would, in fact, constitute deviation from the firm conviction that salvation is a work of God accomplished through grace that is accepted by faith in Jesus as the Christ.

Working through Galatians

Galatians represents Paul's effort to defend his preaching against alternative interpretations and to correct some misrepresentations about the message he preaches. Galatians exhibits the three main parts of a letter: the *address* (1:1–5), the *body* (1:6–6:10), which contains teaching (1:6–4:31) and ethical applications (5:1–6:10), and a *conclusion* (6:11–18). We will comment on these main divisions of Galatians; a more detailed outline is given in the NAB:

- I. Address (1:1–5)
- II. The Body of the Letter (1:6–6:10)
  - A. Defense of Paul's Gospel and Authority (1:6–2:21)
    - 1. Paul's Vocation (1:6–24)
    - 2. Paul and the Jerusalem Authorities (2:1–21)
  - B. Faith, Freedom, and the Scriptures (3:1–4:31)
    - 1. Abraham, Father of Faith (3:6–16)
    - 2. Example of the Human Will (3:17–23)
    - 3. Example of the Child-Minder (3:24–4:11)
    - 4. Assurance of Paul's Affection (4:12–20)
    - 5. Allegory of the Two Wives of Abraham (4:21–31)
  - C. Exhortations for Christian Life (5:1–6:10)
- III. Conclusion (6:11–18)

Reading through Galatians

The Address (1:1–5)

This address, in which Paul greets the recipients, is abbreviated and assertive. It lacks the usual thanksgiving characteristic of the opening of a Pauline letter. Perhaps Paul's eagerness to get to the heart of his message explains this omission. Perhaps, too, he is so distressed at what he has heard about the events in Galatia that he cannot feel thankful. He asserts from the beginning that his credentials are not from any human source, but from God and Jesus Christ.

The Body of the Letter (1:6–6:10)

In Galatians we see Paul on the defensive, strongly insisting on his loyalty to the gospel.

This defense is occasioned by accusations that he seeks only to please other human beings. He develops several themes as part of his defense of the message he preached and that his authority came from God. Key themes in this defense are Paul's vocation, the coherence of his message with that of Jerusalem, and the biblical proofs of the truth of his preaching.

Defense of Paul's Preaching and Authority (1:6–2:21)

Paul expresses amazement that the Galatians have so quickly deserted the one who called them and who remains faithfully rooted in Christ, while they have deserted to "a different gospel" (1:6). He is about to prove to them that they and those who have taught them this way are wrong.

Paul's Vocation (1:6–24). Apparently there were those who accused Paul of lying. They claimed that Paul neglected to inform the Gentiles that their baptism involved following prescriptions of the Jewish Law. According to these opponents, Paul did not fully explain the gospel to his converts. But Paul countered that it was the opponents, rather than he, who were perverting the message of Christ. There cannot be two versions of the true gospel message. Paul understood the challenge to his authority as also a threat to the message he preached. His appeal to the divine origin of his call serves to emphasize that there can only be one true gospel. Even if he himself or any other church leader or an "angel from heaven" (1:8) would teach otherwise, the one true gospel is the one the Galatians heard from Paul. It does not need to be augmented with certain prescriptions from the Jewish Law.

Although we often speak about his conversion, Paul himself describes what happened as a "vocation." This was not merely a personal call as we might think of vocation today. Paul's call from God involves also a mission specifically to the Gentiles. Paul insists that this call came from God and underlines its divine origin by contrasting it with the role played by human beings, including his own initial unwillingness to accept Christ. It is precisely because he was in conflict with many others, including leaders of the church, that Paul begins Galatians by emphasizing that his call is from God. Paul has received an "apocalypse" or "revelation." He did not even go to Jerusalem nor meet any other apostle until three years after his call (which most scholars date around AD 34–35).

Paul uses language from the great prophets to describe his call, suggesting that he stands in their line. He claims that he was called from his "mother's womb," echoing the description of Jeremiah's call (Jer 1:4; see also Is 49:1). Paul reviews his own efforts to destroy the church, insisting that it was zeal for the Jewish Law that caused him to seek the authority to bring to trial in Jerusalem his fellow Jews who believed in Christ. Paul insists that he did not consult nor compromise with "flesh and blood," referring to the church authorities such as Peter, whom he did not even meet until later.

Paul and the Jerusalem Authorities (2:1–21). According to the authentic gospel preaching, faith in Jesus as the Christ is sufficient for salvation, without any other obligations to the Jewish Law. The single gospel message, Paul argues in Galatians 2:1–10, was confirmed by a meeting in Jerusalem with all the leaders of the church. Scholars place this meeting around AD 50 (see Acts 11 and 15). The only stipulation the leaders expressed was that Paul and the Gentiles be mindful of the poor, which probably refers to the collection of money from the Gentile churches for a common fund in Jerusalem (see comment on 2 Cor 8 and 9). Paul insists that he was eager to do this. Nevertheless, the Gentiles probably needed to learn that concern for the poor was a priority of Christian life (see 2 Cor 8:1–9:15). The Gentiles would not have benefited from the long Jewish ethical tradition that mandated taking care of the poor. Although this just concern was part of Jewish Law, the Law is not the reason Paul gives for accepting this stipulation. Rather, he insists that there was neither discussion nor agreement about the Gentiles following any prescriptions of the Law. This account from Paul is quite at odds with the account of presumably the same Jerusalem meeting in Acts 15:20,29, where observance of Jewish marital and sexual customs and basic dietary laws are enjoined on the Gentiles. Scholars have always had difficulty with the two versions, some assuming that Luke invented the cultic observances that the Gentiles were expected to observe, others assuming that Paul ignored them. Here Paul insists that no restrictions were part of the accord but were only added *after* the Jerusalem meeting and only because of pressure from the Jerusalem church headed by James. In Galatians 5:3 Paul will remind the Galatians that those who are circumcised must observe the whole Law, not just selected precepts.

The issue of imposing at least a minimal observance of the Jewish Law, including circumcision, on the Gentiles was introduced, Paul asserts, by "representatives from James," only after the Jerusalem Conference. Paul accuses them of bad faith, saying that they had come to "spy on our freedom . . . in Christ Jesus" (2:4). The notion of Christian freedom will be more developed in Galatians 5. Here it is introduced as characteristic of Christians in the Pauline churches. Paul confronted Peter later in Antioch because Peter caved in to the pressure of the "Judaizing" delegation from James in Jerusalem. The picture Paul paints is of a change of mind on the part of James and Peter after the Jerusalem agreement, which had the impact of undermining Paul's authority in Galatia and elsewhere. The "Judaizers" of Galatia may have been witnesses to this discrepancy and thus felt authorized to challenge Paul's authority there. Paul had accused Peter of influencing the Gentiles to "live like Jews" in the observance of some basics of the Law, including circumcision. Peter, who had also baptized Gentiles (Acts 10), was beginning to compromise the Gentiles' freedom after the Jerusalem meeting.

This historical conflict provides the context for Paul's important concept of "justification by faith." Within the framework of his conflict with Peter and James, Paul reminds Peter as a fellow Jew that "we who are Jews . . . know that a person is not justified by works of the [Jewish] law but through faith in Jesus Christ" (2:15–16). Paul appeals to the faith he has in common with Peter and with other Jewish Christians. All Christians of Jewish descent share the belief that Jesus is the Christ. It is Jesus rather than the Jewish Law that justifies all. Generations later in the church, when the preponderance of believers were of Gentile rather than Jewish origin, the historical context of this dispute was forgotten. Since then, Christians have sometimes mistakenly interpreted Paul's message as somehow considering faith as opposed to works. Furthermore, the word "alone" was added to the formula "justification by faith," and the phrase was understood in an absolute sense. So, for example, Luther portrayed the gospel as "law-free" in his famous objection to indulgences, which were undoubtedly carried to extremes in his day. The Reformers used Paul's doctrine of justification by faith to oppose any notion of salvation as dependent on good works, such as they alleged the Catholic doctrine of salvation taught. They distorted the Catholic teaching of works as a response to faith. For their part, Catholics have sometimes exaggerated the role of meritorious deeds to gain grace. Both Protestants and Catholics have based their arguments on Paul, especially on Galatians and Romans, and both have distorted the Jewish understanding of Law observance as the response of the faithful to the gift of the covenant. As a result, some Christians erroneously read into Paul's message a dichotomy between faith and works that does not accurately interpret Paul's original meaning, and a theological anti-Judaism that characterizes the Jewish way of life as oppressively bound in Law as contrasted to liberating Christian freedom.

We see in all of Paul's letters that his doctrine is consistently followed by ethical applications. Thus Paul teaches that faith is expressed in the moral life. Good works are a response to faith. Even in passages where Paul speaks of freedom (for example, in Galatians 5) he advocates at the same time the practice of good works. Paul's understanding of Christianity includes a highly developed ethic or lifestyle. He would see no opposition between faith and freedom on one side and good works and obedience on the other, as he will show in the next major section of Galatians.

Faith, Freedom, and the Scriptures (Gal 3:1–4:31)

Here Paul begins his theological and biblical explanation of his gospel. He appeals first to the experience of the Galatians, then to the biblical exposition of several texts, then to several human examples.

Paul insists that his converts in Galatia have heard the true and complete gospel message from him and that, as a result of their conversion to Christ, they have received the Spirit of God. He asks them a question to which they all know the answer, in order to shame them into attention: did you receive the Spirit through Law or through faith (3:2)? They know it was through his preaching of faith without Law. In order to emphasize the importance of continuing to live the life of faith, Paul employs a contrast between the "flesh" and the "spirit" designed to show that these are mutually exclusive. Today's reader will find such a contrast problematic unless we understand the Greek philosophical mindset of Paul's audience and the special meanings he attaches to the words.

Today we tend to equate "flesh" with body or material existence, and to affirm the body as a positive and even essential expression of self-fulfillment and human happiness. But the Greeks stressed the tension between the flesh and the spirit, which presupposed the superiority of the spirit and the inferiority of the flesh. For them, the spirit represented the immortal, life-giving aspect of human experience, whereas the body or flesh signified the weaker, sensual, mortal aspect that had to be subordinated to the spirit in order to find happiness. Though the Hebrews did not generally share this mindset, still earlier biblical language will sometimes use "flesh" or "flesh and blood" to mean the weakness and vulnerability of human existence without the assistance of God (see even 1 Cor 15:50). This is usually Paul's meaning for "flesh": human arrogance that tries to live independently of God's grace. To further complicate our task of interpreting Paul's meaning, we note that Paul sometimes refers to the Spirit of God or Holy Spirit (at times simply called the "Spirit"), and at other times he designates the human spirit. Often it is hard for the reader to distinguish the two. In English translations God's Spirit is usually capitalized, but that is at the call of the translator, and sometimes the difference is not clear. Paul asserts that the Spirit of God was conferred upon the Galatians by faith, not by "works of the flesh" such as circumcision. Paul therefore concludes that it would be an absurd regression to "end in the flesh" what had begun in the spirit. Faith transferred the Galatians and all believers from the domain of the flesh to that of the spirit. The Spirit of God enables us to share fully in the inheritance of the promise made to Abraham and fulfilled now in Christ. Thus Paul moves from a review of the Galatian experience of the gospel to an illustration of the validity of that experience taken from the Scriptures.

Abraham, Father of Faith (3, 6–16). Paul reinforces his teaching on justification by faith by giving examples from the Scriptures showing that faith in Christ is sufficient for salvation. Using the exegetical methods in which he was trained, he draws out several biblical passages from different places and puts them together into a new argument to show that Abraham received the promise and was considered to have been justified in God's sight *before* he was given the precept of circumcision (Gen 12:3; 15:6). Then the crucified Christ took upon himself the curse of the Law by hanging on a tree (Dt 27:26; Hb 2:4; Lv 18:5; Dt 21:23). Paul relates the experience of Abraham and his sons to the experience of the Galatians. Through faith the Galatians (a predominantly Gentile community) became the "children of Abraham" (3:7). "Abraham believed God, and it was credited to him as righteousness" (3:6). God gave a promise to Abraham because of his faith. This promise included the "nations" or Gentiles who are blessed through Abraham. Now, Paul says, the Gentiles have received the blessing of Abraham. The promise has been fulfilled in Christ.

Example of the Human Will (3:17–23). Paul then uses the example of a last will or testament (in Greek, the words, will, testament, and covenant are all the same, *diatheke,* which helps make the analogy in a way that is lost in English). Once made and ratified, it cannot be changed by something that comes along later. In like manner, the covenant with Abraham could not be altered by the Mosaic Law that came later. The original covenant through faith is the prior one that cannot be annulled, and this is the one in which all persons of faith belong.

Example of the Child-Minder (3:24–4:11). The next human analogy that Paul uses would have been perfectly comprehensible to his contemporaries, but it needs some explanation today. The "custodian" was a slave in a wealthy family who had authority over the minor son and was responsible for his discipline and education. Once the son came of age and became the heir, the roles were reversed. Paul uses this example to argue that the Law was a temporary custodian until Christ came, which is the time set by the father for our spiritual coming of age. At that point, the Law has no more power over us.

As illustration for this maturity in Christ that

we now have, Paul uses one of his most famous sayings, probably a baptismal formula that he quotes for effect. All who have been baptized in Christ have a new identity, so that there is no longer Jew or Greek, slave or free, male and female, but all are one in Christ Jesus (3:27–28). We would like to know how seriously this proclamation was taken in Paul's day. The tension between Jew and Greek (that is, Gentile) continued, but it was precisely to this that Paul was devoting much of his effort. Nevertheless, Christian persecution of Jews increased rather than decreased in following centuries. Slavery certainly continued for centuries in Christian households and states. Problems between men and women in the church have not yet subsided. Disparities in treatment based on ethnicity, social status, and gender are perennial. This prophetic text remains a challenge for the church in every age.

Assurance of Paul's Affection (4:12–20). In spite of the harsh things Paul had to say to the Galatians in the beginning of the letter, he now softens a bit to express his continued affection for them and his remembrance of how well they treated him when he was there. Verse 15 leads some commentators to suppose that Paul had some kind of eye disease that made him less impressive in person (see 2 Cor 10:10), but this is speculation. He hopes to come again to be with them and to be able to speak more affectionately than he has had to do in this letter.

Allegory of the Two Wives of Abraham (4: 21–31). Paul goes on to illustrate his teaching with yet another scriptural example, namely that of Abraham's two sons by two women. The first, Ishmael, is the son of a slave woman, Hagar, whose name never actually occurs here (but see Gn 21). Isaac is Sarah's son, born free. Ishmael and his mother were expelled from Abraham's sight and did not inherit the promise. Paul develops his commentary as an allegory, understanding Ishmael and Hagar to represent slavery to the covenant on Mount Sinai. Isaac represents the promise fulfilled in the freedom of faith without the restrictions of the Law. The words originally spoken to Sarah, who had been barren, are fulfilled in the believers who inherit the promise (4: 27). Paul says of the Galatians that they, like Isaac, are children of the promise, that is, the promise of grace and with it, freedom from the Law. Thus Paul's reading of the Scriptures reinforces his insistence that the Galatians are justified without the Law and freed from the Law. Therefore, to return to the Law's restrictions would be a great foolishness (see 3:1).

Exhortations for Christian Living (Gal 5:1–6:10)

Paul draws implications for Christian living from his teaching. While insisting on freedom, he shows how faith has its consequences in Christian life. Chapters 5 and 6 exhort believers to exercise their faith in their relationships with one another. These exhortations focus on the responsibilities Christians share for developing the community. We are struck by Paul's emphasis on social responsibility. Note that Paul does not dwell on a believer's personal, interior life so much as on the relationships that should characterize the Christian community, which is living the blessings of the Spirit of God (see 5:21–23). The term "freedom" recurs here (5:1, 13). For Paul freedom is not lawlessness but the liberty to live for God (see Rom 6:4) and to serve one another through love (Gal 5:13). The choice between slavery and freedom is the choice between the works of the Law and the works of the Spirit. For Paul, all humans are under some power—either of "sin" and the "flesh," or of the Spirit of God and faith.

In 5:2–12 Paul refers again to the specific problem that occasioned this urgent letter. The Judaizers are agitating the Galatians, trying to convince them to be circumcised and follow some of the elements of the Jewish Law. Paul reminds the Galatians of a principle certainly upheld by Jews, that circumcision of itself is nothing if not a sign of commitment to follow the whole Law (5:3). The problem Paul confronts is the imposition of circumcision on the Gentiles. Galatians 5, 11 implies that Paul, even as a Christian, did "preach circumcision" for Jews; perhaps he did at one time earlier in his career, and the Galatians have heard of it. Paul does not dispute the role of the Law in Jewish life. Although some accused Paul of undermining the Law for Jews, he considers himself innocent of that charge (see Rom 9:1–5; 1 Cor 9:20; Acts 21: 20–26). The list of "works of the flesh" in 5: 20–21 show that Paul does not equate flesh with the body; many of them are perversions of mind.

In Galatians 6:1–10 Paul continues to reflect on community life, advocating the virtues of charity, service, and humility. Christians are obliged to "bear one another's burdens." Although they are also called to "do good to all," even those outside the church, special priority is given to those in the family of faith (6:10).

Conclusion (6:11–18)

Paul adds a final note for emphasis and concludes with a short prayer. He probably dictated this letter to a scribe. He adds his own closing remarks, beginning at verse 11. Here he adds a new dimension to the arguments against the agitators: they are insincere, since they themselves do not follow the Law. They are only trying to escape persecution by other Jews, or possibly the Romans (see note on 6:12–15). Paul contrasts their cowardice and insincerity with his own boldness and consistency, referring to the "marks of Jesus" on his body. All that matters, Paul says, is that we are created anew (6:15). He concludes with a prayer for peace and mercy, calling down a blessing on his brothers and sisters in Christ.

Concluding Remarks

The letter to the Galatians may be one of the most difficult for us to approach without prior knowledge of the historical circumstances in which it was written, yet no one knows very much about those circumstances. Paul's message here is nevertheless especially appropriate today. Despite painful differences with other leaders, Paul focuses on a single gospel message that all authentic Christian missionaries preach. This message emphasizes the role of faith and the significance of community. Paul's use of Scripture illustrates that this is the same message that has been repeated and refined throughout the Old Testament. Faith is the expression of the bond between God and us, a bond lived out in relationships with others. Paul's exhortation to Christians is to "be free" and therefore responsible for one another. There is no conflict between faith and works, according to Paul. Faith is necessarily expressed in the everyday life of believers. Paul does, however, stress that the works of faith are a result of the gift of the Spirit and a response to it, not a requirement for receiving the Spirit or for meriting salvation.

EPHESIANS

[see pages 1654–1662 of the New Testament]

Before Beginning . . .

Ephesians displays a well-developed theology of the church. The four major epistles of Paul (Romans, 1 and 2 Corinthians, and Galatians) are all addressed to specific congregations in various important locations in the Greco-Roman world. Ephesians envisions not a single congregation but the universal church seen as a spiritual reality entrusted with the worldwide mission of Christ. Here the word "church" *(ekklesia)* acquires that new meaning of universal reality.

There are significant parallels between Ephesians and Colossians. The advanced Christology and ecclesiology, the apparent absence of Jewish-Gentile tensions, and, finally, the unusual vocabulary unique to these two epistles among the Pauline letters prompt many interpreters to assert that Ephesians and Colossians were written in an era after the death of Paul. If that is the case, the disciple who wrote these letters was familiar with Pauline theology and style and adapted Paul's message to new times and circumstances. In our comments we will follow the usual practice of referring to the author of Ephesians and the other "Deutero-Pauline" writings (see "Paul and His Writings," RG 439–40) as "Paul," all the while keeping in mind that nearly all Pauline scholars think of Ephesians as not from Paul himself, and a majority think the same of Colossians.

Working through Ephesians

Ephesians follows the pattern of a Greco-Roman letter, beginning with an *address* (1:1–14) and ending with a *conclusion* (6:21–24). Moreover, it follows the pattern of a Pauline letter, with initial blessing or prayer in the address and conclusion adapted to a liturgical assembly. These stylized elements enclose the *body* of the letter (1:15–6:20), which presents a teaching or doctrine on the church and then applies this teaching to the daily life of believers. We will follow the NAB outline (p. 1655) emphasizing the major themes developed in Ephesians. This outline is as follows:

I. The Address (1:1–14)
II. The Body of the Letter (1:15–6:20)
  A. The Teaching on the Church (1:15–4:24)
    1. Unity of the Church (1:15–2:22)
    2. World Mission of the Church (3:1–4:24)
  B. Ethical Applications (4:25–6:20)
III. Conclusion (6:21–24)

Reading through Ephesians

The Address (1:1–14)

Ephesians identifies the sender as "Paul, an apostle of Christ Jesus by the will of God." The absence from some manuscripts of the designation "in Ephesus" (1:1) is one reason why Ephesians is considered by some to be a circular letter—intended for a wider audience rather than for the specific community at Ephesus alone. No particularities regarding the Ephesian community are mentioned as is customary when Paul writes to a community he knows as well as he should have known the Ephesians (see Acts 19:10). The lack of a personalized greeting further supports the view that this is a letter to all the churches written by a Pauline disciple.

A doxology or blessing of God replaces the personal thanksgiving characteristic of Paul's letters (Eph 1:3–6). As if conscious of the great mystery of the church he is about to describe, the author begins by proclaiming the blessedness of God. The recurrence of the term "blessed" and the many liturgical references suggest that this prayer of praise is inspired by the Jewish liturgies in which believers, mindful of the wondrous works of God, cannot but bless the Creator. The focus is on God's blessing in Christ in whom the divine plan for the salvation of all people is achieved. The Holy Spirit is described as the "first installment" (1:14) of our inheritance toward redemption.

The Body of the Letter (1:15–6:20)

The message of Ephesians has two parts. The first or doctrinal section (1:15–4:24) unfolds the church as the fulfillment of God's plan for salvation, inaugurated in Christ. A second section (4:25–6:20) contains ethical "imperatives" concerning the daily conduct of believers, providing practical applications of Paul's teaching.

The Teaching on the Church (1:15–4:24)

Ephesians develops the New Testament teaching about the unity of the church and the church's worldwide mission. Integral to this mission is the significant role of the apostle in its promotion. We shall briefly consider each of these teachings.

Unity of the Church (1:15–2:22). The ecclesiology, or theology of the church, in Ephesians is integrally linked to its Christology. That is to say that its view of the church follows from its view of Christ and Christ's saving work. Therefore, to understand the emphasis on the unity of the church that occurs in Ephesians, we must see the perspective on Christ developed there. The Christology and ecclesiology in Ephesians and Colossians is developed beyond that in Paul's major letters to the Corinthians and the Romans. Yet this development has its roots in Paul, for whom the image of the church as the body of Christ helps to express the unity of Christians and the salvific work of Christ's death and resurrection.

The description of the church as the Body of Christ appears first in 1 Corinthians 12:12–27 and Romans 12:4–8. Paul urged the Christians in Corinth and Rome to express their unity in mutual love as members of the same body, Christ. But in Ephesians and Colossians there is a major change in the image. Here Christ is referred to as the "head of the body, the church" (Eph 1:22–23; Col 1:18). This shift in the image leads away from the mutual participation and responsibility of all the members to centralized authority in the person of Christ, who is portrayed as above every principality, authority, and dominion (cf. Eph 1:21–22). Nevertheless, the recipients are still reminded that in the body of Christ, we are members of one another (4:15) and of Christ (5:30).

By his resurrection, Paul asserts, Jesus became Lord of all, Jews and Gentiles and every creature (see 1 Cor 12:3). This is so because in Christ's resurrection God has conquered sin and death; it is the beginning of a new era. Paul's writings speak of the humiliation (death) and exaltation (resurrection) of Christ by which God vindicated Jesus because of his obedience. Jesus now sits at God's right hand. At Jesus' name, every knee bends and every tongue proclaims that Jesus is Lord (Phil 2:6–11). This is one of the oldest Christological proclamations (Rom 10:9). Jesus' lordship is an expression of his sovereignty over all created things and his word reconciling the whole of creation to God. Yet even now the universal recognition of Jesus' lordship has not been completed. The mission of preaching Christ's lordship and bringing all creation under God's reign is entrusted to the church.

Some time after AD 50, when Paul was writing Galatians and Romans, it is clear that one of the major problems facing the church was the reconciliation of Jews and Gentiles under one God and one Lord. Distinctions between Jews and Gentiles were symbolized by such practices as circumcision, dietary laws, and restrictions regarding table fellowship, intermarriage, and other forms of social interaction. These, Paul insisted, were obliterated by Christ's death. Yet the apostle himself had to struggle to resolve the tensions between Israel and the Gentiles (see, for example, Romans 9–11). The teaching about the church in Ephesians seems to reflect a time or place in which these tensions are resolved. The Gentiles are portrayed as those who were once "far off . . . strangers to the covenants of promise." Now they have "become near by the blood of Christ" (2:13). The images of the church as the body of Christ and Christ as the head of the church serve to illustrate the intrinsic unity of the church of Jews and Gentiles, that is, of all people in Christ.

World Mission of the Church (3:1–4:24). The author of Ephesians identifies himself as "Paul, a prisoner of Christ [Jesus] for you Gentiles" (3:1). He then abruptly interrupts this self-introduction to elaborate on his role in the mystery of God's plan for the salvation of the world. Now imprisoned, Paul continues the work of intercession. Through prayer Paul brings the Gentiles to God. The church—the body of Christ and the family of God—is entrusted with the work of salvation that is to fill all things "with the fullness of God" (3:19). Paul understands his work to be essential in God's plan, and yet he is unperturbed either by his own imprisonment or by the failure of some to accept the message of Christ. Salvation as well as creation is in God's hands, and God's plan is being fulfilled in inscrutable mystery.

Again the language reflects that introduced by Paul in his earlier writings. But the conception of the divine plan of salvation is more developed. The church, under the impetus of the Spirit, is bringing all to the "one God and Father of all, who is over all and through all and in all" (4:6). Paul's prayer is that "you may be filled with all the fullness of God" (3:19). The mystery of God who ordained that "all Israel will be saved" (Rom 11:26) now prescribes that we "no longer live as the Gentiles do" (Eph 4:17) , but "put on the new self, created in God's way in righteousness and holiness of truth" (4:24). Having described this mystery, Paul goes on to exhort the Ephesians to express their common call to holiness and unity in their daily life.

Ethical Applications (4:25–6:20)

Ephesians 5 illustrates how its teaching on the church has practical consequences in the daily lives of believers. Ephesians 5:1 says, "So be imitators of God, as beloved children, and live in love." This could be the summary of the whole of Christian life. The author of Ephesians draws out some implications of imitating God by living in love. Much of this section consists of general moral exhortation, description of what the ideal Christian life with one another should look like.

Christians relate to one another in ways already established and governed, at least to some extent, by outward society. So, for example, wives and husbands, children and parents, slaves and masters all follow Greco-Roman social norms, which give some direction about the rights and duties of people who are in these kinds of relationships. The author adopts and adapts the traditional philosophical approach to household life that is at least as old as Aristotle and that we call "household rules." In ordinary Greco-Roman society the lines of authority and of subservience were clearly drawn. Husbands, parents, and masters all have great power over wives, children, and slaves in a rigid social hierarchy.

For Paul these rules or principles become practical applications of faith for members of the "household of God" (2:19), giving directives for various segments of society in their relationships to one another. Paul does not offer a radical critique of certain social contracts, such as slavery or male dominance. Yet for him, relationships among Christians must reflect a new perspective. Christians are motivated to a new way of thinking, determined by their common baptism. Christians share the conviction that all are one in Christ and saved by Christ. This leads to innovations in the usual treatment of household rules: here both parties in a relationship are addressed, whereas in the traditional form, only the male authority would be addressed, and here the inferior party is even addressed first. The Ephesians are urged to "live in a manner worthy of the call you have received . . . bearing with one another through love" (Eph 4:1f). They are exhorted to "be subordinate to one another" (5:21), to "nourish and cherish" one another, because they are members of one body (5:29–30). The extra verses spent on the analogy of husband to Christ and wife to the church are the springboard for much later mysticism, even as they also have been justification for continued subordinate positions for women. Such a passage as this, along with the exhortations to slave obedience, are paradoxical combinations of beauty, grace, and what today can only be seen as social oppression in the name of faith. They require careful interpretation both in the context of the author's world and of ours.

If we do not let these thorny problems be major obstacles, reading Ephesians today can inspire us to a powerful vision of the church. It leads us to reassess the ordinary way of approaching one another as colleagues, family, clients, and the like. We, like the Ephesians, are urged to remember our real identity and to respect others by relating to everyone in a way worthy of members of the "household of God." The ordinary hierarchical system that prevails in the world is superseded by a new way of relating to one another in Christ.

Paul finally urges the Ephesians to "pray at every opportunity in the Spirit" (6:18). He again asks for prayers for himself, that he may speak "the mystery of the gospel" with boldness and courage even though he is in chains (6:19–20).

Conclusion (6:21–24)

Ephesians does not exhibit the usual personal tone and greetings of Paul's authentic letters. In the conclusion, however, the author indicates that he sends the letter with Tychicus (6:21), the name of Paul's messenger of Colossians as well (Col 4:7). The final prayers are for peace and love and grace.

Concluding Remarks

Ephesians strikes a balance between reflection on the church as a universal, spiritual reality and application in the daily lives of Christians of their new identity as members of this spiritual creation. The letter also emphasizes the congruence between Christians' personal spirituality and their responsibilities in relationships with one another. Through baptism we are renewed. We have put off the "old humanity," symbolized by Adam; we have been transformed into a "new humanity," in Christ. We are called to be imitators of God and to reflect God's love and compassion in our daily lives.

As part of our Christian Scriptures, Ephesians stands as a continual challenge calling us beyond the present to a deeper reality where all things are in the care of God. The present with its trials, temptations, failures, and limitations can indeed discourage us. The problems of resolving tensions and enduring suffering are temporary. Ephesians is a letter from prison, addressing a church afflicted with oppression from the outside, confusion and dissension from within. Ephesians testifies to the author's faith and by the hope of God's plan for the salvation of the entire world—a plan that will be fulfilled despite, and even by means of, apparent obstacles. When we are confronted by the limitations of our present circumstances or hampered by fear, Ephesians provides encouragement. For us as Christians, the liturgy celebrates a communion with God. Faith is conviction of things unseen, especially about the triumph of God in Christ.

Ephesians is one of the most hope-filled and confident of all the Pauline letters. It may lack the usual personal tone expected of communities Paul knew well. But Ephesians expresses fundamental Christian beliefs that continue to characterize the church today. For example, despite suffering and failures, the church celebrates the reality of salvation already experienced in the daily life of Christians. In our world, where many families are in crisis, we read Paul's advice about mutual relationships with members of God's household and take courage in the admonition to serve one another in love. Like the writer of Ephesians, the modern church at Vatican II complemented reflection on the nature of the church with the role of the church in the modern world. The church as Christ's body, no matter what its limitations, is called and empowered to reconcile the whole world to God. Each of us, as members of the church, has a role in this mission.

PHILIPPIANS

[see pages 1662–1669 of the New Testament]

Before Beginning . . .

Philippians is one of the most appealing of Paul's letters. Along with Ephesians, Colossians, and Philemon, Philippians is traditionally called a "captivity letter" because in all four the author refers to his imprisonment. The authentic Pauline authorship of Philippians and Philemon is never doubted, although there is disagreement regarding the authorship of Ephesians and Colossians.

There are several theories about the location and occasion of the imprisonment from which Paul writes. The oldest and traditional view is that he writes from Rome in his final imprisonment there; this would date the letter to the late fifties or early sixties of the first century. Some have questioned the feasibility of this location, given the apparent frequent exchanges implied in the letter and the great distance from Rome to Philippi. So a second location has been suggested, Caesarea Maritima on the Palestinian coast, during the two years of confinement recorded in Acts 24–26. Still, that is a great distance, requiring a month or more of travel. A third suggestion is that Paul was imprisoned earlier in his life in Ephesus, and that Philippians and Philemon date from that time, perhaps in the middle years of the fifties. The mysterious references to trouble in Asia (Ephesus was the principal city of the Roman province of Asia) in 1 Corinthians 15:32 and 2 Corinthians 1: 8–10 support this idea, as does Paul's avoidance of Ephesus on his journey to Jerusalem (Acts 20: 16). In that case, travel back and forth from Paul's prison to Philippi would have been much easier and faster.

If the Pauline authorship of Philippians is unquestioned, the unity of the letter poses some challenges. The choppy nature of this letter has led many interpreters to suggest that Philippians was originally at least three letters. A later editor (according to this theory), adapting the initial and final greeting, combined the originally separate messages into one edited "letter" for the purpose of later circulation. On the other hand, many more recent interpreters, using methods derived from the principles of ancient rhetoric, argue for the unity of the letter in spite of the rough edges here and there. Whichever is the case, the end result, the "canonical letter," provides the rich spiritual legacy called Philippians, so beloved in the Christian tradition.

Important Pauline themes are developed in Philippians, particularly that of unity. We see in the letter the deep love Paul feels for this community. Disregarding the dangers facing him, Paul focuses on the sufferings of the community caused by external persecution and internal divisions. We hear of Paul's gratitude for the material support he has received from the community. We witness his fears about the problems within the community and the pressure from outside, but he subordinates those concerns to expressions of joy for the strength of the Philippians' church. In a surprisingly vehement outburst against those who advocate a return to the Jewish Law, he reminds us that this issue, so central to Galatians and Romans, is not forgotten elsewhere.

Working through Philippians

We can discuss the main themes of Philippians according to the following outline. The basic letter contains the usual *address* (1:1–11), *body* (1: 12–3:1), and *conclusion* (4:21–23).

I. Address and Thanksgiving (1:1–11)
II. The Body of the Letter (1:12–4:20)
  A. Paul's Situation and the Progress of the Gospel (1:12–26)
  B. Exhortations for Community Unity; Example of Jesus (1:27–2:18)
  C. Travel of Paul and Assistants (2:19–3:1)
  D. Digression and Warning (3:1–4a)
  E. Example of Paul (3:4b–21)
  F. Specific Appeal to Unity (4:1–9)
  G. A Thank-you Note (4:10–20)
III. Conclusion (4:21–23)

Reading through Philippians

The Address (1:1–11)

The opening line names Paul and Timothy as senders of the letter, but the speaker quickly changes to "I" in verse 3, for Paul is really the author. Timothy will be mentioned as an ideal companion in 2:19–24. The address is unique among Pauline letters in its acknowledgment of local leaders by title, "overseers and ministers," which by using later meanings of the words could also mean "bishops and deacons," but there is no evidence that the connotations later brought to those words are active here. Nevertheless, the address shows the beginnings of official titles and functions in the church.

A thanksgiving (1:3–8) and a prayer (1:9–11) complete the address. This is one of the longest and most beautifully developed of the Pauline thanksgivings. It introduces the themes of joy and community, themes that recur throughout Philippians. The paradox expressed in this letter is that the intense suffering experienced by Paul and the Philippians pales in comparison to the confident joy they share. Although separated because of Paul's imprisonment, and threatened on all sides, Paul and the Philippians are "partners," participating together in the spread of the gospel message. Paul draws strength from the Philippians' affection and display of concern for him. He prays (1:9–11) that they will be strengthened and that their love will grow even amid hardships. Together they all await the "day of Christ," which Paul longs for and strains forward to obtain.

The Body of the Letter (1:12–4:20)

Paul's Situation and the Progress of the Gospel (1:12–26)

Paul links faith in suffering and the spread of the gospel. Nowhere is this link more eloquently expressed than in Philippians 1:12–26 where he refers to the effect his own imprisonment has had on the progress of the gospel message. Paul rejoices that even his enemies are using the opportunity represented by his present circumstances to energetically pursue the spread of the Christian message. For him, the priority is that "in every way . . . Christ is being proclaimed" (1:18). This position stands in some contrast to his insistence elsewhere, even in 3:2–3 of this letter, that only he has the right gospel. Paul speaks of joy even though he is in prison and the outcome is uncertain. He could be facing death. As a committed and passionate apostle, Paul worked tirelessly to promote acceptance of the gospel message by Gentiles everywhere. Now, in prison, Paul is equally peaceful, knowing that even should he die the preaching will be continued.

If 1 Corinthians, especially chapters 1 and 2, represents a theoretical development of Paul's theology of the cross, Philippians represents Paul's own faith as he lives this theology. The wisdom of the cross is that God's power is made perfect in weakness. By this transforming power of the cross, Paul's brothers and sisters take encouragement from his imprisonment and preach the gospel all the more fearlessly. By the wisdom of the cross Paul considers death to be "gain," and what he formerly considered "gain" to be "rubbish" (see 3:7–8). Imprisoned, Paul draws strength from the community. He speaks with confidence and joy, expressing hope that is firmly rooted in God.

Exhortations for Community Unity and the Example of Jesus (1:27–2:18)

As he does in several other letters, Paul expresses concern that the opposition the Philippians experience will threaten their faith. He knows of internal divisions among these Christians. By appealing to them to have a common mind and heart, Paul alludes first to his own suffering and imprisonment and then to the example of Christ.

The beautiful hymn about the abasement of Christ of 2:6–11 is probably taken from an already existing piece of early Christian poetry with which the Philippians are familiar. It recalls their source of encouragement, and is a cherished expression of faith in the redemptive aspects of Christ's suffering and death. The example of Christ's death must, above all else, influence the believing community in its own practical acceptance of and obedience to God's will. Thus, Christ who "emptied himself" is the example of behavior for the Philippians who are having trouble preserving unity in the congregation. Further, Christ by his death became "Lord" so that all who profess his Lordship are subject to him. In homage they recognize that they are brothers and sisters, members with one another of one believing community. So Christ is the example and the empowerment of selfless, mutual service in the church. Following the hymn, Paul draws out some implications: the Philippians are to remain blameless and innocent in the midst of adversity and wickedness, waiting for the day of Christ (2: 16). Conceiving of the Christian life as a liturgical sacrifice, Paul says that even though he is "poured out as a libation," (wine that is offered in sacrifice) he rejoices. He asks only that the Philippians share his joy.

Travel of Paul and Assistants (2:19–3:1)

The travel account given here and other indications suggest relatively free and frequent exchanges between the prisoner, Paul, and the Philippians. This would be more easily understood with an imprisonment closer to Philippi than to Rome, hence the Ephesian theory. The news about Epaphroditus's illness and recovery seem to indicate different visits. He probably came from Philippi and was not able to continue his apostolic work because of illness. Timothy is extolled as an ideal assistant, a second example of unity after Jesus. The trust among Paul, Timothy, and Epaphroditus stands in contrast to the squabbling between Euodia and Syntyche and other members of the Philippian community (4:2–3).

Digression and Warning (3:2–4a)

The abrupt change of tone and content between the first two chapters of Philippians and the strong warning in 3:2–4 is one of the strongest arguments that these were originally separate communications. Even so, a skilled rhetorician could also just as abruptly switch topic and tone in order to get his audience's attention. This sudden theme of resistance to those who agitate for the Gentiles to be circumcised, presented in an insulting tone, is brief and does not reappear in this letter.

Example of Paul (3:4b–21)

After presenting the example of Jesus and then in a lesser way of Timothy, Paul now proposes himself as example of one who knows how to give up privilege and status for the good of others. He gives us some of our best biographical information about himself, then reflects on the consequences of his encounter with Christ. Using athletic imagery, Paul encourages the Philippians to strain toward the goal of a "perfect maturity." He urges them not to regress into the past, seeking glory in shame (possible allusions to circumcision) or in other practices of the "flesh" such as observances of certain dietary rules. These, Paul says, are earthly things. Paul himself used to glory in his religious accomplishments, but since his conversion he no longer regards these as significant. Indeed, his former system of valuing is "rubbish" compared with his new way of seeing things in Christ. This is the wisdom of the cross. Those who do not accept this wisdom are "enemies of the cross" (3:18).

Specific Appeal to Unity (4:1–9)

Paul turns to an internal crisis that is just as destructive and threatening to the community. He begins chapter 4 by urging the Philippians to live in harmony, a theme he had already developed in chapters 1 and 2. But now he is specific in his appeal to unity, and all the previous rhetoric on the subject may be leading to this climax. There is a conflict between some leading women of the community, Euodia and Syntyche, and Paul solemnly begs them to stop. What position these women occupy we do not know, but their division is obviously central to the community's problems, so they may be significant leaders. Paul addresses a comrade and enlists the help of an otherwise unknown man named Clement to aid in the reconciliation of these women, for the betterment of the whole community.

A Thank-you Note (4:10–20)

Paul expresses thanks for the help received from the Philippians and sent with Epaphroditus. He adds, however, that his gratitude is not so much that he was personally aided as that the Philippians' generosity is "profit that accrues to your account" (4:17). Paul testifies to his own indifference and ability to do without. Yet he humbly accepted aid not only to alleviate his own need but as a symbol of the affection that linked him to the Philippians. Paul speaks of this aid in liturgical terms, referring to it as "a fragrant aroma . . . a sacrifice, pleasing to God" (4: 18–19; see also 2 Cor 2:14–16). This is the ancient language of liturgical offering and sacrifice. The idea of an offering of mutual love and aid by Christians to one another as a "liturgy" appears also in Romans 12:1–2, and 15:17–20.

Conclusion (4:21–23)

The conclusion of the letter sends greetings to everyone there from everyone here. The reference to "Caesar's household" is to the vast imperial network of civil servants that were present in every major city. We know from this reference that there were Christians among them.

Concluding Remarks

Since the writing of Philippians, the Christian community has been inspired not only by the words of the apostle but by the example of the imprisoned leader who speaks with such affection, hope, and faith. One of the most beautiful and well known of Paul's letters, Philippians represents a reflection on the meaning of fidelity in the midst of trial. Paul's confidence that in all things "Christ is . . . proclaimed" (1:18) transcends the threat of others' jealousy and rivalry. The Christological hymn of Philippians 2 not only inspired the Philippians to greater unity but also continues to invite believers of every age to imitate Christ. Paul's prayer for his fellow Christians is that they always be happy (Phil 4:4–9). This serves as a model for our prayers for one another. Paul puts his own life before the Philippians, encouraging them to follow him in everything that he does and says. Paul then promises that the "God of peace will be with you" (4:9). Such should be our prayer in attracting others to live the Christian life.

COLOSSIANS

[see pages 1670–1676 of the New Testament]

Before Beginning . . .

It is customary to refer to the author of Colossians as Paul, even though many interpreters question whether Paul himself wrote this brief letter. Many characteristics of the letter seem to suggest Paul's presence behind it. The lively style and personal greetings are typical of Paul. Most of the personal names mentioned here also appear in Philemon, a letter that has always been attributed to Paul himself. Yet there are strange speculative expressions, new terminology, and a new understanding of the church that many scholars think indicates a different author here, writing in Paul's name with the hope of using Paul's authority. A compromise position is that Paul entrusted the message to a secretary who composed it in his own terms and with his own style.

Paul himself did not establish the church at Colossae. Possibly Epaphras, a disciple of Paul, was the founding missionary there. The context is that erroneous teachers implied that Christ's work of redemption was incomplete—that certain other religious practices were required to supplement Christ's saving death and resurrection. These suggested practices were drawn from Jewish as well as non-Jewish or pagan religions. They amounted to ascetical and superstitious additions to the message Paul and Epaphras had taught. As in Galatians, but less emotionally, Paul adamantly insists in Colossians that adding to the gospel message is really subtracting from grace. Only as a member of Christ's body and under his headship can we fill up "what is lacking in the afflictions of Christ" (1:24), that is, continuing Christ's redemptive suffering in the world.

At issue in the discussion at Colossae is the primary role of Christ in the salvation of the world. The power and authority of Christ and his relation to the rest of creation are challenged. False teachings at Colossae suggested that other spiritual beings were rivals to Christ's role, and that certain ascetical practices were a means of becoming more spiritual, while also helping to appease these spiritual beings. Using categories and labels present in these false teachings, Paul insists on the primacy of Christ and the sufficiency of his saving action on our behalf. Ethical imperatives follow from this fundamental faith rather than from the necessity of placating angelic spirits or following some ascetical ideals.

Working through Colossians

The *address and thanksgiving* (1:1–14) and *conclusion* (4:7–18) enclose the *body* of this letter in 1:15–4:6. The body of Colossians follows the basic indicative-imperative pattern characteristic of Paul. The structure of Colossians then is the following:

I. Address and Thanksgiving (1:1–14)
II. The Body of the Letter (1:15–4:6)
  A. Instruction about Christ and False Teaching (1:15–2:23)
  B. Ethics Characterizing the True Christian (3:1–4:6)
III. Conclusion (4:7–18)

Reading through Colossians

The Address (1:1–14)

The *address* includes not only the usual greeting (1:1–2) and thanksgiving (1:3–8) but also a prayer for the continued progress of the Colossians (1:9–14). Both the *address* and *conclusion* (4:7–18) contain greetings and personal references that are typical of Paul.

The Body of the Letter (1:15–4:6)

Colossians' main message is correct teaching and warnings against false teachings (1:15–2: 23). This is followed by exhortations to exercise fundamental beliefs in daily Christian living (3: 1–4:6).

Instruction about Christ and False Teaching (1:15–2:23)

Paul is confident that Epaphras has given the community a solid foundation. He reminds the Colossians that by Christ's saving death, "[God] delivered us from the power of darkness and transferred us to the kingdom of his beloved Son" (1:13). This transference from the realm of sin and error into that of grace and truth is effected in baptism and must be lived out in the daily lives of Christians. The doctrinal presentation of the first major part of Colossians falls into three sections: the Christological hymn and its implications (1:15–23), Paul's own ministry and example (1:24–2:3), and warnings against false teachers and their teaching (2:4–23).

The Christological Hymn (1:15–23). In order to teach a correct Christology and clarify errors, Paul quotes a liturgical hymn apparently familiar to the Colossians (1:15–20; see also Phil 2:6–11). Many interpreters believe that this hymn predates Paul and was already in use by the early Christian communities. The poetic rhythm and language suggest that it was a hymn and that it was at home in the liturgy. Since Paul generally writes in prose, the insertion of a hymn here is easily discerned in the Greek. In this hymn Christians profess and celebrate the authority of Christ in whom all "the fullness was pleased to dwell, and through him to reconcile all things for him." Paul stresses the redemption and peace won for us through Christ. He does not badger or scold the Colossians for their errors, but presents Christ's role of reconciling the world to God as the basis of common faith among all believers. The text adapts a variety of traditions about the figure of Wisdom and a cosmic savior to the person of Christ, who begins, as in the prologue of John's Gospel, in the heavenly realm. But he is also the head of the church and firstborn from the dead, so that his saving action works in our history.

Paul's Ministry and Example (1:24–2:3). Emphasis on his own example is a remarkable trait of Paul's letters, one expected of a great teacher in his day (see further 1 Thes 1:6; 2 Cor 11–12). It is also significant that upon reviewing Christ's work of redemption, Paul immediately attaches his own example as a model for the Colossians to emulate. At first this advice may strike us as surprising and almost shocking. How can Paul claim to be a model for all to imitate (see 1 Cor 11:1; Phil 4:8)? It springs from the apostle's humility and transparent confidence. Paul is so firmly rooted in God that he dares to advise his addressees to follow his example. By studying Paul's life, others may know the power of God and be converted. Paul always reveals the source of his confidence, which is not self-reliance but hope in God. This hope is best expressed in Christ's gift of salvation evidenced in the life of the apostle. The apostle glories in his vocation and fidelity while also accentuating his sufferings in the service of the gospel.

In describing his own ministry, Paul adapts categories important to the Colossians and to the false teachers who are disturbing them. They are emphasizing "wisdom" and "perfection," so Paul speaks about the "knowledge of the mystery of God, Christ, in whom are hidden all the treasures of wisdom and knowledge" (2:2–3). Paul identifies the goal of his mission to "present everyone perfect in Christ" (1:28). For this he labors and struggles in accord with God's power "working within me" (1:29).

Warnings against False Teachings (2:4–23). Paul encourages the Colossians in their faith, reminding them of their identity in Christ. He observes the "good order and the firmness of your faith in Christ." He celebrates this fidelity and encourages the Colossians to be grateful, with a thanksgiving rooted in faith. Finally, he warns against the seduction of false teaching that is according to mere human tradition and not grounded in Christ. The false teaching was probably a combination of Jewish and pagan philosophies and pagan ideals. Paul denounces the "circumcision administered by human hands" and the ascetical practices regarding "food and drink" alleged to be required at certain times and days (2:16) . Some teachers flaunted their visions and self-abasement, and were involved in complicated devotions to angelic beings. Paul labeled all these as transitory fads, "shadows of things to come" and "things destined to perish." By contrast, in Christ dwells the fullness of God. All are members of Christ, who is the head of the body, the church. Here and in Ephesians, this specific role of Christ within the church is introduced. Christians are united in one church under one Lord who is Christ. Their common task is the reconciliation of the world to God under Christ.

Ethics Characterizing the True Christian (3:1–4:6)

Paul does not really present a new, uniquely Christian ethical system but draws from several existing systems. Often Paul lists vices or virtues similar to lists found in Stoic or other Greek philosophers. The "household rules" found in Colossians (see Eph 5:21–6:9; Ti 2:1–3:8; 1 Pt 2:11–3:7) have parallels in contemporary Greco-Roman literature where elements of household management are discussed. The submission of wives, children, and slaves to the male household head was an expected part of the social order. A fundamental difference for Paul is the motivation and the empowerment to fulfill these ethical principles. The church as the body of Christ distinguishes itself from the outside world in that the love command operates to create a new way for Christians to relate to one another. Paul says that the Colossians once conducted themselves as pagans who practiced immorality, greed, and passion (see 3:5–7). Now they have "put on the new self, which is being renewed . . . in the image of its creator" (3:10). In Christ the usual sexual, social, and ethnic distinctions do not exist, "but Christ is all and in all" (3:11).

Conclusion (4:7–18)

Tychicus is the messenger entrusted with the letter to the Colossians. Many think that the Onesimus mentioned as his companion (4:9) is the former slave who returned to Colossae with the letter from Paul to Philemon (see Reading Guide to Philemon). The other companions mentioned at the end of Colossians are well-known Christians named in other Pauline letters except for Nympha (4:15), a woman who hosts a house church. This list of personal references reminds us about the common Christian teaching upon which Paul depends and to which he urges the Colossians to hold firm.

Concluding Remarks

Today no less than in the times of the Colossians, Christians are pulled in various directions and people are still searching for spiritual guides and nourishment. The exotic, speculative language in Colossians does not seem so strange to us when we consider the attraction of certain superstitions, the popularity of astrology, the following of television evangelists who promise reprieves from effort in the spiritual life and shortcuts to wholeness and holiness. The epistle to the Colossians stresses the reconciliation of all things in Christ as the fundamental faith assertion with enormous ethical repercussions. As the firstborn of all creation, Christ is a symbol of the value of all creation and a promise of the ultimate salvation of all. That truth translates into the church's responsibility for stewardship in the world, assuming that in preaching reconciliation the rights of all are respected. In carrying out its mission, the church must be a symbol of peace, since Christ is the head of the church and Christ made peace by the blood of the cross.

THE LETTERS TO THE THESSALONIANS

Introduction

As far as we know, the Christian community at Thessalonica was among the earlier ones that Paul established and, although Paul's tone is affectionate in these letters, the apostle experienced a great deal of persecution from both Jews and Gentiles as a result of his preaching there. In his letters to the Thessalonians, Paul addresses real problems that arose in the community, such as mutual charity, the need to be responsible about work, and the issue of the death of Christians. The specific nature of these problems does not in any way detract from the enduring value of these letters as models for the Christian pastor and community. Before turning to the letters themselves, let us briefly describe some of the main elements of Paul's apocalyptic perspective that is so important in the Thessalonian correspondence as well as in Paul's other writings. (For more about apocalyptic literature, see the Reading Guides to Daniel and Revelation.)

Paul's Apocalyptic Perspective

Apocalyptic literature was born of the syncretistic blending of Wisdom and Prophetic traditions from the Bible with some elements of cosmic philosophy and mysticism from the Greco-Roman world. It spoke powerfully to those who were oppressed and suffering, encouraging them in the midst of their suffering. The apocalyptic writer was concerned with why the world was not as it ought to be. Jewish and Christian apocalypticism looked to God to bring about a radical transformation of the present world into something more like what God intended. We can only outline here some of the ways that the apocalyptic perspective influenced Paul.

First, *God's reign is universal.* The Jewish apocalyptic writers interpreted all of history, the good and the bad, as evolving according to a divine plan for the ultimate salvation of Israel, though some also foresaw a definite place for the Gentiles as well. Paul's call taught him to affirm and expand that insight. Throughout his writings Paul emphasizes that salvation is accessible to all now that Christ has come. God shows no partiality (see Rom 1:16; 3:22, 29; 10:12; Eph 2:14; Acts 10:34; 15:9–11). Paul says, "There is neither Jew nor Greek . . . neither slave nor free person . . . not male and female; for you are all one in Christ Jesus" (Gal 3:28). The Gentiles have turned "from idols to serve the living and true God" (1 Thes 1:9).

Second, Paul's thinking, like that of other apocalyptic writers, was characterized by a *dualism* that envisioned the ultimate salvation of the faithful and punishment of the wicked. Paul speaks of those who are "saved" and those who are "perishing" (see 1 Cor 1:18; 2 Thes 2:10). He pictures the judgment seat of Christ before whom we all must appear, "so that each one may receive recompense" (2 Cor 5:10). The faithful are delivered from the wrath of God (1 Thes 1:10), but it will not be withheld forever from the "enemies of the cross" (Phil 3:18; see 1 Thes 2:16). The basis for judgment is acceptance or rejection of the gospel. This dualism also gives rise to tensions and even hostility between the present and the age to come. The Lordship of Christ is a cosmic domain; Christ is in the process of returning all things to God (1 Cor 15:28). The role of believers is to continue in faith and faithful life.

Third, there is language of expectation that the *time of transformation is imminent,* another characteristic of apocalyptic literature, which Paul borrows. For instance, this influences his views on the insignificance of one's marital or social status (for example, 1 Cor 7), his warnings to prayerful vigilance (1 Thes 5:1–11), and his encouragement to endure suffering or oppression while striving to build up the community (Phil 2: 12–18). The just vigilantly await the savior (see Phil 3:20), believing that he is coming to transform their mortal bodies into incorruptibility (Phil 3:21). But we must be careful not to take this kind of language literally. It functioned as a reminder of the radical contingency of time and all things, and the possibility of God's powerful intervention at any time.

Paul adapts these elements, avoiding the extremes of some apocalyptic thinkers. He introduces significant modifications based on his own experience as apostle of the Gentiles, and his conviction that the end-times have already begun in Christ.

1 THESSALONIANS

[see pages 1676–1680 of the New Testament]

Before Beginning . . .

Thessalonica was the capital and major city of the Roman province of Macedonia, about one hundred miles southwest of Philippi along a major Roman road. The communities at Thessalonica and Philippi were among Paul's first converts in Greece. This letter indicates that he encountered many troubles there from both Jews and Greeks. The beginning of Paul's ministry in Thessalonica was characterized by suffering and humiliation. He was "insolently treated at Philippi," an incident to which he does not allude in his letter there (see 2:2; see also Acts 20:34; 1 Cor 4: 12; 9:3–18; 2 Thes 3:7–9). The Thessalonians, too, shared in some of that persecution (2:14–16). Persecution, illness, misunderstanding, and other forms of suffering plague Paul's ministry. Yet he constantly has hope of being found worthy by God to be entrusted with the preaching of the gospel (2:4).

Working through 1 Thessalonians

Following the usual letter format, 1 Thessalonians has an *address and thanksgiving* (1:1–10) and *conclusion* (5:26–28), which envelop the *body* of Paul's message (2:1–5:25). This message falls into two parts: the indicative (2:1–3:13) followed by the ethical exhortations (4:1–5:25).

The structure of 1 Thessalonians can be outlined as follows:

I. The Address (1:1–10)
II. The Body of the Letter (2:1–5:25)
  A. Paul's Account and Defense of His Ministry (2:1–3:13)
  B. Specific Exhortations and Instructions (4:1–5:22)
III. Conclusion (5:23–28)

Reading through 1 Thessalonians

The Address and Thanksgiving (1:1–10)

The address contains a short greeting (1:1) and an extended thanksgiving (1:2–10). A distinctive feature of Paul's letters is that the thanksgiving focuses on what God has done for Paul's addressees. In other correspondence of the time, the thanksgiving normally centers on the health and benefits enjoyed by the sender and a wish for the prosperity of the recipient. Paul's co-authors are Silvanus and Timothy. Following his custom, Paul writes not only in his own name but as a member of a team of Christian missionaries. Unlike many others of his letters that begin with several names, here the second person plural is maintained throughout the letter, Paul's "I" breaking through only at 2:18 and 5:27. In what we believe is the first extant letter from Paul, there is a greeting that will become Paul's trademark: "To the church of __________, grace and peace to you in (or from) God the Father and the Lord Jesus." This greeting is seen in its simplest form here; in later letters Paul will elaborate on this basic form.

A function of the thanksgiving in the address is often to anticipate the themes of a letter. In the case of 1 Thessalonians, thanksgiving itself is a major theme. Paul is grateful for the reception of the word of God by the Thessalonians and for the impact that their faith has had on other communities. Paul claims that he himself does not even have to testify to the fruitfulness of the Thessalonian mission—word of it has spread throughout the Greek world (Macedonia and Achaia include the whole of Greece, 1:8). Besides the initial thanksgiving of 1:2–10 that properly belongs to the address, two other thanksgivings appear in 2:13–16; 3:9–13. In all three places, Paul speaks of the relationship between faith and charity and of the expectation of the *Parousia* or second coming of Jesus Christ. These are the major themes of 1 Thessalonians.

The Body of the Letter (2:1–5:25)

The body contains Paul's main message in two parts; Paul's account and defense (2:1–3:13) followed by teachings and exhortation (4:1–5:25).

Paul's Account and Defense of his Ministry (2:1–3:13)

Paul states clearly that his motives are without guile in his work with them. If we can read between the lines, we can surmise the accusations of unworthy motives on his part against which he defends himself. He stresses his gratitude to God for the success of this community and presents a defense of his ministry among them.

Thanksgiving is a persistent thread that runs throughout 1 Thessalonians. Yet Paul is not a naive optimist. He is aware that this community is experiencing several problems. Although he will return to the theme of gratitude, he launches into a defense of his own ministry with the Thessalonians, thereby implying that some have questioned his authority or actions. Throughout Paul's ministry career, he insists that he is an apostle, called by God to preach the gospel message. Paul's defense of himself and his authority are linked to the call he has from God. He is under a divine compulsion to preach the gospel, and his confidence derives from this vocation. His defense of his ministry is also prompted by some of the dangers represented by false teachers agitating the Thessalonians in Paul's absence. Although this is a painful and threatening problem, Paul interrupts this defense with thanksgivings, as if to say that he is confident in the Thessalonians' perseverance despite the interference of the agitators.

One of the most difficult yet persistent problems that faced the early church was that of false prophets or false teachers. In the ancient world, where travel was difficult and communications took time, often philosophers or religious teachers joined others who traveled for business or personal reasons. News was gathered and disseminated by such traveling groups; new converts were often made along the way. First Thessalonians reflects this kind of mobility where Paul speaks about his own past visits with the Thessalonians as well as his thwarted plans to return. He promises to visit again soon. He warns the Thessalonians about other types of ministers—those who are greedy or who flatter (2:5) or who rely on the community for support (2:9). Paul's own example stands out in contrast to these, for he has been "gentle as a nursing mother" among them (2:7).

Despite his grateful recognition of the sturdy faith of the Thessalonians, Paul found it necessary to remind them of the sacrifices and dedication they saw in him and his companions. Among his characteristic practices, Paul repeatedly notes that he is self-supporting. He "toiled day and night" among them and in so doing, he gave them an example that they ought to imitate. This practice of working with his hands and supporting himself was unusual. The Corinthians misinterpreted it, and he did accept gifts of support from the Philippians (Phil 4:10–20).

Specific Exhortations and Instructions (4:1–5:22)

Concrete ethical applications or "imperatives" follow from Paul's grateful description of the Christian community at Thessalonica. This parenetic or exhortatory section may be considered a specific example of Paul's concern that faith be exercised in practical living, particularly as expressed in charity.

Sexual Conduct (4:3–8). These verses refer to sexual morality, but it is not clear how. The text may refer to a man being faithful to his wife (the usual translation), or to the need for his own sexual control, with no wife mentioned, and verse 6 may refer again to marital fidelity against adultery, or to cheating in business matters. In any case, the text raises a variety of ethical concerns including sexual conduct and business ethics.

For their part, the Jews considered the obligations of marriage and the family to be linked to the covenant relationship with God. This link was an important one Paul wished to adopt for the Gentile Christians. Paul therefore stresses the obligation of believers to develop relationships worthy of them, reflecting respect for one another and for their call to holiness. Charity among believers, in turn, has an effect even on those outside the community who will be impressed with the example of high moral conduct of the Christians.

Death and the Need for Vigilance (4:13–5:11). Paul and other early Christians seem to have believed that the Parousia or return of Jesus was very near. Now members of the Thessalonian community are dying before this event, which was a problem for their faith that Jesus would truly return. They wondered how the dead would participate in the triumphant day of Christ's return. Paul encourages the Thessalonians to persevere in faith and joins to this a warning about continued vigilance. Enthusiastic faith can often wane at the onslaught of opposition, suffering, and frustrated expectations. Paul fears that the death of fellow Christians will so shake the Thessalonians' faith that their grief will give way to doubt, discouragement, and even apostasy.

Paul's view of the second coming is influenced by his apocalyptic perspective. God is perceived as living in heaven, which is "above," beyond the clouds. An archangel and trumpets are standard apocalyptic images accompanying the end of the world and a call to judgment. The second coming of Christ, unlike the first, will be a show of power. It will be cosmic in effect, changing the entire order of creation, not only human existence.

Paul promises that the Christian dead have not been lost or forgotten. They, like us, will be gathered by Christ and judged. The righteous will be restored to God. Paul's emphasis is on the certainty of this event, not on times or manner. The exact manner of the resurrection and of judgment, Paul finally admits in 1 Corinthians 15, is unknown to us (see 1 Thes 5:1; 1 Cor 15:35–57).

The death of loved ones may pose painful faith questions for believers in any age. The death of beloved members of the community seems to have challenged the faith of the Christians at Thessalonica. Because the death of fellow Christians was so threatening, Paul admonished: "console one another with these words" (4:18; 5:11). He reinforced his warning to persevere by speaking again about the certainty of Christ's coming. The images of the pregnant woman and of the thief in the night are ones that appear in Jesus' own preaching, according to the Gospel accounts (see Mt 24:43; Lk 21:23). They stress at once the need for preparedness and vigilance, the certainty of the occurrence, and the threatening aspect of suffering. Continuing his use of stock apocalyptic imagery, Paul envisions a cosmic struggle that differentiates between those who are the children of light and those who remain in darkness.

Spirit and Order (5:12–22). Paul enjoins respect for those who minister among the faithful, an unusual reference to local leaders (see also Phil 1:1). But the more important points are about the way in which believers are to exercise mutual love, not returning evil for evil but consistently seeking the good of all. Joy, prayer, and gratitude characterize their lives as they live according to the Spirit, discerning between good and evil.

Conclusion (5:23–28)

The concluding prayer (5:23–25) and final greetings (5:26–28) suggest that this letter was intended for reading in a liturgical setting. Paul says that the Thessalonians will be kept holy and spotless as they wait for the Lord's return. The "holy kiss" with which they are to greet one another was probably the ritual exchange of peace done during the liturgical assembly.

Concluding Remarks

Actions are an expression of faith. Behavior is a key to the way people think and what they believe. Therefore, if there is carelessness about others, or promiscuity, or indifference to one's role in creating a livable society and universe, we have to examine the underlying faith presuppositions to these actions or omissions. Charity, chastity, and an honest, humble bearing in this life are signs for Paul of conversion to the "living and true God." Paul exhorts Christians to live according to the gospel he preaches. It is not hard to see how the message of 1 Thessalonians is appropriate for today.

2 THESSALONIANS

[see pages 1680–1684 of the New Testament]

Before Beginning . . .

The apocalyptic perspective of 2 Thessalonians (see introduction to the Thessalonian Letters) is more pronounced here than in any other Pauline letter. The Pauline authorship of 2 Thessalonians is widely disputed. This letter may be *pseudepigraphical,* that is, written in Paul's name by someone other than Paul, probably a disciple or admirer. There is a studied attempt on the part of this Pauline disciple to copy Paul's style. For example, the greeting differs only slightly from the greeting of 1 Thessalonians, and the final greeting insists that the letter is based on Paul's authority. There is a rejection of other supposedly Pauline letters circulating (2:1). One could also say that these are signs of Paul's true authorship, but perhaps the insistence on Paul's authority seems more than a little defensive. Writing in Paul's name assured that a letter would be taken seriously. This practice of Paul's disciples was also an attempt to give continuity to the apostle's message, explicitly interpreting the Pauline traditions in a new context. Despite the reservations of interpreters about Pauline authorship, it is customary to refer to the writer of 2 Thessalonians as "Paul."

There is good reason to believe that 2 Thessalonians was written a decade or more after Paul's death. It is addressed to the same community as 1 Thessalonians but a community that is troubled by the mistaken preaching that the Day of the Lord had now arrived. The preoccupation of early Christians with the times and circumstances accompanying the return of Christ is a problem addressed by many of the New Testament writers, including the Gospels of Matthew, Mark, and Luke, and the book of Revelation. The "apocalyptic" message of 2 Thessalonians is not a frightening one that heightens with fear the anticipation of Christ's return, but is instead a message of consolation and hope for the Christians suffering persecution and confusion. The term "apocalyptic" has come into vogue again in our own times as we, like the early Christians, face an uncertain future. We need to understand biblical apocalyptic as emphasizing hope for all those who persevere.

Working through 2 Thessalonians

Second Thessalonians exhibits the usual letter characteristics of an *address and thanksgiving* (1:1–12) and *conclusion* (3:15–18) enclosing the message or *body* of the letter in 2:1–3:16.

I. The Address (1:1–12)
II. The Body of the Letter (2:1–3:15)
III. Conclusion (3:16–18)

Reading through 2 Thessalonians

The Address and Thanksgiving (1:1–12)

The address includes a greeting (1:1–2), a thanksgiving (1:3–10), and a prayer (1:11–12). The greeting is an almost slavish imitation of the greeting of 1 Thessalonians. Paul joins himself with Silvanus and Timothy, fellow missionaries to the Thessalonians (see 1 Thes 1:1). Also similar to 1 Thessalonians is the fact that thanksgiving is not only a part of the initial address as a formal characteristic of a letter; gratitude is also a central theme in the development of Paul's teaching (see 2:13–17).

The Body of the Letter (2:1–3:15)

Paul's message to the Thessalonians can be subdivided into instruction on right thinking (2: 1–17) and right conduct in the daily life of the Christians at Thessalonica (3:1–16).

Paul's Teaching on Right Thinking (2:1–17)

The early Christians' expectation of an imminent return of Christ needed to be adjusted and corrected as the community developed. Unforeseen crises arose, and answers had to be sought in the basics of the Christian preaching. Time passed and the danger was that Christians would become disenchanted and would lose faith, especially in the midst of adversity. First Thessalonians had warned the community about maintaining faith, hope, and love even amid trials such as the death of fellow Christians. There Paul focused on the Day of the Lord, which, he assured them, was coming soon. This reminder served as a warning that behavior would be judged, and the faithful would be rewarded, whereas the unfaithful would be punished.

By the time of the writing of 2 Thessalonians, it seems the eschatological expectation was being taken too seriously, and this caused new problems. As time passed, the early Christians were wondering about the accuracy of their hope that Christ would return soon. They became alarmed by prophecies and by a letter that they thought came from Paul; it seems to have said that the expected "day of the Lord" had arrived (2:2). The author denies this and lists a number of events that must come first. This change in 2 Thessalonians 2:1–10 from the expectation of the near return of Christ seen in 1 Thessalonians is one of the main reasons interpreters suspect that 2 Thessalonians is from a later, second generation Pauline Christian. The early Christians had experienced persecution. History had already shown that any expectation that Christ would speedily return with power, to punish the oppressors of the Christians, was wrong.

The message underlying the apocalyptic references in 2 Thessalonians is "do not be alarmed."

The writer avoids any kind of futile speculation concerning times and circumstances of the Parousia. He uses standard apocalyptic images portraying the conflict between good and evil, and the ultimate victory of God over evil. Yet he studiously avoids any specific description. It is sufficient that his readers focus on the hope of God's victory and that they remain vigilant against deception or alarm.

Paul's Teaching on Right Conduct (3:1–15)

The admonition in 3:10 not to feed anyone who will not work, and the general exhortation against idleness is probably connected to the apocalyptic expectation discussed earlier. Some thought that there was no further point to building the human community. But Paul warns that idlers only disrupt the peace of the community. Thus he connects idleness and a lack of charity. The apostle presents himself as a model to the contrary to be imitated. His work with his hands is apparently a topic of discussion among his converts. Perhaps, like the Corinthians, the Thessalonians despise labor and prefer the leisure that is considered more conducive to the development of the mind and spirit. Paul gives both social and theological reasons showing that he was not constrained to work but does so freely. Part of the legacy he left with the community was his example of working. This may have been a form of self-abasement Paul practiced in order to "be all things to all people" (see 1 Cor 9:21–22). Paul stresses that his aim is to make the gospel accessible to all.

Conclusion (3:16–18)

The author adds a greeting "in his own hand," apparently to insure authenticity. Yet it is such characteristics that make Pauline authorship of 2 Thessalonians suspect. There are no personal greetings and no originality to the abrupt closing of this letter. The author seems to be copying Paul's style rather than adding a more personalized signature as Paul would have done.

Concluding Remarks

Christians today can understand the need for restraint on the belief that the return of Christ was imminent. Perhaps more than ever before, we can appreciate the important balance introduced by 2 Thessalonians between faith that indeed the return of Christ would come, and emphasis on the need to work diligently to create a better society. Second Thessalonians offers us a message of hope and encouragement. The events that must come to pass before the end of the world are opportunities inviting us to a change of heart, expressed in careful stewardship of our lives, of the church, and of the world.

THE PASTORAL LETTERS

Introduction

The two letters to Timothy and the single letter to Titus have been called the "Pastoral Letters" since they deal largely with issues regarding pastoral care in Pauline communities. Most scholars consider them not to have been written by Paul but by a later writer, since they reflect a degree of church organization not present in Paul's day. We are indebted to these communities for preserving this distinctive correspondence that describes the initial development of church offices and organization. The Pastorals might be read as reflections on Christian ministry. In keeping with the tradition of authorship by Paul we will refer to the writer as "Paul," although most interpreters would agree that these letters are written at least a generation after Paul's death. In form they are personal letters written to one disciple, but in reality, they are open letters to communities on church policy in various issues.

Paul himself traveled far and wide preaching the message of Christ, founding churches, and writing letters back to communities he had established. Throughout his missionary career, Paul was joined by others and worked with others. He depended upon others. He kept in touch with local leadership. His letters request prayers and sometimes aid for himself and for his mission. In writing letters, Paul often names co-workers as co-authors. He sends emissaries to communities, sometimes for diplomatic reasons and sometimes because he is prohibited from coming at the time and needs to send a messenger. Among his most trusted and reliable partners in the spread of Christianity were Timothy and Titus.

We have references to the work and reputation of these companions of Paul in the authentic Pauline letters. Galatians 2:2–3 says that Titus accompanied Paul and Barnabas to Jerusalem and that, although he was a Gentile, the Jerusalem authorities did not insist that Titus be circumcised. Luke mentions Timothy as a companion of Paul on the second (Acts 16:1–4) and third (Acts 19:22) missionary journeys. Luke does not mention Titus, but he was a trusted messenger of Paul who eased the apostle's difficult communications, especially with the Corinthians (see 2 Cor 2:12–13; 7:7; 8:16–24).

Timothy and Titus served Christian congregations in ancient Greece. The traditional understanding, reflected in these letters, is that Timothy later became a church leader in Ephesus (1 Tm 1:3) and Titus in Crete (Tit 1:5). Both were struggling with the challenge of those who offered alternatives to the teachings of Paul. Paul writes to reinforce the faith of these pastors and to encourage them, reminding them of their own Christian vocation.

1 TIMOTHY

[see pages 1684–1691 of the New Testament]

Before Beginning . . .

Both of the two letters addressed to Timothy struggle with the nagging threat of false teaching. This is a problem that afflicted the church from the beginning.

Working through 1 Timothy

The content matter of this letter is diverse, and any particular outline seems arbitrary and artificial. Our discussion of 1 Timothy is based on the following structure:

- I. The Address and Thanksgiving (1:1–2, 12–17)
- II. The Body of the Letter (1:3–11; 1:18–6:19)
  - A. Paul's Message to Timothy (1:3–11; 1:18–4:16)
  - B. Duties Toward Others (5:1–6:19)
- III. Conclusion (6:20–21)

Reading through 1 Timothy

The Address and Thanksgiving (1:1–2, 12–17)

The address consists of a brief greeting in Pauline form (1:1–2) with the thanksgiving delayed until 1:12–17. A warning against false doctrines (1:3–11) appears between these two parts of the address. This intrusion breaks the usual structure of a letter but manifests the gravity of the author's concern. The thanksgiving (1:12–17) recalls Paul's former blasphemy and persecution of the church, evidence that his call was unmerited and unsolicited (1:12–17). Paul's example is a primary instance of the transforming power of grace. Because he sinned grievously (though in ignorance), the grace bestowed upon Paul had to be abundant. Notice that the author does not dwell on guilt or remorse. His allusion to Paul's sinful past only serves to illustrate the gratuity of God's mercy. These reflections prompt him to praise God in a short doxology or blessing (1:17).

The Body of the Letter (1:3–11; 1:18–6:19)

The message of 1 Timothy is primarily a warning against the dangers of false teaching. The writer reminds Timothy about the qualities he should look for in assistants who are true ministers of the gospel, and he discusses Christians' duties toward others.

Paul's Message to Timothy (1:3–11; 1:18–4:16)

The Warning Against False Teaching (1:3–11, 18–20). The teaching attacked in 1 Timothy is a form of *gnosis* (knowledge) that involved "myths and . . . genealogies [and] . . . speculations" (1:4). All three Pastorals, but especially 1 Timothy, are aimed at secure knowledge of the truth and secure ways of acting it out. These are reflections on the genuine applications of a teaching or knowledge that Timothy knows well.

The threat Paul combats in 1 Timothy is the pursuit of gnosis without any ethical or practical applications for living (1 Tm 1:4; see 2 Tm 2:14;

3:7; Ti 3:9). Thus the practicalities of Christian living and church life together are emphasized, along with a pastorally oriented theology. This letter attacks those who would reduce Christianity to a mere doctrine or intellectual exercise, to the neglect of the ethical implications. The letter presumes a common fund of knowledge and emphasizes that authentic Christianity should work itself out in everyday life.

Life and Leadership in the Community (2:1–4:16). The primary example of authentic Christian living is the minister of the gospel message. Timothy has a great responsibility entrusted to him by God and verified in the church (1:3, 18–20; 4:6–16; 6:11–16, 20–21). The writer impresses on Timothy the importance of his role as example for the church.

The advice to Timothy in this letter proceeds from the admonition to draw strength from the "prophetic words once spoken about you" (1:18) and the suggestion to "attend to yourself and to your teaching" (4:16). Timothy should concentrate on "righteousness, devotion, faith, love, patience, and gentleness" (6:11). He should ignore the seduction of "profane babbling and the absurdities of so-called knowledge" (6:20). Constancy and perseverance in the faith are required in order to attract and encourage other believers. Timothy is urged to demonstrate to all his reliance on God.

The discussion of how each group of persons should act toward others is an adaptation of the "household codes" used in Eph 5:21–6:9 and Col 3:18–4:1. Here men and women, young and old, male and female should treat each other with the respect due them in traditional society (also 5:1–2; 6:1–2). The duties of bishop and deacons (3:1–13) are drawn from typical descriptions of virtue. The text speaks of a single bishop and a number of deacons, both male and female (or, possibly, of male deacons and their wives, 3:11). We know from Phil 1:1 that these titles were used very early on. Presbyters are not mentioned in this passage (3:1–7), but only in 5:17–19. It does not seem, therefore, that there is as yet a triple-tiered ministry of bishop, presbyters, and deacons, which will come in the next years.

In one way, 1 Timothy may be read as a list of rules for people in various offices and positions within the community. There is, however, a common theme in all of Paul's advice. Members of the Christian community should distinguish themselves by their love for and service to one another. Even the dress and decorum of men and women at the liturgy, for example, should contribute to the building up of the community (2:8–10).

The particular advice to women, which has been controversial throughout Christian history, should be understood in the context of charity and the importance of good example. False teachers advocating asceticism, especially in the form of renunciation of marriage or restrictions on certain foods (4:1–3), were particularly successful with women whom the author of 1 Timothy perceives as especially susceptible. The prevailing male wisdom taught that women were gullible and subject to error, as symbolized in the story of Eve who was seduced by the serpent. Contrary to the false teachers, Paul supports marriage and sees the family as conducive to holiness. He therefore advocates the "submission" of women, which was part of traditional views about the well-run family. This, he insists, is not a lifestyle unworthy of Christian women but a way in which women may, like Timothy, "persevere in faith and love and holiness" (2:15). The same thinking drives the advice to slaves in a later passage to honor and respect their owners (6:1–2), with the warning that believing slaves are not to think of themselves as equal to their owners but to be even more respectful. This kind of thinking, as can be imagined, has caused mayhem in later centuries when those who appeal to the authority of the Bible resist social change. In his own context, however, Paul is simply trying to uphold human dignity within a social structure that he cannot change.

Duties toward Others (5:1–6:19)

This is really a rather artificial division, since the whole letter is preoccupied with community relationships. There is ambiguity in the discussion about widows (5:3–16), perhaps indication of uneven editing. First, widows who have no other means of support are to be supported by the church (5:3–8, 16). Then, there is some kind of enrollment of widows who are at least sixty years old, distinguished for practicing virtue, and resolved to remain unmarried—hardly issues to consider if a widow is starving. Some kind of service organization is envisioned in 5:9–15, returning again in verse 16 to the assistance of needy widows. Given lower life expectancy, few women would live beyond sixty, and younger widows are to remarry, so they could not hope to qualify later to be enrolled as those married only once (5:9).

The concrete advice regarding bishops and deacons and other ministers to the community stresses the power of example. This is especially important in those offices that have visibility in the community and represent a community trust. Many interpreters assume that the degree of development of the offices mentioned suggests a late composition of 1 Timothy. It would seem to have taken some years for the church to develop such a variety of roles and recognized ministries. On the other hand, we know that these ministries were beginning to develop already in Paul's day. They pertain to basic needs that arose as the church struggled to respond to its mission in the world. The office of bishop or overseer developed out of the custom of holding all things in common so that the surplus of the rich would supply the needs of the poor in the Christian community (see 2 Cor 8 and 9). The ministry of deacons reflected the priority of preaching the word, while not neglecting the physical and material needs of the church's members (Rom 16:2; Acts 6:1–6). The earliest writings of Paul, and in fact all of the New Testament, stress the social dimension of the Christian message. Therefore, the stewardships that would assure this dimension were created as soon as the priority was recognized.

Conclusion (6:20–21)

The conclusion (6:20–21) is in the form of a final recommendation and warning. First Timothy ends by restating the main message of the letter: "Guard the trust" (see 1:3–10; 4:7; 6:3–5). Authority is stewardship. Many have been deceived by gnosis or false knowledge. Timothy is urged to hold firm to what he knows and to live it quietly.

Concluding Remarks

First Timothy represents several challenges for the modern interpreter. The author's view that women are more susceptible to error than men, for example, betrays the bias of a male-dominated culture. Changing attitudes throughout history facilitated the education of women, and consequently the underlying premise of their greater gullibility has been proven false. First Timothy stresses the responsibility of leaders to interpret the essentials of the Christian message and to insure charity as distinctive of the Christian community. Interpreters today distinguish between the culturally based bias against women and the essential message that included all in the life of charity to be lived by the community. This is a life in which all may grow and mature, women as well as men. Later generations were able to change oppressive structures of slavery. The responsibility of leaders and pastors is to nurture that life, providing in their own lives a model of charity for other Christians to emulate.

2 TIMOTHY

[see pages 1691–1696 of the New Testament]

Before Beginning . . .

The same preoccupations appear here as we saw in 1 Timothy: warnings about false teachings, and Paul's exhortation to Timothy as a minister of the gospel like himself. Second Timothy is written in a warmer, more personal tone than 1 Timothy, and therefore its lack of formal structure is understandable. It is really a testament in the form of a letter. Like Moses in Deuteronomy 29–30 or Jesus in John 14–16, the elder Paul, imprisoned in Rome (1:16–17), looks back on his life with the knowledge of his imminent death (4:6–8) and gives the younger man the benefit of his experience. He begins and ends the letter with references to his own experiences and the vocation of Timothy, thus linking the two. Their ties of affection and of common vocation are deep and very significant for Paul. The elder apostle speaks of his own life, his loneliness, his lack of confidence in other human beings. Yet he is not discouraged. God is the source of strength for both Paul and Timothy. The deeply personal tone of this letter has led some recent commentators to reevaluate the question of Pauline authorship, and to suggest that while

1 Timothy and Titus are of a later era, perhaps 2 Timothy is not.

Working through 2 Timothy

The *address and thanksgiving* (1:1–5) and *conclusion* (4:9–22) envelop the *body* of the letter in 1:6–4:8. The main themes of 2 Timothy are the minister's experience of God and warnings against false teaching.

I. The Address and Thanksgiving (1:1–5)
II. The Body of the Letter (1:6–4:8)
  A. Instructions to Timothy (1:6–2:13)
  B. Warnings about False Teaching (2:14–3:9)
  C. Final advice (3:10–4:8)
III. Conclusion (4:9–22)

Reading through 2 Timothy

The Address and Thanksgiving (1:1–5)

The address (1:1–5) consists of a greeting (1: 1–2) and a thanksgiving (1:3–5), following the authentic Pauline style.

The Body of the Letter (1:6–4:8)

We have noted previously that Paul generally follows a basic pattern of first presenting his fundamental teaching on various issues and then drawing ethical conclusions from this teaching, though these two parts do not always follow one another in neat order. First Timothy does not follow this pattern very well, and 2 Timothy even less so, primarily because it is more of a personal communication that combines reminders about teaching with advice in an informal way. The informal structure of this letter focuses on two main themes that are developed here: the minister's experience of God and warnings against false teaching.

Instructions to Timothy (1:6–2:13)

Timothy is not to be ashamed of the gospel or his commission to testify to the truth at all times. He also has the responsibility to keep that truth intact as he has received it. The apostle often uses himself as an example, as a source of inspiration and motivation. Paul lives with such integrity that he urges Christians to imitate him in everything (see Phil 4:8–10). Timothy is reminded that those who follow Christ will suffer persecution. This echoes Jesus' warning to his disciples (Mt 24:9–14; Mk 13:9–13; Lk 21:12–19; Jn 15: 11–27). In the face of such pressure, Timothy is to remain constant.

Warnings about False Teaching (2:14–3:9)

Like the other Pastorals, 2 Timothy is aimed at false teachings that promote a certain gnosis or knowledge and a consequent asceticism or strict discipline. The false teachings Paul attacks attach superior value to those who are "enlightened" with such knowledge and practice stringent customs regarding sexuality and diet. These practices set them apart from others, contributing to their sense of superiority. In all three letters, Paul was assuming that his addressees held the right beliefs, so that it was not necessary to review the correct teaching or doctrine that the writer and recipient hold in common. Therefore Paul spoke in vague and abstract terms about the false teaching, concentrating instead on the appropriate ethical applications that follow from true gospel preaching. Paul urges Timothy not to become embroiled in debates: "Charge [people] . . . to stop disputing about words . . . avoid profane [and] idle talk" (2:14, 16). One of the false teachings actually identified is that baptized Christians are already risen with Christ and that there is no future bodily resurrection (see note on 2:14–19). Paul understands Christians as living in the last days when there are many dangers and threats to faith.

While warnings about false teaching are given throughout this section, in verses 1–9 they are concentrated and seem aimed at a specific group of people, although they could also be intended more generally. The disparagement of women's intellectual ability that we have seen surface in 1 Timothy is again present (3:6–7), with perhaps the opposite effect: in fact, the author is telling us that missions among women were very successful, which means that the women were intellectually alert and responsive.

Final Advice (3:10–4:8)

Paul describes his life and impending death as a liturgical sacrifice; he is being poured out like a libation, an offering of wine (4:6). He has run and finished the course (4:7). He awaits with longing the reward of God (4:6–8). Such confidence is based in God and meant to serve as encouragement to Timothy who still runs the course. Like other biblical heroes (including Moses and Jesus), Paul is represented in 2 Timothy as giving a kind of farewell address near the end of his life (4:6–8). In this speech the hero warns his followers about impending dangers and threats to fidelity. They are commissioned with authority and reminded about the source of their confidence. They are promised that God will remain with them and that they will endure. Paul reminds Timothy to hold to the essentials of sound doctrine: Scripture, and the example of Christ and of other Christians. He reminds Timothy that those who live the gospel message will be persecuted. Paul urges Timothy to be faithful in waiting for the appearance of Jesus Christ.

Conclusion (4:9–22)

The personal tone and greetings of 2 Timothy mark this as the closest Pastoral Letter to Paul's own style. Paul often experienced failure in his relationships with others. The author of 2 Timothy experiences similar problems. Like Paul, he says that such difficulties are the occasion for more converts to the gospel message. The letter ends with a prayer for God's spirit to be with Timothy ("your" is singular). The plural in the last line may indicate the letter's being read and reflected upon in the assembly.

Concluding Remarks

The church is not a perfect society nor are its ministers without human faults and failings. Conflicts over a variety of issues have plagued believers from the beginning, making it sometimes difficult to discern right from false teaching and practice. The church has experienced crises of leadership and problems with authority and obedience. Relationships among Christians have often been strained. Paul and other New Testament authors are not strangers to such tensions and problems. The author of 2 Timothy manifests a remarkable vulnerability to the strains in his own relationships with others, but this does not in any way detract from his visions or hopes for the church. In fact, with amazing confidence and humility, the author of 2 Timothy shows that even his failures are opportunities for the spread of the Christian message.

TITUS

[see pages 1696–1699 of the New Testament]

Before Beginning . . .

The third Pastoral Letter is addressed to Titus, who is charged with the administration of the church in the large area of Crete (1:5). The letter to Titus has many parallels with 1 Timothy and manifests the same concerns for the maintenance duties of those entrusted with the care of the local communities. They are to give particular care to the appointment of reliable assistants and to the presentation of sound church teaching, protecting it from the many threats and dangers of false teaching.

Working through Titus

The *address* in 1:1–4 is not followed by the usual thanksgiving, but the text goes directly into the *body* of the letter in 1:5–3:11. This message presents the pastoral charge or responsibilities, especially that of working with others in the preaching of the Christian message. The entire letter may be seen as an exhortation of encouragement from one pastor to another. A short *conclusion* (3:12–15), giving personal information, brings the letter to a close. The simple structure is as follows:

I. Address (1:1–4)
II. The Body of the Letter (1:5–3:11)
  A. Pastoral Charge (1:5–16)
  B. Teaching the Christian Life (2:1–3:11)
III. Conclusion (3:12–15)

Reading through Titus

The Address (1:1–4)

The address follows the usual Pauline pattern, but here it consists of a greeting only. It is slightly more elaborate than Paul's usual greetings but exhibits many of the features of Paul's thinking. As in the other Pastorals, the author emphasizes the apostle's role in the spread of the worldwide mission of Christ. This mission is now entrusted to Paul's "child," Titus, a fellow worker encouraged through this letter to insure the continuing line of good pastors and to preserve the faithful teaching of Christian life. The great dangers that face Titus and the church of Crete are the false teachers and those who would corrupt the Christian message.

The Body of the Letter (1:5–3:11)

Pastoral Charge (1:5–16)

Verses 5 through 9 are parallel to the instruction of 1 Timothy 3:1–7. Paul is an itinerant preacher who, nevertheless, is keenly aware of the need for stabilized leadership, especially to protect the church against heretical or false teaching. Therefore, the instructions given to Titus concerning the administration of the church at Crete are related first to the appointment of trustworthy and reliable pastors for the various duties required for the growth and development of the church there.

One of the important offices was that of *presbyter* (elder, v. 5), a term that in meaning is quite close in this letter to *episkopos* (overseer or bishop, v. 7). The two statements seem to be about the same people, as they could also be in 1 Timothy 3:1–7; 5:17–20. The main function of the bishop was apparently the overseeing of the financial or material matters in the church. Again, as in Philippians 1:1, it is difficult to translate *episkopos* accurately, since the title "bishop" has such different connotations today. This bishop is God's "steward," entrusted with the distribution of goods and accountable to the members of the community. Therefore his own life ought to be exemplary. He must not only avoid excesses but also represent a model Christian life in his own family. As in 1 Timothy 3: 2–13, the description of the virtues of officeholders is taken from typical descriptions in literature on virtue.

Leaders of the church are to offer an alternative example to that of the false teachers who preach for personal gain, living off the community and seeking personal recognition and recompense. These kinds of accusations against one's opponents are also part of traditional rhetoric and should not be taken at face value. The conduct of the presbyters or bishops should, however, be above reproach. Primary among the false teachers are the Judaizers who continue to advocate observance of some aspects of the Jewish Law, a custom that was attractive to some Christians for many centuries. The writer stoops to an ethnic slur by quoting an earlier author to the effect that Cretans are by their very nature prone to deceit, dishonesty, and laziness, thus making them all the more susceptible to falsehoods (1:12).

Teaching the Christian Life (2:1–3:11)

Titus is encouraged to hold on to sound faith in teaching, while resisting pressures from all sides. Since the imagery of moral preaching often depicted the church as the new family, its members are here taught to relate to one another as older and younger people would in a well-ordered family in which respect dominates. Groups singled out include older men and younger men, older and younger women, slaves, and those in authority. Christians must not act in accordance with the world around them. Yet they must survive in an alien world. Paul's instructions focus on how to survive in this world while offering an alternative lifestyle and developing integrity as Christians. The domestic role for women is reinforced. The author reminds them of their duties to be examples within the marital context. Likewise slaves are directed not to rebel against the control of their masters (2:9–10). The author urges them to fidelity and kindness within the context of slavery. Citizens were also inclined to see Christianity as an alternative to obedience to a corrupt state. The author of Titus advocates exemplary citizenship based on the status of Christians as already justified and relying on the mercy of God. Paul summarizes his advice to Titus, reminding him to avoid controversies and to maintain his integrity in the true faith. The false teachers disturb the community and its ministers. Paul exhorts to vigilance and constancy.

Conclusion (3:12–15)

The final lines include very specific travel directives and recommendations for travelers passing through Crete. Titus is told to come with an assistant whom he will send, to join Paul at Nicopolis, a common city name; probably the one in western Greece is intended. Mediterranean Sea travel shut down from November 10 to March 10, and a traveler thus had to "winter" somewhere waiting out the passage of those months. Paul closes with personal greetings. The final greeting "grace be with you all" is the simplest of closing forms. Some manuscripts add "of the Lord" or "of God" and "Amen," which are closer to the usual elaborations of Paul himself.

Concluding Remarks

Christians continue to wrestle with questions relating practice or behavior to belief. Christianity, like Judaism, has always emphasized the importance of deeds rather than mere knowledge or doctrine alone. Ministers of the gospel are entrusted with the responsibility to preserve teaching while also presenting exemplary lives. The letter to Titus reminds us of the difficulties, yet the importance, of working with others for the advance of the gospel message.

The challenge of the Pastoral Letters for today's church can hardly be overestimated. The Catholic view of Paul has long been unduly influenced by his portrait in these letters. Catholic Christians in particular have inherited a long tradition stressing the communal dimensions of Christian teaching. We do not receive the Christian message individually nor can we live it in isolation from each other. This emphasis on communal responsibility is part of the legacy of the Pastoral Letters.

PHILEMON

[see pages 1699–1700 of the New Testament]

Before Beginning . . .

Paul's letter to Philemon is a gem of early Christian exchange, and the only true personal letter that we have from Paul. No one seriously challenges Philemon as an authentic Pauline letter and an integral part of the New Testament. As contrasted with an "epistle" that embodies more stereotypic, stylized forms and features (for instance, Romans), Philemon appears to be a letter between individuals, dealing with a very concrete matter rather than with generalized, abstract theological principles. Neither Paul nor the early Christian community intended to attack slavery directly, so we may well wonder why this letter was preserved at all and why it might be significant for us.

Despite its brevity and apparent succinctness, Paul's letter to Philemon is full of interpretive problems and has been intensively studied in recent years. The traditional story line behind it since the fourth century has been that Onesimus, a slave, had run away from his master, Philemon, and had come to Paul for protection. Paul had converted Onesimus to Christianity, and now sent him back to Philemon, carrying this letter. But more recently, this interpretation has been questioned and several other possible scenarios proposed. One is that, according to Roman law, a slave who goes to a third party to mediate a dispute with his or her owner is not to be considered a fugitive. If one reads the letter from this perspective, it also fits. A third argument is that Onesimus is not a slave at all, but Philemon's brother, whom Philemon is treating like a slave (Phlm 16). Paul asks him to reconcile and treat him as he deserves. The interpretation that Onesimus is indeed a slave is the majority one, but why he went to Paul remains an open question, as does what Paul really wants Philemon to do. But it is clear that the relationship between Philemon and Onesimus is not good, and Paul is trying to patch it up.

The informal conversational tone does not detract from the letter's impressive significance within the Christian context. Each part of this letter underscores its ecclesial or community context and gives us a glimpse into the structure of relationship and exchange in the early Christian church. Because nearly all the names mentioned in the letter also occur in Colossians, the usual supposition is that Philemon's house church is located in Colossae.

Working through Philemon

The letter to Philemon has the usual features of a Pauline letter: an *address and thanksgiving* (1–6), the *body* (7–22) and *conclusion* (23–25). Philemon follows a simple outline:

I. Address and Thanksgiving (1–6)
II. The Body of the Letter (7–22)
III. Conclusion (23–25)

Reading through Philemon

The Address and Thanksgiving (1–6)

It is not Philemon alone who is addressed, but Apphia, perhaps Philemon's wife, Archippus, another member of the household, and the whole "church [that meets] at your house" (1–2). The thanksgiving (4–6) notes the renowned love and faith Philemon has always shown the "holy ones," a reference to his fellow Christians. Paul also names Philemon a "partner" in faith, emphasizing the common life in Christ that they share, which is the basis for the new society that Paul envisions.

The Body of the Letter (7–22)

The varied expressions of Paul's complex relationship with Philemon serve as a model for the new relationships Philemon now has with Onesimus. Their common baptism provides a basis for Philemon and Onesimus (as well as for the whole church) to create an entirely new way of relating to one another and to resolve the tensions between them. In no other Pauline letter is the relationship between the "indicative" or statement of Christian reality (signified by a common baptism) so integrally bound up with the "imperative" implications or exhortations that flow from this reality. From a structural viewpoint, it is impossible to separate the "indicative" from the "imperative" in this letter as we have done in others.

In 1 Corinthians 7:21–23, Paul says that slavery or freedom is indifferent in the Christian life. It is not clear in this letter whether Paul appeals to Philemon to manumit Onesimus, that is, free him from slavery. He may expect that the two of them now continue in a good relationship of master and slave. But if Onesimus is a runaway, normal punitive measures against an errant slave (who perhaps also stole from his master, 18–19) are prohibited by Paul. Master and slave are fellow Christians. The community context should help them work out a new way of relating to one another as "brothers." Because of whatever way Onesimus has wronged Philemon, Philemon is in a delicate position. If he does not punish Onesimus, he is lacking in necessary discipline, and his social peers will think him weak. If he does insist on punishment, he will violate his Christian obligation to forgiveness and Paul's express desires. The whole house church is watching to see what he will do! Unfortunately, we do not know the answer.

Paul describes himself as a prisoner (9), as Philemon's brother (7,20), and as father of Onesimus (10). Paul says he is an old man (9), an anticipated guest of Philemon (22), and one to whom Philemon is indebted (19). These descriptions illustrate the various ways in which the patronage system of the culture interacted with Christian expressions of interdependence and ultimately equality in Christ. They are a way of redefining Paul's relationship to Philemon and to the church in Colossae. They also serve as a model for Philemon to develop a new relationship between himself and Onesimus. The letter is a masterpiece of rhetorical strategy. Paul does not mandate any specific set of actions, but rather appeals to Philemon and to the whole community to read and reflect on this letter in light of their common baptism, and to discern a course of action toward Onesimus that will reflect the Christian faith they share.

Conclusion (23–25)

The final greetings mention names of Paul's co-workers also found in Colossians (1:7; 2:1; 4:12–13) and 2 Timothy (4:9–13). Together with the liturgical blessing (Phlm 25), these greetings underscore once again the communal context in which this letter was written and in which it ought to be reflected upon and acted upon. Philemon draws out some implications of the baptismal formula quoted in Galatians 3:28: "There is neither Jew nor Greek, there is neither slave nor free person, there is not male and female; for you are all one in Christ Jesus" (see also Col 3:11).

Concluding Remarks

The letter to Philemon raises interesting challenges for its original recipients and for us. Apparently Onesimus himself is bearer of this letter from Paul to his master. The letter is to be read at the liturgy when the Christian community will help Philemon reintegrate Onesimus back into his household as a fellow Christian. The very fact that the community preserved this letter—

and that it comes down to us included in the canon of the New Testament—testifies to the spirit of openness, humility, and generosity of Philemon and his congregation that must have successfully resolved this matter. Today the church as a whole and local churches are faced with perplexing social problems, especially with regard to social expectations and their clash with faith values. We can take hope that what was written long ago was written for our instruction. We can well afford to contemplate the role of such a pastoral letter and of the community's reflection on its contents.

FURTHER READING

Dunn, James D. G. *The Theology of Paul the Apostle*. Grand Rapids, MI: Eerdmans, 1998.

Fitzmyer, Joseph A. *According to Paul: Studies in the Theology of the Apostle*. Mahwah, NJ: Paulist, 1993.

Murphy-O'Connor, Jerome. *Paul: A Critical Life*. Oxford: Clarendon, 1996.

Roetzel, Calvin J. *The Letters of Paul: Conversations in Context*. 4th ed. Louisville, KY: Westminster John Knox, 1998.

—. *Paul: The Man and the Myth*. Minneapolis, MN: Fortress, 1999.

Stendahl, Krister. *Paul among Jews and Gentiles*. Philadelphia: Fortress, 1976.

THE GENERAL LETTERS AND REVELATION

LUKE TIMOTHY JOHNSON

HEBREWS

[see pages 1700–1720 of the New Testament]

Before Beginning . . .

Hebrews is not a real letter but a sermon (see introduction, NT, 1700–02) The best way to experience Hebrews is by reading it out loud from beginning to end. Subtle points of Greek rhetoric—such as the alliteration in the opening verses—will still escape the contemporary reader. But oral recitation helps to catch the sermonic rhythms of Hebrews, its use of "we" and "you" (so natural to the sermon), and its alternating pattern of exposition and exhortation. Note, for example, how the opening argument of 1: 5–14 leads naturally to the "therefore, we must attend all the more" in 2:1–5. Reading straight through also enables the reader to grasp the powerful argument that is the outstanding characteristic of this early Christian writing.

Toward Understanding Hebrews

Hebrews has significantly shaped the liturgy, doctrine, and spirituality of the church. Although other New Testament writings speak of Jesus' death as a sacrifice, Hebrews' unique reflection on Melchizedek (chapter 7) and on Jesus as the Great High Priest influenced the development of Catholic liturgy. Hebrews' insistence on Jesus' full divinity and equally full participation in human nature contributed to the understanding of Jesus' identity as God's Son (1–2). And Hebrews' vision of faith as a pilgrimage toward God (11–12) created a symbolic framework for the Christian understanding of discipleship as a "journey." For all its riches, Hebrews resists easy assimilation for two reasons: the first is that it presents a sustained argument from beginning to end; the second is that its symbols are hard to understand. Dealing with these difficulties clears the way to more intelligent and satisfactory reading.

The Argument

Some parts of the New Testament, like the Gospel parables, can be read out of their original context and still make sense. But each part of Hebrews plays a role in a complicated interplay of argument and explanation concerning Jesus and Christian life. Hebrews resists being excerpted. It uses a form of argument, found both in Greek philosophy and rabbinic Judaism, called "from the lesser to the greater." The argument goes, "If something is true in a smaller matter, it is even more true in an analogous greater matter." In Hebrews, the contrast is between the partial revelation of God in the past through angels, law, and priesthood, and the perfect revelation "in the last of these days" through God's Son, Jesus, between that former "lesser" salvation and the present "greater" salvation.

The argument in Hebrews is not theoretical but practical. The real point is the contrast between the response to God's word by the people of the past, and the response demanded of the people today. A greater blessing and hope require a greater degree of obedience and loyalty, just as disobedience carries a greater penalty. The stakes are higher all around.

The Symbols

The symbols of Hebrews are sufficiently strange to shake any assumption that the New Testament world was "just like ours." Hebrews demands of its readers, for example, a far more sophisticated grasp of Scripture than that possessed by most Christians today. Much of its argument, in fact, is based on complex modes of scriptural interpretation that, while strange to us, were common in the first century. The version of Scripture used by Hebrews (as by other New Testament writings) was not Hebrew but Greek. Its citations and allusions are from the Septuagint. This study edition gives some assistance by providing complete Scripture references. Citations in the text are flagged with small letters; passages are identified at the bottom of each page. To fully appreciate Hebrews' virtuosity, study the citations in their original context as well as how Hebrews can turn them to fit its argument (as in 10:5–7).

Hebrews' view of the world is strikingly different from that of present-day Christians in an even more fundamental sense. Hebrews works within a philosophical tradition called Platonism, which saw a great gulf between the spiritual realm and the material world. Spiritual things are eternal, unchanging; material things are transitory. As a result, spiritual things are both more real and better than the material. For Platonic Jews and Christians, the "spiritual" and "material" realms were understood in terms of "heaven" and "earth."

This is the framework for grasping Hebrews' point about the superiority of Jesus' priesthood. By his resurrection, Jesus entered heaven, where he is a "priest forever" (5:6), in contrast to the Jewish priesthood, which could only be temporary. Likewise the "heavenly sanctuary" is superior to the physical tent of worship described in Scripture (8–9). The symbolism at times becomes dense and requires patience to disentangle, but the basic point is clear. The human Messiah Jesus now shares God's life in heaven. His priesthood is therefore both the ultimate and eternal "source of salvation" to others (5:9).

The Readers

The original hearers of this sermon had experienced the loss of property and friends (10: 32–34). They were tempted to lose hope and seek a more stable framework than that offered by a crucified messiah. Hebrews addresses their longing for stability by offering the hope for "a better homeland, a heavenly one" (11:16). The first readers' experience can be translated into that of every age: all of us in various ways experience loss, desperation, alienation, despair. Hebrews' message to us is as sharp as it was to them: "Oh, that today you would hear his voice: Harden not your hearts" (4:7). We also are called to go on pilgrimage through our troubled circumstances, looking to Jesus, who is still and always the "leader and perfecter of faith" (12:2).

The Prologue (1:1–4)

The opening sentence is elegantly constructed and introduces Hebrews' central themes. First is the contrast between God's partial revelation in the past ("to our ancestors") and the perfect revelation now ("to us") made through God's Son, which establishes the basic thesis: Jesus is superior to the old dispensation, or covenant (see 8: 13). Second, Jesus' divine status is clearly if metaphorically expressed by calling him the "imprint" of God. The exalted identity attributed to the Son is similar to that in John and Paul (see, for example, Jn 1:1–4 and 1 Cor 8:6). Third, the prologue states that the way God "spoke" in Jesus was through his death for others (the purification from sins), and his resurrection.

Note the image of enthronement: Jesus "took his seat at the right hand." This alludes to Psalm 110:1, the favorite resurrection psalm of early Christians: "The LORD said to my lord: 'Take your throne at my right hand, while I make your enemies your footstool' " (see also 1:13). Hebrews will also exploit the fourth verse of this psalm when he develops the comparison between Jesus and Melchizedek in chapter 7. The image of enthronement runs throughout the sermon. Jesus is both priest and king. Finally, we notice that Jesus "inherits" a name better than that of the angels. Jesus is here portrayed as a forerunner. If they follow him, Christians also will enter into an inheritance (1:14; 6:12). The mention of angels, in turn, provides a transition to Hebrews' argument.

The Son Is Higher than the Angels (1:5–2:18)

A series of Scripture citations proves that the Son is superior to angels. The notes in the New Testament pp. 1702–04 discuss details of the citations. The pertinent question for us is, why do angels require putting in place, anyway? Our contemporary view of the world has small room for angels! But in the world of the New Testament, especially in the writings of Judaism, angels were regarded as the most powerful intermediaries between God and humans. The tendency to exalt their role is attested in Galatians 4:9 and Colossians 2:18. What concern does the author address? Jesus in his humanity did not appear so impressive as these "spiritual" beings. He was not only human; he suffered and died. Hebrews must overcome the scandal of a "lowly" Messiah.

Citations from Scripture do not by themselves demonstrate the point. As in other New Testament writings (for example, Gal 3:1–5), Hebrews argues "the greater" from the fact of the readers' own *experience*. The work of God's Spirit among them is itself powerful "witness" to the salvation accomplished through Jesus (2:3f). And never content with the speculative, Hebrews drives home the exhortation. This "greater salvation" demands of the readers a greater response of alertness (2:1f).

From the perspective of the power of the Risen Lord, Hebrews takes up the issue of Jesus' "lowliness." On the basis of Psalm 8, the author asserts that Jesus was "lower than the angels" only temporarily. And the reason was so that he could "taste death for everyone," that is, act as priest. On the basis of a messianic reading of Isaiah 8:18f, Hebrews next affirms God's (and the Messiah's) solidarity with humanity. Then, Hebrews turns the tables, and makes Jesus' humanity a positive criterion for authentic priesthood. Because Jesus is one with those he represents before God—he shares the way they are "tested," and the way they "fear death"—he can be a compassionate and merciful priest. It is significant that Hebrews defines priesthood in terms of his personal identity and experience rather than in terms of religious ceremony. Hebrews thereby anticipates an important principle of later doctrine: "what is not assumed [by God] cannot be saved." Precisely *because* he is human, Jesus can save humanity.

Jesus, Faithful and Compassionate High Priest (3:1–5:10)

Moses was so central a figure for Jews that he became a natural point of contrast for Christian claims about Jesus (see, for example, Jn 1:17). Hebrews now contrasts Moses as "the servant of [God's] house," and Jesus as "son over the house" (3:4f). The real contrast in this section, however, is between the people that Moses led and the Christians the author of Hebrews addresses in terms of disobedience and obedient faith (3:7–13). Hebrews agrees with Paul's argument in 1 Corinthians 10:1–13 that what happened to Israel in the desert is a warning for the present.

The argument here uses complex ancient rules for interpreting Scripture. Much is made, for example, of the occurrence of specific words, such as "rest" and "today," without regard for their original contexts. The premise for such a procedure is that Scripture speaks to every age in each of its words, and that every part of Scripture interprets every other part. On that premise, Hebrews asserts that the "rest" to which Moses led the people (the land) was not the "rest of God," namely, God's own life. For that matter, neither did people of old even succeed in entering *that* earthly rest because of their disobedience. Christians in contrast have hope for the real rest—of God's own life—won by Jesus' resurrection. The point? They are to obey the call of God and not fall away (4:6). The message of Hebrews is not a trivial one. The readers are not engaged in a trivial conquest of territory; they are called to a share in God's life, a far more awesome prospect (4:12f).

Hebrews has identified obedient faith as the fundamental response demanded by God. The comparison to the wandering Israelites also establishes Hebrews' basic image of the church as the people of God on *pilgrimage*. The image suggests that the church is not simply an institution like other institutions. It is never fully "at home" in the world. The church exists with reference to a higher goal—the "heavenly city"—toward which it must steadily move like a pilgrim, although this side of death the goal is never reached. Pilgrims need the sort of attentiveness, patience, obedience, and endurance demanded by Hebrews. Above all, they need *hope* (see 6:18). They can move lightly through this worldly existence only if convinced that their destination is truly "greater" than their present abode.

Hebrews points the reader again to the leader of the pilgrimage, the "apostle and high priest of our confession" (3:1). In the description of Jesus as priest (4:14–5:9), Hebrews combines what has come to be called both "high" and "low" Christologies (understandings of Jesus). Jesus is definitely "from above"; he is God's Son in the fullest sense, but he is also fully human, "from below." It is his *human* existence that defines the path "all the children" are to follow. As priest, he is exemplar. Jesus is not only "faithful" (3:1f) as all are called to be; he "learned obedience from what he suffered" (5:8). The full implications of this statement will become clear only later (see 12:1–11), but we already understand that Jesus' suffering deepened his faith, and his obedience was itself a form of suffering. Jesus progressively *became,* in his humanity, perfect Son of God, and therefore the "leader" of all who follow him.

Jesus' Eternal Priesthood and Sacrifice (5:11–10:39)

The long middle section of the sermon argues for the superiority of Jesus' priesthood. It begins with an extended exhortation (5:11–6:20), and then focuses on Jesus' priestly identity and activity (7–10).

Hebrews presupposes the readers' grasp of the "basic teaching about Christ" (6:1), but, in a rebuke as much as an exhortation, he urges them beyond the milk fit for babes to the meat meant for the mature (compare Paul's use of this imagery in 1 Cor 3:1–3). This "mature teaching" is by no means a matter of moving beyond Jesus or abandoning Jesus. Such apostasy from Christ Hebrews calls "recrucifying the Son of God" (6:6). Indeed, God's promise based on Jesus' resurrection is utterly reliable; Jesus is the "anchor of the soul" (6:19), to whose priesthood God has bound himself by oath (6:13). The nature and implications of Jesus' priesthood, however, are precisely what require explication. By it the Christian hope is made secure. By it Christians are able to become "imitators of those who, through faith and patience, are inheriting the promises" (6:12).

The consideration of Jesus as priest is the climax of the "lesser to the greater" argument. But because the procedures and symbols of Jewish cult are foreign to us today, this section makes for some of the hardest reading in the New Testament. It is important to remember from the start that Hebrews' argument is based on the Christian experience of the Spirit and conviction that Jesus is Risen Lord, and he has entered into the life of God (2:3–4). Only this premise makes Hebrews' reinterpretation of Scripture reasonable. Once that premise is granted, then the major turning points of the exposition make sense.

Jesus and Melchizedek (7:1–28)

Why does Hebrews devote so much attention to a figure who appears only twice in Scripture? Because both appearances are understood as pointing forward to Christ. In Genesis 14:17–20, Melchizedek is named a priest of God (although he was a Gentile), whom even Abraham acknowledged by giving him tithes. Logically, then, a priest descended from Melchizedek would be superior to one descended from Abraham! Melchizedek's second scriptural appearance is in verse 4 of the very Psalm 110 that Christians regard as a prophecy of Jesus' resurrection. Melchizedek's being "without beginning or end" (because Scripture records neither his birth nor his death) is therefore an anticipation of the Son of God whose priesthood is eternally valid. Jesus is a priest forever, "like Melchizedek" (Ps 110:4) because through his resurrection, Jesus became priest "by the power of a life that cannot be destroyed" (7:16). He "remains forever" (7:24). His sacrifice is "once for all" (7:27). He "lives forever to make intercession" (7:25). The Jewish priesthood descended from Abraham cannot compete.

The Old and New Covenant (8:1–13)

God's revelation in Jesus does more than continue the story of God's people; it raises it to a new plane. Jesus' death and resurrection mark an absolute beginning. Here, Hebrews' Platonic worldview and its convictions concerning the resurrected Lord converge. In 8:1–6, we see the use of Platonic language, when Moses' desert sanctuary is called "the copy and shadow of the heavenly sanctuary" (8:5). Heaven is greater than earth. More dramatically, Hebrews turns this Platonism into an interpretation of history: the old covenant is likewise a "shadow" of the new, pointing to but replaced by the work of God in Jesus. Hebrews exploits Jeremiah's promise of a new covenant "in the heart" to affirm that the old order is in fact obsolescent.

The Priestly Act of Jesus (9:1–10:18)

The comparison of covenants now becomes a specific contrast between ancient cult and Jesus' death and resurrection. The complexity of the imagery here is daunting. The reader is offered some help by the notes in New Testament pp. 1711–14. Even more helpful would be a careful reading of Exodus 25–27 (which describes the Tent of the Wilderness) and Leviticus 16 (which describes the ritual for the Day of Atonement). Hebrews hammers at two basic points. First, because Jewish sacrifices had to be repeated, it is obvious they were not effective—they could not truly purify the human conscience (9:6, 25; 10: 1–3,11). In contrast, Jesus entered "real" life, so his sacrifice is eternally valid (9:12, 24–28; 10: 10–12). Second, the old cult sacrificed animals, whereas Jesus gave his own life for others in obedience to God (8:12–14; 10:5–10, 19). As both priest and victim, furthermore, he showed himself to be a personal example that others could follow. All believers have "confidence of entrance into the sanctuary by the new and living way he opened for us" (10:19f).

Exhortation to Fidelity (10:19–39)

In the light of this "greater salvation," Hebrews warns again of the consequences of apostasy (10: 26–31). Despite their losses and trials, Christians are called to a still deeper loyalty (10:32–39). By mentioning endurance and faith as requisites for receiving the promises (10:36–38), Hebrews prepares for its final stirring exhortation.

Examples, Discipline, Disobedience (11:1–12:29)

The sermon's long argument reaches its climax in this exhortation to faith, understood as loyalty, endurance, and hope. The recital of heroes and heroines of the past serves to provide *examples* for the readers to imitate. Why? Just as the readers had lost property and had been persecuted, so also had the believers who preceded them. Yet the ancestors persevered in the search for a better homeland (11:14). The repetition of the phrase "by faith" summons the readers to join ranks with those on pilgrimage to God's presence. Unlike the desert generation that fell by the way because of disobedience, these exemplars continued faithful, even though they themselves did not receive the full promise (11:39)! It was left to Jesus, the "leader and perfecter of faith" (12:2) to provide complete access to God through his death and resurrection. Because Christians can now look to him (12:2), there is solid reason to hope while still on the journey.

By summoning such a "cloud of witnesses" (12:1) to support the commitment of the readers, Hebrews states a conviction that eventually became an article of the Christian creed, "the communion of saints." Those struggling for God on earth are not alone. They are joined in a larger fellowship of faith with those who have died and who now support them with their prayers. The people of faith have solidarity in hope.

This is not blind optimism: the alienation, suffering, and persecution experienced by the ancients is not trivialized. And Jesus, before he could sit on the throne, had to "endure the cross, despising its shame" (12:2). Jesus' human response to God is the perfect example for the faith of Christians. Faith is always "evidence of things not seen" (11:1), which means that it is always a risk taken in the face of a pain more palpably present than the promise. Thus, also, the Christian experience of prayer has as an essential component the "dark night" of the soul when God seems more absent than present.

The connection between Sonship and suffering continues in 12:5–13. The remarks about fathers disciplining their children at first seem banal if not regressive. But when we remember that Jesus, "Son though he was, . . . learned obedience from what he suffered" (5:8), we come to appreciate the profound correspondence between Christology and Christian existence. What we suffer in our lives, if we can perceive and accept such suffering in faith, enables God to shape Jesus' own "sonship" in us. Ancient Greeks had the maxim *mathein pathein,* "to learn it is necessary to suffer." Being educated as children of God requires a painful transformation, for the goal is the holy God (12:10).

Hebrews reminds its readers that they have undertaken not a pleasant stroll but a terrible path toward "the city of the living God" (12:22), a pilgrimage whose completion means life eternal but whose abandonment means not seeing the Lord (12:14). Nowhere else does the New Testament give a sterner reminder of life's tragic depths and terrifying heights than in this simple conclusion, "for our God is a consuming fire" (12:29).

Final Exhortation, Blessing, Greetings (13:1–25)

Although the final chapter is mainly practical, it is intimately joined to the theological argument of chapters 1 through 12. Notice, for example, the plea to "imitate the faith" of leaders, and the motivation of that faith being the eternal priesthood of Jesus who is "the same yesterday, today, and forever" (13:7f). The mix of advice about hospitality, marriage, and possessions (13:1–4) with the command to "go to Jesus outside the camp . . . for here we have no lasting city, but we seek the one that is to come" (13:13) is altogether typical of this sermon (see also 10:25) and of the early Christian understanding of existence. Christians live in the world like other people and participate in its structures. But they are not defined by this world or its values, even its religious values (13:9–11). No institutional cult or sacrificial priesthood is legitimated by this severe writing; everything necessary has been accomplished already by Jesus. Christians are defined not by their liturgy but by their following the one who suffered "outside the gate, to consecrate the people by his own blood" (13:12). Christians are never entirely at ease in the world or even in the church. They are pilgrims, struggling toward the "God of peace" into whose care the final blessing (13:20f) entrusts the readers of this profound and powerful sermon.

FURTHER READING

Attridge, H. W. *Epistle to the Hebrews*. Hermeneia. Philadelphia: Fortress Press, 1989.

Koester, C. R. *Hebrews, A New Translation with Introduction and Commentary*. Anchor Bible 36. New York: Doubleday, 2001.

Lane, W. L. *Hebrews*. 2 vols. Word Biblical Commentary. Waco: Word, 1991.

JAMES

[see pages 1721–1728 of the New Testament]

Before Beginning . . .

James as Moral Exhortation

Letter writing was so popular in antiquity that the epistolary form became a package capable of holding many materials. In the case of James (as noted in the introduction, NT, pp. 1721–22), the letter format is the frame for a moral exhortation intended for a general readership.

Before turning to an analysis of the text, it is helpful to consider some of its literary features and major themes. James is not terribly difficult to understand; its style is lucid, its message is straightforward. The reader's task is putting into practice what James teaches. Our task here is simply the deeper appreciation of a clear witness.

The Writing

The form of Greco-Roman moral exhortation called *parenesis* was concerned with reminding readers of traditional values rather than with constructing theory. Such reminders often took the form of short maxims. James's first chapter in particular has such maxims, which are less connected to each other than to other sections of the composition. Chapters 2 through 5 take the form of short essays. The maxims in chapter 1 set themes that are developed in the essays of chapters 2 through 5. Note how the control of the tongue in 1:26 is elaborated by 3:1–12. Moral exhortation also presented models of virtue for readers to imitate. In James, the figures of Abraham, Rahab, Job, and Elijah provide examples from Scripture of the practical virtue James encourages.

James, however, is more than a moral treatise. It is a religious writing that uses the symbols of Scripture. James resembles the *Wisdom* tradition in its use of maxims, and in advocating a "wisdom from above" as the measure of life (3:13–18). James uses the language and perspective of the *Prophets* in its attack on rich oppressors (5:1–6). James also uses the *Law*. For James, both the Decalogue and the Law of Love are binding for Christians. They are to be understood, however, in light of the teachings of Jesus. James has many allusions to the words of Jesus (see, for example, 1:12; 2:5; 3:12; 5:12).

The Message

James advocates living faith and practical love. His concern is behavior. Like other moralists of his age, he is impatient with fine words that go nowhere (see, for example, 1:22–25). Above all, faith that is not expressed in love is a charade.

James's target is the Christian who is "of two minds" (1:8; 4:8). This person wants to live by two standards at once: that of God, and that of the world. James demands a choice. Not only speech but also the use of possessions and the practice of fairness within the community lie within the range of his concern. He especially attacks envy, which perfectly illustrates the morals of "the world" opposed to God (see, for example, 3:13–4:10).

Readers may be surprised to find that Jesus is mentioned only twice (1:1; 2:1), with no reference at all to the messianic message of salvation through Jesus' death and resurrection. But James does not lack theology. He bases his exhortations on the one God who creates and judges all humanity. James centers attention on God rather than on Christ.

This study guide divides the text differently than the *New American Bible*. No major issue is involved, only a judgment concerning what goes better with what. The paragraph headings in the NAB are helpful, as also are the notes.

The Two Measures (1:1–27)

Although chapter 1 is made up of separate aphorisms with only loose internal connections, the chapter does more than simply provide a table of contents for the essays to follow. The opening statements also make clear that humans must live by either one sort of measure or another.

The first verses have some word-linkages, but they don't form an easily followed argument. Like the book of Proverbs, they offer a set of maxims that invite testing against the reader's own experience of life. Although the same Greek word *(peirasmos)* is used in both verses, for example, the meaning of "trial" in 1:2 is not the same as "temptation" in 1:13.

The aphorisms are not, however, simply a random collection of wise sayings. The maxims in chapter 1 provide something of an index to the contents of chapters 2 through 5. The theme of enduring trials (1:2–4, 12–15) is developed in 5:7–11; the opposition between rich and poor (1:9–11) recurs in 4:13–5:6. Control of the tongue (1:19–21) is expanded in 3:1–12. Carrying out words in speech (1:22–26) is enlarged by 2:14–26. The theme of true wisdom (1:5–8,16–18) is argued by 3:13–4:10. The prayer of faith (1:6f) is amplified by 5:12–18.

The aphorisms also introduce the basic pattern that structures the whole of James: the contrast between the measure of the world and the measure of God. The measure of the world is expressed by envy: "desire conceives and brings forth sin, and when sin reaches maturity it gives birth to death" (1:15). The values of the world are self-deceptive (1:16, 27), are expressed in wrathful behavior (1:19), and in every sort of excess (1:21) especially the pursuit of illusory wealth (1:11). These values are based on the perception of life as a closed system; God has no part. Therefore all humans are in competition: one person's gain is another's loss.

The measure of faith is the opposite. All creation—life itself—is a gift: "all good giving and every perfect gift is from above, coming down from the Father of lights" (1:17). Because God has created humans by "the word of truth" (1:18), humans are able to receive the implanted word from him (1:21) and live in the way God does, giving "generously and ungrudgingly" (1:5). In the Greek, these words suggest the opposite of envy, which always grasps for more. Life by God's measure is expressed by "care for orphans and widows in their affliction" (1:27). One is thereby "unstained by the world" by living according to a different value system (1:27).

The greeting in verse 1, "to the twelve tribes in the dispersion," can therefore be understood as referring to the condition of Christians "in the world but not of the world." As in Hebrews and 1 Peter, Christians are regarded as pilgrims and sojourners. They are not hostile to the world but neither are they defined by it. James's whole effort is to persuade those "of two minds" (1:8) to live by God's measure which is the perfect "wisdom from above" (see 3:15).

Discrimination and the Law of Love (2:1–13)

The first essay reveals a voice that resembles Paul in Galatians. James uses the same oral, dialogical style known as the diatribe. Vivid and lively, it is filled with rhetorical questions, exclamations, and abrupt transitions. The effect is a direct challenge to every reader—then and now. The challenge is even more clearly heard when the text is read aloud.

Christians, James says, must live consistently with their convictions. "Faith in our . . . Lord Jesus Christ" (2:1) is incompatible with any form of discrimination within the community. James sketches a lively scene that probably reflects a general situation rather than a local incident. The context is judgment within the community, like that carried out in the diaspora synagogue to settle disputes. In the background is the injunction of Leviticus 19:15 that forbids partiality in judgment. How plausible and true to life is his portrayal of a community pandering to rich members and slighting their poor!

That James intends us to see discrimination as an offense against love as well as faith in his allusion to Leviticus 19:15 is shown immediately by his explicit citation of Leviticus 19:18 in 2:8. The "law of love" is also identified by Jesus as the summation of Scripture. James calls it the "royal" law, and he means the standard regulating relations in the community. It is the "law of the kingdom." James spells out this commandment by alluding to the Ten Commandments (2:11), and also to the specific commandments found in the original context of Leviticus 19 that accompany the original exhortation, "love your neighbor as yourself" (see Jas 4:11; 5:4,9,12,20). James says that breaking any commandment means breaking the whole law, because sin is not against a law but against a lawgiver. Faith in the one God excludes picking and choosing between commandments, just as it excludes picking and choosing between fellow Christians!

Active Faith (2:14–26)

The following section is often misunderstood. Because James speaks of "faith" and "works" (terms often used by Paul), people think James is responding to Paul's teaching. In fact, his perspective is entirely different. James speaks not of the commandments of the law but of active faith. He is a moralist and is concerned with the way speech gets converted to action. Like all moralists, his concern is efficacy: "of what use is it?" The examples of Abraham and Rahab illustrate James's point. Their faith expressed itself in effective action. Abraham was willing to sacrifice his son; Rahab showed hospitality to God's scouts. James is not debating with Paul over the question of how people are saved. His exhortation is intensely practical and arises from the situation pictured in 2:14–16: pious talk does not feed or clothe the needy. Such faith is as "dead" as a corpse; such religion is fraudulent (see 1:26f).

We discover here two distinctive aspects of James. His teaching is not based on what is specifically *Christian,* but on faith in the one God shared by other monotheistic traditions. For James, the "faith of Christ" and teachings of Jesus do not oppose but refine Torah. James therefore also contains the opening to genuine *social ethics*. His moral teaching is not confined to the Christian community; it can be extended to the world. If there is no partiality in the community, based in the law of God, then forms of discrimination in the wider world can be combated on the same basis. If sister and brother in the community are to be fed, then the community as such should also feed the needy of the world in every changing circumstance.

James also warns us that this can cut both ways. If the Christian community does not live up to its own calling, and is unjust, then it bears no witness to the world and is itself subject to condemnation (2:5–7).

The Power of the Tongue (3:1–12)

James's concern for the proper use of speech (see 1:19, 26) now becomes thematic. Preoccupation with speech is typical of ancient moralists. Taciturnity as a sign of wisdom was proverbial (see, for example, Prv 10:19; 11:12). That such "control of the tongue" was almost insurmountably difficult to achieve was also well known. James therefore considers control of speech to be a mark of perfection (3:2).

James makes two related points using conventional imagery from Greek philosophy. The first compares the tongue to a horse's bit or a ship's rudder, showing not only how a small organ can direct a large body but also how much that organ itself, with its disproportionate power, needs to be controlled by someone with a sense of direction! James's second point concerns the potential for *harm* in uncontrolled speech. It is like a flame "setting the entire course of our lives on fire" (3:6).

The capacity of speech to do evil is more impressive than its power for good: "no human being can tame the tongue. It is a restless evil, full of deadly poison" (3:8). Sadly, the story of human discourse from the Garden of Eden to the latest garden party only confirms James's harsh judgment. No wonder the ancients valued taciturnity: better no speech than destructive speech. The dangers inherent in speech also undergird the value of silence in the monastic/contemplative tradition of both the East and the West. Silence is the necessary precondition to "welcome the word that . . . is able to save your souls" (1:21).

The theological implications of speech are central to James's exhortation. In 3:9–12, he contrasts the speech that "blesses God" with that which "curses human beings" who are made in God's image! Once again James combats the "two-minded" person, who thinks that it is possible to have a relationship with God that disregards human obligations. As in 2:14–17, James insists that religious language and practical human care must go together. The same source cannot yield two kinds of water, and a Christian should not speak with two tongues. Action should follow conviction; speech should conform to faith.

The warning is directed most of all at those who desire to be teachers in the faith community (3:1). If care is required for all speech, it is even more necessary for those who shape the minds of others according to the measure of God and not of the world.

Friendship with God or the World (3:13–4:10)

Although the paragraph division of modern translations hides what is clearer in Greek, 3:13–4:10 is a self-contained essay stating the central theological framework for understanding James as a whole.

Formally, it is a call of conversion. In 3:13–4:6, James presents an indictment. In 4:7–10, he exhorts his readers to repentance. A powerful spatial metaphor governs both parts, a contrast between what comes "from above" (true wisdom, God's gift), and that which originates "from below" (false wisdom, human arrogance). Correspondingly, the readers are told to "humble" themselves, so that God can "exalt" them (4:10). The spatial metaphor points to differing measures of reality. That "from below" James calls "the world." It treats life as though God had no claim; human success is measured by human accomplishment and acquisition. But God's measure says that everything comes as a gift from "the Father of lights" (1:17), and that arrogance is empty pretence. James, as always, has as his main target the "two-minded" person (4:8) who wants to live by both measures at once.

Within this call to conversion, James develops the theme of envy as exemplifying the measure of the world. Notice the occurrence of "jealousy" in 3:14, 16; 4:2 and climactically in 4:5. This last verse is notoriously difficult to translate, not least because we have no verse of Scripture saying what James suggests. The best solution is to render 4:5 as two rhetorical questions (a technique common in this essay): "Do you think the scripture speaks in vain? Is the spirit God has made to dwell in us for envy?" The word for "envy" here is never used of God (whereas "jealous" sometimes is), and never occurs in Greek with a positive connotation. The point clearly is that God's spirit has nothing to do with envy. Envy comes from the "wisdom from below." James associates with envy all the vices commonly attributed to it in Greek moral discourse, especially social unrest, murder, and war.

Why is envy so singled out? Because its underlying assumption is that your gain is my loss. This is the opposite of the Spirit of community, where all gain by anyone's growth and all rejoice in anyone's good fortune. Envy causes me to sorrow when another has something that I lack. And when life is measured simply in terms of what I possess—"I am what I have"—then for another to have and me to lack is intolerable. Envy drives the acquisitive instinct: "you covet" (4:2). It is a short step to conflict, war, and murder, between individuals and among nations. Like other Greek moralists, James assigns the cause of war to envy (4:1–3). It is remarkable that this passage, which alone in the New Testament analyzes the causes of human conflict, should play so little role in moral discussions of war and peace.

At the climax of the indictment (4:4), James accuses his readers of being "adulterers" because they have broken covenant both with God and with their fellow humans. The covenant is about loyalty and love. There is no connection between those attitudes and the self-seeking of envy. James also uses the language of Greek philosophy concerning "friendship." He contrasts "friendship with the world" and "friendship with God" as opposing ways of life. James is not condemning the world understood as the place of human activity or God's creation. Rather, it is a system of values that excludes consideration of God. To be "friends with the world" therefore means to live by a measure that leaves God's claim aside.

To this closed system James opposes the measure of faith: God is the source of "all good giving and every perfect gift" (1:17). God gives more grace to the humble even while resisting the arrogant (4:6). God is not envious of humans but gives to all generously and without grudging (see 1:5). Those who submit to God are therefore also lifted up by God (4:10). Their tears of repentance will rapidly turn to joy, because—a remarkable statement—when humans draw near to God, God also draws near to them (4:8).

Against Arrogance (4:11–5:6)

James now turns to three forms of arrogance, which exemplify life according to the measure of the world. The first is the practice of slandering a neighbor (4:11f). Such critical speech naturally involves both a condemnation of the other and an implied assertion of one's own superiority: "I am in a position to judge." James insists that such judgment breaks the law of love (see Lv 19:16) and reminds his readers that the lawgiver is also the judge. God alone can both save and destroy life (see 1:21).

A second form of arrogance is demonstrated by those who make great business plans without ever considering the fragile nature of their own existence (4:13–17). Once more, their speech gives them away; they assume control over the present and the future. James comments: "You are boasting in your arrogance. All such boasting is evil" (4:16). The speech of one living by God's measure is also revealing: "If the Lord wills . . ." This is more than pious talk; it refers all of life and all of life's projects to the one who gives and can alone sustain life.

Finally, with a prophetic rage like that of Amos, James attacks the insolence of the rich who withhold wages from their laborers. The security gained by such fraud is illusory; the rich fatten themselves for the day of judgment (5:5). They sin because they "know the right thing to do but do not do it" (4:17). How do they know? Because the scriptural context for the law of love in Leviticus 19:18 states plainly, "you shall not withhold overnight the wages of your day laborer" (Lv 19:13).

Patience, Plain Speech, Prayer (5:7–20)

Having called the double-minded to conversion and excoriated the arrogant, James turns to the community's inner life. Speech is again the underlying theme, this time with reference to the proper uses of speech in the church.

The attack on oppressors (5:1–6) leads naturally to the condition of those who suffer persecution from without. James recommends patience and extends the example of Job (5:11). Patience is possible for them as it is for a farmer, because the fruitful outcome of their loyalty is certain: "the coming of the Lord is at hand." In the meantime, nothing would be more natural than for the afflicted to turn on each other in resentment and hurt. James again uses Leviticus 19 when he tells them, "Do not complain about one another that you may not be judged" (see Lv 19:17f).

Christians should speak plainly. In 5:12 James repeats the commandment of Jesus (Mt 5:33–37) that speech should be unadorned and straightforward, without oaths. And in his last exhortation, James encourages the sort of mutual correction that can build up the identity of the church (5:20).

Because the church is constituted by the word of truth (1:18), it should above all express that truth in its communal life of prayer. James enumerates the sorts of prayer that are appropriate to the community's diverse circumstances (5:13f) and then elaborates the prayer with anointing for a sick member. This ritual is the basis for the sacrament of anointing for the sick and has roots in the healing ministry of Jesus (see 5:15). James's last example from Torah is the prophet Elijah, whose prayer demonstrates the power of faith for those who live by God's measure (5: 17f; cf. 1:6–8). These final exhortations, down to earth and humane, summarize beautifully the character of James, who from beginning to end finds wisdom in practical faith and active love.

FURTHER READING

Adamson, J. B. *James: The Man and His Message*. Grand Rapids: Eerdmans, 1989.

Harris, Patrick J. *James*. Sacra Pagina. Collegeville, MD: Liturgical Press, 2003.

Johnson, L. T. *The Letter of James*. Anchor Bible 37A. New York: Doubleday, 1995.

Wall, R. W. *Community of the Wise: The Letter of James*. Valley Forge, PA: Trinity Press International, 1997.

1 PETER

[see pages 1728–1735 of the New Testament]

Before Beginning . . .

First Peter bears all the marks of a real letter. It was written to Christians scattered throughout the provinces of Asia Minor. Although written in clear and even elegant Greek, and although containing an exhortation and witness (5:12) at once simple and profound, 1 Peter is given far less attention than it deserves. Partly this is because many contemporary scholars think that the letter is pseudonymous and a product of second generation rather than primitive Christianity (see, for example, introduction, NT, pp. 1728–29). There are, however, excellent reasons for considering Peter the disciple to have been the author of 1 Peter. In any case, the authority of New Testament writings does not derive from the identity of the author. Whether it was the apostle or someone writing in his name, this letter speaks powerfully to a situation of early believers and retains enduring value for readers in every age.

A Letter to the Gentile Christians

The Situation of the Readers

Since the letter is addressed to Christians spread over a large geographical area (1:1), we do not expect the detailed treatment of local problems. By reading between the lines, however, we are able to learn something about their shared characteristics. They seem to have been recently converted. Peter reminds them repeatedly of their former life of vice (1:18–20; 4:3–4), as well as their initiation into the messianic community through baptism (1:3; 1:22–2:3). They seem, furthermore, to be direct converts from paganism rather than from Judaism. They were themselves Gentiles and continued to live among the symbols and social structures of the Empire. They inevitably felt pulled between an allegiance to their new calling and an attraction to the values of the world they had left. They were, finally, converts who were experiencing suffering. On the basis of 4:12, some have considered this to be a state-sponsored persecution such as was later the lot of Christians. But Peter's positive view of the state (2:12–17) does not fit that reconstruction. It is more likely that Peter's readers were experiencing the sort of verbal abuse and social ostracism that Christians experienced from the beginning. The suffering was no less serious. Martyrdom is painful but swift. The corrosion of confidence is slower but terribly effective.

Christian Apologetic

First Peter can best be understood as a form of apologetic literature. This form of writing originated among Diaspora Jews and was taken over by Christians. Ostensibly it explains one's distinctive beliefs to the wider world in terms outsiders can understand. Indirectly, it supports community identity. First Peter has many of the characteristics of this genre. It is positive and open to the dominant culture. Christians are not to flee the world or its structures. They are to be good citizens within those social structures. And they are to be ready to demonstrate by their behavior and their speech that they pose no threat to others (3:15–16).

At the same time, Peter works to build up the identity of the community. He reminds his readers that they are called to holiness and a standard of behavior higher than that of their neighbors (2:11–12; 4:1–2). He reminds them of the fundamental transformation they had undergone in their baptism. He assures them that although they are "sojourners" in the world (2:11), they are part of the "household of God" (2:4–5; 4:17). In so doing, Peter appropriates for these new Gentile believers all the scriptural titles and symbols used of Israel, to give them a sense of continuity with God's people, even though once they were "no people." In 1 Peter we observe a thoroughly Gentile Christianity regarding itself as the "New Israel," taking up a place in the Diaspora not against the world but as a witness to the world.

The Greeting (1:1–2)

The greeting of this circular letter establishes more than the simple identification of author and addressees. No need to elaborate the simple designation, "Peter, apostle of Jesus Christ," for Peter's authority is unquestioned (see, in contrast, 2 Peter). But the "diaspora" of Asia Minor has religious as well as geographical connotations. We see here a theme found also in James and Hebrews and in the Christian literature of the second century: Christians are in exile from their true homeland in heaven so long as they are on earth. They are, in fact, "sojourners" precisely because they have been "chosen" by God and have an identity distinct from that of their neighbors. They should therefore cultivate attitudes appropriate to exiles and pilgrims (see, for example, 2:11). The greeting also reminds the readers of the rich complexity of their experience of God: The Father has chosen them; the Son saved them, by his obedient sacrifice; and the Spirit has sanctified them.

The Gift and Call of God (1:3–21)

The opening prayer (1:3–9) is based on the blessing formula of Jewish worship: God is blessed for his gifts to humans. In this case, Peter gives thanks for the new life his readers have been granted through the resurrection of Jesus. Their new life is real, yet not complete. Their inheritance is one that is kept for them in heaven (1:4f). They, of course, still remain on earth. This tension establishes them as pilgrims and sojourners. As their salvation "waits for them," so also must they "wait for it." In the meantime, they must experience the trials and sufferings inherent to the life of faith (1:6f). Peter places his readers between the "already" of God's grace and the "not yet" of salvation fully achieved (1:9), in a manner typical of New Testament writings. But what they hope for is secure, a "living hope" (1:3) because it is based not simply in human longing but in the "power of God" at work among them (1:5).

Despite the fact that his readers have converted from paganism, Peter inserts them into the story of Israel. In speaking of an "inheritance in heaven," Peter implies a contrast to the "inheritance of the land," which was the hope of Israel. Likewise, 1:10–12 develops a contrast between stages in the story. Peter asserts that the prophets of old did not speak of their own times (1:12) but spoke of the "sufferings destined for Christ and the glories to follow them" (1:11). Three aspects of this striking statement deserve notice. First, the superiority of the Christians' present experience is clearly asserted; as in Hebrews the claims of the earlier covenant are made secondary. What the Christians have received in the gospel transcends even what angels can know (1:12)! Second, Scripture is taken over completely as messianic prophecy. Everything in Scripture points to Jesus. Third, as in Luke-Acts, the pattern of the Messiah is spelled out in terms of "suffering, then glory." That his readers must follow after this same pattern becomes explicit later in the letter.

Having asserted the reality of God's gift, Peter now sketches the demands it places on those who receive it (1:13–21). They are to direct their lives by the new form of existence given to them. This means a radical obedience to the giver of the gift, an obedience spelled out in terms of holiness (1:15f). As their lives have changed, so must their behavior. They must not act as they formerly did but are to become "different." They are to shape themselves in a manner consonant with the one who called them with the gift of the "precious blood of Christ" (1:19). Peter again calls his readers "sojourners" (1:17). Jews of the Diaspora were to be different from pagans; Christians are to be "different" (holy) in the world as they wait for the fulfillment of their salvation (see 1:9). They are not defined by the norms of others (1:14, 18) but by their allegiance to God, so that "your faith and hope are in God" (1:21).

A Gospel People (1:22–2:10)

To strengthen their grasp on their special identity Peter reminds his readers of the basis of their new life in "the living and abiding word of God" (1:23). By this, Peter explicitly means the good news (1:25). This is the message of a crucified

Messiah who was raised to new life. By the obedient acceptance of that strange proclamation, they were given "new birth" (1:23). Immediately, however, Peter asserts the need for them to grow. The "spiritual milk" they now imbibe is appropriate to new converts who have just "tasted and seen that the Lord is good" (see also 1 Cor 3:1–3; Heb 6:13), but they are to mature "in Christ" by patterning their life according to a new standard of moral behavior. They must leave aside deceit in favor of truth, envy for love.

Peter is not only concerned with the transformation of individuals, but, as much as Paul, with the identity of the community also. In 2:4–10, therefore, he reminds them of their communal identity as God's house and people. This section interweaves scriptural passages and allusions. The references at the bottom of New Testament pages 1730–31 provide valuable assistance. The choice of passages is strikingly similar to that in Romans 9:25–33 . It is less likely that Peter used Romans than that both Paul and Peter used community traditions of scriptural interpretation developed from the first days of the church.

The first set of passages (2:6–8) portrays the paradox of Christian faith. The stone that God intended to be the basis for his people Israel was rejected by them; yet the rejected one became the basis of a new people, a "spiritual house" made up of living persons (2:4). The reference here is clearly to the crucified Jesus who was a scandal (a stone of stumbling) to his fellow Jews who expected a messiah with more obvious and impressive credentials than suffering for others (see 1 Cor 1:18–23).

For the Christian community, however, the *rejected* Messiah is the basis for a new life and shared identity. In the second set of texts, Peter strings together the most precious epithets applied to Israel as God's people in Torah. Now, they apply to these Gentiles, "once no people, but now God's people." In the messianic community, these aliens have a home (see also Eph 2:19–22).

Where is the place of the historical Jewish people? It must be confessed that 1 Peter simply does not take them into account. He appropriates the symbols of Torah for the exclusive use of Gentile believers. Readers today cannot expect to find in this text an answer to the many questions concerning the relations of Christians to Jews, for 1 Peter does not address them.

Life within the World's Structures (2:11–3:7)

Christians are to maintain distance from the values of this world as "aliens and sojourners" (2:11). At the same time, they must live within the social structures of the world. Peter is convinced that if they are good citizens, they will turn away from slander and persecution. The practice of "good works" is the community's basic witness (2:12).

Peter uses the traditional form of "household ethics" to sketch the Christians' social obligations. Greek philosophy had elaborated the mutual duties of people who lived in a stratified social order. Over the empire as a whole, the emperor was considered head of the household. In individual families, husbands ruled wives, parents ruled children, and masters ruled slaves. This was simply the conventional arrangement of that time. Neither Paul (see Col 3:18–4:1) nor Peter thought that the Christian message demanded the dismantling of society's structures.

In 2:13–17, Peter portrays the empire and its agents in positive terms. Submission to legitimate authority is both right and expedient, since the state punishes only the wicked: such an outlook is inconceivable if Christians were in fact being harassed by the state as such. Yet, even here, the relationship with God is primary. Social obligations, if they conflict with that relationship, must give way to it: "Be free, yet without using freedom as a pretext for evil, but as slaves of God" (2:16). Obedience to God comes before all; and before God, all are slaves.

We might expect in the next section exhortations to both masters and slaves (compare Col 3:22–4:1). Perhaps the absence of masters says something about the Christians' social status. But since Peter thinks of all Christians as slaves (2:16), this exhortation to servants becomes a general teaching to the community at large. The most striking aspect of this teaching is the invocation of Jesus as an explicit example to be imitated, for all who suffer unjustly (2:21–23). Jesus not only won salvation for others by his death on the cross. In his very manner of suffering, he provided the model for how Christians were to act.

Not only what Jesus did but also how he did it becomes a source of life to the community.

The exhortation to wives (3:1–6) is much more extensive than that to husbands (3:7). Traditional Jewish and Greek motifs, which stress the value of internal virtue over external adornment, are used to support the command to be submissive. Women are to be subordinate, we notice, not to all men, but to their husbands (3: 1,5). In return, men are to regard women as fully equal in their relationship before the Lord. Women are "joint heirs of the gift of life" (3:7).

In these instructions, we do not find a divinely inspired blueprint for the ideal social order or Christian family structure. What we find is the best available moral teaching applied to the real world of that age. Just as the social structures of the past cannot be transferred directly to the present, neither can the relationships appropriate to those structures be directly imitated. Yet for families both ancient and modern, for societies then and now, good order, mutual respect, obedience, and authority are very much required. The style of those structures, happily, is left to human creativity.

Witness in a Hostile World (3:8–4:6)

The Christians of Asia Minor were not suffering persecution, torture, and death. Their suffering was nevertheless real and painful. Social ostracism works a slow and insidious poison into a community's sense of identity. They were being "insulted" (3:9), maligned and defamed (3:16), and "vilified" (4:4). Why? Probably they were abused because they no longer followed the ways of their neighbors (4:3f). They have become different (holy), and people who insist on being different generate resentment.

Peter's response to the community's experience of suffering is remarkable. He does not advocate withdrawal from society or hostility toward outsiders. Instead, Christians are to remain in the world (see 2:13–3:7) and are to engage outsiders in dialogue. They are to be ready to "give an explanation to anyone who asks you for a reason for your hope" (3:15). The expectation that such explanation would be helpful pays a high compliment to the basic reasonableness and goodwill of outsiders. Christians are also to follow the exhortation of Jesus to return a blessing for a curse (see Mt 5:44). In order to act in this way toward outsiders, they must cultivate the same qualities of sympathy and love toward each other in the community (3:8). Within their own hearts, furthermore, they are to "sanctify Christ as Lord" (3:15), which, Peter asserts, will free them from fear of outsiders (3:14). How will this happen?

They are to remember how Jesus not only "suffered for sins once" (3:18) but also how he was raised from the dead in power. Using traditions found in apocalyptic literature (such as 1 Enoch), Peter symbolically expresses the conviction that the resurrection was not simply an event concerning the person Jesus but had cosmic extension. "In the spirit" Jesus went to the spirits in prison to preach the good news (3: 19–22). This dramatic announcement is the basis for the statement in the Apostles' Creed that says Jesus "descended into hell." It means that God's power to save reaches everywhere, even to the farthest reaches of human sin and alienation.

Peter's immediate point, however, is that by baptism (3:21), the Christians of Asia Minor have been given the same power. They need not fear human slander, for the power of God is at work among them. They are like those to whom Jesus preached after his resurrection, "though condemned in the flesh in human estimation . . . alive in the spirit in the estimation of God" (4:6).

Community Attitudes (4:7–5:14)

First Peter does not portray the Christians' moral situation in stark black-and-white tones, but like most New Testament writings it has a keen sense that the time for decision is now. The final exhortations are colored by the conviction that "the end of all things is at hand" (4:7). The time of judgment is soon (4:17). Therefore, Christian life means "resisting the devil" who through affliction such as they are experiencing "seeks to devour them" (5:8f). Such circumstances call for a "serious, sober" attitude and one that is "vigilant" (4:7; 5:8). Those who experience affliction are to regard their sufferings as a share in Christ's own (5:13f), knowing that they will share in his glory (4:13; 5:10). Within the community, attitudes of mutual service are to prevail (4:9–11), demonstrated by good order and humility (5: 1–16).

When exhorting the community's leaders, Peter forbids lording it over the flock. Leaders are rather to provide a positive example (5:3). The image of the shepherd recalls the portrayal of Jesus as the "shepherd and guardian of your souls" (in 2:25). The connection is made explicit in 5:4: with characteristic optimism, Peter promises such good leaders that, "when the chief Shepherd is revealed, you will receive the unfading crown of glory."

The New Testament contains no writing more positive in its evaluation of the world yet more compelling in its call to holiness than 1 Peter. As Martin Luther correctly noted, it is one of the New Testament compositions that truly "show thee Christ."

FURTHER READING

Achtemeier, P. J. *1 Peter: A Commentary on First Peter.* Edited by E. J. Epp. Hermeneia. Minneapolis: Fortress Press, 1996.

Elliot, John H. *1 Peter.* The Anchor Bible 37B. New York: Doubleday, 2000.

Kelly, J. N. D. *A Commentary on the Epistles of Peter and Jude.* Harper New Testament Commentary. New York: Harper & Row, 1969.

Senior, Donald. *1 Peter.* Sacra Pagina. Collegeville, MD: Liturgical Press, 2003.

2 PETER

[see pages 1735–1740 of the New Testament]

Before Beginning . . .

An appreciative understanding of 2 Peter demands more than the normal effort. Hard work is necessary to uncover the situation addressed by the letter. Perhaps even more difficult is the hurdle presented by the letter's sustained argumentative tone. Such effort finds its rewards, however, in the surprising discovery that a writing which at first appears as the New Testament's most irrelevant can emerge as having perennial pertinence.

A Defense of God's Judgment

The circumstances of 2 Peter's composition are obscure (see introduction, NT, pp. 1735–36). The same author did not write both 1 and 2 Peter. The style, outlook, and concerns of the two letters are too disparate for a common authorship. The main thing they have in common is the mention of Noah and the flood. Second Peter has far more in common with Jude (with which it shares the polemical material of chapter 2) than with 1 Peter. In all likelihood, 2 Peter is a pseudonymous composition. Despite the self-presentation of chapter 1, it is not "Symeon Peter" who writes, but someone who invokes his authority as a support for shared traditions being threatened by deviance. This sermon in the form of a letter may have been addressed to a single church, but it may also have been intended for a larger audience, all "those who have received a faith of equal value to ours" (1:1). It is thus considered a "general" epistle. The title "Catholic Epistles" was applied to 1 and 2 Peter, James, 1, 2, 3 John, and Jude because they were written for a broader audience than a local church (in Greek, "catholic" = "pertaining to the whole"). Some readers also consider 2 Peter "catholic" in another sense: its concern for tradition anticipates the emergence of the Catholic Church in the second century.

At first reading, 2 Peter seems to be a loose collection of observations within which talk about Jesus' second coming plays a particularly significant part. Some scholars have therefore thought that the "delay of the *Parousia*" was the crisis that stimulated composition. Closer analysis, however, shows that "Peter" and his opponents are debating a deeper and more perennial problem: does God judge the world? Underlying that issue, in turn, is a still more fundamental one concerning the reality of God and God's relationship to the world. The debate, in short, is between living faith and practical atheism. It is a debate still in progress. The contribution of 2 Peter is worth hearing.

Far from a random collection of statements, the letter as a whole presents a coherent argument. Chapter 1 establishes the authority of the writer and of the Scripture that will be used as the source of proof. Chapter 2 attacks the opponents' "destructive teachings" on the basis of Scripture. Chapter 3 presents the proper understanding of the tradition concerning God's judgment.

The Common Tradition (1:1–21)

The first section of the letter establishes the authority of the writer and of the shared tradition (1:1) that the author represents. Extraordinary emphasis is put on the person of Peter and on the fact that he will soon die (1:13f). These touches recall the literary genre popular in early Christianity called the "Farewell Discourse." In this sort of composition, a figure from the past, speaking shortly before his death, predicts catastrophes to come and enjoins fidelity on his followers. We notice in this case, however, an equally strong emphasis on *memory* (1:9,12,13,15). The opponents "forget" the proper knowledge, and Peter seeks to "remind" his readers of it. The emphasis on memory makes the letter resemble as well the form of moral exhortation called *parenesis*. The connection to parenesis is most obvious in 2 Peter 1:5–8. Parenesis spelled out moral obligations in terms of maxims. Here, Peter lists the sort of qualities that should follow upon the readers' faith. More important even than the specific items is the overall point made by the list: more than knowledge or faith is involved in being Christian. A whole way of life is demanded. Those who have "forgotten" this lead lives that are "idle and unfruitful" (1:8f). There is a sharp polemical edge to this comment. In chapter 2, Peter will show that the opponents' "destructive heresies" bring about destructive behavior, which in turn brings down God's judgment.

A complex statement provides the basis for Peter's overall argument and a transition to his attack on opponents (1:16–21). In a passage that clearly corresponds to the Synoptic Gospels' story of Jesus' transfiguration (see Mt 17:1–8), he asserts the reality of the Christian experience of God. The tradition out of which Peter writes is not speculation ("cleverly devised myths," 1:16), but is a power he and others experience personally; "we" saw and heard on the mountain (1:16–18)! The community's tradition is based not in fancy but in fact. The experience, moreover, was of "the power and coming" of the Lord Jesus Christ. As we will learn, the promise concerning Jesus' return is the bone of contention in chapter 3. Peter claims that the expectation of his return is based on the reality of his already having come.

The disciples' experience of Jesus also grounds the "prophetic message" about Jesus' return for judgment. Peter places this prophecy of Jesus (see Mt 24:29–31) among the prophecies of Scripture. As with scriptural prophecies, interpretation is not to be personal or idiosyncratic but a decision of the community that is guided by the same Spirit that gave utterance in the first place. With this alignment, Peter has provided the basis for arguing the whole issue of God's judgment (and therefore of Jesus' return) on the truthfulness of Scripture as properly interpreted by the tradition.

Condemnation of False Teachers (2:1–22)

The claim to a true "prophetic message" in 1:19 provides a transition to the attack on "false teachers" (2:1) who are placed in the line of "false prophets." As we will learn more fully in chapter 3, the opponents are denying the power of God to judge, that is, to intervene in the affairs of the world (3:4). By denying God's ability to judge, they bring judgment on themselves! Their "destructive heresies" bring on them "destruction" (2:1). But their teaching has proven successful, convincing many (2:2); Peter's response must therefore be vigorous and pointed.

We saw in 1:5–8 that Peter was concerned with the moral consequences of faith. The ancient world knew what our world sometimes ignores, that people act on their ideas, and that bad ideas can lead to bad behavior. A real misconception of what life is about leads to a distorted existence. Showing how certain teachings lead to immoral behavior is a way of proving that the ideas are false. Peter therefore pays particular attention to the *way of life* generated by these doctrines. He attacks the "licentious ways" of the opponents (2:2), their "greed" and "lies" (2:3). They are people of "depraved desires" (2:10), are "irrational" (2:12) and "adulterous" (2:14). The catalogue of vices reaches a rhetorical climax in 2:17f, then takes a sharp turn: "They promise them freedom, though they themselves are slaves of corruption, for a person is a slave of whatever overcomes him" (2:19).

What sort of "freedom" did the opponents promise? Apparently, it was freedom from the fear of punishment. If God does not intervene in human affairs to punish the wicked and reward the good, then (they said) one can live immorally, looking out only for oneself, indulging in antisocial behavior.

Peter's first rebuttal is based on the nature of vice. They are slaves of their dominating appetite, which controls their behavior. They are not sophisticated or liberated. They are as compulsive as dogs returning to their vomit, these Christians who once knew righteousness but have now turned back to a novel version of an old atheism: "Fools say in their hearts, 'There is no God' " (Ps 14:1).

The second part of Peter's rebuttal is based on the conviction that the Bible stories relate the facts of history. When Scripture says therefore that God *did* punish and reward, that is proof of God's ability still to do so. Peter relates the cases of the wicked angels (2:4), of Noah (2:5), of Sodom and Gomorrah (2:6–10) and of Balaam (2:15f) as evidence of God's intervention. In contrast to the letter of Jude (with which much of this material is shared), Peter not only emphasizes punishment; God also rewards those who are faithful. Here, the issue is whether God acts in human history at all. Peter's recitation from Scripture asserts that in fact God does.

The Coming of the Lord (3:1–18)

The specific nature of the debate emerges for the first time in this final section. Here, not simply a question of fact but a matter of principle is at stake.

The question of fact is not really in dispute. Jesus clearly had not yet returned to judge the world as all Christians had been expecting. But quite different conclusions were being drawn from that undisputed fact. The "scoffers" challenge the very *promise* of his coming (3:4).

They base their denial on the immutability of the world "from the beginning." They hold the position of ancient skeptics such as the Epicureans and (among the Jews) Sadducees, who denied divine providence. If there was a god, he did not meddle with the world, which was, therefore, a closed system of natural forces and human desires. God was not a factor to be considered, never had been, never would be. The failure of Jesus to return, therefore, was only one more piece of evidence proving that all such prophecies were empty.

Theirs is a real threat to the whole structure of faith. They challenge not only the reality of the Parousia but the very reality of a living God! Is God, then, merely a figment of the imagination, a projection of human longing, a societal superego? The whole concept of revelation is obviously challenged as well. There can be no real "promise" if there is no living God to speak, or to act.

In this argument, both sides base their position on a claim of *experience,* which then interprets reality as a whole. The skeptics say that experience shows no evidence for God's activity: "nothing has changed." Peter argues that Scripture (which is after all the record of human history) proves that God *does* intervene (see all of chapter 2). God created by a word and can destroy by a word (3:5f). Furthermore—and this is the significance of 1:16–19—Peter and his companions themselves *experienced* such an intervention in the transfiguration of Jesus! Thus, their tradition is based on the prophets, on the Lord Jesus, and on the apostles (3:2).

If God does intervene, how is his apparent absence to be interpreted? Peter invokes the arguments used by other defenders of divine providence. God's time cannot be measured by human time: there is an infinite distance between God and humans (3:7). God's apparent delay is to bring people to repentance (3:8f).

Ultimately, those whose experience is different are not likely to be convinced. Peter appeals not to the opponents but to those attracted to their position. He reasserts the conviction that Jesus will come "like a thief in the night" (see Mt 24: 43; 1 Thes 5:2; Rv 3:3), and that his coming will inaugurate "new heavens and a new earth in which righteousness dwells" (3:13; see Rv 21: 1). His concern throughout this letter, however, has been most of all with the behavior of his readers, and he reasserts "what sort of persons they are to be" during this time of waiting (3:11). After all debate is over, only the truth of human existence validates doctrine.

The letter concludes with a reference to Paul's letters that the opponents are distorting (3:15f). The fact that the author refers to "all" of Paul's letters, that he makes them equivalent to "Scripture," and that there is already a history of interpreting (or misinterpreting) them, are strong indications that this "Peter" is a writer of the second generation who defends a tradition common to the historical Peter and Paul against the threat of doctrinal and behavioral deviance.

FURTHER READING

Bauckham, R. J. *Jude; 2 Peter.* Word Biblical Commentary. Waco, TX: Word, 1983.

Harrington, Daniel, S.J. *Jude and 2 Peter.* Sacra Pagina. Collegeville: Liturgical Press, 2003.

Neyrey, J. H. *2 Peter; Jude* Anchor Bible 37C. New York: Doubleday, 1993.

1 JOHN

[see pages 1740–46 of the New Testament]

Before Beginning . . .

Exhortation to a Divided Church

The New Testament contains three letters attributed to John. How these letters connect to the Gospel according to John and the book of Revelation is not easy to determine. Scholars agree that all came from a community of "Johannine Christianity" in the late first century, but neither their precise authorship nor sequence has been established. We are not even sure of the location of this "Johannine Christianity," although Asia Minor seems most likely. In such a state of ignorance, hypotheses abound. The introductions to each of these letters in the NAB give some sense of the options (cf. New Testament pp. 1740–41, 1746, 1747–48).

What we can learn of "Johannine Christianity" derives from the writings themselves. Apart from the connection to John, what common characteristics marked this version of messianism? First, the figure of Jesus played a central role in the identity of the community. Second, these churches had experienced tragic division. In the Gospel and Revelation, there is conflict between these messianists and the Jews. In the letters and Revelation, there is also evidence of divisions within the churches. Third, this experience of division sharpened the community's symbols into a stark dualism: light and darkness, life and death, truth and falsehood, flesh and spirit.

The Three Letters

In the three letters, we see conflict happening within the churches. Disputes involve the proper understanding of Jesus. The letters provide a window on this early Christian conflict, revealing at once its multiple dimensions and its seriousness. It is impossible to say at this distance exactly how the letters relate to each other or to the situation. Second and 3 John are real letters and claim to come from "the Elder." First John is anonymous and not really a letter so much as a sermonic exhortation.

Some think that the three letters show three stages of the community's conflict. This hypothesis is possible, but a better one is that the three documents were written at the same time by the same author and sent to a single church aligned with "The Elder." Each letter fulfills a specific function: 3 John recommends the mailman, Demetrius, to the church leader, Gaius. Second John is a cover letter to be read publicly to the church. First John is the centerpiece, an exhortation to a community divided by conflict. The Study Guides for 2 and 3 John will describe how they fulfill their functions. Let us concentrate first on 1 John.

The Character of 1 John

Because it is not so closely tied to the particulars of a specific community's life, 1 John lends itself more readily to every time and place. For a document generated by bitter conflict, it is amazingly positive and loving in tone. Christians through the ages have rightly considered it one of the great spiritual witnesses of the New Testament.

The structure of this writing is not obvious. Certainly it is not a genuine letter. Even as a sermon, it tends to wander a bit, repeating the same points. First John at times has the appearance of an argument but none of the substance. Readers are sometimes shocked at the lack of consistency. What is stated positively is sometimes denied only a short time later. The reason for this alternation of ideal and real lies in the circumstances being addressed.

The Johannine Christians saw their lives defined by a choice. Their first and basic choice was to follow Jesus. They considered that truth, life, and light characterized them; while falsehood, darkness, and death characterized those who did not follow Jesus. The Christians were the community of true prophecy. But now, the community finds itself divided into two hostile camps, and the cause of division is precisely what should have been the centerpiece of this unity: the proper understanding of the nature and role of Jesus.

First John's apparent indecisiveness reflects the chastened perspective caused by the trauma of division. The symbols of unity and perfection need reshaping. The author urges his readers away from a smug sense of their own perfection, to an awareness of their need to repent. Not only "those who went out from us" have sinned; all have sinned and need the expiation offered by Jesus.

Opening Exhortation (1:1–2:17)

First John opens with a poetic prologue (1:1–4) that resembles the prologue to the Fourth Gospel (Jn 1:1–8) in its deliberate allusion to Genesis 1:1 ("in the beginning"), and its emphasis on the "word of life." In the epistle's prologue, however, the stress is placed on the community's *experience* of the Word in Jesus. The writer testifies to what he has "seen and heard and touched" (compare Jn 19:35). The experience, furthermore, is one shared by the readers. The language of fellowship dominates 1:3f. The believers have fellowship with God the Father through Jesus. They are also, by that same agency, to have fellowship among themselves. The textual variant in 1:4 illustrates the dense interweaving. Manuscripts differ on reading "your" joy, or "our" joy. For this writer, both meanings coincide.

The section closes with another deliberately rhetorical statement of purpose: "I am writing to you because" (2:12–14). Different groups in the community are addressed, but the message is basically one message and is more clearly spelled out by 2:15–17: the church is to live by the "will of God" and not by the standards of the "world." John's talk about "love of the world" here is very close to that in the letter of James about the "lover of the world" (Jas 4:4) and means much the same thing. The writer does not forbid love for humanity; he denounces the "worldliness" that denies God's claim on his creation and bases existence on "sensual lust, enticement for the eyes, and a pretentious life" (2:16).

Within the framework provided by the prologue and the statement of purpose, the rest of the opening section of this sermon serves to remind the readers of the need to live by the "message we have heard from him and proclaim to you" (1:5).

The community has, to be sure, already heard that "God is light, and in him there is no darkness at all" (1:5). But now, because of the division in this community, a new sense of reality is required. Behavior must match their ideals. They can no longer simply assume that "we are the light" without hesitation. In fact, sin does occur among them, and they need to repent of it. They cannot claim to be "in the light" while their behavior shows that they "walk in darkness" (1:6). That is a lie. Likewise, they cannot claim to "know God" while not keeping God's commandments (2:4).

With a different vocabulary than James, but with a quite similar concern, John seeks to make his readers' actions conform to their convictions. And the great commandment of God that is to govern the life of the community is also—as in James—the law of love for neighbor, the test whether one is "in the light" or "in the darkness." For 1 John, it is not simply doctrinal correctness that spells true fellowship in the community, but ethical consistency.

First John places special emphasis on the role of Jesus as expiation for sin (1:7; 2:2) and advocate for believers (2:1). The community's failure, demonstrated in its division into hostile parties, makes the need for intercession clear. They cannot do it alone. It also makes clear that "love" is not simply a state of mind, but something to be performed. In an atmosphere of hurt and separation, such performance is difficult.

The Divided Community (2:18–3:24)

The severity of the community's crisis is indicated by the fact that the writer thinks the end of all things is at hand. The author calls those who have left the community "antichrists." In apocalyptic literature, the presence of antichrist is a sign of the final tribulation (see Mt 24:24). The theme of Jesus' return occurs again in 2:28 and 3:2. Typical of apocalyptic also is the exhortation to stand fast ("remain in him," 2:24,27,28; 3:6) and to avoid being deceived (2:26).

The threat to the community is the greater because former members make it: "they went out from us." It is impossible for this writer to acknowledge fully that they had ever been of one spirit with the community: "they were not really of our number." What proof does he have? "If they had been, they would have remained" (2:19). This is desperate logic. It indicates the shock given to a church devoted to unity and opposition to a world "out there" when it experiences conflict and division from within. The very identity of the community is called into question.

We cannot be sure exactly what the bone of contention was between those who left and those who stayed, only that it involved the proper understanding of Jesus. The author uses the language of "denial" and "confession" (2:22f), and it seems clear that a formal *doctrinal* issue is at stake (see also 2 Jn 7). The briefest description of the deviance is that they deny "Jesus is the Christ." This obviously qualifies them to be "anti-Christs" in the narrow sense, but it is hard to imagine how such people could ever have been part of the messianic community. Such a denial is more appropriate to nonbelieving Jews. To complicate matters, the author adds other features in 3:23; 4:2f; 5:1, 10. These make it appear that outsiders deny either the full divine origin of Jesus (that he is "God's son") or his full humanity (that he "came in the flesh"). In short, John is convinced his party has the full understanding of Jesus and his opponents do not; beyond that general statement we cannot advance.

Characteristic of this writing, however, is its ability to combine a claim to possession of "the truth" (2:21), with a demand at the same time for transformation. The community is not yet perfect. They are indeed, to use one of their favorite expressions, "children of God" (see Jn 1:12), but they still need to mature. Only when he appears will they become "like him, for we shall see him as he is" (3:2). Having the truth means living the truth, which demands strict ethical norms. In 3:4–18, John develops the strongest possible contrast between the way of the world governed by the devil (4:8; 5:19) and the way revealed by God through the Messiah Jesus. The way of the world is driven by the envy that leads to murder (the example of Cain, 3:12; compare Jas 4:1–5). The way Jesus reveals is exactly the opposite. It does not take away life but gives it, and in the giving of life reveals love: "the way we came to know love was that he laid down his life for us." The moral correlative follows at once: "so we ought to lay down our lives for our brothers" (3:16). The New Testament contains no more direct connection between the work of the Messiah and the pattern of Christian existence. And lest anyone think the giving of life can be accomplished in attitude only or once for all, John spells it out in terms of the sharing of material possessions with the needy, and concludes in a manner familiar to us from Paul and James, "let us love not in word or speech but in deed and truth."

Finally, the claim to be in possession of the truth must be qualified by the deeper statement of humility in 3:19–21. It is because they are in the hands of the one who is "greater than our hearts and knows everything" that they know they belong to the truth. It is not their accomplishment but his gift; their adequate response is to act as he did, in love (3:23f).

The Remnant Community (4:1–5:21)

Because the community is divided, shared symbols are now being interpreted by opposing parties to the dispute. More careful judgment is therefore required. John reminds his readers of the need to "test the spirits to see whether they belong to God" (4:1). As earlier he had spoken of the opponents as "antichrists," now he applies to them the epithet "false prophets," another favorite designation in apocalyptic (see Mt 24:11). In this case, the proper confession of Jesus is the criterion for true and false prophecy, certifying whether the speaker belongs to God or to "the world" (4:2–4; 13–16).

Within the remnant community itself, discernment is also required. How can the church be sure that it lives by the Spirit of God? That it has the right confession of Jesus is taken for granted. But John adds the ethical dimension; keeping the commandment of God shows their love for God (5:2f). What is that commandment? It is that they are to love each other. John indissolubly joins love of God and neighbor; doing one is doing the other: "If anyone says 'I love God' but hates his brother, he is a liar" (4:20). As earlier in 3:15f, John grounds such love in the way God has revealed himself to be for humans in the sending of his son and Jesus' expiatory death: "In this is love: not that we have loved God, but that he loved us and sent his Son as expiation for our sins" (4:10). Since humans do not have direct access to God (4:12; see Jn 1:18), their relationship to God is mediated by their relationships with each other (4:12, 20f).

The last section of this sermon is filled with a mixture of confidence and caution. The community living by God's love and faith is sure of victory "over the world" (5:4f), even though "the whole world is under the power of the evil one" (5:19). This is because the community's testimony is not isolated. It is supported by the testimony of Father, Son, and Spirit, each working in and through the church (5:6–9). The community is confident of its gift of "eternal life" (2:25; 5: 11,13). But the victory over sin and death (see 3: 7–14) is not yet complete. Idolatry is a temptation that needs to be avoided (5:21); perfect love has not yet driven out fear (4:18); mutual correction is required (5:16f). For this divided community, nothing can any longer be taken for granted; division has given new urgency to discernment (5:20).

FURTHER READING

Brown, R. E. *The Epistles of John*. Anchor Bible 30. Garden City, NY: Doubleday, 1982.

Painter, John. *1, 2, and 3 John*. Sacra Pagina. Collegeville: Liturgical Press, 2002.

Rensberger, David. *1 John; 2 John; 3 John*. Abingdon New Testament Commentaries; Nashville: Abingdon, 1997.

Sloyan, G. S. *Walking in the Truth: Preservers and Deserters—The First, Second, and Third Letters of John*. Valley Forge, PA: Trinity Press International, 1995.

2 JOHN

[see pages 1746–1747 of the New Testament]

Before Beginning . . .

A Cover Letter to the Church

Unless 2 and 3 John are connected to the same moment of crisis that generated 1 John, it is hard to explain their preservation by a local church, their exchange between churches, and their eventual inclusion in the New Testament canon. In the Reading Guide to 1 John (RG 513), the suggestion is made that all three letters were sent in a single packet by the emissary Demetrius to the local leader Gaius (see 3 Jn) who was still loyal to "the Elder" in the dispute dividing Johannine Christianity into hostile factions.

Whereas 1 John lacks all epistolary character and appears as a sermon to be delivered aloud to an assembly (or even a number of assemblies), 2 John bears the marks of a genuine letter. It has the formal elements of greeting (1–3), body (4–12) and farewell (13). It mentions the desire of the writer to visit the addressees (12). Unlike 3 John, however, which is addressed to an individual, 2 John is written to the "chosen Lady" and her children (1). The designation is almost certainly an honorary title for the church itself. The argument that it refers to a specific woman leader is doubtful, if the rest of the reconstruction here being suggested makes sense. The "children," of course, are the ones really being addressed; the second-person verbs are predominantly in the plural.

The symbols of Johannine Christianity are very much in evidence. Notice the emphasis on "truth" (1–3) and on "walking in the truth" (4); on "keeping the commandment," which is not new but from the beginning (5); on love for one another as the fulfillment of that commandment (6); on the creation of mutual joy as the mark of fellowship (12). Surely, such a cluster of distinctive themes makes best sense when read together with 1 John.

What distinguishes 2 John is its function. In 3 John 9, the Elder says that he "is writing" (or "wrote") something to the church. In all likelihood, this refers to 1 John, the exhortation to a remnant community. Second John, then, is undoubtedly a letter of introduction to the community as such, to be read before the sermon is delivered, to identify its author, to emphasize its main teaching, and to suggest some practical actions to be taken by the community. These may or may not be fully in accord with the spirit of 1 John, but they are certainly recognizable as a response to the crisis signaled by 3 John.

Strategies for Survival

Again we meet the split between those who "walk in truth" and the "many deceivers who have gone out into the world" (7). As in 1 John, these are designated antichrists because they "do not acknowledge Jesus Christ as coming in the flesh." In the Reading Guide to 1 John, we suggest how difficult it is to determine precisely what this denial implies. For the Elder, however, the opponents appear as "progressives" who have gone too far in their interpretation and no longer "remain in the teaching of the Christ" (or "about" the Christ). The Elder's community is therefore portrayed as defending the traditional understanding of Jesus. The importance of right doctrine is underscored by the equation: having Christ is having God (see 1 Jn 4:3). For Johannine Christianity, the unique mediation of salvation by Jesus is axiomatic. He alone is the "way and the truth and the life" (Jn 14:6). The lesson is clear: misconstruing the mediator means missing the good news entirely. If the Elder's readers do not hold to the proper understanding, they will "lose what they worked for."

The community crisis is so severe that the Elder calls for the extraordinary practice of excommunication. They are neither to offer heretics hospitality nor even to greet them as brothers (10). Notice the connection, everywhere assumed in the New Testament, between message and messenger. Physical fellowship implies spiritual unanimity. Thus, "whoever greets him shares in his evil works" (11). Only those who deliver the proper doctrine (10) are to be welcomed. Here the Elder advocates the same practice of shunning and exclusion of which he accuses Diotrephes in 3 John. The battle is a bitter one.

It is difficult to know what positive instruction one should draw from these ancient fragments of hostile conflicts. Perhaps it is important for the church to remember in every age that it has never been easy to establish or to secure its identity; deviance and dispute are part of community life. Perhaps also, however, it is important for the church in every age to reflect whether proper doctrine is more important than the fellowship of love. Even in an age of ecumenism that issue remains unresolved.

FURTHER READING

See the bibliography for 1 John, and:

Brown, R. E. *The Community of the Beloved Disciple.* New York: Paulist Press, 1979.

Rensberger, D. *1 John; 2 John; 3 John.* Nashville: Abingdon, 1997.

3 JOHN

[see pages 1747–1749 of the New Testament]

Before Beginning . . .

A Letter of Recommendation

The New Testament contains two letters written explicitly to individuals—Paul's letter to Philemon, and the Elder's letter to Gaius, which we know as 3 John. Both Paul and John take up matters of community concern, while having the same specific function, that of recommending the bearer of the letter to the addressee. In the case of Philemon, Paul seeks to return a slave who had run away and to assure his welcome. In the case of 3 John, the Elder recommends to the local church leader his emissary Demetrius. He has a good reputation from all, and "we give our testimonial as well, and you know our testimony is true" (12).

The ancient world had conventions for these letters. They were widely used in early Christianity, as we learn elsewhere in Paul's correspondence (see 2 Cor 3:1; Rom 16). It was natural for a missionary movement to certify its agents (apostles) with such letters, in order to ensure them a safe reception and the hospitality due such "co-workers in the truth" (8). Receiving such messengers, as we see also in 2 John, meant accepting their message as well, an understanding widespread in Judaism and reflected as well in the sayings of Jesus: "Whoever listens to you listens to me. Whoever rejects you rejects me. And whoever rejects me rejects the one who sent me" (Lk 10:16). This principle became problematic when the movement itself divided into hostile parties. Paul complained of the Corinthians' preference for apostles other than himself (2 Cor 10:12; 11:4). 3 John points us directly to such a situation.

Third John is so tied to particular practical problems and so devoid of any real theology that it is doubtful that either it or 2 John would have been preserved or made part of the canon were it not associated with a writing that did transcend those circumstances by its religious message. This Reading Guide has proposed that the three letters of John were all part of the same packet delivered to Gaius from the Elder through Demetrius, and that the two smaller letters owe their preservation to the theological weightiness of 1 John.

But if its survival was accidental and its theology minimal, 3 John is all the more precious to readers today. It provides the key to the historical circumstances presupposed by 2 and 1 John. Without it, their religious emphasis would be less intelligible. And without 3 John, an appreciation for the travails of early Christianity would be appreciably diminished.

The Politics of Ecclesial Power

Third John reveals clearly that the struggle for the soul of Johannine Christianity involved structure as much as symbol, power as much as piety. Indeed, the two levels of conflict were intimately connected. On one side we see the Elder writing to his loyal colleague Gaius. On the other side is Diotrephes, who "loves to dominate." Diotrephes not only asserts authority over Gaius at the local level, but he also refuses to acknowledge the authority of the Elder over the regional church. The author says that when he comes, he will "draw attention to what he is doing" (10), but this is a small threat to a rebellious local chieftain. The position of the Elder is threatened. He needs the personal loyalty of Gaius, and his financial assistance as well.

We are thereby brought to the political maneuvering at the heart of this battle. Diotrephes is not content to "spread evil nonsense" about the Elder. He takes positive action to suppress the Elder's authority. He refuses himself to receive the Elder's delegates, and, even more, Diotrephes expels from the church those who want to receive them (10). We can understand why the Elder appreciates Gaius's reception of Demetrius, and we can grasp the significance of verses 5–8. The Elder needs to provide an alternative source of hospitality and missionary outfitting, since Diotrephes has taken up a position among those who "went out from us" (1 Jn 2:19) and no longer supports the Elder's teaching.

Gaius is being asked to receive Demetrius (and his companions) as well as equip them for their next stage of travel. Perhaps by implication the Elder's future emissaries are also included in the request. Since the Johannine missionaries accept nothing from the "pagans" ("the world"), the need for a network of hospitality and financial support is obvious (7). As in 2 John, financial sharing is tantamount to spiritual fellowship. Helping such missionaries is being "co-workers in the truth" (8). It is clear as well that both parties to the dispute are using the same tactics. Here, Diotrephes is the one shunning and excommunicating. But in 2 John we find the Elder advocating the same actions among his followers.

The internecine struggles of early Christianity are not terribly edifying, but they are instructive. Christians who long for a golden age of harmony should be reminded that there never was one. Among history's benefits is liberation from myth. And edifying or not, these letters testify to another truth. The struggle for identity is never simply a matter of ideas or even symbols. It involves inevitably the messy realities of money and political power.

FURTHER READING

See the bibliographies for 1 and 2 John, and:

Malherbe, A. J. "Hospitality and Inhospitality in the Church." *Social Aspects of Early Christianity.* 2nd ed., 92–112. Philadelphia: Fortress Press, 1983.

Smalley, S. S. *1, 2, 3 John.* Word Biblical Commentary; Waco: Word, 1984.

JUDE

[see pages 1749–1751 of the New Testament]

Before Beginning . . .

The Obscurity of Jude

Although Jude is among the shortest writings in the New Testament, it bristles with difficulties. Some of these have to do with placing the composition in the historical development of early Christianity. Others involve grasping its language, which has a number of obscure allusions. The two sorts of problems are related. Our ignorance of the author and his circumstances prevents us from having a secure context for reading the letter. But because Jude so obviously was responding to some kind of specific crisis, every attempt must be made to construct such a context if the letter is to yield any sense at all.

The introduction in the NAB (New Testament, p. 1749) states the majority scholarly opinion on most of the questions concerning authorship and occasion. Jude is considered a general epistle of relatively late date. It is an attack on false teachers, probably representing some form of Gnosticism (an early deviant form of Christianity stressing "self-fulfillment"). Another reading of the evidence suggests that Jude could have been written at virtually any period and was concerned less with false teaching than with bad behavior. This minority view will be developed in the paragraphs to follow. The main point, of course, is to make as good sense as possible out of the letter.

Literary Connections

Far more puzzling than the identity of Jude is the placement of his letter among other early Christian literature. The author mentions an earlier draft he had begun, when the crisis among his readers demanded his turning attention to the polemic now being read by them (3). What was that earlier version? A not entirely unrelated issue is the relation of Jude to 2 Peter. Everyone recognizes that the material in 2 Peter 2 is similar to that in Jude 5–13. Less clear is whether one author depended on the other, or both relied on a shared earlier tradition. Neither should the resemblance be overstated. Jude is not simply a source for 2 Peter. Each sharpens the material to a different polemical point.

Further literary puzzles are provided by Jude's literary allusions. He cites examples of sinners being punished. Some are readily apparent from the Bible, although a few (like Balaam) may derive as well from Jewish biblical interpretation. Jude also cites the apocryphal writing known as 1 Enoch as though it were Scripture (14). And his version of the dispute between Michael and Satan over the body of Moses appears to derive from another apocryphal writing, The Assumption of Moses (9). His reference to the "words spoken by the apostles" (17) is no clearer, since it is more an amalgam of early Christian statements on the end-time (cf., for example, Mk 13:22; 1 Tim 4:1–3) than a specific citation.

That an author could assume familiarity with such sources among his readers seems to presuppose either a Jewish-Christian readership, or a Gentile one familiar with Jewish apocrypha. What the ancient readers presumably understood, we do not, and the lack of literary context continues to make this letter obscure to present-day readers.

Historical Setting

Writings like 2 Peter and Jude remind us how little we know about early Christianity apart from the chronology provided by Acts and Paul's letters. We cannot fit them into any development we know about and must rely on guesswork. Every hypothesis, furthermore, is based solely on the text itself. Precision concerning what the text does and does not say is obviously critical to the value of any reconstruction.

Jude clearly takes a polemical stand against opponents and exhorts its readers to remain steadfast. Contrary to the usual opinion, however, the text contains no clear indication that Jude was opposing "false teachers" or that they were purveying any "heresy." Their "scorning of Lordship" (4,8) seems to have been practical rather than theoretical. Jude attacks immoral behavior rather than false teaching. So thorough is his disparagement, indeed, that it is hard to know even what they were doing. He specifically accuses them of disrupting the community love feasts. The term is usually taken to mean eucharistic meals. They are also accused of carousing and of looking after only themselves (literally: "shepherding themselves," (12). He also calls their behavior "divisive" (19). Otherwise, Jude uses all the standardized charges common to the polemic of the ancient world: they are sexually immoral (7), greedy (11,16), slanderous (15), and living for their own desires (16). In short, they "live on the natural plane, devoid of the Spirit" (19). They "pervert the grace of our God into licentiousness" (4).

Living by God's Grace

Letters of Paul such as 1 Corinthians attest how difficult it was for the early Christians to translate the gift of God (grace) into consistent patterns of moral behavior. Legitimate disagreement could exist on matters of diet, work, use of possessions, and the like. It was not immediately obvious in all cases what "life in the Spirit" meant behaviorally. In the case of Jude, however, it appears that disagreement has overstepped the boundary into true moral deviance; hence the outrage of the author. The opponents are "perverting the gift."

Jude's first line of defense is an attack on the immoral people. He tries to demonstrate from Scripture how there have always been such troublemakers, and they have always been punished. These will be punished as well. In contrast to 2 Peter 2, in which the emphasis is on the power of God to judge the righteous and unrighteous, in Jude the stress is entirely on the punishment of the rebellious.

The polemic is not random but carefully argued, with some rhetorical polish. Notice the repetition of "these people" in verses 8, 10, 12, 16, and 19, which brings the examples of old to bear on the present circumstances. Jude also plays on the Greek words for "keep" in verses 1, 6, 13, 21, and 24. His opponents fail to "keep their place," but Jude's readers are to "keep themselves in the love of God" who is, in turn, able to "keep them from stumbling."

Jude's second line of defense is to edify ("build up") his readers in their "most holy faith" (20). He reminds them that God dealt with troubles like these from of old, and in fact the apostles of Jesus had foretold the emergence of such rebellious "scoffers" (17f). He reassures them that they are being "kept safe for Jesus Christ" despite this turmoil (1). Jude does not suggest that it is the believers' role to punish the reprobate. He exhorts them to avoid such immoral behavior (23) and to build up their own faith. If the opponents are "devoid of spirit," the believers are to "pray in the holy Spirit" (20). But their love for God is to be demonstrated in an attitude of mercy and care for those who waver and even for those who appear to be lost (22f).

Jude's witness is a limited one. But the use of moral outrage is not entirely exhausted by the circumstances of the first century. The tendency to turn grace into libertinism is a perennial one. Combining justifiable outrage at license with mercy for the licentious is a delicate and difficult art. Few writings have carried it off as well as Jude.

FURTHER READING

Harrington, Daniel, S.J. *Jude and 2 Peter.* Sacra Pagina. Collegeville: Liturgical Press, 2003.

Kelly, J. N. D. *The Epistles of Peter and Jude.* Harper New Testament Commentary. New York: Harper & Row, 1969.

Kraftchick, S. J. *Jude; 2 Peter.* Abingdon New Testament Commentaries. Nashville: Abingdon, 2002.

REVELATION

[see pages 1751–1778 of the New Testament]

Before Beginning . . .

A Book of Christian Prophecy

The book of Revelation makes for difficult reading. Many interpretations of it over the centuries have led to disastrous consequences both for individuals and communities. The fundamental error is to take Revelation as a literal set of predictions from the past about current events. Reading Revelation that way has been popular for a long time, but it has become an obsession for many contemporaries. Such readings have successively been disconfirmed by facts; the "end-time" has been awaited many times without occurring. Such readings have caused the distortion of lives. Many have abandoned livelihood and loved ones to meet the New Jerusalem, only to have their dreams destroyed. Such readings also miss the real religious message of Revelation. They reduce its value to that of an astrological chart.

Although the text itself virtually calls out for such an interpretation, with its promise to reveal "what must happen soon" (22:6), it is critical to recognize that just such statements are standard features of a specific literary genre of the ancient world, called apocalyptic. Two convictions should guide faithful study of Revelation. First, as with all the biblical writings, the Word of God was addressed first to the original audience; a text's "fuller" meaning for successive ages is secondary and never to be divorced from that first, historical, meaning. Second, as in all literature, religious or otherwise, literary genre dictates meaning. Newspapers and poetry do not communicate their respective "truths" in identical ways. Knowing the conventions of a literary form is necessary to intelligent reading.

Revelation as Apocalyptic

Beginning at least with the book of Daniel in the Old Testament, the apocalyptic style was widely used in Judaism during the New Testament period. Generated by persecution from without and the threat of apostasy from within, this "literature of the oppressed" quickly gained certain standard features: revelations about the future are experienced in dreams or visions, and the insights are communicated through a complex symbolism involving numbers, animals, and cosmic phenomena. The element of prediction is actually a fiction. The seer interprets events of his own age, using a figure of the past (such as Enoch) or an angelic being as a spokesperson.

These literary features serve to express an interpretation of history. Apocalyptic defends God's justice. Events appear to be under the control of evil people or even satanic powers, since those devoted to God are being persecuted. Such is the "present age." But apocalyptic places God's blessing in a future time, "the age to come." Just when things become humanly impossible on earth, God will intervene (as through a Messiah) to save his own, and thus inaugurate the "kingdom of God." Apocalyptic reconciles the conviction that God controls history with the experience that suggests God does not. The religious message of apocalyptic is simple. To the faithful, it says, "hold on"; to the wavering, "stand fast." It offers the hope of eventual vindication to those now oppressed but remaining loyal to the one God.

Revelation as Prophecy

Revelation fits the apocalyptic genre well. It has visions, animals, numbers, and cosmic catastrophes. It has a two-age interpretation of history. And its basic religious message is a call for the "endurance of the holy ones" (13:10; 14:12). In other ways, however, Revelation transcends apocalyptic. The author is not a fictional sage from the past but a leader well known to his readers. The voice of prophecy is directed explicitly (and not in coded fashion) to the seven churches of Asia Minor in chapters 2 and 3. Most importantly, the turn of the ages has already begun. The victory of God over evil has in principle been accomplished through the death and resurrection of Jesus; even more impressively, the faithful who have been killed already share in that victory in heaven.

The self-understanding of the church in this writing is thoroughly prophetic. Those who follow Jesus are "servants and prophets and holy ones" (11:18). Their witness is the "spirit of prophecy" (19:10). Jesus is the first and "faithful witness" (1:5) whose mission they continue. The nature of their prophecy is to bear witness to the reality of God in the world. In the letters of chapters 2 and 3, this is expressed as fidelity in face of corruption or apostasy. In the visions of chapters 4 through 21, it is expressed as loyalty in face of the idolatrous claims of the state and even of possible death.

The Opening Vision (1:1–20)

The prologue (1:1–3) and the epilogue (22:6–21) provide an explicit prophetic framework for the entire work and reveal a self-conscious literary awareness as well (cf. 1:3; 22:18). The understanding of prophecy as *witness,* which becomes the major theme of the book, is sounded at once (1:2).

The popularity of letter writing in early Christianity is shown by the fact that this apocalyptic writing contains letters to the seven churches of Asia Minor (Rv 2–3), and even has an epistolary greeting to introduce the work (1:4–8). The author identifies himself as one known to his readers and recounts the vision that provides the basis for the rest of the book. The phrasing of 1: 9 suggests that John is on the Greek island of Patmos as a punishment for his witness to Jesus. The vision that now comforts him becomes an exhortation to all who are likewise oppressed.

The Risen Jesus is encountered as the Son of Man (the central figure in much apocalyptic), described in the most transcendent terms available. The reader is now in the realm of visions, which means the realm of symbols. The terms are obviously not meant literally, any more than the later fantastic descriptions of heaven. The terms used here and elsewhere are not fresh-minted but are the coinage of biblical symbolism. Of all apocalyptic writings, Revelation most artfully weaves together the themes of classical prophecy, especially of the prophet Ezekiel. The footnotes and cross-references in the NAB will repay the effort required. One should quickly realize that Revelation is a self-conscious and complex literary construction.

The Son of Man appears with the stars in his hands, standing amid seven lampstands. Revelation makes clear from the start that it is the risen and powerful Lord (in cosmic control) who is revealed, and that he is present to the churches (1: 20), the concerns of which are taken up in the letters that follow.

Letters to the Seven Churches (2:1–3:22)

In what are literally "spirit letters" (see 2:7) from the Risen Jesus, seven churches of well-known cities in Asia Minor receive individualized prophecies. Revelation understands "prophecy" as exhortations to remain faithful to the integrity of their calling. The trials and lapses of the Christians in these communities are here put on remarkable display. We also hear fragments of sayings (such as in 2:3) that occur elsewhere in the New Testament literature (see 1 Thes 5:2 and Mk 13:33).

The letters all follow the same format. There is a greeting, followed by an elaborate designation of Jesus. The Risen Lord analyzes each community's spiritual condition and concludes with words of warning or of promise. The description of the church's struggles show how they faced opposition from without (as from the Jews), but even more, division within (as with the Nicolaitans). Corruption, too, appears as a vivid possibility. Typical for Johannine literature, the opposition is pictured in terms of false prophecy (2: 20). The focus of praise and of persuasion in these letters is endurance.

The imagery of the letters is lush. Who can resist the almost fairy-tale quality of this statement: "I shall also give a white amulet upon which is inscribed a new name, which no one knows except the one who receives it" (2:17)? Beneath the poetry, however, lies grim reality. The difficulty in these letters of maintaining loyalty in the face of social exclusion and human laxity is raised, in the visions that follow, to the level of a cosmic conflict between the Lord and the forces of evil.

God and the Lamb in Heaven (4:1–5:14)

John is "caught up in spirit" (4:2), and the rest of Revelation consists in the visions he experienced in his ecstatic state. The vision is a staple of apocalyptic. It is found with equal frequency in early Jewish mysticism, called *Merkabah,* or "throne-chariot" mysticism. In prayer, the adept ascended through the heavens to the throne of God's presence. Much of the celestial furniture here resembles that of the *Merkabah:* the jewel-encrusted throne room (4:3f); the sea of glass (4: 6); the angelic creatures (4:6–9), and the numinous hymns sung in praise of God (5:9–13).

A dramatic departure from standard symbolism is the appearance of "the Lamb that seemed to have been slain" (5:6). Jesus is also called "Lamb of God" in John's Gospel (1:29; see also Jn 19:36, a reference to the Passover lamb). It is a bold stroke to picture Jesus in such paradoxical animal terms. The salient aspect of the lamb is its sacrificial function: Jesus was slain. But this lamb is also "the lion of the tribe of Judah," who has triumphed over death (5:5). In a powerful assertion of Jesus' status after his resurrection, the lamb is at "the right hand of the one who sat on the throne" (5:7; see Ps 110:1). Both figures receive the praise of the heavenly creatures (5: 9–11) and indeed of all creation (5:13f).

The special character of the visions of Revelation is shown by the problem of the "scroll" (5: 1). It contains the secrets to be revealed, and because of its use in Ezekiel it is immediately recognizable as a symbol for prophecy (10:8–11 and Ez 2:9–3:4). Because of his resurrection, Jesus is empowered to open the scroll (5:5). What follows, therefore, is both a revelation of and from Jesus Christ (see 1:1). The visions will show "what must happen afterwards" (4:1), but the reader is not frightened, knowing from this first vision that the fundamental victory has already been accomplished.

Visions of Cosmic Conflict (6:1–16:21)

The next section of Revelation is the most difficult to make sense of, and, not surprisingly, the most worked over for signs of the end. The candidates selected to fit the profile of the "Beast" with the number 666 (13:18) have ranged from Nero to Hitler.

The visions are so structured as to give the illusion of temporal sequence, linked together as they are by the phrase "and then I saw. . ." It is indeed tempting to translate a series of visions into a sequence of historical events, so readers have tried to compute the overlapping series of sevens: seals (6:1–17; 8:1), trumpets (8:1–9:21; 11:15), plagues (15:1–8), and bowls (16:1–20). But neither the events reported by headlines nor elaborate literary analyses have ever satisfactorily unlocked this dense poetry. It is in fact more likely that all the visions repeat the same basic message. The saints on earth, locked in conflict with hostile forces, find a cosmic counterpart in the struggle between God and Satan.

Thus, on one side we see all the "beasts" who oppose the faithful: the dragon (12:1–8), the first beast (13:1–10), and the second beast (13: 11–17). These are not separate enemies but successive masks of the one force of evil. As in modern horror films, the destruction of one gives rise to another more horrifying still. Beneath the different manifestations, one visible enemy is most prevalent: the idolatrous state that persecutes the saints, enslaves them, and seeks to kill them (13:7–18).

On the other side are those loyal to God, the "servants, prophets, and holy ones" (11:18; 19: 9f). They continue Jesus' own faithful witness to God by witnessing to Jesus. By so doing, they reject the idolatrous claims of the state on their obeisance. They suffer the consequences, some of them by shedding blood. Revelation establishes the connection between "witness" and "martyr" by the disciples' imitation of Jesus' death. The prophetic self-consciousness of this church is most clearly stated in the account of the two witnesses (11:1–13). This earthly interlude shows two people, who both "witness" and "testify" (the terms are interchangeable). They are killed in imitation of Jesus (11:7). They are also called into heaven (11:12). The vignette describes the conviction of Revelation that those who share Jesus' death also share his triumph in heaven. Thus, alternating with scenes of suffering on earth below are serene descriptions of the saints in heaven celebrating the anticipated and certain victory of the Lamb (5:9f; 6:9–11; 7: 4–7; 14:1–5; 15:2–4). In standard apocalyptic, history moves downward to ever more dismal circumstances, until God finally intervenes. In Revelation, however, the final outcome is not in doubt. Not only Jesus but also those "defeated" with him by evil already share in the resurrection triumph. The earthly conquest is just a matter of tidying up.

It is useless to tease such poetry into a train schedule. The vision here is not one of history unfolding like clockwork; it is a religious vision of God's ultimate conquest despite current appearances. Once the reader lets go of the obsessive "need to know" that twists beauty into charts and tables, it is possible to wonder at the powerful poetic and religious imagination at work in these glorious images. On the side of evil, what genius to make the second beast, who is a "false prophet," mimic the features but betray the nature of the true prophet: "it had two horns like a lamb's but spoke like a dragon" (13:11). On the side of good, what beauty in the prayer that speaks to the suffering of all humankind, that hopes "the Lamb who is in the center of the throne will shepherd them and lead them to springs of life-giving water, and God will wipe away every tear from their eyes" (7:17).

Punishment of Babylon (17:1–20:15)

The masks fall away, revealing as the real enemy of God's people the Roman empire, "the great harlot who lives near the many waters" (17:1). Rome is called Babylon (17:5) because in the biblical tradition it was Babylon above all that symbolized the desecration of the Temple and the exile of the people. In typical apocalyptic fashion, the sequence of events is laid out: God has given temporary rule to this evil empire to accomplish his ends. It does battle against the Lamb and the people.

The persecution and suffering were undoubtedly real. These Christians were faced with the choices of all who suffer oppression. Were they to resist violently and seek the overthrow of Rome? That was futile as well as contrary to their ethos. Were they simply to cooperate? That would be to lose their identity. They chose the path of passive resistance. They did not fight the beast, but neither would they do its bidding. The path of martyrdom, however slow or fast, is not easy. For those who survive, the psychic toll is considerable. Anger at the enemy can easily turn inward; patient endurance is hard. They were convinced that "the Lamb will conquer" (17:14), but in their earthly condition they had not yet seen it happen. Rome's fall is therefore described in delicious detail. The pent-up fury of the oppressed is released in glee over the degradation of the oppressor. Much of this is obviously and literally wish fulfillment, the stuff of fantasy. The anger of a downtrodden people is deflected to a punishing God.

The end-time reveals how "the words of God are accomplished" (17:17). The "Word of God" himself (19:13) leads the climactic battle and inaugurates the messianic age, when the saints "will reign with Christ for a thousand years" (20: 4–6). But this is not yet the end. There is another outbreak of demonic destruction (20:7–10) and the tossing of the Devil into the fire, then the resurrection of the dead for final judgment (20: 11–15). These stages lack poetry, but the final vision overcomes this deficiency.

The New Creation (21:1–22:21)

The conclusion to Revelation is a fitting conclusion to the Bible as a whole. The vision of a new creation (21:1) is central to the New Testament (see, for example, 2 Cor 5:17). The Christian experience of Christ was an absolute beginning, rooted in the ever-new life of God himself. God can say, "Behold, I make all things new" (21:5) because God is "the Alpha and the Omega, the beginning and the end" of all things (21:6; 22: 13). As Genesis began with the creation by a word, so the vision of the end-time recapitulates that beginning: creation is renewed.

The hope expressed by Revelation is not simply that souls be saved after death, or that evil be conquered, or even that saints reign for a thousand years over a burnt-out terrain. The hope is that creation itself be transformed. So the sight of a "New Jerusalem coming down out of heaven from God" is the vision of a civilized order, one that is intrinsically holy in the proper sense. Human society is based on the recognition of God's power and presence. No place for those, now, who refuse the "dwelling place of God with the human race" (21:3, 7f).

In this city, there is not even need for "religion" as a separate compartment of life. The temple of the city is "the Lord God almighty and the Lamb" (21:22). And all the city's people will be priests of [the Lord] God (20:6), showing at last that the fundamental human vocation is praise of God (22:9). There need be no division between peoples. Nothing is here accursed (22:3). The nations will walk by the light of the Lamb (21: 24), and the trees of the city "serve as medicine for the nations" (22:2). And what medicine! There will be "no more death or mourning, wailing or pain, [for] the old order has passed away" (21:4).

Great harm has come to those millenarians who have tried by force to make this vision a reality, and establish a thousand-year reign of the saints on earth. Great despair has come to the utopians who have tried on the basis of goodwill to construct a society like the New Jerusalem.

The vision has its value precisely as challenge, as ever-receding prophecy to all human effort for renewal. This does not come about by human cunning but by God's gift. The transformation is not technical but organic. But so compelling is the vision that no one who hears it can help joining in the plaintive cry of the epilogue, "Amen! Come, Lord Jesus!" The epilogue also reminds us that we are still in the in-between time when the world is not re-created. There is still need for the witness of prophecy and for endurance of the saints, for "the wicked still act wickedly, and the filthy still be filthy. The righteous must still do right, and the holy still be holy" (22:11). Here is a call to the saints.

FURTHER READING

Aune, D. E. *Revelation.* 3 vols. Word Biblical Commentary; Waco: Word, 1997–98.

Boring, M. Eugene. *Revelation.* Interpretation Commentaries. Louisville: John Knox, 1989.

Caird, G. B. *A Commentary of the Revelation of St. John the Divine.* Harper New Testament Commentary. New York: Harper & Row, 1966.

Harrington, Wilfrid J., O.P. *Revelation.* Abington New Testament Commentaries; Nashville: Abingdon, 1998.

Minear, P. *I Saw a New Earth: An Introduction to the Vision of The Apocalypse.* Washington, DC: Corpus Publications, 1968.

Thompson, Leonard L. *Revelation.* Sacra Pagina. Collegeville, MD: Liturgical Press, 1993.

THE OLD TESTAMENT

NEW AMERICAN BIBLE

PREFACE TO THE *NEW AMERICAN BIBLE*

Old Testament

On September 30, 1943, His Holiness Pope Pius XII issued his now famous encyclical on scripture studies, *Divino Afflante Spiritu*. He wrote: "We ought to explain the original text which was written by the inspired author himself and has more authority and greater weight than any, even the very best, translation whether ancient or modern. This can be done all the more easily and fruitfully if to the knowledge of languages be joined a real skill in literary criticism of the same text."

Early in 1944, in conformity with the spirit of the encyclical, and with the encouragement of Archbishop Cicognani, Apostolic Delegate to the United States, the Bishops' Committee of the Confraternity of Christian Doctrine requested members of The Catholic Biblical Association of America to translate the sacred scriptures from the original languages or from the oldest extant form of the text, and to present the sense of the biblical text in as correct a form as possible.

The first English Catholic version of the Bible, the Douay-Rheims (1582–1609/10), and its revision by Bishop Challoner (1750) were based on the Latin Vulgate. In view of the relative certainties more recently attained by textual and higher criticism, it has become increasingly desirable that contemporary translations of the sacred books into English be prepared in which due reverence for the text and strict observance of the rules of criticism would be combined.

The New American Bible has accomplished this in response to the need of the church in America today. It is the achievement of some fifty biblical scholars, the greater number of whom, though not all, are Catholics. In particular, the editors-in-chief have devoted twenty-five years to this work. The collaboration of scholars who are not Catholic fulfills the directive of the Second Vatican Council, not only that "correct translations be made into different languages especially from the original texts of the sacred books," but that, "with the approval of the church authority, these translations be produced in cooperation with separated brothers" so that "all Christians may be able to use them."

The text of the books contained in *The New American Bible* is a completely new translation throughout. From the original and the oldest available texts of the sacred books, it aims to convey as directly as possible the thought and individual style of the inspired writers. The better understanding of Hebrew and Greek, and the steady development of the science of textual criticism, the fruit of patient study since the time of St. Jerome, have allowed the translators and editors in their use of all available materials to approach more closely than ever before the sense of what the sacred authors actually wrote.

Where the translation supposes the received text—Hebrew, Aramaic, or Greek, as the case may be—ordinarily contained in the best-known editions, as the original or the oldest extant form, no additional remarks are necessary. But for those who are happily able to study the original text of the scriptures at firsthand, a supplementary series of textual notes pertaining to the Old Testament was added originally in an appendix to the typical edition. (It is now obtainable in a separate booklet from The Catholic Biblical Association of America, The Catholic University of America, Washington, DC 20064.) These notes furnish a guide in those cases in which the editorial board judges that the manuscripts in the original languages, or the evidence of the ancient versions, or some similar source, furnish the correct reading of a passage, or at least a reading more true to the original than that customarily printed in the available editions.

The Massoretic text of 1 and 2 Samuel has in numerous instances been corrected by the more ancient manuscripts Samuel a, b, and c from Cave 4 of Qumran, with the aid of important evidence from the Septuagint in both its oldest form and its Lucianic recension. Fragments of the lost Book of Tobit in Aramaic and in Hebrew, recovered from Cave 4 of Qumran, are in substantial agreement with the Sinaiticus Greek recension used for the translation of this book. The lost original Hebrew text of 1 Maccabees is replaced by its oldest extant form in Greek. Judith, 2 Maccabees, and parts of Esther are also translated from the Greek.

The basic text for the Psalms is not the Masoretic but one which the editors considered closer to the original inspired form, namely the Hebrew text underlying the new Latin Psalter of the Church, the *Liber Psalmorum* (1944[1], 1945[2]). Nevertheless they retained full liberty to establish the reading of the original text on sound critical principles.

The translation of Sirach, based on the original Hebrew as far as it is preserved and corrected from the ancient versions, is often interpreted in the light of the traditional Greek text. In the Book of Baruch the basic text is the Greek of the Septuagint, with some readings derived from an underlying Hebrew form no longer extant. In the deuterocanonical sections of Daniel (3, 24–90; 13, 1—14, 42), the basic text is the Greek text of Theodotion, occasionally revised according to the Greek text of the Septuagint.

In some instances in the Book of Job, in Proverbs, Sirach, Isaiah, Jeremiah, Ezekiel, Hosea, Amos, Micah, Nahum, Habakkuk, and Zechariah there is good reason to believe that the original order of lines was accidentally disturbed in the transmission of the text. The verse numbers given in such cases are always those of the current Hebrew text, though the arrangement differs. In these instances the textual notes advise the reader of the difficulty. Cases of exceptional dislocation are called to the reader's attention by footnotes.

The Books of *Genesis to Ruth* were first published in 1952; the Wisdom Books, *Job to Sirach,* in 1955; the Prophetic Books, *Isaiah to Malachi,* in 1961; and the Historical Books, *Samuel to Maccabees,* in 1969. In the present edition of *Genesis to Ruth* there are certain new features: a general introduction to the Pentateuch, a retranslation of the text of Genesis with an introduction, cross-references, and revised textual notes, besides new and expanded exegetical notes which take into consideration the various sources or literary traditions.

The revision of *Job to Sirach* includes changes in strophe division in Job and Proverbs and in titles of principal parts and sections of Wisdom and Ecclesiastes. Corrections in the text of Sirach are made in 39, 27—44, 17 on the basis of the Masada text, and in 51, 13–30 on the basis of the occurrence of this canticle in the Psalms scroll from Qumran Cave 11. In this typical edition, new corrections are reflected in the textual notes of Job, Proverbs, Wisdom, and Sirach. In the Psalms, the enumeration found in the Hebrew text is followed instead of the double enumeration, according to both the Hebrew and the Latin Vulgate texts, contained in the previous edition of this book.

In the Prophetic Books *Isaiah to Malachi,* only minor revisions have been made in the structure and wording of the texts, and in the textual notes.

The spelling of proper names in *The New American Bible* follows the customary forms found in most English Bibles since the Authorized Version.

The work of translating the Bible has been characterized as "the sacred and apostolic work of interpreting the word of God and of presenting it to the laity in translations as clear as the difficulty of the matter and the limitations of human knowledge permit" (A. G. Cicognani, Apostolic Delegate, in *The Catholic Biblical Quarterly,* 6, [1944], 389–90). In the appraisal of the present work, it is hoped that the words of the encyclical *Divino afflante Spiritu* will serve as a guide: "Let all the sons of the church bear in mind that the efforts of these resolute laborers in the vineyard of the Lord should be judged not only with equity and justice but also with the greatest charity; all moreover should abhor that intemperate zeal which imagines that whatever is new should for that very reason be opposed or suspected."

Conscious of their personal limitations for the task thus defined, those who have prepared this text cannot expect that it will be considered perfect; but they can hope that it may deepen in its readers "the right understanding of the divinely given Scriptures," and awaken in them "that piety by which it behooves us to be grateful to the God of all providence, who from the throne of his majesty has sent these books as so many personal letters to his own children" *(Divino afflante Spiritu).*

PREFACE TO THE REVISED *NEW AMERICAN BIBLE*

Old Testament

The first step in the genesis of *The New American Bible* was taken in 1936 when His Excellency, the Most Reverend Edwin V. O'Hara, D.D., chairman of the Episcopal Committee of the Confraternity of Christian Doctrine, invited a group of Catholic Scripture scholars to plan for a revised edition of the Challoner-Rheims New Testament, primarily on the basis of the Vulgate; the plans soon expanded to include the revision of the Old Testament. Archbishop O'Hara's initiative resulted in the formation of the Catholic Biblical Association, whose principal activity in its early years was this work of revision and translation. (For information on the work done on the New Testament, see the "Preface to *The New American Bible*: First Edition of the New Testament" and "Preface to the Revised Edition.") In 1943 His Holiness Pope Pius XII issued the encyclical *Divino afflante spiritu*, which encouraged Scripture scholars to translate the Scriptures from the original languages. He wrote: "We ought to explain the original text which was written by the inspired author himself and has more authority and greater weight than any, even the very best, translation whether ancient or modern. This can be done all the more easily and fruitfully if to the knowledge of languages be joined a real skill in literary criticism of the same text." Although at this point work on almost twenty of the Old Testament books was completed or near completion, that work was abandoned and the new project of translating from the Hebrew, Greek, and Aramaic was undertaken.

The completed books of the Old Testament were initially published, as they became available, in four volumes: Genesis–Ruth (1952), Job–Sirach (1955), Isaiah–Malachi (1961), and Samuel–Maccabees (1969). Some fifty scholars collaborated on this project; these were mainly Catholics, but, in accord with the suggestion of Vatican II that "with the approval of the church authority, these translations be produced in cooperation with separated brothers" so that "all Christians may be able to use them" (*Dei Verbum*, No. 22), non-Catholics also participated in the work. To this point the translation had been known under the name of the "Confraternity of Christian Doctrine" or CCD for short, but when these parts of the Old Testament were combined with the New Testament in a single volume, it was given the name "New American Bible," in part to reflect its ecumenical character. In producing the new volume certain changes were made from the original four volumes: a retranslation of the Book of Genesis, cross-references, new and expanded exegetical notes.

New translations and revision of existing translations are required from time to time for various reasons. For example, it is important to keep pace with the discovery and publication of new and better ancient manuscripts (e.g., the Dead Sea scrolls) so that the best possible textual tradition will be followed, as required by *Divino afflante spiritu*. There are advances in linguistics of the biblical languages which make possible a better understanding and more accurate translation of the original languages. And there are changes and developments in vocabulary and the cultural background of the receptor language. An obvious example of this is the abandonment in English of the second person singular (use of "thee," "thou," "sayest," "hearest"), which had a major impact on Bible translations. Other changes are less obvious but are nevertheless present. There have been changes in vocabulary; for example, the term "holocaust" is now normally reserved for the sacrilegious attempt to destroy the Jewish people by the Third Reich. Concerns such as these are reflected in what Pope John Paul II spoke of as the "three pillars" of good biblical translation: "A good translation is based on three pillars that must contemporaneously support the entire work. First, there must be a deep knowledge of the language and the cultural world at the point of origin. Next, there must be a good familiarity with the language and cultural context at the point where the work will arrive. Lastly, to crown the work with success, there must be an adequate mastery of the contents and meaning of what one is translating"—and he praised the translation that "utilizes the vocabulary and idioms of everyday speech" ("le parole e le forme della lingua di tutti i giorni"). (From an address to the United Bible Societies, November 26, 2001.)

This new edition is a thorough revision of the already excellent *New American Bible* Old Testament of 1970. Work on most books of the Old Testament, begun in 1994 and completed in 2001, was done by forty revisers and a board of eight editors. The 1991 revision of the Psalter, the work of thirty revisers and six editors, was further revised by seven revisers and two editors between 2009 and 2010. As suggested in the comments above, the revision aimed at making use of the best manuscript traditions available (see below), translating as accurately as possible, and rendering the result in good contemporary English. In many ways it is a more literal translation than the original NAB and has attempted to be more consistent in rendering Hebrew (or Greek) words and idioms, especially in technical contexts, such as regulations for sacrifices. In translating the Psalter special effort was made to provide a smooth, rhythmic translation for easy singing or recitation, and to retain the concrete imagery of the Hebrew.

Where the Old Testament translation supposes the received text—Hebrew, Aramaic, or Greek, as the case may be—ordinarily contained in the best-known editions, as the original or the oldest extant form, no additional remarks are necessary. Where the translators have departed from those received texts, e.g., by following the Septuagint rather than the Masoretic text, accepting a reading of what is judged to be a better textual tradition, as from a Qumran manuscript, or by emending a reading apparently corrupted in transmission, such changes are recorded in the revised edition of the *Textual Notes on The New American Bible*. Additional information on the textual tradition for some books may be found in the introduction to the book in the same *Textual Notes*.

In particular, important manuscripts from Cave 4 of Qumran, as well as the most useful recensions of the Septuagint, have been consulted in the preparation of 1 and 2 Samuel. Fragments of the lost Book of Tobit in Aramaic and in Hebrew, recovered from Cave 4 of Qumran, are in substantial agreement with the Sinaiticus Greek recension used for the translation of this book. The lost original Hebrew text of 1 Maccabees is replaced by its oldest extant form in Greek. Judith, 2 Maccabees, and parts of Esther are also translated from the Greek. The translation of The Wisdom of Ben Sira is based on the original Hebrew as far as it is preserved, with corrections from the ancient versions; otherwise, the Greek of the Septuagint is followed. In the Book of Baruch the basic text is the Greek of the Septuagint, with some readings derived from an underlying Hebrew form no longer extant. In the deuterocanonical sections of Daniel (3:24–90; 13:1–14:42), the basic text is the Greek text of so-called Theodotion, occasionally revised according to the Greek text of the Septuagint.

THE PENTATEUCH

See RG 85–99

The Pentateuch (Greek for "five books") designates the first five books of the Jewish and Christian Bible (Genesis, Exodus, Leviticus, Numbers, and Deuteronomy). Jewish tradition calls the five books Torah (Teaching, Law) because of the centrality of the Sinai covenant and legislation mediated through Moses.

The unity of the Pentateuch comes from the single story it tells. God creates the world and destines human beings for the blessings of progeny and land possession (Gn 1–3). As the human race expands, its evil conduct provokes God to send the flood to wipe out all but righteous Noah's family. After the flood, the world is repopulated from his three sons, Ham, Shem, and Japheth (Gn 4–9). From them are descended the seventy nations of the civilized world whose offense this time (building a city rather than taking their assigned lands, Gn 10–11) provokes God to elect one family from the rest. Abraham and his wife, Sarah, landless and childless, are promised a child and the land of Canaan. Amid trials and fresh promises, a son (Isaac) is born to them and Abraham takes title to a sliver of Canaanite land, a kind of down payment for later possession (Gn 12–25). Gn 25–36 tells how their descendant Jacob becomes the father of twelve sons (because of which he is called "Israel"), and Gn 37–50 tells how the rejected brother Joseph saves the family from famine and brings them to Egypt.

In Egypt, a pharaoh who knew not Joseph subjects "the seventy sons of Jacob" ("the Hebrews") to hard labor, keeping them from their land and destroying their male progeny (Ex 1). Moses is commissioned to lead the people out of Egypt to their own land (Ex 2–6). In ten plagues, the Lord defeats Pharaoh. Free at last, the Hebrews leave Egypt and journey to Mount Sinai (Ex 7–18), where they enter into a covenant to be the people of the Lord and be shaped by the Ten Commandments and other laws (Ex 19–24). Though the people commit apostasy when Moses goes back to the mountain for the plans of the dwelling (tabernacle), Moses' intercession prevents the abrogation of the covenant by God (Ex 32–34). A principle has been established, however: even the people's apostasy need not end their relationship with God. The book ends with the cloud and the glory taking possession of the tent of meeting (Ex 36:34–38). "The sons of Israel" in Ex 1:1 are the actual sons of Jacob/Israel the patriarch, but at the end of the book they are the nation Israel, for all the elements of nationhood in antiquity have been granted: a god (and temple), a leader, a land, and an authoritative tradition.

Israel remains at the holy mountain for almost a year. The entire block of material from Ex 19:1 to Nm 10:11 is situated at Sinai. The rituals of Leviticus and Numbers are delivered to Moses at the holy mountain, showing that Israel's worship was instituted by God and part of the very fabric of the people's life. Priestly material in the Book of Exodus (chaps. 25–31, 35–40) describes the basic institutions of Israelite worship (the tabernacle, its furniture, and priestly vestments). Leviticus, aptly called in rabbinic tradition the Priests' Manual, lays down the role of priests to teach Israel the distinction between clean and unclean and to see to their holiness. In Nm 10:11–22:1, the journey is resumed, this time from Sinai through the wilderness to Transjordan; Nm 22:2–36:13 tells of events and laws in the plains of Moab.

The final book of the Pentateuch, Deuteronomy, consists of four speeches by Moses to the people who have arrived at the plains of Moab, ready to conquer the land: 1:1–4:43; 4:44–28:68; 29:1–32:52; 33:1–34:12. Each speech is introduced by the formula "This is the law/words/blessing."

The Priestly editor used literary formulas. The formula "These are the generations (the wording can vary) of . . ." occurs five times in the primordial history (Gn 2:4a; 5:1; 6:9; 10:1; 11:10) and five times in the ancestral history (11:27; 25:12; 25:19; 36:1 [v. 9 is secondary]; 37:2). In Exodus and Numbers the formula (with slight variations) "They departed from (place name) and encamped at (place name)" occurs in two groups of six: A. Ex 12:37a; 13:20; 14:1–2; 15:22a; 16:1; 17:1a; and B. 19:2; Nm 10:12; 20:1a; 20:22; 21:10–11; 22:1.

Who wrote the Pentateuch, and when? Up to the seventeenth century, the virtually unanimous answer of Jews and Christians was "Moses." Moses wrote the Pentateuch as David wrote the Psalter and Solomon wrote the wisdom literature. Though scholars had noted inconsistencies (compare Ishmael's age in Gn 16:16 and 21:5, 14) and duplications (Gn 12, 20, and 26), they assumed Mosaic authorship because of the prevalent theory of inspiration: God inspired authors while they wrote. With the rise of historical criticism, scholars began to use the doublets and inconsistencies as clues to different authors and traditions.

By the late nineteenth century, one theory of the sources of the Pentateuch had been worked out that proved acceptable in its main lines to the majority of scholars (apart from Christian and Jewish conservatives) then and now. It can be quickly sketched. In the premonarchic period of the Judges (ca. 1220–1020 B.C.), the twelve tribes had an oral form of their story from creation to the taking of the land. With the beginnings of monarchy in the late eleventh and tenth centuries, the oral material was written down, being known as the Yahwist account (from its use of the divine name Yhwh). Its abbreviation, "J," comes from the German spelling of the divine name. In the following century, another account took shape in the Northern Kingdom (called E after its use of Elohim as a divine name); some believe the E source is simply a supplement to J. After the fall of the Northern Kingdom in 722/721 B.C., the E version was taken to Jerusalem where it was combined with the J version to produce J-E. During the exile (conventionally dated 587–539 B.C.) or thereafter, an editor recast J-E to make it relevant for the exiled population. This editor is conventionally known as P (=Priestly) because of the chronological and ritual interests apparent in the work. P can also designate archival material and chronological notices. The audience for the Priestly edition no longer lived in the land and was deeply concerned about its survival and its claim on the land.

Deuteronomy (=D) stands alone in style, genre (preaching rather than narrative), and content. How did it come to be the fifth book of the Pentateuch? The J-E narrative actually ends in Numbers, when Israel arrives at the plains of Moab. Many scholars believe that Deuteronomy was secondarily attached to Numbers by moving the account of Moses' death from its original place in the J-E version in Numbers to the end of Deuteronomy (chap. 34). Deuteronomy was attached to Genesis–Numbers to link it to another great work, the Deuteronomistic History (Joshua to Kings). Deuteronomy is now the fifth book of the Pentateuch and the first book of the Deuteronomistic History.

In the last three decades, the above consensus on the composition of the Pentateuch has come under attack. Some critics are extremely skeptical about the historical value of the so-called early traditions, and a few doubt there ever was a preexilic monarchy of any substance. For such scholars, the Pentateuch is a retrojection from the fourth or third centuries B.C. Other scholars postulate a different sequence of sources, or understand the sources differently.

How should a modern religiously minded person read the Pentateuch? First, readers have before them the most significant thing, the text of the Pentateuch. It is accurately preserved, reasonably well understood, and capable of touching audiences of every age. Take and read! Second, the controversies are about the sources of the Pentateuch, especially their antiquity and character. Many details will never be known, for the evidence is scanty. Indeed, the origin of many great literary works is obscure.

The Pentateuch witnesses to a coherent story

that begins with the creation of the world and ends with Israel taking its land. The same story is in the historical Ps 44, 77, 78, 80, 105, 114, and 149, and in the confessions Dt 26:5–9, Jos 24:2–13, and 1 Sm 12:7–13. Though the narrative enthralls and entertains, as all great literature does, it is well to remember that it is a theopolitical charter as well, meant to establish how and why descendants of the patriarchs are a uniquely holy people among the world's nations.

The destruction of the Jerusalem Temple and deportation of Israelites in the sixth century B.C. seemed to invalidate the charter, for Israel no longer possessed its land in any real sense. The last chapter of the ancient narrative—Israel dwelling securely in its land—no longer held true. The story had to be reinterpreted, and the Priestly editor is often credited with doing so. A preface (Gn 1) was added, emphasizing God's intent that human beings continue in existence through their progeny and possess their own land. Good news, surely, to a devastated people wondering whether they would survive and repossess their ancestral land. The ending of the old story was changed to depict Israel at the threshold of the promised land (the plains of Moab) rather than in it. Henceforth, Israel would be a people oriented toward the land rather than possessing it. The revised ending could not be more suitable for Jews and Christians alike. Both peoples can imagine themselves on the threshold of the promised land, listening to the word of God in order to be able to enter it in the future. For Christians particularly, the Pentateuch portrays the pilgrim people waiting for the full realization of the kingdom of God.

The Book of Genesis

See RG 100–115

Genesis is the first book of the Pentateuch (Genesis, Exodus, Leviticus, Numbers, Deuteronomy), the first section of the Jewish and the Christian Scriptures. Its title in English, "Genesis," comes from the Greek of Gn 2:4, literally, "the book of the generation (*genesis*) of the heavens and earth." Its title in the Jewish Scriptures is the opening Hebrew word, *Bereshit*, "in the beginning."

The book has two major sections—the creation and expansion of the human race (2:4–11:9), and the story of Abraham and his descendants (11:10–50:26). The first section deals with God and the nations, and the second deals with God and a particular nation, Israel. The opening creation account (1:1–2:3) lifts up two themes that play major roles in each section—the divine command to the first couple (standing for the whole race) to produce offspring and to possess land (1:28). In the first section, progeny and land appear in the form of births and genealogies (chaps. 2–9) and allotment of land (chaps. 10–11), and in the second, progeny and land appear in the form of promises of descendants and land to the ancestors. Another indication of editing is the formulaic introduction, "this is the story; these are the descendants" (Hebrew *tōledôt*), which occurs five times in Section I (2:4; 5:1; 6:9; 10:1; 10:31) and five times in Section II (11:10; 25:12, 19; 36:1 [v. 9 is an addition]; 37:2).

The Composition of the Book. For the literary sources of Genesis, see Introduction to the Pentateuch. As far as the sources of Genesis are concerned, contemporary readers can reasonably assume that ancient traditions (J and E) were edited in the sixth or fifth century B.C. for a Jewish audience that had suffered the effects of the exile and was now largely living outside of Palestine. The editor highlighted themes of vital concern to this audience: God intends that every nation have posterity and land; the ancestors of Israel are models for their descendants who also live in hope rather than in full possession of what has been promised; the ancient covenant with God is eternal, remaining valid even when the human party has been unfaithful. By highlighting such concerns, the editor addressed the worries of exiled Israel and indeed of contemporary Jews and Christians.

Genesis 1–11. The seven-day creation account in Gn 1:1–2:3 tells of a God whose mere word creates a beautiful universe in which human beings are an integral and important part. Though Gn 2:4–3:24 is often regarded as "the second creation story," the text suggests that the whole of 2:4–11:9 tells one story. The plot of Gn 2–11 (creation, the flood, renewed creation) has been borrowed from creation-flood stories attested in Mesopotamian literature of the second and early first millennia. In the Mesopotamian creation-flood stories, the gods created the human race as slaves whose task it was to manage the universe for them—giving them food, clothing, and honor in temple ceremonies. In an unforeseen development, however, the human race grew so numerous and noisy that the gods could not sleep. Deeply angered, the gods decided to destroy the race by a universal flood. One man and his family, however, secretly warned of the flood by his patron god, built a boat and survived. Soon regretting their impetuous decision, the gods created a revised version of humankind. The new race was created mortal so they would never again grow numerous and bother the gods. The authors of Genesis adapted the creation-flood story in accord with their views of God and humanity. For example, they attributed the fault to human sin rather than to divine miscalculation (6:5–7) and had God reaffirm without change the original creation (9:1–7). In the biblical version God is just, powerful, and not needy.

How should modern readers interpret the creation-flood story in Gn 2–11? The stories are neither history nor myth. "Myth" is an unsuitable term, for it has several different meanings and connotes untruth in popular English. "History" is equally misleading, for it suggests that the events actually took place. The best term is creation-flood story. Ancient Near Eastern thinkers did not have our methods of exploring serious questions. Instead, they used narratives for issues that we would call philosophical and theological. They added and subtracted narrative details and varied the plot as they sought meaning in the ancient stories. Their stories reveal a privileged time, when divine decisions were made that determined the future of the human race. The origin of something was thought to explain its present meaning, e.g., how God acts with justice and generosity, why human beings are rebellious, the nature of sexual attraction and marriage, why there are many peoples and languages. Though the stories may initially strike us as primitive and naive, they are in fact told with skill, compression, and subtlety. They provide profound answers to perennial questions about God and human beings.

Genesis 11–50. One Jewish tradition suggests that God, having been rebuffed in the attempt to forge a relationship with the nations, decided to concentrate on one nation in the hope that it would eventually bring in all the nations. The migration of Abraham's family (11:26–31) is part of the general movement of the human race to take possession of their lands (see 10:32–11:9). Abraham, however, must come into possession of his land in a manner different from the nations, for he will not immediately possess it nor will he have descendants in the manner of the nations, for he is old and his wife is childless (12:1–9). Abraham and Sarah have to live with their God in trust and obedience until at last Isaac is born to them and they manage to buy a sliver of the land (the burial cave at Machpelah, chap. 23). Abraham's humanity and faith offer a wonderful example to the exilic generation.

The historicity of the ancestral stories has been much discussed. Scholars have traditionally dated them sometime in the first half of the second millennium, though a few regard them as late (sixth or fifth century B.C.) and purely fictional. There is unfortunately no direct extra-biblical evidence confirming (or disproving) the stories. The ancestral stories have affinities, however, to late second-millennium stories of childless ancestors, and their proper names fit linguistic patterns attested in the second millennium. Given the lack of decisive evidence, it is reasonable to accept the Bible's own chronology that the patriarchs were the ancestors of Israel and that they lived well before the exodus that is generally dated in the thirteenth century.

Gn 25:19–35:43 are about Jacob and his twelve sons. The stories are united by a geographical frame: Jacob lives in Canaan until his theft of the right of the firstborn from his brother Esau forces him to flee to Paddan-Aram (alternately Aram-Naharaim). There his uncle Laban tricks him as he earlier tricked his brother. But Jacob is blessed with wealth and sons. He returns to Canaan to receive the final blessing, land, and on the way is reconciled with his brother Esau. As the sons have reached the number of twelve, the patriarch can be given the name Israel (32:28; 35:10). The blessings given to Abraham are reaffirmed to Isaac and to Jacob.

The last cycle of ancestor stories is about Jacob's son Joseph (37:1–50:26, though in chaps. 48–49 the focus swings back to Jacob). The Joseph stories are sophisticated in theme, deftly plotted, and show keen interest in the psychology of the characters. Jacob's favoring of Joseph, the son of his beloved wife Rachel, provokes his brothers to kill him. Joseph escapes death through the intercession of Reuben, the eldest, and of Judah, but is sold into slavery in Egypt. In the immediately following chap. 38, Judah undergoes experiences similar to Joseph's. Joseph, endowed by God with wisdom, becomes second only to Pharaoh in Egypt. From that powerful position, he encounters his unsuspecting brothers who have come to Egypt because of the famine, and tests them to see if they have repented. Joseph learns that they have given up their hatred because of their love for Israel, their father. Judah, who seems to have inherited the mantle of the failed oldest brother Reuben, expresses the brothers' new and profound appreciation of their father and Joseph (chap. 44). At the end of Genesis, the entire family of Jacob/Israel is in Egypt, which prepares for the events in the Book of Exodus.

Genesis in Later Biblical Books. The historical and prophetic books constantly refer to the covenant with the ancestors Abraham, Isaac, and Jacob. Hos 10 sees the traits of Jacob in the behavior of the Israel of his own day. Is 51:2 cites Abraham and Sarah as a model for his dispirited community, for though only a couple, they became a great nation. Jn 1, "In the beginning was the word," alludes to Gn 1:1 (and Prv 8:22) to show that Jesus is creating a new world. St. Paul interprets Jesus as the New Adam in Rom 5:14 and 1 Cor 15:22, 24, whose obedience brings life just as the Old Adam's disobedience brought death. In Rom 4, Paul cites Abraham as someone who was righteous in God's eyes centuries before the Law was given at Sinai.

Outline of Genesis.

Preamble. The Creation of the World (1:1–2:3)

I. The Story of the Nations (2:4–11:26)
   - A. The Creation of the Man and the Woman, Their Offspring, and the Spread of Civilization (2:4–4:26)
   - B. The Pre-flood Generations (5:1–6:8)
   - C. The Flood and the Renewed Blessing (6:9–9:29)
   - D. The Populating of the World and the Prideful City (10:1–11:9)
   - E. The Genealogy from Shem to Terah (11:10–26)

II. The Story of the Ancestors of Israel (11:27–50:26)
   - A. The Story of Abraham and Sarah (11:27–25:18)
   - B. The Story of Isaac and Jacob (25:19–36:43)
   - C. The Story of Joseph (37:1–50:26)

Preamble. The Creation of the World

CHAPTER 1

See RG 104

The Story of Creation.* 1In the beginning, when God created the heavens and the
earth[a]— 2* and the earth was without form
or shape, with darkness over the abyss and a
mighty wind sweeping over the waters—[b]
3Then God said: Let there be light, and

1:1–2:3 This section, from the Priestly source, functions as an introduction, as ancient stories of the origin of the world (cosmogonies) often did. It introduces the primordial story (2:4–11:26), the stories of the ancestors (11:27–50:26), and indeed the whole Pentateuch. The chapter highlights the goodness of creation and the divine desire that human beings share in that goodness. God brings an orderly universe out of primordial chaos merely by uttering a word. In the literary structure of six days, the creation events in the first three days are related to those in the second three.

1. light (day)/darkness (night)	=	4. sun/moon
2. arrangement of water	=	5. fish + birds from waters
3. a) dry land b) vegetation	=	6. a) animals b) human beings: male/female

The seventh day, on which God rests, the climax of the account, falls outside the six-day structure.

Until modern times the first line was always translated, "In the beginning God created the heavens and the earth." Several comparable ancient cosmogonies, discovered in recent times, have a "when . . . then" construction, confirming the translation "when . . . then" here as well. "When" introduces the pre-creation state and "then" introduces the creative act affecting that state. The traditional translation, "In the beginning," does not reflect the Hebrew syntax of the clause.

1:2 This verse is parenthetical, describing in three phases the pre-creation state symbolized by the chaos out of which God brings order: "earth," hidden beneath the encompassing cosmic waters, could not be seen, and thus had no "form"; there was only darkness; turbulent wind swept over the waters. Commencing with the last-named elements (darkness and water), vv. 3–10 describe the rearrangement of this chaos: light is made (first day) and the water is divided into water above and water below the earth so that the earth appears and is no longer "without outline." **The abyss**: the primordial ocean according to the ancient Semitic cosmogony. After God's creative activity, part of this vast body forms the

a: Gn 2:1, 4; 2 Mc 7:28; Ps 8:4; 33:6; 89:12; 90:2; Wis 11:17; Sir 16:24; Jer 10:12; Acts 14:15; Col 1:16–17; Heb 1:2–3; 3:4; 11:3; Rev 4:11. *b:* Jer 4:23.

there was light.[c] 4 God saw that the light was
good. God then separated the light from the
darkness. 5 God called the light "day," and
the darkness he called "night." Evening
came, and morning followed—the first day.*
6 Then God said: Let there be a dome in
the middle of the waters, to separate one
body of water from the other. 7 God made the
dome,* and it separated the water below the
dome from the water above the dome. And
so it happened.[d] 8 God called the dome "sky."
Evening came, and morning followed—the
second day.
9 Then God said: Let the water under the
sky be gathered into a single basin, so that
the dry land may appear. And so it happened:
the water under the sky was gathered into its
basin, and the dry land appeared.[e] 10 God
called the dry land "earth," and the basin of
water he called "sea." God saw that it was
good. 11[f] Then God said: Let the earth bring
forth vegetation: every kind of plant that
bears seed and every kind of fruit tree on
earth that bears fruit with its seed in it. And
so it happened: 12 the earth brought forth
vegetation: every kind of plant that bears
seed and every kind of fruit tree that bears
fruit with its seed in it. God saw that it was
good. 13 Evening came, and morning followed—the third day.
14 Then God said: Let there be lights in the
dome of the sky, to separate day from night.
Let them mark the seasons, the days and the
years,[g] 15 and serve as lights in the dome of
the sky, to illuminate the earth. And so it happened: 16 God made the two great lights, the
greater one to govern the day, and the lesser
one to govern the night, and the stars.[h] 17 God
set them in the dome of the sky, to illuminate
the earth, 18 to govern the day and the night,
and to separate the light from the darkness.
God saw that it was good. 19 Evening came,
and morning followed—the fourth day.
20[i] Then God said: Let the water teem with
an abundance of living creatures, and on the
earth let birds fly beneath the dome of the
sky. 21 God created the great sea monsters and
all kinds of crawling living creatures with
which the water teems, and all kinds of
winged birds. God saw that it was good,
22 and God blessed them, saying: Be fertile,
multiply, and fill the water of the seas; and let
the birds multiply on the earth.[j] 23 Evening
came, and morning followed—the fifth day.
24[k] Then God said: Let the earth bring forth
every kind of living creature: tame animals,
crawling things, and every kind of wild animal. And so it happened: 25 God made every
kind of wild animal, every kind of tame animal, and every kind of thing that crawls on the
ground. God saw that it was good. 26[l] Then
God said: Let us make* human beings in our
image, after our likeness. Let them have dominion over the fish of the sea, the birds of the
air, the tame animals, all the wild animals, and
all the creatures that crawl on the earth.

27 God created mankind in his image;
in the image of God he created them;
male and female* he created them.

salt-water seas (vv. 9–10); part of it is the fresh water under the earth (Ps 33:7; Ez 31:4), which wells forth on the earth as springs and fountains (Gn 7:11; 8:2; Prv 3:20). Part of it, "the upper water" (Ps 148:4; Dn 3:60), is held up by the dome of the sky (vv. 6–7), from which rain descends on the earth (Gn 7:11; 2 Kgs 7:2, 19; Ps 104:13). **A mighty wind**: literally, "spirit or breath [*ruah*] of God"; cf. Gn 8:1.

1:5 In ancient Israel a day was considered to begin at sunset.

1:7 The dome: the Hebrew word suggests a gigantic metal dome. It was inserted into the middle of the single body of water to form dry space within which the earth could emerge. The Latin Vulgate translation *firmamentum,* "means of support (for the upper waters); firmament," provided the traditional English rendering.

1:26 Let us make: in the ancient Near East, and sometimes in the Bible, God was imagined as presiding over an assembly of heavenly beings who deliberated and decided about matters on earth (1 Kgs 22:19–22; Is 6:8; Ps 29:1–2; 82; 89:6–7; Jb 1:6; 2:1; 38:7). This scene accounts for the plural form here and in Gn 11:7 ("Let us then go down . . ."). Israel's God was always considered "Most High" over the heavenly beings. **Human beings**: Hebrew *'ādām* is here the generic term for humankind; in the first five chapters of Genesis it is the proper name Adam only at 4:25 and 5:1–5. **In our image, after our likeness**: "image" and "likeness" (virtually synonyms) express the worth of human beings who have value in themselves (human blood may not be shed in 9:6 because of this image of God) and in their task, dominion (1:28), which promotes the rule of God over the universe.

1:27 Male and female: as God provided the plants with seeds (vv. 11, 12) and commanded the animals to be fertile

c: 2 Cor 4:6. *d:* Prv 8:27–28; 2 Pt 3:5. *e:* Jb 38:8; Ps 33:7; Jer 5:22. *f:* Ps 104:14. *g:* Jb 26:10; Ps 19:2–3; Bar 3:33. *h:* Dt 4:19; Ps 136:7–9; Wis 13:2–4; Jer 31:35. *i:* Jb 12:7–10. *j:* Gn 8:17. *k:* Sir 16:27–28. *l:* Gn 5:1, 3; 9:6; Ps 8:5–6; Wis 2:23; 10:2; Sir 17:1, 3–4; Mt 19:4; Mk 10:6; Jas 3:7; Eph 4:24; Col 3:10.

The Major Divisions of Genesis

First section: 1:1 to 11:9	Primeval history, the origins of humankind, and failure through sin.
Second section: 11:10 to 25:34	Abraham, his call and response, his blessing and promise, his son Isaac and Isaac's sons Jacob (Israel) and Esau
Third section: 26:1 to 36:43	Isaac, Jacob, and the sons of Jacob (Israel)
Fourth section: 37:1 to 50:26	The sons of Israel, and Jacob and the Israelites in Egypt

[28]God blessed them and God said to them: Be fertile and multiply; fill the earth and subdue it.* Have dominion over the fish of the sea, the birds of the air, and all the living things that crawl on the earth.[m] [29]* [n] God also said: See, I give you every seed-bearing plant on all the earth and every tree that has seed-bearing fruit on it to be your food; [30]and to all the wild animals, all the birds of the air, and all the living creatures that crawl on the earth, I give all the green plants for food. And so it happened. [31]God looked at everything he had made, and found it very good. Evening came, and morning followed—the sixth day.[o]

CHAPTER 2

See RG 104

[1]Thus the heavens and the earth and all their array were completed.[p] [2]* On the seventh day God completed the work he had been doing; he rested on the seventh day from all the work he had undertaken.[q] [3]God blessed the seventh day and made it holy, because on it he rested from all the work he had done in creation.[r]

I. The Story of the Nations

The Garden of Eden. [4]This is the story* of the heavens and the earth at their creation.

and multiply (v. 22), so God gives sexuality to human beings as their means to continue in existence.

1:28 Fill the earth and subdue it: the object of the verb "subdue" may be not the earth as such but earth as the territory each nation must take for itself (chaps. 10–11), just as Israel will later do (see Nm 32:22, 29; Jos 18:1). The two divine commands define the basic tasks of the human race—to continue in existence through generation and to take possession of one's God-given territory. The dual command would have had special meaning when Israel was in exile and deeply anxious about whether they would continue as a nation and return to their ancient territory. **Have dominion**: the whole human race is made in the "image" and "likeness" of God and has "dominion." Comparable literature of the time used these words of kings rather than of human beings in general; human beings were invariably thought of as slaves of the gods created to provide menial service for the divine world. The royal language here does not, however, give human beings unlimited power, for kings in the Bible had limited dominion and were subject to prophetic critique.

1:29 According to the Priestly tradition, the human race was originally intended to live on plants and fruits as were the animals (see v. 30), an arrangement that God will later change (9:3) in view of the human inclination to violence.

2:2 The mention of the seventh day, repeated in v. 3, is outside the series of six days and is thus the climax of the account. The focus of the account is God. The text does not actually institute the practice of keeping the Sabbath, for it would have been anachronistic to establish at this point a custom that was distinctively Israelite (Ex 31:13, 16, 17), but it lays the foundation for the later practice. Similarly, ancient creation accounts often ended with the construction of a temple where the newly created human race provided service to the gods who created them, but no temple is mentioned in this account. As was the case with the Sabbath, it would have been anachronistic to institute the temple at this point, for Israel did not yet exist. In Ex 25–31 and 35–40, Israel builds the tabernacle, which is the precursor of the Temple of Solomon.

2:4 This is the story: the distinctive Priestly formula introduces older traditions, belonging to the tradition called Yahwist, and gives them a new setting. In the first part of Genesis, the formula "this is the story" (or a similar phrase) occurs five times (2:4; 5:1; 6:9; 10:1; 11:10), which corresponds to the five occurrences of the formula in the second part of the book (11:27; 25:12, 19; 36:1[9]; 37:2). Some interpret the formula here as retrospective ("Such is the story"), referring back to chap. 1, but all its other occurrences introduce rather than summarize. It is introductory here; the Priestly source would hardly use the formula to introduce its own material in chap. 1.

The cosmogony that begins in v. 4 is concerned with the nature of human beings, narrating the story of the essential institutions and limits of the human race through their first ancestors. This cosmogony, like 1:1–3 (see note there), uses the "when . . . then" construction common in ancient cos-

m: Gn 8:17; 9:1; Ps 8:6–9; 115:16; Wis 9:2. *n:* Gn 9:3; Ps 104:14–15. *o:* 1 Tm 4:4. *p:* Is 45:12; Jn 1:3. *q:* Ex 20:9–11; 31:17; Heb 4:4, 10. *r:* Ex 20:11; Dt 5:14; Neh 9:14.

When the LORD God made the earth and the
heavens—5there was no field shrub on earth
and no grass of the field had sprouted, for the
LORD God had sent no rain upon the earth
and there was no man* to till the ground, 6but
a stream* was welling up out of the earth and
watering all the surface of the ground—
7then the LORD God formed the man* out of
the dust of the ground and blew into his nostrils the breath of life, and the man became a
living being.[s]

8The LORD God planted a garden in Eden,
in the east,* and placed there the man whom
he had formed.[t] 9* Out of the ground the
LORD God made grow every tree that was
delightful to look at and good for food, with
the tree of life in the middle of the garden
and the tree of the knowledge of good and
evil.[u]

10A river rises in Eden* to water the garden; beyond there it divides and becomes
four branches. 11The name of the first is the
Pishon; it is the one that winds through the
whole land of Havilah, where there is gold.
12The gold of that land is good; bdellium and
lapis lazuli are also there. 13The name of the
second river is the Gihon; it is the one that
winds all through the land of Cush.[v] 14The
name of the third river is the Tigris; it is the
one that flows east of Asshur. The fourth
river is the Euphrates.

15The LORD God then took the man and
settled him in the garden of Eden, to cultivate and care for it.[w] 16The LORD God gave

mogonies. The account is generally attributed to the Yahwist, who prefers the divine name "Yhwh" (here rendered LORD) for God. God in this story is called "the LORD God" (except in 3:1–5); "LORD" is to be expected in a Yahwist account but the additional word "God" is puzzling.

2:5 Man: the Hebrew word *'adam* is a generic term meaning "human being." In chaps. 2–3, however, the archetypal human being is understood to be male (Adam), so the word *'adam* is translated "man" here.

2:6 Stream: the water wells up from the vast flood below the earth. The account seems to presuppose that only the garden of God was irrigated at this point. From this one source of all the fertilizing water on the earth, water will be channeled through the garden of God over the entire earth. It is the source of the four rivers mentioned in vv. 10–14. Later, with rain and cultivation, the fertility of the garden of God will appear in all parts of the world.

2:7 God is portrayed as a potter molding the human body out of earth. There is a play on words in Hebrew between *'adam* ("human being," "man") and *'adama* ("ground"). It is not enough to make the body from earth; God must also breathe into the man's nostrils. A similar picture of divine breath imparted to human beings in order for them to live is found in Ez 37:5, 9–10; Jn 20:22. The Israelites did not think in the (Greek) categories of body and soul.

2:8 Eden, in the east: the place names in vv. 8–14 are mostly derived from Mesopotamian geography (see note on vv. 10–14). Eden may be the name of a region in southern Mesopotamia (modern Iraq), the term derived from the Sumerian word *eden*, "fertile plain." A similar-sounding Hebrew word means "delight," which may lie behind the Greek translation, "The Lord God planted a paradise [= pleasure park] in Eden." It should be noted, however, that the garden was not intended as a paradise for the human race, but as a pleasure park for God; the man tended it for God. The story is not about "paradise lost."

The garden in the precincts of Solomon's Temple in Jerusalem seems to symbolize the garden of God (like gardens in other temples); it is apparently alluded to in Ps 1:3; 80:10; 92:14; Ez 47:7–12; Rev 22:1–2.

2:9 The second tree, the tree of life, is mentioned here and at the end of the story (3:22, 24). It is identified with Wisdom in Prv 3:18; 11:30; 13:12; 15:4, where the pursuit of wisdom gives back to human beings the life that is made inaccessible to them in Gn 3:24. In the new creation described in the Book of Revelation, the tree of life is once again made available to human beings (Rev 2:7; 22:2, 14, 19). **Knowledge of good and evil**: the meaning is disputed. According to some, it signifies moral autonomy, control over morality (symbolized by "good and evil"), which would be inappropriate for mere human beings; the phrase would thus mean refusal to accept the human condition and finite freedom that God gives them. According to others, it is more broadly the knowledge of what is helpful and harmful to humankind, suggesting that the attainment of adult experience and responsibility inevitably means the loss of a life of simple subordination to God.

2:10–14 A river rises in Eden: the stream of water mentioned in v. 6, the source of all water upon earth, comes to the surface in the garden of God and from there flows out over the entire earth. In comparable religious literature, the dwelling of god is the source of fertilizing waters. The four rivers represent universality, as in the phrase "the four quarters of the earth." In Ez 47:1–12; Zec 14:8; Rev 22:1–2, the waters that irrigate the earth arise in the temple or city of God. The place names in vv. 11–14 are mainly from southern Mesopotamia (modern Iraq), where Mesopotamian literature placed the original garden of God. The Tigris and the Euphrates, the two great rivers in that part of the world, both emptied into the Persian Gulf. Gihon is the modest stream issuing from Jerusalem (2 Sm 5:8; 1 Kgs 1:9–10; 2 Chr 32:4), but is here regarded as one of the four great world rivers and linked to Mesopotamia, for Cush here seems to be the territory of the Kassites (a people of Mesopotamia) as in Gn 10:8. The word Pishon is otherwise unknown but is probably formed in imitation of Gihon. Havilah seems, according to Gn 10:7 and 1 Chr 1:9, to be in Cush in southern Mesopotamia though other locations have been suggested.

s: Gn 3:19; 18:27; Tb 8:6; Jb 34:15; Ps 103:14; 104:29; Eccl 3:20; 12:7; Wis 7:1; Sir 33:10; 1 Cor 15:45. *t:* Is 51:3; Ez 31:9. *u:* Gn 3:22; Prv 3:18; Rev 2:7; 22:2, 14. *v:* Sir 24:25. *w:* Sir 7:15.

the man this order: You are free to eat from any of the trees of the garden[x] [17]except the tree of knowledge of good and evil. From that tree you shall not eat; when you eat from it you shall die.[*] [y]

[18]The LORD God said: It is not good for the man to be alone. I will make a helper suited to him.[*] [z] [19]So the LORD God formed out of the ground all the wild animals and all the birds of the air, and he brought them to the man to see what he would call them; whatever the man called each living creature was then its name. [20]The man gave names to all the tame animals, all the birds of the air, and all the wild animals; but none proved to be a helper suited to the man.

[21]So the LORD God cast a deep sleep on the man, and while he was asleep, he took out one of his ribs and closed up its place with flesh.[a] [22]The LORD God then built the rib that he had taken from the man into a woman. When he brought her to the man, [23]the man said:

"This one, at last, is bone of my bones
and flesh of my flesh;
This one shall be called 'woman,'
for out of man this one has been taken."[*]

[24][b] That is why a man leaves his father and mother and clings to his wife, and the two of them become one body.[*]

[25]The man and his wife were both naked, yet they felt no shame.[*]

CHAPTER 3

See RG 104–6

Expulsion from Eden. [1]Now the snake was the most cunning[*] of all the wild animals that the LORD God had made. He asked the woman, "Did God really say, 'You shall not eat from any of the trees in the garden'?" [2]The woman answered the snake: "We may eat of the fruit of the trees in the garden; [3][c] it is only about the fruit of the tree in the middle of the garden that God said, 'You shall not eat it or even touch it, or else you will die.' " [4]But the snake said to the woman: "You certainly will not die![d] [5]God knows well that when you eat of it your eyes will be opened and you will be like gods, who know[*] good and evil." [6]The woman saw that the tree was good for food and pleasing to the eyes, and the tree was desirable for gaining wisdom. So she took some of its fruit and ate it; and she also gave some to her husband, who was with her, and he ate it.[e] [7]Then the eyes of both of them were opened, and they knew that they were naked; so they sewed fig leaves together and made loincloths for themselves.

[8]When they heard the sound of the LORD God walking about in the garden at the breezy time of the day,[*] the man and his wife hid themselves from the LORD God among the trees of the garden.[f] [9]The LORD God then called to the man and asked him: Where are you? [10]He answered, "I heard you in the garden; but I was afraid, because I was naked, so I hid." [11]Then God asked: Who told you that you were naked? Have you eaten from the tree of which I had forbidden you to eat? [12]The man replied, "The woman whom you put here with me—she gave me fruit from the tree, so I ate it." [13]The LORD God then asked the woman: What is this you have

2:17 You shall die: since they do not die as soon as they eat from the forbidden tree, the meaning seems to be that human beings have become mortal, destined to die by virtue of being human.

2:18 Helper suited to him: lit., "a helper in accord with him." "Helper" need not imply subordination, for God is called a helper (Dt 33:7; Ps 46:2). The language suggests a profound affinity between the man and the woman and a relationship that is supportive and nurturing.

2:23 The man recognizes an affinity with the woman God has brought him. Unlike the animals who were made from the ground, she is made from his very self. There is a play on the similar-sounding Hebrew words *'ishsha* ("woman," "wife") and *'ish* ("man," "husband").

2:24 One body: lit., "one flesh." The covenant of marriage establishes kinship bonds of the first rank between the partners.

2:25 They felt no shame: marks a new stage in the drama, for the reader knows that only young children know no shame. This draws the reader into the next episode, where the couple's disobedience results in their loss of innocence.

3:1 Cunning: there is a play on the words for "naked" (2:25) and "cunning/wise" (Heb. *'arum*). The couple seek to be "wise" but end up knowing that they are "naked."

3:5 Like gods, who know: or "like God who knows."

3:8 The breezy time of the day: lit., "the wind of the day." Probably shortly before sunset.

x: Ps 104:14–15. *y:* Gn 3:2–3; Rom 6:23. *z:* Tb 8:6; Sir 36:24; 1 Cor 11:9; 1 Tm 2:13. *a:* Sir 17:1; 1 Cor 11:8–9; 1 Tm 2:13. *b:* Mt 19:5; Mk 10:7; 1 Cor 7:10–11; Eph 5:31. *c:* Gn 2:17; Rom 6:23. *d:* Wis 2:24; Sir 25:14; Is 14:14; Jn 8:44; 2 Cor 11:3. *e:* Gn 3:22; 1 Tm 2:14. *f:* Jer 23:24.

done? The woman answered, "The snake tricked me, so I ate it."[g]
14Then the LORD God said to the snake:

Because you have done this,
cursed are you
among all the animals, tame or wild;
On your belly you shall crawl,
and dust you shall eat
all the days of your life.* [h]
15 I will put enmity between you and the woman,
and between your offspring and hers;
They will strike at your head,
while you strike at their heel.* [i]

16To the woman he said:

I will intensify your toil in childbearing;
in pain* you shall bring forth children.
Yet your urge shall be for your husband,
and he shall rule over you.

17To the man he said: Because you listened to your wife and ate from the tree about which I commanded you, You shall not eat from it,

Cursed is the ground* because of you!
In toil you shall eat its yield
all the days of your life.[j]
18 Thorns and thistles it shall bear for you,
and you shall eat the grass of the field.
19 By the sweat of your brow
you shall eat bread,
Until you return to the ground,
from which you were taken;
For you are dust,
and to dust you shall return.[k]

20The man gave his wife the name "Eve," because she was the mother of all the living.*
21The LORD God made for the man and his wife garments of skin, with which he clothed them. 22Then the LORD God said: See! The man has become like one of us, knowing good and evil! Now, what if he also reaches out his hand to take fruit from the tree of life, and eats of it and lives forever?[l]
23The LORD God therefore banished him from the garden of Eden, to till the ground from which he had been taken. 24He expelled the man, stationing the cherubim and the fiery revolving sword east of the garden of Eden, to guard the way to the tree of life.

CHAPTER 4

See RG 106

Cain and Abel. 1The man had intercourse with his wife Eve, and she conceived and gave birth to Cain, saying, "I have produced a male child with the help of the LORD."** 2Next she gave birth to his brother

3:14 Each of the three punishments (the snake, the woman, the man) has a double aspect, one affecting the individual and the other affecting a basic relationship. The snake previously stood upright, enjoyed a reputation for being shrewder than other creatures, and could converse with human beings as in vv. 1–5. It must now move on its belly, is more cursed than any creature, and inspires revulsion in human beings (v. 15).

3:15 They will strike . . . at their heel: the antecedent for "they" and "their" is the collective noun "offspring," i.e., all the descendants of the woman. Christian tradition has seen in this passage, however, more than unending hostility between snakes and human beings. The snake was identified with the devil (Wis 2:24; Jn 8:44; Rev 12:9; 20:2), whose eventual defeat seemed implied in the verse. Because "the Son of God was revealed to destroy the works of the devil" (1 Jn 3:8), the passage was understood as the first promise of a redeemer for fallen humankind, the protoevangelium. Irenaeus of Lyons (ca. A.D. 130–200), in his *Against Heresies* 5.21.1, followed by several other Fathers of the Church, interpreted the verse as referring to Christ, and cited Gal 3:19 and 4:4 to support the reference. Another interpretive translation is *ipsa*, "she," and is reflected in Jerome's Vulgate. "She" was thought to refer to Mary, the mother of the messiah. In Christian art Mary is sometimes depicted with her foot on the head of the serpent.

3:16 Toil . . . pain: the punishment affects the woman directly by increasing the toil and pain of having children. **He shall rule over you**: the punishment also affects the woman's relationship with her husband. A tension is set up in which her urge (either sexual urge or, more generally, dependence for sustenance) is for her husband but he rules over her. But see Sg 7:11.

3:17–19 Cursed is the ground: the punishment affects the man's relationship to the ground (*'adam* and *'adamah*). **You are dust**: the punishment also affects the man directly insofar as he is now mortal.

3:20 The man gives his wife a more specific name than "woman" (2:23). The Hebrew name *hawwa* ("Eve") is related to the Hebrew word *hay* ("living"); "mother of all the living" points forward to the next episode involving her sons Cain and Abel.

4:1 The Hebrew name *qayin* ("Cain") and the term *qaniti* ("I have produced") present a wordplay that refers to metalworking; such wordplays are frequent in Genesis.

g: 2 Cor 11:3. *h:* Is 65:25; Mi 7:17; Rev 12:9. *i:* Rom 16:20; 1 Jn 3:8; Rev 12:17. *j:* Gn 5:29; Rom 5:12; 8:20; Heb 6:8. *k:* Gn 2:7; Jb 10:9; 34:15; Ps 90:3; 103:14; Eccl 3:20; 12:7; Wis 15:8; Sir 10:9; 17:2; Rom 5:12; 1 Cor 15:21; Heb 9:27. *l:* Gn 2:9; Rev 22:2, 14.

Abel. Abel became a herder of flocks, and Cain a tiller of the ground.* 3 In the course of time Cain brought an offering to the LORD from the fruit of the ground, 4 while Abel, for his part, brought the fatty portion* of the firstlings of his flock.[m] The LORD looked with favor on Abel and his offering, 5 but on Cain and his offering he did not look with favor. So Cain was very angry and dejected. 6 Then the LORD said to Cain: Why are you angry? Why are you dejected? 7 If you act rightly, you will be accepted;* but if not, sin lies in wait at the door: its urge is for you, yet you can rule over it.[n]

8 Cain said to his brother Abel, "Let us go out in the field."* When they were in the field, Cain attacked his brother Abel and killed him.[o] 9 Then the LORD asked Cain, Where is your brother Abel? He answered, "I do not know. Am I my brother's keeper?" 10 God then said: What have you done? Your brother's blood cries out to me from the ground! 11 Now you are banned from the ground* that opened its mouth to receive your brother's blood from your hand.[p] 12 If you till the ground, it shall no longer give you its produce. You shall become a constant wanderer on the earth. 13 Cain said to the LORD: "My punishment is too great to bear. 14 Look, you have now banished me from the ground. I must avoid you and be a constant wanderer on the earth. Anyone may kill me at sight." 15 Not so! the LORD said to him. If anyone kills Cain, Cain shall be avenged seven times. So the LORD put a mark* on Cain, so that no one would kill him at sight. 16 Cain then left the LORD's presence and settled in the land of Nod,* east of Eden.

Descendants of Cain and Seth. 17* Cain had intercourse with his wife, and she conceived and bore Enoch. Cain also became the founder of a city, which he named after his son Enoch. 18 To Enoch was born Irad, and Irad became the father of Mehujael; Mehujael became the father of Methusael, and Methusael became the father of Lamech. 19 Lamech took two wives; the name of the first was Adah, and the name of the second Zillah. 20 Adah gave birth to Jabal, who became the ancestor of those who dwell in tents and keep livestock. 21 His brother's name was Jubal, who became the ancestor of all who play the lyre and the reed pipe. 22 Zillah, on her part, gave birth to Tubalcain, the ancestor of all who forge instruments of bronze and iron. The sister of Tubalcain was Naamah. 23* Lamech said to his wives:

4:2 Some suggest the story reflects traditional strife between the farmer (Cain) and the nomad (Abel), with preference for the latter reflecting the alleged nomadic ideal of the Bible. But there is no disparagement of farming here, for Adam was created to till the soil. The story is about two brothers (the word "brother" occurs seven times) and God's unexplained preference for one, which provokes the first murder. The motif of the preferred younger brother will occur time and again in the Bible, e.g., Isaac, Jacob, Joseph, and David (1 Sm 16:1–13).

4:4 Fatty portion: it was standard practice to offer the fat portions of animals. Others render, less satisfactorily, "the choicest of the firstlings." The point is not that Abel gave a more valuable gift than Cain, but that God, for reasons not given in the text, accepts the offering of Abel and rejects that of Cain.

4:7 You will be accepted: the text is extraordinarily condensed and unclear. "You will be accepted" is a paraphrase of one Hebrew word, "lifting." God gives a friendly warning to Cain that his right conduct will bring "lifting," which could refer to acceptance (*lifting*) of his future offerings or of himself (as in the Hebrew idiom "*lifting* of the face") or *lifting* up of his head in honor (cf. note on 40:13), whereas wicked conduct will make him vulnerable to sin, which is personified as a force ready to attack. In any case, Cain has the ability to do the right thing. **Lies in wait**: sin is personified as a power that "lies in wait" (Heb. *robes*) at a place. In Mesopotamian religion, a related word (*rabisu*) refers to a malevolent god who attacks human beings in particular places like roofs or canals.

4:8 Let us go out in the field: to avoid detection. The verse presumes a sizeable population which Genesis does not otherwise explain.

4:11 Banned from the ground: lit., "cursed." The verse refers back to 3:17 where the ground was cursed so that it yields its produce only with great effort. Cain has polluted the soil with his brother's blood and it will no longer yield any of its produce to him.

4:15 A mark: probably a tattoo to mark Cain as protected by God. The use of tattooing for tribal marks has always been common among the Bedouin of the Near Eastern deserts.

4:16 The land of Nod: a symbolic name (derived from the verb *nûd*, to wander) rather than a definite geographic region.

4:17–24 Cain is the first in a seven-member linear genealogy ending in three individuals who initiate action (Jabal, Jubal, and Tubalcain). Other Genesis genealogies also end in three individuals initiating action (5:32 and 11:26). The purpose of this genealogy is to explain the origin of culture and crafts among human beings. The names in this genealogy are the same (some with different spellings) as those in the ten-member genealogy (ending with Noah), which has a slightly different function. See note on 5:1–32.

4:23–24 Lamech's boast shows that the violence of Cain

m: Ex 34:19; Heb 11:4. *n:* Sir 7:1; Jude 11. *o:* Wis 10:3; Mt 23:35; Lk 11:51; 1 Jn 3:12; Jude 11. *p:* Dt 27:24.

"Adah and Zillah, hear my voice;
wives of Lamech, listen to my
utterance:
I have killed a man for wounding me,
a young man for bruising me.
24 If Cain is avenged seven times,
then Lamech seventy-seven times."

25* Adam again had intercourse with his
wife, and she gave birth to a son whom she
called Seth. "God has granted me another
offspring in place of Abel," she said, "because Cain killed him." 26 To Seth, in turn, a
son was born, and he named him Enosh.
At that time people began to invoke the
LORD by name.[q]

See RG 106

CHAPTER 5

*Generations: Adam to Noah.** 1[r] This
is the record of the descendants of Adam.
When God created human beings, he made
them in the likeness of God; 2 he created
them male and female. When they were created, he blessed them and named them humankind.
3[s] Adam was one hundred and thirty years
old when he begot a son in his likeness, after
his image; and he named him Seth.[t] 4 Adam
lived eight hundred years after he begot
Seth, and he had other sons and daughters.
5 The whole lifetime of Adam was nine hundred and thirty years; then he died.

6 When Seth was one hundred and five
years old, he begot Enosh. 7 Seth lived eight
hundred and seven years after he begot
Enosh, and he had other sons and daughters.
8 The whole lifetime of Seth was nine hundred and twelve years; then he died.
9 When Enosh was ninety years old, he begot Kenan. 10 Enosh lived eight hundred and
fifteen years after he begot Kenan, and he
had other sons and daughters. 11 The whole
lifetime of Enosh was nine hundred and five
years; then he died.
12 When Kenan was seventy years old, he
begot Mahalalel. 13 Kenan lived eight hundred and forty years after he begot Mahalalel, and he had other sons and daughters.
14 The whole lifetime of Kenan was nine
hundred and ten years; then he died.
15 When Mahalalel was sixty-five years
old, he begot Jared. 16 Mahalalel lived eight
hundred and thirty years after he begot Jared, and he had other sons and daughters.
17 The whole lifetime of Mahalalel was eight
hundred and ninety-five years; then he died.
18 When Jared was one hundred and sixty-
two years old, he begot Enoch. 19 Jared lived
eight hundred years after he begot Enoch,
and he had other sons and daughters. 20 The
whole lifetime of Jared was nine hundred
and sixty-two years; then he died.
21 When Enoch was sixty-five years old,
he begot Methuselah. 22 Enoch walked with

continues with his son and has actually increased. The question is posed to the reader: how will God's creation be renewed?

4:25–26 The third and climactic birth story in the chapter, showing that this birth, unlike the other two, will have good results. The name Seth (from the Hebrew verb *shat*, "to place, replace") shows that God has replaced Abel with a worthy successor. From this favored line Enosh ("human being/humankind"), a synonym of Adam, authentic religion began with the worship of Yhwh; this divine name is rendered as "the LORD" in this translation. The Yahwist source employs the name Yhwh long before the time of Moses. Another ancient source, the Elohist (from its use of the term *Elohim*, "God," instead of *Yhwh*, "LORD," for the pre-Mosaic period), makes Moses the first to use Yhwh as the proper name of Israel's God, previously known by other names as well; cf. Ex 3:13–15.

5:1–32 The second of the five Priestly formulas in Part I ("This is the record of the descendants . . ."; see 2:4a; 6:9; 10:1; 11:10) introduces the second of the three linear genealogies in Gn 1–11 (4:17–24 and 11:10–26). In each, a list of individuals (six in 4:17–24, ten in 5:1–32, or nine in 11:10–26) ends in three people who initiate action. Linear genealogies (father to son) in ancient societies had a communicative function, grounding the authority or claim of the last-named individual in the first-named. Here, the genealogy has a literary function as well, advancing the story by showing the expansion of the human race after Adam, as well as the transmission to his descendant Noah of the divine image given to Adam. Correcting the impression one might get from the genealogy in 4:17–24, this genealogy traces the line through Seth rather than through Cain. Most of the names in the series are the same as the names in Cain's line in 4:17–19 (Enosh, Enoch, Lamech) or spelled with variant spellings (Mahalalel, Jared, Methuselah). The genealogy itself and its placement before the flood shows the influence of ancient Mesopotamian literature, which contains lists of cities and kings before and after the flood. Before the flood, the ages of the kings ranged from 18,600 to 36,000 years, but after it were reduced to between 140 and 1,200 years. The biblical numbers are much smaller. There are some differences in the numbers in the Hebrew and Greek manuscripts.

q: 1 Chr 1:1; Lk 3:38. *r:* Gn 1:27; Wis 2:23; Sir 17:1; Jas 3:9. *s:* 1 Chr 1:1–4; Lk 3:36–38. *t:* Gn 4:25.

The *Toledoth* ("Generations") Lists

IN THE TEXT of Genesis, the Hebrew word ***toledoth*** (pronounced "tole-uh-DOTE" and meaning "generations" or "descendants") serves as a marker for the end of one section of the narrative and the beginning of the next. Here are the places where the word occurs:

2:4a	The second creation story
5:1	Introduces the section between the first human family and the days of Noah
6:9	Introduces the story of the flood
10:1	The expansion of people over the earth
11:10	A new list of the nations of the earth
11:27	The beginning of Abraham's story
25:12	The end of the story of Hagar and Ishmael, Abraham's other family
25:19	Introduces Jacob's story
36:1	The end of Esau's story and the beginning of the story of Jacob's children
36:9	The conclusion of the list
37:2	The beginning of the story of Joseph and his brothers

God after he begot Methuselah for three
hundred years, and he had other sons and
daughters. 23The whole lifetime of Enoch
was three hundred and sixty-five years.
24Enoch walked with God,* and he was no
longer here, for God took him.[u]

25When Methuselah was one hundred and
eighty-seven years old, he begot Lamech.
26Methuselah lived seven hundred and
eighty-two years after he begot Lamech, and
he had other sons and daughters. 27The
whole lifetime of Methuselah was nine hundred and sixty-nine years; then he died.

28When Lamech was one hundred and
eighty-two years old, he begot a son 29[v] and
named him Noah, saying, "This one shall
bring us relief from our work and the toil of
our hands, out of the very ground that the
LORD has put under a curse."* 30Lamech
lived five hundred and ninety-five years after he begot Noah, and he had other sons and
daughters. 31The whole lifetime of Lamech
was seven hundred and seventy-seven years;
then he died.

32When Noah was five hundred years old,
he begot Shem, Ham, and Japheth.* [w]

CHAPTER 6

See RG 106-7

Origin of the Nephilim.* 1When human beings began to grow numerous on the

5:24 Enoch is in the important seventh position in the ten-member genealogy. In place of the usual formula "then he died," the change to "Enoch walked with God" implies that he did not die, but like Elijah (2 Kgs 2:11–12) was taken alive to God's abode. This mysterious narrative spurred much speculation and writing (beginning as early as the third century B.C.) about Enoch the sage who knew the secrets of heaven and who could communicate them to human beings (see Sir 44:16; 49:14; Heb 11:5; Jude 14–15 and the apocryphal work 1 Enoch).

5:29 The sound of the Hebrew word *noah*, "Noah," is echoed in the word *yenahamenu*, "he will bring us relief"; the latter refers both to the curse put on the soil because of human disobedience (3:17–19) and to Noah's success in agriculture, especially in raising grapes for wine (9:20–21).

5:32 Shem, Ham, and Japheth: like the genealogies in 4:17–24 and 11:10–26, the genealogy ends in three individuals who engage in important activity. Their descendants will be detailed in chap. 10, where it will be seen that the lineage is political-geographical as well as "ethnic."

6:1–4 These enigmatic verses are a transition between the expansion of the human race illustrated in the genealogy of chap. 5 and the flood depicted in chaps. 6–9. The text, apparently alluding to an old legend, shares a common ancient view that the heavenly world was populated by a multitude of beings, some of whom were wicked and rebellious. It is incorporated here, not only in order to account for the prehistoric giants, whom the Israelites called the Nephilim, but also to introduce the story of the flood with a moral orientation—the constantly increasing wickedness of humanity. This increasing wickedness leads God to reduce the human life span imposed on the first couple. As the ages in the preceding genealogy show, life spans had been exceptionally long in the early period, but God further reduces them to something near the ordinary life span.

u: Wis 4:10–11; Sir 44:16; 49:14; Heb 11:5. *v:* Gn 3:17–19. *w:* Gn 6:10; 10:1.

earth and daughters were born to them, 2the sons of God* saw how beautiful the daughters of human beings were, and so they took for their wives whomever they pleased.[x] 3Then the LORD said: My spirit shall not remain in human beings forever, because they are only flesh. Their days shall comprise one hundred and twenty years.

4The Nephilim appeared on earth in those days, as well as later,* after the sons of God had intercourse with the daughters of human beings, who bore them sons. They were the heroes of old, the men of renown.[y]

Warning of the Flood. 5* When the LORD saw how great the wickedness of human beings was on earth, and how every desire that their heart conceived was always nothing but evil,[z] 6the LORD regretted making human beings on the earth, and his heart was grieved.*

7So the LORD said: I will wipe out from the earth the human beings I have created, and not only the human beings, but also the animals and the crawling things and the birds of the air, for I regret that I made them.* 8But Noah found favor with the LORD.

9These are the descendants of Noah. Noah was a righteous man and blameless in his generation;[a] Noah walked with God. 10Noah begot three sons: Shem, Ham, and Japheth.

11But the earth was corrupt* in the view of God and full of lawlessness.[b] 12When God saw how corrupt the earth had become, since all mortals had corrupted their ways on earth,[c] 13God said to Noah: I see that the end of all mortals has come, for the earth is full of lawlessness because of them. So I am going to destroy them with the earth.[d]

Preparation for the Flood. 14Make yourself an ark of gopherwood,* equip the ark with various compartments, and cover it inside and out with pitch. 15This is how you shall build it: the length of the ark will be three hundred cubits, its width fifty cubits, and its height thirty cubits.* 16Make an opening for daylight* and finish the ark a cubit above it. Put the ark's entrance on its side; you will make it with bottom, second and third decks. 17I, on my part, am about to bring the flood waters on the earth, to destroy all creatures under the sky in which there is the

6:2 The sons of God: other heavenly beings. See note on 1:26.

6:4 As well as later: the belief was common that human beings of gigantic stature once lived on earth. In some cultures, such heroes could make positive contributions, but the Bible generally regards them in a negative light (cf. Nm 13:33; Ez 32:27). The point here is that even these heroes, filled with vitality from their semi-divine origin, come under God's decree in v. 3.

6:5–8:22 The story of the great flood is commonly regarded as a composite narrative based on separate sources woven together. To the Yahwist source, with some later editorial additions, are usually assigned 6:5–8; 7:1–5, 7–10, 12, 16b, 17b, 22–23; 8:2b–3a, 6–12, 13b, 20–22. The other sections are usually attributed to the Priestly writer. There are differences between the two sources: the Priestly source has two pairs of every animal, whereas the Yahwist source has seven pairs of clean animals and two pairs of unclean; the floodwater in the Priestly source is the waters under and over the earth that burst forth, whereas in the Yahwist source the floodwater is the rain lasting forty days and nights. In spite of many obvious discrepancies in these two sources, one should read the story as a coherent narrative. The biblical story ultimately draws upon an ancient Mesopotamian tradition of a great flood, preserved in the Sumerian flood story, the eleventh tablet of the Gilgamesh Epic, and (embedded in a longer creation story) the Atrahasis Epic.

6:6 His heart was grieved: the expression can be misleading in English, for "heart" in Hebrew is the seat of memory and judgment rather than emotion. The phrase is actually parallel to the first half of the sentence ("the LORD regretted . . .").

6:7 Human beings are an essential part of their environment, which includes all living things. In the new beginning after the flood, God makes a covenant with human beings and every living creature (9:9–10). The same close link between human beings and nature is found elsewhere in the Bible; e.g., in Is 35, God's healing transforms human beings along with their physical environment, and in Rom 8:19–23, all creation, not merely human beings, groans in labor pains awaiting the salvation of God.

6:11 Corrupt: God does not punish arbitrarily but simply brings to its completion the corruption initiated by human beings.

6:14 Gopherwood: an unidentified wood mentioned only in connection with the ark. It may be the wood of the cypress, which in Hebrew sounds like "gopher" and was widely used in antiquity for shipbuilding.

6:15 Hebrew "cubit," lit., "forearm," is the distance from the elbow to the tip of the middle finger, about eighteen inches (a foot and a half). The dimensions of Noah's ark were approximately 440 × 73 × 44 feet. The ark of the Babylonian flood story was an exact cube, 120 cubits (180 feet) in length, width, and height.

6:16 Opening for daylight: a conjectural rendering of the Hebrew word *sohar*, occurring only here. The reference is probably to an open space on all sides near the top of the ark to admit light and air. The ark also had a window or hatch, which could be opened and closed (8:6).

x: Mt 24:38; Lk 17:26–27. *y:* Wis 14:6; Bar 3:26. *z:* Ps 14:2–3. *a:* Wis 10:4; Sir 44:17. *b:* Jb 22:15–17. *c:* Ps 14:2. *d:* Sir 40:9–10; 44:17; Mt 24:37–39.

breath of life; everything on earth shall perish.[e] 18I will establish my covenant with you. You shall go into the ark, you and your sons, your wife and your sons' wives with you.[f] 19Of all living creatures you shall bring two of every kind into the ark, one male and one female*, to keep them alive along with you. 20Of every kind of bird, of every kind of animal, and of every kind of thing that crawls on the ground, two of each will come to you, that you may keep them alive. 21Moreover, you are to provide yourself with all the food that is to be eaten, and store it away, that it may serve as provisions for you and for them. 22Noah complied; he did just as God had commanded him.*

See RG 106-7

CHAPTER 7

1Then the LORD said to Noah: Go into the ark, you and all your household, for you alone in this generation have I found to be righteous before me.[g] 2Of every clean animal, take with you seven pairs, a male and its mate; and of the unclean animals, one pair, a male and its mate; 3likewise, of every bird of the air, seven pairs, a male and a female, to keep their progeny alive over all the earth. 4For seven days from now I will bring rain down on the earth for forty days and forty nights, and so I will wipe out from the face of the earth every being that I have made.[h] 5Noah complied, just as the LORD had commanded.

The Great Flood. 6Noah was six hundred years old when the flood came upon the earth. 7Together with his sons, his wife, and his sons' wives, Noah went into the ark because of the waters of the flood.[i] 8Of the clean animals and the unclean, of the birds, and of everything that crawls on the ground, 9two by two, male and female came to Noah into the ark, just as God had commanded him.[j] 10When the seven days were over, the waters of the flood came upon the earth.

11In the six hundredth year of Noah's life, in the second month, on the seventeenth day of the month: on that day

All the fountains of the great abyss* burst forth,
and the floodgates of the sky were opened.

12For forty days and forty nights heavy rain poured down on the earth.

13On the very same day, Noah and his sons Shem, Ham, and Japheth, and Noah's wife, and the three wives of Noah's sons had entered the ark, 14together with every kind of wild animal, every kind of tame animal, every kind of crawling thing that crawls on the earth, and every kind of bird. 15Pairs of all creatures in which there was the breath of life came to Noah into the ark. 16Those that entered were male and female; of all creatures they came, as God had commanded Noah. Then the LORD shut him in.

17The flood continued upon the earth for forty days. As the waters increased, they lifted the ark, so that it rose above the earth. 18The waters swelled and increased greatly on the earth, but the ark floated on the surface of the waters. 19Higher and higher on the earth the waters swelled, until all the highest mountains under the heavens were submerged. 20The waters swelled fifteen cubits higher than the submerged mountains. 21All creatures that moved on earth perished: birds, tame animals, wild animals, and all

6:19–21 You shall bring two of every kind . . . , one male and one female: For the Priestly source (P), there is no distinction between clean and unclean animals until Sinai (Lv 11), no altars or sacrifice until Sinai, and all diet is vegetarian (Gn 1:29–30); even after the flood P has no distinction between clean and unclean, since "any living creature that moves about" may be eaten (9:3). Thus P has Noah take the minimum to preserve all species, one pair of each, without distinction between clean and unclean, but he must also take on provisions for food (6:21). The Yahwist source (J), which assumes the clean-unclean distinction always existed but knows no other restriction on eating meat (Abel was a shepherd and offered meat as a sacrifice), requires additional clean animals ("seven pairs") for food and sacrifice (7:2–3; 8:20).

6:22 Just as God had commanded him: as in the creation of the world in chap. 1 and in the building of the tabernacle in Ex 25–31, 35–40 (all from the Priestly source), everything takes place by the command of God. In this passage and in Exodus, the commands of God are carried out to the letter by human agents, Noah and Moses. Divine speech is important. God speaks to Noah seven times in the flood story.

7:11 Abyss: the subterranean ocean; see note on 1:2.

e: Gn 7:4, 21; 2 Pt 2:5. *f:* Gn 9:9; Wis 14:6; Heb 11:7; 1 Pt 3:20. *g:* Wis 10:4; Sir 44:17; 2 Pt 2:5. *h:* Gn 6:17; 2 Pt 2:5. *i:* Wis 14:6; 1 Pt 3:20; 2 Pt 2:5. *j:* Gn 6:19.

that teemed on the earth, as well as all humankind.[k] [22]Everything on dry land with the breath of life in its nostrils died. [23]The LORD wiped out every being on earth: human beings and animals, the crawling things and the birds of the air; all were wiped out from the earth. Only Noah and those with him in the ark were left.

[24]And when the waters had swelled on the earth for one hundred and fifty days,

CHAPTER 8

See RG 106-7

[1]God remembered Noah and all the animals, wild and tame, that were with him in the ark. So God made a wind sweep over the earth, and the waters began to subside. [2]The fountains of the abyss and the floodgates of the sky were closed, and the downpour from the sky was held back. [3]Gradually the waters receded from the earth. At the end of one hundred and fifty days, the waters had so diminished [4]that, in the seventh month, on the seventeenth day of the month, the ark came to rest on the mountains of Ararat.* [5]The waters continued to diminish until the tenth month, and on the first day of the tenth month the tops of the mountains appeared.

[6]At the end of forty days Noah opened the hatch of the ark that he had made, [7*] and he released a raven. It flew back and forth until the waters dried off from the earth. [8]Then he released a dove, to see if the waters had lessened on the earth. [9]But the dove could find no place to perch, and it returned to him in the ark, for there was water over all the earth. Putting out his hand, he caught the dove and drew it back to him inside the ark. [10]He waited yet seven days more and again released the dove from the ark. [11]In the evening the dove came back to him, and there in its bill was a plucked-off olive leaf! So Noah knew that the waters had diminished on the earth. [12]He waited yet another seven days and then released the dove; but this time it did not come back.

[13*] In the six hundred and first year, in the first month, on the first day of the month, the water began to dry up on the earth. Noah then removed the covering of the ark and saw that the surface of the ground had dried. [14]In the second month, on the twenty-seventh day of the month, the earth was dry.

[15]Then God said to Noah: [16]Go out of the ark, together with your wife and your sons and your sons' wives. [17]Bring out with you every living thing that is with you—all creatures, be they birds or animals or crawling things that crawl on the earth—and let them abound on the earth, and be fertile and multiply on it.[l] [18]So Noah came out, together with his sons and his wife and his sons' wives; [19]and all the animals, all the birds, and all the crawling creatures that crawl on the earth went out of the ark by families.

[20]Then Noah built an altar to the LORD, and choosing from every clean animal and every clean bird, he offered burnt offerings on the altar. [21]When the LORD smelled the sweet odor, the LORD said to himself: Never again will I curse the ground because of human beings, since the desires of the human heart are evil from youth; nor will I ever again strike down every living being, as I have done.[m]

[22] All the days of the earth,
    seedtime and harvest,
    cold and heat,
Summer and winter,
    and day and night
    shall not cease.[n]

CHAPTER 9

See RG 106-7

Covenant with Noah. [1*] God blessed Noah and his sons and said to them: Be fertile and multiply and fill the earth.[o] [2*] Fear

8:4 The mountains of Ararat: the mountain country of ancient Arartu in northwest Iraq, which was the highest part of the world to the biblical writer. There is no Mount Ararat in the Bible.

8:7–12 In the eleventh tablet of the Gilgamesh Epic, Utnapishtim (the equivalent of Noah) released in succession a dove, a swallow, and a raven. When the raven did not return, Utnapishtim knew it was safe to leave the ark. The first century A.D. Roman author Pliny tells of Indian sailors who release birds in order to follow them toward land.

8:13–14 On the first day of the first month, the world was in the state it had been on the day of creation in chap. 1. Noah had to wait another month until the earth was properly dry as in 1:9.

9:1 God reaffirms without change the original blessing and

k: Jb 22:16; Mt 24:39; Lk 17:27; 2 Pt 3:6. *l:* Gn 1:22, 28. *m:* Sir 44:18; Is 54:9; Rom 7:18. *n:* Jer 33:20, 25. *o:* Gn 1:22, 28; 8:17.

and dread of you shall come upon all the animals of the earth and all the birds of the air,
upon all the creatures that move about on the
ground and all the fishes of the sea; into your
power they are delivered. [3][p] Any living creature that moves about shall be yours to eat; I
give them all to you as I did the green plants.
[4][q] Only meat with its lifeblood still in it you
shall not eat.* [5]Indeed for your own
lifeblood I will demand an accounting: from
every animal I will demand it, and from a
human being, each one for the blood of another, I will demand an accounting for human life.[r]

[6] * Anyone who sheds the blood of a
human being,
by a human being shall that one's
blood be shed;
For in the image of God
have human beings been made.[s]

[7]Be fertile, then, and multiply; abound on
earth and subdue it.[t]
[8]* God said to Noah and to his sons with
him: [9]See, I am now establishing my covenant with you and your descendants after
you[u] [10]and with every living creature that
was with you: the birds, the tame animals,
and all the wild animals that were with
you—all that came out of the ark. [11]I will establish my covenant with you, that never
again shall all creatures be destroyed by the
waters of a flood; there shall not be another
flood to devastate the earth.[v] [12]God said:
This is the sign of the covenant that I am
making between me and you and every living creature with you for all ages to come:
[13][w] I set my bow in the clouds to serve as a
sign of the covenant between me and the
earth. [14]When I bring clouds over the earth,
and the bow appears in the clouds, [15]I will
remember my covenant between me and you
and every living creature—every mortal being—so that the waters will never again become a flood to destroy every mortal being.[x]
[16]When the bow appears in the clouds, I will
see it and remember the everlasting covenant between God and every living creature—every mortal being that is on earth.
[17]God told Noah: This is the sign of the covenant I have established between me and
every mortal being that is on earth.

Noah and His Sons. [18]* The sons of Noah
who came out of the ark were Shem, Ham
and Japheth. Ham was the father of Canaan.[y]
[19]These three were the sons of Noah, and
from them the whole earth was populated.

[20]Noah, a man of the soil, was the first to
plant a vineyard. [21]He drank some of the
wine, became drunk, and lay naked inside
his tent.[z] [22]Ham, the father of Canaan, saw
his father's nakedness, and he told his two
brothers outside. [23]Shem and Japheth, however, took a robe, and holding it on their
shoulders, they walked backward and covered their father's nakedness; since their
faces were turned the other way, they did not
see their father's nakedness. [24]When Noah

mandate of 1:28. In the Mesopotamian epic Atrahasis, on which the Genesis story is partly modeled, the gods changed their original plan by restricting human population through such means as childhood diseases, birth demons, and mandating celibacy among certain groups of women.

9:2–3 Pre-flood creatures, including human beings, are depicted as vegetarians (1:29–30). In view of the human propensity to violence, God changes the original prohibition against eating meat.

9:4 Because a living being dies when it loses most of its blood, the ancients regarded blood as the seat of life, and therefore as sacred. Jewish tradition considered the prohibition against eating meat with blood to be binding on all, because it was given by God to Noah, the new ancestor of all humankind; therefore the early Christian Church retained it for a time (Acts 15:20, 29).

9:6 The image of God, given to the first man and woman and transmitted to every human being, is the reason that no violent attacks can be made upon human beings. That image is the basis of the dignity of every individual who, in some sense, "represents" God in the world.

9:8–17 God makes a covenant with Noah and his descendants and, remarkably, with all the animals who come out of the ark: never again shall the world be destroyed by flood. The sign of this solemn promise is the appearance of a rainbow.

9:18–27 The character of the three sons is sketched here. The fault is not Noah's (for he could not be expected to know about the intoxicating effect of wine) but Ham's, who shames his father by looking on his nakedness, and then tells the other sons. Ham's conduct is meant to prefigure the later shameful sexual practices of the Canaanites, which are alleged in numerous biblical passages. The point of the story is revealed in Noah's curse of Ham's son Canaan and his blessing of Shem and Japheth.

p: Gn 1:29–30; Dt 12:15. *q:* Lv 7:26–27; 17:4; Dt 12:16, 23; 1 Sm 14:33; Acts 15:20. *r:* Gn 4:10–11; Ex 21:12. *s:* Gn 1:26–27; Lv 24:17; Nm 35:33; Jas 3:9. *t:* Gn 1:28; 8:17; 9:2; Jas 3:7. *u:* Gn 6:18. *v:* Sir 44:18; Is 54:9. *w:* Sir 43:12. *x:* Is 54:9. *y:* Gn 5:32; 10:1. *z:* Lam 4:21; Hb 2:15.

woke up from his wine and learned what his
youngest son had done to him, 25he said:

"Cursed be Canaan!
The lowest of slaves
shall he be to his brothers."[a]

26He also said:

"Blessed be the LORD, the God of Shem!
Let Canaan be his slave.
27 May God expand Japheth,*
and may he dwell among the tents of
Shem;
and let Canaan be his slave."

28Noah lived three hundred and fifty years
after the flood. 29The whole lifetime of Noah
was nine hundred and fifty years; then he
died.

CHAPTER 10

See RG 107

*Table of the Nations.** 1These are the
descendants of Noah's sons, Shem, Ham and
Japheth, to whom children were born after
the flood.
2[b] The descendants of Japheth: Gomer,*
Magog, Madai, Javan, Tubal, Meshech and
Tiras.[c] 3The descendants of Gomer: Ashkenaz,* Diphath and Togarmah. 4The descendants of Javan: Elishah,* Tarshish, the Kittim and the Rodanim. 5From these branched
out the maritime nations.

These are the descendants of Japheth by
their lands, each with its own language, according to their clans, by their nations.
6The descendants of Ham: Cush,* Mizraim, Put and Canaan. 7The descendants of
Cush: Seba, Havilah, Sabtah, Raamah and
Sabteca. The descendants of Raamah: Sheba
and Dedan.
8Cush* became the father of Nimrod, who
was the first to become a mighty warrior on
earth. 9He was a mighty hunter in the eyes of
the LORD; hence the saying, "Like Nimrod, a
mighty hunter in the eyes of the LORD." 10His
kingdom originated in Babylon, Erech and
Accad, all of them in the land of Shinar.*
11From that land he went forth to Assyria,
where he built Nineveh, Rehoboth-Ir* and
Calah, 12as well as Resen, between Nineveh
and Calah,* the latter being the principal city.

9:27 In the Hebrew text there is a play on the words *yapt* ("expand") and *yepet* ("Japheth").

10:1–32 Verse 1 is the fourth of the Priestly formulas (2:4; 5:1; 6:9; 11:10) that structure Part I of Genesis; it introduces 10:2–11:9, the populating of the world and the building of the city. In a sense, chaps. 4–9 are concerned with the first of the two great commands given to the human race in 1:28, "Be fertile and multiply!" whereas chaps. 10–11 are concerned with the second command, "Fill the earth and subdue it!" ("Subdue it" refers to each nation's taking the land assigned to it by God.) Gn 9:19 already noted that all nations are descended from the three sons of Noah; the same sentiment is repeated in 10:5, 18, 25, 32; 11:8. The presupposition of the chapter is that every nation has a land assigned to it by God (cf. Dt 32:8–9). The number of the nations is seventy (if one does not count Noah and his sons, and counts Sidon [vv. 15, 19] only once), which is a traditional biblical number (Jgs 8:30; Lk 10:1, 17). According to Gn 46:27 and Ex 1:5, Israel also numbered seventy persons, which shows that it in some sense represents the nations of the earth.

This chapter classifies the various peoples known to the ancient Israelites; it is theologically important as stressing the basic family unity of all peoples on earth. It is sometimes called the Table of the Nations. The relationship between the various peoples is based on linguistic, geographic, or political grounds (v. 31). In general, the descendants of Japheth (vv. 2–5) are the peoples of the Indo-European languages to the north and west of Mesopotamia and Syria; the descendants of Ham (vv. 6–20) are the Hamitic-speaking peoples of northern Africa; and the descendants of Shem (vv. 21–31) are the Semitic-speaking peoples of Mesopotamia, Syria and Arabia. But there are many exceptions to this rule; the Semitic-speaking peoples of Canaan are considered descendants of Ham, because at one time they were subject to Hamitic Egypt (vv. 6, 15–19). This chapter is generally considered to be a composite from the Yahwist source (vv. 8–19, 21, 24–30) and the Priestly source (vv. 1–7, 20, 22–23, 31–32). Presumably that is why certain tribes of Arabia are listed under both Ham (v. 7) and Shem (vv. 26–28).

10:2 Gomer: the Cimmerians; **Madai**: the Medes; **Javan**: the Greeks.

10:3 Ashkenaz: an Indo-European people, which later became the medieval rabbinic name for Germany. It now designates one of the great divisions of Judaism, Eastern European Yiddish-speaking Jews.

10:4 Elishah: Cyprus; **the Kittim**: certain inhabitants of Cyprus; **the Rodanim**: the inhabitants of Rhodes.

10:6 Cush: biblical Ethiopia, modern Nubia. **Mizraim**: Lower (i.e., northern) Egypt; **Put**: either Punt in East Africa or Libya.

10:8 Cush: here seems to be Cossea, the country of the Kassites; see note on 2:10–14. **Nimrod**: possibly Tukulti-Ninurta I (thirteenth century B.C.), the first Assyrian conqueror of Babylonia and a famous city-builder at home.

10:10 Shinar: the land of ancient Babylonia, embracing Sumer and Akkad, present-day southern Iraq, mentioned also in 11:2; 14:1.

10:11 Rehoboth-Ir: lit., "wide-streets city," was probably not the name of another city, but an epithet of Nineveh; cf. Jon 3:3.

10:12 Calah: Assyrian Kalhu, the capital of Assyria in the ninth century B.C.

a: Dt 27:16; Wis 12:11. *b:* 1 Chr 1:5–10. *c:* Ez 38:2.

ASHKENAZ (Scythians)
Black Sea
Caspian Sea
JAPHETH
Gomer
Meshech
Tubal
LUD (Lydia)
Togarmah
JAVAN
ASSHUR (Assyria)
Nineveh
Calah
Asshur
Rodanim (Rhodes)
Caphtorim (Crete)
Hamath
Arvad
MADAI (Medes)
Elishah (Cyprus)
Aram
River Euphrates
River Tigris
Sidon
Accad
Mediterranean Sea
Babylon (Babel)
ELAM
Shinar
Gaza
Canaan
Gerar
Erech
Put (Lehabim?) (Libya)
EGYPT
MIDIAN
Persian Gulf
DEDAN
Dedan
SHEM
River Nile
OPHIR
HAM
CUSH (Ethiopia)
Red Sea
SEBA
HAZARMAVETH
SHEBA
0 100 200 Miles
0 100 200 Kilometers
Havilah
Sabtah

Table of Nations

13d Mizraim became the father of the Ludim, the Anamim, the Lehabim, the Naphtuhim, 14 the Pathrusim,* the Casluhim, and the Caphtorim from whom the Philistines came.

15 Canaan became the father of Sidon, his firstborn, and of Heth;* 16 also of the Jebusites, the Amorites, the Girgashites, 17 the Hivites, the Arkites, the Sinites, 18 the Arvadites, the Zemarites, and the Hamathites. Afterward, the clans of the Canaanites spread out, 19 so that the Canaanite borders extended from Sidon all the way to Gerar, near Gaza, and all the way to Sodom, Gomorrah, Admah and Zeboiim, near Lasha.

20 These are the descendants of Ham, according to their clans, according to their languages, by their lands, by their nations.

21 To Shem also, Japheth's oldest brother and the ancestor of all the children of Eber,* children were born. 22e The descendants of Shem: Elam, Asshur, Arpachshad, Lud and Aram. 23 The descendants of Aram: Uz, Hul, Gether and Mash.

24 Arpachshad became the father of Shelah, and Shelah became the father of Eber. 25 To Eber two sons were born: the name of the first was Peleg, for in his time the world was divided;* and the name of his brother was Joktan.

26 Joktan became the father of Almodad, Sheleph, Hazarmaveth, Jerah, 27 Hadoram, Uzal, Diklah, 28 Obal, Abimael, Sheba, 29 Ophir, Havilah and Jobab. All these were descendants of Joktan. 30 Their settlements extended all the way from Mesha to Sephar, the eastern hill country.

31 These are the descendants of Shem, according to their clans, according to their languages, by their lands, by their nations.

32 These are the clans of Noah's sons, according to their origins and by their nations. From these the nations of the earth branched out after the flood.

CHAPTER 11

See RG 107

Tower of Babel.* 1 The whole world had the same language and the same words. 2 When they were migrating from the east, they came to a valley in the land of Shinar* and settled there. 3 They said to one another, "Come, let us mold bricks and harden them with fire." They used bricks for stone, and bitumen for mortar. 4 Then they said, "Come, let us build ourselves a city and a tower with its top in the sky,* and so make a name for ourselves; otherwise we shall be scattered all over the earth."

5 The LORD came down to see the city and the tower that the people had built. 6 Then the LORD said: If now, while they are one people and all have the same language, they have started to do this, nothing they presume to do will be out of their reach. 7 Come, let us go down and there confuse their language, so that no one will understand the speech of another. 8 So the LORD scattered them from there over all the earth, and they stopped building the city. 9 That is why it was called Babel,* because there the LORD confused the speech of all the world. From there the LORD scattered them over all the earth.

Descendants from Shem to Abraham.* 10f These are the descendants of Shem. When Shem was one hundred years old, he begot

10:14 The Pathrusim: the people of Upper (southern) Egypt; cf. Is 11:11; Jer 44:1; Ez 29:14; 30:13. **Caphtorim**: Crete; for Caphtor as the place of origin of the Philistines, cf. Dt 2:23; Am 9:7; Jer 47:4.

10:15 Heth: the biblical Hittites; see note on 23:3.

10:21 Eber: the eponymous ancestor of the Hebrews, that is, the one to whom they traced their name.

10:25 In the Hebrew text there is a play on the name *Peleg* and the word *niplega*, "was divided."

11:1–9 This story illustrates increasing human wickedness, shown here in the sinful pride that human beings take in their own achievements apart from God. Secondarily, the story explains the diversity of languages among the peoples of the earth.

11:2 Shinar: see note on 10:10.

11:4 Tower with its top in the sky: possibly a reference to the chief ziggurat of Babylon, *E-sag-ila*, lit., "the house that raises high its head."

11:9 Babel: the Hebrew form of the name "Babylon"; the Babylonians interpreted their name for the city, *Bab-ili*, as "gate of god." The Hebrew word *balal*, "he confused," has a similar sound.

11:10–26 The second Priestly genealogy goes from Shem to Terah and his three sons Abram, Nahor, and Haran, just as the genealogy in 5:3–32 went from Adam to Noah and his three sons Shem, Ham, and Japheth. This genealogy marks the important transition in Genesis between the story of the nations in 1:1–11:26 and the story of Israel in the person of its ancestors (11:27–50:26). As chaps. 1–11 showed the increase

d: 1 Chr 1:11–16. *e:* 1 Chr 1:17–23. *f:* 1 Chr 1:24–27; Lk 3:34–36.

Arpachshad, two years after the flood. 11Shem
lived five hundred years after he begot
Arpachshad, and he had other sons and daughters. 12When Arpachshad was thirty-five years
old, he begot Shelah.* 13Arpachshad lived four
hundred and three years after he begot Shelah,
and he had other sons and daughters.

14When Shelah was thirty years old, he
begot Eber. 15Shelah lived four hundred and
three years after he begot Eber, and he had
other sons and daughters.

16When Eber* was thirty-four years old,
he begot Peleg. 17Eber lived four hundred
and thirty years after he begot Peleg, and he
had other sons and daughters.

18When Peleg was thirty years old, he begot Reu. 19Peleg lived two hundred and nine
years after he begot Reu, and he had other
sons and daughters.

20When Reu was thirty-two years old, he
begot Serug. 21Reu lived two hundred and
seven years after he begot Serug, and he had
other sons and daughters.

22When Serug was thirty years old, he begot Nahor. 23Serug lived two hundred years
after he begot Nahor, and he had other sons
and daughters.

24When Nahor was twenty-nine years old,
he begot Terah. 25Nahor lived one hundred
and nineteen years after he begot Terah, and
he had other sons and daughters.

26When Terah was seventy years old, he
begot Abram,* Nahor and Haran.[g]

II. The Story of the Ancestors of Israel

Terah. 27These are the descendants of Terah.* Terah begot Abram, Nahor, and Haran,
and Haran begot Lot. 28Haran died before
Terah his father, in his native land, in Ur of
the Chaldeans.* 29Abram and Nahor took
wives; the name of Abram's wife was Sarai,*
and the name of Nahor's wife was Milcah,
daughter of Haran, the father of Milcah and
Iscah.[h] 30Sarai was barren; she had no child.

31Terah took his son Abram, his grandson
Lot, son of Haran, and his daughter-in-law
Sarai, the wife of his son Abram, and
brought them out of Ur of the Chaldeans, to
go to the land of Canaan. But when they
reached Haran, they settled there.[i] 32The
lifetime of Terah was two hundred and five
years; then Terah died in Haran.*

and spread of the nations, so chaps. 12–50 will show the increase and spread of Israel. The contrast between Israel and the nations is a persistent biblical theme. The ages given here are from the Hebrew text; the Samaritan and Greek texts have divergent sets of numbers in most cases. In comparable accounts of the pre-flood period, enormous life spans are attributed to human beings. It may be an attempt to show that the pre-flood generations were extraordinary and more vital than post-flood human beings.

11:12 The Greek text adds Kenan (cf. 5:9–10) between Arpachshad and Shelah. The Greek listing is followed in Lk 3:36.

11:16 Eber: the eponymous ancestor of the Hebrews, "descendants of Eber" (10:21, 24–30); see note on 14:13.

11:26 Abram is a dialectal variant of Abraham. God will change his name in view of his new task in 17:4.

11:27 Descendants of Terah: elsewhere in Genesis the story of the son is introduced by the name of the father (25:12, 19; 36:1; 37:2). The Abraham-Sarah stories begin (11:27–32) and end with genealogical notices (25:1–18), which concern, respectively, the families of Terah and of Abraham. Most of the traditions in the cycle are from the Yahwist source. The so-called Elohist source (E) is somewhat shadowy, denied by some scholars but recognized by others in passages that duplicate other narratives (20:1–18 and 21:22–34). The Priestly source consists mostly of brief editorial notices, except for chaps. 17 and 23.

11:28 Ur of the Chaldeans: Ur was an extremely ancient city of the Sumerians (later, of the Babylonians) in southern Mesopotamia. The Greek text has "the land of the Chaldeans." After a millennium of relative unimportance, Ur underwent a revival during the Neo-Babylonian/Chaldean empire (625–539 B.C.). The sixth-century author here identified the place by its contemporary name. As chap. 24 shows, Haran in northern Mesopotamia is in fact the native place of Abraham. In the Genesis perspective, the human race originated in the East (3:24; 4:16) and migrated from there to their homelands (11:2). Terah's family moved from the East (Ur) and Abraham will complete the journey to the family's true homeland in the following chapters.

11:29 Sarai: like Abram, a dialectal variant of the more usual form of the name Sarah. In 17:15, God will change it to Sarah in view of her new task.

11:32 Since Terah was seventy years old when his son Abraham was born (v. 26), and Abraham was seventy-five when he left Haran (12:4), Terah lived in Haran for sixty years after Abraham's departure. According to the tradition in the Samaritan text, Terah died when he was one hundred and forty-five years old, therefore, in the same year in which Abraham left Haran. This is the tradition followed in Stephen's speech: Abraham left Haran "after his father died" (Acts 7:4).

g: Jos 24:2; 1 Chr 1:26–27. *h:* Gn 17:15. *i:* Jos 24:3; Neh 9:7; Jdt 5:6–9; Acts 7:4.

See RG 110–11

CHAPTER 12

Abram's Call and Migration. [1]The
LORD said to Abram: Go forth[*] from your
land, your relatives, and from your father's
house to a land that I will show you.[j] [2*] I will
make of you a great nation, and I will bless
you; I will make your name great, so that
you will be a blessing.[k] [3l] I will bless those
who bless you and curse those who curse
you. All the families of the earth will find
blessing in you.[*]
[4m] Abram went as the LORD directed him,
and Lot went with him. Abram was seventy-
five years old when he left Haran. [5*] Abram
took his wife Sarai, his brother's son Lot, all
the possessions that they had accumulated,
and the persons they had acquired in Haran,
and they set out for the land of Canaan. When
they came to the land of Canaan, [6*] Abram
passed through the land as far as the sacred
place at Shechem, by the oak of Moreh. The
Canaanites were then in the land.
[7]The LORD appeared to Abram and said:
To your descendants I will give this land. So
Abram built an altar there to the LORD who
had appeared to him.[n] [8]From there he moved
on to the hill country east of Bethel, pitching
his tent with Bethel to the west and Ai to the
east. He built an altar there to the LORD and
invoked the LORD by name. [9]Then Abram
journeyed on by stages to the Negeb.[*]
Abram and Sarai in Egypt.[*] [10]There was
famine in the land; so Abram went down to
Egypt to sojourn there, since the famine in
the land was severe.[o] [11]When he was about
to enter Egypt, he said to his wife Sarai: "I
know that you are a beautiful woman.
[12]When the Egyptians see you, they will say,
'She is his wife'; then they will kill me, but
let you live. [13]Please say, therefore, that you
are my sister,[*] so that I may fare well on your
account and my life may be spared for your
sake."[p] [14]When Abram arrived in Egypt, the
Egyptians saw that the woman was very
beautiful. [15]When Pharaoh's officials saw
her they praised her to Pharaoh, and the
woman was taken into Pharaoh's house.
[16]Abram fared well on her account, and he
acquired sheep, oxen, male and female ser-

12:1–3 Go forth . . . find blessing in you: the syntax of the Hebrew suggests that the blessings promised to Abraham are contingent on his going to Canaan.

12:2 The call of Abraham begins a new history of blessing (18:18; 22:15–18), which is passed on in each instance to the chosen successor (26:2–4; 28:14). This call evokes the last story in the primeval history (11:1–9) by reversing its themes: Abraham goes forth rather than settle down; it is God rather than Abraham who will make a name for him; the families of the earth will find blessing in him.

12:3 Will find blessing in you: the Hebrew conjugation of the verb here and in 18:18 and 28:14 can be either reflexive ("shall bless themselves by you" = people will invoke Abraham as an example of someone blessed by God) or passive ("by you all the families of earth will be blessed" = the religious privileges of Abraham and his descendants ultimately will be extended to the nations). In 22:18 and 26:4, another conjugation of the same verb is used in a similar context that is undoubtedly reflexive ("bless themselves"). Many scholars suggest that the two passages in which the sense is clear should determine the interpretation of the three ambiguous passages: the privileged blessing enjoyed by Abraham and his descendants will awaken in all peoples the desire to enjoy those same blessings. Since the term is understood in a passive sense in the New Testament (Acts 3:25; Gal 3:8), it is rendered here by a neutral expression that admits of both meanings.

12:5 The ancestors appear in Genesis as pastoral nomads living at the edge of settled society, and having occasional dealings with the inhabitants, sometimes even moving into towns for brief periods. Unlike modern nomads such as the Bedouin, however, ancient pastoralists fluctuated between following the herds and sedentary life, depending on circumstances. Pastoralists could settle down and farm and later resume a pastoral way of life. Indeed, there was a symbiotic relationship between pastoralists and villagers, each providing goods to the other. **Persons**: servants and others who formed the larger household under the leadership of Abraham; cf. 14:14.

12:6 Abraham's journey to the center of the land, Shechem, then to Bethel, and then to the Negeb, is duplicated in Jacob's journeys (33:18; 35:1, 6, 27; 46:1) and in the general route of the conquest under Joshua (Jos 7:2; 8:9, 30). Abraham's journey is a symbolic "conquest" of the land he has been promised. In building altars here (vv. 7, 8) and elsewhere, Abraham acknowledges his God as Lord of the land.

12:9 The Negeb: the semidesert land south of Judah.

12:10–13:1 Abraham and Sarah's sojourn in Egypt and encounter with Pharaoh foreshadow their descendants' experience, suggesting a divine design in which they must learn to trust. The story of Sarah, the ancestor in danger, is told again in chap. 20, and also in 26:1–11 with Rebekah instead of Sarah. Repetition of similar events is not unusual in literature that has been orally shaped.

12:13 You are my sister: the text does not try to excuse Abraham's deception, though in 20:12 a similar deception is somewhat excused.

---

j: Acts 7:3; Heb 11:8. *k:* Gn 17:6; Sir 44:20–21; Rom 4:17–22. *l:* Gn 18:18; 22:18; Acts 3:25; Gal 3:8. *m:* Gn 11:31; Jos 24:3; Acts 7:4. *n:* Ex 33:1; Dt 34:4; Acts 7:5. *o:* Gn 26:1. *p:* Gn 20:12–13; 26:7.

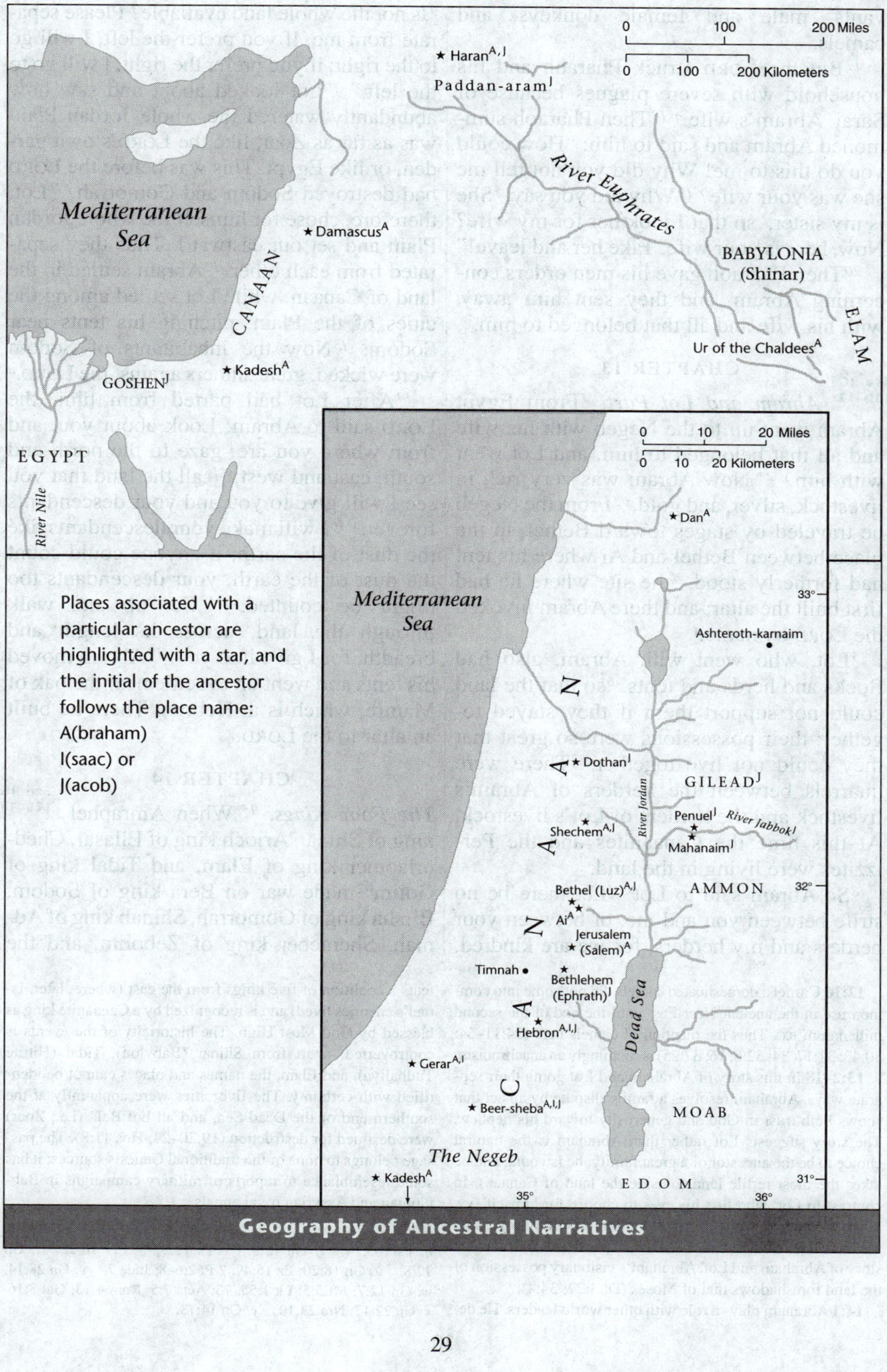
0 100 200 Miles
0 100 200 Kilometers
Haran[A, J]
Paddan-aram[J]
River Euphrates
Mediterranean Sea
Damascus[A]
CANAAN
BABYLONIA (Shinar)
ELAM
Ur of the Chaldees[A]
Kadesh[A]
GOSHEN[J]
EGYPT
River Nile
Places associated with a particular ancestor are highlighted with a star, and the initial of the ancestor follows the place name:
A(braham)
I(saac) or
J(acob)
0 10 20 Miles
0 10 20 Kilometers
Dan[A]
33°
Mediterranean Sea
Ashteroth-karnaim
CANAAN
Dothan[J]
GILEAD[J]
Penuel[J]
River Jabbok[J]
River Jordan
Shechem[A,J]
Mahanaim[J]
AMMON
32°
Bethel (Luz)[A,J]
Ai[A]
Jerusalem (Salem)[A]
Timnah
Bethlehem (Ephrath)[J]
Dead Sea
Hebron[A,I,J]
Gerar[A,I]
Beer-sheba[A,I,J]
MOAB
The Negeb
Kadesh[A]
EDOM
31°
35°
36°
Geography of Ancestral Narratives

vants, male and female donkeys, and camels.*

17 But the LORD struck Pharaoh and his household with severe plagues because of Sarai, Abram's wife.[q] 18 Then Pharaoh summoned Abram and said to him: "How could you do this to me! Why did you not tell me she was your wife? 19 Why did you say, 'She is my sister,' so that I took her for my wife? Now, here is your wife. Take her and leave!"

20 Then Pharaoh gave his men orders concerning Abram, and they sent him away, with his wife and all that belonged to him.

CHAPTER 13

See RG 110–11

Abram and Lot Part. 1 From Egypt Abram went up to the Negeb with his wife and all that belonged to him, and Lot went with him.[r] 2* Now Abram was very rich in livestock, silver, and gold.[s] 3 From the Negeb he traveled by stages toward Bethel, to the place between Bethel and Ai where his tent had formerly stood, 4 the site where he had first built the altar; and there Abram invoked the LORD by name.[t]

5 Lot, who went with Abram, also had flocks and herds and tents, 6 so that the land could not support them if they stayed together; their possessions were so great that they could not live together. 7 There were quarrels between the herders of Abram's livestock and the herders of Lot's livestock. At this time the Canaanites and the Perizzites were living in the land.

8 So Abram said to Lot: "Let there be no strife between you and me, or between your herders and my herders, for we are kindred. 9 Is not the whole land available? Please separate from me. If you prefer the left, I will go to the right; if you prefer the right, I will go to the left." 10 Lot looked about and saw how abundantly watered the whole Jordan Plain was as far as Zoar, like the LORD's own garden, or like Egypt. This was before the LORD had destroyed Sodom and Gomorrah. 11 Lot, therefore, chose for himself the whole Jordan Plain and set out eastward. Thus they separated from each other. 12 Abram settled in the land of Canaan, while Lot settled among the cities of the Plain, pitching his tents near Sodom. 13 Now the inhabitants of Sodom were wicked, great sinners against the LORD.[u]

14 After Lot had parted from him, the LORD said to Abram: Look about you, and from where you are, gaze to the north and south, east and west;[v] 15 all the land that you see I will give to you and your descendants forever.[w] 16 I will make your descendants like the dust of the earth; if anyone could count the dust of the earth, your descendants too might be counted.[x] 17 Get up and walk through the land, across its length and breadth, for I give it to you. 18 Abram moved his tents and went on to settle near the oak of Mamre, which is at Hebron. There he built an altar to the LORD.[y]

CHAPTER 14

See RG 110–11

The Four Kings. 1* When Amraphel king of Shinar, Arioch king of Ellasar, Chedorlaomer king of Elam, and Tidal king of Goiim 2 made war on Bera king of Sodom, Birsha king of Gomorrah, Shinab king of Admah, Shemeber king of Zeboiim, and the

12:16 Camels: domesticated camels did not come into common use in the ancient Near East until the end of the second millennium B.C. Thus the mention of camels here (24:11–64; 30:43; 31:17, 34; 32:8, 16; 37:25) is seemingly an anachronism.

13:2–18 In this story of Abraham and Lot going their separate ways, Abraham resolves a family dispute by an act that shows both trust in God and generosity toward his nephew. The story suggests Lot rather than Abraham is the natural choice to be the ancestor of a great family; he is young and he takes the most fertile land (outside the land of Canaan). In contrast to Lot, who lifts his eyes to choose for himself (vv. 10–11), Abraham waits for God to tell him to lift his eyes and see the land he will receive (v. 14). Chaps. 18–19 continue the story of Abraham and Lot. Abraham's visionary possession of the land foreshadows that of Moses (Dt 3:27; 34:4).

14:1 Abraham plays a role with other world leaders. He defeats a coalition of five kings from the east (where, later, Israel's enemies lived) and is recognized by a Canaanite king as blessed by God Most High. The historicity of the events is controverted; apart from Shinar (Babylon), Tidal (Hittite Tudhaliya), and Elam, the names and places cannot be identified with certainty. The five cities were apparently at the southern end of the Dead Sea, and all but Bela (i.e., Zoar) were destined for destruction (19:20–24; Hos 11:8). The passage belongs to none of the traditional Genesis sources; it has some resemblance to reports of military campaigns in Babylonian and Assyrian royal annals.

---

q: Ps 105:14. *r:* Gn 12:9. *s:* Ps 112:1–3; Prv 10:22. *t:* Gn 12:8. *u:* Gn 18:20; Ez 16:49; 2 Pt 2:6–8; Jude 7. *v:* Gn 28:14. *w:* Gn 12:7; Mt 5:5; Lk 1:55, 73; Acts 7:5; Rom 4:13; Gal 3:16. *x:* Gn 22:17; Nm 23:10. *y:* Gn 14:13.

king of Bela (that is, Zoar), [3]all the latter
kings joined forces in the Valley of Siddim
(that is, the Salt Sea*). [4]For twelve years they
had served Chedorlaomer, but in the thirteenth year they rebelled. [5]In the fourteenth
year Chedorlaomer and the kings allied with
him came and defeated the Rephaim in Ashteroth-karnaim, the Zuzim in Ham, the Emim
in Shaveh-kiriathaim, [6]and the Horites in the
hill country of Seir, as far as El-paran, close
by the wilderness.[z] [7]They then turned back
and came to En-mishpat (that is, Kadesh),
and they subdued the whole country of both
the Amalekites and the Amorites who lived
in Hazazon-tamar. [8]Thereupon the king of
Sodom, the king of Gomorrah, the king of
Admah, the king of Zeboiim, and the king of
Bela (that is, Zoar) marched out, and in the
Valley of Siddim they went into battle
against them: [9]against Chedorlaomer king of
Elam, Tidal king of Goiim, Amraphel king of
Shinar, and Arioch king of Ellasar—four
kings against five. [10]Now the Valley of Siddim was full of bitumen pits; and as the king
of Sodom and the king of Gomorrah fled,
they fell into these, while the rest fled to the
mountains. [11]The victors seized all the possessions and food supplies of Sodom and Gomorrah and then went their way. [12]They took
with them Abram's nephew Lot, who had
been living in Sodom, as well as his possessions, and departed.[a]

[13]A survivor came and brought the news to
Abram the Hebrew,* who was camping at the
oak of Mamre the Amorite, a kinsman of
Eshcol and Aner; these were allies of Abram.
[14]When Abram heard that his kinsman had
been captured, he mustered three hundred
and eighteen of his retainers,* born in his
house, and went in pursuit as far as Dan. [15]He
and his servants deployed against them at
night, defeated them, and pursued them as far
as Hobah, which is north of Damascus. [16]He
recovered all the possessions. He also recovered his kinsman Lot and his possessions,
along with the women and the other people.

[17]When Abram returned from his defeat
of Chedorlaomer and the kings who were allied with him, the king of Sodom went out to
greet him in the Valley of Shaveh (that is, the
King's Valley).

[18]Melchizedek, king of Salem,* brought
out bread and wine. He was a priest of God
Most High. [19]He blessed Abram with these
words:[b]

"Blessed be Abram by God Most High,
the creator of heaven and earth;
[20] And blessed be God Most High,
who delivered your foes into your
hand."

Then Abram gave him a tenth of everything.

[21]The king of Sodom said to Abram,
"Give me the captives; the goods you may
keep." [22]But Abram replied to the king of
Sodom: "I have sworn to the LORD, God
Most High,* the creator of heaven and earth,
[23]that I would not take so much as a thread

14:3 The Salt Sea: the Dead Sea.

14:13 Abram the Hebrew: "Hebrew" was used by biblical writers for the pre-Israelite ancestors. Linguistically, it is an ethnic term; it may be built on the root Eber, who is the eponymous ancestor of the Israelites, that is, the one to whom they traced their name (10:21, 24–25; 11:14–17), or it may reflect the tradition that the ancestors came from beyond (*eber*) the Euphrates. It is used only by non-Israelites, or by Israelites speaking to foreigners.

14:14 Retainers: the Hebrew word *hanik* is used only here in the Old Testament. Cognate words appear in Egyptian and Akkadian texts, signifying armed soldiers belonging to the household of a local leader.

14:18 Melchizedek, king of Salem (Jerusalem, cf. Ps 76:3), appears with majestic suddenness to recognize Abraham's great victory, which the five local kings were unable to achieve. He prepares a feast in his honor and declares him blessed or made powerful by God Most High, evidently the highest God in the Canaanite pantheon. Abraham acknowledges the blessing by giving a tenth of the recaptured spoils as a tithe to Melchizedek. The episode is one of several allusions to David, king at Jerusalem, who also exercised priestly functions (2 Sm 6:17). Heb 7 interprets Melchizedek as a prefiguration of Christ. **God Most High**: in Heb. *El Elyon*, one of several "El names" for God in Genesis, others being *El Olam* (21:33), *El* the God of Israel (33:20), *El Roi* (16:13), *El Bethel* (35:7), and *El Shaddai* (the usual P designation for God in Genesis). All the sources except the Yahwist use El as the proper name for God used by the ancestors. The god El was well-known across the ancient Near East and in comparable religious literature. The ancestors recognized this God as their own when they encountered him in their journeys and in the shrines they found in Canaan.

14:22 In vv. 22–24, Abraham refuses to let anyone but God enrich him. Portrayed with the traits of a later Israelite judge or tribal hero, Abraham acknowledges that his victory is from God alone.

z: Dt 2:12. *a:* Gn 13:10–12. *b:* Ps 110:4; Heb 5:6, 10; 7:1.

or a sandal strap from anything that is yours,
so that you cannot say, 'I made Abram rich.'
24Nothing for me except what my servants
have consumed and the share that is due to
the men who went with me—Aner, Eshcol
and Mamre; let them take their share."

CHAPTER 15

See RG 110-11

The Covenant with Abram.* 1Some
time afterward, the word of the LORD came
to Abram in a vision: Do not fear, Abram! I
am your shield; I will make your reward
very great.

2But Abram said, "Lord GOD, what can
you give me, if I die childless and have only a
servant of my household, Eliezer of Damascus?" 3Abram continued, "Look, you have
given me no offspring, so a servant of my
household will be my heir." 4Then the word
of the LORD came to him: No, that one will
not be your heir; your own offspring will be
your heir.[c] 5He took him outside and said:
Look up at the sky and count the stars, if you
can. Just so, he added, will your descendants
be.[d] 6[e] Abram put his faith in the LORD, who
attributed it to him as an act of righteousness.*

7He then said to him: I am the LORD who
brought you from Ur of the Chaldeans to
give you this land as a possession.[f] 8"Lord
GOD," he asked, "how will I know that I will
possess it?" 9* He answered him: Bring me a
three-year-old heifer, a three-year-old female goat, a three-year-old ram, a turtledove, and a young pigeon.[g] 10He brought
him all these, split them in two, and placed
each half opposite the other; but the birds he
did not cut up. 11Birds of prey swooped
down on the carcasses, but Abram scared
them away. 12As the sun was about to set, a
deep sleep fell upon Abram, and a great,
dark dread descended upon him.

13* Then the LORD said to Abram: Know
for certain that your descendants will reside
as aliens in a land not their own, where they
shall be enslaved and oppressed for four
hundred years.[h] 14But I will bring judgment
on the nation they must serve, and after this
they will go out with great wealth.[i] 15You,
however, will go to your ancestors in peace;
you will be buried at a ripe old age. 16In the
fourth generation* your descendants will return here, for the wickedness of the Amorites is not yet complete.[j]

17When the sun had set and it was dark,
there appeared a smoking fire pot and a flaming torch, which passed between those
pieces. 18* On that day the LORD made a covenant with Abram, saying: To your descen-

15:1–21 In the first section (vv. 1–6), Abraham is promised a son and heir, and in the second (vv. 7–21), he is promised a land. The structure is similar in both: each of the two promises is not immediately accepted; the first is met with a complaint (vv. 2–3) and the second with a request for a sign (v. 8). God's answer differs in each section—a sign in v. 5 and an oath in vv. 9–21. Some scholars believe that the Genesis promises of progeny and land were originally separate and only later combined, but progeny and land are persistent concerns especially of ancient peoples and it is hard to imagine one without the other.

15:6 Abraham's act of faith in God's promises was regarded as an act of righteousness, i.e., as fully expressive of his relationship with God. St. Paul (Rom 4:1–25; Gal 3:6–9) makes Abraham's faith a model for Christians.

15:9–17 Cutting up animals was a well-attested way of making a treaty in antiquity. Jer 34:17–20 shows the rite is a form of self-imprecation in which violators invoke the fate of the animals upon themselves. The eighth-century B.C. Sefire treaty from Syria reads, "As this calf is cut up, thus Matti'el shall be cut up." The smoking fire pot and the flaming torch (v. 17), which represent God, pass between the pieces, making God a signatory to the covenant.

15:13–16 The verses clarify the promise of the land by providing a timetable of its possession: after four hundred years of servitude, your descendants will actually possess the land in the fourth generation (a patriarchal generation seems to be one hundred years). The iniquity of the current inhabitants (called here the Amorites) has not yet reached the point where God must intervene in punishment. Another table is given in Ex 12:40, which is not compatible with this one.

15:16 Generation: the Hebrew term *dor* is commonly rendered as "generation," but it may signify a period of varying length. A "generation" is the period between the birth of children and the birth of their parents, normally about twenty to twenty-five years. The actual length of a generation can vary, however; in Jb 42:16 it is thirty-five and in Nm 32:13 it is forty. The meaning may be life spans, which in Gn 6:3 is one hundred twenty years and in Is 65:20 is one hundred years.

15:18–21 The **Wadi**, i.e., a gully or ravine, **of Egypt** is the Wadi-el-'Arish, which is the boundary between the settled land and the Sinai desert. Some scholars suggest that the boundaries are those of a Davidic empire at its greatest extent; others that they are idealized boundaries. Most lists of the ancient inhabitants of the promised land give three, six, or seven peoples, but vv. 19–21 give a grand total of ten.

c: Gn 17:16. *d:* Gn 22:17; 28:14; Ex 32:13; Dt 1:10; Sir 44:21; Rom 4:18; Heb 11:12. *e:* 1 Mc 2:52; Rom 4:3, 9, 22; Gal 3:6–7; Jas 2:23. *f:* Gn 11:31; 12:1; Ex 32:13; Neh 9:7–8; Acts 7:2–3. *g:* Lv 1:14. *h:* Ex 12:40; Nm 20:15; Jdt 5:9–10; Is 52:4; Acts 13:20; Gal 3:17. *i:* Ex 3:8, 21–22. *j:* 1 Kgs 21:26.

dants I give this land, from the Wadi of Egypt to the Great River, the Euphrates,[k] 19 the land of the Kenites, the Kenizzites, the Kadmonites, 20 the Hittites, the Perizzites, the Rephaim, 21 the Amorites, the Canaanites, the Girgashites, and the Jebusites.

CHAPTER 16

See RG 110–11

*Birth of Ishmael.** 1 Abram's wife Sarai had borne him no children. Now she had an Egyptian maidservant named Hagar.[m] 2 Sarai said to Abram: "The LORD has kept me from bearing children. Have intercourse with my maid; perhaps I will have sons through her." Abram obeyed Sarai.* [n] 3 Thus, after Abram had lived ten years in the land of Canaan, his wife Sarai took her maid, Hagar the Egyptian, and gave her to her husband Abram to be his wife. 4 He had intercourse with her, and she became pregnant. As soon as Hagar knew she was pregnant, her mistress lost stature in her eyes.* [o] 5[p] So Sarai said to Abram: "This outrage against me is your fault. I myself gave my maid to your embrace; but ever since she knew she was pregnant, I have lost stature in her eyes. May the LORD decide between you and me!" 6 Abram told Sarai: "Your maid is in your power. Do to her what you regard as right." Sarai then mistreated her so much that Hagar ran away from her.

7 The LORD's angel* found her by a spring in the wilderness, the spring on the road to Shur,[q] 8 and he asked, "Hagar, maid of Sarai, where have you come from and where are you going?" She answered, "I am running away from my mistress, Sarai." 9 But the LORD's angel told her: "Go back to your mistress and submit to her authority. 10 I will make your descendants so numerous," added the LORD's angel, "that they will be too many to count."[r] 11 Then the LORD's angel said to her:

"You are now pregnant and shall bear a son;
you shall name him Ishmael,*
For the LORD has heeded your affliction.
12 He shall be a wild ass of a man,
his hand against everyone,
and everyone's hand against him;
Alongside* all his kindred
shall he encamp."[s]

13 To the LORD who spoke to her she gave a name, saying, "You are God who sees me";* she meant, "Have I really seen God and remained alive after he saw me?"[t] 14 That is why the well is called Beer-lahai-roi.* It is between Kadesh and Bered.

15 Hagar bore Abram a son, and Abram named the son whom Hagar bore him Ish-

16:1–16 In the previous chapter Abraham was given a timetable of possession of the land, but nothing was said about when the child was to be born. In this chapter, Sarah takes matters into her own hands, for she has been childless ten years since the promise (cf. 12:4 with 16:16). The story is about the two women, Sarah the infertile mistress and Hagar the fertile slave; Abraham has only a single sentence. In the course of the story, God intervenes directly on the side of Hagar, for she is otherwise without resources.

16:2 The custom of an infertile wife providing her husband with a concubine to produce children is widely attested in ancient Near Eastern law; e.g., an Old Assyrian marriage contract states that the wife must provide her husband with a concubine if she does not bear children within two years.

16:4 Because barrenness was at that time normally blamed on the woman and regarded as a disgrace, it is not surprising that Hagar looks down on Sarah. Ancient Near Eastern legal practice addresses such cases of insolent slaves and allows disciplining of them. Prv 30:23 uses as an example of intolerable behavior "a maidservant when she ousts her mistress."

16:7 The LORD's angel: a manifestation of God in human form; in v. 13 the messenger is identified with God. See note on Ex 3:2.

16:11 Ishmael: in Hebrew the name means "God has heard." It is the same Hebrew verb that is translated "heeded" in the next clause. In other ancient Near Eastern texts, the name commemorated the divine answer to the parents' prayer to have a child, but here it is broadened to mean that God has "heard" Hagar's plight. In vv. 13–14, the verb "to see" is similarly broadened to describe God's special care for those in need.

16:12 Alongside: lit., "against the face of"; the same phrase is used of the lands of Ishmael's descendants in 25:18. It can be translated "in opposition to" (Dt 21:16; Jb 1:11; 6:28; 21:31), but here more likely means that Ishmael's settlement was near but not in the promised land.

16:13 God who sees me: Hebrew *el-ro'i* is multivalent, meaning either "God of seeing," i.e., extends his protection to me, or "God sees," which can imply seeing human suffering (29:32; Ex 2:25; Is 57:18; 58:3). It is probable that Hagar means to express both of these aspects. **Remained alive**: for the ancient notion that a person died on seeing God, see Gn 32:31; Ex 20:19; Dt 4:33; Jgs 13:22.

16:14 Beer-lahai-roi: possible translations of the name of

k: Ex 32:13; Neh 9:8; Ps 105:11; Sir 44:21. *l:* Dt 7:1. *m:* Gn 11:30. *n:* Gn 21:8–9; Gal 4:22. *o:* 1 Sm 1:6; Prv 30:23. *p:* Gn 21:10–19. *q:* Ex 15:22. *r:* Gn 17:20; 21:13, 18; 25:12–18. *s:* Gn 21:20; 25:18. *t:* Gn 24:62.

mael.[u] 16 Abram was eighty-six years old when Hagar bore him Ishmael.

CHAPTER 17

See RC 110-11

Covenant of Circumcision.* 1 When Abram was ninety-nine years old, the LORD appeared to Abram and said: I am God the Almighty. Walk in my presence and be blameless.[v] 2 Between you and me I will establish my covenant, and I will multiply you exceedingly.[w]

3 Abram fell face down and God said to him: 4 For my part, here is my covenant with you: you are to become the father of a multitude of nations.[x] 5 No longer will you be called Abram; your name will be Abraham,* for I am making you the father of a multitude of nations.[y] 6 I will make you exceedingly fertile; I will make nations of you; kings will stem from you. 7 I will maintain my covenant between me and you and your descendants after you throughout the ages as an everlasting covenant, to be your God and the God of your descendants after you.[z] 8 I will give to you and to your descendants after you the land in which you are now residing as aliens, the whole land of Canaan, as a permanent possession; and I will be their God.[a] 9 God said to Abraham: For your part, you and your descendants after you must keep my covenant throughout the ages. 10 This is the covenant between me and you and your descendants after you that you must keep: every male among you shall be circumcised.* [b] 11 Circumcise the flesh of your foreskin. That will be the sign of the covenant between me and you.[c] 12 Throughout the ages, every male among you, when he is eight days old, shall be circumcised, including houseborn slaves and those acquired with money from any foreigner who is not of your descendants.[d] 13 Yes, both the houseborn slaves and those acquired with money must be circumcised. Thus my covenant will be in your flesh as an everlasting covenant. 14 If a male is uncircumcised, that is, if the flesh of his foreskin has not been cut away, such a one will be cut off from his people; he has broken my covenant.

15 God further said to Abraham: As for Sarai your wife, do not call her Sarai; her name will be Sarah.* 16 I will bless her, and I will give you a son by her. Her also will I bless; she will give rise to nations, and rulers of peoples will issue from her.[e] 17 Abraham fell face down and laughed* as he said to himself, "Can a child be born to a man who is a hundred years old? Can Sarah give birth at ninety?"[f] 18 So Abraham said to God, "If only Ishmael could live in your favor!" 19 God replied: Even so, your wife Sarah is to bear you a son, and you shall call him Isaac. It is with him that I will maintain my covenant as an everlasting covenant and with his descendants after him.[g] 20 Now as for Ishmael, I will heed you: I hereby bless him. I will make him fertile and will multiply him exceedingly. He will become the father of twelve chieftains,

the well include: "spring of the living one who sees me"; "the well of the living sight"; or "the one who sees me lives." See note on v. 13.

17:1–27 The Priestly source gathers the major motifs of the story so far and sets them firmly within a covenant context; the word "covenant" occurs thirteen times. There are links to the covenant with Noah (v. 1 = 6:9; v. 7 = 9:9; v. 11 = 9:12–17). In this chapter, vv. 1–8 promise progeny and land; vv. 9–14 are instructions about circumcision; vv. 15–21 repeat the promise of a son to Sarah and distinguish this promise from that to Hagar; vv. 22–27 describe Abraham's carrying out the commands. **The Almighty**: traditional rendering of Hebrew *El Shaddai*, which is P's favorite designation of God in the period of the ancestors. Its etymology is uncertain, but its root meaning is probably "God, the One of the Mountains."

17:5 Abram and Abraham are merely two forms of the same name, both meaning, "the father is exalted"; another variant form is Abiram (Nm 16:1; 1 Kgs 16:34). The additional *-ha-* in the form Abraham is explained by popular etymology as coming from *ab-hamon goyim*, "father of a multitude of nations."

17:10 Circumcised: circumcision was widely practiced in the ancient world, usually as an initiation rite for males at puberty. By shifting the time of circumcision to the eighth day after birth, biblical religion made it no longer a "rite of passage" but the sign of the eternal covenant between God and the community descending from Abraham.

17:15 Sarai and Sarah are variant forms of the same name, both meaning "princess."

17:17 Laughed: *yishaq*, which is also the Hebrew form of the name "Isaac"; similar explanations of the name are given in Gn 18:12 and 21:6.

u: Gn 16:2; Gal 4:22. *v:* Gn 35:11; Ex 6:3. *w:* Gn 12:2; 13:16; Ex 32:13. *x:* Sir 44:21; Rom 4:17. *y:* Neh 9:7. *z:* Ps 105:42; Lk 1:72–73; Gal 3:16. *a:* Ex 32:13; Dt 1:8; 14:2; Lk 1:55; Acts 7:5. *b:* Jn 7:22; Acts 7:8; Rom 4:11. *c:* Sir 44:20. *d:* Lv 12:3; Lk 1:59; 2:21. *e:* Gn 18:10; Gal 4:23. *f:* Rom 4:19; Heb 11:11–12. *g:* Gn 11:30; 21:2; Ex 32:13; Sir 44:22.

and I will make of him a great nation.[h] [21]But my covenant I will maintain with Isaac, whom Sarah shall bear to you by this time next year.[i] [22]When he had finished speaking with Abraham, God departed from him.

[23]Then Abraham took his son Ishmael and all his slaves, whether born in his house or acquired with his money—every male among the members of Abraham's household—and he circumcised the flesh of their foreskins on that same day, as God had told him to do. [24]Abraham was ninety-nine years old when the flesh of his foreskin was circumcised,[j] [25]and his son Ishmael was thirteen years old when the flesh of his foreskin was circumcised. [26]Thus, on that same day Abraham and his son Ishmael were circumcised; [27]and all the males of his household, including the slaves born in his house or acquired with his money from foreigners, were circumcised with him.

See RG 110-11

CHAPTER 18

Abraham's Visitors. [1]* The LORD appeared to Abraham by the oak of Mamre, as he sat in the entrance of his tent, while the day was growing hot. [2]Looking up, he saw three men standing near him. When he saw them, he ran from the entrance of the tent to greet them; and bowing to the ground,[k] [3]he said: "Sir,* if it please you, do not go on past your servant. [4]Let some water be brought, that you may bathe your feet, and then rest under the tree. [5]Now that you have come to your servant, let me bring you a little food, that you may refresh yourselves; and afterward you may go on your way." "Very well," they replied, "do as you have said."

[6]Abraham hurried into the tent to Sarah and said, "Quick, three measures* of bran flour! Knead it and make bread." [7]He ran to the herd, picked out a tender, choice calf, and gave it to a servant, who quickly prepared it. [8]Then he got some curds* and milk, as well as the calf that had been prepared, and set these before them, waiting on them under the tree while they ate.

[9]"Where is your wife Sarah?" they asked him. "There in the tent," he replied. [10]One of them* said, "I will return to you about this time next year, and Sarah will then have a son." Sarah was listening at the entrance of the tent, just behind him.[l] [11]Now Abraham and Sarah were old, advanced in years, and Sarah had stopped having her menstrual periods.[m] [12]So Sarah laughed* to herself and said, "Now that I am worn out and my husband is old, am I still to have sexual pleasure?" [13]But the LORD said to Abraham: "Why did Sarah laugh and say, 'Will I really bear a child, old as I am?' [14]Is anything too marvelous for the LORD to do? At the appointed time, about this time next year, I will return to you, and Sarah will have a son."[n] [15]Sarah lied, saying, "I did not laugh," because she was afraid. But he said, "Yes, you did."

Abraham Intercedes for Sodom. [16]With Abraham walking with them to see them on their way, the men set out from there and looked down toward Sodom. [17]The LORD considered: Shall I hide from Abraham what I am about to do, [18]now that he is to become a great and mighty nation, and all the nations of the earth are to find blessing in him?[o] [19]Indeed, I have singled him out that he may direct his children and his household in the future to keep the way of the LORD by doing what is right and just, so that the LORD may

18:1 Chapters 18 and 19 combined form a continuous narrative, concluding the story of Abraham and his nephew Lot that began in 13:2–18. The mysterious men visit Abraham in Mamre to promise him and Sarah a child the following year (18:1–15) and then visit Lot in Sodom to investigate and then to punish the corrupt city (19:1–29). Between the two visits, Abraham questions God about the justice of punishing Sodom (18:16–33). At the end of the destruction of Sodom, there is a short narrative about Lot as the ancestor of Moab and the Ammonites (19:30–38).

18:3 Abraham addresses the leader of the group, whom he does not yet recognize as the Lord; in the next two verses he speaks to all three men. The other two are later (Gn 19:1) identified as angels. The shifting numbers and identification of the visitors are a narrative way of expressing the mysterious presence of God.

18:6 Three measures: Hebrew *seah*; three seahs equal one ephah, about half a bushel.

18:8 Curds: a type of soft cheese or yogurt.

18:10 One of them: i.e., the Lord.

18:12 Sarah laughed: a play on the verb "laugh," which prefigures the name of Isaac; see note on 17:17.

h: Gn 16:10; 21:13, 18; 25:12–16. *i:* Gn 18:14; 21:2; 26:2–5; Rom 9:7. *j:* Gn 17:10; Rom 4:11. *k:* Heb 13:1–2. *l:* Gn 17:19; 21:1; 2 Kgs 4:16; Rom 9:9. *m:* Gn 17:17; Rom 4:19; Heb 11:11–12. *n:* Mt 19:26; Mk 10:27; Lk 1:37; 18:27; Rom 4:21. *o:* Lk 1:55.

put into effect for Abraham the promises he made about him. 20[p] So the LORD said: The outcry against Sodom and Gomorrah is so great, and their sin so grave,* 21 that I must go down to see whether or not their actions are as bad as the cry against them that comes to me. I mean to find out.

22 As the men turned and walked on toward Sodom, Abraham remained standing before the LORD. 23 Then Abraham drew near and said: "Will you really sweep away the righteous with the wicked? 24 Suppose there were fifty righteous people in the city; would you really sweep away and not spare the place for the sake of the fifty righteous people within it? 25 Far be it from you to do such a thing, to kill the righteous with the wicked, so that the righteous and the wicked are treated alike! Far be it from you! Should not the judge of all the world do what is just?"[q] 26 The LORD replied: If I find fifty righteous people in the city of Sodom, I will spare the whole place for their sake. 27 Abraham spoke up again: "See how I am presuming to speak to my Lord, though I am only dust and ashes![r] 28 What if there are five less than fifty righteous people? Will you destroy the whole city because of those five?" I will not destroy it, he answered, if I find forty-five there. 29 But Abraham persisted, saying, "What if only forty are found there?" He replied: I will refrain from doing it for the sake of the forty. 30 Then he said, "Do not let my Lord be angry if I go on. What if only thirty are found there?" He replied: I will refrain from doing it if I can find thirty there. 31 Abraham went on, "Since I have thus presumed to speak to my Lord, what if there are no more than twenty?" I will not destroy it, he answered, for the sake of the twenty. 32 But he persisted: "Please, do not let my Lord be angry if I speak up this last time. What if ten are found there?" For the sake of the ten, he replied, I will not destroy it.[s]

33 The LORD departed as soon as he had finished speaking with Abraham, and Abraham returned home.

CHAPTER 19

See RG 110–11

*Destruction of Sodom and Gomorrah.**

1 The two angels reached Sodom in the evening, as Lot was sitting at the gate of Sodom. When Lot saw them, he got up to greet them; and bowing down with his face to the ground, 2 he said, "Please, my lords,* come aside into your servant's house for the night, and bathe your feet; you can get up early to continue your journey." But they replied, "No, we will pass the night in the town square."[t] 3 He urged them so strongly, however, that they turned aside to his place and entered his house. He prepared a banquet for them, baking unleavened bread, and they dined.

4[u] Before they went to bed, the townsmen of Sodom, both young and old—all the people to the last man—surrounded the house. 5 They called to Lot and said to him, "Where are the men who came to your house tonight? Bring them out to us that we may have sexual relations with them." 6 Lot went out to meet them at the entrance. When he had shut the door behind him, 7 he said, "I beg you, my brothers, do not do this wicked thing! 8 I have two daughters who have never had sexual relations with men. Let me bring them out to you,* and you may do to them as you please. But do not do anything to these men, for they have come under the shelter of

18:20 The immorality of the cities was already hinted at in 13:13, when Lot made his choice to live there. The "outcry" comes from the victims of the injustice and violence rampant in the city, which will shortly be illustrated in the treatment of the visitors. The outcry of the Hebrews under the harsh treatment of Pharaoh (Ex 3:7) came up to God who reacts in anger at mistreatment of the poor (cf. Ex 22:21–23; Is 5:7). Sodom and Gomorrah became types of sinful cities in biblical literature. Is 1:9–10; 3:9 sees their sin as lack of social justice, Ez 16:46–51, as disregard for the poor, and Jer 23:14, as general immorality. In the Genesis story, the sin is violation of the sacred duty of hospitality by the threatened rape of Lot's guests.

19:1–29 The story takes place in one day (counting a day from the previous evening): evening (v. 1), dawn (v. 15), and sunrise (v. 23). The passage resembles Jgs 19:15–25, which suggests dependence of one story on the other.

19:2 My lords: Lot does not yet know that the men are God's messengers; cf. 18:3.

19:8 Let me bring them out to you: the authority of a patriarch within his house was virtually absolute. Lot's extreme response of offering his daughters to a violent mob seems to be motivated by the obligation of hospitality.

p: Gn 19:13; Is 3:9; Lk 17:28; Jude 7. *q:* Dt 32:4; Jb 8:3, 20; Wis 12:15. *r:* Sir 10:9; 17:27. *s:* Jer 5:1; Ez 22:30. *t:* Heb 13:1–2. *u:* Jgs 19:22–25; Jude 7.

my roof." [9]They replied, "Stand back! This man," they said, "came here as a resident alien, and now he dares to give orders! We will treat you worse than them!" With that, they pressed hard against Lot, moving in closer to break down the door.[v] [10]But his guests put out their hands, pulled Lot inside with them, and closed the door; [11]they struck the men at the entrance of the house, small and great, with such a blinding light* that they were utterly unable to find the doorway.

[12]Then the guests said to Lot: "Who else belongs to you here? Sons-in-law, your sons, your daughters, all who belong to you in the city—take them away from this place![w] [13]We are about to destroy this place, for the outcry reaching the LORD against those here is so great that the LORD has sent us to destroy it."[x] [14]So Lot went out and spoke to his sons-in-law, who had contracted marriage with his daughters.* "Come on, leave this place," he told them; "the LORD is about to destroy the city." But his sons-in-law thought he was joking.

[15]As dawn was breaking, the angels urged Lot on, saying, "Come on! Take your wife with you and your two daughters who are here, or you will be swept away in the punishment of the city." [16]When he hesitated, the men, because of the LORD's compassion for him, seized his hand and the hands of his wife and his two daughters and led them to safety outside the city. [17]As soon as they had brought them outside, they said: "Flee for your life! Do not look back or stop anywhere on the Plain. Flee to the hills at once, or you will be swept away."[y] [18]"Oh, no, my lords!" Lot replied to them. [19]"You have already shown favor to your servant, doing me the great kindness of saving my life. But I cannot flee to the hills, or the disaster will overtake and kill me. [20]Look, this town ahead is near enough to escape to. It is only a small place.* Let me flee there—is it not a small place?—to save my life." [21]"Well, then," he replied, "I grant you this favor too. I will not overthrow the town you have mentioned. [22]Hurry, escape there! I cannot do anything until you arrive there." That is why the town is called Zoar.[z]

[23]The sun had risen over the earth when Lot arrived in Zoar, [24]and the LORD rained down sulfur upon Sodom and Gomorrah, fire from the LORD out of heaven.[a] [25]He overthrew* those cities and the whole Plain, together with the inhabitants of the cities and the produce of the soil.[b] [26]But Lot's wife looked back, and she was turned into a pillar of salt.[c]

[27]The next morning Abraham hurried to the place where he had stood before the LORD. [28]As he looked down toward Sodom and Gomorrah and the whole region of the Plain,* he saw smoke over the land rising like the smoke from a kiln.[d]

[29]When God destroyed the cities of the Plain, he remembered Abraham and sent Lot away from the upheaval that occurred when God overthrew the cities where Lot had been living.

Moabites and Ammonites.* [30]Since Lot was afraid to stay in Zoar, he and his two

19:11 Blinding light: an extraordinary flash that temporarily dazed the wicked men and revealed to Lot the true nature of his guests.

19:14 It is uncertain whether Lot's sons-in-law were fully married to his daughters or only "engaged" to them (Israelite "engagement" was the first part of the marriage ceremony), or even whether the daughters involved were the same as, or different from, the two daughters who were still in their father's house.

19:20 A small place: the Hebrew word *misar*, lit., "a little thing," has the same root consonants as the name of the town Zoar in v. 22.

19:25 Overthrew: this term, lit., "turned upside down," is used consistently to describe the destruction of the cities of the Plain. The imagery of earthquake and subsequent fire fits the geology of this region.

19:28–29 In a deft narrative detail, Abraham looks down from the height east of Hebron, from which he could easily see the region at the southern end of the Dead Sea, where the cities of the Plain were probably located.

19:30–38 This Israelite tale about the origin of Israel's neighbors east of the Jordan and the Dead Sea was told partly to ridicule these ethnically related but rival nations and partly to give popular etymologies for their names. The stylized nature of the story is seen in the names of the daughters ("the firstborn" and "the younger"), the ease with which they fool their father, and the identical descriptions of the encounters.

v: Gn 13:12; 2 Pt 2:7–8. *w:* 2 Pt 2:7–9. *x:* Is 1:7, 9; Ez 16:49–50; Zep 2:9. *y:* Wis 10:6. *z:* Wis 10:6. *a:* Ps 9:6; 11:6; 107:34; Wis 10:7; Sir 16:8; Is 1:9; Lk 17:29; 2 Pt 2:6. *b:* Dt 29:22; Is 13:19; Jer 50:40; Lam 4:6; Am 4:11. *c:* Wis 10:7; Lk 17:32. *d:* Rev 9:2; 14:10–11.

daughters went up from Zoar and settled in the hill country, where he lived with his two daughters in a cave. [31]The firstborn said to the younger: "Our father is getting old, and there is not a man in the land to have intercourse with us as is the custom everywhere. [32]Come, let us ply our father with wine and then lie with him, that we may ensure posterity by our father." [33]So that night they plied their father with wine, and the firstborn went in and lay with her father; but he was not aware of her lying down or getting up. [34]The next day the firstborn said to the younger: "Last night I lay with my father. Let us ply him with wine again tonight, and then you go in and lie with him, that we may ensure posterity by our father." [35]So that night, too, they plied their father with wine, and then the younger one went in and lay with him; but he was not aware of her lying down or getting up.

[36]Thus the two daughters of Lot became pregnant by their father. [37]The firstborn gave birth to a son whom she named Moab, saying, "From my father."* He is the ancestor of the Moabites of today.[e] [38]The younger one, too, gave birth to a son, and she named him Ammon, saying, "The son of my kin."* He is the ancestor of the Ammonites of today.[f]

See RG 110–11

CHAPTER 20

Abraham at Gerar.* [1]From there Abraham journeyed on to the region of the Negeb, where he settled between Kadesh and Shur.* While he resided in Gerar as an alien, [2]Abraham said of his wife Sarah, "She is my sister." So Abimelech, king of Gerar, sent and took Sarah. [3]But God came to Abimelech in a dream one night and said to him: You are about to die because of the woman you have taken, for she has a husband. [4]Abimelech, who had not approached her, said: "O Lord, would you kill an innocent man? [5]Was he not the one who told me, 'She is my sister'? She herself also stated, 'He is my brother.' I acted with pure heart and with clean hands." [6]* God answered him in the dream: Yes, I know you did it with a pure heart. In fact, it was I who kept you from sinning against me; that is why I did not let you touch her. [7]So now, return the man's wife so that he may intercede for you, since he is a prophet,* that you may live. If you do not return her, you can be sure that you and all who are yours will die.

[8]Early the next morning Abimelech called all his servants and informed them of everything that had happened, and the men were filled with fear. [9]Then Abimelech summoned Abraham and said to him: "What have you done to us! What wrong did I do to you that you would have brought such great guilt on me and my kingdom? You have treated me in an intolerable way. [10]What did you have in mind," Abimelech asked him, "that you would do such a thing?" [11]Abraham answered, "I thought there would be no fear of God* in this place, and so they would kill me on account of my wife. [12]Besides, she really is my sister,* but only my father's daughter, not my mother's; and so she became my wife. [13]When God sent me wandering from my father's house, I asked her: 'Would you do me this favor? In whatever place we come to, say: He is my brother.' "[g]

19:37 From my father: in Hebrew, *me'abi*, similar in sound to the name "Moab."

19:38 The son of my kin: in Hebrew, *ben-ammi*, similar in sound to the name "Ammonites."

20:1–18 Abraham again passes off his wife Sarah as his sister to escape trouble in a foreign land (cf. 12:10–13:1, the J source). The story appears to be from a different source (according to some, E) and deals with the ethical questions of the incident. Gn 26:6–11 is yet another retelling of the story, but with Isaac and Rebekah as characters instead of Abraham and Sarah.

20:1 Kadesh and Shur: Kadesh-barnea was a major oasis on the southernmost border of Canaan, and Shur was probably the "way to Shur," the road to Egypt. Gerar was a royal city in the area, but has not been identified with certainty.

20:6 Abimelech is exonerated of blame, but by that fact not cleared of the consequences of his act. He is still under the sentence of death for abducting another man's wife; the consequences result from the deed not the intention.

20:7 Prophet: only here is Abraham explicitly called "prophet," Hebrew *nabi* (cf. Ps 105:15).

20:11 Fear of God is the traditional though unsatisfactory rendering of Hebrew *yir'at YHWH*, literally, "revering Yahweh." The phrase refers neither to the emotion of fear nor to religious reverence of a general kind. Rather it refers to adherence to a single deity (in a polytheistic culture), honoring that deity with prayers, rituals, and obedience. The phrase occurs again in 26:24; 43:23; and 50:19. It is very common in the wisdom literature of the Bible.

20:12 My sister: marrying one's half sister was prohibited later in Israel's history.

e: Dt 2:9. *f:* Dt 2:19. *g:* Gn 12:13.

[14]Then Abimelech took flocks and herds and male and female slaves and gave them to Abraham; and he restored his wife Sarah to him. [15]Then Abimelech said, "Here, my land is at your disposal; settle wherever you please." [16]To Sarah he said: "I hereby give your brother a thousand shekels of silver. This will preserve your honor before all who are with you and will exonerate you before everyone." [17]Abraham then interceded with God, and God restored health to Abimelech, to his wife, and his maidservants, so that they bore children; [18]for the LORD had closed every womb in Abimelech's household on account of Abraham's wife Sarah.

See RG 110–11

CHAPTER 21

Birth of Isaac.* [1]The LORD took note of Sarah as he had said he would; the LORD did for her as he had promised.[h] [2]Sarah became pregnant and bore Abraham a son in his old age, at the set time that God had stated.[i] [3]Abraham gave the name Isaac to this son of his whom Sarah bore him.[j] [4]When his son Isaac was eight days old, Abraham circumcised him, as God had commanded.[k] [5]Abraham was a hundred years old when his son Isaac was born to him. [6]Sarah then said, "God has given me cause to laugh,* and all who hear of it will laugh with me.[l] [7]Who would ever have told Abraham," she added, "that Sarah would nurse children! Yet I have borne him a son in his old age." [8]The child grew and was weaned, and Abraham held a great banquet on the day of the child's weaning.

[9]Sarah noticed the son whom Hagar the Egyptian had borne to Abraham playing with her son Isaac; [10]so she demanded of Abraham: "Drive out that slave and her son! No son of that slave is going to share the inheritance with my son Isaac!"[m] [11]Abraham was greatly distressed because it concerned a son of his.* [12]But God said to Abraham: Do not be distressed about the boy or about your slave woman. Obey Sarah, no matter what she asks of you; for it is through Isaac that descendants will bear your name.[n] [13]As for the son of the slave woman, I will make a nation of him also,* since he too is your offspring.

[14]Early the next morning Abraham got some bread and a skin of water and gave them to Hagar. Then, placing the child on her back,* he sent her away. As she roamed aimlessly in the wilderness of Beer-sheba, [15]the water in the skin was used up. So she put the child down under one of the bushes, [16]and then went and sat down opposite him, about a bowshot away; for she said to herself, "I cannot watch the child die." As she sat opposite him, she wept aloud. [17]God heard the boy's voice, and God's angel called to Hagar from heaven: "What is the matter, Hagar? Do not fear; God has heard the boy's voice in this plight of his.[o] [18]Get up, lift up the boy and hold him by the hand; for I will make of him a great nation." [19]Then God opened her eyes, and she saw a well of water. She went and filled the skin with water, and then let the boy drink.

[20]God was with the boy as he grew up. He lived in the wilderness and became an expert

21:1–21 The long-awaited birth of Isaac parallels the birth of Ishmael in chap. 16, precipitating a rivalry and expulsion as in that chapter. Though this chapter is unified, the focus of vv. 1–7 is exclusively on Sarah and Isaac, and the focus of vv. 8–21 is exclusively on Hagar and Ishmael. The promise of a son to the barren Sarah and elderly Abraham has been central to the previous chapters and now that promise comes true with the birth of Isaac. The other great promise, that of land, will be resolved, at least in an anticipatory way, in Abraham's purchase of the cave at Machpelah in chap. 23. The parallel births of the two boys has influenced the Lucan birth narratives of John the Baptist and Jesus (Lk 1–2).

21:6 Laugh: for the third time (cf. 17:17 and 18:12) there is laughter, playing on the similarity in Hebrew between the pronunciation of the name Isaac and words associated with laughter.

21:11 A son of his: Abraham is the father of both boys, but Sarah is the mother only of Isaac. Abraham is very concerned that Ishmael have a sufficient inheritance.

21:13 I will make a nation of him also: Ishmael's descendants are named in 25:12–18.

21:14 Placing the child on her back: a reading based on an emendation of the traditional Hebrew text. In the traditional Hebrew text, Abraham put the bread and the waterskin on Hagar's back, while her son apparently walked beside her. In this way the traditional Hebrew text harmonizes the data of the Priestly source, in which Ishmael would have been at least fourteen years old when Isaac was born; compare 16:16 with 21:5; cf. 17:25. But in the present Elohist (?) story, Ishmael is obviously a little boy, not much older than Isaac; cf. vv. 15, 18.

h: Gn 17:19; 18:10. *i*: Gal 4:23; Heb 11:11. *j*: Mt 1:2; Lk 3:34. *k*: Gn 17:10–14; Acts 7:8. *l*: Gn 17:17. *m*: Jgs 11:2; Gal 4:30. *n*: Rom 9:7; Heb 11:18. *o*: Gn 16:7.

bowman. [21]He lived in the wilderness of Paran. His mother got a wife for him from the
land of Egypt.

The Covenant at Beer-sheba. [22]* At that
time Abimelech, accompanied by Phicol, the
commander of his army, said to Abraham:
"God is with you in everything you do. [23]So
now, swear to me by God at this place* that
you will not deal falsely with me or with my
progeny and posterity, but will act as loyally
toward me and the land in which you reside
as I have acted toward you." [24]Abraham
replied, "I so swear."

[25]Abraham, however, reproached Abimelech about a well that Abimelech's servants
had seized by force. [26]"I have no idea who
did that," Abimelech replied. "In fact, you
never told me about it, nor did I ever hear of
it until now."

[27]Then Abraham took sheep and cattle
and gave them to Abimelech and the two
made a covenant. [28]Abraham also set apart
seven ewe lambs of the flock, [29]and Abimelech asked him, "What is the purpose of
these seven ewe lambs that you have set
apart?" [30]Abraham answered, "The seven
ewe lambs you shall accept from me that
you may be my witness that I dug this well."
[31]This is why the place is called Beer-sheba;
the two of them took an oath there. [32]When
they had thus made the covenant in Beer-
sheba, Abimelech, along with Phicol, the
commander of his army, left to return to the
land of the Philistines.*

[33]Abraham planted a tamarisk at Beer-
sheba, and there he invoked by name the
LORD, God the Eternal.* [34]Abraham resided
in the land of the Philistines for a long time.

CHAPTER 22

See RG 110–11

*The Testing of Abraham.** [1]Some time
afterward, God put Abraham to the test and
said to him: Abraham! "Here I am!" he
replied.[p] [2]Then God said: Take your son
Isaac, your only one, whom you love, and go
to the land of Moriah. There offer him up as a
burnt offering on one of the heights that I will
point out to you.[q] [3]Early the next morning
Abraham saddled his donkey, took with him
two of his servants and his son Isaac, and after cutting the wood for the burnt offering, set
out for the place of which God had told him.
[4]On the third day Abraham caught sight of
the place from a distance. [5]Abraham said to
his servants: "Stay here with the donkey,
while the boy and I go on over there. We will
worship and then come back to you." [6]So
Abraham took the wood for the burnt offering and laid it on his son Isaac, while he himself carried the fire and the knife. As the two
walked on together, [7]Isaac spoke to his father Abraham. "Father!" he said. "Here I
am," he replied. Isaac continued, "Here are
the fire and the wood, but where is the sheep

21:22 Of the two related promises of progeny and land, that of progeny has been fulfilled in the previous chapter. Now the claim on the land begins to be solidified by Abimelech's recognition of Abraham's claim on the well at Beer-sheba; it will be furthered by Abraham's purchase of the cave at Machpelah in chap. 23. Two levels of editing are visible in the story: (1) vv. 22–24, 27, 32, the general covenant with Abimelech; (2) vv. 25–26, 28–30, 31, Abraham's claim on the well. Both versions play on the root of the Hebrew word *sheba'*, which means "seven" and "swear," and the place name Beer-sheba.

21:23 This place: Beer-sheba (v. 31). Abimelech had come from Gerar (20:2), about thirty miles west of Beer-sheba.

21:32 Philistines: one of the Sea Peoples, who migrated from Mycenaean Greece around 1200 B.C. and settled on the coastland of Canaan, becoming a principal rival of Israel. Non-biblical texts do not use the term "Philistine" before ca. 1200 B.C.; it is probable that this usage and those in chap. 26 are anachronistic, perhaps applying a later ethnic term for an earlier, less-known one.

21:33 God the Eternal: in Hebrew, *'el 'olam*, perhaps the name of the deity of the pre-Israelite sanctuary at Beer-sheba, but used by Abraham as a title of God; cf. Is 40:28.

22:1–19 The divine demand that Abraham sacrifice to God the son of promise is the greatest of his trials; after the successful completion of the test, he has only to buy a burial site for Sarah and find a wife for Isaac. The story is widely recognized as a literary masterpiece, depicting in a few lines God as the absolute Lord, inscrutable yet ultimately gracious, and Abraham, acting in moral grandeur as the great ancestor of Israel. Abraham speaks simply, with none of the wordy evasions of chaps. 13 and 21. The style is laconic; motivations and thoughts are not explained, and the reader cannot but wonder at the scene. In vv. 15–18, the angel repeats the seventh and climactic promise. **Moriah**: the mountain is not given a precise geographical location here, though 2 Chr 3:1 identifies Moriah as the mountain of Jerusalem where Solomon built the Temple; Abraham is thus the first to worship there. The word "Moriah" is a play on the verb "to see" (Heb. *ra'ah*); the wordplay is continued in v. 8, "God will provide (lit., "see")" and in v. 14, Yahweh-yireh, meaning "the Lord will see/provide."

p: Sir 44:20. *q:* 2 Chr 3:1; 1 Mc 2:52; Heb 11:17.

for the burnt offering?" 8"My son," Abraham answered, "God will provide the sheep
for the burnt offering." Then the two walked
on together.
9When they came to the place of which
God had told him, Abraham built an altar
there and arranged the wood on it. Next he
bound* his son Isaac, and put him on top of
the wood on the altar.[r] 10Then Abraham
reached out and took the knife to slaughter
his son.[s] 11But the angel of the LORD called
to him from heaven, "Abraham, Abraham!"
"Here I am," he answered. 12"Do not lay
your hand on the boy," said the angel. "Do
not do the least thing to him. For now I know
that you fear God, since you did not withhold from me your son, your only one."[t]
13Abraham looked up and saw a single ram
caught by its horns in the thicket. So Abraham went and took the ram and offered it up
as a burnt offering in place of his son.*
14Abraham named that place Yahweh-
yireh;* hence people today say, "On the
mountain the LORD will provide."
15* A second time the angel of the LORD
called to Abraham from heaven 16[u] and said:
"I swear by my very self—oracle of the
LORD—that because you acted as you did in
not withholding from me your son, your
only one, 17I will bless you and make your
descendants as countless as the stars of the
sky and the sands of the seashore; your descendants will take possession of the gates
of their enemies,[v] 18and in your descendants
all the nations of the earth will find blessing,
because you obeyed my command."[w]
19Abraham then returned to his servants,
and they set out together for Beer-sheba,
where Abraham lived.
Nahor's Descendants.* 20Some time afterward, the news came to Abraham: "Milcah
too has borne sons to your brother Nahor:
21Uz, his firstborn, his brother Buz, Kemuel
the father of Aram, 22Chesed, Hazo, Pildash,
Jidlaph, and Bethuel." 23Bethuel became the
father of Rebekah. These eight Milcah bore to
Nahor, Abraham's brother. 24His concubine,
whose name was Reumah, also bore children:
Tebah, Gaham, Tahash, and Maacah.

CHAPTER 23

See RG 110–11

Purchase of a Burial Plot.* 1The span
of Sarah's life was one hundred and twenty-
seven years. 2She died in Kiriath-arba—now
Hebron—in the land of Canaan, and Abraham proceeded to mourn and weep for her.
3Then he left the side of his deceased wife and
addressed the Hittites:* 4"Although I am a

22:9 Bound: the Hebrew verb is *'aqad,* from which is derived the noun Akedah, "the binding (of Isaac)," the traditional Jewish name for this incident.

22:13 While the Bible recognizes that firstborn males belong to God (Ex 13:11–16; 34:19–20), and provides an alternate sacrifice to redeem firstborn sons, the focus here is on Abraham's being tested by God (v. 1). But the widely attested practice of child sacrifice underscores, for all its horror today, the realism of the test.

22:14 Yahweh-yireh: a Hebrew expression meaning "the Lord will see/provide." See note on vv. 1–19.

22:15–19 The seventh and climactic statement of the blessings to Abraham. Unlike the other statements, which were purely promissory, this one is presented as a reward for Abraham's extraordinary trust.

22:20–24 The descendants to the second generation of Nahor, Abraham's brother, who married Milcah. Of Terah's three sons (11:27), the oldest, Abraham, fathered Isaac (21:1–7), and the youngest, Haran (who died in Ur), fathered Lot. Abraham is now told that Nahor had eight children by Milcah and four by his concubine Reumah. Apart from the notice about the children born to Abraham by his second wife, Keturah (25:1–6), all the information about Terah's family to the second generation is now complete. It is noteworthy that Jacob will, like Nahor, have eight children by his wives and four by his concubines.

23:1–20 The occasion for purchasing the land is the need for a burial site for Sarah, for it would be unthinkable to bury Sarah outside of the promised land. One of the two great promises to Abraham, that of progeny, has been fulfilled (21:1–7). And now the promise of land is to be fulfilled, through a kind of down payment on the full possession that will take place only with the conquest under Joshua and during the reign of David. This purchase has been prepared for by Abimelech's recognition of Abraham's claim to the well at Beer-sheba (21:22–34). Among the ancestral stories this narrative is one of two that are entirely from the P source (chap. 17 being the other). The Priestly writers may have intended to encourage the generation of the exile to a renewed hope of repossessing their land.

23:3 The Hittites: in the Bible the term is applied to several different groups—inhabitants of the second-millennium Hittite empire in Asia Minor and northern Syria, residents of the Neo-Hittite kingdoms in northern Syria in the first part of the first millennium, and (following Assyrian terminology) the inhabitants of Syria and Palestine. The third group is meant here.

---

r: Jas 2:21. *s:* Wis 10:5. *t:* Rom 8:32; 1 Jn 4:9. *u:* Gn 15:5; Ex 32:13; Lk 1:73; Rom 4:13; Heb 6:13–14; 11:12. *v:* Gn 24:60. *w:* Gn 12:3; 18:18; 26:4; Sir 44:21; Acts 3:25; Gal 3:16.

The Family Tree of Abraham

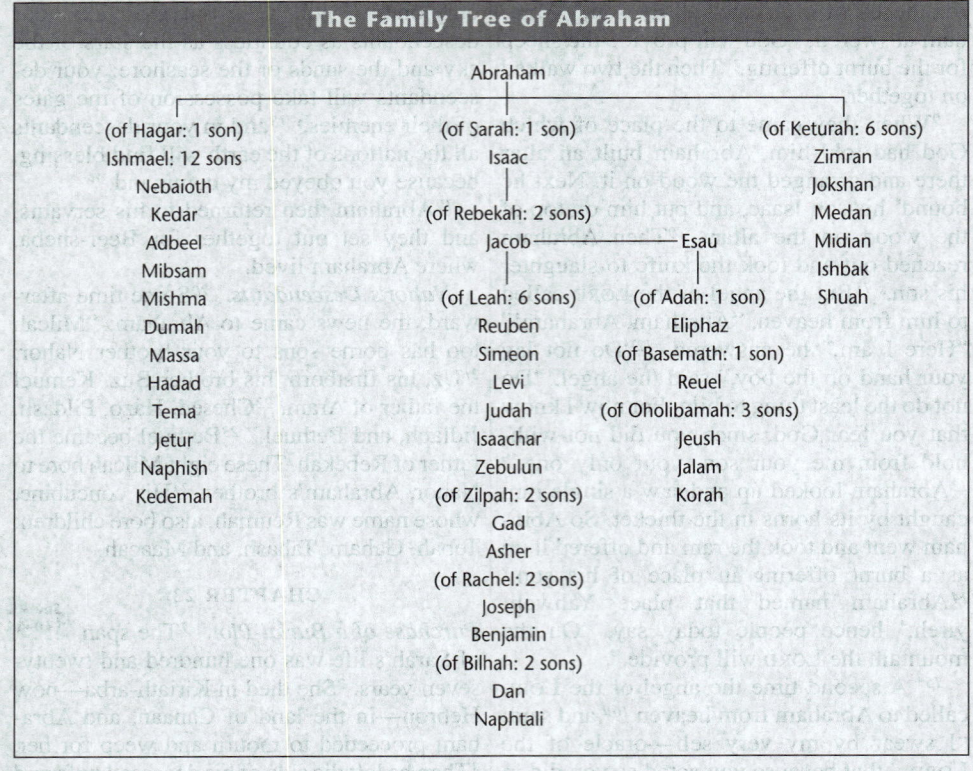

Abraham

- (of Hagar: 1 son)
  - Ishmael: 12 sons
    - Nebaioth
    - Kedar
    - Adbeel
    - Mibsam
    - Mishma
    - Dumah
    - Massa
    - Hadad
    - Tema
    - Jetur
    - Naphish
    - Kedemah
- (of Sarah: 1 son)
  - Isaac
    - (of Rebekah: 2 sons)
      - Jacob
        - (of Leah: 6 sons)
          - Reuben
          - Simeon
          - Levi
          - Judah
          - Isaachar
          - Zebulun
        - (of Zilpah: 2 sons)
          - Gad
          - Asher
        - (of Rachel: 2 sons)
          - Joseph
          - Benjamin
        - (of Bilhah: 2 sons)
          - Dan
          - Naphtali
      - Esau
        - (of Adah: 1 son)
          - Eliphaz
        - (of Basemath: 1 son)
          - Reuel
        - (of Oholibamah: 3 sons)
          - Jeush
          - Jalam
          - Korah
- (of Keturah: 6 sons)
  - Zimran
  - Jokshan
  - Medan
  - Midian
  - Ishbak
  - Shuah

resident alien* among you, sell me from your holdings a burial place, that I may bury my deceased wife."[x] [5]The Hittites answered Abraham: "Please, [6]sir, listen to us! You are a mighty leader among us. Bury your dead in the choicest of our burial sites. None of us would deny you his burial ground for the burial of your dead." [7]Abraham, however, proceeded to bow low before the people of the land, the Hittites, [8]and said to them: "If you will allow me room for burial of my dead, listen to me! Intercede for me with Ephron, son of Zohar, [9]so that he will sell me the cave of Machpelah that he owns; it is at the edge of his field. Let him sell it to me in your presence at its full price for a burial place."

[10]Now Ephron was sitting with the Hittites. So Ephron the Hittite replied to Abraham in the hearing of the Hittites, all who entered the gate of his city: [11]"Please, sir, listen to me! I give you both the field and the cave in it; in the presence of my people I give it to you. Bury your dead!" [12]But Abraham, after bowing low before the people of the land, [13]addressed Ephron in the hearing of these men: "If only you would please listen to me! I will pay you the price of the field. Accept it from me, that I may bury my dead there." [14]Ephron replied to Abraham, "Please, [15]sir, listen to me! A piece of land worth four hundred shekels* of silver—what is that between you and me? Bury your dead!"

23:4 A resident alien: such a one would normally not have the right to own property. The importance of Abraham's purchase of the field in Machpelah, which is worded in technical legal terms, lies in the fact that it gave his descendants their first, though small, land rights in the country that God had promised the patriarch they would one day inherit as their own. Abraham therefore insists on purchasing the field and not receiving it as a gift.

23:15 Four hundred shekels: probably an exorbitant sum; Jeremiah (32:9) paid only seventeen shekels for his field in

x: Gn 33:19; Acts 7:16; Heb 11:9.

16[y] Abraham accepted Ephron's terms; he weighed out to him the silver that Ephron had stipulated in the hearing of the Hittites, four hundred shekels of silver at the current market value.*

17[z] Thus Ephron's field in Machpelah, facing Mamre, together with its cave and all the trees anywhere within its limits, was conveyed 18 to Abraham by purchase in the presence of the Hittites, all who entered the gate of Ephron's city. 19 After this, Abraham buried his wife Sarah in the cave of the field of Machpelah, facing Mamre—now Hebron—in the land of Canaan. 20 Thus the field with its cave was transferred from the Hittites to Abraham as a burial place.

See RG 111–12

CHAPTER 24

Isaac and Rebekah.* 1 Abraham was old, having seen many days, and the LORD had blessed him in every way. 2[a] Abraham said to the senior servant of his household, who had charge of all his possessions: "Put your hand under my thigh,* 3 and I will make you swear by the LORD, the God of heaven and the God of earth, that you will not take a wife for my son from the daughters of the Canaanites among whom I live,[b] 4 but that you will go to my own land and to my relatives to get a wife for my son Isaac." 5 The servant asked him: "What if the woman is unwilling to follow me to this land? Should I then take your son back to the land from which you came?" 6 Abraham told him, "Never take my son back there for any reason! 7 The LORD, the God of heaven, who took me from my father's house and the land of my relatives, and who confirmed by oath the promise he made to me, 'I will give this land to your descendants'—he will send his angel before you, and you will get a wife for my son there.[c] 8 If the woman is unwilling to follow you, you will be released from this oath to me. But never take my son back there!" 9 So the servant put his hand under the thigh of his master Abraham and swore to him concerning this matter.

10 The servant then took ten of his master's camels, and bearing all kinds of gifts from his master, he made his way to the city of Nahor* in Aram Naharaim. 11 Near evening, at the time when women go out to draw water, he made the camels kneel by the well outside the city. 12 Then he said: "LORD, God of my master Abraham, let it turn out favorably for me* today and thus deal graciously with my master Abraham. 13 While I stand here at the spring and the daughters of the townspeople are coming out to draw water, 14 if I say to a young woman, 'Please lower your jug, that I may drink,' and she answers, 'Drink, and I will water your camels, too,' then she is the one whom you have decided upon for your servant Isaac. In this way I will know that you have dealt graciously with my master."

15[d] He had scarcely finished speaking

Anathoth, though the Babylonian invasion no doubt helped to reduce the price.

23:16 The current market value: the standard weight called a shekel varied according to time and place.

24:1–67 The story of Abraham and Sarah is drawing to a close. The promises of progeny (21:1–7) and land (chap. 23) have been fulfilled and Sarah has died (23:1–2). Abraham's last duty is to ensure that his son Isaac shares in the promises. Isaac must take a wife from his own people (vv. 3–7), so the promises may be fulfilled. The extraordinary length of this story and its development of a single theme contrast strikingly with the spare style of the preceding Abraham and Sarah stories. It points ahead to the Jacob and Joseph stories.

The length of the story is partly caused by its meticulous attention to the sign (vv. 12–14), its fulfillment (vv. 15–20), and the servant's retelling of sign and fulfillment to Rebekah's family to win their consent (vv. 34–49).

24:2 Put your hand under my thigh: the symbolism of this act was apparently connected with the Hebrew concept of children issuing from their father's "thigh" (the literal meaning of "direct descendants" in 46:26; Ex 1:5). Perhaps the man who took such an oath was thought to bring the curse of sterility on himself if he did not fulfill his sworn promise. Jacob made Joseph swear in the same way (Gn 47:29). In both these instances, the oath was taken to carry out the last request of a man upon his death.

24:10 Nahor: it is uncertain whether this is the place where Abraham's brother Nahor (11:27) had lived or whether it is the city Nahur, named in the Mari documents (nineteenth and eighteenth centuries B.C.), near the confluence of the Balikh and Middle Euphrates rivers. **Aram Naharaim**: lit., "Aram between the two rivers," is the Yahwist designation for Terah's homeland. The two rivers are the Habur and the Euphrates. The Priestly designation for the area is Paddan-aram, which is from the Assyrian *padana*, "road or garden," and Aram, which refers to the people or land of the Arameans.

24:12 Let it turn out favorably for me: let me have a favorable sign; cf. end of v. 14.

y: Acts 7:16. *z:* Gn 49:29–30. *a:* Gn 47:29. *b:* Gn 24:37; 28:1–2; Jgs 14:3; Tb 4:12. *c:* Gn 12:7; Ex 6:8; Tb 5:17; Gal 3:16. *d:* Gn 22:23.

when Rebekah—who was born to Bethuel,
son of Milcah, the wife of Abraham's brother
Nahor—came out with a jug on her shoulder.
16The young woman was very beautiful, a
virgin, untouched by man. She went down to
the spring and filled her jug. As she came up,
17the servant ran toward her and said,
"Please give me a sip of water from your
jug." 18"Drink, sir," she replied, and quickly
lowering the jug into her hand, she gave him
a drink. 19When she had finished giving him
a drink, she said, "I will draw water for your
camels, too, until they have finished drinking." 20With that, she quickly emptied her
jug into the drinking trough and ran back to
the well to draw more water, until she had
drawn enough for all the camels. 21The man
watched her the whole time, silently waiting
to learn whether or not the LORD had made
his journey successful. 22When the camels
had finished drinking, the man took out a
gold nose-ring weighing half a shekel, and
two gold bracelets weighing ten shekels for
her wrists. 23Then he asked her: "Whose
daughter are you? Tell me, please. And is
there a place in your father's house for us to
spend the night?" 24She answered: "I am the
daughter of Bethuel the son of Milcah,
whom she bore to Nahor. 25We have plenty
of straw and fodder," she added, "and also a
place to spend the night." 26The man then
knelt and bowed down to the LORD, 27say-
ing: "Blessed be the LORD, the God of my
master Abraham, who has not let his kindness and fidelity toward my master fail. As
for me, the LORD has led me straight to the
house of my master's brother."

28Then the young woman ran off and told
her mother's household what had happened.
29[e] Now Rebekah had a brother named Laban. Laban rushed outside to the man at the
spring. 30[*] When he saw the nose-ring and
the bracelets on his sister's arms and when
he heard Rebekah repeating what the man
had said to her, he went to him while he was
standing by the camels at the spring. 31He
said: "Come, blessed of the LORD! Why are
you standing outside when I have made the
house ready, as well as a place for the
camels?" 32The man then went inside; and
while the camels were being unloaded and
provided with straw and fodder, water was
brought to bathe his feet and the feet of the
men who were with him. 33But when food
was set before him, he said, "I will not eat
until I have told my story." "Go ahead," they
replied.

34"I am Abraham's servant," he began.
35"The LORD has blessed my master so
abundantly that he has become wealthy; he
has given him flocks and herds, silver and
gold, male and female slaves, and camels
and donkeys. 36My master's wife Sarah bore
a son to my master in her old age, and he has
given him everything he owns. 37My master
put me under oath, saying: 'You shall not
take a wife for my son from the daughters of
the Canaanites in whose land I live; 38in-
stead, you must go to my father's house, to
my own family, to get a wife for my son.'
39When I asked my master, 'What if the
woman will not follow me?' 40he replied:
'The LORD, in whose presence I have always
walked, will send his angel with you and
make your journey successful, and so you
will get a wife for my son from my own family and my father's house.[f] 41Then you will
be freed from my curse. If you go to my family and they refuse you, then, too, you will be
free from my curse.'[*]

42"When I came to the spring today, I
said: 'LORD, God of my master Abraham,
please make successful the journey I am on.
43While I stand here at the spring, if I say to
a young woman who comes out to draw water, 'Please give me a little water from your
jug,' 44and she answers, 'Drink, and I will
draw water for your camels, too—then she is
the woman whom the LORD has decided
upon for my master's son.'

45"I had scarcely finished saying this to
myself when Rebekah came out with a jug

24:30 Laban becomes hospitable only when he sees the servant's rich gifts, which is in humorous contrast to his sister's spontaneous generosity toward the servant. Laban's opportunism points forward to his behavior in the Jacob stories (31:14–16).

24:41 Curse: this would be the consequence of failing to carry out the oath referred to in v. 3.

e: Gn 27:43. *f:* Tb 5:17; 10:13.

on her shoulder. After she went down to the spring and drew water, I said to her, ‘Please let me have a drink.’ [46]She quickly lowered the jug she was carrying and said, ‘Drink, and I will water your camels, too.’ So I drank, and she watered the camels also. [47]When I asked her, ‘Whose daughter are you?’ she answered, ‘The daughter of Bethuel, son of Nahor, borne to Nahor by Milcah.’ So I put the ring on her nose and the bracelets on her wrists. [48]Then I knelt and bowed down to the LORD, blessing the LORD, the God of my master Abraham, who had led me on the right road to obtain the daughter of my master’s kinsman for his son. [49]Now, if you will act with kindness and fidelity toward my master, let me know; but if not, let me know that too. I can then proceed accordingly.”

[50][g] Laban and Bethuel said in reply: “This thing comes from the LORD; we can say nothing to you either for or against it. [51]Here is Rebekah, right in front of you; take her and go, that she may become the wife of your master’s son, as the LORD has said.” [52]When Abraham’s servant heard their answer, he bowed to the ground before the LORD. [53]Then he brought out objects of silver and gold and clothing and presented them to Rebekah; he also gave costly presents to her brother and mother. [54]After he and the men with him had eaten and drunk, they spent the night there.

When they got up the next morning, he said, “Allow me to return to my master.”[h] [55]Her brother and mother replied, “Let the young woman stay with us a short while, say ten days; after that she may go.” [56]But he said to them, “Do not detain me, now that the LORD has made my journey successful; let me go back to my master.” [57]They answered, “Let us call the young woman and see what she herself has to say about it.” [58]So they called Rebekah and asked her, “Will you go with this man?” She answered, “I will.”* [59]At this they sent off their sister Rebekah and her nurse with Abraham’s servant and his men. [60]They blessed Rebekah and said:

“Sister, may you grow
into thousands of myriads;
And may your descendants gain possession
of the gates of their enemies!”[i]

[61]Then Rebekah and her attendants started out; they mounted the camels and followed the man. So the servant took Rebekah and went on his way.

[62]Meanwhile Isaac had gone from Beer-lahai-roi and was living in the region of the Negeb.[j] [63]One day toward evening he went out to walk in the field, and caught sight of camels approaching. [64]Rebekah, too, caught sight of Isaac, and got down from her camel. [65]She asked the servant, “Who is the man over there, walking through the fields toward us?” “That is my master,” replied the servant. Then she took her veil and covered herself.

[66]The servant recounted to Isaac all the things he had done. [67]Then Isaac brought Rebekah into the tent of his mother Sarah. He took Rebekah as his wife. Isaac loved her and found solace after the death of his mother.

CHAPTER 25

See RG 110-12

Abraham’s Sons by Keturah. [1]*[k]Abraham took another wife, whose name was Keturah. [2]She bore him Zimran, Jokshan, Medan, Midian, Ishbak, and Shuah.* [3]Jokshan became the father of Sheba and Dedan.

24:58 Marriages arranged by the woman’s father did not require the woman’s consent, but marriages arranged by the woman’s brother did. Laban is the brother and Rebekah is therefore free to give her consent or not.

25:1–11 As with the story of Terah in 11:27–32, this section lists all the descendants of Abraham as a means of concluding the story. The Jacob story ends similarly with the listing of the twelve sons (35:22–26), the death of Isaac (35:27–29), and the descendants of Esau (chap. 36). **Abraham took another wife**: though mentioned here, Abraham’s marriage to a “concubine,” or wife of secondary rank, is not to be understood as happening chronologically after the events narrated in the preceding chapter.

25:2 Three of the six names can be identified: the Midianites are a trading people, mentioned in the Bible as dwelling east of the Gulf of Aqaba in northwest Arabia; Ishbak is a north Syrian tribe; Shuah is a city on the right bank of the Middle Euphrates. The other names are probably towns or peoples on the international trade routes.

g: Tb 7:11–12. *h:* Tb 7:14; 8:20. *i:* Gn 22:17. *j:* Gn 16:13–14; 25:11. *k:* 1 Chr 1:32–33.

The descendants of Dedan were the Asshurim, the Letushim, and the Leummim.[l] 4 The descendants of Midian were Ephah, Epher, Hanoch, Abida, and Eldaah. All of these were descendants of Keturah.

5 Abraham gave everything that he owned to his son Isaac.* 6 To the sons of his concubines, however, he gave gifts while he was still living, as he sent them away eastward, to the land of Kedem,* away from his son Isaac.

Death of Abraham. 7 The whole span of Abraham's life was one hundred and seventy-five years. 8 Then he breathed his last, dying at a ripe old age, grown old after a full life; and he was gathered to his people. 9 His sons Isaac and Ishmael buried him in the cave of Machpelah, in the field of Ephron, son of Zohar the Hittite, which faces Mamre,[m] 10 the field that Abraham had bought from the Hittites; there he was buried next to his wife Sarah. 11 After the death of Abraham, God blessed his son Isaac, who lived near Beer-lahai-roi.

Descendants of Ishmael. 12* These are the descendants of Abraham's son Ishmael, whom Hagar the Egyptian, Sarah's slave, bore to Abraham. 13[n] These are the names of Ishmael's sons, listed in the order of their birth: Ishmael's firstborn Nebaioth, Kedar, Adbeel, Mibsam,[o] 14 Mishma, Dumah, Massa, 15 Hadad, Tema, Jetur, Naphish, and Kedemah. 16 These are the sons of Ishmael, their names by their villages and encampments; twelve chieftains of as many tribal groups.[p]

17 The span of Ishmael's life was one hundred and thirty-seven years. After he had breathed his last and died, he was gathered to his people. 18 The Ishmaelites ranged from Havilah, by Shur, which is on the border of Egypt, all the way to Asshur; and they pitched camp* alongside their various kindred.[q]

Birth of Esau and Jacob. 19* These are the descendants of Isaac, son of Abraham; Abraham begot Isaac. 20 Isaac was forty years old when he married Rebekah, the daughter of Bethuel the Aramean of Paddan-aram* and the sister of Laban the Aramean.[r] 21 Isaac entreated the LORD on behalf of his wife, since she was sterile. The LORD heard his entreaty, and his wife Rebekah became pregnant. 22 But the children jostled each other in the womb so much that she exclaimed, "If it is like this,* why go on living!" She went to consult the LORD, 23 and the LORD answered her:

Two nations are in your womb,
two peoples are separating while still within you;
But one will be stronger than the other,
and the older will serve the younger.*[s]

25:5 Amid so many descendants, Abraham takes steps that Isaac will be his favored heir.

25:6 The land of Kedem: or "the country of the East," the region inhabited by the Kedemites or Easterners (29:1; Jgs 6:3, 33; Jb 1:3; Is 11:14). The names mentioned in vv. 2–4, as far as they can be identified, are those of tribes in the Arabian desert.

25:12 Like the conclusion of the Jacob story (chap. 36), where the numerous descendants of the rejected Esau are listed, the descendants of the rejected Ishmael conclude the story.

25:18 Pitched camp: lit., "fell"; the same Hebrew verb is used in Jgs 7:12 in regard to the hostile encampment of desert tribes. The present passage shows the fulfillment of the prediction contained in Gn 16:12.

25:19–36:43 The Jacob cycle is introduced as the family history of Isaac (Jacob's father), just as the Abraham stories were introduced as the record of the descendants of Terah (Abraham's father, 11:27). The cycle, made up of varied stories, is given unity by several recurring themes: birth, blessing and inheritance, which are developed through the basic contrasts of barrenness/fertility, non-blessing/blessing, and inheritance/exile/homeland. The large story has an envelope structure in which Jacob's youth is spent in Canaan striving with his older brother Esau (25:19–28:22), his early adulthood in Paddan-aram building a family and striving with his brother-in-law Laban (chaps. 29–31), and his later years back in Canaan (chaps. 32–36).

25:20 Paddan-aram: the name used by the Priestly tradition for the northwest region of Mesopotamia, between the Habur and the Euphrates rivers. In Assyrian, *padana* is a road or a garden, and Aram refers to the people or the land of the Arameans. The equivalent geographical term in the Yahwist source is Aram Naharaim, "Aram between two rivers."

25:22 If it is like this: in Hebrew, the phrase *lamah zeh* is capable of several meanings; it occurs again in v. 32 ("What good . . . ?"), 32:30 ("Why do you want . . . ?"), and 33:15 ("For what reason?"). It is one of several words and motifs that run through the story, suggesting that a divine pattern (unknown to the actors) is at work.

25:23 The older will serve the younger: Rebekah now knows something that no one else knows, that God favors Jacob over Esau. The text does not say if she shared this knowledge with anyone or kept it to herself, but, from their actions, it seems unlikely that either Isaac or Esau knew. That fact

l: Is 21:13. *m:* Gn 23:3–20. *n:* 1 Chr 1:29–31. *o:* Is 60:7. *p:* Gn 17:20. *q:* Gn 16:12. *r:* Gn 24:67. *s:* Gn 27:29; Nm 24:18; Mal 1:2–5; Rom 9:10–13.

[24]When the time of her delivery came, there were twins in her womb.[t] [25]The first to emerge was reddish,* and his whole body was like a hairy mantle; so they named him Esau. [26]Next his brother came out, gripping Esau's heel;* so he was named Jacob. Isaac was sixty years old when they were born.[u]

[27]When the boys grew up, Esau became a skillful hunter, a man of the open country; whereas Jacob was a simple* man, who stayed among the tents.[v] [28]Isaac preferred Esau, because he was fond of game; but Rebekah preferred Jacob. [29]Once, when Jacob was cooking a stew, Esau came in from the open country, famished. [30]He said to Jacob, "Let me gulp down some of that red stuff;* I am famished." That is why he was called Edom. [31]But Jacob replied, "First sell me your right as firstborn."* [w] [32]"Look," said Esau, "I am on the point of dying. What good is the right as firstborn to me?" [33]But Jacob said, "Swear to me first!" So he sold Jacob his right as firstborn under oath.[x] [34]Jacob then gave him some bread and the lentil stew; and Esau ate, drank, got up, and went his way. So Esau treated his right as firstborn with disdain.

CHAPTER 26

See RG 111-12

Isaac and Abimelech. [1]* [y] There was a famine in the land, distinct from the earlier one that had occurred in the days of Abraham, and Isaac went down to Abimelech, king of the Philistines in Gerar.[z] [2]The LORD appeared to him and said: Do not go down to Egypt, but camp in this land wherever I tell you. [3]Sojourn in this land, and I will be with you and bless you; for to you and your descendants I will give all these lands, in fulfillment of the oath that I swore to your father Abraham.[a] [4]I will make your descendants as numerous as the stars in the sky, and I will give them all these lands, and in your descendants all the nations of the earth will find blessing—[b] [5]this because Abraham obeyed me, keeping my mandate, my commandments, my ordinances, and my instructions.

[6]* So Isaac settled in Gerar. [7]When the men of the place asked questions about his wife, he answered, "She is my sister." He was afraid that, if he called her his wife, the men of the place would kill him on account of Rebekah, since she was beautiful. [8]But when they had been there for a long time, Abimelech, king of the Philistines, looked out of a window and saw Isaac fondling his wife Rebekah. [9]He called for Isaac and said: "She must certainly be your wife! How could you have said, 'She is my sister'?" Isaac replied, "I thought I might lose my life on her account." [10]"How could you have done this to us!" exclaimed Abimelech. "It would have taken very little for one of the people to lie with your wife, and so you would have brought guilt upon us!" [11]Abimelech then commanded all the people: "Anyone who maltreats this man or his wife shall be put to death."

must be borne in mind in assessing Rebekah's role in chap. 27, the theft of Esau's blessing.

25:25 Reddish: in Hebrew, *'admoni*, a reference to Edom, another name for Esau (v. 30; 36:1). Edom was also the name of the country south of Moab (southeast of the Dead Sea) where the descendants of Esau lived. It was called the "red" country because of its reddish sandstone. Moreover, "red" points ahead to the red stew in the next scene. **Hairy**: in Hebrew, *se'ar*, a reference to Seir, another name for Edom (36:8).

25:26 Heel: in Hebrew *'aqeb*, a wordplay on the name Jacob; cf. 27:36. The first of three scenes of striving with Esau. The second is vv. 27–34, and the third, chap. 27. In all the scenes, Jacob values the blessing more than his ardent but unreflective brother Esau does.

25:27 Simple: the Hebrew word denotes soundness, integrity, health, none of which fit here. Whatever its precise meaning, it must be opposite to the qualities of Esau.

25:30 Red stuff: in Hebrew, *'adom*; another play on the word Edom, the "red" land.

25:31 Right as firstborn: the privilege that entitled the firstborn son to a position of honor in the family and to a double share in the possessions inherited from the father. There is a persistent wordplay between *bekorah*, "right of the firstborn," and *berakah*, "the blessing." Contrary to custom, the preference here is for the younger son, as it was in the choice of Isaac over Ishmael.

26:1 The promise of land and numerous descendants given to Abraham (12:1–3; 15; 17; 22:17–18) is renewed for his son Isaac. The divine blessing to Isaac is mentioned also in vv. 12, 24, and 29.

26:6–11 This scene is the third version of the wife-in-danger story (cf. chaps. 12 and 20). The mention of the famine in 26:1 recalls the famine in 12:10; the name Abimelech, king of the Philistines in Gerar, recalls 20:2. The deception, according to all the stories, is the claim that the wife is a sister. This

t: Hos 12:4. *u:* Mt 1:2. *v:* Gn 27:6–7. *w:* Dt 21:17. *x:* Heb 12:16. *y:* Gn 12:10–20. *z:* Gn 12:10. *a:* Gn 12:7; 15:18; Ex 32:13; Ps 105:9; Sir 44:22; Heb 11:9. *b:* Gn 12:3; 22:17–18; 28:14; Ex 32:13.

12* Isaac sowed a crop in that region and reaped a hundredfold the same year. Since the LORD blessed him, 13[c] he became richer and richer all the time, until he was very wealthy. 14 He acquired flocks and herds, and a great work force, and so the Philistines became envious of him. 15[d] The Philistines had stopped up and filled with dirt all the wells that his father's servants had dug back in the days of his father Abraham. 16 So Abimelech said to Isaac, "Go away from us; you have become far too numerous for us." 17 Isaac left there and camped in the Wadi Gerar where he stayed. 18 Isaac reopened the wells which his father's servants had dug back in the days of his father Abraham and which the Philistines had stopped up after Abraham's death; he gave them names like those that his father had given them. 19 But when Isaac's servants dug in the wadi and reached spring water in their well, 20 the shepherds of Gerar argued with Isaac's shepherds, saying, "The water belongs to us!" So he named the well Esek,* because they had quarreled there. 21 Then they dug another well, and they argued over that one too; so he named it Sitnah.* 22 So he moved on from there and dug still another well, but over this one they did not argue. He named it Rehoboth,* and said, "Because the LORD has now given us ample room, we shall flourish in the land."

23 From there Isaac went up to Beer-sheba. 24 The same night the LORD appeared to him and said: I am the God of Abraham, your father. Do not fear, for I am with you. I will bless you and multiply your descendants for the sake of Abraham, my servant.[e] 25 So Isaac built an altar there and invoked the LORD by name. After he had pitched his tent there, Isaac's servants began to dig a well nearby.

26[f] Then Abimelech came to him from Gerar, with Ahuzzath, his councilor, and Phicol, the general of his army. 27 Isaac asked them, "Why have you come to me, since you hate me and have driven me away from you?" 28 They answered: "We clearly see that the LORD has been with you, so we thought: let there be a sworn agreement between our two sides—between you and us. Let us make a covenant with you: 29 you shall do no harm to us, just as we have not maltreated you, but have always acted kindly toward you and have let you depart in peace. So now, may you be blessed by the LORD!" 30 Isaac then made a feast for them, and they ate and drank. 31 Early the next morning they exchanged oaths. Then Isaac sent them on their way, and they departed from him in peace.

32 That same day Isaac's servants came and informed him about the well they had been digging; they told him, "We have reached water!" 33 He called it Shibah;* hence the name of the city is Beer-sheba to this day. 34* When Esau was forty years old, he married Judith, daughter of Beeri the Hittite, and Basemath, daughter of Elon the Hivite.[g] 35 But they became a source of bitterness to Isaac and Rebekah.

CHAPTER 27

See RG 112–14

Jacob's Deception.* 1 When Isaac was so old that his eyesight had failed him, he called his older son Esau and said to him, "My son!" "Here I am!" he replied. 2 Isaac then said, "Now I have grown old. I do not know when I might die. 3 So now take your

story (from the Yahwist source) departs from the two previous accounts in that the wife is not taken into the harem of the foreign king.

26:12–33 The dispute is over water rights. In a sparsely watered land, wells were precious and claims on water could function as a kind of claim on the land. Scholars generally judge the account of the dispute over water rights and its settlement by a legal agreement between Isaac and Abimelech to be a Yahwist version of the similar story about Abraham in 21:22–34. Here, Abimelech realizes that Isaac has brought blessing to his people and thus desires a covenant with him. The feast in v. 30 is part of the covenant ceremony.

26:20 Esek: "quarrel."

26:21 Sitnah: "opposition."

26:22 Rehoboth: "wide spaces," i.e., ample room to live; site is probably SW of modern day Beer-sheba.

26:33 Shibah: the place name Shibah is a play on two Hebrew words, *shebu'ah*, "oath," and *shwebaa'*, "seven." In v. 31, they exchanged oaths.

26:34–35 These verses from the Priestly source introduce the next section on Esau's loss of his right as firstborn by suggesting a motivation for this in Isaac's and Rebekah's dislike for Esau's Canaanite wives.

27:1–45 The chapter, a literary masterpiece, is the third and climactic wresting away of the blessing of Esau. Rebekah manages the entire affair, using perhaps her privileged information about Jacob's status (25:23); Jacob's only qualm is

c: Jb 1:3. *d:* Gn 21:25–31. *e:* Gn 46:3. *f:* Gn 21:22–31; Prv 16:7. *g:* Gn 27:46.

hunting gear—your quiver and bow—and go out into the open country to hunt some game for me. [4]Then prepare for me a dish in the way I like, and bring it to me to eat, so that I may bless you* before I die."

[5]Rebekah had been listening while Isaac was speaking to his son Esau. So when Esau went out into the open country to hunt some game for his father,[h] [6]Rebekah said to her son Jacob, "Listen! I heard your father tell your brother Esau, [7]'Bring me some game and prepare a dish for me to eat, that I may bless you with the LORD's approval before I die.' [8]Now, my son, obey me in what I am about to order you. [9]Go to the flock and get me two choice young goats so that with these I might prepare a dish for your father in the way he likes. [10]Then bring it to your father to eat, that he may bless you before he dies." [11]But Jacob said to his mother Rebekah, "But my brother Esau is a hairy man and I am smooth-skinned![i] [12]Suppose my father feels me? He will think I am making fun of him, and I will bring on myself a curse instead of a blessing." [13]His mother, however, replied: "Let any curse against you, my son, fall on me! Just obey me. Go and get me the young goats."

[14]So Jacob went and got them and brought them to his mother, and she prepared a dish in the way his father liked. [15]Rebekah then took the best clothes of her older son Esau that she had in the house, and gave them to her younger son Jacob to wear; [16]and with the goatskins she covered up his hands and the hairless part of his neck. [17]Then she gave her son Jacob the dish and the bread she had prepared.

[18]Going to his father, Jacob said, "Father!" "Yes?" replied Isaac. "Which of my sons are you?" [19]Jacob answered his father: "I am Esau, your firstborn. I did as you told me. Please sit up and eat some of my game, so that you may bless me." [20]But Isaac said to his son, "How did you get it so quickly, my son?" He answered, "The LORD, your God, directed me." [21]Isaac then said to Jacob, "Come closer, my son, that I may feel you, to learn whether you really are my son Esau or not." [22]So Jacob moved up closer to his father. When Isaac felt him, he said, "Although the voice is Jacob's, the hands are Esau's." [23](He failed to identify him because his hands were hairy, like those of his brother Esau; so he blessed him.) [24]Again Isaac said, "Are you really my son Esau?" And Jacob said, "I am." [25]Then Isaac said, "Serve me, my son, and let me eat of the game so that I may bless you." Jacob served it to him, and Isaac ate; he brought him wine, and he drank. [26]Finally his father Isaac said to him, "Come closer, my son, and kiss me." [27]As Jacob went up to kiss him, Isaac smelled the fragrance of his clothes. With that, he blessed him, saying,

"Ah, the fragrance of my son
is like the fragrance of a field
that the LORD has blessed![j]
[28] May God give to you
of the dew of the heavens
And of the fertility of the earth
abundance of grain and wine.
[29] [k]May peoples serve you,
and nations bow down to you;
Be master of your brothers,
and may your mother's sons bow
down to you.
Cursed be those who curse you,
and blessed be those who bless you."

[30]Jacob had scarcely left his father after Isaac had finished blessing him, when his brother Esau came back from his hunt. [31]Then he too prepared a dish, and bringing it to his father, he said, "Let my father sit up

that if his father discovers the ruse, he will receive a curse instead of a blessing (vv. 11–12). Isaac is passive as he was in chaps. 22 and 24. The deception is effected through clothing (Jacob wears Esau's clothing), which points ahead to a similar deception of a patriarch by means of clothing in the Joseph story (37:21–33). Such recurrent acts and scenes let the reader know a divine purpose is moving the story forward even though the human characters are unaware of it.

27:4 I may bless you: Isaac's blessing confers fertility (vv. 27–28) and dominion (v. 29). The "dew of heaven" is rain that produces grain and wine, two of the principal foodstuffs of the ancient Near East. The "fertility of the earth" may allude to oil, the third basic foodstuff. The full agricultural year may be implied here: the fall rains are followed by the grain harvests of the spring and the grape harvest of late summer, and then the olive harvest of the fall (cf. Dt 11:14; Ps 104:13–15).

h: Gn 25:28. *i:* Gn 25:25. *j:* Gn 22:17–18; Heb 11:20. *k:* Gn 25:23; 49:8; Nm 24:9.

and eat some of his son's game, that you may then give me your blessing." 32His father Isaac asked him, "Who are you?" He said, "I am your son, your firstborn son, Esau." 33Isaac trembled greatly. "Who was it, then," he asked, "that hunted game and brought it to me? I ate it all just before you came, and I blessed him. Now he is blessed!" 34As he heard his father's words, Esau burst into loud, bitter sobbing and said, "Father, bless me too!" 35When Isaac said, "Your brother came here by a ruse and carried off your blessing," 36Esau exclaimed, "He is well named Jacob, is he not! He has supplanted me* twice! First he took away my right as firstborn, and now he has taken away my blessing." Then he said, "Have you not saved a blessing for me?"[l] 37Isaac replied to Esau: "I have already appointed him your master, and I have assigned to him all his kindred as his servants; besides, I have sustained him with grain and wine. What then can I do for you, my son?" 38But Esau said to his father, "Have you only one blessing, father? Bless me too, father!" and Esau wept aloud.[m] 39His father Isaac said in response:

"See, far from the fertile earth
  will be your dwelling;
  far from the dew of the heavens above![n]
40 By your sword you will live,
  and your brother you will serve;
But when you become restless,
  you will throw off his yoke from your
    neck."[o]

41Esau bore a grudge against Jacob because of the blessing his father had given him. Esau said to himself, "Let the time of mourning for my father come, so that I may kill my brother Jacob."[p] 42When Rebekah got news of what her older son Esau had in mind, she summoned her younger son Jacob and said to him: "Listen! Your brother Esau intends to get his revenge by killing you. 43So now, my son, obey me: flee at once to my brother Laban in Haran, 44and stay with him a while until your brother's fury subsides— 45until your brother's anger against you subsides and he forgets what you did to him. Then I will send for you and bring you back. Why should I lose both of you in a single day?"

Jacob Sent to Laban. 46Rebekah said to Isaac: "I am disgusted with life because of the Hittite women. If Jacob also should marry a Hittite woman, a native of the land, like these women, why should I live?"[q]

CHAPTER 28

See RG 112–14

1* Isaac therefore summoned Jacob and blessed him, charging him: "You shall not marry a Canaanite woman![r] 2Go now to Paddan-aram, to the home of your mother's father Bethuel, and there choose a wife for yourself from among the daughters of Laban, your mother's brother.[s] 3May God Almighty bless you and make you fertile, multiply you that you may become an assembly of peoples. 4May God extend to you and your descendants the blessing of Abraham, so that you may gain possession of the land where you are residing, which he assigned to Abraham."[t] 5Then Isaac sent Jacob on his way; he went to Paddan-aram, to Laban, son of Bethuel the Aramean, and brother of Rebekah, the mother of Jacob and Esau.[u]

6Esau noted that Isaac had blessed Jacob when he sent him to Paddan-aram to get himself a wife there, and that, as he gave him

27:36 He has supplanted me: in Hebrew, *wayyaqebeni*, a wordplay on the name Jacob, *ya'aqob*; see Jer 9:3 and Gn 25:26. There is also a play between the Hebrew words *bekorah* ("right of the firstborn") and *berakah* ("blessing").

28:1–9 A glimpse of Rebekah's shrewdness is provided by 27:42–28:2. She is aware of Esau's murderous plot against Jacob (27:42–45) but realizes the episode of the stolen blessing is still painful to Isaac; she therefore uses another motive to persuade Isaac to send Jacob away—he must marry within the family (endogamy), unlike Esau. Esau, unreflective as usual, realizes too late he also should marry within the family but, significantly, marries from Abraham's rejected line. At this point in the story, Jacob (and his mother) have taken the blessing for themselves. Their actions have put Jacob in a precarious position: he must flee the land because of his brother's murderous intent and find a wife in a far country. One might ask how God's blessing can be given to such an unworthy schemer. There is a biblical pattern of preferring the younger brother or sister over the older—Isaac over Ishmael, Jacob over Esau, Rachel over Leah, Joseph over his older brothers, Ephraim over Manasseh (Gn 48:14), David over his older brothers.

28:10–22 As Jacob is leaving the land on his way to an un-

l: Gn 25:26, 29–34; Hos 12:4. *m:* Heb 12:17. *n:* Heb 11:20. *o:* 2 Kgs 8:20, 22; 2 Chr 21:8. *p:* Wis 10:10; Ob 10. *q:* Gn 26:34–35. *r:* Gn 24:3–4; 26:35. *s:* Gn 22:22. *t:* Ex 32:13. *u:* Jdt 8:26.

his blessing, he charged him, “You shall not marry a Canaanite woman,” [7]and that Jacob had obeyed his father and mother and gone to Paddan-aram. [8]Esau realized how displeasing the Canaanite women were to his father Isaac, [9]so Esau went to Ishmael, and in addition to the wives he had, married Mahalath, the daughter of Abraham’s son Ishmael and sister of Nebaioth.[v]

Jacob’s Dream at Bethel.* [10]Jacob departed from Beer-sheba and proceeded toward Haran. [11]When he came upon a certain place,* he stopped there for the night, since the sun had already set. Taking one of the stones at the place, he put it under his head and lay down in that place. [12]Then he had a dream: a stairway* rested on the ground, with its top reaching to the heavens; and God’s angels were going up and down on it.[w] [13]And there was the LORD standing beside him and saying: I am the LORD, the God of Abraham your father and the God of Isaac; the land on which you are lying I will give to you and your descendants.[x] [14]Your descendants will be like the dust of the earth, and through them you will spread to the west and the east, to the north and the south. In you and your descendants all the families of the earth will find blessing.[y] [15]I am with you and will protect you wherever you go, and bring you back to this land. I will never leave you until I have done what I promised you.[z]

[16]When Jacob awoke from his sleep, he said, “Truly, the LORD is in this place and I did not know it!” [17]He was afraid and said: “How awesome this place is! This is nothing else but the house of God, the gateway to heaven!” [18]Early the next morning Jacob took the stone that he had put under his head, set it up as a sacred pillar,* and poured oil on top of it.[a] [19]He named that place Bethel,* whereas the former name of the town had been Luz.[b]

[20]Jacob then made this vow:* “If God will be with me and protect me on this journey I am making and give me food to eat and clothes to wear, [21]and I come back safely to my father’s house, the LORD will be my God. [22]This stone that I have set up as a sacred pillar will be the house of God. Of everything you give me, I will return a tenth part to you without fail.”

CHAPTER 29

See RG 112–14

Arrival in Haran.* [1][c] After Jacob resumed his journey, he came to the land of the

certain future in Paddan-aram, God appears to him at a sacred place that Jacob had visited only to take a night’s rest. Jacob’s unawareness of the holiness of the place underscores the graciousness of the gift. On his return to Canaan, he will again encounter a divine visitor in the form of the mysterious attacker (32:23–33) and, after his return and reconciliation with Esau, he will again go to Bethel (35:1–15).

28:11 Place: the Hebrew word is often used specifically of a sacred site. The ambiguous word “place” is used here, for the text emphasizes that Jacob has no idea the place he has come upon is sacred; only when he wakes up does he realize it is sacred. The place was Bethel (v. 19), a sacred site as early as the time of Abraham (12:8).

28:12 Stairway: in Hebrew, *sullam*, traditionally but inaccurately translated as “ladder.” The corresponding verb, *salal*, means “to heap up” something, such as dirt for a highway or a ramp. The imagery in Jacob’s dream may be derived from the Babylonian ziggurat or temple tower, “with its top in the sky” (11:4), and with brick steps leading up to a small temple at the top.

28:18 Sacred pillar: in Hebrew, *masseba*, a stone which might vary in shape and size, set upright and usually intended for some religious purpose. The custom of erecting such sacred pillars in Palestine went back to its pre-Israelite period; but since their polytheistic associations were often retained, later Israelite religion forbade their erection (Lv 26:1; Dt 16:22) and ordered the destruction of those that were associated with other religions (Ex 34:13; Dt 12:3).

28:19 Bethel: i.e., “house of God”; the reference is to the house of God in v. 17.

28:20 This vow: knowing well that Esau’s murderous wrath stands between him and the possession of the land promised him, Jacob makes his vow very precise. He vows to make the God who appeared to him his own if the God guides him safely to Paddan-aram and back to this land.

29:1–14 Jacob’s arrival in Haran. The sight of Rachel inspires Jacob to the superhuman feat of rolling back the enormous stone by himself. The scene evokes the meeting of Abraham’s steward and Jacob’s mother Rebekah at a well (24:11–27).

The verse begins the story of Jacob’s time in Mesopotamia (29:1–31:54), which is framed on either side by Jacob’s time in Canaan, 25:19–28:22 and 32:1–36:43. In these chapters, Jacob suffers Laban’s duplicity as Esau had to suffer his, though eventually Jacob outwits Laban and leaves Mesopotamia a wealthy man. An elaborate chiastic (or envelope) structure shapes the diverse material: (A) Jacob’s arrival in Haran in 29:1–4; (B) contract with Laban in 29:15–20; (C) Laban’s deception of Jacob in 29:21–30; (D) the center, the

v: Gn 36:2–3. *w:* Jn 1:51. *x:* Dt 1:8; Mi 7:20. *y:* Gn 12:3; 13:14–15; 15:5–6; 18:18; 22:17–18; 26:4; Dt 19:8; Sir 44:21. *z:* Gn 31:3. *a:* Gn 31:13; 35:14–15. *b:* Gn 35:6; 48:3; Jos 18:13; Jgs 1:23; Hos 12:5. *c:* Wis 10:10.

Kedemites. [2]Looking about, he saw a well in the open country, with three flocks of sheep huddled near it, for flocks were watered from that well. A large stone covered the mouth of the well.[d] [3]When all the shepherds were assembled there they would roll the stone away from the mouth of the well and water the sheep. Then they would put the stone back again in its place over the mouth of the well.

[4]Jacob said to them, "My brothers, where are you from?" "We are from Haran," they replied. [5]Then he asked them, "Do you know Laban, son of Nahor?" "We do," they answered.[e] [6]He inquired further, "Is he well?" "He is," they answered; "and here comes his daughter Rachel with the sheep." [7]Then he said: "There is still much daylight left; it is hardly the time to bring the animals home. Water the sheep, and then continue pasturing them." [8]They replied, "We cannot until all the shepherds are here to roll the stone away from the mouth of the well; then can we water the flocks."

[9]While he was still talking with them, Rachel arrived with her father's sheep, for she was the one who tended them. [10]As soon as Jacob saw Rachel, the daughter of his mother's brother Laban, and the sheep of Laban, he went up, rolled the stone away from the mouth of the well, and watered Laban's sheep. [11]Then Jacob kissed Rachel and wept aloud. [12]Jacob told Rachel that he was her father's relative, Rebekah's son. So she ran to tell her father. [13]When Laban heard the news about Jacob, his sister's son, he ran to meet him. After embracing and kissing him, he brought him to his house. Jacob then repeated to Laban all these things, [14]and Laban said to him, "You are indeed my bone and my flesh."*

Marriage to Leah and Rachel. After Jacob had stayed with him a full month, [15]* Laban said to him: "Should you serve me for nothing just because you are a relative of mine? Tell me what your wages should be." [16]Now Laban had two daughters; the older was called Leah, the younger Rachel. [17]Leah had dull eyes,* but Rachel was shapely and beautiful. [18]Because Jacob loved Rachel, he answered, "I will serve you seven years for your younger daughter Rachel."* [19]Laban replied, "It is better to give her to you than to another man. Stay with me." [20]So Jacob served seven years for Rachel, yet they seemed to him like a few days because of his love for her.[f]

[21]Then Jacob said to Laban, "Give me my wife, that I may consummate my marriage with her, for my term is now completed." [22]So Laban invited all the local inhabitants and gave a banquet. [23]At nightfall he took his daughter Leah and brought her to Jacob, and he consummated the marriage with her. [24]Laban assigned his maidservant Zilpah to his daughter Leah as her maidservant. [25]In the morning, there was Leah! So Jacob said to Laban: "How could you do this to me! Was it not for Rachel that I served you? Why did you deceive me?" [26]Laban replied, "It is not the custom in our country to give the younger daughter before the firstborn. [27]Finish the bridal week* for this one, and then the other will also be given to you in return for another seven years of service with me."[g]

[28]Jacob did so. He finished the bridal week for the one, and then Laban gave him his daughter Rachel as a wife. [29]Laban as-

birth of Jacob's children in 29:31–30:24; (C′) Jacob's deception of Laban in 30:25–43; (B′) dispute with Laban in 31:17–42; (A′) departure from Laban in 31:43–54. As the chiasm reverses, so do the fortunes of Laban and Jacob. **Kedemites**: see note on 25:6.

29:14 Bone and . . . flesh: the Hebrew idiom for English "flesh and blood" (cf. 2:23; Jgs 9:2; 2 Sm 5:1 = 1 Chr 11:1).

29:15–30 Laban's deception and Jacob's marriages. There are many ironies in the passage. Jacob's protest to Laban, "How could you do this to me?" echoes the question put to Abraham (20:9) and Isaac (26:10) when their deceptions about their wives were discovered. The major irony is that Jacob, the deceiver of his father and brother about the blessing (chap. 27), is deceived by his uncle (standing in for the father) about his wife.

29:17 Dull eyes: in the language of beauty used here, "dull" probably means lacking in the luster that was the sign of beautiful eyes, as in 1 Sm 16:12 and Sg 4:1.

29:18 Jacob offers to render service (Jos 15:16–17; 1 Sm 17:25; 18:17) to pay off the customary bridal price (Ex 22:15–16; Dt 22:29).

29:27 The bridal week: an ancient wedding lasted for seven days; cf. Jgs 14:12, 17.

d: Gn 24:11–12. *e:* Tb 7:4. *f:* Hos 12:13. *g:* Hos 12:13.

signed his maidservant Bilhah to his daughter Rachel as her maidservant. 30 Jacob then
consummated his marriage with Rachel
also, and he loved her more than Leah. Thus
he served Laban another seven years.[h]

Jacob's Children.* 31 When the LORD saw
that Leah was unloved, he made her fruitful,
while Rachel was barren. 32 Leah conceived
and bore a son, and she named him Reuben;*
for she said, "It means, 'The LORD saw my
misery; surely now my husband will love
me.' "[i] 33 She conceived again and bore a
son, and said, "It means, 'The LORD heard
that I was unloved,' and therefore he has
given me this one also"; so she named him
Simeon.* 34 Again she conceived and bore a
son, and she said, "Now at last my husband
will become attached to me, since I have
now borne him three sons"; that is why she
named him Levi.* 35 Once more she conceived and bore a son, and she said, "This
time I will give thanks to the LORD"; therefore she named him Judah.* Then she
stopped bearing children.[j]

CHAPTER 30

See RG 112–14

1 When Rachel saw that she had not
borne children to Jacob, she became envious
of her sister. She said to Jacob, "Give me
children or I shall die!"[k] 2 Jacob became angry with Rachel and said, "Can I take the
place of God, who has denied you the fruit of
the womb?"[l] 3 She replied, "Here is my
maidservant Bilhah. Have intercourse with
her, and let her give birth on my knees,* so
that I too may have children through her."[m]
4 So she gave him her maidservant Bilhah as
wife,* and Jacob had intercourse with her.
5 When Bilhah conceived and bore a son for
Jacob, 6 Rachel said, "God has vindicated
me; indeed he has heeded my plea and given
me a son." Therefore she named him Dan.*
7 Rachel's maidservant Bilhah conceived
again and bore a second son for Jacob, 8 and
Rachel said, "I have wrestled strenuously
with my sister, and I have prevailed." So she
named him Naphtali.*

9 When Leah saw that she had ceased to
bear children, she took her maidservant Zilpah and gave her to Jacob as wife. 10 So
Leah's maidservant Zilpah bore a son for Jacob. 11 Leah then said, "What good luck!" So
she named him Gad.* 12 Then Leah's maidservant Zilpah bore a second son to Jacob;
13 and Leah said, "What good fortune, because women will call me fortunate!" So she
named him Asher.*

14 One day, during the wheat harvest, Reuben went out and came upon some mandrakes* in the field which he brought home

29:31–30:24 The note of strife, first sounded between Jacob and Esau in chaps. 25–27, continues between the two wives, since Jacob loved Rachel more than Leah (29:30). Jacob's neglect of Leah moves God to make her fruitful (29:31). Leah's fertility provokes Rachel. Leah bears Jacob four sons (Reuben, Levi, Simeon, and Judah) and her maidservant Zilpah, two (Gad and Asher). Rachel's maidservant Bilhah bears two (Dan and Naphtali). After the mandrakes (30:14–17), Leah bears Issachar and Zebulun and a daughter Dinah. Rachel then bears Joseph and, later in the land of Canaan, Benjamin (35:18).

29:32 Reuben: the literal meaning of the Hebrew name is disputed. One interpretation is *re'u ben,* "look, a son!", but here in Genesis (as also with the names of all the other sons of Jacob), it is given a symbolic rather than an etymological interpretation. Name and person were regarded as closely interrelated. The symbolic interpretation of Reuben's name, according to the Yahwist source, is based on the similar-sounding *ra'a be'onyi*, "he saw my misery." In the Elohist source, the name is explained by the similar-sounding *ye'ehabani*, "he will love me."

29:33 Simeon: in popular etymology, related to *shama'*, "he heard."

29:34 Levi: related to *yillaweh*, "he will become attached."

29:35 Judah: related to *'odeh*, "I will give thanks, praise."

30:3 On my knees: in the ancient Near East, a father would take a newborn child in his lap to signify that he acknowledged it as his own; Rachel uses the ceremony in order to adopt the child and establish her legal rights to it.

30:4 As wife: in 35:22 Bilhah is called a "concubine" (Heb. *pilegesh*). In v. 9, Zilpah is called "wife," and in 37:2 both women are called wives. The basic difference between a wife and a concubine was that no bride price was paid for the latter. The interchange of terminology shows that there was some blurring in social status between the wife and the concubine.

30:6 Dan: explained by the term *dannanni*, "he has vindicated me."

30:8 Naphtali: explained by the Hebrew term *naftulim*, lit., "contest" or "struggle."

30:11 Gad: explained by the Hebrew term *begad*, lit., "in luck," i.e., "what good luck!"

30:13 Asher: explained by the term *be'oshri*, lit., "in my good fortune," i.e., "what good fortune," and by the term *ye'ashsheruni*, "they call me fortunate."

30:14 Mandrakes: an herb whose root was thought to promote conception. The Hebrew word for mandrakes, *duda'im*,

h: Dt 21:15–17. *i:* Gn 49:3. *j:* Mt 1:2; Lk 3:33. *k:* Prv 30:16. *l:* 2 Kgs 5:7. *m:* Gn 16:2–4.

to his mother Leah. Rachel said to Leah, "Please give me some of your son's mandrakes." [15]Leah replied, "Was it not enough for you to take away my husband, that you must now take my son's mandrakes too?" Rachel answered, "In that case Jacob may lie with you tonight in exchange for your son's mandrakes." [16]That evening, when Jacob came in from the field, Leah went out to meet him. She said, "You must have intercourse with me, because I have hired you with my son's mandrakes." So that night he lay with her, [17]and God listened to Leah; she conceived and bore a fifth son to Jacob. [18]Leah then said, "God has given me my wages for giving my maidservant to my husband"; so she named him Issachar.* [19]Leah conceived again and bore a sixth son to Jacob; [20]and Leah said, "God has brought me a precious gift. This time my husband will honor me, because I have borne him six sons"; so she named him Zebulun.* [21]Afterwards she gave birth to a daughter, and she named her Dinah.

[22]Then God remembered Rachel. God listened to her and made her fruitful. [23]She conceived and bore a son, and she said, "God has removed my disgrace."[n] [24]She named him Joseph,* saying, "May the LORD add another son for me!"

Jacob Outwits Laban.* [25]After Rachel gave birth to Joseph, Jacob said to Laban: "Allow me to go to my own region and land. [26]Give me my wives and my children for whom I served you and let me go, for you know the service that I rendered you." [27]Laban answered him: "If you will please! I have learned through divination that the LORD has blessed me because of you." [28]He continued, "State the wages I owe you, and I will pay them." [29]Jacob replied: "You know what work I did for you and how well your livestock fared under my care; [30]the little you had before I came has grown into an abundance, since the LORD has blessed you in my company. Now, when can I do something for my own household as well?" [31]Laban asked, "What should I give you?" Jacob answered: "You do not have to give me anything. If you do this thing for me, I will again pasture and tend your sheep. [32]Let me go through your whole flock today and remove from it every dark animal among the lambs and every spotted or speckled one among the goats.* These will be my wages. [33]In the future, whenever you check on my wages, my honesty will testify for me: any animal that is not speckled or spotted among the goats, or dark among the lambs, got into my possession by theft!" [34]Laban said, "Very well. Let it be as you say."

[35]That same day Laban removed the streaked and spotted he-goats and all the speckled and spotted she-goats, all those with some white on them, as well as every dark lamb, and he put them in the care of his sons.* [36]Then he put a three days' journey between himself and Jacob, while Jacob was pasturing the rest of Laban's flock.

[37]Jacob, however, got some fresh shoots

has erotic connotations, since it sounds like the words *daddayim* ("breasts") and *dodim* ("sexual pleasure").

30:18 Issachar: explained by the terms, *sekari*, "my reward," and in v. 16, *sakor sekartika*, "I have hired you."

30:20 Zebulun: explained by the terms, *zebadani . . . zebed tob*, "he has brought me a precious gift," and *yizbeleni*, "he will honor me."

30:24 Joseph: explained by the words *yosep*, "may he add," and in v. 23, *'asap*, "he has removed."

30:25–43 Jacob's deception of Laban. Jacob has been living in Laban's household as an indentured worker paying off the bride price. Having paid off all his obligations, he wants to settle his accounts with Laban. His many children attest to the fulfillment of the Lord's promise of numerous progeny; the birth of Joseph to his beloved Rachel signals the fulfillment in a special way. To enter into the Lord's second promise, the land, he must now return to Canaan.

30:32 Dark . . . lambs . . . spotted or speckled . . . goats: in the Near East the normal color of sheep is light gray, whereas that of goats is dark brown or black. A minority of sheep in that part of the world have dark patches, and a minority of goats, white markings. Laban is quick to agree to the offer, for Jacob would have received only a few animals. But Jacob gets the better of him, using two different means: (1) he separates out the weaker animals and then provides visual impressions to the stronger animals at mating time (a folkloric belief); (2) in 31:8–12, he transmits the preferred characteristics through controlled propagation. It should be noted that Jacob has been told what to do in a dream (31:10) and that God is behind the increase in his flocks.

30:35 By giving the abnormally colored animals to his sons, Laban not only deprived Jacob of his first small wages, but he also schemed to prevent the future breeding of such animals in the flock entrusted to Jacob.

n: Lk 1:25.

of poplar, almond and plane* trees, and he peeled white stripes in them by laying bare the white core of the shoots. [38]The shoots that he had peeled he then set upright in the watering troughs where the animals came to drink, so that they would be in front of them. When the animals were in heat as they came to drink, [39]the goats mated by the shoots, and so they gave birth to streaked, speckled and spotted young. [40]The sheep, on the other hand, Jacob kept apart, and he made these animals face the streaked or completely dark animals of Laban. Thus he produced flocks of his own, which he did not put with Laban's flock. [41]Whenever the hardier animals were in heat, Jacob would set the shoots in the troughs in full view of these animals, so that they mated by the shoots; [42]but with the weaker animals he would not put the shoots there. So the feeble animals would go to Laban, but the hardy ones to Jacob. [43]So the man grew exceedingly prosperous, and he owned large flocks, male and female servants, camels, and donkeys.

CHAPTER 31

See RG 112–14

Flight from Laban. [1]* Jacob heard that Laban's sons were saying, "Jacob has taken everything that belonged to our father, and he has produced all this wealth from our father's property." [2]Jacob perceived, too, that Laban's attitude toward him was not what it had previously been. [3]Then the LORD said to Jacob: Return to the land of your ancestors, where you were born, and I will be with you.[o]

[4]So Jacob sent for Rachel and Leah to meet him in the field where his flock was. [5]There he said to them: "I have noticed that your father's attitude toward me is not as it was in the past; but the God of my father has been with me. [6]You know well that with all my strength I served your father; [7]yet your father cheated me and changed my wages ten times. God, however, did not let him do me any harm.[p] [8]Whenever your father said, 'The speckled animals will be your wages,' the entire flock would bear speckled young; whenever he said, 'The streaked animals will be your wages,' the entire flock would bear streaked young. [9]So God took away your father's livestock and gave it to me. [10]Once, during the flock's mating season, I had a dream in which I saw he-goats mating that were streaked, speckled and mottled. [11]In the dream God's angel said to me, 'Jacob!' and I replied, 'Here I am!' [12]Then he said: 'Look up and see. All the he-goats that are mating are streaked, speckled and mottled, for I have seen all the things that Laban has been doing to you. [13]I am the God of Bethel, where you anointed a sacred pillar and made a vow to me. Get up now! Leave this land and return to the land of your birth.' "[q]

[14]Rachel and Leah answered him: "Do we still have an heir's portion in our father's house? [15]Are we not regarded by him as outsiders?* He not only sold us; he has even used up the money that he got for us! [16]All the wealth that God took away from our father really belongs to us and our children. So do whatever God has told you."[r] [17]Jacob proceeded to put his children and wives on camels, [18]and he drove off all his livestock and all the property he had acquired in Paddan-aram, to go to his father Isaac in the land of Canaan.

[19]Now Laban was away shearing his sheep, and Rachel had stolen her father's household images.*[s] [20]Jacob had hoodwinked* Laban the Aramean by not telling him that he was going

30:37 Plane: also called the Oriental Plane, a deciduous tree found in riverine forests and marshes.

31:1–54 Jacob flees with his family from Laban. The strife that has always accompanied Jacob continues as Laban's sons complain, "he has taken everything that belonged to our father"; the brothers' complaint echoes Esau's in 27:36. Rachel and Leah overcome their mutual hostility and are able to leave together, a harbinger of the reconciliation with Esau in chap. 33.

31:15 Outsiders: lit., "foreign women"; they lacked the favored legal status of native women. **Used up**: lit., "eaten, consumed"; the bridal price that a man received for giving his daughter in marriage was legally reserved as her inalienable dowry. Perhaps this is the reason that Rachel took the household images belonging to Laban.

31:19 Household images: in Hebrew, *teraphim*, figurines used in divination (Ez 21:26; Zec 10:2). Laban calls them his "gods" (v. 30). The traditional translation "idols" is avoided because it suggests false gods, whereas Genesis seems to accept the fact that the ancestors did not always live according to later biblical religious standards and laws.

31:20 Hoodwinked: lit., "stolen the heart of," i.e., lulled the

o: Gn 26:3; 28:15; 32:10. *p:* Jdt 8:26. *q:* Gn 28:18. *r:* Wis 10:10–11. *s:* Gn 31:34; 1 Sm 19:13.

to flee. 21 Thus he fled with all that he had. Once he was across the Euphrates, he headed for the hill country of Gilead.

22 On the third day, word came to Laban that Jacob had fled. 23 Taking his kinsmen with him, he pursued him for seven days* until he caught up with him in the hill country of Gilead. 24 But that night God appeared to Laban the Aramean in a dream and said to him: Take care not to say anything to Jacob.[t]

Jacob and Laban in Gilead. 25 When Laban overtook Jacob, Jacob's tents were pitched in the hill country; Laban also pitched his tents in the hill country of Gilead. 26 Laban said to Jacob, "How could you hoodwink me and carry off my daughters like prisoners of war?* 27 Why did you dupe me by stealing away secretly? You did not tell me! I would have sent you off with joyful singing to the sound of tambourines and harps. 28 You did not even allow me a parting kiss to my daughters and grandchildren! Now what you have done makes no sense. 29 I have it in my power to harm all of you; but last night the God of your father said to me, 'Take care not to say anything to Jacob!' 30 Granted that you had to leave because you were longing for your father's house, why did you steal my gods?" 31 Jacob replied to Laban, "I was frightened at the thought that you might take your daughters away from me by force. 32 As for your gods, the one you find them with shall not remain alive! If, with our kinsmen looking on, you identify anything here as belonging to you, take it." Jacob had no idea that Rachel had stolen the household images.

33 Laban then went in and searched Jacob's tent and Leah's tent, as well as the tents of the two maidservants; but he did not find them. Leaving Leah's tent, he went into Rachel's. 34* Meanwhile Rachel had taken the household images, put them inside the camel's saddlebag, and seated herself upon them. When Laban had rummaged through her whole tent without finding them,[u] 35 she said to her father, "Do not let my lord be angry that I cannot rise in your presence; I am having my period." So, despite his search, he did not find the household images.

36 Jacob, now angered, confronted Laban and demanded, "What crime or offense have I committed that you should hound me? 37 Now that you have rummaged through all my things, what have you found from your household belongings? Produce it here before your kinsmen and mine, and let them decide between the two of us.

38 "In the twenty years that I was under you, no ewe or she-goat of yours ever miscarried, and I have never eaten rams of your flock. 39[v] I never brought you an animal torn by wild beasts; I made good the loss myself. You held me responsible for anything stolen by day or night.* 40 Often the scorching heat devoured me by day, and the frost by night, while sleep fled from my eyes! 41 Of the twenty years that I have now spent in your household, I served you fourteen years for your two daughters and six years for your flock, while you changed my wages ten times. 42 If the God of my father, the God of Abraham and the Fear of Isaac, had not been on my side, you would now have sent me away empty-handed. But God saw my plight and the fruits of my toil, and last night he reproached you."[w]

43* Laban replied to Jacob: "The daughters are mine, their children are mine, and the flocks are mine; everything you see be-

mind of. **Aramean**: the earliest extra-biblical references to the Arameans date later than the time of Jacob, if Jacob is dated to the mid-second millennium; to call Laban an Aramean and to have him speak Aramaic (Jegar-sahadutha, v. 47) is an apparent anachronism. The word may have been chosen to underscore the growing estrangement between the two men and the fact that their descendants will be two different peoples.

31:23 For seven days: lit., "a way of seven days," a general term to designate a long distance; it would actually have taken a camel caravan many more days to travel from Haran to Gilead, the region east of the northern half of the Jordan. The mention of camels in this passage is apparently anachronistic since camels were not domesticated until the late second millennium.

31:26 Prisoners of war: lit., "women captured by the sword"; the women of a conquered people were treated as part of the victor's spoil; cf. 1 Sm 30:2; 2 Kgs 5:2.

31:34 As in chap. 27, a younger child (Rachel) deceives her father to gain what belongs to him.

31:39 Jacob's actions are more generous than the customs suggested in the Code of Hammurabi: "If in a sheepfold an act of god has occurred, or a lion has made a kill, the shepherd shall clear himself before the deity, and the owner of the fold must accept the loss" (par. 266); cf. Ex 22:12.

31:43–54 In this account of the non-aggression treaty between Laban and Jacob, the different objects that serve as wit-

t: Wis 10:12. *u:* Gn 31:19. *v:* Ex 22:12. *w:* Gn 31:24, 29.

longs to me. What can I do now for my own daughters and for the children they have borne? 44* Come, now, let us make a covenant, you and I; and it will be a treaty between you and me."

45Then Jacob took a stone and set it up as a sacred pillar.[x] 46Jacob said to his kinsmen, "Gather stones." So they got stones and made a mound; and they ate there at the mound. 47Laban called it Jegar-sahadutha,* but Jacob called it Galeed. 48Laban said, "This mound will be a witness from now on between you and me." That is why it was named Galeed— 49and also Mizpah,* for he said: "May the LORD keep watch between you and me when we are out of each other's sight. 50If you mistreat my daughters, or take other wives besides my daughters, know that even though no one else is there, God will be a witness between you and me."

51Laban said further to Jacob: "Here is this mound, and here is the sacred pillar that I have set up between you and me. 52This mound will be a witness, and this sacred pillar will be a witness, that, with hostile intent, I may not pass beyond this mound into your territory, nor may you pass beyond it into mine. 53May the God of Abraham and the God of Nahor, the God of their father, judge between us!" Jacob took the oath by the Fear of his father Isaac.* 54He then offered a sacrifice on the mountain and invited his kinsmen to share in the meal. When they had eaten, they passed the night on the mountain.

CHAPTER 32

See RG 112–14

1* Early the next morning, Laban kissed his grandchildren and his daughters and blessed them; then he set out on his journey back home. 2Meanwhile Jacob continued on his own way, and God's angels encountered him. 3When Jacob saw them he said, "This is God's encampment." So he named that place Mahanaim.*

Envoys to Esau. 4Jacob sent messengers ahead to his brother Esau in the land of Seir, the country of Edom,[y] 5ordering them: "Thus you shall say to my lord Esau: 'Thus says your servant Jacob: I have been residing with Laban and have been delayed until now. 6I own oxen, donkeys and sheep, as well as male and female servants. I have sent my lord this message in the hope of gaining your favor.' " 7When the messengers returned to Jacob, they said, "We found your brother Esau. He is now coming to meet you, and four hundred men are with him."

8Jacob was very much frightened. In his anxiety, he divided the people who were with him, as well as his flocks, herds and camels, into two camps. 9"If Esau should come and attack one camp," he reasoned, "the remaining camp may still escape." 10Then Jacob prayed: "God of my father Abraham and God of my father Isaac! You, LORD, who said to me, 'Go back to your land and your relatives, and I will be good to you.'[z] 11I am unworthy of all the acts of kindness and faithfulness that you have performed for your servant: although I crossed the Jordan here with nothing but my staff, I have now grown into two camps. 12Save me from the hand of my brother, from the hand of Esau! Otherwise I fear that he will come and strike me down and the mothers with the children. 13You yourself said, 'I will be very

ness (sacred pillar in v. 45, cairn of stones in v. 46), their different names (Jegar-sahadutha in v. 47, Mizpah in v. 49), and the two references to the covenant meal (vv. 46, 54) suggest that two versions have been fused. One version is the Yahwist source, and another source has been used to supplement it.

31:44–54 The treaty is a typical covenant between two parties: Jacob was bound to treat his wives (Laban's daughters) well, and Laban was bound not to cross Jacob's boundaries with hostile intent.

31:47–48 Jegar-sahadutha: an Aramaic term meaning "mound of witness." **Galeed**: in Hebrew, "the mound of witness."

31:49 Mizpah: a town in Gilead; cf. Jgs 10:17; 11:11, 34; Hos 5:1. The Hebrew name *mispa* ("lookout") is allied to *yisep yhwh* ("may the Lord keep watch"), and also echoes the word *masseba* ("sacred pillar").

31:53 Fear of . . . Isaac: an archaic title for Jacob's God of the Father.

32:1–22 Jacob's negotiations with Esau. Laban kisses his daughters and grandchildren good-bye but not Jacob. On leaving Mesopotamia, Jacob has an encounter with angels of God (vv. 2–3), which provokes him to exclaim, "This is God's encampment," just as he exclaimed upon leaving Canaan, "This is the house of God, the gateway to heaven" (28:11–17).

32:3 Mahanaim: a town in Gilead (Jos 13:26, 30; 21:38; 2 Sm 2:8; etc.). The Hebrew name means "two camps." There are other allusions to the name in vv. 8, 11.

x: Gn 28:18; 35:14. *y:* Gn 36:6. *z:* Gn 31:3.

good to you, and I will make your descendants like the sands of the sea, which are too
numerous to count.' "[a]
14 After passing the night there, Jacob selected from what he had with him a present
for his brother Esau: 15 two hundred she-
goats and twenty he-goats; two hundred
ewes and twenty rams; 16 thirty female
camels and their young; forty cows and ten
bulls; twenty female donkeys and ten male
donkeys. 17 He put these animals in the care
of his servants, in separate herds, and he told
the servants, "Go on ahead of me, but keep
some space between the herds." 18 He ordered the servant in the lead, "When my
brother Esau meets you and asks, 'To whom
do you belong? Where are you going? To
whom do these animals ahead of you belong?' 19 tell him, 'To your servant Jacob, but
they have been sent as a gift to my lord Esau.
Jacob himself is right behind us.' " 20 He also
ordered the second servant and the third and
all the others who followed behind the
herds: "Thus and so you shall say to Esau,
when you reach him; 21 and also tell him,
'Your servant Jacob is right behind us.' " For
Jacob reasoned, "If I first appease him with
a gift that precedes me, then later, when I
face him, perhaps he will forgive me." 22 So
the gifts went on ahead of him, while he
stayed that night in the camp.

Jacob's New Name.* 23 That night, however, Jacob arose, took his two wives, with
the two maidservants and his eleven children, and crossed the ford of the Jabbok.
24 After he got them and brought them across
the wadi and brought over what belonged to
him, 25 Jacob was left there alone. Then a
man* wrestled with him until the break of
dawn. 26 When the man saw that he could not
prevail over him, he struck Jacob's hip at its
socket, so that Jacob's socket was dislocated
as he wrestled with him.[b] 27 The man then
said, "Let me go, for it is daybreak." But Jacob said, "I will not let you go until you
bless me." 28 "What is your name?" the man
asked. He answered, "Jacob."[c] 29 Then the
man said, "You shall no longer be named Jacob, but Israel,* because you have contended
with divine and human beings and have prevailed." 30 Jacob then asked him, "Please tell
me your name." He answered, "Why do you
ask for my name?" With that, he blessed
him. 31 Jacob named the place Peniel,* "because I have seen God face to face," he said,
"yet my life has been spared."[d]
32 At sunrise, as he left Penuel, Jacob
limped along because of his hip. 33 That is
why, to this day, the Israelites do not eat the
sciatic muscle that is on the hip socket, because he had struck Jacob's hip socket at the
sciatic muscle.

CHAPTER 33

See RG 112–14

Jacob and Esau Meet.* 1 Jacob looked
up and saw Esau coming, and with him four
hundred men. So he divided his children
among Leah, Rachel, and the two maidser-

32:23–33 As Jacob crosses over to the land promised him, worried about the impending meeting with Esau, he encounters a mysterious adversary in the night with whom he wrestles until morning. The cunning Jacob manages to wrest a blessing from the night stranger before he departs. There are folkloric elements in the tale—e.g., the trial of the hero before he can return home, the nocturnal demon's loss of strength at sunrise, the demon protecting its river, the power gained by knowledge of an opponent's name—but these have been worked into a coherent though elliptical narrative. The point of the tale seems to be that the ever-striving, ever-grasping Jacob must eventually strive with God to attain full possession of the blessing.

32:25 A man: as with Abraham's three visitors in chap. 18, who appear sometimes as three, two, and one (the latter being God), this figure is fluid; he loses the match but changes Jacob's name (v. 29), an act elsewhere done only by God (17:5, 15). A few deft narrative touches manage to express intimate contact with Jacob while preserving the transcendence proper to divinity.

32:29 Israel: the first part of the Hebrew name *Yisrael* is given a popular explanation in the word *saritha*, "you contended"; the second part is the first syllable of *'elohim*, "divine beings." The present incident, with a similar allusion to the name Israel, is referred to in Hos 12:5, where the mysterious wrestler is explicitly called an angel.

32:31 Peniel: a variant of the word Penuel (v. 32), the name of a town on the north bank of the Jabbok in Gilead (Jgs 8:8–9, 17; 1 Kgs 12:25). The name is explained as meaning "the face of God," *peni-'el*. **Yet my life has been spared**: see note on 16:13.

33:1–20 The truly frightening confrontation seems to have already occurred in Jacob's meeting the divine stranger in the previous chapter. In contrast, this meeting brings reconciliation. Esau, impulsive but largehearted, kisses the cunning Jacob and calls him brother (v. 9). Jacob in return asks Esau to accept his blessing (*berakah*, translated "gift," v. 11), giving

a: Gn 28:14; 48:16; Ex 32:13; Heb 11:12. *b:* Hos 12:5. *c:* Gn 35:10; 1 Kgs 18:31; 2 Kgs 17:34. *d:* Jgs 13:22.

vants, 2putting the maidservants and their
children first, Leah and her children next,
and Rachel and Joseph last. 3He himself
went on ahead of them, bowing to the
ground seven times, until he reached his
brother. 4Esau ran to meet him, embraced
him, and flinging himself on his neck, kissed
him as he wept.
5Then Esau looked up and saw the women
and children and asked, "Who are these with
you?" Jacob answered, "They are the children with whom God has graciously favored
your servant." 6Then the maidservants and
their children came forward and bowed low;
7next, Leah and her children came forward
and bowed low; lastly, Joseph and Rachel
came forward and bowed low. 8Then Esau
asked, "What did you intend with all those
herds that I encountered?" Jacob answered,
"It was to gain my lord's favor." 9Esau
replied, "I have plenty; my brother, you
should keep what is yours." 10"No, I beg
you!" said Jacob. "If you will do me the favor, accept this gift from me, since to see
your face is for me like seeing the face of
God—and you have received me so kindly.
11Accept the gift I have brought you. For
God has been generous toward me, and I
have an abundance." Since he urged him
strongly, Esau accepted.
12Then Esau said, "Let us break camp and
be on our way; I will travel in front of you."
13But Jacob replied: "As my lord knows, the
children are too young. And the flocks and
herds that are nursing are a concern to me; if
overdriven for even a single day, the whole
flock will die. 14Let my lord, then, go before
his servant, while I proceed more slowly at
the pace of the livestock before me and at the
pace of my children, until I join my lord in
Seir." 15Esau replied, "Let me at least put at
your disposal some of the people who are
with me." But Jacob said, "Why is this that I
am treated so kindly, my lord?" 16So on that
day Esau went on his way back to Seir, 17and
Jacob broke camp for Succoth.* There Jacob
built a home for himself and made booths
for his livestock. That is why the place was
named Succoth.
18Jacob arrived safely at the city of Shechem, which is in the land of Canaan, when
he came from Paddan-aram. He encamped
in sight of the city.[e] 19The plot of ground on
which he had pitched his tent he bought for
a hundred pieces of money* from the descendants of Hamor, the father of Shechem.[f]
20He set up an altar there and invoked "El,
the God of Israel."[g]

CHAPTER 34

See RG 112–14

The Rape of Dinah. 1* Dinah, the
daughter whom Leah had borne to Jacob,
went out to visit some of the women of the
land. 2When Shechem, son of Hamor the Hivite,* the leader of the region, saw her, he
seized her and lay with her by force. 3He was
strongly attracted to Dinah, daughter of Jacob, and was in love with the young woman.
So he spoke affectionately to her. 4Shechem
said to his father Hamor, "Get me this young
woman for a wife."
5Meanwhile, Jacob heard that Shechem
had defiled his daughter Dinah; but since his
sons were out in the field with his livestock,
Jacob kept quiet until they came home.
6Now Hamor, the father of Shechem, went

back at least symbolically what he had taken many years before and responding to Esau's erstwhile complaint ("he has taken away my blessing," 27:36). Verses 12–17 show that the reconciliation is not total and, further, that Jacob does not intend to share the ancestral land with his brother.

33:17 Succoth: an important town near the confluence of the Jabbok and the Jordan (Jos 13:27; Jgs 8:5–16; 1 Kgs 7:46). **Booths**: in Hebrew, *sukkot*, of the same sound as the name of the town.

33:19 Pieces of money: in Hebrew, *qesita*, a monetary unit of which the value is unknown. **Descendants of Hamor**: Hamorites, "the people of Hamor"; cf. Jgs 9:28. Hamor was regarded as the eponymous ancestor of the pre-Israelite inhabitants of Shechem.

34:1–31 The story of the rape of Dinah and the revenge of Jacob's sons on the men of the city of Shechem may reflect the relations of the tribes of Simeon and Levi to their Canaanite neighbors around Shechem; the tribes are represented by their eponymous ancestors. Jacob's farewell testament (49:5–7) cites this incident as the reason for the decline of the tribes of Simeon and Levi. Ominously, vv. 30–31 leave the situation unresolved, with Jacob concerned about the welfare of the whole family, and Simeon and Levi concerned only about the honor of their full sister. The danger to the family from narrow self-interest will continue in the Joseph story.

34:2 Hivite: the Greek text has "Horite"; the terms were apparently used indiscriminately to designate the Hurrian or other non-Semitic elements in Palestine.

e: Gn 12:6; Jn 4:5. *f:* Jos 24:32; Jn 4:5; Acts 7:16. *g:* Jgs 6:24.

out to discuss the matter with Jacob, [7]just as Jacob's sons were coming in from the field. When they heard the news, the men were indignant and extremely angry. Shechem had committed an outrage in Israel by lying with Jacob's daughter; such a thing is not done.[h] [8]Hamor appealed to them, saying: "My son Shechem has his heart set on your daughter. Please give her to him as a wife. [9]Intermarry with us; give your daughters to us, and take our daughters for yourselves. [10]Thus you can live among us. The land is open before you. Settle and move about freely in it and acquire holdings here."* [11]Then Shechem appealed to Dinah's father and brothers: "Do me this favor, and whatever you ask from me, I will give. [12]No matter how high you set the bridal price and gift, I will give you whatever you ask from me; only give me the young woman as a wife."

Revenge of Jacob's Sons. [13]Jacob's sons replied to Shechem and his father Hamor with guile, speaking as they did because he had defiled their sister Dinah. [14]They said to them, "We are not able to do this thing: to give our sister to an uncircumcised man. For that would be a disgrace for us. [15]Only on this condition will we agree to that: that you become like us by having every male among you circumcised. [16]Then we will give you our daughters and take your daughters in marriage; we will settle among you and become one people. [17]But if you do not listen to us and be circumcised, we will take our daughter and go."

[18]Their proposal pleased Hamor and his son Shechem. [19]The young man lost no time in acting on the proposal, since he wanted Jacob's daughter. Now he was more highly regarded than anyone else in his father's house. [20]So Hamor and his son Shechem went to the gate of their city and said to the men of their city: [21]"These men are friendly toward us. Let them settle in the land and move about in it freely; there is ample room in the land for them. We can take their daughters in marriage and give our daughters to them. [22]But only on this condition will the men agree to live with us and form one people with us: that every male among us be circumcised as they themselves are. [23]Would not their livestock, their property, and all their animals then be ours? Let us just agree with them, so that they will settle among us."

[24]All who went out of the gate of the city listened to Hamor and his son Shechem, and all the males, all those who went out of the gate of the city,* were circumcised. [25]On the third day, while they were still in pain, two of Jacob's sons, Simeon and Levi, brothers of Dinah, each took his sword, advanced against the unsuspecting city and massacred all the males.[i] [26]After they had killed Hamor and his son Shechem with the sword, they took Dinah from Shechem's house and left.[j] [27]Then the other sons of Jacob followed up the slaughter and sacked the city because their sister had been defiled. [28]They took their sheep, cattle and donkeys, whatever was in the city and in the surrounding country. [29]They carried off all their wealth, their children, and their women, and looted whatever was in the houses.[k]

[30]Jacob said to Simeon and Levi: "You have brought trouble upon me by making me repugnant to the inhabitants of the land, the Canaanites and the Perizzites. I have so few men that, if these people unite against me and attack me, I and my household will be wiped out." [31]But they retorted, "Should our sister be treated like a prostitute?"

CHAPTER 35

See RG 112–14

Bethel Revisited. [1]* God said to Jacob: Go up now to Bethel. Settle there and

34:10 Hamor seems to be making concessions to Jacob's family in the hope of avoiding warfare between the two families.

34:24 All those who went out of the gate of the city: apparently meaning all the residents. By temporarily crippling the men through circumcision, Jacob's sons deprived the city of its defenders.

35:1–7 Jacob returns to Bethel and founds the sanctuary, an event that forms a "bookend" to the first visit to Bethel in 28:10–22. To enter the Lord's sanctuary, one must purify oneself and get rid of all signs of allegiance to other gods (Jos 24:23; Jgs 10:16). Jacob also seems to initiate the custom of making a pilgrimage to Bethel (see Ps 122:1 and Is 2:3, 5).

h: 2 Sm 13:12. *i*: Gn 49:6. *j*: Jdt 9:2. *k*: Jdt 9:3–4.

build an altar there to the God who appeared to you when you were fleeing from your brother Esau.[l] 2So Jacob told his household and all who were with him: "Get rid of the foreign gods* among you; then purify yourselves and change your clothes. 3Let us now go up to Bethel so that I might build an altar there to the God who answered me in the day of my distress and who has been with me wherever I have gone." 4They gave Jacob all the foreign gods in their possession and also the rings they had in their ears* and Jacob buried them under the oak that is near Shechem. 5Then, as they set out, a great terror fell upon the surrounding towns, so that no one pursued the sons of Jacob.

6Thus Jacob and all the people who were with him arrived in Luz (now Bethel) in the land of Canaan.[m] 7There he built an altar and called the place El-Bethel,* for it was there that God had revealed himself to him when he was fleeing from his brother.[n]

8Deborah, Rebekah's nurse, died. She was buried under the oak below Bethel, and so it was named Allon-bacuth.*

9On Jacob's arrival from Paddan-aram, God appeared to him again and blessed him. 10God said to him:

> Your name is Jacob.
> You will no longer be named Jacob,
> but Israel will be your name.[o]

So he was named Israel. 11Then God said to him: I am God Almighty; be fruitful and multiply. A nation, indeed an assembly of nations, will stem from you, and kings will issue from your loins. 12The land I gave to Abraham and Isaac I will give to you; and to your descendants after you I will give the land.[p] 13Then God departed from him. 14In the place where God had spoken with him, Jacob set up a sacred pillar, a stone pillar, and upon it he made a libation and poured out oil.[q] 15Jacob named the place where God spoke to him Bethel.

Jacob's Family. 16Then they departed from Bethel; but while they still had some distance to go to Ephrath, Rachel went into labor and suffered great distress. 17When her labor was most intense, the midwife said to her, "Do not fear, for now you have another son." 18With her last breath—for she was at the point of death—she named him Ben-oni;* but his father named him Benjamin. 19Thus Rachel died; and she was buried on the road to Ephrath (now Bethlehem).*[r] 20Jacob set up a sacred pillar on her grave, and the same pillar marks Rachel's grave to this day.

21Israel moved on and pitched his tent beyond Migdal-eder. 22While Israel was encamped in that region, Reuben went and lay with Bilhah, his father's concubine. When Israel heard of it, he was greatly offended.*[s]

The sons of Jacob were now twelve. 23The sons of Leah: Reuben, Jacob's firstborn, Simeon, Levi, Judah, Issachar, and Zebulun; 24* the sons of Rachel: Joseph and Benjamin; 25the sons of Rachel's maidservant Bilhah: Dan and Naphtali; 26the sons of Leah's maidservant Zilpah: Gad and Asher. These

35:2 Foreign gods: divine images, including those of household deities (see note on 31:19), that Jacob's people brought with them from Paddan-aram.

35:4 Rings . . . their ears: the earrings may have belonged to the gods because earrings were often placed on statues.

35:7 El-Bethel: probably to be translated "the god of Bethel." This is one of several titles of God in Genesis that begin with *El* (= God), e.g., *El Olam* (21:33), *El Elyon* (14:18), *El* the God of Israel (33:20), *El Roi* (16:13), and *El Shaddai*. Most of these (except *El Shaddai*) are tied to specific Israelite shrines.

35:8 Allon-bacuth: the Hebrew name means "oak of weeping."

35:18 Ben-oni: means either "son of my vigor" or, more likely in the context, "son of affliction." **Benjamin**: "son of the right hand," meaning a son who is his father's help and support.

35:19 Bethlehem: the gloss comes from a later tradition that identified the site with Bethlehem, also called Ephrath or Ephratha (Jos 15:59; Ru 4:11; Mi 5:1). But Rachel's grave was actually near Ramah (Jer 31:15), a few miles north of Jerusalem, in the territory of Benjamin (1 Sm 10:2).

35:22 The genealogy in vv. 23–29 is prefaced by a notice about Reuben's sleeping with Bilhah, his father's concubine. Such an act is a serious challenge to the authority of the father (cf. 2 Sm 3:7 and 16:21). In his final testament in chap. 49, Jacob cites this act of Reuben as the reason for Reuben's loss of the authority he had as firstborn son (49:4). Reuben's act is one more instance of strife in the family and of discord between father and son.

35:24–26 Benjamin is here said to have been born in Paddan-aram, apparently because all twelve sons of Jacob are considered as a unit.

l: Gn 28:12–13. *m:* Gn 28:19; Jos 18:13; Jgs 1:22–23. *n:* Gn 28:12–13. *o:* 1 Kgs 18:31; 2 Kgs 17:34. *p:* Ex 32:13; Heb 11:9. *q:* Gn 28:18; 31:45. *r:* Gn 48:7; 1 Sm 10:2; Mi 5:1. *s:* Gn 49:4; 1 Chr 5:1.

are the sons of Jacob who were born to him in Paddan-aram.

27 Jacob went home to his father Isaac at Mamre, in Kiriath-arba (now Hebron), where Abraham and Isaac had resided. 28 The length of Isaac's life was one hundred and eighty years; 29 then he breathed his last. He died as an old man and was gathered to his people. After a full life, his sons Esau and Jacob buried him.

CHAPTER 36

See RG 112–14

*Edomite Lists.** 1 These are the descendants of Esau (that is, Edom). 2* Esau took his wives from among the Canaanite women: Adah, daughter of Elon the Hittite; Oholibamah, the daughter of Anah the son of Zibeon the Hivite;[t] 3 and Basemath, daughter of Ishmael and sister of Nebaioth. 4 Adah bore Eliphaz to Esau; Basemath bore Reuel;[u] 5 and Oholibamah bore Jeush, Jalam and Korah. These are the sons of Esau who were born to him in the land of Canaan.[v]

6 Esau took his wives, his sons, his daughters, and all the members of his household, as well as his livestock, all his cattle, and all the property he had acquired in the land of Canaan, and went to the land of Seir, away from his brother Jacob.[w] 7 Their possessions had become too great for them to dwell together, and the land in which they were residing could not support them because of their livestock. 8 So Esau settled in the highlands of Seir. (Esau is Edom.)[x] 9 These are the descendants of Esau,* ancestor of the Edomites, in the highlands of Seir.

10 These are the names of the sons of Esau: Eliphaz, son of Adah, wife of Esau, and Reuel, son of Basemath, wife of Esau. 11[y] The sons of Eliphaz were Teman, Omar, Zepho, Gatam, and Kenaz. 12 Timna was a concubine of Eliphaz, the son of Esau, and she bore Amalek to Eliphaz. Those were the sons of Adah, the wife of Esau. 13 These were the sons of Reuel: Nahath, Zerah, Shammah, and Mizzah. Those were the sons of Basemath, the wife of Esau.[z] 14 These were the sons of Esau's wife Oholibamah—the daughter of Anah, son of Zibeon—whom she bore to Esau: Jeush, Jalam, and Korah.[a]

15 These are the clans of the sons of Esau. The sons of Eliphaz, Esau's firstborn: the clans of Teman, Omar, Zepho, Kenaz, 16 Korah, Gatam, and Amalek. These are the clans of Eliphaz in the land of Edom; they are the sons of Adah. 17 These are the sons of Reuel, son of Esau: the clans of Nahath, Zerah, Shammah, and Mizzah. These are the clans of Reuel in the land of Edom; they are the sons of Basemath, wife of Esau. 18 These were the sons of Oholibamah, wife of Esau: the clans of Jeush, Jalam, and Korah. These are the clans of Esau's wife Oholibamah, daughter of Anah. 19 These are the sons of Esau—that is, Edom—according to their clans.

20 These are the sons of Seir the Horite,* the inhabitants of the land: Lotan, Shobal, Zibeon, Anah,[b] 21 Dishon, Ezer, and Dishan; those are the clans of the Horites, sons of Seir in the land of Edom. 22[c] The sons of Lotan were Hori and Hemam, and Lotan's sister was Timna. 23 These are the sons of Shobal: Alvan, Mahanath, Ebal, Shepho, and Onam. 24 These are the sons of Zibeon: Aiah and Anah. He is the Anah who found water in the desert while he was pasturing the don-

36:1–43 The line of Esau. In the preceding chapter (35:22–26), the list of Jacob's children completes the narrative of Jacob; in this chapter, the narrative of Esau is complete when his descendants are listed. The notice of Abraham's death and burial in 25:7–10 was followed by a list of the line of his elder son Ishmael (25:12–18) and here Isaac's death and burial are followed by the line of Esau. The lines of both Ishmael and Esau are introduced by the same double formula, "These are the descendants of . . ." (25:12; 36:9) and "These are the names of the sons of . . ." (25:13; 36:10). The chapter consists of diverse material: vv. 1–3, Esau's wives; vv. 9–14, Esau's descendants; vv. 15–19, the clans of Esau; vv. 20–30, the Horites of Seir; vv. 31–39, the Edomite kings; vv. 40–43, the Edomites.

36:2–14 The names of Esau's wives and of their fathers given here differ considerably from their names cited from other old sources in 26:34 and 28:9. **Zibeon the Hivite**: in v. 20 he is called a "Horite"; see note on 34:2.

36:9 These are the descendants of Esau: the original heading of the genealogy is preserved in v. 10 ("These are the names of the sons of Esau"). This use of the Priestly formula is secondary and should not be counted in the list of ten such formulas in Genesis.

36:20 Seir the Horite: according to Dt 2:12, the highlands of Seir were inhabited by Horites before they were occupied by the Edomites.

t: Gn 26:34. *u:* 1 Chr 1:35. *v:* 1 Chr 1:35. *w:* Gn 32:4. *x:* Dt 2:4–5; Jos 24:4. *y:* 1 Chr 1:36. *z:* 1 Chr 1:37. *a:* 1 Chr 1:35. *b:* 1 Chr 1:38. *c:* 1 Chr 1:39–42.

keys of his father Zibeon. [25]These are the children of Anah: Dishon and Oholibamah, daughter of Anah. [26]These are the sons of Dishon: Hemdan, Eshban, Ithran, and Cheran. [27]These are the sons of Ezer: Bilhan, Zaavan, and Akan. [28]These are the sons of Dishan: Uz and Aran. [29]These are the clans of the Horites: the clans of Lotan, Shobal, Zibeon, Anah, [30]Dishon, Ezer, and Dishan; those are the clans of the Horites, clan by clan, in the land of Seir.

[31d] These are the kings who reigned in the land of Edom before any king reigned over the Israelites.* [32]Bela, son of Beor, became king in Edom; the name of his city was Dinhabah. [33]When Bela died, Jobab, son of Zerah, from Bozrah, succeeded him as king. [34]When Jobab died, Husham, from the land of the Temanites, succeeded him as king. [35]When Husham died, Hadad, son of Bedad, succeeded him as king. He is the one who defeated Midian in the country of Moab; the name of his city was Avith. [36]When Hadad died, Samlah, from Masrekah, succeeded him as king. [37]When Samlah died, Shaul, from Rehoboth-on-the-River, succeeded him as king. [38]When Shaul died, Baal-hanan, son of Achbor, succeeded him as king. [39]When Baal-hanan, son of Achbor, died, Hadad succeeded him as king; the name of his city was Pau. His wife's name was Mehetabel, the daughter of Matred, son of Mezahab.

[40]These are the names of the clans of Esau identified according to their families and localities: the clans of Timna, Alvah, Jetheth, [41]Oholibamah, Elah, Pinon, [42]Kenaz, Teman, Mibzar, [43]Magdiel, and Iram. Those are the clans of the Edomites, according to their settlements in their territorial holdings—that is, of Esau, the ancestor of the Edomites.

CHAPTER 37

See RG 114–15

Joseph Sold into Egypt. [1]Jacob settled in the land where his father had sojourned, the land of Canaan.* [2]This is the story of the family of Jacob.* When Joseph was seventeen years old, he was tending the flocks with his brothers; he was an assistant to the sons of his father's wives Bilhah and Zilpah, and Joseph brought their father bad reports about them. [3]Israel loved Joseph best of all his sons, for he was the child of his old age; and he had made him a long ornamented tunic.* [4]When his brothers saw that their father loved him best of all his brothers, they hated him so much that they could not say a kind word to him.

[5]* Once Joseph had a dream, and when he told his brothers, they hated him even more.[e] [6]He said to them, "Listen to this dream I had.

36:31 Before any king reigned over the Israelites: obviously this statement was written after the time of Saul, Israel's first king. According to 1 Sm 14:47, Saul waged war against the Edomites; according to 2 Sm 8:2, 13–14 and 1 Kgs 11:14–17, David made Edom a vassal state and nearly wiped out the royal line. These events reflect the words of the Lord to Rebekah at the birth of the boys, "the older shall serve the younger" (25:23).

37:1 The statement points ahead to 47:27, "Thus Israel settled in the land of Egypt, in the region of Goshen." These two statements frame the Joseph narrative; the later material (47:28–49:33) is about Jacob; chap. 50 brings to a conclusion themes remaining from the earlier story. One aim of the Joseph story is to explain how Israel came to Egypt after sojourning so long in Canaan.

37:2 The Joseph story is great literature not only in its themes but in its art. The stories show an interest in the psychology of the characters; everyone acts "in character" yet there is never a doubt that a divine purpose is bringing events to their conclusion. According to a literary analysis, vv. 1–4 set the scene; vv. 5–36 introduce the dramatic tension in the form of a conflict within the family; chaps. 38–41 describe the journeys away from their family of the eponymous ancestors of the two great tribes of later times, Judah (chap. 38) and Joseph (chaps. 39–41) and their preliminary conclusions; chaps. 42–44 detail the famine and journeys for food (chaps. 42, 43) that bring the brothers and (indirectly) the father into fresh contact with a mature Joseph who now has the power of life and death over them; 45:1–47:27 is the resolution (reconciliation of Joseph to his brothers) and the salvation of the family.

37:3 Jacob's favoring Joseph over his other sons is a cause of the brothers' attempt on his life. Throughout the story, Jacob is unaware of the impact of his favoritism on his other sons (cf. vv. 33–35; 42:36). **Long ornamented tunic**: the meaning of the Hebrew phrase is unclear. In 2 Sm 13:18–19, it is the distinctive dress of unmarried royal daughters. The "coat of many colors" in the Septuagint became the traditional translation. Ancient depictions of Semites in formal dress show them with long, ornamented robes and that is the most likely meaning here. Possibly, the young Joseph is given a coat that symbolizes honor beyond his years. Later, Pharaoh will clothe Joseph in a robe that symbolizes honor (41:42).

37:5–10 Joseph's dreams of ruling his brothers appear at first glance to be merely adolescent grandiosity, and they bring him only trouble. His later successes make it clear, however, that they were from God. Another confirmation of their divine source is the doubling of dreams (cf. 41:32).

d: 1 Chr 1:43–54. *e:* Gn 42:9.

7There we were, binding sheaves in the field,
when suddenly my sheaf rose to an upright
position, and your sheaves formed a ring
around my sheaf and bowed down to it." 8His
brothers said to him, "Are you really going to
make yourself king over us? Will you rule
over us?" So they hated him all the more because of his dreams and his reports.[f]
9Then he had another dream, and told it to
his brothers. "Look, I had another dream," he
said; "this time, the sun and the moon and
eleven stars were bowing down to me."
10When he told it to his father and his brothers, his father reproved him and asked,
"What is the meaning of this dream of yours?
Can it be that I and your mother and your
brothers are to come and bow to the ground
before you?" 11So his brothers were furious
at him but his father kept the matter in mind.
12One day, when his brothers had gone to
pasture their father's flocks at Shechem,
13Israel said to Joseph, "Are your brothers
not tending our flocks at Shechem? Come
and I will send you to them." "I am ready,"
Joseph answered. 14"Go then," he replied;
"see if all is well with your brothers and the
flocks, and bring back word." So he sent him
off from the valley of Hebron. When Joseph
reached Shechem, 15a man came upon him
as he was wandering about in the fields.
"What are you looking for?" the man asked
him. 16"I am looking for my brothers," he
answered. "Please tell me where they are
tending the flocks." 17The man told him,
"They have moved on from here; in fact, I
heard them say, 'Let us go on to Dothan.' "
So Joseph went after his brothers and found
them in Dothan. 18They saw him from a distance, and before he reached them, they plotted to kill him. 19They said to one another:
"Here comes that dreamer! 20Come now, let
us kill him and throw him into one of the cisterns here; we could say that a wild beast devoured him. We will see then what comes of
his dreams."[g]
21* But when Reuben heard this, he tried
to save him from their hands, saying: "We
must not take his life." 22Then Reuben said,
"Do not shed blood! Throw him into this cistern in the wilderness; but do not lay a hand
on him." His purpose was to save him from
their hands and restore him to his father.[h]
23So when Joseph came up to his brothers,
they stripped him of his tunic, the long ornamented tunic he had on; 24then they took him
and threw him into the cistern. The cistern
was empty; there was no water in it.
25Then they sat down to eat. Looking up,
they saw a caravan of Ishmaelites coming
from Gilead, their camels laden with gum,
balm, and resin to be taken down to Egypt.[i]
26Judah said to his brothers: "What is to be
gained by killing our brother and concealing
his blood?[j] 27Come, let us sell him to these
Ishmaelites, instead of doing away with him
ourselves. After all, he is our brother, our
own flesh." His brothers agreed.
28Midianite traders passed by, and they
pulled Joseph up out of the cistern. They
sold Joseph for twenty pieces of silver* to
the Ishmaelites, who took him to Egypt.[k]
29When Reuben went back to the cistern and
saw that Joseph was not in it, he tore his garments,* 30and returning to his brothers, he
exclaimed: "The boy is gone! And I—where
can I turn?" 31They took Joseph's tunic, and
after slaughtering a goat, dipped the tunic in
its blood. 32Then they sent someone to bring
the long ornamented tunic to their father,
with the message: "We found this. See
whether it is your son's tunic or not." 33He
recognized it and exclaimed: "My son's tu-

37:21–36 The chapter thus far is from the Yahwist source, as are also vv. 25–28a. But vv. 21–24 and 28b–36 are from another source (sometimes designated the Elohist source). In the latter, Reuben tries to rescue Joseph, who is taken in Reuben's absence by certain Midianites; in the Yahwist source, it is Judah who saves Joseph's life by having him sold to certain Ishmaelites. Although the two variant forms in which the story was handed down in early oral tradition differ in these minor points, they agree on the essential fact that Joseph was brought as a slave into Egypt because of the jealousy of his brothers.

37:28 They sold Joseph . . . silver: editors tried to solve the confusion, created by different sources, by supposing that it was the Midianite traders who pulled Joseph out of the pit and sold him to Ishmaelites. In all probability, one source had the brothers selling Joseph to Ishmaelites, whereas the other had them cast him into the pit whence he was taken by Midianite traders.

37:29 Tore his garments: the traditional sign of mourning in the ancient Near East.

f: Gn 50:17–18. *g:* Gn 44:28. *h:* Gn 42:22. *i:* Gn 43:11. *j:* Jb 16:18. *k:* Ps 105:17; Wis 10:13; Acts 7:9.

nic! A wild beast has devoured him! Joseph has been torn to pieces!”[l] [34]Then Jacob tore his garments, put sackcloth on his loins, and mourned his son many days. [35]Though his sons and daughters tried to console him, he refused all consolation, saying, “No, I will go down mourning to my son in Sheol.”* Thus did his father weep for him.[m]

[36]The Midianites, meanwhile, sold Joseph in Egypt to Potiphar, an official of Pharaoh and his chief steward.[n]

See RG 114–15

CHAPTER 38

Judah and Tamar.* [1]About that time Judah went down, away from his brothers, and pitched his tent near a certain Adullamite named Hirah. [2]There Judah saw the daughter of a Canaanite named Shua; he married her, and had intercourse with her.[o] [3]She conceived and bore a son, whom she named Er. [4]Again she conceived and bore a son, whom she named Onan. [5]Then she bore still another son, whom she named Shelah. She was in Chezib* when she bore him.[p]

[6]Judah got a wife named Tamar for his firstborn, Er. [7]But Er, Judah’s firstborn, greatly offended the LORD; so the LORD took his life.[q] [8][r] Then Judah said to Onan, “Have intercourse with your brother’s wife, in fulfillment of your duty as brother-in-law, and thus preserve your brother’s line.”* [9]Onan, however, knew that the offspring would not be his; so whenever he had intercourse with his brother’s wife, he wasted his seed on the ground, to avoid giving offspring to his brother. [10]What he did greatly offended the LORD, and the LORD took his life too. [11]Then Judah said to his daughter-in-law Tamar, “Remain a widow in your father’s house until my son Shelah grows up”—for he feared that Shelah also might die like his brothers. So Tamar went to live in her father’s house.

[12]Time passed, and the daughter of Shua, Judah’s wife, died. After Judah completed the period of mourning, he went up to Timnah, to those who were shearing his sheep, in company with his friend Hirah the Adullamite. [13]Then Tamar was told, “Your father-in-law is on his way up to Timnah to shear his sheep.” [14]So she took off her widow’s garments, covered herself with a shawl, and having wrapped herself sat down at the entrance to Enaim, which is on the way to Timnah; for she was aware that, although Shelah was now grown up, she had not been given to him in marriage.[s] [15]When Judah saw her, he thought she was a harlot, since she had covered her face. [16]So he went over to her at the roadside and said, “Come, let me have intercourse with you,” for he did not realize that she was his daughter-in-law. She replied, “What will you pay me for letting you have intercourse with me?” [17]He answered, “I will send you a young goat from the flock.” “Very well,” she said, “provided you leave me a pledge until you send it.” [18]Judah asked, “What pledge should I leave you?” She answered, “Your seal and cord,* and the staff in your hand.” So he gave them to her and had intercourse with her, and she

37:35 Sheol: see note on Ps 6:6.

38:1–30 This chapter has subtle connections to the main Joseph story. It tells of the eponymous founder of the other great tribe of later times, Judah. Having already been introduced as one of the two good brothers in 37:26–27, he appears here as the father-in-law of the twice-widowed Tamar; he has reneged on his promise to provide his son Shelah to her in a levirate marriage. Unjustly treated, Tamar takes matters into her own hands and tricks Judah into becoming the father of her children, Perez and Zerah. Judah ultimately acknowledges that his daughter-in-law was right (“She is in the right rather than I,” v. 26). In contrast to Judah’s expectations, the family line does not continue through his son Shelah, but through the children of Tamar. Similarities relate this little story to the main narrative: the deception involving an article of clothing (the widow’s garments of Tamar, Judah’s seal, cord, and staff) point back to the bloody tunic that deceives Jacob in 37:31–33; a woman attempts the seduction of a man separated from his family, for righteous purposes in chap. 38, for unrighteous purposes in chap. 39.

38:5 Chezib: a variant form of Achzib (Jos 15:44; Mi 1:14), a town in the Judean Shephelah.

38:8 Preserve your brother’s line: lit., “raise up seed for your brother”: an allusion to the law of levirate, or “brother-in-law,” marriage; see notes on Dt 25:5; Ru 2:20. Onan’s violation of this law brought on him God’s punishment (vv. 9–10).

38:18 Seal and cord: the cylinder seal, through which a hole was bored lengthwise so that it could be worn from the neck by a cord, was a distinctive means of identification. Apparently one’s staff could also be marked with some sign of identification (cf. Nm 17:17–18).

l: Gn 44:28. *m:* Gn 42:38. *n:* Ps 105:17. *o:* 1 Chr 2:3. *p:* 1 Chr 4:21. *q:* 1 Chr 2:3. *r:* Dt 25:5; Mt 22:24; Mk 12:19; Lk 20:28. *s:* Prv 7:10.

conceived by him. [19]After she got up and went away, she took off her shawl and put on her widow's garments again.

[20]Judah sent the young goat by his friend the Adullamite to recover the pledge from the woman; but he did not find her. [21]So he asked the men of that place, "Where is the prostitute,* the one by the roadside in Enaim?" But they answered, "No prostitute has been here." [22]He went back to Judah and told him, "I did not find her; and besides, the men of the place said, 'No prostitute has been here.' " [23]"Let her keep the things," Judah replied; "otherwise we will become a laughingstock. After all, I did send her this young goat, but you did not find her."

[24]About three months later, Judah was told, "Your daughter-in-law Tamar has acted like a harlot and now she is pregnant from her harlotry." Judah said, "Bring her out; let her be burned." [25]But as she was being brought out, she sent word to her father-in-law, "It is by the man to whom these things belong that I am pregnant." Then she said, "See whose seal and cord and staff these are." [26]Judah recognized them and said, "She is in the right rather than I, since I did not give her to my son Shelah." He had no further sexual relations with her.

[27]When the time of her delivery came, there were twins in her womb.[t] [28]While she was giving birth, one put out his hand; and the midwife took and tied a crimson thread on his hand, noting, "This one came out first." [29][u] But as he withdrew his hand, his brother came out; and she said, "What a breach you have made for yourself!" So he was called Perez.* [30]Afterward his brother, who had the crimson thread on his hand, came out; he was called Zerah.* [v]

CHAPTER 39

See RG 114–15

Joseph's Temptation. [1]When Joseph was taken down to Egypt, an Egyptian, Potiphar, an official of Pharaoh and his chief steward, bought him from the Ishmaelites who had brought him there. [2][w] The LORD was with Joseph and he enjoyed great success and was assigned to the household of his Egyptian master. [3]When his master saw that the LORD was with him and brought him success in whatever he did, [4]he favored Joseph and made him his personal attendant; he put him in charge of his household and entrusted to him all his possessions.[x] [5]From the moment that he put him in charge of his household and all his possessions, the LORD blessed the Egyptian's house for Joseph's sake; the LORD's blessing was on everything he owned, both inside the house and out. [6]Having left everything he owned in Joseph's charge, he gave no thought, with Joseph there, to anything but the food he ate.

Now Joseph was well-built and handsome. [7]After a time, his master's wife looked at him with longing and said, "Lie with me." [8]But he refused and said to his master's wife, "Look, as long as I am here, my master does not give a thought to anything in the house, but has entrusted to me all he owns. [9]He has no more authority in this house than I do. He has withheld from me nothing but you, since you are his wife. How, then, could I do this great wrong and sin against God?" [10]Although she spoke to him day after day, he would not agree to lie with her, or even be near her.[y]

[11]One such day, when Joseph came into the house to do his work, and none of the household servants were then in the house, [12]she laid hold of him by his cloak, saying, "Lie with me!" But leaving the cloak in her hand, he escaped and ran outside. [13]When she saw that he had left his cloak in her hand as he escaped outside, [14]she cried out to her household servants and told them, "Look! My husband has brought us a Hebrew man to mock us! He came in here to lie with me,

38:21 Prostitute: the Hebrew term *qedesha*, lit., "consecrated woman," designates a woman associated with a sanctuary whose activities could include prostitution; cf. Dt 23:18; Hos 4:14, where the same Hebrew word is used. In 38:15 and 24 the common word for prostitute, *zona*, is used.

38:29 He was called Perez: the Hebrew word means "breach."

38:30 He was called Zerah: a name connected here by popular etymology with a Hebrew word for the red light of dawn, alluding apparently to the crimson thread.

t: 1 Chr 2:4. *u:* Ru 4:12; Mt 1:3; Lk 3:33. *v:* Nm 26:20; 1 Chr 2:4; Mt 1:3. *w:* 1 Sm 3:19; 10:7; 18:14; 2 Sm 5:10; 2 Kgs 18:7; Acts 7:9. *x:* Dn 1:9. *y:* 1 Mc 2:53.

but I cried out loudly. 15When he heard me
scream, he left his cloak beside me and escaped and ran outside."
16She kept the cloak with her until his
master came home. 17Then she told him the
same story: "The Hebrew slave whom you
brought us came to me to amuse himself at
my expense. 18But when I screamed, he left
his cloak beside me and escaped outside."
19When the master heard his wife's story in
which she reported, "Thus and so your servant did to me," he became enraged. 20Jo-
seph's master seized him and put him into
the jail where the king's prisoners were confined.[z] And there he sat, in jail.
21But the LORD was with Joseph, and
showed him kindness by making the chief
jailer well-disposed toward him.[a] 22The
chief jailer put Joseph in charge of all the
prisoners in the jail. Everything that had to
be done there, he was the one to do it. 23The
chief jailer did not have to look after anything that was in Joseph's charge, since the
LORD was with him and was bringing success to whatever he was doing.

CHAPTER 40

See RG 114–15

The Dreams Interpreted. 1* Some
time afterward, the royal cupbearer and
baker offended their lord, the king of Egypt.
2Pharaoh was angry with his two officials,
the chief cupbearer and the chief baker, 3and
he put them in custody in the house of the
chief steward, the same jail where Joseph
was confined. 4The chief steward assigned
Joseph to them, and he became their attendant.
After they had been in custody for some
time, 5the cupbearer and the baker of the
king of Egypt who were confined in the jail
both had dreams on the same night, each his
own dream and each dream with its own
meaning. 6When Joseph came to them in the
morning, he saw that they looked disturbed.
7So he asked Pharaoh's officials who were
with him in custody in his master's house,
"Why do you look so troubled today?"
8They answered him, "We have had dreams,
but there is no one to interpret them." Joseph
said to them, "Do interpretations not come
from God? Please tell me the dreams."[b]
9Then the chief cupbearer told Joseph his
dream. "In my dream," he said, "I saw a vine
in front of me, 10and on the vine were three
branches. It had barely budded when its
blossoms came out, and its clusters ripened
into grapes. 11Pharaoh's cup was in my hand;
so I took the grapes, pressed them out into
his cup, and put it in Pharaoh's hand." 12Jo-
seph said to him: "This is its interpretation.
The three branches are three days; 13within
three days Pharaoh will single you out* and
restore you to your post. You will be handing
Pharaoh his cup as you formerly did when
you were his cupbearer. 14Only think of me
when all is well with you, and please do me
the great favor of mentioning me to Pharaoh,
to get me out of this place. 15The truth is that
I was kidnapped from the land of the Hebrews, and I have not done anything here
that they should have put me into a dungeon."
16When the chief baker saw that Joseph
had given a favorable interpretation, he said
to him: "I too had a dream. In it I had three
bread baskets on my head; 17in the top one
were all kinds of bakery products for Pharaoh, but the birds were eating them out of the
basket on my head." 18Joseph said to him in
reply: "This is its interpretation. The three
baskets are three days; 19within three days
Pharaoh will single you out and will impale
you on a stake, and the birds will be eating
your flesh."
20And so on the third day, which was
Pharaoh's birthday, when he gave a banquet
to all his servants, he singled out the chief
cupbearer and chief baker in the midst of his
servants. 21He restored the chief cupbearer
to his office, so that he again handed the cup
to Pharaoh; 22but the chief baker he impaled—just as Joseph had told them in his
interpretation. 23Yet the chief cupbearer did
not think of Joseph; he forgot him.

40:1 Joseph interprets the dreams of the Pharaoh's two officials. His ability to interpret the dreams shows that God is still with him and points forward to his role of dream interpreter for Pharaoh in chap. 41.

40:13 Single you out: lit., "lift up your head" (see also vv. 19, 20).

z: Ps 105:18. *a:* Acts 7:9–10. *b:* Gn 41:16.

CHAPTER 41

See RG 114–15

Pharaoh's Dream. 1* After a lapse of two years, Pharaoh had a dream. He was standing by the Nile, 2 when up out of the Nile came seven cows, fine-looking and fat; they grazed in the reed grass. 3 Behind them seven other cows, poor-looking and gaunt, came up out of the Nile; and standing on the bank of the Nile beside the others, 4 the poor-looking, gaunt cows devoured the seven fine-looking, fat cows. Then Pharaoh woke up.

5 He fell asleep again and had another dream. He saw seven ears of grain, fat and healthy, growing on a single stalk. 6 Behind them sprouted seven ears of grain, thin and scorched by the east wind; 7 and the thin ears swallowed up the seven fat, healthy ears. Then Pharaoh woke up—it was a dream!

8 Next morning his mind was agitated. So Pharaoh had all the magicians* and sages of Egypt summoned and recounted his dream to them; but there was no one to interpret it for him. 9 Then the chief cupbearer said to Pharaoh: "Now I remember my negligence! 10 Once, when Pharaoh was angry with his servants, he put me and the chief baker in custody in the house of the chief steward. 11 Later, we both had dreams on the same night, and each of our dreams had its own meaning. 12 There was a Hebrew youth with us, a slave of the chief steward; and when we told him our dreams, he interpreted them for us and explained for each of us the meaning of his dream.[c] 13 Things turned out just as he had told us: I was restored to my post, but the other man was impaled."

14 Pharaoh therefore had Joseph summoned, and they hurriedly brought him from the dungeon. After he shaved and changed his clothes, he came to Pharaoh.[d] 15 Pharaoh then said to Joseph: "I had a dream but there was no one to interpret it. But I hear it said of you, 'If he hears a dream he can interpret it.' " 16 "It is not I," Joseph replied to Pharaoh, "but God who will respond for the well-being of Pharaoh."[e]

17 Then Pharaoh said to Joseph: "In my dream, I was standing on the bank of the Nile, 18 when up from the Nile came seven cows, fat and well-formed; they grazed in the reed grass. 19 Behind them came seven other cows, scrawny, most ill-formed and gaunt. Never have I seen such bad specimens as these in all the land of Egypt! 20 The gaunt, bad cows devoured the first seven fat cows. 21 But when they had consumed them, no one could tell that they had done so, because they looked as bad as before. Then I woke up. 22 In another dream I saw seven ears of grain, full and healthy, growing on a single stalk. 23 Behind them sprouted seven ears of grain, shriveled and thin and scorched by the east wind; 24 and the seven thin ears swallowed up the seven healthy ears. I have spoken to the magicians, but there is no one to explain it to me."

25 Joseph said to Pharaoh: "Pharaoh's dreams have the same meaning. God has made known to Pharaoh what he is about to do. 26 The seven healthy cows are seven years, and the seven healthy ears are seven years—the same in each dream. 27 The seven thin, bad cows that came up after them are seven years, as are the seven thin ears scorched by the east wind; they are seven years of famine. 28 Things are just as I told Pharaoh: God has revealed to Pharaoh what he is about to do. 29 Seven years of great abundance are now coming throughout the land of Egypt; 30 but seven years of famine will rise up after them, when all the abundance will be forgotten in the land of Egypt. When the famine has exhausted the land, 31 no trace of the abundance will be found in the land because of the famine that follows it, for it will be very severe. 32 That Pharaoh had the same dream twice means that the

41:1–57 Joseph correctly interprets Pharaoh's dream and becomes second in command over all Egypt.

41:8 Magicians: one of the tasks of the "magicians" was interpreting dreams. The interpretation of dreams was a long-standing practice in Egypt. A manual of dream interpretation has been found, written in the early second millennium and re-published later in which typical dreams are given ("If a man sees himself in a dream . . .") followed by a judgment of "good" or "bad." Interpreters were still needed for dreams, however, and Pharaoh complains that none of his dream interpreters can interpret his unprecedented dream. The same term will be used of Pharaoh's magicians in Exodus.

c: Dn 1:17. *d:* Ps 105:20. *e:* Gn 40:8.

matter has been confirmed by God and that
God will soon bring it about.
33"Therefore, let Pharaoh seek out a discerning and wise man and put him in charge
of the land of Egypt. 34Let Pharaoh act and
appoint overseers for the land to organize it
during the seven years of abundance. 35They
should collect all the food of these coming
good years, gathering the grain under Pharaoh's authority, for food in the cities, and
they should guard it. 36This food will serve
as a reserve for the country against the seven
years of famine that will occur in the land of
Egypt, so that the land may not perish in the
famine."
37This advice pleased Pharaoh and all his
servants.[f] 38"Could we find another like
him," Pharaoh asked his servants, "a man so
endowed with the spirit of God?" 39So Pharaoh said to Joseph: "Since God has made all
this known to you, there is no one as discerning and wise as you are. 40You shall be
in charge of my household, and all my people will obey your command. Only in respect to the throne will I outrank you."[g]
41Then Pharaoh said to Joseph, "Look, I put
you in charge of the whole land of Egypt."
42With that, Pharaoh took off his signet ring*
and put it on Joseph's finger. He dressed him
in robes of fine linen and put a gold chain
around his neck. 43He then had him ride in
his second chariot, and they shouted
"Abrek!"* before him.
Thus was Joseph installed over the whole
land of Egypt. 44"I am Pharaoh," he told Joseph, "but without your approval no one
shall lift hand or foot in all the land of
Egypt." 45Pharaoh also bestowed the name
of Zaphenath-paneah* on Joseph, and he
gave him in marriage Asenath, the daughter
of Potiphera, priest of Heliopolis. And Joseph went out over the land of Egypt. 46Jo-
seph was thirty years old when he entered
the service of Pharaoh, king of Egypt.
After Joseph left Pharaoh, he went
throughout the land of Egypt. 47During the
seven years of plenty, when the land produced abundant crops, 48he collected all the
food of these years of plenty that the land of
Egypt was enjoying and stored it in the cities, placing in each city the crops of the
fields around it. 49Joseph collected grain like
the sands of the sea, so much that at last he
stopped measuring it, for it was beyond
measure.
50Before the famine years set in, Joseph
became the father of two sons, borne to him
by Asenath, daughter of Potiphera, priest of
Heliopolis.[h] 51Joseph named his firstborn
Manasseh,* meaning, "God has made me
forget entirely my troubles and my father's
house"; 52and the second he named
Ephraim,* meaning, "God has made me
fruitful in the land of my affliction."
53When the seven years of abundance enjoyed by the land of Egypt came to an end,
54the seven years of famine set in, just as Joseph had said. Although there was famine in
all the other countries, food was available
throughout the land of Egypt.[i] 55When all the
land of Egypt became hungry and the people
cried to Pharaoh for food, Pharaoh said to all
the Egyptians: "Go to Joseph and do whatever he tells you." 56When the famine had
spread throughout the land, Joseph opened
all the cities that had grain and rationed it to
the Egyptians, since the famine had gripped
the land of Egypt. 57Indeed, the whole world
came to Egypt to Joseph to buy grain, for
famine had gripped the whole world.

41:42 Signet ring: a finger ring in which was set a stamp seal, different from the cylinder seal such as Judah wore; see note on 38:18. By receiving Pharaoh's signet ring, Joseph was made vizier of Egypt (v. 43); the vizier was known as "seal-bearer of the king of Lower Egypt." The gold chain was a symbol of high office in ancient Egypt.

41:43 Abrek: apparently a cry of homage, though the word's derivation and actual meaning are uncertain.

41:45 Zaphenath-paneah: a Hebrew transcription of an Egyptian name meaning "the god speaks and he (the newborn child) lives." **Asenath**: means "belonging to (the Egyptian goddess) Neith." **Potiphera**: means "he whom Ra (the Egyptian god) gave"; a shorter form of the same name was borne by Joseph's master (37:36). **Heliopolis**: in Hebrew, *On*, a city seven miles northeast of modern Cairo, site of the chief temple of the sun god; it is mentioned also in v. 50; 46:20; Ez 30:17.

41:51 Manasseh: an allusion to this name is in the Hebrew expression, *nishshani*, "he made me forget."

41:52 Ephraim: related to the Hebrew expression *hiphrani*, "(God) has made me fruitful." The name originally meant something like "fertile land."

f: Acts 7:10. *g:* 1 Mc 2:53; Ps 105:21; Wis 10:14; Acts 7:10. *h:* Gn 46:20; 48:5. *i:* Ps 105:16; Acts 7:11.

See RG 114–15

CHAPTER 42

The Brothers' First Journey to Egypt.*

[1]When Jacob learned that grain rations were for sale in Egypt, he said to his sons: "Why do you keep looking at one another?" [2]He went on, "I hear that grain is for sale in Egypt. Go down there and buy some for us, that we may stay alive and not die."[j] [3]So ten of Joseph's brothers went down to buy grain from Egypt. [4]But Jacob did not send Joseph's brother Benjamin with his brothers, for he thought some disaster might befall him. [5]And so the sons of Israel were among those who came to buy grain, since there was famine in the land of Canaan.[k]

[6]Joseph, as governor of the country, was the one who sold grain to all the people of the land. When Joseph's brothers came, they bowed down to him with their faces to the ground.[l] [7]He recognized them as soon as he saw them. But he concealed his own identity from them and spoke harshly to them. "Where do you come from?" he asked them. They answered, "From the land of Canaan, to buy food."

[8]When Joseph recognized his brothers, although they did not recognize him, [9]he was reminded of the dreams he had about them. He said to them: "You are spies.[m] You have come to see the weak points* of the land." [10]"No, my lord," they replied. "On the contrary, your servants have come to buy food. [11]All of us are sons of the same man. We are honest men; your servants have never been spies." [12]But he answered them: "Not so! It is the weak points of the land that you have come to see." [13]"We your servants," they said, "are twelve brothers, sons of a certain man in Canaan; but the youngest one is at present with our father, and the other one is no more."[n] [14]"It is just as I said," Joseph persisted; "you are spies. [15]This is how you shall be tested: I swear by the life of Pharaoh that you shall not leave here unless your youngest brother comes here. [16]So send one of your number to get your brother, while the rest of you stay here under arrest. Thus will your words be tested for their truth; if they are untrue, as Pharaoh lives, you are spies!" [17]With that, he locked them up in the guardhouse for three days.

[18]On the third day Joseph said to them: "Do this, and you shall live; for I am a God-fearing man. [19]If you are honest men, let one of your brothers be confined in this prison, while the rest of you go and take home grain for your starving families. [20]But you must bring me your youngest brother. Your words will thus be verified, and you will not die." To this they agreed.[o] [21]To one another, however, they said: "Truly we are being punished because of our brother. We saw the anguish of his heart when he pleaded with us, yet we would not listen. That is why this anguish has now come upon us."[p] [22]Then Reuben responded, "Did I not tell you, 'Do no wrong to the boy'? But you would not listen! Now comes the reckoning for his blood."[q] [23]They did not know, of course, that Joseph understood what they said, since he spoke with them through an interpreter. [24]But turning away from them, he wept. When he was able to speak to them again, he took Simeon from among them and bound him before their eyes. [25]Then Joseph gave orders to have their containers filled with grain, their money replaced in each one's sack, and provisions given them for their journey. After this had been done for them, [26]they loaded their donkeys with the grain and departed.

[27]At the night encampment, when one of them opened his bag to give his donkey some fodder, he saw his money there in the mouth of his bag. [28]He cried out to his brothers, "My money has been returned! Here it is

42:1–38 The first journey of the brothers to Egypt. Its cause is famine, which was also the reason Abraham and Sarah undertook their dangerous journey to Egypt. The brothers bow to Joseph in v. 6, which fulfills Joseph's dream in 37:5–11. Endowed with wisdom, Joseph begins a process of instruction or "discipline" for his brothers that eventually forces them to recognize the enormity of their sin against him and the family. He controls their experience of the first journey with the result that the second journey in chaps. 43–44 leads to full acknowledgment and reconciliation.

42:9, 12 Weak points: lit., "the nakedness of the land"; the military weakness of the land, like human nakedness, should not be seen by strangers.

j: Acts 7:12. *k:* Jdt 5:10; Acts 7:11. *l:* Ps 105:21. *m:* Gn 37:5. *n:* Gn 44:20. *o:* Gn 43:5. *p:* Gn 37:18–27. *q:* Gn 37:22.

in my bag!" At that their hearts sank. Trembling, they asked one another, "What is this that God has done to us?"

29 When they got back to their father Jacob in the land of Canaan, they told him all that had happened to them. 30 "The man who is lord of the land," they said, "spoke to us harshly and put us in custody on the grounds that we were spying on the land. 31 But we said to him: 'We are honest men; we have never been spies. 32 We are twelve brothers, sons of the same father; but one is no more, and the youngest one is now with our father in the land of Canaan.' 33 Then the man who is lord of the land said to us: 'This is how I will know if you are honest men: leave one of your brothers with me, then take grain for your starving families and go. 34 When you bring me your youngest brother, and I know that you are not spies but honest men, I will restore your brother to you, and you may move about freely in the land.' "

35 When they were emptying their sacks, there in each one's sack was his moneybag! At the sight of their moneybags, they and their father were afraid. 36 Their father Jacob said to them: "Must you make me childless? Joseph is no more, Simeon is no more, and now you would take Benjamin away! All these things have happened to me!" 37 Then Reuben told his father: "You may kill my own two sons if I do not return him to you! Put him in my care, and I will bring him back to you." 38 But Jacob replied: "My son shall not go down with you. Now that his brother is dead, he is the only one left. If some disaster should befall him on the journey you must make, you would send my white head down to Sheol in grief."[r]

CHAPTER 43

See RG 114–15

The Second Journey to Egypt.*[*] 1 Now the famine in the land grew severe. 2 So when they had used up all the grain they had brought from Egypt, their father said to them, "Go back and buy us a little more food." 3 But Judah replied: "The man strictly warned us, 'You shall not see me unless your brother is with you.'[s] 4 If you are willing to let our brother go with us, we will go down to buy food for you. 5 But if you are not willing, we will not go down, because the man told us, 'You shall not see me unless your brother is with you.' "[t] 6 Israel demanded, "Why did you bring this trouble on me by telling the man that you had another brother?" 7 They answered: "The man kept asking about us and our family: 'Is your father still living? Do you have another brother?' We answered him accordingly. How could we know that he would say, 'Bring your brother down here'?"

8 Then Judah urged his father Israel: "Let the boy go with me, that we may be off and on our way if you and we and our children are to keep from starving to death.[u] 9 I myself will serve as a guarantee for him. You can hold me responsible for him. If I fail to bring him back and set him before you, I will bear the blame before you forever.[v] 10 Had we not delayed, we could have been there and back twice by now!"

11 Israel their father then told them: "If it must be so, then do this: Put some of the land's best products in your baggage and take them down to the man as gifts: some balm and honey, gum and resin, and pistachios and almonds.[w] 12 Also take double the money along, for you must return the amount that was put back in the mouths of your bags; it may have been a mistake. 13 Take your brother, too, and be off on your way back to the man. 14 May God Almighty grant you mercy in the presence of the man, so that he may let your other brother go, as well as Benjamin. As for me, if I am to suffer bereavement, I shall suffer it."

15 So the men took those gifts and double the money and Benjamin. They made their way down to Egypt and presented themselves before Joseph. 16 When Joseph saw them and Benjamin, he told his steward, "Take the men into the house, and have an animal slaughtered and prepared, for they

43:1–34 The second journey to Egypt. Joseph the sage has carefully prepared the brothers for a possible reconciliation. In this chapter and the following one Judah steps forward as the hero, in contrast to chaps. 37 and 42 where Reuben was the hero. Here Judah serves as guarantee for Benjamin.

r: Gn 37:35. *s:* Gn 44:23. *t:* Gn 42:20. *u:* Gn 42:37. *v:* Gn 44:32. *w:* Gn 45:23.

are to dine with me at noon." [17]Doing as Joseph had ordered, the steward conducted the men to Joseph's house. [18]But they became apprehensive when they were led to his house. "It must be," they thought, "on account of the money put back in our bags the first time, that we are taken inside—in order to attack us and take our donkeys and seize us as slaves." [19]So they went up to Joseph's steward and talked to him at the entrance of the house. [20]"If you please, sir," they said, "we came down here once before to buy food.[x] [21]But when we arrived at a night's encampment and opened our bags, there was each man's money in the mouth of his bag—our money in the full amount! We have now brought it back.[y] [22]We have brought other money to buy food. We do not know who put our money in our bags." [23]He replied, "Calm down! Do not fear! Your God and the God of your father must have put treasure in your bags for you. As for your money, I received it." With that, he led Simeon out to them.

[24]The steward then brought the men inside Joseph's house. He gave them water to wash their feet, and gave fodder to their donkeys. [25]Then they set out their gifts to await Joseph's arrival at noon, for they had heard that they were to dine there. [26]When Joseph came home, they presented him with the gifts they had brought inside, while they bowed down before him to the ground. [27]After inquiring how they were, he asked them, "And how is your aged father, of whom you spoke? Is he still alive?"[z] [28]"Your servant our father is still alive and doing well," they said, as they knelt and bowed down. [29]Then Joseph looked up and saw Benjamin, his brother, the son of his mother. He asked, "Is this your youngest brother, of whom you told me?" Then he said to him, "May God be gracious to you, my son!"[a] [30]With that, Joseph hurried out, for he was so overcome with affection for his brother that he was on the verge of tears. So he went into a private room and wept there.

[31]After washing his face, he reappeared and, now having collected himself, gave the order, "Serve the meal." [32]It was served separately to him,* to the brothers, and to the Egyptians who partook of his board. Egyptians may not eat with Hebrews; that is abhorrent to them. [33]When they were seated before him according to their age, from the oldest to the youngest, they looked at one another in amazement; [34]and as portions were brought to them from Joseph's table, Benjamin's portion was five times as large as* anyone else's. So they drank freely and made merry with him.

CHAPTER 44

See RG 114–15

Final Test.* [1]Then Joseph commanded his steward: "Fill the men's bags with as much food as they can carry, and put each man's money in the mouth of his bag. [2]In the mouth of the youngest one's bag put also my silver goblet, together with the money for his grain." The steward did as Joseph said. [3]At daybreak the men and their donkeys were sent off. [4]They had not gone far out of the city when Joseph said to his steward: "Go at once after the men! When you overtake them, say to them, 'Why did you repay good with evil? Why did you steal my silver goblet? [5]Is it not the very one from which my master drinks and which he uses for divination?* What you have done is wrong.' "

43:32 Separately to him: that Joseph did not eat with the other Egyptians was apparently a matter of rank.

43:34 Five times as large as: probably an idiomatic expression for "much larger than." Cf. 45:22.

44:1–34 Joseph's pressure on his brothers and Judah's great speech. Judah has the longest speech in the Book of Genesis; it summarizes the recent past (vv. 18–29), shows the pain Joseph's actions have imposed on their aged father (vv. 30–32), and ends with the offer to take the place of Benjamin as servant of Joseph (vv. 33–34). The role of Judah in the entire story is exceedingly important and is easily underrated: he tries to rescue Joseph (37:26–27), his "going down away from the brothers" is parallel to Joseph's (chap. 38) and prepares him (as it prepares Joseph) for the reconciliation, his speech in chap. 44 persuades Joseph to reveal himself and be reconciled to his brothers. Here, Judah effectively replaces Reuben as a spokesman for the brothers. Jacob in his testament (chap. 49) devotes the most attention to Judah and Joseph. In one sense, the story can be called the story of Joseph and Judah.

44:5 Divination: seeking omens through liquids poured into a cup or bowl was a common practice in the ancient Near East; cf. v. 15. Even though divination was frowned on in later Israel (Lv 19:31), it is in this place an authentic touch which is ascribed to Joseph, the wisest man in Egypt.

x: Gn 42:3. *y:* Gn 42:27–28. *z:* Tb 7:4. *a:* Gn 42:13.

6 When the steward overtook them and repeated these words to them, 7 they said to him: "Why does my lord say such things? Far be it from your servants to do such a thing! 8 We even brought back to you from the land of Canaan the money that we found in the mouths of our bags. How could we steal silver or gold from your master's house? 9 If any of your servants is found to have the goblet, he shall die, and as for the rest of us, we shall become my lord's slaves." 10 But he replied, "Now what you propose is fair enough, but only the one who is found to have it shall become my slave, and the rest of you can go free." 11 Then each of them quickly lowered his bag to the ground and opened it; 12 and when a search was made, starting with the oldest and ending with the youngest, the goblet turned up in Benjamin's bag. 13 At this, they tore their garments. Then, when each man had loaded his donkey again, they returned to the city.

14 When Judah and his brothers entered Joseph's house, he was still there; so they flung themselves on the ground before him. 15 "How could you do such a thing?" Joseph asked them. "Did you not know that such a man as I could discern by divination what happened?" 16 Judah replied: "What can we say to my lord? How can we plead or how try to prove our innocence? God has uncovered your servants' guilt.* Here we are, then, the slaves of my lord—the rest of us no less than the one in whose possession the goblet was found." 17 Joseph said, "Far be it from me to act thus! Only the one in whose possession the goblet was found shall become my slave; the rest of you may go back unharmed to your father."

18 Judah then stepped up to him and said: "I beg you, my lord, let your servant appeal to my lord, and do not become angry with your servant, for you are the equal of Pharaoh. 19 My lord asked his servants,* 'Have you a father, or another brother?' 20 So we said to my lord, 'We have an aged father, and a younger brother, the child of his old age. This one's full brother is dead, and since he is the only one by his mother who is left, his father is devoted to him.'[b] 21 Then you told your servants, 'Bring him down to me that I might see him.' 22 We replied to my lord, 'The boy cannot leave his father; his father would die if he left him.' 23 But you told your servants, 'Unless your youngest brother comes down with you, you shall not see me again.'[c] 24 When we returned to your servant my father, we reported to him the words of my lord.

25 "Later, our father said, 'Go back and buy some food for us.' 26 So we reminded him, 'We cannot go down there; only if our youngest brother is with us can we go, for we may not see the man if our youngest brother is not with us.' 27 Then your servant my father said to us, 'As you know, my wife bore me two sons. 28 One of them, however, has gone away from me, and I said, "He must have been torn to pieces by wild beasts!" I have not seen him since.[d] 29 If you take this one away from me too, and a disaster befalls him, you will send my white head down to Sheol in grief.'

30 "So now, if the boy is not with us when I go back to your servant my father, whose very life is bound up with his, he will die as soon as he sees that the boy is missing; 31 and your servants will thus send the white head of your servant our father down to Sheol in grief. 32 Besides, I, your servant, have guaranteed the boy's safety for my father by saying, 'If I fail to bring him back to you, father, I will bear the blame before you forever.'[e] 33 So now let me, your servant, remain in place of the boy as the slave of my lord, and let the boy go back with his brothers. 34 How could I go back to my father if the boy were not with me? I could not bear to see the anguish that would overcome my father."

CHAPTER 45

See RG 114–15

The Truth Revealed.* 1 Joseph could no longer restrain himself in the presence of

44:16 Guilt: in trying to do away with Joseph when he was young.

44:19 My lord asked his servants: such frequently repeated expressions in Judah's speech show the formal court style used by a subject in speaking to a high official.

45:1–28 Joseph reveals his identity and the family is reconciled.

b: Gn 42:13. *c:* Gn 43:3. *d:* Gn 37:20, 33. *e:* Gn 43:9.

all his attendants, so he cried out, "Have
everyone withdraw from me!" So no one attended him when he made himself known to
his brothers. 2But his sobs were so loud that
the Egyptians heard him, and so the news
reached Pharaoh's house. 3[f]"I am Joseph,"
he said to his brothers. "Is my father still
alive?" But his brothers could give him no
answer, so dumbfounded were they at him.

4"Come closer to me," Joseph told his
brothers. When they had done so, he said: "I
am your brother Joseph, whom you sold into
Egypt. 5But now do not be distressed, and do
not be angry with yourselves for having sold
me here. It was really for the sake of saving
lives that God sent me here ahead of you.[g]
6The famine has been in the land for two
years now, and for five more years cultivation will yield no harvest. 7God, therefore,
sent me on ahead of you to ensure for you a
remnant on earth and to save your lives in an
extraordinary deliverance. 8So it was not really you but God who had me come here;
and he has made me a father to Pharaoh,*
lord of all his household, and ruler over the
whole land of Egypt.

9* "Hurry back, then, to my father and tell
him: 'Thus says your son Joseph: God has
made me lord of all Egypt; come down to me
without delay.[h] 10You can settle in the region
of Goshen,* where you will be near me—
you and your children and children's children, your flocks and herds, and everything
that you own. 11I will provide for you there
in the five years of famine that lie ahead, so
that you and your household and all that are
yours will not suffer want.' 12Surely, you can
see for yourselves, and Benjamin can see for
himself, that it is I who am speaking to you.
13Tell my father all about my high position
in Egypt and all that you have seen. But
hurry and bring my father down here."
14Then he threw his arms around his brother
Benjamin and wept on his shoulder. 15Jo-
seph then kissed all his brothers and wept
over them; and only then were his brothers
able to talk with him.

16The news reached Pharaoh's house:
"Joseph's brothers have come." Pharaoh
and his officials were pleased. 17So Pharaoh
told Joseph: "Say to your brothers: 'This is
what you shall do: Load up your animals
and go without delay to the land of Canaan.
18There get your father and your households, and then come to me; I will assign
you the best land in Egypt, where you will
live off the fat of the land.'[i] 19Instruct them
further: 'Do this. Take wagons from the
land of Egypt for your children and your
wives and bring your father back here. 20Do
not be concerned about your belongings, for
the best in the whole land of Egypt shall be
yours.' "

21The sons of Israel acted accordingly. Joseph gave them the wagons, as Pharaoh had
ordered, and he supplied them with provisions for the journey. 22He also gave to each
of them a set of clothes, but to Benjamin he
gave three hundred shekels of silver and five
sets of clothes. 23Moreover, what he sent to
his father was ten donkeys loaded with the
finest products of Egypt and another ten
loaded with grain and bread and provisions
for his father's journey. 24As he sent his
brothers on their way, he told them, "Do not
quarrel on the way."

25So they went up from Egypt and came to
the land of Canaan, to their father Jacob.
26When they told him, "Joseph is still
alive—in fact, it is he who is governing all
the land of Egypt," he was unmoved, for he
did not believe them. 27But when they recounted to him all that Joseph had told them,
and when he saw the wagons that Joseph had
sent to transport him, the spirit of their father
Jacob came to life. 28"Enough," said Israel.
"My son Joseph is still alive! I must go and
see him before I die."

45:8 Father to Pharaoh: a term applied to a vizier in ancient Egypt.

45:9–15 In these verses, as in 46:31–47:5a, all from the Yahwist source, Joseph in his own name invites his father and brothers to come to Egypt. Only after their arrival is Pharaoh informed of the fact. On the other hand, in 45:16–20, which scholars have traditionally attributed to the Elohist source, it is Pharaoh himself who invites Joseph's family to migrate to his domain.

45:10 The region of Goshen: the meaning of the term is unknown. It is found in no Egyptian source. It is generally thought to be in the modern Wadi Tumilat in the eastern part of the Nile Delta.

f: Acts 7:13. *g:* Gn 50:20. *h:* Acts 7:14. *i:* Acts 7:14.

CHAPTER 46

See RG 114–15

Migration to Egypt. 1* Israel set out with all that was his. When he arrived at Beer-sheba, he offered sacrifices to the God of his father Isaac. 2 There God, speaking to Israel in a vision by night, called: Jacob! Jacob! He answered, "Here I am." 3 Then he said: I am God,* the God of your father. Do not be afraid to go down to Egypt, for there I will make you a great nation. 4 I will go down to Egypt with you and I will also bring you back here, after Joseph has closed your eyes.

5 So Jacob departed from Beer-sheba, and the sons of Israel put their father and their wives and children on the wagons that Pharaoh had sent to transport him. 6 They took with them their livestock and the possessions they had acquired in the land of Canaan. So Jacob and all his descendants came to Egypt.[j] 7 His sons and his grandsons, his daughters and his granddaughters—all his descendants—he took with him to Egypt.

8 These are the names of the Israelites, Jacob and his children, who came to Egypt.

Reuben, Jacob's firstborn,[k] 9* and the sons of Reuben: Hanoch, Pallu, Hezron, and Carmi.[l] 10 The sons of Simeon: Jemuel, Jamin, Ohad, Jachin, Zohar, and Shaul, son of a Canaanite woman.[m] 11 The sons of Levi: Gershon, Kohath, and Merari.[n] 12 The sons of Judah: Er, Onan, Shelah, Perez, and Zerah—but Er and Onan had died in the land of Canaan; and the sons of Perez were Hezron and Hamul.[o] 13 The sons of Issachar: Tola, Puah, Jashub, and Shimron.[p] 14 The sons of Zebulun: Sered, Elon, and Jahleel.[q] 15 These were the sons whom Leah bore to Jacob in Paddan-aram, along with his daughter Dinah—thirty-three persons in all, sons and daughters.

16 The sons of Gad: Zephon, Haggi, Shuni, Ezbon, Eri, Arod, and Areli.[r] 17 The sons of Asher: Imnah, Ishvah, Ishvi, and Beriah, with their sister Serah; and the sons of Beriah: Heber and Malchiel.[s] 18 These are the children of Zilpah, whom Laban had given to his daughter Leah; these she bore to Jacob—sixteen persons in all.

19 The sons of Jacob's wife Rachel: Joseph and Benjamin. 20 In the land of Egypt Joseph became the father of Manasseh and Ephraim, whom Asenath, daughter of Potiphera, priest of Heliopolis, bore to him.[t] 21 The sons of Benjamin: Bela, Becher, Ashbel, Gera, Naaman, Ahiram, Shupham, Hupham, and Ard.[u] 22 These are the sons whom Rachel bore to Jacob—fourteen persons in all.

23 The sons of Dan: Hushim.[v] 24 The sons of Naphtali: Jahzeel, Guni, Jezer, and Shillem.[w] 25 These are the sons of Bilhah, whom Laban had given to his daughter Rachel; these she bore to Jacob—seven persons in all.

26 Jacob's people who came to Egypt—his direct descendants, not counting the wives of Jacob's sons—numbered sixty-six persons in all.[x] 27 Together with Joseph's sons who were born to him in Egypt—two persons—all the people comprising the household of Jacob who had come to Egypt amounted to seventy persons* in all.[y]

28 Israel had sent Judah ahead to Joseph, so that he might meet him in Goshen. On his arrival in the region of Goshen, 29 Joseph prepared his chariot and went up to meet his father Israel in Goshen. As soon as Israel made his appearance, Joseph threw his arms around him and wept a long time on his

46:1–47:26 Jacob and his family settle in Egypt. Joseph's economic policies.

46:3 I am God: more precisely according to the Hebrew text, "I am El." "El" is here a divine name, not the common noun "god."

46:9–27 This genealogical list is based on the clan lists (Nm 26:5–50) from the Mosaic period.

46:27 Seventy persons: it is difficult to get this exact number by adding up the persons mentioned in the preceding genealogies. One might assume it refers to Jacob and sixty-nine descendants, excluding Er and Onan but including Dinah. Ex 1:5 repeats the number but excludes Jacob. Dt 10:22 refers to seventy persons descending to Egypt. The best solution is to take the number as expressing totality. Since there are seventy nations in chap. 10, it is likely that the text is drawing a parallel between the two entities and suggesting that Israel "represents" the nations before God.

j: Ex 1:1; Jos 24:4; Jdt 5:10; Acts 7:15. *k:* Ex 1:2. *l:* Ex 6:14; Nm 26:5; 1 Chr 5:3. *m:* Ex 6:15; Nm 26:12; 1 Chr 4:24. *n:* Ex 6:16; Nm 3:17; 26:57; 1 Chr 6:1. *o:* Gn 38:3–10, 29–30; Nm 26:19; Ru 4:12; 1 Chr 2:5. *p:* Nm 26:23–24; 1 Chr 7:1. *q:* Nm 26:26. *r:* Nm 26:15–16. *s:* Nm 26:44; 1 Chr 7:30–31. *t:* Gn 41:50; Nm 26:28, 35. *u:* Nm 26:38; 1 Chr 7:6; 8:1–4. *v:* Nm 26:42. *w:* Nm 26:48–49; 1 Chr 7:13. *x:* Ex 1:5. *y:* Ex 1:5; Dt 10:22; Acts 7:14.

shoulder. [30]And Israel said to Joseph, "At last I can die, now that I have seen for myself that you are still alive."

[31]Joseph then said to his brothers and his father's household: "I will go up and inform Pharaoh, telling him: 'My brothers and my father's household, whose home is in the land of Canaan, have come to me. [32]The men are shepherds, having been owners of livestock;* and they have brought with them their flocks and herds, as well as everything else they own.' [33]So when Pharaoh summons you and asks what your occupation is, [34]you must answer, 'We your servants, like our ancestors, have been owners of livestock from our youth until now,' in order that you may stay in the region of Goshen, since all shepherds are abhorrent to the Egyptians."

CHAPTER 47

See RG 114–15

Settlement in Goshen. [1]Joseph went and told Pharaoh, "My father and my brothers have come from the land of Canaan, with their flocks and herds and everything else they own; and they are now in the region of Goshen." [2]He then presented to Pharaoh five of his brothers whom he had selected from their full number. [3]When Pharaoh asked them, "What is your occupation?" they answered, "We, your servants, like our ancestors, are shepherds. [4]We have come," they continued, "in order to sojourn in this land, for there is no pasture for your servants' flocks, because the famine has been severe in the land of Canaan. So now please let your servants settle in the region of Goshen."[z] [5]Pharaoh said to Joseph, "Now that your father and your brothers have come to you, [6]the land of Egypt is at your disposal; settle your father and brothers in the pick of the land. Let them settle in the region of Goshen. And if you know of capable men among them, put them in charge of my livestock." [7]Then Joseph brought his father Jacob and presented him to Pharaoh. And Jacob blessed Pharaoh. [8]Then Pharaoh asked Jacob, "How many years have you lived?" [9]Jacob replied: "The years I have lived as a wayfarer amount to a hundred and thirty. Few and hard have been these years of my life, and they do not compare with the years that my ancestors lived as wayfarers."* [10]Then Jacob blessed Pharaoh and withdrew from his presence.

[11]Joseph settled his father and brothers and gave them a holding in Egypt on the pick of the land, in the region of Rameses,* as Pharaoh had ordered. [12]And Joseph provided food for his father and brothers and his father's whole household, down to the youngest.

Joseph's Land Policy. [13]Since there was no food in all the land because of the extreme severity of the famine, and the lands of Egypt and Canaan were languishing from hunger, [14]Joseph gathered in, as payment for the grain that they were buying, all the money that was to be found in Egypt and Canaan, and he put it in Pharaoh's house. [15]When all the money in Egypt and Canaan was spent, all the Egyptians came to Joseph, pleading, "Give us food! Why should we perish in front of you? For our money is gone." [16]"Give me your livestock if your money is gone," replied Joseph. "I will give you food in return for your livestock." [17]So they brought their livestock to Joseph, and he gave them food in exchange for their horses, their flocks of sheep and herds of cattle, and their donkeys. Thus he supplied them with food in exchange for all their livestock in that year. [18]That year ended, and they came to him in the next one and said: "We cannot hide from my lord that, with our money spent and our livestock made over to my lord, there is nothing left to put at my lord's disposal except our bodies and our land. [19]Why should we and our land perish before your very eyes? Take us and our land in exchange for food, and we will become Pharaoh's slaves and our land his property; only give us seed, that we may survive and not perish, and that our land may not turn into a waste."

46:32 Owners of livestock: the phrase occurs only here and in v. 34. The difference between this term and "shepherds" is not clear, for the brothers do not mention it to Pharaoh in 47:3.

47:9 Wayfarer . . . wayfarers: human beings are merely sojourners on earth; cf. Ps 39:13.

47:11 The region of Rameses: same as the region of Goshen; see note on 45:10.

z: Ex 23:9; Dt 23:8.

[20]So Joseph acquired all the land of Egypt
for Pharaoh. Each of the Egyptians sold his
field, since the famine weighed heavily upon
them. Thus the land passed over to Pharaoh,
[21]and the people were reduced to slavery,
from one end of Egypt's territory to the
other. [22]Only the priests' lands Joseph did
not acquire. Since the priests had a fixed allowance from Pharaoh and lived off the allowance Pharaoh had granted them, they did
not have to sell their land.

[23]Joseph told the people: "Now that I have
acquired you and your land for Pharaoh, here
is your seed for sowing the land. [24]But when
the harvest is in, you must give a fifth of it to
Pharaoh, while you keep four-fifths as seed
for your fields and as food for yourselves and
your households and as food for your children." [25]"You have saved our lives!" they answered. "We have found favor with my lord;
now we will be Pharaoh's slaves." [26]Thus Joseph made it a statute for the land of Egypt,
which is still in force, that a fifth of its produce should go to Pharaoh. Only the land of
the priests did not pass over to Pharaoh.

Israel Blesses Ephraim and Manasseh.
[27]Thus Israel settled in the land of Egypt, in
the region of Goshen. There they acquired
holdings, were fertile, and multiplied
greatly.[a] [28]* Jacob lived in the land of Egypt
for seventeen years; the span of his life came
to a hundred and forty-seven years. [29]When
the time approached for Israel to die, he
called his son Joseph and said to him: "If it
pleases you, put your hand under my thigh as
a sign of your enduring fidelity to me; do not
bury me in Egypt. [30]When I lie down with
my ancestors, take me out of Egypt and bury
me in their burial place."[b] "I will do as you
say," he replied. [31]But his father demanded,
"Swear it to me!" So Joseph swore to him.
Then Israel bowed at the head of the bed.*

CHAPTER 48

See RG 114–15

[1]* Some time afterward, Joseph was
informed, "Your father is failing." So he
took along with him his two sons, Manasseh
and Ephraim. [2]When Jacob was told, "Your
son Joseph has come to you," Israel rallied
his strength and sat up in bed.

[3][c] Jacob then said to Joseph: "God
Almighty appeared to me at Luz* in the land
of Canaan, and blessing me, [4]he said, 'I will
make you fertile and multiply you and make
you into an assembly of peoples, and I will
give this land to your descendants after you
as a permanent possession.' [5]So now your
two sons who were born to you in the land of
Egypt before I joined you here, shall be
mine; Ephraim and Manasseh shall be mine
as much as Reuben and Simeon are mine.
[6]Progeny born to you after them shall remain yours; but their heritage shall be
recorded in the names of their brothers. [7][d] I
do this because, when I was returning from
Paddan, your mother Rachel died, to my sorrow, during the journey in Canaan, while we
were still a short distance from Ephrath; and
I buried her there on the way to Ephrath
[now Bethlehem]."*

[8]When Israel saw Joseph's sons, he asked,
"Who are these?" [9]"They are my sons," Joseph answered his father, "whom God has
given me here." "Bring them to me," said his

47:28–50:26 Supplements to the Joseph story. Most of the material in this section centers on Jacob—his blessing of Joseph's sons, his farewell testament, and his death and burial in Canaan. Only the last verses (50:15–26) redirect attention to Jacob's sons, the twelve brothers; they are assured that the reconciliation will not collapse after the death of the patriarch.

47:31 Israel bowed at the head of the bed: meaning perhaps that he gave a nod of assent and appreciation as he lay on his bed. The oath and gesture are the same as Abraham's in 24:2. Israel's bowing here suggests the fulfillment of Joseph's dreams in 37:9–10, when parents and brothers bowed down to Joseph (cf. 42:6; 43:26). By using different vowels for the Hebrew word for "bed," the Greek version translated it as "staff," and understood the phrase to mean that he bowed in worship, leaning on the top of his staff; it is thus quoted in Heb 11:21.

48:1–22 Jacob continues his preparations for death. In a scene that evokes the nearly blind Isaac blessing Jacob and Esau (chap. 27), Jacob blesses Joseph's two sons. He adopts them, elevating them to a status equal to that of Jacob's first sons Reuben and Simeon (cf. 1 Chr 5:1). The adoption is one more instance of Jacob's favoring Rachel and those born of her. The mention of Jacob's failing eyesight and his selection of the younger son over the older evokes the great deathbed scene in chap. 27. He reaffirms to Joseph the ancient divine promise of progeny and land.

48:3 Luz: an older name of Bethel (28:19).

48:7 Since her early death prevented Rachel from bearing more than two sons, Jacob feels justified in treating her two grandsons as if they were her own offspring.

a: Ex 1:7. *b:* Gn 50:5. *c:* Gn 28:12–15; 35:6. *d:* Gn 35:19.

father, "that I may bless them." 10 Now Israel's eyes were dim from age; he could not
see well. When Joseph brought his sons close
to him, he kissed and embraced them. 11 Then
Israel said to Joseph, "I never expected to see
your face again, and now God has allowed
me to see your descendants as well!"

12 Joseph removed them from his father's
knees and bowed down before him with his
face to the ground. 13 Then Joseph took the
two, Ephraim with his right hand, to Israel's
left, and Manasseh with his left hand, to Israel's right, and brought them up to him.
14 But Israel, crossing his hands, put out his
right hand and laid it on the head of
Ephraim, although he was the younger, and
his left hand on the head of Manasseh, although he was the firstborn. 15 Then he
blessed them with these words:

"May the God in whose presence
my fathers Abraham and Isaac walked,
The God who has been my shepherd
from my birth to this day,[e]
16 The angel who has delivered me from all
harm,
bless these boys
That in them my name be recalled,
and the names of my fathers, Abraham
and Isaac,
And they may become teeming
multitudes
upon the earth!"

17 When Joseph saw that his father had laid
his right hand on Ephraim's head, this
seemed wrong to him; so he took hold of his
father's hand, to remove it from Ephraim's
head to Manasseh's, 18 saying, "That is not
right, father; the other one is the firstborn;
lay your right hand on his head!" 19 But his
father refused. "I know it, son," he said, "I
know. That one too shall become a people,
and he too shall be great. Nevertheless, his
younger brother shall surpass him, and his
descendants shall become a multitude of nations." 20 So he blessed them that day and
said, "By you shall the people of Israel pronounce blessings, saying, 'God make you
like Ephraim and Manasseh.'" Thus he
placed Ephraim before Manasseh.[f]

21 Then Israel said to Joseph: "I am about
to die. But God will be with you and will restore you to the land of your ancestors. 22[g] As
for me, I give to you, as to the one above his
brothers, Shechem, which I captured from
the Amorites with my sword and bow."*

CHAPTER 49

See RG 114–15

Jacob's Testament.* 1 Jacob called his
sons and said: "Gather around, that I may
tell you what is to happen to you in days to
come.

2 "Assemble and listen, sons of Jacob,
listen to Israel, your father.

3 "You, Reuben, my firstborn,
my strength and the first fruit of my
vigor,
excelling in rank and excelling in
power!
4 Turbulent as water, you shall no longer
excel,
for you climbed into your father's bed
and defiled my couch to my sorrow.[h]

5 * "Simeon and Levi, brothers indeed,

48:22 Both the meaning of the Hebrew and the historical reference in this verse are obscure. By taking the Hebrew word for Shechem as a common noun meaning shoulder or mountain slope, some translators render the verse, "I give you one portion more than your brothers, which I captured . . ." The reference may be to the capture of Shechem by the sons of Jacob (34:24–29). Shechem lay near the border separating the tribal territory of Manasseh from that of Ephraim (Jos 16:4–9; 17:1–2, 7).

49:1–27 The testament, or farewell discourse, of Jacob, which has its closest parallel in Moses' farewell in Dt 33:6–25. From his privileged position as a patriarch, he sees the future of his children (the eponymous ancestors of the tribes) and is able to describe how they will fare and so gives his blessing. The dense and archaic poetry is obscure in several places. The sayings often involve wordplays (explained in the notes). The poem begins with the six sons of Leah (vv. 2–15), then deals with the sons of the two secondary wives, and ends with Rachel's two sons, Joseph and Benjamin. Reuben, the oldest son, loses his position of leadership as a result of his intercourse with Bilhah (35:22), and the words about Simeon and Levi allude to their taking revenge for the rape of Dinah (chap. 34). The preeminence of Judah reflects his rise in the course of the narrative (mirroring the rise of Joseph). See note on 44:1–34.

49:5–7 This passage probably refers to their attack on the city of Shechem (Gn 34). Because there is no indication that the warlike tribe of Levi will be commissioned as a priestly

e: Heb 11:21. *f:* Heb 11:21. *g:* Jos 17:14, 17–18; Jn 4:5. *h:* Gn 35:22; 1 Chr 5:1–2.

weapons of violence are their knives.*
6 Let not my person enter their council,
or my honor be joined with their
company;
For in their fury they killed men,
at their whim they maimed oxen.[i]
7 Cursed be their fury so fierce,
and their rage so cruel!
I will scatter them in Jacob,
disperse them throughout Israel.

8 "You, Judah, shall your brothers praise
—your hand on the neck of your
enemies;
the sons of your father shall bow down
to you.
9 Judah is a lion's cub,
you have grown up on prey, my son.
He crouches, lies down like a lion,
like a lioness—who would dare rouse
him?[j]
10 The scepter shall never depart from Judah,
or the mace from between his feet,
Until tribute comes to him,*
and he receives the people's
obedience.
11 He tethers his donkey to the vine,
his donkey's foal to the choicest stem.
In wine he washes his garments,
his robe in the blood of grapes.*
12 His eyes are darker than wine,
and his teeth are whiter than milk.

13 "Zebulun shall dwell by the seashore;
he will be a haven for ships,
and his flank shall rest on Sidon.

14 "Issachar is a rawboned donkey,
crouching between the saddlebags.
15 When he saw how good a settled life was,
and how pleasant the land,
He bent his shoulder to the burden
and became a toiling serf.

16 "Dan shall achieve justice* for his people
as one of the tribes of Israel.
17 Let Dan be a serpent by the roadside,
a horned viper by the path,
That bites the horse's heel,
so that the rider tumbles backward.

18 "I long for your deliverance, O LORD!*

19 "Gad shall be raided by raiders,
but he shall raid at their heels.*

20 "Asher's produce is rich,
and he shall furnish delicacies for kings.

21 "Naphtali is a hind let loose,
which brings forth lovely fawns.

22 "Joseph is a wild colt,
a wild colt by a spring,
wild colts on a hillside.
23 Harrying him and shooting,
the archers opposed him;
24 But his bow remained taut,
and his arms were nimble,
By the power of the Mighty One of
Jacob,
because of the Shepherd, the Rock of
Israel,
25 The God of your father, who helps you,*
God Almighty, who blesses you,
With the blessings of the heavens above,
the blessings of the abyss that
crouches below,
The blessings of breasts and womb,
26 the blessings of fresh grain and
blossoms,
the blessings of the everlasting
mountains,

tribe (Ex 32:26–29; Dt 33:11), this passage reflects an early, independent tradition.

49:5 Knives: if this is the meaning of the obscure Hebrew word here, the reference may be to the knives used in circumcising the men of Shechem (34:24; cf. Jos 5:2).

49:10 Until tribute comes to him: this translation is based on a slight change in the Hebrew text, which, as it stands, would seem to mean, "until he comes to Shiloh." A somewhat different reading of the Hebrew text would be, "until he comes to whom it belongs." This last has been traditionally understood in a messianic sense. In any case, the passage aims at the supremacy of the tribe of Judah and of the Davidic dynasty.

49:11 In wine . . . the blood of grapes: Judah's clothes are poetically pictured as soaked with grape juice from trampling in the wine press, the rich vintage of his land; cf. Is 63:2.

49:16 In Hebrew the verb for "achieve justice" is from the same root as the name Dan.

49:18 This short plea for divine mercy has been inserted into the middle of Jacob's testament.

49:19 In Hebrew there is assonance between the name Gad and the words for "raided," "raiders," and "raid."

49:25–26 A very similar description of the agricultural riches of the tribal land of Joseph is given in Dt 33:13–16.

i: Gn 34:25. *j:* 1 Chr 5:2.

the delights of the eternal hills.
May they rest on the head of Joseph,
on the brow of the prince among his brothers.

27 "Benjamin is a ravenous wolf;
mornings he devours the prey,
and evenings he distributes the spoils."

Farewell and Death. 28 All these are the twelve tribes of Israel, and this is what their father said about them, as he blessed them. To each he gave a suitable blessing. 29 Then he gave them this charge: "Since I am about to be gathered to my people, bury me with my ancestors in the cave that lies in the field of Ephron the Hittite, 30 the cave in the field of Machpelah, facing on Mamre, in the land of Canaan, the field that Abraham bought from Ephron the Hittite for a burial ground.[k] 31 There Abraham and his wife Sarah are buried, and so are Isaac and his wife Rebekah, and there, too, I buried Leah— 32 the field and the cave in it that had been purchased from the Hittites."

33 When Jacob had finished giving these instructions to his sons, he drew his feet into the bed, breathed his last, and was gathered to his people.

CHAPTER 50

See RG 114–15

Jacob's Funeral. 1 Joseph flung himself upon his father and wept over him as he kissed him. 2 Then Joseph ordered the physicians in his service to embalm his father. When the physicians embalmed Israel, 3 they spent forty days at it, for that is the full period of embalming; and the Egyptians mourned him for seventy days. 4 When the period of mourning was over, Joseph spoke to Pharaoh's household. "If you please, appeal to Pharaoh, saying: 5 My father made me swear: 'I am dying. Bury me in my grave that I have prepared for myself in the land of Canaan.' So now let me go up to bury my father. Then I will come back."[l] 6 Pharaoh replied, "Go and bury your father, as he made you promise on oath."

7 So Joseph went up to bury his father; and with him went all of Pharaoh's officials who were senior members of his household and all the other elders of the land of Egypt, 8 as well as Joseph's whole household, his brothers, and his father's household; only their children and their flocks and herds were left in the region of Goshen. 9 Chariots, too, and horsemen went up with him; it was a very imposing retinue.

10 When they arrived at Goren-ha-atad,* which is beyond the Jordan, they held there a very great and solemn memorial service; and Joseph observed seven days of mourning for his father. 11 When the Canaanites who inhabited the land saw the mourning at Goren-ha-atad, they said, "This is a solemn funeral on the part of the Egyptians!" That is why the place was named Abel-mizraim. It is beyond the Jordan.

12 Thus Jacob's sons did for him as he had instructed them. 13 They carried him to the land of Canaan and buried him in the cave in the field of Machpelah, facing on Mamre, the field that Abraham had bought for a burial ground from Ephron the Hittite.[m]

14 After Joseph had buried his father he returned to Egypt, together with his brothers and all who had gone up with him for the burial of his father.

Plea for Forgiveness. 15* Now that their father was dead, Joseph's brothers became fearful and thought, "Suppose Joseph has been nursing a grudge against us and now

50:10–11 Goren-ha-atad: "Threshing Floor of the Brambles." **Abel-mizraim**: although the name really means "watercourse of the Egyptians," it is understood here, by a play on the first part of the term, to mean "mourning of the Egyptians." The site has not been identified through either reading of the name. But it is difficult to see why the mourning rites should have been held in the land beyond the Jordan when the burial was at Hebron. Perhaps an earlier form of the story placed the mourning rites beyond the Wadi of Egypt, the traditional boundary between Canaan and Egypt (Nm 34:5; Jos 15:4, 47).

50:15–26 The final reconciliation of the brothers. Fearful of what may happen after the death of their father, the brothers engage in a final deception, inventing the dying wish of Jacob. Again, Joseph weeps, and, again, his brothers fall down before him, offering to be his slaves (44:16, 33). Joseph's assurance is also a summation of the story: "Even though you meant harm to me, God meant it for good, to achieve this present end, the survival of many people" (v. 20). Joseph's adoption of the children of Manasseh's son

k: Gn 23:17. *l:* Gn 47:30. *m:* Gn 23:16; Jos 24:32; Acts 7:16.

most certainly will pay us back in full for all
the wrong we did him!" [16]So they sent to Joseph and said: "Before your father died, he
gave us these instructions: [17]'Thus you shall
say to Joseph: Please forgive the criminal
wrongdoing of your brothers, who treated
you harmfully.' So now please forgive the
crime that we, the servants of the God of
your father, committed." When they said
this to him, Joseph broke into tears. [18]Then
his brothers also proceeded to fling themselves down before him and said, "We are
your slaves!" [19]But Joseph replied to them:
"Do not fear. Can I take the place of God?
[20]Even though you meant harm to me, God
meant it for good, to achieve this present
end, the survival of many people.[n] [21]So now,
do not fear. I will provide for you and for
your children." By thus speaking kindly to
them, he reassured them.[o]
[22]Joseph remained in Egypt, together with
his father's household. He lived a hundred
and ten years. [23]He saw Ephraim's children
to the third generation, and the children of
Manasseh's son Machir were also born on
Joseph's knees.[p]
Death of Joseph. [24]Joseph said to his brothers: "I am about to die. God will surely take
care of you and lead you up from this land to
the land that he promised on oath to Abraham,
Isaac and Jacob."[q] [25]Then, putting the sons of
Israel under oath, he continued, "When God
thus takes care of you, you must bring my
bones up from this place."[r] [26]Joseph died at
the age of a hundred and ten. He was embalmed and laid to rest in a coffin in Egypt.[s]

Machir recalls Jacob's adoption of his grandchildren (48:5, 13–20); the adoptions reflect tribal history (cf. Jgs 5:14).

n: Gn 45:5. *o:* Gn 47:12. *p:* Nm 32:39; Jos 17:1. *q:* Ex 3:8; Heb 11:22. *r:* Ex 13:19; Heb 11:22. *s:* Sir 49:15.

The Book of Exodus

See RG 115–24

The second book of the Pentateuch is called Exodus, from the Greek word for "departure," because its central event was understood by the Septuagint's translators to be the departure of the Israelites from Egypt. Its Hebrew title, *Shemoth* ("Names"), is from the book's opening phrase, "These are the names . . . ." Continuing the history of Israel from the point where the Book of Genesis leaves off, Exodus recounts the Egyptian oppression of Jacob's ever-increasing descendants and their miraculous deliverance by God through Moses, who led them across the Red Sea to Mount Sinai where they entered into a covenant with the Lord. Covenantal laws and detailed prescriptions for the tabernacle (a portable sanctuary foreshadowing the Jerusalem Temple) and its service are followed by a dramatic episode of rebellion, repentance, and divine mercy. After the broken covenant is renewed, the tabernacle is constructed, and the cloud signifying God's glorious presence descends to cover it.

These events made Israel a nation and confirmed their unique relationship with God. The "law" (Hebrew *torah*) given by God through Moses to the Israelites at Mount Sinai constitutes the moral, civil, and ritual legislation by which they were to become a holy people. Many elements of it were fundamental to the teaching of Jesus (Mt 5:21–30; 15:4) as well as to New Testament and Christian moral teaching (Rom 13:8–10; 1 Cor 10:1–5; 1 Pt 2:9).

The principal divisions of Exodus are:

I. Introduction: The Oppression of the Israelites in Egypt (1:1–2:22)
II. The Call and Commission of Moses (2:23–7:7)
III. The Contest with Pharaoh (7:8–13:16)
IV. The Deliverance of the Israelites from Pharaoh and Victory at the Sea (13:17–15:21)
V. The Journey in the Wilderness to Sinai (15:22–18:27)
VI. Covenant and Legislation at Mount Sinai (19:1–31:18)
VII. Israel's Apostasy and God's Renewal of the Covenant (32:1–34:35)
VIII. The Building of the Tabernacle and the Descent of God's Glory upon It (35:1–40:38)

I. Introduction: The Oppression of the Israelites in Egypt

CHAPTER 1

See RG 117–18

Jacob's Descendants in Egypt. 1These are the names of the sons of Israel* who, accompanied by their households, entered into Egypt with Jacob: 2* Reuben, Simeon, Levi and Judah; 3Issachar, Zebulun and Benjamin; 4Dan and Naphtali; Gad and Asher. 5The total number of Jacob's direct descendants* was seventy.[a] Joseph was already in Egypt.

6Now Joseph and all his brothers and that whole generation died.[b] 7But the Israelites were fruitful and prolific. They multiplied and became so very numerous that the land was filled with them.*

The Oppression. 8[c] Then a new king, who knew nothing of Joseph,* rose to power in Egypt. 9He said to his people, "See! The Israelite people have multiplied and become more numerous than we are! 10Come, let us deal shrewdly with them to stop their increase;* otherwise, in time of war they too may join our enemies to fight against us, and so leave the land."

11Accordingly, they set supervisors over the Israelites to oppress them with forced labor.[d] Thus they had to build for Pharaoh* the garrison cities of Pithom and Raamses. 12Yet the more they were oppressed, the more they multiplied and spread, so that the Egyptians began to loathe the Israelites. 13So the Egyptians reduced the Israelites to cruel slavery, 14making life bitter for them with hard labor, at mortar* and brick and all kinds of field work—cruelly oppressed in all their labor.

Command to the Midwives. 15The king of Egypt told the Hebrew midwives, one of whom was called Shiphrah and the other Puah, 16"When you act as midwives for the Hebrew women, look on the birthstool:* if it is a boy, kill him; but if it is a girl, she may live." 17The midwives, however, feared God; they did not do as the king of Egypt had ordered them, but let the boys live. 18So the king of Egypt summoned the midwives and asked them, "Why have you done this, allowing the boys to live?" 19The midwives answered Pharaoh, "The Hebrew women are not like the Egyptian women. They are robust and give birth before the midwife arrives." 20Therefore God dealt well with the midwives; and the people multiplied and grew very numerous. 21And because the midwives feared God, God built up families for them. 22Pharaoh then commanded all his people, "Throw into the Nile every boy that is born,[e] but you may let all the girls live."

1:1 Sons of Israel: here literally the first-generation sons of Jacob/Israel. Cf. v. 5. However, beginning with v. 7 the same Hebrew phrase refers to Jacob's more remote descendants; hence, from there on, it is ordinarily rendered "the Israelites." **Households**: the family in its fullest sense, including wives, children and servants.

1:2 Jacob's sons are listed here according to their respective mothers. Cf. Gn 29:31; 30:20; 35:16–26.

1:5 Direct descendants: lit., "persons coming from Jacob's loins"; hence, wives of Jacob's sons and servants are not included. Cf. Gn 46:26. **Seventy**: Gn 46:26, along with the Septuagint for the verse, agrees on a total of sixty-six coming down to Egypt with Jacob, but in v. 27 the Hebrew text adds the two sons born to Joseph in Egypt and presupposes Jacob himself and Joseph for a total of seventy; the Septuagint adds "nine sons" born to Joseph to get a total of seventy-five. This is the figure the Septuagint and 4QEx[a] have here in Ex 1:5.

1:7 Fruitful . . . multiplied . . . the land was filled with them: the language used here to indicate the fecundity of the Israelite population echoes the divine blessing bestowed upon humanity at creation (Gn 1:28) and after the flood (Gn 9:1) as well as suggesting fulfillment of the promises to the ancestors Abraham, Isaac, and Jacob (Gn 12:2; 13:16; 15:5; 28:14; passim).

1:8 Who knew nothing of Joseph: the nuance intended by the Hebrew verb "know" here goes beyond precise determination. The idea may be not simply that a new king came to power who had not heard of Joseph but that this king ignored the services that Joseph had rendered to Egypt, repudiating the special relationship that existed between Joseph and his predecessor on the throne.

1:10 Increase: Pharaoh's actions thereby immediately pit him against God's will for the Israelites to multiply; see note on v. 7 above.

1:11 Pharaoh: not a personal name, but a title common to all the kings of Egypt.

1:14 Mortar: either the wet clay with which the bricks were made, as in Na 3:14, or the cement used between the bricks in building, as in Gn 11:3.

1:16 Birthstool: apparently a pair of stones on which the mother is seated for childbirth opposite the midwife. The Hebrew word elsewhere is used to refer to the stones of a potter's wheel.

a: Gn 46:26–27; Dt 10:22; Acts 7:14. *b:* Gn 50:26. *c:* Acts 7:18–19. *d:* Dt 26:6. *e:* Acts 7:19.

See RG 118–19

CHAPTER 2

Birth and Adoption of Moses. [1]Now a man* of the house of Levi married a Levite woman,[f] [2]and the woman conceived and bore a son. Seeing what a fine child he was, she hid him for three months.[g] [3]But when she could no longer hide him, she took a papyrus basket,* daubed it with bitumen and pitch, and putting the child in it, placed it among the reeds on the bank of the Nile. [4]His sister stationed herself at a distance to find out what would happen to him.

[5]Then Pharaoh's daughter came down to bathe at the Nile, while her attendants walked along the bank of the Nile. Noticing the basket among the reeds, she sent her handmaid to fetch it. [6]On opening it, she looked, and there was a baby boy crying! She was moved with pity for him and said, "It is one of the Hebrews' children." [7]Then his sister asked Pharaoh's daughter, "Shall I go and summon a Hebrew woman to nurse the child for you?" [8]Pharaoh's daughter answered her, "Go." So the young woman went and called the child's own mother. [9]Pharaoh's daughter said to her, "Take this child and nurse him for me, and I will pay your wages."* So the woman took the child and nursed him. [10]When the child grew,* she brought him to Pharaoh's daughter, and he became her son.[h] She named him Moses; for she said, "I drew him out of the water."

Moses' Flight to Midian. [11][i] On one occasion, after Moses had grown up,* when he had gone out to his kinsmen and witnessed their forced labor, he saw an Egyptian striking a Hebrew, one of his own kinsmen. [12]Looking about and seeing no one, he struck down the Egyptian and hid him in the sand. [13]The next day he went out again, and now two Hebrews were fighting! So he asked the culprit, "Why are you striking your companion?" [14]But he replied, "Who has appointed you ruler and judge over us? Are you thinking of killing me as you killed the Egyptian?" Then Moses became afraid and thought, "The affair must certainly be known." [15]When Pharaoh heard of the affair, he sought to kill Moses. But Moses fled from Pharaoh and went to the land of Midian.*[j] There he sat down by a well.

[16]Now the priest of Midian had seven daughters, and they came to draw water and fill the troughs to water their father's flock. [17]But shepherds came and drove them away. So Moses rose up in their defense and watered their flock. [18]When they returned to

2:1 Now a man: the chapter begins abruptly, without names for the man or woman (in contrast to the midwives of 1:15), who in 6:20 are identified as Amram and Jochebed.

2:3 Basket: the same Hebrew word is used in Gn 6:14 and throughout the flood narrative for Noah's ark, but nowhere else in the Bible. Here, however, the "ark" or "chest" was made of papyrus stalks. Presumably the allusion to Genesis is intentional. Just as Noah and his family were preserved safe from the threatening waters of the flood in the ark he built, so now Moses is preserved from the threatening waters of the Nile in the ark prepared by his mother. **Among the reeds**: the Hebrew noun for "reed" is overwhelmingly used in the phrase "Reed Sea," traditionally translated "Red Sea."

2:9 And I will pay your wages: the idea that the child's mother will be paid for nursing her child—and by Pharaoh's own daughter—heightens the narrative's irony.

2:10 When the child grew: while v. 9 implies that the boy's mother cared for him as long as he needed to be nursed (presumably, between two and four years), the same verb appears in v. 11 to describe the attainment of adulthood. **And he became her son**: Pharaoh's daughter adopts Moses, thus adding to the irony of the account. The king of Egypt had ordered the killing of all the sons of the Hebrews, and one now becomes the son of his own daughter! **Moses**: in Hebrew, *mosheh*. There is a play on words here: Hebrew *mosheh* echoes *meshithihu* ("I drew him out"). However, the name Moses actually has nothing to do with that Hebrew verb, but is probably derived from Egyptian "beloved" or "has been born," preserved in such Pharaonic names as Thutmoses (meaning approximately "Beloved of the god Thoth" or "The god Thoth is born, has given birth to [the child]"). The original meaning of Moses' name was no longer remembered (if it was Egyptian, it may have contained an Egyptian divine element as well, perhaps the name of the Nile god Hapi), and a secondary explanation was derived from this story (or gave rise to it, if the drawing from the water of the Nile was intended to foreshadow the Israelites' escape from Egypt through the Red Sea).

2:11 After Moses had grown up: cf. 7:7, where Moses is said to be eighty years old at the time of his mission to Pharaoh. **Striking**: probably in the sense of "flogging"; in v. 12, however, the same verb is used in the sense of "killing."

2:15 Land of Midian: the territory under the control of a confederation made up, according to Nm 31:8, of five Midianite tribes. According to Gn 25:1–2, Midian was a son of Abraham by Keturah. In view of the extreme hostility in later periods between Israel and Midian (cf. Nm 31; Jgs 6–8), the relationship is striking, as is the account here in Exodus of good relations between Moses and no less than a Midianite priest.

f: Ex 6:20; Nm 26:59. *g:* Acts 7:20; Heb 11:23. *h:* Acts 7:21; Heb 11:24. *i:* Acts 7:23–28. *j:* Acts 7:29; Heb 11:27.

their father Reuel,* he said to them, "How is
it you have returned so soon today?" 19 They
answered, "An Egyptian* delivered us from
the shepherds. He even drew water for us
and watered the flock!" 20 "Where is he?" he
asked his daughters. "Why did you leave the
man there? Invite him to have something to
eat." 21 Moses agreed to stay with him, and
the man gave Moses his daughter Zipporah
in marriage. 22 She conceived and bore a son,
whom he named Gershom;* for he said, "I
am a stranger residing in a foreign land."[k]

II. The Call and Commission of Moses

The Burning Bush. 23 A long time passed,
during which the king of Egypt died. The Israelites groaned under their bondage and
cried out, and from their bondage their cry
for help went up to God.[l] 24 God heard their
moaning and God was mindful of his
covenant[m] with Abraham, Isaac and Jacob.
25 God saw the Israelites, and God knew . . . .*

CHAPTER 3

See RG 118–19

1* Meanwhile Moses was tending the
flock of his father-in-law Jethro, the priest of
Midian. Leading the flock beyond the wilderness, he came to the mountain of God,
Horeb.* 2 There the angel of the LORD* appeared to him as fire flaming out of a bush.[n]
When he looked, although the bush was on
fire, it was not being consumed. 3 So Moses
decided, "I must turn aside to look at this remarkable sight. Why does the bush not burn
up?" 4 When the LORD saw that he had turned
aside to look, God called out to him from the
bush: Moses! Moses! He answered, "Here I
am." 5 God said: Do not come near! Remove
your sandals from your feet, for the place
where you stand is holy ground.[o] 6 I am the
God of your father,* he continued, the God
of Abraham, the God of Isaac, and the God

2:18 Reuel: also called Jethro. Cf. 3:1; 4:18; 18:1.

2:19 An Egyptian: Moses was probably wearing Egyptian dress, or spoke Egyptian to Reuel's daughters.

2:22 Gershom: the name is explained unscientifically as if it came from the Hebrew word *ger*, "sojourner, resident alien," and the Hebrew word *sham*, "there." **Stranger residing**: Hebrew *ger*, one who seeks and finds shelter and a home away from his or her own people or land.

2:25 God knew: in response to the people's cry, God, mindful of the covenant, looks on their plight and acknowledges firsthand the depth of their suffering (see 3:7). In vv. 23–25, traditionally attributed to the Priestly writer, God is mentioned five times, in contrast to the rest of chaps. 1–2, where God is rarely mentioned. These verses serve as a fitting transition to Moses' call in chap. 3.

3:1–4:17 After the introduction to the narrative in 2:23–25, the commissioning itself falls into three sections: God's appearance under the aspect of a burning bush (3:1–6); the explicit commission (3:7–10); and an extended dialogue between Moses and God, in the course of which Moses receives the revelation of God's personal name. Although in the J source of the Pentateuch people have known and invoked God's personal name in worship since the time of Seth (Gn 4:26), for the E and P sources (see 6:2–4) God first makes this name publicly available here through Moses.

3:1 The mountain of God, Horeb: traditionally, "Horeb" is taken to be an alternate name in E source material and Deuteronomy (e.g., Dt 1:2) for what in J and P is known as Mount Sinai, the goal of the Israelites' journey after leaving Egypt and the site of the covenant God makes with Israel. However, it is not clear that originally the two names reflect the same mountain, nor even that "Horeb" refers originally to a mountain and not simply the dry, ruined region (from Hebrew *horeb*, "dryness, devastation") around the mountain. Additionally, the position of "Horeb" at the end of the verse may indicate that the identification of the "mountain of God" with Horeb (= Sinai?) represents a later stage in the evolution of the tradition about God's meeting with Moses. The phrase "mountain of God" simply anticipates the divine apparitions which would take place there, both on this occasion and after the Israelites' departure from Egypt; alternatively, it means that the place was already sacred or a place of pilgrimage in pre-Israelite times. In any case, the narrative offers no indications of its exact location.

3:2 The angel of the LORD: Hebrew *mal'ak* or "messenger" is regularly translated *angelos* by the Septuagint, from which the English word "angel" is derived, but the Hebrew term lacks connotations now popularly associated with "angel" (such as wings). Although angels frequently assume human form (cf. Gn 18–19), the term is also used to indicate the visual form under which God occasionally appeared and spoke to people, referred to indifferently in some Old Testament texts either as God's "angel," *mal'ak*, or as God. Cf. Gn 16:7, 13; Ex 14:19, 24–25; Nm 22:22–35; Jgs 6:11–18. **The bush**: Hebrew *seneh*, perhaps "thorny bush," occurring only here in vv. 2–4 and in Dt 33:16. Its use here is most likely a wordplay on Sinai (Hebrew *sinay*), implying a popular etymology for the name of the sacred mountain.

3:6 God of your father: a frequently used epithet in Genesis (along with the variants "my father" and "your father") for God as worshiped by the ancestors. As is known from its usage outside of the Bible in the ancient Near East, it suggests a close, personal relationship between the individual and the particular god in question, who is both a patron and a protector, a god traditionally revered by the individual's family and

k: Ex 18:3. *l:* Ex 3:7, 9; Dt 26:7. *m:* Ex 6:5; Ps 105:8–9; 106:44–45. *n:* Acts 7:30–35. *o:* Jos 5:15.

of Jacob.[p] Moses hid his face, for he was
afraid to look at God.
The Call and Commission of Moses. [7]But
the LORD said: I have witnessed the affliction
of my people in Egypt and have heard their
cry against their taskmasters, so I know well
what they are suffering. [8]Therefore I have
come down* to rescue them from the power
of the Egyptians and lead them up from that
land into a good and spacious land, a land
flowing with milk and honey, the country of
the Canaanites, the Hittites, the Amorites, the
Perizzites, the Girgashites, the Hivites and
the Jebusites.[q] [9]Now indeed the outcry of the
Israelites has reached me, and I have seen
how the Egyptians are oppressing them.
[10]Now, go! I am sending you to Pharaoh to
bring my people, the Israelites, out of Egypt.
[11]But Moses said to God, "Who am I* that
I should go to Pharaoh and bring the Israelites
out of Egypt?" [12]God answered: I will be with
you; and this will be your sign* that I have
sent you. When you have brought the people
out of Egypt, you will serve God at this
mountain. [13]"But," said Moses to God, "if I
go to the Israelites and say to them, 'The God
of your ancestors has sent me to you,' and
they ask me, 'What is his name?' what do I
tell them?" [14]God replied to Moses: I am who
I am.* Then he added: This is what you will
tell the Israelites: I AM has sent me to you.
[15]God spoke further to Moses: This is
what you will say to the Israelites: The
LORD, the God of your ancestors, the God of
Abraham, the God of Isaac, and the God of
Jacob, has sent me to you.

whose worship is passed down from father to son. **The God of Abraham . . . Jacob**: this precise phrase (only here and in v. 15; 4:5) stresses the continuity between the new revelation to Moses and the earlier religious experience of Israel's ancestors, identifying the God who is now addressing Moses with the God who promised land and numerous posterity to the ancestors. Cf. Mt 22:32; Mk 12:26; Lk 20:37. **Afraid to look at God**: the traditions about Moses are not uniform in regard to his beholding or not being able to look at God (cf. 24:11; 33:11, 18–23; 34:29–35). Here Moses' reaction is the natural and spontaneous gesture of a person suddenly confronted with a direct experience of God. Aware of his human frailty and the gulf that separates him from the God who is holy, he hides his face. To encounter the divine was to come before an awesome and mysterious power unlike any other a human being might experience and, as such, potentially threatening to one's very identity or existence (see Gn 32:30).

3:8 I have come down: cf. Gn 11:5, 7; 18:21. **Flowing with milk and honey**: an expression denoting agricultural prosperity, which seems to have been proverbial in its application to the land of Canaan. Cf. Ex 13:5; Nm 13:27; Jos 5:6; Jer 11:5; 32:22; Ez 20:6, 15.

3:11 Who am I: this question is always addressed by an inferior to a superior (to the ruler in 1 Sm 18:18; to God in 2 Sm 7:18 and its parallel, 1 Chr 17:16; 1 Chr 29:14; 2 Chr 2:5). In response to some special opportunity or invitation, the question expresses in a style typical of the ancient Near East the speaker's humility or gratitude or need of further assistance, but never unwillingness or an outright refusal to respond. Instead the question sets the stage for further support from the superior should that be needed (as here).

3:12 Sign: a visible display of the power of God. The ancient notion of a sign from God does not coincide with the modern understanding of "miracle," which suggests some disruption in the laws governing nature. While most any phenomenon can become a vehicle for displaying the purposes and providence of God, here the sign intended to confirm Moses' commission by God seems to be the burning bush itself. Since normally the giving of such a sign would follow the commission rather than precede it (see Jgs 6:11–24), some see Israel's service of God at Sinai after the exodus from Egypt as the confirmatory sign, albeit retroactively. It is more likely, however, that its mention here is intended to establish the present episode with Moses alone as a prefigurement of God's fiery theophany to all Israel on Mount Sinai. **Serve God**: Hebrew *'-b-d*, "serve," includes among its meanings both the notion of "serving or working for another" and the notion of "worship." The implication here is that the Israelites' service/worship of God is incompatible with their service to Pharaoh.

3:14 I am who I am: Moses asks in v. 13 for the name of the One speaking to him, but God responds with a wordplay which preserves the utterly mysterious character of the divine being even as it appears to suggest something of the inner meaning of God's name: *'ehyeh* "I am" or "I will be(come)" for "*Yhwh*," the personal name of the God of Israel. While the phrase "I am who I am" resists unraveling, it nevertheless suggests an etymological linking between the name "Yhwh" and an earlier form of the Hebrew verbal root *h-y-h* "to be." On that basis many have interpreted the name "Yhwh" as a third-person form of the verb meaning "He causes to be, creates," itself perhaps a shortened form of a longer liturgical name such as "(God who) creates (the heavenly armies)." Note in this connection the invocation of Israel's God as "LORD (*Yhwh*) of Hosts" (e.g., 1 Sm 17:45). In any case, out of reverence for God's proper name, the term *Adonai*, "my Lord," was later used as a substitute. The word LORD (in small capital letters) indicates that the Hebrew text has the sacred name (*Yhwh*), the tetragrammaton. The word "Jehovah" arose from a false reading of this name as it is written in the current Hebrew text. The Septuagint has *egō eimi ho ōn*, "I am the One who is" (ōn being the participle of the verb "to be"). This can be taken as an assertion of God's aseity or self-existence, and has been understood as such by the Church, since the time of the Fathers, as a true expression of God's being, even though it is not precisely the meaning of the Hebrew.

p: Ex 4:5; Mt 22:32; Mk 12:26; Lk 20:37. *q:* Gn 15:19–21.

This is my name forever;[r]
this is my title for all generations.

16 Go and gather the elders of the Israelites, and tell them, The LORD, the God of your ancestors, the God of Abraham, Isaac, and Jacob, has appeared to me and said: I have observed you and what is being done to you in Egypt; 17 so I have decided to lead you up out of your affliction in Egypt into the land of the Canaanites, the Hittites, the Amorites, the Perizzites, the Girgashites, the Hivites and the Jebusites, a land flowing with milk and honey. 18 They will listen to you. Then you and the elders of Israel will go to the king of Egypt and say to him:[s] The LORD, the God of the Hebrews, has come to meet us. So now, let us go a three days' journey in the wilderness to offer sacrifice to the LORD, our God. 19 Yet I know that the king of Egypt will not allow you to go unless his hand is forced. 20 So I will stretch out my hand and strike Egypt with all the wondrous deeds I will do in its midst. After that he will let you go. 21[t] I will even make the Egyptians so well-disposed toward this people that, when you go, you will not go empty-handed. 22 Every woman will ask her neighbor and the resident alien in her house for silver and gold articles* and for clothing, and you will put them on your sons and daughters. So you will plunder the Egyptians.

CHAPTER 4

See RG 118–19

1 "But," objected Moses, "suppose they do not believe me or listen to me? For they may say, 'The LORD did not appear to you.'" 2 The LORD said to him: What is in your hand? "A staff," he answered. 3 God said: Throw it on the ground. So he threw it on the ground and it became a snake,[u] and Moses backed away from it. 4 Then the LORD said to Moses: Now stretch out your hand and take hold of its tail. So he stretched out his hand and took hold of it, and it became a staff in his hand. 5 That is so they will believe that the LORD, the God of their ancestors, the God of Abraham, the God of Isaac, and the God of Jacob, did appear to you.

6 Again the LORD said to him: Put your hand into the fold of your garment. So he put his hand into the fold of his garment, and when he drew it out, there was his hand covered with scales, like snowflakes. 7 Then God said: Put your hand back into the fold of your garment. So he put his hand back into the fold of his garment, and when he drew it out, there it was again like his own flesh. 8 If they do not believe you or pay attention to the message of the first sign, they should believe the message of the second sign. 9 And if they do not believe even these two signs and do not listen to you, take some water from the Nile and pour it on the dry land. The water you take from the Nile will become blood on the dry land.[v]

Aaron's Office as Assistant. 10 Moses, however, said to the LORD, "If you please, my Lord, I have never been eloquent, neither in the past nor now that you have spoken to your servant; but I am slow of speech and tongue."[w] 11 The LORD said to him: Who gives one person speech? Who makes another mute or deaf, seeing or blind? Is it not I, the LORD? 12 Now go, I will assist you in speaking* and teach you what you are to say. 13 But he said, "If you please, my Lord, send someone else!"* 14 Then the LORD became angry with Moses and said: I know there is your brother, Aaron the Levite, who is a good speaker; even now he is on his way to meet you. When he sees you, he will truly be glad. 15 You will speak to him and put the words in his mouth. I will assist both you and him in speaking and teach you both what you are to do. 16 He will speak to the people for you: he will be your spokesman,* and you will be as God to him.[x] 17 Take this staff* in your hand; with it you are to perform the signs.

3:22 Articles: probably jewelry.

4:12 Assist you in speaking: lit., "be with your mouth"; cf. v. 15, lit., "be with your mouth and with his mouth."

4:13 Send someone else: lit., "send by means of him whom you will send," that is, "send whom you will."

4:16 Spokesman: lit., "mouth"; Aaron was to serve as a mouthpiece for Moses, as a prophet does for God; hence the relation between Moses and Aaron is compared to that between God and his prophet: Moses "will be as God to," i.e., lit., "will become God for him." Cf. 7:1.

4:17 This staff: probably the same as that of vv. 2–4; but some understand that a new staff is now given by God to Moses.

r: Ps 135:13. *s:* Ex 5:3. *t:* Ex 11:2–3; 12:35–36. *u:* Ex 7:10. *v:* Ex 7:17, 19–20. *w:* Ex 6:12. *x:* Ex 7:1.

Moses' Return to Egypt. 18 After this Moses returned to Jethro* his father-in-law and
said to him, "Let me return to my kindred in
Egypt, to see whether they are still living."
Jethro replied to Moses, "Go in peace."
19 Then the LORD said to Moses in Midian:
Return to Egypt, for all those who sought
your life are dead. 20 So Moses took his wife
and his sons, mounted them on the donkey,
and started back to the land of Egypt. Moses
took the staff of God with him. 21 The LORD
said to Moses: On your return to Egypt, see
that you perform before Pharaoh all the
wonders I have put in your power. But I will
harden his heart* and he will not let the people go. 22[y] So you will say to Pharaoh, Thus
says the LORD: Israel is my son, my firstborn. 23 I said to you: Let my son go, that he
may serve me. Since you refused to let him
go, I will kill your son, your firstborn.[z]
24* On the journey, at a place where they
spent the night, the LORD came upon Moses
and sought to put him to death. 25[a] But Zipporah took a piece of flint and cut off her
son's foreskin and, touching his feet,* she
said, "Surely you are a spouse of blood to
me." 26 So God let Moses alone. At that time
she said, "A spouse of blood," in regard to
the circumcision.
27 The LORD said to Aaron: Go into the wilderness to meet Moses. So he went; when
meeting him at the mountain of God, he kissed
him. 28 Moses told Aaron everything the LORD
had sent him to say, and all the signs he had
commanded him to do. 29 Then Moses and
Aaron went and gathered all the elders of the
Israelites. 30 Aaron told them everything the
LORD had said to Moses, and he performed the
signs before the people. 31 The people believed, and when they heard that the LORD had
observed the Israelites and had seen their affliction,* they knelt and bowed down.

CHAPTER 5

See RG 119–20

Pharaoh's Hardness of Heart. 1 Afterwards, Moses and Aaron went to Pharaoh
and said, "Thus says the LORD, the God of Israel: Let my people go, that they may hold a
feast* for me in the wilderness." 2 Pharaoh answered, "Who is the LORD, that I should obey
him and let Israel go? I do not know the
LORD,* and I will not let Israel go." 3 They

4:18 Jethro: the Hebrew text has "Jether," apparently a variant form of "Jethro" found in the same verse. **To see whether they are still living**: Moses did not tell his father-in-law his main reason for returning to Egypt.

4:21 Harden his heart: in the biblical view, the heart, whose actual function in the circulation of blood was unknown, typically performs functions associated today more with the brain than with the emotions. Therefore, while it may be used in connection with various emotional states ranging from joy to sadness, it very commonly designates the seat of intellectual and volitional activities. For God to harden Pharaoh's heart is to harden his resolve against the Israelites' desire to leave. In the ancient world, actions which are out of character are routinely attributed not to the person but to some "outside" superhuman power acting upon the person (Jgs 14:16; 1 Sm 16:10). Uncharacteristically negative actions or states are explained in the same way (1 Sm 16:14). In this instance, the opposition of Pharaoh, in the face of God's displays of power, would be unintelligible to the ancient Israelites unless he is seen as under some divine constraint. But this does not diminish Pharaoh's own responsibility. In the anthropology of the ancient Israelites there is no opposition between individual responsibility and God's sovereignty over all of creation. Cf. Rom 9:17–18.

4:24–26 This story continues to perplex commentators and may have circulated in various forms before finding its place here in Exodus. Particularly troublesome is the unique phrase "spouse of blood." Nevertheless, v. 26, which apparently comes from the hand of a later commentator on the original story, is intended to offer some clarification. It asserts that when Zipporah used the problematic expression (addressing it either to Moses or her son), she did so with reference to the circumcision performed on her son—the only place in the Bible where this rite is performed by a woman. Whatever the precise meaning of the phrase "spouse of blood," circumcision is the key to understanding it as well as the entire incident. One may conclude, therefore, that God was angry with Moses for having failed to keep the divine command given to Abraham in Gn 17:10–12 and circumcise his son. Moses' life is spared when his wife circumcises their son.

4:25 Touching his feet: a euphemism most probably for the male sexual organ (see 2 Kgs 18:27; Is 7:20); whether the genitals of the child (after Zipporah circumcised him) or of Moses (after the circumcision of his son) is not clear.

4:31 Observed . . . their affliction: the same phrases used in God's dialogue with Moses in 3:16–17.

5:1 Hold a feast: the Hebrew verb used here, *hagag* ("to celebrate a feast or a festival"; see 12:14; 23:14), refers to a community celebration marked above all by a procession to the sanctuary. It is used especially of three major feasts: Unleavened Bread, Pentecost (in 23:16, "the Feast of Harvest," but customarily "the Feast of Weeks" [*Shavuot*]), and Succoth/Sukkoth (in 34:16, "the Feast of Ingathering," but more frequently "of Booths, or Tabernacles," as in Dt 16:13, 16; 31:10; Lv 23:34; Zec 14:16; passim) and—along with the related noun *hag*—the Passover in 12:14. See 23:14–18; 34:18–25.

5:2 I do not know the LORD: whether or not he had heard of the Lord, the God of Israel, Pharaoh here refuses to acknowledge the Lord's authority. See note on 1:8.

y: Sir 36:11. *z:* Ex 11:5; 12:29. *a:* Is 6:2; 7:20.

replied, "The God of the Hebrews has come to meet us. Let us go a three days' journey in the wilderness, that we may offer sacrifice to the LORD, our God,[b] so that he does not strike us with the plague or the sword." 4The king of Egypt answered them, "Why, Moses and Aaron, do you make the people neglect their work? Off to your labors!" 5Pharaoh continued, "Look how they are already more numerous* than the people of the land, and yet you would give them rest from their labors!"

6That very day Pharaoh gave the taskmasters of the people and their foremen* this order: 7"You shall no longer supply the people with straw for their brickmaking* as before. Let them go and gather their own straw! 8Yet you shall levy upon them the same quota of bricks as they made previously. Do not reduce it. They are lazy; that is why they are crying, 'Let us go to offer sacrifice to our God.' 9Increase the work for the men, so that they attend to it and not to deceitful words."

10So the taskmasters of the people and their foremen went out and told the people, "Thus says Pharaoh,* 'I will not provide you with straw. 11Go and get your own straw from wherever you can find it. But there will not be the slightest reduction in your work.' " 12The people, then, scattered throughout the land of Egypt to gather stubble for straw, 13while the taskmasters kept driving them on, saying, "Finish your work, the same daily amount as when the straw was supplied to you." 14The Israelite foremen, whom the taskmasters of Pharaoh had placed over them, were beaten, and were asked, "Why have you not completed your prescribed amount of bricks yesterday and today, as before?"

Complaint of the Foremen. 15Then the Israelite foremen came and cried out to Pharaoh:* "Why do you treat your servants in this manner? 16No straw is supplied to your servants, and still we are told, 'Make bricks!' Look how your servants are beaten! It is you who are at fault." 17He answered, "Lazy! You are lazy! That is why you keep saying, 'Let us go and offer sacrifice to the LORD.' 18Now off to work! No straw will be supplied to you, but you must supply your quota of bricks."

19The Israelite foremen realized they were in trouble, having been told, "Do not reduce your daily amount of bricks!" 20So when they left Pharaoh they assailed Moses and Aaron, who were waiting to meet them, 21and said to them, "The LORD look upon you and judge! You have made us offensive to Pharaoh and his servants, putting a sword into their hands to kill us."

Renewal of God's Promise. 22Then Moses again had recourse to the LORD and said, "LORD, why have you treated this people badly? And why did you send me? 23From the time I went to Pharaoh to speak in your name, he has treated this people badly, and you have done nothing to rescue your people."

CHAPTER 6

See RG 119–20

1The LORD answered Moses: Now you will see what I will do to Pharaoh. For by a strong hand, he will let them go; by a strong hand,* he will drive them from his land.

Confirmation of the Promise to the Ancestors. 2* Then God spoke to Moses, and said to him: I am the LORD. 3As God the Almighty* I appeared[c] to Abraham, Isaac, and Jacob, but

5:5 They are already more numerous: a recollection of Pharaoh's earlier words to his subjects in 1:9.

5:6 The taskmasters of the people and their foremen: the former were higher officials and probably Egyptians; the latter were lower officials (perhaps recordkeepers or clerks), chosen from the Israelites themselves. Cf. v. 14.

5:7 Straw was mixed with clay to give sun-dried bricks greater cohesion and durability.

5:10 Thus says Pharaoh: the standard formula for prophetic oracles, but with Pharaoh rather than the Lord as the subject. This heightens the sense of personal conflict between Pharaoh, who acts as if he were God, and the Lord, whose claims are spurned by Pharaoh.

5:15 Cried out to Pharaoh: the Hebrew verb translated "cry out" and its related noun are normally used of appeals to God by Moses (8:8; 14:15; 15:25; 17:4), the people (3:7, 9; 14:10), or an oppressed individual (22:22, 26). Here, by implication, these minor Israelite officials appeal to Pharaoh as if he were their God. See v. 10.

6:1 By a strong hand: by God's hand or Pharaoh's hand? The Hebrew is ambiguous; although it may be an allusion to God's hand of 3:19–20, both interpretations are possible.

6:2–7:7 According to the standard source criticism of the Pentateuch, 6:2–7:7 represents a Priestly version of the JE call narrative in 3:1–4:17. But in context the present account does more than simply repeat the earlier passage. See note below.

6:3 God the Almighty: in Hebrew, *El Shaddai*. This traditional translation does not have a firm philological basis. **But**

b: Ex 3:18. *c:* Gn 17:1; 35:11.

by my name, LORD, I did not make myself known to them. [4]I also established my covenant with them, to give them the land of Canaan, the land in which they were residing as aliens.[d] [5]Now that I have heard the groaning of the Israelites, whom the Egyptians have reduced to slavery, I am mindful of my covenant.[e] [6]Therefore, say to the Israelites: I am the LORD. I will free you from the burdens of the Egyptians and will deliver you from their slavery. I will redeem you by my outstretched arm and with mighty acts of judgment. [7]I will take you as my own people, and I will be your God;[f] and you will know that I, the LORD, am your God who has freed you from the burdens of the Egyptians [8]and I will bring you into the land which I swore to give to Abraham, Isaac, and Jacob. I will give it to you as your own possession—I, the LORD! [9]But when Moses told this to the Israelites, they would not listen to him because of their dejection and hard slavery.

[10]Then the LORD spoke to Moses: [11]Go, tell Pharaoh, king of Egypt, to let the Israelites leave his land. [12]However, Moses protested to the LORD, "If the Israelites did not listen to me, how is it possible that Pharaoh will listen to me, poor speaker* [g] that I am!" [13]But the LORD spoke to Moses and Aaron regarding the Israelites and Pharaoh, king of Egypt, and charged them to bring the Israelites out of the land of Egypt.

Genealogy of Moses and Aaron. [14]These are the heads of their ancestral houses.* The sons of Reuben,[h] the firstborn of Israel: Hanoch, Pallu, Hezron and Carmi; these are the clans of Reuben. [15]The sons of Simeon:[i] Jemuel, Jamin, Ohad, Jachin, Zohar and Shaul, the son of a Canaanite woman; these are the clans of Simeon. [16]These are the names of the sons of Levi,[j] in their genealogical order: Gershon, Kohath and Merari. Levi lived one hundred and thirty-seven years.

[17]The sons of Gershon,[k] by their clans: Libni and Shimei. [18]The sons of Kohath:[l] Amram, Izhar, Hebron and Uzziel. Kohath lived one hundred and thirty-three years. [19]The sons of Merari:[m] Mahli and Mushi. These are the clans of Levi in their genealogical order.

[20]Amram married his aunt* Jochebed,[n] who bore him Aaron, Moses, and Miriam. Amram lived one hundred and thirty-seven years. [21]The sons of Izhar: Korah, Nepheg and Zichri. [22]The sons of Uzziel: Mishael, Elzaphan and Sithri. [23]Aaron married Elisheba, Amminadab's[o] daughter, the sister of Nahshon; she bore him Nadab, Abihu, Eleazar and Ithamar. [24]The sons of Korah: Assir, Elkanah and Abiasaph. These are the clans of the Korahites. [25]Eleazar, Aaron's son, married one of Putiel's daughters, who bore him Phinehas.* These are the heads of the ancestral houses of the Levites by their clans. [26]These are the Aaron and the Moses to whom the LORD said, "Bring the Israelites out from the land of Egypt, company by company." [27]They are the ones who spoke to Pharaoh, king of Egypt, to bring the Israelites out of Egypt—the same Moses and Aaron.

[28]When the LORD spoke to Moses in the land of Egypt [29]the LORD said to Moses: I am the LORD. Say to Pharaoh, king of Egypt, all that I tell you. [30]But Moses protested to the LORD, "Since I am a poor speaker, how is it possible that Pharaoh will listen to me?"

by my name . . . I did not make myself known to them: although the text implies that the name LORD was unknown previously, in context the emphasis in the passage falls on the understanding of God that comes with knowledge of the name. In this way God responds to the worsening plight of the Israelites and Moses' complaint in 5:23 that God has done nothing at all to rescue them.

6:12 Poor speaker: lit., "uncircumcised of lips": a metaphor expressing the hindrance of good communication expressed as "slow of speech and tongue" (4:10). Also used as a metaphor for impeded "heart" (Lv 26:41; Dt 10:16).

6:14 The purpose of the genealogy here is to give the line from which Moses and Aaron sprang, with special emphasis placed on the line of Aaron. Reuben and Simeon are mentioned first because, as older brothers of Levi, their names occur before his in the genealogy.

6:20 His aunt: more exactly, "his father's sister." Later on such a marriage was forbidden. Cf. Lv 18:12. Hence, the Greek and Latin versions render here, "his cousin."

6:25 Phinehas: according to Nm 25:13, Phinehas was given by God "the covenant of an everlasting priesthood" because of his zeal for God when the Israelites committed apostasy by worshiping the Baal of Peor in the plains of Moab (see Nm 25:1–18).

d: Gn 15:18; 17:4–8. *e:* Ex 2:24. *f:* Lv 26:12. *g:* Ex 4:10. *h:* Nm 26:5–6; 1 Chr 5:3. *i:* Nm 26:12; 1 Chr 4:24. *j:* Nm 3:17; 1 Chr 6:1; 23:6. *k:* Nm 3:21; 1 Chr 6:2; 23:7. *l:* Nm 3:27; 1 Chr 6:3, 18. *m:* Nm 3:20; 1 Chr 6:4, 14; 23:21. *n:* Nm 26:59. *o:* Ru 4:19–20; 1 Chr 2:10.

CHAPTER 7

See RG 119–20

1The LORD answered Moses: See! I have made you a god to Pharaoh,[p] and Aaron your brother will be your prophet.* 2You will speak all that I command you. In turn, your brother Aaron will tell Pharaoh to let the Israelites go out of his land. 3Yet I will make Pharaoh so headstrong that, despite the many signs and wonders that I work in the land of Egypt, 4Pharaoh will not listen to you. Therefore I will lay my hand on Egypt and with mighty acts of judgment I will bring my armies, my people the Israelites, out of the land of Egypt. 5All Egyptians will know that I am the LORD, when I stretch out my hand against Egypt and bring the Israelites out of their midst.

6This, then, is what Moses and Aaron did. They did exactly as the LORD had commanded them. 7Moses was eighty years old, and Aaron eighty-three, when they spoke to Pharaoh.

III. The Contest with Pharaoh

The Staff Turned into a Serpent. 8The LORD spoke to Moses and Aaron: 9When Pharaoh demands of you, "Produce a sign or wonder," you will say to Aaron: "Take your staff and throw it down before Pharaoh, and it will turn into a serpent."[q] 10Then Moses and Aaron went to Pharaoh and did just as the LORD had commanded. Aaron threw his staff down before Pharaoh and his servants, and it turned into a serpent. 11Pharaoh, in turn, summoned the wise men and the sorcerers, and they also, the magicians[r] of Egypt, did the same thing by their magic arts. 12Each one threw down his staff, and they turned into serpents. But Aaron's staff swallowed their staffs. 13Pharaoh, however, hardened his heart and would not listen to them, just as the LORD had foretold.

First Plague: Water Turned into Blood.* 14Then the LORD said to Moses: Pharaoh is obstinate* in refusing to let the people go. 15In the morning, just when he sets out for the water, go to Pharaoh and present yourself by the bank of the Nile, holding in your hand the staff that turned into a snake.* 16Say to him: The LORD, the God of the Hebrews, sent me to you with the message: Let my people go to serve me in the wilderness. But as yet you have not listened. 17Thus says the LORD: This is how you will know that I am the LORD. With the staff here in my hand, I will strike the water in the Nile and it will be changed into blood.[s] 18The fish in the Nile will die, and the Nile itself will stink so that the Egyptians will be unable to drink water from the Nile.

19The LORD then spoke to Moses: Speak to Aaron: Take your staff and stretch out your hand over the waters of Egypt—its streams, its canals, its ponds, and all its supplies of water—that they may become blood. There will be blood throughout the land of Egypt, even in the wooden pails and stone jars.

20This, then, is what Moses and Aaron did, exactly as the LORD had commanded. Aaron raised his staff and struck the waters in the Nile in full view of Pharaoh and his servants, and all the water in the Nile was changed into blood. 21The fish in the Nile died, and the Nile itself stank so that the Egyptians could not drink water from it. There was blood throughout the land of Egypt. 22But the

7:1 Prophet: Hebrew *nabi*, one who can legitimately speak for God and in God's name to another or others. Just as God spoke to Moses, so Moses will speak to Aaron, who will be a "prophet" to Pharaoh. Cf. 4:16.

7:14–12:30 After a brief preface (vv. 8–13) drawn from the Priestly source, a narrative depicting the series of ten disasters that God brings upon Pharaoh because of his stubbornness ensues. Although most of these disasters, known traditionally as the "ten plagues of Egypt," could be interpreted as naturally occurring phenomena, they are clearly represented by the biblical authors as extraordinary events indicative of God's intervention on behalf of Israel and as occurring exactly according to Moses' commands. See Ps 78:43–51 and 105:27–36 for poetic versions of these plagues, which also differ significantly from the account here.

7:14 Pharaoh is obstinate: lit., "Pharaoh's heart is heavy" (*kabed*); thus not precisely the same Hebrew idiom as found in vv. 13 and 22, "stubborn," lit., "Pharaoh's heart was hard(ened)" (*hazaq*) (cf. the related idiom with Pharaoh as the object, e.g., 4:21).

7:15 The staff that turned into a snake: the allusion is to 4:2–4 rather than 7:9–12. The latter comes from the hand of the Priestly writer and features Aaron—with his staff—as the principal actor.

p: Ex 4:15–16. *q:* Ex 4:3. *r:* 2 Tm 3:8. *s:* Ex 4:9; Ps 78:44; 105:29; Wis 11:5–7.

Egyptian magicians did the same* by their
magic arts. So Pharaoh hardened his heart
and would not listen to them, just as the LORD
had said. 23Pharaoh turned away and went
into his house, with no concern even for this.
24All the Egyptians had to dig round about
the Nile for drinking water, since they could
not drink any water from the Nile.

Second Plague: the Frogs. 25Seven days
passed after the LORD had struck the Nile.
26Then the LORD said to Moses: Go to Pharaoh and tell him:[t] Thus says the LORD: Let
my people go to serve me. 27If you refuse to
let them go, then I will send a plague of frogs
over all your territory. 28The Nile will teem
with frogs. They will come up and enter into
your palace and into your bedroom and onto
your bed, into the houses of your servants,
too, and among your people, even into your
ovens and your kneading bowls. 29The frogs
will come up over you and your people and
all your servants.

CHAPTER 8

See RG 119–20

1The LORD then spoke to Moses:
Speak to Aaron: Stretch out your hand with
your staff over the streams, the canals, and
the ponds, and make frogs overrun the land
of Egypt. 2So Aaron stretched out his hand
over the waters of Egypt, and the frogs came
up and covered the land of Egypt. 3But the
magicians did the same by their magic arts
and made frogs overrun the land of Egypt.

4Then Pharaoh summoned Moses and
Aaron and said, "Pray to the LORD to remove
the frogs from me and my people, and I will
let the people go to sacrifice to the LORD."
5Moses answered Pharaoh, "Please designate for me the time when I am to pray for
you and your servants and your people, to
get rid of the frogs from you and your
houses. They will be left only in the Nile."
6"Tomorrow," he said. Then Moses replied,
"It will be as you have said, so that you may
know that there is none like the LORD, our
God. 7The frogs will leave you and your
houses, your servants and your people; they
will be left only in the Nile."

8After Moses and Aaron left Pharaoh's
presence, Moses cried out to the LORD on account of the frogs that he had inflicted on
Pharaoh; 9and the LORD did as Moses had
asked. The frogs died off in the houses, the
courtyards, and the fields. 10Heaps of them
were piled up, and the land stank. 11But
when Pharaoh saw there was a respite, he
became obstinate and would not listen to
them, just as the LORD had said.

Third Plague: the Gnats. 12Thereupon the
LORD spoke to Moses: Speak to Aaron:
Stretch out your staff and strike the dust of
the earth, and it will turn into gnats*[u]
throughout the land of Egypt. 13They did so.
Aaron stretched out his hand with his staff
and struck the dust of the earth, and gnats
came upon human being and beast alike. All
the dust of the earth turned into gnats
throughout the land of Egypt. 14Though the
magicians did the same thing to produce
gnats by their magic arts, they could not do
so.[v] The gnats were on human being and
beast alike, 15and the magicians said to Pharaoh, "This is the finger of God."* Yet Pharaoh hardened his heart and would not listen
to them, just as the LORD had said.

Fourth Plague: the Flies. 16Then the LORD
spoke to Moses: Early tomorrow morning
present yourself to Pharaoh when he sets out
toward the water, and say to him: Thus says
the LORD: Let my people go to serve me.

7:22 The Egyptian magicians did the same: this is an exaggeration, presumably influenced by the similar statement in v. 11; whereas the magicians could turn their staffs into snakes after Aaron had done so, after Aaron's sign there should not have been any water in Egypt still unchanged to blood for the magicians "to do the same" with it (cf. v. 24).

8:12, 17 Gnats, flies: it is uncertain what species of troublesome insects are meant here in vv. 12–14 and then in vv. 17–27, the identification as "gnat" (vv. 12–14) and as "fly" (vv. 17–27) being based on the rendering of the Septuagint. Others suggest "lice" in vv. 12–14, while rabbinic literature renders Hebrew *'arob* in vv. 17–27 as a "mixture of wild animals." In the Hebrew of the Old Testament, the word occurs only in the context of the plagues (see also Ps 78:45 and 105:31).

8:15 The finger of God: previously the magicians had, for the most part, been able to replicate the signs and wonders Moses performed to manifest God's power—turning their staffs into snakes (7:11–12), turning water into blood (7:22), and producing frogs to overrun the land of Egypt (8:3). But now for the first time they are unable to compete, and confess a power greater than their own is at work. Cf. Lk 11:20.

t: Ps 78:45; 105:30. *u:* Ps 105:31. *v:* Wis 17:7.

17For if you do not let my people go, I will send swarms of flies upon you and your servants and your people and your houses. The houses of the Egyptians and the very ground on which they stand will be filled with swarms of flies. 18But on that day I will make an exception of the land of Goshen, where my people are, and no swarms of flies will be there, so that you may know that I the LORD am in the midst of the land. 19I will make a distinction* between my people and your people. This sign will take place tomorrow. 20This the LORD did. Thick swarms of flies entered the house of Pharaoh and the houses of his servants; throughout Egypt the land was devastated on account of the swarms of flies.[w]

21Then Pharaoh summoned Moses and Aaron and said, "Go sacrifice to your God within the land." 22But Moses replied, "It is not right to do so, for what we sacrifice to the LORD, our God, is abhorrent to the Egyptians.* If we sacrifice what is abhorrent to the Egyptians before their very eyes, will they not stone us? 23We must go a three days' journey in the wilderness and sacrifice to the LORD, our God, as he commands us." 24Pharaoh said, "I will let you go to sacrifice to the LORD, your God, in the wilderness, provided that you do not go too far away. Pray for me." 25Moses answered, "As soon as I leave you I will pray to the LORD that the swarms of flies may depart tomorrow from Pharaoh, his servants, and his people. Pharaoh, however, must not act deceitfully again and refuse to let the people go to sacrifice to the LORD." 26When Moses left Pharaoh, he prayed to the LORD; 27and the LORD did as Moses had asked, removing the swarms of flies from Pharaoh, his servants, and his people. Not one remained. 28But once more Pharaoh became obstinate and would not let the people go.

CHAPTER 9

See RG 119–20

Fifth Plague: the Pestilence. 1Then the LORD said to Moses: Go to Pharaoh and tell him: Thus says the LORD, the God of the Hebrews: Let my people go to serve me. 2For if you refuse to let them go and persist in holding them, 3the hand of the LORD will strike your livestock in the field—your horses, donkeys, camels, herds and flocks—with a very severe pestilence. 4But the LORD will distinguish between the livestock of Israel and that of Egypt, so that nothing belonging to the Israelites will die. 5And the LORD set a definite time, saying: Tomorrow the LORD will do this in the land. 6And on the next day the LORD did it. All the livestock of the Egyptians died,[x] but not one animal belonging to the Israelites died. 7But although Pharaoh found upon inquiry that not even so much as one of the livestock of the Israelites had died, he remained obstinate and would not let the people go.

Sixth Plague: the Boils. 8So the LORD said to Moses and Aaron: Each of you take handfuls of soot from a kiln, and in the presence of Pharaoh let Moses scatter it toward the sky. 9It will turn into fine dust over the whole land of Egypt and cause festering boils* on human being and beast alike throughout the land of Egypt.

10So they took the soot from a kiln and appeared before Pharaoh. When Moses scattered it toward the sky, it caused festering boils on human being and beast alike. 11Because of the boils the magicians could not stand in Moses' presence, for there were boils on the magicians as well as on the rest of the Egyptians. 12But the LORD hardened

8:19 A distinction: while some uncertainty surrounds the Hebrew here rendered as "distinction," it is clear that now the Israelites begin to be set apart from the Egyptians, a separation that reaches a climax in the death of the Egyptian firstborn (11:7).

8:22 Perhaps Moses is deceiving the Pharaoh much like the "God-fearing" midwives (1:16–20), although ancient historians writing about Egypt some time after the period in which the exodus is set do note Egyptian prohibitions on sacrificing cattle or slaughtering sacred animals. As such, the Egyptians might well have fiercely resented certain sacrificial practices of the Israelites. Certain animals were held sacred in Egypt, as the representations of various deities.

9:9 Boils: the exact nature of the disease is not clear. Semitic cognates, for example, suggest the Hebrew root means "to be hot" and thus point to some sort of inflammation. The fact that soot taken from the kiln is the agent of the disease would point in the same direction. See further Lv 13:18–23; Dt 28:35; 2 Kgs 20:7.

w: Ps 78:45; 105:31; Wis 16:9. *x:* Ps 78:48.

Pharaoh's heart, and he would not listen to them, just as the LORD had said to Moses.

Seventh Plague: the Hail. [13]Then the LORD spoke to Moses: Early tomorrow morning present yourself to Pharaoh and say to him: Thus says the LORD, the God of the Hebrews: Let my people go to serve me, [14]for this time I will unleash all my blows upon you and your servants and your people, so that you may know that there is none like me anywhere on earth. [15]For by now I should have stretched out my hand and struck you and your people with such pestilence that you would have vanished from the earth. [16]But this is why I have let you survive: to show you* my power and to make my name resound throughout the earth![y] [17]Will you continue to exalt yourself over my people and not let them go? [18]At this time tomorrow, therefore, I am going to rain down such fierce hail as there has never been in Egypt from the day it was founded up to the present. [19]Therefore, order your livestock and whatever else you have in the open fields to be brought to a place of safety. Whatever human being or animal is found in the fields and is not brought to shelter will die when the hail comes down upon them. [20]Those of Pharaoh's servants who feared the word of the LORD hurried their servants and their livestock off to shelter. [21]But those who did not pay attention to the word of the LORD left their servants and their livestock in the fields.

[22]The LORD then said to Moses: Stretch out your hand toward the sky, that hail may fall upon the entire land of Egypt, on human being and beast alike and all the vegetation of the fields in the land of Egypt. [23]So Moses stretched out his staff toward the sky, and the LORD sent forth peals of thunder and hail.[z] Lightning flashed toward the earth, and the LORD rained down hail upon the land of Egypt. [24]There was hail and lightning flashing here and there through the hail, and the hail was so fierce that nothing like it had been seen in Egypt since it became a nation. [25]Throughout the land of Egypt the hail struck down everything in the fields, human being and beast alike; it struck down all the vegetation of the fields and splintered every tree in the fields. [26]Only in the land of Goshen, where the Israelites were, was there no hail.

[27]Then Pharaoh sent for Moses and Aaron and said to them, "I have sinned this time! The LORD is the just one, and I and my people are the ones at fault. [28]Pray to the LORD! Enough of the thunder* and hail! I will let you go; you need stay no longer." [29]Moses replied to him, "As soon as I leave the city I will extend my hands to the LORD; the thunder will cease, and there will be no more hail so that you may know that the earth belongs to the LORD. [30]But as for you and your servants, I know that you do not yet fear the LORD God."

[31]Now the flax and the barley were ruined, because the barley was in ear and the flax in bud. [32]But the wheat and the spelt were not ruined, for they grow later.

[33]When Moses had left Pharaoh and gone out of the city, he extended his hands to the LORD. The thunder and the hail ceased, and the rain no longer poured down upon the earth. [34]But Pharaoh, seeing that the rain and the hail and the thunder had ceased, sinned again and became obstinate, both he and his servants. [35]In the hardness of his heart, Pharaoh would not let the Israelites go, just as the LORD had said through Moses.

CHAPTER 10

See RG 119–20

Eighth Plague: the Locusts. [1]Then the LORD said to Moses: Go to Pharaoh, for I have made him and his servants obstinate in order that I may perform these signs of mine among them [2]and that you may recount to your son and grandson how I made a fool of the Egyptians and what signs I did among them, so that you may know that I am the LORD.[a]

[3]So Moses and Aaron went to Pharaoh and told him, "Thus says the LORD, the God of the Hebrews: How long will you refuse to submit to me? Let my people go to serve me.

9:16 To show you: some ancient versions such as the Septuagint read, "to show through you." Cf. Rom 9:17.

9:28 Thunder: lit., "divine voices," "voices of God," or the like.

y: Rom 9:17. *z:* Ps 78:47; 105:32–33. *a:* Dt 6:20–25.

[4]For if you refuse to let my people go, tomorrow I will bring locusts into your territory. [5]They will cover the surface of the earth, so that the earth itself will not be visible. They will eat up the remnant you saved undamaged from the hail, as well as all the trees that are growing in your fields. [6]They will fill your houses and the houses of your servants and of all the Egyptians—something your parents and your grandparents have not seen from the day they appeared on this soil until today." With that he turned and left Pharaoh.

[7]But Pharaoh's servants said to him, "How long will he be a snare for us? Let the people go to serve the LORD, their God. Do you not yet realize that Egypt is being destroyed?" [8]So Moses and Aaron were brought back to Pharaoh, who said to them, "Go, serve the LORD, your God. But who exactly will go?" [9]Moses answered, "With our young and old we must go; with our sons and daughters, with our flocks and herds we must go. It is a pilgrimage feast of the LORD for us." [10]"The LORD help you,"* Pharaoh replied, "if I let your little ones go with you! Clearly, you have some evil in mind. [11]By no means! Just you men go and serve the LORD.* After all, that is what you have been asking for." With that they were driven from Pharaoh's presence.

[12][b] The LORD then said to Moses: Stretch out your hand over the land of Egypt for the locusts, that they may come upon it and eat up all the land's vegetation, whatever the hail has left. [13]So Moses stretched out his staff over the land of Egypt, and the LORD drove an east wind* over the land all that day and all night. When it was morning, the east wind brought the locusts. [14]The locusts came up over the whole land of Egypt and settled down over all its territory. Never before had there been such a fierce swarm of locusts, nor will there ever be again. [15]They covered the surface of the whole land, so that it became black. They ate up all the vegetation in the land and all the fruit of the trees the hail had spared. Nothing green was left on any tree or plant in the fields throughout the land of Egypt.

[16]Pharaoh hurriedly summoned Moses and Aaron and said, "I have sinned against the LORD, your God, and against you. [17]But now, do forgive me my sin only this once, and pray to the LORD, your God, only to take this death from me." [18]When Moses left Pharaoh, he prayed to the LORD, [19]and the LORD caused the wind to shift to a very strong west wind, which took up the locusts and hurled them into the Red Sea.* Not a single locust remained within the whole territory of Egypt. [20]Yet the LORD hardened Pharaoh's heart, and he would not let the Israelites go.

Ninth Plague: the Darkness. [21][c] Then the LORD said to Moses: Stretch out your hand toward the sky, that over the land of Egypt there may be such darkness* that one can feel it. [22]So Moses stretched out his hand toward the sky, and there was dense darkness throughout the land of Egypt for three days. [23]People could not see one another, nor could they get up from where they were, for three days. But all the Israelites had light where they lived.

[24]Pharaoh then summoned Moses and Aaron and said, "Go, serve the LORD. Only your flocks and herds will be detained. Even your little ones may go with you." [25]But Moses replied, "You also must give us sacrifices and burnt offerings to make to the LORD, our God. [26]Our livestock also must go with us.

10:10 The LORD help you . . .: lit., "May the Lord be with you in the same way as I let you . . ."; a sarcastic blessing intended as a curse.

10:11 Pharaoh realized that if the men alone went they would have to return to their families. He suspected that the Hebrews had no intention of returning.

10:13 East wind: coming across the desert from Arabia, the strong east wind brings Egypt the burning sirocco and, at times, locusts. Cf. 14:21.

10:19 The Red Sea: the traditional translation, cf. Septuagint and other Versions; but the Hebrew literally means "sea of reeds" or "reedy sea," which could probably be applied to a number of bodies of shallow water, most likely somewhat to the north of the present deep Red Sea.

10:21 Darkness: commentators note that at times a storm from the south, called the *khamsin*, blackens the sky of Egypt with sand from the Sahara; the dust in the air is then so thick that the darkness can, in a sense, "be felt." But such observations should not obscure the fact that for the biblical author what transpires in each of the plagues is clearly something extraordinary, an event which witnesses to the unrivaled power of Israel's God.

b: Ps 78:46; 105:34–35. *c:* Ps 105:28.

Not an animal must be left behind, for some of them we will select for service* to the LORD, our God; but we will not know with which ones we are to serve the LORD until we arrive there." 27But the LORD hardened Pharaoh's heart, and he was unwilling to let them go. 28Pharaoh said to Moses, "Leave me, and see to it that you do not see my face again! For the day you do see my face you will die!" 29Moses replied, "You are right! I will never see your face again."

CHAPTER 11

See RG 119–20

Tenth Plague: the Death of the Firstborn. 1Then the LORD spoke to Moses: One more plague I will bring upon Pharaoh and upon Egypt. After that he will let you depart. In fact, when he finally lets you go, he will drive you away. 2[d] Instruct the people that every man is to ask his neighbor, and every woman her neighbor, for silver and gold articles and for clothing. 3The LORD indeed made the Egyptians well-disposed toward the people; Moses himself was very highly regarded by Pharaoh's servants and the people in the land of Egypt.

4Moses then said, "Thus says the LORD: About midnight I will go forth through Egypt.[e] 5[f] Every firstborn in the land of Egypt will die, from the firstborn of Pharaoh who sits on his throne to the firstborn of the slave-girl who is at the handmill,* as well as all the firstborn of the animals. 6Then there will be loud wailing throughout the land of Egypt, such as has never been, nor will ever be again. 7But among all the Israelites, among human beings and animals alike, not even a dog will growl, so that you may know that the LORD distinguishes between Egypt and Israel. 8All these servants of yours will then come down to me and bow down before me, saying: Leave, you and all your followers![g] Then I will depart." With that he left Pharaoh's presence in hot anger.

9The LORD said to Moses: Pharaoh will not listen to you so that my wonders may be multiplied in the land of Egypt. 10Thus, although Moses and Aaron performed all these wonders in Pharaoh's presence, the LORD hardened Pharaoh's heart, and he would not let the Israelites go from his land.

CHAPTER 12

See RG 119–20

The Passover Ritual Prescribed.* 1The LORD said to Moses and Aaron in the land of Egypt: 2* This month will stand at the head of your calendar; you will reckon it the first month of the year.[h] 3Tell the whole community of Israel: On the tenth of this month every family must procure for itself a lamb, one apiece for each household. 4If a household is too small for a lamb, it along with its nearest neighbor will procure one, and apportion the lamb's cost* in proportion to the number of persons, according to what each household consumes. 5Your lamb must be a year-old male and without blemish. You may take it from either the sheep or the goats. 6You will keep it until the fourteenth day of this month, and then, with the whole community of Israel assembled, it will be slaughtered during the evening twilight. 7They will take some of its blood and apply it to the two doorposts and the lintel of the houses in which they eat it. 8They will consume its meat that same night, eating it roasted with unleavened bread and bitter herbs. 9Do not eat any of it raw or even boiled in water, but

10:26 Service: as is obvious from v. 25, the service in question here is the offering of sacrifice. The continued use of the verb *'bd* "to serve" and related nouns for both the people's bondage in Egypt and their subsequent service to the Lord dramatizes the point of the conflict between Pharaoh and the God of Israel, who demands from the Israelites an attachment which is exclusive. See Lv 25:55.

11:5 Handmill: two pieces of stone were used to grind grain. A smaller upper stone was moved back and forth over a larger stationary stone. This menial work was done by slaves and captives.

12:1–20 This section, which interrupts the narrative of the exodus, contains later legislation concerning the celebration of Passover.

12:2 As if to affirm victory over Pharaoh and sovereignty over the Israelites, the Lord proclaims a new calendar for Israel. **This month**: Abib, the month of "ripe grain." Cf. 13:4; 23:15; 34:18; Dt 16:1. It occurred near the vernal equinox, March–April. Later it was known by the Babylonian name of Nisan. Cf. Neh 2:1; Est 3:7.

12:4 The lamb's cost: some render the Hebrew, "reckon for the lamb the number of persons required to eat it." Cf. v. 10.

d: Ex 3:21–22; 12:35–36. *e:* Ex 12:12. *f:* Ex 12:29–30. *g:* Ex 12:31–33. *h:* Lv 23:5–8; Nm 9:2–5; 28:16–25; Dt 16:1–8.

roasted, with its head and shanks and inner organs. [10]You must not keep any of it beyond the morning; whatever is left over in the morning must be burned up.

[11]This is how you are to eat it: with your loins girt, sandals on your feet and your staff in hand, you will eat it in a hurry. It is the LORD's Passover. [12]For on this same night I will go through Egypt, striking down every firstborn in the land, human being and beast alike, and executing judgment on all the gods of Egypt—I, the LORD![i] [13]But for you the blood will mark the houses where you are. Seeing the blood, I will pass over you; thereby, when I strike the land of Egypt, no destructive blow will come upon you.[j]

[14]This day will be a day of remembrance for you, which your future generations will celebrate with pilgrimage to the LORD; you will celebrate it as a statute forever. [15]For seven days you must eat unleavened bread. From the very first day you will have your houses clear of all leaven. For whoever eats leavened bread from the first day to the seventh will be cut off* from Israel. [16]On the first day you will hold a sacred assembly, and likewise on the seventh. On these days no sort of work shall be done, except to prepare the food that everyone needs. [17]Keep, then, the custom of the unleavened bread,[k] since it was on this very day that I brought your armies out of the land of Egypt. You must observe this day throughout your generations as a statute forever. [18]From the evening of the fourteenth day of the first month until the evening of the twenty-first day of this month you will eat unleavened bread. [19]For seven days no leaven may be found in your houses; for anyone, a resident alien or a native, who eats leavened food will be cut off from the community of Israel. [20]You shall eat nothing leavened; wherever you dwell you may eat only unleavened bread.

Promulgation of the Passover. [21]Moses summoned all the elders of Israel and said to them, "Go and procure lambs for your families, and slaughter the Passover victims. [22][l] Then take a bunch of hyssop,* and dipping it in the blood that is in the basin, apply some of this blood to the lintel and the two doorposts. And none of you shall go outdoors until morning. [23]For when the LORD goes by to strike down the Egyptians, seeing the blood on the lintel and the two doorposts, the LORD will pass over that door and not let the destroyer come into your houses to strike you down.

[24]"You will keep this practice forever as a statute for yourselves and your descendants. [25]Thus, when you have entered the land which the LORD will give you as he promised, you must observe this rite. [26][m] When your children ask you, 'What does this rite of yours mean?' [27]you will reply, 'It is the Passover sacrifice for the LORD, who passed over the houses of the Israelites in Egypt; when he struck down the Egyptians, he delivered our houses.' "

Then the people knelt and bowed down, [28]and the Israelites went and did exactly as the LORD had commanded Moses and Aaron.

Death of the Firstborn. [29][n] And so at midnight the LORD struck down every firstborn in the land of Egypt, from the firstborn of Pharaoh sitting on his throne to the firstborn of the prisoner in the dungeon, as well as all the firstborn of the animals. [30]Pharaoh arose in the night, he and all his servants and all the Egyptians; and there was loud wailing throughout Egypt, for there was not a house without its dead.

Permission to Depart. [31]During the night Pharaoh summoned Moses and Aaron and said, "Leave my people at once, you and the Israelites! Go and serve the LORD as you said. [32]Take your flocks, too, and your herds, as you said, and go; and bless me, too!"*

[33]The Egyptians, in a hurry to send them

12:15 Cut off: a common Priestly term, not easily reduced to a simple English equivalent, since its usage appears to involve a number of associated punishments, some or all of which may come into play in any instance of the term's use. These included the excommunication of the offender from the Israelite community, the premature death of the offender, the eventual eradication of the offender's posterity, and finally the loss by the offender of all ancestral holdings.

12:22 Hyssop: a plant with many small woody branches that was convenient for a sprinkling rite.

12:32 Bless me, too: in a final and humiliating admission of defeat, once again Pharaoh asks Moses to intercede for

i: Nm 33:4. *j:* Heb 11:28. *k:* Ex 13:3. *l:* Ex 12:7, 13. *m:* Ex 13:8, 14–15; Dt 6:20–25. *n:* Ex 11:4–6; Nm 33:4; Ps 78:51; 105:36; 136:10; Wis 18:10–16.

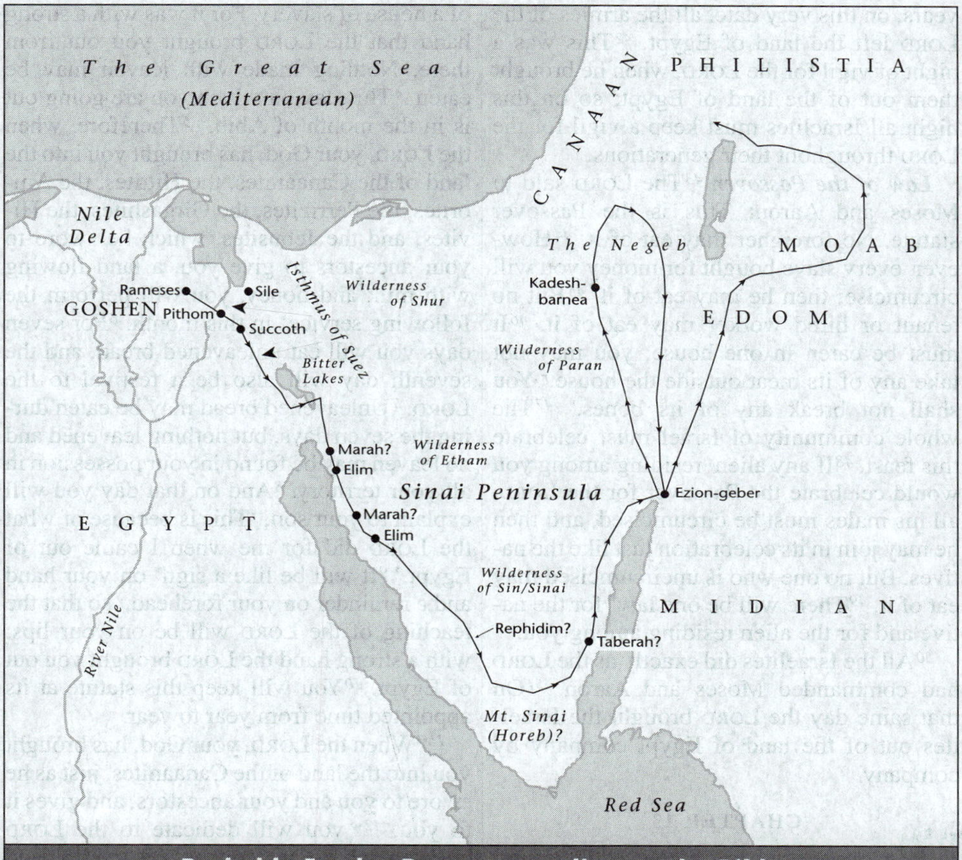

Probable Exodus Routes according to the Bible

away from the land, urged the people on, for they said, "All of us will die!" 34 The people, therefore, took their dough before it was leavened, in their kneading bowls wrapped in their cloaks on their shoulders. 35[o] And the Israelites did as Moses had commanded: they asked the Egyptians for articles of silver and gold and for clothing. 36 Indeed the LORD had made the Egyptians so well-disposed toward the people that they let them have whatever they asked for. And so they despoiled the Egyptians.

Departure from Egypt. 37 The Israelites set out from Rameses[p] for Succoth, about six hundred thousand men on foot, not counting the children. 38 A crowd of mixed ancestry[*] also went up with them, with livestock in great abundance, both flocks and herds. 39 The dough they had brought out of Egypt they baked into unleavened loaves. It was not leavened, because they had been driven out of Egypt and could not wait. They did not even prepare food for the journey.

40 The time the Israelites had stayed in Egypt[*] was four hundred and thirty years.[q] 41 At the end of four hundred and thirty

him (cf. 8:24). However, Pharaoh may be speaking sarcastically.

12:38 Mixed ancestry: not simply descendants of Jacob; cf. Nm 11:4; Lv 24:10–11.

12:40 In Egypt: according to the Septuagint and the Samaritan Pentateuch "in Canaan and Egypt," thus reckoning from the time of Abraham. Cf. Gal 3:17.

o: Ex 3:21–22; 11:2–3; Ps 105:37–38. *p:* Nm 33:3–5. *q:* Gn 15:13; Acts 7:6; Gal 3:17.

years, on this very date, all the armies of the LORD left the land of Egypt. [42]This was a night of vigil for the LORD, when he brought them out of the land of Egypt; so on this night all Israelites must keep a vigil for the LORD throughout their generations.

Law of the Passover. [43]The LORD said to Moses and Aaron: This is the Passover statute. No foreigner may eat of it. [44]However, every slave bought for money you will circumcise; then he may eat of it. [45]But no tenant or hired worker may eat of it. [46]It must be eaten in one house; you may not take any of its meat outside the house.[r] You shall not break any of its bones.* [47]The whole community of Israel must celebrate this feast. [48]If any alien[s] residing among you would celebrate the Passover for the LORD, all his males must be circumcised, and then he may join in its celebration just like the natives. But no one who is uncircumcised may eat of it. [49]There will be one law* for the native and for the alien residing among you.

[50]All the Israelites did exactly as the LORD had commanded Moses and Aaron. [51]On that same day the LORD brought the Israelites out of the land of Egypt company by company.

CHAPTER 13

See RG 120–21

Consecration of Firstborn. [1]The LORD spoke to Moses and said: [2]Consecrate to me every firstborn; whatever opens the womb among the Israelites,[t] whether of human being or beast, belongs to me.

[3u] Moses said to the people, "Remember this day on which you came out of Egypt, out of a house of slavery. For it was with a strong hand that the LORD brought you out from there. Nothing made with leaven may be eaten. [4]This day on which you are going out is in the month of Abib.* [5]Therefore, when the LORD, your God, has brought you into the land of the Canaanites, the Hittites, the Amorites, the Perrizites, the Girgashites, the Hivites, and the Jebusites, which he swore to your ancestors to give you, a land flowing with milk and honey, you will perform the following service* in this month. [6]For seven days you will eat unleavened bread, and the seventh day will also be a festival to the LORD. [7]Unleavened bread may be eaten during the seven days, but nothing leavened and no leaven may be found in your possession in all your territory. [8]And on that day you will explain to your son, 'This is because of what the LORD did for me when I came out of Egypt.' [9]It will be like a sign* on your hand and a reminder on your forehead,[v] so that the teaching of the LORD will be on your lips: with a strong hand the LORD brought you out of Egypt. [10]You will keep this statute at its appointed time from year to year.

[11]"When the LORD, your God, has brought you into the land of the Canaanites, just as he swore to you and your ancestors, and gives it to you, [12w] you will dedicate to the LORD every newborn that opens the womb; and every firstborn male of your animals will belong to the LORD. [13]Every firstborn of a donkey you will ransom with a sheep. If you do not ransom it, you will break its neck. Every human firstborn of your sons you must ransom. [14]And when your son asks you later on,

12:46 You shall not break any of its bones: the application of these words to Jesus on the cross (Jn 19:36) sees the Paschal lamb as a prophetic type of Christ, sacrificed to free men and women from the bondage of sin. Cf. also 1 Cor 5:7; 1 Pt 1:19.

12:49 One law: the first appearance of the word torah, traditionally translated as "law," though it can have the broader meaning of "teaching" or "instruction." Elsewhere, too, it is said that the "alien" is to be accorded the same treatment as the Israelite (e.g., Lv 19:34).

13:4 Abib: lit., "ear (of grain)," the old Canaanite name for this month; Israel later called it "Nisan." It was the first month in their liturgical calendar (cf. Ex 12:2).

13:5 The following service: the celebration of the feast of Unleavened Bread now constitutes the Israelites' service, in contrast to the "service" they performed for Pharaoh as his slaves.

13:9 Sign: while here observance of the feast of Unleavened Bread is likened only metaphorically to a physical sign of one's piety that can be worn as a kind of badge in commemoration of the exodus, from ancient times Jews have seen in this verse also the basis for the wearing of phylacteries. These are small receptacles for copies of biblical verses which Jewish men bind to the arms and forehead as a kind of mnemonic device for the observance of the Law.

13:17 By way of the Philistines' land: the most direct route from Egypt to Palestine, along the shore of the Mediterranean.

---

r: Nm 9:12; Jn 19:36. *s:* Nm 9:14. *t:* Ex 13:12–15. *u:* Ex 12:2–20. *v:* Ex 13:16; Dt 6:8; 11:18. *w:* Ex 13:2; 22:28–29; 34:19–20; Nm 3:12–13; 8:16–17; 18:15; Dt 15:19.

'What does this mean?' you will tell him, 'With a strong hand the LORD brought us out of Egypt, out of a house of slavery. [15]When Pharaoh stubbornly refused to let us go, the LORD killed every firstborn in the land of Egypt, the firstborn of human being and beast alike. That is why I sacrifice to the LORD every male that opens the womb, and why I ransom every firstborn of my sons.' [16]It will be like a sign on your hand and a band on your forehead that with a strong hand the LORD brought us out of Egypt."[x]

IV. The Deliverance of the Israelites from Pharaoh and Victory at the Sea

Toward the Red Sea. [17]Now, when Pharaoh let the people go, God did not lead them by way of the Philistines' land,* though this was the nearest; for God said: If the people see that they have to fight, they might change their minds and return to Egypt. [18]Instead, God rerouted them toward the Red Sea by way of the wilderness road, and the Israelites went up out of the land of Egypt arrayed for battle. [19]Moses also took Joseph's bones[y] with him, for Joseph had made the Israelites take a solemn oath, saying, "God will surely take care of you, and you must bring my bones up with you from here."

[20]Setting out from Succoth, they camped at Etham[z] near the edge of the wilderness.

[21][a] The LORD preceded them, in the daytime by means of a column of cloud to show them the way, and at night by means of a column of fire* to give them light. Thus they could travel both day and night. [22]Neither the column of cloud by day nor the column of fire by night ever left its place in front of the people.

CHAPTER 14

See RG 120–21

[1]Then the LORD spoke to Moses: [2]Speak to the Israelites: Let them turn about and camp before Pi-hahiroth, between Migdol and the sea.[b] Camp in front of Baal-zephon,* just opposite, by the sea. [3]Pharaoh will then say, "The Israelites are wandering about aimlessly in the land. The wilderness has closed in on them." [4]I will so harden Pharaoh's heart that he will pursue them. Thus I will receive glory through Pharaoh and all his army, and the Egyptians will know that I am the LORD.

This the Israelites did. [5][c] When it was reported to the king of Egypt that the people had fled, Pharaoh and his servants had a change of heart about the people. "What in the world have we done!" they said. "We have released Israel from our service!" [6]So Pharaoh harnessed his chariots and took his army with him. [7]He took six hundred select chariots and all the chariots of Egypt, with officers* on all of them. [8]The LORD hardened the heart of Pharaoh, king of Egypt, so that he pursued the Israelites while they were going out in triumph. [9]The Egyptians pursued them—all Pharaoh's horses, his chariots, his horsemen,* and his army—and caught up with them as they lay encamped by the sea, at Pi-hahiroth, in front of Baal-zephon.

Crossing the Red Sea. [10]Now Pharaoh was near when the Israelites looked up and saw that the Egyptians had set out after them. Greatly frightened, the Israelites cried out to the LORD. [11]To Moses they said, "Were there no burial places in Egypt that you brought us

13:21 A column of cloud . . . a column of fire: probably one and the same extraordinary phenomenon, a central nucleus of fire surrounded by smoke; only at night was its luminous nature visible; cf. 40:38.

14:2 Pi-hahiroth . . . Migdol . . . Baal-zephon: these places have not been definitively identified. Even the relative position of Pi-hahiroth and Baal-zephon is not clear; perhaps the former was on the west shore of the sea, where the Israelites were, and the latter on the opposite shore.

14:7 Officers: cf. 1 Kgs 9:22; Ez 23:15. The Hebrew word *shalish*, rendered in 1 Kgs 9:22 as "adjutant," has yet to have its meaning convincingly established. Given the very possible etymological connection with the number "three," others suggest the translation "three-man crew" or, less likely, the "third man in the chariot" although Egyptian chariots carried two-man crews. The author of the text may have been describing the chariots of his experience without direct historical knowledge of Egyptian ways.

14:9 Horsemen: the usage here may be anachronistic, since horsemen, or cavalry, play a part in warfare only at the end of the second millennium B.C.

x: Ex 13:9. *y:* Gn 50:25; Jos 24:32. *z:* Nm 33:6. *a:* Ex 40:38; Nm 9:15–22; Dt 1:33; Neh 9:19; Ps 78:14; 105:39; Wis 10:17. *b:* Nm 33:7–8. *c:* Wis 19:3; 1 Mc 4:9.

to die in the wilderness? What have you
done to us, bringing us out of Egypt? [12]Did
we not tell you this in Egypt, when we said,
'Leave us alone that we may serve the Egyptians'? Far better for us to serve the Egyptians than to die in the wilderness." [13]But
Moses answered the people, "Do not fear!
Stand your ground and see the victory the
LORD will win for you today. For these
Egyptians whom you see today you will
never see again. [14]The LORD will fight for
you; you have only to keep still."

[15]Then the LORD said to Moses: Why are
you crying out to me? Tell the Israelites to
set out. [16]And you, lift up your staff and
stretch out your hand over the sea, and split
it in two, that the Israelites may pass through
the sea on dry land. [17]But I will harden the
hearts of the Egyptians so that they will go in
after them, and I will receive glory through
Pharaoh and all his army, his chariots and his
horsemen. [18]The Egyptians will know that I
am the LORD, when I receive glory through
Pharaoh, his chariots, and his horsemen.

[19]The angel of God,* who had been leading Israel's army, now moved and went
around behind them. And the column of
cloud, moving from in front of them, took up
its place behind them, [20]so that it came between the Egyptian army and that of Israel.
And when it became dark, the cloud illumined the night; and so the rival camps did
not come any closer together all night long.*
[21][d] Then Moses stretched out his hand over
the sea; and the LORD drove back the sea
with a strong east wind all night long and
turned the sea into dry ground. The waters
were split, [22]so that the Israelites entered
into the midst of the sea on dry land, with the
water as a wall to their right and to their left.

Rout of the Egyptians. [23]The Egyptians followed in pursuit after them—all Pharaoh's
horses and chariots and horsemen—into the
midst of the sea. [24]But during the watch just
before dawn, the LORD looked down from a
column of fiery cloud upon the Egyptian
army and threw it into a panic; [25]and he so
clogged their chariot wheels that they could
drive only with difficulty. With that the Egyptians said, "Let us flee from Israel, because
the LORD is fighting for them against Egypt."

[26]Then the LORD spoke to Moses: Stretch
out your hand over the sea, that the water
may flow back upon the Egyptians, upon
their chariots and their horsemen. [27]So Moses stretched out his hand over the sea, and
at daybreak the sea returned to its normal
flow. The Egyptians were fleeing head on toward it when the LORD cast the Egyptians
into the midst of the sea. [28][e] As the water
flowed back, it covered the chariots and the
horsemen. Of all Pharaoh's army which had
followed the Israelites into the sea, not even
one escaped. [29]But the Israelites had walked
on dry land through the midst of the sea,
with the water as a wall to their right and to
their left. [30]Thus the LORD saved Israel on
that day from the power of Egypt. When Israel saw the Egyptians lying dead on the
seashore [31]and saw the great power that the
LORD had shown against Egypt, the people
feared the LORD. They believed in the LORD[f]
and in Moses his servant.

CHAPTER 15

See RG 120–21

[1]Then Moses and the Israelites sang[g]
this song to the LORD:*

I will sing to the LORD, for he is
gloriously triumphant;

14:19 Angel of God: Hebrew *mal'ak ha'elohim* (Septuagint *ho angelos tou theou*) here refers not to an independent spiritual being but to God's power at work in the world; corresponding to the column of cloud/fire, the expression more clearly preserves a sense of distance between God and God's creatures. The two halves of the verse are parallel and may come from different narrative sources.

14:20 The reading of the Hebrew text here is uncertain. The image is of a darkly glowing storm cloud, ominously bright, keeping the two camps apart.

15:1–21 This poem, regarded by many scholars as one of the oldest compositions in the Bible, was once an independent work. It has been inserted at this important juncture in the large narrative of Exodus to celebrate God's saving power, having miraculously delivered the people from their enemies, and ultimately leading them to the promised land.

Although the victory it describes over the Egyptians at the sea bears a superficial resemblance in v. 8 to the preceding depiction of the water standing like a wall (14:22), the poem (as opposed to the following prose verse, v. 19) suggests a

d: Ex 15:19; Ps 66:6; 78:13; 136:13–14; Wis 10:18; 19:7–8; Is 63:12–13; Heb 11:29. *e:* Dt 11:4; Ps 106:11. *f:* Ex 4:31; Ps 106:12; Wis 10:20. *g:* Ex 15:21.

horse and chariot he has cast into the
sea.
2 My strength and my refuge is the LORD,
and he has become my savior.[h]
This is my God, I praise him;
the God of my father, I extol him.
3 The LORD is a warrior,
LORD is his name!
4 Pharaoh's chariots and army he hurled
into the sea;
the elite of his officers were drowned
in the Red Sea.*
5 The flood waters covered them,
they sank into the depths like a stone.[i]
6 Your right hand, O LORD, magnificent in
power,
your right hand, O LORD, shattered the
enemy.
7 In your great majesty you overthrew your
adversaries;
you loosed your wrath to consume
them like stubble.
8 At the blast of your nostrils the waters
piled up,
the flowing waters stood like a mound,
the flood waters foamed in the midst
of the sea.
9 The enemy boasted, "I will pursue and
overtake them;
I will divide the spoils and have my
fill of them;
I will draw my sword; my hand will
despoil them!"
10 When you blew with your breath, the sea
covered them;
like lead they sank in the mighty
waters.
11 Who is like you among the gods,
O LORD?
Who is like you, magnificent among
the holy ones?
Awe-inspiring in deeds of renown,
worker of wonders,
12 when you stretched out your right
hand, the earth swallowed them!
13 In your love* you led the people you
redeemed;
in your strength you guided them to
your holy dwelling.
14 The peoples heard and quaked;
anguish gripped the dwellers in
Philistia.
15 Then were the chieftains of Edom
dismayed,
the nobles of Moab seized by
trembling;
All the inhabitants of Canaan melted
away;
16 [j] terror and dread fell upon them.
By the might of your arm they became
silent like stone,
while your people, LORD, passed over,
while the people whom you created
passed over.*
17 You brought them in, you planted them
on the mountain that is your own—
The place you made the base of your
throne, LORD,
the sanctuary, LORD, your hands
established.
18 May the LORD reign forever and ever!

19 When Pharaoh's horses and chariots and
horsemen entered the sea, the LORD made

different version of the victory at sea than that found in chap. 14. There is no splitting of the sea in an act reminiscent of the Lord's combat at creation with the sea monsters Rahab and Leviathan (Jb 9:13; 26:12; Ps 74:13–14; 89:11; Is 51:9–10); nor is there mention of an east wind driving the waters back so that the Israelites can cross. In this version it is by means of a storm at sea, caused by a ferocious blast from his nostrils, that the Lord achieves a decisive victory against Pharaoh and his army (vv. 1–12). The second half of the poem (vv. 13–18) describes God's guidance into the promised land.

15:4 Red Sea: the traditional translation of the Hebrew *yam suph*, which actually means "Sea of Reeds" or "reedy sea." The location is uncertain, though in view of the route taken by the Israelites from Egypt to Sinai, it could not have been the Red Sea, which is too far south. It was probably a smaller body of water south of the Gulf of Suez. The term occurs also in Exodus at 10:19; 13:18; and 23:31.

15:13 Love: the very important Hebrew term *hesed* carries a variety of nuances depending on context: love, kindness, faithfulness. It is often rendered "steadfast love." It implies a relationship that generates an obligation and therefore is at home in a covenant context. Cf. 20:6.

15:16 Passed over: an allusion to the crossing of the Jordan River (cf. Jos 3–5), written as if the entry into the promised land had already occurred. This verse suggests that at one time there was a ritual enactment of the conquest at a shrine near the Jordan River which included also a celebration of the victory at the sea.

h: Ps 118:14; Is 12:2. *i:* Neh 9:11. *j:* Ps 78:53–55.

the waters of the sea flow back upon them, though the Israelites walked on dry land through the midst of the sea.[k] 20 Then the prophet Miriam, Aaron's sister, took a tambourine in her hand, while all the women went out after her with tambourines, dancing; 21 and she responded* to them:

Sing to the LORD, for he is gloriously
triumphant;
horse and chariot he has cast into the
sea.[l]

V. The Journey in the Wilderness to Sinai

At Marah and Elim. 22 [m] Then Moses led Israel forward from the Red Sea,* and they marched out to the wilderness of Shur. After traveling for three days through the wilderness without finding water, 23 they arrived at Marah, where they could not drink its water, because it was too bitter. Hence this place was called Marah. 24 As the people grumbled against Moses, saying, "What are we to drink?" 25 he cried out to the LORD, who pointed out to him a piece of wood. When he threw it into the water, the water became fresh.[n]

It was here that God, in making statutes and ordinances for them, put them to the test. 26 He said: If you listen closely to the voice of the LORD, your God, and do what is right in his eyes: if you heed his commandments and keep all his statutes, I will not afflict you with any of the diseases with which I afflicted the Egyptians;[o] for I, the LORD, am your healer.

27 Then they came to Elim, where there were twelve springs of water and seventy palm trees, and they camped there near the water.[p]

CHAPTER 16

See RG 121–22

The Wilderness of Sin. 1 Having set out from Elim, the whole Israelite community came into the wilderness of Sin, which is between Elim and Sinai, on the fifteenth day of the second month* after their departure from the land of Egypt. 2 Here in the wilderness the whole Israelite community grumbled against Moses and Aaron. 3 The Israelites said to them, "If only we had died at the LORD's hand in the land of Egypt, as we sat by our kettles of meat and ate our fill of bread! But you have led us into this wilderness to make this whole assembly die of famine!"

The Quail and the Manna. 4 Then the LORD said to Moses:[q] I am going to rain down bread from heaven* for you. Each day the people are to go out and gather their daily portion; thus will I test them, to see whether they follow my instructions or not. 5 On the sixth day, however, when they prepare what they bring in, let it be twice as much as they gather on the other days. 6 So Moses and Aaron told all the Israelites,[r] "At evening you will know that it was the LORD who brought you out of the land of Egypt; 7 and in the morning you will see the glory of the LORD, when he hears your grumbling against him. But who are we that you should grumble against us?" 8 And Moses said, "When the LORD gives you meat to eat in the evening and in the morning your fill of bread, and hears the grumbling you utter against him, who then are we? Your grumbling is not against us, but against the LORD."

9 Then Moses said to Aaron, "Tell the whole Israelite community: Approach the LORD, for he has heard your grumbling." 10 But while Aaron was speaking to the whole

15:21 She responded: Miriam's refrain echoes the first verse of this song and was probably sung as an antiphon after each verse.

15:22 Red Sea: see note on Ex 15:4.

16:1 On the fifteenth day of the second month: just one full month after their departure from Egypt. Cf. 12:2, 51; Nm 33:3–4. The Septuagint takes the date to be the beginning of the Israelites' grumbling.

16:4 Bread from heaven: as a gift from God, the manna is said to come down from the sky. Cf. Ps 78:24–25; Wis 16:20. Perhaps it was similar to a natural substance that is still found in small quantities on the Sinai peninsula—probably the honey-like resin from the tamarisk tree—but here it is, at least in part, clearly an extraordinary sign of God's providence. With reference to Jn 6:32, 49–52, the Christian tradition has regarded the manna as a type of the Eucharist. **Test**: as the text stands, it seems to leave open the question whether the test concerns trusting in God to provide them with the daily gift of food or observing the sabbath instructions.

k: Ex 14:21–29. *l:* Ex 15:1. *m:* Nm 33:8. *n:* Sir 38:5. *o:* Dt 7:15. *p:* Nm 33:9. *q:* Ps 78:24–25; 105:40; Jn 6:31–32; 1 Cor 10:3. *r:* Ex 16:12.

Israelite community, they turned in the direction of the wilderness, and there the glory of the LORD appeared in the cloud! 11The LORD said to Moses: 12I have heard the grumbling of the Israelites. Tell them: In the evening twilight you will eat meat, and in the morning you will have your fill of bread, and then you will know that I, the LORD, am your God.

13In the evening, quail[s] came up and covered the camp. In the morning there was a layer of dew all about the camp, 14and when the layer of dew evaporated, fine flakes were on the surface of the wilderness, fine flakes like hoarfrost on the ground. 15On seeing it, the Israelites asked one another, "What is this?"* for they did not know what it was. But Moses told them, "It is the bread which the LORD has given you to eat.[t]

Regulations Regarding the Manna. 16"Now, this is what the LORD has commanded. Gather as much of it as each needs to eat, an omer* for each person for as many of you as there are, each of you providing for those in your own tent." 17The Israelites did so. Some gathered a large and some a small amount. 18* But when they measured it out by the omer, the one who had gathered a large amount did not have too much, and the one who had gathered a small amount did not have too little. They gathered as much as each needed to eat. 19Moses said to them, "Let no one leave any of it over until morning." 20But they did not listen to Moses, and some kept a part of it over until morning, and it became wormy and stank. Therefore Moses was angry with them.

21Morning after morning they gathered it, as much as each needed to eat; but when the sun grew hot, it melted away. 22On the sixth day they gathered twice as much food, two omers for each person. When all the leaders of the community came and reported this to Moses, 23he told them, "That is what the LORD has prescribed. Tomorrow is a day of rest, a holy sabbath of the LORD. Whatever you want to bake, bake; whatever you want to boil, boil; but whatever is left put away and keep until the morning." 24When they put it away until the morning, as Moses commanded, it did not stink nor were there worms in it. 25Moses then said, "Eat it today, for today is the sabbath of the LORD. Today you will not find any in the field. 26Six days you will gather it, but on the seventh day, the sabbath, it will not be there." 27Still, on the seventh day some of the people went out to gather it, but they did not find any. 28Then the LORD said to Moses: How long will you refuse to keep my commandments and my instructions? 29Take note! The LORD has given you the sabbath. That is why on the sixth day he gives you food for two days. Each of you stay where you are and let no one go out on the seventh day. 30After that the people rested on the seventh day.

31The house of Israel named this food manna.[u] It was like coriander seed,* white, and it tasted like wafers made with honey.

32Moses said, "This is what the LORD has commanded. Keep a full omer of it for your future generations, so that they may see the food I gave you to eat in the wilderness when I brought you out of the land of Egypt." 33Moses then told Aaron, "Take a jar* and put a full omer of manna in it. Then place it before the LORD to keep it for your future generations." 34As the LORD had commanded Moses, Aaron placed it in front of the covenant* to keep it.

35The Israelites ate the manna for forty years, until they came to settled land;[v] they ate the manna until they came to the borders of Canaan. 36(An omer is one tenth of an ephah.)*

16:15 What is this: the Hebrew *man hu* is thus rendered by the ancient versions, which understood the phrase as a popular etymology of the Hebrew word *man*, "manna"; but some render *man hu*, "This is manna."

16:16 Omer: a dry measure of approximately two quarts.

16:18 Paul cites this passage as an example of equitable sharing (2 Cor 8:15).

16:31 Coriander seed: small, round, aromatic seeds of bright brown color; the comparison, therefore, refers merely to the size and shape, not to the taste or color of the manna.

16:33 Jar: according to the Greek translation, which is followed in Heb 9:4, this was a golden vessel.

16:34 The covenant: i.e., the ark of the covenant, in which were placed the two tablets of the Ten Commandments. Cf. 25:16, 21–22.

16:36 Omer . . . ephah: see note on Is 5:10.

s: Nm 11:31; Ps 78:27–28. *t:* Dt 8:3. *u:* Nm 11:7. *v:* Jos 5:12.

CHAPTER 17

See RG 121–22

Water from the Rock. [1]From the wilderness of Sin the whole Israelite community journeyed by stages, as the LORD directed, and encamped at Rephidim.[w]

But there was no water for the people to drink, [2][x]and so they quarreled with Moses and said, "Give us water to drink." Moses replied to them, "Why do you quarrel with me? Why do you put the LORD to a test?" [3]Here, then, in their thirst for water, the people grumbled against Moses, saying, "Why then did you bring us up out of Egypt? To have us die of thirst with our children and our livestock?" [4]So Moses cried out to the LORD, "What shall I do with this people? A little more and they will stone me!" [5]The LORD answered Moses: Go on ahead of the people, and take along with you some of the elders of Israel, holding in your hand, as you go, the staff with which you struck the Nile. [6]I will be standing there in front of you on the rock in Horeb. Strike the rock, and the water will flow from it for the people to drink.[y] Moses did this, in the sight of the elders of Israel. [7]The place was named Massah and Meribah,* because the Israelites quarreled there and tested the LORD, saying, "Is the LORD in our midst or not?"[z]

Battle with Amalek. [8]Then Amalek* came and waged war against Israel in Rephidim.[a] [9]So Moses said to Joshua, "Choose some men for us, and tomorrow go out and engage Amalek in battle. I will be standing on top of the hill with the staff of God in my hand." [10]Joshua did as Moses told him: he engaged Amalek in battle while Moses, Aaron, and Hur climbed to the top of the hill. [11]As long as Moses kept his hands raised up, Israel had the better of the fight, but when he let his hands rest, Amalek had the better of the fight. [12]Moses' hands, however, grew tired; so they took a rock and put it under him and he sat on it. Meanwhile Aaron and Hur supported his hands, one on one side and one on the other, so that his hands remained steady until sunset. [13]And Joshua defeated Amalek and his people with the sword.

[14]Then the LORD said to Moses: Write this down in a book as something to be remembered, and recite it to Joshua:[b] I will completely blot out the memory of Amalek from under the heavens. [15]Moses built an altar there, which he named Yahweh-nissi;* [16]for he said, "Take up the banner of the LORD!* The LORD has a war against Amalek through the ages."

CHAPTER 18

See RG 121–22

Meeting with Jethro. [1]Now Moses' father-in-law Jethro, the priest of Midian, heard of all that God had done for Moses and for his people Israel: how the LORD had brought Israel out of Egypt. [2]So his father-in-law Jethro took along Zipporah, Moses' wife—now this was after Moses had sent her back—* [3]and her two sons. One of these was named Gershom;[c] for he said, "I am a resident alien in a foreign land." [4]The other was named Eliezer; for he said, "The God of my father is my help; he has rescued me from Pharaoh's sword." [5]Together with Moses' wife and sons, then, his father-in-law Jethro came to him in the wilderness where he was encamped at the mountain of God,* [6]and he sent word to Moses, "I, your father-in-law Jethro, am coming to you, along with your wife and her two sons."

17:7 Massah . . . Meribah: Hebrew words meaning, respectively, "the place of the test" and "the place of strife, of quarreling."

17:8 Amalek: the Amalekites appear in the Bible as early inhabitants of southern Palestine and the Sinai peninsula prior to the appearance of the Israelites in the region. Cf. Nm 24:20.

17:15 Yahweh-nissi: meaning, "the Lord is my banner."

17:16 Take up the banner of the LORD: lit., "a hand on the LORD's banner," apparently a war cry for the Israelite troops in the conduct of Holy War; however, the Hebrew text is difficult to interpret.

18:2 Moses had sent her back: a later gloss which attempts to harmonize Zipporah's presence with Jethro here in this story and the account of Moses' return to Egypt with Zipporah in 4:20.

18:5 The allusion to meeting Moses encamped at the mountain of God, prior to the arrival of the Israelites at Sinai in chap. 19, might well suggest a different narrative context for this story from an earlier stage of the biblical tradition's development. It is noteworthy that immediately after the Sinai pericope (Ex 19:1–Nm 10:28), recounting the theophany at Sinai and the giving of the law, the narrative of Israel's march through the wilderness resumes with an apparent doublet of the visit by Moses' father-in-law (Nm 10:29–32).

w: Nm 33:12–14. *x:* Nm 20:2–13. *y:* Dt 8:15; Ps 78:15–16; 105:41; Wis 11:4; Is 43:20; 48:21. *z:* Ps 95:8–9. *a:* Dt 25:17–19; 1 Sm 15:2. *b:* Nm 24:20; 1 Sm 15:3, 20. *c:* Ex 2:22.

[7]Moses went out to meet his father-in-law, bowed down, and then kissed him. Having greeted each other, they went into the tent. [8]Moses then told his father-in-law of all that the LORD had done to Pharaoh and the Egyptians for the sake of Israel, and of all the hardships that had beset them on their journey, and how the LORD had rescued them. [9]Jethro rejoiced over all the goodness that the LORD had shown Israel in rescuing them from the power of the Egyptians. [10]"Blessed be the LORD," he said, "who has rescued you from the power of the Egyptians and of Pharaoh. [11]Now I know that the LORD is greater than all the gods; for he rescued the people from the power of the Egyptians when they treated them arrogantly." [12]Then Jethro, the father-in-law of Moses, brought a burnt offering* and sacrifices for God, and Aaron came with all the elders of Israel to share with Moses' father-in-law in the meal before God.

Appointment of Minor Judges. [13]The next day Moses sat in judgment for the people, while they stood around him from morning until evening. [14]When Moses' father-in-law saw all that he was doing for the people, he asked, "What is this business that you are conducting for the people? Why do you sit alone while all the people have to stand about you from morning till evening?" [15]Moses answered his father-in-law, "The people come to me to consult God. [16]Whenever they have a disagreement, they come to me to have me settle the matter between them and make known to them God's statutes and instructions."

[17]"What you are doing is not wise," Moses' father-in-law replied. [18]"You will surely wear yourself out, both you and these people with you. The task is too heavy for you;[d] you cannot do it alone. [19]* Now, listen to me, and I will give you some advice, and may God be with you. Act as the people's representative before God, and bring their disputes to God. [20]Enlighten them in regard to the statutes and instructions, showing them how they are to conduct themselves and what they are to do. [21]But you should also look among all the people for able and God-fearing men, trustworthy men who hate dishonest gain, and set them over the people as commanders of thousands, of hundreds, of fifties, and of tens.[e] [22]Let these render decisions for the people in all routine cases. Every important case they should refer to you, but every lesser case they can settle themselves. Lighten your burden by letting them bear it with you! [23]If you do this, and God so commands you,* you will be able to stand the strain, and all these people, too, will go home content."

[24]Moses listened to his father-in-law and did all that he had said. [25]He picked out able men from all Israel and put them in charge of the people as commanders of thousands, of hundreds, of fifties, and of tens. [26]They rendered decisions for the people in all routine cases. The more difficult cases they referred to Moses, but all the lesser cases they settled themselves. [27]Then Moses said farewell to his father-in-law, who went off to his own country.

VI. Covenant and Legislation at Mount Sinai

CHAPTER 19

See RG 122

Arrival at Sinai. [1f] In the third month after the Israelites' departure from the land of Egypt, on the first day, they came to the wilderness of Sinai. [2]After they made the journey from Rephidim and entered the wilderness of Sinai, they then pitched camp in the wilderness.*

18:12 That a non-Israelite, such as Jethro, should bless Israel's God by way of acknowledging what God had done for Israel (v. 10) is not entirely surprising; but the Midianite priest's sacrifice to the God of Israel, including his presiding over a sacrificial meal with Aaron and the elders of Israel, is unusual, suggesting that he was himself already a worshiper of Yhwh, Israel's God. Note further in this connection the role Jethro takes in the following narrative (vv. 13–27) in instituting a permanent judiciary for the Israelites. **Burnt offering**: a sacrifice wholly burnt up as an offering to God.

18:19–20 By emphasizing Moses' mediatorial role for the people before God in regard to God's statutes and instructions, this story about the institution of Israel's judiciary prepares for Moses' role in the upcoming revelation of the law at Sinai.

18:23 And God so commands you: i.e., and God approves.

19:2 Apparently from a different source (P) than v. 1, which notes the date, v. 2 from the J source includes a second notice of the arrival in the wilderness of Sinai. The Israelites now will be

d: Nm 11:14. *e:* Dt 1:15; 16:18. *f:* Nm 33:15.

While Israel was encamped there in front of the mountain, 3 Moses went up to the mountain of God. Then the LORD called to him from the mountain, saying: This is what you will say to the house of Jacob; tell the Israelites: 4 You have seen how I treated the Egyptians and how I bore you up on eagles' wings and brought you to myself.[g] 5 Now, if you obey me completely and keep my covenant,* you will be my treasured possession among all peoples,[h] though all the earth is mine. 6 You will be to me a kingdom of priests,* a holy nation.[i] That is what you must tell the Israelites. 7 So Moses went and summoned the elders of the people. When he set before them all that the LORD had ordered him to tell them, 8 all the people answered together, "Everything the LORD has said, we will do." Then Moses brought back to the LORD the response of the people.

9 The LORD said to Moses: I am coming to you now in a dense cloud,[j] so that when the people hear me speaking with you, they will also remain faithful to you.

When Moses, then, had reported the response of the people to the LORD, 10 the LORD said to Moses: Go to the people and have them sanctify themselves today and tomorrow. Have them wash their garments 11 and be ready for the third day; for on the third day the LORD will come down on Mount Sinai in the sight of all the people. 12 Set limits for the people all around,[k] saying: Take care not to go up the mountain, or even to touch its edge. All who touch the mountain must be put to death. 13 No hand shall touch them, but they must be stoned to death or killed with arrows. Whether human being or beast, they must not be allowed to live. Only when the ram's horn sounds may they go up on the mountain.* 14 Then Moses came down from the mountain to the people and had them sanctify themselves, and they washed their garments. 15 He said to the people, "Be ready for the third day. Do not approach a woman."

The Great Theophany. 16[l] On the morning of the third day there were peals of thunder and lightning, and a heavy cloud over the mountain, and a very loud blast of the shofar,* so that all the people in the camp trembled. 17 But Moses led the people out of the camp to meet God, and they stationed themselves at the foot of the mountain. 18 Now Mount Sinai was completely enveloped in smoke, because the LORD had come down upon it in fire. The smoke rose from it as though from a kiln, and the whole mountain trembled violently. 19 The blast of the shofar grew louder and louder, while Moses was speaking and God was answering him with thunder.

20* When the LORD came down upon Mount Sinai, to the top of the mountain, the LORD summoned Moses to the top of the mountain, and Moses went up. 21 Then the LORD told Moses: Go down and warn the people not to break through to the LORD in order to see him; otherwise many of them will be struck down. 22 For their part, the

camped at Sinai from this point on all the way to Nm 10:10. This is a striking indication of the centrality and importance of the Sinai narrative in the overall composition of the Pentateuch.

19:5 Covenant: while covenants between individuals and between nations are ubiquitous in the ancient Near East, the adaptation of this concept to express the relationship that will henceforth characterize God's relationship to Israel represents an important innovation of biblical faith. Other gods might "choose" nations to fulfill a special destiny or role in the world; but only Israel's God is bound to a people by covenant. Thereby Israel's identity as a people is put upon a foundation that does not depend upon the vicissitudes of Israelite statehood or the normal trappings of national existence. Israel will be a covenant people.

19:6 Kingdom of priests: inasmuch as this phrase is parallel to "holy nation," it most likely means that the whole Israelite nation is set apart from other nations and so consecrated to God, or holy, in the way priests are among the people (cf. Is 61:6; 1 Pt 2:5, 9).

19:13 May they go up on the mountain: in vv. 12–13a, a later Priestly reshaping of an earlier version of the instructions governing how the people are to prepare for the encounter with God (vv. 10–11, 13b), the people are to be restrained from ascending the mountain, which is suffused with the holiness of God and too dangerous for their approach. In the earlier version, as v. 13b suggests, the sanctified people must come near, in order to hear God speaking with Moses (v. 9) and in this way receive confirmation of his special relationship with God.

19:16 Shofar: a ram's horn used like a trumpet for signaling both for liturgical and military purposes.

19:20–25 At this point the Priestly additions of vv. 12–13a are elaborated with further Priestly instructions, which include the priests' sanctifying themselves apart from the people (v. 22) and Aaron accompanying Moses to the top of the mountain (v. 24).

g: Dt 32:11–12. *h:* Dt 7:6; 14:2; 26:18–19; 32:8–9. *i:* 1 Pt 2:9. *j:* Ex 20:21; 24:15–18. *k:* Ex 34:3; Heb 12:18–19. *l:* Dt 4:10–12.

priests, who approach the LORD must sanctify themselves; else the LORD will break out in anger against them. 23 But Moses said to the LORD, "The people cannot go up to Mount Sinai, for you yourself warned us, saying: Set limits around the mountain to make it sacred." 24 So the LORD said to him: Go down and come up along with Aaron. But do not let the priests and the people break through to come up to the LORD; else he will break out against them." 25 So Moses went down to the people and spoke to them.

CHAPTER 20

See RG 122

*The Ten Commandments.** 1 Then God spoke all these words:

2[m] I am the LORD your God, who brought you out of the land of Egypt,[n] out of the house of slavery. 3 You shall not have other gods beside me.* 4 You shall not make for yourself an idol[o] or a likeness of anything* in the heavens above or on the earth below or in the waters beneath the earth; 5 you shall not bow down before them or serve them.[p] For I, the LORD, your God, am a jealous God, inflicting punishment for their ancestors' wickedness on the children of those who hate me, down to the third and fourth generation*; 6 but showing love down to the thousandth generation of those who love me and keep my commandments.

7 You shall not invoke the name of the LORD, your God, in vain.* [q] For the LORD will not leave unpunished anyone who invokes his name in vain.

8 Remember the sabbath day—keep it holy.* 9 Six days you may labor and do all your work, 10 but the seventh day is a sabbath of the LORD your God.[r] You shall not do any work, either you, your son or your daughter, your male or female slave, your work animal, or the resident alien within your gates. 11 For in six days the LORD made the heavens and the earth, the sea and all that is in them;

20:1–17 The precise numbering and division of these precepts into "ten commandments" is somewhat uncertain. Traditionally among Catholics and Lutherans vv. 1–6 are considered as only one commandment, and v. 17 as two. The Anglican, Greek Orthodox, and Reformed churches count vv. 1–6 as two, and v. 17 as one. Cf. Dt 5:6–21. The traditional designation as "ten" is not found here but in 34:28 (and also Dt 4:13 and 10:4), where these precepts are alluded to literally as "the ten words." That they were originally written on two tablets appears in Ex 32:15–16; 34:28–29; Dt 4:13; 10:2–4.

The present form of the commands is a product of a long development, as is clear from the fact that the individual precepts vary considerably in length and from the slightly different formulation of Dt 5:6–21 (see especially vv. 12–15 and 21). Indeed they represent a mature formulation of a traditional morality. Why this specific selection of commands should be set apart is not entirely clear. None of them is unique in the Old Testament and all of the laws which follow are also from God and equally binding on the Israelites. Even so, this collection represents a privileged expression of God's moral demands on Israel and is here set apart from the others as a direct, unmediated communication of God to the Israelites and the basis of the covenant being concluded on Sinai.

20:3 Beside me: this commandment is traditionally understood as an outright denial of the existence of other gods except the God of Israel; however, in the context of the more general prohibitions in vv. 4–5, v. 3 is, more precisely, God's demand for Israel's exclusive worship and allegiance.

The Hebrew phrase underlying the translation "beside me" is, nonetheless, problematic and has been variously translated, e.g., "except me," "in addition to me," "in preference to me," "in defiance of me," and "in front of me" or "before my face." The latter translation, with its concrete, spatial nuances, has suggested to some that the prohibition once sought to exclude from the Lord's sanctuary the cult images or idols of other gods, such as the asherah, or stylized sacred tree of life, associated with the Canaanite goddess Asherah (34:13). Over the course of time, as vv. 4–5 suggest, the original scope of v. 3 was expanded.

20:4 Or a likeness of anything: compare this formulation to that found in Dt 5:8, which understands this phrase and the following phrases as specifications of the prohibited idol (Hebrew *pesel*), which usually refers to an image that is carved or hewn rather than cast.

20:5 Jealous: demanding exclusive allegiance. **Inflicting punishment . . . the third and fourth generation**: the intended emphasis is on God's mercy by the contrast between punishment and mercy ("to the thousandth generation"—v. 6). Other Old Testament texts repudiate the idea of punishment devolving on later generations (cf. Dt 24:16; Jer 31:29–30; Ez 18:2–4). Yet it is known that later generations may suffer the punishing effects of sins of earlier generations, but not the guilt.

20:7 In vain: i.e., to no good purpose, a general framing of the prohibition which includes swearing falsely, especially in the context of a legal proceeding, but also goes beyond it (cf. Lv 24:16; Prv 30:8–9).

20:8 Keep it holy: i.e., to set it apart from the other days of the week, in part, as the following verse explains, by not doing work that is ordinarily done in the course of a week. The special importance of this command can be seen in the fact that, together with vv. 9–11, it represents the longest of the Decalogue's precepts.

m: Dt 5:6–21. *n:* Lv 26:13; Ps 81:11; Hos 13:4. *o:* Ex 34:17; Lv 26:1; Dt 4:15–19; 27:15. *p:* Ex 34:7, 14; Nm 14:18; Dt 4:24; 6:15. *q:* Lv 19:12; 24:16. *r:* Ex 23:12; 31:13–16; 34:21; 35:2; Lv 23:3.

but on the seventh day he rested.[s] That is why the LORD has blessed the sabbath day and made it holy.*

12* [t] Honor your father and your mother, that you may have a long life in the land the LORD your God is giving you.[u]

13 You shall not kill.* [v]

14 You shall not commit adultery.[w]

15 You shall not steal.[x]

16 You shall not bear false witness against your neighbor.[y]

17 You shall not covet your neighbor's house. You shall not covet your neighbor's wife, his male or female slave, his ox or donkey, or anything that belongs to your neighbor.[z]

Moses Accepted as Mediator. 18 Now as all the people witnessed the thunder and lightning, the blast of the shofar and the mountain smoking, they became afraid and trembled.[a] So they took up a position farther away 19 and said to Moses, "You speak to us, and we will listen; but do not let God speak to us, or we shall die." 20 Moses answered the people, "Do not be afraid, for God has come only to test you and put the fear of him upon you so you do not sin." 21 So the people remained at a distance, while Moses approached the dark cloud where God was.

The Covenant Code. 22* The LORD said to Moses: This is what you will say to the Israelites: You have seen for yourselves that I have spoken to you from heaven. 23 You shall not make alongside of me gods of silver, nor shall you make for yourselves gods of gold.[b] 24 An altar of earth make for me, and sacrifice upon it your burnt offerings and communion sacrifices, your sheep and your oxen.[c] In every place where I cause my name to be invoked* I will come to you and bless you. 25 But if you make an altar of stone for me,[d] do not build it of cut stone, for by putting a chisel to it you profane it. 26 You shall not ascend to my altar by steps, lest your nakedness be exposed.

CHAPTER 21

See RG 122

Laws Regarding Slaves. 1 These are the ordinances* you shall lay before them. 2[e] When you purchase a Hebrew slave,* he is to serve you for six years, but in the seventh year he shall leave as a free person without any payment. 3 If he comes into service alone, he shall leave alone; if he comes with a wife, his wife shall leave with him. 4 But if his master gives him a wife and she bears him sons or daughters, the woman and her children belong to her master and the man shall leave alone. 5 If, however, the slave declares, 'I love my master and my wife and children; I will not leave as a free person,'

20:11 Here, in a formulation which reflects Priestly theology, the veneration of the sabbath is grounded in God's own hallowing of the sabbath in creation. Compare 31:13; Dt 5:15.

20:12–17 The Decalogue falls into two parts: the preceding precepts refer to God, the following refer primarily to one's fellow Israelites.

20:13 Kill: as frequent instances of killing in the context of war or certain crimes (see vv. 12–18) demonstrate in the Old Testament, not all killing comes within the scope of the commandment. For this reason, the Hebrew verb translated here as "kill" is often understood as "murder," although it is in fact used in the Old Testament at times for unintentional acts of killing (e.g., Dt 4:41; Jos 20:3) and for legally sanctioned killing (Nm 35:30). The term may originally have designated any killing of another Israelite, including acts of manslaughter, for which the victim's kin could exact vengeance. In the present context, it denotes the killing of one Israelite by another, motivated by hatred or the like (Nm 35:20; cf. Hos 6:9).

20:22–23:33 This collection consists of the civil and religious laws, both apodictic (absolute) and casuistic (conditional), which were given to the people through the mediation of Moses. They will be written down by Moses in 24:4.

20:24 Where I cause my name to be invoked: i.e., at the sacred site where God wishes to be worshiped. Dt 12 will demand the centralization of all sacrificial worship in one place chosen by God.

21:1 Ordinances: judicial precedents to be used in settling questions of law and custom. More than half of the civil and religious laws in this collection (20:22–23:33), designated in 24:7 as "the book of the covenant," have parallels in the cuneiform laws of the ancient Near East. It is clear that Israel participated in a common legal culture with its neighbors.

21:2 Slave: an Israelite could become a slave of another Israelite as a means of paying a debt, or an Israelite could be born into slavery due to a parent's status as a slave. Here a time limit is prescribed for such slavery; other stipulations (vv. 20–21, 26–27) tried to reduce the evils of slavery, but slavery itself is not condemned in the Old Testament.

s: Ex 31:17; Gn 2:2–3. *t:* Mt 19:18–19; Mk 10:19; Lk 18:20; Rom 13:9. *u:* Lv 20:9; Mt 15:4; Mk 7:10; Eph 6:2–3. *v:* Mt 5:21. *w:* Lv 18:20; 20:10; Dt 22:22; Mt 5:27. *x:* Lv 19:11. *y:* Ex 23:1; Dt 19:16–19; Prv 19:5, 9; 24:28. *z:* Rom 7:7. *a:* Dt 4:11; 5:22–27; 18:16; Heb 12:18–19. *b:* Ex 20:3–4. *c:* Dt 12:5, 11; 14:23; 16:6. *d:* Dt 27:5; Jos 8:31. *e:* Lv 25:39–55; Dt 15:12–18; Jer 34:14.

[6]his master shall bring him to God* and there, at the door or doorpost, he shall pierce his ear with an awl, thus keeping him as his slave forever.

[7]When a man sells his daughter as a slave, she shall not go free as male slaves do. [8]But if she displeases her master, who had designated her* for himself, he shall let her be redeemed. He has no right to sell her to a foreign people, since he has broken faith with her. [9]If he designates her for his son, he shall treat her according to the ordinance for daughters. [10]If he takes another wife, he shall not withhold her food, her clothing, or her conjugal rights. [11]If he does not do these three things for her, she may leave without cost, without any payment.

Personal Injury. [12]* Whoever strikes someone a mortal blow must be put to death.[f] [13]However, regarding the one who did not hunt another down, but God caused death to happen by his hand, I will set apart for you a place to which that one may flee. [14]But when someone kills a neighbor after maliciously scheming to do so, you must take him even from my altar and put him to death. [15]Whoever strikes father or mother shall be put to death.*

[16]A kidnaper, whether he sells the person or the person is found in his possession, shall be put to death.[g]

[17]Whoever curses* father or mother shall be put to death.[h]

[18]When men quarrel and one strikes the other with a stone or with his fist, not mortally, but enough to put him in bed, [19]the one who struck the blow shall be acquitted, provided the other can get up and walk around with the help of his staff. Still, he must compensate him for his recovery time and make provision for his complete healing.

[20]When someone strikes his male or female slave with a rod so that the slave dies under his hand, the act shall certainly be avenged. [21]If, however, the slave survives for a day or two, he is not to be punished, since the slave is his own property.

[22]* When men have a fight and hurt a pregnant woman, so that she suffers a miscarriage, but no further injury, the guilty one shall be fined as much as the woman's husband demands of him, and he shall pay in the presence of the judges. [23][i] But if injury ensues, you shall give life for life, [24]eye for eye, tooth for tooth, hand for hand, foot for foot, [25]burn for burn, wound for wound, stripe for stripe.

[26]When someone strikes his male or female slave in the eye and destroys the use of the eye, he shall let the slave go free in compensation for the eye. [27]If he knocks out a tooth of his male or female slave, he shall let the slave go free in compensation for the tooth.

[28]When an ox gores a man or a woman to death, the ox must be stoned; its meat may not be eaten. The owner of the ox, however, shall be free of blame. [29]But if an ox was

21:6 To God: the ritual of the piercing of the slave's ear, which signified a lifetime commitment to the master, probably took place at the door of the household, where God as protector of the household was called upon as a witness. Another possible location for the ritual would have been the door of the sanctuary, where God or judges would have witnessed the slave's promise of lifetime obedience to his master.

21:8 Designated her: intended her as a wife of second rank.

21:12–14 Unintentional homicide is to be punished differently from premeditated, deliberate murder. One who kills unintentionally can seek asylum by grasping the horns of the altar at the local sanctuary. In later Israelite history, when worship was centralized in Jerusalem, cities throughout the realm were designated as places of refuge. Apparently the leaders of the local community were to determine whether or not the homicide was intentional.

21:15 The verb used most often signifies a violent, sometimes deadly, attack. The severe penalty assigned is intended to safeguard the integrity of the family.

21:17 Curses: not merely an angrily uttered expletive at one's parents, but a solemn juridical formula of justifiable retribution which was considered to be legally binding and guaranteed by God.

21:22–25 This law of talion is applied here in the specific case of a pregnant woman who, as an innocent bystander, is injured by two fighting men. The law of talion is not held up as a general principle to be applied throughout the book of the covenant. (But see note on Lv 24:19–20.) Here this principle of rigorous accountability aimed to prevent injury to a woman about to give birth by apparently requiring the assailant to have his own wife injured as she was about to bring new life into his family. However, it is debatable whether talion was ever understood or applied literally in Israel. In his Sermon on the Mount, Jesus challenges his audience to find a deeper form of justice than the supposed equilibrium offered by talion (Mt 5:38–40).

f: Lv 24:17; Nm 35:15–29; Dt 4:41–42; 19:2–5. *g:* Dt 24:7. *h:* Lv 20:9; Prv 20:20; Mt 15:4; Mk 7:10. *i:* Lv 24:18–21; Dt 19:21; Mt 5:38.

previously in the habit of goring people and its owner, though warned, would not watch it; should it then kill a man or a woman, not only must the ox be stoned, but its owner also must be put to death. [30]If, however, a fine is imposed on him, he must pay in ransom* for his life whatever amount is imposed on him. [31]This ordinance applies if it is a boy or a girl that the ox gores. [32]But if it is a male or a female slave that it gores, he must pay the owner of the slave thirty shekels of silver, and the ox must be stoned.

Property Damage. [33]When someone uncovers or digs a cistern and does not cover it over again, should an ox or a donkey fall into it, [34]the owner of the cistern must make good by restoring the value of the animal to its owner, but the dead animal he may keep.

[35]When one man's ox hurts another's ox and it dies, they shall sell the live ox and divide this money as well as the dead animal equally between them. [36]But if it was known that the ox was previously in the habit of goring and its owner would not watch it, he must make full restitution, an ox for an ox; but the dead animal he may keep.

[37]When someone steals an ox or a sheep and slaughters or sells it, he shall restore five oxen for the one ox, and four sheep for the one sheep.[j]

CHAPTER 22

See RG 122

[1][If a thief is caught* in the act of housebreaking and beaten to death, there is no bloodguilt involved. [2]But if after sunrise he is thus beaten, there is bloodguilt.] He must make full restitution. If he has nothing, he shall be sold to pay for his theft. [3]If what he stole is found alive in his possession, be it an ox, a donkey or a sheep, he shall make twofold restitution.

[4]When someone causes a field or a vineyard to be grazed over, by sending his cattle to graze in another's field, he must make restitution with the best produce of his own field or vineyard. [5]If a fire breaks out, catches on to thorn bushes, and consumes shocked grain, standing grain, or the field itself, the one who started the fire must make full restitution.

Trusts and Loans. [6]When someone gives money or articles to another for safekeeping and they are stolen from the latter's house, the thief, if caught, must make twofold restitution. [7]If the thief is not caught, the owner of the house shall be brought to God,* to swear that he himself did not lay hands on his neighbor's property. [8]In every case of dishonest appropriation, whether it be about an ox, or a donkey, or a sheep, or a garment, or anything else that has disappeared, where another claims that the thing is his, the claim of both parties shall be brought before God; the one whom God convicts must make twofold restitution to the other.

[9]When someone gives an ass, or an ox, or a sheep, or any other animal to another for safekeeping, if it dies, or is maimed or snatched away, without anyone witnessing the fact, [10]there shall be an oath before the LORD between the two of them that the guardian did not lay hands on his neighbor's property; the owner must accept the oath, and no restitution is to be made. [11]But if the guardian has actually stolen from it, then he must make restitution to the owner. [12]If it has been killed by a wild beast, let him bring it as evidence; he need not make restitution for the mangled animal.[k]

[13]When someone borrows an animal from a neighbor, if it is maimed or dies while the owner is not present, that one must make restitution. [14]But if the owner is present, that one need not make restitution. If it was hired, this was covered by the price of its hire.

Social Laws. [15][l] When a man seduces a virgin who is not betrothed, and lies with her, he shall make her his wife by paying the

21:30 Ransom: the amount of money or material goods required to restore the relationship between the relatives of the victim and the negligent owner of the goring ox.

22:1–2 If a thief is caught: this seems to be a fragment of what was once a longer law on housebreaking, which has been inserted here into the middle of a law on stealing animals. At night the householder would be justified in killing a burglar outright, but not so in the daytime, when the burglar could more easily be caught alive. **He must make full restitution**: this stood originally immediately after 21:37.

22:7 Brought to God: either within the household or at the sanctuary, the owner of the house is required to take an oath before God.

j: 2 Sm 12:6. *k:* Gn 31:39. *l:* Dt 22:28–29.

bride price. [16]If her father refuses to give her to him, he must still pay him the bride price for virgins.*

[17]You shall not let a woman who practices sorcery live.[m]

[18]Anyone who lies with an animal shall be put to death.[n]

[19]Whoever sacrifices to any god, except to the LORD alone, shall be put under the ban.[o]

[20]You shall not oppress or afflict a resident alien, for you were once aliens residing in the land of Egypt.[p] [21]You shall not wrong any widow or orphan. [22]If ever you wrong them and they cry out to me, I will surely listen to their cry. [23]My wrath will flare up, and I will kill you with the sword; then your own wives will be widows, and your children orphans.

[24][q] If you lend money to my people, the poor among you, you must not be like a money lender; you must not demand interest from them. [25]If you take your neighbor's cloak as a pledge, you shall return it to him before sunset; [26]for this is his only covering; it is the cloak for his body. What will he sleep in? If he cries out to me, I will listen; for I am compassionate.[r]

[27]You shall not despise God,* nor curse a leader of your people.[s]

[28]You shall not delay the offering of your harvest and your press. You shall give me the firstborn of your sons. [29]You must do the same with your oxen and your sheep; for seven days the firstling may stay with its mother, but on the eighth day you must give it to me.[t]

[30]You shall be a people sacred to me. Flesh torn to pieces in the field you shall not eat; you must throw it to the dogs.[u]

CHAPTER 23

See RG 122

[1]You shall not repeat a false report. Do not join your hand with the wicked to be a witness supporting violence.[v] [2]You shall not follow the crowd in doing wrong. When testifying in a lawsuit, you shall not follow the crowd in perverting justice. [3]You shall not favor the poor in a lawsuit.[w]

[4]When you come upon your enemy's ox or donkey going astray, you must see to it that it is returned.[x] [5]When you notice the donkey of one who hates you lying down under its burden, you should not desert him; you must help him with it.

[6]You shall not pervert justice for the needy among you in a lawsuit. [7]You shall keep away from anything dishonest. The innocent and the just you shall not put to death, for I will not acquit the guilty. [8]Never take a bribe, for a bribe blinds the clear-sighted and distorts the words of the just.[y]

[9]You shall not oppress a resident alien; you well know how it feels to be an alien, since you were once aliens yourselves in the land of Egypt.[z]

Religious Laws. [10][a] For six years you may sow your land and gather in its produce. [11]But the seventh year you shall let the land lie untilled and fallow, that the poor of your people may eat of it and their leftovers the wild animals may eat. So also shall you do in regard to your vineyard and your olive grove.

[12]For six days you may do your work, but on the seventh day you must rest,[b] that your ox and your donkey may have rest, and that the son of your maidservant and the resident alien may be refreshed. [13]Give heed to all that I have told you.

You shall not mention the name of any other god; it shall not be heard from your lips.

[14][c] Three times a year you shall celebrate a pilgrim feast to me.* [15]You shall keep the feast of Unleavened Bread. As I have commanded you, you must eat unleavened bread for seven days at the appointed time in the month of Abib, for it was then that you came

22:16 The bride price for virgins: fifty shekels according to Dt 22:29.

22:27 Despise God: a turning away from God's authority and so failing to honor God (cf. 1 Sm 2:30).

23:14 These three feasts—Passover/Unleavened Bread, Weeks (Pentecost), and Booths (Tabernacles or Succoth/Sukkoth)—are also listed in 34:18–26; Lv 23; Dt 16.

---

m: Lv 19:26, 31; 20:6, 27; Dt 18:10–11. *n:* Lv 18:23; Dt 27:21. *o:* Dt 13; 17:2–7. *p:* Ex 23:9; Lv 19:33–34; Dt 10:18–19; 24:17–18; 27:19; Zec 7:10. *q:* Lv 25:35–38; Dt 23:19–20; 24:10–13; Ez 18:7–8, 17–18. *r:* Dt 24:10–13; Jb 22:6; Prv 20:16; 27:13; Am 2:8. *s:* Acts 23:5. *t:* Ex 13:2; 34:19; Lv 22:27; Dt 15:19. *u:* Lv 7:24; 17:15; 22:8. *v:* Dt 19:16–21. *w:* Lv 19:15. *x:* Dt 22:1–4. *y:* Dt 16:19; 27:25; Sir 20:28. *z:* Ex 22:20. *a:* Lv 25:3–7. *b:* Ex 20:8–10. *c:* Ex 34:18, 22–24; Lv 23; Dt 16:1–17.

out of Egypt. No one shall appear before me*
empty-handed. 16 You shall also keep the
feast of the grain harvest with the first fruits
of the crop that you sow in the field; and finally, the feast of Ingathering at the end of
the year, when you collect your produce
from the fields. 17 Three times a year shall all
your men appear before the LORD God.
18 You shall not offer the blood of my sacrifice with anything leavened;[d] nor shall the
fat of my feast be kept overnight till the next
day. 19 The choicest first fruits of your soil
you shall bring to the house of the LORD,
your God.

You shall not boil a young goat in its
mother's milk.*

Reward of Fidelity. 20 See, I am sending an
angel[e] before you, to guard you on the way
and bring you to the place I have prepared.
21 Be attentive to him and obey him. Do not
rebel against him, for he will not forgive
your sin. My authority is within him.* 22 If
you obey him and carry out all I tell you, I
will be an enemy to your enemies and a foe
to your foes.

23 My angel will go before you and bring
you to the Amorites, Hittites, Perizzites,
Canaanites, Hivites and Jebusites; and I will
wipe them out. 24 Therefore, you shall not
bow down to their gods and serve them, nor
shall you act as they do; rather, you must demolish them and smash their sacred stones.*[f]
25 You shall serve the LORD, your God; then
he will bless your food and drink, and I will
remove sickness from your midst; 26 no
woman in your land will be barren or miscarry; and I will give you a full span of life.
27 I will have the terror of me precede you,
so that I will throw into panic every nation
you reach.[g] I will make all your enemies turn
from you in flight, 28 and ahead of you I will
send hornets* to drive the Hivites, Canaanites and Hittites out of your way. 29 But I will
not drive them all out before you in one year,
lest the land become desolate and the wild
animals multiply against you. 30 Little by little I will drive them out before you, until you
have grown numerous enough to take possession of the land. 31[h] I will set your boundaries from the Red Sea to the sea of the Philistines,* and from the wilderness to the
Euphrates; all who dwell in this land I will
hand over to you and you shall drive them
out before you. 32 You shall not make a covenant with them or their gods. 33 They must
not live in your land. For if you serve their
gods, this will become a snare to you.[i]

CHAPTER 24

See RG 122

Ratification of the Covenant. 1 Moses
himself was told: Come up to the LORD, you
and Aaron, with Nadab, Abihu, and seventy
of the elders of Israel. You shall bow down
at a distance. 2 Moses alone is to come close
to the LORD; the others shall not come close,
and the people shall not come up with them.
3 When Moses came to the people and related all the words and ordinances of the
LORD, they all answered with one voice,
"We will do everything that the LORD has
told us."[j] 4 Moses then wrote down all the
words of the LORD and, rising early in the
morning, he built at the foot of the mountain
an altar and twelve sacred stones* for the

23:15 Appear before me: the original expression was "see my face"; so also in several other places, as 23:17; 34:23–24; Dt 16:16; 31:11.

23:19 Boil a young goat in its mother's milk: this command, repeated in 34:26 and Dt 14:21, is difficult to understand. It may originate from a taboo that forbade killing the young that were still nursing from the mother, or that forbade the mixing of life and death: the slaughtered young goat with the milk that previously had nourished its life. The Jewish dietary custom of keeping meat and dairy products separate is based on this command.

23:21 My authority is within him: lit., "My name is within him."

23:24 Sacred stones: objects that symbolized the presence of Canaanite deities. In general, standing stones served as memorials for deities, persons, or significant events such as military victories or covenant-making. See 24:4.

23:28 Hornets: the Hebrew *sir'ah* is a disputed term, but according to ancient interpreters it refers to hornets that were unleashed against the enemy to sting them and cause panic (cf. Dt 7:20; Jos 24:12; Wis 12:8). Others associate the word with plagues or troublesome afflictions.

23:31 The sea of the Philistines: the Mediterranean. Only in the time of David and Solomon did the territory of Israel come near to reaching such distant borders.

24:4 Sacred stones: stone shafts or slabs, erected as symbols of the fact that each of the twelve tribes had entered into this covenant with God; see 23:24; Gn 28:18.

d: Ex 34:25–26. *e:* Ex 14:19; 32:34; 33:2. *f:* Ex 34:10–16; Nm 33:51–52; Dt 7:24–26. *g:* Dt 2:25; 7:20–22. *h:* Gn 15:18; Dt 11:24; Jos 1:4. *i:* Ex 34:12–16; Dt 7:2–6. *j:* Ex 19:8.

Calendar

THE YEAR WAS COMPOSED of twelve lunar months (beginning on the day of the new moon), with an intercalary month added periodically (see perhaps 1 Kgs 12:33). In some traditions, and perhaps originally, the year began in the fall, at the autumnal equinox (see Ex 23:16; 34:22). In others, following Babylonian practice, the new year was celebrated in the spring. The fall new year became standard in postbiblical Judaism.

Months in the Bible are usually identified by ordinal numbers, beginning with the spring new year. Some months (in boldface in the following list) are also designated with names derived either from a Canaanite calendar or, in postexilic texts, from a Babylonian one; the names of months not found in the Bible are known from other ancient sources.

	Canaanite Name	Babylonian/Aramaic Name	Modern Equivalent
First	**Abib**	**Nisan**	March–April
Second	**Ziv**	Iyar	April–May
Third		**Sivan**	May–June
Fourth		Tammuz	June–July
Fifth		Av	July–August
Sixth		**Elul**	August–September
Seventh	**Ethanim**	Tishri	September–October
Eighth	**Bul**	Marheshvan	October–November
Ninth		Chislev	November–December
Tenth		**Tebeth**	December–January
Eleventh		**Shebat**	January–February
Twelfth		**Adar**	February–March

The Jewish calendar is based on the lunar month, which is a bit longer than 29½ days, so Jewish lunar months are 29 or 30 days long. Twelve lunar months usually amount to 354 days, 11 days short of a solar year. In order for the festivals to stay in the correct season in relation to the solar year, an extra month is added every few years. Following ancient Babylonian models, the calendar runs on a 19-year cycle: years 3, 6, 8, 11, 14, 17, and 19 of the cycle are intercalated or "leap" years, containing an extra month of Adar, sometimes called ***Adar Sheni*** (second Adar). Adar was chosen for intercalation because it is the last month of the Babylonian year and of the biblical year beginning in Nisan (an alternate calendar, the one now in use, begins the year in Tishri with Rosh Ha-Shanah). The next 19-year intercalation cycle began in 5768 (2007–2008 A.D.).

Observances fall within the calendar as follows:

Rosh Ha-Shanah (the New Year)	1–2 Tishri
Yom Kippur (the Day of Atonement)	10 Tishri
Succoth (Booths) begins	15 Tishri
Hanukkah begins	25 Chislev
Purim	14 Adar (15 Adar in Jerusalem and other ancient walled cites)
Passover begins	15 Nisan
Shavuot (Weeks) begins	6 Sivan
Tish'ah be'av	9 Ab

twelve tribes of Israel. 5[k] Then, having sent
young men of the Israelites to offer burnt offerings and sacrifice young bulls as communion offerings to the LORD, 6Moses took
half of the blood and put it in large bowls;
the other half he splashed on the altar. 7Tak-
ing the book of the covenant, he read it aloud
to the people, who answered, "All that the
LORD has said, we will hear and do." 8Then
he took the blood and splashed it on the people, saying, "This is the blood of the covenant which the LORD has made with you according to all these words."

9Moses then went up with Aaron, Nadab,
Abihu, and seventy elders of Israel, 10and
they beheld the God of Israel. Under his feet
there appeared to be sapphire tilework, as
clear as the sky itself. 11Yet he did not lay a
hand on these chosen Israelites. They saw
God,* and they ate and drank.

Moses on the Mountain. 12The LORD said
to Moses: Come up to me on the mountain
and, while you are there, I will give you the
stone tablets[l] on which I have written the
commandments intended for their instruction. 13So Moses set out with Joshua, his assistant, and went up to the mountain of God.
14He told the elders, "Wait here for us until
we return to you. Aaron and Hur are with
you. Anyone with a complaint should approach them." 15Moses went up the mountain. Then the cloud covered the mountain.
16The glory of the LORD settled upon Mount
Sinai. The cloud covered it for six days, and
on the seventh day he called to Moses from
the midst of the cloud.[m] 17To the Israelites
the glory of the LORD was seen as a consuming fire on the top of the mountain.[n]
18But Moses entered into the midst of the
cloud and went up on the mountain. He was
on the mountain for forty days and forty
nights.[o]

CHAPTER 25

See RG 123

Collection of Materials. 1The LORD
spoke to Moses:[p] 2Speak to the Israelites:
Let them receive contributions for me. From
each you shall receive the contribution that
their hearts prompt them to give me. 3These
are the contributions you shall accept from
them: gold, silver, and bronze;[q] 4violet, purple, and scarlet yarn; fine linen and goat
hair; 5rams' skins dyed red, and tahash*
skins; acacia wood; 6oil for the light; spices
for the anointing oil and for the fragrant incense; 7onyx stones and other gems for
mounting on the ephod and the breastpiece.
8They are to make a sanctuary for me, that I
may dwell in their midst.[r] 9According to all
that I show you regarding the pattern of the
tabernacle and the pattern of its furnishings,
so you are to make it.[s]

Plan of the Ark. 10You shall make an ark
of acacia wood,[t] two and a half cubits* long,
one and a half cubits wide, and one and a
half cubits high. 11Plate it inside and outside
with pure gold, and put a molding of gold
around the top of it. 12Cast four gold rings
and put them on the four supports of the ark,
two rings on one side and two on the opposite side. 13Then make poles of acacia wood
and plate them with gold. 14These poles you
are to put through the rings on the sides of
the ark, for carrying it; 15they must remain in
the rings of the ark and never be withdrawn.
16In the ark you are to put the covenant
which I will give you.

17You shall then make a cover* of pure
gold, two and a half cubits long, and one and
a half cubits wide. 18Make two cherubim* of

24:11 They saw God: the ancients thought that the sight of God would bring instantaneous death. Cf. 33:20; Gn 16:13; 32:31; Jgs 6:22–23; 13:22. **Ate and drank**: partook of the sacrificial meal.

25:5 Tahash: perhaps a kind of specially finished leather. The Greek and Latin versions took it for the color hyacinth.

25:10 Cubits: the distance between the elbow and tip of the middle finger of an average-size person, about eighteen inches. The dimensions of the ark of the covenant were approximately 3 3/4 feet long, 2 1/4 feet wide, and 2 1/4 feet high.

25:17 Cover: the Hebrew term, *kapporet*, has been connected with *kippur*, as in the feast of Yom Kippur or Day of Atonement (Lv 16; 23:26–32): hence, influenced by the Greek and Latin versions, and Luther's German, English translations have rendered it "propitiatory," "mercy seat," and the like.

25:18–20 Cherubim: probably in the form of human-headed winged lions. The cherubim over the ark formed the throne for the invisible Lord. Cf. Ps 80:2. For a more detailed description of the somewhat different cherubim in the

k: Heb 9:18–20. *l:* Ex 31:18; 32:15–16; Dt 5:22. *m:* Sir 45:5. *n:* Ex 19:18; Heb 12:18. *o:* Ex 34:28; Dt 9:9. *p:* Ex 35:4–9, 20–29. *q:* Ex 35:4–9. *r:* Ex 26:1–30; 36:8–38. *s:* Acts 7:44. *t:* Ex 37:1–9; Heb 9:1–5.

beaten gold for the two ends of the cover;
19 make one cherub at one end, and the other
at the other end, of one piece with the cover,
at each end. 20 The cherubim shall have their
wings spread out above, sheltering the cover
with them; they shall face each other, with
their faces looking toward the cover. 21 This
cover you shall then place on top of the ark.
In the ark itself you are to put the covenant
which I will give you. 22 There I will meet
you and there, from above the cover, between the two cherubim on the ark of the
covenant, I will tell you all that I command
you regarding the Israelites.

The Table. 23 You shall also make a table of
acacia[u] wood, two cubits long, a cubit wide,
and a cubit and a half high. 24 Plate it with
pure gold and make a molding of gold
around it. 25 Make a frame* for it, a handbreadth high, and make a molding of gold
around the frame. 26 You shall also make four
rings of gold for it and fasten them at the
four corners, one at each leg. 27 The rings
shall be alongside the frame as holders for
the poles to carry the table. 28 These poles for
carrying the table you shall make of acacia
wood and plate with gold. 29 You shall make
its plates* and cups, as well as its pitchers
and bowls for pouring libations; make them
of pure gold. 30 On the table you shall always
keep showbread set before me.[v]

The Menorah. 31 You shall make a menorah* of pure beaten gold[w]—its shaft and
branches—with its cups and knobs and
petals springing directly from it. 32 Six
branches are to extend from its sides, three
branches on one side, and three on the other.
33* On one branch there are to be three cups,
shaped like almond blossoms, each with its
knob and petals; on the opposite branch
there are to be three cups, shaped like almond blossoms, each with its knob and
petals; and so for the six branches that extend from the menorah. 34 On the menorah
there are to be four cups,* shaped like almond blossoms, with their knobs and petals.
35 The six branches that go out from the
menorah are to have a knob under each pair.
36 Their knobs and branches shall so spring
from it that the whole will form a single
piece of pure beaten gold. 37* You shall then
make seven lamps[x] for it and so set up the
lamps that they give their light on the space
in front of the menorah. 38 These, as well as
the trimming shears and trays,* must be of
pure gold. 39 Use a talent* of pure gold for the
menorah and all these utensils. 40 See that
you make them according to the pattern
shown you on the mountain.[y]

CHAPTER 26

See RG 123

The Tent Cloth. 1 The tabernacle itself
you shall make out of ten sheets* woven of
fine linen twined and of violet, purple, and
scarlet yarn, with cherubim embroidered on
them.[z] 2 The length of each shall be twenty-
eight cubits, and the width four cubits; all
the sheets shall be of the same size. 3 Five of
the sheets are to be joined one to another;
and the same for the other five. 4 Make loops

Temple of Solomon, see 1 Kgs 6:23–28; 2 Chr 3:10–13.

25:25 A frame: probably placed near the bottom of the legs to keep them steady. The golden table of Herod's Temple is pictured thus on the Arch of Titus.

25:29–30 The plates held the showbread, that is, the holy bread which was placed upon the table every sabbath as an offering to God, and was later eaten by the priests. The cups held the incense which was strewn upon the bread. Cf. Lv 24:5–9. The libation wine was poured from the pitchers into the bowls. All these vessels were kept on the golden table.

25:31 Menorah: this traditional lampstand is still used today in Jewish liturgy.

25:33 In keeping with the arrangement of the ornaments on the shaft, the three sets of ornaments on each branch were probably so placed that one was at the top and the other two equally spaced along the length of the branch. **Knob**: the cup-shaped seed capsule at the base of a flower.

25:34–35 Of the four ornaments on the shaft, one was at the top and one was below each of the three sets of side branches.

25:37 The lamps were probably shaped like small boats, with the wick at one end; the end with the wick was turned toward the front of the menorah.

25:38 Trays: small receptacles for the burnt-out wicks.

25:39 Talent: Heb. *kikkar*. The largest unit of weight used in the Bible, equivalent to 3,000 shekels (see 38:24). It is difficult to be precise about biblical weights; the Israelite talent may have weighed between 75–80 pounds.

26:1 Sheets: strips of tapestry, woven of white linen, the colored threads being used for the cherubim which were embroidered on them. These sheets were stretched across the top of the tabernacle to form a roof, their free ends hanging down inside the framework that formed the walls.

u: Ex 37:10–16. *v:* Lv 24:5–9. *w:* Ex 37:17–24. *x:* Lv 24:2–4; Nm 8:2. *y:* Heb 8:5. *z:* Ex 36:8–19.

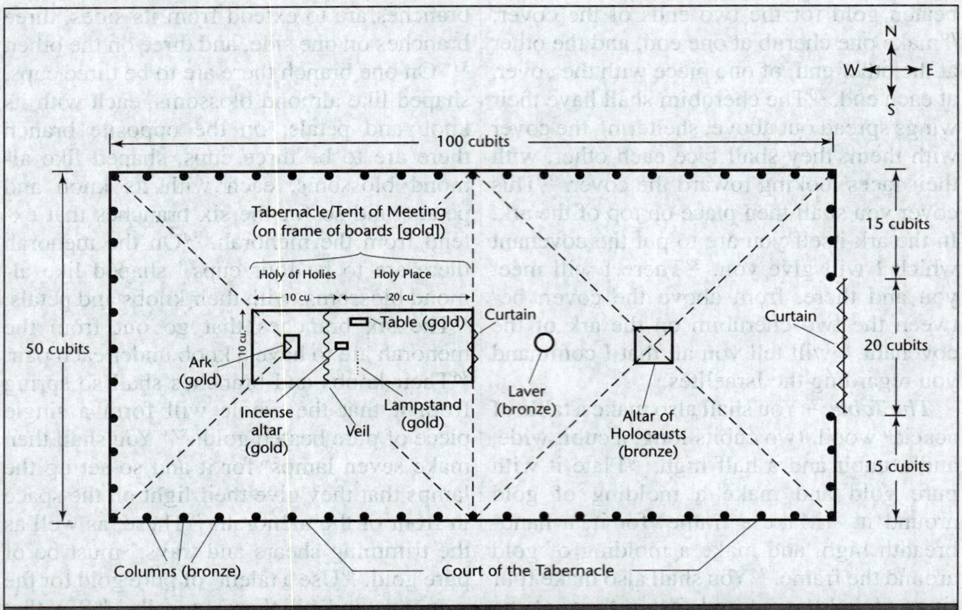

Structure of the Tabernacle

of violet yarn along the edge of the end sheet
in one set, and the same along the edge of the
end sheet in the other set. [5]Make fifty loops
along the edge of the end sheet in the first
set, and fifty loops along the edge of the corresponding sheet in the second set, and so
placed that the loops are directly opposite
each other. [6]Then make fifty clasps of gold
and join the two sets of sheets, so that the
tabernacle forms one whole.

[7]Also make sheets woven of goat hair for
a tent* over the tabernacle. Make eleven
such sheets; [8]the length of each shall be
thirty cubits, and the width four cubits: all
eleven sheets shall be of the same size. [9]Join
five of the sheets into one set, and the other
six sheets into another set. Use the sixth
sheet double at the front of the tent.* [10]Make
fifty loops along the edge of the end sheet in
one set, and fifty loops along the edge of the
end sheet in the second set. [11]Also make
fifty bronze clasps and put them into the
loops, to join the tent into one whole.
[12]There will be an extra half sheet of tent
covering, which shall be allowed to hang
down over the rear of the tabernacle. [13]Like-
wise, the sheets of the tent will have an extra cubit's length to be left hanging down on
either side of the tabernacle to cover it.
[14]Over the tent itself make a covering of
rams' skins dyed red, and above that, a covering of tahash skins.

The Framework. [15a]You shall make
frames for the tabernacle, acacia-wood uprights. [16]The length of each frame is to be ten
cubits, and its width one and a half cubits.
[17]Each frame shall have two arms* joined
one to another; so you are to make all the
frames of the tabernacle. [18]Make the frames
of the tabernacle as follows: twenty frames
on the south side, [19]with forty silver pedestals under the twenty frames, two ped-

26:7 Tent: the cloth made of sheets of goat hair to cover the tabernacle.

26:9 Half the width of the end strip was folded back at the front of the tabernacle, thus leaving another half-strip to hang down at the rear. Cf. v. 12.

26:17 Arms: lit., "hands." According to some, they served as "tongue and groove" to mortise the structural elements; according to others, they were pegs that fitted into sockets in the pedestals.

a: Ex 36:20–34.

estals under each frame for its two arms; 20 twenty frames on the other side of the tabernacle, the north side, 21 with their forty silver pedestals, two pedestals under each frame. 22 At the rear of the tabernacle, to the west, six frames, 23 and two frames for the corners of the tabernacle, at its rear. 24 These two shall be double at the bottom, and likewise double at the top, to the first ring. That is how both corner frames are to be made. 25 Thus, there shall be eight frames, with their sixteen silver pedestals, two pedestals under each frame. 26 Also make bars of acacia wood: five for the frames on one side of the tabernacle, 27 five for those on the other side, and five for those at the rear, to the west. 28 The center bar, at the middle of the frames, shall reach across from end to end. 29 Plate the frames with gold, and make gold rings on them as holders for the bars, which are also to be plated with gold. 30 You shall set up the tabernacle according to its plan, which you were shown on the mountain.

The Veils. 31 You shall make a veil woven of violet, purple, and scarlet yarn,[b] and of fine linen twined, with cherubim embroidered on it.[c] 32 It is to be hung on four gold-plated columns of acacia wood, which shall have gold hooks* and shall rest on four silver pedestals. 33 Hang the veil from clasps. The ark of the covenant you shall bring inside, behind this veil which divides the holy place from the holy of holies. 34 Set the cover on the ark of the covenant in the holy of holies.

35 Outside the veil you shall place the table and the menorah, the latter on the south side of the tabernacle, opposite the table, which is to be put on the north side. 36 For the entrance of the tent make a variegated* curtain of violet, purple, and scarlet yarn and of fine linen twined. 37 Make five columns of acacia wood for this curtain; plate them with gold, with their hooks of gold; and cast five bronze pedestals for them.

CHAPTER 27

See RG 123

The Altar for Burnt Offerings. 1 You shall make an altar[d] of acacia wood, on a square, five cubits long and five cubits wide; it shall be three cubits high. 2 At the four corners make horns* that are of one piece with the altar. You shall then plate it with bronze. 3 Make pots for removing the ashes, as well as shovels, basins, forks, and fire pans; all these utensils you shall make of bronze. 4 Make for it a grating,* a bronze network; make four bronze rings for it, one at each of its four corners. 5 Put it down around the altar, on the ground. This network is to be half as high as the altar. 6 You shall also make poles of acacia wood for the altar, and plate them with bronze. 7 These poles are to be put through the rings, so that they are on either side of the altar when it is carried. 8 Make the altar itself in the form of a hollow* box. Just as it was shown you on the mountain, so it is to be made.

Court of the Tabernacle. 9[e] You shall also make a court for the tabernacle. On the south side the court shall have hangings, of fine linen twined, a hundred cubits long, 10 with twenty columns and twenty pedestals of bronze; the hooks and bands on the columns shall be of silver. 11 On the north side there shall be similar hangings, a hundred cubits long, with twenty columns and twenty pedestals of bronze; the hooks and bands on the columns shall be of silver. 12 On the west side, across the width of the court, there shall be hangings, fifty cubits long, with ten columns and ten pedestals. 13 The width of the court on the east side shall be fifty cubits. 14 On one side there shall be hangings to the extent of fifteen cubits, with three columns and three pedestals; 15 on the other side there shall be hangings to the extent of fifteen cubits, with three columns and three pedestals. 16 At the gate of the court there shall be a variegated curtain, twenty cubits long, wo-

26:32 Hooks: probably placed near the tops of the columns, to hold the rope from which the veils and curtains hung.

26:36 Variegated: without definite designs such as the cherubim on the inner veil.

27:2 Horns: the horn of a ram, goat or ox is a common Old Testament figure for strength and dignity; they represent the divine character of the altar itself or the deity worshiped there.

27:4 Grating: it is not clear whether this was flush with the altar or at some small distance from it; in the latter case the space between the altar and the grating would be filled with stones and serve as a platform around the altar, which would otherwise be too high for the priest to reach conveniently.

27:8 Hollow: probably filled with earth or stones when in use. Cf. 20:24–25.

b: 2 Chr 3:14. *c:* Ex 36:35–38. *d:* Ex 38:1–7. *e:* Ex 38:9–20.

ven of violet, purple, and scarlet yarn and of fine linen twined. It shall have four columns and four pedestals.

17All the columns around the court shall have bands and hooks of silver, and pedestals of bronze. 18The court is to be one hundred cubits long, fifty cubits wide, and five cubits high. Fine linen twined must be used, and the pedestals must be of bronze. 19All the fittings of the tabernacle, whatever be their use, as well as all its tent pegs and all the tent pegs of the court, must be of bronze.

Oil for the Lamps. 20You shall command the Israelites to bring you clear oil of crushed olives, to be used for the light, so that you may keep lamps burning always.[f] 21From evening to morning Aaron and his sons shall maintain them before the LORD in the tent of meeting, outside the veil which hangs in front of the covenant. This shall be a perpetual statute for the Israelites throughout their generations.

See RG 123

CHAPTER 28

The Priestly Vestments. 1[g] Have your brother Aaron, and with him his sons, brought to you, from among the Israelites, that they may be my priests: Nadab and Abihu, Eleazar and Ithamar, Aaron's sons. 2For the glorious adornment of your brother Aaron you shall have sacred vestments made. 3Therefore, tell the various artisans whom I have endowed with skill* to make vestments for Aaron to consecrate him as my priest. 4These are the vestments they shall make: a breastpiece, an ephod, a robe, a brocade tunic, a turban, and a sash. In making these sacred vestments which your brother Aaron and his sons are to wear in serving as my priests, 5they shall use gold, violet, purple, and scarlet yarn and fine linen.

The Ephod and Breastpiece. 6The ephod* they shall make of gold thread and of violet, purple, and scarlet yarn, embroidered on cloth of fine linen twined.[h] 7It shall have a pair of shoulder straps joined to its two upper ends. 8The embroidered belt of the ephod shall extend out from it and, like it, be made of gold thread, of violet, purple, and scarlet yarn, and of fine linen twined.

9Get two onyx stones and engrave on them the names of the sons of Israel: 10six of their names on one stone, and the names of the remaining six on the other stone, in the order of their birth. 11As a gem-cutter engraves a seal, so shall you have the two stones engraved with the names of the sons of Israel and then mounted in gold filigree work. 12Set these two stones on the shoulder straps of the ephod as memorial stones of the sons of Israel. Thus Aaron shall bear their names on his shoulders as a reminder before the LORD. 13Make filigree rosettes of gold,[i] 14as well as two chains of pure gold, twisted like cords, and fasten the cordlike chains to the filigree rosettes.

15[j] The breastpiece* of decision you shall also have made, embroidered like the ephod with gold thread and violet, purple, and scarlet yarn on cloth of fine linen twined. 16It is to be square when folded double, a span high and a span wide. 17* On it you shall mount four rows of precious stones: in the first row, a carnelian, a topaz, and an emerald; 18in the second row, a garnet, a sapphire, and a beryl; 19in the third row, a jacinth, an agate, and an amethyst; 20in the fourth row, a chrysolite, an onyx, and a jasper. These stones are to be mounted in gold filigree work, 21twelve of them to match the names of the sons of Israel, each stone engraved like a seal with the name of one of the twelve tribes.

22When the chains of pure gold, twisted

28:3 Artisans . . . endowed with skill: lit., "wise of heart," and "filled with a spirit of wisdom." In Hebrew wisdom includes practical skills. Cf. 35:35; 36:1–2.

28:6 Ephod: this Hebrew word is retained in the translation because it is the technical term for a peculiar piece of the priestly vestments, the exact nature of which is uncertain. It seems to have been a sort of apron that hung from the shoulders of the priest by shoulder straps (v. 7) and was tied around his waist by the loose ends of the attached belt (v. 8).

28:15–30 Breastpiece: an approximately nine-inch square, pocketlike receptacle for holding the Urim and Thummim (v. 30). It formed an integral part of the ephod, to which it was attached by an elaborate system of rings and chains. Both the ephod and its breastpiece were made of brocaded linen. **Span**: Heb. *zeret*, the distance between the top of the little finger and the thumb; one half a cubit, approximately nine inches.

28:17–20 The translation of the Hebrew names of some of these gems is quite conjectural.

f: Lv 24:1–4. *g:* Ex 39:1; Sir 45:7. *h:* Ex 39:2–7; Sir 45:8–14. *i:* Ex 28:22, 25; 39:15, 18. *j:* Ex 39:15–21.

like cords, have been made for the breastpiece, [23]you shall then make two rings of gold for it and fasten them to the two upper ends of the breastpiece. [24]The gold cords are then to be fastened to the two rings at the upper ends of the breastpiece, [25]the other two ends of the cords being fastened in front to the two filigree rosettes which are attached to the shoulder straps of the ephod. [26]Make two other rings of gold and put them on the two lower ends of the breastpiece, on its edge that faces the ephod. [27]Then make two more rings of gold and fasten them to the bottom of the shoulder straps next to where they join the ephod in front, just above its embroidered belt. [28]Violet ribbons shall bind the rings of the breastpiece to the rings of the ephod, so that the breastpiece will stay right above the embroidered belt of the ephod and not swing loose from it.

[29]Whenever Aaron enters the sanctuary, he will thus bear the names of the sons of Israel on the breastpiece of decision over his heart as a constant reminder before the LORD. [30]In this breastpiece of decision[k] you shall put the Urim and Thummim,* that they may be over Aaron's heart whenever he enters the presence of the LORD. Thus he shall always bear the decisions for the Israelites over his heart in the presence of the LORD.

Other Vestments. [31]The robe of the ephod[l] you shall make entirely of violet material. [32]It shall have an opening for the head in the center, and around this opening there shall be a selvage, woven as at the opening of a shirt, to keep it from being torn. [33]At the hem at the bottom you shall make pomegranates, woven of violet, purple, and scarlet yarn and fine linen twined, with gold bells between them; [34]a gold bell, a pomegranate, a gold bell, a pomegranate, all around the hem of the robe. [35]Aaron shall wear it when ministering, that its sound may be heard as he enters and leaves the LORD's presence in the sanctuary; else he will die.

[36]You shall also make a plate of pure gold and engrave on it, as on a seal engraving, "Sacred to the LORD." [37]This plate is to be tied over the turban with a violet ribbon in such a way that it rests on the front of the turban,[m] [38]over Aaron's forehead. Since Aaron bears whatever guilt the Israelites may incur in consecrating any of their sacred gifts, this plate must always be over his forehead, so that they may find favor with the LORD.

[39][n] The tunic of fine linen shall be brocaded. The turban shall be made of fine linen. The sash shall be of variegated work.

[40]Likewise, for the glorious adornment of Aaron's sons you shall have tunics and sashes and skullcaps made, for glorious splendor. [41]With these you shall clothe your brother Aaron and his sons. Anoint and install them,* consecrating them as my priests. [42]You must also make linen pants for them, to cover their naked flesh from their loins to their thighs.[o] [43]Aaron and his sons shall wear them whenever they go into the tent of meeting or approach the altar to minister in the sanctuary, lest they incur guilt and die. This shall be a perpetual ordinance for him and for his descendants.

CHAPTER 29

See RG 123

Consecration of the Priests. [1]This is the rite you shall perform in consecrating them as my priests.[p] Procure a young bull and two unblemished rams. [2]With bran flour make unleavened cakes mixed with oil, and unleavened wafers spread with oil, [3]and put them in a basket. Take the basket of them along with the bull and the two rams. [4]Aaron and his sons you shall also bring to the entrance of the tent of meeting, and there wash them with water. [5]Take the vestments and clothe Aaron with the tunic, the robe of the ephod, the ephod itself, and the breastpiece, fastening the embroidered belt of the ephod around him. [6]Put the turban on his head, the sacred diadem on the turban. [7]Then take the

28:30 Urim and Thummim: both the meaning of these Hebrew words and the exact nature of the objects so designated are uncertain. They were apparently lots of some kind which were drawn or cast by the priest to ascertain God's decision on particular questions. Hence, the pocket in which they were kept was called "the breastpiece of decision."

28:41 Install them: lit., "fill their hands," a technical expression used for the installation of priests.

k: Lv 8:8; Sir 45:11. *l:* Ex 39:20–25; Lv 8:9; Sir 45:10. *m:* Ex 39:31; Lv 8:9. *n:* Ex 39:27–31. *o:* Ez 44:18. *p:* Lv 8:1–9.

anointing oil and pour it on his head, and
anoint him. [8]Bring forward his sons also and
clothe them with the tunics, [9]gird them with
the sashes, and tie the skullcaps on them.[q]
Thus shall the priesthood be theirs by a perpetual statute, and thus shall you install
Aaron and his sons.

Installation Sacrifices. [10r] Now bring forward the bull in front of the tent of meeting.
There Aaron and his sons shall lay their
hands on its head. [11]Then slaughter the bull
before the LORD, at the entrance of the tent of
meeting. [12]Take some of its blood and with
your finger put it on the horns of the altar. All
the rest of the blood you shall pour out at the
base of the altar. [13]All the fat that covers its
inner organs, as well as the lobe of its liver
and its two kidneys, together with the fat that
is on them, you shall take and burn on the altar. [14]But the meat and hide and dung of the
bull you must burn up outside the camp,
since this is a purification offering.[s]

[15]Then take one of the rams, and after
Aaron and his sons have laid their hands on
its head, [16]slaughter it. The blood you shall
take and splash on all the sides of the altar.
[17]Cut the ram into pieces; you shall wash its
inner organs and shanks and put them with
the pieces and with the head. [18]Then you
shall burn the entire ram on the altar, since it
is a burnt offering, a sweet-smelling oblation
to the LORD.

[19]After this take the other ram, and when
Aaron and his sons have laid their hands on
its head, [20]slaughter it. Some of its blood you
shall take and put on the tip of Aaron's right
ear and on the tips of his sons' right ears and
on the thumbs of their right hands and the
great toes of their right feet. Splash the rest
of the blood on all the sides of the altar.
[21]Then take some of the blood that is on the
altar, together with some of the anointing
oil, and sprinkle this on Aaron and his vestments, as well as on his sons and their vestments, that he and his sons and their vestments may be sacred.

[22]Now, from this ram you shall take its
fat: its fatty tail,* the fat that covers its inner
organs, the lobe of its liver, its two kidneys
with the fat that is on them, and its right
thigh, since this is the ram for installation;
[23]then, out of the basket of unleavened food
that you have set before the LORD, you shall
take one of the loaves of bread, one of the
cakes made with oil, and one of the wafers.
[24]All these things you shall put into the
hands of Aaron and his sons, so that they
may raise them as an elevated offering* before the LORD. [25]After you receive them
back from their hands, you shall burn them
on top of the burnt offering on the altar as a
sweet-smelling oblation to the LORD. [26]Fi-
nally, take the brisket of Aaron's installation
ram and raise it as an elevated offering before the LORD; this is to be your own portion.

[27*] Thus shall you set aside the brisket of
whatever elevated offering is raised,[t] as well
as the thigh of whatever contribution is
raised up, whether this be the installation ram
or anything else belonging to Aaron or to his
sons. [28]Such things are due to Aaron and his
sons from the Israelites by a perpetual statute
as a contribution. From their communion offerings, too, the Israelites shall make a contribution, their contribution to the LORD.

[29]The sacred vestments[u] of Aaron shall be
passed down to his sons after him, that in
them they may be anointed and installed.
[30]The son who succeeds him as priest and
who is to enter the tent of meeting to minister in the sanctuary shall be clothed with
them for seven days.

[31v] You shall take the installation ram and
boil its meat in a holy place. [32]At the entrance of the tent of meeting Aaron and his
sons shall eat the meat of the ram and the
bread that is in the basket. [33]They themselves are to eat of these things by which

29:22 Fatty tail: the thick layer of fat surrounding the tails of sheep and rams bred in the Middle East. It is regarded as a choice food. Cf. Lv 3:9.

29:24–26 Elevated offering: the portions of a communion offering, brisket and right thigh, which the officiating priest raised in the presence of the Lord. They were reserved for Aaron and his sons.

29:27–30 These verses are a parenthetical interruption of the installation ritual; v. 31 belongs logically immediately after v. 26.

q: Lv 8:13. *r:* Lv 8:14–30. *s:* Heb 13:11. *t:* Lv 7:31–34; 10:14–15; Nm 18:18–19; Dt 18:3. *u:* Nm 20:26, 28. *v:* Lv 8:31–32.

atonement was made at their installation and
consecration; but no unauthorized person
may eat of them, since they are sacred. 34 If
some of the meat of the installation sacrifice
or some of the bread remains over on the
next day, this remnant you must burn up; it
is not to be eaten, since it is sacred.
35 Carry out all these commands in regard
to Aaron and his sons just as I have given
them to you.[w] Seven days you shall spend
installing them, 36[x] sacrificing a bull each
day as a purification offering, to make atonement. Thus you shall purify the altar* by
purging it, and you shall anoint it in order to
consecrate it. 37 Seven days you shall spend
in purging the altar and in consecrating it.
Then the altar will be most sacred, and whatever touches it will become sacred.
38* Now, this is what you shall regularly
offer on the altar: two yearling lambs[y] as the
sacrifice established for each day; 39 one lamb
in the morning and the other lamb at the
evening twilight. 40 With the first lamb there
shall be a tenth of an ephah of bran flour
mixed with a fourth of a hin* of oil of crushed
olives and, as its libation, a fourth of a hin of
wine. 41 The other lamb you shall offer at the
evening twilight, with the same grain offering and libation as in the morning. You shall
offer this as a sweet-smelling oblation to the
LORD. 42 Throughout your generations this
regular burnt offering shall be made before
the LORD at the entrance of the tent of meeting, where I will meet you and speak to you.
43 There, at the altar, I will meet the Israelites; hence, it will be made sacred by my
glory.[z] 44 Thus I will consecrate the tent of
meeting and the altar, just as I also consecrate Aaron and his sons to be my priests. 45 I
will dwell in the midst of the Israelites and
will be their God. 46 They shall know that I,
the LORD, am their God who brought them
out of the land of Egypt, so that I, the LORD,
their God, might dwell among them.

CHAPTER 30

See RG 123

Altar of Incense. 1 For burning incense
you shall make an altar of acacia wood,[a]
2 with a square surface, a cubit long, a cubit
wide, and two cubits high, with horns that
are of one piece with it. 3 Its grate on top, its
walls on all four sides, and its horns you
shall plate with pure gold. Put a gold molding around it. 4 Underneath the molding you
shall put gold rings, two on one side and two
on the opposite side, as holders for the poles
used in carrying it. 5 Make the poles, too, of
acacia wood and plate them with gold. 6 This
altar you are to place in front of the veil that
hangs before the ark of the covenant where I
will meet you.[b]
7 On it Aaron shall burn fragrant incense.
Morning after morning, when he prepares
the lamps, 8 and again in the evening twilight, when he lights the lamps, he shall burn
incense. Throughout your generations this
shall be the regular incense offering before
the LORD. 9 On this altar you shall not offer
up any profane incense, or any burnt offering or grain offering; nor shall you pour out
a libation upon it. 10 Once a year Aaron shall
purge its horns.[c] Throughout your generations he is to purge it once a year with the
blood of the atoning purification offering.
This altar is most sacred to the LORD.
Census Tax. 11 The LORD also told Moses:
12 When you take a census[d] of the Israelites
who are to be enrolled, each one, as he is enrolled, shall give the LORD a ransom for his
life, so that no plague may come upon them
for being enrolled. 13 This is what everyone
who is enrolled must pay: a half-shekel, according to the standard of the sanctuary
shekel—twenty gerahs to the shekel—a half-
shekel contribution to the LORD.[e] 14 Everyone
who is enrolled, of twenty years or more,
must give the contribution to the LORD. 15 The
rich need not give more, nor shall the poor

29:36–37 Purify the altar: the purpose of the purification offering here is to cleanse, or purify, the newly constructed altar of any defilement resulting from presumably minor and inadvertent sins, but the text is not explicit about what the offenses were or who committed them. So various theories have been proposed to explain the cause of the altar's contamination. Note, however, that the offering appears to be demanded of Aaron and his sons; they are the ones who lay hands upon it (v. 10).

29:38–42 A parenthesis inserted into the rubrics for consecrating the altar; v. 43 belongs directly after v. 37.

29:40 Hin: see note on Ez 45:24.

w: Lv 8:36. *x:* Lv 8:33–35. *y:* Nm 28:3–8. *z:* Ex 25:22. *a:* Ex 37:25–28. *b:* Ex 40:26. *c:* Lv 16:18. *d:* Nm 1:2–3; 26:2. *e:* Mt 17:24–27.

give less, than a half-shekel in this contribution to the LORD to pay the ransom for their lives. [16][f]When you receive this ransom money from the Israelites, you shall donate it to the service of the tent of meeting, that there it may be a reminder of the Israelites before the LORD of the ransom paid for their lives.

The Basin. [17]The LORD told Moses: [18]For ablutions you shall make a bronze basin with a bronze stand. Place it between the tent of meeting and the altar, and put water in it.[g] [19]Aaron and his sons shall use it in washing their hands and feet.[h] [20]When they are about to enter the tent of meeting, they must wash with water, lest they die. Likewise when they approach the altar to minister, to offer an oblation to the LORD, [21]they must wash their hands and feet, lest they die. This shall be a perpetual statute for him and his descendants throughout their generations.

The Anointing Oil. [22]The LORD told Moses: [23]Take the finest spices: five hundred shekels of free-flowing myrrh; half that amount, that is, two hundred and fifty shekels, of fragrant cinnamon; two hundred and fifty shekels of fragrant cane; [24]five hundred shekels of cassia—all according to the standard of the sanctuary shekel; together with a hin of olive oil; [25]and blend them into sacred anointing oil,[i] perfumed ointment expertly prepared.[j] With this sacred anointing oil [26]you shall anoint the tent of meeting and the ark of the covenant, [27]the table and all its utensils, the menorah and its utensils, the altar of incense [28]and the altar for burnt offerings with all its utensils, and the basin with its stand. [29]When you have consecrated them, they shall be most sacred; whatever touches them shall be sacred. [30]Aaron and his sons you shall also anoint and consecrate as my priests.[k] [31]Tell the Israelites: As sacred anointing oil this shall belong to me throughout your generations. [32]It may not be used in any ordinary anointing of the body, nor may you make any other oil of a like mixture. It is sacred, and shall be treated as sacred by you. [33]Whoever prepares a perfume like this, or whoever puts any of this on an unauthorized person, shall be cut off from his people.

The Incense. [34][l]The LORD told Moses: Take these aromatic substances: storax and onycha and galbanum, these and pure frankincense in equal parts; [35]and blend them into incense. This fragrant powder, expertly prepared, is to be salted and so kept pure and sacred. [36]Grind some of it into fine dust and put this before the covenant in the tent of meeting where I will meet you. This incense shall be treated as most sacred by you. [37]You may not make incense of a like mixture for yourselves; you must treat it as sacred to the LORD. [38]Whoever makes an incense like this for his own enjoyment of its fragrance, shall be cut off from his people.

CHAPTER 31

See RG 123

Choice of Artisans. [1][m]The LORD said to Moses: [2]See, I have singled out* Bezalel, son of Uri, son of Hur, of the tribe of Judah, [3]and I have filled him with a divine spirit of skill and understanding and knowledge in every craft: [4]in the production of embroidery, in making things of gold, silver, or bronze, [5]in cutting and mounting precious stones, in carving wood, and in every other craft. [6]As his assistant I myself have appointed Oholiab, son of Ahisamach, of the tribe of Dan. I have also endowed all the experts with the necessary skill to make all the things I have commanded you: [7][n]the tent of meeting, the ark of the covenant with its cover, all the furnishings of the tent, [8]the table with its utensils, the pure gold menorah with all its utensils, the altar of incense, [9]the altar for burnt offerings with all its utensils, the basin with its stand, [10]the service cloths,* the sacred vestments for Aaron the priest, the vestments for his sons in their ministry, [11]the anointing oil, and the fragrant incense for the sanctuary. According to all I have commanded you, so shall they do.

31:2 Singled out: lit., "called by name"; cf. 35:30.

31:10 The service cloths: so the Greek. They were perhaps the colored cloths mentioned in Nm 4:4–15.

f: Ex 38:25. *g:* Ex 38:8; 40:7, 30. *h:* Ex 40:31–32. *i:* Ex 37:29. *j:* Ex 40:9–11; Lv 8:10; Nm 7:1. *k:* Ex 29:7; Lv 8:12. *l:* Ex 25:6; 37:29. *m:* Ex 35:30–35. *n:* Ex 35:10–19.

Sabbath Laws. 12[o] The LORD said to Moses: 13 You must also tell the Israelites: Keep my sabbaths, for that is to be the sign between you and me throughout the generations, to show that it is I, the LORD, who make you holy. 14* Therefore, you must keep the sabbath for it is holiness for you. Whoever desecrates it shall be put to death. If anyone does work on that day, that person must be cut off from the people. 15 Six days there are for doing work, but the seventh day is the sabbath of complete rest, holy to the LORD. Anyone who does work on the sabbath day shall be put to death. 16 So shall the Israelites observe the sabbath, keeping it throughout their generations as an everlasting covenant. 17 Between me and the Israelites it is to be an everlasting sign; for in six days the LORD made the heavens and the earth, but on the seventh day he rested at his ease.

18 When the LORD had finished speaking to Moses on Mount Sinai, he gave him the two tablets of the covenant, the stone tablets inscribed by God's own finger.[p]

VII. Israel's Apostasy and God's Renewal of the Covenant

CHAPTER 32

See RG 123

The Golden Calf. 1 When the people saw that Moses was delayed in coming down from the mountain, they gathered around Aaron and said to him, "Come, make us a god who will go before us; as for that man Moses who brought us out of the land of Egypt, we do not know what has happened to him."[q] 2 Aaron replied, "Take off the golden earrings that your wives, your sons, and your daughters are wearing, and bring them to me." 3 So all the people took off their earrings and brought them to Aaron. 4 He received their offering, and fashioning it with a tool, made a molten calf. Then they cried out, "These are your gods, Israel, who brought you* up from the land of Egypt."[r] 5 On seeing this, Aaron built an altar in front of the calf and proclaimed, "Tomorrow is a feast of the LORD." 6 Early the next day the people sacrificed burnt offerings and brought communion sacrifices. Then they sat down to eat and drink, and rose up to revel.[s]

7[t] Then the LORD said to Moses: Go down at once because your people, whom you brought out of the land of Egypt, have acted corruptly. 8 They have quickly turned aside from the way I commanded them, making for themselves a molten calf and bowing down to it, sacrificing to it and crying out, "These are your gods, Israel, who brought you up from the land of Egypt!" 9[u] I have seen this people, how stiff-necked they are, continued the LORD to Moses. 10 Let me alone, then, that my anger may burn against them to consume them. Then I will make of you a great nation.

11* But Moses implored the LORD, his God, saying,[v] "Why, O LORD, should your anger burn against your people, whom you brought out of the land of Egypt with great power and with a strong hand? 12 Why should the Egyptians say, 'With evil intent he brought them out, that he might kill them in the mountains and wipe them off the face of the earth'? Turn from your burning wrath; change your mind about punishing your people. 13 Remember your servants Abraham, Isaac, and Israel, and how you swore to them by your own self, saying,[w] 'I will make your descendants as numerous as the stars in the sky; and all this land that I promised, I will give your descendants as their perpetual her-

31:14–15 For the distinction between work proscribed on certain festivals and weekly Sabbaths, see note on Lv 23:3.

32:4–5 Who brought you . . . a feast of the LORD: it seems that the golden calf was intended as an image, not of another god, but of the Lord, whose strength was symbolized by the strength of a young bull. The Israelites, however, had been forbidden to represent the Lord under any visible form. Cf. 20:4. In the tenth century Jeroboam made golden calves for the shrines at Bethel and Dan, presumably to function as thrones for the Lord as the ark did in Jerusalem (see 1 Kgs 12:27–30).

32:11–13 Moses uses three arguments to persuade the Lord to remain faithful to the Sinai covenant even though the people have broken it: (1) they are God's own people, redeemed with God's great power; (2) God's reputation will suffer if they are destroyed; (3) the covenant with Abraham still stands. The Lord's change of mind is a testimony to Israel's belief in the power of intercessory prayer.

o: Ex 20:8–11; 35:1–3. *p:* Ex 24:12; 32:15–16; Dt 5:22. *q:* Ex 32:23; Acts 7:40. *r:* Ex 32:8; 1 Kgs 12:28. *s:* 1 Cor 10:7. *t:* Dt 9:12, 16. *u:* Dt 9:13. *v:* Nm 14:13–19; Dt 9:28–29; Ps 106:23. *w:* Gn 22:16–17.

itage.’ ” 14So the LORD changed his mind
about the punishment he had threatened to
inflict on his people.
15Moses then turned and came down the
mountain with the two tablets of the covenant in his hands,[x] tablets that were written
on both sides, front and back. 16The tablets
were made by God; the writing was the writing of God, engraved on the tablets.[y] 17Now,
when Joshua heard the noise of the people
shouting, he said to Moses, “That sounds like
a battle in the camp.” 18But Moses answered,

“It is not the noise of victory,
it is not the noise of defeat;
the sound I hear is singing.”

19As he drew near the camp, he saw the calf
and the dancing. Then Moses’ anger burned,
and he threw the tablets down and broke
them on the base of the mountain.[z] 20Taking
the calf they had made, he burned it in the
fire and then ground it down to powder,
which he scattered on the water* and made
the Israelites drink.[a]
21* Moses asked Aaron, “What did this
people do to you that you should lead them
into a grave sin?” 22Aaron replied, “Do not
let my lord be angry. You know how the people are prone to evil. 23They said to me,
‘Make us a god to go before us; as for this
man Moses who brought us out of the land of
Egypt, we do not know what has happened to
him.’ 24So I told them, ‘Whoever is wearing
gold, take it off.’ They gave it to me, and I
threw it into the fire, and this calf came out.”
25Moses saw that the people were running
wild because Aaron had lost control—to the
secret delight of their foes. 26Moses stood at
the gate of the camp and shouted, “Whoever
is for the LORD, come to me!” All the Levites[b] then rallied to him, 27and he told them,
“Thus says the LORD, the God of Israel:
Each of you put your sword on your hip! Go
back and forth through the camp, from gate
to gate, and kill your brothers, your friends,
your neighbors!” 28The Levites did as Moses
had commanded, and that day about three
thousand of the people fell. 29Then Moses
said, “Today you are installed as priests* for
the LORD, for you went against your own
sons and brothers, to bring a blessing upon
yourselves this day.”

The Atonement. 30On the next day Moses
said to the people,[c] “You have committed a
grave sin. Now I will go up to the LORD; perhaps I may be able to make atonement for
your sin.” 31So Moses returned to the LORD
and said, “Ah, this people has committed a
grave sin in making a god of gold for themselves! 32Now if you would only forgive
their sin! But if you will not, then blot me
out of the book that you have written.”*
33The LORD answered Moses: Only the one
who has sinned against me will I blot out of
my book. 34Now, go and lead the people
where I have told you. See, my angel will go
before you. When it is time for me to punish,
I will punish them for their sin.
35Thus the LORD struck the people for
making the calf, the one that Aaron made.

CHAPTER 33

See RG 123

1The LORD spoke to Moses: Go! You
and the people whom you have brought up
from the land of Egypt are to go up from
here to the land about which I swore to Abraham, Isaac, and Jacob: I will give it to your
descendants.[d] 2Driving out the Canaanites,
Amorites, Hittites, Perizzites, Hivites and
Jebusites, I will send an angel before you[e]
3to a land flowing with milk and honey. But
I myself will not go up in your company, because you are a stiff-necked people; otherwise I might consume you on the way.
4When the people heard this painful news,
they mourned, and no one wore any ornaments.
5The LORD spoke to Moses: Speak to the

32:20 The water: according to Dt 9:21, this was the stream that flowed down Mount Sinai.

32:21–24 Aaron attempts to persuade Moses not to act in anger, just as Moses persuaded the Lord. He also shifts the blame from himself to the people.

32:29 Installed as priests: lit., “fill your hands,” a term for the ordination of priests (see 28:41; 29:9, 29, 33, 35; Nm 3:3). Because of their zeal for the true worship of the Lord, the Levites were chosen to be special ministers of the ritual service.

32:32 The book that you have written: a symbolic reference to the list of God’s faithful people.

x: Dt 9:15. *y:* Ex 31:18. *z:* Dt 9:16–17. *a:* Dt 9:21. *b:* Dt 33:8–9. *c:* Dt 9:18–19. *d:* Gn 12:7. *e:* Ex 23:23.

Israelites: You are a stiff-necked people. Were I to go up in your company even for a moment, I would destroy you. Now off with your ornaments! Let me think what to do with you. [6]So, from Mount Horeb onward, the Israelites stripped off their ornaments.

Moses' Intimacy with God. [7]Moses used to pitch a tent[f] outside the camp at some distance. It was called the tent of meeting. Anyone who wished to consult the LORD would go to the tent of meeting outside the camp. [8]Whenever Moses went out to the tent, the people would all rise and stand at the entrance of their own tents, watching Moses until he entered the tent. [9]As Moses entered the tent, the column of cloud would come down and stand at its entrance while the LORD spoke with Moses. [10]On seeing the column of cloud stand at the entrance of the tent, all the people would rise and bow down at the entrance of their own tents. [11]The LORD used to speak to Moses face to face,[g] as a person speaks to a friend. Moses would then return to the camp, but his young assistant, Joshua, son of Nun, never left the tent. [12]Moses said to the LORD, "See, you are telling me: Lead this people.[h] But you have not let me know whom you will send with me. Yet you have said: You are my intimate friend;* You have found favor with me. [13]Now, if I have found favor with you, please let me know your ways so that, in knowing you, I may continue to find favor with you. See, this nation is indeed your own people. [14]The LORD answered: I myself* will go along, to give you rest. [15]Moses replied, "If you are not going yourself, do not make us go up from here. [16]For how can it be known that I and your people have found favor with you, except by your going with us? Then we, your people and I, will be singled out from every other people on the surface of the earth." [17]The LORD said to Moses: This request, too, which you have made, I will carry out, because you have found favor with me and you are my intimate friend.

[18]Then Moses said, "Please let me see your glory!" [19]The LORD answered: I will make all my goodness pass before you, and I will proclaim my name, "LORD," before you; I who show favor to whom I will, I who grant mercy to whom I will.[i] [20]But you cannot see my face,[j] for no one can see me and live.* [21]Here, continued the LORD, is a place near me where you shall station yourself on the rock. [22]When my glory passes I will set you in the cleft of the rock and will cover you with my hand until I have passed by. [23]Then I will remove my hand, so that you may see my back; but my face may not be seen.

CHAPTER 34

See RG 123

Renewal of the Tablets. [1]The LORD said to Moses: "Cut two stone tablets like the former,[k] that I may write on them the words* which were on the former tablets that you broke. [2]Get ready for tomorrow morning, when you are to go up Mount Sinai and there present yourself to me on the top of the mountain. [3]No one shall come up with you, and let no one even be seen on any part of the mountain;[l] even the sheep and the cattle are not to graze in front of this mountain." [4]Moses then cut two stone tablets like the former, and early the next morning he went up Mount Sinai as the LORD had commanded him, taking in his hand the two stone tablets.

[5]The LORD came down in a cloud and stood with him there and proclaimed the name, "LORD." [6]So the LORD passed before him and proclaimed: The LORD, the LORD, a God gracious and merciful, slow to anger and abounding in love and fidelity,* [7]contin-

33:12 Intimate friend: lit., "know by name." The root word meaning "know" or "make known" appears four times in vv. 12–13.

33:14 I myself: lit., "my face," that is, "my presence." The making of the calf (32:1–4) is an attempt to control the Lord's presence. In response the Lord refuses to accompany the people (33:3) until Moses persuades him.

33:20 No one can see me and live: reflecting the tradition that to see God meant instant death. This is contradicted by the statements that Hagar (Gn 16:13), Jacob (Gn 32:31), and Manoah and his wife (Jgs 13:22) all "see God" and yet live (see also Ex 24:10–11).

34:1 Words: a common term for commandments, especially the Decalogue (see v. 28). In v. 27 "words" connotes the commands given in vv. 11–26.

34:6 Gracious . . . fidelity: this succinct poetic description

f: Ex 29:42–43. *g:* Nm 12:8; Dt 34:10; Sir 45:4–5. *h:* Ex 32:34. *i:* Rom 9:15. *j:* Jn 1:18; 1 Tm 6:16. *k:* Dt 10:1–2. *l:* Ex 19:12–13, 21.

uing his love for a thousand generations, and forgiving wickedness, rebellion, and sin; yet not declaring the guilty guiltless, but bringing punishment for their parents' wickedness on children and children's children to the third and fourth generation![m] 8 Moses at once knelt and bowed down to the ground. 9 Then he said, "If I find favor with you, Lord, please, Lord, come along in our company. This is indeed a stiff-necked people; yet pardon our wickedness and sins, and claim us as your own."

Religious Laws. 10 The LORD said: Here is the covenant I will make. Before all your people I will perform marvels never before done* in any nation anywhere on earth, so that all the people among whom you live may see the work of the LORD. Awe-inspiring are the deeds I will perform with you! 11 As for you, observe what I am commanding you today.[n]

See, I am about to drive out before you the Amorites, Canaanites, Hittites, Perizzites, Hivites and Jebusites. 12[o] Take care not to make a covenant with the inhabitants of the land that you are to enter; lest they become a snare among you. 13 Tear down their altars; smash their sacred stones, and cut down their asherahs.* 14 You shall not bow down to any other god, for the LORD—"Jealous"* his name—is a jealous God. 15 Do not make a covenant with the inhabitants of the land; else, when they prostitute themselves with their gods and sacrifice to them, one of them may invite you and you may partake of the sacrifice. 16 And when you take their daughters as wives for your sons, and their daughters prostitute themselves with their gods, they will make your sons do the same.

17 You shall not make for yourselves molten gods.[p]

18 You shall keep the festival of Unleavened Bread.[q] For seven days at the appointed time in the month of Abib you are to eat unleavened bread, as I commanded you; for in the month of Abib you came out of Egypt.

19 To me belongs every male that opens the womb among all your livestock, whether in the herd or in the flock.[r] 20 The firstling of a donkey you shall redeem with a lamb; if you do not redeem it, you must break its neck. The firstborn among your sons you shall redeem.

No one shall appear before me empty-handed.

21 Six days you may labor,[s] but on the seventh day you shall rest; even during the seasons of plowing and harvesting you must rest.

22[t] You shall keep the feast of Weeks with the first fruits of the wheat harvest, likewise, the feast of the Ingathering at the close of the year.* 23 Three times a year all your men shall appear before the Lord, the LORD God of Israel. 24 Since I will drive out the nations before you and enlarge your territory, no one will covet your land when you go up three times a year to appear before the LORD, your God.

25 You shall not offer me the blood of sacrifice with anything leavened, nor shall the sacrifice of the Passover feast be kept overnight for the next day.

26 The choicest first fruits of your soil you shall bring to the house of the LORD, your God.

You shall not boil a young goat in its mother's milk.[u]

Radiance of Moses' Face. 27 Then the LORD said to Moses: Write down these words, for in accordance with these words I have made a covenant with you and with Israel. 28 So Moses was there with the LORD for

of God is an often-repeated statement of belief (see Nm 14:18; Ps 103:8; 145:8; Jl 2:13; Jon 4:2). All the terms describe God's relationship to the covenant people.

34:10 Never before done: lit., "created." The verb used here (Heb. *bara'*) is predicated only of God (see Gn 1:1, 21, 27; Ps 51:12). These wonders are a new creation and can be performed only by God.

34:13 Asherah was the name of a Canaanite goddess. In her honor wooden poles (*asherot*) were erected, just as stone pillars (*massebot*) were erected in honor of the god Baal. Both were placed near the altar in a Canaanite shrine.

34:14 Jealous: see note on 20:5. Some, by a slight emendation, render, "The Lord is jealous for his name." Cf. Ez 39:25.

34:22 Feast of Weeks: the festival of thanksgiving for the harvest, celebrated seven weeks or fifty days after the beginning of the harvest. It was also called Pentecost (fiftieth) and coincided with the giving of the law on Mount Sinai, fifty days after the offering of the first fruits; cf. Lv 23:10–11; Dt 16:9. **Feast of the Ingathering**: feast of Booths.

m: Ex 20:5–6; Nm 14:18; Dt 5:9–10; Jer 32:18. *n:* Ex 13:5; 33:2. *o:* Ex 23:32–33; Dt 7:1–5; 12:2–3. *p:* Lv 19:4; Dt 5:8–9. *q:* Ex 12:15–20; 13:3–4. *r:* Ex 13:2, 12–13; 23:15. *s:* Ex 20:9–10. *t:* Ex 23:16–17; Dt 16:10, 13, 16. *u:* Ex 23:18–19.

forty days and forty nights,[v] without eating any food or drinking any water, and he wrote on the tablets the words of the covenant, the ten words.

29 As Moses came down from Mount Sinai with the two tablets of the covenant in his hands, he did not know that the skin of his face had become radiant* while he spoke with the LORD. 30 When Aaron, then, and the other Israelites saw Moses and noticed how radiant the skin of his face had become, they were afraid to come near him. 31 Only after Moses called to them did Aaron and all the leaders of the community come back to him. Moses then spoke to them. 32 Later, all the Israelites came up to him, and he enjoined on them all that the LORD had told him on Mount Sinai. 33 When Moses finished speaking with them, he put a veil over his face. 34 Whenever Moses entered the presence of the LORD to speak with him, he removed the veil until he came out again.[w] On coming out, he would tell the Israelites all that he had been commanded. 35 Then the Israelites would see that the skin of Moses' face was radiant; so he would again put the veil over his face until he went in to speak with the LORD.

VIII. The Building of the Tabernacle and the Descent of God's Glory upon It

CHAPTER 35

See RG 123

Sabbath Regulations. 1 Moses assembled the whole Israelite community and said to them,[x] "These are the words the LORD has commanded to be observed. 2 On six days work may be done, but the seventh day shall be holy to you as the sabbath of complete rest to the LORD. Anyone who does work on that day shall be put to death. 3 You shall not even light a fire in any of your dwellings on the sabbath day."

Collection of Materials. 4 Moses said to the whole Israelite community, "This is what the LORD has commanded: 5[y] Receive from among you contributions for the LORD. Everyone, as his heart prompts him, shall bring, as a contribution to the LORD, gold, silver, and bronze; 6 violet, purple, and scarlet yarn; fine linen and goat hair; 7 rams' skins dyed red, and tahash skins; acacia wood; 8 oil for the light; spices for the anointing oil and for the fragrant incense; 9 onyx stones and other gems for mounting on the ephod and on the breastpiece.

Call for Artisans. 10[z] "Let every artisan among you come and make all that the LORD has commanded: 11 the tabernacle, with its tent, its covering, its clasps, its frames, its bars, its columns, and its pedestals; 12 the ark, with its poles, the cover, and the curtain veil; 13 the table, with its poles and all its utensils, and the showbread; 14 the menorah, with its utensils, the lamps, and the oil for the light; 15 the altar of incense, with its poles; the anointing oil, and the fragrant incense; the entrance curtain for the entrance of the tabernacle; 16 the altar for burnt offerings, with its bronze grating, its poles, and all its utensils; the basin, with its stand; 17 the hangings of the court, with their columns and pedestals; the curtain for the gate of the court; 18 the tent pegs for the tabernacle and for the court, with their ropes; 19 the service cloths for use in the sanctuary; the sacred vestments for Aaron, the priest, and the vestments for his sons in their ministry."

The Contribution. 20 When the whole Israelite community left Moses' presence, 21 all, as their hearts moved them and their spirit prompted, brought a contribution to the LORD for the work of the tent of meeting, for all its services, and for the sacred vestments. 22 Both the men and the women, all as their heart prompted them, brought brooches, earrings, rings, necklaces, and various other gold articles.[a] Everyone who could presented an offering of gold to the LORD. 23 Everyone who happened to have violet, purple, or scarlet yarn, fine linen or goat hair, rams' skins dyed red or tahash skins, brought them. 24 Whoever could make a contribution of sil-

34:29 Radiant: the Hebrew word translated "radiant" is spelled like the term for "horns." Thus the artistic tradition of portraying Moses with horns.

v: Ex 24:18; Dt 9:9, 18; 10:2, 4. *w:* 2 Cor 3:13, 16. *x:* Ex 31:13–17. *y:* Ex 25:2–7. *z:* Ex 31:6–11. *a:* Ex 25:3–7.

ver or bronze offered it to the LORD; and everyone who happened to have acacia wood for any part of the work, brought it. 25All the women who were expert spinners brought hand-spun violet, purple, and scarlet yarn and fine linen thread. 26All the women, as their hearts and skills moved them, spun goat hair. 27The tribal leaders brought onyx stones and other gems for mounting on the ephod and on the breastpiece; 28as well as spices, and oil for the light, anointing oil, and fragrant incense. 29Every Israelite man and woman brought to the LORD such voluntary offerings as they thought best, for the various kinds of work which the LORD, through Moses, had commanded to be done.

The Artisans. 30Moses said to the Israelites:[b] "See, the LORD has singled out Bezalel, son of Uri, son of Hur, of the tribe of Judah, 31and has filled him with a divine spirit of skill and understanding and knowledge in every craft: 32in the production of embroidery, in making things of gold, silver, or bronze, 33in cutting and mounting precious stones, in carving wood, and in every other craft. 34He has also given both him and Oholiab, son of Ahisamach, of the tribe of Dan, the ability to teach others. 35He has endowed them with skill to execute all types of work: engraving, embroidering, the making of variegated cloth of violet, purple, and scarlet yarn and fine linen thread, weaving, and all other arts and crafts.

CHAPTER 36

See RG 123

1"Bezalel, therefore, will set to work with Oholiab and with all the artisans whom the LORD has endowed with skill and understanding in knowing how to do all the work for the service of the sanctuary, just as the LORD has commanded."[c]

2Moses then called Bezalel and Oholiab and all the other artisans whom the LORD had endowed with skill, men whose hearts moved them to come and do the work. 3They received from Moses all the contributions which the Israelites had brought for the work to be done for the sanctuary service. Still, morning after morning the people continued to bring their voluntary offerings to Moses. 4Thereupon all the artisans who were doing the work for the sanctuary came from the work each was doing, 5and told Moses, "The people are bringing much more than is needed to carry out the work which the LORD has commanded us to do." 6Moses, therefore, ordered a proclamation to be made throughout the camp: "Let neither man nor woman make any more contributions for the sanctuary." So the people stopped bringing their offerings; 7there was already enough at hand, and more than enough, to complete the work to be done.

The Tent Cloth and Coverings. 8[d] The various artisans who were doing the work made the tabernacle with its ten sheets woven of fine linen twined, having cherubim embroidered on them with violet, purple, and scarlet yarn. 9The length of each sheet was twenty-eight cubits, and the width four cubits; all the sheets were the same size. 10Five of the sheets were joined together, edge to edge; and the other five sheets likewise, edge to edge. 11Loops of violet yarn were made along the edge of the end sheet in the first set, and the same along the edge of the end sheet in the second set. 12Fifty loops were thus put on one inner sheet, and fifty loops on the inner sheet in the other set, with the loops directly opposite each other. 13Then fifty clasps of gold were made, with which the sheets were joined so that the tabernacle formed one whole.

14Sheets of goat hair were also woven as a tent over the tabernacle. Eleven such sheets were made. 15The length of each sheet was thirty cubits and the width four cubits; all eleven sheets were the same size. 16Five of these sheets were joined into one set, and the other six sheets into another set. 17Fifty loops were made along the edge of the end sheet in one set, and fifty loops along the edge of the corresponding sheet in the other set. 18Fifty bronze clasps were made with which the tent was joined so that it formed one whole. 19A covering for the tent was made of rams' skins dyed red and, above that, a covering of tahash skins.

---

b: Ex 31:1–6. *c:* Ex 31:1, 6. *d:* Ex 26:1–14.

The Framework. 20[e] Frames were made for the tabernacle, acacia-wood uprights. 21The length of each frame was ten cubits, and the width one and a half cubits. 22Each frame had two arms, fastening them one to another. In this way all the frames of the tabernacle were made. 23The frames for the tabernacle were made as follows: twenty frames on the south side, 24with forty silver pedestals under the twenty frames, two pedestals under each frame for its two arms; 25twenty frames on the other side of the tabernacle, the north side, 26with their forty silver pedestals, two pedestals under each frame. 27At the rear of the tabernacle, to the west, six frames were made, 28and two frames were made for the corners of the tabernacle, at its rear. 29These were double at the bottom, and likewise double at the top, to the first ring. That is how both corner frames were made. 30Thus, there were eight frames, with their sixteen silver pedestals, two pedestals under each frame. 31Bars of acacia wood were also made, five for the frames on one side of the tabernacle, 32five for those on the other side, and five for those at the rear, to the west. 33The center bar, at the middle of the frames, was made to reach across from end to end. 34The frames were plated with gold, and gold rings were made on them as holders for the bars, which were also plated with gold.

The Veil. 35[f] The veil was made of violet, purple, and scarlet yarn, and of fine linen twined, with cherubim embroidered on it. 36Four gold-plated columns of acacia wood, with gold hooks, were made for it, and four silver pedestals were cast for them.

37The curtain for the entrance of the tent was made of violet, purple, and scarlet yarn, and of fine linen twined, woven in a variegated manner. 38Its five columns, with their hooks as well as their capitals and bands, were plated with gold; their five pedestals were of bronze.

CHAPTER 37

See RG 123

The Ark. 1Bezalel made the ark of acacia wood, two and a half cubits long, one and a half cubits wide, and one and a half cubits high. 2The inside and outside were plated with gold, and a molding of gold was put around it. 3Four gold rings were cast for its four supports, two rings on one side and two on the opposite side. 4Poles of acacia wood were made and plated with gold; 5these poles were put through the rings on the sides of the ark, for carrying it.

6The cover was made of pure gold, two and a half cubits long and one and a half cubits wide. 7Two cherubim of beaten gold were made for the two ends of the cover; 8one cherub was at one end, the other at the other end, made of one piece with the cover, at each end. 9The cherubim had their wings spread out above, sheltering the cover. They faced each other, with their faces looking toward the cover.[g]

The Table. 10[h] The table was made of acacia wood, two cubits long, a cubit wide, and a cubit and a half high. 11It was plated with pure gold, and a molding of gold was put around it. 12A frame a handbreadth high was also put around it, with a molding of gold around the frame. 13Four rings of gold were cast for it and fastened at the four corners, one at each leg. 14The rings were alongside the frame as holders for the poles to carry the table. 15These poles for carrying the table were made of acacia wood and plated with gold. 16The vessels that were set on the table, its plates and cups, as well as its pitchers and bowls for pouring libations, were made of pure gold.

The Menorah. 17[i] The menorah was made of pure beaten gold—its shaft and branches—with its cups and knobs and petals springing directly from it. 18Six branches extended from its sides, three branches on one side and three on the other. 19On one branch there were three cups, shaped like almond blossoms, each with its knob and petals; on the opposite branch there were three cups, shaped like almond blossoms, each with its knob and petals; and so for the six branches that extended from the menorah. 20On the menorah there were four cups, shaped like almond blossoms, with their knobs and petals. 21The six

e: Ex 26:15–29. *f:* Ex 26:31–37. *g:* Ex 25:10–22. *h:* Ex 25:23–30. *i:* Ex 25:31–39.

branches that went out from the menorah had a knob under each pair. [22]The knobs and branches so sprang from it that the whole formed but a single piece of pure beaten gold. [23]Its seven lamps, as well as its trimming shears and trays, were made of pure gold. [24]A talent of pure gold was used for the menorah and its various utensils.

The Altar of Incense. [25][j] The altar of incense was made of acacia wood, on a square, a cubit long, a cubit wide, and two cubits high, having horns that sprang directly from it. [26]Its grate on top, its walls on all four sides, and its horns were plated with pure gold; and a gold molding was put around it. [27]Underneath the molding gold rings were placed, two on one side and two on the opposite side, as holders for the poles used in carrying it. [28]The poles, too, were made of acacia wood and plated with gold.

[29]The sacred anointing oil and the fragrant incense were prepared in their pure form by a perfumer.[k]

CHAPTER 38

See RG 123

The Altar for Burnt Offerings. [1]The altar for burnt offerings[l] was made of acacia wood, on a square, five cubits long and five cubits wide; its height was three cubits. [2]At the four corners horns were made that sprang directly from the altar. It was then plated with bronze. [3]All the utensils of the altar, the pots, shovels, basins, forks and fire pans, were likewise made of bronze. [4]A grating, a bronze network, was made for the altar and placed around it, on the ground, half as high as the altar itself. [5]Four rings were cast for the four corners of the bronze grating, as holders for the poles, [6]which were made of acacia wood and plated with bronze. [7]The poles were put through the rings on the sides of the altar for carrying it. The altar was made in the form of a hollow box.

[8]The bronze basin,[m] with its bronze stand, was made from the mirrors of the women who served* at the entrance of the tent of meeting.

The Court of the Tabernacle. [9][n] The court was made as follows. On the south side the hangings of the court were of fine linen twined, a hundred cubits long, [10]with twenty columns and twenty pedestals of bronze, the hooks and bands of the columns being of silver. [11]On the north side there were similar hangings, a hundred cubits long, with twenty columns and twenty pedestals of bronze; the hooks and bands of the columns were of silver. [12]On the west side there were hangings, fifty cubits long, with ten columns and ten pedestals; the hooks and bands of the columns were of silver. [13]On the east side the court was fifty cubits. [14]On one side there were hangings to the extent of fifteen cubits, with three columns and three pedestals; [15]on the other side, beyond the gate of the court, there were likewise hangings to the extent of fifteen cubits, with three columns and three pedestals. [16]The hangings on all sides of the court were woven of fine linen twined. [17]The pedestals of the columns were of bronze, while the hooks and bands of the columns were of silver; the capitals were silver-plated, and all the columns of the court were banded with silver.

[18]At the gate of the court there was a variegated curtain, woven of violet, purple, and scarlet yarn and of fine linen twined, twenty cubits long and five cubits wide, in keeping with the hangings of the court. [19]There were four columns and four pedestals of bronze for it, while their hooks were of silver, and their capitals and their bands silver-plated. [20]All the tent pegs for the tabernacle and for the court around it were of bronze.

Amount of Metal Used. [21]The following is an account of the various amounts used on the tabernacle, the tabernacle of the covenant, drawn up at the command of Moses by the Levites under the direction of Ithamar, son of Aaron the priest. [22]However, it was Bezalel, son of Uri,[o] son of Hur, of the tribe of Judah, who made all that the LORD commanded Moses, [23]and he was assisted by Oholiab, son of Ahisamach, of the tribe of Dan, who was an engraver, an embroiderer, and a weaver of variegated cloth of

38:8 The reflecting surface of ancient mirrors was usually of polished bronze. **The women who served**: cf. 1 Sm 2:22.

j: Ex 30:1–5. *k:* Ex 30:23–25, 34–36. *l:* Ex 27:1–8; 2 Chr 1:5. *m:* Ex 30:18–21. *n:* Ex 27:9–19. *o:* Ex 31:2, 6; 35:30, 34; 36:1.

violet, purple, and scarlet yarn and of fine linen.

[24]All the gold used in the entire construction of the sanctuary, having previously been given as an offering, amounted to twenty-nine talents and seven hundred and thirty shekels, according to the standard of the sanctuary shekel. [25]The silver of those of the community who were enrolled was one hundred talents and one thousand seven hundred and seventy-five shekels, according to the standard of the sanctuary shekel; [26]one bekah apiece, that is, a half-shekel, according to the standard of the sanctuary shekel, was received from everyone who was enrolled, of twenty years or more, namely, six hundred and three thousand five hundred and fifty men.[p] [27]One hundred talents of silver were used for casting the pedestals of the sanctuary and the pedestals of the veil, one talent for each pedestal, or one hundred talents for the one hundred pedestals. [28]The remaining one thousand seven hundred and seventy-five shekels were used for making the hooks on the columns, for plating the capitals, and for banding them with silver. [29]The bronze, given as an offering, amounted to seventy talents and two thousand four hundred shekels. [30]With this were made the pedestals at the entrance of the tent of meeting, the bronze altar with its bronze gratings, and all the utensils of the altar, [31]the pedestals around the court, the pedestals at the gate of the court, and all the tent pegs for the tabernacle and for the court around it.

See RG 123

CHAPTER 39

The Priestly Vestments. [1]With violet, purple, and scarlet yarn were woven the service cloths for use in the sanctuary, as well as the sacred vestments[q] for Aaron, as the LORD had commanded Moses.

[2r]The ephod was woven of gold thread and of violet, purple, and scarlet yarn and of fine linen twined. [3]Gold was first hammered into gold leaf and then cut up into threads, which were woven with the violet, purple, and scarlet yarn into an embroidered pattern on the fine linen. [4]Shoulder straps were made for it and joined to its two upper ends. [5]The embroidered belt on the ephod extended out from it, and like it, was made of gold thread, of violet, purple, and scarlet yarn, and of fine linen twined, as the LORD had commanded Moses. [6]The onyx stones were prepared and mounted in gold filigree work; they were engraved like seal engravings with the names of the sons of Israel. [7]These stones were set on the shoulder straps of the ephod as memorial stones of the sons of Israel, just as the LORD had commanded Moses.

[8s]The breastpiece was embroidered like the ephod, with gold thread and violet, purple, and scarlet yarn on cloth of fine linen twined. [9]It was square and folded double, a span high and a span wide in its folded form. [10]Four rows of precious stones were mounted on it: in the first row a carnelian, a topaz, and an emerald; [11]in the second row, a garnet, a sapphire, and a beryl; [12]in the third row a jacinth, an agate, and an amethyst; [13]in the fourth row a chrysolite, an onyx, and a jasper. They were mounted in gold filigree work. [14]These stones were twelve, to match the names of the sons of Israel, and each stone was engraved like a seal with the name of one of the twelve tribes.

[15t]Chains of pure gold, twisted like cords, were made for the breastpiece, [16]together with two gold filigree rosettes and two gold rings. The two rings were fastened to the two upper ends of the breastpiece. [17]The two gold chains were then fastened to the two rings at the ends of the breastpiece. [18]The other two ends of the two chains were fastened in front to the two filigree rosettes, which were attached to the shoulder straps of the ephod. [19]Two other gold rings were made and put on the two lower ends of the breastpiece, on the edge facing the ephod. [20]Two more gold rings were made and fastened to the bottom of the two shoulder straps next to where they joined the ephod in front, just above its embroidered belt. [21]Violet ribbons bound the rings of the breastpiece to the rings of the ephod, so that the breastpiece stayed right above the embroidered

p: Nm 1:46. *q:* Ex 31:10. *r:* Ex 28:6–12. *s:* Ex 28:15–21. *t:* Ex 28:31–35.

belt of the ephod and did not swing loose from it. All this was just as the LORD had commanded Moses.

Other Vestments. [22]The robe of the ephod was woven entirely of violet yarn, [23]with an opening in its center like the opening of a shirt, with selvage around the opening to keep it from being torn. [24]At the hem of the robe pomegranates were made of violet, purple, and scarlet yarn and of fine linen twined; [25]bells of pure gold were also made and put between the pomegranates all around the hem of the robe: [26]a bell, a pomegranate, a bell, a pomegranate, all around the hem of the robe which was to be worn in performing the ministry—all this, just as the LORD had commanded Moses.

[27]For Aaron and his sons there were also woven tunics of fine linen;[u] [28]the turban of fine linen; the ornate skullcaps of fine linen; linen pants of fine linen twined; [29]and sashes of variegated work made of fine linen twined and of violet, purple, and scarlet yarn, as the LORD had commanded Moses. [30][v] The plate of the sacred diadem was made of pure gold and inscribed, as on a seal engraving: "Sacred to the LORD." [31]It was tied over the turban with a violet ribbon, as the LORD had commanded Moses.

Presentation of the Work to Moses. [32]Thus the entire work of the tabernacle of the tent of meeting was completed. The Israelites did the work just as the LORD had commanded Moses; so it was done. [33]They then brought to Moses the tabernacle, the tent with all its furnishings, the clasps, the frames, the bars, the columns, the pedestals, [34]the covering of rams' skins dyed red, the covering of tahash skins, the curtain veil; [35]the ark of the covenant with its poles, the cover, [36]the table with all its utensils and the showbread, [37]the pure gold menorah with its lamps set up on it and with all its utensils, the oil for the light, [38]the golden altar, the anointing oil, the fragrant incense; the curtain for the entrance of the tent, [39]the altar of bronze with its bronze grating, its poles and all its utensils, the basin with its stand, [40]the hangings of the court with their columns and pedestals, the curtain for the gate of the court with its ropes and tent pegs, all the equipment for the service of the tabernacle of the tent of meeting; [41]the service cloths for use in the sanctuary, the sacred vestments for Aaron the priest, and the vestments to be worn by his sons in their ministry. [42]Just as the LORD had commanded Moses, so the Israelites had carried out all the work. [43]So when Moses saw that all the work was done just as the LORD had commanded, he blessed them.

CHAPTER 40

See RG 123

Setting up the Tabernacle. [1]Then the LORD said to Moses: [2][w] On the first day of the first month* you shall set up the tabernacle of the tent of meeting.[x] [3]Put the ark of the covenant in it, and screen off the ark with the veil.[y] [4]Bring in the table and set it. Then bring in the menorah and set up the lamps on it. [5]Put the golden altar of incense in front of the ark of the covenant, and hang the curtain at the entrance of the tabernacle. [6]Put the altar for burnt offerings in front of the entrance of the tabernacle of the tent of meeting. [7]Place the basin between the tent of meeting and the altar, and put water in it. [8]Set up the court round about, and put the curtain at the gate of the court.

[9][z] Take the anointing oil and anoint the tabernacle and everything in it, consecrating it and all its furnishings, so that it will be sacred. [10]Anoint the altar for burnt offerings and all its utensils, consecrating it, so that it will be most sacred. [11]Likewise, anoint the basin with its stand, and thus consecrate it.

[12][a] Then bring Aaron and his sons to the entrance of the tent of meeting, and there wash them with water. [13]Clothe Aaron with the sacred vestments and anoint him, thus consecrating him as my priest. [14]Bring forward his sons also, and clothe them with the tunics. [15]As you have anointed their father, anoint them also as my priests. Thus, by be-

40:2 On the first day of the first month: almost a year after the departure of the Israelites from Egypt. Cf. v. 17.

u: Ex 28:39–42. *v:* Ex 28:36–37. *w:* Ex 40:16–33. *x:* Ex 26:30. *y:* Ex 26:33–37. *z:* Ex 30:26–29. *a:* Ex 28:41; 29:4–9; Lv 8:1–13.

ing anointed, shall they receive a perpetual priesthood throughout all future generations. [16]Moses did just as the LORD had commanded him. [17]On the first day of the first month of the second year the tabernacle was set up. [18]It was Moses who set up the tabernacle. He placed its pedestals, set up its frames, put in its bars, and set up its columns. [19]He spread the tent over the tabernacle and put the covering on top of the tent, as the LORD had commanded him. [20][b] He took the covenant and put it in the ark; he placed poles alongside the ark and set the cover upon it. [21]He brought the ark into the tabernacle and hung the curtain veil, thus screening off the ark of the covenant, as the LORD had commanded him. [22]He put the table in the tent of meeting, on the north side of the tabernacle, outside the veil, [23]and arranged the bread on it before the LORD, as the LORD had commanded him.[c] [24]He placed the menorah in the tent of meeting, opposite the table, on the south side of the tabernacle, [25]and he set up the lamps before the LORD, as the LORD had commanded him. [26]He placed the golden altar in the tent of meeting, in front of the veil, [27]and on it he burned fragrant incense, as the LORD had commanded him. [28]He hung the curtain at the entrance of the tabernacle. [29]He put the altar for burnt offerings in front of the entrance of the tabernacle of the tent of meeting, and sacrificed burnt offerings and grain offerings on it, as the LORD had commanded him. [30][d] He placed the basin between the tent of meeting and the altar, and put water in it for washing. [31]Moses and Aaron and his sons used to wash their hands and feet there, [32]for they washed themselves whenever they went into the tent of meeting or approached the altar, as the LORD had commanded Moses. [33]Finally, he set up the court around the tabernacle and the altar and hung the curtain at the gate of the court.

Thus Moses finished all the work.

God's Presence in the Tabernacle. [34][e] Then the cloud covered the tent of meeting, and the glory of the LORD filled the tabernacle. [35]Moses could not enter the tent of meeting, because the cloud settled down upon it and the glory of the LORD filled the tabernacle. [36]Whenever the cloud rose from the tabernacle, the Israelites would set out on their journey. [37]But if the cloud did not lift, they would not go forward; only when it lifted did they go forward. [38]The cloud of the LORD was over the tabernacle by day, and fire in the cloud at night, in the sight of the whole house of Israel in all the stages of their journey.

b: Ex 25:16, 21; 26:33–37. *c:* Ex 25:30. *d:* Ex 30:18–21. *e:* Nm 9:15–22.

The Book of Leviticus

See RG 125–33

The name "Leviticus" was given to the third book of the Pentateuch by the ancient Greek translators because a good part of this book deals with concerns of the priests, who are of the tribe of Levi.

The book mainly treats cultic matters (i.e., sacrifices and offerings, purity and holiness, the priesthood, the operation of the sanctuary, and feast days) but is also interested in various behavioral, ethical, and economic issues (e.g., sexual practices, idolatrous worship, treatment of others, the sale of land, slavery). The goal of the laws is not merely legislative. For the most part they cohere as a system and attempt to inculcate a way of life in the book's hearers and readers. In addition to these concerns, Leviticus, comprising as it does the center of the Pentateuch, carries forward the narrative of Exodus (cf. chaps. 1, 8–9, 10, 16, 24).

The book is part of the Priestly tradition (P) of the Pentateuch, to which belong various narratives and legal passages (e.g., Gn 1:1–2:4; 9:1–17; 17:1–27; Ex 12:1–20, 40–50; 25:1–31:18; 35:1–40:38; Nm 1:1–10:28; 15:1–14; 17:1–19:22; 25:6–31:54). Within the Priestly material itself there are signs of variant traditions and development.

The main divisions of Leviticus are:

- I. Ritual of Sacrifices (1:1–7:38)
  - A. Instructions for the Israelites (1:1–5:26)
  - B. Instructions for the Priests (6:1–7:38)
- II. Ceremony of Ordination (8:1–10:20)
- III. Laws Regarding Ritual Purity (11:1–16:34)
- IV. Holiness Laws (17:1–26:46)
- V. Redemption of Offerings (27:1–34)

I. Ritual of Sacrifices

A. Instructions for the Israelites

CHAPTER 1

See RG 128

Burnt Offerings. 1The LORD called
Moses, and spoke to him from the tent of
meeting:[a] 2Speak to the Israelites and tell
them: When any one of you* brings an offering of livestock to the LORD, you shall bring
your offering from the herd or from the flock.[b]
3* [c] If a person's offering is a burnt offering* from the herd, the offering must be a
male without blemish.[d] The individual shall
bring it to the entrance of the tent of meeting
to find favor with the LORD, 4and shall lay a
hand* on the head[e] of the burnt offering, so
that it may be acceptable[f] to make atonement[g] for the one who offers it. 5The bull
shall then be slaughtered* before the LORD,
and Aaron's sons, the priests, shall offer its
blood by splashing it on all the sides of the
altar which is at the entrance of the tent of
meeting.[h] 6Then the burnt offering shall be
flayed and cut into pieces. 7After Aaron's
sons, the priests, have put burning embers on
the altar and laid wood on them, 8they shall
lay the pieces of meat, together with the
head and the suet, on top of the wood and the
embers on the altar; 9but the inner organs
and the shanks shall be washed with water.
The priest shall then burn all of it on the altar as a burnt offering, a sweet-smelling
oblation to the LORD.[i]
10If a person's burnt offering is from the
flock, that is, a sheep or a goat, the offering
must be a male without blemish. 11It shall be
slaughtered on the north side of the altar before the LORD, and Aaron's sons, the priests,
shall splash its blood on all the sides of the
altar. 12When it has been cut into pieces, the
priest shall lay these, together with the head
and suet, on top of the wood and the embers
on the altar; 13but the inner organs and the
shanks shall be washed with water. The
priest shall then offer all of it, burning it on
the altar. It is a burnt offering, a sweet-
smelling oblation to the LORD.
14If a person offers a bird as a burnt offering to the LORD, the offering brought must be
a turtledove or a pigeon.[j] 15Having brought it
to the altar, the priest shall wring its head off
and burn it on the altar. The blood shall be
drained out against the side of the altar.[k] 16He
shall remove its crissum* by means of its

1:2 Any one of you: women as well as men bring sacrifices (see 12:6–8; 15:28–30) and are explicitly obligated in other ritual matters (e.g., 13:29, 38; Nm 5:6; 6:2; Lk 2:24). Thus, though the Hebrew formulates sacrificial and other law with male reference, the translation reflects the inclusion of women in ritual requirements. **From the herd or from the flock**: the only animals which could be used as sacrificial victims were domestic animals either of the bovine class (bulls, cows and calves) or the ovine class (sheep and lambs, goats and kids). Excluded, therefore, were not only all wild animals, but also such "unclean" domestic animals as the camel and the donkey (cf. 11:1–47; 27:26–27).

1:3–5 Entrance of the tent of meeting . . . before the LORD: probably the forecourt from the entrance of the court to the entrance of the tent (cf. Ex 27). Thus the altar in front of the tent was entirely accessible to the laity.

1:3 The burnt offering is used for regular daily (6:1–6) offerings, public festivals (Nm 28–29), purification rituals (Lv 12:6–8; 14:19–20; 15:15, 30), and individuals' vows and voluntary offerings (22:18–20).

1:4 Lay a hand: the imposition of a single hand for the sacrifices in chaps. 1–5 may be a means of designating the animal as belonging to the offerer. See note on 16:21. **Atonement**: see note on 16:6.

1:5 Shall then be slaughtered: lit., "he shall slaughter the bull." Slaughtering is not something the offerer must do (as opposed to, for example, hand placement [v. 4] or the presentation of sacrificial portions as an elevated offering [7:29–34]). Thus the verb is construed impersonally here.

1:16 Crissum: the area around the anus of the bird, lying beneath the bird's tail.

a: Ex 40. *b:* Lv 1:3, 10; 3:1, 6, 12. *c:* Lv 6:1–6; 22:18–19; *d:* Lv 22:17–25; Ex 12:5. *e:* Lv 3:2, 8, 13; 4:4, 15, 24, 29, 33; 8:14, 18, 22; Nm 8:12; 2 Chr 29:23; cf. Lv 16:21; 24:14; Nm 27:18, 23; Dt 34:9. *f:* Lv 19:5; 22:19–29; Gn 4:3–5; Mal 1:8–14. *g:* Lv 9:7; 14:20; Jb 1:5; 42:8; cf. Gn 32:21; Ex 29:36–37; 30:15; Lv 16:16–20; 17:11; Ez 43:20, 26. *h:* Lv 1:11, 15; 3:2, 8, 13; cf. Lv 4:5–7, 25. *i:* Lv 2:2; 3:5; 4:31; 26:31; Gn 8:20–21; Nm 28:2; cf. Lv 3:11; 21:6, 21; 22:25. *j:* Lv 5:7; 12:8; 15:14–15; Lk 2:24. *k:* Lv 5:8–9.

feathers and throw it on the ash heap at the east side of the altar. 17 Then, having torn the bird open by its wings without separating the halves, the priest shall burn it on the altar, on the wood and the embers. It is a burnt offering, a sweet-smelling oblation to the LORD.

CHAPTER 2

See RG 128

Grain Offerings. 1* [l] When anyone brings a grain offering to the LORD, the offering must consist of bran flour. The offerer shall pour oil on it and put frankincense[m] over it, 2 and bring it to Aaron's sons, the priests. A priest shall take a handful of the bran flour and oil, together with all the frankincense, and shall burn it on the altar as a token of the offering,* a sweet-smelling oblation to the LORD.[n] 3 The rest of the grain offering belongs to Aaron and his sons,[o] a most holy[p] portion from the oblations to the LORD.

4 When you offer a grain offering baked in an oven, it must be in the form of unleavened cakes made of bran flour mixed with oil, or of unleavened wafers spread with oil.[q] 5 If your offering is a grain offering that is fried on a griddle,[r] it must be of bran flour mixed with oil and unleavened. 6 Break it into pieces, and pour oil over it. It is a grain offering. 7 If your offering is a grain offering that is prepared in a pan, it must be made of bran flour, fried in oil. 8 A grain offering that is made in any of these ways you shall bring to the LORD. It shall be presented to the priest, who shall take it to the altar. 9 The priest shall then remove from the grain offering a token and burn it on the altar as a sweet-smelling oblation to the LORD. 10 The rest of the grain offering belongs to Aaron and his sons, a most holy portion from the oblations to the LORD.

11* Every grain offering that you present to the LORD shall be unleavened, for you shall not burn any leaven or honey as an oblation to the LORD.[s] 12 Such you may present to the LORD in the offering of the first produce that is processed,[t] but they are not to be placed on the altar for a pleasing odor. 13 You shall season all your grain offerings with salt. Do not let the salt of the covenant with your God* be lacking from your grain offering. On every offering you shall offer salt.[u]

14 If you offer a grain offering of first ripe fruits to the LORD, you shall offer it in the form of fresh early grain, roasted by fire and crushed as a grain offering of your first ripe fruits. 15 You shall put oil on it and set frankincense on it. It is a grain offering. 16 The priest shall then burn some of the groats and oil, together with all the frankincense, as a token of the offering, an oblation to the LORD.

CHAPTER 3

See RG 128

Communion Sacrifices. 1* [v] If a person's offering is a communion sacrifice, if it is brought from the herd, be it a male or a female animal, it must be presented without blemish[w] before the LORD. 2 The one offering it shall lay a hand on the head[x] of the offering. It shall then be slaughtered at the entrance of the tent of meeting. Aaron's sons, the priests, shall splash its blood on all the sides of the altar. 3[y] From the communion sacrifice the individual shall offer as an obla-

2:1 Grain offerings are used as independent offerings (those in this chapter and cf. 6:12–16; 8:26–27; 23:10–11), as substitutes for other offerings in a case of poverty (5:11–13), and as accompaniments to animal offerings (cf. Nm 15:1–12; 28:1–29:39; Lv 14:20; 23:12, 18, 37). Chapter 2 describes two basic types of grain offering: uncooked (vv. 1–3) and cooked (vv. 4–10). The flour (*sōlet*) used was made of wheat (Ex 29:2) and Jewish tradition and Semitic cognates indicate that it is a coarse rather than a fine flour.

2:2 Token of the offering: lit., "reminder." Instead of burning the whole grain offering, only this part is burned on the altar.

2:11–12 No grain offering that is leavened can be offered on the altar. Those in 7:13 and 23:17 are leavened but not offered on the altar. The Hebrew word for "honey" may refer to fruit syrup as well as to bee honey.

2:13 The salt of the covenant with your God: partaking of salt in common was an ancient symbol of friendship and alliance. Cf. Mark 9:49–50 and Col 4:6.

3:1 The exact meaning of Hebrew *shelamim*, "communion sacrifice," is not clear. It has also been rendered "gift," "(re)payment," "peace," "well-being," or "covenant" offering. This offering may be brought for a vow or voluntary offering

l: Lv 5:11–13; 6:7–16; 7:9–14; 24:5–9; Nm 15:1–21; cf. Gn 4:3–5. *m:* Cf. Ex 30:1–10; Lv 16:11–13; Prv 27:9. *n:* Lv 1:9. *o:* Lv 6:9; 7:9–10. *p:* Lv 6:10, 18, 22; 10:12, 17; 24:9. *q:* 1 Chr 23:29. *r:* Lv 6:14. *s:* Mt 16:12; Mk 8:15; Lk 12:1; 1 Cor 5:7; Gal 5:9. *t:* Nm 18:12–13, 27; 15:20–21. *u:* Nm 18:19; Ezr 6:9; 7:22; Ez 43:24. *v:* Lv 7:11–36. *w:* Lv 22:21. *x:* Lv 1:4. *y:* Lv 3:9–10, 14–16; 4:8–9, 31, 35; 6:5; 7:3–4, 30–31; 8:16, 25; 16:25; 17:6; Ex 29:13, 22; cf. Ez 44:15.

tion to the LORD the fat* that covers the inner organs, and all the fat that adheres to them, 4 as well as the two kidneys, with the fat on them near the loins, and the lobe of the liver, which is removed with the kidneys. 5 Aaron's sons shall burn this on the altar with the burnt offering that is on the wood and the embers, as a sweet-smelling oblation to the LORD.[z]

6 If the communion sacrifice one offers to the LORD is from the flock, be it a male or a female animal, it must be presented without blemish. 7 If one presents a lamb as an offering, that person shall bring it before the LORD, 8 and after laying a hand on the head of the offering, it shall then be slaughtered before the tent of meeting. Aaron's sons shall splash its blood on all the sides of the altar. 9 From the communion sacrifice the individual shall present as an oblation to the LORD its fat: the whole fatty tail, which is removed close to the spine, the fat that covers the inner organs, and all the fat that adheres to them, 10 as well as the two kidneys, with the fat on them near the loins, and the lobe of the liver, which is removed with the kidneys. 11 The priest shall burn this on the altar as food,[a] an oblation to the LORD.

12 If a person's offering is a goat, the individual shall bring it before the LORD, 13 and after laying a hand on its head, it shall then be slaughtered before the tent of meeting. Aaron's sons shall splash its blood on all the sides of the altar. 14 From this the one sacrificing shall present an offering as an oblation to the LORD: the fat that covers the inner organs, and all the fat that adheres to them, 15 as well as the two kidneys, with the fat on them near the loins, and the lobe of the liver, which is removed with the kidneys. 16 The priest shall burn these on the altar as food, a sweet-smelling oblation.

All the fat belongs to the LORD. 17 This shall be a perpetual ordinance for your descendants wherever they may dwell. You shall not eat any fat or any blood.* [b]

CHAPTER 4

See RG 128

Purification Offerings. 1 The LORD said to Moses: 2 [c] Tell the Israelites: When a person inadvertently* does wrong by violating any one of the LORD's prohibitions—

For the Anointed Priest. 3 If it is the anointed priest* who thus does wrong and thereby makes the people guilty, he shall offer to the LORD an unblemished bull of the herd as a purification offering for the wrong he committed. 4 Bringing the bull to the entrance of the tent of meeting, before the LORD, he shall lay his hand on its head[d] and slaughter it before the LORD. 5* The anointed priest shall then take some of the bull's blood and bring it into the tent of meeting, 6 where, dipping his finger in the blood, he shall sprinkle some of it seven times before the LORD, toward the veil of the sanctuary.[e] 7 The priest shall also put some of the blood on the horns of the altar of fragrant incense which stands before the LORD in the tent of meeting. The rest of the bull's blood he shall pour out at the base of the altar for burnt of-

(cf. 22:21). A distinct version of the communion sacrifice is the thanksgiving offering (7:11–15 vis-à-vis vv. 16–18).

3:3–5 Fat: only part of the offering is devoted to God, as opposed to the burnt offering (chap. 1), which is wholly burnt (except for the skin). The meat is distributed among the offerer (and the offerer's party) and the priests (cf. 7:11–36).

3:17 Any fat or any blood: this prohibition is mentioned here because portions of this offering could be eaten by lay Israelites, who may not be entirely familiar with the prohibition (cf. 7:22–27; 19:26). The fat prohibited is only the visceral fat mentioned in 3:9–10, 14–15, not muscular fat.

4:2 Inadvertently: the concern in this chapter, and much of chap. 5, is wrongs done unintentionally. Intentional ("high-handed") sins are punished with being "cut off" from the people (Nm 15:30–31). See note on Lv 7:20. **LORD's prohibitions**: not included in the faults figured here is failure to perform positive commandments. Failing to perform positive commands, however, still renders the individual liable to other punishment (e.g., failing to observe the Passover, Nm 9:13). Cf. Nm 15:22–31.

4:3 The anointed priest: the chapter presents four cases of inadvertent wrong, arranged in descending order according to the status of the wrongdoer: high priest (vv. 3–12), entire community (vv. 13–21), tribal leader (vv. 22–26), and general populace (vv. 27–35). The higher one's position, the more deeply the sin affects the sanctuary (vv. 5–7, 17–18 versus vv. 25, 29, 34). See note on 16:6. **Purification offering**: the Hebrew verb *ḥiṭṭēʾ* means "remove sin, purify" (Lv 8:15; Ez 43:20–23; 45:18–19; cf. Ex 29:36). The offering cleansed the various places to which the blood was applied or the rooms in which it was sprinkled.

4:5–7 On the structure of the sanctuary, see Ex 26–27.

z: Lv 1:9. *a:* Lv 9:19. *b:* Lv 17:10. *c:* Lv 6:17–23; Nm 15:22–31. *d:* Lv 1:4. *e:* Lv 4:17–18; 16:16; cf. 4:25.

ferings which is at the entrance of the tent of
meeting. [8]He shall remove all the fat of the
bull of the purification offering: the fat that
covers the inner organs, and all the fat that
adheres to them, [9]as well as the two kidneys,
with the fat on them near the loins, and the
lobe of the liver, which is removed with the
kidneys, [10]just as the fat pieces are removed
from the ox of the communion sacrifice.[f]
The priest shall burn these on the altar for
burnt offerings. [11]* But the hide of the bull
and its meat, with its head, shanks, inner organs and dung, [12]that is, the whole bull, shall
be brought outside the camp to a clean place*
where the ashes are deposited and there be
burned in a wood fire. At the place of the ash
heap, there it must be burned.[g]

For the Community. [13]If the whole community of Israel errs* inadvertently and
without even being aware of it violates any
of the LORD's prohibitions, and thus are
guilty, [14]when the wrong that was committed becomes known, the community shall
offer a bull of the herd as a purification offering. They shall bring it before the tent of
meeting. [15]The elders of the community
shall lay their hands on the bull's head before the LORD. When the bull has been
slaughtered before the LORD, [16]the anointed
priest shall bring some of its blood into the
tent of meeting, [17]and dipping his finger in
the blood, he shall sprinkle it seven times before the LORD, toward the veil. [18]He shall
also put some of the blood on the horns of
the altar which is before the LORD in the tent
of meeting. The rest of the blood he shall
pour out at the base of the altar for burnt offerings which is at the entrance of the tent of
meeting. [19]He shall remove all of its fat and
burn it on the altar, [20]doing with this bull just
as he did with the other bull of the purification offering; he will do the same thing. Thus
the priest shall make atonement[h] on their behalf, that they may be forgiven. [21]This bull
shall also be brought outside the camp and
burned,[i] just as the first bull. It is a purification offering for the assembly.

For the Tribal Leader. [22]Should a tribal
leader[j] do wrong inadvertently by violating
any one of the prohibitions of the LORD his
God, and thus be guilty, [23]when he learns of
the wrong he committed, he shall bring as
his offering an unblemished male goat. [24]He
shall lay his hand on its head and it shall be
slaughtered in the place where the burnt offering is slaughtered, before the LORD. It is a
purification offering. [25]The priest shall then
take some of the blood of the purification offering on his finger and put it on the horns[k]
of the altar for burnt offerings. The rest of
the blood he shall pour out at the base of the
altar. [26]All of its fat he shall burn on the altar
like the fat of the communion sacrifice. Thus
the priest shall make atonement on the tribal
leader's behalf for his wrong, that he may be
forgiven.

For the General Populace. [27]If anyone of
the general populace does wrong inadvertently by violating one of the LORD's prohibitions, and thus is guilty, [28]upon learning of
the wrong committed, that person shall bring
an unblemished she-goat as the offering for
the wrong committed. [29]The wrongdoer
shall lay a hand on the head of the purification offering, and the purification offering
shall be slaughtered at the place of the burnt
offerings. [30]The priest shall then take some
of its blood on his finger and put it on the
horns of the altar for burnt offerings. The
rest of the blood he shall pour out at the base
of the altar. [31]He shall remove all the fat, just
as the fat is removed from the communion
sacrifice. The priest shall burn it on the altar
for a sweet odor to the LORD. Thus the priest
shall make atonement, so that the individual
may be forgiven.

[32]If, however, a person brings a lamb as a
purification offering, that person shall bring
an unblemished female, and [33]lay a hand on
its head. It shall be slaughtered as a purifica-

4:11–12 See note on 6:17–23.

4:12 Clean place: i.e., ritually "clean" or pure. It has nothing to do with the presence of dirt or waste. See 6:4.

4:13 Whole community . . . errs: this case probably complements that of vv. 3–12. There the high priest sins so that the people become guilty. Those verses deal with his requirements for atonement; vv. 13–21 deal with the people's requirements.

f: Lv 3:3. *g:* Lv 6:23. *h:* Lv 1:4. *i:* Lv 6:23. *j:* Nm 10:4; 25:14. *k:* Lv 4:30, 34; 8:15; 9:9; 16:18; Ex 29:12; Ez 43:20; cf. Lv 4:7.

tion offering in the place where the burnt offering is slaughtered. [34]The priest shall then take some of the blood of the purification offering on his finger and put it on the horns of the altar for burnt offerings. The rest of the blood he shall pour out at the base of the altar. [35]He shall remove all its fat just as the fat is removed from the lamb of the communion sacrifice. The priest shall burn these on the altar with the other oblations for the LORD. Thus the priest shall make atonement on the person's behalf for the wrong committed, that the individual may be forgiven.

CHAPTER 5

See RG 128

Special Cases for Purification Offerings.*
[1]If a person, either having seen or come to know something, does wrong by refusing as a witness under oath to give information,[l] that individual shall bear the penalty; [2]or if someone, without being aware of it, touches any unclean thing, such as the carcass of an unclean wild animal, or an unclean domestic animal, or an unclean swarming creature,* and thus is unclean and guilty;[m] [3]or if someone, without being aware of it, touches some human uncleanness,[n] whatever kind of uncleanness this may be, and then subsequently becomes aware of guilt; [4]or if someone, without being aware of it, rashly utters an oath with bad or good intent,[o] whatever kind of oath this may be, and then subsequently becomes aware of guilt in regard to any of these matters— [5]when someone is guilty in regard to any of these matters, that person shall confess the wrong committed, [6]and make reparation to the LORD for the wrong committed: a female animal from the flock, a ewe lamb or a she-goat, as a purification offering. Thus the priest shall make atonement on the individual's behalf for the wrong.

[7]If, however, the person cannot afford an animal of the flock,[p] that person shall bring to the LORD as reparation for the wrong committed two turtledoves or two pigeons, one for a purification offering and the other for a burnt offering. [8]The guilty party shall bring them to the priest, who shall offer the one for the purification offering first.[q] Wringing its head at the neck, yet without breaking it off, [9]he shall sprinkle some of the blood of the purification offering against the side of the altar. The rest of the blood shall be drained out against the base of the altar. It is a purification offering. [10]The other bird he shall offer as a burnt offering according to procedure. Thus the priest shall make atonement on the person's behalf for the wrong committed, so that the individual may be forgiven.

[11]If the person is unable to afford even two turtledoves or two pigeons, that person shall bring as an offering for the wrong committed one tenth of an ephah* of bran flour for a purification offering. The guilty party shall not put oil or place frankincense on it, because it is a purification offering.[r] [12]The individual shall bring it to the priest, who shall take a handful as a token of the offering and burn it on the altar with the other oblations for the LORD. It is a purification offering. [13]Thus the priest shall make atonement on the person's behalf for the wrong committed in any of the above cases, so that the individual may be forgiven. The rest of the offering, like the grain offering, shall belong to the priest.

Reparation Offerings.* [14]The LORD said to Moses: [15][s] When a person commits sacrilege

5:1–13 This differs from the prescriptions for purification offerings in chap. 4 by listing four specific wrongs for which a purification offering is brought and allowing the substitution of birds and grain offerings in the case of poverty.

5:2 Swarming creature: a rather imprecise categorization that includes various small creatures in the seas, such as fish that go about in large groups or swarms (Gn 1:20; Lv 11:10); or, similarly, various winged insects that mass in the skies (Lv 11:20; Dt 14:19); and, finally, various small creatures that move in swarms on land, whether crawlers, quadrupeds, or of the multilegged variety (Lv 11:41–42). According to 11:29–30, even various rodents and lizards can be included in this category.

5:11 Ephah: see note on Is 5:10.

5:14–26 This last half of the chapter deals with a distinct sacrifice, the reparation offering (Heb. *'asham*). The Hebrew root for this term has a basic meaning of "be guilty." The noun can have a consequential sense of "that which is due from guilt," i.e., "compensation, indemnification, reparation"; hence the translation "reparation offering," rather than the alternatives "guilt offering" or "trespass offering." This offering is brought most often in cases of sacrilege.

l: Jgs 17:2–3; Prv 29:24. *m:* Lv 11:1–45; 15:31; 17:15–16. *n:* Lv 12:4; 13:35–36; 15:2–12, 19–27; Nm 19:14–22. *o:* Nm 30:3; Jgs 11:30–36; 1 Sm 14:24–30; Mk 6:23–26; Acts 23:12. *p:* Cf. Lv 5:11; 12:8; 14:21. *q:* Lv 1:14–17. *r:* Lv 2:1–3; Nm 5:15. *s:* Lv 7:1–6; Nm 5:5–8.

by inadvertently misusing any of the LORD's sacred objects,[t] the wrongdoer shall bring to the LORD as reparation an unblemished ram from the flock, at the established value* in silver shekels according to the sanctuary shekel, as a reparation offering. [16]The wrongdoer shall also restore what has been misused of the sacred objects, adding a fifth of its value,[u] and give this to the priest. Thus the priest shall make atonement for the person with the ram of the reparation offering, so that the individual may be forgiven.

[17]If someone does wrong and violates one of the LORD's prohibitions without realizing it, that person is guilty[v] and shall bear the penalty. [18]The individual shall bring to the priest an unblemished ram of the flock, at the established value, for a reparation offering. The priest shall then make atonement on the offerer's behalf for the error inadvertently and unknowingly committed so that the individual may be forgiven. [19]It is a reparation offering. The individual must make reparation to the LORD.

[20]The LORD said to Moses: [21]When someone does wrong and commits sacrilege against the LORD by deceiving[w] a neighbor about a deposit or a pledge or a stolen article, or by otherwise retaining a neighbor's goods unjustly;[x] [22]or if, having found a lost article, the person lies about it, swearing falsely about any of the things that a person may do wrong— [23]when someone has thus done wrong and is guilty, that person shall restore the thing that was stolen, the item unjustly retained, the item left as deposit, or the lost article that was found [24]or whatever else the individual swore falsely about. That person shall make full restitution of the thing itself, and add one fifth of its value to it, giving it to its owner at the time of reparation. [25]Then that person shall bring to the priest as reparation to the LORD an unblemished ram of the flock, at the established value, as a reparation offering. [26]The priest shall make atonement on the person's behalf before the LORD, so that the individual may be forgiven for whatever was done to incur guilt.

B. Instructions for the Priests

CHAPTER 6

See RG 128

The Daily Burnt Offering. [1]The LORD said to Moses: [2]*[y] Give Aaron and his sons the following command: This is the ritual* for the burnt offering—the burnt offering that is to remain on the hearth of the altar all night until the next morning, while the fire is kept burning on the altar. [3]The priest, clothed in his linen robe and wearing linen pants underneath, shall take away the ashes to which the fire has reduced the burnt offering on the altar, and lay them at the side of the altar. [4]Then, having taken off these garments and put on other garments, he shall carry the ashes to a clean place outside the camp. [5]The fire on the altar is to be kept burning; it must not go out. Every morning the priest shall put firewood on it. On this he shall lay out the burnt offering[z] and burn the fat of the communion offering. [6]The fire is to be kept burning continuously on the altar; it must not go out.

The Grain Offering.* [7]This is the ritual of the grain offering. Aaron's sons shall offer it before the LORD, in front of the altar. [8]A priest shall then take from the grain offering a handful of bran flour and oil, together with all the frankincense that is on it,[a] and this he shall burn on the altar as a token of the offering, a sweet aroma to the LORD. [9]The rest of it Aaron and his sons may eat; but it must be eaten unleavened in a sacred place:[b] in the court of the tent of meeting they shall eat it. [10]It shall not be baked with leaven. I have given it to them as their portion from the

5:15 At the established value: the Hebrew term *'erkēkā*, which in context means "(established) value," may indicate that a person could bring the monetary equivalent of a ram instead of an actual animal. See vv. 18, 25.

6:2–6 This passage may have reference to the burnt offering that is offered in the morning and late afternoon each day (cf. Ex 29:38–42; Nm 28:3–8).

6:2 Ritual: Hebrew *torah*, which also has the broader meaning of "instruction." The treatment of sacrifices in chaps. 6–7 recapitulates the offerings treated in 1–5 but now with more emphasis on priestly duties and prerogatives.

6:7–11 The passage is apparently concerned with the raw grain offering of 2:1–3.

t: Lv 22:14. *u:* Lv 22:14; 27:13, 15, 19, 27. *v:* Ps 19:13; Jb 1:5. *w:* Ps 59:13; Hos 4:2. *x:* Ex 22:6–12. *y:* Lv 1. *z:* Lv 9:17. *a:* Lv 2:1–3. *b:* Lv 6:19; 7:6; 10:13, 17; 24:9.

oblations for the LORD; it is most holy,[c] like the purification offering and the reparation offering. 11 Every male of Aaron's descendants may eat of it perpetually throughout your generations as their rightful due from the oblations for the LORD. Whatever touches the oblations becomes holy.

*High Priest's Daily Grain Offering.** 12 The LORD said to Moses: 13 This is the offering that Aaron and his sons shall present to the LORD on the day he is anointed: one tenth of an ephah of bran flour for the regular grain offering, half of it in the morning and half of it in the evening. 14 You shall bring it well kneaded and fried in oil on a griddle.[d] Having broken the offering into pieces, you shall present it as a sweet aroma to the LORD. 15 The anointed priest descended from Aaron who succeeds him shall do likewise. This is the LORD's due forever. The offering shall be wholly burned.[e] 16 Every grain offering of a priest shall be a whole offering; it may not be eaten.

*Purification Offerings.** 17 The LORD said to Moses: 18 [f] Tell Aaron and his sons: This is the ritual for the purification offering. At the place where the burnt offering is slaughtered, there also, before the LORD, shall the purification offering be slaughtered. It is most holy.[g] 19 The priest who offers the purification offering shall eat of it; it shall be eaten in a sacred place,[h] in the court of the tent of meeting. 20 Whatever touches its flesh becomes holy. If any of its blood spatters on a garment, the stained part must be washed in a sacred place. 21 A clay vessel in which it has been boiled shall be broken; if it is boiled in a copper vessel, this shall be scoured afterward and rinsed with water.[i] 22 Every male of the priestly line may eat it. It is most holy. 23 But no purification offering of which some blood has been brought into the tent of meeting[j] to make atonement in the sanctuary shall be eaten; it must be burned with fire.[k]

CHAPTER 7

See RG 128–29

Reparation Offerings. 1 *[l] This is the ritual for the reparation offering. It is most holy. 2 At the place where the burnt offering is slaughtered, the reparation offering shall also be slaughtered.[m] Its blood shall be splashed on all the sides of the altar. 3 [n] All of its fat shall be offered: the fatty tail, the fat that covers the inner organs, and all the fat that adheres to them, 4 as well as the two kidneys with the fat on them near the loins, and the lobe of the liver, which is removed with the kidneys. 5 The priest shall burn these on the altar as an oblation to the LORD. It is a reparation offering. 6 Every male of the priestly line may eat of it; but it must be eaten in a sacred place.[o] It is most holy.[p]

7 Because the purification offering and the reparation offering are alike, both have the same ritual. The reparation offering belongs to the priest who makes atonement with it. 8 As for the priest who offers someone's burnt offering, to him belongs the hide of the burnt offering that is offered. 9 * [q] Also, every grain offering that is baked in an oven or made in a pan or on a griddle shall belong to the priest who offers it, 10 whereas all grain offerings[r] that are mixed with oil or are dry shall belong to all of Aaron's sons without distinction.

*Communion Sacrifices.** 11 [s] This is the rit-

6:12–16 This seems to refer to a grain offering offered twice daily by the high priest, perhaps identical to the regular grain offering in Nm 4:16 (cf. Neh 10:34). This offering is distinct from the grain offering that accompanies the daily burnt offering.

6:17–23 There are two types of purification offering: one whose blood is used inside the tent sanctuary (4:1–12, 13–21) and another whose blood was only used at the outer sacrificial altar (4:22–26, 27–31, 32–35). The carcasses of the former, as well as of purification offerings brought by the priests themselves (cf. 8:14–17; 9:8–11), are not eaten by priests but disposed of at the ash heap outside the camp, which itself is set up around the sanctuary (Ex 29:14; Lv 4:11–12, 21; 6:23; 8:17; 9:11; 16:27). The Letter to the Hebrews compares Jesus' suffering "outside the gate" to the disposal of purification offering carcasses outside the camp (Heb 13:11–13).

7:1–6 These prescriptions may appear here rather than in 5:14–26 where this offering is first treated because the monetary equivalent of the offering might have been brought instead of an actual animal. See note on 5:15.

7:9–10 For the distinction between uncooked and cooked grain offerings, see 2:1–10 and note on 2:1. The contradiction between v. 9 and 2:10 may reflect a development in custom, with the distribution in v. 9 coming from earlier times, when sanctuary personnel was more limited.

7:11–36 This section discusses three types of communion sacrifice: the thanksgiving offering (vv. 12–15), a votive of-

c: Lv 2:3. *d:* Lv 2:5. *e:* Lv 2:9. *f:* Lv 4:1–5:13. *g:* Lv 2:3. *h:* Lv 6:9. *i:* Lv 11:32–33; 15:12. *j:* Lv 4:5; Heb 13:11. *k:* Lv 4:11–12, 21; 8:17; 9:11; 16:27. *l:* Lv 5:14–26. *m:* Lv 6:18. *n:* Lv 3:4. *o:* Lv 6:9. *p:* Lv 2:3. *q:* Lv 2:3–10; Nm 18:9; Ez 44:29. *r:* Lv 2:14–15. *s:* Lv 3.

ual for the communion sacrifice that is offered
to the LORD. 12* If someone offers it for
thanksgiving, that person shall offer it with
unleavened cakes mixed with oil, unleavened
wafers spread with oil, and cakes made of
bran flour mixed with oil and well kneaded.
13 One shall present this offering together with
loaves of leavened bread along with the
thanksgiving communion sacrifice. 14 From
this the individual shall offer one bread of
each type of offering as a contribution* to the
LORD; this shall belong to the priest who
splashes the blood of the communion offering.

15* [t] The meat of the thanksgiving communion sacrifice shall be eaten on the day it
is offered; none of it may be kept till the next
morning.[u] 16 However, if the sacrifice offered
is a votive or a voluntary offering,* it shall be
eaten on the day the sacrifice is offered, and
on the next day what is left over may be
eaten.[v] 17 But what is left over of the meat of
the sacrifice on the third day must be burned
in the fire. 18 If indeed any of the flesh of the
communion sacrifice is eaten on the third
day, it shall not be accepted; it will not be
reckoned to the credit of the one offering it.
Rather it becomes a desecrated meat. Anyone who eats of it shall bear the penalty.*

19* Should the meat touch anything unclean, it may not be eaten, but shall be burned
in the fire.[w] As for other meat, all who are
clean may eat of it. 20 If, however, someone in
a state of uncleanness eats the meat of a communion sacrifice belonging to the LORD, that
person shall be cut off* [x] from the people.
21 Likewise, if someone touches anything unclean, whether it be human uncleanness or an
unclean animal or an unclean loathsome
creature, and then eats the meat of the communion sacrifice belonging to the LORD, that
person, too, shall be cut off from the people.

Prohibition Against Blood and Fat. 22 The
LORD said to Moses: 23 Tell the Israelites:
You shall not eat the fat of any ox or sheep
or goat.[y] 24 Although the fat of an animal that
has died a natural death or has been killed by
wild beasts may be put to any other use, you
may not eat it.[z] 25 If anyone eats the fat of an
animal from which an oblation is made to
the LORD, that person shall be cut off from
the people. 26[a] Wherever you dwell, you
shall not eat any blood, whether of bird or of
animal. 27 Every person who eats any blood
shall be cut off from the people.

***Portions from the Communion Sacrifice
for Priests.*** 28 The LORD said to Moses: 29 Tell
the Israelites: The person who offers a communion sacrifice to the LORD shall be the
one to bring from it the offering to the LORD.
30 The offerer's own hands shall carry the
oblations for the LORD: the person shall
bring the fat together with the brisket, which
is to be raised as an elevated[b] offering* before the LORD. 31 The priest shall burn the fat
on the altar,[c] but the brisket belongs to Aaron
and his sons. 32 Moreover, from your com-

fering, and a voluntary offering (vv. 16–18). The latter two are similar and are thus mentioned together. Verses 19–36 apply to all types of communion sacrifice.

7:12–13 Four types of breads accompany the thanksgiving offering. Three types are cooked grain offerings comparable to those in 2:4–10. Also required are loaves of leavened bread (see 2:11).

7:14 Contribution: Hebrew *terumah*. This does not indicate a particular ritual action. The word simply means "gift, something set apart."

7:15–18 Sacrifices must be properly consumed for them to be effective (cf. also 19:5–8; 22:30). Similar rules obtain for the Passover offering (Ex 12:10; Nm 9:12; cf. Ex 23:18; 34:25; Dt 16:4) and the ordination offering (Ex 29:34; Lv 8:32).

7:16 Votive or a voluntary offering: these are not specific types of offerings but rather motivations for bringing the communion sacrifice (cf. 22:18). A votive offering is brought as the consequence of a promise (vow) made to God. A voluntary offering is a spontaneous gift to God independent of a prior promise. See note on 27:2–13.

7:18 Bear the penalty: this refers in many cases to punishment by God (cf. 17:16; 19:8; 20:17, 19; Nm 18:1, 23; 30:16).

7:19–21 For ritual impurity, see note on 11:1–15:33.

7:20 Cut off: a common term in the Priestly source that cannot always be reduced to a simple English equivalent, since its usage appears to involve a number of associated punishments, some or all of which may come into play in any one instance (see Ex 12:15 and note). All the same, as a punishment from God, to be "cut off" (from one's people) frequently appears to refer to termination of the offender's family line (and perhaps in some cases an early death); see Lv 20:2–3, 20–21; Ru 4:10; Ps 109:13; Mal 2:12.

7:30 Raised as an elevated offering: these portions of the sacrifices were specially dedicated by lifting them in presentation before God's abode. The sanctifying effect of this action is clearly seen in 23:17–20; Nm 6:19–20.

---

t: Lv 19:6–7. *u:* Lv 22:29–30. *v:* Lv 19:5–8. *w:* Lv 12:4. *x:* Lv 17:4, 9–10, 14; 18:29; 20:3, 5–6, 17–18; Gn 17:14; Ex 30:33; Nm 15:31; Ps 37:9, 28, 34; 109:13. *y:* Lv 3:17. *z:* Lv 22:8. *a:* Lv 17:10. *b:* Lv 8:27, 29; 9:21; 10:15; 14:12, 21, 24; 23:17, 20; Nm 6:20; 8:13; 18:18. *c:* Lv 3:11, 16.

munion sacrifices you shall give to the priest
the right leg as a contribution. [33]The one
among Aaron's sons who offers the blood
and the fat of the communion offering shall
have the right leg as his portion, [34]for from
the communion sacrifices of the Israelites I
have taken the brisket that is elevated and
the leg that is a contribution, and I have
given them to Aaron, the priest, and to his
sons as their due from the Israelites forever.[d]
[35]This is the priestly share from the oblations for the LORD, allotted to Aaron and his
sons on the day they were brought forth to be
the priests of the LORD, [36]which the LORD
ordered to be given them from the Israelites
on the day they were anointed, as their due
throughout their generations forever.

Summary. [37]This is the ritual for the burnt
offering, the grain offering, the purification
offering, the reparation offering, the ordination offering,[e] and the communion sacrifice,
[38]which the LORD enjoined on Moses at
Mount Sinai at the time when he commanded the Israelites in the wilderness of Sinai to bring their offerings to the LORD.[f]

II. Ceremony of Ordination

CHAPTER 8

See RG 129

*Ordination of Aaron and His Sons.**

[1g] The LORD said to Moses: [2]Take Aaron
along with his sons, the vestments, the
anointing oil, the bull for a purification offering, the two rams, and the basket of unleavened bread, [3]then assemble the whole
community* at the entrance of the tent of
meeting. [4]Moses did as the LORD had commanded. When the community[h] had assembled at the entrance of the tent of meeting,
[5]Moses told them: "This is what the LORD
has ordered to be done." [6]Bringing forward
Aaron and his sons, Moses first washed
them with water. [7]* Then he put the tunic on
Aaron,[i] girded him with the sash, clothed
him with the robe, placed the ephod on him,
and girded him with the ephod's embroidered belt, fastening the ephod on him with
it. [8]He then set the breastpiece on him, putting the Urim and Thummim* in it. [9]He put
the turban on his head, attaching the gold
medallion, the sacred headband,* on the
front of the turban, as the LORD had commanded Moses to do.

[10]* Taking the anointing oil, Moses
anointed and consecrated the tabernacle and
all that was in it.[j] [11]Then he sprinkled some of
the oil seven times on the altar, and anointed
the altar, with all its utensils, and the laver,
with its base, to consecrate them. [12]He also
poured some of the anointing oil on Aaron's
head and anointed him, to consecrate him.[k]
[13]Moses likewise brought forward Aaron's
sons, clothed them with tunics, girded them
with sashes, and put skullcaps on them, as
the LORD had commanded him to do.

Ordination Sacrifices. [14]He brought forward the bull for a purification offering, and
Aaron and his sons laid their hands on its
head. [15]When it was slaughtered, Moses
took the blood* and with his finger he put it
on the horns around the altar, thus purifying
the altar.[l] He poured out the rest of the blood
at the base of the altar. Thus he consecrated
it so that atonement could be made on it.
[16]Taking all the fat that was over the inner
organs, as well as the lobe of the liver and

8:1–2 This chapter presents the fulfillment of the commands in Ex 28–29; 30:26–30; and 40:9–15.

8:3–4 Community: this word (Heb. *'edah*) may refer to tribal leaders, all adult males, or the entire nation. The last is probably intended here.

8:7–9, 13 On the priestly clothing, see Ex 28–29. **Ephod**: according to Ex 28:6–14, the term for one of Aaron's special vestments made of gold thread, with multicolored woolen thread woven into it as well as fine linen. In appearance it resembled a kind of apron, hung on the priest by shoulder straps and secured by an embroidered belt. A somewhat simpler "apron" was presumably worn by other priests (1 Sm 22:18).

8:8 The Urim and Thummim: see Ex 28:30 and note there. Although these terms and the object(s) they refer to are still unexplained, they appear to be small objects that functioned like dice or lots to render a decision for those making an inquiry of God, perhaps originally in legal cases where the guilt of the accused could not otherwise be determined (cf. Ex 28:30; Nm 27:21; Dt 33:8; 1 Sm 28:6; Ezr 2:63; Neh 7:65).

8:9 Headband: see Ex 39:30–31. The gold medallion, together with its cords, comprises the sacred headband.

8:10–12 Anointing with the specially prepared oil (cf. Ex 30:22–33) is one of the means of making objects and persons holy by setting them apart for a special function or purpose.

8:15 Moses took the blood: Moses is acting as a priest in this chapter.

d: Ex 29:27–28. *e:* Lv 8:22. *f:* Lv 26:46; 27:34. *g:* Cf. Ex 28–29; 39; 40:12–15. *h:* Nm 27:19. *i:* Sir 45:8–13; Heb 5:1–4; 7:1–28. *j:* Ex 30:26. *k:* Sir 45:15. *l:* Heb 9:22.

the two kidneys with their fat,[m] Moses
burned them on the altar. 17 The bull, however, with its hide and flesh and dung he
burned in the fire outside the camp, as the
LORD had commanded Moses to do.[n]
18 He next brought forward the ram of the
burnt offering,[o] and Aaron and his sons laid
their hands on its head. 19 When it was
slaughtered, Moses splashed the blood on all
sides of the altar. 20 After the ram was cut up
into pieces, Moses burned the head, the cut-
up pieces and the suet. 21 After the inner organs and the shanks were washed with water, Moses burned these remaining parts of
the ram on the altar. It was a burnt offering
for a sweet aroma, an oblation to the LORD,
as the LORD had commanded Moses.
22* Then he brought forward the second
ram, the ordination ram,[p] and Aaron and his
sons laid their hands on its head. 23 When it
was slaughtered, Moses took some of its
blood and put it on the lobe of Aaron's right
ear, on the thumb of his right hand, and on the
big toe* of his right foot.[q] 24 Moses had the
sons of Aaron also come forward, and he put
some of the blood on the lobes of their right
ears, on the thumbs of their right hands, and
on the big toes of their right feet. The rest of
the blood he splashed on all the sides of the
altar. 25 He then took the fat: the fatty tail and
all the fat over the inner organs, the lobe of
the liver and the two kidneys with their fat,
and likewise the right thigh; 26 from the basket
of unleavened bread that was set before the
LORD he took one unleavened cake, one loaf
of bread made with oil, and one wafer; these
he placed on top of the portions of fat and the
right thigh. 27 He then put all these things upon
the palms of Aaron and his sons, whom he
had raise them as an elevated offering before
the LORD.[r] 28 When Moses had removed them
from their palms, he burned them on the altar
with the burnt offering. They were an ordination offering for a sweet aroma, an oblation to
the LORD. 29 He then took the brisket and
raised it as an elevated offering before the
LORD; this was Moses' own portion of the ordination ram, as the LORD had commanded
Moses. 30 Taking some of the anointing oil
and some of the blood that was on the altar,
Moses sprinkled it upon Aaron and his vestments, as well as his sons and their vestments,
thus consecrating both Aaron and his vestments and his sons and their vestments.[s]
31 Moses said to Aaron and his sons, "Boil
the meat at the entrance of the tent of meeting, and there eat it with the bread that is in
the basket of the ordination offering, in keeping with the command I have received:
'Aaron and his sons shall eat of it.' 32 What is
left over of the meat and the bread you shall
burn in the fire. 33 Moreover, you are not to
depart* from the entrance of the tent of meeting for seven days, until the days of your ordination are completed; for your ordination
is to last for seven days. 34 What has been
done today the LORD has commanded be
done, to make atonement for you. 35 You must
remain at the entrance of the tent of meeting
day and night for seven days, carrying out the
prescriptions of the LORD, so that you do not
die, for this is the command I have received."[t] 36 So Aaron and his sons did all that
the LORD had commanded through Moses.

CHAPTER 9

See RG 129

Octave of the Ordination. 1 On the
eighth day* [u] Moses summoned Aaron and
his sons, together with the elders of Israel,
2 and said to Aaron, "Take a calf of the herd
for a purification offering and a ram for a
burnt offering, both without blemish, and offer them before the LORD. 3* Tell the Israelites, too: Take a he-goat for a purification of-

8:22–32 The priestly ordination offering is a unique type of sacrifice but similar in many respects to the communion sacrifice (chap. 3; 7:11–34).

8:23–24 Lobe . . . thumb . . . toe: these parts of the body are meant to represent the body as a whole. The application of the blood symbolizes the priests' passing from a profane to a holy state. Cf. 14:14–17.

8:33–35 You are not to depart: the tenor and context of this requirement in vv. 33 and 35 seem to indicate that the priests are not to leave the sanctuary precincts for any reason. **Your ordination is to last for seven days . . . what has been done today . . . be done**: the consecration rites in Exodus are to be performed every day for seven days (cf. Ex 29:30, 35–37).

9:1 Eighth day: this is the conclusion of the priestly initiation ceremony.

9:3–4 The seven-day consecration of the priests in chap. 8

m: Lv 3:4–5; 4:8–11. *n:* Lv 6:23. *o:* Lv 1:10–13. *p:* Lv 7:37. *q:* Lv 14:14, 17. *r:* Lv 7:30. *s:* Ex 40:15. *t:* Lv 10:7. *u:* Lv 8:33.

fering, a calf and a lamb, both unblemished yearlings, for a burnt offering, 4and an ox and a ram for a communion sacrifice, to sacrifice before the LORD, along with a grain offering mixed with oil; for today the LORD will appear to you." 5So they brought what Moses had ordered before the tent of meeting. When the whole community had come forward and stood before the LORD, 6* Moses said, "This is what the LORD orders you to do, that the glory of the LORD may appear to you. 7Approach the altar," Moses then told Aaron, "and make your purification offering and your burnt offering in atonement for yourself and for your household;* then make the offering of the people in atonement for them, as the LORD has commanded."[v]

8Approaching the altar, Aaron first slaughtered the calf of the purification offering that was his own offering. 9When his sons presented the blood to him, he dipped his finger in the blood and put it on the horns of the altar.[w] The rest of the blood he poured out at the base of the altar. 10He then burned on the altar the fat, the kidneys and the lobe of the liver from the purification offering, as the LORD had commanded Moses; 11but the flesh and the hide he burned in the fire outside the camp.[x] 12Then Aaron slaughtered the burnt offering. When his sons brought him the blood, he splashed it on all sides of the altar. 13They then brought him the pieces and the head of the burnt offering, and he burned them on the altar. 14Having washed the inner organs and the shanks, he burned these also with the burnt offering on the altar.[y]

15Then he had the people's offering brought. Taking the goat that was for the people's purification offering, he slaughtered it and offered it as a purification offering as before. 16Then he brought forward the burnt offering and offered it according to procedure. 17He then presented the grain offering; taking a handful of it, he burned it on the altar, in addition to the morning burnt offering.[z] 18Finally he slaughtered the ox and the ram, the communion sacrifice of the people. When his sons brought him the blood, Aaron splashed it on all sides of the altar.[a] 19The portions of fat from the ox and from the ram, the fatty tail, the covering fat, the kidneys, and the lobe of the liver 20they placed on top of the briskets. Aaron burned the fat pieces on the altar, 21but the briskets and the right thigh he raised as an elevated offering[b] before the LORD, as the LORD had commanded Moses.

Revelation of the Lord's Glory. 22* Aaron then raised his hands over the people and blessed[c] them. When he came down from offering the purification offering, the burnt offering, and the communion offering, 23Moses and Aaron went into the tent of meeting. On coming out they blessed the people. Then the glory of the LORD appeared to all the people. 24* Fire came forth from the LORD's presence and consumed the burnt offering and the fat on the altar.[d] Seeing this, all the people shouted with joy and fell prostrate.

CHAPTER 10

See RG 129

Nadab and Abihu. 1* Aaron's sons Nadab and Abihu took their censers and, putting incense on the fire they had set in them,[e] they offered before the LORD unauthorized fire, such as he had not commanded. 2Fire therefore came forth from the LORD's presence and consumed them,[f] so that they died in the

did not require sacrifices from the community. Now communal sacrifices as well as priestly sacrifices are required.

9:6–21 Aaron and his sons now perform the offerings, instead of Moses (see note on 8:15).

9:7 For your household: unlike the Septuagint, the Hebrew reads *be'ad ha'am*, "for the people."

9:22–23 The people are blessed twice. For the possible content of the blessing, compare the priestly blessing in Nm 6:22–27. Solomon offers a double blessing at the dedication of the Temple (1 Kgs 8:14–21, 55–61).

9:24 The theophany consists of a fire that apparently comes from the tent of meeting. God's fiery glory is also manifested in the pillar of cloud and fire that led the Israelites and rested over the tent of meeting (Ex 13:21; 40:38; Nm 9:15–23; 10:11). On God's fiery glory, see also Ex 24:17; Ez 1:27–28.

10:1–2 Nadab and Abihu are the older sons of Aaron (Ex 6:23–24). Their sin apparently involves using embers from an unapproved source instead of the altar (cf. 16:12). The fire that destroys them is the same type found in 9:24.

v: Lv 16:3–5. *w:* Lv 4:25, 30, 34. *x:* Lv 6:23. *y:* Lv 1:5–9. *z:* Nm 28:23; 2 Kgs 16:15; Ez 46:13–15. *a:* Lv 3:2. *b:* Lv 7:30–34. *c:* Nm 6:22–27. *d:* 1 Kgs 18:38; 2 Chr 7:1; 2 Mc 2:10; cf. Ex 24:16–17. *e:* Lv 16:1; Nm 3:4; 26:61; 1 Chr 24:2. *f:* Nm 16:35; cf. Lv 9:24.

LORD's presence. [3]Moses then said to Aaron, "This is as the LORD said:

> Through those near to me I will be sanctified;
> in the sight of all the people I will obtain glory."* [g]

But Aaron said nothing. [4]* Then Moses summoned Mishael and Elzaphan, the sons of Aaron's uncle Uzziel, with the order, "Come, carry your kinsmen from before the sanctuary to a place outside the camp." [5]So they drew near and carried them by means of their tunics outside the camp, as Moses had commanded.

Conduct of the Priests. [6]Moses said to Aaron and his sons Eleazar and Ithamar, "Do not dishevel your hair[h] or tear your garments,[i] lest you die and bring God's wrath also on the whole community. While your kindred, the rest of the house of Israel, may mourn for those whom the LORD's fire has burned up, [7]you shall not go beyond the entrance of the tent of meeting,[j] else you shall die; for the anointing oil of the LORD is upon you." So they did as Moses told them.

[8]The LORD said to Aaron: [9]When you are to go to the tent of meeting, you and your sons are forbidden, by a perpetual statute throughout your generations, to drink any wine or strong drink, lest you die.[k] [10]You must be able to distinguish between what is sacred and what is profane, and between what is clean and what is unclean;* [l] [11]and you must be able to teach the Israelites all the statutes that the LORD has given them through Moses.

The Eating of the Priestly Portions. [12]Moses said to Aaron and his surviving sons, Eleazar and Ithamar, "Take the grain offering* left over from the oblations to the LORD, and eat it beside the altar in the form of unleavened cakes, since it is most holy. [13]You must eat it in a sacred place because it is your and your sons' due from the oblations to the LORD; such is the command I have received. [14][m] The brisket of the elevated offering and the leg* of the contribution, however, you and your sons and daughters may eat, in a clean place; for these have been assigned to you and your children as your due from the communion sacrifices of the Israelites. [15]The leg of the contribution and the brisket of the elevated offering shall be brought in with the oblations of fat to be raised as an elevated offering before the LORD. They shall belong to you and your children as your due forever, as the LORD has commanded."

[16]Moses inquired closely about the goat of the purification offering* and discovered that it had all been burned. So he was angry with the surviving sons of Aaron, Eleazar and Ithamar, and said, [17][n] "Why did you not eat the purification offering in the sacred place, since it is most holy? It has been given to you that you might remove the guilt of the community and make atonement for them before the LORD. [18]Since its blood was not brought inside the sanctuary, you should certainly have eaten the offering in the sanctuary, as I was commanded." [19]Aaron answered Moses, "Even though they presented their purification offering and burnt offering before the LORD today, still this misfortune

10:3 The explanation for the divine reaction indicates that improper cultic actions desecrate God and compromise God's glory. Desecration evokes divine punishment (cf. Ex 28:43; Nm 4:15, 19–20). **Those near to me**: i.e., cultic officials.

10:4–5 Moses has lay people remove the bodies so that the priests can continue their cultic activities free of contamination by a corpse (cf. Nm 19).

10:10 Sacred and . . . profane . . . clean and . . . unclean: something or someone may be either sacred or profane (i.e., ordinary, not set apart), and at the same time clean or unclean. Priests would be particularly concerned about keeping what is unclean away from the sacred.

10:12–13 Grain offering: this is the grain offering of the people of 9:4, 17. Only the token offering had been offered; the rest was for the priests' consumption.

10:14 Brisket . . . leg: these are from the Israelites' communion sacrifices in 9:4, 18–21.

10:16–20 Goat of the purification offering: this is the people's purification offering of 9:3, 15. Since its blood is not brought into the sanctuary, then, according to 6:17–23, this is the type of purification offering which is to be eaten by the priests in a holy place. **Eleazar and Ithamar**: they burned the entire goat of the people's purification offering (9:15) instead of eating it in a sacred place (6:19) to remove ritually the sin of the community by the ingestion of the meat of the offering. Aaron's defense of this action of his sons is somewhat vague: he merely alludes to the loss suffered in the death of Nadab and Abihu, without giving an explicit reason for Eleazar and Ithamar's not eating the people's purification offering, as required.

g: Lv 21:17, 21; Nm 20:12. *h:* Lv 13:45. *i:* Lv 21:5–6, 10–12. *j:* Lv 8:33–35; 21:12. *k:* Ez 44:21. *l:* Lv 11:47; 20:25; Ez 22:26; 44:23. *m:* Lv 7:34. *n:* Lv 6:18–19.

has befallen me. Had I then eaten of the purification offering today, would it have been pleasing to the LORD?" [20]On hearing this, Moses was satisfied.

III. Laws Regarding Ritual Purity*

CHAPTER 11

See RG 129–31

*Clean and Unclean Meats.** [1][o]The LORD said to Moses and Aaron: [2]Speak to the Israelites and tell them: Of all land animals these are the ones you may eat: [3]Any animal that has hoofs you may eat, provided it is cloven-footed and chews the cud. [4]But you shall not eat[p] any of the following from among those that only chew the cud or only have hoofs: the camel, which indeed chews the cud, but does not have hoofs and is therefore unclean for you; [5]the rock hyrax,* which indeed chews the cud, but does not have hoofs and is therefore unclean for you; [6]the hare, which indeed chews the cud, but does not have hoofs and is therefore unclean for you; [7]and the pig,[q] which does indeed have hoofs and is cloven-footed, but does not chew the cud and is therefore unclean for you. [8]You shall not eat their meat, and you shall not touch their carcasses; they are unclean for you.

[9]Of the various creatures that live in the water, you may eat the following: whatever in the seas or in river waters that has both fins and scales you may eat.[r] [10]But of the creatures that swarm in the water or of animals that otherwise live in the water, whether in the sea or in the rivers, all those that lack either fins or scales are loathsome for you, [11]and shall always be loathsome to you. Their meat you shall not eat, and their carcasses you shall loathe. [12]Every water creature that lacks fins or scales is loathsome for you.

[13]Of the birds,* these you shall loathe; they shall not be eaten, they are loathsome: the griffon vulture, the bearded vulture, the black vulture, [14]the kite, the various species of falcons, [15]the various species of crows, [16]the eagle owl, the kestrel, the long-eared owl, the various species of hawks, [17]the little owl, the cormorant, the screech owl, [18]the barn owl, the horned owl, the osprey, [19]the stork, the various species of herons, the hoopoe, and the bat.

[20]The various winged insects that walk on all fours are loathsome for you. [21]But of the various winged insects that walk on all fours you may eat those that have legs jointed above their feet for leaping on the ground; [22]hence of these you may eat the following: the various kinds of locusts, the various kinds of bald locusts, the various kinds of crickets, and the various kinds of grasshoppers.[s] [23]All other winged insects that have four legs are loathsome for you.

[24]You become unclean by the following—anyone who touches their carcasses shall be unclean until evening,[t] [25]and anyone who carries any part of their carcasses shall wash his garments and be unclean until evening—[26]by all hoofed animals that are not cloven-footed or do not chew the cud; they are unclean for you; anyone who touches them becomes unclean. [27]Also by the various quadrupeds that walk on paws; they are unclean for you; anyone who touches their carcasses shall be

11:1–15:33 Priestly legislation manifests two types of impurity or uncleanness: tolerated and prohibited. Prohibited impurity arises from various sins (e.g., 4:1–5; 5:2–3; 18:6–23; 20:2–5; Nm 5:13–14; 6:6–7). Tolerated impurity has three main sources: certain dead bodies (animal and human; cf. Lv 11 and Nm 19), various regular and abnormal genital discharges (Lv 12; 15), and diseases (specifically "scaly infection," chaps. 13–14). An additional tolerated impurity is that generated by the cult in order to rectify the effect of these impurities or sins (cf. chap. 4; 16:26, 28).

11:1–47 Apart from the introduction and conclusion (vv. 1–2a, 46–47), this chapter has three sections: (1) prohibitions against eating certain land, water, and air animals (vv. 2b–23); (2) consequences of contact with various animals (vv. 24–41); (3) a prohibition against eating small land animals, which is motivated by the requirement that Israel be holy as God is holy (vv. 41–45). These animals are impure only when dead. Cf. Dt 14:3–21.

11:5–6 According to modern zoology, *the rock hyrax* (*hyrax Syriacus*) is classified as an ungulate, and *the hare* as a rodent; neither is a ruminant. They appear to chew their food as the true ruminants do, and it is upon this appearance that the classification in the text is based.

11:13–23, 30 Birds: the term is broader, including all animals that fly (including bats, v. 19, and flying insects, vv. 20–23). The identification of the various Hebrew names for these birds and reptiles is in many cases uncertain.

o: Lv 27:11, 27; Gn 7:2–3, 8–9; Dt 14:3–21. *p:* Jgs 13:4, 7; Is 66:17; Ez 4:12–14. *q:* Prv 11:22; Is 65:4; 66:17; Mt 7:6; 8:30–32; Mk 5:11–16; Lk 8:32–33; 15:15–16. *r:* Jn 21:9–13. *s:* Mt 3:4; Mk 1:6. *t:* Lv 5:2; 7:21.

Purity, Cleanliness, and Ritual

IN THE THINKING of the ancient Israelites, there were certain boundaries within nature that should not be crossed or confused. These boundaries separated things of one kind from things of another kind, and things that went together were seen to have certain characteristics in common. Take, for instance, the category of "creatures that live in the water" (11:9): along with living in the water, these creatures were supposed to have fins and scales. If a creature—such as an oyster or a lobster—lived in the waters but did not have fins and scales, it did not fulfill all of the characteristics of its kind, and it therefore confused the boundaries of "creatures that live in the water" and was unclean. In the same way, the Israelites believed that animals that chewed the cud—ruminants, such as the cow—should have cloven, or divided, hoofs. The cow has divided hoofs, so it is clean. But the pig, which has divided hoofs, does not chew the cud, so it is unclean. It has confused a natural category, and is therefore to be avoided. See also Deuteronomy 14:3-21.

The clearest and strongest boundary was the one between life and death, and one had to be very careful when dealing with anything that was dead.

unclean until evening, [28]and anyone who carries their carcasses shall wash his garments and be unclean until evening. They are unclean for you.

[29]Of the creatures that swarm on the ground, the following are unclean for you: the rat, the mouse, the various kinds of lizards, [30]the gecko, the spotted lizard, the agama, the skink, and the chameleon. [31]Among the various swarming creatures, these are unclean for you. Everyone who touches them when they are dead shall be unclean until evening. [32]Everything on which one of them falls when dead becomes unclean, including any article of wood, cloth, leather or goat hair—any article of which use can be made. It must be immersed in water and remain unclean until evening, when it again becomes clean. [33]Should any of these creatures fall into a clay vessel, everything in it becomes unclean, and the vessel itself you must break. [34]Any food that can be eaten which makes contact with water, and any liquid that may be drunk, in any such vessel become unclean. [35]Any object on which any part of their carcasses falls becomes unclean; if it is an oven or stove, this must be broken to pieces; they are unclean and shall always be unclean to you. [36]However, a spring or a cistern for collecting water remains clean; but whoever touches such an animal's carcass becomes unclean. [37]If any part of their carcasses falls on any sort of grain that is to be sown, it remains clean; [38]but if the grain has become moistened, it becomes unclean to you when any part of their carcasses falls on it.

[39]* [u] When one of the animals that you could otherwise eat dies of itself, anyone who touches its carcass shall be unclean until evening; [40]and anyone who eats any part of its carcass shall wash his garments and be unclean until evening;[v] so also, anyone who carries its carcass shall wash his garments and be unclean until evening.

[41]All the creatures that swarm on the ground are loathsome and shall not be eaten. [42]Whether it crawls on its belly, goes on all fours, or has many legs—any creature that swarms on the earth—you shall not eat them; they are loathsome. [43]Do not make yourselves loathsome by any swarming creature nor defile yourselves with them and so become unclean by them.[w] [44]For I, the LORD, am your God. You shall make and keep yourselves holy,* because I am holy.[x] You shall not make yourselves unclean,

11:39–40 These animals create uncleanness, but are not prohibited as food (cf. 17:15–16). Priests who have a higher degree of holiness than other Israelites may not eat these animals (22:8; cf. Ez 44:31). Cf. Ex 22:30; Dt 14:21.

11:44–45 Keep yourselves holy . . . you shall be holy: a similar idea is expressed in 20:25–26. There, distinguishing

u: Lv 17:15–16; 22:8; Ex 22:30; Ez 4:12–14; 44:31. *v:* Lv 17:15; 22:8. *w:* Lv 20:25–26. *x:* Lv 19:2; 20:7, 26; Mt 5:48; 1 Pt 1:16.

then, by any swarming creature that crawls on the ground. 45 Since I, the LORD, am the one who brought you up from the land of Egypt that I might be your God, you shall be holy, because I am holy.

46 This is the instruction for land animals, birds, and all the creatures that move about in the water, as well as any animal that swarms on the ground, 47 that you may distinguish between the clean and the unclean, and between creatures that may be eaten and those that may not be eaten.[y]

CHAPTER 12

See RG 129–31

Uncleanness of Childbirth. 1 The LORD said to Moses: 2 Tell the Israelites: When a woman has a child, giving birth to a boy, she shall be unclean* for seven days, with the same uncleanness as during her menstrual period.[z] 3 On the eighth day, the flesh of the boy's foreskin shall be circumcised,*[a] 4 and then she shall spend thirty-three days more in a state of blood purity; she shall not touch anything sacred nor enter the sanctuary till the days of her purification are fulfilled. 5 If she gives birth to a girl, for fourteen days she shall be as unclean as during her menstrual period, after which she shall spend sixty-six days* in a state of blood purity.

6* When the days of her purification for a son or for a daughter are fulfilled,[b] she shall bring to the priest at the entrance of the tent of meeting a yearling lamb for a burnt offering and a pigeon or a turtledove for a purification offering. 7 The priest shall offer them before the LORD to make atonement for her, and thus she will be clean again after her flow of blood. Such is the ritual for the woman who gives birth to a child, male or female. 8 If, however, she cannot afford a lamb,[c] she may take two turtledoves or two pigeons,[d] the one for a burnt offering and the other for a purification offering. The priest shall make atonement for her, and thus she will again be clean.

CHAPTER 13

See RG 129–31

Scaly Infection.* 1 The LORD said to Moses and Aaron: 2[e] When someone has on the skin a mark, lesion, or blotch which appears to develop into a scaly infection, the person shall be brought to Aaron, the priest, or to one of the priests among his sons. 3 If the priest, upon examination of the skin's infection, finds that the hair on the infection has turned white and the infection itself appears to be deeper than the skin,* it is indeed a scaly infection; the priest, on seeing this,

between the animals is compared to God's distinguishing between the peoples and choosing Israel.

12:2–5 The mother has two stages of uncleanness or impurity: the first where her uncleanness is as severe as during her menstrual period and is contagious to profane persons and objects (cf. 15:19–24), and the second where she does not contaminate persons and objects but is still impure to what is holy, such as the sanctuary (12:4) or sacrifices. The implication is that in the second stage she may resume sexual relations with her husband (which would be prohibited in the first stage according to 18:19).

12:3 Circumcision is the sign of the covenant between God and Israel (Gn 17:1–27) and allows full participation in the religious community (Ex 12:43–49; Jos 5:2–10). This command was fulfilled after Jesus' birth (Lk 2:21).

12:5 If she gives birth to a girl . . . sixty-six days: while the longer period of uncleanness following the birth of a girl, compared to that following the birth of a boy, might reflect the relative disparity in social status between men and women in ancient Israel (and attested in other cultures), this is by no means certain. There is no simple correlation in the Bible between the worth of something and the degree of impurity it can occasion.

12:6–8 Certain tolerated impurities (see note on 11:1–15:33) are strong enough to pollute the sanctuary and require purification offerings, including the parturient (see also 14:10–32; 15:13–15, 28–30). Cf. note on 4:3. Mary fulfilled the command of bringing sacrifices after the birth of Jesus (Lk 2:22–24).

13:1–14:57 These chapters deal with scaly or fungal infections (Hebrew *ṣāraʻat*). The older translation "leprosy" is misleading because *ṣāraʻat* refers to not just one but several chronic and enduring skin diseases in human beings. The disease known as "leprosy" (Hansen's disease) is probably not included among the conditions described in the chapter. Also the term *ṣāraʻat* refers to fungal growths in fabrics and on the walls of houses. The reason why these conditions, and not other diseases, were considered unclean may be that they were quite visible, associated with death (cf. Nm 12:9–12), and traditionally connected with punishment by the deity (Lv 14:34; Dt 28:27, 35; 2 Sm 3:29; 2 Kgs 5:26–27; 2 Chr 26:16–21).

13:3 The symptoms of white hair and depth (perhaps a subcutaneous lesion) do not clearly correlate with known skin diseases or lesions. It may be that the symptoms are a hybrid ideal that do not reflect reality and are the result of priestly systematization. The same judgment applies to the conditions in vv. 10–11, 20, 25; cf. note on vv. 12–17.

y: Lv 10:10. *z:* Lv 15:19. *a:* Gn 17:12; Jn 7:22. *b:* Lk 2:22–24. *c:* Lv 14:21–22. *d:* Lv 1:14; Lk 2:24. *e:* Lv 22:4; Ex 4:6; Nm 5:2–3; Dt 24:8; 2 Sm 3:29; 2 Kgs 5:1, 3–7, 11, 27; Mk 1:40–45.

shall declare the person unclean. [4]* If, however, the blotch on the skin is white, but does not seem to be deeper than the skin, nor has the hair turned white, the priest shall quarantine the afflicted person for seven days.* [5]Should the priest, upon examination on the seventh day, find that the infection has remained unchanged in color and has not spread on the skin, the priest shall quarantine the person for another seven days. [6]Should the priest, upon examination again on the seventh day, find that the infection is now faded and has not spread on the skin, the priest shall declare the person clean; it was merely a scab. The person shall wash his garments* and so become clean. [7]But if, after the person was examined by the priest and declared clean, the scab spreads at all on the skin, the person shall once more be examined by the priest. [8]Should the priest, upon examination, find that the scab has indeed spread on the skin, he shall declare the person unclean; it is a scaly infection.

[9]When someone is afflicted with a scaly infection, that person shall be brought to the priest. [10]Should the priest, upon examination, find that there is a white mark on the skin which has turned the hair white and that there is raw flesh in it, [11]it is a chronic scaly infection on the skin. The priest shall declare the person unclean without quarantine, since the individual is certainly unclean. [12]* If the scaly infection breaks out on the skin and, as far as the priest can see, covers all the skin of the afflicted person from head to foot, [13]should the priest then, upon examination, find that the scaly infection does cover the whole body, he shall declare the afflicted person clean; since the person has turned completely white; that individual is clean. [14]But as soon as raw flesh appears, the individual is unclean; [15]on observing the raw flesh, the priest shall declare the person unclean, because raw flesh is unclean; it is a scaly infection. [16]If, however, the raw flesh again turns white, the person shall return to the priest; [17]should the latter, upon examination, find that the infection has indeed turned white, he shall declare the afflicted person clean; the individual is clean.

[18]If a boil appeared on a person's skin which later healed, [19]should now in the place of the boil a white mark or a reddish white blotch develop, the person shall be examined by the priest. [20]If the latter, upon examination, finds that it is deeper than the skin and that the hair has turned white, he shall declare the person unclean; it is a scaly infection that has broken out in the boil. [21]But if the priest, upon examination, finds that there is no white hair in it and that it is not deeper than the skin and is faded, the priest shall quarantine the person for seven days. [22]If it has then spread on the skin, the priest shall declare the person unclean; it is an infection. [23]But if the blotch remains the same without spreading, it is merely the scar of the boil; the priest shall therefore declare the person clean.

[24]If there was a burn on a person's skin, and the burned area now becomes a reddish white or a white blotch, [25]when the priest, upon examination, finds that the hair has turned white in the blotch and this seems to be deeper than the skin, it is a scaly infection that has broken out in the burn; the priest shall therefore declare the person unclean; it is a scaly infection. [26]But if the priest, upon examination, finds that there is no white hair in the blotch and that this is not deeper than the skin and is faded, the priest shall quarantine the person for seven days. [27]Should the priest, upon examination on the seventh day, find that it has spread at all on the skin, he shall declare the person unclean; it is a scaly infection. [28]But if the blotch remains the same without spreading on the skin and is

13:4–8 The symptoms here involve a flaky patch of skin that spreads after one week or stays the same after two. This correlates with many skin diseases, such as psoriasis, seborrhoeic dermatitis, certain mycotic infections, patchy eczema, and pityriasis rosea.

13:4 Quarantine . . . seven days: unless lesions have unmistakable symptoms of scaly infection, time is needed to distinguish disease from a condition which is following the natural course of healing and remission. Cf. vv. 5, 21, 26, 27, 31, 33, 50, 54; 14:38.

13:6 Wash his garments: even suspected scaly infections create some impurity, not just diagnosed infections (vv. 45–46).

13:12–17 This is not a paradox, namely where a limited lesion is impure but one that covers the whole body is pure. Rather, a white lesion that lacks ulcerated skin ("raw flesh") is pure, even if it covers the whole body. This formulation reflects priestly interest in systematization.

faded, it is merely the spot of the burn; the priest shall therefore declare the person clean, since it is only the scar of the burn.

29* When a man or a woman has an infection on the head or in the beard, 30 should the priest, upon examination, find that the infection appears to be deeper than the skin and that there is fine yellow hair in it, the priest shall declare the person unclean; it is a scall. It is a scaly infection of the head or beard. 31 But if the priest, upon examining the scall infection, finds that it does not appear to be deeper than the skin, though the hair in it may not be black, the priest shall quarantine the scall-stricken person for seven days. 32 Should the priest, upon examining the infection on the seventh day find that the scall has not spread and has no yellow hair in it and does not seem to be deeper than the skin, 33 the person shall shave, but not the scall spot. Then the priest shall quarantine the scall-diseased person for another seven days. 34 If the priest, upon examining the scall on the seventh day, finds that it has not spread on the skin and that it does not appear to be deeper than the skin, he shall declare the person clean; the latter shall wash his garments, and will thus be clean. 35 But if the scall spreads at all on the skin after the person has been declared clean— 36 should the priest, upon examination, find that the scall has indeed spread on the skin, he need not look for yellow hair; the individual is unclean. 37 If, however, the scall has remained unchanged in color and black hair has grown in it, the disease has been healed; the person is clean, and the priest shall declare the individual clean.

38* When the skin of a man or a woman is spotted with several white blotches, 39 if the priest, upon examination, finds that the blotches on the skin are pale white, it is only tetter that has broken out on the skin, and the person therefore is clean.

40 When a man loses the hair of his head, he is simply bald on the crown and not unclean.[f] 41 So too, if he loses the hair on the front of his head, he is simply bald on the forehead and not unclean. 42 But when there is a reddish white infection on his bald crown or bald forehead, it is a scaly infection that is breaking out there. 43 If the priest, upon examination, finds that the infection spot on the bald area on the crown or forehead has the same reddish white appearance as that of a scaly infection of the skin, 44 the man has a scaly infection and is unclean. The priest shall declare him unclean; his infection is on his head.

45* The garments of one afflicted with a scaly infection shall be rent and the hair disheveled,[g] and the mustache covered.[h] The individual shall cry out, "Unclean, unclean!" 46 As long as the infection is present, the person shall be unclean. Being unclean, that individual shall dwell apart, taking up residence outside the camp.[i]

Fungal Infection of Fabrics and Leather. 47 When a fungal infection is on a garment of wool or of linen, 48 or on the warp and woof* of linen or wool, or on a hide or anything made of leather, 49 if the infection on the garment or hide, or on the warp or woof, or on any leather article is greenish or reddish, the thing is indeed a fungal infection and must be examined by the priest. 50 Having examined the infection, the priest shall quarantine the infected article for seven days. 51 If the priest, upon inspecting the infection on the seventh day, finds that it has spread on the garment, or on the warp or woof, or on the leather, whatever be its use, the infection is a harmful fungus; the article is unclean. 52 He shall

13:29–37 The symptoms in this unit may include either favus (a mycotic infection) or a protein deficiency syndrome (Kwashiorkor) where the hair may be fine and copper-red to yellow.

13:38–39 This may refer to vitiligo, where patches of the skin and hair lose pigmentation.

13:45–46 The symbolic association with death is found in the mourning activities in which those diagnosed with these afflictions engage: rending clothes, disheveling the hair, and covering the mouth. They are also excluded from the camp. Cf. examples of exclusion in Nm 5:1–4; 12:14–15; 2 Kgs 7:3–10; 15:5; 2 Chr 26:21. Persons with scaly infections must have been able to pollute others in the priestly system, though this is not stated. Hence, they must cry out "Unclean, unclean!" to warn others of their presence.

13:48 Warp and woof: it is possible that the nature of the weave allowed fungus to grow separately along warp or woof. Otherwise, this may refer to the yarns before they are woven together.

f: 2 Kgs 2:23. *g:* Lv 10:6. *h:* Mi 3:7. *i:* Lv 14:3; Nm 5:2; 12:14–15; 2 Kgs 7:3–10; 15:5; 2 Chr 26:21; Mt 26:6; Mk 14:3; Lk 17:11–19.

therefore burn up the garment, or the warp or woof, be it of wool or linen, or any leather article which is infected; since it is a harmful fungus, it must be destroyed by fire. [53]But if the priest, upon examination, finds that it has not spread on the garment, or on the warp or woof, or on the leather article, [54]he shall give orders to have the infected article washed and then quarantined for another seven days. [55]If the priest, upon examination after the infection was washed, finds that it has not changed its color, even though it may not have spread, the article is unclean. You shall burn it with fire. It is a fray, be it on its inner or outer side. [56]But if the priest, upon examination, finds that the infection has faded after the washing, he shall cut it out of the garment, or the leather, or the warp or woof. [57]If, however, the infection again appears on the garment, or on the warp or woof, or on the leather article, it is still virulent and you shall burn the thing infected with fire. [58]But if, after the washing, the infection has disappeared from the garment, or the warp or woof, or the leather article, the thing shall be washed a second time, and thus it will be clean. [59]This is the instruction for a fungal[j] infection on a garment of wool or linen, or on a warp or woof, or on any leather article, to determine whether it is clean or unclean.

See RG 129–31

CHAPTER 14

Purification After Scaly Infection.

[1]* The LORD said to Moses: [2][k] This is the ritual for someone that had a scaly infection at the time of that person's purification.[l] The individual shall be brought to the priest, [3]who is to go outside the camp.[m] If the priest, upon inspection, finds that the scaly infection has healed in the afflicted person, [4]he shall order that two live, clean birds,* as well as some cedar wood, scarlet yarn, and hyssop be obtained for the one who is to be purified.[n] [5]* The priest shall then order that one of the birds be slaughtered over an earthen vessel with fresh water in it. [6]Taking the living bird with the cedar wood, the scarlet yarn and the hyssop, the priest shall dip them, including the live bird, in the blood of the bird that was slaughtered over the fresh water, [7]and then sprinkle seven times on the person to be purified from the scaly infection. When he has thus purified that person, he shall let the living bird fly away over the countryside.[o] [8]The person being purified shall then wash his garments, shave off all hair, and bathe in water,* and so become clean. After this the person may come inside the camp, but shall still remain outside his or her tent for seven days.[p] [9]On the seventh day this individual shall again shave off all hair, of the head, beard, and eyebrows—all hair must be shaved—and also wash his garments and bathe the body in water, and so become clean.

[10]On the eighth day the individual shall take two unblemished male lambs, one unblemished yearling ewe lamb, three tenths of an ephah of bran flour mixed with oil for a grain offering, and one log* of oil. [11]The priest who performs the purification ceremony shall place the person who is being purified, as well as all these offerings, before the LORD at the entrance of the tent of meeting. [12]Taking one of the male lambs, the priest shall present it as a reparation offering,[q] along with the log of oil, raising them as an elevated[r] offering before the LORD. [13]This lamb shall be slaughtered in the sacred place

14:1–32 The rites here are for purification from human scaly infections after recovery, not for healing (but cf. 2 Kgs 5:10–14).

14:4–7 The bird rite is also found for purifying a house from a fungus (vv. 49–53). The rite apparently removes impurity from the individual and, by means of the live bird, sends it away to unpopulated areas (v. 7). This is similar to the dispatch of a goat laden with sins on the Day of Atonement (16:21–22).

14:5–7 The blood from the bird serves as a ritual detergent, much like the blood from the purification offering (see notes on 4:3). It is not a sacrifice, however, since it is not performed at the sanctuary. **Fresh water**: lit., "living water," taken from some source of running water, not from a cistern.

14:8 Bathe in water: This phrase occurs frequently in Lv 14–16 and is imprecise. It can refer to both ordinary and cultic washing. The context will determine the meaning. At this early period in Israel's history it is probably not a reference to cultic immersion in a Mikveh—a Second Temple period ritual.

14:10 Log: a liquid measure of capacity attested in the Bible only here. It is apparently equal in capacity to one-half liter.

j: Lv 14:54–57. *k:* 2 Kgs 5:10, 14; Mt 8:4; 10:8; Mk 1:44; Lk 4:27; 5:14. *l:* Lv 14:48–53. *m:* Lv 13:46. *n:* Nm 19:6. *o:* Lv 16:21–22. *p:* Lv 15:13, 28. *q:* Lv 7:1–10. *r:* Lv 7:30.

where the purification offering and the burnt offering are slaughtered, because the reparation offering is like the purification offering; it belongs to the priest and is most holy. 14* [s] Then the priest shall take some of the blood of the reparation offering and put it on the lobe of the right ear, the thumb of the right hand, and the big toe of the right foot of the person being purified. 15The priest shall also take the log of oil and pour some of it into the palm of his own left hand; 16then, dipping his right finger in the oil on his left palm, he shall sprinkle some of it with his finger seven times before the LORD. 17Of the oil left in his hand the priest shall put some on the lobe of the right ear, the thumb of the right hand, and the big toe of the right foot of the person being purified, over the blood of the reparation offering. 18The rest of the oil in his hand the priest shall put on the head[t] of the one being purified. Thus shall the priest make atonement for the individual before the LORD. 19The priest shall next offer the purification offering,[u] thus making atonement on behalf of the one being purified from the uncleanness. After this the burnt offering shall be slaughtered. 20The priest shall offer the burnt offering[v] and the grain offering on the altar before the LORD. Thus shall the priest make atonement for the person, and the individual will become clean.

Poor Person's Sacrifices. 21If a person is poor and cannot afford so much,[w] that person shall take one male lamb for a reparation offering, to be used as an elevated offering in atonement, one tenth of an ephah of bran flour mixed with oil for a grain offering, a log of oil, 22and two turtledoves or pigeons, which the individual can more easily afford, the one as a purification offering and the other as a burnt offering. 23On the eighth day of purification the person shall bring them to the priest, at the entrance of the tent of meeting before the LORD. 24Taking the lamb of the reparation offering, along with the log of oil, the priest shall raise them as an elevated offering before the LORD. 25When the lamb of the reparation offering has been slaughtered, the priest shall take some of its blood, and put it on the lobe of the right ear, on the thumb of the right hand, and on the big toe of the right foot of the person being purified. 26The priest shall then pour some of the oil into the palm of his own left hand 27and with his right finger sprinkle some of the oil in his left palm seven times before the LORD. 28Some of the oil in his hand the priest shall also put on the lobe of the right ear, the thumb of the right hand, and the big toe of the right foot of the person being purified, where he had sprinkled the blood of the reparation offering. 29The rest of the oil in his hand the priest shall put on the head of the one being purified. Thus shall he make atonement for the individual before the LORD. 30Then, of the turtledoves or pigeons, such as the person can afford, 31the priest shall offer one as a purification offering and the other as a burnt offering,[x] along with the grain offering. Thus shall the priest make atonement before the LORD for the person who is being purified. 32This is the ritual for one afflicted with a scaly infection who has insufficient means for purification.

Fungal Infection of Houses. 33*The LORD said to Moses and Aaron: 34When you come into the land of Canaan, which I am giving you to possess, if I put[y] a fungal infection in any house of the land you occupy, 35the owner of the house shall come and report to the priest, "Something like an infection has appeared in my house." 36The priest shall then order the house to be cleared out before he goes in to examine the infection, lest everything in the house become unclean. Only after this is he to go in to examine the house. 37If the priest, upon inspection, finds that the infection on the walls of the house

14:14–17 The application of blood and oil here facilitates the movement of the person from the severely impure to the pure profane sphere; it reintegrates him or her into the community. Cf. 8:23–24.

14:33–53 Discussion of fungi in houses is probably delayed until here because it deals with a case pertaining to living in the land (v. 34) as opposed to the foregoing cases which apply even in the wilderness. The rules on fabrics (13:47–58) apply to the tent dwellings in the wilderness.

s: Lv 8:23–24. *t:* Lv 8:12, 30. *u:* Lv 4. *v:* Lv 1. *w:* Lv 5:7, 11; 12:8. *x:* Lv 1:14–17; 5:7–10. *y:* Nm 12:9–15; 2 Kgs 15:4–5; 2 Chr 26:16–21.

consists of greenish or reddish spots[z] which seem to go deeper than the surface of the wall, [38]he shall go out of the house to the doorway and quarantine the house for seven days. [39]On the seventh day the priest shall return. If, upon inspection, he finds that the infection has spread on the walls, [40]he shall order the infected stones to be pulled out and cast in an unclean place outside the city. [41]The whole inside of the house shall then be scraped, and the mortar that has been scraped off shall be dumped in an unclean place outside the city. [42]Then other stones shall be brought and put in the place of the old stones, and new mortar obtained and plastered on the house. [43]If the infection breaks out once more in the house after the stones have been pulled out and the house has been scraped and replastered, [44]the priest shall come; and if, upon inspection, he finds that the infection has spread in the house, it is a corrosive fungus in the house, and it is unclean. [45]It shall be pulled down, and all its stones, beams and mortar shall be hauled away to an unclean place outside the city. [46a] Whoever enters a house while it is quarantined shall be unclean until evening. [47]Whoever sleeps or eats in such a house shall also wash his garments.

[48b] If the priest finds, when he comes to the house, that the infection has in fact not spread in the house after the plastering, he shall declare the house clean, since the infection has been healed. [49]To purify the house, he shall take two birds, as well as cedar wood, scarlet yarn, and hyssop. [50]One of the birds he shall slaughter over an earthen vessel with fresh water in it. [51]Then, taking the cedar wood, the hyssop and the scarlet yarn, together with the living bird, he shall dip them all in the blood of the slaughtered bird and the fresh water, and sprinkle the house seven times. [52]Thus he shall purify the house with the bird's blood and the fresh water, along with the living bird, the cedar wood, the hyssop, and the scarlet yarn. [53]He shall then let the living bird fly away over the countryside outside the city. Thus he shall make atonement for the house, and it will be clean.

[54]This is the ritual for every kind of human scaly infection and scall, [55]and for fungus diseases in garments and houses— [56]for marks, lesions and blotches— [57]to give direction when there is a state of uncleanness and when a state of cleanness. This is the ritual for scaly infection.

CHAPTER 15

See RG 129–31

Sexual Uncleanness.* [1]The LORD said to Moses and Aaron: [2]* Speak to the Israelites and tell them: When any man has a genital discharge, he is thereby unclean.[c] [3]Such is his uncleanness from this discharge, whether his body* drains freely with the discharge or is blocked up from the discharge. His uncleanness is on him all the days that his body discharges or is blocked up from his discharge; this is his uncleanness. [4]Any bed on which the man with the discharge lies is unclean, and any article on which he sits is unclean. [5]Anyone who touches his bed shall wash his garments, bathe in water, and be unclean until evening. [6]Whoever sits on an article on which the man with the discharge was sitting shall wash his garments, bathe in water, and be unclean until evening. [7]Whoever touches the body of the man with the discharge shall wash his garments, bathe in water, and be unclean until evening. [8]If the man with the discharge spits on a clean person, the latter shall wash his garments, bathe in water, and be unclean until evening. [9]Any saddle on which the man with the discharge rides is unclean. [10]Whoever touches anything that was under him shall be unclean until evening; whoever carries any such thing shall wash his garments, bathe in water, and be unclean until evening.[d] [11]Anyone whom the man with the discharge touches with his unrinsed hands shall wash his garments, bathe in water, and be unclean until evening. [12]Earthenware touched by the man with the discharge shall be broken; and

15:1–33 Sexual discharges may be unclean partly because they involve the loss of life fluids or are otherwise involved with phenomena at the margins of life and death.

15:2–3 The uncleanness here is perhaps a discharge of pus because of urethritis (often but not solely associated with gonorrhea).

15:3 Body: here a euphemism in the Hebrew for "penis."

z: Lv 13:49. *a:* cf. Lv 15:10. *b:* Lv 14:2–9. *c:* Nm 5:2. *d:* Lv 11:24–25, 27–28, 39–40; 14:46–47.

every wooden article shall be rinsed with water.

13 When a man with a discharge becomes clean* of his discharge, he shall count seven days[e] for his purification. Then he shall wash his garments and bathe his body in fresh water, and so he will be clean. 14 On the eighth day he shall take two turtledoves or two pigeons,[f] and going before the LORD, to the entrance of the tent of meeting, he shall give them to the priest, 15 who shall offer them up, the one as a purification offering and the other as a burnt offering. Thus shall the priest make atonement before the LORD for the man because of his discharge.

16* When a man has an emission of semen, he shall bathe his whole body in water and be unclean until evening.[g] 17 Any piece of cloth or leather with semen on it shall be washed with water and be unclean until evening.

18 If a man has sexual relations with a woman, they shall both bathe in water and be unclean until evening.

19* When a woman has a flow of blood from her body, she shall be in a state of menstrual uncleanness for seven days. Anyone who touches her shall be unclean until evening.[h] 20 Anything on which she lies or sits during her menstrual period shall be unclean. 21 Anyone who touches her bed shall wash his garments, bathe in water, and be unclean until evening. 22 Whoever touches any article on which she was sitting shall wash his garments, bathe in water, and be unclean until evening. 23 Whether an object* is on the bed or on something she sat upon, when the person touches it, that person shall be unclean until evening. 24 If a man lies with her, he contracts her menstrual uncleanness and shall be unclean for seven days;[i] every bed on which he then lies also becomes unclean.

25* When a woman has a flow of blood for several days outside her menstrual period, or when her flow continues beyond the ordinary period, as long as she suffers this unclean flow she shall be unclean, just as during her menstrual period.[j] 26 Any bed on which she lies during such a flow becomes unclean, as it would during her menstrual period, and any article on which she sits becomes unclean just as during her menstrual period. 27 Anyone who touches them becomes unclean; that person shall wash his garments, bathe in water, and be unclean until evening.

28[k] When she becomes clean from her flow, she shall count seven days; after this she becomes clean. 29 On the eighth day she shall take two turtledoves or two pigeons and bring them to the priest at the entrance of the tent of meeting. 30 The priest shall offer one of them as a purification offering and the other as a burnt offering. Thus shall the priest make atonement before the LORD for her because of her unclean flow.

31 You shall warn the Israelites of their uncleanness, lest they die through their uncleanness by defiling my tabernacle,[l] which is in their midst.

32 This is the ritual for the man with a discharge, or who has an emission of semen, and thereby becomes unclean; 33 as well as for the woman who has her menstrual period; or one who has a discharge, male or female; and also for the man who lies with an unclean woman.

15:13 Becomes clean: i.e., when his discharge ceases. The rite that follows is for purification, not a cure; see note on 14:1–32.

15:16–18 Menstrual blood, semen, and other impurities in Lv 11–15 are considered "impure" either because they are force of life whose "loss" represents death or because, as uniquely human conditions, they are symbolically incompatible with the deity and the divine abode, the sanctuary. Lv 15:16 refers to a spontaneous nocturnal emission, and either because this marks life and death boundaries or because of its uniquely human (versus divine) character, any contact with it renders the object or person ritually unclean. Thus, in 15:18 it is not the marital act itself that is polluting, but only semen.

15:19–24 This is normal menstruation.

15:23 An object: the Hebrew is unclear. This translation means that even an object on the woman's unclean bed or chair can mediate uncleanness to another, but only if all the object touched is still on the bed or article sat upon, thus forming a chain of simultaneous contact.

15:25–30 This is menstruation outside the normal cycle or for periods longer than normal. A woman with a chronic blood flow was healed by touching the tassel of Jesus' cloak (Mt 9:20–22; Mk 5:25–34; Lk 8:43–48).

e: Lv 14:8. *f:* Lv 12:8; 14:22. *g:* Ex 19:15; Dt 23:11–12; 1 Sm 21:6. *h:* Lv 12:2, 5; 2 Sm 11:4; Ez 36:17. *i:* Lv 18:19; 20:18; Ez 18:6. *j:* Mt 9:20–22; Mk 5:25–34; Lk 8:43–48. *k:* Lv 15:13–15. *l:* Lv 5:2–3; 22:9; Nm 19:13, 20.

See RG 131

CHAPTER 16

The Day of Atonement. [1]* After the death of Aaron's two sons,[m] who died when they encroached on the LORD's presence, the LORD spoke to Moses [2]and said to him: Tell your brother Aaron that he is not to come whenever he pleases* into the inner sanctuary, inside the veil,[n] in front of the cover on the ark, lest he die, for I reveal myself in a cloud above the ark's cover. [3]Only in this way may Aaron enter the inner sanctuary. He shall bring a bull of the herd for a purification offering and a ram for a burnt offering. [4]He shall wear the sacred linen tunic, with the linen pants underneath, gird himself with the linen sash and put on the linen turban.[o] But since these vestments are sacred, he shall not put them on until he has first bathed his body in water.[p] [5]From the Israelite community he shall receive two male goats for a purification offering and one ram for a burnt offering.

[6]Aaron shall offer the bull, his purification offering, to make atonement* for himself and for his household. [7]Taking the two male goats and setting them before the LORD at the entrance of the tent of meeting, [8]he shall cast lots[q] to determine which one is for the LORD and which for Azazel.* [r] [9]The goat that is determined by lot for the LORD, Aaron shall present and offer up as a purification offering. [10]But the goat determined by lot for Azazel he shall place before the LORD alive, so that with it he may make atonement by sending it off to Azazel in the desert.

[11]Thus shall Aaron offer his bull for the purification offering, to make atonement for himself and for his family. When he has slaughtered it, [12]he shall take a censer full of glowing embers from the altar before the LORD, as well as a double handful of finely ground fragrant incense, and bringing them inside the veil, [13]there before the LORD he shall put incense on the fire, so that a cloud of incense may shield the cover that is over the covenant, else he will die. [14]Taking some of the bull's blood, he shall sprinkle it with his finger on the front of the ark's cover and likewise sprinkle some of the blood with his finger seven times in front of the cover.

[15]Then he shall slaughter the goat of the people's purification offering, and bringing its blood inside the veil, he shall do with it as he did with the bull's blood, sprinkling it on the ark's cover and in front of it. [16]Thus he shall purge the inner sanctuary* of all the Israelites' impurities and trespasses, including all their sins. He shall do the same for the tent of meeting,[s] which is set up among them in the midst of their uncleanness. [17]No one else may be in the tent of meeting from the time he enters the inner sanctuary to make atonement until he departs. When he has made atonement for himself and his household, as well as for the whole Israelite assembly, [18]* he shall come out to the altar before the LORD and purge it also. Taking some of the

16:1–34 This is the narrative sequel of the story in chap. 10. The ritual in chapter 16 originally may have been an emergency rite in response to unexpected pollution of the sanctuary.

16:2 Not to come whenever he pleases: access to the various parts of the sanctuary is strictly controlled. Only the high priest can enter the most holy place, and only once a year. **The veil**: the Letter to the Hebrews makes use of the imagery of the Day of Atonement (in Hebrew *Yom Kippur*) to explain Jesus' sacrifice (Heb 9:1–14, 23–28). **Ark's cover**: the meaning of *kappōret* is not certain. It may be connected with the verb *kipper* "to atone, purge" (see note on v. 6) and thus refer to this part of the ark as a focus of atonement or purification.

16:6 Make atonement: the Hebrew verb *kipper* refers specifically to the removal of sin and impurity (cf. Ex 30:10; Lv 6:23; 8:15; 16:16, 18, 20, 27, 33; Ez 43:20, 26; 45:20), thus "to purge" in vv. 16, 18, 20, and 33, and more generally to the consequence of the sacrificial procedure, which is atonement (cf. Lv 17:11). "Atonement" is preeminently a function of the purification sacrifice, but other sacrifices, except apparently for the communion sacrifice, achieve this as well.

16:8 Azazel: a name for a demon (meaning something like "angry/fierce god"). See note on 17:7.

16:16 Inner sanctuary: this refers to the most holy room (vv. 2, 11–15). **Trespasses, including all their sins**: the term for "trespasses" (Heb. *pesha'im*), which has overtones of rebellion, and the phrase "all their sins" indicate that even sins committed intentionally are included (such as when the sinner "acts defiantly," as in Nm 15:30–31). This complements the scheme found in Lv 4 (see note on 4:3): intentional sins pollute the sanctuary more and penetrate even further than inadvertent sins, namely to the most holy place. **The same for the tent of meeting**: this rite may be that found in 4:5–7, 16–18 where blood is sprinkled in the anterior room and blood is placed on the horns of the incense altar there. Cf. Ex 30:10.

16:18–19 Thus a third locale in the sanctuary complex, the open-air altar, is purified. See the summaries in 16:20, 33.

m: Lv 10:1–5. *n:* Lv 23:26–32; Nm 29:7–11; Heb 9:6–28. *o:* Lv 8:7; Ex 28:1–40. *p:* Lv 8:6. *q:* Jos 7:14–20; Acts 1:26. *r:* Lv 17:7. *s:* Lv 4:5–7, 16–18.

bull's and the goat's blood, he shall put it on the horns around the altar, [19]and with his finger sprinkle some of the blood on it seven times.[t] Thus he shall purify it and sanctify it from the impurities of the Israelites.

The Scapegoat. [20]When he has finished purging the inner sanctuary, the tent of meeting and the altar, Aaron shall bring forward the live goat. [21]Laying both hands* on its head, he shall confess over it all the iniquities of the Israelites and their trespasses, including all their sins, and so put them on the goat's head.[u] He shall then have it led into the wilderness by an attendant. [22]The goat will carry off all their iniquities to an isolated region.[v]

When the goat is dispatched into the wilderness, [23]Aaron shall go into the tent of meeting, strip off the linen vestments he had put on when he entered the inner sanctuary, and leave them in the tent of meeting. [24]After bathing his body with water in a sacred place, he shall put on his regular vestments, and then come out and offer his own and the people's burnt offering, in atonement for himself and for the people, [25]and also burn the fat of the purification offering on the altar.

[26]The man who led away the goat for Azazel shall wash his garments and bathe his body in water; only then may he enter the camp. [27]The bull and the goat of the purification offering whose blood was brought to make atonement in the inner sanctuary, shall be taken outside the camp,[w] where their hides and flesh and dung shall be burned in the fire. [28]The one who burns them shall wash his garments and bathe his body in water; only then may he enter the camp.

The Fast. [29][x] This shall be an everlasting statute for you: on the tenth day of the seventh month every one of you, whether a native or a resident alien, shall humble yourselves* and shall do no work. [30]For on this day atonement is made for you to make you clean; of all your sins you will be cleansed before the LORD. [31]It shall be a sabbath of complete rest for you, on which you must humble yourselves—an everlasting statute.

[32]This atonement is to be made by the priest who has been anointed and ordained to the priesthood in succession to his father. He shall wear the linen garments, the sacred vestments, [33]and purge the most sacred part of the sanctuary, as well as the tent of meeting, and the altar. He shall also make atonement for the priests and all the people of the assembly. [34]This, then, shall be an everlasting statute for you: once a year atonement shall be made on behalf of the Israelites for all their sins. And Moses did as the LORD had commanded him.

IV. Holiness Laws

CHAPTER 17

See RG 131–32

Sacredness of Blood. [1]The LORD said to Moses: [2]Speak to Aaron and his sons, as well as to all the Israelites, and tell them: This is what the LORD has commanded: [3]* Any Israelite who slaughters an ox or a sheep or a goat, whether in the camp or outside of it, [4]without first bringing it to the entrance of the tent of meeting to present it as an offering to the LORD in front of the LORD's tabernacle, shall be judged guilty of bloodshed*[y]—that individual has shed blood, and shall be cut off[z] from the people. [5]This is so that such sacrifices as they used to offer in the open field the Israelites shall henceforth bring to the LORD at the entrance of the tent of meeting, to the priest, and sac-

16:21 Both hands: this gesture is for transferring sins to the head of the goat and is apparently different in meaning from the one-handed gesture that precedes the slaughtering of sacrificial animals (1:4; 3:2; 4:4; see note on 1:4).

16:29 Humble yourselves: also v. 31. The idiom used here (Heb. *'innâ nephesh*) involves mainly fasting (Ps 35:13), but probably prohibits other activities such as anointing (Dn 10:3) and sexual intercourse (2 Sm 12:15–24). Such acts of self-denial display the need for divine favor. Fasting is often undertaken in times of emergency and mourning (cf. 1 Sm 14:24; 2 Sm 1:12; 3:35; cf. Mk 2:18–22).

17:3–4 Any animal slaughtered must be brought to the tent of meeting as an offering. This differs from Dt 12:15–28, which allows those living too far from the temple to slaughter an animal for food at home without offering it as a sacrifice.

17:4 Guilty of bloodshed: human beings and animals can incur blood guilt for killing human beings (cf. Gn 9:5–6); human beings can incur blood guilt for killing animals (see note on Lv 24:17–22).

t: Lv 4:25, 30, 34. *u:* Is 53:6; 2 Cor 5:21. *v:* Lv 14:7, 53; Is 53:11–12; Jn 1:29; 1 Pt 2:24. *w:* Lv 4:11–12; 6:23; Heb 13:11–13. *x:* Lv 23:27, 32; Nm 29:7. *y:* Lv 24:18. *z:* Lv 7:20.

rifice them there as communion sacrifices to the LORD.[a] 6 The priest will splash the blood on the altar of the LORD at the entrance of the tent of meeting and burn the fat for an odor pleasing to the LORD. 7 No longer shall they offer their sacrifices to the demons* with whom they prostituted themselves.[b] This shall be an everlasting statute for them and their descendants.

8 Tell them, therefore: Anyone, whether of the house of Israel or of the aliens residing among them, who offers a burnt offering or sacrifice 9 without bringing it to the entrance of the tent of meeting to offer it to the LORD, shall be cut off from the people. 10[c] As for anyone, whether of the house of Israel or of the aliens residing among them, who consumes any blood, I will set myself against that individual and will cut that person off from among the people, 11 since the life of the flesh is in the blood,[d] and I have given it to you to make atonement* on the altar for yourselves, because it is the blood as life that makes atonement. 12 That is why I have told the Israelites: No one among you, not even a resident alien, may consume blood.

13 Anyone hunting,* whether of the Israelites or of the aliens residing among them, who catches an animal or a bird that may be eaten, shall pour out its blood and cover it with earth,[e] 14 since the life of all flesh is its blood. I have told the Israelites: You shall not consume the blood of any flesh. Since the life of all flesh is its blood, anyone who consumes it shall be cut off.

15 Everyone, whether a native or an alien, who eats of an animal that died of itself or was killed by a wild beast, shall wash his garments, bathe in water, and be unclean until evening, and then become clean.[f] 16 If one does not wash his garments and bathe, that person shall bear the penalty.

CHAPTER 18

See RG 131–32

Laws Concerning Sexual Behavior.

1 The LORD said to Moses: 2 Speak to the Israelites and tell them: I, the LORD, am your God.* 3 You shall not do as they do in the land of Egypt, where you once lived, nor shall you do as they do in the land of Canaan, where I am bringing you; do not conform to their customs.[g] 4 My decrees you shall carry out, and my statutes you shall take care to follow. I, the LORD, am your God. 5 Keep, then, my statutes and decrees, for the person who carries them out will find life* through them. I am the LORD.[h]

6* None of you shall approach a close relative* to have sexual intercourse. I am the LORD. 7* You shall not disgrace your father by having intercourse with your mother.[i] She is your own mother; you shall not have intercourse with her. 8 You shall not have intercourse with your father's wife, for that would be a disgrace to your father. 9 You shall not have intercourse with your sister,*[j] your father's daughter or your mother's daughter, whether she was born in your own household or born elsewhere. 10 You shall not have intercourse with your son's daugh-

17:7 Demons: for Hebrew *śe'îrîm*, lit., "goats." Like the demon Azazel (cf. 16:8, 10, 21–22), they dwell in the open country (17:5). Cf. Is 13:21; 34:14.

17:11 To make atonement: this is probably to be understood in the context of liability for shedding animal blood (cf. v. 4). Placing the blood on the altar exonerates the slaughterer from guilt for the killing. See note on 16:6.

17:13 Hunting: game animals are not permitted as offerings. One nonetheless has to treat the blood of these animals carefully by covering it with earth. Cf. Dt 12:16, 24.

18:2 I, the LORD, am your God: this declaration appears frequently elsewhere throughout chaps. 17–26, sometimes with a statement of God's holiness or his sanctifying activity. It emphasizes the importance of the laws and the relationship of the divine lawgiver to the people.

18:5 Find life: in Dt 30:15–20 Moses sets before the people life and death. The alternatives are set out in detail in Lv 26 and Dt 28. Cf. Ez 20:11, 13, 21.

18:6–23 These laws deal with illicit sexual behavior. Lv 20:10–21 reiterates most of these cases, with penalties. Cf. also Dt 27:15–26; Ez 22:7–12. The ordering of the cases in Lv 18 seems to be: blood relatives (vv. 6–13), those related by marriage (vv. 14–18), then other cases (vv. 19–23).

18:6 Close relative: this refers to a blood relative and includes those not specifically mentioned in the list, such as one's own daughter and a full sister. **Have sexual intercourse**: lit., "to uncover nakedness."

18:7–8 Cf. the story of Reuben lying with Bilhah, his father's concubine and Rachel's maid (Gn 35:22; 49:4).

18:9, 11 Cf. actual or possible marriage to a half sister in Gn 20:12 and 2 Sm 13:13.

a: Lv 3:1–2, 7–8, 13. *b:* Ex 34:15; Dt 32:17; 2 Chr 11:15; 1 Cor 10:20. *c:* Lv 3:17; 7:26–27; Gn 9:4; Dt 12:16, 23–24. *d:* Gn 9:4. *e:* Dt 12:15–16. *f:* Lv 11:39–40; 22:8. *g:* Lv 20:22–23. *h:* Ez 20:11, 13, 21; Gal 3:12. *i:* Lv 20:11; Dt 23:1; 27:20; 1 Cor 5:1. *j:* Lv 20:17; Dt 27:22.

ter or with your daughter's daughter,* for that would be a disgrace to you. 11You shall not have intercourse with the daughter whom your father's wife bore to him in his household,[k] since she, too, is your sister. 12You shall not have intercourse with your father's sister,[l] since she is your father's relative. 13You shall not have intercourse with your mother's sister, since she is your mother's relative. 14You shall not disgrace your father's brother by having sexual relations with his wife,[m] since she, too, is your aunt. 15You shall not have intercourse with your daughter-in-law;* [n] she is your son's wife; you shall not have intercourse with her. 16You shall not have intercourse with your brother's wife;* [o] that would be a disgrace to your brother. 17You shall not have intercourse with a woman and also with her daughter, nor shall you marry and have intercourse with her son's daughter or her daughter's daughter;[p] they are related to her. This would be shameful. 18While your wife is still living you shall not marry her sister as her rival and have intercourse with her.[q]

19You shall not approach a woman to have intercourse with her while she is in her menstrual uncleanness.[r] 20You shall not have sexual relations with your neighbor's wife,* [s] defiling yourself with her. 21[t] You shall not offer any of your offspring for immolation to Molech,* thus profaning the name of your God. I am the LORD. 22You shall not lie with a male as with a woman;[u] such a thing is an abomination. 23You shall not have sexual relations with an animal, defiling yourself with it; nor shall a woman set herself in front of an animal to mate with it; that is perverse.[v]

24Do not defile yourselves by any of these things, because by them the nations whom I am driving out of your way have defiled themselves. 25And so the land has become defiled, and I have punished it for its wickedness, and the land has vomited out its inhabitants.[w] 26You, however, must keep my statutes and decrees, avoiding all these abominations, both the natives and the aliens resident among you— 27because the previous inhabitants did all these abominations and the land became defiled; 28otherwise the land will vomit you out also for having defiled it, just as it vomited out the nations before you. 29For whoever does any of these abominations shall be cut off from the people. 30Heed my charge, then, not to observe the abominable customs that have been observed before your time, and thus become impure by them.[x] I, the LORD, am your God.

CHAPTER 19

See RG 131–32

Various Rules of Conduct. 1The LORD said to Moses: 2Speak to the whole Israelite community and tell them: Be holy, for I, the LORD your God, am holy.* [y] 3* Each of you revere your mother and father,[z] and keep my sabbaths.[a] I, the LORD, am your God.

4Do not turn aside to idols, nor make molten gods for yourselves.[b] I, the LORD, am your God.

18:10 Daughter incest is found in the story of Lot (Gn 19:30–38).

18:15 Judah had intercourse with his daughter-in-law Tamar (Gn 38), but did not know her true identity until her pregnancy was discovered.

18:16 This refers to cohabiting with one's sister-in-law not only while the brother is alive, but also after he is dead. Dt 25:5–10 allows for the marriage to the wife of a brother when that brother died without a male heir. Cf. Gn 38:6–14. It was the violation of this law of Leviticus which aroused the wrath of John the Baptist against Herod Antipas (Mt 14:4; Mk 6:18).

18:20 Adultery in the Hebrew Bible and the ancient Near East is intercourse between a married or betrothed woman and any male. In the Bible it is generally punishable by the death of both individuals (20:10; cf. Dt 22:22–27). Intercourse with an unmarried or unbetrothed woman is not prohibited but carries responsibilities and fines (cf. Ex 22:15–16; Dt 22:28–29). Cf. Lv 19:20–22.

18:21 Immolation to Molech: the reference is to the custom of sacrificing children to the god Molech. Cf. Ez 16:20–21; 20:26, 31; 23:37. See note on Lv 20:1–5.

19:2 Be holy, for I . . . am holy: in the writings commonly attributed to the Priestly collection, Israel is called to be holy through obeying God's precepts (11:44–45; 20:7–8, 24–26; Nm 15:40–41). Cf. Dt 14:2, 21; 26:19; and Ex 19:6.

19:3–4 Cf. the Decalogue laws on revering parents (Ex

k: Lv 20:17. *l:* Lv 20:19. *m:* Lv 20:20. *n:* Lv 20:12. *o:* Lv 20:21; Dt 25:5–10; Mt 14:3–4; Mk 6:18. *p:* Lv 20:14; Dt 27:23. *q:* Gn 29:27–28. *r:* Lv 15:24, 33; 20:18; Ez 18:6; 22:10. *s:* Lv 20:10; Ex 20:14; Dt 5:18; 22:22; Mt 5:27–30; Jn 8:4–5. *t:* Lv 20:2–5; Dt 18:10; 1 Kgs 11:7; 2 Kgs 16:3. *u:* Lv 20:13; Gn 19:4–11; Jgs 19:22–30; Rom 1:27; 1 Cor 6:9. *v:* Lv 20:15–16; Ex 22:18; Dt 27:21. *w:* Lv 20:22. *x:* Lv 20:23; Dt 18:9. *y:* Lv 11:44. *z:* Lv 20:9; Ex 20:12. *a:* Lv 23:3. *b:* Lv 26:1; Ex 20:3–5; 34:17; Dt 5:8; 27:15.

5 When you sacrifice your communion sacrifice to the LORD, you shall sacrifice it so that it is acceptable on your behalf. 6 It must be eaten on the day of your sacrifice or on the following day. Whatever is left over until the third day shall be burned in fire. 7 If any of it is eaten on the third day, it will be a desecrated offering and not be accepted;[c] 8 whoever eats of it then shall bear the penalty for having profaned what is sacred to the LORD. Such a one shall be cut off[d] from the people.

9* When you reap the harvest of your land, you shall not be so thorough that you reap the field to its very edge, nor shall you gather the gleanings of your harvest.[e] 10 Likewise, you shall not pick your vineyard bare, nor gather up the grapes that have fallen. These things you shall leave for the poor and the alien. I, the LORD, am your God.

11* You shall not steal. You shall not deceive or speak falsely to one another.[f] 12 You shall not swear falsely by my name, thus profaning the name of your God.[g] I am the LORD.

13 You shall not exploit your neighbor. You shall not commit robbery. You shall not withhold overnight the wages of your laborer.[h] 14* You shall not insult the deaf, or put a stumbling block in front of the blind, but you shall fear your God. I am the LORD.

15 You shall not act dishonestly in rendering judgment. Show neither partiality to the weak nor deference to the mighty, but judge your neighbor justly.[i] 16 You shall not go about spreading slander among your people; nor shall you stand by idly when your neighbor's life is at stake. I am the LORD.

17* You shall not hate any of your kindred in your heart. Reprove your neighbor openly so that you do not incur sin because of that person.[j] 18 Take no revenge and cherish no grudge against your own people. You shall love your neighbor as yourself. I am the LORD.[k]

19* Keep my statutes: do not breed any of your domestic animals with others of a different species; do not sow a field of yours with two different kinds of seed; and do not put on a garment woven with two different kinds of thread.[l]

20* [m] If a man has sexual relations with a female slave who has been acquired by another man but has not yet been redeemed or given her freedom, an investigation shall be made. They shall not be put to death, because she has not been freed. 21 The man shall bring to the entrance of the tent of meeting as his reparation to the LORD a ram as a reparation offering.[n] 22 With the ram of the reparation offering the priest shall make atonement before the LORD for the wrong the man has committed, so that he will be forgiven for the wrong he has committed.

23 When you come into the land and plant any fruit tree there,[o] first look upon its fruit as if it were uncircumcised. For three years, it shall be uncircumcised for you; it may not be eaten. 24 In the fourth year, however, all of its fruit shall be dedicated to the LORD in joyous celebration. 25 Not until the fifth year may you eat its fruit, to increase the yield for you. I, the LORD, am your God.

26 Do not eat anything with the blood still

20:12; Dt 5:16), keeping sabbaths (Ex 20:8–11; Dt 5:12–15), and not making or worshiping idols (Ex 20:2–6; Dt 5:7–10).

19:9–10 The Israelites maintain the poor in part by letting them gather unharvested portions of fields and vineyards. Cf. 23:22; Ru 2:1–10.

19:11–13 Cf. the Decalogue commandments against stealing (Ex 20:15; Dt 5:19), wrongly using God's name (Ex 20:7; Dt 5:11), and swearing falsely against another (Ex 20:16; Dt 5:20).

19:14 In Dt 27:18 a curse falls on the head of the one who misleads the blind.

19:17–18 These verses form a unit and describe different attitudes and actions towards one's fellow Israelites. A separate passage is necessary to advise a similar attitude toward aliens (vv. 33–34). Cf. 25:39–46. The admonition at the end of v. 18 came to be viewed in Judaism and Christianity as one of the central commandments. (See Mt 22:34–40; Mk 12:28–34; Lk 10:25–28; cf. Mt 19:19; Rom 13:8–10; Gal 5:14). The New Testament urges love for enemies as well as neighbors (Mt 5:43–48; Lk 6:27–36; cf. Prv 25:21–22).

19:19 One reason why mixtures are prohibited seems to be that they are holy (see Dt 22:9, 10–11). Israelites are allowed mixtures in the wearing of fringes on the edges or corners of their clothing (Nm 15:37–41; Dt 22:12). Some mixtures are considered abominations (cf. Lv 18:23; Dt 22:5).

19:20–22 On adultery, see note on 18:20. Here it is not adultery in the technical sense since the woman is not free. A reparation offering is required as a penalty (see 5:14–26).

c: Lv 7:15–18. *d:* Lv 7:20. *e:* Lv 23:22; Dt 24:19–22. *f:* Ex 20:15–16. *g:* Ex 20:7; Mt 5:33–37. *h:* Dt 24:14–15. *i:* Ex 23:2–3; Dt 1:17; 16:19; Ps 82:2; Prv 24:23. *j:* Mt 18:15; Lk 17:3; Gal 6:1. *k:* Mt 5:43; 19:19; 22:39; Mk 12:31; Rom 13:9; Gal 5:14; Jas 2:8; 1 Jn 3:14. *l:* Dt 22:9–12. *m:* Dt 22:22–29. *n:* Lv 5:14–26. *o:* Dt 20:19–20.

in it.[p] Do not recite charms or practice soothsaying.* [q] 27Do not clip your hair at the temples, nor spoil the edges of your beard. 28Do
not lacerate your bodies for the dead, and do
not tattoo yourselves.* [r] I am the LORD.
29You shall not degrade your daughter by
making a prostitute of her;[s] otherwise the
land will prostitute itself and become full of
lewdness. 30Keep my sabbaths, and reverence my sanctuary.[t] I am the LORD.
31Do not turn to ghosts or consult spirits,
by which you will be defiled.[u] I, the LORD,
am your God.
32Stand up in the presence of the aged,
show respect for the old, and fear your God.
I am the LORD.
33When an alien resides with you in your
land, do not mistreat such a one.[v] 34You shall
treat the alien who resides with you no differently than the natives born among you;
you shall love the alien as yourself; for you
too were once aliens in the land of Egypt.[w] I,
the LORD, am your God.
35Do not act dishonestly in using measures
of length or weight or capacity. 36You shall
have a true scale and true weights, an honest
ephah and an honest hin.* [x] I, the LORD, am
your God, who brought you out of the land of
Egypt. 37Be careful, then, to observe all my
statutes and decrees. I am the LORD.

See RG 131–32

CHAPTER 20

Penalties for Various Sins. 1* The
LORD said to Moses: 2Tell the Israelites:
Anyone, whether an Israelite or an alien residing in Israel, who gives offspring to Molech shall be put to death.[y] The people of the
land shall stone that person. 3[z] I myself will
turn against and cut off[a] that individual from
among the people; for in the giving of offspring to Molech, my sanctuary was defiled[b]
and my holy name was profaned. 4If the people of the land condone the giving of offspring to Molech, by failing to put the
wrongdoer to death, 5I myself will turn
against that individual and his or her family,
and I will cut off from their people both the
wrongdoer and all who follow this person by
prostituting themselves with Molech.
6Should anyone turn to ghosts and spirits
and prostitute oneself with them,[c] I will turn
against that person and cut such a one off
from among the people. 7Sanctify yourselves,
then, and be holy; for I, the LORD, your God,[d]
am holy. 8Be careful, therefore, to observe my
statutes. I, the LORD, make you holy.
9Anyone who curses father or mother
shall be put to death;* [e] and having cursed father or mother, such a one will bear the
bloodguilt.* 10* If a man commits adultery
with his neighbor's wife,[f] both the adulterer
and the adulteress shall be put to death. 11If
a man disgraces his father by lying with his
father's wife,[g] the two of them shall be put to
death; their bloodguilt is upon them. 12If a
man lies with his daughter-in-law,[h] both of
them shall be put to death; they have done
what is perverse; their bloodguilt is upon

19:26 Recite charms . . . soothsaying: methods of divination (cf. Gn 44:5, 15; Is 2:6; Ez 21:26–28). Legitimate means of learning the future or God's will were through the Urim and Thummim stones (see Lv 8:8), lots (see Lv 16:8) and prophets (cf. Dt 18:9–22; 1 Sm 28:6–7).

19:28 Do not tattoo yourselves: see note on Gn 4:15. This prohibition probably refers only to the common ancient Near Eastern practice of branding a slave with its owner's name as well as branding the devotees of a god with its name.

19:36 Ephah: see note on Is 5:10; **hin**: see note on Ez 45:24.

20:1–5 The term Molech may refer to a deity, perhaps with an underworld association, and the activity forbidden here may be connected with divination. Cf. Dt 18:10; 2 Kgs 17:17; 21:6. In the kingdom of Judah the cult appears to have been practiced in the Valley of Hinnom, just outside Jerusalem on the west and south (2 Kgs 23:10; Jer 32:35).

20:9 Curses father or mother . . . put to death: this is more than a simple expletive uttered in anger against one's parents. See note on Ex 21:17.

20:9–21 Bloodguilt: these penalties, beginning with cursing one's parents, reflect the concerns of a patriarchal society that the breakdown of one's relations with one's parents can lead to the breakdown of all other familial relationships, resulting in the breakdown of society.

20:10–21 See 18:6–23 and notes there. It appears that the inclusion of various penalties in 20:10–21 accounts for the different order of the cases here compared to the order found in 18:6–23. The reason why the offenses in 20:10–21 carry different penalties, however, is not clear. Perhaps the cases in vv. 17–21 were considered slightly less serious, being condemned but not criminally prosecuted.

p: Lv 17:10. *q:* Dt 18:10; 2 Kgs 17:17; 21:6; 2 Chr 33:6. *r:* Lv 21:5. *s:* Lv 21:7, 14. *t:* Lv 19:3. *u:* Lv 20:6, 27; Dt 18:11; Is 8:19. *v:* Ex 22:20; 23:9; Jer 22:3; Mal 3:5. *w:* Dt 10:19. *x:* Dt 25:13–16; Prv 16:11; Am 8:5; Mi 6:10–11. *y:* Lv 18:21; Dt 12:31; 18:10; 2 Kgs 16:3; 17:17; 21:6; 23:10; Jer 32:35. *z:* Ez 23:39. *a:* Lv 7:20. *b:* Lv 15:31. *c:* Lv 19:31. *d:* Lv 11:44. *e:* Lv 19:3; Ex 21:17; Dt 21:18–21; Prv 20:20; Mt 15:4; Mk 7:10. *f:* Lv 18:20. *g:* Lv 18:8. *h:* Lv 18:15.

them. 13If a man lies with a male as with a woman,[i] they have committed an abomination; the two of them shall be put to death; their bloodguilt is upon them. 14If a man marries a woman and her mother also,[j] that is shameful conduct; the man and the two women as well shall be burned to death, so that shamefulness may not be found among you. 15If a man has sexual relations with an animal,[k] the man shall be put to death, and you shall kill the animal. 16If a woman goes up to any animal to mate with it,[l] you shall kill the woman and the animal; they shall both be put to death; their bloodguilt is upon them. 17If a man marries his sister,[m] his father's daughter or his mother's daughter, and they have intercourse with each other, that is disgraceful; they shall be publicly cut off* from the people; the man shall bear the penalty of having had intercourse with his own sister. 18If a man lies with a woman during her menstrual period and has intercourse with her, he has laid bare the source of her flow and she has uncovered it.[n] The two of them shall be cut off from the people. 19You shall not have intercourse with your mother's sister or your father's sister,[o] because that dishonors one's own flesh; they shall bear their penalty. 20If a man lies with his uncle's wife, he disgraces his uncle;[p] they shall bear the penalty; they shall die childless. 21If a man takes his brother's wife, it is severe defilement and he has disgraced his brother;[q] they shall be childless.

22Be careful to observe all my statutes and all my decrees; otherwise the land where I am bringing you to dwell will vomit you out.[r] 23Do not conform, therefore, to the customs of the nations[s] whom I am driving out of your way, because all these things that they have done have filled me with disgust for them. 24But to you I have said:[t] You shall take possession of their land. I am giving it to you to possess, a land flowing with milk and honey. I, the LORD, am your God, who have set you apart from other peoples. 25[u] You, too, must set apart, then, the clean animals from the unclean, and the clean birds from the unclean, so that you do not make yourselves detestable through any beast or bird or any creature which creeps on the ground that I have set apart for you as unclean. 26To me, therefore, you shall be holy; for I, the LORD, am holy,[v] and I have set you apart from other peoples to be my own.

27A man or a woman who acts as a medium or clairvoyant[w] shall be put to death. They shall be stoned to death; their bloodguilt is upon them.

CHAPTER 21

See RG 131–32

Sanctity of the Priesthood. 1* The LORD said to Moses: Speak to the priests, Aaron's sons, and tell them: None of you shall make himself unclean for any dead person among his kindred,[x] 2except for his nearest relatives, his mother or father, his son or daughter, his brother[y] 3or his unmarried sister, who is of his own family while she remains single; for these he may make himself unclean. 4But as a husband among his kindred* he shall not make himself unclean and thus profane himself.

5The priests shall not make bald the crown of their head, nor shave the edges of their beard, nor lacerate their body.[z] 6They shall be holy to their God, and shall not profane their God's name, since they offer the oblations of the LORD, the food of their God; so they must be holy.

7* A priest shall not marry a woman debased by prostitution, nor a woman who has

20:17 Cut off: see note on 7:20.

21:1–12 While off duty the regular priests are not to become corpse-contaminated except for the close relatives listed in vv. 2–3. While on duty they presumably could not become impure at all. The high priest is restricted from all corpse contamination, on or off duty (vv. 11–12). Lay Israelites are not restricted from corpse contamination, except when in contact with what is holy (cf. Dt 26:14). See note on Lv 11:39–40. Israelites who undertake a nazirite vow enter into a sanctified state and cannot contact corpses (Nm 6:6–12). Cf. Ez 44:25–27.

21:4 Husband among his kindred: this probably refers to relatives by marriage and may even include his wife.

21:7 The ideal seems to be that a priest marry a virgin. This is explicitly stated for the high priest (cf. vv. 13–14; so also

i: Lv 18:22. *j:* Lv 18:17. *k:* Lv 18:23. *l:* Lv 18:23. *m:* Lv 18:9. *n:* Lv 18:19. *o:* Lv 18:12–13. *p:* Lv 18:14. *q:* Lv 18:16. *r:* Lv 18:25, 28. *s:* Lv 18:30. *t:* Ex 3:8, 17. *u:* Lv 11:2–47; Dt 14:4–20. *v:* Lv 11:44. *w:* Lv 19:31; Ex 22:17; Dt 18:11. *x:* Ez 44:25–27. *y:* Lv 10:6–7. *z:* Lv 19:27–28; Ez 44:20.

been divorced by her husband; for the priest is holy to his God.[a] 8Honor him as holy for he offers the food[b] of your God; he shall be holy to you, because I, the LORD, am holy who make you holy.

9If a priest's daughter debases herself by prostitution, she thereby debases her father; she shall be burned with fire.[c]

10The most exalted of the priests, upon whose head the anointing oil has been poured and who has been ordained to wear the special vestments, shall not dishevel his hair or rend his garments, 11nor shall he go near any dead person.[d] Not even for his father or mother may he thus become unclean; 12nor shall he leave the sanctuary and profane the sanctuary of his God, for the consecration of the anointing oil of his God is upon him.[e] I am the LORD.

13He shall marry only a woman who is a virgin. 14He shall not marry a widow or a woman who has been divorced or one who has been debased by prostitution, but only a virgin, taken from his kindred, he shall marry,[f] 15so that he not profane his offspring among his kindred. I, the LORD, make him holy.

Priestly Blemishes.* 16The LORD said to Moses: 17Say to Aaron: None of your descendants, throughout their generations, who has any blemish shall come forward to offer the food of his God. 18Anyone who has any of the following blemishes may not come forward:[g] he who is blind, or lame, or who has a split lip, or a limb too long, 19or a broken leg or arm, 20or who is a hunchback or dwarf or has a growth in the eye, or who is afflicted with sores, scabs, or crushed testicles. 21No descendant of Aaron the priest who has any such blemish may draw near to offer the oblations of the LORD; on account of his blemish he may not draw near to offer the food of his God. 22He may, however, eat the food of his God: of the most sacred as well as sacred offerings.[h] 23Only, he may not enter through the veil nor draw near to the altar on account of his blemish; he shall not profane my sacred precincts, for it is I, the LORD, who make them holy.

24Moses, therefore, told this to Aaron and his sons and to all the Israelites.

CHAPTER 22

See RG 131–32

Priestly Purity.* 1The LORD said to Moses: 2Tell Aaron and his sons to treat with respect the sacred offerings which the Israelites consecrate to me; otherwise they will profane my holy name. I am the LORD.

3* Tell them: If any one of you, or of your descendants in any future generation, dares, while he is in a state of uncleanness, to draw near the sacred offerings which the Israelites consecrate to the LORD, such a one shall be cut off from my presence.[i] I am the LORD.

4No descendant of Aaron who is stricken with a scaly infection,[j] or who suffers from a genital discharge,[k] may eat of the sacred offerings, until he again becomes clean. Moreover, if anyone touches a person who has become unclean by contact with a corpse,[l] or if anyone has had an emission of semen,[m] 5or if anyone touches any swarming creature[n] whose uncleanness is contagious or any person whose uncleanness, of whatever kind it may be, is contagious—[o] 6the one who touches such as these shall be unclean until evening and may not eat of the sacred portions until he has first bathed his body in water.[p] 7Then, when the sun sets, he shall be clean.[q] Only then may he eat of the sacred offerings, for they are his food. 8* He shall not make himself unclean by eating of any animal that has died of itself or has been killed by wild beasts.[r] I am the LORD.

9They shall keep my charge so that they

Ez 44:22, except there priests may marry widows of priests). The high priest has the added limitation that his wife must come from his kindred, i.e., the priestly family (cf. Ez 44:22).

21:16–23 Though priests with certain bodily imperfections cannot serve at the altar (vv. 18–20), they are not impure, since they may still eat of the offerings, which are holy, and do so within the sanctuary precincts since it is there the most holy offerings are to be eaten (v. 22).

22:1–16 While priests with bodily imperfections may eat the holy sacrifices (21:16–23), those impure and those not of the priestly household may not.

22:3–8 On uncleanness, see chaps. 11–15 and notes there.

22:8 See note on 11:39–40.

a: Lv 19:29; Ez 44:22. *b:* Lv 1:9. *c:* Gn 38:24. *d:* Lv 10:4–7. *e:* Lv 10:7. *f:* Ez 44:22. *g:* Lv 22:19–25; Dt 23:2–9. *h:* Lv 2:3, 10; 6:29; 7:6, 34. *i:* Lv 7:20–21. *j:* Lv 13–14. *k:* Lv 15:2–18. *l:* Nm 19:14–22. *m:* Lv 15:16. *n:* Lv 11:29–31. *o:* Lv 15:2–12, 18–27. *p:* Lv 17:15; Nm 19:7–8, 19; Heb 10:22. *q:* Dt 23:12. *r:* Lv 11:39–40; Ez 44:31.

will not bear the punishment in this matter and die[s] for their profanation. I am the LORD who makes them holy.

[10]Neither an unauthorized person nor a priest's tenant or laborer may eat of any sacred offering.[t] [11]But a slave* whom a priest acquires by purchase or who is born in his house may eat of his food. [12]* A priest's daughter who is married to an unauthorized person may not eat of the sacred contributions. [13]But if a priest's daughter is widowed or divorced and, having no children, returns to her father's house, she may then eat of her father's food as in her youth. No unauthorized person, however, may eat of it. [14][u] If such a one eats of a sacred offering through inadvertence, that person shall make restitution to the priest for the sacred offering, with an increment of one fifth of the amount. [15]The priests shall not allow the sacred offerings which the Israelites contribute to the LORD to be profaned[v] [16]nor make them incur a penalty when they eat their sacred offerings. For I, the LORD, make them holy.

Unacceptable Victims. [17]* The LORD said to Moses: [18]Speak to Aaron and his sons and to all the Israelites, and tell them: When anyone of the house of Israel, or any alien residing in Israel, who presents an offering, brings a burnt offering[w] as a votive offering or as a voluntary offering to the LORD, [19]if it is to be acceptable for you, it must be an unblemished male of the herd, of the sheep or of the goats.[x] [20]You shall not offer one that has any blemish, for such a one would not be acceptable on your behalf.[y] [21]When anyone presents a communion sacrifice[z] to the LORD from the herd or the flock in fulfillment of a vow, or as a voluntary offering, if it is to find acceptance, it must be unblemished; it shall not have any blemish. [22]One that is blind or lame or maimed, or one that has running lesions or sores or scabs, you shall not offer to the LORD; do not put such an animal on the altar as an oblation to the LORD. [23]* An ox or a sheep that has a leg that is too long or is stunted you may indeed present as a voluntary offering, but it will not be acceptable as a votive offering. [24]One that has its testicles bruised or crushed or torn out or cut off you shall not offer to the LORD. You shall neither do this in your own land [25]nor receive from a foreigner any such animals to offer up as the food of your God; since they are deformed or blemished, they will not be acceptable on your behalf.

[26]* The LORD said to Moses: [27]When an ox or a lamb or a goat is born, it shall remain with its mother for seven days; only from the eighth day onward will it be acceptable, to be offered as an oblation to the LORD.[a] [28]You shall not slaughter an ox or a sheep on one and the same day with its young. [29]Whenever you offer a thanksgiving sacrifice to the LORD, so offer it that it may be acceptable on your behalf; [30]it must be eaten on the same day; none of it shall be left over until morning.[b] I am the LORD.

[31]Be careful to observe my commandments. I am the LORD. [32]Do not profane my holy name, that in the midst of the Israelites I may be hallowed. I, the LORD, make you holy, [33]who led you out of the land of Egypt to be your God. I am the LORD.

CHAPTER 23

See RG 131–32

Holy Days.* [1]The LORD said to Moses: [2]Speak to the Israelites and tell them:

22:11 Slave: in contrast to the tenant or hired worker of v. 10, the slave, who is by definition a foreigner, is part of the priest's household and therefore may eat of sacrifices.

22:12–13 A priest's daughter, when a dependent of her father, may eat of the lesser holy offerings.

22:17–25 This passage complements the section on the bodily imperfections of priests in 21:16–23. The laws taken together indicate that whoever and whatever approaches and contacts the altar needs to be physically unimpaired.

22:23 Burnt offerings and communion sacrifices brought as voluntary offerings may have slight defects, probably because they are freely given and do not depend upon a prior promise as do votive offerings.

22:26–30 Other activities and procedures that would impair sacrifice are appended here. The rules in vv. 27–28 are reminiscent of the rule not to boil a young goat in its mother's milk (Ex 23:19; 34:26; Dt 14:21) and not to take a bird and its eggs (Dt 22:6–7), all of which have a humanitarian tenor.

23:1–44 This is paralleled by another calendar from the Priestly tradition, in Nm 28–29. Non-Priestly resumes of festal and holy observances are found in Ex 23:10–17; 34:18–24 and Dt 16:1–17.

s: Lv 15:31. *t:* Mt 12:4. *u:* Lv 5:15–16. *v:* Lv 19:8; Nm 18:32. *w:* Lv 1:3. *x:* Lv 21:16–23. *y:* Dt 15:21; 17:1; Mal 1:7–14. *z:* Lv 3:1; 7:11. *a:* Ex 22:29; 23:19. *b:* Lv 7:15.

The following are the festivals[c] of the LORD, which you shall declare holy days. These are my festivals:

3 For six days work may be done; but the seventh day is a sabbath of complete rest,* a declared holy day; you shall do no work. It is the LORD's sabbath wherever you dwell.[d]

Passover. 4 These are the festivals of the LORD, holy days which you shall declare at their proper time.[e] 5 The Passover of the LORD* falls on the fourteenth day of the first month, at the evening twilight.[f] 6 The fifteenth day of this month is the LORD's feast of Unleavened Bread. For seven days you shall eat unleavened bread.[g] 7 On the first of these days you will have a declared holy day; you shall do no heavy work. 8 On each of the seven days you shall offer an oblation to the LORD. Then on the seventh day you will have a declared holy day; you shall do no heavy work.

9* The LORD said to Moses: 10 Speak to the Israelites and tell them: When you come into the land which I am giving you, and reap its harvest, you shall bring the first sheaf of your harvest to the priest, 11 who shall elevate[h] the sheaf before the LORD that it may be acceptable on your behalf.[i] On the day after the sabbath* the priest shall do this. 12 On this day, when your sheaf is elevated, you shall offer to the LORD for a burnt offering an unblemished yearling lamb. 13 Its grain offering shall be two tenths of an ephah of bran flour mixed with oil, as a sweet-smelling oblation to the LORD; and its libation shall be a fourth of a hin of wine. 14 You shall not eat any bread or roasted grain or fresh kernels until this day, when you bring the offering for your God. This shall be a perpetual statute throughout your generations wherever you dwell.

Pentecost. 15 Beginning with the day after the sabbath, the day on which you bring the sheaf for elevation, you shall count seven full weeks;[j] 16 you shall count to the day after the seventh week, fifty days.*[k] Then you shall present a new grain offering to the LORD. 17 For the elevated offering of your first-ripened fruits to the LORD, you shall bring with you from wherever you live two loaves of bread made of two tenths of an ephah of bran flour and baked with leaven. 18 Besides the bread, you shall offer to the LORD a burnt offering of seven unblemished yearling lambs, one bull of the herd, and two rams, along with their grain offering and libations, as a sweet-smelling oblation to the LORD. 19 One male goat shall be sacrificed as a purification offering, and two yearling lambs as a communion sacrifice. 20 The priest shall elevate them—that is, the two lambs—with the bread of the first-ripened fruits as an elevated offering before the LORD; these shall be sacred to the LORD and belong to the priest. 21 On this same day you shall make a proclamation: there shall be a declared holy day for you; no heavy work may be done. This shall be a perpetual statute through all your generations wherever you dwell.

22[l] When you reap the harvest of your land, you shall not be so thorough that you reap the field to its very edge, nor shall you

23:3 Sabbath of complete rest: the sabbath and the Day of Atonement are called "sabbaths of complete rest" (Ex 16:23; 31:15; 35:2; Lv 16:31; 23:32). Work of any sort is prohibited on these days (Lv 23:3, 28; Nm 29:7) as opposed to other holy days where only laborious work is prohibited but light work, such as preparing food, is allowed (Ex 12:16; cf. Lv 23:7, 8, 21, 25, 35, 36; Nm 28:18, 25, 26; 29:1, 12, 35).

23:5–6 The Passover of the LORD . . . feast of Unleavened Bread: the two occasions were probably separate originally. Combined they celebrate the exodus from Egypt. Cf. Ex 12:1–20, 43–49; Nm 28:16–25.

23:9–14 Around Passover a first fruits offering is to be brought (see 2:14), consisting of a sheaf of barley, the crop that matures at this time of year.

23:11 Day after the sabbath: the singular term *shabbat* "sabbath" may mean "week" here and refer to the seven-day period of the feast of Unleavened Bread. According to this interpretation, the barley sheaf is offered the day after the week of Unleavened Bread. Others understand it as referring to the first or last day of Unleavened Bread.

23:16–21 Fifty days: Pentecost. This festival occurs on a single day, fifty days after the feast of Unleavened Bread, elsewhere called the "feast of the Harvest" (Ex 23:16), "Day of First Fruits" (Nm 28:26), and "feast of Weeks" (Ex 34:22; Dt 16:10, 16). The name Pentecost comes from the later Greek term for the holy day (cf. Acts 2:1; 20:16; 1 Cor 16:8), referring to the fiftieth day. This is the occasion for bringing the first fruits of the wheat harvest.

c: Nm 28–29; Dt 16:1–17. *d:* Lv 19:3; 26:2; Ex 20:8–11; 23:12; 31:14–15; 34:21; Nm 28:9–10; Dt 5:12–15; Lk 13:14. *e:* Ex 23:14–19. *f:* Ex 12:1–51; Nm 9:1–8; 28:16–25; Dt 16:1–8. *g:* Ex 12:18; 13:3–10; 23:15; 34:18. *h:* Lv 7:30. *i:* Dt 26:2. *j:* Ex 23:16; 34:22; Nm 28:26–31; Dt 16:9–12. *k:* Acts 2:1. *l:* Lv 19:9–10.

gather the gleanings of your harvest. These things you shall leave for the poor and the alien. I, the LORD, am your God.

New Year's Day. [23]The LORD said to Moses: [24]Tell the Israelites: On the first day of the seventh month*[m] you will have a sabbath rest, with trumpet blasts as a reminder, a declared holy day; [25]you shall do no heavy work, and you shall offer an oblation to the LORD.

The Day of Atonement. [26]The LORD said to Moses: [27]Now the tenth day of this seventh month is the Day of Atonement.*[n] You will have a declared holy day. You shall humble yourselves and offer an oblation to the LORD. [28]On this day you shall not do any work, because it is the Day of Atonement, when atonement is made for you before the LORD, your God. [29]Those who do not humble themselves on this day shall be cut off from the people. [30]If anyone does any work on this day, I will remove that person from the midst of the people. [31]You shall do no work; this is a perpetual statute throughout your generations wherever you dwell; [32]it is a sabbath of complete rest for you. You shall humble yourselves. Beginning on the evening of the ninth of the month, you shall keep your sabbath from evening to evening.

The Feast of Booths. [33]The LORD said to Moses: [34]Tell the Israelites: The fifteenth day of this seventh month is the LORD's feast of Booths,*[o] which shall continue for seven days. [35]On the first day, a declared holy day, you shall do no heavy work. [36]For seven days you shall offer an oblation to the LORD, and on the eighth day you will have a declared holy day. You shall offer an oblation to the LORD. It is the festival closing. You shall do no heavy work.

[37]*These, therefore, are the festivals of the LORD which you shall declare holy days, in order to offer as an oblation to the LORD burnt offerings and grain offerings, sacrifices and libations, as prescribed for each day, [38]in addition to the LORD's sabbaths, your donations, your various votive offerings, and the voluntary offerings that you present to the LORD.

[39]On the fifteenth day, then, of the seventh month, when you have gathered in the produce of the land, you shall celebrate the feast of the LORD* for a whole week. The first and the eighth day shall be days of rest. [40]On the first day you shall gather fruit of majestic trees, branches of palms, and boughs* of leafy trees and valley willows. Then for a week you shall make merry before the LORD, your God. [41]You shall keep this feast of the LORD for one whole week in the year. By perpetual statute throughout your generations in the seventh month of the year, you shall keep it. [42]You shall dwell in booths for seven days; every native-born Israelite shall dwell in booths, [43]that your descendants may realize that, when I led the Israelites out of the land of Egypt, I made them dwell in booths. I, the LORD, am your God.

[44]Thus did Moses announce to the Israelites the festivals of the LORD.

CHAPTER 24

See RG 131–32

*The Sanctuary Light.** [1]The LORD said to Moses: [2]Order the Israelites to bring you clear oil of crushed olives for the light, so that you may keep the lamp burning regularly.[p]

23:24 First day of the seventh month: the seventh new moon is counted from a new year beginning in the spring (cf. v. 5). Like the seventh day in the week, it is preeminent among the new moon days (cf. Nm 28:11–15; 29:1–6).

23:27 Day of Atonement: see chap. 16 and notes there.

23:34 Feast of Booths: this is the final harvest festival of the year celebrating the remaining harvest. It is called the "feast of Ingathering" (Ex 23:16; 34:22), the "feast of Booths" (Lv 23:34; Dt 16:13), or simply the "feast" (1 Kgs 8:65). It is a seven-day festival with an eighth closing day. The first and eighth days are rest days (see note on v. 3).

23:37–38 This appears to be the original conclusion of the chapter.

23:39–43 The feast of the LORD: the feast of Booths, the preeminent festival. This section supplements vv. 33–36 by prescribing the popular activities for the festival.

23:40–43 Fruit . . . branches . . . boughs: the fruit and/or foliage from these trees is to be gathered, but it is not said how they are used. The command to make merry suggests they may have been used in a procession or even circumambulation of the altar (cf. Ps 26:6). Later tradition understood these prescriptions as referring to making the booths out of the foliage (Neh 8:15).

24:1–4 On the lamp, see Ex 25:31–40; 26:35; 27:20–21; 37:17–24; 40:24–25; Nm 8:1–4. It occupies the south side of the anterior room of the sanctuary tent and provides light for that room.

---

m: Nm 29:1–6. *n:* Lv 16:1–34; 25:9; Nm 29:7–11. *o:* Ex 23:16; 34:22; Dt 16:13–15; 31:10; 2 Mc 1:9, 18; Jn 7:2. *p:* Ex 25:31–40; 27:20–21.

3 In the tent of meeting, outside the veil that hangs in front of the covenant, Aaron shall set up the lamp to burn before the LORD regularly, from evening till morning, by a perpetual statute throughout your generations. 4 He shall set up the lamps on the pure gold menorah to burn regularly before the LORD.

The Showbread.* 5 You shall take bran flour and bake it into twelve cakes,[q] using two tenths of an ephah of flour for each cake. 6 These you shall place in two piles, six in each pile, on the pure gold table before the LORD. 7 With each pile put some pure frankincense, which shall serve as an oblation to the LORD, a token of the bread offering. 8 Regularly on each sabbath day the bread[r] shall be set out before the LORD on behalf of the Israelites by an everlasting covenant. 9 It shall belong to Aaron and his sons, who must eat it in a sacred place, since it is most sacred,[s] his as a perpetual due from the oblations to the LORD.

Punishment of Blasphemy.* 10 A man born of an Israelite mother and an Egyptian father went out among the Israelites, and in the camp a fight broke out between the son of the Israelite woman and an Israelite man. 11 The son of the Israelite woman uttered the LORD's name in a curse and blasphemed. So he was brought to Moses—now his mother's name was Shelomith, daughter of Dibri, of the tribe of Dan— 12 and he was kept in custody till a decision from the LORD should settle the case for them.[t] 13 The LORD then said to Moses: 14 Take the blasphemer outside the camp, and when all who heard him have laid their hands* on his head,[u] let the whole community stone him. 15 Tell the Israelites: Anyone who blasphemes God shall bear the penalty; 16 whoever utters the name of the LORD in a curse shall be put to death.[v] The whole community shall stone that person; alien and native-born alike must be put to death for uttering the LORD's name in a curse.

17* Whoever takes the life of any human being shall be put to death;[w] 18 whoever takes the life of an animal shall make restitution of another animal, life for a life.[x] 19* Anyone who inflicts a permanent injury on his or her neighbor shall receive the same in return: 20 fracture for fracture, eye for eye, tooth for tooth. The same injury that one gives another shall be inflicted in return.[y] 21 Whoever takes the life of an animal shall make restitution, but whoever takes a human life shall be put to death. 22 You shall have but one rule, for alien and native-born alike.[z] I, the LORD, am your God.

23 When Moses told this to the Israelites, they took the blasphemer outside the camp and stoned him;[a] they did just as the LORD commanded Moses.

CHAPTER 25

See RG 131–32

The Sabbatical Year. 1 The LORD said to Moses on Mount Sinai: 2* Speak to the Israelites and tell them: When you enter the land that I am giving you, let the land, too, keep a sabbath for the LORD. 3 For six years you may sow your field, and for six years

24:5–9 On the bread table, see Ex 25:23–29; 26:35; 37:10–16; 40:22–23. It occupies the north side of the anterior room of the sanctuary tent. The bread is a type of grain offering (see note on 2:1).

24:10–22 This is a narrative where an offense leads to clarifying revelation similar to the cases in Lv 10:1–7 and 16:1–34; Nm 9:6–14 and 15:32–36.

24:14 Laid their hands: see notes on 1:4 and 16:21. It may be that blasphemy generated a type of pollution which the hearers return to the culprit by this gesture.

24:17–22 A digression dealing with bodily injury follows the blasphemy rules. It may have been appended since the first case is another example of the death penalty. But the section develops according to its own logic. All legal traditions require death for homicide: Gn 9:5–6; Ex 21:12–14; Nm 35:9–34; Dt 19:1–13; cf. Ex 20:13 and Dt 5:17.

24:19–20 The phrase "life for a life" in v. 18 leads to introducing the law of talion in vv. 19–20. Some have interpreted the law here and the similar expressions in Ex 21:23–25 and Dt 19:21 to mean that monetary compensation equal to the injury is to be paid, though the wording of the law here and the context of Dt 19:21 indicate an injury is to be inflicted upon the injurer.

25:2–7 As every seventh day is to be a day of rest (cf. 23:3), so every seventh year is a year of rest (cf. 26:34–35, 43). The rest consists in not doing agricultural work. The people are to live off what grows naturally in the fields (vv. 6–7). Verses 19–22 add insurance by saying that God will make the sixth-year crop abundant such that its excess will stretch over the seventh sabbatical year as well as the eighth year when new crops are not yet harvested (cf. 26:10). Cf. Ex 23:10–11.

q: Ex 25:23–30; 1 Kgs 7:48; 2 Chr 13:11; Heb 9:2. *r:* 1 Chr 9:32. *s:* 1 Sm 21:5. *t:* Nm 15:34. *u:* Lv 16:21. *v:* Ex 22:27; 1 Kgs 21:10, 13; Mt 26:65–66; Jn 10:33. *w:* Gn 9:5–6; Ex 21:12–14; Nm 35:9–34; Dt 19:11–13. *x:* Ex 21:33–34; cf. Lv 17:4. *y:* Ex 21:23–25; Dt 19:21; Mt 5:38. *z:* Lv 19:34; Ex 12:49; Nm 15:16. *a:* Acts 7:57–58.

prune your vineyard, gathering in their produce.[b] 4But during the seventh year the land shall have a sabbath of complete rest, a sabbath for the LORD,[c] when you may neither sow your field nor prune your vineyard. 5The aftergrowth of your harvest you shall not reap, nor shall you pick the grapes of your untrimmed vines. It shall be a year of rest for the land. 6While the land has its sabbath, all its produce will be food to eat for you yourself and for your male and female slave, for your laborer and the tenant who live with you, 7and likewise for your livestock and for the wild animals on your land.

The Jubilee Year. 8* You shall count seven weeks of years—seven times seven years—such that the seven weeks of years amount to forty-nine years. 9Then, on the tenth day of the seventh month* let the ram's horn resound; on this, the Day of Atonement,[d] the ram's horn blast shall resound throughout your land. 10You shall treat this fiftieth year as sacred. You shall proclaim liberty in the land for all its inhabitants.[e] It shall be a jubilee for you, when each of you shall return to your own property, each of you to your own family. 11This fiftieth year is your year of jubilee; you shall not sow, nor shall you reap the aftergrowth or pick the untrimmed vines, 12since this is the jubilee. It shall be sacred for you. You may only eat what the field yields of itself.

13In this year of jubilee, then, each of you shall return to your own property. 14Therefore, when you sell any land to your neighbor or buy any from your neighbor, do not deal unfairly with one another. 15On the basis of the number of years since the last jubilee you shall purchase the land from your neighbor;[f] and so also, on the basis of the number of years of harvest, that person shall sell it to you. 16When the years are many, the price shall be so much the more; when the years are few, the price shall be so much the less. For it is really the number of harvests that the person sells you. 17Do not deal unfairly with one another, then; but stand in fear of your God. I, the LORD, am your God.

18Observe my statutes and be careful to keep my ordinances, so that you will dwell securely in the land. 19The land will yield its fruit and you will eat your fill, and live there securely.[g] 20And if you say, "What shall we eat in the seventh year, if we do not sow or reap our crop?"[h] 21I will command such a blessing for you in the sixth year that there will be crop enough for three years, 22and when you sow in the eighth year, you will still be eating from the old crop; even into the ninth year, until the crop comes in, you will still be eating from the old crop.[i]

Redemption of Property.* 23The land shall not be sold irrevocably; for the land is mine, and you are but resident aliens and under my authority. 24Therefore, in every part of the country that you occupy, you must permit the land to be redeemed. 25When one of your kindred is reduced to poverty and has to sell some property, that person's closest relative,* who has the duty to redeem it, shall come and redeem what the relative has sold.[j] 26If, however, the person has no relative to redeem it, but later on acquires sufficient means to redeem it, 27the person shall calculate the years since the sale, return the balance to the one to whom it was sold, and thus regain the property.[k] 28But if the person does not acquire sufficient means to buy back the land, what was sold shall remain in the possession of the purchaser until the year of the

25:8–17 The fiftieth year is the jubilee, determined by counting off "seven weeks of years." It is sacred, like the sabbath day. Specifically, in it indentured Israelites return to their own households and land that has been sold returns to its original owner. Different laws are found in Ex 21:1–6; Dt 15:1–3, 12–18 (cf. Jer 34:8–22).

25:9 Seventh month: the priestly laws reflect the use of two calendars, one starting in the spring (cf. chap. 23) and one in the fall. The jubilee is calculated on the basis of the latter. **Ram's horn**: Hebrew *shophar*. The name for the year, jubilee (Heb. *yobel*), also means "ram's horn" and comes from the horn blown to announce the occasion.

25:23–55 This is a series of laws dealing mainly with situations of poverty in which one has to sell land, obtain a loan, or become indentured. Many of the laws are connected with the release of debts in the jubilee year.

25:25 A close family member is responsible for redemption. Some of these are specified in v. 49.

b: Ex 23:10–11. *c:* Lv 26:34; 1 Mc 6:49, 53. *d:* Lv 16:29. *e:* Nm 36:4; Is 61:2; Jer 34:8–22; Ez 46:17; Lk 4:19. *f:* Lv 27:18, 23. *g:* Lv 26:5–6. *h:* Mt 6:25, 31–34; Lk 12:22, 29. *i:* Lv 26:10. *j:* Ru 2:20; 4:4, 6; Jer 32:7–8. *k:* Lv 27:18, 23.

jubilee, when it must be released and returned to the original owner.[l]

29* When someone sells a dwelling in a walled town, it can be redeemed up to a full year after its sale—the redemption period is one year. 30 But if such a house in a walled town has not been redeemed at the end of a full year, it shall belong irrevocably to the purchaser throughout the generations; it shall not be released in the jubilee. 31 However, houses in villages that are not encircled by walls shall be reckoned as part of the surrounding farm land; they may be redeemed, and in the jubilee they must be released.

32* In levitical cities[m] the Levites shall always have the right to redeem the houses in the cities that are in their possession. 33 As for levitical property that goes unredeemed—houses sold in cities of their possession shall be released in the jubilee; for the houses in levitical cities are their possession in the midst of the Israelites. 34 Moreover, the pasture land[n] belonging to their cities shall not be sold at all; it must always remain their possession.

35 When one of your kindred is reduced to poverty and becomes indebted to you, you shall support that person like a resident alien; let your kindred live with you. 36 Do not exact interest in advance or accrued interest,* but out of fear of God let your kindred live with you. 37[o] Do not give your money at interest or your food at a profit. 38 I, the LORD, am your God, who brought you out of the land of Egypt to give you the land of Canaan and to be your God.

39* When your kindred with you, having been so reduced to poverty, sell themselves to you, do not make them work as slaves.[p] 40 Rather, let them be like laborers or like your tenants, working with you until the jubilee year, 41 when, together with any children, they shall be released from your service and return to their family and to their ancestral property. 42 Since they are my servants, whom I brought out of the land of Egypt, they shall not sell themselves as slaves are sold. 43 Do not lord it over them harshly, but stand in fear of your God.

44* The male and female slaves that you possess—these you shall acquire from the nations round about you.[q] 45 You may also acquire them from among the resident aliens who reside with you, and from their families who are with you, those whom they bore in your land. These you may possess, 46 and bequeath to your children as their hereditary possession forever. You may treat them as slaves. But none of you shall lord it harshly over any of your fellow Israelites.[r]

47 When your kindred, having been so reduced to poverty, sell themselves to a resident alien who has become wealthy or to descendants of a resident alien's family, 48 even after having sold themselves, they still may be redeemed by one of their kindred, 49 by an uncle or cousin, or by some other relative from their family; or, having acquired the means, they may pay the redemption price themselves. 50 With the purchaser they shall compute the years from the sale to the jubilee, distributing the sale price over these years as though they had been hired as laborers. 51 The more years there are, the more of the sale price they shall pay back as the redemption price; 52 the fewer years there are before the jubilee year, the more they have as credit; in proportion to the years of ser-

25:29–31 Not being able to redeem a house in a walled city after one year is probably due to the demographic and economic situation of large towns as opposed to small villages and open agricultural areas. The agricultural lands associated with the latter were the foundation for the economic viability of the Israelite family, and as such, God—who is the ultimate owner of the land (25:23)—has assigned them to the Israelites as permanent holdings.

25:32–34 An exception to the rule in vv. 29–31 is made for levitical cities (Nm 35:1–8), since the Levites have no broad land holdings. Their houses can be redeemed and are to be released in the jubilee year.

25:36 Interest in advance or accrued interest: two types of interest are mentioned here. The former may refer to interest subtracted from the loaned amount in advance, and the latter, to interest or a payment in addition to the loaned amount.

25:39–43 Here the individual Israelite has no assets and must become indentured to another Israelite for economic survival. No provision is given for redemption before the jubilee year, though such is probably allowed.

25:44–46 While Israelites may not be held as permanent slaves (vv. 39–43, 47–55), foreigners may be. They are not released in the jubilee, but may be bequeathed to one's children. They may be treated as "slaves," i.e., harshly (cf. Ex 21:20–21).

l: Lv 27:24. *m:* Nm 35:1–8. *n:* Nm 35:3. *o:* Ex 22:24; Dt 23:20. *p:* Ex 21:2–11; Dt 15:12–18; 1 Kgs 9:22; Jer 34:8–22. *q:* Dt 21:10–14. *r:* Is 14:1–2.

vice they shall pay the redemption price.
53 The tenant alien shall treat those who sold
themselves as laborers hired on an annual
basis, and the alien shall not lord it over
them harshly before your very eyes. 54 And if
they are not redeemed by these means, they
shall nevertheless be released, together with
any children, in the jubilee year. 55 For the Israelites belong to me as servants; they are
my servants, whom I brought out of the land
of Egypt, I, the LORD, your God.

CHAPTER 26

See RG 132–33

The Reward of Obedience. 1* Do not
make idols for yourselves. You shall not
erect a carved image or a sacred stone for
yourselves, nor shall you set up a carved
stone for worship in your land;[s] for I, the
LORD, am your God. 2 Keep my sabbaths,[t]
and reverence my sanctuary. I am the LORD.
3* [u] If you live in accordance with my statutes and are careful to observe my commandments, 4 I will give you your rains in
due season, so that the land will yield its
crops, and the trees their fruit;[v] 5 your threshing will last till vintage time, and your vintage till the time for sowing, and you will eat
your fill of food, and live securely in your
land.[w] 6 I will establish peace in the land, and
you will lie down to rest with no one to cause
you anxiety. I will rid the country of ravenous beasts, and no sword shall sweep across
your land. 7 You will rout your enemies, and
they shall fall before your sword. 8 Five of
you will put a hundred of your foes to flight,
and a hundred of you will put to flight ten
thousand, till your enemies fall before your
sword.[x] 9 I will look with favor upon you,
and make you fruitful and numerous,[y] as I
carry out my covenant with you. 10 You shall
eat the oldest stored harvest, and have to discard it to make room for the new.[z] 11 [a] I will
set my tabernacle in your midst, and will not
loathe you. 12 Ever present in your midst, I
will be your God, and you will be my people; 13 I, the LORD, am your God, who
brought you out of the land of Egypt to be
their slaves no more, breaking the bars of
your yoke and making you walk erect.[b]

*The Punishment of Disobedience.** 14 [c] But
if you do not heed me and do not keep all
these commandments, 15 if you reject my
statutes and loathe my decrees, refusing to
obey all my commandments and breaking
my covenant, 16 then I, in turn, will do this to
you: I will bring terror upon you—with consumption and fever to dim the eyes and sap
the life. You will sow your seed in vain, for
your enemies will consume the crop. 17 I will
turn against you, and you will be beaten
down before your enemies[d] and your foes
will lord it over you. You will flee though no
one pursues you.

18 If even after this you do not obey me, I
will increase the chastisement for your sins
sevenfold,[e] 19 to break your proud strength. I
will make the sky above you as hard as iron,
and your soil as hard as bronze, 20 so that
your strength will be spent in vain; your land
will bear no crops, and its trees no fruit.

21 If then you continue hostile, unwilling
to obey me, I will multiply my blows sevenfold, as your sins deserve. 22 I will unleash
wild beasts against you, to rob you of your
children and wipe out your livestock, till
your population dwindles away and your
roads become deserted.

23 If, with all this, you still do not accept
my discipline and continue hostile to me,
24 [f] I, too, will continue to be hostile to you

26:1–46 This chapter concludes the revelation of laws at Mount Sinai (cf. v. 46). Blessings and curses are also found at the end of Deuteronomy's law collection (Dt 28). Similar lists of blessings and curses appear in the conclusions of ancient Near Eastern treaties.

26:3–13 The blessings are concerned with the well-being of the nation and its land and involve agricultural bounty, national security, military success and population growth.

26:14–46 To encourage obedience, the list of punishments is longer than the blessings (cf. a similar proportion in Dt 28). The punishments are presented in waves (vv. 14–17, 18–20, 21–22, 23–26, 27–39), one group following another if the people do not return to obedience. Punishments involve sickness, pestilence, agricultural failure and famine, attack of wild animals, death of the people's children, destruction of illicit and even licit cults, military defeat, panic, and exile.

s: Lv 19:4; Nm 33:52. *t:* Lv 23:3. *u:* Dt 28:1–69. *v:* Dt 11:14; Ps 85:13; Ez 34:26–27. *w:* Lv 25:18–19; Dt 12:10. *x:* Dt 32:30; Jos 23:10. *y:* Gn 1:28; Ex 1:7. *z:* Lv 25:22. *a:* Ex 29:45; Ez 37:26–28; 2 Cor 6:16. *b:* Ez 34:27; Na 1:13. *c:* Dt 28:15–69. *d:* 2 Kgs 8:33–34. *e:* Ps 79:12; Prv 6:31. *f:* Jer 2:30; Ez 5:17; 14:17.

and I, for my part, will smite you for your sins sevenfold. 25 I will bring against you the sword, the avenger of my covenant. Though you then huddle together in your cities, I will send pestilence among you, till you are delivered to the enemy. 26 When I break your staff of bread, ten women will need but one oven for baking your bread, and they shall dole it out to you by weight;[g] and though you eat, you shall not be satisfied.

27 If, despite all this, you disobey and continue hostile to me, 28 I will continue in my hostile rage toward you, and I myself will discipline you for your sins sevenfold, 29 till you begin to eat the flesh of your own sons and daughters.[h] 30 I will demolish your high places, overthrow your incense stands, and cast your corpses upon the corpses of your idols.[i] In my loathing of you, 31 I will lay waste your cities and desolate your sanctuaries, refusing your sweet-smelling offerings. 32 So devastated will I leave the land that your enemies who come to live there will stand aghast at the sight of it.[j] 33 And you I will scatter among the nations[k] at the point of my drawn sword, leaving your countryside desolate and your cities deserted. 34 Then shall the land, during the time it lies waste, make up its lost sabbaths, while you are in the land of your enemies; then shall the land have rest and make up for its sabbaths[l] 35 during all the time that it lies desolate, enjoying the rest that you would not let it have on your sabbaths when you lived there.

36 Those of you who survive in the lands of their enemies, I will make so fainthearted that the sound of a driven leaf will pursue them, and they shall run as if from the sword, and fall though no one pursues them; 37 stumbling over one another as if to escape a sword, while no one is after them—so helpless will you be to take a stand against your foes! 38 You shall perish among the nations, swallowed up in your enemies' country. 39 Those of you who survive will waste away in the lands of their enemies, for their own and their ancestors' guilt.[m]

40* They will confess[n] their iniquity and the iniquity of their ancestors in their treachery against me and in their continued hostility toward me, 41 so that I, too, had to be hostile to them and bring them into their enemies' land. Then, when their uncircumcised hearts are humbled and they make amends for their iniquity, 42 I will remember my covenant with Jacob, and also my covenant with Isaac; and also my covenant with Abraham I will remember.[o] The land, too, I will remember. 43 The land will be forsaken by them, that in its desolation without them, it may make up its sabbaths, and that they, too, may make good the debt of their guilt for having spurned my decrees and loathed my statutes. 44 Yet even so, even while they are in their enemies' land, I will not reject or loathe them to the point of wiping them out, thus making void my covenant with them; for I, the LORD, am their God. 45 I will remember for them the covenant I made with their forebears, whom I brought out of the land of Egypt before the eyes of the nations,[p] that I might be their God. I am the LORD.

46 These are the statutes, decrees and laws which the LORD established between himself and the Israelites through Moses on Mount Sinai.[q]

V. Redemption of Offerings

CHAPTER 27

Votive Offerings and Dedications. See RG 133

1 The LORD said to Moses: 2* Speak to the Is-

26:40–45 Even though the people may be severely punished, God will remember the covenant when the people repent.

27:2–13 Vows are conditional promissory oaths. One covenants to do something for the benefit of God, usually to make a dedication, if God fulfills the individual's accompanying request (cf. Gn 28:20–21; Jgs 11:30–31; 1 Sm 1:11; 2 Sm 15:7–8; Ps 56:13–14). Vows must be fulfilled (Nm 30:3; Dt 23:22; cf. Ps 66:13–15). Verses 2–8 deal with votive offerings involving human beings. Actual dedication of human beings (cf. Jgs 11:30–31, 34–40; 1 Sm 1:11, 24–28) is obviated by payment of the person's value (mentioned in the temple income in 2 Kgs 12:5). The values reflect the different economic and administrative roles of people in different age and gender groups within ancient Israelite society. Verses 9–13 concern the bringing of animals for a vow.

g: Is 9:19; Ez 4:16; 5:16; 14:13; Mi 6:14. *h:* Lam 2:20. *i:* 2 Chr 14:5; 34:3–4, 7; Ez 6:3–6. *j:* 1 Kgs 9:8; Jer 9:11; 18:16; 19:8; 25:18. *k:* Ps 44:12; Jer 15:7; Ez 6:8. *l:* Lv 25:2; 2 Chr 36:21. *m:* Ez 4:17; 24:23; 33:10. *n:* Lv 16:21; Nm 5:7; Neh 1:6. *o:* Ex 6:5; 2 Kgs 13:23; Ps 106:45; Ez 16:60. *p:* Ex 12:51. *q:* Lv 7:38; Nm 36:13.

raelites and tell them: When anyone makes a vow to the LORD[r] with respect to the value of a human being, 3 the value for males between the ages of twenty and sixty shall be fifty silver shekels, by the sanctuary shekel; 4 and for a female, the value shall be thirty shekels. 5 For persons between the ages of five and twenty, the value for a male shall be twenty shekels, and for a female, ten shekels. 6 For persons between the ages of one month and five years, the value for a male shall be five silver shekels, and for a female, three shekels. 7 For persons of sixty or more, for a male the value shall be fifteen shekels, and ten shekels for a female. 8 However, if the one who made the vow is too poor to meet the sum,[s] the person must be set before the priest, who shall determine a value; the priest will do this in keeping with the means of the one who made the vow.

9 If the offering vowed to the LORD is an animal that may be sacrificed, every such animal given to the LORD becomes sacred.[t] 10 The offerer shall not substitute or exchange another for it, either a worse or a better one. If the offerer exchanges one animal in place of another, both the original and its substitute shall become sacred. 11 If any unclean animal which is unfit for sacrifice[u] to the LORD is vowed, it must be set before the priest, 12 who shall determine its value* in keeping with its good or bad qualities, and the value set by the priest shall stand. 13 If the offerer wishes to redeem the animal, the person shall pay one fifth more than this valuation.[v]

14* When someone dedicates a house as sacred to the LORD,* the priest shall determine its value in keeping with its good or bad qualities, and the value set by the priest shall stand. 15 A person dedicating a house who then wishes to redeem it shall pay one fifth more than the price thus established, and then it will again belong to that individual.[w]

16 If someone dedicates to the LORD a portion of hereditary land, its valuation shall be made according to the amount of seed required to sow it, the acreage sown with a homer* of barley seed being valued at fifty silver shekels. 17 If the dedication of a field is made at the beginning of a jubilee period, the full valuation shall hold; 18 but if it is some time after this, the priest shall estimate its money value according to the number of years left until the next jubilee year, with a corresponding reduction on the valuation.[x] 19 A person dedicating a field who then wishes to redeem* [y] it shall pay one fifth more than the price thus established, and so reclaim it. 20 If, instead of redeeming such a field, one sells it* to another, it may no longer be redeemed; 21 but at the jubilee it shall be released[z] as sacred* to the LORD; like a field that is put under the ban, it shall become priestly property.

22 If someone dedicates to the LORD a field that was purchased and was not part of hereditary property, 23 the priest shall compute its value in proportion to the number of years until the next jubilee, and on the same day the person shall pay the price thus established, a sacred donation to the LORD; 24 at the jubilee the field shall revert to the hered-

27:12 Determine its value: in contrast to human beings (vv. 3–7) there are no set values for unclean animals, and the condition of the animal is taken into consideration (cf. vv. 14, 27).

27:14–24 These verses deal with dedications. They take effect when uttered and, unlike vows, they are not conditional. They are related to the jubilee year laws in 25:23–31.

27:14 House as sacred to the LORD: the house becomes sanctuary property and presumably may be sold to another if the owner does not redeem it (cf. notes on vv. 20 and 21). While 25:31 requires that unredeemed houses in unwalled towns be returned to the original owners at the jubilee, in the laws here such houses apparently become the property of the sanctuary (cf. v. 21). It is likely that dedicated houses in a walled city needed to be redeemed within one year, following 25:29–30.

27:16 Homer: see note on Is 5:10.

27:19 Redeem: the person apparently can redeem the land up to the jubilee year, following 25:23–28. See note on v. 21.

27:20 If . . . one sells it: the verse is difficult since the person should not be able to sell the land after it is dedicated. The verb "sells" may be construed impersonally here: "If . . . it is sold," i.e., by the sanctuary.

27:21 Released as sacred: the dedication changes the ownership of the land. It now belongs to the sanctuary. It returns to the sanctuary's possession after leasing it out (v. 20). Presumably if the land remained in the sanctuary's possession until the jubilee, and it was not redeemed, the land would belong permanently to the sanctuary and priests.

r: Dt 23:22–24; Jgs 11:30–31; Eccl 5:3–4. *s:* Lv 5:7, 11. *t:* Lv 27:11, 27. *u:* Lv 11:2–8; Ex 13:13; 34:20. *v:* Lv 5:16, 24. *w:* Lv 22:14. *x:* Lv 25:15–16, 26–27, 50–52. *y:* Lv 25:25. *z:* Lv 25:28, 31.

itary owner of this land from whom it had been purchased.*

[25]Every valuation shall be made according to the standard of the sanctuary shekel. There are twenty gerahs to the shekel.

Irredeemable Offerings. [26*] Note that a firstborn animal,[a] which as such already belongs to the LORD, may not be dedicated. Whether an ox or a sheep, it is the LORD's. [27]But if it is an unclean animal,* it may be redeemed by paying one fifth more than its value. If it is not redeemed, it shall be sold at its value.

[28]Note, also, that any possession which someone puts under the ban* for the LORD, whether it is a human being, an animal, or a hereditary field, shall be neither sold nor redeemed; everything that is put under the ban becomes most holy to the LORD.[b] [29]All human beings that are put under the ban cannot be redeemed; they must be put to death.[c]

[30*] All tithes of the land, whether in grain from the fields or in fruit from the trees, belong to the LORD; they are sacred to the LORD.[d] [31]If someone wishes to redeem any of the tithes, the person shall pay one fifth more than their value. [32]The tithes of the herd and the flock, every tenth animal that passes under the herdsman's rod, shall be sacred to the LORD. [33]It shall not matter whether good ones or bad ones are thus chosen, and no exchange may be made. If any exchange is made, both the original animal and its substitute become sacred and cannot be redeemed.

[34]These are the commandments which the LORD gave Moses on Mount Sinai for the Israelites.[e]

27:24 In contrast to the cases in vv. 14–15 and 16–21, this land returns to the original owner since that individual did not personally make the dedication. The principle is that one cannot permanently dedicate what one does not own. Cf. 2 Sm 24:22–25.

27:26 Firstborn animals and human beings already belong to God (cf. Ex 13:1–2, 12; 34:19); they cannot be vowed or dedicated. Cf. Nm 18:15–18; Dt 15:19–23.

27:27 An unclean animal: such as the firstborn of a donkey, which was unfit for sacrifice. According to Ex 13:13; 34:20, a firstborn donkey was to be redeemed by offering a sheep in its stead, or was to have its neck broken.

27:28 Puts under the ban: this is a higher form of dedication to God than that found in vv. 14–24. Anything so dedicated is beyond redemption and cannot be sold by the sanctuary and priests (contrast vv. 15, 19, 20). This type of dedication is found mostly in contexts of war (e.g., Jos 6:17–21; 8:26; 10:1, 28). Lv 27:28 shows that the ban can apply to one's own property.

27:30–33 On the regulation concerning the tithes see Dt 14:22–29.

a: Ex 13:2. *b:* Nm 18:14; Dt 7:26; Jos 7:1; 1 Sm 15:21; Ez 44:29. *c:* 1 Kgs 20:42. *d:* Nm 18:25–32; Dt 14:22–24; Mal 3:8, 10. *e:* Lv 7:38.

See RG 133–41

The Book of Numbers

The Book of Numbers derives its name from the account of the two censuses taken of the Hebrew people, one near the beginning and the other toward the end of the journey in the wilderness (chaps. 1 and 26). It continues the story of that journey begun in Exodus, and describes briefly the experiences of the Israelites for a period of thirty-eight years, from the end of their encampment at Sinai to their arrival at the border of the promised land. Numerous legal ordinances are interspersed in the account, making the book a combination of law and history.

The book divides neatly into two parts. Each part begins with a census of the people (chaps. 1 and 26) and inaugurates a period of preparation prior to entering the promised land. In the first case these preparations come to a tragic end when scouts are sent forth to survey the promised land (chaps. 13–14). Upon their return, the people are so disheartened by the description of the native inhabitants and the seemingly impossible task that lies in front of them that they refuse to enter the land. This results in a decision to doom that entire generation to death and to allow another generation the chance to enter. After the death of the first generation, then, a second census is taken (chap. 26) and again preparations are made to enter the land. In this case, however, the birth of a new generation suggests these preparations will not be in vain. The book ends with the Israelites across the Jordan outside the land of Canaan, underscoring a chief theme of the Pentateuch as a whole: the people anticipating the fulfillment of God's promise of the land.

In the New Testament numerous allusions to incidents in the Book of Numbers appear: the bronze serpent (Jn 3:14–15), the sedition of Korah and its consequences (1 Cor 10:10), the prophecies of Balaam (2 Pt 2:15–16), and the water gushing from the rock (1 Cor 10:4).

The chief divisions of the Book of Numbers are as follows:

I. Census and Preparation for the Departure from Sinai (1:1–10:10)
II. Departure, Rebellion, and Wandering in the Wilderness for Forty Years (10:11–25:18)
III. Second Census of a New Generation and Preparation to Enter the Promised Land (25:19–36:13)

I. Census and Preparation for the Departure from Sinai

CHAPTER 1

See RG 134–35
The Census. [1]In the second year after
the Israelites' departure from the land of
Egypt, on the first day of the second month,
the LORD said to Moses at the tent of meeting in the wilderness of Sinai: [2]* Take a census of the whole community of the Israelites,[a] by clans and ancestral houses,
registering by name each male individually.
[3]You and Aaron shall enroll in companies all
the men in Israel of twenty years or more
who are fit for military service.
Moses' Assistants. [4]With you there shall
be a man from each tribe, each the head of
his ancestral house. [5][b] These are the names
of those who are to assist you:

from Reuben: Elizur, son of Shedeur;
[6] from Simeon: Shelumiel, son of Zurishaddai;
[7] from Judah:[c] Nahshon, son of Amminadab;
[8] from Issachar: Nethanel, son of Zuar;
[9] from Zebulun: Eliab, son of Helon;
[10] for the descendants of Joseph: from Ephraim: Elishama, son of Ammihud; and from Manasseh: Gamaliel, son of Pedahzur;
[11] from Benjamin: Abidan, son of Gideoni;
[12] from Dan: Ahiezer, son of Ammishaddai;
[13] from Asher: Pagiel, son of Ochran;
[14] from Gad: Eliasaph, son of Reuel;
[15] from Naphtali: Ahira, son of Enan.

[16][d] These were the elect of the community, leaders of their ancestral tribes, heads
of the clans of Israel. [17]So Moses and Aaron
took these men who had been designated by
name, [18]and assembled the whole community on the first day of the second month.
Every man of twenty years or more then registered individually his name and lineage according to clan and ancestral house, [19]as the
LORD had commanded Moses. So he enrolled them in the wilderness of Sinai.
Count of the Twelve Tribes. [20]Of the descendants of Reuben, the firstborn of Israel,
registered individually by name and lineage
according to their clans and ancestral
houses, every male of twenty years or more,
everyone fit for military service: [21]those enrolled from the tribe of Reuben were forty-
six thousand five hundred.
[22]Of the descendants of Simeon, registered individually by name and lineage according to their clans and ancestral houses,
every male of twenty years or more, everyone fit for military service: [23]those enrolled
from the tribe of Simeon were fifty-nine
thousand three hundred.
[24]Of the descendants of Gad, registered by
name and lineage according to their clans and
ancestral houses, every male of twenty years
or more, everyone fit for military service:
[25]those enrolled from the tribe of Gad were
forty-five thousand six hundred and fifty.
[26]Of the descendants of Judah, registered
by name and lineage according to their clans
and ancestral houses, every male of twenty
years or more, everyone fit for military service: [27]those enrolled from the tribe of Judah
were seventy-four thousand six hundred.

1:2 All Israel was divided into tribes, each tribe into clans, and each clan into ancestral houses.

a: Nm 14:29; 26:2–51. *b:* Nm 10:14–28. *c:* Mt 1:4; Lk 3:32–33. *d:* Ex 18:21, 25.

[28]Of the descendants of Issachar, registered by name and lineage according to their clans and ancestral houses, every male of twenty years or more, everyone fit for military service: [29]those enrolled from the tribe of Issachar were fifty-four thousand four hundred.

[30]Of the descendants of Zebulun, registered by name and lineage according to their clans and ancestral houses, every male of twenty years or more, everyone fit for military service: [31]those enrolled from the tribe of Zebulun were fifty-seven thousand four hundred.

[32]Of the descendants of Joseph:

Of the descendants of Ephraim, registered by name and lineage according to their clans and ancestral houses, every male of twenty years or more, everyone fit for military service: [33]those enrolled from the tribe of Ephraim were forty thousand five hundred.

[34]Of the descendants of Manasseh, registered by name and lineage according to their clans and ancestral houses, every male of twenty years or more, everyone fit for military service: [35]those enrolled from the tribe of Manasseh were thirty-two thousand two hundred.

[36]Of the descendants of Benjamin, registered by name and lineage according to their clans and ancestral houses, every male of twenty years or more, everyone fit for military service: [37]those enrolled from the tribe of Benjamin were thirty-five thousand four hundred.

[38]Of the descendants of Dan, registered by name and lineage according to their clans and ancestral houses, every male of twenty years or more, everyone fit for military service: [39]those enrolled from the tribe of Dan were sixty-two thousand seven hundred.

[40]Of the descendants of Asher, registered by name and lineage according to their clans and ancestral houses, every male of twenty years or more, everyone fit for military service: [41]those enrolled from the tribe of Asher were forty-one thousand five hundred.

[42]Of the descendants of Naphtali, registered by name and lineage according to their clans and ancestral houses, every male of twenty years or more, everyone fit for military service: [43]those enrolled from the tribe of Naphtali were fifty-three thousand four hundred.

[44]It was these who were enrolled, each according to his ancestral house, by Moses and Aaron and the twelve leaders of Israel. [45]The total enrollment of the Israelites of twenty years or more, according to their ancestral houses, everyone fit for military service in Israel— [46]the total enrollment was six hundred and three thousand, five hundred and fifty.

Levites Omitted in the Census. [47]Now the Levites were not enrolled[e] by their ancestral tribe with the others.* [48]For the LORD had told Moses, [49]The tribe of Levi alone you shall not enroll nor include in the census along with the other Israelites. [50]You are to give the Levites charge of the tabernacle of the covenant with all its equipment and all that belongs to it. It is they who shall carry the tabernacle with all its equipment and who shall be its ministers;[f] and they shall camp all around the tabernacle. [51]When the tabernacle is to move on, the Levites shall take it down; when the tabernacle is to be pitched, it is the Levites who shall set it up. Any unauthorized person who comes near* it shall be put to death.[g] [52]The other Israelites shall camp according to their companies, each in their own divisional camps,[h] [53]but the Levites shall camp around the tabernacle of the covenant to ensure that God's wrath will not fall upon the Israelite community. The Levites shall keep guard over the tabernacle of the covenant.[i] [54]The Israelites complied; they did just as the LORD had commanded Moses.

CHAPTER 2

See RG 134–35

Arrangement of the Tribes. [1]The LORD said to Moses and Aaron: [2]The Israelites shall camp, each in their own divisions, under the ensigns of their ancestral houses.[j]

1:47 The Levites were not enrolled in this census, which was principally for military purposes, but a separate census was made of them. Cf. 3:15–16, 39.

1:51 Comes near: here and in 3:10, 38; 17:5; 18:4, 7 the Hebrew word rendered "comes near" is very nearly a technical term for someone who intrudes upon or violates a space set apart as holy and for which they have not been qualified by priesthood.

e: Nm 2:33; 3:14–39; 26:57–62. *f:* Nm 3:7–8; 4:2–49; 1 Chr 6:33. *g:* Nm 3:10, 38; 18:7; 2 Sm 6:6–7; 1 Chr 13:10. *h:* Nm 2:2, 34. *i:* Nm 3:7–8, 38; 8:19; 18:4–5. *j:* Nm 1:52.

Tribal Lists in Genesis, Numbers, and Deuteronomy

THE LISTS OF the names of the tribes that made up the people of Israel are not always identical. This indicates that there were slight variations in the traditions that stand behind these lists. The list in Numbers 34 omits the tribes of Reuben and Gad, who did not cross the Jordan. The lists in Numbers also do not include the names of Joseph or Levi, but instead substitute the names of Joseph's sons, Ephraim and Manasseh. (For purposes of comparison, the order of the names is the same in each of these lists, but the numbers beneath each name show its position in the list given in the biblical text.)

Genesis 49:1–22	Numbers 1:5–15	Numbers 1:20–43	Numbers 2:3–29 7:12–83	Numbers 13:4–15	Numbers 26:5–50	Numbers 34:19–28	Deuteronomy 33:1–29
Reuben 1	Reuben 1	Reuben 1	Reuben 4	Reuben 1	Reuben 1	—	Reuben 1
Simeon 2	Simeon 2	Simeon 2	Simeon 5	Simeon 2	Simeon 2	Simeon 2	Levi 3
Judah 4	Judah 3	Judah 4	Judah 1	Judah 3	Judah 4	Judah 1	Judah 2
Issachar 6	Issachar 4	Issachar 5	Issachar 2	Issachar 4	Issachar 5	Issachar 8	Issachar 8
Zebulun 5	Zebulun 5	Zebulun 6	Zebulun 3	Zebulun 7	Zebulun 6	Zebulun 7	Zebulun 7
Joseph 11	Ephraim 6	Ephraim 7	Ephraim 7	Ephraim 5	Ephraim 8	Ephraim 6	Ephraim 5
Levi 3	Manasseh 7	Manasseh 8	Manasseh 8	Manasseh 8	Manasseh 7	Manasseh 5	Manasseh 6
Benjamin 12	Benjamin 8	Benjamin 9	Benjamin 9	Benjamin 6	Benjamin 9	Benjamin 3	Benjamin 4
Dan 7	Dan 9	Dan 10	Dan 10	Dan 9	Dan 10	Dan 4	Dan 10
Asher 9	Asher 10	Asher 11	Asher 11	Asher 10	Asher 11	Asher 9	Asher 12
Gad 8	Gad 11	Gad 3	Gad 6	Gad 12	Gad 3	—	Gad 9
Naphtali 10	Naphtali 12	Naphtali 12	Naphtali 12	Naphtali 11	Naphtali 12	Naphtali 10	Naphtali 11

They shall camp at some distance all around
the tent of meeting.
[3]* Encamped on the east side, toward the
sunrise, shall be the divisional camp of Judah, arranged in companies. The leader of
the Judahites is Nahshon, son of Amminadab, [4]and the enrollment of his company is
seventy-four thousand six hundred. [5]En-
camped beside it is the tribe of Issachar. The
leader of the Issacharites is Nethanel, son of
Zuar, [6]and the enrollment of his company is
fifty-four thousand four hundred. [7]Also the
tribe of Zebulun. The leader of the Zebulunites is Eliab, son of Helon, [8]and the enrollment of his company is fifty-seven thousand
four hundred. [9]The total enrollment of the
camp of Judah by companies is one hundred
and eighty-six thousand four hundred. They
shall be first on the march.
[10]The divisional camp of Reuben shall be

2:3–31 A similar arrangement of the tribes around the central sanctuary in the ideal Israel is given in Ez 48.

on the south side, by companies. The leader of the Reubenites is Elizur, son of Shedeur, 11 and the enrollment of his company is forty-six thousand five hundred. 12 Encamped beside it is the tribe of Simeon. The leader of the Simeonites is Shelumiel, son of Zurishaddai, 13 and the enrollment of his company is fifty-nine thousand three hundred. 14 Next is the tribe of Gad. The leader of the Gadites is Eliasaph, son of Reuel, 15 and the enrollment of his company is forty-five thousand six hundred and fifty. 16 The total enrollment of the camp of Reuben by companies is one hundred and fifty-one thousand four hundred and fifty. They shall be second on the march.

17 Then the tent of meeting and the camp of the Levites shall set out in the midst of the divisions. As they camp, so also they will march, each in place, by their divisions.

18 The divisional camp of Ephraim shall be on the west side, by companies. The leader of the Ephraimites is Elishama, son of Ammihud, 19 and the enrollment of his company is forty thousand five hundred. 20 Beside it shall be the tribe of Manasseh. The leader of the Manassites is Gamaliel, son of Pedahzur, 21 and the enrollment of his company is thirty-two thousand two hundred. 22 Also the tribe of Benjamin. The leader of the Benjaminites is Abidan, son of Gideoni, 23 and the enrollment of his company is thirty-five thousand four hundred. 24 The total enrollment of the camp of Ephraim by companies is one hundred and eight thousand one hundred. They shall be third on the march.

25 The divisional camp of Dan shall be on the north side, by companies. The leader of the Danites is Ahiezer, son of Ammishaddai, 26 and the enrollment of his company is sixty-two thousand seven hundred. 27 Encamped beside it shall be the tribe of Asher. The leader of the Asherites is Pagiel, son of Ochran, 28 and the enrollment of his company is forty-one thousand five hundred. 29 Also the tribe of Naphtali. The leader of the Naphtalites is Ahira, son of Enan, 30 and the enrollment of his company is fifty-three thousand four hundred. 31 The total enrollment of the camp of Dan is one hundred and fifty-seven thousand six hundred. They shall be the last on the march, by divisions.

32[k] These are the enrollments of the Israelites according to their ancestral houses. The total enrollment of the camps by companies is six hundred and three thousand five hundred and fifty. 33 The Levites, however, were not enrolled with the other Israelites, just as the LORD had commanded Moses. 34 The Israelites did just as the LORD had commanded Moses; both in camp and on the march they were in their own divisions, everyone by clan and according to ancestral house.

CHAPTER 3

See RG 134–35

The Sons of Aaron. 1 These are the offspring of Aaron and Moses at the time the LORD spoke to Moses on Mount Sinai. 2 These are the names of Aaron's sons: Nadab, the firstborn, Abihu, Eleazar, and Ithamar.[l] 3 These are the names of Aaron's sons, the anointed priests whom he ordained to serve as priests. 4 But Nadab and Abihu died[m] in the presence of the LORD when they offered unauthorized fire before the LORD in the wilderness of Sinai; and they left no sons. So only Eleazar and Ithamar served as priests during the lifetime of their father Aaron.

Levites in Place of the Firstborn. 5 Now the LORD said to Moses: 6 Summon the tribe of Levi and station them before Aaron the priest to serve him.[n] 7 They shall discharge his obligations and those of the whole community before the tent of meeting[o] by maintaining the tabernacle. 8 They shall have responsibility for all the furnishings of the tent of meeting and discharge the obligations of the Israelites by maintaining the tabernacle. 9 You shall assign the Levites to Aaron and his sons;[p] they have been assigned unconditionally to him from among the Israelites. 10 But you will appoint only Aaron and his descendants to exercise the priesthood.[q] Any unauthorized person who comes near shall be put to death.

11 The LORD said to Moses: 12 I hereby take

k: Nm 1:44–49. *l:* Ex 6:23; 1 Chr 24:1. *m:* Nm 26:61; Lv 10:1–2; 1 Chr 24:2. *n:* Nm 18:2. *o:* Nm 8:24. *p:* Nm 8:19. *q:* Nm 1:51; 18:7.

the Levites from the Israelites in place of every firstborn that opens the womb among the Israelites.[r] The Levites, therefore, are mine, 13because every firstborn is mine. When I struck down all the firstborn in the land of Egypt, I consecrated to me every firstborn in Israel, human being and beast alike. They belong to me; I am the LORD.

Census of the Levites. 14The LORD said to Moses in the wilderness of Sinai: 15Enroll the Levites by their ancestral houses and clans, enrolling every male of a month or more.[s] 16Moses, therefore, enrolled them at the direction of the LORD, just as the LORD had charged.

17[t] These were the sons of Levi by name: Gershon, Kohath and Merari. 18These were the names of the sons of Gershon, by their clans: Libni and Shimei. 19The sons of Kohath, by their clans, were Amram, Izhar, Hebron and Uzziel. 20The sons of Merari, by their clans, were Mahli and Mushi. These were the clans of the Levites by their ancestral houses.

Duties of the Levitical Clans. 21To Gershon belonged the clan of the Libnites and the clan of the Shimeites; these were the clans of the Gershonites. 22Their enrollment, registering every male of a month or more, was seven thousand five hundred. 23The clans of the Gershonites camped behind the tabernacle, to the west. 24The leader of the ancestral house of the Gershonites was Eliasaph, son of Lael. 25[u] At the tent of meeting their responsibility was the tabernacle:* the tent and its covering, the curtain at the entrance of the tent of meeting, 26the hangings of the court, the curtain at the entrance of the court enclosing both the tabernacle and the altar, and the ropes—whatever pertained to their maintenance.

27To Kohath belonged the clans of the Amramites, the Izharites, the Hebronites, and the Uzzielites; these were the clans of the Kohathites. 28Their enrollment, registering every male of a month or more, was eight thousand three hundred. They were the ones who performed the duties of the sanctuary. 29The clans of the Kohathites camped on the south side of the tabernacle. 30And the leader of their ancestral house of the clan of the Kohathites was Elizaphan, son of Uzziel. 31Their responsibility was the ark, the table, the menorah, the altars, the utensils of the sanctuary with which the priests minister, the veil, and everything pertaining to their maintenance.* 32The chief of the leaders of the Levites, however, was Eleazar, son of Aaron the priest; he was in charge of those who performed the duties of the sanctuary.

33To Merari belonged the clans of the Mahlites and the Mushites; these were the clans of Merari. 34Their enrollment, registering every male of a month or more, was six thousand two hundred. 35The leader of the ancestral house of the clans of Merari was Zuriel, son of Abihail. They camped at the north side of the tabernacle. 36* The Merarites were assigned responsibility for the boards of the tabernacle, its bars, columns, pedestals, and all its fittings—and everything pertaining to their maintenance, 37as well as the columns of the surrounding court with their pedestals, pegs and ropes.

38East of the tabernacle, that is, in front of the tent of meeting, toward the sunrise, were camped Moses and Aaron and the latter's sons, performing the duties of the sanctuary incumbent upon the Israelites. Any unauthorized person who came near was to be put to death.

39The total enrollment of the Levites whom Moses and Aaron enrolled at the direction of the LORD, by clans, every male a month old or more, was twenty-two thousand.

3:25–26 The Gershonites had two wagons for transporting these things; cf. 7:7. For a description of the tabernacle, see Ex 26:1–6; the tent, Ex 26:7–13; its covering, Ex 26:14; the curtain at the entrance, Ex 26:36; the hangings of the court, Ex 27:9–15; the curtain at the entrance of the court, Ex 27:16; the ropes of the tabernacle, Ex 35:18.

3:31 The Kohathites had to carry these sacred objects on their shoulders; cf. 7:9. For a description of the ark, see Ex 25:10–22; the table, Ex 25:23–30; the menorah, Ex 25:31–40; the altars, Ex 27:1–8; 30:1–10.

3:36–37 The Merarites had four wagons for transporting this heavy material; cf. 7:8. For a description of the boards, bars, etc., of the tabernacle, see Ex 26:15–30; the columns, pedestals, etc., of the court, Ex 27:9–19.

r: Nm 3:41; 8:16–18; Ex 13:2, 12, 15. *s:* Nm 3:39; 26:62. *t:* Nm 26:57; Gn 46:11; Ex 6:16–19; 1 Chr 6:1–2, 16–19. *u:* Ex 26:7, 14, 36; 36:14.

Census and Ransom of Firstborn. 40The LORD then said to Moses: Enroll every firstborn male of the Israelites a month old or more, and count the number of their names. 41Then take the Levites for me—I am the LORD—in place of all the firstborn of the Israelites, as well as the Levites' cattle, in place of all the firstborn among the cattle of the Israelites. 42So Moses enrolled all the firstborn of the Israelites, as the LORD had commanded him. 43All the firstborn males, registered by name, of a month or more, numbered twenty-two thousand two hundred and seventy-three.

44The LORD said to Moses: 45Take the Levites in place of all the firstborn of the Israelites, and the Levites' cattle in place of their cattle, that the Levites may belong to me. I am the LORD. 46As a redemption-price for the two hundred and seventy-three firstborn of the Israelites over and above the number of the Levites, 47you shall take five shekels for each individual, according to the sanctuary shekel, twenty gerahs to the shekel.[v] 48Give this money to Aaron and his sons as a redemption-price for the extra number. 49So Moses took the redemption money for those over and above the ones redeemed by the Levites. 50From the firstborn of the Israelites he took the money, one thousand three hundred and sixty-five shekels according to the sanctuary shekel. 51He then gave this redemption money to Aaron and his sons, at the direction of the LORD, just as the LORD had commanded Moses.

CHAPTER 4

See RG 134–35

Duties Further Defined. 1The LORD said to Moses and Aaron: 2Take a census among the Levites of the Kohathites, by clans and ancestral houses, 3all between thirty* and fifty years of age, who will join the personnel for doing tasks in the tent of meeting.[w]

4This is the task of the Kohathites in the tent of meeting: the most sacred objects. 5In breaking camp, Aaron and his sons shall go in and take down the screening curtain* and cover the ark of the covenant with it. 6Over these they shall put a cover of yellow-orange skin, and on top of this spread an all-violet cloth and put the poles in place. 7On the table of the Presence they shall spread a violet cloth and put on it the plates and cups, as well as the bowls and pitchers for libations; the established bread offering shall remain on the table. 8Over these they shall spread a scarlet cloth and cover it with a covering of yellow-orange skin, and put the poles in place. 9They shall use a violet cloth to cover the menorah of the light with its lamps, tongs, and trays, as well as the various containers of oil from which it is supplied. 10The menorah with all its utensils they shall then put in a covering of yellow-orange skin, and place on a litter. 11Over the golden altar* they shall spread a violet cloth, and cover this also with a covering of yellow-orange skin, and put the poles in place. 12Taking the utensils of the sanctuary service, they shall put them all in violet cloth and cover them with a covering of yellow-orange skin. They shall then place them on a litter. 13After cleansing the altar* of its ashes, they shall spread a purple cloth over it. 14On this they shall put all the utensils with which it is served: the fire pans, forks,* shovels, basins, and all the utensils of the altar. They shall then spread a covering of yellow-orange skin over this, and put the poles in place.

15Only after Aaron and his sons have finished covering the sacred objects and all their utensils on breaking camp, can the Kohathites enter to carry them. But they shall not touch the sacred objects; if they do they will die.[x] These, then, are the objects in the tent of meeting that the Kohathites shall carry.

16Eleazar, son of Aaron the priest, shall be in charge of the oil for the light, the fragrant

4:3 Thirty: according to other passages the Levites began to serve when they were twenty-five (8:24) or even only twenty years old (1 Chr 23:24, 27; 2 Chr 31:17; Ezr 3:8; but cf. 1 Chr 23:3).

4:5 The screening curtain: the veil between the inner and the outer rooms of the sanctuary. Cf. Ex 26:31–33.

4:11 The golden altar: the altar of incense. Cf. Ex 30:1–6.

4:13 The altar: the bronze altar for animal sacrifices. Cf. Ex 27:1–8.

4:14 Forks: used in turning over the sacrificed animal on the fire of the altar. **Basins**: to receive the sacrificial blood; cf. Zec 9:15.

v: Nm 18:16; Ex 30:13; Lv 27:25; Ez 45:12. *w:* Nm 8:24; 1 Chr 23:24–27. *x:* 2 Sm 6:6–7; 1 Chr 13:9–10.

incense, the established grain offering, and the anointing oil. He shall be in charge of the whole tabernacle with all the sacred objects and utensils that are in it.

[17]The LORD said to Moses and Aaron: [18]Do not let the group of Kohathite clans perish from among the Levites. [19]That they may live and not die when they approach the most sacred objects, this is what you shall do for them: Aaron and his sons shall go in and assign to each of them his task and what he must carry; [20]but the Kohathites shall not go in to look upon the sacred objects even for an instant, or they will die.[y]

[21]The LORD said to Moses: [22]Take a census of the Gershonites also, by ancestral houses and clans, [23]enrolling all between thirty and fifty years of age who will join the personnel to do the work in the tent of meeting. [24]This is the task of the clans of the Gershonites, what they must do and what they must carry: [25]they shall carry the curtains of the tabernacle, the tent of meeting with its covering and the outer wrapping of yellow-orange skin, the curtain at the entrance of the tent of meeting, [26]the hangings of the court, the curtain at the entrance to the gate of the court that encloses both the tabernacle and the altar, together with their ropes and all other objects necessary for their use. Whatever is to be done to maintain these things, they shall do. [27]The service of the Gershonites shall be entirely under the direction of Aaron and his sons, with regard to what they must carry and what they must do; you shall list for them by name what they are to carry. [28]This, then, is the task of the clans of the Gershonites in the tent of meeting; and they shall be under the supervision of Ithamar, son of Aaron the priest.

[29]The Merarites, too, you shall enroll by clans and ancestral houses, [30]enrolling all between thirty and fifty years of age who will join the personnel to maintain the tent of meeting. [31][z] This is what they shall be responsible for carrying, with respect to all their service in the tent of meeting: the boards of the tabernacle with its bars, columns and pedestals, [32]and the columns of the surrounding court with their pedestals, pegs and ropes, including all their accessories and everything for their maintenance. You shall list by name the objects they shall be responsible for carrying. [33]This, then, is the task of the clans of the Merarites with respect to all their service in the tent of meeting under the supervision of Ithamar, son of Aaron the priest.

Number of Adult Levites. [34]So Moses and Aaron and the leaders of the community enrolled the Kohathites, by clans and ancestral houses, [35]all between thirty and fifty years of age who will join the personnel to work in the tent of meeting; [36]their enrollment by clans was two thousand seven hundred and fifty. [37]Such was the enrollment of the clans of the Kohathites, everyone who was to serve in the tent of meeting, whom Moses enrolled, together with Aaron, as the LORD directed through Moses.

[38]As for the enrollment of the Gershonites, by clans and ancestral houses, [39]all between thirty and fifty years of age who will join the personnel to work in the tent of meeting— [40]their enrollment by clans and ancestral houses was two thousand six hundred and thirty. [41]Such was the enrollment of the clans of the Gershonites, everyone who was to serve in the tent of meeting, whom Moses enrolled, together with Aaron, as the LORD directed.

[42]As for the enrollment of the clans of the Merarites, by clans and ancestral houses, [43]all from thirty up to fifty years of age who will join the personnel to work in the tent of meeting— [44]their enrollment by clans was three thousand two hundred. [45]Such was the enrollment of the clans of the Merarites, whom Moses enrolled, together with Aaron, as the LORD directed through Moses.

[46]As for the total enrollment of the Levites, which Moses and Aaron and the Israelite leaders had made, by clans and ancestral houses, [47]all between thirty and fifty years of age who were to undertake tasks of service or transport for the tent of meeting— [48]their total enrollment was eight thousand five hundred and eighty. [49]As the LORD directed

y: 1 Sm 6:19–20. *z:* Nm 3:36–37.

through Moses, they gave each of them their assignments for service and for transport; just as the LORD had commanded Moses.

See RG 134–35

CHAPTER 5

The Unclean Expelled. 1The LORD said to Moses: 2Order the Israelites to expel from camp everyone with a scaly infection, and everyone suffering from a discharge, and everyone who has become unclean by contact with a corpse.* [a] 3Male and female alike, you shall expel them. You shall expel them from the camp so that they do not defile their camp, where I dwell in their midst.[b] 4This the Israelites did, expelling them from the camp; just as the LORD had commanded Moses, so the Israelites did.

Unjust Possession.* 5The LORD said to Moses: 6[c] Tell the Israelites: If a man or a woman commits any offense against another person, thus breaking faith with the LORD, and thereby becomes guilty, 7that person shall confess the wrong that has been done, make restitution in full, and in addition give one fifth of its value to the one that has been wronged. 8However, if there is no next of kin,* one to whom restitution can be made, the restitution shall be made to the LORD and shall fall to the priest; this is apart from the ram of atonement with which the priest makes atonement for the guilty individual. 9Likewise, every contribution among the sacred offerings that the Israelites present to the priest will belong to him.[d] 10Each shall possess his own sacred offerings; what is given to a priest shall be his.[e]

Ordeal for Suspected Adultery. 11The LORD said to Moses: 12Speak to the Israelites and tell them: If a man's wife goes astray and becomes unfaithful to him 13by virtue of a man having intercourse with her[f] in secret from her husband and she is able to conceal the fact that she has defiled herself for lack of a witness who might have caught her in the act; 14or if a man is overcome by a feeling of jealousy that makes him suspect his wife, and she has defiled herself; or if a man is overcome by a feeling of jealousy that makes him suspect his wife and she has not defiled herself— 15then the man shall bring his wife to the priest as well as an offering on her behalf, a tenth of an ephah* of barley meal. However, he shall not pour oil on it nor put frankincense over it, since it is a grain offering of jealousy, a grain offering of remembrance which recalls wrongdoing.

16The priest shall first have the woman come forward and stand before the LORD. 17In an earthen vessel he shall take holy water,* as well as some dust from the floor of the tabernacle and put it in the water.[g] 18Making the woman stand before the LORD, the priest shall uncover her head and place in her hands the grain offering of remembrance, that is, the grain offering of jealousy, while he himself shall hold the water of bitterness that brings a curse. 19Then the priest shall adjure the woman, saying to her, "If no other man has had intercourse with you, and you have not gone astray by defiling yourself while under the authority of your husband, be immune to this water of bitterness that brings a curse. 20But if you have gone astray while under the authority of your husband, and if you have defiled yourself and a man other than your husband has had intercourse with you"— 21so shall the priest adjure the woman with this imprecation—"may the LORD make you a curse and malediction* among your people by causing your uterus to fall and your belly to swell! 22May this water, then, that brings a curse, enter your bowels to

5:2 For the laws regarding victims of skin disease, see Lv 13–14; those suffering from a discharge, Lv 15; those unclean by contact with a corpse, Nm 19:11–22; Lv 21:1–4.

5:5–10 The basic law on unjust possession is given in Lv 5:14–26. The new item here concerns the case where the injured party has died and left no heirs, in which case the restitution must be made to the priest.

5:8 Next of kin: Hebrew *go'el* ("redeemer"), a technical term denoting the nearest relative, upon whom devolved the obligation of "redeeming" the family property, in order to keep it within the family. Cf. Lv 25:25; Ru 4:1–6.

5:15 Ephah: see note on Is 5:10.

5:17 Holy water: water from the basin that stood in the court of the tabernacle.

5:21 Curse and malediction: the woman's name would be used in curses and oaths to invoke a similar misfortune on another person or on oneself. Cf. Is 65:15; Jer 29:22.

a: Nm 19:11, 13; Lv 13:46; 21:1; 22:4. *b:* Nm 35:34. *c:* Lv 5:21–25. *d:* Dt 18:3–4; Ez 44:29–30. *e:* Lv 10:12–15. *f:* Lv 18:20; Jn 8:4. *g:* Nm 19:17.

make your belly swell and your uterus fall!"[h] And the woman shall say, "Amen, amen!"* 23The priest shall put these curses in writing and shall then wash them off into the water of bitterness, 24and he will have the woman drink the water of bitterness that brings a curse, so that the water that brings a curse may enter into her to her bitter hurt. 25But first the priest shall take the grain offering of jealousy from the woman's hand, and having elevated the grain offering before the LORD, shall bring it to the altar, 26where he shall take a handful of the grain offering as a token offering and burn it on the altar.[i] Only then shall he have the woman drink the water. 27Once he has had her drink the water, if she has defiled herself and been unfaithful to her husband, the water that brings a curse will enter into her to her bitter hurt, and her belly will swell and her uterus will fall, so that she will become a curse among her people. 28If, however, the woman has not defiled herself, but is still pure, she will be immune and will still be fertile.

29This, then, is the ritual for jealousy when a woman goes astray while under the authority of her husband and defiles herself, 30or when such a feeling of jealousy comes over a man that he becomes suspicious of his wife; he shall have her stand before the LORD, and the priest shall perform this entire ritual for her. 31The man shall be free from punishment,* but the woman shall bear her punishment.

CHAPTER 6

See RG 134–35

Laws Concerning Nazirites. 1The LORD said to Moses: 2Speak to the Israelites and tell them: When men or women solemnly take the nazirite* vow to dedicate themselves to the LORD, 3they shall abstain from wine and strong drink;[j] they may neither drink wine vinegar, other vinegar, or any kind of grape juice, nor eat either fresh or dried grapes. 4As long as they are nazirites they shall not eat anything of the produce of the grapevine; not even the seeds or the skins. 5While they are under the nazirite vow, no razor shall touch their hair.[k] Until the period of their dedication to the LORD is over, they shall be holy, letting the hair of their heads grow freely. 6As long as they are dedicated to the LORD, they shall not come near a dead person.[l] 7Not even for their father or mother, sister or brother, should they defile themselves, when these die, since their heads bear their dedication to God. 8As long as they are nazirites they are holy to the LORD.

9If someone dies very suddenly in their presence, defiling their dedicated heads, they shall shave their heads on the day of their purification, that is, on the seventh day. 10On the eighth day they shall bring two turtledoves or two pigeons to the priest at the entrance of the tent of meeting. 11The priest shall offer up the one as a purification offering and the other as a burnt offering, thus making atonement for them for the sin they committed with respect to the corpse. On the same day they shall reconsecrate their heads 12and rededicate themselves to the LORD for the period of their dedication, bringing a yearling lamb as a reparation offering. The previous period is not valid, because they defiled their dedicated heads.

13This is the ritual for the nazirites:[m] When the period of their dedication is complete they shall go to the entrance of the tent of meeting, 14bringing their offerings to the LORD, one unblemished yearling lamb for a

5:22 Amen: a Hebrew word meaning "certainly, truly," used to give assent to a statement, a curse, a blessing, a prayer, or the like, in the sense of "so be it."

5:31 Free from punishment: the point is that a husband will not suffer a harmful consequence if his accusation is not borne out by the ordeal; if he's right, his wife's punishment vindicates him. For her part, the woman (if guilty) must bear her punishment.

6:2–21 Nazirite: from the Hebrew word *nazir*, meaning "set apart as sacred, dedicated, vowed." The nazirite vow could be either for a limited period or for life. Those bound by this vow had to abstain from all the products of the grapevine, from cutting or shaving their hair, and from contact with a corpse. They were regarded as men and women of God like the prophets; cf. Am 2:11–12. Examples of lifelong nazirites were Samson (Jgs 13:4–5, 7; 16:17), Samuel (1 Sm 1:11), and John the Baptist (Lk 1:15). At the time of Jesus the practice of taking the nazirite vow for a limited period seems to have been quite common, even among the early Christians; cf. Acts 18:18; 21:23–24, 26.

h: Ps 109:18. *i:* Lv 5:12. *j:* Jgs 13:7, 14. *k:* Jgs 13:5; 16:17; 1 Sm 1:11. *l:* Nm 19:11, 16; Lv 21:11. *m:* Acts 21:24, 26.

burnt offering, one unblemished yearling ewe lamb for a purification offering, one unblemished ram as a communion offering, 15 and a basket of unleavened cakes of bran flour mixed with oil and of unleavened wafers spread with oil, along with their grain offerings and libations. 16 The priest shall present them before the LORD, and shall offer up the purification offering and the burnt offering for them. 17 He shall then offer up the ram as a communion sacrifice to the LORD, along with the basket of unleavened cakes, and the priest will offer the grain offering and libation. 18 Then at the entrance of the tent of meeting the nazirite shall shave his or her dedicated head, take the hair of the dedicated head, and put it in the fire under the communion sacrifice. 19 After the nazirite has shaved off the dedicated hair, the priest shall take a boiled shoulder of the ram, as well as one unleavened cake from the basket and one unleavened wafer, and shall put them in the hands of the nazirite. 20 The priest shall then elevate them as an elevated offering before the LORD. They are an offering belonging to the priest, along with the brisket of the elevated offering and the leg of the contribution. Only after this may the nazirite drink wine.

21 This, then, is the law for the nazirites, that is, what they vow as their offering to the LORD in accord with their dedication, apart from anything else which their means may allow. In keeping with the vow they take so shall they do, according to the law of their dedication.

The Priestly Blessing. 22 The LORD said to Moses: 23 Speak to Aaron and his sons and tell them: This is how you shall bless the Israelites. Say to them:

24 The LORD bless you and keep you!
25 The LORD let his face shine upon you,
and be gracious to you!
26 The LORD look upon you kindly and give
you peace!*

27 So shall they invoke my name upon the Israelites, and I will bless them.

CHAPTER 7

See RG 134–35

Offerings of the Tribal Leaders. 1 Now, when Moses had completed the erection of the tabernacle, he anointed and consecrated it with all its equipment,[n] as well as the altar with all its equipment. After he anointed and consecrated them, 2 an offering was made by the tribal leaders of Israel, who were heads of ancestral houses, the same leaders of the tribes who supervised those enrolled. 3 The offering they brought before the LORD consisted of six wagons for baggage and twelve oxen, that is, a wagon for every two tribal leaders, and an ox for each. These they presented before the tabernacle.

4 The LORD then said to Moses: 5 Accept their offering, that these things may be put to use to maintain the tent of meeting. Assign them to the Levites, to each according to his duties. 6 So Moses accepted the wagons and oxen, and assigned them to the Levites. 7 He gave two wagons and four oxen to the Gershonites[o] according to their duties, 8 and four wagons and eight oxen to the Merarites according to their duties, under the supervision of Ithamar, son of Aaron the priest. 9 He gave none to the Kohathites, because they were responsible for maintenance of the sacred objects that had to be carried on their shoulders.[p]

10 For the dedication of the altar also, the tribal leaders brought offerings when it was anointed;[q] the leaders presented their offering before the altar. 11 But the LORD said to Moses: Let one leader each day present his offering for the dedication of the altar.

12* The one who presented his offering on the first day was Nahshon, son of Amminadab, of the tribe of Judah. 13 His offering consisted of one silver plate weighing a hundred and thirty shekels and one silver basin weighing seventy shekels according to the sanctuary shekel, both filled with bran flour mixed with oil for a grain offering; 14 one

6:26 Peace: the Hebrew word *Shalom* includes the idea of happiness, good health, prosperity, friendship, and general well-being. To use this term as a greeting was to pray for all these things upon the one greeted.

7:12–88 The repetitious account of the same offerings brought by each of the twelve tribal leaders and the summary of them are characteristic of an official registration.

n: Ex 40:17. *o:* Nm 4:24–33. *p:* Nm 3:31; 4:4–15. *q:* Nm 7:84.

gold cup of ten shekels' weight filled with incense; [15]one bull from the herd, one ram, and one yearling lamb for a burnt offering; [16]one goat for a purification offering; [17]and two bulls, five rams, five he-goats, and five yearling lambs for a communion sacrifice. This was the offering of Nahshon, son of Amminadab.

[18]On the second day Nethanel, son of Zuar, tribal leader of Issachar, made his offering. [19]He presented as his offering one silver plate weighing a hundred and thirty shekels and one silver basin weighing seventy shekels according to the sanctuary shekel, both filled with bran flour mixed with oil for a grain offering; [20]one gold cup of ten shekels' weight filled with incense; [21]one bull from the herd, one ram, and one yearling lamb for a burnt offering; [22]one goat for a purification offering; [23]and two bulls, five rams, five he-goats, and five yearling lambs for a communion sacrifice. This was the offering of Nethanel, son of Zuar.

[24]On the third day it was the turn of the tribal leader of the Zebulunites, Eliab, son of Helon. [25]His offering consisted of one silver plate weighing a hundred and thirty shekels and one silver basin weighing seventy shekels according to the sanctuary shekel, both filled with bran flour mixed with oil for a grain offering; [26]one gold cup of ten shekels' weight filled with incense; [27]one bull from the herd, one ram, and one yearling lamb for a burnt offering; [28]one goat for a purification offering; [29]and two bulls, five rams, five he-goats, and five yearling lambs for a communion sacrifice. This was the offering of Eliab, son of Helon.

[30]On the fourth day it was the turn of the tribal leader of the Reubenites, Elizur, son of Shedeur. [31]His offering consisted of one silver plate weighing a hundred and thirty shekels and one silver basin weighing seventy shekels according to the sanctuary shekel, both filled with bran flour mixed with oil for a grain offering; [32]one gold cup of ten shekels' weight filled with incense; [33]one bull from the herd, one ram, and one yearling lamb for a burnt offering; [34]one goat for a purification offering; [35]and two bulls, five rams, five he-goats, and five yearling lambs for a communion sacrifice. This was the offering of Elizur, son of Shedeur.

[36]On the fifth day it was the turn of the tribal leader of the Simeonites, Shelumiel, son of Zurishaddai. [37]His offering consisted of one silver plate weighing a hundred and thirty shekels and one silver basin weighing seventy shekels according to the sanctuary shekel, both filled with bran flour mixed with oil for a grain offering; [38]one gold cup of ten shekels' weight filled with incense; [39]one bull from the herd, one ram, and one yearling lamb for a burnt offering; [40]one goat for a purification offering; [41]and two bulls, five rams, five he-goats, and five yearling lambs for a communion sacrifice. This was the offering of Shelumiel, son of Zurishaddai.

[42]On the sixth day it was the turn of the tribal leader of the Gadites, Eliasaph, son of Reuel. [43]His offering consisted of one silver plate weighing a hundred and thirty shekels and one silver basin weighing seventy shekels according to the sanctuary shekel, both filled with bran flour mixed with oil for a grain offering; [44]one gold cup of ten shekels' weight filled with incense; [45]one bull from the herd, one ram, and one yearling lamb for a burnt offering; [46]one goat for a purification offering; [47]and two bulls, five rams, five he-goats, and five yearling lambs for a communion sacrifice. This was the offering of Eliasaph, son of Reuel.

[48]On the seventh day it was the turn of the tribal leader of the Ephraimites, Elishama, son of Ammihud. [49]His offering consisted of one silver plate weighing a hundred and thirty shekels and one silver basin weighing seventy shekels according to the sanctuary shekel, both filled with bran flour mixed with oil for a grain offering; [50]one gold cup of ten shekels' weight filled with incense; [51]one bull from the herd, one ram, and one yearling lamb for a burnt offering; [52]one goat for a purification offering; [53]and two bulls, five rams, five he-goats, and five yearling lambs for a communion sacrifice. This was the offering of Elishama, son of Ammihud.

[54]On the eighth day it was the turn of the tribal leader of the Manassites, Gamaliel, son of Pedahzur. [55]His offering consisted of one silver plate weighing a hundred and thirty

shekels and one silver basin weighing seventy shekels according to the sanctuary shekel, both filled with bran flour mixed with oil for a grain offering; [56]one gold cup of ten shekels' weight filled with incense; [57]one bull from the herd, one ram, and one yearling lamb for a burnt offering; [58]one goat for a purification offering; [59]and two bulls, five rams, five he-goats, and five yearling lambs for a communion sacrifice. This was the offering of Gamaliel, son of Pedahzur.

[60]On the ninth day it was the turn of the tribal leader of the Benjaminites, Abidan, son of Gideoni. [61]His offering consisted of one silver plate weighing a hundred and thirty shekels and one silver basin weighing seventy shekels according to the sanctuary shekel, both filled with bran flour mixed with oil for a grain offering; [62]one gold cup of ten shekels' weight filled with incense; [63]one bull from the herd, one ram, and one yearling lamb for a burnt offering; [64]one goat for a purification offering; [65]and two bulls, five rams, five he-goats, and five yearling lambs for a communion sacrifice. This was the offering of Abidan, son of Gideoni.

[66]On the tenth day it was the turn of the tribal leader of the Danites, Ahiezer, son of Ammishaddai. [67]His offering consisted of one silver plate weighing a hundred and thirty shekels and one silver basin weighing seventy shekels according to the sanctuary shekel, both filled with bran flour mixed with oil for a grain offering; [68]one gold cup of ten shekels' weight filled with incense; [69]one bull from the herd, one ram, and one yearling lamb for a burnt offering; [70]one goat for a purification offering; [71]and two bulls, five rams, five he-goats, and five yearling lambs for a communion sacrifice. This was the offering of Ahiezer, son of Ammishaddai.

[72]On the eleventh day it was the turn of the tribal leader of the Asherites, Pagiel, son of Ochran. [73]His offering consisted of one silver plate weighing one hundred and thirty shekels and one silver basin weighing seventy shekels according to the sanctuary shekel, both filled with bran flour mixed with oil for a grain offering; [74]one gold cup of ten shekels' weight filled with incense; [75]one bull from the herd, one ram, and one yearling lamb for a burnt offering; [76]one goat for a purification offering; [77]and two bulls, five rams, five he-goats, and five yearling lambs for a communion sacrifice. This was the offering of Pagiel, son of Ochran.

[78]On the twelfth day it was the turn of the tribal leader of the Naphtalites, Ahira, son of Enan. [79]His offering consisted of one silver plate weighing a hundred and thirty shekels and one silver basin weighing seventy shekels according to the sanctuary shekel, both filled with bran flour mixed with oil for a grain offering; [80]one gold cup of ten shekels' weight filled with incense; [81]one bull from the herd, one ram, and one yearling lamb for a burnt offering; [82]one goat for a purification offering; [83]and two bulls, five rams, five he-goats, and five yearling lambs for a communion sacrifice. This was the offering of Ahira, son of Enan.

[84]These were the offerings for the dedication of the altar, given by the tribal leaders of Israel on the occasion of its anointing: twelve silver plates, twelve silver basins, and twelve gold cups. [85]Each silver plate weighed a hundred and thirty shekels, and each silver basin seventy, so that all the silver of these vessels amounted to two thousand four hundred shekels, according to the sanctuary shekel. [86]The twelve gold cups that were filled with incense weighed ten shekels apiece, according to the sanctuary shekel, so that all the gold of the cups amounted to one hundred and twenty shekels. [87]The animals for the burnt offerings were, in all, twelve bulls, twelve rams, and twelve yearling lambs, with their grain offerings; those for the purification offerings were twelve goats. [88]The animals for the communion sacrifices were, in all, twenty-four bulls, sixty rams, sixty he-goats, and sixty yearling lambs. These, then, were the offerings for the dedication of the altar after it was anointed.

The Voice. [89]When Moses entered the tent of meeting to speak with God, he heard the voice addressing him from above the cover[r]

r: Ex 25:22.

on the ark of the covenant, from between the two cherubim; and so it spoke to him.

CHAPTER 8

See RG 134–35

The Menorah. 1The LORD said to Moses: 2Speak to Aaron and say: "When you set up the menorah-lamps,[s] have the seven lamps throw their light in front of the menorah."* 3Aaron did so, setting up the menorah-lamps to face the area in front of the menorah, just as the LORD had commanded Moses. 4This is the construction of the menorah: hammered gold,[t] from its base to its bowls* it was hammered; according to the pattern which the LORD had shown Moses, so he made the menorah.

Purification of the Levites. 5The LORD said to Moses: 6Take the Levites from among the Israelites and cleanse them.* 7This is what you shall do to them to cleanse them. Sprinkle them with the water of purification, have them shave their whole bodies and wash their garments, and so cleanse themselves. 8Then they shall take a bull from the herd, along with its grain offering of bran flour mixed with oil; and you shall take another bull from the herd for a purification offering. 9Bringing the Levites before the tent of meeting, you shall assemble also the whole community of the Israelites. 10When you have brought the Levites before the LORD, the Israelites shall lay their hands upon them. 11Aaron shall then present the Levites before the LORD as an elevated offering from the Israelites, that they may perform the service of the LORD. 12The Levites in turn shall lay their hands on the heads of the bulls, offering one as a purification offering and the other as a burnt offering to the LORD, to make atonement for the Levites. 13Then you shall have the Levites stand before Aaron and his sons, and you shall present them as an elevated offering to the LORD; 14thus you shall separate the Levites from the rest of the Israelites, and the Levites shall belong to me.[u]

15Only then shall the Levites enter upon their service in the tent of meeting, when you have cleansed them and presented them as an elevated offering. 16For they, among the Israelites, are totally dedicated to me; I have taken them for myself in place of everyone that opens the womb, the firstborn of all the Israelites.[v] 17Indeed, all the firstborn among the Israelites, human being and beast alike, belong to me; I consecrated them to myself on the day I killed all the firstborn in the land of Egypt.[w] 18But I have taken the Levites in place of all the firstborn Israelites; 19and from among the Israelites I have given to Aaron and his sons these Levites, who are to be dedicated,[x] to perform the service of the Israelites in the tent of meeting and to make atonement for them, so that no plague may strike among the Israelites should they come too near the sanctuary.

20This, then, is what Moses and Aaron and the whole community of the Israelites did with respect to the Levites; the Israelites did exactly as the LORD had commanded Moses concerning them. 21When the Levites had purified themselves* and washed their garments, Aaron presented them as an elevated offering before the LORD, and made atonement for them to cleanse them. 22Only then did they enter upon their service in the tent of meeting under the supervision of Aaron and his sons. Exactly as the LORD had commanded Moses concerning the Levites, so it was done with regard to them.

Age Limits for Levitical Service. 23The LORD said to Moses: 24This is the rule for the Levites. Everyone twenty-five years old or more shall join the personnel in the service of the tent of meeting.[y] 25But everyone fifty on up shall retire from the work force and serve no more. 26They shall assist their fellow Levites in the tent of meeting in per-

8:2 Menorah: a seven-branched lampstand; see Ex 25:31–40; 37:17–24.

8:4 Bowls: lit., "blossom," a designation for the blossom-shaped cups holding the lamps of the menorah.

8:6 Cleanse them: in the language of the Pentateuch only the priests were "consecrated," that is, made sacred or set aside for the Lord, in an elaborate ceremony described in Ex 29 and in this chapter. The Levites were "cleansed," that is, made ritually clean for their special work.

8:21 Purified themselves: by having the "water of purification" sprinkled on them as prescribed in v. 7.

s: Ex 25:37. *t:* Ex 25:31, 40. *u:* Nm 3:45. *v:* Nm 3:12, 45. *w:* Nm 3:13; Lk 2:23. *x:* Nm 3:9–10. *y:* Nm 4:3, 23.

forming their duties, but they shall not do the work. This, then, is how you are to regulate the duties of the Levites.

CHAPTER 9

See RG 134–35

Second Passover. 1The LORD said to Moses in the wilderness of Sinai, in the first month of the second year following their departure from the land of Egypt: 2Tell the Israelites to celebrate the Passover at the prescribed time. 3In the evening twilight of the fourteenth day of this month[z] you shall celebrate it at its prescribed time, in accord with all its statutes and regulations. 4So Moses told the Israelites to celebrate the Passover, 5and they did celebrate the Passover on the fourteenth day of the first month during the evening twilight in the wilderness of Sinai. Just as the LORD had commanded Moses, so the Israelites did.

6There were some, however, who were unclean because of a human corpse and so could not celebrate the Passover that day. These men came up to Moses and Aaron that same day 7and they said to them, "Although we are unclean because of a human corpse, why should we be deprived of presenting the LORD's offering at its prescribed time along with other Israelites?" 8Moses answered them, "Wait so that I can learn what the LORD will command in your regard."

9The LORD then said to Moses: 10Speak to the Israelites: "If any one of you or of your descendants is unclean because of a human corpse, or is absent on a journey, you may still celebrate the LORD's Passover. 11But you shall celebrate it in the second month,[a] on the fourteenth day of that month during the evening twilight, eating it with unleavened bread and bitter herbs, 12and not leaving any of it over till morning, nor breaking any of its bones,[b] but observing all the statutes of the Passover. 13However, anyone who is clean and not away on a journey, who yet fails to celebrate the Passover, shall be cut off from the people, for not presenting the LORD's offering at the prescribed time. That person shall bear the consequences of this sin.

14"If an alien* who lives among you would celebrate the LORD's Passover, it shall be celebrated according to the statutes and regulations for the Passover. You shall have the same law for the resident alien as for the native of the land."[c]

The Fiery Cloud. 15On the day when the tabernacle was erected, the cloud* covered the tabernacle, the tent of the covenant; but from evening until morning it took on the appearance of fire over the tabernacle.[d] 16It was always so: during the day the cloud covered the tabernacle and at night had the appearance of fire. 17Whenever the cloud rose from the tent, the Israelites would break camp; wherever the cloud settled, the Israelites would pitch camp.[e] 18At the direction of the LORD the Israelites broke camp, and at the LORD's direction they pitched camp.[f] As long as the cloud stayed over the tabernacle, they remained in camp.

19Even when the cloud lingered many days over the tabernacle, the Israelites kept the charge of the LORD and would not move on. 20Yet if it happened the cloud was over the tabernacle only for a few days, at the direction of the LORD they stayed in camp; and at the LORD's direction they broke camp. 21If it happened the cloud remained there only from evening until morning, when the cloud rose in the morning, they would break camp. Whether the cloud lifted during the day or the night they would then break camp. 22Whether the cloud lingered over the tabernacle for two days or for a month or longer, the Israelites remained in camp and did not break camp; but when it lifted, they broke camp. 23At the direction of the LORD they pitched camp, and at the LORD's direction they broke camp; they kept the charge of the LORD, as the LORD directed them through Moses.

CHAPTER 10

See RG 134–35

The Silver Trumpets. 1The LORD said to Moses: 2Make two trumpets of silver,

9:14 An alien: compare this passage with the Passover legislation in Ex 12:48, where circumcision is required of the alien who would celebrate the feast.

9:15 The cloud: already mentioned at the departure from Egypt; cf. Ex 13:21–22.

z: Ex 12:6; Lv 23:5. *a:* 2 Chr 30:2–15. *b:* Ex 12:46; Jn 19:36. *c:* Ex 12:48–49. *d:* Ex 13:21. *e:* Wis 18:3. *f:* 1 Cor 10:1.

making them of hammered silver, for you to use in summoning the community and in breaking camp. 3When both are blown, the whole community shall gather round you at the entrance of the tent of meeting; 4but when one of them is blown, only the tribal leaders, the heads of the clans of Israel, shall gather round you. 5When you sound the signal, those encamped on the east side shall break camp; 6when you sound a second signal, those encamped on the south side shall break camp; when you sound a third signal, those encamped on the west side shall break camp; when you sound a fourth signal, those encamped on the north side shall break camp. Thus shall the signal be sounded for them to break camp. 7But in calling forth an assembly you are to blow a blast, without sounding the signal.

8The sons of Aaron, the priests, shall blow the trumpets; this is prescribed forever for you and your descendants. 9[g] When in your own land you go to war against an enemy that is attacking you, you shall sound the alarm on the trumpets, and you shall be remembered before the LORD, your God, and be saved from your foes. 10And when you rejoice* on your festivals, and your new-moon feasts, you shall blow the trumpets over your burnt offerings and your communion sacrifices,[h] so that this serves as a reminder of you before your God. I, the LORD, am your God.

II. Departure, Rebellion, and Wandering in the Wilderness for Forty Years

Departure from Sinai. 11In the second year, on the twentieth day of the second month, the cloud rose from the tabernacle of the covenant, 12and the Israelites moved on from the wilderness of Sinai by stages, until the cloud came to rest in the wilderness of Paran.

13The first time that they broke camp at the direction of the LORD through Moses, 14[i] the divisional camp of the Judahites, arranged in companies, was the first to set out. Over its whole company was Nahshon, son of Amminadab, 15with Nethanel, son of Zuar, over the company of the tribe of Issacharites, 16and Eliab, son of Helon, over the company of the tribe of Zebulunites. 17Then, after the tabernacle was dismantled, the Gershonites and Merarites who carried the tabernacle set out. 18The divisional camp of the Reubenites, arranged in companies, was the next to set out. Over its whole company was Elizur, son of Shedeur, 19with Shelumiel, son of Zurishaddai, over the company of the tribe of Simeonites, 20and Eliasaph, son of Reuel, over the company of the tribe of Gadites. 21The Kohathites, who carried the sacred objects, then set out. Before their arrival the tabernacle would be erected. 22The divisional camp of the Ephraimites set out next, arranged in companies. Over its whole company was Elishama, son of Ammihud, 23with Gamaliel, son of Pedahzur, over the company of the tribe of Manassites, 24and Abidan, son of Gideoni, over the company of the tribe of Benjaminites. 25Finally, as rear guard for all the camps, the divisional camp of the Danites set out, arranged in companies. Over its whole company was Ahiezer, son of Ammishaddai, 26with Pagiel, son of Ochran, over the company of the tribe of Asherites, 27and Ahira, son of Enan, over the company of the tribe of Naphtalites. 28This was the order of march for the Israelites, company by company, when they set out.

Hobab as Guide. 29Moses said to Hobab,* son of Reuel the Midianite, Moses' father-in-law, "We are setting out for the place concerning which the LORD has said, 'I will give it to you.' Come with us, and we will be generous toward you, for the LORD has prom-

10:10 When you rejoice: cf. Dt 16:14. **Festivals**: the great annual feasts of the Passover, Pentecost and Booths described in Lv 23; Nm 28–29.

10:29–32 Hobab: one of three names for the father-in-law of Moses (see Ex 2:18; 4:18; 18:6; Jgs 4:11). Here perhaps Hobab's initial refusal indicates he wished to be coaxed before granting the favor. From Jgs 1:16 it seems probable that he did accede to Moses' request. However, Ex 18:27 suggests Moses' father-in-law returned to his own land. Indeed, to the extent Nm 10:29–32 appears to repeat Ex 18:27, it may indicate a resumption of the narrative of Israel's march through the wilderness after the "digression" formed by the Israelite sojourn at Sinai, Ex 19:1–Nm 10:28.

g: 2 Chr 13:14. *h:* Nm 29:1; 2 Chr 29:26–28. *i:* Nm 2:3, 5, 7.

ised prosperity to Israel." [30]But he answered, "No, I will not come. I am going instead to the land of my birth." [31]Moses said, "Please, do not leave us; you know where we can camp in the wilderness, and you can serve as our guide. [32]If you come with us, we will share with you the prosperity the LORD will bestow on us."

Into the Wilderness. [33j]From the mountain of the LORD* they made a journey of three days, and the ark of the covenant of the LORD went before them for the three-day journey to seek out a resting place for them. [34]And the cloud of the LORD was over them by day when they set out from camp.

[35]Whenever the ark set out, Moses would say,

"Arise, O LORD, may your enemies be
  scattered,
 and may those who hate you flee
  before you."

[36]And when it came to rest, he would say,

"Bring back, O LORD, the myriads of
  Israel's troops!"

CHAPTER 11

See RG 135–36

Discontent of the People. [1]Now the people complained bitterly in the hearing of the LORD;[k] and when he heard it his wrath flared up, so that the LORD's fire burned among them and consumed the outskirts of the camp. [2]But when the people cried out to Moses, he prayed to the LORD and the fire died out. [3]Hence that place was called Taberah,* because there the fire of the LORD burned among them.

[4]The riffraff among them were so greedy for meat that even the Israelites lamented again,[l] "If only we had meat for food! [5]We remember the fish we used to eat without cost in Egypt, and the cucumbers, the melons, the leeks, the onions, and the garlic. [6]But now we are famished; we have nothing to look forward to but this manna."[m]

[7n]Manna was like coriander seed* and had the appearance of bdellium. [8]When they had gone about and gathered it up, the people would grind it between millstones or pound it in a mortar, then cook it in a pot and make it into loaves, with a rich creamy taste. [9]At night, when the dew fell upon the camp, the manna also fell.[o]

[10]When Moses heard the people, family after family, crying at the entrance of their tents, so that the LORD became very angry, he was grieved. [11]"Why do you treat your servant so badly?" Moses asked the LORD. "Why are you so displeased with me that you burden me with all this people? [12]Was it I who conceived all this people? or was it I who gave them birth, that you tell me to carry them at my breast, like a nurse carrying an infant, to the land you have promised under oath to their fathers? [13]Where can I get meat to give to all this people? For they are crying to me, 'Give us meat for our food.' [14]I cannot carry all this people by myself, for they are too heavy for me. [15]If this is the way you will deal with me, then please do me the favor of killing me at once, so that I need no longer face my distress."

The Seventy Elders. [16]Then the LORD said to Moses: Assemble for me seventy of the elders of Israel, whom you know to be elders and authorities among the people, and bring them to the tent of meeting. When they are in place beside you, [17]I will come down and speak with you there. I will also take some of the spirit that is on you and will confer it on them, that they may share the burden of the people with you. You will then not have to bear it by yourself.

[18]To the people, however, you shall say: "Sanctify yourselves for tomorrow, when you shall have meat to eat. For in the hearing of the LORD you have cried, 'If only we had

10:33 The mountain of the LORD: Sinai (Horeb), elsewhere always called "the mountain of God."

11:3 Taberah: means "the burning."

11:7 Coriander seed: see note on Ex 16:31. **Bdellium**: a transparent, amber-colored gum resin, which is also mentioned in Gn 2:12.

---

j: Dt 1:33. *k:* Dt 9:22. *l:* Ps 78:18. *m:* Nm 21:5; Ex 16:3; Acts 7:39. *n:* Ex 16:14–15, 31; Ps 78:24; Wis 16:20; Jn 6:31. *o:* Ex 16:14–15.

meat for food! Oh, how well off we were in Egypt!' Therefore the LORD will give you meat to eat, 19and you will eat it, not for one day, or two days, or five, or ten, or twenty days, 20but for a whole month—until it comes out of your very nostrils and becomes loathsome to you. For you have rejected the LORD who is in your midst, and in his presence you have cried, 'Why did we ever leave Egypt?' "

21But Moses said, "The people around me include six hundred thousand soldiers; yet you say, 'I will give them meat to eat for a whole month.' 22Can enough sheep and cattle be slaughtered for them? If all the fish of the sea were caught for them, would they have enough?" 23The LORD answered Moses: Is this beyond the LORD's reach? You shall see now whether or not what I have said to you takes place.

The Spirit on the Elders. 24So Moses went out and told the people what the LORD had said. Gathering seventy elders of the people, he had them stand around the tent. 25The LORD then came down in the cloud and spoke to him. Taking some of the spirit that was on Moses, he bestowed it on the seventy elders; and as the spirit came to rest on them, they prophesied* but did not continue.

26Now two men, one named Eldad and the other Medad, had remained in the camp, yet the spirit came to rest on them also. They too had been on the list, but had not gone out to the tent; and so they prophesied in the camp. 27So, when a young man ran and reported to Moses, "Eldad and Medad are prophesying in the camp," 28Joshua, son of Nun, who from his youth had been Moses' aide, said, "My lord, Moses, stop them." 29But Moses answered him, "Are you jealous for my sake? If only all the people of the LORD were prophets! If only the LORD would bestow his spirit on them!" 30Then Moses retired to the camp, along with the elders of Israel.

The Quail. 31There arose a wind[p] from the LORD that drove in quail from the sea and left them all around the camp site, to a distance of a day's journey and at a depth of two cubits upon the ground.* 32[q] So all that day, all night, and all the next day the people set about to gather in the quail. Even the one who got the least gathered ten homers* of them. Then they spread them out all around the camp. 33But while the meat was still between their teeth, before it could be chewed, the LORD's wrath flared up against the people, and the LORD struck them with a very great plague. 34So that place was named Kibroth-hattaavah,* because it was there that the greedy people were buried.

35From Kibroth-hattaavah the people set out for Hazeroth, where they stayed.

CHAPTER 12

See RG 135–36

Jealousy of Aaron and Miriam. 1Miriam and Aaron spoke against Moses on the pretext of the Cushite woman he had married; for he had in fact married a Cushite woman.* 2They complained,* "Is it through Moses alone that the LORD has spoken? Has he not spoken through us also?" And the LORD heard this. 3[r] Now the man Moses was very humble, more than anyone else on earth. 4So at once the LORD said to Moses and Aaron and Miriam: Come out, you three, to the tent of meeting. And the three of them went. 5Then the LORD came down in a column of cloud, and standing at the entrance of the tent, called, "Aaron and Miriam." When both came forward, 6the LORD said: Now listen to my words:

If there are prophets among you,
in visions I reveal myself to them,

11:25 They prophesied: in the sense, not of foretelling the future, but of speaking in enraptured enthusiasm. Such manifestations are mentioned in the early days of Hebrew prophecy (1 Sm 10:10–12; 19:20–21; Jl 3:1) and in the first years of the Church (Acts 2:6–11, 17; 19:6; 1 Cor 12–14).

11:31 The heaps of quail lying upon the ground all around the Israelites' camp suggest the ambiguity of God's response to the people's lament for meat in v. 4 and foreshadow the plague which God will now bring upon Israel (v. 33). Their request had been nothing less than a rejection of what God has done for them (v. 20).

11:32 Homers: see note on Is 5:10. **They spread them out**: to cure by drying.

11:34 Kibroth-hattaavah: means "graves of greed."

12:1 Cushite woman: apparently Zipporah, the Midianite, is meant; cf. Ex 2:21.

12:2 The apparent reason for Miriam's and Aaron's quarrel with their brother Moses was jealousy of his authority; his Cushite wife served only as an occasion for the dispute.

p: Ps 78:26–28. *q:* Ps 78:26–31. *r:* Sir 45:1–2.

in dreams I speak to them;
7 Not so with my servant Moses!
Throughout my house he is worthy of
trust:*[s]
8 face to face I speak to him,[t]
plainly and not in riddles.
The likeness of the LORD he beholds.

Why, then, do you not fear to speak against
my servant Moses? 9 And so the LORD's
wrath flared against them, and he departed.
Miriam's Punishment. 10 Now the cloud
withdrew from the tent, and there was Miriam,[u] stricken with a scaly infection, white
as snow!* When Aaron turned toward Miriam and saw her stricken with snow-white
scales, 11 he said to Moses, "Ah, my lord!
Please do not charge us with the sin that we
have foolishly committed! 12 Do not let her
be like the stillborn baby that comes forth
from its mother's womb with its flesh half
consumed." 13 Then Moses cried to the
LORD, "Please, not this! Please, heal her!"
14 But the LORD answered Moses: Suppose
her father had spit in her face, would she not
bear her shame for seven days? Let her be
confined outside the camp for seven days;
afterwards she may be brought back. 15 So
Miriam was confined outside the camp for
seven days, and the people did not start out
again until she was brought back.
16 After that the people set out from Hazeroth and encamped in the wilderness of Paran.

CHAPTER 13

See RG 135–36

The Twelve Scouts. 1 The LORD said to
Moses: 2 Send men to reconnoiter the land of
Canaan, which I am giving the Israelites.
You shall send one man from each ancestral
tribe, every one a leader among them. 3[v] So
Moses sent them from the wilderness of Paran, at the direction of the LORD. All of them
were leaders among the Israelites. 4 These
were their names:

from the tribe of Reuben, Shammua, son
of Zaccur;
5 from the tribe of Simeon, Shaphat, son of
Hori;
6 from the tribe of Judah, Caleb, son of
Jephunneh;
7 from the tribe of Issachar, Igal;
8 for the Josephites, from the tribe of
Ephraim, Hoshea, son of Nun;
9 from the tribe of Benjamin, Palti, son of
Raphu;
10 from the tribe of Zebulun, Gaddiel, son
of Sodi;
11 for the Josephites, from the tribe of
Manasseh, Gaddi, son of Susi;
12 from the tribe of Dan, Ammiel, son of
Gemalli;
13 from the tribe of Asher, Sethur, son of
Michael;
14 from the tribe of Naphtali, Nahbi, son of
Vophsi;
15 from the tribe of Gad, Geuel, son of Machi.

16 These are the names of the men whom
Moses sent to reconnoiter the land. But Hoshea, son of Nun, Moses called Joshua.*
17 In sending them to reconnoiter the land
of Canaan, Moses said to them, "Go up there
in the Negeb, up into the highlands, 18 and
see what kind of land it is and whether the
people living there are strong or weak, few
or many. 19 Is the country in which they live
good or bad? Are the towns in which they
dwell open or fortified? 20 Is the soil fertile or
barren, wooded or clear? And do your best to
get some of the fruit of the land." It was then
the season for early grapes.
21 So they went up and reconnoitered the
land from the wilderness of Zin* as far as
where Rehob adjoins Lebo-hamath. 22[w] Go-

12:7 Worthy of trust: the text is open to a variety of interpretations. Thus, the word of Moses may be relied upon by Israel because God speaks to him directly; or, Moses alone is worthy of God's trust in God's household (heavenly or earthly). An alternative translation, however, is: "with all my house he is entrusted."

12:10 Stricken with a scaly infection, white as snow: see note on Lv 13:1–14:47. The point of the simile lies either in the flakiness or the whiteness of snow.

13:16 Joshua: in Hebrew, "Jehoshua," which was later modified to "Jeshua," the Hebrew name for "Jesus." Hoshea and Joshua are variants of one original name meaning "the LORD saves." Cf. Mt 1:21.

13:21 The wilderness of Zin: north of Paran and southwest of the Dead Sea. It is quite distinct from "the wilderness of Sin" near the border of Egypt (Ex 16:1; 17:1; Nm 33:11). **Lebo-hamath**: a town near Riblah (Jer 39:5–6) at the south-

s: Heb 3:2, 5. *t:* Ex 33:1; Dt 34:10; Sir 45:3. *u:* Dt 24:9. *v:* Dt 1:22–28. *w:* Jos 11:21–22.

ing up by way of the Negeb, they reached Hebron, where Ahiman, Sheshai and Talmai, descendants of the Anakim,* were. (Now Hebron had been built seven years before Zoan in Egypt.) [23]They also reached the Wadi Eshcol,* where they cut down a branch with a single cluster of grapes on it, which two of them carried on a pole, as well as some pomegranates and figs. [24]It was because of the cluster the Israelites cut there that they called the place Wadi Eshcol.[x]

Their Report. [25]They returned from reconnoitering the land forty days later. [26y] Proceeding directly to Moses and Aaron and the whole community of the Israelites in the wilderness of Paran at Kadesh, they made a report to them and to the whole community, showing them the fruit of the land. [27]They told Moses: "We came to the land to which you sent us. It does indeed flow with milk and honey, and here is its fruit. [28]However, the people who are living in the land are powerful, and the towns are fortified and very large.[z] Besides, we saw descendants of the Anakim there. [29]Amalekites live in the region of the Negeb; Hittites, Jebusites and Amorites dwell in the highlands, and Canaanites along the sea and the banks of the Jordan."

[30]Caleb, however, quieted the people before Moses and said, "We ought to go up and seize the land, for we can certainly prevail over it." [31]But the men who had gone up with him said, "We cannot attack these people; they are too strong for us." [32]They spread discouraging reports[a] among the Israelites about the land they had reconnoitered, saying, "The land that we went through and reconnoitered is a land that consumes its inhabitants. And all the people we saw there are huge. [33b] There we saw the Nephilim* (the Anakim are from the Nephilim); in our own eyes we seemed like mere grasshoppers, and so we must have seemed to them."

CHAPTER 14

See RG 135–36

Threats of Revolt. [1]At this, the whole community broke out with loud cries, and the people wept into the night. [2c] All the Israelites grumbled against Moses and Aaron, the whole community saying to them, "If only we had died in the land of Egypt," or "If only we would die here in the wilderness! [3]Why is the LORD bringing us into this land only to have us fall by the sword? Our wives and little ones will be taken as spoil. Would it not be better for us to return to Egypt?" [4]So they said to one another, "Let us appoint a leader and go back to Egypt."

[5]But Moses and Aaron fell prostrate before the whole assembled community of the Israelites; [6]while Joshua, son of Nun, and Caleb, son of Jephunneh, who had been among those that reconnoitered the land, tore their garments [7]and said to the whole community of the Israelites,[d] "The land which we went through and reconnoitered is an exceedingly good land. [8]If the LORD is pleased with us, he will bring us in to this land and give it to us, a land which flows with milk and honey. [9e] Only do not rebel against the LORD! You need not be afraid of the people of the land, for they are but food for us!* Their protection has left them, but the LORD is with us. Do not fear them."

The Lord's Sentence. [10]The whole community threatened to stone them. But the glory of the LORD appeared at the tent of meeting to all the Israelites. [11]And the LORD said to Moses: How long will this people spurn me? How long will they not trust me, despite all the signs I have performed among them?[f] [12]I will strike them with pestilence

ern border of Hamath, an independent kingdom in southern Syria. David's conquests extended as far as Hamath (2 Sm 8:9–11), and Lebo-hamath thus formed the northern border of the ideal extent of Israel's possessions (Nm 34:7–9; Ez 47:15; 48:1). This may suggest that this verse was inserted precisely to extend the scope of the reconnaissance; cf. Dt 1:24.

13:22, 28 Anakim: an aboriginal race in southern Palestine, largely absorbed by the Canaanites. Either because of their tall stature or because of the massive stone structures left by them, the Israelites regarded them as giants.

13:23 Eshcol: means "cluster."

13:33 Nephilim: i.e., "fallen ones" (in the Septuagint, "giants"), a reference to fallen heroes of old. Cf. Gn 6:4.

14:9 They are but food for us: lit., "for they are our bread." "Bread" (Heb. *lechem*) is here used in the sense of "prey, spoils" to be consumed by an invader. This is the answer to the pessimistic report that this land "consumes its inhabitants" (13:32).

x: Nm 32:9; Dt 1:24–25. *y:* Ex 3:8, 17. *z:* Dt 9:1–2. *a:* Nm 32:9; Jos 14:8. *b:* Dt 2:10. *c:* Ex 16:3; Ps 106:25. *d:* Dt 1:25. *e:* Dt 7:18. *f:* Ps 78:22, 32.

and disown them. Then I will make of you a
nation greater and mightier than they.[g]
13[h] But Moses said to the LORD: "The
Egyptians will hear of this, for by your power
you brought out this people from among
them. 14They will tell the inhabitants of this
land, who have heard that you, LORD, are in
the midst of this people; you, LORD, who directly revealed yourself! Your cloud stands
over them, and you go before them by day in
a column of cloud and by night in a column of
fire.[i] 15If now you slay this people all at once,
the nations who have heard such reports of
you will say, 16'The LORD was not able to
bring this people into the land he swore to
give them; that is why he slaughtered them in
the wilderness.'[j] 17Now then, may my Lord's
forbearance be great, even as you have said,
18[k] 'The LORD is slow to anger and abounding
in kindness, forgiving iniquity and rebellion;
yet certainly not declaring the guilty guiltless,
but punishing children to the third and fourth
generation for their parents' iniquity.' 19Par-
don, then, the iniquity of this people in keeping with your great kindness, even as you
have forgiven them from Egypt until now."[l]
20The LORD answered: I pardon them as
you have asked. 21Yet, by my life and the
LORD's glory that fills the whole earth, 22of
all the people who have seen my glory and
the signs I did in Egypt and in the wilderness,[m] and who nevertheless have put me to
the test ten times already and have not
obeyed me, 23not one shall see the land
which I promised on oath to their ancestors.
None of those who have spurned me shall
see it. 24But as for my servant Caleb, because he has a different spirit and follows me
unreservedly,[n] I will bring him into the land
which he entered, and his descendants shall
possess it. 25But now, since the Amalekites
and Canaanites are living in the valleys,*
turn away tomorrow and set out into the wilderness by way of the Red Sea road.
26The LORD also said to Moses and Aaron:
27How long will this wicked community
grumble against me?[o] I have heard the grumblings of the Israelites against me. 28Tell
them:* "By my life"—oracle of the LORD—
"I will do to you just what I have heard you
say. 29Here in the wilderness[p] your dead
bodies shall fall. Of all your men of twenty
years or more, enrolled in your registration,
who grumbled against me, 30not one of you
shall enter the land where I solemnly swore
to settle you, except Caleb, son of Jephunneh, and Joshua, son of Nun. 31Your little
ones, however, who you said would be taken
as spoil, I will bring in, and they shall know
the land you rejected.[q] 32But as for you, your
bodies shall fall here in the wilderness,
33while your children will wander for forty
years, suffering for your infidelity, till the
last of you lies dead in the wilderness.[r]
34Corresponding to the number of days you
spent reconnoitering the land—forty days—
you shall bear your punishment one year for
each day: forty years. Thus you will realize
what it means to oppose me. 35I, the LORD,
have spoken; and I will surely do this to this
entire wicked community that conspired
against me: here in the wilderness they shall
come to their end and there they will die."
36And the men whom Moses had sent to
reconnoiter the land[s] and who on returning
had set the whole community grumbling
against him by spreading discouraging reports about the land— 37these men who had
spread discouraging reports about the land
were struck down by the LORD and died.
38Only Joshua, son of Nun, and Caleb, son
of Jephunneh, survived of all the men who
had gone to reconnoiter the land.[t]
Unsuccessful Invasion. 39When Moses repeated these words to all the Israelites, the
people mourned greatly. 40Early the next
morning they started up high into the hill
country, saying, "Here we are, ready to go

14:25 The valleys: the low-lying plains in the Negeb and along the seacoast and in the Jordan depression, as well as the higher valleys in the mountains farther north: cf. v. 45.

14:28–29 God punished the grumblers by giving them their wish; cf. v. 2. Their lack of trust in God is cited in 1 Cor 10:10 and Heb 3:12–18 as a warning for Christians.

g: Ex 32:10. *h:* Ex 32:12; Dt 9:26–29; Ps 106:23. *i:* Ex 13:21; Jos 2:9–10. *j:* Ex 32:12; Dt 9:28. *k:* Ex 20:5; 34:6–7; Ps 103:8; 145:8. *l:* Ps 78:38. *m:* Dt 1:35. *n:* Jos 14:8–9. *o:* Ex 16:7, 12. *p:* Dt 1:35; Heb 3:17. *q:* Dt 1:39. *r:* Nm 13:26; 32:13; Ps 95:10; Ez 4:6. *s:* Nm 13:17, 32–33; 1 Cor 10:10. *t:* Nm 26:65.

up to the place that the LORD spoke of:[u] for we did wrong." 41 But Moses said, "Why are you now transgressing the LORD's order? This cannot succeed. 42 Do not go up, because the LORD is not in your midst; do not allow yourself to be struck down by your enemies.[v] 43 For there the Amalekites and Canaanites will face you, and you will fall by the sword. You have turned back from following the LORD; therefore the LORD will not be with you."

44 Yet they dared to go up high into the hill country,[w] even though neither the ark of the covenant of the LORD nor Moses left the camp. 45 And the Amalekites and Canaanites who dwelt in that hill country came down and defeated them, beating them back as far as Hormah.*

CHAPTER 15

See RG 135–36

Secondary Offerings. 1 The LORD spoke to Moses: 2* Speak to the Israelites and say to them: When you enter the land that I am giving you for your settlements, 3 if you make to the LORD an oblation from the herd or from the flock—either a burnt offering or a sacrifice, to fulfill a vow, or as a voluntary offering, or for one of your festivals—to produce a pleasing aroma for the LORD, 4 the one presenting the offering shall also present to the LORD a grain offering, a tenth of a measure* of bran flour mixed with a fourth of a hin of oil, 5 as well as wine for a libation, a fourth of a hin. You will do this with the burnt offering or the sacrifice, for each lamb. 6 Alternatively for a ram you shall make a grain offering of two tenths of a measure of bran flour mixed with a third of a hin of oil, 7 and for a libation, a third of a hin of wine, thereby presenting a pleasing aroma to the LORD. 8 If you make an offering from the herd—either a burnt offering, or a sacrifice, to fulfill a vow, or as a communion offering to the LORD, 9 with it a grain offering of three tenths of a measure of bran flour mixed with half a hin of oil will be presented; 10 and you will present for a libation, half a hin of wine—a sweet-smelling oblation to the LORD. 11 The same is to be done for each ox, ram, lamb or goat. 12 Whatever the number you offer, do the same for each of them.

13 All the native-born shall make these offerings in this way, whenever they present a sweet-smelling oblation to the LORD. 14 Likewise, in any future generation, any alien residing with you or anyone else in your midst, who presents an oblation of pleasing aroma to the LORD, must do as you do. 15 There is but one statute for you and for the resident alien, a perpetual statute throughout your generations. You and the resident alien will be alike before the LORD; 16 you and the alien residing with you will have the same rule and the same application of it.

17 The LORD spoke to Moses: 18 Speak to the Israelites and say to them: When you enter the land into which I am bringing you 19 and eat of the bread of the land, you shall offer the LORD a contribution. 20 A round loaf from your first batch of dough* you shall offer as a contribution. Just like a contribution from the threshing floor you shall offer it.[x] 21 Throughout your generations you shall give a contribution to the LORD from your first batch of dough.

Purification Offerings.* 22 If through inadvertence you fail to do any of these commandments which the LORD has given to

---

14:45 Hormah: one of the Canaanite royal cities in southern Judah, according to the tradition attested in Jos 12:14, although Nm 21:1–3 gives it as the new name for the city of Arad when it was destroyed by Israel. According to the list of conquered cities preserved in Jgs 1, the earlier name for the city of Hormah was Zephath. The precise location is unknown.

15:2–16 These laws on sacrifice are complementary to those of Lv 1–3. Since the food of the Israelites consisted not only of meat but also of bread, oil and wine, they offered flour, wine and oil in sacrifice to the Lord besides the animal oblations.

15:4 Measure: the word, supplied from the context, does not appear in the Hebrew (as also in vv. 6, 9; 28:9, 12, 20, 28; 29:3, 9, 14). Probably the ephah (which is named in 5:15; 28:5) is intended. **Hin**: see note on Ez 45:24.

15:20 Dough: the meaning of the Hebrew term is uncertain; some render, "baking utensils." This word is used elsewhere only in Ez 44:30 and Neh 10:33; a related Hebrew word is used in Lv 2:14.

15:22–31 See note on Lv 4:2. Although Lv 4–5 and Nm 15:22–31 both concern inadvertent sins, the emphasis here, as opposed to Lv 4–5, is on the failure of the community to perform "positive commands" rather than on doing what is prohibited.

u: Nm 13:18; Dt 1:41. *v*: Dt 1:42. *w*: Dt 1:43. *x*: Ez 44:30.

Moses—[y] [23]anything the LORD commanded you through Moses from the time the LORD first gave the command down through your generations— [24]if it was done inadvertently without the community's knowledge, the whole community shall sacrifice one bull from the herd as a burnt offering of pleasing aroma to the LORD, along with its prescribed grain offering and libation, as well as one he-goat as a purification offering. [25][z] Then the priest shall make atonement for the whole Israelite community; and they will be forgiven, since it was inadvertence, and for their inadvertence they have brought their offering: an oblation to the LORD as well as their purification offering before the LORD. [26]Not only the whole Israelite community but also the aliens residing among you shall be forgiven, since the inadvertent fault affects all the people.

[27]If it is an individual who sins inadvertently,[a] this person shall bring a yearling she-goat as a purification offering. [28]And the priest shall make atonement before the LORD for the one who erred, since the sin was inadvertent, making atonement for the person to secure forgiveness. [29]You shall have but one rule for the person who sins inadvertently, whether a native-born Israelite or an alien residing among you.

[30]But anyone who acts defiantly,[b] whether a native or an alien, reviles the LORD, and shall be cut off from among the people. [31][c] For having despised the word of the LORD and broken his commandment, he must be cut off entirely and bear the punishment.

The Sabbath-breaker. [32]While the Israelites were in the wilderness, a man was discovered gathering wood on the sabbath day. [33]Those who caught him at it brought him to Moses and Aaron and the whole community. [34]But they put him in custody, for there was no clear decision* as to what should be done with him.[d] [35]Then the LORD said to Moses: This man shall be put to death; let the whole community stone him outside the camp. [36]So the whole community led him outside the camp and stoned him to death, as the LORD had commanded Moses.

Tassels on the Cloak. [37]The LORD said to Moses: [38]Speak to the Israelites and tell them that throughout their generations they are to make tassels* for the corners of their garments, fastening a violet cord to each corner.[e] [39]When you use these tassels, the sight of the cord will remind you of all the commandments of the LORD and you will do them, without prostituting yourself going after the desires of your hearts and your eyes. [40]Thus you will remember to do all my commandments and you will be holy to your God. [41]I, the LORD, am your God who brought you out of the land of Egypt to be your God: I, the LORD your God.[f]

CHAPTER 16

See RG 135–36

Rebellion of Korah. [1]* Korah, son of Izhar, son of Kohath, son of Levi, and the Reubenites Dathan and Abiram, sons of Eliab, and On, son of Peleth,* son of Reuben took [2]two hundred and fifty Israelites who were leaders in the community, members of

15:34 No clear decision: either it was not clear that gathering wood constituted "work" and as such a willful violation of the sabbath and a capital offense; or they did not yet know how the death penalty was to be inflicted.

15:38 Tassels: at the time of Jesus these tassels were worn by all pious Jews, including Jesus (Mt 9:20–21; Mk 6:56); some Pharisees wore very large ones in a display of their zeal for the law (Mt 23:5).

16:1–3 The evidence seems to show that accounts of two, if not more, distinct rebellions have been combined in this chapter. The most obvious are the rebellions of Korah and his faction (Nm 27:3) and of Dathan and Abiram (Dt 11:6); cf. Ps 106. The present account combines both events into one narrative; but even here it is rather easy to separate the two. The rebellion of the Reubenites, Dathan and Abiram, was more political in character, against Moses alone as the civil leader (cf. v. 13); these rebels were punished by being swallowed alive in an earthquake. The rebellion of Korah was more religious in character, directed primarily against the religious leadership of Aaron (though in vv. 19–22 it is Korah and the whole community against both Moses and Aaron). About two hundred and fifty malcontents joined Korah's faction, and they are punished by fire. The parts of the present section which refer to the rebellion of Dathan and Abiram are vv. 12–15 and vv. 25–34 of chap. 16; the rest of chap. 16 and all of chap. 17 chiefly concern the rebellion of Korah.

16:1 The Reubenites . . . son of Peleth: some suggest on the basis of 26:5, 8 and Gn 46:9 reading instead of the traditional Hebrew text: "son of Levi, and Dathan and Abiram, sons of Eliab, son of Pallu, son of Reuben."

y: Lv 4:13–14. *z:* Lv 4:20. *a:* Lv 4:27–28. *b:* Dt 17:12. *c:* Prv 13:13. *d:* Lv 24:12. *e:* Dt 22:12. *f:* Lv 22:32–33.

the council and men of note, and confronted
Moses. [3]Holding an assembly against Moses
and Aaron, they said,[g] "You go too far! The
whole community, all of them, are holy; the
LORD is in their midst. Why then should you
set yourselves over the LORD's assembly?"
[4]When Moses heard this, he fell prostrate.
[5]Then he said to Korah and to all his faction,
"May the LORD make known tomorrow
morning who belongs to him and who is the
holy one and whom he will have draw near
to him! The one whom he chooses, he will
have draw near to him. [6]Do this: take your
censers, Korah and all his faction, [7]and put
fire in them and place incense in them before
the LORD tomorrow. He whom the LORD
then chooses is the holy one. You Levites go
too far!"
[8]Moses also said to Korah, "Hear, now,
you Levites! [9][h] Are you not satisfied that the
God of Israel has singled you out from the
community of Israel, to have you draw near
him to maintain the LORD's tabernacle, and to
attend upon the community and to serve
them? [10]He has allowed you and your Levite
kinsmen with you to approach him, and yet
you seek the priesthood too. [11]It is therefore
against the LORD that you and all your faction
are conspiring. As for Aaron, what has he
done that you should grumble against him?"
Rebellion of Dathan and Abiram. [12]Moses
summoned Dathan and Abiram, sons of
Eliab, but they answered, "We will not go.*
[13]Are you not satisfied that you have brought
us here from a land flowing with milk and
honey to have us perish in the wilderness,
that now you must also lord it over us? [14]Far
from bringing us to a land flowing with milk
and honey, or giving us fields and vineyards
for our inheritance, will you gouge out our
eyes?* No, we will not go."
[15]Then Moses became very angry and said
to the LORD, "Pay no attention to their offering. I have never taken a single donkey from
them, nor have I wronged any one of them."[i]
Korah. [16]Moses said to Korah, "You and
all your faction shall appear before the LORD
tomorrow—you and they and Aaron too.
[17]Then each of you take his own censer, put
incense in it, and present it before the LORD,
two hundred and fifty censers; and you and
Aaron, each with his own censer, do the
same." [18]So each of them took their censers,
and laying incense on the fire they had put in
them, they took their stand by the entrance
of the tent of meeting along with Moses and
Aaron. [19]Then, when Korah had assembled
all the community against them at the entrance of the tent of meeting, the glory of the
LORD appeared to the entire community,
[20]and the LORD said to Moses and Aaron:
[21]Stand apart from this community, that I
may consume them at once. [22]But they fell
prostrate and exclaimed, "O God, God of the
spirits of all living creatures, if one man sins
will you be angry with the whole community?" [23]The LORD answered Moses:
[24]Speak to the community and tell them:
Withdraw from the area around the tent* of
Korah, Dathan and Abiram.
Punishment of Dathan and Abiram. [25]Mo-
ses, followed by the elders of Israel, arose
and went to Dathan and Abiram.* [26]Then he
spoke to the community, "Move away from
the tents of these wicked men and do not
touch anything that is theirs: otherwise you
too will be swept away because of all their
sins." [27]So they withdrew from the area
around the tents of Korah, Dathan and Abiram. When Dathan and Abiram had come out
and were standing at the entrance of their
tents with their wives, their children, and
their little ones, [28]Moses said, "This is how
you shall know that the LORD sent me to do
all I have done, and that it was not of my own
devising: [29]if these die an ordinary death,

16:12 We will not go: to appear before Moses' "tribunal."

16:14 Gouge out our eyes: blind us to the real state of affairs.

16:24 Withdraw from the area around the tent: the word for "tent," *mishkan*, here and in v. 27, is otherwise used in the singular only for the tent of meeting, suggesting possibly the erection of a rival sanctuary by the rebels. Note further, as an indication of the fact that various accounts of rebellion have been fused here, that in v. 19 the entire community had been assembled by Korah at the tent of meeting.

16:25 Since Dathan and Abiram had refused to go to Moses (vv. 12–14), he, with the elders as witnesses, was obliged to go to their tents.

g: Ps 106:16–18; Sir 45:19. *h:* Dt 10:8. *i:* 1 Sm 12:3.

merely suffering the fate common to all humanity, the LORD has not sent me. 30But if the LORD makes a chasm, and the ground opens its mouth and swallows them with all belonging to them, and they go down alive to Sheol,* then you will know that these men have spurned the LORD." 31[j] No sooner had he finished saying all this than the ground beneath them split open, 32and the earth opened its mouth and swallowed them and their families and all of Korah's people* with all their possessions. 33They went down alive to Sheol with all belonging to them; the earth closed over them, and they disappeared from the assembly. 34But all the Israelites near them fled at their shrieks, saying, "The earth might swallow us too!"

Punishment of Korah. 35And fire from the LORD came forth which consumed the two hundred and fifty men who were offering the incense.

CHAPTER 17

See RG 135–36

1The LORD said to Moses: 2Tell Eleazar, son of Aaron the priest, to remove the censers from the embers; and scatter the fire some distance away, for they have become holy— 3* the censers of those who sinned at the cost of their lives. Have them hammered into plates to cover the altar, because in being presented before the LORD they have become holy. In this way they shall serve as a sign to the Israelites. 4So taking the bronze censers which had been presented by those who were burned, Eleazar the priest had them hammered into a covering for the altar, 5just as the LORD had directed him through Moses. This was to be a reminder to the Israelites that no unauthorized person, no one who was not a descendant of Aaron, should draw near to offer incense before the LORD, lest he meet the fate of Korah and his faction.

6The next day the whole Israelite community grumbled against Moses and Aaron, saying, "You have killed the people of the LORD." 7But while the community was assembling against them, Moses and Aaron turned toward the tent of meeting, and the cloud now covered it and the glory of the LORD appeared. 8Then Moses and Aaron came to the front of the tent of meeting, 9and the LORD said to Moses: 10Remove yourselves from this community, that I may consume them at once. But they fell prostrate.

11Then Moses said to Aaron, "Take your censer, put fire from the altar in it, lay incense on it, and bring it quickly to the community to make atonement for them; for wrath has come forth from the LORD and the plague has begun."[k] 12Aaron took his censer just as Moses directed and ran in among the assembly, where the plague had already begun among the people. Then he offered the incense and made atonement for the people, 13while standing there between the living and the dead. And so the scourge was checked. 14There were fourteen thousand seven hundred dead from the scourge, in addition to those who died because of Korah. 15When the scourge had been checked, Aaron returned to Moses at the entrance of the tent of meeting.

Aaron's Staff. 16The LORD now said to Moses: 17Speak to the Israelites and get from them a staff* for each ancestral house, twelve staffs in all, from all the leaders of their ancestral houses. Write each man's name on his staff; 18and write Aaron's name on Levi's staff.* For each head of an ances-

16:30 Sheol: see note on Ps 6:6.

16:32 And all of Korah's people: the implication of this secondary addition to the text is, on the one hand, that Korah met his death elsewhere, presumably with the two hundred and fifty offering incense (vv. 16–17, 35); or, on the other hand, he died along with Dathan and Abiram in the splitting of the earth.

17:3 Whatever was brought into intimate contact with something holy shared in its holiness. See note on 19:20.

17:17 The staff was not merely an article of practical use, but also a symbol of authority; cf. Gn 49:10; Nm 24:17; Jer 48:17. Therefore, the staff of a leader of a tribe was considered the emblem of the tribe; in fact, certain Hebrew words such as *matteh*, the word for "staff" here, also mean "tribe." Perhaps for this reason, to avoid confusion, the author here uses the term *bet'ab*, "ancestral house," for "tribe" instead of one of the ordinary words for "tribe."

17:18 Levi's staff: it is not clear whether this is considered as one of the twelve mentioned in the preceding verse, or as a thirteenth staff. Sometimes Levi is reckoned as one of the twelve tribes (e.g., Dt 27:12–13), but more often the number twelve is arrived at by counting the two sub-tribes of Joseph, i.e., Ephraim and Manasseh, as distinct tribes. In this passage also it seems probable that the tribe of Levi is considered apart from the other twelve tribes.

j: Nm 26:10; Lv 10:2; Dt 11:6; Ps 106:17–18. *k:* Wis 18:20–21.

tral house shall have a staff. 19Then deposit
them in the tent of meeting, in front of the
covenant, where I meet you. 20The staff of
the man whom I choose shall sprout. Thus I
will rid myself of the Israelites' grumbling
against you.

21So Moses spoke to the Israelites, and all
their leaders gave him staffs, twelve in all,
one from each leader of their ancestral
houses; and Aaron's staff was among them.
22Then Moses deposited the staffs before the
LORD in the tent of the covenant. 23The next
day, when Moses entered the tent of the covenant, Aaron's staff, representing the house
of Levi, had sprouted. It had put forth
sprouts, produced blossoms, and borne ripe
almonds! 24So Moses brought out all the
staffs from the LORD's presence to all the Israelites, and each one identified his own
staff and took it. 25Then the LORD said to
Moses: Put back Aaron's staff in front of the
covenant, for safe keeping as a sign to the rebellious, so that their grumbling against me
may cease and they might not die. 26Moses
did this. Just as the LORD had commanded
him, so he did.

Charge of the Sacred Things. 27* Then the
Israelites exclaimed to Moses, "We will perish; we are lost, we are all lost! 28Anyone who
approaches the tabernacle of the LORD will
die! Will there be no end to our perishing?"

CHAPTER 18

See RG 135–36

1The LORD said to Aaron:* You and
your sons as well as your ancestral house
with you* shall be responsible for any sin
with respect to the sanctuary; but only you
and your sons with you shall be responsible
for any sin with respect to your priesthood.
2You shall also present with you your kinsmen of the tribe of Levi, your ancestral tribe,
that they may be joined to you* and assist
you, while you and your sons with you are in
front of the tent of the covenant. 3They shall
discharge your obligations and those with
respect to the whole tent; however, they
shall not come near the utensils of the sanctuary or the altar, or else both they and you
will die. 4They will be joined to you to perform the duties associated with the tent of
meeting, all the labor pertaining to the tent.
But no unauthorized person* shall come near
you. 5You shall perform the duties of the
sanctuary and of the altar, that wrath may not
fall again upon the Israelites.

6I hereby take your kinsmen, the Levites,
from among the Israelites; they are a gift to
you,[l] dedicated to the LORD for the labor
they perform for the tent of meeting. 7[m] But
you and your sons with you must take care to
exercise your priesthood in whatever concerns the altar and the area within the veil.* I
give you your priesthood as a gift. Any
unauthorized person who comes near shall
be put to death.

The Priests' Share of the Sacrifices. 8The
LORD said to Aaron:* I hereby give to you
charge of the contributions made to me, including the various holy offerings of the Israelites;[n] I assign them to you and to your
sons as a perquisite, a perpetual due. 9This is
what you shall have from the oblations that
are most holy: every offering of theirs—
namely, all their grain offerings, purification
offerings, and reparation offerings which
they must return to me—shall be most holy
for you and for your sons. 10You shall eat
them in a most holy place;* every male may
partake of them. As holy, they belong to you.

11This also you shall have: the contribu-

17:27–28 The people's distress here echoes their panic in 16:34, and may be heightened further by the death of the two hundred and fifty leaders offering incense in 16:35.

18:1–3 This law, which kept unqualified persons from contact with holy things, is in response to the Israelites' cry in 17:28. It is followed by other laws concerning priests and Levites.

18:1 With you: not only in the present but also those of his house in the future.

18:2 Be joined to you: in Hebrew a pun on the popular etymology of the name "Levi." Cf. Gn 29:34.

18:4 Unauthorized person: here, "one who is not a Levite"; in v. 7, "one who is not a priest."

18:7 Veil: the outer veil, or "curtain," is probably meant.

18:8–10 Two classes of offerings are here distinguished: the most holy offering, which only the male members of the priestly families could eat (vv. 8–10), and the other offerings, which the women of the priestly families could eat (vv. 11–19).

18:10 In a most holy place: in the court of the tabernacle, according to Lv 6:9, 19.

l: Nm 3:9; 8:19. *m:* Nm 3:10. *n:* Nm 5:9.

tions that are their gifts, including the elevated offering* of the Israelites; I assign them to you and to your sons and daughters with you as a perpetual due.[o] All in your household who are clean may eat them. [12]I also assign to you all the best[p] of the new oil and of the new wine and grain that they give to the LORD as their first produce that has been processed. [13]The first-ripened fruits of whatever is in their land, which they bring to the LORD, shall be yours; all of your household who are clean may eat them. [14]Whatever is under the ban* in Israel shall be yours. [15]Every living thing that opens the womb, human being and beast alike, such as are to be offered to the LORD, shall be yours;[q] but you must redeem the firstborn of human beings, as well as redeem the firstborn of unclean animals. [16]For the redemption price of a son, when he is a month old, you shall pay the equivalent of five silver shekels according to the sanctuary shekel, that is, twenty gerahs. [17]But the firstborn of cattle, or the firstborn of sheep or the firstborn of goats you shall not redeem; they are holy. Their blood you must splash on the altar and their fat you must burn as an oblation of pleasing aroma to the LORD. [18r] Their meat, however, shall be yours, just as the brisket of the elevated offering and the right thigh belong to you. [19]As a perpetual due I assign to you and to your sons and daughters with you all the contributions of holy things which the Israelites set aside for the LORD; this is a covenant of salt* to last forever before the LORD, for you and for your descendants with you. [20s] Then the LORD said to Aaron:* You shall not have any heritage in their land nor hold any portion among them; I will be your portion and your heritage among the Israelites.

Tithes Due the Levites. [21]To the Levites, however, I hereby assign all tithes in Israel as their heritage in recompense for the labor they perform, the labor pertaining to the tent of meeting.[t] [22]The Israelites may no longer approach the tent of meeting, thereby incurring the penalty of death. [23]Only the Levites are to perform the labor pertaining to the tent of meeting, and they shall incur the penalty for the Israelites' sin;* this is a permanent statute for all your generations. But they shall not have any heritage among the Israelites, [24]for I have assigned to the Levites as their heritage the tithes which the Israelites put aside as a contribution to the LORD. That is why I have said, they will not have any heritage among the Israelites.

Tithes Paid by the Levites. [25]The LORD said to Moses: [26]Speak to the Levites and say to them: When you take from the Israelites the tithes I have assigned you from them as your heritage, you are to make a contribution from them to the LORD, a tithe of the tithe; [27]and your contribution will be credited to you as if it were grain from the threshing floor or new wine from the vat. [28]Thus you too shall make a contribution to the LORD from all the tithes you take from the Israelites, handing over to Aaron the priest the contribution to the LORD. [29]From all the gifts to you, you shall make every contribution due to the LORD—from their best parts, that is the part to be consecrated from them.

[30]Say to them also: Once you have made your contribution from the best part, the rest of the tithe will be credited to the Levites as if it were produce of the threshing floor or

18:11 Elevated offering: this included the brisket and right thigh (v. 18), the shoulder of the peace offering (Lv 7:30–34), and portions of the nazirite sacrifice (Nm 6:19–20). **With you**: see note on v. 1. Aaron had no daughters; see also v. 19.

18:14 Under the ban: in Hebrew, *herem*, which means here "set aside from profane use and made sacred to the Lord." Cf. Lv 27:21, 28.

18:19 A covenant of salt: cf. 2 Chr 13:5. The reference may perhaps be to the preservative power of salt (cf. Mt 5:13); but more likely the phrase refers to the custom of eating salt together to render a contract unbreakable. See note on Lv 2:13.

18:20 The priests and Levites were forbidden to own hereditary land such as the other Israelites possessed; therefore in the allotment of the land (chap. 34) they did not receive any portion of it. Certain cities, however, were assigned to them for their residence; cf. 35:1–8.

18:23 Incur the penalty for the Israelites' sin: the Levites are responsible for protecting the sanctuary from illegitimate encroachment and in this sense pay the penalty for the Israelites' iniquity. This responds further to the fears of the people expressed in 17:27–28.

o: Ex 29:27–28; Lv 7:34; 10:14. *p:* Dt 18:4; 26:2. *q:* Ex 13:2. *r:* Lv 7:31–34. *s:* Dt 10:9; 18:1–2; Jos 13:33; Ez 44:28. *t:* Heb 7:5.

the produce of the vat. [31]You and your households may eat it anywhere, since it is your recompense in exchange for labor in the tent of meeting. [32]You will incur no punishment when you contribute the best part of it. But do not profane the holy offerings of the Israelites or else you shall die.

CHAPTER 19

See RG 135–36

Ashes of the Red Heifer. [1]The LORD spoke to Moses and Aaron: [2]This is the statute for the ritual which the LORD has commanded. Tell the Israelites to procure for you a red heifer without defect and free from every blemish and on which no yoke has ever been laid. [3]You will give it to Eleazar the priest, and it will be led outside the camp* and slaughtered in his presence. [4]Eleazar the priest will take some of its blood on his finger and sprinkle it seven times toward the front of the tent of meeting.* [5]Then the heifer will be burned in his sight; it will be burned with its hide and flesh, its blood and dung; [6]and the priest will take cedar wood, hyssop and scarlet yarn and throw them into the fire in which the heifer is being burned. [7]The priest shall then wash his garments and bathe his body in water, afterward he may enter the camp. The priest remains unclean until the evening. [8]Likewise, the one who burned the heifer shall wash his garments in water, bathe his body in water, and be unclean until evening. [9]Then somebody who is clean shall gather up the ashes of the heifer and deposit them in a clean place outside the camp. There they are to be kept to prepare purification water for the Israelite community. This is a purification offering. [10]The one who has gathered up the ashes of the heifer shall also wash his garments and be unclean until evening. This is a permanent statute, both for the Israelites and for the alien residing among them.

Use of the Ashes. [11]Those who touch the corpse of any human being will be unclean for seven days; [12]they shall purify themselves with the water on the third and on the seventh day, and then be clean. But if they fail to purify themselves on the third and on the seventh day, they will not become clean. [13u] Those who touch the corpse of a human being who dies and who fail to purify themselves defile the tabernacle of the LORD and these persons shall be cut off from Israel. Since the purification water has not been splashed over them, they remain unclean: their uncleanness is still on them.

[14]This is the ritual: When someone dies in a tent, everyone who enters the tent, as well as everyone already in it, will be unclean for seven days; [15]and every open vessel with its lid unfastened will be unclean. [16]Moreover, everyone who in the open country touches a person who has been slain by the sword or who has died naturally, or who touches a human bone or a grave, will be unclean for seven days. [17]For anyone who is thus unclean, ashes shall be taken from the burnt purification offering, and spring water will be poured on them from a vessel.[v] [18]Then someone who is clean will take hyssop, dip it in this water, and sprinkle it on the tent and on all the vessels and persons that were in it, or on the one who touched the bone, the slain person or the other corpse, or the grave. [19]The clean will sprinkle the unclean on the third and on the seventh day, and thus purify them on the seventh day. Then they will wash their garments and bathe in water, and in the evening be clean. [20]* Those who become unclean and fail to purify themselves—those people will be cut off from the assembly, because they defile the sanctuary of the LORD. The purification water has not been splashed over them; they remain unclean. [21]This will be a permanent statute for you.

Those who sprinkle the purification water will wash their garments, and those who come in contact with the purification water will be

19:3 Outside the camp: several early Christian writers saw in this a prefiguring of the sacrificial death of Jesus outside the walls of Jerusalem; cf. Jn 19:20; Heb 13:12; in the purifying water, into which the ashes of the red heifer were put, they saw a type of the water of Baptism.

19:4 Toward the front of the tent of meeting: since the tabernacle faced the east (Ex 26:15–30), the killing of the heifer would take place east of the camp; in later times it was done on the Mount of Olives, east of the Temple.

19:20 Ritual uncleanness is, as it were, contagious; so also sacredness; see note on 17:3.

u: Lv 15:31. *v:* Heb 9:13–14.

unclean until evening. 22 Moreover, anything that the unclean person touches becomes unclean itself, and the one who touches such a person becomes unclean until evening.

CHAPTER 20*

See RG 135–36

Death of Miriam. 1 The Israelites, the whole community, arrived in the wilderness of Zin* in the first month, and the people stayed at Kadesh. It was here that Miriam died, and here that she was buried.

Need for Water at Kadesh. 2 Since the community had no water, they held an assembly against Moses and Aaron. 3 The people quarreled with Moses, exclaiming, "Would that we had perished when our kindred perished before the LORD! 4 Why have you brought the LORD's assembly into this wilderness for us and our livestock to die here? 5 Why have you brought us up out of Egypt, only to bring us to this wretched place? It is not a place for grain nor figs nor vines nor pomegranates! And there is no water to drink!" 6 But Moses and Aaron went away from the assembly to the entrance of the tent of meeting, where they fell prostrate.

Sin of Moses and Aaron. Then the glory of the LORD appeared to them, 7 and the LORD said to Moses: 8 Take the staff and assemble the community, you and Aaron your brother, and in their presence command the rock to yield its waters. Thereby you will bring forth water from the rock for them, and supply the community and their livestock with water. 9 So Moses took the staff from its place before the LORD, as he was ordered. 10 Then Moses and Aaron gathered the assembly in front of the rock, where he said to them,[w] "Just listen, you rebels! Are we to produce water for you out of this rock?" 11[x] Then, raising his hand, Moses struck the rock twice* with his staff, and water came out in abundance, and the community and their livestock drank. 12* But the LORD said to Moses and Aaron: Because you did not have confidence in me, to acknowledge my holiness before the Israelites, therefore you shall not lead this assembly into the land I have given them.

13 These are the waters of Meribah,[y] where the Israelites quarreled with the LORD, and through which he displayed his holiness.

Edom's Refusal. 14 From Kadesh Moses sent messengers to the king of Edom: "Thus says your brother Israel:* You know of all the hardships that have befallen us, 15 how our ancestors went down to Egypt, and we stayed in Egypt a long time, and the Egyptians treated us and our ancestors harshly. 16 When we cried to the LORD,[z] he heard our cry and sent an angel who led us out of Egypt. Now here we are at Kadesh, a town at the edge of your territory. 17 Please let us pass through your land. We will not cross any fields or vineyards, nor drink any well water, but we will go straight along the King's Highway* without turning to the right or to the left, until we have passed through your territory."

18 But Edom answered him, "You shall not pass through here; if you do, I will advance against you with the sword." 19 The Israelites said to him, "We will go up along the highway. If we or our livestock drink any of your water, we will pay for it. It is nothing—just let us pass through on foot." 20 But Edom replied, "You shall not pass through,"[a] and advanced against them with a large and

20:1–29 In this chapter the deaths of the three wilderness leaders are either intimated or explicitly reported: Miriam, v. 1; Moses, v. 12; Aaron, vv. 12, 22–29.

20:1 The wilderness of Zin: a barren region with a few good oases, southwest of the Dead Sea. See note on 13:21. **The first month**: we would expect the mention also of the day and of the year (after the exodus) when this took place; cf. similar dates in 1:1; 10:11; 33:38; Dt 1:3. Here the full date is left unspecified. According to one chronology, the Israelites arrived in Kadesh in the third year after the exodus (cf. Dt 1:46). But the itinerary in chap. 33 would suggest the fortieth year, the year in which Aaron died (33:38).

20:11 Twice: perhaps because he did not have sufficient faith to work the wonder with the first blow. Cf. v. 12.

20:12–13 What lay behind Moses and Aaron's lack of confidence is not made explicit in the text. **Holiness**: an allusion to the name of the place, Kadesh, which means "holy, sanctified, sacred." Meribah means "contention." Cf. Ex 17:7.

20:14 Your brother Israel: according to biblical tradition, the Edomites were descended from Esau, the brother of Jacob. Their country, to the southeast of the Dead Sea, was also known as Seir; cf. Gn 25:24–26; 36:1, 8–9.

20:17 The King's Highway: an important highway, running north and south along the plateau east of the Dead Sea. In ancient times it was much used by caravans and armies; later it was improved by the Romans, and large stretches of it are still clearly recognizable.

w: Ex 17:5–6. *x:* Ps 78:15–16; Wis 11:4; 1 Cor 10:4. *y:* Nm 27:14; Ex 17:7. *z:* Ex 2:23. *a:* Jgs 11:17.

heavily armed force. [21]Therefore, since
Edom refused to let Israel pass through their
territory, Israel turned away from them.
Death of Aaron. [22][b] Setting out from Kadesh, the Israelites, the whole community,
came to Mount Hor.* [23]There at Mount Hor,
on the border of the land of Edom, the LORD
said to Moses and Aaron: [24]Let Aaron be
gathered to his people, for he shall not enter
the land I have given to the Israelites, because you both rebelled against my directions at the waters of Meribah. [25]Take Aaron
and Eleazar his son and bring them up on
Mount Hor.[c] [26]Then strip Aaron of his garments and put them on Eleazar, his son; but
there Aaron shall be gathered up in death.
[27]Moses did as the LORD commanded.
When they had climbed Mount Hor in view
of the whole community, [28]Moses stripped
Aaron of his garments and put them on Eleazar his son. Then Aaron died there on top of
the mountain.[d] When Moses and Eleazar
came down from the mountain, [29]all the
community understood that Aaron had
breathed his last; and for thirty days the
whole house of Israel mourned Aaron.

CHAPTER 21

See RG 136–37

Victory over Arad. [1]When the
Canaanite, the king of Arad,* who ruled over
the Negeb,[e] heard that the Israelites were
coming along the way of Atharim, he engaged Israel in battle and took some of them
captive. [2]Israel then made this vow to the
LORD: "If you deliver this people into my
hand, I will put their cities under the ban."[f]
[3]The LORD paid attention to Israel and delivered up the Canaanites,[g] and they put them
and their cities under the ban. Hence that
place was named Hormah.*
The Bronze Serpent. [4]From Mount Hor they
set out by way of the Red Sea, to bypass the
land of Edom, but the people's patience was
worn out by the journey; [5]so the people complained[h] against God and Moses, "Why have
you brought us up from Egypt to die in the
wilderness, where there is no food or water?
We are disgusted with this wretched food!"*
[6]So the LORD sent among the people seraph* serpents, which bit[i] the people so that
many of the Israelites died. [7]Then the people
came to Moses and said, "We have sinned in
complaining against the LORD and you. Pray
to the LORD to take the serpents from us." So
Moses prayed for the people, [8]and the LORD
said to Moses: Make a seraph and mount it
on a pole, and everyone who has been bitten
will look at it and recover.* [9]Accordingly
Moses made a bronze serpent* and mounted
it on a pole, and whenever the serpent bit
someone, the person looked at the bronze
serpent and recovered.[j]
Journey Around Moab. [10]The Israelites
moved on and encamped in Oboth.[k] [11]Then
they moved on from Oboth and encamped in
Iye-abarim* in the wilderness facing Moab
on the east. [12]Moving on from there, they encamped in the Wadi Zered. [13]Moving on
from there, they encamped on the other side
of the Arnon, in the wilderness that extends
from the territory of the Amorites; for the
Arnon forms Moab's boundary, between
Moab and the Amorites. [14]Hence it is said in
the "Book of the Wars of the LORD":*

20:22 Mount Hor: not definitively identified, but probably to be sought in the vicinity of Kadesh. According to Dt 10:6, Aaron died at Moserah (cf. "Moseroth" in Nm 33:30–31), which is apparently the name of the region in which Mount Hor is situated.

21:1–3 The account of this episode seems to be a later insertion here, since logically v. 4 belongs immediately after 20:29. Perhaps this is the same event as that mentioned in Jgs 1:16–17.

21:3 Hormah: related to the Hebrew word *herem*, meaning "put under the ban." See notes on 14:45; 18:14.

21:5 This wretched food: apparently the manna is meant.

21:6 Seraph: the Hebrew name for a certain species of venomous snake; etymologically the word might signify "the fiery one." Compare the winged throne guardians in Is 6:2, 6; see also Is 14:29; 30:6.

21:8 Everyone who has been bitten will look at it and recover: in the Gospel of John this scene is regarded as a type for the crucifixion of Jesus (Jn 3:14–15).

21:9 King Hezekiah, in his efforts to reform Israelite worship, "smashed the bronze serpent Moses had made" (2 Kgs 18:4).

21:11 Iye-abarim: probably means "the ruins in the Abarim (Mountains)." See note on 27:12.

21:14 The "Book of the Wars of the LORD": an ancient collection of Israelite songs, now lost. **Waheb in Suphah**: since neither place is mentioned elsewhere, it is uncertain whether these Hebrew words are to be considered as place

b: Nm 33:37. *c:* Dt 32:50. *d:* Nm 33:38. *e:* Nm 33:40. *f:* Jos 6:17; Jgs 1:17. *g:* Nm 14:45. *h:* Nm 11:6; Ex 16:3. *i:* Dt 8:15; Wis 16:5; 1 Cor 10:9. *j:* Wis 16:6–7, 10; Jn 3:14–15. *k:* Nm 33:43–44.

"Waheb in Suphah and the wadies,
15 Arnon and the wadi gorges
That reach back toward the site of Ar*
and lean against the border of Moab."

[16]From there they went to Beer,* which is the
well of which the LORD said to Moses,
Gather the people together so that I may give
them water. [17]Then Israel sang this song:

Spring up, O well!—so sing to it—
18 The well that the princes sank,
that the nobles of the people dug,
With their scepters and their staffs—
from the wilderness, a gift.

[19]From Beer to Nahaliel, from Nahaliel to
Bamoth, [20]from Bamoth to the valley in the
country of Moab at the headland of Pisgah
that overlooks Jeshimon.*

Victory over Sihon. [21]Now Israel sent
messengers to Sihon, king of the Amorites,
with the message, [22]"Let us pass through
your land. We will not turn aside into any
field or vineyard, nor will we drink any well
water, but we will go straight along the
King's Highway until we have passed
through your territory." [23]Sihon,[l] however,
would not permit Israel to pass through his
territory, but mustered all his forces and advanced against Israel into the wilderness.
When he reached Jahaz, he engaged Israel in
battle. [24]But Israel put him to the sword, and
took possession of his land from the Arnon
to the Jabbok and as far as Jazer of the Ammonites, for Jazer is the boundary of the
Ammonites. [25][m] Israel seized all the towns
here, and Israel settled in all the towns of the
Amorites, in Heshbon and all its dependencies. [26]For Heshbon was the city of Sihon,
king of the Amorites, who had fought
against the former king of Moab and had
taken all his land from him as far as the Arnon. [27]That is why the poets say:

"Come to Heshbon, let it be rebuilt,
let Sihon's city be firmly constructed.
28 For fire went forth from Heshbon
and a blaze from the city of Sihon;
It consumed Ar of Moab
and swallowed up the high places of
the Arnon.
29 Woe to you, Moab!
You are no more, people of Chemosh!*
He let his sons become fugitives
and his daughters be taken captive by
the Amorite king Sihon.
30 From Heshbon to Dibon their dominion
is no more;
Ar is laid waste; fires blaze as far as
Medeba."

[31]So Israel settled in the land of the Amorites. [32]Moses sent spies to Jazer; and the Israelites captured it with its dependencies and
dispossessed the Amorites who were there.

Victory over Og. [33][n] Then they turned and
went up along the road to Bashan. But Og,
king of Bashan, advanced against them with
all his forces to give battle at Edrei. [34]The
LORD, however, said to Moses: Do not fear
him; for into your hand I deliver him with all
his forces and his land. You will do to him as
you did to Sihon, king of the Amorites, who
reigned in Heshbon.[o] [35]So they struck him
down with his sons and all his forces, until
not a survivor was left to him, and they took
possession of his land.

CHAPTER 22

See RG 136–37

[1]Then the Israelites moved on and encamped in the plains of Moab* on the other
side of the Jordan opposite Jericho.

Balaam Summoned. [2]Now Balak, son of

names; some Hebrew words, now lost, must have preceded this phrase.

21:15 Ar: a city or district in Moab, located on the Arnon; see v. 28; Dt 2:18.

21:16 Beer: "a well," here used as a place name.

21:20 Jeshimon: "the wasteland"; in 1 Sm 23:19, 24 and 26:1, 3, this is the wilderness of Judah on the western side of the Dead Sea, but here and in Nm 23:28, it seems to refer to the southern end of the Jordan valley where Beth-jeshimoth was situated.

21:29 Chemosh: the chief god of the Moabites, mentioned in the famous inscription of Mesha, king of Moab, who ruled at the same time as the Omrides in Israel. Cf. 1 Kgs 11:7, 33; 2 Kgs 23:13; Jer 48:7, 13.

22:1 The plains of Moab: the lowlands to the northeast of the Dead Sea, between the Jordan and the foothills below Mount Nebo. Here the Israelites remained until they crossed the Jordan, according to Jos 1–4. Jericho lay to the west of the Jordan.

l: Dt 2:32; Jgs 11:20. *m:* Jos 21:39; Jgs 11:26. *n:* Dt 3:1–7. *o:* Ps 136:17–22.

Zippor, saw all that Israel did to the Amorites, [3]and Moab feared the Israelites greatly
because they were numerous. Moab was in
dread of the Israelites. [4]So Moab said to the
elders of Midian, "Now this horde will devour everything around us as an ox devours
the grass of the field." At that time Balak, son
of Zippor, was king of Moab; [5]and he sent
messengers to Balaam, son of Beor, at Pethor
on the river, in the land of the Ammonites,* to
summon him with these words, "A people
has come out of Egypt! They have covered
up the earth and are settling down opposite
me! [6]Now come, curse this people for me,*
since they are stronger than I am. Perhaps I
may be able to defeat them and drive them
out of the land. For I know that whoever you
bless is blessed and whoever you curse is
cursed." [7]So the elders of Moab and the elders of Midian, themselves experts in divination,* left and went to Balaam, to whom they
gave Balak's message. [8]He said to them,
"Stay here overnight, and I will give you
whatever answer the LORD gives me." So the
princes of Moab lodged with Balaam.
[9]Then God came to Balaam and said: Who
are these men with you? [10]Balaam answered
God, "Balak, son of Zippor, king of Moab,
sent me the message: [11]'This people that has
come out of Egypt has covered up the earth.
Now come, lay a curse on them for me; perhaps I may be able to fight them and drive
them out.' " [12]But God said to Balaam: Do
not go with them and do not curse this people, for they are blessed. [13]The next morning
Balaam arose and told the princes of Balak,
"Go back to your own country, for the LORD
has refused to let me go with you." [14]So the
princes of Moab went back to Balak with the
report, "Balaam refused to come with us."

Second Appeal to Balaam. [15]Balak yet
again sent princes, who were more numerous and more distinguished than the others.
[16]On coming to Balaam they told him, "Thus
says Balak, son of Zippor: Please do not refuse to come to me. [17]I will reward you very
handsomely and will do anything you ask of
me. Come, lay a curse on this people for
me." [18][p] But Balaam replied to Balak's servants, "Even if Balak gave me his house full
of silver and gold, I could not do anything,
small or great, contrary to the command of
the LORD, my God. [19]But, you too stay here
overnight, so that I may learn what else the
LORD may say to me." [20]That night God
came to Balaam and said to him: If these
men have come to summon you, go back
with them; yet only on the condition that you
do exactly as I tell you. [21]So the next morning when Balaam arose, he saddled his donkey,* and went off with the princes of Moab.

The Talking Donkey. [22]But now God's
anger flared up* at him for going, and the angel of the LORD took up a position on the
road as his adversary. As Balaam was riding
along on his donkey, accompanied by two of
his servants, [23]the donkey saw the angel of
the LORD standing in the road with sword
drawn. The donkey turned off the road and
went into the field, and Balaam beat the donkey to bring her back on the road. [24]Then the
angel of the LORD stood in a narrow lane between vineyards with a stone wall on each
side. [25]When the donkey saw the angel of
the LORD there, she pressed against the wall;
and since she squeezed Balaam's leg against
the wall, he beat her again. [26]Then the angel
of the LORD again went ahead, and stood
next in a passage so narrow that there was no
room to move either to the right or to the left.

22:5 In the land of the Ammonites: the translation rests on a slight emendation of the traditional Hebrew text in accordance with the tradition represented by the Vulgate. While Pethor remains unidentified, this verse supports an identification of Balaam's homeland in the Transjordan (cf. the Deir 'Alla Inscriptions), over against other traditions in the text which connect Balaam with Syria (23:7; Dt 23:5).

22:6 Curse this people for me: Balak believed that Balaam, known in the tradition as a diviner (cf. Jos 13:22), could utter a curse upon Israel which would come to pass.

22:7 Experts in divination: lit., "divination was in their hand," i.e., "in their possession"; cf. Ezr 7:25.

22:21 Donkey: technically a she-donkey; Heb. *aton*.

22:22 God's anger flared up: God's apparent change of mind became a source of much speculation in the tradition. So, for example, God was angry, not merely because Balaam was going to Balak, for he had God's permission for the journey (v. 20), but perhaps because he was tempted by greed to curse Israel against God's command (cf. 2 Pt 2:15; Jude 11; compare Nm 22:32). **Adversary**: Heb. *satan*; see also v. 32; cf. 1 Sm 29:4; 2 Sm 19:22; 1 Kgs 11; Jb 1–2; Ps 109:6; Zec 3:1–2; 1 Chr 21:1.

p: Nm 24:13.

27When the donkey saw the angel of the LORD there, she lay down under Balaam. Balaam's anger flared up and he beat the donkey with his stick.

28[q] Then the LORD opened the mouth of the donkey, and she asked Balaam, "What have I done to you that you beat me these three times?" 29"You have acted so willfully against me," said Balaam to the donkey, "that if I only had a sword at hand, I would kill you here and now." 30But the donkey said to Balaam, "Am I not your donkey, on which you have always ridden until now? Have I been in the habit of treating you this way before?" "No," he replied.

31Then the LORD opened Balaam's eyes, so that he saw the angel of the LORD standing on the road with sword drawn; and he knelt and bowed down to the ground. 32But the angel of the LORD said to him: "Why have you beaten your donkey these three times? I have come as an adversary because this rash journey of yours is against my will. 33When the donkey saw me, she turned away from me these three times. If she had not turned away from me, you are the one I would have killed, though I would have spared her." 34Then Balaam said to the angel of the LORD, "I have sinned. Yet I did not know that you took up a position to oppose my journey. Since it has displeased you, I will go back home." 35But the angel of the LORD said to Balaam: "Go with the men; but you may say only what I tell you." So Balaam went on with the princes of Balak.

36When Balak heard that Balaam was coming, he went out to meet him at Ar-Moab on the border formed by the Arnon, at its most distant point. 37And Balak said to Balaam, "Did I not send an urgent summons to you? Why did you not come to me? Did you think I could not reward you?" 38Balaam answered Balak, "Well, I have come to you after all. But what power have I to say anything? I can speak only what God puts in my mouth." 39Then Balaam went with Balak, and they came to Kiriath-huzoth. 40Here Balak sacrificed oxen and sheep, and sent portions to Balaam and to the princes who were with him.

The First Oracle. 41The next morning Balak took Balaam up on Bamoth-baal, and from there he could see some of the people.

CHAPTER 23

See RG 136–37

1Then Balaam said to Balak, "Build me seven altars here, and here prepare seven bulls and seven rams for me." 2So Balak did as Balaam had ordered, and Balak and Balaam offered a bull and a ram on each altar. 3Balaam said to Balak, "Stand here by your burnt offering while I go over there. Perhaps the LORD will meet me, and then I will tell you whatever he lets me see." And so he went out on the barren height. 4Then God met Balaam, and Balak said to him: "I have erected the seven altars, and have offered a bull and a ram on each altar." 5The LORD put an utterance in Balaam's mouth, and said: Go back to Balak, and speak accordingly. 6So he went back to Balak, who was still standing by his burnt offering together with all the princes of Moab. 7Then Balaam recited his poem:

From Aram* Balak has led me here,
    Moab's king, from the mountains of
        Qedem:[r]
"Come, curse for me Jacob,
    come, denounce Israel."
8 How can I lay a curse on the one whom
        God has not cursed?
    How denounce the one whom the
        LORD has not denounced?
9 For from the top of the crags I see him,
    from the heights I behold him.
Here is a people that lives apart*
    and does not reckon itself among the
        nations.
10 Who has ever counted the dust of Jacob,
    who numbered Israel's dust-cloud?*

23:7 Aram: the ancient name of the region later known as Syria. **The mountains of Qedem**: Qedem is the name for a region in northern Syria. Qedem also means "eastern." Perhaps this designates the low ranges in the Syrian desert. The "mountains of old" is also a possible translation.

23:9 A people that lives apart: that is, "securely"; cf. Dt 33:28.

23:10 The dust of Jacob . . . Israel's dust-cloud: the Israelites will be as numerous as the dust kicked up by Israel in its march through the wilderness.

q: 2 Pt 2:15–16. *r:* Nm 22:6.

May I die the death of the just,
may my end be like theirs!

11“What have you done to me?” cried Balak to Balaam. “It was to lay a curse on my
foes that I brought you here; but instead, you
have blessed them!” 12Balaam replied, “Is it
not what the LORD puts in my mouth that I
take care to repeat?”

The Second Oracle. 13Then Balak said to
him, “Please come with me to another place*
from which you can see them; but you will
see only some, not all of them, and from
there lay a curse on them for me.” 14So he
brought him to a lookout post on the top of
Pisgah, where he built seven altars and offered a bull and a ram on each of them. 15Ba-
laam then said to Balak, “Stand here by your
burnt offering, while I seek a meeting over
there.” 16Then the LORD met Balaam, and,
having put an utterance in his mouth, said to
him: Return to Balak, and speak accordingly. 17So he went to Balak, who was still
standing by his burnt offering together with
the princes of Moab. When Balak asked
him, “What did the LORD say?” 18Balaam recited his poem:

Rise, Balak, and listen;
give ear to my testimony, son of
Zippor!
19 God is not a human being who speaks
falsely,
nor a mortal, who feels regret.
Is God one to speak and not act,
to decree and not bring it to pass?
20 I was summoned to bless;
I will bless; I cannot revoke it!
21 Misfortune I do not see in Jacob,
nor do I see misery* in Israel.
The LORD, their God, is with them;
among them is the war-cry of their
King.
22 They have the like of a wild ox’s horns:*
God who brought them out of Egypt.[s]
23 No, there is no augury against Jacob,
nor divination against Israel.
Now it is said of Jacob,
of Israel, “Look what God has done!”
24 Here is a people that rises up like a
lioness,
and gets up like a lion;
It does not rest till it has devoured its
prey
and has drunk the blood of the slain.[t]

25“Neither lay a curse on them nor bless
them,” said Balak to Balaam. 26But Balaam
answered Balak, “Did I not tell you, ‘Everything the LORD tells me I must do’?”

The Third Oracle. 27Then Balak said to
Balaam, “Come, let me bring you to another
place; perhaps God will approve of your laying a curse on them for me from there.” 28So
he took Balaam to the top of Peor, that overlooks Jeshimon. 29Balaam then said to Balak, “Build me seven altars here; and here
prepare for me seven bulls and seven rams.”
30And Balak did as Balaam had ordered, offering a bull and a ram on each altar.

CHAPTER 24

See RG 136–37

1Balaam, however, perceiving that
the LORD was pleased to bless Israel, did not
go aside as before to seek omens, but turned
his gaze toward the wilderness. 2When Balaam looked up and saw Israel encamped,
tribe by tribe, the spirit of God came upon
him, 3and he recited his poem:

The oracle of Balaam, son of Beor,
the oracle of the man whose eye is
true,
4 The oracle of one who hears what God
says,
and knows what the Most High knows,
Of one who sees what the Almighty sees,
in rapture* and with eyes unveiled:
5 How pleasant are your tents, Jacob;
your encampments, Israel!

23:13 To another place: Balak thought that if Balaam would view Israel from a different site, he could deliver a different kind of omen.

23:21 Misfortune . . . misery: Balaam states that he is unable to see any evils for Israel.

23:22 A wild ox’s horns: Israel possesses the strength of a wild ox because of God’s presence among them. Compare the claim by the psalmist, the Lord is “my rock . . . my saving horn” (Ps 18:3).

24:4 In rapture: lit., “falling,” therefore possibly “in a trance.” However, this interpretation is uncertain.

s: Nm 24:8. *t:* Nm 24:9; Gn 49:9.

6 Like palm trees spread out,
like gardens beside a river,
Like aloes the LORD planted,
like cedars beside water;
7 Water will drip from their buckets,
their seed will have plentiful water;
Their king will rise higher than Agag*
and their dominion will be exalted.
8 They have the like of a wild ox's horns:
God who brought them out of Egypt.
They will devour hostile nations,
break their bones, and crush their
loins.[u]
9 Crouching, they lie like a lion,
or like a lioness; who will arouse
them?
Blessed are those who bless you,
and cursed are those who curse you![v]

10 In a blaze of anger at Balaam, Balak
clapped his hands* and said to him, "It was
to lay a curse on my foes that I summoned
you here; yet three times now you have actually blessed them![w]
11 Now flee to your
home. I promised to reward you richly, but
the LORD has withheld the reward from
you!"
12 Balaam replied to Balak, "Did I not
even tell the messengers whom you sent to
me,
13 'Even if Balak gave me his house full
of silver and gold, I could not of my own accord do anything, good or evil, contrary to
the command of the LORD'? Whatever the
LORD says I must say.[x]

The Fourth Oracle.
14 "But now that I am
about to go to my own people, let me warn
you what this people will do to your people
in the days to come."
15 Then he recited his
poem:

The oracle of Balaam, son of Beor,
the oracle of the man whose eye is true,
16 The oracle of one who hears what God
says,
and knows what the Most High knows,
Of one who sees what the Almighty sees,
in rapture and with eyes unveiled.
17 I see him, though not now;
I observe him, though not near:
A star shall advance from Jacob,
and a scepter* shall rise from Israel,
That will crush the brows of Moab,[y]
and the skull of all the Sethites,
18 Edom will be dispossessed,
and no survivor is left in Seir.
Israel will act boldly,
19 and Jacob will rule his foes.

20 Upon seeing Amalek, Balaam recited his
poem:

First* of the nations is Amalek,
but their end is to perish forever.[z]

21 Upon seeing the Kenites,* he recited his
poem:

Though your dwelling is safe,
and your nest is set on a cliff;

24:7 Agag: during Saul's reign, king of Amalek (1 Sm 15:8), fierce enemy of Israel during the wilderness period; see v. 20 (Ex 17:8–16).

24:10 Balak clapped his hands: a gesture suggesting contempt or derision, apparently made in anger (cf. Jb 27:23; Lam 2:15).

24:17 A star . . . a scepter: some early Christian writers, as well as rabbinic interpreters, understood this prophecy in messianic terms. So, for example, Rabbi Akiba designates Bar Kosiba the messiah in the early second century A.D. by calling him Bar Kokhba, i.e., son of the star, alluding to this passage. Although this text is not referred to anywhere in the New Testament, in a Christian messianic interpretation the star would refer to Jesus, as also the scepter from Israel; cf. Is 11:1. But it is doubtful whether this passage is to be connected with the "star of the Magi" in Mt 2:1–12. **The brows of Moab, and the skull of all the Sethites**: under the figure of a human being, Moab is specified as the object of conquest by a future leader of Israel. The personification of peoples or toponyms is common enough in the Old Testament; see, e.g., Hos 11:1; Ps 98:8. In Jer 48:45, which paraphrases the latter part of our verse, Moab is depicted as someone whose boasting warrants its ruin. In view of the use of Heb. *pe'ah* (here "brows") in Nm 34:3 to indicate a boundary, some see in the "brows" of Moab and the "skull" of the Sethites a representation of features of Moab's topography, i.e., the borderlands and the interior plateau. **The Sethites**: cf. Gn 4:25; here probably a general designation for nomadic/tribal groups on the borders of Palestine, unless they are to be identified with the Shutu mentioned in Execration texts of the early second millennium B.C. and the fourteenth century Amarna tablets from Egypt; however, the Shutu are not attested in Moab. On the basis of Gn 4:25 and Gn 25, one might also think of a reference to humanity in general.

24:20 First: lit., "the beginning." In the Bible, Amalek is a people indigenous to Palestine and therefore considered as of great antiquity. There is a deliberate contrast here between the words "first" and "end."

24:21 The Kenites lived in high strongholds in the mountains of southern Palestine and the Sinai Peninsula, and were skilled in working the various metals found in their territory.

u: Nm 23:22. *v:* Nm 23:24; Gn 12:3; 27:29; 49:9. *w:* Nm 23:11. *x:* Nm 22:18. *y:* 2 Sm 8:2. *z:* Ex 17:14; 1 Sm 15:3.

22 Yet Kain will be destroyed
when Asshur* takes you captive.

23 Upon seeing* [the Ishmaelites?] he recited
his poem:

Alas, who shall survive of Ishmael,
24 to deliver them from the hands of the
Kittim?
When they have conquered Asshur and
conquered Eber,
They too shall perish forever.

25 Then Balaam set out on his journey
home; and Balak also went his way.

CHAPTER 25

See RG 136–37

Worship of Baal of Peor. 1 While Israel
was living at Shittim,* the people profaned
themselves by prostituting themselves with
the Moabite women.[a] 2 These then invited the
people to the sacrifices of their god, and the
people ate of the sacrifices[b] and bowed down
to their god. 3 Israel thereby attached itself to
the Baal of Peor,[c] and the LORD's anger flared
up against Israel. 4[d] The LORD said to Moses:
Gather all the leaders of the people, and publicly execute them* before the LORD, that the
blazing wrath of the LORD may turn away from
Israel. 5 So Moses told the Israelite judges,
"Each of you kill those of his men who have
attached themselves to the Baal of Peor."*

Zeal of Phinehas. 6 At this a certain Israelite came and brought in a Midianite woman*
to his kindred in the view of Moses and of
the whole Israelite community, while they
were weeping at the entrance of the tent of
meeting. 7[e] When Phinehas, son of Eleazar,
son of Aaron the priest, saw this, he rose up
from the assembly, and taking a spear in his
hand, 8 followed the Israelite into the tent
where he pierced the two of them, the Israelite and the woman. Thus the plague upon the
Israelites was checked; 9 but the dead from
the plague were twenty-four thousand.

10 Then the LORD said to Moses: 11 Phinehas, son of Eleazar, son of Aaron the priest,
has turned my anger from the Israelites by
his being as jealous among them as I am;
that is why I did not put an end to the Israelites in my jealousy.* 12[f] Announce, therefore,
that I hereby give him my covenant of
peace,* 13 which shall be for him and for his
descendants after him the covenant of an
everlasting priesthood, because he was jealous on behalf of his God and thus made expiation for the Israelites.

14* The name of the slain Israelite, the one
slain with the Midianite woman, was Zimri,
son of Salu, prince of a Simeonite ancestral
house. 15 The name of the slain Midianite
woman was Cozbi, daughter of Zur, who was
head of a clan, an ancestral house, in Midian.

Their name is connected, at least by popular etymology, with the Hebrew word for "smith"; of similar sound to *qayin*, i.e., "Kain" or "smith," is the Hebrew word for "nest," *qen*—hence the play on words in the present passage.

24:22 Asshur: the mention of Asshur, i.e., Assyria, is not likely before the ninth or eighth centuries B.C.

24:23–24 Upon seeing: this phrase, lacking the Hebrew text, is found in the Septuagint, but without "the Ishmaelites" designated as the subject of the oracle. The Hebrew text of the oracle itself shows considerable disarray; the translation therefore relies on reconstruction of the putative original and is quite uncertain.

25:1 Shittim: the full name was Abel-shittim, a locality at the foot of the mountains in the northeastern corner of the plains of Moab (33:49). **Prostituting themselves**: the application to men of such traditional language for apostasy clearly suggests apostasy was taken to be an inevitable consequence of intermarriage with the Midianite women.

25:4 Publicly execute them: the same phrase occurs in 2 Sm 21:6–14, where the context shows that at least a part of the penalty consisted in being denied honorable burial. In both passages, dismemberment or impalement (perhaps subsequent to the actual execution) as a punishment for the breaking of covenant pledges, is a possible interpretation of the Hebrew phrase.

25:5 Thereby Moses apparently alters the Lord's command to execute all the leaders.

25:6 Midianite woman: according to 22:4, 7, the Midianites were allied with the Moabites in opposing Israel, while 31:16 claims that Balaam had induced the Midianite women to lure the Israelites away from the Lord. **They were weeping**: on account of the plague that had struck them; cf. v. 8.

25:11 My jealousy: God's desire to maintain an exclusive hold on the allegiance of the Israelites.

25:12 Covenant of peace: by means of this covenant between God and Phinehas, Phinehas can expect God's protection, especially from any threat of reprisal for his action; cf. Is 54:10; Ez 34:25; 37:26.

25:14–15 The noble lineage of the slain couple is mentioned in order to stress the courage of Phinehas in punishing them. The zeal of Phinehas became proverbial; cf. Ps 106:30; Sir 45:23; 1 Mc 2:26, 54.

a: Nm 31:16. *b:* Ex 34:15–16. *c:* Ps 106:28; Hos 9:10. *d:* Dt 4:3. *e:* Ps 106:30. *f:* 1 Mc 2:26, 54; Ps 106:31; Sir 45:23–24.

Vengeance on the Midianites. 16* The LORD then said to Moses: 17[g] Treat the Midianites as enemies and strike them, 18 for they have been your enemies by the deceitful dealings they had with you regarding Peor and their kinswoman Cozbi, the daughter of a Midianite prince, who was slain at the time of the plague because of Peor.

III. Second Census of a New Generation and Preparation to Enter the Promised Land

CHAPTER 26

See RG 136–37

The Second Census. 19 After the plague 1 the LORD said to Moses and Eleazar, son of Aaron the priest: 2 Take a census, by ancestral houses, throughout the community of the Israelites of all those of twenty years or more who are eligible for military service in Israel.[h] 3 So on the plains of Moab along the Jordan at Jericho, Moses and Eleazar the priest enrolled them, 4 those of twenty years or more, as the LORD had commanded Moses.

The Israelites who came out of the land of Egypt were as follows:*

5[i] Reuben, the firstborn of Israel. The descendants of Reuben by their clans were: through Hanoch, the clan of the Hanochites; through Pallu, the clan of the Palluites; 6 through Hezron, the clan of the Hezronites; through Carmi, the clan of the Carmites. 7 These were the clans of the Reubenites, and those enrolled numbered forty-three thousand seven hundred and thirty.

8 From Pallu descended Eliab. 9 The sons of Eliab were Nemuel, Dathan, and Abiram[j]—the same Dathan and Abiram, ones designated by the community, who contended with Moses and Aaron as part of Korah's faction when they contended with the LORD. 10 The earth opened its mouth and swallowed them, along with Korah, as a warning. The faction was destroyed when the fire consumed two hundred and fifty men. 11 The descendants of Korah, however, did not die out.

12 The descendants of Simeon by clans were: through Nemuel,* the clan of the Nemuelites; through Jamin, the clan of the Jaminites; through Jachin, the clan of the Jachinites; 13 through Zerah, the clan of the Zerahites; through Shaul, the clan of the Shaulites. 14 These were the clans of the Simeonites, twenty-two thousand two hundred.

15 The descendants of Gad by clans were: through Zephon, the clan of the Zephonites; through Haggi, the clan of the Haggites; through Shuni, the clan of the Shunites; 16 through Ozni, the clan of the Oznites; through Eri, the clan of the Erites; 17 through Arod, the clan of the Arodites; through Areli, the clan of the Arelites. 18 These were the clans of the descendants of Gad, of whom there were enrolled forty thousand five hundred.

19 The sons of Judah were Er and Onan. Er and Onan died in the land of Canaan.[k] 20 The descendants of Judah by their clans were: through Shelah, the clan of the Shelahites; through Perez, the clan of the Perezites; through Zerah, the clan of the Zerahites. 21 The descendants of Perez were: through Hezron, the clan of the Hezronites; through Hamul, the clan of the Hamulites. 22 These were the clans of Judah, of whom there were enrolled seventy-six thousand five hundred.

23 The descendants of Issachar by their clans were: through Tola, the clan of the Tolaites; through Puvah, the clan of the Puvahites; 24 through Jashub, the clan of the Jashubites; through Shimron, the clan of the Shimronites. 25 These were the clans of Issachar, of whom there were enrolled sixty-four thousand three hundred.

26 The descendants of Zebulun by their

25:16–18 The account of the execution of this command is given in 31:1–18.

26:4 This introduction to the census seems to contradict vv. 64–65 by including those who came out of Egypt.

26:12 Nemuel: so also in 1 Chr 4:24. In Gn 46:10 and Ex 6:15, a son of Simeon with the same position in the genealogy bears the name "Jemuel"; it is uncertain which form is correct. See above, v. 9, where the name "Nemuel" occurs for a person descended from Pallu. Some speculate this name was inserted from v. 12 to provide a continuing line for Pallu.

g: Nm 31:2–12. *h:* Nm 1:2–3. *i:* 1 Chr 5:3. *j:* Nm 16:1, 32. *k:* Gn 38:7, 10; 46:12; 1 Chr 2:3.

clans were: through Sered, the clan of the Seredites; through Elon, the clan of the Elonites; through Jahleel, the clan of the Jahleelites. [27]These were the clans of the Zebulunites, of whom there were enrolled sixty thousand five hundred.

[28]The sons of Joseph were Manasseh and Ephraim. [29]The descendants of Manasseh by clans were: through Machir, the clan of the Machirites. Now Machir begot Gilead: through Gilead, the clan of the Gileadites. [30]The descendants of Gilead were: through Iezer, the clan of the Iezrites; through Helek, the clan of the Helekites; [31]through Asriel, the clan of the Asrielites; through Shechem, the clan of the Shechemites; [32]through Shemida, the clan of the Shemidaites; through Hepher, the clan of the Hepherites. [33][l] As for Zelophehad, son of Hepher—he had no sons, but only daughters. The names of the daughters of Zelophehad were Mahlah, Noah, Hoglah, Milcah and Tirzah. [34]These were the clans of Manasseh, and those enrolled numbered fifty-two thousand seven hundred.

[35]These were the descendants of Ephraim by their clans: through Shuthelah, the clan of the Shuthelahites; through Becher, the clan of the Becherites; through Tahan, the clan of the Tahanites. [36]These were the descendants of Shuthelah: through Eran, the clan of the Eranites. [37]These were the clans of the Ephraimites, of whom there were enrolled thirty-two thousand five hundred.

These were the descendants of Joseph by their clans.

[38]The descendants of Benjamin by their clans were: through Bela, the clan of the Belaites; through Ashbel, the clan of the Ashbelites; through Ahiram, the clan of the Ahiramites; [39]through Shupham, the clan of the Shuphamites; through Hupham, the clan of the Huphamites. [40]The sons of Bela were Ard and Naaman: through Ard, the clan of the Ardites; through Naaman, the clan of the Naamites. [41]These were the descendants of Benjamin by their clans, of whom there were enrolled forty-five thousand six hundred.

[42]These were the descendants of Dan by their clans: through Shuham the clan of the Shuhamites. These were the clans of Dan, [43]of whom there were enrolled sixty-four thousand four hundred.

[44]The descendants of Asher by their clans were: through Imnah, the clan of the Imnites; through Ishvi, the clan of the Ishvites; through Beriah, the clan of the Beriites; [45]through Heber, the clan of the Heberites; through Malchiel, the clan of the Malchielites. [46]The name of Asher's daughter was Serah. [47]These were the clans of the descendants of Asher, of whom there were enrolled fifty-three thousand four hundred.

[48]The descendants of Naphtali by their clans were: through Jahzeel, the clan of the Jahzeelites; through Guni, the clan of the Gunites; [49]through Jezer, the clan of the Jezerites; through Shillem, the clan of the Shillemites. [50]These were the clans of Naphtali, of whom there were enrolled forty-five thousand four hundred.

[51]These were the Israelites who were enrolled: six hundred and one thousand seven hundred and thirty.

Allotment of the Land.* [52]The LORD said to Moses: [53][m] Among these the land shall be divided as their heritage in keeping with the number of people named. [54][n] To a large tribe you shall assign a large heritage, to a small tribe a small heritage, each receiving its heritage in proportion to the number enrolled in it. [55]But the land shall be divided by lot, all inheriting according to the lists of their ancestral tribes. [56]As the lot falls the heritage of each tribe, large or small, will be assigned.

Census of the Levites. [57]These were the Levites enrolled by clans: through Gershon, the clan of the Gershonites; through Kohath, the clan of the Kohathites; through Merari, the clan of the Merarites. [58]These were clans of Levi: the clan of the Libnites, the clan of

26:52–56 The division of Canaan among the various tribes and clans and families was determined not only by the size of each group but also by lot. Perhaps the lots determined the respective locality of each tribal land and the section reserved for each clan, while the relative size of the allotted locality and section depended on the numerical strength of each group. The Israelites considered the outcome of the drawing of lots as an expression of God's will; cf. Lv 16:8–10; Jos 14:2; 15:1; etc.; Acts 1:23–26.

l: Nm 27:1; 36:11; Jos 17:3. *m:* Jos 11:23. *n:* Nm 33:54; 35:8.

the Hebronites, the clan of the Mahlites, the clan of the Mushites, the clan of the Korahites.*

Now Kohath begot Amram, [59]whose wife was named Jochebed. She was the daughter of Levi, born to Levi in Egypt. To Amram she bore Aaron and Moses and Miriam their sister. [60]To Aaron were born Nadab and Abihu, Eleazar and Ithamar. [61]But Nadab and Abihu died when they offered unauthorized fire before the LORD. [62]The Levites enrolled were twenty-three thousand, every male one month or more of age.[o] They were not enrolled with the other Israelites, however, for no heritage was given them among the Israelites.

[63]These, then, were those enrolled by Moses and Eleazar the priest, when they enrolled the Israelites on the plains of Moab along the Jordan at Jericho. [64]Among them there was not one of those who had been enrolled by Moses and Aaron the priest, when they enrolled the Israelites in the wilderness of Sinai. [65][p] For the LORD had told them that they would surely die in the wilderness, and not one of them was left except Caleb, son of Jephunneh, and Joshua, son of Nun.

CHAPTER 27

See RG 136–37

Zelophehad's Daughters. [1]The daughters of Zelophehad, son of Hepher, son of Gilead, son of Machir, son of Manasseh, came forward. (Zelophehad belonged to the clans of Manasseh, son of Joseph.) The names of his daughters were Mahlah, Noah, Hoglah, Milcah and Tirzah.[q] [2]Standing before Moses, Eleazar the priest, the princes, and the whole community at the entrance of the tent of meeting, they said: [3]"Our father died in the wilderness. Although he did not join the faction of those who conspired against the LORD,* Korah's faction, he died for his own sin without leaving any sons. [4]But why should our father's name be cut off from his clan merely because he had no son? Give us land among our father's kindred."

Laws Concerning Heiresses.* [5]So Moses laid their case before the LORD, [6]and the LORD said to him: [7]The plea of Zelophehad's daughters is just; you shall give them hereditary land among their father's kindred and transfer their father's heritage to them. [8]Tell the Israelites: If a man dies without leaving a son, you shall transfer his heritage to his daughter; [9]if he has no daughter, you shall give his heritage to his brothers; [10]if he has no brothers, you shall give his heritage to his father's brothers; [11]if his father had no brothers, you shall give his heritage to his nearest relative in his clan, who shall then take possession of it.

This will be the statutory procedure for the Israelites, as the LORD commanded Moses.[r]

Joshua to Succeed Moses. [12]The LORD said to Moses: Go up into this mountain of the Abarim range* and view the land that I have given to the Israelites.[s] [13]When you have viewed it, you will be gathered to your people, as was Aaron your brother.[t] [14]For in the rebellion of the community in the wilderness of Zin you both rebelled against my order to acknowledge my holiness before them by means of the water.[u] (These were the waters of Meribah of Kadesh in the wilderness of Zin.)

[15]Then Moses said to the LORD, [16]"May the LORD, the God of the spirits of all humanity,* set over the community someone [17]who will be their leader in battle and who will lead them out and bring them in, that the LORD's community may not be like sheep without a shepherd." [18]And the LORD replied

26:58 Compare 3:18–20 for a different listing.

27:3 He did not join . . . against the LORD: had he done so, he and his heirs could have been deprived of a portion in the promised land.

27:5–11 The purpose of this law, as also that of the related laws in 36:2–10 (marriage within the same tribe), Dt 25:5–10 (levirate marriage), and Lv 25:10 (return of property in the jubilee year), was to keep the landed property within the proper domain of each tribe.

27:12 The Abarim range: the mountains on the eastern side of the Dead Sea. The peak of this chain is Mount Nebo where Moses views the promised land before he dies (Dt 32:49).

27:16 The God of the spirits of all humanity: the sense is that God knows the character and abilities of all people and therefore knows best whom to appoint (cf. Jgs 6:34; 11:29; 1 Sm 16:13); see the same phrase in Nm 16:22, where "spirit" evidently means the life principle.

o: Nm 3:39. *p:* Nm 14:22–24, 29. *q:* Nm 26:33; Jos 17:3. *r:* Jer 32:6–9. *s:* Dt 3:27; 32:49; 34:1. *t:* Nm 20:12, 24. *u:* Dt 32:51.

to Moses: Take Joshua, son of Nun,[v] a man of spirit,* and lay your hand upon him. [19]Have him stand before Eleazar the priest and the whole community, and commission him in their sight. [20]Invest him with some of your own power, that the whole Israelite community may obey him. [21]He shall present himself to Eleazar the priest, who will seek for him the decision of the Urim* in the LORD's presence; and as it directs, Joshua, all the Israelites with him, and the whole community will go out for battle; and as it directs, they will come in.

[22]Moses did as the LORD had commanded him. Taking Joshua and having him stand before Eleazar the priest and the whole community, [23]he laid his hands on him and commissioned him, as the LORD had directed through Moses.

See RG 136–37

CHAPTER 28

General Sacrifices. [1]The LORD said to Moses: [2]Give the Israelites this commandment: At their prescribed times, you will be careful to present to me the food offerings that are due me, oblations of pleasing aroma to me.

Each Morning and Evening. [3][w] You will tell them therefore: This is the oblation which you will offer to the LORD: two unblemished yearling lambs each day as the regular burnt offering,* [4]offering one lamb in the morning and the other during the evening twilight, [5]each with a grain offering of one tenth of an ephah of bran flour mixed with a fourth of a hin of oil of crushed olives.* [6]This is the regular burnt offering that was made at Mount Sinai for a pleasing aroma, an oblation to the LORD. [7]And as the libation for the first lamb, you will make a libation to the LORD in the sanctuary* of a fourth of a hin of strong drink. [8]The other lamb you will offer during the evening twilight, making the same grain offering and the same libation as in the morning, as an oblation of pleasing aroma to the LORD.

On the Sabbath. [9]On the sabbath day: two unblemished yearling lambs, with a grain offering of two tenths of an ephah of bran flour mixed with oil, and its libation. [10]This is the sabbath burnt offering each sabbath, in addition to the regular burnt offering and its libation.

At the New Moon Feast. [11]On your new moons* you will offer as a burnt offering to the LORD two bulls of the herd, one ram, and seven unblemished yearling lambs, [12]with three tenths of an ephah of bran flour mixed with oil as the grain offering for each bull, two tenths of an ephah of bran flour mixed with oil as the grain offering for the ram, [13]and one tenth of an ephah of bran flour mixed with oil as the grain offering for each lamb, a burnt offering with a pleasing aroma, an oblation to the LORD. [14]Their libations will consist of a half a hin of wine for each bull, a third of a hin for the ram, and a fourth of a hin for each lamb. This is the burnt offering for the new moon, for every new moon through the months of the year. [15]Moreover, there will be one goat for a purification offering to the LORD; it will be offered in addition to the regular burnt offering and its libation.

At the Passover. [16]The fourteenth day* of the first month is the Passover of the LORD,[x] [17]and the fifteenth day of this month is the pilgrimage feast. For seven days unleavened bread is to be eaten. [18]On the first day you will declare a holy day, and you shall do no

27:18 A man of spirit: lit., "a man in whom there is spirit," that is, probably one who is endowed with a courageous spirit (Jos 2:11); compare Gn 41:38; Dt 34:9.

27:21 The Urim: certain sacred objects which Israelite priests employed to discern the divine will, probably by obtaining a positive or negative answer to a given question. The full expression was "the Urim and Thummim"; cf. Ex 28:30; Lv 8:8; Dt 33:8; Ezr 2:63; Neh 7:65. Joshua ordinarily did not receive direct revelations from God as Moses had received them.

28:3 The regular burnt offering: "the *tamid* burnt offering," the technical term for the daily sacrifice. The lambs—as well as the goats for the purification offering (vv. 15, 22, 30)—are all specified as males.

28:5 Oil of crushed olives: this oil, probably made in a mortar, was purer and more expensive than oil extracted in the olive press.

28:7 In the sanctuary: i.e., the tent of meeting. But according to Sir 50:15, the libation was poured at the base of the outer altar.

28:11 On your new moons: beginning on the evening when the crescent of the new moon first appeared. The beginning of the month is reckoned according to the new moon.

28:16 The fourteenth day: toward evening at the end of this day; cf. Ex 12:6, 18.

v: Dt 34:9. *w:* Ex 29:38–42. *x:* Ex 12:18; Lv 23:5; Dt 16:1.

heavy work.* [y] [19]You will offer an oblation, a burnt offering to the LORD: two bulls of the herd, one ram, and seven yearling lambs that you are sure are unblemished. [20]Their grain offerings will be of bran flour mixed with oil; you will offer three tenths of an ephah for each bull and two tenths for the ram. [21]You will offer one tenth for each of the seven lambs; [22]and one goat as a purification offering to make atonement for yourselves. [23]These offerings you will make in addition to the morning burnt offering which is part of the regular burnt offering. [24]You will make exactly the same offerings each day for seven days as food offerings, oblations of pleasing aroma to the LORD; they will be offered in addition to the regular burnt offering with its libation. [25]On the seventh day you will declare a holy day: you shall do no heavy work.[z]

At Pentecost. [26]On the day of first fruits,* on your feast of Weeks,[a] when you present to the LORD an offering of new grain, you will declare a holy day: you shall do no heavy work. [27]You will offer burnt offering for a pleasing aroma to the LORD: two bulls of the herd, one ram, and seven yearling lambs that you are sure are unblemished. [28]Their grain offerings will be of bran flour mixed with oil: three tenths of an ephah for each bull, two tenths for the ram, [29]and one tenth for each of the seven lambs. [30]One goat will be for a purification offering to make atonement for yourselves. [31]You will make these offerings, together with their libations, in addition to the regular burnt offering with its grain offering.

CHAPTER 29

See RG 136–37

On New Year's Day. [1]In the seventh month on the first day* you will declare a holy day, and do no heavy work; it shall be a day on which you sound the trumpet.[b] [2]You will offer a burnt offering for a pleasing aroma to the LORD: one bull of the herd, one ram, and seven unblemished yearling lambs. [3]Their grain offerings will be of bran flour mixed with oil: three tenths of an ephah for the bull, two tenths for the ram, [4]and one tenth for each of the seven lambs. [5]One goat will be a purification offering to make atonement for yourselves. [6]These are in addition to the burnt offering for the new moon with its grain offering, and in addition to the regular burnt offering with its grain offering, together with the libations prescribed for them, for a pleasing aroma, an oblation to the LORD.

On the Day of Atonement. [7]On the tenth day of this seventh month* you will declare a holy day, humble yourselves, and do no sort of work.[c] [8]You will offer a burnt offering to the LORD, a pleasing aroma: one bull of the herd, one ram, and seven yearling lambs that you are sure are unblemished. [9]Their grain offerings of bran flour mixed with oil: three tenths of an ephah for the bull, two tenths for the one ram, [10]and one tenth for each of the seven lambs. [11]One goat will be a purification offering. These are in addition to the purification offering for purging,* the regular burnt offering with its grain offering, and their libations.

On the Feast of Booths. [12]* On the fifteenth day of the seventh month you will declare a holy day:[d] you shall do no heavy work. For the following seven days you will celebrate a pilgrimage feast to the LORD. [13]You will offer a burnt offering, an oblation of pleasing aroma to the LORD: thirteen bulls* of the herd, two rams, and fourteen yearling lambs that are unblemished. [14]Their grain offerings will

28:18 Heavy work: apparently, some sorts of activity are permitted on a day such as this, whereas "any work" is prohibited by 29:7 on the Day of Atonement. See note on Lv 23:3.

28:26 The day of first fruits: a unique term for this feast, which is usually called "the feast of Weeks"; it was celebrated as a thanksgiving for the wheat harvest seven weeks after the barley harvest (Passover). In the time of Jesus it was commonly known by the Greek word "Pentecost," that is, "fiftieth" (day after the Passover); see note on Lv 23:16–21.

29:1 In the seventh month on the first day: (about September–October) now the Jewish New Year's Day. In the older calendar the year began with the first of Nisan (March–April), which is still known as the first month; cf. Ex 12:2.

29:7 The tenth day of this seventh month: the Day of Atonement. **Humble yourselves**: that is, with fasting.

29:11 The purification offering for purging: the bull prescribed in Lv 16:11–12 for the purging of the tent sanctuary.

29:12 This feast of Booths (Tabernacles or Sukkot) celebrating the vintage harvest was the most popular of all and therefore had the most elaborate ritual. See note on Lv 23:34.

29:13 Thirteen bulls: the number of bulls sacrificed before the octave day was seventy, arranged on a descending

y: Ex 12:16; Lv 23:7. *z:* Ex 12:16; 13:6; Lv 23:8. *a:* Ex 34:22. *b:* Nm 10:10; Lv 23:24. *c:* Lv 16:29; 23:27–28, 32. *d:* Lv 23:34–35.

be of bran flour mixed with oil: three tenths of an ephah for each of the thirteen bulls, two tenths for each of the two rams, [15]and one tenth for each of the fourteen lambs. [16]One goat will be a purification offering. These are in addition to the regular burnt offering with its grain offering and libation.

[17]On the second day: twelve bulls of the herd, two rams, and fourteen unblemished yearling lambs, [18]with the grain offerings and libations for the bulls, rams and lambs in their prescribed number, [19]as well as one goat as a purification offering, besides the regular burnt offering with its grain offering and libation.

[20]On the third day: eleven bulls, two rams, and fourteen unblemished yearling lambs, [21]with the grain offerings and libations for the bulls, rams and lambs in their prescribed number, [22]as well as one goat for a purification offering, besides the regular burnt offering with its grain offering and libation.

[23]On the fourth day: ten bulls, two rams, and fourteen unblemished yearling lambs, [24]the grain offerings and libations for the bulls, rams and lambs in their prescribed number, [25]as well as one goat as a purification offering, besides the regular burnt offering, its grain offering and libation.

[26]On the fifth day: nine bulls, two rams, and fourteen unblemished yearling lambs, [27][e] with the grain offerings and libations for the bulls, rams and lambs in their prescribed number, [28]as well as one goat as a purification offering, besides the regular burnt offering with its grain offering and libation.

[29]On the sixth day: eight bulls, two rams, and fourteen unblemished yearling lambs, [30]with the grain offerings and libations for the bulls, rams and lambs in their prescribed number, [31]as well as one goat as a purification offering, besides the regular burnt offering, its grain offering and libation.

[32]On the seventh day: seven bulls, two rams, and fourteen unblemished yearling lambs, [33]with the grain offerings and libations for the bulls, rams and lambs in their prescribed number, [34]as well as one goat as a purification offering, besides the regular burnt offering, its grain offering and libation.

[35]On the eighth day[f] you will hold a public assembly:* you shall do no heavy work. [36]You will offer a burnt offering, an oblation of pleasing aroma to the LORD: one bull, one ram, and seven unblemished yearling lambs, [37]with the grain offerings and libations for the bulls, rams and lambs in their prescribed number, [38]as well as one goat as a purification offering, besides the regular burnt offering with its grain offering and libation.

[39]These are the offerings you will make to the LORD on your festivals, besides your votive or voluntary offerings of burnt offerings, grain offerings, libations, and communion offerings.

CHAPTER 30

See RG 136–37

[1]So Moses instructed the Israelites exactly as the LORD had commanded him.

Validity and Annulment of Vows. [2]Moses said to the heads of the Israelite tribes, "This is what the LORD has commanded: [3]When a man makes a vow to the LORD or binds himself under oath to a pledge,* he shall not violate his word, but must fulfill exactly the promise he has uttered.[g]

[4]"When a woman makes a vow to the LORD, or binds herself to a pledge, while still in her father's house in her youth, [5]and her father learns of her vow or the pledge to which she bound herself and says nothing to her about it, then any vow or any pledge to which she bound herself remains valid. [6]But if on the day he learns of it her father opposes her, then any vow or any pledge to which she bound herself becomes invalid;

scale so that the number on the seventh day was the sacred number seven.

29:35 A public assembly: the Hebrew word is the technical term for the closing celebration of the three major feasts of the Passover, Pentecost and Booths, or of other special feasts that lasted for a week. Cf. Lv 23:36; Dt 16:8; 2 Chr 7:9; Neh 8:18.

30:3 A vow . . . a pledge: here the former signifies the promise to dedicate either a person, an animal, or a thing or their equivalent to the sanctuary upon the fulfillment of some specified conditions (Lv 27:1–13); the latter signifies the assumption of either a positive or a negative obligation—that is, the promise either to do something or to abstain from something; cf. v. 14.

e: Nm 29:30, 37. *f:* Lv 23:36; Jn 7:37. *g:* Dt 23:22; Eccl 5:3–4.

and the LORD will release her from it, since her father opposed her.

7“If she marries while under a vow or under a rash pledge to which she bound herself, 8and her husband learns of it, yet says nothing to her on the day he learns it, then the vows or the pledges to which she bound herself remain valid. 9But if on the day her husband learns of it he opposes her, he thereby annuls the vow she had made or the rash pledge to which she had bound herself, and the LORD will release her from it. 10(The vow of a widow or of a divorced woman, however, any pledge to which such a woman binds herself, is valid.)

11“If it is in her husband's house* that she makes a vow or binds herself under oath to a pledge, 12and her husband learns of it yet says nothing to her to oppose her, then all her vows remain valid or any pledge to which she has bound herself. 13But if on the day he learns of them her husband annuls them, then whatever she has expressly promised in her vows or in her pledge becomes invalid; since her husband has annulled them, the LORD will release her from them.

14“Any vow or any pledge that she makes under oath to humble herself, her husband may either confirm or annul. 15But if her husband, day after day, says nothing at all to her, he thereby confirms all her vows or all the pledges incumbent upon her; he has confirmed them, because on the day he learned of them he said nothing to her. 16If, however, he annuls them* some time after he first learned of them, he will be responsible for her guilt.”

17These are the statutes which the LORD commanded Moses concerning a husband and his wife, as well as a father and his daughter while she is still in her youth in her father's house.

CHAPTER 31

See RG 136–37

Campaign Against the Midianites. 1The LORD said to Moses:* 2Avenge the Israelites on the Midianites, and then you will be gathered to your people. 3So Moses told the people, “Arm some men among you for the campaign, to attack Midian and to execute the LORD's vengeance on Midian. 4From each of the tribes of Israel you will send a thousand men to the campaign.” 5From the contingents of Israel, therefore, a thousand men of each tribe were levied, so that there were twelve thousand men armed for war. 6Moses sent them out on the campaign, a thousand from each tribe, with Phinehas, son of Eleazar, the priest for the campaign, who had with him the sacred vessels and the trumpets for sounding the alarm. 7They waged war against the Midianites, as the LORD had commanded Moses, and killed every male. 8Besides those slain in battle, they killed the kings of Midian: Evi, Rekem, Zur, Hur and Reba, the five kings of Midian;* and they also killed Balaam, son of Beor, with the sword. 9But the Israelites took captive the women of the Midianites with their children, and all their herds and flocks and wealth as loot, 10while they set on fire all the towns where they had settled and all their encampments. 11Then they took all the plunder, with the people and animals they had captured, and brought the captives, together with the spoils and plunder, 12to Moses and Eleazar the priest and to the Israelite community at their camp on the plains of Moab by the Jordan opposite Jericho.

Treatment of the Captives. 13When Moses and Eleazar the priest, with all the leaders of the community, went outside the camp to meet them, 14Moses became angry with the officers of the army, the commanders of thousands and the commanders of hundreds, who were returning from the military campaign. 15“So you have spared all the women!” he exclaimed. 16“These are the very ones who on Balaam's advice were behind the Israelites' unfaithfulness to the LORD in the affair at Peor,[h] so that plague

30:11 In her husband's house: after her marriage. This contrasts with the case given in vv. 7–9.

30:16 He annuls them: he prevents their fulfillment. Since he has first allowed the vows to remain valid, he can no longer annul them.

31:1–3 The narrative of Israel's campaign against Midian, which was interrupted after 25:18, is now resumed.

31:8 The five kings of Midian: they are called Midianite princes, Sihon's vassals, in Jos 13:21.

h: 2 Pt 2:15; Rev 2:14.

struck the LORD's community. [17]* Now kill, therefore, every male among the children and kill every woman who has had sexual relations with a man. [18]But you may spare for yourselves all the girls who have not had sexual relations.

Purification After Combat. [19]"Moreover, remain outside the camp for seven days; every one of you who has killed anyone or touched someone killed will purify yourselves on the third and on the seventh day—both you and your captives. [20]You will also purify every garment, every article of leather, everything made of goats' hair, and every article of wood."

[21]Eleazar the priest told the soldiers who had taken part in the battle: "This is the prescribed ritual which the LORD has commanded Moses: [22]gold, silver, bronze, iron, tin and lead— [23]whatever can stand fire—you shall put into the fire, that it may become clean; however, it must also be purified with water of purification.* But whatever cannot stand fire you must put into the water. [24]On the seventh day you will wash your garments, and then you will again be clean. After that you may enter the camp."

Division of the Spoils. [25]The LORD said to Moses: [26]With the help of Eleazar the priest and of the heads of the ancestral houses of the community, inventory all the spoils captured, human being and beast alike; [27]then divide the spoils* between the warriors who went on the campaign and the whole community. [28]You will levy a tax for the LORD on the soldiers who went on the campaign: one out of every five hundred persons, oxen, donkeys, and sheep. [29]From their half you will take it and give it to Eleazar the priest as a contribution to the LORD. [30]From the Israelites' half you will take one captive from every fifty human beings, oxen, donkeys, and sheep—all the animals—and give them to the Levites, who perform the duties of the LORD's tabernacle. [31]So Moses and Eleazar the priest did this, as the LORD had commanded Moses.

Amount of the Plunder. [32]This plunder, what was left of the loot which the troops had taken, amounted to six hundred and seventy-five thousand sheep, [33]seventy-two thousand oxen, [34]sixty-one thousand donkeys, [35]and thirty-two thousand women who had not had sexual relations.

[36]The half-share that fell to those who had gone out on the campaign was in number: three hundred and thirty-seven thousand five hundred sheep, [37]of which six hundred and seventy-five fell as tax to the LORD; [38]thirty-six thousand oxen, of which seventy-two fell as tax to the LORD; [39]thirty thousand five hundred donkeys, of which sixty-one fell as tax to the LORD; [40]and sixteen thousand persons, of whom thirty-two persons fell as tax to the LORD. [41]Moses gave the taxes contributed to the LORD to Eleazar the priest, exactly as the LORD had commanded Moses.

[42]As for the Israelites' half, which Moses had taken from the men who had fought—[43]the community's half was three hundred and thirty-seven thousand five hundred sheep, [44]thirty-six thousand oxen, [45]thirty thousand five hundred donkeys, [46]and sixteen thousand persons. [47]From the Israelites' half, Moses took one captive from every fifty, from human being and beast alike, and gave them to the Levites, who performed the duties of the LORD's tabernacle, exactly as the LORD had commanded Moses.

Gifts of the Officers. [48]Then those who were officers over the contingents of the army, commanders of thousands and commanders of hundreds, came up to Moses [49]and said to him, "Your servants have counted the soldiers under our command, and not one of us is missing. [50]* So, we have brought as an offering to the LORD articles of gold that each of us has picked up—anklets,

31:17 There are later references to Midian in Jgs 6–8; 1 Kgs 11:18; Is 60:6. The present raid was only against those Midianites who were dwelling at this time near the encampment of the Israelites.

31:23 Water of purification: water mixed with the ashes of the red heifer as prescribed in 19:9.

31:27 Divide the spoils: for a similar division of the plunder into two equal parts, between those who engaged in the battle and those who stayed with the baggage, cf. 1 Sm 30:24. But note that here the tax on the plunder of the noncombatants is ten times as much as that on the soldiers' plunder.

31:50 The precise nature and use of some of these articles of gold is not certain.

bracelets, rings, earrings, or pendants—to make atonement for ourselves before the LORD." [51]Moses and Eleazar the priest accepted the gold from them, all fashioned pieces. [52]The gold that was given as a contribution to the LORD—from the commanders of thousands and the commanders of hundreds—amounted in all to sixteen thousand seven hundred and fifty shekels. [53]What the common soldiers had looted each one kept for himself.* [54]So Moses and Eleazar the priest accepted the gold from the commanders of thousands and of hundreds, and put it in the tent of meeting as a reminder on behalf of the Israelites before the LORD.

CHAPTER 32

See RG 136–37

Request of Gad and Reuben. [1]Now the Reubenites and Gadites had a very large number of livestock. Noticing that the land of Jazer and of Gilead* was a place suited to livestock, [2]the Gadites and Reubenites came to Moses and Eleazar the priest and to the leaders of the community and said, [3*]"The region of Ataroth, Dibon, Jazer, Nimrah, Heshbon, Elealeh, Sebam, Nebo and Baal-meon— [4]the land which the LORD has laid low before the community of Israel, is a land for livestock, and your servants have livestock." [5]They continued, "If we find favor with you, let this land be given to your servants as their possession. Do not make us cross the Jordan."

Moses' Rebuke. [6]But Moses answered the Gadites and Reubenites: "Are your kindred, then, to go to war, while you remain here? [7]Why do you wish to discourage the Israelites from crossing to the land the LORD has given them? [8]That is just what your ancestors did when I sent them from Kadesh-barnea to reconnoiter the land.[i] [9]They went up to the Wadi Eshcol and reconnoitered the land, then so discouraged the Israelites that they would not enter the land the LORD had given them. [10j] At that time the anger of the LORD flared up, and he swore: [11]None of the men twenty years old or more who have come up from Egypt will see the land I promised under oath to Abraham and Isaac and Jacob, because they have not followed me unreservedly— [12k] except the Kenizzite* Caleb, son of Jephunneh, the Kenizzite, and Joshua, son of Nun, since they have followed the LORD unreservedly. [13]So the anger of the LORD flared up against the Israelites and he made them wander in the wilderness forty years, until the whole generation that had done evil in the sight of the LORD had disappeared. [14]And now here you are, offspring of sinful stock, rising up in your ancestors' place to add still more to the LORD's blazing anger against the Israelites. [15]If you turn away from following him, he will again abandon them in the wilderness, and you will bring about the ruin of this entire people."

Counter Proposal. [16]But they approached him and said: "We will only build sheepfolds here for our flocks and towns for our families; [17]but we ourselves will march as troops in the vanguard before the Israelites,[l] until we have led them to their destination. Meanwhile our families will remain in the fortified towns because of the land's inhabitants. [18]We will not return to our homes until all the Israelites have taken possession of their heritage. [19m] But we will not claim any heritage with them across the Jordan and beyond, because we have received a heritage for ourselves on the eastern side of the Jordan."

Agreement Reached. [20*] Moses said to them in reply: "If you do this—if you march as troops before the LORD into battle [21]and

31:53 Apparently because of the commanders' generosity the common troops were under no sort of obligation to make their own offerings and could keep their loot.

32:1 Gilead: the name of the western part of the plateau east of the Jordan, sometimes signifying the whole region from the Yarmuk to the Jordan, sometimes only the northern part of this region, and sometimes, as here, only its southern part. Jazer lay to the east of southern Gilead.

32:3 The places named in this verse, as well as the additional ones given in vv. 34–38, were all in the former kingdom of Sihon, that is, in the region between the Jabbok and the Arnon. Cf. 21:23–24; Jos 13:19–21, 24–27.

32:12 Kenizzite: a member of the clan of Kenaz, which, according to Gn 36:11, 15, 42, was Edomite; but, according to Nm 13:6; 34:19, Caleb belonged to the tribe of Judah; cf. also Jos 14:6, 14.

32:20–22 Since the ark of the Lord was carried into battle with the Israelite army, the vanguard was said to march before the Lord (see Jos 6:6–9).

i: Nm 13:31–33; Dt 1:22. *j:* Dt 1:34–35. *k:* Nm 14:24; Dt 1:36. *l:* Jos 4:12–13. *m:* Jos 13:8.

cross the Jordan in full force before the
LORD until he has driven his enemies out of
his way 22 and the land is subdued before the
LORD, then you may return here, free from
every obligation to the LORD and to Israel,
and this land will be your possession before
the LORD.[n] 23 But if you do not do this, you
will have sinned against the LORD, and you
can be sure that the consequences of your sin
will overtake you. 24 Build the towns, then,
for your families, and the folds for your
flocks, but fulfill what you have promised."

25 The Gadites and Reubenites answered
Moses, "Your servants will do as my lord
commands. 26[o] While our wives and children, our livestock and other animals remain
there in the towns of Gilead, 27 all your servants will go across as armed troops before
the LORD to battle, just as my lord says."

28 So Moses gave this command in their regard to Eleazar the priest, to Joshua, son of
Nun, and to the heads of the ancestral houses
of the Israelite tribes: 29 He said to them, "If all
the Gadites and Reubenites cross the Jordan
with you in full force before the LORD into
battle, the land will be subdued before you,
and you will give them Gilead as a possession. 30 But if they will not go across in force
with you before the LORD, you will bring their
wives and children and livestock across before you into Canaan, and they will possess a
holding among you in the land of Canaan."

31 To this the Gadites and Reubenites
replied, "We will do what the LORD has ordered your servants. 32 We ourselves will go
across in force before the LORD into the land
of Canaan, but we will retain our hereditary
property on this side of the Jordan."* 33 So
Moses gave them—*the Gadites and Reubenites, as well as half the tribe of Manasseh, son of Joseph—the kingdom of Sihon,
king of the Amorites, and the kingdom of
Og, king of Bashan, the land with its towns,
and the districts of the surrounding towns.[p]

34 The Gadites rebuilt the cities of Dibon,
Ataroth, Aroer, 35 Atroth-shophan, Jazer, Jogbehah, 36 Beth-nimrah and Beth-haran—fortified cities—and sheepfolds. 37 The Reubenites rebuilt Heshbon, Elealeh, Kiriathaim,
38 Nebo, Baal-meon (names to be changed!),*
and Sibmah. These towns, which they rebuilt, they called by their old names.

Other Conquests. 39 The descendants of
Machir, son of Manasseh, went to Gilead
and captured it, dispossessing the Amorites
who were there. 40 (Moses gave Gilead to
Machir,[q] son of Manasseh, and he settled
there.) 41 Jair,[r] a descendant of Manasseh,
went and captured their tent villages, and
called them Havvoth-jair.* 42 Nobah went
and captured Kenath with its dependencies
and called it Nobah after his own name.

CHAPTER 33

See RG 136–37

Stages of the Journey. 1 The following
are the stages by which the Israelites went
out by companies from the land of Egypt under the guidance of Moses and Aaron.* 2 Moses recorded the starting points of the various stages at the direction of the LORD.
These are the stages according to their starting points: 3 They set out from Rameses in
the first month, on the fifteenth day of the
first month. On the day after the Passover

32:32 This side of the Jordan: lit., "beyond the Jordan"; the perspective in Hebrew is from the west bank looking toward the east bank where the Reubenites and Gadites finally settled.

32:33 The preceding is concerned solely with the two tribes of Gad and Reuben and with the land of the former kingdom of Sihon; it seems probable that the sudden reference here to the half-tribe of Manasseh and to their territory in Bashan, the former kingdom of Og, is a later addition to the text.

32:38 The phrase in parentheses is probably a gloss, warning the reader perhaps to substitute some other word for Nebo and Baal, the names of foreign deities mentioned in the last two city names. **They called by their old names**: lit., "they called by their names"; however, some understand the current Hebrew text to mean, "they called by new names," or "their own names."

32:41 Havvoth-jair: that is, "villages of Jair."

33:1–3 According to v. 2, this list of camping sites was drawn up by Moses as an itinerary recording Israel's trek through the wilderness. Comparison with the more detailed accounts of the journey as given elsewhere suggests that the list is not necessarily comprehensive. It records just forty camping sites, not counting the starting place, Rameses, and the terminus, the plains of Moab. This number, which corresponds exactly to the forty years of wandering in the wilderness, is probably a schematic device. Moreover, it seems that in its present form the order of some of the names has been disturbed. Several names listed here are not recorded elsewhere.

n: Jos 1:15. *o:* Jos 1:14. *p:* Dt 3:12; 29:7; Jos 12:6; 13:8. *q:* Dt 3:15. *r:* Dt 3:14.

the Israelites went forth in triumph, in view of all Egypt, [4]while the Egyptians buried those whom the LORD had struck down, every firstborn; on their gods, too, the LORD executed judgments.[s]

From Egypt to Sinai. [5]Setting out from Rameses, the Israelites camped at Succoth. [6]Setting out from Succoth, they camped at Etham near the edge of the wilderness. [7]Setting out from Etham, they turned back to Pi-hahiroth, which is opposite Baal-zephon, and they camped opposite Migdol.[t] [8]Setting out from Pi-hahiroth, they crossed over through the sea into the wilderness,[u] and after they traveled a three days' journey in the wilderness of Etham, they camped at Marah. [9]Setting out from Marah, they came to Elim; at Elim there were twelve springs of water and seventy palm trees, and they camped there.[v] [10]Setting out from Elim, they camped beside the Red Sea. [11]Setting out from the Red Sea, they camped in the wilderness of Sin. [12]Setting out from the wilderness of Sin, they camped at Dophkah. [13]Setting out from Dophkah, they camped at Alush. [14]Setting out from Alush, they camped at Rephidim, where there was no water for the people to drink.[w] [15]Setting out from Rephidim, they camped in the wilderness of Sinai.[x]

From Sinai to Kadesh. [16]Setting out from the wilderness of Sinai, they camped at Kibroth-hattaavah. [17]Setting out from Kibroth-hattaavah, they camped at Hazeroth.[y] [18]Setting out from Hazeroth, they camped at Rithmah. [19]Setting out from Rithmah, they camped at Rimmon-perez. [20]Setting out from Rimmon-perez, they camped at Libnah. [21]Setting out from Libnah, they camped at Rissah. [22]Setting out from Rissah, they camped at Kehelathah. [23]Setting out from Kehelathah, they camped at Mount Shepher. [24]Setting out from Mount Shepher, they camped at Haradah. [25]Setting out from Haradah, they camped at Makheloth. [26]Setting out from Makheloth, they camped at Tahath. [27]Setting out from Tahath, they camped at Terah. [28]Setting out from Terah, they camped at Mithkah. [29]Setting out from Mithkah, they camped at Hashmonah. [30]* Setting out from Hashmonah, they camped at Moseroth. [31]Setting out from Moseroth, they camped at Bene-jaakan. [32]Setting out from Bene-jaakan, they camped at Mount Gidgad. [33]Setting out from Mount Gidgad, they camped at Jotbathah. [34]Setting out from Jotbathah, they camped at Abronah. [35]Setting out from Abronah, they camped at Ezion-geber.* [36]Setting out from Ezion-geber, they camped in the wilderness of Zin, that is, Kadesh.[z]

From Kadesh to the Plains of Moab. [37]Setting out from Kadesh, they camped at Mount Hor on the border of the land of Edom.

[38]Aaron the priest ascended Mount Hor[a] at the LORD's direction, and there he died in the fortieth year after the departure of the Israelites from the land of Egypt, on the first day of the fifth month. [39]Aaron was a hundred and twenty-three years old when he died on Mount Hor.

[40]* When the Canaanite, the king of Arad, who ruled over the Negeb in the land of Canaan, heard that the Israelites were coming . . . .

[41]* Setting out from Mount Hor, they camped at Zalmonah. [42]Setting out from Zalmonah, they camped at Punon. [43]Setting out from Punon, they camped at Oboth. [44]Setting out from Oboth, they camped at Iye-abarim on the border of Moab. [45]Setting out from Iye-abarim, they camped at Dibon-gad. [46]Setting out from Dibon-gad, they camped at Almon-diblathaim. [47]Setting out from Almon-diblathaim, they camped in the

33:30–36 Moseroth is mentioned in Dt 10:6 (in the form of "Moserah") as the place where Aaron died, apparently a variant of the tradition here in v. 38 regarding the place of Aaron's death; so also Nm 20:22–24 and Dt 32:50. Perhaps Moseroth was close to Mount Hor.

33:35 Ezion-geber: Solomon conducted sea trade with Ophir from this port (1 Kgs 9:26), today probably identified on the northern coast of the Gulf of Elath between the Jordanian city of Aqabah and the Israeli city of Elath.

33:40 The verse repeats almost verbatim the same introduction to the account of the victory over Arad as is given in 21:1–3, where it also follows the account of Aaron's death. Perhaps the isolated verse here is intended by the editor(s) of Numbers to point the reader to the fuller account given there.

33:41b–49 It seems that this section stood originally immediately after v. 36a.

s: Ex 12:12, 29, 37. *t:* Ex 14:2. *u:* Ex 15:22. *v:* Ex 15:27. *w:* Ex 17:1. *x:* Ex 19:2. *y:* Nm 11:34–35. *z:* Nm 20:1, 22. *a:* Nm 20:25; Dt 32:50.

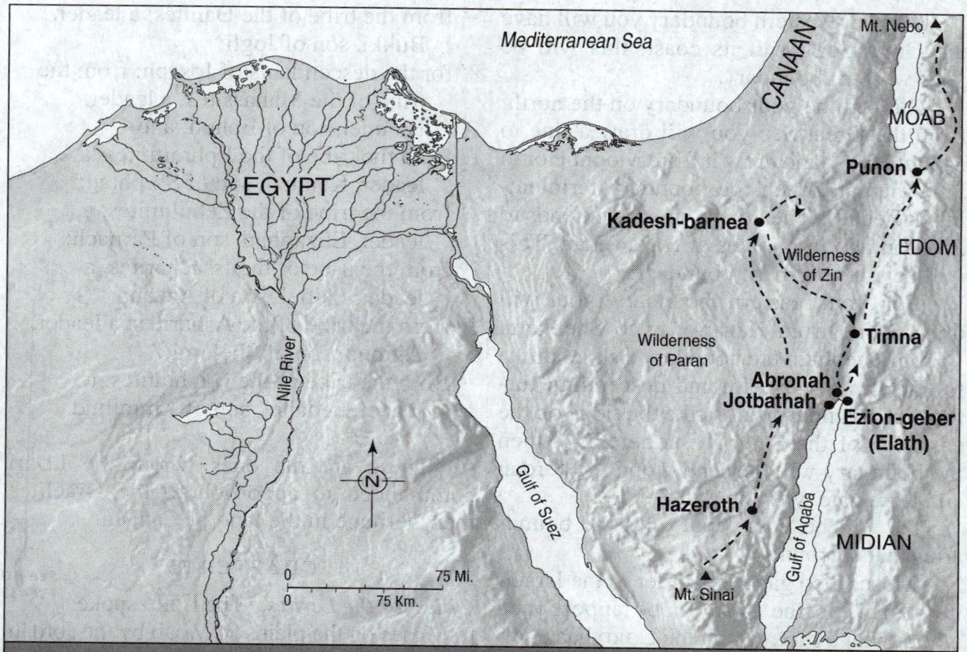

Journey from the Wilderness to Canaan

Abarim range opposite Nebo. [48]Setting out from the Abarim range, they camped on the plains of Moab by the Jordan opposite Jericho. [49]They camped by the Jordan on the plains of Moab extended from Beth-jeshimoth to Abel-shittim.

Conquest and Division of Canaan. [50]The LORD spoke to Moses on the plains of Moab by the Jordan opposite Jericho: [51]Speak to the Israelites and say to them: When you go across the Jordan into the land of Canaan, [52]dispossess all the inhabitants of the land before you; destroy all their stone figures, destroy all their molten images, and demolish all their high places.[b]

[53]You will take possession of the land and settle in it, for I have given you the land to possess. [54]You will apportion the land among yourselves by lot, clan by clan, assigning a large heritage to a large clan and a small heritage to a small clan.[c] Wherever anyone's lot falls, there will his possession be; you will apportion these shares within your ancestral tribe.

[55]But if you do not dispossess the inhabitants of the land before you, those whom you allow to remain will become barbs in your eyes and thorns in your sides, and they will harass you in the land where you live,[d] [56]and I will treat you as I had intended to treat them.

CHAPTER 34

The Boundaries. [1]The LORD spoke to Moses: [2]Give the Israelites this order: When you enter the land of Canaan, this is the territory that shall fall to you as your heritage—the land of Canaan with its boundaries:

[3]Your southern boundary will be at the wilderness of Zin along the border of Edom;[e] on the east your southern boundary will begin at the end of the Salt Sea. [4]Then your boundary will turn south of the Akrabbim Pass and cross Zin. Terminating south of Kadesh-barnea, it extends to Hazar-addar and crosses to Azmon.[f] [5]Then the boundary will turn from Azmon to the Wadi of Egypt and terminate at the Sea.[g]

---

b: Ex 23:31; 34:13; Dt 7:5; 12:3. *c:* Nm 26:53–56. *d:* Jos 23:13; Jgs 2:3. *e:* Jos 15:1–2. *f:* Jos 15:3. *g:* Jos 15:4.

6 For your western boundary you will have
the Great Sea* with its coast; this will be
your western boundary.
7 This will be your boundary on the north:
from the Great Sea you will draw a line to
Mount Hor,* 8 and draw it from Mount Hor to
Lebo-hamath, with the boundary terminating at Zedad. 9 Then the boundary extends to
Ziphron and terminates at Hazar-enan. This
will be your northern boundary.
10 For your eastern boundary you will
draw a line from Hazar-enan to Shepham.
11 From Shepham the boundary will go down
to Riblah, east of Ain, and descending further, the boundary will strike the ridge on the
east side of the Sea of Chinnereth;* 12 then
the boundary will descend along the Jordan
and terminate with the Salt Sea.

This will be your land, with the boundaries that surround it.

13 Moses also gave this order to the Israelites: "This is the land, to be apportioned
among you by lot, which the LORD has commanded to be given to the nine and a half
tribes. 14 For the tribe of the Reubenites according to their ancestral houses, and the
tribe of the Gadites according to their ancestral houses, as well as half of the tribe of Manasseh, have already received their heritage;
15 these two and a half tribes have received
their heritage across the Jordan opposite Jericho, in the east, toward the sunrise."

Supervisors of the Allotment. 16 The LORD
spoke to Moses: 17 These are the names of
the men who shall apportion the land among
you: Eleazar the priest, and Joshua, son of
Nun; 18h and you will designate one leader
from each of the tribes to apportion the land.
19 These are the names of the men:

from the tribe of Judah: Caleb, son of Jephunneh,
20 from the tribe of the Simeonites: Samuel, son of Ammihud;
21 from the tribe of Benjamin: Elidad, son of Chislon;
22 from the tribe of the Danites: a leader, Bukki, son of Jogli;
23 for the descendants of Joseph: from the tribe of the Manassites: a leader, Hanniel, son of Ephod; and
24 from the tribe of the Ephraimites: a leader, Kemuel, son of Shiphtan;
25 from the tribe of the Zebulunites: a leader, Elizaphan, son of Parnach;
26 from the tribe of the Issacharites: a leader, Paltiel, son of Azzan;
27 from the tribe of the Asherites: a leader, Ahihud, son of Shelomi;
28 from the tribe of the Naphtalites: a leader, Pedahel, son of Ammihud.

29 These are the ones whom the LORD commanded to apportion to the Israelites their heritage in the land of Canaan.

CHAPTER 35

See RG 136–37

Cities for the Levites. 1 The LORD spoke
to Moses on the plains of Moab by the Jordan
opposite Jericho: 2i Command the Israelites
out of the heritage they possess to give the Levites cities to dwell in; you will also give the
Levites the pasture lands around the cities.
3 The cities will be for them to dwell in, and the
pasture lands will be for their cattle, their
flocks, and all their other animals. 4 The pasture
lands of the cities to be assigned the Levites
shall extend a thousand cubits out from the city
walls in every direction. 5 You will measure out
two thousand cubits outside the city along the
east side, two thousand cubits along the south
side, two thousand cubits along the west side,
and two thousand cubits along the north side,
with the city lying in the center. These will be
the pasture lands of their cities.
6j Now these are the cities you will give to
the Levites: the six cities of asylum which
you must establish for the homicide to run
to, and in addition forty-two other cities— 7 a
total of forty-eight cities with their pasture
lands which you will assign to the Levites.
8* In assigning the cities from what the Isra-

34:6 The Great Sea: the Mediterranean.

34:7–8 Mount Hor: different from the one where Aaron died; cf. 20:22; 33:37–38.

34:11 Sea of Chinnereth: in the New Testament known as the Sea of Galilee; today called Lake Kinneret.

35:8 This provision was hardly observed in the actual assignment of the levitical cities as narrated in Jos 21.

h: Nm 1:4. *i:* Jos 14:3–4; 21:2. *j:* Dt 4:41–42; Jos 20:2.

elites possess, take more from a larger group and fewer from a smaller one, so that each will cede cities to the Levites in proportion to the heritage which it receives.

Cities of Asylum. [9][k] The LORD spoke to Moses: [10]Speak to the Israelites and say to them: When you go across the Jordan into the land of Canaan, [11]select for yourselves cities to serve as cities of asylum, where a homicide who has killed someone inadvertently may flee. [12]These cities will serve you as places of asylum from the avenger of blood,* so that a homicide will not be put to death until tried before the community. [13]As for the cities you assign, you will have six cities of asylum: [14]you will designate three cities beyond the Jordan, and you will designate three cities in the land of Canaan. These will be cities of asylum. [15]These six cities will serve as places of asylum for the Israelites, and for the resident or transient aliens among them, so that anyone who has killed a person inadvertently may flee there.

Murder and Manslaughter. [16]* If someone strikes another with an iron instrument and causes death, that person is a murderer, and the murderer must be put to death.[l] [17]If someone strikes another with a death-dealing stone in the hand and death results, that person is a murderer, and the murderer must be put to death. [18]Or if someone strikes another with a death-dealing club in the hand and death results, that person is a murderer, and the murderer must be put to death. [19]The avenger of blood is the one who will kill the murderer, putting the individual to death on sight.

[20]If someone pushes another out of hatred, or throws something from an ambush, and death results,[m] [21]or strikes another with the hand out of enmity and death results, the assailant must be put to death as a murderer. The avenger of blood will kill the murderer on sight.

[22][n] However, if someone pushes another without malice aforethought, or without lying in ambush throws some object at another, [23]or without seeing drops upon another some death-dealing stone and death results, although there was neither enmity nor malice— [24]then the community will judge between the assailant and the avenger of blood in accordance with these norms. [25]The community will deliver the homicide from the avenger of blood and the community will return the homicide to the city of asylum where the latter had fled;[o] and the individual will stay there until the death of the high priest who has been anointed with sacred oil. [26]If the homicide leaves at all the bounds of the city of asylum to which flight had been made, [27]and is found by the avenger of blood beyond the bounds of the city of asylum, and the avenger of blood kills the homicide, the avenger incurs no bloodguilt; [28]for the homicide was required to stay in the city of asylum until the death of the high priest. Only after the death of the high priest may the homicide return to the land of the homicide's possession.

[29]This is the statute for you throughout all your generations, wherever you live, for rendering judgment.

Judgment. [30]Whenever someone kills another, the evidence of witnesses is required to kill the murderer.[p] A single witness does not suffice for putting a person to death.

No Indemnity. [31]You will not accept compensation in place of the life of a murderer who deserves to die, but that person must be put to death. [32]Nor will you accept compensation to allow one who has fled to a city of asylum to return to live in the land before the death of the high priest. [33]You will not pollute the land where you live. For bloodshed pollutes the land, and the land can have no expiation for the blood shed on it except through the blood of the one who shed it. [34]Do not defile the land in which you live and in the midst of which I dwell;[q] for I the LORD dwell in the midst of the Israelites.

35:12 The avenger of blood: Hebrew, *go'el*, often translated as "redeemer," one who, as next of kin to the slain (2 Sm 14:7), and here, as executor of public justice, had the right and duty to take the life of the murderer; cf. Dt 19:6, 12; Jos 20:3, 5, 9.

35:16–25 Here, as also in Dt 19:1–13, there is a casuistic development of the original law as stated in Ex 21:12–14.

k: Dt 19:2; Jos 20:2–6. *l:* Ex 21:12; Lv 24:17. *m:* Ex 21:14; Dt 19:11. *n:* Jos 20:3. *o:* Jos 20:6. *p:* Dt 17:6; 19:15; Jn 8:17; 2 Cor 13:1; 1 Tm 5:19. *q:* Ex 29:45.

CHAPTER 36

See RG 136–37

Inheritance of Daughters. [1]The heads of the ancestral houses in a clan of the descendants of Gilead, son of Machir, son of Manasseh—one of the Josephite clans—came up and spoke before Moses and Eleazar the priest and before the leaders who were the heads of the ancestral houses of the Israelites. [2]They said: "The LORD commanded my lord to apportion the land by lot for a heritage among the Israelites;[r] and my lord was commanded by the LORD to give the heritage of Zelophehad our kinsman to his daughters. [3]But if they marry into one of the other Israelite tribes, their heritage will be withdrawn from our ancestral heritage and will be added to that of the tribe into which they marry; thus the heritage that fell to us by lot will be diminished. [4]When the Israelites celebrate the jubilee year,* the heritage of these women will be added to that of the tribe into which they marry and their heritage will be withdrawn from that of our ancestral tribe."

[5]* So Moses commanded the Israelites at the direction of the LORD: "The tribe of the Josephites are right in what they say. [6]This is what the LORD commands with regard to the daughters of Zelophehad: They may marry anyone they please, provided they marry into a clan of their ancestral tribe, [7]so that no heritage of the Israelites will pass from one tribe to another, but all the Israelites will retain their own ancestral heritage. [8]Every daughter who inherits property in any of the Israelite tribes will marry someone belonging to a clan of her own ancestral tribe, in order that all the Israelites may remain in possession of their own ancestral heritage. [9]Thus, no heritage will pass from one tribe to another, but all the Israelite tribes will retain their own ancestral heritage."

[10]The daughters of Zelophehad did exactly as the LORD commanded Moses. [11]Mahlah, Tirzah, Hoglah, Milcah and Noah, Zelophehad's daughters, married sons of their uncles on their father's side. [12]They married within the clans of the descendants of Manasseh, son of Joseph; hence their heritage remained in the tribe of their father's clan.

Conclusion. [13]These are the commandments and decisions which the LORD commanded the Israelites through Moses, on the plains of Moab beside the Jordan opposite Jericho.

36:4 Before the jubilee year various circumstances, such as divorce, could make such property revert to its original tribal owners; but in the jubilee year it became irrevocably attached to its new owners.

36:5–9 This is a supplement to the law given in 27:5–11.

r: Nm 26:55; 27:6; Jos 17:3–4.

See RG 141–48

The Book of Deuteronomy

The title of Deuteronomy in Hebrew is *Debarim*, "words," from its opening phrase. The English title comes from the Septuagint of 17:18, *deuteronomion*, "copy of the law"; this title is appropriate because the book replicates much of the legal content of the previous books, serving as a "second law." It brings to a close the five books of the Torah or Pentateuch with a retrospective account of Israel's past—the exodus, the Sinai covenant, and the wilderness wanderings—and a look into Israel's future as they stand poised to enter the land of Canaan and begin their life as a people there.

The book consists of three long addresses by Moses. Each of these contains narrative, law, and exhortation, in varying proportions. In an expansion of the first commandment of the decalogue (Ex 20:5–6; Dt 5:9–10), Moses tells the Israelites how to make a success of their life as a people once they are settled in the land. The choice presented to Israel is to love the Lord and keep his commandments, or to serve "other gods." That choice will determine what kind of life they will make for themselves in the land. Whichever choice they make as a people carries consequences, which Deuteronomy terms "blessing" and "curse." Thus the book can be seen as a kind of survival manual for Israel in their life as a people: how to live and what to avoid. This gives the book its hortatory style and tone of life-or-death urgency.

One defining concern of the book is centralization of worship. As Israel's God is one (6:4–5), so its worship must be focused in one place, which the Lord "will choose from among your tribes"; there the Lord will "make his name dwell" (see note on 12:5). Thus the privileged status of the Jerusalem Temple is asserted; all other places and all other modes of worship of the God of Israel (the local shrines, the "high places," "under every green tree") are proscribed.

The book was probably composed over the course of three centuries, from the eighth century to the exile and beyond. It bears some relation to "the Book of the Law" discovered in the Jerusalem Temple around 622 B.C. during the reign of King Josiah (2 Kgs 22:8–13). It gives evidence of later editing: cf. the references to exile in 4:1–40; 28:63–68; 29:21–28; 30:1–10.

Over the book looms the disaster of 722/721, the fall of the Northern Kingdom, Israel. The detailed description of siege (28:49–57) especially echoes the fate the North suffered at the hands of the Assyrian invader. The book draws the minds of its intended readers back to a time before disastrous mistakes were made and their disastrous effects felt, and serves to explain the political and theological dynamics that led to the destruction of the North as well as to warn the surviving Southern Kingdom, Judah, to reform by keeping faith with Israel's covenant Lord.

The characteristic and highly recognizable language and theology of Deuteronomy are seen in editorial comments structuring the works that follow it in the Hebrew canon, the Books of Joshua, Judges, Samuel, and Kings. Together with Deuteronomy, these present a history of Israel from Moses to the time of the Babylonian exile. Conventionally this great multivolume work is termed the Deuteronomistic History. The Book of Deuteronomy itself was also incorporated into the Torah as its fifth volume.

The book presents three discourses by Moses, as follows:

I. First Address (1:1–4:43)
II. Second Address (4:44–28:69)
  A. The Lord's Covenant with Israel (4:44–11:32)
  B. The Deuteronomic Code (12:1–28:69)
III. Third Address (29:1–33:29)
IV. The Death of Moses (34:1–12)

I. First Address

CHAPTER 1

See RG 141–48

Introduction. [1]* These are the words that Moses spoke to all Israel beyond the Jordan in the wilderness, in the Arabah, opposite Suph, between Paran and Tophel, Laban, Hazeroth, and Dizahab. [2]It is a journey of eleven days from Horeb* to Kadesh-barnea by way of the highlands of Seir.

[3]In the fortieth year,* on the first day of the eleventh month, Moses spoke to the Israelites according to all that the LORD had commanded him to speak to them, [4]after he had defeated Sihon, king of the Amorites, who reigned in Heshbon,[a] and Og, king of Bashan, who reigned in Ashtaroth and in Edrei. [5]Beyond the Jordan, in the land of Moab, Moses undertook to explain this law:

Departure from Horeb. [6]* [b] The LORD, our God, said to us at Horeb:* You have stayed long enough at this mountain. [7]Leave here and go to the hill country of the Amorites* and to all the surrounding regions, the Arabah, the mountains, the Shephelah, the

1:1 The entire book of Deuteronomy is set "beyond the Jordan," in the land of Moab (cf. v. 5; Nm 36:13), on the eve of the Israelites' crossing of the Jordan (Jos 3). **The Arabah**: the valley of the Jordan and the depression south of the Dead Sea.

1:2 Horeb: an alternative name for Mount Sinai, the wilderness mountain where the Israelites received revelation from God (cf. Ex 3; 19). **Kadesh-barnea**: the southern gateway to the land of Canaan, from which Moses sent spies to reconnoiter the land (cf. Nm 13:26; 32:8). **Seir**: Edom, the land just south of Moab.

1:3 Fortieth year: counting from the exodus from Egypt (cf. Ex 12:2; 13:20–22).

1:6–3:29 Throughout this section Moses is reviewing the events following the departure from Horeb, as a basis for the exhortation beginning in 4:1. Most of these events are narrated with some variation in the Book of Numbers.

1:6 Horeb: the name given to the mountain of revelation in the Elohist and Deuteronomic traditions; this mountain is called Sinai in the Yahwist and Priestly traditions.

1:7 The hill country of the Amorites: the central moun-

a: Dt 2:24–3:11; Nm 21:21–35. *b*: Ex 32:34–33:3.

Negeb and the seacoast—the land of the Canaanites and the Lebanon as far as the Great River, the Euphrates. [8]See, I have given that land over to you.[c] Go now and possess the land that the LORD swore to your ancestors, Abraham, Isaac, and Jacob, to give to them and to their descendants after them.

Appointment of Elders. [9d] At that time I said to you, "I am unable to carry you by myself.[e] [10]The LORD, your God, has made you numerous, and now you are as numerous as the stars of the heavens.[f] [11]May the LORD, the God of your ancestors, increase you a thousand times over, and bless you as he promised! [12]But how can I, by myself, bear the weight, the contentiousness of you? [13]Provide wise, discerning, and reputable persons for each of your tribes, that I may appoint them as your leaders." [14]You answered me, "What you have proposed is good." [15]So I took the leaders of your tribes, wise and reputable, and set them as leaders over you, commanders over thousands, over hundreds, over fifties and over tens, and other tribal officers. [16g] I charged your judges at that time, "Listen to complaints among your relatives, and administer true justice to both parties even if one of them is a resident alien. [17]In rendering judgment, do not consider who a person is; give ear to the lowly and to the great alike, fearing no one, for the judgment is God's. Any case that is too difficult for you bring to me and I will hear it." [18]Thus I charged you, at that time, with all the things you were to do.

The Twelve Scouts. [19h] Then we set out from Horeb and journeyed through that whole vast and fearful wilderness that you have seen, in the direction of the hill country of the Amorites, as the LORD, our God, had commanded; and we came to Kadesh-barnea.[i] [20]I said to you, "You have come to the hill country of the Amorites, which the LORD, our God, is giving us. [21]See, the LORD, your God, has given this land over to you. Go up and take possession of it, as the LORD, the God of your ancestors, has promised you. Do not fear or be dismayed." [22]Then all of you approached me and said, "Let us send men ahead to spy out the land for us and report to us on the road we should follow and the cities we will come upon." [23]Agreeing with the proposal, I took twelve men from your number, one from each tribe. [24]They set out into the hill country as far as the Wadi Eshcol, and explored it. [25]Then, taking along some of the fruit of the land, they brought it down to us and reported, "The land the LORD, our God, is giving us is good."

Threats of Revolt. [26j] But you refused to go up;[k] you defied the command of the LORD, your God. [27]You set to murmuring in your tents, "Out of hatred for us the LORD has brought us out of the land of Egypt,[l] to deliver us into the power of the Amorites and destroy us. [28]What shall we meet with up there? Our men have made our hearts melt by saying, 'The people are bigger and taller than we, and their cities are large and fortified to the sky; besides, we saw the Anakim* there.' "[m]

[29]But I said to you, "Have no dread or fear of them. [30n] The LORD, your God, who goes before you, is the one who will fight for you, just as he acted with you before your very eyes in Egypt, [31]as well as in the wilderness, where you saw how the LORD, your God, carried you, as one carries his own child, all along your journey until you arrived at this place." [32]Despite this, you would not trust the LORD, your God, [33]who journeys before you to find you a place to camp—by night in the fire, and by day in the cloud, to show you

tain range of Palestine. **The Negeb**: the arid land in southern Palestine. **The Lebanon**: the mountain range of Phoenicia, north of Palestine. This is an idealized presentation of the land the Israelites were to occupy; Israel never held power as far as the "Great River" (the Euphrates). The Amorites and the Canaanites were only two of several different peoples occupying the land (cf. 7:1).

1:28 Anakim: a people proverbially notable for height, mentioned in pre-Israelite Egyptian texts, and in the biblical tradition associated with the region of Hebron and the hill country of Judah (Nm 13:22, 28, 33; Jos 11:21; 14:12, 15).

c: Dt 6:10, 23; 9:5, 27; 29:13; 30:20; 34:4; Gn 12:7; 13:14–15; 15:18–21; 17:8; 26:3–5; 28:13–14. *d:* Ex 18:13–26; Nm 11:16–30. *e:* Dt 1:31. *f:* Dt 10:22; Gn 15:5; 22:17; 26:3–4; Ex 32:13. *g:* Dt 10:17–18; 16:18–20. *h:* Nm 13:1–27. *i:* Nm 11:11–36. *j:* Nm 13:28–14:38. *k:* Dt 9:23. *l:* Dt 9:28. *m:* Dt 1:28; 2:10–11, 21; 9:2; Nm 13:22, 28, 33; Jos 11:21–22; 14:12, 15; 15:13–14; 21:11; Jgs 1:20. *n:* Dt 3:22; 8:15; 32:10; Ex 14:13–14.

the way to go.[o] 34When the LORD heard your words, he was angry, and took an oath: 35Not a single one of this evil generation shall look upon the good land I swore to give to your ancestors, 36except Caleb,* son of Jephunneh. He shall see it, for to him and to his descendants I will give the land he trod upon,[p] because he has fully followed the LORD.

37The LORD was angered against me also on your account, and said, You shall not enter there either,[q] 38but Joshua,[r] son of Nun, your attendant, shall enter. Encourage him, for he is the one who is to give Israel its possession. 39Your little ones, who you said would become plunder, and your children, who as yet do not know good from evil—they shall enter there; to them I will give it, and they shall take possession of it. 40But as for yourselves: turn back and proceed into the wilderness on the Red Sea road.

Unsuccessful Invasion. 41[s]In reply you said to me, "We have sinned against the LORD. We will go up ourselves and fight, just as the LORD, our God, commanded us." And each of you girded on his weapons, making light of going up into the hill country. 42But the LORD said to me, Warn them: Do not go up and fight—for I will not be in your midst—lest you be beaten down before your enemies. 43I gave you this warning but you would not listen. You defied the LORD's command and arrogantly went off into the hill country. 44Then the Amorites living in that hill country came out against you and put you to flight the way bees do, cutting you down in Seir as far as Hormah. 45On your return you wept before the LORD, but the LORD did not listen to your voice or give ear to you. 46That is why you had to stay as long as you did at Kadesh.

CHAPTER 2

See RG 141–48

Northward Along Edom. 1[t]Then we turned and proceeded into the wilderness on the Red Sea road,[u] as the LORD had told me, and circled around the highlands of Seir for a long time. 2Finally the LORD said to me, 3You have wandered round these highlands long enough; turn and go north. 4Command the people: You are now about to pass through the territory of your relatives, the descendants of Esau, who live in Seir. Though they are afraid of you, be very careful 5not to come in conflict with them, for I will not give you so much as a foot of their land, since I have already given Esau possession of the highlands of Seir.[v] 6You shall purchase from them with money the food you eat; even the water you drink you shall buy from them with money. 7Surely, the LORD, your God, has blessed you in all your undertakings; he has been concerned* about your journey through this vast wilderness. It is now forty years that the LORD, your God, has been with you, and you have lacked nothing.[w] 8So we passed by our relatives, the descendants of Esau who live in Seir, leaving behind us the Arabah route, Elath, and Ezion-geber.

Along Moab. Then we turned and passed on toward the wilderness of Moab. 9[x]And the LORD said to me, Do not show hostility to the Moabites or engage them in battle, for I will not give you possession of any of their land, since I have given Ar to the descendants of Lot as their possession.[y] 10(Formerly the Emim lived there, a people great and numerous and as tall as the Anakim;[z] 11like the Anakim they are considered Rephaim, though the Moabites call them Emim.[a] 12In Seir, however, the former inhabitants were the Horites;[b] the descendants of Esau dispossessed them, clearing them out of the way and dwelling in their place, just as Israel has done in the land of its possession which the LORD gave it.) 13Now get ready to cross the Wadi Zered.

So we crossed the Wadi Zered. 14[c]Now thirty-eight years had elapsed between our departure from Kadesh-barnea and the crossing of the Wadi Zered; in the meantime

1:36 Except Caleb: and Joshua (v. 38).

2:7 Concerned: lit., "known"; cf. Ex 2:25.

o: Ex 13:21; 40:38; Nm 9:15–16; 10:33–34; 14:14. *p:* Jos 14:6–14. *q:* Dt 4:21; 34:4; Nm 20:12. *r:* Dt 31:3, 7–8; Nm 27:18–23; 34:17; Jos 1:1–9. *s:* Nm 14:39–45. *t:* Nm 20:14–21; Jgs 11:15–17. *u:* Dt 1:40; Nm 14:25. *v:* Gn 36:6–8. *w:* Dt 8:2–5. *x:* Nm 21:12–15; Jgs 11:17–18. *y:* Gn 19:36–38. *z:* Dt 1:28. *a:* Dt 2:20; 3:11, 13; Gn 14:5; 15:20; Jos 12:4; 13:12; 17:15. *b:* Gn 14:6; 36:20–30. *c:* Nm 14:28–35.

the whole generation of soldiers had perished from the camp, as the LORD had sworn they should. [15]Indeed the LORD's own hand was against them, to rout them from the camp completely.

Along Ammon. [16][d] When at length death had put an end to all the soldiers among the people, [17]the LORD said to me, [18]You are now about to leave Ar and the territory of Moab behind. [19]As you come opposite the Ammonites,[e] do not show hostility or come in conflict with them, for I will not give you possession of any land of the Ammonites, since I have given it to the descendants of Lot as their possession. [20](This also is considered a country of the Rephaim; formerly the Rephaim dwelt there. The Ammonites call them Zamzummim,[f] [21]a people great and numerous and as tall as the Anakim. But these, too, the LORD cleared out of the way for the Ammonites, so that they dispossessed them and dwelt in their place.[g] [22]He did the same for the descendants of Esau, who live in Seir, by clearing the Horites out of their way, so that they dispossessed them and dwelt in their place down to the present.[h] [23]As for the Avvim, who once lived in villages in the vicinity of Gaza,* the Caphtorim, migrating from Caphtor, cleared them away and dwelt in their place.)[i]

Defeat of Sihon. [24][j] Advance now across the Wadi Arnon. I now deliver into your power Sihon, the Amorite king of Heshbon, and his land. Begin to take possession; engage him in battle.[k] [25]This day I will begin to put a fear and dread of you into the peoples everywhere under heaven, so that at the mention of your name they will quake and tremble before you.

[26]So I sent messengers from the wilderness of Kedemoth to Sihon, king of Heshbon, with this offer of peace: [27]"Let me pass through your country. I will travel only on the road. I will not turn aside either to the right or to the left. [28]The food I eat you will sell me for money, and the water I drink, you will give me for money. Only let me march through, [29]as the descendants of Esau who dwell in Seir and the Moabites who dwell in Ar have done, until I cross the Jordan into the land the LORD, our God, is about to give us."[l] [30]But Sihon, king of Heshbon, refused to let us pass through his land, because the LORD, your God, made him stubborn in mind and obstinate in heart that he might deliver him into your power, as indeed he has now done.

[31]Then the LORD said to me, Now that I have already begun to give over to you Sihon and his land, begin to take possession. [32]So Sihon and all his people advanced against us to join battle at Jahaz; [33]but since the LORD, our God, had given him over to us, we defeated him and his sons and all his people. [34][m] At that time we captured all his cities and put every city under the ban,* men, women and children; we left no survivor. [35]Our only plunder was the livestock and the spoils of the captured cities. [36]From Aroer on the edge of the Wadi Arnon and from the town in the wadi itself, as far as Gilead,[n] no city was too well fortified for us. All of them the LORD, our God, gave over to us. [37]However, just as the LORD, our God, commanded us, you did not encroach upon any of the Ammonite land, neither the region bordering on the Wadi Jabbok, nor the cities of the highlands.[o]

CHAPTER 3

See RG 141–48

Defeat of Og. [1]Then we turned and proceeded up the road to Bashan. But Og, king of Bashan,[p] came out against us with all his people to give battle at Edrei. [2]The LORD said to me, Do not be afraid of him, for I have delivered him into your power with all

2:23 Gaza: later a stronghold of the Philistines (cf. Jos 13:3). **Caphtor**: the island of Crete.

2:34 Under the ban: in Hebrew, *herem*, which means to devote to the Lord (cf. 7:1–5; 20:10–18). The biblical text often presents *herem* as the total extermination of a population as a manifestation of the will of the Lord. It is historically doubtful that Israel ever literally carried out this theological program.

---

d: Nm 21:24. *e:* Gn 19:36–38. *f:* Dt 2:11; 3:11, 13; Gn 14:5; 15:20; Jos 12:4; 13:12; 17:15. *g:* Dt 1:28. *h:* Gn 14:6; 36:6–8, 20–30. *i:* Gn 10:14; Jos 13:3; 18:23; 1 Chr 1:12; Jer 47:4; Am 9:7. *j:* Dt 1:4; 29:7; 31:4; Jos 2:10; 9:10; 12:1–6; Neh 9:22; Ps 135:10–12; 136:17–22. *k:* Nm 21:21–32; Jgs 11:19–22. *l:* Dt 2:4–9. *m:* Dt 3:6; 7:2, 26; 13:16, 18; 20:16–18; Jos 10:40; 11:11–12. *n:* Dt 3:12–13; Jos 13:8–13, 15–23. *o:* Nm 21:24; Jos 12:2. *p:* Nm 21:33–35.

his people and his land. Do to him as you did to Sihon, king of the Amorites, who reigned in Heshbon. [3]And thus the LORD, our God, delivered into our power also Og, king of Bashan, with all his people. We defeated him so completely that we left him no survivor. [4]At that time we captured all his cities; there was no town we did not take: sixty cities in all, the whole region of Argob, the kingdom of Og in Bashan— [5]all these cities were fortified with high walls and gates and bars—besides a great number of unwalled towns. [6q] As we had done to Sihon, king of Heshbon, so also here we put all the towns under the ban, men, women and children; [7]but all the livestock and the spoils of each city we took as plunder for ourselves.

[8]And so at that time we took from the two kings of the Amorites beyond the Jordan the territory from the Wadi Arnon to Mount Hermon [9](the Sidonians call Hermon Sirion and the Amorites call it Senir), [10]all the towns of the plateau, all of Gilead, and all of Bashan as far as Salecah and Edrei, towns of the kingdom of Og in Bashan. [11](Og, king of Bashan, was the last remaining survivor of the Rephaim. He had a bed of iron,* nine regular cubits long and four wide, which is still preserved in Rabbah of the Ammonites.)[r]

Allotment of the Conquered Lands. [12s] As for the land we took possession of at that time, I gave Reuben and Gad the territory from Aroer, on the edge of the Wadi Arnon, halfway up into the highlands of Gilead, with its cities. [13]The rest of Gilead and all of Bashan, the kingdom of Og, I gave to the half-tribe of Manasseh. (The whole Argob region, all that part of Bashan, was once called a land of the Rephaim.[t] [14]Jair, a Manassite,[u] took all the region of Argob as far as the border of the Geshurites and Maacathites, and named them—Bashan, that is—after himself, Havvoth-jair, the name it bears today.) [15]To Machir* I gave Gilead, [16]and to Reuben and Gad the territory from Gilead to the Wadi Arnon—the middle of the wadi being its boundary—and to the Wadi Jabbok, which is the border of the Ammonites, [17]as well as the Arabah with the Jordan and its banks from Chinnereth* to the Salt Sea of the Arabah, under the slopes of Pisgah on the east.

[18v] At that time I charged you: The LORD, your God, has given you this land as your possession. But all your troops equipped for battle must cross over in the vanguard of your fellow Israelites. [19]But your wives and children, as well as your livestock, of which I know you have a large number, shall remain behind in the towns I have given you, [20]until the LORD has settled your relatives as well, and they too possess the land which the LORD, your God, will give them on the other side of the Jordan. Then you may all return to the possessions I have given you.

[21]And I charged Joshua as well, "Your own eyes have seen all that the LORD, your God, has done to both these kings; so, too, will the LORD do to all the kingdoms into which you will cross over. [22]Do not fear them, for it is the LORD, your God, who will fight for you."[w]

Moses Excluded from the Promised Land. [23x] It was then that I entreated the LORD, [24]"Lord GOD, you have begun to show to your servant your greatness and your mighty hand. What god in heaven or on earth can perform deeds and powerful acts like yours? [25]Ah, let me cross over and see the good land beyond the Jordan, that fine hill country, and the Lebanon!" [26]But the LORD was angry with me on your account* and would not hear

3:11 Bed of iron: some translate, "a sarcophagus of basalt"; its dimensions would be approximately thirteen and a half feet by six feet.

3:15 Machir: a clan of the tribe of Manasseh (cf. Gn 50:23).

3:17 Chinnereth: later known as the Lake of Gennesaret and the Sea of Galilee. **The Salt Sea**: the Dead Sea. **Pisgah**: a mountain range to the northeast of the Salt Sea; Mount Nebo, from which Moses viewed the promised land, is in this range (cf. v. 27; 34:1).

3:26 On your account: that Moses saw but never entered the promised land is attested by every Pentateuchal tradition, but different reasons are given in different places. Nm 20:12 and Dt 32:51 present Moses as being at fault. Here, as in 1:37 and 4:21, the fault lies in the people but affects Moses.

q: Dt 2:34–35; 7:2, 26; 13:16, 18; 20:16–18; Jos 10:40; 11:11–12. *r:* Dt 2:11, 20; 3:13; Gn 14:5; 15:20; Jos 12:4; 13:12; 17:15. *s:* Nm 32:1–42; Jos 13:8–33. *t:* Dt 2:11, 20; 3:11; Gn 14:5; 15:20; Jos 12:4; 13:12; 17:15. *u:* Nm 32:41; Jgs 10:4; 1 Chr 2:23. *v:* Jos 1:12–15; 4:12; 22:1–4. *w:* Dt 1:30; Ex 14:13–14. *x:* Nm 27:12–23.

me.[y] The LORD said to me, Enough! Speak to me no more of this. 27 Go up to the top of Pisgah and look out to the west, and to the north, and to the south, and to the east. Look well, for you shall not cross this Jordan.[z] 28 Commission Joshua,[a] and encourage and strengthen him, for it is he who will cross at the head of this people and he who will give them possession of the land you are to see.

29 So we remained in the valley opposite Beth-peor.

CHAPTER 4

See RG 141–48

Advantages of Fidelity. 1 Now therefore, Israel, hear the statutes and ordinances I am teaching you to observe, that you may live, and may enter in and take possession of the land which the LORD, the God of your ancestors, is giving you.[b] 2 In your observance of the commandments of the LORD, your God,[c] which I am commanding you, you shall not add to what I command you nor subtract from it. 3 You have seen with your own eyes what the LORD did at Baal-peor:[d] the LORD, your God, destroyed from your midst everyone who followed the Baal of Peor; 4 but you, who held fast to the LORD, your God, are all alive today. 5 See, I am teaching you the statutes and ordinances as the LORD, my God, has commanded me, that you may observe them in the land you are entering to possess. 6 Observe them carefully, for this is your wisdom and discernment in the sight of the peoples, who will hear of all these statutes and say, "This great nation is truly a wise and discerning people."[e] 7 [f] For what great nation is there that has gods so close to it as the LORD, our God, is to us whenever we call upon him? 8 Or what great nation has statutes and ordinances that are as just as this whole law which I am setting before you today?[g]

Revelation at Horeb. 9 However, be on your guard and be very careful not to forget the things your own eyes have seen, nor let them slip from your heart as long as you live, but make them known to your children[h] and to your children's children, 10 that day you stood before the LORD, your God, at Horeb, when the LORD said to me: Assemble the people for me, that I may let them hear my words, that they may learn to fear* me as long as they live in the land and may so teach their children. 11 [i] You came near and stood at the foot of the mountain, while the mountain blazed to the heart of the heavens with fire and was enveloped in a dense black cloud. 12 Then the LORD spoke to you from the midst of the fire.[j] You heard the sound of the words, but saw no form; there was only a voice. 13 He proclaimed to you his covenant, which he commanded you to keep: the ten words,* which he wrote on two stone tablets.[k] 14 At that time the LORD charged me to teach you the statutes and ordinances for you to observe in the land you are about to cross into and possess.

Danger of Idolatry. 15 Because you saw no form at all on the day the LORD spoke to you at Horeb from the midst of the fire, be strictly on your guard 16 not to act corruptly by fashioning an idol for yourselves to represent any figure, whether it be the form of a man or of a woman,[l] 17 the form of any animal on the earth, the form of any bird that flies in the sky, 18 the form of anything that crawls on the ground, or the form of any fish in the waters under the earth. 19 And when you look up to the heavens and behold the sun or the moon or the stars, the whole heavenly host, do not be led astray into bowing down to them and serving them.[m] These the LORD, your God, has apportioned to all the other nations under the heavens; 20 but you the LORD has taken and led out of that iron foundry, Egypt, that you might be his people, his heritage, as you are today.[n] 21 But the LORD was angry with me on your account[o] and swore that I should not cross the Jordan nor enter the good land which the LORD,

4:10 Fear: not in the sense of "be terrified," but rather "manifest reverence or awe."

4:13 Ten words: the ten commandments, or decalogue (cf. 5:22; Ex 34:28).

y: Dt 4:21. *z:* Dt 3:17; 32:48–52; 34:1–4. *a:* Dt 1:38; 31:7–8. *b:* Dt 4:45; 5:1, 31; 6:1, 17, 20; 11:32; 12:1; 26:16. *c:* Dt 13:1. *d:* Nm 25:1–13; Ps 106:28; Hos 9:10. *e:* Dt 26:5; Gn 12:2; 18:18; 46:3; Ex 32:10. *f:* 2 Sm 7:23. *g:* Dt 4:44. *h:* Dt 6:7, 20–25; 11:19–21; 29:29; 31:12–13; Ps 78:3–6. *i:* Ex 19:7–20:21. *j:* Dt 4:33, 36; 5:4. *k:* Dt 5:6–21; 10:4; Ex 20:1–17; 24:12; 31:18; 34:27–28. *l:* Dt 5:8; Ex 20:4. *m:* Dt 17:3; Jb 31:26–28. *n:* 1 Kgs 8:51; Is 48:10; Jer 11:4. *o:* Dt 1:37; 3:26.

your God, is giving you as a heritage. [22]I myself shall die in this country; I shall not cross the Jordan; but you are going to cross over and take possession of that good land.[p] [23]Be careful, therefore, lest you forget the covenant which the LORD, your God, has made with you, and fashion for yourselves against his command an idol in any form whatsoever.[q] [24]For the LORD, your God, is a consuming fire, a jealous God.*[r]

God's Fidelity and Love. [25][s] When you have children and children's children, and have grown old in the land, should you then act corruptly by fashioning an idol in the form of anything, and by this evil done in his sight provoke the LORD, your God, [26]I call heaven and earth this day to witness against you, that you shall all quickly perish from the land which you are crossing the Jordan to possess. You shall not live in it for any length of time but shall be utterly wiped out.[t] [27]The LORD will scatter you among the peoples, and there shall remain but a handful of you among the nations to which the LORD will drive you. [28]There you shall serve gods that are works of human hands, of wood and stone, gods which can neither see nor hear, neither eat nor smell.[u] [29]Yet when you seek the LORD, your God, from there, you shall indeed find him if you search after him with all your heart and soul.[v] [30]In your distress, when all these things shall have come upon you, you shall finally return to the LORD, your God, and listen to his voice. [31]Since the LORD, your God, is a merciful God, he will not abandon or destroy you, nor forget the covenant with your ancestors that he swore to them.[w]

[32]Ask now of the days of old, before your time, ever since God created humankind upon the earth; ask from one end of the sky to the other: Did anything so great ever happen before? Was it ever heard of? [33]Did a people ever hear the voice of God speaking from the midst of fire, as you did, and live?[x] [34]Or did any god venture to go and take a nation for himself from the midst of another nation, by testings, by signs and wonders,[y] by war, with strong hand and outstretched arm, and by great terrors, all of which the LORD, your God, did for you in Egypt before your very eyes? [35]All this you were allowed to see that you might know that the LORD is God; there is no other.[z] [36]Out of the heavens he let you hear his voice to discipline you; on earth he let you see his great fire, and you heard him speaking out of the fire. [37]For love of your ancestors he chose their descendants after them and by his presence and great power led you out of Egypt, [38]dispossessing before you nations greater and mightier than you, so as to bring you in and to give their land to you as a heritage, as it is today. [39]This is why you must now acknowledge, and fix in your heart, that the LORD is God in the heavens above and on earth below, and that there is no other.[a] [40]And you must keep his statutes and commandments which I command you today, that you and your children after you may prosper, and that you may have long life on the land which the LORD, your God, is giving you forever.[b]

Cities of Refuge. [41][c] Then Moses set apart three cities in the region east of the Jordan, [42]to which a homicide might flee who killed a neighbor unintentionally, where there had been no hatred previously, so that the killer might flee to one of these cities and live: [43]Bezer in the wilderness, in the region of

4:24 A jealous God: Hebrew *'el qanna*. The root of the adjective *qanna* expresses the idea of intense feeling focused on solicitude for someone or something; see, e.g., Ps 69:10; Sg 8:6; Is 9:6; 37:32; Ez 39:25. The Septuagint translated the adjective as *zelotes*, and the Vulgate followed suit; hence the traditional English rendering "jealous" (and sometimes "zealous") found in the Douai-Rheims and King James versions. In modern usage, however, "jealous" denotes unreasonable, petty possessiveness, a meaning, even as nuance, wanting in the Hebrew. In the first commandment (5:6–10; Ex 20:2–6) and passages derived from it (like 4:24; 6:15; Ex 34:14; Jos 24:19; Na 1:2), Israel's God is represented as totally committed to his purpose, and Israel is put on notice to take him and his directives for their life as a people with equal seriousness.

p: Dt 3:27; 34:1–12; Jos 1–12. *q:* Dt 4:16; 9:12–14; Ex 32:1–10. *r:* Dt 5:9; 6:15; 9:3; Ex 24:17; 34:14. *s:* Dt 28:64–67. *t:* Dt 30:19; 31:28; 32:1; Is 1:2. *u:* Dt 28:64; 29:17; Lv 26:30–39; Ps 115:4–8; 135:15–18; Is 44:9–20. *v:* Dt 6:5; Jer 29:13–14. *w:* Dt 31:8; Gn 9:9–17; 15:18–21; 17:1–21; Ex 34:6–7. *x:* Dt 4:36; 5:24, 26; Ex 20:19. *y:* Dt 7:19; 26:8; 29:2; Ex 7:3; 15:3–10; Jer 32:21. *z:* Dt 4:39; 32:39; 1 Kgs 8:60; Is 43:10–13; Jl 2:27. *a:* Dt 4:35; 32:39; 1 Kgs 8:60; Is 43:10–13; Jl 2:27. *b:* Dt 6:3; 12:28. *c:* Dt 19:1–13; Nm 35:10–28; Jos 20:1–9.

the plateau, for the Reubenites; Ramoth in Gilead for the Gadites; and Golan in Bashan for the Manassites.

II. Second Address

A. The Lord's Covenant with Israel

Introduction. 44 This is the law* which Moses set before the Israelites.[d] 45 These are the decrees, and the statutes and ordinances* which Moses proclaimed to the Israelites after they came out of Egypt,[e] 46[f] beyond the Jordan in the valley opposite Beth-peor, in the land of Sihon, king of the Amorites, who reigned in Heshbon, whom Moses and the Israelites defeated after they came out of Egypt.[g] 47 They took possession of his land and the land of Og, king of Bashan, as well—the land of these two kings of the Amorites in the region beyond the Jordan to the east: 48 from Aroer on the edge of the Wadi Arnon to Mount Sion* (that is, Hermon) 49 and all the Arabah beyond the Jordan to the east, as far as the Arabah Sea* under the slopes of Pisgah.

CHAPTER 5

See RG 141–48

The Covenant at Horeb. 1 Moses summoned all Israel and said to them, Hear, O Israel, the statutes and ordinances which I proclaim in your hearing this day, that you may learn them and take care to observe them.[h] 2 The LORD, our God, made a covenant with us at Horeb; 3 not with our ancestors* did the LORD make this covenant, but with us, all of us who are alive here this day. 4[i] Face to face, the LORD spoke with you on the mountain from the midst of the fire,[j] 5 while I was standing between the LORD and you at that time, to announce to you these words of the LORD, since you were afraid of the fire and would not go up the mountain:

The Decalogue. 6[k] I am the LORD your God, who brought you out of the land of Egypt,[l] out of the house of slavery. 7[m] You shall not have other gods beside me. 8 You shall not make for yourself an idol or a likeness of anything in the heavens above or on the earth below or in the waters beneath the earth; 9* you shall not bow down before them or serve them. For I, the LORD, your God, am a jealous* God, bringing punishment for their parents' wickedness on the children of those who hate me, down to the third and fourth generation, 10 but showing love down to the thousandth generation of those who love me and keep my commandments.

11 You shall not invoke the name of the LORD, your God, in vain.[n] For the LORD will not leave unpunished anyone who invokes his name in vain.

12[o] Observe the sabbath day—keep it holy, as the LORD, your God, commanded you. 13 Six days you may labor and do all your work, 14 but the seventh day is a sabbath of the LORD your God. You shall not do any work, either you, your son or your daughter, your male or female slave, your ox or don-

4:44 Law: Hebrew *torah,* meaning "instruction," "law," "teaching"; the standard translation "law" comes from the influence of the Septuagint's *nomos*, "law," and the extensive legislation in Ex 20–Nm 10.

4:45 Statutes and ordinances: terms referring to the legal corpus in 12:1–26:19.

4:48 Sion: another name for Mount Hermon, besides those mentioned in 3:9 (to be distinguished from the Mount Zion of Jerusalem).

4:49 The Arabah Sea: the Dead Sea, cf. 3:17.

5:3 Not with our ancestors: in fact, the covenant was made with the ancestors, but these had died out during the "forty" years. The covenant is considered to be ongoing—for Israel in Moab and beyond.

5:9–10 Israel is confronted with a choice, to "love" or to "hate" the Lord, and with the consequences of each choice. "Wickedness" works destruction not only on those who do it but also down the generations, in a sort of ripple effect. Yet, if Israel keeps the commandments, they will experience the Lord's *hesed* ("love") down to the thousandth generation. Thus the Lord's merciful love is disproportionate to the evil results of iniquity ("down to the third and fourth generation"). **To the thousandth generation**: lit., "to thousands"; cf. 7:9.

5:9 Jealous: see note on 4:24.

d: Dt 4:8; 17:18–19; 30:10; 31:11–12. *e:* Dt 4:1; 5:1, 31; 6:1, 17, 20; 11:32; 12:1; 26:16; Ps 25:10. *f:* Dt 2:24–3:29. *g:* Dt 3:29; 34:6. *h:* Dt 4:1, 45; 5:31; 6:1, 17, 20; 11:32; 12:1; 26:16. *i:* Ex 19:3–25; 20:18–19; 24:2. *j:* Dt 34:10; Nm 12:8. *k:* Ex 20:2–17. *l:* Ex 20:2; Ps 81:11. *m:* Dt 4:23–24, 31; 6:4–5; 7:9–10; 12:2–13:18; 17:3; 18:20; 24:16; 27:15; Ex 20:3–6; 34:6–7, 14; Lv 26:1; Nm 14:18; Ps 81:10; 97:7; Jer 7:9; 31:29–30; 32:18–19; Ez 18:1–24. *n:* Dt 6:13; 10:20; 18:20; 23:21–23; Ex 20:7; Lv 19:12; 24:10–23; Ps 24:4; Jer 29:23; Mt 5:33–37. *o:* Dt 14:22–16:17; 24:18, 22; Ex 20:8–11; 23:12; 31:12–17; 34:21; Is 58:13–14; Jer 17:21–27; Mt 12:1–14; Mk 2:23–3:6; Lk 6:1–11; 13:10–17; 14:1–6; Jn 5:2–18; 7:22–23.

key or any work animal, or the resident alien
within your gates, so that your male and female slave may rest as you do. 15Remember
that you too were once slaves in the land of
Egypt, and the LORD, your God, brought you
out from there with a strong hand and outstretched arm. That is why the LORD, your
God, has commanded you to observe the
sabbath day.

16[p] Honor your father and your mother, as
the LORD, your God, has commanded you,
that you may have a long life and that you
may prosper in the land the LORD your God
is giving you.

17[q] You shall not kill.*

18[r] You shall not commit adultery.

19[s] You shall not steal.

20[t] You shall not bear dishonest witness
against your neighbor.

21[u] You shall not covet your neighbor's
wife.

You shall not desire your neighbor's
house or field, his male or female slave, his
ox or donkey, or anything that belongs to
your neighbor.

Moses as Mediator. 22These words the
LORD spoke with a loud voice to your entire
assembly on the mountain from the midst of
the fire and the dense black cloud, and added
no more. He inscribed them on two stone
tablets and gave them to me.[v] 23But when
you heard the voice from the midst of the
darkness, while the mountain was ablaze
with fire, you came near to me, all your
tribal heads and elders, 24and said, "The
LORD, our God, has indeed let us see his
glory and his greatness, and we have heard
his voice from the midst of the fire.[w] Today
we have found out that God may speak to a
mortal and that person may still live. 25Now,
why should we die? For this great fire will
consume us. If we hear the voice of the
LORD, our God, any more, we shall die.[x]
26For what mortal has heard the voice of the
living God speaking from the midst of fire,
as we have, and lived? 27You go closer and
listen to all that the LORD, our God, will say,
and then tell us what the LORD, our God,
tells you; we will listen and obey."[y]

28The LORD heard your words as you were
speaking to me and said to me, I have heard
the words these people have spoken to you,
which are all well said.[z] 29Would that they
might always be of such a mind, to fear me
and to keep all my commandments! Then
they and their descendants would prosper
forever. 30Go, tell them: Return to your tents.
31Then you stand here near me and I will
give you all the commandments, the statutes
and the ordinances; you must teach them,
that they may observe them in the land I am
giving them to possess.[a]

32Be careful, therefore, to do as the LORD,
your God, has commanded you, not turning
aside to the right or to the left, 33but following exactly the way that the LORD, your God,
commanded you that you may live and prosper, and may have long life in the land which
you are to possess.[b]

CHAPTER 6

See RG 141–48

1This then is the commandment, the
statutes and the ordinances,[c] which the
LORD, your God, has commanded that you
be taught to observe in the land you are
about to cross into to possess, 2so that you,
that is, you, your child, and your grandchild,
may fear the LORD, your God, by keeping, as
long as you live, all his statutes and commandments[d] which I enjoin on you, and thus
have long life. 3Hear then, Israel, and be
careful to observe them, that it may go well

5:17 Kill: see note on Ex 20:13.

p: Dt 21:18–21; 27:16; Ex 20:12; 21:15, 17; Sir 3:1–16; Mt 10:34–39; 12:46–50; 15:4; 19:19; Mk 3:31–35; 7:10; 10:19; Lk 8:19–21; 14:26; 18:20, 28–30; Eph 6:1–4. *q:* Dt 4:41–43; 19:1–13; 20:1–21:9; 21:18–23; Gn 4:8–16; Ex 20:13; 21:12–14; Nm 35:16–34; Jer 7:9; Hos 4:2; Mt 5:21–26; 19:18; Mk 10:19; Lk 18:20; Jas 2:11. *r:* Dt 22:13–23:1; Gn 20:1–18; 39:7–20; Ex 20:14; Lv 18:20; 20:10; 2 Sm 11:1–12:25; Jer 7:9; Hos 4:2; Mt 5:27–30; 19:18; Mk 10:19; Lk 18:20; Jas 2:11. *s:* Dt 23:24; 24:7; Gn 40:15; Ex 20:15; 21:16, 37; 22:1–3, 12; Lv 19:11, 13; 1 Kgs 21:1–19; Jer 7:9; Hos 4:2; Mt 19:18; Mk 10:19; Lk 18:20. *t:* Dt 19:15–19; Ex 20:16; 23:1–3; Lv 19:11, 15–16; 1 Kgs 21:1–19; Ps 5:6–10; 10:7–9; 27:12; Prv 25:18; 30:8–10; Jer 7:9; Hos 4:2; Mt 19:18; 26:59–60; Mk 10:19; Lk 18:20. *u:* Dt 7:25; Ex 20:17; Jos 7:21; 2 Sm 11:1–12:25; 1 Kgs 21:1–19; Is 5:8; Mi 2:2; Mt 5:27–30; Lk 12:13–21; Eph 5:5; Col 3:5. *v:* Dt 4:13; 9:9–11, 17; 10:1–5; Ex 24:12; 31:18; 32:15–20; 34:1–5. *w:* Dt 4:33, 36; Ex 20:19. *x:* Dt 18:16. *y:* Ex 20:19. *z:* Dt 18:17. *a:* Dt 4:1, 45; 5:1; 6:1, 17, 20; 11:32; 12:1; 26:16. *b:* Dt 4:40. *c:* Dt 4:1, 45; 5:1, 31; 6:17, 20; 11:32; 12:1; 26:16. *d:* Dt 4:10, 40; 5:29; 6:24; 10:12–13.

"Hear, O Israel"

THIS STATEMENT OF belief (6:4–9) is the most important one for Israel, and is also partly quoted in the New Testament by Jesus (Mark 12:29-30). It is known as the *Shema*, from its first word in Hebrew, the command "Hear!"

with you and that you may increase greatly;
for the LORD, the God of your ancestors,
promised you a land flowing with milk and
honey.[e]
*The Great Commandment.** 4[f] Hear, O Israel!* The LORD is our God, the LORD alone!
5 Therefore, you shall love the LORD, your
God, with your whole heart, and with your
whole being, and with your whole strength.[g]
6[h] Take to heart these words which I command you today.[i] 7 Keep repeating them to
your children. Recite them when you are at
home and when you are away, when you lie
down and when you get up.[j] 8 Bind them on
your arm as a sign* and let them be as a pendant on your forehead.[k] 9 Write them on the
doorposts of your houses and on your gates.[l]
Fidelity in Prosperity. 10[m] When the LORD,
your God, brings you into the land which he
swore to your ancestors, to Abraham, Isaac,
and Jacob, that he would give you, a land
with fine, large cities that you did not build,[n]
11 with houses full of goods of all sorts that
you did not garner, with cisterns that you did
not dig, with vineyards and olive groves that
you did not plant; and when, therefore, you
eat and are satisfied,[o] 12[p] be careful not to
forget the LORD, who brought you out of the
land of Egypt, that house of slavery. 13[q] The
LORD, your God, shall you fear; him shall
you serve,* and by his name shall you swear.
14[r] You shall not go after other gods, any of
the gods of the surrounding peoples—15 for
the LORD, your God who is in your midst, is
a passionate God—lest the anger of the
LORD, your God, flare up against you and he
destroy you from upon the land.
16 You shall not put the LORD, your God, to
the test, as you did at Massah.[s] 17 But keep
the commandments of the LORD, your God,
and the decrees and the statutes he has commanded you. 18 Do what is right and good in
the sight of the LORD, that it may go well
with you, and you may enter in and possess
the good land which the LORD promised on
oath to your ancestors, 19 driving all your enemies out of your way, as the LORD has
promised.[t]
Instruction to Children. 20[u] Later on, when
your son asks you, "What do these decrees
and statutes and ordinances mean?"[v] which
the LORD, our God, has enjoined on you,
21[w] you shall say to your son, "We were once
slaves of Pharaoh in Egypt, but the LORD
brought us out of Egypt with a strong hand[x]
22 and wrought before our eyes signs and won-

6:4–5 This passage, an expansion of the first commandment (5:6–10), contains the basic principle of the whole Mosaic law, the keynote of the Book of Deuteronomy: since the Lord alone is God, Israel must love him with an undivided heart. Jesus cited these words as "the greatest and the first commandment," embracing in itself the whole law of God (Mt 22:37–38; Mk 12:29–30; Lk 10:27).

6:4 Hear, O Israel!: in Hebrew, *shema yisra'el*; hence this passage (vv. 4–9), containing the Great Commandment, is called the Shema. In later Jewish tradition, 11:13–21 and Nm 15:37–41 were added to form a prayer recited every evening and morning. **The LORD is our God, the LORD alone**: other possible translations are "the Lord our God is one Lord"; "the Lord our God, the Lord is one"; "the Lord is our God, the Lord is one."

6:8 Bind them . . . as a sign: these injunctions were probably meant merely in a figurative sense; cf. Ex 13:9, 16. In the late postexilic period, they were taken quite literally, and devout Jews tied on their arms and foreheads "phylacteries," boxes containing strips of parchment on which these words were inscribed; cf. Mt 23:5.

6:13 Him shall you serve: the verb could be translated as either "serve" or "worship" (cf. 5:9).

e: Ex 3:8. *f:* Dt 4:35, 39; 5:6–10; 6:13–14; 10:17; 1 Kgs 8:60; 18:39; 2 Kgs 5:15; 19:15, 19; Is 44:6; 45:5–6; Mt 22:37–38; Mk 12:29–30; Lk 10:27. *g:* Dt 4:29; 10:12; 11:13; 13:4; 26:16; 30:2, 10; 1 Sm 7:3; 2 Kgs 23:3, 25. *h:* Dt 11:18–21. *i:* Dt 11:18; 30:14; 32:46; Ps 37:31; Prv 3:3; Is 51:7; Jer 31:33. *j:* Dt 4:9–10; 6:20–25; 11:1–7, 19; 31:13; 32:46; Prv 6:22. *k:* Dt 11:18; Ex 13:9, 16; Prv 3:3; 6:21. *l:* Dt 11:20. *m:* Dt 5:6–10. *n:* Dt 1:8. *o:* Dt 8:7–14; 32:11–14; Jos 24:13; Neh 9:25. *p:* Dt 5:6. *q:* Dt 10:20; Is 48:1; Jer 4:2; 12:16; Mt 4:10; Lk 4:8. *r:* Dt 4:23–26; 8:19–20; 11:16–17, 28; 29:18–28; 30:17–18; 2 Kgs 17:7–18. *s:* Ex 17:1–7; Ps 95:8–9; Mt 4:7; Lk 4:12. *t:* Ex 23:27; 34:11; Jos 1–12. *u:* Dt 6:6–9. *v:* Ex 12:26; 13:14; Jos 4:6, 21. *w:* Dt 26:5–10. *x:* Dt 5:3, 6.

ders, great and dire, against Egypt and against Pharaoh and his whole house. [23]He brought us from there to bring us in and give us the land he had promised on oath to our ancestors.[y] [24][z] The LORD commanded us to observe all these statutes in fear of the LORD, our God, that we may always have as good a life as we have today. [25]This is our justice before the LORD, our God: to observe carefully this whole commandment he has enjoined on us."

See RG 141–48

CHAPTER 7

Destruction of the Nations in the Land. [1][a] When the LORD, your God, brings you into the land which you are about to enter to possess, and removes many nations before you—the Hittites, Girgashites, Amorites, Canaanites, Perizzites, Hivites, and Jebusites,[b] seven nations more numerous and powerful than you—[2]and when the LORD, your God, gives them over to you and you defeat them, you shall put them under the ban. Make no covenant with them[c] and do not be gracious to them. [3][d] You shall not intermarry with them, neither giving your daughters to their sons nor taking their daughters for your sons. [4]For they would turn your sons from following me to serving other gods, and then the anger of the LORD would flare up against you and he would quickly destroy you.

[5]But this is how you must deal with them:[e] Tear down their altars, smash their sacred pillars, chop down their asherahs,* and destroy their idols by fire. [6]For you are a people holy to the LORD, your God; the LORD, your God, has chosen you from all the peoples on the face of the earth to be a people specially his own.[f] [7]It was not because you are more numerous than all the peoples that the LORD set his heart on you and chose you; for you are really the smallest of all peoples.[g] [8]It was because the LORD loved you and because of his fidelity to the oath he had sworn to your ancestors, that the LORD brought you out with a strong hand and redeemed you from the house of slavery, from the hand of Pharaoh, king of Egypt.[h] [9][i] Know, then, that the LORD, your God, is God: the faithful God who keeps covenant mercy to the thousandth generation toward those who love him and keep his commandments,[j] [10]but who repays with destruction those who hate him; he does not delay with those who hate him, but makes them pay for it. [11]Therefore carefully observe the commandment, the statutes and the ordinances which I command you today.

Blessings of Obedience. [12][k] As your reward for heeding these ordinances and keeping them carefully, the LORD, your God, will keep with you the covenant mercy he promised on oath to your ancestors. [13]He will love and bless and multiply you; he will bless the fruit of your womb and the produce of your soil, your grain and wine and oil, the young of your herds and the offspring of your flocks, in the land which he swore to your ancestors he would give you. [14]You will be blessed above all peoples; no man or woman among you shall be childless nor shall your livestock be barren. [15]The LORD will remove all sickness from you; he will not afflict you with any of the malignant diseases that you know from Egypt, but will leave them with all those who hate you.

[16]You shall consume all the peoples which the LORD, your God, is giving over to you. You are not to look on them with pity, nor serve their gods, for that would be a

7:5 Sacred pillars . . . asherahs: cut or uncut stones and wooden poles or trees (cf. 16:21) that had some cultic function. Fairly common religious artifacts, their association with the non-Israelite cults of Canaan and perhaps with Canaanite gods and goddesses, specifically the goddess Asherah, led to their condemnation in the Deuteronomic reform and possibly earlier.

y: Dt 1:8. *z:* Dt 4:1–4; 30:15–20. *a:* Ex 23:23–33; 34:11–16; Nm 33:51–56. *b:* Dt 1:7; Gn 10:16–17; 13:7; 15:19–21; 23:3–20; 34:2, 30; 49:29–30; Ex 3:8; 23:23; 33:2; Nm 13:29; Jos 1:4; 3:10; 9:1–7; 15:63; 17:15; 24:11; Jgs 1:4–5; 3:3, 5; 2 Sm 5:6–10; 1 Kgs 9:20; Ez 16:3, 45. *c:* Dt 2:34–35; 3:6; 7:26; 13:16, 18; 20:16–18; Ex 23:32–33; 34:12, 15; Jos 9:3–27; 10:40; 11:11–12; Jgs 2:2. *d:* Gn 34:9–10; Ex 34:16; Jos 23:12–13; Jgs 3:5–6; 1 Kgs 11:1–6. *e:* Dt 12:2–3, 29–31; 16:21–22; Ex 34:13; 2 Kgs 18:4; 23:4–24. *f:* Dt 14:2, 21; 26:18–19; 32:8–14; Ex 19:5–6; Ps 135:4; Mal 3:17. *g:* Dt 10:15. *h:* Dt 5:6; 9:26; 13:5; 15:15; 21:8; 24:18; Ps 78:42. *i:* Dt 4:31; 5:9–10; 24:16; Ex 20:5–6; 34:6–7; Nm 14:18; Jer 31:29–30; 32:18–19; Ez 18:1–24; Jn 9:1–3. *j:* Dt 5:9–10; 7:12; 32:4; 1 Kgs 8:23–24; Neh 1:5; 9:32; Ps 89:1–2, 24, 28, 33–34; 98:3; Is 49:7; 54:10; 55:3; Dn 9:4; Jon 4:2; Mi 7:20. *k:* Dt 15:6; 28:1–14; 30:1–10; Ex 23:22–33; Lv 26:3–13.

snare to you.[l] 17[m] If you say to yourselves, "These nations are more numerous than we. How can we dispossess them?" 18 do not be afraid of them. Rather, remember clearly what the LORD, your God, did to Pharaoh and to all Egypt: 19 the great testings which your own eyes have seen, the signs and wonders, the strong hand and outstretched arm with which the LORD, your God, brought you out. The same also will he do to all the peoples of whom you are now afraid. 20 Moreover, the LORD, your God, will send hornets among them, until those who are left and those who are hiding from you are destroyed.[n] 21 Therefore, do not be terrified by them, for the LORD, your God, who is in your midst, is a great and awesome God. 22 He will remove these nations before you little by little. You cannot finish with them quickly, lest the wild beasts become too numerous for you.[o] 23 The LORD, your God, will give them over to you and throw them into utter panic until they are destroyed.[p] 24 He will deliver their kings into your power, that you may make their names perish from under the heavens. No one will be able to stand up against you,[q] till you have destroyed them. 25[r] The images of their gods you shall destroy by fire. Do not covet the silver or gold on them, nor take it for yourselves, lest you be ensnared by it; for it is an abomination to the LORD, your God.[s] 26 You shall not bring any abominable thing into your house, so as to be, like it, under the ban; loathe and abhor it utterly for it is under the ban.*

CHAPTER 8

See RG 141–48

God's Care. 1 Be careful to observe this whole commandment[t] that I enjoin on you today, that you may live and increase, and may enter in and possess the land which the LORD promised on oath to your ancestors. 2 Remember how for these forty years the LORD, your God, has directed all your journeying in the wilderness,[u] so as to test you by affliction, to know what was in your heart: to keep his commandments, or not. 3 He therefore let you be afflicted with hunger, and then fed you with manna,[v] a food unknown to you and your ancestors, so you might know that it is not by bread alone* that people live, but by all that comes forth from the mouth of the LORD. 4 The clothing did not fall from you in tatters, nor did your feet swell these forty years.[w] 5 So you must know in your heart that, even as a man disciplines his son, so the LORD, your God, disciplines you.[x] 6 Therefore, keep the commandments of the LORD, your God, by walking in his ways and fearing him.

Cautions About Prosperity. 7[y] For the LORD, your God, is bringing you into a good country, a land with streams of water, with springs and fountains welling up in the hills and valleys, 8 a land of wheat and barley, of vines and fig trees and pomegranates, of olive trees and of honey, 9 a land where you will always have bread and where you will lack nothing, a land whose stones contain iron and in whose hills you can mine copper. 10 But when you have eaten and are satisfied, you must bless the LORD, your God, for the good land he has given you. 11[z] Be careful not to forget the LORD, your God, by failing to keep his commandments and ordinances and statutes which I enjoin on you today: 12 lest, when you have eaten and are satisfied, and have built fine houses and lived in them, 13 and your herds and flocks have increased, your silver and gold has increased, and all your property has increased, 14 you then become haughty of heart and forget the LORD, your God, who brought you out of the land of Egypt, that house of slavery; 15 he guided you

7:26 Under the ban: and therefore doomed to destruction; see note on 2:34.

8:3 Not by bread alone: Deuteronomic theology puts the good things promised faithful Israel into the context of the Lord's gratuitous love. As in 6:10–12, the goods of life must be seen as gift. Israel is to seek what really matters; all else will be added (cf. Mt 6:33).

l: Dt 5:7–10. *m:* Dt 1:28–31; 3:22; 4:34, 37–38; 9:1–3; 20:1; 29:2–3; Jos 23:3, 9–10. *n:* Ex 23:28. *o:* Ex 23:29–30; Jgs 3:1–6. *p:* Dt 7:2. *q:* Dt 11:25; Jos 12:7–24. *r:* Dt 5:8–9; 9:21; Jos 6:18–19; 7:1, 20–21; Jgs 8:24–27; 17:2–4; 1 Kgs 15:13; 2 Kgs 23:4. *s:* Dt 12:31; 17:1; 18:12; 22:5; 23:18; 24:4; 25:16; Prv 6:16; 15:8–9, 26. *t:* Dt 4:1; 6:1. *u:* Dt 1:3; 2:7; 29:4; Ps 95:10; Am 2:10. *v:* Ex 16:11–36; Nm 11:5–9; Jos 5:12; Mt 4:4; Lk 4:4. *w:* Dt 29:4; Neh 9:21. *x:* Dt 4:36; 11:2; 21:18–21; Ps 94:12; Prv 3:11–12. *y:* Dt 1:25; 11:10–12; 32:13–14; 33:28. *z:* Dt 6:10–12.

through the vast and terrible wilderness with
its saraph* serpents and scorpions, its
parched and waterless ground; he brought
forth water for you from the flinty rock[a]
[16]and fed you in the wilderness with manna,
a food unknown to your ancestors, that he
might afflict you and test you, but also make
you prosperous in the end. [17]Otherwise, you
might say in your heart,[b] "It is my own power
and the strength of my own hand that has got
me this wealth." [18]Remember then the LORD,
your God, for he is the one who gives you the
power to get wealth, by fulfilling, as he has
now done, the covenant he swore to your ancestors. [19]But if you do forget the LORD, your
God, and go after other gods, serving and
bowing down to them,[c] I bear witness to you
this day that you will perish utterly. [20]Like
the nations which the LORD destroys before
you, so shall you too perish for not listening
to the voice of the LORD, your God.

CHAPTER 9

See RG 141–48

Unmerited Success. [1]Hear, O Israel!
You are now about to cross the Jordan to enter in and dispossess nations greater and
stronger than yourselves, having large cities
fortified to the heavens,[d] [2]the Anakim, a
people great and tall.[e] You yourselves know
of them and have heard it said of them,
"Who can stand up against the Anakim?"
[3]Know, then, today that it is the LORD, your
God, who will cross over before you as a
consuming fire; he it is who will destroy
them and subdue them before you, so that
you can dispossess and remove them
quickly, as the LORD promised you.[f] [4]After
the LORD, your God, has driven them out of
your way, do not say in your heart, "It is because of my justice the LORD has brought me
in to possess this land,[g] and because of the
wickedness of these nations the LORD is dispossessing them before me."* [5]No, it is not
because of your justice or the integrity of
your heart that you are going in to take possession of their land; but it is because of their
wickedness that the LORD, your God, is dispossessing these nations before you and in
order to fulfill the promise he made on oath
to your ancestors, Abraham, Isaac, and Jacob.[h] [6]Know this, therefore: it is not because
of your justice that the LORD, your God, is
giving you this good land to possess, for you
are a stiff-necked people.[i]

The Golden Calf. [7]Remember and do not
forget how you angered the LORD, your God,
in the wilderness. From the day you left the
land of Egypt until you came to this place,
you have been rebellious toward the LORD.[j]
[8k] At Horeb you so provoked the LORD that
he was angry enough to destroy you,[l] [9]when
I had gone up the mountain to receive the
stone tablets of the covenant which the LORD
made with you.[m] Meanwhile I stayed on the
mountain forty days and forty nights; I ate
no food and drank no water. [10]The LORD
gave me the two stone tablets inscribed, by
God's own finger,[n] with a copy of all the
words that the LORD spoke to you on the
mountain from the midst of the fire on
the day of the assembly. [11]Then, at the end
of the forty days and forty nights, when the
LORD had given me the two stone tablets, the
tablets of the covenant, [12o] the LORD said to
me, Go down from here now, quickly, for
your people whom you have brought out of
Egypt are acting corruptly; they have already turned aside from the way I commanded them and have made for themselves
a molten idol. [13]I have seen now how stiff-
necked this people is, the LORD said to me.
[14]Let me be, that I may destroy them and
blot out their name from under the heavens.
I will then make of you a nation mightier and
greater than they.

[15]When I had come down again from the
blazing, fiery mountain, with the two tablets
of the covenant in both my hands,[p] [16]I saw
how you had sinned against the LORD, your
God, by making for yourselves a molten

8:15 Saraph: see note on Nm 21:6.

9:4 Before me: Hebrew reads "before you."

---

a: Dt 32:13; Ex 17:6; Nm 20:8–11; 21:6–9; Ps 114:8; Wis 11:4. *b:* Dt 9:4–5. *c:* Dt 4:25–26; 30:18; 2 Kgs 17:7–18. *d:* Dt 1:28; 4:38. *e:* Dt 1:28; 2:10–11, 21; Nm 13:22, 28, 33; Jos 11:21–22; 14:12, 15; 15:13–14; 21:11; Jgs 1:20. *f:* Dt 4:24; 31:3. *g:* Dt 8:17. *h:* Dt 1:8. *i:* Dt 9:13; 10:16; 31:27; Ex 32:9; 33:3; 34:9; Is 48:4; Jer 17:23; 19:15. *j:* Dt 31:27; Ex 14:10–14; 2 Kgs 21:15; Jer 7:25–26. *k:* Ex 32:1–34:29. *l:* Ex 32:10. *m:* Dt 4:13–14; 5:22; 9:11, 18, 25; 10:10; Ex 24:12–18; 34:28. *n:* Dt 5:22; 10:4; Ex 31:18. *o:* Dt 5:6–10; Ex 32:7–10. *p:* Ex 32:15.

calf. You had already turned aside from the
way which the LORD had commanded you.[q]
17I took hold of the two tablets and with both
hands cast them from me and broke them before your eyes.[r] 18Then, as before, I lay prostrate before the LORD for forty days and
forty nights; I ate no food, I drank no water,
because of all the sin you had committed in
the sight of the LORD, doing wrong and provoking him.[s] 19For I dreaded the fierce anger
of the LORD against you: his wrath would
destroy you.[t] Yet once again the LORD listened to me. 20With Aaron, too, the LORD
was deeply angry, and would have destroyed
him; but I prayed for Aaron also at that
time.[u] 21Then, taking the calf, the sinful object you had made, I burnt it and ground it
down to powder as fine as dust, which I
threw into the wadi that went down the
mountainside.[v]

22At Taberah, at Massah, and at Kibroth-
hattaavah likewise, you enraged the LORD.[w]
23And when the LORD sent you up from Kadesh-barnea saying, Go up and take possession of the land I have given you, you rebelled
against this command of the LORD, your God,
and would not believe him or listen to his
voice.[x] 24You have been rebels against the
LORD from the day I first knew you.

25[y]Those forty days, then, and forty
nights, I lay prostrate before the LORD, because he had threatened to destroy you.
26And I prayed to the Lord and said: O Lord
GOD, do not destroy your people, the heritage you redeemed in your greatness and
have brought out of Egypt with your strong
hand.[z] 27Remember your servants, Abraham,
Isaac, and Jacob. Do not look upon the stubbornness of this people nor upon their
wickedness and sin,[a] 28lest the land from
which you have brought us say, "The LORD
was not able to bring them into the land he
promised them, and out of hatred for them,
he brought them out to let them die in the
wilderness."[b] 29They are your people and
your heritage, whom you have brought out
by your great power and with your outstretched arm.[c]

CHAPTER 10

See RG 141–48

1[d]At that time the LORD said to me,
Cut two stone tablets like the first ones[e] and
come up the mountain to me. Also make an
ark out of wood. 2I will write upon the
tablets the words that were on the tablets that
you broke, and you shall place them in the
ark. 3So I made an ark of acacia wood, and
cut two stone tablets like the first ones, and
went up the mountain with the two tablets in
my hand.[f] 4[g]The LORD then wrote on the
tablets, as he had written before, the ten
words* that the LORD had spoken to you on
the mountain from the midst of the fire on
the day of the assembly; and the LORD gave
them to me. 5Then I turned and came down
from the mountain, and placed the tablets in
the ark I had made.[h] There they have remained, as the LORD commanded me.

6[i]The Israelites set out from Beeroth
Bene-jaakan for Moserah; Aaron died there
and was buried. His son Eleazar succeeded
him as priest.[j] 7From there they set out for
Gudgodah, and from Gudgodah for Jotbathah, a region where there is water in the
wadies. 8At that time the LORD set apart the
tribe of Levi to carry the ark of the covenant
of the LORD,[k] to stand before the LORD to
minister to him, and to bless in his name, as
they have done to this day. 9For this reason,
Levi has no hereditary portion with his relatives;[l] the LORD himself is his portion, as the
LORD, your God, promised him.

10Meanwhile I stayed on the mountain as
I did before, forty days and forty nights, and
once again the LORD listened to me. The
LORD was unwilling to destroy you. 11The
LORD said to me, Go now and set out at the
head of the people,[m] that they may enter in

10:4 Ten words: the ten commandments (cf. 4:13).

q: Dt 5:6–10; Ex 32:1–6; Ps 106:19–22. *r:* Ex 32:19. *s:* Dt 10:10; Ex 32:31; 34:28. *t:* Dt 10:10; Ex 32:11–14. *u:* Ex 32:1–6, 21–25, 35. *v:* Ex 32:20. *w:* Dt 6:16; Ex 17:1–7; Nm 11:1–34. *x:* Dt 1:19–33. *y:* Ex 32:11–14. *z:* Dt 4:20; 7:8. *a:* Dt 7:8. *b:* Dt 32:26–27; Nm 14:13–16. *c:* Dt 4:20; Ex 6:6–7. *d:* Ex 34:1–28. *e:* Ex 34:1. *f:* Ex 34:4. *g:* Dt 4:13; 5:22; Ex 20:1–17; 34:1–4, 27–29. *h:* Ex 40:20; 1 Kgs 8:9. *i:* Nm 33:31–33. *j:* Nm 3:1–4, 32; 20:22–29. *k:* Dt 21:5; 33:8–11; Ex 32:25–29; Nm 3:6–10; 6:22–27; 8:23–26. *l:* Dt 18:1–8; Nm 18:20. *m:* Dt 1:6; Ex 32:34; 33:1.

and possess the land that I swore to their ancestors I would give them.

The Lord's Majesty and Compassion. 12[n] Now, therefore, Israel, what does the LORD, your God, ask of you but to fear the LORD, your God, to follow in all his ways, to love and serve the LORD, your God, with your whole heart and with your whole being,[o] 13 to keep the commandments and statutes of the LORD that I am commanding you today for your own well-being?[p] 14 Look, the heavens, even the highest heavens, belong to the LORD, your God, as well as the earth and everything on it.[q] 15 Yet only on your ancestors did the LORD set his heart to love them. He chose you, their descendants, from all the peoples, as it is today.[r] 16 Circumcise therefore the foreskins of your hearts,* and be stiff-necked no longer. 17 For the LORD, your God, is the God of gods, the Lord of lords, the great God, mighty and awesome, who has no favorites, accepts no bribes,[s] 18 who executes justice for the orphan and the widow, and loves the resident alien, giving them food and clothing.[t] 19 So you too should love the resident alien, for that is what you were in the land of Egypt.[u] 20 The LORD, your God, shall you fear, and him shall you serve; to him hold fast and by his name shall you swear.[v] 21 He is your praise; he is your God, who has done for you those great and awesome things that your own eyes have seen.[w] 22 Seventy strong your ancestors went down to Egypt,[x] and now the LORD, your God, has made you as numerous as the stars of heaven.

CHAPTER 11

See RG 141–48

Recalling the Wonders of the Lord. 1 Love the LORD, your God, therefore, and keep his charge, statutes, ordinances, and commandments always.[y] 2 Recall today that it was not your children, who have neither known nor seen the discipline of the LORD, your God—his greatness, his strong hand and outstretched arm;[z] 3 the signs and deeds he wrought in the midst of Egypt, on Pharaoh, king of Egypt, and on all his land;[a] 4 what he did to the Egyptian army and to their horses and chariots, engulfing them in the waters of the Red Sea* as they pursued you,[b] so that the LORD destroyed them even to this day; 5 what he did for you in the wilderness until you came to this place; 6 and what he did to the Reubenites Dathan and Abiram, sons of Eliab, when the earth opened its mouth and swallowed them up out of the midst of Israel, with their families and tents and every living thing that belonged to them—[c] 7 but it was you who saw with your own eyes all these great deeds that the LORD has done.

The Gift of Rain. 8[d] So keep all the commandments I give you today, that you may be strong enough to enter in and take possession of the land that you are crossing over to possess, 9 and that you may have long life on the land which the LORD swore to your ancestors he would give to them and their descendants, a land flowing with milk and honey. 10 The land you are to enter and possess is not like the land of Egypt from which you have come, where you would sow your seed and then water it by hand,* as in a vegetable garden. 11[e] No, the land into which you are crossing to take possession is a land of mountains and valleys that drinks in rain from the heavens, 12 a land which the LORD, your God, looks after; the eyes of the LORD, your God, are upon it continually through the year, from beginning to end.

10:16 Circumcise therefore the foreskins of your hearts: cf. 30:6; Jer 4:4; Rom 2:29. The "uncircumcised heart" (Lv 26:41; Jer 9:25; Ez 44:7, 9) is closed and unreceptive to God, just as "uncircumcised ears" (Jer 6:10) are closed to the word of the Lord, and "uncircumcised lips" (Ex 6:12, 30) are a hindrance to speaking on behalf of the Lord.

11:4 The Red Sea: Hebrew *yam suph*, that is, "sea of reeds" or "reedy sea."

11:10 By hand: lit., "by foot," probably referring to a kind of mechanism for irrigation from the Nile.

n: Ps 15; 24:3–5; Mi 6:6–8. *o:* Dt 6:5, 13; 8:6; 11:13. *p:* Dt 4:1; 5:10, 29–33; 6:2; 7:9; 11:1, 13, 22. *q:* 1 Kgs 8:27; Neh 9:6; Ps 148:4. *r:* Dt 7:6–8; Ex 19:5–6. *s:* Dt 1:17; 16:19; Ex 15:11; 2 Chr 19:7; Jb 34:19; Ps 47:2; 136:2–3; Dn 2:47; Acts 10:34; Rom 2:11; Gal 2:6; 1 Tm 6:15; Rev 17:14; 19:16. *t:* Ps 68:5–6; 99:4; 146:7–9. *u:* Dt 24:17–22; Ex 22:21–24; 23:9; Lv 19:33–34. *v:* Dt 6:13; Mt 4:10; Lk 4:8. *w:* Ps 109:1; Jer 17:14. *x:* Dt 1:10; Gn 46:8–27; Ex 1:5; Acts 7:14. *y:* Gn 26:5; 1 Kgs 2:3. *z:* Dt 4:9; 6:20–25. *a:* Dt 6:22; 7:18–19; 26:8; 29:1–2; 34:11; Ps 78:42–51. *b:* Ex 14:26–31; 15:1–10; Jos 24:6–7; Ps 78:53; 106:9–11. *c:* Nm 16:1–35; Ps 106:16–17. *d:* Dt 5:33; 6:1–3. *e:* Dt 8:7–10.

[13]*[f] If, then, you truly listen to my commandments which I give you today, loving
and serving the LORD, your God, with your
whole heart and your whole being, [14]I will
give the seasonal rain to your land, the early
rain* and the late rain, that you may have
your grain, wine and oil to gather in; [15]and I
will bring forth grass in your fields for your
animals. Thus you may eat and be satisfied.
[16][g] But be careful lest your heart be so lured
away that you serve other gods and bow
down to them.[h] [17]For then the anger of the
LORD will flare up against you and he will
close up the heavens, so that no rain will fall,
and the soil will not yield its crops, and you
will soon perish from the good land the
LORD is giving you.

Need for Fidelity. [18][i] Therefore, take these
words of mine into your heart and soul. Bind
them on your arm as a sign, and let them be as
a pendant on your forehead. [19]Teach them to
your children, speaking of them when you are
at home and when you are away, when you lie
down and when you get up, [20]and write them
on the doorposts of your houses and on your
gates, [21]so that, as long as the heavens are
above the earth, you and your children may
live on in the land which the LORD swore to
your ancestors he would give them.

[22][j] For if you are careful to observe this
entire commandment I am giving you, loving the LORD, your God, following his ways
exactly, and holding fast to him, [23]the LORD
will dispossess all these nations before you,
and you will dispossess nations greater and
mightier than yourselves. [24][k] Every place
where you set foot shall be yours: from the
wilderness and the Lebanon, from the Euphrates River to the Western Sea,* shall be
your territory. [25]None shall stand up against
you; the LORD, your God, will spread the
fear and dread of you through any land
where you set foot, as he promised you.[l]

Blessing and Curse. [26][m] See, I set before
you this day a blessing and a curse: [27]a blessing for obeying the commandments of the
LORD, your God, which I give you today; [28]a
curse if you do not obey the commandments
of the LORD, your God, but turn aside from
the way I command you today, to go after
other gods, whom you do not know.[n]
[29]When the LORD, your God, brings you into
the land which you are to enter and possess,
then on Mount Gerizim you shall pronounce
the blessing,[o] on Mount Ebal, the curse.*
[30](These are beyond the Jordan, on the other
side of the western road in the land of the
Canaanites who live in the Arabah, opposite
Gilgal beside the oak of Moreh.)[p] [31]Now you
are about to cross the Jordan to enter and
possess the land which the LORD, your God,
is giving you. When, therefore, you take
possession of it and settle there, [32]be careful
to observe all the statutes and ordinances
that I set before you today.

B. The Deuteronomic Code

CHAPTER 12

See RG 141–48

One Center of Worship. [1]These are
the statutes and ordinances which you must
be careful to observe in the land which the
LORD, the God of your ancestors, has given
you to possess, throughout the time you live
on its soil.[q] [2][r] Destroy entirely all the places
where the nations you are to dispossess
serve their gods, on the high mountains, on
the hills, and under every green tree.[s] [3]Tear

11:13–15 Here as elsewhere Moses shifts between speaking of the Lord in the third person and speaking for the Lord in the first person.

11:14 The early rain: the rains which begin in October or November and continue intermittently throughout the winter. **The late rain**: the heavy showers of March and April. In Palestine crops are sown in autumn and harvested in spring and summer.

11:24 The Western Sea: the Mediterranean.

11:29 For the full ceremony of blessing and curse, see chaps. 27–28. Gerizim and Ebal are mountains in Samaria, separated by a deep ravine.

---

f: Dt 7:12–14; 10:12–13; 28:1–14; Lv 26:3–5; Jer 5:24; Ps 104:14. *g:* Dt 4:25–27; 6:14–15; 28:15–68. *h:* Dt 5:6–10; 7:1–6; 13:2–19; 1 Kgs 8:35–36. *i:* Dt 6:6–9. *j:* Dt 7:1; 9:1–3; 10:12–13. *k:* Dt 1:7; Ex 23:31; Jos 1:3. *l:* Dt 2:25; 7:23–24; Ex 23:27. *m:* Dt 28:1–68; 30:1, 15–20; Lv 26:3–45. *n:* Dt 32:16–18. *o:* Dt 27:12–13; Jos 8:30–35. *p:* Gn 12:6; 35:4. *q:* Dt 4:44–45. *r:* Dt 5:7–10; Ex 20:24–26; 2 Kgs 18:3–6, 22; 23:4–9. *s:* Dt 7:5, 24–25; Ex 23:23–24; 34:11–14; Nm 33:51–52; Jgs 17:3–5; 1 Kgs 12:28–30; 14:22–24; 2 Kgs 16:4; 17:7–12; Jer 2:20; 3:6–10; Hos 4:12–13.

down their altars, smash their sacred pillars,
burn up their asherahs, and chop down the
idols of their gods, that you may destroy the
very name of them from that place.

4 That is not how you are to act toward the
LORD, your God. 5 Instead,[t] you shall seek
out the place which the LORD, your God,
chooses out of all your tribes and designates
as his dwelling to put his name there.* [u]
There you shall go, 6 bringing your burnt offerings and sacrifices, your tithes and personal contributions, your votive and voluntary offerings, and the firstlings of your
herds and flocks.[v] 7 There, too, in the presence of the LORD, your God, you and your
families shall eat and rejoice in all your undertakings, in which the LORD, your God,
has blessed you.[w]

8 You shall not do as we are doing here today, everyone doing what is right in their own
sight,[x] 9 since you have not yet reached your
resting place, the heritage which the LORD,
your God, is giving you. 10 But after you have
crossed the Jordan and dwell in the land
which the LORD, your God, is giving you as a
heritage, when he has given you rest from all
your enemies round about and you live there
in security,[y] 11* [z] then to the place which the
LORD, your God, chooses as the dwelling
place for his name you shall bring all that I
command you: your burnt offerings and sacrifices, your tithes and personal contributions,
and every special offering you have vowed to
the LORD. 12 You shall rejoice in the presence
of the LORD, your God, with your sons and
daughters, your male and female slaves, as
well as with the Levite within your gates, who
has no hereditary portion with you.

13 [a] Be careful not to sacrifice your burnt
offerings in any place you like, 14 but offer
them in the place which the LORD chooses in
one of your tribal territories; there you shall
do what I command you.

Profane and Sacred Slaughter. 15* However, in any of your communities you may
slaughter and eat meat freely, according to
the blessing that the LORD, your God, has
given you; the unclean as well as the clean
may eat it, as they do the gazelle or the deer.[b]
16* Only, you shall not eat of the blood, but
must pour it out on the ground like water.[c]
17 Moreover, you may not, in your own communities, partake of your tithe of grain or
wine or oil, of the firstborn of your herd or
flock, of any offering you have vowed, of
your voluntary offerings, or of your personal
contributions. 18 These you must eat in the
presence of the LORD, your God, in the place
that the LORD, your God, chooses, along
with your son and daughter, your male and
female slave, and the Levite within your
gates; and there, in the presence of the LORD,
you shall rejoice in all your undertakings.
19 Be careful, also, that you do not neglect the
Levite as long as you live in your land.[d]

20 [e] After the LORD, your God, has enlarged your territory, as he promised you,[f]
and you think, "I will eat meat," as it is your
desire to eat meat, you may eat it freely;
21 and if the place where the LORD, your God,
chooses to put his name is too far, you may
slaughter in the manner I have commanded

12:5 The place . . . to put his name there: Moses thus designates Jerusalem (Mt. Zion), in accordance with the Deuteronomic doctrine that the Lord "chooses" Zion, as the place where eventually the Temple will be built, as he chooses the house of David to reign over Israel; see 2 Sm 7; 1 Kgs 8; Ps 132. But the Lord's presence in Jerusalem consists in putting his "name" there (12:11, 21; 14:23–24; 16:2, 6, 11; 26:2; 1 Kgs 8:44, 49; 9:3; 11:36; 14:21; 2 Kgs 17:34; 21:4, 7; 23:27). The Lord himself "cannot be contained" in an earthly dwelling (1 Kgs 8:27), but because he says of the Jerusalem Temple that "my name will be there" (1 Kgs 8:16, 29; 2 Kgs 23:27), he is present. This theology allows God in a way to dwell with Israel and at the same time preserves divine transcendence. See note on 1 Kgs 8:12–13.

12:11 Sacrifice is to be confined to the single place that the Lord has chosen; eventually this was Jerusalem.

12:15 At this point a distinction is being made between cultic sacrifice and slaughter of animals for food. **In any of your communities**: lit., "within your gates."

12:16 The blood was understood to be the source or vehicle of life and so was not to be consumed. Cf. Gn 9:4.

t: Dt 12:11–12; 14:22–26; 15:19–20; 16:2, 6, 10–11, 14–15; 26:2. *u:* 2 Sm 7:13; 1 Kgs 8:16–21, 27–30. *v:* Dt 14:22–27; 15:19–23; 23:21–23; 26:12–15; Lv 1:3–17; 3:1–17; 6:2–6; 7:29–36; 27:1–8; Nm 15:18–21; 28:2–8; 30:2–15; Am 4:4–5; 5:22. *w:* Dt 12:12, 18–19; 14:26–27; 15:20; 16:11, 14; 26:11. *x:* Dt 6:18; 12:28; Jgs 17:6; 21:25. *y:* Dt 3:18–20; 11:22–25; Jos 23:1; 2 Sm 7:1; 1 Kgs 5:17–18; 8:56. *z:* Dt 12:5–7; 14:22–26; 15:19–20; 16:2, 6, 10–11, 14–15; 26:2. *a:* Jos 22:10–34. *b:* Dt 12:20–22; 15:22; Lv 7:19–21. *c:* Dt 12:23–27; 15:23; Gn 9:4; Lv 3:17; 17:10–14; 19:26; 1 Sm 14:31–35. *d:* Dt 14:27. *e:* Lv 17:3–9. *f:* Dt 19:8; Gn 28:14; Ex 34:24.

you any of your herd or flock that the LORD has given you, and eat it freely in your own community. 22 You may eat it as you would the gazelle or the deer: the unclean and the clean eating it together. 23[g] But make sure that you do not eat of the blood; for blood is life; you shall not eat that life with the flesh. 24 Do not eat of the blood, therefore, but pour it out on the ground like water. 25 Do not eat of it, that you and your children after you may prosper for doing what is right in the sight of the LORD. 26 However, any sacred gifts or votive offerings that you may have, you shall bring with you to the place which the LORD chooses, 27 and there you must sacrifice your burnt offerings, both the flesh and the blood, on the altar of the LORD, your God; of your other sacrifices the blood indeed must be poured out against the altar of the LORD, your God,[h] but their flesh you may eat.

28 Be careful to heed all these words I command you today, that you and your descendants after you may forever prosper for doing what is good and right in the sight of the LORD, your God.[i]

Warning Against Abominable Practices. 29[j] When the LORD, your God, cuts down from before you the nations you are going in to dispossess, and you have dispossessed them and are settled in their land, 30 be careful that you not be trapped into following them after they have been destroyed before you. Do not inquire regarding their gods, "How did these nations serve their gods, so I might do the same." 31 You shall not worship the LORD, your God, that way, because they offered to their gods every abomination that the LORD detests, even burning their sons and daughters to their gods.[k]

CHAPTER 13

See RG 141–48

Penalties for Enticing to Idolatry. 1 Every word that I command you, you shall be careful to observe, neither adding to it nor subtracting from it.

2[l] If there arises in your midst a prophet or a dreamer* who promises you a sign or wonder, 3 saying, "Let us go after other gods," whom you have not known, "and let us serve them," and the sign or wonder foretold to you comes to pass, 4 do not listen to the words of that prophet or that dreamer; for the LORD, your God, is testing you to know whether you really love the LORD, your God, with all your heart and soul.[m] 5 The LORD, your God, shall you follow, and him shall you fear; his commandments shall you observe, and to his voice shall you listen; him you shall serve, and to him you shall hold fast.[n] 6 But that prophet or that dreamer shall be put to death, because, in order to lead you astray from the way which the LORD, your God, has commanded you to take, the prophet or dreamer has spoken apostasy against the LORD, your God, who brought you out of the land of Egypt and redeemed you from the house of slavery. Thus shall you purge the evil from your midst.[o]

7 If your brother, your father's child or your mother's child, your son or daughter, your beloved spouse, or your intimate friend entices you secretly, saying, "Come, let us serve other gods," whom you and your ancestors have not known, 8 any of the gods of the surrounding peoples, near to you or far away, from one end of the earth to the other: 9 do not yield or listen to any such person; show no pity or compassion and do not shield such a one,[p] 10[q] but kill that person. Your hand shall be the first raised to put such a one to death; the hand of all the people shall follow. 11 You shall stone that person to death, for seeking to lead you astray from the LORD, your God, who brought you out of the land of Egypt, out of the house of slavery. 12 And all Israel shall hear of it and fear, and never again do such evil as this in your midst.[r]

13:2, 4, 6 Dreamer: a false prophet who pretended to have received revelations from God in a dream; cf. Jer 23:25–32; 27:9; Zec 10:2. But dreams could also be a means of true prophecy (Nm 12:6; Jl 3:1) and of genuine revelations (Gn 20:3, 6; 31:11, 24; 37:5, 9; Mt 1:20; 2:12, 13, 19; etc.).

g: Dt 12:16; 15:23; Gn 9:4; Lv 3:17; 17:10–14; 19:26; 1 Sm 14:31–35. *h:* Lv 17:11. *i:* Dt 4:40; 5:29; 6:2–3, 17–18; 12:25. *j:* Dt 7:1–5, 25; Ex 23:33; 34:12; Jgs 2:2–3. *k:* Dt 18:10; Lv 18:21; 20:2–5; 2 Kgs 3:27; 16:3; 21:6; 23:10; Jer 7:31; 19:5. *l:* Dt 6:4, 14–15; 17:2–7. *m:* Dt 8:2, 16. *n:* Dt 6:4–5; 10:20; 11:22. *o:* Dt 17:7, 12; 19:19; 21:21; 22:21–22, 24; 24:7; Jer 28:16; 29:32. *p:* Dt 7:16; 19:13, 21; 25:12. *q:* Dt 17:5–7; 21:21; 22:20–24; Jos 7:25–26; 1 Kgs 21:13–14. *r:* Dt 17:13; 21:21.

[13]If you hear it said concerning one of the cities which the LORD, your God, gives you to dwell in, [14]that certain scoundrels have sprung up in your midst and have led astray the inhabitants of their city, saying, "Come, let us serve other gods," whom you have not known, [15]you must inquire carefully into the matter and investigate it thoroughly. If you find that it is true and an established fact that this abomination has been committed in your midst,[s] [16][t] you shall put the inhabitants of that city to the sword, placing the city and all that is in it, even its livestock, under the ban. [17]Having heaped up all its spoils in the middle of its square, you shall burn the city with all its spoils as a whole burnt offering to the LORD, your God. Let it be a heap of ruins forever, never to be rebuilt. [18]You shall not hold on to anything that is under the ban; then the LORD will turn from his burning anger and show you mercy, and in showing you mercy multiply you as he swore to your ancestors, [19]because you have listened to the voice of the LORD, your God, keeping all his commandments, which I give you today, doing what is right in the sight of the LORD, your God.

CHAPTER 14

See RG 141–48

Improper Mourning Rites. [1]You are children of the LORD, your God. You shall not gash yourselves nor shave the hair above your foreheads for the dead.[u] [2]For you are a people holy to the LORD, your God; the LORD, your God, has chosen you from all the peoples on the face of the earth to be a people specially his own.[v]

Clean and Unclean Animals. [3]You shall not eat any abominable thing.[w] [4][x] These are the animals you may eat: the ox, the sheep, the goat, [5]the deer, the gazelle, the roebuck, the wild goat, the ibex, the antelope, and the mountain sheep. [6]Any among the animals that has divided hooves, with the foot cloven in two, and that chews the cud you may eat. [7]But you shall not eat any of the following that chew the cud or have cloven hooves: the camel, the hare, and the rock badger, which indeed chew the cud, but do not have divided hooves; they are unclean for you. [8]And the pig, which indeed has divided hooves, with cloven foot, but does not chew the cud, is unclean for you. Their flesh you shall not eat, and their dead bodies you shall not touch.

[9]These you may eat, of all that live in the water: whatever has both fins and scales you may eat, [10]but all those that lack either fins or scales you shall not eat; they are unclean for you.

[11]You may eat all clean birds. [12]* But you shall not eat any of the following: the griffon vulture, the bearded vulture, the black vulture, [13]the various kites and falcons, [14]all kinds of crows, [15]the eagle owl, the kestrel, the long-eared owl, all species of hawks, [16]the little owl, the screech owl, the barn owl, [17]the horned owl, the osprey, the cormorant, [18]the stork, any kind of heron, the hoopoe, and the bat. [19]* All winged insects are also unclean for you and shall not be eaten. [20]Any clean winged creatures you may eat.

[21]You shall not eat the carcass of any animal that has died of itself; but you may give it to a resident alien within your gates to eat, or you may sell it to a foreigner. For you are a people holy to the LORD, your God.[y]

You shall not boil a young goat in its mother's milk.*

Tithes. [22]Each year you shall tithe all the produce of your seed that grows in the field;[z] [23]then in the place which the LORD, your God, chooses as the dwelling place of his

14:12–18 The identification of several of the birds in these verses is uncertain.

14:19–20 Lv 11:20–23 suggests that the unclean winged insects are those that walk on the ground; the clean winged creatures are those that leap on the ground, such as certain species of locusts.

14:21 Boil a young goat in its mother's milk: the meaning of this regulation is obscure but it may have a humane concern similar to the prohibitions against slaughtering an animal and its young on the same day (Lv 22:27–28) and capturing a mother bird along with her fledgling or eggs (Dt 22:6–7). See note on Ex 23:19.

s: Dt 17:4; 19:18. *t:* Dt 20:16–18; Jos 6:17, 24; 7:25–26; 8:28. *u:* Dt 32:5–6, 18–20; Lv 19:27–28; 21:5; Ps 103:13; Is 1:2, 4; 30:1; Jer 3:14, 19, 22; 16:6; 31:9, 20; 41:4–5; Hos 2:1; 11:1–4. *v:* Dt 7:6; Ex 19:5–6. *w:* Acts 10:14. *x:* Lv 11:2–23. *y:* Ex 22:30; 23:19; 34:26; Lv 17:15; 22:8; Ez 44:31. *z:* Gn 14:20; 28:22; Lv 27:30–33; Nm 18:21–32; 1 Sm 8:15, 17; 2 Chr 31:2–19; Neh 12:44; Am 4:4.

name[a] you shall eat in his presence the tithe of your grain, wine and oil, as well as the firstlings of your herd and flock, that you may learn always to fear the LORD, your God. [24b] But if, when the LORD, your God, blesses you, the journey is too much for you and you are not able to bring your tithe, because the place which the LORD, your God, chooses to put his name is too far for you, [25]you may exchange the tithe for money, and with the money securely in hand, go to the place which the LORD, your God, chooses. [26]You may then exchange the money for whatever you desire, oxen or sheep, wine or beer, or anything else you want, and there in the presence of the LORD, your God, you shall consume it and rejoice, you and your household together.[c] [27]But do not neglect the Levite within your gates, for he has no hereditary portion with you.[d]

[28e] At the end of every third year you shall bring out all the tithes of your produce for that year and deposit them within your own communities, [29]that the Levite who has no hereditary portion with you, and also the resident alien, the orphan and the widow within your gates, may come and eat and be satisfied; so that the LORD, your God, may bless you in all that you undertake.

CHAPTER 15

See RG 141–48

Debts and the Poor. [1]At the end of every seven-year period* you shall have a remission of debts,[f] [2]and this is the manner of the remission. Creditors shall remit all claims on loans made to a neighbor, not pressing the neighbor, one who is kin, because the LORD's remission has been proclaimed. [3]You may press a foreigner, but you shall remit the claim on what your kin owes to you.[g] [4h] However, since the LORD, your God, will bless you abundantly in the land the LORD, your God, will give you to possess as a heritage, there shall be no one of you in need [5]if you but listen to the voice of the LORD, your God, and carefully observe this entire commandment which I enjoin on you today. [6]Since the LORD, your God, will bless you as he promised, you will lend to many nations, and borrow from none;[i] you will rule over many nations, and none will rule over you.

[7j] If one of your kindred is in need in any community in the land which the LORD, your God, is giving you, you shall not harden your heart nor close your hand against your kin who is in need. [8]Instead, you shall freely open your hand and generously lend what suffices to meet that need.[k] [9]Be careful not to entertain the mean thought, "The seventh year, the year of remission, is near," so that you would begrudge your kin who is in need and give nothing, and your kin would cry to the LORD against you and you would be held guilty.[l] [10]When you give, give generously and not with a stingy heart; for that, the LORD, your God, will bless you in all your works and undertakings. [11]The land will never lack for needy persons; that is why I command you: "Open your hand freely to your poor and to your needy kin in your land."[m]

Hebrew Slaves. [12n] If your kin, a Hebrew man or woman, sells himself or herself to you, he or she is to serve you for six years, but in the seventh year you shall release him or her as a free person. [13o] When you release a male from your service, as a free person, you shall not send him away empty-handed, [14]but shall weigh him down with gifts from your flock and threshing floor and wine press; as the LORD, your God, has blessed you, so you shall give to him. [15]For remember that you too were slaves in the land of Egypt, and the LORD, your God, redeemed you. That is why I am giving you this command today.[p] [16q] But if he says to you, "I do not wish to leave you," because he loves you and your household,

15:1 At the end of every seven-year period: in every seventh, or sabbatical, year. Cf. 15:9; 31:10; and compare Jer 34:14 with Dt 15:12. **A remission of debts**: it is debated whether a full cancellation of debts is meant, or merely a suspension of payment on them or on their interest, but the former is more likely. Cf. Ex 23:11 where the same Hebrew root is used of a field that is "let lie fallow" in the sabbatical year.

a: Dt 12:5–7, 11–12, 17–18; 15:19–20. *b:* Mk 11:15; Jn 2:13–14. *c:* Dt 12:7. *d:* Dt 12:12, 19. *e:* Dt 26:12–15. *f:* Dt 31:10; Lv 25:1–55; Neh 10:31. *g:* Dt 23:20. *h:* Dt 7:12–14; 28:1–14. *i:* Dt 28:12. *j:* Ex 22:25. *k:* Dt 24:19; Lv 25:35; Ps 37:21–22; Prv 19:17; Sir 29:1–2; Mt 5:42. *l:* Dt 24:15; Ex 22:23–24, 27. *m:* Dt 15:8; Mt 26:11. *n:* Ex 21:2–11; Jer 34:8–22. *o:* Ex 3:21–22; 12:35–36. *p:* Dt 5:15; 10:19; 16:12; 24:18, 22. *q:* Ex 21:5–6.

since he is well off with you, [17]you shall take an awl and put it through his ear[*] into the door, and he shall be your slave forever. Your female slave, also, you shall treat in the same way. [18]Do not be reluctant when you let them go free, since the service they have given you for six years was worth twice a hired laborer's salary; and the LORD, your God, will bless you in everything you do.

Firstlings. [19r] You shall consecrate to the LORD, your God, every male firstling born in your herd and in your flock. You shall not work the firstlings of your cattle, nor shear the firstlings of your flock. [20]In the presence of the LORD, your God, you shall eat them year after year, you and your household, in the place that the LORD will choose.[s] [21t] But if a firstling has any defect, lameness or blindness, any such serious defect, you shall not sacrifice it to the LORD, your God, [22]but in your own communities you may eat it, the unclean and the clean eating it together, as you would a gazelle or a deer. [23]Only, you must not eat of its blood; you shall pour it out on the ground like water.

CHAPTER 16

See RG 141–48

Feast of the Passover. [1]Observe the month of Abib[*] by keeping the Passover of the LORD, your God,[u] since it was in the month of Abib that the LORD, your God, brought you out of Egypt by night. [2]You shall offer the Passover sacrifice from your flock and your herd to the LORD, your God, in the place the LORD will choose as the dwelling place of his name.[v] [3w] You shall not eat leavened bread with it. For seven days you shall eat with it only unleavened bread, the bread of affliction, so that you may remember as long as you live the day you left the land of Egypt; for in hurried flight you left the land of Egypt. [4]No leaven is to be found with you in all your territory for seven days, and none of the meat which you sacrificed on the evening of the first day shall be kept overnight for the next day.

[5]You may not sacrifice the Passover in any of the communities which the LORD, your God, gives you; [6]only at the place which the LORD, your God, will choose as the dwelling place of his name, and in the evening at sunset, at the very time when you left Egypt, shall you sacrifice the Passover.[x] [7]You shall cook and eat it at the place the LORD, your God, will choose; then in the morning you may return to your tents. [8]For six days you shall eat unleavened bread, and on the seventh day there shall be a solemn assembly for the LORD, your God; on that day you shall do no work.[y]

Feast of Weeks. [9z] You shall count off seven weeks; begin to count the seven weeks from the day when the sickle is first put to the standing grain. [10]You shall then keep the feast of Weeks[*] for the LORD, your God, and the measure of your own voluntary offering which you will give shall be in proportion to the blessing the LORD, your God, has given you. [11]You shall rejoice in the presence of the LORD, your God, together with your son and daughter, your male and female slave, and the Levite within your gates, as well as the resident alien, the orphan, and the widow among you, in the place which the LORD, your God, will choose as the dwelling place of his name.[a] [12]Remember that you too were slaves in Egypt, so carry out these statutes carefully.

Feast of Booths. [13b] You shall celebrate the feast of Booths[*] for seven days, when

15:17 His ear: cf. Ex 21:6 and note there.

16:1 Abib: "ear of grain, ripe grain," the name of the month in which the barley harvest fell, corresponding to our March and April; at a later period this month received the Babylonian name of "Nisan."

16:10 Feast of Weeks: a celebration of the grain harvest, later known as "Pentecost"; cf. Acts 2:1.

16:13 Feast of Booths: also called Tabernacles; a harvest festival at the end of the agricultural year. In later times, during the seven days of the feast the Israelites camped in booths made of branches erected on the roofs of their houses or in the streets in commemoration of their wanderings in the wilderness, where they dwelt in such temporary shelters.

---

r: Ex 13:2, 11–16; 22:29–30; 34:19–20; Lv 22:27; 27:26; Nm 18:15–18. *s:* Dt 12:6–7, 17–18; 14:23. *t:* Dt 12:15–16, 22–24; 17:1; Lv 22:17–25; Mal 1:8. *u:* Ex 12:2–13:10; 23:15; 34:18; Lv 23:5–8; Nm 28:16–25; Jos 5:10–12; 2 Kgs 23:21–23; 2 Chr 30:1–27; 35:1–19; Ez 45:21–24. *v:* Dt 12:5, 11; 16:6. *w:* Ex 12:34, 39; 13:6–7; 34:18. *x:* Dt 12:5, 11; 16:2. *y:* Ex 13:6; Lv 23:36; Nm 29:35; Is 1:13; Am 5:21. *z:* Ex 23:16; 34:22; Lv 23:15–21; Nm 28:26–31. *a:* Dt 12:5–7, 11–12, 18. *b:* Dt 31:10–13; Ex 23:16; 34:22; Lv 23:34–43; Nm 29:12–38; 1 Kgs 8:2, 62–66; Ezr 3:4; Neh 8:14; Ez 45:25.

you have gathered in the produce from your threshing floor and wine press. [14]You shall rejoice at your feast,[c] together with your son and daughter, your male and female slave, and also the Levite, the resident alien, the orphan and the widow within your gates. [15]For seven days you shall celebrate this feast for the LORD, your God, in the place which the LORD will choose; since the LORD, your God, has blessed you in all your crops and in all your undertakings, you will be full of joy.

[16]Three times a year,[d] then, all your males shall appear before the LORD, your God, in the place which he will choose: at the feast of Unleavened Bread, at the feast of Weeks, and at the feast of Booths. They shall not appear before the LORD empty-handed, [17]but each with his own gift, in proportion to the blessing which the LORD, your God, has given to you.

Justice. [18][e] In all the communities which the LORD, your God, is giving you, you shall appoint judges and officials throughout your tribes to administer true justice for the people. [19]You must not distort justice: you shall not show partiality;[f] you shall not take a bribe, for a bribe blinds the eyes even of the wise and twists the words even of the just. [20]Justice, justice alone shall you pursue, so that you may live and possess the land the LORD, your God, is giving you.

Illicit Worship. [21][g] You shall not plant an asherah* of any kind of wood next to the altar of the LORD, your God, which you will build;[h] [22]nor shall you erect a sacred pillar, such as the LORD, your God, hates.

CHAPTER 17

See RG 141–48

[1]You shall not sacrifice to the LORD, your God, an ox or a sheep with any serious defect;[i] that would be an abomination to the LORD, your God.

[2][j] If there is found in your midst, in any one of the communities which the LORD, your God, gives you, a man or a woman who does evil in the sight of the LORD, your God, and transgresses his covenant,[k] [3]by going to serve other gods, by bowing down to them, to the sun or the moon or any of the host of heaven, contrary to my command;[l] [4]and if you are told or hear of it, you must investigate it thoroughly. If the truth of the matter is established that this abomination has been committed in Israel, [5]you shall bring the man or the woman who has done this evil deed out to your gates* and stone the man or the woman to death. [6]Only on the testimony of two or three witnesses shall a person be put to death;[m] no one shall be put to death on the testimony of only one witness. [7]The hands of the witnesses shall be the first raised to put the person to death, and afterward the hands of all the people.[n] Thus shall you purge the evil from your midst.

Judges. [8][o] If there is a case for judgment which proves too baffling for you to decide, in a matter of bloodshed or of law or of injury, matters of dispute within your gates, you shall then go up to the place which the LORD, your God, will choose, [9]to the levitical priests or to the judge who is in office at that time. They shall investigate the case and then announce to you the decision.[p] [10]You shall act according to the decision they announce to you in the place which the LORD will choose, carefully observing everything as they instruct you. [11]You shall carry out the instruction they give you and the judgment they pronounce, without turning aside either to the right or left from the decision they announce to you. [12]Anyone who acts presumptuously and does not obey the priest* who officiates there in the ministry of the LORD, your God, or the judge, shall die. Thus shall

16:21–22 Asherah . . . sacred pillar: see note on 7:5; Ex 34:13.

17:5 Out to your gates: outside the gates, so as not to defile the city; cf. Lv 24:14; Nm 15:36; Acts 7:58; Heb 12:13.

17:12 The priest: the high priest; **the judge**: a layman. The court system here, involving lay and priestly officials, resembles the one whose establishment is attributed to King Jehoshaphat in 2 Chr 19:8–11 (cf. Ex 18:17–23 and Dt 1:17).

---

c: Dt 16:11. *d:* Dt 12:7; 16:11, 14; Ex 23:14–15, 17; 34:23–24; 2 Chr 8:13. *e:* Dt 1:13–17; 17:8–13; 19:17; 21:5; Ex 18:13–26; 2 Chr 19:5–11. *f:* Dt 1:16–17; 10:17–18; Ex 23:2–3, 6–8; Lv 19:15; Prv 17:23; 18:5; 24:23; Is 1:23; Mi 7:3; Jn 7:24; Jas 2:9. *g:* Dt 5:7–10; 6:4–5; 12:29–14:2. *h:* Dt 7:5; Ex 34:13; 1 Kgs 14:15; 2 Kgs 23:6, 15; 2 Chr 33:3. *i:* Lv 22:20. *j:* Dt 13:2–19. *k:* Jos 7:11, 15; 23:16; Jgs 2:20; 2 Kgs 18:12; Jer 34:18; Hos 6:7; 8:1. *l:* Dt 4:19; 2 Kgs 17:16; 21:3; 23:5; Jer 8:2; Ez 8:16. *m:* Dt 19:15; Nm 35:30; Jn 8:17; 2 Cor 13:1. *n:* Dt 13:6, 10. *o:* Ex 18:13–26. *p:* Dt 21:5; 2 Chr 19:8; Ezr 7:25.

you purge the evil from Israel. 13 And all the people, on hearing of it, shall fear, and will never again act presumptuously.[q]

The King. 14[r] When you have come into the land which the LORD, your God, is giving you, and have taken possession of it and settled in it, should you then decide, "I will set a king over me, like all the surrounding nations,"[s] 15 you may indeed set over you a king whom the LORD, your God, will choose.[t] Someone from among your own kindred you may set over you as king; you may not set over you a foreigner, who is no kin of yours. 16* But he shall not have a great number of horses; nor shall he make his people go back again to Egypt to acquire many horses, for the LORD said to you, Do not go back that way again.[u] 17 Neither shall he have a great number of wives, lest his heart turn away,[v] nor shall he accumulate a vast amount of silver and gold. 18 When he is sitting upon his royal throne, he shall write a copy of this law* upon a scroll from the one that is in the custody of the levitical priests.[w] 19*[x] It shall remain with him and he shall read it as long as he lives, so that he may learn to fear the LORD, his God, and to observe carefully all the words of this law and these statutes, 20 so that he does not exalt himself over his kindred or turn aside from this commandment to the right or to the left, and so that he and his descendants may reign long in Israel.

See RG 141–48

CHAPTER 18

Priests. 1 The levitical priests, the whole tribe of Levi, shall have no hereditary portion with Israel; they shall eat the fire offerings of the LORD and the portions due to him.[y] 2 They shall have no heritage among their kindred; the LORD himself is their heritage, as he has told them.[z] 3 This shall be the due of the priests from the people: those who are offering a sacrifice, whether an ox or a sheep, shall give the priest the shoulder, the jowls and the stomach. 4 The first fruits of your grain, your wine, and your oil,[a] as well as the first shearing of your flock, you shall also give him. 5 For the LORD, your God, has chosen him out of all your tribes to be in attendance to minister in the name of the LORD, him and his descendants for all time.[b]

6 When a Levite goes from one of your communities anywhere in Israel in which he has been residing, to visit, as his heart may desire, the place which the LORD will choose, 7 and ministers there in the name of the LORD, his God, like all his fellow Levites who stand before the LORD there, 8 he shall receive the same portions to eat, along with his stipends and patrimony.*

Prophets. 9 When you come into the land which the LORD, your God, is giving you, you shall not learn to imitate the abominations of the nations there.[c] 10[d] Let there not be found among you anyone who causes their son or daughter to pass through the fire,* or practices divination, or is a soothsayer, augur, or sorcerer, 11 or who casts spells, consults ghosts and spirits, or seeks oracles from the dead. 12 Anyone who does such things is an abomination to the LORD, and because of such abominations the LORD, your God, is

17:16–17 This restriction on royal acquisitions may have in mind the excesses of Solomon's reign mentioned in 1 Kgs 10:1–11:6. **Horses**: chariotry for war. Egypt engaged in horse trading, and the danger envisioned here is that some king might make Israel a vassal of Egypt for military aid.

17:18 A copy of this law: the source of the name Deuteronomy, which in Hebrew is literally "double" or "copy"; in the Septuagint translated as *deuteronomion*, literally "a second law." In Jerome's Latin Vulgate as *deuteronium*.

17:19 The only positive requirement imposed upon the king is strict adherence to the Mosaic or Deuteronomic law. In that respect, the king's primary task was to be a model Israelite.

18:8 His stipends and patrimony: meaning of the Hebrew is uncertain.

18:10–11 Causes their son or daughter to pass through the fire: to Molech. See note on Lv 18:21. Such human sacrifices are classed here with various occult and magical practices because they were believed to possess powers for averting a calamity; cf. 2 Kgs 3:27. Three other categories of magic are listed here: divination of the future (by a soothsayer or augur); black magic (by a sorcerer or one who casts spells); and necromancy (by one who consults ghosts and spirits, or seeks oracles from the dead to divine the future).

q: Dt 13:12. *r:* 1 Sm 10–25. *s:* Dt 26:1; 1 Sm 8:5, 19–20. *t:* 1 Sm 9:16; 10:24; 16:1–13; 1 Kgs 19:15–16; 2 Kgs 9:1–13. *u:* Dt 28:68; 1 Sm 8:10–12; 1 Kgs 4:26; 10:26–29; Is 2:7. *v:* 1 Kgs 10:10–25; 11:1–8; Neh 13:26; Is 2:7. *w:* Dt 31:9, 24–26; Jos 8:32. *x:* Dt 5:32–6:3; 2 Sm 7:12–16; 1 Kgs 2:4; Ps 132:11–18. *y:* Nm 18:8–9, 20–24; Jos 13:14; 18:7; 2 Chr 31:2–19; 1 Cor 9:13. *z:* Nm 18:20; Jos 13:33. *a:* Dt 26:1–11; Nm 18:12; 2 Chr 31:5; Neh 13:10–13. *b:* Dt 10:8; Jer 33:18. *c:* Dt 12:29–31; Lv 18:24–30. *d:* Dt 12:31; Ex 22:18; Lv 18:21; 19:31; 20:6, 27; 1 Sm 28:7–19; 2 Kgs 17:17; 21:6; 23:10, 24; Is 8:19–20; Ez 21:21.

dispossessing them before you.[e] [13]You must be altogether sincere with the LORD, your God. [14]Although these nations whom you are about to dispossess listen to their soothsayers and diviners, the LORD, your God, will not permit you to do so.

[15]A prophet like me* will the LORD, your God, raise up for you from among your own kindred; that is the one to whom you shall listen.[f] [16]This is exactly what you requested of the LORD, your God, at Horeb on the day of the assembly, when you said, "Let me not again hear the voice of the LORD, my God, nor see this great fire any more, or I will die."[g] [17]And the LORD said to me, What they have said is good. [18]I will raise up for them a prophet like you from among their kindred, and will put my words into the mouth of the prophet; the prophet shall tell them all that I command.[h] [19]Anyone who will not listen to my words which the prophet speaks in my name, I myself will hold accountable for it.[i] [20]But if a prophet presumes to speak a word in my name[j] that I have not commanded, or speaks in the name of other gods, that prophet shall die.

[21]Should you say to yourselves, "How can we recognize that a word is one the LORD has not spoken?", [22]if a prophet speaks in the name of the LORD but the word does not come true, it is a word the LORD did not speak. The prophet has spoken it presumptuously; do not fear him.

CHAPTER 19

See RG 141–48

Cities of Refuge. [1][k] When the LORD, your God, cuts down the nations whose land the LORD, your God, is giving you, and you have dispossessed them and settled in their cities and houses,[l] [2]you shall set apart three cities* in the land the LORD, your God, is giving you to possess. [3]You shall measure the distances and divide into three regions the land of which the LORD, your God, is giving you possession, so that every homicide will be able to find a refuge.

[4]This is the case of a homicide who may take refuge there and live: when someone strikes down a neighbor unintentionally and not out of previous hatred. [5]For example, if someone goes with a neighbor to a forest to cut wood, wielding an ax to cut down a tree, and its head flies off the handle and hits the neighbor a mortal blow, such a person may take refuge in one of these cities and live. [6]Should the distance be too great, the avenger of blood* might in hot anger pursue, overtake, and strike the killer dead, even though that one does not deserve the death penalty since there had been no previous hatred; [7]for this reason I command you: Set apart three cities.

[8][m] But if the LORD, your God, enlarges your territory, as he swore to your ancestors, and gives you all the land he promised your ancestors he would give, [9]because you carefully observe this whole commandment which I give you today, loving the LORD, your God, and ever walking in his ways, then add three more cities to these three. [10]Thus, in the land which the LORD, your God, is giving you as a heritage, innocent blood will not be shed and you will not become guilty of bloodshed.[n]

[11]However, if someone, hating a neighbor, lies in wait, attacks, and strikes the neighbor dead, and then flees to one of these cities, [12]the elders of the killer's own city shall send and have the killer taken from there, to be handed over to the avenger of blood and slain. [13]Do not show pity, but purge from Israel the innocent blood, so that it may go well with you.[o]

18:15 A prophet like me: from the context (opposition to the practices described in vv. 10–11) it seems that Moses is referring in general to all the true prophets who were to succeed him. This passage came to be understood in a quasi-Messianic sense in the New Testament (Mt 17:5; Jn 6:14; 7:40; Acts 3:22; 7:37).

19:2 Set apart three cities: the Israelites were to have at least six cities of refuge, three in the land east of the Jordan and three in the land of Canaan west of the Jordan (Nm 35:9–34); but since the three cities east of the Jordan had now been appointed (Dt 4:41–43), reference is made here only to the three west of the Jordan. The execution of this command is narrated in Jos 20.

19:6 The avenger of blood: see note on Nm 35:12.

e: Dt 9:4. *f:* Mt 17:5; Mk 9:7; Lk 9:35; Jn 1:45; 6:14; 7:40; Acts 3:22; 7:37. *g:* Ex 20:19. *h:* Ex 4:10–16; Jer 1:9; 15:19; Ez 3:1–4. *i:* Jer 11:21–23; Am 7:10–17; Acts 3:23. *j:* Dt 13:2–6; 1 Kgs 22:1–40; Jer 14:13–16; 23:9–40; 28:1–17; Ez 13:1–23. *k:* Dt 4:41–43; Ex 21:12–14; Nm 35:9–34; Jos 20:1–9. *l:* Dt 6:10–11; 12:29. *m:* Dt 11:22–25; 12:20; Gn 15:18–21; 28:14; Ex 23:31. *n:* Dt 21:8–9. *o:* Dt 13:6, 9.

Removal of Landmarks. 14You shall not move your neighbor's boundary markers* erected by your forebears in the heritage that will be allotted to you in the land the LORD, your God, is giving you to possess.[p]

False Witnesses. 15[q]One witness alone shall not stand against someone in regard to any crime or any offense that may have been committed; a charge shall stand only on the testimony of two or three witnesses.[r]

16If a hostile witness rises against someone to accuse that person of wrongdoing, 17the two parties in the dispute shall appear in the presence of the LORD, in the presence of the priests and judges in office at that time,[s] 18[t]and the judges must investigate it thoroughly. If the witness is a false witness and has falsely accused the other,[u] 19you shall do to the false witness just as that false witness planned to do to the other. Thus shall you purge the evil from your midst. 20The rest shall hear and be afraid, and never again do such an evil thing as this in your midst.[v] 21Do not show pity. Life for life,* eye for eye, tooth for tooth, hand for hand, and foot for foot![w]

CHAPTER 20

See RG 141–48

Courage in War. 1When you go out to war against your enemies and you see horses and chariots and an army greater than your own, you shall not be afraid of them, for the LORD, your God, who brought you up from the land of Egypt, will be with you.

2When you are drawing near to battle, the priest shall come forward and speak to the army, 3and say to them, "Hear, O Israel! Today you are drawing near for battle against your enemies. Do not be weakhearted or afraid, alarmed or frightened by them. 4For it is the LORD, your God, who goes with you to fight for you against your enemies and give you victory."[x]

5Then the officials shall speak to the army:[y] "Is there anyone who has built a new house and not yet dedicated it? Let him return home, lest he die in battle and another dedicate it. 6Is there anyone who has planted a vineyard and not yet plucked its fruit? Let him return home, lest he die in battle and another pluck its fruit. 7Is there anyone who has betrothed a woman and not yet married her? Let him return home, lest he die in battle and another marry her."[z] 8The officials shall continue to speak to the army: "Is there anyone who is afraid and weakhearted?[a] Let him return home, or else he might make the hearts of his fellows melt as his does."

9When the officials have finished speaking to the army, military commanders shall be appointed over them.

Cities of the Enemy. 10[b]When you draw near a city to attack it, offer it terms of peace. 11If it agrees to your terms of peace and lets you in, all the people to be found in it shall serve you in forced labor. 12[c]But if it refuses to make peace with you and instead joins battle with you, lay siege to it, 13and when the LORD, your God, delivers it into your power, put every male in it to the sword; 14but the women and children and livestock and anything else in the city—all its spoil—you may take as plunder for yourselves, and you may enjoy this spoil of your enemies, which the LORD, your God, has given you.

15* That is how you shall deal with any city at a considerable distance from you, which does not belong to these nations here. 16[d]But in the cities of these peoples that the LORD, your God, is giving you as a heritage, you shall not leave a single soul alive. 17You must put them all under the ban—the Hittites, Amorites, Canaanites, Perizzites, Hivites, and Jebusites—just as the LORD, your God, has commanded you, 18so that they do

19:14 Move your neighbor's boundary markers: a prohibition against furtively extending one's property by moving a neighbor's boundary stone.

19:21 Life for life . . .: this phrasing of the *lex talionis* may seem exaggerated, but the law itself is meant to ensure equity and proportional punishment; cf. note on Ex 21:22–25.

20:15 Deuteronomy makes a distinction between treatment of nations far away and those close at hand whose abhorrent religious practices might, or did, influence Israel's worship. This harsh policy was to make sure the nations nearby did not pass their practices on to Israel (cf. chap. 7).

p: Dt 27:17; Jb 24:2; Prv 22:28; 23:10; Hos 5:10. *q:* Dt 5:20; Ex 20:16; 23:1. *r:* Dt 17:6; Nm 35:30; Mt 18:16; Jn 8:17; 2 Cor 13:1. *s:* Dt 1:17; 17:8–12. *t:* Dn 13:61–62. *u:* Dt 13:15; 17:4. *v:* Dt 13:11. *w:* Ex 21:23–25; Lv 24:19–20; Mt 5:38. *x:* Dt 1:30; 3:22; Ex 14:14; 15:3; Jos 23:10; Jgs 4:14. *y:* 1 Mc 3:56. *z:* Dt 24:5. *a:* Jgs 7:3. *b:* Jos 9:23–27; 11:19; 2 Sm 10:19. *c:* Nm 31:7, 9, 11; Jos 22:8. *d:* Dt 7:1–2; 12:29–31; Jos 10:40; 11:11, 14.

not teach you to do all the abominations that they do for their gods, and you thus sin against the LORD, your God.

Trees of a Besieged City. 19[e] When you are at war with a city and have to lay siege to it for a long time before you capture it, you shall not destroy its trees by putting an ax to them. You may eat of them, but you must not cut them down. Are the trees of the field human beings, that they should be included in your siege? 20 However, those trees which you know are not fruit trees you may destroy. You may cut them down to build siegeworks against the city that is waging war with you, until it falls.

CHAPTER 21

See RG 141-48

*Absolution of Untraced Murder.** 1 If the corpse of someone who has been slain is found lying in the open, in the land the LORD, your God, is giving you to possess, and it is not known who killed the person, 2 your elders and judges shall go out and measure the distances to the cities that are in the neighborhood of the corpse. 3[f] When it is established which city is nearest the corpse, the elders of that city shall take a heifer that has never been put to work or worn a yoke; 4 the elders of that city shall bring the heifer down to a wadi with an everflowing stream at a place that has not been plowed or sown, and shall break the heifer's neck there in the wadi. 5 The priests, the descendants of Levi, shall come forward, for the LORD, your God, has chosen them to minister to him and to bless in the name of the LORD, and every case of dispute or assault shall be for them to decide. 6 Then all the elders of that city nearest the corpse shall wash their hands* over the heifer whose neck was broken in the wadi, 7 and shall declare, "Our hands did not shed this blood,* and our eyes did not see the deed. 8 Absolve, O LORD, your people Israel, whom you have redeemed, and do not let the guilt of shedding innocent blood remain in the midst of your people Israel." Thus they shall be absolved from the guilt of bloodshed, 9 and you shall purge the innocent blood from your midst, and do what is right in the eyes of the LORD.[g]

Marriage with a Female Captive. 10[h] When you go out to war against your enemies and the LORD, your God, delivers them into your power, so that you take captives, 11 if you see a beautiful woman among the captives and become so enamored of her that you wish to have her as a wife, 12 and so you take her home to your house, she must shave her head,* cut her nails, 13 lay aside her captive's garb, and stay in your house, mourning her father and mother for a full month. After that, you may come to her, and you shall be her husband and she shall be your wife. 14 If later on you lose your liking for her, you shall give her her freedom, if she wishes it; you must not sell her for money. Do not enslave her, since you have violated her.[i]

Rights of the Firstborn. 15[j] If a man has two wives, one loved and the other unloved, and if both the loved and the unloved bear him sons, but the firstborn is the son of the unloved wife: 16 when he comes to bequeath his property to his sons he may not consider as his firstborn the son of the wife he loves, in preference to the son of the wife he does not love, the firstborn. 17 On the contrary, he shall recognize as his firstborn the son of the unloved wife, giving him a double share of whatever he happens to own, since he is the first fruits of his manhood, and to him belong the rights of the firstborn.[k]

The Stubborn and Rebellious Son. 18[l] If someone has a stubborn and rebellious son who will not listen to his father or mother, and will not listen to them even though they discipline him,[m] 19 his father and mother

21:1–9 This law has to do with absolving the community of bloodguilt that accrues to it and to the land when a homicide occurs and the murderer cannot be identified and punished.

21:6 Wash their hands: a symbolic gesture in protestation of one's own innocence when human blood is unjustly shed; cf. Mt 27:24.

21:7 This blood: the blood of the slain, or the bloodguilt effected by the killing.

21:12–13 Shave her head . . .: these symbolic actions probably signified the transition or change of status of the woman or perhaps the end of her period of mourning for her previous husband or family.

e: 2 Kgs 3:18, 25. *f:* Nm 19:2–3. *g:* Dt 19:13. *h:* Dt 20:14. *i:* Dt 15:12–18; 22:13–19, 28–29; 24:1–3; Jer 34:15–16. *j:* Gn 21:9–13; 1 Kgs 1:5–21. *k:* Gn 49:3–4. *l:* Dt 5:16; 27:16; Ex 20:12; 21:15, 17; Lv 20:9. *m:* Ps 78:8; Jer 5:23.

shall take hold of him and bring him out to the elders at the gate* of his home city, [20]where they shall say to the elders of the city, "This son of ours is a stubborn and rebellious fellow who will not listen to us; he is a glutton and a drunkard."[n] [21]Then all his fellow citizens shall stone him to death. Thus shall you purge the evil from your midst, and all Israel will hear and be afraid.[o]

Corpse of a Criminal. [22p] If a man guilty of a capital offense is put to death and you hang him on a tree,* [23]his corpse shall not remain on the tree overnight.[q] You must bury it the same day; anyone who is hanged is a curse of God.* You shall not defile the land which the LORD, your God, is giving you as a heritage.

CHAPTER 22

See RG 141–48

Concern for the Neighbor. [1r] You shall not see your neighbor's ox or sheep going astray and ignore it; you must bring it back. [2]If this neighbor does not live near you, or you do not know who the owner may be, take it to your own house and keep it with you until your neighbor claims it; then return it. [3]You shall do the same with a donkey; you shall do the same with a garment; and you shall do the same with anything else which your neighbor loses and you happen to find. You may not ignore them.

[4]You shall not see your neighbor's donkey or ox fallen on the road and ignore it; you must help in lifting it up.

Various Precepts. [5]A woman shall not wear a man's garment, nor shall a man put on a woman's clothing; for anyone who does such things is an abomination to the LORD, your God.[s]

[6t] If, while walking along, you come across a bird's nest with young birds or eggs in it, in any tree or on the ground, and the mother bird is sitting on them, you shall not take away the mother bird along with her brood. [7]You must let the mother go, taking only her brood, in order that you shall prosper and have a long life.

[8]When you build a new house, put a parapet around the roof, so that you do not bring bloodguilt upon your house if someone falls off.[u]

[9* v] You shall not sow your vineyard with two different kinds of seed, or else its produce shall become forfeit, both the crop you have sown and the yield of the vineyard. [10]You shall not plow with an ox and a donkey harnessed together. [11]You shall not wear cloth made from wool and linen woven together.

[12]You shall put tassels on the four corners of the cloak that you wrap around yourself.[w]

Marriage Legislation. [13]If a man, after marrying a woman and having relations with her, comes to dislike her,[x] [14]and accuses her of misconduct and slanders her by saying, "I married this woman, but when I approached her I did not find evidence of her virginity," [15]the father and mother of the young woman shall take the evidence of her virginity* and bring it to the elders at the city gate. [16]There the father of the young woman shall say to the elders, "I gave my daughter to this man in marriage, but he has come to dislike her, [17]and now accuses her of misconduct, saying: 'I did not find evidence of your daughter's virginity.' But here is the evidence of my daughter's virginity!" And they shall spread out the cloth before the elders of the city. [18]Then these city elders shall take the man and discipline him,* [19]and fine him one hundred silver shekels, which they shall give to the young woman's father, because the

21:19 The gate: in the city walls. This open space served as the forum for the administration of justice. Cf. 22:15; 25:7; Ruth 4:1, 2, 11; Is 29:21; Am 5:10, 12, 15.

21:22 You hang him on a tree: some understand, "impaled on a stake." In any case the hanging or impaling was not the means used to execute the criminal; he was first put to death by the ordinary means, stoning, and his corpse was then exposed on high as a warning for others. Cf. Jos 8:29; 10:26; 1 Sm 31:10; 2 Sm 21:9.

21:23 Gal 3:13 applies these words to the crucifixion of Jesus, who "redeemed us from the curse of the law, becoming a curse for us."

22:9–11 Some understand these laws as serving to preserve distinctions set by God in the creation. **Become forfeit**: to the sanctuary; lit., "be holy"; cf. Lv 19:19; Jos 6:19.

22:15 The evidence of her virginity: the bridal garment or sheet stained with blood from the first nuptial relations.

22:18 Discipline him: whip him, as prescribed in 25:1–3.

n: Prv 23:20–21; 28:7; Mt 11:19; Lk 7:34. *o:* Dt 13:6, 11–12; 22:21, 24; Lv 20:2; 24:14–16. *p:* Jos 8:29; 10:26–27; 1 Sm 31:8–13; 2 Sm 4:12. *q:* Gal 3:13. *r:* Ex 23:4–5. *s:* Dt 7:25–26. *t:* Lv 22:28. *u:* Dt 19:10. *v:* Lv 19:19. *w:* Nm 15:38–41; Mt 23:5. *x:* Dt 24:1.

man slandered a virgin in Israel. She shall remain his wife, and he may not divorce her as long as he lives. 20But if this charge is true, and evidence of the young woman's virginity is not found, 21they shall bring the young woman to the entrance of her father's house and there the men of her town shall stone her to death, because she committed a shameful crime in Israel by prostituting herself in her father's house. Thus shall you purge the evil from your midst.[y]

22If a man is discovered lying with a woman who is married to another, they both shall die, the man who was lying with the woman as well as the woman.[z] Thus shall you purge the evil from Israel.

23If there is a young woman, a virgin who is betrothed,* and a man comes upon her in the city and lies with her, 24you shall bring them both out to the gate of the city and there stone them to death: the young woman because she did not cry out though she was in the city, and the man because he violated his neighbor's wife. Thus shall you purge the evil from your midst. 25But if it is in the open fields that a man comes upon the betrothed young woman, seizes her and lies with her, only the man who lay with her shall die. 26You shall do nothing to the young woman, since the young woman is not guilty of a capital offense. As when a man rises up against his neighbor and murders him, so in this case:*[a] 27it was in the open fields that he came upon her, and though the betrothed young woman may have cried out, there was no one to save her.

28[b] If a man comes upon a young woman, a virgin who is not betrothed, seizes her and lies with her, and they are discovered, 29the man who lay with her shall give the young woman's father fifty silver shekels and she will be his wife, because he has violated her. He may not divorce her as long as he lives.

CHAPTER 23

See RG 141–48

1A man shall not marry his father's wife,* nor shall he dishonor his father's bed.[c]

Membership in the Assembly. 2* No one whose testicles have been crushed or whose penis has been cut off may come into the assembly of the LORD.[d] 3No one born of an illicit union may come into the assembly of the LORD, nor any descendant of such even to the tenth generation may come into the assembly of the LORD.[e] 4[f] No Ammonite or Moabite may ever come into the assembly of the LORD, nor may any of their descendants even to the tenth generation come into the assembly of the LORD, 5because they would not come to meet you with food and water on your journey after you left Egypt, and because they hired Balaam, son of Beor, from Pethor in Aram Naharaim, to curse you. 6The LORD, your God, would not listen to Balaam but turned his curse into a blessing for you, because the LORD, your God, loves you. 7Never seek their welfare or prosperity as long as you live.[g] 8[h] Do not abhor the Edomite: he is your brother. Do not abhor the Egyptian: you were a resident alien in his country. 9Children born to them may come into the assembly of the LORD in the third generation.

Cleanliness in Camp. 10When in camp during an expedition against your enemies, you shall keep yourselves from anything bad. 11[i] If one of you becomes unclean because of a nocturnal emission, he shall go outside the camp; he shall not come back into the camp. 12Toward evening, he shall bathe in water; then, when the sun has set, he may come back into the camp. 13Outside the camp you shall have a place set aside where you shall go. 14You shall keep a trowel in your equipment and, when you go outside to relieve yourself, you shall dig a hole with it and then

22:23 A young woman, a virgin who is betrothed: a girl who is married but not yet brought to her husband's home and whose marriage is therefore still unconsummated.

22:26 So in this case: in the absence of witnesses ("in the open field"), the presumption must be that the woman is the victim, and so guiltless.

23:1 Father's wife: stepmother.

23:2 Exclusion of an emasculated male may have had to do with association of emasculation with the practices of other peoples, or it may have been rejection of someone with a significant blemish who was thus not suitable for participation in the sacral assembly.

y: Dt 13:6; Gn 34:7; 2 Sm 13:12. *z:* Dt 5:18; Ex 20:14; Lv 20:10; Ez 16:38–40; Jn 8:3–5. *a:* Dt 19:4–6. *b:* Dt 22:19; Ex 22:16–17. *c:* Dt 27:20; Gn 9:20–27; 49:4; Lv 18:6–19; 20:11; Ez 22:10. *d:* Lv 21:16–24. *e:* Gn 19:30–38; Lv 18:6–18. *f:* Nm 22:1–24:25; Ru 4:9–17; Ezr 10:10–44; Neh 13:1–3, 23–27. *g:* Ezr 9:12. *h:* Dt 2:2–8; 26:5; Gn 12:10–20; 25:19–26; 36:6–9; 46:5–7; 47:27. *i:* Lv 15:16–17.

cover up your excrement. [15]Since the LORD, your God, journeys along in the midst of your camp to deliver you and to give your enemies over to you, your camp must be holy, so that he does not see anything indecent in your midst and turn away from you.[j]

Various Precepts. [16k] You shall not hand over to their master any slaves who have taken refuge with you from their master. [17]Let them live among you in any place they choose, in any one of your communities* that seems good to them. Do not oppress them.

[18]There shall be no temple prostitute* among the Israelite women, nor a temple prostitute among the Israelite men.[l] [19]You shall not offer a prostitute's fee or a dog's pay* as any kind of votive offering in the house of the LORD, your God; both these things are an abomination to the LORD, your God.[m]

[20n] You shall not demand interest from your kindred on a loan of money or of food or of anything else which is loaned. [21]From a foreigner you may demand interest, but you may not demand interest from your kindred, so that the LORD, your God, may bless you in all your undertakings on the land you are to enter and possess.

[22o] When you make a vow to the LORD, your God, you shall not delay in fulfilling it; for the LORD, your God, will surely require it of you and you will be held guilty. [23]Should you refrain from making a vow, you will not be held guilty. [24]But whatever your tongue utters you must be careful to do, just as you freely vowed to the LORD, your God, with your own mouth.

[25]When you go through your neighbor's vineyard, you may eat as many grapes as you wish, until you are satisfied, but do not put them in your basket. [26]When you go through your neighbor's grainfield, you may pluck some of the ears with your hand, but do not put a sickle to your neighbor's grain.

CHAPTER 24

See RG 141–48

*Marriage Legislation.** [1p] When a man, after marrying a woman, is later displeased with her because he finds in her something indecent, and he writes out a bill of divorce and hands it to her, thus dismissing her from his house, [2]if on leaving his house she goes and becomes the wife of another man, [3]and the second husband, too, comes to dislike her and he writes out a bill of divorce and hands it to her, thus dismissing her from his house, or if this second man who has married her dies, [4]then her former husband, who dismissed her, may not again take her as his wife after she has become defiled. That would be an abomination before the LORD, and you shall not bring such guilt upon the land the LORD, your God, is giving you as a heritage.[q]

[5r] When a man is newly wed, he shall not go out on a military expedition, nor shall any duty be imposed on him. He shall be exempt for one year for the sake of his family, to bring joy to the wife he has married.

Pledges and Kidnappings. [6*] No one shall take a hand mill or even its upper stone as a

23:17 In any one of your communities: from this it would seem that the slave in question is a fugitive from a foreign country.

23:18–19 Temple prostitute: Heb. *qedesha*, lit., "holy one," a title of the goddess of fertility. The role or function of the *qedesha* is debated; some see this as simply a term for a prostitute (Heb. *zona*). Others see it as designating a cultic role but not necessarily one involving sexual activity. The evidence is insufficient to give a final answer.

23:19 Dog's pay: "dog" is a derogatory term for a male temple prostitute.

24:1–4 This law is directly concerned only with forbidding a divorced man from remarrying his former wife, and indirectly with checking hasty divorces, by demanding sufficient cause and certain legal formalities. Divorce itself is taken for granted and tolerated as an existing custom whose potential evils this law seeks to lessen. Cf. 22:19, 29; Mal 2:14–16. **Something indecent**: a rather indefinite phrase, meaning perhaps "immodest conduct," but possibly including any kind of objectionable conduct. By New Testament times Jewish opinion differed concerning what was sufficient ground for divorce; cf. Mt 19:3.

24:6 Since the Israelites ground their grain into flour only in sufficient quantity for their current need, to deprive a debtor of his hand mill was equivalent to condemning him to starvation.

j: Dt 1:30; 20:4; 31:6, 8; 2 Sm 7:6. *k:* 1 Kgs 2:39–40. *l:* Gn 38:21–22; 1 Kgs 14:24; 15:12; 22:46; 2 Kgs 23:7; Hos 4:14. *m:* Dt 7:25–26; Is 23:17–18. *n:* Dt 15:1–11; 24:10–13; Ex 22:25; Lv 25:35–38; Ez 18:8, 13, 17; 22:12; Lk 6:34–35. *o:* Gn 28:20–22; Nm 21:2–3; 30:1–15; Jgs 11:30–40; 1 Sm 1:11; Ps 56:12–13; 66:13–15; 132:1–5; Eccl 5:3–5. *p:* Dt 22:13–19, 28–29; Sir 7:26; Jer 3:1; Mt 5:31–32; 19:3–9. *q:* Dt 7:25–26. *r:* Dt 20:7.

pledge for debt, for that would be taking as a pledge the debtor's life.

7 If anyone is caught kidnapping a fellow Israelite, enslaving or selling the victim, that kidnapper shall be put to death.[s] Thus shall you purge the evil from your midst.

Skin Diseases. 8[t] In an attack of scaly infection* you shall be careful to observe exactly and to carry out all the instructions the levitical priests give you, as I have commanded them: observe them carefully. 9[u] Remember what the LORD, your God, did to Miriam on the journey after you left Egypt.

Loans and Wages. 10 When you make a loan of any kind to your neighbor, you shall not enter the neighbor's house to receive the pledge, 11 but shall wait outside until the person to whom you are making the loan brings the pledge outside to you. 12 If the person is poor, you shall not sleep in the pledged garment, 13 but shall definitely return it at sunset, so that your neighbor may sleep in the garment[v] and bless you. That will be your justice before the LORD, your God.

14[w] You shall not exploit a poor and needy hired servant, whether one of your own kindred or one of the resident aliens who live in your land, within your gates.[x] 15 On each day you shall pay the servant's wages before the sun goes down, since the servant is poor and is counting on them. Otherwise the servant will cry to the LORD against you, and you will be held guilty.[y]

Individual Responsibility. 16 Parents shall not be put to death for their children, nor shall children be put to death for their parents; only for one's own crime shall a person be put to death.[z]

Rights of the Unprotected. 17[a] You shall not deprive the resident alien or the orphan of justice, nor take the clothing of a widow as pledge. 18 For, remember, you were slaves in Egypt, and the LORD, your God, redeemed you from there; that is why I command you to do this.

19[b] When you reap the harvest in your field and overlook a sheaf in the field, you shall not go back to get it; let it be for the resident alien, the orphan, and the widow, so that the LORD, your God, may bless you in all your undertakings. 20 When you knock down the fruit of your olive trees, you shall not go over the branches a second time; let what remains be for the resident alien, the orphan, and the widow. 21 When you pick your grapes, you shall not go over the vineyard a second time; let what remains be for the resident alien, the orphan, and the widow. 22 For remember that you were slaves in the land of Egypt; that is why I command you to do this.

CHAPTER 25

See RG 141–48

Limits on Punishments. 1 When there is a dispute and the parties draw near for judgment, and a decision is given, declaring one party in the right and the other in the wrong, 2 if the one in the wrong deserves whipping, the judge shall have him lie down and in the presence of the judge receive the number of lashes the crime warrants. 3 Forty lashes* may be given, but no more;[c] or else, if more lashes are added to these many blows, your brother will be degraded in your sight.

Treatment of Oxen.* 4 You shall not muzzle an ox when it treads out grain.[d]

Levirate Marriage. 5[e] When brothers live together* and one of them dies without a son,

24:8 Scaly infection: the Hebrew word seems to have to do with one or more skin diseases that produce scales, such as psoriasis. Its precise meaning is uncertain. See note on Lv 13:1–14:57.

25:3 Forty lashes: while the punishment is severe, the law seeks to limit it from being overly harsh and inhumane. Later Jewish practice limited the number to thirty-nine; cf. 2 Cor 11:24.

25:4 This is comparable in spirit to 22:6–7; Israelites are not to be grasping and calculating. St. Paul argues from this verse that laborers have the right to live on the fruits of their labor; cf. 1 Cor 9:9; 1 Tm 5:18.

25:5 When brothers live together: when relatives of the same clan, though married, hold their property in common. It was only in this case that the present law was to be observed, since one of its purposes was to keep the property of the deceased within the same clan. Such a marriage of a widow with

s: Dt 13:6; Ex 21:16. *t:* Lv 13:1–14:57. *u:* Nm 12:10–15. *v:* Dt 6:25; Ex 22:25–26; Am 2:8. *w:* Lv 19:13; Sir 34:26–27; Jer 22:13. *x:* Dt 1:16. *y:* Dt 15:9; Mt 20:1–16. *z:* Dt 7:10; 2 Kgs 14:6; 2 Chr 25:4; Jer 31:29–30; Ez 18:20. *a:* Dt 10:17–19; 15:15; 24:22; 27:19; Ex 22:21–24; 23:9. *b:* Ex 23:10–11; Lv 19:9–10; 23:22; Ru 2:1–23. *c:* 2 Cor 11:24. *d:* Prv 12:10; 1 Cor 9:9; 1 Tm 5:18. *e:* Gn 38:1–30; Ru 4:5–10; Lk 20:27–33.

the widow of the deceased shall not marry anyone outside the family; but her husband's brother shall come to her, marrying her and performing the duty of a brother-in-law.[f] 6 The firstborn son she bears shall continue the name of the deceased brother, that his name may not be blotted out from Israel. 7 But if a man does not want to marry his brother's wife, she shall go up to the elders at the gate and say, "My brother-in-law refuses to perpetuate his brother's name in Israel and does not intend to perform his duty toward me." 8 Thereupon the elders of his city shall summon him and speak to him. If he persists in saying, "I do not want to marry her," 9* his sister-in-law, in the presence of the elders, shall go up to him and strip his sandal from his foot and spit in his face, declaring, "This is how one should be treated who will not build up his brother's family!" 10 And his name shall be called in Israel, "the house of the man stripped of his sandal."

Various Precepts. 11 When two men are fighting and the wife of one intervenes to save her husband from the blows of his opponent, if she stretches out her hand and seizes the latter by his genitals, 12 you shall chop off her hand; show no pity.

13[g] You shall not keep two differing weights in your bag, one heavy and the other light; 14 nor shall you keep two different ephahs* in your house, one large and the other small. 15 But use a full and just weight, a full and just ephah, so that you may have a long life on the land the LORD, your God, is giving you. 16 For everyone who does these things, everyone who does what is dishonest, is an abomination to the LORD, your God.[h]

17*[i] Bear in mind what Amalek did to you on the journey after you left Egypt, 18 how he surprised you along the way, weak and weary as you were, and struck down at the rear all those who lagged behind; he did not fear God. 19 Therefore, when the LORD, your God, gives you rest from all your enemies round about in the land which the LORD, your God, is giving you to possess as a heritage, you shall blot out the memory of Amalek from under the heavens. Do not forget!

CHAPTER 26

See RG 141–48

Thanksgiving for the Harvest. 1[j] When you have come into the land which the LORD, your God, is giving you as a heritage, and have taken possession and settled in it, 2 you shall take some first fruits[k] of the various products of the soil which you harvest from the land the LORD, your God, is giving you; put them in a basket and go to the place which the LORD, your God, will choose as the dwelling place for his name. 3 There you shall go to the priest in office at that time and say to him, "Today I acknowledge to the LORD, my God, that I have indeed come into the land which the LORD swore to our ancestors to give us."[l] 4 The priest shall then take the basket from your hands and set it in front of the altar of the LORD, your God. 5 Then you shall declare in the presence of the LORD, your God, "My father was a refugee Aramean* who went down to Egypt with a small household and lived there as a resident alien.[m] But there he became a nation great, strong and numerous. 6[n] When the Egyptians maltreated and oppressed us, imposing harsh servitude upon us, 7 we cried to the LORD, the God of our ancestors, and the LORD heard our cry and saw our affliction, our toil and our oppression. 8 Then the LORD brought us out of Egypt with a strong hand and outstretched arm, with terrifying power, with signs and wonders,[o] 9 and brought us to this place, and gave us this

her brother-in-law is known as a "levirate" marriage from the Latin word *levir*, meaning "a husband's brother."

25:9–10 The penalty decreed for a man who refuses to comply with this law of family loyalty is public disgrace; the widow is to spit in his face. Some commentators connect this symbolic act with the ceremony mentioned in Ru 4:7, 8.

25:14 Ephahs: see note on Is 5:10.

25:17–19 This attack on Israel by Amalek is not mentioned elsewhere in the Old Testament, although it probably was connected with the battle mentioned in Ex 17:8. A campaign against Amalek was carried out by Saul; cf. 1 Sm 15.

26:5 Aramean: probably in reference to the origin of the patriarchs from Aram Naharaim (cf. Gn 24:10; 25:20; 28:5; 31:20, 24).

f: Mt 22:24; Mk 12:19; Lk 20:28. *g:* Lv 19:35–36; Prv 16:11; 20:23; Ez 45:10; Hos 12:7; Mi 6:11. *h:* Dt 7:25–26. *i:* Ex 17:8–16; 1 Sm 15:2–33. *j:* Dt 14:22–29; 16:1–17; Ex 22:29; Lv 23:9–21; Nm 28:26–31. *k:* Dt 12:5, 11; 18:4; Ex 23:19; 34:26; Tb 1:6–7. *l:* Dt 1:8, 20–21. *m:* Gn 46:5–7, 26–27; Ex 1:7, 9; Acts 7:14–15. *n:* Ex 1:8–22; 2:23–25; 3:7–10; 6:9; Nm 20:15–16; 1 Kgs 12:4. *o:* Dt 4:34; 6:21–22; Ex 12:51.

land, a land flowing with milk and honey.[p]
[10]Now, therefore, I have brought the first
fruits of the products of the soil which you,
LORD, have given me." You shall set them before the LORD, your God, and you shall bow
down before the LORD, your God. [11]Then you
and your household, together with the Levite
and the resident aliens who live among you,
shall celebrate with all these good things
which the LORD, your God, has given you.[q]

Declaration Concerning Tithes. [12]When
you have finished setting aside all the tithes of
your produce in the third year,[r] the year of the
tithes, and have given them to the Levite, the
resident alien, the orphan and the widow, that
they may eat and be satisfied in your own
communities, [13]you shall declare before the
LORD, your God, "I have purged my house of
the sacred portion and I have given it to the
Levite, the resident alien, the orphan and the
widow, just as you have commanded me. I
have not transgressed any of your commandments, nor forgotten any. [14*] I have not eaten
any of the tithe while in mourning; I have not
brought any of it while unclean; I have not offered any of it to the dead. I have thus obeyed
the voice of the LORD, my God, and done just
as you have commanded me.[s] [15]Look down,
then, from heaven, your holy abode, and bless
your people Israel and the fields you have
given us, as you promised on oath to our ancestors, a land flowing with milk and honey."[t]

The Covenant. [16u] This day the LORD,
your God, is commanding you to observe
these statutes and ordinances. Be careful,
then, to observe them with your whole heart
and with your whole being. [17]Today you
have accepted the LORD's agreement: he will
be your God, and you will walk in his ways,
observe his statutes, commandments, and
ordinances, and obey his voice. [18]And today
the LORD has accepted your agreement: you
will be a people specially his own, as he
promised you, you will keep all his commandments, [19]and he will set you high in
praise and renown and glory above all nations he has made, and you will be a people
holy to the LORD, your God, as he promised.

CHAPTER 27

See RG 141–48

The Altar on Mount Ebal. [1]Then Moses, with the elders of Israel, commanded the
people, saying: Keep this whole commandment which I give you today. [2]On the day
you cross the Jordan into the land which the
LORD, your God, is giving you, set up some
large stones and coat them with plaster.
[3]Write on them,[v] at the time you cross, all the
words of this law, so that you may enter the
land which the LORD, your God, is giving
you, a land flowing with milk and honey,
just as the LORD, the God of your ancestors,
promised you. [4]When you cross the Jordan,
on Mount Ebal you shall set up these stones
concerning which I command you today,
and coat them with plaster, [5w] and you shall
build there an altar to the LORD, your God,
an altar made of stones that no iron tool has
touched. [6]You shall build this altar of the
LORD, your God, with unhewn stones, and
shall offer on it burnt offerings to the LORD,
your God. [7]You shall also offer communion
sacrifices[*] and eat them there, rejoicing in
the presence of the LORD, your God. [8]On the
stones you shall inscribe all the words of this
law very clearly.

[9]Moses, with the levitical priests, then
said to all Israel: Be silent, Israel, and listen!
This day you have become the people of the
LORD, your God.[x] [10]You shall obey the voice
of the LORD, your God, and keep his commandments and statutes which I am giving
you today.

Preparation for Blessings and Curses.
[11]That same day Moses commanded the
people, saying: [12y] When you cross the Jordan, these shall stand on Mount Gerizim to
bless the people: Simeon, Levi, Judah, Issa-

26:14 These are allusions to foreign religious practices. **To the dead**: to feed the spirits of the dead, or perhaps to worship Baal.

27:7 Communion sacrifices: The principal feature of this ritual (see Lv 3:1–17) is the sharing of the sacrifice with God, the priest and the person offering the sacrifice, who eat it as a holy thing (cf. Ex 24:5).

---

p: Ex 3:8. *q:* Dt 12:7, 12. *r:* Dt 14:28–29. *s:* Dt 14:1; Lv 11:24–25; 22:3; Jer 16:7. *t:* 1 Kgs 8:39, 43, 49; Ps 102:19. *u:* Dt 7:6; 8:6; 10:12–13; 11:22; 14:2; 27:9; 28:1, 9; 29:12–13; Ex 6:7; 19:5–6; 24:7; Lv 26:12; 2 Sm 7:24; Jer 7:23; 31:33; Ez 11:20; Hos 2:23. *v:* Jos 8:32. *w:* Ex 20:24–25; Jos 8:30–31. *x:* Dt 26:17–19. *y:* Dt 11:26–29; Jos 8:33–35.

char, Joseph and Benjamin. 13 And these shall stand on Mount Ebal for the curse: Reuben, Gad, Asher, Zebulun, Dan and Naphtali.

The Twelve Curses. 14 The Levites shall proclaim in a loud voice to all the Israelites: 15* "Cursed be anyone who makes a carved or molten idol,[z] an abomination to the LORD, the work of a craftsman's hands, and sets it up in secret!" And all the people shall answer, "Amen!"

16 "Cursed be anyone who dishonors father or mother!"[a] And all the people shall answer, "Amen!"

17 "Cursed be anyone who moves a neighbor's boundary markers!"[b] And all the people shall answer, "Amen!"

18 "Cursed be anyone who misleads the blind on their way!"[c] And all the people shall answer, "Amen!"

19 "Cursed be anyone who deprives the resident alien, the orphan or the widow of justice!"[d] And all the people shall answer, "Amen!"

20 "Cursed be anyone who has relations with his father's wife, for he dishonors his father's bed!"[e] And all the people shall answer, "Amen!"

21 "Cursed be anyone who has relations with any animal!"[f] And all the people shall answer, "Amen!"

22 "Cursed be anyone who has relations with his sister, whether his father's daughter or his mother's daughter!"[g] And all the people shall answer, "Amen!"

23 "Cursed be anyone who has relations with his mother-in-law!"[h] And all the people shall answer, "Amen!"

24 "Cursed be anyone who strikes down a neighbor in secret!"[i] And all the people shall answer, "Amen!"

25 "Cursed be anyone who accepts payment to kill an innocent person!"[j] And all the people shall answer, "Amen!"

26 "Cursed be anyone whose actions do not uphold the words of this law!"[k] And all the people shall answer, "Amen!"

CHAPTER 28

See RG 141–48

Blessings for Obedience. 1 Now,[l] [m] if you diligently obey the voice of the LORD, your God, carefully observing all his commandments which I give you today, the LORD, your God, will set you high above all the nations of the earth.[n] 2 All these blessings will come upon you and overwhelm you when you obey the voice of the LORD, your God:

3 [o] May you be blessed in the city,
and blessed in the country!
4 Blessed be the fruit of your womb,
the produce of your soil and the
offspring of your livestock,
the issue of your herds and the young
of your flocks![p]
5 Blessed be your grain basket and your
kneading bowl!
6 May you be blessed in your coming in,
and blessed in your going out!* [q]

Victory and Prosperity. 7 The LORD will beat down before you the enemies that rise up against you; they will come out against you from one direction, and flee before you in seven.* [r] 8 The LORD will affirm the blessing upon you, on your barns and on all your undertakings; he will bless you in the land that the LORD, your God, is giving you. 9 The

27:15–26 The ceremony described here reflects the structure of covenant. The people assent to the directives their covenant Lord sets forth; their "Amen" ratifies the proscription of idolatry, injustice, incest, murder, and infidelity in general. Thus the "love" of the Lord which is at the heart of Israel's existence as his covenant people (6:4–5) is spelled out in terms of particular actions. The "Amen" is an acceptance of the curses or sanctions entailed by breaking faith with the Lord. Cf. 30:15–20, a concise statement of covenant theology.

28:6 In your coming in . . . in your going out: at the beginning and end of every action, or in all actions in general. The rhetorical figure is called merismus. See also 6:7.

28:7 From one direction . . . in seven: in one disciplined body, contrasted with many scattered groups.

z: Dt 4:15–20; 5:8–9; Ex 20:4, 23; 34:17; Lv 19:4; 26:1; Ps 115:4–8; Wis 14:8. *a:* Dt 5:16; 21:18–21; Ex 20:12; 21:17; Lv 20:9. *b:* Dt 19:14. *c:* Lv 19:14. *d:* Dt 24:17–18; Ex 22:21–24; 23:9; Lv 19:33–34. *e:* Dt 23:1; Lv 18:7–8; 20:11. *f:* Ex 22:18; Lv 18:23; 20:15–16. *g:* Lv 18:9; 20:17. *h:* Lv 18:17; 20:14. *i:* Dt 5:17; 21:1; Ex 20:13; 21:12; Nm 35:20–21. *j:* Dt 16:19; Ex 23:7–8. *k:* Jer 11:3; Gal 3:10. *l:* Lv 26:3–45. *m:* Dt 7:12–16; 11:13–15. *n:* Dt 26:19; Ps 89:27; Is 55:3–5. *o:* Dt 28:16–19. *p:* Dt 7:13–14; 30:9; Ex 23:26; Lv 26:9. *q:* Ps 121:8. *r:* Dt 9:1–3; Ex 23:27–28; Lv 26:6–8.

LORD will establish you as a holy people, as he swore to you,[s] if you keep the commandments of the LORD, your God, and walk in his ways. 10 All the peoples of the earth will see that the name of the LORD is proclaimed over you,* and they will be afraid of you.[t] 11 The LORD will generously increase the fruit of your womb, the offspring of your livestock, and the produce of your soil, upon the land which the LORD swore to your ancestors he would give you.[u] 12 The LORD will open up for you his rich storehouse, the heavens, to give your land rain in due season and to bless all the works of your hands. You will lend to many nations but borrow from none.[v] 13 The LORD will make you the head not the tail, the top not the bottom, if you obey the commandments of the LORD, your God, which I am giving you today, observing them carefully, 14 not turning aside, either to the right or to the left, from any of the words which I am giving you today, following other gods and serving them.[w]

Curses for Disobedience. 15 But if you do not obey the voice of the LORD, your God,[x] carefully observing all his commandments and statutes which I give you today, all these curses shall come upon you and overwhelm you:

16[y] May you be cursed in the city, and cursed in the country! 17 Cursed be your grain basket and your kneading bowl! 18 Cursed be the fruit of your womb, the produce of your soil and the offspring of your livestock, the issue of your herds and the young of your flocks! 19 May you be cursed in your coming in, and cursed in your going out!

Sickness and Defeat. 20 The LORD will send on you a curse, panic, and frustration in everything you set your hand to, until you are speedily destroyed and perish for the evil you have done in forsaking me. 21[z] The LORD will make disease cling to you until he has made an end of you from the land you are entering to possess. 22 The LORD will strike you with consumption, fever, and inflammation, with fiery heat and drought, with blight and mildew, that will pursue you until you perish. 23 The heavens over your heads will be like bronze and the earth under your feet like iron.[a] 24 For rain the LORD will give your land powdery dust, which will come down upon you from the heavens until you are destroyed. 25 The LORD will let you be beaten down before your enemies; though you advance against them from one direction, you will flee before them in seven,* so that you will become an object of horror to all the kingdoms of the earth.[b] 26 Your corpses will become food for all the birds of the air and for the beasts of the field, with no one to frighten them off.[c] 27 The LORD will strike you with Egyptian boils[d] and with tumors, skin diseases and the itch, from none of which you can be cured. 28[e] And the LORD will strike you with madness, blindness and panic, 29 so that even at midday you will grope in the dark as though blind, unable to find your way.

Despoilment. You will be oppressed and robbed continually, with no one to come to your aid. 30 Though you betroth a wife, another will have her. Though you build a house, you will not live in it. Though you plant a vineyard, you will not pluck its fruits.[f] 31[g] Your ox will be slaughtered before your eyes, but you will not eat its flesh. Your donkey will be stolen in your presence, but you will never get it back. Your flocks will be given to your enemies, with no one to come to your aid. 32 Your sons and daughters will be given to another people while you strain your eyes looking for them every day, having no power to do anything. 33 A people you do not know will consume the fruit of your soil and of all your labor, and you will be thoroughly oppressed and continually

28:10 The name of the LORD is proclaimed over you: an expression signifying ownership and protection. Cf. 2 Sm 12:28; 1 Kgs 8:43; Is 4:1; 63:19; Jer 7:10–11; 14:9; 15:16; 25:29; Am 9:12.

28:25 From one direction . . . in seven: see note on v. 7.

s: Dt 26:18–19; Ex 19:5–6. *t:* Dt 2:25; 11:25; Is 61:9. *u:* Dt 28:4. *v:* Dt 15:6. *w:* Dt 5:32. *x:* Bar 1:20; Dn 9:11; Mal 2:2. *y:* Dt 28:3–6. *z:* Lv 26:16, 25; Jer 14:12; Am 4:9–10; Hg 2:17. *a:* Lv 26:19. *b:* Dt 1:44; 28:7; Lv 26:17, 37. *c:* Ps 79:2; Jer 7:33; 34:20. *d:* Dt 7:15; 28:60; Ex 9:8–12. *e:* Is 59:10. *f:* Dt 20:5–7; Am 5:11. *g:* Jer 5:17; Lam 5:1–18; Am 7:17.

crushed, 34until you are driven mad by what your eyes must look upon. 35The LORD will strike you with malignant boils of which you cannot be cured, on your knees and legs, and from the soles of your feet to the crown of your head.

Exile. 36[h] The LORD will bring you, and your king whom you have set over you, to a nation which you and your ancestors have not known, and there you will serve other gods, of wood and stone, 37and you will be a horror, a byword, a taunt among all the peoples to which the LORD will drive you.

Fruitless Labors. 38[i] Though you take out seed to your field, you will harvest but little, for the locusts will devour it. 39Though you plant and cultivate vineyards, you will not drink or store up the wine, for the worms will eat them. 40Though you have olive trees throughout your country, you will have no oil for ointment, for your olives will drop off. 41Though you beget sons and daughters, they will not remain with you, for they will go into captivity. 42Buzzing insects will take possession of all your trees and the crops of your soil. 43[j] The resident aliens among you will rise above you higher and higher, while you sink lower and lower. 44They will lend to you, not you to them. They will become the head, you the tail.

45All these curses will come upon you, pursuing you and overwhelming you, until you are destroyed, because you would not obey the voice of the LORD, your God, by keeping his commandments and statutes which he gave you.[k] 46They will be a sign and a wonder* for you and your descendants for all time. 47Since you would not serve the LORD, your God, with heartfelt joy for abundance of every kind, 48in hunger and thirst, in nakedness and utter want, you will serve the enemies whom the LORD will send against you. He will put an iron yoke on your neck, until he destroys you.[l]

Invasion and Siege. 49[m] The LORD will raise up against you a nation from afar, from the end of the earth, that swoops down like an eagle, a nation whose language you do not understand, 50a nation of fierce appearance, that shows neither respect for the aged nor mercy for the young. 51They will consume the offspring of your livestock and the produce of your soil, until you are destroyed; they will leave you no grain or wine or oil, no issue of herd, no young of flock, until they have brought about your ruin. 52They will besiege you in each of your communities, until the great, fortified walls, in which you trust, come tumbling down all over your land. They will besiege you in every community throughout the land which the LORD, your God, has given you, 53[n] and because of the siege and the distress to which your enemy subjects you, you will eat the fruit of your womb, the flesh of your own sons and daughters whom the LORD, your God, has given you. 54The most refined and fastidious man among you will begrudge his brother and his beloved wife and his surviving children, 55any share in the flesh of his children that he himself is using for food because nothing else is left him—such the siege and distress to which your enemy will subject you in all your communities. 56The most fastidious woman among you, who would not venture to set the sole of her foot on the ground, so refined and fastidious is she, will begrudge her beloved husband and her son and daughter 57the afterbirth that issues from her womb and the infants she brings forth because she secretly eats them for want of anything else—such the siege and distress to which your enemy will subject you in your communities.

Plagues. 58If you are not careful to observe all the words of this law which is written in this book, and to fear this glorious and awesome name, the LORD, your God,[o] 59[p] the LORD will bring upon you and your descendants wondrous calamities, severe and constant calamities, and malignant and constant sicknesses. 60He will bring back upon you

28:46 A sign and a wonder: an ominous example, attracting attention; cf. 29:21–28.

h: Dt 4:27–28; 1 Kgs 9:6–9; 2 Kgs 25:6–7, 11; 2 Chr 7:19–22; 33:11; 36:6, 20; Jer 16:13; 24:8–9; 25:8–11; Ez 17:12. *i:* Dt 28:18; Lv 26:20; Lam 1:5; Mi 6:15; Zep 1:13; Hg 1:6. *j:* Dt 15:6; 28:12–13. *k:* Dt 28:15. *l:* Jer 28:14. *m:* Jer 5:15–17; 6:22–26; Bar 4:15–16. *n:* Lv 26:29; 2 Kgs 6:28–29; Jer 19:9; Lam 2:20; 4:10; Bar 2:3. *o:* Dt 6:13; Jos 24:14. *p:* Dt 7:15; 28:21–22, 27.

all the diseases of Egypt* which you dread, and they will cling to you. [61]Even any sickness or calamity not written in this book of the law, that too the LORD will bring upon you until you are destroyed. [62]You who were numerous as the stars of the heavens[q] will be left few in number, because you would not obey the voice of the LORD, your God.

Exile. [63r] Just as the LORD once took delight in making you prosper and grow, so will the LORD now take delight in ruining and destroying you, and you will be plucked out of the land you are now entering to possess. [64]The LORD will scatter you among all the peoples from one end of the earth to the other, and there you will serve other gods, of wood and stone, which you and your ancestors have not known. [65]Among these nations you will find no rest, not even a resting place for the sole of your foot, for there the LORD will give you an anguished heart and wearied eyes* and a trembling spirit. [66]Your life will hang in suspense and you will stand in dread both day and night, never sure of your life. [67]In the morning you will say, "Would that it were evening!" and in the evening you will say, "Would that it were morning!" because of the dread that your heart must feel and the sight that your eyes must see. [68]The LORD will send you back in ships to Egypt, by a route which I told you that you would never see again;[s] and there you will offer yourselves for sale to your enemies as male and female slaves, but there will be no buyer.

[69]These are the words of the covenant which the LORD commanded Moses to make with the Israelites in the land of Moab, in addition to the covenant he made with them at Horeb.

III. Third Address

CHAPTER 29

See RC 141–48

Past Favors Recalled. [1]Moses summoned all Israel and said to them, You have seen with your own eyes all that the LORD did in the land of Egypt to Pharaoh and all his servants and to all his land, [2]the great testings your own eyes have seen, and those great signs and wonders.[t] [3]But the LORD has not given you a heart to understand, or eyes to see, or ears to hear until this day.[u] [4v] I led you for forty years in the wilderness. Your clothes did not fall from you in tatters nor your sandals from your feet; [5]it was not bread that you ate, nor wine or beer that you drank—so that you might know that I, the LORD, am your God. [6w] When you came to this place, Sihon, king of Heshbon, and Og, king of Bashan, came out to engage us in battle, but we defeated them [7]and took their land, and gave it as a heritage to the Reubenites, Gadites, and the half-tribe of Manasseh.[x] [8]Observe carefully the words of this covenant, therefore, in order that you may succeed in whatever you do.[y]

All Israel Bound by Covenant. [9]You are standing today, all of you, in the presence of the LORD, your God—your tribal heads, elders, and officials, all of the men of Israel, [10]your children, your wives, and the resident alien who lives in your camp, from those who cut wood to those who draw water for you— [11]to enter into the covenant of the LORD, your God, which the LORD, your God, is making with you today, with its curse, [12]so that he may establish you today as his people and he may be your God, as he promised you and as he swore to your ancestors, to Abraham, Isaac and Jacob. [13z] But it is not with you alone that I am making this covenant, with its curse, [14]but with those who are standing here with us today in the presence of the LORD, our God, and with those who are not here with us* today.

Warning Against Idolatry. [15]You know that we lived in the land of Egypt and that we passed through the nations, that you too passed through [16]and saw the loathsome

28:60 He will bring back upon you all the diseases of Egypt: such as the Lord had promised to remove from the people (7:15); cf. v. 27.

28:65 Wearied eyes: cf. v. 32.

q: Dt 1:10; 10:22; 26:5; Jer 42:2. *r:* Dt 4:26–28; 30:9; Lv 26:33–39. *s:* Jer 42–44; Hos 8:13; 9:3, 6; 11:5. *t:* Dt 4:34, 37–38; 6:21–23; 7:19; 26:5–9. *u:* Is 6:9–10; Jer 5:21; Ez 12:2; Mt 13:14–15; Mk 4:12; Lk 8:10; Jn 12:40; Acts 28:26–27. *v:* Dt 8:2–4. *w:* Dt 1:4; 2:31–33; 3:1–3; Nm 21:23–24, 33–35. *x:* Dt 3:16–17; Nm 32:33. *y:* Jos 1:7–8; 1 Kgs 2:3. *z:* Dt 5:3.

things and idols of wood and stone, of gold
and silver, that they possess. 17 There may be
among you a man or woman, or a clan or
tribe, whose heart is now turning away from
the LORD, our God, to go and serve the gods
of these nations; there may be among you a
root bearing poison and wormwood; 18 if any
such persons, after hearing the words of this
curse, should congratulate themselves, saying in their hearts, "I am safe, even though I
walk in stubbornness of heart," thereby
sweeping away moist and dry alike,* [a] 19 the
LORD will never consent to pardon them. Instead, the LORD's burning wrath will flare up
against them; every curse written in this
book will pounce on them, and the LORD
will blot out their names from under the
heavens.[b] 20 The LORD will single them out
from all the tribes of Israel for doom, in
keeping with all the curses of the covenant
written in this book of the law.

Punishment for Idolatry. 21 [c] Future generations, your descendants who will rise up after you, as well as the foreigners who will
come here from distant lands, when they see
the calamities of this land and the ills the
LORD has inflicted upon it—22 all its soil
burned out by sulphur and salt, unsown and
unfruitful, without a blade of grass, like the
catastrophe of Sodom and Gomorrah,[d] Admah and Zeboiim,* which the LORD overthrew in his furious wrath— 23 [e] they and all
the nations will ask, "Why has the LORD
dealt thus with this land? Why this great outburst of wrath?" 24 And they will say, "Because they abandoned the covenant of the
LORD, the God of their ancestors, which he
had made with them when he brought them
out of the land of Egypt, 25 and they went and
served other gods and bowed down to them,
gods whom they did not know and whom he
had not apportioned to them.[f] 26 [g] So the
anger of the LORD flared up against this land
and brought on it every curse written in this
book. 27 The LORD uprooted them from their
soil in anger, fury, and great wrath, and cast
them out into another land, as they are today." 28 The hidden things* belong to the
LORD our God, but the revealed things are
for us and for our children forever, to observe all the words of this law.

CHAPTER 30

See RG 141–48

Compassion for the Repentant.
1* [h] When all these things, the blessing and
the curse which I have set before you, come
upon you,[i] and you take them to heart in any
of the nations where the LORD, your God,
has dispersed you, 2 [j] and return to the LORD,
your God, obeying his voice, according to
all that I am commanding you today, you
and your children, with your whole heart
and your whole being, 3 the LORD, your God,
will restore your fortunes and will have
compassion on you; he will again gather you
from all the peoples where the LORD, your
God, has scattered you. 4 Though you may
have been dispersed to the farthest corner of
the heavens, even from there will the LORD,
your God, gather you; even from there will
he bring you back.[k] 5 The LORD, your God,
will then bring you into the land your ancestors once possessed, that you may possess it;
and he will make you more prosperous and
numerous than your ancestors.[l] 6 The LORD,
your God, will circumcise your hearts* and
the hearts of your descendants,[m] so that you
will love the LORD, your God, with your

29:14 Not here with us: this includes future generations. This attitude appears also in 5:3.

29:18 Sweeping away moist and dry alike: possibly a proverbial expression: because of Israel's infidelity the Lord will punish the just with the wicked (cf. Gn 18:25), rooting out good plants in irrigated soil, together with worthless plants growing in dry ground.

29:22 Admah and Zeboiim: neighboring cities of Sodom and Gomorrah in the Jordan Plain and identified in the tradition as destroyed with them. Cf. Hos 11:8; Jer 50:40.

29:28 The hidden things: probably the events of the future. **The revealed things**: the covenant and its provisions, including the sanctions of blessing and curse. This aphorism may mean: leave "hidden things" to God; what matters is to keep the law.

30:1–5 Text such as this suggests a postexilic perspective; cf. also chaps. 31–32.

30:6 Circumcise your hearts: see note on 10:16.

a: Jer 7:10. *b:* Dt 9:14; 25:19. *c:* Dt 4:25–28. *d:* Gn 19:24–25; Hos 11:8. *e:* 1 Kgs 9:8–9; Jer 5:19; 9:12–16; 16:10–13; 22:8–9. *f:* Dt 4:19; 32:8–9. *g:* Dt 29:20–21; Dn 9:11–14. *h:* Dt 4:29–31; Lv 26:40–45. *i:* Dt 11:26–28; 27:11–28:69. *j:* Dt 4:29–30; 6:5; 30:10; 1 Kgs 8:47–48; Jer 24:7; 29:14; 33:26; Ez 39:25; Am 9:14; Zep 3:20. *k:* Neh 1:9; Is 43:5–7; Jer 31:10; 32:37; Ez 36:24; 37:21. *l:* Jer 23:3. *m:* Dt 6:5; 10:16; Ez 11:19–20; 36:26–28.

whole heart and your whole being, in order that you may live. 7The LORD, your God, will put all those curses on your enemies and the foes who pursued you.[n] 8You, however, shall again obey the voice of the LORD and observe all his commandments which I am giving you today. 9Then the LORD, your God, will generously increase your undertakings, the fruit of your womb, the offspring of your livestock, and the produce of your soil;[o] for the LORD, your God, will again take delight in your prosperity, just as he took delight in your ancestors', 10because you will obey the voice of the LORD, your God, keeping the commandments and statutes that are written in this book of the law, when you return to the LORD, your God, with your whole heart and your whole being.

11[p] For this command which I am giving you today is not too wondrous or remote for you. 12It is not in the heavens, that you should say, "Who will go up to the heavens to get it for us and tell us of it, that we may do it?" 13Nor is it across the sea, that you should say, "Who will cross the sea to get it for us and tell us of it, that we may do it?" 14No, it is something very near to you, in your mouth* and in your heart, to do it.

The Choice Before Israel. 15See, I have today set before you life and good, death and evil.[q] 16If you obey the commandments of the LORD, your God, which I am giving you today, loving the LORD, your God, and walking in his ways, and keeping his commandments, statutes and ordinances, you will live and grow numerous, and the LORD, your God, will bless you in the land you are entering to possess.[r] 17[s] If, however, your heart turns away and you do not obey, but are led astray and bow down to other gods and serve them, 18I tell you today that you will certainly perish; you will not have a long life on the land which you are crossing the Jordan to enter and possess. 19I call heaven and earth today to witness against you:[t] I have set before you life and death, the blessing and the curse. Choose life, then, that you and your descendants may live, 20by loving the LORD, your God, obeying his voice, and holding fast to him. For that will mean life for you, a long life for you to live on the land which the LORD swore to your ancestors, to Abraham, Isaac, and Jacob, to give to them.[u]

CHAPTER 31

See RG 141–48

The Lord's Leadership. 1When Moses had finished speaking these words to all Israel, 2he said to them, I am now one hundred and twenty years old[v] and am no longer able to go out and come in; besides, the LORD has said to me, Do not cross this Jordan. 3It is the LORD, your God, who will cross before you; he will destroy these nations before you, that you may dispossess them.[w] (It is Joshua who will cross before you, as the LORD promised.) 4[x] The LORD will deal with them just as he dealt with Sihon and Og, the kings of the Amorites, and with their country, when he destroyed them. 5When, therefore, the LORD delivers them up to you, you shall deal with them according to the whole commandment which I have given you.[y] 6Be strong and steadfast; have no fear or dread of them, for it is the LORD, your God, who marches with you; he will never fail you or forsake you.[z]

Call of Joshua. 7Then Moses summoned Joshua and in the presence of all Israel said to him,[a] "Be strong and steadfast, for you shall bring this people into the land which the LORD swore to their ancestors he would give them; it is you who will give them possession of it. 8It is the LORD who goes before you; he will be with you and will never fail you or forsake you. So do not fear or be dismayed."[b]

The Reading of the Law. 9[c] When Moses had written down this law, he gave it to the levitical priests who carry the ark of the covenant of the LORD, and to all the elders of Is-

30:14 In your mouth: that is, memorized and recited; cf. 6:7; 11:19. **And in your heart**: internalized and appropriated; cf. 6:6; 11:18.

n: Dt 7:15. *o:* Dt 28:4, 11; 30:2. *p:* Dt 6:6; 11:18; Jer 1:9; Bar 3:29–31; Rom 10:6–8. *q:* Dt 11:26–28; Jer 21:8. *r:* Dt 4:1; 8:1; 11:22. *s:* Dt 5:7; 6:4; 8:19–20. *t:* Dt 4:26; 11:26–28; 28:2, 15; 31:28. *u:* Dt 1:8; 4:1, 40. *v:* Dt 1:37; 3:23–28; 4:21–24; 34:7; Gn 6:3; Ex 7:7; Nm 20:12; Acts 7:23, 30. *w:* Dt 1:30–33; 3:22, 28; 9:3. *x:* Dt 2:26–3:7; 3:21–22; Nm 21:21–35. *y:* Dt 7:1–5; 20:16–18. *z:* Dt 1:29; 20:3–4. *a:* Dt 1:21; 31:23; Jos 1:6–9; 10:25. *b:* Ex 3:12; Jos 1:5, 17; 3:7; 2 Sm 7:9. *c:* Dt 31:24–27.

rael.[d] [10]Moses commanded them, saying, On the feast of Booths,[e] at the prescribed time in the year for remission* which comes at the end of every seven-year period, [11]when all Israel goes to appear before the LORD, your God, in the place which he will choose, you shall read this law aloud in the presence of all Israel. [12]Assemble the people—men, women and children, as well as the resident aliens who live in your communities—that they may hear and so learn to fear the LORD, your God, and to observe carefully all the words of this law. [13]Their children also, who do not know it yet, shall hear and learn to fear the LORD, your God, as long as you live on the land which you are about to cross the Jordan to possess.

Commission to Joshua. [14f] The LORD said to Moses, The time is now approaching for you to die. Summon Joshua, and present yourselves at the tent of meeting that I may commission him. So Moses and Joshua went and presented themselves at the tent of meeting. [15]And the LORD appeared at the tent in a column of cloud; the column of cloud stood at the entrance of the tent.

A Command to Moses. [16]The LORD said to Moses, Soon you will be at rest with your ancestors, and then this people will prostitute themselves* by following the foreign gods among whom they will live in the land they are about to enter.[g] They will forsake me and break the covenant which I have made with them. [17h] At that time my anger will flare up against them; I will forsake them and hide my face from them; they will become a prey to be devoured, and much evil and distress will befall them. At that time they will indeed say, "Is it not because our God is not in our midst that these evils have befallen us?" [18]Yet I will surely hide my face at that time because of all the evil they have done in turning to other gods. [19]Now, write out this song[i] for yourselves. Teach it to the Israelites and have them recite it, so that this song may be a witness for me against the Israelites. [20]For when I have brought them into the land flowing with milk and honey which I promised on oath to their ancestors, and they have eaten and are satisfied and have grown fat, if they turn to other gods and serve them, despising me and breaking my covenant, [21]then, when great evil and distress befall them, this song will speak to them as a witness, for it will not be forgotten if their descendants recite it. For I know what they are inclined to do even at the present time, before I have brought them into the land which I promised on oath. [22]So Moses wrote this song that same day, and he taught it to the Israelites.

Commission of Joshua. [23]Then he commissioned Joshua, son of Nun, and said to him, Be strong and steadfast, for it is you who will bring the Israelites into the land which I promised them on oath.[j] I myself will be with you.

The Law Placed in the Ark. [24]When Moses had finished writing out on a scroll the words of this law in their entirety, [25]Moses gave the Levites[k] who carry the ark of the covenant of the LORD this order: [26]Take this book of the law and put it beside the ark of the covenant of the LORD, your God, that there it may be a witness against you.[l] [27]For I already know how rebellious and stiff-necked you will be. Why, even now, while I am alive among you, you have been rebels against the LORD! How much more, then, after I am dead![m] [28n] Assemble all your tribal elders and your officials before me, that I may speak these words for them to hear and so may call heaven and earth to witness against them. [29o] For I know that after my death you are sure to act corruptly and to turn aside from the way along which I commanded you, so that evil will befall you in time to come because you have done what is evil in the LORD's sight, and provoked him by your deeds.

31:10 The year for remission: cf. 15:1–3 and note there.

31:16 Prostitute themselves: lit., "whore after," a play on the phrase "go after," viz. after other gods.

d: Dt 10:1–5, 8. *e:* Dt 12:5; 15:1–11; 16:13–15; 2 Kgs 23:2; Neh 8:1–8. *f:* Ex 33:7–11; Nm 12:5. *g:* Dt 32:16–17; Ex 34:15–16; Jgs 2:11–23; 8:27, 33; 1 Kgs 11:1–10; 2 Kgs 17:7–41; Jer 11:9–10; Hos 4:12; 9:1. *h:* Dt 1:42; 32:19–25; Nm 14:42. *i:* Dt 6:6–9; 31:21; 32:1–43. *j:* Dt 31:7–8; Nm 27:15–23; Jos 1:1–9. *k:* Dt 31:9. *l:* Dt 10:1–5; Ex 40:20; 1 Kgs 8:9. *m:* Dt 9:6–7, 22–24. *n:* Dt 31:12–13, 19–22; 30:19; 32:1–43. *o:* Jgs 2:11–23.

The Song of Moses. [30]Then Moses recited the words of this song in their entirety, for the whole assembly of Israel to hear:

CHAPTER 32

See RG 141–48

[1]* Give ear, O heavens, and let me speak;
let the earth hear the words of my mouth![p]
[2] May my teaching soak in like the rain,
and my utterance drench like the dew,
Like a downpour upon the grass,
like a shower upon the crops.
[3] For I will proclaim the name of the LORD,
praise the greatness of our God!

[4] The Rock—how faultless are his deeds,
how right all his ways!
A faithful God, without deceit,
just and upright is he![q]
[5] Yet his degenerate children have treated him basely,
a twisted and crooked generation![r]
[6] Is this how you repay the LORD,
so foolish and unwise a people?
Is he not your father who begot you,
the one who made and established you?[s]
[7] Remember the days of old,
consider the years of generations past.
Ask your father, he will inform you,
your elders, they will tell you:[t]
[8] When the Most High allotted each nation its heritage,
when he separated out human beings,[u]
He set up the boundaries of the peoples
after the number of the divine beings;*
[9] But the LORD's portion was his people;
his allotted share was Jacob.[v]
[10] He found them in a wilderness,
a wasteland of howling desert.
He shielded them, cared for them,
guarded them as the apple of his eye.[w]
[11] As an eagle incites its nestlings,
hovering over its young,
So he spread his wings, took them,
bore them upon his pinions.[x]
[12] The LORD alone guided them,
no foreign god was with them.[y]
[13] [z] He had them mount the summits of the land,*
fed them the produce of its fields;
He suckled them with honey from the crags
and olive oil from the flinty rock;
[14] Butter from cows and milk from sheep,
with the best of lambs;
Bashan* bulls and goats,
with the cream of finest wheat;
and the foaming blood of grapes you drank.

[15] So Jacob ate and was satisfied,
Jeshurun* grew fat and kicked;
you became fat and gross and gorged.
They forsook the God who made them
and scorned the Rock of their salvation.[a]
[16] With strange gods they incited him,
with abominations provoked him to anger.[b]
[17] They sacrificed to demons, to "no-gods,"
to gods they had never known,
Newcomers from afar,

32:1–43 The whole song is a poetic sermon, having for its theme the Lord's benefits to Israel (vv. 1–14) and Israel's ingratitude and idolatry in turning to the gods of the nations; these sins will be punished by the nations themselves (vv. 15–29); in turn, the foolish pride of the nations will be punished, and the Lord's honor will be vindicated (vv. 30–43).

32:8 Divine beings: lit., "sons of God" (see also v. 43); members of the divine assembly; cf. 1 Kgs 22:19; Jb 1:6; 2:1; 38:7; Ps 82; 89:6–7. The nations are portrayed as having their respective tutelary deities.

32:13 The land: Canaan.

32:14 Bashan: a fertile grazing land east of the Jordan, famous for its sleek, strong cattle. Cf. Ps 22:13; Ez 39:18; Am 4:1.

32:15 Jeshurun: a term for Israel from *yashar*, meaning "upright"; its use here is possibly ironic.

p: Dt 4:26; 30:19; 31:28. *q:* Dt 7:9; 32:15, 18, 30–31; 2 Sm 22:3; Ps 18:2, 31, 46; 92:15; Is 17:10; Hb 1:12; Rev 15:3. *r:* Dt 9:12; 14:1; 31:29; Ps 78:8; Is 1:2–4; Lk 9:41. *s:* Ex 4:22–23; Is 63:16; 64:8; Jer 31:9; Hos 11:1–4. *t:* Dt 4:32–34. *u:* Gn 14:18–22; Nm 24:16; Jb 1:6; 2:1; Ps 29:1; 47:2; 82:6; 83:18; 89:5–7; Is 14:14; Acts 17:26. *v:* Dt 7:6; Ex 19:5–6; Ps 33:12; Sir 17:17; Jer 10:16; Zec 2:16. *w:* Dt 1:31; 2:7; 8:15; Ps 17:8; Prv 7:2; Jer 2:2–3, 6; Hos 2:15; 13:5–6; Zec 2:12. *x:* Ex 19:4. *y:* Ex 15:13; Is 43:12; Hos 13:4. *z:* Dt 8:7–10; Ps 81:16. *a:* Dt 8:12–18; 31:20; 33:5, 26; Neh 9:25; Is 44:2. *b:* Dt 31:16; Ps 78:58; 81:9; 106:34–39.

before whom your ancestors had never trembled.
18 You were unmindful of the Rock that begot you,
you forgot the God who gave you birth.[c]

19 The LORD saw and was filled with loathing,
provoked by his sons and daughters.[d]
20 He said, I will hide my face from them,
and see what becomes of them.
For they are a fickle generation,
children with no loyalty in them![e]
21 Since they have incited me with a "no-god,"
and provoked me with their empty idols,
I will incite them with a "no-people";*
with a foolish nation I will provoke them.[f]
22 For by my wrath a fire is kindled
that has raged to the depths of Sheol,
It has consumed the earth with its yield,
and set on fire the foundations of the mountains.[g]
23 I will heap evils upon them
and exhaust all my arrows against them:[h]
24 Emaciating hunger and consuming fever
and bitter pestilence,
And the teeth of wild beasts I will send among them,
with the venom of reptiles gliding in the dust.[i]
25 Out in the street the sword shall bereave,
and at home the terror
For the young man and the young woman alike,
the nursing babe as well as the gray beard.[j]
26 I said: I will make an end of them
and blot out their name from human memory,
27 Had I not feared the provocation by the enemy,
that their foes might misunderstand,
And say, "Our own hand won the victory;
the LORD had nothing to do with any of it."[k]
28 For they are a nation devoid of reason,*
having no understanding.
29 If they had insight they would realize this,
they would understand their end:
30 "How could one rout a thousand,
or two put ten thousand to flight,
Unless it was because their Rock sold them,
the LORD delivered them up?"

31 Indeed, their "rock" is not like our Rock;
our enemies are fools.
32 For their vine is from the vine of Sodom,
from the vineyards of Gomorrah.
Their grapes are grapes of poison,
and their clusters are bitter.[l]
33 Their wine is the venom of serpents,
the cruel poison of vipers.
34 Is not this stored up with me,
sealed up in my storehouses?
35 Vengeance is mine and recompense,
for the time they lose their footing;
Because the day of their disaster is at hand
and their doom is rushing upon them![m]

36 Surely, the LORD will do justice for his people;
on his servants he will have pity.
When he sees their strength is gone,
and neither bond nor free* is left,[n]
37 He will say, Where are their gods,[o]
the rock in whom they took refuge,

32:21 "No-god" . . . "no-people": worship of the gods of the nations brings destruction at the hands of a foreign invader. A false god cannot sustain or protect (cf. Jer 14:22); and though the nations seem "foolish" (see their characterization in such passages as Ps 114:1; Is 28:11; 33:19), they will prove to be anything but nonentities when the Lord stirs them up against Israel (Is 9:10–12). For the "no-" or "not-" construction, see Hos 1:6, 9; 2:1, 25.

32:28–35 The reference is to the nations, not to Israel.

32:36 Neither bond nor free: an all-inclusive expression; cf. 1 Kgs 14:10; 2 Kgs 9:8.

c: Is 49:15; Jer 2:32. *d:* Dt 4:24. *e:* Dt 31:17–18; Nm 6:25–26. *f:* Dt 28:49–50; Jgs 2:14–15; Is 9:11–12; Rom 10:19. *g:* Dt 4:24; Ps 18:7–8; 50:3; Lam 4:11. *h:* Dt 32:42; Ps 7:12–13; 18:14; Ez 5:16. *i:* Dt 28:21–22. *j:* Lv 26:25; Jer 6:11; Lam 1:20; 2:21; Ez 7:15. *k:* Dt 9:26–29; Ex 32:11–14; Ps 74:18. *l:* Dt 29:23. *m:* Ps 94:1; Is 59:18; 61:2; Hos 9:7. *n:* Ps 9:8; 135:14; 2 Mc 7:6. *o:* Jgs 10:14; 1 Kgs 18:27; Jer 2:28.

38 Who ate the fat of their sacrifices
and drank the wine of their libations?
Let them rise up now and help you!
Let them be your protection!
39 See now that I, I alone, am he,
and there is no god besides me.
It is I who bring both death and life,
I who inflict wounds and heal them,
and from my hand no one can deliver.[p]
40 For I raise my hand to the heavens
and will say: As surely as I live
forever,
41 When I sharpen my flashing sword,
and my hand lays hold of judgment,
With vengeance I will repay my foes
and requite those who hate me.[q]
42 I will make my arrows drunk with blood,
and my sword shall devour flesh—
With the blood of the slain and the
captured,
from the long-haired heads of the
enemy.
43 Exult with him, you heavens,
bow to him, all you divine beings!
For he will avenge the blood of his
servants,
take vengeance on his foes;
He will requite those who hate him,
and purge his people's land.[r]

44 So Moses, together with Hoshea,* son of
Nun, went and spoke all the words of this
song in the hearing of the people.[s]
Final Appeal. 45 When Moses had finished
speaking all these words to all Israel, 46 he
said to them,[t] Take to heart all the words that
I am giving in witness against you today,
words you should command your children,
that they may observe carefully every word
of this law. 47 For this is no trivial matter for
you, but rather your very life; by this word
you will enjoy a long life on the land you are
crossing the Jordan to possess.[u]
Moses Looks upon Canaan. 48 On that
very day the LORD said to Moses, 49 Ascend
this mountain of the Abarim,* Mount Nebo
in the land of Moab facing Jericho, and view
the land of Canaan, which I am giving to the
Israelites as a possession.[v] 50 Then you shall
die on the mountain you are about to ascend,
and shall be gathered to your people, just as
your brother Aaron died on Mount Hor* and
there was gathered to his people,[w] 51 because
both of you broke faith with me among the
Israelites at the waters of Meribath-kadesh
in the wilderness of Zin: you did not manifest my holiness among the Israelites.*[x]
52 You may indeed see the land from a distance, but you shall not enter that land which
I am giving to the Israelites.[y]

CHAPTER 33

See RG 141–48

Blessing upon the Tribes.* 1 This is the
blessing with which Moses, the man of God,
blessed the Israelites before he died.[z]
2[a] He said:

The LORD came from Sinai
and dawned on his people from Seir;
he shone forth from Mount Paran.
With him were myriads of holy ones;
at his right hand advanced the gods.*
3 Indeed, lover of the peoples,
all the holy ones are at your side;
They follow at your heels,
carry out your decisions.

32:44 Hoshea: a variant of "Joshua." Cf. note on Nm 13:16.

32:49 Abarim: probably the mountain range to the east of the Dead Sea.

32:50 Mount Hor: on the western border of Seir or Edom; cf. Nm 20:23–28; 33:37–38. Dt 10:6 locates elsewhere the place of Aaron's death.

32:51 Cf. note on 3:26.

33:1–29 This poem, called the Blessing of Moses, consists of a series of poetic characterizations of each of the tribes of Israel (vv. 6–25), introduced (vv. 2–3) and concluded (vv. 26–27) by a theophany; vv. 4–5 lead into the blessing proper; and the poem ends with a blessing on Israel as a whole (vv. 28–29). This catalog of the tribal units of the people Israel resembles the Blessing of Jacob (Gn 49) and the Song of Deborah (Jgs 5, especially vv. 14–18); all three poems seem to date from the early premonarchic period.

33:2 Gods: the divine beings who constitute the armies of the Lord, the heavenly hosts (Sabaoth); see note on 32:8. These "holy ones" (v. 3) are the retinue of the Lord, the warrior God, in his march from the southern mountains (Sinai, Seir, Paran).

p: Dt 4:35; 6:4; 1 Sm 2:6–8; Jb 5:18; Tb 13:2; Wis 16:13; Is 30:26; 43:10–13; 44:6; Hos 6:1–2. *q:* Is 1:24; Na 1:2. *r:* Dt 32:1, 8; Is 49:13. *s:* Dt 31:14–15, 23. *t:* Dt 4:9. *u:* Dt 4:40; 6:1–2. *v:* Dt 34:1; Nm 27:12. *w:* Dt 10:6; Nm 20:23–29; 27:13; 33:38–39. *x:* Ex 17:1–7; Nm 20:1–13; 27:14; Ps 106:32–33. *y:* Dt 3:27; 34:4. *z:* Jos 14:6; Ps 90:1. *a:* Ex 15:14–17; 19:18–20; Nm 10:36; Jgs 5:4–5; Ps 68:7–8, 17; 89:7; Hb 3:3–6.

4 Moses charged us with the law,
as a possession for the assembly of Jacob.[b]
5 A king arose* in Jeshurun
when the chiefs of the people assembled,
and the tribes of Israel united.[c]
6 May Reuben live and not die out,[d]
but let his numbers be few.

7 Of Judah he said this:

Hear, LORD, the voice of Judah,
and bring him to his people.*
His own hands defend his cause;
be a help against his foes.[e]

8 Of Levi he said:[f]

Give to Levi your Thummim,
your Urim* to your faithful one;
Him you tested at Massah,
contended against him at the waters of Meribah.[g]
9 * He said of his father and mother,
"I have no regard for them";
His brothers he would not acknowledge,
and his own children he did not recognize.
For they kept your words,
and your covenant they upheld.[h]
10 [i] They teach your ordinances to Jacob,
your law to Israel.
They bring incense to your nostrils,
and burnt offerings to your altar.
11 Bless, LORD, his strength,
be pleased with the work of his hands.
Crush the loins of his adversaries
and of his foes, that they may not rise.

12 Of Benjamin he said:

The beloved of the LORD,
he abides in safety beside him;
He shelters him all day long;
the beloved abides at his breast.* [j]

13 Of Joseph he said:[k]

Blessed by the LORD is his land
with the best of heaven above
and of the abyss crouching beneath;
14 With the best of the produce of the sun,
and the choicest yield of the months;
15 With the finest gifts of the ancient mountains
and the best from the everlasting hills;
16 With the best of the earth and its fullness,
and the favor of the one who dwells on Sinai.
Let these come upon the head of Joseph
and upon the brow of the prince among his brothers.[l]
17 His firstborn bull, majesty is his!
His horns are the horns of a wild ox;
With them he gores the peoples,
attacks the ends of the earth.
These are the myriads of Ephraim,
and these the thousands of Manasseh.

18 Of Zebulun he said:[m]

Rejoice, Zebulun, in your expeditions,
exult, Issachar, in your tents!
19 They invite peoples to the mountain
where they offer right sacrifices,
Because they suck up the abundance of the seas*
and the hidden treasures of the sand.

20 Of Gad he said:[n]

Blessed be the one who has made Gad so vast!

33:5 A king arose: it is unclear whether this refers to divine kingship or the beginning of the monarchy in Israel. **Jeshurun**: see note on 32:15.

33:7 Bring him to his people: this probably refers to the isolated position of the tribe of Judah (cf. Jgs 1:17–19); according to some commentators the reference is to the divided kingdom.

33:8 Thummim . . . Urim: devices priests used for divination (cf. note on Ex 28:30).

33:9 The reference is probably to the Levites' slaughter of other Israelites after the incident of the golden calf; cf. Ex 32:27–29.

33:12 Abides at his breast: an image of security under divine protection.

33:19 The abundance of the seas: perhaps the wealth that comes from sea trade or from fishing. **The hidden treasures of the sand**: possibly an allusion to the valuable purple dye extracted from certain marine shells found on the coast of northern Palestine.

b: Dt 4:44; Jn 1:17; 7:19. *c:* Dt 32:15. *d:* Gn 49:3–4. *e:* Gn 49:8–12. *f:* Gn 49:5–7. *g:* Dt 6:16; 9:22; 32:51; Ex 17:1–7; 28:30; Lv 8:8; Nm 20:1–13; 1 Sm 14:41–42. *h:* Lk 14:26. *i:* Dt 10:8; 17:9–11; 18:1–8; Ex 30:7–8; Lv 10:11; 2 Kgs 17:27–28; Mal 2:4–9. *j:* Gn 49:27. *k:* Gn 49:22–26. *l:* Ex 3:1–6; Jgs 5:6. *m:* Gn 49:13–15. *n:* Gn 49:19.

He lies there like a lion;
he tears the arm, the head as well.
21 He saw that the best should be his,
for there the commander's portion was assigned;
he came at the head of the people.
He carried out the justice of the LORD
and his ordinances for Israel.[o]

22 Of Dan he said:

Dan is a lion's cub,[p]
that springs away from a viper!

23 Of Naphtali he said:

Naphtali, abounding with favor,
filled with the blessing of the LORD,
take possession of the west and south.[q]

24 Of Asher he said:[r]

Most blessed* of sons be Asher!
May he be the favorite among his brothers,
and may he dip his foot in oil!
25 May the bolts of your gates be iron and bronze;
may your strength endure through all your days!

26 There is none like the God of Jeshurun,
who rides the heavens in his power,
who rides the clouds in his majesty;[s]
27 The God of old is a refuge;
a support are the arms of the Everlasting.
He drove the enemy out of your way
and he said, "Destroy!"[t]
28 Israel abides securely,
Jacob dwells apart,
In a land of grain and wine,
where the heavens drip with dew.[u]
29 Happy are you, Israel! Who is like you,
a people delivered by the LORD,
Your help and shield,
and the sword of your glory.
Your enemies cringe before you;
you stride upon their backs.[v]

IV. The Death of Moses

CHAPTER 34

See RG 141–48

1 Then Moses went up from the plains
of Moab to Mount Nebo,[w] the peak of Pisgah
which faces Jericho, and the LORD showed
him all the land—Gilead, and as far as Dan,
2 all Naphtali, the land of Ephraim and Manasseh, all the land of Judah as far as the
Western Sea,[x] 3 the Negeb, the plain (the valley of Jericho, the City of Palms), and as far
as Zoar. 4 The LORD then said to him, This is
the land[y] about which I promised on oath to
Abraham, Isaac, and Jacob, "I will give it to
your descendants." I have let you see it with
your own eyes, but you shall not cross over.
5 So there, in the land of Moab, Moses, the
servant of the LORD, died[z] as the LORD had
said; 6 and he was buried in a valley in the
land of Moab, opposite Beth-peor; to this
day no one knows the place of his burial.[a]
7 Moses was one hundred and twenty years
old[b] when he died, yet his eyes were
undimmed and his vigor unabated. 8 The Israelites wept for Moses in the plains of
Moab for thirty days, till they had completed
the period of grief and mourning for Moses.

9 Now Joshua, son of Nun,[c] was filled with
the spirit of wisdom, since Moses had laid
his hands upon him; and so the Israelites
gave him their obedience, just as the LORD
had commanded Moses.

10[d] Since then no prophet has arisen in Israel like Moses, whom the LORD knew face
to face, 11[e] in all the signs and wonders the
LORD sent him to perform in the land of
Egypt against Pharaoh and all his servants
and against all his land, 12 and all the great
might and the awesome power that Moses
displayed in the sight of all Israel.

33:24 Most blessed: Hebrew *baruk*; but the name Asher may suggest a play on the Hebrew *'ashre*, "happy"; cf., e.g., v. 29; Ps 1:1. **Oil**: the land of the tribe of Asher was covered with olive groves.

o: Nm 32:1–32; Jos 1:12–15; 1 Chr 5:18–22; 12:8–15. *p:* Gn 49:16–17. *q:* Gn 49:21; Jos 19:32–39. *r:* Gn 49:20. *s:* Dt 32:15; Ps 18:10; 68:4, 33; 104:3; Is 19:1. *t:* Dt 7:1, 17–24. *u:* Dt 7:12–16; Gn 27:28; Nm 23:9. *v:* Dt 4:7–8; Gn 15:1; 2 Sm 22:3; Ps 28:7; 119:114. *w:* Dt 3:27; 32:49. *x:* Dt 11:24. *y:* Dt 1:8; 3:27; 32:52; Gn 12:7; 15:18–21. *z:* Dt 32:50; Ex 14:31; Nm 12:7–8; Jos 1:1–2, 7, 13, 15; 1 Kgs 8:53, 56; Mal 3:22. *a:* Dt 3:29. *b:* Dt 31:2. *c:* Nm 27:18–23; Jos 1:17. *d:* Dt 5:4; 18:15; Ex 33:11; Nm 12:8; Sir 45:5. *e:* Dt 4:34; Ex 4:21; 7:1, 8–12.

THE HISTORICAL BOOKS

See RG 169–234

Where the Hebrew Bible comprises three sections—Torah or Pentateuch; Prophetic Books, both the Former and the Latter Prophets; and the Writings, including everything else in the Hebrew Canon—the Christian Old Testament has traditionally been arranged along different lines. After the Pentateuch comes a series of books that continue, in roughly chronological order, the history of Israel. The Book of Joshua depicts Israel taking possession of the land of Canaan. Judges collects stories about the leaders of early Israel in the two hundred years before the emergence of the monarchy. After the tale of Ruth, a sort of interlude in the narrative sweep of these books, 1 and 2 Samuel tell of the rise and fall of Saul, Israel's first king, and the succession and successes of David. The Books of Kings take us from the death of David and the enthronement of Solomon, through the division of the people into the two kingdoms of Israel and Judah, to the destruction of the Northern Kingdom, Israel, at the hands of the Assyrian invader (722/721 B.C.), and the fall of Judah, the Southern Kingdom, to the Babylonians (587 B.C.) and its ensuing exile, the Babylonian captivity.

Except for Ruth, these writings bear the marks of a specific theological outlook, that of the Book of Deuteronomy, and together with that book as its introductory volume constitute what is called the Deuteronomistic History. In this theology, what has characterized Israel's history, in the six hundred years from Moses to the Babylonian exile, has been a dynamic of fidelity or infidelity to Israel's covenant Lord, and the consequent destiny Israel forges for itself of covenant blessing or covenant curse. This dynamic of choice and consequences serves to explain the disasters Israel incurs throughout its history, from the so-called conquest and the days of the Judges to the fall of the North. In its preexilic edition, the Deuteronomistic History would have stood also as warning and wake-up call to the surviving Southern Kingdom.

The Books of Chronicles recycle much of the material found in the previous works, but the author ("the Chronicler") treats it selectively, with a characteristic theological point of view; its focus is the Jerusalem Temple and its cultic arrangements, which by way of legitimation are attributed to David, the ideal king. The Chronicler's interests carry through the Books of Ezra and Nehemiah, which recount the restoration of Jewish worship and life in the period of Persian rule following release from exile in Babylon.

The Books of Maccabees give us two overlapping but somewhat differing accounts of Jewish resistance to Seleucid persecution in the early second century B.C., and the assumption of power by the leaders of the resistance, the Maccabees or Hasmoneans.

The traditional designation of these books as "historical" describes their scope and contents, and is not meant to assert factual verifiability; while they contain much valuable historical information, in the narrow sense, their purpose is theological rather than historiographic.

The Books of Tobit, Judith, and Esther are sometimes reckoned among the historical books, but they differ from the writings sketched above, and call for special treatment; see the introduction to those books.

See RG 149–56

The Book of Joshua

The Book of Joshua presents a narrative of the way Israel took possession of the land of Canaan, making it the land of Israel. This process is swift and inexorable, and is followed by an orderly division and disposition of the land among the twelve tribes, with a concluding ceremony of covenant renewal.

The theological message of the book is unmistakable. God has been faithful to the promise of the land. If Israel relies totally on the Lord for victory; if Israel is united as a people; if the law of *herem* is kept and no one grows rich from victory in war—then and only then will Israel possess the land.

The Israelites are led by Joshua, the successor of Moses, and the book is at pains to show not only how Joshua carries on the work of Moses but how the "conquest" of Canaan is continuous with the exodus from Egypt. This is seen in the repeated insistence that, as the Lord was with Moses, so he is with Joshua; and, especially, in the crossing of the Jordan River, which is patterned after the crossing of the Red Sea.

The book preserves older traditions of Israel's settlement in the land, especially in the division of the land among the tribes. As with Deuteronomy and the whole Deuteronomistic History (see introduction to Deuteronomy), the fall of the Northern Kingdom in 722/721 B.C. shows its influence throughout. As addressed to the needs of a late preexilic audience, then, the book should be read not so much as imparting information about how Israel took over the land of Canaan, many centuries before the composition of the book, as teaching a lesson about how Israel is to avoid losing the land.

Modern readers may be put off by the description of battles and their aftermath, the destruction of everyone and everything in the cities taken under the "ban" (*herem*). The ban was practiced in the ancient Near East, in Israel and elsewhere, but in Joshua the wholesale destruction of the Canaanites is an idealization of the deuteronomic idea that pagans are to be wiped out so they will not be an occasion for apostasy from the Lord (cf. Dt 7:1–6); note in particular the artificial, formalized description of destruction of towns in Jos 10:28–39. It should be remembered that by the time the book was written, the Canaanites were long gone. Progressive revelation throughout Israel's history produced far more lofty ideals, as when the prophets see all the nations embracing faith in Yahweh, being joined to Israel, and living in peace with one another (Is 2:2–4; 19:23–25; 45:22–25; Zec 8:22–23), and the New Testament teaches us to love even our enemies (Mt 5:43–45).

A comparison of Joshua with the account of Israel's early history found in the first chapter of the Book of Judges shows that Israel's emergence as the dominant presence in the land was a slow and piecemeal affair, not achieved at one stroke and with great ease: the Book of Joshua, with its highly idealized depiction of the "conquest," is a theologically programmatic cautionary tale about what the people are to do and not do in order to avoid the fate of the Northern Kingdom in losing the land.

The Book of Joshua may be divided as follows:

I. Conquest of Canaan (1:1–12:24)
II. Division of the Land (13:1–21:45)
III. Return of the Transjordan Tribes and Joshua's Farewell (22:1–24:33)

I. Conquest of Canaan

CHAPTER 1

See RG 150

Divine Promise of Assistance. 1 After
Moses, the servant of the LORD, had died,
the LORD said to Moses' aide Joshua, son of
Nun: 2* Moses my servant is dead. So now,
you and the whole people with you, prepare
to cross the Jordan to the land that I will give

1:2–9 The beginning of the Book of Joshua strongly emphasizes the credentials of Joshua as Moses' worthy successor (vv. 2, 3, 4, 7; cf. v. 17; 3:7; 4:14; 5:15). The movement Joshua leads, whereby the Israelites take possession of the land of Canaan, is thus made continuous with the exodus from Egypt, even though (except for Joshua and Caleb) the generation that left Egypt under Moses' leadership has died out (5:4, 6), and the people who will make the land of Canaan the land of Israel are a new generation. Thus the book is at pains to establish the continuity between exodus and conquest.

the Israelites. [3][a] Every place where you set foot I have given you, as I promised Moses. [4]* All the land of the Hittites, from the wilderness and the Lebanon east to the great river Euphrates and west to the Great Sea, will be your territory.[b] [5]No one can withstand you as long as you live. As I was with Moses, I will be with you:[c] I will not leave you nor forsake you. [6]Be strong and steadfast, so that you may give this people possession of the land I swore to their ancestors that I would give them. [7][d] Only be strong and steadfast, being careful to observe the entire law which Moses my servant enjoined on you. Do not swerve from it either to the right or to the left, that you may succeed wherever you go. [8]Do not let this book of the law depart from your lips. Recite it by day and by night,[e] that you may carefully observe all that is written in it; then you will attain your goal; then you will succeed. [9]I command you: be strong and steadfast! Do not fear nor be dismayed, for the LORD, your God, is with you wherever you go.

[10][f] So Joshua commanded the officers of the people: [11]"Go through the camp and command the people, 'Prepare your provisions, for three days from now you shall cross the Jordan here, to march in and possess the land the LORD, your God, is giving as your possession.' "

The Transjordan Tribes. [12][g] Joshua addressed the Reubenites, the Gadites, and the half-tribe of Manasseh: [13]"Remember what Moses, the servant of the LORD, commanded you when he said, 'The LORD, your God, is about to give you rest; he will give you this land.' [14]Your wives, your children, and your livestock may remain in the land Moses gave you here beyond the Jordan. But all the warriors among you must cross over armed, ahead of your kindred, and you must help them [15]until the LORD has settled your kindred, and they like you possess the land the LORD, your God, is giving them. Afterward you may return and possess your own land, which Moses, the servant of the LORD, has given you east of the Jordan."[h] [16]They answered Joshua, "We will do all you have commanded us, and we will go wherever you send us. [17]As completely as we obeyed Moses, we will obey you. Only, may the LORD, your God, be with you as God was with Moses. [18]Anyone who rebels against your orders and does not obey all your commands shall be put to death. Only be strong and steadfast."

CHAPTER 2

See RG 150

Spies Saved by Rahab. [1]Then Joshua, son of Nun, secretly sent out two spies from Shittim, saying, "Go, reconnoiter the land and Jericho." When the two reached Jericho, they went into the house of a prostitute named Rahab,[i] where they lodged. [2]But a report was brought to the king of Jericho: "Some men came here last night, Israelites, to spy out the land." [3]So the king of Jericho sent Rahab the order, "Bring out the men who have come to you and entered your house, for they have come to spy out the entire land." [4]The woman[j] had taken the two men and hidden them, so she said, "True, the men you speak of came to me, but I did not know where they came from. [5]At dark, when it was time to close the gate, they left, and I do not know where they went. You will have to pursue them quickly to overtake them." [6]Now, she had led them to the roof, and hidden them among her stalks of flax spread out* there. [7]But the pursuers set out along the way to the fords of the Jordan. As soon as they had left to pursue them, the gate was shut.

[8]Before the spies lay down, Rahab went up to them on the roof [9]and said:* "I know that the LORD has given you the land, that a dread of you has come upon us, and that all

1:4 The frontiers are as follows: in the south the wilderness of Sinai, in the north the Lebanon range, in the east the Euphrates, and in the west the Great Sea, the Mediterranean. These boundaries are ideal rather than actual.

2:6 Stalks of flax spread out: to dry in the sun, after they had been soaked in water, according to the ancient process of preparing flax for linen-making. In the Near East the flax harvest occurs near the time of the feast of the Passover (4:19; 5:10); cf. Ex 9:31.

2:9–11 Rahab's speech is Deuteronomic in content and style. Through her, the author expresses a theological conviction: the Lord, the God of Israel, is God above all gods; the

a: Jos 14:9; Gn 15:18; Dt 11:24–25; 34:4. *b:* Gn 10:19; Nm 13:17, 21–22; 34:3–12. *c:* Dt 3:21–22; 31:8, 23; Heb 13:5. *d:* Dt 2:27; 5:29; 17:11, 20; 28:14; Ps 1:1–3. *e:* Ps 1:2. *f:* Dt 20:5–9. *g:* Nm 32; Dt 3:12–20. *h:* Jos 22:4; Dt 3:20. *i:* Dt 1:22; Mt 1:5; Jas 2:25. *j:* Jos 6:17; Heb 11:31.

the inhabitants of the land tremble with fear because of you.[k] 10 For we have heard how the LORD dried up the waters of the Red Sea before you when you came out of Egypt,[l] and what you did to Sihon and Og, the two kings of the Amorites beyond the Jordan, whom you destroyed under the ban. 11 We heard, and our hearts melted within us; everyone is utterly dispirited because of you, since the LORD, your God, is God in heaven above and on earth below.[m] 12[n] Now then, swear to me by the LORD that, since I am showing kindness to you, you in turn will show kindness to my family.[o] Give me a reliable sign 13 that you will allow my father and mother, brothers and sisters, and my whole family to live, and that you will deliver us from death." 14 "We pledge our lives for yours," they answered her. "If you do not betray our mission, we will be faithful in showing kindness to you when the LORD gives us the land."

15 Then she let them down through the window with a rope; for she lived in a house built into the city wall.* 16 "Go up into the hill country," she said, "that your pursuers may not come upon you. Hide there for three days, until they return; then you may go on your way." 17 They answered her, "We are free of this oath that you made us take, unless, 18 when we come into the land, you tie this scarlet cord in the window through which you are letting us down. Gather your father and mother, your brothers, and all your family into your house. 19 Should any of them pass outside the doors of your house, their blood will be on their own heads, and we will be guiltless. But if anyone in your house is harmed, their blood will be on our heads. 20 If, however, you betray our mission, we will be free of the oath you have made us take." 21 "Let it be as you say," she replied, and sent them away. When they were gone, she tied the scarlet cord in the window.

22 They went up into the hill country, where they stayed three days until their pursuers, who had sought them all along the road without finding them, returned. 23 Then the two came back down from the hills, crossed the Jordan to Joshua, son of Nun, and told him all that had happened to them. 24 They assured Joshua, "The LORD has given all this land into our power; indeed, all the inhabitants of the land tremble with fear because of us."

CHAPTER 3

See RG 150

Preparations for Crossing the Jordan.

1 Early the next morning, Joshua and all the Israelites moved from Shittim and came to the Jordan, where they stayed before crossing over. 2[p] Three days later the officers went through the camp 3[q] and issued these commands to the people: "When you see the ark of the covenant of the LORD, your God, which the levitical priests will carry, you must break camp and follow it, 4 that you may know the way to take, for you have not gone over this road before. But let there be a space of two thousand cubits between you and the ark: do not come nearer to it." 5 Joshua also said to the people, "Sanctify yourselves, for tomorrow the LORD will perform wonders among you." 6 And he told the priests, "Take up the ark of the covenant and cross ahead of the people"; so they took up the ark of the covenant and went before the people.

7[r] Then the LORD said to Joshua: Today I will begin to exalt you in the sight of all Israel, that they may know that, as I was with Moses, so I will be with you.[s] 8 Now command the priests carrying the ark of the covenant, "When you come to the edge of the waters of the Jordan, there take your stand."

9 So Joshua said to the Israelites, "Come here and listen to the words of the LORD, your God." 10 He continued: "By this you will know that there is a living God in your

formation of the people Israel and its success is the Lord's doing; and all the rulers of the neighboring nations do well to panic at what the Lord is doing (cf. 5:1). Rahab the prostitute is pointedly mentioned in the Matthean genealogy of Jesus (Mt 1:5) and in Jas 2:25.

2:15 A house built into the city wall: the city wall formed the back wall of the house; remains of such houses have been found at ancient sites. The upper story of Rahab's house was evidently higher than the city wall. It was through the window of such a house that St. Paul escaped from Damascus; cf. Acts 9:25; 2 Cor 11:33.

k: Ex 15:15–16; 23:27. *l:* Jos 4:23; Ex 14:21; Nm 21:23–26, 33–35. *m:* Jos 5:1; Dt 4:39; Rom 10:9. *n:* Jgs 1:22–26. *o:* Jos 2:18; 6:23, 25. *p:* Jos 2:1. *q:* Nm 10:33. *r:* Jos 1:5; Dt 31:23. *s:* Jos 1:5; 4:14.

midst: he will certainly dispossess before you the Canaanites, Hittites, Hivites, Perizzites, Girgashites, Amorites, and Jebusites.[t] 11 The ark of the covenant of the Lord of the whole earth will cross the Jordan before you. 12 Now choose twelve men,[u] one from each of the tribes of Israel. 13 When the soles of the feet of the priests carrying the ark of the LORD, the Lord of the whole earth, touch the waters of the Jordan, it will cease to flow; the water flowing down from upstream will halt in a single heap."*

The Crossing Begun. 14 The people set out from their tents to cross the Jordan, with the priests carrying the ark of the covenant ahead of them. 15 When those bearing the ark came to the Jordan and the feet of the priests bearing the ark were immersed in the waters of the Jordan—which overflows all its banks during the entire season of the harvest—* 16 the waters flowing from upstream halted, standing up in a single heap[v] for a very great distance indeed, from Adam, a city in the direction of Zarethan; those flowing downstream toward the Salt Sea of the Arabah disappeared entirely.* Thus the people crossed over opposite Jericho. 17 The priests carrying the ark of the covenant of the LORD stood on dry ground in the Jordan riverbed[w] while all Israel crossed on dry ground, until the whole nation had completed the crossing of the Jordan.

CHAPTER 4

See RG 150

Memorial Stones. 1 After the entire nation had completed the crossing of the Jordan, 2 the LORD said to Joshua: Choose twelve men[x] from the people, one from each tribe, 3 and command them, "Take up twelve stones from this spot in the Jordan riverbed where the priests have been standing.[y] Carry them over with you, and place them where you are to stay tonight."

4 Summoning the twelve men he had selected from among the Israelites, one from each tribe, 5 Joshua said to them: "Go to the Jordan riverbed in front of the ark of the LORD, your God; lift to your shoulders one stone apiece, so that they will equal in number the tribes of the Israelites. 6 In the future, these are to be a sign among you. When your children ask you,* 'What do these stones mean to you?'[z] 7 you shall answer them, 'The waters of the Jordan ceased to flow before the ark of the covenant of the LORD when it crossed the Jordan.'[a] Thus these stones are to serve as a perpetual memorial to the Israelites." 8 The twelve Israelites did as Joshua had commanded: they took up twelve stones from the Jordan riverbed as the LORD had said to Joshua, one for each of the tribes of the Israelites. They carried them along to the camp site, and there they placed them. 9 Joshua set up the twelve stones that had been in the Jordan riverbed on the spot where the priests stood who were carrying the ark of the covenant. They are there to this day.

10* The priests carrying the ark stood in the Jordan riverbed until everything had been done that the LORD had commanded Joshua to tell the people, just as Moses had commanded Joshua. The people crossed over quickly, 11 and when all the people had completed the crossing, the ark of the LORD also crossed; and the priests were now in front of them. 12 The Reubenites, Gadites, and half-tribe of Manasseh, armed, marched in the vanguard of the Israelites, as Moses

3:13 Heap: Heb. *nēd*, the same word found in Ex 15:8; the narrative echoes the ancient Song of Miriam (Ex 15:1–18), which celebrates the crossing of the Red Sea. Thus the language provides another parallel between Joshua and Moses, conquest and exodus.

3:15 Season of the harvest: toward the end of March and the beginning of April, when the barley and other crops that grew during the rainy season of winter were reaped. The crossing took place "on the tenth day of the first month" of the Hebrew year, which began with the first new moon after the spring equinox; cf. 4:19. At this time of the year the Jordan would be swollen as a result of the winter rains and the melting snow of Mount Hermon.

3:16 Some scholars have suggested that this account may reflect an annual ritual reenactment of the event near the sanctuary of Gilgal.

4:6 When your children ask you: reminiscent of the question and response at the Passover meal, Ex 12:26–27.

4:10–18 After the digression about the memorial stones, the author resumes the narrative by briefly repeating the story of the crossing, which had already been told in 3:14–17.

t: Ex 33:2; Dt 7:1. *u:* Jos 4:2, 4. *v:* Ps 114:3. *w:* Jos 4:7, 22. *x:* Jos 3:12. *y:* Jos 3:13; 4:8–9; Dt 27:2. *z:* Ex 12:26–27; Dt 6:7, 20–25. *a:* Jos 3:13, 16.

had ordered. 13About forty thousand troops,
equipped for battle, crossed over before the
LORD to the plains of Jericho for war.
14That day the LORD exalted Joshua in the
sight of all Israel,[b] and so during his whole
life they feared him as they had feared Moses.
15Then the LORD said to Joshua: 16Com-
mand the priests carrying the ark of the covenant to come up from the Jordan. 17Joshua
commanded the priests, "Come up from the
Jordan," 18and when the priests carrying the
ark of the covenant of the LORD had come up
from the Jordan riverbed, as the soles of
their feet regained the dry ground, the waters
of the Jordan resumed their course and as
before overflowed all its banks.
19The people came up from the Jordan on
the tenth day of the first month, and camped
in Gilgal on the eastern limits of Jericho.[c]
20At Gilgal Joshua set up the twelve stones
that had been taken from the Jordan, 21say-
ing to the Israelites, "In the future, when
your children ask their parents, 'What do
these stones mean?' 22you shall inform
them, 'Israel crossed the Jordan here on dry
ground.' 23For the LORD, your God, dried up
the waters of the Jordan in front of you until
you crossed over, just as the LORD, your
God, had done at the Red Sea, drying it up in
front of us until we crossed over,[d] 24in order
that all the peoples of the earth may know
that the hand of the LORD is mighty, and that
you may fear the LORD, your God, forever."[e]

CHAPTER 5

See RG 150–51

Rites at Gilgal. 1When all the kings of
the Amorites to the west of the Jordan and all
the kings of the Canaanites by the sea heard
that the LORD had dried up the waters of the
Jordan before the Israelites until they crossed
over, their hearts melted and they were utterly dispirited because of the Israelites.
2[f]On this occasion the LORD said to
Joshua: Make flint knives and circumcise Israel for the second time. 3So Joshua made
flint knives and circumcised the Israelites at
Gibeath-haaraloth.* 4This was the reason for
the circumcision: Of all the people who had
come out of Egypt, every male of military
age had died in the wilderness[g] during the
journey after they came out of Egypt.
5Though all the men who came out were circumcised, none of those born in the wilderness during the journey after the departure
from Egypt were circumcised. 6Now the Israelites wandered forty years in the wilderness, until all the warriors among the people
that came forth from Egypt died off because
they had not listened to the voice of the
LORD. For the LORD swore[h] that he would not
let them see the land he had sworn to their ancestors to give us, a land flowing with milk
and honey. 7[i] It was the children God raised
up in their stead whom Joshua circumcised,
for these were yet with foreskins, not having
been circumcised on the journey. 8When the
circumcision of the entire nation was complete, they remained in camp where they
were, until they recovered. 9Then the LORD
said to Joshua: Today I have removed the reproach of Egypt from you.[j] Therefore the
place is called Gilgal* to the present day.
10[k] While the Israelites were encamped at
Gilgal on the plains of Jericho, they celebrated the Passover on the evening of the
fourteenth day of the month.* 11On the day
after the Passover they ate of the produce of
the land in the form of unleavened cakes and
parched grain. On that same day 12after they
ate of the produce of the land, the manna
ceased. No longer was there manna for the
Israelites, who that year ate of the yield of
the land of Canaan.[l]

Siege at Jericho. 13* While Joshua was
near Jericho, he raised his eyes and saw one
who stood facing him, drawn sword in

5:3 Gibeath-haaraloth: "Hill of the Foreskins."

5:9 The place is called Gilgal: by popular etymology, because of the similarity of sound with the Hebrew word *gallothi*, "I have removed." Gilgal probably means "circle," i.e., the place of the circle of standing stones. Cf. 4:4–8.

5:10 The month: the first month of the year, later called Nisan; see note on 3:15. The crossing of the Jordan occurred, therefore, about the same time of the year as did the crossing of the Red Sea; cf. Ex 12–14.

5:13–6:26 The account of the siege of Jericho embraces: (1) the command of the Lord to Joshua (5:13–6:5); (2) Joshua's instructions to the Israelites, with a brief summary of how these orders were carried out (6:6–11); (3) a description

b: Jos 3:7. *c:* Ex 12:2–3. *d:* Ex 14:21. *e:* Ex 9:3; 14:31; 16:3. *f:* Gn 17; 34; Ex 4:24–26. *g:* Nm 14:29; 26:64–65; 1 Cor 10:5. *h:* Nm 14:33–34; Heb 3:11, 17. *i:* Gn 17:8–14. *j:* Jos 4:19; Eph 2:11–22. *k:* Ex 12:6; Nm 9:3–5. *l:* Ex 16:35.

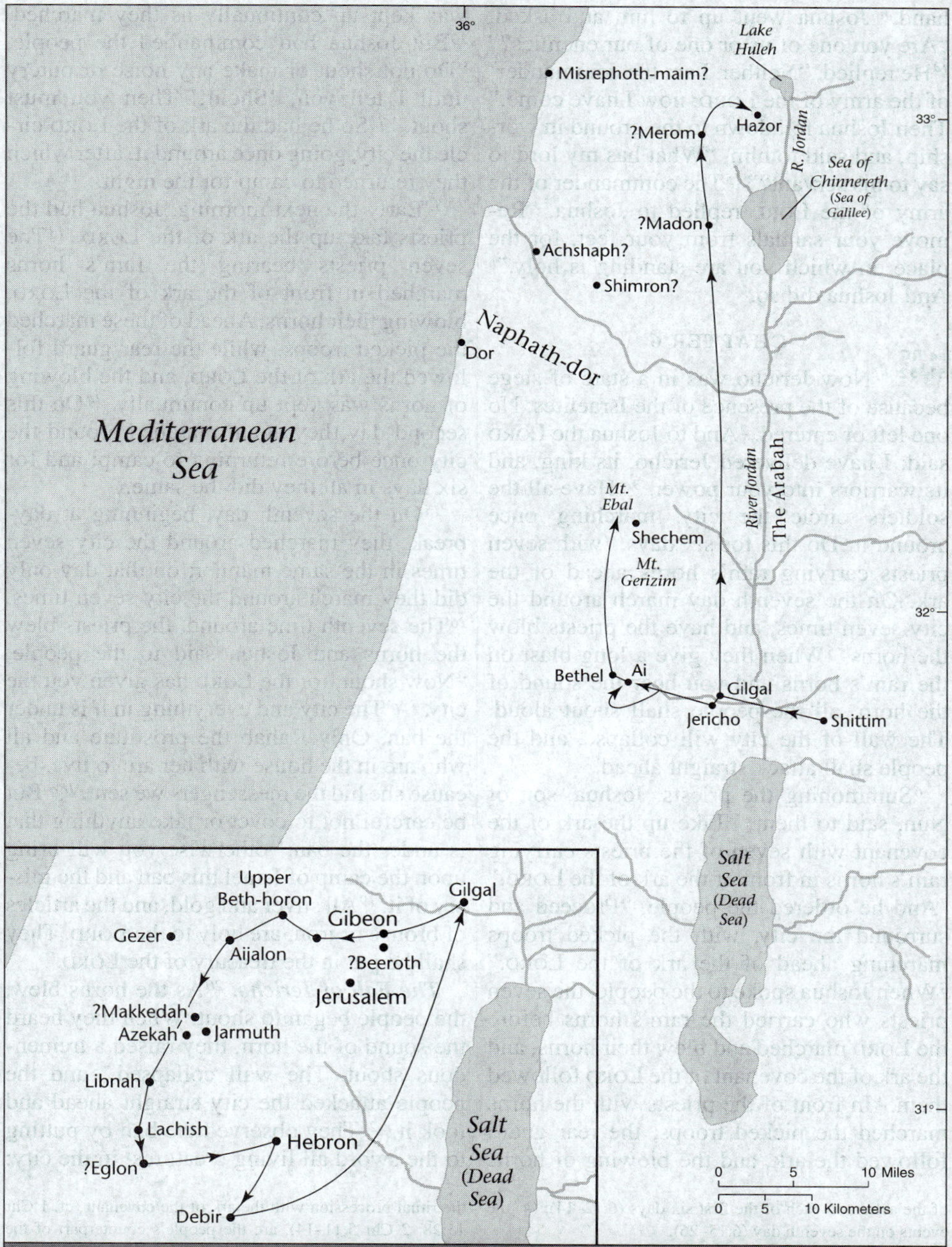

Conquest of Canaan according to the Book of Joshua

hand.[m] Joshua went up to him and asked, "Are you one of us or one of our enemies?" 14 He replied, "Neither. I am the commander* of the army of the LORD: now I have come." Then Joshua fell down to the ground in worship, and said to him, "What has my lord to say to his servant?" 15 The commander of the army of the LORD replied to Joshua, "Remove your sandals from your feet, for the place on which you are standing is holy."[n] And Joshua did so.

CHAPTER 6

See RG 151–52

1 Now Jericho was in a state of siege because of the presence of the Israelites. No one left or entered. 2 And to Joshua the LORD said: I have delivered Jericho, its king, and its warriors into your power. 3[o] Have all the soldiers circle the city, marching once around it. Do this for six days, 4 with seven priests carrying ram's horns ahead of the ark. On the seventh day march around the city seven times, and have the priests blow the horns. 5 When they give a long blast on the ram's horns and you hear the sound of the horn, all the people shall shout aloud. The wall of the city will collapse, and the people shall attack straight ahead.

6 Summoning the priests, Joshua, son of Nun, said to them, "Take up the ark of the covenant with seven of the priests carrying ram's horns in front of the ark of the LORD." 7 And he ordered the people, "Proceed and surround the city, with the picked troops marching ahead of the ark of the LORD." 8 When Joshua spoke to the people, the seven priests who carried the ram's horns before the LORD marched and blew their horns, and the ark of the covenant of the LORD followed them. 9 In front of the priests with the horns marched the picked troops; the rear guard followed the ark, and the blowing of horns was kept up continually as they marched. 10 But Joshua had commanded the people, "Do not shout or make any noise or outcry until I tell you, 'Shout!' Then you must shout." 11 So he had the ark of the LORD circle the city, going once around it, after which they returned to camp for the night.

12 Early the next morning, Joshua had the priests take up the ark of the LORD. 13 The seven priests bearing the ram's horns marched in front of the ark of the LORD, blowing their horns. Ahead of these marched the picked troops, while the rear guard followed the ark of the LORD, and the blowing of horns was kept up continually. 14 On this second day they again marched around the city once before returning to camp; and for six days in all they did the same.

15 On the seventh day, beginning at daybreak, they marched around the city seven times in the same manner; on that day only did they march around the city seven times. 16 The seventh time around, the priests blew the horns and Joshua said to the people, "Now shout, for the LORD has given you the city. 17[p] The city and everything in it is under the ban. Only Rahab the prostitute and all who are in the house with her are to live, because she hid the messengers we sent. 18[q] But be careful not to covet or take anything that is under the ban;* otherwise you will bring upon the camp of Israel this ban and the misery of it. 19 All silver and gold, and the articles of bronze or iron, are holy to the LORD. They shall be put in the treasury of the LORD."

The Fall of Jericho. 20 As the horns blew, the people began to shout. When they heard the sound of the horn, they raised a tremendous shout. The wall collapsed,* and the people attacked the city straight ahead and took it.[r] 21 They observed the ban by putting to the sword all living creatures[s] in the city:

of the action on each of the first six days (6:12–14); (4) the events on the seventh day (6:15–26).

5:14 Commander: the leader of the heavenly army of the Lord of hosts is either the Lord or an angelic warrior; if the latter, he is a messenger who speaks in the person of the one who sent him. **I have come**: the solemn language of theophany; cf., e.g., Ps 50:3; 96:13.

6:18 Under the ban: doomed to destruction; see notes on Lv 27:28; Nm 18:14; 21:3.

6:20 The blowing of the horns and the shouting, features of the ritual procession with the ark of the covenant (cf. 1 Chr 15:28; 2 Chr 5:11–14), are the people's counterpart of the Lord's theophany; cf. note on Jgs 5:4–5; and Jgs 7:15–22; 2 Chr 13:15. The Lord gives the victory; this is the theological point of the story.

m: Ex 23:20. *n:* Ex 3:5; Acts 7:33. *o:* Nm 10:2–9; 2 Sm 6:15–16. *p:* Jos 2:4; Dt 20:17; Heb 11:31. *q:* Jos 7:12, 25; Dt 13:18. *r:* 2 Mc 12:15; Heb 11:30. *s:* Gn 15:16; Dt 7:2.

men and women, young and old, as well as oxen, sheep and donkeys.

[22][t] To the two men who had spied out the land, Joshua said, "Go into the prostitute's house and bring out the woman with all her family, as you swore to her you would do." [23]The spies entered and brought out Rahab, with her father, mother, brothers, and all her family; her entire family they led forth and placed outside the camp of Israel. [24]The city itself they burned with all that was in it;[u] but the silver, gold, and articles of bronze and iron they placed in the treasury of the house of the LORD. [25]* Because Rahab the prostitute had hidden the messengers whom Joshua had sent to reconnoiter Jericho, Joshua let her live, along with her father's house and all her family, who dwell in the midst of Israel to this day.

[26][v] On that occasion Joshua imposed the oath: Cursed before the LORD be the man who attempts to rebuild this city, Jericho. At the cost of his firstborn will he lay its foundation, and at the cost of his youngest son will he set up its gates.*

[27]Thus the LORD was with Joshua so that his fame spread throughout the land.[w]

CHAPTER 7

See RG 151–52

Defeat at Ai. [1]But the Israelites acted treacherously with regard to the ban; Achan, son of Carmi, son of Zabdi, son of Zerah of the tribe of Judah, took goods that were under the ban,[x] and the anger of the LORD flared up against the Israelites.

[2][y] Joshua next sent men from Jericho to Ai, which is near Beth-aven and east of Bethel, with the order, "Go up and reconnoiter the land." When they had explored Ai, [3]they returned to Joshua and advised, "Do not send all the people up; if only about two or three thousand go up, they can attack and overcome Ai. You need not tire all the people: the enemy there are few." [4]About three thousand of the people made the attack, but they fled before the army at Ai, [5]who killed some thirty-six of them. They pursued them from the city gate to the Shebarim, and defeated them on the descent, so that the confidence of the people melted away like water.

[6]Joshua, together with the elders of Israel, tore their garments and fell face down before the ark of the LORD until evening; and they threw dust on their heads. [7]"Alas, Lord GOD," Joshua prayed, "why did you ever allow this people to cross over the Jordan, delivering us into the power of the Amorites, that they might destroy us? Would that we had been content to dwell on the other side of the Jordan. [8]Please, Lord, what can I say, now that Israel has turned its back to its enemies? [9]When the Canaanites and the other inhabitants of the land hear of it, they will close in around us and efface our name from the earth. What will you do for your great name?"[z]

[10]The LORD replied to Joshua: Stand up. Why are you lying there? [11][a] Israel has sinned: they have transgressed the covenant* which I enjoined on them. They have taken goods subject to the ban. They have stolen and lied, placing the goods in their baggage. [12]If the Israelites cannot stand up to their enemies, but must turn their back to them, it is because they are under the ban. I will not continue to be with you unless you remove that which is banned from among you. [13]Get up, sanctify the people.[b] Tell them, "Sanctify yourselves before tomorrow, for thus says the LORD, the God of Israel: That which is banned is in your midst, Israel. You cannot stand up to your enemies until you remove it from among you. [14]In the morning you must come forward by tribes. The tribe which the LORD designates shall come forward by clans; the clan which the LORD designates shall come forward by families; the family which the LORD designates shall come forward one by one. [15]Whoever is designated as

6:25 The genealogy of Jesus in Matthew (1:2–16) presents Rahab the prostitute as the wife of Salmon (1:5) and so the ancestor of David (Ru 4:18–22) and of Jesus.

6:26 At the cost of his firstborn . . . its gates: this curse was fulfilled when Hiel rebuilt Jericho as a fortified city during the reign of Ahab, king of Israel; cf. 1 Kgs 16:34.

7:11 Transgressed the covenant: the Hebrew word translated "transgressed" appears frequently in the first five chapters where it is used to describe how Israel "crossed" the Jordan River. There is a wordplay here to emphasize Israel's responsibility to follow God to the promised land and so to obey and not transgress the divine command.

t: Jos 2:13–14. *u:* Jos 8:2. *v:* Jos 9:23; 1 Kgs 16:34. *w:* Jos 1:5. *x:* Jos 6:18; 22:20; 1 Chr 2:7. *y:* Nm 13:17–20. *z:* Nm 14:13–19. *a:* Jos 6:17–19. *b:* Jos 3:5; Lv 20:7; 1 Sm 16:5.

having incurred the ban shall be destroyed by fire, with all that is his, because he has trangressed the covenant of the LORD and has committed a shameful crime in Israel."[c]

Achan's Guilt and Punishment. [16]Early the next morning Joshua had Israel come forward by tribes, and the tribe of Judah was designated.* [17]Then he had the clans of Judah come forward, and the clan of Zerah was designated. He had the clan of Zerah[d] come forward by families, and Zabdi was designated. [18]Finally he had that family come forward one by one, and Achan, son of Carmi, son of Zabdi, son of Zerah of the tribe of Judah, was designated. [19]Joshua said to Achan, "My son, give glory to the LORD, the God of Israel, and praise him by telling me what you have done; do not hide it from me." [20]Achan answered Joshua, "I have indeed sinned against the LORD, the God of Israel. This is what I have done: [21]Among the spoils, I saw a beautiful Babylonian mantle, two hundred shekels of silver, and a bar of gold fifty shekels in weight; I coveted them and I took them. They are now hidden in the ground inside my tent, with the silver underneath." [22]Joshua sent messengers and they ran to the tent and there they were, hidden in the tent, with the silver underneath. [23]They took them from the tent, brought them to Joshua and all the Israelites, and spread them out before the LORD.

[24]Then Joshua and all Israel took Achan, son of Zerah, with the silver, the mantle, and the bar of gold, and with his sons and daughters, his ox, his donkey and his sheep, his tent, and all his possessions, and led them off to the Valley of Achor. [25]Joshua said, "What misery have you caused us? May the LORD bring misery upon you today!"[e] And all Israel stoned him to death. They burnt them with fire and they stoned them. [26]Over Achan they piled a great heap of stones, which remains to the present day.[f] Then the LORD turned from his anger. That is why the place is called the Valley of Achor* to this day.

See RG 151–52

CHAPTER 8

Capture of Ai. [1][g] The LORD then said to Joshua: Do not be afraid or dismayed. Take all the army with you and prepare to attack Ai.[h] I have delivered the king of Ai into your power, with his people, city, and land. [2]Do to Ai and its king what you did to Jericho and its king—except that you may take its spoil and livestock as plunder.[i] Set an ambush behind the city. [3]So Joshua and all the soldiers prepared to attack Ai. Picking out thirty thousand warriors,* Joshua sent them off by night [4]with these orders: "See that you ambush the city from the rear. Do not be very far from the city. All of you must be ready. [5]The rest of the people and I will come up to the city, and when they make a sortie against us as they did the last time, we will flee from them. [6]They will keep coming out after us until we have drawn them away from the city, for they will think, 'They are fleeing from us as they did the last time.' When we flee, [7]then you rise from ambush and take possession of the city, which the LORD, your God, will deliver into your power. [8]When you have taken the city, set it on fire in obedience to the LORD's command. These are my orders to you."[j] [9]Then Joshua sent them away. They went to the place of ambush, taking up their position to the west of Ai, toward Bethel. Joshua, however, spent that night with the army.

[10]Early the next morning Joshua mustered the army and went up to Ai at its head, with the elders of Israel. [11]When all the troops he led were drawn up in position before the city, they pitched camp north of Ai, on the other side of the ravine. [12]He took about five thousand warriors and set them in ambush

7:16–18 Was designated: probably by means of the Urim and Thummim; cf. 1 Sm 14:38–42. See note on Ex 28:30.

7:26 Achor: "misery," or "disaster." The reference is to the saying of Joshua in v. 25, with an allusion also to the similar-sounding name of Achan.

8:3 Thirty thousand warriors: this figure of the Hebrew text, which seems extremely high, may be due to a copyist's error; some manuscripts of the Septuagint have "three thousand," which is the number of the whole army in the first, unsuccessful attack (7:4); the variant reading in v. 12 mentions "five thousand." More likely, the word for "thousand" here and in other military contexts may designate a squad or fighting unit, itself composed of significantly fewer warriors.

c: Dt 13:15–16. *d:* Nm 26:20. *e:* Jos 6:18; 22:20; Dt 13:15–16; 1 Chr 2:7. *f:* Jos 8:29; Dt 13:18. *g:* Jgs 20:20–38. *h:* Jos 2:24; Dt 1:21. *i:* Jos 6:21, 24; Dt 20:14. *j:* Jos 6:24.

between Bethel and Ai, west of the city. [13]Thus the people took up their stations, with the main body north of the city and the ambush west of it, and Joshua waited overnight in the valley. [14]The king of Ai saw this, and he and all his army came out very early in the morning to engage Israel in battle at the place in front of the Arabah, not knowing that there was an ambush behind the city. [15]Joshua and the main body of the Israelites fled toward the wilderness, pretending defeat, [16]until the last of the soldiers in the city had been called out to pursue them. Since they were drawn away from the city, with everyone pursuing Joshua, [17]not a soldier remained in Ai or Bethel. They abandoned the city, leaving it open, as they pursued Israel.

[18]Then the LORD directed Joshua: Stretch out the javelin in your hand toward Ai, for I will deliver it into your power. Joshua stretched out the javelin in his hand toward the city, [19]and as soon as he did so, the men in ambush rose from their post, rushed in, captured the city, and immediately set it on fire. [20]By the time the army of Ai looked back, the smoke from the city was going up to the heavens. Escape in any direction was impossible, because the Israelites retreating toward the wilderness now turned on their pursuers; [21]for when Joshua and the main body of Israelites saw that the city had been taken by ambush and was going up in smoke, they struck back at the forces of Ai. [22]Since those in the city came out to intercept them, Ai's army was hemmed in by Israelites on both sides, who cut them down without any fugitives or survivors[k] [23]except the king, whom they took alive and brought to Joshua.

[24]When Israel finished killing all the inhabitants of Ai in the open, who had pursued them into the wilderness, and all of them to the last man fell by the sword, then all Israel returned and put to the sword those inside the city. [25]There fell that day a total of twelve thousand men and women, the entire population of Ai. [26][l] Joshua kept the javelin in his hand stretched out until he had carried out the ban on all the inhabitants of Ai. [27]However, the Israelites took for themselves as plunder the livestock and the spoil of that city, according to the command of the LORD issued to Joshua. [28]Then Joshua destroyed Ai by fire, reducing it to an everlasting mound of ruins, as it remains today.[m] [29]He had the king of Ai hanged on a tree until evening;[n] then at sunset Joshua ordered the body removed from the tree and cast at the entrance of the city gate, where a great heap of stones was piled up over it, which remains to the present day.

Altar on Mount Ebal. [30*][o] Later, on Mount Ebal, Joshua built to the LORD, the God of Israel, an altar [31]of unhewn stones on which no iron tool had been used,[p] just as Moses, the servant of the LORD, had commanded the Israelites, as recorded in the book of the law. On this altar they sacrificed burnt offerings to the LORD and made communion sacrifices. [32]There, in the presence of the Israelites, Joshua inscribed upon the stones a copy of the law written by Moses. [33]And all Israel, resident alien and native alike, with their elders, officers and judges, stood on either side of the ark facing the levitical priests who were carrying the ark of the covenant of the LORD.[q] Half of them were facing Mount Gerizim and half Mount Ebal, just as Moses, the servant of the LORD, had first commanded for the blessing of the people of Israel. [34][r] Then were read aloud all the words of the law, the blessings and the curses, exactly as written in the book of the law. [35][s] Every single word that Moses had commanded, Joshua read aloud to the entire assembly, including the women and children, and the resident aliens among them.

CHAPTER 9

See RG 151–52

Confederacy Against Israel. [1]When the news reached all the kings west of the Jordan, in the mountain regions and in the Shephelah, and all along the coast of the Great Sea as far as the Lebanon: Hittites,

8:30–35 These ceremonies were prescribed in Dt 11:29 and 27:2–26.

k: Dt 7:2. *l:* Ex 17:11–13. *m:* Dt 13:16. *n:* Jos 10:26–27; Dt 21:22–23; Jn 19:31. *o:* Dt 27:1–8, 12–13. *p:* Ex 20:24–25. *q:* Jos 3:3; Dt 11:27; 31:9, 12. *r:* Dt 28:2–68; 30:19; 31:11; Neh 8:2–3. *s:* Dt 31:12.

Amorites, Canaanites, Perizzites, Hivites, and Jebusites,[t] [2]they gathered together to launch a common attack against Joshua and Israel.

The Gibeonite Deception. [3]On hearing what Joshua had done to Jericho and Ai, the inhabitants of Gibeon[u] [4]formed their own scheme. They chose provisions for a journey, making use of old sacks for their donkeys, and old wineskins, torn and mended. [5]They wore old, patched sandals and shabby garments; and all the bread they took was dry and crumbly. [6]Thus they journeyed to Joshua in the camp at Gilgal, where they said to him and to the Israelites, "We have come from a far-off land; now, make a covenant with us."[v] [7]But the Israelites replied to the Hivites,* "You may be living in land that is ours. How, then, can we make a covenant with you?" [8]But they answered Joshua, "We are your servants." Then Joshua asked them, "Who are you? Where do you come from?" [9]They answered him, "Your servants have come from a far-off land, because of the fame of the LORD, your God. For we have heard reports of all that he did in Egypt[w] [10]and all that he did to the two kings of the Amorites beyond the Jordan,[x] Sihon, king of Heshbon, and Og, king of Bashan, who lived in Ashtaroth. [11]So our elders and all the inhabitants of our land said to us, 'Take along provisions for the journey and go to meet them. Say to them: "We are your servants; now make a covenant with us." ' [12]This bread of ours was still warm when we brought it from home as provisions the day we left to come to you, but now it is dry and crumbly. [13]Here are our wineskins, which were new when we filled them, but now they are torn. Look at our garments and sandals; they are worn out from the very long journey." [14]Then the Israelite leaders partook of their provisions, without inquiring of the LORD.[y] [15]So Joshua made peace with them and made a covenant to let them live,[z] which the leaders of the community sealed with an oath.

Gibeonites Made Vassals. [16]Three days after the covenant was made, the Israelites heard that these people were from nearby, and would be living in Israel. [17]The third day on the road, the Israelites came to their cities of Gibeon, Chephirah, Beeroth, and Kiriath-jearim, [18]but did not attack them, because the leaders of the community had sworn to them by the LORD, the God of Israel. When the entire community grumbled against the leaders, [19]these all remonstrated with the community, "We have sworn to them by the LORD, the God of Israel, and so we cannot harm them. [20]Let us therefore let them live, and so deal with them that no wrath fall upon us because of the oath we have sworn to them."[a] [21]Thus the leaders said to them, "Let them live, and become hewers of wood and drawers of water* for the entire community." So the community did as the leaders advised them.[b]

[22]Joshua summoned the Gibeonites and said to them, "Why did you deceive us and say, 'We live far off from you'?—You live among us! [23]Now are you accursed: every one of you shall always be a slave, hewers of wood and drawers of water, for the house of my God." [24]They answered Joshua, "Your servants were fully informed of how the LORD, your God, commanded Moses his servant that you be given the entire land and that all its inhabitants be destroyed before you. Since, therefore, at your advance, we were in great fear for our lives, we acted as we did.[c] [25]And now that we are in your power, do with us what is good and right in your eyes." [26]* Joshua did what he had decided: while he saved them from being killed by the Israelites, [27]on that day he made them, as they still are, hewers of wood and drawers of water for the community and for the altar of the LORD, in the place the LORD would choose.

9:7 The Hivites: apparently the Gibeonites belonged to this larger ethnic group (cf. also 11:19), although in 2 Sm 21:2 they are classed as Amorites; both groups are listed among the seven nations of Canaan whom, according to Dt 7:1–2, the Israelites were to dispossess.

9:21 Hewers of wood and drawers of water: proverbial terms for those who do menial work; cf. Dt 29:10–11.

9:26–27 Later on, Saul violated the immunity of the Gibeonites, but David vindicated it; cf. 2 Sm 21:1–9.

t: Jos 3:10; 5:1; Ex 3:8, 17; 23:23; Dt 1:7. *u:* Jos 6:21, 24. *v:* Ex 23:32; Dt 7:2. *w:* Jos 2:10–11. *x:* Nm 21:25, 33–35; Dt 1:4. *y:* Nm 27:21. *z:* Jos 11:19; 2 Sm 21:2. *a:* Jos 22:20. *b:* Dt 29:11. *c:* Ex 23:27–28; Dt 7:1–2.

CHAPTER 10

See RG 151–52

The Siege of Gibeon. 1Now when Adonizedek, king of Jerusalem, heard that Joshua had captured Ai and put it under the ban, and had done to that city and its king as he had done to Jericho and its king,[d] and that the inhabitants of Gibeon had made their peace with Israel, remaining among them, 2there was great fear abroad, because Gibeon was a great city, like one of the royal cities, greater even than Ai, and all its men were warriors. 3So Adonizedek, king of Jerusalem, sent to Hoham, king of Hebron, Piram, king of Jarmuth, Japhia, king of Lachish, and Debir, king of Eglon, with this message: 4"Come and help me attack Gibeon, for it has made peace with Joshua and the Israelites."[e] 5The five Amorite kings, of Jerusalem, Hebron, Jarmuth, Lachish, and Eglon,* gathered with all their forces, and marched against Gibeon to make war on it. 6Thereupon, the Gibeonites sent an appeal to Joshua in his camp at Gilgal: "Do not abandon your servants. Come up here quickly and save us. Help us, because all the Amorite kings of the mountain country have joined together against us."[f]

Joshua's Victory. 7So Joshua marched up from Gilgal with all his army and all his warriors. 8The LORD said to Joshua: Do not fear them, for I have delivered them into your power. Not one of them will be able to withstand you. 9After an all-night march from Gilgal, Joshua made a surprise attack upon them, 10and the LORD threw them into disorder before Israel. The Israelites inflicted a great slaughter on them at Gibeon and pursued them down the Beth-horon slope, attacking them as far as Azekah and Makkedah.

11While they fled before Israel along the descent of Beth-horon, the LORD hurled great stones from the heavens* above them all the way to Azekah, killing many.[g] More died from these hailstones than the Israelites killed with the sword. 12It was then, when the LORD delivered up the Amorites to the Israelites, that Joshua prayed to the LORD, and said in the presence of Israel:

Sun, stand still at Gibeon,
  Moon, in the valley of Aijalon!
13 The sun stood still,
  the moon stayed,
  while the nation took vengeance on its foes.[h]

This is recorded* in the Book of Jashar. The sun halted halfway across the heavens; not for an entire day did it press on. 14Never before or since was there a day like this, when the LORD obeyed the voice of a man; for the LORD fought for Israel. 15Then Joshua and all Israel returned to the camp at Gilgal.

Execution of Amorite Kings. 16The five kings who had fled hid in the cave at Makkedah. 17When Joshua was told, "The five kings have been found, hiding in the cave at Makkedah," 18he said, "Roll large stones to the mouth of the cave and post guards over it. 19But do not remain there yourselves. Pursue your enemies, and harry them in the rear. Do not allow them to reach their cities, for the LORD, your God, has delivered them into your power."

20Once Joshua and the Israelites had finally inflicted the last blows in this very great slaughter, and the survivors had escaped from them into the fortified cities, 21all the army returned to Joshua and the camp at Makkedah in victory; no one uttered a sound against the Israelites. 22Then Joshua said, "Open the mouth of the cave and bring me those five kings from the cave." 23They did so; they brought out to him from the cave the five kings, of Jerusalem, Hebron, Jarmuth, Lachish, and Eglon. 24When they brought the five kings out to Joshua, he summoned all the army of Israel and said to the

10:5 Hebron . . . Eglon: these four cities were to the south and southwest of Jerusalem.

10:11 Great stones from the heavens: the hailstones mentioned in the next sentence.

10:13 This is recorded: the reference is to the preceding poetic passage. Evidently the *Book of Jashar*, like the *Book of the Wars of the Lord* (Nm 21:14), recounted in epic style the exploits of Israel's early heroes. **The sun halted**: lit., "the sun stood"; this obscure passage may suppose a longer than natural day caused when the sun stopped moving across the sky, or it may refer to the sun stopping its light-giving function, perhaps through an eclipse. In any case it was seen as a sign that God fought Israel's battle (v. 42; cf. Ex 14:14).

d: Jos 6:21, 24; 8:26–29. *e:* Jos 9:15. *f:* Jos 9:6. *g:* Jb 38:22–23. *h:* Sir 46:4; Is 28:21.

commanders of the soldiers who had
marched with him, “Come forward and put
your feet on the necks of these kings.” They
came forward and put their feet upon their
necks. 25[i] Then Joshua said to them, “Do not
be afraid or dismayed, be firm and steadfast.
This is what the LORD will do to all the enemies against whom you fight.” 26[j] Thereupon Joshua struck and killed the kings, and
hanged them on five trees, where they remained hanging until evening. 27 At sunset
Joshua commanded that they be taken down
from the trees and be thrown into the cave
where they had hidden; over the mouth of
the cave large stones were placed, which remain until this very day.
Conquest of Southern Canaan. 28[k] Makkedah, too, Joshua captured and put to the
sword at that time. He put the city, its king,
and every person in it under the ban, leaving
no survivors. Thus he did to the king of
Makkedah what he had done to the king of
Jericho. 29 Joshua then passed on with all Israel from Makkedah to Libnah, and attacked
it, 30 and the LORD delivered it, with its king,
into the power of Israel. He put it to the
sword with every person there, leaving no
survivors. Thus he did to its king what he
had done to the king of Jericho. 31 Joshua
next passed on with all Israel from Libnah to
Lachish, where they set up a camp during
the attack. 32 The LORD delivered Lachish
into the power of Israel, so that on the second day Joshua captured it and put it to the
sword with every person in it, just as he had
done to Libnah. 33 At that time Horam, king
of Gezer, came up to help Lachish, but
Joshua defeated him and his people, leaving
him no survivors. 34 From Lachish, Joshua
passed on with all Israel to Eglon; encamp-
ing near it, they attacked it 35 and captured it
the same day, putting it to the sword. On that
day he put under the ban every person in it,
just as he had done at Lachish. 36 From Eglon, Joshua went up with all Israel to Hebron, which they attacked 37 and captured.
They put it to the sword with its king, all its
cities, and every person there, leaving no
survivors, just as Joshua had done to Eglon.
He put it under the ban and every person in
it. 38 Then Joshua and all Israel turned back
to Debir and attacked it, 39 capturing it with
its king and all its cities. They put them to
the sword and put under the ban every person in it, leaving no survivors. Thus he did to
Debir and its king what he had done to Hebron, as well as to Libnah and its king.
40[l] Joshua conquered the entire land; the
mountain regions, the Negeb, the Shephelah, and the mountain slopes, with all their
kings. He left no survivors, but put under the
ban every living being, just as the LORD, the
God of Israel, had commanded. 41 Joshua
conquered them from Kadesh-barnea to
Gaza, and all the land of Goshen* to Gibeon.
42 All these kings and their lands Joshua captured all at once, for the LORD, the God of Israel, fought for Israel. 43 Thereupon Joshua
with all Israel returned to the camp at Gilgal.

CHAPTER 11

See RG 151–52

Northern Confederacy. 1 When Jabin,
king of Hazor,* learned of this, he sent a message to Jobab, king of Madon, to the king of
Shimron, to the king of Achshaph, 2 and to the
northern kings in the mountain regions and in
the Arabah near Chinneroth, in the Shephelah, and in Naphath-dor to the west.[m] 3 These
were Canaanites to the east and west, Amorites, Hittites, Perizzites, and Jebusites in the
mountain regions, and Hivites at the foot of
Hermon in the land of Mizpah.[n] 4 They came
out with all their troops, an army numerous
as the sands on the seashore, and with a multitude of horses and chariots.[o] 5 All these
kings made a pact and together they marched
to the waters of Merom,* where they encamped to fight against Israel.

10:41 Goshen: a town and its surrounding district at the southern end of the Judean mountains (cf. 11:16; 15:51); not to be confused with the land of Goshen in northeastern Egypt (Gn 45:10).

11:1–3 Hazor, Madon, Shimron, and **Chinneroth**: cities and their surrounding districts in eastern Galilee. **Achshaph** and **Naphath-dor**: southwest of Galilee. **The mountain regions**: in central and northern Galilee.

11:5 The waters of Merom: of uncertain identification, perhaps Tel Qarnei Hittin, about seven and a half kilometers west of modern Tiberias.

i: Jos 1:9. *j:* Jos 8:29; Dt 21:22–23. *k:* Jos 6:21. *l:* Dt 20:16–17. *m:* Jos 12:3. *n:* Jos 3:10. *o:* Ex 15:1, 21.

6 The LORD said to Joshua, "Do not fear them, for by this time tomorrow I will present them slain to Israel. You must hamstring their horses and burn their chariots." 7 Joshua with his whole army came upon them suddenly at the waters of Merom and fell upon them. 8 The LORD delivered them into the power of the Israelites, who defeated them and pursued them to Greater Sidon, to Misrephoth-maim,[p] and eastward to the valley of Mizpeh. They struck them all down, leaving no survivors. 9 Joshua did to them as the LORD had commanded: he hamstrung their horses and burned their chariots.

Conquest of Northern Canaan. 10 At that time Joshua, turning back, captured Hazor and struck down its king with the sword; for Hazor formerly was the chief of all those kingdoms. 11 He also struck down with the sword every person there, carrying out the ban, till none was left alive. Hazor itself he burned. 12 All the cities of those kings, and the kings themselves, Joshua captured and put to the sword, carrying out the ban on them, as Moses, the servant of the LORD, had commanded.[q] 13 However, Israel did not destroy by fire any of the cities built on their mounds, except Hazor, which Joshua burned. 14 All the spoil and livestock of these cities the Israelites took as plunder; but the people they put to the sword, until they had destroyed the last of them, leaving none alive. 15 As the LORD had commanded his servant Moses, so Moses commanded Joshua, and Joshua acted accordingly.[r] He left nothing undone that the LORD had commanded Moses should be done.

Survey of the Conquest. 16 So Joshua took all this land: the mountain regions, the entire Negeb, all the land of Goshen, the Shephelah, the Arabah, as well as the mountain regions and Shephelah of Israel,[s] 17 from Mount Halak that rises toward Seir[t] as far as Baal-gad in the Lebanon valley at the foot of Mount Hermon. All their kings he captured and put to death. 18 Joshua waged war against all these kings for a long time. 19 With the exception of the Hivites who lived in Gibeon, no city made peace with the Israelites; all were taken in battle.[u] 20 For it was the LORD's doing to make their hearts obstinate to meet Israel in battle, that they might be put under the ban without mercy, and be destroyed as the LORD had commanded Moses.[v]

21* At that time Joshua penetrated the mountain regions and exterminated the Anakim in Hebron,[w] Debir, Anab, the entire mountain region of Judah, and the entire mountain region of Israel. Joshua put them and their cities under the ban, 22 so that no Anakim were left in the land of the Israelites. However, some survived in Gaza, in Gath, and in Ashdod. 23[x] Thus Joshua took the whole land, just as the LORD had said to Moses. Joshua gave it to Israel as their heritage, apportioning it among the tribes. And the land had rest from war.*

CHAPTER 12*

See RG 152–53

Lists of Conquered Kings. 1 These are the kings of the land whom the Israelites conquered and whose lands they occupied, east of the Jordan, from the River Arnon to Mount Hermon, including all the eastern section of the Arabah: 2[y] First, Sihon, king of the Amorites, who lived in Heshbon. His domain extended from Aroer, which is on the bank of the Wadi Arnon, to include the wadi itself, and the land northward through half of Gilead to the Wadi Jabbok at the border with the Ammonites, 3 as well as the Arabah from the eastern side of the Sea of Chinnereth, as far south as the eastern side of the Salt Sea of the Arabah in the direction of Beth-jeshimoth,[z] southward under the slopes of Pisgah.

11:21–23 Most of the land assigned to the tribe of Judah was not conquered by it until the early period of the Judges. See note on Jgs 1:1–36.

11:23 The land had rest from war: later passages (15:13–17; 17:12–13) show individual tribes still fighting against the remaining Canaanites. This verse forms the conclusion to the first part of the book.

12:1–24 This chapter, inserted between the two principal parts of the book (chaps. 1–11 and 13–21), resembles the lists of conquered cities which are inscribed on monuments of Egyptian and Assyrian rulers. Perhaps this list was copied here from some such public Israelite record.

p: Jos 13:6. *q:* Dt 7:2; 20:16–17. *r:* Dt 7:2; 31:7–8. *s:* Jos 10:41; 12:8. *t:* Jos 12:7; Dt 7:24. *u:* Jos 9:3, 7, 15. *v:* Dt 2:30; 20:16–17. *w:* Jos 15:13–14; Nm 13:22; Dt 1:28; 9:1–3. *x:* Jos 14:1–19:51; Nm 34:2–12; Heb 4:8–10. *y:* Nm 21:21–35; Dt 1:4; 2:24–37. *z:* Jos 13:20.

4 Secondly, the border of Og, king of Bashan, a survivor of the Rephaim, who lived at Ashtaroth and Edrei.[a] 5 He ruled over Mount Hermon, Salecah, and all Bashan as far as the boundary of the Geshurites and Maacathites, and over half of Gilead as far as the territory of Sihon, king of Heshbon. 6 It was Moses, the servant of the LORD, and the Israelites who conquered them; Moses, the servant of the LORD, gave possession of their land to the Reubenites, the Gadites, and the half-tribe of Manasseh.[b]

7 This is a list of the kings of the land whom Joshua and the Israelites conquered west of the Jordan, from Baal-gad in the Lebanon valley to Mount Halak which rises toward Seir; Joshua apportioned their land and gave possession of it to the tribes of Israel; 8 it included the mountain regions and Shephelah, the Arabah, the slopes, the wilderness, and the Negeb, belonging to the Hittites, Amorites, Canaanites, Perizzites, Hivites, and Jebusites: 9 The king of Jericho, one;[c] the king of Ai, which is near Bethel, one; 10 the king of Jerusalem, one; the king of Hebron, one; 11 the king of Jarmuth, one; the king of Lachish, one;[d] 12 the king of Eglon, one; the king of Gezer, one;[e] 13 the king of Debir, one; the king of Geder, one;[f] 14 the king of Hormah, one; the king of Arad, one; 15 the king of Libnah, one; the king of Adullam, one;[g] 16 the king of Makkedah, one; the king of Bethel, one;[h] 17 the king of Tappuah, one; the king of Hepher, one;[i] 18 the king of Aphek, one; the king of Lasharon, one;[j] 19 the king of Madon, one; the king of Hazor, one;[k] 20 the king of Shimron, one; the king of Achshaph, one;[l] 21 the king of Taanach, one; the king of Megiddo, one;[m] 22 the king of Kedesh, one; the king of Jokneam, at Carmel, one;[n] 23 the king of Dor, in Naphath-dor, one; the king of Goyim at Gilgal, one;[o] 24 and the king of Tirzah, one—thirty-one kings in all.

II. Division of the Land

CHAPTER 13

See RG 152–53

Division of Land Commanded. 1 When Joshua was old and advanced in years, the LORD said to him:[p] Though now you are old and advanced in years, a very large part of the land still remains to be possessed. 2 This is the remaining land: all Geshur* and all the districts of the Philistines 3 (from the stream adjoining Egypt to the boundary of Ekron in the north is reckoned Canaanite territory, though held by the five lords of the Philistines in Gaza, Ashdod, Ashkelon, Gath, and Ekron); 4 also where the Avvim are in the south;[q] all the land of the Canaanites from Mearah of the Sidonians to Aphek, and the boundaries of the Amorites;[r] 5 and the Gebalite territory; and all the Lebanon on the east, from Baal-gad at the foot of Mount Hermon to Lebo-hamath. 6 All the inhabitants of the mountain regions between Lebanon and Misrephoth-maim, all Sidonians, I will drive out before the Israelites;[s] at least include these areas in the division of the Israelite heritage, just as I have commanded you. 7 Now, therefore, apportion among the nine tribes and the half-tribe of Manasseh the land which is to be their heritage.

The Eastern Tribes. 8[t] Now the other half of the tribe of Manasseh, as well as the Reubenites and Gadites, had taken as their heritage what Moses, the servant of the LORD, had given them east of the Jordan: 9 from Aroer on the bank of the Wadi Arnon and the city in the wadi itself, through the tableland of Medeba and Dibon, 10 with the rest of the cities of Sihon, king of the Amorites, who reigned in Heshbon, to the boundary of the Ammonites; 11 also Gilead and the territory of the Geshurites and Maacathites, all Mount Hermon, and all Bashan as far as Salecah, 12 the entire kingdom in Bashan of Og,

13:2 Geshur: not to be confused with the large Aramean district of the same name in Bashan (vv. 11–13; Dt 3:14); here it is a region to the south of the Philistine country, since vv. 2–5 list the unconquered lands along the coast from south to north; cf. also 1 Sm 27:8.

a: Nm 34:11–12. *b:* Nm 32:33; Dt 3:12–13. *c:* Jos 6:2; 8:23. *d:* Jos 10:23. *e:* Jos 10:23, 33. *f:* Jos 10:38–39; 15:36. *g:* Jos 10:29–30; 15:35. *h:* Jos 8:17; 10:28. *i:* Jos 15:34. *j:* Jos 15:53. *k:* Jos 11:1, 10. *l:* Jos 11:1. *m:* Jos 17:11. *n:* Jos 19:37. *o:* Jos 11:2. *p:* Jos 23:1. *q:* Jgs 3:3. *r:* Jos 1:4. *s:* Jos 11:8. *t:* Jos 12:6; Nm 32:33.

who was king at Ashtaroth and Edrei (he was a holdover from the remnant of the Rephaim). These Moses defeated and dispossessed. [13]But the Israelites did not dispossess the Geshurites and Maacathites, so that Geshur and Maacath dwell in the midst of Israel to this day. [14u] However, Moses assigned no heritage to the tribe of Levi; the LORD, the God of Israel, is their heritage, as the LORD had promised them.

Reuben. [15v] This is what Moses gave to the tribe of the Reubenites by their clans:[w] [16]Their territory reached from Aroer, on the bank of the Wadi Arnon, and the city in the wadi itself, through the tableland about Medeba, [17]to include Heshbon and all its towns on the tableland, Dibon, Bamoth-baal, Beth-baal-meon, [18]Jahaz, Kedemoth, Mephaath, [19]Kiriathaim, Sibmah, Zereth-shahar on the knoll within the valley, [20]Beth-peor, the slopes of Pisgah, Beth-jeshimoth, [21]and the other cities of the tableland and of the whole kingdom of Sihon. This Amorite king, who reigned in Heshbon, Moses had defeated, with the princes of Midian, vassals of Sihon who were settled in the land: Evi, Rekem, Zur, Hur, and Reba;[x] [22]Balaam, son of Beor, the diviner, the Israelites killed with the sword, together with those they struck down.[y] [23]The boundary of the Reubenites was the Jordan. These cities and their villages were the heritage of the Reubenites by their clans.

Gad. [24z] This is what Moses gave to the tribe of the Gadites by their clans: [25]Their territory included Jazer, all the cities of Gilead, and half the land of the Ammonites as far as Aroer, toward Rabbah [26](that is, from Heshbon to Ramath-mizpeh and Betonim, and from Mahanaim to the boundary of Lodebar); [27]and in the Jordan valley: Beth-haram, Beth-nimrah, Succoth, Zaphon, the other part of the kingdom of Sihon, king of Heshbon, with the bank of the Jordan to the southeastern tip of the Sea of Chinnereth. [28]These cities and their villages were the heritage of the clans of the Gadites.

Manasseh. [29a] This is what Moses gave to the half-tribe of Manasseh; the half-tribe of the Manassites, by their clans, had [30]territory including Mahanaim, all of Bashan, the entire kingdom of Og, king of Bashan, and all the villages of Jair, which are sixty cities in Bashan. [31]Half of Gilead, with Ashtaroth and Edrei, royal cities of Og in Bashan, fell to the descendants of Machir, son of Manasseh, to half the Machirites, by their clans.

[32]These are the heritages which Moses gave when he was in the plains of Moab, beyond the Jordan east of Jericho. [33]But Moses gave no heritage to the tribe of Levi: the LORD, the God of Israel, is their heritage, as he had promised them.[b]

CHAPTER 14

See RG 152–53

The Western Tribes. [1]These are the portions which the Israelites received as heritage in the land of Canaan.[c] Eleazar the priest, Joshua, son of Nun, and the heads of families in the tribes of the Israelites determined [2]their heritage by lot, as the LORD had commanded through Moses concerning the remaining nine and a half tribes.[d] [3]To two and a half tribes Moses had already given a heritage beyond the Jordan; to the Levites he had given no heritage among them:[e] [4]the descendants of Joseph formed two tribes, Manasseh and Ephraim. But the Levites were given no share of the land except cities to live in, with their pasture lands for the herds and flocks.[f]

[5]As the LORD had commanded Moses, so the Israelites did: they apportioned the land.

Caleb's Portion. [6g] When the Judahites approached Joshua in Gilgal, the Kenizzite Caleb, son of Jephunneh, said to him: "You know the word the LORD spoke to Moses, the man of God, concerning you and concerning me in Kadesh-barnea. [7h] I was forty years old when Moses, the servant of the LORD, sent me from Kadesh-barnea to reconnoiter the land; and I brought back to him a frank report. [8i] My fellow scouts who went up with me made the people's confidence melt away, but I was completely loyal

u: Jos 14:3–4; Nm 18:20–24. *v:* Dt 3:12–17. *w:* Nm 21:25–31; 32:37–38. *x:* Nm 21:24; 31:8; Dt 3:10. *y:* Nm 31:8. *z:* Nm 32:34–36. *a:* Nm 32:39–42. *b:* Jos 18:7; Nm 18:20. *c:* Jos 17:4; 21:1; Nm 27:19–22; 34:17–18. *d:* Nm 26:55; 33:54; 34:13. *e:* Jos 13:8, 14, 33. *f:* Jos 21:3–40; Gn 48:5. *g:* Nm 14:24, 30; 32:12; Dt 1:36, 38. *h:* Nm 14:6–9. *i:* Nm 13:31–33; 14:24; 32:12; Dt 1:36.

to the LORD, my God. 9On that occasion Moses swore this oath, 'The land where you have set foot shall become your heritage and that of your descendants forever, because you have been completely loyal to the LORD, my God.' 10Now, as he promised, the LORD has preserved me these forty-five years since the LORD spoke thus to Moses while Israel journeyed in the wilderness; and now I am eighty-five years old,[j] 11but I am still as strong today as I was the day Moses sent me forth, with no less vigor whether it be for war or for any other tasks.* [k] 12Now give me this mountain region which the LORD promised me that day, as you yourself heard. True, the Anakim are there, with large fortified cities, but if the LORD is with me I shall be able to dispossess them, as the LORD promised."[l] 13Joshua blessed Caleb, son of Jephunneh, and gave him Hebron as his heritage.[m] 14Therefore Hebron remains the heritage of the Kenizzite Caleb, son of Jephunneh, to the present day, because he was completely loyal to the LORD, the God of Israel. 15Hebron was formerly called Kiriath-arba, for Arba, the greatest among the Anakim.[n] And the land had rest from war.

CHAPTER 15

See RG 152–53

Boundaries of Judah. 1The lot for the tribe of Judah by their clans fell toward the boundary of Edom, the wilderness of Zin in the Negeb, in the extreme south.[o] 2[p] Their southern boundary ran from the end of the Salt Sea,* from the tongue of land that faces the Negeb, 3and went southward below the pass of Akrabbim, across through Zin, up to a point south of Kadesh-barnea, across to Hezron, and up to Addar; from there, looping around Karka, 4it crossed to Azmon and then joined the Wadi of Egypt* before coming out at the sea. (This is your southern boundary.) 5The eastern boundary was the Salt Sea as far as the mouth of the Jordan.

The northern boundary climbed northward from the tongue of the sea, toward the mouth of the Jordan, 6[q] up to Beth-hoglah, and ran north of Beth-arabah, up to Eben-Bohan-ben-Reuben. 7Thence the boundary climbed to Debir, north of the Valley of Achor,[r] in the direction of the Gilgal that faces the pass of Adummim, on the south side of the wadi; from there it crossed to the waters of En-shemesh and emerged at En-rogel. 8Climbing again to the Valley of Ben-hinnom* on the southern flank of the Jebusites (that is, Jerusalem), the boundary rose to the top of the mountain at the northern end of the Valley of Rephaim,[s] which bounds the Valley of Hinnom on the west. 9From the top of the mountain it ran to the fountain of waters of Nephtoah,[t] extended to the cities of Mount Ephron, and continued to Baalah, or Kiriath-jearim. 10From Baalah the boundary curved westward to Mount Seir and passed north of the ridge of Mount Jearim (that is, Chesalon); it descended to Beth-shemesh, and ran across to Timnah. 11It then extended along the northern flank of Ekron, continued through Shikkeron, and across to Mount Baalah, from there to include Jabneel, before it came out at the sea. 12The western boundary was the Great Sea* and its coast. This was the complete boundary of the Judahites by their clans.

Conquest by Caleb. 13[u] As the LORD had commanded, Joshua gave Caleb, son of Jephunneh,[v] a portion among the Judahites, namely, Kiriath-arba (Arba was the father of Anak), that is, Hebron. 14[w] And Caleb dispossessed from there the three Anakim, the descendants of Anak: Sheshai, Ahiman, and Talmai. 15From there he marched up against the inhabitants of Debir,[x] which was formerly called Kiriath-sepher. 16Caleb said,

14:11 War . . . other tasks: lit., "to go forth and to come in," i.e., to conduct military expeditions and to return after victory; cf. 1 Sm 18:16; 2 Sm 5:2.

15:2 Salt Sea: the Dead Sea. The "tongue," a prominent feature of the landscape, is a spit of land thrusting into the Dead Sea from its eastern shore; it is now called by its Arabic name, *'el lisân*, "tongue."

15:4 Wadi of Egypt: the natural boundary between Gaza and the Sinai Peninsula.

15:8 The Valley of Ben-hinnom: the southern limit of Jerusalem. *Ben-hinnom* means "son of Hinnom." The place was also called Valley of Hinnom, in Hebrew *ge-hinnom*, whence the word "Gehenna" is derived.

15:12 Great Sea: the Mediterranean.

j: Nm 14:30. *k:* Sir 46:1–10. *l:* Jos 11:21–22. *m:* Jos 10:36–37; 15:13–19; 21:11–12. *n:* Jgs 1:10. *o:* Nm 34:3. *p:* Nm 34:3–12. *q:* Jos 18:18–19, 22. *r:* Jos 7:26; 18:16–18. *s:* Jos 18:16. *t:* Jos 18:15. *u:* Jgs 1:10–15. *v:* Jos 14:13–15. *w:* Nm 13:22; Jgs 1:20. *x:* Jos 10:38.

"To the man who attacks Kiriath-sepher and
captures it, I will give my daughter Achsah in
marriage." 17* Othniel captured it, the son of
Caleb's brother Kenaz; so Caleb gave him
his daughter Achsah in marriage. 18 When she
came to him, she induced him to ask her father for some land. Then, as she alighted
from the donkey, Caleb asked her, "What do
you want?" 19 She answered, "Give me a
present! Since you have assigned to me land
in the Negeb, give me also pools of water."
So he gave her the upper and the lower pools.

Cities of Judah.* 20 This is the heritage of
the tribe of Judahites by their clans: 21 The
cities of the tribe of the Judahites in the extreme southern district toward Edom were:
Kabzeel, Eder, Jagur, 22 Kinah, Dimonah,
Adadah, 23 Kedesh, Hazor, and Ithnan;
24 Ziph, Telem, Bealoth, 25 Hazor-hadattah,
and Kerioth-hezron (that is, Hazor);
26 Amam, Shema, Moladah, 27 Hazar-gaddah,
Heshmon, Beth-pelet, 28 Hazar-shual, Beer-
sheba, and Biziothiah; 29 Baalah, Iim, Ezem,
30 Eltolad, Chesil, Hormah, 31 Ziklag, Madmannah, Sansannah, 32 Lebaoth, Shilhim,
and Ain and Rimmon; a total of twenty-nine
cities with their villages.

33 In the Shephelah: Eshtaol, Zorah, Ashnah, 34 Zanoah, Engannim, Tappuah, Enam,
35 Jarmuth, Adullam, Socoh, Azekah, 36 Shaaraim, Adithaim, Gederah, and Gederothaim;
fourteen cities and their villages. 37 Zenan,
Hadashah, Migdal-gad, 38 Dilean, Mizpeh,
Joktheel, 39 Lachish, Bozkath, Eglon, 40 Cab-
bon, Lahmas, Chitlish, 41 Gederoth, Beth-dagon, Naamah, and Makkedah; sixteen cities
and their villages. 42 Libnah, Ether, Ashan,
43 Iphtah, Ashnah, Nezib, 44 Keilah, Achzib,
and Mareshah; nine cities and their villages.
45 Ekron and its towns and villages; 46 from
Ekron to the sea, all the towns that lie alongside Ashdod, and their villages; 47 Ashdod
and its towns and villages; Gaza and its
towns and villages, as far as the Wadi of
Egypt and the coast of the Great Sea.

48 In the mountain regions: Shamir, Jattir,
Socoh, 49 Dannah, Kiriath-sannah (that is,
Debir), 50 Anab, Eshtemoh, Anim, 51 Goshen,
Holon, and Giloh; eleven cities and their villages. 52 Arab, Dumah, Eshan, 53 Janim, Beth-
tappuah, Aphekah, 54 Humtah, Kiriath-arba
(that is, Hebron), and Zior; nine cities and
their villages. 55 Maon, Carmel, Ziph, Juttah,
56 Jezreel, Jokdeam, Zanoah, 57 Kain,
Gibbeah, and Timnah; ten cities and their villages. 58 Halhul, Beth-zur, Gedor, 59 Maarath,
Beth-anoth, and Eltekon; six cities and their
villages. Tekoa, Ephrathah (that is, Bethlehem), Peor, Etam, Kulom, Tatam, Zores,
Karim, Gallim, Bether, and Manoko; eleven
cities and their villages. 60 Kiriath-baal (that
is, Kiriath-jearim) and Rabbah; two cities
and their villages.[y]

61 In the wilderness:* Beth-arabah, Middin, Secacah, 62 Nibshan, Ir-hamelah, and
En-gedi; six cities and their villages. 63 But
the Jebusites who lived in Jerusalem the Judahites could not dispossess; so the Jebusites dwell in Jerusalem beside the Judahites
to the present day.[z]

CHAPTER 16

See RG 152–53

The Joseph Tribes.* 1 The lot that fell
to the Josephites extended from the Jordan at
Jericho to the waters of Jericho east of the
wilderness; then the boundary went up from
Jericho to the heights at Bethel.* 2 Leaving
Bethel for Luz, it crossed the ridge to the
border of the Archites at Ataroth, 3 and descended westward to the border of the
Japhletites, to that of the Lower Beth-horon,
and to Gezer, and from there to the sea.[a]

Ephraim. 4 Within the heritage of Manasseh and Ephraim, sons of Joseph, 5 the divid-

15:17–19 The story of Othniel is told again in Jgs 1:13–15; cf. also Jgs 3:9–11.

15:20–62 This elaborate list of the cities of Judah was probably taken from a document made originally for administrative purposes; the cities are divided into four provincial districts, some of which have further subdivisions. For similar lists of the cities of Judah, cf. 19:2–7; 1 Chr 4:28–32; Neh 11:25–30. This list has suffered in transmission, so that the totals given in vv. 32 and 36 are not exact; many of the cities cannot be identified.

15:61 In the wilderness: in the Jordan rift near the Dead Sea.

16:1–17:18 After the boundaries and cities of Judah, the most important tribe, are given, the land of the next most important group, the two Joseph tribes of Ephraim and Manasseh, is described, though it was separated from Judah by the territories of Benjamin (18:11–20) and Dan (19:40–48).

16:1–3 This line formed the southern boundary of Ephraim and the northern boundaries of Benjamin and of Dan.

y: Jos 18:14. *z*: Jgs 1:21; 2 Sm 5:6. *a*: Jos 10:10, 33.

ing line* for the heritage of the Ephraimites by their clans ran from east of Ataroth-addar to Upper Beth-horon[b] 6and thence to the sea. From Michmethath[c] on the north, their boundary curved eastward around Taanath-shiloh, and continued east of it to Janoah; 7from there it descended to Ataroth and Naarah, and reaching Jericho, it ended at the Jordan. 8From Tappuah the boundary ran westward to the Wadi Kanah and ended at the sea. This was the heritage of the Ephraimites by their clans, 9including the villages that belonged to each city set aside for the Ephraimites within the heritage of the Manassites. 10But they did not dispossess the Canaanites living in Gezer;[d] they live within Ephraim to the present day, though they have been put to forced labor.

See RG 152–53

CHAPTER 17

Manasseh. 1[e] Now as for the lot that fell to the tribe of Manasseh[f] as the firstborn of Joseph: since Manasseh's eldest son, Machir, the father of Gilead, was a warrior, who had already obtained Gilead and Bashan, 2the allotment was now made to the rest of the Manassites by their clans: the descendants of Abiezer, Helek, Asriel, Shechem, Hepher, and Shemida; these are the other male children of Manasseh, son of Joseph, by their clans.

3[g] Furthermore, Zelophehad, son of Hepher, son of Gilead, son of Machir, son of Manasseh, had no sons, but only daughters, whose names were Mahlah, Noah, Hoglah, Milcah, and Tirzah. 4These presented themselves to Eleazar the priest, to Joshua, son of Nun, and to the leaders, saying, "The LORD commanded Moses to give us a heritage among our relatives." So in accordance with the command of the LORD a heritage was given them among their father's relatives. 5Thus ten shares fell to Manasseh apart from the land of Gilead and Bashan beyond the Jordan,[h] 6since these female descendants of Manasseh received each a portion among his sons. The land of Gilead fell to the rest of the Manassites.

7Manasseh bordered on Asher.* From Michmethath, near Shechem, another boundary ran southward to include the inhabitants of En-Tappuah, 8because the district of Tappuah belonged to Manasseh, although Tappuah itself was an Ephraimite city on the border of Manasseh. 9This same boundary continued down to the Wadi Kanah.[i] The cities that belonged to Ephraim from among the cities in Manasseh were those to the south of that wadi; thus the territory of Manasseh ran north of the wadi and ended at the sea. 10The land on the south belonged to Ephraim and that on the north to Manasseh; with the sea as their common boundary, they reached Asher on the north and Issachar on the east.

11[j] Moreover, in Issachar and in Asher Manasseh was awarded Beth-shean and its towns, Ibleam and its towns, the inhabitants of Dor and its towns, the inhabitants of Endor and its towns, the inhabitants of Taanach and its towns, the inhabitants of Megiddo and its towns (the third is Naphath-dor). 12Since the Manassites were not able to dispossess these cities, the Canaanites continued to inhabit this region. 13When the Israelites grew stronger they put the Canaanites to forced labor, but they did not dispossess them.

Protest of Joseph Tribes. 14The descendants of Joseph said to Joshua, "Why have you given us only one lot and one share as our heritage?[k] Our people are too many, because of the extent to which the LORD has blessed us." 15Joshua answered them, "If you are too many, go up to the forest and clear out a place for yourselves there in the land of the Perizzites and Rephaim, since the mountain regions of Ephraim are so narrow." 16For the Josephites said, "Our moun-

16:5 The dividing line: separating Ephraim from Manasseh. Ephraim's northern border (v. 5) is given in an east-to-west direction; its eastern border (vv. 6–7) in a north-to-south direction.

17:7 Manasseh bordered on Asher: only at the extreme northwestern section of Manasseh's territory. The boundary given in the following sentences (vv. 7–10) is a more detailed description of the one already mentioned in 16:5–7, as separating Manasseh from Ephraim.

b: Jos 18:13. *c:* Jos 17:7–9. *d:* Jgs 1:29. *e:* Nm 26:29–33. *f:* Gn 41:51; 46:20; 48:18; 50:23; Dt 3:13, 15. *g:* Nm 27:1–7; 36:2. *h:* Nm 13:30–31. *i:* Jos 16:8–9. *j:* 1 Chr 7:29. *k:* Jos 16:4; Gn 48:19–22.

tain regions are not enough for us; on the other hand, the Canaanites living in the valley region all have iron chariots, in particular those in Beth-shean and its towns, and those in the valley of Jezreel." 17Joshua therefore said to Ephraim and Manasseh, the house of Joseph, "You are a numerous people and very strong. You shall not have merely one share, 18for the mountain region which is now forest shall be yours when you clear it. Its adjacent land shall also be yours if, despite their strength and iron chariots, you dispossess the Canaanites."

CHAPTER 18

See RG 152-53

1The whole community of the Israelites assembled at Shiloh, where they set up the tent of meeting; and the land was subdued before them.[l]

The Seven Remaining Portions. 2There remained seven tribes among the Israelites that had not yet received their heritage. 3Joshua therefore said to the Israelites, "How much longer will you put off taking steps to possess the land which the LORD, the God of your ancestors, has given you? 4Choose three representatives from each of your tribes; I will send them to go throughout the land and describe it for purposes of acquiring their heritage. When they return to me 5you shall divide it into seven parts. Judah is to retain its territory in the south,[m] and the house of Joseph its territory in the north. 6You shall bring to me here the description of the land in seven sections. I will then cast lots for you here before the LORD, our God. 7For the Levites have no share among you,[n] because the priesthood of the LORD is their heritage; while Gad, Reuben, and the half-tribe of Manasseh have already received the heritage east of the Jordan which Moses, the servant of the LORD, gave them."

8When those who were to describe the land were ready for their journey, Joshua commanded them, "Go throughout the land and describe it; return to me and I will cast lots for you here before the LORD in Shiloh." 9So they went through the land, described its cities in writing in seven sections, and returned to Joshua in the camp at Shiloh. 10Joshua then cast lots for them before the LORD in Shiloh, and divided up the land for the Israelites into their separate shares.

Benjamin. 11One lot fell to the tribe of Benjaminites by their clans. The territory allotted them lay between the descendants of Judah and those of Joseph. 12[o] Their northern boundary* began at the Jordan and went over the northern flank of Jericho, up westward into the mountains, until it reached the wilderness of Beth-aven. 13From there it crossed over to the southern flank of Luz (that is, Bethel). Then it ran down to Ataroth-addar, on the mountaintop south of Lower Beth-horon.[p] 14For the western border, the boundary line swung south from the mountaintop opposite Beth-horon until it reached Kiriath-baal (that is, Kiriath-jearim; this city belonged to the Judahites). This was the western boundary. 15The southern boundary began at the limits of Kiriath-jearim and projected to the spring at Nephtoah. 16[q] It went down to the edge of the mountain on the north of the Valley of Rephaim, where it faces the Valley of Ben-hinnom; and continuing down the Valley of Hinnom along the southern flank of the Jebusites, reached En-rogel. 17Inclining to the north, it extended to En-shemesh, and thence to Geliloth, opposite the pass of Adummim. Then it dropped to Eben-Bohan-ben-Reuben, 18across the northern flank of the Arabah overlook, down into the Arabah. 19From there the boundary continued across the northern flank of Beth-hoglah and extended northward to the tongue of the Salt Sea, toward the southern end of the Jordan. This was the southern boundary. 20The Jordan bounded it on the east. This was how the heritage of the Benjaminites by their clans was bounded on all sides.

21Now the cities belonging to the tribe of the Benjaminites by their clans were: Jericho, Beth-hoglah, Emek-keziz, 22Beth-arabah, Zemaraim, Bethel, 23Avvim, Parah,

18:12–20 Benjamin's northern boundary (vv. 12–13) corresponded to part of the southern boundary of Ephraim (16:1–2). Their western border (v. 14) was the eastern border of Dan (cf. 19:40–47). Their southern boundary (vv. 15–19) corresponded to part of the northern boundary of Judah (15:5–9).

l: Jos 11:23; 14:15; 19:51. *m:* Jos 15:1–17:18. *n:* Jos 13:8, 33. *o:* Jos 16:1–5. *p:* Gn 28:19. *q:* Jos 15:6–8.

Ophra, [24]Chephar-ammoni, Ophni, and Geba; twelve cities and their villages. [25]Also Gibeon, Ramah, Beeroth, [26]Mizpeh, Chephirah, Mozah, [27]Rekem, Irpeel, Taralah, [28]Zela, Haeleph, the Jebusite city (that is, Jerusalem), Gibeah, and Kiriath; fourteen cities and their villages. This was the heritage of the clans of Benjaminites.

CHAPTER 19

See RG 152–53

Simeon. [1]The second lot fell to Simeon. The heritage of the tribe of Simeonites by their clans lay within that of the Judahites. [2][r] For their heritage they received Beer-sheba, Shema, Moladah, [3]Hazar-shual, Balah, Ezem, [4]Eltolad, Bethul, Hormah, [5]Ziklag, Bethmar-caboth, Hazar-susah, [6]Beth-lebaoth, and Sharuhen; thirteen cities and their villages. [7]Also Ain, Rimmon, Ether, and Ashan; four cities and their villages, [8]besides all the villages around these cities as far as Baalath-beer (that is, Ramoth-negeb). This was the heritage of the tribe of the Simeonites by their clans. [9]This heritage of the Simeonites was within the confines of the Judahites; for since the portion of the latter was too large for them, the Simeonites obtained their heritage within it.

Zebulun. [10]* The third lot fell to the Zebulunites by their clans. The boundary of their heritage was at Sarid. [11]Their boundary went up west and through Mareal, reaching Dabbesheth and the wadi that is near Jokneam. [12]From Sarid eastward it ran to the district of Chisloth-tabor, on to Daberath, and up to Japhia. [13]From there it continued eastward to Gath-hepher and to Eth-kazin, extended to Rimmon, and turned to Neah. [14]Skirting north of Hannathon, the boundary ended at the valley of Iphtahel. [15]Thus, with Kattath, Nahalal, Shimron, Idalah, and Bethlehem, there were twelve cities and their villages. [16]This was the heritage of the Zebulunites by their clans, these cities and their villages.

Issachar. [17]* The fourth lot fell to Issachar. The territory of the Issacharites by their clans [18]included Jezreel, Chesulloth, Shunem, [19]Hapharaim, Shion, Anaharath, [20]Rabbith, Kishion, Ebez, [21]Remeth, En-gannim, Enhaddah, and Beth-pazzez. [22]The boundary reached Tabor, Shahazumah, and Beth-shemesh, ending at the Jordan: sixteen cities and their villages. [23]This was the heritage of the Issacharites by their clans, these cities and their villages.

Asher. [24]* The fifth lot fell to the Asherites by their clans. [25]Their territory included Helkath, Hali, Beten, Achshaph, [26]Allammelech, Amad, and Mishal, and reached Carmel on the west, and Shihor-libnath. [27]In the other direction, it ran eastward of Beth-dagon, reached Zebulun and the valley of Iphtahel; then north of Beth-emek and Neiel, it extended northward to Cabul, [28]Ebron, Rehob,[s] Hammon, and Kanah, near Greater Sidon. [29]Then the boundary turned back to Ramah and to the fortress city of Tyre; thence it cut back to Hosah and ended at the sea. Thus, with Mahalab, Achzib, [30]Ummah, Acco, Aphek, and Rehob, there were twenty-two cities and their villages. [31]This was the heritage of the tribe of the Asherites by their clans, these cities and their villages.

Naphtali. [32]* The sixth lot fell to the Naphtalites. [33]Their boundary extended from Heleph, from the oak at Zaanannim, including Adami-nekeb and Jabneel, to Lakkum, and ended at the Jordan. [34]In the opposite direc-

19:10–16 Zebulun's territory was in the central section of the Jezreel Valley and of southern Galilee; it was bounded on the south by Manasseh, on the southeast by Issachar, on the northeast and north by Naphtali, and on the west by Asher. The site of the later city of Nazareth was within its borders. Bethlehem of Zebulun was, of course, distinct from the city of the same name in Judah. **Twelve cities**: apparently seven of the names are missing from v. 15, unless some of the places mentioned in vv. 12–14 are to be included in the number.

19:17–23 Issachar's land was on the eastern watershed of the Jezreel Valley, but also included the southeastern end of the Galilean mountains. It was surrounded by Manasseh on the south and east, by Naphtali on the north, and by Zebulun on the west. Jezreel (v. 18) dominated the valley to which it gave its name, the later form of which was Esdraelon.

19:24–31 Asher inherited the western slope of the Galilean hills as far as the Mediterranean, with Manasseh to the south, Zebulun and Naphtali to the east, and Phoenicia to the north.

19:32–39 Naphtali received eastern Galilee; Asher was to the west and Zebulun and Issachar were to the south, while the upper Jordan and Mount Hermon formed the eastern border. Part of the tribe of Dan later on occupied the northern extremity of Naphtali's lands, at the sources of the Jordan (v. 47).

r: 1 Chr 4:28–33. *s:* Jgs 1:31.

tion, westerly, it ran through Aznoth-tabor and from there extended to Hukkok; it reached Zebulun on the south, Asher on the west, and the Jordan on the east. 35 The fortified cities were Ziddim, Zer, Hammath, Rakkath, Chinnereth, 36 Adamah, Ramah, Hazor, 37 Kedesh, Edrei, En-hazor, 38 Yiron, Migdal-el, Horem, Beth-anath, and Beth-shemesh;[t] nineteen cities and their villages. 39 This was the heritage of the tribe of the Naphtalites by their clans, these cities and their villages.

Dan. 40* The seventh lot fell to the tribe of Danites by their clans. 41 Their heritage was the territory of Zorah, Eshtaol, Ir-shemesh, 42 Shaalabbin, Aijalon, Ithlah,[u] 43 Elon, Timnah, Ekron, 44 Eltekoh, Gibbethon, Baalath, 45 Jehud, Bene-berak, Gath-rimmon, 46 Mejarkon, and Rakkon, with the coast at Joppa. 47[v] But the territory of the Danites was too small for them; so the Danites marched up and attacked Leshem,* which they captured and put to the sword. Once they had taken possession of Leshem, they dwelt there and named it after their ancestor Dan. 48 This was the heritage of the tribe of the Danites by their clans, these cities and their villages.

Joshua's City. 49 When the last of them had received the portions of the land they were to inherit, the Israelites assigned a heritage in their midst to Joshua, son of Nun. 50 According to the command of the LORD, they gave him the city he requested, Timnah-serah[w] in the mountain region of Ephraim. He rebuilt the city and made it his home.

51 These are the heritages which Eleazar the priest, Joshua, son of Nun, and the heads of families in the tribes of the Israelites apportioned by lot in the presence of the LORD, at the door of the tent of meeting in Shiloh. Thus they finished dividing the land.

CHAPTER 20

See RG 153–54

Cities of Refuge. 1[x] The LORD said to Joshua:* 2 Tell the Israelites: Designate for yourselves the cities of refuge of which I spoke to you through Moses, 3 to which anyone guilty of inadvertent and unintentional homicide may flee for asylum from the avenger of blood. 4 To one of these cities the killer shall flee, and standing at the entrance of the city gate, shall plead his case in the hearing of the elders of the city, who must receive him and assign him a place in which to live among them. 5 Though the avenger of blood pursues him, they shall not deliver up to him the one who killed a neighbor unintentionally, when there had been no hatred previously. 6 Once he has stood judgment before the community, he shall live on in that city until the death of the high priest who is in office at the time. Then the killer may return home to the city from where he originally fled.

List of Cities. 7 So they set apart Kedesh in Galilee in the mountain region of Naphtali, Shechem in the mountain region of Ephraim, and Kiriath-arba (that is, Hebron) in the mountain region of Judah.[y] 8 And beyond the Jordan east of Jericho they designated Bezer in the wilderness on the tableland in the tribe of Reuben, Ramoth in Gilead in the tribe of Gad, and Golan in Bashan in the tribe of Manasseh.[z] 9 These are the designated cities to which any Israelite or alien residing among them who had killed a person unintentionally might flee to escape death at the hand of the avenger of blood, until the killer could appear before the community.

CHAPTER 21

See RG 153–54

Levitical Cities. 1 The heads of the Levite families* approached Eleazar the priest, Joshua, son of Nun, and the heads of families of the other tribes of the Israelites[a] 2 at Shiloh in the land of Canaan, and said to them, "The LORD commanded, through Moses, that cities be given us to dwell in, with pasture lands for our livestock."[b] 3 Out of

19:40–46 The original territory of Dan was a small enclave between Judah, Benjamin, Ephraim, and the Philistines.

19:47 Leshem: called Laish in Jgs 18, where the story of the migration of the Danites is told at greater length.

20:1–9 The laws concerning the cities of refuge are given in Nm 35:9–28; Dt 19:1–13; see notes on Nm 35:16–25; Dt 19:2.

21:1 The order to establish special cities for the Levites is given in Nm 35:1–8. The forty-eight cities listed here were hardly the exclusive possession of the Levites; at least the

t: Jgs 1:33. *u:* Jgs 1:35. *v:* Jgs 18:27–29. *w:* Jos 24:30; Jgs 2:9. *x:* Ex 21:12–14; Nm 35:9–15; Dt 4:41–43; 19:1–10. *y:* Jos 15:13; 19:37; 21:21. *z:* Jos 21:27, 36. *a:* Ex 6:16–19; Nm 3:17–20. *b:* Nm 35:1–8.

their own heritage, according to the command of the LORD, the Israelites gave the Levites the following cities with their pasture lands.

4 When the first lot among the Levites fell to the clans of the Kohathites, the descendants of Aaron the priest obtained by lot from the tribes of Judah, Simeon, and Benjamin, thirteen cities. 5 From the clans of the tribe of Ephraim, from the tribe of Dan, and from the half-tribe of Manasseh, the rest of the Kohathites obtained by lot ten cities.[c] 6 From the clans of the tribe of Issachar, from the tribe of Asher, from the tribe of Naphtali, and from the half-tribe of Manasseh, the Gershonites obtained by lot thirteen cities. 7 From the tribes of Reuben, Gad, and Zebulun, the clans of the Merarites obtained twelve cities. 8 These cities with their pasture lands the Israelites gave by lot to the Levites, as the LORD had commanded through Moses.

Cities of the Priests. 9[d] From the tribes of the Judahites and Simeonites they gave the following cities 10 and assigned them to the descendants of Aaron in the Kohathite clan of the Levites, since the first lot fell to them: 11 first, Kiriath-arba (Arba was the father of Anak), that is, Hebron, in the mountain region of Judah, with the adjacent pasture lands, 12 although the open country and villages belonging to the city had been given to Caleb, son of Jephunneh, as his holding.[e] 13 Thus to the descendants of Aaron the priest were given the city of refuge for homicides at Hebron, with its pasture lands; also, Libnah with its pasture lands, 14 Jattir with its pasture lands, Eshtemoa with its pasture lands, 15 Holon with its pasture lands, Debir with its pasture lands, 16 Ain with its pasture lands, Juttah with its pasture lands, and Beth-shemesh with its pasture lands: nine cities from these two tribes. 17 From the tribe of Benjamin they obtained Gibeon with its pasture lands, Geba with its pasture lands, 18 Anathoth[f] with its pasture lands, and Almon with its pasture lands: four cities. 19 These cities which with their pasture lands belonged to the priestly descendants of Aaron, were thirteen in all.

Cities of the Other Kohathites. 20[g] The rest of the Kohathite clans among the Levites obtained by lot, from the tribe of Ephraim, four cities. 21 They were assigned, with its pasture lands, the city of refuge for homicides at Shechem in the mountain region of Ephraim; also Gezer with its pasture lands, 22 Kibzaim with its pasture lands, and Beth-horon with its pasture lands. 23 From the tribe of Dan they obtained Elteke with its pasture lands, Gibbethon with its pasture lands, 24 Aijalon with its pasture lands, and Gath-rimmon with its pasture lands: four cities. 25 From the half-tribe of Manasseh, Taanach with its pasture lands, and Gath-rimmon with its pasture lands: two cities. 26 These cities which with their pasture lands belonged to the rest of the Kohathite clans were ten in all.

Cities of the Gershonites. 27[h] The Gershonite clan of the Levites received from the half-tribe of Manasseh the city of refuge for homicides at Golan in Bashan, with its pasture lands; and also Beth-Astharoth with its pasture lands: two cities. 28 From the tribe of Issachar they obtained Kishion with its pasture lands, Daberath with its pasture lands, 29 Jarmuth with its pasture lands, and En-gannim with its pasture lands: four cities. 30 From the tribe of Asher, Mishal with its pasture lands, Abdon with its pasture lands, 31 Helkath with its pasture lands, and Rehob with its pasture lands: four cities. 32 From the tribe of Naphtali, the city of refuge for homicides at Kedesh in Galilee, with its pasture lands; also Hammath with its pasture lands, and Kartan with its pasture lands: three cities. 33 The cities which belonged to the Gershonite clans, with their pasture lands, were thirteen in all.

Cities of the Merarites. 34[i] The Merarite clans, the last of the Levites, received, from the tribe of Zebulun, Jokneam with its pasture lands, Kartah with its pasture lands, 35 Dimnah with its pasture lands, and Nahalal with its pasture lands: four cities. 36 Also,

more important of them, such as Hebron, Shechem, and Ramoth in Gilead, were certainly peopled for the most part by the tribe in whose territory they were situated. But in all these cities the Levites had special property rights which they did not possess in other cities; cf. Lv 25:32–34.

c: Gn 46:11. *d:* 1 Chr 6:39–66. *e:* Jos 14:14; 15:13. *f:* Jer 1:1. *g:* 1 Chr 6:51–55. *h:* 1 Chr 6:56–61. *i:* 1 Chr 6:62–66.

Mediterranean Sea
ASHER
NAPHTALI
Kedesh
Abdon
MANASSEH
Rehob
Rimmon (Dimnah)
Hammath-dor
Golan
ZEBULUN
Daberath
BASHAN
Helkath
Jokneam
Kishion
ISSACHAR
Jarmuth
Taanach
Ramoth-gilead?
MANASSEH
GILEAD
GAD
Shechem
Mahanaim
Gath-rimmon
Shiloh
DAN
EPHRAIM
Jazer
Beth-horon
Elteke?
Gibeon
Geba
Gibbethon
Gezer
Aijalon
BENJAMIN
Almon
Anathoth
Heshbon
Bezer?
Beth-shemesh
Holon?
REUBEN
Libnah
Hebron (Kiriath-arba)
Kedemoth?
JUDAH
Dead Sea
Juttah
Debir
Eshtemoa
Jattir
SIMEON
33°
32°
31°
35°
36°
0 10 20 Miles
0 10 20 Kilometers

Levitical Cities

across the Jordan, from the tribe of Reuben,
the city of refuge for homicides at Bezer with
its pasture lands, Jahaz with its pasture lands,
37 Kedemoth with its pasture lands, and
Mephaath with its pasture lands: four cities.
38 From the tribe of Gad, the city of refuge for
homicides at Ramoth in Gilead with its pasture lands, Mahanaim with its pasture lands,
39 Heshbon with its pasture lands, and Jazer
with its pasture lands: four cities in all. 40 The
cities allotted to the Merarite clans, the last of
the Levites, were therefore twelve in all.

41 Thus the total number of cities[j] within
the territory of the Israelites which, with
their pasture lands, belonged to the Levites,
was forty-eight. 42 With each and every one
of these cities went the pasture lands round
about it.

43 And so the LORD gave Israel the entire
land he had sworn to their ancestors he
would give them.[k] Once they had taken possession of it, and dwelt in it, 44 the LORD gave
them peace on every side, just as he had
promised their ancestors. Not one of their
enemies could withstand them; the LORD
gave all their enemies into their power. 45 Not
a single word of the blessing[l] that the LORD
had promised to the house of Israel failed; it
all came true.

III. Return of the Transjordan Tribes and Joshua's Farewell

CHAPTER 22

See RG 154

The Eastern Tribes Dismissed. 1 At
that time Joshua summoned the Reubenites,
the Gadites, and the half-tribe of Manasseh
2 and said to them:[m] "You have observed all
that Moses, the servant of the LORD, commanded you, and have listened to my voice
in everything I commanded you. 3 For many
years now, even until today, you have not
abandoned your allies, but have taken care
to observe the commands of the LORD, your
God. 4 Now that the LORD, your God, has settled your allies as he promised them, you
may return to your tents, to your own land,
which Moses, the servant of the LORD, gave
you, across the Jordan.[n] 5 But be very careful
to observe the commandment and the law
which Moses, the servant of the LORD, commanded you: love the LORD, your God,[o] follow him in all his ways, keep his commandments, hold fast to him, and serve him with
your whole heart and your whole self."
6 Joshua then blessed them and sent them
away, and they went to their tents.

7 (For, to half of the tribe of Manasseh Moses had assigned land in Bashan;[p] and to the
other half Joshua had given a portion along
with their allies west of the Jordan.) When
Joshua sent them away to their tents and
blessed them, 8 he said, "Now that you are returning to your own tents with great wealth,
with abundant livestock, with silver, gold,
bronze and iron, and with a very large supply of clothing, divide these spoils of your
enemies with your allies there."[q] 9 So the
Reubenites, the Gadites, and the half-tribe of
Manasseh left the other Israelites at Shiloh
in the land of Canaan and returned to the
land of Gilead, their own land, which they
had received according to the LORD's command through Moses.[r]

The Altar Beside the Jordan. 10 When the
Reubenites, the Gadites, and the half-tribe of
Manasseh came to the region of the Jordan
in the land of Canaan, they built an altar
there at the Jordan, an impressively large altar. 11 The other Israelites heard the report:[s]
"The Reubenites, the Gadites, and the half-
tribe of Manasseh have built an altar" in the
region of the Jordan facing the land of Canaan,* across from the Israelites. 12 When the
Israelites heard this, they assembled at Shiloh, as the entire Israelite community to take
military action against them.*

22:11 In the region of the Jordan facing the land of Canaan: on the eastern side of the Jordan valley. The river itself formed the boundary between these eastern tribes and the rest of the tribes who lived in what was formerly Canaan—though the term "Canaan" could also be used of both sides of the Jordan valley (cf. v. 10). The Transjordan tribes naturally built their altar in their own territory.

22:12 To take military action against them: the western

j: Nm 35:7. *k:* Gn 12:7; 13:15; 15:18; 26:3; 28:4, 13. *l:* Jos 23:14–15. *m:* Jos 1:12–17; Nm 32:20–32; Dt 3:18–20. *n:* Jos 13:8. *o:* Dt 6:5–6, 17; 10:12; 11:1, 13, 22. *p:* Jos 17:5. *q:* Nm 31:27. *r:* Jos 18:1; Nm 32:1, 26, 29. *s:* Dt 12:5, 11–14; 13:13–17.

Accusation of the Western Tribes. [13]The Israelites sent Phinehas, son of Eleazar the priest, to the Reubenites, the Gadites, and the half-tribe of Manasseh in the land of Gilead,[t] [14]and with him ten leaders, one from each tribe of Israel, each one the head of an ancestral house among the clans of Israel. [15]When these came to the Reubenites, the Gadites, and the half-tribe of Manasseh in the land of Gilead, they said to them: [16]"Thus says the whole community of the LORD: What act of treachery is this you have committed against the God of Israel? This day you have turned from following the LORD; by building an altar of your own you have rebelled against the LORD this day. [17]Is the iniquity of Peor not enough, by which we made ourselves impure, even to this day, and a plague came upon the community of the LORD?[u] [18]If today you turn away from following the LORD, and rebel against the LORD, tomorrow he will be angry with the whole community of Israel! [19]If you consider the land you now possess unclean,* cross over to the land the LORD possesses, where the tabernacle of the LORD stands, and share that with us. But do not rebel against the LORD, nor involve us in rebellion, by building an altar of your own in addition to the altar of the LORD, our God. [20]When Achan, son of Zerah,[v] acted treacherously by violating the ban, was it not upon the entire community of Israel that wrath fell? Though he was but a single man, he did not perish alone* for his guilt!"

Reply of the Eastern Tribes. [21]The Reubenites, the Gadites, and the half-tribe of Manasseh replied to the heads of the Israelite clans: [22]"The LORD is the God of gods. The LORD, the God of gods,* knows and Israel shall know. If now we have acted out of rebellion or treachery against the LORD, our God, do not try to save us this day, [23]and if we have built an altar of our own to turn from following the LORD, or to sacrifice burnt offerings, grain offerings, or communion sacrifices upon it, the LORD himself will exact the penalty. [24]We did it rather out of our anxious concern lest in the future your children should say to our children: 'What have you to do with the LORD, the God of Israel? [25]For the LORD has placed the Jordan as a boundary between you and us, you Reubenites and Gadites. You have no share in the LORD.' Thus your children would prevent ours from revering the LORD. [26]So we thought, 'Let us act for ourselves by building this altar of our own'—not for burnt offerings or sacrifice, [27][w] but as witness between us and you and our descendants, that we have the right to provide for the service of the LORD in his presence with our burnt offerings, sacrifices, and communion sacrifices. Now in the future your children cannot say to our children, 'You have no share in the LORD.' [28]Our thought was that, if in the future they should speak thus to us or to our descendants, we could answer: 'Look at the copy of the altar of the LORD which our ancestors made, not for burnt offerings or for sacrifices, but to witness* between you and us.' [29]Far be it from us to rebel against the LORD or to turn now from following the LORD by building an altar for burnt offering, grain offering, or sacrifice in addition to the altar of the LORD, our God, which stands before his tabernacle."

[30]When Phinehas the priest and the leaders of the community, the heads of the Israelite clans, heard what the Reubenites, the Gadites, and the Manassites had to say, they were satisfied. [31]Phinehas, son of Eleazar

Israelites considered this altar, which seemed to violate the customary unity of the sanctuary (cf. Lv 17:1–9; Dt 12:4–14), as constituting rebellion against the Lord and compromising national unity.

22:19 Unclean: not sanctified by the tabernacle.

22:20 Achan . . . did not perish alone: his guilt caused the failure of the first attack on Ai (7:4–23); this fact is adduced as an argument for the solidarity and mutual responsibility of all the Israelites.

22:22 The LORD, the God of gods: the Hebrew, which cannot be adequately rendered in English here, adds to the divine name Yhwh ("the LORD") two synonymous words for "God," *'el* and *'elohim*. The repetition of these three sacred words adds force to the protestations of fidelity and innocence.

22:28 To witness: far from being destined to form a rival sanctuary, the copy of the altar is intended by the eastern tribes solely as a means of teaching their children to be faithful to the one true sanctuary beyond the Jordan.

t: Ex 6:25; Sir 45:23–24. *u:* Nm 25:3–4; Dt 4:3. *v:* Jos 7:1, 5. *w:* Ex 27:1–8; Dt 12:5–6, 11–14.

the priest, said to the Reubenites, the Gadites, and the Manassites, "Today we know
that the LORD is in our midst. Since you have
not rebelled against the LORD by this act of
treachery, you have delivered the Israelites
from the hand of the LORD."
32Phinehas, son of Eleazar the priest, and
the leaders returned from the Reubenites and
the Gadites in the land of Gilead to the Israelites in the land of Canaan, and reported the
matter to them. 33The report satisfied the Israelites, who blessed God and decided not to
take military action against the Reubenites
and Gadites nor to ravage the land where
they lived.
34The Reubenites and the Gadites gave
the altar its name* as a witness among them
that the LORD is God.

See RG 154

CHAPTER 23

Joshua's Final Plea. 1Many years
later, after the LORD had given the Israelites
rest from all their enemies round about
them, and when Joshua was old and advanced in years,[x] 2he summoned all Israel,
including their elders, leaders, judges, and
officers, and said to them: "I am old and advanced in years.[y] 3You have seen all that the
LORD, your God, has done for you against all
these nations; for it has been the LORD, your
God, who fought for you. 4[z] See, I have apportioned among your tribes as their heritage the nations that survive, as well as
those I destroyed, between the Jordan and
the Great Sea in the west. 5The LORD, your
God, will drive them out and dispossess
them at your approach, so that you will take
possession of their land as the LORD, your
God, promised you. 6Therefore be strong
and be careful to observe all that is written in
the book of the law of Moses, never turning
from it right or left,[a] 7or mingling with these
nations that survive among you. You must
not invoke their gods by name, or swear by
them, or serve them, or bow down to them,[b]
8but you must hold fast to the LORD, your
God, as you have done up to this day. 9At
your approach the LORD has dispossessed
great and strong nations; not one has withstood you up to this day. 10One of you puts
to flight a thousand, because it is the LORD,
your God, himself who fights for you,[c] as he
promised you. 11As for you, take great care
to love the LORD, your God. 12For if you
ever turn away from him and join with the
remnant of these nations that survive among
you, by intermarrying and intermingling
with them,[d] 13know for certain that the
LORD, your God, will no longer dispossess
these nations at your approach. Instead they
will be a snare and a trap for you, a scourge
for your sides and thorns for your eyes, until
you perish from this good land which the
LORD, your God, has given you.[e]
14"Today, as you see, I am going the way
of all the earth.* So now acknowledge with
your whole heart and soul that not one of all
the promises the LORD, your God, made concerning you has failed. Every one has come
true for you; not one has failed. 15[f] But just
as every promise the LORD, your God, made
to you has come true for you, so will he
bring upon you every threat,* even so far as
to exterminate you from this good land
which the LORD, your God, has given you.
16If you transgress the covenant of the LORD,
your God, which he enjoined on you, to go
and serve other gods and bow down to them,
the anger of the LORD will flare up against
you and you will quickly perish from the
good land he has given you."

CHAPTER 24

See RG 154

Covenant Ceremony. 1[g] Joshua gathered together all the tribes of Israel at Shechem, summoning the elders, leaders, judges,
and officers of Israel. When they stood in
ranks before God, 2Joshua addressed all the

22:34 The name of this altar was the Hebrew word for "witness," *ed.*
23:14 Going the way of all the earth: drawing near to death, the inevitable end of all; cf. 1 Kgs 2:1–2.
23:15 Every threat: mentioned especially in the list of curses in Dt 28:15–68.
24:2 Beyond the River: east of the Euphrates; cf. Gn 11:28–31.

---

x: Jos 13:1. *y:* Dt 29:10. *z:* Jos 13:2–7; 14:2; 18:10; Ps 78:55. *a:* Jos 1:7. *b:* Ex 20:3–6; Dt 5:7–10; 7:2–11. *c:* Ex 14:14; Lv 26:8; Dt 3:22. *d:* Ex 34:16; Dt 7:3. *e:* Nm 33:55. *f:* Lv 26:14–39; Dt 28:15–68. *g:* Ex 19:17.

people: "Thus says the LORD, the God of Israel: In times past your ancestors, down to Terah,[h] father of Abraham and Nahor, lived beyond the River* and served other gods. 3But I brought your father Abraham from the region beyond the River and led him through the entire land of Canaan.[i] I made his descendants numerous, and gave him Isaac. 4To Isaac I gave Jacob and Esau.[j] To Esau I assigned the mountain region of Seir to possess, while Jacob and his children went down to Egypt.

5"Then I sent Moses and Aaron, and struck Egypt with the plagues and wonders that I wrought in her midst.[k] Afterward I led you out. 6And when I led your ancestors out of Egypt, you came to the sea, and the Egyptians pursued your ancestors to the Red Sea with chariots and charioteers.[l] 7When they cried out to the LORD,[m] he put darkness between you and the Egyptians, upon whom he brought the sea so that it covered them. Your eyes saw what I did to Egypt. After you dwelt a long time in the wilderness, 8[n] I brought you into the land of the Amorites who lived east of the Jordan. They fought against you, but I delivered them into your power. You took possession of their land, and I destroyed them at your approach. 9[o] Then Balak, son of Zippor, king of Moab, prepared to war against Israel. He summoned Balaam, son of Beor, to curse you, 10[p] but I would not listen to Balaam. Instead, he had to bless you, and I delivered you from his power. 11Once you crossed the Jordan[q] and came to Jericho, the citizens of Jericho fought against you, but I delivered them also into your power. 12And I sent the hornets* ahead of you which drove them—the Amorites, Perizzites, Canaanites, Hittites, Girgashites, Hivites, and Jebusites—out of your way; it was not your sword or your bow.[r] 13I gave you a land you did not till and cities you did not build, to dwell in; you ate of vineyards and olive groves you did not plant.[s]

14[t] "Now, therefore, fear the LORD and serve him completely and sincerely. Cast out the gods your ancestors served beyond the River and in Egypt, and serve the LORD. 15[u] If it is displeasing to you to serve the LORD, choose today whom you will serve, the gods your ancestors served beyond the River or the gods of the Amorites in whose country you are dwelling. As for me and my household, we will serve the LORD."

16But the people answered, "Far be it from us to forsake the LORD to serve other gods. 17For it was the LORD, our God, who brought us and our ancestors up out of the land of Egypt, out of the house of slavery. He performed those great signs before our very eyes and protected us along our entire journey and among all the peoples through whom we passed. 18At our approach the LORD drove out all the peoples, including the Amorites who dwelt in the land. Therefore we also will serve the LORD, for he is our God."

19Joshua in turn said to the people, "You may not be able to serve the LORD, for he is a holy God; he is a passionate God[v] who will not forgive your transgressions or your sins. 20If you forsake the LORD and serve strange gods, he will then do evil to you and destroy you, after having done you good."

21But the people answered Joshua, "No! We will serve the LORD." 22Joshua therefore said to the people, "You are witnesses against yourselves that you have chosen to serve the LORD." They replied, "We are witnesses!" 23"Now, therefore, put away the foreign gods that are among you and turn your hearts to the LORD, the God of Israel." 24Then the people promised Joshua, "We will serve the LORD, our God, and will listen to his voice."

25So Joshua made a covenant with the people that day and made statutes and ordinances for them at Shechem. 26Joshua wrote these words in the book of the law of God. Then he took a large stone and set it up there under the terebinth that was in the sanctuary of the LORD.[w] 27And Joshua said to all the

24:12 The hornets: see note on Ex 23:28.

h: Gn 11:26, 31; 31:53. *i:* Gn 12:1; Acts 7:2–4. *j:* Gn 36:8; 46:1, 6; Acts 7:15. *k:* Ex 3:10; 7:14; 12:30. *l:* Ex 12:37, 51; 14:9. *m:* Ex 14:10, 20, 27–28. *n:* Nm 21:21–35. *o:* Nm 22:2–5. *p:* Nm 23:1–24:25. *q:* Jos 3:14; 6:1. *r:* Jos 3:10; 11:20; Ex 23:28; Dt 7:20; Ps 44:3. *s:* Dt 6:10–11. *t:* Dt 10:12; 1 Sm 7:3; 12:24; Tb 14:9. *u:* Dt 30:15–19; Jgs 2:11–13. *v:* Ex 20:5; 23:21; 34:14; Lv 19:2; Dt 5:9. *w:* Gn 28:18; 31:45; Jgs 9:6.

people, "This stone shall be our witness,[x] for
it has heard all the words which the LORD
spoke to us. It shall be a witness against you,
should you wish to deny your God." [28]Then
Joshua dismissed the people, each to their
own heritage.[y]

Death of Joshua. [29z] After these events,
Joshua, son of Nun, servant of the LORD,
died at the age of a hundred and ten, [30]and
they buried him within the borders of his
heritage at Timnath-serah[a] in the mountain
region of Ephraim north of Mount Gaash.*
[31]Israel served the LORD during the entire
lifetime of Joshua, and of those elders who
outlived Joshua and who knew all the work
the LORD had done for Israel. [32b] The bones
of Joseph,* which the Israelites had brought
up from Egypt, were buried in Shechem in
the plot of ground Jacob had bought from
the sons of Hamor, father of Shechem, for a
hundred pieces of money. This was a heritage of the descendants of Joseph. [33]When
Eleazar, son of Aaron, also died, he was
buried on the hill which had been given to
his son Phinehas[c] in the mountain region of
Ephraim.

24:30 Following this verse the Greek translation of the Bible (the Septuagint) adds: "They laid with him there, in the tomb where they buried him, the flint knives with which he had circumcised the Israelites at Gilgal, when he brought them out of Egypt, as Yhwh commanded them. There they are to this very day."

24:32 Joseph's bones (Gn 50:24–26) and Jacob's purchase of the burial ground (Gn 33:18–20) relate Joshua with Genesis. **A hundred pieces of money**: see note on Gn 33:19.

x: Jos 4:1–9; Gn 31:48, 52; Dt 31:19, 21, 26. *y:* Jgs 2:6. *z:* Jgs 2:7–9. *a:* Jos 19:50. *b:* Gn 33:19; 50:24; Ex 13:19. *c:* Jos 22:13.

See RG 156–64

The Book of Judges

The Hebrew word translated "Judges" in the English title of the book refers not to specialized judicial officers or magistrates but to leaders in general. According to the biblical narrative these judges led Israel from the end of the conquest of Canaan until the beginning of the monarchy. The period of the Judges, therefore, extended from the death of Joshua (Jos 24:29–31; cf. Jgs 1:1) until the installation of Saul as Israel's first king by the prophet Samuel, who was also the last judge (see 1 Sm 7:15–17).

The Book of Judges begins with two introductory passages. The first (chap. 1) gives a description of the situation in Canaan after the Israelite conquest. It emphasizes the continued existence of the indigenous inhabitants of Canaan in many parts of the land because of Israel's inability to drive them out completely. The second passage (2:1–3:6) is a thematic introduction to the period of the Judges, describing a cyclical pattern of infidelity, oppression, "crying out," and deliverance (see note on 2:10–19).

The main part of the book (3:7–16:31) consists of a series of stories about thirteen leaders whose careers are described in greater or lesser detail. The exploits of six of these—Othniel, Ehud, Deborah, Gideon, Jephthah, and Samson—are related at length, and all are shown to have delivered Israel from oppression or danger. They are customarily called "major judges," whereas the other six—Shamgar, Tola, Jair, Ibzan, Elon, and Abdon—who appear only in brief notices, are designated "minor judges." The thirteenth, Abimelech, is included in neither group, since his story is essentially a continuation of that of Gideon and his career is presented as deplorable, a cautionary tale of royal ambition.

The final section of the book consists of two episodes, one about the migration of the tribe of Dan (chaps. 17–18) and the other about an intertribal war directed against the tribe of Benjamin (chaps. 19–21). These stories illustrate the religious and political disorder that prevailed at the time when, as yet, "there was no king in Israel" (see note on 17:6).

The principal contribution of the Deuteronomistic historian to the Book of Judges is the thematic introduction to—and theological evaluation of—the period of the Judges in 2:1–3:6, as well as editorial comments structuring the narrative throughout, e.g., 3:7; 4:1; etc. The historian drew the stories of the judges themselves from older sources, which could have existed in written form but derive ultimately from oral tradition.

Thus the principal divisions of the book in outline are as follows:

I. The Situation in Canaan Following the Israelite Conquest (1:1–3:6)
II. Stories of the Judges (3:7–16:31)
III. Further Stories of the Tribes of Dan and Benjamin (17:1–21:25)

I. The Situation in Canaan Following the Israelite Conquest

CHAPTER 1

See RG 157–58

Canaanites in Palestine. [1*] After the death of Joshua the Israelites consulted the LORD, asking, "Who shall be first among us to attack the Canaanites and to do battle with them?" [2]The LORD answered: Judah shall attack: I have delivered the land into his power.[a] [3]Judah then said to his brother Simeon, "Come up with me into the territory allotted to me, and let us do battle with the Canaanites. I will likewise go with you into the territory allotted to you." So Simeon went with him.[b]

[4]When Judah attacked, the LORD delivered the Canaanites and Perizzites into their power, and they struck down ten thousand of them in Bezek. [5c] They came upon Adonibezek in Bezek and fought against him. When they struck down the Canaanites and Perizzites, [6]Adonibezek fled. They pursued him, and when they caught him, they cut off his thumbs and big toes. [7]"Seventy kings," said Adonibezek, "used to pick up scraps under my table with their thumbs and big toes cut off. As I have done, so has God repaid me." He was brought to Jerusalem, and he died there. [8*] The Judahites fought against Jerusalem, captured it, and put it to the sword, setting the city itself on fire.[d]

[9]Afterward the Judahites went down to fight against the Canaanites who lived in the mountain region, in the Negeb, and in the foothills.[e] [10]Judah also marched against the Canaanites who lived in Hebron, which was formerly called Kiriath-arba, and defeated Sheshai, Ahiman, and Talmai.[f] [11]They marched from there against the inhabitants of Debir, which was formerly called Kiriath-sepher. [12]Caleb said, "To the man who attacks Kiriath-sepher and captures it, I will give my daughter Achsah in marriage." [13g] Othniel captured it, the son of Caleb's younger brother Kenaz; so Caleb gave him his daughter Achsah in marriage. [14]When she came to him, she induced him to ask her father for some land. Then, as she alighted from the donkey, Caleb asked her, "What do you want?" [15]She answered, "Give me a present. Since you have put me in the land of the Negeb, give me pools of water." So Caleb gave her what she wanted, both the upper and the lower pool.

[16h] The descendants of Hobab the Kenite, Moses' father-in-law,* came up with the Judahites from the City of Palms to the wilderness of Arad, which is in the Negeb, and they settled among the Amalekites. [17i] Then Judah went with his brother Simeon, and they defeated the Canaanites who lived in Zephath. They put the city under the ban and renamed it Hormah.* [j] [18]Judah captured Gaza with its territory, Ashkelon with its territory, Ekron

1:1–36 The chapter depicts the Israelite settlement of Canaan as a gradual and incomplete process (cf. Ex 23:29–30; Dt 7:22). This picture contrasts sharply with that found in Joshua, where the conquest is rapid and total. Accordingly, some scholars believe that Jgs 1 derives from an early account, which is less idealized and more realistic than that on which Joshua is based. Others, noting that Judah is presented as the only tribe that was completely successful in driving foreigners from its territory, think that the account was written at a late date and reflects suspicion in Judah about foreign elements in the Israelite populations of outlying areas (cf. 2 Kgs 17:24–33).

1:8 See note on 1:21 below.

1:16 Hobab the Kenite, Moses' father-in-law: as in 4:11. However, in Nm 10:29 Hobab is identified as Moses' brother-in-law, while Reuel is identified as Moses' father-in-law (see also Ex 2:18). The more common name of Moses' father-in-law is Jethro, also a Midianite (e.g., Ex 3:1). It is impossible to sort out the relationships among these three men in the ancient traditions. **City of Palms**: Jericho (cf. Dt 34:3) or a town in the Negeb.

1:17 The ban . . . Hormah: the narrator relates the city-name "Hormah" to "the ban" (Hebrew *herem*), which commanded the Israelites to devote to the Lord—and thus to destroy—whatever was captured within the land (cf. Dt 20:10–18).

---

a: Jgs 20:18. *b:* Jgs 1:17. *c:* Jos 10:1. *d:* Jos 10:1–27; 2 Sm 5:6–9. *e:* Jos 10:40; 11:16; 12:8. *f:* Jos 15:13–19; Nm 13:22; Jos 14:15. *g:* Jgs 3:9. *h:* Jgs 4:11; Nm 10:29–32. *i:* Jos 1:3. *j:* Nm 21:3; Jos 12:14.

with its territory, and Ashdod* with its territory.[k] 19 The LORD was with Judah, so they gained possession of the mountain region. But they could not dispossess those who lived on the plain, because they had iron chariots. 20[l] As Moses had commanded, they gave Hebron to Caleb, who then drove the three sons of Anak away from there.

21* As for the Jebusites dwelling in Jerusalem, the Benjaminites did not dispossess them, so that the Jebusites live with the Benjaminites in Jerusalem to the present day.[m]

22 The house of Joseph, too, went up against Bethel, and the LORD was with them. 23 The house of Joseph reconnoitered Bethel, which formerly was called Luz.[n] 24 The scouts saw a man coming out of the city and said to him, "Tell us the way into the city, and we will show you mercy." 25 He showed them the way into the city, and they put the city to the sword; but they let the man and his whole clan go free. 26 The man then went to the land of the Hittites, where he built a city and called it Luz, which is its name to this day.

27[o] Manasseh did not take possession of Beth-shean with its towns or of Taanach with its towns. Nor did they dispossess the inhabitants of Dor and its towns, those of Ibleam and its towns, or those of Megiddo and its towns. The Canaanites continued to live in this district. 28 When Israel grew stronger, they conscripted the Canaanites as laborers, but did not actually drive them out. 29[p] Ephraim did not drive out the Canaanites living in Gezer, and so the Canaanites lived among them in Gezer.

30[q] Nor did Zebulun dispossess the inhabitants of Kitron or those of Nahalol; the Canaanites lived among them and became forced laborers.

31[r] Nor did Asher dispossess the inhabitants of Acco or those of Sidon, or take possession of Mahaleb, Achzib, Helbah, Aphik, or Rehob. 32 So the Asherites settled among the Canaanite inhabitants of the land, for they had not dispossessed them.

33[s] Nor did Naphtali drive out the inhabitants of Beth-shemesh or those of Beth-anath. They settled among the Canaanite inhabitants of the land and the inhabitants of Beth-shemesh and Beth-anath became forced laborers for them.

34 The Amorites hemmed in the Danites in the mountain region, not permitting them to come down onto the plain. 35 So the Amorites continued to live in Harheres, Aijalon, and Shaalbim, but as the power of the house of Joseph grew, they were conscripted as laborers. 36 The territory of the Amorites extended from the Akrabbim pass, from Sela and upward.

CHAPTER 2

See RG 157–58

Infidelities of the Israelites. 1 A messenger of the LORD went up from Gilgal to Bochim and said, I brought you up from Egypt and led you into the land which I promised on oath to your ancestors. I said, I will never break my covenant with you, 2 but you must not make a covenant with the inhabitants of this land; you must pull down their altars.[t] But you did not listen to me. Look what you have done! 3 For I also said,* I will not clear them out of your way; they will become traps for you, and their gods a snare for you.[u]

4 When the messenger of the LORD had spoken these things to all the Israelites, the people wept aloud. 5 They named that place Bochim,* and they offered sacrifice there to the LORD.

6[v] Then Joshua dismissed the people, and the Israelites went, each to their own her-

1:18 Gaza . . . Ashkelon . . . Ekron . . . Ashdod: four of the five major cities of the Philistines (see note on 3:3). Since these cities were on the coastal plain, the statement that Judah captured them is contrary to v. 19, which notes Judah's failure to drive out the inhabitants of the lowlands. In the Septuagint the problem is removed by changing the beginning of this verse to read "Judah did not dispossess . . . ."

1:21 According to Jos 18:16, Jerusalem was assigned to the tribe of Benjamin. According to the notice in 1:8 above, the city was burned by the Judahites, but elsewhere (2 Sm 5:6–9) we learn that it was not actually taken from the Jebusites until David captured it and made it his capital.

2:3 I also said: the Lord explicitly warned the Israelites of the consequences of disobedience; see Nm 33:55 and especially Jos 23:13.

2:5 Bochim: Hebrew for "weepers."

k: Jos 11:22. *l:* Jos 14:6–15. *m:* Jos 15:63; 18:16; 2 Sm 5:6–9. *n:* Gn 28:19; Jos 18:13. *o:* Jos 17:11–13. *p:* Jos 16:10. *q:* Jos 19:10–16. *r:* Jos 19:24–31. *s:* Jos 19:32–39. *t:* Ex 23:32; 34:12–13; Dt 7:2, 5; 12:2–3. *u:* Ex 23:33; Dt 7:16; Jos 23:13. *v:* Jos 24:28–31.

itage, to take possession of the land. [7]The people served the LORD during the entire lifetime of Joshua, and of those elders who outlived Joshua and who had seen all the great work the LORD had done for Israel. [8]Joshua, son of Nun, the servant of the LORD, died at the age of a hundred and ten, [9]and they buried him within the borders of his heritage at Timnath-heres in the mountain region of Ephraim north of Mount Gaash.[w]

[10]* When the rest of that generation were also gathered to their ancestors, and a later generation arose that did not know the LORD or the work he had done for Israel, [11][x] the Israelites did what was evil in the sight of the LORD. They served the Baals,* [12]and abandoned the LORD, the God of their ancestors, the one who had brought them out of the land of Egypt. They followed other gods, the gods of the peoples around them, and bowed down to them, and provoked the LORD.

[13]Because they had abandoned the LORD and served Baal and the Astartes,* [14]the anger of the LORD flared up against Israel, and he delivered them into the power of plunderers who despoiled them. He sold them into the power of the enemies around them, and they were no longer able to withstand their enemies. [15]Whenever they marched out, the hand of the LORD turned against them, as the LORD had said, and as the LORD had sworn to them;[y] and they were in great distress. [16]But the LORD raised up judges to save them from the power of their plunderers; [17]but they did not listen to their judges either, for they prostituted themselves by following other gods, bowing down to them. They were quick to stray from the way their ancestors had taken, who obeyed the commandments of the LORD; but these did not. [18]When the LORD raised up judges for them, he would be with the judge and save them from the power of their enemies as long as the judge lived. The LORD would change his mind when they groaned in their affliction under their oppressors. [19]But when the judge died, they would again do worse than their ancestors, following other gods, serving and bowing down to them, relinquishing none of their evil practices or stubborn ways.[z]

[20][a]The anger of the LORD flared up against Israel, and he said: Because this nation has transgressed my covenant, which I enjoined on their ancestors, and has not listened to me, [21]I for my part will not clear away for them any more of the nations Joshua left when he died. [22][b] They will be made to test Israel, to see whether or not they will keep to the way of the LORD and continue in it as their ancestors did. [23]Therefore the LORD allowed these nations to remain instead of expelling them immediately. He had not delivered them into the power of Joshua.

CHAPTER 3

See RG 157–59

[1]These are the nations the LORD allowed to remain, so that through them he might test Israel, all those who had not experienced any of the Canaanite wars— [2]to teach warfare to those generations of Israelites who had never experienced it: [3][c] the five lords of the Philistines,* and all the Canaanites, the Sidonians, and the Hivites who lived in the mountain region of the Lebanon between Baal-hermon and Lebo-hamath. [4]These served as a test for Israel, to know whether they would obey the command-

2:10–19 This long thematic passage establishes the cyclical pattern for the stories found in the rest of the book. When the Israelites are secure, they forsake the Lord and worship other gods. In punishment the Lord places them in the power of a foreign oppressor. But when they cry out in distress, the Lord takes pity on them and raises up a judge, who delivers them from the oppressor. The Israelites remain faithful to the Lord during the lifetime of the judge, but when the judge dies they again abandon the Lord, and the cycle begins anew.

2:11 The Baals: the title "Baal," meaning "lord" or "master," belonged to a large number of Canaanite, Phoenician, and Syrian deities, including especially the great storm god Hadad Baal, widely revered as lord of the earth. The plural form, which occurs here, was used by the biblical writers to refer to foreign gods in general.

2:13 The Astartes: Ashtoreth, or Astarte, was an important Canaanite and Phoenician goddess. The plural form used here probably refers to foreign goddesses in general.

3:3 The Philistines: a people of Aegean origin who settled on the coastal plain of southern Canaan in the twelfth century B.C.; from their name derives the geographic designation Palestine. Israel competed for control of the country against a group of their cities: Gaza, Ashkelon, Ashdod, Gath, and Ekron.

---

w: Jos 19:49–50. *x:* Jgs 3:7–8, 12; 4:1–2; 6:1; 10:6–8; 13:1. *y:* Lv 26:14–39; Dt 28:15–68. *z:* Jgs 3:12; 4:1; 8:33–34. *a:* Jos 23:13; Jgs 2:2–3. *b:* Jgs 3:1, 4. *c:* Jos 13:2–5.

ments the LORD had enjoined on their ancestors through Moses. 5So the Israelites settled among the Canaanites, Hittites, Amorites, Perizzites, Hivites, and Jebusites.[d] 6They took their daughters in marriage, and gave their own daughters to their sons in marriage,[e] and served their gods.

II. Stories of the Judges

Othniel. 7[f]Then the Israelites did what was evil in the sight of the LORD; they forgot the LORD, their God, and served the Baals and the Asherahs,* 8and the anger of the LORD flared up against them. He sold them into the power of Cushan-rishathaim,* king of Aram Naharaim; and the Israelites served Cushan-rishathaim for eight years. 9But when the Israelites cried out to the LORD,[g] he raised up a savior for them, to save them. It was Othniel, son of Caleb's younger brother Kenaz.[h] 10The spirit of the LORD came upon him,[i] and he judged Israel. When he marched out to war, the LORD delivered Cushan-rishathaim, king of Aram, into his power, and his hold on Cushan-rishathaim was firm. 11So the land was at rest for forty years,[j] until Othniel, son of Kenaz, died.

Ehud. 12Again the Israelites did what was evil in the sight of the LORD, so he strengthened Eglon, king of Moab, against Israel because they did what was evil in the sight of the LORD. 13Taking the Ammonites and Amalek as allies, he went and defeated Israel, taking possession of the City of Palms. 14So the Israelites served Eglon, king of Moab, for eighteen years.

15But when the Israelites cried out to the LORD, he raised up for them a savior, Ehud, son of Gera, a Benjaminite who was left-handed.* The Israelites would send their tribute to Eglon, king of Moab, by him. 16Ehud made himself a two-edged dagger a foot long, and strapped it under his clothes on his right thigh. 17He presented the tribute to Eglon, king of Moab; now Eglon was a very fat man. 18When he had finished presenting the tribute, he dismissed the troops who had carried the tribute. 19But he himself turned back at the sculptured stones near Gilgal, and said, "I have a secret message for you, O king." And the king said, "Silence!" Then when all his attendants had left his presence, 20Ehud went in to him where he sat alone in his cool upper room. Ehud said, "I have a word from God for you." So the king rose from his throne. 21Then Ehud with his left hand drew the dagger from his right thigh, and thrust it into Eglon's belly. 22The hilt also went in after the blade, and the fat closed over the blade because he did not withdraw the dagger from the body.

23Then Ehud went out onto the porch, shutting the doors of the upper room on Eglon and locking them. 24When Ehud had left and the servants had come, they saw that the doors of the upper room were locked, and thought, "He must be easing himself in the cool chamber." 25They waited until they were at a loss when he did not open the doors of the upper room. So they took the key and opened them, and there was their lord lying on the floor, dead.

26During their delay Ehud escaped and, passing the sculptured stones, took refuge in Seirah. 27On his arrival he sounded the horn in the mountain region of Ephraim, and the Israelites went down from the mountains with him as their leader. 28"Follow me," he said to them, "for the LORD has delivered your enemies the Moabites into your power."[k] So they followed him down and seized the fords of the Jordan against the Moabites, permitting no one to cross. 29On that occasion they slew about ten thousand Moabites, all of them strong warriors. Not one escaped. 30So Moab was brought under

3:7 The Asherahs: Asherah was an important goddess, whose presence in the cult was represented by a wooden pole, also called an "asherah"; see notes on Ex 34:13 and Dt 7:5. Here the plural is used to refer to goddesses in general.

3:8 Cushan-rishathaim: this king is not known from other biblical or extrabiblical sources. His title, "king of Aram Naharaim," indicates that he was a Mesopotamian ruler.

3:15 Left-handed: this detail is important because it shows why Ehud is able to conceal a weapon on his right thigh (3:16). There is also a wordplay involved, since "Benjaminite" in Hebrew could also mean "right-handed man."

d: Ex 3:8, 17; 23:23; 33:2; 34:11; Dt 7:1; 20:17; Jos 3:10; 24:11. *e:* Ex 34:16; Dt 7:3; Jos 23:12. *f:* Jgs 2:11–14. *g:* Jgs 3:15; 4:3; 6:6, 7; 10:10; 1 Sm 12:8, 10. *h:* Jgs 1:13. *i:* Jgs 6:34; 11:29; 13:25; 14:6, 19; 15:14; 1 Sm 11:6. *j:* Jgs 3:30; 5:31; 8:28. *k:* Nm 21:34; Dt 2:24; Jos 2:24; Jgs 4:7, 14; 7:7, 9, 15.

the power of Israel[l] at that time; and the land had rest for eighty years.[m]

Shamgar. 31 After him there was Shamgar,* son of Anath,[n] who slew six hundred Philistines with an oxgoad.[o] He, too, was a savior for Israel.

See RG 159

CHAPTER 4

Deborah and Barak. 1[p] The Israelites again did what was evil in the sight of the LORD; Ehud was dead. 2 So the LORD sold them into the power of the Canaanite king, Jabin, who reigned in Hazor. The general of his army was Sisera, who lived in Harosheth-ha-goiim.[q] 3[r] But the Israelites cried out to the LORD; for with his nine hundred iron chariots Jabin harshly oppressed the Israelites for twenty years.

4 At that time the prophet Deborah, wife of Lappidoth, was judging Israel. 5 She used to sit under Deborah's palm tree, between Ramah and Bethel in the mountain region of Ephraim, where the Israelites came up to her for judgment. 6 She had Barak, son of Abinoam,[s] summoned from Kedesh of Naphtali. She said to him, "This is what the LORD, the God of Israel, commands: Go, march against Mount Tabor, and take with you ten thousand men from Naphtali and Zebulun. 7 I will draw Sisera, the general of Jabin's army, out to you at the Wadi Kishon,[t] together with his chariots and troops, and I will deliver them into your power." 8 But Barak answered her, "If you come with me, I will go; if you do not come with me, I will not go." 9 "I will certainly go with you," she replied, "but you will not gain glory for the expedition on which you are setting out, for it is into a woman's power that the LORD is going to sell Sisera." So Deborah arose and went with Barak and journeyed with him to Kedesh.

10 Barak summoned Zebulun and Naphtali to Kedesh, and ten thousand men followed him.[u] Deborah also went up with him. 11* Now Heber the Kenite had detached himself from Cain, the descendants of Hobab, Moses' father-in-law,[v] and had pitched his tent by the terebinth of Zaanannim, which was near Kedesh.

12 It was reported to Sisera that Barak, son of Abinoam, had gone up to Mount Tabor. 13 So Sisera called out all nine hundred of his iron chariots and all his forces from Harosheth-ha-goiim to the Wadi Kishon. 14 Deborah then said to Barak, "Up! This is the day on which the LORD has delivered Sisera into your power. The LORD marches before you." So Barak went down Mount Tabor, followed by his ten thousand men. 15 And the LORD threw Sisera and all his chariots and forces into a panic before Barak.[w] Sisera himself dismounted from his chariot and fled on foot, 16 but Barak pursued the chariots and the army as far as Harosheth-ha-goiim. The entire army of Sisera fell beneath the sword, not even one man surviving.

17 Sisera fled on foot to the tent of Jael, wife of Heber the Kenite, for there was peace between Jabin, king of Hazor, and the family of Heber the Kenite. 18 Jael went out to meet Sisera and said to him, "Turn aside, my lord, turn aside with me; do not be afraid." So he went into her tent, and she covered him with a rug. 19 He said to her, "Please give me a little water to drink. I am thirsty." So she opened a skin of milk, gave him a drink, and then covered him.[x] 20 "Stand at the entrance of the tent," he said to her. "If anyone comes and asks, 'Is there someone here?' say, 'No!' " 21 Jael, wife of Heber, got a tent peg and took a mallet in her hand. When Sisera was in a deep sleep from exhaustion, she approached him stealthily and drove the peg through his temple and down into the ground, and he died.[y] 22 Then when Barak came in pursuit of Sisera, Jael went

3:31 Shamgar is the first of the so-called minor judges; cf. Introduction.

4:11 It was characteristic of the Kenites that they encamped alongside or among other nomadic groups, such as the Amalekites (cf. 1:16; 1 Sm 15:6). They are most often mentioned in connection with tribes living in the southern part of Judah, but Heber's group seems to have moved north and pitched its tents in the lower Galilee. **Cain**: in this case a collective term for the Kenites. For Hobab, see 1:16.

l: Jgs 8:28; 11:23; 1 Sm 7:13. *m:* Jgs 3:11; 5:31; 8:28. *n:* Jgs 5:6. *o:* Jgs 15:15; 2 Sm 23:8, 18. *p:* Jgs 2:19; 3:12; 8:33–34. *q:* Jos 11:1–15; Ps 83:10; 1 Sm 12:9. *r:* Jgs 3:9, 15; 6:6, 7; 10:10; 1 Sm 12:8, 10. *s:* Heb 11:32. *t:* Jgs 5:21; Ps 83:10. *u:* Jgs 5:18. *v:* Nm 10:29; Jgs 1:16. *w:* Ex 14:24; Jos 10:10; 1 Sm 7:10. *x:* Jgs 5:25. *y:* Jgs 5:26.

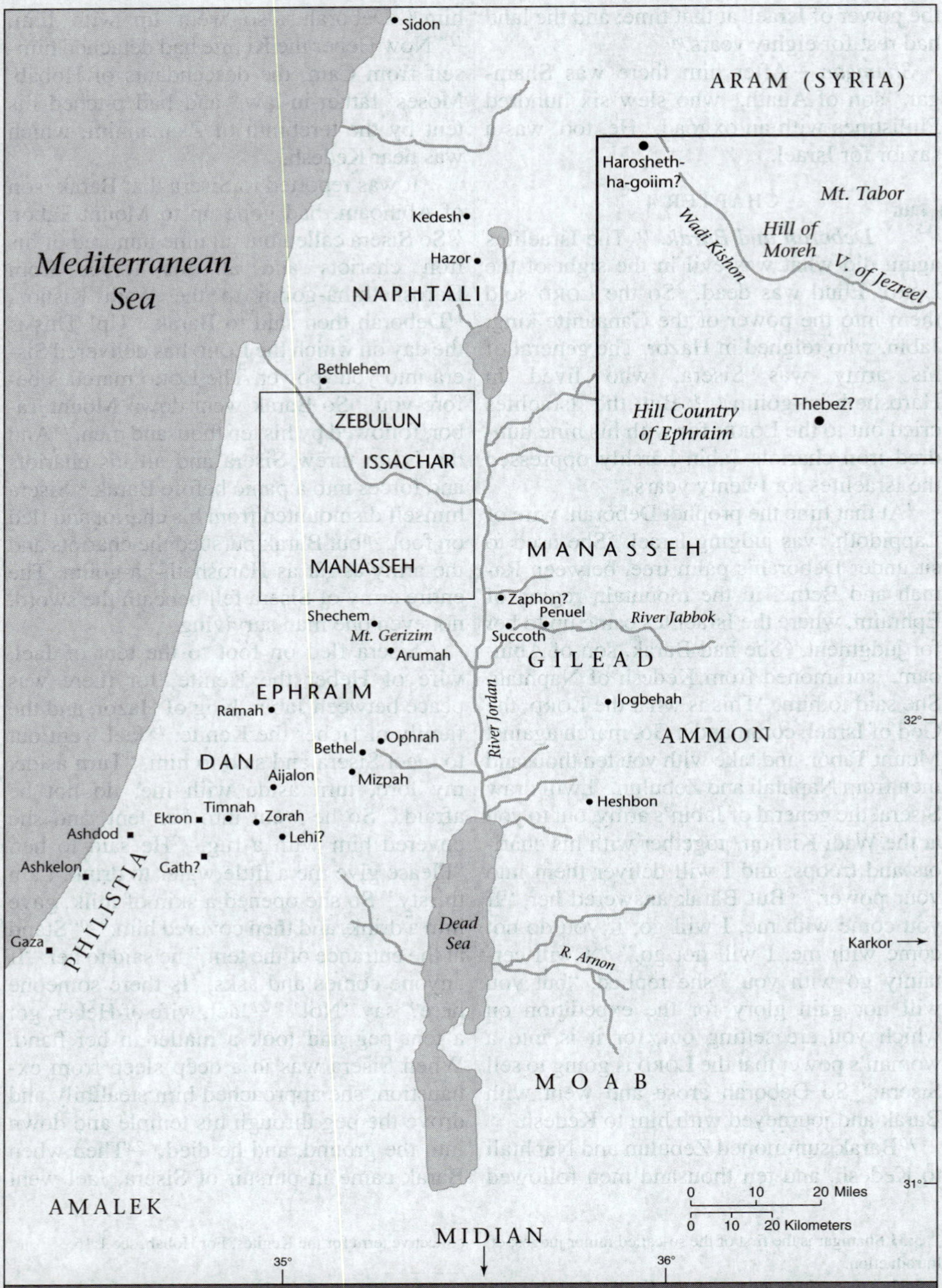

Important Cities Mentioned in Judges

out to meet him and said to him, "Come, I will show you the man you are looking for." So he went in with her, and there lay Sisera dead, with the tent peg through his temple.

23 Thus on that day God humbled the Canaanite king, Jabin, before the Israelites;
24 their power weighed ever more heavily on him, until at length they finished off the Canaanite king, Jabin.

CHAPTER 5

See RG 159

Song of Deborah. 1 [z] On that day Deborah sang this song—and Barak, son of Abinoam:

2 * When uprising broke out in Israel,
when the people rallied for duty—
bless the LORD!
3 Hear, O kings! Give ear, O princes!
I will sing, I will sing to the LORD,
I will make music to the LORD, the
God of Israel.
4 * [a] LORD, when you went out from Seir,
when you marched from the plains of
Edom,
The earth shook, the heavens poured,
the clouds poured rain,
5 The mountains streamed,
before the LORD, the One of Sinai,
before the LORD, the God of Israel.
6 In the days of Shamgar, son of Anath,[b]
in the days of Jael, caravans ceased:
Those who traveled the roads
now traveled by roundabout paths.[c]
7 Gone was freedom beyond the walls,
gone indeed from Israel.
When I, Deborah, arose,
when I arose, a mother in Israel.*
8 New gods were their choice;
then war was at the gates.
No shield was to be found, no spear,
among forty thousand in Israel!
9 My heart is with the leaders of Israel,
with the dedicated ones of the
people—bless the LORD;
10 Those who ride on white donkeys,
seated on saddle rugs,
and those who travel the road,
Sing of them
11 to the sounds of musicians at the wells.
There they recount the just deeds of the
LORD,
his just deeds bringing freedom to
Israel.
12 Awake, awake, Deborah!
Awake, awake, strike up a song!
Arise, Barak!
Take captive your captors, son of
Abinoam!
13 Then down went Israel against the
mighty,
the army of the LORD went down for
him against the warriors.
14 * From Ephraim, their base in the valley;
behind you, Benjamin, among your
troops.
From Machir came down commanders,
from Zebulun wielders of the
marshal's staff.
15 The princes of Issachar were with
Deborah,
Issachar, faithful to Barak;
in the valley they followed at his heels.
Among the clans of Reuben
great were the searchings of heart!
16 Why did you stay beside your hearths
listening to the lowing of the herds?
Among the clans of Reuben
great were the searchings of heart!
17 Gilead stayed beyond the Jordan;
Why did Dan spend his time in ships?
Asher remained along the shore,

5:2–31 This canticle is an excellent example of early Hebrew poetry, even though some of its verses are now obscure.

5:4–5 The Lord himself marches to war in support of Israel. Storm and earthquake are part of the traditional imagery of theophany; cf. Ex 19:16, 18–20; Dt 33:2–3; Ps 18:7–15; 77:17–20; 144:5–7.

5:7 A mother in Israel: the precise meaning of the term "mother" is unclear, except that it seems to indicate Deborah's position of leadership, and so may be a title (cf. 2 Sm 20:19).

5:14–22 The poet praises the tribes that participated in the war against Sisera: Ephraim, Benjamin, Machir (later regarded as a clan of Manasseh), Zebulun, Issachar, and Naphtali, the tribe of Barak (cf. 4:6). By contrast, the tribes of Reuben, Gilead (elsewhere a region occupied by Reubenites and Gadites), Dan, and Asher are chided for their lack of participation. The more distant tribes of Judah and Simeon are not mentioned, and some historians believe they were not part of Israel at this time.

z: Ex 15:1. *a:* Dt 33:2; Ps 68:8–9; Hb 3:3–15. *b:* Jgs 3:31. *c:* Is 33:8.

he stayed in his havens.
18 Zebulun was a people who defied death,
Naphtali, too, on the open heights![d]
19 The kings came and fought;
then they fought, those kings of Canaan,
At Taanach by the waters of Megiddo;
no spoil of silver did they take.
20 From the heavens the stars* fought;
from their courses they fought against Sisera.[e]
21 The Wadi Kishon swept them away;
the wadi overwhelmed them, the Wadi Kishon.[f]
Trample down the strong!*
22 Then the hoofs of the horses hammered,
the galloping, galloping of steeds.
23 "Curse Meroz,"* says the messenger of the LORD,
"curse, curse its inhabitants!
For they did not come when the LORD helped,
the help of the LORD against the warriors."
24 Most blessed of women is Jael,[g]
the wife of Heber the Kenite,
blessed among tent-dwelling women!
25 He asked for water, she gave him milk,
in a princely bowl she brought him curds.[h]
26 [i] With her hand she reached for the peg,
with her right hand, the workman's hammer.
She hammered Sisera, crushed his head;
she smashed, pierced his temple.
27 At her feet he sank down, fell, lay still;
down at her feet he sank and fell;
where he sank down, there he fell, slain.
28 * From the window she looked down,
the mother of Sisera peered through the lattice:
"Why is his chariot so long in coming?
why are the hoofbeats of his chariots delayed?"
29 The wisest of her princesses answers her;
she even replies to herself,
30 "They must be dividing the spoil they took:
a slave woman or two for each man,
Spoil of dyed cloth for Sisera,
spoil of ornate dyed cloth,
a pair of ornate dyed cloths for my neck in the spoil."

31 So perish all your enemies, O LORD![j]
But may those who love you be like
the sun rising in its might!
And the land was at rest for forty years.[k]

CHAPTER 6

See RG 159–60

The Call of Gideon. 1 The Israelites
did what was evil in the sight of the LORD,
who therefore delivered them into the power
of Midian for seven years, 2 so that Midian
held Israel subject. From fear of Midian the
Israelites made dens in the mountains, the
caves, and the strongholds.[l] 3 For it used to
be that whenever the Israelites had completed sowing their crops, Midian, Amalek,
and the Kedemites* would come up, 4 en-
camp against them, and lay waste the produce of the land as far as the outskirts of
Gaza, leaving no sustenance in Israel, and no
sheep, ox, or donkey. 5 For they would come
up with their livestock, and their tents would
appear as thick as locusts. They would be
too many to count when they came into the
land to lay it waste. 6 [m] Israel was reduced to
utter poverty by Midian, and so the Israelites
cried out to the LORD.
7 When Israel cried out to the LORD because of Midian, 8 [n] the LORD sent a prophet

5:20–21 Stars: the heavenly host, or angelic army. The roles played by the stars and the flash floods underscore the divine involvement in the battle (cf. 5:4–5).

5:21 Trample down the strong!: the meaning of these words is obscure. If this interpretation is correct, Deborah is the one addressed.

5:23 Meroz: an unknown locality in which Israelites probably resided, since its inhabitants are cursed for their failure to participate in the battle.

5:28–30 The scene shifts to the household of the slain Canaanite general, where the anxious foreboding of Sisera's mother is countered by the assurances of the noblewomen.

6:3 Midian, Amalek, and the Kedemites: three groups of camel nomads, whose raids were a constant threat to settled peoples like the Israelites during the period of the Judges.

d: Jgs 4:10. *e:* Jgs 4:15. *f:* Jgs 4:7, 13; Ps 83:10. *g:* Jgs 4:17; Jdt 13:18; Lk 1:42. *h:* Jgs 4:19. *i:* Jgs 4:21. *j:* Ps 83. *k:* Jgs 3:11, 30; 8:28. *l:* 1 Sm 13:6. *m:* Jgs 3:9, 15; 4:3; 10:10; 1 Sm 12:8, 10. *n:* Jgs 2:1–3; 10:11–14.

to the Israelites who said to them: Thus says the LORD, the God of Israel: I am the one who brought you up from Egypt; I brought you out of the house of slavery. [9]I rescued you from the power of Egypt and all your oppressors. I drove them out before you and gave you their land. [10]And I said to you: I, the LORD, am your God; you shall not fear the gods of the Amorites in whose land you are dwelling. But you did not listen to me.

[11]Then the messenger of the LORD came and sat under the terebinth in Ophrah that belonged to Joash the Abiezrite. Joash's son Gideon[o] was beating out wheat in the wine press to save it from the Midianites, [12]and the messenger of the LORD appeared to him and said: The LORD is with you, you mighty warrior! [13]"My lord," Gideon said to him, "if the LORD is with us, why has all this happened to us? Where are his wondrous deeds about which our ancestors told us when they said, 'Did not the LORD bring us up from Egypt?' For now the LORD has abandoned us and has delivered us into the power of Midian." [14p] The LORD turned to him and said: Go with the strength you have, and save Israel from the power of Midian. Is it not I who send you? [15]But he answered him, "Please, my Lord, how can I save Israel? My family is the poorest in Manasseh, and I am the most insignificant in my father's house."[q] [16]The LORD said to him: I will be with you,* and you will cut down Midian to the last man. [17]He answered him, "If you look on me with favor, give me a sign that you are the one speaking with me. [18]Please do not depart from here until I come to you and bring out my offering and set it before you." He answered: I will await your return.

[19]So Gideon went off and prepared a young goat and an ephah* of flour in the form of unleavened cakes. Putting the meat in a basket and the broth in a pot, he brought them out to him under the terebinth and presented them. [20r] The messenger of God said to him: Take the meat and unleavened cakes and lay them on this rock; then pour out the broth. When he had done so, [21]the messenger of the LORD stretched out the tip of the staff he held. When he touched the meat and unleavened cakes, a fire came up from the rock and consumed the meat and unleavened cakes. Then the messenger of the LORD disappeared from sight. [22]* Gideon, now aware that it had been the messenger of the LORD, said, "Alas, Lord GOD, that I have seen the messenger of the LORD face to face!"[s] [23]The LORD answered him: You are safe. Do not fear. You shall not die. [24]So Gideon built there an altar to the LORD and called it Yahweh-shalom.* [t] To this day it is still in Ophrah of the Abiezrites.

[25]That same night the LORD said to him: Take your father's bull, the bull fattened for seven years, and pull down your father's altar to Baal. As for the asherah* beside it, cut it down [26]and build an altar to the LORD, your God, on top of this stronghold with the pile of wood. Then take the fattened bull and offer it as a whole-burnt sacrifice on the wood from the asherah you have cut down. [27]So Gideon took ten of his servants and did as the LORD had commanded him. But he was too afraid of his family and of the townspeople to do it by day; he did it at night. [28]Early the next morning the townspeople found that the altar of Baal had been dismantled, the asherah beside it cut down, and the fattened bull offered on the altar that was built. [29]They asked one another, "Who did this?" They inquired and searched until they were told, "Gideon, son of Joash, did it." [30]So the townspeople said to Joash, "Bring out your son that he may die, for he has dismantled the altar of Baal and cut down the asherah that was beside it." [31]But

6:16 I will be with you: narratives telling how the Lord commissions someone for a task depict the person's reactions of reluctance, confusion, or sense of inadequacy, and the Lord's reassurance ("I will be with you"), sometimes accompanied by a sign (cf. Ex 3:12; Jer 1:8). Lk 1:28–37 is modeled on this pattern.

6:19 Ephah: see note on Is 5:10.

6:22 Ancient Israel thought that seeing God face to face meant mortal danger, as Ex 33:20 indicates and as Gideon's reaction here shows. Compare the reaction of Samson's parents (13:22–23) when they realize they have been conversing with the Lord.

6:24 Yahweh-shalom: a reference to the Lord's words, "You are safe" (v. 23), lit., "Peace be to you!"

6:25 The asherah: see note on Ex 34:13.

o: Heb 11:32. *p:* Ex 3:10–12. *q:* 1 Sm 9:21. *r:* Jgs 13:19–22. *s:* Gn 32:31; Dt 5:24–26; Jgs 13:22. *t:* Gn 33:20; 35:7; Ex 7:15.

Joash replied to all who were standing
around him, "Is it for you to take action for
Baal, or be his savior? Anyone who takes action for him shall be put to death by morning. If he is a god, let him act for himself,[u]
since his altar has been dismantled!" [32]So on
that day Gideon was called Jerubbaal,* [v] because of the words, "Let Baal take action
against him, since he dismantled his altar."
[33]Then all Midian and Amalek and the
Kedemites mustered and crossed over into
the valley of Jezreel, where they encamped.
[34]And Gideon was clothed with the spirit of
the LORD,* [w] and he blew the horn summoning Abiezer to follow him. [35]He sent messengers throughout Manasseh, and they, too,
were summoned to follow him; he also sent
messengers throughout Asher, Zebulun, and
Naphtali, and they advanced to meet the others. [36]Gideon said to God, "If indeed you are
going to save Israel through me, as you have
said, [37]I am putting this woolen fleece on the
threshing floor, and if dew is on the fleece
alone, while all the ground is dry, I shall
know that you will save Israel through me, as
you have said." [38]That is what happened.
Early the next morning when he wrung out
the fleece, he squeezed enough dew from it
to fill a bowl. [39]Gideon then said to God, "Do
not be angry with me if I speak once more.
Let me make just one more test with the
fleece. Let the fleece alone be dry, but let
there be dew on all the ground." [40]That is
what God did that night: the fleece alone was
dry, but there was dew on all the ground.

CHAPTER 7

See RG 159–60

Defeat of Midian. [1]Early the next
morning Jerubbaal[x] (that is, Gideon) encamped by the spring of Harod with all his

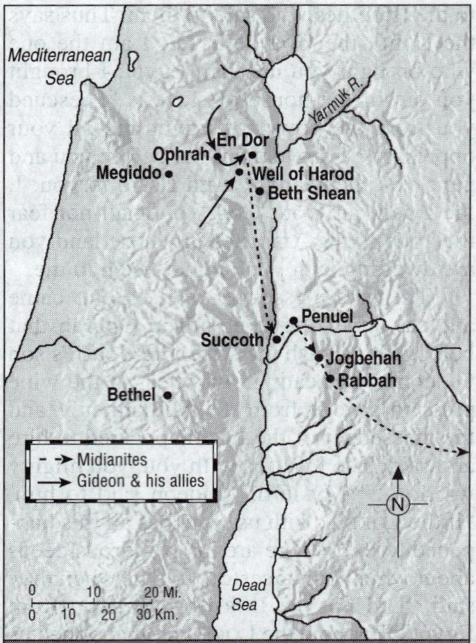

Battles of Gideon

soldiers. The camp of Midian was north of
him, beside the hill of Moreh in the valley.
[2]The LORD said to Gideon: You have too
many soldiers with you for me to deliver
Midian into their power, lest Israel vaunt itself against me and say, "My own power
saved me."* [y] [3]So announce in the hearing of
the soldiers, "If anyone is afraid or fearful,
let him leave![z] Let him depart from Mount
Gilead!"* Twenty-two thousand of the soldiers left, but ten thousand remained. [4]The
LORD said to Gideon: There are still too
many soldiers. Lead them down to the water
and I will test them for you there. If I tell you
that a certain man is to go with you, he must

6:32 Jerubbaal: similar in sound to the Hebrew words meaning, "Let Baal take action."

6:34 Clothed with the spirit of the LORD: narratives about the selection of leaders in early Israel typically attribute their prowess to "the spirit of the Lord," not to their own qualities (cf. v. 15). The Lord's spirit "comes upon" them (3:10; 11:29; 13:25) or "rushes upon" them (14:6, 19; 15:14; 1 Sm 11:6), and they are transformed into effective leaders. Here, Gideon is "clothed" with the Lord's spirit; cf. the clothing or vesture imagery in Is 59:17; 61:10; Ez 16:10–14; Jb 29:14.

7:2 My own power saved me: Deuteronomic theology constantly warns Israel against attributing success to their own efforts; cf. Dt 6:10–12; 8:17.

7:3 Mount Gilead: since the well-known highlands of Gilead were east of the Jordan River, some other hill of Gilead must be intended here. Perhaps its name is preserved in Ain Jalud (or Galud), the modern Arabic name of the spring of Harod, where Gideon's army is encamped (v. 1). The narrator plays on the Hebrew word "fearful" (*hared*) and the name of the spring, *harod*.

u: 1 Kgs 18:27. *v:* 1 Sm 12:11. *w:* Jgs 3:10; 11:29; 13:25; 14:6, 19; 15:14; 1 Sm 11:6. *x:* Jgs 6:32. *y:* Dt 8:17; 9:4. *z:* Dt 20:8.

go with you. But no one is to go if I tell you he must not. [5*] When Gideon led the soldiers down to the water, the LORD said to him: Everyone who laps up the water as a dog does with its tongue you shall set aside by himself; and everyone who kneels down to drink raising his hand to his mouth you shall set aside by himself. [6]Those who lapped up the water with their tongues numbered three hundred, but all the rest of the soldiers knelt down to drink the water. [7]The LORD said to Gideon: By means of the three hundred who lapped up the water I will save you and deliver Midian into your power. So let all the other soldiers go home. [8]They took up such supplies as the soldiers had with them, as well as their horns, and Gideon sent the rest of the Israelites to their tents, but kept the three hundred men. Now the camp of Midian was below him in the valley.

[9]That night the LORD said to Gideon: Go, descend on the camp, for I have delivered it into your power. [10]If you are afraid to attack, go down to the camp with your aide Purah [11]and listen to what they are saying. After that you will have the courage to descend on the camp. So he went down with his aide Purah to the outposts of the armed men in the camp. [12a] The Midianites, Amalekites, and all the Kedemites were lying in the valley, thick as locusts. Their camels could not be counted, for they were as many as the sands on the seashore. [13*] When Gideon arrived, one man was telling another about a dream. "I had a dream," he said, "that a round loaf of barley bread was rolling into the camp of Midian. It came to a certain tent and struck it and turned it upside down, and the tent collapsed." [14]"This can only be the sword of the Israelite Gideon, son of Joash," the other replied. "God has delivered Midian and all the camp into his power." [15]When Gideon heard the account of the dream and its explanation, he bowed down. Then returning to the camp of Israel, he said, "Arise, for the LORD has delivered the camp of Midian into your power."

[16]He divided the three hundred men into three companies, and provided them all with horns and with empty jars and torches inside the jars. [17]"Watch me and follow my lead," he told them. "I shall go to the edge of the camp, and as I do, you must do also. [18]When I and those with me blow horns, you too must blow horns all around the camp and cry out, 'For the LORD and for Gideon!' " [19]So Gideon and the hundred men who were with him came to the edge of the camp at the beginning of the middle watch,* just after the posting of the guards. They blew the horns and broke the jars they were holding. [20]When the three companies had blown their horns and broken their jars, they took the torches in their left hands, and in their right the horns they had been blowing, and cried out, "A sword for the LORD and for Gideon!" [21]They all remained standing in place around the camp, while the whole camp began to run and shout and flee. [22]When they blew the three hundred horns, the LORD set the sword of one against another throughout the camp, and they fled as far as Beth-shittah in the direction of Zeredah, near the border of Abel-meholah at Tabbath.

[23b] The Israelites were called to arms from Naphtali, from Asher, and from all Manasseh, and they pursued Midian. [24]Gideon also sent messengers throughout the mountain region of Ephraim to say, "Go down to intercept Midian, and seize the water courses against them as far as Beth-barah, as well as the Jordan." So all the Ephraimites were called to arms, and they seized the water courses as far as Beth-barah, and the Jordan as well. [25c] They captured the two princes of Midian, Oreb and Zeeb, killing Oreb at the rock of Oreb and Zeeb at the wine press of Zeeb. Then they pursued Midian, but they

7:5 The point of this selection process is clear: the battle against the nomadic raiders is going to be won not because of the numerical superiority of the Israelite troops but because of the power of the Lord.

7:13 The dream seems to foretell the victory of the agricultural Israelites (the barley loaf) over the nomadic Midianites (the tent).

7:19 At the beginning of the middle watch: at the start of the second of the three watches into which the night was divided. The sentinels were changed at the beginning of a watch, thus making the camp momentarily vulnerable.

a: Jgs 6:3. *b:* Jgs 6:35. *c:* Ps 83:12; Is 10:26.

had the heads of Oreb and Zeeb brought to Gideon beyond the Jordan.

CHAPTER 8

See RG 159–60

1[d] But the Ephraimites said to him, "What have you done to us, not summoning us when you went to fight against Midian?" And they quarreled bitterly with him. 2But he answered them, "What have I done in comparison with you? Is not the gleaning of Ephraim better than the vintage of Abiezer?[e] 3It was into your power God delivered the princes of Midian, Oreb and Zeeb.[f] What have I been able to do in comparison with you?" When he said this, their anger against him subsided.

4When Gideon reached the Jordan and crossed it, he and his three hundred men were exhausted and famished. 5So he said to the people of Succoth, "Will you give my followers some loaves of bread? They are exhausted, and I am pursuing Zebah and Zalmunna, kings of Midian." 6But the princes of Succoth replied, "Are the hands of Zebah and Zalmunna already in your possession, that we should give food to your army?"* 7Gideon said, "Very well; when the LORD has delivered Zebah and Zalmunna into my power, I will thrash your bodies with desert thorns and briers." 8He went up from there to Penuel and made the same request of them, but the people of Penuel answered him as had the people of Succoth. 9So to the people of Penuel, too, he said, "When I return in peace, I will demolish this tower."

10Now Zebah and Zalmunna were in Karkor with their force of about fifteen thousand men; these were all who were left of the whole Kedemite army, a hundred and twenty thousand swordsmen having fallen. 11Gideon went up by the route of the tent-dwellers east of Nobah and Jogbehah, and attacked the force when it felt secure. 12Zebah and Zalmunna fled and Gideon pursued them. He captured the two kings of Midian, Zebah and Zalmunna, terrifying the entire force.

13Then Gideon, son of Joash, returned from battle by the pass of Heres. 14He captured a young man of Succoth and questioned him, and he wrote down for him the seventy-seven princes and elders of Succoth. 15So he went to the princes of Succoth and said, "Here are Zebah and Zalmunna, with whom you taunted me, 'Are the hands of Zebah and Zalmunna already in your possession, that we should give food to your weary men?' " 16He seized the elders of the city, and with desert thorns and briers he thrashed the people of Succoth. 17He also demolished the tower of Penuel and killed the people of the city.

18Then he said to Zebah and Zalmunna, "What about the men you killed at Tabor?" "They were all like you," they replied. "They appeared to be princes." 19"They were my brothers, my mother's sons," he said. "As the LORD lives, if you had spared their lives, I would not kill you." 20Then he said to his firstborn, Jether, "Go, kill them." But the boy did not draw his sword, for he was afraid, for he was still a boy. 21[g] Zebah and Zalmunna said, "Come, kill us yourself, for as a man is, so is his strength." So Gideon stepped forward and killed Zebah and Zalmunna. He also took the crescents that were on the necks of their camels.

22[h] The Israelites then said to Gideon, "Rule over us—you, your son, and your son's son—for you saved us from the power of Midian." 23But Gideon answered them, "I will not rule over you, nor shall my son rule over you. The LORD must rule over you."[i]

24Gideon went on to say, "Let me make a request of you. Give me, each of you, a ring from his spoils." (Since they were Ishmaelites,* the enemy had gold rings.) 25"We will certainly give them," they replied, and they spread out a cloak into which everyone threw a ring from his spoils. 26The gold rings

8:6 Are the hands . . . already in your possession . . . ?: i.e., can you already boast of victory? The hands of slain enemies were sometimes cut off and counted as trophies.

8:24 Ishmaelites: evidently used here as a general term for nomads, whose wealth was in the form of gold and flocks. The genealogies in Genesis place the Midianites as descendants of Abraham and his wife Keturah (Gn 25:1–2), and the Ishmaelites as the descendants of Ishmael, son of Abraham and Hagar, Sarah's Egyptian slave (Gn 25:12–16).

d: Jgs 12:1. *e:* Jgs 6:34. *f:* Jgs 7:25. *g:* Ps 83:12. *h:* 1 Sm 8:5; Hos 13:10. *i:* 1 Sm 8:7; 10:19; 12:12.

he had requested weighed seventeen hundred gold shekels, apart from the crescents
and pendants, the purple garments worn by
the kings of Midian, and apart from the trappings that were on the necks of their camels.
27[j] Gideon made an ephod out of the gold
and placed it in his city, Ophrah. All Israel
prostituted themselves there, and it became a
snare to Gideon and his household.
28 Midian was brought into subjection by
the Israelites; they no longer held their heads
high, and the land had rest for forty years,[k]
during the lifetime of Gideon.

Gideon's Son Abimelech. 29 Then Jerubbaal, son of Joash, went to live in his house.
30[l] Now Gideon had seventy sons, his own
offspring, for he had many wives. 31 His concubine* who lived in Shechem also bore him
a son, whom he named Abimelech. 32 At a
good old age Gideon, son of Joash, died and
was buried in the tomb of Joash his father in
Ophrah of the Abiezrites. 33[m] But after Gideon was dead, the Israelites again prostituted
themselves by following the Baals, making
Baal-berith* their god. 34 The Israelites did
not remember the LORD, their God, who had
delivered them from the power of their enemies all around them. 35 Nor were they loyal
to the house of Jerubbaal (Gideon) for all the
good he had done for Israel.

CHAPTER 9

See RG 160-61

1 Abimelech, son of Jerubbaal, went to
his mother's kin in Shechem,[n] and said to
them and to the whole clan to which his
mother's family belonged, 2 "Put this question to all the lords of Shechem: 'Which is
better for you: that seventy men, all Jerubbaal's sons, rule over you, or that one man
rule over you?' You must remember that I
am your own flesh and bone."[o] 3 When his
mother's kin repeated these words on his behalf to all the lords of Shechem, they set
their hearts on Abimelech, thinking, "He is
our kin." 4 They also gave him seventy
pieces of silver from the temple of Baal-berith, with which Abimelech hired worthless
men and outlaws as his followers. 5 He then
went to his father's house in Ophrah, and
killed his brothers, the seventy sons of
Jerubbaal, on one stone. Only the youngest
son of Jerubbaal, Jotham, escaped, for he
was hidden. 6 Then all the lords of Shechem
and all Beth-millo came together and made
Abimelech king by the terebinth at the memorial pillar in Shechem.
7 When this was reported to Jotham, he
went and stood at the top of Mount Gerizim
and cried out in a loud voice:

"Hear me, lords of Shechem,
and may God hear you!
8 One day the trees went out
to anoint a king over themselves.
So they said to the olive tree,
'Reign over us.'
9 But the olive tree answered them,
'Must I give up my rich oil,
whereby gods and human beings are
honored,*
and go off to hold sway over the trees?'
10 Then the trees said to the fig tree,
'Come; you reign over us!'
11 But the fig tree answered them,
'Must I give up my sweetness
and my sweet fruit,
and go off to hold sway over the trees?'
12 Then the trees said to the vine,
'Come you, reign over us.'
13 But the vine answered them,
'Must I give up my wine
that cheers gods* and human beings,
and go off to hold sway over the trees?'
14 Then all the trees said to the buckthorn,
'Come; you reign over us!'
15 The buckthorn answered the trees,
'If you are anointing me in good faith,
to make me king over you,

8:31 Concubine: a wife of secondary rank.

8:33 Baal-berith: a divine epithet meaning "lord of the covenant." The same deity is called El-berith, "god of the covenant," in 9:46.

9:9 Whereby gods and human beings are honored: olive oil had a variety of cultic uses (e.g., Lv 2:1, 6, 15; 24:2), and it was also used in the consecration of priests and kings for office (e.g., Ex 30:25, 30; 1 Sm 10:1; 16:13).

9:13 Cheers gods: wine was part of a number of types of offerings in the Israelite cult (cf. Ex 29:40; Lv 23:13; Nm 15:7, 10), and it was also used widely in the worship of foreign gods (cf. Dt 32:37–38; Is 65:11).

j: Jgs 17:5; 18:14. *k:* Jgs 3:11, 30; 5:31. *l:* Jgs 9:2, 5; 10:4; 12:9, 14. *m:* Jgs 2:19; 3:12; 4:1. *n:* Jgs 8:31. *o:* 2 Sm 5:1; 19:12, 13.

come, and take refuge in my shadow.
But if not, let fire come from the
buckthorn
and devour the cedars of Lebanon.'[p]

[16]"Now then, if you have acted in good faith and integrity in appointing Abimelech your king, if you have acted with good will toward Jerubbaal and his house, and if you have treated him as he deserved— [17]for my father fought for you at the risk of his life when he delivered you from the power of Midian, [18]but you have risen against my father's house today and killed his seventy sons upon one stone and made Abimelech, the son of his maidservant,[q] king over the lords of Shechem, because he is your kin— [19]if, then, you have acted in good faith and integrity toward Jerubbaal and his house today, then rejoice in Abimelech and may he in turn rejoice in you! [20]But if not, let fire come forth from Abimelech and devour the lords of Shechem and Beth-millo, and let fire come forth from the lords of Shechem and Beth-millo and devour Abimelech." [21]Then Jotham fled and escaped to Beer, where he remained for fear of his brother Abimelech.

[22]When Abimelech had ruled Israel for three years, [23]God put an evil spirit[r] between Abimelech and the lords of Shechem, and the lords of Shechem broke faith with the house of Abimelech. [24]This was to repay the violence done to the seventy sons of Jerubbaal and to avenge their blood upon their brother Abimelech, who killed them, and upon the lords of Shechem, who encouraged him to kill his brothers. [25]The lords of Shechem then set men in ambush for him on the mountaintops, and they robbed all who passed them on the road. It was reported to Abimelech.

[26]Now Gaal, son of Ebed, and his kin came, and when they passed through Shechem, the lords of Shechem put their trust in him. [27]They went out into the fields, harvested the grapes from their vineyards, trod them out, and held a festival. Then they went to the temple of their god, where they ate and drank and cursed Abimelech. [28][s] Gaal, son of Ebed, said, "Who is Abimelech? And who is Shechem that we should serve him? Did not the son of Jerubbaal and his lieutenant Zebul serve the men of Hamor, father of Shechem?[t] So why should we serve him? [29]Would that these troops were entrusted to my command! I would depose Abimelech. I would say to Abimelech, 'Get a larger army and come out!' "

[30]When Zebul, the ruler of the city, heard what Gaal, son of Ebed, had said, he was angry [31]and sent messengers to Abimelech in Arumah to say, "Gaal, son of Ebed, and his kin have come to Shechem and are stirring up the city against you. [32]So take action tonight, you and the troops who are with you, and set an ambush in the fields. [33]Promptly at sunrise tomorrow morning, make a raid on the city. When he and the troops who are with him come out against you, deal with him as best you can."

[34]During the night Abimelech went into action with all his soldiers and set up an ambush outside of Shechem in four companies. [35]Gaal, son of Ebed, went out and stood at the entrance of the city gate. When Abimelech and his soldiers rose from their place of ambush, [36]Gaal saw the soldiers and said to Zebul, "There are soldiers coming down from the mountaintops!" But Zebul answered him, "It is the shadow of the hills that you see as men." [37]But Gaal went on to say, "Soldiers are coming down from the region of Tabbur-haarez, and one company is coming by way of Elon-meonenim." [38]Zebul said to him, "Where now is your boast, when you said, 'Who is Abimelech that we should serve him?' Are these not the troops for whom you expressed contempt? Go out now and fight with them." [39]So Gaal went out at the head of the lords of Shechem to fight against Abimelech; [40]but when Abimelech went after him, he fled from him. Many fell slain right up to the entrance of the gate. [41]Abimelech returned to Arumah, and Zebul drove Gaal and his kin away so that they could no longer remain at Shechem.

[42]The next day, the army marched out into the field, and it was reported to Abim-

p: 2 Kgs 14:9. *q:* Jgs 8:31. *r:* 1 Sm 16:14; 18:10; 19:9; 1 Kgs 22:19–23. *s:* 1 Sm 25:10. *t:* Gn 33:19; 34:2.

elech. 43 He divided the troops he had into three companies, and set up an ambush in the fields. He watched until he saw the army leave the city and then went on the attack against them. 44 Abimelech and the company with him rushed in and stood by the entrance of the city gate, while the other two companies rushed upon all who were in the field and attacked them. 45 That entire day Abimelech fought against the city. He captured it, killed the people who were in it, and demolished the city itself, sowing it with salt.*[u]

46 When they heard of this, all the lords of the Migdal-shechem went into the crypt of the temple of El-berith. 47 It was reported to Abimelech that all the lords of the Migdal-shechem were gathered together. 48 So he went up Mount Zalmon with all his soldiers, took his ax in his hand, and cut down some brushwood. This he lifted to his shoulder, then said to the troops with him, "Hurry! Do just as you have seen me do." 49 So all the soldiers likewise cut down brushwood and, following Abimelech, placed it against the crypt. Then they set the crypt on fire over them, so that every one of the people of the Migdal-shechem, about a thousand men and women, perished.

50 Abimelech proceeded to Thebez, encamped, and captured it. 51 Now there was a strong tower in the middle of the city, and all the men and women and all the lords of the city fled there, shutting themselves in and going up to the roof of the tower. 52 Abimelech came up to the tower and fought against it. When he came close to the entrance of the tower to set it on fire, 53 a certain woman cast the upper part of a millstone* down on Abimelech's head, and it fractured his skull.[v] 54 He immediately called his armor-bearer and said to him, "Draw your sword and put me to death so they will not say about me, 'A woman killed him.' "[w] So his attendant ran him through

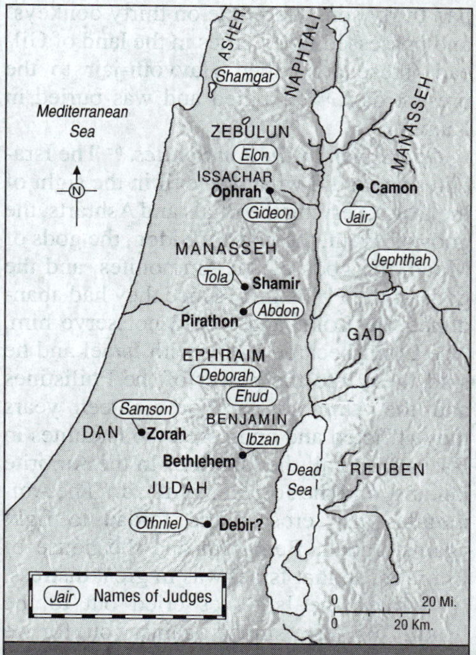

The Twelve Judges

and he died. 55 When the Israelites saw that Abimelech was dead, they all left for their homes.

56 Thus did God repay the evil that Abimelech had done to his father in killing his seventy brothers. 57 God also brought all the wickedness of the people of Shechem back on their heads, for the curse of Jotham, son of Jerubbaal, overtook them.

CHAPTER 10

See RG 161

Tola. 1 After Abimelech, Tola,* son of Puah, son of Dodo, a man of Issachar, rose up to save Israel; he lived in Shamir in the mountain region of Ephraim. 2 When he had judged Israel twenty-three years, he died and was buried in Shamir.

Jair. 3 Jair the Gileadite came after him and judged Israel twenty-two years. 4[x] He

9:45 Sowing it with salt: a severe measure, since it rendered the soil barren and useless.

9:53 The upper part of a millstone: a common hand mill consisted of a large flat stone base and a smaller upper stone (cf. Dt 24:6) shaped so that it could be held in the hands and rolled or ground against the lower stone. It is an upper stone that the woman hurls over the wall to kill Abimelech.

10:1–5 Tola . . . Jair: two more of the so-called "minor judges"; see Introduction.

u: Dt 29:23; Jer 17:6; Ps 107:34. *v:* 2 Sm 11:21. *w:* 1 Sm 31:4; 2 Sm 1:9; 1 Chr 10:4. *x:* Jgs 8:30; 9:2, 5; 12:9, 14.

had thirty sons who rode on thirty donkeys* and possessed thirty cities in the land of Gilead (these are called Havvoth-jair to the present day).[y] [5]Jair died and was buried in Kamon.

Oppression by the Ammonites. [6z]The Israelites again did what was evil in the sight of the LORD, serving the Baals and Ashtarts, the gods of Aram, the gods of Sidon, the gods of Moab, the gods of the Ammonites, and the gods of the Philistines. Since they had abandoned the LORD and would not serve him, [7]the LORD became angry with Israel and he sold them into the power of the Philistines and the Ammonites. [8]For eighteen years they afflicted and oppressed the Israelites in Bashan, and all the Israelites in the Amorite land beyond the Jordan in Gilead. [9]The Ammonites also crossed the Jordan to fight against Judah, Benjamin and the house of Ephraim, so that Israel was in great distress.

[10a]Then the Israelites cried out to the LORD, "We have sinned against you, for we have abandoned our God and served the Baals." [11b]The LORD answered the Israelites: Did not the Egyptians, the Amorites,[c] the Ammonites, the Philistines, [12]the Sidonians, the Amalekites, and the Midianites[d] oppress you? Yet when you cried out to me, and I saved you from their power, [13]you still abandoned me and served other gods. Therefore I will save you no more.[e] [14]Go and cry out to the gods you have chosen; let them save you in your time of distress. [15]But the Israelites said to the LORD, "We have sinned. Do to us whatever is good in your sight. Only deliver us this day!" [16]And they cast out the foreign gods from their midst and served the LORD, so that he grieved over the misery of Israel.

[17]The Ammonites were called out for war and encamped in Gilead, while the Israelites assembled and encamped at Mizpah. [18]The captains of the army of Gilead said to one another, "The one who begins the war against the Ammonites shall be leader of all the inhabitants of Gilead."[f]

CHAPTER 11

See RG 161

Jephthah. [1]Jephthah[g] the Gileadite was a warrior. He was the son of a prostitute, fathered by Gilead. [2]Gilead's wife had also borne him sons. When they grew up the sons of the wife had driven Jephthah away, saying to him, "You shall inherit nothing in our father's house, for you are the son of another woman." [3]So Jephthah had fled from his brothers and taken up residence in the land of Tob.[h] Worthless men had joined company with him, and went out with him on raids.[i]

[4]Some time later, the Ammonites went to war with Israel. [5]As soon as the Ammonites were at war with Israel, the elders of Gilead went to bring Jephthah from the land of Tob. [6]"Come," they said to Jephthah, "be our commander so that we can fight the Ammonites." [7]"Are you not the ones who hated me and drove me from my father's house?" Jephthah replied to the elders of Gilead, "Why do you come to me now, when you are in distress?" [8j]The elders of Gilead said to Jephthah, "This is the reason we have come back to you now: if you go with us to fight against the Ammonites, you shall be the leader of all of the inhabitants of Gilead." [9]Jephthah answered the elders of Gilead, "If you bring me back to fight against the Ammonites and the LORD delivers them up to me, I will be your leader." [10]The elders of Gilead said to Jephthah, "The LORD is witness between us that we will do as you say." [11]So Jephthah went with the elders of Gilead, and the army made him their leader and commander. Jephthah gave all his orders in the presence of the LORD in Mizpah.

[12]Then he sent messengers to the king of the Ammonites to say, "What do you have against me that you come to fight with me in my land?" [13]The king of the Ammonites answered the messengers of Jephthah, "Israel took away my land from the Arnon to the Jabbok and the Jordan when they came up from Egypt.[k] Now restore it peaceably."

10:4 Donkeys: mounts signifying rank and wealth; cf. 5:10; 12:14.

y: Dt 3:14. *z:* Jgs 2:11–14; 3:7–8, 12; 4:1–2; 6:1; 13:1. *a:* Jgs 3:9, 15; 4:3; 6:6, 7; 1 Sm 12:8, 10. *b:* Jgs 2:1–3; 6:8–10. *c:* Nm 21:21–32. *d:* Jgs 6:1–6. *e:* Jgs 2:21. *f:* Jgs 11:5–11. *g:* Heb 11:32. *h:* 2 Sm 10:6, 8. *i:* Jgs 9:4; 1 Sm 22:2. *j:* Jgs 10:18. *k:* Nm 21:24.

14 Again Jephthah sent messengers to the king of the Ammonites, 15 saying to him, "This is what Jephthah says: 'Israel did not take the land of Moab or the land of the Ammonites.[l] 16 For when they came up from Egypt, Israel went through the wilderness to the Red Sea and came to Kadesh. 17 Israel then sent messengers to the king of Edom saying, "Let me pass through your land." But the king of Edom did not give consent.[m] They also sent to the king of Moab, but he too was unwilling. So Israel remained in Kadesh.[n]
18 Then they went through the wilderness, and bypassing the land of Edom and the land of Moab, they arrived east of the land of Moab and encamped across the Arnon.[o] Thus they did not enter the territory of Moab, for the Arnon is the boundary of Moab.[p] 19[q] Then Israel sent messengers to the Amorite king Sihon, who was king of Heshbon. Israel said to him, "Let me pass through your land to my own place." 20 But Sihon refused to let Israel pass through his territory. He gathered all his soldiers, and they encamped at Jahaz and fought Israel. 21 But the LORD, the God of Israel, delivered Sihon and his entire army into the power of Israel, who defeated them and occupied all the land of the Amorites who lived in that region. 22 They occupied all of the Amorite territory from the Arnon to the Jabbok and the wilderness to the Jordan.[r]
23 Now, then, it was the LORD, the God of Israel, who dispossessed the Amorites for his people, Israel. And you are going to dispossess them? 24 Should you not take possession of that which your god Chemosh* gave you to possess, and should we not take possession of all that the LORD, our God, has dispossessed for us? 25 Now, then, are you any better than Balak, son of Zippor, king of Moab? Did he ever quarrel with Israel or make war against them?[s] 26 Israel has dwelt in Heshbon and its villages, Aroer and its villages, and all the cities on the banks of the Arnon for three hundred years.[t] Why did you not recover them during that time? 27 As for me, I have not sinned against you, but you wrong me by making war against me. Let the LORD, who is judge, decide this day between the Israelites and the Ammonites!' " 28 But the king of the Ammonites paid no heed to the message Jephthah sent him.

Jephthah's Vow. 29 The spirit of the LORD came upon Jephthah.[u] He passed through Gilead and Manasseh, and through Mizpah of Gilead as well, and from Mizpah of Gilead he crossed over against the Ammonites.
30* Jephthah made a vow to the LORD.[v] "If you deliver the Ammonites into my power," he said, 31 "whoever comes out of the doors of my house to meet me when I return from the Ammonites in peace shall belong to the LORD. I shall offer him up as a burnt offering."

32 Jephthah then crossed over against the Ammonites to fight against them, and the LORD delivered them into his power. 33 He inflicted a very severe defeat on them from Aroer to the approach of Minnith—twenty cities in all—and as far as Abel-keramin. So the Ammonites were brought into subjection by the Israelites. 34 When Jephthah returned to his house in Mizpah, it was his daughter who came out to meet him, with tambourine-playing and dancing. She was his only child: he had neither son nor daughter besides her. 35 When he saw her, he tore his garments and said, "Ah, my daughter! You have struck me

11:24 Chemosh: the god of the Moabites (1 Kgs 11:7; 2 Kgs 23:13) not the Ammonites, whose god was Milcom (1 Kgs 11:5; 2 Kgs 23:13). Much of the disputed land, which lay between the Jabbok and Arnon Rivers, was actually in Moab, and many of the details of this passage (vv. 12–28) seem more applicable to a quarrel with the king of the Moabites than with the king of the Ammonites.

11:30–40 Jephthah's rash vow and its tragic consequences reflect a widespread folklore motif, most familiar in the Greek story of Iphigenia and her father, Agamemnon. The sacrifice of children was strictly forbidden by Mosaic law (Lv 18:21; 20:2–5), and when the biblical writers report its occurrence, they usually condemn it in strong terms (2 Kgs 16:3; 21:6; Jer 7:31; 19:5). In this case, however, the narrator simply records the old story, offering no comment on the acceptability of Jephthah's extreme gesture. The story may have been preserved because it provided an explanation of the custom described in vv. 39–40 according to which Israelite women mourned Jephthah's daughter annually in a four-day ceremony.

l: Dt 2:9, 19. *m:* Nm 21:14–21. *n:* Dt 1:46. *o:* Nm 20:21; 21:4, 10–12; Dt 2:8. *p:* Nm 21:13; 22:36. *q:* Nm 21:21–26; Dt 2:26–36. *r:* Jgs 11:13. *s:* Nm 22–24; Jos 24:9–10; Mi 6:5. *t:* Nm 21:25; Dt 2:36. *u:* Jgs 3:10; 6:34; 13:25; 14:6, 19; 15:14; 1 Sm 11:6. *v:* Gn 28:20–22; 1 Sm 1:11; 2 Sm 15:7–8.

down and brought calamity upon me. For I have made a vow* to the LORD and I cannot take it back.”[w] 36“Father,” she replied, “you have made a vow to the LORD. Do with me as you have vowed, because the LORD has taken vengeance for you against your enemies the Ammonites.” 37Then she said to her father, “Let me have this favor. Do nothing for two months, that I and my companions may go wander in the mountains to weep for my virginity.” 38“Go,” he replied, and sent her away for two months. So she departed with her companions and wept for her virginity in the mountains. 39At the end of the two months she returned to her father, and he did to her as he had vowed. She had not had relations with any man.

It became a custom in Israel 40for Israelite women to go yearly to mourn the daughter of Jephthah the Gileadite for four days of the year.

CHAPTER 12

See RG 161–62

The Shibboleth Incident. 1The men of Ephraim were called out, and they crossed over to Zaphon. They said to Jephthah, “Why did you go to fight with the Ammonites without calling us to go with you?[x] We will burn your house on top of you.” 2Jephthah answered them, “My soldiers and I were engaged in a contest with the Ammonites. They were pressing us hard, and I cried out to you, but you did not come to save me from their power. 3When I saw that you were not coming to save me, I took my life in my own hand and crossed over against the Ammonites, and the LORD delivered them into my power. Why, then, should you come up against me this day to fight with me?”

4Then Jephthah gathered together all the men of Gilead and fought against Ephraim. The men of Gilead defeated Ephraim, 5and Gilead seized the fords of the Jordan against Ephraim. When any of the fleeing Ephraimites said, “Let me pass,” the men of Gilead would say to him, “Are you an Ephraimite?” If he answered, “No!” 6they would ask him to say “Shibboleth.”* If he said “Sibboleth,” not pronouncing it exactly right, they would seize him and kill him at the fords of the Jordan. Forty-two thousand Ephraimites fell at that time.

7Jephthah judged Israel for six years, and Jephthah the Gileadite died and was buried in his city in Gilead.[y]

Ibzan. 8After him Ibzan* of Bethlehem judged Israel. 9[z] He had thirty sons and thirty daughters whom he gave in marriage outside the family, while bringing in thirty wives for his sons from outside the family. He judged Israel for seven years. 10Ibzan died and was buried in Bethlehem.

Elon. 11After him Elon the Zebulunite judged Israel; he judged Israel for ten years. 12Elon the Zebulunite died and was buried at Aijalon in the land of Zebulun.

Abdon. 13After him Abdon, son of Hillel, the Pirathonite, judged Israel. 14[a] He had forty sons and thirty grandsons, who rode on seventy donkeys. He judged Israel for eight years. 15Abdon, son of Hillel, the Pirathonite, died and was buried in Pirathon in the land of Ephraim in the mountain region of the Amalekites.

CHAPTER 13

See RG 162

The Birth of Samson. 1[b] The Israelites again did what was evil in the sight of the LORD, who therefore delivered them into the power of the Philistines for forty years.

2There was a certain man from Zorah, of the clan of the Danites,* whose name was Manoah. His wife was barren and had borne no children.[c] 3[d] An angel of the LORD appeared to the woman and said to her: Though you are barren and have had no children, you

11:35 Made a vow: lit., “opened my mouth”; so in v. 36.

12:6 Shibboleth: Hebrew meaning “ear of grain” or “torrent of water.” Though the Ephraimites probably spoke the same dialect of Hebrew as their Gileadite neighbors, there was enough regional variation in their pronunciation of the initial sound of this word to betray them to their enemies.

12:8–15 Ibzan . . . Elon . . . Abdon: three more of the so-called “minor judges”; see Introduction.

13:2 The clan of the Danites: before the migration described in chap. 18 the tribe of Dan occupied a small territory west of Benjamin, adjacent to the Philistine plain; see note on 3:3.

w: Nm 30:3; Dt 23:22; Eccl 5:4. *x:* Jgs 8:1. *y:* Jgs 10:2, 5; 12:10, 12, 15; 15:20. *z:* Jgs 8:30; 9:2, 5; 10:4; 12:14. *a:* Jgs 9:2, 5; 10:4; 12:9. *b:* Jgs 2:11–14; 3:7–8, 12; 4:1–2; 6:1; 10:6–8. *c:* 1 Sm 1:2; Lk 1:7. *d:* 1 Sm 1:20; Lk 1:13, 31.

will conceive and bear a son. 4[e] Now, then, be careful to drink no wine or beer and to eat nothing unclean, 5 for you will conceive and bear a son. No razor shall touch his head, for the boy is to be a nazirite for God* from the womb. It is he who will begin to save Israel from the power of the Philistines.

6 The woman went and told her husband, "A man of God came to me; he had the appearance of an angel of God, fearsome indeed. I did not ask him where he came from, nor did he tell me his name. 7 But he said to me, 'You will conceive and bear a son. So drink no wine or beer, and eat nothing unclean. For the boy shall be a nazirite for God from the womb, until the day of his death.' " 8 Manoah then prayed to the LORD. "Please, my Lord," he said, "may the man of God whom you sent return to us to teach us what to do for the boy who is to be born."

9 God heard the prayer of Manoah, and the angel of God came again to the woman as she was sitting in the field; but her husband Manoah was not with her. 10 The woman ran quickly and told her husband. "The man who came to me the other day has appeared to me," she said to him; 11 so Manoah got up and followed his wife. When he reached the man, he said to him, "Are you the one who spoke to my wife?" I am, he answered. 12 Then Manoah asked, "Now, when what you say comes true, what rules must the boy follow? What must he do?" 13 The angel of the LORD answered Manoah: Your wife must be careful about all the things of which I spoke to her. 14 She must not eat anything that comes from the vine, she must not drink wine or beer, and she must not eat anything unclean. Let her observe all that I have commanded her. 15 Then Manoah said to the angel of the LORD, "Permit us to detain you, so that we may prepare a young goat for you." 16 But the angel of the LORD answered Manoah: Though you detained me, I would not eat your food. But if you want to prepare a burnt offering, then offer it up to the LORD. For Manoah did not know that he was the angel of the LORD. 17* Then Manoah said to the angel of the LORD, "What is your name, that we may honor you when your words come true?" 18[f] The angel of the LORD answered him: Why do you ask my name? It is wondrous. 19[g] Then Manoah took a young goat with a grain offering and offered it on the rock to the LORD, who works wonders. While Manoah and his wife were looking on, 20 as the flame rose to the heavens from the altar, the angel of the LORD ascended in the flame of the altar. When Manoah and his wife saw this, they fell on their faces to the ground; 21 but the angel of the LORD was seen no more by Manoah and his wife.[h] Then Manoah, realizing that it was the angel of the LORD, 22 said to his wife, "We will certainly die,* for we have seen God." 23 But his wife said to him, "If the LORD had meant to kill us, he would not have accepted a burnt offering and grain offering from our hands! Nor would he have let us see all this, or hear what we have heard."

24 The woman bore a son and named him Samson, and when the boy grew up the LORD blessed him. 25 The spirit of the LORD came upon him for the first time[i] in Mahaneh-dan, between Zorah and Eshtaol.

CHAPTER 14

See RG 162

Marriage of Samson. 1 Samson went down to Timnah where he saw one of the Philistine women. 2 On his return he told his father and mother, "I saw in Timnah a woman, a Philistine. Get her for me as a wife." 3[j] His father and mother said to him, "Is there no woman among your kinsfolk or among all your people, that you must go and take a woman from the uncircumcised Phi-

13:5 A nazirite for God: according to the rules for nazirites set forth in Nm 6:2–8, Samson's vows would have obliged him to abstain from wine and other products of the vine and to keep his hair uncut. As the story that follows shows, the last requirement proved especially fateful in Samson's life.

13:17–19 Manoah asks for a name so that he will know how to acknowledge the help of the visitor, but the angel will say only that his name is "wondrous," i.e., beyond human comprehension. Manoah's response is to dedicate his offering to "the Lord, who works wonders."

13:22 We will certainly die: seeing God face to face was believed to be fatal, as explained in note on 6:22, where Gideon's reaction is similar to that of Manoah here.

e: Nm 6:1–5; 1 Sm 1:11; Lk 1:15. *f:* Gn 32:30. *g:* Jgs 6:19–21. *h:* Jgs 6:22–23. *i:* Jgs 3:10; 6:34; 11:29; 14:6, 19; 15:14; 1 Sm 11:6. *j:* Gn 24:3–4; 26:34–35; 28:1–2, 6–9.

listines?" But Samson answered his father,
"Get her for me, for she is the one I want."
[4][k] Now his father and mother did not know
that this had been brought about by the
LORD, who was seeking an opportunity
against the Philistines;* for at that time they
ruled over Israel.[l]
[5]So Samson went down to Timnah with
his father and mother. When he turned aside
to the vineyards of Timnah, a young lion
came roaring out toward him. [6][m] But the
spirit of the LORD rushed upon Samson, and
he tore the lion apart barehanded,[n] as one
tears a young goat. Without telling his father
or mother what he had done, [7]he went down
and spoke to the woman. He liked her.
[8]Later, when he came back to marry her, he
turned aside to look at the remains of the
lion, and there was a swarm of bees in the
lion's carcass, and honey. [9]So he scooped
the honey out into his hands and ate it as he
went along. When he came to his father and
mother, he gave them some to eat, but he did
not tell them that he had scooped the honey
from the lion's carcass.
[10]His father also went down to the
woman, and Samson gave a feast there,
since it was customary for the young men to
do this. [11]Out of their fear of him, they
brought thirty men to be his companions.
[12]Samson said to them, "Let me propose a
riddle to you. If within the seven days of the
feast you solve it for me, I will give you
thirty linen tunics and thirty sets of garments. [13]But if you cannot answer it for me,
you must give me thirty tunics and thirty sets
of garments." "Propose your riddle," they
responded, "and we will listen to it." [14]So he
said to them,

"Out of the eater came food,
out of the strong came sweetness."

For three days they were unable to answer the
riddle, [15]and on the fourth day they said to
Samson's wife,[o] "Trick your husband into
solving the riddle for us, or we will burn you
and your family.[p] Did you invite us here to reduce us to poverty?" [16]* [q] So Samson's wife
wept at his side and said, "You just hate me!
You do not love me! You proposed a riddle to
my people, but did not tell me the answer."
He said to her, "If I did not tell even my father
or my mother, must I tell you?" [17]But she
wept beside him during the seven days the
feast lasted, and on the seventh day, he told
her the answer, because she pressed him, and
she explained the riddle to her people.[r]
[18]On the seventh day, before the sun set,
the men of the city said to him,

"What is sweeter than honey,
what is stronger than a lion?"

He replied to them,

"If you had not plowed with my heifer,
you would not have solved my riddle."

[19][s] The spirit of the LORD rushed upon
him, and he went down to Ashkelon, where
he killed thirty of their men and stripped
them; he gave their garments to those who
had answered the riddle. Then he went off to
his own family in anger, [20]and Samson's
wife was married to the companion who had
been his best man.[t]

CHAPTER 15

See RG 162

Samson Defeats the Philistines. [1]Af-
ter some time, in the season of the wheat
harvest, Samson visited his wife, bringing a
young goat. But when he said, "Let me go
into my wife's room," her father would not
let him go in. [2]He said, "I thought you hated
her, so I gave her to your best man. Her
younger sister is better; you may have her

14:4 An opportunity against the Philistines: although the story of Samson's first love might be taken as an illustration of the danger of foreign marriages, the narrator explains it differently. Samson's infatuation with the Timnite woman was the Lord's way of creating an opportunity to punish the Philistines for their oppression of Israel.

14:16 The story of Samson and the Timnite woman is very similar in its narrative structure to the better-known story of Samson and Delilah (16:1–22). In both, Samson's success in his conflict with the Philistines depends on keeping a secret. In both stories Samson is betrayed by the Philistine woman he loves when she importunes him to reveal the secret to her and then, when he gives in, divulges it to her people.

k: 1 Sm 10:14–16; Lk 2:41–51. *l:* 2 Kgs 5:7. *m:* Jgs 3:10; 6:34; 11:29; 13:25; 14:19; 15:14; 1 Sm 11:6. *n:* 1 Sm 17:34–36; 2 Sm 23:20. *o:* Jgs 16:5. *p:* Jgs 15:6. *q:* Jgs 16:15. *r:* Jgs 16:16–18. *s:* Jgs 3:10; 6:34; 11:29; 13:25; 14:6; 15:14; 1 Sm 11:6. *t:* Jgs 15:2, 6.

instead." 3Samson said to him, "This time I
am guiltless if I harm the Philistines." 4So
Samson went and caught three hundred
jackals, and turning them tail to tail, he took
some torches and tied one between each pair
of tails. 5He then kindled the torches and set
the jackals loose in the standing grain of the
Philistines, thus burning both the shocks and
standing grain, the vineyards and olive
groves.
6[u] When the Philistines asked, "Who has
done this?" they were told, "Samson, the
son-in-law of the Timnite, because his wife
was taken and given to his best man." So the
Philistines went up and destroyed her and
her family by fire.[v] 7Samson said to them,
"If this is how you act, I will not stop until I
have taken revenge on you." 8And he struck
them hip and thigh—a great slaughter. Then
he went down and stayed in a cleft of the
crag of Etam.
9The Philistines went up and encamped in
Judah, deploying themselves against Lehi.[w]
10When the men of Judah asked, "Why have
you come up against us?" they answered,
"To take Samson prisoner; to do to him as he
has done to us." 11Three thousand men of Judah went down to the cleft of the crag of
Etam and said to Samson, "Do you not know
that the Philistines are our rulers? Why, then,
have you done this to us?" He answered
them, "As they have done to me, so have I
done to them." 12They said to him, "We have
come down to bind you and deliver you to
the Philistines." Samson said to them,
"Swear to me that you will not attack me
yourselves." 13"No," they replied, "we will
only bind you and hand you over to them.
We will certainly not kill you." So they
bound him with two new ropes and brought
him up from the crag. 14When he reached
Lehi, and the Philistines came shouting to
meet him,[x] the spirit of the LORD rushed
upon him: the ropes around his arms became
like flax that is consumed by fire, and his
bonds melted away from his hands. 15Com-

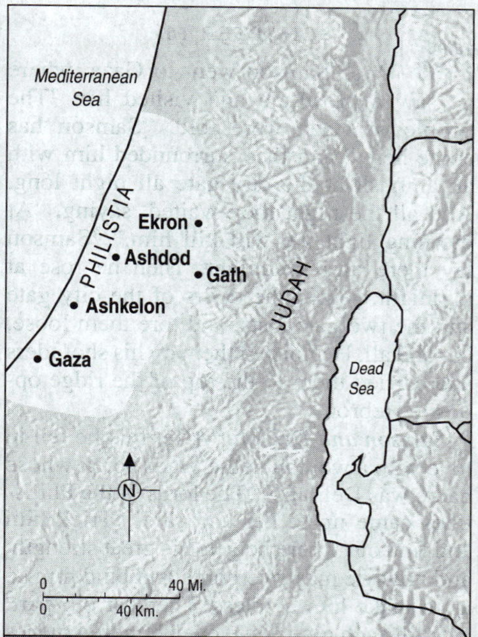

Five Cities of the Philistines

ing upon the fresh jawbone of an ass, he
reached out, grasped it, and with it killed a
thousand men.[y] 16Then Samson said,

"With the jawbone of an ass
I have piled them in a heap;
With the jawbone of an ass
I have slain a thousand men."

17As he finished speaking he threw the
jawbone from him; and so that place was
named Ramath-lehi.* 18Being very thirsty,
he cried to the LORD and said, "You have put
this great victory into the hand of your servant. Must I now die of thirst and fall into
the hands of the uncircumcised?" 19Then
God split the cavity in Lehi, and water issued from it, and Samson drank till his spirit
returned and he revived. Hence it is called
En-hakkore* in Lehi to this day.
20Samson judged Israel for twenty years
in the days of the Philistines.[z]

15:17 Ramath-lehi: "Jawbone Height"; in Hebrew *lehi* means "jawbone." The Hebrew also means "Partridge Spring."

15:19 En-hakkore: understood as "the spring of the crier," an allusion to Samson's cry in v. 18. The story is used to explain the name of a well-known spring in Lehi.

u: Jgs 14:20. *v:* Jgs 14:15. *w:* 2 Sm 23:11–12. *x:* Jgs 3:10; 6:34; 11:29; 13:25; 14:6, 19; 1 Sm 11:6. *y:* Jgs 3:31; 2 Sm 23:12. *z:* Jgs 10:2, 5; 12:7, 10, 12, 15; 16:31.

CHAPTER 16

See RG 162–64

1 Once Samson went to Gaza, where he saw a prostitute and visited her. 2 The people of Gaza were told, "Samson has come here," and they surrounded him with an ambush at the city gate all night long. And all the night they waited, saying, "At morning light we will kill him." 3 Samson lay there until midnight. Then he rose at midnight, seized the doors of the city gate and the two gateposts, and tore them loose, bar and all. He hoisted them on his shoulders and carried them to the top of the ridge opposite Hebron.

Samson and Delilah. 4 After that he fell in love with a woman in the Wadi Sorek whose name was Delilah. 5[a] The lords of the Philistines came up to her and said, "Trick him and find out where he gets his great strength, and how we may overcome and bind him so as to make him helpless. Then for our part, we will each give you eleven hundred pieces of silver."

6 So Delilah said to Samson, "Tell me where you get your great strength and how you may be bound so as to be made helpless." 7 "If they bind me with seven fresh bowstrings that have not dried," Samson answered her, "I shall grow weaker and be like anyone else." 8 So the lords of the Philistines brought her seven fresh bowstrings that had not dried, and she bound him with them. 9 She had men lying in wait in the room, and she said to him, "The Philistines are upon you, Samson!" But he snapped the bowstrings as a thread of tow is snapped by a whiff of flame; and his strength remained unexplained.

10 Delilah said to Samson, "You have mocked me and told me lies. Now tell me how you may be bound." 11 "If they bind me tight with new ropes, with which no work has been done," he answered her, "I shall grow weaker and be like anyone else." 12 So Delilah took new ropes and bound him with them. Then she said to him, "The Philistines are upon you, Samson!" For there were men lying in wait in the room. But he snapped the ropes off his arms like thread.

13 Delilah said to Samson again, "Up to now you have mocked me and told me lies. Tell me how you may be bound." He said to her, "If you weave the seven locks of my hair into the web and fasten them with the pin, I shall grow weaker and be like anyone else." 14 So when he went to bed, Delilah took the seven locks of his hair and wove them into the web, and fastened them with the pin. Then she said, "The Philistines are upon you, Samson!" Awakening from his sleep, he pulled out both the loom and the web.

15[b] Then she said to him, "How can you say 'I love you' when your heart is not mine? Three times already you have mocked me, and not told me where you get your great strength!" 16[c] She pressed him continually and pestered him till he was deathly weary of it. 17 So he told her all that was in his heart and said, "No razor has touched my head, for I have been a nazirite for God from my mother's womb.[d] If I am shaved, my strength will leave me, and I shall grow weaker and be like anyone else." 18 When Delilah realized that he had told her all that was in his heart, she summoned the lords of the Philistines, saying, "Come up this time, for he has told me all that is in his heart." So the lords of the Philistines came to her and brought the money with them.[e] 19 She put him to sleep on her lap, and called for a man who shaved off the seven locks of his hair. He immediately became helpless, for his strength had left him.* 20 When she said "The Philistines are upon you, Samson!" he woke from his sleep and thought, "I will go out as I have done time and again and shake myself free." He did not realize that the LORD had left him. 21 But the Philistines seized him and gouged out his eyes. Then they brought him down to Gaza and bound him with bronze fetters, and he was put to grinding grain in the prison. 22 But the hair of his head began to grow as soon as it was shaved.

The Death of Samson. 23[f] The lords of the Philistines assembled to offer a great sacrifice

16:19 See note on 13:5.

a: Jgs 14:15. *b:* Jgs 14:16. *c:* Jgs 14:17. *d:* Jgs 13:5. *e:* Jgs 16:5. *f:* 1 Sm 5:2–5.

to their god Dagon* and to celebrate. They said, "Our god has delivered Samson our enemy into our power." [24]When the people saw him, they praised their god. For they said,

"Our god has delivered into our power
our enemy, the ravager of our land,
the one who has multiplied our slain."

[25]When their spirits were high, they said, "Call Samson that he may amuse us." So they called Samson from the prison, and he provided amusement for them. They made him stand between the columns, [26]and Samson said to the attendant who was holding his hand, "Put me where I may touch the columns that support the temple, so that I may lean against them." [27]The temple was full of men and women: all the lords of the Philistines were there, and from the roof about three thousand men and women looked on as Samson provided amusement. [28]Samson cried out to the LORD and said, "Lord GOD, remember me! Strengthen me only this once that I may avenge myself on the Philistines at one blow for my two eyes." [29]Samson grasped the two middle columns on which the temple rested and braced himself against them, one at his right, the other at his left. [30]Then saying, "Let me die with the Philistines!" Samson pushed hard, and the temple fell upon the lords and all the people who were in it. Those he killed by his dying were more than those he had killed during his lifetime.

[31]His kinsmen and all his father's house went down and bore him up for burial in the grave of Manoah his father between Zorah and Eshtaol. He had judged Israel for twenty years.[g]

III. Further Stories of the Tribes of Dan and Benjamin

CHAPTER 17

See RG 163–64

Micah and the Levite. [1]There was a man from the mountain region of Ephraim whose name was Micah. [2]* He said to his mother, "The eleven hundred pieces of silver that were taken from you, about which you pronounced a curse and even said it in my hearing—I have that silver. I took it. So now I will restore it to you." Then his mother said, "May my son be blessed by the LORD!" [3]When he restored the eleven hundred pieces of silver to his mother, she said, "I consecrate the silver to the LORD from my own hand on behalf of my son to make an idol overlaid with silver."*[h] [4]So when he restored the silver to his mother, she took two hundred pieces and gave them to the silversmith, who made of them an idol overlaid with silver. So it remained in the house of Micah. [5]The man Micah had a shrine, and he made an ephod and teraphim,*[i] and installed one of his sons, who became his priest.[j] [6]* In those days there was no king in Israel; everyone did what was right in their own eyes.[k]

[7]There was a young man from Bethlehem of Judah, from the clan of Judah; he was a Levite residing there.[l] [8]The man set out from the city, Bethlehem of Judah, to take up residence wherever he could find a place. On his journey he came into the mountain region of Ephraim as far as the house of Micah. [9]"Where do you come from?" Micah asked him. He answered him, "I am a Levite, from Bethlehem in Judah, and I am on my way to take up residence wherever I can find

16:23 Dagon: an ancient Syrian grain deity (cf. Hebrew *dagan*, "grain") whom the Philistines adopted as their national god after their arrival on the coast of Canaan.

17:2 The narrator picks up the story after a number of events, including a theft and a mother's curse, have already taken place.

17:3 An idol overlaid with silver: two nouns in Hebrew, one indicating a wooden image and the other denoting an image cast from metal. The probable interpretation is that the woman intends for her silver to be recast as a covering for an image of a god, possibly the Lord. This was forbidden in Mosaic law (cf. Ex 20:4 and Dt 5:8).

17:5 An ephod and teraphim: cultic paraphernalia. An ephod was a priestly garment, especially that worn by the high priest (cf. Ex 28 and 39), which contained a pocket for objects used for divination. Teraphim were household idols (Gn 31:19, 34–35; 1 Sm 19:13), which may also have had a divinatory function.

17:6 This refrain, which will be repeated fully or in part three more times (18:1; 19:1; 21:25), calls attention to the disorder and lawlessness that prevailed before the establishment of kingship in Israel. In this case the problem is cultic impropriety, seen not only in the making of an idol but in the establishment of a local temple, complete with an ephod and teraphim.

g: Jgs 10:2, 5; 12:7, 10, 12, 15; 15:20. *h:* Ex 20:4; Lv 19:4; Dt 5:8. *i:* Jgs 18:14, 18. *j:* 1 Sm 7:1. *k:* Jgs 18:1; 19:1; 21:25. *l:* Jgs 19:1.

a place.” 10“Stay with me,” Micah said to
him. “Be father and priest to me,[m] and I will
give you ten silver pieces a year, a set of garments, and your living.” He pressed the Levite, 11and he agreed to stay with the man.
The young man became like one of his own
sons. 12* Micah installed the Levite, and the
young man became his priest, remaining in
the house of Micah. 13Then Micah said,
“Now I know that the LORD will prosper me,
since I have the Levite as my priest.”

CHAPTER 18

See RG 162–64

Migration of the Danites. 1In those
days there was no king in Israel.[n] In those
days the tribe of the Danites were in search
of a heritage to dwell in, for up to that time
no heritage had been allotted* to them
among the tribes of Israel.[o]
2So the Danites sent from their clans five
powerful men of Zorah and Eshtaol, to reconnoiter the land and scout it. “Go, scout
the land,” they were told. They went into the
mountain region of Ephraim, and they spent
the night there. 3While they were near the
house of Micah,[p] they recognized the voice*
of the young Levite,[q] so they turned aside.
They asked him, “Who brought you here?
What are you doing here? What is your interest here?” 4“This is what Micah has done
for me,” he replied to them. “He has hired
me and I have become his priest.”[r] 5They
said to him, “Consult God, that we may
know whether the journey we are making
will lead to success.”[s] 6The priest said to
them, “Go in peace! The journey you are
making is under the eye of the LORD.”
7So the five men went on and came to Laish. They saw the people there living securely after the manner of the Sidonians,
quiet and trusting, with no lack of any natural resource. They were distant from the
Sidonians and had no dealings with the Arameans.* 8When the five returned to their kin
in Zorah and Eshtaol, they were asked,
“What do you have to report?” 9They
replied, “Come, let us attack them, for we
have seen the land and it is very good. Are
you going to hesitate? Do not be slow to go
in and take possession of the land! 10When
you go you will come to a trusting people.
The land stretches out in both directions, and
God has indeed given it into your power—a
place where no natural resource is lacking.”[t]
11So six hundred of the clan of the Danites,
men armed with weapons of war, set out from
Zorah and Eshtaol. 12They marched up into
Judah and encamped near Kiriath-jearim; for
this reason the place is called Mahaneh-dan*
to this day (it lies west of Kiriath-jearim).[u]
13From there they passed on into the
mountain region of Ephraim and came to the
house of Micah. 14Then the five men who
had gone to reconnoiter the land spoke up
and said to their kindred, “Do you know that
in these houses there are an ephod, teraphim,
and an idol overlaid with silver?[v] Now decide what you must do!” 15So turning in that
direction, they went to the house of the
young Levite at the home of Micah and
greeted him. 16The six hundred Danites stationed themselves at the entrance of the gate
armed with weapons of war. 17The five men
who had gone to reconnoiter the land went
up 18and entered the house of Micah with the
priest standing there. They took the idol, the

17:12–13 Previously one of Micah’s sons served as priest (v. 5). But Micah’s family were probably Ephraimites (cf. v. 1) rather than Levites, and the story reflects a sense that only Levites were to be consecrated as priests; cf. Nm 18:7, where descent from Aaron is further specified as a requirement to be a priest. Thus Micah believes it will be to his advantage to retain the itinerant Levite.

18:1 No heritage . . . allotted: according to Jos 19:40–48, the Danites received an allotment in the central part of the country (cf. note on 13:2 above). The point here may be that since they were unable to take full possession of that original allotment, as indicated by the notice in Jgs 1:34, they are now seeking territory elsewhere.

18:3 Recognized the voice: this might indicate that the Danite scouts were personally acquainted with the young Levite, but it is more likely to mean that, being originally from Judah, his dialect or accent was noticeably different from others in Micah’s household.

18:7 The Sidonians . . . the Arameans: the people of Laish were not in regular contact with their neighbors, including the Sidonians or Phoenicians in the coastal district to the west and the Arameans in the regions to the north and east. This isolation is mentioned to underscore the vulnerability of the peaceful and unfortified city.

18:12 Mahaneh-dan: Hebrew, “camp of Dan.”

m: Jgs 18:19. *n:* Jgs 17:6; 19:1; 21:25. *o:* Jgs 1:34; Jos 19:40–48. *p:* Jgs 17:1. *q:* Jgs 17:7–12. *r:* Jgs 17:10. *s:* Jgs 1:1; 1 Sm 14:18–19, 36–44; 23:2, 4, 9–12; 30:7–8. *t:* 1 Chr 5:40. *u:* Jgs 13:25. *v:* Jgs 17:4–5.

ephod, the teraphim and the metal image. When the priest said to them, "What are you doing?" [19]they said to him, "Be still! Put your hand over your mouth! Come with us and be our father and priest.[w] Is it better for you to be priest for the family of one man or to be priest for a tribe and a clan in Israel?" [20]The priest, agreeing, took the ephod, the teraphim, and the idol, and went along with the troops. [21]As they turned to depart, they placed their little ones, their livestock, and their goods at the head of the column.

[22][x] When the Danites had gone some distance from the house of Micah, Micah and the men in the houses nearby mustered and overtook them. [23]They called to the Danites, who turned and said to Micah, "What do you want that you have called this muster?" [24]"You have taken my god, which I made for myself, and you have gone off with my priest as well," he answered. "What is left for me? How, then, can you ask me, 'What do you want?' " [25]The Danites said to him, "Do not let your voice be heard near us, or aggravated men will attack you, and you will have forfeited your life and the lives of your family!" [26]Then the Danites went on their way, and Micah, seeing that they were too strong for him, turned back and went home.

[27][y] Having taken what Micah had made and his priest, they marched against Laish, a quiet and trusting people; they put them to the sword and destroyed the city by fire. [28]No one came to their aid, since the city was far from Sidon and they had no dealings with the Arameans; the city was in the valley that belongs to Beth-rehob. The Danites then rebuilt the city and occupied it. [29]They named it Dan after their ancestor Dan, who was born to Israel.[z] But Laish was the name of the city formerly. [30]* The Danites set up the idol for themselves, and Jonathan, son of Gershom, son of Moses,[a] and his descendants were priests for the tribe of the Danites until the time the land went into captivity. [31]They maintained the idol Micah had made as long as the house of God was in Shiloh.*

CHAPTER 19

See RG 162–64

The Levite from Ephraim. [1]In those days, when there was no king in Israel,* [b] there was a Levite residing in remote parts of the mountain region of Ephraim[c] who had taken for himself a concubine from Bethlehem of Judah. [2]But his concubine spurned him and left him for her father's house in Bethlehem of Judah, where she stayed for some four months. [3]Her husband then set out with his servant and a pair of donkeys, and went after her to soothe her and bring her back. He arrived at her father's house, and when the young woman's father saw him, he came out joyfully to meet him. [4]His father-in-law, the young woman's father, urged him to stay, and so he spent three days eating and drinking and passing the night there. [5]On the fourth day they rose early in the morning and he prepared to go. But the young woman's father said to his son-in-law, "Fortify yourself with a little food; you can go later on." [6]So they stayed and the two men ate and drank together. Then the young woman's father said to the husband, "Why not decide to spend the night here and enjoy yourself?" [7]The man made a move to go, but when his father-in-law pressed him he went back and spent the night there.

[8]On the fifth morning he rose early to de-

18:30 Micah's shrine is now reinstalled at Laish-Dan. In the time of the kings of Israel and Judah, Dan was the site of one of the two national sanctuaries of the Northern Kingdom, both of which are strongly condemned by the editors of the Books of Kings, who regarded Jerusalem as the only acceptable place for a temple (1 Kgs 12:26–30). This verse draws a direct connection between Micah's temple and the later royal sanctuary at Dan. Seen in this light the account of the establishment of Micah's shrine, with its idol cast from stolen silver, becomes a highly polemical foundation story for the temple at Dan. **Jonathan, son of Gershom, son of Moses**: Micah's Levite is now identified as the son or descendant of Gershom, Moses' eldest son (Ex 2:22; 18:3). In the traditional Hebrew text an additional letter has been suspended over the name "Moses" to alter it to "Manasseh," thus protecting Moses from association with idol worship. **Captivity**: although Samaria fell in 722/721 B.C., much of the northern part of the country, probably including Dan, had been subjugated about a decade earlier by the Assyrian emperor Tilgath-pileser III.

18:31 Shiloh: a major sanctuary which has a role in the final episode of Judges (21:12, 21).

19:1 No king in Israel: see note on 17:6. The violent story that follows is offered as another example of the disorder that prevailed before the inauguration of the monarchy.

w: Jgs 17:10. *x:* Gn 31:22–32:1. *y:* Jos 19:47. *z:* Gn 30:5–6. *a:* Ex 2:22; 18:3. *b:* Jgs 17:6; 18:1; 21:25. *c:* Jgs 17:7.

part, but the young woman's father said, "Fortify yourself!" He coaxed him, and he tarried until the afternoon, and the two of them ate. 9 Then when the husband was ready to go with his concubine and servant, the young woman's father said to him, "See, the day is wearing on toward evening. Stay for the night. See, the day is coming to an end. Spend the night here and enjoy yourself. Early tomorrow you can start your journey home." 10 The man, however, refused to stay another night; he and his concubine set out with a pair of saddled donkeys, and traveled until they came opposite Jebus, which is Jerusalem. 11 Since they were near Jebus with the day far gone, the servant said to his master, "Come, let us turn off to this city of the Jebusites and spend the night in it." 12 But his master said to him, "We will not turn off to a foreigner's city,[d] where there are no Israelites. We will go on to Gibeah. 13 Come," he said to his servant, "let us make for some other place and spend the night in either Gibeah or Ramah."[e] 14 So they continued on their way until the sun set on them when they were opposite Gibeah of Benjamin.

15* There they turned off to enter Gibeah for the night.[f] The man went in and sat down in the town square, but no one took them inside to spend the night. 16 In the evening, however, an old man came from his work in the field; he was from the mountain region of Ephraim, though he was living in Gibeah where the local people were Benjaminites. 17[g] When he noticed the traveler in the town square, the old man asked, "Where are you going, and where have you come from?" 18 He said to him, "We are traveling from Bethlehem of Judah far up into the mountain region of Ephraim, where I am from. I have been to Bethlehem of Judah, and now I am going home; but no one has taken me into his house. 19 We have straw and fodder for our donkeys, and bread and wine for myself and for your maidservant and the young man who is with your servant; there is nothing else we need." 20 "Rest assured," the old man said to him, "I will provide for all your needs, but do not spend the night in the public square." 21 So he led them to his house and mixed fodder for the donkeys. Then they washed their feet, and ate and drank.[h]

The Outrage at Gibeah. 22*[i] While they were enjoying themselves, the men of the city, a bunch of scoundrels, surrounded the house and beat on the door. They said to the old man who was the owner of the house, "Bring out the man who has come into your house, so that we may get intimate with him." 23 The man who was the owner of the house went out to them and said, "No, my brothers; do not be so wicked. This man has come into my house; do not commit this terrible crime. 24 Instead, let me bring out my virgin daughter and this man's concubine. Humiliate them, or do whatever you want; but against him do not commit such a terrible crime." 25 But the men would not listen to him. So the man seized his concubine and thrust her outside to them. They raped her and abused her all night until morning, and let her go as the sun was coming up. 26 At the approach of morning the woman came and collapsed at the entrance of the house in which her husband was, and lay there until morning. 27 When her husband rose in the morning and opened the door of the house to start out again on his journey, there was the woman, his concubine, collapsed at the entrance of the house with her hands on the threshold. 28 "Come, let us go," he said to her, but there was no answer. So the man placed her on a donkey and started out again for home.

29* On reaching home, he got a knife and took hold of the body of his concubine. He cut her up limb by limb into twelve pieces and sent them throughout the territory of Is-

19:15–21 The narrative casts a very unfavorable light on Gibeah of Benjamin, the town from which Israel's first king would come (cf. 1 Sm 9:1–2). No Benjaminite offers hospitality to the Levite and his travel party, who are obliged to wait at night in the town square until an Ephraimite residing in Gibeah welcomes them into his home.

19:22–25 This part of the grim story closely parallels that of the assault on Lot's angelic visitors in Gn 19:4–8.

19:29 The Levite's gruesome way of summoning the tribes is a drastic version of that used by Saul in 1 Sm 11:7, where he dismembers a yoke of oxen.

d: Jgs 1:21; 2 Sm 5:6. *e:* Jos 18:25. *f:* Jgs 20:4. *g:* Gn 19:1–3. *h:* Gn 18:4; 24:32; 43:24. *i:* Gn 19:4–9.

rael.[j] 30He instructed the men whom he sent, "Thus you shall say to all the men of Israel: 'Has such a thing ever happened from the day the Israelites came up from the land of Egypt to this day?* [k] Take note of it; form a plan and give orders.' "

See RG 162–64

CHAPTER 20

Assembly of Israelites. 1So all the Israelites came out as one, from Dan to Beer-sheba* [l] including the land of Gilead, and the assembly gathered to the LORD at Mizpah. 2The leaders of all the people, all the staff-bearers of Israel,* presented themselves in the assembly of the people of God—four hundred thousand foot soldiers who carried swords. 3Meanwhile, the Benjaminites heard that the Israelites had gone up to Mizpah. The Israelites asked, "How did this evil thing happen?" 4and the Levite, the husband of the murdered woman, testified: "It was at Gibeah of Benjamin, which my concubine and I had entered for the night.[m] 5[n] The lords of Gibeah rose up against me and surrounded me in the house at night. I was the one they intended to kill, but they abused my concubine and she died. 6[o] So I took my concubine and cut her up and sent her through every part of the territory of Israel, because of the terrible thing they had done in Israel. 7So now, all you Israelites, give your judgment and counsel in this matter."[p] 8All the people rose as one to say, "None of us will leave for our tents or return to our homes. 9Now as for Gibeah, this is what we will do: We will go up against it by lot, 10taking from all the tribes of Israel ten men for every hundred, a hundred for every thousand, a thousand for every ten thousand, and procuring supplies for the soldiers who will go to exact from Gibeah of Benjamin the full measure of the terrible thing it committed in Israel."

11So all the men of Israel gathered against the city, united as one. 12The tribes of Israel sent men throughout the tribe of Benjamin to say, "What is this evil that has occurred among you? 13Now give up the men, the scoundrels who are in Gibeah, that we may put them to death and thus purge the evil from Israel." But the Benjaminites refused to listen to their kindred, the Israelites. 14Instead, the Benjaminites assembled from their cities at Gibeah, to march out to battle with the Israelites. 15On that day the Benjaminites mustered from their cities twenty-six thousand swordsmen, in addition to the inhabitants of Gibeah, who mustered seven hundred picked men 16* who were left-handed, every one of them able to sling a stone at a hair without missing. 17The men of Israel, without Benjamin, mustered four hundred thousand swordsmen, all of them warriors. 18They went up to Bethel and consulted God. When the Israelites asked, "Who shall go up first for us to do battle with the Benjaminites?" the LORD said: Judah first.* [q] 19* The Israelites rose in the morning and encamped against Gibeah.

War with Benjamin. 20The men of Israel marched out to do battle with Benjamin and drew up in battle array against them at Gibeah. 21The Benjaminites marched out of Gibeah that day and felled twenty-two thousand men of Israel. 22* But the army of the men of Israel took courage and again drew up for battle in the place where they had drawn up on the previous day. 23Then the Israelites went up and wept before the LORD until evening. "Shall I again engage my brother Benjamin in battle?" they asked the

19:30 Has such a thing ever happened . . . ?: the outrage became a byword in Israel, so that in the eighth century the prophet Hosea could invoke "the days of Gibeah" (Hos 9:9; cf. 10:9) to signify corruption and wrongdoing.

20:1 From Dan to Beer-sheba: the entire country, from north to south. **The land of Gilead**: Israelite territory east of the Jordan.

20:2 The staff-bearers of Israel: the tribal leaders.

20:16 The strange notice that the Gibeahite warriors were left-handed was probably added here under the influence of the Ehud story; cf. 3:15 and the note there.

20:18 Judah first: as in 1:2, where the enemy is the Canaanites. This time the attack is against fellow Israelites, an indication of how far things have deteriorated in these days when as yet "there was no king in Israel"; see note on 17:6.

20:19–25 The Israelites are defeated twice by the Benjaminites.

20:22–23 These two verses seem to be transposed. The day of supplication described in v. 23 must have preceded the assembly for battle reported in v. 22.

j: 1 Sm 11:7. *k:* Hos 9:9; 10:9. *l:* 1 Sm 3:20; 2 Sm 3:10; 17:11; 24:2, 15; 1 Kgs 5:5. *m:* Jgs 19:15. *n:* Jgs 19:22–28. *o:* Jgs 19:29. *p:* Jgs 19:30. *q:* Jgs 1:1–2.

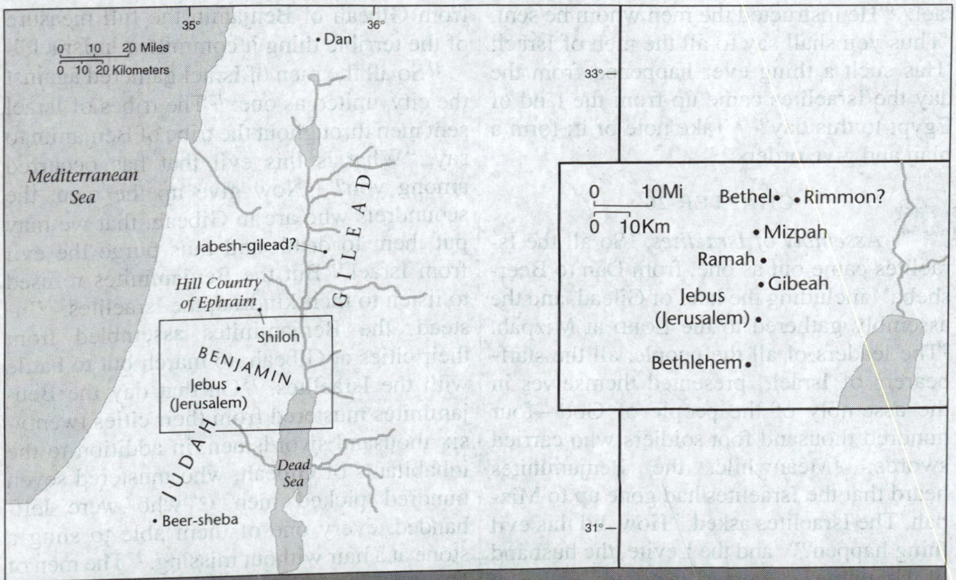

Sites Mentioned in Benjaminite War

LORD; and the LORD answered: Attack!
24When the Israelites drew near to the Benjaminites on the second day, 25Benjamin
marched out of Gibeah against them again
and felled eighteen thousand Israelites, all of
them swordsmen. 26So the entire Israelite
army went up and entered Bethel, where
they sat weeping before the LORD. They
fasted that day until evening and presented
burnt offerings and communion offerings
before the LORD. 27The Israelites consulted
the LORD (for the ark of the covenant of the
LORD was there in those days, 28and Phinehas, son of Eleazar, son of Aaron,* was
standing in his presence in those days), and
asked, "Shall I again go out to battle with my
brother Benjamin, or shall I stop?" The
LORD said: Attack! For tomorrow I will deliver him into your power. 29* r So Israel set
men in ambush around Gibeah.
30When the Israelites went up against the
Benjaminites on the third day, they drew up
against Gibeah as on other occasions.
31When the Benjaminites marched out to
meet the army, they began, as on other occasions, to strike down some of the troops
along the highways, one of which goes up to
Bethel and one to Gibeah in the open country; about thirty Israelites were slain. 32The
Benjaminites thought, "They are routed before us as previously." The Israelites, however, were thinking, "We will flee and draw
them out from the city onto the highways."
33And then all the men of Israel rose from
their places, forming up at Baal-tamar, and
the Israelites in ambush rushed from their
place west of Gibeah 34and advanced against
Gibeah with ten thousand picked men from
all Israel. The fighting was severe, but no
one knew that a disaster was closing in.
35The LORD defeated Benjamin before Israel; and on that day the Israelites killed

20:28 Phinehas, son of Eleazar, son of Aaron: the main line of the priesthood was traced through a grandson of Aaron by this name; see Ex 6:25 and Nm 25:10–13. Whether the priest identified here is the same man or his lineal descendant, the mention of his name adds authority to the sanctuary at Bethel. The reference to the ark of the covenant in the preceding verse has the same effect.

20:29–46 The Israelites are successful in their third attempt to defeat Benjamin. Leaving an ambush behind, they decoy the enemy troops out of the city by pretending to be routed as on the two previous occasions. The stratagem is strongly reminiscent of that employed in the conquest of Ai (Jos 8). Two accounts of the present battle against Gibeah are preserved, one in 20:29–36a and another in 20:36b–46.

r: Jos 8:3–24.

twenty-five thousand one hundred men of Benjamin, all of them swordsmen.

[36]Then the Benjaminites saw that they were defeated. The men of Israel gave ground to Benjamin, trusting in the ambush they had set at Gibeah. [37]Then the men in ambush, having made a sudden dash against Gibeah, marched in and put the whole city to the sword. [38]The arrangement the men of Israel had with the men in ambush was that they would send up a smoke signal from the city, [39]and the men of Israel would then wheel about in the battle. Benjamin, having begun by killing off some thirty of the men of Israel, thought, "Surely they are completely routed before us, as in the earlier fighting." [40]But when the signal, the column of smoke, began to rise up from the city, Benjamin looked back and there was the whole city going up in smoke toward heaven. [41]Then when the men of Israel wheeled about, the men of Benjamin were thrown into confusion, for they realized that disaster was closing in on them. [42]They retreated before the men of Israel in the direction of the wilderness, but the fighting kept pace with them, and those who had been in the city were spreading destruction in between. [43]They surrounded the men of Benjamin, pursued them from Nohah and drove them along to a point east of Gibeah. [44]Eighteen thousand from Benjamin fell, all of them warriors. [45]They turned and fled into the wilderness to the crag of Rimmon. The Israelites picked off five thousand men on the highways and kept pace with them as far as Gidom, where they struck down another two thousand of them. [46]The total of those from Benjamin who fell that day was twenty-five thousand swordsmen, all of them warriors. [47]Six hundred men turned and fled into the wilderness to the crag of Rimmon, where they remained for four months.[s]

[48]Then the men of Israel turned back against the Benjaminites, putting them to the sword—the inhabitants of the cities, the livestock, and all they came upon.[t] Moreover they destroyed by fire all the cities they came upon.

CHAPTER 21

Ensuring a Future for Benjamin.

See RG 162–64

[1*] The men of Israel took an oath at Mizpah: "None of us will give his daughter in marriage to anyone from Benjamin." [2]So the people went to Bethel and remained there before God until evening, raising their voices in bitter weeping.[u] [3]They said, "LORD, God of Israel, why has this happened in Israel that today one tribe of Israel should be lacking?" [4]Early the next day the people built an altar there and offered burnt offerings and communion offerings. [5]Then the Israelites asked, "Are there any among all the tribes of Israel who did not come up to the LORD for the assembly?" For there was a solemn oath that anyone who did not go up to the LORD at Mizpah should be put to death.[v]

[6]The Israelites were disconsolate over their brother Benjamin and said, "Today one tribe has been cut off from Israel. [7]What can we do about wives for the survivors, since we have sworn by the LORD not to give them any of our daughters in marriage?" [8]And when they asked, "Is there one among the tribes of Israel who did not come up to the LORD in Mizpah?" they found that none of the men of Jabesh-gilead had come to the encampment for the assembly. [9]A roll call of the people was taken, and none of the inhabitants of Jabesh-gilead[w] was present. [10]So the assembly sent twelve thousand warriors there with orders, "Go put the inhabitants of Jabesh-gilead to the sword. [11]This is what you are to do: Every male and every woman who has had relations with a male you shall put under the ban."* [x] [12]Finding among the inhabitants of Jabesh-gilead four hundred young virgin women, who had not had relations with a

21:1–7 The victorious Israelites now become concerned about the survival of the tribe they have defeated. Despite the large number of Benjaminites killed in the final battle (20:46) and the general carnage that followed (20:48), there does not seem to be a shortage of men. The problem is rather a shortage of wives for the surviving men, the result of a previously unmentioned vow the Israelites took not to permit their daughters to marry Benjaminites.

21:11 Under the ban: see note on 1:17. In this case the sanction is imposed not because of the rules for the conquest of the promised land (cf. Dt 20:10–18) but because of the failure of the men of Jabesh-gilead to honor their oath and report for the assembly.

s: Jgs 21:13. *t:* Dt 13:15–17. *u:* Jgs 20:26. *v:* Jgs 20:8–10. *w:* 1 Sm 11:1–11; 31:11–13; 2 Sm 2:4–7; 21:11–14. *x:* Nm 31:17.

man, they brought them to the camp at Shiloh, in the land of Canaan.[y] 13 Then the whole assembly sent word to the Benjaminites at the crag of Rimmon,[z] offering them peace. 14* So Benjamin returned at that time, and they were given as wives the women of Jabesh-gilead who had been spared; but these proved to be not enough for them.

15 The people had regrets about Benjamin because the LORD had made a breach among the tribes of Israel.[a] 16 The elders of the assembly said, "What shall we do for wives for the survivors? For the women of Benjamin have been annihilated."[b] 17 They said, "There must be heirs for the survivors of Benjamin, so that a tribe will not be wiped out from Israel. 18 Yet we cannot give them any of our daughters in marriage." For the Israelites had taken an oath, "Cursed be he who gives a wife to Benjamin!" 19 Then they thought of the yearly feast of the LORD at Shiloh,[c] north of Bethel, east of the highway that goes up from Bethel to Shechem, and south of Lebonah. 20 And they instructed the Benjaminites, "Go and set an ambush in the vineyards. 21 When you see the women of Shiloh come out to join in the dances, come out of the vineyards and catch a wife for each of you from the women of Shiloh; then go on to the land of Benjamin. 22 When their fathers or their brothers come to complain to us, we shall say to them, 'Release them to us as a kindness, since we did not take a woman for every man in battle. Nor did you yourselves give your daughters to them, thus incurring guilt.' "*

23 The Benjaminites did this; they carried off wives for each of them from the dancers they had seized, and they went back each to his own heritage, where they rebuilt the cities and settled them. 24 At that time the Israelites dispersed from there for their own tribes and clans; they set out from there each to his own heritage.

25* In those days there was no king in Israel; everyone did what was right in their own sight.[d]

21:14 Very strong political ties existed between the people of Jabesh-gilead and the Benjaminites, especially those involving Saul, the Benjaminite king of Israel. See 1 Sm 11, where Saul rescues Jabesh from an Ammonite siege, and 1 Sm 31:11–13, where the people of Jabesh exert themselves to ensure that the bodies of Saul and his sons should receive honorable burial.

21:22 Release them . . . guilt: this verse is difficult. Evidently the elders intend to make two arguments in support of their request that the men of Shiloh release their claims on the abducted women. The first argument seems to be that an insufficient number of women were taken "in battle"—i.e., the raid on Jabesh-gilead—to provide "a woman for every man"—i.e., a wife for every Benjaminite. The second argument is that since the women have been kidnapped, the men of Shiloh will not be guilty of having violated the oath mentioned above in 21:1, 7, and 18.

21:25 See note on 17:6. This final editorial comment calls attention to the chaos that followed the Benjaminite civil war and the near anarchy that characterized the various efforts to meet the need for wives for the Benjaminites.

y: Jos 21:2; 22:9. *z:* Jgs 20:47. *a:* 2 Sm 6:8. *b:* Jgs 20:48. *c:* 1 Sm 1:3, 21. *d:* Jgs 17:6; 18:1; 19:1.

See RG 164–69

The Book of Ruth

The Book of Ruth is named for the Moabite woman who commits herself to the Israelite people by an oath to her mother-in-law Naomi and becomes the great-grandmother of David by marriage to Boaz of Bethlehem. Thus she is an ancestor in the messianic line that leads to Jesus (Mt 1:5).

The book portrays the love and loyalty of human beings in working their way through tragic circumstances to participation in the community of the faithful people of God. The key is responsible and loving decision-making: Ruth's loyalty (2:11), her generosity (1:15–17; 2:2, 7) and her willingness to take risks for the sake of righteousness set in motion a chain of beneficial events, while behind the scenes God blesses each step in the developing drama. Ruth is so frequently designated "the Moabite" in the book that the audience of the story is constantly reminded of the universality of the embrace of salvation.

In the Greek and Latin canons, Ruth follows Judges, to which it is related by its opening time reference ("Once back in the time of the judges . . ."), and precedes Samuel, serving as transition from Israel as tribal union to monarchy. In the present sequence of the Hebrew canon it is placed among the "Writings" immediately after the

Book of Proverbs, which ends with a powerful portrayal of "the woman of worth" (Prv 31:10–31; cf. Ru 3:11). Ruth is the primary liturgical text in Judaism for the celebration of the feast of Weeks (Shabuot).

The beauty of the story's construction, its use of dialogue (nearly two thirds of the text), and the sheer drama of its content mark it as one of the classic short stories of world literature. Based on the recollection of an historical figure, a story is developed which grips its audience with profound insight into divine and human relationships. The story is presented from a point some time after the course of events, as is indicated by the explanation of an obscure custom in 4:7. Wherever and whenever it was told, its claim of God's universal concern for humankind and the attractiveness of caring human responsibility shines forth.

The date of composition is disputed. Many authors date it early in the monarchy, and valid arguments can be presented for that position. Others argue for a postexilic date; they see the favorable presentation of a Moabite woman who became David's grandmother as a counter to the stringent measures of Ezra and Nehemiah against marriage with Moabites and other non-Jews (Ezr 9–10; Neh 13:23–29).

CHAPTER 1

See RG 167–68

Naomi in Moab. [1]Once back in the time of the judges* there was a famine in the land; so a man from Bethlehem of Judah left home with his wife and two sons to reside on the plateau of Moab. [2]The man was named Elimelech, his wife Naomi, and his sons Mahlon and Chilion; they were Ephrathites from Bethlehem of Judah. Some time after their arrival on the plateau of Moab, [3]Elimelech, the husband of Naomi, died, and she was left with her two sons. [4]They married

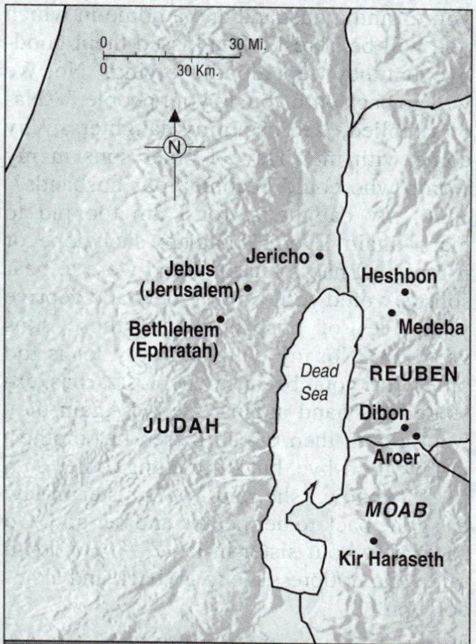

Places in Ruth

Moabite women, one named Orpah, the other Ruth. When they had lived there about ten years, [5]both Mahlon and Chilion died also, and the woman was left with neither her two boys* nor her husband.

[6]She and her daughters-in-law then prepared to go back from the plateau of Moab because word had reached her there that the LORD had seen to his people's needs* and given them food. [7]She and her two daughters-in-law left the place where they had been living. On the road back to the land of Judah, [8]Naomi said to her daughters-in-law, "Go back, each of you to your mother's house.* May the LORD show you the same kindness as you have shown to the deceased and to me. [9a] May the LORD guide each of

1:1–2 Back in the time of the judges: the story looks back three generations before King David (4:17) into the time of the tribal confederation described in the Book of Judges. David's Moabite connections are implied in 1 Sm 22:3–4. **Bethlehem of Judah**: Bethlehem, a town in which part of the Judean clan-division called Ephrathah lived; cf. 1 Chr 2:50–51; 4:4; Mi 5:1. Jos 19:15 mentions a different Bethlehem in the north. **The plateau of Moab**: on the east side of the Jordan valley rift, where the hills facing west get more rain, and where agricultural conditions differ from those in Judah. **Ephrathites**: a reminder of David's origins; cf. Mi 5:1.

1:5 Boys: the way the storyteller chooses certain words as guides is shown here; "boy" will not appear again until 4:16.

1:6 Had seen to his people's needs: lit., "had visited his people."

1:8 Mother's house: the women's part of the home, but also perhaps the proper location for arranging marriage; Sg 3:4; 8:2; Gn 24:28. **Kindness**: Hebrew *hesed*. The powerful

a: Ru 3:1.

you to find a husband and a home in which you will be at rest." She kissed them good-bye, but they wept aloud, 10 crying, "No! We will go back with you, to your people." 11 Naomi replied, "Go back, my daughters. Why come with me? Have I other sons in my womb who could become your husbands?* 12 Go, my daughters, for I am too old to marry again. Even if I had any such hope, or if tonight I had a husband and were to bear sons, 13 would you wait for them and deprive yourselves of husbands until those sons grew up? No, my daughters, my lot is too bitter for you, because the LORD has extended his hand against me." 14 Again they wept aloud; then Orpah kissed her mother-in-law good-bye, but Ruth clung to her.

15 "See now," she said, "your sister-in-law has gone back to her people and her god. Go back after your sister-in-law!" 16* But Ruth said, "Do not press me to go back and abandon you!

Wherever you go I will go,
    wherever you lodge I will lodge.
Your people shall be my people
    and your God, my God.
17 Where you die I will die,
    and there be buried.

May the LORD do thus to me, and more, if even death separates me from you!" 18 Naomi then ceased to urge her, for she saw she was determined to go with her.

The Return to Bethlehem. 19 So they went on together until they reached Bethlehem. On their arrival there, the whole town was excited about them, and the women asked: "Can this be Naomi?" 20[b] But she said to them, "Do not call me Naomi ['Sweet']. Call me Mara ['Bitter'], for the Almighty has made my life very bitter. 21*[c] I went away full, but the LORD has brought me back empty. Why should you call me 'Sweet,' since the LORD has brought me to trial, and the Almighty has pronounced evil sentence on me." 22 Thus it was that Naomi came back with her Moabite daughter-in-law Ruth, who accompanied her back from the plateau of Moab. They arrived in Bethlehem at the beginning of the barley harvest.*

CHAPTER 2

See RG 167–68

The Meeting. 1* Naomi had a powerful relative named Boaz,[d] through the clan of her husband Elimelech. 2* Ruth the Moabite said to Naomi, "I would like to go and glean grain in the field of anyone who will allow me." Naomi said to her, "Go ahead, my daughter." 3 So she went. The field she entered to glean after the harvesters happened to be the section belonging to Boaz, of the clan of Elimelech. 4* Soon, along came Boaz from Beth-

relationship term used here will recur in 2:20 and 3:10; kindness operates on both the divine-human and human-human level in Ruth.

1:11 Other sons . . . husbands: a reference to a customary practice known from Dt 25:5–10, levirate marriage, which assigns responsibility to the brother-in-law to produce heirs in order to perpetuate the name and hold the patrimonial land of a man who died childless. How far the responsibility extended beyond blood brothers is unclear; cf. Gn 38:8 and the upcoming scene in Ru 4:5–6. Naomi imagines the impossible: were she to have more sons they could take Ruth and Orpah as their wives.

1:16–17 Ruth's adherence to her mother-in-law in 1:14 is now expressed in a profound oath of loyalty, culminating in a formulary found frequently in Samuel and Kings; cf. especially 1 Sm 20:13. **Even death**: burial in Naomi's family tomb means that not even death will separate them.

1:21 Naomi's despair is made clear by her play on the meaning of her name in v. 20 and now by her accusation, like that in many psalms and in Job, that God has acted harshly toward her. The language belongs to the realm of judicial proceedings. By crying out in this way, the faithful Israelite opens the door to change, since the cry assumes that God hears and will do something about such seemingly unjust circumstances.

1:22 Barley and wheat harvests come in succession, from as early as April–May into June–July; Dt 16:9–12 suggests that the grain harvest lasts about seven weeks. The time reference leads effectively to the next episode.

2:1 Kinship ties and responsibilities now become very important. Boaz is introduced as one of a group surrounding Naomi through her husband's kin who are expected to extend care. The particular term used here (*moda'*, "relative") is picked up in 3:2; otherwise, most of the terminology about this responsibility to care will use the vocabulary of redeeming (*go'el*, "redeemer").

2:2 Israelite custom made provision for the poor, the widow, the stranger and the orphan to gather what was left behind by the harvesters, and instructed farmers not to cut to the edges of their fields, for the sake of these marginalized; Lv 19:9–10; 23:22; Dt 24:19–22.

2:4 The story brings Boaz upon the scene quickly, but he moves among his workers with the grace of a man of prominence, greeting them and being received with courtesy. The

b: Ex 15:23. *c:* Ru 3:17; 1 Kgs 17:20. *d:* Ru 3:2, 12; Mt 1:5.

lehem and said to the harvesters, "The LORD
be with you," and they replied, "The LORD
bless you." 5 Boaz asked the young man overseeing his harvesters, "Whose young woman
is this?" 6 The young man overseeing the harvesters answered, "She is the young Moabite
who came back with Naomi from the plateau
of Moab.[e] 7* She said, 'I would like to gather
the gleanings into sheaves after the harvesters.' Ever since she came this morning
she has remained here until now, with
scarcely a moment's rest."
8 Boaz then spoke to Ruth, "Listen, my
daughter. Do not go to glean in anyone else's
field; you are not to leave here. Stay here
with my young women. 9 Watch to see which
field is to be harvested, and follow them.
Have I not commanded the young men to do
you no harm? When you are thirsty, go and
drink from the vessels the young people
have filled." 10 Casting herself prostrate
upon the ground, she said to him, "Why
should I, a foreigner, be favored with your
attention?" 11[f] Boaz answered her: "I have
had a complete account of what you have
done for your mother-in-law after your husband's death; you have left your father and
your mother and the land of your birth, and
have come to a people whom previously you
did not know. 12[g] May the LORD reward what
you have done! May you receive a full reward from the LORD, the God of Israel, under whose wings you have come for refuge."
13 She said, "May I prove worthy of your favor, my lord. You have comforted me. You
have spoken to the heart of your servant*—
and I am not even one of your servants!"
14 At mealtime Boaz said to her, "Come here
and have something to eat; dip your bread in
the sauce." Then as she sat near the harvesters, he handed her some roasted grain
and she ate her fill and had some left over.
15 As she rose to glean, Boaz instructed his
young people: "Let her glean among the
sheaves themselves without scolding her,
16 and even drop some handfuls and leave
them for her to glean; do not rebuke her."
17 She gleaned in the field until evening,
and when she beat out what she had gleaned
it came to about an ephah* of barley, 18 which
she took into the town and showed to her
mother-in-law. Next she brought out what
she had left over from the meal and gave it
to her. 19 So her mother-in-law said to her,
"Where did you glean today? Where did you
go to work? May the one who took notice of
you be blessed!" Then she told her mother-
in-law with whom she had worked. "The
man at whose place I worked today is named
Boaz," she said. 20[h] "May he be blessed by
the LORD, who never fails to show kindness
to the living and to the dead," Naomi exclaimed to her daughter-in-law. She continued, "This man is a near relative of ours, one
of our redeemers."* 21 "He even told me,"
added Ruth the Moabite, "Stay with my
young people until they complete my entire
harvest." 22 "You would do well, my daughter," Naomi rejoined, "to work with his
young women; in someone else's field you
might be insulted." 23 So she stayed gleaning
with Boaz's young women until the end of
the barley and wheat harvests.

CHAPTER 3

See RG 168

Ruth Again Presents Herself. When
Ruth was back with her mother-in-law, 1 Naomi said to her, "My daughter, should I not
be seeking a pleasing home for you?[i]
2* Now! Is not Boaz,[j] whose young women

Hebrew blessing formulas used are frequent in Jewish and Christian liturgies.

2:7 The verse is somewhat garbled, but the points are clear that Ruth has been appropriately deferential in seeking permission to glean, and has worked steadily since arriving. Or perhaps she has waited patiently until Boaz arrives to gain permission.

2:13 Servant: only here is the language of servanthood used. Ruth has spoken with very deferential words to Boaz, but then seems to think that she has assumed too much.

2:17 Ephah: see note on Is 5:10.

2:20 For the first time, the story uses the Hebrew word *go'el*, "redeemer," for the responsibilities of the circle of kinship surrounding Naomi and Ruth and their deceased relatives. Involved are the recovery or retention of family land (Lv 25:25; 27:9–33; Jer 32:6–25), release of a relative from voluntary servitude to pay debts (Lv 25:47–55), and "redeeming blood" or vengeance, attested in passages which regulate such vengeance. No explicit connection is made elsewhere in the Bible between marriage responsibilities and redeeming.

3:2 Ruth's determined action to bring relief to Naomi's and

e: Ru 1:22. *f:* Ru 1:14–17. *g:* Ru 3:9; Dt 32:37; Ps 91:4. *h:* Gn 24:27; Lv 25:25; 27:9–33. *i:* Ru 1:9. *j:* Ru 2:1.

you were working with, a relative of ours? This very night he will be winnowing barley at the threshing floor. 3 Now, go bathe and anoint yourself; then put on your best attire and go down to the threshing floor. Do not make yourself known to the man before he has finished eating and drinking. 4 But when he lies down, take note of the place where he lies; then go uncover a place at his feet* and you lie down. He will then tell you what to do." 5 "I will do whatever you say," Ruth replied. 6 She went down to the threshing floor and did just as her mother-in-law had instructed her.

7 Boaz ate and drank to his heart's content, and went to lie down at the edge of the pile of grain. She crept up, uncovered a place at his feet, and lay down. 8 Midway through the night, the man gave a start and groped about, only to find a woman lying at his feet. 9 "Who are you?" he asked. She replied, "I am your servant Ruth. Spread the wing of your cloak* over your servant, for you are a redeemer." 10 He said, "May the LORD bless you, my daughter! You have been even more loyal now than before in not going after the young men, whether poor or rich. 11 Now rest assured, my daughter, I will do for you whatever you say; all my townspeople know you to be a worthy woman.* 12[k] Now, I am in fact a redeemer, but there is another redeemer closer than I.* 13 Stay where you are for tonight, and tomorrow, if he will act as redeemer for you, good. But if he will not, as the LORD lives, I will do it myself. Lie there until morning."[l] 14 So she lay at his feet until morning, but rose before anyone could recognize another, for Boaz had said, "Let it not be known that this woman came to the threshing floor." 15 Then he said to her, "Take off the shawl you are wearing; hold it firmly." When she did so, he poured out six measures of barley and helped her lift the bundle; then he himself left for the town.

16 She, meanwhile, went home to her mother-in-law, who asked, "How did things go, my daughter?" So she told her all the man had done for her, 17 and concluded, "He gave me these six measures of barley and said, 'Do not go back to your mother-in-law empty.' "[m] 18 Naomi then said, "Wait here, my daughter, until you learn what happens, for the man will not rest, but will settle the matter today."

CHAPTER 4

See RG 168–69

Boaz Marries Ruth. 1 Boaz went to the gate* and took a seat there. Along came the other redeemer[n] of whom he had spoken. Boaz called to him by name, "Come, sit here." And he did so. 2 Then Boaz picked out ten of the elders* of the town and asked them to sit nearby. When they had done this, 3 he said to the other redeemer: "Naomi, who has come back from the plateau of Moab, is putting up for sale the piece of land that belonged to our kinsman Elimelech. 4* So I thought I would inform you. Before those here present, including the elders of my people, purchase the field; act as redeemer.[o] But if you do not want to do it, tell me so, that I may know, for no one has a right of redemp-

her own circumstances now impels Naomi to move, using means available in Israelite custom which no one in the story has up to this point brought into play.

3:4 Uncover a place at his feet: Naomi advocates a course of action that will lead Boaz to act. Israelite custom and moral expectations strongly suggest that there is no loss of virtue involved in the scene.

3:9 Spread the wing of your cloak: Ez 16:8 makes it clear that this is a request for marriage. Ruth connects it to "redeemer" responsibility. A wordplay on "wing" links what Boaz is asked to do to what he has asked God to do for Ruth in 2:12.

3:11 Worthy woman: the language corresponds to the description of Boaz in 2:1 (lit., "strong and worthy"); the two worthy people are linked in character to one another, as they have already proven to be in their generous behavior toward the ones in need of their care. The townspeople, lit., "all the gate of my people," will ratify this at the gate in the sequel.

3:12 Another redeemer closer than I: Boaz knows of a closer relative who would have a prior right to buy the field and marry Ruth.

4:1 The gate of an Israelite town was the place where commercial and other legal matters were dealt with in publicly witnessed fashion.

4:2 Ten of the elders: to serve as judges in legal matters as well as witnesses of the settlement of business affairs; cf. Dt 25:7–9.

4:4 Although the laws governing inheritance by Israelite widows are not specified in the Bible, Naomi seems to have the right of disposal of a piece of Elimelech's land. The redemption custom in Lv 25:25 would then guide the procedure.

k: Ru 4:1. *l:* Ru 1:16; 4:5. *m:* Ru 1:21. *n:* Ru 3:12. *o:* Lv 25:25.

tion prior to yours, and mine is next." He answered, "I will act as redeemer."
5* Boaz continued, "When you acquire the
field from Naomi, you also acquire responsibility for Ruth the Moabite,[p] the widow of
the late heir, to raise up a family for the deceased on his estate." 6 The redeemer replied,
"I cannot exercise my right of redemption for
that would endanger my own estate. You do
it in my place, for I cannot." 7[q] Now it used
to be the custom in Israel that, to make binding a contract of redemption or exchange,
one party would take off a sandal* and give it
to the other. This was the form of attestation
in Israel. 8 So the other redeemer, in saying to
Boaz, "Acquire it for yourself," drew off his
sandal. 9 Boaz then said to the elders and to
all the people, "You are witnesses today that
I have acquired from Naomi all the holdings
of Elimelech, Chilion and Mahlon. 10 I also
acquire Ruth the Moabite, the widow of
Mahlon, as my wife, in order to raise up a
family for her late husband on his estate, so
that the name of the deceased may not perish
from his people and his place. Do you witness this today?" 11[r] All those at the gate, including the elders, said, "We do. May the
LORD make this woman come into your
house like Rachel and Leah, who between
them built up the house of Israel. Prosper in
Ephrathah! Bestow a name in Bethlehem!
12 With the offspring the LORD will give you
from this young woman, may your house become like the house of Perez, whom Tamar
bore to Judah."*
13 Boaz took Ruth. When they came together as husband and wife, the LORD enabled her to conceive and she bore a son.
14 Then the women said to Naomi, "Blessed
is the LORD who has not failed to provide
you today with a redeemer. May he become
famous in Israel! 15 He will restore your life
and be the support of your old age, for his
mother is the daughter-in-law who loves
you. She is worth more to you than seven
sons!" 16 Naomi took the boy, cradled him*
against her breast, and cared for him. 17 The
neighbor women joined the celebration: "A
son has been born to Naomi!"[s] They named
him Obed. He was the father of Jesse, the father of David.
18[t] These are the descendants of Perez: Perez was the father of Hezron,[u] 19 Hezron was
the father of Ram, Ram was the father of
Amminadab, 20[v] Amminadab was the father
of Nahshon, Nahshon was the father of
Salma, 21 Salma was the father of Boaz, Boaz
was the father of Obed, 22[w] Obed was the father of Jesse, and Jesse became the father of
David.

4:5–6 Although redemption and levirate practices are not otherwise linked in the Bible, they belong in the same area of need. Boaz claims that buying Elimelech's field obligates the other redeemer to produce an heir for Mahlon, who would then inherit the land. That would jeopardize this redeemer's overall holdings, since he would lose the land he had paid for. He can afford the first step but not the second, and cedes his responsibility to Boaz, who is willing to do both.

4:7 Take off a sandal: the legislation in Dt 25:8–10 provides that if a "redeemer" refuses to carry out the obligation of marrying his brother's wife, the woman shall strip off his sandal as a gesture of insult. In later years, when the obligation of carrying out this function of the "redeemer" was no longer keenly felt, the removal of the sandal may have become a formalized way of renouncing the rights/obligations of the "redeemer," as in this text.

4:12 Gn 38 contains a story about Tamar similar to Ruth's in levirate marriage. Judah, under less laudable circumstances, fulfills the same role as Boaz will, and Perez, son of Judah and Tamar, perpetuates the line. Thus two non-Israelite women, Tamar and Ruth, are important links in David's genealogy.

4:16 Cradled him: the child belongs to Naomi in the sense that he now becomes the redeemer in the family, as stated in 4:14. This tender act by Naomi is not necessarily adoptive and differs from the relationship in Gn 30:3; cf. Nm 11:12. Naomi now has a "boy" to replace her two lost "boys" in 1:5.

p: Ru 3:13. *q:* Dt 25:9. *r:* Gn 29:31–30:24; 35:16–19. *s:* Lk 1:58. *t:* 1 Chr 2:4–15; Mt 1:3–6. *u:* Gn 46:12; Nm 26:21; 1 Chr 4:1. *v:* Ex 6:23; Nm 1:7; 2:3; 7:12–17; 10:14. *w:* 1 Sm 16:2–13.

See RG 169-83

The Books of Samuel

These books describe the rise and development of kingship in Israel. Samuel is a pivotal figure. He bridges the gap between the period of the Judges and the monarchy, and guides Israel's transition to kingship. A Deuteronomistic editor presents both positive and negative traditions about the monarchy, portraying it both as evidence of Israel's rejection of the Lord as their sovereign (1 Sm 8:6–22; 12:1–25) and as part of God's plan to deliver the people (1 Sm 9:16; 10:17–27; 2 Sm 7:8–17). Samuel's misgivings about abuse of royal power foreshadow the failures and misdeeds of Saul and David and the failures of subsequent Israelite kings.

Although the events described in 1 and 2 Samuel move from the last of the judges to the decline of David's reign and the beginning of a legendary "Golden Age" under Solomon's rule, this material does not present either a continuous history or a systematic account of this period. The author/editor developed a narrative timeline around freely composed speeches, delivered by prophets like Samuel (e.g., 1 Sm 15:10–31; 28:15–19) and Nathan (2 Sm 12:1–12), who endorse Deuteronomistic perspectives regarding the establishment of the monarchy, the relationship between worship and obedience, and the divine covenant established with the house of David.

These books include independent blocks (e.g., the Ark Narrative [1 Sm 4:1–7:1], Saul's rise to power [1 Sm 9:1–11:15], David's ascendancy over Saul [1 Sm 16–31], the Succession Narrative [2 Sm 9–20; 1 Kgs 1–2]), which the editor shaped into three narrative cycles, the last two marked by transitional passages in 1 Sm 13:1 and 2 Sm 1:1. Each section focuses on a major figure in the development of the monarchy: Samuel, the reluctant king maker (1 Sm 1–12); Saul, the king whom the Lord rejects (1 Sm 13–31); David, the king after the Lord's own heart (2 Sm 1–24). A common theme unites these narratives: Israel's God acts justly, prospering those who remain faithful and destroying those who reject his ways (1 Sm 2:9). Along with the rest of the Deuteronomistic History, the Books of Samuel become an object lesson for biblical Israel as it tries to re-establish its religious identity after the destruction of Jerusalem and the loss of its homeland (587/586 B.C.).

The contents of the Books of Samuel may be divided as follows:

I. The Last Judges, Eli and Samuel (1 Sm 1:1–7:17)
II. Establishment of the Monarchy (1 Sm 8:1–12:25)
III. Saul and David (1 Sm 13:1–2 Sm 2:7)
IV. The Reign of David (2 Sm 2:8–20:26)
V. Appendixes (2 Sm 21:1–24:25)

The First Book of Samuel

I. The Last Judges, Eli and Samuel

CHAPTER 1

See RG 170

Elkanah and His Family at Shiloh.
1 There was a certain man from Ramathaim,
a Zuphite from the hill country of Ephraim.
His name was Elkanah, the son of Jeroham,
son of Elihu, son of Tohu, son of Zuph, an
Ephraimite.[a] 2 He had two wives, one named
Hannah, the other Peninnah; Peninnah had
children, but Hannah had no children. 3 Each
year this man went up from his city to worship and offer sacrifice to the LORD of hosts
at Shiloh, where the two sons of Eli, Hophni
and Phinehas, were ministering as priests of
the LORD.[b] 4 When the day came for Elkanah
to offer sacrifice, he used to give portions to
his wife Peninnah and to all her sons and
daughters, 5 but he would give a double por-

a: 1 Chr 6:19–20. *b:* Ex 23:14–17; 34:23; Dt 16:16; Jgs 21:19.

tion to Hannah because he loved her, though the LORD had closed her womb.[c] [6]Her rival,* to upset her, would torment her constantly, since the LORD had closed her womb.[d] [7]Year after year, when she went up to the house of the LORD, Peninnah would provoke her, and Hannah would weep and refuse to eat.* [8]Elkanah, her husband, would say to her: "Hannah, why are you weeping? Why are you not eating? Why are you so miserable? Am I not better for you than ten sons?"[e]

Hannah's Prayer. [9]Hannah rose after one such meal at Shiloh, and presented herself before the LORD; at the time Eli the priest was sitting on a chair near the doorpost of the LORD's temple. [10]In her bitterness she prayed to the LORD, weeping freely, [11]and made this vow: "O LORD of hosts, if you look with pity on the hardship of your servant, if you remember me and do not forget me, if you give your handmaid a male child, I will give him to the LORD all the days of his life. No razor shall ever touch his head."* [f] [12]As she continued praying before the LORD, Eli watched her mouth, [13]for Hannah was praying silently; though her lips were moving, her voice could not be heard. Eli, thinking she was drunk, [14]said to her, "How long will you make a drunken spectacle of yourself? Sober up from your wine!" [15]"No, my lord!" Hannah answered. "I am an unhappy woman. I have had neither wine nor liquor; I was only pouring out my heart to the LORD. [16]Do not think your servant a worthless woman; my prayer has been prompted by my deep sorrow and misery." [17]Eli said, "Go in peace, and may the God of Israel grant you what you have requested." [18]She replied, "Let your servant find favor in your eyes," and left. She went to her quarters, ate and drank with her husband, and no longer appeared downhearted. [19]Early the next morning they worshiped before the LORD, and then returned to their home in Ramah. When they returned Elkanah had intercourse with his wife Hannah, and the LORD remembered her.

Hannah Bears a Son. [20]She conceived and, at the end of her pregnancy, bore a son whom she named Samuel.* "Because I asked the LORD for him. [21]The next time her husband Elkanah was going up with the rest of his household to offer the customary sacrifice to the LORD and to fulfill his vows, [22]Hannah did not go, explaining to her husband, "Once the child is weaned, I will take him to appear before the LORD and leave him there forever."* [23]Her husband Elkanah answered her: "Do what you think best; wait until you have weaned him. Only may the LORD fulfill his word!" And so she remained at home and nursed her son until she had weaned him.[g]

Hannah Presents Samuel to the Lord. [24]Once he was weaned, she brought him up with her, along with a three-year-old bull, an ephah* of flour, and a skin of wine, and presented him at the house of the LORD in Shiloh. [25]After they had slaughtered the bull, they brought the child to Eli. [26]Then Hannah spoke up: "Excuse me, my lord! As you live, my lord, I am the woman who stood here near you, praying to the LORD. [27]I prayed for this child, and the LORD granted my request. [28]Now I, in turn, give him to the LORD; as long as he lives, he shall be dedicated to the LORD." Then they worshiped there before the LORD.

1:6 Her rival: Hebrew *sara*, "rival wife, co-wife"; in the Talmud, a technical term for a second or co-wife.

1:7 In biblical narrative, the social status gained by producing children, especially males, often set woman against woman; cf. e.g., Gn 16, 21, 30. Peninnah's provocations may be the arrogant boasting mentioned in 2:3.

1:11 No razor . . . : the Septuagint adds "he shall drink neither wine nor liquor." This addition is a further suggestion that Samuel is dedicated to God under a nazirite vow (Nm 6:4–5); see note on v. 22.

1:20 Samuel: Hannah's explanation associates her son's name with the narrative's wordplay on the Hebrew verbs *s'l* ("ask," vv. 17, 27), *his'il* ("hand over, dedicate," v. 28), *sa'ul* ("dedicated," v. 28), and the noun *se'elah* ("request," vv. 17, 27). The name, however, is related to the Hebrew root *s'l* only through assonance. It means "his name is El/God," not "the one requested of or dedicated (*sa'ul*) to God" (v. 28), which is the meaning of the name Saul. The author may have lifted the *s'l* wordplay from a narrative about Saul to portray Samuel as God's gracious answer to Hannah's request.

1:22 Leave him there forever: a Qumran manuscript adds "I will give him as a nazirite forever"; it interprets v. 11 to mean that Hannah dedicates Samuel under a nazirite vow (cf. Nm 6:4–5).

1:24 Ephah: see note on Is 5:10.

c: Dt 21:15–17. *d:* Gn 16:4–5; 29:31; Jgs 13:2; Lk 1:7. *e:* Ru 4:15. *f:* Nm 6:1–5; Jgs 13:2–5; 16:17; Lk 1:15. *g:* Dt 9:5; 2 Sm 7:25; 1 Kgs 2:4.

See RG 170–71

CHAPTER 2

1 And Hannah prayed:*

"My heart exults in the LORD,
my horn is exalted by my God.
I have swallowed up my enemies;
I rejoice in your victory.[h]
2 There is no Holy One like the LORD;
there is no Rock like our God.[i]
3 Speak boastfully no longer,
Do not let arrogance issue from your mouths.*
For an all-knowing God is the LORD,
a God who weighs actions.[j]

4 "The bows of the mighty are broken,
while the tottering gird on strength.[k]
5 The well-fed hire themselves out for bread,
while the hungry no longer have to toil.
The barren wife bears seven sons,
while the mother of many languishes.[l]
6 "The LORD puts to death and gives life,
casts down to Sheol and brings up again.[m]
7 The LORD makes poor and makes rich,
humbles, and also exalts.
8 He raises the needy from the dust;
from the ash heap lifts up the poor,
To seat them with nobles
and make a glorious throne their heritage.

"For the pillars of the earth are the LORD's,
and he has set the world upon them.[n]
9 He guards the footsteps of his faithful ones,
but the wicked shall perish in the darkness;
for not by strength does one prevail.
10 The LORD's foes shall be shattered;
the Most High in heaven thunders;
the LORD judges the ends of the earth.
May he give strength to his king,
and exalt the horn of his anointed!"[o]

11 When Elkanah returned home to Ramah,
the child remained in the service of the LORD
under the priest Eli.

Wickedness of Eli's Sons. 12 Now the sons
of Eli were wicked; they had respect neither
for the LORD 13 nor for the priests' duties toward the people. When someone offered a
sacrifice, the priest's servant would come
with a three-pronged fork, while the meat
was still boiling,[p] 14 and would thrust it into
the basin, kettle, caldron, or pot. Whatever
the fork brought up, the priest would take for
himself. They treated all the Israelites who
came to the sanctuary at Shiloh in this way.
15 In fact, even before the fat was burned, the
priest's servant would come and say to the
one offering the sacrifice, "Give me some
meat to roast for the priest. He will not accept boiled meat from you, only raw meat."
16 And if this one protested, "Let the fat be
burned first, then take whatever you wish,"
he would reply, "No, give it to me now, or
else I will take it by force."[q] 17 Thus the
young men sinned grievously in the presence of the LORD, treating the offerings to
the LORD with disdain.

The Lord Rewards Hannah. 18 Meanwhile
the boy Samuel, wearing a linen ephod,* was
serving in the presence of the LORD. 19 His
mother used to make a little garment for
him, which she would bring him each time
she went up with her husband to offer the
customary sacrifice. 20 And Eli would bless
Elkanah and his wife, as they were leaving
for home. He would say, "May the LORD re-

2:1–10 Hannah appeals to a God who maintains order by keeping human affairs in balance, reversing the fortunes of the arrogant, who, like Peninnah, boast of their good fortune (vv. 1, 3, 9) at the expense of those like Hannah who receive less from the Lord. Hannah's admission places her among the faithful who trust that God will execute justice on their behalf. The reference "his king . . . his anointed" (v. 10) recalls the final sentence of the Book of Judges and introduces the kingship theme that dominates the Books of Samuel.

2:3 Speak . . . mouths: addressed to the enemies mentioned in v. 1.

2:18 Linen ephod: not the same as the high priest's ephod (Ex 28:6–14) or the ephod used in divination (v. 28). Samuel wore the same kind of a ceremonial garment as the priests did (1 Sm 22:18). David also wore an ephod when he danced before the ark (2 Sm 6:14).

h: Dt 33:17; 2 Sm 22:3; Ps 18:2; 89:18; Is 61:10; Lk 1:47, 69. *i:* 2 Sm 22:3; Ps 18:2. *j:* Ps 75:5–6. *k:* Is 40:29. *l:* Ru 4:15; Jer 15:9. *m:* Dt 32:39; Tb 4:19; Jb 5:11; Ps 30:4; Wis 16:13; Lk 1:52. *n:* Jb 9:6; 38:6; Ps 75:4; 104:5; 113:8; 121:3. *o:* Ps 98:9. *p:* Ex 29:27–28; Lv 7:29–36; Dt 18:3. *q:* Lv 3:3–5; Nm 18:17.

pay you with children from this woman for the gift she has made to the LORD!" 21 The LORD favored Hannah so that she conceived and gave birth to three more sons and two daughters, while young Samuel grew up in the service of the LORD.[r]

Eli's Futile Rebuke. 22 When Eli was very old, he kept hearing how his sons were treating all Israel, and that they were behaving promiscuously* with the women serving at the entry of the meeting tent. 23 So he said to them: "Why are you doing such things? I hear from everyone that your behavior is depraved. 24 Stop this, my sons! The report that I hear the LORD's people spreading is not good. 25 If someone sins against another, anyone can intercede for the sinner with the LORD; but if anyone sins against the LORD, who can intercede* for the sinner?" But they disregarded their father's warning, since the LORD wanted them dead. 26 Meanwhile, young Samuel was growing in stature and in worth in the estimation of the LORD and the people.[s]

The Fate of Eli's House.* 27 A man of God came to Eli and said to him: "Thus says the LORD: I went so far as to reveal myself to your father's house when they were in Egypt as slaves to the house of Pharaoh. 28 I chose them out of all the tribes of Israel to be my priests, to go up to my altar, to burn incense, and to wear the ephod* in my presence; and I assigned all the fire offerings of the Israelites to your father's house.[t] 29 Why do you stare greedily at my sacrifices and at the offerings that I have prescribed? Why do you honor your sons more than you honor me, fattening yourselves with the choicest part of every offering of my people Israel? 30[u] This, therefore, is the oracle of the LORD, the God of Israel: I said in the past that your family and your father's house should minister in my presence forever. But now—oracle of the LORD: Far be it from me! I will honor those who honor me, but those who despise me shall be cursed. 31 Yes, the days are coming when I will break your strength and the strength of your father's house, so that no one in your family lives to old age. 32 You shall witness, like a disappointed rival, all the benefits enjoyed by Israel, but no member of your household shall ever grow old. 33 I will leave you one man at my altar to wear out his eyes and waste his strength, but the rest of your family shall die by the sword. 34 This is a sign for you—what happens to your two sons, Hophni and Phinehas. Both of them will die on the same day.[v] 35 I will choose a faithful priest who shall do what I have in heart and mind. I will establish a lasting house for him and he shall serve in the presence of my anointed forever. 36 Then whoever is left of your family will grovel before him for a piece of silver or a loaf of bread, saying: Please assign me a priestly function, that I may have a crust of bread to eat."[w]

CHAPTER 3

See RG 171

Revelation to Samuel. 1 During the time young Samuel was minister to the LORD under Eli, the word of the LORD was scarce and vision infrequent. 2* One day Eli was asleep in his usual place. His eyes had lately grown so weak that he could not see. 3 The lamp of God was not yet extinguished,* and Samuel was sleeping in the temple of the LORD where the ark of God was.[x] 4 The LORD

2:22 Behaving promiscuously: this part of the verse, which recalls Ex 38:8, is a gloss; it is lacking in the oldest Greek translation, and in 4QSam[a].

2:25 Who can intercede: Eli's sons fail to understand that their crime is directly against God and that God will punish them for it. Their behavior is set in sharp contrast to Samuel's, which meets with God's approval.

2:27–36 These verses describe the punishment of Eli from a point of view contemporary with the reform of Josiah (2 Kgs 23:9; cf. v. 36); they hint at the events recorded in 1 Sm 22:18–23 and 1 Kgs 2:27. The older story of this divine warning occurs in 1 Sm 3:11–14. **A man of God**: often an anonymous figure whose speech foreshadows events in the near future. Cf. 1 Sm 9:6; 1 Kgs 13:1; 2 Kgs 23:16–17.

2:28 Ephod: a portable container, presumably of cloth, for the lots used in ritual consultation of God during the days of the Judges (Jgs 17:5; 18:14–15) and into the time of David (1 Sm 14:3; 23:6–9; 30:7–8). Attached to the ephod of the high priest described in Ex 28:6–8 is a "breastpiece of decision" which symbolized, but did not facilitate, such consultation. The Exodus text codifies a later form of the tradition.

3:2–18 The call of Samuel: This section may be divided as follows: 1. the triple summons (vv. 2–9); 2. God's revelation (vv. 10–14); 3. Samuel informs Eli (vv. 15–18).

3:3 Not yet extinguished: referring to the nighttime setting of this narrative (cf. Ex 27:20–21) and foreshadowing a

r: 1 Sm 3:19. *s:* Lk 2:52. *t:* 1 Sm 23:9; 30:7–8; Jgs 17:5. *u:* 2 Sm 22:26; 1 Kgs 2:27; Ps 18:25. *v:* 1 Sm 4:11. *w:* 2 Kgs 23:9. *x:* Ex 27:20–22.

called to Samuel, who answered, "Here I am." [5]He ran to Eli and said, "Here I am. You called me." "I did not call you," Eli answered. "Go back to sleep." So he went back to sleep. [6]Again the LORD called Samuel, who rose and went to Eli. "Here I am," he said. "You called me." But he answered, "I did not call you, my son. Go back to sleep."

[7]Samuel did not yet recognize the LORD, since the word of the LORD had not yet been revealed to him. [8]The LORD called Samuel again, for the third time. Getting up and going to Eli, he said, "Here I am. You called me." Then Eli understood that the LORD was calling the youth. [9]So he said to Samuel, "Go to sleep, and if you are called, reply, 'Speak, LORD, for your servant is listening.' " When Samuel went to sleep in his place, [10]the LORD came and stood there, calling out as before: Samuel, Samuel! Samuel answered, "Speak, for your servant is listening." [11]The LORD said to Samuel: I am about to do something in Israel that will make the ears of everyone who hears it ring.[y] [12]On that day I will carry out against Eli everything I have said about his house, beginning to end. [13]I announce to him that I am condemning his house once and for all, because of this crime: though he knew his sons were blaspheming God, he did not reprove them.[z] [14]Therefore, I swear to Eli's house: No sacrifice or offering will ever expiate its crime.* [15]Samuel then slept until morning, when he got up early and opened the doors of the temple of the LORD. He was afraid to tell Eli the vision, [16]but Eli called to him, "Samuel, my son!" He replied, "Here I am." [17]Then Eli asked, "What did he say to you? Hide nothing from me! May God do thus to you, and more,* if you hide from me a single thing he told you." [18]So Samuel told him everything, and held nothing back. Eli answered, "It is the LORD. What is pleasing in the LORD's sight, the LORD will do."

Samuel Acknowledged as Prophet. [19]Samuel grew up, and the LORD was with him, not permitting any word of his to go unfulfilled.[a] [20b] Thus all Israel from Dan to Beer-sheba came to know that Samuel was a trustworthy prophet of the LORD. [21]The LORD continued to appear at Shiloh, manifesting himself to Samuel at Shiloh through his word. Samuel's word spread throughout Israel.

CHAPTER 4

See RG 171–72

Defeat of the Israelites.* [1]At that time, the Philistines gathered for an attack on Israel. Israel went out to engage them in battle and camped at Ebenezer, while the Philistines camped at Aphek. [2]The Philistines then drew up in battle formation against Israel. After a fierce struggle Israel was defeated by the Philistines, who killed about four thousand men on the battlefield. [3]When the troops retired to the camp, the elders of Israel said, "Why has the LORD permitted us to be defeated today by the Philistines? Let us fetch the ark of the LORD from Shiloh that it may go into battle among us and save us from the grasp of our enemies."[c]

Loss of the Ark. [4]So the people sent to Shiloh and brought from there the ark of the LORD of hosts, who is enthroned upon the cherubim.* The two sons of Eli, Hophni and Phinehas, accompanied the ark of God.[d] [5]When the ark of the LORD arrived in the camp, all Israel shouted so loudly that the earth shook. [6]The Philistines, hearing the uproar, asked, "What does this loud shouting in the camp of the Hebrews mean?" On learning that the ark of the LORD had come into the camp, [7]the Philistines were frightened, crying

permanently extinguished lamp when the ark is captured and Shiloh destroyed.

3:14 Lv 4:3–12 presents another view: the offering of a bull can expiate priestly sin.

3:17 May God do thus to you, and more: an oath formula which strengthens Eli's demand by threatening divine punishment if Samuel does not obey. Cf. 14:44; 20:13; 25:22; 2 Sm 3:9, 35; 19:14.

4:1–7:1 The Ark Narrative: A striking indication that this is an independent narrative is the absence of any mention of Samuel. **The Philistines**: one of the Sea Peoples, of Aegean origin, who occupied the coastal plain of Palestine and threatened the Israelites who settled the inland hills.

4:4 Enthroned upon the cherubim: this divine title first occurs in the Old Testament at the sanctuary at Shiloh (cf. 2 Sm 6:2); God is represented seated upon a throne borne through the heavens by cherubim, creatures partly human being, partly beast (cf. Ez 1 and 10).

y: 2 Kgs 21:12. *z:* 1 Sm 2:27–36. *a:* 1 Sm 2:21. *b:* Jgs 20:1; 2 Sm 3:10; 17:11; 24:2. *c:* Nm 10:35; 14:42–44. *d:* Ex 25:21–22.

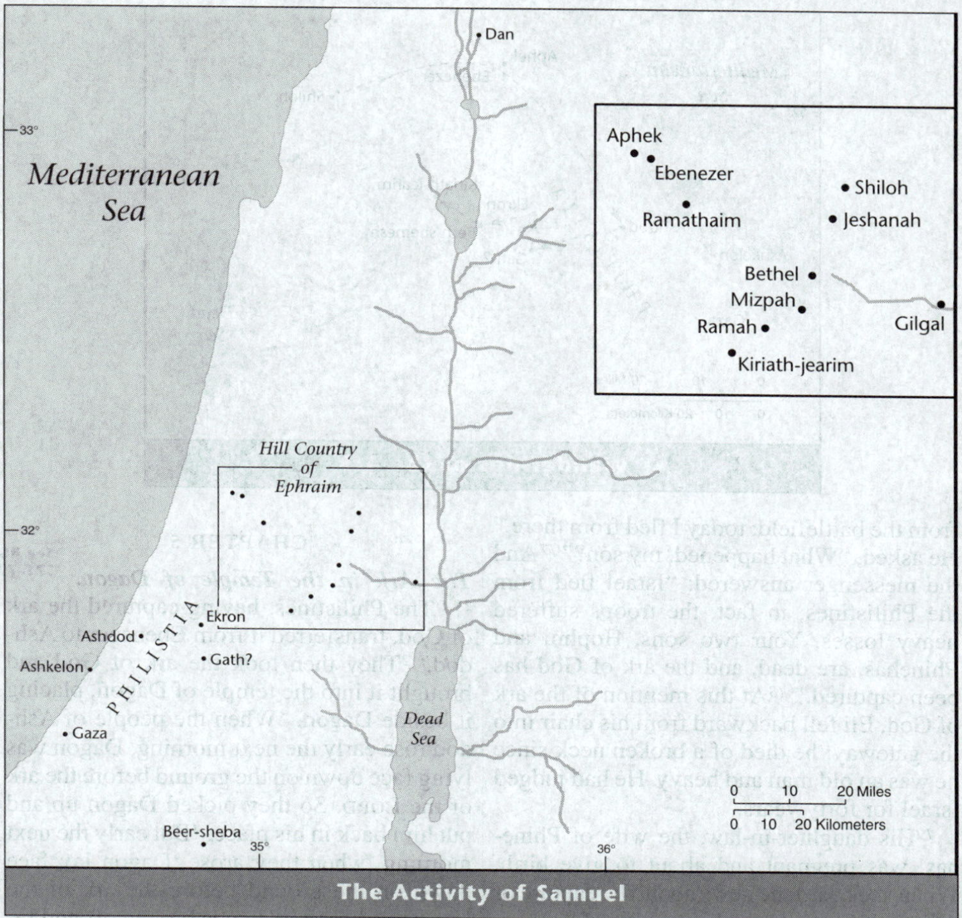

out, "Gods have come to their camp. Woe to
us! This has never happened before. 8 Woe to
us! Who can deliver us from the power of
these mighty gods?* These are the gods who
struck the Egyptians with various plagues in
the desert. 9 Take courage and act like soldiers, Philistines; otherwise you will become
slaves to the Hebrews, as they were your
slaves. Fight like soldiers!" 10 The Philistines
fought and Israel was defeated; everyone fled
to their own tents.* It was a disastrous defeat;
Israel lost thirty thousand foot soldiers. 11 The
ark of God was captured, and Eli's two sons,
Hophni and Phinehas, were dead.[e]

Death of Eli. 12 A Benjaminite fled from
the battlefield and reached Shiloh that same
day, with his clothes torn and his head covered with dirt.[f] 13 When he arrived, Eli was
sitting in his chair beside the gate, watching
the road, for he was troubled at heart about
the ark of God. The man, however, went into
the city to announce his news; then the
whole city cried out. 14 When Eli heard the
uproar, he wondered why there was such
commotion. Just then the man rushed up to
inform him. 15 Eli was ninety-eight years old,
and his eyes would not focus. So he could
not see. 16 The man said to Eli: "I have come

4:8 These mighty gods: the Philistines, who were polytheists, presume that the Israelites also honored several gods.

4:10 To their own tents: the defeat is so catastrophic that the soldiers abandon the army for home; cf. 2 Sm 18:17.

e: 1 Sm 2:34. *f:* Jos 7:6; 2 Sm 1:2; Jer 7:12.

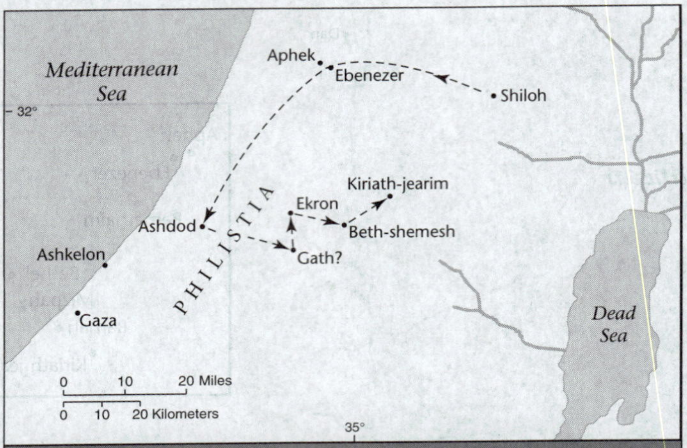

Wanderings of the Ark

from the battlefield; today I fled from there."
He asked, "What happened, my son?" 17 And
the messenger answered: "Israel fled from
the Philistines; in fact, the troops suffered
heavy losses. Your two sons, Hophni and
Phinehas, are dead, and the ark of God has
been captured." 18 At this mention of the ark
of God, Eli fell backward from his chair into
the gateway; he died of a broken neck since
he was an old man and heavy. He had judged
Israel for forty years.

19 His daughter-in-law, the wife of Phinehas, was pregnant and about to give birth.
When she heard the news about the capture of
the ark of God and the deaths of her father-in-
law and her husband, she crouched down in
labor, and gave birth. 20 She was about to die
when the women standing around her said to
her, "Do not be afraid, you have given birth to
a son." Yet she neither answered nor paid any
attention.[g] 21 She named the child Ichabod,
saying, "Gone is the glory from Israel," referring to the capture of the ark of God and to her
father-in-law and her husband. 22 She said,
"Gone is the glory from Israel," because the
ark of God had been captured.[h]

CHAPTER 5

See RG 171–72

The Ark in the Temple of Dagon.
1* [i] The Philistines, having captured the ark
of God, transferred it from Ebenezer to Ashdod.[j] 2 They then took the ark of God and
brought it into the temple of Dagon, placing
it beside Dagon. 3 When the people of Ashdod rose early the next morning, Dagon was
lying face down on the ground before the ark
of the LORD. So they picked Dagon up and
put him back in his place. 4 But early the next
morning, when they arose, Dagon lay face
down on the ground before the ark of the
LORD, his head and hands broken off and lying on the threshold, his trunk alone intact.
5 For this reason, neither the priests of Dagon
nor any others who enter the temple of Dagon tread on the threshold of Dagon in Ashdod to this very day.

The Ark Is Carried About. 6 Now the hand
of the LORD weighed heavily on the people
of Ashdod, ravaging them and afflicting the
city and its vicinity with tumors.* [k] 7 On seeing how matters stood, the people of Ashdod
decided, "The ark of the God of Israel must

5:1–12 The Philistines take the ark to Dagon's temple in Ashdod to confirm their victory. Their action, however, underscores Dagon's impotence and the Lord's power. The narrator relates the transfer of the ark from Ashdod to Gath and then Ekron as the progress of a conquering warrior king through the Philistine cities along the central plain. The Philistines' humiliation recalls the climax of the Samson story (Jgs 16:13–21).

5:6 Tumors: the Septuagint adds that mice, suggestive of bubonic plague, infested their fields, thus anticipating the golden mice in 6:4–5. One symptom of bubonic plague is swollen lymph nodes ("tumors").

g: 1 Sm 14:3; Gn 35:16–20. *h:* Ps 78:61. *i:* Jgs 16:23–30; Is 45:5–6, 20–21. *j:* Jos 13:3. *k:* Ps 32:4.

not remain with us, for his hand weighs heavily on us and Dagon our god." 8So they summoned all the Philistine leaders and inquired of them, "What shall we do with the ark of the God of Israel?" The people of Gath replied, "Let them move the ark of the God of Israel to us." So they moved the ark of the God of Israel to Gath. 9But after it had been brought there, the hand of the LORD was against the city, resulting in utter turmoil: the LORD afflicted its inhabitants, young and old, and tumors broke out on them. 10The ark of God was next sent to Ekron; but as it entered that city, the people there cried out, "Why have they brought the ark of the God of Israel here to kill us and our kindred?" 11Then they, too, sent a summons to all the Philistine leaders and pleaded: "Send away the ark of the God of Israel. Send it back to its place so it does not kill us and our kindred." A deadly panic had seized the whole city, since the hand of God lay heavy upon it. 12Those who escaped death were afflicted with tumors. Thus the outcry from the city went up to the heavens.

CHAPTER 6

See RG 171–72

The Ark Is Returned. 1The ark of the LORD had been in the land of the Philistines seven months 2when they summoned priests and diviners to ask, "What shall we do with the ark of the LORD? Tell us what we should send back with it." 3They replied: "If you intend to send back the ark of the God of Israel, you must not send it alone, but must, by all means, make amends to God through a reparation offering.* Then you will be healed, and will learn why God continues to afflict you." 4When asked further, "What reparation offering should be our amends to God?" they replied: "Five golden tumors and five golden mice to correspond to the number of Philistine leaders, since the same plague has struck all of you and your leaders. 5Therefore, make images of the tumors and of the mice that are devastating your land and so give glory to the God of Israel. Perhaps then God will lift his hand from you, your gods, and your land. 6Why should you become stubborn, the way the Egyptians and Pharaoh were stubborn? Was it not after he had dealt ruthlessly with them that the Israelites were released and departed?[l] 7So now set to work and make a new cart. Then take two milk cows that have not borne the yoke; hitch them to the cart, but drive their calves indoors away from them.*[m] 8You shall next take the ark of the LORD and place it on the cart, putting the golden articles that you are offering as reparation for your guilt in a box beside it. Start it on its way, and let it go. 9Then watch! If it goes up to Beth-shemesh* along the route to the LORD's territory, then it was the LORD who brought this great calamity upon us; if not, we will know that it was not the LORD's hand, but a bad turn, that struck us."

The Ark in Beth-shemesh. 10They acted upon this advice. Taking two milk cows, they hitched them to the cart but shut up their calves indoors. 11Then they placed the ark of the LORD on the cart, along with the box containing the golden mice and the images of the tumors. 12The cows went straight for the route to Beth-shemesh and continued along this road, mooing as they went, turning neither right nor left. The Philistine leaders followed them as far as the border of Beth-shemesh. 13The people of Beth-shemesh were harvesting the wheat in the valley. They looked up and rejoiced when they saw the ark. 14The cart came to the field of Joshua the Beth-shemite and stopped there. At a large stone in the field, the wood of the cart was split up and the cows were offered as a burnt offering to the LORD.[n] 15The Levites, meanwhile, had taken down the ark of God and the box beside it, with the golden articles, and had placed them on the great stone. The people of Beth-shemesh also of-

6:3 A reparation offering: an offering to make amends for unwitting transgressions against holy things or property rights; cf. Lv 6:1–3.

6:7 But drive their calves indoors away from them: a test to confirm the source of the Philistines' trouble. Left to their instincts, milk cows would remain near their calves rather than head for the road to Beth-shemesh.

6:9 Beth-shemesh: a border city (about twenty-four miles west of Jerusalem) between Philistine and Israelite territory.

l: Ex 7:14; 8:15; 9:34. *m:* Nm 19:2; Dt 21:3; 2 Sm 6:3. *n:* 2 Sm 24:21–25.

fered other burnt offerings and sacrifices to the LORD that day.[o] 16 After witnessing this, the five Philistine leaders returned to Ekron the same day.

17 The golden tumors the Philistines sent back as a reparation offering to the LORD were as follows: one for Ashdod, one for Gaza, one for Ashkelon, one for Gath, and one for Ekron. 18 The golden mice, however, corresponded to the number of all the cities of the Philistines belonging to the five leaders, including fortified cities and open villages.* The large stone on which the ark of the LORD was placed is still in the field of Joshua the Beth-shemite at the present time.[p]

Penalty for Irreverence. 19 The descendants of Jeconiah did not join in the celebration with the inhabitants of Beth-shemesh when they saw the ark of the LORD, and seventy of them were struck down. The people mourned over this great calamity which the LORD had inflicted upon them. 20 The men of Beth-shemesh asked, "Who can stand in the presence of the LORD, this Holy God? To whom can the ark go so that we are rid of it?" 21 They then sent messengers to the inhabitants of Kiriath-jearim, saying, "The Philistines have returned the ark of the LORD; come down and get it."

CHAPTER 7

See RG 171–73

1 So the inhabitants of Kiriath-jearim came for the ark of the LORD and brought it into the house of Abinadab on the hill, appointing his son Eleazar as guardian of the ark of the LORD.

Samuel the Judge. 2 From the day the ark came to rest in Kiriath-jearim, a long time, twenty years, elapsed, and the whole house of Israel turned to the LORD. 3 Then Samuel addressed the whole house of Israel: "If you would return to the LORD with your whole heart, remove your foreign gods and your Astartes, fix your hearts on the LORD, and serve him alone, then the LORD will deliver you from the hand of the Philistines."[q] 4 So the Israelites removed their Baals and Astartes,* and served the LORD alone. 5 Samuel then gave orders, "Gather all Israel to Mizpah, that I may pray to the LORD for you."[r] 6 When they had gathered at Mizpah, they drew water and poured it out* on the ground before the LORD, and they fasted that day, saying, "We have sinned against the LORD." It was at Mizpah that Samuel began to judge the Israelites.[s]

Rout of the Philistines. 7 When the Philistines heard that the Israelites had gathered at Mizpah, their leaders went up against Israel. Hearing this, the Israelites became afraid of the Philistines 8 and appealed to Samuel, "Do not stop crying out to the LORD our God for us, to save us from the hand of the Philistines."[t] 9 Samuel therefore took an unweaned lamb and offered it whole as a burnt offering to the LORD.[u] He cried out to the LORD for Israel, and the LORD answered him. 10 While Samuel was sacrificing the burnt offering, the Philistines drew near for battle with Israel. That day, however, the LORD thundered loudly against the Philistines, and threw them into such confusion that they were defeated by Israel.[v] 11 Thereupon the Israelites rushed out from Mizpah and pursued the Philistines, striking them down even beyond Beth-car. 12 Samuel then took a stone and placed it between Mizpah and Jeshanah; he named it Ebenezer,* explaining, "As far as this place the LORD has been our help." 13 Thus were the Philistines subdued, never again to enter the territory of Israel, for the hand of the LORD was against them as long as Samuel lived.[w] 14 The cities from Ekron to Gath which the Philistines had taken from

6:18 Open villages: the plague devastated both fortified cities and villages, an indication of the Lord's power over the Philistines.

7:4 Baals and Astartes: a Deuteronomistic phrase; cf. Jgs 2:13; 10:6; 1 Sm 12:10. Baal and Astarte were Canaanite divinities.

7:6 Drew water and poured it out: this ritual act does not appear elsewhere in the Old Testament. Linked with fasting and admission of sin, it seems to function as a purification ritual that washes away the guilt incurred by worshiping the Canaanite Baal and his consort Astarte. Its effectiveness is immediately evident when the Lord thunders a response to Samuel's offering.

7:12 Ebenezer: "stone of the helper," i.e., the Lord.

o: Dt 31:25; 1 Chr 15:2. *p:* 1 Sm 7:12; Gn 31:52; Jos 24:27. *q:* 1 Sm 12:10, 20, 24; Jos 24:23; Jgs 6:6–10; 10:10–16. *r:* 1 Sm 10:17; Jgs 20:1. *s:* Jgs 20:26; Ps 22:14; Lam 2:19. *t:* Jos 24:7; Jgs 3:9, 15; 6:6; 10:15. *u:* 2 Sm 22:14–15; Sir 46:16–18. *v:* Ex 9:23; 2 Sm 22:14. *w:* Jgs 3:20; 8:28; 11:33.

Israel were restored to them. Israel also
freed the territory of these cities from Philistine domination. There was also peace between Israel and the Amorites.*
[15]Samuel judged Israel as long as he lived.
[16]He made a yearly circuit, passing through
Bethel, Gilgal and Mizpah* and judging Israel at each of these places. [17]Then he used
to return to Ramah, for that was his home.
There, too, he judged Israel and built an altar to the LORD.[x]

II. Establishment of the Monarchy

CHAPTER 8

See RG 172–73

Request for a King. [1]* In his old age
Samuel appointed his sons judges over Israel.[y] [2]His firstborn was named Joel, his second son, Abijah; they judged at Beer-sheba.
[3]His sons did not follow his example, but
looked to their own gain, accepting bribes
and perverting justice.[z] [4]Therefore all the
elders of Israel assembled and went to Samuel at Ramah [5]and said to him, "Now that
you are old, and your sons do not follow
your example, appoint a king over us, like
all the nations, to rule us."[a]
[6]Samuel was displeased when they said,
"Give us a king to rule us." But he prayed to
the LORD. [7]The LORD said: Listen to whatever the people say. You are not the one they
are rejecting. They are rejecting me as their
king.[b] [8]They are acting toward you just as
they have acted from the day I brought them
up from Egypt to this very day, deserting me
to serve other gods. [9]Now listen to them; but
at the same time, give them a solemn warning and inform them of the rights of the king
who will rule them.
The Governance of the King. [10]Samuel delivered the message of the LORD in full to
those who were asking him for a king. [11]He
told them: "The governance of the king who
will rule you will be as follows: He will take
your sons and assign them to his chariots
and horses, and they will run before his chariot.[c] [12]He will appoint from among them his
commanders of thousands and of hundreds.
He will make them do his plowing and harvesting and produce his weapons of war and
chariotry.[d] [13]He will use your daughters as
perfumers, cooks, and bakers. [14]He will take
your best fields, vineyards, and olive groves,
and give them to his servants.[e] [15]He will
tithe your crops and grape harvests to give to
his officials* and his servants.[f] [16]He will take
your male and female slaves, as well as your
best oxen and donkeys, and use them to do
his work. [17]He will also tithe your flocks. As
for you, you will become his slaves.[g] [18]On
that day you will cry out because of the king
whom you have chosen, but the LORD will
not answer you on that day."
Persistent Demand. [19]The people, however, refused to listen to Samuel's warning
and said, "No! There must be a king over
us.[h] [20]We too must be like all the nations,
with a king to rule us, lead us in warfare, and
fight our battles." [21]Samuel listened to all
the concerns of the people and then repeated
them to the LORD. [22]The LORD said: Listen
to them! Appoint a king to rule over them.
Then Samuel said to the people of Israel,
"Return, each one of you, to your own city."*

CHAPTER 9

See RG 173–74

Saul. [1]There was a powerful man
from Benjamin named Kish, who was the
son of Abiel, son of Zeror, son of Becorath,
son of Aphiah, a Benjaminite.[i] [2]He had a son
named Saul, who was a handsome young
man. There was no other Israelite more

7:14 The Amorites: enemies in Transjordan. Israel is now secure, safe from external and internal threat.

7:16 Bethel, Gilgal and Mizpah: Bethel and Mizpah are located about five and eight miles north of Jerusalem respectively, in the district around Ramah, Samuel's home. Perhaps Gilgal, which has not been definitively located, was also in this area.

8:1–22 From this chapter on, the editors of 1 Samuel provide two and sometimes three perspectives on the same event: e.g., the selection of Saul as king is recounted in chap. 8; 10:17–24; chap. 12.

8:15 Officials: lit., eunuchs. These high-ranking administrators were not necessarily emasculated.

8:22 To your own city: Samuel will later reassemble the people at Mizpah (10:17) to acclaim Saul as their king.

x: 1 Sm 9:12; 14:35. *y:* 1 Chr 6:13. *z:* 1 Sm 2:12–17; Ex 23:8; Dt 16:19; Prv 17:23. *a:* Dt 17:14–15; Hos 13:10; Acts 13:21. *b:* 1 Sm 12:1, 12–13; Jgs 8:22–23; 10:13; 1 Kgs 9:9. *c:* 1 Sm 10:25; Dt 17:14–20; 1 Kgs 12. *d:* 2 Sm 15:1; 1 Kgs 1:5. *e:* Dt 14:22–23. *f:* 1 Sm 22:7; 1 Kgs 21:1–24; Ez 46:18. *g:* 1 Kgs 12:4. *h:* 1 Sm 10:19. *i:* 1 Sm 14:51; 1 Chr 8:33.

handsome than Saul; he stood head and shoulders above the people.[j]

The Lost Donkeys. 3Now the donkeys of Saul's father, Kish, had wandered off. Kish said to his son Saul, "Take one of the servants with you and go out and hunt for the donkeys." 4So they went through the hill country of Ephraim, and through the land of Shalishah. Not finding them there, they continued through the land of Shaalim without success. They also went through the land of Benjamin, but they failed to find the animals. 5When they came to the land of Zuph, Saul said to the servant who was with him, "Come, let us turn back, lest my father forget about the donkeys and become anxious about us." 6The servant replied, "Listen! There is a man of God in this city, a man held in high esteem; everything he says comes true. Let us go there now! Perhaps he can advise us about the journey we have undertaken." 7[k] But Saul said to his servant, "If we go, what can we offer the man? The food in our bags has run out; we have no present to give the man of God. What else do we have?" 8Again the servant answered Saul, "I have a quarter shekel of silver.* If I give that to the man of God, he will advise us about the journey." 9[l] (In former times in Israel, anyone who went to consult God used to say, "Come, let us go to the seer." For the one who is now called prophet was formerly called seer.) 10Saul then said to his servant, "You are right! Come on, let us go!" So they headed toward the city where the man of God lived.

Meeting the Young Women. 11[m] As they were going up the path to the city, they met some young women coming out to draw water and they asked them, "Is the seer in town?" 12[n] The young women answered, "Yes, there—straight ahead. Hurry now; just today he came to the city, because the people have a sacrifice today on the high place.* 13When you enter the city, you may reach him before he goes up to the high place to eat. The people will not eat until he arrives; only after he blesses the sacrifice will the invited guests eat. Go up immediately, for you should find him right now."

Saul Meets Samuel. 14So they went up to the city. As they entered it—there was Samuel coming toward them on his way to the high place. 15The day before Saul's arrival, the LORD had revealed to Samuel:[o] 16At this time tomorrow I will send you a man from the land of Benjamin whom you are to anoint as ruler of my people Israel. He shall save my people from the hand of the Philistines. I have looked upon my people; their cry has come to me.[p] 17When Samuel caught sight of Saul, the LORD assured him: This is the man I told you about; he shall govern my people. 18Saul met Samuel in the gateway and said, "Please tell me where the seer lives." 19Samuel answered Saul: "I am the seer. Go up ahead of me to the high place and eat with me today. In the morning, before letting you go, I will tell you everything on your mind. 20As for your donkeys that were lost three days ago, do not worry about them, for they have been found. Whom should Israel want if not you and your father's family?" 21Saul replied: "Am I not a Benjaminite, from the smallest of the tribes of Israel,* and is not my clan the least among the clans of the tribe of Benjamin? Why say such things to me?"[q]

*The Meal.** 22Samuel then took Saul and his servant and brought them into the room. He seated them at the head of the guests, of whom there were about thirty. 23He said to the cook, "Bring the portion I gave you and told you to put aside." 24So the cook took up the leg and what went with it, and placed it before Saul. Samuel said: "This is a reserved

9:8 A quarter shekel of silver: about a tenth of an ounce of silver.

9:12 On the high place: the local sanctuary on the top of a hill, where the sacrifice was offered and the sacrificial meal eaten.

9:21 Smallest of the tribes of Israel: Saul's objection is a common element in call narrative, e.g., Ex 3:11; 4:10; Jgs 6:15.

9:22–24 At this ritual meal, Samuel treats the youthful Saul as if he were already king. Saul receives the part of the sacrificed animal reserved for the priest and his family, perhaps the sheep's fat tail. Legal texts (Ex 29:22; Lv 3:9; 7:3–4) require the priest to burn this portion of the sheep on the altar.

j: 1 Sm 10:23; 16:12. *k:* Nm 22:7; 1 Kgs 14:3; 2 Kgs 4:42; 5:15; 8:8–9. *l:* Sir 46:15. *m:* Gn 24:11–14; Ex 2:16. *n:* 1 Sm 7:17; 16:2, 5; 20:6, 29; Dt 12:13; 1 Kgs 3:2, 4. *o:* Acts 13:21. *p:* 1 Sm 10:1; Jgs 6:14. *q:* 1 Sm 15:17.

portion that is set before you. Eat, for it was kept for you until this time; I explained that I was inviting some guests." Thus Saul dined with Samuel that day. [25]When they came down from the high place into the city, a mattress was spread for Saul on the roof, [26]and he slept there.

Saul's Anointing. At daybreak Samuel called to Saul on the roof, "Get up, and I will send you on your way." Saul got up, and he and Samuel went outside the city together. [27]As they were approaching the edge of the town, Samuel said to Saul, "Tell the servant to go on ahead of us, but you stay here for a moment, that I may give you a word from God."

See RG 173–74

CHAPTER 10

[1]Then, from a flask he had with him, Samuel poured oil on Saul's head and kissed him, saying: "The LORD anoints you ruler over his people Israel. You are the one who will govern the LORD's people and save them from the power of their enemies all around them.[r]

The Signs Foretold. "This will be the sign* for you that the LORD has anointed you ruler over his heritage: [2]When you leave me today, you will meet two men near Rachel's tomb* at Zelzah in the territory of Benjamin. They will say to you, 'The donkeys you went to look for have been found. Now your father is no longer worried about the donkeys, but is anxious about you and says: What shall I do about my son?'[s] [3]Farther on, when you arrive at the oak of Tabor,* three men will meet you as they go up to God at Bethel; one will be bringing three young goats, another three loaves of bread, and the third a skin of wine. [4]They will greet you and offer you two elevated offerings of bread, which you should accept from them. [5][t] After that you will come to Gibeath-elohim, where the Philistine garrison* is located. As you enter that city, you will meet a band of prophets coming down from the high place. They will be preceded by lyres, tambourines, flutes, and harps, and will be in prophetic ecstasy. [6]The spirit of the LORD will rush upon you, and you will join them in their prophetic ecstasy and will become a changed man.[u] [7]When these signs have come to pass, do whatever lies to hand, because God is with you. [8][v] Now go down ahead of me to Gilgal, for I shall come down to you, to offer burnt offerings and to sacrifice communion offerings. Wait seven days until I come to you; I shall then tell you what you must do.'"*

The Signs Come to Pass. [9]As Saul turned to leave Samuel, God changed his heart. That very day all these signs came to pass . . . . [10]* From there they arrived at Gibeah, where a band of prophets met Saul, and the spirit of God rushed upon him, so that he joined them in their prophetic ecstasy.[w] [11]When all who had known him previously saw him in a prophetic state among the prophets, they said to one another, "What has happened to the son of Kish? Is Saul also among the prophets?"[x] [12]And someone from that district responded, "And who is their father?" Thus the saying arose, "Is Saul also among the prophets?" [13]When he came out of the prophetic ecstasy, he went home.

Silence About the Kingship. [14]Saul's uncle asked him and his servant, "Where have you been?" Saul replied, "Looking for the donkeys. When we could not find them, we went to Samuel." [15]Saul's uncle said, "Tell me,

10:1 The sign: the role of the new ruler is confirmed by specific signs; cf. Ex 7:9.

10:2 Here, as in Jer 31:15, Rachel's tomb is placed at Ramah, north of Jerusalem. Later tradition understood Ephrath (Gn 35:19–20) as Bethlehem and placed the tomb farther south (Mt 2:16–18).

10:3 Oak of Tabor: or terebinth. Such a tree often indicates a shrine.

10:5 The Philistine garrison: the Hebrew word for "garrison" has been explained alternatively to mean a stele established to mark the Philistine occupation, or an inspector or officer for the collection of taxes. **Prophetic ecstasy**: a condition of religious enthusiasm often induced by communal rituals of music and dancing.

10:8 By inserting this verse, with its seven days, an editor has named in the very context of Saul's anointing the condition which in a later narrative will be the grounds for the rejection of the dynastic character of Saul's kingship (13:8–15).

10:10 An editor has abridged a longer version of this story by omitting mention of the first two signs Samuel has given (vv. 2–4).

r: 1 Sm 9:16–17; 16:13; 24:7; Jgs 9:9; 1 Kgs 1:39; Acts 13:21. *s:* Jer 31:15; Mk 14:13. *t:* 1 Sm 13:3; 16:13; 19:20–21. *u:* 1 Sm 11:6; 16:13; Jgs 14:6, 19; 15:14; 2 Kgs 3:15. *v:* 1 Sm 13:8; Lv 3:1. *w:* 1 Sm 19:20–24; Nm 11:25. *x:* 1 Sm 19:24.

then, what Samuel said to you." [16]Saul said to his uncle, "He assured us that the donkeys had been found." But Saul told him nothing about what Samuel had said about the kingship.

Saul Chosen King. [17]Samuel called the people together to the LORD at Mizpah[y] [18]and addressed the Israelites: "Thus says the LORD, the God of Israel: It was I who brought Israel up from Egypt and delivered you from the power of the Egyptians and from the power of all the kingdoms that oppressed you.[z] [19]But today you have rejected your God, who saves you from all your evils and calamities, by saying, 'No! You must appoint a king over us.' Now, therefore, take your stand before the LORD according to your tribes and families."[a] [20]So Samuel had all the tribes of Israel come forward, and the tribe of Benjamin was chosen.* [21]Next he had the tribe of Benjamin come forward by clans, and the clan of Matri was chosen, and finally Saul, son of Kish, was chosen. But when they went to look for him, he was nowhere to be found. [22][b] Again they consulted the LORD, "Is there still someone else to come forward?" The LORD answered: He is hiding among the baggage. [23]They ran to bring him from there; when he took his place among the people, he stood head and shoulders above all the people.[c] [24]Then Samuel addressed all the people, "Do you see the man whom the LORD has chosen? There is no one like him among all the people!" Then all the people shouted out, "Long live the king!"[d]

[25]Samuel next explained to the people the rules of the monarchy,* wrote them in a book, and placed them before the presence of the LORD. Samuel then sent the people back to their own homes.[e] [26]Saul also went home to Gibeah, accompanied by warriors whose hearts the LORD had touched. [27]But some worthless people said, "How can this fellow save us?" They despised him and brought him no tribute.* [f]

CHAPTER 11

See RG 173–74

Defeat of the Ammonites. [1]* About a month later, Nahash the Ammonite went up and besieged Jabesh-gilead. All the people of Jabesh begged Nahash, "Make a treaty with us, and we will serve you."[g] [2]But Nahash the Ammonite replied, "This is my condition for making a treaty with you: I will gouge out the right eye of every man,* and thus bring shame on all Israel." [3]The elders of Jabesh said to him: "Give us seven days to send messengers throughout the territory of Israel. If there is no one to save us, we will surrender to you." [4]When the messengers arrived at Gibeah of Saul and reported the news in the people's hearing, they all wept aloud. [5]Just then Saul came in from the field, behind his oxen. "Why are the people weeping?" he asked. They repeated the message of the inhabitants of Jabesh for him. [6]As he listened to this report, the spirit of God rushed upon him and he became very angry.[h] [7]Taking a yoke of oxen, he cut them into pieces and sent them throughout the territory of Israel* by messengers saying, "If anyone does not come out to follow Saul and Samuel, the same thing will be done to his oxen!" The dread of the LORD came upon the people and they went forth as one.[i] [8]When Saul reviewed them in Bezek,* there were three

10:20 Was chosen: probably by casting lots; cf. 14:40–42; Jos 7:14, 17.

10:25 Rules of the monarchy: a charter describing the relationship between the king and the people.

10:27 Tribute: a gift to honor a new ruler as a pledge of one's loyalty; see Gn 32:14; Jgs 3:15; 2 Sm 8:2.

11:1 A text from Qumran (1QSam[a]) introduces this chapter with the report that Nahash, king of the Ammonites, had attacked the Gadites and the Reubenites, gouging out their right eyes. Seven thousand of them had fled to Jabesh-gilead. This additional information would explain why Nahash besieged Jabesh-gilead. There is no consensus among scholars whether the Qumran text represents an original reading or a secondary expansion.

11:2 Right eye of every man: thus rendering them incapable of military action.

11:7 Throughout the territory of Israel: Saul's gesture summons the Israelite confederacy to a coordinated response against Nahash; cf. Jgs 19:29 for a similar action. **Dread of the LORD**: often a panic that immobilizes Israel's enemies; here, however, it has the opposite effect and incites the Israelites to battle.

11:8 Bezek: probably modern Khirbet Ibziq, northeast of Shechem, on the west slope of the Jordan valley, opposite Jabesh-gilead.

---

y: 1 Sm 7:5. *z:* Ex 20:2; Lv 11:45; 25:38; Nm 15:41; Dt 5:6; Jgs 6:8–9. *a:* 1 Sm 8:19. *b:* 1 Sm 30:24. *c:* 1 Sm 9:2; 16:7. *d:* 2 Sm 16:16; 1 Kgs 1:25; 2 Kgs 11:12. *e:* 1 Sm 8:11; Dt 17:14–20. *f:* 1 Sm 11:12. *g:* 1 Sm 12:12; 31:11; 2 Sm 10:2. *h:* 1 Sm 16:13; Jgs 14:6, 19; 15:14. *i:* 1 Kgs 11:30; 2 Kgs 13:18.

hundred thousand Israelites and seventy thousand Judahites.

9 To the messengers who had come he said, "Tell the inhabitants of Jabesh-gilead that tomorrow, when the sun grows hot, they will be saved." The messengers went and reported this to the inhabitants of Jabesh, and they rejoiced. 10 The men of Jabesh said to Nahash, "Tomorrow we will surrender to you, and you may do with us whatever you want." 11 The next day, Saul arranged his troops in three companies and invaded the camp during the dawn watch. They slaughtered Ammonites until the day had gotten hot; by then the survivors were so scattered that no two of them were left together.

Saul Accepted as King. 12* The people then said to Samuel: "Who questioned whether Saul should rule over us? Hand them over and we will put them to death."[j] 13 But Saul objected, "No one will be put to death this day, for today the LORD has rescued Israel."[k] 14 Samuel said to the people, "Come, let us go to Gilgal to renew the kingship there." 15 So all the people went to Gilgal, and there they made Saul king in the LORD's presence. They also sacrificed communion offerings there before the LORD, and Saul and all the Israelites rejoiced greatly.

CHAPTER 12*

See RG 173–74

Samuel's Integrity. 1* Samuel addressed all Israel: "I have granted your request in every respect," he said. "I have set a king over you[l] 2 and now the king will lead you. As for me, I am old and gray, and my sons are among you. I was your leader from my youth to the present day. 3 Here I stand! Answer me in the presence of the LORD and the LORD's anointed. Whose ox have I taken? Whose donkey have I taken? Whom have I cheated? Whom have I wronged? From whom have I accepted a bribe and shut my eyes because of it? I will make restitution to you."[m] 4 They replied, "You have neither cheated us, nor oppressed us, nor accepted anything from anyone." 5 So he said to them, "The LORD is witness against you this day, and the LORD's anointed is witness, that you have found nothing in my possession." "The LORD is witness," they said.

Samuel Admonishes the People. 6 Samuel continued: "The LORD is witness, who appointed Moses and Aaron and brought your ancestors up from the land of Egypt.[n] 7 Now take your stand, that I may judge you in the presence of the LORD according to all the gracious acts that the LORD has done for you and your ancestors. 8 When Jacob and his sons went to Egypt and the Egyptians oppressed them, your ancestors cried out to the LORD. The LORD then sent Moses and Aaron to bring them out of Egypt and settled them in this place.[o] 9 But they forgot the LORD their God; and so the LORD sold them into the power of Sisera, the captain of the army of Hazor, the power of the Philistines, and the power of the king of Moab, who made war against them.[p] 10 They cried out to the LORD and said, 'We have sinned because we abandoned the LORD and served the Baals and Astartes. Now deliver us from the power of our enemies, and we will serve you.'[q] 11 The LORD sent Jerubbaal, Barak, Jephthah, and Samuel; he delivered you from the power of your enemies on every side, so that you could live in security.[r] 12 Yet, when you saw Nahash, king of the Ammonites, advancing against you, you said to me, 'No! A king must rule us,' even though the LORD your God is your king.[s]

Warnings for People and King. 13 "Now

11:12–14 With the defeat of the Ammonites, Saul demonstrates his ability to command Israel's army and defend the land. At Gilgal, Saul's kingship is ratified; ironically, he loses his kingship at the same place (13:7).

12:1–25 This chapter narrates the transition from the leadership of the judges to the rule of the king. The Deuteronomistic redactor has Samuel contrast the wickedness of Israel's ancestors with the Lord's gracious deliverance (vv. 6–12). The people realize that their demand for a king has compounded that wickedness. Now that the Lord has given them a king, Samuel urges the people and their king to serve the Lord wholeheartedly (vv. 13–25).

12:1–5 Samuel's upright leadership is set in sharp contrast to the despotic powers of the king described in chap. 8. By their testimony, the people witness to Samuel's righteousness.

j: 1 Sm 10:27. *k:* 2 Sm 19:23. *l:* 1 Sm 8:7, 9, 22. *m:* Ex 20:17; 23:8; Nm 16:15; Dt 16:19; Sir 46:19. *n:* Mi 6:4. *o:* Gn 46:5; Ex 1:11; 2:23–25. *p:* Jgs 3:12–15; 4:2–3; 10:7; 13:1. *q:* 1 Sm 7:3–4; Jgs 10:10. *r:* Jgs 6:14, 32; 11:1. *s:* 1 Sm 8:6–7, 19; 11:1–2; Jgs 8:23.

here is the king you chose. See! The LORD has given you a king.[t] 14 If you fear and serve the LORD, if you listen to the voice of the LORD and do not rebel against the LORD's command, if both you and the king, who rules over you, follow the LORD your God—well and good. 15 But if you do not listen to the voice of the LORD and if you rebel against the LORD's command, the hand of the LORD will be against you and your king. 16 Now then, stand ready to witness the great marvel the LORD is about to accomplish before your eyes. 17 Are we not in the harvest time for wheat?* Yet I will call upon the LORD, and he will send thunder and rain. Thus you will see and understand how great an evil it is in the eyes of the LORD that you have asked for a king."[u] 18 Samuel called upon the LORD, and the LORD sent thunder and rain that day.

Assistance Promised. Then all the people feared the LORD and Samuel. 19 They said to Samuel, "Pray to the LORD your God for us, your servants, that we may not die for having added to all our other sins the evil of asking for a king." 20 "Do not fear," Samuel answered them. "You have indeed committed all this evil! Yet do not turn from the LORD, but serve him with your whole heart. 21 Do not turn aside to gods who are nothing,* who cannot act and deliver. They are nothing.[v] 22 For the sake of his own great name* the LORD will not abandon his people, since the LORD has decided to make you his people.[w] 23 As for me, far be it from me to sin against the LORD by ceasing to pray for you and to teach you the good and right way.[x] 24 But you must fear the LORD and serve him faithfully with all your heart, for you have seen the great things the LORD has done among you. 25 If instead you continue to do evil, both you and your king shall be swept away."

III. Saul and David

CHAPTER 13

See RG 174

1 [Saul was . . . years old when he became king and he reigned . . . -two years over Israel.]*

Saul Offers Sacrifice. 2 Saul chose three thousand of Israel, of whom two thousand remained with him in Michmash and in the hill country of Bethel, and one thousand were with Jonathan in Gibeah of Benjamin. He sent the rest of the army back to their tents. 3 Now Jonathan struck the Philistine garrison* in Gibeah, and the Philistines got word of it. Then Saul sounded the horn throughout the land, saying, "Let the Hebrews hear!"[y] 4 Then all Israel heard the report, "Saul has struck the garrison of the Philistines! Israel has become odious to the Philistines!" Then the army was called up to Saul in Gilgal. 5 The Philistines also assembled for battle against Israel, with thirty thousand chariots,* six thousand horsemen, and foot soldiers as numerous as the sand on the seashore.[z] They came up and encamped in Michmash, east of Beth-aven.[a] 6 When the soldiers saw they were in danger because the army was hardpressed, they hid themselves in caves, thickets, rocks, caverns, and cisterns. 7 Other Hebrews crossed the Jordan into the land of Gad and Gilead. Saul, however, held out in Gilgal, all his army trembling in fear behind him.* 8 He waited seven

12:17 Harvest time for wheat: in May–June. Since this is a period of little or no rainfall in Israel, the people will not mistake the sign for a natural phenomenon.

12:21 Gods who are nothing: Hebrew *tohu*, lit., "emptiness," cf. Gn 1:2 (. . . *webohu*); here, idols without power or substance, as in Is 41:29.

12:22 His own great name: were the Lord to abandon his people, even if they abandon him, he would diminish his stature or reputation in the divine council or among the nations (e.g., Ez 20:9). Throughout the Old Testament the Lord is encouraged to deliver Israel, despite its evil, "for the sake of his name."

13:1 A formula like that of 2 Sm 5:4 was introduced here at some time; but the age of Saul when he became king remains a blank, and the two years assigned for his reign in the Masoretic text cannot be correct. Acts 13:21 offers the round number of forty years.

13:3–4 The Philistine garrison: see note on 10:5. **Let the Hebrews hear**: a different reading of these verses, based on the Greek, would yield: "And the Philistines heard that the Hebrews (or: the slaves) had revolted. Saul in the meantime sounded the trumpet throughout all the land (v. 4), and all Israel heard that Saul . . . ."

13:5 Thirty thousand chariots: some Greek manuscripts read "three thousand chariots."

13:7–15 These verses, like 10:8, anticipate the rejection of

t: 1 Sm 8:7. *u:* Ex 9:23, 28–30; 1 Kgs 18:1. *v:* Dt 32:37–39; Is 41:29; 44:9–10. *w:* Ex 18:10; Dt 4:34; Jos 7:9; Is 48:9; Jer 14:21; Dn 3:34. *x:* Ex 32:11. *y:* 1 Sm 14:1–15; Jgs 3:27; 6:34; 2 Sm 20:1–2. *z:* Gn 22:17; 41:49; Jgs 7:12. *a:* 1 Sm 14:22.

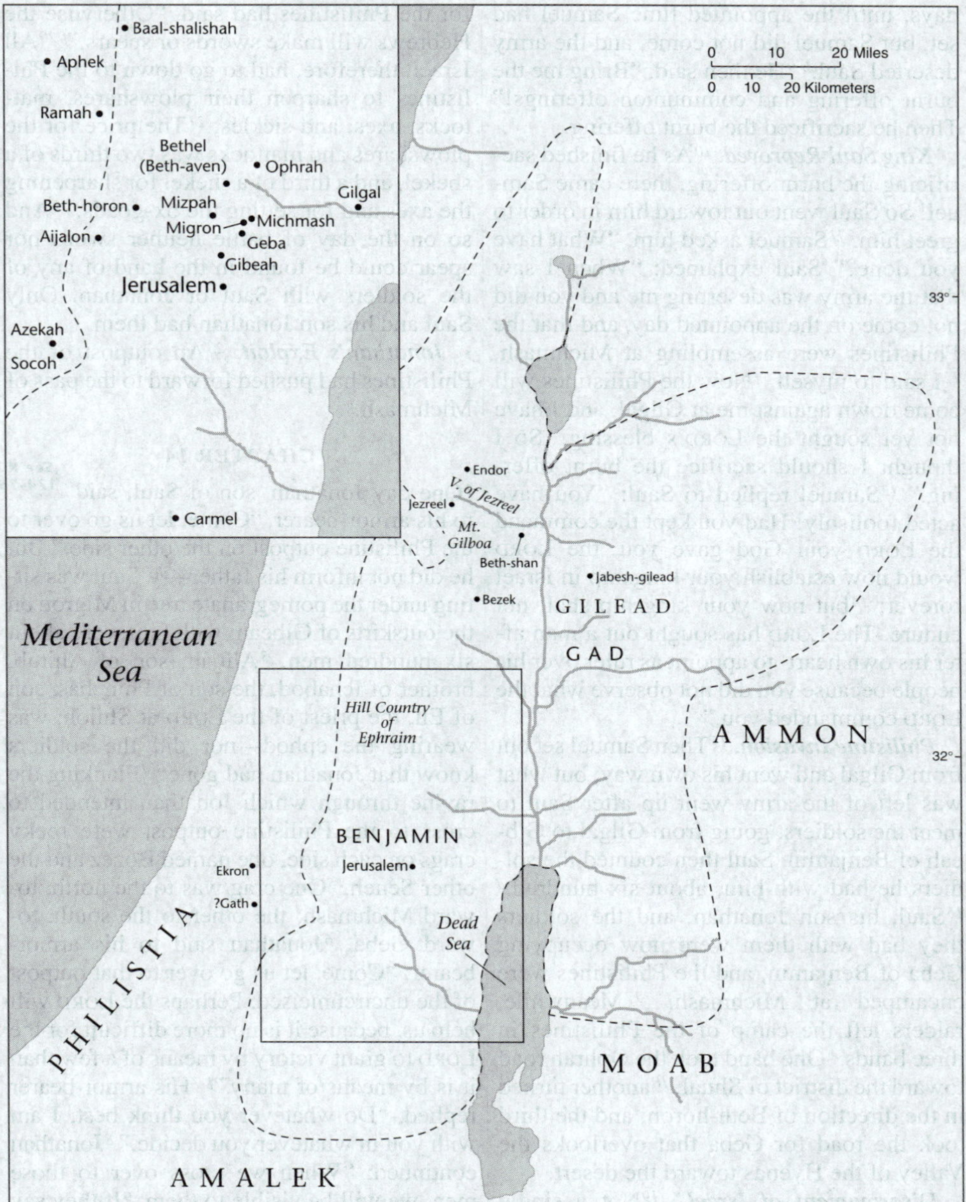

0 10 20 Miles
0 10 20 Kilometers
Baal-shalishah
Aphek
Ramah
Bethel
(Beth-aven)
Ophrah
Gilgal
Mizpah
Beth-horon
Michmash
Migron
Geba
Aijalon
Gibeah
Jerusalem
Azekah
Socoh
Carmel
Endor
V. of Jezreel
Jezreel
Mt. Gilboa
Beth-shan
Jabesh-gilead
Bezek
GILEAD
GAD
Mediterranean Sea
Hill Country of Ephraim
AMMON
BENJAMIN
Ekron
Jerusalem
?Gath
Dead Sea
PHILISTIA
MOAB
AMALEK
EDOM
33°
32°
31°
35°
36°

The Kingdom of Saul according to 1 Samuel

days, until the appointed time Samuel had set, but Samuel did not come, and the army deserted Saul.[b] 9 He then said, "Bring me the burnt offering and communion offerings!" Then he sacrificed the burnt offering.

King Saul Reproved. 10 As he finished sacrificing the burnt offering, there came Samuel! So Saul went out toward him in order to greet him. 11 Samuel asked him, "What have you done?" Saul explained: "When I saw that the army was deserting me and you did not come on the appointed day, and that the Philistines were assembling at Michmash, 12 I said to myself, 'Now the Philistines will come down against me at Gilgal, and I have not yet sought the LORD's blessing.' So I thought I should sacrifice the burnt offering." 13 Samuel replied to Saul: "You have acted foolishly! Had you kept the command the LORD your God gave you, the LORD would now establish your kingship in Israel forever; 14 but now your kingship shall not endure. The LORD has sought out a man after his own heart* to appoint as ruler over his people because you did not observe what the LORD commanded you."[c]

Philistine Invasion. 15 Then Samuel set out from Gilgal and went his own way; but what was left of the army went up after Saul to meet the soldiers, going from Gilgal to Gibeah of Benjamin. Saul then counted the soldiers he had with him, about six hundred.[d] 16 Saul, his son Jonathan, and the soldiers they had with them were now occupying Geba of Benjamin, and the Philistines were encamped at Michmash. 17 Meanwhile, raiders left the camp of the Philistines in three bands.[e] One band took the Ophrah road toward the district of Shual; 18 another turned in the direction of Beth-horon; and the third took the road for Geba that overlooks the Valley of the Hyenas toward the desert.

Disarmament of Israel.* 19 Not a single smith was to be found anywhere in Israel, for the Philistines had said, "Otherwise the Hebrews will make swords or spears."[f] 20 All Israel, therefore, had to go down to the Philistines to sharpen their plowshares, mattocks, axes, and sickles. 21 The price for the plowshares and mattocks was two thirds of a shekel, and a third of a shekel for sharpening the axes and for setting the ox-goads. 22 And so on the day of battle neither sword nor spear could be found in the hand of any of the soldiers with Saul or Jonathan. Only Saul and his son Jonathan had them.

Jonathan's Exploit. 23 An outpost of the Philistines had pushed forward to the pass of Michmash.[g]

CHAPTER 14

See RG 174–75

1 One day Jonathan, son of Saul, said to his armor-bearer, "Come, let us go over to the Philistine outpost on the other side." But he did not inform his father—[h] 2 Saul was sitting under the pomegranate tree in Migron on the outskirts of Gibeah; with him were about six hundred men. 3 Ahijah, son of Ahitub, brother of Ichabod, the son of Phinehas, son of Eli, the priest of the LORD at Shiloh, was wearing the ephod—nor did the soldiers know that Jonathan had gone.[i] 4 Flanking the ravine through which Jonathan intended to cross to the Philistine outpost were rocky crags on each side, one named Bozez and the other Seneh. 5 One crag was to the north, toward Michmash; the other to the south, toward Geba. 6 Jonathan said to his armor-bearer: "Come, let us go over to that outpost of the uncircumcised. Perhaps the LORD will help us, because it is no more difficult for the LORD to grant victory by means of a few than it is by means of many."[j] 7 His armor-bearer replied, "Do whatever you think best; I am with you in whatever you decide." 8 Jonathan continued: "When we cross over to those men, we will be visible to them. 9 If they say to us, 'Stay there until we can come to you,'

Saul; a different occasion and motivation for this are given in chap. 15 and 28:17–18.

13:14 After his own heart: i.e., of his choosing, for his purpose. While the verse undoubtedly refers to David, it concerns the Lord's decision to continue the kingship, even though he has rejected Saul, by selecting the heir to Saul's throne.

13:19–22 These details emphasize the Philistines' military power and superior technology, a reminder that an Israelite victory depends on God.

b: 1 Sm 10:8. *c:* 1 Sm 15:28; 25:30; 2 Sm 7:15–16; Ps 78:70; Acts 13:22. *d:* 1 Sm 14:2. *e:* 1 Sm 14:15. *f:* Jgs 5:8. *g:* 1 Sm 14:15. *h:* 1 Sm 13:3. *i:* 1 Sm 2:28; 4:21; 14:18; 23:9; 30:7. *j:* 1 Sm 17:26, 36, 47; Jgs 14:3; Sir 39:18; 1 Mc 3:19.

we will stop where we are; we will not go up to them. [10]But if they say, ‘Come up to us,’ we will go up, because the LORD has delivered them into our hand. That will be our sign.”* [k] [11]When the two of them came into the view of the Philistine outpost, the Philistines remarked, “Look, some Hebrews* are coming out of the holes where they have been hiding.” [12]The men of the outpost called to Jonathan and his armor-bearer. “Come up here,” they said, “and we will teach you a lesson.” So Jonathan said to his armor-bearer, “Climb up after me, for the LORD has delivered them into the hand of Israel.” [13]Jonathan clambered up with his armor-bearer behind him. As the Philistines fell before Jonathan, his armor-bearer, who followed him, would finish them off. [14]In this first attack Jonathan and his armor-bearer killed about twenty men within half a furlong. [15]Then terror spread through the camp and the countryside; all the soldiers in the outpost and in the raiding parties shuddered in terror. The earth shook with an awesome shuddering.* [l]

Rout of the Philistines. [16]Saul’s sentinels in Gibeah of Benjamin saw that the enemy camp had scattered and were running in all directions. [17]Saul said to those around him, “Count the troops and find out if any of us are missing.” When they had taken the count, they found Jonathan and his armor-bearer missing. [18]Saul then said to Ahijah, “Bring the ephod here.” (Ahijah was wearing the ephod before the Israelites at that time.) [19]While Saul was speaking to the priest, the uproar in the Philistine camp kept increasing. So he said to the priest, “Withdraw your hand.” [20]And Saul and all his men rallied and rushed into the fight, where the Philistines, wholly confused, were thrusting swords at one another.[m] [21]The Hebrews who had previously sided with the Philistines and had gone up with them to their camp turned to join the Israelites under Saul and Jonathan.[n] [22]Likewise, all the Israelites who were hiding in the hill country of Ephraim, hearing that the Philistines were fleeing, kept after them in the battle.[o] [23]* Thus the LORD saved Israel that day.

Saul’s Oath. The battle continued past Beth-aven. [24]Even though the Israelites were exhausted that day, Saul laid an oath on them, saying, “Cursed be the one who takes food before evening, before I am able to avenge myself on my enemies.” So none of the people tasted food. [25]Now there was a honeycomb lying on the ground, [26]and when the soldiers came to the comb the honey was flowing; yet no one raised a hand from it to his mouth, because the people feared the oath.

Violation of the Oath. [27]Jonathan, who had not heard that his father had put the people under oath, thrust out the end of the staff he was holding and dipped it into the honeycomb. Then he raised it to his mouth and his eyes brightened. [28]At this, one of the soldiers spoke up: “Your father put the people under a strict oath, saying, ‘Cursed be the one who takes food today!’ As a result the people are weakened.” [29][p] Jonathan replied: “My father brings trouble to the land. Look how bright my eyes are because I had this little taste of honey. [30]What is more, if the army had eaten freely of the enemy’s plunder when they came across it today, surely the slaughter of the Philistines would have been the greater by now!”

Consuming the Blood. [31]After the Philistines were routed that day from Michmash to Aijalon, the people were completely exhausted. [32]So the army pounced upon the plunder and took sheep, oxen, and calves, slaughtering them on the ground and eating the meat with the blood in it.[q] [33]Informed that the army was sinning against the LORD by eating the meat with blood in it, Saul

14:10 That will be our sign: Jonathan acknowledges that the battle is in God’s hands.

14:11 Hebrews: while this term is often used by foreigners of Israelites, in this verse it seems to be a derogatory epithet for soldiers who deserted Saul’s army while he was waiting for Samuel to arrive in Gilgal.

14:15 Awesome shuddering: lit., “shuddering caused by God”; the panic in the Philistine camp is the work of Israel’s warrior God.

14:23 The victory apparently cleared the Philistines off the main ridge of mountains in the territories of Benjamin and Ephraim.

k: Jos 8:1; 10:8; Jgs 12:3. *l:* 2 Sm 22:8; Jl 2:10–11. *m:* Jgs 7:22. *n:* 1 Sm 29:4. *o:* 1 Sm 13:6. *p:* Jos 7:25; 1 Kgs 18:17–18. *q:* 1 Sm 15:19, 21; Gn 4:9; Lv 3:17; 7:26–27; 17:10–14; Acts 15:20, 29.

said: "You have broken faith. Roll a large stone here for me." [34]He continued: "Mingle with the people and tell each of them, 'Bring an ox or sheep to me. Slaughter them here and then eat. But you must not sin against the LORD by eating meat with blood in it.' " So that night they all brought whatever oxen they had seized, and they slaughtered them there; [35]and Saul built an altar to the LORD—this was the first time he built an altar to the LORD.[r]

Jonathan in Danger of Death. [36]Then Saul said, "Let us go down in pursuit of the Philistines by night, to plunder them until daybreak and leave no one alive." They replied, "Do what you think best." But the priest said, "Let us consult God." [37]So Saul inquired of God: "Shall I go down in pursuit of the Philistines? Will you deliver them into the hand of Israel?" But he received no answer on this occasion.[s] [38]"All officers of the army," Saul announced, "come forward. Find out how this sin was committed today. [39]As the LORD lives who has given victory to Israel, even if my son Jonathan has committed it, he shall surely die!" But none of the people answered him. [40]So he said to all Israel, "Stand on one side, and my son Jonathan and I will stand on the other." The people responded, "Do what you think best."[t] [41]And Saul said to the LORD, the God of Israel: "Why did you not answer your servant this time? If the blame for this resides in me or my son Jonathan, LORD, God of Israel, respond with Urim; but if this guilt is in your people Israel, respond with Thummim."* Jonathan and Saul were designated, and the people went free.[u] [42]Saul then said, "Cast lots between me and my son Jonathan." And Jonathan was designated. [43]Saul said to Jonathan, "Tell me what you have done." Jonathan replied, "I only tasted a little honey from the end of the staff I was holding. Am I to die for this?" [44]Saul declared, "May God do thus to me, and more, if you do not indeed die, Jonathan!"[v]

Rescue of Jonathan. [45]But the soldiers protested to Saul: "Is Jonathan to die, the man who won this great victory for Israel? This must not be! As the LORD lives, not a single hair of his head shall fall to the ground, for God was with him in what he did today!" Thus the soldiers rescued* Jonathan and he did not die.[w] [46]After that Saul gave up the pursuit of the Philistines, who returned to their own territory.

Saul's Victories. [47]After taking possession of the kingship over Israel, Saul waged war on its enemies all around—Moab, the Ammonites, Edom, the kings of Zobah, and the Philistines. Wherever he turned, he was successful[x] [48]and fought bravely. He defeated Amalek and delivered Israel from the hand of those who were plundering them.[y]

Saul's Family. [49]The sons of Saul were Jonathan, Ishvi, and Malchishua; the name of his firstborn daughter was Merob; the name of the younger was Michal.[z] [50]The name of Saul's wife was Ahinoam, daughter of Ahimaaz. The name of his general was Abner, son of Ner, Saul's uncle; [51]Kish, Saul's father, and Ner, Abner's father, were sons of Abiel.[a]

[52]There was heavy fighting with the Philistines during Saul's lifetime. Whenever Saul saw any strong or brave man, he took him into his service.

CHAPTER 15*

See RG 175

Disobedience of Saul. [1]Samuel said to Saul: "It was I the LORD sent to anoint you king over his people Israel. Now, therefore, listen to the message of the LORD.[b] [2]Thus says the LORD of hosts: I will punish what

14:41 Urim . . . Thummim: objects, one representing a positive response and the other a negative response, kept in the front pocket of the priest's ephod, a garment worn as a breastplate, and used to ascertain God's will in certain instances, e.g., whether Saul should help rout the Philistines. Saul consults the priest but is too impatient to finish the consultation and hurries impulsively into battle.

14:45 Rescued: the Hebrew word used is that for the "redemption" of the firstborn (Ex 13:13–15).

15:1–35 The rejection of Saul sets the stage for the remainder of 1 Samuel. The audience knows that, in the ensuing struggle between David and Saul, David will triumph as king.

r: 1 Sm 7:17; Jgs 6:24. *s:* 1 Sm 28:6, 15. *t:* Jos 7:13–15. *u:* 1 Sm 10:20; 28:6; Ex 28:30; Dt 33:8. *v:* 1 Sm 3:17; Ru 1:17. *w:* 2 Sm 14:11; 1 Kgs 1:52. *x:* 2 Sm 1:22; 8:2–5. *y:* 1 Sm 15:7. *z:* 1 Sm 18:20, 25; 31:2; 1 Chr 8:33; 9:39; 10:2. *a:* 1 Sm 9:1. *b:* Jos 3:9; 2 Kgs 20:16; Is 28:14.

Amalek did to the Israelites when he barred
their way as they came up from Egypt.[c] [3]Go,
now, attack Amalek, and put under the ban*
everything he has. Do not spare him; kill
men and women, children and infants, oxen
and sheep, camels and donkeys."[d]
[4]Saul alerted the army, and at Telaim reviewed two hundred thousand foot soldiers
and ten thousand men of Judah.* [5]Saul went
to the city of Amalek and set up an ambush
in the wadi. [6e]He warned the Kenites:
"Leave Amalek, turn aside and come down
so I will not have to destroy you with them,
for you were loyal to the Israelites when
they came up from Egypt."* After the Kenites left, [7]Saul routed Amalek from Havilah
to the approaches of Shur, on the frontier of
Egypt.[f] [8]He took Agag, king of Amalek,
alive, but the rest of the people he destroyed
by the sword, putting them under the ban.
[9]He and his troops spared Agag and the best
of the fat sheep and oxen, and the lambs.
They refused to put under the ban anything
that was worthwhile, destroying only what
was worthless and of no account.

Samuel Rebukes Saul. [10]Then the word of
the LORD came to Samuel: [11]I regret having
made Saul king, for he has turned from me
and has not kept my command. At this Samuel grew angry and cried out to the LORD all
night.[g] [12]Early in the morning he went to
meet Saul, but was informed that Saul had
gone to Carmel, where he set up a monument in his own honor, and that on his return
he had gone down to Gilgal. [13]When Samuel
came to him, Saul greeted him: "The LORD
bless you! I have kept the command of the
LORD." [14]But Samuel asked, "What, then, is
this bleating of sheep that comes to my ears,
the lowing of oxen that I hear?" [15]Saul
replied: "They were brought from Amalek.
The people spared the best sheep and oxen
to sacrifice to the LORD, your God; but the
rest we destroyed, putting them under the
ban." [16]Samuel said to Saul: "Stop! Let me
tell you what the LORD said to me last
night." "Speak!" he replied. [17]Samuel then
said: "Though little in your own eyes, are
you not chief of the tribes of Israel? The
LORD anointed you king of Israel[h] [18]and sent
you on a mission, saying: Go and put the sinful Amalekites under a ban of destruction.
Fight against them until you have exterminated them.[i] [19]Why then have you disobeyed
the LORD? You have pounced on the spoil,
thus doing what was evil in the LORD's
sight."[j] [20]Saul explained to Samuel: "I did
indeed obey the LORD and fulfill the mission
on which the LORD sent me. I have brought
back Agag, the king of Amalek, and, carrying out the ban, I have destroyed the
Amalekites. [21]But from the spoil the army
took sheep and oxen, the best of what had
been banned, to sacrifice to the LORD your
God in Gilgal."[k] [22l]But Samuel said:

"Does the LORD delight in burnt
offerings and sacrifices
as much as in obedience to the LORD's
command?
Obedience is better than sacrifice,
to listen, better than the fat of rams.*
[23] For a sin of divination is rebellion,
and arrogance, the crime of idolatry.
Because you have rejected the word of
the LORD,
the LORD in turn has rejected you as
king."[m]

Rejection of Saul. [24]Saul admitted to Samuel: "I have sinned, for I have transgressed
the command of the LORD and your instructions. I feared the people and obeyed them.[n]
[25]Now forgive my sin, and return with me,
that I may worship the LORD." [26]But Samuel
said to Saul, "I will not return with you, because you rejected the word of the LORD and

15:3 Put under the ban: this terminology mandates that all traces of the Amalekites (people, cities, animals, etc.) be exterminated. No plunder could be seized for personal use. In the light of Dt 20:16–18, this injunction would eliminate any tendency toward syncretism. The focus of this chapter is that Saul fails to execute this order.

15:4 The numbers here are not realistic; compare 14:2.

15:6 The Kenites honored the terms of an alliance with Israel.

15:22 Samuel's reprimand echoes that of the prophets. Cultic practice is meaningless, even hypocritical, unless accompanied by an attentiveness to God's will.

c: Ex 17:8–10, 16; Dt 25:17–19. *d:* 1 Sm 27:8; 30:17; Ex 17:16; Nm 24:20; Jos 6:17. *e:* Nm 24:21. *f:* 1 Sm 27:8. *g:* 1 Sm 15:35; Gn 6:6–7. *h:* 1 Sm 9:21. *i:* 1 Sm 28:18. *j:* 1 Sm 14:32. *k:* Lv 27:28. *l:* Prv 21:3; Hos 6:6; Am 5:21–25; Zec 10:2; Mt 9:13; 12:7; Heb 10:9. *m:* Dt 18:10. *n:* 1 Sm 26:21.

the LORD has rejected you as king of Israel."[o] 27 As Samuel turned to go, Saul seized a loose end of his garment, and it tore off.[p] 28 So Samuel said to him: "The LORD has torn the kingdom of Israel from you this day, and has given it to a neighbor of yours, who is better than you.[q] 29 The Glory of Israel neither deceives nor repents,* for he is not a mortal who repents."[r] 30 But Saul answered: "I have sinned, yet honor me now before the elders of my people and before Israel. Return with me that I may worship the LORD your God." 31 And so Samuel returned with him, and Saul worshiped the LORD.

Samuel Executes Agag. 32 Afterward Samuel commanded, "Bring Agag, king of Amalek, to me." Agag came to him struggling and saying, "So it is bitter death!" 33 And Samuel said,

"As your sword has made women
childless,
so shall your mother be childless
among women."

Then he cut Agag to pieces before the LORD in Gilgal.[s] 34 Samuel departed for Ramah, while Saul went up to his home in Gibeah of Saul. 35 Never again, as long as he lived, did Samuel see Saul. Yet he grieved over Saul, because the LORD repented that he had made him king of Israel.[t]

CHAPTER 16

See RG 175

Samuel Is Sent to Bethlehem. 1[u] The LORD said to Samuel: How long will you grieve for Saul, whom I have rejected as king of Israel? Fill your horn with oil, and be on your way. I am sending you to Jesse of Bethlehem, for from among his sons I have decided on a king.* 2 But Samuel replied: "How can I go? Saul will hear of it and kill me." To this the LORD answered: Take a heifer along and say, "I have come to sacrifice to the LORD." 3 Invite Jesse to the sacrifice, and I myself will tell you what to do; you are to anoint for me the one I point out to you.[v]

Samuel Anoints David. 4 Samuel did as the LORD had commanded him. When he entered Bethlehem, the elders of the city came trembling to meet him and asked, "Is your visit peaceful, O seer?" 5 He replied: "Yes! I have come to sacrifice to the LORD. So purify yourselves and celebrate with me today." He also had Jesse and his sons purify themselves and invited them to the sacrifice.[w] 6 As they came, he looked at Eliab and thought, "Surely the anointed is here before the LORD." 7 But the LORD said to Samuel: Do not judge from his appearance or from his lofty stature, because I have rejected him. God does not see as a mortal, who sees the appearance. The LORD looks into the heart.[x] 8[y] Then Jesse called Abinadab and presented him before Samuel, who said, "The LORD has not chosen him." 9 Next Jesse presented Shammah, but Samuel said, "The LORD has not chosen this one either." 10 In the same way Jesse presented seven sons before Samuel, but Samuel said to Jesse, "The LORD has not chosen any one of these." 11 Then Samuel asked Jesse, "Are these all the sons you have?" Jesse replied, "There is still the youngest, but he is tending the sheep." Samuel said to Jesse, "Send for him; we will not sit down to eat until he arrives here."[z] 12 Jesse had the young man brought to them. He was ruddy, a youth with beautiful eyes, and good looking. The LORD said: There—anoint him, for this is the one![a] 13 Then Samuel, with the horn of oil in hand, anointed him in the midst of his brothers, and from that day on, the spirit of the LORD rushed upon David. Then Samuel set out for Ramah.[b]

15:29 Nor repents: the apparent contradiction between this verse and vv. 11, 35 leads some scholars to consider it a gloss (cf. Nm 23:19). However, this phrase can be understood to underscore the definitive character of Samuel's declaration that Saul has lost the kingship.

16:1 David is anointed two more times after Saul's death (2 Sm 2:4; 5:3). In 17:28, his brother Eliab is not aware of David's selection. These repetitions and inconsistencies reflect the final editor's use of multiple sources.

o: 1 Kgs 11:11, 30–31. *p:* 1 Sm 24:6; 1 Kgs 11:29–31. *q:* 1 Sm 28:17; 2 Sm 7:15–16. *r:* Nm 23:19. *s:* Ex 21:23; Jgs 8:21. *t:* 1 Sm 28:15. *u:* Ru 4:17–22; 1 Kgs 1:39; 1 Chr 11:3; Is 11:1; Mt 2:6; Lk 2:4. *v:* 1 Sm 9:13, 22, 24. *w:* 1 Sm 9:12–13; 20:26; Ex 19:10; Jb 1:5. *x:* 1 Sm 10:23–24; 1 Kgs 11:4; 1 Chr 28:9; Prv 15:11; Jer 17:10; 20:12; Lk 16:15; Acts 1:24. *y:* 1 Sm 17:12–13; 1 Chr 2:13–15. *z:* 1 Sm 17:15, 28, 34; 2 Sm 7:8; Ps 78:70–71. *a:* 1 Sm 9:2. *b:* 1 Sm 10:6; 11:6; Jgs 3:10; 9:9; Sir 46:13.

David Wins Saul's Approval. [14*][c] The spirit of the LORD had departed from Saul, and he was tormented by an evil spirit from the LORD. [15]So the servants of Saul said to him: "Look! An evil spirit from God is tormenting you. [16]If your lordship will order it, we, your servants here attending to you, will look for a man skilled in playing the harp. When the evil spirit from God comes upon you, he will play and you will feel better." [17]Saul then told his servants, "Find me a good harpist and bring him to me." [18][d] One of the servants spoke up: "I have observed that a son of Jesse of Bethlehem is a skillful harpist. He is also a brave warrior, an able speaker, and a handsome young man. The LORD is certainly with him."

David Made Armor-Bearer. [19]Accordingly, Saul dispatched messengers to ask Jesse to send him his son David, who was with the flock. [20]Then Jesse took five loaves of bread, a skin of wine, and a young goat, and sent them to Saul with his son David.[e] [21]Thus David came to Saul and entered his service. Saul became very fond of him and made him his armor-bearer.[f] [22]Saul sent Jesse the message, "Let David stay in my service, for he meets with my approval." [23]Whenever the spirit from God came upon Saul, David would take the harp and play, and Saul would be relieved and feel better, for the evil spirit would leave him.

CHAPTER 17

See RG 175–76

The Challenge of Goliath. [1]The Philistines rallied their forces for battle at Socoh in Judah and camped between Socoh and Azekah at Ephes-dammim. [2]Saul and the Israelites rallied and camped in the valley of the Elah, drawing up their battle line to meet the Philistines. [3]The Philistines were stationed on one hill and the Israelites on an opposite hill, with a valley between them.

[4]A champion named Goliath of Gath came out from the Philistine camp; he was six cubits and a span* tall. [5]He had a bronze helmet on his head and wore a bronze breastplate of scale armor weighing five thousand shekels, [6]bronze greaves, and had a bronze scimitar slung from his shoulders. [7]The shaft of his javelin was like a weaver's beam, and its iron head weighed six hundred shekels.* His shield-bearer went ahead of him.[g] [8]He stood and shouted to the ranks of Israel: "Why come out in battle formation? I am a Philistine, and you are Saul's servants. Choose one of your men, and have him come down to me. [9]If he beats me in combat and kills me, we will be your vassals; but if I beat him and kill him, you shall be our vassals and serve us." [10]The Philistine continued: "I defy the ranks of Israel today. Give me a man and let us fight together." [11]When Saul and all Israel heard this challenge of the Philistine, they were stunned and terrified.

David Comes to the Camp.* [12]David was the son of an Ephrathite named Jesse from Bethlehem in Judah who had eight sons. In the days of Saul Jesse was old and well on in years.[h] [13]The three oldest sons of Jesse had followed Saul to war; the names of these three sons who had gone off to war were Eliab the firstborn; Abinadab the second; and Shammah the third. [14]David was the youngest. While the three oldest had joined Saul, [15]David would come and go from Saul's presence to tend his father's sheep at Bethlehem.[i]

[16]Meanwhile the Philistine came forward and took his stand morning and evening for forty days.

16:14–23 These verses explain Saul's loss of divine favor and David's rise to power. By approving the young man, Saul identifies David as his legitimate successor. Of the two traditions in the Hebrew text about David's entry into Saul's service, the Greek translation retains only the one found in vv. 14–23; 17:1–11, 32–54. **An evil spirit from the LORD**: Saul's erratic behavior is attributed to a change in the Lord's relationship with him. Cf. Jgs 9:23, where the Lord puts an evil spirit between Abimelech and the citizens of Shechem.

17:4 Six cubits and a span: about nine feet nine inches (a cubit equals about eighteen inches; a span equals about eight inches). The Greek text and 4QSam[a] read: "four cubits and a span" (six feet nine inches). The description of the Philistine's might and his powerful weapons contrasts with the picture of the youthful David who trusts in God.

17:7 Six hundred shekels: over fifteen pounds.

17:12–31 Here the final editor begins an alternative account of David's encounter with the Philistine hero, which continues in vv. 50–51 and concludes in 17:55–18:5.

c: 1 Sm 18:10–11. *d:* 1 Sm 18:12, 14, 28; 2 Sm 5:10; 17:8; Jn 3:2. *e:* 1 Sm 9:7–8; 10:3–4; 16:1; 17:17–19. *f:* 1 Sm 18:2. *g:* 2 Sm 21:19; 1 Chr 11:23; 20:5. *h:* 1 Sm 16:1, 10; Ru 1:2. *i:* 1 Sm 16:11; 18:2; 2 Sm 7:8; Ps 78:70–71.

17 Now Jesse said to his son David: "Take
this ephah of roasted grain and these ten
loaves for your brothers, and bring them
quickly to your brothers in the camp. 18 Also
take these ten cheeses for the field officer.
Greet your brothers and bring home some
token from them. 19 Saul and your brothers,
together with all Israel, are at war with the
Philistines in the valley of the Elah." 20 Early
the next morning, having left the flock with
a shepherd, David packed up and set out, as
Jesse had commanded him. He reached the
barricade of the camp just as the army, on
their way to the battleground, were shouting
their battle cry.[j] 21 The Israelites and the Philistines drew up opposite each other in battle
array. 22 David entrusted what he had
brought to the keeper of the baggage and
hastened to the battle line, where he greeted
his brothers.[k] 23 While he was talking with
them, the Philistine champion, by name Goliath of Gath, came up from the ranks of the
Philistines and spoke as before, and David
listened. 24 When the Israelites saw the man,
they all retreated before him, terrified. 25 The
Israelites had been saying: "Do you see this
man coming up? He comes up to insult Israel. The king will make whoever kills him a
very wealthy man. He will give his daughter
to him and declare his father's family exempt from taxes in Israel."[l] 26 David now
said to the men standing near him: "How
will the man who kills this Philistine and
frees Israel from disgrace be rewarded? Who
is this uncircumcised Philistine that he
should insult the armies of the living God?"[m]
27 They repeated the same words to him and
said, "That is how the man who kills him
will be rewarded." 28 When Eliab, his oldest
brother, heard him speaking with the men,
he grew angry with David and said: "Why
did you come down? With whom have you
left those sheep in the wilderness? I know
your arrogance and dishonest heart. You
came down to enjoy the battle!"[n] 29 David
protested, "What have I done now? I was
only talking." 30 He turned from him to another and asked the same question; and
everyone gave him the same answer as before. 31 The words that David had spoken
were overheard and reported to Saul, who
sent for him.

David Challenges Goliath. 32 Then David
spoke to Saul: "My lord should not lose
heart. Let your servant go and fight this
Philistine." 33 But Saul answered David,
"You cannot go up against this Philistine and
fight with him, for you are only a youth,
while he has been a warrior from his youth."
34[o] Then David told Saul: "Your servant
used to tend his father's sheep, and whenever a lion or bear came to carry off a sheep
from the flock, 35 I would chase after it, attack it, and snatch the prey from its mouth. If
it attacked me, I would seize it by the throat,
strike it, and kill it. 36 Your servant has killed
both a lion and a bear. This uncircumcised
Philistine will be as one of them, because he
has insulted the armies of the living God."

37 David continued: "The same LORD who
delivered me from the claws of the lion and
the bear will deliver me from the hand of this
Philistine." Saul answered David, "Go! the
LORD will be with you."[p]

Preparation for the Encounter. 38 Then
Saul dressed David in his own tunic, putting
a bronze helmet on his head and arming him
with a coat of mail. 39 David also fastened
Saul's sword over the tunic. He walked with
difficulty, however, since he had never worn
armor before. He said to Saul, "I cannot go
in these, because I am not used to them." So
he took them off. 40 Then, staff in hand, David selected five smooth stones from the
wadi and put them in the pocket of his shepherd's bag. With his sling in hand, he approached the Philistine.

David's Victory. 41* With his shield-bearer
marching before him, the Philistine advanced closer and closer to David. 42 When
he sized David up and saw that he was
youthful, ruddy, and handsome in appearance, he began to deride him. 43 He said to
David, "Am I a dog that you come against

17:41–47 The two combatants trade theological taunts. God uses the most unlikely opponent to destroy Goliath.

j: 1 Sm 26:5. *k:* 1 Sm 25:13. *l:* 1 Sm 18:17; Jos 15:16. *m:* 1 Sm 18:25; Dt 5:26; Jgs 15:18; 2 Kgs 19:4; Is 37:4; Jer 10:10.
n: 1 Sm 16:6. *o:* Jgs 14:6; Sir 47:3. *p:* Prv 28:1.

me with a staff?" Then the Philistine cursed David by his gods 44and said to him, "Come here to me, and I will feed your flesh to the birds of the air and the beasts of the field."[q] 45David answered him: "You come against me with sword and spear and scimitar, but I come against you in the name of the LORD of hosts, the God of the armies of Israel whom you have insulted. 46Today the LORD shall deliver you into my hand; I will strike you down and cut off your head. This very day I will feed your dead body and the dead bodies of the Philistine army to the birds of the air and the beasts of the field; thus the whole land shall learn that Israel has a God. 47All this multitude, too, shall learn that it is not by sword or spear that the LORD saves. For the battle belongs to the LORD, who shall deliver you into our hands."[r]

48The Philistine then moved to meet David at close quarters, while David ran quickly toward the battle line to meet the Philistine. 49David put his hand into the bag and took out a stone, hurled it with the sling, and struck the Philistine on the forehead. The stone embedded itself in his brow, and he fell on his face to the ground. 50Thus David triumphed over the Philistine with sling and stone; he struck the Philistine dead, and did it without a sword in his hand.[s] 51Then David ran and stood over him; with the Philistine's own sword which he drew from its sheath he killed him, and cut off his head.[t]

Flight of the Philistines. When the Philistines saw that their hero was dead, they fled. 52Then the men of Israel and Judah sprang up with a battle cry and pursued them to the approaches of Gath and to the gates of Ekron, and Philistines fell wounded along the road from Shaaraim as far as Gath and Ekron. 53When they returned from their pursuit of the Philistines, the Israelites looted their camp. 54[u] David took the head of the Philistine and brought it to Jerusalem; but he kept Goliath's armor in his own tent.*

David Presented to Saul. 55As Saul watched David go out to meet the Philistine, he asked his general Abner, "Abner, whose son is that young man?" Abner replied, "On your life, O king, I have no idea."[v] 56And the king said, "Find out whose son the lad is." 57So when David returned from slaying the Philistine, Abner escorted him into Saul's presence. David was still holding the Philistine's head. 58Saul then asked him, "Whose son are you, young man?" David replied, "I am the son of your servant Jesse of Bethlehem."

CHAPTER 18

See RG 175–76

David and Jonathan. 1By the time David finished speaking with Saul, Jonathan's life became bound up with David's life; he loved him as his very self.[w] 2Saul retained David on that day and did not allow him to return to his father's house.[x] 3Jonathan and David made a covenant, because Jonathan loved him as his very self. 4Jonathan took off* the cloak he was wearing and handed it over to David, along with his military dress, even his sword, bow, and belt.[y] 5David then carried out successfully every mission on which Saul sent him. So Saul put him in charge of his soldiers; this met with the approval of the whole army, even Saul's officers.

Saul's Jealousy. 6At the approach of Saul and David, on David's return after striking down the Philistine, women came out from all the cities of Israel to meet Saul the king, singing and dancing, with tambourines, joyful songs, and stringed instruments.* [z] 7The women played and sang:

"Saul has slain his thousands,
David his tens of thousands."[a]

8Saul was very angry and resentful of the song, for he thought: "They give David tens

17:54 Jerusalem was a Jebusite city; it came under Israelite control only at the beginning of David's rule. As a young shepherd, David would not have had a military tent. In 21:10, Goliath's sword is in the Nob temple.

18:4 Jonathan took off: with the details in this verse, the narrator identifies David as Jonathan's replacement and Saul's heir to the throne. Cf. 23:17 and Gn 41:39–43.

18:6 Stringed instruments: perhaps a lute-like instrument with three strings; the Hebrew word, *shalshim*, perhaps related to the root *shlsh* ("three"), occurs only here in the Old Testament.

q: Dt 28:26; Ps 79:2–3; Is 18:6; Jer 7:33; 15:3. *r:* 1 Sm 14:6, 10; Ps 33:16. *s:* 1 Mc 4:30; Sir 47:4. *t:* 1 Sm 21:10. *u:* 1 Sm 31:9. *v:* 1 Sm 14:50. *w:* 1 Sm 19:1–7; 20:17; 23:16; 2 Sm 1:26; 9:1. *x:* 1 Sm 16:21; 17:15. *y:* 2 Sm 1:22. *z:* Ex 15:20–21; Jgs 11:34; Jdt 15:12. *a:* 1 Sm 21:12; 29:5; Ps 91:7; Sir 47:6–7.

of thousands, but only thousands to me. All that remains for him is the kingship." [9]From that day on, Saul kept a jealous eye on David.

[10b] The next day an evil spirit from God rushed upon Saul, and he raged in his house. David was in attendance, playing the harp as at other times, while Saul was holding his spear. [11]Saul poised the spear, thinking, "I will nail David to the wall!" But twice David escaped him. [12]Saul then began to fear David because the LORD was with him but had turned away from Saul. [13]Saul sent him out of his presence and appointed him a field officer. So David led the people on their military expeditions [14]and prospered in all his ways, for the LORD was with him. [15]Seeing how he prospered, Saul feared David. [16]But all Israel and Judah loved David, since he led them on their expeditions.* [c]

Saul Plots Against David. [17]Saul said to David, "Look, I will give you my older daughter, Merob, in marriage if you become my warrior and fight the battles of the LORD." Saul thought, "I will not lay a hand on him. Let the hand of the Philistines strike him."[d] [18]But David answered Saul: "Who am I? And who are my kindred or my father's clan in Israel that I should become the king's son-in-law?" [19]But when the time came for Saul's daughter Merob to be given to David, she was given as wife to Adriel the Meholathite instead.[e]

[20]Now Saul's daughter Michal loved David. When this was reported to Saul, he was pleased.[f] [21]He thought, "I will offer her to him as a trap, so that the hand of the Philistines may strike him." So for the second time Saul said to David, "You shall become my son-in-law today." [22]Saul then ordered his servants, "Speak to David privately and say: The king favors you, and all his officers love you. You should become son-in-law to the king." [23]But when Saul's servants mentioned this to David, he said: "Is becoming the king's son-in-law a trivial matter in your eyes? I am poor and insignificant." [24]When his servants reported David's answer to him, [25]Saul commanded them, "Say this to David: The king desires no other price for the bride than the foreskins of one hundred Philistines, that he may thus take vengeance on his enemies." Saul intended to have David fall into the hands of the Philistines.[g] [26]When the servants reported this offer to David, he was pleased with the prospect of becoming the king's son-in-law. Before the year was up, [27]David arose and went with his men and slew two hundred Philistines. He brought back their foreskins and counted them out before the king that he might become the king's son-in-law. So Saul gave him his daughter Michal as wife. [28]Then Saul realized that the LORD was with David and that his own daughter Michal loved David. [29]So Saul feared David all the more and was his enemy ever after.

[30]The Philistine chiefs continued to make forays, but each time they took the field, David was more successful against them than any of Saul's other officers, and his name was held in great esteem.

CHAPTER 19

See RG 176–77

Persecution of David. [1]Saul discussed his intention to kill David with his son Jonathan and with all his servants. But Saul's son Jonathan, who was very fond of David,[h] [2]told him: "My father Saul is trying to kill you. Therefore, please be on your guard tomorrow morning; stay out of sight and remain in hiding. [3]I, however, will go out and stand beside my father in the countryside where you are, and will speak to him about you. If I learn anything, I will let you know."

[4]Jonathan then spoke well of David to his father Saul, telling him: "The king should not harm his servant David. He has not harmed you, but has helped you very much by his deeds.* [5]When he took his life in his hands and killed the Philistine, and the LORD won a great victory for all Israel, you were glad to see it. Why, then, should you become

18:16 Led them on their expeditions: lit., "go out and come in," i.e., through the city gates; an idiom for military victory.
19:4 Jonathan reminds Saul that David has served him loyally and done nothing to earn a traitor's death. Cf. 24:18–20.

b: 1 Sm 16:14; 19:9–10; 20:33; 22:6; 26:8. *c:* 2 Sm 5:2. *d:* 1 Sm 14:49; 17:25. *e:* 1 Sm 21:8; 24:16. *f:* 1 Sm 14:49; 25:44; 26:23; 2 Sm 3:13. *g:* 1 Sm 17:26; Gn 34:12. *h:* 1 Sm 18:1; 20:1–3.

guilty of shedding innocent blood by killing David without cause?"[i] 6Saul heeded Jonathan's plea and swore, "As the LORD lives, he shall not be killed." 7So Jonathan summoned David and repeated the whole conversation to him. He then brought David to Saul, and David served him as before.

David Escapes from Saul. 8When war broke out again, David went out to fight against the Philistines and inflicted such a great defeat upon them that they fled from him. 9[j] Then an evil spirit from the LORD came upon Saul as he was sitting in his house with spear in hand while David was playing the harp nearby. 10Saul tried to pin David to the wall with the spear, but David eluded Saul, and the spear struck only the wall, while David got away safely.

11The same night, Saul sent messengers to David's house to guard it, planning to kill him in the morning. David's wife Michal informed him, "Unless you run for your life tonight, tomorrow you will be killed."* 12Then Michal let David down through a window, and he made his escape in safety.[k] 13Michal took the teraphim* and laid it in the bed, putting a tangle of goat's hair at its head and covering it with a blanket.[l] 14When Saul sent officers to arrest David, she said, "He is sick." 15Saul, however, sent the officers back to see David and commanded them, "Bring him up to me in his bed, that I may kill him." 16But when the messengers entered, they found the teraphim in the bed, with the tangle of goat's hair at its head. 17Saul asked Michal: "Why did you lie to me like this? You have helped my enemy to get away!" Michal explained to Saul: "He threatened me, saying 'Let me go or I will kill you.' "

David and Saul in Ramah. 18When David got safely away, he went to Samuel in Ramah, informing him of all that Saul had done to him. Then he and Samuel went to stay in Naioth.* 19When Saul was told that David was at Naioth in Ramah, 20he sent officers to arrest David. But when they saw the band of prophets presided over by Samuel in a prophetic state, the spirit of God came upon them and they too fell into the prophetic ecstasy.[m] 21Informed of this, Saul sent other messengers, who also fell into the prophetic ecstasy. For the third time Saul sent messengers, but they too fell into a prophetic ecstasy.

Saul Among the Prophets. 22Finally Saul went to Ramah himself. Arriving at the large cistern in Secu, he asked, "Where are Samuel and David?" Someone answered, "At Naioth in Ramah." 23As he walked from there to Naioth in Ramah, the spirit of God came upon him also, and he continued on, acting like a prophet until he reached Naioth in Ramah. 24Then he, too, stripped himself of his garments and remained in a prophetic state in the presence of Samuel;* all that day and night he lay naked. That is why they say, "Is Saul also among the prophets?"[n]

CHAPTER 20

See RG 176–77

David Consults with Jonathan. 1David fled from Naioth in Ramah, and went to Jonathan. "What have I done?" he asked him. "What crime or what offense does your father hold against me that he seeks my life?"[o] 2Jonathan answered him: "Heaven forbid that you should die! My father does nothing, great or small, without telling me. Why, then, should my father conceal this from me? It cannot be true!" 3But David replied: "Your father is well aware that I am favored with your friendship, so he has decided, 'Jonathan must not know about this or he will be grieved.' Nevertheless, as the LORD lives and as you live, there is only a step between me and death." 4Jonathan then said to David, "I

19:11 This story may have originally followed 18:29, placing the episode of David's escape on the night of his marriage with Michal.

19:13 Teraphim: a life-sized image of a household god in human form; cf. also note on Gn 31:19. Elsewhere in the Deuteronomistic History, use of teraphim is condemned (15:23; 2 Kgs 23:24).

19:18 Naioth: meaning "the pastures." This place appears only in chaps. 19–20 and is associated with Ramah.

19:24 In the presence of Samuel: this verse, which disagrees with 15:35, is further evidence of the diverse origins of these accounts. **"Is Saul also among the prophets?"**: although similar to the story of Saul's prophetic ecstasy in 10:10–13, this account offers a more disparaging portrait of Saul.

i: 1 Sm 17:55–56; Dt 19:10; Ps 119:109. *j:* 1 Sm 16:14; 18:10–11. *k:* Jos 2:15; Acts 9:25; 2 Cor 11:33. *l:* Gn 31:19; Jgs 17:5; 18:14, 18, 20; Ez 21:26. *m:* 1 Sm 10:5–6, 10; Nm 11:25. *n:* 1 Sm 10:10–12; 2 Sm 6:20. *o:* 1 Sm 19:1–7, 11–17; 21:11; 27:4; Gn 31:36.

will do whatever you say." 5David answered: "Tomorrow is the new moon, when I should in fact dine with the king. Let me go and hide in the open country until evening.[p] 6If it turns out that your father misses me, say, 'David urged me to let him go on short notice to his city Bethlehem, because his whole clan is holding its seasonal sacrifice there.'[q] 7If he says, 'Very well,' your servant is safe. But if he becomes quite angry, you can be sure he has planned some harm. 8[r] Do this kindness for your servant because of the LORD's covenant into which you brought us: if I am guilty, kill me yourself! Why should you give me up to your father?" 9But Jonathan answered: "Not I! If ever I find out that my father is determined to harm you, I will certainly let you know." 10David then asked Jonathan, "Who will tell me if your father gives you a harsh answer?"

Mutual Agreement. 11Jonathan replied to David, "Come, let us go out into the field." When they were out in the open country together, 12Jonathan said to David: "As the LORD, the God of Israel, lives, I will sound out my father about this time tomorrow. Whether he is well disposed toward David or not, I will inform you. 13[s] Should it please my father to bring any harm upon you, may the LORD do thus to Jonathan and more,* if I do not inform you of it and send you on your way in peace. May the LORD be with you even as he was with my father. 14Only this: if I am still alive, may you show me the kindness of the LORD. But if I die, 15never cut off your kindness from my house. And when the LORD cuts off all the enemies of David from the face of the land, 16the name of Jonathan must never be cut off from the family of David, or the LORD will make you answer for it." 17And in his love for David, Jonathan renewed his oath to him, because he loved him as he loved himself.

18Jonathan then said to him: "Tomorrow is the new moon; you will be missed, since your place will be vacant. 19On the third day you will be missed all the more. Go to the spot where you hid on the other occasion and wait near the mound there.[t] 20On the third day of the month I will shoot arrows to the side of it, as though aiming at a target. 21I will then send my attendant to recover the arrows. If in fact I say to him, 'Look, the arrow is this side of you; pick it up,' come, for you are safe. As the LORD lives, there will be nothing to fear. 22But if I say to the boy, 'Look, the arrow is beyond you,' go, for the LORD sends you away. 23However, in the matter which you and I have discussed, the LORD shall be between you and me forever." 24So David hid in the open country.

David's Absence. On the day of the new moon, when the king sat down at the feast to dine, 25he took his usual place against the wall. Jonathan sat facing him, while Abner sat at the king's side. David's place was vacant. 26[u] Saul, however, said nothing that day, for he thought, "He must have become unclean by accident."* 27On the next day, the second day of the month, David's place was still vacant. So Saul asked his son Jonathan, "Why has the son of Jesse not come to table yesterday or today?" 28Jonathan explained to Saul: "David pleaded with me to let him go to Bethlehem. 29'Please let me go,' he begged, 'for we are having a clan sacrifice in our city, and my brothers insist on my presence. Now then, if you think well of me, give me leave to visit my brothers.' That is why he has not come to the king's table." 30But Saul grew angry with Jonathan and said to him: "Son of a rebellious woman, do I not know that, to your own disgrace and to the disgrace of your mother's nakedness, you are the companion of Jesse's son? 31For as long as the son of Jesse lives upon the earth, you cannot make good your claim to the kingship!* Now send for him, and bring him

20:13 See note on 3:17.

20:26 The meal on the first day of the month would have had religious overtones, and a ritual impurity (Lv 15:16; Dt 23:10–12) would have barred David from sharing in it.

20:31 Your claim to the kingship: Saul admits his intention that Jonathan should succeed him and that David is a threat to his lineage (cf. 23:17). However Jonathan has already acknowledged David's kingship (18:3–4) and his own subservient role (20:13–16).

p: Nm 10:10; 28:11–15; Ezr 3:5; Neh 10:34. *q:* 1 Sm 17:12. *r:* 1 Sm 18:3; 23:17–18. *s:* 1 Sm 10:7; 17:37; 18:12, 14; 24:22–23; 2 Sm 9:1–13; 21:7. *t:* 1 Sm 19:1–7. *u:* 1 Sm 16:5; Lv 7:20–21; 15:1–3.

to me, for he must die."[v] 32 But Jonathan argued with his father Saul: "Why should he die? What has he done?" 33 At this Saul brandished his spear to strike him, and thus Jonathan learned that his father was determined to kill David.[w] 34 Jonathan sprang up from the table in a rage and ate nothing that second day of the month, because he was grieved on David's account, and because his father had humiliated him.

Jonathan's Farewell. 35 The next morning Jonathan, accompanied by a young boy, went out into the field for his appointment with David. 36 There he said to the boy, "Run and find the arrows." And as the boy ran, he shot an arrow past him. 37 When the boy made for the spot where Jonathan had shot the arrow, Jonathan called after him, "The arrow is farther on!" 38 Again he called to the boy, "Hurry, be quick, don't delay!" Jonathan's boy picked up the arrow and brought it to his master. 39 The boy suspected nothing; only Jonathan and David knew what was meant. 40 Then Jonathan gave his weapons to his boy and said to him, "Go, take them to the city." 41 When the boy had gone, David rose from beside the mound and fell on his face to the ground three times in homage. They kissed each other and wept aloud together. 42[x] At length Jonathan said to David, "Go in peace, in keeping with what the two of us have sworn by the name of the LORD: 'The LORD shall be between you and me, and between your offspring and mine forever.' "

CHAPTER 21

See RG 176–77

1 Then David departed on his way, while Jonathan went back into the city.

The Holy Bread. 2 David went to Ahimelech, the priest of Nob, who came trembling to meet him. He asked, "Why are you alone? Is there no one with you?"*[y] 3 David answered the priest: "The king gave me a commission and told me, 'Do not let anyone know anything about the business on which I have sent you or the commission I have given you.' For that reason I have arranged a particular meeting place with my men. 4[z] Now what do you have on hand? Give me five loaves, or whatever you can find." 5* But the priest replied to David, "I have no ordinary bread on hand, only holy bread; if the men have abstained from women, you may eat some of that." 6 David answered the priest: "We have indeed stayed away from women. In the past whenever I went out on a campaign, all the young men were consecrated—even for an ordinary campaign. All the more so are they consecrated with their weapons today!" 7 So the priest gave him holy bread, for no other bread was on hand except the showbread which had been removed from before the LORD and replaced by fresh bread when it was taken away.[a] 8 One of Saul's servants was there that day, detained before the LORD;* his name was Doeg the Edomite, the chief of Saul's shepherds.[b]

The Sword of Goliath. 9 David then asked Ahimelech: "Do you have a spear or a sword on hand? I brought along neither my sword nor my weapons, because the king's business was urgent." 10 The priest replied: "The sword of Goliath the Philistine, whom you killed in the Valley of Elah, is here wrapped in a garment behind an ephod.* If you wish to take it, do so; there is no sword here except that one." "There is none like it," David cried, "give it to me!"[c]

David a Fugitive. 11 That same day David fled from Saul, going to Achish, king of Gath.[d] 12 But the servants of Achish said to him, "Is this not David, the king of the land? Is it not for him that during their dances they sing out,

21:2 Ahimelech realizes that he risks incurring Saul's anger if David has come to Nob as a fugitive.

21:5–6 According to Lv 24:5–9, the showbread consisted of twelve loaves that were replaced each sabbath. Since the old bread was to be consumed by the priests, Ahimelech questions David regarding the ritual purity of his men (see 2 Sm 11:11). David's answer supposes the discipline of a military campaign under the conditions of "holy war" (Dt 23:10–15).

21:8 Detained before the LORD: perhaps to fulfill a ritual obligation. David's arrival at Nob seems to coincide with a festival day, since the showbread has recently been replaced with fresh bread. **Shepherds**: i.e., Saul's palace guard. Cf. 22:9–10, where Doeg has easy access to Saul.

21:10 Ephod: here an object or image large enough to conceal Goliath's sword. Cf. Gideon's ephod in Jgs 8:27.

v: 2 Sm 12:5. *w:* 1 Sm 18:11. *x:* 2 Sm 9:1; 21:7. *y:* 1 Sm 16:4; Is 10:32; Mk 2:26. *z:* Lv 24:5, 9. *a:* Lv 24:5–9; Mt 12:3–4; Mk 2:26; Lk 6:3–5. *b:* 1 Sm 22:9. *c:* 1 Sm 17:51, 54. *d:* 1 Sm 27:2; 29:5.

'Saul has slain his thousands,
David his tens of thousands'?"[e]

13 David took note of these remarks and became very much afraid of Achish, king of Gath.* 14 So, he feigned insanity in front of them and acted like a madman in their custody, drumming on the doors of the gate and drooling onto his beard. 15 Finally Achish said to his servants: "You see the man is mad. Why did you bring him to me? 16 Do I not have enough madmen, that you bring this one to rant in my presence? Should this fellow come into my house?"

CHAPTER 22

See RG 176–77

1 David left Gath and escaped to the cave of Adullam. When his brothers and the rest of his family heard about it, they came down to him there.[f] 2 He was joined by all those in difficulties or in debt, or embittered,* and became their leader. About four hundred men were with him.

3 From there David went to Mizpeh of Moab and said to the king of Moab, "Let my father and mother stay with you, until I learn what God will do for me." 4 He left them with the king of Moab; they stayed with him as long as David remained in the stronghold.*

5 But Gad the prophet said to David: "Do not remain in the stronghold! Leave! Go to the land of Judah." And so David left and went to the forest of Hereth.[g]

Doeg Betrays Ahimelech. 6 Now Saul heard that David and his men had been located. At the time he was sitting in Gibeah under a tamarisk tree on the high place, holding his spear, while all his servants stood by him.[h] 7 So he said to them: "Listen, men of Benjamin! Will the son of Jesse give all of you fields and vineyards? Will he appoint any of you an officer over a thousand or a hundred men?[i] 8 Is that why you have all conspired against me? Why no one told me that my son had made a pact with the son of Jesse? None of you has shown compassion for me by revealing to me that my son has incited my servant to ambush me, as is the case today."[j] 9[k] Then Doeg the Edomite, who was standing with Saul's officers, spoke up: "I saw the son of Jesse come to Ahimelech, son of Ahitub, in Nob. 10 He consulted the LORD for him, furnished him with provisions, and gave him the sword of Goliath the Philistine."

Slaughter of the Priests. 11 So the king summoned Ahimelech the priest, son of Ahitub, and all his family, the priests in Nob. They all came to the king. 12 "Listen, son of Ahitub!" Saul declared. "Yes, my lord," he replied. 13 Saul questioned him, "Why have you conspired against me with the son of Jesse by giving him food and a sword and by consulting God for him, that he might rise up against me in ambush, as is the case today?" 14 Ahimelech answered the king: "Who among all your servants is as loyal as David, the king's son-in-law, captain of your bodyguard, and honored in your own house? 15 Is this the first time I have consulted God for him? No indeed! Let not the king accuse his servant or anyone in my family of such a thing. Your servant knows nothing at all, great or small, about the whole matter." 16 But the king said, "You shall certainly die, Ahimelech, with all your family." 17 The king then commanded his guards standing by him: "Turn and kill the priests of the LORD, for they gave David a hand. They knew he was a fugitive and yet failed to inform me." But the king's servants refused to raise a hand to strike the priests of the LORD.[l]

18 The king therefore commanded Doeg, "You, turn and kill the priests!" So Doeg the Edomite himself turned and killed the priests that day—eighty-five who wore the linen ephod. 19 Saul also put the priestly city of Nob to the sword, including men and women, children and infants, and oxen, donkeys and sheep.

21:13 Gath: a Philistine city (see note on 5:1–12), the home of Goliath.

22:2 Embittered: Hebrew *mar-nephesh*, "bitter of spirit," used of Hannah, deprived of a child, in 1:10, and of David's soldiers, whose women and children the Amalekites had seized (30:6). Cf. also 2 Sm 17:8. David becomes a hero for those who have endured loss or deprivation.

22:4–5 Stronghold: seemingly connected with the cave complex in v. 1.

e: 1 Sm 18:7; 29:5. *f:* 2 Sm 23:13; Ps 63; Mi 1:15. *g:* 2 Sm 24:11–13. *h:* 1 Sm 14:2; Jgs 4:5. *i:* 1 Sm 8:14. *j:* 1 Sm 18:3; 20:8; 23:18. *k:* 1 Sm 21:2–10; Ps 52. *l:* 1 Sm 2:31, 33; 21:7.

Abiathar Escapes. [20]One son of Ahimelech, son of Ahitub, named Abiathar,* escaped and fled to David.[m] [21]When Abiathar told David that Saul had slain the priests of the LORD, [22]David said to him: "I knew that day, when Doeg the Edomite was there, that he would certainly tell Saul. I am responsible for the slaughter of all your family. [23]Stay with me. Do not be afraid; whoever seeks your life must seek my life also. You are under my protection."*

CHAPTER 23

See RG 176–77

Keilah Liberated. [1]David was informed that the Philistines were attacking Keilah and plundering the threshing floors.[n] [2]So he consulted the LORD, asking, "Shall I go and attack these Philistines?" The LORD answered, Go, attack them, and free Keilah.[o] [3]But David's men said to him: "Even in Judah we have reason to fear. How much more so if we go to Keilah against the forces of the Philistines!" [4]Again David consulted the LORD, who answered: Go down to Keilah, for I will deliver the Philistines into your power.[p] [5]So David went with his men to Keilah and fought against the Philistines. He drove off their cattle and inflicted a severe defeat on them, and freed the inhabitants of Keilah.

[6]Abiathar, son of Ahimelech, who had fled to David, went down with David to Keilah, taking the ephod with him.[q]

Flight from Keilah. [7]When Saul was told that David had entered Keilah, he thought: "God has put him in my hand, for he has boxed himself in by entering a city with gates and bars." [8]Saul then called all the army to war, in order to go down to Keilah and besiege David and his men. [9]When David found out that Saul was planning to harm him, he said to the priest Abiathar, "Bring the ephod here."[r] [10]"LORD God of Israel," David prayed, "your servant has heard that Saul plans to come to Keilah, to destroy the city on my account. [11]Will they hand me over? Will Saul come down as your servant has heard? LORD God of Israel, tell your servant." The LORD answered: He will come down. [12]David then asked, "Will the citizens of Keilah deliver me and my men into the hand of Saul?" The LORD answered: They will deliver you. [13]So David and his men, about six hundred in number, left Keilah and wandered from place to place. When Saul was informed that David had fled from Keilah, he did not go forth.

David and Jonathan in Horesh. [14]David now lived in the strongholds in the wilderness, or in the barren hill country near Ziph. Though Saul sought him continually, the LORD did not deliver David into his hand. [15]While David was in the wilderness of Ziph at Horesh he was afraid that Saul had come out to seek his life. [16]Then Saul's son, Jonathan, came down to David at Horesh and encouraged him in the LORD.[s] [17]He said to him: "Have no fear, my father Saul shall not lay a hand to you. You shall be king of Israel* and I shall be second to you. Even my father Saul knows this."[t] [18]The two of them made a covenant before the LORD in Horesh, where David remained, while Jonathan returned to his home.[u]

Treachery of the Ziphites. [19]Some of the Ziphites went up to Saul in Gibeah and said, "David is hiding among us in the strongholds at Horesh on the hill of Hachilah, south of Jeshimon.[v] [20]Therefore, whenever the king wishes to come down, let him do so. It will be our task to deliver him into the king's hand." [21]Saul replied: "The LORD bless you for your compassion toward me.[w] [22]Go now and make sure once more! Take note of the place where he sets foot for I am told that he is very cunning. [23]Look around and learn in which of all the various hiding places he is holding out. Then come back to

22:20 Abiathar: the sole survivor of Eli's household (2:27–36). David now has in his service the only priest of the Lord left in the land and exclusive access to the ephod for consulting the Lord (cf. 23:9–13). David later appoints Abiathar co-high priest with Zadok in Jerusalem (2 Sm 20:25), but Solomon exiles Abiathar to Anathoth when the priest does not support his bid for the throne. Cf. 1 Kgs 2:26–27.

22:23 You are under my protection: once again a sharp contrast is drawn between Saul, who kills the Lord's priests, and David, who protects the lone survivor.

23:17 King of Israel: to emphasize the inevitability of the Lord's plan, the narrator frames Jonathan's statement with two accounts of David's mercy toward Saul.

m: 1 Sm 23:6; 30:7; 2 Sm 20:25; 1 Kgs 2:26–27. *n:* Jos 15:44. *o:* 1 Sm 28:6. *p:* 1 Sm 17:47. *q:* 1 Sm 22:20; 30:7. *r:* 1 Sm 2:28. *s:* 1 Sm 18:1. *t:* 1 Sm 20:14–16. *u:* 1 Sm 18:3; 20:8. *v:* 1 Sm 26:1–3; Ps 54. *w:* 2 Sm 2:5.

me with reliable information, and I will go with you. If he is in the region, I will track him down out of all the families of Judah." 24 So they went off to Ziph ahead of Saul. At this time David and his men were in the wilderness below Maon, in the Arabah south of the wasteland.[x]

Escape from Saul. 25 When Saul and his men came looking for him, David got word of it and went down to the gorge in the wilderness below Maon. Saul heard of this and pursued David into the wilderness below Maon. 26 As Saul moved along one side of the gorge, David and his men took to the other. David was anxious to escape Saul, while Saul and his men were trying to outflank David and his men in order to capture them. 27 Then a messenger came to Saul, saying, "Come quickly, because the Philistines have invaded the land." 28 Saul interrupted his pursuit of David and went to meet the Philistines. This is how that place came to be called the Rock of Divisions.

CHAPTER 24

See RG 176–77

*David Spares Saul.** 1 David then went up from there and stayed in the strongholds of Engedi. 2 When Saul returned from the pursuit of the Philistines, he was told that David was in the desert near Engedi. 3 So Saul took three thousand of the best men from all Israel and went in search of David and his men in the direction of the wild goat crags. 4 When he came to the sheepfolds along the way, he found a cave, which he entered to relieve himself. David and his men were occupying the inmost recesses of the cave.[y]

5 David's servants said to him, "This is the day about which the LORD said to you: I will deliver your enemy into your hand; do with him as you see fit." So David moved up and stealthily cut off an end of Saul's robe. 6 Afterward, however, David regretted that he had cut off an end of Saul's robe.[z] 7 He said to his men, "The LORD forbid that I should do such a thing to my master, the LORD's anointed, to lay a hand on him, for he is the LORD's anointed."[a] 8 With these words David restrained his men and would not permit them to attack Saul. Saul then left the cave and went on his way. 9 David also stepped out of the cave, calling to Saul, "My lord the king!" When Saul looked back, David bowed, his face to the ground in homage, 10 and asked Saul: "Why do you listen to those who say, 'David is trying to harm you'? 11 You see for yourself today that the LORD just now delivered you into my hand in the cave. I was told to kill you, but I took pity on you instead. I decided, 'I will not raise a hand against my master, for he is the LORD's anointed.' 12 Look here, my father. See the end of your robe which I hold. I cut off an end of your robe and did not kill you. Now see and be convinced that I plan no harm and no rebellion. I have done you no wrong, though you are hunting me down to take my life.[b] 13 May the LORD judge between me and you. May the LORD exact justice from you in my case. I shall not lay a hand on you. 14 As the old proverb says, 'From the wicked comes wickedness.' Thus I will not lay a hand on you. 15 What is the king of Israel attacking? What are you pursuing? A dead dog! A single flea![c] 16 The LORD will be the judge to decide between us. May the LORD see this, defend my cause, and give me justice against you!"[d]

Saul's Remorse. 17 When David finished saying these things to Saul, Saul answered, "Is that your voice, my son David?" And he wept freely. 18 Saul then admitted to David: "You are more in the right than I am. You have treated me graciously, while I have treated you badly. 19 You have declared this day how you treated me graciously: the LORD delivered me into your hand and you did not kill me. 20 For if someone comes upon an enemy, do they send them graciously on their way? So may the LORD reward you graciously for what you have done this day. 21 And now, since I know that you

24:1 The first of two accounts (see chap. 26) in which David spares Saul's life. The two accounts, which do not make reference to each other, are probably alternative versions of the same story.

x: 1 Sm 25:2. *y:* Ps 57. *z:* 1 Sm 15:27. *a:* 1 Sm 10:1; 26:9; 31:4; 2 Sm 1:14. *b:* Rom 12:19. *c:* 2 Sm 9:8; 16:9. *d:* 1 Sm 18:19, 31; 26:19; Ps 35:1–3; 43:1.

will certainly become king and that the kingship over Israel shall come into your possession,[e] 22 swear to me by the LORD that you will not cut off my descendants and that you will not blot out my name from my father's house."[f] 23 David gave Saul his oath and Saul returned home, while David and his men went up to the stronghold.

See RG 176–77

CHAPTER 25

Death of Samuel. 1 Samuel died, and all Israel gathered to mourn him; they buried him at his home in Ramah.[g] Then David went down to the wilderness of Paran.

Nabal and Abigail. 2 There was a man of Maon who had property in Carmel; he was very wealthy, owning three thousand sheep and a thousand goats. At the time, he was present for the shearing of his flock in Carmel.[h] 3 The man's name was Nabal and his wife was Abigail. The woman was intelligent and attractive, but Nabal, a Calebite, was harsh and bad-mannered.[i] 4 While in the wilderness, David heard that Nabal was shearing his flock, 5 so he sent ten young men, instructing them: "Go up to Carmel. Pay Nabal a visit and greet him in my name. 6 Say to him, 'Peace be with you, my brother, and with your family, and with all who belong to you. 7 I have just heard that shearers are with you. Now, when your shepherds were with us, we did them no injury, neither did they miss anything while they were in Carmel. 8 Ask your servants and they will tell you. Look kindly on these young men, since we come at a festival time. Please give your servants and your son David* whatever you can.' "

9 When David's young men arrived, they delivered the entire message to Nabal in David's name, and then waited. 10 But Nabal answered the servants of David: "Who is David? Who is the son of Jesse? Nowadays there are many servants who run away from their masters. 11 Must I take my bread, my wine, my meat that I have slaughtered for my own shearers, and give them to men who come from who knows where?" 12 So David's young men retraced their steps and on their return reported to him all that had been said. 13 Thereupon David said to his men, "Let everyone strap on his sword." And everyone did so, and David put on his own sword. About four hundred men went up after David, while two hundred remained with the baggage.

14 Abigail, Nabal's wife, was informed of this by one of the servants, who said: "From the wilderness David sent messengers to greet our master, but he screamed at them. 15 Yet these men were very good to us. We were not harmed, neither did we miss anything all the while we were living among them during our stay in the open country. 16 Day and night they were a wall of protection for us, the whole time we were pasturing the sheep near them. 17 Now, see what you can do, for you must realize that otherwise disaster is in store for our master and for his whole house. He is such a scoundrel that no one can talk to him." 18 Abigail quickly got together two hundred loaves, two skins of wine, five dressed sheep, five seahs of roasted grain, a hundred cakes of pressed raisins, and two hundred cakes of pressed figs, and loaded them on donkeys. 19 She then said to her servants, "Go on ahead; I will follow you." But to her husband Nabal she said nothing.

20 Hidden by the mountain, she came down riding on a donkey, as David and his men were coming down from the opposite direction. When she met them, 21 David had just been saying: "Indeed, it was in vain that I guarded all this man's possessions in the wilderness, so that nothing of his was missing. He has repaid good with evil. 22 May God do thus to David, and more, if by morning I leave a single male alive among all those who belong to him."[j] 23 As soon as Abigail saw David, she dismounted quickly from the donkey and, falling down, bowed low to the ground before David in homage.

25:8 Your son David: this kinship language may reflect a political or social relationship between Nabal and David. Nabal, however, does not acknowledge it.

e: 1 Sm 26:25. *f:* 2 Sm 9:1–3. *g:* 1 Sm 28:3; Sir 46:13–20. *h:* 1 Sm 23:24; Jos 15:55. *i:* 1 Sm 27:3; Dt 1:35–36; Jos 14:6–15; 1 Chr 2:42, 45. *j:* 1 Kgs 16:11; 21:21; 2 Kgs 9:8.

24 As she fell at his feet she said: "My lord,
let the blame be mine. Please let your maidservant speak to you; listen to the words of
your maidservant.[k] 25 My lord, do not pay
any attention to that scoundrel Nabal, for he
is just like his name. His name means fool,*
and he acts the fool. I, your maidservant, did
not see the young men whom my lord sent.
26 Now, therefore, my lord, as the LORD lives,
and as you live, the LORD has kept you from
shedding blood and from avenging yourself
by your own hand. May your enemies and
those who seek to harm my lord become as
Nabal!* [l] 27 Accept this gift, then, which your
maidservant has brought for my lord, and let
it be given to the young men who follow my
lord. 28 Please forgive the offense of your
maidservant, for the LORD shall certainly establish a lasting house for my lord, because
my lord fights the battles of the LORD. Let no
evil be found in you your whole life long.[m]
29 If any adversary pursues you to seek your
life, may the life of my lord be bound in the
bundle of the living* in the care of the LORD
your God; may God hurl out the lives of
your enemies as from the hollow of a sling.[n]
30 And when the LORD fulfills for my lord the
promise of success he has made concerning
you, and appoints you as ruler over Israel,[o]
31 you shall not have any regrets or burdens
on your conscience, my lord, for having
shed innocent blood or for having rescued
yourself. When the LORD bestows good on
my lord, remember your maidservant."
32 David said to Abigail: "Blessed is the
LORD, the God of Israel, who sent you to
meet me today. 33 Blessed is your good judgment and blessed are you yourself. Today
you have prevented me from shedding blood
and rescuing myself with my own hand.
34 Otherwise, as the LORD, the God of Israel,
lives, who has kept me from harming you, if
you had not come so promptly to meet me,
by dawn Nabal would not have had so much
as one male left alive." 35 David then took
from her what she had brought him and said
to her: "Go to your home in peace! See, I
have listened to your appeal and have
granted your request."

Nabal's Death. 36 When Abigail came to
Nabal, he was hosting a banquet in his house
like that of a king, and Nabal was in a festive
mood and very drunk. So she said not a word
to him until daybreak the next morning.
37 But then, when Nabal was sober, his wife
told him what had happened. At this his
heart died within him, and he became like a
stone. 38 About ten days later the LORD struck
Nabal and he died. 39 Hearing that Nabal was
dead, David said: "Blessed be the LORD,
who has defended my cause against the insult from Nabal, and who restrained his servant from doing evil, but has repaid Nabal
for his evil deeds."

David Marries Abigail and Ahinoam. David then sent a proposal of marriage to Abigail.[p] 40 When David's servants came to Abigail in Carmel, they said to her, "David has
sent us to make his proposal of marriage to
you." 41 Rising and bowing to the ground,
she answered, "Let your maidservant be the
slave who washes the feet of my lord's servants." 42 She got up immediately, mounted a
donkey, and followed David's messengers,
with her five maids attending her. She became his wife. 43 [q] David also married Ahinoam of Jezreel. Thus both of them were his
wives. 44 But Saul gave David's wife Michal,
Saul's own daughter, to Palti, son of Laish,
who was from Gallim.[r]

CHAPTER 26

See RG 176–77

David Spares Saul Again.* 1 [s] Men
from Ziph came to Saul in Gibeah, reporting

25:25 Hebrew *nabal* means "fool" (cf. Is 32:5–7). Abigail, on the other hand, acts wisely to save herself and her household by offering prudent counsel to the future king of Israel.

25:26 Abigail, encouraging David to trust in God's promise, anticipates that some misfortune will shortly overtake Nabal, as in fact it does (vv. 37–38).

25:29 The bundle of the living: the figure is perhaps taken from the practice of tying up valuables in a kerchief or bag for safekeeping. Abigail desires that David enjoy permanent peace and security, but that his enemies be subject to constant agitation and humiliation like a stone whirled about, cast out of the sling, and thereafter disregarded.

26:1 The second account of David sparing Saul's life; cf. note on 24:1.

k: 2 Sm 14:9. *l:* Dt 20:4; Jgs 7:2. *m:* 1 Kgs 11:38. *n:* Ps 69:28. *o:* 1 Sm 13:14; 2 Sm 3:10. *p:* 1 Kgs 2:44. *q:* 1 Sm 27:3. *r:* 1 Sm 18:20; 27:3; 30:5; 2 Sm 2:2, 13–16; 1 Chr 3:1. *s:* 1 Sm 23:19–20; Ps 54.

that David was hiding on the hill of Hachilah at the edge of Jeshimon. [2]So Saul went down to the wilderness of Ziph with three thousand of the best warriors of Israel, to search for David in the wilderness of Ziph. [3]Saul camped beside the road on the hill of Hachilah, at the edge of Jeshimon. David, who was living in the wilderness, saw that Saul had come into the wilderness after him [4]and sent out scouts, who confirmed Saul's arrival. [5]David then went to the place where Saul was encamped and saw the spot where Saul and his general, Abner, son of Ner, had their sleeping quarters. Saul was lying within the camp, and all his soldiers were bivouacked around him.[t] [6]David asked Ahimelech the Hittite, and Abishai, son of Zeruiah and brother of Joab, "Who will go down into the camp with me to Saul?" Abishai replied, "I will."[u] [7]So David and Abishai reached Saul's soldiers by night, and there was Saul lying asleep within the camp, his spear thrust into the ground at his head and Abner and his troops sleeping around him.

[8]Abishai whispered to David: "God has delivered your enemy into your hand today. Let me nail him to the ground with one thrust of the spear; I will not need to strike him twice!"[v] [9]But David said to Abishai, "Do not harm him, for who can lay a hand on the LORD's anointed and remain innocent? [10]As the LORD lives," David declared, "only the LORD can strike him: either when the time comes for him to die, or when he goes out and perishes in battle.* [w] [11]But the LORD forbid that I lay a hand on the LORD's anointed! Now take the spear at his head and the water jug, and let us be on our way." [12]So David took the spear and the water jug from their place at Saul's head, and they withdrew without anyone seeing or knowing or awakening. All remained asleep, because a deep slumber* from the LORD had fallen upon them.[x]

David Taunts Abner. [13]Crossing over to an opposite slope, David stood on a distant hilltop. With a great distance between them [14]David called to the army and to Abner, son of Ner, "Will you not answer, Abner?" Then Abner shouted back, "Who is it that calls me?" [15]David said to Abner: "Are you not a man? Who in Israel is your equal? Why were you not guarding your lord the king when one of his subjects came to assassinate the king, your lord? [16]What you have done is not right. As the LORD lives, you people deserve death because you have not guarded your lord, the anointed of the LORD. Go, look: where are the king's spear and the water jug that was at his head?"

Saul Admits His Guilt. [17]Saul recognized David's voice and asked, "Is that your voice, David my son?"* David answered, "Yes, my lord the king." [18]He continued: "Why does my lord pursue his servant? What have I done? What evil am I planning? [19]Please, now, let my lord the king listen to the words of his servant. If the LORD has incited you against me, may an offering please the LORD. But if it is the people who have done so, may they be cursed before the LORD. They have driven me away so that today I have no share in the LORD's heritage,* but am told: 'Go serve other gods!'[y] [20]Do not let my blood spill on the ground far from the presence of the LORD. For the king of Israel has come out to seek a single flea as if he were hunting partridge* in the mountains." [21]Then Saul said: "I have done wrong. Come back, David, my son! I will not harm you again, because you considered my life pre-

26:10 Perishes in battle: David's words foreshadow how Saul will die (31:3–4). They also emphasize that David, unlike Saul, knows his proper place before God. David comes to the kingship innocent of Saul's blood, although the king pursues him like an enemy and David has had two opportunities to kill him.

26:12 Deep slumber: as in Gn 2:21; 15:12; Is 29:10. The Lord aids David's foray into Saul's camp and allows David to come and go undetected.

26:17 David my son: Saul's reference to David as his son, which appears three times in this chapter (vv. 17, 21, 25), alludes to David's role as his successor.

26:19 The LORD's heritage: the land and people of Israel (Dt 32:8–9; Ps 33:12). If driven from the land, David could not take part in worship of Israel's God; nonetheless, God has blessed David (cf. v. 25).

26:20 Partridge: lit., "the caller." The metaphor is built on clever wordplay: in v. 14, David calls out to the army and Abner asks the caller's identity. David calls out the answer: "the caller" is the object of the king's pursuit.

t: 1 Sm 17:20. *u:* 2 Sm 3:30; 1 Chr 2:16. *v:* 1 Sm 18:11; 19:10; 20:33. *w:* Ps 37:13. *x:* Gn 2:21; 15:12. *y:* 1 Sm 24:16.

cious today even though I have been a fool and have made a serious mistake." 22But David answered: "Here is the king's spear. Let an attendant come over to get it. 23The LORD repays everyone's righteousness and faithfulness. Although the LORD delivered you into my hands today, I could not lay a hand on the LORD's anointed.[z] 24Just as I regarded your life as precious today, so may the LORD regard my life as precious and deliver me from all dangers." 25Then Saul said to David: "Blessed are you, my son David! You shall certainly succeed in whatever you undertake." David went his way, and Saul returned to his place.[a]

CHAPTER 27

See RG 176–77

David Flees to the Philistines. 1David said to himself: "I shall perish some day at the hand of Saul. I have no choice but to escape to the land of the Philistines; then Saul will give up his continual search for me throughout the land of Israel, and I will be out of his reach." 2Accordingly, David departed with his six hundred soldiers and went over to Achish, son of Maoch, king of Gath.[b] 3David and his men lived in Gath with Achish; each one had his family, and David had his two wives, Ahinoam from Jezreel and Abigail, the widow of Nabal from Carmel.[c] 4When Saul learned that David had fled to Gath, he no longer searched for him.

5David said to Achish: "If I meet with your approval, let me have a place to live in one of the country towns. Why should your servant live with you in the royal city?" 6That same day Achish gave him Ziklag, which has, therefore, belonged to the kings of Judah* up to the present time.[d] 7In all, David lived a year and four months in Philistine territory.[e]

David Raids Israel's Foes. 8David and his men went out on raids against the Geshurites, Girzites, and Amalekites—peoples living in the land between Telam, on the approach to Shur, and the land of Egypt.[f] 9In attacking the land David would not leave a man or woman alive, but would carry off sheep, oxen, donkeys, camels, and clothes. Then he would return to Achish, 10who would ask, "Against whom did you raid this time?" David would reply, "Against the Negeb of Judah,"* or "Against the Negeb of Jerahmeel," or "Against the Negeb of the Kenites."[g] 11David never left a man or woman alive to be brought to Gath. He thought, "They will betray us and say, 'This is what David did.' " This was his custom as long as he lived in Philistine territory. 12Achish trusted David, thinking, "His people Israel must certainly detest him. I shall have him as my vassal forever."

CHAPTER 28

See RG 176–78

1In those days the Philistines mustered their military forces to fight against Israel. So Achish said to David, "You realize, of course, that you and your warriors* must march out for battle with me." 2David answered Achish, "Good! Now you shall learn what your servant can do." Then Achish said to David, "I shall appoint you as my permanent bodyguard."

3Now, Samuel was dead. All Israel had mourned him and buried him in his city, Ramah. Meanwhile Saul had driven mediums and diviners out of the land.[h]

Saul in Despair. 4The Philistines rallied and, coming to Shunem, they encamped. Saul, too, mustered all Israel; they camped on Gilboa. 5When Saul saw the Philistine camp, he grew afraid and lost heart completely. 6He consulted the LORD; but the LORD gave no answer, neither in dreams nor by Urim nor through prophets.[i] 7Then Saul said to his servants, "Find me a medium* through whom I can seek counsel." His ser-

27:6 Ziklag was a royal city and not part of Israel's tribal land holdings. Jerusalem later enjoyed a similar status (2 Sm 5:7–9).

27:10 The Negeb of Judah: David deceives Achish by assuring him that he has attacked Israelite territory.

28:1 You and your warriors: David is faced with a potentially dangerous dilemma: either to reveal his continuing loyalty to his own people or to obey Achish and fight against his own people.

28:7 A medium: Saul's own prohibition of necromancy and divination (v. 3) was in keeping with the consistent teaching of the Old Testament (cf. Lv 19:31; 20:6, 27; Dt 18:10).

z: 1 Sm 18:20. *a:* 1 Sm 18:14; 24:21. *b:* 1 Sm 21:11–16. *c:* 1 Sm 25:3, 44; 30:3–5; 2 Sm 2:3. *d:* 1 Sm 30:1. *e:* 1 Sm 29:3. *f:* 1 Sm 15:3, 7; Jos 13:2–3. *g:* 1 Sm 30:14, 29; 1 Chr 2:9, 25, 42. *h:* 1 Sm 25:1; Sir 46:20. *i:* 1 Sm 14:37, 41; Ex 28:30; Lv 8:8.

vants answered him, "There is a woman in Endor who is a medium."[j]

The Medium at Endor. 8 So he disguised himself, putting on other clothes, and set out with two companions. They came to the woman at night, and Saul said to her, "Divine for me; conjure up the spirit I tell you."[k] 9 But the woman answered him, "You know what Saul has done, how he expelled the mediums and diviners from the land. Then why are you trying to entrap me and get me killed?" 10 But Saul swore to her by the LORD, "As the LORD lives, you shall incur no blame for this." 11 "Whom do you want me to conjure up?" the woman asked him. "Conjure up Samuel for me," he replied.

Samuel Appears. 12 When the woman saw Samuel, she shrieked at the top of her voice and said to Saul, "Why have you deceived me? You are Saul!" 13 But the king said to her, "Do not be afraid. What do you see?" "I see a god rising from the earth," she replied. 14 "What does he look like?" asked Saul. "An old man is coming up wrapped in a robe," she replied. Saul knew that it was Samuel, and so he bowed his face to the ground in homage.

Saul's Doom. 15* Samuel then said to Saul, "Why do you disturb me by conjuring me up?" Saul replied: "I am in great distress, for the Philistines are waging war against me and God has turned away from me. Since God no longer answers me through prophets or in dreams, I have called upon you to tell me what I should do."[l] 16 To this Samuel said: "But why do you ask me, if the LORD has abandoned you for your neighbor?[m] 17 The LORD has done to you what he declared through me: he has torn the kingdom from your hand and has given it to your neighbor David.

18 "Because you disobeyed the LORD's directive and would not carry out his fierce anger against Amalek, the LORD has done this to you today.[n] 19 Moreover, the LORD will deliver Israel, and you as well, into the hands of the Philistines. By tomorrow you and your sons will be with me, and the LORD will have delivered the army of Israel into the hands of the Philistines."[o]

20 Immediately Saul fell full length on the ground, in great fear because of Samuel's message. He had no strength left, since he had eaten nothing all that day and night. 21 Then the woman came to Saul and, seeing that he was quite terror-stricken, said to him: "Remember, your maidservant obeyed you: I took my life in my hands and carried out the request you made of me. 22 Now you, in turn, please listen to your maidservant. Let me set out a bit of food for you to eat, so that you are strong enough to go on your way." 23 But he refused, saying, "I will not eat." However, when his servants joined the woman in urging him, he listened to their entreaties, got up from the ground, and sat on a couch. 24 The woman had a stall-fed calf in the house, which she now quickly slaughtered. Then taking flour, she kneaded it and baked unleavened bread. 25 She set the meal before Saul and his servants, and they ate. Then they got up and left the same night.

CHAPTER 29

See RG 177–78

David's Aid Rejected. 1 Now the Philistines had mustered all their forces in Aphek, and the Israelites were encamped at the spring in Jezreel.[p] 2 As the Philistine lords were marching their units of a hundred and a thousand, David and his warriors were marching in the rear guard with Achish. 3 The Philistine commanders asked, "What are those Hebrews doing here?" Achish answered them: "Why, that is David, the officer of Saul, king of Israel. He has been with me for a year or two, and from the day he came over to me until now I have never found fault in him."[q] 4 But the Philistine commanders were angered at this and said to him: "Send that man back! Let him return to the place you picked out for him. He must not go down into battle with us; during the battle he might become our enemy. For how else can he win back his master's favor, if

28:15–19 The consultation with the medium serves to remind the reader that the Lord's plan for David marches onward; no sorcery can thwart it.

j: Lv 19:31; 20:27; Dt 18:10–12; 2 Kgs 21:6; 1 Chr 10:13–14; Acts 16:16. *k:* 1 Sm 15:23; 1 Kgs 14:2. *l:* 1 Sm 14:37; Sir 46:20. *m:* 1 Sm 15:27–28. *n:* 1 Sm 15:18–19, 26. *o:* 1 Sm 31:2–6; Sir 46:20. *p:* 1 Sm 4:1. *q:* 1 Sm 27:7.

not at the expense of our soldiers?[r] 5Is this not the David for whom they sing during their dances,

'Saul has slain his thousands,
David his tens of thousands'?"[s]

6So Achish summoned David and said to him: "As the LORD lives, you are honest, and I would want you with me in all my battles. To this day I have found nothing wrong with you since you came to me. But in the view of the chiefs you are not welcome. 7Leave peacefully, now, and do nothing that might displease the Philistine chiefs." 8But David said to Achish: "What have I done? What fault have you found in your servant from the day I entered your service until today, that I cannot go to fight against the enemies of my lord the king?" 9"I recognize," Achish answered David, "that you are trustworthy, like an angel of God. But the Philistine commanders are saying, 'He must not go with us into battle.' 10So the first thing tomorrow, you and your lord's servants who came with you, go to the place I picked out for you. Do not take to heart their worthless remarks; for you have been valuable in my service. But make an early morning start, as soon as it grows light, and be on your way." 11So David and his warriors left early in the morning to return to the land of the Philistines, and the Philistines went on up to Jezreel.

CHAPTER 30

See RG 177–78

Ziklag in Ruins. 1Before David and his men reached Ziklag on the third day, the Amalekites had raided the Negeb and Ziklag. They stormed Ziklag, and set it on fire.[t] 2They took captive the women and all who were in the city, young and old, killing no one, and they herded them off when they left. 3David and his men arrived at the city to find it burned to the ground and their wives, sons, and daughters taken captive. 4Then David and those who were with him wept aloud until they could weep no more. 5David's two wives, Ahinoam of Jezreel and Abigail, the widow of Nabal from Carmel, had also been carried off.[u] 6Now David found himself in great danger, for the soldiers spoke of stoning him, so bitter were they over the fate of their sons and daughters. David took courage in the LORD his God 7[v] and said to Abiathar, the priest, son of Ahimelech, "Bring me the ephod!" When Abiathar brought him the ephod, 8David inquired of the LORD, "Shall I pursue these raiders? Can I overtake them?" The LORD answered him: Go in pursuit, for you will certainly overtake them and bring about a rescue.

Raid on the Amalekites. 9So David went off with his six hundred as far as the Wadi Besor, where those who were to remain behind halted. 10David continued the pursuit with four hundred, but two hundred were too exhausted to cross the Wadi Besor and remained behind. 11An Egyptian was found in the open country and brought to David. They gave him food to eat and water to drink; 12they also offered a cake of pressed figs and two cakes of pressed raisins. When he had eaten, he revived, for he had not taken food nor drunk water for three days and three nights. 13Then David asked him, "To whom do you belong? Where did you come from?" "I am an Egyptian, the slave of an Amalekite," he replied. "My master abandoned me three days ago because I fell sick. 14We raided the Negeb of the Cherethites, the territory of Judah, and the Negeb of Caleb; and we set Ziklag on fire."[w] 15David then asked him, "Will you lead me down to these raiders?" He answered, "Swear to me by God that you will not kill me or hand me over to my master, and I will lead you down to the raiders." 16So he led them down, and there were the Amalekites lounging all over the ground, eating, drinking, and celebrating because of all the rich plunder they had taken from the land of the Philistines and from the land of Judah.

The Plunder Recovered. 17From dawn to sundown the next day David attacked them, allowing no one to escape except four hundred young men, who mounted their camels and fled.[x] 18David recovered everything the Amalekites had taken, and he rescued his

r: 1 Chr 12:19–20. *s:* 1 Sm 18:6–7; 21:12. *t:* 1 Sm 15:2; 27:6, 10; 1 Chr 12:21. *u:* 1 Sm 25:42; 27:3; 30:5. *v:* 1 Sm 2:28; 23:6; Ex 28:30. *w:* 1 Sm 27:10; Ez 25:16. *x:* 1 Sm 15:3; Jos 6:17; Jgs 7:12.

two wives. [19]Nothing was missing, small or great, plunder or sons or daughters, of all that the Amalekites had taken. David brought back everything. [20]Moreover, David took all the sheep and oxen, and as they drove these before him, they shouted, "This is David's plunder!"

Division of the Plunder. [21]When David came to the two hundred men who had been too exhausted to follow him, whom he had left behind at the Wadi Besor, they came out to meet David and the men with him. As David approached, he greeted them. [22]But all the greedy and worthless among those who had accompanied David said, "Since they did not accompany us, we will not give them anything from the plunder, except for each man's wife and children." [23]But David said: "You must not do this, my brothers, after what the LORD has given us. The LORD has protected us and delivered into our hands the raiders that came against us.[y] [24]Who could agree with this proposal of yours? Rather, the share of the one who goes down to battle shall be the same as that of the one who remains with the baggage—they share alike."[z] [25]And from that day forward he made this a law and a custom in Israel, as it still is today.[a]

David's Gifts to Judah. [26]When David came to Ziklag, he sent part of the plunder to his friends, the elders of Judah,* saying, "This is a gift to you from the plunder of the enemies of the LORD," namely, [27]to those in Bethel, Ramoth-negeb, Jattir, [28]Aroer, Siphmoth, Eshtemoa, [29]Racal, Jerahmeelite cities and Kenite cities,[b] [30]Hormah, Borashan, Athach, [31]Hebron, and to all the places that David and his men had frequented.[c]

See RG 177–78

CHAPTER 31

Death of Saul and His Sons. [1][d] Now the Philistines went to war against Israel, and the Israelites fled before them, and fell, slain on Mount Gilboa. [2]The Philistines pressed hard after Saul and his sons. When the Philistines had struck down Jonathan, Abinadab, and Malchishua, sons of Saul,[e] [3]the fury of the battle converged on Saul. Then the archers hit him, and he was severely wounded. [4]Saul said to his armor-bearer, "Draw your sword and run me through; otherwise these uncircumcised will come and abuse me." But the armor-bearer, badly frightened, refused, so Saul took his own sword and fell upon it.[f] [5][g] When the armor-bearer saw that Saul was dead, he too fell upon his sword and died with him. [6]Thus Saul, his three sons, and his armor-bearer died together on that same day. [7]When the Israelites on the slope of the valley and those along the Jordan saw that the men of Israel had fled and that Saul and his sons were dead, they abandoned their cities and fled. Then the Philistines came and lived in those cities.

[8]On the following day, when the Philistines came to strip the slain, they found Saul and his three sons fallen on Mount Gilboa. [9]They cut off Saul's head and stripped him of his armor; these they sent throughout the land of the Philistines to bring the good news to the temple of their idols and to the people.[h] [10]They put his armor in the temple of Astarte but impaled his body on the wall of Beth-shan.

Burial of Saul. [11][i] When the inhabitants of Jabesh-gilead heard what the Philistines had done to Saul, [12]all their warriors set out and traveled through the night; they removed the bodies of Saul and his sons from the wall of Beth-shan, and, returning to Jabesh, burned them.* [13]Then they took their bones and buried them under the tamarisk tree in Jabesh, and fasted for seven days.

30:26 Elders of Judah: David consolidates his power in southern Judah in preparation for his anointing at Hebron (2 Sm 5:3).

31:12 Burned them: cremation was not an Israelite custom. The people of Jabesh-gilead repay Saul's victory over the Ammonites on their behalf (chap. 11) by providing burial and funeral rites for him and his sons. Probably the damaged state of the corpus necessitated cremation.

y: Dt 20:4, 14. *z:* 1 Sm 17:22; 25:13. *a:* Nm 31:27. *b:* 1 Sm 27:10. *c:* 2 Sm 2:1–4. *d:* 2 Sm 1:1–16; 4:4; 1 Chr 10:1–12. *e:* 1 Sm 14:49; 28:19; 1 Chr 10:2–3. *f:* 1 Sm 24:6; Jgs 9:54; 1 Chr 10:4. *g:* 1 Sm 10:1; 26:9; 2 Mc 14:42. *h:* 1 Sm 17:54; 2 Sm 1:20; 2 Mc 15:35. *i:* 1 Sm 11:1–11; 2 Sm 2:4–7; 21:12–14.

See RG 177–83

The Second Book of Samuel

CHAPTER 1

See RG 177–78

Report of Saul's Death. 1After the death of Saul, David returned from his victory over the Amalekites and stayed in Ziklag two days.[a] 2On the third day a man came from the field of battle, one of Saul's people, with his garments torn and his head covered with dirt. Going to David, he fell to the ground in homage. 3David asked him, "Where have you come from?" He replied, "From the Israelite camp: I have escaped." 4"What happened?" David said. "Tell me." He answered that the soldiers had fled the battle and many of them had fallen and were dead; and that Saul and his son Jonathan were dead. 5Then David said to the youth who was reporting to him, "How do you know that Saul and his son Jonathan are dead?" 6[b] The youth reporting to him replied: "I happened to find myself on Mount Gilboa and saw Saul leaning on his spear, with chariots and horsemen closing in on him. 7He turned around and saw me, and called me to him. When I said, 'Here I am,' 8he asked me, 'Who are you?' and I replied, 'An Amalekite.' 9Then he said to me, 'Stand over me, please, and put me to death, for I am in great suffering, but still alive.' 10So I stood over him and put him to death, for I knew that he could not survive his wound. I removed the crown from his head and the armlet from his arm and brought them here to my lord."

11David seized his garments and tore them, and so did all the men who were with him.[c] 12They mourned and wept and fasted until evening for Saul and his son Jonathan, and for the people of the LORD and the house of Israel, because they had fallen by the sword.[d] 13David said to the youth who had reported to him, "Where are you from?" He replied, "I am the son of a resident alien, an Amalekite." 14David said to him, "How is it that you were not afraid to put forth your hand to desecrate the LORD's anointed?"[e] 15David then called one of the attendants and said to him, "Come, strike him down"; so he struck him and he died. 16David said to him, "Your blood is on your head, for you testified against yourself when you said, 'I put the LORD's anointed to death.' "

Lament for Saul and Jonathan. 17Then David chanted this lament for Saul and his son Jonathan 18(he commanded that it be taught to the Judahites; it is recorded in the Book of Jashar):[f]

19 Alas! the glory of Israel,
  slain upon your heights!
How can the warriors have fallen!
20 Do not report it in Gath,
  as good news in Ashkelon's streets,
Lest Philistine women rejoice,
  lest the women of the uncircumcised
    exult![g]
21 O mountains of Gilboa,
  upon you be neither dew nor rain,
  nor surging from the deeps!*
Defiled there the warriors' shields,
  the shield of Saul—no longer anointed
    with oil![h]
22 From the blood of the slain,
  from the bodies of the warriors,
The bow of Jonathan did not turn back,
  nor the sword of Saul return
    unstained.* [i]
23 Saul and Jonathan, beloved and dear,
  separated neither in life nor death,
  swifter than eagles, stronger than
    lions!
24 Women of Israel, weep over Saul,
  who clothed you in scarlet and in
    finery,

1:21 Surging from the deeps: this conjectural reading of the Hebrew yields a parallelism with dew and rain: the mountains where the warriors have fallen in battle are to be desiccated, deprived of water from above (rain, dew) and below (the primordial deeps).

1:22 Unstained: lit., "empty." The sword was conceived as a devouring mouth; see, e.g., 2:26.

a: 1 Sm 30:17–20; 31:1–13. *b:* 2 Sm 4:10; 1 Sm 31:1–4; 1 Chr 10:1–4. *c:* 2 Sm 13:31. *d:* 1 Sm 31:13. *e:* 1 Sm 10:1; 24:7; Ps 105:15. *f:* Jos 10:13. *g:* Jgs 16:23; 1 Sm 31:9; Mi 1:10. *h:* Gn 27:28. *i:* 1 Sm 14:47.

covered your clothing with ornaments
of gold.
25 How can the warriors have fallen
in the thick of battle!
Jonathan—slain upon your heights!
26 I grieve for you, Jonathan my brother!
Most dear have you been to me;
More wondrous your love to me
than the love of women.[j]
27 How can the warriors have fallen,
the weapons of war have perished!

CHAPTER 2

See RG 178–79

David Is Anointed King. 1After this,
David inquired of the LORD, "Shall I go up
into one of the cities of Judah?" The LORD
replied to him: Go up. Then David asked,
"Where shall I go?" He replied: To Hebron.
2So David went up there, with his two wives,
Ahinoam of Jezreel and Abigail, the wife of
Nabal of Carmel.[k] 3David also brought up
his men with their families, and they dwelt
in the towns of Hebron. 4Then the men of Judah came there and anointed David king
over the house of Judah.

A report reached David that the people of
Jabesh-gilead had buried Saul.[l] 5So David
sent messengers to the people of Jabesh-gilead and said to them: "May you be blessed
by the LORD for having done this kindness to
your lord Saul in burying him. 6And now
may the LORD show you kindness and fidelity. For my part, I will show generosity to
you for having done this. 7So take courage
and prove yourselves valiant, for though
your lord Saul is dead, the house of Judah
has anointed me king over them."

IV. The Reign of David

Ishbaal King of Israel. 8Abner, son of Ner,
captain of Saul's army, took Ishbaal,* son of
Saul, and brought him over to Mahanaim,[m]
9where he made him king over Gilead, the
Asherites, Jezreel, Ephraim, Benjamin, and
the rest of Israel. 10Ishbaal, son of Saul, was
forty years old when he became king over
Israel, and he reigned two years; but the
house of Judah followed David. 11In all, David was king in Hebron over the house of Judah seven years and six months.[n]

Combat near Gibeon. 12Now Abner, son
of Ner, and the servants of Ishbaal, Saul's
son, set out from Mahanaim for Gibeon.
13Joab, son of Zeruiah, and the servants of
David also set out and encountered them at
the pool of Gibeon. And they sat down, one
group on one side of the pool and the other
on the opposite side. 14Then Abner said to
Joab, "Let the young men rise and perform
for us."* Joab replied, "All right." 15So they
rose and were counted off: twelve of the
Benjaminites of Ishbaal, son of Saul, and
twelve of David's servants. 16Then each one
grasped his opponent's head and thrust his
sword into his opponent's side, and they all
fell down together.* And so that place was
named the Field of the Sides; it is in Gibeon.

Death of Asahel. 17The battle that day was
very fierce, and Abner and the men of Israel
were defeated by David's servants. 18The
three sons of Zeruiah were there—Joab,
Abishai, and Asahel.[o] Asahel, who was as
fleet of foot as a gazelle in the open field,
19set out after Abner, turning neither right
nor left in his pursuit. 20Abner turned around
and said, "Is that you, Asahel?" He replied,
"Yes." 21Abner said to him, "Turn right or
left; seize one of the young men and take
what you can strip from him." But Asahel
would not stop pursuing him. 22Once more
Abner said to Asahel: "Stop pursuing me!
Why must I strike you to the ground? How
could I show my face to your brother
Joab?"[p] 23Still he refused to stop. So Abner
struck him in the abdomen with the heel of
his spear, and the weapon protruded from his
back. He fell there and died on the spot. All
who came to the place where Asahel had
fallen and died, halted. 24But Joab and
Abishai continued the pursuit of Abner. The

2:8 Ishbaal: here and elsewhere in the Hebrew text, his name appears as "Ishbosheth"; the second part of Ishbaal, -*baal*, refers to the Canaanite god Baal, and is therefore suppressed, replaced by *bosheth*, "shame."

2:14 Perform: lit., "play."

2:16 The nature of this gruesome game is not clear, and the place name is variously given in the older texts.

j: 1 Sm 18:1–4. *k:* 1 Sm 25:42–43. *l:* 1 Sm 31:11–13. *m:* 1 Sm 14:50. *n:* 2 Sm 5:5; 1 Kgs 2:11. *o:* 2 Sm 23:24; 1 Chr 2:16; 27:7. *p:* 2 Sm 3:27–28, 30.

sun had gone down when they came to the hill of Ammah which lies east of the valley toward the wilderness near Geba.

Truce Between Joab and Abner. 25Here the Benjaminites rallied around Abner, forming a single group, and made a stand on a hilltop. 26Then Abner called to Joab and said: "Must the sword devour forever? Do you not know that afterward there will be bitterness? How long before you tell the people to stop pursuing their brothers?" 27Joab replied, "As God lives, if you had not spoken, it would be morning before the people would be stopped from pursuing their brothers." 28Joab then sounded the horn, and all the people came to a halt, pursuing Israel no farther and fighting no more. 29Abner and his men marched all night long through the Arabah, crossed the Jordan, marched all through the morning, and came to Mahanaim. 30Joab, coming from the pursuit of Abner, assembled all the men. Nineteen other servants of David were missing, besides Asahel. 31But David's servants had struck down and killed three hundred and sixty men of Benjamin, followers of Abner. 32They took up Asahel and buried him in his father's tomb in Bethlehem. Joab and his men made an all-night march, and dawn found them in Hebron.

CHAPTER 3

See RG 178–79

1There followed a long war between the house of Saul and the house of David, in which David grew ever stronger, but the house of Saul ever weaker.

Sons Born in Hebron. 2[q] Sons were born to David in Hebron: his firstborn, Amnon, of Ahinoam from Jezreel; 3the second, Chileab, of Abigail the wife of Nabal of Carmel; the third, Absalom, son of Maacah, who was the daughter of Talmai, king of Geshur;[r] 4the fourth, Adonijah, son of Haggith; the fifth, Shephatiah, son of Abital;[s] 5and the sixth, Ithream, by David's wife Eglah. These were born to David in Hebron.

Ishbaal and Abner Quarrel. 6During the war between the house of Saul and the house of David, Abner was gaining power in the house of Saul. 7Now Saul had had a concubine, Rizpah, the daughter of Aiah. And Ishbaal, son of Saul, said to Abner, "Why have you slept with my father's concubine?"*[t] 8Enraged at the words of Ishbaal, Abner said, "Am I a dog's head from Judah? As of today, I have been loyal to the house of Saul your father, to his brothers and his friends, and I have kept you out of David's clutches; and today you charge me with a crime involving a woman! 9May God do thus to Abner, and more, if I do not carry out for David what the LORD swore to him—[u] 10that is, take away the kingdom from the house of Saul and establish the throne of David over Israel as well as Judah, from Dan to Beersheba."[v] 11Ishbaal was no longer able to say a word to Abner, he feared him so.

Abner and David Reconciled. 12Then Abner sent messengers to David in Telam, where he was at the moment, to say, "Make a covenant with me, and you have me on your side, to bring all Israel over to you." 13He replied, "Good, I will make a covenant with you. But one thing I require of you. You must not appear before me unless you bring back Michal, Saul's daughter, when you come to present yourself to me."[w] 14At the same time David sent messengers to Ishbaal, son of Saul, to say, "Give me my wife Michal, whom I betrothed by paying a hundred Philistine foreskins." 15Ishbaal sent for her and took her away from her husband Paltiel, son of Laish,[x] 16who followed her weeping as far as Bahurim. But Abner said to him, "Go back!" So he turned back.

17Abner then had a word with the elders of Israel: "For some time you have been wanting David as your king. 18Now take action, for the LORD has said of David: By David my servant I will save my people Israel from the power of the Philistines and from the power of all their enemies." 19Abner also spoke with Benjamin, and then went to speak with David in Hebron concerning all that would be agreeable to Israel and to the whole house

3:7 Asserting a right to the late king's harem was tantamount to claiming his kingship; cf. 16:21–22; 1 Kgs 2:21–22.

q: 1 Chr 3:1–4. *r:* 2 Sm 13:37; 15:8. *s:* 1 Kgs 1:5. *t:* 2 Sm 16:21–22; 21:8–10; 1 Kgs 2:21–22. *u:* Ru 1:17. *v:* 2 Sm 5:2; 1 Sm 25:30. *w:* 1 Sm 18:20–27. *x:* 1 Sm 25:44.

of Benjamin. 20When Abner, accompanied by twenty men, came to David in Hebron, David prepared a feast for Abner and for the men who were with him. 21Then Abner said to David, "I will now go to assemble all Israel for my lord the king, that they may make a covenant with you; you will then be king over all whom you wish to rule." So David let Abner go on his way in peace.

Death of Abner. 22Just then David's servants and Joab were coming in from an expedition, bringing much plunder with them. Abner, having been dismissed by David, was no longer with him in Hebron but had gone on his way in peace. 23When Joab and the whole force he had with him arrived, he was informed, "Abner, son of Ner, came to David, and he let him go on his way in peace." 24So Joab went to the king and said: "What have you done? Abner came to you! Why did you let him get away? 25Don't you know Abner? He came to trick you, to learn your comings and goings, to learn everything you do." 26Joab then left David and sent messengers after Abner to bring him back from the cistern of Sirah; but David did not know. 27When Abner returned to Hebron, Joab took him aside within the city gate to speak with him privately. There he stabbed him in the abdomen, and he died for the blood of Asahel, Joab's brother.[y] 28Later David heard of it and said: "Before the LORD, I and my kingdom are forever innocent.[z] 29May the blood of Abner, son of Ner, be on the head of Joab and all his family. May Joab's family never be without one suffering from a discharge, or one with a skin disease, or a man who holds the distaff, or one falling by the sword, or one in need of food!"* 30Joab and Abishai his brother had been lying in wait for Abner because he killed Asahel their brother in battle at Gibeon.

David Mourns Abner. 31Then David said to Joab and to all the people who were with him, "Tear your garments, put on sackcloth, and mourn over Abner." King David himself followed the bier.[a] 32When they had buried Abner in Hebron, the king wept aloud at the grave of Abner, and all the people wept. 33And the king sang this lament over Abner:

Should Abner have died like a fool?
34 Your hands were not bound with chains,
nor your feet placed in fetters;
As one falls before the wicked, you fell.

And all the people continued to weep for him. 35Then they went to console David with food while it was still day. But David swore, "May God do thus to me, and more, if before the sun goes down I eat bread or anything else."[b] 36All the people noted this with approval, just as everything the king did met with their approval. 37So on that day all the people and all Israel came to know that it was not the king's doing that Abner, son of Ner, was put to death. 38The king then said to his servants: "Do you not know that a prince, a great man, has fallen today in Israel. 39Although I am the anointed king, I am weak this day, and these men, the sons of Zeruiah, are too ruthless for me. May the LORD repay the evildoer in accordance with his evil deed."[c]

CHAPTER 4

See RG 178–79

Death of Ishbaal. 1When Ishbaal, son of Saul, heard that Abner was dead in Hebron, he lost his resolve and all Israel was alarmed. 2Ishbaal, son of Saul, had two company leaders named Baanah and Rechab, sons of Rimmon the Beerothite, of the tribe of Benjamin—Beeroth, too, was ascribed to Benjamin:[d] 3the Beerothites fled to Gittaim, where they have been resident aliens to this day.[e] 4(Jonathan, son of Saul, had a son with crippled feet. He was five years old when the news about Saul and Jonathan came from Jezreel; his nurse took him and fled, but in their hasty flight, he fell and became lame. His name was Meribbaal.)* [f] 5The sons of Rimmon the Beerothite, Rechab and Baanah, came into the house of Ishbaal during

3:29 An assortment of imprecations, consisting of physical ailments, weakness, violent death, and poverty.

4:4 Meribbaal: Hebrew has *mephiboseth*; see note on 2:8. His name, in fact, is Meribbaal; cf. 1 Chr 8:34; 9:40. He is the subject of chap. 9 below. The text of this verse may owe its present place to the fact that ancient copies of the Books of Samuel tended to confuse his name with that of his uncle Ishbaal, Saul's son and successor, a principal figure in chaps. 2–4.

y: 2 Sm 2:17–23; 1 Kgs 2:5, 31–33. *z:* 2 Sm 2:22–23. *a:* 2 Sm 21:10. *b:* Ru 1:17. *c:* Ps 28:4; Is 3:11. *d:* 2 Sm 9:3; Jos 9:17–18. *e:* Jos 18:25. *f:* 2 Sm 9:3; 19:25.

the heat of the day, while he was lying on his bed in the afternoon. 6 The gatekeeper of the house had dozed off while sifting wheat, and was asleep. So Rechab and his brother Baanah slipped past her 7 and entered the house while Ishbaal was lying asleep in his bedroom. They struck and killed him, and cut off his head. Then, taking the head, they traveled on the Arabah road all night long.

The Murder Avenged. 8 They brought the head of Ishbaal to David in Hebron and said to the king: "This is the head of Ishbaal, son of your enemy Saul, who sought your life. Thus has the LORD this day avenged my lord the king on Saul and his posterity." 9 But David replied to Rechab and his brother Baanah, sons of Rimmon the Beerothite: "As the LORD lives, who rescued me from every distress: 10 the man who reported to me, 'Saul is dead,' and thought he was bringing good news, that man I seized and killed in Ziglag: that was the reward I gave him.[g] 11 How much more now, when wicked men have slain an innocent man in bed at home, must I require his blood from you and purge you from the land!" 12 So at David's command, the young men killed them and cut off their hands and feet, hanging them up near the pool in Hebron. But he took the head of Ishbaal and buried it in Abner's grave in Hebron.[h]

See RG 178–79

CHAPTER 5

David King of Israel. 1[i] All the tribes of Israel came to David in Hebron, and they said: "Look! We are your bone and your flesh. 2 In days past, when Saul was still our king, you were the one who led Israel out in all its battles and brought it back. And the LORD said to you: You shall shepherd my people Israel; you shall be ruler over Israel."[j] 3 Then all the elders of Israel came to the king in Hebron, and at Hebron King David made a covenant with them in the presence of the LORD; and they anointed David king over Israel. 4 David was thirty years old when he became king, and he reigned forty years: 5 in Hebron he was king over Judah seven years and six months, and in Jerusalem he was king thirty-three years over all Israel and Judah.[k]

*Capture of Zion.** 6[l] Then the king and his men went to Jerusalem against the Jebusites who inhabited the land. They told David, "You shall not enter here: the blind and the lame will drive you away!" which was their way of saying, "David shall not enter here."[m] 7 David nevertheless captured the fortress of Zion, which is the City of David. 8 On that day David said: "All who wish to strike at the Jebusites must attack through the water shaft. The lame and the blind shall be the personal enemies of David." That is why it is said, "The blind and the lame shall not enter the palace."[n] 9 David took up residence in the fortress which he called the City of David. David built up the city on all sides, from the Millo toward the center.[o] 10 David became ever more powerful, for the LORD of hosts was with him.[p] 11[q] Hiram, king of Tyre, sent envoys to David along with cedar wood, and carpenters and masons, who built a house for David.[r] 12 David now knew* that the LORD had truly established him as king over Israel and had exalted his kingdom for the sake of his people Israel.

David's Family in Jerusalem. 13[s] David took more concubines and wives in Jerusalem after he had come from Hebron, and more sons and daughters were born to him. 14 These are the names of those who were born to him in Jerusalem: Shammua, Shobab, Nathan, Solomon, 15 Ibhar, Elishua, Ne-

5:6–12 David's most important military exploit, the taking of Jerusalem, is here presented before his battles with the Philistines, vv. 17–25, which took place earlier. The sense of vv. 6 and 8 is in doubt. Perhaps the Jebusites boasted that Jerusalem was impregnable, using a metaphorical or proverbial expression that claimed the city was defensible even by people not suited for military action. The saying then received a different sense (v. 8), to the effect that "the blind and the lame" were David's enemies. Mt 21:14 and Lk 14:13 seem to play off, and transform, this saying.

5:12 David now knew: Hiram's carpenters and masons built David a house of cedar, the very model of a Canaanite king's palace. This house then represented the consolidation of David's royal power, in the Canaanite mode, with Jerusalem as David's personal fiefdom and capital city.

g: 2 Sm 1:6–10, 14, 16. *h:* Dt 21:22–23; 1 Sm 31:10. *i:* 1 Chr 11:1–3. *j:* 2 Sm 3:10; Dt 17:15; 1 Sm 18:16. *k:* 2 Sm 2:11; 1 Kgs 2:11; 1 Chr 3:4. *l:* 1 Chr 11:4–9. *m:* Jos 15:63; Jgs 1:19, 21; Is 29:3. *n:* Lv 21:18; Mt 21:14–15. *o:* 1 Kgs 3:1; 9:15; 11:27. *p:* Ps 78:70–72; 89; 132:13. *q:* 1 Chr 14:1–16. *r:* 1 Kgs 5:15; 1 Chr 14:1–2. *s:* 1 Chr 3:5–8; 14:3–7.

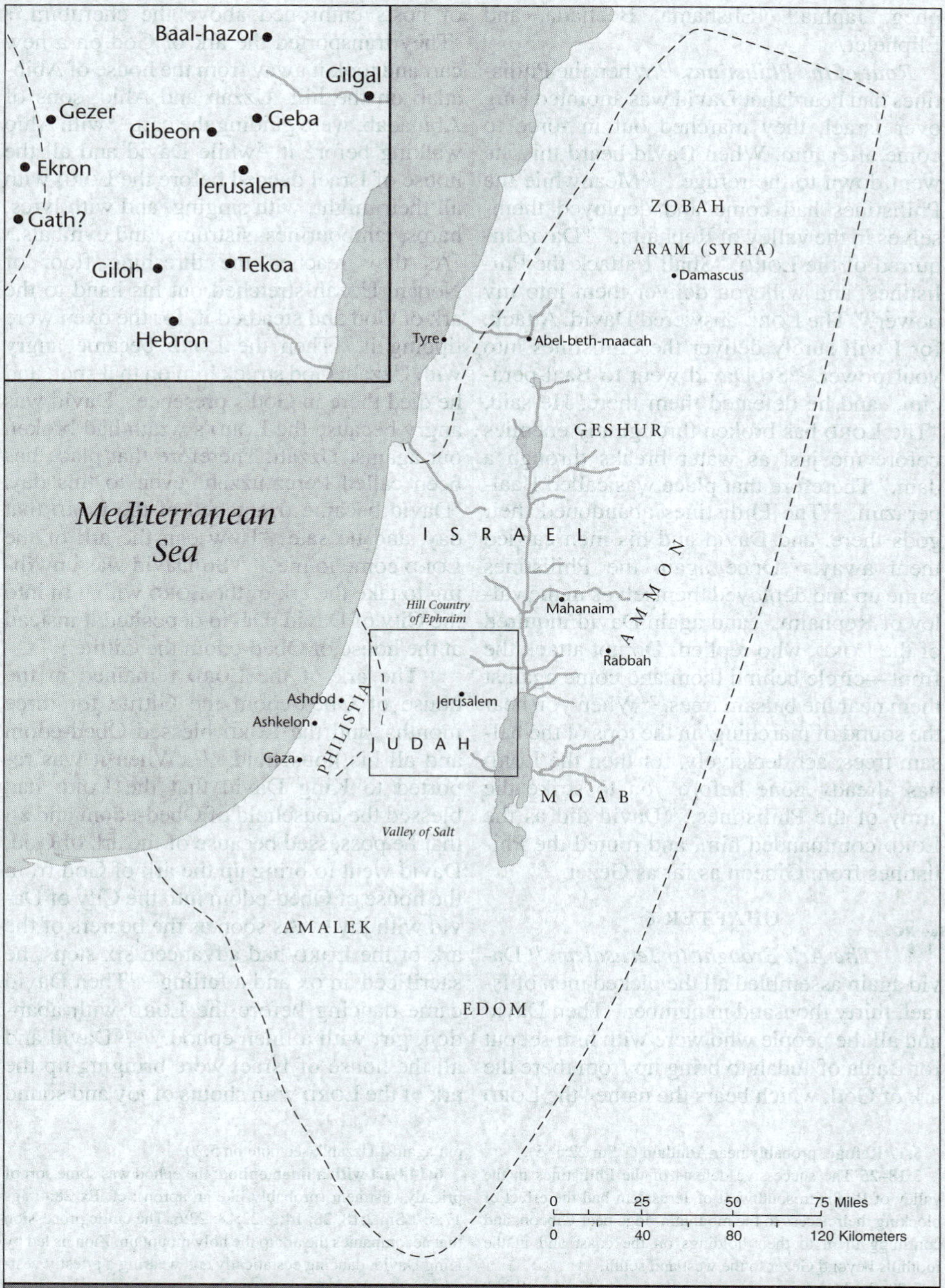

The Kingdom of David according to 2 Samuel

pheg, Japhia, 16 Elishama, Beeliada, and Eliphelet.

Rout of the Philistines. 17 When the Philistines had heard that David was anointed king over Israel, they marched out in force to come after him. When David heard this, he went down to the refuge.* 18 Meanwhile the Philistines had come and deployed themselves in the valley of Rephaim.* 19 David inquired of the LORD, "Shall I attack the Philistines, and will you deliver them into my power?" The LORD answered David: Attack, for I will surely deliver the Philistines into your power. 20 So David went to Baal-perazim,* and he defeated them there. He said, "The LORD has broken through my enemies before me just as water breaks through a dam." Therefore that place was called Baal-perazim. 21 The Philistines abandoned their gods there, and David and his men carried them away. 22 Once again the Philistines came up and deployed themselves in the valley of Rephaim, 23 and again David inquired of the LORD, who replied: Do not attack the front—circle behind them and come against them near the balsam trees. 24 When you hear the sound of marching* in the tops of the balsam trees, act decisively, for then the LORD has already gone before you to strike the army of the Philistines. 25 David did as the LORD commanded him, and routed the Philistines from Gibeon as far as Gezer.

CHAPTER 6

See RG 179

The Ark Brought to Jerusalem. 1[t] David again assembled all the picked men of Israel, thirty thousand in number. 2 Then David and all the people who were with him set out for Baala of Judah to bring up from there the ark of God, which bears the name "the LORD of hosts enthroned above the cherubim."[u] 3 They transported the ark of God on a new cart and took it away from the house of Abinadab on the hill. Uzzah and Ahio, sons of Abinadab, were guiding the cart,[v] 4 with Ahio walking before it, 5 while David and all the house of Israel danced before the LORD with all their might, with singing, and with lyres, harps, tambourines, sistrums, and cymbals.[w] 6 As they reached the threshing floor of Nodan, Uzzah stretched out his hand to the ark of God and steadied it, for the oxen were tipping it. 7 Then the LORD became angry with Uzzah; God struck him on that spot, and he died there in God's presence. 8 David was angry because the LORD's wrath had broken out against Uzzah. Therefore that place has been called Perez-uzzah* even to this day. 9 David became frightened of the LORD that day, and he said, "How can the ark of the LORD come to me?" 10 So David was unwilling to take the ark of the LORD with him into the City of David. David deposited it instead at the house of Obed-edom the Gittite.

11 The ark of the LORD remained in the house of Obed-edom the Gittite for three months, and the LORD blessed Obed-edom and all his household.[x] 12[y] When it was reported to King David that the LORD had blessed the household of Obed-edom and all that he possessed because of the ark of God, David went to bring up the ark of God from the house of Obed-edom into the City of David with joy.[z] 13 As soon as the bearers of the ark of the LORD had advanced six steps, he sacrificed an ox and a fatling. 14 Then David came dancing before the LORD with abandon, girt with a linen ephod.*[a] 15 David and all the house of Israel were bringing up the ark of the LORD with shouts of joy and sound

5:17 Refuge: probably near Adullam (1 Sm 22:1–5).

5:18–25 The successive defeats of the Philistines in the valley of Rephaim southwest of Jerusalem had the effect of blocking their access to the mountain ridge near Gibeon, and confining them to their holdings on the coast and in the foothills beyond Gezer to the west and south.

5:20 Baal-perazim: here the title *ba'al*, "master, lord," refers to the Lord; *perazim* is the plural of *perez*, which means "breaking" or "bursting," as in 6:8.

5:24 Sound of marching: the wind in the treetops suggestive of the footsteps of the Lord and the heavenly host.

6:8 Perez-uzzah: this Hebrew phrase means "the breaking out against Uzzah"; see note on 5:20.

6:14 Girt with a linen ephod: the ephod was some sort of priestly vestment (probably like an apron); cf. Ex 28:4; Jgs 17:5; 1 Sm 2:18, 28; 14:3; 22:18; 23:6. The cultic procession that accompanies the ark to the holy mountain, Zion, is led by King David, dancing ecstatically and wearing a priestly vestment.

t: 1 Chr 13:1–14. *u:* Ex 25:10; Jos 15:9; 1 Chr 13:6; Ps 132:8–10. *v:* 1 Sm 4:3–4; 6:7–8; 7:1; Dn 3:55. *w:* Ps 68:24–25; 150:3–5. *x:* 1 Chr 26:4. *y:* 1 Chr 15:1–29; Ps 24:7–10. *z:* 1 Kgs 8:1. *a:* 1 Sm 2:18.

of horn. 16 As the ark of the LORD was entering the City of David, Michal, daughter of Saul, looked down from her window, and when she saw King David jumping and dancing before the LORD, she despised him in her heart. 17[b] They brought in the ark of the LORD and set it in its place within the tent which David had pitched for it. Then David sacrificed burnt offerings and communion offerings before the LORD. 18 When David had finished sacrificing burnt offerings and communion offerings, he blessed the people in the name of the LORD of hosts, 19 and distributed among all the people, the entire multitude of Israel, to every man and every woman, one loaf of bread, one piece of meat, and one raisin cake. Then all the people returned to their homes.

20* When David went home to bless his own house,[c] Michal, the daughter of Saul, came out to meet him and said, "How well the king of Israel has honored himself today, exposing himself to the view of the slave girls of his followers, as a commoner might expose himself!" 21 But David replied to Michal: "I was dancing before the LORD. As the LORD lives, who chose me over your father and all his house when he appointed me ruler over the LORD's people, Israel, not only will I make merry before the LORD,[d] 22 but I will demean myself even more. I will be lowly in your eyes, but in the eyes of the slave girls you spoke of I will be somebody." 23 Saul's daughter Michal was childless to the day she died.

CHAPTER 7

See RG 179–80

The Oracle of Nathan. 1[e] After the king had taken up residence in his house, and the LORD had given him rest from his enemies on every side,[f] 2 the king said to Nathan the prophet, "Here I am living in a house of cedar, but the ark of God dwells in a tent!"[g] 3 Nathan answered the king, "Whatever is in your heart, go and do, for the LORD is with you."[h] 4 But that same night the word of the LORD came to Nathan: 5 Go and tell David my servant, Thus says the LORD: Is it you who would build me a house to dwell in?[i] 6 I have never dwelt in a house from the day I brought Israel up from Egypt to this day, but I have been going about in a tent or a tabernacle. 7 As long as I have wandered about among the Israelites, did I ever say a word to any of the judges whom I commanded to shepherd my people Israel: Why have you not built me a house of cedar?

8 Now then, speak thus to my servant David, Thus says the LORD of hosts:* I took you from the pasture, from following the flock, to become ruler over my people Israel.[j] 9 I was with you wherever you went, and I cut down all your enemies before you. And I will make your name like that of the greatest on earth.[k] 10 I will assign a place for my people Israel and I will plant them in it to dwell there; they will never again be disturbed, nor shall the wicked ever again oppress them, as they did at the beginning, 11 and from the day when I appointed judges over my people Israel. I will give you rest from all your enemies. Moreover, the LORD also declares to you that the LORD will make a house for you:[l] 12[m] when your days have been completed and you rest with your ancestors, I will raise up your offspring after you, sprung from your loins, and I will establish his kingdom. 13 He it is* who shall build a house for my name, and I will establish his royal

6:20–23 Michal's reaction to David's dancing comes from her conception of how a king should comport himself. David rejects this understanding, saying he needs no instruction from the house of the failed king, Saul.

7:8–16 The message Nathan delivers to David, called the Dynastic Oracle, is prompted by David's intention to build a house (i.e., a temple) for the Lord, like David's own house (i.e., palace) of cedar. David is told, in effect, not to bother building a house for the Lord; rather, the Lord will make a house for him—a dynasty, the House of David. Not only will he have descendants (v. 12) who will sit upon the throne of Israel (v. 13), their rule will last forever (vv. 13, 16); and even if they transgress the Lord's commands, the line of David will never be removed from kingship as Saul was (cf. 1 Sm 13; 15). The oracle establishes the Davidic king as standing in relationship to the Lord as a son to a father (v. 14; cf. Ps 2:7; 89:27). The Dynastic Oracle, with cognate texts in the Scriptures, is the basis for Jewish expectations of an anointed king (1 Sm 12:3, 5), son of David (Mt 21:9); cf. Acts 2:30; Heb 1:5.

7:13 He it is: Solomon, in the event.

b: Lv 1:1–17; 3:1–17; 1 Chr 16:1–3. *c:* 1 Chr 16:43. *d:* 1 Sm 13:14; 15:28. *e:* 1 Chr 17:1–27. *f:* Dt 12:10; 25:19; 1 Kgs 5:4. *g:* Ex 39:32. *h:* Ps 132:1–5. *i:* 1 Kgs 5:3; 8:16, 27; 1 Chr 22:8; 28:3; Is 66:1; Acts 7:48–49. *j:* 1 Sm 16:13; 17:15–20; Ps 78:70–71; Am 7:14–15. *k:* Ps 89:27. *l:* 2 Sm 23:5; 1 Kgs 2:4–24. *m:* 1 Kgs 5:19; 8:19; 1 Chr 22:10; 2 Chr 7:18; Ps 89:4, 26–29, 36–37; Lk 1:32; Heb 1:5.

throne forever. 14I will be a father to him, and he shall be a son to me. If he does wrong, I will reprove him with a human rod and with human punishments;[n] 15but I will not withdraw my favor from him as I withdrew it from Saul who was before you.[o] 16Your house and your kingdom are firm forever before me; your throne shall be firmly established forever.* [p] 17In accordance with all these words and this whole vision Nathan spoke to David.

David's Thanksgiving. 18Then King David went in and sat in the LORD's presence and said, "Who am I, Lord GOD, and what is my house, that you should have brought me so far?[q] 19And yet even this is too little in your sight, Lord GOD! For you have made a promise regarding your servant's house reaching into the future, and giving guidance to the people, Lord GOD! 20What more can David say to you? You know* your servant, Lord GOD! 21For your servant's sake and as you have had at heart, you have brought about this whole magnificent disclosure to your servant. 22Therefore, great are you, Lord GOD! There is no one like you, no God but you, as we have always heard.[r] 23What other nation on earth is there like your people Israel? What god has ever led a nation, redeeming it as his people and making a name by great and awesome deeds, as you drove out the nations and their gods before your people, whom you redeemed for yourself from Egypt?[s] 24[t] You have established for yourself your people Israel as your people forever, and you, LORD, have become their God. 25Now, LORD God, confirm the promise that you have spoken concerning your servant and his house forever. Bring about what you have promised 26so that your name may be forever great. People will say: 'The LORD of hosts is God over Israel,' when the house of your servant David is established in your presence. 27Because you, LORD of hosts, God of Israel, have revealed to your servant, 'I will build you a house,' your servant now finds the courage to make this prayer before you. 28Since you, Lord GOD, are truly God and your words are truth and you have made this generous promise to your servant,[u] 29do, then, bless the house of your servant, that it may be in your presence forever—since you, Lord GOD, have promised, and by your blessing the house of your servant shall be blessed forever."

CHAPTER 8

See RG 180

Summary of David's Wars. 1[v] After this, David defeated the Philistines and subdued them; and David took . . .* from the Philistines. 2He also defeated Moab and measured them with a line. Making them lie down on the ground, he measured two lengths of line for death, and a full length for life.* Thus the Moabites became subject to David, paying tribute. 3[w] David then defeated Hadadezer, son of Rehob, king of Zobah, when he went to re-establish his dominion at the River.[x] 4David captured from him one thousand seven hundred horsemen and twenty thousand foot soldiers. David hamstrung all the chariot horses, but left one hundred for his chariots.[y] 5The Arameans of Damascus came to help Hadadezer, king of Zobah, but David also defeated twenty-two thousand of them in Aram. 6David then placed garrisons in the Damascus region of Aram, and the Arameans became David's subjects, paying tribute. The LORD brought David victory in all his undertakings. 7David took the golden shields that were car-

7:16 The unconditional promise made here, and reflected in Ps 89:34–35, stands in contrast to the tradition in Ps 132:12, where the continuation of the line of David depends on their fidelity to the Lord; cf. also 1 Kgs 2:4; 6:12; 8:25.

7:20 Know: give recognition, choose, single out: cf. Gn 18:19; Ex 33:12; Am 3:2.

8:1 David took . . .: the original Hebrew seems irretrievable. The transmitted text gives "the bridle of the cubit"; 1 Chr 18:1 understood "Gath and its towns"; others implausibly read "dominion of the capital city."

8:2 Two lengths . . . a full length for life: usually taken to mean that two-thirds of them were executed; but it could mean that two-thirds were spared, if the line was used full length in their case but doubled on itself to make "two lines" for those to be put to death. Note the contrasting good relations in 1 Sm 22:3–4.

n: Ps 2:7; 89:26; Prv 3:12. *o:* 2 Sm 23:5; 1 Sm 13:14; 15:26, 28; 2 Kgs 19:34; 1 Chr 17:11–14; Ps 89:33–34. *p:* 2 Sm 23:5; Dn 2:44; 1 Mc 2:57; Mk 11:10; Lk 1:32–33; Heb 1:8. *q:* 1 Chr 17:16. *r:* Ex 15:11; Is 45:5. *s:* Dt 4:7, 34. *t:* Ex 6:7; Dt 7:6; 26:17; 29:13. *u:* Nm 23:19; Jn 17:17. *v:* 1 Chr 18:1–17. *w:* 2 Sm 10:15–19. *x:* 2 Sm 10:6; 1 Kgs 11:23. *y:* Jos 11:6, 9.

ried by Hadadezer's attendants and brought them to Jerusalem. (These Shishak, king of Egypt, took away when he came to Jerusalem in the days of Rehoboam, son of Solomon.) [8]From Tebah and Berothai, cities of Hadadezer, King David removed a very large quantity of bronze. [9]When Toi, king of Hamath, heard that David had defeated the entire army of Hadadezer, [10]Toi sent his son Hadoram to wish King David well and to congratulate him on having waged a victorious war against Hadadezer; for Hadadezer had been at war with Toi. Hadoram also brought with him articles of silver, gold, and bronze. [11]These also King David consecrated to the LORD along with the silver and gold that he had taken for this purpose from all the nations he had subdued: [12]from Edom, Moab, the Ammonites, the Philistines, and Amalek, and from the spoils of Hadadezer, son of Rehob, king of Zobah.

[13]On his return,* David made a name for himself by defeating eighteen thousand Edomites in the Valley of Salt.[z] [14]He set up garrisons in Edom, and all the Edomites became David's subjects. Thus the LORD brought David victory in all his undertakings.

David's Officials. [15][a] David was king over all Israel; he dispensed justice and right to all his people. [16]Joab, son of Zeruiah, was in command of the army. Jehoshaphat, son of Ahilud, was chancellor. [17]Zadok, son of Ahitub, and Ahimelech, son of Abiathar, were priests.* Shavsha was scribe. [18]Benaiah, son of Jehoiada, was in command of the Cherethites and the Pelethites; and David's sons were priests.[b]

CHAPTER 9

See RG 180–82

David and Meribbaal. [1]David asked, "Is there any survivor of Saul's house to whom I may show kindness for the sake of Jonathan?"[c] [2]Now there was an official of the house of Saul named Ziba. He was summoned to David, and the king asked him, "Are you Ziba?" He replied, "Your servant."[d] [3]Then the king asked, "Is there any survivor of Saul's house to whom I may show God's kindness?" Ziba answered the king, "There is still Jonathan's son, the one whose feet are crippled."[e] [4]The king asked him, "Where is he?" and Ziba answered the king, "He is in the house of Machir, son of Ammiel, in Lodebar."[f] [5]So King David sent for him and had him brought from the house of Machir, son of Ammiel, from Lodebar. [6]When Meribbaal, son of Jonathan, son of Saul, came to David, he fell face down in homage. David said, "Meribbaal," and he answered, "Your servant." [7]"Do not be afraid," David said to him, "I will surely be kind to you for the sake of Jonathan your father. I will restore to you all the lands of Saul your grandfather, and you shall eat at my table always." [8]Bowing low, he answered, "What am I, your servant, that you should pay attention to a dead dog like me?"[g] [9]The king then called Ziba, Saul's attendant, and said to him: "All that belonged to Saul and to his entire house, I am giving to your lord's son. [10]You and your sons and servants must till the land for him. You shall bring in the produce, which shall be food for your lord's household to eat. But Meribbaal, your lord's son, shall always eat at my table." Now Ziba had fifteen sons and twenty servants. [11]Ziba answered the king, "Whatever my lord the king commands his servant, so shall your servant do." And so Meribbaal ate at David's table like one of the king's sons.[h] [12]Meribbaal had a young son whose name was Mica; and all the tenants of Ziba's household

8:13 On his return: possibly to Jerusalem, after the revolt of Absalom (chaps. 15–18), which this catalogue of victories would avoid mentioning. 1 Chr 18:12 attributes the defeat of the Edomites to Abishai, while the superscription of Ps 60 attributes it to Joab.

8:17 Zadok . . . Ahimelech, son of Abiathar, were priests: the names of Abiathar and Ahimelech are frequently associated with David (1 Sm 22:20; 23:6; 30:7; 2 Sm 15:24, 29, 35; 17:15; 19:12; 20:25), but they show Abiathar acting as priest, not Ahimelech: Abiathar shared the priestly office with Zadok in David's reign and even during Solomon's early years (1 Kgs 2:26; 4:4). Ahimelech was the name of Abiathar's father. This verse and 1 Chr 18:16 may indicate that Abiathar had a son named Ahimelech who also acted as a priest, like his father and his namesake grandfather, in the last years of David.

z: 2 Kgs 14:7. *a:* 2 Sm 20:23–26; 1 Kgs 4:1–6; 1 Chr 18:14–17. *b:* 2 Sm 15:18; 20:7, 23; 23:20. *c:* 2 Sm 21:7; 1 Sm 18:1–4; 20:8–10, 15–17, 42. *d:* 2 Sm 16:1–4; 19:27. *e:* 2 Sm 4:4. *f:* 2 Sm 17:27. *g:* 1 Sm 24:15. *h:* 2 Sm 19:29.

worked for Meribbaal.[i] 13But Meribbaal lived in Jerusalem, because he always ate at the king's table. He was lame in both feet.[j]

CHAPTER 10

See RG 180–82

Campaigns Against Ammon. 1[k] After this,* the king of the Ammonites died, and Hanun his son succeeded him as king. 2David said, "I will show kindness to Hanun, the son of Nahash, as his father showed kindness to me." Therefore David sent his servants to Hanun to console him concerning his father. But when David's servants had entered the land of the Ammonites, 3the Ammonite princes said to their lord Hanun, "Do you think David is doing this—sending you these consolers—to honor your father? Is it not rather to explore the city, to spy on it, and to overthrow it, that David has sent his servants to you?" 4So Hanun seized David's servants, shaved off half their beards, cut away the lower halves of their garments at the buttocks, and sent them away.[l] 5David was told of it and he sent word for them to be intercepted, for the men had been greatly disgraced. "Remain at Jericho," the king told them, "until your beards have grown again; then come back here."

6* When the Ammonites realized that they were in bad odor with David, they sent for and hired twenty thousand Aramean foot soldiers from Beth-rehob and Zobah, as well as the king of Maacah with one thousand men, and twelve thousand men from Tob.[m]

7When David heard of this, he sent Joab and his whole army of warriors against them.[n] 8The Ammonites marched out and lined up for battle at the entrance of their city gate, while the Arameans of Zobah and Rehob and the men of Tob and Maacah remained apart in the open field. 9When Joab saw that there was a battle line both in front of and behind him, he chose some of the best fighters of Israel and lined them up against the Arameans; 10the rest of the army he placed under the command of his brother Abishai and lined up to oppose the Ammonites. 11And he said, "If the Arameans prove too strong for me, you must come and save me; and if the Ammonites prove too strong for you, I will come to save you. 12Hold firm and let us show ourselves courageous for the sake of our people and the cities of our God; and may the LORD do what is good in his sight." 13Joab therefore advanced with his men for battle with the Arameans, but they fled before him. 14And when the Ammonites saw that the Arameans had fled, they too fled before Abishai, and reentered their city. Joab then ceased his attack on the Ammonites and came to Jerusalem. 15[o] Seeing themselves vanquished by Israel, the Arameans held a full muster of troops. 16Hadadezer sent for and brought Arameans from beyond the River. They came to Helam, with Shobach, the captain of Hadadezer's army, at their head. 17When this was reported to David, he gathered all Israel together, crossed the Jordan, and went to Helam. The Arameans drew up in formation against David and gave battle. 18But the Arameans fled before Israel, and David killed seven hundred of their chariot fighters and forty thousand of their foot soldiers. He struck down Shobach, commander of the army, and he died on the field. 19When Hadadezer's vassal kings saw themselves vanquished by Israel, they made peace with the Israelites and became their subjects. After this, the Arameans were afraid to give further aid to the Ammonites.

CHAPTER 11

See RG 180–82

David's Sin. 1At the turn of the year,* the time when kings go to war, David sent out Joab along with his officers and all Israel, and they laid waste the Ammonites and besieged Rabbah. David himself remained

10:1 After this: early in the reign of David, since Hanun's father Nahash (1 Chr 19:1) had been ruling in Ammon at the beginning of Saul's reign (1 Sm 11) and Solomon was not yet born (2 Sm 11:1; 12:24).

10:6–9 A Hebrew text from Qumran (4QSam[a]) comes closer in these verses to what is given in 1 Chr 19:6–9. The scene of the conflict is more likely the Ammonite capital, Rabbath-Ammon (v. 8; cf. Josephus *Ant.*, vii, 123), than Medeba (1 Chr 19:7).

11:1 At the turn of the year: in the spring.

i: 1 Chr 8:34. *j:* 2 Sm 21:7. *k:* 1 Chr 19:1–19. *l:* Is 20:4. *m:* 2 Sm 8:3; 1 Sm 14:47. *n:* 2 Sm 11:1. *o:* 2 Sm 8:3–8; 1 Chr 9:16–19.

in Jerusalem.[p] 2One evening David rose from his bed and strolled about on the roof of the king's house. From the roof he saw a woman bathing; she was very beautiful. 3David sent people to inquire about the woman and was told, "She is Bathsheba, daughter of Eliam, and wife of Uriah the Hittite, Joab's armor-bearer."[q] 4Then David sent messengers and took her. When she came to him, he took her to bed, at a time when she was just purified after her period; and she returned to her house.[r] 5But the woman had become pregnant; she sent a message to inform David, "I am pregnant."

6So David sent a message to Joab, "Send me Uriah the Hittite." Joab sent Uriah to David. 7And when he came, David asked him how Joab was, how the army was, and how the war was going, and Uriah answered that all was well. 8David then said to Uriah, "Go down to your house and bathe your feet." Uriah left the king's house, and a portion from the king's table was sent after him. 9But Uriah slept at the entrance of the king's house with the other officers of his lord, and did not go down to his own house. 10David was told, "Uriah has not gone down to his house." So he said to Uriah, "Have you not come from a journey? Why, then, did you not go down to your house?" 11Uriah answered David, "The ark and Israel and Judah are staying in tents, and my lord Joab and my lord's servants are encamped in the open field. Can I go home to eat and to drink and to sleep with my wife? As the LORD lives and as you live, I will do no such thing."[s] 12Then David said to Uriah, "Stay here today also, and tomorrow I will send you back." So Uriah stayed in Jerusalem that day. On the following day, 13David summoned him, and he ate and drank with David, who got him drunk. But in the evening he went out to sleep on his bed among his lord's servants, and did not go down to his house. 14The next morning David wrote a letter to Joab which he sent by Uriah. 15This is what he wrote in the letter: "Place Uriah up front, where the fighting is fierce. Then pull back and leave him to be struck down dead." 16So while Joab was besieging the city, he assigned Uriah to a place where he knew the defenders were strong. 17When the men of the city made a sortie against Joab, some officers of David's army fell, and Uriah the Hittite also died.

18Then Joab sent David a report of all the details of the battle, 19instructing the messenger, "When you have finished giving the king all the details of the battle, 20the king may become angry and say to you: 'Why did you go near the city to fight? Did you not know that they would shoot from the wall above? 21Who killed Abimelech, son of Jerubbaal? Was it not a woman who threw a millstone down on him from the wall above, so that he died in Thebez? Why did you go near the wall?' Then you in turn are to say, 'Your servant Uriah the Hittite is also dead.' "[t] 22The messenger set out, and on his arrival he reported to David everything Joab had sent him to tell.* 23He told David: "The men had the advantage over us and came out into the open against us, but we pushed them back to the entrance of the city gate. 24Then the archers shot at your servants from the wall above, and some of the king's servants died; and your servant Uriah the Hittite is also dead." 25David said to the messenger: "This is what you shall say to Joab: 'Do not let this be a great evil in your sight, for the sword devours now here and now there. Strengthen your attack on the city and destroy it.' Encourage him."

26When the wife of Uriah heard that her husband had died, she mourned her lord. 27But once the mourning was over, David sent for her and brought her into his house. She became his wife and bore him a son. But in the sight of the LORD what David had done was evil.

CHAPTER 12

See RG 180–82

Nathan's Parable. * 1The LORD sent Nathan to David, and when he came to him,

11:22–24 In these verses the Greek text has David, angry with Joab, repeat exactly the questions Joab had foreseen in vv. 20–21. In v. 24 of our oldest Greek text, the messenger specifies that about eighteen men were killed. The Greek is considerably longer than the transmitted Hebrew text, suggesting that the Hebrew may have lost some sentences.

12:1–7 David has committed adultery with Bathsheba and

p: 2 Sm 10:7; 1 Chr 20:1. *q:* 2 Sm 23:39. *r:* Lv 15:19. *s:* 1 Sm 4:3–4. *t:* Jgs 9:50–54.

he said: "Tell me how you judge this case: In a certain town there were two men, one rich, the other poor.[u]
2The rich man had flocks and herds in great numbers.
3But the poor man had nothing at all except one little ewe lamb that he had bought. He nourished her, and she grew up with him and his children. Of what little he had she ate; from his own cup she drank; in his bosom she slept; she was like a daughter to him.
4Now, a visitor came to the rich man, but he spared his own flocks and herds to prepare a meal for the traveler who had come to him: he took the poor man's ewe lamb and prepared it for the one who had come to him."
5David grew very angry with that man and said to Nathan: "As the LORD lives, the man who has done this deserves death!
6He shall make fourfold restitution* for the lamb because he has done this and was unsparing."[v]
7Then Nathan said to David: "You are the man!

Nathan's Indictment. "Thus says the LORD God of Israel: I anointed you king over Israel. I delivered you from the hand of Saul.[w]
8I gave you your lord's house and your lord's wives for your own. I gave you the house of Israel and of Judah. And if this were not enough, I could count up for you still more.
9Why have you despised the LORD and done what is evil in his sight? You have cut down Uriah the Hittite with the sword; his wife you took as your own, and him you killed with the sword of the Ammonites.
10Now, therefore, the sword shall never depart from your house, because you have despised me and have taken the wife of Uriah the Hittite to be your wife.[x]
11Thus says the LORD: I will bring evil upon you out of your own house. I will take your wives before your very eyes, and will give them to your neighbor: he shall lie with your wives in broad daylight.* [y]
12You have acted in secret, but I will do this in the presence of all Israel, in the presence of the sun itself."

David's Repentance.
13Then David said to Nathan, "I have sinned against the LORD." Nathan answered David: "For his part, the LORD has removed your sin. You shall not die,[z]
14but since you have utterly spurned the LORD by this deed, the child born to you will surely die."
15Then Nathan returned to his house.

The LORD struck the child that the wife of Uriah had borne to David, and it became desperately ill.
16David pleaded with God on behalf of the child. He kept a total fast, and spent the night lying on the ground clothed in sackcloth.
17The elders of his house stood beside him to get him to rise from the ground; but he would not, nor would he take food with them.
18On the seventh day, the child died. David's servants were afraid to tell him that the child was dead, for they said: "When the child was alive, we spoke to him, but he would not listen to what we said. How can we tell him the child is dead? He may do some harm!"
19But David noticed his servants whispering among themselves and realized that the child was dead. He asked his servants, "Is the child dead?" They said, "Yes."
20Rising from the ground, David washed and anointed himself, and changed his clothes. Then he went to the house of the LORD and worshiped. He returned to his own house and asked for food; they set it before him, and he ate.
21His servants said to him: "What is this you are doing? While the child was living, you fasted and wept and kept vigil; now that the child is dead, you rise and take food."
22He replied: "While the child was living, I fasted and wept, thinking, 'Who knows? The LORD may grant me the child's life.'
23But now he is dead. Why should I fast? Can I bring him back again? I shall go to him, but he will not return to

arranged the death of her husband. Instead of directly indicting the king for this criminal abuse of his royal authority, the prophet Nathan tells David a story. In the story, a parable of David's own actions, a powerful man takes cruel advantage of his vulnerable neighbor. Hearing the story, David is outraged and denounces the rich man—thus unwittingly pronouncing judgment on himself ("You are the man," v. 7).

12:6 Fourfold restitution: David's judgment foreshadows the deaths of four of his own sons: the child born of his adulterous union with Bathsheba (v. 18); Amnon (13:28–29); Absalom (18:15; 19:1); and Adonijah (1 Kgs 2:24–25).

12:11 In broad daylight: lit., "before the eyes of the sun"; the phrase echoes "before your very eyes" and anticipates "in the presence of the sun itself" (v. 12). The reference is to Absalom's action in appropriating his father's harem (16:22).

u: Sir 47:1. *v:* Ex 21:37; Lk 19:8. *w:* 1 Sm 16:13. *x:* 2 Sm 13:28–29; 18:14. *y:* 2 Sm 16:21–22. *z:* 1 Kgs 21:29; Ps 32:5; 51:4; Sir 47:11.

me."[a] [24]Then David consoled Bathsheba his wife. He went and slept with her; and she conceived and bore him a son, who was named Solomon. The LORD loved him [25]and sent the prophet Nathan to name him Jedidiah,* on behalf of the LORD.

End of the Ammonite War. [26][b] Joab fought against Rabbah of the Ammonites and captured that royal city. [27]He sent messengers to David to say: "I have fought against Rabbah and have taken the water-city. [28]Therefore, assemble the rest of the soldiers, join the siege against the city, and capture it, lest I be the one to capture the city and mine be the name people mention, not yours." [29]So David assembled the rest of the soldiers, went to Rabbah, fought against it, and captured it. [30]He took the crown of Milcom from the idol's head, a talent* of gold in weight, with precious stones; this crown David wore on his own head. He also brought out a great amount of spoil from the city. [31]He deported the people of the city and set them to work with saws, iron picks, and iron axes, or put them to work at the brickmold. He dealt thus with all the cities of the Ammonites. Then David and his whole army returned to Jerusalem.

CHAPTER 13

See RG 180–82

Amnon's Rape of Tamar. [1]After this, the following occurred. David's son Absalom had a beautiful sister named Tamar, and David's son Amnon loved her.[c] [2]He was in such anguish over his sister Tamar that he became sick; she was a virgin, and Amnon thought it impossible to do anything to her. [3]Now Amnon had a friend named Jonadab, son of David's brother Shimeah, who was very clever.* [d] [4]He asked him, "Prince, why are you so dejected morning after morning? Why not tell me?" So Amnon said to him, "I am in love with Tamar, my brother Absalom's sister." [5]Then Jonadab replied, "Lie down on your bed and pretend to be sick. When your father comes to visit you, say to him, 'Please let my sister Tamar come and encourage me to take food. If she prepares something in my presence, for me to see, I will eat it from her hand.' " [6]So Amnon lay down and pretended to be sick. When the king came to visit him, Amnon said to the king, "Please let my sister Tamar come and prepare some fried cakes before my eyes, that I may take food from her hand."

[7]David then sent home a message to Tamar, "Please go to the house of your brother Amnon and prepare some food for him." [8]Tamar went to the house of her brother Amnon, who was in bed. Taking dough and kneading it, she twisted it into cakes before his eyes and fried the cakes. [9]Then she took the pan and set out the cakes before him. But Amnon would not eat; he said, "Have everyone leave me." When they had all left him, [10]Amnon said to Tamar, "Bring the food into the bedroom, that I may have it from your hand." So Tamar picked up the cakes she had prepared and brought them to her brother Amnon in the bedroom. [11]But when she brought them close to him so he could eat, he seized her and said to her, "Come! Lie with me, my sister!" [12]But she answered him, "No, my brother! Do not force me! This is not done in Israel. Do not commit this terrible crime.[e] [13]Where would I take my shame? And you would be labeled a fool in Israel.* So please, speak to the king; he will not keep me from you."[f] [14]But he would not listen to her; he was too strong for her: he forced her down and raped her. [15]Then Amnon felt intense hatred for her; the hatred he felt for her far surpassed the love he had had for her. Amnon said to her, "Get up, leave." [16]She replied, "No, brother, because sending me away would be far worse than this evil thing you have done to me." He would not listen to her, [17]but called the youth who was his attendant and said, "Send this girl outside, away

12:25 Jedidiah: the name means "beloved of Yhwh."

12:30 A talent: since this would normally be more than seventy-five pounds, the report may have been embellished.

13:3 Clever: lit., "wise." Jonadab's "wisdom" extends only to sly cleverness in getting things done; he devises the plan that will enable Amnon to pursue his infatuation. In the categories of the Old Testament wisdom tradition, Jonadab is a fool.

13:13 A fool in Israel: a play on *nebala* (v. 12), "terrible crime," lit., "folly."

a: Jb 7:9–10. *b:* 1 Chr 20:1–3. *c:* 2 Sm 3:2–3; 1 Chr 3:9. *d:* 2 Sm 21:21. *e:* Lv 18:9; 20:17; Dt 22:21; 27:22. *f:* Gn 34:7–8.

from me, and bar the door after her." [18]Now she had on a long tunic, for that is how virgin princesses dressed in olden days. When his attendant put her out and barred the door after her, [19]Tamar put ashes on her head and tore the long tunic in which she was clothed. Then, putting her hands to her head, she went away crying loudly. [20]Her brother Absalom said to her: "Has your brother Amnon been with you? Keep still now, my sister; he is your brother. Do not take this so to heart." So Tamar remained, devastated, in the house of her brother Absalom. [21]King David, when he heard of the whole affair, became very angry. He would not, however, antagonize Amnon, his high-spirited son; he loved him, because he was his firstborn. [22]And Absalom said nothing, good or bad, to Amnon; but Absalom hated Amnon for having humiliated his sister Tamar.

Absalom's Plot. [23]Two years went by. It was sheep-shearing time for Absalom in Baal-hazor near Ephraim, and Absalom invited all the king's sons. [24]Absalom went to the king and said: "Your servant has hired the shearers. Please, may the king come with all his servants to your servant." [25]But the king said to Absalom, "No, my son, all of us should not go lest we be a burden to you." And though Absalom urged him, he would not go but began to bid him good-bye. [26]Absalom then said, "If not you, then please let my brother Amnon come with us." The king asked him, "Why should he go with you?" [27]But at Absalom's urging, the king sent Amnon and with him all his other sons. Absalom prepared a banquet fit for a king. [28][g] But Absalom had instructed his attendants: "Now watch! When Amnon is merry with wine and I say to you, 'Kill Amnon,' put him to death. Do not be afraid, for it is I who order you to do it. Be strong and act like warriors."

Death of Amnon. [29]When the attendants did to Amnon as Absalom had commanded, all the king's other sons rose up, mounted their mules, and fled. [30]While they were still on the road, a report reached David: "Absalom has killed all the king's sons and not one of them is left." [31]The king stood up, tore his garments, and lay on the ground. All his servants standing by him also tore their garments.[h] [32]But Jonadab, son of David's brother Shimeah, spoke up: "Let not my lord think that all the young men, the king's sons, have been killed! Amnon alone is dead, for Absalom was set on this ever since Amnon humiliated his sister Tamar. [33]Now let my lord the king not take so to heart that report, 'All the king's sons are dead.' Amnon alone is dead." [34]Meanwhile, Absalom had taken flight. Then the servant on watch looked out and saw a large group coming down the slope from the direction of Bahurim. He came in and reported this to the king: "I saw some men coming down the mountainside from the direction of Bahurim." [35]So Jonadab said to the king: "There! The king's sons have come. It is as your servant said." [36]No sooner had he finished speaking than the king's sons came in, weeping aloud. The king, too, and all his servants wept very bitterly. [37]But Absalom, who had taken flight, went to Talmai, son of Ammihud, king of Geshur,[i] [38]and stayed in Geshur for three years. [39]All that time the king continued to mourn his son; but his intention of going out against Absalom abated as he was consoled over the death of Amnon.

CHAPTER 14

See RG 180–82

The Wise Woman of Tekoa. [1]Now Joab, son of Zeruiah, knew how the king felt toward Absalom. [2]Joab sent to Tekoa and brought from there a wise woman, to whom he said: "Pretend to be in mourning. Put on mourning apparel and do not anoint yourself with oil, that you may appear to be a woman who has long been mourning someone dead. [3]Then go to the king and speak to him in this manner." And Joab told her what to say.

[4]So the woman of Tekoa went to the king and fell to the ground in homage, saying, "Help, O king!" [5][j] The king said to her,

14:7 Hope: lit., "glowing coal." The image is similar to that of a lighted lamp, e.g., Ps 132:17, or small hearth fire, to keep alive the ancestral name.

g: 2 Sm 12:10. *h:* 2 Sm 1:11. *i:* 2 Sm 3:3; 15:8. *j:* 2 Kgs 6:26–28.

"What do you want?" She replied: "Alas, I
am a widow; my husband is dead. [6]Your servant had two sons, who quarreled in the field,
with no one to part them, and one of them
struck his brother and killed him. [7]Then the
whole clan confronted your servant and demanded: 'Give up the one who struck down
his brother. We must put him to death for the
life of his brother whom he has killed; we
must do away with the heir also.' Thus they
will quench my remaining hope* and leave
my husband neither name nor posterity upon
the earth."[k] [8]The king then said to the
woman: "Go home. I will issue a command
on your behalf." [9]The woman of Tekoa answered him, "Upon me and my family be the
blame, my lord king; the king and his throne
are innocent." [10]Then the king said, "If anyone says a word to you, have him brought to
me, and he shall not touch you again." [11]But
she said, "Please, let the king remember the
LORD your God, that the avenger of blood
may not go too far in destruction and that my
son may not be done away with." He replied,
"As the LORD lives, not a hair of your son
shall fall to the ground."

[12]But the woman continued, "Please let
your servant say still another word to my
lord the king." He replied, "Speak." [13]So the
woman said: "Why, then, do you think the
way you do against the people of God? In
pronouncing as he has, the king shows himself guilty, in not bringing back his own banished son. [14]We must indeed die; we are then
like water that is poured out on the ground
and cannot be gathered up. Yet, though God
does not bring back to life, he does devise
means so as not to banish* anyone from him.[l]
[15]And now, if I have presumed to speak to
the king of this matter, it is because the people have given me cause to fear. And so your
servant thought: 'Let me speak to the king.
Perhaps he will grant the petition of his servant. [16]For the king must surely listen and
rescue his servant from the grasp of one who
would destroy both me and my son from the
heritage of God.' [17]And your servant says,
'Let the word of my lord the king lead to
rest;* indeed, my lord the king is like an angel of God, discerning good and evil. The
LORD your God be with you.' "[m]

[18]The king answered the woman, "Now
do not conceal from me anything I may ask
you!" The woman said, "Let my lord the
king speak." [19]So the king asked, "Is the
hand of Joab with you in all this?" And
the woman answered: "As you live, my lord
the king, it is just as my lord has said, and
not otherwise. It was your servant Joab who
instructed me and told your servant all these
things she was to say. [20]Your servant Joab
did this in order to approach the matter in a
roundabout way. But my lord is wise with
the wisdom of an angel of God, knowing all
things on earth."

Absalom's Return. [21]Then the king said to
Joab: "I am granting this request. Go and
bring back young Absalom." [22]Falling to the
ground in homage and blessing the king,
Joab said, "This day your servant knows that
I am in good favor with you, my lord king,
since the king has granted the request of
your servant." [23]Joab then went off to Geshur and brought Absalom to Jerusalem.
[24]But the king said, "Let him go off to his
own house; he shall not appear before* me."
So Absalom went off to his house and did
not appear before the king.

[25]In all Israel there was no man more
praised for his beauty than Absalom, flaw-
less from the sole of his foot to the crown of
his head. [26]When he shaved his head—as he
used to do at the end of every year, because
his hair became too heavy for him—the hair
weighed two hundred shekels according to
the royal standard. [27]Absalom had three sons
born to him, besides a daughter named Tamar, who was a beautiful woman.[n]

Absalom Is Pardoned. [28]Absalom lived in
Jerusalem for two years without appearing
before the king. [29]Then he sent a message
asking Joab to send him to the king, but Joab

14:14 Not to banish: a possible allusion to the religious institution of cities of refuge for involuntary murderers; see Nm 35:9–15.

14:17 Rest: cf. Ru 1:9; Ps 95:11; Mi 2:10. The reference here is to a return home for Absalom.

14:24 Appear before: lit., "see the face of," a term from court etiquette; so also in vv. 28, 32.

k: Nm 35:19. *l:* Jb 7:9; 14:7–12; Ps 88:4, 10–12. *m:* 1 Sm 29:9. *n:* 2 Sm 18:18.

would not come to him. Although he asked him a second time, Joab would not come. [30]He therefore instructed his servants: "You see Joab's field that borders mine, where he has barley. Go, set it on fire." And so Absalom's servants set the field on fire.[o] Joab's farmhands came to him with torn garments and told him, "Absalom's servants set your field on fire." [31]Joab went to Absalom in his house and asked him, "Why have your servants set my field on fire?" [32]Absalom answered Joab: "I sent you a message: Come here, that I may send you to the king to say: 'Why did I come back from Geshur? I would be better off if I were still there!' Now, let me appear before the king. If I am guilty, let him put me to death." [33]Joab went to the king and reported this. The king then called Absalom; he came to him and in homage fell on his face to the ground before the king. Then the king kissed Absalom.

CHAPTER 15

See RG 180–82

Absalom's Ambition. [1]After this, Absalom provided himself with chariots, horses, and a retinue of fifty.[p] [2]Moreover, Absalom used to rise early and stand alongside the road leading to the gate. If someone had a lawsuit to be decided by the king, Absalom would call to him and say, "From what city are you?" And when he replied, "Your servant is of such and such a tribe of Israel," [3]Absalom would say to him, "Your case is good and just, but there is no one to hear you in the king's name." [4]And he would continue: "If only I could be appointed judge in the land! Then everyone who has a lawsuit to be decided might come to me and I would render him justice." [5]Whenever a man approached him to show homage, he would extend his hand, hold him, and kiss him. [6]By behaving in this way toward all the Israelites who came to the king for judgment, Absalom was stealing the heart of Israel.

Conspiracy in Hebron. [7]After a period of four years, Absalom said to the king: "Please let me go to Hebron and fulfill a vow I made to the LORD. [8]For while living in Geshur in Aram, your servant made this vow: 'If the LORD ever brings me back to Jerusalem, I will worship him in Hebron.' "[q] [9]The king said to him, "Go in peace," and he went off to Hebron. [10]Then Absalom sent agents throughout the tribes of Israel to say, "When you hear the sound of the horn, say, 'Absalom is king in Hebron!' " [11]Two hundred men had accompanied Absalom from Jerusalem. They had been invited and went in all innocence, knowing nothing. [12]Absalom also sent to Ahithophel the Gilonite, David's counselor, an invitation to come from his town, Giloh, for the sacrifices he was about to offer. So the conspiracy gained strength, and the people with Absalom increased in numbers.[r]

David Flees Jerusalem. [13]An informant came to David with the report, "The Israelites have given their hearts to Absalom,[s] and they are following him." [14]At this, David said to all his servants who were with him in Jerusalem: "Get up, let us flee, or none of us will escape from Absalom. Leave at once, or he will quickly overtake us, and then bring disaster upon us, and put the city to the sword." [15]The king's servants answered him, "Whatever our lord the king chooses to do, we are your servants." [16]Then the king set out, accompanied by his entire household, except for ten concubines whom he left behind to care for the palace.[t] [17]As the king left the city, with all his officers accompanying him, they halted opposite the ascent of the Mount of Olives, at a distance, [18]while the whole army marched past him.

David and Ittai. As all the Cherethites and Pelethites, and the six hundred Gittites who had entered his service from that city, were passing in review before the king,[u] [19]the king said to Ittai the Gittite: "Why should you also go with us? Go back and stay with the king, for you are a foreigner and you, too, are an exile from your own country. [20]You came only yesterday, and today shall I have you wander off with us wherever I have to go? Return and take your brothers with you, and may the LORD show you kindness and fidelity." [21]But Ittai answered the king, "As the LORD lives, and as my lord the king lives, your servant shall be wherever my lord the

o: Jgs 15:4–5. *p:* 1 Sm 8:11; 1 Kgs 1:5. *q:* 2 Sm 3:3; 13:37. *r:* 2 Sm 16:23. *s:* Ps 3. *t:* 2 Sm 16:21–22; 20:3. *u:* 2 Sm 8:18.

king is, whether for death or for life."[v] 22 So the king said to Ittai, "Go, then, march on." And Ittai the Gittite, with all his men and all the dependents that were with him, marched on. 23 The whole land wept aloud as the last of the soldiers went by, and the king crossed the Wadi Kidron with all the soldiers moving on ahead of him by way of the ascent of the Mount of Olives, toward the wilderness.

David and the Priests. 24 Zadok, too, and all the Levites bearing the ark of the covenant of God set down the ark of God until the whole army had finished marching out of the city; and Abiathar came up. 25 Then the king said to Zadok: "Take the ark of God back to the city. If I find favor with the LORD, he will bring me back and permit me to see it and its lodging place. 26 But if he should say, 'I am not pleased with you,' I am ready; let him do to me as he sees fit."[w] 27 The king also said to Zadok the priest: "Look, you and Abiathar return to the city in peace, and both your sons with you, your own son Ahimaaz, and Abiathar's son Jonathan. 28 Remember, I shall be waiting at the fords near the wilderness until a report from you comes to me." 29 So Zadok and Abiathar took the ark of God back to Jerusalem and remained there.

30 As David went up the ascent of the Mount of Olives, he wept without ceasing. His head was covered, and he was walking barefoot. All those who were with him also had their heads covered and were weeping as they went.[x] 31 When David was told, "Ahithophel is among the conspirators with Absalom," he said, "O LORD, turn the counsel of Ahithophel to folly!"[y]

David and Hushai. 32 When David reached the top, where God was worshiped, Hushai the Archite was there to meet him, with garments torn and dirt upon his head.[z] 33 David said to him: "If you come with me, you will be a burden to me; 34 but if you return to the city and say to Absalom, 'Let me be your servant, O king; I was formerly your father's servant, but now I will be yours,' you will thwart for me the counsel of Ahithophel.[a] 35 You will have the priests Zadok and Abiathar there with you. If you hear anything from the king's house, you shall report it to the priests Zadok and Abiathar, 36 who have there with them their two sons, Zadok's son Ahimaaz and Abiathar's son Jonathan. Through them you shall send on to me whatever you hear." 37 So David's friend Hushai went into the city, Jerusalem, as Absalom was about to enter it.

CHAPTER 16

See RG 180–82

David and Ziba. 1 David went a little beyond the top and Ziba, the servant of Meribbaal, was there to meet him with saddled donkeys laden with two hundred loaves of bread, an ephah of cakes of pressed raisins, an ephah of summer fruits, and a skin of wine.[b] 2 The king said to Ziba, "What are you doing with all this?" Ziba replied: "The donkeys are for the king's household to ride on. The bread and summer fruits are for your servants to eat, and the wine to drink when they grow weary in the wilderness." 3 Then the king said, "And where is your lord's son?" Ziba answered the king, "He is staying in Jerusalem, for he said, 'Today the house of Israel will restore to me my father's kingdom.' "[c] 4 The king therefore said to Ziba, "So! Everything Meribbaal had is yours." Then Ziba said: "I pay you homage, my lord the king. May I find favor with you!"[d]

David and Shimei. 5 As King David was approaching Bahurim, there was a man coming out; he was of the same clan as the house of Saul, and his name was Shimei, son of Gera. He kept cursing as he came out,[e] 6 and throwing stones at David and at all King David's officers, even though all the soldiers, including the royal guard, were on David's right and on his left. 7 Shimei was saying as he cursed: "Get out! Get out! You man of blood, you scoundrel! 8 The LORD has paid you back for all the blood shed from the family of Saul,* whom you replaced as king, and the LORD has handed over the kingdom to your son Absalom. And now look at you: you suffer ruin because you are a man of

16:8 Blood shed . . . Saul: probably refers to the episode recounted in 21:1–14.

v: Ru 1:16–17. *w:* 2 Sm 16:10. *x:* 2 Sm 19:5; Mi 1:8. *y:* 2 Sm 16:23; 17:14, 23. *z:* 2 Sm 16:16. *a:* 2 Sm 16:19. *b:* 2 Sm 4:4; 9:1–13; 19:18, 25. *c:* 2 Sm 19:26–27. *d:* 2 Sm 19:30. *e:* 2 Sm 3:16; 19:17, 22–23; 1 Kgs 2:8.

blood." 9Abishai, son of Zeruiah, said to the
king: "Why should this dead dog curse my
lord the king? Let me go over and take off
his head."[f] 10But the king replied: "What
business is it of mine or of yours, sons of
Zeruiah, that he curses? Suppose the LORD
has told him to curse David; who then will
dare to say, 'Why are you doing this?' "[g]
11Then David said to Abishai and to all his
servants: "If my own son, who came forth
from my loins, is seeking my life, how much
more might this Benjaminite do so! Let him
alone and let him curse, for the LORD has
told him to.[h] 12Perhaps the LORD will look
upon my affliction and repay me with good
for the curses he is uttering this day." 13Da-
vid and his men continued on the road, while
Shimei kept up with them on the hillside, all
the while cursing and throwing stones and
dirt as he went.[i] 14The king and all the soldiers with him arrived at the Jordan tired out,
and stopped there to rest.

Absalom's Counselors. 15In the meantime
Absalom, with all the Israelites, entered
Jerusalem, and Ahithophel was with him.
16When David's friend Hushai the Archite
came to Absalom, he said to him: "Long live
the king! Long live the king!"[j] 17But Absalom asked Hushai: "Is this your devotion to
your friend? Why did you not go with your
friend?" 18Hushai replied to Absalom: "On
the contrary, I am his whom the LORD and all
this people and all Israel have chosen, and
with him I will stay. 19Furthermore, as I was
in attendance upon your father, so will I be
before you. Whom should I serve, if not his
son?"[k]

20Then Absalom said to Ahithophel, "Offer your counsel on what we should do."
21Ahithophel replied to Absalom: "Go to
your father's concubines, whom he left behind to take care of the palace. When all Israel hears how odious you have made yourself to your father, all those on your side will
take courage."[l] 22So a tent was pitched on
the roof for Absalom, and Absalom went to
his father's concubines in view of all Israel.[m]

Counsel of Ahithophel. 23Now the counsel given by Ahithophel at that time was as
though one sought the word of God. Such
was all the counsel of Ahithophel both to
David and to Absalom.[n]

CHAPTER 17

See RG 180–82

1Ahithophel went on to say to Absalom: "Let me choose twelve thousand men
and be off in pursuit of David tonight. 2If I
come upon him when he is weary and discouraged, I shall cause him panic, and all the
people with him will flee, and I shall strike
down the king alone. 3Then I can bring back
the rest of the people to you, as a bride returns to her husband. It is the death of only
one man you are seeking; then all the people
will be at peace." 4This plan sounded good
to Absalom and to all the elders of Israel.

Counsel of Hushai. 5Then Absalom said,
"Now call Hushai the Archite also; let us
hear what he too has to say." 6When Hushai
came to Absalom, Absalom said to him:
"This is Ahithophel's plan. Shall we follow
his plan? If not, give your own." 7Hushai
replied to Absalom, "This time Ahithophel
has not given good counsel." 8And he went
on to say: "You know that your father and
his men are warriors, and that they are as
fierce as a bear in the wild robbed of her
cubs. Moreover, since your father is a skilled
fighter, he will not spend the night with the
army.[o] 9Even now he lies hidden in one of
the caves or in one of his other places. And
if some of our soldiers should fall at the first
attack, whoever hears of it will say, 'Absalom's followers have been slaughtered.'
10Then even the brave man with the heart of
a lion—his heart will melt. For all Israel
knows that your father is a fighter and those
who are with him are brave. 11This is what I
counsel: Let all Israel be assembled, from
Dan to Beer-sheba, as numerous as the sands
by the sea, and you yourself go with them.
12We can then attack him wherever we find
him, settling down upon him as dew alights
on the ground. None shall survive—neither
he nor any of his followers. 13And if he re-
tires into a city, all Israel shall bring ropes to

f: 2 Sm 19:22; 1 Sm 24:15; 26:6. *g:* 2 Sm 15:25–26; 19:23. *h:* 2 Sm 12:11. *i:* 2 Sm 19:19–24. *j:* 2 Sm 15:32–37. *k:* 2 Sm 15:34. *l:* 2 Sm 15:16; 20:3. *m:* 2 Sm 12:11–12. *n:* 2 Sm 15:12, 31; 17:23. *o:* Hos 13:8.

that city and we can drag it into the gorge, so that not even a pebble of it can be found." [14]Then Absalom and all the Israelites said, "The counsel of Hushai the Archite is better than the counsel of Ahithophel." For the LORD had commanded that Ahithophel's good counsel should be thwarted, so that he might bring Absalom to ruin.[p]

David Told of the Plan. [15]Then Hushai said to the priests Zadok and Abiathar: "This is the counsel Ahithophel gave Absalom and the elders of Israel, and this is what I counseled. [16]So send a warning to David immediately: 'Do not spend the night at the fords near the wilderness, but cross over without fail. Otherwise the king and all the people with him will be destroyed.' " [17]Now Jonathan and Ahimaaz were staying at En-rogel. A maidservant was to come with information for them, and they in turn were to go and report to King David. They could not risk being seen entering the city, [18]but an attendant did see them and informed Absalom. They hurried on their way and reached the house of a man in Bahurim who had a cistern in his courtyard. They let themselves down into it, [19]and the woman took the cover and spread it over the mouth of the cistern, strewing crushed grain on the cover so that nothing could be noticed. [20]When Absalom's servants came to the woman at the house, they asked, "Where are Ahimaaz and Jonathan?" The woman replied, "They went by a short while ago toward the water." They searched, but found no one, and so returned to Jerusalem. [21]As soon as they left, Ahimaaz and Jonathan came up out of the cistern and went on to report to King David. They said to him: "Leave! Cross the water at once, for Ahithophel has given such and such counsel in regard to you." [22]So David and all his people moved on and crossed the Jordan. By daybreak, there was no one left who had not crossed.

[23]When Ahithophel saw that his counsel was not acted upon, he saddled his donkey and departed, going to his home in his own city. Then, having left orders concerning his household, he hanged himself. And so he died and was buried in his father's tomb.[q]

[24]Now David had arrived at Mahanaim while Absalom crossed the Jordan accompanied by all the Israelites. [25]Absalom had put Amasa in command of the army in Joab's place. Amasa was the son of an Ishmaelite named Ithra, who had married Abigail, daughter of Jesse and sister of Joab's mother Zeruiah.[r] [26]Israel and Absalom encamped in the land of Gilead.

[27]When David came to Mahanaim, Shobi, son of Nahash from Rabbah of the Ammonites, Machir, son of Ammiel from Lodebar, and Barzillai, the Gileadite from Rogelim,[s] [28]brought beds and covers, basins and pottery, as well as wheat, barley, flour, roasted grain, beans, lentils, [29]honey, and butter and cheese from the flocks and herds, for David and those who were with him to eat; for they said, "The people will be hungry and tired and thirsty in the wilderness."

CHAPTER 18

See RG 180–82

Preparation for Battle. [1]After mustering the troops he had with him, David placed officers in command of units of a thousand and units of a hundred. [2]David then divided the troops three ways, a third under Joab, a third under Abishai, son of Zeruiah and brother of Joab, and a third under Ittai the Gittite. The king said to the troops, "I intend to go out with you myself." [3]But they replied: "You must not come out with us. For if we flee, no one will care; even if half of us die, no one will care. But you are worth ten thousand of us. Therefore it is better that we have you to help us from the city." [4]The king said to them, "I will do what you think best." So the king stood by the gate as all the soldiers marched out in units of a hundred and a thousand. [5]But the king gave this command to Joab, Abishai, and Ittai: "Be gentle with young Absalom for my sake." All the soldiers heard as the king gave commands to the various leaders with regard to Absalom.

Defeat of Absalom's Forces. [6]David's army then took the field against Israel, and a battle was fought in the forest near Mahanaim. [7]The forces of Israel were defeated by David's servants, and the casualties there

---

p: 2 Sm 15:31, 34. *q:* 2 Sm 15:31; 16:23. *r:* 2 Sm 19:14; 20:4–13. *s:* 2 Sm 9:4; 19:32; 1 Kgs 2:7; Ezr 2:61.

that day were heavy—twenty thousand men.
[8]The battle spread out over that entire region, and the forest consumed more combatants that day than did the sword.

Death of Absalom. [9]Absalom unexpectedly came up against David's servants. He
was mounted on a mule, and, as the mule
passed under the branches of a large oak
tree, his hair caught fast in the tree. He hung
between heaven and earth while the mule
under him kept going. [10]Someone saw this
and reported to Joab, "I saw Absalom hanging from an oak tree." [11]Joab said to the man
who told him this: "If you saw him, why did
you not strike him to the ground on the spot?
Then it would have been my duty to give
you fifty pieces of silver and a belt." [12]But
the man replied to Joab: "Even if I already
held a thousand pieces of silver in my two
hands, I would not lay a hand on the king's
son, for in our hearing the king gave you and
Abishai and Ittai a command: 'Protect the
youth Absalom for my sake.' [13]Had I been
disloyal and killed him, it would all have
come out before the king, and you would
stand aloof." [14]Joab replied, "I will not
waste time with you in this way." And taking
three pikes in hand, he thrust for the heart of
Absalom. He was still alive in the tree.[t]
[15]When ten of Joab's young armor-bearers
closed in on Absalom, and killed him with
further blows, [16]Joab then sounded the horn,
and the soldiers turned back from the pursuit
of the Israelites, because Joab called them to
halt. [17]They took Absalom and cast him into
a deep pit in the forest, and built up a very
large mound of stones over him. And all the
Israelites fled to their own tents.[u]

[18]During his lifetime Absalom had taken a
pillar and set it up for himself in the King's
Valley, for he said, "I have no son to perpetuate my name." The pillar which he named
for himself is called Absalom's Monument
to the present day.[v]

David Told of Absalom's Death. [19]Then
Ahimaaz, son of Zadok, said, "Let me run to
take the good news to the king that the LORD
has set him free from the power of his enemies." [20]But Joab said to him: "You are not
the man to bring the news today. On some
other day you may take the good news, but
today you would not be bringing good news,
for in fact the king's son is dead." [21]Then
Joab said to a Cushite, "Go, tell the king what
you have seen." The Cushite bowed to Joab
and ran off. [22]But Ahimaaz, son of Zadok,
said to Joab again, "Come what may, permit
me also to run after the Cushite." Joab
replied: "Why do you want to run, my son?
You will receive no reward." [23]But he insisted, "Come what may, I want to run." Joab
said to him, "Run." Ahimaaz took the way of
the Jordan plain and outran the Cushite.

[24]Now David was sitting between the two
gates, and a lookout mounted to the roof of
the gate above the city wall, where he looked
out and saw a man running all alone. [25]The
lookout shouted to inform the king, who
said, "If he is alone, he has good news to report." As he kept coming nearer, [26]the lookout spied another runner. From his place
atop the gate he cried out, "There is another
man running by himself." And the king responded, "He, too, is bringing good news."
[27]Then the lookout said, "I notice that the
first one runs like Ahimaaz, son of Zadok."
The king replied, "He is a good man; he
comes with good news."[w] [28]Then Ahimaaz
called out and greeted the king. With face to
the ground he paid homage to the king and
said, "Blessed be the LORD your God, who
has delivered up the men who rebelled
against my lord the king." [29]But the king
asked, "Is young Absalom safe?" And Ahimaaz replied, "I saw a great disturbance when
the king's servant Joab sent your servant on,
but I do not know what it was." [30]The king
said, "Step aside and remain in attendance
here." So he stepped aside and remained
there. [31]When the Cushite came in, he said,
"Let my lord the king receive the good news
that this day the LORD has freed you from the
power of all who rose up against you." [32]But
the king asked the Cushite, "Is young Absalom all right?" The Cushite replied, "May
the enemies of my lord the king and all who
rebel against you with evil intent be as that
young man!"

t: 2 Sm 12:10; 13:28–29. *u:* Jos 7:26; 8:29; 10:27. *v:* 2 Sm 14:27. *w:* 2 Kgs 9:20.

See RG 180–82

CHAPTER 19

1 The king was shaken, and went up to the room over the city gate and wept. He said as he wept, "My son Absalom! My son, my son Absalom! If only I had died instead of you, Absalom, my son, my son!"

Joab Reproves David. 2 Joab was told, "The king is weeping and mourning for Absalom," 3 and that day's victory was turned into mourning for the whole army when they heard, "The king is grieving for his son." 4 The soldiers stole into the city that day like men shamed by flight in battle. 5 Meanwhile the king covered his face and cried out in a loud voice, "My son Absalom! Absalom! My son, my son!"[x] 6 So Joab went to the king's residence and said: "Though they saved your life and your sons' and daughters' lives, and the lives of your wives and your concubines, you have put all your servants to shame today 7 by loving those who hate you and hating those who love you. For you have announced today that officers and servants are nothing to you. Indeed I am now certain that if Absalom were alive today and all of us dead, that would be fine with you. 8 Now then, get up! Go out and speak kindly to your servants. I swear by the LORD that if you do not go out, not a single man will remain with you overnight, and this will be a far greater disaster for you than any that has come upon you from your youth until now." 9 So the king got up and sat at the gate. When all the people were told, "The king is sitting at the gate," they came into his presence.

The Reconciliation. Now the Israelites had fled to their separate tents, 10 but throughout the tribes of Israel all the people were arguing among themselves, saying to one another: "The king delivered us from the grasp of our enemies, and it was he who rescued us from the grasp of the Philistines. Now, he has fled the country before Absalom, 11 but Absalom, whom we anointed over us, has died in battle. Why, then, should you remain silent about restoring the king to his palace?" When the talk of all Israel reached the king, 12 David sent word to the priests Zadok and Abiathar: "Say to the elders of Judah: 'Why should you be last to restore the king to his palace? 13 You are my brothers, you are my bone and flesh. Why should you be last to restore the king?' 14 Also say to Amasa: 'Are you not my bone and flesh? May God do thus to me, and more, if you do not become commander of my army permanently in place of Joab.' "[y] 15 He won the hearts of the Judahites all together, and so they sent a message to the king: "Return, with all your servants."

David and Shimei. 16 So the king returned, and when he reached the Jordan, Judah had come to Gilgal to meet him and to bring him across the Jordan. 17 Shimei, son of Gera, the Benjaminite from Bahurim, hurried down with the Judahites to meet King David,[z] 18 accompanied by a thousand men from Benjamin. Ziba, too, the servant of the house of Saul, accompanied by his fifteen sons and twenty servants, hastened to the Jordan before the king.[a] 19[b] They crossed over the ford to bring the king's household over and to do whatever he wished. When Shimei, son of Gera, crossed the Jordan, he fell down before the king 20 and said to him: "May my lord not hold me guilty; do not remember or take to heart the wrong that your servant did the day my lord the king left Jerusalem. 21 For your servant knows that I have done wrong. But I now am the first of the whole house of Joseph to come down today to meet my lord the king." 22 But Abishai, son of Zeruiah, countered: "Shimei must be put to death for this. He cursed the anointed of the LORD." 23 David replied: "What has come between you and me, sons of Zeruiah, that you would become my adversaries this day? Should anyone die today in Israel? Am I not aware that today I am king over Israel?"[c] 24 Then the king said to Shimei, "You shall not die." And the king gave him his oath.

David and Meribbaal. 25 Meribbaal, son of Saul, also went down to meet the king. He had not cared for his feet nor trimmed his mustache nor washed his clothes from the

x: 2 Sm 15:30. *y:* 2 Sm 17:25; 20:4. *z:* 2 Sm 16:5–13. *a:* 2 Sm 16:1–4; 19:25–31. *b:* 2 Sm 16:13; Ex 22:27; 1 Kgs 2:8–9. *c:* 2 Sm 16:9–10; 1 Sm 11:13; 1 Kgs 2:8–9, 36–46.

day the king left until he returned safely.
26 When he came from Jerusalem to meet the
king, the king asked him, "Why did you not
go with me, Meribbaal?"[d] 27 He replied: "My
lord king, my servant deceived me. For your
servant said to him, 'Saddle the donkey for
me, that I may ride on it and go with the
king'; your servant is lame.[e] 28 But he slandered your servant before my lord the king.
But my lord the king is like an angel of God.
Do whatever seems good to you. 29 For
though my father's entire house deserved
only death from my lord the king, yet you
placed your servant among those who eat at
your table. What right do I still have to make
further appeal to the king?"[f] 30 But the king
said to him: "Why do you go on talking? I
say, 'You and Ziba shall divide the property.' "[g] 31 Meribbaal answered the king, "Indeed let him take it all, now that my lord the
king has returned safely to his house."

David and Barzillai. 32 Barzillai the Gileadite also came down from Rogelim and escorted the king to the Jordan for his crossing,
taking leave of him at the Jordan.[h] 33 It was
Barzillai, a very old man of eighty, who had
provided for the king during his stay in Mahanaim; he was a very great man. 34 The king
said to Barzillai, "Cross over with me, and I
will provide for your old age as my guest in
Jerusalem." 35 But Barzillai answered the
king: "How much longer have I to live, that I
should go up to Jerusalem with the king? 36 I
am now eighty years old. Can I distinguish
between good and evil? Can your servant
taste what he eats and drinks, or still hear the
voices of men and women singers? Why
should your servant be any further burden to
my lord the king? 37 In escorting the king
across the Jordan, your servant is doing little
enough! Why should the king give me this reward? 38 Please let your servant go back to die
in my own city by the tomb of my father and
mother. Here is your servant Chimham. Let
him cross over with my lord the king. Do for
him whatever seems good to you." 39 Then the
king said to him, "Chimham shall cross over
with me, and for him I will do whatever
seems good to you. And anything else you
would like me to do for you, I will do."
40 Then all the people crossed over the Jordan
but the king remained; he kissed Barzillai and
bade him farewell as he returned to his own
place. 41 Finally the king crossed over to Gilgal, accompanied by Chimham.

Israel and Judah Quarrel. All of the people of Judah and half of the people of Israel
had escorted the king across. 42 But then all
these Israelites began coming to the king and
saying, "Why did our brothers the Judahites
steal you away and bring the king and his
household across the Jordan, along with all
David's men?" 43 All the Judahites replied to
the men of Israel: "Because the king is our
relative. Why are you angry over this? Have
we had anything to eat at the king's expense? Or have portions from his table been
given to us?" 44 The Israelites answered the
Judahites: "We have ten shares in the king.
Also, we are the firstborn* rather than you.
Why do you slight us? Were we not first to
speak of restoring our king?" Then the Judahites in turn spoke even more fiercely than
the Israelites.[i]

CHAPTER 20

See RG 180–82

Sheba's Rebellion. 1 Now a scoundrel
named Sheba, the son of Bichri, a Benjaminite, happened to be there. He sounded the
horn and cried out,

"We have no share in David,
nor any heritage in the son of Jesse.
Everyone to your tents, O Israel!"[j]

2 So all the Israelites left David to follow
Sheba, son of Bichri. But the Judahites, from
the Jordan to Jerusalem, remained loyal to
their king. 3 David came to his house in Jerusalem, and the king took the ten concubines
whom he had left behind to care for the
palace and placed them under guard. He
provided for them, but never again saw
them. And so they remained shut away to the
day of their death, lifelong widows.[k]

19:44 The firstborn had special rights over the other siblings.

d: 2 Sm 16:3. *e:* 2 Sm 9:2–13. *f:* 2 Sm 9:9–11. *g:* 2 Sm 16:4. *h:* 2 Sm 17:27–29; 1 Kgs 2:7; Ezr 2:61. *i:* 1 Kgs 11:31. *j:* 1 Kgs 12:16. *k:* 2 Sm 15:16; 16:20–22.

Amasa's Death. 4 Then the king said to Amasa: "Summon the Judahites for me within three days. Then present yourself here."[l] 5 Accordingly Amasa set out to summon Judah, but delayed beyond the time set for him. 6 Then David said to Abishai: "Sheba, son of Bichri, may now do us more harm than Absalom did. Take your lord's servants and pursue him, lest he find fortified cities and take shelter while we look on." 7 So Joab and the Cherethites and Pelethites and all the warriors marched out behind Abishai from Jerusalem to campaign in pursuit of Sheba, son of Bichri.[m] 8* They were at the great stone in Gibeon when Amasa met them. Now Joab had a belt over his tunic, from which was slung a sword in its sheath at his thigh; the sword would slide out downwards.[n] 9 Joab asked Amasa, "Is everything all right, my brother?" and with his right hand held Amasa's beard as if to kiss him. 10 And since Amasa was not on his guard against the sword in Joab's other hand, Joab stabbed him in the abdomen with it, so that his entrails burst forth to the ground, and he died; there was no second thrust. Then Joab and Abishai his brother pursued Sheba, son of Bichri.[o] 11 One of Joab's attendants stood by Amasa and said, "Let him who favors Joab and is for David follow Joab." 12 Amasa lay covered with blood in the middle of the highroad, and the man noticed that all the soldiers were stopping. So he rolled Amasa away from the road to the field and spread a garment over him, because he saw how all who came upon him were stopping. 13 When he had been removed from the road, everyone went on after Joab in pursuit of Sheba, son of Bichri.

Joab Pursues Sheba. 14 Sheba had passed through all the tribes of Israel to Abel Beth-maacah. Then all the Bichrites assembled and they too entered the city after him. 15 So all Joab's troops came and besieged him in Abel Beth-maacah. They built up a mound against the city, so that it stood against the rampart, and were battering the wall to knock it down. 16 Then a wise woman from the city called out, "Listen, listen! Tell Joab, 'Come here, so I can speak with you.'" 17 When Joab had come near her, the woman said, "Are you Joab?" And he replied, "Yes." She said to him, "Listen to what your servant has to say." He replied, "I am listening." 18 Then she went on to say: "There is a saying from long ago,* 'Let them ask if they will in Abel or in Dan whether loyalty is finished 19 or ended in Israel.' You are seeking to batter down a city that is a mother in Israel. Why do you wish to swallow up the heritage of the LORD?"[p] 20 Joab answered, "Not at all, not at all! I do not wish to swallow or batter anything. 21 That is not the case at all. A man from the hill country of Ephraim, whose name is Sheba, son of Bichri, has rebelled against King David. Give him up, just him, and I will withdraw from the city." Then the woman said to Joab, "His head shall be thrown to you across the wall." 22 In her wisdom, the woman went to all the people, and they cut off the head of Sheba, son of Bichri, and threw it out to Joab. He then sounded the horn, and they scattered from the city to their own tents, while Joab returned to Jerusalem to the king.

David's Officials. 23 Joab was in command of the whole army of Israel. Benaiah, son of Jehoiada, was in command of the Cherethites and Pelethites.[q] 24 Adoram was in charge of the forced labor. Jehoshaphat, son of Ahilud, was the chancellor. 25 Shawsha was the scribe. Zadok and Abiathar were priests.[r] 26 Ira the Jairite was also David's priest.

V. Appendixes

CHAPTER 21

See RG 182–83

Gibeonite Vengeance. 1 In David's time there was a famine for three years, year after year. David sought the presence of the LORD, who said: There is bloodguilt on Saul and his family because he put the Gibeonites to

20:8 The text of this verse is quite uncertain.

20:18–19 This proverbial expression is obscure but seems to reflect a tradition that this Danite town was associated with oracles or other sorts of revelation. Cf. Mt 16:13–17; and the intertestamental *Testament of Levi* 2:3.

l: 2 Sm 17:25; 19:14. *m:* 2 Sm 8:18. *n:* 2 Sm 2:13. *o:* 1 Kgs 2:5. *p:* Gn 49:16. *q:* 2 Sm 8:16–18; 23:20. *r:* 2 Sm 8:17–18.

death.[s] [2]So the king called the Gibeonites and spoke to them. (Now the Gibeonites were not Israelites, but survivors of the Amorites; and although the Israelites had given them their oath, Saul had sought to kill them off in his zeal for the Israelites and for Judah.)[t] [3]David said to the Gibeonites, "What must I do for you and how must I make atonement, that you may bless the heritage of the LORD?" [4]The Gibeonites answered him, "We have no claim against Saul and his house for silver or gold, nor is it our place to put anyone to death in Israel." Then he said, "I will do for you whatever you propose." [5]They said to the king, "As for the man who was exterminating us and who intended to destroy us that we might have no place in all the territory of Israel, [6]let seven men from among his descendants be given to us, that we may execute them before the LORD in Gibeon, on the LORD's mountain." The king replied, "I will give them up." [7]The king, however, spared Meribbaal, son of Jonathan, son of Saul, because of the LORD's oath that formed a bond between David and Saul's son Jonathan.[u] [8]But the king took Armoni and Meribbaal, the two sons that Aiah's daughter Rizpah had borne to Saul, and the five sons of Saul's daughter Merob that she had borne to Adriel, son of Barzillai the Meholathite,[v] [9]and delivered them into the power of the Gibeonites, who then executed them on the mountain before the LORD. The seven fell at the one time; they were put to death during the first days of the harvest—that is, at the beginning of the barley harvest.

[10]Then Rizpah, Aiah's daughter, took sackcloth and spread it out for herself on the rock from the beginning of the harvest until rain came down on them from the heavens, fending off the birds of the heavens from settling on them by day, and the wild animals by night.[w] [11]When David was informed of what Rizpah, Aiah's daughter, the concubine of Saul, had done, [12]he went and obtained the bones of Saul and of his son Jonathan from the citizens of Jabesh-gilead, who had stolen them away secretly from the public square of Beth-shan, where the Philistines had hanged them at the time they defeated Saul on Gilboa.[x] [13]When he had brought up from there the bones of Saul and of his son Jonathan, the bones of those who had been executed were also gathered up. [14]Then the bones of Saul and of his son Jonathan were buried in the land of Benjamin, at Zela, in the tomb of his father Kish. After all that the king commanded had been carried out, God granted relief to the land.[y]

Exploits in Philistine Wars. [15]There was another battle between the Philistines and Israel. David went down with his servants and fought the Philistines, but David grew tired. [16]Dadu, a descendant of the Rephaim, whose bronze spear weighed three hundred shekels, was about to take him captive. Dadu was girt with a new sword and thought he would kill David, [17]but Abishai, son of Zeruiah, came to help him, and struck and killed the Philistine. Then David's men swore to him, "You must not go out to battle with us again, lest you quench the lamp of Israel."[z]

[18a] After this, there was another battle with the Philistines, in Gob. On that occasion Sibbecai the Hushathite struck down Saph, a descendant of the Rephaim.[b] [19c] There was another battle with the Philistines, in Gob, and Elhanan, son of Jair from Bethlehem, killed Goliath of Gath, whose spear shaft was like a weaver's beam. [20]There was another battle, at Gath, and there was a giant, who had six fingers on each hand and six toes on each foot—twenty-four in all. He too was descended from the Rephaim. [21]And when he insulted Israel, Jonathan, son of David's brother Shimei, struck him down.[d] [22]These four were descended from the Rephaim in Gath, and they fell at the hands of David and his servants.

CHAPTER 22

See RG 182–83

Song of Thanksgiving.* [1]David proclaimed the words of this song to the LORD

22:1–51 This psalm of thanksgiving also appears in the Psalter, with a few small variants, as Ps 18. In both places it is attributed to David. Two main sections can be distinguished. In the first part, after an introductory stanza of praise to God (vv.

s: 2 Sm 24:13. *t:* Jos 9:3–27. *u:* 2 Sm 9:13; 1 Sm 18:3; 20:8–10, 15–16, 42. *v:* 2 Sm 3:7. *w:* 2 Sm 3:31; 12:16. *x:* 1 Sm 31:10–13. *y:* 2 Sm 24:25. *z:* 1 Kgs 11:36; 15:4; 2 Kgs 8:19. *a:* 1 Chr 20:4–8. *b:* 2 Sm 23:27. *c:* 1 Sm 17:4, 7. *d:* 2 Sm 13:3.

when the LORD had rescued him from the
grasp of all his enemies and from the grasp
of Saul.[e] 2 He said:[f]

O LORD, my rock, my fortress, my
deliverer,
3 my God, my rock of refuge!
My shield, my saving horn,*
my stronghold, my refuge,
my savior, from violence you keep me
safe.[g]
4 Praised be the LORD, I exclaim!
I have been delivered from my enemies.
5 The breakers of death surged round
about me,
the menacing floods* terrified me;
6 The cords of Sheol tightened;
the snares of death lay in wait for me.
7 In my distress I called out: LORD!
I cried out to my God;
From his temple* he heard my voice,
my cry reached his ears.

8 The earth rocked and shook;*
the foundations of the heavens
trembled;
they shook as his wrath flared up.
9 Smoke rose in his nostrils,
a devouring fire from his mouth;
it kindled coals into flame.
10 He parted the heavens and came down,
a dark cloud under his feet.[h]
11 Mounted on a cherub* he flew,
borne along on the wings of the wind.[i]
12 He made darkness the cover about him,
a mass of water, heavy thunderheads.
13 From the brightness of his presence
coals were kindled to flame.
14 The LORD thundered from heaven;
the Most High made his voice resound.
15 He let fly arrows and scattered them;
lightning, and dispersed them.[j]
16 Then the bed of the sea appeared;
the world's foundations lay bare,
At the roar of the LORD,
at the storming breath of his nostrils.[k]
17 He reached down from on high and
seized me,
drew me out of the deep waters.[l]
18 He rescued me from my mighty enemy,
from foes too powerful for me.
19 They attacked me on a day of distress,
but the LORD came to my support.
20 He set me free in the open;
he rescued me because he loves me.

21 The LORD acknowledged my
righteousness;
rewarded my clean hands.
22 For I kept the ways of the LORD;
I was not disloyal to my God.
23 His laws were all before me,
his decrees I did not cast aside.
24 I was honest toward him;
I was on guard against sin.
25 So the LORD rewarded my righteousness,
the cleanness of my hands in his sight.
26[m] Toward the faithful you are faithful;*
to the honest you are honest;
27 Toward the sincere you are sincere;
but to the perverse you are devious.
28 Humble people you save,
though on the haughty your eyes look
down.

2–4), the writer describes the peril he was in (vv. 5–7), and then poetically depicts, under the form of a theophany, God's intervention in his behalf (vv. 8–20), concluding with an acknowledgment of God's justice (vv. 21–31). In the second part, God is praised for having prepared the psalmist for war (vv. 32–35), given him victory over his enemies (vv. 36–39), whom he put to flight (vv. 40–43), and bestowed on him dominion over many peoples (vv. 44–46). The entire song ends with an expression of grateful praise (vv. 47–51).

22:3 My saving horn: my strong savior. The horn, such as that of an enraged bull, was a symbol of strength; cf. Lk 1:69.

22:5–6 Breakers . . . floods: traditional Old Testament imagery for lethal danger, from which the Lord is uniquely able to rescue; cf. Ps 69:2, 15–16; 89:10–11; Jon 2:3–6.

22:7 His temple: his heavenly abode.

22:8–10 The Lord's coming is depicted by means of a storm theophany, including earthquake (vv. 8, 16) and thunderstorm (vv. 9–15); cf. Jgs 5:4–5; Ps 29; 97:2–6; Hb 3.

22:11 Mounted on a cherub: in the traditional storm theophany, as here, the Lord appears with thunder, lightning, earthquake, rain, darkness, cloud, and wind. Sometimes these are represented as his retinue; sometimes he is said to ride upon the clouds or "the wings of the wind" (Ps 104:3). The parallelism in v. 11 suggests that the winged creatures called cherubim are imagined as bearing the Lord aloft. In the iconography of the ark of the covenant, the Lord was "enthroned upon the cherubim"; cf. Ex 37:7–9; 1 Sm 4:4; 2 Sm 6:2; 2 Kgs 19:15; Ps 80:2; 99:1.

22:26–27 People are treated by God in the same way they treat him and other people.

e: Ps 18:1. *f:* Ps 18:3–51. *g:* 1 Sm 2:1–2. *h:* Ps 144:5. *i:* Ex 25:18–22. *j:* Ps 144:6. *k:* Ex 15:8. *l:* Ps 144:7. *m:* 1 Sm 2:30.

[29] You are my lamp, O LORD!
My God brightens the darkness about me.
[30] With you I can rush an armed band,
with my God to help I can leap a wall.
[31] God's way is unerring;
the LORD's promise is tried and true;
he is a shield for all who trust in him.[n]

[32] Truly, who is God except the LORD?
Who but our God is the rock?
[33] This God who girded me with might,
kept my way unerring,
[34] Who made my feet swift as a deer's,
set me safe on the heights,[o]
[35] Who trained my hands for war,
my arms to bend even a bow of bronze.

[36] You have given me your protecting shield,
and your help has made me great.
[37] You gave me room to stride;
my feet never stumbled.
[38] I pursued my enemies and overtook them;
I did not turn back till I destroyed them.
[39] I struck them down, and they did not rise;
they fell dead at my feet.
[40] You girded me with strength for war;
subdued adversaries at my feet.
[41] My foes you put to flight before me;
those who hated me I destroyed.
[42] They cried for help, but no one saved them,
cried to the LORD but got no answer.
[43] I ground them fine as the dust of the earth;
like mud in the streets I trod them down.
[44] You rescued me from the strife of my people;
you made me head over nations.
A people I had not known became my slaves;
[45] Foreigners cringed before me;
as soon as they heard of me they obeyed.
[46] Their courage failed;
they came trembling from their fortresses.
[47] The LORD lives! Blessed be my rock!
Exalted be God, the rock of my salvation.
[48] O God who granted me vindication,
subdued peoples under me,
[49] and helped me escape from my enemies,
Truly you have exalted me above my adversaries,
from the violent you have rescued me.
[50] Thus I will proclaim you, LORD, among the nations;
I will sing the praises of your name.[p]
[51] You have given great victories to your king,
and shown kindness to your anointed,
to David and his posterity forever.

CHAPTER 23

See RG 182–83

The Last Words of David.* [1] These are the last words of David:

The oracle of David, son of Jesse;
the oracle of the man God raised up,
Anointed of the God of Jacob,
favorite of the Mighty One of Israel.[q]
[2] The spirit of the LORD spoke through me;
his word was on my tongue.[r]
[3] The God of Israel spoke;
of me the Rock of Israel said,
"One who rules over humankind with justice,
who rules in the fear of God,[s]
[4] Is like the light at sunrise
on a cloudless morning,
making the land's vegetation glisten after rain."[t]
[5] Is not my house firm before God?
He has made an eternal covenant with me,
set forth in detail and secured.[u]
Will he not bring to fruition

* **23:1–7 The last words of David**: the text of this short composition is difficult in places; it views David's career in retrospect.

n: Prv 30:5. *o:* Ps 62:3; Hb 3:19. *p:* Ps 22:23; Rom 15:9. *q:* 1 Kgs 2:1–9; Sir 47:8. *r:* Is 59:21; Jer 1:9. *s:* Ps 72:1–4. *t:* Jgs 5:31; Ps 72:6. *u:* 2 Sm 7:11, 15–16; Ps 89:30; Is 55:3.

all my salvation and my every desire?
6 But the wicked are all like thorns to be
cast away;
they cannot be taken up by hand.[v]
7 One wishing to touch them
must be armed with iron or the shaft of
a spear.
They must be utterly consumed by fire.

David's Warriors. 8These are the names of
David's warriors.* Ishbaal, the son of Hachamoni, chief of the Three. He brandished his
spear over eight hundred whom he had slain
in a single encounter.[w] 9Next to him was Eleazar, the son of Dodo the Ahohite, one of the
Three warriors with David at Ephes-dammim, when they insulted the Philistines who
had massed there for battle. The Israelites
had retreated,[x] 10but he stood there and struck
down the Philistines until his hand grew tired
from clutching the sword. The LORD brought
about a great victory on that day; the army
turned back to rejoin Eleazar, but only to
strip the slain. 11Next to him was Shammah,
son of Agee the Hararite. The Philistines had
assembled at Lehi, where there was a plot of
land full of lentils. The people were fleeing
before the Philistines,[y] 12but he took his stand
in the middle of the plot, kept it safe, and cut
down the Philistines. Thus the LORD brought
about a great victory. Such deeds as these the
Three warriors performed.

13Three of the Thirty chiefs went down to
David in the cave of Adullam during the harvest, while a Philistine clan was encamped in
the Valley of Rephaim.[z] 14David was then in
the stronghold, and there was a garrison of
Philistines in Bethlehem. 15Now David had a
craving and said, "If only someone would
give me a drink of water from the cistern by
the gate of Bethlehem!" 16Thereupon the three
warriors broke through the encampment of the
Philistines, drew water from the cistern by the
gate of Bethlehem, and carried it back to David. But he refused to drink it, and instead
poured it out* to the LORD, 17saying: "The
LORD forbid that I do such a thing! Could I
drink the blood of these men who went at the
risk of their lives?" So he refused to drink it.

18Abishai, the brother of Joab, son of Zeruiah, was the chief of the Thirty; he brandished his spear over three hundred whom
he had slain. He made a name among the
Thirty, 19but was more famous than any of
the Thirty, becoming their leader. However,
he did not attain to the Three.

20Benaiah, son of Jehoiada, a valiant man
of mighty deeds, from Kabzeel, killed the
two sons of Ariel of Moab. Also, he went
down and killed the lion in the cistern on a
snowy day.[a] 21He likewise slew an Egyptian,
a huge man. The Egyptian carried a spear, but
Benaiah came against him with a staff; he
wrested the spear from the Egyptian's hand,
and killed him with that spear. 22Such deeds
as these Benaiah, the son of Jehoiada, performed; and he made a name among the
Thirty warriors 23but was more famous than
any of the Thirty. However, he did not attain
to the Three. David put him in charge of his
bodyguard.[b] 24Asahel,[c] brother of Joab, was
among the Thirty; Elhanan, son of Dodo,
from Bethlehem; 25Shammah, from En-harod; Elika, from En-harod; 26Helez, from
Beth-pelet; Ira, son of Ikkesh, from Tekoa;
27Abiezer, from Anathoth; Sibbecai, from
Husha;[d] 28Zalmon, from Ahoh; Maharai,
from Netophah; 29Heled, son of Baanah,
from Netophah; Ittai, son of Ribai, from Gibeah of Benjamin; 30Benaiah, from Pirathon;
Hiddai, from the valley of Gaash; 31Abibaal,
from Beth-arabah; Azmaveth, from Bahurim;
32Eliahba, from Shaalbon; Jashen the Gunite;
Jonathan, 33son of Shammah the Hararite;
Ahiam, son of Sharar the Hararite;
34Eliphelet, son of Ahasbai, from Beth-maacah; Eliam, son of Ahithophel, from Gilo;
35Hezrai, from Carmel; Paarai the Arbite;

23:8–39 There are thirty-seven warriors in all named in this list. First there are the Three warriors most noted for single-handed exploits (vv. 8–12). Then comes the story of a daring adventure by three unnamed members of the larger group of the Thirty (vv. 13–17). Next come the commanders of the king's bodyguard, Abishai (vv. 18–19) and Benaiah (vv. 20–23), with whom must be counted Asahel (v. 24) and Joab (vv. 18, 24, 37), and finally the group of the Thirty (vv. 24–39).

23:16 Poured it out: as a libation.

v: Dt 13:14. *w:* 1 Chr 11:11–41; 27:1–15. *x:* 1 Sm 17:1. *y:* Jgs 15:9. *z:* 1 Sm 22:1; Mi 1:15. *a:* 2 Sm 8:18; 20:23; Jgs 14:6; 1 Kgs 2:29–30. *b:* 1 Sm 22:14. *c:* 2 Sm 2:18–23. *d:* 2 Sm 21:18.

[36]Igal, son of Nathan, from Zobah; Bani the Gadite; [37]Zelek the Ammonite; Naharai, from Beeroth, the armor-bearer of Joab, son of Zeruiah; [38]Ira, from Jattir; Gareb, from Jattir; [39]Uriah the Hittite—thirty-seven in all.[e]

CHAPTER 24

See RG 182–83

David's Census; the Plague. [1]The LORD's anger against Israel flared again,[f] and he incited David against them: "Go, take a census of Israel and Judah." [2]The king therefore said to Joab and the leaders of the army who were with him, "Tour all the tribes of Israel from Dan to Beer-sheba and register the people, that I may know their number." [3]But Joab replied to the king: "May the LORD your God increase the number of people a hundredfold for my lord the king to see it with his own eyes. But why does it please my lord to do a thing of this kind?" [4]However, the king's command prevailed over Joab and the leaders of the army, so they left the king's presence in order to register the people of Israel. [5]Crossing the Jordan, they began near Aroer, south of the city in the wadi, and turned in the direction of Gad toward Jazer. [6]They continued on to Gilead and to the district below Mount Hermon. Then they proceeded to Dan; from there they turned toward Sidon, [7]going to the fortress of Tyre and to all the cities of the Hivites and Canaanites, and ending up in the Negeb of Judah, at Beer-sheba. [8]Thus they toured the whole land, reaching Jerusalem again after nine months and twenty days. [9]Joab then reported the census figures to the king: of men capable of wielding a sword, there were in Israel eight hundred thousand, and in Judah five hundred thousand.

[10]Afterward, however, David regretted having numbered the people. David said to the LORD: "I have sinned grievously in what I have done.[g] Take away, LORD, your servant's guilt, for I have acted very foolishly."* [11]When David rose in the morning, the word of the LORD came to the prophet Gad, David's seer, saying: [12]Go, tell David: Thus says the LORD: I am offering you three options; choose one of them, and I will give you that. [13]Gad then went to David to inform him. He asked: "Should three years of famine come upon your land; or three months of fleeing from your enemy while he pursues you; or is it to be three days of plague in your land? Now consider well: what answer am I to give to him who sent me?"[h] [14]David answered Gad: "I am greatly distressed. But let us fall into the hand of God, whose mercy is great, rather than into human hands." [15]Thus David chose the plague. At the time of the wheat harvest it broke out among the people. The LORD sent plague over Israel from morning until the time appointed, and from Dan to Beer-sheba seventy thousand of the people died. [16]But when the angel stretched forth his hand toward Jerusalem to destroy it, the LORD changed his mind about the calamity, and said to the angel causing the destruction among the people: Enough now! Stay your hand.[i] The angel of the LORD was then standing at the threshing floor of Araunah the Jebusite.[j] [17]When David saw the angel who was striking the people, he said to the LORD: "It is I who have sinned; it is I, the shepherd, who have done wrong. But these sheep, what have they done? Strike me and my father's family!"

David Offers Sacrifices. [18]On the same day Gad went to David and said to him, "Go and set up an altar to the LORD on the threshing floor of Araunah the Jebusite." [19]According to Gad's word, David went up as the LORD had commanded. [20]Now Araunah looked down and saw the king and his servants coming toward him while he was threshing wheat. So he went out and bowed down before the king, his face to the ground. [21]Then Araunah asked, "Why does my lord the king come to his servant?" David replied, "To buy the threshing floor from

24:10 The narrative supposes that since the people belonged to the Lord rather than to the king, only the Lord should know their exact number. Further, since such an exact numbering of the people would make it possible for the king to exercise centralized power, imposing taxation, conscription, and expropriation upon Israel, the story shares the view of monarchy found in 1 Sm 8:4–18. See also Nm 3:44–51, where census taking requires an apotropaic offering.

e: 2 Sm 11:3. *f:* 1 Chr 21:1–27. *g:* 1 Sm 24:6; 1 Chr 21:7–8. *h:* 2 Sm 21:1. *i:* Gn 6:6; Ex 32:14; 1 Chr 21:15; Jon 3:10. *j:* Ex 12:23; 2 Kgs 19:35.

you, to build an altar to the LORD, that the
plague may be withdrawn from the people."
22[k] But Araunah said to David: "Let my lord
the king take it and offer up what is good in
his sight. See, here are the oxen for burnt offerings, and the threshing sledges and the
yokes of oxen for wood. 23 All this does
Araunah give to the king." Araunah then
said to the king, "May the LORD your God
accept your offering." 24 The king, however,
replied to Araunah, "No, I will buy it from
you at the proper price, for I cannot sacrifice
to the LORD my God burnt offerings that cost
me nothing." So David bought the threshing
floor and the oxen for fifty silver shekels.
25 Then David built an altar to the LORD
there, and sacrificed burnt offerings and
communion offerings. The LORD granted relief to the land, and the plague was withdrawn from Israel.

k: 1 Sm 6:14; 1 Kgs 19:21.

See RG 183–98

The Books of Kings

The two Books of Kings are regarded by many as the last part of a work commonly known as the Deuteronomistic History. The latter tells the story of Israel from its settlement in the land (Joshua and Judges) through the transition from judgeship to monarchy under Samuel, Saul, and David (1 and 2 Samuel) to the reign of Solomon, the disintegration of the united kingdom into the kingdoms of Israel and Judah and the eventual downfall of both kingdoms (1 and 2 Kings). The Deuteronomistic History along with the Pentateuch forms a single historical narrative stretching from creation to exile.

The Books of Kings can be approached in several ways. They contain history and are an important source of information about the Israelite kingdoms. They are also narrative that calls for careful reading; historical accuracy is sometimes sacrificed to the demands of compelling characterization and dramatic tension. Most importantly, both historical presentation and narrative creativity are shaped by a particular religious worldview.

The multifaceted character of the work means that it has a variety of focal points. The historical events themselves, of course, are important, but the patterns according to which the author organizes those events give a unity to the author's historical reconstruction. The northern kings are condemned without exception, and the royal line degenerates from the divine election of Jeroboam I through a succession of short-lived dynasties to the bloodbath of Jehu's coup d'état, and finally dies out in a series of assassinations. (It must be admitted that the author at times skews the story to preserve the pattern: the relatively prosperous forty-one-year reign of Jeroboam II is dismissed in seven verses!) Judah's kings, on the other hand, follow a cyclic pattern of infidelity followed by reform, with each reformer king (Asa, Joash, Hezekiah, Josiah) greater than the last. Unfortunately the apostate kings also progress in wickedness, until the evil of Manasseh is so great that even Josiah's fidelity cannot turn away the Lord's wrath (2 Kgs 23:26).

As a literary work, the Books of Kings are admirable. Some of the brilliance is accessible only in Hebrew: wordplays, the sounds and rhythms of poetic passages, verbal allusions to other passages of the Hebrew Bible. Scenes are drawn with a vibrancy and immediacy that English cannot reproduce without sounding overdone. But other literary techniques survive translation: symmetrical structures for narrative units (and the disruptions of symmetry at significant points), rich ambiguities (see 1 Kgs 3:26), foreshadowings (such as the way the prophet of Bethel and the man of God of Judah in 1 Kgs 13 portend the destinies of their respective kingdoms). Characterization is rich and complex (Solomon, Jeroboam, Elijah, Ahab, Elisha, Jehu, etc.), revealing deep insight into human nature.

In offering a theological interpretation of history, 1–2 Kings upholds a double principle: the justification of the political disintegration of the Davidic empire, and the necessity of the religious unity of the Lord's people. This double principle is, practically speaking, unrealistic; see Jeroboam I's reasonable assessment in 1 Kgs 12:26–27. But for the Deuteronomistic historian, that is irrelevant. Just as the separation of the kingdoms is the

Lord's will (1 Kgs 12:22–24), so too is the centralization of worship at the Temple in Jerusalem (1 Kgs 9:3; see Dt 12). 1–2 Kings reflects that double principle in its organization. The story of each king is told integrally, whether the king is of Israel or Judah: both lines of kings are legitimate. But the stories of the two lines are recounted in the order in which each king came to the throne, irrespective of which kingdom he ruled: there is only one people of God, though they are under two different royal jurisdictions. Moreover, each king is evaluated on theological grounds, with no allowance made for political or economic successes or failures. All Israelite kings are condemned because they did not reverse Jeroboam I's sin of setting up sanctuaries outside Jerusalem. Judahite kings are condemned for apostasy or praised for reform, as the case may be; but a continuing source of irritation to the Deuteronomistic historian is the failure of even the praiseworthy kings to do anything about local shrines outside Jerusalem (the "high places").

Into the stories of the kings, almost as a counterpoint, are woven numerous stories of prophets, named and great (Elijah, Elisha, Isaiah), and less known or anonymous (1 Kgs 13; 22). Many of the stories are anecdotal, reflecting the everyday life of prophets and prophetic guilds (1 Kgs 17; 2 Kgs 4). But the volatile dynamics of prophetic involvement in the political realm are prominent: prophets in opposition to kings (1 Kgs 14; 21; 2 Kgs 9), prophets in support of kings (1 Kgs 20:1–34; 2 Kgs 19–20; 22:14–20). This too is part of the theological worldview of the Deuteronomistic historian. The destiny of Israel is in God's hand. Through prophets, the divine will is made known on earth to kings and people and the future consequences of their response to God's will are spelled out. It is perhaps indicative of the importance prophets have in 1 and 2 Kings that the structural center of the two books is the story of Elisha's succession to Elijah's prophetic ministry (2 Kgs 2), and that this is one of the few passages in Kings that occurs outside the account of any king's reign. Behind the temporal realm of kings and reigns lies the continuing realm of the divine word and its servants, the prophets.

1–2 Kings draws on older sources (perhaps on archival records, certainly on works called "The Book of the Chronicles of the Kings"; see, for example, 1 Kgs 14:19, 29), which it uses for its own theological purpose. The so-called Deuteronomistic History itself underwent a complex process of editorial revision whose stages are disputed by scholars. There may have been an edition sometime late in the reign of Josiah (640–609 B.C.), but in the form we have it the work comes from the time of the exile (see 2 Kgs 25:27–30). In its turn the Deuteronomistic History was one of the sources used by the Chronicler in postexilic times to compile the history presented in 1 and 2 Chronicles. Though Chronicles has little interest in the Northern Kingdom, much of the material in Kings about the kingdom of Judah reappears, sometimes in altered form, in Chronicles.

The Books of Kings may be divided as follows:

I. The Reign of Solomon (1 Kgs 1:1–11:43)
II. The Reign of Jeroboam (1 Kgs 12:1–14:20)
III. Kings of Judah and Israel (1 Kgs 14:21–16:34)
IV. The Story of Elijah (1 Kgs 17:1–19:21)
V. The Story of Ahab (1 Kgs 20:1–2 Kgs 1:18)
VI. Elisha Succeeds Elijah (2 Kgs 2:1–25)
VII. Stories of Elisha and Joram (2 Kgs 3:1–9:13)
VIII. The End of the Omrid Dynasty (2 Kgs 9:14–11:20)
IX. Kings of Judah and Israel (2 Kgs 12:1–17:5)
X. The End of Israel (2 Kgs 17:6–41)
XI. The End of Judah (2 Kgs 18:1–25:30)

See RG 183–91

The First Book of Kings

I. The Reign of Solomon*

CHAPTER 1

See RG 184–85

David's Old Age. 1* When King David
was old and advanced in years, though they
covered him with blankets he could not get
warm. 2His servants therefore said to him,
"Let a young virgin be sought to attend my
lord the king,* and to nurse him. If she sleeps
with you, my lord the king will be warm."
3So they sought for a beautiful girl throughout the territory of Israel, and found Abishag
the Shunamite. So they brought her to the
king. 4The girl was very beautiful indeed,
and she nursed the king and took care of
him. But the king did not have relations with
her.

Adonijah's Ambition. 5Adonijah, son of
Haggith, boasted, "I shall be king!" and he
provided himself with chariots, horses, and a
retinue of fifty to go before him.[a] 6Yet his father would never antagonize him by asking,
"Why are you doing this?" Adonijah was
also very handsome, and next in age to Absalom by the same mother. 7He consulted
with Joab, son of Zeruiah, and with Abiathar
the priest, and they became Adonijah's supporters. 8However, Zadok the priest, Benaiah, son of Jehoiada, Nathan the prophet,
Shimei and Rei, and David's warriors did
not support Adonijah.

9Adonijah slaughtered sheep, oxen, and
fatlings at the stone Zoheleth near En-rogel*
and invited all his brothers, the king's sons,
and all the royal officials of Judah; 10but he
did not invite Nathan the prophet, or Benaiah, or the warriors, or Solomon his brother.

Solomon Proclaimed King. 11Then Nathan
said to Bathsheba, Solomon's mother:
"Have you not heard that Adonijah, son of
Haggith, has become king, and our lord David does not know? 12Come now, let me advise you so that you may save your life and
the life of your son Solomon. 13Go, visit
King David, and say to him, 'Did you not,
my lord king, swear to your handmaid: Your
son Solomon shall be king after me; it is he
who shall sit upon my throne? Why, then,
has Adonijah become king?' 14And while
you are still there speaking to the king, I will
come in after you and confirm your words."

15So Bathsheba visited the king in his room.
The king was very old, and Abishag the Shunamite was caring for the king.* 16Bathsheba
bowed in homage to the king. The king said to
her, "What do you wish?"* 17She answered
him: "My lord, you swore to your servant by
the LORD, your God, 'Solomon your son will
be king after me; it is he who shall sit upon my

1:1–11:43 The story of the reign of Solomon comprises twelve major units, organized concentrically. That is, the first unit (1:1–2:12a) balances the last (11:26–43), the second (2:12b–46) balances the second last (11:14–25), and so forth. (See the structural notes at the beginning of each major unit.) The center of the whole story is a diptych that narrates the construction of the Temple (6:1–7:51) and its dedication (8:1–9:10).

1:1–2:12a The first major unit of the Solomon story concludes the so-called Succession Narrative (2 Sm 9–20; 1 Kgs 1–2). This unit tells how Solomon, a younger son, came to succeed David on the throne of Israel through the intervention of the prophet Nathan. Compare the last unit of the Solomon story, 11:26–43, where the prophet Ahijah begins the process whereby Jeroboam becomes king of the northern tribes after Solomon's death. The story of Solomon's accession is itself concentrically arranged: David's decline, Adonijah's rise, Solomon's supporters, David's decision, Solomon's inauguration, Adonijah's fall, David's death. Chronicles has no developed parallel to this story (see 1 Chr 23:1).

1:2 The fulsome use of royal titles and the elaborate etiquette in the Succession Narrative suggest the raw ambition of the contending parties and the oppressive atmosphere of the court.

1:9 En-rogel: the modern Job's Well just southeast of Jerusalem. It marked the ancient boundary between the tribes of Benjamin and Judah (Jos 15:7; 18:16).

1:15 Entering the king's chambers, Bathsheba confronts two realities: he is very old; and she herself, the woman for whom David once committed adultery and murder, has been replaced at the king's side and in his bed.

1:16 Throughout 1 Kgs 1 the key question is "Who shall be king (*malak*)?" David's feeble, two-syllable question to Bathsheba is an ironic echo of that key word: "What do you wish?" renders the Heb. *mahlak?*

a: 2 Sm 15:1.

throne.’ [18]But now Adonijah has become king, and you, my lord king, do not know it.* [19]He has sacrificed bulls, fatlings, and sheep in great numbers; he has invited all the king’s sons, Abiathar the priest, and Joab, the commander of the army, but not your servant Solomon. [20]* Now, my lord king, all Israel is looking to you to declare to them who is to sit upon the throne of my lord the king after him. [21]If this is not done, when my lord the king rests with his ancestors, I and my son Solomon will be considered criminals.”

[22]While she was still speaking to the king, Nathan the prophet came in. [23]They told the king, “Nathan the prophet is here.” He entered the king’s presence and did him homage, bowing to the floor. [24]Then Nathan said: “My lord king, did you say, ‘Adonijah shall be king after me and shall sit upon my throne’? [25]For today he went down and sacrificed bulls, fatlings, and sheep in great numbers; he invited all the king’s sons, the commanders of the army, and Abiathar the priest, and even now they are eating and drinking in his company and saying, ‘Long live King Adonijah!’ [26]But me, your servant, he did not invite; nor Zadok the priest, nor Benaiah, son of Jehoiada, nor your servant Solomon. [27]If this was done by order of my lord the king, you did not tell me, your servant, who is to sit upon the throne of my lord the king after him.”

[28]King David answered, “Call Bathsheba here.” When she entered the king’s presence and stood before him, [29]the king swore, “As the LORD lives, who has redeemed my life from all distress, [30]this very day I will fulfill the oath I swore to you by the LORD, the God of Israel, ‘Your son Solomon shall be king after me and shall sit upon my throne in my place.’ ” [31]Bowing to the floor in homage to the king, Bathsheba said, “May my lord, King David, live forever!”

[32]Then King David said, “Call Zadok the priest, Nathan the prophet, and Benaiah, son of Jehoiada.” When they had entered the king’s presence, [33]he said to them: “Take with you the royal officials. Mount my son Solomon upon my own mule and escort him down to Gihon. [34]There Zadok the priest and Nathan the prophet shall anoint him king over Israel, and you shall blow the ram’s horn and cry, ‘Long live King Solomon!’ [35]When you come back up with him, he is to go in and sit upon my throne. It is he that shall be king in my place: him I designate ruler of Israel and of Judah.” [36]Benaiah, son of Jehoiada, answered the king: “So be it! May the LORD, the God of my lord the king, so decree! [37]As the LORD has been with my lord the king, so may he be with Solomon, and make his throne even greater than that of my lord, King David!”

[38]So Zadok the priest, Nathan the prophet, Benaiah, son of Jehoiada, and the Cherethites and Pelethites* went down, and mounting Solomon on King David’s mule, escorted him to Gihon. [39]Then Zadok the priest took the horn of oil from the tent and anointed Solomon. They blew the ram’s horn and all the people shouted, “Long live King Solomon!” [40]Then all the people went up after him, playing flutes and rejoicing so much the earth split with their shouting.

Adonijah Submits to Solomon. [41]Adonijah and all the guests who were with him heard it, just as they ended their banquet. When Joab heard the sound of the ram’s horn, he asked, “Why this uproar in the city?” [42]As he was speaking, Jonathan, son of Abiathar the priest, arrived. Adonijah said, “Come, you are a man of worth and must bring good news.” [43]Jonathan answered Adonijah, “Hardly!* Our lord, King David, has made Solomon king. [44]The king sent with him Za-

1:18 Bathsheba uses a clever wordplay to conceal the rivalry between Solomon and Adonijah and imply that the real rivalry is between David and Adonijah. She repeatedly addresses David as “my lord king” (*’adoni hammelek*), but claims that “Adonijah has become king” (*’adoniya malak*). **Know**: the term means both “be aware of” and “recognize, acknowledge, ratify.”

1:20 There was no precedent for determining succession to the throne of Israel. Adonijah and his supporters assumed that primogeniture would assure the succession as it did in the monarchies of the surrounding nations. But Bathsheba persuades David that he is free to name anyone he chooses.

1:38 Cherethites and Pelethites: mercenaries in David’s bodyguard. They became part of his retinue after he defeated the Philistines and established himself in Jerusalem; cf. 2 Sm 8:18; 15:18; 20:23.

1:43 Hardly: Jonathan’s first word, *’abal*, whose meaning (such as “indeed,” “on the contrary”) must be discerned from the context, may be ironic. This irony is deepened by an untranslatable wordplay in Hebrew: a very similar word means

dok the priest, Nathan the prophet, Benaiah, son of Jehoiada, and the Cherethites and Pelethites, and they mounted him upon the king's own mule. [45]Zadok the priest and Nathan the prophet anointed him king at Gihon, and they went up from there rejoicing, so that the city is in an uproar. That is the noise you hear. [46]Moreover, Solomon has taken his seat on the royal throne, [47]and moreover the king's servants have come to pay their respects to our lord, King David, saying, 'May your God make Solomon's name more famous than your name, his throne greater than your throne!' And the king in his bed did homage. [48]This is what the king said: 'Blessed be the LORD, the God of Israel, who has this day provided one to sit upon my throne, so that I see it with my own eyes.' " [49]All the guests of Adonijah got up trembling, and went each their way, [50]but Adonijah, in fear of Solomon, got up and went to grasp the horns of the altar.*

[51]It was reported to Solomon: "Adonijah, in fear of King Solomon, is clinging to the horns of the altar and saying, 'Let King Solomon first swear that he will not kill me, his servant, with the sword.' " [52]Solomon answered, "If he proves worthy, not a hair of his shall fall to the ground. But if evil is found in him, he shall die." [53]King Solomon sent to have him brought down from the altar, and he came and paid homage to King Solomon. Solomon then said to him, "Go to your house."

See RG 184–85

CHAPTER 2

David's Last Instructions and Death.

[1]When the time of David's death drew near, he gave these instructions to Solomon his son: [2]"I am going the way of all the earth. Be strong and be a man! [3 b] Keep the mandate of the LORD, your God, walking in his ways and keeping his statutes, commands, ordinances, and decrees as they are written in the law of Moses, that you may succeed in whatever you do, and wherever you turn, [4 c] and that the LORD may fulfill the word he spoke concerning me: If your sons so conduct themselves that they walk before me in faithfulness with their whole heart and soul, there shall never be wanting someone of your line on the throne of Israel.

[5* d] "You yourself know what Joab, son of Zeruiah, did to me—what he did to the two commanders of Israel's armies, Abner, son of Ner, and Amasa, son of Jether: he killed them and brought the blood of war into a time of peace, and put the blood of war on the belt about his waist and the sandal on his foot. [6]Act with all the wisdom you possess; do not let his gray head go down to Sheol in peace. [7 e] But be true to the sons of Barzillai the Gileadite, and have them among those who eat at your table. For they were loyal to me when I was fleeing from your brother Absalom. [8 f] You also have with you Shimei, son of Gera, the Benjaminite of Bahurim, who cursed me bitterly the day I was going to Mahanaim. When he came down to meet me at the Jordan, I swore to him by the LORD: 'I will not kill you by the sword.' [9]But you must not let him go unpunished. You are wise; you will know what to do to send his gray head down to Sheol in blood."

[10 g] David rested with his ancestors and was buried in the City of David. [11 h] David was king over Israel for forty years: he was king seven years in Hebron and thirty-three years in Jerusalem.

The Kingdom Made Secure.* [12]Then Solomon sat on the throne of David his father, and his kingship was established.

"to mourn," which is an appropriate comment about the death of Adonijah's hopes for the throne.

1:50 Horns of the altar: the protuberances on each of the four corners of the altar (Ex 27:2; 29:12). By grasping the horns of the altar Adonijah is claiming asylum (Ex 21:13–14; 1 Kgs 2:28).

2:5–9 David urges Solomon to purge Joab and Shimei and supplies him with justification for doing so. Joab had killed Abner (2 Sm 3:22–30) and Amasa (2 Sm 20:4–12), thereby bringing blood guilt upon himself and perhaps upon his master David. Shimei had cursed David (2 Sm 16:5–8), though David pledged that Shimei would not be killed for it (2 Sm 19:16–24). David's motives, however, may have been more personal. Joab also killed David's son Absalom and chided David for his untimely public display of grief (2 Sm 18:9–19:8), and David may have felt himself free of the promise he made to Shimei because that promise was coerced by the presence of Shimei's thousand partisans backing him at the time.

2:12–46 The second major unit of the Solomon story shows how Solomon eliminated people he considered threats

b: Dt 17:18–19. *c:* 2 Sm 7:11–16; Ps 132:11–12. *d:* 2 Sm 3:22–30; 20:8–10. *e:* 2 Sm 17:27–29; 19:32–41. *f:* 2 Sm 16:5–13; 19:17–24. *g:* Acts 2:29. *h:* 2 Sm 2:1–4; 5:1–5.

[13]Adonijah, son of Haggith, came to Bathsheba, the mother of Solomon. "Do you come in peace?" she asked. "In peace," he answered, [14]and he added, "I have something to say to you." She replied, "Speak." [15]So he said: "You know that the kingship was mine, and all Israel expected me to be king. But the kingship passed me by and went to my brother; by the LORD's will it went to him. [16]But now there is one favor I would ask of you. Do not refuse me." And she said, "Speak on." [17*] He said, "Please ask King Solomon, who will not refuse you, to give me Abishag the Shunamite to be my wife." [18]Bathsheba replied, "Very well, I will speak to the king for you."

[19]Then Bathsheba went to King Solomon to speak to him for Adonijah, and the king stood up to meet her and paid her homage. Then he sat down upon his throne, and a throne was provided for the king's mother, who sat at his right. [20]She said, "There is one small favor I would ask of you. Do not refuse me." The king said to her, "Ask it, my mother, for I will not refuse you." [21]So she said, "Let Abishag the Shunamite be given to your brother Adonijah to be his wife." [22]King Solomon answered his mother, "And why do you ask that Abishag the Shunamite be given to Adonijah? Ask the kingship for him as well, for he is my older brother! Ask for him, for Abiathar the priest, for Joab, son of Zeruiah!" [23]And King Solomon swore by the LORD: "May God do thus to me and more, if Adonijah has not spoken this word at the cost of his life. [24i] And now, as the LORD lives, who has established me and set me on the throne of David my father and made for me a house as he promised, this day shall Adonijah be put to death." [25]Then King Solomon sent Benaiah, son of Jehoiada, who struck him dead.

[26j] The king said to Abiathar the priest: "Go to your estate in Anathoth. Though you deserve to die, I will not put you to death at this time, because you carried the ark of the Lord GOD before David my father and shared in all the hardships my father endured."* [27k] So Solomon dismissed Abiathar from the office of priest of the LORD, thus fulfilling the word the LORD had spoken in Shiloh against the house of Eli.

[28]When the news came to Joab, since he had sided with Adonijah, though not with Absalom, he fled to the tent of the LORD and clung to the horns of the altar. [29]King Solomon was told, "Joab has fled to the tent of the LORD and is by the altar." He sent Benaiah, son of Jehoiada, with the order, "Go, strike him down." [30]Benaiah went to the tent of the LORD and said to him, "The king says, 'Come out.' " But he answered, "No! I will die here." Benaiah reported to the king, "This is what Joab said to me in reply." [31]The king answered him: "Do as he has said. Strike him down and bury him, and remove from me and from my father's house the blood which Joab shed without provocation. [32l] The LORD will bring blood upon his own head, because he struck down two men better and more just than himself, and slew them with the sword without my father David's knowledge: Abner, son of Ner, commander of Israel's army, and Amasa, son of Jether, commander of Judah's army. [33]Their blood will be upon the head of Joab and his descendants. But upon David and his descendants, upon his house and his throne, there shall be peace forever from the LORD." [34]Benaiah, son of Jehoiada, went back, struck him down and killed him; he was buried in his house in the wilderness. [35]The king appointed Benaiah, son of Jehoiada, over the army in his place; Zadok the priest the king put in place of Abiathar.

[36]Then the king summoned Shimei and said to him: "Build yourself a house in Jerusalem and stay there. Do not go anywhere

to the security of his throne. It is marked by a device called "inclusion," where the text repeats a word, phrase, or idea at the beginning and end of a literary unit (see vv. 12b, 46b). Compare 11:14–25, where Solomon is unable to eliminate other threats to his security.

2:17–25 Abishag had belonged to David's harem (1:3–4), which Solomon inherited. Adonijah's request could imply a challenge to Solomon's accession and so exposes Adonijah to the suspicion of insurrection that will cost him his life; cf. 2 Sm 3:6–11; 16:21–22.

2:26 The narrator indulges in a subtle wordplay: Abiathar's exile to Anathoth (*'anatot*) continues the series of hardships he has endured (*hit'annita*).

i: 2 Sm 7:11–16. *j:* 1 Sm 22:20–23. *k:* 1 Sm 2:27–33. *l:* 2 Sm 3:22–30; 20:8–10.

else. [37]For the day you leave, and cross the Wadi Kidron, be certain you shall surely die. Your blood shall be upon your own head." [38]Shimei answered the king: "I accept. Your servant will do just as my lord the king has said." So Shimei stayed in Jerusalem for a long time. [39]But three years later, two of Shimei's servants ran away to Achish, son of Maacah, king of Gath, and Shimei was told, "Your servants are in Gath." [40]So Shimei rose, saddled his donkey, and went to Achish in Gath in search of his servants; and Shimei returned from Gath with his servants. [41]When Solomon was told that Shimei had gone from Jerusalem to Gath, and had returned, [42]the king summoned Shimei and said to him: "Did I not have you swear by the LORD and warn you clearly, 'The day you leave and go anywhere else, be certain you shall surely die'? And you answered, 'I accept and obey.'* [43]Why, then, have you not kept the oath of the LORD and the command that I gave you?" [44][m] And the king said to Shimei: "In your heart you know very well the evil that you did to David my father. Now the LORD is bringing your own evil upon your head. [45]But King Solomon shall be blessed, and David's throne shall be established before the LORD forever." [46]The king then gave the order to Benaiah, son of Jehoiada, who went out and struck him dead.

And the royal power was established in Solomon's hand.

CHAPTER 3

See RG 185-86

*Early Promise of Solomon's Reign.**

[1][n] Solomon allied himself by marriage with Pharaoh, king of Egypt. He married the daughter of Pharaoh and brought her to the City of David, until he should finish building his own house, and the house of the LORD, and the wall around Jerusalem. [2]The people were sacrificing on the high places, however, for up to that time no house had been built for the name of the LORD. [3]Although Solomon loved the LORD, walking in the statutes of David his father, he offered sacrifice and burned incense on the high places.

[4]The king went to Gibeon to sacrifice there, because that was the great high place. Upon its altar Solomon sacrificed a thousand burnt offerings. [5]In Gibeon the LORD appeared to Solomon in a dream at night. God said: Whatever you ask I shall give you. [6]Solomon answered: "You have shown great kindness to your servant, David my father, because he walked before you with fidelity, justice, and an upright heart; and you have continued this great kindness toward him today, giving him a son to sit upon his throne. [7]Now, LORD, my God, you have made me, your servant, king to succeed David my father; but I am a mere youth, not knowing at all how to act— [8]I, your servant, among the people you have chosen, a people so vast that it cannot be numbered or counted. [9]Give your servant, therefore, a listening heart to judge your people and to distinguish between good and evil. For who is able to give judgment for this vast people of yours?"

[10]The Lord was pleased by Solomon's request. [11]So God said to him: Because you asked for this—you did not ask for a long life for yourself, nor for riches, nor for the life of your enemies—but you asked for discernment to know what is right— [12]I now do as you request. I give you a heart so wise and discerning that there has never been anyone like you until now, nor after you will there be anyone to equal you. [13][o] In addition, I give you what you have not asked for: I give you such riches and glory that among kings there will be no one like you all your days. [14]And if you walk in my ways, keeping my statutes and commandments, as David your father did, I will give you a long life. [15]Solomon awoke; it was a

2:42–44 In his charge against Shimei, Solomon misrepresents the truth in two ways. He did not make Shimei take an oath. And he imposed capital punishment only on crossing the Wadi Kidron, to the east of Jerusalem. This was presumably to prevent Shimei from returning to his home, Bahurim, which lay in that direction; Gath, however, is southwest of Jerusalem. Solomon's next words to Shimei reveal that he is really being punished for cursing David, not for violating Solomon's command.

3:1–15 The third major unit of the Solomon story depicts the bright beginning of his reign. It includes the narrator's remarks about Solomon's marriage and his building projects, and a divine appearance to Solomon. Compare 11:1–13, where the same themes recur, but in negative fashion. The story of the divine appearance is told also in 2 Chr 1:1–13.

m: 2 Sm 16:5–13; 19:17–24. *n:* 1 Kgs 7:8; 9:24. *o:* Eccl 1:12–13; Wis 7:7–11; Mt 6:29.

dream! He went to Jerusalem, stood before the ark of the covenant of the Lord, sacrificed burnt offerings and communion offerings, and gave a feast for all his servants.

Solomon's Listening Heart.* 16 Later, two prostitutes came to the king and stood before him. 17 One woman said: "By your leave, my lord, this woman and I live in the same house, and I gave birth in the house while she was present. 18 On the third day after I gave birth, this woman also gave birth. We were alone; no one else was in the house with us; only the two of us were in the house. 19 This woman's son died during the night when she lay on top of him. 20 So in the middle of the night she got up and took my son from my side, as your servant was sleeping. Then she laid him in her bosom and laid her dead son in my bosom. 21 I rose in the morning to nurse my son, and he was dead! But when I examined him in the morning light, I saw it was not the son I had borne." 22 The other woman answered, "No! The living one is my son, the dead one is yours." But the first kept saying, "No! the dead one is your son, the living one is mine!" Thus they argued before the king. 23 Then the king said: "One woman claims, 'This, the living one, is my son, the dead one is yours.' The other answers, 'No! The dead one is your son, the living one is mine.' " 24 The king continued, "Get me a sword." When they brought the sword before the king, 25 he said, "Cut the living child in two, and give half to one woman and half to the other." 26* The woman whose son was alive, because she was stirred with compassion for her son, said to the king, "Please, my lord, give her the living baby—do not kill it!" But the other said, "It shall be neither mine nor yours. Cut it in two!" 27 The king then answered, "Give her the living baby! Do not kill it! She is the mother." 28 When all Israel heard the judgment the king had given, they were in awe of him, because they saw that the king had in him the wisdom of God for giving right judgment.

CHAPTER 4

See RG 186

Solomon's Riches: Domestic Affairs.* 1 Solomon was king over all Israel, 2 and these were the officials he had in his service:

Azariah, son of Zadok, the priest;
3 Elihoreph and Ahijah, sons of Shisha, scribes;
Jehoshaphat, son of Ahilud, the chancellor;
4 Benaiah, son of Jehoiada, in charge of the army;
Zadok and Abiathar, priests;
5 Azariah, son of Nathan, in charge of the governors;
Zabud, son of Nathan, priest and companion to the king;
6 Ahishar, master of the palace; and
Adoniram, son of Abda, in charge of the forced labor.

7* Solomon had twelve governors over all Israel who supplied food for the king and his household, each having to provide for one month in the year. 8 Their names were:*

the son of Hur in the hill country of Ephraim;
9 the son of Deker in Makaz, Shaalbim, Beth-shemesh, and Elon Beth-hanan;
10 the son of Hesed in Arubboth, as well as in Socoh and the whole region of Hepher;

3:16–5:14 The fourth major unit of the Solomon story shows how Solomon used the three gifts that the Lord gave him in 3:12–13: a listening heart (3:16–28), riches (4:1–5:8), universal renown (5:9–14). In each case his gifts benefited the populace, from the lowest classes (3:16–28) to his whole people (4:20; 5:5) to the whole world (5:9–14). Compare 9:26–10:29, where the same three gifts all redound to the benefit of Solomon himself.

3:26–27 The true mother reveals herself by an uncommon and tender word for the child, "baby." With this, and the woman's willingness to give up her child, Solomon realizes that she is the true mother, and quotes her words exactly in rendering his judgment.

4:1–5:8 The sub-unit on Solomon's riches is organized around domestic affairs (4:1–20) and international affairs (5:1–5), with a short appendix on Solomon's horses and chariots (5:6–8). Compare 9:26–10:29, where comparable elements reappear.

4:7–19 The administration of the kingdom thus initiated by Solomon continued in its main features for the duration of the monarchy in Israel and Judah. Note the use of "all Israel" to mean only the northern tribes (see also 5:27). Solomon's exactions did not fall evenly on the whole people, but favored his own southern tribe of Judah. Eventually this inequity would lead to the dissolution of the union of Israel and Judah (12:1–19).

4:8–19 Several of the governors are identified only by their fathers' names.

Solomon's Twelve Administrative Districts

11 the son of Abinadab, in all Naphath-dor;
he was married to Taphath, Solomon's
daughter;
12 Baana, son of Ahilud, in Taanach and
Megiddo and all Beth-shean near
Zarethan below Jezreel, from Beth-
shean to Abel-meholah to beyond
Jokmeam;
13 the son of Geber in Ramoth-gilead,
having charge of the villages of Jair,
son of Manasseh, in Gilead; and of the
district of Argob in Bashan—sixty
large walled cities with gates barred
with bronze;
14 Ahinadab, son of Iddo, in Mahanaim;
15 Ahimaaz, in Naphtali; he was married to
Basemath, another daughter of
Solomon;
16 Baana, son of Hushai, in Asher and Aloth;
17 Jehoshaphat, son of Paruah, in Issachar;
18 Shimei, son of Ela, in Benjamin;
19 Geber, son of Uri, in the land of Gilead,
the land of Sihon, king of the
Amorites, and of Og, king of Bashan.

There was one governor besides, in the
land of Judah.* 20p Judah and Israel were as
numerous as the sands by the sea; they ate
and drank and rejoiced.

CHAPTER 5

See RG 186

Solomon's Riches: International Af-
fairs. 1* Solomon ruled over all the kingdoms from the River* to the land of the Philistines, down to the border of Egypt; they
paid Solomon tribute and served him as long
as he lived. 2* Solomon's provisions for each
day were thirty kors of fine flour, sixty kors
of meal, 3ten fatted oxen, twenty pasture-fed
oxen, and a hundred sheep, not counting
harts, gazelles, roebucks, and fatted fowl.
4He had dominion over all the land west of
the River, from Tiphsah to Gaza, and all its
kings, and he had peace on all his borders
round about. 5q Thus Judah and Israel lived
in security, everyone under their own vine
and fig tree from Dan to Beer-sheba, as long
as Solomon lived.

Solomon's Riches: Chariots and Horses.
6r Solomon had forty thousand stalls for
horses for chariots and twelve thousand
horsemen. 7* The governors, one for each
month, provided food for King Solomon and
for all the guests at King Solomon's table.
They left nothing unprovided. 8For the chariot horses and draft animals also, each
brought his quota of barley and straw to the
required place.

Solomon's Renown. 9s Moreover, God
gave Solomon wisdom, exceptional understanding, and knowledge, as vast as the sand
on the seashore. 10Solomon's wisdom surpassed that of all the peoples of the East and
all the wisdom of Egypt. 11He was wiser than
anyone else—wiser than Ethan the Ezrahite,
or Heman, Chalcol, and Darda, the musicians—and his fame spread throughout the
neighboring peoples. 12Solomon also uttered
three thousand proverbs, and his songs numbered a thousand and five. 13He spoke of
plants, from the cedar on Lebanon to the hyssop growing out of the wall, and he spoke
about beasts, birds, reptiles, and fishes.
14t People from all nations came to hear Solomon's wisdom, sent by all the kings of the
earth who had heard of his wisdom.

*Preparations for the Temple.** 15When Hiram, king of Tyre, heard that Solomon had

4:19 One governor . . . land of Judah: the royal territory of Judah had its own peculiar administration different from that of the twelve northern districts, each of which had to supply the king and his household with a month's provisions of food each year (v. 7).

5:1–32 This translation follows the numeration of the Hebrew Bible, rather than the Vulgate; in many English translations, 5:1–14 is 4:21–34, and 5:15 is 5:1.

5:1 The River: that is, the Euphrates. This claim may be exaggerated, but "from the Euphrates to the border of Egypt" was the traditional description of the extent of the Davidic holdings.

5:2 The list of Solomon's supplies may have originally belonged with the list of governors in 4:7–19, but the author has placed it here to imply that Solomon's vassal kingdoms, not his own citizenry, supplied his vast daily needs. The daily provisions listed could have supported several thousand people. **Kors**: see note on Ez 45:14.

5:7 This verse suggests that the governors also saw to the provender for Solomon's animals (v. 8).

5:15–32 The fifth major unit of the Solomon story explains the preparations Solomon made for the construction of the Temple. He negotiates with Hiram of Tyre for materiel

p: Gn 22:17; 32:13; Dn 3:36; Hos 1:10; Heb 11:12. *q:* Sir 47:13. *r:* 1 Kgs 10:26; Dt 17:16; 2 Chr 1:14; 9:25. *s:* Sir 47:15–17. *t:* 1 Kgs 10:1.

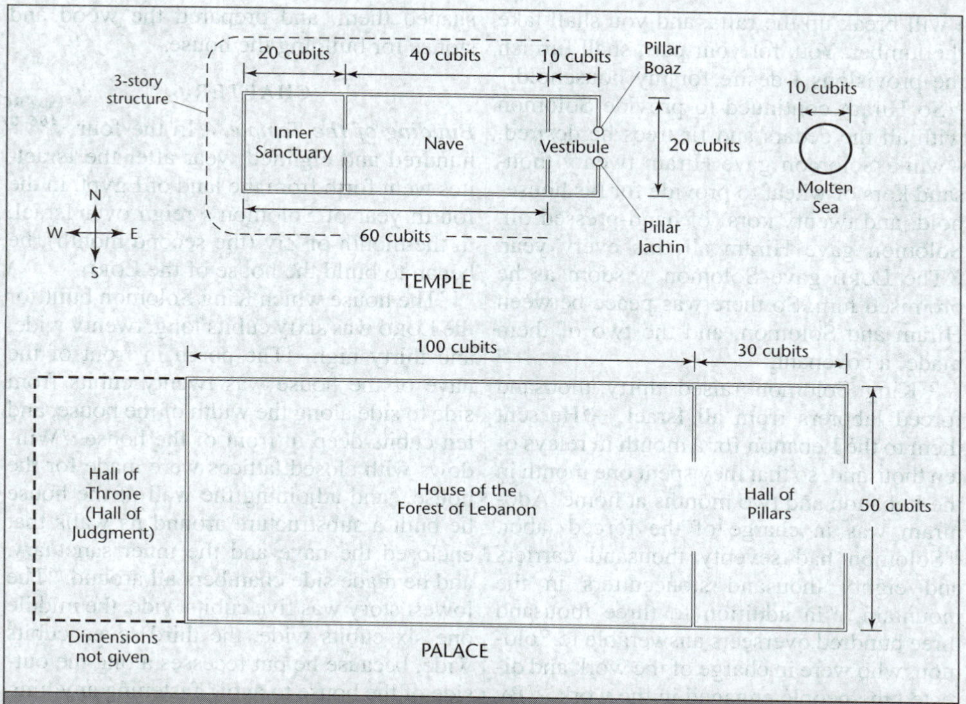

The Temple and Palace of Solomon

been anointed king in place of his father, he
sent an embassy to him; for Hiram had always been David's friend.* 16Solomon sent
back this message to Hiram: 17u "You know
that David my father, because of the wars
that beset him, could not build a house for
the name of the LORD his God until such
time as the LORD should put his enemies under the soles of his feet. 18But now the LORD,
my God, has given me rest on all sides, without adversary or misfortune. 19v So I intend
to build a house for the name of the LORD,
my God, as the LORD said to David my father: Your son whom I will put upon your
throne in your place shall build the house for
my name. 20Give orders, then, to have cedars
from the Lebanon cut down for me. My servants shall accompany yours, and I will pay
you whatever you say for your servants'
wages. For you know that there is no one
among us who is skilled in cutting timber
like the Sidonians." 21When Hiram had
heard the words of Solomon, he was overjoyed, and said, "Blessed be the LORD this
day, who has given David a wise son over
this numerous people." 22* Hiram then sent
word to Solomon, "I have heard the proposal
you sent me, and I will provide all the cedars
and fir trees you desire. 23My servants shall
bring them down from the Lebanon to the
sea, and I will arrange them into rafts in the
sea and bring them wherever you say. There

(5:15–26), and conscripts a labor force for personnel (5:27–32). Compare 9:11–23, which returns to the same two themes after the Temple has been built and dedicated. 2 Chr 2:1–17 presents another version of the same material.

5:15 David's friend: the term "to be a friend," lit., "to love," is political, and means that David and Hiram had been allies. The purpose of Hiram's embassy is to determine whether Solomon is willing to continue the alliance. This unspoken agenda lies behind the negotiations about materials for the Temple, as the concluding v. 26 makes clear.

5:22–23 Although his reply is couched in polite, diplomatic language, Hiram renegotiates Solomon's terms in his own favor. No Israelites are to enter Tyrian territory, and Solomon is not to pay the salary of Hiram's laborers but rather to furnish "provisions" for his household—the same language used of the tribute Solomon received from his own vassals in v. 2.

u: 2 Sm 7:5–7; 1 Chr 22:7–8. *v:* 2 Sm 7:12–13.

I will break up the rafts, and you shall take the lumber. You, for your part, shall furnish the provisions I desire for my household." 24So Hiram continued to provide Solomon with all the cedars and fir trees he desired, 25while Solomon gave Hiram twenty thousand kors of wheat to provide for his household, and twenty kors* of hand-pressed oil. Solomon gave Hiram all this every year. 26The LORD gave Solomon wisdom as he promised him. So there was peace between Hiram and Solomon, and the two of them made* a covenant.

27King Solomon raised thirty thousand forced laborers from all Israel.* 28He sent them to the Lebanon for a month in relays of ten thousand, so that they spent one month in the Lebanon and two months at home. Adoniram was in charge of the forced labor. 29Solomon had seventy thousand carriers and eighty thousand stonecutters in the mountain, 30in addition to three thousand three hundred overseers answerable to Solomon, who were in charge of the work and directed the people engaged in the work. 31By order of the king, fine, large blocks of stone were quarried to give the house a foundation of hewn stone. 32Solomon's and Hiram's builders, along with others from Gebal,* shaped them, and prepared the wood and stones for building the house.

CHAPTER 6

See RG 186–87

*Building of the Temple.** 1In the four hundred and eightieth year after the Israelites went forth from the land of Egypt, in the fourth year of Solomon's reign over Israel, in the month of Ziv (the second month), he began to build the house of the LORD.*

2The house which King Solomon built for the LORD was sixty cubits long, twenty wide, and thirty high. 3The porch in front of the nave of the house was twenty cubits from side to side along the width of the house, and ten cubits deep in front of the house. 4Windows with closed lattices were made for the house, 5and adjoining the wall of the house he built a substructure around its walls that enclosed the nave and the inner sanctuary, and he made side chambers all around. 6The lowest story was five cubits wide, the middle one six cubits wide, the third seven cubits wide, because he put recesses along the outside of the house to avoid fastening anything into the walls of the house. 7The house was built of stone dressed at the quarry, so that no hammer or ax, no iron tool, was to be heard in the house during its construction. 8The en-

5:25 Twenty kors: this means about two thousand gallons of the finest olive oil available, hand-pressed rather than produced in large olive presses, so that no debris (such as crushed olive pits, powder from the grinding stones) would contaminate the oil. Also see note on 2 Chr 2:9.

5:26 Made: lit., "cut." The story of Solomon's arrangements with Hiram is framed by references to political alliance between Israel and Tyre (vv. 15, 26). Since, in Hebrew idiom, Hiram and Solomon "cut" a covenant, this suggests that the agreement they reach for "cutting" wood (which clearly favors Hiram) reflects the terms of the larger treaty.

5:27 All Israel: see note on 4:7–19.

5:32 Gebal: Byblos.

6:1–7:51 The central units of the Solomon story describe the building of the Temple (6:1–7:51) and its dedication ceremony (8:1–9:10). The account of the construction of the Temple ("the house") is organized to give the reader a guided tour. Approaching from a distance, we see ground plans (6:2–3) and structural work in stone (6:4–8) and wood (6:9–10). After a brief interruption that recounts a divine word to Solomon (6:11–13), we enter the Temple to view the paneling and ornamentation of the nave (6:14–18), the gilded walls and golden entrance of the inner sanctuary or holy of holies (6:19–22), with its priceless interior decoration and furnishings (6:23–28). As we leave, we admire the interior carvings and gilded floor of the inner sanctuary (6:29–30), return to the nave through carved and gilded doors (6:31–32), and exit from the nave through another set of carved and gilded doors (6:33–35) to the courtyard (6:36). Our guide briefly points out the nearby palace complex (7:1–12); then we walk around the courtyard to marvel at Hiram's heroic works in bronze: the two columns (7:15–22), the "sea" (7:23–26), and the ten stands and basins set along either side of the Temple buildings (7:27–39). The account ends with the smaller bronze vessels Hiram made for the Temple services (7:40–47) and the gold vessels that Solomon made (7:48–50). Unfortunately, several factors make it impossible to use the account to produce a satisfactory model of Solomon's Temple. Throughout the account there are numerous technical architectural terms whose meaning is lost to us; and it is moreover likely that the author is describing the Temple as it stood in his own time, centuries after Solomon's day. The Chronicler also describes the construction of the Temple in 2 Chr 3:1–4:22 and its dedication in 2 Chr 5:1–7:22.

6:1 Construction of the Temple is here dated in relation to the traditional date of the exodus from Egypt, rounded off to a conventional twelve generations of forty years each. This chronology means that the Temple was built approximately midway between Israel's two foundational deliverances, the exodus and the return from the Babylonian exile. The schematization of history implied in these figures recommends caution in using them for historical reconstruction.

trance to the middle story was on the south side of the house; stairs led up to the middle story and from the middle story to the third. [9]When he had finished building the house, it was roofed in with rafters and boards of cedar. [10]He built the substructure five cubits high all along the outside of the house, to which it was joined by cedar beams.

[11]The word of the LORD came to Solomon: [12][w] As to this house you are building—if you walk in my statutes, carry out my ordinances, and observe all my commands, walking in them, I will fulfill toward you my word which I spoke to David your father. [13]I will dwell in the midst of the Israelites and will not forsake my people Israel.

[14]When Solomon finished building the house, [15]its inside walls were lined with cedar paneling: he covered the interior with wood from floor to ceiling, and he covered its floor with fir planking. [16]At the rear of the house a space of twenty cubits was set off by cedar panels from the floor to the ceiling, enclosing the inner sanctuary, the holy of holies. [17]The house was forty cubits long, that is, the nave, the part in front. [18]The cedar in the interior of the house was carved in the form of gourds and open flowers; all was of cedar, and no stone was to be seen.

[19]In the innermost part of the house* he set up the inner sanctuary to house the ark of the LORD's covenant. [20]In front of the inner sanctuary (it was twenty cubits long, twenty wide, and twenty high, and he covered it with pure gold), he made an altar of cedar. [21]Solomon covered the interior of the house with pure gold, and he drew golden chains across in front of the inner sanctuary, and covered it with gold. [22]He covered the whole house with gold, until the whole house was done, and the whole altar that belonged to the inner sanctuary he covered with gold. [23]In the inner sanctuary he made two cherubim, each ten cubits high, made of pine. [24]Each wing of a cherub was five cubits so that the span from wing tip to wing tip was ten cubits. [25]The second cherub was also ten cubits: the two cherubim were identical in size and shape; [26]the first cherub was ten cubits high, and so was the second. [27]He placed the cherubim in the inmost part of the house; the wings of the cherubim were spread wide, so that one wing of the first touched the side wall and the wing of the second touched the other wall; the wings pointing to the middle of the room touched each other. [28]He overlaid the cherubim with gold.

[29]The walls of the house on all sides of both the inner and the outer rooms had carved figures of cherubim, palm trees, and open flowers. [30]The floor of the house of both the inner and the outer rooms was overlaid with gold. [31]At the entrance of the inner sanctuary, doors of pine were made; the doorframes had five-sided posts. [32]The two doors were of pine, with carved figures of cherubim, palm trees, and open flowers. The doors were overlaid with gold, and the cherubim and the palm trees were also covered with beaten gold. [33]He did the same at the entrance to the nave, where the doorposts were of pine and were four-sided. [34]The two doors were of fir wood, each door consisting of two panels hinged together; [35]and he carved cherubim, palm trees, and open flowers, and plated them with gold. [36]He walled off the inner court with three courses of hewn stones and one course of cedar beams.

[37]The foundations of the LORD's house were laid in the month of Ziv in the fourth year, [38]and it was finished, in all particulars, exactly according to plan, in the month of Bul, the eighth month, in the eleventh year. Thus Solomon built it in seven years.

CHAPTER 7

See RG 187

[1]* [x] To finish the building of his own house Solomon took thirteen years. [2]He built

6:19 The innermost part of the house: the inner sanctuary or holy of holies reserved exclusively for the Lord, enthroned upon the cherubim over the ark of the covenant (2 Chr 3:10–13). See note on Ex 25:18–20.

7:1–12 The account of Solomon's building of the Temple (the Lord's "house") is interrupted by an account of his building of the palace (Solomon's "house"), which contained also the main buildings of public administration. The passage is anachronistic, since 6:38–7:1 and 9:10 imply that the palace was not begun until the Temple was completed. By placing the account here, the narrator highlights the fact that Solomon spent almost twice as long on his own "house" as on the Lord's.

w: 2 Sm 7:13–16. *x:* 1 Kgs 9:10.

the House of the Forest of Lebanon one hundred cubits long, fifty wide, and thirty high; it was supported by four rows of cedar columns, with cedar beams upon the columns. [3]Moreover, it had a ceiling of cedar above the rafters resting on the columns; these rafters numbered forty-five, fifteen to a row. [4]There were lattices in three rows, each row facing the next, [5]and all the openings and doorposts were squared with lintels, each facing across from the next. [6]He also made the Porch of Columns, fifty cubits long and thirty wide. The porch extended across the front, and there were columns with a canopy in front of them. [7]He also made the Porch of the Throne where he gave judgment—that is, the Porch of Judgment; it was paneled with cedar from floor to ceiling beams. [8][y] The house in which he lived was in another court, set in deeper than the Porch and of the same construction. (Solomon made a house like this Porch for Pharaoh's daughter, whom he had married.)* [9]All these buildings were of fine stones, hewn to size and trimmed front and back with a saw, from the foundation to the bonding course and outside as far as the great court. [10]The foundation was made of fine, large blocks, some ten cubits and some eight cubits. [11]Above were fine stones hewn to size, and cedar wood. [12]The great court had three courses of hewn stones all around and a course of cedar beams. So also were the inner court of the house of the LORD and its porch.

[13]King Solomon brought Hiram* from Tyre. [14]He was a bronze worker, the son of a widow from the tribe of Naphtali; his father had been from Tyre. He was endowed with wisdom, understanding, and knowledge for doing any work in bronze. He came to King Solomon and did all his metal work.

[15]* [z] He fashioned two bronze columns, each eighteen cubits high and twelve cubits in circumference. [16]He also made two capitals cast in bronze, to be placed on top of the columns, each of them five cubits high. [17]There were meshes made like netting and braid made like chains for the capitals on top of the columns, seven for each capital. [18]* He also cast pomegranates, two rows around each netting to cover the capital on top of the columns. [19]The capitals on top of the columns (in the porch) were made like lilies, four cubits high. [20]And the capitals on the two columns, both above and adjoining the bulge where it crossed out of the netting, had two hundred pomegranates in rows around each capital. [21]He set up the columns at the temple porch; one he set up to the south, and called it Jachin, and the other to the north, and called it Boaz.* [22]The top of the columns was made like a lily. Thus the work on the columns was completed.

[23]Then he made the molten sea;* it was made with a circular rim, and measured ten cubits across, five in height, and thirty in circumference. [24]Under the brim, gourds encircled it for ten cubits around the compass of the sea; the gourds were in two rows and were cast in one mold with the sea. [25]This rested on twelve oxen, three facing north, three facing west, three facing south, and three facing east, with their haunches all toward the center; upon them was set the sea. [26]It was a handbreadth thick, and its brim resembled that of a cup, being lily-shaped. Its capacity was two thousand baths.*

[27]He also made ten stands of bronze, each

7:8 Solomon did not build the house for Pharaoh's daughter until Temple and palace were finished (3:1). By mentioning this marriage, the narrator keeps before the reader a developing theme in the Solomon story: the king's building activities for his foreign wives, which eventually implicate him in idolatry (3:1; 7:8; 9:24; 11:1–8).

7:13 Hiram: a craftsman, not the king of Tyre (5:15–26).

7:15 The two bronze columns were called Jachin and Boaz (v. 21; also 2 Chr 3:17); the significance of the names is unclear. The columns stood to the right and left of the Temple porch, and may have been intended to mark the entrance to the building as the entrance to God's private dwelling. Their extraordinary size and elaborate decoration would have made them the most impressive parts of the Temple visible to the ordinary viewer, who was not permitted into the nave, let alone into the innermost sanctuary. According to Jer 52:21, the columns were hollow, the bronze exterior being "four fingers thick."

7:18–20 The Hebrew text is corrupt in many places here, and alternative readings attested in the ancient versions are secondary attempts to make sense of the text. A clearer description of the columns and their decoration is found in vv. 41–42.

7:21 Jachin . . . Boaz: see note on 7:15.

7:23–26 The molten sea: this was a large circular tank containing about twelve thousand gallons of water.

7:26 Baths: see note on Is 5:10.

y: 1 Kgs 3:1; 9:24. *z:* Jer 52:21–23.

four cubits long, four wide, and three high. [28]When these stands were constructed, panels were set within the framework. [29]On the panels within the frames there were lions, oxen, and cherubim; and on the frames likewise, above and below the lions and oxen, there were wreaths in hammered relief. [30]Each stand had four bronze wheels and bronze axles. The four legs of each stand had cast braces, which were under the basin; they had wreaths on each side. [31]The mouth of the basin was inside, and a cubit above, the crown, whose opening was round, made like a receptacle, a cubit and a half in depth. There was carved work at the opening, on panels that were square, not circular. [32]The four wheels were below the paneling, and the axletrees of the wheels and the stand were of one piece. Each wheel was a cubit and a half high. [33]The wheels were constructed like chariot wheels; their axletrees, rims, spokes, and hubs were all cast. [34]The four braces reached the four corners of each stand, and formed part of the stand. [35]At the top of the stand there was a raised collar half a cubit high, and the handles and panels on top of the stand formed part of it. [36]On the flat ends of the handles and on the panels, wherever there was a bare space, cherubim, lions, and palm trees were carved, as well as wreaths all around. [37]This was how he made the ten stands, all of the same casting, the same size, the same shape. [38]He made ten bronze basins, each four cubits in diameter with a capacity of forty baths, one basin atop each of the ten stands.

[39]He placed the stands, five on the south side of the house and five on the north. The sea he placed off to the southeast from the south side of the house.

[40]When Hiram had made the pots, shovels, and bowls, he finished all his work for King Solomon in the house of the LORD: [41]two columns; two nodes for the capitals on top of the columns; two pieces of netting covering the two nodes for the capitals on top of the columns; [42]four hundred pomegranates in double rows on both pieces of netting that covered the two nodes of the capitals on top of the columns; [43]ten stands; ten basins on the stands; [44]one sea; twelve oxen supporting the sea; [45]pots, shovels, and bowls. All these articles which Hiram made for King Solomon in the house of the LORD were of burnished bronze. [46]The king had them cast in the neighborhood of the Jordan, between Succoth and Zarethan, in thick clay molds. [47]Solomon did not weigh all the articles because they were so numerous; the weight of the bronze, therefore, was not determined.

[48]Solomon made all the articles that were for the house of the LORD: the golden altar; the table on which the showbread lay; [49]the lampstands of pure gold, five to the right and five to the left before the inner sanctuary; their flowers, lamps, and tongs of gold; [50]basins, snuffers, bowls, cups, and firepans of pure gold; hinges of gold for the doors of the innermost part of the house, or holy of holies, and for the doors of the outer room, the nave. [51][a] When all the work undertaken by King Solomon in the house of the LORD was completed,* he brought in the votive offerings of his father David, and put the silver, gold, and other articles in the treasuries of the house of the LORD.

CHAPTER 8

See RG 187

*Dedication of the Temple.** [1]Then Solomon assembled the elders of Israel and all the heads of the tribes, the princes in the ancestral houses of the Israelites. They came to King Solomon in Jerusalem, to bring up the ark of the LORD's covenant from the city of David (which is Zion). [2]All the people of Israel assembled before King Solomon dur-

7:51 The account of the Temple's construction has been punctuated by references to "building" (*banah*) or "finishing" (*killah*) it (6:1b, 9a, 14, 38; 7:40). Here, at the end of the account, the narrator uses a different verb for its "completion," *shillem*, which allows him to play on the name of Solomon (*shelomo*).

8:1–66 The account of the Temple's dedication ceremony is organized concentrically: Solomon gathers the assembly (vv. 1–13), blesses it (vv. 14–21), utters a long dedicatory prayer (vv. 22–53), blesses the assembly again (vv. 54–61), and dismisses it (vv. 62–66). To this account is appended an appearance of the Lord to Solomon (9:2–9) that balances the divine word to Solomon in the account of the Temple's construction (6:11–13).

a: 2 Sm 8:9–12.

ing the festival in the month of Ethanim (the seventh month).* 3 When all the elders of Israel had arrived, the priests took up the ark; 4 and they brought up the ark of the LORD and the tent of meeting with all the sacred vessels that were in the tent. The priests and Levites brought them up. 5 King Solomon and the entire community of Israel, gathered for the occasion before the ark, sacrificed sheep and oxen too many to number or count. 6* The priests brought the ark of the covenant of the LORD to its place, the inner sanctuary of the house, the holy of holies, beneath the wings of the cherubim. 7 The cherubim had their wings spread out over the place of the ark, sheltering the ark and its poles from above. 8[b] The poles were so long that their ends could be seen from the holy place in front of the inner sanctuary. They cannot be seen from outside, but they remain there to this day. 9[c] There was nothing in the ark but the two stone tablets which Moses had put there at Horeb, when the LORD made a covenant with the Israelites after they went forth from the land of Egypt. 10[d] When the priests left the holy place, the cloud filled the house of the LORD 11 so that the priests could no longer minister because of the cloud, since the glory of the LORD had filled the house of the LORD. 12*[e] Then Solomon said,

"The LORD intends to dwell in the dark
cloud;
13 I have indeed built you a princely house,
the base for your enthronement
forever."

14 The king turned and blessed the whole assembly of Israel, while the whole assembly of Israel stood. 15 He said: "Blessed be the LORD, the God of Israel, who with his own mouth spoke a promise to David my father and by his hand fulfilled it, saying: 16[f] Since the day I brought my people Israel out of Egypt, I have not chosen a city out of any tribe of Israel for the building of a house, that my name might be there; but I have chosen David to rule my people Israel. 17 When David my father wished to build a house for the name of the LORD, the God of Israel, 18 the LORD said to him: In wishing to build a house for my name, you did well. 19 But it is not you who will build the house, but your son, who comes from your loins; he shall build the house for my name. 20 Now the LORD has fulfilled the word he spoke: I have succeeded David my father, and I sit on the throne of Israel, as the LORD has spoken, and I have built this house for the name of the LORD, the God of Israel. 21 I have provided there a place for the ark in which is the covenant of the LORD that he made with our ancestors when he brought them out of the land of Egypt."

Solomon's Prayer. 22 Solomon stood before the altar of the LORD in the presence of the whole assembly of Israel, and stretching forth his hands toward heaven, 23 he said, "LORD, God of Israel, there is no God like you in heaven above or on earth below; you keep covenant and love toward your servants who walk before you with their whole heart, 24 the covenant that you kept toward your servant, David my father, what you promised him;

8:2 "The seventh month" ("Ethanim" in the Canaanite calendar) corresponded to late September/early October. The great festival at that time of year is the feast of Booths, or Succoth/Sukkoth (see Lv 23:33–43; Dt 16:13–15). The feast was important enough to warrant holding the dedication ceremony either a month before or eleven months after the Temple was completed in the eighth month (6:38).

8:6–9 The transfer of the ark of the covenant into the newly constructed Temple building, God's act of possession (8:10–13), and Solomon's dedicatory prayer and sacrifices constituted the Temple's solemn dedication and made of it the place of God's presence in the midst of Israel for which David had hoped (2 Sm 6:12–15; 7:1–3). Later God expresses approval of the Temple with an oracle (1 Kgs 9:3–9).

8:12–13 This brief poem is rich in layered meanings. The "dark cloud" in which the Lord intends to dwell refers not only to the cloud that filled the Temple (v. 10) but to the darkness of the windowless holy of holies and to the mystery of the God enthroned invisibly upon the cherubim as well. Solomon calls the Temple he offers God a firm base, using terminology similar to that used for God's firm establishment of Solomon's own kingdom (2:12, 46). Finally, Solomon intends this as a place for God to *yashab*, but the Hebrew word *yashab* can mean "to dwell" or "to sit." In other words, the Temple can be understood both as a place where God resides and as the earthly foundation of God's heavenly throne. The double meaning allows an understanding of the divine presence as both transcendent and graciously immanent. See Solomon's sentiments in 8:27, and the frequent reference in 8:30–52 to God's hearing in heaven prayers that were offered in or toward the Temple.

b: Ex 25:13–15. *c:* Ex 25:16; 34:27–28; Dt 10:5; Heb 9:4. *d:* Ex 13:21; 40:34–38. *e:* Ex 20:21; Dt 4:11; 5:22; Ps 97:2. *f:* 2 Sm 7:5–8, 12–13.

your mouth has spoken and your hand has fulfilled this very day. [25g] And now, LORD, God of Israel, keep toward your servant, David my father, what you promised: There shall never be wanting someone from your line to sit before me on the throne of Israel, provided that your descendants keep to their way, walking before me as you have. [26]Now, God of Israel, may the words you spoke to your servant, David my father, be confirmed.

[27]"Is God indeed to dwell on earth? If the heavens and the highest heavens cannot contain you, how much less this house which I have built! [28]Regard kindly the prayer and petition of your servant, LORD, my God, and listen to the cry of supplication which I, your servant, utter before you this day. [29]May your eyes be open night and day toward this house, the place of which you said, My name shall be there; listen to the prayer your servant makes toward this place. [30]Listen to the petition of your servant and of your people Israel which they offer toward this place. Listen, from the place of your enthronement, heaven, listen and forgive.

[31h] "If someone sins in some way against a neighbor and is required to take an oath sanctioned by a curse, and comes and takes the oath before your altar in this house, [32]listen in heaven; act and judge your servants. Condemn the wicked, requiting their ways; acquit the just, rewarding their justice.

[33]"When your people Israel are defeated by an enemy because they sinned against you, and then they return to you, praise your name, pray to you, and entreat you in this house, [34]listen in heaven and forgive the sin of your people Israel, and bring them back to the land you gave their ancestors.

[35]"When the heavens are closed, so that there is no rain, because they have sinned against you, but they pray toward this place and praise your name, and turn from their sin because you have afflicted them, [36]listen in heaven and forgive the sin of your servants, your people Israel (for you teach them the good way in which they should walk). Give rain to this land of yours which you have given to your people as their heritage.

[37]"If there is famine in the land or pestilence; or if blight comes, or mildew, or locusts, or caterpillars; if an enemy of your people presses upon them in the land and at their gates; whatever plague or sickness there may be; [38]whatever prayer or petition any may make, any of your people Israel, who know heartfelt remorse and stretch out their hands toward this house, [39]listen in heaven, the place of your enthronement; forgive and take action. Render to each and all according to their ways, you who know every heart; for it is you alone who know the heart of every human being. [40]So may they revere you as long as they live on the land you gave our ancestors.

[41]"To the foreigners, likewise, who are not of your people Israel, but who come from a distant land for the sake of your name [42](since people will hear of your great name and your mighty hand and your outstretched arm), when they come and pray toward this house, [43]listen in heaven, the place of your enthronement. Do all that the foreigner asks of you, that all the peoples of the earth may know your name, may revere you as do your people Israel, and may know that your name has been invoked upon this house that I have built.

[44]"When your people go out to war against their enemies, by whatever way you send them, and they pray to the LORD toward the city you have chosen and the house I have built for your name, [45]listen in heaven to their prayer and petition, and uphold their cause.

[46i] "When they sin against you (for there is no one who does not sin), and in your anger against them you deliver them to an enemy, so that their captors carry them off to the land of the enemy, far or near, [47]and they have a change of heart in the land of their captivity and they turn and entreat you in the land of their captors and say, 'We have sinned and done wrong; we have been wicked'; [48]if with their whole heart and soul they turn back to you in the land of their enemies who took them captive, and pray to you toward the land you gave their ancestors, the city you have chosen, and the house I have built for your name, [49]listen in heaven, your dwelling place, to their prayer

g: 1 Kgs 2:4; 9:5; 2 Sm 7:14–16; Jer 33:17. *h:* Ex 22:6–10. *i:* Eccl 7:20; 1 Jn 1:8.

and petition, and uphold their cause. [50]Forgive your people who have sinned against you and all the offenses they have committed against you, and grant them mercy in the sight of their captors, so that these will be merciful to them. [51]For they are your people and your heritage, whom you brought out of Egypt, from the midst of the iron furnace.

[52]"Thus may your eyes be open to the petition of your servant and to the petition of your people Israel; thus may you listen to them whenever they call upon you. [53]For you have set them apart from all the peoples of the earth to be your heritage, as you declared through Moses your servant when you brought our ancestors out of Egypt, Lord my GOD."

[54]After Solomon finished offering this entire prayer and petition to the LORD, he rose from before the altar of the LORD, where he had been kneeling, hands outstretched toward heaven. [55]He stood and blessed the whole assembly of Israel, saying in a loud voice: [56]"Blessed be the LORD who has given rest to his people Israel, just as he promised. Not a single word has gone unfulfilled of the entire gracious promise he made through Moses his servant. [57]May the LORD, our God, be with us as he was with our ancestors and may he not forsake us nor cast us off. [58]May he draw our hearts to himself, that we may walk in his ways and keep the commands, statutes, and ordinances that he enjoined on our ancestors. [59]May these words of mine, the petition I have offered before the LORD, our God, be present to the LORD our God day and night, that he may uphold the cause of his servant and the cause of his people Israel as each day requires, [60]so that all the peoples of the earth may know that the LORD is God and there is no other. [61*] Your heart must be wholly devoted to the LORD, our God, observing his statutes and keeping his commandments, as on this day."

[62]The king and all Israel with him offered sacrifices before the LORD. [63*] Solomon offered as communion offerings to the LORD twenty-two thousand oxen and one hundred twenty thousand sheep. Thus the king and all the Israelites dedicated the house of the LORD. [64]On that day the king consecrated the middle of the court facing the house of the LORD; he offered there the burnt offerings, the grain offerings, and the fat of the communion offerings, because the bronze altar before the LORD was too small to hold the burnt offering, the grain offering, and the fat of the communion offering. [65]On this occasion Solomon and all Israel with him, a great assembly from Lebo-hamath to the Wadi of Egypt, celebrated the festival before the LORD, our God, for seven days. [66]On the eighth day he dismissed the people, who blessed the king and went to their tents, rejoicing and glad of heart because of all the blessings the LORD had given to David his servant and to his people Israel.

CHAPTER 9

See RG 187–88

Promise and Warning to Solomon. [1]After Solomon finished building the house of the LORD, the house of the king, and everything else that he wanted to do, [2][j] the LORD appeared to Solomon a second time, as he had appeared to him in Gibeon. [3]The LORD said to him: I have heard the prayer of petition which you offered in my presence. I have consecrated this house which you have built and I set my name there forever; my eyes and my heart shall be there always. [4]As for you, if you walk before me as David your father did, wholeheartedly and uprightly, doing all that I have commanded you, keeping my statutes and ordinances, [5][k] I will establish your royal throne over Israel forever, as I promised David your father: There shall never be wanting someone from your line on the throne of Israel. [6]But if ever you and your descendants turn from following me, fail to keep my commandments and statutes which I set before you, and proceed to serve other gods and bow down to them, [7]I will cut off Israel from the land I gave them and repudiate the house I have consecrated for my name. Israel shall become a proverb and a byword among all

8:61 In urging the people to be "wholly devoted" (*shalem*), Solomon plays on his own name (*shelomo*), as if to imply that he himself exemplifies perfect fidelity to God.

8:63 "Communion offerings" (*shelamim*) is another wordplay on the name of Solomon.

j: 1 Kgs 3:4–15; 6:11–13; 11:9–13. *k:* 2 Sm 7:16.

nations, [8l] and this house shall become a heap of ruins. Every passerby shall gasp in horror and ask, "Why has the LORD done such things to this land and to this house?" [9]And the answer will come: "Because they abandoned the LORD, their God, who brought their ancestors out of the land of Egypt, and they embraced other gods, bowing down to them and serving them. That is why the LORD has brought upon them all this evil."

After Building the Temple.* [10m] After the twenty years during which Solomon built the two houses, the house of the LORD and the house of the king— [11]Hiram, king of Tyre, supplying Solomon with all the cedar wood, fir wood, and gold he wished, and King Solomon giving Hiram in return twenty cities in the land of Galilee— [12]Hiram left Tyre to see the cities Solomon had given him, but he was not satisfied with them. [13]So he said, "What are these cities you have given me, my brother?"* And he called them the land of Cabul, as they are called to this day. [14]Hiram, however, had sent King Solomon one hundred and twenty talents of gold.*

[15]This is an account of the conscript labor force King Solomon raised in order to build the house of the LORD, his own house, Millo,* the wall of Jerusalem, Hazor, Megiddo, Gezer [16](Pharaoh, king of Egypt, had come up and taken Gezer and, after destroying it by fire and slaying all the Canaanites living in the city, had given it as a farewell gift to his daughter, Solomon's wife; [17]Solomon then rebuilt Gezer), Lower Beth-horon, [18]Baalath, Tamar in the desert of Judah, [19]all his cities for supplies, cities for chariots and cities for cavalry, and whatever Solomon desired to build in Jerusalem, in Lebanon, and in the entire land under his dominion. [20]All the people who were left of the Amorites, Hittites, Perizzites, Hivites, and Jebusites, who were not Israelites— [21]those of their descendants who were left in the land and whom the Israelites had not been able to destroy under the ban—these Solomon conscripted as forced laborers, as they are to this day. [22]But Solomon made none of the Israelites forced laborers, for they were his fighting force, his ministers, commanders, adjutants, chariot officers, and cavalry. [23]There were five hundred fifty overseers answerable to Solomon's governors for the work, directing the people engaged in the work.

[24n] As soon as Pharaoh's daughter went up from the City of David to her house, which he had built for her, Solomon built Millo. [25]Three times a year Solomon used to offer burnt offerings and communion offerings on the altar which he had built to the LORD, and to burn incense before the LORD.

Thus he completed the temple.*

Solomon's Gifts.* [26]King Solomon also built a fleet at Ezion-geber, which is near Elath on the shore of the Red Sea in the land of Edom.* [27]To this fleet Hiram sent his own servants, expert sailors, with the servants of Solomon. [28]They went to Ophir, and obtained four hundred and twenty talents of gold and brought it to King Solomon.

9:10–25 This unit of the Solomon story corresponds to 5:15–32. It comprises the same two themes, negotiations with Hiram of Tyre (vv. 10–14) and use of conscripted labor (vv. 15–23); the last two verses mark the end of the account of Solomon's building projects (vv. 24–25). Chronicles has an incomplete parallel in 2 Chr 8:1–13.

9:13 Brother: a term for a treaty partner; cf. 20:32–33. **Cabul**: the meaning is uncertain; perhaps "of no value."

9:14 The talent was a measure of weight that varied in the course of ancient Israel's history from forty-five to one hundred thirty pounds. This would mean that, at the least, Hiram sent five thousand pounds of gold to Solomon, and the figure may be as much as three times that amount.

9:15 Millo: probably means ground fill, and may refer to an artificial earthwork or platform of stamped ground south of the Temple area. It was begun by David (2 Sm 5:9); cf. 1 Kgs 9:24; 11:27.

9:25 With these words the account of the construction and dedication of the Temple, which began in 6:1, comes to a close. The verb "complete" (*shillem*) is a play on Solomon's name (*shelomo*); see also the note on 7:51.

9:26–10:29 The next major unit of the Solomon story returns to the theme of the three gifts the Lord gave Solomon in 3:12–13: a listening heart (10:1–13), riches (9:26–27; 10:14–22, 26–29), universal renown (10:23–25). In 3:16–5:14, where the same three themes structure the passage, the emphasis was on the benefits these gifts brought to the whole nation; here it is on the luxury they afford to Solomon's own court. The material in 9:26–28; 10:11–12, 22 dealing with Solomon's commercial fleet corresponds to the material on Solomon's international affairs in 5:1–5. Chronicles has a partial parallel to this material in 2 Chr 9:17–28; see also 2 Chr 1:14–17.

l: Dt 29:23; Jer 22:8. *m:* 1 Kgs 6:38–7:1. *n:* 1 Kgs 3:1; 7:8.

See RG 188

CHAPTER 10

*Solomon's Listening Heart: the Queen of Sheba.** [1][o]The queen of Sheba,* having heard a report of Solomon's fame, came to test him with subtle questions. [2]She arrived in Jerusalem with a very numerous retinue, and with camels bearing spices, a large amount of gold, and precious stones. She came to Solomon and spoke to him about everything that she had on her mind. [3]King Solomon explained everything she asked about, and there was nothing so obscure that the king could not explain it to her. [4]When the queen of Sheba witnessed Solomon's great wisdom, the house he had built, [5]the food at his table, the seating of his ministers, the attendance and dress of his waiters, his servers, and the burnt offerings he offered in the house of the LORD, it took her breath away. [6]"The report I heard in my country about your deeds and your wisdom is true," she told the king. [7]"I did not believe the report until I came and saw with my own eyes that not even the half had been told me. Your wisdom and prosperity surpass the report I heard. [8]Happy are your servants, happy these ministers of yours, who stand before you always and listen to your wisdom. [9]Blessed be the LORD, your God, who has been pleased to place you on the throne of Israel. In his enduring love for Israel, the LORD has made you king to carry out judgment and justice." [10]Then she gave the king one hundred and twenty gold talents, a very large quantity of spices, and precious stones. Never again did anyone bring such an abundance of spices as the queen of Sheba gave to King Solomon.

[11]Hiram's fleet, which used to bring gold from Ophir, also brought from there a very large quantity of almug* wood and precious stones. [12]With this wood the king made supports for the house of the LORD and for the house of the king, and harps and lyres for the singers. Never again was any such almug wood brought or seen to the present day.

[13]King Solomon gave the queen of Sheba everything she desired and asked for, besides what King Solomon gave her from Solomon's royal bounty. Then she returned with her servants to her own country.

*Solomon's Riches: Domestic Affairs.** [14][p]The gold that came to Solomon in one year weighed six hundred and sixty-six gold talents, [15]in addition to what came from the tolls on travelers, from the traffic of merchants, and from all the kings of Arabia and the governors of the country. [16][q]King Solomon made two hundred shields of beaten gold (six hundred shekels of gold went into each shield) [17]and three hundred bucklers of beaten gold (three minas of gold went into each buckler); and the king put them in the house of the Forest of Lebanon. [18]The king made a large ivory throne, and overlaid it with refined gold. [19]The throne had six steps, a back with a round top, and an arm on each side of the seat, with two lions standing next to the arms, [20]and twelve other lions standing there on the steps, two to a step, one on either side of each step. Nothing like this was made in any other kingdom. [21]All King Solomon's drinking vessels were gold, and

9:26 Ezion-geber . . . Edom: the first mention of maritime commerce in the Israelite kingdom; Edom was subject after David conquered it; cf. 2 Sm 8:13–14.

10:1–13 The sub-unit on Solomon's wisdom contrasts with 3:16–28. There Solomon's gifts led him to listen to the humblest of his subjects; he accomplished justice and was revered by all his people. Here the emphasis is on his clever speech to a foreign monarch. She is duly impressed by the glory of his court, but it is she, not Solomon, who recalls the monarch's duty of establishing justice (v. 9). The unit is interrupted briefly by a remark about Solomon's maritime commerce (10:11–12).

10:1 Queen of Sheba: women rulers among the Arabs are recorded in eighth-century B.C. Assyrian inscriptions. Sheba was for centuries the leading principality in what is now Yemen.

10:11–12 Almug: the identification of this wood is unknown.

10:14–29 The material on Solomon's riches, like that in 4:1–5:8, is organized around domestic affairs, international affairs, and chariots and horses (see note on 4:1–5:8), but contrasts with that earlier passage. There, Solomon's domestic administration produced prosperity for all Judah and Israel (4:20); here the focus is on the wealth and luxury of Solomon's own palace (10:14–21). There his international hegemony assured peace for all Judah and Israel (5:5); here his maritime ventures simply bring him more and more wealth (9:26–28; 10:11–12, 22). There even his livestock benefited from his prudent administration; here chariotry and horses are just another commodity to be traded (10:26–29).

o: Mt 12:42; Lk 11:31. *p:* Dt 17:17; Sir 47:18. *q:* 1 Kgs 14:26–28; 2 Sm 8:7.

all the utensils in the house of the Forest of Lebanon were pure gold. There was no silver, for in Solomon's time silver was reckoned as nothing. [22]For the king had a fleet of Tarshish ships* at sea with Hiram's fleet. Once every three years the fleet of Tarshish ships would come with a cargo of gold, silver, ivory, apes, and peacocks.

Solomon's Renown. [23]Thus King Solomon surpassed all the kings of the earth in riches and wisdom. [24]And the whole world sought audience with Solomon, to hear the wisdom God had put into his heart. [25]They all brought their yearly tribute: vessels of silver and gold, garments, weapons, spices, horses and mules—what was due each year.

Solomon's Riches: Chariots and Horses. [26r] Solomon amassed chariots and horses; he had one thousand four hundred chariots and twelve thousand horses; these he allocated among the chariot cities and to the king's service in Jerusalem. [27s] The king made silver as common in Jerusalem as stones, and cedars as numerous as the sycamores of the Shephelah. [28]Solomon's horses were imported from Egypt and from Cilicia, where the king's merchants purchased them. [29]A chariot imported from Egypt cost six hundred shekels of silver, a horse one hundred and fifty shekels; they were exported at these rates to all the Hittite and Aramean kings.

See RG 188

CHAPTER 11

The End of Solomon's Reign.* [1t] King Solomon loved many foreign women besides the daughter of Pharaoh—Moabites, Ammonites, Edomites, Sidonians, Hittites—[2u] from nations of which the LORD had said to the Israelites: You shall not join with them and they shall not join with you, lest they turn your hearts to their gods. But Solomon held them* close in love. [3]He had as wives seven hundred princesses and three hundred concubines, and they turned his heart.

[4]When Solomon was old his wives had turned his heart to follow other gods, and his heart was not entirely with the LORD, his God, as the heart of David his father had been. [5]Solomon followed Astarte, the goddess of the Sidonians, and Milcom, the abomination of the Ammonites. [6]Solomon did what was evil in the sight of the LORD, and he did not follow the LORD unreservedly as David his father had done. [7]Solomon then built a high place to Chemosh, the abomination of Moab, and to Molech, the abomination of the Ammonites, on the mountain opposite Jerusalem. [8]He did the same for all his foreign wives who burned incense and sacrificed to their gods.

[9v] The LORD became angry with Solomon, because his heart turned away from the LORD, the God of Israel, who had appeared to him twice [10]and commanded him not to do this very thing, not to follow other gods. But he did not observe what the LORD commanded. [11]So the LORD said to Solomon: Since this is what you want, and you have not kept my covenant and the statutes which I enjoined on you, I will surely tear the kingdom away from you and give it to your servant. [12w] But I will not do this during your lifetime, for the sake of David your father; I will tear it away from your son's hand. [13]Nor will I tear away the whole kingdom. I will give your son one tribe for the sake of David my servant and for the sake of Jerusalem, which I have chosen.

Threats to Solomon's Kingdom.* [14]The

10:22 Tarshish ships: large, strong vessels for long voyages. Tarshish was probably the ancient Tartessus, a Phoenician colony in southern Spain. **Ivory, apes, and peacocks**: the Hebrew words are obscure and the translations conjectural; however, the reference is certainly to exotic luxury items.

11:1–13 The next major unit of the Solomon story corresponds to 3:1–15. Like the earlier passage it includes the narrator's remarks about Solomon's foreign wives and his building projects, and a divine word commenting on Solomon's conduct. However, where 3:1–15 is generally positive toward Solomon, the present passage is unrelievedly negative. Chronicles has no parallel to this material.

11:2 Them: both the nations and their gods.

11:14–25 This unit of the Solomon story corresponds to 2:12b–46, where Solomon secured his kingdom by eliminating three men he perceived as threats. In this passage, we learn of two foreigners the Lord raised up as "adversaries" to Solomon as early as the beginning of his reign (despite Solomon's complacent claim to Hiram in 5:18 that he had no adversary). In the next section we will learn of a third opponent, Israelite rather than foreign, who turns out to be the "servant of Solomon" announced by the Lord in 11:11. Chronicles has no parallel to this material.

r: 1 Kgs 5:6; Dt 17:16; 2 Chr 1:14; 9:25. *s:* Dt 17:17; Sir 47:18. *t:* Dt 17:17; Sir 47:19–20. *u:* Ex 34:16. *v:* 1 Kgs 3:4–15; 6:11–13; 9:2–9. *w:* 1 Kgs 11:34–36.

LORD then raised up an adversary* against Solomon: Hadad the Edomite, who was of the royal line in Edom. [15x] Earlier, when David had conquered Edom, Joab, the commander of the army, while going to bury the slain, killed every male in Edom. [16]Joab and all Israel remained there six months until they had killed off every male in Edom. [17]But Hadad, with some Edomite servants of his father, fled toward Egypt. Hadad was then a young boy. [18]They left Midian and came to Paran; they gathered men from Paran and came to Egypt, to Pharaoh, king of Egypt; he gave Hadad a house, appointed him rations, and assigned him land. [19]Hadad won great favor with Pharaoh, so that he gave him in marriage his sister-in-law, the sister of Queen Tahpenes, his own wife. [20]Tahpenes' sister bore Hadad a son, Genubath. Tahpenes weaned him in Pharaoh's palace. And Genubath lived in Pharaoh's house, with Pharaoh's own sons. [21]When Hadad in Egypt heard that David rested with his ancestors and that Joab, the commander of the army, was dead, he said to Pharaoh, "Give me leave to return to my own land." [22]Pharaoh said to him, "What do you lack with me, that you are seeking to return to your own land?" He answered, "Nothing, but please let me go!"

[23]God raised up against Solomon another adversary, Rezon, the son of Eliada, who had fled from his lord, Hadadezer, king of Zobah, [24y] when David was slaughtering them. Rezon gathered men about him and became leader of a marauding band. They went to Damascus, settled there, and made him king in Damascus. [25]Rezon was an adversary of Israel as long as Solomon lived, in addition to the harm done by Hadad, and he felt contempt for Israel. He became king over Aram.

Ahijah Announces Jeroboam's Kingship.* [26]Solomon had a servant, Jeroboam, son of Nebat, an Ephraimite from Zeredah with a widowed mother named Zeruah. He rebelled against the king. [27]This is how he came to rebel. King Solomon was building Millo, closing up the breach of the City of David, his father. [28]Jeroboam was a very able man, and when Solomon saw that the young man was also a good worker, he put him in charge of all the carriers conscripted from the house of Joseph.

[29]At that time Jeroboam left Jerusalem, and the prophet Ahijah the Shilonite met him on the road. The prophet was wearing a new cloak,* and when the two were alone in the open country, [30z] Ahijah took off his new cloak, tore it into twelve pieces, [31a] and said to Jeroboam: "Take ten pieces for yourself. Thus says the LORD, the God of Israel: I am about to tear the kingdom out of Solomon's hand and will give you ten of the tribes. [32]He shall have one tribe for the sake of my servant David, and for the sake of Jerusalem, the city I have chosen out of all the tribes of Israel. [33]For they have forsaken me and have bowed down to Astarte, goddess of the Sidonians, Chemosh, god of Moab, and Milcom, god of the Ammonites. They have not walked in my ways or done what is right in my eyes, according to my statutes and my ordinances, as David his father did. [34]Yet I will not take any of the kingdom from Solomon himself, but will keep him a prince as long as he lives, for the sake of David my servant, whom I have chosen, who kept my commandments and statutes.

[35]But I will take the kingdom from his son's hand and give it to you—that is, the ten tribes. [36]I will give his son one tribe, that David my servant may always have a holding

11:14 Adversary: Hebrew *Satan*, one who stands in opposition; in this context a political opponent.

11:26–43 The last major unit of the Solomon story tells how the prophet Ahijah announces the divine intention to take the larger part of Solomon's kingdom from his control and give it to Jeroboam, Solomon's servant. This counterbalances the first unit of the story, 1:1–2:12a, where another prophet, Nathan, managed to influence the royal succession and obtain the throne for Solomon. The unit is also the first part of the story of Jeroboam (11:26–14:20). It thus acts as a literary hinge connecting the two stories. Chronicles contains a death notice for Solomon in 2 Chr 9:29–31.

11:29 The narrator uses a powerful wordplay here. In the Hebrew consonantal text, Ahijah's cloak (*slmh*) is indistinguishable from Solomon's name (*slmh*). Since a prophetic gesture such as Ahijah's was understood as effecting the event it announced, Ahijah's tearing of his cloak embodies the divine action that will tear Solomon's kingdom apart (cf. vv. 11–13).

x: 2 Sm 8:13–14. *y:* 2 Sm 8:3–6. *z:* 1 Sm 15:27–28. *a:* 1 Kgs 12:20.

before me in Jerusalem, the city I have chosen, to set my name there. [37]You I will take and you shall reign over all that you desire and shall become king of Israel. [38]If, then, you heed all that I command you, walking in my ways, and do what is right in my eyes by keeping my statutes and my commandments like David my servant, I will be with you. I will build a lasting house for you, just as I did for David; I will give Israel to you. [39]I will humble David's line for this, but not forever."

[40]When Solomon tried to have Jeroboam killed, Jeroboam fled to Shishak, king of Egypt. He remained in Egypt until Solomon's death.

[41]The rest of the acts of Solomon, with all that he did and his wisdom, are recorded in the book of the acts of Solomon. [42]Solomon was king in Jerusalem over all Israel for forty years. [43]Solomon rested with his ancestors and was buried in the City of David, his father, and Rehoboam his son succeeded him as king.

II. The Reign of Jeroboam*

CHAPTER 12

See RG 188–89

*Political Disunity.** [1]Rehoboam went to Shechem,* where all Israel had come to make him king. [2]When Jeroboam, son of Nebat, heard about it, he was still in Egypt. He had fled from King Solomon and remained in Egypt, [3]and they sent for him.

Then Jeroboam and the whole assembly of Israel came and they said to Rehoboam, [4]"Your father put a heavy yoke on us. If you now lighten the harsh servitude and the heavy yoke your father imposed on us, we will be your servants." [5]He answered them, "Come back to me in three days," and the people went away.

[6]King Rehoboam asked advice of the elders who had been in his father Solomon's service while he was alive, and asked, "How do you advise me to answer this people?" [7]They replied, "If today you become the servant of this people and serve them, and give them a favorable answer, they will be your servants forever." [8]But he ignored the advice the elders had given him, and asked advice of the young men who had grown up with him and were in his service. [9]He said to them, "What answer do you advise that we should give this people, who have told me, 'Lighten the yoke your father imposed on us'?" [10]The young men who had grown up with him replied, "This is what you must say to this people who have told you, 'Your father made our yoke heavy; you lighten it for us.' You must say, 'My little finger is thicker than my father's loins. [11]My father put a heavy yoke on you, but I will make it heavier. My father beat you with whips, but I will beat you with scorpions.' " [12]Jeroboam and the whole people came back to King Rehoboam on the third day, as the king had instructed them: "Come back to me in three days." [13]Ignoring the advice the elders had given him, the king gave the people a harsh answer. [14]He spoke to them as the young men had advised: "My father made your yoke heavy, but I will make it heavier. My father beat you with whips, but I will beat you with scorpions." [15b] The king did not listen to the people, for this turn of events was from the LORD: he fulfilled the word the LORD had spoken through Ahijah the Shilonite to Jeroboam, son of Nebat.

12:1–14:20 Like the story of the reign of Solomon, the story of the reign of Jeroboam is concentrically organized. Ahijah's oracle of promise to Jeroboam (11:26–43) belongs to both stories, ending that of Solomon (see note on 1:1–11:43) and beginning that of Jeroboam; it corresponds to Ahijah's oracle of condemnation in 14:1–20. Within those literary boundaries are accounts of political (12:1–20) and religious (13:11–34) disunity between Israel and Judah. The center of the story is the account of Jeroboam's heterodox cultic innovations (12:26–31).

12:1–20 The first major unit of the Jeroboam story was Ahijah's oracle (11:26–40), followed by the notice of Solomon's death (11:41–43). This is the second major unit. It tells how Jeroboam came to the throne of Israel after the intransigence of Solomon's son Rehoboam provoked the northern tribes to secede from Jerusalem. The political disunity of the two kingdoms fulfills the word spoken by Ahijah. Compare 13:11–32, where Jeroboam's improper cultic innovations produce religious disunity as well. The scene is concentrically arranged: narrative introduction, first interview, first consultation, second consultation, second interview, narrative conclusion. Chronicles has a parallel version of this story in 2 Chr 10:1–19.

12:1 Shechem: chief city of the northern tribes, where a covenant had previously been made between the Lord and his people and a stone of witness had been erected in memory of the event (Jos 24:25–27). **All Israel**: see note on 4:7–19.

b: 1 Kgs 11:26–39.

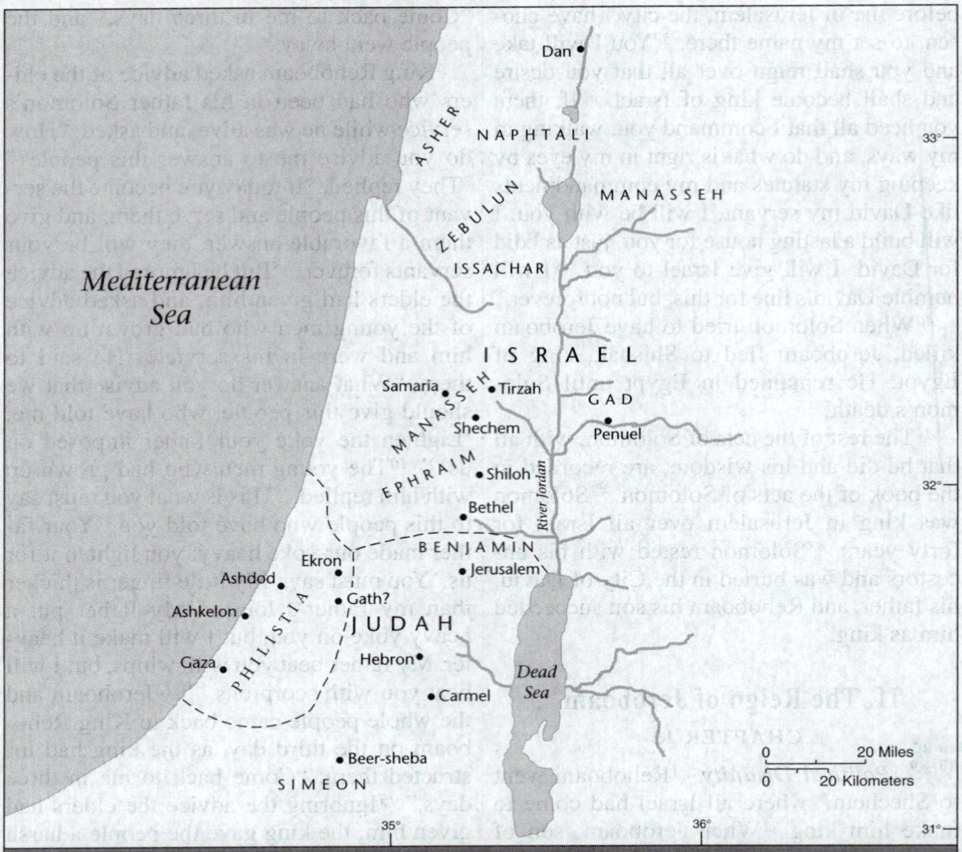

The Divided Monarchy

16c When all Israel saw that the king did not
listen to them, the people answered the king:

> "What share have we in David?*
> We have no heritage in the son of Jesse.
> To your tents, Israel!
> Now look to your own house, David."

So Israel went off to their tents. 17 But Rehoboam continued to reign over the Israelites
who lived in the cities of Judah.
18 King Rehoboam then sent out Adoram,*
who was in charge of the forced labor, but all
Israel stoned him to death. King Rehoboam
then managed to mount his chariot and flee
to Jerusalem. 19 And so Israel has been in rebellion against the house of David to this
day. 20 When all Israel heard that Jeroboam
had returned, they summoned him to an assembly and made him king over all Israel.
None remained loyal to the house of David
except the tribe of Judah alone.

12:16 What share have we in David?: even in David's time the northern tribes seemed ready to withdraw from the union with Judah (2 Sm 20:1). The unreasonable attitude of Rehoboam toward them intensified the discontent caused by the oppression of Solomon (v. 4) and thus precipitated the political separation of the two kingdoms. In the view of the Deuteronomistic historian (1 Kgs 11:35–36; 12:24), this was by the Lord's decree.

12:18 Adoram: the name is a shortened form of "Adoniram" (see 4:6; 5:28). If this is the same Adoram who held the position in David's day (2 Sm 20:24), he would have been a very old man.

c: 2 Sm 20:1.

Divine Approval. * [21]On his arrival in Jerusalem, Rehoboam assembled all the house of Judah and the tribe of Benjamin—one hundred and eighty thousand elite warriors—to wage war against the house of Israel, to restore the kingdom to Rehoboam, son of Solomon. [22]However, the word of God came to Shemaiah, a man of God: [23]Say to Rehoboam, son of Solomon, king of Judah, and to all the house of Judah and to Benjamin, and to the rest of the people: [24]Thus says the LORD: You must not go out to war against your fellow Israelites. Return home, each of you, for it is I who have brought this about. They obeyed the word of the LORD and turned back, according to the word of the LORD.

[25]Jeroboam built up Shechem in the hill country of Ephraim and lived there. Then he left it and built up Penuel.

Jeroboam's Cultic Innovations. * [26]Jeroboam thought to himself: "Now the kingdom will return to the house of David. [27]If this people go up to offer sacrifices in the house of the LORD in Jerusalem, the hearts of this people will return to their master, Rehoboam, king of Judah, and they will kill me and return to Rehoboam, king of Judah." [28][d] The king took counsel, made two calves of gold, and said to the people: "You have been going up to Jerusalem long enough. Here are your gods, O Israel, who brought you up from the land of Egypt." [29][e] And he put one in Bethel, the other in Dan.* [30]This led to sin, because the people frequented these calves in Bethel and in Dan. [31]He also built temples on the high places and made priests from among the common people who were not Levites.

Divine Disapproval. * [32]Jeroboam established a feast in the eighth month on the fifteenth day of the month like the pilgrimage feast in Judah, and he went up to the altar. He did this in Bethel, sacrificing to the calves he had made. He stationed in Bethel the priests of the high places he had built. [33]Jeroboam went up to the altar he built in Bethel on the fifteenth day of the eighth month, the month he arbitrarily chose. He established a feast for the Israelites, and he went up to the altar to burn incense.

CHAPTER 13

See RG 189

[1]A man of God came from Judah to Bethel by the word of the LORD, while Jeroboam was standing at the altar to burn incense. [2][f] He cried out against the altar by the word of the LORD: "Altar, altar, thus says the LORD: A child shall be born to the house of David, Josiah by name, who shall slaughter upon you the priests of the high places who burn incense upon you, and they shall burn human bones upon you." [3][g] He also gave a sign that same day and said: "This is the sign that the LORD has spoken: The altar shall be torn apart and the ashes on it shall be scattered." [4]When the king heard the word of the man of God which he was crying out against the altar in Bethel, Jeroboam stretched forth his hand from the altar and said, "Seize

12:21–25 The center of this unit is a divine oracle delivered by a man of God of the Southern Kingdom in which the Lord affirms his approval of the secession of the northern tribes. Compare 13:1–10, where another man of God from Judah proclaims the Lord's condemnation of Jeroboam's religious separatism. Chronicles has a very similar version of Shemaiah's oracle in 2 Chr 11:1–4.

12:26–31 At the center of the story of Jeroboam the narrator describes how the king went beyond the political separation of Israel from Judah to create a separatist religious system as well. Jeroboam feared that continued worship in the single Temple in Jerusalem would threaten the political independence of his kingdom. To prevent this he established sanctuaries with non-levitical clergy in his own territory. At two of the sanctuaries he set up golden calves, which the narrator depicts as idols. Thus begins what will later be called "the sin of Jeroboam" (13:34), a theme that will be echoed throughout 1–2 Kings in the condemnations of almost every king of the Northern Kingdom. Historically, Jeroboam's innovations were not as heterodox as our narrative portrays them. Bethel was an ancient and traditional site for worship of the Lord; and the calves were probably intended to be a dais for the deity invisibly enthroned upon them, rather like the cherubim atop the ark of the covenant.

12:29 Bethel . . . Dan: at the southern and northern boundaries of the separate kingdom of Israel, where sanctuaries had existed in the past (Gn 12:8; 13:3–4; 28:10–22; 35:1–15; Jgs 18:1–31).

12:32–13:10 This unit of the Jeroboam story corresponds to 12:21–25. Before Jeroboam's cultic innovations, a man of God from Judah proclaimed the Lord's approval of the political separation of the kingdoms. After Jeroboam's cultic innovations, a man of God from Judah proclaims the Lord's disapproval of Israel's religious separatism. The unit begins with a long, detailed introduction about the dedication festival Jeroboam holds at Bethel (12:32–33); then follows the scene of the ceremony disrupted by the oracle of the man of God (13:1–10).

d: Ex 32:1–10. *e:* Tb 1:5. *f:* 2 Kgs 23:16. *g:* 2 Kgs 23:15.

Chronology of the Two Kingdoms

DIFFICULTIES ARISE IN comparing the chronology of the two kingdoms, Israel and Judah. Before the modern system of numbering years was adopted in the fifth century A.D., events were usually dated by the reigns of kings, beginning a new series with each new king. In some instances the remaining months of the year of a king's death were counted as the first year of his successor; in others the new series of numbers did not begin until the next full year. Frequently a king associated his son with him on the throne, so that the year could be designated by either king; in such cases one writer might begin the new king's reign when this occurred, whereas another writer might not begin the enumeration until after the father's death. Interest in precise chronology is comparatively recent. Until modern times the year was commenced at different dates in various countries. When these facts are recognized, most of the chronological discrepancies in the narratives of the two kingdoms can be resolved.

The total length of the kingdoms of Israel and Judah can be learned from events mentioned in the history of other countries. A much larger sum is reached by adding together the number of years of each king's reign, because fractions of a year would appear as full years in each reign.

From 1050–931 B.C. the united kingdom was ruled by Saul, David, and Solomon. The approximate dates of the reigns of the kings of Israel and Judah are shown in the table below:

Israel	*Reign*	*Co-Regency*	*Judah*	*Reign*	*Co-Regency*
Jeroboam I	931–910 B.C.		Rehoboam	931–913 B.C.	
			Abijah	913–911	
Nadab	910–909		Asa	911–870	
Baasha	909–886				
Elah	886–885				
Zimri	885				
Omri	885–874	885–880 B.C.			
Ahab	874–853		Jehoshaphat	870–848	873–870 B.C.
Ahaziah	853–852		Jehoram	848–841	853–848
Joram	852–841		Ahaziah	841	
Jehu	841–814		Athaliah	841–835	
Jehoahaz	814–798		Joash	835–796	
Jehoash	798–782		Amaziah	796–767	
Jeroboam II	782–753	793–782	Azariah	767–740	791–767
Zechariah	753–752				
Shallum	752				
Menahem	752–742		Jotham	740–732	750–740
Pekahiah	742–740				
Pekah	740–732	752–740	Ahaz	732–716	
Hoshea	732–721				
			Hezekiah	716–687	
			Manasseh	687–642	696–687
			Amon	642–640	
			Josiah	640–608	
			Jehoahaz	608	
			Jehoiakim	608–597	
			Jehoiachin	597	
			Zedekiah	597–586	

him!" But the hand he stretched forth against
him withered, so that he could not draw it
back. 5(The altar was torn apart and the
ashes from the altar were scattered, in accordance with the sign the man of God gave by
the word of the LORD.)
6Then the king said to the man of God,
"Entreat the LORD, your God, and intercede
for me that my hand may be restored." So
the man of God entreated the LORD, and the
king's hand was restored as it was before.
7The king told the man of God, "Come with
me to the house for some refreshment so that
I may give you a present." 8The man of God
said to the king, "If you gave me half your
palace, I would not go with you, nor eat
bread or drink water in this place. 9For I was
instructed by the word of the LORD: Do not
eat bread or drink water, and do not return by
the way you came." 10So he departed by another road and did not go back the way he
had come to Bethel.
Prophetic Disunity. * 11There was an old
prophet living in Bethel, whose son came
and told him all that the man of God had done
that day in Bethel. When his sons repeated to
their father the words the man of God had
spoken to the king, 12the father asked them,
"Which way did he go?" So his sons pointed
out to him the road taken by the man of God
who had come from Judah. 13Then he said to
his sons, "Saddle the donkey for me." When
they had saddled it, he mounted 14and followed the man of God, whom he found
seated under a terebinth. When he asked him,
"Are you the man of God who came from Judah?" he answered, "Yes." 15Then he said,
"Come home with me and have some bread."
16"I cannot return with you or go with you,
and I cannot eat bread or drink water with
you in this place," he answered, 17"for I was
told by the word of the LORD: You shall not
eat bread or drink water there, and do not go
back the way you came." 18But he said to
him, "I, too, am a prophet like you, and an
angel told me by the word of the LORD: Bring
him back with you to your house to eat bread
and drink water." But he was lying to him.
19So he went back with him, and ate bread
and drank water in his house. 20But while
they were sitting at table, the word of the
LORD came to the prophet who had brought
him back, 21and he cried out to the man of
God who had come from Judah: "Thus says
the LORD: Because you rebelled against the
charge of the LORD and did not keep the command which the LORD, your God, gave you,
22but returned and ate bread and drank water
in the place where he told you, Do not eat
bread or drink water, your corpse shall not be
brought to the grave of your ancestors." 23Af-
ter he had eaten bread and drunk, they saddled for him the donkey that belonged to the
prophet who had brought him back, 24and he
set out. But a lion met him on the road, and
killed him. His body lay sprawled on the
road, and the donkey remained standing by
it, and so did the lion.
25Some passersby saw the body lying in
the road, with the lion standing beside it, and
carried the news to the city where the old
prophet lived. 26On hearing it, the prophet
who had brought him back from his journey
said: "It is the man of God who rebelled
against the charge of the LORD. The LORD
has delivered him to a lion, which mangled
and killed him, according to the word which
the LORD had spoken to him." 27Then he said
to his sons, "Saddle the donkey for me," and
they saddled it. 28He went off and found the
body sprawled on the road with the donkey
and the lion standing beside it. The lion had
not eaten the body nor had it harmed the
donkey. 29The prophet lifted up the body of
the man of God and put it on the donkey, and
brought him back to the city to mourn and to
bury him. 30He laid the man's body in his
own grave, and they mourned over it: "Alas,
my brother!" 31[h] After he had buried him, he
said to his sons, "When I die, bury me in the

13:11–34 The next major unit illustrates how Jeroboam's cultic innovations begin to alienate prophetic figures of the two kingdoms. Nevertheless, the Lord's word is stronger than any human attempt to thwart it. The two prophets also foreshadow the destinies of their respective kingdoms. Israel's experiment with idolatry can tempt Judah to abandon its faithfulness to the Lord. If Judah succumbs, and no longer speaks the word that can call Israel back to the true God, then the only hope for reuniting the two kingdoms will be when they have both died the death of exile.

h: 2 Kgs 23:17–18.

grave where the man of God is buried. Lay my bones beside his. [32][i] For the word which he proclaimed by the word of the LORD against the altar in Bethel and against all the temples on the high places in the cities of Samaria shall certainly come to pass."

[33]Even after this, Jeroboam did not turn from his evil way, but again made priests for the high places from among the common people. Whoever desired it was installed as a priest of the high places. [34]This is the account of the sin of the house of Jeroboam for which it was to be cut off and destroyed from the face of the earth.

CHAPTER 14

See RG 189

Ahijah Announces Jeroboam's Downfall.* [1] At that time Abijah, son of Jeroboam, took sick. [2][j] So Jeroboam said to his wife, "Go and disguise yourself so that no one will recognize you as Jeroboam's wife. Then go to Shiloh, where you will find Ahijah the prophet. It was he who spoke the word that made me king over this people. [3]Take along ten loaves, some cakes, and a jar of honey, and go to him. He will tell you what will happen to the child." [4]The wife of Jeroboam did so. She left and went to Shiloh and came to the house of Ahijah.

Now Ahijah could not see because age had dimmed his sight. [5]But the LORD said to Ahijah: Jeroboam's wife is coming to consult you about her son, for he is sick. Thus and so you must tell her. When she comes, she will be in disguise. [6]So Ahijah, hearing the sound of her footsteps as she entered the door, said, "Come in, wife of Jeroboam. Why are you in disguise? For my part, I have been commissioned to give you bitter news. [7]Go, tell Jeroboam, 'Thus says the LORD, the God of Israel: I exalted you from among the people and made you ruler of my people Israel. [8]I tore the kingdom away from the house of David and gave it to you. Yet you have not been like my servant David, who kept my commandments and followed me with his whole heart, doing only what is right in my sight. [9]You have done more evil than all who were before you: you have gone and made for yourself other gods and molten images to provoke me; but me you have cast behind your back. [10][k] Therefore, I am bringing evil upon the house of Jeroboam:

I will cut off from Jeroboam's line every male
—bond or free—in Israel;
I will burn up what is left of the house of Jeroboam
as dung is burned, completely.
[11][l] Anyone of Jeroboam's line who dies in the city,
dogs will devour;
anyone who dies in the field,
the birds of the sky will devour.

For the LORD has spoken!' [12]As for you, leave, and go home! As you step inside the city, the child will die, [13]and all Israel will mourn him and bury him, for he alone of Jeroboam's line will be laid in the grave, since in him alone of Jeroboam's house has something pleasing to the LORD, the God of Israel, been found. [14]The LORD will raise up for himself a king over Israel who will cut off the house of Jeroboam—today, at this very moment! [15]The LORD will strike Israel like a reed tossed about in the water and will pluck out Israel from this good land which he gave their ancestors, and will scatter them beyond the River,* because they made asherahs for themselves, provoking the LORD. [16]He will give up Israel because of the sins Jeroboam has committed and caused Israel to commit." [17]So Jeroboam's wife left and went back; when she came to Tirzah and crossed the threshold of her house, the child died. [18]He was buried and all Israel mourned him, according to the word of the LORD spoken through his servant Ahijah the prophet.

[19]The rest of the acts of Jeroboam, how he

14:1–20 The last major unit of the Jeroboam story recounts the story of Ahijah of Shiloh's oracle condemning the entire house of Jeroboam; this is followed by a formulaic notice of Jeroboam's death and the succession of his son. Compare the first unit of the Jeroboam story, 11:26–43, which recounted Ahijah's oracle proclaiming Jeroboam's kingship, followed by the formulaic notice of the death of Solomon.

14:15 The River: the Euphrates; see note on 5:1.

i: 2 Kgs 23:19–20. *j:* 1 Kgs 11:29–39. *k:* 1 Kgs 15:29–30. *l:* 1 Kgs 16:4; 21:22.

fought and how he reigned, these are
recorded in the book of the chronicles of the
kings of Israel. [20]The length of Jeroboam's
reign was twenty-two years. He rested with
his ancestors, and Nadab his son succeeded
him as king.

III. Kings of Judah and Israel*

Reign of Rehoboam. [21]* Rehoboam, son of
Solomon, became king in Judah. Rehoboam
was forty-one years old when he became king,
and he reigned seventeen years in Jerusalem,
the city in which, out of all the tribes of Israel,
the LORD chose to set his name. His mother's
name was Naamah the Ammonite.
[22]Judah did evil in the LORD's sight and
they angered him even more than their ancestors had done. [23]They, too, built for themselves high places, sacred pillars, and asherahs,* upon every high hill and under every
green tree. [24]There were also pagan priests in
the land. Judah imitated all the abominable
practices of the nations whom the LORD had
driven out of the Israelites' way. [25]* In the
fifth year of King Rehoboam, Shishak, king
of Egypt, attacked Jerusalem. [26]m He took
everything, including the treasures of the
house of the LORD and the treasures of the
house of the king, even the gold shields Solomon had made. [27]To replace them, King Rehoboam made bronze shields, which he entrusted to the officers of the guard on duty at
the entrance of the royal house. [28]Whenever
the king visited the house of the LORD, those
on duty would carry the shields, and then return them to the guardroom.
[29]The rest of the acts of Rehoboam, with
all that he did, are recorded in the book of
the chronicles of the kings of Judah. [30]There
was war between Rehoboam and Jeroboam
all their days. [31]Rehoboam rested with his
ancestors; he was buried with his ancestors
in the City of David. His mother's name was
Naamah the Ammonite. His son Abijam succeeded him as king.

CHAPTER 15

See RG 189–90

Reign of Abijam. [1]In the eighteenth
year of King Jeroboam, son of Nebat, Abijam became king of Judah; [2]he reigned three
years in Jerusalem. His mother's name was
Maacah, daughter of Abishalom.
[3]He followed all the sins his father had
committed before him, and his heart was not
entirely with the LORD, his God, as was the
heart of David his father. [4]Yet for David's
sake the LORD, his God, gave him a holding
in Jerusalem, raising up his son after him
and permitting Jerusalem to endure, [5]n because David had done what was right in the
sight of the LORD and did not disobey any of
his commands as long as he lived, except in
the case of Uriah the Hittite.
[6]There was war between Rehoboam and
Jeroboam all their days. [7]The rest of the acts
of Abijam, with all that he did, are recorded
in the book of the chronicles of the kings of
Judah. There was war between Abijam and
Jeroboam. [8]Abijam rested with his ancestors; they buried him in the City of David,
and his son Asa succeeded him as king.
Reign of Asa. [9]In the twentieth year of Jeroboam, king of Israel, Asa, king of Judah,
became king; [10]he reigned forty-one years in
Jerusalem. His mother's* name was Maacah,
daughter of Abishalom. [11]Asa did what was

14:21–16:34 The treatment of the events of Jeroboam's reign shows that the author believes that the political division of the kingdoms embodies the Lord's will, but that their religious separation is undesirable. The Israelites are, in effect, one people of God under two royal administrations. This complex arrangement is reflected in the way 1–2 Kings organizes the history of the divided kingdoms. Each reign is treated as a unity: the kings, whether of Israel or Judah, are legitimate rulers. But the accounts of northern and southern kings are interwoven in the order in which each came to the throne, without regard to which kingdom they ruled: the people of God is one.

14:21 The account of each king's reign follows the same basic pattern: a formulaic introduction, a theological evaluation based on religious fidelity, a brief account of an event from the king's reign, and a formulaic conclusion.

14:23 Asherahs: see note on Ex 34:13.

14:25–28, 30 The narrator recounts Shishak's campaign here to imply that it was punishment for Judah's evil, and perhaps to cast him as supporting Jeroboam in his constant warfare with Rehoboam. (Shishak was named as Jeroboam's protector and patron in 11:40.) Egyptian records of the campaign list one hundred fifty cities conquered in Israel as well as Judah, but Jerusalem is not one of them. Chronicles has a parallel version of this account in 2 Chr 12:9–11.

15:10 Maacah was in fact Asa's grandmother (see v. 2), but "king's mother" was perhaps a title for the *gebira*, the "Great Lady" or "queen mother" (see, for instance, 2:19). This influ-

m: 1 Kgs 10:16–17. *n:* 2 Sm 11:1–27.

right in the sight of the LORD like David his father, [12]banishing the pagan priests from the land and removing all the idols his ancestors had made. [13]He also deposed his grandmother Maacah from her position as queen mother, because she had made an outrageous object for Asherah. Asa cut down this object and burned it in the Wadi Kidron. [14]The high places did not disappear; yet Asa's heart was entirely with the LORD as long as he lived. [15]He brought into the house of the LORD his father's and his own votive offerings of silver and gold and various vessels. [16]There was war between Asa and Baasha, king of Israel, all their days. [17]Baasha, king of Israel, attacked Judah and fortified Ramah to blockade Asa, king of Judah. [18]Asa then took all the silver and gold remaining in the treasuries of the house of the LORD and the house of the king. Entrusting them to his ministers, King Asa sent them to Ben-hadad, son of Tabrimmon, son of Hezion, king of Aram,* who ruled in Damascus. He said: [19]"There is a treaty between you and me, as there was between your father and my father. I am sending you a present of silver and gold. Go, break your treaty with Baasha, king of Israel, that he may withdraw from me." [20]Ben-hadad agreed with King Asa and sent the leaders of his troops against the cities of Israel. They attacked Ijon, Dan, Abel-beth-maacah, and all Chinnereth, besides all the land of Naphtali. [21]When Baasha heard of it, he left off fortifying Ramah, and stayed in Tirzah. [22]Then King Asa summoned all Judah without exception, and they carried away the stones and beams with which Baasha was fortifying Ramah. With them King Asa built Geba of Benjamin and Mizpah. [23]All the rest of the acts of Asa, with all his valor and all that he did, and the cities he built, are recorded in the book of the chronicles of the kings of Judah. But in his old age, Asa had an infirmity in his feet. [24]Asa rested with his ancestors; he was buried with his ancestors in the City of David his father, and his son Jehoshaphat succeeded him as king.

Reign of Nadab. [25]Nadab, son of Jeroboam, became king of Israel in the second year of Asa, king of Judah. For two years he reigned over Israel.

[26]He did what was evil in the LORD's sight, walking in the way of his father and the sin he had caused Israel to commit. [27]Baasha, son of Ahijah, of the house of Issachar, plotted against him and struck him down at Gibbethon of the Philistines, which Nadab and all Israel were besieging. [28]Baasha killed him in the third year of Asa, king of Judah, and succeeded him as king. [29][o] Once he was king, he killed the entire house of Jeroboam, not leaving a single soul but destroying Jeroboam utterly, according to the word of the LORD spoken through his servant, Ahijah the Shilonite, [30]because of the sins Jeroboam committed and caused Israel to commit, by which he provoked the LORD, the God of Israel, to anger.

[31]The rest of the acts of Nadab, with all that he did, are recorded in the book of the chronicles of the kings of Israel. [32]There was war between Asa and Baasha, king of Israel, all their days.

Reign of Baasha. [33]In the third year of Asa, king of Judah, Baasha, son of Ahijah, became king of all Israel in Tirzah for twenty-four years.

[34]He did what was evil in the LORD's sight, walking in the way of Jeroboam and the sin he had caused Israel to commit.

CHAPTER 16

See RG 190

[1]The word of the LORD came to Jehu, son of Hanani, against Baasha: [2]Inasmuch as I exalted you from the dust and made you ruler of my people Israel, but you have walked in the way of Jeroboam and have caused my people Israel to sin, provoking me to anger by their sins, [3][p] I will burn up what is

ential position was usually held by the king's biological mother, but Maacah may have retained it after the early death of her son Abijam.

15:18 Ben-hadad . . . king of Aram: Ben-hadad I, third successor of Rezon, who had thrown off the yoke of the Israelites during the reign of Solomon and become king of Aram (11:23–24). Chronicles has a parallel version of this account in 2 Chr 16:1–6. **Who ruled**: lit., "sitting," i.e., enthroned, possibly also meaning "resident" or "residing."

o: 1 Kgs 14:10–11. *p:* 1 Kgs 16:11; 21:22.

left of Baasha and his house; I will make your house like that of Jeroboam, son of Nebat:

4 [q] One of Baasha's line who dies in the city,
dogs will devour;
One who dies in the field,
the birds of the sky will devour.

5 The rest of the acts of Baasha, what he did and his valor, are recorded in the book of the chronicles of the kings of Israel. 6 Baasha rested with his ancestors; he was buried in Tirzah, and his son Elah succeeded him as king. 7 (Through the prophet Jehu, son of Hanani, the word of the LORD came against Baasha and his house, because of all the evil Baasha did in the sight of the LORD, provoking him to anger by his deeds so that he became like the house of Jeroboam, and because of what he destroyed.)

Reign of Elah. 8 In the twenty-sixth year of Asa, king of Judah, Elah, son of Baasha, became king of Israel in Tirzah for two years.

9 His servant Zimri, commander of half his chariots, plotted against him. As he was in Tirzah, drinking to excess in the house of Arza, master of his palace in Tirzah, 10 [r] Zimri entered; he struck and killed him in the twenty-seventh year of Asa, king of Judah, and succeeded him as king. 11 Once he was king, seated on the throne, he killed the whole house of Baasha, not sparing a single male relative or friend of his. 12 [s] Zimri destroyed the entire house of Baasha, according to the word the LORD spoke against Baasha through Jehu the prophet, 13 because of all the sins which Baasha and his son Elah committed and caused Israel to commit, provoking the LORD, the God of Israel, to anger by their idols.

14 The rest of the acts of Elah, with all that he did, are recorded in the book of the chronicles of the kings of Israel.

Reign of Zimri. 15 In the twenty-seventh year of Asa, king of Judah, Zimri became king for seven days in Tirzah.

The army was encamped at Gibbethon of the Philistines 16 when they heard, "Zimri has formed a conspiracy and has killed the king." So that day in the camp all Israel made Omri, commander of the army, king of Israel. 17 Omri and all Israel with him marched up from Gibbethon and besieged Tirzah. 18 When Zimri saw that the city was captured, he entered the citadel of the king's house and burned it down over him. He died 19 because of the sins he had committed, doing what was evil in the LORD's sight by walking in the way of Jeroboam and the sin he had caused Israel to commit.

20 The rest of the acts of Zimri, with the conspiracy he carried out, are recorded in the book of the chronicles of the kings of Israel.

Civil War. 21 At that time the people of Israel were divided in two, half following Tibni, son of Ginath, to make him king, and half for Omri. 22 The partisans of Omri prevailed over those of Tibni, son of Ginath. Tibni died and Omri became king.

Reign of Omri. 23 In the thirty-first year of Asa, king of Judah, Omri became king of Israel for twelve years; the first six of them he reigned in Tirzah.

24 He then bought the mountain of Samaria from Shemer for two silver talents and built upon the mountain the city he named Samaria, after Shemer, the former owner. 25 But Omri did what was evil in the LORD's sight, more than any of his predecessors. 26 In every way he imitated the sinful conduct of Jeroboam, son of Nebat, and the sin he had caused Israel to commit, thus provoking the LORD, the God of Israel, to anger by their idols.

27 The rest of the acts of Omri, what he did and his valor, are recorded in the book of the chronicles of the kings of Israel. 28 Omri rested with his ancestors; he was buried in Samaria, and Ahab his son succeeded him as king.

Reign of Ahab. 29 Ahab, son of Omri, became king of Israel in the thirty-eighth year of Asa, king of Judah. Ahab, son of Omri, reigned over Israel in Samaria for twenty-two years.

30 Ahab, son of Omri, did what was evil in the LORD's sight more than any of his predecessors. 31 It was not enough for him to follow the sins of Jeroboam, son of Nebat. He even married Jezebel, daughter of Ethbaal, king of

q: 1 Kgs 14:11. *r:* 2 Kgs 9:31. *s:* 1 Kgs 16:2–4.

the Sidonians, and began to serve Baal, and worship him. [32]Ahab set up an altar to Baal in the house of Baal which he built in Samaria, [33]and also made an asherah. Ahab did more to provoke the LORD, the God of Israel, to anger than any of the kings of Israel before him. [34t] During his reign, Hiel from Bethel rebuilt Jericho. At the cost of Abiram, his firstborn son, he laid the foundation, and at the cost of Segub, his youngest son, he set up the gates, according to the word of the LORD spoken through Joshua, son of Nun.*

IV. The Story of Elijah*

CHAPTER 17

See RG 190

Elijah Proclaims a Drought.* [1]Elijah the Tishbite,* [u] from Tishbe in Gilead, said to Ahab: "As the LORD, the God of Israel, lives, whom I serve, during these years there shall be no dew or rain except at my word." [2]The word of the LORD came to Elijah: [3]Leave here, go east and hide in the Wadi Cherith, east of the Jordan. [4]You shall drink of the wadi, and I have commanded ravens to feed you there. [5]So he left and did as the LORD had commanded. He left and remained by the Wadi Cherith, east of the Jordan. [6v] Ravens brought him bread and meat in the morning, and bread and meat in the evening, and he drank from the wadi.

[7]After some time, however, the wadi ran dry, because no rain had fallen in the land. [8w] So the word of the LORD came to him: [9]Arise, go to Zarephath of Sidon and stay there. I have commanded a widow there to feed you. [10]He arose and went to Zarephath. When he arrived at the entrance of the city, a widow was there gathering sticks; he called out to her, "Please bring me a small cupful of water to drink." [11]She left to get it, and he called out after her, "Please bring along a crust of bread." [12]She said, "As the LORD, your God, lives, I have nothing baked; there is only a handful of flour in my jar and a little oil in my jug. Just now I was collecting a few sticks, to go in and prepare something for myself and my son; when we have eaten it, we shall die." [13]Elijah said to her, "Do not be afraid. Go and do as you have said. But first make me a little cake and bring it to me. Afterwards you can prepare something for yourself and your son. [14]For the LORD, the God of Israel, says: The jar of flour shall not go empty, nor the jug of oil run dry, until the day when the LORD sends rain upon the earth." [15]She left and did as Elijah had said. She had enough to eat for a long time—he and she and her household. [16]The jar of flour did not go empty, nor the jug of oil run dry, according to the word of the LORD spoken through Elijah.

[17x] Some time later the son of the woman, the owner of the house, fell sick, and his sick-

16:34 See note on Jos 6:26.

17:1–19:21 The central section of 1–2 Kings tells the story of the dynasty of Omri. That dynasty begins and ends in civil war (1 Kgs 16:21–22; 2 Kgs 9–11). Most of the story is set during the reigns of Ahab of Israel (1 Kgs 16:29–22:40) and his son Joram (2 Kgs 3:1–9:26) and focuses particularly on the interaction of the king with various prophets, especially Ahab with Elijah and Joram with Elisha. The story of Ahab itself contains two large complexes, a series of narratives about Elijah (1 Kgs 17:1–19:21) and a series about hostility between Ahab and the prophets (1 Kgs 20:1–22:38).

17:1–24 The story of Elijah is in three parts. The first (chap. 17) describes how Elijah proclaimed a drought on God's authority and how he survived during the drought. The second (chap. 18) describes how he ends the drought by bringing the populace back to exclusive worship of the Lord. The third (chap. 19) describes Elijah's despair at the failure of his prophetic mission and his consequent attempt to resign from the prophetic office.

17:1 This verse introduces the enigmatic figure of Elijah the Tishbite. (The name "Elijah" means "the Lord is my God." The meaning of "Tishbite" is unknown; it may refer to a place or to a social class.) His appearance before Ahab is abrupt and involves several matters that will unify the whole Elijah story. His claim to "serve the Lord" (lit., to "stand before the Lord") points forward to 19:13, where he refuses to do so; the center of narrative tension on this level is the question of the prophet's autonomy in God's service. His proclamation of a drought points forward to 18:41–45 where he announces the drought's end; the center of narrative tension on this level is the struggle between the Lord and the Canaanite fertility god Baal for the loyalties of Israel. His claim that the drought is due to his own word of power ("except at my word") points forward to 17:24 where the widow acknowledges the divine source of the word Elijah speaks; the center of narrative tension on this level is the gradual characterization of the prophet as one who receives a divine word (vv. 2, 8), obeys it (v. 5), conveys an effective divine word of threat (v. 1) or promise (vv. 14, 16), and even speaks an effective human word of entreaty to God (vv. 20, 22).

t: Jos 6:26. *u:* Sir 48:1–12; Jas 5:17–18. *v:* Ex 16:8, 12. *w:* 2 Kgs 4:1–7; Lk 4:25–26. *x:* 2 Kgs 4:18–37; Lk 7:11–16.

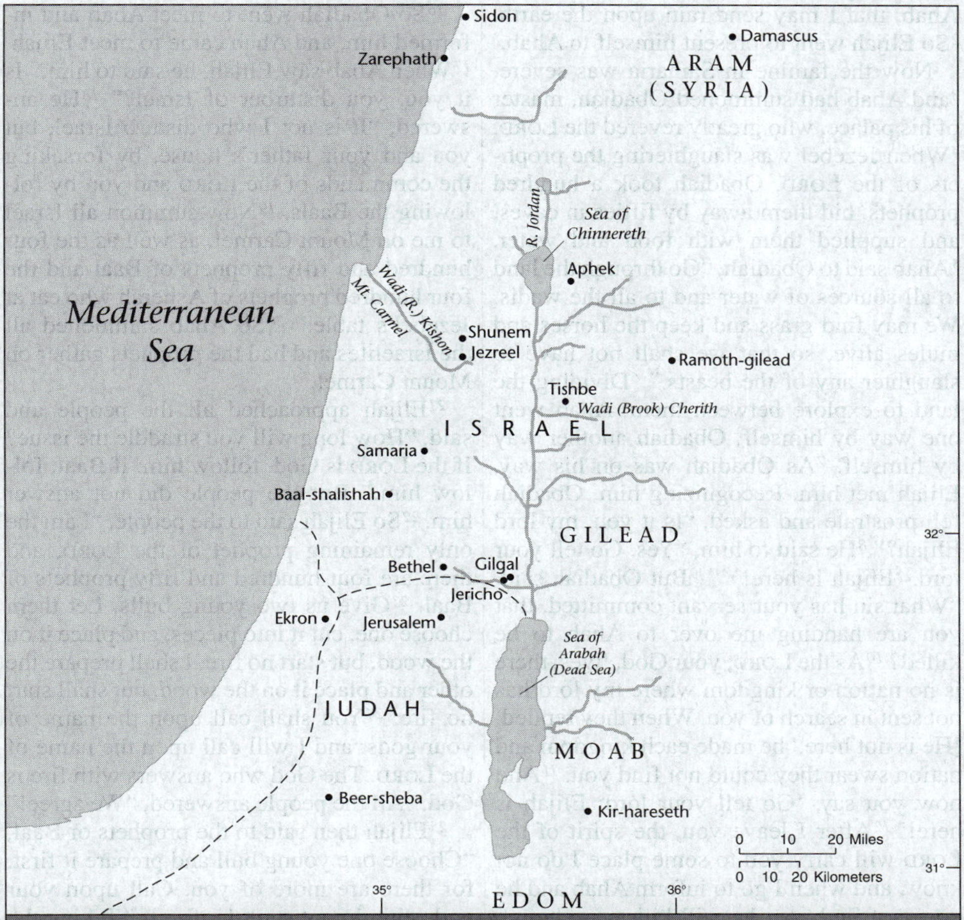

Places Associated with Elijah

ness grew more severe until he stopped
breathing. 18So she said to Elijah, "Why have
you done this to me, man of God? Have you
come to me to call attention to my guilt and
to kill my son?" 19Elijah said to her, "Give
me your son." Taking him from her lap, he
carried him to the upper room where he was
staying, and laid him on his own bed. 20He
called out to the LORD: "LORD, my God, will
you afflict even the widow with whom I am
staying by killing her son?" 21Then he
stretched himself out upon the child three
times and he called out to the LORD: "LORD,
my God, let the life breath return to the body
of this child." 22The LORD heard the prayer of
Elijah; the life breath returned to the child's
body and he lived. 23Taking the child, Elijah
carried him down into the house from the upper room and gave him to his mother. Elijah
said, "See! Your son is alive." 24The woman
said to Elijah, "Now indeed I know that you
are a man of God, and it is truly the word of
the LORD that you speak."

CHAPTER 18

See RG 190

Elijah Ends the Drought.* 1Long afterward, in the third year, the word of the
LORD came to Elijah: Go, present yourself to

18:1–45 The story of the conflict with the prophets of Baal (vv. 21–40) is embedded in the story of the drought and its

Ahab, that I may send rain upon the earth. [2]So Elijah went to present himself to Ahab.

Now the famine in Samaria was severe, [3]and Ahab had summoned Obadiah, master of his palace, who greatly revered the LORD. [4]When Jezebel was slaughtering the prophets of the LORD, Obadiah took a hundred prophets, hid them away by fifties in caves, and supplied them with food and water. [5]Ahab said to Obadiah, "Go through the land to all sources of water and to all the wadis. We may find grass and keep the horses and mules alive, so that we shall not have to slaughter any of the beasts." [6]Dividing the land to explore between them, Ahab went one way by himself, Obadiah another way by himself. [7]As Obadiah was on his way, Elijah met him. Recognizing him, Obadiah fell prostrate and asked, "Is it you, my lord Elijah?" [8]He said to him, "Yes. Go tell your lord, 'Elijah is here!' "* [9]But Obadiah said, "What sin has your servant committed, that you are handing me over to Ahab to be killed? [10]As the LORD, your God, lives, there is no nation or kingdom where my lord has not sent in search of you. When they replied, 'He is not here,' he made each kingdom and nation swear they could not find you. [11]And now you say, 'Go tell your lord: Elijah is here!' [12]After I leave you, the spirit of the LORD will carry you to some place I do not know, and when I go to inform Ahab and he does not find you, he will kill me—though your servant has revered the LORD from his youth! [13]Have you not been told, my lord, what I did when Jezebel was murdering the prophets of the LORD—that I hid a hundred of the prophets of the LORD, fifty each in caves, and supplied them with food and water? [14]And now you say, 'Go tell your lord: Elijah is here!' He will kill me!" [15]Elijah answered, "As the LORD of hosts lives, whom I serve, I will present myself to him today."

[16]So Obadiah went to meet Ahab and informed him, and Ahab came to meet Elijah. [17]When Ahab saw Elijah, he said to him, "Is it you, you disturber of Israel?" [18]He answered, "It is not I who disturb Israel, but you and your father's house, by forsaking the commands of the LORD and you by following the Baals. [19]Now summon all Israel to me on Mount Carmel, as well as the four hundred and fifty prophets of Baal and the four hundred prophets of Asherah who eat at Jezebel's table." [20]So Ahab summoned all the Israelites and had the prophets gather on Mount Carmel.

[21]Elijah approached all the people and said, "How long will you straddle the issue? If the LORD is God, follow him; if Baal, follow him." But the people did not answer him. [22]So Elijah said to the people, "I am the only remaining prophet of the LORD, and there are four hundred and fifty prophets of Baal. [23]Give us two young bulls. Let them choose one, cut it into pieces, and place it on the wood, but start no fire. I shall prepare the other and place it on the wood, but shall start no fire. [24]You shall call upon the name of your gods, and I will call upon the name of the LORD. The God who answers with fire is God." All the people answered, "We agree!"

[25]Elijah then said to the prophets of Baal, "Choose one young bull and prepare it first, for there are more of you. Call upon your gods, but do not start the fire." [26]Taking the young bull that was turned over to them, they prepared it and called upon Baal from morning to noon, saying, "Baal, answer us!" But there was no sound, and no one answering. And they hopped around the altar they had prepared. [27]When it was noon, Elijah taunted them: "Call louder, for he is a god; he may be busy doing his business, or may be on a journey. Perhaps he is asleep and must be awakened." [28]They called out

ending (vv. 1–20, 41–45). The connection between the two stories is found in Canaanite theology, in whose pantheon Baal, "the Cloud Rider," the god of rain and storm, was recognized as the one who brings fertility. Worship of many gods was virtually universal in the ancient world; the Israelite requirement of exclusive worship of the Lord (Ex 20:3) was unique. The people of Israel had apparently become comfortable worshiping both Baal and the Lord, perhaps assigning mutually exclusive spheres of influence to each. By claiming authority over the rain (17:1; 18:1), the Lord was challenging Baal's power in Baal's own domain. The entire drought story in chaps. 17–18 implies what becomes explicit in 18:21–40: this is a struggle between the Lord and Baal for the loyalties of the people of Israel.

18:8 Elijah is here: the Hebrew *hinneh 'eliyahu* involves a pun. The sentence means both "Elijah is here," informing Ahab that the prophet has been found, and "Behold, Yhwh is my God" (the meaning of the name "Elijah").

louder and slashed themselves with swords and spears according to their ritual until blood gushed over them. [29]Noon passed and they remained in a prophetic state until the time for offering sacrifice. But there was no sound, no one answering, no one listening.

[30]Then Elijah said to all the people, "Come here to me." When they drew near to him, he repaired the altar of the LORD which had been destroyed. [31]He took twelve stones, for the number of tribes of the sons of Jacob, to whom the LORD had said: Israel shall be your name. [32]He built the stones into an altar to the name of the LORD, and made a trench around the altar large enough for two measures of grain. [33]When he had arranged the wood, he cut up the young bull and laid it on the wood. [34]He said, "Fill four jars with water and pour it over the burnt offering and over the wood." "Do it again," he said, and they did it again. "Do it a third time," he said, and they did it a third time. [35]The water flowed around the altar; even the trench was filled with the water. [36]At the time for offering sacrifice, Elijah the prophet came forward and said, "LORD, God of Abraham, Isaac, and Israel, let it be known this day that you are God in Israel and that I am your servant and have done all these things at your command. [37][y] Answer me, LORD! Answer me, that this people may know that you, LORD, are God and that you have turned their hearts back to you." [38]The LORD's fire came down and devoured the burnt offering, wood, stones, and dust, and lapped up the water in the trench. [39]Seeing this, all the people fell prostrate and said, "The LORD is God! The LORD is God!" [40][z] Then Elijah said to them, "Seize the prophets of Baal. Let none of them escape!" They seized them, and Elijah brought them down to the Wadi Kishon and there he slaughtered them. [41]Elijah then said to Ahab, "Go up, eat and drink, for there is the sound of a heavy rain." [42]So Ahab went up to eat and drink, while Elijah went up to the top of Carmel, crouched down to the earth, and put his head between his knees. [43]He said to his servant, "Go up and look out to sea." He went up and looked, but reported, "There is nothing." Seven times he said, "Go look again!" [44]And the seventh time the youth reported, "There is a cloud as small as a man's hand rising from the sea." Elijah said, "Go and say to Ahab, 'Harness up and go down the mountain before the rain stops you.' " [45]All at once the sky grew dark with clouds and wind, and a heavy rain fell. Ahab mounted his chariot and headed for Jezreel. [46]But the hand of the LORD was on Elijah. He girded up his clothing and ran before Ahab as far as the approaches to Jezreel.

CHAPTER 19

See RG 190–91

Flight to Horeb. * [1]Ahab told Jezebel all that Elijah had done—that he had murdered all the prophets by the sword. [2]Jezebel then sent a messenger to Elijah and said, "May the gods do thus to me and more, if by this time tomorrow I have not done with your life what was done to each of them." [3]Elijah was afraid and fled for his life, going to Beer-sheba of Judah. He left his servant there [4][a] and went a day's journey into the wilderness, until he came to a solitary broom tree and sat beneath it. He prayed for death: "Enough, LORD! Take my life, for I am no better than my ancestors." [5]He lay down and fell asleep under the solitary broom tree, but suddenly a messenger* touched him and said, "Get up and eat!" [6]He looked and there at his head was a hearth cake and a jug of water. After he ate and drank, he lay down again, [7]but the angel of the LORD came back a second time, touched him, and said, "Get up and eat or the journey will be too much for you!" [8][b] He got up, ate, and drank; then strengthened by that food, he walked forty days and forty nights to the mountain of God, Horeb.

19:1–21 The story of Elijah's journey to Mount Horeb begins as a flight from danger, but takes a surprising turn. The prophet makes his solitary way to the mountain where the Lord had appeared to Moses and the Israelites ("Horeb" is an alternate name for "Sinai"). Like Moses on the holy mountain, Elijah experiences a theophany and receives a commission.

19:5–7 Sound asleep, Elijah is startled awake by an unspecified "messenger." Only in v. 7 is the figure identified as a messenger (or "angel") of the Lord.

y: Ex 32:13. *z:* Ex 32:26–28. *a:* Jon 4:6–9. *b:* Ex 34:28.

[9]There he came to a cave, where he took shelter. But the word of the LORD came to him: Why are you here, Elijah? [10]He answered: "I have been most zealous for the LORD, the God of hosts, but the Israelites have forsaken your covenant. They have destroyed your altars and murdered your prophets by the sword. I alone remain, and they seek to take my life." [11c] Then the LORD said: Go out and stand on the mountain before the LORD;* the LORD will pass by. There was a strong and violent wind rending the mountains and crushing rocks before the LORD—but the LORD was not in the wind; after the wind, an earthquake—but the LORD was not in the earthquake; [12]after the earthquake, fire—but the LORD was not in the fire; after the fire, a light silent sound.*

[13]When he heard this, Elijah hid his face in his cloak and went out and stood at the entrance of the cave. A voice said to him, Why are you here, Elijah? [14d] He replied, "I have been most zealous for the LORD, the God of hosts, but the Israelites have forsaken your covenant. They have destroyed your altars and murdered your prophets by the sword. I alone remain, and they seek to take my life." [15*e] The LORD said to him: Go back! Take the desert road to Damascus. When you arrive, you shall anoint Hazael as king of Aram. [16f] You shall also anoint Jehu, son of Nimshi, as king of Israel, and Elisha, son of Shaphat of Abel-meholah, as prophet to succeed you. [17]Anyone who escapes the sword of Hazael, Jehu will kill. Anyone who escapes the sword of Jehu, Elisha will kill. [18g] But I will spare seven thousand in Israel—every knee that has not bent to Baal, every mouth that has not kissed him.

[19*] Elijah set out, and came upon Elisha, son of Shaphat, as he was plowing with twelve yoke of oxen; he was following the twelfth. Elijah went over to him and threw his cloak on him. [20h] Elisha left the oxen, ran after Elijah, and said, "Please, let me kiss my father and mother good-bye, and I will follow you." Elijah answered, "Go back! What have I done to you?" [21]Elisha left him and, taking the yoke of oxen, slaughtered them; he used the plowing equipment for fuel to boil their flesh, and gave it to the people to eat. Then he left and followed Elijah to serve him.

V. The Story of Ahab*

CHAPTER 20

See RG 191

Ahab's Victories over Aram.* [1]Ben-hadad, king of Aram, gathered all his forces and, accompanied by thirty-two kings with horses and chariotry, set out to besiege and

19:11–13 To "stand before the Lord" is a literal translation of a Hebrew idiom meaning "to serve the Lord"; Elijah has used this idiom twice before to describe himself as the Lord's servant (17:1; 18:15). The Lord's command, then, means that Elijah is to take up once again the prophetic service to which he has been appointed. The Lord's question, "Why are you here?" (v. 9, repeated in v. 13), could imply an accusation that he is abandoning his prophetic office. In v. 15, the Lord tells him to go back.

19:12 Compare these divine manifestations to Elijah with those to Moses on the same mountain (Ex 19:16–19; 33:18–23; 34:5–6; Dt 4:10–15). Though various phenomena, such as wind, storms, earthquakes, fire, accompany the divine presence, they do not constitute the presence itself which, like the "silent sound," is mysterious and ultimately ungraspable. Moses and Elijah, the two figures who experienced God's theophany on this mountain, reappear with Jesus on another mountain at his transfiguration (Mt 17:1–9; Mk 9:2–9; Lk 9:28–36).

19:15–17 Elijah himself carried out only the last of the three commissions entrusted to him (vv. 19–21); Elisha performed the first himself (2 Kgs 8:7–19), and the second, the anointing of Jehu, through one of his followers (2 Kgs 9:1–10).

19:19–21 Elijah's act of throwing his mantle over the shoulders of Elisha associates him with Elijah as a servant (v. 21). Elisha will later succeed to Elijah's position and prophetic power (2 Kgs 2:1–15). Elisha's prompt response, destroying his plow and oxen, signifies a radical change from his former manner of living.

20:1–22:54 Although coverage of Ahab's reign began in 16:29, he was only a secondary character in the chapters about Elijah. Now attention focuses on Ahab. Each of these chapters tells a story of the king (20:1–34; 21:1–16; 22:1–4, 29–38), to which is attached a scene of prophetic condemnation (20:30–42; 21:17–29; 22:5–28). As relations between Ahab and the prophets of the Lord deteriorate, the scenes of prophetic condemnation get longer and the condemnations themselves become more pointed. Some historians doubt that the stories of hostility between Israel and Aram (chaps. 20 and 22) originally pertained to the reign of Ahab. If this is correct, their original setting may have been several decades later.

20:1–34 This story recounts two battles through which Ahab won freedom for Israel from vassalage to Ben-hadad of Syria. The story is chiastically arranged: negotiations (vv. 1–12), battle (vv. 13–21), battle (vv. 22–30), negotiations (vv. 31–34). The ensuing prophetic condemnation is surprising, since the portrait of Ahab in vv. 1–34 is apparently quite positive.

c: Ex 33:18–23; 34:5–6. *d:* Rom 11:3. *e:* 2 Kgs 8:7–15. *f:* 2 Kgs 2:1–15; 9:1–10. *g:* Rom 11:4. *h:* Lk 9:61–62.

attack Samaria. [2]He sent messengers to Ahab, king of Israel, within the city, [3]and said to him, "This is Ben-hadad's message: 'Your silver and gold are mine, and your wives and your fine children are mine.' " [4]The king of Israel answered, "Just as you say, my lord king, I and all I have are yours." [5]But the messengers came again and said, "This is Ben-hadad's message: 'I sent you word: Give me your silver and gold, your wives and your children. [6]But now I say: At this time tomorrow I will send my servants to you, and they shall ransack your house and the houses of your servants. They shall seize and take away whatever you consider valuable.' " [7]The king of Israel then summoned all the elders of the land and said: "Understand clearly that this man is intent on evil. When he sent to me for my wives and children, my silver and my gold, I did not refuse him." [8]All the elders and all the people said to him, "Do not listen. Do not give in." [9]Accordingly he directed the messengers of Ben-hadad, "Say this: 'To my lord the king: I will do all that you demanded of your servant the first time. But this I cannot do.' " The messengers left and reported this. [10]Ben-hadad then responded, "May the gods do thus to me and more, if there will remain enough dust in Samaria to make handfuls for all my followers." [11]The king of Israel replied, "Tell him, 'Let not one who puts on armor boast like one who takes it off.' " [12]Ben-hadad was drinking in the pavilions with the kings when he heard this reply. He commanded his servants, "Get ready!"; and they got ready to storm the city.

[13]Then a prophet came up to Ahab, king of Israel, and said: "The LORD says, Do you see all this vast army? Today I am giving it into your power, that you may know that I am the LORD." [14]But Ahab asked, "Through whom will it be given over?" He answered, "The LORD says, Through the aides of the provincial governors." Then Ahab asked, "Who is to attack?" He replied, "You are." [15]So Ahab mustered the aides of the provincial governors, two hundred thirty-two of them. Behind them he mustered all the Israelite soldiery, who numbered seven thousand in all. [16]* They marched out at noon, while Ben-hadad was drinking heavily in the pavilions with the thirty-two kings who were his allies. [17]When the aides of the provincial governors marched out first, Ben-hadad received word, "Some men have marched out of Samaria." [18]He answered, "Whether they have come out for peace or for war, take them alive." [19]But when these had come out of the city—the aides of the provincial governors with the army following them— [20]each of them struck down his man. The Arameans fled with Israel pursuing them, while Ben-hadad, king of Aram, escaped on a chariot horse. [21]Then the king of Israel went out and destroyed the horses and chariots. Thus he inflicted a severe defeat on Aram.

[22]Then the prophet approached the king of Israel and said to him: "Go, regroup your forces. Understand clearly what you must do, for at the turning of the year* the king of Aram will attack you." [23]Meanwhile the servants of the king of Aram said to him: "Their gods are mountain gods. That is why they defeated us. But if we fight them on level ground, we shall be sure to defeat them. [24]This is what you must do: Take the kings from their posts and put prefects in their places. [25]Raise an army as large as the army you have lost, horse for horse, chariot for chariot. Let us fight them on level ground, and we shall surely defeat them." He took their advice and did this. [26]At the turning of the year, Ben-hadad mustered Aram and went up to Aphek to fight against Israel. [27]The Israelites, too, were mustered and supplied with provisions; then they went out to meet the enemy. The Israelites, encamped opposite, looked like little flocks of goats, while Aram covered the land. [28]A man of God approached and said to the king of Is-

20:16–19 The narrator uses a sort of verbal split-screen technique to show us two separate and simultaneous scenes. At the gates of Samaria, the Israelite forces are coming out to battle (v. 16a): first the aides (lit., "young men"; v. 17a), then the whole army (v. 19). Meanwhile in the Aramean camp Ben-hadad is getting drunk (v. 16b), receiving reports (v. 17b) and issuing commands (v. 18).

20:22 At the turning of the year: the idiom may mean "next year about this time" or "at the beginning of the year," i.e., the spring (cf. 2 Sm 11:1).

rael: "The LORD says, Because Aram has said the LORD is a god of mountains, not a god of plains, I will give all this vast army into your power that you may know I am the LORD." 29 They were encamped opposite each other for seven days. On the seventh day battle was joined, and the Israelites struck down one hundred thousand foot soldiers of Aram in one day. 30 The survivors fled into the city of Aphek, where the wall collapsed on twenty-seven thousand of them. Ben-hadad, too, fled, and took refuge within the city, in an inner room.

31 His servants said to him: "We have heard that the kings of the house of Israel are merciful kings. Allow us, therefore, to garb ourselves in sackcloth, with cords around our heads, and go out to the king of Israel. Perhaps he will spare your life." 32 Dressed in sackcloth girded at the waist and wearing cords around their heads, they went to the king of Israel and said, "Your servant Ben-hadad says, 'Spare my life!'" He asked, "Is he still alive? He is my brother."[*] 33 Hearing this as a good omen, the men quickly took him at his word and said, "Ben-hadad is your brother." He answered, "Go and get him." When Ben-hadad came out to him, the king had him mount his chariot. 34 Ben-hadad said to him, "The cities my father took from your father I will restore, and you may set up bazaars for yourself in Damascus, as my father did in Samaria." Ahab replied, "For my part, I will set you free on those terms." So he made a covenant with him and then set him free.

Prophetic Condemnation. 35 Acting on the word of the LORD, one of the guild prophets said to his companion, "Strike me." But he refused to strike him. 36 Then he said to him, "Since you did not obey the voice of the LORD, a lion will attack you when you leave me." When he left him, a lion came upon him and attacked him.[i] 37 Then the prophet met another man and said, "Strike me." The man struck him a blow and wounded him. 38 The prophet went on and waited for the king on the road, disguising himself with a bandage over his eyes. 39 As the king was passing, he called out to the king and said: "Your servant went into the thick of the battle, and suddenly someone turned and brought me a man and said, 'Guard this man. If he is missing, you shall have to pay for his life with your life or pay out a talent of silver.'[*] 40 But while your servant was occupied here and there, the man disappeared." The king of Israel said to him, "That is your sentence. You have decided it yourself." 41 He quickly removed the bandage from his eyes, and the king of Israel recognized him as one of the prophets. 42[j] He said to him: "The LORD says, Because you have set free the man I put under the ban,[*] your life shall pay for his life, your people for his people." 43[k] Disturbed and angry, the king of Israel set off for home and entered Samaria.

CHAPTER 21

See RG 191

Seizure of Naboth's Vineyard.[*] 1 Naboth the Jezreelite had a vineyard in Jezreel next to the palace of Ahab, king of Samaria. Some time later, 2 Ahab said to Naboth, "Give me your vineyard to be my vegetable garden, since it is close by, next to my house. I will give you a better vineyard in exchange, or, if you prefer, I will give you its value in money." 3 Naboth said to Ahab, "The LORD forbid that I should give you my ancestral heritage."[*] 4 Ahab went home disturbed and angry at the answer Naboth the Jezreelite had

20:32 He is my brother: cf. note on 9:13.

20:39 The "man" is ostensibly a prisoner of war, to be kept or sold as a slave. In the event he escapes, the one charged with guarding him would be obliged either to pay a fine or to take his place as a slave. The fine, however, is exorbitant: a talent of silver is roughly one hundred times the price of an ordinary slave (see Ex 21:32). This is the only clue Ahab will get that he is being set up and that the story is really about himself in his dealings with Ben-hadad. In 2 Sm 14:1–20, the wise woman of Tekoa uses the same technique with King David: she tells a story that elicits a reaction from the king; David is tricked into pronouncing judgment on himself, as the story parallels his own situation. The prophet Nathan (2 Sm 12:1–7) likewise uses a story that leads David to see his sin for what it is.

20:42 Under the ban: cf. note on Dt 2:34.

21:1–16 The story tells how Jezebel manipulates important structures of Israelite social order, law, and religious observance to eliminate a faithful Israelite landowner who frustrates Ahab's will.

21:3 Heritage: Hebrew *nahalah*. Naboth is unwilling to sell or exchange his vineyard. According to the Israelite system of land tenure and distribution, land was held in common

i: 1 Kgs 13:24. *j:* 1 Kgs 22:35. *k:* 1 Kgs 21:4.

given him: "I will not give you my ancestral heritage." Lying down on his bed, he turned away and would not eat. [5]His wife Jezebel came to him and said to him, "Why are you so sullen that you will not eat?" [6]He answered her, "Because I spoke to Naboth the Jezreelite and said to him, 'Sell me your vineyard, or, if you prefer, I will give you a vineyard in exchange.' But he said, 'I will not give you my vineyard.' " [7]Jezebel his wife said to him, "What a king of Israel you are! Get up! Eat and be cheerful. I will give you the vineyard of Naboth the Jezreelite."

[8]So she wrote letters in Ahab's name and, having sealed them with his seal, sent them to the elders and to the nobles who lived in the same city with Naboth. [9]This is what she wrote in the letters: "Proclaim a fast and set Naboth at the head of the people. [10]Next, set two scoundrels opposite him to accuse him: 'You have cursed God and king.' Then take him out and stone him to death."

[11]His fellow citizens—the elders and the nobles who dwelt in his city—did as Jezebel had ordered in the letters she sent them. [12]They proclaimed a fast and set Naboth at the head of the people. [13]Two scoundrels came in and sat opposite Naboth, and the scoundrels accused him in the presence of the people, "Naboth has cursed God and king." And they led him out of the city and stoned him to death. [14]Then they sent word to Jezebel: "Naboth has been stoned to death."

[15]When Jezebel learned that Naboth had been stoned to death, she said to Ahab, "Go, take possession of the vineyard of Naboth the Jezreelite which he refused to sell you, because Naboth is not alive, but dead." [16]When Ahab heard that Naboth was dead, he started on his way down to the vineyard of Naboth the Jezreelite, to take possession of it.

Prophetic Condemnation. [17]Then the word of the LORD came to Elijah the Tishbite: [18]Go down to meet Ahab, king of Israel, who is in Samaria. He will be in the vineyard of Naboth, where he has gone to take possession. [19][l] Tell him: "Thus says the LORD: After murdering, do you also take possession?" And tell him, "Thus says the LORD: In the place where the dogs licked up the blood of Naboth, the dogs shall lick up your blood, too."

[20*] Ahab said to Elijah, "Have you found me out, my enemy?" He said, "I have found you. Because you have given yourself up to doing evil in the LORD's sight, [21][m] I am bringing evil upon you: I will consume you and will cut off every male belonging to Ahab, whether bond or free, in Israel. [22]I will make your house like that of Jeroboam, son of Nebat, and like the house of Baasha, son of Ahijah, because you have provoked me by leading Israel into sin."

[23]Against Jezebel, too, the LORD declared: The dogs shall devour Jezebel in the confines of Jezreel.

[24] Anyone of Ahab's line who dies in the city,
dogs will devour;
Anyone who dies in the field,
the birds of the sky will devour.

[25]Indeed, no one gave himself up to the doing of evil in the sight of the LORD as did Ahab, urged on by his wife Jezebel. [26]He became completely abominable by going after idols, just as the Amorites had done, whom the LORD drove out of the Israelites' way.

[27]When Ahab heard these words, he tore his garments and put on sackcloth over his bare flesh. He fasted, slept in the sackcloth, and went about subdued. [28]Then the word of the LORD came to Elijah the Tishbite, [29][n] Have you seen how Ahab has humbled himself before me? Since he has humbled himself before me, I will not bring the evil in

within a social unit. The ancestral *nahalah* was not private property, to be alienated at will.

21:20–26 In these verses the narrator uses against the third Israelite dynasty the same condemnation formula that was uttered against the first two dynasties, those of Jeroboam (14:9–11) and Baasha (16:2–4). Part of the formula is put in Elijah's mouth, in an oracle against Ahab and his descendants (vv. 21–22), and part of it in an aside to the reader that extends the condemnation to Ahab's wife, Jezebel, and his whole household (vv. 23–24). The oracle against Jezebel will be fulfilled in 2 Kgs 9:36; the obliteration of the dynasty will be recounted in the bloody stories of 2 Kgs 9–11.

l: 1 Kgs 22:38; 2 Kgs 9:26. *m:* 1 Kgs 14:10–11; 15:29; 16:3–4, 11; 2 Kgs 9:8–10, 36. *n:* 2 Kgs 9:25–26.

his time. I will bring the evil upon his house in his son's time.

See RG 191

CHAPTER 22

Ahab's Defeat by Aram. * [1]Three years passed without war between Aram and Israel. [2]In the third year, however, King Jehoshaphat of Judah came down to the king of Israel. [3]The king of Israel said to his servants, "Do you not know that Ramoth-gilead is ours and we are doing nothing to take it from the king of Aram?" [4]He asked Jehoshaphat, "Will you come with me to fight against Ramoth-gilead?" Jehoshaphat answered the king of Israel, "You and I are as one, and your people and my people, your horses and my horses as well."

Prophetic Condemnation. [5]Jehoshaphat also said to the king of Israel, "Seek the word of the LORD at once." [6]The king of Israel assembled the prophets, about four hundred of them, and asked, "Shall I go to fight against Ramoth-gilead or shall I refrain?" They said, "Attack. The Lord will give it into the power of the king."* [7]But Jehoshaphat said, "Is there no other prophet of the LORD here we might consult?" [8]The king of Israel answered, "There is one other man through whom we might consult the LORD; but I hate him because he prophesies not good but evil about me. He is Micaiah, son of Imlah." Jehoshaphat said, "Let not the king say that." [9]So the king of Israel called an official and said to him, "Get Micaiah, son of Imlah, at once."

[10]The king of Israel and Jehoshaphat, king of Judah, were seated, each on his throne, clothed in their robes of state in the square at the entrance of the gate of Samaria, and all the prophets were prophesying before them. [11][o]Zedekiah, son of Chenaanah, made himself two horns of iron* and said, "The LORD says, With these you shall gore Aram until you have destroyed them." [12]The other prophets prophesied in a similar vein, saying: "Attack Ramoth-gilead and conquer! The LORD will give it into the power of the king."

[13]Meanwhile, the messenger who had gone to call Micaiah said to him, "Look now, the prophets are unanimously predicting good for the king. Let your word be the same as any of theirs; speak a good word." [14]Micaiah said, "As the LORD lives, I shall speak whatever the LORD tells me."

[15]When he came to the king, the king said to him, "Micaiah, shall we go to fight at Ramoth-gilead, or shall we refrain?" He said, "Attack and conquer! The LORD will give it into the power of the king." [16]But the king answered him, "How many times must I adjure you to tell me nothing but the truth in the name of the LORD?" [17]* So Micaiah said:

"I see all Israel
scattered on the mountains,
like sheep without a shepherd,
And the LORD saying,
These have no master!
Let each of them go back home in peace."

[18]The king of Israel said to Jehoshaphat, "Did I not tell you, he does not prophesy good about me, but only evil?" [19]* Micaiah continued: "Therefore hear the word of the LORD: I saw the LORD seated on his throne, with the whole host of heaven standing to

22:1–40 This chapter presents a contrasting parallel to chap. 20, where Ahab enjoyed victories over Aram's aggression. Here Ahab is the aggressor, but falls in battle against Aram. Like the preceding chapters, it contains a story of Ahab plus an episode of prophetic condemnation. The story ends with the formulaic conclusion to Ahab's reign (vv. 39–40). Chronicles has a parallel version of this account in 2 Chr 18:1–34. After the story of Ahab's death come accounts of the reign of Jehoshaphat (paralleled in 2 Chr 20:31–37) and of the beginning of the reign of Ahaziah.

22:6 Though Ahab is clearly intended to understand the oracle as prophesying his success, the prophets' words are ambiguous. "The lord" (not "the LORD," i.e., the proper name of Israel's God) who will give victory is unidentified, as is the king to whom it will be given.

22:11 The "two" horns probably symbolize the coalition of two kings, Ahab and Jehoshaphat.

22:17 Micaiah's oracle uses the common ancient metaphor of "shepherd" for the king. It means that the Israelite forces will be left leaderless because the king (or perhaps both kings: the word "master" could be singular or plural in Hebrew) will die in battle.

22:19–23 Since Ahab's intention to attack Ramoth-gilead is unshaken, Micaiah reveals God's plan to trick Ahab to his death, and thus virtually dares Ahab to walk into the trap with his eyes open. The work of the "lying spirit" explains the ambiguities of the prophets' original oracle in v. 6. Prophets "stand in the council of the Lord" and are privy to its deliberations; cf. Jer 23:22.

o: Dt 33:17.

his right and to his left. [20]The LORD asked: Who will deceive Ahab, so that he will go up and fall on Ramoth-gilead?* And one said this, another that, [21]until this spirit came forth and stood before the LORD, saying, 'I will deceive him.' The LORD asked: How? [22]He answered, 'I will go forth and become a lying spirit in the mouths of all his prophets.' The LORD replied: You shall succeed in deceiving him. Go forth and do this. [23]So now, the LORD has put a lying spirit in the mouths of all these prophets of yours; the LORD himself has decreed evil against you."

[24]Thereupon Zedekiah, son of Chenaanah, came up and struck Micaiah on the cheek, saying, "Has the spirit of the LORD, then, left me to speak with you?" [25]Micaiah said, "You shall find out on the day you go into an inner room to hide." [26]The king of Israel then said, "Seize Micaiah and take him back to Amon, prefect of the city, and to Joash, the king's son, [27]and say, 'This is the king's order: Put this man in prison and feed him scanty rations of bread and water until I come back in safety.' " [28][p] But Micaiah said, "If you return in safety, the LORD has not spoken through me." (He also said, "Hear, O peoples, all of you.")*

Ahab at Ramoth-gilead. [29]The king of Israel and Jehoshaphat, king of Judah, went up to Ramoth-gilead, [30]and the king of Israel said to Jehoshaphat, "I will disguise myself and go into battle, but you put on your own robes." So the king of Israel disguised himself and entered the battle. [31]In the meantime the king of Aram had given his thirty-two chariot commanders the order, "Do not fight with anyone, great or small, except the king of Israel alone."

[32]When the chariot commanders saw Jehoshaphat, they cried out, "There is the king of Israel!" and wheeled to fight him. But Jehoshaphat cried out, [33]and the chariot commanders, seeing that he was not the king of Israel, turned away from him. [34]But someone drew his bow at random, and hit the king of Israel between the joints of his breastplate. He ordered his charioteer, "Rein about and take me out of the ranks, for I am wounded."

[35][q] The battle grew fierce during the day, and the king, who was propped up in his chariot facing the Arameans, died in the evening. The blood from his wound flowed to the bottom of the chariot. [36]At sunset a cry went through the army, "Every man to his city, every man to his land!"

[37]And so the king died, and came back to Samaria, and they buried him there. [38][r] When they washed out the chariot at the pool of Samaria, the dogs licked up his blood and prostitutes bathed there, as the LORD had prophesied.

[39]The rest of the acts of Ahab, with all that he did, including the ivory house he built and all the cities he built, are recorded in the book of the chronicles of the kings of Israel. [40]Ahab rested with his ancestors, and his son Ahaziah succeeded him as king.

Reign of Jehoshaphat. [41]Jehoshaphat, son of Asa, became king of Judah in the fourth year of Ahab, king of Israel. [42]Jehoshaphat was thirty-five years old when he became king, and he reigned twenty-five years in Jerusalem. His mother's name was Azubah, daughter of Shilhi.

[43]He walked in the way of Asa his father unceasingly, doing what was right in the LORD's sight. [44]Nevertheless, the high places did not disappear, and the people still sacrificed on the high places and burned incense there. [45]Jehoshaphat also made peace with the king of Israel.

[46]The rest of the acts of Jehoshaphat, with his valor, what he did and how he fought, are recorded in the book of the chronicles of the kings of Judah. [47]He removed from the land the rest of the pagan priests who had remained in the reign of Asa his father. [48]There was no king in Edom, but an appointed regent. [49]Jehoshaphat made Tarshish ships to go to Ophir for gold; but in fact the ships did

22:20 Fall on Ramoth-gilead: lit., "heights of Gilead"; even the Lord's words are double-meaning. God wants Ahab to "fall on" (that is, attack) Ramoth-gilead so that he will "fall on" (that is, die on) Ramoth-gilead.

22:28 The last words of the verse are a scribal gloss attributing to Micaiah, son of Imlah, the opening words of the book of a different Micaiah (Micah), the prophet of Moresheth, the sixth of the twelve minor prophets of the Old Testament canon.

p: Mi 1:2. *q:* 1 Kgs 20:42. *r:* 1 Kgs 21:19.

not go, because they were wrecked at Ezion-geber. [50]That was the time when Ahaziah, son of Ahab, had said to Jehoshaphat, "Let my servants accompany your servants in the ships." But Jehoshaphat would not agree. [51]Jehoshaphat rested with his ancestors; he was buried with his ancestors in the City of David his father, and his son Jehoram succeeded him as king.

Reign of Ahaziah.* [52]Ahaziah, son of Ahab, became king over Israel in Samaria in the seventeenth year* of Jehoshaphat, king of Judah; he reigned two years over Israel. [53]He did what was evil in the sight of the LORD, walking in the way of his father, his mother, and Jeroboam, son of Nebat, who caused Israel to sin. [54]He served Baal and worshiped him, thus provoking the LORD, the God of Israel, just as his father had done.

22:52–54 The account of Ahaziah's reign continues in 2 Kings.

22:52 Seventeenth year: so the present Hebrew text. This is consistent with the figures in 2 Kgs 3:1, but together those figures conflict with information in 1 Kgs 22:42 and 2 Kgs 1:17. The problem of the chronology of the kings of Israel and Judah has never been convincingly resolved; it is complicated by the fact that the ancient Greek translation sometimes has different lengths of reign and different accession dates. See further note on 2 Kgs 3:1.

See RG 191–98

The Second Book of Kings

CHAPTER 1

See RG 191

Reign of Ahaziah, Continued. [1]After Ahab's death, Moab rebelled against Israel.[a]

[2]Ahaziah fell through the lattice of his roof terrace at Samaria and was injured. So he sent out messengers with the instructions: "Go and inquire of Baalzebub,* the god of Ekron, whether I shall recover from this injury."

[3]Meanwhile, the messenger of the LORD said to Elijah the Tishbite: Go and meet the messengers of Samaria's king, and tell them: "Is it because there is no God in Israel that you are going to inquire of Baalzebub, the god of Ekron?" [4]For this, the LORD says: You shall not leave the bed upon which you lie; instead, you shall die. And Elijah departed. [5]The messengers then returned to Ahaziah, who asked them, "Why have you returned?" [6]They answered, "A man met us and said to us, 'Go back to the king who sent you and tell him: The LORD says: Is it because there is no God in Israel that you are sending to inquire of Baalzebub, the god of Ekron? For this you shall not leave the bed upon which you lie; instead, you shall die.' " [7]The king asked them, "What was the man like who met you and said these things to you?" [8]They replied, "He wore a hairy garment* with a leather belt around his waist." "It is Elijah the Tishbite!" he exclaimed.

[9]Then the king sent a captain with his company of fifty men after Elijah. The prophet was seated on a hilltop when he found him. He said, "Man of God, the king commands you, 'Come down.' " [10]Elijah answered the captain, "Well, if I am a man of God, may fire come down from heaven and consume you and your fifty men." And fire came down from heaven and consumed him and his fifty men.[b] [11]The king sent another captain with his company of fifty men after Elijah. He shouted up and said, "Man of God, the king says, 'Come down immediately!' " [12]Elijah answered them, "If I am a man of God, may fire come down from heaven and consume you and your fifty men." And divine fire* came down from

1:2 Baalzebub: in this form, "Baal of flies." The name in the Hebrew text is a derisive alteration of Baalzebul, "Prince Baal." The best New Testament evidence supports the latter form in Mt 10:25; Lk 11:15.

1:8 Hairy garment: a sign of prophetic calling; see Zec 13:4. John the Baptizer wore a similarly distinctive mantle; see Mt 3:4; Mk 1:6.

1:12 Divine fire: lit., "fire of God," which in Hebrew sounds quite like "man of God." The play on words is the basis for Elijah's retort. This story was told among the people to enhance the dignity of the prophet and to reflect the power of God whom he served. A similar phrase, "the LORD's fire," described the miraculous divine fire that fell from a cloudless sky to consume Elijah's offering in 1 Kgs 18:38.

a: 2 Kgs 3:4–27. *b:* Lv 10:1–2; Sir 48:3; Lk 9:51–55.

heaven and consumed him and his fifty men. 13The king sent a third captain with his company of fifty men. When the third captain had climbed the hill, he fell to his knees before Elijah, pleading with him. He said, "Man of God, let my life and the lives of these fifty men, your servants, count for something in your sight! 14Already fire has come down from heaven, consuming the first two captains with their companies of fifty men. But now, let my life count for something in your sight!" 15Then the messenger of the LORD said to Elijah: Go down with him; you need not be afraid of him. So Elijah left and went down with him to the king. 16He declared to the king: "Thus says the LORD: Because you sent messengers to inquire of Baalzebub, the god of Ekron—do you think there is no God in Israel to inquire of?—you shall not leave the bed upon which you lie; instead you shall die."[c]

17Ahaziah died according to the word of the LORD spoken by Elijah. Since he had no son, Joram* succeeded him as king, in the second year of Joram, son of Jehoshaphat, king of Judah.

18The rest of the acts of Ahaziah, which he did, are recorded in the book of chronicles of the kings of Israel.

VI. Elisha Succeeds Elijah*

CHAPTER 2

See RG 192

Elijah's Journey. 1When the LORD was about to take Elijah up to heaven in a whirlwind, he and Elisha were on their way from Gilgal.* 2Elijah said to Elisha, "Stay here, please. The LORD has sent me on to Bethel." Elisha replied, "As the LORD lives, and as you yourself live, I will not leave you." So they went down to Bethel. 3The guild prophets who were in Bethel went out to Elisha and asked him, "Do you know that today the LORD will take your master from you?" He replied, "Yes, I know that. Be still."

4Elijah said to him, "Elisha, stay here, please. The LORD has sent me on to Jericho." Elisha replied, "As the LORD lives, and as you yourself live, I will not leave you." So they came to Jericho. 5The guild prophets who were in Jericho approached Elisha and asked him, "Do you know that today the LORD will take your master from you?" He replied, "Yes, I know that. Be still."

6Elijah said to him, "Stay here, please. The LORD has sent me on to the Jordan." Elisha replied, "As the LORD lives, and as you yourself live, I will not leave you." So the two went on together. 7Fifty of the guild prophets followed and stood facing them at a distance, while the two of them stood next to the Jordan.

Elisha Succeeds Elijah. 8Elijah took his mantle, rolled it up and struck the water: it divided, and the two of them crossed over on dry ground.[d]

9[e] When they had crossed over, Elijah said to Elisha, "Request whatever I might do for you, before I am taken from you." Elisha answered, "May I receive a double portion of your spirit."* 10He replied, "You have asked something that is not easy. Still, if you see me taken up from you, your wish will be granted; otherwise not." 11As they walked

1:17 Joram: in 2 Kings the name "Joram" (*yoram*) and its variant "Jehoram" (*yehoram*) are used interchangeably. To avoid the impression that they are different names and designate different people, both forms are rendered "Joram" in this translation. Confusion arises, however, because the king of Israel whose reign is recounted beginning in 3:1 and the contemporary king of Judah whose reign is recounted beginning in 8:16 share this name. On the relationship of Joram of Israel to Joram of Judah, see note on 3:1.

2:1–25 The story of Elisha's succession to Elijah's prophetic office is oddly set between the death of Ahaziah (1:17) and the accession of his successor (3:1). The effect is to place this scene, which is the central scene in the whole of 1–2 Kings, outside of time. It thereby becomes almost mythic in its import and reminds us that, behind the transitory flow of kings and kingdoms, stand the eternal word of God and the prophets who give it voice. Just as 1–2 Kings pivots on this chapter, so this scene too is concentrically constructed. Together Elijah and Elisha journey to Bethel, thence to Jericho, and thence across the Jordan. There Elijah is taken up in the whirlwind and Elijah's mantle of power comes to Elisha. Now alone, Elisha crosses the Jordan again, returns to Jericho and thence back to Bethel.

2:1 Gilgal: there are several places in the Hebrew Bible named Gilgal; the word probably means "circle," viz. of stones. Here the route of the prophets' journey rules out the most famous Gilgal (Jos 4–5), the one near Jericho. This Gilgal may have been located in the area of modern Jiljulieh, approximately seven miles north of Bethel, which seems to preserve the ancient name.

2:9 Double portion of your spirit: as the firstborn son in-

c: Sir 48:6. *d:* Ex 14:15–22; Jos 3:14–17. *e:* Nm 11:16–17, 24–29.

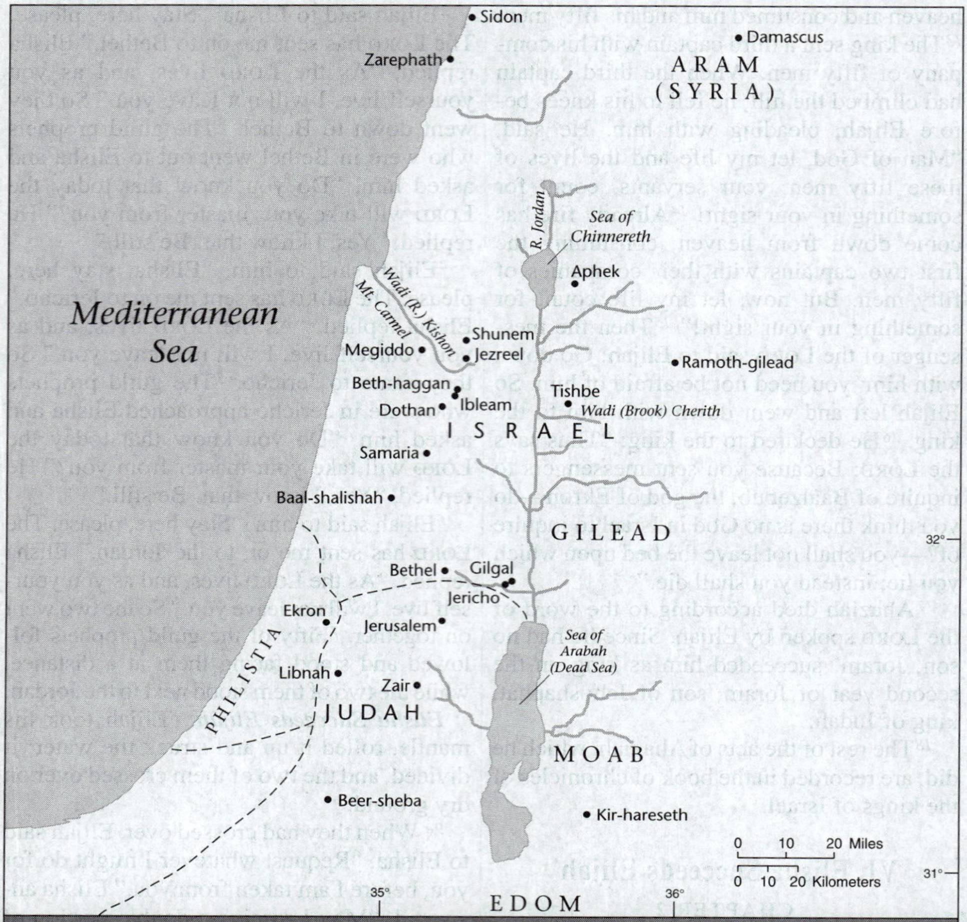

Places Associated with Elisha

on still conversing, a fiery chariot and fiery
horses came between the two of them, and
Elijah went up to heaven in a whirlwind,[f]
[12]and Elisha saw it happen. He cried out,
"My father! my father!* Israel's chariot and
steeds!" Then he saw him no longer.

He gripped his own garment, tore it into
two pieces, [13]and picked up the mantle
which had fallen from Elijah. Then he went
back and stood at the bank of the Jordan.
[14]Wielding the mantle which had fallen from
Elijah, he struck the water and said, "The
LORD, the God of Elijah—where is he
now?"* He struck the water: it divided, and
he crossed over.

Elisha's Journey. [15]The guild prophets in
Jericho, who were on the other side, saw him
and said, "The spirit of Elijah rests on Eli-

herited a double portion of his father's property (Dt 21:17), so Elisha asks to inherit from Elijah his spirit of prophecy in the degree befitting his principal disciple. In Nm 11:17–25, God bestows some of the spirit of Moses on others.

2:12 My father: a religious title accorded prophetic leaders; cf. 6:21; 8:9; and 13:14, where King Joash of Israel reacts to Elisha's own impending death with the same words Elisha uses here.

2:14 The LORD, the God of Elijah—where is he now?: the words in Hebrew have an incantatory quality, as if Elisha is invoking both the divine name and the name of his departed master in an attempt to duplicate Elijah's miracle.

f: Gn 5:24; 1 Mc 2:58; Sir 48:9–12; Acts 1:9.

sha." They went to meet him, bowing to the
ground before him.[g] 16 They said, "Among
your servants are fifty brave men. Let them
go in search of your master. Perhaps the spirit
of the LORD has lifted him up and left him on
some mountain or in some valley." He answered, "Do not send them."[h] 17 But they kept
urging him, until he was embarrassed and
said, "Send them." So they sent the fifty men,
who searched for three days without finding
him.[i] 18 When they returned to Elisha in Jericho, where he was staying, he said to them,
"Did I not tell you not to go?"
19[j] The inhabitants of the city complained
to Elisha, "The site of the city is fine indeed,
as my lord can see, but the water is bad and
the land sterile." 20 Elisha said, "Bring me a
new bowl and put salt into it." When they had
brought it to him, 21 he went out to the spring
and threw salt into it, saying, "Thus says the
LORD: I have purified this water. Never again
shall death or sterility come from it." 22 And
the water has stayed pure even to this day, according to the word Elisha had spoken.
23* From there Elisha went up to Bethel.
While he was on the way, some little boys
came out of the city and jeered at him: "Go
away, baldy; go away, baldy!" 24 The prophet
turned and saw them, and he cursed them in
the name of the LORD. Then two she-bears
came out of the woods and tore forty-two of
the children to pieces.
25 From there he went to Mount Carmel,
and returned to Samaria from there.

VII. Stories of Elisha and Joram*

CHAPTER 3

See RG 192

Reign of Joram of Israel. 1 Joram, son
of Ahab, became king over Israel in Samaria
in the eighteenth year of Jehoshaphat, king
of Judah, and he reigned twelve years.*
2[k] He did what was evil in the LORD's
sight, though not like his father and mother.
He did away with the pillar of Baal that his
father had made, 3 but he still held fast unceasingly to the sins which Jeroboam, son of
Nebat, caused Israel to commit.
War Against Moab: Drought. 4* Now Mesha, king of Moab, who raised sheep, used to
pay the king of Israel as tribute a hundred
thousand lambs and the wool of a hundred
thousand rams. 5 But when Ahab died, the
king of Moab rebelled against the king of Israel. 6 King Joram set out from Samaria and
mustered all Israel. 7[l] Then he sent Jehoshaphat, the king of Judah, the message: "The
king of Moab has rebelled against me. Will

2:23–24 This story probably was told to warn children of the importance of respect for prophets.

3:1–9:13 After the formulaic introduction to the reign of Joram of Israel, this section falls into two parts. The first contains several stories about the prophet Elisha, both in private and in public life. There are four longer stories, arranged in an ABBA pattern: drought during war with Moab (vv. 4–27), restoration of the Shunammite's son (4:8–37), healing of Naaman (5:1–27), famine during war with Aram (6:24–7:20). The last three of these stories are each preceded and followed by short anecdotal tales about Elisha. The second part of this section turns to the political realm. Elisha carries out the Lord's commissions to Elijah (1 Kgs 19:15–17) to anoint Hazael king of Aram (2 Kgs 8:7–15) and Jehu king of Israel (9:1–13). To prepare for the story of Jehu's insurrection (9:14–11:20), the narrator places between those two narratives notices about the royal succession in Judah (8:16–24, 25–29). The formulaic conclusions to the reigns of Joram of Israel and Ahaziah of Judah (8:25–29) are missing, since the deaths of both will be recounted in the story of Jehu's insurrection.

3:1 The contradiction between 1:17 and v. 1 regarding the year when Joram succeeded Ahaziah of Israel makes any reconstruction of the chronology of Israel's and Judah's kings uncertain. Some scholars think that one or the other notice is simply incorrect. Others propose to explain the discrepancy by a co-regency: Jehoshaphat of Judah would have shared the throne with his son Joram from Jehoshaphat's seventeenth year until he died in the twenty-fifth year of his reign (1 Kgs 22:42; see also 2 Kgs 8:16). The issue is further complicated by the speculation of some historians that "Joram of Israel" ("son" of Ahab of Israel: v. 1) and "Joram of Judah" ("son-in-law" of Ahab of Israel: 8:18) were in fact the same person, in whom the royal houses and separate realms of Israel and Judah were briefly reunited.

3:4 In the period of oral tradition, it seems that stories of kings were often told without identifying the kings by name. (Vestiges of this anonymity are still visible in 1 Kgs 3:16–28; 20:4–43; 22:1–38; 2 Kgs 6:8–7:20.) Names (such as "Ahab" in 1 Kgs 20:13–14; 22:20) were added later. As a consequence, the historical attachment of such stories to the kings about whom they are told is open to question. (See note on 1 Kgs 20:1–22:54.) The present story about a campaign against Moab by Joram and Jehoshaphat has several striking similarities to the campaign against Ramoth-gilead by Ahab and Jehoshaphat in 1 Kgs 22:1–38. There exists a Moabite inscription that contains Mesha's self-aggrandizing account of his successful rebellion against Israel, but the times and places it mentions are different from those implied in vv. 4–27.

g: 1 Kgs 19:19; Sir 48:12. *h:* 1 Kgs 18:12. *i:* 1 Kgs 17:2; 18:10. *j:* 2 Kgs 4:38–41. *k:* 1 Kgs 16:32. *l:* 1 Kgs 22:3–8.

you come with me to Moab to fight?" He replied, "I will. You and I are as one, your people and my people, and your horses and my horses as well." 8 He said, "By what route shall we attack?" and the other said, "By way of the wilderness of Edom."

9 So the king of Israel set out, accompanied by the king of Judah and the king of Edom. After a roundabout journey of seven days the water gave out for the army and for the animals with them. 10 The king of Israel exclaimed, "Alas! The LORD has called three kings together only to deliver us into the power of Moab." 11 But Jehoshaphat asked, "Is there no prophet of the LORD here through whom we may inquire of the LORD?" One of the servants of the king of Israel replied, "Elisha, son of Shaphat, who poured water on the hands of Elijah,* is here." 12 Jehoshaphat agreed, "He has the word of the LORD." So the king of Israel, along with Jehoshaphat and the king of Edom, went down to Elisha. 13 Elisha asked the king of Israel, "What do you want with me? Go to the prophets of your father and to the prophets of your mother." The king of Israel replied, "No, the LORD has called these three kings together only to deliver us into the power of Moab." 14 Then Elisha said, "As the LORD of hosts lives, whom I serve, were it not that I respect Jehoshaphat, the king of Judah, I should neither look at you nor notice you at all. 15 Now get me a minstrel." When the minstrel played, the hand of the LORD came upon Elisha, 16 and he announced: "Thus says the LORD: Provide many catch basins in this wadi. 17 For the LORD says: Though you will see neither wind nor rain, yet this wadi will be filled with water for you to drink, and for your livestock and pack animals. 18 And since the LORD does not consider this enough, he will also deliver Moab into your power. 19 You shall destroy every fortified city and every choice city, fell every fruit tree, stop up all the springs, and ruin every fertile field with stones."[m]

20 In the morning, at the time of the sacrifice, water came from the direction of Edom and filled the land.

21 Meanwhile, all Moab had heard that the kings had come to war against them; troops from the youngest on up were mobilized and stationed at the border. 22 When they rose early that morning, the sun was shining across the water. The Moabites saw the water as red as blood, 23 and said, "This is blood! The kings have fought among themselves and killed one another. Quick! To the spoils, Moab!" 24 But when they reached the camp of Israel, the Israelites rose up and attacked the Moabites, who fled from them. They ranged through the countryside destroying Moab— 25 leveling the cities, each one casting the stones onto every fertile field and filling it, stopping up every spring, felling every fruit tree, until only the stones of Kir-hareseth* remained. Then the slingers surrounded and attacked it. 26 When he saw that the battle was going against him, the king of Moab took seven hundred swordsmen to break through to the king of Edom, but he failed. 27 So he took his firstborn, who was to succeed him as king, and offered him as a burnt offering upon the wall. The wrath against Israel* was so great that they gave up the siege and returned to their own land.[n]

CHAPTER 4

See RG 192

The Widow's Oil. 1[o] A certain woman, the widow of one of the guild prophets, cried out to Elisha: "My husband, your servant, is dead. You know that he revered the LORD, yet now his creditor has come to take my two children into servitude."* 2 Elisha answered her, "What am I to do for you? Tell me what you have in the house." She replied, "This servant of yours has nothing in the house but a jug of oil." 3 He said, "Go

3:11 Poured water on the hands of Elijah: possibly a metaphor for "was Elijah's servant." But the phrase occurs nowhere else in the Old Testament and its meaning is not certain.

3:25 Kir-hareseth: a major city of Moab, identified with modern Kerak, east of the Dead Sea; cf. Is 16:7, 11; Jer 48:31, 36.

3:27 The wrath against Israel: probably the wrath of Chemosh, the Moabite god to whom the child was offered. The Israelites, intimidated by this wrath, retreat.

4:1 His creditor . . . into servitude: Israelite law permitted the selling of wife and children into slavery for debt; cf. Ex 21:7; Am 2:6; 8:6; Is 50:1.

m: Dt 20:19. *n:* Jgs 11:30–31. *o:* 1 Kgs 17:8–16.

out, borrow vessels from all your neighbors—as many empty vessels as you can. 4 Then come back and close the door on yourself and your children; pour the oil into all the vessels, and as each is filled, set it aside." 5 So she went out. She closed the door on herself and her children and, as they handed her the vessels, she would pour in oil. 6 When all the vessels were filled, she said to her son, "Bring me another vessel." He answered, "There is none left." And then the oil stopped. 7 She went and told the man of God, who said, "Go sell the oil to pay off your creditor; with what remains, you and your children can live."

Elisha Raises the Shunammite's Son. 8 One day Elisha came to Shunem, where there was a woman of influence, who pressed him to dine with her. Afterward, whenever he passed by, he would stop there to dine. 9 So she said to her husband, "I know that he is a holy man of God. Since he visits us often, 10 let us arrange a little room on the roof and furnish it for him with a bed, table, chair, and lamp, so that when he comes to us he can stay there."[p]

11 One day Elisha arrived and stayed in the room overnight. 12 Then he said to his servant Gehazi, "Call this Shunammite woman." He did so, and when she stood before Elisha, 13 he told Gehazi, "Say to her, 'You have troubled yourself greatly for us; what can we do for you? Can we say a good word for you to the king or to the commander of the army?' " She replied, "I am living among my own people."[*] 14 Later Elisha asked, "What can we do for her?" Gehazi answered, "She has no son, and her husband is old." 15 Elisha said, "Call her." He did so, and when she stood at the door, 16 Elisha promised, "This time next year you will be cradling a baby son." She said, "My lord, you are a man of God; do not deceive your servant."[q] 17 Yet the woman conceived, and by the same time the following year she had given birth to a son, as Elisha had promised; 18 and the child grew up healthy.[r]

One day the boy went out to his father among the reapers. 19 He said to his father, "My head! My head!" And his father said to the servant, "Carry him to his mother." 20 The servant picked him up and carried him to his mother; he sat in her lap until noon, and then died. 21 She went upstairs and laid him on the bed of the man of God. Closing the door on him, she went out 22 and called to her husband, "Let me have one of the servants and a donkey. I must go quickly to the man of God, and I will be back." 23 He asked, "Why are you going to him today? It is neither the new moon nor the sabbath." But she said, "It is all right." 24 When the donkey was saddled, she said to her servant, "Lead on! Do not stop my donkey unless I tell you." 25 She kept going till she reached the man of God on Mount Carmel. When he saw her at a distance, the man of God said to his servant Gehazi: "There is the Shunammite! 26 Hurry to meet her, and ask if everything is all right with her, with her husband, and with the boy." "Everything is all right," she replied. 27 But when she reached the man of God on the mountain, she clasped his feet. Gehazi came near to push her away, but the man of God said: "Let her alone, she is in bitter anguish; the LORD hid it from me and did not let me know." 28 She said, "Did I ask my lord for a son? Did I not say, 'Do not mislead me'?" 29 He said to Gehazi, "Get ready for a journey. Take my staff with you and be off; if you meet anyone, give no greeting,[*] and if anyone greets you, do not answer. Lay my staff upon the boy." 30 But the boy's mother cried out: "As the LORD lives and as you yourself live, I will not release you." So he started back with her.

31 Meanwhile, Gehazi had gone on ahead and had laid the staff upon the boy, but there was no sound, no response. He returned to meet Elisha and told him, "The boy has not

4:13 I am living among my own people: the Shunammite woman declines Elisha's offer. Surrounded by the support of her family and her clan, she is secure. Ironically, at some point in the future Elisha's advice will send her to live among foreigners (see 8:1–2).

4:29 Give no greeting: a profuse exchange of greetings and compliments would normally surround the chance encounter of acquaintances on the road. This would, however, take time, and Gehazi's mission was urgent. Compare Lk 10:4.

p: 1 Kgs 17:9. *q:* Gn 18:9–15. *r:* 1 Kgs 17:17–24; Lk 7:11–16; Acts 20:10–12.

awakened.” 32 When Elisha reached the house, he found the boy dead, lying on the bed. 33 He went in, closed the door on them both, and prayed to the LORD. 34 Then he lay upon the child on the bed, placing his mouth upon the child’s mouth, his eyes upon the eyes, and his hands upon the hands. As Elisha stretched himself over the child, the boy’s flesh became warm.[s] 35 He arose, paced up and down the room, and then once more stretched himself over him, and the boy sneezed seven times and opened his eyes.[t] 36 Elisha summoned Gehazi and said, “Call the Shunammite.” He called her, and she came to him, and Elisha said to her, “Take your son.” 37 She came in and fell at his feet in homage; then she took her son and left.

The Poisoned Stew. 38[u] When Elisha returned to Gilgal, there was a famine in the land. Once, when the guild prophets were seated before him, he said to his servant, “Put the large pot on, and make some vegetable stew for the guild prophets.” 39 Someone went out into the field to gather herbs and found a wild vine, from which he picked a sackful of poisonous wild gourds. On his return he cut them up into the pot of vegetable stew without anybody’s knowing it. 40 The stew was served, but when they began to eat it, they cried, “Man of God, there is death in the pot!” And they could not eat it. 41 He said, “Bring some meal.” He threw it into the pot and said, “Serve it to the people to eat.” And there was no longer anything harmful in the pot.

The Barley Loaves. 42[v] A man came from Baal-shalishah bringing the man of God twenty barley loaves made from the first fruits, and fresh grain in the ear. Elisha said, “Give it to the people to eat.” 43 But his servant objected, “How can I set this before a hundred?” Elisha again said, “Give it to the people to eat, for thus says the LORD: You will eat and have some left over.” 44 He set it before them, and when they had eaten, they had some left over, according to the word of the LORD.

CHAPTER 5

See RG 192

Elisha Cures Naaman’s Leprosy. 1 Naaman, the army commander of the king of Aram, was highly esteemed and respected by his master, for through him the LORD had brought victory to Aram. But valiant as he was, the man was a leper.* 2 Now the Arameans had captured from the land of Israel in a raid a little girl, who became the servant of Naaman’s wife. 3 She said to her mistress, “If only my master would present himself to the prophet in Samaria! He would cure him of his leprosy.”

4 Naaman went and told his master, “This is what the girl from the land of Israel said.” 5 The king of Aram said, “Go. I will send along a letter to the king of Israel.” So Naaman set out, taking along ten silver talents, six thousand gold pieces, and ten festal garments.

6 He brought the king of Israel the letter, which read: “With this letter I am sending my servant Naaman to you, that you may cure him of his leprosy.” 7 When he read the letter, the king of Israel tore his garments and exclaimed: “Am I a god with power over life and death, that this man should send someone for me to cure him of leprosy? Take note! You can see he is only looking for a quarrel with me!”[w] 8 When Elisha, the man of God, heard that the king of Israel had torn his garments, he sent word to the king: “Why have you torn your garments? Let him come to me and find out that there is a prophet in Israel.”

9 Naaman came with his horses and chariot and stopped at the door of Elisha’s house. 10 Elisha sent him the message: “Go and wash seven times in the Jordan, and your flesh will heal, and you will be clean.”[x] 11 But Naaman went away angry, saying, “I thought that he would surely come out to me and stand there to call on the name of the LORD his God, and would move his hand

5:1 Leper: the terms traditionally translated “leper” and “leprosy” covered a wide variety of skin disorders like psoriasis, eczema, and seborrhea, but probably not Hansen’s disease (modern “leprosy”); there is no clear evidence of its existence in biblical times.

s: Sir 48:13. *t:* Heb 11:35. *u:* 2 Kgs 2:19–22. *v:* Mt 14:13–21; 15:32–38; Mk 6:34–44; 8:1–9; Lk 9:10–17; Jn 6:1–13. *w:* 1 Sm 2:6; Jn 5:21. *x:* Jn 9:7.

over the place, and thus cure the leprous
spot. 12 Are not the rivers of Damascus, the
Abana and the Pharpar, better than all the
waters of Israel? Could I not wash in them
and be cleansed?"'[*] With this, he turned
about in anger and left.

13 But his servants came up and reasoned
with him: "My father, if the prophet told you
to do something extraordinary, would you
not do it? All the more since he told you,
'Wash, and be clean'?" 14 So Naaman went
down and plunged into the Jordan seven
times, according to the word of the man of
God. His flesh became again like the flesh of
a little child, and he was clean.[y]

15 He returned with his whole retinue to
the man of God. On his arrival he stood before him and said, "Now I know that there is
no God in all the earth, except in Israel.
Please accept a gift from your servant."[z]
16 Elisha replied, "As the LORD lives whom I
serve, I will not take it." And despite Naaman's urging, he still refused. 17 Naaman
said: "If you will not accept, please let me,
your servant, have two mule-loads of earth,[*]
for your servant will no longer make burnt
offerings or sacrifices to any other god except the LORD. 18 But may the LORD forgive
your servant this: when my master enters the
temple of Rimmon to bow down there, as he
leans upon my arm, I too must bow down in
the temple of Rimmon. When I bow down in
the temple of Rimmon, may the LORD please
forgive your servant this." 19 Elisha said to
him, "Go in peace."[*]

Naaman had gone some distance 20 when
Gehazi, the servant of Elisha, the man of
God, thought to himself: "My master was too
easy on this Aramean Naaman, not accepting
what he brought. As the LORD lives, I will run
after him and get something out of him."
21 So Gehazi hurried after Naaman. Seeing
that someone was running after him, Naaman alighted from his chariot to wait for him.
He asked, "Is everything all right?" 22 Gehazi
replied, "Yes, but my master sent me to say,
'Two young men have just come to me, guild
prophets from the hill country of Ephraim.
Please give them a talent of silver and two
festal garments.' " 23 Naaman said, "I insist!
Take two talents," and he pressed him. He
tied up two silver talents in bags and gave
them, with two festal garments, to two of his
servants, who carried them before Gehazi.
24 When he reached the hill, Gehazi received
these things, appropriated them for his
house, and sent the men on their way.

25 He went in and stood by Elisha his master, who asked him, "Where have you been,
Gehazi?" He answered, "Your servant has
not gone anywhere." 26 But Elisha said to
him: "Was I not present in spirit when someone got down from his chariot to wait for
you? Is this a time to take money or to take
garments, olive orchards or vineyards, sheep
or cattle, male or female servants? 27 The leprosy of Naaman shall cling to you and your
descendants forever." And Gehazi went out,
a leper with skin like snow.[*]

CHAPTER 6

See RG 192–93

The Lost Ax. 1 The guild prophets
once said to Elisha: "This place where we
live with you is too cramped for us. 2 Let us
go to the Jordan, where by getting one beam
apiece we can build ourselves a place to
live." Elisha said, "Go." 3 One of them requested, "Please agree to accompany your
servants." He replied, "Yes, I will come."

4 So he went with them, and when they arrived at the Jordan they began to cut down
trees. 5 While one of them was felling a tree
trunk, the iron ax blade slipped into the water. He cried out, "Oh, no, master! It was
borrowed!" 6 "Where did it fall?" asked the
man of God. When he pointed out the spot,

5:12 Wash in them and be cleansed: typical of the ambiguity in ritual healing or cleanliness. The muddy waters of the Jordan are no match hygienically for the mountain spring waters of Damascus; ritually, it is the other way around.

5:17 Two mule-loads of earth: worship of the Lord is associated with the soil of the Holy Land, where he is present.

5:19 Go in peace: Elisha understands and approves the situation of Naaman who, though now a worshiper of the God of Israel, is required by his courtly office to assist his master, the king ("leans upon my arm," v. 18), worshiping in the temple of the Canaanite god Baal-Rimmon.

5:27 With skin like snow: "snow" is often used to describe the skin conditions covered by the term "leprosy" (Ex 4:6; Nm 12:10; see note on 5:1). It is unclear whether the comparison is with the white color, dry flakes, or moist shine, any of which can occur in the relevant skin diseases.

y: Lk 4:27. *z:* Lk 17:17–19.

Elisha cut off a stick, threw it into the water,
and brought the iron to the surface. [7]He said,
"Pick it up." And the man stretched out his
hand and grasped it.
The Aramean Ambush. [8]When the king of
Aram was waging war on Israel, he would
make plans with his servants: "I will bivouac
at such and such a place." [9]But the man of
God would send word to the king of Israel,
"Be careful! Do not pass by this place, for
Aram will attack there." [10]So the king of Israel would send word to the place which the
man of God had indicated, and alert it; then
they would be on guard. This happened several times.
[11]Greatly disturbed over this, the king of
Aram called together his officers and asked
them, "Will you not tell me who among us is
for the king of Israel?" [12]"No one, my lord
king," answered one of the officers. "The Israelite prophet Elisha can tell the king of Israel the very words you speak in your bedroom." [13]He said, "Go, find out where he is,
so that I may take him captive."
Informed that Elisha was in Dothan, [14]he
sent there a strong force with horses and
chariots. They arrived by night and encircled
the city. [15]Early the next morning, when the
servant of the man of God arose and went
out, he saw the force with its horses and chariots surrounding the city. "Alas!" he said to
Elisha. "What shall we do, my lord?" [16]Eli-
sha answered, "Do not be afraid. Our side
outnumbers theirs." [17]Then he prayed, "O
LORD, open his eyes, that he may see." And
the LORD opened the eyes of the servant, and
he saw that the mountainside was filled with
fiery chariots and horses around Elisha.[a]
[18]When the Arameans came down to get
him, Elisha prayed to the LORD, "Strike this
people blind, I pray you." And the LORD
struck them blind, according to Elisha's
word. [19]Then Elisha said to them: "This is
the wrong road, and this is the wrong city.
Follow me! I will take you to the man you
want." And he led them to Samaria. [20]When
they entered Samaria, Elisha prayed, "O
LORD, open their eyes that they may see."
The LORD opened their eyes, and they saw
that they were inside Samaria. [21]When the
king of Israel saw them, he asked, "Shall I
kill them, my father? Shall I kill them?"
[22]Elisha replied, "You must not kill them.
Do you slay those whom you have taken
captive with your sword or bow?[*] Serve
them a meal. Let them eat and drink, and
then go back to their master." [23]The king
spread a great feast for them. When they had
eaten and drunk he sent them away, and they
went back to their master. No more Aramean
raiders came into the land of Israel.
War Against Aram: Famine. [24]After this,
Ben-hadad, king of Aram, mustered his
whole army and laid siege to Samaria. [25]Be-
cause of the siege the famine in Samaria was
so severe that a donkey's head sold for eighty
pieces of silver, and a fourth of a kab of
"dove droppings"[*] for five pieces of silver.
[26b] One day, as the king of Israel was
walking on the city wall, a woman cried out
to him, "Save us, my lord king!" [27]He
replied, "If the LORD does not save you,
where could I find means to save you? On
the threshing floor? In the wine press?"
[28]Then the king asked her, "What is your
trouble?" She replied: "This woman said to
me, 'Give up your son that we may eat him
today; then tomorrow we will eat my son.'
[29]So we boiled my son and ate him. The next
day I said to her, 'Now give up your son that
we may eat him.' But she hid her son."
[30]When the king heard the woman's words,
he tore his garments. And as he was walking
on the wall, the people saw that he was wearing sackcloth underneath, next to his skin.
[31]The king exclaimed, "May God do thus
to me, and more, if the head of Elisha, son of
Shaphat, stays on him today!"
[32]Meanwhile, Elisha was sitting in his
house in conference with the elders. The

6:22 With your sword or bow: since the king would not slay prisoners who had surrendered to his power, much less should he slay prisoners captured by God's power. This wartime practice stands in contrast to that of holy war, where prisoners were placed under the ban and so devoted to destruction (see 1 Kgs 20:35–43).

6:25 "Dove droppings": it is unclear whether this phrase is to be read literally (e.g., dung used as fuel) or as the nickname of a type of edible plant, as attested in Arabic. A kab was probably around a quart.

a: 2 Kgs 2:11; 7:6; Ps 68:18. *b:* Dt 28:53–57.

king had sent one of his courtiers; but before the messenger reached him, Elisha said to the elders: "Do you know that this murderer is sending someone to cut off my head? When the messenger comes, see that you close the door and hold it fast against him. His master's footsteps are echoing behind him." 33 While Elisha was still speaking, the messenger came down to him and said, "This evil is from the LORD. Why should I trust in the LORD any longer?"[*]

See RG 193

CHAPTER 7

1 Elisha replied: "Hear the word of the LORD! Thus says the LORD: At this time tomorrow a seah of fine flour will sell for a shekel, and two seahs of barley for a shekel, in the market[*] of Samaria." 2 But the adjutant, upon whose arm the king leaned, answered the man of God, "Even if the LORD were to make windows in heaven, how could this happen?" Elisha said, "You shall see it with your own eyes, but you shall not eat of it."

3 At the city gate four lepers were asking one another, "Why should we sit here until we die?[c] 4 If we decide to go into the city, we shall die there, for there is famine in the city. If we remain here, we shall die too. So come, let us desert to the camp of the Arameans. If they let us live, we live; if they kill us, we die." 5 At twilight they left for the Arameans; but when they reached the edge of the camp, no one was there. 6[d] The Lord had caused the army of the Arameans to hear the sound of chariots and horses, the sound of a large army, and they had reasoned among themselves, "The king of Israel has hired the kings of the Hittites and the kings of Egypt to fight us." 7 Then in the twilight they had fled, abandoning their tents, their horses, and their donkeys, the whole camp just as it was, and fleeing for their lives.

8 After the lepers reached the edge of the camp, they went first into one tent, ate and drank, and took silver, gold, and clothing from it, and went out and hid them. Back they came into another tent, took things from it, and again went out and hid them. 9 Then they said to one another: "We are not doing right. This is a day of good news, and we are keeping silent. If we wait until morning breaks, we will be blamed. So come, let us go and inform the palace." 10 They came and summoned the city gatekeepers. They said, "We went to the camp of the Arameans, but no one was there—not a human voice, only the horses and donkeys tethered, and the tents just as they were left." 11 The gatekeepers announced this and it was reported within the palace.

12 Though it was night, the king got up; he said to his servants, "Let me tell you what the Arameans have done to us. Knowing that we are starving, they have left their camp to hide in the field. They are thinking, 'The Israelites will leave the city and we will take them alive and enter it.' " 13[*] One of his servants, however, suggested: "Let some of us take five of the horses remaining in the city—they are just like the whole throng of Israel that has reached its limit—and let us send scouts to investigate." 14 They took two chariots, and horses, and the king sent them to reconnoiter the Aramean army with the order, "Go and find out." 15 They followed the Arameans as far as the Jordan, and the whole route was strewn with garments and other objects that the Arameans had thrown away in their haste. The messengers returned and told the king. 16 The people went out and plundered the camp of the Arameans.

Then a seah of fine flour sold for a shekel and two seahs of barley for a shekel, according to the word of the LORD. 17 The king had put in charge of the gate the officer upon whose arm he leaned; but the people trampled him to death at the gate, just as the man of God had predicted when the messenger came down to him. 18 This was in accordance with the word the man of God spoke to the king: "Two seahs of barley will sell for a

6:33 The messenger speaks in the king's name. Similarly, Elisha's response in the next verse can be spoken of as delivered to the king (7:18).

7:1 Market: lit., "gate," the principal place of trading in ancient walled cities in time of peace.

7:13 The Hebrew of this verse is difficult and its meaning is uncertain.

c: Lv 13:46. *d:* 2 Kgs 6:17; 2 Sm 5:24.

shekel, and a seah of fine flour for a shekel at this time tomorrow in the market of Samaria." 19The adjutant had answered the man of God, "Even if the LORD were to make windows in heaven, how could this happen?" And Elisha had replied, "You shall see it with your own eyes, but you shall not eat of it." 20And that is what happened to him, for the people trampled him to death at the gate.

CHAPTER 8

See RG 193

The Shunammite's Return. 1Elisha once said to the woman whose son he had restored to life: "Get ready! Leave with your household and live wherever you can, because the LORD has decreed a seven-year famine which is coming upon the land."[e] 2The woman got ready and did as the man of God said, setting out with her household, and living in the land of the Philistines for seven years.

3At the end of the seven years, the woman returned from the land of the Philistines and went out to the king to appeal for her house and her field. 4The king was talking with Gehazi, the servant of the man of God: "Tell me all the great things that Elisha has done." 5Just as he was telling the king how his master had restored a dead person to life, the very woman whose son Elisha had restored to life came to the king appealing for her house and field. Gehazi said, "My lord king, this is the woman, and this is that son of hers whom Elisha restored to life." 6The king questioned the woman, and she told him her story. With that the king placed an official* at her disposal, saying, "Restore all her property to her, with all that the field produced from the day she left the land until now."

Elisha and Hazael of Aram.* 7[f] Elisha came to Damascus at a time when Ben-hadad, king of Aram, lay sick. When he was told, "The man of God has come here," 8the king said to Hazael, "Take a gift with you and go call on the man of God. Consult the LORD through him, 'Will I recover from this sickness?' "[g] 9Hazael went to visit him, carrying a present, and with forty camel loads of the best goods of Damascus. On his arrival, he stood before Elisha and said, "Your son Ben-hadad, king of Aram, has sent me to you to ask, 'Will I recover from my sickness?' " 10Elisha answered, "Go and tell him, 'You will surely recover.' But the LORD has showed me that he will surely die." 11Then he stared him down until he became ill at ease. The man of God wept, 12and Hazael asked, "Why are you weeping, my lord?" Elisha replied, "Because I know the evil that you will inflict upon the Israelites. You will burn their fortresses, you will slay their youth with the sword, you will dash their little children to pieces, you will rip open their pregnant women."[h] 13Hazael exclaimed, "How can your servant, a dog* like me, do anything so important?" Elisha replied, "The LORD has showed you to me as king over Aram."

14Hazael left Elisha and returned to his master, who asked, "What did Elisha tell you?" Hazael replied, "He said, 'You will surely recover.' " 15The next day, however, Hazael took a cloth, dipped it in water, and spread it over the king's face, so that he died. And Hazael succeeded him as king.

Reign of Joram of Judah. 16* In the fifth year of Joram, son of Ahab, king of Israel, Joram, son of Jehoshaphat, king of Judah, became king. 17He was thirty-two years old when he became king, and he reigned eight years in Jerusalem.

18He walked in the way of the kings of Israel as the house of Ahab had done, since the daughter of Ahab was his wife; and he did what was evil in the LORD's sight. 19Even so, the LORD was unwilling to destroy Judah, for the sake of his servant David. For he had promised David that he would leave him a holding in the LORD's presence for all time.[i]

8:6 An official: lit., "eunuch," and perhaps actually so in this instance.

8:7–15 Elisha carries out the commission the Lord gave Elijah in 1 Kgs 19:15. See note on 2 Kgs 3:1–9:13.

8:13 To call oneself a "dog" is to admit one's insignificance (1 Sm 24:15; 2 Sm 9:8); it is not necessarily a term of contempt, as in English. Hazael focuses on the question of his power, making no comment on the atrocities Elisha predicts he will commit.

8:16 On the apparent contradictions among 1:17, 3:1, and this verse, see note on 3:1.

---

e: 2 Kgs 4:18–37. *f:* 1 Kgs 19:15. *g:* 1 Kgs 14:1–3. *h:* 2 Kgs 13:3–7. *i:* 2 Sm 7:12–16; 1 Kgs 11:36; 15:4.

[20]During Joram's reign, Edom revolted against the rule of Judah and installed a king of its own. [21]Thereupon Joram with all his chariots crossed over to Zair. He arose by night and broke through the Edomites when they had surrounded him and the commanders of his chariots. Then his army fled homeward. [22]To this day Edom has been in revolt against the rule of Judah. Libnah also revolted at that time.[j]

[23]The rest of the acts of Joram, with all that he did, are recorded in the book of the chronicles of the kings of Judah. [24]Joram rested with his ancestors; he was buried with his ancestors in the City of David, and his son Ahaziah succeeded him as king.

Reign of Ahaziah of Judah.* [25]In the twelfth year of Joram, son of Ahab, king of Israel, Ahaziah, son of Joram, king of Judah, became king. [26]Ahaziah was twenty-two years old when he became king, and he reigned one year in Jerusalem. His mother's name was Athaliah, daughter of Omri, king of Israel.*

[27]He walked in the way of the house of Ahab and did what was evil in the LORD's sight like the house of Ahab, since he was related to them by marriage. [28]He joined Joram, son of Ahab, in battle against Hazael, king of Aram, at Ramoth-gilead, where the Arameans wounded Joram.[k] [29]King Joram returned to Jezreel to be healed of the wounds which the Arameans had inflicted on him at Ramah in his battle against Hazael, king of Aram. Then Ahaziah, son of Joram, king of Judah, went down to Jezreel to visit Joram, son of Ahab, for he was sick.

CHAPTER 9

See RG 193–94

Elisha and Jehu of Israel.* [1][l] Elisha the prophet called one of the guild prophets and said to him: "Get ready for a journey. Take this flask of oil with you, and go to Ramoth-gilead. [2]When you get there, look for Jehu, son of Jehoshaphat, son of Nimshi. Enter and take him away from his companions and bring him into an inner chamber. [3]From the flask you have, pour oil on his head, and say, 'Thus says the LORD: I anoint you king over Israel.' Then open the door and flee without delay."

[4]The aide (the prophet's aide) went to Ramoth-gilead. [5]When he arrived, the commanders of the army were in session. He said, "I have a message for you, commander." Jehu asked, "For which one of us?" "For you, commander," he answered. [6]Jehu got up and went into the house. Then the prophet's aide poured the oil on his head and said, "Thus says the LORD, the God of Israel: I anoint you king over the people of the LORD, over Israel. [7]* You shall destroy the house of Ahab your master; thus will I avenge the blood of my servants the prophets, and the blood of all the other servants of the LORD shed by Jezebel. [8][m] The whole house of Ahab shall perish:

> I will cut off from Ahab's line every male,
> whether bond or free in Israel.

[9]I will make the house of Ahab like that of Jeroboam, son of Nebat, and like that of Baasha, son of Ahijah. [10]In the confines of Jezreel, the dogs shall devour Jezebel so that no one can bury her." Then he opened the door and fled.

[11]When Jehu rejoined his master's servants, they asked him, "Is all well? Why did that madman come to you?" He replied, "You know that kind of man and his talk." [12]But they said, "Tell us another lie!" So he told them, "This is what the prophet's aide said to me, 'Thus says the LORD: I anoint you king over Israel.' " [13]At once each took his gar-

8:25–29 The narrative of Ahaziah's reign, like that of Joram of Israel, lacks the standard formulaic conclusion. The deaths of both kings, and indeed the obliteration of the whole house of Omri, will be recounted in the story of Jehu's insurrection.

8:26 It is unclear whether Athaliah was Omri's daughter (v. 26) or his granddaughter (v. 18). Perhaps "daughter" here is being used loosely for "female descendant."

9:1–13 Elisha carries out the commission the Lord gave Elijah in 1 Kgs 19:16. See note on 2 Kgs 3:1–9:13.

9:7–10 The author has Elisha's emissary expand considerably the speech Elisha told him to deliver by adding the same type of prophetic indictments and sanctions as were invoked on previous occasions against the dynasties of Jeroboam (1 Kgs 14:10–11), of Baasha (1 Kgs 16:3–4), and of Ahab himself (1 Kgs 21:21–24).

j: Gn 27:40. *k:* 2 Kgs 9:14–15. *l:* 1 Kgs 19:16. *m:* 1 Kgs 14:10–11; 16:3–4; 21:21–24.

ment, spread it under Jehu on the bare steps, blew the horn, and cried out, "Jehu is king!"

VIII. The End of the Omrid Dynasty*

Death of Joram of Israel. [14][n] Jehu, son of Jehoshaphat, son of Nimshi, formed a conspiracy against Joram. (Joram, with all Israel, had been besieging Ramoth-gilead against Hazael, king of Aram, [15]but had returned to Jezreel to be healed of the wounds the Arameans had inflicted on him in the battle against Hazael, king of Aram.)

Jehu said to them, "If this is what you really want, see that no one escapes from the city to report in Jezreel."

[16]Then Jehu mounted his chariot and drove to Jezreel, where Joram lay ill and Ahaziah, king of Judah, had come to visit him. [17]The watchman standing on the tower in Jezreel saw the troop of Jehu coming and reported, "I see chariots." Joram said, "Get a driver and send him to meet them and to ask whether all is well." [18]So a horseman went out to meet him and said, "The king asks, 'Is everything all right?' " Jehu said, "What does it matter to you how things are? Get behind me." The watchman reported to the king, "The messenger has reached them, but is not returning." [19]Joram sent a second horseman, who went to them and said, "The king asks, 'Is everything all right?' " "What does it matter to you how things are?" Jehu replied. "Get behind me." [20]The watchman reported, "He has reached them, but is not returning. The driving is like that of Jehu, son of Nimshi; he drives like a madman." [21][o] "Hitch up my chariot," said Joram, and they hitched up his chariot. Then Joram, king of Israel, and Ahaziah, king of Judah, set out, each in his own chariot, to meet Jehu. They reached him near the plot of ground of Naboth the Jezreelite. [22]When Joram recognized Jehu, he asked, "Is everything all right, Jehu?" Jehu replied, "How could everything be all right as long as all the harlotry and sorcery* of your mother Jezebel continues?" [23]Joram reined about and fled, crying to Ahaziah, "Treason, Ahaziah!" [24]But Jehu had drawn his bow and he shot Joram between the shoulders, so that the arrow went through his heart and he collapsed in his chariot. [25]Then Jehu said to his adjutant Bidkar, "Take him and throw him into the plot of ground in the field of Naboth the Jezreelite. For remember when you and I were driving teams behind Ahab his father, the LORD delivered this oracle against him: [26]As surely as I saw yesterday the blood of Naboth and the blood of his sons—oracle of the LORD—I will repay you for it in that very plot of ground—oracle of the LORD. So now take him and throw him into this plot of ground, in keeping with the word of the LORD."

Death of Ahaziah of Judah. [27][p] Seeing what was happening, Ahaziah, king of Judah, fled toward Beth-haggan. Jehu pursued him, shouting, "Him too!" They struck him as he rode through the pass of Gur near Ibleam, but he continued his flight as far as Megiddo and died there. [28]His servants brought him in a chariot to Jerusalem and they buried him in his grave with his ancestors in the City of David. [29]In the eleventh year of Joram, son of Ahab, Ahaziah became king over Judah.

Death of Jezebel. [30]Jehu came to Jezreel, and when Jezebel heard of it, she shadowed her eyes, adorned her hair, and looked down from her window. [31]As Jehu came through the gate, she cried out, "Is all well, you Zimri, murderer of your master?"[q] [32]Jehu looked up to the window and shouted, "Who is on my side? Who?" At this, two or three eunuchs looked down toward him. [33]"Throw her down," he ordered. They threw her

9:14–11:20 Death pervades this section. The dynasty founded by Omri (1 Kgs 16:23) drowns in a bloodbath, taking numberless others along with it. The scenes are in three parallel sets of three: death comes (1) to Joram of Israel, Ahab's son; to Ahaziah of Judah, his son-in-law; and to Jezebel, the Baalist queen mother of Israel; (2) then to seventy descendants of Ahab; to forty-two relatives of Ahaziah of Judah; and to numerous Baal worshipers; (3) finally to Jehu of Israel; to the blood royal of Judah; and to Athaliah, the Baalist queen mother of Judah and last of the Omrids.

9:22 Harlotry and sorcery: both terms are metaphors referring to Jezebel's worship of the foreign god Baal.

n: 2 Kgs 8:28–29. *o:* 1 Kgs 21:1–24. *p:* 2 Chr 22:7–9. *q:* 1 Kgs 16:8–13.

down, and some of her blood spurted against the wall and against the horses. Jehu trod over her body [34]and, after eating and drinking, he said: "Attend to that accursed woman and bury her; for she was the daughter of a king." [35]But when they went to bury her, they found nothing of her but the skull, the feet, and the hands. [36]They returned to Jehu, and when they told him, he said, "This is the word the LORD spoke through his servant Elijah the Tishbite: In the confines of Jezreel the dogs shall devour the flesh of Jezebel.[r] [37]The corpse of Jezebel shall be like dung in the field in the confines of Jezreel, so that no one can say: This was Jezebel."

See RG 194

CHAPTER 10

Death of the Sons of Ahab of Israel. [1][s] Ahab had seventy sons in Samaria. Jehu wrote letters and sent them to Samaria, to the elders who were rulers of Jezreel and to Ahab's guardians. Jehu wrote: [2]"Since your master's sons are with you, as well as his chariots, horses, fortified city, and weaponry, when this letter reaches you [3]decide which is the best and the fittest of your master's sons, place him on his father's throne, and fight for your master's house." [4]They were overcome with fright and said, "If the two kings could not withstand him, how can we?" [5]So the master of the palace and the chief of the city, along with the elders and the guardians, sent this message to Jehu: "We are your servants, and we will do everything you tell us. We will proclaim no one king; do whatever you think best." [6]So Jehu wrote them a second letter: "If you are on my side and will obey me, bring along the heads of your master's sons* and come to me in Jezreel at this time tomorrow." (The seventy princes were in the care of prominent men of the city, who were rearing them.)

[7]When the letter arrived, they took the princes and slew all seventy of them, put their heads in baskets, and sent them to Jehu in Jezreel. [8]A messenger came in and told him, "They have brought the heads of the princes." He said, "Pile them in two heaps at the gate of the city until morning."

[9]In the morning he came outside, stood there, and said to all the people: "You are guiltless, for it was I who conspired against my lord and slew him. But who killed all these? [10]Know that not a single word which the LORD has spoken against the house of Ahab shall fail. The LORD has accomplished what he decreed through his servant Elijah."[t] [11](And so Jehu slew all who were left of the house of Ahab in Jezreel, as well as all his powerful supporters, intimates, and priests, leaving him no survivor.)[u] [12]Then he went back inside.

Death of the Relatives of Ahaziah of Judah. He set out for Samaria and, at Beth-eked-haroim on the way, [13]Jehu came across relatives of Ahaziah, king of Judah. "Who are you?" he asked, and they said, "We are relatives of Ahaziah. We are going down to visit the princes and the family of the queen mother."* [14]"Take them alive," Jehu ordered. They were taken alive, forty-two in number, then slain at the pit of Beth-eked. Not one of them survived.

[15]When he set out from there, Jehu met Jehonadab, son of Rechab, on the road. He greeted him and asked, "Are you with me wholeheartedly, as I am with you?" "Yes," he replied. "If you are, give me your hand." He gave him his hand, and he had him mount his chariot,[v] [16]and said, "Come with me and see my zeal for the LORD." And they took him along in his chariot.

Slaughter of the Worshipers of Baal. [17]When he arrived in Samaria, Jehu slew all

10:6 Heads of your master's sons: Jehu's command is cleverly ambiguous. He allows the Samarian leaders to understand "heads" either literally or metaphorically as "most important individuals." Then, when the leaders decapitate Ahab's potential successors, Jehu can claim to be innocent of their blood (v. 9).

10:13 Since Athaliah, the queen mother in Judah, was of the Israelite royal house (8:18, 26), both the "princes" (lit., the "king's sons") and the queen mother's "family" (lit., her "sons") would belong to the royal houses of both kingdoms. They may thus be numbered among the seventy "sons of Ahab" killed in vv. 1–7. Because "sons" can refer to more remote offspring, the queen mother's "sons" may include Ahaziah's brothers, sons, nephews, as well as the "relatives" (lit., the "brothers") of Ahaziah who are speaking in this scene.

---

r: 1 Kgs 21:23. *s:* Jgs 9:5; 1 Kgs 15:29; 16:11–12; 21:8. *t:* 1 Kgs 21:17–29. *u:* Hos 1:4. *v:* 1 Kgs 20:33; 1 Chr 2:55; Jer 35:1–19.

who were left of Ahab's line in Samaria, doing away with them completely, according
to the word the LORD spoke to Elijah.
18 Jehu gathered all the people together
and said to them: "Ahab served Baal to some
extent, but Jehu will serve him yet more.[w]
19 Now summon for me all Baal's prophets,
all his servants, and all his priests. See that
no one is absent, for I have a great sacrifice
for Baal. Whoever is absent shall not live."
This Jehu did as a ruse, so that he might destroy the servants of Baal.[x]
20 Jehu said further, "Proclaim a solemn
assembly in honor of Baal." They did so,
21 and Jehu sent word of it throughout all Israel. All the servants of Baal came; there was
no one who did not come; they came to the
temple of Baal, and it was filled from wall to
wall. 22 Then Jehu said to the custodian of the
wardrobe, "Bring out garments for all the
servants of Baal." When he had brought out
the garments for them, 23 Jehu, with Jehonadab, son of Rechab, entered the temple
of Baal and said to the servants of Baal,
"Search and be sure that there is no one who
serves the LORD here with you, but only servants of Baal." 24 Then they proceeded to offer sacrifices and burnt offerings. Now Jehu
had stationed eighty troops outside with this
warning, "Any of you who lets someone escape of those whom I shall deliver into your
hands shall pay life for life."
25 As soon as he finished offering the burnt
offering, Jehu said to the guards and aides,
"Go in and slay them. Let no one escape."
So the guards and aides put them to the
sword and cast them out. Afterward they
went into the inner shrine of the temple of
Baal, 26 and took out the pillars of the temple
of Baal. They burned the shrine, 27 tore down
the pillar of Baal, tore down the temple of
Baal, and turned it into a latrine, as it remains today.
28 Thus Jehu destroyed Baal in Israel.
Death of Jehu of Israel. 29 However, Jehu
did not desist from the sins which Jeroboam,
son of Nebat, had caused Israel to commit,
the golden calves at Bethel and at Dan.[y]
30 The LORD said to Jehu: Because you
have done well what is right in my eyes, and
have done to the house of Ahab all that was
in my heart, your sons to the fourth generation shall sit upon the throne of Israel.[z] 31 But
Jehu was not careful to walk in the law of the
LORD, the God of Israel, with all his heart,
since he did not desist from the sins which
Jeroboam had caused Israel to commit.
32[a] At that time the LORD began to dismem-
ber Israel. Hazael defeated the Israelites
throughout their territory 33 east of the Jordan
(all the land of Gilead, of the Gadites, Reubenites, and Manassites), from Aroer on the
wadi Arnon up through Gilead and Bashan.
34 The rest of the acts of Jehu, with all that
he did and all his valor, are recorded in the
book of the chronicles of the kings of Israel.
35 Jehu rested with his ancestors and was
buried in Samaria, and his son Jehoahaz
succeeded him as king. 36 The length of
Jehu's reign over Israel was twenty-eight
years in Samaria.

CHAPTER 11

See RG 194

*Death of the Heirs of Ahaziah of Ju-
dah.* 1[b] When Athaliah, the mother of Ahaziah, saw that her son was dead, she began to
kill off the whole royal family. 2 But Jehosheba,* daughter of King Joram and sister
of Ahaziah, took Joash, Ahaziah's son, and
spirited him away, along with his nurse, from
the bedroom where the princes were about to
be slain. He was concealed from Athaliah,
and so he did not die. 3 For six years he remained hidden with her in the house of the
LORD, while Athaliah ruled as queen over the
land.
Death of Athaliah. 4 But in the seventh
year, Jehoiada summoned the captains of the
Carians* and of the guards. He had them
come to him in the house of the LORD, made
a covenant with them, exacted an oath from
them in the house of the LORD, and then

11:2 According to 2 Chr 22:11, Jehosheba was the wife of Jehoiada, the high priest. If this is historical, it would explain her access to the Temple's residential precincts.

11:4 Carians: foreign mercenaries serving as the royal bodyguard. Compare "Cherethites and Pelethites" in 1 Kgs 1:38.

w: 1 Kgs 16:30–33. *x:* 1 Kgs 18:19, 40. *y:* 1 Kgs 12:28–30. *z:* 2 Kgs 15:12. *a:* 2 Kgs 8:12; Am 1:3. *b:* Jgs 9:5.

showed them the king's son. 5He gave them
these orders: "This is what you must do: one
third of you who come on duty on the sabbath shall guard the king's house; 6another
third shall be at the gate Sur; and the last
third shall be at the gate behind the guards.
You shall guard the palace on all sides,
7while the two of your divisions who are going off duty that week shall keep guard over
the house of the LORD for the king. 8You
shall surround the king, each with drawn
weapons, and anyone who tries to approach
the guard detail is to be killed; stay with the
king, wherever he goes."

9The captains did just as Jehoiada the
priest commanded. Each took his troops,
both those going on duty for the week and
those going off duty that week, and came to
Jehoiada the priest. 10[c] He gave the captains
King David's spear and quivers, which were
in the house of the LORD. 11And the guards,
with drawn weapons, lined up from the
southern to the northern limit of the enclosure, surrounding the altar and the temple on
the king's behalf. 12Then Jehoiada brought
out the king's son and put the crown and the
testimony* upon him. They proclaimed him
king and anointed him, clapping their hands
and shouting, "Long live the king!"

13When Athaliah heard the noise made by
the people, she came before them in the
house of the LORD. 14When she saw the king
standing by the column,* as was the custom,
and the captains and trumpeters near the
king, and all the people of the land rejoicing
and blowing trumpets, Athaliah tore her garments and cried out, "Treason, treason!"
15Then Jehoiada the priest instructed the
captains in command of the force: "Escort
her with a guard detail. If anyone follows
her, let him die by the sword." For the priest
had said, "She must not die in the house of
the LORD." 16So they seized her, and when
she reached the Horse Gate of the king's
house, she was put to death.

17[d] Then Jehoiada made a covenant between the LORD and the king and the people,* by which they would be the LORD's
people; and another between the king and
the people. 18Thereupon all the people of the
land went to the temple of Baal and demolished it. They shattered its altars and images
completely, and slew Mattan, the priest of
Baal, before the altars. Jehoiada the priest
appointed a detachment for the house of the
LORD, 19and took the captains, the Carians,
the guards, and all the people of the land,
and they led the king down from the house
of the LORD; they came through the guards'
gate to the king's house, and Joash took his
seat on the royal throne. 20All the people of
the land rejoiced and the city was quiet, now
that Athaliah had been slain with the sword
at the king's house.

IX. Kings of Judah and Israel*

CHAPTER 12

See RG 194

Reign of Joash of Judah. 1Joash was
seven years old when he became king. 2In
the seventh year of Jehu, Joash became king,
and he reigned forty years in Jerusalem. His
mother's name was Zibiah, from Beer-
sheba.

3Joash did what was right in the LORD's
sight as long as he lived, because Jehoiada
the priest guided him, 4though the high
places did not disappear; the people continued to sacrifice and to burn incense on the
high places.

11:12 Testimony: that is, the two tablets of the law preserved in the ark in the Temple. Presumably they were placed upon the king during his installation ceremony as a reminder of the law he was to uphold.

11:14 By the column: the king's special place in the Temple court; cf. 23:3; 2 Chr 23:13. **People of the land**: in this period, the phrase referred to the important citizenry, whose influence sometimes extended to the selection of royal successors (cf. 2 Kgs 11:14–20; 15:5; 16:15; 21:24; 23:6, 30–35; 24:14; 25:3, 19). In postexilic times, by contrast, the phrase was used of the poor.

11:17 There are two covenants. One is between the Lord as one party and the people, headed by the king, as the other. The second covenant, between king and people, is comparable to that made between David and the elders of Israel at Hebron (2 Sm 5:3).

12:1–17:5 This section recounts briefly the reigns of the last several kings of Israel and the kings of Judah contemporary with them. As always, the accounts of the kings are given in the order in which each came to the throne, without regard to which kingdom they ruled. See note on the similar section that begins in 1 Kgs 14:21.

c: 2 Sm 8:7. *d:* 2 Kgs 23:3.

5 Joash said to the priests: "All the funds for sacred purposes that are brought to the house of the LORD—the census tax, personal redemption money—and all funds that are freely brought to the house of the LORD, 6 the priests may take for themselves, each from his own vendor. However, they must make whatever repairs on the temple may prove necessary." 7 Nevertheless, as late as the twenty-third year of the reign of King Joash, the priests had not made needed repairs on the temple. 8 Accordingly, King Joash summoned the priest Jehoiada and the other priests. He asked, "Why do you not repair the temple? You must no longer take funds from your vendors, but you shall turn them over for the repairs." 9 So the priests agreed that they would neither take funds from the people nor make the repairs on the temple.

10 Jehoiada the priest then took a chest, bored a hole in its lid, and set it beside the altar, on the right as one entered the house of the LORD. The priests who kept the doors would put into it all the silver that was brought to the house of the LORD. 11[e] When they noticed that there was a large amount of silver in the chest, the royal scribe would come up with the high priest, and they would gather up and weigh all the silver that was in the house of the LORD. 12 The amount thus realized they turned over to the workers assigned to the house of the LORD. They in turn would pay it to the carpenters and builders working in the house of the LORD, 13 and to the masons and stone cutters, and for the purchase of the wood and hewn stone used in repairing the breaches, and for any other expenses that were necessary to repair the house of the LORD. 14 None of the valuables brought to the house of the LORD were used there to make silver basins, snuffers, bowls, trumpets, or any gold or silver article. 15 Instead, they were given to the workers, and with them they repaired the house of the LORD. 16 Moreover, no reckoning was asked of those who were provided with the funds to give to the workers, because they held positions of trust. 17 The funds from reparation offerings and from purification offerings, however, were not brought to the house of the LORD; they belonged to the priests.

18 Then Hazael, king of Aram, came up and attacked Gath. When he had taken it, Hazael resolved to go on to attack Jerusalem. 19 Joash,* king of Judah, took all the sacred offerings presented by his forebears, Jehoshaphat, Jehoram, and Ahaziah, kings of Judah, as well as his own, and all the gold there was in the treasuries of the house of the LORD and the king's house, and sent them to King Hazael of Aram, who then turned away from Jerusalem.

20 The rest of the acts of Joash, with all that he did, are recorded in the book of the chronicles of the kings of Judah. 21 Certain of his officials* entered into a conspiracy and struck Joash down at Beth-millo. 22 Jozacar, son of Shimeath, and Jehozabad, son of Shomer, were the officials who struck and killed him. He was buried with his ancestors in the City of David, and his son Amaziah succeeded him as king.

CHAPTER 13

See RG 194

Reign of Jehoahaz of Israel. 1 In the twenty-third year of Joash, son of Ahaziah, king of Judah, Jehoahaz, son of Jehu, became king over Israel in Samaria for seventeen years.

2 He did what was evil in the LORD's sight: he did not depart from following the sins that Jeroboam, son of Nebat, had caused Israel to commit. 3 The LORD was angry with Israel and for a long time gave them into the power of Hazael, king of Aram, and of Ben-hadad, son of Hazael. 4 Then Jehoahaz entreated the LORD, who heard him, since he saw the oppression to which the king of Aram had subjected Israel.[f] 5 So the LORD gave Israel a savior,* and the Israelites, freed from the power

12:19 Joash: in 2 Kings the name "Joash" and its variant "Jehoash" are interchangeable (see note on "Joram" and "Jehoram" at 1:17), whether in reference to the king of Judah (vv. 1–22) or his slightly later contemporary, Joash of Israel (13:10–25). Both forms are rendered "Joash" in this translation.

12:21 Officials: lit., "servants." The Hebrew *ebed* ("servant") has a wide range of meanings, always including service to another.

13:5 A savior: i.e., a military leader (cf. Jgs 3:9, 15). Here the identity of the savior is unclear, but the reappearance of a

e: 2 Kgs 22:3–7. *f:* 2 Kgs 14:26–27.

of Aram, dwelt in their own tents as formerly. 6Nevertheless, they did not desist from the sins the house of Jeroboam had caused Israel to commit, but persisted in them. The Asherah* remained even in Samaria.[g] 7No army was left to Jehoahaz, except fifty horses with ten chariots and ten thousand foot soldiers, since the king of Aram had destroyed them and trampled them like dust.

8The rest of the acts of Jehoahaz, with all that he did and his valor, are recorded in the book of the chronicles of the kings of Israel. 9Jehoahaz rested with his ancestors; he was buried in Samaria and his son Joash succeeded him as king.

Reign of Joash of Israel. 10In the thirty-seventh year of Joash, king of Judah, Joash, son of Jehoahaz, became king over Israel in Samaria sixteen years.

11He did what was evil in the LORD's sight; he did not desist from any of the sins Jeroboam, son of Nebat, had caused Israel to commit, but persisted in them.

12* The rest of the acts of Joash, with all that he did and his valor, and how he fought with Amaziah, king of Judah, are recorded in the book of the chronicles of the kings of Israel. 13Joash rested with his ancestors. Then Jeroboam sat on his throne. Joash was buried in Samaria with the kings of Israel.

Elisha's Deathbed Prophecy. 14When Elisha was suffering from the sickness of which he was to die, Joash, king of Israel, went down to weep over him. "My father, my father!"* he exclaimed, "Israel's chariot and steeds!"[h] 15Elisha said to him, "Take bow and arrows," and he took bow and arrows. 16* Elisha said to the king of Israel, "Rest your hand on the bow," and he rested his hand on it. Elisha placed his hands over the king's hands 17and said, "Open the window toward the east." He opened it. Elisha said, "Shoot," and he shot. He said,

"An arrow of victory for the LORD!
An arrow of victory over Aram!
You will beat Aram at Aphek and finish him!"

18Then he said to the king of Israel, "Take the arrows," which he did. Elisha said to the king of Israel, "Beat the ground!" He beat the ground three times and stopped. 19The man of God became angry with him and said, "You should have beat five or six times. You would have beaten Aram and finished him. Now you will beat Aram only three times."

20And so Elisha died and was buried.

At that time of year, bands of Moabites used to raid the land. 21Once some people were burying a man, when suddenly they saw such a raiding band. So they cast the man into the grave of Elisha, and everyone went off. But when the man came in contact with the bones of Elisha, he came back to life and got to his feet.[i]

22King Hazael of Aram oppressed Israel all the days of Jehoahaz. 23But the LORD was gracious with Israel and looked on them with compassion because of his covenant with Abraham, Isaac, and Jacob. He was unwilling to destroy them or to cast them out from his presence even up to now. 24So when King Hazael of Aram died and his son Ben-hadad succeeded him as king, 25Joash, son of Jehoahaz, took back from Ben-hadad, son of Hazael, the cities Hazael had taken in battle from Jehoahaz, his father. Three times Joash beat him, and thus recovered the cities of Israel.

militant Elisha in this chapter after an absence of several chapters and nearly thirty years suggests the narrator may have had him in mind. Two generations later Joash's grandson, Jeroboam II, will also "save" Israel (14:27).

13:6 Asherah: see note on Ex 34:13.

13:12–13 The conclusion to the reign of Joash is given again in 14:15–16. In both places it disrupts the standard pattern followed in the Books of Kings. The account of Joash's reign ends in vv. 12–13; this leaves the story of Elisha's last illness (in which Joash figures prominently) suspended between regnal accounts, much as the story of Elisha's succession to Elijah's prophetic office (chap. 2) was suspended between the accounts of Ahaziah and Joram. In 14:15–16 the concluding formula for Joash's reign interrupts the account of the reign of Amaziah of Judah (14:1–22), much as Joash himself invaded Amaziah's kingdom (14:11–14).

13:14 My father, my father: the way the king addresses the dying Elisha echoes Elisha's address to Elijah in 2:12.

13:16–19 Symbolic acts, like prophetic oracles, were understood to unleash the power they expressed. Similar symbolic acts are seen in Ex 17:8–13; Jos 8:18–20; Ez 4:1–3.

g: Ex 34:13; 1 Kgs 16:33. *h:* 2 Kgs 2:12. *i:* Sir 48:14.

CHAPTER 14

See RG 195

Reign of Amaziah of Judah. [1]In the second year* of Joash, son of Jehoahaz, king of Israel, Amaziah, son of Joash, king of Judah, became king. [2]He was twenty-five years old when he became king, and he reigned twenty-nine years in Jerusalem. His mother's name was Jehoaddin, from Jerusalem.

[3]He did what was right in the LORD's eyes, though not like David his father. He did just as his father Joash had done, [4]though the high places did not disappear, and the people continued to sacrifice and to burn incense on the high places.

[5]When Amaziah had the kingdom firmly in hand, he struck down the officials who had struck down the king, his father. [6]But their children he did not put to death, according to what is written in the book of the law of Moses, which the LORD commanded: "Parents shall not be put to death for their children, nor shall children be put to death for their parents; only for one's own crimes shall a person be put to death."[j]

[7]Amaziah struck down ten thousand Edomites in the Salt Valley. He took Sela in battle and renamed it Joktheel, the name it has to this day.[k]

[8]Then Amaziah sent messengers to Joash, son of Jehoahaz, son of Jehu, king of Israel, with this message: "Come, let us meet face to face." [9]Joash, king of Israel, sent this reply to Amaziah, king of Judah: "A thistle of Lebanon sent word to a cedar of Lebanon, 'Give your daughter to my son in marriage,' but an animal of Lebanon passed by and trampled the thistle underfoot.[l] [10]You have indeed struck down Edom, and your heart is lifted up; enjoy your glory, but stay home! Why bring misfortune and failure on yourself and on Judah with you?" [11]But Amaziah did not listen. So Joash, king of Israel, advanced, and he and Amaziah, king of Judah, met face to face at Beth-shemesh of Judah, [12]and Judah was defeated by Israel, and all fled to their tents. [13]But Amaziah, king of Judah, son of Joash, son of Ahaziah, was captured by Joash, king of Israel, at Beth-shemesh. When they came to Jerusalem Joash tore down the wall of Jerusalem, from the Gate of Ephraim to the Corner Gate, four hundred cubits. [14]He took all the gold and silver and all the vessels found in the house of the LORD and in the treasuries of the king's house, and hostages as well. Then he returned to Samaria.

[15]* The rest of the acts of Joash, what he did and his valor, and how he made war against Amaziah, king of Judah, are recorded in the book of the chronicles of the kings of Israel. [16]Joash rested with his ancestors; he was buried in Samaria with the kings of Israel, and his son Jeroboam succeeded him as king.

[17]* Amaziah, son of Joash, king of Judah, survived Joash, son of Jehoahaz, king of Israel, by fifteen years. [18]The rest of the acts of Amaziah are recorded in the book of the chronicles of the kings of Judah. [19]When a conspiracy was formed against him in Jerusalem, he fled to Lachish. But he was pursued to Lachish and killed there. [20]He was brought back on horses and was buried in Jerusalem with his ancestors in the City of David. [21]Thereupon all the people of Judah* took Azariah, who was only sixteen years old, and made him king to succeed Amaziah, his father. [22]It was he who rebuilt Elath and restored it to Judah, after the king rested with his ancestors.

Reign of Jeroboam II of Israel. [23]In the fifteenth year of Amaziah, son of Joash, king of Judah, Jeroboam, son of Joash, king of Israel, became king in Samaria for forty-one years.

14:1–2 In the second year . . . twenty-nine years in Jerusalem: as they stand, the chronological data in the introductions to the reigns of the kings of Judah and Israel are incompatible with one another. The kings of Judah between Athaliah and Ahaz are assigned too many years in all to correspond to the reigns in Israel from Jehu to the fall of Samaria. Various theories have been proposed in an attempt to explain the discrepancy, such as co-regencies, or textual corruption in the process of transmission.

14:15–16 See note on 13:12–13.

14:17 See note on vv. 1–2.

14:21 All the people of Judah: this phrase may refer to the army (compare, for example, "all Israel" in 1 Kgs 16:16–17). If this is its meaning here, then Amaziah's assassination and Azariah's succession are owing to a military coup. **Azariah**: also called Uzziah in many texts.

j: Dt 24:16; Ez 18:20. *k:* 2 Sm 8:13–14. *l:* Jgs 9:8–15.

[24]He did evil in the LORD's sight; he did
not desist from any of the sins that Jeroboam, son of Nebat, had caused Israel to
commit. [25]He restored the boundaries of Israel from Lebo-hamath to the sea of the Arabah,* as the LORD, the God of Israel, had
foretold through his servant, the prophet Jonah, son of Amittai, from Gath-hepher. [26]For
the LORD saw the very bitter affliction of Israel, where there was neither bond nor free,
no one at all to help Israel. [27]Since the LORD
had not resolved to wipe out the name of Israel from under the heavens, he saved them
through Jeroboam, son of Joash.
[28]The rest of the acts of Jeroboam, with all
that he did and his valor, how he fought, and
how he regained Damascus and Hamath for
Israel, are recorded in the book of the chronicles of the kings of Israel. [29]Jeroboam rested
with his ancestors, the kings of Israel, and his
son Zechariah succeeded him as king.

CHAPTER 15

See RG 195

Reign of Azariah of Judah. [1]In the
twenty-seventh year* of Jeroboam, king of
Israel, Azariah, son of Amaziah, king of Judah, became king. [2]He was sixteen years old
when he became king, and he reigned fifty-
two years in Jerusalem. His mother's name
was Jecholiah, from Jerusalem.
[3]He did what was right in the LORD's
sight, just as his father Amaziah had done,
[4]though the high places did not disappear,
and the people continued to sacrifice and to
burn incense on the high places. [5]The LORD
afflicted the king, and he was a leper until
the day he died. He lived in a house apart,
while Jotham, the king's son, was master of
the palace and ruled the people of the land.*
[6]The rest of the acts of Azariah, and all
that he did, are recorded in the book of the
chronicles of the kings of Judah. [7]Azariah
rested with his ancestors, and was buried
with them in the City of David, and his son
Jotham succeeded him as king.
Reign of Zechariah of Israel. [8]In the
thirty-eighth year of Azariah, king of Judah,
Zechariah, son of Jeroboam, became king
over Israel in Samaria for six months.
[9]He did what was evil in the LORD's sight,
as his ancestors had done, and did not desist
from the sins that Jeroboam, son of Nebat,
had caused Israel to commit. [10]Shallum, son
of Jabesh, plotted against him and struck
him down at Ibleam. He killed him and
reigned in his place.
[11]As for the rest of the acts of Zechariah,
these are recorded in the book of the chronicles of the kings of Israel. [12]This was the
word the LORD had spoken to Jehu: Sons of
your line to the fourth generation shall sit
upon the throne of Israel; and so it was.[m]
Reign of Shallum of Israel. [13]Shallum, son
of Jabesh, became king in the thirty-ninth
year of Uzziah, king of Judah; he reigned
one month in Samaria.
[14]Menahem, son of Gadi, came up from
Tirzah to Samaria, and struck down Shallum, son of Jabesh, in Samaria. He killed
him and reigned in his place.
[15]As for the rest of the acts of Shallum,
with the conspiracy he carried out, these are
recorded in the book of the chronicles of the
kings of Israel. [16]At that time, Menahem attacked Tappuah, all its inhabitants, and its
whole district as far as Tirzah, because they
did not let him in. He attacked them; he even
ripped open all their pregnant women.
Reign of Menahem of Israel. [17]In the
thirty-ninth year of Azariah, king of Judah,
Menahem, son of Gadi, became king over
Israel for ten years in Samaria. [18]He did
what was evil in the LORD's sight as long as
he lived, not desisting from the sins that Jeroboam, son of Nebat, had caused Israel to
commit. [19]Pul,* king of Assyria, came
against the land. But Menahem gave Pul a
thousand talents of silver to have his help in
holding onto his kingdom. [20]Menahem paid
out silver on behalf of Israel, that is, for all
the people of substance, by giving the king
of Assyria fifty shekels of silver for each
one. So the king of Assyria went home and
did not stay in the land.

14:25 Sea of the Arabah: the Dead Sea. **Jonah, son of Amittai**: see note on Jon 1:1.

15:1 Twenty-seventh year: see note on 14:1–2.

15:5 People of the land: see note on 11:14.

15:19 Pul: the Babylonian throne name of the Assyrian Tiglath-pileser III; cf. v. 29.

m: 2 Kgs 10:30.

[21]The rest of the acts of Menahem, with all that he did, are recorded in the book of the chronicles of the kings of Israel. [22]Menahem rested with his ancestors, and his son Pekahiah succeeded him as king.

Reign of Pekahiah of Israel. [23]In the fiftieth year of Azariah, king of Judah, Pekahiah, son of Menahem, became king over Israel in Samaria for two years.

[24]He did what was evil in the LORD's sight, not desisting from the sins that Jeroboam, son of Nebat, had caused Israel to commit. [25]His adjutant Pekah, son of Remaliah, conspired against him, and struck him down at Samaria within the palace stronghold; he had with him fifty men from Gilead. He killed him and reigned in his place. [26]As for the rest of the acts of Pekahiah, with all that he did, these are recorded in the book of the chronicles of the kings of Israel.

Reign of Pekah of Israel. [27]* In the fifty-second year of Azariah, king of Judah, Pekah, son of Remaliah, became king over Israel in Samaria for twenty years.

[28]He did what was evil in the LORD's sight, not desisting from the sins that Jeroboam, son of Nebat, had caused Israel to commit. [29]In the days of Pekah, king of Israel, Tiglath-pileser, king of Assyria, came and took Ijon, Abel-beth-maacah, Janoah, Kedesh, Hazor, Gilead, and Galilee—all the land of Naphtali—deporting the inhabitants to Assyria. [30]* Hoshea, son of Elah, carried out a conspiracy against Pekah, son of Remaliah; he struck and killed him, and succeeded him as king in the twentieth year of Jotham, son of Uzziah.

[31]As for the rest of the acts of Pekah, with all that he did, these are recorded in the book of the chronicles of the kings of Israel.

Reign of Jotham of Judah. [32]In the second year of Pekah, son of Remaliah, king of Israel, Jotham, son of Uzziah, king of Judah, became king. [33]He was twenty-five years old when he became king, and he reigned sixteen years in Jerusalem. His mother's name was Jerusha, daughter of Zadok.

[34]He did what was right in the LORD's sight, just as his father Uzziah had done, [35]though the high places did not disappear, and the people continued to sacrifice and to burn incense on the high places. It was he who built the Upper Gate* of the LORD's house.

[36]The rest of the acts of Jotham, with what he did, are recorded in the book of the chronicles of the kings of Judah. [37]It was at that time that the LORD began to unleash Rezin, king of Aram, and Pekah, son of Remaliah, against Judah.[n] [38]Jotham rested with his ancestors; he was buried with his ancestors in the City of David his father, and his son Ahaz succeeded him as king.

CHAPTER 16

See RG 196

Reign of Ahaz of Judah.* [1]In the seventeenth year of Pekah, son of Remaliah, Ahaz, son of Jotham, king of Judah, became king. [2]Ahaz was twenty years old when he became king, and he reigned sixteen years in Jerusalem.

He did not do what was right in the sight of the LORD his God, as David his father had done. [3]He walked in the way of the kings of Israel; he even immolated his child by fire, in accordance with the abominable practices of the nations whom the LORD had dispossessed before the Israelites.[o] [4]Further, he sacrificed and burned incense on the high places, on hills, and under every green tree.[p]

15:27 The twenty years here ascribed to Pekah are difficult to reconcile with other chronological notices about the kings. One theory would see Pekah and Menahem as rival kings over parts of a divided Israelite territory; this could explain Menahem's concern for Assyrian support (vv. 19–20) and Assyria's attack on Pekah (v. 29). See 16:1 and note on 14:1–2.

15:30 The twenty years here reckoned to Jotham of Judah may include his co-regency with Azariah (v. 5); otherwise they are impossible to reconcile with v. 33, which ascribes him only sixteen years. The verse also appears to contradict 16:1, which has Jotham's son and successor, Ahaz, coming to the throne while Pekah still reigns in Israel, and 17:1, which dates Hoshea's accession to the throne to the twelfth year of Ahaz.

15:35 The Upper Gate: also called the Gate of Benjamin; cf. Jer 20:2; Ez 9:2.

16:1–20 Firmly dated events bearing on chaps. 16–20 are: the fall of Damascus (16:9) in 732 B.C., the fall of Samaria (18:9–11) in 722/721 B.C., and Sennacherib's invasion of Judah (18:13) in 701 B.C., which both in Kings and in Is 36:1 occurs in the fourteenth year of Hezekiah. These data make it possible to connect the chronology of Israel and Judah to the larger chronology of ancient Near Eastern history, but they also complicate further the already vexed problem of inconsistencies in the biblical data about accession years and lengths of reign.

n: Is 7:1–16. *o:* Lv 18:21; Dt 18:10. *p:* Dt 12:2.

5Then Rezin, king of Aram, and Pekah, son of Remaliah, king of Israel, came up to Jerusalem to attack it. Although they besieged Ahaz, they were unable to do battle. 6(In those days Rezin, king of Aram, recovered Elath for Aram, and drove the Judahites out of it. The Edomites then entered Elath, which they have occupied until the present.)

7Meanwhile, Ahaz sent messengers to Tiglath-pileser, king of Assyria, with the plea: "I am your servant and your son. Come up and rescue me from the power of the king of Aram and the king of Israel, who are attacking me." 8Ahaz took the silver and gold that were in the house of the LORD and in the treasuries of the king's house and sent them as a present to the king of Assyria. 9The king of Assyria listened to him and moved against Damascus, captured it, deported its inhabitants to Kir, and put Rezin to death.

10King Ahaz went to Damascus to meet Tiglath-pileser, king of Assyria. When he saw the altar in Damascus, King Ahaz sent to Uriah the priest a model of the altar and a detailed design of its construction. 11Uriah the priest built an altar according to the plans which King Ahaz sent him from Damascus, and had it completed by the time King Ahaz returned from Damascus. 12On his arrival from Damascus, the king inspected the altar; the king approached the altar, went up 13and sacrificed his burnt offering and grain offering, pouring out his libation, and sprinkling the blood of his communion offerings on the altar. 14The bronze altar that stood before the LORD he brought from the front of the temple—that is, from the space between the new altar and the house of the LORD—and set it on the north side of his altar. 15[q] King Ahaz commanded Uriah the priest, "Upon the large altar sacrifice the morning burnt offering and the evening grain offering, the king's burnt offering and grain offering, and the burnt offering and grain offering of the people of the land.* Their libations you must sprinkle on it along with all the blood of burnt offerings and sacrifices. But the old bronze altar shall be mine for consultation." 16Uriah the priest did just as King Ahaz had commanded. 17King Ahaz detached the panels from the stands and removed the basins from them; he also took down the bronze sea from the bronze oxen that supported it, and set it on a stone pavement. 18In deference to the king of Assyria he removed the sabbath canopy that had been set up in the house of the LORD and the king's outside entrance* to the temple.

19The rest of the acts of Ahaz, with what he did, are recorded in the book of the chronicles of the kings of Judah. 20Ahaz rested with his ancestors; he was buried with his ancestors in the City of David, and his son Hezekiah succeeded him as king.

CHAPTER 17

See RG 196

Reign of Hoshea of Israel. 1In the twelfth year of Ahaz, king of Judah, Hoshea, son of Elah, became king in Samaria over Israel for nine years.

2He did what was evil in the LORD's sight, yet not to the extent of the kings of Israel before him. 3Shalmaneser,* king of Assyria, advanced against him, and Hoshea became his vassal and paid him tribute.[r] 4But the king of Assyria found Hoshea guilty of conspiracy for sending messengers to the king of Egypt at Sais, and for failure to pay the annual tribute to the king of Assyria. So the king of Assyria arrested and imprisoned him. 5Then the king of Assyria* occupied the whole land and attacked Samaria, which he besieged for three years.

16:15 People of the land: see note on 11:14. **For consultation**: perhaps the introduction into Judah of the Babylonian practice of reading omens from animal sacrifices; cf. Ez 21:26.

16:18 Sabbath canopy . . . outside entrance: the Hebrew is obscure, but as a vassal Ahaz must have had to divest himself of signs of sovereignty.

17:3 Shalmaneser: son and successor of the Assyrian king Tiglath-pileser III. **Vassal**: lit., "servant"; cf. 16:7; so also in 24:1.

17:5 The king of Assyria: Shalmaneser was succeeded by Sargon II, who usurped the Assyrian throne in 722/721 B.C. In his inscriptions, Sargon claims to have captured Samaria during the first year of his reign.

17:6–41 This brief section is the Deuteronomistic historian's theological reflection on the causes and aftermath of Assyria's conquest of the Northern Kingdom. The text contrasts the Israelites, who were deported (v. 6) because they abandoned the worship of the Lord (vv. 7–23), with the foreigners who were brought into the land (v. 24) and undertook,

q: Ex 29:38–41; Nm 28:3–8. *r*: 2 Kgs 18:9.

X. The End of Israel*

Israelites Deported. 6 In Hoshea's ninth year, the king of Assyria took Samaria, deported the Israelites to Assyria, and settled them in Halah, and at the Habor, a river of Gozan, and in the cities of the Medes.[s] 7 This came about because the Israelites sinned against the LORD, their God, who had brought them up from the land of Egypt, from under the hand of Pharaoh, king of Egypt. They venerated other gods, 8[t] they followed the rites of the nations whom the LORD had dispossessed before the Israelites and those that the kings of Israel had practiced. 9 They adopted unlawful practices toward the LORD, their God. They built high places in all their cities, from guard post to garrisoned town. 10 They set up pillars and asherahs* for themselves on every high hill and under every green tree. 11 They burned incense there, on all the high places, like the nations whom the LORD had sent into exile at their coming. They did evil things that provoked the LORD, 12 and served idols, although the LORD had told them: You must not do this.

13[u] The LORD warned Israel and Judah by every prophet and seer: Give up your evil ways and keep my commandments and statutes, in accordance with the entire law which I enjoined on your ancestors and which I sent you by my servants the prophets. 14 But they did not listen. They grew as stiff-necked as their ancestors, who had not believed in the LORD, their God.[v] 15 They rejected his statutes, the covenant he had made with their ancestors, and the warnings he had given them. They followed emptiness and became empty; they followed the surrounding nations whom the LORD had commanded them not to imitate.[w] 16 They abandoned all the commandments of the LORD, their God: they made for themselves two molten calves; they made an asherah; they bowed down to all the host of heaven; they served Baal.[x] 17[y] They immolated their sons and daughters by fire. They practiced augury and divination. They surrendered themselves to doing what was evil in the LORD's sight, and provoked him.

18[z] The LORD became enraged, and removed them from his presence. Only the tribe of Judah was left. 19 Even the people of Judah did not keep the commandments of the LORD, their God, but followed the rites practiced by Israel. 20 So the LORD rejected the entire people of Israel: he afflicted them and delivered them over to plunderers, finally casting them from his presence.[a] 21 When he tore Israel away from the house of David, they made Jeroboam, son of Nebat, king; but Jeroboam lured the Israelites away from the LORD, causing them to commit a great sin.[b] 22 The Israelites imitated Jeroboam in all the sins he committed; they would not depart from them.

23 Finally, the LORD removed Israel from his presence, just as he had declared through all his servants, the prophets. Thus Israel went into exile from their native soil to Assyria until this very day.

Foreigners Deported to Israel. 24 The king of Assyria brought people from Babylon, Cuthah, Avva, Hamath, and Sepharvaim, and settled them in the cities of Samaria in place of the Israelites. They took possession of Samaria and dwelt in its cities. 25 When they first settled there, they did not venerate the LORD, so he sent lions among them that killed some of them. 26 A report reached the king of Assyria: "The nations you deported and settled in the cities of Samaria do not know the proper worship of the god of the land, so he has sent lions among them that are killing them, since they do not know the law of the god of the land." 27 The king of Assyria gave the order, "Send back some of the priests you deported, to go there and settle,

however imperfectly, to worship the Lord alongside their own traditional deities (vv. 25–34a). The last verses recapitulate the apostasy of the Israelites (vv. 34b–40) and the syncretism of the foreigners (v. 41). This is a deliberately disparaging, and not wholly accurate, account of the origin of the Samaritans; it reflects the hostility the Judahites continued to hold toward the inhabitants of the northern territories.

17:10 Asherahs: see note on Ex 34:13.

s: 2 Kgs 18:10–11; Tb 1:2. *t:* Ex 23:24; 34:13; Dt 12:2. *u:* Jer 25:5. *v:* Dt 9:13. *w:* Jer 2:5. *x:* Ex 34:13; Dt 4:19; 17:2–3; 1 Kgs 12:28; 16:33. *y:* Lv 18:21; Dt 18:10. *z:* Sir 48:15. *a:* Jer 25:9. *b:* 1 Kgs 12:20, 26–33; 13:34.

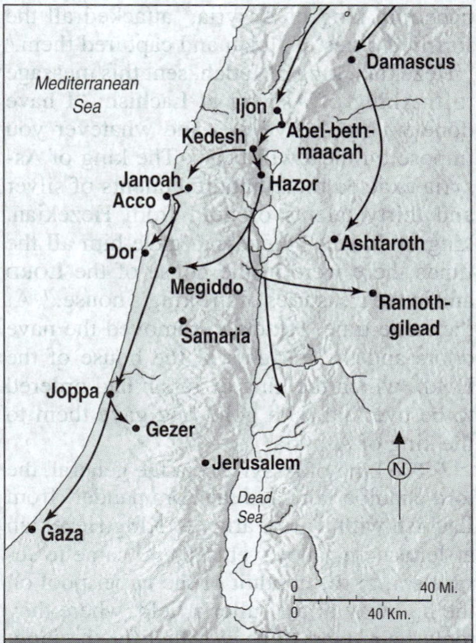

Campaign of Tiglath-pileser III

to teach them the proper worship of the god of the land." 28So one of the priests who had been deported from Samaria returned and settled in Bethel, and began to teach them how to venerate the LORD.

29Thus each of these nations continued to make its own gods, setting them up in the shrines of the high places the Samarians had made: each nation in the cities in which they dwelt. 30The Babylonians made Sukkot-Benot;[*] the people of Cuth made Nergal; those from Hamath made Ashima; 31those from Avva made Nibhaz and Tartak; and those from Sepharvaim immolated their children by fire to their city gods, King Hadad and King Anu. 32At the same time, they were venerating the LORD, appointing from their own number priests for the high places to officiate for them in the shrines on the high places. 33They were both venerating the LORD and serving their own gods. They followed the custom of the nations from among whom they had been deported.

34To this very day they continue to act according to their former customs, not venerating the LORD nor observing the statutes and regulations, the law and commandment, that the LORD enjoined on the descendants of Jacob, whom he had named Israel.[c] 35When the LORD made a covenant with them, he commanded them: You must not venerate other gods, nor bow down to them, nor serve them, nor offer sacrifice to them,[d] 36but only to the LORD, who brought you up from the land of Egypt with great power and outstretched arm. Him shall you venerate, to him shall you bow down, and to him shall you offer sacrifice. 37You must be careful always to observe the statutes and ordinances, the law and commandment, which he wrote for you; you must not venerate other gods. 38The covenant I made with you, you must not forget; you must not venerate other gods. 39You must venerate only the LORD, your God; it is he who will deliver you from the power of all your enemies. 40But they did not listen; they continued to act according to their former customs.

41But these nations were both venerating the LORD and serving their own idols. Their children and children's children are still acting like their ancestors, to this very day.

XI. The End of Judah[*]

CHAPTER 18

See RG 196

Reign of Hezekiah. 1In the third year of Hoshea, son of Elah, king of Israel, Hezekiah, son of Ahaz, king of Judah, became king. 2He was twenty-five years old when he became king, and he reigned twenty-nine

17:30 Sukkot-Benot: several of the divine names in vv. 30–31 are problematic or conjectural. Sukkot-Benot is unknown, but the name may have been corrupted from that of Sarpanitu, the consort of the Babylonian god Marduk.

18:1–25:30 The Books of Kings end, as they began, with the people of the Lord in a single kingdom, Judah, centered on the capital, Jerusalem, and the Solomonic Temple. The reigns of two reformer kings, both praised, are recounted at length: Hezekiah (chaps. 18–20) and Josiah (22:1–23:30). Each is followed by shorter accounts of two kings who are condemned: Manasseh and Amon (chap. 21) and Jehoahaz and Jehoiakim (23:31–24:7). The book ends with the last days of Judah under Jehoiachin and Zedekiah and the beginning of the Babylonian exile.

c: Gn 32:29; 35:10. *d:* Ex 20:3–6.

years in Jerusalem. His mother's name was Abi, daughter of Zechariah.

3 He did what was right in the LORD's sight, just as David his father had done. 4 It was he who removed the high places, shattered the pillars, cut down the asherah,* and smashed the bronze serpent Moses had made, because up to that time the Israelites were burning incense to it. (It was called Nehushtan.)[e] 5 He put his trust in the LORD, the God of Israel; and neither before nor after him was there anyone like him among all the kings of Judah. 6 Hezekiah held fast to the LORD and never turned away from following him, but observed the commandments the LORD had given Moses. 7 The LORD was with him, and he succeeded in all he set out to do. He rebelled against the king of Assyria and did not serve him. 8 It was he who struck the Philistines as far as Gaza, and all its territory from guard post to garrisoned town.

9* In the fourth year of King Hezekiah, which was the seventh year of Hoshea, son of Elah, king of Israel, Shalmaneser, king of Assyria, attacked Samaria and laid siege to it, 10[f] and after three years they captured it. In the sixth year of Hezekiah, the ninth year of Hoshea, king of Israel, Samaria was taken. 11 The king of Assyria then deported the Israelites to Assyria and led them off to Halah, and the Habor, a river of Gozan, and the cities of the Medes. 12 This happened because they did not obey the LORD, their God, but violated his covenant; they did not obey nor do all that Moses, the servant of the LORD, commanded.[g]

Sennacherib and Hezekiah. 13* In the fourteenth year of King Hezekiah, Sennacherib, king of Assyria,* attacked all the fortified cities of Judah and captured them.[h] 14 Hezekiah, king of Judah, sent this message to the king of Assyria at Lachish: "I have done wrong. Leave me, and whatever you impose on me I will bear." The king of Assyria exacted three hundred talents of silver and thirty talents of gold from Hezekiah, king of Judah. 15 Hezekiah gave him all the funds there were in the house of the LORD and in the treasuries of the king's house. 16 At the same time, Hezekiah removed the nave doors and the uprights of the house of the LORD, which the king of Judah had ordered to be overlaid with gold, and gave them to the king of Assyria.[i]

17 The king of Assyria sent the general, the lord chamberlain, and the commander* from Lachish with a great army to King Hezekiah at Jerusalem. They went up and came to Jerusalem, to the conduit of the upper pool on the highway of the fuller's field, where they took their stand. 18 They called for the king, but Eliakim, son of Hilkiah, the master of the palace, came out, along with Shebnah the scribe and the chancellor Joah, son of Asaph.[j]

19 The commander said to them, "Tell Hezekiah, 'Thus says the great king, the king of Assyria: On what do you base this trust of yours? 20 Do you think mere words substitute for strategy and might in war? In whom, then, do you place your trust, that you rebel against me? 21 Do you trust in Egypt, that broken reed of a staff, which pierces the hand of anyone who leans on it? That is what Pharaoh, king of Egypt, is to all who trust in him.[k] 22 Or do you people say to me, "It is in the

18:4 Asherah: see note on Ex 34:13. **Nehushtan**: the name *nehushtan* contains several wordplays in Hebrew. It recalls the word "serpent" (*nahash*), the word "bronze" (*nehoshet*), and the word "to read omens" (*nihesh*). The sentence is also unclear about who named the bronze serpent "Nehushtan"—whether Moses when he made it, or the people when they venerated it, or Hezekiah when he destroyed it.

18:9 The correlations between the reigns of Hezekiah and Hoshea in vv. 9–10 conflict with other biblical data and with the date for the fall of Samaria, 722/721 B.C. (see note on 16:1–20). Since Sennacherib's invasion in the fourteenth year of Hezekiah (v. 13) took place in 701, Hezekiah cannot have been on the throne twenty years earlier. Various solutions have been proposed: scribal errors in writing the numbers; a Hezekian co-regency with his father Ahaz beginning in 729; etc. None of the solutions has won a consensus among historians.

18:13–20:19 This material is found also in Is 36–39, with one long addition (Is 38:9–20) and only a few other changes.

18:13 Sennacherib succeeded Sargon II as king of Assyria. His Judean campaign was waged in 701 B.C. See notes on 16:1–20 and 18:9.

18:17 General, the lord chamberlain . . . commander: the text lists three major functionaries by their Assyrian titles, of which only the first, more nearly "lord lieutenant," is military in origin; the commander was technically the king's chief butler.

e: Ex 23:24; 34:13; Nm 21:4–9; Dt 12:2; Wis 16:5–7; Jn 3:14. *f:* 2 Kgs 17:5–6; Tb 1:2. *g:* 2 Kgs 17:6–23; Ex 24:7. *h:* Sir 48:18–21. *i:* 1 Kgs 6:31–35. *j:* Is 22:15–25. *k:* Is 30:1–7; 31:1–3; Ez 29:6–7.

LORD our God we trust!"? Is it not he whose high places and altars Hezekiah has removed, commanding Judah and Jerusalem, "Worship before this altar in Jerusalem"?'

[23]"Now, make a wager with my lord, the king of Assyria: I will give you two thousand horses if you are able to put riders on them. [24]How then can you turn back even a captain, one of the least servants of my lord, trusting, as you do, in Egypt for chariots and horses? [25]Did I come up to destroy this place without the LORD? The LORD himself said to me: Go up and destroy that land!"

[26]Then Eliakim, son of Hilkiah, and Shebnah and Joah said to the commander: "Please speak to your servants in Aramaic; we understand it. Do not speak to us in the language of Judah within earshot of the people who are on the wall." [27]But the commander replied: "Was it to your lord and to you that my lord sent me to speak these words? Was it not rather to those sitting on the wall, who, with you, will have to eat their own excrement and drink their urine?"*

[28]Then the commander stepped forward and cried out in a loud voice in the language of Judah, "Listen to the words of the great king, the king of Assyria. [29]Thus says the king: Do not let Hezekiah deceive you, for he cannot rescue you from my hand. [30]And do not let Hezekiah induce you to trust in the LORD, saying, 'The LORD will surely rescue us, and this city will not be handed over to the king of Assyria.' [31]Do not listen to Hezekiah, for thus says the king of Assyria: Make peace with me, and surrender to me! Eat, each of you, from your vine, each from your own fig tree. Drink water, each from your own well, [32]until I arrive and take you to a land like your own, a land of grain and wine, a land of bread and vineyards, a land of rich olives and honey. Live, and do not die! And do not listen to Hezekiah when he would incite you by saying, 'The LORD will rescue us.' [33]Has any of the gods of the nations ever rescued his land from the power of the king of Assyria? [34]Where are the gods of Hamath and Arpad? Where are the gods of Sepharvaim, Hena, and Ivvah? Did they indeed rescue Samaria from my power?* [35]Which of the gods for all these lands ever rescued his land from my power? Will the LORD then rescue Jerusalem from my power?" [36]But the people remained silent and did not answer at all, for the king's command was, "Do not answer him."

[37]Then the master of the palace, Eliakim, son of Hilkiah, Shebnah the scribe, and the chancellor Joah, son of Asaph, came to Hezekiah with their garments torn, and reported to him the words of the commander.

CHAPTER 19

See RG 196

Hezekiah and Isaiah. [1]When King Hezekiah heard this, he tore his garments, covered himself with sackcloth, and went into the house of the LORD. [2]He sent Eliakim, the master of the palace, Shebnah the scribe, and the elders of the priests, covered with sackcloth, to tell the prophet Isaiah, son of Amoz, [3]"Thus says Hezekiah:

A day of distress and rebuke,
  a day of disgrace is this day!
Children are due to come forth,
  but the strength to give birth is lacking.*

[4]Perhaps the LORD, your God, will hear all the words of the commander, whom his lord, the king of Assyria, sent to taunt the living God, and will rebuke him for the words which the LORD, your God, has heard. So lift up a prayer for the remnant that is here." [5]When the servants of King Hezekiah had come to Isaiah, [6]he said to them, "Tell this to your lord: Thus says the LORD: Do not be frightened by the words you have heard, by which the deputies of the king of Assyria have blasphemed me.[l] [7]I am putting in him

18:27 Excrement . . . urine: the reference is to the famine that results from a prolonged siege (compare 6:24–25; Dt 28:53–57). For public reading, ancient tradition (e.g., the Qere reading of the Masoretic text) softened the terms to "eat their own waste and drink their own bodies' water."

18:34 Did they indeed . . . power?: some time after the fall of Samaria in 722/721 B.C., Hamath, Arpad, and other small states in the region formed an anti-Assyrian coalition. If the coalition had succeeded, it could have broken Assyrian control over the whole region, including Samaria, and allowed the kingdom of Israel to free itself. When Assyria crushed the coalition, it also crushed Israel's hopes for liberation.

19:3 See note on Is 37:3.

l: Is 10:5–14.

such a spirit that when he hears a report he
will return to his land. I will make him fall
by the sword in his land."
8 When the commander, on his return, heard
that the king of Assyria had withdrawn from
Lachish, he found him besieging Libnah.
Sennacherib, Hezekiah, and Isaiah. 9 The
king of Assyria heard a report: "Tirhakah,
king of Ethiopia, has come out to fight
against you." Again he sent messengers to
Hezekiah to say: 10 "Thus shall you say to
Hezekiah, king of Judah: Do not let your
God in whom you trust deceive you by saying, 'Jerusalem will not be handed over to
the king of Assyria.' 11 You, certainly, have
heard what the kings of Assyria have done to
all the lands: they put them under the ban!
And are you to be rescued? 12 [m] Did the gods
of the nations whom my fathers destroyed
deliver them—Gozan, Haran, Rezeph, or the
Edenites in Telassar? 13 Where are the king
of Hamath, the king of Arpad, or the kings of
the cities Sepharvaim, Hena and Ivvah?"
14 Hezekiah took the letter from the hand of
the messengers and read it; then he went up to
the house of the LORD, and spreading it out before the LORD, 15 Hezekiah prayed in the
LORD's presence: "LORD, God of Israel, enthroned on the cherubim! You alone are God
over all the kingdoms of the earth. It is you
who made the heavens and the earth.[n] 16 Incline your ear, LORD, and listen! Open your
eyes, LORD, and see! Hear the words Sennacherib has sent to taunt the living God.
17 Truly, O LORD, the kings of Assyria have
laid waste the nations and their lands. 18 They
gave their gods to the fire—they were not
gods at all, but the work of human hands—
wood and stone, they destroyed them.
19 Therefore, LORD, our God, save us from this
man's power, that all the kingdoms of the earth
may know that you alone, LORD, are God."[o]
20 Then Isaiah, son of Amoz, sent this message to Hezekiah: "Thus says the LORD, the
God of Israel, to whom you have prayed
concerning Sennacherib, king of Assyria: I
have listened! 21* This is the word the LORD
has spoken concerning him:

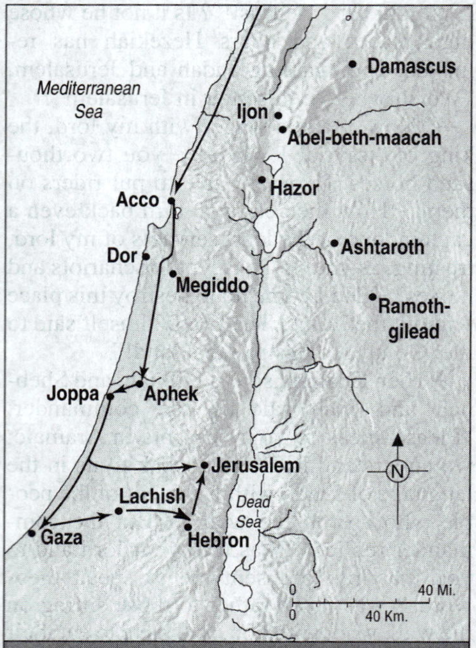

Campaign of Sennacherib

She despises you, laughs you to scorn,
the virgin daughter Zion!
Behind you she wags her head,
daughter Jerusalem.
22 Whom have you insulted and
blasphemed,
at whom have you raised your voice
And lifted up your eyes on high?
At the Holy One of Israel!
23 Through the mouths of your messengers
you insulted the Lord when you said,
'With my many chariots I went up
to the tops of the peaks,
to the recesses of Lebanon,
To cut down its lofty cedars,
its choice cypresses;
I reached to the farthest shelter,
the forest ranges.
24 I myself dug wells
and drank foreign waters,
Drying up all the rivers of Egypt
beneath the soles of my feet.'

19:21–31 Verses 21–28 are addressed to Sennacherib, vv. 29–31 to Judah.

m: 2 Kgs 17:6, 24; 18:34. *n:* Ex 25:17–22; 1 Kgs 6:23–28; 8:6–7. *o:* 1 Kgs 18:36.

25 “Have you not heard?
A long time ago I prepared it,
from days of old I planned it.
Now I have brought it about:
You are here to reduce
fortified cities to heaps of ruins,
26 Their people powerless,
dismayed and distraught.
They are plants of the field,
green growth,
thatch on the rooftops,
Grain scorched by the east wind.
27 I know when you stand or sit,
when you come or go[p]
and how you rage against me.
28 Because you rage against me,
and your smugness has reached my ears,
I will put my hook in your nose
and my bit in your mouth,
And make you leave by the way you came.

29 “This shall be a sign for you:
This year you shall eat the aftergrowth,
next year, what grows of itself;
But in the third year, sow and reap,
plant vineyards and eat their fruit!
30 The remaining survivors of the house of Judah
shall again strike root below
and bear fruit above.
31 For out of Jerusalem shall come a remnant,
and from Mount Zion, survivors.
The zeal of the LORD of hosts shall do this.

32 “Therefore, thus says the LORD about the king:

He shall not come as far as this city,
nor shoot there an arrow,
nor confront it with a shield,
Nor cast up a siege-work against it.
33 By the way he came he shall leave,
never coming as far as this city,
oracle of the LORD.
34 I will shield and save this city
for my own sake and the sake of David
my servant.”[q]

35 That night the angel of the LORD went
forth and struck down one hundred and
eighty-five thousand men in the Assyrian
camp. Early the next morning, there they
were, dead, all those corpses![r] 36 So Sennacherib, the king of Assyria, broke camp,
departed, returned home, and stayed in Nineveh.

37 When he was worshiping in the temple
of his god Nisroch, his sons Adrammelech
and Sharezer struck him down with the
sword and fled into the land of Ararat. His
son Esarhaddon reigned in his place.

CHAPTER 20

See RG 196

End of Hezekiah’s Reign. 1[s] In those
days, when Hezekiah was mortally ill, the
prophet Isaiah, son of Amoz, came and said
to him: “Thus says the LORD: Put your house
in order, for you are about to die; you shall
not recover.” 2 He turned his face to the wall
and prayed to the LORD: 3 “Ah, LORD, remember how faithfully and wholeheartedly I
conducted myself in your presence, doing
what was good in your sight!” And Hezekiah
wept bitterly. 4 Before Isaiah had left the central courtyard, the word of the LORD came to
him: 5 Go back and tell Hezekiah, the leader
of my people: “Thus says the LORD, the God
of David your father:

I have heard your prayer;
I have seen your tears.
Now I am healing you.
On the third day you shall go up
to the house of the LORD.
6 I will add to your life fifteen years.
I will rescue you and this city
from the hand of the king of Assyria;
I will be a shield to this city
for my own sake and the sake of David
my servant.”

7 Then Isaiah said, “Bring a poultice of figs
and apply it to the boil for his recovery.”
8 Hezekiah asked Isaiah, “What is the sign
that the LORD will heal me and that I shall go
up to the house of the LORD on the third
day?” 9 Isaiah replied, “This will be the sign
for you from the LORD that he will carry out

p: Ps 139:2–3. *q:* 2 Sm 7:12. *r:* 1 Mc 7:41; 2 Mc 8:19. *s:* Sir 48:23.

the word he has spoken: Shall the shadow go forward or back ten steps?" [10]"It is easy for the shadow to advance ten steps," Hezekiah answered. "Rather, let it go back ten steps." [11]So Isaiah the prophet invoked the LORD. He made the shadow go back the ten steps it had descended on the staircase to the terrace of Ahaz.

[12]At that time, Berodach-baladan,* son of Baladan, king of Babylon, sent letters and gifts to Hezekiah when he heard that he had been ill. [13]Hezekiah listened to the envoys and then showed off his whole treasury: his silver, gold, spices and perfumed oil, his armory, and everything in his storerooms; there was nothing in his house or in all his realm that Hezekiah did not show them. [14]Then Isaiah the prophet came to King Hezekiah and asked him: "What did these men say to you? Where did they come from?" Hezekiah replied, "They came from a distant land, from Babylon." [15]He asked, "What did they see in your house?" Hezekiah answered, "They saw everything in my house. There is nothing in my storerooms that I did not show them." [16]Then Isaiah said to Hezekiah: "Hear the word of the LORD: [17]The time is coming when all that is in your house, everything that your ancestors have stored up until this day, shall be carried off to Babylon; nothing shall be left, says the LORD. [18]Some of your own descendants, your offspring, your progeny, shall be taken and made attendants in the palace of the king of Babylon." [19]Hezekiah replied to Isaiah, "The word of the LORD which you have spoken is good." For he thought, "There will be peace and stability in my lifetime."

[20]The rest of the acts of Hezekiah, with all his valor, and how he constructed the pool and conduit* and brought water into the city, are recorded in the book of the chronicles of the kings of Judah.[t] [21]Hezekiah rested with his ancestors, and his son Manasseh succeeded him as king.

CHAPTER 21

See RG 196–97

Reign of Manasseh. [1]Manasseh was twelve years old when he became king, and he reigned fifty-five years in Jerusalem. His mother's name was Hephzibah.

[2]He did what was evil in the LORD's sight, following the abominable practices of the nations whom the LORD had dispossessed before the Israelites. [3]He rebuilt the high places which Hezekiah his father had destroyed. He set up altars to Baal and also made an asherah, as Ahab, king of Israel, had done. He bowed down to the whole host of heaven and served them.[u] [4]He built altars in the house of the LORD, of which the LORD had said: In Jerusalem I will set my name. [5]And he built altars for the whole host of heaven in the two courts of the house of the LORD. [6]He immolated his child by fire. He practiced soothsaying and divination, and reintroduced the consulting of ghosts and spirits.

He did much evil in the LORD's sight and provoked him to anger.[v] [7]The Asherah idol he had made, he placed in the LORD's house, of which the LORD had said to David and to his son Solomon: In this house and in Jerusalem, which I have chosen out of all the tribes of Israel, I shall set my name forever.[w] [8]I will no longer make Israel step out of the land I gave their ancestors, provided that they are careful to observe all I have commanded them and the entire law which Moses my servant enjoined upon them. [9]But they did not listen.

Manasseh misled them into doing even greater evil than the nations the LORD had destroyed at the coming of the Israelites. [10]Then the LORD spoke through his servants the prophets: [11]"Because Manasseh, king of Judah, has practiced these abominations, and has done greater evil than all that was done by the Amorites before him, and has led Judah into sin by his idols,[x] [12]therefore, thus says the LORD, the God of Israel: I am about

20:12 Berodach-baladan: this famous king's name is more correctly recorded in Is 39:1 as "Merodach-baladan." The Babylonian form, Marduk-apal-idinna, means "Marduk has granted a son." Historically, any embassy from him to Hezekiah must have been aimed at establishing an anti-Assyrian strategy of cooperation.

20:20 Pool and conduit: Hezekiah's tunnel is described in more detail in 2 Chr 32:30.

t: Sir 48:17. *u:* 2 Kgs 17:16; 1 Kgs 16:31–33. *v:* Lv 18:21; 19:26; Dt 18:10–14; 1 Sm 28:3. *w:* 2 Sm 7:13; 1 Kgs 8:16; 9:3. *x:* Jer 15:4.

to bring such evil on Jerusalem and Judah that, when any hear of it, their ears shall ring: 13I will measure Jerusalem with the same cord as I did Samaria, and with the plummet I used for the house of Ahab. I will wipe Jerusalem clean as one wipes a dish, wiping it inside and out.[y] 14I will cast off the survivors of my inheritance. I will deliver them into enemy hands, to become prey and booty for all their enemies, 15because they have done what is evil in my sight and provoked me from the day their ancestors came forth from Egypt until this very day." 16Manasseh shed so much innocent blood that it filled the length and breadth of Jerusalem, in addition to the sin he caused Judah to commit by doing what was evil in the LORD's sight.

17The rest of the acts of Manasseh, with all that he did and the sin he committed, are recorded in the book of the chronicles of the kings of Judah. 18Manasseh rested with his ancestors; he was buried in his palace garden, the garden of Uzza, and his son Amon succeeded him as king.

Reign of Amon. 19Amon was twenty-two years old when he became king, and he reigned two years in Jerusalem. His mother's name was Meshullemeth, daughter of Haruz, from Jotbah.

20He did what was evil in the LORD's sight, as his father Manasseh had done. 21He walked in all the ways of his father; he served the idols his father had served, and bowed down to them. 22He abandoned the LORD, the God of his ancestors, and did not walk in the way of the LORD.

23Officials of Amon plotted against him and killed the king in his palace, 24but the people of the land* then slew all who had plotted against King Amon, and the people of the land made his son Josiah king in his stead. 25The rest of the acts of Amon, which he did, are recorded in the book of the chronicles of the kings of Judah. 26He was buried in his own grave in the garden of Uzza, and his son Josiah succeeded him as king.

CHAPTER 22

See RG 197

Reign of Josiah. 1Josiah was eight years old when he became king, and he reigned thirty-one years in Jerusalem. His mother's name was Jedidah, daughter of Adaiah, from Bozkath.

2He did what was right in the LORD's sight, walking in the way of David his father, not turning right or left.

The Book of the Law. 3[z] In his eighteenth year, King Josiah sent the scribe Shaphan,* son of Azaliah, son of Meshullam, to the house of the LORD with these orders: 4"Go to the high priest Hilkiah and have him calculate the valuables that have been brought to the house of the LORD, which the doorkeepers have collected from the people. 5Then have him turn them over to the master workers in the house of the LORD, and have them give them to the ordinary workers who are in the house of the LORD to repair its breaches: 6to the carpenters, the builders, and the masons, and to purchase wood and hewn stone. 7No reckoning shall be asked of them regarding the funds provided to them, because they hold positions of trust."

8The high priest Hilkiah informed the scribe Shaphan, "I have found the book of the law* in the temple of the LORD." Hilkiah gave the book to Shaphan, who read it. 9Then the scribe Shaphan went to the king and reported, "Your servants have smelted down the silver deposited in the temple and have turned it over to the master workers in the house of the LORD." 10The scribe Shaphan also informed the king, "Hilkiah the priest has given me a book," and then Shaphan read it in the presence of the king. 11When the king heard the words of the book of the law, he tore his garments.

12The king then issued this command to Hilkiah the priest, Ahikam, son of Shaphan, Achbor, son of Micaiah, Shaphan the scribe, and Asaiah the king's servant: 13"Go, consult the LORD for me, for the people, and for

21:24 People of the land: see note on 11:14.

22:3 Shaphan: head of a prominent family in the reign of Josiah, secretary to the king, bearer and reader of the newly found book of the law (vv. 3–13; 25:22). He and his sons favored the reform of King Josiah and supported the prophet Jeremiah; cf. Jer 26:24; 29:1–3; 36:10–12; 39:14.

22:8 Book of the law: probably an early edition of material now found in the Book of Deuteronomy.

y: Is 34:11; Lam 2:8; Am 7:7–9. *z:* 2 Kgs 12:11–16.

all Judah, about the words of this book that has been found, for the rage of the LORD has been set furiously ablaze against us, because our ancestors did not obey the words of this book, nor do what is written for us." [14]So Hilkiah the priest, Ahikam, Achbor, Shaphan, and Asaiah went to Huldah the prophet, wife of Shallum, son of Tikvah, son of Harhas, keeper of the wardrobe; she lived in Jerusalem, in the Second Quarter. When they had spoken to her, [15]she said to them, "Thus says the LORD, the God of Israel: Say to the man who sent you to me, [16]Thus says the LORD: I am about to bring evil upon this place and upon its inhabitants—all the words of the book which the king of Judah has read. [17]Because they have abandoned me and have burned incense to other gods, provoking me by all the works of their hands, my rage is ablaze against this place and it cannot be extinguished.

[18]"But to the king of Judah who sent you to consult the LORD, give this response: Thus says the LORD, the God of Israel: As for the words you have heard, [19]because you were heartsick and have humbled yourself before the LORD when you heard what I have spoken concerning this place and its inhabitants, that they would become a desolation and a curse; and because you tore your garments and wept before me, I in turn have heard, oracle of the LORD. [20]I will therefore gather you to your ancestors; you shall go to your grave in peace, and your eyes shall not see all the evil I am about to bring upon this place." This they reported to the king.

CHAPTER 23

See RG 197

[1]The king then had all the elders of Judah and of Jerusalem summoned before him. [2]The king went up to the house of the LORD with all the people of Judah and all the inhabitants of Jerusalem: priests, prophets, and all the people, great and small. He read aloud to them all the words of the book of the covenant that had been found in the house of the LORD.[a] [3]The king stood by the column and made a covenant in the presence of the LORD to follow the LORD and to observe his commandments, statutes, and decrees with his whole heart and soul, and to re-establish the words of the covenant written in this book. And all the people stood by the covenant.

Josiah's Religious Reform. [4]Then the king commanded the high priest Hilkiah, his assistant priests, and the doorkeepers to remove from the temple of the LORD all the objects that had been made for Baal, Asherah, and the whole host of heaven. These he burned outside Jerusalem on the slopes of the Kidron; their ashes were carried to Bethel.[b] [5]He also put an end to the idolatrous priests whom the kings of Judah had appointed to burn incense on the high places in the cities of Judah and in the vicinity of Jerusalem, as well as those who burned incense to Baal, to the sun, moon, and signs of the zodiac, and to the whole host of heaven.[c] [6]From the house of the LORD he also removed the Asherah to the Wadi Kidron, outside Jerusalem; he burned it and beat it to dust, in the Wadi Kidron, and scattered its dust over the graveyard of the people of the land.* [d] [7]He tore down the apartments of the cult prostitutes in the house of the LORD, where the women wove garments for the Asherah.[e] [8]He brought in all the priests from the cities of Judah, and then defiled, from Geba to Beer-sheba, the high places where they had offered incense. He also tore down the high places of the gates, which were at the entrance of the Gate of Joshua, governor of the city, north of the city gate. [9](The priests of the high places could not function at the altar of the LORD in Jerusalem; but they, along with their relatives, ate the unleavened bread.)

[10]The king also defiled Topheth in the Valley of Ben-hinnom, so that there would no longer be any immolation of sons or daughters by fire* in honor of Molech.[f] [11]He

23:6 People of the land: see note on 11:14.

23:10 Topheth . . . by fire: Topheth was a cultic site probably in the Hinnom Valley just west of Jerusalem where, apparently, children were immolated to the deity Molech (Hebrew *melek*, "king," deformed in the biblical tradition to "Molech"). The practice was condemned by Deuteronomic law and denounced by Jeremiah (Dt 12:31; Jer 7:29–31). In Jer 19 the deity is identified as the Canaanite god Baal.

a: Dt 17:18–19. *b:* Sir 49:3. *c:* Dt 4:19; 17:2–7. *d:* Dt 16:21. *e:* Dt 23:18–19. *f:* Lv 18:21; Dt 18:10–12.

did away with the horses which the kings of Judah had dedicated to the sun; these were at the entrance of the house of the LORD, near the chamber of Nathan-melech the official, which was in the large building. The chariots of the sun he destroyed by fire. 12He also demolished the altars made by the kings of Judah on the roof (the roof terrace of Ahaz), and the altars made by Manasseh in the two courts of the LORD's house. He pulverized them and threw the dust into the Wadi Kidron.[g] 13The king defiled the high places east of Jerusalem, south of the Mount of the Destroyer,* which Solomon, king of Israel, had built in honor of Astarte, the Sidonian horror, of Chemosh, the Moabite horror, and of Milcom, the Ammonites' abomination.[h] 14He broke to pieces the pillars, cut down the asherahs, and filled the places where they had been with human bones.[i]

15Likewise the altar which was at Bethel, the high place built by Jeroboam, son of Nebat, who caused Israel to sin—this same altar and high place he tore down and burned, grinding the high place to powder and burning the asherah.[j] 16When Josiah turned and saw the graves there on the mountainside, he ordered the bones taken from the graves and burned on the altar, and thus defiled it, according to the LORD's word proclaimed by the man of God as Jeroboam stood by the altar on the feast day. When the king looked up and saw the grave of the man of God who had proclaimed these words, 17he asked, "What is that marker I see?" The people of the city replied, "The grave of the man of God who came from Judah and proclaimed the very things you have done to the altar in Bethel." 18"Let him be," he said, "let no one move his bones." So they left his bones undisturbed together with the bones of the prophet who had come from Samaria.* 19Josiah also removed all the temples on the high places in the cities of Samaria which the kings of Israel had built, provoking the LORD; he did the very same to them as he had done in Bethel. 20He slaughtered upon the altars all the priests of the high places that were there, and burned human bones upon them. Then he returned to Jerusalem.

21The king issued a command to all the people: "Observe the Passover of the LORD, your God, as it is written in this book of the covenant."[k] 22No Passover such as this had been observed during the period when the judges ruled Israel, or during the entire period of the kings of Israel and the kings of Judah, 23until the eighteenth year of King Josiah, when this Passover of the LORD was kept in Jerusalem.

24Further, Josiah purged the consultation of ghosts and spirits, with the household gods, idols,* and all the other horrors to be seen in the land of Judah and in Jerusalem, so that he might carry out the words of the law that were written in the book that Hilkiah the priest had found in the house of the LORD.[l]

25Before him there had been no king who turned to the LORD as he did, with his whole heart, his whole being, and his whole strength, in accord with the entire law of Moses; nor did any king like him arise after him.[m] 26Yet the LORD did not turn from his fiercely burning anger against Judah, because of all the provocations that Manasseh had given. 27The LORD said: Even Judah will I put out of my sight as I did Israel. I will reject this city, Jerusalem, which I chose, and the house of which I said: There shall my name be.

28The rest of the acts of Josiah, with all that he did, are recorded in the book of the chronicles of the kings of Judah. 29In his

23:13 Mount of the Destroyer: the name of the mountain in Hebrew is a wordplay. "The Mount of the *mashchit*" means "the Mount of the Destroyer" or perhaps "the Mount of Destruction." The word plays on *mishchah*, "anointment," and on *mashiach*, "anointed one," both of which are references to the ceremony that consecrated the king. The mountain in question was the Mount of Olives, whose trees produced oil for the royal anointing. In the present context, both sides of the wordplay allude to Solomon, the anointed king (*mashiach*), whose building of non-Yahwistic shrines on this very mountain resulted in the destruction (*mashchit*) of the Davidic realm (see 1 Kgs 11:4–13). **Horror . . . abomination**: all three idols are described with pejorative terms.

23:18 From Samaria: an anachronistic use of the name of the later capital city for the whole region. The prophet was from Bethel; cf. 1 Kgs 13:11.

23:24 Household gods, idols: teraphim. See note on Gn 31:19.

g: 2 Kgs 20:11; 21:5. *h:* 1 Kgs 11:4–8. *i:* Dt 16:21; 1 Kgs 14:23. *j:* 1 Kgs 12:26–13:34. *k:* Dt 16:1–8. *l:* 2 Kgs 21:6; Gn 31:19; Dt 18:10–14; Jgs 18:14. *m:* Dt 6:5; Sir 49:1–3.

time Pharaoh Neco, king of Egypt, went up toward the Euphrates River against the king of Assyria.[*] King Josiah set out to meet him, but was slain at Megiddo at the first encounter. 30His servants brought his body on a chariot from Megiddo to Jerusalem, where they buried him in his own grave. Then the people of the land took Jehoahaz, son of Josiah, anointed him, and proclaimed him king to succeed his father.

Reign of Jehoahaz. 31Jehoahaz was twenty-three years old when he became king, and he reigned three months in Jerusalem. His mother's name was Hamutal, daughter of Jeremiah, from Libnah.[n]

32He did what was evil in the LORD's sight, just as his ancestors had done. 33Pharaoh Neco took him prisoner at Riblah in the land of Hamath, thus ending his reign in Jerusalem. He imposed a fine upon the land of a hundred talents of silver and a talent of gold.[*] 34Pharaoh Neco then made Eliakim, son of Josiah, king in place of Josiah his father; he changed his name to Jehoiakim. Jehoahaz he took away with him to Egypt, where he died. 35Jehoiakim gave the silver and gold to Pharaoh, but taxed the land to raise the amount Pharaoh demanded. He exacted the silver and gold from the people of the land, from each proportionately, to pay Pharaoh Neco.

Reign of Jehoiakim. 36Jehoiakim was twenty-five years old when he became king, and he reigned eleven years in Jerusalem. His mother's name was Zebidah, daughter of Pedaiah, from Rumah.

37He did what was evil in the LORD's sight, just as his ancestors had done.

CHAPTER 24

See RG 197

1During Jehoiakim's reign Nebuchadnezzar, king of Babylon, attacked, and Jehoiakim became his vassal for three years. Then Jehoiakim turned and rebelled against him. 2The LORD loosed against him bands of Chaldeans, Arameans, Moabites, and Ammonites; he unleashed them against Judah to destroy him, according to the LORD's word spoken through his servants the prophets. 3This befell Judah because the LORD had stated that he would put them out of his sight for the sins Manasseh had committed in all that he did, 4and especially because of the innocent blood he shed; he filled Jerusalem with innocent blood, and the LORD would not forgive.[o]

5The rest of the acts of Jehoiakim, with all that he did, are recorded in the book of the chronicles of the kings of Judah. 6Jehoiakim rested with his ancestors, and his son Jehoiachin succeeded him as king. 7The king of Egypt did not again leave his own land, for the king of Babylon had taken all that belonged to the king of Egypt from the wadi of Egypt to the Euphrates River.

Reign of Jehoiachin. 8Jehoiachin was eighteen years old when he became king, and he reigned three months in Jerusalem. His mother's name was Nehushta, daughter of Elnathan, from Jerusalem.

9He did what was evil in the LORD's sight, just as his father had done.

10[p] At that time officers of Nebuchadnezzar, king of Babylon, attacked Jerusalem, and the city came under siege. 11Nebuchadnezzar, king of Babylon, himself arrived at the city while his officers were besieging it. 12Then Jehoiachin, king of Judah, together with his mother, his ministers, officers, and functionaries, surrendered to the king of Babylon, who, in the eighth year of his reign,[*] took him captive. 13He carried off all the treasures of the house of the LORD and the treasures of the king's house, and broke up all the gold utensils that Solomon, king of Israel, had provided in the house of the LORD, as the LORD had decreed.[q] 14He deported all Jerusalem: all the officers and warriors of the army, ten thousand in num-

23:29 Against the king of Assyria: the narrator depicts Neco's advance as an attack on Assyrian forces. The Babylonian record of the event, however, implies that Neco intended to support the remnant of Assyrian forces against a Babylonian onslaught in order to prop up a buffer state between Egypt and Babylon and assure Egyptian control of the Syro-Palestinian region.

23:33 A talent of gold: unless the fine imposed was a mere token, this figure seems too low; cf. 18:14. A number may have dropped from the Hebrew text; various ancient translations read "ten" or "one hundred" here.

24:12 The eighth year of his reign: that is, of Nebuchadnezzar's reign, not Jehoiachin's. The year was 597 B.C.

n: 2 Kgs 24:18. *o:* 2 Kgs 21:16. *p:* Dn 1:1–2. *q:* 2 Kgs 20:17.

ber, and all the artisans and smiths. Only the lowliest of the people of the land* were left. [15]He deported Jehoiachin to Babylon, and the king's mother, his wives, his functionaries, and the chiefs of the land he led captive from Jerusalem to Babylon.[r] [16]All seven thousand soldiers of the army, and a thousand artisans and smiths, all of them trained warriors, these too the king of Babylon brought captive to Babylon. [17]In place of Jehoiachin the king of Babylon made Mattaniah, Jehoiachin's uncle, king; he changed his name to Zedekiah.[s]

Reign of Zedekiah. [18]* Zedekiah was twenty-one years old when he became king, and he reigned eleven years in Jerusalem. His mother's name was Hamutal, daughter of Jeremiah, from Libnah.[t]

[19]He did what was evil in the sight of the LORD, just as Jehoiakim had done. [20]This befell Jerusalem and Judah because the LORD was so angry that he cast them out of his sight.

Zedekiah rebelled against the king of Babylon.

CHAPTER 25

See RG 197–98

[1]In the tenth month of the ninth year of Zedekiah's reign, on the tenth day of the month, Nebuchadnezzar, king of Babylon, and his whole army advanced against Jerusalem, encamped around it, and built siege walls on every side. [2]The siege of the city continued until the eleventh year of Zedekiah. [3]On the ninth day of the month,* when famine had gripped the city, and the people of the land had no more food, [4]the city walls were breached. That night, all the soldiers came to the gate between the two walls near the king's garden (the Chaldeans had the city surrounded), while the king went toward the Arabah.* [5]But the Chaldean army pursued the king and overtook him in the desert near Jericho, abandoned by his whole army. [6]The king was therefore arrested and brought to Riblah to the king of Babylon, who pronounced sentence on him. [7]They slew Zedekiah's sons before his eyes; then they put out his eyes, bound him with fetters, and brought him to Babylon.

[8]On the seventh day of the fifth month (this was in the nineteenth year of Nebuchadnezzar, king of Babylon), Nebuzaradan, captain of the bodyguard, came to Jerusalem as the agent of the king of Babylon. [9]He burned the house of the LORD, the house of the king, and all the houses of Jerusalem (every noble house); he destroyed them by fire.[u] [10]The Chaldean troops who were with the captain of the guard tore down the walls that surrounded Jerusalem, [11]and Nebuzaradan, captain of the guard, led into exile the last of the army remaining in the city, and those who had deserted* to the king of Babylon, and the last of the commoners. [12]But some of the country's poor the captain of the guard left behind as vinedressers and farmers.

[13]The bronze columns that belonged to the house of the LORD, and the stands and the bronze sea in the house of the LORD, the Chaldeans broke into pieces; they carried away the bronze to Babylon.[v] [14]They took also the pots, the shovels, the snuffers, the cups and all the bronze articles used for service.[w] [15]The fire pans and the bowls that were of solid gold or silver the captain of the guard also carried off.[x] [16]The two columns, the one bronze sea, and the stands, which Solomon had made for the house of the LORD—the weight in bronze of all these articles was never calculated.[y] [17]Each of the columns was eighteen cubits high; a bronze capital three cubits high surmounted each column, and a netting with pomegranates encircled the capital, all of bronze; and they were duplicated on the other column, on the netting.[z]

[18]The captain of the guard also took Sera-

24:14 People of the land: see note on 11:14.

24:18–25:30 Much of this material closely parallels Jer 52; some of the events are also recounted in Jer 39.

25:3 Ninth day of the month: the text does not say which month, but Jer 39:2 and 52:6 set the breaching of the city walls in the fourth month; in later times that was the date of a fast commemorating the event (cf. Zec 8:19). **People of the land**: the influential citizens (see note on 11:14); even they, whose resources went beyond those of the ordinary people, were starving.

25:4 The Hebrew text of this verse is missing some words. The present translation is based on a likely reconstruction.

25:11 Those who had deserted: perhaps on the advice of Jeremiah; cf. Jer 38:2–3.

r: Est A:3; 2:6. *s:* Jer 37:1. *t:* 2 Kgs 23:31. *u:* Ps 74:2–7. *v:* 2 Kgs 16:17; 1 Kgs 7:15–39; Jer 27:19–23. *w:* 1 Kgs 7:40–45. *x:* 1 Kgs 7:50. *y:* 1 Kgs 7:47. *z:* 1 Kgs 7:15–20; Jer 52:21–23.

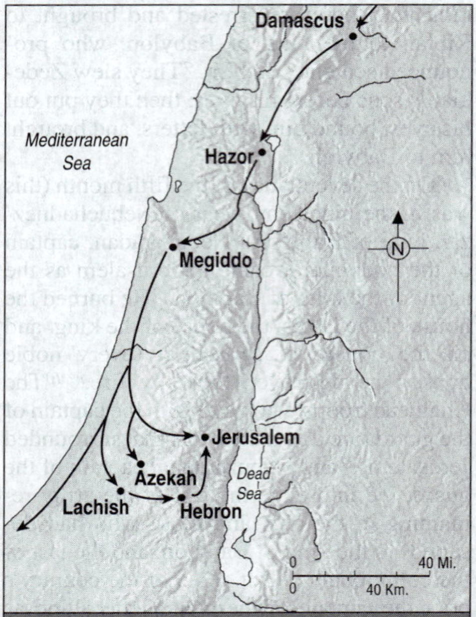

Nebuchadnezzar's Campaign

iah, the chief priest, Zephaniah, an assistant
priest, and the three doorkeepers. [19]And from
the city he took one officer who was a commander of soldiers, five courtiers in the personal service of the king who were still in the
city, the scribe in charge of the army who mustered the people of the land,* and sixty of the
people of the land still remaining in the city.
[20]The captain of the guard, Nebuzaradan, arrested these and brought them to the king of
Babylon at Riblah, and [21]the king of Babylon
struck them down and put them to death in
Riblah, in the land of Hamath. And thus Judah
went into exile from their native soil.

Governorship of Gedaliah. [22][a] As for the
people whom he had allowed to remain in the
land of Judah, Nebuchadnezzar, king of Babylon, appointed Gedaliah, son of Ahikam,
son of Shaphan, over them. [23]Hearing that
the king of Babylon had appointed Gedaliah
over them, all the army commanders and the
troops came to him at Mizpah: Ishmael, son
of Nethaniah, Johanan, son of Kareah, Seraiah, son of Tanhumeth the Netophathite, and
Jaazaniah, son of the Maakite, each with his
troops. [24]Gedaliah gave the commanders and
their troops his oath. He said to them, "Do
not be afraid of the Chaldean officials. Remain in the country and serve the king of
Babylon, so that all will be well with you."
[25]But in the seventh month Ishmael, son
of Nethaniah, son of Elishama, of royal descent, came with ten others, attacked Gedaliah and killed him, along with the Judahites
and Chaldeans who were in Mizpah with
him. [26]Then all the people, great and small,
left with the army commanders and went to
Egypt for fear of the Chaldeans.

Release of Jehoiachin. [27]In the thirty-seventh year of the exile of Jehoiachin, king of
Judah, on the twenty-seventh day of the
twelfth month, Evil-merodach, king of Babylon, in the inaugural year of his own reign,
raised up Jehoiachin, king of Judah, from
prison. [28]He spoke kindly to him and gave
him a throne higher than that of the other
kings who were with him in Babylon. [29]Je-
hoiachin took off his prison garb; he ate regularly in the king's presence as long as he
lived; [30]and for his allowance the king
granted him a regular allowance, in fixed
daily amounts, for as long as he lived.

25:19 People of the land: see note on 11:14.

a: Jer 40:7–41:18.

See RG 199–203

The First Book of Chronicles

The Greek title, *paraleipomena*, means "things omitted," or "passed over" (i.e., in the accounts found in Samuel and Kings). The Books of Chronicles, however, are much more than a supplement to Samuel and Kings; a comparison of the two histories discloses striking differences of scope and purpose. The Books of Chronicles record in some detail the lengthy span (some five hundred fifty years) from the death of King Saul to the return from the exile. Unlike today's history writing, wherein factual accuracy and impartiality of judgment are the norm, biblical history, with rare exceptions, was less concerned with reporting in precise detail all the facts of a situation than with drawing out the meaning of those facts. Biblical history was thus primarily interpretative, and its purpose was to disclose the action of the living God in human affairs. For this reason we speak of it as "sacred history."

These characteristics are apparent when we examine the primary objective of the Chronicler (the conventional designation for the anonymous author) in compiling his work. Given the situation which confronted the Jewish people at this time (the end of the fifth century B.C.), the Chronicler realized that Israel's political greatness was a thing of the past. Yet, for the Chronicler, Israel's past held the key to the people's future. In particular, the Chronicler aimed to establish and defend the legitimate claims of the Davidic monarchy in Israel's history, and to underscore the status of Jerusalem and its divinely established Temple worship as the center of religious life for the Jewish people. If Judaism was to survive and prosper, it would have to heed the lessons of the past and devoutly serve its God in the place where he had chosen to dwell, the Temple in Jerusalem. From the Chronicler's point of view, the reigns of David and Solomon were the ideal to which all subsequent rule in Judah must aspire. The Chronicler was much more interested in David's religious and cultic influence than in his political power, however. He saw David's (and Solomon's) primary importance as deriving rather from their roles in the establishment of Jerusalem and its Temple as the center of the true worship of the Lord. Furthermore, he presents David as the one who prescribed the Temple's elaborate ritual (which, in point of fact, only gradually evolved in the Second Temple period) and who appointed the Levites to supervise the liturgical services there.

The Chronicler used a variety of sources in writing his history. Besides the canonical Books of Genesis, Exodus, Numbers, Joshua, and Ruth, and especially the Books of Samuel and Kings (specifically 1 Sm 31–2 Kings 25), he cites the titles of many other works which have not come down to us, e.g., "The Books of the Kings of Israel," or "The Books of the Kings of Israel and Judah," and "The History of Gad the Seer." In addition, the Chronicler's work contains early preexilic material not found in the Books of Kings.

The principal divisions of 1 Chronicles are as follows:

I. Genealogical Tables (1:1–9:34)
II. The History of David (9:35–29:30)

I. Genealogical Tables*

CHAPTER 1

See RG 200

From Adam to Abraham. 1 Adam,
Seth, Enosh,[a] 2 Kenan, Mahalalel, Jared,[b]
3 Enoch, Methuselah, Lamech,[c] 4 Noah,
Shem, Ham, and Japheth.[d] 5 The sons of Japheth were Gomer, Magog, Madai, Javan,
Tubal, Meshech, and Tiras.[e] 6 The sons of
Gomer were Ashkenaz, Riphath, and Togarmah. 7 The sons of Javan were Elishah, Tarshish, the Kittim, and the Rodanim.

8 The sons of Ham were Cush, Mizraim,
Put, and Canaan. 9 The sons of Cush were
Seba, Havilah, Sabta, Raama, and Sabteca.
The sons of Raama were Sheba and Dedan.
10 Cush became the father of Nimrod, who
was the first to be a warrior on the earth.[f]
11 [g] Mizraim became the father of the Ludim,
Anamim, Lehabim, Naphtuhim, 12 Pathrusim, Casluhim, and Caphtorim, from whom
the Philistines sprang. 13 Canaan became the
father of Sidon, his firstborn, and Heth,
14 and the Jebusites, the Amorites, the Girgashites, 15 the Hivites, the Arkites, the Sinites,
16 the Arvadites, the Zemarites, and the
Hamathites.

17 [h] The sons of Shem were Elam, Asshur,
Arpachshad, Lud, and Aram. The sons of

1:1–9:34 The Chronicler's intention seems to have been to retell, from his particular viewpoint, the story of God's people from creation down to his own day. Since his primary interest was the history of David and the Davidic dynasty of Judah, he hurries through everything that preceded the death of Saul, David's predecessor as king, by the use of genealogical lists. The sources for these genealogies are mostly the books, already largely in their present form in the Chronicler's time, that eventually formed the Hebrew canon. For any given portion of these chapters, see the cross-references to their scriptural sources.

a: Gn 5:3, 6, 9. *b:* Gn 5:9–32; 10:2–32. *c:* Gn 4:24. *d:* Gn 5:32; 6:10; 9:18. *e:* Gn 10:2–4. *f:* Gn 10:8. *g:* Gn 10:13–18. *h:* Gn 10:22–29; 11:10–18.

Aram were Uz, Hul, Gether, and Mash.
[18]Arpachshad became the father of Shelah,
and Shelah became the father of Eber. [19]Two
sons were born to Eber; the first was named
Peleg (for in his time the world was divided),* and his brother was named Joktan.
[20]Joktan became the father of Almodad,
Sheleph, Hazarmaveth, Jerah, [21]Hadoram,
Uzal, Diklah, [22]Ebal, Abimael, Sheba,
[23]Ophir, Havilah, and Jobab; all these were
the sons of Joktan.

[24][i] Shem, Arpachshad, Shelah, [25]Eber, Peleg, Reu, [26]Serug, Nahor, Terah, [27]Abram,
that is, Abraham.[j]

From Abraham to Jacob. [28]The sons of
Abraham were Isaac and Ishmael.[k] [29]These
were their generations:

Nebaioth, the firstborn of Ishmael, then
Kedar, Adbeel, Mibsam, [30]Mishma, Dumah,
Massa, Hadad, Tema, [31]Jetur, Naphish, and
Kedemah. These were the sons of Ishmael.[l]

[32]The sons of Keturah, Abraham's concubine: she bore Zimran, Jokshan, Medan, Midian, Ishbak, and Shuah. The sons of Jokshan
were Sheba and Dedan. [33]The sons of Midian
were Ephah, Epher, Hanoch, Abida, and Eldaah. All these were the sons of Keturah.[m]

[34]Abraham begot Isaac. The sons of Isaac
were Esau and Israel.[n]

[35]The descendants of Esau were Eliphaz,
Reuel, Jeush, Jalam, and Korah. [36]The de-
scendants of Eliphaz were Teman, Omar,
Zephi, Gatam, Kenaz, Timna, and Amalek.
[37]The descendants of Reuel were Nahath,
Zerah, Shammah, and Mizzah.[o]

[38]The sons of Seir* were Lotan, Shobal,
Zibeon, Anah, Dishon, Ezer, and Dishan.
[39]The sons of Lotan were Hori and Homam;
Timna was the sister of Lotan. [40]The sons of
Shobal were Alian, Manahath, Ebal, Shephi,
and Onam. The sons of Zibeon were Aiah
and Anah. [41]The sons of Anah: Dishon. The
sons of Dishon were Hemdan, Eshban, Ithran, and Cheran. [42]The sons of Ezer were
Bilhan, Zaavan, and Jaakan. The sons of Dishan were Uz and Aran.[p]

[43][q] The kings who reigned in the land of
Edom before the Israelites had kings were
the following: Bela, son of Beor, the name of
whose city was Dinhabah. [44]When Bela died,
Jobab, son of Zerah, from Bozrah, succeeded
him as king.[r] [45]When Jobab died, Husham,
from the land of the Temanites, succeeded
him as king.[s] [46]Husham died and Hadad, son
of Bedad, succeeded him as king. He overthrew the Midianites on the Moabite plateau,
and the name of his city was Avith. [47]Hadad
died and Samlah of Masrekah succeeded him
as king. [48]Samlah died and Shaul from Rehoboth on the Euphrates succeeded him as
king. [49]When Shaul died, Baalhanan, son of
Achbor, succeeded him as king. [50]Baalhanan
died and Hadad succeeded him as king. The
name of his city was Pai, and his wife's name
was Mehetabel. She was the daughter of Matred, who was the daughter of Mezahab.
[51][t] After Hadad died, there were chiefs in
Edom: the chiefs of Timna, Aliah, Jetheth,
[52]Oholibamah, Elah, Pinon, [53]Kenaz, Teman,
Mibzar, [54]Magdiel, and Iram were the chiefs
of Edom.

CHAPTER 2

See RG 200

[1]These were the sons of Israel: Reuben, Simeon, Levi, Judah, Issachar, Zebulun,[u] [2]Dan, Joseph, Benjamin, Naphtali,
Gad, and Asher.[v]

Judah. [3]The sons of Judah* were: Er,
Onan, and Shelah; these three Bathshua, a
Canaanite woman, bore to him. But Judah's
firstborn, Er, was wicked in the sight of the
LORD, so he took his life.[w] [4]Judah's daughter-in-law Tamar bore him Perez and Zerah,
so that he had five sons in all.[x]

1:19 Divided: see note on Gn 10:25.

1:38 Seir: another name for Esau (v. 35) or Edom (v. 43).

2:3–4:23 The Chronicler had two reasons for placing his genealogy of the tribe of Judah before those of the other tribes, and for making it longer than all the others: his interest in David, who was of the tribe of Judah; and the prominence of descendants of that tribe among the Jews of the Chronicler's time.

i: Gn 11:10–26; Lk 3:34–36. *j:* Gn 17:5; Neh 9:7. *k:* Gn 16:11, 15; 21:2–3; Gal 4:22–23; Heb 11:11. *l:* Gn 25:13–16. *m:* Gn 25:1–4. *n:* Gn 21:2–3; 25:19, 25–26; 32:28–29; Mt 1:2; Lk 3:34. *o:* Gn 36:4–5, 10–13, 15–19. *p:* Gn 36:20–28. *q:* Gn 36:31–43. *r:* Is 34:6; 63:1; Jer 49:13, 22. *s:* Gn 36:11; Jb 2:11; Jer 49:7, 20. *t:* Gn 36:40–43. *u:* Gn 29:32–35; 30:18, 20; 35:23. *v:* Gn 30:6, 8, 11, 13, 24; 35:18, 24–26. *w:* 1 Chr 4:21; Gn 38:1–5; 46:12. *x:* Gn 38:7, 13–30; 46:12; Mt 1:3.

5The sons of Perez were Hezron and Hamul.[y] 6The sons of Zerah were Zimri, Ethan, Heman, Calcol, and Darda—five in all.[z] 7The sons of Zimri: Carmi. The sons of Carmi: Achar, who brought trouble upon Israel by violating the ban.[a] 8The sons of Ethan: Azariah. 9The sons born to Hezron were Jerahmeel, Ram, and Chelubai.* [b]

10* Ram became the father of Amminadab, and Amminadab became the father of Nahshon, a prince of the Judahites.[c] 11[d] Nahshon became the father of Salmah. Salmah became the father of Boaz. 12Boaz became the father of Obed. Obed became the father of Jesse. 13[e] Jesse became the father of Eliab, his firstborn, of Abinadab, the second son, Shimea, the third,[f] 14Nethanel, the fourth, Raddai, the fifth, 15Ozem, the sixth, and David, the seventh. 16Their sisters were Zeruiah and Abigail. Zeruiah had three sons: Abishai, Joab, and Asahel.[g] 17Abigail bore Amasa, whose father was Jether the Ishmaelite.[h]

18* By his wife Azubah, Caleb, son of Hezron, became the father of a daughter, Jerioth. Her sons were Jesher, Shobab, and Ardon.[i] 19When Azubah died, Caleb married Ephrath, who bore him Hur.[j] 20Hur became the father of Uri, and Uri became the father of Bezalel.[k] 21Then Hezron had relations with the daughter of Machir, the father of Gilead, whom he married when he was sixty years old. She bore him Segub.[l] 22Segub became the father of Jair, who possessed twenty-three cities in the land of Gilead.[m] 23Geshur and Aram took from them the villages of Jair, that is, Kenath and its towns, sixty cities in all, which had belonged to the sons of Machir, the father of Gilead.[n] 24After the death of Hezron, Caleb had relations with Ephrathah, the widow of his father Hezron, and she bore him Ashhur, the father of Tekoa.[o]

25The sons of Jerahmeel,* the firstborn of Hezron, were Ram, the firstborn, then Bunah, Oren, and Ozem, his brothers.[p] 26Jerahmeel also had another wife, named Atarah, who was the mother of Onam. 27The sons of Ram, the firstborn of Jerahmeel, were Maaz, Jamin, and Eker. 28The sons of Onam were Shammai and Jada. The sons of Shammai were Nadab and Abishur. 29Abishur's wife, who was named Abihail, bore him Ahban and Molid. 30The sons of Nadab were Seled and Appaim. Seled died childless. 31The sons of Appaim: Ishi. The sons of Ishi: Sheshan. The sons of Sheshan: Ahlai.[q] 32The sons of Jada, the brother of Shammai, were Jether and Jonathan. Jether died childless. 33The sons of Jonathan were Peleth and Zaza. These were the sons of Jerahmeel. 34Sheshan had no sons, only daughters; he had an Egyptian slave named Jarha. 35Sheshan gave his daughter in marriage to his slave Jarha, and she bore him Attai. 36Attai became the father of Nathan. Nathan became the father of Zabad. 37Zabad became the father of Ephlal. Ephlal became the father of Obed. 38Obed became the father of Jehu. Jehu became the father of Azariah. 39Azariah became the father of Helez. Helez became the father of Eleasah. 40Eleasah became the father of Sismai. Sismai became the father of Shallum. 41Shallum became the father of Jekamiah. Jekamiah became the father of Elishama.

42The sons of Caleb,* the brother of Jerahmeel: Mesha his firstborn, who was the father of Ziph. Then the sons of Mareshah, who was the father of Hebron. 43The sons of Hebron were Korah, Tappuah, Rekem, and

2:9 Chelubai: a variant form of the name Caleb (vv. 18, 42), a different person from the Chelub mentioned in 4:11.

2:10–17 These verses list the immediate ancestors of David. A similar list appears in Ru 4:18–22.

2:18–24 These verses record the descendants of Caleb. In 4:15 as well as frequently in the Pentateuch (see Nm 13:6; 14:6, 30; 26:65; etc.), Caleb is called the son of Jephunneh. Here his father is called Hezron, perhaps because the Calebites were reckoned as part of the clan of the Hezronites.

2:25–41 The Jerahmeelites were a clan living in the Negeb of Judah.

2:42–49 Another list (see vv. 18–24) of the Calebites, a clan inhabiting the south of Judah.

y: Gn 46:12. *z:* 1 Kgs 5:11. *a:* Jos 7:1, 18–21, 24–25; 22:20. *b:* Mt 1:3. *c:* Mt 1:4. *d:* Nm 1:7; Mt 1:4–5. *e:* 1 Sm 16:6–13; 17:13–14. *f:* 2 Chr 11:18. *g:* 2 Sm 2:18. *h:* 2 Sm 17:25; 19:14; 20:4–13. *i:* 1 Chr 2:24. *j:* 1 Chr 2:24. *k:* Ex 24:14; 31:2; 35:30; 2 Chr 1:5. *l:* Nm 26:29; 27:1; 32:39; Jos 13:31; Jgs 5:14. *m:* Nm 32:41; 1 Kgs 4:13. *n:* Dt 3:14; Jos 13:30. *o:* 1 Chr 2:19; 2 Sm 14:2; 2 Chr 11:6. *p:* 1 Sm 27:10; 30:29; Jb 32:2. *q:* 1 Chr 4:20.

Shema. 44 Shema became the father of Raham, who was the father of Jorkeam. Rekem became the father of Shammai. 45 The son of Shammai: Maon, who was the father of Beth-zur. 46 Ephah, Caleb's concubine, bore Haran, Moza, and Gazez. Haran became the father of Gazez. 47 The sons of Jahdai were Regem, Jotham, Geshan, Pelet, Ephah, and Shaaph. 48 Maacah, Caleb's concubine, bore Sheber and Tirhanah. 49 She also bore Shaaph, the father of Madmannah, Sheva, the father of Machbenah, and the father of Gibea. Achsah was Caleb's daughter.[r]

50 These were sons of Caleb, sons of Hur,* the firstborn of Ephrathah: Shobal, the father of Kiriath-jearim, 51 Salma, the father of Bethlehem, and Hareph, the father of Bethgader. 52 The sons of Shobal, the father of Kiriath-jearim, were Reaiah, half of the Manahathites, 53 and the clans of Kiriath-jearim: the Ithrites, the Puthites, the Shumathites, and the Mishraites. From these the Zorahites and the Eshtaolites derived.[s] 54 The sons of Salma were Bethlehem, the Netophathites, Atroth-beth-Joab, half of the Manahathites, and the Zorites. 55 The clans of the Sopherim dwelling in Jabez were the Tirathites, the Shimeathites, and the Sucathites. They were the Kenites, who descended from Hammath, the ancestor of the Rechabites.[t]

CHAPTER 3

See RG 200

1*[u] These were the sons of David born to him in Hebron: the firstborn, Amnon, by Ahinoam of Jezreel; the second, Daniel,* by Abigail of Carmel; 2 the third, Absalom, son of Maacah, who was the daughter of Talmai, king of Geshur; the fourth, Adonijah, son of Haggith; 3 the fifth, Shephatiah, by Abital; the sixth, Ithream, by his wife Eglah. 4 Six in all were born to him in Hebron, where he reigned seven years and six months. Then he reigned thirty-three years in Jerusalem.[v] 5[w] In Jerusalem the following were born to him: Shimea,* Shobab, Nathan, Solomon—four by Bathsheba, the daughter of Ammiel;[x] 6 Ibhar, Elishua, Eliphelet, 7 Nogah, Nepheg, Japhia, 8 Elishama, Eliada, and Eliphelet—nine. 9 All these were sons of David, in addition to other sons by concubines; and Tamar was their sister.[y]

10*[z] The son of Solomon was Rehoboam, whose son was Abijah, whose son was Asa, whose son was Jehoshaphat,[a] 11 whose son was Joram, whose son was Ahaziah, whose son was Joash,[b] 12 whose son was Amaziah, whose son was Azariah, whose son was Jotham,[c] 13 whose son was Ahaz, whose son was Hezekiah, whose son was Manasseh,[d] 14 whose son was Amon, whose son was Josiah.[e] 15 The sons of Josiah were: the firstborn Johanan; the second, Jehoiakim; the third, Zedekiah; the fourth, Shallum.*[f] 16 The sons of Jehoiakim were: Jeconiah, his son; Zedekiah, his son.[g]

17 The sons of Jeconiah* the captive were: Shealtiel,[h] 18 Malchiram, Pedaiah, Shenazzar,* Jekamiah, Hoshama, and Nedabiah.

2:50–55 The Hurites were a clan dwelling to the south and west of Jerusalem and related to the Calebites.

3:1–9 A list of David's sons.

3:1 Daniel: he is called Chileab in 2 Sm 3:3.

3:5 Shimea: he bears the name Shammua in 2 Sm 5:14. **Ammiel**: Bathsheba's father is called Eliam in 2 Sm 11:3.

3:10–16 The kings of Judah from Solomon down to the destruction of Jerusalem by the Babylonians.

3:15 Shallum: another name for Jehoahaz, Josiah's immediate successor; cf. Jer 22:11.

3:17–24 The descendants of King Jeconiah down to the time of the Chronicler. If twenty-five years are allowed for each generation, the ten generations between Jeconiah and Anani (the last name on the list) would put the birth of the latter at about 405 B.C.—an important item in establishing the approximate date of the Chronicler's work in its final form.

3:18 Shenazzar: presumably he is the same as Sheshbazzar (Ezr 1:8, 11; 5:14–16), the prince of Judah who was the first Jewish governor of Judah after the exile. Both forms of the name probably go back to the Babylonian name Sin-ab-ussar, meaning "O [god] Sin, protect [our] father!"

3:19 Zerubbabel: here called the son of Pedaiah, though elsewhere (Hg 1:12, 14; 2:2, 23; Ezr 3:2, 8; 5:2; Neh 12:1) his father's name is given as Shealtiel. The latter indication may merely point to the fact that Zerubbabel succeeded Shealtiel as head of the house of David.

r: Jos 15:16; Jgs 1:12. *s:* Jgs 18:2. *t:* Nm 24:21; Jgs 1:16; 4:11; 1 Sm 15:6; Jer 35. *u:* 2 Sm 3:2–5. *v:* 2 Sm 2:11; 5:5. *w:* 2 Sm 5:14–16. *x:* 2 Sm 11:3. *y:* 2 Sm 13:1–2. *z:* Mt 1:7–12. *a:* 1 Kgs 11:43; 14:31; 15:1, 8, 24; 2 Chr 9:31; 12:16; 13:23; 17:1. *b:* 1 Kgs 22:51; 2 Chr 21:1; 22:1; 24:1, 27. *c:* 2 Kgs 12:21; 14:21; 15:7; 2 Chr 25:1; 26:1, 23; 27:1. *d:* 2 Kgs 15:38; 16:20; 20:21; 2 Chr 28:1, 27; 32:33. *e:* 2 Kgs 21:18, 26; 2 Chr 33:20, 25. *f:* 2 Kgs 23:34; 24:17; 2 Chr 36:4, 10. *g:* 2 Kgs 24:6, 17; 2 Chr 36:8, 10. *h:* Ezr 2:2; 3:2, 8; 5:2; Sir 49:11; Hg 1:1, 12, 14; Mt 1:12–13; Lk 3:27.

19 The sons of Pedaiah were Zerubbabel* and Shimei. The sons of Zerubbabel were Meshullam and Hananiah; Shelomith was their sister. 20 The sons of Meshullam were Hashubah, Ohel, Berechiah, Hasadiah, Jushab-hesed—five. 21 The sons of Hananiah were Pelatiah, Jeshaiah, Rephaiah, Arnan, Obadiah, and Shecaniah. 22 The sons of Shecaniah were Shemaiah, Hattush, Igal, Bariah, Neariah, Shaphat—six.[i] 23 The sons of Neariah were Elioenai, Hizkiah, and Azrikam—three. 24 The sons of Elioenai were Hodaviah, Eliashib, Pelaiah, Akkub, Johanan, Delaiah, and Anani—seven.

CHAPTER 4

See RG 200

1* The sons of Judah were: Perez, Hezron, Carmi, Hur, and Shobal.[j] 2 Reaiah, the son of Shobal, became the father of Jahath, and Jahath became the father of Ahumai and Lahad. These were the clans of the Zorathites.

3 These were the sons of Hareph, the father of Etam: Jezreel, Ishma, and Idbash; their sister was named Hazzelelponi. 4 Penuel was the father of Gedor, and Ezer the father of Hushah. These were the sons of Hur, the first-born of Ephrathah, the father of Bethlehem.

5 Ashhur, the father of Tekoa, had two wives, Helah and Naarah.[k] 6 Naarah bore him Ahuzzam, Hepher, the Temenites, and the Ahashtarites. These were the sons of Naarah. 7 The sons of Helah were Zereth, Izhar, Ethnan, and Koz. 8 Koz became the father of Anub and Zobebah, as well as of the clans of Aharhel, son of Harum. 9 Jabez was the most distinguished of his brothers. His mother had named him Jabez, saying, "I bore him with pain." 10 Jabez prayed to the God of Israel: "Oh, that you may truly bless me and extend my boundaries! May your hand be with me and make me free of misfortune, without pain!" And God granted his prayer.

11 Chelub, the brother of Shuhah, became the father of Mehir, who was the father of Eshton. 12 Eshton became the father of Bethrapha, Paseah, and Tehinnah, the father of the city of Nahash. These were the men of Recah.

13 The sons of Kenaz were Othniel and Seraiah. The sons of Othniel were Hathath and Meonothai;[l] 14 Meonothai became the father of Ophrah. Seraiah became the father of Joab, the father of Geharashim, so called because they were artisans. 15 The sons of Caleb, son of Jephunneh, were Ir, Elah, and Naam. The sons of Elah: Kenaz.[m] 16 The sons of Jehallelel were Ziph, Ziphah, Tiria, and Asarel. 17 The sons of Ezrah were Jether, Mered, Epher, and Jalon. Jether became the father of Miriam, Shammai, and Ishbah, the father of Eshtemoa.[n] 18 Mered's Egyptian wife bore Jered, the father of Gedor, Heber, the father of Soco, and Jekuthiel, the father of Zanoah. These were the sons of Bithiah, the daughter of Pharaoh, whom Mered married. 19 The sons of his Jewish wife, the sister of Naham, the father of Keilah, were Shimon the Garmite and Ishi the Maacathite. 20 The sons of Shimon were Amnon, Rinnah, Benhanan, and Tilon. The son of Ishi was Zoheth and the son of Zoheth. . . .

21 The sons of Shelah, son of Judah, were: Er, the father of Lecah; Laadah, the father of Mareshah; the clans of the linen weavers' guild in Bethashbea;[o] 22 Jokim; the people of Cozeba; and Joash and Saraph, who held property in Moab, but returned to Bethlehem. (These are events of old.) 23 They were potters and inhabitants of Netaim and Gederah, where they lived in the king's service.

Simeon. 24 The sons of Simeon were Nemuel, Jamin, Jachin, Zerah, and Shaul,[p] 25 whose son was Shallum, whose son was Mibsam, whose son was Mishma. 26 The sons of Mishma were his son Hammuel, whose son was Zaccur, whose son was Shimei. 27 Shimei had sixteen sons and six daughters. His brothers, however, did not have many sons, and as a result all their clans did not equal the number of the Judahites.

28 They dwelt in Beer-sheba, Moladah, Hazar-shual, 29 Bilhah, Ezem, Tolad, 30 Bethuel, Hormah, Ziklag, 31 Beth-marcaboth, Hazar-

4:1–43 Genealogies of the southern tribes, Judah and Simeon.

i: Neh 3:29. *j:* 1 Chr 2:4–5, 7, 9, 50; Gn 38:29; 46:12; Mt 1:3. *k:* 1 Chr 2:24. *l:* Jos 15:17; Jgs 1:13; 3:9, 11. *m:* Nm 13:6; 14:6; 32:12; Jos 14:6, 14. *n:* 1 Sm 30:28. *o:* 1 Chr 2:3; Gn 38:5; 46:12; Nm 26:20. *p:* Gn 46:10; Ex 6:15; Nm 26:12–13.

susim, Bethbiri, and Shaaraim. Until the reign of David, these were their cities 32 and their villages. Etam, also, and Ain, Rimmon, Tochen, and Ashan—five cities,[q] 33 together with all their outlying villages as far as Baal. Here is where they dwelt, and so it was inscribed of them in their family records.

34 Meshobab, Jamlech, Joshah, son of Amaziah, 35 Joel, Jehu, son of Joshibiah, son of Seraiah, son of Asiel, 36 Elioenai, Jaakobah, Jeshohaiah, Asaiah, Adiel, Jesimiel, Benaiah, 37 Ziza, son of Shiphi, son of Allon, son of Jedaiah, son of Shimri, son of Shemaiah— 38 these just named were princes in their clans, and their ancestral houses spread out to such an extent[r] 39 that they went to the approaches of Gedor,* east of the valley, seeking pasture for their flocks. 40 They found abundant and good pastures, and the land was spacious, quiet, and peaceful—for the Hamites dwelt there formerly. 41 They who have just been listed by name set out during the reign of Hezekiah, king of Judah, and attacked their tents and also the Meunites who were there. They put them under the ban that is still in force to this day and dwelt in their place because they found pasture there for their flocks.[s]

42 Five hundred of them (the Simeonites) went to Mount Seir, with Pelatiah, Neariah, Rephaiah, and Uzziel, sons of Ishi, at their head. 43 They attacked the surviving Amalekites who had escaped, and have lived there to the present day.[t]

See RG 200

CHAPTER 5

Reuben. 1* The sons of Reuben, the firstborn of Israel. (He was indeed the firstborn, but because he defiled the couch of his father his birthright was given to the sons of Joseph, son of Israel, so that he is not listed in the family records according to his birthright.[u] 2 Judah, in fact, became powerful among his brothers, so that the ruler came from him, though the birthright had been Joseph's.)[v] 3 The sons of Reuben, the firstborn of Israel, were Hanoch, Pallu, Hezron, and Carmi.[w] 4 His son was Joel, whose son was Shemaiah, whose son was Gog, whose son was Shimei, 5 whose son was Micah, whose son was Reaiah, whose son was Baal, 6 whose son was Beerah, whom Tilgath-pileser, the king of Assyria, took into exile; he was a prince of the Reubenites.[x] 7 His brothers who belonged to his clans, when they were listed in the family records according to their descendants, were: Jeiel, the chief, and Zechariah, 8 and Bela, son of Azaz, son of Shema, son of Joel. The Reubenites lived in Aroer and as far as Nebo and Baal-meon;[y] 9 toward the east they dwelt as far as the wilderness which extends from the Euphrates River, for they had much livestock in the land of Gilead.[z] 10 In Saul's time they waged war with the Hagrites, and when they had defeated them they dwelt in their tents throughout the region east of Gilead.[a]

Gad. 11 The Gadites lived alongside them in the land of Bashan as far as Salecah.[b] 12 Joel was chief, Shapham was second in command, and Janai was judge in Bashan.[c] 13 Their brothers, according to their ancestral houses, were: Michael, Meshullam, Sheba, Jorai, Jacan, Zia, and Eber—seven. 14 These were the sons of Abihail, son of Huri, son of Jaroah, son of Gilead, son of Michael, son of Jeshishai, son of Jahdo, son of Buz. 15 Ahi, son of Abdiel, son of Guni, was the head of their ancestral houses. 16 They dwelt in Gilead, in Bashan and its towns, and in all the pasture lands of Sirion to the borders. 17 All were listed in the family records in the time of Jotham, king of Judah, and of Jeroboam, king of Israel.

18 The Reubenites, Gadites, and the half-tribe of Manasseh were warriors, men who bore shield and sword and who drew the bow, trained in warfare—forty-four thousand seven hundred and sixty men fit for military service. 19 When they waged war against the

4:39 Gedor: the Greek reads Gerar, probably correctly.

5:1–26 Genealogies of the Transjordanian tribes, Reuben, Gad, and the half-tribe of Manasseh.

q: Jos 19:2–8. *r:* Nm 1:2. *s:* 2 Kgs 18:1–2; 2 Chr 29:1. *t:* Ex 17:8, 14; Dt 25:17–19; 1 Sm 14:48; 15:3, 7–8; 2 Sm 8:12. *u:* Gn 35:22; 48:5, 15–22; 49:3–4; Dt 33:6. *v:* 1 Chr 28:4; Gn 49:8–12. *w:* Gn 46:9; Ex 6:14; Nm 26:5–6. *x:* 2 Kgs 15:29. *y:* Jos 13:9, 16–17; Nm 32:3, 38. *z:* Jos 22:9. *a:* Ps 83:6–7. *b:* Jos 13:11, 24–28. *c:* Gn 46:16.

Hagrites and against Jetur, Naphish, and Nodab,[d] [20]they received help so that the Hagrites and all who were with them were delivered into their power. For during the battle they cried out to God, and he heard them because they had put their trust in him.[e] [21]Along with one hundred thousand persons they also captured their livestock: fifty thousand camels, two hundred fifty thousand sheep, and two thousand donkeys. [22]Many were slain and fell; for "From God the victory." They dwelt in their place until the time of the exile.[f]

The Half-tribe of Manasseh. [23]The half-tribe of Manasseh lived in the land of Bashan as far as Baal-hermon, Senir, and Mount Hermon; they were numerous. [24]The following were the heads of their ancestral houses: Epher, Ishi, Eliel, Azriel, Jeremiah, Hodaviah, and Jahdiel—men who were warriors, famous men, and heads over their ancestral houses.

[25]However, they acted treacherously toward the God of their ancestors by prostituting themselves to follow the gods of the peoples of the land, whom God had destroyed before them.[g] [26]Therefore the God of Israel stirred up against them the anger of Pul,* king of Assyria, and the anger of Tilgath-pilneser [sic], king of Assyria, who deported the Reubenites, the Gadites, and the half-tribe of Manasseh and brought them to Halah, Habor, and Hara, and to the river Gozan, where they have remained to this day.[h]

Levi.* [27]The sons of Levi were Gershon, Kohath, and Merari.[i] [28]The sons of Kohath were Amram, Izhar, Hebron, and Uzziel.[j] [29]The children of Amram were Aaron, Moses, and Miriam. The sons of Aaron were Nadab, Abihu, Eleazar, and Ithamar.[k] [30]* Eleazar became the father of Phinehas. Phinehas became the father of Abishua. [31]Abishua became the father of Bukki. Bukki became the father of Uzzi. [32]Uzzi became the father of Zerahiah. Zerahiah became the father of Meraioth. [33]Meraioth became the father of Amariah. Amariah became the father of Ahitub. [34]Ahitub became the father of Zadok. Zadok became the father of Ahimaaz. [35]Ahimaaz became the father of Azariah. Azariah became the father of Johanan. [36]Johanan became the father of Azariah, who served as priest in the temple Solomon built in Jerusalem. [37]Azariah became the father of Amariah. Amariah became the father of Ahitub. [38]Ahitub became the father of Zadok. Zadok became the father of Shallum. [39]Shallum became the father of Hilkiah. Hilkiah became the father of Azariah. [40]Azariah became the father of Seraiah. Seraiah became the father of Jehozadak. [41]Jehozadak was one of those who went into the exile which the LORD inflicted on Judah and Jerusalem through Nebuchadnezzar.

CHAPTER 6

See RG 200

[1]The sons of Levi were Gershon, Kohath, and Merari.[l] [2]The sons of Gershon were named Libni and Shimei.[m] [3]The sons of Kohath were Amram, Izhar, Hebron, and Uzziel.[n] [4]The sons of Merari were Mahli and Mushi.[o]

These were the clans of Levi, according to their ancestors. [5]Of Gershon: his son Libni, whose son was Jahath, whose son was Zimmah, [6]whose son was Joah, whose son was Iddo, whose son was Zerah, whose son was Jetherai.

[7]The sons of Kohath: his son Amminadab, whose son was Korah, whose son was Assir, [8]whose son was Elkanah, whose son was Ebiasaph, whose son was Assir, [9]whose son was Tahath, whose son was Uriel, whose son was Uzziah, whose son was Shaul. [10]The sons of Elkanah were Amasai and Ahimoth,

5:26 Pul: the Chronicler seems to speak of two different kings here, but Pul was the name which the Assyrian king Tilgath-pileser III (745–727 B.C.) adopted as king of Babylon.

5:27–6:66 The tribe of Levi. The Chronicler's list gives special prominence to Levi's son Kohath, from whom were descended both the Aaronite priests (vv. 28–41) and the leading group of Temple singers (6:18–23).

5:30–41 The line of preexilic high priests. The list seems to become confused in vv. 36–38, which repeat the same names, mostly in inverse order, that occur in vv. 34–36. A similar but shorter list occurs, with variations, in Ezr 7:1–5.

d: 1 Chr 1:31; 5:10; Gn 25:15; Ps 83:6–7. *e:* Dt 33:20–21. *f:* Nm 32:39; Dt 3:8–10; Jgs 3:3. *g:* Ex 34:14–16; 2 Kgs 17:7. *h:* 2 Kgs 15:9, 29; 17:6. *i:* 1 Chr 6:1; 23:6; Gn 46:11; Ex 6:16; Nm 26:57. *j:* 1 Chr 6:3; Ex 6:18. *k:* Ex 6:20; Nm 26:59–60. *l:* 1 Chr 5:27; 23:6; Gn 46:11; Ex 6:16; Nm 26:57. *m:* Ex 6:17. *n:* Ex 6:18; Nm 3:19; 26:59. *o:* 1 Chr 6:14; Ex 6:19; Nm 3:20; 26:58.

[11]whose son was Elkanah, whose son was
Zophai, whose son was Nahath, [12]whose son
was Eliab, whose son was Jeroham, whose
son was Elkanah, whose son was Samuel.
[13]The sons of Samuel were Joel, the firstborn, and Abijah, the second.

[14]The sons of Merari: Mahli, whose son
was Libni, whose son was Shimei, whose
son was Uzzah,[p] [15]whose son was Shimea,
whose son was Haggiah, whose son was
Asaiah.

[16]The following were established by David for the service of song* in the LORD's
house at the time when the ark had a resting
place. [17]They served as singers before the
tabernacle of the tent of meeting until Solomon built the house of the LORD in Jerusalem, and they performed their services according to the order prescribed for them.
[18]Those who so performed are the following, together with their sons.

Among the Kohathites: Heman, the
chanter, son of Joel, son of Samuel, [19]son of
Elkanah, son of Jeroham, son of Eliel, son of
Toah, [20]son of Zuph, son of Elkanah, son of
Mahath, son of Amasi, [21]son of Elkanah, son
of Joel, son of Azariah, son of Zephaniah,
[22]son of Tahath, son of Assir, son of Ebiasaph, son of Korah,[q] [23]son of Izhar, son of
Kohath, son of Levi, son of Israel.

[24]His brother Asaph stood at his right
hand. Asaph was the son of Berechiah, son
of Shimea, [25]son of Michael, son of Baase-
iah, son of Malchijah, [26]son of Ethni, son of
Zerah, son of Adaiah, [27]son of Ethan, son of
Zimmah,[r] son of Shimei, [28]son of Jahath,
son of Gershon, son of Levi.

[29]Their brothers, the Merarites, stood at
the left: Ethan, son of Kishi, son of Abdi, son
of Malluch, [30]son of Hashabiah, son of Amaziah, son of Hilkiah, [31]son of Amzi, son of
Bani, son of Shemer, [32]son of Mahli, son of
Mushi, son of Merari, son of Levi.[s]

[33]Their brother Levites were appointed to
all the other services of the tabernacle of the
house of God.[t] [34]However, it was Aaron and
his sons who made the sacrifice on the altar
for burnt offerings and on the altar of incense; they alone had charge of the holy of
holies and of making atonement for Israel,
as Moses, the servant of God, had commanded.[u]

[35]These were the sons of Aaron: his son
Eleazar, whose son was Phinehas, whose son
was Abishua, [36]whose son was Bukki, whose
son was Uzzi, whose son was Zerahiah,
[37]whose son was Meraioth, whose son was
Amariah, whose son was Ahitub, [38]whose
son was Zadok, whose son was Ahimaaz.

[39]* The following were their dwelling
places, by encampments in their territories.
To the sons of Aaron who belonged to the
clan of the Kohathites, since the lot fell to
them, [40]was assigned Hebron in the land of
Judah, with its adjacent pasture lands.
[41]However, the open country and the villages belonging to the city had been given to
Caleb, the son of Jephunneh. [42]There were
assigned to the sons of Aaron: Hebron a city
of refuge, Libnah with its pasture lands, Jattir with its pasture lands, Eshtemoa with its
pasture lands, [43]Holon with its pasture lands,
Debir with its pasture lands, [44]Ashan with its
pasture lands, Jetta with its pasture lands,
and Beth-shemesh with its pasture lands.
[45]Also from the tribe of Benjamin: Gibeon
with its pasture lands, Geba with its pasture
lands, Almon with its pasture lands, Anathoth with its pasture lands. In all, they had
thirteen cities with their pasture lands. [49]The
Israelites assigned these cities with their
pasture lands to the Levites, [50]designating
them by name and assigning them by lot
from the tribes of the Judahites, Simeonites,
and Benjaminites.

[46]The other Kohathites obtained ten cities
by lot for their clans from the tribe of
Ephraim, from the tribe of Dan, and from the
half-tribe of Manasseh. [47]The clans of the
Gershonites obtained thirteen cities from the

6:16–32 The cultic functions performed by the levitical families in the postexilic Temple at the time of the Chronicler are here traced back to David, in a way analogous to that in which all the laws in the Pentateuch are attributed to Moses.

6:39–66 For the rights of the Levites in the cities assigned to them, see note on Jos 21:1.

p: 1 Chr 6:4; Ex 6:19; Nm 3:20; 26:58. *q:* Ex 6:24. *r:* 1 Chr 6:2, 5. *s:* Ex 6:19; Nm 26:58. *t:* 1 Chr 15:17, 19; 16:41–42; 2 Chr 5:12. *u:* 1 Chr 16:39–40.

tribes of Issachar, Asher, and Naphtali, and from the half-tribe of Manasseh in Bashan. [48]The clans of the Merarites obtained twelve cities by lot from the tribes of Reuben, Gad, and Zebulun.

[51]The clans of the Kohathites obtained cities by lot from the tribe of Ephraim. [52]They were assigned cities of refuge: Shechem in the mountain region of Ephraim, with its pasture lands, Gezer with its pasture lands, [53]Kibzaim with its pasture lands, and Beth-horon with its pasture lands. [54]From the tribe of Dan: Elteke with its pasture lands, Gibbethon with its pasture lands, Aijalon with its pasture lands, and Gath-rimmon with its pasture lands. [55]From the half-tribe of Manasseh: Taanach with its pasture lands and Ibleam with its pasture lands. These belonged to the rest of the Kohathite clan.

[56]The clans of the Gershonites received from the half-tribe of Manasseh: Golan in Bashan with its pasture lands and Ashtaroth with its pasture lands. [57]From the tribe of Issachar: Kedesh with its pasture lands, Daberath with its pasture lands, [58]Ramoth with its pasture lands, and Engannim with its pasture lands. [59]From the tribe of Asher: Mashal with its pasture lands, Abdon with its pasture lands, [60]Hilkath with its pasture lands, and Rehob with its pasture lands. [61]From the tribe of Naphtali: Kedesh in Galilee with its pasture lands, Hammon with its pasture lands, and Kiriathaim with its pasture lands.

[62]The rest of the Merarites received from the tribe of Zebulun: Jokneam with its pasture lands, Kartah with its pasture lands, Rimmon with its pasture lands, and Tabor with its pasture lands. [63]Across the Jordan at Jericho (that is, east of the Jordan) they received from the tribe of Reuben: Bezer in the desert with its pasture lands, Jahzah with its pasture lands, [64]Kedemoth with its pasture lands, and Mephaath with its pasture lands. [65]From the tribe of Gad: Ramoth in Gilead with its pasture lands, Mahanaim with its pasture lands, [66]Heshbon with its pasture lands, and Jazer with its pasture lands.

CHAPTER 7

See RG 200

Issachar. [1*] The sons of Issachar were Tola, Puah, Jashub, and Shimron: four.[v] [2]The sons of Tola were Uzzi, Rephaiah, Jeriel, Jahmai, Ibsam, and Shemuel, heads of the ancestral houses of Tola, mighty warriors in their generations. In the time of David they numbered twenty-two thousand six hundred.[w] [3]The sons of Uzzi: Izarahiah. The sons of Izarahiah were Michael, Obadiah, Joel, and Isshiah. All five of these were chiefs. [4]Along with them, in their generations, according to ancestral houses, were thirty-six thousand men in organized military troops, since they had more wives and children [5]than their fellow tribesmen. In all the clans of Issachar there was a total of eighty-seven thousand warriors listed in their family records.

Benjamin. [6]The sons of Benjamin were Bela, Becher, and Jediael—three.[x] [7]The sons of Bela were Ezbon, Uzzi, Uzziel, Jerimoth, and Iri—five. They were heads of their ancestral houses and warriors. Their family records listed twenty-two thousand and thirty-four. [8]The sons of Becher were Zemirah, Joash, Eliezer, Elioenai, Omri, Jeremoth, Abijah, Anathoth, and Alemeth—all these were sons of Becher.[y] [9]Their family records listed twenty thousand two hundred of their kindred who were heads of their ancestral houses and warriors. [10]The sons of Jediael: Bilhan. The sons of Bilhan were Jeush, Benjamin, Ehud, Chenaanah, Zethan, Tarshish, and Ahishahar. [11]All these were sons of Jediael, heads of ancestral houses and warriors. They numbered seventeen thousand two hundred men fit for military service . . .* [12]Shupham and Hupham.[z]

Dan, Naphtali and Manasseh. The sons of Dan: Hushim. [13]The sons of Naphtali were Jahziel, Guni, Jezer, and Shallum. These were sons of Bilhah.[a] [14]The sons of Manasseh, whom his Aramean concubine bore:[b]

7:1–40 The seven northern tribes.
7:11 The Hebrew text appears to be defective.

v: Gn 46:13. *w:* Nm 26:23–24; Jgs 10:1. *x:* Gn 46:21; Nm 26:38. *y:* Gn 46:21. *z:* Nm 26:39. *a:* Gn 46:24; Nm 26:48–49. *b:* Nm 26:29–32.

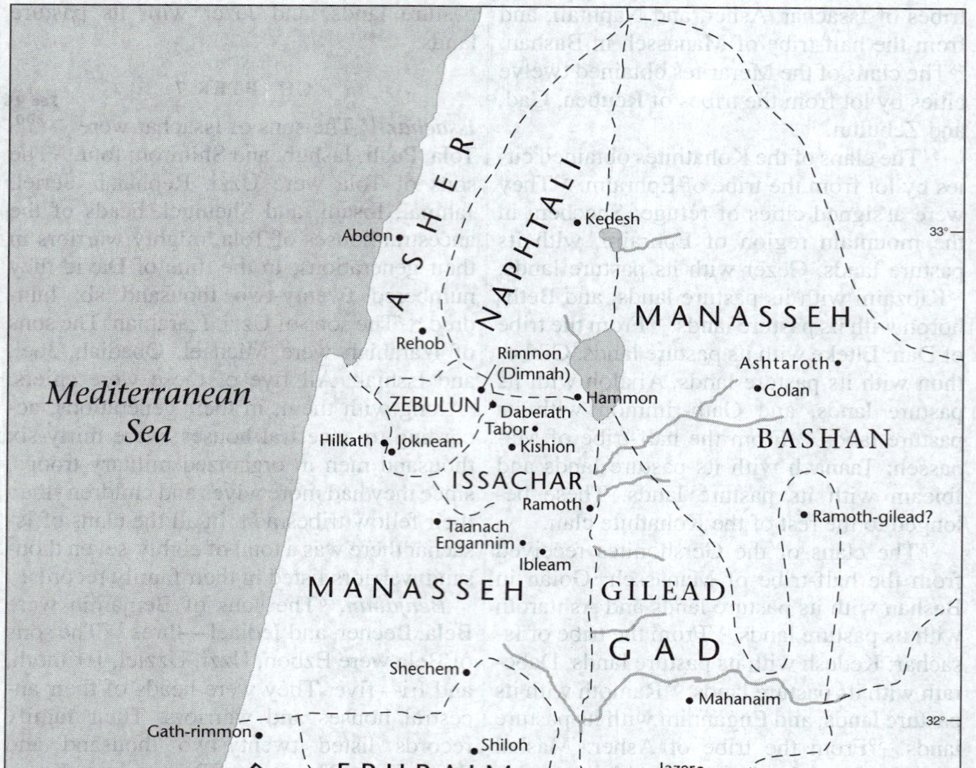
Mediterranean Sea
ASHER
NAPHTALI
MANASSEH
Kedesh
Abdon
Rehob
Rimmon (Dimnah)
Ashtaroth
Golan
Hammon
ZEBULUN
Daberath
Tabor
Hilkath
Jokneam
Kishion
BASHAN
ISSACHAR
Ramoth
Ramoth-gilead?
Taanach
Engannim
Ibleam
MANASSEH
GILEAD
GAD
Shechem
Mahanaim
Gath-rimmon
Shiloh
DAN
EPHRAIM
Jazer
Elteke?
Beth-horon
Gibeon
Geba
Gibbethon
Gezer
Aijalon
BENJAMIN
Almon
Anathoth
Heshbon
Bezer?
Beth-shemesh
Kiriathaim
Holon?
REUBEN
Libnah
Hebron (Kiriath-arba)
Jahzah
Kedemoth?
JUDAH
Dead Sea
Debir
Jetta
Eshtemoa
Jattir
Ashan
SIMEON
0 10 20 Miles
0 10 20 Kilometers
33°
32°
31°
35°
36°

The Levitical Cities according to 1 Chronicles

she bore Machir, the father of Gilead.[c] 15 Machir took a wife whose name was Maacah; his sister's name was Molecheth. Manasseh's second son was named Zelophehad, who had only daughters.[d] 16 Maacah, Machir's wife, bore a son whom she named Peresh. He had a brother named Sheresh, whose sons were Ulam and Rakem. 17 The sons of Ulam: Bedan. These were the sons of Gilead, the son of Machir, the son of Manasseh. 18 His sister Molecheth bore Ishhod, Abiezer, and Mahlah. 19 The sons of Shemida were Ahian, Shechem, Likhi, and Aniam.

Ephraim. 20[e] The sons of Ephraim: Shuthelah, whose son was Bered, whose son was Tahath, whose son was Eleadah, whose son was Tahath, 21 whose son was Zabad. Ephraim's son Shuthelah, and Ezer and Elead, who were born in the land, were killed by the inhabitants of Gath because they had gone down to take away their livestock. 22 Their father Ephraim mourned a long time, but after his relatives had come and comforted him, 23 he had relations with his wife, who conceived and bore a son whom he named Beriah, since evil* had befallen his house.[f] 24 He had a daughter, Sheerah, who built Lower and Upper Beth-horon and Uzzen-sheerah. 25 Zabad's son was Rephah, whose son was Resheph, whose son was Telah, whose son was Tahan, 26 whose son was Ladan, whose son was Ammihud, whose son was Elishama,[g] 27 whose son was Nun, whose son was Joshua.

28 Their property and their dwellings were in Bethel and its towns, Naaran to the east, Gezer and its towns to the west, and also Shechem and its towns as far as Ayyah and its towns.[h] 29 Manasseh, however, had possession of Beth-shean and its towns, Taanach and its towns, Megiddo and its towns, and Dor and its towns. In these dwelt the sons of Joseph, the son of Israel.[i]

Asher. 30 The sons of Asher were Imnah, Ishvah, Ishvi, and Beriah; their sister was Serah.[j] 31 Beriah's sons were Heber and Malchiel, who was the father of Birzaith. 32 Heber became the father of Japhlet, Shomer, Hotham, and their sister Shua. 33 The sons of Japhlet were Pasach, Bimhal, and Ashvath; these were the sons of Japhlet. 34 The sons of Shomer were Ahi, Rohgah, Jehubbah, and Aram. 35 The sons of his brother Hotham were Zophah, Imna, Shelesh, and Amal. 36 The sons of Zophah were Suah, Harnepher, Shual, Beri, Imrah, 37 Bezer, Hod, Shamma, Shilshah, Ithran, and Beera. 38 The sons of Jether were Jephunneh, Pispa, and Ara. 39 The sons of Ulla were Arah, Hanniel, and Rizia. 40 All these were sons of Asher, heads of ancestral houses, distinguished men, warriors, and chiefs among the princes. Their family records numbered twenty-six thousand men fit for military service.

CHAPTER 8

See RG 200

Benjamin. 1* Benjamin became the father of Bela, his firstborn, Ashbel, the second son, Aharah, the third,[k] 2 Nohah, the fourth, and Rapha, the fifth. 3 The sons of Bela were Addar and Gera, the father of Ehud. 4 The sons of Ehud were Abishua, Naaman, Ahoah,[l] 5 Gera, Shephuphan, and Huram. 6 These were the sons of Ehud, family heads over those who dwelt in Geba and were deported to Manahath. 7 Also Naaman, Ahijah, and Gera. The last, who led them into exile, became the father of Uzza and Ahihud. 8 Shaharaim became a father on the Moabite plateau after he had put away his wives Hushim and Baara. 9 By his wife Hodesh he begot Jobab, Zibia, Mesha, Malcam, 10 Jeuz, Sachia, and Mirmah. These were his sons, family heads. 11 By Hushim he begot Abitub and Elpaal. 12 The sons of Elpaal were Eber, Misham, Shemed (who built Ono and Lod with its nearby towns),[m] 13 and Beriah, and Shema. They were family heads of those who dwelt in Aijalon, and they put the inhabitants of Gath to flight. 14 Their relatives were Elpaal, Shashak, and Jeremoth. 15 Zebadiah, Arad, Eder, 16 Michael, Ishpah, and Joha were the sons of Beriah. 17 Zebadiah,

7:23 Beriah . . . evil: the name sounds like the Hebrew word for "evil," with the preposition *be*.
8:1–40 A second, variant list (cf. 7:6–11) of the Benjaminites, highlighting the family of Saul (vv. 33–40).

c: Nm 26:29; Jos 17:1. *d:* Nm 26:33; Jos 17:3. *e:* Nm 26:35. *f:* 1 Chr 8:13. *g:* Nm 1:10; 2:18; 7:48; 10:22. *h:* Gn 12:8; 1 Kgs 9:16. *i:* Jos 17:11. *j:* Gn 46:17; Nm 26:44–46. *k:* 1 Chr 7:6; Gn 46:21; Nm 26:38–44. *l:* Jgs 3:15. *m:* Neh 11:35.

Meshullam, Hizki, Heber, [18]Ishmerai, Izliah,
and Jobab were the sons of Elpaal. [19]Jakim,
Zichri, Zabdi, [20]Elienai, Zillethai, Eliel,
[21]Adaiah, Beraiah, and Shimrath were the
sons of Shimei. [22]Ishpan, Eber, Eliel, [23]Ab-
don, Zichri, Hanan, [24]Hananiah, Elam, An-
thothijah, [25]Iphdeiah, and Penuel were the
sons of Shashak. [26]Shamsherai, Shehariah,
Athaliah, [27]Jaareshiah, Elijah, and Zichri
were the sons of Jeroham. [28]These were family heads in their generations, chiefs who
dwelt in Jerusalem.

[29][n] In Gibeon dwelt Jeiel, the founder of
Gibeon, whose wife's name was Maacah;
[30]also his firstborn son, Abdon, and Zur, Kish,
Baal, Ner, Nadab, [31]Gedor, Ahio, Zecher, and
Mikloth. [32]Mikloth became the father of
Shimeah. These, too, dwelt with their relatives in Jerusalem, opposite their fellow
tribesmen. [33][o] Ner became the father of Kish,
and Kish became the father of Saul. Saul became the father of Jonathan, Malchishua,
Abinadab, and Eshbaal.[p] [34]The son of Jonathan was Meribbaal, and Meribbaal became
the father of Micah.[q] [35]The sons of Micah
were Pithon, Melech, Tarea, and Ahaz.
[36]Ahaz became the father of Jehoaddah, and
Jehoaddah became the father of Alemeth, Azmaveth, and Zimri. Zimri became the father
of Moza.[r] [37]Moza became the father of Binea,
whose son was Raphah, whose son was Eleasah, whose son was Azel. [38]Azel had six sons,
whose names were Azrikam, his firstborn,
Ishmael, Sheariah, Azariah, Obadiah, and
Hanan; all these were the sons of Azel.[s] [39]The
sons of Eshek, his brother, were Ulam, his
firstborn, Jeush, the second son, and
Eliphelet, the third. [40]The sons of Ulam were
warriors, skilled with the bow, and they had
many sons and grandsons: one hundred and
fifty. All these were the sons of Benjamin.

CHAPTER 9

See RG 200

[1]Thus all Israel was listed in family
lists, and these are recorded in the book of
the kings of Israel.[t]

Now Judah had been exiled to Babylon
because of its treachery. [2*][u] The first to settle again in their cities and dwell there were
certain Israelites, the priests, the Levites,
and the temple servants.[v]

Jerusalemites. [3]In Jerusalem lived Judahites and Benjaminites; also Ephraimites
and Manassites. [4]Among the Judahites was
Uthai, son of Ammihud, son of Omri, son of
Imri, son of Bani, one of the sons of Perez,
son of Judah. [5]Among the Shelanites were
Asaiah, the firstborn, and his sons. [6]Among
the Zerahites were Jeuel and six hundred and
ninety of their relatives. [7]Among the Benjaminites were Sallu, son of Meshullam, son
of Hodaviah, son of Hassenuah, [8]as well as
Ibneiah, son of Jeroham; Elah, son of Uzzi,
son of Michri; Meshullam, son of Shephatiah, son of Reuel, son of Ibnijah. [9]Their kindred of various families were nine hundred
and fifty-six. All those named were heads of
their ancestral houses.

[10]Among the priests were Jedaiah; Jehoiarib; Jachin; [11]Azariah, son of Hilkiah,
son of Meshullam, son of Zadok, son of Meraioth, son of Ahitub, the ruler of the house
of God; [12]Adaiah, son of Jeroham, son of
Pashhur, son of Malchijah; Maasai, son of
Adiel, son of Jahzerah, son of Meshullam,
son of Meshillemith, son of Immer. [13]Their
brothers, heads of their ancestral houses,
were one thousand seven hundred and sixty,
valiant in the work of the service of the
house of God.

[14]Among the Levites were Shemaiah, son
of Hasshub, son of Azrikam, son of
Hashabiah, one of the sons of Merari; [15]Bak-
bakkar; Heresh; Galal; Mattaniah, son of
Mica, son of Zichri, a descendant of Asaph;
[16]Obadiah, son of Shemaiah, son of Galal, a
descendant of Jeduthun; and Berechiah, son
of Asa, son of Elkanah, whose family lived
in the villages of the Netophathites.

[17]The gatekeepers were Shallum, Akkub,
Talmon, Ahiman, and their brothers; Shallum was the chief. [18]Previously they had

9:2–34 The inhabitants of Jerusalem after the exile. A similar list, though with many variants in the names, occurs in Neh 11:3–24.

n: 1 Chr 9:35–38. *o:* 1 Chr 9:39–44. *p:* 1 Chr 10:2; 1 Sm 9:1; 14:49, 51; 31:2. *q:* 2 Sm 4:4; 9:6; 10:12. *r:* 1 Chr 9:42. *s:* 1 Chr 9:43. *t:* 2 Chr 16:11; 20:34; 25:26; 27:7; 33:18; 36:8. *u:* Neh 11:3–24. *v:* Ezr 2:70; 7:7; Neh 11:3.

stood guard at the king's gate on the east side; now they became gatekeepers for the encampments of the Levites. [19]Shallum, son of Kore, son of Ebiasaph, a descendant of Korah, and his brothers of the same ancestral house of the Korahites had as their assigned task the guarding of the threshold of the tent, just as their fathers had guarded the entrance to the encampment of the LORD. [20]Phinehas, son of Eleazar, had been their chief in times past; the LORD was with him.[w] [21]Zechariah, son of Meshelemiah, guarded the gate of the tent of meeting.[x] [22]In all, those who were chosen for gatekeepers at the threshold were two hundred and twelve. They were inscribed in the family records of their villages. David and Samuel the seer had established them in their position of trust. [23]Thus they and their sons kept guard over the gates of the house of the LORD, the house which was then a tent. [24]The gatekeepers were stationed at the four sides, to the east, the west, the north, and the south.[y] [25]Their brothers who lived in their own villages took turns in assisting them for seven-day periods,[z] [26]while the four chief gatekeepers were on permanent duty. These were the Levites who also had charge of the chambers and treasures of the house of God. [27]They would spend the night near the house of God, for it was in their charge and they had the duty of opening it each morning.

[28]Some of them had charge of the vessels used there, tallying them as they were brought in and taken out. [29]Others were appointed to take care of the utensils and all the sacred vessels, as well as the fine flour, the wine, the oil, the frankincense, and the spices. [30]It was the sons of priests, however, who mixed the spiced ointments.[a] [31][b] Mattithiah, one of the Levites, the firstborn of Shallum the Korahite, was entrusted with preparing the cakes. [32]Benaiah the Kohathite, one of their brothers, was in charge of setting out the showbread each sabbath.[c]

[33]These were the singers and the gatekeepers, family heads over the Levites. They stayed in the chambers when free of duty, for day and night they had to be ready for service. [34]These were the levitical family heads by their generations, chiefs who dwelt in Jerusalem.

II. The History of David

Genealogy of Saul. [35][d] Jeiel, the founder of Gibeon, dwelt in Gibeon; his wife's name was Maacah. [36]His firstborn son was Abdon; then came Zur, Kish, Baal, Ner, Nadab, [37]Gedor, Ahio, Zechariah, and Mikloth. [38]Mikloth became the father of Shimeam. These, too, with their relatives, dwelt opposite their relatives in Jerusalem. [39]Ner became the father of Kish, and Kish became the father of Saul. Saul became the father of Jonathan, Malchishua, Abinadab, and Eshbaal. [40]The son of Jonathan was Meribbaal, and Meribbaal became the father of Micah. [41]The sons of Micah were Pithon, Melech, Tahrea, and Ahaz. [42]Ahaz became the father of Jehoaddah, and Jehoaddah became the father of Alemeth, Azmaveth, and Zimri. Zimri became the father of Moza. [43]Moza became the father of Binea, whose son was Rephaiah, whose son was Eleasah, whose son was Azel. [44]Azel had six sons, whose names were Azrikam, his firstborn, Ishmael, Sheariah, Azariah, Obadiah, and Hanan; these were the sons of Azel.

CHAPTER 10

See RG 200–203

Death of Saul and His Sons. [1][e] Now the Philistines went to war against Israel, and Israel fled before them, and they fell, slain on Mount Gilboa. [2]The Philistines pressed hard after Saul and his sons. When the Philistines had struck down Jonathan, Abinadab, and Malchishua, sons of Saul, [3]the fury of the battle converged on Saul. Then the archers hit him, and he was severely wounded.

[4]Saul said to his armor-bearer, "Draw your sword and run me through; otherwise these uncircumcised will come and abuse me." But the armor-bearer, badly frightened, refused, so Saul took his own sword and fell upon it. [5]When the armor-bearer saw that Saul was dead, he too fell upon his sword

w: Ex 6:25; Nm 25:7, 11; Jgs 20:28. *x:* 1 Chr 26:2, 14. *y:* 1 Chr 26:13. *z:* 2 Chr 23:4–5. *a:* Ex 30:20–33. *b:* 1 Chr 23:29; Lv 2:1–15; 6:13–16; 7:11. *c:* Ex 25:30; Lv 24:5–8. *d:* 1 Chr 8:29–38. *e:* 1 Sm 31:1–13.

and died. [6]Thus Saul, and his three sons, his whole house, died together. [7]When all the Israelites in the valley saw that Saul and his sons had fled and that they had died, they abandoned their cities and fled. Then the Philistines came and lived in those cities.

[8]On the following day, when the Philistines came to strip the slain, they found Saul and his sons fallen on Mount Gilboa. [9]They stripped him, and took his head and his armor; these they sent throughout the land of the Philistines to bring the good news to their idols and to the people. [10]They put his armor in the temple of their gods, but his skull they impaled at the temple of Dagon.

Burial of Saul. [11]When all the inhabitants of Jabesh-gilead heard all that the Philistines had done to Saul, [12]all their warriors set out, recovered the corpses of Saul and his sons, and brought them to Jabesh. They buried their bones under the oak of Jabesh, and fasted for seven days.[f]

[13*] Thus Saul died because of his treason against the LORD in disobeying his word, and also because he had sought counsel from a ghost,[g] [14]rather than from the LORD. Therefore the LORD took his life, and turned his kingdom over to David, the son of Jesse.[h]

See RG 200–203

CHAPTER 11

David Is Made King. [1 i] Then all Israel gathered around David in Hebron, and they said: "Look! We are your bone and your flesh. [2]In days past, when Saul was still the king, it was you who led Israel in all its battles. And now the LORD, your God, has said to you: You shall shepherd my people Israel; you shall be ruler over my people Israel."[j] [3]Then all the elders of Israel came to the king at Hebron, and at Hebron David made a covenant with them in the presence of the LORD; and they anointed David king over Israel, in accordance with the word of the LORD given through Samuel.[k]

Jerusalem Captured. [4]Then David and all Israel went to Jerusalem, that is, Jebus, where the inhabitants of the land were called Jebusites.[l] [5]The inhabitants of Jebus said to David, "You shall not enter here." David nevertheless captured the fortress of Zion, which is the City of David. [6]David said, "Whoever strikes the Jebusites first shall be made chief and captain." Joab, the son of Zeruiah, was the first to attack; and so he became chief.[m] [7]David took up residence in the fortress, which therefore was called the City of David. [8]He built up the city on all sides, from the Millo all the way around, while Joab restored the rest of the city.[n] [9]David became ever more powerful, for the LORD of hosts was with him.

David's Warriors. [10 o] These were David's chief warriors who, together with all Israel, supported him in his reign in order to make him king, according to the LORD's word concerning Israel.

[11]Here is the list of David's warriors:

Ishbaal, the son of Hachamoni, chief of the Three.* He brandished his spear over three hundred, whom he had slain in a single encounter.

[12]Next to him was Eleazar, the son of Dodo the Ahohite, one of the Three warriors.[p] [13]He was with David at Pas-dammim, where the Philistines had massed for battle. There was a plot of land full of barley. The people were fleeing before the Philistines,[q] [14]but he took his stand in the middle of the plot, kept it safe, and cut down the Philistines. Thus the LORD brought about a great victory.

[15]Three of the Thirty chiefs went down to the rock, to David, who was in the cave of Adullam while the Philistines were encamped in the valley of Rephaim.[r] [16]David was then in the stronghold, and a Philistine garrison was at Bethlehem. [17]David had a strong craving, and said, "If only someone would give me a drink of water from the cis-

10:13–14 The Chronicler explains why Saul met his tragic end: he had disobeyed the Lord's command given through the prophet Samuel (1 Sm 15:3–9), and had consulted a necromancer (1 Sm 28:6–19), contrary to the Mosaic law (Dt 18:10–11).

11:11 The Three: the Chronicler actually names only two of these figures, Ishbaal and Eleazar. According to 2 Sm 23:11, the third member of the Three was Shammah.

---

f: 2 Sm 2:5. *g:* Dt 18:10–14; 1 Sm 13:13–14; 15:3, 11, 26. *h:* 1 Sm 15:28; 2 Sm 3:9–10. *i:* 2 Sm 5:1–10. *j:* 1 Sm 18:5, 13–16, 30; 19:8. *k:* 1 Sm 16:1, 13; 2 Sm 2:4. *l:* Jos 15:8; Jgs 1:21; 19:10–11. *m:* 2 Sm 8:16. *n:* 1 Kgs 9:15, 24; 11:27; 2 Chr 32:5. *o:* 2 Sm 23:8–39. *p:* 1 Chr 27:4. *q:* 1 Sm 17:1. *r:* 1 Chr 14:9; 2 Sm 5:18, 22.

tern by the gate of Bethlehem!" [18]Thereupon
the Three broke through the encampment of
the Philistines, drew water from the cistern by
the gate of Bethlehem, and carried it back to
David. But David refused to drink it. Instead,
he poured it out* to the LORD, [19]saying, "God
forbid that I should do such a thing! Could I
drink the blood of these men who risked their
lives? For at the risk of their lives they
brought it." So he refused to drink it. Such
deeds as these the Three warriors performed.
[20][s] Abishai, the brother of Joab, was the
chief of the Thirty;* he brandished his spear
over three hundred, whom he had slain. He
made a name beside the Three,[t] [21]but was
twice as famous as any of the Thirty, becoming their leader. However, he did not attain to the Three.
[22]Benaiah, son of Jehoiada, a valiant man
of mighty deeds, from Kabzeel, killed the
two sons of Ariel of Moab. Also, he went
down and killed the lion in the cistern on a
snowy day. [23]He likewise slew the Egyptian,
a huge man five cubits tall. The Egyptian
carried a spear that was like a weaver's
beam, but Benaiah came against him with a
staff; he wrested the spear from the Egyptian's hand, and killed him with that spear.
[24]Such deeds as these Benaiah, the son of Jehoiada, performed, and he made a name beside the Three warriors, [25]but was more famous than any of the Thirty. However, he
did not attain to the Three. David put him in
charge of his bodyguard.[u]
[26]Also these warriors: Asahel, the brother
of Joab; Elhanan, son of Dodo, from Bethlehem;[v] [27]Shammoth, from En-harod; Helez,
from Beth-pelet; [28]Ira, son of Ikkesh, from
Tekoa; Abiezer, from Anathoth; [29]Sibbecai,
from Husha; Ilai, from Ahoh;[w] [30]Maharai,
from Netophah; Heled, son of Baanah, from
Netophah;[x] [31]Ithai, son of Ribai, from Gibeah
of Benjamin; Benaiah, from Pirathon;[y] [32]Hu-
rai, from Nahale-gaash; Abiel, from Beth-arabah; [33]Azmaveth, from Bahurim; Eliahba,
from Shaalbon; [34]Jashen the Gunite; Jonathan, son of Shagee the Hararite; [35]Ahiam,
son of Sachar the Hararite; Elipheleth, son of
[36]Ahasbai, from Beth-maacah; Ahijah, from
Gilo; [37]Hezro, from Carmel; Naarai, the son
of Ezbai; [38]Joel, brother of Nathan, from Rehob, the Gadite; [39]Zelek the Ammonite; Naharai, from Beeroth, the armor-bearer of
Joab, son of Zeruiah; [40]Ira, from Jattir; Gareb,
from Jattir; [41]Uriah the Hittite; Zabad, son of
Ahlai, [42]and, in addition to the Thirty, Adina,
son of Shiza, the Reubenite, chief of the tribe
of Reuben; [43]Hanan, son of Maacah;
Joshaphat the Mithnite; [44]Uzzia, the
Ashterathite; Shama and Jeiel, sons of Hotham, from Aroer; [45]Jediael, son of Shimri,
and Joha, his brother, the Tizite; [46]Eliel the
Mahavite; Jeribai and Joshaviah, sons of El-
naam; Ithmah, from Moab; [47]Eliel, Obed, and
Jaasiel the Mezobian.

CHAPTER 12

See RG 200–203

David's Early Followers. [1]The following men came to David in Ziklag while he
was still under banishment from Saul, son of
Kish; they, too, were among the warriors
who helped him in his battles.[z] [2]They were
archers who could use either the right or the
left hand, both in slinging stones and in
shooting arrows with the bow. They were
some of Saul's kinsmen, from Benjamin.
[3]Ahiezer was their chief, along with Joash,
both sons of Shemaah of Gibeah; also Jeziel
and Pelet, sons of Azmaveth; Beracah; Jehu,
from Anathoth;[a] [4]Ishmaiah the Gibeonite, a
warrior among the Thirty, and over the
Thirty; [5]Jeremiah; Jahaziel; Johanan; Jozabad from Gederah; [6]Eluzai; Jerimoth; Bea-
liah; Shemariah; Shephatiah the Haruphite;
[7]Elkanah, Isshiah, Azarel, Joezer, and
Jashobeam, who were Korahites; [8]Joelah
and Zebadiah, sons of Jeroham, from Gedor.
[9]Some of the Gadites also went over to
David when he was at the stronghold in the
wilderness. They were valiant warriors, ex-

11:18 Poured it out: as a libation.

11:20 The Thirty: they are listed by name in vv. 26–47. The parallel list in 2 Sm 23:8–39 often differs in names and spellings; for the numbers, see note on 2 Sm 23:8–39.

s: 2 Sm 23:18–19. *t:* 1 Chr 18:12; 1 Sm 26:6–10; 2 Sm 16:9; 18:2; 21:17. *u:* 2 Sm 8:18; 20:23. *v:* 1 Chr 2:16; 27:7. *w:* 1 Chr 27:11. *x:* 1 Chr 27:13. *y:* 1 Chr 27:14. *z:* 1 Sm 27:1–7. *a:* 1 Chr 27:12.

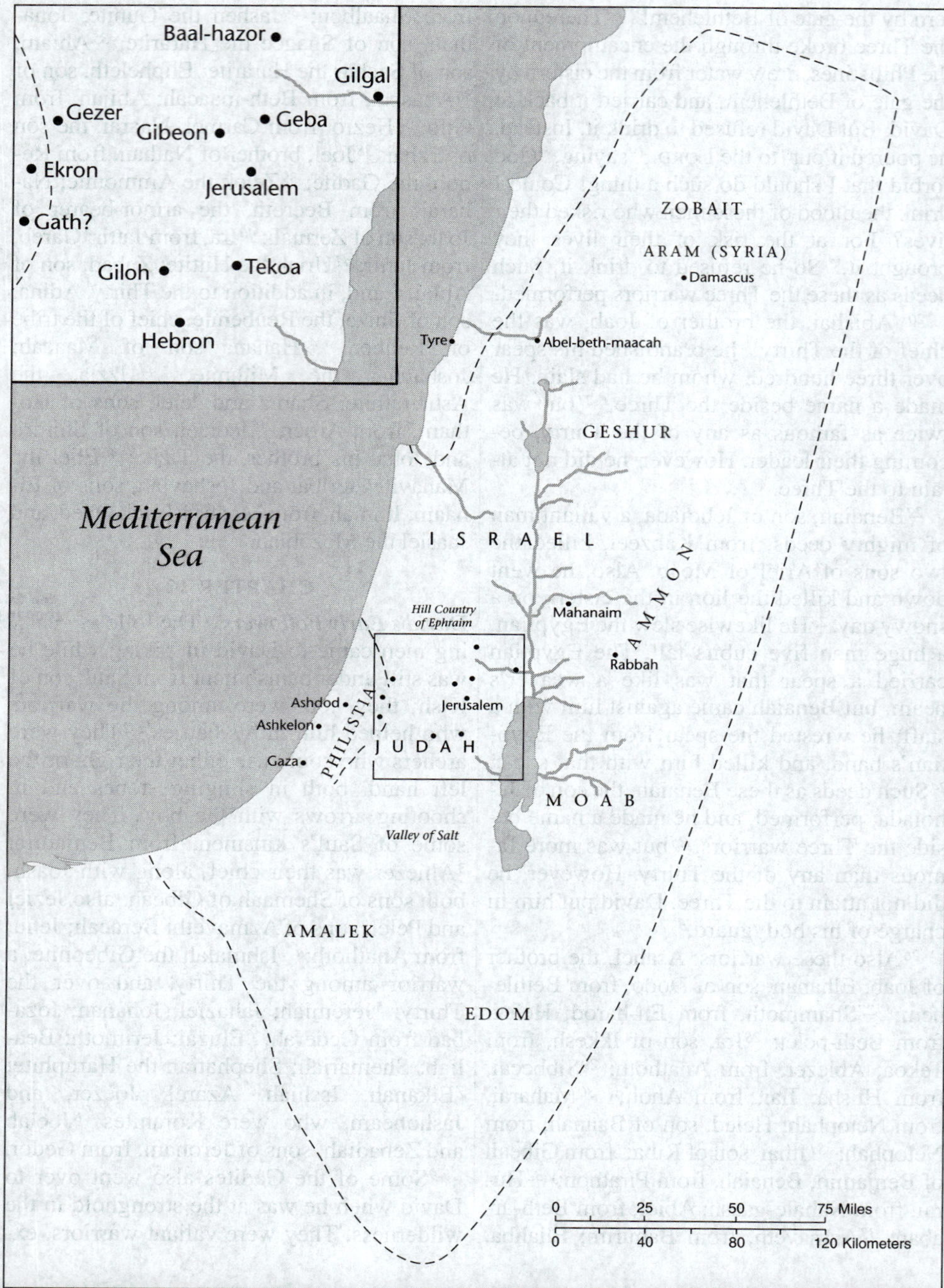

The Kingdom of David according to 1 Chronicles

perienced soldiers equipped with shield and spear, fearsome as lions, swift as gazelles on the mountains.[b] 10Ezer was their chief, Obadiah was second, Eliab third, 11Mishmannah fourth, Jeremiah fifth, 12Attai sixth, Eliel seventh, 13Johanan eighth, Elzabad ninth, 14Jeremiah tenth, and Machbannai eleventh. 15These Gadites were army commanders, the lesser over hundreds and the greater over thousands. 16It was they who crossed over the Jordan in the first month, when it was overflowing both its banks, and chased away all who were in the valleys to the east and to the west.

17Some Benjaminites and Judahites also came to David at the stronghold. 18David went out to meet them and addressed them in these words: "If you come peacefully, to help me, I am of a mind to have you join me. But if you have come to betray me to my enemies though my hands have done no wrong, may the God of our ancestors see and punish you."

19Then a spirit clothed Amasai, the chief of the Thirty, and he answered David:

"We are yours, O David,
  we are with you, son of Jesse.
Peace, peace to you,
  and peace to him who helps you;
  may your God be your helper!"

So David received them and placed them among the leaders of his troops.

20Men from Manasseh also deserted to David when he came with the Philistines to battle against Saul. However, he did not help the Philistines, for their lords took counsel and sent him home, saying, "At the cost of our heads he will desert to his master Saul." 21As he was returning to Ziklag, therefore, these deserted to him from Manasseh: Adnah, Jozabad, Jediael, Michael, Jozabad, Elihu, and Zillethai, chiefs of thousands of Manasseh.* 22They helped David by taking charge of his troops, for they were all warriors and became commanders of his army. 23And from day to day men kept coming to David's help until there was a vast encampment, like God's own encampment.

The Assembly at Hebron. 24This is the muster of the detachments of armed troops that came to David at Hebron to bring Saul's kingdom over to him, as the LORD had ordained. 25* Judahites bearing shields and spears: six thousand eight hundred armed troops. 26Of the Simeonites, warriors fit for battle: seven thousand one hundred. 27Of the Levites: four thousand six hundred, 28along with Jehoiada, leader of the line of Aaron, with another three thousand seven hundred, 29and Zadok, a young warrior, with twenty-two princes of his father's house. 30Of the Benjaminites, the kinsmen of Saul: three thousand—until this time, most of them had kept their allegiance to the house of Saul. 31Of the Ephraimites: twenty thousand eight hundred warriors, men renowned in their ancestral houses. 32Of the half-tribe of Manasseh: eighteen thousand, designated by name to come and make David king. 33Of the Issacharites, their chiefs who were endowed with an understanding of the times and who knew what Israel had to do: two hundred chiefs, together with all their kinsmen under their command. 34From Zebulun, men fit for military service, set in battle array with every kind of weapon for war: fifty thousand men rallying with a single purpose. 35From Naphtali: one thousand captains, and with them, armed with shield and lance, thirty-seven thousand men. 36Of the Danites, set in battle array: twenty-eight thousand six hundred. 37From Asher, fit for military service and set in battle array: forty thousand. 38From the other side of the Jordan, of the Reubenites, Gadites, and the half-tribe of Manasseh, men equipped with every kind of weapon of war: one hundred and twenty thousand.

39All these soldiers, drawn up in battle order, came to Hebron with the resolute intention of making David king over all Israel. The rest of Israel was likewise of one mind to make David king. 40They remained with David for three days, eating and drinking, for their relatives had prepared for them. 41Moreover, their neighbors from as far as Issachar, Zebulun, and Naphtali came bring-

12:21 See note on 27:1–15.

12:25–38 The Chronicler here takes the brief account of David's installation as king in 2 Sm 5:1–3 (= 1 Chr 11:1–3) and expands it in line with his exaltation of David and his dynasty.

b: Dt 33:20.

ing food on donkeys, camels, mules, and oxen—provisions in great quantity of meal, pressed figs, raisins, wine, oil, oxen, and sheep. For there was rejoicing in Israel.

CHAPTER 13

See RG 200–203

Transfer of the Ark. 1[c] After David had taken counsel with his commanders of thousands and of hundreds, that is, with every leader, 2he said to the whole assembly of Israel: "If it seems good to you, and is so decreed by the LORD our God, let us send to the rest of our kindred from all the districts of Israel, and also the priests and the Levites from their cities with pasture lands, that they may join us;[d] 3and let us bring the ark of our God here among us, for in the days of Saul we did not consult it." 4And the whole assembly agreed to do it, for it seemed right in the eyes of all the people.

5Then David assembled all Israel, from Shihor of Egypt* to Lebo-hamath, to bring the ark of God from Kiriath-jearim.[e] 6David and all Israel went up to Baalah, that is, to Kiriath-jearim, of Judah, to bring up from there the ark of God, which was known by the name "LORD enthroned upon the cherubim."[f] 7They transported the ark of God on a new cart from the house of Abinadab; Uzzah and Ahio were guiding the cart, 8while David and all Israel danced before God with all their might, with singing, and with lyres, harps, tambourines, cymbals, and trumpets.

9As they reached the threshing floor of Chidon,* Uzzah stretched out his hand to steady the ark, for the oxen were tipping it. 10Then the LORD became angry with Uzzah and struck him, because he had laid his hand on the ark; he died there in God's presence. 11David was angry because the LORD's anger had broken out against Uzzah. Therefore that place has been called Perez-uzzah* even to this day. 12David was afraid of God that day, and he said, "How can I bring in the ark of God to me?" 13Therefore he did not take the ark with him into the City of David, but deposited it instead at the house of Obed-edom the Gittite. 14The ark of God remained in the house of Obed-edom with his family for three months, and the LORD blessed Obed-edom's household and all that he possessed.[g]

CHAPTER 14

See RG 200–203

David in Jerusalem. 1[h] Hiram, king of Tyre, sent envoys to David along with cedar wood, and masons and carpenters to build him a house.*[i] 2David now knew* that the LORD had truly established him as king over Israel, for his kingdom was greatly exalted for the sake of his people Israel. 3David took other wives in Jerusalem and became the father of more sons and daughters. 4These are the names of those who were born to him in Jerusalem: Shammua, Shobab, Nathan, Solomon, 5Ibhar, Elishua, Elpelet, 6Nogah, Nepheg, Japhia, 7Elishama, Beeliada, and Eliphelet.[j]

The Philistine Wars. 8When the Philistines had heard that David was anointed king over all Israel, they marched out in force looking for him. But when David heard of this, he went out against them. 9Meanwhile the Philistines had come and raided the valley of Rephaim.[k] 10David inquired of God, "Shall I attack the Philistines, and will you deliver them into my power?" The LORD answered him, "Attack, for I have delivered them into your power." 11So they attacked, at Baal-perazim, and David defeated them there. Then David said, "By my hand God has broken through my enemies just as water breaks through a dam." Therefore that place was called Baal-perazim.* 12The Philistines abandoned their gods there, and David ordered them to be burnt.[l]

13:5 Shihor of Egypt: the eastern branch of the Nile delta. **Lebo-hamath**: in southern Syria.

13:9 Chidon: in 2 Sm 6:6 the name is Nodan (variant: Nacon).

13:11 Perez-uzzah: this Hebrew phrase means "the breaking out against Uzza."

14:1 The Chronicler's account of David's establishment as king and his victories over the Philistines follows 2 Sm 5:11–25, but makes David's rule even more prominent.

14:2 David now knew: see note on 2 Sm 5:12.

14:11 See note on 2 Sm 5:20.

c: 2 Sm 6:1–11. *d:* Nm 35:1–8; Jos 14:4; 21:2–42. *e:* 1 Chr 15:3; Jos 13:3, 5; 1 Sm 6:21; 7:1–2; 2 Sm 6:1–11. *f:* Jos 15:9; 18:14; 1 Sm 4:4; 7:1. *g:* 1 Chr 26:4–5. *h:* 2 Sm 5:11–25. *i:* 2 Sm 5:11; 2 Chr 2:4. *j:* 1 Chr 3:5–8; 2 Sm 5:13–16. *k:* 1 Chr 11:15. *l:* Dt 7:5, 25.

[13]Once again the Philistines raided the valley, [14]and again David inquired of God. But God answered him: Do not try to pursue them, but go around them and come against them near the balsam trees. [15]When you hear the sound of marching in the tops of the balsam trees, then go forth to battle, for God has already gone before you to strike the army of the Philistines. [16]David did as God commanded him, and they routed the Philistine army from Gibeon to Gezer.

[17]Thus David's fame was spread abroad through every land, and the LORD put the fear of him on all the nations.

CHAPTER 15

See RG 200–203

Preparations for Moving the Ark. [1]David built houses for himself in the City of David and prepared a place for the ark of God, pitching a tent for it there. [2]At that time he said, "No one may carry the ark of God except the Levites, for the LORD chose them to carry the ark of the LORD and to minister to him forever."[m] [3]Then David assembled all Israel to Jerusalem to bring up the ark of the LORD to its place, which he had prepared for it.[n] [4]David also convened the sons of Aaron and the Levites: [5]of the sons of Kohath, Uriel, their chief, and one hundred and twenty of his brothers; [6]of the sons of Merari, Asaiah, their chief, and two hundred and twenty of his brothers; [7]of the sons of Gershon, Joel, their chief, and one hundred and thirty of his brothers; [8]of the sons of Elizaphan, Shemaiah, their chief, and two hundred of his brothers; [9]of the sons of Hebron, Eliel, their chief, and eighty of his brothers; [10]of the sons of Uzziel, Amminadab, their chief, and one hundred and twelve of his brothers.

[11]David summoned the priests Zadok and Abiathar, and the Levites Uriel, Asaiah, Joel, Shemaiah, Eliel, and Amminadab,[o] [12]and said to them: "You heads of the levitical houses, sanctify yourselves along with your brothers to bring up the ark of the LORD, the God of Israel, to the place which I have prepared for it.[p] [13]Because you were not with us the first time, the LORD our God broke out against us, for we did not seek him aright."[q] [14]Accordingly, the priests and the Levites sanctified themselves to bring up the ark of the LORD, the God of Israel. [15]The Levites carried the ark of God on their shoulders with poles, as Moses had commanded according to the word of the LORD.[r]

[16]David commanded the commanders of the Levites to appoint their brothers as singers and to play on musical instruments, harps, lyres, and cymbals, to make a loud sound of rejoicing.[s] [17]Therefore the Levites appointed Heman, son of Joel, and, among his brothers, Asaph, son of Berechiah; and among the sons of Merari, their brothers, Ethan, son of Kushaiah;[t] [18]and, together with these, their brothers of the second rank: the gatekeepers Zechariah, Uzziel, Shemiramoth, Jehiel, Unni, Eliab, Benaiah, Maaseiah, Mattithiah, Eliphelehu, Mikneiah, Obed-edom, and Jeiel. [19]The singers, Heman, Asaph, and Ethan, sounded brass cymbals. [20]Zechariah, Uzziel, Shemiramoth, Jehiel, Unni, Eliab, Maaseiah, and Benaiah played on harps set to "Alamoth."* [21]But Mattithiah, Eliphelehu, Mikneiah, Obed-edom, and Jeiel led the song on lyres set to "sheminith." [22]Chenaniah was the chief of the Levites in the singing; he directed the singing, for he was skillful.[u] [23]Berechiah and Elkanah were gatekeepers before the ark. [24]The priests, Shebaniah, Joshaphat, Nethanel, Amasai, Zechariah, Benaiah, and Eliezer, sounded the trumpets before the ark of God.[v] Obed-edom and Jeiel were also gatekeepers before the ark.

The Ark Comes to Jerusalem. [25][w] Thus David, the elders of Israel, and the commanders of thousands went to bring up the ark of the covenant of the LORD with joy from the house of Obed-edom. [26]While God

15:20–21 Alamoth . . . sheminith: musical terms of uncertain meaning. *Alamoth*, lit., "young women," occurs in the superscription to Ps 46. The term *sheminith*, in v. 21, might mean "bass" or "octave"; cf. Ps 6:1; 12:1.

m: Nm 1:50; 7:9; Dt 10:8; 31:25; 1 Sm 6:15; Jos 3:8. *n:* 1 Chr 13:5; 2 Sm 6:15, 17. *o:* 1 Chr 16:39; 2 Sm 8:17; 15:29, 35. *p:* 2 Chr 29:5, 15, 34; 30:3, 15, 24. *q:* 1 Chr 13:3. *r:* Ex 25:10–22; Nm 1:50; 7:9; 2 Chr 35:3. *s:* 1 Chr 13:8; 16:5; 2 Chr 5:12; 29:25; Neh 12:27. *t:* 1 Chr 6:31–47; 25:1–8. *u:* 1 Chr 26:29. *v:* Nm 10:8; Jos 6:4–8. *w:* 2 Sm 6:12–16.

helped the Levites to carry the ark of the
covenant of the LORD, they sacrificed seven
bulls and seven rams.[x] 27 David was vested in
a robe of fine linen, as were all the Levites
who carried the ark, the singers, and
Chenaniah, the leader of song; David was
also wearing a linen ephod.[y] 28 Thus all Israel
brought up the ark of the covenant of the
LORD with joyful shouting, to the sound of
horns, trumpets, and cymbals, and the music
of harps and lyres. 29 But as the ark of the
covenant of the LORD was entering the City
of David, Michal, daughter of Saul, looked
down from her window, and when she saw
King David leaping and dancing, she despised him in her heart.[z]

CHAPTER 16

See RG 200–203

1 [a] They brought in the ark of God and
set it within the tent which David had
pitched for it.[b] Then they sacrificed burnt offerings and communion offerings to God.
2 When David had finished sacrificing the
burnt offerings and communion offerings,
he blessed the people in the name of the
LORD, 3 and distributed to every Israelite, to
every man and every woman, a loaf of
bread, a piece of meat, and a raisin cake.

David's Directives for the Levites. 4 He
then appointed certain Levites to minister
before the ark of the LORD, to celebrate,
thank, and praise the LORD, the God of Israel.[c] 5 Asaph was their chief, and second to
him were Zechariah, Uzziel, Shemiramoth,
Jehiel, Mattithiah, Eliab, Benaiah, Obed-
edom, and Jeiel. These were to play on harps
and lyres, while Asaph was to sound the
cymbals, 6 and the priests Benaiah and Jahaziel were to be the regular trumpeters before
the ark of the covenant of God.

7 On that same day, David appointed
Asaph and his brothers to sing for the first
time these praises of the LORD:

8 * Give thanks to the LORD, invoke his
name;[d]
make known among the peoples his
deeds.
9 Sing praise, play music;
proclaim all his wondrous deeds.
10 Glory in his holy name;
rejoice, O hearts that seek the LORD!
11 Rely on the mighty LORD;
constantly seek his face.
12 Recall the wondrous deeds he has done,
his signs, and his words of judgment,
13 You sons of Israel, his servants,
offspring of Jacob, the chosen ones!
14 The LORD is our God;
who rules the whole earth.
15 He remembers forever his covenant
the pact imposed for a thousand
generations—
16 Which was made with Abraham,
confirmed by oath to Isaac,
17 And ratified as binding for Jacob,
an everlasting covenant for Israel:
18 "To you will I give the land of Canaan,
your own allotted heritage."
19 When they were few in number,
a handful, and strangers there,
20 Wandering from nation to nation,
from one kingdom to another,
21 He let no one oppress them;
for their sake he rebuked kings:
22 "Do not touch my anointed,
to my prophets do no harm."
23 [e] Sing to the LORD, all the earth,
announce his salvation, day after
day.
24 Tell his glory among the nations;
among all peoples, his wondrous
deeds.
25 For great is the LORD and highly to be
praised;
to be feared above all gods.
26 For the gods of the nations all do
nothing,
but the LORD made the heavens.
27 Splendor and majesty go before him;
power and rejoicing are in his holy
place.

16:8–36 A hymn composed of parts of several psalms: vv. 8–22 = Ps 105:1–15; vv. 23–33 = Ps 96:1–13; vv. 34–36 = Ps 106:1, 47–48. There are minor textual variants between this hymn and the psalms it is drawn from.

x: 2 Sm 6:17; 2 Chr 29:21. *y:* 1 Sm 2:18; 2 Sm 6:14. *z:* 2 Sm 6:20–23. *a:* 2 Sm 6:17–19. *b:* 1 Chr 15:1. *c:* Sir 47:9. *d:* Ps 105:1–15. *e:* Ps 96:1–13.

28 Give to the LORD, you families of
nations,
give to the LORD glory and might;
29 Give to the LORD the glory due his name!
Bring gifts, and come before him;
bow down to the LORD, splendid in
holiness.
30 Tremble before him, all the earth;
the world will surely stand fast, never
to be moved.
31 Let the heavens be glad and the earth
rejoice;
let them say among the nations: The
LORD is king.
32 Let the sea and what fills it resound;
let the plains be joyful and all that is in
them!
33 Then let all the trees of the forest exult
before the LORD, who comes,
who comes to rule the earth.
34 [f] Give thanks to the LORD, who is good,
whose love endures forever;
35 And say, "Save us, O God, our savior,
gather us and deliver us from among
the nations,
That we may give thanks to your holy
name
and glory in praising you."
36 Blessed be the LORD, the God of Israel,
from everlasting to everlasting!
Let all the people say, Amen! Hallelujah.

37 Then David left Asaph and his brothers
there before the ark of the covenant of the
LORD to minister before the ark regularly according to the daily ritual; 38 he also left there
Obed-edom and sixty-eight of his brothers,
including Obed-edom, son of Jeduthun, and
Hosah, to be gatekeepers.[g]
39 But the priest Zadok and his priestly
brothers he left before the tabernacle of the
LORD on the high place at Gibeon,[h] 40 to
make burnt offerings to the LORD on the altar for burnt offerings regularly, morning
and evening, and to do all that is written in
the law of the LORD which he commanded
Israel.[i] 41 With them were Heman and Jeduthun and the others who were chosen and
designated by name to give thanks to the
LORD, "whose love endures forever,"[j] 42 with
trumpets and cymbals for accompaniment,
and instruments for sacred song. The sons of
Jeduthun kept the gate.[k]
43 Then all the people departed, each to
their own homes, and David returned to
bless his household.[l]

CHAPTER 17

See RG 200–203

The Oracle of Nathan. 1 [m] After David
had taken up residence in his house, he said
to Nathan the prophet, "See, I am living in a
house of cedar, but the ark of the covenant of
the LORD is under tentcloth."[n] 2 Nathan
replied to David, "Whatever is in your heart,
go and do, for God is with you."
3 But that same night the word of God
came to Nathan: 4 Go and tell David my servant, Thus says the LORD: It is not you who
are to build the house for me to dwell in.[o]
5 For I have never dwelt in a house, from the
day I brought Israel up, even to this day, but
I have been lodging in tent or tabernacle. 6 As
long as I have wandered about with all Israel,
did I ever say a word to any of the judges of
Israel whom I commanded to shepherd my
people, Why have you not built me a house
of cedar? 7 Now then, speak thus to my servant David, Thus says the LORD of hosts: I
took you from the pasture, from following
the flock, to become ruler over my people Israel.[p] 8 I was with you wherever you went,
and I cut down all your enemies before you.
I will make your name like that of the greatest on the earth. 9 I will assign a place for my
people Israel and I will plant them in it to
dwell there; they will never again be disturbed, nor shall the wicked ever again oppress them, as they did at the beginning,
10 and during all the time when I appointed
judges over my people Israel. And I will subdue all your enemies. Moreover, I declare to
you that the LORD will build you a house:
11 when your days have been completed and
you must join your ancestors, I will raise up
your offspring after you who will be one of
your own sons, and I will establish his king-

f: Ps 106:1, 47–48. *g:* 1 Chr 15:24. *h:* 1 Kgs 3:4. *i:* Ex 29:38–42; Lv 6:9; Nm 28:3, 6; 2 Chr 13:11. *j:* 2 Chr 5:12; 7:3, 6; 20:21; Ezr 3:11. *k:* 2 Chr 29:27. *l:* 2 Sm 6:19–20. *m:* 2 Sm 7:1–29. *n:* 1 Chr 15:1; 2 Sm 5:11. *o:* 1 Chr 28:3; 1 Kgs 8:19. *p:* 1 Sm 16:11.

dom.[q] [12]He it is who shall build me a house, and I will establish his throne forever.[r] [13]I will be a father to him, and he shall be a son to me, and I will not withdraw my favor from him as I withdrew it from the one who was before you;[s] [14]but I will maintain him in my house and in my kingdom forever, and his throne shall be firmly established forever.

[15]In accordance with all these words and this whole vision Nathan spoke to David.

David's Thanksgiving. [16]Then King David came in and sat in the LORD's presence, and said: "Who am I, LORD God, and what is my house, that you should have brought me so far? [17]And yet, even this is too little in your sight, O God! For you have made a promise regarding your servant's house reaching into the future, and you have looked on me as henceforth the most notable of men, LORD God.[t] [18]What more can David say to you? You have known* your servant. [19]LORD, for your servant's sake and in keeping with your purpose, you have done this great thing. [20]LORD, there is no one like you, no God but you, just as we have always heard.[u]

[21]"Is there, like your people Israel, whom you redeemed from Egypt, another nation on earth whom a god went to redeem as his people? You won for yourself a name for great and awesome deeds by driving out the nations before your people.[v] [22]You made your people Israel your own forever, and you, LORD, became their God. [23]Now, LORD, may the promise that you have spoken concerning your servant and his house remain firm forever. Bring about what you have promised, [24]that your name, LORD of hosts, God of Israel, may be great and abide forever, while the house of your servant is established in your presence.

[25]"Because you, my God, have revealed to your servant that you will build him a house, your servant dares to pray before you.[w] [26]Since you, LORD, are truly God and have made this generous promise to your servant, [27]do, then, bless the house of your servant, that it may be in your presence forever—since it is you, LORD, who blessed it, it is blessed forever."[x]

CHAPTER 18

See RG 200–203

David's Victories. [1][y] After this, David defeated the Philistines and subdued them; and he took Gath and its towns away from the Philistines. [2]He also defeated Moab, and the Moabites became David's subjects, paying tribute.

[3]David then defeated Hadadezer, king of Zobah, toward Hamath, who was on his way to set up his victory stele at the river Euphrates. [4]David captured from him one thousand chariots, seven thousand horsemen, and twenty thousand foot soldiers. David hamstrung all the chariot horses, but left one hundred for his chariots.[z] [5]The Arameans of Damascus came to help Hadadezer, king of Zobah, but David also defeated twenty-two thousand of their men in Aram. [6]Then David set up garrisons in the Damascus region of Aram, and the Arameans became David's subjects, paying tribute. Thus the LORD made David victorious in all his campaigns.

[7]David took the golden shields that were carried by Hadadezer's attendants and brought them to Jerusalem. [8]David likewise took away from Tibhath and Cun, cities of Hadadezer, large quantities of bronze; Solomon later used it to make the bronze sea and the pillars and the vessels of bronze.[a]

[9]When Tou, king of Hamath, heard that David had defeated the entire army of Hadadezer, king of Zobah, [10]he sent his son Hadoram to wish King David well and to congratulate him on having waged a victorious war against Hadadezer; for Hadadezer had been at war with Tou. He also brought gold, silver and bronze articles of every sort.[b] [11]These also King David consecrated to the LORD along with all the silver and gold that he had taken from the nations: from Edom, Moab, the Ammonites, the Philistines, and Amalek.

[12]Abishai, the son of Zeruiah, also defeated eighteen thousand Edomites in the

17:18 Known: given David recognition, chosen him, singled him out; cf. Gn 18:19; Ex 33:12; Am 3:2.

q: 2 Sm 7:12–13. *r:* 1 Chr 22:10; 28:6, 10. *s:* 2 Sm 7:14. *t:* 2 Sm 7:19. *u:* Sir 36:4. *v:* Dt 4:7; 2 Sm 7:23. *w:* 2 Sm 7:27. *x:* Nm 22:6. *y:* 2 Sm 8:1–14. *z:* 2 Sm 8:14; Jos 11:6, 9. *a:* 2 Sm 8:8; 1 Kgs 7:15, 23, 27. *b:* 2 Sm 8:10.

Valley of Salt.[c] [13]He set up garrisons in Edom, and all the Edomites became David's subjects. Thus the LORD brought David victory in all his undertakings.

David's Officials. [14d] David was king over all Israel; he dispensed justice and right to all his people. [15]Joab, son of Zeruiah, was in command of the army; Jehoshaphat, son of Ahilud, was chancellor;[e] [16]Zadok, son of Ahitub, and Ahimelech, son of Abiathar, were priests;* Shavsha was scribe;[f] [17]Benaiah, son of Jehoiada, was in command of the Cherethites and the Pelethites; and David's sons were the chief assistants to the king.* [g]

CHAPTER 19

See RG 200–203

Campaigns Against Ammon. [1h] Afterward Nahash, king of the Ammonites, died and his son succeeded him as king. [2]David said, "I will show kindness to Hanun, the son of Nahash, for his father showed kindness to me." Therefore he sent envoys to console him over his father. But when David's servants had entered the land of the Ammonites to console Hanun, [3]the Ammonite princes said to Hanun, "Do you think David is doing this—sending you these consolers—to honor your father? Have not his servants rather come to you to explore the land, spying it out for its overthrow?" [4]So Hanun seized David's servants and had them shaved and their garments cut off halfway at the hips. Then he sent them away. [5]David was told about the men, and he sent word for them to be intercepted, for the men had been greatly disgraced. "Remain at Jericho," the king told them, "until your beards have grown again; then come back here."

[6]When the Ammonites realized that they had put themselves in bad odor with David, Hanun and the Ammonites sent a thousand talents of silver to hire chariots and horsemen from Aram Naharaim, from Aram-maacah, and from Zobah. [7]They hired thirty-two thousand chariots along with the king of Maacah and his army, who came and encamped before Medeba. The Ammonites also assembled from their cities and came out for war.

[8]When David heard of this, he sent Joab and his whole army of warriors against them. [9]The Ammonites marched out and lined up for battle at the entrance of the city, while the kings who had come to their help remained apart in the open field. [10]When Joab saw that there was a battle line both in front of and behind him, he chose some of the best fighters among the Israelites and lined them up against the Arameans; [11]the rest of the army, which he placed under the command of his brother Abishai, then lined up to oppose the Ammonites. [12]And he said: "If the Arameans prove too strong for me, you must come and save me; and if the Ammonites prove too strong for you, I will save you. [13]Hold firm and let us show ourselves courageous for the sake of our people and the cities of our God; and may the LORD do what is good in his sight." [14]Joab therefore advanced with his men to engage the Arameans in battle; but they fled before him. [15]And when the Ammonites saw that the Arameans had fled, they too fled before his brother Abishai, and entered their city. Joab then came to Jerusalem.

[16]Seeing themselves vanquished by Israel, the Arameans sent messengers to bring out the Arameans from beyond the Euphrates, with Shophach, the commander of Hadadezer's army, at their head. [17]When this was reported to David, he gathered all Israel together, crossed the Jordan, and met them. With the army of David drawn up to fight the Arameans, they gave battle. [18]But the Arameans fled before Israel, and David killed seven thousand of their chariot fighters and forty thousand of their foot soldiers; he also put to death Shophach, the commander of the army. [19]When the vassals of Hadadezer saw themselves vanquished by Israel, they made peace with David and became his sub-

18:16 Zadok . . . and Ahimelech, son of Abiathar, were priests: emendation—the Masoretic text here reads "Abimelech," not "Ahimelech"; but 2 Sm 8:17, the Chronicler's source, has "Ahimelech." See note there.

18:17 Chief assistants to the king: according to 2 Sm 8:18, the Chronicler's source here, David's sons were priests. The Chronicler's modification reflects his conviction that only Aaron's descendants could be priests.

c: 2 Sm 8:13; 2 Kgs 14:7. *d:* 2 Sm 8:15–18. *e:* 1 Chr 11:6; 2 Sm 8:16; 1 Kgs 4:3. *f:* 1 Chr 24:3, 6, 31; 2 Sm 8:17. *g:* 1 Chr 11:22; 2 Sm 8:18; 1 Kgs 1:38, 44. *h:* 2 Sm 10:1–19.

jects. After this, the Arameans refused to come to the aid of the Ammonites.

CHAPTER 20

See RG 200–203

1 At the turn of the year,* the time when kings go to war, Joab led the army out in force, laid waste the land of the Ammonites, and went on to besiege Rabbah; David himself remained in Jerusalem. When Joab had attacked Rabbah and destroyed it, 2 David took the crown of Milcom from the idol's head. It was found to weigh a talent of gold, with precious stones on it; this crown David wore on his own head. He also brought out a great amount of spoil from the city. 3 He deported the people of the city and set them to work with saws, iron picks, and axes. David dealt thus with all the cities of the Ammonites. Then David and his whole army returned to Jerusalem.[i]

Victories over the Philistines. 4 [j] Afterward there was another battle with the Philistines, at Gezer. At that time, Sibbecai the Hushathite struck down Sippai, one of the descendants of the Rephaim, and the Philistines were subdued.[k]

5 There was another battle with the Philistines, and Elhanan, the son of Jair, slew Lahmi, the brother of Goliath* of Gath, whose spear shaft was like a weaver's beam.[l]

6 There was another battle, at Gath, and there was a giant, who had six fingers to each hand and six toes to each foot; twenty-four in all. He too was descended from the Rephaim. 7 He defied Israel, and Jonathan, the son of Shimea, David's brother, slew him. 8 These were the descendants of the Rephaim of Gath who died at the hands of David and his servants.

CHAPTER 21

See RG 200–203

David's Census; the Plague. 1 [m] A satan* rose up against Israel, and he incited David to take a census of Israel.[n] 2 David therefore said to Joab and to the other generals of the army, "Go, number the Israelites from Beer-sheba to Dan, and report back to me that I may know their number." 3 But Joab replied: "May the LORD increase his people a hundredfold! My lord king, are not all of them my lord's subjects? Why does my lord seek to do this thing? Why should he bring guilt upon Israel?" 4 However, the king's command prevailed over Joab, who departed and traversed all of Israel, and then returned to Jerusalem. 5 Joab reported the census figures to David: of men capable of wielding a sword, there were in all Israel one million one hundred thousand, and in Judah four hundred and seventy thousand. 6 Levi and Benjamin, however, he did not include in the census, for the king's command was repugnant to Joab.[o] 7 This command was evil in the sight of God, and he struck Israel. 8 Then David said to God, "I have sinned greatly in doing this thing. Take away your servant's guilt, for I have acted very foolishly."

9 Then the LORD spoke to Gad, David's seer, in these words:[p] 10 Go, tell David: Thus says the LORD: I am laying out three options; choose one of them, and I will inflict it on you. 11 Accordingly, Gad went to David and said to him: "Thus says the LORD: Decide now— 12 will it be three years of famine; or three months of fleeing your enemies, with the sword of your foes ever at your back; or three days of the LORD's own sword, a plague in the land, with the LORD's destroying angel in every part of Israel? Now con-

20:1 At the turn of the year: thus in 2 Sm 11 begins the story of David's adultery with Bathsheba and his murder of her husband Uriah, but the Chronicler omits it.

20:5 Elhanan . . . slew Lahmi, the brother of Goliath: with this notice the Chronicler solves the difficulty of the apparent contradiction between 1 Sm 17:49, 51 (David killed Goliath) and 2 Sm 21:19 (Elhanan killed Goliath).

21:1 A satan: in the parallel passage (2 Sm 24:1) David is led astray because of the Lord's anger. The Chronicler's modification reflects the changed theological outlook of postexilic Israel, when evil was no longer attributed directly to God. At an earlier period the Hebrew word *satan* ("adversary," or, especially in a court of law, "accuser") designated both human beings (1 Kgs 11:14) and a "son of God" who accused people before God (Jb 1:6–12; 2:1–7; Zec 3:1–2). In later Judaism (cf. Wis 2:24) and in the New Testament, *satan*, or the "devil" (from *diablos*, the Greek translation of the Hebrew word), designates an evil spirit who tempts people to do wrong.

i: 2 Sm 12:30–31. *j:* 2 Sm 21:18–22. *k:* 1 Chr 11:29; 27:11. *l:* 1 Chr 11:26; 1 Sm 17:4, 23. *m:* 2 Sm 24:1–25. *n:* Zec 3:1–2. *o:* 1 Chr 27:24; Nm 1:49. *p:* 1 Chr 29:29; 1 Sm 9:9; 2 Chr 29:25.

sider: What answer am I to give him who
sent me?" [13]Then David said to Gad: "I am
in serious trouble. But let me fall into the
hand of the LORD, whose mercy is very
great, rather than into hands of men."
[14]Therefore the LORD sent a plague upon
Israel, and seventy thousand Israelites died.
[15]God also sent an angel to Jerusalem to destroy it; but as the angel was on the point of
destroying it, the LORD saw and changed his
mind about the calamity, and said to the destroying angel, "Enough now! Stay your
hand!"[q]

Ornan's Threshing Floor. The angel of the
LORD was then standing by the threshing
floor of Ornan the Jebusite. [16]When David
raised his eyes, he saw the angel of the LORD
standing between earth and heaven, drawn
sword in hand stretched out against Jerusalem.[r] David and the elders, clothed in sackcloth, fell face down, [17]and David prayed to
God: "Was it not I who ordered the census of
the people? I am the one who sinned, I did
this wicked thing. But these sheep, what
have they done? O LORD, my God, strike me
and my father's family, but do not afflict
your people with this plague!"
[18]Then the angel of the LORD commanded
Gad to tell David to go up and set up an altar to the LORD on the threshing floor of Ornan the Jebusite.[s] [19]David went up at the
word of Gad, which he spoke in the name of
the LORD. [20]Ornan turned around and saw
the king; his four sons who were with him
hid themselves, but Ornan kept on threshing
wheat. [21]But as David came toward Ornan,
he looked up and saw that it was David, and
left the threshing floor and bowed down before David, his face to the ground. [22]David
said to Ornan: "Sell me the site of this
threshing floor, that I may build on it an altar to the LORD. Sell it to me at its full price,
that the plague may be withdrawn from the
people." [23]But Ornan said to David: "Take it
as your own, and let my lord the king do
what is good in his sight. See, I also give you
the oxen for the burnt offerings, the threshing sledges for the wood, and the wheat for
the grain offering. I give it all to you." [24]But
King David replied to Ornan: "No! I will
buy it from you properly, at its full price. I
will not take what is yours for the LORD, nor
bring burnt offerings that cost me nothing."
[25]So David paid Ornan six hundred shekels
of gold* for the place.

Altar for Burnt Offerings. [26]David then
built an altar there to the LORD, and sacrificed burnt offerings and communion offerings. He called upon the LORD, who answered him by sending down fire from
heaven upon the altar for burnt offerings.[t]
[27]Then the LORD gave orders to the angel to
return his sword to its sheath.
[28]Once David saw that the LORD had answered him at the threshing floor of Ornan
the Jebusite, he continued to offer sacrifices
there. [29]The tabernacle of the LORD, which
Moses had made in the wilderness, and the
altar for burnt offerings were at that time on
the high place at Gibeon.[u] [30]But David could
not go into his presence to inquire of God,
for he was fearful of the sword of the angel
of the LORD.

CHAPTER 22

See RG 200–203

[1]Thus David said, "This is the house
of the LORD God, and this is the altar for
burnt offerings for Israel."[v] [2]* David then ordered that the resident aliens in the land of
Israel should be brought together, and he appointed them stonecutters to hew out stone
blocks for building the house of God.[w] [3]Da-
vid also laid up large stores of iron to make
nails for the doors of the gates, and clamps,
together with so much bronze that it could
not be weighed,[x] [4]and cedar trees without
number. The Sidonians and Tyrians brought
great stores of cedar logs to David.[y] [5]David

21:25 Six hundred shekels of gold: according to 2 Sm 24:24, David paid only fifty shekels of silver for Ornan's threshing floor; the Chronicler's higher figure reflects the value the site of the future Temple had in his eyes.

22:2–4 According to 1 Kgs 5:15–32, Solomon himself made the material preparations for building the Temple, even though David had wished to do so (1 Kgs 5:17–19). The Chronicler, however, seeks to enhance David's role in the building of the Temple.

q: Gn 6:6; Ex 32:14; 2 Sm 24:16; Jon 3:10. *r:* Jos 5:13. *s:* 2 Chr 3:1. *t:* Lv 9:24; Jgs 6:21; 1 Kgs 18:38; 2 Chr 7:1; 2 Mc 2:10–12. *u:* 1 Chr 16:39; 1 Kgs 8:4; 2 Chr 1:3. *v:* 1 Chr 21:18, 26, 28; 2 Chr 3:1. *w:* 1 Kgs 5:31–32; 9:20–21; 2 Chr 2:16–17. *x:* 1 Chr 18:8; 1 Kgs 7:47. *y:* Ezr 3:7; 2 Chr 2:9.

said: "My son Solomon is young and inexperienced; but the house that is to be built for the LORD must be made so magnificent that it will be renowned and glorious in all lands. Therefore I will make preparations for it." Thus before his death David laid up materials in abundance.[z]

Charge to Solomon. 6 Then he summoned his son Solomon and commanded him to build a house for the LORD, the God of Israel. 7[a] David said to Solomon: "My son, it was my purpose to build a house myself for the name of the LORD, my God. 8 But this word of the LORD came to me: You have shed much blood, and you have waged great wars. You may not build a house for my name, because you have shed too much blood upon the earth in my sight. 9 However, a son will be born to you. He will be a peaceful man, and I will give him rest from all his enemies on every side. For Solomon shall be his name, and in his time I will bestow peace* and tranquility on Israel.[b] 10 It is he who shall build a house for my name; he shall be a son to me, and I will be a father to him,[c] and I will establish the throne of his kingship over Israel forever.

11 "Now, my son, the LORD be with you, and may you succeed in building the house of the LORD your God, as he has said you shall. 12 But may the LORD give you prudence and discernment when he gives you command over Israel, so that you keep the law of the LORD, your God. 13 Only then shall you succeed, if you are careful to observe the statutes and ordinances which the LORD commanded Moses for Israel. Be strong and steadfast; do not fear or be dismayed.[d] 14 See, with great effort I have laid up for the house of the LORD a hundred thousand talents of gold,* a million talents of silver, and bronze and iron in such great quantities that they cannot be weighed. I have also laid up wood and stones, to which you must add.[e] 15 Moreover, you have available workers, stonecutters, masons, carpenters, and experts in every craft, 16 without number, skilled with gold, silver, bronze, and iron. Set to work, therefore, and the LORD be with you!"

Charge to the Officials. 17 David also commanded all of the officials of Israel to help his son Solomon: 18 "Is not the LORD your God with you? Has he not given you rest on every side? Indeed, he has delivered the inhabitants of the land into my power, and the land is subdued before the LORD and his people.[f] 19 Therefore, devote your hearts and souls to seeking the LORD your God. Proceed to build the sanctuary of the LORD God, that the ark of the covenant of the LORD and God's sacred vessels may be brought into the house built for the name of the LORD."[g]

CHAPTER 23

See RG 200–203

The Levitical Divisions. 1 When David had grown old and was near the end of his days, he made his son Solomon king over Israel.[h] 2 He then gathered together all the officials of Israel, along with the priests and the Levites.

3 The Levites thirty years old and above were counted, and their total number was found to be thirty-eight thousand.[i] 4 Of these, twenty-four thousand were to direct the service of the house of the LORD, six thousand were to be officials and judges, 5 four thousand were to be gatekeepers,[j] and four thousand were to praise the LORD with the instruments which [David] had devised for praise. 6 David apportioned them into divisions according to the sons of Levi: Gershon, Kohath, and Merari.[k]

22:9 The Hebrew word for peace, *shalom*, is reflected in the name Solomon, in Hebrew, *Shelomo*. The Chronicler draws a contrast here between Solomon, the "peaceful man," and David, who "waged great wars" (v. 8). David was prevented from building the Temple, not only because his time was taken up in waging war (1 Kgs 5:17), but also because he shed much blood (1 Chr 22:8), thereby making himself, in the Chronicler's view, ritually unfit for the task.

22:14 A hundred thousand talents of gold: about 3,775 tons of gold. **A million talents of silver**: about 37,750 tons of silver. These highly exaggerated figures are intended to stress the inestimable value of the Temple as the center of Israelite worship. More modest figures are given in 1 Kgs 9:14, 28; 10:10, 14.

z: 1 Chr 29:1. *a:* 1 Chr 17:1–14; 28:2–7; 2 Sm 7:1–16; 1 Kgs 5:17–19; 8:17–21. *b:* 2 Sm 12:24. *c:* Heb 1:5. *d:* 1 Chr 28:7, 20; Dt 31:6, 23; Jos 1:6–7, 9; 1 Kgs 2:2–3. *e:* 1 Chr 29:2–5. *f:* 1 Chr 23:25; Jos 21:44; 23:1; 2 Sm 7:1. *g:* 1 Kgs 8:6, 21; 2 Chr 5:7; 6:11. *h:* 1 Chr 28:5; 1 Kgs 1:30. *i:* Nm 4:3, 23, 30, 35, 39, 43, 47; 8:23–26; 2 Chr 31:17. *j:* 1 Chr 9:22. *k:* 1 Chr 6:1, 16–30; 26:1–19; Ex 6:16; Nm 3:17; 26:57.

[7]To the Gershonites belonged Ladan and Shimei. [8]The sons of Ladan: Jehiel the chief, then Zetham and Joel; three in all.[l] [9]The sons of Shimei were Shelomoth, Haziel, and Haran; three. These were the heads of the families of Ladan. [10]The sons of Shimei were Jahath, Zizah, Jeush, and Beriah; these were the sons of Shimei, four in all. [11]Jahath was the chief and Zizah was second to him; but Jeush and Beriah had few sons, and therefore they were classed as a single family, exercising a single office.

[12]The sons of Kohath: Amram, Izhar, Hebron, and Uzziel; four in all.[m] [13]The sons of Amram were Aaron and Moses. Aaron was set apart to be consecrated as most holy, he and his sons forever, to offer sacrifice before the LORD, to minister to him, and to bless in his name forever.[n] [14]As for Moses, however, the man of God, his sons were counted as part of the tribe of Levi. [15]The sons of Moses were Gershom and Eliezer.[o] [16]The sons of Gershom: Shubael the chief.[p] [17]The sons of Eliezer were Rehabiah the chief—Eliezer had no other sons, but the sons of Rehabiah were very numerous. [18]The sons of Izhar: Shelomith the chief. [19]The sons of Hebron: Jeriah, the chief, Amariah, the second, Jahaziel, the third, and Jekameam, the fourth.[q] [20]The sons of Uzziel: Micah, the chief, and Isshiah, the second.[r]

[21]The sons of Merari: Mahli and Mushi. The sons of Mahli: Eleazar and Kish.[s] [22]Eleazar died leaving no sons, only daughters; the sons of Kish, their kinsmen, married them.[t] [23]The sons of Mushi: Mahli, Eder, and Jeremoth; three in all.[u]

[24]These were the sons of Levi according to their ancestral houses, the family heads as they were enrolled one by one according to their names. They performed the work of the service of the house of the LORD beginning at twenty years of age.[v]

[25]David said: "The LORD, the God of Israel, has given rest to his people, and has taken up his dwelling in Jerusalem forever.[w] [26]Henceforth the Levites need not carry the tabernacle or any of the equipment for its service."[x] [27]For by David's last words the Levites were enlisted from the time they were twenty years old. [28]Their duty is to assist the sons of Aaron in the service of the house of the LORD, having charge of the courts, the chambers, and the preservation of everything holy: they take part in the service of the house of God. [29]They also have charge of the showbread, of the fine flour for the grain offering, of the wafers of unleavened bread, and of the baking and mixing, and of all measures of quantity and size.[y] [30]They are to be present every morning to offer thanks and to praise the LORD, and likewise in the evening;[z] [31]and at every sacrifice of burnt offerings to the LORD on sabbaths, new moons, and feast days, in such numbers as are prescribed, they must always be present before the LORD[a] [32]and observe what is prescribed for them concerning the tent of meeting, the sanctuary, and the sons of Aaron, their kinsmen, in the service of the house of the LORD.[b]

CHAPTER 24

See RG 200-203

The Priestly Divisions. [1]There were also divisions for the sons of Aaron. The sons of Aaron were Nadab, Abihu, Eleazar, and Ithamar.[c] [2]Nadab and Abihu died before their father, leaving no sons; therefore only Eleazar and Ithamar served as priests.[d] [3]David, with Zadok, a descendant of Eleazar, and Ahimelech, a descendant of Ithamar, apportioned them their offices in the priestly service.[e] [4]But since the sons of Eleazar were found to be more numerous by male heads than those of Ithamar, the former were divided into sixteen groups, and the latter into eight groups, each under its family heads. [5]Their functions were assigned impartially by lot, for there were officers of the holy place, and officers of God, descended both from Eleazar and from Ithamar. [6]The scribe

24:6 Ahimelech, son of Abiathar: see note on 18:16.

l: 1 Chr 26:21–22; 29:8. *m:* 1 Chr 26:23; Ex 6:18; Nm 3:19; 26:58–61. *n:* 1 Chr 6:49; Ex 6:20; 28:1; Nm 6:23. *o:* Ex 2:22; 18:3–4. *p:* 1 Chr 26:24. *q:* 1 Chr 24:23. *r:* 1 Chr 24:24–25. *s:* 1 Chr 6:29; 24:26, 28–29; Ex 6:19; Nm 3:20, 33. *t:* 1 Chr 24:28–29. *u:* 1 Chr 6:47; 24:30. *v:* 2 Chr 31:17; Ezr 3:8. *w:* 1 Chr 22:18; Ps 132:13. *x:* 1 Chr 15:15; 2 Chr 35:3. *y:* 1 Chr 9:29, 31–32; Lv 2:1, 4–5; 24:5–8. *z:* Nm 28:3–8. *a:* Nm 28:2–29:39. *b:* Nm 3:6–9; 18:2–5. *c:* Ex 6:23; Nm 3:2–4; 26:60. *d:* Lv 10:1–7, 12; Nm 3:2, 4. *e:* 1 Chr 18:16; 2 Sm 8:17; 2 Chr 8:14.

Shemaiah, son of Nethanel, a Levite, recorded them in the presence of the king, and of the officials, of Zadok the priest, and of Ahimelech, son of Abiathar,* and of the heads of the ancestral houses of the priests and of the Levites, listing two successive family groups from Eleazar before each one from Ithamar.[f]

7[g] The first lot fell to Jehoiarib, the second to Jedaiah, 8 the third to Harim, the fourth to Seorim, 9 the fifth to Malchijah, the sixth to Mijamin, 10 the seventh to Hakkoz, the eighth to Abijah,[h] 11 the ninth to Jeshua, the tenth to Shecaniah, 12 the eleventh to Eliashib, the twelfth to Jakim, 13 the thirteenth to Huppah, the fourteenth to Ishbaal, 14 the fifteenth to Bilgah, the sixteenth to Immer, 15 the seventeenth to Hezir, the eighteenth to Happizzez, 16 the nineteenth to Pethahiah, the twentieth to Jehezkel, 17 the twenty-first to Jachin, the twenty-second to Gamul, 18 the twenty-third to Delaiah, the twenty-fourth to Maaziah. 19 This was the appointed order of their service when they functioned in the house of the LORD according to the precepts given them by Aaron, their father, as the LORD, the God of Israel, had commanded him.[i]

Other Levites. 20[j] Of the remaining Levites, there were Shubael, of the sons of Amram, and Jehdeiah, of the sons of Shubael; 21 Isshiah, the chief, of the sons of Rehabiah; 22 Shelomith of the Izharites, and Jahath of the sons of Shelomith. 23 The sons of Hebron were Jeriah, the chief, Amariah, the second, Jahaziel, the third, Jekameam, the fourth. 24 The sons of Uzziel were Micah; Shamir, of the sons of Micah; 25 Isshiah, the brother of Micah; and Zechariah, a descendant of Isshiah. 26 The sons of Merari were Mahli, Mushi, and the sons of his son Uzziah. 27 The sons of Merari through his son Uzziah: Shoham, Zaccur, and Ibri. 28 The sons of Mahli were Eleazar, who had no sons, 29 and Jerahmeel, of the sons of Kish. 30 The sons of Mushi were Mahli, Eder, and Jerimoth.

These were the sons of the Levites according to their ancestral houses. 31 They too, in the same manner as their kinsmen, the sons of Aaron, cast lots in the presence of King David, Zadok, Ahimelech, and the heads of the priestly and levitical families; the more important family did so in the same way as the less important one.[k]

CHAPTER 25

See RG 200–203

The Singers. 1 David and the leaders of the liturgy set apart for the service the sons of Asaph, Heman, and Jeduthun, who prophesied* to the accompaniment of lyres and harps and cymbals.[l]

This is the list of those who performed this service: 2 Of the sons of Asaph: Zaccur, Joseph, Nethaniah, and Asharelah, sons of Asaph, under the direction of Asaph, who prophesied under the guidance of the king. 3 Of Jeduthun, these sons of Jeduthun: Gedaliah, Zeri, Jeshaiah, Shimei, Hashabiah, and Mattithiah; six, under the direction of their father Jeduthun, who prophesied to the accompaniment of a lyre, to give thanks and praise to the LORD. 4 Of Heman, these sons of Heman: Bukkiah, Mattaniah, Uzziel, Shubael, and Jerimoth; Hananiah, Hanani, Eliathah, Giddalti, Romamti-ezer, Joshbekashah, Mallothi, Hothir, and Mahazioth. 5 All these were the sons of Heman, the king's seer for divine matters; to exalt him God gave Heman fourteen sons and three daughters.[m] 6 All these, whether of Asaph, Jeduthun, or Heman, were under their fathers' direction in the singing in the house of the LORD to the accompaniment of cymbals, harps and lyres, serving in the house of God, under the guidance of the king.[n] 7 Their number, together with that of their kinsmen who were trained in singing to the LORD, all of them skilled

25:1 This list of twenty-four classes of Temple singers balances the list of the twenty-four classes of priests (24:4–19). The last nine names in v. 4, which seem to form a special group, were perhaps originally fragments or incipits (the opening words) of hymns. With some slight changes in the vocalization, these names would mean: "Have mercy on me, O LORD," "Have mercy on me," "You are my God," "I magnify," "I extol the help of . . . ," "Sitting in adversity," "I have fulfilled," "He made abundant," and "Visions."

f: 1 Chr 18:16; 2 Sm 8:17. *g:* 1 Chr 9:10–13; Ezr 2:36–38; Neh 7:39–42; 11:10–14. *h:* Lk 1:5. *i:* 2 Chr 23:8. *j:* 1 Chr 23:7–23. *k:* 1 Chr 25:8; 26:13. *l:* 1 Chr 6:16–32; 15:16–17, 19; 16:37; 2 Chr 5:12; 35:15; Neh 12:27, 45. *m:* 2 Chr 35:15. *n:* 1 Chr 15:16.

men, was two hundred and eighty-eight. 8They cast lots for their functions equally, young and old, master and pupil alike.[o]

9The first lot fell to Asaph, to the family of Joseph; he and his sons and his kinsmen were twelve. Gedaliah was the second; he and his kinsmen and his sons were twelve. 10The third was Zaccur, his sons, and his kinsmen: twelve. 11The fourth fell to Izri, his sons, and his kinsmen: twelve. 12The fifth was Nethaniah, his sons, and his kinsmen: twelve. 13The sixth was Bukkiah, his sons, and his kinsmen: twelve. 14The seventh was Jesarelah, his sons, and his kinsmen: twelve. 15The eighth was Jeshaiah, his sons, and his kinsmen: twelve. 16The ninth was Mattaniah, his sons, and his kinsmen: twelve. 17The tenth was Shimei, his sons, and his kinsmen: twelve. 18The eleventh was Uzziel, his sons, and his kinsmen: twelve. 19The twelfth fell to Hashabiah, his sons, and his kinsmen: twelve. 20The thirteenth was Shubael, his sons, and his kinsmen: twelve. 21The fourteenth was Mattithiah, his sons, and his kinsmen: twelve. 22The fifteenth fell to Jeremoth, his sons, and his kinsmen: twelve. 23The sixteenth fell to Hananiah, his sons, and his kinsmen: twelve. 24The seventeenth fell to Joshbekashah, his sons, and his kinsmen: twelve. 25The eighteenth fell to Hanani, his sons, and his kinsmen: twelve. 26The nineteenth fell to Mallothi, his sons, and his kinsmen: twelve. 27The twentieth fell to Eliathah, his sons, and his kinsmen: twelve. 28The twenty-first fell to Hothir, his sons, and his kinsmen: twelve. 29The twenty-second fell to Giddalti, his sons, and his kinsmen: twelve. 30The twenty-third fell to Mahazioth, his sons, and his kinsmen: twelve. 31The twenty-fourth fell to Romamti-ezer, his sons, and his kinsmen: twelve.

CHAPTER 26

See RG 200–203

Divisions of Gatekeepers. 1[p] As for the divisions of gatekeepers: Of the Korahites was Meshelemiah, the son of Kore, one of the sons of Abiasaph. 2Meshelemiah's sons: Zechariah, the firstborn, Jediael, the second son, Zebadiah, the third, Jathniel, the fourth, 3Elam, the fifth, Jehohanan, the sixth, Eliehoenai, the seventh. 4Obed-edom's sons: Shemaiah, the firstborn, Jehozabad, a second son, Joah, the third, Sachar, the fourth, Nethanel, the fifth, 5Ammiel, the sixth, Issachar, the seventh, Peullethai, the eighth, for God blessed him. 6To his son Shemaiah were born sons who ruled over their family, for they were warriors. 7The sons of Shemaiah were Othni, Rephael, Obed, and Elzabad; also his kinsmen who were men of substance, Elihu and Semachiah. 8All these were the sons of Obed-edom, who, together with their sons and their kinsmen, were men of substance, fit for the service. Of Obed-edom, sixty-two. 9Of Meshelemiah, eighteen sons and kinsmen, men of substance.

10Hosah, a descendant of Merari, had these sons: Shimri, the chief (for though he was not the firstborn, his father made him chief),[q] 11Hilkiah, the second son, Tebaliah, the third, Zechariah, the fourth. All the sons and kinsmen of Hosah were thirteen.

12To these divisions of the gatekeepers, by their chief men, were assigned watches for them to minister in the house of the LORD, for each group in the same way. 13They cast lots for each gate, small and large families alike. 14When the lot was cast for the east side, it fell to Meshelemiah. Then they cast lots for his son Zechariah, a prudent counselor, and the north side fell to his lot.[r] 15To Obed-edom fell the south side, and to his sons the storehouse. 16To Hosah fell the west side with the Shallecheth gate at the ascending highway. For each family, watches were established. 17On the east, six watched each day, on the north, four each day, on the south, four each day, and at the storehouse they were two and two; 18as for the large building* on the west, there were four at the highway and two at the large building. 19These were the classes of the gatekeepers, sons of Korah and Merari.

Treasurers. 20Their brother Levites had oversight of the treasuries of the house of

26:18 The large building: *parbar*, mentioned also in 2 Kgs 23:11; the meaning of the word is unclear.

o: 1 Chr 24:31. *p:* 1 Chr 9:19; 2 Chr 8:14; 23:19; 35:15; Neh 12:45. *q:* 1 Chr 16:38. *r:* 1 Chr 9:21.

God and the treasures of votive offerings.[s] 21 Among the sons of Ladan the Gershonite, the family heads were sons of Jehiel:[t] 22 [u] the sons of Jehiel, Zetham and his brother Joel, who oversaw the treasures of the house of the LORD. 23 Of the Amramites, Izharites, Hebronites, and Uzzielites, 24 Shubael, son of Gershom, son of Moses, was principal overseer of the treasures. 25 [v] His associate was of the line of Eliezer, whose son was Rehabiah, whose son was Jeshaiah, whose son was Joram, whose son was Zichri, whose son was Shelomith. 26 This Shelomith and his kinsmen oversaw all the treasures of the votive offerings dedicated by King David, the heads of the families, the commanders of thousands and of hundreds, and the commanders of the army;[w] 27 what came from wars and from spoils, they dedicated for the support of the house of the LORD. 28 Also, whatever Samuel the seer, Saul, son of Kish, Abner, son of Ner, Joab, son of Zeruiah, and all others had consecrated, was under the charge of Shelomith and his kinsmen.

Magistrates. 29 Among the Izharites, Chenaniah and his sons were in charge of Israel's civil affairs* as officials and judges.[x] 30 Among the Hebronites, Hashabiah[y] and his kinsmen, one thousand seven hundred men of substance, had the administration of Israel on the western side of the Jordan for all the work of the LORD and the service of the king. 31 Among the Hebronites, Jerijah was their chief according to their family records. In the fortieth year of David's reign search was made, and there were found among them warriors at Jazer of Gilead.[z] 32 His kinsmen were also men of substance, two thousand seven hundred heads of families. King David appointed them to the administration of the Reubenites, the Gadites, and the half-tribe of Manasseh for everything pertaining to God and to the king.

CHAPTER 27

See RG 200–203

Army Commanders.* 1 This is the list of the Israelite family heads, commanders of thousands and of hundreds, and other officers who served the king in all that pertained to the divisions, of twenty-four thousand men each, that came and went month by month throughout the year.

2 Over the first division for the first month was Ishbaal, son of Zabdiel, and in his division were twenty-four thousand men; 3 a descendant of Perez, he was chief over all the commanders of the army for the first month. 4 Over the division of the second month was Eleazar, son of Dodo, from Ahoh, and in his division were twenty-four thousand men.[a] 5 [b] The third army commander, for the third month, was Benaiah, son of Jehoiada the chief priest, and in his division were twenty-four thousand men. 6 This Benaiah was a warrior among the Thirty and over the Thirty. His son Ammizabad was over his division. 7 Fourth, for the fourth month, was Asahel, brother of Joab, and after him his son Zebadiah, and in his division were twenty-four thousand men.[c] 8 Fifth, for the fifth month, was the commander Shamhuth, a descendant of Zerah, and in his division were twenty-four thousand men. 9 Sixth, for the sixth month, was Ira, son of Ikkesh, from Tekoa, and in his division were twenty-four thousand men. 10 Seventh, for the seventh month, was Hellez, from Beth-pelet, of the Ephraimites, and in his division were twenty-four thousand men. 11 Eighth, for the eighth month, was Sibbecai the Hushathite, a descendant of Zerah, and in his division were twenty-four thousand men.[d] 12 Ninth, for the ninth month, was Abiezer from Anathoth, of Benjamin, and in his division were twenty-four thousand men. 13 Tenth, for the tenth month, was Maharai from Netophah, a descendant of Zerah, and in his division were twenty-four thousand men.

26:29 Civil affairs: lit., "external work," i.e., conduct of affairs external to the Temple.

27:1–15 This list of army commanders is similar to, but distinct from, the list of David's warriors given in 11:10–47. The schematic enumeration of the soldiers presented here appears artificial and exaggerated (12 x 24,000 = 288,000 men!). However, the Hebrew word (*'eleph*) translated "thousand" might also designate a military unit of much smaller size.

s: 1 Chr 28:12; 1 Kgs 7:51. *t:* 1 Chr 23:7–8; 29:8. *u:* 1 Chr 23:8, 12, 16. *v:* 1 Chr 23:17–18; 24:21. *w:* 2 Sm 8:11. *x:* 1 Chr 23:4. *y:* 1 Chr 27:17; Neh 11:15–16. *z:* 1 Chr 23:19; 29:27; Jos 13:25. *a:* 1 Chr 11:12; 2 Sm 23:9. *b:* 1 Chr 11:22–25; 18:17; 2 Sm 23:20–23. *c:* 2 Sm 2:18; 23:24. *d:* 1 Chr 11:29; 20:4; 2 Sm 21:18.

14 Eleventh, for the eleventh month, was Benaiah the Pirathonite, of the Ephraimites, and in his division were twenty-four thousand men. 15 Twelfth, for the twelfth month, was Heldai the Netophathite, of the family of Othniel, and in his division were twenty-four thousand men.

Tribal Leaders. 16 Over the tribes of Israel, for the Reubenites the leader was Eliezer, son of Zichri; for the Simeonites, Shephatiah, son of Maacah; 17 for Levi, Hashabiah, son of Kemuel; for Aaron, Zadok; 18 for Judah, Eliab,[e] one of David's brothers; for Issachar, Omri, son of Michael; 19 for Zebulun, Ishmaiah, son of Obadiah; for Naphtali, Jeremoth, son of Azriel; 20 for the Ephraimites, Hoshea, son of Azaziah; for the half-tribe of Manasseh, Joel, son of Pedaiah; 21 for the half-tribe of Manasseh in Gilead, Iddo, son of Zechariah; for Benjamin, Jaasiel, son of Abner; 22 for Dan, Azarel, son of Jeroham. These were the commanders of the tribes of Israel.

23 David did not count those who were twenty years of age or younger, for the LORD had promised to multiply Israel like the stars of the heavens.[f] 24 Joab, son of Zeruiah, began to take the census, but he did not complete it, for because of it wrath fell upon Israel. Therefore the number was not recorded in the book of chronicles of King David.[g]

Overseers. 25 Over the treasuries of the king was Azmaveth,[h] the son of Adiel. Over the treasuries in the country, the cities, the villages, and the towers was Jonathan, son of Uzziah. 26 Over the farm workers who tilled the soil was Ezri, son of Chelub. 27 Over the vineyards was Shimei from Ramah, and over their produce for the wine cellars was Zabdi the Shiphmite. 28 Over the olive trees and sycamores of the Shephelah was Baal-hanan the Gederite, and over the stores of oil was Joash. 29 Over the cattle that grazed in Sharon was Shitrai the Sharonite, and over the cattle in the valleys was Shaphat, the son of Adlai; 30 over the camels was Obil the Ishmaelite; over the donkeys was Jehdeiah the Meronothite; 31 and over the flocks was Jaziz the Hagrite. All these were the overseers of King David's possessions.

David's Court. 32 Jonathan, David's uncle and a man of intelligence, was counselor and scribe; he and Jehiel, the son of Hachmoni, attended the king's sons. 33 Ahithophel was also the king's counselor, and Hushai the Archite was the king's friend.[i] 34 After Ahithophel* came Jehoiada, the son of Benaiah, and Abiathar. The commander of the king's army was Joab.

CHAPTER 28

See RG 200–203

The Assembly at Jerusalem. 1 David assembled at Jerusalem all the commanders of Israel, the tribal commanders, the commanders of the divisions who were in the service of the king, the commanders of thousands and of hundreds, those in command of all the king's estates and possessions, and his sons, together with the courtiers, the warriors, and every person of substance.[j] 2[k] King David rose to his feet and said: "Hear me, my kinsmen and my people. It was my purpose to build a house of repose myself for the ark of the covenant of the LORD, the footstool for the feet of our God;* and I was preparing to build it. 3 But God said to me, You may not build a house for my name, for you are a man who waged wars and shed blood. 4 However, the LORD, the God of Israel, chose me from all my father's family to be king over Israel forever. For he chose Judah as leader, then one family of Judah, that of my father; and finally, among all the sons of my father, it pleased him to make me king over all Israel.[l] 5 And of all my sons—for the LORD has given me many sons—he has chosen my son Solomon to sit

27:34 After Ahithophel: after Ahithophel's suicide (2 Sm 17:23), Jehoiada succeeded him as the king's counselor. **Abiathar**: David's priest, along with Zadok. See note on 18:16.

28:2 The ark . . . the footstool . . . of our God: the Lord, who was invisibly enthroned upon the cherubim associated with the ark of the covenant at Shiloh and later in the Jerusalem Temple, had the ark as his footstool; cf. Ps 99:5; 132:7. There was no ark in the postexilic Temple. Cf. note on 2 Chr 5:9.

e: 1 Chr 2:13. *f:* Gn 22:17. *g:* 2 Sm 24:10. *h:* 2 Sm 23:31. *i:* 2 Sm 15:12, 32–37; 16:16–19, 23; 17:5–16, 23. *j:* 1 Chr 27:2–22, 25–31; 11:10–47. *k:* 1 Chr 17:4; 22:7–10; 2 Sm 7:5; 1 Kgs 5:3; Ps 132:3–7. *l:* 1 Chr 17:23; Gn 49:8–12; 1 Sm 16:6–13.

on the throne of the LORD's kingship over Israel.[m] 6For he said to me: It is your son Solomon who shall build my house and my courts, for I have chosen him for my son, and I will be a father to him.[n] 7I will establish his kingdom forever, if he perseveres in carrying out my commandments and ordinances as he does now. 8Therefore, in the sight of all Israel, the assembly of the LORD, and in the hearing of our God: keep and carry out all the commandments of the LORD, your God, that you may continue to possess this good land and afterward leave it as an inheritance to your children forever.[o]

9"As for you, Solomon, my son, know the God of your father and serve him with a whole heart and a willing soul, for the LORD searches all hearts and understands all the mind's thoughts. If you search for him, he will be found; but if you abandon him, he will cast you off forever.[p] 10See, then! The LORD has chosen you to build a house as his sanctuary. Be strong and set to work."

Temple Plans Given to Solomon. 11Then David gave to his son Solomon the design of the portico and of the house itself, with its storerooms, its upper rooms and inner chambers, and the shrine containing the cover of the ark.[q] 12He provided also the design for all else that he had in mind by way of courts for the house of the LORD, with the surrounding compartments for the treasuries of the house of God and the treasuries for the votive offerings, 13as well as for the divisions of the priests and Levites, for all the work of the service of the house of the LORD, and for all the liturgical vessels of the house of the LORD. 14He specified the weight of gold to be used in the golden vessels for the various services and the weight of silver to be used in the silver vessels for the various services; 15likewise for the golden menorahs and their lamps he specified the weight of gold for each menorah and its lamps, and for the silver menorahs he specified the weight of silver for each menorah and its lamps, depending on the use to which each menorah was to be put.[r] 16He specified the weight of gold for each table that was to hold the showbread, and the silver for the silver tables; 17the pure gold for the forks, basins, and pitchers; the weight of gold for each golden bowl and the weight of silver for each silver bowl; 18the refined gold, and its weight, to be used for the altar of incense; and, finally, gold to fashion the chariot:* the cherubim spreading their wings and covering the ark of the covenant of the LORD.[s] 19All this he wrote down, by the hand of the LORD, to make him understand it—the working out of the whole design.

20Then David said to his son Solomon: "Be strong and steadfast, and go to work; do not fear or be dismayed, for the LORD God, my God, is with you. He will not fail you or abandon you before you have completed all the work for the service of the house of the LORD.[t] 21The divisions of the priests and Levites are ready for all the service of the house of God; they will be with you in all the work with all those who are eager to show their skill in every kind of craftsmanship. Also the commanders and all the people will do everything that you command."[u]

CHAPTER 29

See RG 200-203

Offerings for the Temple. 1King David then said to the whole assembly: "My son Solomon, whom alone God has chosen, is still young and inexperienced; the work, however, is great, for this palace is not meant for human beings, but for the LORD God.[v] 2For this reason I have stored up for the house of my God, as far as I was able, gold for what will be made of gold, silver for what will be made of silver, bronze for what will be made of bronze, iron for what will be made of iron, wood for what will be made of wood, onyx stones and settings for them, carnelian and mosaic stones, every other kind of precious stone, and great quantities of marble.[w] 3But now, because of the delight

28:18 Chariot: this reference is probably inspired by the vision account in Ez 1:4–24; 10:1–22.

m: 1 Chr 3:1–9; 14:3–7; 22:9; 23:1; Wis 9:7. *n:* 1 Chr 17:11–14; 22:9–10; 2 Sm 7:12–13. *o:* Dt 4:5. *p:* 1 Chr 29:17; 2 Chr 15:2; 1 Kgs 8:61. *q:* Ex 25:9, 40; 26:30. *r:* Ex 25:31–37. *s:* Ex 25:18–22; 30:1–10; 1 Kgs 6:23–28. *t:* 1 Chr 22:13; Jos 1:5. *u:* Ex 36:1–5. *v:* 1 Chr 22:5; 28:5. *w:* 1 Chr 22:14.

I take in the house of my God, in addition to
all that I stored up for the holy house, I give
to the house of my God my personal fortune
in gold and silver: [4]three thousand talents of
Ophir gold, and seven thousand talents of refined silver, for overlaying the walls of the
rooms,[x] [5]for the various utensils to be made
of gold and silver, and for every work that is
to be done by artisans. Now, who else will
contribute generously and consecrate themselves this day to the LORD?"[y]

[6]Then the heads of the families, the tribal
commanders of Israel, the commanders of
thousands and of hundreds, and those who
had command of the king's affairs came forward willingly[z] [7]and contributed for the service of the house of God five thousand talents and ten thousand darics of gold, ten
thousand talents of silver, eighteen thousand
talents of bronze, and one hundred thousand
talents of iron.[a] [8]Those who had precious
stones gave them into the keeping of Jehiel
the Gershonite for the treasury of the house
of the LORD.[b] [9]The people rejoiced over
these free-will offerings, for they had been
contributed to the LORD wholeheartedly.
King David also rejoiced greatly.[c]

David's Prayer. [10]Then David blessed the
LORD in the sight of the whole assembly. David said:

"Blessed are you, LORD,
God of Israel our father,
from eternity to eternity.
[11] Yours, LORD, are greatness and might,
majesty, victory, and splendor.
For all in heaven and on earth is yours;
yours, LORD, is kingship;
you are exalted as head over all.
[12] Riches and glory are from you,
and you have dominion over all.
In your hand are power and might;
it is yours to give greatness and
strength to all.[d]
[13] Therefore, our God, we give you thanks
and we praise the majesty of your name.

[14]"But who am I, and who are my people,
that we should have the means to contribute
so freely? For everything is from you, and
what we give is what we have from you.
[15]For before you we are strangers and travelers, like all our ancestors. Our days on
earth are like a shadow, without a future.[e]
[16]LORD our God, all this wealth that we have
brought together to build you a house for
your holy name comes from you and is entirely yours. [17]I know, my God, that you put
hearts to the test and that you take pleasure
in integrity. With a whole heart I have willingly given all these things, and now with
joy I have seen your people here present also
giving to you generously. [18]LORD, God of
our ancestors Abraham, Isaac, and Israel,[f]
keep such thoughts in the hearts and minds
of your people forever, and direct their
hearts toward you. [19]Give to my son Solomon a wholehearted desire to keep your
commandments, precepts, and statutes, that
he may carry out all these plans and build the
palace for which I have made preparation."

[20]Then David told the whole assembly,
"Now bless the LORD your God!" And the
whole assembly blessed the LORD, the God
of their ancestors, bowing down in homage
before the LORD and before the king. [21]On
the following day they brought sacrifices
and burnt offerings to the LORD, a thousand
bulls, a thousand rams, and a thousand
lambs, together with their libations and
many other sacrifices for all Israel; [22]and on
that day they ate and drank in the LORD's
presence with great rejoicing.

Solomon Anointed. Then for a second
time* they proclaimed David's son Solomon
king, and they anointed him for the LORD as
ruler, and Zadok as priest. [23]Thereafter Solomon sat on the throne of the LORD as king
succeeding his father David; he prospered,
and all Israel obeyed him.[g] [24]All the commanders and warriors, and also all the other
sons of King David, swore allegiance to
King Solomon. [25]And the LORD exalted

29:22 For a second time: the first time is in 23:1 where David appoints Solomon his successor. Now there is a solemn public ratification of that appointment.

x: 2 Chr 9:10; 1 Kgs 9:28; 10:11. *y:* Ex 25:2; 35:5–6. *z:* 1 Chr 27:1, 25–31; 28:1. *a:* Ezr 2:69; 8:27; Neh 7:70–71. *b:* 1 Chr 23:8; 26:21. *c:* 2 Kgs 12:4. *d:* 2 Chr 20:6; Wis 6:3. *e:* Lv 25:23; Wis 2:5; 5:9. *f:* Ex 3:6, 15; 4:5; 1 Kgs 18:36. *g:* 1 Chr 28:5; 2 Chr 9:8; 1 Kgs 2:12.

Solomon greatly in the eyes of all Israel, giving him a glorious reign such as had not been enjoyed by any king over Israel before him.[h]

David's Death. [26]Thus David, the son of Jesse, had reigned over all Israel. [27]He was king over Israel for forty years: he was king seven years in Hebron and thirty-three years in Jerusalem.[i] [28]He died at a ripe old age, rich in years and wealth and glory, and his son Solomon succeeded him as king.[j]

[29]Now the deeds of King David, first and last, are recorded in the history of Samuel the seer, the history of Nathan the prophet, and the history of Gad the seer,[k] [30]together with the particulars of his reign and valor, and of the events that affected him and all Israel and all the kingdoms of the earth.

h: 2 Chr 1:12; 1 Kgs 3:13. *i:* 2 Sm 5:5; 1 Kgs 2:11. *j:* 1 Chr 23:1. *k:* 1 Chr 21:9; 1 Sm 22:5.

See RG 203–7

The Second Book of Chronicles

The Second Book of Chronicles takes up the history of the monarchy where the First Book leaves off. It begins with the account of the reign of Solomon (chaps. 1–9) from the special viewpoint of the Chronicler. The portrait of Solomon is an idealized one; he appears as second only to David. Solomon's building of the Temple and the magnificence of his court are described in detail while the serious defects of his reign as cited in 1 Kings are simply not mentioned. This procedure is in keeping with the Chronicler's purpose of stressing the supreme importance of the Temple and its worship. He wishes to impress on his readers the splendor of God's dwelling and the magnificence of the liturgy of sacrifice, prayer, and praise offered there. Judah's kings are judged by their attitude toward the Temple and its cult. To this ideal of one people, united in the worship of the one true God at the Temple of Jerusalem founded by David and Solomon, the restored community is to conform.

In treating the period of divided monarchy (chaps. 10–36), the Chronicler gives practically all his attention to the kingdom of Judah. His virtual omission of the northern Israelite kings is significant. In his view, the northern tribes of Israel were guilty of religious schism as long as they worshiped the Lord in a place other than the Temple of Jerusalem. The Chronicler makes no mention of the important sanctuaries of Yhwh at Dan and Bethel—as though they had never existed. Nevertheless, he retains the ancient ideal of "all Israel" (a phrase occurring forty-one times in Chronicles) as the people of God. This unity, however, can exist only if the worship of "the whole congregation of Israel" takes place exclusively in the Jerusalem Temple. This requirement explains the Chronicler's praise of Kings Hezekiah and Josiah for striving, after the fall of Samaria, to unite the remnants of the northern tribes of Israel with the kingdom of Judah. Nevertheless, after Josiah's death, Judah quickly careens toward its demise at the hands of the Babylonians. That catastrophe is reversed by the edict of Cyrus allowing a return to Jerusalem and rebuilding of the Temple. Thus 2 Chronicles ends.

The Second Book of Chronicles can be divided into two major segments as follows:

I. The Reign of Solomon (1:1–9:31)
II. The Post-Solomonic Monarchy of Judah (10:1–36:23)

I. The Reign of Solomon

CHAPTER 1

Solomon at Gibeon. [1]Solomon, son of David, strengthened his hold on the kingdom, for the LORD, his God, was with him, making him ever greater. [2]Solomon summoned all Israel, the commanders of thousands and of hundreds, the judges, the princes of all Israel, and the family heads; [3a] and, accompanied by the whole assembly, Solomon went to the high place at Gibeon, because the tent

a: 1 Kgs 3:4–15; 1 Chr 21:29.

of meeting of God, made in the wilderness by Moses, the LORD's servant, was there. [4]David had, however, brought up the ark of God from Kiriath-jearim to Jerusalem, where he had provided a place and pitched a tent for it; [5]the bronze altar made by Bezalel, son of Uri, son of Hur, he put in front of the tabernacle of the LORD.* There Solomon and the assembly sought out the LORD,[b] [6]and Solomon offered sacrifice in the LORD's presence on the bronze altar at the tent of meeting; he sacrificed a thousand burnt offerings upon it.

[7]That night God appeared to Solomon and said to him: Whatever you ask, I will give you. [8]Solomon answered God: "You have shown great favor to David my father, and you have made me king to succeed him. [9]Now, LORD God, may your word to David my father be confirmed, for you have made me king over a people as numerous as the dust of the earth.[c] [10]Give me, therefore, wisdom and knowledge to govern this people, for otherwise who could rule this vast people of yours?" [11]God then replied to Solomon: Because this has been your wish—you did not ask for riches, treasures, and glory, or the life of those who hate you, or even for a long life for yourself, but you have asked for wisdom and knowledge in order to rule my people over whom I have made you king— [12]wisdom and knowledge are given you. I will also give you riches, treasures, and glory, such as kings before you never had, nor will those who come after you.

Solomon's Wealth. [13]Solomon returned to Jerusalem from the high place at Gibeon, from before the tent of meeting, and became king over Israel. [14]Solomon amassed chariots and horses: he had one thousand four hundred chariots and twelve thousand horses; these he allocated among the chariot cities and to the king's service in Jerusalem.[d] [15]The king made silver and gold as common in Jerusalem as stones, and cedars as numerous as the sycamores of the Shephelah.[e] [16]Solomon's horses were imported from Egypt and Cilicia,* where the king's agents purchased them at the prevailing price.[f] [17]A chariot imported from Egypt cost six hundred shekels of silver, a horse one hundred and fifty shekels; so they were exported to all the Hittite and Aramean kings.[g]

Preparations for the Temple. [18]Solomon gave orders for the building of a house for the name of the LORD and also a king's house for himself.

CHAPTER 2

See RG 203

[1]Solomon conscripted seventy thousand men to carry stones and eighty thousand to cut the stones in the mountains, and over these he placed three thousand six hundred overseers.[h] [2][i] Moreover, Solomon sent this message to Huram, king of Tyre: "As you dealt with David my father, and sent him cedars to build a house for his dwelling— [3]now I am going to build a house for the name of the LORD, my God, and to consecrate it to him, for the burning of fragrant incense in his presence, for the perpetual display of the showbread, for burnt offerings morning and evening, and for the sabbaths, new moons, and festivals of the LORD, our God: such is Israel's perpetual obligation.[j] [4]And the house I am going to build must be great, for our God is greater than all other gods. [5]Yet who is really able to build him a house, since the heavens and even the highest heavens cannot contain him? And who am I that I should build him a house,[k] unless it be to offer incense in his presence? [6]Now, send me men skilled at work in gold, silver,

1:5 The bronze altar . . . the tabernacle of the LORD: by this notice, the Chronicler justifies Solomon's worship at the high place of Gibeon. He pictures the tabernacle, i.e., the Mosaic meeting tent, and the bronze altar made at Moses' command (Ex 31:1–9) as remaining at Gibeon after David had installed the ark of the covenant in another tent in Jerusalem (1 Chr 15:1, 25; 16:1). Bezalel's altar was made of acacia wood plated with bronze (Ex 27:1–2). Later, Solomon made an all-bronze altar for the Temple in Jerusalem (2 Chr 4:1).

1:16–17 Egypt and Cilicia: it seems likely that the horses came from Cilicia and the chariots from Egypt. Some scholars find a reference to Musur, a mountain district north of Cilicia, rather than to Egypt (Misrayim) in 1 Kgs 10:28–29, the Chronicler's source for this notice. The Chronicler himself probably understood the source to be speaking of Egypt; cf. 2 Chr 9:28.

b: Ex 27:1–2; 31:2; 1 Chr 2:20. *c:* Gn 13:16; 28:14. *d:* 2 Chr 9:25; 1 Kgs 10:26–29. *e:* 1 Kgs 10:27. *f:* 1 Kgs 10:28. *g:* 1 Kgs 10:29. *h:* 2 Chr 2:17; 5:29–30. *i:* 1 Kgs 5:15–20; 1 Chr 14:1. *j:* Lv 24:5–8; Nm 28–29. *k:* 2 Chr 6:18.

bronze, and iron, in purple, crimson, and violet fabrics, and who know how to do engraved work, to join the skilled craftsmen who are with me in Judah and Jerusalem, whom David my father appointed. [7]Also send me boards of cedar, cypress and cabinet wood from Lebanon, for I realize that your servants know how to cut the wood of Lebanon. My servants will work with yours [8]in order to prepare for me a great quantity of wood, since the house I intend to build must be great and wonderful. [9]I will furnish as food for your servants, the woodcutters, twenty thousand kors of wheat, twenty thousand kors of barley, twenty thousand baths of wine, and twenty thousand baths of oil."* [l]

[10]Huram, king of Tyre, wrote an answer which he sent to Solomon: "Because the LORD loves his people, he has placed you over them as king." [11]He added: "Blessed be the LORD, the God of Israel, who made heaven and earth, for having given King David a wise son of intelligence and understanding, who will build a house for the LORD and also his own royal house.[m] [12n] I am now sending you a craftsman of great skill, Huram-abi, [13]son of a Danite woman* and of a father from Tyre; he knows how to work with gold, silver, bronze, and iron, with stone and wood, with purple, violet, fine linen, and crimson, and also how to do all kinds of engraved work and to devise every type of design that may be given him and your craftsmen and the craftsmen of my lord David your father. [14o] And now, let my lord send to his servants the wheat, barley, oil, and wine which he has promised. [15]For our part, we will cut trees on Lebanon, as many as you need, and send them down to you in rafts to the port of Joppa, whence you may take them up to Jerusalem."[p]

[16q] Thereupon Solomon took a census of all the alien men resident in the land of Israel (following the census David his father had taken of them); they were found to number one hundred fifty-three thousand six hundred. [17]Of these he made seventy thousand carriers and eighty thousand cutters in the mountains, and three thousand six hundred overseers to keep the people working.[r]

CHAPTER 3

See RG 203

Building of the Temple. [1s] Then Solomon began to build the house of the LORD in Jerusalem on Mount Moriah,* which had been shown to David his father, in the place David had prepared, the threshing floor of Ornan the Jebusite. [2]He began to build in the second month of the fourth year of his reign. [3]These were the specifications laid down by Solomon for building the house of God: the length was sixty cubits according to the old measure, and the width was twenty cubits;[t] [4]the front porch along the width of the house was also twenty cubits, and it was twenty cubits high.* He covered its interior with pure gold.[u] [5]The nave he overlaid with cypress wood and overlaid that with fine gold, embossing on it palms and chains.[v] [6]He also covered the house with precious stones for splendor; the gold was from Parvaim. [7]The house, its beams and thresholds, as well as its walls and its doors, he overlaid with gold, and he engraved cherubim upon the walls. [8]He also made the room of the holy of holies. Its length corresponded to the width of the house, twenty cubits, and its width was also twenty cubits. He overlaid it with

2:9 There is probably some exaggeration here. The parallel passage in 1 Kgs 5:25 does not list the barley or the wine, and mentions only twenty kors of olive oil. **Kors**: see note on Ez 45:14; **baths**: see note on Is 5:10. The amount given in Chronicles would be one hundred times as much (20,000 baths equals 2,000 kors).

2:13 A Danite woman: in 1 Kgs 7:14 she is called a widow of the tribe of Naphtali. The Danites had settled in the northern section of Naphtali's territory (Jgs 18:27–29). Bezalel, the head artisan in the time of Moses, had as his assistant a member of the tribe of Dan (Ex 31:6).

3:1 Mount Moriah: Gn 22:2 speaks of a "height in the land of Moriah." This is the only place in the Bible where the Temple mount is identified with the site where Abraham was to have sacrificed Isaac.

3:4 The front porch . . . twenty cubits high: this figure, not given in 1 Kgs 7, is based on a variant Greek text that may be due to a later revision. The Hebrew text itself has "one hundred and twenty cubits high." The Chronicler nearly doubles the height of the two free-standing columns adjacent to the porch in 2 Chr 3:15 as compared with the source, 1 Kgs 7:15–16.

l: 1 Kgs 5:25; Ezr 3:7. *m:* 1 Kgs 5:21. *n:* Ex 31:1–5; 1 Kgs 7:13–14. *o:* 1 Kgs 5:22–26. *p:* Ezr 3:7. *q:* 1 Chr 22:2. *r:* 2 Chr 2:1. *s:* Gn 22:2; 1 Kgs 6:1; 1 Chr 21:22–26; 22:1. *t:* 1 Kgs 6:2. *u:* 1 Kgs 6:3. *v:* 1 Kgs 6:15; Ez 41:1.

fine gold to the amount of six hundred talents.[w] [9]The weight of the nails was fifty gold shekels. The upper chambers he likewise overlaid with gold.

[10x] For the room of the holy of holies he made two cherubim of carved workmanship, which were then covered with gold. [11]The wings of the cherubim spanned twenty cubits: one wing of each cherub, five cubits in length, extended to a wall of the house, while the other wing, also five cubits in length, touched the corresponding wing of the other cherub. [12]The wing of the cherub, five cubits, touched the wall of the house, and the other wing, five cubits, was joined to the wing of the other cherub. [13]The combined wingspread of the two cherubim was thus twenty cubits. They stood upon their own feet, facing toward the nave. [14]He made the veil* of violet, purple, crimson, and fine linen, and had cherubim embroidered upon it.[y]

[15z] In front of the house he set two columns thirty-five cubits high; the capital of each was five cubits. [16]He devised chains in the form of a collar with which he encircled the capitals of the columns, and he made a hundred pomegranates which he set on the chains. [17]He set up the columns to correspond with the nave, one for the right side and the other for the left, and he called the one to the right Jachin and the one to the left Boaz.

CHAPTER 4

See RG 203

[1]Then he made a bronze altar twenty cubits long, twenty cubits wide and ten cubits high.[a] [2b] He also made the molten sea. It was made with a circular rim, and measured ten cubits across, five in height, and thirty in circumference. [3]Under the brim a ring of figures of oxen* encircled it for ten cubits, all the way around the compass of the sea; there were two rows of oxen cast in one mold with the sea. [4]This rested on twelve oxen, three facing north, three facing west, three facing south, and three facing east, with their haunches all toward the center; upon them was set the sea. [5]It was a handbreadth thick, and its brim resembled that of a cup, being lily-shaped. It had a capacity of three thousand baths.*

[6]Then he made ten basins for washing, placing five of them to the right and five to the left. In these the victims for the burnt offerings were washed; but the sea was for the priests to wash in.[c]

[7]He made the menorahs of gold, ten of them as was prescribed, and placed them in the nave, five to the right and five to the left.[d] [8]He made ten tables and had them set in the nave, five to the right and five to the left; and he made a hundred golden bowls.[e] [9]He made the court of the priests and the great courtyard[f] and the gates of the courtyard; the gates he covered with bronze. [10]The sea he placed off to the southeast from the south side of the house.[g]

[11h] When Huram had made the pots, shovels, and bowls, he finished all his work for King Solomon in the house of God: [12]two columns; two nodes for the capitals on top of the columns; and two pieces of netting covering the two nodes for the capitals on top of the columns; [13]four hundred pomegranates in double rows on both pieces of netting that covered the two nodes of the capitals on top of the columns. [14]He made the stands, and the basins on the stands; [15]one sea, and the twelve oxen under it; [16]pots, shovels, forks, and all the articles Huram-abi made for King Solomon for the house of the LORD; they were of burnished bronze. [17]The king had them cast in the neighborhood of the Jordan, between Succoth and Zeredah, in thick clay molds. [18]Solomon made all these vessels, so

3:14 The veil: this was suspended at the entrance of the holy of holies, in imitation of the veil of the Mosaic meeting tent (Ex 26:31–32). Solomon's Temple had doors at this point, according to 1 Kgs 6:31. Apparently the Temple of the Chronicler's time did have a veil, just as did Herod's Temple (Mt 27:51; Mk 15:38; Lk 23:45).

4:3 Oxen: in 1 Kgs 7:24 this double row of ornaments is described as consisting of gourds. The text of Kings available to the Chronicler may have been corrupt at this point since the two words sound similar in Hebrew. In 4:16 the Chronicler speaks of forks while 1 Kgs 7:40 refers to bowls.

4:5 Three thousand baths: two thousand baths according to 1 Kgs 7:26; see note on 1 Kgs 7:23–26.

w: 1 Kgs 6:16–17, 20. *x:* 1 Kgs 6:23–27. *y:* Mt 27:51. *z:* 1 Kgs 7:15–20; Ez 40:49. *a:* Ez 43:13–17. *b:* 1 Kgs 7:23–26. *c:* 1 Kgs 7:38–39; Ez 40:38. *d:* 1 Kgs 7:49. *e:* 1 Kgs 7:50; 1 Chr 28:16. *f:* 1 Kgs 7:12. *g:* 1 Kgs 7:39. *h:* 1 Kgs 7:40–51.

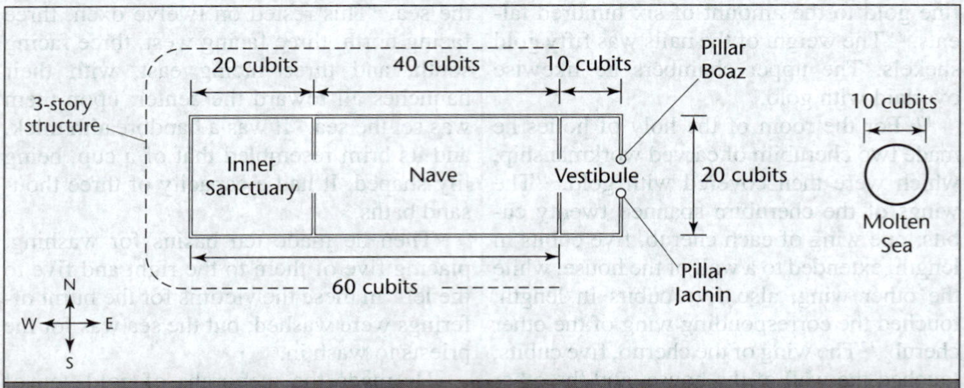

The Temple of Solomon according to 2 Chronicles

many in number that the weight of the
bronze could not be determined.
[19]Solomon made all the articles that were
for the house of God: the golden altar, the tables on which the showbread lay, [20]the
menorahs and their lamps of pure gold
which were to burn as prescribed before the
inner sanctuary, [21]flowers, lamps, and gold
tongs (this was of purest gold), [22]snuffers,
bowls, cups, and firepans of pure gold. As
for the entrance to the house, its inner doors
to the holy of holies, as well as the doors to
the nave of the temple, were of gold.

CHAPTER 5

See RG 203

Dedication of the Temple. [1i] When all
the work undertaken by Solomon for the
house of the LORD was completed, he brought
in the votive offerings of David his father,
putting the silver, the gold, and other articles
in the treasuries of the house of God. [2]Then
Solomon assembled the elders of Israel and
all the heads of the tribes, the princes in the
ancestral houses of the Israelites, to Jerusalem to bring up the ark of the LORD's covenant from the City of David, which is Zion.
[3]All the people of Israel assembled before the
king during the festival of the seventh
month.* [4j] When all the elders of Israel had arrived, the Levites* took up the ark; [5]and they
brought up the ark and the tent of meeting
with all the sacred vessels that were in the
tent. The levitical priests brought them up.
[6]King Solomon and the entire community
of Israel, gathered for the occasion before
the ark, sacrificed sheep and oxen too many
to number or count. [7]The priests brought the
ark of the covenant of the LORD to its place:
the inner sanctuary of the house, the holy of
holies, beneath the wings of the cherubim.
[8]The cherubim had their wings spread out
over the place of the ark, covering the ark
and its poles from above. [9]The poles were so
long that their ends could be seen from the
holy place in front of the inner sanctuary.
(They cannot be seen from outside, but they
remain there to this day.)* [10]There was nothing in the ark but the two tablets which Moses had put there at Horeb when the LORD
made a covenant with the Israelites after
they went forth from Egypt.
[11]When the priests left the holy place (all
the priests who were present had purified
themselves regardless of the rotation of their
various divisions), [12]the Levites who were
singers, all who belonged to Asaph, Heman,

5:3 Festival of the seventh month: feast of Booths (Tabernacles); cf. notes on 7:9–10; 1 Kgs 8:2.

5:4 The Levites: the parallel passage in 1 Kgs 8:3 reads "the priests"; but in 2 Chr 5:5 the Deuteronomic expression "levitical priests" is used, as it is in 23:18; 30:27.

5:9 They remain there to this day: the Chronicler must have copied this notice from his source (1 Kgs 8:8), losing sight of the fact that there was no ark in the Temple of his own day. (According to 2 Mc 2:4–8, the ark of Solomon's Temple was concealed by Jeremiah at the time of the Babylonian destruction of Jerusalem.)

i: 1 Kgs 7:51–8:13. *j*: 2 Chr 35:3.

Jeduthun, and their sons and brothers, clothed in fine linen, with cymbals, harps, and lyres, stood east of the altar, and with them a hundred and twenty priests blowing trumpets.

13 When the trumpeters and singers were heard as a single voice praising and giving thanks to the LORD, and when they raised the sound of the trumpets, cymbals, and other musical instruments to "Praise the LORD, who is so good, whose love endures forever," the cloud filled the house of the LORD.[k] 14 The priests could no longer minister because of the cloud, since the glory of the LORD had filled the house of God.[l]

CHAPTER 6

See RG 203

1[m] Then Solomon said:

"The LORD intends to dwell in the dark cloud;
2 I have built you a princely house,
the base for your enthronement forever."

3[n] The king turned and blessed the whole assembly of Israel, while the whole assembly of Israel stood. 4 He said: "Blessed be the LORD, the God of Israel, who with his own mouth spoke a promise to David my father and by his hand fulfilled it, saying: 5 Since the day I brought my people out of the land of Egypt, I have not chosen a city out of any tribe of Israel for the building of a house, that my name might be there; nor have I chosen any man to be ruler of my people Israel; 6 but now I have chosen Jerusalem, that my name may be there, and I have chosen David* to rule my people Israel. 7 When David my father wished to build a house for the name of the LORD, the God of Israel, 8 the LORD said to him: In wishing to build a house for my name, you did well. 9 But it is not you who will build the house, but your son, who comes from your loins: he shall build the house for my name.

10 "Now the LORD has fulfilled the word he spoke. I have succeeded David my father, and I sit on the throne of Israel, as the LORD has said, and I have built this house for the name of the LORD, the God of Israel. 11 I have placed there the ark, in which is the covenant of the LORD that he made with the Israelites."

Solomon's Prayer. 12[o] Then he stood before the altar of the LORD in the presence of the whole assembly of Israel and stretched forth his hands. 13* Solomon had made a bronze platform five cubits long, five cubits wide, and three cubits high, which he had placed in the middle of the courtyard. Having ascended it, Solomon knelt in the presence of the whole assembly of Israel and stretched forth his hands toward heaven. 14 He said: "LORD, God of Israel, there is no God like you in heaven or on earth; you keep the covenant and love toward your servants who walk before you with their whole heart, 15 the covenant that you kept toward your servant, David my father. That which you promised him, your mouth has spoken and your hand has fulfilled this very day. 16 And now, LORD, God of Israel, keep toward your servant, David my father, what you promised: There shall never be wanting someone from your line to sit before me on the throne of Israel, provided that your descendants keep to their way, walking by my law, as you have. 17 Now, LORD, God of Israel, may the words which you spoke to David your servant be confirmed.

18 "Is God indeed to dwell with human beings on earth? If the heavens and the highest heavens cannot contain you, how much less this house which I have built! 19 Regard kindly the prayer and petition of your servant, LORD, my God, and listen to the cry of supplication which I, your servant, utter before you. 20 May your eyes be open day and night toward this house, the place where you have decreed your name shall be; listen to the prayer your servant makes toward this place. 21 Listen to the petition of your servant and of

6:6 Jerusalem . . . David: Ps 132:11, 13 puts in parallel the Lord's choice of David and Zion, the royal house of David and the mountain in Jerusalem as the site for the Lord's house.

6:13 This verse has no equivalent in 1 Kgs 8:22–23, the Chronicler's source. Solomon is depicted as praying on "a bronze platform . . . in the middle of the courtyard" because in the time of the Chronicler only priests were permitted to pray before the altar.

k: Ps 136; Jer 33:11. *l:* 2 Chr 7:2; 1 Kgs 8:10–11. *m:* 1 Kgs 8:12–13. *n:* 1 Kgs 8:14–21. *o:* 1 Kgs 8:22–53.

your people Israel which they offer toward this place. Listen, from the place of your enthronement, heaven, and listen and forgive.

22“If someone sins against a neighbor and is required to take an oath sanctioned by a curse, and comes and takes the oath before your altar in this house, 23listen in heaven: act and judge your servants. Condemn the wicked, requiting their ways; acquit the just, rewarding their justice. 24When your people Israel are defeated by an enemy because they have sinned against you, and then they turn, praise your name, pray to you, and entreat you in this house, 25listen from heaven and forgive the sin of your people Israel, and bring them back to the land you gave them and their ancestors. 26When the heavens are closed so that there is no rain, because they have sinned against you, but they pray toward this place and praise your name, and turn from their sin because you have afflicted them, 27listen in heaven and forgive the sin of your servants, your people Israel. (For you teach them the good way in which they should walk.) Give rain upon this land of yours which you have given to your people as their heritage.

28“If there is famine in the land or pestilence; or if blight comes, or mildew, or locusts swarm, or caterpillars; when their enemies besiege them at any of their gates; whatever plague or sickness there may be; 29whatever prayer of petition any may make, any of your people Israel, who know affliction and pain and stretch out their hands toward this house, 30listen from heaven, the place of your enthronement, and forgive. Render to each and all according to their ways, you who know every heart; for it is you alone who know the heart of every human being. 31So may they revere you and walk in your ways as long as they live on the land you gave our ancestors.

32“To the foreigners, likewise, who are not of your people Israel, but who come from a distant land for the sake of your great name, your mighty hand and outstretched arm, and come in prayer to this house, 33listen from heaven, the place of your enthronement. Do all that the foreigner asks of you, that all the peoples of the earth may know your name, may revere you as do your people Israel, and may know that your name has been invoked upon this house that I have built.

34“When your people go out to war against their enemies, by whatever way you send them, and they pray to you toward the city you have chosen and the house I have built for your name, 35listen from heaven to their prayer and petition, and uphold their cause. 36When they sin against you (for there is no one who does not sin), and in your anger against them you deliver them to an enemy, so that their captors carry them off to another land, far or near, 37and they have a change of heart in the land of their captivity and they turn and entreat you in the land of their captors and say, ‘We have sinned and done wrong; we have been wicked,’ 38if with all their heart and soul they turn back to you in the land of those who took them captive, and pray toward their land which you gave their ancestors, the city you have chosen, and the house which I have built for your name, 39listen from heaven, the place of your enthronement, to their prayer and petitions, and uphold their cause. Forgive your people who have sinned against you. 40Now, my God, may your eyes be open and your ears be attentive to the prayer of this place. 41And now:

“Arise, LORD God, come to your resting place,
you and your majestic ark.
Your priests, LORD God, will be clothed with salvation,
your faithful ones rejoice in good things.
42 LORD God, do not reject the plea of your anointed,
remember the devotion of David, your servant.”[p]

CHAPTER 7

See RG 203

1[q] When Solomon had ended his prayer, fire came down from heaven and consumed the burnt offerings and the sacrifices, and the glory of the LORD filled the

p: Ps 132:8–10. *q:* Jgs 6:21; 1 Kgs 8:54–66; 1 Chr 21:26; 2 Mc 2:10.

house. [2]But the priests could not enter the
house of the LORD, for the glory of the LORD
filled the house of the LORD.[r] [3]All the Israelites looked on while the fire came down and
the glory of the LORD was upon the house,
and they fell down upon the pavement with
their faces to the earth and worshiped, praising the LORD, "who is so good, whose love
endures forever." [4]The king and all the people offered sacrifices before the LORD.[s]
[5]King Solomon offered as sacrifice twenty-
two thousand oxen, and one hundred twenty
thousand sheep.[t]

End of the Dedication. Thus the king and
all the people dedicated the house of God.
[6]The priests were standing at their stations,
as were the Levites, with the musical instruments of the LORD which King David had
made to give thanks to the LORD, "whose
love endures forever," when David offered
praise through them. The priests opposite
them blew the trumpets and all Israel stood.[u]

[7]Then Solomon consecrated the middle of
the court facing the house of the LORD; he
offered there the burnt offerings and the fat
of the communion offerings, since the
bronze altar which Solomon had made could
not hold the burnt offering, the grain offering, and the fat.[v]

[8]On this occasion Solomon and with him
all Israel, a great assembly from Lebo-hamath to the Wadi of Egypt, celebrated the
festival for seven days.[w] [9][x] On the eighth day
they held a solemn assembly, for they had
celebrated the dedication of the altar for
seven days and the feast* for seven days.
[10]On the twenty-third day of the seventh
month he dismissed the people to their tents,
rejoicing and glad of heart because of all the
blessings the LORD had given to David, to
Solomon, and to his people Israel. [11][y] Solomon finished building the house of the
LORD, the house of the king, and everything
else he wanted to do in regard to the house of
the LORD and his own house.

God's Promise to Solomon. [12]The LORD
appeared to Solomon during the night and
said to him: I have heard your prayer, and I
have chosen this place for my house of sacrifice. [13]If I close heaven so that there is no
rain, if I command the locust to devour the
land, if I send pestilence among my people,
[14]if then my people, upon whom my name
has been pronounced, humble themselves
and pray, and seek my face and turn from
their evil ways, I will hear them from heaven
and pardon their sins and heal their land.
[15]Now, therefore, my eyes shall be open and
my ears attentive to the prayer of this place;
[16]now I have chosen and consecrated this
house that my name may be there forever;
my eyes and my heart shall be there always.

[17]As for you, if you walk before me as David your father did, doing all that I have
commanded you and keeping my statutes
and ordinances, [18]I will establish the throne
of your kingship as I covenanted with David
your father when I said, There shall never be
wanting someone from your line as ruler in
Israel. [19]But if ever you turn away and forsake my commandments and statutes which
I set before you, and proceed to serve other
gods, and bow down to them, [20]I will uproot
the people from the land I gave and repudiate the house I have consecrated for my
name. I will make it a proverb and a byword
among all nations. [21]And this house which is
so exalted—every passerby shall be horrified and ask: "Why has the LORD done such
things to this land and to this house?" [22]And
the answer will come: "Because they abandoned the LORD, the God of their ancestors,
who brought them out of the land of Egypt,
and they embraced other gods, bowing down
to them and serving them. That is why he has
brought upon them all this evil."

7:9–10 The feast: Booths, celebrated on the fifteenth day of the seventh month and followed by a solemn octave lasting through the twenty-second day (Lv 23:33–36; Nm 29:12–35); the people are therefore sent home on the twenty-third day of the month (v. 10). The festival (v. 8) marking the dedication of the altar and of the Temple was held during the seven days prior to the feast of Booths, i.e., from the seventh to the fourteenth day of the seventh month. According to 1 Kgs 8:3, 65–66 the dedication of the Temple was celebrated concomitantly with the seven days of the feast of Booths, after which the people were dismissed on the eighth day.

r: 2 Chr 5:14; Ex 24:16; 1 Kgs 8:10–11. *s:* 2 Chr 5:13; 1 Kgs 8:62; Ps 136:1. *t:* 1 Kgs 8:63. *u:* Nm 10:8, 10; Ps 136:1. *v:* 1 Kgs 8:64. *w:* 1 Kgs 8:65. *x:* 1 Kgs 8:66. *y:* 1 Kgs 9:1–9.

CHAPTER 8

See RG 203

Public Works. [1][z] After the twenty years during which Solomon built the house of the LORD and his own house, [2]he built up the cities which Huram had given him,* and settled Israelites there. [3]Then Solomon went to Hamath of Zoba and conquered it. [4]He built Tadmor* in the wilderness and all the supply cities, which he built in Hamath. [5][a] He built Upper Beth-horon and Lower Beth-horon, fortified cities with walls, gates, and bars; [6]also Baalath, all the supply cities belonging to Solomon, and all the cities for the chariots, the cities for horses, and whatever else Solomon desired to build in Jerusalem, in Lebanon, and in the entire land under his dominion. [7]All the people who were left of the Hittites, Amorites, Perizzites, Hivites, and Jebusites who were not Israelites—[8]those of their descendants who were left in the land and whom the Israelites had not destroyed—Solomon conscripted as forced laborers, as they are to this day. [9]But Solomon made none of the Israelites forced laborers for his works, for they were his fighting force, commanders, adjutants, chariot officers, and cavalry. [10]They were also King Solomon's two hundred and fifty overseers who directed the people.

Solomon's Piety. [11]Solomon brought the daughter of Pharaoh up from the City of David to the house which he had built for her, for he said, "No wife of mine shall dwell in the house of David, king of Israel, for the places where the ark of the LORD has come are holy."

[12]In those times Solomon sacrificed burnt offerings to the LORD upon the altar of the LORD which he had built in front of the porch, [13]as was required to be done day by day according to the command of Moses, especially on the sabbaths, at the new moons, and on the fixed festivals three times a year: on the feast of the Unleavened Bread, the feast of Weeks, and the feast of Booths.[b] [14]And according to the ordinance of David his father he appointed the various divisions of the priests for their service, and the Levites according to their functions of praise and attendance upon the priests, as the daily duty required. The gatekeepers by their divisions stood guard at each gate, since such was the command of David, the man of God.[c] [15]There was no deviation from the king's command in whatever related to the priests and Levites or the treasuries. [16]All of Solomon's work was carried out successfully from the day the foundation of the house of the LORD was laid until its completion. The house of the LORD was finished.

Glories of the Court. [17]In those times Solomon went to Ezion-geber and to Elath on the seashore of the land of Edom.[d] [18]Huram had his servants send him ships and his own servants, expert seamen; they went with Solomon's servants to Ophir, and obtained there four hundred and fifty talents of gold and brought it to King Solomon.[e]

CHAPTER 9

See RG 203

The Queen of Sheba. [1][f] The queen of Sheba, having heard a report of Solomon's fame, came to Jerusalem to test him with subtle questions, accompanied by a very numerous retinue and by camels bearing spices, a large amount of gold, and precious stones. She came to Solomon and spoke to him about everything that she had on her mind. [2]Solomon explained to her everything she asked about, and there was nothing so obscure that Solomon could not explain it to her.[g]

[3][h] When the queen of Sheba witnessed Solomon's great wisdom, the house he had built, [4]the food at his table, the seating of his ministers, the attendance and dress of his

8:2 The cities which Huram had given him: according to 1 Kgs 9:10–14, it was Solomon who ceded the cities to the king of Tyre as payment for the timber and gold received from him. Since, however, 1 Kgs 9:12 states that Hiram was not satisfied with the cities, the Chronicler may have inferred that he gave them back to Solomon.

8:4 Tadmor: later known as Palmyra, an important caravan city in the Syrian desert. The parallel passage in 1 Kgs 9:18 has "Tamar," in southern Judah; cf. Ez 47:19; 48:28. But Solomon may well have fortified Tadmor against the Arameans.

z: 1 Kgs 9:10–11. *a:* 1 Kgs 9:17–25. *b:* Ex 23:14; Nm 28–29; 1 Kgs 9:25. *c:* 1 Chr 23–26; Neh 12:46. *d:* 1 Kgs 9:26. *e:* 1 Kgs 9:27–28. *f:* 1 Kgs 10:1–2. *g:* 1 Kgs 10:3. *h:* 1 Kgs 10:4–9.

waiters, his cupbearers and their dress, and the burnt offerings he sacrificed in the house of the LORD, it took her breath away. 5“The report I heard in my country about your deeds and your wisdom is true,” she told the king. 6“I did not believe the report until I came and saw with my own eyes that not even the half of your great wisdom had been told me. You have surpassed the report I heard. 7Happy your servants, happy these ministers of yours, who stand before you always and listen to your wisdom. 8Blessed be the LORD, your God, who was pleased to set you on his throne as king for the LORD, your God. In the love your God has for Israel, to establish them forever, he has made you king over them to carry out judgment and justice.” 9Then she gave the king one hundred and twenty gold talents, a very large quantity of spices, and precious stones. Never again did anyone bring such an abundance of spices as the queen of Sheba gave to King Solomon.

10The servants of Huram and of Solomon who brought gold from Ophir also brought cabinet wood and precious stones. 11With the cabinet wood the king made stairs for the house of the LORD and the house of the king, and harps and lyres for the chanters. The like of these had not been seen before in the land of Judah.[i]

12King Solomon gave the queen of Sheba everything she desired and asked for, more than she had brought to the king. Then she returned with her servants to her own country.[j]

13[k] The gold that came to Solomon in one year weighed six hundred and sixty-six gold talents, 14in addition to what came from the tolls on travelers and what the merchants brought. All the kings of Arabia also, and the governors of the country, brought gold and silver to Solomon.

15King Solomon made two hundred large shields of beaten gold (six hundred shekels of gold went into each shield) 16and three hundred bucklers of beaten gold (three hundred shekels of gold went into each buckler); and the king put them in the house of the Forest of Lebanon.

17The king made a large ivory throne, and overlaid it with fine gold. 18The throne had six steps; a footstool of gold was fastened to the throne, and there was an arm on each side of the seat, with two lions standing next to the arms, 19and twelve other lions standing there on the steps, two to a step. Nothing like this was made in any other kingdom. 20All King Solomon’s drinking vessels were gold, and all the utensils in the house of the Forest of Lebanon were pure gold. There was no silver, for in Solomon’s time silver was reckoned as nothing. 21For the king had ships that went to Tarshish with the servants of Huram. Once every three years the fleet of Tarshish ships would come with a cargo of gold, silver, ivory, apes, and monkeys.

Solomon’s Renown. 22Thus King Solomon surpassed all the kings of the earth in riches and wisdom.

23All the kings of the earth sought audience with Solomon, to hear the wisdom God had put into his heart. 24They all brought their tribute: vessels of silver and gold, garments, weapons, spices, horses, and mules—what was due each year. 25Solomon had four thousand stalls for horses, chariots, and twelve thousand horses; these he allocated among the chariot cities and to the king’s service in Jerusalem. 26He was ruler over all the kings from the River to the land of the Philistines and down to the border of Egypt. 27The king made silver as common in Jerusalem as stones, and cedars as numerous as the sycamores of the Shephelah. 28* Solomon’s horses were imported from Egypt and from all the lands.

The Death of Solomon. 29[l] The remainder of the acts of Solomon, first and last, are recorded in the acts of Nathan the prophet, in the prophecy of Ahijah the Shilonite, and in the visions of Iddo the seer concerning Jeroboam, son of Nebat. 30Solomon was king in Jerusalem over all Israel for forty years. 31Solomon rested with his ancestors and was buried in the City of David, his father, and Rehoboam his son succeeded him as king.

9:28 See note on 1:16–17.

i: 1 Kgs 10:11–12. *j:* 1 Kgs 10:13. *k:* 1 Kgs 10:14–28. *l:* 1 Kgs 11:41–43.

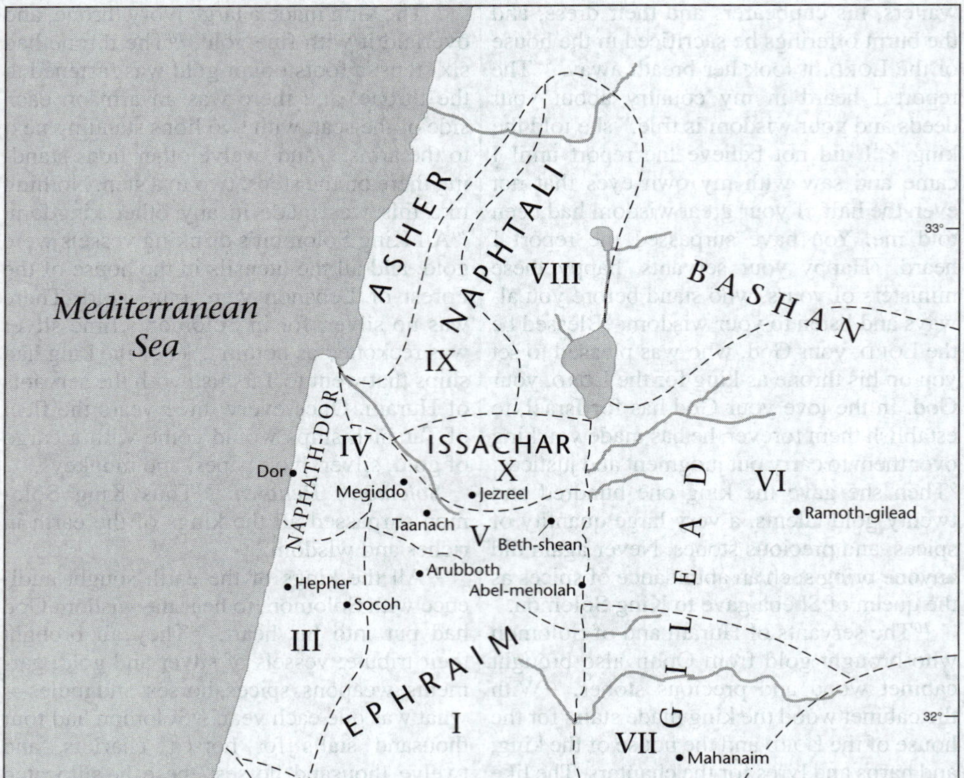

The Kingdom of Solomon according to 2 Chronicles

II. The Post-Solomonic Monarchy of Judah

CHAPTER 10

See RG 203-4

Division of the Kingdom. 1[m] Rehoboam went to Shechem, where all Israel* had come to make him king. 2When Jeroboam, son of Nebat, heard about it, he was in Egypt where he had fled from King Solomon; and he returned from Egypt. 3They sent for him; Jeroboam and all Israel came and said to Rehoboam: 4"Your father put on us a heavy yoke. If you now lighten the harsh servitude and the heavy yoke your father imposed on us, we will be your servants." 5He answered them, "Come back to me in three days," and the people went away.

6King Rehoboam asked advice of the elders who had been in his father Solomon's service while he was still alive, and asked, "How do you advise me to answer this people?" 7They replied, "If you will deal kindly with this people and please them, giving them a favorable reply, they will be your servants forever." 8But he ignored the advice the elders had given him and asked advice of the young men who had grown up with him and were in his service. 9He said to them, "What answer do you advise us to give this people, who have told me, 'Lighten the yoke your father imposed on us'?" 10The young men who had grown up with him replied: "This is what you must say to this people who have told you, 'Your father laid a heavy yoke on us; lighten it for us.' You must say, 'My little finger is thicker than my father's loins. 11My father put a heavy yoke on you; I will make it heavier. My father beat you with whips; I will use scorpions!' "

12On the third day, Jeroboam and the whole people came back to King Rehoboam as the king had instructed them: "Come back to me in three days." 13Ignoring the advice the elders had given him, King Rehoboam gave the people a harsh answer. 14He spoke to them as the young men had advised: "My father laid a heavy yoke on you; I will make it heavier. My father beat you with whips; I will use scorpions." 15The king did not listen to the people, for this turn of events was from God: the LORD fulfilled the word he had spoken through Ahijah the Shilonite to Jeroboam, the son of Nebat.[n]

16[o] When all Israel saw that the king did not listen to them, the people answered the king:

"What share have we in David?
  We have no heritage in the son of Jesse.
Everyone to your tents, Israel!
  Now look to your own house, David!"

So all Israel went off to their tents, 17but the Israelites who lived in the cities of Judah had Rehoboam as their king. 18King Rehoboam then sent out Hadoram, who was in charge of the forced labor, but the Israelites stoned him to death. King Rehoboam, however, managed to mount his chariot and flee to Jerusalem. 19And so Israel has been in rebellion against the house of David to this day.

CHAPTER 11

See RG 203-4

1[p] On his arrival in Jerusalem, Rehoboam assembled the house of Judah and Benjamin—one hundred and eighty thousand elite warriors—to wage war against Israel and restore the kingdom to Rehoboam. 2However, the word of the LORD came to Shemaiah, a man of God: 3Say to Rehoboam, son of Solomon, king of Judah, and to all the Israelites in Judah and Benjamin: 4"Thus says the LORD: You must not go out to war against your kinsmen. Return home, each of you, for it is I who have brought this about." They obeyed the word of the LORD and turned back from going against Jeroboam.

Rehoboam's Works.* 5Rehoboam took up residence in Jerusalem and built fortified cities in Judah. 6He built up Bethlehem, Etam,

10:1 All Israel: as in the source (1 Kgs 12:1), this term designates the northern tribes, as distinct from Judah and Benjamin. Elsewhere the Chronicler, writing on his own, speaks comprehensively of "those Israelites who lived in the cities of Judah" (10:17), and "all the Israelites [lit., all Israel] in Judah and Benjamin" (11:3).

11:5–12 These verses have no parallel in 1 Kings; they are apparently based on a separate source.

m: 1 Kgs 12:1–14. *n:* 1 Kgs 11:29–39; 12:15. *o:* 1 Kgs 12:16–19. *p:* 1 Kgs 12:21–24.

Tekoa, [7]Beth-zur, Soco, Adullam, [8]Gath, Mareshah, Ziph, [9]Adoraim, Lachish, Azekah, [10]Zorah, Aijalon, and Hebron; these were fortified cities in Judah and Benjamin. [11]Then he strengthened the fortifications and put commanders in them, along with supplies of food, oil, and wine. [12]In every city were shields and spears, and he made them very strong. Thus Judah and Benjamin remained his.

Refugees from the North. [13]Now the priests and Levites throughout Israel presented themselves to him from all parts of their land, [14]for the Levites left their assigned pasture lands and their holdings and came to Judah and Jerusalem, because Jeroboam and his sons rejected them as priests of the LORD.[q] [15]In their place, he himself appointed priests for the high places as well as for the satyrs and calves he had made.[r] [16]After them, all those, of every tribe of Israel, who set their hearts to seek the LORD, the God of Israel, came to Jerusalem to sacrifice to the LORD, the God of their ancestors. [17]Thus they strengthened the kingdom of Judah and made Rehoboam, son of Solomon, prevail for three years; for they walked in the way of David and Solomon three years.

Rehoboam's Family. [18]Rehoboam married Mahalath, daughter of Jerimoth, son of David and of Abihail, daughter of Eliab, son of Jesse. [19]She bore him sons: Jehush, Shemariah, and Zaham. [20]After her, he married Maacah, daughter of Absalom, who bore him Abijah,[s] Attai, Ziza, and Shelomith. [21]Rehoboam loved Maacah, daughter of Absalom, more than all his other wives and concubines; he had taken eighteen wives and sixty concubines, and he fathered twenty-eight sons and sixty daughters. [22]Rehoboam put Abijah, son of Maacah, first among his brothers, as leader, for he intended to make him king. [23]He acted prudently, distributing his various sons throughout all the districts of Judah and Benjamin, in all the fortified cities; and he gave them generous provisions and sought an abundance of wives for them.

CHAPTER 12

See RG 203-4

Rehoboam's Apostasy. [1]Once Rehoboam had established himself as king and was firmly in charge, he abandoned the law of the LORD, and so did all Israel with him.[t] [2]So in the fifth year of King Rehoboam, Shishak, king of Egypt, attacked Jerusalem, for they had acted treacherously toward the LORD.[u] [3]He had twelve hundred chariots and sixty thousand horsemen, and there was no counting the army that came with him from Egypt—Libyans, Sukkites,* and Ethiopians. [4]They captured the fortified cities of Judah and came as far as Jerusalem. [5]Then Shemaiah[v] the prophet came to Rehoboam and the commanders of Judah who had gathered at Jerusalem because of Shishak, and said to them: "Thus says the LORD: You have abandoned me, and so I have abandoned you to the power of Shishak."

[6]Then the commanders of Israel and the king humbled themselves saying, "The LORD is in the right." [7]When the LORD saw that they had humbled themselves, the word of the LORD came to Shemaiah: Because they have humbled themselves, I will not destroy them; I will give them some deliverance, and my wrath shall not be poured out upon Jerusalem through Shishak. [8]But they shall be his servants. Then they will know what it is to serve me and what it is to serve the kingdoms of the earth. [9][w] Thereupon Shishak, king of Egypt, attacked Jerusalem and took away the treasures of the house of the LORD and the treasures of the house of the king. He took everything, including the gold shields that Solomon had made. [10]To replace them, King Rehoboam made bronze shields, which he entrusted to the officers of the attendants on duty at the entrance of the king's house. [11]Whenever the king visited the house of the LORD, the attendants would carry them, and then return them to the guardroom. [12]Because he had humbled himself, the anger of the LORD turned from him so as not to destroy him

12:3 Sukkites: foreign mercenaries in the Egyptian army.

---

q: 1 Kgs 12:32. *r:* Lv 17:7; 1 Kgs 12:32. *s:* 1 Kgs 15:2. *t:* 1 Kgs 11:4; 14:22. *u:* 1 Kgs 14:25. *v:* 2 Chr 11:2. *w:* 1 Kgs 14:25–28.

completely; in Judah, moreover, there was some good.

13 King Rehoboam was firmly in power in Jerusalem and continued to rule. Rehoboam was forty-one years old when he became king, and he reigned seventeen years in Jerusalem, the city in which, out of all the tribes of Israel, the LORD chose to set his name. His mother's name was Naamah, the Ammonite.[x] 14 He did evil, for he had not set his heart to seek the LORD. 15[y] The acts of Rehoboam, first and last, are recorded in the history of Shemaiah the prophet and of Iddo the seer (his family record). There were wars between Rehoboam and Jeroboam all their days. 16 Rehoboam rested with his ancestors; he was buried in the City of David. His son Abijah* succeeded him as king.

CHAPTER 13

See RG 203-4

War Between Abijah and Jeroboam. 1[z] In the eighteenth year of King Jeroboam, Abijah became king of Judah; 2 he reigned three years in Jerusalem. His mother was named Micaiah, daughter of Uriel of Gibeah. There was war between Abijah and Jeroboam.

3* Abijah joined battle with a force of four hundred thousand picked warriors, while Jeroboam lined up against him in battle with eight hundred thousand picked and valiant warriors. 4 Abijah stood on Mount Zemaraim, which is in the highlands of Ephraim, and said: "Listen to me, Jeroboam and all Israel! 5 Do you not know that the LORD, the God of Israel, has given David kingship over Israel forever, to him and to his sons, by a covenant of salt?* 6 Yet Jeroboam, son of Nebat, the servant of Solomon, son of David, arose and rebelled against his lord![a] 7 Worthless men, scoundrels, joined him and overcame Rehoboam, son of Solomon, when Rehoboam was young and inexperienced, and no match for them. 8 But now, do you think you are a match for the kingdom of the LORD led by the descendants of David, simply because you are a huge multitude and have with you the golden calves which Jeroboam made you for gods? 9 Have you not expelled the priests of the LORD, the sons of Aaron, and the Levites, and made for yourselves priests like the peoples of other lands? Everyone who comes to consecrate himself with a young bull and seven rams becomes a priest of no-gods. 10 But as for us, the LORD is our God, and we have not abandoned him. The priests ministering to the LORD are sons of Aaron, and the Levites also have their offices. 11 They sacrifice burnt offerings to the LORD and fragrant incense morning after morning and evening after evening; they set out the showbread on the pure table, and the lamps of the golden menorah burn evening after evening; for we observe our duties to the LORD, our God, but you have abandoned him. 12 See, God is with us, at our head, and his priests are here with trumpets to sound the attack against you. Israelites, do not fight against the LORD, the God of your ancestors, for you will not succeed!"

13 But Jeroboam had an ambush go around them to come at them from the rear; so that while his army faced Judah, his ambush lay behind them. 14 When Judah turned and saw that they had to battle on both fronts, they cried out to the LORD and the priests sounded the trumpets. 15 Then the Judahites shouted; and when they shouted, God struck down Jeroboam and all Israel before Abijah and Judah. 16 The Israelites fled before Judah, and God delivered them into their power. 17 Abijah and his people inflicted a severe defeat upon them; five hundred thousand picked men of Israel fell slain. 18 The Israelites were humbled on that occasion, while the Judahites were victorious because they relied on the LORD, the God of their ancestors. 19 Abijah pursued Jeroboam and seized cities from him: Bethel and its dependencies, Jeshanah and its dependencies, and Ephron and its dependencies. 20 Jeroboam did not regain power during Abijah's

12:16 Abijah: in 1 Kgs 14:31–15:8 this king is called Abijam.

13:3–21 This passage is a free composition of the Chronicler based on the reference in 1 Kgs 15:6 to the war between Abijam (so in Kings, "Abijah" in Chronicles) and Jeroboam.

13:5 Covenant of salt: see note on Nm 18:19.

x: 1 Kgs 14:21. *y:* 1 Kgs 14:29–31. *z:* 1 Kgs 15:1–2. *a:* 1 Kgs 11:26.

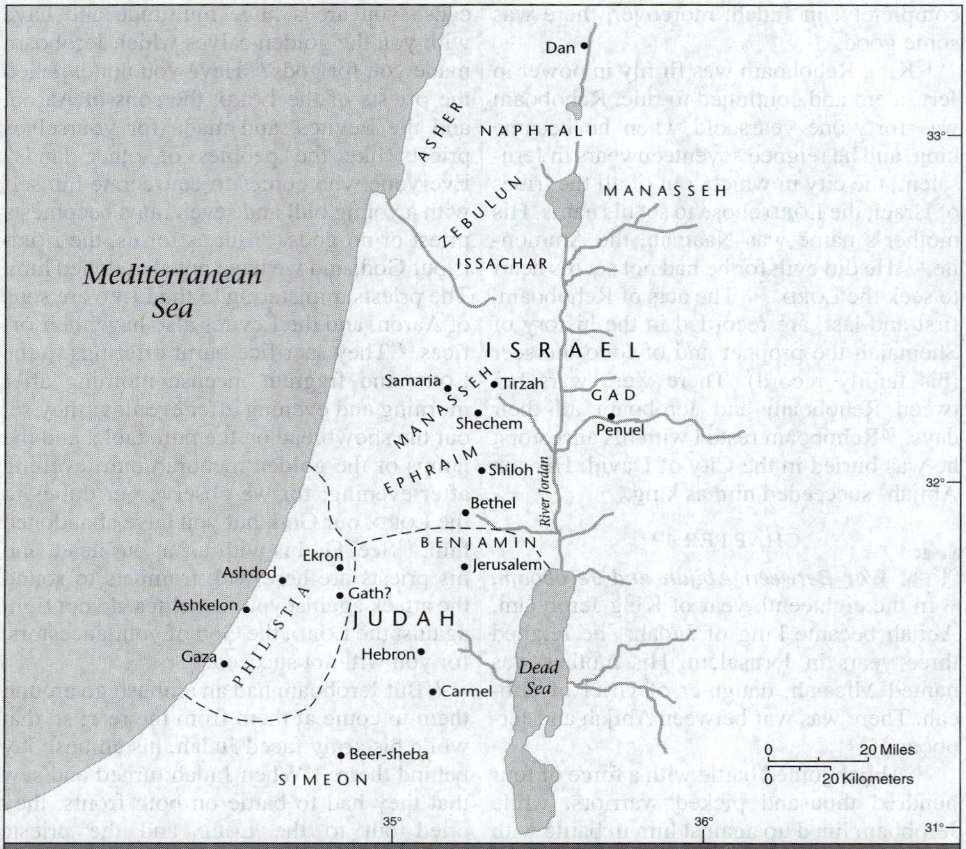

The Divided Monarchy according to 2 Chronicles

time; the LORD struck him down and he died,
[21]while Abijah continued to grow stronger.
He married fourteen wives and fathered
twenty-two sons and sixteen daughters.

Death of Abijah. [22b] The rest of the acts of
Abijah, his deeds and his words, are
recorded in the midrash of the prophet Iddo.
[23]Abijah rested with his ancestors; they
buried him in the City of David and his son
Asa succeeded him as king. During his time,
the land had ten years of peace.

CHAPTER 14

See RG 203–4

Asa's Initial Reforms. [1c] Asa did what
was good and right in the sight of the LORD,
his God. [2]He removed the illicit altars and
the high places, smashed the sacred pillars,
and cut down the asherahs. [3]He told Judah to
seek the LORD, the God of their ancestors,
and to observe the law and the commandment. [4]He removed the high places and incense stands from all the cities of Judah, and
under him the kingdom had peace. [5]He built
fortified cities in Judah, for the land had
peace and no war was waged against him
during these years, because the LORD had
given him rest. [6]He said to Judah: "Let us
build these cities and surround them with
walls, towers, gates and bars. The land is
still ours, for we have sought the LORD, our
God; we sought him, and he has given us rest
on every side." So they built and prospered.

b: 2 Chr 12:15–16; 1 Kgs 15:7–8. *c:* 2 Chr 33:15; Ex 23:24; 34:13; 1 Kgs 15:11–12.

The Ethiopian Invasion. * 7 Asa had an army of three hundred thousand shield- and lance-bearers from Judah, and from Benjamin two hundred and eighty thousand who carried bucklers and were archers, all of them valiant warriors. 8 Zerah the Ethiopian advanced against them with a force of one million men and three hundred chariots, and he came as far as Mareshah.[d] 9 Asa went out to meet him and they drew up for battle in the valley of Zephathah, near Mareshah. 10 Asa called upon the LORD, his God: "LORD, there is none like you to help the powerless against the strong. Help us, LORD, our God, for we rely on you, and in your name we have come against this multitude. You are the LORD, our God; do not let men prevail against you."[e] 11 And so the LORD defeated the Ethiopians before Asa and Judah, and the Ethiopians fled. 12 Asa and those with him pursued them as far as Gerar, and the Ethiopians fell until there were no survivors, for they were crushed before the LORD and his army, which carried away enormous spoils. 13 Then the Judahites conquered all the cities around Gerar, for the fear of the LORD was upon them; they plundered all the cities, for there was much plunder in them. 14 They also attacked the tents of the cattle-herders and carried off a great number of sheep and camels. Then they returned to Jerusalem.

CHAPTER 15

See RG 203-4

Further Reforms. 1 The spirit of God came upon Azariah, son of Oded. 2 He went forth to meet Asa and said to him: "Hear me, Asa and all Judah and Benjamin! The LORD is with you when you are with him, and if you seek him he will be found; but if you abandon him, he will abandon you.[f] 3 For a long time Israel was without a true God, without a priest-teacher, without instruction, 4 but when in their distress they turned to the LORD, the God of Israel, and sought him, he was found by them.[g] 5 At that time there was no peace for anyone to go or come; rather, there were many terrors upon the inhabitants of the lands. 6 Nation crushed nation and city crushed city,[h] for God overwhelmed them with every kind of distress. 7 But as for you, be strong and do not slack off, for there shall be a reward for what you do."[i]

8 When Asa heard these words and the prophecy (Oded the prophet), he was encouraged to remove the detestable idols from the whole land of Judah and Benjamin and from the cities he had taken in the highlands of Ephraim, and to restore the altar of the LORD which was before the vestibule of the LORD. 9 Then he gathered all Judah and Benjamin, together with those of Ephraim, Manasseh, and Simeon who were resident with them; for many had defected to him from Israel when they saw that the LORD, his God, was with him. 10 They gathered at Jerusalem in the third month* of the fifteenth year of Asa's reign, 11 and sacrificed to the LORD on that day seven hundred oxen and seven thousand sheep from the spoils they had brought. 12[j] They entered into a covenant to seek the LORD, the God of their ancestors, with all their heart and soul; 13 and everyone who would not seek the LORD, the God of Israel, was to be put to death, from least to greatest, man or woman. 14 They swore an oath to the LORD with a loud voice, with shouting and with trumpets and horns. 15 All Judah rejoiced over the oath, for they had sworn it with their whole heart and sought him with complete desire. The LORD was found by them,[k] and gave them rest on every side.

16[l] He also deposed Maacah, the mother* of King Asa, from her position as queen

14:7–14 This Ethiopian invasion of Judah is not mentioned in 1 Kings. The account is likely a legend intended to show the pious King Asa being rewarded with divine assistance. It could, however, reflect an incursion by nomads from the Negeb in Asa's time.

15:10–12 With this description of a covenant ceremony in "the third month" of a year beginning in the spring, the Chronicler provides a basis for the later understanding of the ancient Jewish spring feast of Weeks as a commemoration of the covenant on Mount Sinai; see Ex 19:1–3; Lv 23:16 and note on Lv 23:16–21. In the Greek period the feast came to be called Pentecost, from the Greek word for "fifty," i.e., fifty days or seven weeks after Passover. The Chronicler's presentation here has also influenced the celebration of Christian Pentecost as the "birthday of the Church"; cf. Acts 2.

15:16 Mother: see note on 1 Kgs 15:10.

d: 2 Chr 16:8. *e:* 2 Chr 32:8. *f:* Jer 29:13–14; Hos 3:4–5. *g:* Dt 4:29–30. *h:* Is 19:2. *i:* Is 7:4; Jer 31:16. *j:* Neh 10:29–30. *k:* Dt 4:29. *l:* 1 Kgs 15:13–15.

mother because she had made an obscene object for Asherah; Asa cut down this object, smashed it, and burnt it in the Wadi Kidron. [17]The high places did not disappear from Israel, yet Asa's heart was undivided as long as he lived. [18]He brought into the house of God his father's and his own votive offerings: silver, gold, and vessels. [19]There was no war until the thirty-fifth year of Asa's reign.

CHAPTER 16

See RG 203-4

Asa's Infidelity. [1][m]In the thirty-sixth year of Asa's reign, Baasha, king of Israel, attacked Judah and fortified Ramah to block all movement for Asa, king of Judah. [2]Asa then brought out silver and gold from the treasuries of the house of the LORD and the house of the king and sent them to Ben-hadad, king of Aram, who ruled in Damascus. He said: [3]"There is a treaty between you and me, as there was between your father and my father. I am sending you silver and gold. Go, break your treaty with Baasha, king of Israel, that he may withdraw from me." [4]Ben-hadad agreed with King Asa and sent the leaders of his troops against the cities of Israel. They attacked Ijon, Dan, Abel-maim, besides all the store cities of Naphtali. [5]When Baasha heard of it, he left off fortifying Ramah, putting an end to his work. [6]Then King Asa commandeered all Judah and they carried away the stones and beams with which Baasha was fortifying Ramah. With them he fortified Geba and Mizpah.

[7]At that time Hanani the seer came to Asa, king of Judah, and said to him: "Because you relied on the king of Aram and did not rely on the LORD, your God, the army of the king of Aram has escaped* your power. [8][n]Were not the Ethiopians and Libyans a vast army, with great numbers of chariots and horses? And yet, because you relied on the LORD, he delivered them into your power. [9]The eyes of the LORD roam over the whole earth,[o] to encourage those who are devoted to him wholeheartedly. You have acted foolishly in this matter, for from now on you will have wars." [10]But Asa became angry with the seer and imprisoned him in the stocks, so greatly was he enraged at him over this. Asa also oppressed some of his people at this time.

[11][p]Now the acts of Asa, first and last, are recorded in the book of the kings of Judah and Israel. [12]In the thirty-ninth year of his reign, Asa contracted disease in his feet; it became worse, but even with this disease he did not seek the LORD, only physicians. [13]Asa rested with his ancestors; he died in the forty-first year of his reign. [14]They buried him in the tomb he had hewn for himself in the City of David, after laying him on a couch that was filled with spices and various kinds of aromatics compounded into an ointment; and they kindled a huge fire for him.

CHAPTER 17

See RG 203-4

Jehoshaphat's Zeal for the Law. [1]His son Jehoshaphat succeeded him as king and strengthened his position against Israel.[q] [2]He placed armed forces in all the fortified cities of Judah, and set garrisons in the land of Judah and in the cities of Ephraim which Asa his father had taken. [3]The LORD was with Jehoshaphat,* for he walked in the earlier ways of David his father, and did not seek the Baals. [4]Rather, he sought the God of his father and walked in his commands, and not the practices of Israel. [5]Through him, the LORD made the kingdom secure, and all Judah gave Jehoshaphat gifts, so that great wealth and glory was his. [6]Thus he was encouraged* to follow the LORD's ways, and once again he removed the high places and the asherahs from Judah.[r]

[7]In the third year of his reign he sent his officials, Ben-hail, Obadiah, Zechariah, Nethanel, and Micaiah, to teach in the cities of

16:7 The king of Aram has escaped: the Lucianic recension of the Septuagint reads, "the king of Israel escaped." This may well be the original reading, since according to the story Asa hired the king of Aram as an ally against Israel.

17:3 The LORD was with Jehoshaphat: along with his successors Hezekiah and Josiah, Jehoshaphat is one of the Chronicler's exemplary kings.

17:6 Thus he was encouraged: lit., "his heart was high," a phrase that ordinarily describes arrogance and rebelliousness; in this case, however, it introduces a notice of Jehoshaphat's fidelity to the Lord.

m: 1 Kgs 15:16–21. *n:* 2 Chr 14:8–14. *o:* Ps 33:13–15. *p:* 1 Kgs 15:23–24. *q:* 1 Kgs 15:24. *r:* 2 Chr 20:33; Ex 34:13.

Judah. 8With them he sent the Levites Shemaiah, Nethaniah, Zebadiah, Asahel, Shemiramoth, Jehonathan, Adonijah, and Tobijah, together with Elishama and Jehoram the priests.[s] 9They taught in Judah, having with them the book of the law of the LORD; they traveled through all the cities of Judah and taught among the people.[t]

His Power. 10Now the fear of the LORD was upon all the kingdoms of the countries surrounding Judah, so that they did not war against Jehoshaphat. 11Some of the Philistines brought Jehoshaphat gifts and a tribute of silver; the Arabians also brought him a flock of seven thousand seven hundred rams and seven thousand seven hundred he-goats.

12Jehoshaphat grew ever greater. He built strongholds and store cities in Judah. 13He carried out many works in the cities of Judah, and he had soldiers, valiant warriors, in Jerusalem. 14This was their mustering according to their ancestral houses. From Judah, the commanders of thousands: Adnah the commander, and with him three hundred thousand valiant warriors. 15Next to him, Jehohanan the commander, and with him two hundred eighty thousand. 16Next to him, Amasiah, son of Zichri, who offered himself to the LORD, and with him two hundred thousand valiant warriors. 17From Benjamin: Eliada, a valiant warrior, and with him two hundred thousand armed with bow and buckler. 18Next to him, Jehozabad, and with him one hundred and eighty thousand equipped for war. 19These attended the king; in addition to those whom the king had stationed in the fortified cities throughout all Judah.

CHAPTER 18

See RG 203–4

Alliance with Israel. 1[u] Jehoshaphat therefore had wealth and glory in abundance; but he became related to Ahab by marriage. 2After some years he went down to Ahab at Samaria; Ahab slaughtered numerous sheep and oxen for him and for the people with him, and incited him to go up against Ramoth-gilead. 3Ahab, king of Israel, asked Jehoshaphat, king of Judah, "Will you come with me to Ramoth-gilead?" He answered, "You and I are as one, and your people and my people as well. We will be with you in the battle." 4Jehoshaphat also said to the king of Israel, "Seek the word of the LORD at once."

Prophets in Conflict. 5The king of Israel assembled the prophets, four hundred of them, and asked, "Shall we go to fight against Ramoth-gilead, or shall I refrain?" They said, "Attack. God will give it into the power of the king." 6But Jehoshaphat said, "Is there no other prophet of the LORD here we might consult?" 7The king of Israel answered, "There is one other man through whom we may consult the LORD; but I hate him, because he prophesies not good but always evil about me. He is Micaiah, son of Imlah." Jeshoshaphat said, "Let not the king say that." 8So the king of Israel called an official, and said to him, "Get Micaiah, son of Imlah, at once." 9The king of Israel and Jehoshaphat, king of Judah, were seated, each on his throne, clothed in their robes of state in the square at the entrance of the gate of Samaria, and all the prophets were prophesying before them.

10Zedekiah, son of Chenaanah, made himself two horns of iron and said: "The LORD says: With these you shall gore Aram until you have destroyed them." 11The other prophets prophesied in the same vein, saying: "Attack Ramoth-gilead, and conquer! The LORD will give it into the power of the king." 12* Meanwhile the messenger who had gone to call Micaiah said to him: "Look now, the words of the prophets are as one in speaking good for the king. Let your word be at one with theirs; speak a good word." 13Micaiah said, "As the LORD lives, I shall speak whatever my God says."

14When he came to the king, the king said to him, "Micah, shall we go to fight at Ramoth-gilead, or shall I refrain?" He said, "Attack and conquer! They will be delivered into your power." 15But the king answered

18:12–22 See note on 1 Kgs 22:19–23.

s: 2 Chr 19:8. *t:* Ezr 7:25. *u:* 1 Kgs 22:1–35.

him, "How many times must I adjure you to tell me nothing but the truth in the name of the LORD?" [16]So Micaiah said:

"I see all Israel
  scattered on the mountains,
  like sheep without a shepherd,
And the LORD saying,
  These have no masters!
  Let each of them go back home in
    peace."

[17]The king of Israel said to Jehoshaphat, "Did I not tell you, he does not prophesy good about me, but only evil?" [18]Micaiah continued: "Therefore hear the word of the LORD. I saw the LORD seated on his throne, with the whole host of heaven standing to his right and to his left. [19]The LORD asked: Who will deceive Ahab, king of Israel, so that he will go up and fall on Ramoth-gilead? And one said this, another that, [20]until this spirit came forth and stood before the LORD, saying, 'I will deceive him.' The LORD asked: How? [21]He answered, 'I will go forth and become a lying spirit in the mouths of all his prophets.' The LORD replied: You shall succeed in deceiving him. Go forth and do this. [22]So now the LORD has put a lying spirit in the mouths of these prophets of yours; but the LORD himself has decreed evil against you."

[23]Thereupon Zedekiah, son of Chenaanah, came up and struck Micaiah on the cheek, saying, "Has the spirit of the LORD, then, passed from me to speak with you?" [24]Micaiah said, "You shall find out on the day you go into an innermost room to hide." [25]The king of Israel then said: "Seize Micaiah and take him back to Amon, prefect of the city, and to Joash the king's son, [26]and say, 'This is the king's order: Put this man in prison and feed him scanty rations of bread and water until I come back in safety!' " [27]But Micaiah said, "If ever you return in safety, the LORD has not spoken through me." (He also said, "Hear, O peoples, all of you!")*

Ahab's Death. [28]The king of Israel and Jehoshaphat, king of Judah, went up to Ramoth-gilead, [29]and the king of Israel said to Jehoshaphat, "I will disguise myself and go into battle. But you, put on your own robes." So the king of Israel disguised himself and they entered the battle. [30]In the meantime, the king of Aram had given his chariot commanders the order, "Fight with no one, great or small, except the king of Israel alone." [31]When the chariot commanders saw Jehoshaphat, they thought, "There is the king of Israel!" and wheeled to fight him. But Jehoshaphat cried out and the LORD helped him; God induced them to leave him alone. [32]The chariot commanders, seeing that he was not the king of Israel, turned away from him. [33]But someone drew his bow at random and hit the king of Israel between the joints of his breastplate. He ordered his charioteer, "Rein about and take me out of the ranks, for I am wounded."[v] [34]The battle grew fierce during the day, and the king of Israel braced himself up in his chariot facing the Arameans until evening. He died as the sun was setting.

CHAPTER 19

See RG 203–4

Jehoshaphat Rebuked. [1]Jehoshaphat king of Judah returned in safety to his house in Jerusalem. [2]Jehu the seer, son of Hanani,* went out to meet King Jehoshaphat and said to him: "Should you help the wicked and love those who hate the LORD? For this reason, wrath is upon you from the LORD. [3]Yet some good has been found* in you, since you have removed the asherahs from the land and have set your heart to seek God."

Judges Appointed. [4]Jehoshaphat dwelt in Jerusalem; but he went out again among the people from Beer-sheba to the highlands of Ephraim and brought them back to the LORD, the God of their ancestors. [5]He appointed judges in the land, in all the fortified cities of Judah, city by city, [6]and he said to them: "Take care what you do, for the judgment you

18:27 "Hear, O peoples, all of you!": this quotation, which also appears in 1 Kgs 22:28, ascribes to the prophet Micaiah ben Imlah the opening words of the book of the prophet Micah of Moresheth (Mi 1:2), who was active a century later.

19:2 Jehu the seer, son of Hanani: probably not the Jehu, son of Hanani, who prophesied against Baasha of Israel almost fifty years earlier (1 Kgs 16:1).

19:3 Has been found: theological passive, i.e., God is the implied agent.

v: 2 Chr 35:23; 1 Kgs 22:34.

give is not human but divine; for when it comes to judgment God will be with you.[w] 7 And now, let the fear of the LORD be upon you. Act carefully, for with the LORD, our God, there is no injustice, no partiality, no bribe-taking."[x] 8 In Jerusalem also, Jehoshaphat appointed some Levites and priests and some of the family heads of Israel for the LORD's judgment and the disputes of those who dwell in Jerusalem.[y] 9 He gave them this command: "Thus you shall act: in the fear of the LORD, with fidelity and with an undivided heart. 10 And in every dispute that comes to you from your kin living in their cities, whether it concerns bloodguilt or questions of law, command, statutes, or ordinances, warn them lest they incur guilt before the LORD and his wrath come upon you and your kin. Do that and you shall not incur guilt.[z] 11 See now, Amariah is chief priest over you for everything that pertains to the LORD, and Zebadiah, son of Ishmael, is leader of the house of Judah in all that pertains to the king; and the Levites will be your officials. Take firm action, and the LORD will be with the good."

CHAPTER 20

See RG 203–4

Invasion from Edom. 1* After this the Moabites, the Ammonites, and with them some Meunites came to fight against Jehoshaphat. 2 Jehoshaphat was told: "A great multitude is coming against you from across the sea, from Edom; they are already in Hazazon-tamar" (which is En-gedi). 3 Frightened, Jehoshaphat resolved to consult the LORD. He proclaimed a fast throughout all Judah. 4 Then Judah gathered to seek the LORD's help; from every one of the cities of Judah they came to seek the LORD.[a]

Jehoshaphat's Prayer. 5 Jehoshaphat stood up in the assembly of Judah and Jerusalem in the house of the LORD before the new court, 6 and he said: "LORD, God of our ancestors, are you not God in heaven, and do you not rule over all the kingdoms of the nations? In your hand is power and might, and no one can withstand you.[b] 7 Was it not you, our God, who dispossessed the inhabitants of this land before your people Israel and gave it forever to the descendants of Abraham, your friend? 8 They have dwelt in it and they built in it a sanctuary for your name. They have said: 9 'If evil comes upon us, the sword of judgment, or pestilence, or famine, we will stand before this house and before you, for your name is in this house, and we will cry out to you in our affliction, and you will hear and save!'[c] 10 And now, see the Ammonites, Moabites, and those of Mount Seir whom you did not allow Israel to invade when they came from the land of Egypt, but instead they passed them by and did not destroy them:[d] 11 See how they are now repaying us by coming to drive us out of the possession you have given us. 12 O our God, will you not bring judgment on them? We are powerless before this vast multitude that is coming against us. We ourselves do not know what to do, so our eyes are turned toward you."

Victory Prophesied. 13 All Judah was standing before the LORD, with their little ones, their wives, and their children. 14 And the spirit of the LORD came upon Jahaziel, son of Zechariah, son of Benaiah, son of Jeiel, son of Mattaniah, a Levite of the clan of Asaph, in the midst of the assembly, 15 and he said: "Pay attention, all of Judah, inhabitants of Jerusalem, and King Jehoshaphat! The LORD says to you: Do not fear or be dismayed at the sight of this vast multitude, for the battle is not yours but God's. 16 Go down against them tomorrow. You will see them coming up by the ascent of Ziz, and you will come upon them at the end of the wadi which opens on the wilderness of Jeruel. 17 You will not have to fight in this encounter. Take your places, stand firm, and see the salvation of the LORD; he will be with you, Judah and Jerusalem. Do not fear or be dismayed. Tomorrow go out to meet them, and

20:1–30 This account seems to be a free composition of the Chronicler. However, there could well have been a raid of nomads against Judah in the reign of Jehoshaphat, similar to the one that occurred under Asa (14:8–14). The story may also be connected in some way with the campaign of Israel and Judah against Moab launched through the territory of Edom (2 Kgs 3:4–27).

w: Dt 1:16–18; 16:19–20. *x:* Dt 10:17. *y:* 2 Chr 17:8–9; Dt 17:8–13; Ps 122:3–5. *z:* Dt 17:8–13. *a:* Jer 36:6. *b:* 2 Chr 32:7; Dt 4:39. *c:* 2 Chr 6:28–31; 7:13–14; 1 Kgs 8:37–40. *d:* Dt 2:4–5, 9–10, 18–19.

the LORD will be with you."[e] 18 Then Jehoshaphat knelt down with his face to the ground,
and all Judah and the inhabitants of Jerusalem fell down before the LORD in worship.
19 Levites from among the Kohathites and
Korahites stood up to sing the praises of the
LORD, the God of Israel, their voices ever
louder.

The Invaders Destroyed. 20 Early in the
morning they went out to the wilderness of
Tekoa. As they were going out, Jehoshaphat
halted and said: "Listen to me, Judah and
inhabitants of Jerusalem! Let your faith in
the LORD, your God, be firm, and you will be
firm.[f] Have faith in his prophets and you will
succeed." 21* After taking counsel with the
people, he appointed some to sing to the
LORD and some to praise the holy Splendor
as it went forth at the head of the army. They
sang: "Give thanks to the LORD, whose love
endures forever."[g] 22 At the moment they began their jubilant praise, the LORD laid an
ambush against the Ammonites, Moabites,
and those of Mount Seir who were coming
against Judah, so that they were defeated.
23 For the Ammonites and Moabites set upon
the inhabitants of Mount Seir and exterminated them according to the ban.[h] And when
they had finished with the inhabitants of
Seir, each helped to destroy the other.

24 When Judah came to the watchtower of
the wilderness and looked toward the throng,
there were only corpses fallen on the ground,
with no survivors. 25 Jehoshaphat and his
people came to gather the spoils, and they
found an abundance of cattle and personal
property, garments and precious vessels.
They took so much that they were unable to
carry it all; it took them three days to gather
the spoils, there was so much of it. 26 On the
fourth day they held an assembly in the Valley of Berakah*—for there they blessed the
LORD; that is why the place is called the Valley of Berakah to this day. 27 Then all the men
of Judah and Jerusalem, with Jehoshaphat at
their head, returned to Jerusalem with joy;
for the LORD had given them joy over their
enemies. 28 They came to Jerusalem, with
harps, lyres, and trumpets, to the house of the
LORD. 29 And the fear of God came upon all
the kingdoms of the surrounding lands when
they heard how the LORD had fought against
the enemies of Israel. 30 Thereafter Jehoshaphat's kingdom had peace, for his God gave
him rest on every side.

Jehoshaphat's Other Deeds. 31[i] Thus Jehoshaphat reigned over Judah. He was
thirty-five years old when he became king,
and he reigned twenty-five years in
Jerusalem. His mother's name was Azubah,
daughter of Shilhi. 32 He walked in the way
of Asa his father unceasingly, doing what
was right in the LORD's sight. 33 Nevertheless, the high places did not disappear and
the people had not yet set their hearts on the
God of their ancestors.

34 The rest of the acts of Jehoshaphat, first
and last, are recorded in the chronicle of
Jehu, son of Hanani, which was incorporated into the book of the kings of Israel.
35 After this, Jehoshaphat king of Judah
joined with Ahaziah king of Israel—he acted
wickedly. 36[j] He joined with him in building
ships to go to Tarshish; the fleet was built at
Ezion-geber. 37 But Eliezer, son of Dodavahu
from Mareshah, prophesied against Jehoshaphat. He said: "Because you have joined
with Ahaziah, the LORD will shatter your
work." And the ships were wrecked and
were unable to sail to Tarshish.

CHAPTER 21

See RG 203–4

1 Jehoshaphat rested with his ancestors; he was buried with them in the City of
David. Jehoram, his son, succeeded him as
king.[k] 2 He had brothers, Jehoshaphat's sons:

20:21 In accordance with Israelite conceptions of Holy War (cf. Ex 14:13–14), this highly stylized narrative presents the Lord as active in battle, while the people have only to sing hymns of praise; the enemy, in panic, fight among themselves to their mutual destruction (v. 23). **Splendor**: the Lord "goes before," i.e., leads, the army of Israel (cf. 2 Sm 5:24) with the heavenly hosts. Israel's God is depicted as present "enthroned upon the cherubim" atop the ark of the covenant. By postexilic times, the ark had disappeared, but the Lord was still present to his people. Here that presence is described as "holy Splendor," a phrase found in Ps 29:2; 96:9. Cf. the cognate image of cloud and fire that led Israel in the wilderness (Ex 13:21–22), or the cloud of the Lord's glory that fills the sanctuary (Ex 40:34; 1 Kgs 8:10–11).

20:26 Berakah: the Hebrew word for "blessing."

e: Ex 14:13–14; Is 8:10. *f:* Is 7:9. *g:* Ps 136:1. *h:* Jos 6:17. *i:* 1 Kgs 22:41–45. *j:* 1 Kgs 22:48–49. *k:* 1 Kgs 22:51.

Azariah, Jehiel, Zechariah, Azariah, Michael, and Shephatiah; all these were sons of King Jehoshaphat of Judah. 3 Their father gave them many gifts of silver, gold, and precious objects, together with fortified cities in Judah, but the kingship he gave to Jehoram because he was the firstborn.

Jehoram's Evil Deeds. 4 When Jehoram had acceded to his father's kingdom and was firmly in power, he killed all his brothers with the sword, and also some of the princes of Israel. 5[l] Jehoram was thirty-two years old when he became king, and he reigned eight years in Jerusalem. 6 He walked in the way of the kings of Israel as the house of Ahab had done, since the daughter of Ahab* was his wife; and he did what was evil in the LORD's sight. 7 Even so, the LORD was unwilling to destroy the house of David because of the covenant he had made with David and because of his promise to leave him and his sons a holding for all time.[m]

8[n] During his time Edom revolted against the rule of Judah and installed its own king. 9 Thereupon Jehoram with his officers and all his chariots crossed over. He arose by night and broke through the Edomites when they had surrounded him and the commanders of his chariots. 10 To this day Edom has been in revolt against the rule of Judah. Libnah also revolted at that time against his rule because he had abandoned the LORD, the God of his ancestors. 11 He also set up high places in the mountains of Judah, prostituting the inhabitants of Jerusalem, leading Judah astray.

Jehoram Punished. 12 A letter came to him from Elijah* the prophet with this message: "Thus says the LORD, the God of David your father: Because you have not walked in the way of your father Jehoshaphat, nor of Asa, king of Judah, 13 but instead have walked in the way of the kings of Israel, leading Judah and the inhabitants of Jerusalem into prostitution, like the harlotries of the house of Ahab, and because you have killed your brothers of your father's house, who were better than you, 14 the LORD will strike your people, your children, your wives, and all that is yours with a great plague. 15 You shall have severe pains from a disease in your bowels, which will fall out because of the disease, day after day."

16 Then the LORD stirred up against Jehoram the animosity of the Philistines and of the Arabians who were neighbors of the Ethiopians. 17 They came up against Judah, breached it, and carried away all the wealth found in the king's house, along with his sons and his wives. He was left with only one son, Jehoahaz, his youngest. 18 After these events, the LORD afflicted him with a disease of the bowels for which there was no cure. 19 Some time later, after a period of two years had elapsed, his bowels fell out because of the disease and he died in great pain. His people did not make a fire for him as they had for his ancestors.[o] 20 He was thirty-two years old when he became king, and he reigned eight years in Jerusalem. He departed unloved; and they buried him in the City of David, though not in the tombs of the kings.[p]

CHAPTER 22

See RG 203-4

Ahaziah. 1[q] Then the inhabitants of Jerusalem made Ahaziah, his youngest son, king to succeed him, since all the older sons had been killed by the band that had come into the camp with the Arabians. Thus Ahaziah, son of Jehoram, reigned as the king of Judah. 2 Ahaziah was twenty-two years old when he became king, and he reigned one year in Jerusalem. His mother's name was Athaliah, daughter of Omri. 3 He, too, walked in the ways of the house of Ahab, because his mother was his counselor in doing evil. 4 To his own destruction, he did what was evil in the sight of the LORD, like the house of Ahab, since they were his counselors after the death of his father.

21:6 The daughter of Ahab: her name was Athaliah. In 22:2 (and its source, 2 Kgs 8:26) she is called the daughter of Ahab's father Omri, but this should probably be understood in the sense of granddaughter.

21:12 Elijah: this is the Chronicler's only mention of this prophet of the Northern Kingdom. It is doubtful that Elijah was still living in the reign of Jehoram of Judah; in any case, the attribution of the letter to him has a folkloristic quality.

l: 1 Kgs 8:17–19. *m:* 1 Kgs 11:36; 2 Kgs 8:19. *n:* Gn 27:40; 2 Kgs 8:20–22. *o:* 2 Chr 16:14. *p:* 2 Kgs 8:24. *q:* 2 Kgs 8:24–29.

5 He was also following their counsel when he joined Jehoram, son of Ahab, king of Israel, in battle against Hazael, king of Aram, at Ramoth-gilead, where the Arameans wounded Jehoram. 6 He returned to Jezreel to be healed of the wounds that had been inflicted on him at Ramah in his battle against Hazael, king of Aram. Then Ahaziah, son of Jehoram, king of Judah, went down to Jezreel to visit Jehoram, son of Ahab, for he was sick. 7 Now from God came Ahaziah's downfall, that he should join Jehoram; for after his arrival he rode out with Jehoram to Jehu, son of Nimshi, whom the LORD had anointed to cut down the house of Ahab.[r] 8 While Jehu was executing judgment on the house of Ahab, he also came upon the princes of Judah and the nephews of Ahaziah who were his attendants, and he killed them.[s] 9 Then he looked for Ahaziah himself. They caught him hiding in Samaria and brought him to Jehu, who put him to death. They buried him, for they said, "He was the grandson of Jehoshaphat, who sought the LORD with his whole heart."[t] Now the house of Ahaziah did not retain the power of kingship.*

Usurpation of Athaliah. 10[u] When Athaliah, the mother of Ahaziah, saw that her son was dead, she began to kill off the whole royal family of the house of Judah. 11 But Jehosheba, a daughter of the king, took Joash, Ahaziah's son, and spirited him away from among the king's sons who were about to be slain, and put him and his nurse in a bedroom. In this way Jehosheba, the daughter of King Jehoram, a sister of Ahaziah and wife of Jehoiada the priest, concealed the child from Athaliah, so that she did not put him to death. 12 For six years he remained hidden with them in the house of God, while Athaliah ruled as queen over the land.

CHAPTER 23

See RG 203-4

Athaliah Overthrown. 1[v] In the seventh year, Jehoiada took courage and brought into covenant with himself the captains: Azariah, son of Jehoram; Ishmael, son of Jehohanan; Azariah, son of Obed; Maaseiah, son of Adaiah; and Elishaphat, son of Zichri. 2 They journeyed about Judah, gathering the Levites from all the cities of Judah and also the heads of the Israelite families, and they came to Jerusalem. 3 The whole assembly made a covenant with the king in the house of God. Jehoiada said to them: "Here is the king's son who must reign, as the LORD promised concerning the sons of David. 4 This is what you must do: a third of your number, both priests and Levites, who come on duty on the sabbath must guard the thresholds, 5 another third must be at the king's house, and the final third at the Foundation Gate, when all the people will be in the courts of the LORD's house. 6 Let no one enter the LORD's house except the priests and those Levites who are ministering. They may enter because they are holy; but all the other people must observe the prescriptions of the LORD. 7 The Levites shall surround the king on all sides, each with drawn weapon. Whoever tries to enter the house is to be killed. Stay with the king wherever he goes."

8 The Levites and all Judah did just as Jehoiada the priest commanded. Each took his troops, both those going on duty for the week and those going off duty that week, since Jehoiada the priest had not dismissed any of the divisions.[w] 9 Jehoiada the priest gave to the captains the spears, shields, and bucklers of King David which were in the house of God. 10 He stationed all the people, each with spear in hand, from the southern to the northern limit of the enclosure, surrounding the altar and the temple on the king's behalf. 11 Then they brought out the king's son and put the crown and the testimony upon him, and proclaimed him king. Jehoiada and his sons anointed him, and they cried, "Long live the king!"

12 When Athaliah heard the noise of the people running and acclaiming the king, she came before them in the house of the LORD. 13 When she saw the king standing by his

22:9 This account of the death of Ahaziah of Judah does not agree with that given in 2 Kgs 9:27–28.

r: 2 Kgs 9:21. *s:* 2 Kgs 10:12–14. *t:* 2 Kgs 9:27–28. *u:* 2 Kgs 11:1–3. *v:* 2 Kgs 11:4–20. *w:* 2 Kgs 11:9; 1 Chr 24:19.

column* at the entrance, the captains and the trumpeters near the king, and all the people of the land rejoicing and blowing trumpets, while the singers with their musical instruments were leading the acclaim, Athaliah tore her garments, saying, "Treason! treason!" 14 Then Jehoiada the priest brought out the captains in command of the force: "Escort her with a guard detail. If anyone follows her, let him die by the sword." For the priest had said, "You must not put her to death in the house of the LORD." 15 So they seized her, and when she reached the Horse Gate of the royal palace, they put her to death.

16 Then Jehoiada made a covenant between himself and all the people and the king, that they should be the LORD's people. 17 Thereupon all the people went to the temple of Baal and demolished it. They shattered its altars and images completely, and killed Mattan, the priest of Baal, before the altars. 18 Then Jehoiada gave the charge of the LORD's house into the hands of the levitical priests, to whom David had assigned turns in the LORD's house for sacrificing the burnt offerings of the LORD, as is written in the law of Moses, with rejoicing and song, as David had provided.[x] 19 Moreover, he stationed guards at the gates of the LORD's house so that no one unclean in any respect might enter. 20 Then he took the captains, the nobles, the rulers among the people, and all the people of the land, and led the king out of the LORD's house; they came within the upper gate of the king's house, and seated the king upon the royal throne. 21 All the people of the land rejoiced and the city was quiet, now that Athaliah had been slain with the sword.

CHAPTER 24

See RG 203–4

The Temple Restored. 1 [y] Joash was seven years old when he became king, and he reigned forty years in Jerusalem. His mother's name was Zibiah, from Beer-sheba. 2 Joash did what was right in the LORD's sight as long as Jehoiada the priest lived. 3 Jehoiada provided him with two wives, and he became the father of sons and daughters.

4 After some time, Joash decided to restore the house of the LORD. 5 He gathered together the priests and Levites and said to them: "Go out to all the cities of Judah and gather money* from all Israel that you may repair the house of your God over the years. You must hurry this project." But the Levites did not. 6 Then the king summoned Jehoiada, who was in charge, and said to him: "Why have you not required the Levites to bring in from Judah and Jerusalem the tax levied by Moses, the servant of the LORD, and by the assembly of Israel, for the tent of the testimony?"[z] 7 For the wicked Athaliah and her sons had damaged the house of God and had even turned over to the Baals the holy things of the LORD's house.

8 At the king's command, therefore, they made a chest, which they put outside the gate of the LORD's house.[a] 9 They had it proclaimed throughout Judah and Jerusalem that the tax which Moses, the servant of God, had imposed on Israel in the wilderness should be brought to the LORD.[b] 10 All the princes and the people rejoiced; they brought what was asked and cast it into the chest until it was filled. 11 Whenever the chest was brought to the royal officials by the Levites and they noticed that there was a large amount of money, the royal scribe and an overseer for the chief priest would come up, empty the chest, and then take it back and return it to its place. This they did day after day until they had collected a large sum of money. 12 Then the king and Jehoiada gave it to the workers in charge of the labor on the LORD's house, who hired masons and carpenters to restore the LORD's house, and also iron- and bronze-smiths to repair it. 13 The workers labored, and the task of

23:13 By his column: there was a special place reserved for the king in the eastern gateway of the Temple court where the altar for burnt offerings stood. The king occupied this place on feasts and sabbaths at the time of the prescribed offerings, or when he came to make voluntary offerings of his own; cf. 2 Kgs 11:14 and Ez 46:1–8.

24:5 Gather money: according to 2 Kgs 12:5 the people themselves brought the money, consisting at least in part of voluntary contributions, to the Temple. By the time of the Chronicler, a fixed head tax for the upkeep of the Temple had been introduced; see 2 Chr 34:9; Neh 10:32; Ex 30:12–16. This was still in force in New Testament times (Mt 17:24–25).

x: 1 Chr 23:13. *y:* 2 Kgs 12:1–13. *z:* Ex 25:1–9; Neh 10:33. *a:* 2 Chr 34:9. *b:* Ex 30:13.

restoration progressed under their hands. They restored the house of God according to its original form, and reinforced it. 14 After they had finished, they brought the rest of the money to the king and to Jehoiada, who had it made into utensils for the house of the LORD, utensils for the service and the burnt offerings, and basins and other gold and silver utensils.* They sacrificed burnt offerings in the LORD's house continually all the days of Jehoiada. 15 Jehoiada grew old, full of years, and died; he was a hundred and thirty years old. 16 They buried him in the City of David with the kings, because of the good he had done in Israel, especially for God and his house.

Joash's Apostasy. 17 After the death of Jehoiada, the princes of Judah came and paid homage to the king; then the king listened to them. 18 They abandoned the house of the LORD, the God of their ancestors, and began to serve the asherahs and the idols;[c] and because of this crime of theirs, wrath came upon Judah and Jerusalem. 19 Although prophets were sent to them to turn them back to the LORD and to warn them, the people would not listen. 20[d] Then the spirit of God clothed Zechariah, son of Jehoiada the priest. He took his stand above the people and said to them: "Thus says God, Why are you transgressing the LORD's commands, so that you cannot prosper? Because you have abandoned the LORD, he has abandoned you." 21 But they conspired against him, and at the king's command they stoned him in the court of the house of the LORD. 22 Thus King Joash was unmindful of the devotion shown him by Jehoiada, Zechariah's father, and killed the son. As he was dying, he said, "May the LORD see and avenge."

Joash Punished. 23 At the turn of the year a force of Arameans came up against Joash. They invaded Judah and Jerusalem, killed all the princes of the people, and sent all their spoil to the king of Damascus.[e] 24 Though the Aramean force was small, the LORD handed over a very large force into their power,[f] because Judah had abandoned the LORD, the God of their ancestors. So judgment was meted out to Joash. 25[g] After the Arameans had departed from him, abandoning him to his many injuries, his servants conspired against him because of the murder of the son of Jehoiada the priest. They killed him on his sickbed. He was buried in the City of David, but not in the tombs of the kings.

26 Those who conspired against him were Zabad, son of Shimeath from Ammon, and Jehozabad, son of Shimrith from Moab. 27 An account of his sons, the great tribute imposed on him, and his rebuilding of the house of God is written in the midrash of the book of the kings. His son Amaziah succeeded him as king.[h]

CHAPTER 25

See RG 203-4

Amaziah's Good Start. 1[i] Amaziah was twenty-five years old when he became king, and he reigned twenty-nine years in Jerusalem. His mother's name was Jehoaddan, from Jerusalem. 2 He did what was right in the LORD's sight, though not wholeheartedly. 3 When he had the kingdom firmly in hand, he struck down the officials who had struck down the king, his father. 4 But their children he did not put to death, for he acted according to what is written in the law, in the Book of Moses, which the LORD commanded: "Parents shall not be put to death for their children, nor shall children be put to death for their parents; they shall each die for their own sin."[j]

5 Amaziah gathered Judah and placed them, out of all Judah and Benjamin according to their ancestral houses, under leaders of thousands and of hundreds. When he made a count of those twenty years old and over, he found that there were three hundred thousand picked men fit for war, capable of handling lance and shield. 6 He also hired a hundred thousand valiant warriors from Israel for a hundred talents of silver. 7 But a man of God came to him and said: "O king, let not the army of Israel go with you, for the

24:14 See the parallel in 2 Kgs 12:14–15; the passages are difficult to reconcile.

c: Ex 34:13. *d:* Jgs 6:34. *e:* 2 Kgs 12:17–18. *f:* Dt 32:30. *g:* 2 Kgs 12:21–22. *h:* 2 Kgs 12:19, 22. *i:* 2 Kgs 14:1–6. *j:* Dt 24:16; 2 Kgs 14:5–6; Ez 18:20.

LORD is not with Israel—with any Ephraimite. [8]Instead, go on your own, strongly prepared for the battle; why should the LORD hinder you in the face of the enemy: for with God is power to help or to hinder." [9]Amaziah answered the man of God, "But what is to be done about the hundred talents that I paid for the troops of Israel?" The man of God replied, "The LORD can give you much more than that." [10]Amaziah then disbanded the troops that had come to him from Ephraim, and sent them home. But they became furiously angry with Judah, and returned home blazing with anger.

[11]Amaziah now assumed command of his army. They proceeded to the Valley of Salt, where they killed ten thousand men of Seir.[k] [12]The Judahites also brought back another ten thousand alive, led them to the summit of Sela, and then threw them down from that rock* so that their bodies split open. [13]Meanwhile, the troops Amaziah had dismissed from going into battle with him raided the cities of Judah from Samaria to Beth-horon. They struck down three thousand of the inhabitants and carried off much plunder.

Amaziah's Apostasy. [14]When Amaziah returned from his conquest of the Edomites he brought back with him the gods of the people of Seir. He set these up as his own gods; he bowed down before them and offered sacrifice to them. [15]Then the anger of the LORD blazed out against Amaziah, and he sent a prophet to him who said: "Why have you sought this people's gods that could not deliver their own people from your power?" [16]While he was still speaking, however, the king said to him: "Have you been appointed the king's counselor? Stop! Why should you have to be killed?" Therefore the prophet stopped. But he said, "I know that God's counsel is your destruction, for by doing this you have refused to listen to my counsel."

Amaziah Punished. [17][l]Having taken counsel, Amaziah, king of Judah, sent word to Joash, son of Jehoahaz, son of Jehu, the king of Israel, saying, "Come, let us meet face to face." [18]Joash, king of Israel, sent this reply to Amaziah, king of Judah: "A thistle of Lebanon sent word to a cedar of Lebanon, 'Give your daughter to my son in marriage,' but an animal of Lebanon passed by and trampled the thistle underfoot.[m] [19]You are thinking,

'See, I have struck down Edom!'
Your heart is lifted up,
And glories in it. Stay home!
Why bring misfortune and failure
on yourself and on Judah with you?"

[20]But Amaziah did not listen; for it was God's doing that they be handed over because they sought the gods of Edom.

[21]So Joash, king of Israel, advanced, and he and Amaziah, king of Judah, met face to face at Beth-shemesh of Judah, [22]and Judah was defeated by Israel, and all fled to their tents. [23]But Amaziah, king of Judah, son of Joash, son of Jehoahaz, was captured by Joash, king of Israel, at Beth-shemesh. Joash brought him to Jerusalem and tore down the wall of Jerusalem from the Gate of Ephraim to the Corner Gate, four hundred cubits. [24]He took all the gold and silver and all the vessels found in the house of God with Obed-edom,* and in the treasuries of the king's house, and hostages as well. Then he returned to Samaria.

[25][n]Amaziah, son of Joash, king of Judah, survived Joash, son of Jehoahaz, king of Israel, by fifteen years. [26]The rest of the acts of Amaziah, first and last, are recorded in the book of the kings of Judah and Israel. [27]Now from the time that Amaziah turned away from the LORD, a conspiracy was formed against him in Jerusalem, and he fled to Lachish. But he was pursued to Lachish and killed there. [28]He was brought back on horses and was buried with his ancestors in the City of Judah.*

25:12 Sela . . . rock: a pun—the name of the city, Sela, in Hebrew means "rock."

25:24 With Obed-edom: perhaps an Edomite priest (cf. v. 14), or possibly a member of a levitical family of gatekeepers; cf. 1 Chr 15:18; 26:12–15.

25:28 The City of Judah: i.e., Jerusalem, the capital of Judah; the parallel passage (2 Kgs 14:20) reads "the City of David."

k: 2 Kgs 14:7. *l*: 2 Kgs 14:8–14. *m*: Jgs 9:7–15; 2 Kgs 14:9. *n*: 2 Kgs 14:17–20.

CHAPTER 26

See RG 203-4

Uzziah's Projects. 1[o] All the people of Judah took Uzziah, who was only sixteen years old, and made him king to succeed Amaziah his father. 2 It was he who rebuilt Elath and restored it to Judah, after the king rested with his ancestors. 3 Uzziah was sixteen years old when he became king, and he reigned fifty-two years in Jerusalem. His mother's name was Jecoliah, from Jerusalem. 4 He did what was right in the LORD's sight, just as his father Amaziah had done.

5 He was prepared to seek God as long as Zechariah* lived,[p] who taught him to fear God; and as long as he sought the LORD, God made him prosper. 6 He went out and fought the Philistines and razed the walls of Gath, Jabneh, and Ashdod, and built cities in the district of Ashdod and in Philistia.[q] 7 God helped him against the Philistines, against the Arabians who dwelt in Gurbaal, and against the Meunites. 8 The Ammonites paid tribute to Uzziah and his fame spread as far as Egypt, for he grew stronger and stronger. 9 Moreover, Uzziah built towers in Jerusalem at the Corner Gate, at the Valley Gate, and at the Angle, and he fortified them. 10 He built towers in the wilderness and dug numerous cisterns, for he had many cattle. He had plowmen in the Shephelah and the plains, farmers and vinedressers in the highlands and the garden land. He was a lover of the soil.

11 Uzziah also had a standing army of fit soldiers divided into bands according to the number in which they were mustered by Jeiel the scribe and Maaseiah the recorder, under the command of Hananiah, one of the king's officials. 12 The entire number of family heads over these valiant warriors was two thousand six hundred, 13 and at their disposal was a mighty army of three hundred seven thousand five hundred fighting men of great valor to help the king against his enemies. 14 Uzziah provided for them—for the entire army—bucklers, lances, helmets, breastplates, bows, and slingstones. 15 He also built machines in Jerusalem, devices designed to stand on the towers and at the angles of the walls to shoot arrows and cast large stones. His name spread far and wide; the help he received was wondrous, so strong did he become.

Pride and Fall. 16 But after he had become strong, he became arrogant to his own destruction and acted treacherously with the LORD, his God. He entered the temple of the LORD to make an offering on the altar of incense. 17 But Azariah the priest, and with him eighty other priests of the LORD, courageous men, followed him. 18 They stood up to King Uzziah, saying to him: "It is not for you, Uzziah, to burn incense to the LORD, but for the priests, the sons of Aaron, who have been consecrated for this purpose.[r] Leave the sanctuary, for you have acted treacherously and no longer have a part in the glory that comes from the LORD God." 19 Uzziah, who was holding a censer for burning the incense, became angry. But at the very moment he showed his anger to the priests, while they were looking at him in the house of the LORD beside the altar of incense, leprosy broke out on his forehead.[s] 20 Azariah the chief priest and all the other priests examined him, and when they saw that his forehead was leprous, they rushed him out. He let himself be expelled, for the LORD had afflicted him. 21[t] King Uzziah remained a leper till the day he died. As a leper he lived in a house apart, for he was excluded from the house of the LORD. Therefore his son Jotham was master of the palace and ruled the people of the land.

22 The rest of the acts of Uzziah, first and last, were written by Isaiah the prophet, son of Amoz. 23 Uzziah rested with his ancestors and was buried with them in the field adjoining the royal cemetery, for they said, "He was a leper." His son Jotham succeeded him as king.

CHAPTER 27

See RG 203-4

Jotham. 1[u] Jotham was twenty-five years old when he became king, and he

26:5 Zechariah: not otherwise identified, but cf. 29:1.

o: 2 Kgs 14:21–22; 15:1–3. *p:* 2 Chr 24:2. *q:* Am 1:8. *r:* Ex 30:7. *s:* Nm 12:10. *t:* 2 Kgs 15:5–7; Lv 13:46; Nm 19:20. *u:* 2 Kgs 15:32–35.

reigned sixteen years in Jerusalem. His mother's name was Jerusha, daughter of Zadok. 2He did what was right in the LORD's sight, just as his father Uzziah had done, though he did not enter the temple of the LORD. The people, however, continued to act corruptly.

3It was he who built the Upper Gate of the LORD's house and did much construction on the wall of Ophel. 4Moreover, he built cities in the hill country of Judah, and in the wooded areas he set up fortresses and towers. 5He fought with the king of the Ammonites and conquered them. That year the Ammonites paid him one hundred talents of silver, together with ten thousand kors of wheat and ten thousand of barley. They brought the same to him also in the second and in the third year. 6Thus Jotham continued to grow strong because he made sure to walk before the LORD, his God. 7[v] The rest of the acts of Jotham, his wars and his activities, are recorded in the book of the kings of Israel and Judah. 8He was twenty-five years old when he became king, and he reigned sixteen years in Jerusalem. 9Jotham rested with his ancestors and was buried in the City of David, and his son Ahaz succeeded him as king.

CHAPTER 28

See RG 203–4

Ahaz's Misdeeds. 1[w] Ahaz was twenty years old when he became king, and he reigned sixteen years in Jerusalem. He did not do what was right in the sight of the LORD as David his father had done. 2He walked in the ways of the kings of Israel and even made molten idols for the Baals. 3Moreover, he offered sacrifice in the Valley of Ben-hinnom, and immolated his children by fire in accordance with the abominable practices of the nations whom the LORD had dispossessed before the Israelites.[x] 4He sacrificed and burned incense on the high places, on hills, and under every green tree.

Ahaz Punished. 5* Therefore the LORD, his God, delivered him into the power of the king of Aram. The Arameans defeated him and carried away captive a large number of his people, whom they brought to Damascus. He was also delivered into the power of the king of Israel, who defeated him with great slaughter.[y] 6For Pekah, son of Remaliah, killed one hundred and twenty thousand of Judah in a single day, all of them valiant men, because they had abandoned the LORD, the God of their ancestors. 7Zichri, an Ephraimite warrior, killed Maaseiah, the king's son, and Azrikam, the master of the palace, and also Elkanah, who was second to the king. 8The Israelites took away as captives two hundred thousand of their kinfolk's wives, sons, and daughters; they also took from them much plunder, which they brought to Samaria.

Oded's Prophecy. 9In Samaria there was a prophet of the LORD by the name of Oded. He went out to meet the army returning to Samaria and said to them: "It was because the LORD, the God of your ancestors, was angry with Judah that he delivered them into your power. You, however, have killed them with a fury that has reached up to heaven. 10And now you are planning to subjugate the people of Judah and Jerusalem as your slaves and bondwomen. Are not you yourselves, therefore, guilty of a crime against the LORD, your God? 11Now listen to me: send back the captives you have carried off from among your kin, for the burning anger of the LORD is upon you."

12At this, some of the Ephraimite leaders, Azariah, son of Johanan, Berechiah, son of Meshillemoth, Jehizkiah, son of Shallum, and Amasa, son of Hadlai, themselves stood up in opposition to those who had returned from the war. 13They said to them: "Do not bring the captives here, for what you are planning will make us guilty before the

28:5–8, 16–23 The account of Ahaz's reign in 2 Kings refers to hostilities of Syria (Aram) and Israel against Judah, the revolt of the Edomites, submission to Tiglath-pileser, king of Assyria, the stripping of Temple treasures to pay him tribute, and, in deference to him, shaping the cult of the Jerusalem Temple according to patterns seen in Damascus (2 Kgs 16:5–18; cf. Is 7:1–2). The account in Kings relates all this to an attack of Syria and Israel on Judah (735 B.C.), as they attempted to force Judah into an anti-Assyrian coalition; but the Chronicler, who does not mention the attack, depicts these troubles as the result of, or examples of, Ahaz's infidelity.

v: 2 Kgs 15:36–38. *w:* 2 Kgs 16:1–4. *x:* Lv 18:21; 2 Kgs 16:3. *y:* 2 Kgs 16:5; Is 7:1–9.

LORD and increase our sins and our guilt. Great is our guilt, and there is burning anger upon Israel." [14]Therefore the soldiers left their captives and the plunder before the princes and the whole assembly. [15]Then the men just named proceeded to help the captives. All of them who were naked they clothed from the spoils; they clothed them, put sandals on their feet, gave them food and drink, anointed them, and all who were weak they set on donkeys. They brought them to Jericho, the City of Palms, to their kinfolk. Then they returned to Samaria.[z]

Further Sins of Ahaz. [16]At that time King Ahaz sent an appeal for help to the kings of Assyria.[a] [17]The Edomites had returned, attacked Judah, and carried off captives.[b] [18]The Philistines too had raided the cities of the Shephelah and the Negeb of Judah; they captured Beth-shemesh, Aijalon, Gederoth, Soco and its dependencies, Timnah and its dependencies, and Gimzo and its dependencies, and settled there. [19]For the LORD had brought Judah low because of Ahaz, king of Israel,* who let Judah go its own way and committed treachery against the LORD. [20]Tiglath-pileser, king of Assyria, did indeed come to him, but to oppress him rather than to lend strength.[c] [21]Though Ahaz plundered the LORD's house and the houses of the king and the princes to pay off the king of Assyria, it was no help to him.[d]

[22]While he was already in distress, the same King Ahaz increased his treachery to the LORD. [23]He sacrificed to the gods of Damascus who had defeated him, saying, "Since it was the gods of the kings of Aram who helped them, I will sacrifice to them that they may help me also." However, they only furthered his downfall and that of all Israel.[e] [24]Ahaz gathered up the utensils of God's house and broke them in pieces. He closed the doors of the LORD's house and made altars for himself in every corner of Jerusalem.[f] [25]In every city throughout Judah he set up high places to offer sacrifice to other gods. Thus he provoked the LORD, the God of his ancestors, to anger.

[26][g] The rest of his words and his deeds, first and last, are recorded in the book of the kings of Judah and Israel. [27]Ahaz rested with his ancestors and was buried in Jerusalem—in the city, for they did not bring him to the tombs of the kings of Israel. His son Hezekiah succeeded him as king.

CHAPTER 29

See RG 203–4

Hezekiah's Reforms. [1][h] Hezekiah was twenty-five years old when he became king, and he reigned twenty-nine years in Jerusalem. His mother's name was Abijah, daughter of Zechariah. [2]He did what was right in the LORD's sight, just as David his father had done. [3]In the first month of the first year of his reign, he opened the doors of the LORD's house and repaired them.[i] [4]He summoned the priests and Levites, gathering them in the open space to the east, [5]and said to them: "Listen to me, you Levites! Sanctify yourselves now and sanctify the house of the LORD, the God of your ancestors, and clean out the filth from the sanctuary. [6]Our ancestors acted treacherously and did what was evil in the eyes of the LORD, our God. They abandoned him, turned away their faces from the LORD's dwelling, and turned their backs on him. [7]They also closed the doors of the vestibule, extinguished the lamps, and failed to burn incense and sacrifice burnt offerings in the sanctuary to the God of Israel.[j] [8][k] Therefore the anger of the LORD has come upon Judah and Jerusalem; he has made them an object of terror, horror, and hissing, as you see with your own eyes. [9]For our ancestors fell by the sword, and our sons, our daughters, and our wives have been taken captive because of this. [10]Now, I intend to make a covenant with the LORD, the God of Israel, that his burning anger may turn away from us. [11]My sons, do not be neg-

28:19 Ahaz, king of Israel: in his account of the period of the divided monarchy, the Chronicler regularly uses the term "Israel" as here to designate, not the Northern Kingdom, but the entire people. See note on 10:1.

z: Lk 10:25–37. *a:* 2 Kgs 16:7. *b:* 2 Kgs 16:6. *c:* 2 Kgs 16:10; Is 7:17–20; 8:5–8. *d:* 2 Kgs 16:8. *e:* 2 Kgs 16:12–13; Is 10:20. *f:* 2 Chr 29:3; 30:14; 2 Kgs 16:17. *g:* 2 Kgs 16:19–20. *h:* 2 Kgs 18:2–3. *i:* 2 Chr 28:24. *j:* 2 Kgs 16:15. *k:* Lv 26:32–33; Dt 28:25; Jer 25:18.

ligent any longer, for it is you whom the LORD has chosen to stand before him, to minister to him, to be his ministers and to offer incense."

[12]Then the Levites arose: Mahath, son of Amasai, and Joel, son of Azariah, of the Kohathites; of the descendants of Merari: Kish, son of Abdi, and Azariah, son of Jehallel; of the Gershonites: Joah, son of Zimmah, and Eden, son of Joah; [13]of the sons of Elizaphan: Shimri and Jeuel; of the sons of Asaph: Zechariah and Mattaniah; [14]of the sons of Heman: Jehuel and Shimei; of the sons of Jeduthun: Shemiah and Uzziel. [15]They gathered their kinfolk together and sanctified themselves; then they came as the king had ordered, in keeping with the words of the LORD, to cleanse the LORD's house.

[16]The priests entered the interior of the LORD's house to cleanse it. Whatever they found in the LORD's temple that was unclean they brought out to the court of the LORD's house, where the Levites took it from them and carried it out to the Wadi Kidron. [17]They began the work of consecration on the first day of the first month, and on the eighth day of the month they reached the vestibule of the LORD; they consecrated the LORD's house over an eight-day period, and on the sixteenth day of the first month, they had finished.

[18]Then they went inside to King Hezekiah and said: "We have cleansed the entire house of the LORD, the altar for burnt offerings with all its utensils, and the table for the showbread with all its utensils. [19]We have restored and consecrated all the articles which King Ahaz had thrown away during his reign because of his treachery; they are now before the LORD's altar."

The Rite of Expiation. [20]Then King Hezekiah hastened to convoke the princes of the city and went up to the LORD's house. [21]Seven bulls, seven rams, seven lambs, and seven he-goats were presented as a purification offering for the kingdom, for the sanctuary, and for Judah. Hezekiah ordered the sons of Aaron, the priests, to offer them on the altar of the LORD. [22]They slaughtered the bulls, and the priests collected the blood and splashed it on the altar. Then they slaughtered the rams and splashed the blood on the altar; then they slaughtered the lambs and splashed the blood on the altar. [23]Then the he-goats for the purification offering were led before the king and the assembly, who laid their hands upon them. [24]The priests then slaughtered them and offered their blood on the altar to atone for the sin of all Israel. For the king had said, "The burnt offering and the purification offering are for all Israel."

[25]He stationed the Levites in the LORD's house with cymbals, harps, and lyres, according to the command of David, of Gad the king's seer, and of Nathan the prophet; for this command was from the LORD through his prophets. [26]The Levites were stationed with the instruments of David, and the priests with the trumpets. [27]Then Hezekiah ordered the burnt offering to be sacrificed on the altar. At the very moment the burnt offering began, they also began the song of the LORD, to the accompaniment of the trumpets and the instruments of David, king of Israel. [28]The entire assembly bowed down, and the song was sung and the trumpets sounded until the burnt offering had been completed. [29]Once the burnt offering was completed, the king and all who were with him knelt and worshiped. [30]King Hezekiah and the princes then told the Levites to sing the praises of the LORD in the words of David and of Asaph the seer. They sang praises till their joy was full, then fell down and worshiped.

[31]Hezekiah then said: "You have dedicated yourselves to the LORD. Approach, and bring forward the sacrifices and thank offerings for the house of the LORD." Then the assembly brought forward the sacrifices and thank offerings and all their voluntary burnt offerings. [32]The number of burnt offerings that the assembly brought forward was seventy oxen, one hundred rams, and two hundred lambs: all of these as a burnt offering to the LORD. [33]As consecrated gifts there were six hundred oxen and three thousand sheep. [34]Since there were too few priests to skin all the victims for the burnt offerings, their fellow Levites assisted them until the task was completed and the priests had sanctified themselves. The Levites, in fact, were more careful than the priests to sanctify them-

selves.[l] [35]The burnt offerings were indeed many, along with the fat of the communion offerings and the libations for the burnt offerings. Thus the service of the house of the LORD was re-established. [36]Hezekiah and all the people rejoiced over what God had re-established for the people, and at how suddenly this had been done.

See RG 203–4

CHAPTER 30

Invitation to Passover. [1]Hezekiah sent word to all Israel and Judah, and even wrote letters to Ephraim and Manasseh, saying that they should come to the house of the LORD in Jerusalem to celebrate the Passover to the LORD, the God of Israel.[m] [2][n]The king, his princes, and the entire assembly in Jerusalem had agreed to celebrate the Passover during the second month. [3]They could not celebrate it at the regular time because the priests had not sanctified themselves in sufficient numbers, and the people were not gathered at Jerusalem. [4]This seemed right to the king and the entire assembly, [5]and they issued a decree to be proclaimed throughout all Israel from Beer-sheba to Dan, that everyone should come to celebrate the Passover to the LORD, the God of Israel, in Jerusalem; for not many had kept it in the prescribed manner. [6]By the king's command, the couriers, with the letters written by the king and his princes, went through all Israel and Judah. They said: "Israelites, return to the LORD, the God of Abraham, Isaac, and Israel, that he may return to you, the remnant left from the hands of the Assyrian kings. [7]Do not be like your ancestors and your kin who acted treacherously toward the LORD, the God of their ancestors, so that he handed them over to desolation, as you yourselves now see.[o] [8]Do not be stiff-necked, as your ancestors were; stretch out your hands to the LORD and come to his sanctuary that he has consecrated forever, and serve the LORD, your God, that he may turn his burning anger from you. [9]If you return to the LORD, your kinfolk and your children will find mercy with their captors and return to this land. The LORD, your God, is gracious and merciful and he will not turn away his face from you if you return to him."[p]

[10]So the couriers passed from city to city in the land of Ephraim and Manasseh and as far as Zebulun, but they were derided and scoffed at. [11]Nevertheless, some from Asher, Manasseh, and Zebulun humbled themselves and came to Jerusalem. [12]In Judah, however, the hand of God brought it about that the people were of one heart to carry out the command of the king and the princes by the word of the LORD. [13]Thus many people gathered in Jerusalem to celebrate the feast of Unleavened Bread in the second month; it was a very great assembly.

Passover Celebrated. [14]They proceeded to remove the altars that were in Jerusalem as well as all the altars of incense, and cast them into the Wadi Kidron.[q] [15]They slaughtered the Passover on the fourteenth day of the second month. The priests and Levites were shamed into sanctifying themselves and brought burnt offerings into the house of the LORD. [16]They stood in the places prescribed for them according to the law of Moses, the man of God. The priests splashed the blood given them by the Levites; [17]for many in the assembly had not sanctified themselves, and the Levites were in charge of slaughtering the Passover victims for all who were unclean so as to consecrate them to the LORD.[r] [18]The greater part of the people, in fact, chiefly from Ephraim, Manasseh, Issachar, and Zebulun, had not cleansed themselves. Nevertheless they ate the Passover, contrary to the prescription; because Hezekiah prayed for them, saying, "May the good LORD grant pardon to [19]all who have set their heart to seek God, the LORD, the God of their ancestors, even though they are not clean as holiness requires." [20]The LORD heard Hezekiah and healed the people.

[21]Thus the Israelites who were in Jerusalem celebrated the feast of Unleavened Bread with great rejoicing for seven days, and the Levites and the priests sang the praises of the LORD day after day with all

l: 1 Chr 15:12. *m:* Ex 12:1–28. *n:* Nm 9:6–13. *o:* Acts 7:51. *p:* 1 Kgs 8:50. *q:* 2 Chr 28:24–25. *r:* 2 Chr 35:6.

their strength. 22 Hezekiah spoke encouragingly to all the Levites who had shown themselves well skilled in the service of the LORD. And when they had completed the seven days of festival, sacrificing communion offerings and singing praises to the LORD, the God of their ancestors, 23 the whole assembly agreed to celebrate another seven days. So with joy they celebrated seven days more. 24 King Hezekiah of Judah had contributed a thousand bulls and seven thousand sheep to the assembly, and the princes a thousand bulls and ten thousand sheep. The priests sanctified themselves in great numbers, 25 and the whole assembly of Judah rejoiced, together with the priests and Levites and the rest of the assembly that had come from Israel, as well as the resident aliens from the land of Israel and those that lived in Judah. 26 There was great rejoicing in Jerusalem, for since the days of Solomon, son of David, king of Israel, there had been nothing like it in the city. 27 Then the levitical priests rose and blessed the people; their voice was heard and their prayer reached heaven, God's holy dwelling.

See RG 203–4

CHAPTER 31

Liturgical Reforms. 1 After all this was over, those Israelites who had been present went forth to the cities of Judah and smashed the sacred pillars, cut down the asherahs, and tore down the high places and altars throughout Judah, Benjamin, Ephraim, and Manasseh, until they were all destroyed.[s] Then the Israelites returned to their cities, each to his own possession.

2 Hezekiah re-established the divisions of the priests and the Levites according to their former divisions, assigning to each priest and Levite his proper service, whether in regard to burnt offerings or communion offerings, thanksgiving or praise, or ministering in the gates of the encampment of the LORD. 3 From his own wealth the king allotted a portion for burnt offerings, those of morning and evening and those on sabbaths, new moons, and festivals, as is written in the law of the LORD.[t] 4 He also commanded the people living in Jerusalem to provide for the support of the priests and Levites, that they might firmly adhere to the law of the LORD.

5 As soon as the order was promulgated, the Israelites brought, in great quantities, the best of their grain, wine, oil, and honey, and all the produce of the fields; they gave a generous tithe of everything.[u] 6 Israelites and Judahites living in other cities of Judah also brought in tithes of oxen, sheep, and votive offerings consecrated to the LORD, their God; these they brought in and heaped up in piles.[v] 7 It was in the third month that they began to establish these heaps, and they completed them in the seventh month.* 8 When Hezekiah and the princes had come and seen the piles, they blessed the LORD and his people Israel. 9 Then Hezekiah questioned the priests and the Levites concerning the piles, 10 and the priest Azariah, head of the house of Zadok, answered him, "Since they began to bring the offerings to the house of the LORD, we have eaten, been satisfied, and had much left over, for the LORD has blessed his people. This great supply is what was left over."[w]

11 Hezekiah then gave orders that chambers be constructed in the house of the LORD. When this had been done, 12 they deposited the offerings, tithes, and votive offerings there for safekeeping. The overseer of these things was Conaniah the Levite, and his brother Shimei was second in command. 13 Jehiel, Azaziah, Nahath, Asahel, Jerimoth, Jozabad, Eliel, Ismachiah, Mahath, and Benaiah were supervisors subject to Conaniah the Levite and his brother Shimei by appointment of King Hezekiah and of Azariah, the prefect of the house of God. 14 Kore, the son of Imnah, a Levite and the keeper of the eastern gate, was in charge of the voluntary offerings made to God; he distributed the offerings made to the LORD and the most holy of the votive offerings. 15 Under him in the

31:7 Third month . . . seventh month: between the late spring feast of Weeks or Pentecost and the fall feast of Booths or Tabernacles, there is seldom any rain in Palestine; at the end of this dry period the problem of storage (v. 11) would become acute.

s: 2 Chr 34:3–4; 2 Kgs 18:4. *t:* Nm 28–29; 1 Chr 29:3; Ez 45:17. *u:* Nm 18:18–24; Dt 14:22–23. *v:* Neh 12:44–47; 13:10–13. *w:* Lv 25:19–22.

priestly cities were Eden, Miniamin, Jeshua, Shemaiah, Amariah, and Shecaniah, who faithfully made the distribution to their brothers, great and small alike, according to their divisions.

16There was also a register by ancestral houses of males three years of age* and over, for all priests who were eligible to enter the house of the LORD according to the daily schedule to fulfill their service in the order of their divisions.[x] 17The priests were inscribed in their family records according to their ancestral houses, as were the Levites twenty years of age and over according to their various offices and divisions.[y] 18A distribution was also made to all who were inscribed in the family records, for their little ones, wives, sons and daughters—thus for the entire assembly, since they were to sanctify themselves by sharing faithfully in the votive offerings. 19The sons of Aaron, the priests who lived on the lands attached to their cities, had in every city men designated by name to distribute portions to every male of the priests and to every Levite listed in the family records.

20Hezekiah did this in all Judah. He did what was good, upright, and faithful before the LORD, his God. 21Everything that he undertook, for the service of the house of God or for the law and the commandment, was to seek his God. He did this with all his heart, and he prospered.[z]

CHAPTER 32

See RG 203-4

Sennacherib's Invasion. 1But after all this and all Hezekiah's fidelity, there came Sennacherib, king of Assyria. He invaded Judah and besieged the fortified cities, intending to breach and take them.[a] 2When Hezekiah saw that Sennacherib was coming with the intention of attacking Jerusalem, 3he took the advice of his princes and warriors to stop the waters of the springs outside the city; they promised their help. 4[b] A large force was gathered and stopped all the springs and also the stream running nearby. For they said, "Why should the kings of Assyria come and find an abundance of water?" 5He then looked to his defenses: he rebuilt the wall where it was broken down, raised towers upon it, and built another wall outside.[c] He strengthened the Millo of the City of David and made a great number of spears and shields. 6Then he appointed army commanders over the people. He gathered them together in his presence in the open space at the gate of the city and encouraged them with these words: 7"Be strong and steadfast; do not be afraid or dismayed because of the king of Assyria and all the horde coming with him, for there is more with us than with him.[d] 8He has only an arm of flesh, but we have the LORD, our God, to help us and to fight our battles."[e] And the people took confidence from the words of Hezekiah, king of Judah.

Threat of Sennacherib. 9[f] After this, while Sennacherib, king of Assyria, himself remained at Lachish with all his forces, he sent his officials to Jerusalem with this message for Hezekiah, king of Judah, and all the Judahites who were in Jerusalem: 10"Thus says Sennacherib, king of Assyria: In what are you trusting, now that you are under siege in Jerusalem? 11Is not Hezekiah deceiving you, delivering you over to a death of famine and thirst, by his claim that 'the LORD, our God, will rescue us from the grasp of the king of Assyria'? 12Has not this same Hezekiah removed the Lord's own high places and altars and commanded Judah and Jerusalem, 'You shall bow down before one altar only, and on it alone you shall offer incense'? 13Do you not know what my fathers and I have done to all the peoples of other lands? Were the gods of the nations in those lands able to rescue their lands from my hand? 14Who among all the gods of those nations which my fathers put under the ban was able to rescue their people from my hand? Will your god, then, be able to rescue you from my hand? 15Let not Hezekiah mislead you further and deceive you in

31:16 Three years of age: this may be a textual error for "thirty years." According to Nm 4:3, 23, 30, men of the priestly clans served from the ages of thirty to fifty.

x: 1 Chr 23:3–4. *y:* 1 Chr 23:6–24. *z:* Ps 119:2. *a:* 2 Kgs 18:13. *b:* Is 22:9, 11. *c:* Neh 2:17–18. *d:* 2 Chr 14:10; 20:6–12. *e:* Is 31:3. *f:* 2 Kgs 18:17–37; Is 36:1–22.

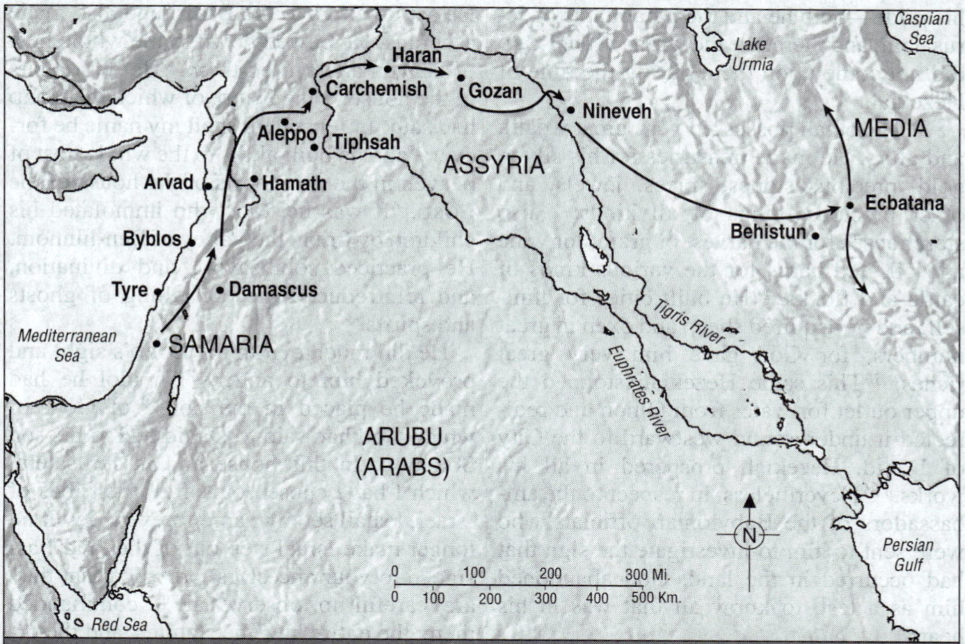

Exile of Northern Kingdom

any such way. Do not believe him! Since no
other god of any other nation or kingdom has
been able to rescue his people from my hand
or the hands of my fathers, how much the less
shall your god rescue you from my hand!"
16 His officials said still more against the
LORD God and against his servant Hezekiah,
17 for he had written letters to deride the
LORD, the God of Israel, speaking of him in
these terms: "As the gods of the nations in
other lands have not rescued their people
from my hand, neither shall Hezekiah's god
rescue his people from my hand."[g] 18 In a
loud voice they shouted in the language of
Judah to the people of Jerusalem who were
on the wall, to frighten and terrify them so
that they might capture their city. 19 They
spoke of the God of Israel as though he were
one of the gods of the other peoples of the
earth, a work of human hands. 20 But because
of this, King Hezekiah and Isaiah the
prophet, son of Amoz, prayed and cried out
to heaven.[h]

Sennacherib's Defeat. 21 Then the LORD
sent an angel, who destroyed every warrior,
leader, and commander in the camp of the
Assyrian king, so that he had to return
shamefaced to his own country. And when
he entered the temple of his god, some of his
own offspring struck him down there with
the sword.[i] 22 Thus the LORD saved Hezekiah
and the inhabitants of Jerusalem from the
hand of Sennacherib, king of Assyria, as
from every other power; he gave them rest
on every side. 23 Many brought gifts for the
LORD to Jerusalem and costly objects for
Hezekiah, king of Judah, who thereafter was
exalted in the eyes of all the nations.[j]

Hezekiah's Later Reign. 24 In those days
Hezekiah became mortally ill. He prayed to
the LORD, who answered him by giving him
a sign.[k] 25 Hezekiah, however, did not respond with like generosity, for he had become arrogant. Therefore wrath descended
upon him and upon Judah and Jerusalem.
26[l] But then Hezekiah humbled himself for

g: 2 Kgs 19:9–13; Is 37:9–13. *h:* 2 Kgs 19:14–19; Is 37:14–20. *i:* 2 Kgs 19:35–37; Is 37:36–38. *j:* 2 Chr 17:10–11. *k:* 2 Kgs 20:1–11; Is 38:1–8. *l:* 2 Kgs 20:12–19; Is 39:1–8.

his pride—both he and the inhabitants of Jerusalem; and therefore the wrath of the LORD did not come upon them during the time of Hezekiah.

[27][m] Hezekiah possessed very great wealth and glory. He made treasuries for his silver, gold, precious stones, spices, jewels, and other precious things of all kinds; [28]also storehouses for the harvest of grain, for wine and oil, and barns for the various kinds of cattle and flocks. [29]He built cities for himself, and he acquired sheep and oxen in great numbers, for God gave him very great riches. [30]This same Hezekiah stopped the upper outlet for water from Gihon and redirected it underground westward to the City of David. Hezekiah prospered in all his works.[n] [31]Nevertheless, in respect to the ambassadors of the Babylonian officials who were sent to him to investigate the sign that had occurred in the land, God abandoned him as a test, to know all that was in his heart.

[32]The rest of Hezekiah's acts, including his good deeds, are recorded in the vision of Isaiah the prophet, son of Amoz, and in the book of the kings of Judah and Israel. [33]Hezekiah rested with his ancestors; he was buried at the approach to the tombs* of the descendants of David. All Judah and the inhabitants of Jerusalem paid him honor at his death. His son Manasseh succeeded him as king.

CHAPTER 33

See RG 203-4

Manasseh's Impiety. [1][o] Manasseh was twelve years old when he became king, and he reigned fifty-five years in Jerusalem. [2]He did what was evil in the LORD's sight, following the abominable practices of the nations whom the LORD dispossessed before the Israelites. [3]He rebuilt the high places which Hezekiah his father had torn down. He set up altars to the Baals, and also made asherahs. He bowed down to the whole host of heaven and served them. [4]He built altars in the house of the LORD, of which the LORD had said: In Jerusalem shall my name be forever; [5]and he built altars to the whole host of heaven in the two courts of the house of the LORD. [6]It was he, too, who immolated his children by fire in the Valley of Ben-hinnom. He practiced soothsaying and divination, and reintroduced the consulting of ghosts and spirits.

He did much evil in the LORD's sight and provoked him to anger. [7]An idol he had made he placed in the house of God, of which God had said to David and to his son Solomon: In this house and in Jerusalem, which I have chosen out of all the tribes of Israel, I shall set my name forever. [8]I will no longer make Israel step out of the land I assigned to your ancestors, provided that they are careful to observe all I commanded them, the entire law, the statutes, and the ordinances given by Moses.

[9]Manasseh misled Judah and the inhabitants of Jerusalem into doing even greater evil than the nations the LORD had destroyed at the coming of the Israelites. [10]The LORD spoke to Manasseh and his people, but they paid no attention.

Manasseh's Conversion. [11][p] Therefore the LORD brought against them the army commanders of the Assyrian king; they captured Manasseh with hooks, shackled him with chains, and transported him to Babylon.* [12]In his distress, he began to appease the LORD, his God. He humbled himself abjectly before the God of his ancestors, [13]and prayed to him.* The LORD let himself be won over: he heard his prayer and restored him to his kingdom in Jerusalem. Then Manasseh knew that the LORD is indeed God.

[14]Afterward he built an outer wall for the

32:33 The approach to the tombs: lit., "the ascent of the tombs," perhaps "the upper section of the tombs," i.e., their most prominent and honored place.

33:11 There is no evidence elsewhere for such an imprisonment of King Manasseh in Babylon. According to the Assyrian inscriptions, however, Manasseh did pay tribute to the Assyrian kings Esarhaddon (680–669 B.C.) and Asshurbanipal (668–627 B.C.). He may well then have been obliged to go to Nineveh, Assyria's capital (rather than to Babylon as the Chronicler has it), to take his oath of allegiance as vassal to the king of Assyria.

33:13 And prayed to him: these words inspired an unknown writer to compose the apocryphal "Prayer of Manasseh," which since the Council of Trent appears as an appendix to many editions of the Vulgate Bible and is used in the Church's liturgy.

m: 2 Kgs 20:13; Is 39:2. *n:* 2 Kgs 20:20–21. *o:* 2 Kgs 21:1–9. *p:* Jb 36:8; Ez 19:9.

City of David to the west of Gihon in the valley, extending to the Fish Gate and encircling Ophel; he built it very high. He stationed army officers in all the fortified cities
of Judah. 15He removed the foreign gods and
the idol from the LORD's house and all the altars he had built on the mount of the LORD's
house and in Jerusalem, and cast them outside the city.[q] 16He restored the altar of the
LORD, and sacrificed on it communion offerings and thank offerings, and commanded
Judah to serve the LORD, the God of Israel.
17Though the people continued to sacrifice
on the high places, they now did so to the
LORD, their God.

18[r] The rest of the acts of Manasseh, his
prayer to his God, and the words of the seers
who spoke to him in the name of the LORD,
the God of Israel, are written in the chronicles of the kings of Israel. 19His prayer and
how his supplication was heard, all his sins
and his treachery, the sites where he built
high places and set up asherahs and carved
images before he humbled himself, all this is
recorded in the chronicles of his seers. 20Ma-
nasseh rested with his ancestors and was
buried in his own palace. His son Amon succeeded him as king.

Reign of Amon. 21[s] Amon was twenty-
two years old when he became king, and he
reigned two years in Jerusalem. 22He did
what was evil in the LORD's sight, as his father Manasseh had done. Amon offered
sacrifice to all the idols his father Manasseh
had made, and served them. 23Moreover, he
did not humble himself before the LORD as
his father Manasseh had humbled himself;
on the contrary, Amon only increased his
guilt. 24His officials plotted against him
and put him to death in his palace, 25but the
people of the land then slew all who had
plotted against King Amon, and the people
of the land made his son Josiah king in his
stead.

CHAPTER 34

See RG 203-4

Josiah's Reforms. 1[t] Josiah was eight
years old when he became king, and he
reigned thirty-one years in Jerusalem. 2He
did what was right in the LORD's sight, walking in the way of David his father, not turning right or left. 3[u] In the eighth year of his
reign, while he was still a youth, he began to
seek after the God of David his father. Then
in his twelfth year* he began to purify Judah
and Jerusalem of the high places, the asherahs, and the carved and molten images. 4In
his presence, the altars of the Baals were
torn down; the incense stands erected above
them he broke down; the asherahs and the
carved and molten images he smashed and
beat into dust, which he scattered over the
tombs of those who had sacrificed to them;
5and the bones of the priests he burned upon
their altars. Thus he purified Judah and Jerusalem. 6He did likewise in the cities of Manasseh, Ephraim, Simeon, and in the ruined
villages of the surrounding country as far as
Naphtali; 7he tore down the altars and asherahs, and the carved images he beat into
dust, and broke down the incense stands
throughout the land of Israel. Then he returned to Jerusalem.

The Temple Restored. 8[v] In the eighteenth
year of his reign, in order to purify the land
and the temple, he sent Shaphan, son of Azaliah, Maaseiah, the ruler of the city, and
Joah, son of Joahaz, the chancellor, to restore the house of the LORD, his God. 9They
came to Hilkiah the high priest and turned
over the money brought to the house of God
which the Levites, the guardians of the
threshold, had collected from Manasseh,
Ephraim, and all the remnant of Israel, as
well as from all of Judah, Benjamin, and the
inhabitants of Jerusalem.[w] 10They turned it
over to the master workers in the house of
the LORD, and these in turn used it to pay the

34:3 In his twelfth year: ca. 628 B.C., i.e., around the time of the Assyrian emperor Asshurbanipal's death, which enabled Judah to free itself from Assyrian domination. On the basis of 2 Kgs 22:1–23:25 alone, one might suppose that Josiah's reform began only after and as a result of the discovery of the book of the law in the Temple, in the eighteenth year of his reign (622 B.C.). But the Chronicler is no doubt right in placing the beginning of the reform at an earlier period. The repair of the Temple itself, which led to the finding of the book of the law, was likely part of a cultic reform initiated by Josiah.

q: 2 Chr 14:2. *r:* 2 Kgs 21:17–18. *s:* 2 Kgs 21:19–26. *t:* 2 Kgs 22:1–2. *u:* 2 Chr 14:1–4; 31:1; 2 Kgs 23:4–20. *v:* 2 Kgs 22:3–7. *w:* 2 Chr 24:8–9.

workers in the LORD's house who were restoring and repairing it. [11]They also gave it to the carpenters and the masons to buy hewn stone and timber for the tie beams and rafters of the buildings which the kings of Judah had allowed to fall into ruin. [12]The men worked faithfully at their task; their overseers were Jahath and Obadiah, Levites of the line of Merari, and Zechariah and Meshullam, of the Kohathites, who directed them. All those Levites who were skillful with musical instruments [13]were in charge of the men who carried the burdens, and they directed all the workers in every kind of labor. Some of the other Levites were scribes, officials, and gatekeepers.

The Finding of the Law. [14x] When they brought out the money that had been deposited in the house of the LORD, Hilkiah the priest found the book of the law of the LORD given through Moses. [15]He reported this to Shaphan the scribe, saying, "I have found the book of the law in the house of the LORD." Hilkiah gave the book to Shaphan, [16]who brought it to the king at the same time that he made his report to him. He said, "Your servants are doing everything that has been entrusted to them; [17]they have smelted down the silver deposited in the LORD's house and have turned it over to the overseers and the workers." [18]Then Shaphan the scribe also informed the king, "Hilkiah the priest has given me a book," and then Shaphan read it in the presence of the king.

[19]When the king heard the words of the law, he tore his garments. [20]The king then issued this command to Hilkiah, to Ahikam, son of Shaphan, to Abdon, son of Michah, to Shaphan the scribe, and to Asaiah, the king's servant: [21]"Go, consult the LORD for me and for those who are left in Israel and Judah, about the words of the book that has been found, for the anger of the LORD burns furiously against us, because our ancestors did not keep the word of the LORD and have not done all that is written in this book." [22]Then Hilkiah and others from the king went to Huldah the prophet, wife of Shallum, son of Tokhath, son of Hasrah, keeper of the wardrobe; she lived in Jerusalem, in the Second Quarter. They spoke to her as they had been instructed, [23]and she said to them: "Thus says the LORD, the God of Israel: Say to the man who sent you to me, [24]Thus says the LORD: I am about to bring evil upon this place and upon its inhabitants, all the curses written in the book that was read before the king of Judah. [25]Because they have abandoned me and have burned incense to other gods, provoking me by all the works of their hands, my anger burns against this place and it cannot be extinguished.

[26]"But to the king of Judah who sent you to consult the LORD, give this response: Thus says the LORD, the God of Israel: As for the words you have heard, [27]because you were heartsick and have humbled yourself before God when you heard his words concerning this place and its inhabitants; because you humbled yourself before me, tore your garments, and wept before me, I in turn have heard—oracle of the LORD. [28]I will gather you to your ancestors and you shall go to your grave in peace, and your eyes shall not see all the evil I am about to bring upon this place and upon its inhabitants."

This they reported to the king.

Covenant Renewal. [29y] The king then had all the elders of Judah and of Jerusalem summoned before him. [30]The king went up to the house of the LORD with all the people of Judah and the inhabitants of Jerusalem: priests, Levites, and all the people, great and small. He read aloud to them all the words of the book of the covenant that had been found in the house of the LORD. [31]The king stood by the column* and made a covenant in the presence of the LORD to follow the LORD and to observe his commandments, statutes, and decrees with his whole heart and soul, carrying out the words of the covenant written in this book. [32]He thereby committed all who were in Jerusalem and Benjamin, and the inhabitants of Jerusalem acted according to the covenant of God, the God of their ancestors. [33]Josiah removed every abomination

34:31 The column: see note on 23:13.

x: 2 Kgs 22:8–20. *y:* 2 Kgs 23:1–3.

from all the territories belonging to the Israelites, and he obliged all who were in Israel to serve the LORD, their God. During his lifetime they did not turn away from following the LORD, the God of their ancestors.[z]

CHAPTER 35

See RG 203-4

The Passover. 1[a] Josiah celebrated in Jerusalem a Passover to honor the LORD; the Passover sacrifice was slaughtered on the fourteenth day of the first month.[b] 2 He reappointed the priests to their duties and confirmed them in the service of the LORD's house. 3 He said to the Levites who were to instruct all Israel, and who were consecrated to the LORD: "Put the holy ark in the house built by Solomon, son of David, king of Israel. It shall no longer be a burden on your shoulders. Serve now the LORD, your God, and his people Israel.[c] 4 Prepare yourselves by your ancestral houses and your divisions according to the prescriptions of David, king of Israel, and the prescriptions of his son Solomon. 5 Stand in the sanctuary according to the branches of the ancestral houses of your kin, the common people, so that the distribution of the Levites and the families may be the same.[d] 6 Slaughter the Passover sacrifice, sanctify yourselves, and be at the disposition of your kin, that all may be done according to the word of the LORD given through Moses."[e]

7 Josiah contributed to the common people a flock of lambs and young goats,[f] thirty thousand in number, each to serve as a Passover victim for all who were present, and also three thousand oxen; these were from the king's property. 8 His princes also gave a voluntary offering to the people, the priests, and the Levites. Hilkiah, Zechariah, and Jehiel, prefects of the house of God, gave to the priests two thousand six hundred Passover victims along with three hundred oxen.[g] 9 Conaniah and his brothers Shemaiah, Nethanel, Hashabiah, Jehiel, and Jozabad, the rulers of the Levites, contributed to the Levites five thousand Passover victims, together with five hundred oxen.

10 When the service had been arranged, the priests took their places, as did the Levites in their divisions according to the king's command. 11 The Passover sacrifice was slaughtered, whereupon the priests splashed some of the blood and the Levites proceeded with the skinning. 12 They separated out what was destined for the burnt offering and gave it to various groups of the ancestral houses of the common people to offer to the LORD, as is written in the book of Moses. They did the same with the oxen. 13 They cooked the Passover on the fire as prescribed, and also cooked the sacred portions in pots, caldrons, and pans, then brought them quickly to all the common people.[h] 14 Afterward they prepared the Passover for themselves and for the priests. Indeed the priests, the sons of Aaron, were busy sacrificing burnt offerings and the fatty portions until night; therefore the Levites prepared for themselves and for the priests, the sons of Aaron. 15 The singers, the sons of Asaph, were at their posts as commanded by David and by Asaph, Heman, and Jeduthun, the king's seer. The gatekeepers were at every gate; there was no need for them to leave their stations, for their fellow Levites prepared for them. 16 Thus the entire service of the LORD was arranged that day so that the Passover could be celebrated and the burnt offerings sacrificed on the altar of the LORD, as King Josiah had commanded. 17 The Israelites who were present on that occasion kept the Passover and the feast of the Unleavened Bread for seven days. 18[i] No such Passover had been observed in Israel since the time of Samuel the prophet; no king of Israel had observed a Passover like that celebrated by Josiah, the priests, and Levites, all of Judah and Israel that were present, and the inhabitants of Jerusalem. 19 It was in the eighteenth year of Josiah's reign that this Passover was observed.

Josiah's End. 20 After Josiah had done all this to restore the temple, Neco, king of Egypt, came up to fight at Carchemish on the Euphrates, and Josiah went out to meet him. 21 Neco sent messengers to him, saying: "What quarrel is between us, king of Judah? I

z: 2 Kgs 23:4–20. *a:* 2 Kgs 23:21–23. *b:* Ex 12:1–28; 2 Kgs 23:21. *c:* 2 Chr 5:4; 1 Chr 15:12, 15. *d:* 1 Chr 24–26. *e:* 2 Chr 30:17. *f:* Ex 12:5. *g:* Nm 7:1–83. *h:* Ex 12:8–9. *i:* 2 Kgs 23:22–23.

have not come against you this day, for my war is with another kingdom, and God has told me to hasten. Do not interfere with God who is with me; let him not destroy you." [22]But Josiah would not withdraw from him, for he was seeking a pretext to fight with him. Therefore he would not listen to the words of Neco that came from the mouth of God, but went out to fight in the plain of Megiddo. [23]Then the archers shot King Josiah, who said to his servants, "Take me away, I am seriously wounded."[j] [24]His servants took him from his own chariot, placed him in the one he had in reserve, and brought him to Jerusalem, where he died. He was buried in the tombs of his ancestors, and all Judah and Jerusalem mourned him. [25]Jeremiah also composed a lamentation for Josiah, which is recited to this day by all the male and female singers in their lamentations for Josiah. These have been made an ordinance for Israel, and can be found written in the Lamentations.*

[26][k] The rest of the acts of Josiah, his good deeds in accord with what is written in the law of the LORD, [27]and his words, first and last, are recorded in the book of the kings of Israel and Judah.

CHAPTER 36

See RG 203–4

Jehoahaz. [1][l] The people of the land took Jehoahaz, son of Josiah, and made him king in Jerusalem to succeed his father. [2]Jehoahaz was twenty-three years old when he became king, and he reigned three months in Jerusalem. [3]The king of Egypt deposed him in Jerusalem and fined the land one hundred talents of silver and a talent of gold. [4]Then the king of Egypt made Eliakim, the brother of Jehoahaz, king over Judah and Jerusalem, changing his name to Jehoiakim. Neco took Jehoahaz his brother away and brought him to Egypt.

Jehoiakim. [5]Jehoiakim was twenty-five years old when he became king, and he reigned eleven years in Jerusalem. He did what was evil in the sight of the LORD, his God.[m] [6][n] Nebuchadnezzar, king of Babylon, attacked and bound him in chains to take him to Babylon.* [7]Nebuchadnezzar also carried away to Babylon some of the vessels of the house of the LORD and put them in his palace in Babylon. [8]The rest of the acts of Jehoiakim, the abominable things that he did, and what therefore happened to him, are recorded in the book of the kings of Israel and Judah. His son Jehoiachin succeeded him as king.[o]

Jehoiachin. [9]Jehoiachin was eighteen years old when he became king, and he reigned three months and ten days in Jerusalem. He did what was evil in the LORD's sight.[p] [10]At the turn of the year, King Nebuchadnezzar sent for him and had him brought to Babylon, along with precious vessels from the house of the LORD. He made his brother Zedekiah* king over Judah and Jerusalem.[q]

Zedekiah. [11]Zedekiah was twenty-one years old when he became king, and he reigned eleven years in Jerusalem.[r] [12]He did what was evil in the sight of the LORD, his God, and he did not humble himself before Jeremiah the prophet, who spoke for the LORD.[s] [13]He also rebelled against King Nebuchadnezzar, who had made him swear by God. He became stiff-necked and hardened his heart rather than return to the LORD, the God of Israel.[t] [14]Likewise all the princes of Judah, the priests, and the people added treachery to treachery, practicing all the abominations of the nations and defiling the LORD's house which he had consecrated in Jerusalem.

The Fall of Judah. [15]Early and often the LORD, the God of their ancestors, sent his messengers to them, for he had compassion on his people and his dwelling place.[u] [16]But they mocked God's messengers, despised his words, and scoffed at his prophets, until the LORD's anger against his people blazed up beyond remedy.[v] [17]Then he brought up against them the king of the Chaldeans, who killed their young men with the sword in their own sanctuary, with compassion for

j: 2 Chr 18:33–34. *k:* 2 Kgs 23:28. *l:* 2 Kgs 23:30–34; 1 Chr 3:15–16. *m:* 2 Kgs 23:36–37; Jer 22:18–19. *n:* 2 Kgs 24:1–2. *o:* 2 Kgs 24:5. *p:* 2 Kgs 24:8–9. *q:* 2 Kgs 24:10–17. *r:* 2 Kgs 24:18–19; Jer 52:1. *s:* Jer 37:1–2. *t:* 2 Kgs 24:20; Jer 52:4; Ez 17:13–16. *u:* Jer 7:25; Heb 1:1. *v:* Mt 23:34–37.

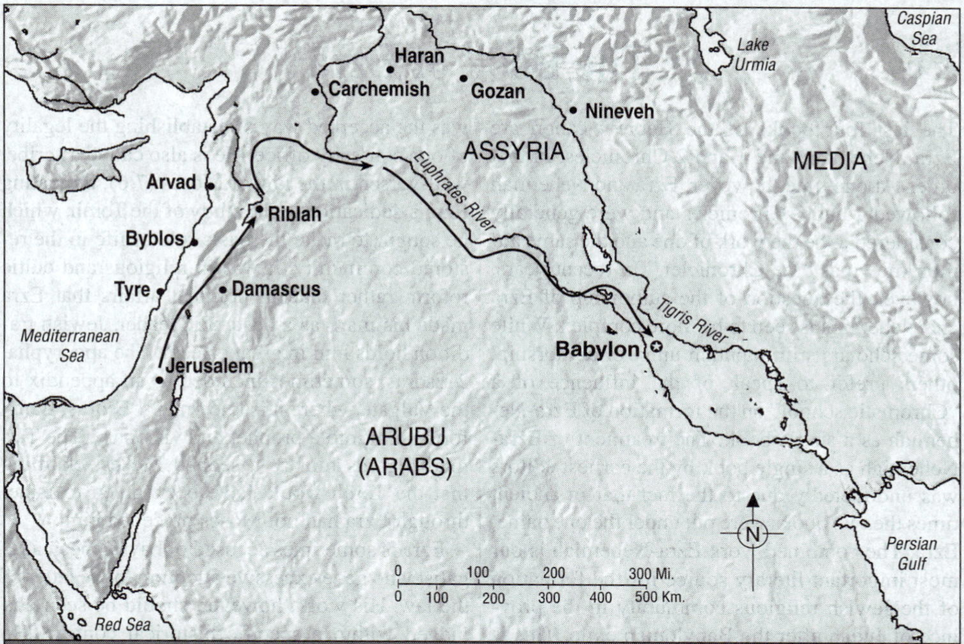

Exile of Southern Kingdom

neither young men nor young women, neither the old nor the infirm; all of them he delivered into his power.[w] 18 All the utensils of
the house of God, large and small, the treasures of the LORD's house, and the treasures
of the king and his princes, all these he
brought to Babylon.[x] 19 They burnt the house
of God, tore down the walls of Jerusalem,
burnt down all its palaces, and destroyed all
its precious objects.[y] 20 Those who escaped
the sword he carried captive to Babylon,
where they became servants to him and his
sons until the Persian kingdom came to
power. 21 All this was to fulfill the word of
the LORD spoken by Jeremiah: Until the land
has retrieved its lost sabbaths, during all the
time it lies waste it shall have rest while seventy years are fulfilled.

Decree of Cyrus. 22* In the first year of
Cyrus, king of Persia, in order to realize the
word of the LORD spoken by Jeremiah, the
LORD roused the spirit of Cyrus, King of
Persia, to spread this proclamation throughout his kingdom, both by word of mouth and
in writing:[z] 23 "Thus says Cyrus, king of Persia: The LORD, the God of heaven, has given
to me all the kingdoms of the earth. He has
also charged me to build him a house in
Jerusalem, which is in Judah. All among
you, therefore, who belong to his people,
may their God be with them; let them go
up."

35:25 There is no mention of such a lamentation for Josiah composed by Jeremiah in either 2 Kings or Jeremiah; but see note on Zec 12:11. **Lamentations**: probably a reference to the Book of Lamentations.

36:6 Nebuchadnezzar . . . bound him in chains to take him to Babylon: the Chronicler does not state that Jehoiakim was actually taken to Babylon. According to 2 Kgs 24:1–6, Jehoiakim revolted after being Nebuchadnezzar's vassal for three years; he died in Jerusalem before the city surrendered to the Babylonians. Dn 1:1–2, apparently based on 2 Chr 36:6–7, does speak of Jehoiakim's deportation to Babylon.

36:10 His brother Zedekiah: Zedekiah was actually the brother of Jehoiakim and the uncle of Jehoiachin (2 Kgs 24:17; Jer 37:1), though scarcely older than his nephew (2 Kgs 24:8, 18; 2 Chr 36:9, 11).

36:22–23 These verses are identical with those of Ezr 1:1–3a and were to prevent the work from ending on a note of doom.

w: Lam 1:15; 5:11–14. *x:* 2 Kgs 25:14–15. *y:* 2 Kgs 25:9–10; Lam 2:8. *z:* Ezr 1:1–4.

See RG 207–11

The Book of Ezra

The last four books of the Hebrew canon are Ezra, Nehemiah, and 1 and 2 Chronicles, in that order. At one time, however, Ezra and Nehemiah followed 1 and 2 Chronicles and were generally considered to be the work of one and the same author known as "the Chronicler." In recent years, however, the question of the authorship of Ezra and Nehemiah is seen to be more complex. While some scholars still maintain unity of authorship, others prefer to speak of the influence of a "Chronistic school" on the formation of Ezra-Nehemiah as a single book. The treatment of Ezra-Nehemiah as a single book by the earliest editors was undoubtedly due to the fact that in ancient times the two books were put under the one name, Ezra. The combined work Ezra-Nehemiah is our most important literary source for the formation of the Jewish religious community in the province of Judah after the Babylonian exile. This is known as the period of the Restoration, and the two men most responsible for the reorganization of Jewish life at this time were Ezra and Nehemiah.

In the present state of the Ezra-Nehemiah text, there are several dislocations of large sections so that the chronological or logical sequence is disrupted. The major instance is Ezra's public reading of the law in Neh 8; others will be pointed out in the footnotes. Since arguments in favor of the chronological priority of Nehemiah to Ezra are indecisive, we accept the order in the text according to which Ezra's activity preceded that of Nehemiah.

What is known of Ezra and his work is derived almost exclusively from Ezr 7–10 (the "Ezra Memoirs") and Neh 8–9. Strictly speaking, the term "Ezra Memoirs" should be used only of that section in which Ezra speaks in the first person, i.e., Ezr 7:27–9:15. Compare the "Nehemiah Memoirs" in Neh 1:1–7:72a; 11:1, 2; 12:27–43; 13:4–31. The author combined this material with other sources at his disposal. The personality of Ezra is not so well-known as that of Nehemiah. Ben Sira, in his praise of the fathers (Sir 44–49), omits mention of Ezra, perhaps for polemical reasons. The genealogy of Ezra (7:1–5) traces his priesthood back to Aaron, brother of Moses. This was the accepted way of establishing the legality of one's priestly office. He is also called a scribe, well-versed in the law of Moses (7:6), indicating Ezra's dedication to the study of the Torah, which he sought to make the basic rule of life in the restored community. It was in religious and cultic reform rather than in political affairs that Ezra made his mark as a postexilic leader. Jewish tradition holds him in great esteem. The apocryphal 2 Esdras, sometimes included as an appendix to the Vulgate, where it is known as 4 Esdras, transforms him into a prophet and visionary. The Talmud regards him as a second Moses, claiming that the Torah would have been given to Israel through Ezra had not Moses preceded him.

Ezra is sometimes accused of having been a legalist who gave excessive attention to the letter of the law. His work, however, should be seen and judged within a specific historical context. He gave to his people a cohesion and spiritual unity which helped to prevent the disintegration of the small Jewish community settled in the province of Judah. Had it not been for the intransigence of Ezra and of those who adopted his ideal, it is doubtful that Judaism would have so effectively resisted Hellenism in later centuries. Ezra set the tone of the postexilic community, and it was characterized by fidelity to the Torah, Judaism's authentic way of life. It is in this light that we can judge most fairly the work of Ezra during the Restoration.

The Book of Ezra is divided as follows:

I. The Return from Exile (1:1–6:22)
II. The Work of Ezra (7:1–10:44)

The following list of the kings of Persia, with the dates of their reigns, will be useful for dating the events mentioned in Ezra-Nehemiah:

Cyrus	539–530 B.C.
Cambyses	530–522 B.C.
Darius I	522–486 B.C.
Xerxes I	486–465 B.C.
Artaxerxes I	465–424 B.C.
Darius II	423–404 B.C.
Artaxerxes II	404–358 B.C.
Artaxerxes III	358–337 B.C.
End of the Persian Empire (Defeat of Darius III)	331 B.C.

I. The Return from Exile

CHAPTER 1

See RG 208

The Decree of Cyrus. [1][a] In the first year of Cyrus,* king of Persia, in order to fulfill the word of the LORD spoken by Jeremiah, the LORD stirred up the spirit of Cyrus king of Persia to issue a proclamation throughout his entire kingdom, both by word of mouth and in writing: [2]"Thus says Cyrus, king of Persia: 'All the kingdoms of the earth the LORD, the God of heaven,* has given to me, and he has charged me to build him a house in Jerusalem, which is in Judah. [3]Those among you who belong to any part of his people, may their God be with them! Let them go up to Jerusalem in Judah to build the house of the LORD the God of Israel, that is, the God who is in Jerusalem. [4]Let all those who have survived, in whatever place they may have lived, be assisted by the people of that place with silver, gold, goods, and livestock, together with voluntary offerings for the house of God in Jerusalem.' "

[5]Then the heads of ancestral houses* of Judah and Benjamin and the priests and Levites—everyone, that is, whose spirit had been stirred up by God—prepared to go up to build the house of the LORD in Jerusalem. [6][b] All their neighbors gave them help in every way, with silver, gold, goods, livestock, and many precious gifts, besides all their voluntary offerings. [7][c] King Cyrus, too, had the vessels of the house of the LORD brought forth that Nebuchadnezzar had taken from Jerusalem and placed in the house of his god. [8]Cyrus, king of Persia, had them brought forth by the treasurer Mithredath, who counted them out to Sheshbazzar, prince of Judah.* [9]This was the inventory: baskets of goldware, thirty; baskets of silverware, one thousand and twenty-nine; [10]golden bowls, thirty; silver bowls, four hundred and ten; other vessels, one thousand. [11]Total of the gold and silver vessels: five thousand four hundred.* All these Sheshbazzar took with him when the exiles were brought up from Babylon to Jerusalem.

CHAPTER 2

See RG 208-9

A Census of the Returned Exiles. [1]* [d] These are the inhabitants of the province who returned from the captivity of the exiles, whom Nebuchadnezzar, king of Babylon, had carried away to Babylon, and who came back to Jerusalem and Judah, to their various cities [2](those who returned with Zerubbabel, Jeshua, Nehemiah, Seraiah, Reelaiah, Mordecai, Bilshan, Mispar, Bigvai, Rehum, and Baanah):

The census of the people of Israel: [3]descendants of Parosh, two thousand one hundred and seventy-two; [4]descendants of Shephatiah, three hundred and seventy-two; [5]descendants of Arah, seven hundred and seventy-five; [6]descendants of Pahath-moab, who were descendants of Jeshua and Joab, two thousand eight hundred and twelve; [7]descendants of Elam, one thousand two hundred and fifty-four; [8]descendants of Zattu, nine hundred and forty-five; [9]descendants of Zaccai, seven hundred and sixty; [10]descendants of Bani, six hundred and forty-two; [11]descendants of Bebai, six hundred and twenty-three; [12]descendants of Azgad, one thousand two hundred and

1:1 In the first year of Cyrus: the first regnal year of Cyrus was 539 B.C., but his first year as ruler of Babylon, after the conquest of that city, was 538 B.C., the year in which he issued an edict, replicated on the famous Cyrus cylinder, permitting the repatriation of peoples deported by the Babylonians.

1:2 The God of heaven: this title, used as in 7:12, 21, 23, corresponds to a title of the Zoroastrian supreme deity Ahura Mazda, though it is not certain that Cyrus was a Zoroastrian.

1:5 Heads of ancestral houses: the ancestral house was the basic organizational unit of the postexilic community, consisting of an extended kinship group claiming descent from a common ancestor. The patriarchs of these units played an important role in civic government.

1:8 Sheshbazzar, prince of Judah: often identified with Shenassar, fourth son of Jehoiachin, king of Judah, exiled in 598 B.C. (see 1 Chr 3:17–18), and therefore the uncle of Zerubbabel (Ezr 3:2–4). This identification is uncertain.

1:11 Five thousand four hundred: either this figure or the figures given for one or more of the items listed have been corrupted in the transmission of the text.

2:1–67 As it now stands, this list, which also appears at Neh 7:6–72, is an expanded form of lists of Babylonian repatriates from the sixth century B.C. It served to establish membership in the reconstituted Temple community; civic status and perhaps also title to property depended on this membership.

a: Ezr 6:3–5; 2 Chr 36:22–23; Jer 25:11–12; 29:10; Zec 1:12. *b:* Ex 3:21–22; 11:2; 12:35. *c:* 2 Kgs 25:14–15. *d:* Neh 7:6–72.

The Kings of Persia

Cyrus	539–530 B.C.	Xerxes	486–465 B.C.	Artaxerxes II	404–358 B.C.
Cambyses	530–522 B.C.	Artaxerxes I	465–424 B.C.	Artaxerxes III	358–337 B.C.
Darius I	522–486 B.C.	Darius II	424–404 B.C.	Darius III	336–331 B.C.

(Darius III was defeated by Alexander, and the Persian empire came to an end, in 331 B.C.)

twenty-two; 13 descendants of Adonikam, six
hundred and sixty-six; 14 descendants of Bigvai, two thousand and fifty-six; 15 descendants
of Adin, four hundred and fifty-four; 16 descendants of Ater, who were descendants of
Hezekiah, ninety-eight; 17 descendants of Bezai, three hundred and twenty-three; 18 descendants of Jorah, one hundred and twelve; 19 descendants of Hashum, two hundred and
twenty-three; 20 descendants of Gibeon,
ninety-five; 21 descendants of Bethlehem, one
hundred and twenty-three; 22 people of Netophah, fifty-six; 23 people of Anathoth, one hundred and twenty-eight; 24 people of Beth-azmaveth, forty-two; 25 people of Kiriath-jearim,
Chephirah, and Beeroth, seven hundred and
forty-three; 26 people of Ramah and Geba, six
hundred and twenty-one; 27 people of Michmas, one hundred and twenty-two; 28 people of
Bethel and Ai, two hundred and twenty-three;
29 descendants of Nebo, fifty-two; 30 descendants of Magbish, one hundred and fifty-six;
31 descendants of the other Elam, one thousand
two hundred and fifty-four; 32 descendants of
Harim, three hundred and twenty; 33 descendants of Lod, Hadid, and Ono, seven hundred
and twenty-five; 34 descendants of Jericho,
three hundred and forty-five; 35 descendants of
Senaah, three thousand six hundred and thirty.

36 The priests: descendants of Jedaiah, of
the house of Jeshua, nine hundred and seventy-three; 37 descendants of Immer, one
thousand and fifty-two; 38 descendants of
Pashhur, one thousand two hundred and
forty-seven; 39 descendants of Harim, one
thousand and seventeen.

40[e] The Levites: descendants of Jeshua
and Kadmiel, of the descendants of Hodaviah, seventy-four.

41 The singers:* descendants of Asaph, one
hundred and twenty-eight.

42 The gatekeepers:* descendants of Shallum, descendants of Ater, descendants of
Talmon, descendants of Akkub, descendants
of Hatita, descendants of Shobai, one hundred and thirty-nine in all.

43 The temple servants: descendants of
Ziha, descendants of Hasupha, descendants
of Tabbaoth, 44 descendants of Keros, descendants of Siaha, descendants of Padon,
45 descendants of Lebanah, descendants of
Hagabah, descendants of Akkub, 46 descen-
dants of Hagab, descendants of Shamlai, de-
scendants of Hanan, 47 descendants of Giddel, descendants of Gahar, descendants of
Reaiah, 48 descendants of Rezin, descendants
of Nekoda, descendants of Gazzam, 49 descendants of Uzza, descendants of Paseah,
descendants of Besai, 50 descendants of As-
nah, descendants of the Meunites, descendants of the Nephusites, 51 descendants of
Bakbuk, descendants of Hakupha, descendants of Harhur, 52 descendants of Bazluth,
descendants of Mehida, descendants of Harsha, 53 descendants of Barkos, descendants
of Sisera, descendants of Temah, 54 descendants of Neziah, descendants of Hatipha.

55 Descendants of Solomon's servants:
descendants of Sotai, descendants of Has-
sophereth, descendants of Peruda, 56 de-
scendants of Jaalah, descendants of Darkon, descendants of Giddel, 57 descendants
of Shephatiah, descendants of Hattil, descendants of Pochereth-hazzebaim, descen-

2:41 The singers: the term covers the composition as well as the rendition of liturgical music. Since they are listed as distinct from Levites (2:40), they had not yet attained levitical status, as in Chronicles (e.g., 1 Chr 9:33–34; 23:3–6).

2:42 The gatekeepers: their principal task was to protect the ritual purity of the temple area (e.g., 2 Chr 23:19). The author assumes that they were established by David as a distinct levitical category (1 Chr 15:18; 26:1–19).

e: Neh 12:23.

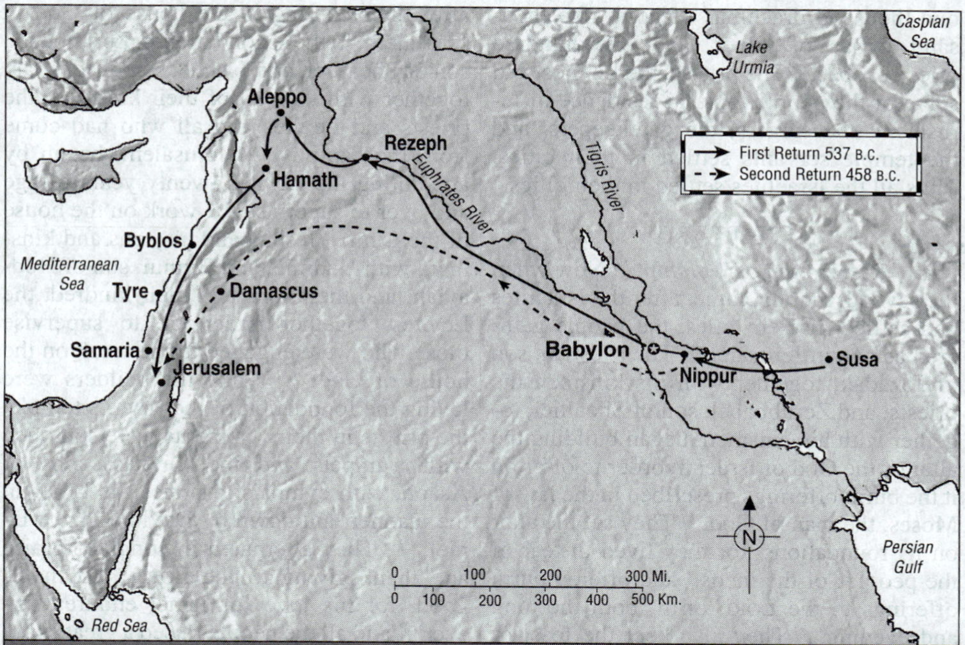

The Return from Exile

dants of Ami. 58The total of the temple servants together with the descendants of Solomon's servants was three hundred and
ninety-two.
59The following who returned from Tel-
melah, Tel-harsha, Cherub, Addan, and Immer were unable to prove that their ancestral
houses and their descent were Israelite: 60de-
scendants of Delaiah, descendants of Tobiah, descendants of Nekoda, six hundred
and fifty-two. 61f Also, of the priests: descendants of Habaiah, descendants of Hakkoz, descendants of Barzillai (he had married one of the daughters of Barzillai the
Gileadite and was named after him). 62These
searched their family records, but their
names could not be found there, and they
were excluded from the priesthood. 63g The
governor* ordered them not to partake of the
most holy foods until there should be a priest
to consult the Urim and Thummim.
64The entire assembly taken together
came to forty-two thousand three hundred
and sixty, 65not counting their male and female servants, who numbered seven thousand three hundred and thirty-seven. They
also had two hundred male and female
singers. 66Their horses numbered seven hundred and thirty-six, their mules two hundred
and forty-five, 67their camels four hundred
and thirty-five, their donkeys six thousand
seven hundred and twenty.
68When they arrived at the house of the
LORD in Jerusalem, some of the heads of ancestral houses made voluntary offerings for
the house of God, to rebuild it in its place.
69According to their means they contributed
to the treasury for the temple service: sixty-

2:63 The governor: the honorific title was also held by Nehemiah (Neh 8:9; 10:2). The identity of the governor is unknown; both Sheshbazzar (Ezr 5:14) and Zerubbabel (Hg 1:1, 14; 2:2, 21) are identified as governors of Judah in the early Persian period. Mal 1:8 refers to an unnamed governor, and the names of other occupants of the office (Yehoezer, Ahzai, Elnathan) occur on seal impressions, though their date is uncertain. **Urim and Thummim**: cf. Ex 28:30.

f: 2 Sm 17:27; 19:32–33; 1 Kgs 2:7. *g:* Nm 27:21; Dt 33:8; 1 Sm 14:41–42; 28:6.

one thousand drachmas of gold, five thousand minas of silver, and one hundred priestly robes. [70]The priests, the Levites, and some of the people took up residence in Jerusalem; the singers, the gatekeepers, and the temple servants settled in their cities. Thus all the Israelites settled in their cities.

CHAPTER 3

See RG 209

Restoration of Worship. [1h] Now when the seventh month* came, after the Israelites had settled in their cities, the people gathered as one in Jerusalem. [2]Then Jeshua, son of Jozadak, together with his kinsmen the priests, and Zerubbabel, son of Shealtiel, together with his kinsmen, began building the altar of the God of Israel in order to offer on it the burnt offerings prescribed in the law of Moses, the man of God. [3i] They set the altar on its foundations, for they lived in fear of the peoples of the lands,* and offered burnt offerings to the LORD on it, both morning and evening. [4j] They also kept the feast of Booths in the manner prescribed, and they offered the daily burnt offerings in the proper number required for each day. [5]Thereafter they offered regular burnt offerings, the sacrifices prescribed for the new moons and all the festivals sacred to the LORD, and those which anyone might bring as a voluntary offering to the LORD.

Laying the Foundations of the Temple. [6]From the first day of the seventh month they reinstituted the burnt offering to the LORD, though the foundation of the LORD's temple had not yet been laid. [7k] Then they hired stonecutters and carpenters, and sent food and drink and oil to the Sidonians and Tyrians that they might ship cedar trees from the Lebanon to the port of Joppa, as Cyrus, king of Persia, had authorized. [8]In the year after their coming to the house of God in Jerusalem, in the second month, Zerubbabel, son of Shealtiel, and Jeshua, son of Jozadak, together with the rest of their kinsmen, the priests and Levites and all who had come from the captivity to Jerusalem, began by appointing the Levites twenty years of age and over to supervise the work on the house of the LORD. [9]Jeshua and his sons and kinsmen, with Kadmiel and Binnui, son of Hodaviah, and their sons and their kindred, the Levites, together undertook to supervise those who were engaged in the work on the house of God. [10l] While the builders were laying the foundation of the LORD's temple, the priests in their vestments were stationed with trumpets and the Levites, sons of Asaph, with cymbals to praise the LORD in the manner laid down by David, king of Israel. [11m] They alternated in songs of praise and thanksgiving to the LORD, "for he is good, for his love for Israel endures forever";* and all the people raised a great shout of joy, praising the LORD because the foundation of the LORD's house had been laid. [12n] Many of the priests, Levites, and heads of ancestral houses, who were old enough to have seen the former house, cried out in sorrow as they watched the foundation of the present house being laid. Many others, however, lifted up their voices in shouts of joy. [13]No one could distinguish the sound of the joyful shouting from the sound of those who were weeping; for the people raised a mighty clamor which was heard far away.

CHAPTER 4

See RG 209

Outside Interference. [1]When the enemies of Judah and Benjamin heard that the exiles were building a temple for the LORD, the God of Israel, [2o] they approached Zerub-

3:1–2 The seventh month: Tishri (September–October), apparently of the first year of the return (538 B.C.), followed by events in the second year (v. 8). In that case it was Sheshbazzar who laid the foundations of the Temple (5:16), and it was in the second year of Darius I (520 B.C.) that Jeshua and Zerubbabel resumed work on the Temple that had been temporarily interrupted (Ezr 4:24–5:1; Hg 1:1; 2:1). The author, or a later editor, has set the construction and dedication of the Temple under Darius I back into the earliest period of the return. Shealtiel was the oldest son of King Jehoiachin (1 Chr 3:17–19); Zerubbabel was therefore Jehoiachin's grandson; see note on Ezr 1:8.

3:3 Peoples of the lands: referring either to those who had never left Judah or to neighboring peoples—Edomites, Arabs, inhabitants of Samaria—who opposed those who returned.

3:11 "For he is good . . . forever": a refrain occurring frequently in liturgies of ancient Israel (cf. Ps 136).

h: Neh 7:7–78. *i:* Dt 9:25; 1 Kgs 8:64. *j:* Ex 23:16; Nm 28:3–8; Dt 16:13–15. *k:* 1 Chr 22:4; 2 Chr 2:9. *l:* Ezr 2:41 *m:* 1 Chr 16:34; 2 Chr 5:13; 7:3; Ps 106:1; 136:1; Jer 33:11. *n:* Hg 2:3. *o:* Ezr 4:10.

babel and the heads of ancestral houses and said to them, "Let us build with you, for we seek your God just as you do, and we have sacrificed to him since the days of Esarhaddon, king of Assyria,* who brought us here." [3]But Zerubbabel, Jeshua, and the rest of the heads of ancestral houses of Israel answered them, "It is not your responsibility to build with us a house for our God, but we alone must build it for the LORD, the God of Israel, as Cyrus king of Persia has commanded us." [4]Thereupon the local inhabitants* discouraged the people of Judah and frightened them off from building. [5]They also bribed counselors to work against them and to frustrate their plans during all the years of Cyrus, king of Persia, and even into the reign of Darius,* king of Persia.

Later Hostility. [6]In the reign of Ahasuerus,* at the beginning of his reign, they prepared a written accusation against the inhabitants of Judah and Jerusalem.

[7]* Again, in the time of Artaxerxes, Tabeel and the rest of his fellow officials, in concert with Mithredath, wrote to Artaxerxes, king of Persia. The document was written in Aramaic and was accompanied by a translation.

[8]* Then Rehum, the governor, and Shimshai, the scribe, wrote the following letter against Jerusalem to King Artaxerxes: [9]"Rehum, the governor, Shimshai, the scribe, and their fellow officials, judges, legates, and agents from among the Persians, Urukians, Babylonians, Susians (that is, Elamites), [10]and the other peoples whom the great and illustrious Osnappar* transported and settled in the city of Samaria and elsewhere in the province West-of-Euphrates, as follows . . . ." [11]This is a copy of the letter that they sent to him:

"To King Artaxerxes, your servants, the men of West-of-Euphrates, as follows: [12]Let it be known to the king that the Jews who came up from you to us have arrived at Jerusalem and are now rebuilding this rebellious and evil city. They are completing its walls, and the foundations have already been laid. [13]Now let it be known to the king that if this city is rebuilt and its walls completed, they will no longer pay taxes, tributes, or tolls; eventually the throne will be harmed. [14]Now, since we eat the salt of the palace* and it is not fitting for us to look on while the king is being dishonored, we have sent this message to inform the king, [15]so that inquiry may be made in the historical records of your fathers. In the historical records you will discover and verify that this is a rebellious city, harmful to kings and provinces; its people have been acting seditiously there since ancient times. That is why this city was destroyed. [16]We therefore inform the king, that if this city is rebuilt and its walls completed again, you will thereupon not have a portion in the province West-of-Euphrates."

[17]The king sent this answer: "To Rehum, the governor, Shimshai, the scribe, and their fellow officials living in Samaria and elsewhere in the province West-of-Euphrates, greetings: [18]The communication which you sent us has been read in translation in my presence. [19]When at my command inquiry was made, it was verified that from ancient times this city has risen up against kings and that rebellion and sedition have been fostered there. [20]Powerful kings once ruled in Jerusalem who controlled all West-of-Euphrates, and taxes, tributes, and tolls were paid to them. [21]Give orders, therefore, to stop these

4:2 Esarhaddon, king of Assyria: the enemies represent themselves as descendants of foreigners forcibly resettled in the Samaria region after the incorporation of the Northern Kingdom into the Assyrian empire (722 B.C.; cf. 2 Kgs 17:24). We have no record of a settlement under Esarhaddon (681–669 B.C.); the Aramaic source (Ezr 4:10) refers to a different resettlement under Osnappar/Ashurbanipal (668–627 B.C.).

4:4 Local inhabitants: lit., "the people of the land."

4:5 Darius: Darius I (522–486 B.C.). The Temple-building narrative continues in v. 24. In between (vv. 6–23) is a series of notices about opposition to the returned exiles voiced at the Persian court in the early fifth century B.C., after the Temple had been built.

4:6 Ahasuerus: Xerxes (486–465 B.C.); the early years of his reign were occupied with revolts in several parts of the empire.

4:7 There is a note placed in the original text to indicate a change from Hebrew to Aramaic. The Aramaic section beginning here ends with 6:18; in 7:12–26 a royal letter is cited in Aramaic.

4:8–23 The letter to Artaxerxes I (465–424 B.C.) deals with the building of the fortification walls of Jerusalem, not the building of the Temple. The interruption of the work on the city wall some time before 445 B.C. was the occasion for the arrival of Nehemiah in the province (Neh 1:1–4; 2:1–5).

4:10 Osnappar: probably Ashurbanipal; see note on 4:2.

4:14 Eat the salt of the palace: the idiom signifies sharing in the benefits of the palace.

men. This city may not be rebuilt until a further decree has been issued by me. [22]Take care that you do not neglect this matter. Why should evil increase to harm the throne?"

[23p] As soon as a copy of King Artaxerxes' letter had been read before Rehum, the governor, Shimshai, the scribe, and their fellow officials, they immediately went to the Jews in Jerusalem and stopped their work by force of arms. [24]As a result, work on the house of God in Jerusalem ceased. This interruption lasted until the second year of the reign of Darius,* king of Persia.

CHAPTER 5

See RG 209

The Work Resumed Under Darius; Further Problems. [1q] Then the prophets Haggai and Zechariah,* son of Iddo, began to prophesy to the Jews in Judah and Jerusalem in the name of the God of Israel. [2]Thereupon Zerubbabel, son of Shealtiel, and Jeshua, son of Jozadak, began again to build the house of God in Jerusalem, with the prophets of God giving them support. [3]At that time Tattenai, governor of West-of-Euphrates, came to them, along with Shethar-bozenai, and their fellow officials, and asked of them: "Who issued the decree for you to build this house and complete this edifice? [4]What are the names of the men who are building this structure?" [5]But the eye of their God was upon the elders of the Jews, and they were not delayed during the time a report went to Darius and a written order came back concerning this matter.

[6]A copy of the letter which Tattenai, governor of West-of-Euphrates, along with Shethar-bozenai and their fellow officials from West-of-Euphrates, sent to King Darius; [7]they sent him a report in which was written the following:

"To King Darius, all good wishes! [8]Let it be known to the king that we have visited the province of Judah and the house of the great God: it is being rebuilt of cut stone and the walls are being reinforced with timber; the work is being carried out diligently, prospering under their hands. [9]We then questioned the elders, addressing to them the following words: 'Who issued the decree for you to build this house and complete this edifice?' [10]We also asked them their names, in order to give you a list of the men who are their leaders. [11]This was their answer to us: 'We are the servants of the God of heaven and earth, and we are rebuilding the house built here many years ago, which a great king of Israel built and completed. [12]But because our ancestors provoked the wrath of the God of heaven, he delivered them into the power of the Chaldean, Nebuchadnezzar, king of Babylon, who destroyed this house and exiled the people to Babylon. [13r] However, in the first year of Cyrus, king of Babylon, King Cyrus issued a decree for the rebuilding of this house of God. [14]Moreover, the gold and silver vessels of the house of God, which Nebuchadnezzar had taken from the temple in Jerusalem and carried off to the temple in Babylon, King Cyrus ordered to be removed from the temple in Babylon, and they were given to a certain Sheshbazzar, whom he named governor. [15]He commanded him: Take these vessels and deposit them in the temple of Jerusalem, and let the house of God be rebuilt on its former site. [16]Then this same Sheshbazzar came and laid the foundations of the house of God in Jerusalem. Since that time to the present the building has been going on, and is not yet completed.' [17]Now, if it please the king, let a search be made in the royal archives of Babylon to discover whether a decree really was issued by King Cyrus for the rebuilding of this house of God in Jerusalem. And may the king's decision in this matter be communicated to us."

CHAPTER 6

See RG 209

The Decree of Darius. [1*] Thereupon King Darius issued an order to search the ar-

4:24 The second year . . . of Darius: that is, 520 B.C.; it marks the beginning of the successful restoration of the Temple, completed within the five years following (5:1–6:18).

5:1 The prophets Haggai and Zechariah: Haggai and Zechariah were active during the early years of Darius I. They document the rebuilding of the Temple and the messianic expectations associated with the Davidic descendant Zerubbabel.

6:1–2 Babylon was the capital city of the satrapy to which Judah belonged; it was therefore the natural place to look. The decree was discovered eventually, however, in Ecbatana

p: Neh 1:3. *q:* Hg 1:14–2:9; Zec 4:9. *r:* Ezr 1:1–5.

chives in which the treasures were stored in Babylon. [2s] However, a scroll was found in Ecbatana, the stronghold in the province of Media, containing the following text: "Memorandum. [3]In the first year of his reign, King Cyrus issued a decree: With regard to the house of God in Jerusalem: the house is to be rebuilt as a place for offering sacrifices and bringing burnt offerings. Its height is to be sixty cubits and its width sixty cubits. [4]It shall have three courses of cut stone for each one of timber. The costs are to be borne by the royal house. [5]Also, let the gold and silver vessels of the house of God which Nebuchadnezzar took from the temple of Jerusalem and brought to Babylon be sent back; let them be returned to their place in the temple of Jerusalem and deposited in the house of God."

[6]"Now, therefore, Tattenai, governor of West-of-Euphrates, and Shethar-bozenai, and you, their fellow officials in West-of-Euphrates, stay away from there. [7]Let the governor and the elders of the Jews continue the work on that house of God; they are to rebuild it on its former site. [8]I also issue this decree concerning your dealing with these elders of the Jews in the rebuilding of that house of God: Let these men be repaid for their expenses, in full and without delay from the royal revenue, deriving from the taxes of West-of-Euphrates, so that the work not be interrupted. [9]Whatever else is required—young bulls, rams, and lambs for burnt offerings to the God of heaven, wheat, salt, wine, and oil, according to the requirements of the priests who are in Jerusalem—let that be delivered to them day by day without fail, [10]that they may continue to offer sacrifices of pleasing odor to the God of heaven and pray for the life of the king and his sons. [11]I also issue this decree: if any man alters this edict, a beam is to be taken from his house, and he is to be lifted up and impaled on it; and his house is to be reduced to rubble for this offense. [12]And may the God who causes his name to dwell there overthrow every king or people who may undertake to alter this decree or to destroy this house of God in Jerusalem. I, Darius, have issued this decree; let it be diligently executed."

The Task Finally Completed. [13]Then Tattenai, the governor of West-of-Euphrates, and Shethar-bozenai, and their fellow officials carried out with all diligence the instructions King Darius had sent them. [14]The elders of the Jews continued to make progress in the building, supported by the message of the prophets, Haggai and Zechariah, son of Iddo. They finished the building according to the command of the God of Israel and the decrees of Cyrus and Darius, and of Artaxerxes, king of Persia. [15]They completed this house on the third day of the month Adar, in the sixth year of the reign of King Darius. [16]The Israelites—priests, Levites, and the other returned exiles—celebrated the dedication of this house of God with joy. [17]For the dedication of this house of God, they offered one hundred bulls, two hundred rams, and four hundred lambs, together with twelve he-goats as a sin offering for all Israel, in keeping with the number of the tribes of Israel. [18]Finally, they set up the priests in their classes and the Levites in their divisions for the service of God in Jerusalem, as is prescribed in the book of Moses.

The Passover. [19t] The returned exiles kept the Passover on the fourteenth day of the first month. [20]The Levites, every one of whom had purified himself for the occasion, sacrificed the Passover for all the exiles, for their colleagues the priests, and for themselves. [21]The Israelites who had returned from the exile and all those who had separated themselves from the uncleanness of the Gentiles in the land shared in it, seeking the LORD, the God of Israel. [22u] They joyfully kept the feast of Unleavened Bread for seven days, for the LORD had filled them with joy by making the king of Assyria* favorable to them, so that he gave them help in

(Hamadan), the former capital of the Medes and summer residence of the Persian kings. Cf. the Hebrew version of the decree (1:2–4).

6:22 The king of Assyria: "Assyria" is perhaps used in a broad sense for the Persian empire; or the editor may have in mind the account of Hezekiah's Passover which refers to those who had escaped the hand of the king of Assyria (2 Chr 30:6).

s: Ezr 1:4–11. *t:* Ex 12:1–20; 2 Chr 30:14–27; 35:1–19. *u:* 2 Chr 30:6.

their work on the house of God, the God of Israel.

II. The Work of Ezra

CHAPTER 7

See RG 209

Ezra, Priest and Scribe. [1*] [v] After these events, during the reign of Artaxerxes, king of Persia, Ezra, son of Seraiah, son of Azariah, son of Hilkiah, [2]son of Shallum, son of Zadok, son of Ahitub, [3]son of Amariah, son of Azariah, son of Meraioth, [4]son of Zerahiah, son of Uzzi, son of Bukki, [5]son of Abishua, son of Phinehas, son of Eleazar, son of Aaron, the high priest— [6][w] this Ezra came up from Babylon. He was a scribe, well-versed in the law of Moses given by the LORD, the God of Israel. The king granted him all that he requested, because the hand of the LORD, his God, was over him.

[7]Some of the Israelites and some priests, Levites, singers, gatekeepers, and temple servants also came up to Jerusalem in the seventh year of King Artaxerxes. [8]Ezra came to Jerusalem in the fifth month of that seventh year of the king. [9]On the first day of the first month he began the journey up from Babylon, and on the first day of the fifth month he arrived at Jerusalem, for the favoring hand of his God was over him. [10][x] Ezra had set his heart on the study and practice of the law of the LORD and on teaching statutes and ordinances in Israel.

The Decree of Artaxerxes. [11]This is a copy of the rescript which King Artaxerxes gave to Ezra the priest-scribe, the scribe versed in matters concerning the LORD's commandments and statutes for Israel:

[12][y] "Artaxerxes, king of kings, to Ezra the priest, scribe of the law of the God of heaven, greetings! And now, [13]I have issued this decree, that anyone in my kingdom belonging to the people of Israel, its priests or Levites, who is willing to go up to Jerusalem with you, may go, [14]for you are the one sent by the king and his seven counselors to supervise Judah and Jerusalem with regard to the law of your God which is in your possession, [15]and to bring the silver and gold which the king and his counselors have freely contributed to the God of Israel, whose dwelling is in Jerusalem, [16]as well as all the silver and gold which you may receive throughout the province of Babylon, together with the voluntary offerings the people and priests freely contribute for the house of their God in Jerusalem. [17]Therefore, you must use this money with all diligence to buy bulls, rams, lambs, and the grain offerings and libations proper to these, and offer them on the altar of the house of your God in Jerusalem. [18]You and your kinsmen may do whatever seems best to you with the remainder of the silver and gold, as your God wills. [19]The vessels given to you for the service of the house of your God you are to deposit before the God of Jerusalem. [20]Whatever else you may be required to supply for the needs of the house of your God, you may draw from the royal treasury. [21]I, Artaxerxes the king, issue this decree to all the treasurers of West-of-Euphrates: Whatever Ezra the priest, scribe of the law of the God of heaven, requests of you, let it be done with all diligence, [22]within these limits: silver, one hundred talents; wheat, one hundred kors;* wine, one hundred baths; oil, one hundred baths; salt, without limit. [23]Let everything that is decreed by the God of heaven be carried out exactly for the house of the God of heaven, that wrath may not come upon the realm of the king and his sons. [24]We also inform you that it is not permitted to impose taxes, tributes, or tolls on any priest, Levite, singer, gatekeeper, temple servant, or any other servant of that house of God.

[25][z] "As for you, Ezra, in accordance with

7:1–10 The editor's introduction to Ezra's autobiographical narrative. The context suggests the seventh year of Artaxerxes I, therefore, 458 B.C., as the date of Ezra's arrival in Jerusalem. The arguments often advanced for 398 B.C., the seventh year of Artaxerxes II, or less often for the thirty-seventh year of Artaxerxes I, that is, 428 B.C., are inconclusive. For Ezra's descent from Aaron, the editor has drawn selectively on 1 Chr 5:27–41. Seraiah, the chief priest executed by the Babylonians after the fall of Jerusalem (2 Kgs 25:18–21), cannot be Ezra's father in a literal sense, and Ezra was not himself high priest.

7:22 Kors: see note on Ez 45:14; **baths**: see note on Is 5:10.

v: 1 Chr 5:27–41. *w:* Ezr 7:28; 8:18; Neh 2:8, 18. *x:* Ps 119:45. *y:* Ezr 1:2–4. *z:* Dt 4:6; 2 Chr 17:7–9; Ps 37:30–31; 119:98.

the wisdom of your God* which is in your possession, appoint magistrates and judges to administer justice to all the people in West-of-Euphrates, to all, that is, who know the laws of your God. Instruct those who do not know these laws. [26]All who will not obey the law of your God and the law of the king, let judgment be executed upon them with all diligence, whether death, or corporal punishment, or confiscation of goods, or imprisonment."

Ezra Prepares for the Journey. [27]Blessed be the LORD, the God of our ancestors, who put it into the heart of the king thus to glorify the house of the LORD in Jerusalem, [28][a] and who let me find favor with the king, with his counselors, and with all the most influential royal officials. I therefore took courage and, with the hand of the LORD, my God, over me, I gathered together Israelite leaders to make the return journey with me.

CHAPTER 8

See RG 209

Ezra's Caravan. [1]These are the heads of the ancestral houses and the genealogies of those who returned with me from Babylon during the reign of King Artaxerxes:

[2]Of the descendants of Phinehas, Gershon; of the descendants of Ithamar, Daniel; of the descendants of David, Hattush, [3]son of Shecaniah; of the descendants of Parosh, Zechariah, and with him one hundred and fifty males were enrolled; [4]of the descendants of Pahath-moab, Eliehoenai, son of Zerahiah, and with him two hundred males; [5]of the descendants of Zattu, Shecaniah, son of Jahaziel, and with him three hundred males; [6]of the descendants of Adin, Ebed, son of Jonathan, and with him fifty males; [7]of the descendants of Elam, Jeshaiah, son of Athaliah, and with him seventy males; [8]of the descendants of Shephatiah, Zebadiah, son of Michael, and with him eighty males; [9]of the descendants of Joab, Obadiah, son of Jehiel, and with him two hundred and eighteen males; [10]of the descendants of Bani, Shelomoth, son of Josiphiah, and with him one hundred and sixty males; [11]of the descendants of Bebai, Zechariah, son of Bebai, and with him twenty-eight males; [12]of the descendants of Azgad, Johanan, son of Hakkatan, and with him one hundred and ten males; [13]of the descendants of Adonikam, younger sons, whose names were Eliphelet, Jeiel, and Shemaiah, and with them sixty males; [14]of the descendants of Bigvai, Uthai, son of Zakkur, and with him seventy males.

Final Preparations for the Journey. [15]I assembled them by the river that flows toward Ahava,* where we camped for three days. There I perceived that both laymen and priests were present, but I could not discover a single Levite. [16]So I sent for discerning leaders, Eliezer, Ariel, Shemaiah, Jarib, Elnathan, Nathan, Zechariah, and Meshullam, [17]with a command for Iddo, the leader in the place Casiphia, instructing them what to say to Iddo and his kinsmen, and to the temple servants in Casiphia, in order to procure for us ministers for the house of our God. [18][b] Since the favoring hand of our God was over us, they sent to us a well-instructed man, one of the descendants of Mahli, son of Levi, son of Israel, namely Sherebiah, with his sons and kinsmen, eighteen men. [19]They also sent us Hashabiah, and with him Jeshaiah, descendants of Merari, and their kinsmen and their sons, twenty men. [20][c] Of the temple servants, those whom David and the princes appointed to serve the Levites, there were two hundred and twenty. All these were enrolled by name.

[21]Then I proclaimed a fast, there by the river of Ahava, that we might humble ourselves before our God to seek from him a safe journey for ourselves, our children, and all our possessions. [22][d] For I was ashamed to ask the king for troops and horsemen to protect us against enemies along the way, since we had said to the king, "The favoring hand

7:25 The wisdom of your God: with reference to the law (cf. Dt 4:6). The law in question was certainly not new, since it was assumed to be known by Jews in Judah and elsewhere. It corresponded to Pentateuchal law, though perhaps this had not yet been given its final form.

8:15 Ahava: an unidentified location near Babylon; also the name of the river or canal on which it stood (vv. 21, 31). A location near water was dictated by ritual as well as practical reasons (cf. Ps 137:1; Ez 1:1, 3; 3:15).

a: Ezr 7:6. *b:* Ezr 7:6. *c:* Ezr 2:43. *d:* Neh 2:9.

of our God is over all who seek him, but his fierce anger is against all who forsake him." [23]So we fasted, seeking this from our God, and it was granted. [24]Next I selected twelve of the priestly leaders along with Sherebiah, Hashabiah, and ten of their kinsmen, [25]and I weighed out before them the silver and the gold and the vessels offered for the house of our God by the king, his counselors, his officials, and all the Israelites of that region. [26]I weighed out into their hands these amounts: silver, six hundred and fifty talents; silver vessels, one hundred; gold, one hundred talents; [27]twenty golden bowls valued at a thousand darics; two vases of excellent polished bronze, as precious as gold. [28]I addressed them in these words: "You are consecrated to the LORD, and the vessels are also consecrated; the silver and the gold are a voluntary offering to the LORD, the God of your ancestors. [29]Watch over them carefully until you weigh them out in Jerusalem in the presence of the chief priests and Levites and the leaders of ancestral houses of Israel, in the chambers of the house of the LORD." [30]The priests and the Levites then took over the silver, the gold, and the vessels that had been weighed out, to bring them to Jerusalem, to the house of our God.

Arrival in Jerusalem. [31]We set out from the river of Ahava on the twelfth day of the first month to go to Jerusalem. The hand of our God remained over us, and he protected us from enemies and robbers along the way. [32]We arrived in Jerusalem, where we rested for three days. [33]On the fourth day, the silver, the gold, and the vessels were weighed out in the house of our God and given to the priest Meremoth, son of Uriah, with whom was Eleazar, son of Phinehas; they were assisted by the Levites Jozabad, son of Jeshua, and Noadiah, son of Binnui. [34]Everything was in order as to number and weight, and the total weight was registered. At that same time, [35]those who had returned from the captivity, the exiles, offered as burnt offerings to the God of Israel twelve bulls for all Israel, ninety-six rams, seventy-seven lambs, and twelve goats as sin offerings: all these as a burnt offering to the LORD. [36]* Finally, the orders of the king were presented to the king's satraps and to the governors in West-of-Euphrates, who gave their support to the people and to the house of God.

CHAPTER 9

See RG 209-10

The Crisis of Mixed Marriages. [1][e] When these matters had been concluded, the leaders approached me with this report: "Neither the Israelite laymen nor the priests nor the Levites have kept themselves separate from the peoples of the lands and their abominations—Canaanites, Hittites, Perizzites, Jebusites, Ammonites, Moabites, Egyptians, and Amorites— [2]for they have taken some of their daughters as wives for themselves and their sons, thus intermingling the holy seed with the peoples of the lands. Furthermore, the leaders and rulers have taken a prominent part in this apostasy!"

Ezra's Reaction. [3][f] When I had heard this, I tore my cloak and my mantle, plucked hair from my head and beard, and sat there devastated. [4][g] Around me gathered all who were in dread of the sentence of the God of Israel* on the apostasy of the exiles, while I remained devastated until the evening sacrifice. [5]Then, at the time of the evening sacrifice, I rose in my wretchedness, and with cloak and mantle torn I fell on my knees, stretching out my hands to the LORD, my God.

A Penitential Prayer. [6]* [h] I said: "My God, I am too ashamed and humiliated to raise my face to you, my God, for our wicked deeds are heaped up above our heads and our guilt reaches up to heaven. [7]From the time of our ancestors even to this day our guilt has been great, and for our wicked deeds we have

8:36 The story of Ezra's mission is apparently continued from this point by Neh 7:72b–8:18, which may be read before Ezr 9:1.

9:4 All who were in dread . . . God of Israel: lit., "all who trembled"; these people are also mentioned at 10:3, and a similar designation occurs at Is 66:2, 5, a text more or less contemporary with this passage. The allusion may be to a distinct social group of rigorist tendencies who supported Ezra's marriage reform.

9:6–15 The prayer attributed to Ezra is a communal confession of sin, of a kind characteristic of the Second Temple period (cf. Neh 9:6–37; Dn 9:4–19; 1QS 1:4–2:1), but adapted to the present situation.

e: Dt 7:1; Neh 9:2. *f:* Ps 119:136. *g:* Ezr 10:3; Is 66:2, 5. *h:* Neh 9:6–37; Ps 38:4; Dn 9:4–19.

been delivered, we and our kings and our priests, into the hands of the kings of foreign lands, to the sword, to captivity, to pillage, and to disgrace, as is the case today.

[8i] "And now, only a short time ago, mercy came to us from the LORD, our God, who left us a remnant and gave us a stake in his holy place; thus our God has brightened our eyes and given us relief in our slavery. [9j] For slaves we are, but in our slavery our God has not abandoned us; rather, he has turned the good will of the kings of Persia toward us. Thus he has given us new life to raise again the house of our God and restore its ruins, and has granted us a protective wall in Judah and Jerusalem. [10]But now, our God, what can we say after all this? For we have abandoned your commandments, [11k] which you gave through your servants the prophets: The land which you are entering to take as your possession is a land unclean with the filth of the peoples of the lands, with the abominations with which they have filled it from one end to the other by their uncleanness. [12l] Do not, then, give your daughters to their sons in marriage, and do not take their daughters for your sons. Never promote their welfare and prosperity; thus you will grow strong, enjoy the produce of the land, and leave it as an inheritance to your children forever.

[13]"After all that has come upon us for our evil deeds and our great guilt—though you, our God, have made less of our sinfulness than it deserved and have allowed us to survive as we do— [14]shall we again violate your commandments by intermarrying with these abominable peoples? Would you not become so angered with us as to destroy us without remnant or survivor? [15]LORD, God of Israel, you are just; yet we have been spared, the remnant we are today. Here we are before you in our sins. Because of all this, we can no longer stand in your presence."

CHAPTER 10

See RG 209

Response to the Crisis. [1]While Ezra prayed and acknowledged their guilt, weeping and prostrate before the house of God, a very large assembly of Israelites gathered about him, men, women, and children; and the people wept profusely. [2]Then Shecaniah, the son of Jehiel, one of the descendants of Elam, made this appeal to Ezra: "We have indeed betrayed our God by taking as wives foreign women of the peoples of the land. Yet in spite of this there still remains a hope for Israel. [3]Let us therefore enter into a covenant before our God to dismiss all our foreign wives and the children born of them, in keeping with what you, my lord, advise, and those who are in dread of the commandments of our God. Let it be done according to the law! [4]Rise, then, for this is your duty! We are with you, so have courage and act!"

[5]Ezra stood and demanded an oath from the leaders of the priests, from the Levites and from all Israel that they would do as had been proposed; and they swore it. [6]Then Ezra left his place before the house of God and entered the chamber of Johanan, son of Eliashib,* where he spent the night neither eating food nor drinking water, for he was in mourning over the apostasy of the exiles. [7]A proclamation was made throughout Judah and Jerusalem that all the exiles should gather together in Jerusalem, [8]and that whoever failed to appear within three days would, according to the judgment of the leaders and elders, suffer the confiscation of all his possessions, and would be excluded from the assembly of the exiles.

[9]All the men of Judah and Benjamin gathered together in Jerusalem within the three-day period: it was in the ninth month,* on the twentieth day of the month. All the people, sitting in the open place before the house of God, were trembling both over the matter at hand and because it was raining. [10m] Then

10:6 Johanan, son of Eliashib: if this Eliashib is identical with the high priest of that name during Nehemiah's mission (Neh 3:1), it would be difficult to avoid the conclusion that Ezra followed Nehemiah. But Eliashib is a common name, and, on the hypothesis of Nehemiah's chronological priority, it would be unlikely that Ezra would consort with a family which had "defiled the priesthood" (Neh 13:28–29).

10:9 The ninth month: Kislev (November–December), during the first of two rainy seasons in Palestine.

i: Is 4:3. *j:* Ps 106:46. *k:* Lv 18:24–25; Ez 36:17. *l:* Dt 7:3. *m:* Neh 9:2.

Ezra, the priest, stood up and said to them: "Your apostasy in taking foreign women as wives has added to Israel's guilt. [11]But now, give praise to the LORD, the God of your ancestors, and do his will: separate yourselves from the peoples of the land and from the foreign women." [12]In answer, the whole assembly cried out with a loud voice: "Yes, it is our duty to do as you say! [13]But the people are numerous and it is the rainy season, so that we cannot remain outside; besides, this is not a task that can be performed in a single day or even two, for those of us who have sinned in this regard are many. [14]Let our leaders represent the whole assembly; then let all those in our cities who have taken foreign women for wives appear at appointed times, accompanied by the elders and magistrates of each city in question, till we have turned away from us our God's burning anger over this affair." [15]Only Jonathan, son of Asahel, and Jahzeiah, son of Tikvah, were against this proposal, with Meshullam and Shabbethai the Levite supporting them.

[16]* The exiles did as agreed. Ezra the priest appointed as his assistants men who were heads of ancestral houses, one for each ancestral house, all of them designated by name. They held sessions to examine the matter, beginning with the first day of the tenth month. [17]By the first day of the first month they had finished dealing with all the men who had taken foreign women for wives.

The List of Transgressors. [18]Among the priests, the following were found to have taken foreign women for wives: Of the descendants of Jeshua, son of Jozadak, and his kinsmen: Maaseiah, Eliezer, Jarib, and Gedaliah. [19]They pledged themselves to dismiss their wives, and as a guilt offering for their guilt they gave a ram from the flock. [20]Of the descendants of Immer: Hanani and Zebadiah; [21]of the descendants of Harim: Maaseiah, Elijah, Shemaiah, Jehiel, and Uzziah; [22]of the descendants of Pashhur: Elioenai, Maaseiah, Ishmael, Nethanel, Jozabad, and Elasah.

[23][n] Of the Levites: Jozabad, Shimei, Kelaiah (also called Kelita), Pethahiah, Judah, and Eliezer.

[24]Of the singers: Eliashib; of the gatekeepers: Shallum, Telem, and Uri.

[25]Of the people of Israel: Of the descendants of Parosh: Ramiah, Izziah, Malchijah, Mijamin, Eleazar, Malchijah, and Benaiah; [26]of the descendants of Elam: Mattaniah, Zechariah, Jehiel, Abdi, Jeremoth, and Elijah; [27]of the descendants of Zattu: Elioenai, Eliashib, Mattaniah, Jeremoth, Zabad, and Aziza; [28]of the descendants of Bebai: Jehohanan, Hananiah, Zabbai, and Athlai; [29]of the descendants of Bani: Meshullam, Malluch, Adaiah, Jashub, Sheal, and Jeremoth; [30]of the descendants of Pahath-moab: Adna, Chelal, Benaiah, Maaseiah, Mattaniah, Bezalel, Binnui, and Manasseh; [31]of the descendants of Harim: Eliezer, Isshijah, Malchijah, Shemaiah, Shimeon, [32]Benjamin, Malluch, Shemariah; [33]of the descendants of Hashum: Mattenai, Mattattah, Zabad, Eliphelet, Jeremai, Manasseh, Shimei; [34]of the descendants of Begui: Maadai, Amram, Uel, [35]Benaiah, Bedeiah, Cheluhi, [36]Vaniah, Meremoth, Eliashib, [37]Mattaniah, Mattenai, and Jaasu; [38]of the descendants of Binnui: Shimei, [39]Shelemiah, Nathan, and Adaiah; [40]of the descendants of Zachai: Shashai, Sharai, [41]Azarel, Shelemiah, Shemariah, [42]Shallum, Amariah, Joseph; [43]of the descendants of Nebo: Jeiel, Mattithiah, Zabad, Zebina, Jaddai, Joel, Benaiah.

[44]* All these had taken foreign wives; but they sent them away, both the women and their children.

10:16–17 The work of the committee lasted three months, from the first day of the tenth month, Tebeth (December–January), to the first day of the first month, Nisan (March–April), of the following year.

10:44 Some scholars find the continuation of the account of the marriage reform in Neh 9:1–5, though the date given at Neh 9:1 would fit better after Ezr 10:15; cf. Hg 2:10–14. The abrupt conclusion to Ezr 9–10 suggests that the policy of forced separation from foreign wives, not mandated by any law known to us, did not succeed. Assuming the chronological priority of Ezra, marriage outside the community was still prevalent during Nehemiah's administration, and the remarkable demographic expansion of Judaism in the following centuries would be difficult to explain if Ezra's measures had been put into effect.

n: Neh 8:7; 10:11.

See RG 211-15

The Book of Nehemiah

Problems common to the combined books Ezra-Nehemiah have been pointed out in the Introduction to the Book of Ezra. The achievements of the two men were complementary; each helped to make it possible for Judaism to maintain its identity during the difficult days of the Restoration. Ezra was the great religious reformer who succeeded in establishing the Torah as the constitution of the returned community. Nehemiah, governor of the province of Judah, was the man of action who rebuilt the walls of Jerusalem and introduced necessary administrative reforms.

The biblical sources for Nehemiah's life and work are the autobiographical portions scattered through the book. They are called the "Memoirs of Nehemiah," and have been used more effectively by the editor than the "Memoirs of Ezra." The substantial authenticity of Nehemiah's memoirs is widely accepted. From these and other sources, the picture emerges of a man dedicated to the single purpose of the welfare of his people. While serving as cupbearer to the king at the Persian court in Susa, Nehemiah received permission from Artaxerxes I to fortify Jerusalem, and served as governor of Judah for two terms, the first lasting twelve years (445–432 B.C.), the second of unknown length (Neh 5:14; 13:6). Despite temperamental shortcomings, Nehemiah was a man of good practical sense combined with deep faith in God. He used his influence as governor of Judah to serve God and the fledgling Jewish community in Jerusalem.

The Book of Nehemiah is divided as follows:

I. The Deeds of Nehemiah (1:1–7:72)
II. Promulgation of the Law (8:1–10:40)
III. Dedication of the Wall; Other Reforms (11:1–13:31)

I. The Deeds of Nehemiah

CHAPTER 1

See RG 211-12

Nehemiah Hears Bad News. [1*] The
words of Nehemiah, son of Hacaliah.
In the month Kislev of the twentieth year,
I was in the citadel of Susa [2]when Hanani,
one of my brothers, came with other men
from Judah. I asked them about the Jews, the
remnant preserved after the captivity, and
about Jerusalem. [3]They answered me: "The
survivors of the captivity there in the province are in great distress and under reproach.
The wall of Jerusalem has been breached, its
gates gutted by fire." [4]When I heard this report, I began to weep and continued mourning for several days, fasting and praying before the God of heaven.
[5*] [a] I prayed: "LORD, God of heaven, great
and awesome God, you preserve your covenant of mercy with those who love you and
keep your commandments. [6b] May your ears
be attentive, and your eyes open, to hear the
prayer that I, your servant, now offer in your
presence day and night for your servants the
Israelites, confessing the sins we have committed against you, I and my ancestral house
included. [7c] We have greatly offended you,
not keeping the commandments, the statutes, and the ordinances you entrusted to
your servant Moses. [8d] But remember the
admonition which you addressed to Moses,
your servant, when you said: If you prove
faithless, I will scatter you among the peoples; [9]but if you return to me and carefully
keep my commandments, even though your
outcasts have been driven to the farthest corner of the world, I will gather them from
there, and bring them back to the place I

1:1 The first mission of Nehemiah, from the twentieth year of Artaxerxes I, lasted from the spring (2:1) of 445 B.C. until 433 B.C. (5:14). It is recounted in 1:1–6:15; 12:27–43; 6:16–7:5; 11:1–21; in terms of chronology, these texts may usefully be read in that order. **Kislev**: the ninth month (November–December). **Susa**: the winter residence of the Persian kings, in southwest Iran.

1:5 Nehemiah's prayer is a communal confession of sin, characteristic of Second Temple piety; cf. Ezr 9:6–15; Neh 9:6–37; Dn 9:4–19.

a: Dt 7:9, 12; Dn 9:4. *b:* 2 Chr 6:40. *c:* Dn 3:29–30. *d:* Dt 30:1–5.

The Four Stages of Return from Exile

THE CHRONOLOGY OF Ezra and Nehemiah is not completely clear. The following list of stages outlines the possibilities.

Stage 1:	Return of the people by permission of the Persian emperor Cyrus in 538 B.C. The leader of the people was Sheshbazzar, and the group he led began to rebuild the temple but abandoned the project when there was local opposition.
Stage 2:	Return by permission of the Persian emperor Darius I (late 6th century/early 5th century). The leaders were Zerubbabel and Jeshua, and the group completed the rebuilding of the temple.
Stage 3:	A group under the leadership of Ezra, in either 458 or 398 B.C. This group brought a copy of the Law of Moses.
Stage 4:	A group returning by permission of the Persian emperor Artaxerxes I in 445 B.C. Nehemiah came as the governor with a retinue, and worked with other reurning groups to rebuild the walls of Jerusalem and re-establish worship and the Jewish community.

have chosen as the dwelling place for my name. [10e] They are your servants, your people, whom you freed by your great might and strong hand. [11f] LORD, may your ears be attentive to the prayer of your servant and that of all your servants who willingly revere your name. Grant success to your servant this day, and let him find favor with this man"—for I was cupbearer to the king.*

CHAPTER 2

See RG 212

Appointment by the King. [1]In the month Nisan of the twentieth year of King Artaxerxes, when the wine was in my charge, I took some and offered it to the king. Because I had never before been sad in his presence, [2]the king asked me, "Why do you look sad? If you are not sick, you must be sad at heart." Though I was seized with great fear, [3]I answered the king: "May the king live forever! How could I not look sad when the city where my ancestors are buried lies in ruins, and its gates consumed by fire?" [4]The king asked me, "What is it, then, that you wish?" I prayed to the God of heaven [5]and then answered the king: "If it please the king, and if your servant is deserving of your favor, send me to Judah, to the city where my ancestors are buried, that I may rebuild it." [6]Then the king, with the queen seated beside him, asked me, "How long will your journey take and when will you return?" My answer was acceptable to the king and he agreed to let me go; I set a date for my return.

[7]I asked the king further: "If it please the king, let letters be given to me for the governors of West-of-Euphrates, that they may give me safe-conduct till I arrive in Judah; [8g] also a letter for Asaph, the keeper of the royal woods, that he may give me timber to make beams for the gates of the temple citadel, for the city wall and the house that I will occupy." Since I enjoyed the good favor of my God, the king granted my requests. [9h] Thus I proceeded to the governors of West-of-Euphrates and presented the king's letters to them. The king also sent with me army officers and cavalry.

[10]When Sanballat the Horonite* and Tobiah the Ammonite official had heard of this,

1:11 Cupbearer to the king: an important official in the royal household.

2:10 Sanballat the Horonite: the governor of the province of Samaria (3:33–34), apparently a native of one of the Beth-horons. A letter from the Jews living at Elephantine in southern Egypt, dated 408–407 B.C., mentions "Delayah and Shelemyah, the sons of Sanballat, the governor of Samaria," and papyri discovered in the Wadi ed-Dâliyeh in the Jordan Valley refer to a Sanballat, governor of Samaria, during the last years of Persian rule. Although his own name was Babylonian—Sin-uballit, i.e., "Sin (the moon god) has given life"—his two sons had names based on the divine name Yhwh. **Tobiah the Ammonite offi-**

e: Dt 9:29. *f:* Ps 118:25. *g:* Ezr 7:6. *h:* Ezr 8:22.

they were very much displeased that someone had come to improve the lot of the Israelites.

Circuit of the City. [11][i] When I arrived in Jerusalem, and had been there three days, [12]I set out by night with only a few other men and with no other animals but my own mount (for I had not told anyone what my God had inspired me to do for Jerusalem). [13*] I rode out at night by the Valley Gate, passed by the Dragon Spring, and came to the Dung Gate, observing how the walls of Jerusalem were breached and its gates consumed by fire. [14]Then I passed over to the Fountain Gate and to the King's Pool. Since there was no room here for my mount to pass with me astride, [15]I continued on foot up the wadi by night, inspecting the wall all the while, until I once more reached the Valley Gate, by which I went back in. [16]The magistrates knew nothing of where I had gone or what I was doing, for as yet I had disclosed nothing to the Jews, neither to the priests, nor to the nobles, nor to the magistrates, nor to the others who were to do the work.

Decision to Rebuild the City Wall. [17]Afterward I said to them: "You see the trouble we are in: how Jerusalem lies in ruins and its gates have been gutted by fire. Come, let us rebuild the wall of Jerusalem, so that we may no longer be a reproach!" [18][j] Then I explained to them how God had shown his gracious favor to me, and what the king had said to me. They replied, "Let us begin building!" And they undertook the work with vigor.

[19]When they heard about this, Sanballat the Horonite, Tobiah the Ammonite official, and Geshem the Arab* mocked and ridiculed us. "What are you doing?" they asked. "Are you rebelling against the king?" [20]My answer to them was this: "It is the God of heaven who will grant us success. We, his servants, shall set about the rebuilding; but you have neither share nor claim nor memorial* in Jerusalem."

CHAPTER 3

See RG 212

List of Workers. [1*][k] Eliashib the high priest and his priestly kinsmen took up the task of rebuilding the Sheep Gate. They consecrated it and set up its doors, its bolts, and its bars, then continued the rebuilding to the Tower of the Hundred, the Tower of Hananel. [2]At their side the men of Jericho were rebuilding, and next to them was Zaccur, son of Imri. [3][l] The Fish Gate was rebuilt by the people of Hassenaah; they timbered it and set up its doors, its bolts, and its bars. [4]At their side Meremoth, son of Uriah, son of Hakkoz, carried out the work of repair; next to him was Meshullam, son of Berechiah, son of Meshezabel; and next to him was Zadok, son of Baana. [5]Next to him the Tekoites carried out the work of repair; however, some of their most powerful men would not submit to the labor asked by their masters. [6]The Mishneh Gate* was repaired by Joiada, son of Paseah; and Meshullam, son of Besodeiah; they timbered it and set up its doors, its bolts, and its

cial: the governor of the province of Ammon in Transjordan. His title, "official," lit., "servant" (in Hebrew, *'ebed*), could also be understood as "slave," and Nehemiah perhaps meant it in this derogatory sense. The Tobiads remained a powerful family even in Maccabean times, and something of their history is known from 2 Maccabees (3:11; 12:17), Josephus (*Ant.* 12:160–236), the Zeno papyri of the third century B.C., and excavation at 'Araq el-'Emir in Jordan. Sanballat and Tobiah, together with Geshem the Arab (Neh 2:19; 6:1–2), who was probably in charge of Edom and the regions to the south and southeast of Judah, opposed the rebuilding of Jerusalem's walls on political grounds; the city was the capital of a rival province.

2:13–15 Nehemiah left Jerusalem by the Valley Gate near the northwestern end of the old City of David and went south down the Tyropoean Valley toward the Dragon Spring (or the En-rogel [Jos 15:7; 18:16; 2 Sm 17:17; 1 Kgs 1:9], now known as Job's Well) at the juncture of the Valley of Hinnom and the Kidron Valley. He then turned north at the Dung Gate (or the Potsherd Gate of Jer 19:2) at the southern end of the city and proceeded up the wadi, that is, the Kidron Valley, passing the Fountain Gate (at the Spring of Gihon) and the King's Pool (unidentified); finally he turned west and then south to his starting point.

2:19 Geshem the Arab: see also 6:1–2; in 6:6 the name occurs as Gashmu. He is known from a contemporary inscription as ruler of the Kedarite Arabs, who were threatening Judah from the south and east.

2:20 Neither share nor claim nor memorial: although Sanballat and Tobiah worshiped Yhwh, Nehemiah would not let them participate in any of the activities of the religious community in Jerusalem.

3:1–32 The construction work on the gates and walls of the city is described in counterclockwise direction, beginning and ending at the Sheep Gate (to the north of the Temple). The exact locations of many of the topographical points mentioned are uncertain.

3:6 The Mishneh Gate: the gate leading into the second, expanded quarter of the city; cf. 2 Kgs 22:14; Zep 1:10.

i: Ezr 8:32. *j:* Ezr 7:6. *k:* Jer 31:38. *l:* Ezr 2:35; Zep 1:10.

bars. 7 At their side Melatiah the Gibeonite did the repairing, together with Jadon the Meronothite, and the men of Gibeon and of Mizpah, who were under the jurisdiction of the governor of West-of-Euphrates. 8 Next to them the work of repair was carried out by Uzziel, son of Harhaiah, a member of the goldsmiths' guild, and at his side was Hananiah, one of the perfumers' guild. They restored Jerusalem as far as the Broad Wall.* 9 Next to them the work of repair was carried out by Rephaiah, son of Hur, administrator of half the district of Jerusalem, 10 and at his side was Jedaiah, son of Harumaph, who repaired opposite his own house. Next to him Hattush, son of Hashabneiah, carried out the work of repair. 11 The adjoining sector, as far as the Oven Tower, was repaired by Malchijah, son of Harim, and Hasshub, son of Pahath-moab. 12 At their side the work of repair was carried out by Shallum, son of Hallohesh, administrator of half the district of Jerusalem, together with his daughters. 13 The Valley Gate was repaired by Hanun and the inhabitants of Zanoah; they rebuilt it and set up its doors, its bolts, and its bars. They also repaired a thousand cubits of the wall up to the Dung Gate. 14 The Dung Gate was repaired by Malchijah, son of Rechab, administrator of the district of Beth-haccherem; he rebuilt it and set up its doors, its bolts, and its bars. 15 The Fountain Gate was repaired by Shallum, son of Colhozeh, administrator of the district of Mizpah; he rebuilt it, roofed it, and set up its doors, its bolts, and its bars. He also repaired the wall of the Aqueduct Pool near the King's Garden as far as the steps that lead down from the City of David. 16 After him, the work of repair was carried out by Nehemiah, son of Azbuk, administrator of half the district of Beth-zur, to a place opposite the tombs of David, as far as the Artificial Pool and the barracks.

17 After him, these Levites carried out the work of repair: Rehum, son of Bani, and next to him, for his own district, was Hashabiah, administrator of half the district of Keilah. 18 After him, their kinsmen carried out the work of repair: Binnui, son of Henadad, administrator of half the district of Keilah; 19 next to him Ezer, son of Jeshua, administrator of Mizpah, who repaired the adjoining sector, the Corner, opposite the ascent to the arsenal. 20 After him, Baruch, son of Zabbai, repaired the adjoining sector from the Corner to the entrance of the house of Eliashib, the high priest. 21 After him, Meremoth, son of Uriah, son of Hakkoz, repaired the adjoining sector from the entrance of Eliashib's house to its end.

22 After him, the work of repair was carried out by the priests, men of the surrounding country. 23 After them, Benjamin and Hasshub carried out the repair in front of their houses; after them, Azariah, son of Maaseiah, son of Ananiah, made the repairs alongside his house. 24 After him, Binnui, son of Henadad, repaired the adjoining sector from the house of Azariah to the Corner (that is, to the Angle). 25 After him, Palal, son of Uzai, carried out the work of repair opposite the Corner and the tower projecting from the Upper Palace at the quarters of the guard. After him, Pedaiah, son of Parosh, carried out the work of repair 26 to a point opposite the Water Gate on the east, and the projecting tower. 27 After him, the Tekoites repaired the adjoining sector opposite the great projecting tower, to the wall of Ophel.

28 Above the Horse Gate the priests carried out the work of repair, each opposite his own house. 29[m] After them Zadok, son of Immer, carried out the repair opposite his house, and after him the repair was carried out by Shemaiah, son of Shecaniah, keeper of the East Gate. 30 After him, Hananiah, son of Shelemiah, and Hanun, the sixth son of Zalaph, repaired the adjoining sector; after them, Meshullam, son of Berechiah, repaired the place opposite his own lodging. 31 After him, Malchijah, a member of the goldsmiths' guild, carried out the work of repair as far as the quarters of the temple servants and the merchants, in front of the Gate of Inspection and as far as the upper chamber of the Angle. 32 Between the upper chamber of the Angle and the Sheep Gate, the

3:8 The Broad Wall: perhaps identical with the wall, seven meters thick, discovered in the Jewish quarter of the Old City.

m: Ez 40:6.

goldsmiths and the merchants carried out the
work of repair.

Opposition from Judah's Enemies.
33When Sanballat heard that we were rebuilding the wall, he became angry and very
much incensed. He ridiculed the Jews, 34say-
ing in the presence of his associates and the
troops of Samaria: "What are these miserable Jews trying to do? Will they complete
their restoration in a single day? Will they
recover these stones, burnt as they are, from
the heaps of dust?" 35Tobiah the Ammonite
was beside him, and he said: "Whatever they
are building—if a fox attacks it, it will
breach their wall of stones!" 36Hear, our
God, how we were mocked! Turn back their
reproach upon their own heads and deliver
them up as plunder in a land of captivity!
37[n] Do not hide their crime and do not let
their sin be blotted out in your sight, for they
insulted the builders to their faces! 38We,
however, continued to build the wall, and
soon it was completed up to half its height.
The people worked enthusiastically.

CHAPTER 4

See RG 212

1When Sanballat, Tobiah, the Arabs,
the Ammonites, and the Ashdodites heard
that the restoration of the walls of Jerusalem
was progressing—for the gaps were beginning to be closed up—they became extremely angry. 2They all plotted together to
come and fight against Jerusalem and to
throw us into confusion. 3We prayed to our
God and posted a watch against them day
and night for fear of what they might do.
4Meanwhile the Judahites were saying:

"Slackened is the bearers' strength,
there is no end to the rubbish;
Never will we be able
to rebuild the wall."

5Our enemies thought, "Before they are
aware of it or see us, we will come into their
midst, kill them, and put an end to the work."
6When the Jews who lived near them had
come to us from one place after another, and
had told us ten times over that they were
about to attack us, 7I stationed guards down
below, behind the wall, near the exposed
points, assigning them by family groups with
their swords, spears, and bows. 8I made an
inspection, then addressed these words to the
nobles, the magistrates, and the rest of the
people: "Do not fear them! Keep in mind the
LORD, who is great and to be feared, and fight
for your kindred, your sons and daughters,
your wives and your homes." 9When our enemies realized that we had been warned and
that God had upset their plan, we all went
back, each to our own task at the wall.
10[o] From that time on, however, only half
my work force took a hand in the work,
while the other half, armed with spears,
bucklers, bows, and breastplates, stood
guard behind the whole house of Judah 11as
they rebuilt the wall. The load carriers, too,
were armed; each worked with one hand and
held a weapon with the other. 12Every builder, while working, had a sword tied at his
side. A trumpeter stood beside me, 13for I
had said to the nobles, the magistrates, and
the rest of the people: "Our work is scattered
and extensive, and we are widely separated
from one another along the wall; 14wherever
you hear the trumpet sound, join us there;
our God will fight with us." 15Thus we went
on with the work, half with spears in hand,
from daybreak till the stars came out.
16At the same time I told the people to
spend the nights inside Jerusalem, each with
an attendant, so that they might serve as a
guard by night and a working force by day.
17Neither I, nor my kindred, nor any of my
attendants, nor any of the bodyguard that accompanied me took off our clothes; everyone kept a weapon at hand.

CHAPTER 5

See RG 212

Social and Economic Problems.
1[p] Then there rose a great outcry of the people
and their wives against certain of their Jewish
kindred.* 2Some said: "We are forced to pawn
our sons and daughters in order to get grain to

5:1 Certain of their Jewish kindred: probably Jews who had returned from Babylonia who formed the social and economic elite in the province.

n: Neh 6:14; 13:29; Jer 18:23. *o:* Ps 149:6. *p:* Jer 34:8–22.

eat that we may live." [3]Others said: "We are forced to pawn our fields, our vineyards, and our houses, that we may have grain during the famine." [4]Still others said: "To pay the king's tax we have borrowed money on our fields and vineyards. [5][q] And though these are our own kindred, and our children are as good as theirs, we have had to reduce our sons and daughters to slavery, and violence has been done to some of our daughters! Yet we can do nothing about it, for our fields and vineyards belong to others."

[6]I was extremely angry when I heard the reasons for their complaint. [7][r] After some deliberation, I called the nobles and magistrates to account, saying to them, "You are exacting interest from your own kindred!"* I then rebuked them severely, [8][s] saying to them: "As far as we were able, we bought back our Jewish kindred who had been sold to Gentiles; you, however, are selling your own kindred, to have them bought back by us." They remained silent, for they could find no answer. [9]I continued: "What you are doing is not good. Should you not conduct yourselves out of fear of our God rather than fear of the reproach of our Gentile enemies? [10]I myself, my kindred, and my attendants have lent the people money and grain without charge. Let us put an end to this usury! [11]Return to them this very day their fields, vineyards, olive groves, and houses, together with the interest on the money, the grain, the wine, and the oil that you have lent them." [12]They answered: "We will return everything and exact nothing further from them. We will do just what you ask." Then I called for the priests to administer an oath to them that they would do as they had promised. [13]I shook out the folds of my garment, saying, "Thus may God shake from home and fortune every man who fails to keep this promise, and may he thus be shaken out and emptied!" And the whole assembly answered, "Amen," and praised the LORD. Then the people did as they had promised.

Nehemiah's Record. [14]Moreover, from the time that King Artaxerxes appointed me governor in the land of Judah, from his twentieth to his thirty-second year—during these twelve years neither I nor my kindred lived off the governor's food allowance. [15]The earlier governors,* my predecessors, had laid a heavy burden on the people, taking from them each day forty silver shekels for their food; then, too, their attendants oppressed the people. But I, because I feared God, did not do this. [16]In addition, though I had acquired no land of my own, I did my part in this work on the wall, and all my attendants were gathered there for the work. [17]Though I set my table for a hundred and fifty persons, Jews and magistrates, as well as the neighboring Gentiles who came to us, [18]and though the daily preparations were made at my expense—one ox, six choice sheep, poultry—besides all kinds of wine in abundance every ten days, despite this I did not claim the governor's allowance, for the labor lay heavy upon this people. [19]Keep in mind, my God, to my credit all that I did for this people.

CHAPTER 6

See RG 212

Plots Against Nehemiah. [1]When it had been reported to Sanballat, Tobiah, Geshem the Arab, and our other enemies that I had rebuilt the wall and that there was no breach left in it (though up to that time I had not yet set up the doors in the gates), [2]Sanballat and Geshem sent me this message: "Come, let us hold council together at Chephirim in the plain of Ono." They were planning to do me harm. [3]I sent messengers to them with this reply: "I am engaged in a great enterprise and am unable to come down. Why should the work stop, while I leave it to come down to you?" [4]Four times they sent me this same proposal, and each time I gave the same reply. [5]Then, the fifth time, Sanballat sent me the same message by one of his servants, who bore an unsealed letter [6]containing this text: "Among the nations it has been re-

5:7 You are exacting interest from your own kindred!: contrary to the Mosaic law (Dt 23:20).

5:15 The earlier governors: both Sheshbazzar (Ezr 5:14) and Zerubbabel (Hg 1:1, 14; 2:2, 21) are said to be governors, and Mal 1:8 mentions a governor but does not name him. Other names are known from seal impressions of uncertain date.

q: Ex 21:7; Lv 25:39. *r*: Dt 23:20. *s*: Lv 25:48.

ported—Gashmu* is witness to this—that you and the Jews are planning a rebellion; that for this reason you are rebuilding the wall; and that you are to be their king. [7]Also, that you have set up prophets in Jerusalem to proclaim you king of Judah. Now, since matters like these will reach the ear of the king, come, let us hold council together." [8]I sent him this answer: "Nothing of what you report is happening; rather, it is the invention of your own mind." [9]They were all trying to intimidate us, thinking, "They will be discouraged from continuing with the work, and it will never be completed." But instead, I then redoubled my efforts.

[10]I went to the house of Shemaiah, son of Delaiah, son of Mehetabel, who was confined to his house, and he said: "Let us meet in the house of God, inside the temple building; let us lock the doors of the temple. For they are coming to kill you—by night they are coming to kill you." [11]My answer was: "A man like me take flight? Should a man like me enter the temple to save his life? I will not go!" [12]For on consideration, it was plain to me that God had not sent him; rather, because Tobiah and Sanballat had bribed him, he voiced this prophecy concerning me, [13]that I might act on it out of fear and commit this sin. Then they would have had a shameful story with which to discredit me. [14t] Keep in mind Tobiah and Sanballat, my God, because of these things they did; keep in mind as well Noadiah the woman prophet and the other prophets who were trying to intimidate me.

Completion of the Work. [15]The wall was finished on the twenty-fifth day of Elul;* the work had taken fifty-two days. [16u] When all our enemies had heard of this, and all the neighboring Gentiles round about had taken note of it, they were very discouraged, for they knew that it was with our God's help that this work had been completed. [17]At that same time, however, many letters were going to Tobiah from the nobles of Judah, and Tobiah's letters were reaching them, [18]for many in Judah were in league with him, since he was the son-in-law of Shecaniah, son of Arah, and his son Jehohanan had married the daughter of Meshullam, son of Berechiah. [19]They would praise his good deeds in my presence and relate to him whatever I said; and Tobiah sent letters trying to intimidate me.

CHAPTER 7

See RG 212

[1]Now that the wall had been rebuilt, I had the doors set up, and the gatekeepers, the singers, and the Levites were put in charge of them. [2]Over Jerusalem I placed Hanani, my brother, and Hananiah, the commander of the citadel, who was more trustworthy and God-fearing than most. [3]I said to them: "The gates of Jerusalem are not to be opened until the sun is hot, and while the sun is still shining they shall shut and bar the doors. Appoint as sentinels the inhabitants of Jerusalem, some at their watch posts, and others in front of their own houses."

Census of the Province. [4]Now, the city was quite wide and spacious, but its population was small, and none of the houses had been rebuilt. [5]When my God had inspired me to gather together the nobles, the magistrates, and the people, and to examine their family records, I came upon the family list of those who had returned in the earliest period. There I found the following written:

[6* v] These are the inhabitants of the province who returned from the captivity of the exiles whom Nebuchadnezzar, king of Babylon, had carried away, and who came back to Jerusalem and Judah, to their own cities: [7]They returned with Zerubbabel, Jeshua, Nehemiah, Azariah, Raamiah, Nahamani, Mordecai, Bilshan, Mispereth, Bigvai, Nehum, and Baanah.

The census of the people of Israel: [8]descendants of Parosh, two thousand one hundred and seventy-two; [9]descendants of Shephatiah, three hundred and seventy-two; [10]descendants of Arah, six hundred

6:6 Gashmu: elsewhere (vv. 1–2; 2:19) the name is given as Geshem.

6:15 Elul: the sixth month (August–September). **Fifty-two days**: according to Josephus (*Ant.* 11:174–183), the rebuilding of the walls of Jerusalem by Nehemiah took two years and four months.

7:6–72 See note on Ezr 2:1–67.

t: Jer 23:9–40; Zec 13:3. *u:* Ps 118:22–23; 127:1. *v:* Ezr 2:1–70.

and fifty-two; 11 descendants of Pahath-
moab who were descendants of Jeshua and
Joab, two thousand eight hundred and
eighteen; 12 descendants of Elam, one thousand two hundred and fifty-four; 13 descendants of Zattu, eight hundred and forty-
five; 14 descendants of Zaccai, seven
hundred and sixty; 15 descendants of Binnui, six hundred and forty-eight; 16 descendants of Bebai, six hundred and twenty-
eight; 17 descendants of Azgad, two
thousand three hundred and twenty-two;
18 descendants of Adonikam, six hundred
and sixty-seven; 19 descendants of Bigvai,
two thousand and sixty-seven; 20 descendants of Adin, six hundred and fifty-five;
21 descendants of Ater who were descendants of Hezekiah, ninety-eight; 22 descendants of Hashum, three hundred and
twenty-eight; 23 descendants of Bezai, three
hundred and twenty-four; 24 descendants of
Hariph, one hundred and twelve; 25 descendants of Gibeon, ninety-five; 26 people of
Bethlehem and Netophah, one hundred and
eighty-eight; 27 people of Anathoth, one
hundred and twenty-eight; 28 people of
Beth-azmaveth, forty-two; 29 people of Kiriath-jearim, Chephirah, and Beeroth, seven
hundred and forty-three; 30 people of Ramah and Geba, six hundred and twenty-
one; 31 people of Michmas, one hundred and
twenty-two; 32 people of Bethel and Ai, one
hundred and twenty-three; 33 people of
Nebo, fifty-two; 34 descendants of the other
Elam, one thousand two hundred and fifty-
four; 35 descendants of Harim, three hundred and twenty; 36 descendants of Jericho,
three hundred and forty-five; 37 descendants
of Lod, Hadid, and Ono, seven hundred and
twenty-one; 38 descendants of Senaah, three
thousand nine hundred and thirty.

39 The priests: descendants of Jedaiah of
the house of Jeshua, nine hundred and seventy-three; 40 descendants of Immer, one
thousand and fifty-two; 41 descendants of
Pashhur, one thousand two hundred and
forty-seven; 42 descendants of Harim, one
thousand and seventeen.

43 The Levites: descendants of Jeshua,
Kadmiel of the descendants of Hodeviah,
seventy-four.

44 The singers: descendants of Asaph, one
hundred and forty-eight.

45 The gatekeepers: descendants of Shallum, descendants of Ater, descendants of
Talmon, descendants of Akkub, descendants
of Hatita, descendants of Shobai, one hundred and thirty-eight.

46 The temple servants: descendants of
Ziha, descendants of Hasupha, descendants
of Tabbaoth, 47 descendants of Keros, descendants of Sia, descendants of Padon,
48 descendants of Lebana, descendants of
Hagaba, descendants of Shalmai, 49 descen-
dants of Hanan, descendants of Giddel, de-
scendants of Gahar, 50 descendants of Reaiah, descendants of Rezin, descendants of
Nekoda, 51 descendants of Gazzam, descendants of Uzza, descendants of Paseah, 52 descendants of Besai, descendants of the Meunites, descendants of the Nephusites,
53 descendants of Bakbuk, descendants of
Hakupha, descendants of Harhur, 54 descen-
dants of Bazlith, descendants of Mehida, de-
scendants of Harsha, 55 descendants of Barkos, descendants of Sisera, descendants of
Temah, 56 descendants of Neziah, descendants of Hatipha.

57 Descendants of Solomon's servants: descendants of Sotai, descendants of Sophereth, descendants of Perida, 58 descendants of Jaala, descendants of Darkon,
descendants of Giddel, 59 descendants of
Shephatiah, descendants of Hattil, descendants of Pochereth-hazzebaim, descendants
of Amon. 60 The total of the temple servants
and the descendants of Solomon's servants
was three hundred and ninety-two.

61 The following who returned from Tel-
melah, Tel-harsha, Cherub, Addon, and Immer were unable to prove that their ancestral
houses and their descent were Israelite: 62 descendants of Delaiah, descendants of Tobiah,
descendants of Nekoda, six hundred and
forty-two. 63 Also, of the priests: descendants
of Hobaiah, descendants of Hakkoz, descendants of Barzillai (he had married one of the
daughters of Barzillai the Gileadite and was
named after him). 64 These men searched
their family records, but their names could
not be found written there; hence they were
disqualified from the priesthood, 65 and the

governor* ordered them not to partake of the most holy foods until there should be a priest to consult the Urim and Thummim.

[66]The entire assembly taken together came to forty-two thousand three hundred and sixty, [67]not counting their male and female servants, who were seven thousand three hundred and thirty-seven. They also had two hundred male and female singers. Their horses were seven hundred and thirty-six, their mules two hundred and forty-five, [68]their camels four hundred and thirty-five, their donkeys six thousand seven hundred and twenty.

[69]Certain of the heads of ancestral houses contributed to the temple service. The governor put into the treasury one thousand drachmas of gold, fifty basins, thirty vestments for priests, and five hundred minas of silver. [70]Some of the heads of ancestral houses contributed to the treasury for the temple service: twenty thousand drachmas of gold and two thousand two hundred minas of silver. [71]The contributions of the rest of the people amounted to twenty thousand drachmas of gold, two thousand minas of silver, and sixty-seven vestments for priests.

[72]The priests, the Levites, the gatekeepers, the singers, the temple servants, and all Israel took up residence in their cities.

II. Promulgation of the Law

CHAPTER 8

See RG 212–14

Ezra Reads the Law. [1*][w] Now when the seventh month came, the whole people gathered as one in the square in front of the Water Gate, and they called upon Ezra the scribe to bring forth the book of the law of Moses which the LORD had commanded for Israel. [2x] On the first day of the seventh month, therefore, Ezra the priest brought the law before the assembly, which consisted of men, women, and those children old enough to understand. [3]In the square in front of the Water Gate, Ezra read out of the book from daybreak till midday, in the presence of the men, the women, and those children old enough to understand; and all the people listened attentively to the book of the law. [4]Ezra the scribe stood on a wooden platform that had been made for the occasion; at his right side stood Mattithiah, Shema, Anaiah, Uriah, Hilkiah, and Maaseiah, and on his left Pedaiah, Mishael, Malchijah, Hashum, Hashbaddanah, Zechariah, Meshullam. [5]Ezra opened the scroll so that all the people might see it, for he was standing higher than any of the people. When he opened it, all the people stood. [6]Ezra blessed the LORD, the great God, and all the people, their hands raised high, answered, "Amen, amen!" Then they knelt down and bowed before the LORD, their faces to the ground. [7y] The Levites Jeshua, Bani, Sherebiah, Jamin, Akkub, Shabbethai, Hodiah, Maaseiah, Kelita, Azariah, Jozabad, Hanan, and Pelaiah explained the law to the people, who remained in their places. [8z] Ezra read clearly from the book of the law of God, interpreting it so that all could understand what was read. [9]Then Nehemiah, that is, the governor, and Ezra the priest-scribe, and the Levites who were instructing the people said to all the people: "Today is holy to the LORD your God. Do not lament, do not weep!"—for all the people were weeping as they heard the words of the law. [10a] He continued: "Go, eat rich foods and drink sweet drinks, and allot portions to those who had nothing prepared; for today is holy to our LORD. Do not be saddened this day, for rejoicing in the LORD is your strength!" [11]And the Levites quieted all the people, saying, "Silence! Today is holy, do not be saddened." [12]Then all the people began to eat and drink, to distribute portions, and to celebrate with great joy, for they understood the words that had been explained to them.

The Feast of Booths. [13]On the second day, the heads of ancestral houses of the whole people, and also the priests and the Levites, gathered around Ezra the scribe to study the

7:65, 69 The governor: see note on Ezr 2:63.

8:1–18 Chronologically this belongs after Ezr 8:36. The gloss mentioning Nehemiah in Neh 8:9 was inserted in this Ezra section after the dislocation of several parts of Ezra-Nehemiah had occurred. There is no clear evidence of a simultaneous presence of Nehemiah and Ezra in Jerusalem; Neh 12:26, 36 are also scribal glosses.

w: Ezr 3:1. *x:* Lv 23:23–25; Nm 29:1–6. *y:* Neh 10:10–13. *z:* Ezr 7:6. *a:* Est 9:19.

words of the law. [14b] They found it written in
the law commanded by the LORD through
Moses that the Israelites should dwell in
booths during the feast of the seventh
month; [15c] and that they should have this
proclamation made throughout their cities
and in Jerusalem: "Go out into the hill country and bring in branches of olive, oleaster,
myrtle, palm, and other trees in leaf, to make
booths, as it is written." [16]The people went
out and brought in branches with which they
made booths for themselves, on the roof of
their houses, in their courtyards, in the
courts of the house of God, and in the
squares of the Water Gate and the Gate of
Ephraim. [17d] So the entire assembly of the
returned exiles made booths and dwelt in
them. Now the Israelites had done nothing
of this sort from the days of Jeshua, son of
Nun, until this occasion; therefore there was
very great joy. [18]Ezra read from the book of
the law of God day after day, from the first
day to the last. They kept the feast for seven
days, and the solemn assembly on the eighth
day, as was required.

CHAPTER 9

See RG 212–14

Public Confession of Sin. [1* e] On the
twenty-fourth day of this month, the Israelites gathered together while fasting and
wearing sackcloth, their heads covered with
dust. [2f] Those of Israelite descent separated
themselves from all who were of foreign ex-
traction, then stood forward and confessed
their sins and the guilty deeds of their ancestors. [3]When they had taken their places, they
read from the book of the law of the LORD
their God, for a fourth of the day, and during
another fourth they made their confession
and bowed down before the LORD their God.
[4]Standing on the platform of the Levites
were Jeshua, Binnui, Kadmiel, Shebaniah,
Bunni, Sherebiah, Bani, and Chenani, who
cried out to the LORD their God, with a loud
voice. [5g] The Levites Jeshua, Kadmiel, Bani,
Hashabneiah, Sherebiah, Hodiah, Shebaniah, and Pethahiah said,

"Arise, bless the LORD, your God,
from eternity to eternity!"
"And may they bless your glorious name,
which is exalted above all blessing and
praise."
[6 *] "You are the LORD, you alone;
You made the heavens,
the highest heavens and all their host,
The earth and all that is upon it,
the seas and all that is in them.
To all of them you give life,
the heavenly hosts bow down before
you.
[7 h] You are the LORD God
who chose Abram,
Who brought him from Ur of the
Chaldees,
who named him Abraham.
[8 i] You found his heart faithful in your sight,
you made the covenant with him
To give the land of the Canaanites,
Hittites, Amorites,
Perizzites, Jebusites, and Girgashites
to him and his descendants.
You fulfilled your promises,
for you are just.
[9 j] You saw the affliction of our ancestors
in Egypt,
you heard their cry by the Red Sea;
[10 k] You worked signs and wonders against
Pharaoh,
against all his servants and the people
of his land,
Because you knew of their insolence
toward them;
thus you made for yourself a name
even to this day.
[11 l] The sea you divided before them,
on dry ground they passed through the
midst of the sea;
Their pursuers you hurled into the depths,
like a stone into the mighty waters.

9:1–5 The feast of Booths is followed by a penitential liturgy. Since it includes separation from foreigners, some read it as a sequel to Ezr 9–10.

9:6–37 The Septuagint attributes the prayer to Ezra; cf. Ezr 9:6–15.

b: Ex 23:14–16; Lv 23:33–36; Nm 29:1–38; Ez 45:25. *c:* Ps 118:27. *d:* 2 Chr 30:26; 35:18. *e:* Dn 9:3. *f:* Ezr 9:1–2; 10:11. *g:* Ps 41:14; 106:48; Dn 2:20; 3:52. *h:* Gn 12:1; 17:5. *i:* Gn 15:18–19. *j:* Ex 2:23–24. *k:* Ex 7–11; 14. *l:* Ex 15:5, 10.

12 [m] With a column of cloud you led them
by day,
and by night with a column of fire,
To light the way of their journey,
the way in which they must travel.
13 [n] On Mount Sinai you came down,
you spoke with them from heaven;
You gave them just ordinances, true laws,
good statutes and commandments;
14 [o] Your holy sabbath you made known to
them,
commandments, statutes, and law you
prescribed for them,
by the hand of Moses your servant.
15 [p] Food from heaven you gave them in
their hunger,
water from a rock you sent them in
their thirst.
You told them to enter and occupy the
land
which you had sworn to give them.
16 But they, our ancestors, proved to be
insolent;
they were obdurate* and did not obey
your commandments.
17 [q] They refused to obey and no longer
remembered
the wonders you had worked for them.
They were obdurate and appointed a
leader
in order to return to their slavery in
Egypt.
But you are a forgiving God, gracious
and merciful,
slow to anger and rich in mercy;
you did not forsake them.
18 [r] Though they made for themselves a
molten calf,
and proclaimed, 'Here is your God
who brought you up from Egypt,'
and were guilty of great insults,
19 Yet in your great mercy
you did not forsake them in the desert.
By day the column of cloud did not cease
to lead them on their journey,
by night the column of fire did not cease
to light the way they were to travel.
20 [s] Your good spirit you bestowed on them,
to give them understanding;
Your manna you did not withhold from
their mouths,
and you gave them water in their thirst.
21 [t] Forty years in the desert you sustained
them:
they did not want;
Their garments did not become worn,
and their feet did not swell.
22 [u] You gave them kingdoms and peoples,
which you divided among them as
border lands.
They possessed the land of Sihon, king
of Heshbon,
and the land of Og, king of Bashan.
23 [v] You made their children as numerous as
the stars of the heavens,
and you brought them into the land
which you had commanded their
ancestors to enter and possess.
24 The children went in to possess the land;
you humbled before them the
Canaanite inhabitants
and gave them into their power,
Their kings and the peoples of the land,
to do with them as they wished.
25 [w] They captured fortified cities and fertile
land;
they took possession of houses filled
with all good things,
Cisterns already dug, vineyards, olive
groves,
and fruit trees in abundance.
They ate and had their fill,
fattened and feasted on your great
goodness.
26 [x] But they were contemptuous and
rebelled against you:
they cast your law behind their backs.
They murdered your prophets
who bore witness against them to
bring them back to you:
they were guilty of great insults.
27 [y] Therefore you gave them into the power
of their enemies,
who oppressed them.

9:16 They were obdurate: lit., "they stiffened their necks."

m: Ex 13:21–22. *n:* Ex 19–24. *o:* Ex 20:8. *p:* Ex 16:4; 17:1–2. *q:* Ex 34:6; Nm 14:1–4; Dt 9:9. *r:* Ex 32:4, 8. *s:* Dt 2:7. *t:* Dt 8:4. *u:* Nm 21:21–35; Dt 1:4; 2:26–3:11. *v:* Dt 1:10. *w:* Dt 3:5; 6:10–11; 11:11; 32:15. *x:* Wis 2:10–20. *y:* Dn 9:19.

But in the time of their oppression they
would cry out to you,
and you would hear them from heaven,
And according to your great mercy give
them saviors
to deliver them from the power of their
enemies.
28 As soon as they had relief,
they would go back to doing evil in
your sight.
Again you abandoned them to the power
of their enemies,
who crushed them.
Once again they cried out to you, and
you heard them from heaven
and delivered them according to your
mercy, many times over.
29 [z] You bore witness against them,
to bring them back to your law.
But they were insolent
and would not obey your
commandments;
They sinned against your ordinances,
which give life to those who keep them.
They turned stubborn backs, stiffened
their necks,
and would not obey.
30 You were patient with them for many
years,
bearing witness against them through
your spirit, by means of your
prophets;
Still they would not listen.
Therefore you delivered them into the
power of the peoples of the lands.
31 Yet in your great mercy you did not
completely destroy them
and did not forsake them, for you are a
gracious and merciful God.
32 [a] Now, our God, great, mighty, and
awesome God,
who preserves the covenant of mercy,
do not discount all the hardship that
has befallen us,
Our kings, our princes, our priests,
our prophets, our ancestors, and your
entire people,
from the time of the kings of Assyria
until this day!
33 [b] In all that has come upon us you have
been just,
for you kept faith while we have done
evil.
34 Yes, our kings, our princes, our priests,
and our ancestors
have not kept your law;
They paid no attention to your
commandments
and the warnings which you gave them.
35 While they were still in their kingdom,
in the midst of the many good things
that you had given them
And in the wide, fertile land
that you had spread out before them,
They did not serve you
nor turn away from their evil deeds.
36 Today we are slaves!
As for the land which you gave our
ancestors
That they might eat its fruits and good
things—
see, we have become slaves upon it!
37 Its rich produce goes to the kings
you set over us because of our sins,
Who rule over our bodies and our cattle
as they please.
We are in great distress!"

CHAPTER 10

See RG 212–14

Signatories to the Pact. 1* In view of
all this, we are entering into a firm pact,
which we are putting into writing. On the
sealed document appear the names of our
princes, our Levites, and our priests.
2 On the sealed document: the governor
Nehemiah, son of Hacaliah, and Zedekiah.
3 [c] Seraiah, Azariah, Jeremiah, 4 Pashhur,
Amariah, Malchijah, 5 Hattush, Shebaniah,
Malluch, 6 Harim, Meremoth, Obadiah,
7 Daniel, Ginnethon, Baruch, 8 Meshullam,
Abijah, Mijamin, 9 Maaziah, Bilgai, Shemaiah: these are the priests.
10 The Levites: Jeshua, son of Azaniah;
Binnui, of the descendants of Henadad;

10:1–39 This section belongs to the Nehemiah narrative rather than to that of Ezra. It is best read after Neh 13:31, since the stipulations of the pact seem to presuppose Nehemiah's measures recorded in Neh 13. **In view of all this**: considering the situation described in Neh 13:4–31.

z: Lv 18:5; Dt 30:16; 32:47. *a:* Lam 5. *b:* Dn 3:27; 9:14. *c:* Neh 12:1–7, 12–26.

Kadmiel; [11d] and their kinsmen Shebaniah, Hodiah, Kelita, Pelaiah, Hanan, [12]Mica, Rehob, Hashabiah, [13]Zaccur, Sherebiah, Shebaniah, [14]Hodiah, Bani, Beninu.

[15]The leaders of the people: Parosh, Pahath-moab, Elam, Zattu, Bani, [16]Bunni, Azgad, Bebai, [17]Adonijah, Bigvai, Adin, [18]Ater, Hezekiah, Azzur, [19]Hodiah, Hashum, Bezai, [20]Hariph, Anathoth, Nebai, [21]Magpiash, Meshullam, Hezir, [22]Meshezabel, Zadok, Jaddua, [23]Pelatiah, Hanan, Anaiah, [24]Hoshea, Hananiah, Hasshub, [25]Hallhohesh, Pilha, Shobek, [26]Rehum, Hashabnah, Maaseiah, [27]Ahiah, Hanan, Anan, [28]Malluch, Harim, Baanah.

Provisions of the Pact. [29]The rest of the people, priests, Levites, gatekeepers, singers, temple servants, and all others who have separated themselves from the local inhabitants in favor of the law of God, with their wives, their sons, their daughters, all who are of the age of discretion, [30e] join their influential kindred, and with the sanction of a curse take this oath to follow the law of God given through Moses, the servant of God, and to observe carefully all the commandments of the LORD, our Lord, his ordinances and his statutes.

[31f] We will not marry our daughters to the local inhabitants, and we will not accept their daughters for our sons.

[32g] When the local inhabitants bring in merchandise or any kind of grain for sale on the sabbath day, we will not buy from them on the sabbath or on any other holy day. In the seventh year we will forgo the produce, and forgive every kind of debt.

[33h] We impose these commandments on ourselves: to give a third of a shekel each year for the service of the house of our God, [34]for the showbread, the daily grain offering, the daily burnt offering, for the sabbaths, new moons, and festivals, for the holy offerings and sin offerings to make atonement for Israel, for every service of the house of our God. [35i] We, priests, Levites, and people, have determined by lot concerning the procurement of wood: it is to be brought to the house of our God by each of our ancestral houses at stated times each year, to be burnt on the altar of the LORD, our God, as the law prescribes. [36j] We have agreed to bring each year to the house of the LORD the first fruits of our fields and of our fruit trees, of every kind; [37]also, as is prescribed in the law, to bring to the house of our God, to the priests who serve in the house of our God, the firstborn of our children and our animals, including the firstborn of our flocks and herds. [38k] The first batch of our dough, and our offerings of the fruit of every tree, of wine and oil, we will bring to the priests, to the chambers of the house of our God. The tithe of our fields we will bring to the Levites; they, the Levites, shall take the tithe in all the cities of our service. [39]An Aaronite priest shall be with the Levites when they take the tithe, and the Levites shall bring the tithe of the tithes to the house of our God, to the chambers of the treasury. [40]For to these chambers the Israelites and Levites bring the offerings of grain, wine, and oil; there also are housed the vessels of the sanctuary, and the ministering priests, the gatekeepers, and the singers. We will not neglect the house of our God.

III. Dedication of the Wall; Other Reforms

CHAPTER 11

See RG 214

Resettlement of Jerusalem. [1*][l] The administrators took up residence in Jerusalem, and the rest of the people cast lots to bring one man in ten to reside in Jerusalem, the holy city, while the other nine would remain in the other cities. [2]The people blessed all those who willingly agreed to take up residence in Jerusalem.

[3m] These are the heads of the province who took up residence in Jerusalem. In the cities of Judah dwelt Israelites, priests, Le-

11:1–19 This list of the family heads who lived in Jerusalem at the time of Nehemiah is best read after Neh 7:72. It parallels at many points the list of early settlers in 1 Chr 9:2–17.

d: Ezr 10:23. *e:* Neh 13:23–27. *f:* Dt 7:2–4; Ezr 9:2, 12; Neh 13:15–22. *g:* Neh 5:1–13; 13:15–22; Ex 20:8; Lv 25:2–7. *h:* Lv 24:5–9; 2 Chr 24:6, 9–10. *i:* Neh 13:31. *j:* Ex 13:1, 11–16; Dt 26:1. *k:* Neh 13:10–14; Nm 18:21–32. *l:* Neh 7:4. *m:* 1 Chr 9:2–34.

vites, temple servants, and the descendants
of Solomon's servants, each on the property
they owned in their own cities.
[4]In Jerusalem dwelt both Judahites and
Benjaminites. Of the Judahites: Athaiah, son
of Uzziah, son of Zechariah, son of Amariah,
son of Shephatiah, son of Mehallalel, of the
sons of Perez; [5]Maaseiah, son of Baruch, son
of Colhozeh, son of Hazaiah, son of Adaiah,
son of Joiarib, son of Zechariah, a son of the
Shelanites. [6]The total of the descendants of
Perez who dwelt in Jerusalem was four hundred and sixty-eight people of substance.
[7]These were the Benjaminites: Sallu, son
of Meshullam, son of Joed, son of Pedaiah,
son of Kolaiah, son of Maaseiah, son of Ith-
iel, son of Jeshaiah, [8]and his kinsmen, warriors, nine hundred and twenty-eight in
number. [9]Joel, son of Zichri, was their commander, and Judah, son of Hassenuah, was
second in command of the city.
[10]Among the priests were: Jedaiah; Joiarib; Jachin; [11]Seraiah, son of Hilkiah, son of
Meshullam, son of Zadok, son of Meraioth,
son of Ahitub, the ruler of the house of God,
[12]and their kinsmen who carried out the temple service, eight hundred and twenty-two;
Adaiah, son of Jeroham, son of Pelaliah, son
of Amzi, son of Zechariah, son of Pashhur,
son of Malchijah, [13]and his kinsmen, heads
of ancestral houses, two hundred and forty-
two; and Amasai, son of Azarel, son of Ahzai, son of Meshillemoth, son of Immer,
[14]and his kinsmen, warriors, one hundred
and twenty-eight. Their commander was
Zabdiel, son of Haggadol.
[15]Among the Levites were Shemaiah, son
of Hasshub, son of Azrikam, son of
Hashabiah, son of Bunni; [16]Shabbethai and
Jozabad, levitical chiefs who were placed
over the external affairs of the house of God;
[17]Mattaniah, son of Micah, son of Zabdi, son
of Asaph, director of the psalms, who led the
thanksgiving at prayer; Bakbukiah, second
in rank among his kinsmen; and Abda, son
of Shammua, son of Galal, son of Jeduthun.
[18]The total of the Levites in the holy city was
two hundred and eighty-four.
[19]The gatekeepers were Akkub, Talmon,
and their kinsmen, who kept watch over the
gates; one hundred and seventy-two in number.
[20]The rest of Israel, including priests and
Levites, were in all the other cities of Judah
in their own inheritances.
[21]The temple servants lived on Ophel.
Ziha and Gishpa were in charge of the temple servants.
[22][n] The prefect of the Levites in Jerusalem
was Uzzi, son of Bani, son of Hashabiah,
son of Mattaniah, son of Micah; he was one
of the descendants of Asaph, the singers appointed to the service of the house of God—
[23]for they had been appointed by royal decree, and there was a fixed schedule for the
singers assigning them their daily duties.
[24]Pethahiah, son of Meshezabel, a descendant of Zerah, son of Judah, was royal deputy
in all affairs that concerned the people.
Other Settlements. [25]As concerns their
villages with their fields: Judahites lived in
Kiriath-arba and its dependencies, in Dibon
and its dependencies, in Jekabzeel and its
villages, [26]in Jeshua, Moladah, Beth-pelet,
[27]in Hazarshual, in Beer-sheba and its dependencies, [28]in Ziklag, in Meconah and its
dependencies, [29]in En-rimmon, Zorah, Jarmuth, [30]Zanoah, Adullam, and their villages,
Lachish and its fields, Azekah and its dependencies. They were settled from Beer-
sheba to Ge-hinnom.
[31]Benjaminites were in Geba, Michmash,
Aija, Bethel and its dependencies, [32]Ana-
thoth, Nob, Ananiah, [33]Hazor, Ramah, Gittaim, [34]Hadid, Zeboim, Neballat, [35]Lod,
Ono, and the Valley of the Artisans.
[36]Some divisions of the Levites from Judah were attached to Benjamin.

CHAPTER 12

See RG 214

Priests and Levites at the Time of Ze-
rubbabel. [1][o] The following are the priests and
Levites who returned with Zerubbabel, son of
Shealtiel, and Jeshua: Seraiah, Jeremiah,
Ezra, [2]Amariah, Malluch, Hattush, [3]Sheca-
niah, Rehum, Meremoth, [4]Iddo, Ginnethon,
Abijah, [5]Mijamin, Maadiah, Bilgah, [6]Shema-
iah, and Joiarib, Jedaiah, [7]Sallu, Amok, Hil-

n: 2 Chr 20:14. *o:* Neh 12:12–22.

kiah, Jedaiah. These were the priestly heads and their kinsmen in the days of Jeshua.

8 The Levites were Jeshua, Binnui, Kadmiel, Sherebiah, Judah, Mattaniah, who, together with his kinsmen, was in charge of the thanksgiving hymns, 9 while Bakbukiah and Unno and their kinsmen ministered opposite them by turns.

High Priests. 10* Jeshua became the father of Joiakim, Joiakim the father of Eliashib, and Eliashib the father of Joiada; 11 Joiada the father of Johanan, and Johanan the father of Jaddua.

Priests and Levites Under Joiakim. 12p In the days of Joiakim these were the priestly family heads: for Seraiah, Meraiah; for Jeremiah, Hananiah; 13 for Ezra, Meshullam; for Amariah, Jehohanan; 14 for Malluchi, Jonathan; for Shebaniah, Joseph; 15 for Harim, Adna; for Meremoth, Helkai; 16 for Iddo, Zechariah; for Ginnethon, Meshullam; 17 for Abijah, Zichri; for Miamin, . . . ; for Moadiah, Piltai; 18 for Bilgah, Shammua; for Shemaiah, Jehonathan; 19 and for Joiarib, Mattenai; for Jedaiah, Uzzi; 20 for Sallu, Kallai; for Amok, Eber; 21 for Hilkiah, Hashabiah; for Jedaiah, Nethanel.

22 In the time of Eliashib, Joiada, Johanan, and Jaddua, the heads of ancestral houses of the priests were written down in the Book of Chronicles, up until the reign of Darius the Persian. 23 The sons of Levi: the family heads were written down in the Book of Chronicles, up until the time of Johanan, the son of Eliashib.

24q The heads of the Levites were Hashabiah, Sherebiah, Jeshua, Binnui, Kadmiel. Their kinsmen who stood opposite them to sing praises and thanksgiving in fulfillment of the command of David, the man of God, one section opposite the other, 25r were Mattaniah, Bakbukiah, Obadiah. Meshullam, Talmon, and Akkub were gatekeepers. They guarded the storerooms at the gates.

26 All these lived in the time of Joiakim, son of Jeshua, son of Jozadak (and in the time of Nehemiah the governor and of Ezra the priest-scribe).

Dedication of the Wall. 27* At the dedication of the wall of Jerusalem, the Levites were sought out wherever they lived and were brought to Jerusalem to celebrate a joyful dedication with thanksgiving hymns and the music of cymbals, harps, and lyres. 28 The levitical singers gathered together from the region about Jerusalem, from the villages of the Netophathites, 29 from Beth-gilgal, and from the plains of Geba and Azmaveth (for the singers had built themselves settlements about Jerusalem). 30 The priests and Levites first purified themselves, then they purified the people, the gates, and the wall.

31 I had the administrators of Judah go up on the wall, and I arranged two great choirs. The first of these proceeded to the right, along the top of the wall, in the direction of the Dung Gate, 32 followed by Hoshaiah and half the administrators of Judah, 33 along with Azariah, Ezra, Meshullam, 34 Judah, Benjamin, Shemaiah, and Jeremiah, 35 priests with the trumpets, and also Zechariah, son of Jonathan, son of Shemaiah, son of Mattaniah, son of Micaiah, son of Zaccur, son of Asaph, 36 and his kinsmen Shemaiah, Azarel, Milalai, Gilalai, Maai, Nethanel, Judah, and Hanani, with the musical instruments of David, the man of God. Ezra the scribe was at their head. 37 At the Fountain Gate they went straight up by the steps of the City of David and continued along the top of the wall above the house of David until they came to the Water Gate on the east.

38 The second choir proceeded to the left, followed by myself and the other half of the

12:10–11 Jeshua was the high priest when Zerubbabel was governor, in the last decades of the sixth century B.C. (Hg 1:1, 12, 14; 2:2, 4). He was the grandfather of Eliashib, the high priest early in Nehemiah's governorship (445–433 B.C.; Neh 3:1, 20, 21) and perhaps later. Eliashib, the grandfather of Johanan, was a grown man, if not yet a high priest, at the time of Ezra, ca. 400 B.C. (Ezr 10:6; and note). According to Josephus (*Ant.* 11:120–183), whose testimony here is doubtful, Jaddua, son of Johanan, died as an old man about the time that Alexander the Great died, 323 B.C. If, as seems probable, this list of the postexilic high priests, at least as far as Johanan, comes from the author himself (cf. Neh 12:23) and not from a later scribe, it is of prime importance for dating the author's work in the first decades of the fourth century B.C.

12:27–43 The dedication of the wall of Jerusalem took place, no doubt, soon after the restoration of the wall and its gates had been completed. This section, therefore, is best read after Neh 6:15.

p: Neh 10:3–9; 12:1–6. *q:* Ezr 2:40. *r:* Neh 11:17.

administrators, along the top of the wall past the Oven Tower as far as the Broad Wall, [39]then past the Ephraim Gate to the Mishneh Gate, the Fish Gate, the Tower of Hananel, and the Hundred Tower, as far as the Sheep Gate. They came to a halt at the Prison Gate.

[40]Both choirs took up a position in the house of God; I, too, and half the magistrates with me, [41]together with the priests Eliakim, Maaseiah, Minjamin, Micaiah, Elioenai, Zechariah, Hananiah, with the trumpets, [42]and Maaseiah, Shemaiah, Eleazar, Uzzi, Jehohanan, Malchijah, Elam, and Ezer. The singers were heard under the leadership of Jezrahiah. [43]Great sacrifices were offered on that day, and they rejoiced, for God had given them cause for great rejoicing. The women and the children joined in, and the rejoicing at Jerusalem could be heard from far off.

[44*] [s] At that time men were appointed over the chambers set aside for stores, offerings, first fruits, and tithes; in them they were to collect from the fields of the various cities the portions legally assigned to the priests and Levites. For Judah rejoiced in its appointed priests and Levites [45]who carried out the ministry of their God and the ministry of purification (as did the singers and the gatekeepers) in accordance with the prescriptions of David and Solomon, his son. [46t] For in the days of David and Asaph, long ago, there were leaders of singers for songs of praise and thanksgiving to God. [47u] All Israel, in the days of Zerubbabel and in the days of Nehemiah, gave the singers and the gatekeepers their portions, according to their daily needs. They made their consecrated offering to the Levites, and the Levites made theirs to the descendants of Aaron.

CHAPTER 13

See RG 214

[1*] [v] At that time, when the book of Moses was being read in the hearing of the people, it was found written there: "No Ammonite or Moabite may ever be admitted into the assembly of God; [2w] for they did not meet the Israelites with food and water, but they hired Balaam to curse them, though our God turned the curse into a blessing." [3x] When they had heard the law, they separated all those of mixed descent from Israel.

Reform in the Temple. [4*] Before this, the priest Eliashib, who had been placed in charge of the chambers of the house of our God and who was an associate of Tobiah, [5y] had set aside for the latter's use a large chamber in which had previously been stored the grain offerings, incense and vessels, the tithes in grain, wine, and oil allotted to the Levites, singers, and gatekeepers, and the offerings due the priests. [6]During all this time I had not been in Jerusalem, for in the thirty-second year of Artaxerxes,* king of Babylon, I had gone back to the king. After a suitable period of time, however, I asked leave of the king [7]and returned to Jerusalem, where I discovered the evil thing that Eliashib had done for Tobiah, in setting aside for him a chamber in the courts of the house of God. [8]This displeased me very much, so I had all of Tobiah's household goods thrown outside the chamber. [9]Then I gave orders to purify the chambers, and I brought back the vessels of the house of God, the grain offerings, and the incense.

[10]I learned, too, that the portions due the Levites were no longer being given, so that the Levites and the singers who should have been carrying out the services had deserted to their own fields. [11]I reprimanded the magistrates, demanding, "Why is the house of God neglected?" Then I brought the Levites together and had them resume their stations. [12z] All Judah once more brought in the tithes of grain, wine, and oil to the storerooms. [13]In charge of the storerooms I appointed Shele-

12:44–47 This account of the provisions made for the Temple services is a composition either of the author or of a later scribe. The gloss mentioning Nehemiah is not in the Septuagint.

13:1–3 These verses serve as an introduction to the reforms Nehemiah instituted during his second mission in Jerusalem (vv. 4–31). The part of the Book of Moses read to the people is freely quoted here from Dt 23:3–6.

13:4–31 This is part of the "Memoirs of Nehemiah"; it is continued in 10:1–40.

13:6 In the thirty-second year of Artaxerxes: Artaxerxes I, therefore 433 B.C. **After . . . time**: it is not known when Nehemiah returned to Jerusalem or how long his second period of activity there lasted.

s: 1 Chr 23–26; 2 Chr 8:14. *t:* 2 Chr 29:30; 35:15. *u:* Neh 10:39; 13:10–11; Nm 18:26. *v:* Dt 23:3–6. *w:* Nm 22–24. *x:* Neh 13:23–28. *y:* Neh 12:44. *z:* Neh 10:38–39; 12:44–45, 47; 2 Chr 31:6.

miah the priest, Zadok the scribe, and Pedaiah, one of the Levites, together with Hanan, son of Zaccur, son of Mattaniah, as their assistant; for they were considered trustworthy. It was their duty to make the distribution to their kinsmen. 14Remember this to my credit, my God! Do not forget the good deeds I have done for the house of my God and its services!

Sabbath Observance. 15a In those days I perceived that people in Judah were treading the wine presses on the sabbath; that they were bringing in sheaves of grain, loading them on their donkeys, together with wine, grapes, figs, and every other kind of load, and bringing them to Jerusalem on the sabbath day. I warned them to sell none of these provisions. 16In Jerusalem itself the Tyrians residing there were importing fish and every other kind of merchandise and selling it to the Judahites on the sabbath. 17I reprimanded the nobles of Judah, demanding: "What is this evil thing you are doing, profaning the sabbath day? 18Did not your ancestors act in this same way, with the result that our God has brought all this evil upon us and upon this city? Would you add to the wrath against Israel by once more profaning the sabbath?"

19When the shadows were falling on the gates of Jerusalem before the sabbath, I ordered the doors to be closed and prohibited their reopening until after the sabbath. I posted some of my own people at the gates so that no load might enter on the sabbath day. 20The merchants and sellers of various kinds of merchandise spent the night once or twice outside Jerusalem, 21but then I warned them: "Why do you spend the night alongside the wall? If you keep this up, I will beat you!" From that time on, they did not return on the sabbath. 22Then I ordered the Levites to purify themselves and to watch the gates, so that the sabbath day might be kept holy. This, too, remember in my favor, my God, and have mercy on me in accordance with your great mercy!

Mixed Marriages. 23b Also in those days I saw Jews who had married women of Ashdod, Ammon, or Moab. 24Of their children, half spoke the language of Ashdod,* or of one of the other peoples, and none of them knew how to speak the language of Judah. 25So I reprimanded and cursed them; I beat some of their men and pulled out their hair; and I adjured them by God: "You shall not marry your daughters to their sons nor accept any of their daughters for your sons or for yourselves! 26c Did not Solomon, the king of Israel, sin because of them? Though among the many nations there was no king like him, and though he was beloved of his God and God had made him king over all Israel, yet even he was led into sin by foreign women. 27Must it also be heard of you that you have done this same terrible evil, betraying our God by marrying foreign women?"

28d One of the sons of Joiada, son of Eliashib the high priest, was the son-in-law of Sanballat the Horonite! I drove him from my presence. 29Remember against them, my God, how they defiled the priesthood and the covenant of the priesthood and the Levites!

30So I cleansed them of all foreign contamination. I established the various functions for the priests and Levites, so that each had an appointed task. 31e I also provided for the procurement of wood at stated times and for the first fruits. Remember this in my favor, my God!

13:24 Language of Ashdod: more likely an Aramaic rather than a Philistine dialect. **The language of Judah**: probably Hebrew.

---

a: Neh 10:32; Ex 20:8. *b:* Neh 10:31; 13:1–3; Dt 23:3; Ezr 9–10. *c:* 1 Kgs 11:1–13. *d:* Neh 2:10; 13:4–5, 7–9. *e:* Neh 10:35–36.

Biblical Novellas

The Bible conveys the Word of God in many literary forms: historical narrative, poetry, prophetic exhortation, wisdom sayings, and novellas (edifying stories). In the Constitution on Divine Revelation from Vatican II (*Dei Verbum*), the council fathers give instruction on how to approach this variety: "Attention must be paid to literary forms, for the fact is that truth is differently presented and expressed in the various types of historical writing, in prophetical and poetical texts, and in other forms of literary expression. Hence the interpreter must look for that meaning which the sacred writer intended to express and did in fact express through the medium of a contemporary literary form" (DV 12).

The Books of Tobit, Judith, and Esther are often grouped together. They are stories told to instruct the people concerning the ways of God, to encourage them in critical times, and to entertain. They are aids to the imagination. While they may contain kernels of historical fact, these stories are told primarily to illustrate truths that transcend history.

The author of the Book of Tobit, writing in the second century B.C., tells a story about the life of a devout family in seventh-century Assyria. He gives the people of his own time an example to follow as they struggle with the tensions of living a faithful Jewish life in the midst of a non-Jewish civilization. Tobit, suffering from the affliction of blindness, perseveres in good works and prayer, as do the other characters in the story. God sends an angel who, while hidden from them, leads them to health and happiness. The conclusion demonstrates that God does answer prayer and that perseverance in good works does not go unrewarded.

The author of the Book of Judith gives many clues that this story is beyond history. All the worst enemies of the people—the Assyrians of the eighth and seventh centuries, the sixth-century Babylonian king Nebuchadnezzar—are rolled into one terror. The hero, Judith, is modeled on the heroes of the Book of Judges, yet her story is also reminiscent of a second-century hero, Judas Maccabeus (1–2 Maccabees). Even the conflation of time indications—the eighteenth year of Nebuchadnezzar (2:1; the year 587 B.C., when he destroyed Jerusalem and took the Jews into exile) with the return from exile and rededication of the Temple (4:3; the events of 538 and 515 respectively)—suggests God's deliverance from the most terrible circumstances. The story may be set in a time long past, but it is meant to encourage the people of the late second century to trust in God when their way of life is threatened. God can use even the most unlikely means, such as a widow, a biblical figure of powerlessness and vulnerability, to deliver them from their enemies.

The Book of Esther includes several historical elements. The Persian king Xerxes (486–465 B.C.), the city of Susa, a court official named Marduka, are all known from other sources. But further investigation shows this is not meant to be a historical account. There is no record of Xerxes having any other queen than Amestris and no mention of such a massacre during his reign. The book has a different purpose: to suggest a historical basis to the festival of Purim, perhaps originally a Persian feast. Through the story of Esther, Purim becomes a celebration of God's rescue of the people from persecution and certain death.

The message conveyed in these stories is not confined to one geographic place or historical period. It remains a valid expression of God's care for faithful people in every time and place.

See RG 215–18

The Book of Tobit

The Book of Tobit, named after its principal character, combines Jewish piety and morality with folklore in a fascinating story that has enjoyed wide popularity in both Jewish and Christian circles. Prayers, psalms, and words of wisdom, as well as the skillfully constructed story itself, provide valuable insights into the faith and the religious milieu of its unknown author. The book was probably written early in the second century B.C.; it is not known where.

Tobit, a devout and wealthy Israelite living among the captives deported to Nineveh from the Northern Kingdom of Israel in 722/721 B.C., suffers severe reverses and is finally blinded. Because of his misfortunes he begs the Lord to let him die. But recalling the large sum he had formerly deposited in far-off Media, he sends his son Tobiah there to bring back the money. In Media, at this same time, a young woman, Sarah, also prays for death, because she has lost seven husbands, each killed in turn on his wedding night by the demon Asmodeus. God hears the prayers of Tobit and Sarah and sends the angel Raphael in human form to aid them both.

Raphael makes the trip to Media with Tobiah. When Tobiah is attacked by a large fish as he bathes in the Tigris River, Raphael orders him to seize it and to remove its gall, heart, and liver because they are useful for medicine. Later, at Raphael's urging, Tobiah marries Sarah, and uses the fish's heart and liver to drive Asmodeus from the bridal chamber. Returning to Nineveh with his wife and his father's money, Tobiah rubs the fish's gall into his father's eyes and cures him. Finally, Raphael reveals his true identity and returns to heaven. Tobit then utters his beautiful hymn of praise. Before dying, Tobit tells his son to leave Nineveh because God will destroy that wicked city. After Tobiah buries his father and mother, he and his family depart for Media, where he later learns that the destruction of Nineveh has taken place.

The inspired author of the book used the literary form of religious novel (as in Esther and Judith) for the purpose of instruction and edification. The seemingly historical data, names of kings, cities, etc., are used as vivid details not only to create interest and charm, but also to illustrate the negative side of the theory of retribution: the wicked are indeed punished.

Although the Book of Tobit is usually listed with the historical books, it more correctly stands midway between them and the wisdom literature. It contains numerous maxims like those found in the wisdom books (cf. 4:3–19, 21; 12:6–10; 14:7, 9) as well as standard wisdom themes: fidelity to the law, intercessory function of angels, piety toward parents, purity of marriage, reverence for the dead, and the value of almsgiving, prayer, and fasting. The book makes Tobit a relative of Ahiqar, a noted hero of ancient Near Eastern wisdom literature and folklore.

Written most likely in Aramaic, the original of the book was lost for centuries. Fragments of four Aramaic texts and of one Hebrew text were discovered in Qumran Cave 4 in 1952 and have only recently been published. These Semitic forms of the book are in substantial agreement with the long Greek recension of Tobit found in Codex Sinaiticus, which had been recovered from St. Catherine's Monastery (Mount Sinai) only in 1844, and in mss. 319 and 910. Two other Greek forms of Tobit have long been known: the short recension, found mainly in the mss. Alexandrinus, Vaticanus, Venetus, and numerous cursive mss.; and an intermediate Greek recension, found in mss. 44, 106, 107. The Book of Tobit has also been known from two Latin versions: the long recension in the Vetus Latina, which is closely related to the long Greek recension and sometimes is even closer to the Aramaic and Hebrew texts than the Greek is; and the short recension in the Vulgate, related to the short Greek recension. The present English translation has been based mainly on Sinaiticus, which is the most complete form of the long Greek recension, despite two lacunae (4:7–19b and 13:6i–10b) and some missing phrases, which make succeeding verses difficult to understand and make it necessary to supplement Sinaiticus from the Vetus Latina or from the short Greek recension. Occasionally, phrases or words have been introduced from the Aramaic or Hebrew texts, when they are significantly different. Forms of the Book of Tobit are also extant in ancient Arabic, Armenian, Coptic (Sahidic), Ethiopic, and Syriac, but these are almost all secondarily derived from the short Greek recension.

The divisions of the Book of Tobit are:

I. Tobit's Ordeals (1:3–3:6)
II. Sarah's Plight (3:7–17)
III. Preparation for the Journey (4:1–6:1)
IV. Tobiah's Journey to Media (6:2–18)
V. Marriage and Healing of Sarah (7:1–9:6)
VI. Tobiah's Return Journey to Nineveh and the Healing of Tobit (10:1–11:18)
VII. Raphael Reveals His Identity (12:1–22)
VIII. Tobit's Song of Praise (13:1–18)
IX. Epilogue (14:1–15)

See RG 215

CHAPTER 1

Tobit. 1This book tells the story of Tobit,* son of Tobiel, son of Hananiel, son of Aduel, son of Gabael, son of Raphael, son of Raguel, of the family of Asiel and the tribe of Naphtali. 2During the days of Shalmaneser,* king of the Assyrians, he was taken captive from Thisbe, which is south of Kedesh Naphtali in upper Galilee, above and to the west of Asher, north of Phogor.[a]

I. Tobit's Ordeals

His Virtue. 3I, Tobit, have walked all the days of my life on paths of fidelity and righteousness. I performed many charitable deeds for my kindred and my people who had been taken captive with me to Nineveh, in the land of the Assyrians. 4When I lived as a young man in my own country, in the land of Israel, the entire tribe of my ancestor Naphtali broke away from the house of David, my ancestor, and from Jerusalem, the city that had been singled out of all Israel's tribes that all Israel might offer sacrifice there. It was the place where the temple, God's dwelling, had been built and consecrated for all generations to come. 5[b] All my kindred, as well as the house of Naphtali, my ancestor, used to offer sacrifice on every hilltop in Galilee to the calf that Jeroboam, king of Israel, had made in Dan.*

6[c] But I alone used to go often to Jerusalem for the festivals, as was prescribed for all Israel by longstanding decree.* Bringing with me the first fruits of crops, the firstlings of the flock, the tithes of livestock, and the first shearings of sheep,[d] I used to hasten to Jerusalem 7[e] and present them to the priests, Aaron's sons, at the altar. To the Levites ministering in Jerusalem I used to give the tithe of grain, wine, olive oil, pomegranates, figs, and other fruits. Six years in a row, I used to give a second tithe in money, which each year I would go to pay in Jerusalem. 8The third-year tithe I gave to orphans, widows, and converts who had joined the Israelites. Every third year I would bring them this offering, and we ate it in keeping with the decree laid down in the Mosaic law concerning it, and according to the commands of Deborah, the mother of my father Tobiel; for my father had died and left me an orphan.

9When I reached manhood, I married Anna, a woman of our ancestral family. By her I had a son whom I named Tobiah. 10Now, after I had been deported to the Assyrians and came as a captive to Nineveh, all my kindred and my people used to eat the food of the Gentiles,[f] 11but I refrained from eating that Gentile food. 12Because I was mindful of God with all my heart, 13the Most High granted me favor and status with Shalmaneser, so that I became purchasing agent for all his needs.[g] 14Until he died, I would go to Media to buy goods for him there. I also deposited pouches of silver worth ten talents* in trust with my kinsman Gabael, son of Gabri, who lived at Rages, in the land of Media. 15When Shalmaneser died and his son Sennacherib* came to rule in his stead, the roads to Media became unsafe, so I could no longer go to Media.

1:1 Tobit: in the Aramaic text the name is given as Tobi, an abbreviated form of Tobiyah (Ezr 2:60) or of Tobiyahu (2 Chr 17:8), a name that means "Yhwh is my welfare." **Tobiel**: "El [God] is my welfare." **Hananiel**: "El [God] has shown mercy." The book abounds in theophoric names.

1:2 Shalmaneser (V) (727–722 B.C.): began the siege of Samaria; the inhabitants of the Northern Kingdom were taken into captivity by his successor, Sargon II (722–705); cf. 2 Kgs 17:1–6. **Thisbe** and **Phogor**: unidentified towns of Galilee. **Kedesh Naphtali**: cf. Jos 20:7; 2 Kgs 15:29. **Asher**: probably Hazor (Jos 11:1).

1:5 Jeroboam established sanctuaries in Dan and Bethel so that the people would no longer have to go to Jerusalem for the festivals. The gold statues of calves that he placed in the sanctuaries were considered the throne of Yhwh; but the people may have tended to worship the images themselves. Jeroboam also encouraged high places or hilltop shrines (1 Kgs 12:26–33).

1:6–8 Longstanding decree: Dt 12:11, 13–14. Refusing to worship at Jeroboam's shrines, the faithful Tobit continued to bring his offerings to Jerusalem; see 2 Chr 11:16. For the various tithes, cf. Lv 27:30–33; Nm 18:20–32; 2 Chr 31:4–6; Dt 14:22–29; 26:12–13.

1:14 Silver worth ten talents: a great sum of money; about ten thousand dollars, at least. **Rages**: modern Rai, about five miles southeast of Tehran. **Media**: the northwestern part of modern Iran.

1:15 Sennacherib (705–681 B.C.): the son of Sargon II; neither was descended from Shalmaneser. On such historical inconsistencies, see Introduction; also notes on 5:6; 6:2; 9:2; 14:15.

a: 2 Kgs 17:3; 18:9–12. *b:* 1 Kgs 12:26–32. *c:* Ex 23:14–15, 17; 34:23. *d:* Dt 16:16. *e:* Nm 18:12–13, 24; Dt 14:22–29; 18:4–5. *f:* Lv 11; Dt 14:3–21; Acts 15:29; 1 Cor 8:7–13. *g:* Dn 2:48–49.

Courage in Burying the Dead. 16 In the days of Shalmaneser I had performed many charitable deeds for my kindred, members of my people. 17[h] I would give my bread to the hungry and clothing to the naked. If I saw one of my people who had died and been thrown behind the wall of Nineveh, I used to bury him.* 18 Sennacherib returned from Judea, having fled during the days of the judgment enacted against him by the King of Heaven because of the blasphemies he had uttered; whomever he killed I buried. For in his rage he killed many Israelites, but I used to take their bodies away by stealth and bury them. So when Sennacherib looked for them, he could not find them. 19 But a certain Ninevite went and informed the king about me, that I was burying them, and I went into hiding. When I realized that the king knew about me and that I was being hunted to be put to death, I became afraid and took flight. 20 All my property was confiscated; I was left with nothing. All that I had was taken to the king's palace, except for my wife Anna and my son Tobiah.*

21 But forty days did not pass before two of the king's sons assassinated him and fled to the mountains of Ararat. A son of his, Esarhaddon,* succeeded him as king. He put Ahiqar, my kinsman Anael's son, in charge of all the credit accounts of his kingdom, and he took control over the entire administration.[i] 22 Then Ahiqar interceded on my behalf, and I returned to Nineveh. Ahiqar had been chief cupbearer, keeper of the signet ring, treasury accountant, and credit accountant under Sennacherib, king of the Assyrians; and Esarhaddon appointed him as Second to himself. He was, in fact, my nephew, of my father's house, and of my own family.

CHAPTER 2

See RG 216

1 Thus under King Esarhaddon I returned to my home, and my wife Anna and my son Tobiah were restored to me. Then on our festival of Pentecost, the holy feast of Weeks,* a fine dinner was prepared for me, and I reclined to eat.[j] 2 The table was set for me, and the dishes placed before me were many. So I said to my son Tobiah: "Son, go out and bring in whatever poor person you find among our kindred exiled here in Nineveh who may be a sincere worshiper of God to share this meal with me. Indeed, son, I shall wait for you to come back."*

3 Tobiah went out to look for some poor person among our kindred, but he came back and cried, "Father!" I said to him, "Here I am, son." He answered, "Father, one of our people has been murdered! He has been thrown out into the market place, and there he lies strangled." 4 I sprang to my feet, leaving the dinner untouched, carried the dead man from the square, and put him in one of the rooms until sundown, so that I might bury him. 5 I returned and washed* and in sorrow ate my food.[k] 6 I remembered the oracle pronounced by the prophet Amos against Bethel:[l]

"I will turn your feasts into mourning,
and all your songs into dirges."

7 Then I wept. At sunset I went out, dug a grave, and buried him.

8 My neighbors mocked me, saying: "Does he have no fear? Once before he was hunted, to be executed for this sort of deed, and he ran away; yet here he is again burying the dead!"

1:17–18 Tobit risked his own life to bury the dead. Deprivation of burial was viewed with horror by the Jews. Cf. 4:3–4; 6:15; 14:12–13.

1:20 Tobiah: the son bears the fuller form of his father's name; see note on 1:1.

1:21 Esarhaddon: 681–669 B.C. **Ahiqar**: a hero of ancient folklore, known for his outstanding wisdom. *The Story (or Wisdom) of Ahiqar* was very popular in antiquity and is extant in many different forms: Aramaic, Syriac, Armenian, Arabic (*Arabian Nights*), Greek (*Aesop's Fables*), Slavonic, Ethiopic, and Romanian. The sacred author makes Tobit the uncle of the famous Ahiqar in order to enhance Tobit's own prestige. See note on 14:10.

2:1 Feast of Weeks: also called by its Greek name, Pentecost, was celebrated fifty days after the Passover. Cf. Lv 23:15–21; Dt 16:9–12.

2:2 Almsgiving and charity to the poor are important virtues taught by the book (4:7–11, 16–17; 12:8–9; 14:10–11). **A sincere worshiper of God**: lit., "who is mindful of God with the whole heart."

2:5 Washed: because of ritual defilement from touching a corpse (Nm 19:11–13).

h: Jb 31:16–20. *i:* 2 Kgs 19:37; 2 Chr 32:21; 2 Mc 8:19; Sir 48:21; Is 37:38. *j:* Lv 23:15–21; Nm 28:26–31; Dt 16:9–12. *k:* Nm 19:11–22. *l:* 1 Mc 1:39; Am 8:10.

Tobit's Blindness. 9 That same night I
washed and went into my courtyard, where I
lay down to sleep beside the wall. Because
of the heat I left my face uncovered. 10 I did
not know that sparrows were perched on the
wall above me; their warm droppings settled
in my eyes, causing white scales* on them. I
went to doctors for a cure, but the more they
applied ointments, the more my vision was
obscured by the white scales, until I was totally blind. For four years I was unable to
see, and all my kindred were distressed at
my condition. Ahiqar, however, took care of
me for two years, until he left for Elam.
11 At that time my wife Anna worked for
hire at weaving cloth, doing the kind of work
women do. 12 When she delivered the material to her employers, they would pay her a
wage. On the seventh day of the month of
Dystrus,* she finished the woven cloth and
delivered it to her employers. They paid her
the full salary and also gave her a young goat
for a meal. 13 On entering my house, the goat
began to bleat. So I called to my wife and
said: "Where did this goat come from? It
was not stolen, was it? Give it back to its
owners; we have no right to eat anything
stolen!" 14[m] But she said to me, "It was given
to me as a bonus over and above my wages."
Yet I would not believe her and told her to
give it back to its owners. I flushed with
anger at her over this. So she retorted:
"Where are your charitable deeds now?
Where are your righteous acts? Look! All
that has happened to you is well known!"*

CHAPTER 3

See RG 216–17

1 Then sad at heart, I groaned and wept
aloud. With sobs I began to pray:*

Tobit's Prayer for Death

2 "You are righteous, Lord,
and all your deeds are just;
All your ways are mercy and fidelity;
you are judge of the world.[n]
3 And now, Lord, be mindful of me
and look with favor upon me.
Do not punish me for my sins,
or for my inadvertent offenses,
or for those of my ancestors.[o]

"They sinned against you,
4 and disobeyed your commandments.
So you handed us over to plunder,
captivity, and death,
to become an object lesson, a byword,
and a reproach
in all the nations among whom you
scattered us.[p]

5 "Yes, your many judgments are right
in dealing with me as my sins,
and those of my ancestors, deserve.
For we have neither kept your
commandments,
nor walked in fidelity before you.

6 "So now, deal with me as you please;
command my life breath to be taken
from me,
that I may depart from the face of the
earth and become dust.
It is better for me to die than to live,*
because I have listened to undeserved
reproaches,
and great is the grief within me.[q]
"Lord, command that I be released from
such anguish;
let me go to my everlasting abode;

2:10 White scales: or white films. A primitive way of describing an eye ailment that results in blindness. **Elam**: or in Greek, *Elymais*, an ancient district northeast of the head of the Persian Gulf.

2:12 Seventh day of the month of Dystrus: late in winter. The Macedonian month Dystros corresponds to the Jewish month of Shebat (January–February). **A meal**: lit., "for the hearth"; the gift had probably been made in view of some springtime festival like the Jewish Purim.

2:14 Anna's sharp rebuke calls to mind the words of Job's wife (Jb 2:9).

3:1 Pray: prayer is a significant theme, occurring at six major turning points in the story (3:2–6, 11–15; 8:5–8, 15–17; 11:14–15; 13:1–18).

3:6 It is better for me to die than to live: in his distress Tobit uses the words of the petulant Jonah (Jon 4:3, 8), who wished to die because God did not destroy the hated Ninevites. In similar circumstances, Moses (Nm 11:15), Elijah (1 Kgs 19:4), and Job (Jb 7:15) also prayed for death. **Everlasting abode**: a reference to Sheol, the dismal abode of the dead from which no one returns (Jb 7:9–10; 14:12; Is 26:14). See note on Tb 4:6.

m: Jb 2:9. *n:* Ps 25:10; 119:137; Dn 3:27. *o:* Ex 34:7. *p:* Dt 28:15; Bar 1:16–22; 2:4–5; 3:8; Dn 9:5–6. *q:* Nm 11:15; 1 Kgs 19:4; Jb 7:15; Jon 4:3, 8.

Do not turn your face away from me,
Lord.
For it is better for me to die
than to endure so much misery in life,
and to listen to such reproaches!"

II. Sarah's Plight

Sarah Falsely Accused. 7* On that very day, at
Ecbatana in Media, it so happened that
Raguel's daughter Sarah also had to listen to
reproaches from one of her father's maids.
8 For she had been given in marriage to seven
husbands, but the wicked demon Asmodeus*
kept killing them off before they could have
intercourse with her, as is prescribed for wives.
The maid said to her: "You are the one who
kills your husbands! Look! You have already
been given in marriage to seven husbands, but
you do not bear the name of a single one of
them. 9 Why do you beat us? Because your
husbands are dead? Go, join them! May we
never see son or daughter of yours!"
10 That day Sarah was sad at heart. She
went in tears to an upstairs room in her father's house and wanted to hang herself. But
she reconsidered, saying to herself: "No! May
people never reproach my father and say to
him, 'You had only one beloved daughter, but
she hanged herself because of her misfortune.' And thus would I bring my father laden
with sorrow in his old age to Hades. It is far
better for me not to hang myself, but to beg
the Lord that I might die, and no longer have
to listen to such reproaches in my lifetime."[r]
11 At that same time, with hands outstretched toward the window,* she implored
favor:

Sarah's Prayer for Death

"Blessed are you, merciful God!
Blessed be your holy and honorable
name forever!
May all your works forever bless you.[s]
12 Now to you, Lord, I have turned my face
and have lifted up my eyes.
13 Bid me to depart from the earth,
never again to listen to such
reproaches.
14 "You know, Master, that I am clean
of any defilement with a man.
15 I have never sullied my own name
or my father's name in the land of my
captivity.
"I am my father's only daughter,
and he has no other child to be his heir,
Nor does he have a kinsman or close
relative
whose wife I should wait to become.
Seven husbands of mine have already
died.
Why then should I live any longer?
But if it does not please you, Lord, to
take my life,
look favorably upon me and have pity
on me,
that I may never again listen to such
reproaches!"

An Answer to Prayer. 16 At that very time,
the prayer of both of them was heard in the
glorious presence of God. 17[t] So Raphael was
sent to heal them both: to remove the white
scales from Tobit's eyes, so that he might
again see with his own eyes God's light; and
to give Sarah, the daughter of Raguel, as a
wife to Tobiah, the son of Tobit, and to rid her
of the wicked demon Asmodeus. For it fell to
Tobiah's lot* to claim her before any others
who might wish to marry her.
At that very moment Tobit turned from
the courtyard to his house, and Raguel's
daughter Sarah came down from the upstairs
room.

3:7 From here on, the story is told in the third person. Verse 7 relates one of the several marvelous coincidences that the storyteller uses to suggest divine providence; see also vv. 16–17; 4:1; 5:4. **Ecbatana**: Hamadan in modern Iran; this was the capital of ancient Media. **Raguel**: the Greek form of the Hebrew name *Re'u'el*, "friend of God."

3:8 Asmodeus: in Persian *aeshma daeva*, "demon of wrath," adopted into Aramaic with the sense of "the Destroyer." It will be subdued (8:3) by Raphael (v. 17), whose name means "God has healed."

3:11 Toward the window: that is, looking in prayer toward Jerusalem; cf. Dn 6:11. "Blessed are you" and "Blessed be God" are traditional openings of Jewish prayers (Tb 8:5, 15; 11:14; 13:1).

3:17 It fell to Tobiah's lot: according to the patriarchal custom of marriage within the family group. Tobiah was Sarah's closest eligible relative (6:12). Cf. 4:12–13; Gn 24:4; 28:2; Ru 3:9–12; 4:1–12.

r: Tb 6:15; Gn 37:35; 42:38; 44:29, 31. *s:* 1 Kgs 8:44, 48; Ps 28:2; 134:2; Dn 6:11. *t:* Tb 4:12–13; 6:12–13; Gn 24:3–4.

III. Preparation for the Journey

CHAPTER 4

See RG 217

A Father's Instruction. 1 That same day Tobit remembered the money he had deposited in trust with Gabael at Rages in Media. 2 He thought to himself, "Now that I have asked for death, why should I not call my son Tobiah and let him know about this money before I die?" 3 So he called his son Tobiah; and when he came, he said to him:* "Son, when I die, give me a decent burial. Honor your mother, and do not abandon her as long as she lives. Do whatever pleases her, and do not grieve her spirit in any way.[u] 4 Remember, son, how she went through many dangers for you while you were in her womb. When she dies, bury her in the same grave with me.

5 "Through all your days, son, keep the Lord in mind, and do not seek to sin or to transgress the commandments. Perform righteous deeds all the days of your life, and do not tread the paths of wickedness. 6[v] For those who act with fidelity, all who practice righteousness, will prosper in their affairs.*

7 "Give alms from your possessions. Do not turn your face away from any of the poor, so that God's face will not be turned away from you.[w] 8 Give in proportion to what you own. If you have great wealth, give alms out of your abundance; if you have but little, do not be afraid to give alms even of that little. 9 You will be storing up a goodly treasure for yourself against the day of adversity.[x] 10 For almsgiving delivers from death and keeps one from entering into Darkness. 11 Almsgiving is a worthy offering in the sight of the Most High for all who practice it.[y]

12 "Be on your guard, son, against every kind of fornication, and above all, marry a woman of your own ancestral family. Do not marry a foreign woman, one who is not of your father's tribe, because we are descendants of the prophets, who were the first to speak the truth. Noah prophesied first, then Abraham, Isaac, and Jacob, our ancestors from the beginning of time. Son, remember that all of them took wives from among their own kindred and were blessed in their children, and that their posterity would inherit the land.[z] 13 Therefore, son, love your kindred. Do not act arrogantly toward any of them, the sons and daughters of your people, by refusing to take a wife for yourself from among them. For in arrogance there is ruin and great instability. In idleness there is loss and dire poverty, for idleness is the mother of famine.

14 "Do not keep with you overnight the wages of those who have worked for you, but pay them at once. If you serve God thus, you will receive your reward. Be on your guard, son, in everything you do; be wise in all that you say and discipline yourself in all your conduct.[a] 15 Do to no one what you yourself hate. Do not drink wine till you become drunk or let drunkenness accompany you on your way.[b]

16[c] "Give to the hungry some of your food, and to the naked some of your clothing. Whatever you have left over, give away as alms; and do not let your eye begrudge the alms that you give. 17[d] Pour out your wine and your bread on the grave of the righteous, but do not share them with sinners.*

18 "Seek counsel from every wise person, and do not think lightly of any useful advice. 19[e] At all times bless the Lord, your God, and ask him that all your paths may be straight and all your endeavors and plans may pros-

4:3–19 A collection of maxims that parallel those in the wisdom literature, especially Proverbs and Sirach (see Introduction): duties toward parents (vv. 3–4; cf. also 14:13); perseverance in virtue and avoidance of evil (vv. 5–6, 14b); necessity and value of almsgiving and charity (vv. 7–11, 16–17); marriage within the clan (vv. 12–13a); industry (v. 13b); prompt payment of wages (v. 14a); the golden rule (v. 15a); temperance (v. 15b); docility (v. 18); prayer (v. 19).

4:6 It was commonly thought in the Old Testament that virtue guaranteed earthly prosperity, and sin earthly disaster (Prv 10:2; cf. Dt 28).

4:17 Tobit counsels his son to give alms in honor of the dead or, more probably, to give the "bread of consolation" to the family of the deceased. Cf. Jer 16:7; Ez 24:17.

u: Ex 20:12; Prv 23:22; Sir 7:27. *v:* Tb 13:6; Jn 3:21; Eph 4:15. *w:* Tb 12:8–10; Dt 15:7–8, 11; Prv 19:17; Sir 4:1–6; 14:13; Lk 14:13; 1 Jn 3:17. *x:* Mt 6:20–21. *y:* Sir 3:30; 29:12. *z:* Tb 3:15, 17; 6:12; Gn 11:29, 31; 25:20; 28:1–4; 29:15–30; Ex 34:16; Dt 7:3; Jgs 14:3. *a:* Lv 19:3; Dt 24:15. *b:* Mt 7:12; Lk 6:31. *c:* Dt 15:10; Is 58:7; Mt 25:35–36; 2 Cor 9:7. *d:* Jer 16:7; Lk 14:13. *e:* Dt 4:6; Ps 119:10.

per. For no other nation possesses good counsel, but it is the Lord who gives all good things. Whomever the Lord chooses to raise is raised; and whomever the Lord chooses to cast down is cast down to the recesses of Hades. So now, son, keep in mind these my commandments, and never let them be erased from your heart.

20 "Now, I must tell you, son, that I have deposited in trust ten talents of silver with Gabael, the son of Gabri, at Rages in Media. 21 Do not fear, son, that we have lived in poverty. You will have great wealth, if you fear God, avoid all sin, and do what is good before the Lord your God."[f]

CHAPTER 5

See RG 217

The Angel Raphael. 1 Then Tobiah replied to his father Tobit: "Everything that you have commanded me, father, I shall do. 2 But how will I be able to get that money from him, since he does not know me, and I do not know him? What sign can I give him so that he will recognize and trust me, and give me the money? I do not even know the roads to Media, in order to go there." 3 Tobit answered his son Tobiah: "He gave me his bond,* and I gave him mine; I divided his into two parts, and each of us took one part; I put one part with the money. It is twenty years since I deposited that money! So, son, find yourself a trustworthy person who will make the journey with you, and we will give him wages when you return; but bring back that money from Gabael while I am still alive."

4 Tobiah went out to look for someone who would travel with him to Media, someone who knew the way. He went out and found the angel Raphael standing before him (though he did not know* that this was an angel of God).[g] 5 Tobiah said to him, "Where do you come from, young man?" He replied, "I am an Israelite, one of your kindred. I have come here to work." Tobiah said to him, "Do you know the way to Media?" 6 "Yes," he replied, "I have been there many times. I know the place well and am acquainted with all the routes. I have often traveled to Media; I used to stay with our kinsman Gabael, who lives at Rages in Media. It is a good two days' journey from Ecbatana to Rages,* for Rages is situated in the mountains, but Ecbatana is in the middle of the plain." 7 Tobiah said to him, "Wait for me, young man, till I go in and tell my father; for I need you to make the journey with me. I will pay you your wages."[h] 8 He replied, "Very well, I will wait; but do not be long."

9 Tobiah went in and informed his father Tobit: "I have found someone of our own Israelite kindred who will go with me!" Tobit said, "Call the man in, so that I may find out from what family and tribe he comes, and whether he is trustworthy enough to travel with you, son."

10 Tobiah went out to summon him, saying, "Young man, my father is calling for you." When Raphael entered the house, Tobit greeted him first. He replied, "Joyful greetings to you!" Tobit answered, "What joy is left for me? Here I am, a blind man who cannot see the light of heaven, but must remain in darkness, like the dead who no longer see the light! Though alive, I am among the dead. I can hear people's voices, but I do not see them." The young man said, "Take courage! God's healing is near; so take courage!" Tobit then said: "My son Tobiah wants to go to Media. Can you go with him to show him the way? I will pay you your wages, brother." He answered: "Yes, I will go with him, and I know all the routes. I have often traveled to Media and crossed all its plains so I know well the mountains and

5:3 Bond: a document called in Greek *cheirographon*. In the Middle Ages, notably in England, a deed and its duplicate were written on one piece of parchment, with the Latin word *chirographum* inscribed across the top of the sheet or between the two copies of the text. The document was then cut in two in either a straight or a wavy line, the parts being given to the persons concerned. Perhaps this procedure was derived from the present verse of Tobit. Duplicate documents, usually one part open and the other sealed, are well known from the ancient Near East.

5:4 He did not know: the theme of an angel in disguise occurs frequently in folklore as well as in the Old Testament (Gn 18; cf. Heb 13:2).

5:6 It is a good two days' journey from Ecbatana to Rages: Alexander's army took eleven days in forced marches to cover this distance, about 180 miles. (See notes on 1:15; 3:7 and Introduction.)

f: 1 Tm 6:6–10. *g:* Heb 13:2. *h:* Tb 12:2.

all its roads.” 11 Tobit asked him, “Brother,
tell me, please, from what family and tribe
are you?” 12 He replied, “Why? What need
do you have for a tribe? Aren’t you looking
for a hired man?” Tobit replied, “I only want
to know, brother, whose son you truly are
and what your name is.”[i]
13 He answered, “I am Azariah,* son of the
great Hananiah, one of your own kindred.”
14 Tobit exclaimed: “Welcome! God save
you, brother! Do not be provoked with me,
brother, for wanting to learn the truth about
your family. It turns out that you are a kinsman, from a noble and good line! I knew
Hananiah and Nathan, the two sons of the
great Shemeliah. They used to go to Jerusalem with me, where we would worship together. They were not led astray; your kindred are good people. You are certainly of
good lineage. So welcome!”
15 Then he added: “For each day I will give
you a drachma as wages,* as well as expenses for you and for my son. So go with
my son, and 16 I will even add a bonus to your
wages!” The young man replied: “I will go
with him. Do not fear. In good health we will
leave you, and in good health we will return
to you, for the way is safe.” 17 Tobit said,
“Blessing be upon you, brother.” Then he
called his son and said to him: “Son, prepare
whatever you need for the journey, and set
out with your kinsman. May God in heaven
protect you on the way and bring you back to
me safe and sound; may his angel accompany you for your safety, son.”
Tobiah left to set out on his journey, and
he kissed his father and mother. Tobit said to
him, “Have a safe journey.” 18 But his mother
began to weep and she said to Tobit: “Why
have you sent my child away? Is he not the
staff of our hands, as he goes in and out before us? 19 Do not heap money upon money!
Rather relinquish it in exchange for our
child! 20 What the Lord has given us to live
on is certainly enough for us.” 21 Tobit reassured her: “Do not worry! Our son will leave
in good health and come back to us in good
health. Your own eyes will see the day when
he returns to you safe and sound. So, do not
worry; do not fear for them, my sister.* 22 For
a good angel* will go with him, his journey
will be successful, and he will return in good
health.” 1 Then she stopped weeping.

IV. Tobiah’s Journey to Media

CHAPTER 6

See RG 216

On the Way to Rages. 2 When the
young man left home, accompanied by the
angel, the dog followed Tobiah out and went
along with them. Both journeyed along, and
when the first night came, they camped beside the Tigris River.* 3 When the young man
went down to wash his feet in the Tigris
River, a large fish leaped out of the water
and tried to swallow his foot. He shouted in
alarm. 4 But the angel said to the young man,
“Grab the fish and hold on to it!” He seized
the fish and hauled it up on dry land. 5 The
angel then told him: “Slit the fish open and
take out its gall, heart, and liver, and keep
them with you; but throw away the other entrails. Its gall, heart, and liver are useful for
medicine.”* 6 After Tobiah had slit the fish
open, he put aside the gall, heart, and liver.
Then he roasted and ate part of the fish; the
rest he salted and kept for the journey.
Raphael’s Instructions. Afterward the two
of them traveled on together till they drew
near to Media. 7 Then the young man asked
the angel this question: “Brother Azariah,
what medicine is in the fish’s heart, liver,
and gall?” 8 He answered: “As for the fish’s
heart and liver, if you burn them to make

5:13–14 Azariah, “Yhwh has helped”; Hananiah, “Yhwh has shown mercy”; Nathan is a shortened form of Nathaniah, “Yhwh has given”; Shemeliah may be a Greek corruption of the Hebrew name, Shemaiah, “Yhwh has heard.”

5:15 A drachma as wages: the normal wages, about seventeen cents, a day’s wage for a laborer.

5:21 My sister: “sister” was a term of endearment used in antiquity even for one’s wife; similarly “brother” for one’s husband. Cf. 7:11, 15; 8:4, 21; 10:6, 13; Sg 4:9–10, 12; 5:1–2.

5:22 A good angel: a reference to a guardian angel, though Tobit does not know, of course, that Raphael himself, disguised as Azariah, is the good angel in this case.

6:2 Tigris River: this river is actually west of Nineveh, so they would not have come to it on their way to Media. See note on 1:15 and the Introduction.

6:5 Its gall . . . medicine: belief in the healing power of these organs was common among the physicians of antiquity.

i: Jgs 13:17–18.

smoke in the presence of a man or a woman who is afflicted by a demon or evil spirit, any affliction will flee and never return. [9]As for the gall, if you apply it to the eyes of one who has white scales, blowing right into them, sight will be restored."

[10]When they had entered Media and were getting close to Ecbatana, [11]Raphael said to the young man, "Brother Tobiah!" He answered, "Here I am!" Raphael continued, "Tonight we must stay in the house of Raguel, who is a relative of yours. He has a beautiful daughter named Sarah, [12]but no other son or daughter apart from Sarah. Since you are Sarah's closest relative, you more than any other have the right to marry her. Moreover, her father's estate is rightfully yours to inherit. The girl is wise, courageous, and very beautiful; and her father is a good man who loves her dearly."[j] [13]He continued: "You have the right to marry her. So listen to me, brother. Tonight I will speak to her father about the girl so that we may take her as your bride. When we return from Rages, we will have the wedding feast for her. I know that Raguel cannot keep her from you or promise her to another man; he would incur the death penalty as decreed in the Book of Moses.* For he knows that you, more than anyone else, have the right to marry his daughter. Now listen to me, brother; we will speak about this girl tonight, so that we may arrange her engagement to you. Then when we return from Rages, we will take her and bring her back with us to your house."

[14]But Tobiah said to Raphael in reply, "Brother Azariah, I have heard that she has already been given in marriage to seven husbands, and that they have died in the bridal chamber. On the very night they approached her, they would die. I have also heard it said that it was a demon that killed them. [15]So now I too am afraid of this demon, because it is in love with her and does not harm her; but it kills any man who wishes to come close to her. I am my father's only child. If I should die, I would bring the life of my father and mother down to their grave in sorrow over me; they have no other son to bury them!"[k]

[16]Raphael said to him: "Do you not remember your father's commands? He ordered you to marry a woman from your own ancestral family. Now listen to me, brother; do not worry about that demon. Take Sarah. I know that tonight she will be given to you as your wife! [17]When you go into the bridal chamber, take some of the fish's liver and the heart, and place them on the embers intended for incense, and an odor will be given off. [18]As soon as the demon smells the odor, it will flee and never again show itself near her. Then when you are about to have intercourse with her, both of you must first get up to pray.* Beg the Lord of heaven that mercy and protection be granted you. Do not be afraid, for she was set apart for you before the world existed. You will save her, and she will go with you. And I assume that you will have children by her, and they will be like brothers for you. So do not worry."

When Tobiah heard Raphael's words that she was his kinswoman, and of the lineage of his ancestral house, he loved her deeply, and his heart was truly set on her.

V. Marriage and Healing of Sarah

CHAPTER 7

See RG 215–18

At the House of Raguel. [1]When they entered Ecbatana, Tobiah said, "Brother Azariah, bring me straight to the house of our kinsman Raguel." So he did, and they came to the house of Raguel, whom they found seated by his courtyard gate. They greeted him first, and he answered, "Many greetings to you, brothers! Welcome! You have come in peace! Now enter in peace!" And he brought them into his house. [2]He said to his wife Edna, "How this young man resembles Tobit, the son of my uncle!" [3]So Edna asked them, saying, "Where are you from, brothers?" They answered, "We are descendants

6:13 Raguel . . . Book of Moses: Nm 36:6–8 prescribed marriage within the ancestral tribe for daughters who had no brothers who might inherit the ancestral property, but no death penalty is mentioned.

6:18 Get up to pray: prayer, combined with ritual action, drives out the demon.

j: Tb 4:12–13; Nm 36:8. *k:* Tb 3:10.

of Naphtali, now captives in Nineveh." [4]She said to them, "Do you know our kinsman Tobit?" They answered her, "Indeed, we do know him!" She asked, "Is he well?" [5]They answered, "Yes, he is alive and well." Then Tobiah said, "He is my father!" [6]Raguel jumped up, kissed him, and broke into tears. [7]Then, finding words, he said, "A blessing upon you, son! You are the son of a good and noble father. What a terrible misfortune that a man so righteous and charitable has been afflicted with blindness!" He embraced his kinsman Tobiah and continued to weep. [8]His wife Edna also wept for Tobit; and their daughter Sarah also began to weep.

Marriage of Tobiah and Sarah. [9]Afterward, Raguel slaughtered a ram from the flock and gave them a warm reception. When they had washed, bathed, and reclined to eat and drink, Tobiah said to Raphael, "Brother Azariah, ask Raguel to give me my kinswoman Sarah." [10]Raguel overheard the words; so he said to the young man: "Eat and drink and be merry tonight, for no man has a greater right to marry my daughter Sarah than you, brother. Besides, not even I have the right to give her to anyone but you, because you are my closest relative. However, son, I must frankly tell you the truth. [11]I have given her in marriage to seven husbands who were kinsmen of ours, and all died on the very night they approached her. But now, son, eat and drink. The Lord will look after you both." Tobiah answered, "I will neither eat nor drink anything here until you settle what concerns me."

Raguel said to him: "I will do it. She is yours as decreed by the Book of Moses. It has been decided in heaven that she be given to you! Take your kinswoman; from now on you are her brother, and she is your sister.* She is given to you today and here ever after. May the Lord of heaven prosper you both tonight, son, and grant you mercy and peace." [12]Then Raguel called his daughter Sarah, and she came to him. He took her by the hand and gave her to Tobiah with these words: "Take her according to the law. According to the decree written in the Book of Moses I give her to be your wife. Take her and bring her safely to your father. And may the God of heaven grant both of you a safe journey in peace!"[l] [13]He then called her mother and told her to bring writing materials. He wrote out a copy of a marriage contract stating that he gave Sarah to Tobiah as his wife as decreed by the law of Moses. Her mother brought the material, and he drew up the contract, to which he affixed his seal.[m]

[14]Afterward they began to eat and drink. [15]Later Raguel called his wife Edna and said, "My sister, prepare the other bedroom and bring Sarah there." [16]She went, made the bed in the room, as he had told her, and brought Sarah there. After she had cried over her, she wiped away her tears and said, [17]"Take courage, my daughter! May the Lord of heaven grant you joy in place of your grief! Courage, my daughter!" Then she left.

CHAPTER 8

See RG 216

Expulsion of the Demon. [1]When they had finished eating and drinking, they wanted to retire. So they brought the young man out and led him to the bedroom. [2]Tobiah, mindful of Raphael's instructions, took the fish's liver and heart from the bag where he had them, and put them on the embers intended for incense.* [3]The odor of the fish repulsed the demon, and it fled to the upper regions of Egypt;* Raphael went in pursuit of it and there bound it hand and foot. Then Raphael returned immediately.

[4]When Sarah's parents left the bedroom and closed the door behind them, Tobiah rose from bed and said to his wife, "My sister,

7:11 You are her brother, and she is your sister: the marriage formula is similar to a marriage contract from the fifth century B.C. found at Elephantine in Egypt: "She is my wife and I am her husband from this day forever."

8:2–3 The manner of coping with demonic influences among the ancients seems strange to us. However, the fish here is a folktale element, suggesting the hero's fight with a dragon, and not a recipe for exorcism. It is clear that the author places primary emphasis on the value of prayer to God (6:18; 8:4–8), on the role of the angel as God's agent, and on the pious disposition of Tobiah.

8:3 The desert was considered the dwelling place of demons. Cf. Is 13:21; 34:14; Mt 4:1; 12:43.'

l: Gn 24:50–51. *m:* Tb 6:12.

come, let us pray and beg our Lord to grant us mercy and protection." [5]She got up, and they started to pray and beg that they might be protected. He began with these words:

"Blessed are you, O God of our ancestors;
blessed be your name forever and ever!
Let the heavens and all your creation bless you forever.[n]
[6] You made Adam, and you made his wife Eve
to be his helper and support;
and from these two the human race has come.
You said, 'It is not good for the man to be alone;
let us make him a helper like himself.'[o]
[7] Now, not with lust,
but with fidelity I take this kinswoman as my wife.
Send down your mercy on me and on her,
and grant that we may grow old together.
Bless us with children."

[8]They said together, "Amen, amen!" [9]Then they went to bed for the night.

But Raguel got up and summoned his servants. They went out with him and dug a grave, [10]for he said, "Perhaps Tobiah will die; then we would be a laughingstock and an object of mockery." [11]When they had finished digging the grave, Raguel went back into the house and called his wife, [12]saying, "Send one of the maids in to see whether he is alive. If he has died, let us bury him without anyone knowing about it." [13]They sent the maid, lit a lamp, and opened the bedroom door; she went in and found them sleeping together. [14]The maid came out and told them that Tobiah was alive, and that nothing was wrong. [15]Then they praised the God of heaven in these words:

"Blessed are you, God, with every pure blessing!
Let all your chosen ones bless you forever!
[16] Blessed are you, for you have made me happy;
what I feared did not happen.
Rather you have dealt with us
according to your abundant mercy.
[17] Blessed are you, for you have shown mercy
toward two only children.
Grant them, Master, mercy and protection,
and bring their lives to fulfillment
with happiness and mercy."

[18]Then Raguel told his servants to fill in the grave before dawn.

Wedding Feast. [19]He asked his wife to bake many loaves of bread; he himself went out to the herd and brought two steers and four rams, which he ordered to be slaughtered. So they began to prepare the feast. [20]He summoned Tobiah and said to him, "For fourteen days* you shall not stir from here, but shall remain here eating and drinking with me; you shall bring joy to my daughter's afflicted spirit. [21]Now take half of what I own here; go back in good health to your father. The other half will be yours when I and my wife die. Take courage, son! I am your father, and Edna is your mother; we belong to you and to your sister both now and forever. So take courage, son!"

CHAPTER 9

See RG 215–18

The Money Recovered. [1]Then Tobiah called Raphael and said to him: [2]"Brother Azariah, take along with you from here four servants and two camels and travel to Rages.* Go to Gabael's house and give him this bond. Get the money and then bring him along with you to the wedding celebration. [3]For you know that my father will be counting the days. If I should delay even by a single day, I would cause him intense grief. [4]You have witnessed the oath that Raguel has sworn; I cannot violate his oath." [5]So

8:20 For fourteen days: because of the happy, and unexpected, turn of events, Raguel doubles the time of the wedding feast. When Tobiah returns home, the usual seven-day feast is held (11:18). Cf. Jgs 14:12.

9:2 To Rages: see note on 5:6.

n: Dn 3:26. *o:* Gn 2:18–23.

Raphael, together with the four servants and two camels, traveled to Rages in Media, where they stayed at Gabael's house. Raphael gave Gabael his bond and told him about Tobit's son Tobiah, that he had married and was inviting him to the wedding celebration. Gabael got up and counted out for him the moneybags with their seals, and they packed them on the camels.

6 The following morning they both got an early start and traveled to the wedding celebration. When they entered Raguel's house, they found Tobiah reclining at table. He jumped up and greeted Gabael, who wept and blessed him, exclaiming: "Good and noble child, son of a good and noble, righteous and charitable man, may the Lord bestow a heavenly blessing on you and on your wife, and on your wife's father and mother. Blessed be God, because I have seen the very image of my cousin Tobit!"

VI. Tobiah's Return Journey to Nineveh and the Healing of Tobit

CHAPTER 10

See RG 215–18

Anxiety of the Parents. 1 Meanwhile, day by day, Tobit was keeping track of the time Tobiah would need to go and to return. When the number of days was reached and his son did not appear, 2 he said, "Could it be that he has been detained there? Or perhaps Gabael has died, and there is no one to give him the money?" 3 And he began to grieve. 4 His wife Anna said, "My son has perished and is no longer among the living!" And she began to weep aloud and to wail over her son: 5 "Alas, child, light of my eyes, that I have let you make this journey!" 6 But Tobit kept telling her: "Be still, do not worry, my sister; he is safe! Probably they have to take care of some unexpected business there. The man who is traveling with him is trustworthy and one of our kindred. So do not grieve over him, my sister. He will be here soon." 7 But she retorted, "You be still, and do not try to deceive me! My son has perished!" She would rush out and keep watch every day at the road her son had taken. She ate nothing. After the sun had set, she would go back home to wail and cry the whole night through, getting no sleep at all.[p]

Departure from Ecbatana. Now when the fourteen days of the wedding celebration, which Raguel had sworn to hold for his daughter, had come to an end, Tobiah went to him and said: "Send me off, now, since I know that my father and mother do not believe they will ever see me again. So I beg you, father, let me depart and go back to my own father. I have already told you how I left him." 8 Raguel said to Tobiah: "Stay, son, stay with me. I am sending messengers to your father Tobit, and they will give him news of you." 9 But Tobiah insisted, "No, I beg you to send me back to my father."

10 Raguel then promptly handed over to Tobiah his wife Sarah, together with half of all his property: male and female slaves, oxen and sheep, donkeys and camels, clothing, money, and household goods. 11 He saw them safely off. Embracing Tobiah, he said to him: "Farewell, son. Have a safe journey. May the Lord of heaven grant prosperity to you and to your wife Sarah. And may I see children of yours before I die!" 12 Then he said to his daughter Sarah, "My daughter, honor your father-in-law and your mother-in-law, because from now on they are as much your parents as the ones who brought you into the world. Go in peace, daughter; let me hear a good report about you as long as I live." Finally he said good-bye to them and let them go.

Edna also said to Tobiah: "My child and beloved kinsman, may the Lord bring you back safely, and may I live long enough to see children of you and of my daughter Sarah before I die. Before the Lord, I entrust my daughter to your care. Never cause her grief all the days of your life. Go in peace, son. From now on I am your mother, and Sarah is your sister. Together may we all prosper throughout the days of our lives." She kissed them both and saw them safely off.

13 Tobiah left Raguel, full of happiness and joy, and he blessed the Lord of heaven

p: Gn 45:26.

and earth, the King of all, for making his journey so successful. Finally he blessed Raguel and his wife Edna, and added, "I have been commanded by the Lord to honor you all the days of your life!"

See RG 216

CHAPTER 11

Homeward Journey. 1 As they drew near to Kaserin, which is opposite Nineveh, 2 Raphael said: "You know how we left your father. 3 Let us hurry on ahead of your wife to prepare the house while they are still on the way." 4 So both went on ahead together, and Raphael said to him, "Take the gall in your hand!" And the dog ran along behind them.

5 Meanwhile, Anna sat watching the road by which her son was to come. 6 When she saw him coming, she called to his father, "Look, your son is coming, and the man who traveled with him!"

7 Raphael said to Tobiah before he came near to his father: "I know that his eyes will be opened. 8 Apply the fish gall to his eyes, and the medicine will make the white scales shrink and peel off from his eyes; then your father will have sight again and will see the light of day."

Sight Restored. 9 Then Anna ran up to her son, embraced him, and said to him, "Now that I have seen you again, son, I am ready to die!" And she sobbed aloud.[q] 10 Tobit got up and stumbled out through the courtyard gate to meet his son. Tobiah went up to him 11 with the fish gall in his hand and blew into his eyes. Holding him firmly, he said, "Courage, father." Then he applied the medicine to his eyes, and it made them sting. 12,13 Tobiah used both hands to peel the white scales from the corners of his eyes. Tobit saw his son and threw his arms around him. 14 Weeping, he exclaimed, "I can see you, son, the light of my eyes!" Then he prayed,

"Blessed be God,
blessed be his great name,
and blessed be all his holy angels.
May his great name be with us,
and blessed be all the angels
throughout all the ages.
15 God it was who afflicted me,
and God who has had mercy on me.
Now I see my son Tobiah!"

Then Tobit went back in, rejoicing and praising God with full voice. Tobiah related to his father how his journey had been a success; that he had brought back the money; and that he had married Raguel's daughter Sarah, who was about to arrive, for she was near the gate of Nineveh.[r]

16 Rejoicing and blessing God, Tobit went out to the gate of Nineveh to meet his daughter-in-law. When the people of Nineveh saw him coming, walking along briskly, with no one leading him by the hand, they were amazed. 17 Before them all Tobit proclaimed how God had shown mercy to him and opened his eyes. When Tobit came up to Sarah, the wife of his son Tobiah, he blessed her and said: "Welcome, my daughter! Blessed be your God for bringing you to us, daughter! Blessed are your father and your mother. Blessed be my son Tobiah, and blessed be you, daughter! Welcome to your home with blessing and joy. Come in, daughter!" That day there was joy for all the Jews who lived in Nineveh. 18 Ahiqar and his nephew Nadin* were also on hand to rejoice with Tobit. Tobiah's wedding feast was celebrated with joy for seven days, and many gifts were given to him.

VII. Raphael Reveals his Identity

CHAPTER 12

See RG 216–17

Raphael's Wages.* 1 When the wedding celebration came to an end, Tobit called his son Tobiah and said to him, "Son, see to it that you pay his wages to the man who made the journey with you and give him a bonus too." 2 Tobiah said: "Father, how much shall I pay him? It would not hurt to give him half the wealth he brought back with me.[s] 3 He led me back safe and sound,

11:18 Nadin: see note on 14:10.
12:1–5 Tobit and his son generously agree to give Raphael far more than the wages agreed upon in 5:15–16.

q: Gn 33:4; 45:14; 46:29–30; Lk 15:20. *r:* Tb 13:2; Dt 32:39; 1 Sm 2:6. *s:* Tb 5:3, 7, 15–16.

healed my wife, brought the money back with me, and healed you. How much should I pay him?” 4Tobit answered, “It is only fair, son, that he should receive half of all that he brought back.” 5So Tobiah called Raphael and said, “Take as your wages half of all that you have brought back, and farewell!”

Exhortation. * 6Raphael called the two of them aside privately and said to them: “Bless God and give him thanks before all the living for the good things he has done for you, by blessing and extolling his name in song. Proclaim before all with due honor the deeds of God, and do not be slack in thanking him.* 7A king’s secret should be kept secret, but one must declare the works of God and give thanks with due honor. Do good, and evil will not overtake you. 8Prayer with fasting is good. Almsgiving with righteousness is better than wealth with wickedness. It is better to give alms than to store up gold,[t] 9for almsgiving saves from death, and purges all sin. Those who give alms will enjoy a full life,[u] 10but those who commit sin and do evil are their own worst enemies.

Raphael’s Identity. 11“I shall now tell you the whole truth and conceal nothing at all from you. I have already said to you, ‘A king’s secret should be kept secret, but one must declare the works of God with due honor.’ 12[v] Now when you, Tobit, and Sarah prayed, it was I who presented the record of your prayer before the Glory of the Lord; and likewise whenever you used to bury the dead.* 13When you did not hesitate to get up and leave your dinner in order to go and bury that dead man, 14I was sent to put you to the test. At the same time, however, God sent me to heal you and your daughter-in-law Sarah. 15I am Raphael, one of the seven angels who stand and serve before the Glory of the Lord.”[w]

16Greatly shaken, the two of them fell prostrate in fear. 17But Raphael said to them: “Do not fear; peace be with you! Bless God now and forever. 18As for me, when I was with you, I was not acting out of any favor on my part, but by God’s will. So bless God every day; give praise with song. 19Even though you saw me eat and drink, I did not eat or drink anything; what you were seeing was a vision. 20So now bless the Lord on earth and give thanks to God. Look, I am ascending to the one who sent me. Write down all that has happened to you.”[x] And he ascended. 21They stood up but were no longer able to see him. 22They kept blessing God and singing his praises, and they continued to give thanks for these marvelous works that God had done, because an angel of God appeared to them.

VIII. Tobit’s Song of Praise

CHAPTER 13

See RG 217–18

1* Then Tobit spoke and composed a song of joyful praise; he said:

Blessed be God who lives forever,
because his kingship lasts for all ages.[y]
2 For he afflicts and shows mercy,
casts down to the depths of Hades,
brings up from the great abyss.
What is there that can snatch from his hand?[z]
3 Give thanks to him, you Israelites, in the presence of the nations,
for though he has scattered you among them,
4 even there recount his greatness.

12:6–10 In the fashion of a wisdom teacher, Raphael gives the two men a short exhortation similar to the one Tobit gave his son in 4:3–19.

12:6–7 The faithful considered the praise of God their most esteemed privilege. Without it, life was meaningless; cf. Is 38:16–20.

12:12 Raphael is one of the seven Angels of the Presence, specially designated intercessors who present prayers to God. Angelology was developing in this period. The names of two other of these seven angels are given in the Bible: Gabriel (Dn 8:16; 9:21; Lk 1:19, 26) and Michael (Dn 10:13, 21; 12:1; Jude 9; Rev 12:7). See 1 Enoch for the names of the rest.

13:1–18 Tobit’s hymn of praise is divided into two parts. The first part (vv. 1–8) is a song of praise that echoes themes from the psalms; the second (vv. 9–18) is addressed to Jerusalem in the style of those prophets who spoke of a new and ideal Jerusalem (Is 60; cf. Rev 21). **Joyful praise**: words for joy and gladness occur throughout this prayer (vv. 1, 7, 10, 11, 13, 14, 16, 18).

t: Tb 4:7–11; Sir 29:8–13. *u:* Dn 4:24. *v:* Jb 33:23–24; Acts 10:4; Rev 8:3–4. *w:* Lk 1:19; Rev 8:2. *x:* Jgs 13:20. *y:* Tb 3:11; 8:5, 15; 1 Chr 29:10; Dn 3:26. *z:* Tb 11:15; 13:9; Dt 32:39; 1 Sm 2:6; Wis 16:13.

Exalt him before every living being,
because he is your Lord, and he is your God,
our Father and God forever and ever!
5 He will afflict you for your iniquities,
but will have mercy on all of you.
He will gather you from all the nations
among whom you have been scattered.[a]

6 When you turn back to him with all your heart,
and with all your soul do what is right before him,
Then he will turn to you,
and will hide his face from you no longer.[b]

Now consider what he has done for you,
and give thanks with full voice.
Bless the Lord of righteousness,
and exalt the King of the ages.

In the land of my captivity I give thanks,
and declare his power and majesty to a sinful nation.
According to your heart do what is right before him:
perhaps there will be pardon for you.

7 As for me, I exalt my God,
my soul exalts the King of heaven,
and rejoices all the days of my life.
Let all sing praise to his greatness,
8 let all speak and give thanks in Jerusalem.

9 Jerusalem, holy city,
he will afflict you for the works of your hands,*
but will again pity the children of the righteous.[c]
10 Give thanks to the Lord with righteousness,
and bless the King of the ages,
so that your tabernacle may be rebuilt in you with joy.
May he gladden within you all who are captives;
may he cherish within you all who are distressed
for all generations to come.[d]

11 A bright light will shine to the limits of the earth.
Many nations will come to you from afar,
And inhabitants of all the ends of the earth
to your holy name,
Bearing in their hands gifts for the King of heaven.
Generation after generation will offer
joyful worship in you;
your name will be great forever and ever.[e]

12 Cursed be all who despise you and revile you;
cursed be all who hate you and speak a harsh word against you;
cursed be all who destroy you
and pull down your walls,
And all who overthrow your towers
and set fire to your homes.
But blessed forever be all those who respect you.[f]

13 Go, then, rejoice and exult over the children of the righteous,
for they will all be gathered together
and will bless the Lord of the ages.
14 Happy are those who love you,
and happy are those who rejoice in your peace.
Happy too are all who grieve
over all your afflictions,
For they will rejoice over you
and behold all your joy forever.[g]

15 My soul, bless the Lord, the great King;
16 for Jerusalem will be rebuilt as his house forever.
Happy too will I be if a remnant of my offspring survives
to see your glory and to give thanks to the King of heaven!

13:9 Works of your hands: idols.

a: Dt 30:3; Neh 1:9. *b:* Dt 30:2. *c:* Tb 11:15; Mi 7:19; Rev 21. *d:* Is 44:26, 28; Am 9:11; Zec 1:16. *e:* Is 2:3–4; 9:1; 49:6; 60:1; Mi 4:2; Zec 8:22. *f:* Bar 4:31–32. *g:* Ps 122:6; Is 66:10.

The gates of Jerusalem will be built with
sapphire and emerald,
and all your walls with precious
stones.
The towers of Jerusalem will be built
with gold,
and their battlements with purest
gold.[h]
17 The streets of Jerusalem will be paved
with rubies and stones of Ophir;
18 The gates of Jerusalem will sing hymns
of gladness,
and all its houses will cry out,
Hallelujah!
Blessed be the God of Israel for all ages!
For in you the blessed will bless the holy
name forever and ever.

IX. Epilogue

CHAPTER 14

See RG 215–16

Parting Advice. 1 So the words of Tobit's hymn of praise came to an end. Tobit
died in peace at the age of a hundred and
twelve and was buried with honor in Nineveh. 2 He was fifty-eight years old when he
lost his eyesight, and after he recovered it he
lived in prosperity, giving alms; he continued to fear God and give thanks to the divine
Majesty.
3 As he was dying, he summoned his son
Tobiah and Tobiah's seven sons, and commanded him, "Son, take your children[i] 4 and
flee into Media, for I believe God's word
that Nahum* spoke against Nineveh. It will
all happen and will overtake Assyria and
Nineveh; indeed all that was said by Israel's
prophets whom God sent will come to pass.
Not one of all their words will remain unfulfilled, but everything will take place in the
time appointed for it. So it will be safer in
Media than in Assyria or Babylon. For I
know and believe that whatever God has
said will be accomplished. It will happen,
and not a single word of the prophecies will
fail.
As for our kindred who dwell in the land
of Israel, they will all be scattered and taken
into captivity from the good land. All the
land of Israel will become a wilderness; even
Samaria and Jerusalem will be a wilderness!
For a time, the house of God will be desolate
and will be burned.[j] 5 But God will again have
mercy on them and bring them back to the
land of Israel. They will build the house
again, but it will not be like the first until the
era when the appointed times will be completed.* Afterward all of them will return
from their captivity, and they will rebuild Jerusalem with due honor. In it the house of
God will also be rebuilt, just as the prophets
of Israel said of it.[k] 6[l] All the nations of the
world will turn and reverence God in truth;
all will cast away their idols, which have deceitfully led them into error.* 7 They will
bless the God of the ages in righteousness.
All the Israelites truly mindful of God, who
are to be saved in those days, will be gathered
together and will come to Jerusalem; in security will they dwell forever in the land of
Abraham, which will be given to them.
Those who love God sincerely will rejoice,
but those who commit sin and wickedness
will disappear completely from the land.[m]
8,9 "Now, my children, I give you this command: serve God sincerely and do what is
pleasing in his sight; you must instruct your
children to do what is right and to give alms,
to be mindful of God and at all times to bless
his name sincerely and with all their strength.
Now, as for you, son, leave Nineveh; do not
stay here. 10 The day you bury your mother
next to me, do not even stay overnight within
the confines of the city. For I see that there is
much wickedness in it, and much treachery is
practiced in it, and people are not ashamed.

14:4–5 Nahum: one of the minor prophets, whose book contains oracles of doom against Nineveh. Here, in keeping with the period in which the story is set, the author makes Tobit speak as if the punishment of Nineveh, the destruction of Jerusalem (587 B.C.), the exile from Judah and the return, would all take place in the future. The technique of using the facts of past history as seemingly future predictions is a frequent device of apocalyptic writers. **The good land**: a favorite name for the promised land. Cf. Dt 1:35; 3:25; 4:21–22.

14:5 Until the era . . . completed: a reference to the coming of the day of the Lord, when a new, more perfect temple was to be expected. Cf. Heb 9:1–14.

14:6 Conversion of the nations is also to come with the day of the Lord.

h: Tb 14:5; Is 54:11–13; 62:2; Rev 21:10–21. *i:* Gn 47:29–30. *j:* Na 2:2–3:19. *k:* Neh 12:27; Jer 31:38. *l:* Is 60:1–4. *m:* Is 60:21; Jer 32:37; Ez 34:28; 37:25; 39:26.

See, my son, all that Nadin[*] did to Ahiqar, the very one who reared him. Was not Ahiqar brought down alive into the earth? Yet God made Nadin's disgraceful crime rebound against him. Ahiqar came out again into the light, but Nadin went into the everlasting darkness, for he had tried to kill Ahiqar. Because Ahiqar had given alms he escaped from the deadly trap Nadin had set for him. But Nadin fell into the deadly trap himself, and it destroyed him.[n] 11 So, my children, see what almsgiving does, and also what wickedness does—it kills! But now my spirit is about to leave me."

Death of Tobit and Tobiah. They laid him on his bed, and he died; and he was buried with honor. 12 When Tobiah's mother died, he buried her next to his father. He then departed with his wife and children for Media, where he settled in Ecbatana with his father-in-law Raguel.[o] 13 He took respectful care of his aging father-in-law and mother-in-law; and he buried them at Ecbatana in Media. Then he inherited Raguel's estate as well as that of his father Tobit. 14 He died highly respected at the age of one hundred seventeen. 15 But before he died, he saw and heard of the destruction of Nineveh. He saw the inhabitants of the city being led captive into Media by Cyaxares,[*] the king of Media. Tobiah blessed God for all that he had done against the Ninevites and Assyrians. Before dying he rejoiced over Nineveh, and he blessed the Lord God forever and ever.

14:10 Nadin: in the *Story of Ahiqar*, the hero Ahiqar, chancellor under the Assyrian kings Sennacherib and Esarhaddon, adopts his nephew Nadin and prepares him to become his successor. But Nadin treacherously plots to have his uncle put to death. Ahiqar hides in a friend's house and is finally vindicated when Nadin's scheme is discovered. Thereupon Nadin is thrown into a dungeon where he dies. It was Ahiqar's almsgiving that delivered him from death; see note on 2:2. The Greek and Latin versions of the Book of Tobit read the name as Nadab, but the Aramaic form has the ancient name Nadin, which is also found in the fifth-century B.C. Aramaic *Story of Ahiqar*.

14:15 Cyaxares: Nabopolassar, king of Babylon, and Cyaxares conquered and destroyed Nineveh in 612 B.C.; see note on 1:15.

n: Tb 1:21–22. *o*: Tb 4:4.

See RG 218–22

The Book of Judith

The Book of Judith relates the story of God's deliverance of the Jewish people. This was accomplished "by the hand of a female"—a constant motif (cf. 8:33; 9:9, 10; 12:4; 13:4, 14, 15; 15:10; 16:5) meant to recall the "hand" of God in the Exodus narrative (cf. Ex 15:6). The work may have been written around 100 B.C., but its historical range is extraordinary. Within the reign of Nebuchadnezzar (1:1; 2:1), it telescopes five centuries of historical and geographical information with imaginary details. There are references to Nineveh, the Assyrian capital destroyed in 612 B.C., to Nebuchadnezzar, the ruler not of Assyria but of Babylon (605/604–562), and to the second Temple, built around 515. The postexilic period is presumed (e.g., governance by the High Priest). The Persian period is represented by two characters, Holofernes and Bagoas, who appear together in the military campaigns of Artaxerxes III Ochus (358–338); there seem to be allusions to the second-century Seleucid ruler Antiochus IV Epiphanes. Several mysteries remain: Judith herself, Arphaxad, and others are otherwise unknown. The geographical details, such as the narrow defile into Bethulia (an unidentified town which gives access to the heart of the land), are fanciful. The simple conclusion from these and other details is that the work is historical fiction, written to exalt God as Israel's deliverer from foreign might, not by an army, but by means of a simple widow.

There are four Greek recensions of Judith (Septuagint codices Vaticanus, Sinaiticus, Alexandrinus, and Basiliano-Vaticanus), four ancient translations (Old Latin, Syriac, Sahidic, and Ethiopic), and some late Hebrew versions, apparently translated from the Vulgate. Despite Jerome's claim to have translated an Aramaic text, no ancient Aramaic or Hebrew manuscripts have been found. The oldest extant text of Judith is the preservation of 15:1–7 inscribed on a third-century A.D. potsherd. Whatever the reasons, the rabbis did not count Judith among their scriptures, and the Reformation adopted that position. The early Church, however, held this book in high honor. The first-century Pope, St. Clement of Rome, proposes Judith as an example of courageous love (1 Corinthians 55). St. Jerome holds her up as an example of a holy widow and a type of the Church (To Salvina: Letter 79, par. 10; see also To Furia: Letter 54, par. 16) and, in another place, describes Mary as a new Judith (To Eustochium: Letter 22, par. 21). The Council of Trent (1546) included Judith in the canon; thus it is one of the seven deuterocanonical books.

Inner-biblical references are noteworthy: as God acted through Moses' hand (Ex 10:21–22; 14:27–30), so God delivers "by the hand of a female," Judith. Like Jael, who drove a tent peg through the head of Sisera (Jgs 4), Judith kills an enemy general. Like Deborah (Jgs 4–5), Judith "judges" Israel in the time of military crisis. Like Sarah, the mother of Israel's future (Gn 17:6), Judith's beauty deceives foreigners, with the result that blessings redound to Israel (Gn 12:11–20). Her Hebrew name means "Jewish woman." Her exploits captured the imagination of liturgists, artists, and writers through the centuries. The book is filled with double entendres and ironic situations, e.g., Judith's conversation with Holofernes in 11:5–8, 19, where "my lord" is ambiguous, and her declaration to Holofernes that she will lead him through Judea to Jerusalem (his head goes on such a journey).

The book can be divided into five parts:

I. Assyrian Threat (1:1–3:10)
II. Siege of Bethulia (4:1–7:32)
III. Judith, Instrument of the Lord (8:1–10:10)
IV. Judith Goes Out to War (10:11–13:20)
V. Victory and Thanksgiving (14:1–16:25)

I. Assyrian Threat*

CHAPTER 1

See RG 219

*Nebuchadnezzar Against Arphaxad.**

1 It was the twelfth year* of the reign of Nebuchadnezzar, who ruled over the Assyrians
in the great city of Nineveh. At that time Arphaxad was ruling over the Medes in Ecbatana.[a] 2* Around Ecbatana he built a wall of
hewn stones, three cubits thick and six cubits long. He made the walls seventy cubits
high and fifty cubits wide. 3 At its gates he
raised towers one hundred cubits high with
foundations sixty cubits wide. 4 He made its
gates seventy cubits high and forty cubits
wide to allow passage of his mighty forces,
with his infantry in formation. 5 At that time
King Nebuchadnezzar waged war against
King Arphaxad in the vast plain that borders
Ragau.* 6 Rallying to him were all who lived
in the hill country, all who lived along the
Euphrates, the Tigris, and the Hydaspes, as
well as Arioch, king of the Elamites, in the
plains. Thus many nations joined the ranks
of the Chelodites.*[b]

7 Then Nebuchadnezzar, king of the Assyrians, contacted all the inhabitants of Persia* and all who lived in the west, the inhabitants of Cilicia and Damascus, Lebanon and

1:1–3:10 This section consists of an introduction to Nebuchadnezzar (1:1–16), his commissioning of Holofernes (2:1–13), and a description of the campaigns Holofernes leads against the disobedient vassal nations of the west (2:14–3:10).

1:1–16 Introduction to Nebuchadnezzar and his campaign against Arphaxad. Nebuchadnezzar (605/4–562 B.C.), the most famous Neo-Babylonian king, destroyed Jerusalem in 587 B.C., the eighteenth year of his reign (see Jer 32:1). His depiction here as an Assyrian is an invention of the author, as is the description of Arphaxad, an otherwise unknown king of the Medes, in Ecbatana.

1:1 Twelfth year: in the twelfth year of Nebuchadnezzar (593 B.C.) Zedekiah, king of Judah, refused to join a revolt against him (see Jer 27:3; 28:1). **Nineveh**: capital of Assyria, destroyed in 612 B.C.

1:2–4 Since a cubit was the distance from the elbow to the fingertip (approximately eighteen inches), these dimensions are prodigious. The massive wall around Ecbatana is described as 105 feet high and 75 feet thick, with each stone measuring four and a half feet thick and nine feet long. The tower gates are 150 feet high and 60 feet wide. Such unlikely massive structures have never been found at Ecbatana, which lies beneath the modern city of Hamadan, located in the Zagros mountains of northwest Iran. Ecbatana is mentioned in vv. 1, 2, 14 as Arphaxad's headquarters. Tradition claims Esther and Mordecai are buried there.

1:5 Ragau, the place where Arphaxad is slain (v. 15), one of the oldest settlements in Iran, is located on a plain one hundred miles northeast of Ecbatana. In the Book of Tobit it is the home of Gabael (Tb 1:14; 4:1, 20; 5:6; 6:13; 9:2, 5).

1:6 Chelodites: Greek *Cheleoud*, probably a corruption of "Chaldeans," i.e., the Neo-Babylonians.

1:7 Mention of Persia suggests a postexilic setting for the book, since this area would have been designated Media before the middle of the fifth century B.C.

a: Gn 10:22; Ezr 6:2; Tb 3:7; 5:6; 6:10; 7:1; 14:12–13; 2 Mc 9:3; Jon 1:2; 3:2–3. *b:* Gn 14:1, 9.

Antilebanon, and all who lived along the seacoast, 8the peoples of Carmel, Gilead, Upper Galilee, and the vast plain of Esdraelon, 9and all in Samaria and its cities, and west of the Jordan as far as Jerusalem, Bethany, Chelous, Kadesh,[c] and the river of Egypt; Tahpanhes,[d] Raamses, all the land of Goshen, 10Tanis, Memphis[e] and beyond, and all the inhabitants of Egypt as far as the borders of Ethiopia.

11But all the inhabitants of the whole land* made light of the summons of Nebuchadnezzar, king of the Assyrians, and would not join him in the war. They were not afraid of him, since he was only a single opponent. So they sent back his envoys empty-handed and disgraced.[f] 12Then Nebuchadnezzar fell into a violent rage against all the land, and swore by his throne and his kingdom that he would take revenge on all the territories of Cilicia, Damascus, and Syria, and would destroy with his sword all the inhabitants of Moab, Ammon, the whole of Judea, and all those living in Egypt as far as the coasts of the two seas.*

Defeat of Arphaxad. 13In the seventeenth year* he mustered his forces against King Arphaxad and was victorious in his campaign. He routed the whole force of Arphaxad, his entire cavalry, and all his chariots, 14and took possession of his cities. He pressed on to Ecbatana, took its towers, sacked its marketplaces, and turned its glory into shame. 15He captured Arphaxad in the mountains of Ragau, ran him through with spears, and utterly destroyed him once and for all. 16Then he returned to Nineveh with all his consolidated forces, a very great multitude of warriors; and there he and his forces relaxed and feasted for one hundred and twenty days.[g]

CHAPTER 2

See RG 219

Revenge Planned Against the Western Nations.* 1In the eighteenth year,* on the twenty-second day of the first month, there was a discussion in the palace of Nebuchadnezzar, king of the Assyrians, about taking revenge on all the land, as he had threatened.[h] 2He summoned all his attendants and officers, laid before them his secret plan, and with his own lips recounted in full detail the wickedness of all the land. 3They decided to destroy all who had refused to obey the order he had issued.

4When he had fully recounted his plan, Nebuchadnezzar, king of the Assyrians, summoned Holofernes, the ranking general* of his forces, second only to himself in command, and said to him: 5"Thus says the great king, the lord of all the earth: Go forth from my presence, take with you men of proven valor, one hundred and twenty thousand infantry and twelve thousand cavalry,[i] 6and proceed against all the land of the west, because they disobeyed the order I issued. 7Tell them to have earth and water* ready, for I will come against them in my wrath; I will cover all the land with the feet of my soldiers, to whom I will deliver them as spoils. 8Their wounded will fill their ravines and wadies, the swelling river will be choked with their dead; 9and I will deport them as exiles to the very ends of the earth.

10"Go before me and take possession of all their territories for me. If they surrender

1:11 References to "the whole land," "all the land" are used ten times in the first two chapters (vv. 11, 12; 2:1, 2, 5, 6, 7, 9, 10, 19). This signifies all the nations west of Persia as far as Egypt that were subject to Nebuchadnezzar, i.e., the whole earth or world (esp. 2:9). These and similar formulations throughout the book build the case that the "God of heaven" (5:8; 6:19; 11:17) is the true "Master of heaven and earth" (9:12).

1:12 The two seas: probably the Mediterranean to the Persian Gulf, though possibly the Red Sea and Mediterranean.

1:13 Seventeenth year: 588 B.C. Without help from the vassal nations, Nebuchadnezzar defeats Arphaxad.

2:1–13 Nebuchadnezzar commissions Holofernes to take vengeance on the vassal nations that refused him auxiliary military support (see 1:7–12).

2:1 Eighteenth year: 587 B.C. Most of the story is set in the catastrophic year when the historical Nebuchadnezzar, king of Babylon, destroyed Jerusalem.

2:4 The ranking general: Holofernes is so identified six times in Judith. See also 4:1; 5:1; 6:1; 10:13; 13:15. Holofernes and Bagoas (12:11) are Persian names; two officers of Artaxerxes III Ochos (358–338 B.C.) were so named.

2:7 Earth and water: in the Persian period, offering these to a conqueror was a symbolic gesture signifying humble submission of one asking for a treaty.

c: Nm 34:4; Dt 32:51; Jos 15:23. *d:* Jer 2:16; 43:7–9; 44:1; 46:14. *e:* Is 19:13; Jer 2:16; 44:1; 46:14, 19; Ez 30:13, 15; Hos 9:6. *f:* 2 Sm 17:3; Ez 33:24. *g:* Est 1:3–4. *h:* Jer 32:1; 52:29. *i:* 2 Kgs 18:19, 28; 1 Mc 15:13; Is 36:4, 13; Hos 5:13; 10:6.

to you, guard them for me until the day of their sentencing. 11 As for those who disobey, show them no mercy, but deliver them up to slaughter and plunder in all the land you occupy.[j] 12 For as I live,* and by the strength of my kingdom, what I have spoken I will accomplish by my own hand.[k] 13 Do not disobey a single one of the orders of your lord; fulfill them exactly as I have commanded you, and do it without delay."

Campaigns of Holofernes.* 14 So Holofernes left the presence of his lord, and summoned all the commanders, generals, and officers of the Assyrian forces. 15 He mustered one hundred and twenty thousand picked troops, as his lord had commanded, and twelve thousand mounted archers, 16 and drew them up as a vast force organized for battle. 17 He took along a very large number of camels, donkeys, and mules for carrying their supplies; innumerable sheep, cattle, and goats for their food;[l] 18 abundant provisions for each man, and much gold and silver from the royal palace.

19 Then he and all his forces set out on their expedition in advance of King Nebuchadnezzar, to overrun all the lands of the western region with their chariots, cavalry, and picked infantry. 20 A huge, irregular force, too many to count, like locusts, like the dust of the earth, went along with them.[m] 21 After a three-day march* from Nineveh, they reached the plain of Bectileth, and camped opposite Bectileth near the mountains to the north of Upper Cilicia. 22 From there Holofernes took all his forces, the infantry, cavalry, and chariots, and marched into the hill country. 23 He devastated Put and Lud,* and plundered all the Rassisites and the Ishmaelites on the border of the wilderness toward the south of the Chelleans.[n]

24 Then, following the Euphrates, he went through Mesopotamia, and battered down every fortified city along the Wadi Abron, until he reached the sea. 25 He seized the territory of Cilicia, and cut down everyone who resisted him. Then he proceeded to the southern borders of Japheth, toward Arabia. 26 He surrounded all the Midianites, burned their tents, and sacked their encampments.[o] 27 Descending to the plain of Damascus at the time of the wheat harvest, he set fire to all their fields, destroyed their flocks and herds, looted their cities, devastated their plains, and put all their young men to the sword.[p]

28[q] Fear and dread of him fell upon all the inhabitants of the coastland, upon those in Sidon and Tyre,[r] and those who dwelt in Sur and Ocina, and the inhabitants of Jamnia. Those in Azotus and Ascalon also feared him greatly.*

CHAPTER 3

See RG 219

Submission of the Vassal Nations. 1 So they sent messengers to him to sue for peace in these words: 2 "We, the servants of Nebuchadnezzar the great king, lie prostrate before you; do with us as you will. 3 See, our dwellings and all our land and every wheat field, our flocks and herds, and all our encampments are at your disposal; make use of them as you please. 4 Our cities and their inhabitants are also at your service; come and deal with them as you see fit."

5 After the spokesmen had reached Holofernes and given him this message, 6 he went down with his forces to the seacoast, stationed garrisons in the fortified cities, and

2:12 As I live: an oath proper to God; see the promissory oath of God the divine warrior in Dt 32:39–42; cf. Is 49:18; Jer 22:24; Ez 5:11. **By my own hand**: in his pride, Nebuchadnezzar claims to do this by his own hand (cf. Is 10:13). In contrast, Judith claims that God will deliver Israel "by my hand" (8:33; 12:4).

2:14–3:10 As Holofernes attacks the western nations, terror sweeps across the empire at large (2:28), then Judea (4:1–2), and finally Bethulia (7:1). In these verses, the line of advance is from Nineveh to Damascus and all who submit are nonetheless devastated and forced to worship Nebuchadnezzar.

2:21 A three-day march: no ancient army could have traveled three hundred miles from Nineveh to Cilicia in three days.

2:23 Put and Lud: mentioned together in Jer 46:9; Ez 27:10; 30:5. Put is thought to be in Libya in Africa; Lud is usually identified with Lydia in Asia Minor. Rather than indicating definite localities here, Put and Lud add assonance and prophetic overtones to the narrative.

2:28 Symbolic of the completeness of the terror that descended on the area, seven towns are listed: Tyre, Sidon, Sur, Ocina, Jamnia, Ashdod, and Ashkelon.

j: Dt 7:2; Jos 11:20; Is 13:18. *k:* Dt 32:39–41. *l:* Gn 41:49. *m:* Ex 10:4, 13, 14; Jgs 6:5; 7:12; Ps 105:34; Jl 1:4. *n:* Gn 2:2; 10:6, 22; Is 66:19; Ez 30:5. *o:* Gn 37:36; Ex 2:15; Jgs 6–8. *p:* Gn 34:26; Jos 6:21; 1 Sm 15:8. *q:* Ex 15:16; Ps 55:6. *r:* Ez 26:7–14; 29:17–20.

took selected men from them as auxiliaries. 7The people of these cities and all the inhabitants of the countryside received him with garlands and dancing to the sound of timbrels. 8But he devastated their whole territory and cut down their sacred groves, for he was allowed to destroy all the gods of the land, so that every nation might worship only Nebuchadnezzar, and all their tongues and tribes should invoke him as a god.* [s] 9At length Holofernes reached Esdraelon in the neighborhood of Dothan,* the approach to the main ridge of the Judean mountains; 10he set up his camp between Geba* and Scythopolis, and stayed there a whole month to replenish all the supplies of his forces.

II. Siege of Bethulia*

CHAPTER 4

See RG 219

Israel Prepares for War.* 1When the Israelites who lived in Judea heard of all that Holofernes, the ranking general of Nebuchadnezzar king of the Assyrians, had done to the nations, and how he had looted all their shrines* and utterly destroyed them, 2they were in very great fear of him, and greatly alarmed for Jerusalem and the temple of the Lord, their God. 3Now, they had only recently returned from exile, and all the people of Judea were just now reunited, and the vessels, the altar, and the temple had been purified from profanation.* [t] 4So they sent word to the whole region of Samaria, to Kona, Beth-horon, Belmain, and Jericho, to Choba and Aesora, and to the valley of Salem.* 5The people there secured all the high hilltops, fortified the villages on them, and since their fields had recently been harvested, stored up provisions in preparation for war.

6Joakim, who was high priest* in Jerusalem in those days, wrote to the inhabitants of Bethulia and Betomesthaim, which is opposite Esdraelon, facing the plain near Dothan,[u] 7and instructed them to keep firm hold of the mountain passes, since these offered access to Judea. It would be easy to stop those advancing, as the approach was only wide enough for two at a time.* 8The Israelites carried out the orders given them by Joakim, the high priest, and the senate of the whole people of Israel, in session in Jerusalem.[v]

Israel at Prayer. 9All the men of Israel cried to God with great fervor and humbled themselves. 10They, along with their wives, and children, and domestic animals, every resident alien, hired worker, and purchased

3:8 Invoke him as a god: Holofernes violates Nebuchadnezzar's instructions (see 2:5–13). No Assyrian, Neo-Babylonian, or Persian king is known to have claimed divinity. During Hellenistic times, Ptolemy V (203–181 B.C.) and the Seleucid Antiochus IV made claims to divinity. In Dn 3 and 6, divinity is ascribed to Nebuchadnezzar and Darius, respectively.

3:9 Dothan: a town in Ephraimite territory fourteen miles north of Shechem, mentioned elsewhere only twice (Gn 37:17 and 2 Kgs 6:13), but five times in Judith (3:9; 4:6; 7:3, 18; 8:3). Destroyed in 810 B.C. by Aramean invasions, Dothan was deserted until the Hellenistic period when a small settlement was constructed. Because it is mentioned so often, Dothan is sometimes thought to be the author's home.

3:10 Geba: location uncertain. Scythopolis, the Greek name for ancient Beth-shean (Jos 17:11), the only city in Judith given its Greek name, strategically guarded the eastern end of the Valley of Jezreel.

4:1–7:32 In this section the focus narrows to Judea and specifically the little town of Bethulia. The scenes alternate between the Assyrian camp (5:1–6:13; 7:1–3, 6–18) and Judea/Bethulia (4:1–15; 6:14–21; 7:4–5, 19–32).

4:1–15 Here the scene shifts to Judea where Israel hears and is greatly terrified about Holofernes' destruction of the neighboring places of worship. At Joakim's instruction they take defensive measures and then pray fervently that God will not allow their sanctuary to be destroyed.

4:1 Shrines: the Greek word *hiera* is used only here and may mean holy places or things. By contrast, the sanctuary in Jerusalem is *naos*, "temple" (v. 2); *oikos*, "house" (v. 3); and *hagia*, lit., "holy things" (v. 12).

4:3 Returned from exile . . . purified from profanation: conflated historical references associated with events in 538 B.C. (return from exile) and 515 B.C. (dedication of the Second Temple) or perhaps even 164 B.C. (the rededication of the Second Temple in the Maccabean period).

4:4 Of the eight cities listed, only the locations of Beth-horon, Jericho, and Samaria are known. Salem, mentioned in Gn 17:17, is thought to be an ancient name of Jerusalem.

4:6 Joakim, who was high priest: see also vv. 8, 14; 15:8. Joakim exercises religious and military authority comparable to that of Jonathan in Maccabean times (cf. 1 Mc 10:18–21). **Bethulia and Betomesthaim**: unknown locations mentioned only in Judith. Bethulia may mean "House of God" (*byt 'l/yh*) or "House of Ascent" (*byt 'lyh*), perhaps a reference to either Bethel or Shechem.

4:7 Only wide enough for two at a time: such a narrow pass near Esdraelon cannot be identified.

s: Ex 34:13; 2 Kgs 18:4; 23:14–15; 2 Chr 14:2; 17:6; 31:1; 34:4. *t:* 1 Mc 4:36–61; 2 Mc 10:3–5. *u:* Dn 13:1, 4, 28, 29, 63. *v:* 2 Mc 11:27.

slave, girded themselves with sackcloth.*[w]
11 And all the Israelite men, women, and children who lived in Jerusalem fell prostrate in
front of the temple*[x] and sprinkled ashes on
their heads, spreading out their sackcloth before the Lord.[y] 12 The altar, too, they draped in
sackcloth;* and with one accord they cried
out fervently to the God of Israel not to allow
their children to be seized, their wives to be
taken captive, the cities of their inheritance to
be ruined, or the sanctuary to be profaned
and mocked for the nations to gloat over.
13 The Lord heard their cry* and saw their
distress. The people continued fasting for
many days throughout Judea and before the
sanctuary of the Lord Almighty in Jerusalem.[z] 14 Also girded with sackcloth, Joakim,
the high priest, and all the priests in attendance before the Lord, and those who ministered to the Lord offered the daily burnt offering, the votive offerings, and the
voluntary offerings of the people.[a] 15 With
ashes upon their turbans, they cried to the
Lord with all their strength to look with favor on the whole house of Israel.[b]

See RG 219

CHAPTER 5

*Achior in the Assyrian War Council.**

1 It was reported to Holofernes, the ranking
general of the Assyrian forces, that the Israelites were ready for battle, had blocked the
mountain passes, fortified the high hilltops,
and placed roadblocks in the plains. 2 In great
anger he summoned all the rulers of Moab,
the governors of Ammon, and all the satraps
of the coastland[c] 3 and said to them: "Now
tell me, you Canaanites, what sort of people
is this that lives in the hill country? Which
cities do they inhabit? How large is their
force? In what does their power and strength
consist? Who has set himself up as their king
and the leader of their army? 4 Why have
they alone of all the inhabitants of the west
refused to come out to meet me?"
5* Then Achior, the leader of all the Ammonites, said to him: "My lord, please listen
to a report from your servant. I will tell you
the truth about this people that lives in the
hill country near here. No lie shall escape
your servant's lips.
6 "These people are descendants of the
Chaldeans. 7 They formerly lived in Mesopotamia, for they did not wish to follow the
gods of their ancestors who were in the land
of the Chaldeans.[d] 8 Since they abandoned
the way of their ancestors, and worshiped
the God of heaven,* the God whom they had
come to know, their ancestors expelled them
from the presence of their gods. So they fled
to Mesopotamia and lived there a long time.
9 Their God told them to leave the place
where they were living and go to the land of
Canaan. Here they settled, and grew very
rich in gold, silver, and a great abundance of
livestock.[e] 10 Later, when famine had gripped
the land of Canaan, they went down into
Egypt. They stayed there as long as they
found sustenance and there they grew into
such a great multitude that the number of
their people could not be counted.[f] 11[g] The
king of Egypt, however, rose up against
them, and shrewdly forced them to labor at
brickmaking; they were oppressed and made
into slaves. 12 But they cried to their God,
and he struck the whole land of Egypt with
plagues for which there was no remedy. So
the Egyptians drove them out. 13 Then God
dried up the Red Sea before them[h] 14 and led

4:10 Sackcloth: traditional sign of penitence and supplication is here taken to the extreme. Cf. Jon 3:8.

4:11 Fell prostrate in front of the temple: for a parallel to this ceremony of entreaty see Jl 1:13, 14; 2:15–17.

4:12 The altar . . . draped in sackcloth: attested nowhere else in the Bible.

4:13 The Lord heard their cry: this anticipates the role of Judith, the instrument of deliverance (chap. 16), though the people believe God has abandoned them (7:25).

5:1–6:13 The scene shifts to the Assyrian camp below Bethulia where Holofernes talks with Achior and then expels him to the foot of the hill below the little town.

5:5–21 Achior (Heb. "brother of light") traces the covenant of Israel from Abraham to the exile and defends the inviolability of the people because their powerful God will defend them if they do not sin. He later identifies the head Judith displays as that of Holofernes (14:6–10). He may be modeled on the famous sage, Ahiqar (see note on Tb 1:21). Achior is wise, but the wisdom granted Judith by God is more effective than his.

5:8 God of heaven: a common expression in Persian times; see also 6:19; 11:17 (cf. 7:28; 9:12; 13:18).

w: Neh 9:1; Est 4:1–4; Jl 1:13, 14; Jon 3:5, 6, 8. *x:* 1 Chr 29:20; 2 Mc 3:15. *y:* 2 Sm 21:10. *z:* Est 4:16; Jl 2:15. *a:* Ex 29:38–46; Nm 28:1–8; Ezr 3:4. *b:* Lv 16:4; Ez 24:23; 44:18; Zec 3:5. *c:* Dt 2:21; 2 Kgs 24:2. *d:* Gn 11:31. *e:* Gn 11:31–12:5; 13:2. *f:* Gn 42:1–5; 46:1–7; Ex 1:7. *g:* Ex 1:10–14; 5:1–21; 7:1–11:10. *h:* Ex 14:21; Jos 2:10; 4:23; Ps 106:9; Wis 19:7; Heb 11:29.

them along the route to Sinai and Kadesh-barnea. They drove out all the inhabitants of the wilderness 15 and settled in the land of the Amorites. By their strength they destroyed all the Heshbonites,[i] crossed the Jordan, and took possession of all the hill country.[j] 16 They drove out before them the Canaanites, the Perizzites, the Jebusites, the Shechemites,* and all the Gergesites,[k] and they lived there a long time.

17 [l] "As long as the Israelites did not sin in the sight of their God, they prospered, for their God, who hates wickedness, was with them. 18* But when they abandoned the way he had prescribed for them, they were utterly destroyed by frequent wars, and finally taken as captives into foreign lands. The temple of their God was razed to the ground, and their cities were occupied by their enemies.[m] 19 But now they have returned to their God, and they have come back from the Diaspora where they were scattered. They have reclaimed Jerusalem, where their sanctuary is, and have settled again in the hill country, because it was unoccupied.

20 [n] "So now, my master* and lord, if these people are inadvertently at fault, or if they are sinning against their God, and if we verify this offense of theirs, then we will be able to go up and conquer them. 21 But if they are not a guilty nation, then let my lord keep his distance; otherwise their Lord and God will shield them, and we will be mocked in the eyes of all the earth."

22 Now when Achior had finished saying these things, all the people standing round about the tent murmured; and the officers of Holofernes and all the inhabitants of the seacoast and of Moab alike said he should be cut to pieces. 23 [o] "We are not afraid of the Israelites," they said, "for they are a powerless people, incapable of a strong defense. 24 Therefore let us attack, master Holofernes. They will become fodder for your great army."

CHAPTER 6

See RG 219

1 When the noise of the crowd surrounding the council had subsided, Holofernes, the ranking general of the Assyrian forces, said to Achior, in the presence of the whole throng of foreigners, of the Moabites, and of the Ammonite mercenaries: 2 "Who are you,* Achior and the mercenaries of Ephraim, to prophesy among us as you have done today, and to tell us not to fight against the people of Israel because their God shields them? Who is God beside Nebuchadnezzar? He will send his force and destroy them from the face of the earth. Their God will not save them;[p] 3 but we, the servants of Nebuchadnezzar, will strike them down with one blow, for they will be unable to withstand the force of our cavalry. 4 We will overwhelm them with it, and their mountains shall be drunk with their blood, and their plains filled with their corpses. Not a trace of them shall survive our attack; they will utterly perish. So says King Nebuchadnezzar, lord of all the earth. For he has spoken, and his words will not be in vain. 5 As for you, Achior, you Ammonite mercenary, for saying these things in a moment of perversity, you will not see my face after today, until I have taken revenge on this people that came out of Egypt. 6 Then at my return, the sword of my army or the spear of my attendants will pierce your sides, and you will fall among their wounded. 7 My servants will now conduct you to the hill country, and leave you at one of the cities beside the passes. 8 You will not die until you are destroyed together with them. 9 If you still harbor the hope that they will not be taken, then there is no need for you to be downcast.[q] I

5:16 Shechemites: perhaps anticipates the allusion in Judith's prayer (9:2) to Simeon's revenge on these people.

5:18–19 Knowledge of the Babylonian exile is presupposed; cf. also 4:3.

5:20 Master: the Greek word *despota*, usually applied to God in the Septuagint, is applied to Holofernes five times in the Book of Judith (vv. 20, 24; 7:9, 11; 11:10), and only once to God (9:12).

6:2 Who are you: repeated by Judith in 8:12 to the officials of Bethulia and modified in 12:14 in her response to Bagoas' invitation on Holofernes' behalf. The question, "Who is God?" motivates the entire narrative. Holofernes defends Nebuchadnezzar; Judith defends the Lord.

i: Nm 21:25–28, 30, 34; Dt 1:4; 2:24, 26, 30; 3:2, 6; 4:46. *j:* Jos 3. *k:* Gn 10:16; 15:20; Dt 7:1; Jos 3:10; 24:12; 1 Chr 1:14. *l:* Dt 28–30; Jgs 2:11–15; Ps 106:40–46. *m:* 2 Kgs 25. *n:* Jdt 8:18–23; 11:10; Tb 3:3. *o:* Jdt 6:2; 9:7–8; 16:2. *p:* Jdt 3:8; 9:7–8; 1 Kgs 22:15–17; 2 Kgs 18:32–35; Is 36:18–20; Dn 3:14–18. *q:* Gn 4:5; 40:7.

have spoken, and not one of my words will fail to be fulfilled."

10Then Holofernes ordered the servants who were standing by in his tent to seize Achior, conduct him to Bethulia, and hand him over to the Israelites. 11So the servants seized him and took him out of the camp into the plain. From the plain they led him up into the hill country until they reached the springs below Bethulia.

12When the men of the city saw them, they seized their weapons and ran out of the city to the top of the hill, and all the slingers kept them from coming up by hurling stones at them. 13So, taking cover below the hill, they bound Achior and left him lying at the foot of the hill; then they returned to their lord.

Achior in Bethulia.* 14The Israelites came down from their city and found him, untied him, and brought him into Bethulia. They placed him before the rulers of the city, 15who in those days were Uzziah,* son of Micah of the tribe of Simeon, and Chabris, son of Gothoniel, and Charmis, son of Melchiel.[r] 16They then convened all the elders of the city, and all their young men, as well as the women, gathered in haste at the place of assembly. They placed Achior in the center of the people, and Uzziah questioned him about what had happened. 17He replied by giving them an account of what was said in the council of Holofernes, and of all his own words among the Assyrian rulers, and of all the boasting threats of Holofernes against the house of Israel.

18At this the people fell prostrate and worshiped God,* and they cried out: 19"Lord, God of heaven, look at their arrogance! Have mercy on our people in their abject state, and look with favor this day on the faces of those who are consecrated to you." 20Then they reassured Achior and praised him highly. 21Uzziah brought him from the place of assembly to his home, where he gave a banquet for the elders. That whole night they called upon the God of Israel for help.

CHAPTER 7

See RG 219

The Campaign Against Israel.* 1The following day Holofernes ordered his whole army, and all the troops who had come to join him, to break camp and move against Bethulia, seize the passes into the hills, and make war on the Israelites. 2That same day all their fighting men went into action. Their forces numbered a hundred and seventy thousand infantry and twelve thousand cavalry, not counting the baggage train or the men who accompanied it on foot, a very great army. 3They encamped at the spring in the valley near Bethulia, and spread crosswise toward Dothan as far as Balbaim, and lengthwise from Bethulia to Cyamon, which faces Esdraelon.

4When the Israelites saw how many there were, they were greatly distressed and said to one another, "Soon they will strip the whole land bare. Neither the high mountains nor the valleys nor the hills will bear their weight." 5Yet they all seized their weapons, lighted fires on their towers, and kept watch throughout the night.[s]

The Siege of Bethulia.* 6On the second day Holofernes led out all his cavalry in the sight of the Israelites who were in Bethulia. 7He reconnoitered the ascents to their city and located their springs of water; these he seized, stationing armed detachments around them, while he himself returned to his troops.

8All the rulers of the Edomites, all the leaders of the Moabites, together with the generals of the coastal region, came to Holofernes and said:[t] 9"Master, please listen to what we have to say, that there may be no

6:14–21 The scene shifts back to Bethulia where Achior tells the town leaders and citizens all that Holofernes has planned against them. The people cry out to God for help.

6:15 Uzziah: *Ozeias* is the Greek equivalent of the Hebrew *'uzziyyah*, "Yah-is-my-strength." His compromise in 7:30 highlights the irony of his name. **Chabris . . . Charmis**: unknown outside Judith.

6:18 The people fell prostrate and worshiped God: here in response to Achior's report, the people properly turn to God in their distress. See 4:12.

7:1–5 The scene returns to the Assyrian camp (vv. 1–3) and then shifts back to Bethulia (vv. 4–5). Holofernes orders war preparations; Israel sees and is greatly terrified.

7:6–32 The scene is set first in the Assyrian camp where Holofernes moves against Bethulia (vv. 6–18), and then in Bethulia where the people cry out to God and, when their courage fails, determine it is time to surrender (vv. 19–32).

r: Gn 29:33; 34:25, 30; 35:23. *s:* 1 Mc 12:28–29; 2 Mc 10:36. *t:* Gn 36:1; 1 Mc 5:3.

losses among your forces. 10These Israelite troops do not rely on their spears, but on the height of the mountains where they dwell, for it is not easy to reach the summit of their mountains.[u] 11Therefore, master, do not attack them in regular formation, and not a single one of your troops will fall. 12Stay in your camp, and spare every man of your force. Have some of your servants keep control of the spring of water that flows out at the base of the mountain, 13for that is where the inhabitants of Bethulia get their water. Then thirst will destroy them, and they will surrender their city. Meanwhile, we and our troops will go up to the nearby hilltops and encamp there to guard against anyone's leaving the city. 14They and their wives and children will languish with hunger, and even before the sword strikes them they will be laid low in the streets where they live. 15Thus you will render them dire punishment for their rebellion and their refusal to meet you peacefully."

16Their words pleased Holofernes and all his attendants, and he ordered their proposal to be carried out. 17So the Ammonites moved camp, together with five thousand Assyrians. They encamped in the valley and held the water supply and the springs of the Israelites. 18The Edomites and the Ammonites went up and encamped in the hill country opposite Dothan; and they sent some of their men to the southeast opposite Egrebel, near Chusi, which is on Wadi Mochmur. The rest of the Assyrian army was encamped in the plain, covering all the land. Their tents and equipment were spread out in profusion everywhere, and they formed a vast multitude.

The Distress of the Israelites. 19The Israelites cried to the Lord, their God, for they were disheartened, since all their enemies had them surrounded, and there was no way of escaping from them.* 20The whole Assyrian army, infantry, chariots, and cavalry, kept them thus surrounded for thirty-four days.* All the reservoirs of water failed the inhabitants of Bethulia, 21and the cisterns ran dry, so that on no day did they have enough water to drink, for their drinking water was rationed. 22Their children were listless, and the women and youths were fainting from thirst and were collapsing in the streets and gateways of the city, with no strength left in them.

23So all the people, including youths, women, and children, went in a crowd to Uzziah and the rulers of the city. They cried out loudly and said before all the elders: 24"May God judge between you and us! You have done us grave injustice in not making peace with the Assyrians.[v] 25There is no one to help us now! God has sold us into their hands by laying us prostrate before them in thirst and utter exhaustion.[w] 26So now, summon them and deliver the whole city as plunder to the troops of Holofernes and to all his forces; 27we would be better off to become their prey. Although we would be made slaves, at least we would live, and not have to see our little ones dying before our eyes, and our wives and children breathing their last.[x] 28We adjure you by heaven and earth and by our God, the Lord of our ancestors, who is punishing us for our sins and the sins of our ancestors,* that this very day you do as we have proposed."[y]

29All in the assembly with one accord broke into shrill wailing and cried loudly to the Lord their God. 30But Uzziah said to them, "Courage, my brothers and sisters! Let us endure patiently five days more for the Lord our God to show mercy toward us; for God will not utterly forsake us. 31But if these days pass and help does not come to us, I will do as you say." 32Then he dismissed the people. The men returned to their posts on the walls and towers of the city, the women and

7:19 The prayers of the Israelites shift focus from concern for the Temple and Jerusalem (4:12), to concern that God see the arrogance of the enemy and show pity on the covenant people (6:18), to expression of fear and loss of courage regarding their own safety (7:19).

7:20 Thirty-four days: the Bethulians lose heart after being without water; Judith will spend four days in the enemy camp (12:10) and the Israelites will plunder the enemy camp for thirty days (15:11).

7:28 In keeping with the deuteronomic theme of retribution, the Bethulians interpret their persecution as punishment for their sins and the sins of their ancestors (see Ex 20:5; 34:7; Ez 18). In 8:18–27, Judith argues that they are being tested.

u: 1 Kgs 20:23, 28; 2 Kgs 19:23; Ps 95:4; Is 37:24. *v:* Ex 5:21. *w:* Est 7:4. *x:* Ex 14:12; 16:3; 1 Mc 1:62–63. *y:* Ps 106:6; Lam 5:7.

children went back to their homes. Throughout the city they were in great misery.

III. Judith, Instrument of the Lord*

CHAPTER 8

See RG 219

Description of Judith. [1*] [z] Now in those days Judith, daughter of Merari,[a] son of Ox, son of Joseph, son of Oziel, son of Elkiah, son of Ananias, son of Gideon, son of Raphain, son of Ahitub, son of Elijah, son of Hilkiah, son of Eliab, son of Nathanael, son of Salamiel, son of Sarasadai, son of Simeon, son of Israel, heard of this. [2]Her husband, Manasseh,* of her own tribe and clan, had died at the time of the barley harvest. [3]While he was supervising those who bound the sheaves in the field, he was overcome by the heat; and he collapsed on his bed and died in Bethulia, his native city. He was buried with his ancestors in the field between Dothan and Balamon. [4][b] Judith was living as a widow* in her home for three years and four months. [5]She set up a tent for herself on the roof of her house, put sackcloth about her waist, and wore widow's clothing.[c] [6]She fasted all the days of her widowhood, except sabbath eves and sabbaths, new moon eves and new moons, feastdays and holidays of the house of Israel.[d] [7]She was beautiful in appearance and very lovely to behold.[e] Her husband, Manasseh, had left her gold and silver, male and female servants, livestock and fields, which she was maintaining. [8]No one had a bad word to say about her, for she feared God greatly.

Judith and the Elders.* [9]So when Judith heard of the harsh words that the people, discouraged by their lack of water, had spoken against their ruler, and of all that Uzziah had said to them in reply, swearing that he would hand over the city to the Assyrians at the end of five days, [10]she sent her maid who was in charge of all her things* to summon Uzziah, Chabris, and Charmis, the elders of her city. [11]When they came, she said to them: "Listen to me, you rulers of the people of Bethulia. What you said to the people today is not right. You pronounced this oath, made between God and yourselves, and promised to hand over the city to our enemies unless within a certain time the Lord comes to our aid. [12]Who are you to put God to the test today, setting yourselves in the place of God in human affairs?* [f] [13]And now it is the Lord Almighty you are putting to the test, but you will never understand anything! [14]You cannot plumb the depths of the human heart or grasp the workings of the human mind; how then can you fathom God, who has made all these things, or discern his mind, or understand his plan?[g]

"No, my brothers, do not anger the Lord our God. [15*] For if he does not plan to come to our aid within the five days, he has it equally within his power to protect us at such time as he pleases, or to destroy us in

8:1–10:10 In this section the hero is introduced (8:1–8) and prepares to deliver Israel (8:9–10:10).

8:1 Judith has the longest genealogy accorded any biblical woman, with family ties back to Israel/Jacob.

8:2 Manasseh: Judith's marriage was endogamous, within her own tribe. The tribe and clan are identified as hers, though usually it is the husband's tribe and clan that are noted.

8:4 Widow: in a reversal of traditional property law, Judith holds title to her husband's estate (see v. 7). However, she will give a part of her inheritance to her late husband's family before her death (16:24); she chooses not to remarry (16:22).

8:9–10:10 This section opens with a repetition of the information that Judith heard about the discouragement of the people and about Uzziah's vow (cf. v. 1). Judith's plan to save Israel then takes shape. In her own home, she meets with the elders of Bethulia (vv. 9–36), prays (9:1–14), prepares herself and the food she will need in the Assyrian camp (10:1–5), goes out to meet the elders again at the gate of Bethulia (10:6–8), and sets out with her maid for the Assyrian camp (10:9–10).

8:10 Her maid who was in charge of all her things: cf. Gn 15:2; 24:2; 39:4. Judith's first act in the story is to send this unnamed maid (*habra*, lit., "graceful one" or "favorite slave," v. 33; 10:2, 5, 17; 13:9; 16:23) to summon the town officials (see also other terms for female servants, *paidiske* in 10:10 and *doule* in 12:15; 13:3). Her last act in the story will be to give this woman her freedom (16:23).

8:12 Judith reprimands the leaders for putting God to the test (cf. Dt 6:16). She will argue that the right to test belongs to God (vv. 25–27).

8:15–16 God's plans are in opposition to Nebuchadnezzar's plans (2:2, 4). **To protect . . . or to destroy**: Judith defends God's freedom (cf. Jb 1:21; 2:10).

z: Gn 26:34; Jer 36:14, 21, 23. *a:* Gn 46:11; Ex 6:16; Nm 3:17. *b:* 1 Sm 25:39–42; 2 Sm 11:27; Is 54:4; Lam 1:1; 5:3. *c:* Jos 2:6, 8; Jgs 3:20–25; 1 Sm 9:25–26; 2 Sm 11:2; 16:22; 2 Kgs 4:10; 23:12; Ps 102:8; Acts 10:9. *d:* Lk 2:37. *e:* Gn 12:11; 29:17; Est 2:7. *f:* Dt 6:16; Jb 38:2; 40:2, 7–8; Ps 106:14; Mal 3:15. *g:* Ps 139:17–18; Wis 9:13; Is 40:13; Rom 11:33–34; 1 Cor 2:11.

the sight of our enemies. 16Do not impose conditions on the plans of the Lord our God. God is not like a human being to be moved by threats, nor like a mortal to be cajoled.

17"So while we wait for the salvation that comes from him, let us call upon him to help us, and he will hear our cry if it pleases him. 18For there has not risen among us in recent generations, nor does there exist today, any tribe, or clan, or district, or city of ours that worships gods made by hands, as happened in former days.[h] 19It was for such conduct that our ancestors were handed over to the sword and to pillage, and fell with great destruction before our enemies.[i] 20But since we acknowledge no other god but the Lord, we hope that he will not disdain us or any of our people. 21If we are taken, then all Judea will fall, our sanctuary will be plundered, and God will demand an account from us for their profanation. 22For the slaughter of our kindred, for the taking of exiles from the land, and for the devastation of our inheritance, he will hold us responsible among the nations. Wherever we are enslaved, we will be a scandal and a reproach in the eyes of our masters. 23Our servitude will not work to our advantage, but the Lord our God will turn it to disgrace.

24"Therefore, my brothers, let us set an example* for our kindred. Their lives depend on us, and the defense of the sanctuary, the temple, and the altar rests with us. 25[j] Besides all this, let us give thanks to the Lord our God for putting us to the test as he did our ancestors.[k] 26Recall how he dealt with Abraham, and how he tested Isaac, and all that happened to Jacob in Syrian Mesopotamia while he was tending the flocks of Laban, his mother's brother. 27He has not tested us with fire, as he did them, to try their hearts, nor is he taking vengeance on us. But the Lord chastises those who are close to him in order to admonish them."

28Then Uzziah said to her: "All that you have said you have spoken truthfully, and no one can deny your words. 29For today is not the first time your wisdom has been evident, but from your earliest days all the people have recognized your understanding, for your heart's disposition is right. 30The people, however, were so thirsty that they forced us to do for them as we have promised, and to bind ourselves by an oath that we cannot break.* [l] 31But now, since you are a devout woman, pray for us that the Lord may send rain to fill up our cisterns. Then we will no longer be fainting from thirst."

32Then Judith said to them: "Listen to me! I will perform a deed that will go down from generation to generation among our descendants. 33Stand at the city gate tonight to let me pass through with my maid; and within the days you have specified before you will surrender the city to our enemies, the Lord will deliver Israel by my hand. 34You must not inquire into the affair, for I will not tell you what I am doing until it has been accomplished." 35Uzziah and the rulers said to her, "Go in peace, and may the Lord God go before you to take vengeance upon our enemies!" 36Then they withdrew from the tent and returned to their posts.

CHAPTER 9

See RG 219

*The Prayer of Judith.** 1Judith fell prostrate, put ashes upon her head, and uncovered the sackcloth she was wearing. Just as the evening incense was being offered in the temple of God in Jerusalem, Judith cried loudly to the Lord:[m] 2"Lord, God of my father Simeon, into whose hand you put a

8:24 Let us set an example: when Judith says "us," she includes herself. She proposes that she together with Uzziah, Chabris, and Charmis model a faithful response to God's test for the wavering people. "Let us give thanks to the Lord our God for putting us to the test" (v. 25) repeats her intention. "Us" for Uzziah does not include her (see vv. 30, 31).

8:30–31 An oath that we cannot break: Uzziah's request that Judith pray for rain underscores his lack of imagination concerning how God's deliverance might come.

9:1–14 Judith prepares to confront the enemy by turning to God, the source of her strength. Her prayer, an individual lament, moves from a remembrance of God's saving deeds of the past to an appeal to God to exercise the same power in the present. Judith contrasts the empty pride of the Assyrians with God's surpassing might, powerful enough to be exercised in unlikely ways, even through the hand of a woman.

h: Jdt 5:20–21; 11:10. *i:* Ps 78:56–57; 106:13–14; Jer 7:16–20. *j:* Dt 8:5; Tb 12:14; Ps 94:12; Prv 3:11–12; Wis 3:4–6; Sir 2:1–6; Heb 12:5–6. *k:* Gn 22:1–19; 32:22–32; Ex 20:20; Dt 8:16. *l:* Ex 32:22; 1 Sm 15:20–24. *m:* Ex 30:7–8; 1 Chr 28:18; Ezr 9:5; Ps 141:2; Dn 9:21.

sword to take revenge upon the foreigners* who had defiled a virgin by violating her, shaming her by uncovering her thighs, and dishonoring her by polluting her womb. You said, 'This shall not be done!' Yet they did it. 3 Therefore you handed over their rulers to slaughter; and you handed over to bloodshed the bed in which they lay deceived, the same bed that had felt the shame of their own deceiving. You struck down the slaves together with their masters, and the masters upon their thrones.* 4 Their wives you handed over to plunder, and their daughters to captivity, and all the spoils you divided among your favored children, who burned with zeal for you and in their abhorrence of the defilement of their blood called on you for help. O God, my God, hear me also, a widow.

5 "It is you who were the author of those events and of what preceded and followed them. The present and the future you have also planned.[n] Whatever you devise comes into being. 6 The things you decide come forward and say, 'Here we are!' All your ways are in readiness, and your judgment is made with foreknowledge.[o]

7 "Here are the Assyrians, a vast force, priding themselves on horse and chariot, boasting of the power of their infantry, trusting in shield and spear, bow and sling.[p] They do not know that you are the Lord who crushes wars;* 8 Lord is your name. Shatter their strength in your might, and crush their force in your wrath.[q] For they have resolved to profane your sanctuary, to defile the tent where your glorious name resides, and to break off the horns of your altar with the sword. 9* See their pride, and send forth your fury upon their heads.[r] Give me, a widow, a strong hand to execute my plan.[s] 10 By the deceit of my lips, strike down slave together with ruler, and ruler together with attendant. Crush their arrogance by the hand of a female.[t]

11* [u] "Your strength is not in numbers, nor does your might depend upon the powerful.[v] You are God of the lowly, helper of those of little account, supporter of the weak, protector of those in despair, savior of those without hope.

12 "Please, please, God of my father, God of the heritage of Israel, Master of heaven and earth, Creator of the waters, King of all you have created, hear my prayer! 13 Let my deceitful words* [w] wound and bruise those who have planned dire things against your covenant, your holy temple, Mount Zion, and the house your children possess.[x] 14 Make every nation and every tribe know clearly that you are God, the God of all power and might, and that there is no other who shields the people of Israel but you alone."

CHAPTER 10

See RG 219

Judith Prepares to Depart. 1 As soon as Judith had ceased her prayer to the God of Israel and finished all these words, 2 she rose from the ground. She called her maid and they went down into the house, which she used only on sabbaths and feast days. 3 She took off the sackcloth she had on, laid aside

9:2 The foreigners: Shechem, the Hivite, violated Dinah, Jacob and Leah's daughter (Gn 34:2). **Defiled a virgin by violating her**: meaning of the Greek is unclear; lit., "who loosened the virgin's womb (*metran*) to defilement." Some read "headdress" or "girdle" (*mitran*) instead of "womb" (*metran*).

9:3 Because Shechem had deceived and violated Dinah, her brothers, Simeon and Levi, tricked Shechem and the men of his city into being circumcised, and then killed them while they were recovering from the circumcision (Gn 34:13–29).

9:7–8 You are the Lord who crushes wars; Lord is your name: cf. Ex 15:3, "The Lord is a warrior; Lord is his name" and Jdt 16:2, "The Lord is a God who crushes wars."

9:9–10 In a five-fold petition, Judith asks that God see their pride, send fury on their heads, give her a strong hand, strike down the enemy through her deceit, and crush their pride by the hand of a female (*theleia*, see also 13:15 and 16:5, rather than the more usual *gyne*, *woman*). In an androcentric society, there was no greater dishonor for a male than that he die at the hand of a female (see Jgs 9:53–54). Nine verses emphasize that by her hand God's deliverance is accomplished: 8:33; 9:9, 10; 12:4; 13:4, 14, 15; 15:10; and 16:5.

9:11–12 Ten titles for God are arranged in two groups of five on either side of the repeated Greek particle, *nai nai* ("verily" or "please"). The title "Master of heaven and earth" (v. 12; see notes on 1:11 and 5:20) is unique to Judith in the Septuagint, as are also "God of the heritage of Israel" and "Creator of the waters."

9:13 Deceitful words: twice Judith asks God to make her a successful liar in order to preserve her people (vv. 10, 13).

n: Is 41:22–23; 42:9; 43:9; 44:7; 46:10. *o:* Jb 38:35; Is 46:9–13; Bar 3:35. *p:* Ex 15:1, 21. *q:* Ex 15:3; Ps 46:9–10; 76:4–5. *r:* Ex 15:7. *s:* Ex 3:19–20; 4:2, 4, 6, 7, 17, 20; 5:21; 6:1; 7:4, 5, 15, 17, 19; 8:1, 2, 12, 13; 9:3, 22; 10:12, 21, 22; 12:11; 13:3, 9, 14, 16; 14:16, 21, 26, 27; 15:6, 9, 12, 20; Jgs 5:26. *t:* Jgs 4:9. *u:* Ps 33:16–17. *v:* Ex 15:2; Jgs 7:2; 1 Sm 17:45–47; 2 Chr 16:8–9. *w:* Jdt 10:4; 11:20, 23; 16:6, 9; Est C:24. *x:* Dn 11:28.

the garments of her widowhood, washed her body with water, and anointed herself with rich ointment. She arranged her hair, put on a diadem, and dressed in the festive attire she had worn while her husband, Manasseh, was living.[y] 4 She chose sandals for her feet, and put on her anklets, bracelets, rings, earrings, and all her other jewelry.[z] Thus she made herself very beautiful, to entice the eyes of all the men who should see her.*

5 She gave her maid a skin of wine and a jug of oil. She filled a bag with roasted grain, dried fig cakes, and pure bread.* [a] She wrapped all her dishes and gave them to the maid to carry.[b]

6 Then they went out to the gate of the city of Bethulia and found Uzziah and the elders of the city, Chabris and Charmis, standing there. 7 When they saw Judith transformed in looks and differently dressed, they were very much astounded at her beauty and said to her, 8 "May the God of our ancestors grant you favor and make your design successful, for the glory of the Israelites and the exaltation of Jerusalem." 9 Judith bowed down to God.

Judith and Her Maid Leave Bethulia. Then she said to them, "Order the gate of the city opened for me, that I may go to accomplish the matters we discussed." So they ordered the young men to open the gate for her, as she had requested, 10 and they did so. Then Judith and her maidservant went out. The men of the city kept her in view as she went down the mountain and crossed the valley; then they lost sight of her.

IV. Judith Goes out to War*

See RG 219

11 As Judith and her maid walked directly across the valley, they encountered the Assyrian patrol. 12 The men took her in custody and asked her, "To what people do you belong? Where do you come from, and where are you going?"[c] She replied: "I am a daughter of the Hebrews, and I am fleeing from them, because they are about to be delivered up to you as prey. 13 I have come to see Holofernes, the ranking general of your forces, to give him a trustworthy report; in his presence I will show him the way by which he can ascend and take possession of the whole hill country without a single one of his men suffering injury or loss of life."[d]

14 When the men heard her words and gazed upon her face, which appeared marvelously beautiful to them, they said to her, 15 "By hastening down to see our master, you have saved your life. Now go to his tent; some of us will accompany you to hand you over to him. 16 When you stand before him, have no fear in your heart; give him the report you have given us, and he will treat you well." 17 So they selected a hundred of their men as an escort for her and her maid, and these conducted them to the tent of Holofernes.

18 As the news of her arrival spread among the tents, a crowd gathered in the camp. They came and stood around her as she waited outside the tent of Holofernes, while he was being informed about her. 19 They marveled at her beauty, regarding the Israelites with wonder because of her, and they said to one another, "Who can despise this people who have such women among them? It is not good to leave one of their men alive, for if any were to be spared they could beguile the whole earth."

Judith Meets Holofernes. 20 Then the guards of Holofernes and all his attendants came out and ushered her into the tent. 21 Holofernes was reclining on his bed under a canopy* woven of purple, gold, emeralds, and other precious stones. 22 When they announced her to him, he came out to the front part of the tent, preceded by silver lamps. 23 When Judith came before Holofernes and his attendants, they all marveled at the beauty

10:4 Judith's beauty overcomes all who meet her (8:7; 10:7, 14, 19, 23; 11:21, 23; 12:13).

10:5 Concern for Israel's dietary laws, reflected in her selection of wine, roasted grain, and bread, emphasizes Judith's religious fidelity (cf. 1 Sm 25:18 and Dn 1:8–16).

10:11–13:20 In this section Judith and her maid arrive in the Assyrian camp (10:11–19), where Judith meets (10:20–12:9) and triumphs over Holofernes (12:10–13:10a). Then she and her maid return to Bethulia and announce the victory (13:10b–20).

10:21 Canopy: netting for protection against insects. A prized possession in this story (cf. 13:15; 16:19).

y: Gn 43:24; Lv 8:6; 22:6; Tb 6:3; Ez 16:4, 9. *z:* Gn 24:47, 53; 35:4; Ex 3:22; 12:35; 32:3; 35:22; Nm 31:50; Is 3:18, 21; Hos 2:15. *a:* 1 Sm 25:18. *b:* Jdt 12:2; Est C:28. *c:* Gn 16:8. *d:* Jdt 11:5–6.

of her face. She fell prostrate and paid homage to him, but his servants raised her up.[e]

CHAPTER 11

See RG 219

1 Then Holofernes said to her: "Take courage, woman! Have no fear in your heart! I have never harmed anyone who chose to serve Nebuchadnezzar, king of all the earth. 2 As for your people who live in the hill country, I would never have raised my spear against them, had they not insulted me. They have brought this upon themselves. 3 But now tell me why you have fled from them and come to us? In any case, you have come to safety. Take courage! Your life is spared tonight and for the future.[f] 4 No one at all will harm you. Rather, you will be well treated, as are the servants of my lord, King Nebuchadnezzar."

5 Judith answered him: "Listen to the words of your servant, and let your maidservant speak in your presence! I will say nothing false to my lord* this night. 6 If you follow the words of your maidservant, God will successfully perform a deed through you, and my lord will not fail to achieve his designs.* 7 I swear by the life of Nebuchadnezzar, king of all the earth, and by the power of him who has sent you to guide all living things, that not only do human beings serve him through you; but even the wild animals, and the cattle, and the birds of the air, because of your strength, will live for Nebuchadnezzar and his whole house.[g] 8 Indeed, we have heard of your wisdom and cleverness.[h] The whole earth is aware that you above all others in the kingdom are able, rich in experience, and distinguished in military strategy.

9[i] "As for Achior's speech in your council, we have heard it. When the men of Bethulia rescued him, he told them all he had said to you. 10 So then, my lord and master, do not disregard his word, but bear it in mind, for it is true. Indeed our people are not punished, nor does the sword prevail against them, except when they sin against their God.[j] 11 But now their sin* has caught up with them, by which they will bring the wrath of their God upon them when they do wrong; so that my lord will not be repulsed and fail, but death will overtake them. 12 Because their food has given out and all their water is running low, they have decided to kill their animals, and are determined to consume all the things which God in his laws has forbidden them to eat. 13 They have decided that they would use the first fruits of grain and the tithes of wine and oil, which they had consecrated and reserved for the priests who minister in the presence of our God in Jerusalem—things which the people should not so much as touch with their hands.[k] 14 They have sent messengers to Jerusalem to bring back permission from the senate, for even there people have done these things.[l] 15 On the very day when the response reaches them and they act upon it, they will be handed over to you for destruction.

16 "As soon as I, your servant, learned all this, I fled from them. God has sent me to perform with you such deeds as will astonish people throughout the whole earth who hear of them. 17 Your servant is, indeed, a God-fearing woman, serving the God of heaven night and day. Now I will remain with you, my lord; but each night your servant will go out into the valley and pray to God. He will tell me when they have committed their offenses. 18 Then I will come and let you know, so that you may march out with all your forces, and not one of them will be able to withstand you. 19 I will lead you through the heart of Judea until you come to Jerusalem, and there in its center I will set up your throne. You will drive them like sheep that have no shepherd, and not even a dog will growl at you.[m] This was told to me in

11:5–6 Here the word "lord" has a double meaning, indicating both Holofernes and God. Much irony is evident in Judith's conversation with Holofernes (e.g., 12:4).

11:6 Designs: cf. 10:8; 11:6; 13:5 where this word is used as a synonym for Judith's "affair" (8:34), which she kept secret as she carried out the plan of her God (8:15, 16), unlike her counterpart Nebuchadnezzar, who told all the details of his plan (2:2, 4).

11:11 Sin: but in 8:18–20 Judith asserts that the people have not committed idolatry in recent generations.

e: Ru 2:10; 1 Sm 25:41; 2 Sm 14:4. *f:* 2 Mc 11:19. *g:* Jgs 8:19; 1 Sm 14:45; 25:26; 28:10; 2 Sm 11:11; Ez 17:16; Dn 2:38. *h:* Sir 1:6; 42:18. *i:* Jdt 5:5. *j:* Jdt 5:21; 8:18. *k:* Nm 18:8–9. *l:* 1 Mc 2:31–41. *m:* Ex 11:7.

advance and announced to me, and I have been sent to tell you."

[20]Her words pleased Holofernes and all his attendants. They marveled at her wisdom and exclaimed, [21]"No other woman from one end of the earth to the other looks so beautiful and speaks so wisely!" [22]Then Holofernes said to her: "God has done well in sending you ahead of your people, to bring victory to our hands, and destruction to those who have despised my lord. [23]You are not only beautiful in appearance, but you are also eloquent. If you do as you have said, your God will be my God;* you will live in the palace of King Nebuchadnezzar and be renowned throughout the whole earth."

CHAPTER 12

See RG 219

[1]Then he ordered them to lead her into the room where his silver dinnerware was kept, and ordered them to set a table for her with his own delicacies to eat and his own wine to drink. [2]But Judith said, "I cannot eat any* of them, because it would be a scandal.[n] Besides, I will have enough with the things I brought with me." [3]Holofernes asked her, "But if your provisions give out, where can we get more of the same to provide for you? None of your people are with us." [4]Judith answered him, "As surely as you live, my lord, your servant will not use up her supplies before the Lord accomplishes by my hand what he has determined."

[5]Then the attendants of Holofernes led her to her tent, where she slept until the middle of the night. Toward the early morning watch, she rose[o] [6]and sent this message to Holofernes, "Give orders, my lord, to let your servant go out for prayer." [7]So Holofernes ordered his guards not to hinder her. Thus she stayed in the camp three days. Each night she went out to the valley of Bethulia, where she bathed herself* at the spring of the camp.[p] [8]After bathing, she prayed to the Lord, the God of Israel, to direct her way for the triumph of her people. [9]Then she returned purified to the tent and remained there until her food was brought to her toward evening.[q]

Judith at the Banquet of Holofernes. [10]On the fourth day Holofernes gave a banquet for his servants alone, to which he did not invite any of the officers. [11]And he said to Bagoas, the eunuch in charge of his personal affairs, "Go and persuade the Hebrew woman in your care to come and to eat and drink with us. [12]It would bring shame on us to be with such a woman without enjoying her. If we do not seduce her, she will laugh at us."[r]

[13]So Bagoas left the presence of Holofernes, and came to Judith and said, "So lovely a maidservant should not be reluctant to come to my lord to be honored by him, to enjoy drinking wine with us, and to act today like one of the Assyrian women who serve in the palace of Nebuchadnezzar." [14]Judith replied, "Who am I to refuse my lord? Whatever is pleasing to him I will promptly do. This will be a joy* for me until the day of my death."

[15]So she proceeded to put on her festive garments and all her finery. Meanwhile her servant went ahead and spread out on the ground opposite Holofernes the fleece Bagoas had furnished for her daily use in reclining while eating.[s] [16]Then Judith came in and reclined. The heart of Holofernes was in rapture over her and his passion was aroused. He was burning with the desire to possess her, for he had been biding his time to seduce her from the day he saw her.[t] [17]Holofernes said to her, "Drink and be happy with us!" [18]Judith replied, "I will gladly drink, my lord, for today is the greatest day of my whole life." [19]She then took the things her servant had prepared and ate and drank in his presence. [20]Holofernes,

11:23 Your God will be my God: in 3:8, Holofernes insisted that Nebuchadnezzar alone is god.

12:2 Cannot eat any: the food of Gentiles was avoided by pious Jews (see Dn 1:8, 13, 15; Tb 1:10–11) because it might have been prohibited as unclean (see Lv 11:13–44), sacrificed to idols (see Ex 34:15; Dt 32:37–38), or contaminated with blood (see Lv 7:26–27). In addition, eating together symbolized the sharing of life.

12:7 Bathed herself: she bathes to purify herself after contact with the Gentiles. Her nightly departure from the camp provides for her escape (cf. 13:10).

12:14 Joy: the irony of this response is obvious; see also the joy of 14:9 and Judith's "new song" in chap. 16.

n: Tb 1:10–11; Est C:28; 1 Mc 1:62–63; 2 Mc 5:27; 6:18–7:2; Dn 1:8. *o:* Ex 14:24; 1 Sm 11:11. *p:* Tb 7:9. *q:* 2 Sm 3:35. *r:* Dn 13:37, 54, 57–58. *s:* Tb 9:6; Ez 23:41. *t:* Dn 13:20, 39.

charmed by her, drank a great quantity of
wine, more than he had ever drunk on any
day since he was born.

See RG 219

CHAPTER 13

Judith Beheads Holofernes. 1 When it
grew late, his servants quickly withdrew.
Bagoas closed the tent from the outside and
dismissed the attendants from their master's
presence. They went off to their beds, for
they were all tired because the banquet had
lasted so long. 2 Judith was left alone in the
tent with Holofernes, who lay sprawled on
his bed, for he was drunk with wine. 3 Judith
had ordered her maidservant to stand outside
the bedchamber and to wait, as on the other
days, for her to come out; she had said she
would be going out for her prayer. She had
also said this same thing to Bagoas.
4 When all had departed, and no one, small
or great, was left in the bedchamber, Judith
stood by Holofernes' bed and prayed
silently, "O Lord, God of all might, in this
hour look graciously on the work of my
hands for the exaltation of Jerusalem. 5 Now
is the time for aiding your heritage and for
carrying out my design to shatter the enemies who have risen against us."[u] 6 She went
to the bedpost near the head of Holofernes,
and taking his sword from it, 7 she drew close
to the bed, grasped the hair of his head, and
said, "Strengthen me this day, Lord, God of
Israel!" 8 Then with all her might she struck
his neck twice and cut off his head.[v] 9 She
rolled his body off the bed and took the
canopy from its posts. Soon afterward, she
came out and handed over the head of
Holofernes to her maid, 10 who put it into her
food bag. Then the two went out together for
prayer as they were accustomed to do.

Judith and Her Maid Return to Bethulia.
They passed through the camp, and skirting
that valley, went up the mountain to Bethulia, and approached its gates. 11 From a distance, Judith shouted to the guards at the
gates: "Open! Open the gate! God, our God,
is with us. Once more he has shown his
strength in Israel and his power against the
enemy, as he has today!"

Judith Displays the Head of Holofernes.
12* When the citizens heard her voice, they
hurried down to their city gate and summoned
the elders of the city. 13 All the people, from
the least to the greatest, hurriedly assembled,
for her return seemed unbelievable. They
opened the gate and welcomed the two
women. They made a fire for light and gathered around the two. 14 Judith urged them with
a loud voice: "Praise God, give praise! Praise
God, who has not withdrawn his mercy from
the house of Israel, but has shattered our enemies by my hand this very night!" 15 Then she
took the head out of the bag, showed it to
them, and said: "Here is the head of
Holofernes, the ranking general of the Assyrian forces, and here is the canopy under
which he lay in his drunkenness. The Lord
struck him down by the hand of a female!*
16 Yet I swear by the Lord, who has protected
me in the way I have walked, that it was my
face that seduced Holofernes to his ruin, and
that he did not defile me with sin or shame."
17 All the people were greatly astonished.
They bowed down and worshiped God, saying with one accord, "Blessed are you, our
God, who today have humiliated the enemies
of your people." 18 Then Uzziah said to her,
"Blessed are you, daughter, by the Most High
God, above all the women on earth; and
blessed be the Lord God, the creator of heaven
and earth, who guided your blow at the head
of the leader of our enemies.[w] 19 Your deed of
hope will never be forgotten by those who recall the might of God.[x] 20 May God make this
redound to your everlasting honor, rewarding
you with blessings, because you risked your
life when our people were being oppressed,
and you averted our disaster, walking in the
straight path before our God." And all the people answered, "Amen! Amen!"[y]

13:12–20 Elements from chaps. 8–9 are echoed here. The assembly of the people at Judith's return parallels the meeting of the town officials summoned by Judith in 8:10. Uzziah blesses Judith in 8:5 and again in 13:18–20.

13:15 By the hand of a female: cf. 16:5 and note on 9:9–10.

u: Gn 24:45; 1 Sm 1:13. *v:* Jgs 4:21; 1 Sm 17:51; 31:9. *w:* Jgs 5:24; Lk 1:42. *x:* Sir 35:9. *y:* Dt 27:15–26; Ps 41:14; 72:19; 89:53.

V. Victory and Thanksgiving*

CHAPTER 14

See RG 219

Judith's Plan of Attack. 1 Then Judith said to them: "Listen to me,* my brothers and sisters. Take this head and hang it on the parapet of your wall.[z] 2 At daybreak, when the sun rises on the earth, each of you seize your weapons, and let all the able-bodied men rush out of the city under command of a captain, as if about to go down into the valley against the Assyrian patrol, but without going down. 3 The Assyrians will seize their weapons and hurry to their camp to awaken the generals of the army. When they run to the tent of Holofernes and do not find him, panic will seize them, and they will flee before you.[a] 4 Then you and all the other inhabitants of the whole territory of Israel will pursue them and strike them down in their tracks. 5 But before doing this, summon for me Achior the Ammonite, that he may see and recognize the one who despised the house of Israel and sent him here to meet his death."

Achior's Conversion.* 6 So they called Achior from the house of Uzziah. When he came and saw the head of Holofernes in the hand of one of the men in the assembly of the people, he collapsed in a faint. 7 Then, after they lifted him up, he threw himself at the feet of Judith in homage, saying: "Blessed are you in every tent of Judah! In every nation, all who hear your name will be struck with terror.[b] 8 But now, tell me all that you did during these days." So Judith told him, in the midst of the people, all that she had done, from the day she left until the time she began speaking to them. 9 When she had finished her account, the people cheered loudly, so that the city resounded with shouts of joy. 10 Now Achior, seeing all that the God of Israel had done, believed firmly in God. He circumcised the flesh of his foreskin and he has been united with the house of Israel to the present day.[c]

Panic in the Assyrian Camp. 11 At daybreak they hung the head of Holofernes on the wall. Then all the Israelite men took up their weapons and went out by groups to the mountain passes.[d] 12 When the Assyrians saw them, they notified their commanders, who, in turn, went to their generals, their division leaders, and all their other leaders. 13 They came to the tent of Holofernes and said to the one in charge of all his things, "Awaken our lord, for the slaves have dared come down against us in battle, to their utter destruction." 14 So Bagoas went in and knocked at the entry of the tent, presuming that Holofernes was sleeping with Judith. 15 When no one answered, he parted the curtains, entered the bedchamber, and found him thrown on the floor dead, with his head gone! 16 He cried out loudly, weeping, groaning, and howling, and tore his garments. 17 Then he entered the tent where Judith had her quarters; and, not finding her, he rushed out to the troops and cried: 18 "The slaves have duped us! One Hebrew woman has brought shame on the house of King Nebuchadnezzar. Look! Holofernes on the ground—without a head!"[e]

19 When the leaders of the Assyrian forces heard these words, they tore their tunics and were overcome with great distress. Their

14:1–16:25 This section describes Judith's plan to attack the Assyrian camp (14:1–5) and its execution (14:11–15:7). Between the plan and its execution, Achior identifies the head of Holofernes and is converted to Judaism. The book concludes with the victory celebration (15:8–14), hymn of thanksgiving (16:1–20), and a description of Judith's final days (16:21–25). Elements from chaps. 8–9 recur here: Judith, widow of Manasseh (8:2; 16:22), lived alone in Bethulia on her estate (8:4; 16:22), with servants and property (8:7; 16:21). Judith's instructions begin with the words "listen to me" (8:11; 14:1). Her prayer for success (9:1–14) is balanced by a prayer and display of success in 14:14–16.

14:1–5 Listen to me: an imperative (used also in 8:11, 32) opens Judith's instruction that the people display the head of Holofernes on the parapet and themselves in ranks before the enemy at daybreak. The strategy is to throw the Assyrians into panic and strike them down in their confusion; cf. 15:1–3.

14:6–10 Recognizing the head of Holofernes, Achior faints. Then he throws himself down before Judith, acclaiming her blessed in Judah and every nation. After listening to all she had done, Achior is circumcised and joins the house of Israel. Since this violates the prohibition of Dt 23:4 that no Ammonite or Moabite shall enter the assembly, even to the tenth generation, some suggest that the book was not included in the Hebrew scriptures for this reason. However, see Is 56:3–6.

z: 1 Sm 17:54; 31:9–10; 2 Sm 20:21; 2 Kgs 10:7–8; 1 Mc 7:47; 2 Mc 15:30; Mt 14:8. *a:* 1 Mc 7:44. *b:* Jgs 5:24. *c:* Dt 23:4. *d:* 2 Mc 8:23; 12:20. *e:* Jgs 9:54.

loud cries and shouts were heard throughout
the camp.

CHAPTER 15

See RG 219

1 On hearing what had happened,
those still in their tents were horrified.
2 Overcome with fear and dread, no one kept
ranks any longer. They scattered in all directions, and fled along every path, both
through the valley and in the hill country.[f]
3 Those who were stationed in the hill country around Bethulia also took to flight. Then
the Israelites, every warrior among them,
came charging down upon them.
4 Uzziah sent messengers to Betomas-
thaim, to Choba and Kona, and to the whole
territory of Israel to report what had happened and to urge them all to attack the enemy and destroy them. 5 On hearing this, all
the Israelites, with one accord, attacked
them and cut them down as far as Choba.
Even those from Jerusalem and the rest of
the hill country took part in this, for they too
had been notified of the happenings in the
camp of their enemy. The Gileadites and the
Galileans struck the enemy's flanks with
great slaughter, even beyond Damascus and
its borders. 6 The remaining people of Bethulia swept down on the camp of the Assyrians, plundered it, and acquired great riches.
7 The Israelites, when they returned from the
slaughter, took possession of what was left.
Even the towns and villages in the hill country and on the plain got an enormous quantity of spoils, for there was a tremendous
amount of it.
Israel Celebrates Judith's Victory. 8 Then
the high priest Joakim and the senate of the
Israelites who lived in Jerusalem came to see
for themselves the good things that the Lord
had done for Israel, and to meet and congratulate Judith. 9 When they came to her, all
with one accord blessed her, saying:

"You are the glory of Jerusalem!*
You are the great pride of Israel!
You are the great boast of our nation!
10 By your own hand you have done all
this.
You have done good things for Israel,
and God is pleased with them.
May the Almighty Lord bless you
forever!"

And all the people said, "Amen!"
11 For thirty days* all the people plundered
the camp, giving Judith the tent of Holofernes, with all his silver, his beds, his
dishes, and all his furniture. She took them
and loaded her mule, hitched her carts, and
loaded these things on them.
12 All the women of Israel gathered to see
her, and they blessed her and performed a
dance in her honor.[g] She took branches in
her hands and distributed them to the women
around her, 13 and she and the other women
crowned themselves with olive leaves.
Then, at the head of all the people, she led
the women in the dance, while the men of Israel followed, bearing their weapons, wearing garlands and singing songs of praise.
14* Judith led all Israel in this song of thanksgiving, and the people loudly sang this hymn
of praise:

CHAPTER 16

Judith's Hymn of Deliverance

See RG 219

1 And Judith sang:

"Strike up a song to my God with
tambourines,[h]
sing to the Lord with cymbals;
Improvise for him a new song,
exalt and acclaim his name.
2 For the Lord is a God who crushes wars;[i]

15:9 In the Lectionary of the Catholic Church, this passage is one of several choices for feasts of Mary (e.g., the Presentation of Mary). These words of praise are also echoed in antiphons for the Liturgy of the Hours on Marian feasts.

15:11 Thirty days: the central actions in each half of the book are accomplished in a total of thirty-four days. Bethulia was without water for thirty-four days (7:20). Judith spent four days in the enemy camp and the Israelites plunder the Assyrian camp for thirty days.

15:14–16:17 Judith's hymn of deliverance is patterned on the Song of Miriam (Ex 15:20–21).

f: Gn 9:2; Dt 11:25; 1 Mc 7:18; Sir 4:17. *g:* Ex 15:20; Jgs 11:34; 1 Sm 18:6; Jer 31:4. *h:* Gn 31:27; Ex 15:20; 1 Sm 18:6; 2 Sm 6:5; 1 Chr 13:8; Ps 68:26; 81:3; 149:3; Jer 31:4. *i:* Ex 15:3; Ps 46:10.

he sets his encampment among his
people;
he delivered me from the hands of my
pursuers.

3 "The Assyrian came from the mountains
of the north,
with myriads of his forces he came;
Their numbers blocked the wadis,
their cavalry covered the hills.
4 He threatened to burn my territory,
put my youths to the sword,
Dash my infants to the ground,
seize my children as plunder.
And carry off my virgins as spoil.

5 "But the Lord Almighty thwarted them,
by the hand of a female!
6 Not by youths was their champion struck
down,[j]
nor did Titans bring him low,
nor did tall giants attack him;[k]
But Judith, the daughter of Merari,
by the beauty of her face brought him
down.
7 She took off her widow's garb
to raise up the afflicted in Israel.
She anointed her face with fragrant oil;
8 fixed her hair with a diadem,
and put on a linen robe to beguile him.
9 Her sandals ravished his eyes,[l]
her beauty captivated his mind,
the sword cut through his neck![m]

10 "The Persians trembled at her boldness,
the Medes were daunted at her daring.
11 When my lowly ones shouted,
and my weak ones cried out,
The enemy was terrified,
screamed and took to flight.
12 Sons of maidservants pierced them
through;
wounded them like deserters' children.
They perished before the ranks of my
Lord.

13 "I will sing a new song to my God.[n]
O Lord, great are you and glorious,
marvelous in power and unsurpassable.
14 Let your every creature serve you;
for you spoke, and they were made.
You sent forth your spirit, and it created
them;[o]
no one can resist your voice.[p]
15 For the mountains to their bases
are tossed with the waters;
the rocks, like wax, melt before your
glance.[q]

"But to those who fear you,
you will show mercy.
16 Though the sweet fragrance of every
sacrifice is a trifle,
and the fat of all burnt offerings but
little in your sight,
one who fears the Lord is forever
great.
17 "Woe to the nations that rise against my
people!
the Lord Almighty will requite them;
in the day of judgment he will punish
them:
He will send fire and worms into their
flesh,[r]
and they will weep and suffer forever."

18 When they arrived at Jerusalem, they
worshiped God. As soon as the people were
purified, they offered their burnt offerings,
voluntary offerings, and donations.[s] 19 Judith
dedicated to God all the things of Holofernes
that the people had given her, putting under
the ban the canopy that she herself had taken
from his bedchamber.[t] 20 For three months
the people continued their celebration in Jerusalem before the sanctuary, and Judith remained with them.

The Renown and Death of Judith. 21 When
those days were over, all of them returned to
their inheritance. Judith went back to Bethulia and remained on her estate. For the rest of
her life she was renowned throughout the
land. 22 Many wished to marry her, but she
gave herself to no man all the days of her life
from the time her husband, Manasseh, died
and was gathered to his people. 23 Her fame
continued to increase, and she lived in the

j: 1 Sm 17:4, 51. *k:* Gn 6:1–4; Dt 2:10, 21; 2 Sm 21:16–22; 1 Chr 20:4–8. *l:* Sg 7:2; Ez 16:10. *m:* Jgs 5:26. *n:* Ps 33:3; 40:4; 96:1; 98:1; 144:9; 149:1; Is 42:10. *o:* Gn 1; Ps 104:30; 148:5. *p:* Est C:3–4; Ps 33:9; Is 55:11. *q:* Ps 97:5; Mi 1:4; Na 1:5. *r:* Sir 7:17; Is 66:24; Mk 9:48. *s:* Nm 19:11–22; 31:19. *t:* Lv 7:16.

house of her husband, reaching the advanced age of one hundred and five.* [u] She set her maid free. And when she died in Bethulia, they buried her in the cave of her husband, Manasseh;[v]
24 and the house of Israel mourned her for seven days.* [w] Before she died, she distributed her property to the relatives of her husband, Manasseh, and to her own relatives.[x]
25y During the lifetime of Judith and for a long time after her death, no one ever again spread terror* among the Israelites.

16:23 One hundred and five: long life was a sign of blessing (see Jb 42:16; Prv 16:31; 20:29). The fact that the Maccabean period was one hundred and five years long (168–63 B.C.) may account for assigning this age to Judith.

16:24 Seven days: the customary period for mourning the dead (1 Sm 31:13).

16:25 Spread terror: Judith is compared to the heroes of the Book of Judges (cf. Jgs 3:11, 30).

u: Jb 42:16; Prv 16:31; 20:29; Sir 18:9; Lk 2:36. *v:* Gn 23:19; 25:9; 49:29–32; 50:13. *w:* Gn 50:3; 1 Sm 31:13; 1 Chr 10:12; Sir 22:12. *x:* Nm 27:6–11. *y:* Jgs 3:11, 30; 5:31; 8:28.

See RG 222-26

The Book of Esther

The Book of Esther tells a story of the deliverance of the Jewish people. We are shown a Persian emperor, Ahasuerus (loosely based on Xerxes, 485–464 B.C.), who makes momentous decisions for trivial reasons, and his wicked minister, Haman, who takes advantage of the king's compliance to pursue a personal vendetta against the Jews by having a royal decree issued ordering their destruction. The threat is averted by two Jews, Esther and Mordecai. Their influence and intervention allow the Jews to turn the tables on their enemies and rout their attackers. This deliverance is commemorated by the inauguration of the Jewish festival of Purim on the fourteenth and fifteenth of Adar (mid-February through mid-March). The book confronts the modern reader with important themes, the evils of genocide and racism.

Esther's character matures over the course of the narrative. As a girl she is recruited for the king's harem because of her physical beauty. But at a key moment in the book (chap. 4), she rises to the challenge to risk her life for the salvation of her people. At that point, she transforms her status as queen from a position of personal privilege to one of power and public responsibility.

Esther's uncle, Mordecai, appears first as an adoptive father, whose solicitude for Esther leads him to the king's gate, where he foils a plot to assassinate the king. When he learns of the edict against the Jews, he encourages Esther to confront the king. The book ends with Mordecai as the king's chief minister.

The book is a free composition, not a historical document. Its fictional character can be illustrated by many examples of literary motifs: the use of extensive conversation to move the plot along; the motif of concealment (Esther is a Jew, related to Mordecai, but Haman does not know it, even as he comes to her banquet in chap. 7). A whole series of banquets structure the work: two by the king, one by Vashti, three by Esther, and the joyful banqueting that ends the book. Further artificialities are clear in the way characters are paired (e.g., Mordecai and Esther) and in the delays and the speed of the action (Esther delays the banquet in 5:3–8, but the tempo of chaps. 5–6 is particularly fast); Mordecai passes from the threat of death (5:9–14) to royal honors (6:10–11) within twenty-four hours. There are many exaggerations, and even sarcastic implausibilities (cf. the effect of Vashti's disobedience in 1:17–18), and huge ironies (e.g., Haman in 6:6, 10). The work is a composite of reversals (cf. 9:1) in the lives of individuals and communities.

The book was probably written in the third or second century B.C. It has come down to us in two versions: an older Hebrew version, and a Greek version based on a text similar to the Hebrew, but with additions and alterations as described below.

One striking feature of the Hebrew version of the Book of Esther is that no divine names or titles are employed here; God is not mentioned at all. This would not be unusual in a book whose subject matter or outlook was more secular, but Esther is a book in which the religious element is prominent: the Jews fast in order to be delivered from imminent peril, experience deliverance at the eleventh hour, and commemorate their deliverance with an annual festival. Moreover, there are indirect references to divine activity (for example, in 4:14).

The Greek additions to Esther have many explicit references to God, as well as explicit descriptions of the beliefs and emotional states of Esther and Mordecai. They also elaborate on the content of the edicts from Ahasuerus as illustrations of Gentile attitudes toward Jews. While there are only a few contradictions between these Greek additions and the older Hebrew text, reading the book with these additions is a very different experience from reading the book without them. The additions to Esther are an excellent example of a process that occurs throughout the Bible: further reflections on the story become part of the story itself. Although the Book of Esther was questioned by some early Christians, even St. Jerome, the whole book, including the Greek additions, was included in the canon of Scripture by the Council of Trent.

The Greek version of the book dates from ca. 116 to 48 B.C. (see note on F:11). In the present translation, the Greek additions are indicated by the letters A through F. The regular chapter numbers apply to the Hebrew text.

The book may be divided as follows:

I. Prologue (A:1–17)
II. Esther Becomes Queen (1:1–2:23)
III. Haman's Plot Against the Jews (3:1–13; B:1–7; 3:14–15)
IV. Esther and Mordecai Plead for Help (4:1–16; C:1–D:16; 5:1–5)
V. Haman's Downfall (5:6–8:2)
VI. The Jewish Victory and the Feast of Purim (8:3–12; E:1–24; 8:13–9:23)
VII. Epilogue: The Rise of Mordecai (9:24–10:3; F:1–11)

The order of the Vulgate text in relation to the order of the Greek text is as follows:

Vulg. 11:2–12:6	=	A:1–17 at the beginning of the book.
13:1–7	=	B:1–7 after 3:13.
13:8–15:3–19	=	C:1–D:16 after 4:16.
15:1–2	=	B:8, 9 after 4:8.
16:1–24	=	E:1–24 after 8:12.
10:4–13	=	F:1–10 after 10:3.

I. Prologue

CHAPTER A

See RG 222–26

Dream of Mordecai. [1]In the second year of the reign of Ahasuerus the great, on the first day of Nisan, Mordecai, son of Jair, son of Shimei, son of Kish, of the tribe of Benjamin, had a dream.* [a] [2]* He was a Jew residing in the city of Susa, a prominent man who served at the king's court, [3]and one of the captives whom Nebuchadnezzar, king of Babylon, had taken from Jerusalem with Jeconiah, king of Judah.[b]

[4c] This was his dream.* There was noise and tumult, thunder and earthquake—confusion upon the earth. [5]Two great dragons advanced, both poised for combat. They uttered a mighty cry, [6]and at their cry every nation prepared for war, to fight against the nation of the just. [7]It was a dark and gloomy day. Tribulation and distress, evil and great confusion, lay upon the earth. [8]The whole nation of the just was shaken with fear at the evils to come upon them, and they expected to perish. [9d] Then they cried out to God, and from their crying there arose, as though from a tiny spring, a mighty river, a flood of water. [10]The light of the sun broke forth; the lowly were exalted and they devoured the boastful.

[11]Having seen this dream and what God intended to do, Mordecai awoke. He kept it in mind, and tried in every way, until night, to understand its meaning.

Mordecai Thwarts an Assassination.* [12e] Mordecai lodged in the courtyard with

A:1 The genealogy of Mordecai is designed to reflect opposition to Israel's enemy Haman, an Agagite (v. 17). In 1 Sm 15:1–9, Saul (whose father's name was Kish, of the tribe of Benjamin) conquered Agag the Amalekite.

A:2–3 Repeats information from 2:5–6, on which see note, but states that Mordecai is already a court official. In the Hebrew text, Mordecai is not given this rank until 7:10–8:2.

A:4 An interpretation of the dream that relates its features to the plot of the book is given in F:1–6.

A:12–17 Retells the story in 2:21–23, but with several differences. Addition A has Mordecai inform the king directly, whereas in 2:22 Mordecai informs the king through Esther after she has become queen. A:16 has Mordecai rewarded immediately after his service, whereas the Hebrew text defers

a: Est 2:5. *b:* Est 2:6; 2 Kgs 24:15; 2 Chr 36:9–10; Jer 22:24–30; 24:1; 29:1–2. *c:* Est F:2, 4–6. *d:* Est F:3. *e:* Est 2:21–23; 6:1–3.

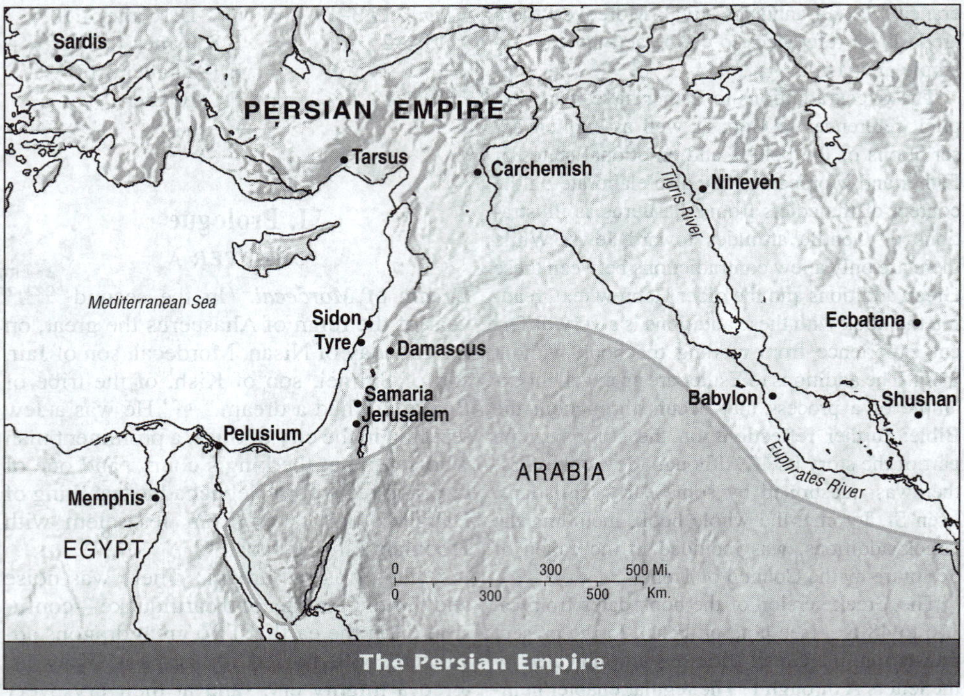

The Persian Empire

Bigthan and Teresh, two eunuchs of the king who guarded the courtyard. [13]He overheard them plotting, investigated their plans, and discovered that they were preparing to assassinate King Ahasuerus. So he informed the king about them. [14]The king had the two eunuchs questioned and, upon their confession, put to death. [15]Then the king had these things recorded; Mordecai, too, put them into writing. [16]The king also appointed Mordecai to serve at the court, and rewarded him for his actions.[f]

[17]Haman, however, son of Hammedatha, a Bougean,* who was held in high honor by the king, sought to harm Mordecai and his people because of the two eunuchs of the king.[g]

II. Esther Becomes Queen

CHAPTER 1

See RG 222–26

The Banquet of Ahasuerus. [1]* During the reign of Ahasuerus—the same Ahasuerus who ruled over a hundred and twenty-seven provinces from India to Ethiopia— [2]while he was occupying the royal throne in the royal precinct of Susa,* [3]in the third year of his reign, he gave a feast for all his officials and ministers: the Persian and Median army officers, the nobles, and the governors of the provinces.[h] [4]For as many as a hundred and eighty days, he displayed the glorious riches of his kingdom and the resplendent wealth of his royal estate.

the reward of Mordecai to 6:3–13. In A:17, the failure of the eunuchs' plot becomes Haman's reason for seeking the destruction of Mordecai and his people, something which the Hebrew text attributes to Mordecai's refusal to bow to Haman (see note on 3:2).

A:17 A Bougean: the origin of this term is unknown; it may represent a garbled attempt to render the Hebrew "Agagite" (3:1). In the Greek additions Haman not only knows the plot to assassinate the king, but is apparently a co-conspirator.

1:1 The Hebrew text opens with a portrait of the power and luxury of the Persian king Ahasuerus (Xerxes I, whose empire consisted of only about thirty provinces).

1:2 Susa was the winter capital of the Persian empire. The "royal precinct" (sometimes translated "stronghold" or "citadel") was a well-fortified section of the city that included the king's residence. The Book of Esther depicts other citizens living in this section as well.

f: Est 6:3. *g:* Est 3:1–15; B:1–7; E:13. *h:* Jdt 1:16.

5At the end of this time the king gave a
feast of seven days in the garden court of the
royal palace for all the people, great and
small, who were in the royal precinct of
Susa. 6There were white cotton draperies
and violet hangings, held by cords of fine
crimson linen from silver rings on marble
pillars. Gold and silver couches were on a
mosaic pavement, which was of porphyry,
marble, mother-of-pearl, and colored stones.
7Drinks were served in a variety of golden
cups, and the royal wine flowed freely, as
befitted the king's liberality. 8By ordinance
of the king the drinking was unstinted, for he
had instructed all the stewards of his household to comply with the good pleasure of
everyone. 9Queen Vashti also gave a feast
for the women in the royal palace of King
Ahasuerus.

Refusal of Vashti. 10On the seventh day,
when the king was merry with wine, he instructed Mehuman, Biztha, Harbona, Big-
tha, Abagtha, Zethar, and Carkas, the seven
eunuchs who attended King Ahasuerus,[i] 11to
bring Queen Vashti into his presence wearing the royal crown, that he might display
her beauty to the populace and the officials,
for she was lovely to behold. 12But Queen
Vashti refused to come at the royal order issued through the eunuchs. At this the king's
wrath flared up, and he burned with fury.
13He conferred with the sages who understood the times, because the king's business
was conducted in general consultation with
lawyers and jurists. 14He summoned Car-
shena, Shethar, Admatha, Tarshish, Meres,
Marsena, and Memucan, the seven Persian
and Median officials who were in the king's
personal service and held first rank in the
realm,[j] 15and asked them, "What is to be
done by law with Queen Vashti for disobeying the order of King Ahasuerus issued
through the eunuchs?"

16In the presence of the king and of the officials, Memucan answered: "Queen Vashti
has not wronged the king alone, but all the
officials and the populace throughout the
provinces of King Ahasuerus. 17For the
queen's conduct will become known to all
the women, and they will look with disdain
upon their husbands when it is reported,
'King Ahasuerus commanded that Queen
Vashti be ushered into his presence, but she
would not come.' 18This very day the Persian and Median noblewomen who hear of
the queen's conduct will recount it to all the
royal officials, and disdain and rancor will
abound. 19If it please the king, let an irrevocable royal decree* be issued by him and inscribed among the laws of the Persians and
Medes, forbidding Vashti to come into the
presence of King Ahasuerus and authorizing
the king to give her royal dignity to one
more worthy than she.[k] 20Thus, when the decree that the king will issue is published
throughout his realm, vast as it is, all wives
will honor their husbands, from the greatest
to the least."

21This proposal pleased the king and the
officials, and the king acted on the advice of
Memucan. 22He sent letters to all the royal
provinces, to each province in its own script
and to each people in its own language, to
the effect that every man should be lord in
his own home.

CHAPTER 2

See RG 222–26

The Search for a New Queen. 1After
this, when King Ahasuerus' wrath had
cooled, he thought over what Vashti had
done and what had been decreed against her.
2Then the king's personal attendants suggested: "Let beautiful young virgins be
sought for the king. 3Let the king appoint
emissaries in all the provinces of his realm
to gather all beautiful young virgins into the
harem in the royal precinct of Susa. Under
the care of the royal eunuch Hegai, guardian
of the women, let cosmetics be given them.
4Then the young woman who pleases the
king shall reign in place of Vashti." This suggestion pleased the king, and he acted accordingly.

5There was in the royal precinct of Susa a

1:19 An irrevocable royal decree: the first of several in the book. In a satiric portrayal, even a minor domestic disagreement is resolved through a sweeping international edict. The irrevocable nature of the decree is intended to increase its force, but creates problems if the king needs to adapt to new information or conditions. See note on 8:8.

i: Dn 5:1. *j:* 1 Chr 12:32; Ezr 7:14. *k:* Est 8:5, 8; Dn 6:8–9.

certain Jew named Mordecai,* son of Jair,
son of Shimei, son of Kish, a Benjaminite,
6who had been exiled from Jerusalem with
the captives taken with Jeconiah, king of Judah, whom Nebuchadnezzar, king of Babylon, had deported.[l] 7He became foster father to his cousin Hadassah, that is, Esther,*
when she lost both father and mother. The
young woman was beautifully formed and
lovely to behold. On the death of her father
and mother, Mordecai adopted her as his
own daughter.[m]
8When the king's order and decree had
been proclaimed and many young women
brought together to the royal precinct of
Susa under the care of Hegai, Esther also
was brought in to the royal palace under the
care of Hegai, guardian of the women. 9The
young woman pleased him and won his favor. So he promptly furnished her with cosmetics and provisions. Then choosing seven
maids for her from the royal palace, he transferred both her and her maids to the best
place in the harem. 10Esther did not reveal
her nationality or family, for Mordecai had
commanded her not to do so.
11Day by day Mordecai would walk about
in front of the court of the harem to learn
how Esther was faring and what was to become of her.
12After the twelve months' preparation
decreed for the women, each one went in
turn to visit King Ahasuerus. During this period of beautifying treatment, six months
were spent with oil of myrrh, and the other
six months with perfumes and cosmetics.
13Then, when each one was to visit the king,
she was allowed to take with her from the
harem to the royal palace whatever she
chose. 14She would go in the evening and return in the morning to a second harem under
the care of the royal eunuch Shaashgaz,
guardian of the concubines. She could not
return to the king unless he was pleased with
her and had her summoned by name.[n] 15As
for Esther, daughter of Abihail and adopted
daughter of his nephew Mordecai, when her
turn came to visit the king, she did not ask
for anything but what the royal eunuch
Hegai, guardian of the women, suggested.
And she won the admiration of all who saw
her.

Ahasuerus Chooses Esther. 16Esther was
led to King Ahasuerus in his palace in the
tenth month, Tebeth, in the seventh year of
his reign. 17The king loved Esther more than
all other women, and of all the virgins she
won his favor and good will. So he placed
the royal crown on her head and made her
queen in place of Vashti. 18Then the king
gave a great feast in honor of Esther to all his
officials and servants, granting a holiday to
the provinces and bestowing gifts with royal
generosity.

Mordecai Thwarts an Assassination.*
19[o] As was said, from the time the virgins
had been brought together, and while Mordecai was passing his time at the king's gate,
20Esther had not revealed her family or nationality, because Mordecai had told her not
to; and Esther continued to follow Mordecai's instructions, just as she had when she
was being brought up by him. 21[p] During the
time that Mordecai spent at the king's gate,
Bigthan and Teresh, two of the royal eunuchs who guarded the entrance, became angry and plotted to assassinate King Ahasuerus. 22When the plot became known to
Mordecai, he told Queen Esther, who in turn
informed the king in Mordecai's name.
23The matter was investigated and verified,
and both of them were impaled on stakes.*
This was written in the annals in the king's
presence.

2:5 Mordecai: a Babylonian name, deriving from the god Marduk. Like Esther, Mordecai may have had a Jewish name as well, although in his case we do not know what it is. The chronology of the book makes him well over one hundred years old, since he was deported with Jehoiachin about 598 B.C.; cf. A:1.

2:7 Esther: a Babylonian name, deriving from the goddess Ishtar. She is given a Hebrew name as well, "Hadassah," which means "myrtle."

2:19–23 This story is retold and placed at the beginning of the book in Greek addition A:12–17, with significant differences (see note). The Greek also has a translation of the account in 2:19–23 at this point in the narrative.

2:23 Impaled on stakes: a method of execution used by the Persians, known from ancient records and reliefs.

l: Est A:3; 2 Kgs 24:15; 2 Chr 36:9–10; Jer 22:24–30; 24:1; 29:1–2. *m:* Est 2:15. *n:* Est 2:19–20; 4:11, 16. *o:* Est 2:14. *p:* Est A:12–15; 6:1–3.

III. Haman's Plot Against the Jews

CHAPTER 3

See RG 222–26

Mordecai Refuses to Honor Haman.
1After these events King Ahasuerus promoted Haman, son of Hammedatha the Agagite, to high rank, seating him above all his
fellow officials.[q] 2All the king's servants
who were at the royal gate would kneel and
bow down to Haman, for that is what the
king had ordered in his regard.[r] Mordecai,
however, would not kneel and bow down.*
3The king's servants who were at the royal
gate said to Mordecai, "Why do you disobey
the king's order?"[s] 4When they had reminded him day after day and he would not
listen to them, they informed Haman, to see
whether Mordecai's explanation would prevail, since he had told them that he was a
Jew.
Haman's Reprisal. 5When Haman observed that Mordecai would not kneel and
bow down to him, he was filled with anger.
6But he thought it was beneath him to attack
only Mordecai. Since they had told Haman
of Mordecai's nationality, he sought to destroy all the Jews, Mordecai's people,
throughout the realm of King Ahasuerus. 7In
the first month, Nisan, in the twelfth year of
King Ahasuerus, the *pur*, or lot,* was cast in
Haman's presence to determine the day and
the month for the destruction of Mordecai's
people on a single day, and the lot fell on the
thirteenth day of the twelfth month, Adar.[t]
Decree Against the Jews. 8Then Haman
said to King Ahasuerus: "Dispersed among
the nations throughout the provinces of your
kingdom, there is a certain people living
apart. Their laws differ from those of every
other people and they do not obey the laws
of the king; so it is not proper for the king to
tolerate them.[u] 9If it please the king, let a decree be issued to destroy them; and I will deliver to the procurators ten thousand silver
talents for deposit in the royal treasury."[v]
10The king took the signet ring* from his
hand and gave it to Haman, son of Hammedatha the Agagite, the enemy of the Jews.[w]
11The king said to Haman, "The silver is
yours, as well as the people, to do with as
you please."*
12So the royal scribes were summoned on
the thirteenth day of the first month, and
they wrote, at the dictation of Haman, an order to the royal satraps, the governors of
every province, and the officials of every
people, to each province in its own script
and to each people in its own language. It
was written in the name of King Ahasuerus
and sealed with the royal signet ring. 13Let-
ters were sent by couriers to all the royal
provinces, to destroy, kill and annihilate all
the Jews, young and old, including women
and children in one day, the thirteenth day of
the twelfth month, Adar, and to seize their
goods as spoil.[x]

CHAPTER B

See RG 222–26

1This is a copy of the letter:
"The great King Ahasuerus writes to the
satraps of the hundred and twenty-seven
provinces from India to Ethiopia, and the
governors subordinate to them, as follows:
2When I came to rule many peoples and to
hold sway over the whole world, not being
carried away by a sense of my own authority
but always acting fairly and with mildness, I
determined to provide for my subjects a life
of lasting tranquility; and, by making my
kingdom civilized and safe for travel to its
farthest borders, to restore the peace desired

3:2 We are not told the reasons for Mordecai's refusal to bow. It may be the result of a form of Jewish piety that refuses to offer such homage to any mortal; see also Greek addition C:5–7.

3:7 The pur, or lot: the Hebrew text preserves the Akkadian word *pur* because its plural, *purim*, became the name of the feast of Purim commemorating the deliverance of the Jews; cf. 9:24, 26. The lot functions as a kind of horoscope to determine the most favorable day for the pogrom.

3:10 Signet ring: a ring containing a seal that was impressed on documents to authenticate them. With this ring, Haman can issue decrees in the king's name.

3:11 Although Ahasuerus seems to refuse the bribe, this is probably a polite way of accepting it that makes him appear munificent (compare Gn 23:11–15, where Ephron tells Abraham that he "gives" him the field and, after a few more pleasantries, sets a very high price for it). Both 4:7 and 7:4 seem to assume Ahasuerus has accepted the money.

q: Est B:3; 5:11; E:11. *r:* Est C:5; 5:9, 13; 6:10, 12. *s:* Est 4:16. *t:* Est 9:24–32; F:10. *u:* Est 3:13; B:4; E:24; Wis 2:14–15; Dn 3:8–12. *v:* Est 7:4. *w:* Gn 41:42. *x:* Est B:6; 7:4.

by all people.[y] 3When I consulted my counselors as to how this might be accomplished, Haman, who excels among us in discretion, who is outstanding for constant good will and steadfast loyalty, and who has gained a place in the kingdom second only to me,[z] 4brought it to our attention that, mixed among all the nations throughout the world, there is one people of ill will, which by its laws is opposed to every other people and continually disregards the decrees of kings, so that the unity of empire blamelessly designed by us cannot be established.[a]

5"Having noted, therefore, that this nation, and it alone, is continually at variance with all people, lives by divergent and alien laws, is inimical to our government, and does all the harm it can to undermine the stability of the kingdom, 6we hereby decree that all those who are indicated to you in the letters of Haman, who is in charge of the administration and is a second father to us, shall, together with their wives and children, be utterly destroyed by the swords of their enemies, without any pity or mercy, on the fourteenth day* of the twelfth month, Adar, of the current year;[b] 7so that when these people, whose present ill will is of long standing, have gone down into Hades by a violent death on a single day, they may leave our government completely stable and undisturbed for the future."

See RG 222–26

(CHAPTER 3)

14A copy of the decree to be promulgated as law in every province was published to all the peoples, that they might be prepared for that day. 15The couriers set out in haste at the king's command; meanwhile, the decree was promulgated in the royal precinct of Susa. The king and Haman then sat down to drink, but the city of Susa was thrown into confusion.

IV. Esther and Mordecai Plead for Help

CHAPTER 4

See RG 222–26

Mordecai Exhorts Esther. 1When Mordecai learned all that was happening, he tore his garments, put on sackcloth and ashes, and went through the city crying out loudly and bitterly,[c] 2till he came before the royal gate, which no one clothed in sackcloth might enter. 3Likewise in each of the provinces, wherever the king's decree and law reached, the Jews went into deep mourning, with fasting, weeping, and lament; most of them lay on sackcloth and ashes.

4Esther's maids and eunuchs came and told her. Overwhelmed with anguish, the queen sent garments for Mordecai to put on, so that he might take off his sackcloth; but he refused. 5Esther then summoned Hathach, one of the king's eunuchs whom he had placed at her service, and commanded him to find out what this action of Mordecai meant and the reason for it. 6So Hathach went out to Mordecai in the public square in front of the royal gate, 7and Mordecai recounted all that had happened to him, as well as the exact amount of silver Haman had promised to pay to the royal treasury for the slaughter of the Jews. 8He also gave him a copy of the written decree for their destruction that had been promulgated in Susa, to show and explain to Esther. Hathach was to instruct her to go to the king and to plead and intercede with him on behalf of her people.*

9Hathach returned to Esther and told her what Mordecai had said. 10Then Esther replied to Hathach and gave him this message for Mordecai: 11"All the servants of the king and the people of his provinces know that any man or woman who goes to the king in the inner court without being summoned

B:6 Fourteenth day: only the Greek text here names the fourteenth of Adar as the day set aside for the destruction of the Jews. The Hebrew text consistently gives the date as the thirteenth of Adar (e.g., 3:13) as does Greek addition E:20; see note on 9:17–19.

4:8 The Greek text adds the following to Mordecai's message to Esther: "Remember the days of your lowly estate, when you were brought up in my charge; for Haman, who is second to the king, has asked for our death. Invoke the Lord and speak to the king for us: save us from death."

y: Est E:8–9. *z:* Est 3:1; 5:11; E:11. *a:* Est 3:8; E:24. *b:* Est 3:13; 7:4; E:11. *c:* Jdt 4:12.

is subject to the same law—death. Only if the king extends the golden scepter will such a person live. Now as for me, I have not been summoned to the king for thirty days."[d]

12 When Esther's words were reported to Mordecai, 13 he had this reply brought to her: "Do not imagine that you are safe in the king's palace, you alone of all the Jews. 14 Even if you now remain silent, relief and deliverance will come to the Jews from another source;* but you and your father's house will perish. Who knows—perhaps it was for a time like this that you became queen?"

15 Esther sent back to Mordecai the response: 16 "Go and assemble all the Jews who are in Susa; fast on my behalf, all of you, not eating or drinking night or day for three days. I and my maids will also fast in the same way. Thus prepared, I will go to the king, contrary to the law. If I perish, I perish!"[e] 17 Mordecai went away and did exactly as Esther had commanded.

See RG 222–26

CHAPTER C

Prayer of Mordecai. 1 Recalling all that the Lord had done, Mordecai prayed to the Lord 2 and said: "Lord, Lord, King and Ruler of all, everything is in your power, and there is no one to oppose you when it is your will to save Israel. 3 You made heaven and earth and every wonderful thing under heaven. 4 You are Lord of all, and there is no one who can resist you, the Lord. 5[f] You know all things. You know, Lord, that it was not out of insolence or arrogance or desire for glory that I acted thus in not bowing down to the arrogant Haman. 6 I would have gladly kissed the soles of his feet for the salvation of Israel. 7 But I acted as I did so as not to place the honor of a mortal above that of God. I will not bow down to anyone but you, my Lord. It is not out of arrogance that I am acting thus. 8 And now, Lord God, King, God of Abraham, spare your people, for our enemies regard us with deadly envy and are bent upon destroying the inheritance that was yours from the beginning. 9 Do not spurn your portion, which you redeemed for yourself out of the land of Egypt. 10 Hear my prayer; have pity on your inheritance and turn our mourning into feasting, that we may live to sing praise to your name, Lord. Do not silence the mouths of those who praise you."

11 All Israel, too, cried out with all their strength, for death was staring them in the face.

Prayer of Esther. 12[g] Queen Esther, seized with mortal anguish, fled to the Lord for refuge. 13 Taking off her splendid garments, she put on garments of distress and mourning. In place of her precious ointments she covered her head with dung and ashes. She afflicted her body severely and in place of her festive adornments, her tangled hair covered her.

14 Then she prayed to the Lord, the God of Israel, saying: "My Lord, you alone are our King. Help me, who am alone and have no help but you, 15 for I am taking my life in my hand.[h] 16 From birth, I have heard among my people that you, Lord, chose Israel from among all nations, and our ancestors from among all their forebears, as a lasting inheritance, and that you fulfilled all your promises to them.[i] 17 But now we have sinned in your sight, and you have delivered us into the hands of our enemies, 18 because we worshiped their gods. You are just, O Lord. 19 But now they are not satisfied with our bitter servitude, but have sworn an oath to their idols 20 to do away with the decree you have pronounced, to destroy your inheritance, to close the mouths of those who praise you, to extinguish the glory of your house and your altar, 21 to open the mouths of the nations to acclaim their worthless gods, and to extol a mortal king forever.

22 "Lord, do not relinquish your scepter to those who are nothing. Do not let our foes gloat over our ruin, but turn their own counsel against them and make an example of the one who began this against us. 23 Be mindful of us, Lord. Make yourself known in the time of our distress and give me courage, King of gods and Ruler of every power. 24 Put in my mouth persuasive words in the presence of the lion, and turn his heart to ha-

4:14 From another source: probably Mordecai refers to divine aid; the Greek additions (C) are explicit about this.

d: Est 2:14; 4:12; D:12. *e:* Est C:12–13. *f:* Est 3:2; 5:9. *g:* Est 4:16. *h:* Est 4:16. *i:* Dt 4:20; 7:6; 9:29; 14:2; 26:18; 32:9.

tred for our enemy, so that he and his co-conspirators may perish. 25 Save us by your power, and help me, who am alone and have no one but you, Lord.

26 "You know all things. You know that I hate the pomp of the lawless, and abhor the bed of the uncircumcised or of any foreigner. 27 You know that I am under constraint, that I abhor the sign of grandeur that rests on my head when I appear in public. I abhor it like a polluted rag, and do not wear it in private. 28 I, your servant, have never eaten at the table of Haman, nor have I graced the banquet of the king or drunk the wine of libations.* 29 From the day I was brought here till now, your servant has had no joy except in you, Lord, God of Abraham. 30 O God, whose power is over all, hear the voice of those in despair. Save us from the power of the wicked, and deliver me from my fear."

CHAPTER D

See RG 222–26

*Esther Goes to Ahasuerus.** 1 On the third day, ending her prayers, she took off her prayer garments and arrayed herself in her splendid attire. 2 In making her appearance, after invoking the all-seeing God and savior, she took with her two maids; 3 on the one she leaned gently for support, 4 while the other followed her, bearing her train. 5 She glowed with perfect beauty and her face was as joyous as it was lovely, though her heart was pounding with fear. 6 She passed through all the portals till she stood before the king, who was seated on his royal throne, clothed in full robes of state, and covered with gold and precious stones, so that he inspired great awe. 7 As he looked up in extreme anger, his features fiery and majestic, the queen staggered, turned pale and fainted, collapsing against the maid in front of her. 8 But God changed the king's anger to gentleness. In great anxiety he sprang from his throne, held her in his arms until she recovered, and comforted her with reassuring words. 9 "What is it, Esther?" he said to her. "I am your brother.* Take courage! 10 You shall not die; this order of ours applies only to our subjects. 11 Come near!" 12 Raising the golden scepter, he touched her neck with it, embraced her, and said, "Speak to me."[j]

13 She replied: "I saw you, my lord, as an angel of God, and my heart was shaken by fear of your majesty. 14 For you are awesome, my lord, though your countenance is full of mercy." 15 As she said this, she fainted. 16 The king was shaken and all his attendants tried to revive her.

CHAPTER 5

See RG 222–26

1* [Now on the third day, Esther put on her royal garments and stood in the inner courtyard, looking toward the royal palace, while the king was seated on his royal throne in the audience chamber, facing the palace doorway. 2 When he saw Queen Esther standing in the courtyard, she won his favor and he extended toward her the golden scepter he held. She came up to him, and touched the top of the scepter.]

3 Then the king said to her, "What is it, Queen Esther? What is your request? Even if it is half of my kingdom, it shall be granted you."[k] 4 Esther replied, "If it please your majesty, come today with Haman to a banquet I have prepared." 5 The king ordered, "Have Haman make haste to fulfill the wish of Esther."

V. Haman's Downfall

First Banquet of Esther. So the king went with Haman to the banquet Esther had prepared. 6 During the drinking of the wine, the king said to Esther, "Whatever you ask for shall be granted, and whatever request you make shall be honored, even if it is for half my kingdom."[l] 7 Esther replied: "This is my petition and request: 8 if I have found favor

C:28 Wine of libations: offered in sacrifice to the gods.

D:1–16 Addition D expands on and replaces 5:1–2 of the Hebrew text.

D:9 Brother: along with "sister," a common term of affection between lovers or husband and wife. See, e.g., Sg 4:9–12; 8:1; Tb 5:22; 7:11.

5:1–2 The Hebrew text translated here is a short form of the account which is in Greek addition D.

6:4–13 Haman's presumption that the king wants to honor him creates the irony that Haman himself prescribes and fulfills the elaborate terms of Mordecai's reward. This comic reversal mirrors the fatal reversal to come: Haman and those who hate the Jews find that their plot to destroy them recoils on their own head.

j: Est 4:11. *k:* Est 5:6; 7:2; 9:12. *l:* Est 5:3.

with the king and if it pleases your majesty
to grant my petition and honor my request,
let the king come with Haman tomorrow to
a banquet I will prepare; and tomorrow I will
do as the king asks."

Haman's Plot Against Mordecai. 9 That
day Haman left happy and in good spirits.
But when he saw that Mordecai at the royal
gate did not rise, and showed no fear of him,
he was filled with anger toward him.[m] 10 Haman restrained himself, however, and went
home, where he summoned his friends and
his wife Zeresh. 11 He recounted the greatness of his riches, the large number of his
sons, and how the king had promoted him
and placed him above the officials and royal
servants.[n] 12 "Moreover," Haman added,
"Queen Esther invited no one but me to
come with the king to the banquet she prepared; again tomorrow I am to be her guest
with the king. 13 Yet none of this satisfies me
as long as I continue to see the Jew Mordecai sitting at the royal gate."[o] 14 His wife Zeresh and all his friends said to him, "Have a
stake set up, fifty cubits in height, and in the
morning ask the king to have Mordecai impaled on it. Then go to the banquet with the
king in good spirits." This suggestion
pleased Haman, and he had the stake
erected.[p]

CHAPTER 6

See RG 222–26

Mordecai's Reward from the King.
1 That night the king, unable to sleep, asked
that the chronicle of notable events be
brought in. While this was being read to him,
2 the passage occurred in which Mordecai reported Bigthan and Teresh, two of the royal
eunuchs who guarded the entrance, for seeking to assassinate King Ahasuerus.[q] 3 The
king asked, "What was done to honor and
exalt Mordecai for this?" The king's attendants replied, "Nothing was done for him."[r]

4* "Who is in the court?" the king asked.
Now Haman had entered the outer court of
the king's palace to suggest to the king that
Mordecai should be impaled on the stake he
had raised for him.[s] 5 The king's attendants
answered him, "Haman is waiting in the
court." The king said, "Let him come in."
6 When Haman entered, the king said to him,
"What should be done for the man whom the
king wishes to reward?" Now Haman
thought to himself, "Whom would the king
wish to honor more than me?" 7 So he replied
to the king: "For the man whom the king
wishes to honor 8 there should be brought the
royal robe the king wore and the horse the
king rode with the royal crest placed on its
head. 9 The robe and the horse should be
given to one of the noblest of the king's officials, who must clothe the man the king
wishes to reward, have him ride on the horse
in the public square of the city, and cry out
before him, 'This is what is done for the man
whom the king wishes to honor!' "[t] 10 Then
the king said to Haman: "Hurry! Take the
robe and horse as you have proposed, and do
this for the Jew Mordecai, who is sitting at
the royal gate. Do not omit anything you
proposed."[u] 11 So Haman took the robe and
horse, clothed Mordecai, had him ride in the
public square of the city, and cried out before him, "This is what is done for the man
whom the king wishes to honor!"

12 Mordecai then returned to the royal
gate, while Haman hurried home grieving,
with his head covered.[v] 13 When he told his
wife Zeresh and all his friends everything
that had happened to him, his advisers and
his wife Zeresh said to him, "If Mordecai,
before whom you are beginning to fall, is of
Jewish ancestry, you will not prevail against
him, but will surely be defeated by him."

Esther's Second Banquet. 14 While they
were speaking with him, the king's eunuchs
arrived and hurried Haman off to the banquet Esther had prepared.

CHAPTER 7

See RG 222–26

1 So the king and Haman went to the
banquet with Queen Esther. 2 Again, on this
second day, as they were drinking wine, the
king said to Esther, "Whatever you ask,
Queen Esther, shall be granted you. Whatever request you make, even for half the

m: Est 3:2–3; C:5–7; 6:10, 12. *n:* Est 3:1; B:3; E:11; 9:6–10. *o:* Est 3:2–3; 6:10, 12. *p:* Est 6:4; 7:9–10. *q:* Est A:12–14; 2:21–23. *r:* Est A:16. *s:* Est 5:14; 7:9–10. *t:* Gn 41:42–43; 1 Kgs 1:33; Dn 5:29. *u:* Est 2:21; 3:2–3; 5:9, 13. *v:* Est 2:21; 3:2–3; 5:9, 13.

kingdom, shall be honored."[w] 3 Queen Esther replied: "If I have found favor with you, O king, and if it pleases your majesty, I ask that my life be spared, and I beg that you spare the lives of my people. 4 For we have been sold, I and my people, to be destroyed, killed, and annihilated. If we were only to be sold into slavery I would remain silent, for then our distress would not have been worth troubling the king."[x] 5 King Ahasuerus said to Queen Esther, "Who and where is the man who has dared to do this?"[y] 6 Esther replied, "The enemy oppressing us is this wicked Haman." At this, Haman was seized with dread of the king and queen.

7 The king left the banquet in anger and went into the garden of the palace, but Haman stayed to beg Queen Esther for his life, since he saw that the king had decided on his doom. 8 When the king returned from the palace garden to the banquet hall, Haman had thrown himself on the couch on which Esther was reclining; and the king exclaimed, "Will he also violate the queen while she is with me in my own house!" Scarcely had the king spoken when the face of Haman was covered over.

Punishment of Haman. 9[z] Harbona, one of the eunuchs who attended the king, said, "At the house of Haman stands a stake fifty cubits high. Haman made it for Mordecai, who gave the report that benefited the king." The king answered, "Impale him on it." 10 So they impaled Haman on the stake he had set up for Mordecai, and the anger of the king abated.

See RG 222-26

CHAPTER 8

1 That day King Ahasuerus gave the house of Haman, enemy of the Jews, to Queen Esther; and Mordecai was admitted to the king's presence, for Esther had revealed his relationship to her.[a] 2 The king removed his signet ring that he had taken away from Haman, and gave it to Mordecai; and Esther put Mordecai in charge of the house of Haman.[b]

VI. The Jewish Victory and the Feast of Purim

See RG 222-26

The Second Royal Decree. 3 Esther again spoke to the king. She fell at his feet and tearfully implored him to revoke the harm done by Haman the Agagite and the plan he had devised against the Jews. 4 The king stretched forth the golden scepter to Esther. So she rose and, standing before him, 5 said: "If it seems good to the king and if I have found favor with him, if the thing seems right to the king and I am pleasing in his eyes, let a document be issued to revoke the letters that the schemer Haman, son of Hammedatha the Agagite, wrote for the destruction of the Jews in all the royal provinces.[c] 6 For how can I witness the evil that is to befall my people, and how can I behold the destruction of my kindred?"

7 King Ahasuerus then said to Queen Esther and to the Jew Mordecai: "Now that I have given Esther the house of Haman, and they have impaled him on the stake because he was going to attack the Jews, 8[d] you in turn may write in the king's name what you see fit concerning the Jews and seal the letter with the royal signet ring." For a decree written in the name of the king and sealed with the royal signet ring cannot be revoked.*

9 At that time, on the twenty-third day of the third month, Sivan, the royal scribes were summoned. Exactly as Mordecai dictated, they wrote to the Jews and to the satraps, governors, and officials of the hundred and twenty-seven provinces from India to Ethiopia: to each province in its own script and to each people in its own language, and to the Jews in their own script and language. 10 These letters, which he wrote in the name of King Ahasuerus and sealed with the royal

8:8 A decree written . . . cannot be revoked: the king cannot directly grant Esther's request (v. 5) to revoke the previous decree against the Jews because of the irrevocable character of the laws of the Medes and Persians (see 1:19 and note). He can, however, empower Esther to issue another decree in his name to counteract the earlier one. The second decree authorizes the Jews to defend themselves against those who would kill them, which is what they do in 9:2. This is why the outcome of the two decrees is that the attackers are killed instead of the Jews, rather than a simple cancellation of all hostilities.

w: Est 5:3. *x:* Est 3:13; B:6. *y:* Est 3:8–9. *z:* Est 5:14; 6:4. *a:* Est 9:1; Prv 11:8; 26:27; Mt 7:2. *b:* Prv 13:22; Dn 2:48–49. *c:* Est 1:19. *d:* Est 1:19.

signet ring, he sent by mounted couriers riding thoroughbred royal steeds. [11e] In these letters the king authorized the Jews in each and every city to gather and defend their lives, to destroy, kill, and annihilate every armed group of any nation or province that might attack them, along with their wives and children, and to seize their goods as spoil [12]on a single day throughout the provinces of King Ahasuerus, the thirteenth day of the twelfth month, Adar.

CHAPTER E

See RG 222–26

[1]The following is a copy of the letter: "The great King Ahasuerus to the governors of the provinces in the hundred and twenty-seven satrapies from India to Ethiopia, and to those who are loyal to our government: Greetings!

[2]"Many have become more ambitious the more they were showered with honors through the bountiful generosity of their patrons. [3]Not only do they seek to do harm to our subjects but, incapable of dealing with such greatness, they even begin plotting against their own benefactors. [4]Not only do they drive out gratitude from among humankind but, with the arrogant boastfulness of those to whom goodness has no meaning, they suppose they will escape the stern judgment of the all-seeing God.

[5]"Often, too, the fair speech of friends entrusted with the administration of affairs has induced many placed in authority to become accomplices in the shedding of innocent blood, and has involved them in irreparable calamities [6]by deceiving with malicious slander the sincere good will of rulers. [7]This can be verified in the ancient stories that have been handed down to us, but more fully when you consider the wicked deeds perpetrated in your midst by the pestilential influence of those undeserving of authority. [8f] We must provide for the future, so as to render the kingdom undisturbed and peaceful for all people, [9]taking advantage of changing conditions and always deciding matters coming to our attention with equitable treatment.

[10]"For instance, Haman, son of Hammedatha, a Macedonian,* certainly not of Persian blood, and very different from us in generosity, was hospitably received by us. [11]He benefited so much from the good will we have toward all peoples that he was proclaimed 'our father,' before whom everyone was to bow down; and he attained a position second only to the royal throne.[g] [12]But, unable to control his arrogance, he strove to deprive us of kingdom and of life, [13]and by weaving intricate webs of deceit he demanded the destruction of Mordecai, our savior and constant benefactor, and of Esther, our blameless royal consort, together with their whole nation.[h] [14]For by such measures he hoped to catch us defenseless and to transfer the rule of the Persians to the Macedonians. [15]But we find that the Jews, who were doomed to extinction by this archcriminal, are not evildoers, but rather are governed by very just laws [16]and are the children of the Most High, the living God of majesty, who has maintained the kingdom in a flourishing condition for us and for our forebears.

[17]"You will do well, then, to ignore the letter sent by Haman, son of Hammedatha, [18]for he who composed it has been impaled, together with his entire household, before the gates of Susa. Thus swiftly has God, who governs all, brought just punishment upon him.[i]

[19]"You shall exhibit a copy of this letter publicly in every place to certify that the Jews may follow their own laws [20]and that you may help them on the day set for their ruin, the thirteenth day of the twelfth month, Adar, to defend themselves against those who attack them. [21]For God, the ruler of all, has turned that day from one of destruction of the chosen people into one of joy for them. [22]Therefore, you too must celebrate

E:10 Macedonian: throughout the book Haman is identified with terms of contempt—in the Hebrew text as an Agagite (3:1, 10; 8:3, 5; 9:24; cf. note on A:17), thus making him a descendant of Agag, king of the Amalekites, a group hated by the Israelites; in the Greek additions Haman is identified as a Macedonian, reflecting the enmity between the Persians and the Macedonians after Macedonia's conquest of Persia in the fourth century B.C.

---

e: Est 9:1–4. *f:* Est B:2. *g:* Est B:3, 6. *h:* Est A:17. *i:* Est 7:10; 9:14.

this memorable day among your designated feasts with all rejoicing, [23]so that both now and in the future it may be a celebration of deliverance for us and for Persians of good will, but for those who plot against us a reminder of destruction.

[24]"Every city and province without exception that does not observe this decree shall be ruthlessly destroyed with fire and sword, so that it will be left not merely untrodden by people, but even shunned by wild beasts and birds forever."[j]

See RG 222–26

(CHAPTER 8)

[13]A copy of the letter to be promulgated as law in each and every province was published among all the peoples, so that the Jews might be prepared on that day to avenge themselves on their enemies. [14]Couriers mounted on royal steeds sped forth in haste at the king's order, and the decree was promulgated in the royal precinct of Susa.

[15]Mordecai left the king's presence clothed in a royal robe of violet and of white cotton, with a large crown of gold and a mantle of fine crimson linen. The city of Susa shouted with joy,[k] [16]and for the Jews there was splendor and gladness, joy and triumph. [17]In each and every province and in each and every city, wherever the king's order arrived, there was merriment and joy, banqueting and feasting for the Jews. And many of the peoples of the land identified themselves as Jews, for fear of the Jews fell upon them.[l]

See RG 222–26

CHAPTER 9

The Massacre Reversed. [1][m] When the day arrived on which the order decreed by the king was to be carried out, the thirteenth day of the twelfth month, Adar, on which the enemies of the Jews had expected to overpower them, the situation was reversed: the Jews overpowered those who hated them. [2]The Jews mustered in their cities throughout the provinces of King Ahasuerus to attack those who sought to do them harm, and no one could withstand them, for fear of them fell upon all the peoples. [3]Moreover, all the officials of the provinces, the satraps, governors, and royal procurators supported the Jews out of fear of Mordecai; [4]for Mordecai was powerful in the royal palace, and the report was spreading through all the provinces that he was continually growing in power.

[5]The Jews struck down all their enemies with the sword, killing and destroying them; they did to those who hated them as they pleased.[n] [6][o] In the royal precinct of Susa, the Jews killed and destroyed five hundred people. [7]They also killed Parshandatha, Dalphon, Aspatha, [8]Poratha, Adalia, Aridatha, [9]Parmashta, Arisai, Aridai, and Vaizatha, [10][p] the ten sons of Haman, son of Hammedatha, the foe of the Jews. However, they did not engage in plundering.

[11]On the same day, when the number of those killed in the royal precinct of Susa was reported to the king, [12]he said to Queen Esther: "In the royal precinct of Susa the Jews have killed and destroyed five hundred people, as well as the ten sons of Haman. What must they have done in the other royal provinces! You shall again be granted whatever you ask, and whatever you request shall be honored." [13]So Esther said, "If it pleases your majesty, let the Jews in Susa be permitted again tomorrow to act according to today's decree, and let the ten sons of Haman be impaled on stakes." [14]The king then gave an order that this be done, and the decree was published in Susa. So the ten sons of Haman were impaled,[q] [15]and the Jews in Susa mustered again on the fourteenth of the month of Adar and killed three hundred people in Susa. However, they did not engage in plundering.[r]

[16]The other Jews, who dwelt in the royal provinces, also mustered and defended themselves, and obtained rest from their enemies. They killed seventy-five thousand of those who hated them, but they did not engage in plunder.[s] [17]This happened on the thirteenth day of the month of Adar.

j: Est 3:8–9; B:4. *k:* Dn 5:7. *l:* Est 9:27. *m:* Est 8:11–12. *n:* Jdt 15:6. *o:* Est 5:11; B:3; E:11. *p:* Est 9:15; Jdt 15:7, 11. *q:* Est 7:10; E:18. *r:* Est 9:10. *s:* Jdt 15:6.

The Feast of Purim.* On the fourteenth of the month they rested, and made it a day of feasting and rejoicing.
[18]The Jews in Susa, however, mustered on the thirteenth and fourteenth of the month. But on the fifteenth they rested, and made it a day of joyful banqueting. [19]That is why the rural Jews, who dwell in villages, celebrate the fourteenth of the month of Adar as a day of joyful banqueting, a holiday on which they send food to one another.
[20]Mordecai recorded these events and sent letters to all the Jews, both near and far, in all the provinces of King Ahasuerus. [21*] He ordered them to celebrate every year both the fourteenth and the fifteenth of the month of Adar [22]as the days on which the Jews obtained rest from their enemies and as the month which was turned for them from sorrow into joy, from mourning into celebration. They were to observe these days with joyful banqueting, sending food to one another and gifts to the poor. [23*] The Jews adopted as a custom what they had begun doing and what Mordecai had written to them.[t]

VII. Epilogue: The Rise of Mordecai

Summary of the Story. [24u] Haman, son of Hammedatha the Agagite, the foe of all the Jews, had planned to destroy them and had cast the *pur*, or lot, for the time of their defeat and destruction. [25]Yet, when the plot became known to the king, the king ordered in writing that the wicked plan Haman had devised against the Jews should instead be turned against Haman and that he and his sons should be impaled on stakes.[v] [26]And so these days have been named Purim after the word *pur*.

Thus, because of all that was contained in this letter, and because of what they had witnessed and experienced in this event, [27]the Jews established and adopted as a custom for themselves, their descendants, and all who should join them, the perpetual obligation of celebrating these two days every year in the manner prescribed by this letter, and at the time appointed.[w] [28]These days were to be commemorated and kept in every generation, by every clan, in every province, and in every city. These days of Purim were never to be neglected among the Jews, nor forgotten by their descendants.

Esther and Mordecai Act in Concert.*
[29]Queen Esther, daughter of Abihail, and Mordecai the Jew, wrote to confirm with full authority this second letter about Purim, [30]and Mordecai sent documents concerning peace and security to all the Jews in the hundred and twenty-seven provinces of Ahasuerus' kingdom.[x] [31]Thus were established, for their appointed time, these days of Purim which Mordecai the Jew and Queen Esther had designated for the Jews, just as they had previously enjoined upon themselves and upon their descendants the duty of fasting and supplication. [32]The command of Esther confirmed these prescriptions for Purim and was recorded in the book.

CHAPTER 10

See RG 222–26

The Rise of Mordecai Completed.
[1]King Ahasuerus levied a tax on the land and on the islands of the sea. [2]All the acts of his power and valor, as well as a detailed account of the greatness of Mordecai, whom the king promoted, are recorded in the chronicles of the kings of Media and Persia. [3]The Jew Mordecai was next in rank to King Ahasuerus, in high standing among the Jews, pop-

9:17–19 According to Esther, Jewish feasting on the day after the defeat of their enemies establishes the date of the holiday. Since in Susa the fighting lasts for two days, the Jews of that community initially celebrate Purim a day later than Jews elsewhere.

9:21 Mordecai creates a compromise among the Jews by making Purim a two-day festival.

9:23 According to the story, the two-day celebration has its roots in popular observance, which Mordecai's leadership reinforces and regularizes.

9:29–32 In attempting to give the impression of concerted action between Esther and Mordecai, the Hebrew text here presents several unresolved difficulties. Verse 29 makes Mordecai and Esther joint authors of a letter that is ascribed in v. 32 to Esther alone. Verse 31 makes Mordecai and Esther joint authors of a letter that is ascribed in vv. 20–22 to Mordecai alone. Finally, it is difficult to see the purpose of confirming a second letter in the second letter itself.

t: Est 9:29. *u:* Est 3:7; F:10. *v:* Est 6:5–13. *w:* Est 8:12, 17. *x:* Est 9:23–26.

ular with many of his kindred, seeking the good of his people and speaking out on behalf of the welfare of all its descendants.[y]

CHAPTER F

See RG 222–26

Mordecai's Dream Fulfilled. [1z] Then Mordecai said: "This is the work of God. [2] I recall the dream I had about these very things, and not a single detail has been left unfulfilled— [3] the tiny spring that grew into a river, and there was light, and sun, and many waters. The river is Esther, whom the king married and made queen. [4] The two dragons are myself and Haman. [5] The nations are those who assembled to destroy the name of the Jews, [6] but my people is Israel, who cried to God and was saved.

"The Lord saved his people and delivered us from all these evils. God worked signs and great wonders, such as have not occurred among the nations. [7] For this purpose he arranged two lots:* one for the people of God, the second for all the other nations. [8] These two lots were fulfilled in the hour, the time, and the day of judgment before God and among all the nations. [9] God remembered his people and rendered justice to his inheritance.

[10a] "Gathering together with joy and happiness before God, they shall celebrate these days on the fourteenth and fifteenth of the month Adar throughout all future generations of his people Israel."

Colophon.* [11] In the fourth year of the reign of Ptolemy and Cleopatra, Dositheus, who said he was a priest and Levite, and his son Ptolemy brought the present letter of Purim, saying that it was genuine and that Lysimachus, son of Ptolemy, of the community of Jerusalem, had translated it.

F:7 Two lots: this passage of the Greek text gives an additional interpretation of the feast. The two lots are drawn by God to determine, respectively, the destiny of Israel and that of the nations; contrast with 3:7 of the Hebrew text.

F:11 Several "Ptolemies" (Greek kings reigning in Egypt) had wives named Cleopatra. This postscript dates the Greek version somewhere between 116 B.C. and 48 B.C.

y: 2 Mc 15:14. *z:* Est A:4–10. *a:* Est 3:7; 9:17–18, 21, 24–28.

See RG 226–31

The First Book of Maccabees

The name Maccabee, probably meaning "hammer," is actually applied in the Books of Maccabees to only one man, Judas, third son of the priest Mattathias and first leader of the revolt against the Seleucid kings who persecuted the Jews (1 Mc 2:4, 66; 2 Mc 8:5, 16; 10:1, 16). Traditionally the name has come to be extended to the brothers of Judas, his supporters, and even to other Jewish heroes of the period, such as the seven brothers (2 Mc 7).

The two Books of Maccabees contain independent accounts of events (in part identical) that accompanied the attempted suppression of Judaism in Palestine in the second century B.C. The vigorous reaction to this attempt established for a time the religious and political independence of the Jews.

First Maccabees was written about 100 B.C., in Hebrew, but the original has not come down to us. Instead, we have an early, pre-Christian, Greek translation full of Hebrew idioms. The author, probably a Palestinian Jew, is unknown. He was familiar with the traditions and sacred books of his people and had access to much reliable information on their recent history (from 175 to 134 B.C.). He may well have played some part in it himself in his youth. His purpose in writing is to record the deliverance of Israel that God worked through the family of Mattathias (5:62)—especially through his three sons, Judas, Jonathan, and Simon, and his grandson, John Hyrcanus. The writer compares their virtues and their exploits with those of Israel's ancient heroes, the Judges, Samuel, and David.

There are seven poetic sections in the book that imitate the style of classical Hebrew poetry: four laments (1:25–28, 36–40; 2:7–13; 3:45), and three hymns of praise of "our fathers" (2:51–64), of Judas (3:3–9), and of Simon (14:4–15). The doctrine expressed in the book is the customary belief of Israel, without the new developments which appear in 2 Maccabees and Daniel. The people of Israel have been specially chosen by the one true God as covenant-partner, and they alone are privileged to know and worship God, their eternal benefactor and unfailing source of help. The people, in turn, must worship the Lord alone and observe exactly the precepts of the law given to them. The rededication of the Jerusalem Temple described in 4:36–59 (see 2 Mc 10:1–8) is the origin of the Jewish feast of Hanukkah.

Unlike the Second Book of Maccabees, there is no doctrine of individual immortality except in the survival of one's name and fame, nor does the book express any messianic expectation, though messianic images are applied historically to "the days of Simon" (1 Mc 14:4–17). In true Deuteronomic tradition, the author insists on fidelity to the law as the expression of Israel's love for God. The contest which he describes is a struggle, not simply between Jew and Gentile, but between those who would uphold the law and those, Jews or Gentiles, who would destroy it. His severest condemnation goes, not to the Seleucid politicians, but to the lawless apostates among his own people, adversaries of Judas and his brothers, who are models of faith and loyalty.

The first and second Books of Maccabees, though regarded by Jews and Protestants as apocryphal, i.e., not inspired Scripture, because not contained in the Jewish list of books drawn up at the end of the first century A.D., have always been accepted by the Catholic Church as inspired and are called "deuterocanonical" to indicate that they are canonical even though disputed by some.

First Maccabees can be divided as follows:

I. Crisis and Response (1:1–2:70)
II. Leadership of Judas Maccabeus (3:1–9:22)
III. Leadership of Jonathan (9:23–12:53)
IV. Leadership of Simon (13:1–16:24)

I. Crisis and Response

CHAPTER 1

See RG 227

From Alexander to Antiochus. 1a After Alexander the Macedonian, Philip's son,
who came from the land of Kittim,* had defeated Darius, king of the Persians and
Medes, he became king in his place, having
first ruled in Greece. 2 He fought many battles, captured fortresses, and put the kings of
the earth to death. 3 He advanced to the ends
of the earth, gathering plunder from many
nations; the earth fell silent before him, and
his heart became proud and arrogant. 4 He
collected a very strong army and won dominion over provinces, nations, and rulers,
and they paid him tribute.
5 But after all this he took to his bed, realizing that he was going to die. 6 So he summoned his noblest officers, who had been
brought up with him from his youth, and divided his kingdom among them while he
was still alive. 7 Alexander had reigned
twelve years* when he died.
8 So his officers took over his kingdom,
each in his own territory, 9 and after his death
they all put on diadems,* and so did their
sons after them for many years, multiplying
evils on the earth.
10 There sprang from these a sinful offshoot, Antiochus Epiphanes, son of King
Antiochus, once a hostage at Rome. He became king in the one hundred and thirty-seventh year* of the kingdom of the Greeks.
Lawless Jews. 11b In those days there appeared in Israel transgressors of the law who
seduced many, saying: "Let us go and make
a covenant with the Gentiles all around us;

1:1 Land of Kittim: Greece. The name referred originally to inhabitants of Kiti, capital of the isle of Cyprus, then to any Cypriots (Is 23:1; Jer 2:10), later to Greeks in general, and finally even to Romans. See note on Dn 11:30. **Darius**: Darius III, Codoman (336–331 B.C.).

1:7 Twelve years: 336–323 B.C. The division of the empire was not fully settled until 305 B.C.

1:9 Diadems: decorated bands of white cloth worn around the head, symbolizing kingship. The Ptolemies, based in Egypt, controlled Judea until 198 B.C., when they were replaced by the Seleucids, based in Syria.

1:10 The one hundred and thirty-seventh year: Antiochus IV seized the throne in September, 175 B.C. Dates are given in this book according to the beginning of the Seleucid era, which however was reckoned in two different ways. Antiochians considered this date to be October, 312 B.C. (Syrian calendar), while Babylonians and Jewish priests accepted April, 311 B.C. as the commencement of the era (Temple calendar). The author of 1 Maccabees dates political events by the Syrian calendar but religious events by the Temple calendar. Accordingly, the civil New Year occurred variously in September or October, the religious New Year in March or April.

a: Dn 8:20–22; 11:3–4, 21. *b:* 2 Mc 4:12–17.

since we separated from them, many evils have come upon us." 12 The proposal was agreeable; 13 some from among the people promptly went to the king, and he authorized them to introduce the ordinances of the Gentiles. 14 Thereupon they built a gymnasium* in Jerusalem according to the Gentile custom. 15 They disguised their circumcision and abandoned the holy covenant; they allied themselves with the Gentiles and sold themselves to wrongdoing.

Antiochus in Egypt. 16[c] When his kingdom seemed secure, Antiochus undertook to become king of the land of Egypt and to rule over both kingdoms. 17 He invaded Egypt with a strong force, with chariots, elephants* and cavalry, and with a large fleet, 18 to make war on Ptolemy,* king of Egypt. Ptolemy was frightened at his presence and fled, and many were wounded and fell dead. 19 The fortified cities in the land of Egypt were captured, and Antiochus plundered the land of Egypt.

Robbery of the Temple. 20[d] After Antiochus had defeated Egypt in the one hundred and forty-third year,* he returned and went up against Israel and against Jerusalem with a strong force. 21 He insolently entered the sanctuary* and took away the golden altar, the lampstand for the light with all its utensils, 22 the offering table, the cups and bowls, the golden censers, and the curtain. The cornices and the golden ornament on the facade of the temple—he stripped it all off. 23 And he took away the silver and gold and the precious vessels; he also took all the hidden treasures he could find. 24 Taking all this, he went back to his own country. He shed much blood and spoke with great arrogance.

25 And there was great mourning
throughout all Israel,
26 and the rulers and the elders groaned.
Young women and men languished,
and the beauty of the women faded.
27 Every bridegroom took up lamentation,
while the bride sitting in her chamber
mourned,
28 And the land quaked on account of its
inhabitants,
and all the house of Jacob was clothed
with shame.

Attack and Occupation. 29[e] Two years later, the king sent the Mysian commander* to the cities of Judah, and he came to Jerusalem with a strong force. 30 He spoke to them deceitfully in peaceful terms, and they believed him. Then he attacked the city suddenly, in a great onslaught, and destroyed many of the people in Israel. 31 He plundered the city and set fire to it, demolished its houses and its surrounding walls. 32 And they took captive the women and children, and seized the animals. 33 Then they built up the City of David with a high, strong wall and strong towers, and it became their citadel.* 34 There they installed a sinful race, transgressors of the law, who fortified themselves inside it. 35 They stored up weapons and provisions, depositing there the plunder they had collected from Jerusalem, and they became a great snare.

36 The citadel became an ambush against
the sanctuary,
and a wicked adversary to Israel at all
times.
37 They shed innocent blood around the
sanctuary;
they defiled the sanctuary.

1:14 Gymnasium: symbol and center of Greek athletic and intellectual life, it was the chief instrument of Hellenistic culture. Jewish youth were attracted by sports and encouraged to join youth clubs. They received training in military skills and in the duties of citizens. Many were won over to paganism, and some even sought surgical correction of their circumcision (since physical exercise was carried out in nudity).

1:17 Elephants: an important part of Seleucid armament (cf. 6:34–37).

1:18 Ptolemy VI Philometer, a nephew of Antiochus.

1:20 Defeated Egypt in the one hundred and forty-third year: 169 B.C. No mention is made in 1 Maccabees of the second expedition to Egypt a year later, described in 2 Mc 5:1, 11; Dn 11:25, 29 records both.

1:21 Entered the sanctuary: to pay his soldiers, Antiochus seized the sacred vessels and the money deposited at the Temple (see 2 Mc 3:10–11).

1:29 Mysian commander: in 2 Mc 5:24 he is identified as "Apollonius, commander of the Mysians" (mercenaries from Asia Minor). The Greek text of 1 Mc 1:29 ("chief collector of tribute") reflects a misreading of the Hebrew original.

1:33 Citadel: literally, *akra* means fortress. This was a garrison for foreign troops and renegade Jews that was established near the Temple area and fell to Simon only in 141 B.C. (13:49–50).

c: 2 Mc 5:1–10; Dn 11:25–30. *d:* 2 Mc 5:11–21. *e:* 2 Mc 5:24–26.

38 Because of them the inhabitants of
Jerusalem fled away,
she became the abode of strangers.
She became a stranger to her own
offspring,
and her children forsook her.
39 [f] Her sanctuary became desolate as a
wilderness;
her feasts were turned into mourning,
Her sabbaths to shame,
her honor to contempt.
40 As her glory had been, so great was her
dishonor:
her exaltation was turned into
mourning.

Religious Persecution. 41 [g] Then the king wrote to his whole kingdom that all should be one people, 42 and abandon their particular customs. All the Gentiles conformed to the command of the king, 43 and many Israelites delighted in his religion; they sacrificed to idols and profaned the sabbath.

44 The king sent letters by messenger to Jerusalem and to the cities of Judah, ordering them to follow customs foreign to their land; 45 to prohibit burnt offerings, sacrifices, and libations in the sanctuary, to profane the sabbaths and feast days, 46 to desecrate the sanctuary and the sacred ministers, 47 to build pagan altars and temples and shrines, to sacrifice swine and unclean animals, 48 to leave their sons uncircumcised, and to defile themselves with every kind of impurity and abomination; 49 so that they might forget the law and change all its ordinances. 50 Whoever refused to act according to the command of the king was to be put to death.[h]

51 In words such as these he wrote to his whole kingdom. He appointed inspectors over all the people, and he ordered the cities of Judah to offer sacrifices, each city in turn. 52 Many of the people, those who abandoned the law, joined them and committed evil in the land. 53 They drove Israel into hiding, wherever places of refuge could be found.

54 On the fifteenth day of the month Kislev, in the year one hundred and forty-five,* the king erected the desolating abomination upon the altar of burnt offerings, and in the surrounding cities of Judah they built pagan altars.[i] 55 They also burned incense at the doors of houses and in the streets. 56 Any scrolls of the law* that they found they tore up and burned. 57 Whoever was found with a scroll of the covenant, and whoever observed the law, was condemned to death by royal decree. 58 So they used their power against Israel, against those who were caught, each month, in the cities. 59 On the twenty-fifth day of each month they sacrificed on the pagan altar that was over the altar of burnt offerings. 60 In keeping with the decree, they put to death women who had their children circumcised, 61 and they hung their babies from their necks; their families also and those who had circumcised them were killed.

62 But many in Israel were determined and resolved in their hearts not to eat anything unclean; 63 they preferred to die rather than to be defiled with food or to profane the holy covenant; and they did die. 64 And very great wrath came upon Israel.

CHAPTER 2

See RG 227–28

Mattathias and His Sons. 1 In those days Mattathias, son of John, son of Simeon, a priest of the family of Joarib,[j] left Jerusalem and settled in Modein.* 2 He had five sons: John, who was called Gaddi; 3 Simon, who was called Thassi; 4 Judas, who was called Maccabeus; 5 Eleazar, who was called Avaran; and Jonathan, who was called Apphus. 6 When he saw the sacrileges that were being committed in Judah and in Jerusalem, 7 he said:

1:54 Fifteenth day of the month Kislev, in the year one hundred and forty-five: December 6, 167 B.C. **Desolating abomination**: in the original Hebrew, a contemptuous pun on the title "Lord of heaven" given to the god to whom an image or perhaps an altar was erected upon the altar of burnt offerings in the Temple of Jerusalem; cf. Dn 9:27; 11:31.

1:56 Scrolls of the law: one or more of the first five books of the Old Testament, the traditional law of Israel.

2:1 Modein: a village about twenty miles northwest of Jerusalem, the family's ancestral home (see 2:70; 9:19).

f: Am 8:10; Tb 2:6. *g:* 2 Mc 6:1–11. *h:* 1 Mc 2:29–38; 2 Mc 6:18–7:42. *i:* Dn 9:27; 11:31; Mk 13:14. *j:* 1 Chr 9:10; 24:7.

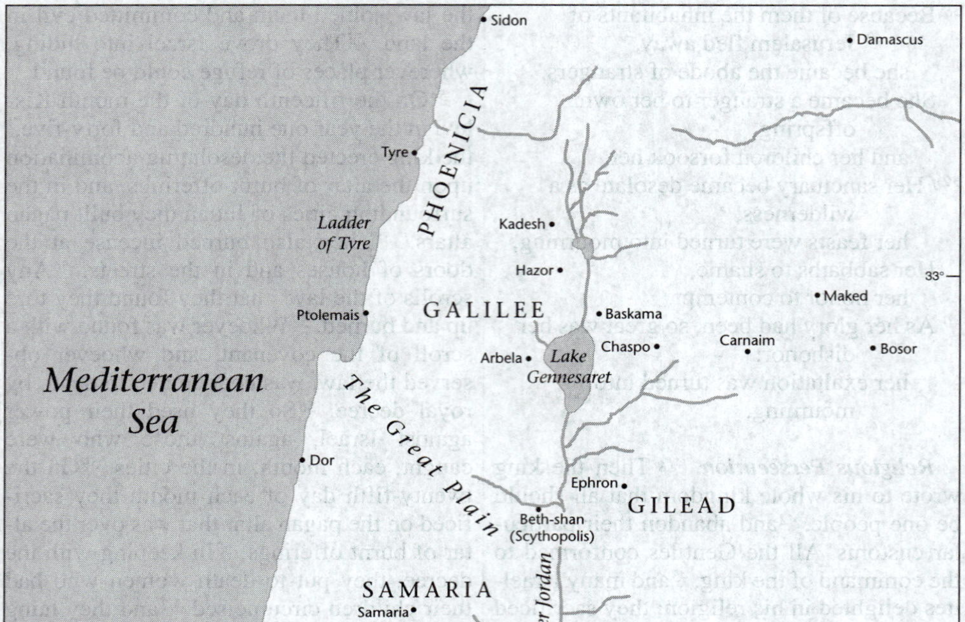

The Campaigns of the Maccabees and Hasmoneans

"Woe is me! Why was I born
to see the ruin of my people,
the ruin of the holy city—
To dwell there
as it was given into the hands of enemies,
the sanctuary into the hands of
strangers?

8 Her temple has become like a man
disgraced,
9 her glorious vessels carried off as spoils,
Her infants murdered in her streets,
her youths by the sword of the enemy.[k]
10 What nation has not taken its share of her
realm,

k: Lam 2:11, 21.

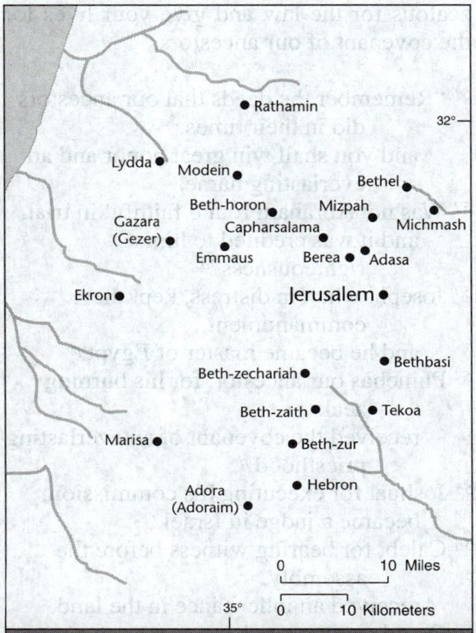

The Jerusalem Vicinity

and laid its hand on her spoils?
11 All her adornment has been taken away.
Once free, she has become a slave.
12 We see our sanctuary laid waste,
our beauty, our glory.
The Gentiles have defiled them!
13 Why are we still alive?"

14 Then Mattathias and his sons tore their
garments, put on sackcloth, and mourned
bitterly.

Pagan Worship Refused and Resisted.
15 The officers of the king in charge of enforcing the apostasy came to the city of
Modein to make them sacrifice. 16 Many of
Israel joined them, but Mattathias and his
sons drew together. 17 Then the officers of
the king addressed Mattathias: "You are a
leader, an honorable and great man in this
city, supported by sons and kindred. 18 Come
now, be the first to obey the king's command, as all the Gentiles and Judeans and
those who are left in Jerusalem have done.
Then you and your sons shall be numbered
among the King's Friends,* and you and
your sons shall be honored with silver and
gold and many gifts."

19 But Mattathias answered in a loud voice:
"Although all the Gentiles in the king's realm
obey him, so that they forsake the religion of
their ancestors and consent to the king's orders, 20 yet I and my sons and my kindred will
keep to the covenant of our ancestors.
21 Heaven forbid that we should forsake the
law and the commandments. 22 We will not
obey the words of the king by departing from
our religion in the slightest degree."

23 As he finished saying these words, a certain Jew came forward in the sight of all to
offer sacrifice on the altar in Modein according to the king's order. 24 When Mattathias
saw him, he was filled with zeal; his heart
was moved and his just fury was aroused; he
sprang forward and killed him upon the altar.
25 At the same time, he also killed the messenger of the king who was forcing them to
sacrifice, and he tore down the altar. 26 Thus
he showed his zeal for the law, just as Phinehas did with Zimri, son of Salu.[l]

27 Then Mattathias cried out in the city, "Let
everyone who is zealous for the law and who
stands by the covenant follow me!" 28 Then he
and his sons fled to the mountains, leaving
behind in the city all their possessions.[m]

29 At that time many who sought righteousness and justice went out into the wilderness* to settle there, 30 they and their children, their wives and their animals, because
misfortunes pressed so hard on them. 31 It
was reported to the officers and soldiers of
the king who were in the City of David, in
Jerusalem, that those who had flouted the
king's order had gone out to secret refuges in
the wilderness. 32[n] Many hurried out after
them, and having caught up with them,
camped opposite and prepared to attack
them on the sabbath. 33 The pursuers said to

2:18 The King's Friends: a regular order of nobility at Hellenistic courts (see 10:65; 11:27).

2:29 The wilderness: the sparsely inhabited mountain country southward from Jerusalem and west of the Dead Sea, in the region where the Dead Sea Scrolls were found.

l: Nm 25:6–15; Ps 106:28–31; Sir 45:23–24; 1 Mc 2:54. *m:* 2 Mc 5:27. *n:* 2 Mc 6:11.

them, "Enough of this! Come out and obey
the king's command, and you will live."
34 But they replied, "We will not come out,
nor will we obey the king's command to profane the sabbath." 35 Then the enemy attacked them at once. 36 But they did not retaliate; they neither threw stones, nor
blocked up their secret refuges. 37 They said,
"Let us all die in innocence; heaven and
earth are our witnesses that you destroy us
unjustly." 38 So the officers and soldiers attacked them on the sabbath, and they died
with their wives, their children and their animals, to the number of a thousand persons.
39 When Mattathias and his friends heard
of it, they mourned deeply for them. 40 They
said to one another, "If we all do as our kindred have done, and do not fight against the
Gentiles for our lives and our laws, they will
soon destroy us from the earth." 41 So on that
day they came to this decision: "Let us fight
against anyone who attacks us on the sabbath, so that we may not all die as our kindred died in their secret refuges."
42 Then they were joined by a group of
Hasideans,* mighty warriors of Israel, all of
them devoted to the law. 43 And all those who
were fleeing from the persecutions joined
them and supported them. 44 They gathered
an army and struck down sinners in their
wrath and the lawless in their anger, and the
survivors fled to the Gentiles for safety.
45 Mattathias and his friends went about and
tore down the pagan altars; 46 they also
forcibly circumcised any uncircumcised
boys whom they found in the territory of Israel. 47 They put to flight the arrogant, and
the work prospered in their hands. 48 They
saved the law from the hands of the Gentiles
and of the kings and did not let the sinner triumph.

Farewell of Mattathias. 49 When the time
came for Mattathias to die, he said to his
sons: "Arrogance and scorn have now
grown strong; it is a time of disaster and violent wrath. 50 Therefore, my children, be
zealous for the law and give your lives for
the covenant of our ancestors.

51 "Remember the deeds that our ancestors
did in their times,
and you shall win great honor and an
everlasting name.
52 Was not Abraham found faithful in trial,
and it was credited to him as
righteousness?[o]
53 Joseph, when in distress, kept the
commandment,
and he became master of Egypt.[p]
54 Phinehas our ancestor, for his burning
zeal,
received the covenant of an everlasting
priesthood.[q]
55 Joshua, for executing his commission,
became a judge in Israel.[r]
56 Caleb, for bearing witness before the
assembly,
received an inheritance in the land.[s]
57 David, for his loyalty,
received as a heritage a throne of
eternal kingship.[t]
58 Elijah, for his burning zeal for the law,
was taken up to heaven.[u]
59 Hananiah, Azariah and Mishael, for their
faith,
were saved from the fire.[v]
60 Daniel, for his innocence,
was delivered from the mouths of
lions.[w]
61 And so, consider this from generation to
generation,
that none who hope in Heaven shall
fail in strength.
62 Do not fear the words of sinners,
for their glory ends in corruption and
worms.[x]
63 Today exalted, tomorrow not to be found,
they have returned to dust,
their schemes have perished.
64 Children! be courageous and strong in
keeping the law,
for by it you shall be honored.

2:42 Hasideans: in Hebrew *hasidim*, "pious ones," a militant religious group devoted to the strict observance of the law. They first supported the Maccabean movement, but subsequently opposed it, regarding it as too political (see 7:12–18).

o: Gn 15:6; 22:1–18. *p:* Gn 39:7–10; 41:39–43. *q:* Nm 25:6–15. *r:* Jos 1, 2, 5. *s:* Nm 13:30; 14:6–9, 24; Jos 14:14. *t:* 2 Sm 2:4; 7:16. *u:* 1 Kgs 19:10, 14; 2 Kgs 2:11. *v:* Dn 3:26. *w:* Dn 6:23. *x:* 2 Mc 9:5–10, 28.

65“Here is your brother Simeon who I
know is a wise counselor; listen to him always, and he will be a father to you. 66And
Judas Maccabeus, a mighty warrior from his
youth, shall be the leader of your army and
wage the war against the nations. 67Gather
about you all who observe the law, and
avenge your people. 68Pay back the Gentiles
what they deserve, and observe the precepts
of the law.”

69Then he blessed them, and he was gathered to his ancestors. 70He died in the year
one hundred and forty-six,* and was buried
in the tombs of his ancestors in Modein, and
all Israel mourned him greatly.

II. Leadership of Judas Maccabeus

CHAPTER 3

See RG 229

Judas and His Early Victories. 1Then
his son Judas, who was called Maccabeus,
took his place. 2All his brothers and all who
had joined his father supported him, and
they gladly carried on Israel’s war.

3 He spread abroad the glory of his people,
and put on his breastplate like a giant.
He armed himself with weapons of war;
he fought battles and protected the
camp with his sword.
4 In his deeds he was like a lion,
like a young lion roaring for prey.
5 He pursued the lawless, hunting them
out,
and those who troubled his people he
destroyed by fire.
6 The lawless were cowed by fear of him,
and all evildoers were dismayed.
By his hand deliverance was happily
achieved,
7 and he afflicted many kings.
He gave joy to Jacob by his deeds,
and his memory is blessed forever.
8 He went about the cities of Judah
destroying the renegades there.
He turned away wrath from Israel,
9 was renowned to the ends of the earth;
and gathered together those who were
perishing.

10Then Apollonius* gathered together the
Gentiles, along with a large army from
Samaria, to fight against Israel. 11When Judas learned of it, he went out to meet him
and struck and killed him. Many fell
wounded, and the rest fled. 12They took their
spoils, and Judas took the sword of Apollonius and fought with it the rest of his life.

13But Seron, commander of the Syrian
army, heard that Judas had mustered an assembly of faithful men ready for war. 14So he
said, “I will make a name for myself and win
honor in the kingdom. I will wage war against
Judas and his followers, who have despised
the king’s command.” 15And again a large
company of renegades advanced with him to
help him take revenge on the Israelites.

16When he reached the ascent of Beth-horon,* Judas went out to meet him with a few
men. 17But when they saw the army coming
against them, they said to Judas: “How can
we, few as we are, fight such a strong host as
this? Besides, we are weak since we have
not eaten today.” 18But Judas said: “Many
are easily hemmed in by a few; in the sight
of Heaven there is no difference between deliverance by many or by few; 19for victory in
war does not depend upon the size of the
army, but on strength that comes from
Heaven.[y] 20With great presumption and lawlessness they come against us to destroy us
and our wives and children and to despoil
us; 21but we are fighting for our lives and our
laws. 22He* will crush them before us; so do
not fear them.” 23When he finished speaking, he rushed suddenly upon Seron and his
army, who were crushed before him. 24He
pursued Seron down the descent of Beth-horon into the plain. About eight hundred* of
their men fell, and the rest fled to the land of

2:70 In the year one hundred and forty-six: 166 B.C.

3:10 Apollonius: the Mysian commander mentioned in 1 Mc 1:29; 2 Mc 5:24.

3:16 Beth-horon: the famous pass leading up from the coastal plain to the Judean hill country. Here Joshua won an important battle (Jos 10:10–11), and in A.D. 66 a Roman force under Cestius was trapped and massacred.

3:22 He: out of reverence for God, the author of 1 Maccabees prefers to use the pronoun and other expressions, such as “Heaven,” instead of the divine name. Cf. v. 50.

3:24 About eight hundred: the figures given in this book for strength of armies and number of casualties are not always

y: 1 Sm 14:6.

the Philistines. [25]Then Judas and his brothers began to be feared, and dread fell upon the Gentiles about them. [26]His fame reached the king, and the Gentiles talked about the battles of Judas.

The King's Strategy. [27]When King Antiochus heard these reports, he was filled with rage; so he ordered that all the forces of his kingdom be gathered, a very strong army. [28]He opened his treasury, gave his soldiers a year's pay, and commanded them to be prepared for anything. [29]But then he saw that this exhausted the money in his treasury; moreover the tribute from the province was small because of the dissension and distress he had brought upon the land by abolishing the laws which had been in effect from of old. [30]He feared that, as had happened once or twice, he would not have enough for his expenses and for the gifts that he was accustomed to give with a lavish hand—more so than all previous kings. [31]Greatly perplexed, he decided to go to Persia and levy tribute on those provinces, and so raise a large sum of money.

[32]He left Lysias, a noble of royal descent, in charge of the king's affairs from the Euphrates River to the frontier of Egypt, [33]and commissioned him to take care of his son Antiochus until his return. [34]He entrusted to him half of his forces, and the elephants, and gave him instructions concerning everything he wanted done. As for the inhabitants of Judea and Jerusalem, [35]Lysias was to send an army against them to crush and destroy the power of Israel and the remnant of Jerusalem and efface their memory from the place. [36]He was to settle foreigners in all their territory and distribute their land by lot. [37]* The king took the remaining half of the army and set out from Antioch, his capital, in the year one hundred and forty-seven; he crossed the Euphrates River and went through the provinces beyond.

Preparations for Battle. [38][z] Lysias chose Ptolemy, son of Dorymenes, and Nicanor* and Gorgias, powerful men among the King's Friends, [39]and with them he sent forty thousand foot soldiers and seven thousand cavalry to invade and ravage the land of Judah according to the king's orders. [40]Setting out with their whole force, they came and pitched their camp near Emmaus* in the plain. [41]When the merchants of the region heard of their prowess, they came to the camp, bringing a huge sum of silver and gold, along with fetters, to buy the Israelites as slaves. A force from Edom and from Philistia joined with them.

[42]Judas and his brothers saw that evils had multiplied and that armies were encamped within their territory. They learned of the orders which the king had given to destroy and utterly wipe out the people. [43]So they said to one another, "Let us raise our people from their ruin and fight for them and for our sanctuary!"

[44]The assembly gathered together to prepare for battle and to pray and ask for mercy and compassion.

[45] Jerusalem was uninhabited, like a
    wilderness;
  not one of her children came in or
    went out.
The sanctuary was trampled on,
  and foreigners were in the citadel;
  it was a habitation for Gentiles.
Joy had disappeared from Jacob,
  and the flute and the harp were silent.

[46]*Thus they assembled and went to Mizpah near Jerusalem, because formerly at Mizpah there was a place of prayer for Israel.[a] [47]That day they fasted and wore sackcloth; they sprinkled ashes on their heads and tore their garments. [48]They unrolled the scroll of the law, to learn about the things for

to be taken literally. In accordance with biblical usage, they indicate rather the importance of the battle described or the greatness of the victory.

3:37 This expedition, in the spring of 165 B.C., resulted in failure; cf. chap. 6.

3:38 Nicanor: perhaps the leader of another attack against the Jews four years later; he was finally killed by Judas; cf. 7:26–46.

3:40 Emmaus: probably not the village mentioned in Lk 24:13 but a settlement about twenty miles west of Jerusalem at the edge of the hill country.

3:46 Mizpah . . . a place of prayer for Israel: a holy place of great antiquity eight miles north and slightly west of Jerusalem. It was here that Samuel began to judge the Israelites (1 Sm 7:5–11; 10:17).

z: 2 Mc 8:9–23. *a:* Jgs 20:1; 1 Sm 7:5–9; 10:17.

which the Gentiles consulted the images of
their idols.* 49They brought with them the
priestly garments, the first fruits, and the
tithes; and they brought forward the
nazirites* [b] who had completed the time of
their vows. 50And they cried aloud to
Heaven: "What shall we do with these, and
where shall we take them? 51For your sanctuary has been trampled on and profaned,
and your priests are in mourning and humbled. 52Now the Gentiles are gathered together against us to destroy us. You know
what they plot against us. 53How shall we be
able to resist them unless you help us?"
54Then they blew the trumpets and cried out
loudly.

55After this Judas appointed officers for
the people, over thousands, over hundreds,
over fifties, and over tens. 56He proclaimed
that those who were building houses, or
were just married, or were planting vineyards, and those who were afraid, could each
return home, according to the law.[c] 57Then
the army moved off, and they camped to the
south of Emmaus. 58Judas said: "Arm yourselves and be brave; in the morning be ready
to fight these Gentiles who have assembled
against us to destroy us and our sanctuary.
59It is better for us to die in battle than to witness the evils befalling our nation and our
sanctuary. 60Whatever is willed in heaven
will be done."

See RG 229

CHAPTER 4

Victory over Gorgias. 1Now Gorgias
took five thousand infantry and a thousand
picked cavalry, and this detachment set out
at night 2in order to fall upon the camp of the
Jews in a surprise attack. Some from the
citadel were his guides. 3Judas heard of it
and himself set out with his soldiers to attack
the king's army at Emmaus 4while these
forces were still scattered away from the
camp. 5During the night Gorgias came into
the camp of Judas, and found no one there;
so he sought them in the mountains, saying,
"They are fleeing from us."

6But at daybreak Judas appeared in the
plain with three thousand men; furthermore
they lacked the helmets and swords they
wanted. 7They saw the army of the Gentiles,* strong, breastplated, and flanked with
cavalry, and made up of experienced soldiers. 8[d] Judas said to the men with him: "Do
not fear their numbers or dread their attack.
9Remember how our ancestors were saved
in the Red Sea, when Pharaoh pursued them
with an army.[e] 10So now let us cry to Heaven
in the hope that he will favor us, remember
the covenant with our ancestors, and destroy
this army before us today. 11All the Gentiles
shall know that there is One who redeems
and delivers Israel."

12When the foreigners looked up and saw
them marching toward them, 13they came
out of their camp for battle. The men with
Judas blew the trumpet, and 14joined the battle. They crushed the Gentiles, who fled toward the plain. 15Their whole rear guard fell
by the sword, and they were pursued as far
as Gazara* and the plains of Idumaea, to
Azotus and Jamnia. About three thousand of
their men fell.

16When Judas and the army returned from
the pursuit, 17he said to the people: "Do not
be greedy for plunder; for there is a fight
ahead of us, 18and Gorgias and his army are
near us on the mountain. But now stand firm
against our enemies and fight them. Afterward you can freely take the plunder."

19As Judas was finishing this speech, a detachment* appeared, looking down from the
mountain. 20They saw that their army had
been put to flight and their camp was burning. The smoke they saw revealed what had
happened. 21When they realized this, they
completely lost heart; and when they also
saw the army of Judas in the plain ready to

3:48 To learn . . . idols: favorable omens for the coming battle. A contrast is intended between the idol worship of the pagans and the consultation of the word of God by the Jews; cf. 2 Mc 8:23.

3:49 Nazirites: see note on Nm 6:2–21.

4:7 Army of the Gentiles: the main force; cf. 3:39–40; 4:1–2.

4:15 Gazara: Gezer of the Hebrew Bible, five miles northwest of Emmaus; **Azotus**, Hebrew Ashdod, lay to the southwest; **and Jamnia**, Hebrew Jabneel (Jos 15:11) or Jabneh (2 Chr 26:6), to the west of Gazara.

4:19 A detachment: i.e., Gorgias' force; cf. vv. 1–5.

b: Nm 6:1–21. *c:* Dt 20:5–8. *d:* Dt 20:3–4; Jgs 7:2–3. *e:* Ex 14:21–31.

attack, 22they all fled to the land of the foreigners.*

23Then Judas went back to plunder the camp, and they took much gold and silver, cloth dyed blue and marine purple, and great treasure. 24As they returned, they were singing hymns and glorifying Heaven, "who is good, whose mercy endures forever."[f] 25Thus Israel experienced a great deliverance that day.

Victory over Lysias. 26[g] But those of the foreigners who had escaped went and told Lysias all that had occurred. 27When he heard it he was disturbed and discouraged, because things had not turned out in Israel as he intended and as the king had ordered.

28So the following year he gathered together sixty thousand picked men and five thousand cavalry, to fight them. 29They came into Idumea and camped at Beth-zur,* and Judas met them with ten thousand men. 30Seeing that the army was strong, he prayed thus:

"Blessed are you, Savior of Israel, who crushed the attack of the mighty one by the hand of your servant David and delivered the foreign camp into the hand of Jonathan, the son of Saul, and his armor-bearer.[h] 31Give this army into the hands of your people Israel; make them ashamed of their troops and their cavalry. 32Strike them with cowardice, weaken the boldness of their strength, and let them tremble at their own destruction. 33Strike them down by the sword of those who love you, that all who know your name may sing your praise."

34Then they engaged in battle, and about five thousand of Lysias' army fell in hand-to-hand fighting. 35* When Lysias saw the tide of the battle turning, and the increased boldness of Judas, whose men were ready either to live or to die nobly, he withdrew to Antioch and began to recruit mercenaries so as to return to Judea with greater numbers.[i]

Purification and Rededication of the Temple. 36[j] Then Judas and his brothers said, "Now that our enemies have been crushed, let us go up to purify the sanctuary* and rededicate it." 37So the whole army assembled, and went up to Mount Zion. 38They found the sanctuary desolate, the altar desecrated, the gates burnt, weeds growing in the courts as in a thicket or on some mountain, and the priests' chambers demolished.[k] 39Then they tore their garments and made great lamentation; they sprinkled their heads with ashes 40and prostrated themselves. And when the signal was given with trumpets, they cried out to Heaven.

41Judas appointed men to attack those in the citadel, while he purified the sanctuary. 42He chose blameless priests, devoted to the law; 43these purified the sanctuary and carried away the stones of the defilement to an unclean place. 44They deliberated what ought to be done with the altar for burnt offerings that had been desecrated.[l] 45They decided it best to tear it down, lest it be a lasting shame to them that the Gentiles had defiled it; so they tore down the altar. 46They stored the stones in a suitable place on the temple mount, until the coming of a prophet who could determine what to do with them.[m] 47Then they took uncut stones, according to the law, and built a new altar like the former one.[n] 48They also repaired the sanctuary and the interior of the temple and consecrated the courts. 49They made new sacred vessels and brought the lampstand, the altar of incense, and the table into the temple.[o] 50Then they burned incense on the altar and lighted the lamps on the lampstand, and these illuminated the temple. 51They also put loaves on the table and hung up the curtains. Thus they finished all the work they had undertaken.

52They rose early on the morning of the twenty-fifth day of the ninth month, that is,

4:22 The land of the foreigners: i.e., territory controlled by the Syrians. The Greek term used here is the same as that used throughout 1–2 Samuel in Greek for Philistine territory and intends to compare Maccabean victories to those of Saul and David.

4:29 Beth-zur: an important frontier city (between Judea and Idumea) in the mountain area, fifteen miles south of Jerusalem.

4:35 According to 2 Mc 11:13–15, peace negotiations followed between Lysias and Judas.

4:36 The sanctuary: the whole Temple area with its walls, courts and outbuildings, to be distinguished from the Temple proper, the oblong edifice with porch, main room and inner shrine.

f: Ps 118:1–4, 29; 136. *g:* 2 Mc 11:1–15. *h:* 1 Sm 17:48–58. *i:* 1 Mc 6:28–31. *j:* 2 Mc 10:1–8. *k:* Ps 74:2–7. *l:* 1 Kgs 8:64. *m:* 1 Mc 14:41; Dt 18:15. *n:* Ex 20:25. *o:* Ex 25:23–39; 30:1–6.

the month of Kislev, in the year one hundred and forty-eight,* [53]and offered sacrifice according to the law on the new altar for burnt offerings that they had made.[p] [54]On the anniversary of the day on which the Gentiles had desecrated it, on that very day it was rededicated with songs, harps, lyres, and cymbals. [55]All the people prostrated themselves and adored and praised Heaven, who had given them success.

[56]For eight days they celebrated the dedication of the altar and joyfully offered burnt offerings and sacrifices of deliverance and praise. [57]They ornamented the facade of the temple with gold crowns and shields; they repaired the gates and the priests' chambers and furnished them with doors. [58]There was great joy among the people now that the disgrace brought by the Gentiles was removed. [59]Then Judas and his brothers and the entire assembly of Israel decreed that every year for eight days, from the twenty-fifth day of the month Kislev,[q] the days of the dedication* of the altar should be observed with joy and gladness on the anniversary.

[60]At that time they built high walls and strong towers around Mount Zion, to prevent the Gentiles from coming and trampling it as they had done before. [61]Judas also placed a garrison there to protect it, and likewise fortified Beth-zur, that the people might have a stronghold facing Idumea.

CHAPTER 5

See RG 229

*Victories over Hostile Neighbors.**

[1][r] When the nations round about heard that the altar had been rebuilt and the sanctuary restored as before, they were enraged. [2]So they decided to destroy the descendants of Jacob who were among them, and they began to kill and eradicate the people. [3][s] Then Judas attacked the Edomites* at Akrabattene in Idumea, because they were blockading Israel; he dealt them a heavy blow, humbled and despoiled them. [4]He also remembered the malice of the Baeanites,* who had become a snare and a stumbling block to the people by ambushing them along the roads. [5]He forced them to take refuge in towers, which he besieged; he put them under the ban and burned down their towers along with all who were in them. [6]*[t] Then he crossed over to the Ammonites, where he found a strong army and a large body of people with Timothy as their leader. [7]He fought many battles with them, routed them, and struck them down. [8]After seizing Jazer and its villages, he returned to Judea.

Liberation of Jews in Galilee and Gilead.

[9]The Gentiles in Gilead assembled to destroy the Israelites who were in their territory; these then fled to the stronghold of Dathema.* [10]They sent a letter to Judas and his brothers saying: "The Gentiles around us have assembled against us to destroy us, [11]and they are preparing to come and seize this stronghold to which we have fled. Timothy is the leader of their army. [12]Come at once to rescue us from them, for many of us have fallen. [13]All our kindred who were in the territory of the Tobiads* have been killed; the Gentiles have captured their wives, their children and their goods, and they have slain there about a thousand men."[u]

[14]While they were reading this letter, suddenly other messengers, with garments torn, arrived from Galilee to deliver a similar message: [15]that "the inhabitants of Ptolemais,*

4:52 Twenty-fifth day of the ninth month . . . in the year one hundred and forty-eight: December 14, 164 B.C.

4:59 Days of the dedication: institution of the feast of Hanukkah, also called the feast of Dedication (Jn 10:22). Josephus calls it the feast of Lights (*Ant.* 12:325).

5:1 The events of this chapter occurred within the year 163 B.C.

5:3 Edomites: lit., "sons of Esau"; here a pejorative term for the Idumeans. Cf. also 5:65. **Akrabattene**: either a district southwest of the Dead Sea or on the eastern border of Judea and Samaria.

5:4 Baeanites: 2 Mc 10:15–23 calls them simply Idumeans.

5:6–8 This summary anticipates the order of events and would fit better between vv. 36 and 37. It corresponds to 2 Mc 12:17–23. The action was probably a reprisal for the massacre referred to in 1 Mc 5:13. Timothy may have been a local ruler, or the Seleucid governor of Transjordan. **Jazer**: a town on the road from the Jordan to Amman.

5:9 Dathema: the exact location is uncertain; it was east of the Jordan (in Gilead) and a night's journey from Bozrah (v. 29).

5:13 Tobiads: a prominent Jewish family that settled east of the Jordan.

5:15 Ptolemais: Hebrew *Acco* (Jgs 1:31), modern Acre, on the coast north of Haifa.

p: Ex 30:10; Ez 43:18–27. *q:* Jn 10:22. *r:* 1 Mc 13:6. *s:* 2 Mc 10:15–23. *t:* 2 Mc 8:30–33. *u:* 2 Mc 12:17.

Tyre, and Sidon, and the whole of Gentile
Galilee have joined forces to destroy us."
16When Judas and the people heard this, a
great assembly convened to consider what
they should do for their kindred who were in
distress and being attacked by enemies.

17Judas said to his brother Simon:
"Choose men for yourself, and go, rescue
your kindred in Galilee; my brother Jonathan
and I will go to Gilead."

18He left Joseph, son of Zechariah, and
Azariah, leader of the people, with the rest
of the army in Judea to guard it. 19He commanded them, "Take charge of these people,
but do not join battle against the Gentiles until we return." 20Three thousand men were
allotted to Simon to go into Galilee, and
eight thousand men to Judas, for Gilead.

21Simon went into Galilee and fought
many battles with the Gentiles. They were
crushed before him, 22and he pursued them
to the very gate of Ptolemais. About three
thousand of the Gentiles fell, and he gathered their spoils. 23He took with him the
Jews who were in Galilee and in Arbatta,*
with their wives and children and all that
they had, and brought them to Judea with
great rejoicing.

24[v] Judas Maccabeus and his brother Jonathan crossed the Jordan and marched for
three days through the wilderness. 25There
they met some Nabateans,* who received
them peaceably and told them all that had
happened to their kindred in Gilead:
26"Many of them are shut up in Bozrah, in
Bosor near Alema, in Chaspho, Maked, and
Carnaim"—all of these are large, fortified
cities— 27"and some are shut up in other cities of Gilead. Tomorrow their enemies plan
to attack the strongholds and to seize and destroy all these people in one day."

28Thereupon Judas suddenly changed direction with his army, marched across the
wilderness to Bozrah, and captured the city.
He put every male to the sword, took all their
spoils, and set fire to the city. 29* He led his
army from that place by night, and they
marched toward the stronghold. 30When
morning came, they looked ahead and saw a
countless multitude, with ladders and machines for capturing the stronghold, beginning to attack. 31When Judas perceived that
the struggle had begun and that the noise of
the battle was resounding to heaven with
trumpet blasts and loud shouting, 32he said
to the men of his army, "Fight for our kindred today." 33He came up behind them with
three columns blowing their trumpets and
crying out in prayer. 34When the army of
Timothy realized that it was Maccabeus,
they fled before him, and he inflicted on
them a great defeat. About eight thousand of
their men fell that day.

35Then he turned toward Alema* and attacked and captured it; he killed every male,
took spoils, and burned it down. 36From
there he moved on and took Chaspho,
Maked, Bosor, and the other cities of Gilead.

37[w] After these events Timothy assembled
another army and camped opposite Raphon,
on the other side of the wadi. 38Judas sent
men to spy on the camp, and they reported to
him: "All the Gentiles around us have rallied
to him, making a very large force; 39they
have also hired Arabians to help them, and
have camped beyond the wadi, ready to attack you." So Judas went forward to meet
them.

40As Judas and his army were approaching
the flowing wadi, Timothy said to the officers of his army: "If he crosses over to us
first, we shall not be able to resist him; he
will certainly defeat us.[x] 41But if he is hesitant and camps on the other side of the river,
we will cross over to him and defeat him."
42But when Judas reached the flowing wadi,
he stationed the officers of the people beside
it and gave them this order: "Do not allow

5:23 Arbatta: (or, Narbatta), probably south of Mount Carmel.

5:25 Nabateans: an Arab people who acquired wealth and power as caravan merchants in the final two centuries B.C. They established Petra as their capital and for a time controlled all of Transjordan, even as far as Damascus. It was from a Nabatean governor of Damascus that Paul escaped (2 Cor 11:32–33).

5:29 Cf. v. 9.

5:35 Alema: see v. 26; other manuscripts read Maapha, which may be Mizpah of Gilead (Jgs 11:29).

v: 2 Mc 12:10–16. *w:* 2 Mc 12:17–25. *x:* 1 Sm 14:9–10.

anyone to encamp; all must go into battle." [43]He was the first to cross to the attack, with all the people behind him, and all the Gentiles were crushed before them. They threw away their arms and fled to the temple enclosure at Carnaim. [44]But Judas' troops captured the city and burnt the temple enclosure with all who were in it. So Carnaim was subdued, and Judas met with no more resistance.

Return to Jerusalem. [45][y] Then Judas assembled all the Israelites, great and small, who were in Gilead, with their wives and children and their goods, a very large company, to go into the land of Judah. [46]When they reached Ephron,* a large and strongly fortified city along the way, they found it impossible to go around it on either the right or the left; they would have to march right through it.[z] [47]But the people in the city shut them out and blocked up the gates with stones. [48]Then Judas sent them this peaceful message: "Let us cross your territory in order to reach our own; no one will harm you; we will only march through." But they would not open to him. [49]So Judas ordered a proclamation to be made in the camp that everyone should take up positions where they were. [50]When the men of the army took up their positions, he assaulted the city all that day and night, and it was delivered into his hand. [51]He put every male to the sword, leveled the city, took spoils and passed through it over the slain.

[52]Then they crossed the Jordan to the great plain in front of Beth-shan; [53]and Judas kept gathering the stragglers and encouraging the people the whole way, until he reached the land of Judah. [54]They ascended Mount Zion in joy and gladness and sacrificed burnt offerings, because not one of them had fallen; they had returned in safety.

Joseph and Azariah Defeated. [55]In those days when Judas and Jonathan were in the land of Gilead, and Simon his brother was in Galilee opposite Ptolemais, [56]Joseph, son of Zechariah, and Azariah, the leaders of the army, heard about the brave deeds and the fighting that they were doing. [57]They said, "Let us also make a name for ourselves by going out and fighting against the Gentiles around us." [58]They gave orders to those of their army who were with them, and marched against Jamnia.* [59]But Gorgias and his men came out of the city to meet them in battle. [60]Joseph and Azariah were routed and were pursued to the frontiers of Judea, and about two thousand Israelites fell that day. [61]It was a great setback for the people, because they had not obeyed Judas and his brothers, thinking that they would do brave deeds. [62]But they were not of the family through whom Israel's deliverance was given.

Victories at Hebron and Azotus. [63]The valiant Judas and his brothers were greatly honored in all Israel and among all the Gentiles, wherever their name was heard; [64]and people gathered about them and praised them.

[65][a] Then Judas and his brothers went out and attacked the Edomites in the land toward the south; he took Hebron and its villages, and he destroyed its strongholds and burned the towers around it. [66]He then set out for the land of the foreigners and passed through Marisa. [67]On that day some priests fell in battle who had gone out rashly to fight in their desire to do brave deeds. [68]Judas then turned toward Azotus in the land of the foreigners. He destroyed their altars and burned the carved images of their gods; and after plundering their cities he returned to the land of Judah.

CHAPTER 6

See RG 229

[1][b] As King Antiochus passed through the eastern provinces, he heard that in Persia there was a city, Elam,* famous for its wealth in silver and gold, [2]and that its temple was

5:46 Ephron: a city in Transjordan opposite Beth-shan (v. 52), about nine miles east of the Jordan River. Situated on a height, it dominated the valleys of the two tributaries of the Jordan.

5:58 Jamnia: Yavneh (see 10:69), the capital of the province of Azotus (Ashdod).

6:1 Elam: in fact, the mountainous region north of the Persian Gulf, rather than a city. The city may have been Persepolis. This section continues the story from 3:37 and pertains to events preceding those in 4:37–39.

y: 2 Mc 12:26–31. *z:* Nm 20:17–21; 21:21–25. *a:* 2 Mc 12:36–46. *b:* 2 Mc 1:13–17; 9:1–29; Dn 11:40–45.

very rich, containing gold helmets, breastplates, and weapons left there by the first king of the Greeks, Alexander, son of Philip, king of Macedon. [3]He went therefore and tried to capture and loot the city. But he could not do so, because his plan became known to the people of the city [4]who rose up in battle against him. So he fled and in great dismay withdrew from there to return to Babylon.

[5]While he was in Persia, a messenger brought him news that the armies that had gone into the land of Judah had been routed; [6]that Lysias had gone at first with a strong army and been driven back; that the people of Judah had grown strong by reason of the arms, wealth, and abundant spoils taken from the armies they had cut down; [7]that they had pulled down the abomination which he had built upon the altar in Jerusalem; and that they had surrounded with high walls both the sanctuary, as it had been before, and his city of Beth-zur.[c]

[8]When the king heard this news, he was astonished and very much shaken. Sick with grief because his designs had failed, he took to his bed. [9]There he remained many days, assailed by waves of grief, for he thought he was going to die. [10]So he called in all his Friends and said to them: "Sleep has departed from my eyes, and my heart sinks from anxiety. [11]I said to myself: 'Into what tribulation have I come, and in what floods of sorrow am I now! Yet I was kindly and beloved in my rule.' [12]But I now recall the evils I did in Jerusalem, when I carried away all the vessels of silver and gold that were in it, and for no cause gave orders that the inhabitants of Judah be destroyed. [13]I know that this is why these evils have overtaken me; and now I am dying, in bitter grief, in a foreign land."

[14]Then he summoned Philip, one of his Friends, and put him in charge of his whole kingdom. [15]He gave him his diadem, his robe, and his signet ring, so that he might guide the king's son Antiochus and bring him up to be king. [16]So King Antiochus died there in the one hundred and forty-ninth year.* [17]When Lysias learned that the king was dead, he set up the king's son Antiochus,* whom he had reared as a child, to be king in his place; and he gave him the title Eupator.[d]

Siege of the Citadel. [18]Those in the citadel were hemming Israel in around the sanctuary, continually trying to harm them and to strengthen the Gentiles.[e] [19]And so Judas planned to destroy them, and assembled the people to besiege them. [20]So in the one hundred and fiftieth year* they assembled and besieged the citadel, for which purpose he constructed platforms and siege engines. [21]But some of the besieged escaped, and some renegade Israelites joined them. [22]They went to the king and said: "How long will you fail to do justice and to avenge our kindred? [23]We agreed to serve your father and to follow his orders and obey his edicts. [24]And for this our own people have become our enemies; they have put to death as many of us as they could find and have seized our inheritances. [25]They have acted aggressively not only against us, but throughout their whole territory. [26]Look! Today they have besieged the citadel in Jerusalem in order to capture it, and they have fortified the sanctuary and Beth-zur. [27]Unless you act quickly to prevent them, they will do even worse things than these, and you will not be able to stop them."

[28f]When the king heard this he was enraged, and he called together all his Friends, the officers of his army, and the commanders of the cavalry. [29]Mercenary forces also came to him from other kingdoms and from the islands of the seas. [30]His army numbered a hundred thousand footsoldiers, twenty thousand cavalry, and thirty-two elephants trained for war. [31]They passed through Idu-

6:16 The one hundred and forty-ninth year: September 22, 164, to October 9, 163 B.C. A Babylonian list of the Seleucid kings indicates that Antiochus died in November or early December of 164, about the same time as the rededication of the Temple.

6:17 The king's son Antiochus: Antiochus V Eupator ("of a good father"), then about nine years old. He was in Antioch, still in the charge of Lysias, who proceeded to govern and wage wars in his name. Both were put to death two years later, when Demetrius, brother of Antiochus IV, arrived to claim the kingship; cf. 7:1–3.

6:20 The one hundred and fiftieth year: October, 163, to September, 162 B.C.

c: 1 Mc 1:54; 4:41–61. *d:* 2 Mc 10:10–11. *e:* 1 Mc 1:33–36. *f:* 2 Mc 13:1–26.

mea and camped before Beth-zur. For many days they attacked it; they constructed siege engines, but the besieged made a sortie and burned these, and they fought bravely.

Battle of Beth-zechariah. 32 Then Judas marched away from the citadel and moved his camp to Beth-zechariah,* opposite the king's camp. 33 The king, rising before dawn, moved his force hastily along the road to Beth-zechariah; and the troops prepared for battle and sounded the trumpet. 34 They made the elephants drunk on the juice of grapes and mulberries to get them ready to fight. 35 The beasts were distributed along the phalanxes, each elephant having assigned to it a thousand men in coats of mail, with bronze helmets on their heads, and five hundred picked cavalry. 36 These accompanied the beast wherever it was; wherever it moved, they moved too and never left it. 37 Each elephant was outfitted with a strong wooden tower, fastened to it by a harness; each tower held three soldiers who fought from it, besides the Indian driver. 38 The remaining cavalry were stationed on one or the other of the two flanks of the army, to harass the enemy and to be protected by the phalanxes. 39 When the sun shone on the gold and bronze shields, the mountains gleamed with their brightness and blazed like flaming torches. 40 Part of the king's army spread out along the heights, while some were on low ground, and they marched forward steadily in good order. 41 All who heard the noise of their numbers, the tramp of their marching, and the clanging of the arms, trembled; for the army was very great and strong.

42 Judas with his army advanced to fight, and six hundred men of the king's army fell. 43 Eleazar, called Avaran, saw one of the beasts covered with royal armor and bigger than any of the others, and so he thought the king was on it.[g] 44 He gave up his life to save his people and win an everlasting name for himself. 45 He dashed courageously up to it in the middle of the phalanx, killing men right and left, so that they parted before him. 46 He ran under the elephant, stabbed it and killed it. The beast fell to the ground on top of him, and he died there. 47 But when Judas' troops saw the strength of the royal army and the ardor of its forces, they retreated from them.

The Siege of Jerusalem. 48 Some of the king's army went up to Jerusalem to attack them, and the king established camps in Judea and at Mount Zion. 49 He made peace with the people of Beth-zur, and they evacuated the city, because they had no food there to enable them to withstand a siege, for that was a sabbath year in the land.* [h] 50 The king took Beth-zur and stationed a garrison there to hold it. 51 For many days he besieged the sanctuary, setting up platforms and siege engines, fire-throwers, catapults and mechanical bows for shooting arrows and projectiles. 52 The defenders countered by setting up siege engines of their own, and kept up the fight a long time. 53 But there were no provisions in the storerooms, because it was the seventh year, and the reserves had been eaten up by those who had been rescued from the Gentiles and brought to Judea. 54 Few men remained in the sanctuary because the famine was too much for them; the rest scattered, each to his own home.

Peace Treaty. 55 [i] Lysias heard that Philip, whom King Antiochus, before his death, had appointed to train his son Antiochus to be king, 56 had returned from Persia and Media with the army that accompanied the king, and that he was seeking to take over the government. 57 So he hastily decided to withdraw. He said to the king, the leaders of the army, and the soldiers: "We are growing weaker every day, our provisions are scanty, the place we are besieging is strong, and it is our duty to take care of the affairs of the kingdom.[j] 58 Therefore let us now come to terms with these people and make peace with them and all their nation. 59 Let us grant them freedom to live according to their own laws as formerly; it was on account of their

6:32 Beth-zechariah: south of Jerusalem, and six miles north of Beth-zur.

6:49 A sabbath year in the land: when sowing and reaping were prohibited (Ex 23:10–11; Lv 25:2–7). The year without a harvest (autumn of 164 to autumn of 163) was followed by a food shortage.

g: 2 Mc 13:15. *h:* Lv 25:1–7. *i:* 2 Mc 13:23–26. *j:* 2 Mc 11:13–15.

laws, which we abolished, that they became enraged and did all these things."

60 The proposal pleased the king and the leaders; he sent peace terms to the Jews, and they accepted. 61 So the king and the leaders swore an oath to them, and on these terms the Jews evacuated the fortification. 62 But when the king entered Mount Zion and saw how the place was fortified, he broke the oath he had sworn and gave orders to tear down the encircling wall. 63 Then he departed in haste and returned to Antioch, where he found Philip in control of the city. He fought against him and took the city by force.

See RG 229

CHAPTER 7

Expedition of Bacchides and Alcimus.

1[k] In the one hundred and fifty-first year,* Demetrius, son of Seleucus, set out from Rome, arrived with a few men at a coastal city, and began to rule there. 2 As he was entering the royal palace of his ancestors, the soldiers seized Antiochus and Lysias to bring them to him. 3 When he was informed of this, he said, "Do not show me their faces." 4 So the soldiers killed them, and Demetrius assumed the royal throne.

5 Then all the lawless men and renegades of Israel came to him. They were led by Alcimus,* who desired to be high priest. 6 They made this accusation to the king against the people: "Judas and his brothers have destroyed all your friends and have driven us out of our land. 7 So now, send a man whom you trust to go and see all the destruction Judas has wrought on us and on the king's territory, and let him punish them and all their supporters."

8 So the king chose Bacchides, one of the King's Friends, who ruled the province of West-of-Euphrates, a great man in the kingdom, and faithful to the king. 9 He sent him and the renegade Alcimus, to whom he granted the high priesthood, with orders to take revenge on the Israelites. 10 They set out and, on arriving in the land of Judah with a great army, sent messengers who spoke deceitfully to Judas and his brothers in peaceful terms. 11 But these paid no attention to their words, seeing that they had come with a great army.

12 A group of scribes, however, gathered about Alcimus and Bacchides to ask for a just agreement. 13[l] The Hasideans were the first among the Israelites to seek peace with them, 14 for they said, "A priest of the line of Aaron has come with the army, and he will not do us any wrong." 15 He spoke with them peacefully and swore to them, "We will not seek to injure you or your friends." 16 So they trusted him. But he arrested sixty of them and killed them in one day, according to the words that he wrote:*

17 "The flesh of your faithful,
and their blood they have spilled all
around about Jerusalem,
and no one was left to bury them."[m]

18 Then fear and dread of them came upon all the people, who said: "There is no truth or justice among them; they violated the agreement and the oath that they swore."

19 Bacchides withdrew from Jerusalem and camped in Beth-zaith.* He had many of the men who deserted to him arrested and some of the people. He killed them and threw them into a great cistern. 20 He handed the province over to Alcimus, leaving troops to help him, while he himself returned to the king.

21 Alcimus struggled to maintain his high priesthood, 22 and all those who were troubling the people gathered about him. They took possession of the land of Judah and caused great distress in Israel. 23 When Judas

7:1–3 The one hundred and fifty-first year: the spring of 161 B.C. Demetrius, son of Seleucus, was the lawful heir to the kingdom; but when only nine years old, he was taken as a hostage to Rome in place of his uncle, who ruled as Antiochus IV Epiphanes. At the age of twenty-five Demetrius fled secretly from Rome and, with the support of the Syrians, overcame his rival Antiochus V and put him to death. **The royal palace**: at Antioch.

7:5–6 Alcimus: a Jew hostile to the Maccabees, who became high priest after the death of Menelaus (2 Mc 14:3). He received confirmation in his office from the new king Demetrius (1 Mc 7:9), and brought malicious charges against Judas and his brothers and the people (1 Mc 7:6).

7:16 The words that he wrote: based on Ps 79:2–3. But who is "he"—David, Alcimus, Judas, or someone else?

7:19 Beth-zaith: about three miles north of Beth-zur and twelve miles south of Jerusalem.

k: 2 Mc 14:1–11. *l:* 1 Mc 2:42. *m:* Ps 79:2–3.

saw all the evils that Alcimus and those with
him were bringing upon the Israelites, even
more than the Gentiles had, 24he went about
all the borders of Judea and took revenge on
the men who had deserted, preventing them
from going out into the country. 25But when
Alcimus saw that Judas and his followers
were gaining strength and realized that he
could not resist them, he returned to the king
and accused them of grave crimes.

Defeat of Nicanor. 26n Then the king sent
Nicanor, one of his honored officers, who
was a bitter enemy of Israel, with orders to
destroy the people. 27Nicanor came to
Jerusalem with a large force and deceitfully
sent to Judas* and his brothers this peaceable
message: 28"Let there be no fight between
me and you. I will come with a few men to
meet you face to face in peace."

29So he came to Judas, and they greeted
one another peaceably. But Judas' enemies
were prepared to seize him. 30When he became aware that Nicanor had come to him
with deceit in mind, Judas was afraid of him
and would not meet him again.o 31When Nicanor saw that his plan had been discovered,
he went out to fight Judas near Capharsalama.* 32About five hundred men of Nicanor's army fell; the rest fled to the City of
David.*

33p After this, Nicanor went up to Mount
Zion. Some of the priests from the sanctuary
and some of the elders of the people came
out to greet him peaceably and to show him
the burnt offering that was being sacrificed
for the king. 34But he mocked and ridiculed
them, defiled them,* and spoke arrogantly.
35In a rage he swore: "If Judas and his army
are not delivered to me at once, when I return victorious I will burn this temple
down." He went away in great anger. 36q The
priests, however, went in and stood before
the altar and the sanctuary. They wept and
said: 37"You have chosen this house to bear
your name, to be a house of prayer and supplication for your people. 38Take revenge on
this man and his army, and let them fall by
the sword. Remember their blasphemies,
and do not let them continue."

39Nicanor left Jerusalem and camped at
Beth-horon, where the Syrian army joined
him. 40But Judas camped in Adasa* with
three thousand men. Here Judas uttered this
prayer: 41r "When they who were sent by the
king* blasphemed, your angel went out and
killed a hundred and eighty-five thousand of
them.s 42In the same way, crush this army
before us today, and let the rest know that
Nicanor spoke wickedly against your sanctuary; judge him according to his wickedness."

43The armies met in battle on the thirteenth day of the month Adar. Nicanor's
army was crushed, and he himself was the
first to fall in the battle.t 44When his army
saw that Nicanor had fallen, they threw
down their weapons and fled. 45The Jews
pursued them a day's journey from Adasa to
near Gazara, blowing the trumpets behind
them as signals. 46From all the surrounding
villages of Judea people came out and out-
flanked them. They turned them back, and
all the enemies fell by the sword; not a single one escaped.

47Then the Jews collected the spoils and
the plunder; they cut off Nicanor's head and
his right arm, which he had lifted up so arrogantly. These they brought and displayed in
the sight of Jerusalem. 48The people rejoiced
greatly, and observed that day as a day of
much joy. 49They decreed that it should be
observed every year on the thirteenth of

7:27 Nicanor . . . deceitfully sent to Judas: a more favorable picture of Nicanor, as an honest man who became a personal friend of Judas, is given in 2 Mc 14:17–25. Their friendship was broken by the intrigues of Alcimus (2 Mc 14:26–30).

7:31 Capharsalama: a village north of Jerusalem whose precise location is disputed.

7:32 City of David: the citadel occupied by the Seleucid garrison in Jerusalem.

7:34 Defiled them: spitting on the priests caused them to become legally defiled.

7:40 Adasa: a village between Jerusalem and Beth-horon.

7:41 They who were sent by the king: 2 Kgs 18:19–25, 29–35; 19:10–13 recount in detail the boastful threats made by Sennacherib, the Assyrian king, through his emissaries. **Your angel**: a reference to 2 Kgs 19:35, which describes the fate of the Assyrian army which besieged Jerusalem in the days of Hezekiah, king of Judah.

n: 1 Mc 3:38; 2 Mc 8:9; 14:12–13. *o:* 2 Mc 14:30. *p:* 2 Mc 14:31–36. *q:* 1 Kgs 8:29–30, 33–34, 43. *r:* 2 Mc 8:19; 15:22–24. *s:* 2 Kgs 19:35–36; Is 37:36–37. *t:* 2 Mc 15:25–36.

Adar.* 50 And so for a few days* the land of Judah was at rest.

CHAPTER 8

See RG 229

Eulogy of the Romans. 1* Judas had heard of the reputation of the Romans. They were valiant fighters and acted amiably to all who took their side. They established a friendly alliance with all who applied to them. 2 He was also told of their battles and the brave deeds that they performed against the Gauls,* conquering them and forcing them to pay tribute; 3 and what they did in Spain to get possession of the silver and gold mines there. 4 By planning and persistence they subjugated the whole region, although it was very remote from their own. They also subjugated the kings who had come against them from the far corners of the earth until they crushed them and inflicted on them severe defeat. The rest paid tribute to them every year. 5 Philip* and Perseus, king of the Macedonians, and the others who opposed them in battle they overwhelmed and subjugated. 6 Antiochus* the Great, king of Asia, who fought against them with a hundred and twenty elephants and with cavalry and chariots and a very great army, was defeated by them. 7 They took him alive and obliged him and the kings who succeeded him to pay a heavy tribute, to give hostages and to cede 8 Lycia, Mysia, and Lydia* from among their best provinces. The Romans took these from him and gave them to King Eumenes. 9* When the Greeks planned to come and destroy them, 10 the Romans discovered it, and sent against the Greeks a single general who made war on them. Many were wounded and fell, and the Romans took their wives and children captive. They plundered them, took possession of their land, tore down their strongholds and reduced them to slavery even to this day. 11 All the other kingdoms and islands that had ever opposed them they destroyed and enslaved; with their friends, however, and those who relied on them, they maintained friendship. 12 They subjugated kings both near and far, and all who heard of their fame were afraid of them. 13 Those whom they wish to help and to make kings, they make kings; and those whom they wish, they depose; and they were greatly exalted. 14 Yet with all this, none of them put on a diadem or wore purple as a display of grandeur. 15 But they made for themselves a senate chamber, and every day three hundred and twenty men took counsel, deliberating on all that concerned the people and their well-being. 16 They entrust their government to one man* every year, to rule over their en-

7:49 The thirteenth of Adar: March 27, 160 B.C. This day in the Jewish calendar was called the "Day of Nicanor" (2 Mc 15:36), but it was not long celebrated by the Jews.

7:50 For a few days: about one month following the death of Nicanor. After that began the attack of Bacchides resulting in the death of Judas (9:1–18).

8:1 This chapter contains the account of the embassy which Judas sent to Rome, probably before the death of Nicanor, to conclude a treaty of alliance between Rome and the Jewish nation. Without precise chronology, the pertinent data are gathered into a unified theme.

The image of the Roman Republic greatly impressed the smaller Eastern peoples seeking support against their overlords (vv. 1–16), because of Roman success in war (vv. 2–11) and effective aid to their allies (vv. 12–13). Numerous interventions by Rome in the politics of the Near East bear witness to its power and prestige in the second century B.C. See 1:10; 7:2; 12:3; 15:15–24; 2 Mc 11:34. With the increased Roman control of Palestine after 63 B.C., the Republic and later the Empire became heartily detested. The eulogy of Rome in this chapter is one of the reasons why 1 Maccabees was not preserved by the Palestinian Jews of the century that followed.

8:2 Gauls: probably the Celts of northern Italy and southern France, subdued by the Romans in 222 B.C., and again in 200–191 B.C.; but also those in Asia Minor (the Galatians), whom the Romans defeated in 189 B.C.

8:5 Philip: Philip V of Macedonia, defeated by a Graeco-Roman alliance at Cynoscephalae in 197 B.C. Perseus, his son, was defeated at Pydna in 168 B.C., and died a prisoner. With this, the kingdom of Macedonia came to an end.

8:6 Antiochus: Antiochus III, greatest of the Seleucid kings. He was defeated at Magnesia in 190 B.C. By the Treaty of Apamea in 189 B.C., he was obliged to pay Rome a crushing indemnity of 15,000 talents. The weakening of Antiochene power and the growing military and economic influence of Rome may have led Antiochus IV to adopt the policy of political, religious, and cultural unification of Syria and Palestine.

8:8 Lycia, Mysia, and Lydia: regions in western Asia Minor. "Lycia" and "Mysia" are restored here by conjectural emendation; the Greek text has "India, Media," most likely through scribal error. **Eumenes**: Eumenes II (197–158 B.C.), king of Pergamum, an ally of Rome who benefited greatly from Antiochus' losses.

8:9–10 The revolt of the Achaean League, inserted here, occurred in 146 B.C., after Judas' time. It was crushed by the Roman consul Lucius Mummius and marked the end of Greek independence.

8:16 They entrust their government to one man: actually the Roman Republic had two consuls chosen yearly as joint heads of the government.

tire land, and they all obey that one, and there is no envy or jealousy among them.

Treaty with the Romans. 17So Judas chose Eupolemus, son of John, son of Accos, and Jason, son of Eleazar, and sent them to Rome to establish friendship and alliance with them.[u] 18He did this to lift the yoke from Israel, for it was obvious that the kingdom of the Greeks was subjecting them to slavery. 19After making a very long journey to Rome, the envoys entered the senate chamber and spoke as follows: 20"Judas, called Maccabeus, and his brothers, with the Jewish people, have sent us to you to establish alliance and peace with you, and to be enrolled among your allies and friends." 21The proposal pleased the Romans, 22and this is a copy of the reply they inscribed on bronze tablets and sent to Jerusalem,* to remain there with the Jews as a record of peace and alliance:[v]

23"May it be well with the Romans and the Jewish nation at sea and on land forever; may sword and enemy be far from them. 24But if war is first made on Rome, or any of its allies in any of their dominions, 25the Jewish nation will fight along with them wholeheartedly, as the occasion shall demand; 26and to those who wage war they shall not give or provide grain, weapons, money, or ships, as seems best to Rome. They shall fulfill their obligations without receiving any recompense. 27In the same way, if war is made first on the Jewish nation, the Romans will fight along with them willingly, as the occasion shall demand, 28and to those who attack them there shall not be given grain, weapons, money, or ships, as seems best to Rome. They shall fulfill their obligations without deception. 29On these terms the Romans have made an agreement with the Jewish people. 30But if both parties hereafter agree to add or take away anything, they shall do as they choose, and whatever they shall add or take away shall be valid.

31"Moreover, concerning the wrongs that King Demetrius is doing to them, we have written to him thus: 'Why have you made your yoke heavy upon our friends and allies the Jews? 32If they petition against you again, we will enforce justice and make war on you by sea and land.' "

CHAPTER 9

See RG 229

Death of Judas. 1When Demetrius heard that Nicanor and his army had fallen in battle, he again sent Bacchides and Alcimus into the land of Judah, along with the right wing of his army. 2They took the road to Galilee, and camping opposite the ascent at Arbela, they captured it* and killed many people. 3In the first month of the one hundred and fifty-second year,* they encamped against Jerusalem. 4Then they set out for Berea with twenty thousand men and two thousand cavalry. 5Judas, with three thousand picked men, had camped at Elasa. 6When they saw the great number of the troops, they were very much afraid; and many slipped away from the camp, until only eight hundred of them remained.

7When Judas saw that his army was melting away just as the battle was imminent, he was brokenhearted, because he had no time to gather them together. 8In spite of his discouragement he said to those who remained: "Let us go forward to meet our enemies; perhaps we can put up a good fight against them." 9They tried to dissuade him, saying: "We certainly cannot. Let us save our own lives now, and come back with our kindred, and then fight against them. Now we are too few." 10But Judas said: "Far be it from me to do such a thing as to flee from them! If our time has come, let us die bravely for our kindred and not leave a stain upon our honor!"

11Then the army of Bacchides moved out of camp and took its position for combat.

8:22 The reply . . . on bronze tablets and sent to Jerusalem: the decree of the Senate would be inscribed on bronze and kept in the Roman Capitol, with only a copy in letter form sent to Jerusalem.

9:2 They took the road . . . Arbela, they captured it: this passage is restored, in part, by conjectural emendation. The present Greek text could be translated, "They took the road to Gilgal, and camping opposite Mesaloth at Arbela, they captured it." But Arbela (modern Khirbet Irbid) was in Galilee, on a high hill overlooking the western shore of the Sea of Galilee. Gilgal, on the contrary, was in the Jordan valley near Jericho. "Mesaloth" is probably a corrupt form of a Hebrew word meaning "steps, ascent." It is possible, however, that all these terms referred to places in the Judean hills.

9:3 The first month of the one hundred and fifty-second year: April/May 160 B.C., by the Temple calendar.

u: 1 Mc 12:1–4; 15:15–22. *v:* 1 Mc 14:17–18.

The cavalry were divided into two squadrons, and the slingers and the archers came on ahead of the army, and in the front line were all the best warriors. Bacchides was on the right wing. 12Flanked by the two squadrons, the phalanx attacked as they blew their trumpets. Those who were on Judas' side also blew their trumpets. 13The earth shook with the noise of the armies, and the battle raged from morning until evening.

14When Judas saw that Bacchides was on the right, with the main force of his army, all the most stouthearted rallied to him, 15and the right wing was crushed; Judas pursued them as far as the mountain slopes.* 16But when those on the left wing saw that the right wing was crushed, they closed in behind Judas and those with him. 17The battle became intense, and many on both sides fell wounded. 18Then Judas fell, and the rest fled.

19Jonathan and Simon took their brother Judas and buried him in the tomb of their ancestors at Modein. 20All Israel wept for him with great lamentation. They mourned for him many days, and they said, 21"How the mighty one has fallen, the savior of Israel!"[w] 22The other acts of Judas, his battles, the brave deeds he performed, and his greatness have not been recorded; but they were very many.

III. Leadership of Jonathan

Jonathan Succeeds Judas. 23After the death of Judas, the lawless raised their heads in every part of Israel, and all kinds of evildoers appeared. 24In those days there was a very great famine, and the country deserted to them. 25Bacchides chose renegades and made them masters of the country. 26These sought out and hunted down the friends of Judas and brought them to Bacchides, who punished and derided them. 27There was great tribulation in Israel, the like of which had not been since the time prophets ceased to appear among them.

28Then all the friends of Judas came together and said to Jonathan: 29"Ever since your brother Judas died, there has been no one like him to lead us against our enemies, both Bacchides and those of our nation who are hostile to us. 30Now therefore we have chosen you today to be our ruler and leader in his place, to fight our battle." 31From that moment Jonathan accepted the leadership, and took the place of Judas his brother.

Bacchides Pursues Jonathan. 32When Bacchides learned of it, he sought to kill him. 33But Jonathan and his brother Simon and all who were with him discovered this, and they fled to the wilderness of Tekoa* and camped by the waters of the pool of Asphar. 34*

35Jonathan sent his brother* as leader of the convoy to implore his friends, the Nabateans, to let them deposit with them their great quantity of baggage.[x] 36But the tribe of Jambri from Medaba* made a raid and seized and carried off John and everything he had.

37After this, word was brought to Jonathan and his brother Simon: "The tribe of Jambri are celebrating a great wedding, and with a large escort they are bringing the bride, the daughter of one of the great princes of Canaan, from Nadabath." 38Remembering the blood of John their brother, they went up and hid themselves under cover of the mountain. 39As they watched there appeared a noisy throng with much baggage; then the bridegroom and his friends and kinsmen had come out to meet them with tambourines and musicians with their instruments. 40Jonathan and his party rose up against them from their ambush and killed them. Many fell wounded; the rest fled toward the mountain; all their spoils were taken. 41Thus the wedding was turned into mourning, and the sound of their music into lamentation. 42Having taken their revenge for the blood of their brother, they returned to the marshes of the Jordan.

9:15 As far as the mountain slopes: conjectural emendation. The Greek text has "as far as Mount Azotus"; this is most unlikely. Apparently the Greek translator mistook the Hebrew word *ashdot*, "slopes," for *ashdod*, "Azotus."

9:33 Tekoa: home of the prophet Amos in the wild country above the Dead Sea, southeast of Jerusalem.

9:34 Omitted, it is a dittography of v. 43.

9:35 Jonathan sent his brother: this was John who was called Gaddi (2:2; cf. 9:36, 38).

9:36 Medaba: northeast of the Dead Sea.

w: 2 Sm 1:19, 25, 27; Jgs 3:9. *x:* 1 Mc 5:25.

[43]When Bacchides heard of it, he came on the sabbath to the banks of the Jordan with a large force. [44]Then Jonathan said to his companions, "Let us rise up now and fight for our lives, for today is not like yesterday and the day before. [45]The battle is before us, behind us are the waters of the Jordan, on either side of us, marsh and thickets; there is no way of escape.* [46]Cry out now to Heaven so that you may be delivered from the hand of our enemies." [47]When they joined battle, Jonathan raised his hand to strike Bacchides, but Bacchides backed away from him. [48]Jonathan and those with him jumped into the Jordan and swam across to the other side, but the enemy did not pursue them across the Jordan. [49]About a thousand men on Bacchides' side fell that day.

[50]On returning to Jerusalem, Bacchides built strongholds in Judea: the Jericho fortress, as well as Emmaus, Beth-horon, Bethel, Timnath, Pharathon, and Tephon, with high walls and gates and bars.* [51]In each he put a garrison to harass Israel. [52]He fortified the city of Beth-zur, Gazara and the citadel, and put troops in them and stores of provisions. [53]He took as hostages the sons of the leading people of the country and put them in custody in the citadel at Jerusalem.[y]

[54]In the one hundred and fifty-third year, in the second month,* Alcimus ordered the wall of the inner court of the sanctuary to be torn down, thus destroying the work of the prophets. But he only began to tear it down. [55]Just at that time Alcimus was stricken, and his work was interrupted; his mouth was closed and he was paralyzed, so that he could no longer utter a word or give orders concerning his household. [56]Alcimus died in great agony at that time. [57]Seeing that Alcimus was dead, Bacchides returned to the king, and the land of Judah was at rest for two years.

[58]Then all the lawless took counsel and said: "Jonathan and those with him are living in peace and security. Now then, let us have Bacchides return, and he will capture all of them in a single night." [59]So they went and took counsel with him. [60]When Bacchides was setting out with a large force, he sent letters secretly to all his allies in Judea, telling them to seize Jonathan and his companions. They were not able to do this, however, because their plan became known. [61]In fact, Jonathan's men seized about fifty of the men of the country who were leaders in the conspiracy and put them to death.

[62]Then Jonathan and those with him, along with Simon, withdrew to Bethbasi* in the wilderness; he rebuilt its ruins and fortified it. [63]When Bacchides learned of this, he gathered together his whole force and sent word to those who were in Judea. [64]He came and camped before Bethbasi, and constructing siege engines, he fought against it for many days.

[65]Leaving his brother Simon in the city, Jonathan, accompanied by a small group of men, went out into the countryside. [66]He struck down Odomera and his kindred and the tribe of Phasiron in their encampment; these men had begun to attack and they were going up with their forces. [67]Simon and those with him then sallied forth from the city and set fire to the siege engines. [68]They fought against Bacchides, and he was crushed. They caused him great distress, because the enterprise he had planned was in vain. [69]He was enraged with the lawless men who had advised him to invade the province. He killed many of them and resolved to return to his own country.

[70]Jonathan learned of this and sent ambassadors to agree on peace with him and to obtain the release of the prisoners. [71]He agreed to do as Jonathan asked. He swore an oath to him that he would never try to do him any harm for the rest of his life; [72]and he released to him the prisoners he had previously taken

9:45 Jonathan's force may have been trapped in one of the many oxbows of the lower Jordan. Bacchides had crossed and caught them still on the east bank.

9:50 These sites constitute a ring on the edges of the province of Judea.

9:54 In the one hundred and fifty-third year, in the second month: May, 159 B.C. **The work of the prophets**: probably Haggai and Zechariah, who were instrumental in building the Second Temple after the Babylonian exile; cf. Hg 1:12–14; Zec 4:8–10; Ezr 5:1–2.

9:62 Bethbasi: two miles east of Bethlehem and six miles north of Tekoa.

y: 1 Mc 10:9.

from the land of Judah. Thereupon he returned to his own land and never came into
their territory again. 73Then the sword
ceased from Israel. Jonathan settled in Michmash;* he began to judge the people and he
eliminated the renegades from Israel.

CHAPTER 10

See RG 229

Jonathan Becomes High Priest. 1In
the one hundred and sixtieth year,* Alexander Epiphanes, son of Antiochus, came up
and took Ptolemais. They accepted him as
king and he began to reign there. 2When
King Demetrius heard of it, he mustered a
very large army and marched out to engage
him in battle. 3Demetrius sent a letter to Jonathan written in peaceful terms, to exalt him;
4for he said: "Let us be the first to make
peace with him, before he makes peace with
Alexander against us, 5since he will remember all the wrongs we have done to him, his
brothers, and his nation."

6So Demetrius authorized him to gather
an army and procure arms as his ally; and he
ordered that the hostages in the citadel be released to him. 7Accordingly Jonathan went
to Jerusalem and read the letter to all the
people and to those who were in the citadel.
8They were struck with fear when they heard
that the king had given him authority to
gather an army. 9Those in the citadel released the hostages to Jonathan, and he gave
them back to their parents.[z] 10Thereafter Jonathan dwelt in Jerusalem, and began to build
and restore the city. 11He ordered those doing the work to build the walls and to encircle Mount Zion with square stones for its
fortification, and they did so. 12The foreigners in the strongholds that Bacchides had
built took flight; 13all of them left their
places and returned to their own lands.
14Only in Beth-zur did some remain of those
who had abandoned the law and the commandments, for it was a place of refuge.

15King Alexander heard of the promises
that Demetrius had made to Jonathan; he
was also told of the battles and brave deeds
of Jonathan and his brothers and of the troubles that they had endured. 16He said, "Shall
we ever find another man like him? Let us
now make him our friend and ally." 17So he
sent Jonathan a letter written in these terms:
18"King Alexander sends greetings to his
brother Jonathan. 19We have heard of you,
that you are a mighty warrior and worthy to
be our friend. 20We have therefore appointed
you today to be high priest of your nation;
you are to be called the King's Friend, and
you are to look after our interests and preserve friendship with us." He also sent him a
purple robe and a crown of gold.[a] 21Jonathan
put on the sacred vestments in the seventh
month of the one hundred and sixtieth year
at the feast of Booths,* and he gathered an
army and procured many weapons.

A Letter from Demetrius to Jonathan.
22When Demetrius heard of these things, he
was distressed and said: 23"Why have we allowed Alexander to get ahead of us by gaining
the friendship of the Jews and thus strengthening himself? 24I too will write them encouraging words and offer honors and gifts, so that
they may support me." 25So he sent them this
message: "King Demetrius sends greetings to
the Jewish nation. 26We have heard how you
have kept the treaty with us and continued in
our friendship and not gone over to our enemies, and we are glad. 27Continue, therefore,
to keep faith with us, and we will reward you
with favors in return for what you do in our
behalf. 28We will grant you many exemptions
and will bestow gifts on you.

9:73 Michmash, southeast of Bethel, famous for the exploits of Jonathan, son of Saul; see 1 Sm 14. It was Jonathan's base from 157 to 152 B.C. **Began to judge**: exercise the governing authority as in the Book of Judges. With Jerusalem and the garrison towns (v. 50) firmly in Seleucid hands, Jonathan's freedom of action was greatly restricted.

10:1 The one hundred and sixtieth year: 152 B.C. **Alexander . . . Antiochus**: Alexander Balas claimed to be a son of Antiochus IV. He had the backing of the Romans, who had never forgiven Demetrius for becoming king without their permission. The latter meanwhile had become unpopular with his own people as well as with the Jews.

10:21 Jonathan . . . feast of Booths: Jonathan began to discharge the office of high priest in October 152 B.C. For seven years after the death of Alcimus there had been no high priest in Jerusalem. It was taken for granted that the king, though a Gentile, had the power to appoint one (2 Mc 4:7, 23–24). The Maccabees, though a priestly family (1 Mc 2:1), were not of the line of Zadok, and some in Israel (perhaps the Qumran community) regarded Jonathan's tenure as a usurpation.

z: 1 Mc 9:53. *a:* 1 Mc 2:18.

[29b] "I now free you and exempt all the
Jews from the tribute, the salt tax, and the
crown levies. [30]Instead of collecting the third
of the grain and the half of the fruit of the
trees that should be my share, I renounce the
right from this day forward. Neither now nor
in the future will I collect them from the land
of Judah or from the three districts annexed
from Samaria.* [31]Let Jerusalem and her territory, her tithes and her tolls, be sacred and
free from tax. [32]I also yield my authority over
the citadel in Jerusalem, and I transfer it to
the high priest, that he may put in it such men
as he shall choose to guard it. [33]Every Jew
who has been carried into captivity from the
land of Judah into any part of my kingdom I
set at liberty without ransom; and let all their
taxes, even those on their cattle, be canceled.
[34]Let all feast days, sabbaths, new moon
festivals, appointed days, and the three days
that precede each feast day, and the three days
that follow, be days of immunity and exemption for all Jews in my kingdom. [35]No one
will have authority to exact payment from
them or to harass any of them in any matter.
[36]"Let thirty thousand Jews be enrolled in
the king's army and allowances be given
them, as is due to all the king's soldiers.
[37]Let some of them be stationed in the king's
principal strongholds, and of these let some
be given positions of trust in the affairs of
the kingdom. Let their superiors and their
rulers be chosen from among them, and let
them follow their own laws, as the king has
commanded in the land of Judah.
[38]"Let the three districts that have been
added to Judea from the province of Samaria
be annexed to Judea so that they may be under one rule and obey no other authority than
the high priest. [39]Ptolemais and its confines
I give as a present to the sanctuary in Jerusalem for the necessary expenses of the sanctuary. [40]I make a yearly personal grant of fifteen thousand silver shekels out of the royal
revenues, taken from appropriate places.
[41]All the additional funds that the officials
did not hand over as they had done in the
first years shall henceforth be handed over
for the services of the temple. [42]Moreover,
the dues of five thousand silver shekels that
used to be taken from the revenue of the
sanctuary every year shall be canceled, since
these funds belong to the priests who perform the services. [43]All who take refuge in
the temple of Jerusalem or in any of its
precincts, because of money they owe the
king, or because of any other debt, shall be
released, together with all the goods they
possess in my kingdom. [44]The cost of rebuilding and restoring the structures of the
sanctuary shall be covered out of the royal
revenue. [45]Likewise the cost of building the
walls of Jerusalem and fortifying it all
around, and of building walls in Judea, shall
be donated from the royal revenue."
[46]When Jonathan and the people heard
these words, they neither believed nor accepted them, for they remembered the great
evil that Demetrius had done in Israel, and
the great tribulation he had brought upon
them. [47]They therefore decided in favor of
Alexander, for he had been the first to address them peaceably, and they remained his
allies for the rest of his life.
[48]Then King Alexander gathered together
a large army and encamped opposite Demetrius. [49]The two kings joined battle, and
when the army of Demetrius fled, Alexander
pursued him, and overpowered his soldiers.
[50]He pressed the battle hard until sunset, and
Demetrius fell that day.

Treaty of Ptolemy and Alexander.
[51]Alexander sent ambassadors to Ptolemy,
king of Egypt, with this message: [52]"Now
that I have returned to my realm, taken my
seat on the throne of my ancestors, and established my rule by crushing Demetrius
and gaining control of my country— [53]for I
engaged him in battle, he and his army were
crushed by us, and we assumed his royal
throne— [54]let us now establish friendship
with each other. Give me now your daughter
for my wife; and as your son-in-law, I will
give to you and to her gifts worthy of you."

10:30 The three districts annexed from Samaria: mentioned by name in 11:34. The present Greek text, by a scribal error, has added "and Galilee" after "Samaria."

b: 1 Mc 11:28, 34.

55King Ptolemy answered in these words:
“Happy the day on which you returned to the
land of your ancestors and took your seat on
their royal throne! 56I will do for you what
you have written; but meet me in Ptolemais,
so that we may see each other, and I will become your father-in-law as you have proposed.”
57So Ptolemy with his daughter Cleopatra* set out from Egypt and came to Ptolemais in the one hundred and sixty-second
year. 58There King Alexander met him, and
Ptolemy gave him his daughter Cleopatra in
marriage. Their wedding was celebrated at
Ptolemais with great splendor according to
the custom of kings.
59King Alexander also wrote to Jonathan
to come and meet him. 60So he went with
pomp to Ptolemais, where he met the two
kings and gave them and their friends silver
and gold and many gifts and thus won their
favor.[c] 61Some villainous men of Israel,
transgressors of the law, united against him
to accuse him, but the king paid no heed to
them. 62The king ordered Jonathan to be di-
vested of his garments and to be clothed in
royal purple; and so it was done. 63The king
also had him seated at his side. He said to his
magistrates: “Go with him to the center of
the city and make a proclamation that no one
is to bring charges against him on any
grounds or be troublesome to him for any
reason.” 64[d] When his accusers saw the
honor paid to him according to the king’s
proclamation, and him clothed in purple,
they all fled. 65And so the king honored him,
enrolling him among his Chief Friends, and
he made him governor and chief of the province. 66So Jonathan returned in peace and
happiness to Jerusalem.

Jonathan Defeats Apollonius. 67In the one
hundred and sixty-fifth year,* Demetrius,
son of Demetrius, came from Crete to the
land of his ancestors. 68When King Alexander heard of it he was greatly troubled, and
returned to Antioch. 69Demetrius set Apollonius over Coelesyria.* Having gathered a
large army, Apollonius encamped at Jamnia.
From there he sent this message to Jonathan
the high priest:
70“You are the only one who resists us. I
am laughed at and put to shame on your account. Why are you exercising authority
against us in the mountains? 71If you have
confidence in your forces, come down now
to us in the plain, and let us test each other’s
strength there; for the forces of the cities are
on my side. 72Inquire and find out who I am
and who the others are who are helping me.
People are saying that you cannot make a
stand against us because your ancestors
were twice put to flight* in their own land.
73Now you too will be unable to withstand
our cavalry and such a force as this in the
plain, where there is not a stone or a pebble
or a place to flee.”
74When Jonathan heard the message of
Apollonius, he was provoked. Choosing ten
thousand men, he set out from Jerusalem,
and Simon his brother joined him to help
him. 75He encamped near Joppa, but the
people of the city shut him out because
Apollonius had a garrison in Joppa. When
they attacked it, 76the people of the city became afraid and opened the gates, and so
Jonathan took possession of Joppa.*
77When Apollonius heard of it, he drew up
three thousand cavalry and a large force of
infantry. He marched toward Azotus as
though he were going on through, but at the
same time he was advancing into the plain,
because he had such a large number of cavalry to rely on. 78Jonathan pursued him toward Azotus, and the armies engaged in battle. 79Apollonius, however, had left a
thousand cavalry in hiding behind them.

10:57 Cleopatra: Cleopatra Thea, then about fifteen years old. She later married Demetrius II, and later still, his brother Antiochus VII. Ptolemais (Acco) on the coast of Palestine was a neutral site. **The one hundred and sixty-second year**: 151/150 B.C.

10:67 The one hundred and sixty-fifth year: 147 B.C. **Demetrius**: Demetrius II Nicator.

10:69 Coelesyria: originally the region between the Lebanon and anti-Lebanon mountains, it came later to refer to Palestine also. **Jamnia**: on the coast, also known as Yavneh (5:58).

10:72 Twice put to flight: the reference is unclear.

10:76 Joppa: about forty miles northwest of Jerusalem. For the first time the Maccabees took possession of a seaport, though nominally it was on behalf of King Alexander.

c: 1 Mc 2:18. *d:* 1 Mc 2:18; 11:27.

80 Jonathan discovered that there was an ambush behind him; his army was surrounded.
From morning until evening they showered
his troops with arrows. 81 But his troops held
their ground, as Jonathan had commanded,
while the enemy's horses became tired out.
82 Then Simon brought forward his force,
and engaged the phalanx in battle. Since the
cavalry were exhausted, the phalanx was
crushed by him and fled, 83 while the cavalry
too were scattered over the plain. They fled
to Azotus and entered Beth-dagon, the temple of their idol, to save themselves. 84 But
Jonathan burned and plundered Azotus with
its neighboring towns, and destroyed by fire
both the temple of Dagon and those who had
taken refuge in it.[e] 85 Those who fell by the
sword, together with those who were burned
alive, came to about eight thousand.
86 Then Jonathan left there and encamped
at Askalon, and the people of that city came
out to meet him with great pomp. 87 Jonathan
and those with him then returned to Jerusalem, with much spoil. 88 When King Alexander heard of these events, he accorded new
honors to Jonathan. 89 He sent him a gold
buckle, such as is usually given to King's
Kinsmen;* he also gave him Ekron and all its
territory as a possession.

CHAPTER 11

See RG 229

Alliance of Ptolemy and Demetrius II.

1 Then the king of Egypt gathered forces as
numerous as the sands of the seashore, and
many ships; and he sought by deceit to take
Alexander's kingdom and add it to his own.
2 He set out for Syria with peaceful words,
and the people in the cities opened their
gates to welcome him, as King Alexander
had ordered them to do, since Ptolemy was
his father-in-law. 3 But when Ptolemy entered the cities, he stationed a garrison of
troops in each one.
4 As they neared Azotus, they showed him
the temple of Dagon destroyed by fire, Azotus and its suburbs demolished, corpses lying
about, and the charred bodies of those burned
in the war, for they had heaped them up along
his route.[f] 5 They told the king what Jonathan
had done in order to denigrate him; but the
king said nothing. 6 Jonathan met the king
with pomp at Joppa, and they greeted each
other and spent the night there. 7 Jonathan accompanied the king as far as the river called
Eleutherus* and then returned to Jerusalem.
8 And so King Ptolemy took possession of
the cities along the seacoast as far as Seleucia by the sea,* plotting evil schemes against
Alexander all the while. 9 He sent ambassadors to King Demetrius, saying: "Come, let
us make a covenant with each other; I will
give you my daughter whom Alexander has
married, and you shall reign over your father's kingdom. 10 I regret that I gave him my
daughter, for he has sought to kill me."* 11 He
was criticizing Alexander, however, because
he coveted his kingdom. 12 After taking his
daughter away, Ptolemy gave her to Demetrius and broke with Alexander; the enmity
between them was now evident. 13 Then
Ptolemy entered Antioch and assumed the
crown* of Asia; thus he set upon his head
two crowns, that of Egypt and that of Asia.
14 Now King Alexander was in Cilicia at
that time, because the people of that region
had revolted. 15 When Alexander heard the
news, he came against Ptolemy in battle.
Ptolemy marched out and met him with a
strong force and routed him. 16 When Alexander fled to Arabia to seek protection, King
Ptolemy was triumphant. 17 Zabdiel the Arabian cut off Alexander's head and sent it to
Ptolemy. 18 But three days later King
Ptolemy himself died, and his troops in the
strongholds were killed by the inhabitants of
the strongholds. 19 Thus Demetrius became
king in the one hundred and sixty-seventh
year.*

10:89 Kinsmen: a rank higher than Chief Friends.

11:7 Eleutherus: two hundred miles north of Joppa, in the second century B.C. the northern limit of Coelesyria.

11:8 Seleucia by the sea: at the mouth of the Orontes, the port city of Antioch.

11:10 I regret . . . to kill me: according to Josephus, Ammonius, a friend of Alexander, had tried to assassinate Ptolemy, and the latter claimed that Alexander was the instigator, thus calumniating him to gain his kingdom (v. 11).

11:13 Crown: lit., diadem.

11:19 The one hundred and sixty-seventh year: 146/145 B.C. The two deaths (vv. 17–18) occurred in the summer of 145 B.C.

e: 1 Mc 11:4; 1 Sm 5:2–5. *f*: 1 Mc 10:84.

Alliance of Jonathan and Demetrius II.
20In those days Jonathan gathered together
the people of Judea to attack the citadel in
Jerusalem, and they set up many siege engines against it. 21But some transgressors of
the law, enemies of their own nation, went to
the king and informed him that Jonathan was
besieging the citadel. 22When Demetrius
heard this, he was enraged; and as soon as he
heard it, he set out and came to Ptolemais.
He wrote to Jonathan to discontinue the
siege and to meet him for a conference at
Ptolemais as soon as possible.
23On hearing this, Jonathan ordered the
siege to continue. He selected some elders
and priests of Israel and put himself at risk.
24Taking with him silver, gold and apparel,
and many other presents, he went to the king
at Ptolemais, and found favor with him.
25Although certain renegades of his own nation kept on bringing charges against him,
26the king treated him just as his predecessors had done and exalted him in the presence of all his Friends. 27He confirmed him
in the high priesthood and in the other honors he had previously held, and had him enrolled among his Chief Friends.
28Jonathan asked the king to exempt Judea
and the three districts of Samaria from tribute,
promising him in return three hundred talents.[g] 29The king agreed and wrote a letter to
Jonathan about all these matters as follows:
30[h]"King Demetrius sends greetings to
his brother* Jonathan and to the Jewish nation. 31We are sending you, for your information, a copy of the letter that we wrote to
Lasthenes* our Kinsman concerning you.
32'King Demetrius sends greetings to his father Lasthenes. 33Upon the Jewish nation,
who are our friends and observe their obligations to us, we have decided to bestow
benefits because of the good will they show
us. 34[i] Therefore we confirm their possession, not only of the territory of Judea, but
also of the three districts of Aphairema,*
Lydda, and Ramathaim. These districts, together with all their dependencies, are
hereby transferred from Samaria to Judea
for those who offer sacrifices in Jerusalem in
lieu of the royal taxes the king used to receive yearly from the produce of earth and
trees. 35From payment of the other things
that would henceforth be due to us, namely,
the tithes and taxes, as well as the salt tax,
and the crown tax—from all these we grant
them release. 36Henceforth and forever not
one of these provisions shall ever be revoked. 37See to it, therefore, that a copy of
these instructions be made and given to Jonathan. Let it be displayed on the holy mountain in a conspicuous place.' "

The Intrigue of Trypho. 38When King
Demetrius saw that the land was peaceful under his rule and that he had no opposition, he
dismissed his entire army, each to his own
home, except the foreign troops which he
had hired from the islands of the nations. So
all the soldiers who had served under his
predecessors became hostile to him. 39When
a certain Trypho, who had previously supported Alexander, saw that all the troops
were grumbling against Demetrius, he went
to Imalkue the Arabian, who was raising
Alexander's young son Antiochus.[j] 40Trypho
kept urging Imalkue to hand over the boy to
him, so that he might succeed his father as
king. He told him of all that Demetrius had
done and of the hostility his soldiers had for
him; and he remained there for many days.

Jonathan Aids Demetrius II. 41Mean-
while Jonathan sent the request to King
Demetrius to withdraw the troops in the
citadel from Jerusalem and from the other
strongholds, for they were constantly waging war on Israel. 42Demetrius, in turn, sent
this word to Jonathan: "I will do not only

11:30 Brother: this term and "father" in v. 32 are honorific expressions used of the Kinsmen.

11:31 Lasthenes: leader of the mercenary troops who had come with Demetrius from Crete. He was now the young king's chief minister and was apparently responsible for the disastrous policy (v. 38) of disbanding the national army.

11:34 Aphairema: the Ophrah of Jos 18:23; 1 Sm 13:17; the Ephron of 2 Chr 13:19; and the Ephraim of Jn 11:54—modern et-Taiyibeh, five miles northeast of Bethel. **Lydda**: the Lod of the postexilic Jews (Ezr 2:33; Neh 11:35) and the hometown of Aeneas, who was cured by Peter (Acts 9:32–34). It is ten miles southeast of Joppa. **Ramathaim**: the Ramathaim-zophim of 1 Sm 1:1, and the Arimathea of Mt 27:57, modern Rentis, nine miles northeast of Lydda.

g: 1 Mc 10:29; 11:34–35. *h:* 1 Mc 10:25–45. *i:* 1 Mc 10:29; 11:28. *j:* 1 Mc 12:39.

this for you and your nation, but I will greatly honor you and your nation when I find the opportunity. [43]Now, therefore, you will do well to send men to fight for me, because all my troops have revolted."

[44]So Jonathan sent three thousand good fighting men to him at Antioch. When they came to the king, he was delighted over their arrival. [45]The populace, one hundred and twenty thousand strong, massed in the center of the city in an attempt to kill the king. [46]So the king took refuge in the palace, while the populace gained control of the main streets of the city and prepared for battle. [47]Then the king called the Jewish force to his aid. They all rallied around him and spread out through the city. On that day they killed about a hundred thousand in the city. [48]At the same time, they set the city on fire and took much spoil. Thus they saved the king. [49]When the populace saw that the Jewish force controlled the city, they lost courage and cried out to the king in supplication, [50]"Extend the hand of friendship to us, and make the Jews stop attacking us and the city." [51]So they threw down their weapons and made peace. The Jews thus gained honor in the eyes of the king and all his subjects, and they became renowned throughout his kingdom. Finally they returned to Jerusalem with much plunder.

[52]But when King Demetrius was sure of his royal throne, and the land was peaceful under his rule, [53]he broke all his promises and became estranged from Jonathan. Instead of repaying Jonathan for all the favors he had received from him, he caused him much distress.

Alliance of Jonathan and Antiochus VI. [54]After this, Trypho returned and brought with him the young boy Antiochus, who became king and put on the diadem.[k] [55]All the soldiers whom Demetrius had discharged rallied around Antiochus and fought against Demetrius, who was routed and fled. [56]Trypho captured the elephants and occupied Antioch. [57]Then young Antiochus wrote to Jonathan: "I confirm you in the high priesthood and appoint you ruler over the four districts, and to be one of the King's Friends." [58]He also sent him gold dishes and a table service, gave him the right to drink from gold cups, to dress in royal purple, and to wear a gold buckle.[l] [59]Likewise, he made Jonathan's brother Simon governor of the region from the Ladder of Tyre* to the borders of Egypt.

Campaigns of Jonathan and Simon. [60]Jonathan set out and traveled through the province of West-of-Euphrates* and its cities, and all the forces of Syria espoused his cause as allies. When he arrived at Askalon, the citizens welcomed him with pomp. [61]But when he set out for Gaza, the people of Gaza shut him out. So he besieged it, and burned and plundered its suburbs. [62]Then the people of Gaza appealed to Jonathan, and he granted them terms of peace. He took the sons of their leaders as hostages and sent them to Jerusalem. He then traveled on through the province as far as Damascus.

[63]Jonathan heard that the generals of Demetrius had come with a strong force to Kadesh in Galilee, intending to remove him from office. [64]So he went to meet them, leaving his brother Simon in the province. [65][m] Simon encamped against Beth-zur, attacked it for many days, and shut in the inhabitants. [66]They appealed to him, and he granted them terms of peace. He expelled them from the city, took possession of it, and put a garrison there.

[67]Meanwhile, Jonathan and his army pitched their camp near the waters of Gennesaret, and at daybreak they went to the plain of Hazor.* [68]There the army of the foreigners met him on the plain. Having first detached an ambush in the mountains, this army mounted a frontal attack. [69]Then those in ambush rose out of their places and joined

11:59 Ladder of Tyre: modern Ras en-Naqurah, where the mountains reach the sea, so that the coastal road must ascend in a series of steps. Thus the Maccabees controlled the coastal area from Syria to Egypt.

11:60 The province of West-of-Euphrates: refers here to the territory of Palestine and Coelesyria, but not Upper Syria; cf. 7:8.

11:67 Plain of Hazor: the site of the ancient Canaanite city (Jos 11:10), ten miles north of the Lake of Gennesaret.

k: 1 Mc 11:39; 12:39. *l*: 1 Mc 2:18. *m*: 1 Mc 9:52; 10:14.

in the battle. 70 All of Jonathan's men fled; no one stayed except the army commanders Mattathias, son of Absalom, and Judas, son of Chalphi. 71 Jonathan tore his clothes, threw dust on his head, and prayed. 72 Then he went back to the battle and routed them, and they fled. 73 Those of his men who were running away saw it and returned to him; and with him they pursued the enemy as far as their camp in Kadesh, and there they encamped. 74 About three thousand of the foreign troops fell on that day. Then Jonathan returned to Jerusalem.

See RG 229

CHAPTER 12

Alliances with Rome and Sparta. 1 When Jonathan saw that the time was right, he chose men and sent them to Rome to confirm and renew the friendship with the Romans.[n] 2 He also sent letters to the Spartans and other places to the same effect.

3 After reaching Rome, the men entered the senate chamber and said, "The high priest Jonathan and the Jewish people have sent us to renew the friendship and alliance of earlier times with them." 4 The Romans gave them letters addressed to authorities in various places, with the request to provide them with safe conduct to the land of Judah.

5 This is a copy of the letter that Jonathan wrote to the Spartans: 6 "Jonathan the high priest, the senate of the nation, the priests, and the rest of the Jewish people send greetings to their brothers the Spartans. 7 Long ago a letter was sent* to the high priest Onias from Arius, who then reigned over you, stating that you are our brothers, as the attached copy shows.[o] 8 Onias welcomed the envoy with honor and received the letter, which spoke clearly of alliance and friendship. 9 Though we have no need of these things, since we have for our encouragement the holy books that are in our possession,*[p] 10 we have ventured to send word to you for the renewal of brotherhood and friendship, lest we become strangers to you; a long time has passed since you sent your message to us. 11 We, on our part, have unceasingly remembered you in the sacrifices and prayers that we offer on our feasts and other appropriate days, as it is right and proper to remember brothers. 12 We likewise rejoice in your renown. 13 But many tribulations and many wars have beset us, and the kings around us have attacked us. 14 We did not wish to be troublesome to you and to the rest of our allies and friends in these wars. 15 For we have the help of Heaven for our support, and we have been saved from our enemies, and our enemies have been humbled. 16 So we have chosen Numenius, son of Antiochus, and Antipater, son of Jason, and we have sent them to the Romans to renew with them the friendship and alliance of earlier times.[q] 17 We have also ordered them to come to you and greet you, and to deliver to you our letter concerning the renewal of our brotherhood. 18 Therefore kindly send us an answer on this matter."

19 This is a copy of the letter that they sent to Onias: 20[r] "Arius, king of the Spartans, sends greetings to Onias the high priest. 21 A document has been found stating that the Spartans and the Jews are brothers and that they are of the family of Abraham. 22 Now that we have learned this, kindly write to us about your welfare. 23 We, for our part, declare to you that your animals and your possessions are ours, and ours are yours. We have, therefore, given orders that you should be told of this."

More Campaigns of Jonathan and Simon. 24 Then Jonathan heard that the officers of Demetrius had returned to attack him with a stronger army than before. 25 So he set out from Jerusalem and met them in the territory of Hamath,* giving them no opportunity to enter his province. 26 The spies he had sent into their camp came back and reported to

12:7 Long ago a letter was sent: i.e., a century and a half before. **Onias**: Onias I, high priest from 323 to 300 or 290 B.C. **Arius**: Arius I, king from 309 to 265 B.C.

12:9 The holy books . . . in our possession: a reference to "the law, the prophets and other books," as mentioned in the Prologue to Sirach.

12:25 Territory of Hamath: the Seleucid territory of Upper Syria northeast of Coelesyria and separated from it by the Eleutherus River. The latter territory was under the command of Jonathan (11:59–60).

n: 1 Mc 8:17. *o:* 1 Mc 12:20–23. *p:* 2 Mc 2:14. *q:* 1 Mc 14:22; 15:15. *r:* 1 Mc 12:7.

him that the enemy were preparing to attack them that night. [27]Therefore, when the sun set, Jonathan ordered his men to keep watch, with their weapons at the ready for battle, throughout the night; and he set outposts around the camp. [28]When the enemy heard that Jonathan and his men were ready for battle, their hearts sank with fear and dread. They lighted fires in their camp and then withdrew. [29]But because Jonathan and his men were watching the campfires burning, they did not know until the morning what had happened. [30]Then Jonathan pursued them, but he could not overtake them, for they had crossed the river Eleutherus. [31]So Jonathan turned aside against the Arabians who are called Zabadeans, and he struck them down and plundered them. [32]Then he broke camp, marched on toward Damascus and traveled through the whole region.

[33]Simon also set out and traveled as far as Askalon and its neighboring strongholds. He then turned to Joppa and took it by surprise, [34]for he heard that its people intended to hand over the stronghold to the supporters of Demetrius. He left a garrison there to guard it.

[35]When Jonathan returned, he assembled the elders of the people, and with them he made plans for building strongholds in Judea, [36]for making the walls of Jerusalem still higher, and for erecting a high barrier between the citadel and the city, to separate it from the city and isolate it, so that its garrison could neither buy nor sell. [37]The people therefore gathered together to build up the city, for part of the wall of the eastern valley had collapsed. And Jonathan repaired the quarter called Chaphenatha. [38]Simon likewise built up Adida in the Shephelah, and fortified it by installing gates and bars.

Capture of Jonathan. [39]Then Trypho sought to become king of Asia, assume the diadem, and do violence to King Antiochus.[s] [40]But he was afraid that Jonathan would not permit him, but would fight against him. Looking for a way to seize and kill him, he set out and came to Beth-shan. [41]Jonathan marched out to meet him with forty thousand picked fighting men and came to Beth-shan. [42]But when Trypho saw that Jonathan had arrived with a large army he was afraid to do him violence. [43]Instead, he received him with honor, introduced him to all his friends, and gave him presents. He also ordered his friends and soldiers to obey him as they would himself. [44]Then he said to Jonathan: "Why have you put all these people to so much trouble when we are not at war? [45]Now pick out a few men to stay with you, send the rest to their homes, and then come with me to Ptolemais. I will hand it over to you together with other strongholds and the remaining troops, as well as all the officials; then I will turn back and go home. That is why I came here."

[46]Jonathan trusted him and did as he said. He dismissed his troops, and they returned to the land of Judah. [47]But he kept with him three thousand men, of whom he left two thousand in Galilee while one thousand accompanied him. [48]Then as soon as Jonathan entered Ptolemais, the people of Ptolemais closed the gates and seized him; all who had entered with him, they killed with the sword.[t]

[49]Then Trypho sent soldiers and cavalry to Galilee and the Great Plain* to destroy all Jonathan's men. [50]These, upon learning that Jonathan had been captured and killed along with his companions, encouraged one another and went out in close formation, ready to fight. [51]As their pursuers saw that they were ready to fight for their lives, they turned back. [52]Thus all Jonathan's men came safely into the land of Judah. They mourned Jonathan and those who were with him. They were in great fear, and all Israel fell into deep mourning. [53]All the nations round about sought to crush them. They said, "Now that they have no leader or helper, let us make war on them and wipe out their memory from the earth."[u]

IV. Leadership of Simon

CHAPTER 13

See RG 229

Simon as Leader. [1]When Simon heard that Trypho was gathering a large army to in-

12:49 The Great Plain: of Beth-shan (v. 41), where Jonathan's disbanded troops remained.

s: 1 Mc 11:39–40, 54–55. *t:* 1 Mc 5:15, 22, 55. *u:* 1 Mc 5:2; 13:6.

vade and ravage the land of Judah, [2]and saw that the people were trembling with terror, he went up to Jerusalem. There he assembled the people [3]and exhorted them in these words: "You know what I, my brothers, and my father's house have done for the laws and the sanctuary; what battles and hardships we have seen. [4]For the sake of this, for the sake of Israel, all my brothers have perished, and I alone am left. [5]Far be it from me, then, to save my own life in any time of distress, for I am not better than my brothers. [6]But I will avenge my nation and the sanctuary, as well as your wives and children, for out of hatred all the Gentiles have united to crush us."[v]

[7]As the people heard these words, their spirit was rekindled. [8]They shouted in reply: "You are our leader in place of your brothers Judas and Jonathan. [9]Fight our battles, and we will do everything that you tell us." [10]So Simon mustered all the men able to fight, and hastening to complete the walls of Jerusalem, fortified it on every side. [11]He sent Jonathan, son of Absalom, to Joppa with a strong force; Jonathan drove out the occupants and remained there.

Trypho's Deceit. [12]Then Trypho moved from Ptolemais with a large army to invade the land of Judah, bringing Jonathan with him as a prisoner. [13]Simon encamped at Adida, facing the plain. [14]When Trypho learned that Simon had succeeded his brother Jonathan, and that he intended to fight him, he sent ambassadors to him with this message: [15]"It was on account of the money your brother Jonathan owed the royal treasury in connection with the offices that he held, that we have detained him. [16]Now send a hundred talents of silver, and two of his sons as hostages to guarantee that when he is set free he will not revolt against us, and we will release him."

[17]Simon knew that they were speaking deceitfully to him. Nevertheless, for fear of provoking much hostility among the people, he sent for the money and the boys, [18]lest the people say "Jonathan perished because I would not send Trypho the money and the boys." [19]So he sent the boys and the hundred talents; but Trypho broke his promise and would not release Jonathan.

[20]* Next Trypho moved to invade and ravage the country. His troops went around by the road that leads to Adora, but Simon and his army moved along opposite him everywhere he went. [21]The people in the citadel kept sending emissaries to Trypho, pressing him to come to them by way of the wilderness, and to send them provisions. [22]Although Trypho got all his cavalry ready to go, there was a very heavy snowfall that night, and he could not go on account of the snow. So he left for Gilead. [23]When he was approaching Baskama,* he had Jonathan killed and buried him there. [24]Then Trypho returned to his own land.

Jonathan's Tomb. [25]Simon sent for the remains of his brother Jonathan, and buried him in Modein, the city of his ancestors. [26]All Israel bewailed him with solemn lamentation, mourning over him for many days. [27]Then Simon erected over the tomb of his father and his brothers a monument of stones, polished front and back, and raised high enough to be seen at a distance. [28]He set up seven pyramids facing one another for his father and his mother and his four brothers.[w] [29]For the pyramids he devised a setting of massive columns, which he adorned with suits of armor as a perpetual memorial, and next to the armor carved ships, which could be seen by all who sailed the sea. [30]This tomb which he built at Modein is there to the present day.

Alliance of Simon and Demetrius II. [31]Trypho dealt treacherously with the young King Antiochus. He killed him [32]and became king in his place, putting on the crown of Asia. Thus he brought much evil on the land.[x] [33]Simon, for his part, built up the strongholds of Judea, fortifying them all around with high towers, thick walls, and gates with bars, and he stored up provisions in the strongholds. [34]Simon also chose men

13:20–21 The invaders made a wide flanking movement to invade Judea from the south (see 4:29; 6:31). Adora was a few miles southwest of Beth-zur. They would avoid Beth-zur itself and other strongholds of the Maccabees by following the way of the wilderness.

13:23 Baskama: perhaps northeast of the Sea of Galilee.

v: 1 Mc 5:2; 12:53. *w*: 2 Sm 18:18. *x*: 1 Mc 8:6.

and sent them to King Demetrius to obtain for the land an exemption from taxation, since Trypho did nothing but plunder. [35]King Demetrius replied favorably and sent him the following letter:

[36]"King Demetrius sends greetings to Simon, high priest and friend of kings, and to the elders and the Jewish people. [37]We have received the gold crown and the palm branch that you sent. We are ready to make a lasting peace with you and to write to our officials to grant you exemption. [38]Whatever decrees we have made in your regard remain in force, and the strongholds that you have built you may keep. [39]We pardon any oversights and offenses committed up to now, as well as the crown tax that you owe. Any other tax that used to be collected in Jerusalem shall no longer be collected there. [40]Any of you qualified for enrollment in our service may be enrolled. Let there be peace between us."

[41]Thus in the one hundred and seventieth year,* the yoke of the Gentiles was removed from Israel, [42]and the people began to write in their records and contracts, "In the first year of Simon, great high priest, governor, and leader of the Jews."

Simon Captures Gazara. [43][y] In those days Simon besieged Gazara* and surrounded it with troops. He made a siege machine, brought it up against the city, and attacked and captured one of the towers. [44]Those in the siege machine leaped down into the city and a great tumult arose there. [45]Those in the city, together with their wives and children, went up on the wall, with their garments rent, and cried out in loud voices, begging Simon to grant them terms of peace. [46]They said, "Treat us not according to our evil deeds but according to your mercy." [47]So Simon came to terms with them and did not attack them. He expelled them from the city, however, and he purified the houses in which there were idols. Then he entered the city with hymns and songs of praise. [48]After removing from it everything that was impure, he settled there people who observed the law. He improved its fortifications and built himself a residence.

Simon Captures the Citadel. [49]The people in the citadel in Jerusalem were prevented from going out into the country and back to buy or sell; they suffered greatly from hunger, and many of them died of starvation. [50]They finally cried out to Simon, and he gave them terms of peace. He expelled them from the citadel and cleansed it of impurities. [51]On the twenty-third day of the second month,* in the one hundred and seventy-first year, the Jews entered the citadel with shouts of praise, the waving of palm branches, the playing of harps and cymbals and lyres, and the singing of hymns and canticles, because a great enemy of Israel had been crushed.[z] [52]Simon decreed that this day should be celebrated every year with rejoicing. He also strengthened the fortifications of the temple mount alongside the citadel, and he and his people dwelt there. [53]Seeing that his son John* was now a grown man, Simon made him commander of all his soldiers, and he dwelt in Gazara.

CHAPTER 14

See RG 229–30

Capture of Demetrius II. [1]In the one hundred and seventy-second year,* King Demetrius assembled his army and marched into Media to obtain help so that he could fight Trypho. [2]When Arsaces,* king of Persia and Media, heard that Demetrius had entered his territory, he sent one of his generals to take him alive. [3]The general went forth and attacked the army of Demetrius; he captured him and brought him to Arsaces, who put him under guard.

13:41 The one hundred and seventieth year: March, 142, to April, 141 B.C., by the Temple calendar.

13:43 Gazara: ancient Gezer, a key position in the Shephelah, fortified by Bacchides in 160 B.C.; cf. 9:52.

13:51 The twenty-third day of the second month: June 3, 141 B.C.

13:53 John: John Hyrcanus, who was to succeed his father as ruler and high priest; cf. 16:23–24.

14:1 The one hundred and seventy-second year: 141/140 B.C. The expedition began most probably in the spring of 140.

14:2 Arsaces: Arsaces VI, also called Mithridates I, the Parthian king (171–138 B.C.). Parthians had overrun Persia and now held Babylonia, both of which had hitherto belonged to the Seleucid empire. The Greeks and Macedonians in these countries had appealed to Demetrius for help.

y: 2 Mc 10:32–38. *z:* 1 Mc 1:36.

Praise of Simon

4 The land was at rest all the days of
Simon,
who sought the good of his nation.
His rule delighted his people
and his glory all his days.[a]
5 As his crowning glory he took Joppa for
a port
and made it a gateway to the isles of
the sea.[b]
6 He enlarged the borders of his nation
and gained control of the country.
7 He took many prisoners of war
and made himself master of Gazara,
Beth-zur, and the citadel.
He cleansed the citadel of its impurities;
there was no one to withstand him.
8 The people cultivated their land in peace;
the land yielded its produce,
the trees of the field their fruit.[c]
9 Old men sat in the squares,
all talking about the good times,
while the young men put on the
glorious raiment of war.[d]
10 He supplied the cities with food
and equipped them with means of
defense,
till his glorious name reached the ends
of the earth.
11 He brought peace to the land,
and Israel was filled with great joy.[e]
12 Every one sat under his vine and fig tree,
with no one to disturb them.[f]
13 No attacker was left in the land;
the kings in those days were crushed.
14 He strengthened all the lowly among his
people
and was zealous for the law;
he destroyed the lawless and the
wicked.
15 The sanctuary he made splendid
and multiplied its furnishings.

Alliance with Rome and Sparta. 16When
people in Rome and even in Sparta heard
that Jonathan had died, they were deeply
grieved.* 17But when they heard that his
brother Simon had become high priest in his
place and was master of the territory and its
cities, 18they sent him inscribed tablets of
bronze to renew with him the friendship and
alliance that they had established with his
brothers Judas and Jonathan.[g] 19These were
read before the assembly in Jerusalem.
20This is a copy of the letter that the Spartans sent: "The rulers and the city of the
Spartans send greetings to Simon the high
priest, the elders, the priests, and the rest of
the Jewish people, our brothers. 21The ambassadors sent to our people have informed
us of your glory and renown, and we rejoiced at their coming. 22In accordance with
what they said we have recorded the following in the public decrees: Numenius, son of
Antiochus, and Antipater, son of Jason, ambassadors of the Jews, have come to us to renew their friendship with us.[h] 23The people
have resolved to receive these men with
honor, and to deposit a copy of their words
in the public archives, so that the people of
Sparta may have a record of them. A copy of
this decree has been made for Simon the
high priest."
24After this, Simon sent Numenius to
Rome with a large gold shield weighing a
thousand minas, to confirm the alliance with
the Romans.

Official Honors for Simon. 25When the
people heard of these things, they said,
"How shall we thank Simon and his sons?
26He and his brothers and his father's house
have stood firm and repulsed Israel's enemies, and so have established its freedom."
So they made an inscription on bronze
tablets, which they affixed to pillars on
Mount Zion.
27The following is a copy of the inscription: "On the eighteenth day of Elul,* in the
one hundred and seventy-second year, that
is, the third year under Simon the great high
priest in Asaramel, 28in a great assembly of
the people of God."

14:16 The embassy to Rome and Sparta was sent soon after Simon's accession to power, and the replies were received before Demetrius' expedition (vv. 1–3), probably in 142 B.C.

14:27 Eighteenth day of Elul: September 13, 140 B.C. **Asaramel**: perhaps a Hebrew name meaning "court of the people of God."

a: 1 Mc 3:3–9. *b:* 1 Mc 12:33; 13:11. *c:* Lv 26:3–4; Zec 8:12. *d:* Zec 8:4–5. *e:* Lv 26:6. *f:* Mi 4:4; Zec 3:10. *g:* 1 Mc 8:22. *h:* 1 Mc 12:16; 15:15.

priests, people, rulers of the nation, and elders of the region, the following proclamation was made to us:

29" 'Since there have often been wars in our country, Simon, son of the priest Mattathias, descendant of Joarib, and his brothers have put themselves in danger and resisted the enemies of their nation, so that their sanctuary and law might be maintained, and they have thus brought great glory to their nation. 30Jonathan rallied the nation, became their high priest, and was gathered to his people. 31When their enemies sought to invade and ravage their country and to violate their sanctuary, 32Simon rose up and fought for his nation, spending large sums of his own money to equip his nation's forces and give them their pay. 33He fortified the cities of Judea, especially the border city of Bethzur, formerly the site of the enemy's weaponry, and he stationed there a garrison of Jewish soldiers. 34He also fortified Joppa by the sea and Gazara on the border of Azotus, a place previously occupied by the enemy; these cities he settled with Jews and furnished them with all that was necessary for their restoration. 35When the people saw Simon's fidelity and the glory he planned to bring to his nation, they made him their leader and high priest because of all he had accomplished and the justice and fidelity he had shown his nation. In every way he sought to exalt his people.

36" 'In his time and under his guidance they succeeded in driving the Gentiles out of their country and those in the City of David in Jerusalem, who had built for themselves a citadel from which they used to sally forth to defile the environs of the sanctuary and inflict grave injury on its purity. 37In this citadel he stationed Jewish soldiers, and he strengthened its fortifications for the security of the land and the city, while he also built up the wall of Jerusalem to a greater height. 38Consequently, King Demetrius confirmed him in the high priesthood, 39made him one of his Friends, and conferred great honor on him.[i] 40This was because he had heard that the Romans had addressed the Jews as friends, allies, and brothers, that they had received Simon's envoys with honor, 41and that the Jewish people and their priests had decided the following: Simon shall be their leader and high priest forever until a trustworthy prophet arises.[j] 42He shall act as governor over them, and shall have charge of the sanctuary, to make regulations concerning its functions and concerning the country, its weapons and strongholds. 43He shall be obeyed by all. All contracts in the country shall be written in his name, and he shall be clothed in purple and gold.[k] 44It shall not be lawful for any of the people or priests to nullify any of these decisions, or to contradict the orders given by him, or to convene an assembly in the country without his consent, to be clothed in purple or wear a gold buckle. 45Whoever acts otherwise or violates any of these prescriptions shall be liable to punishment.

46" 'Thus all the people approved of granting Simon the right to act in accord with these decisions, 47and Simon accepted and agreed to be high priest, governor, and ethnarch* of the Jewish people and priests, and to have authority over all.' "

48It was decreed that this inscription should be engraved on bronze tablets, to be set up in a conspicuous place in the precincts of the sanctuary, 49and that copies of it should be deposited in the treasury, where they would be available to Simon and his sons.

CHAPTER 15

See RG 229–30

Letter of Antiochus VII. 1Antiochus,* son of King Demetrius, sent a letter from the islands of the sea to Simon, the priest and ethnarch of the Jews, and to all the nation, 2which read as follows:

"King Antiochus sends greetings to Simon, the high priest and ethnarch, and to the

14:47 Ethnarch: a subordinate ruler over an ethnic group whose office needed confirmation by a higher authority within the empire.

15:1 Antiochus: Antiochus VII Sidetes, son of Demetrius I, and younger brother of Demetrius II (now a prisoner of the Parthians). At the age of twenty he set out from the island of Rhodes to take his brother's place and drive out the usurper Trypho.

i: 1 Mc 2:18. *j:* 1 Mc 4:46; 9:27. *k:* 1 Mc 10:20, 89.

Jewish nation. [3]Whereas certain villains have gained control of the kingdom of our ancestors, I intend to reclaim it, that I may restore it to its former state. I have recruited a large number of mercenary troops and equipped warships. [4]I intend to make a landing in the country so that I may take revenge on those who have ruined our country and laid waste many cities in my kingdom.

[5]"Now, therefore, I confirm to you all the tax exemptions that the kings before me granted you and whatever other privileges they conceded to you. [6]I authorize you to coin your own money, as legal tender in your country. [7]Jerusalem and its sanctuary shall be free. All the weapons you have prepared and all the strongholds you have built and now occupy shall remain in your possession. [8]All debts, present or future, due to the royal treasury shall be canceled for you, now and for all time. [9]When we establish our kingdom, we will greatly honor you and your nation and the temple, so that your glory will be manifest in all the earth."

[10]In the one hundred and seventy-fourth year* Antiochus invaded the land of his ancestors, and all the troops rallied to him, so that few were left with Trypho. [11]Pursued by Antiochus, Trypho fled to Dor, by the sea,* [12]realizing what troubles had come upon him now that his soldiers had deserted him. [13]Antiochus encamped before Dor with a hundred and twenty thousand infantry and eight thousand cavalry. [14]While he surrounded the city, his ships closed from the sea, so that he pressed it hard by land and sea and let no one go in or out.

Roman Alliance Renewed. [15]Meanwhile, Numenius and his companions came from Rome with letters containing this message to various kings and countries:[l] [16]"Lucius,* Consul of the Romans, sends greetings to King Ptolemy. [17]Ambassadors of the Jews, our friends and allies, have come to us to renew their earlier friendship and alliance. They had been sent by Simon the high priest and the Jewish people, [18]and they brought with them a gold shield of a thousand minas.[m] [19]Therefore we have decided to write to various kings and countries, that they are not to venture to harm them, or wage war against them or their cities or their country, and are not to assist those who fight against them. [20]We have also decided to accept the shield from them. [21]If, then, any troublemakers from their country take refuge with you, hand them over to Simon the high priest, so that he may punish them according to their law."

[22]The consul sent identical letters to Kings Demetrius, Attalus,* Ariarthes and Arsaces; [23]to all the countries—Sampsames, the Spartans, Delos, Myndos, Sicyon, Caria, Samos, Pamphylia, Lycia, Halicarnassus, Rhodes, Phaselis, Cos, Side, Aradus, Gortyna, Cnidus, Cyprus, and Cyrene. [24]A copy of the letter was also sent to Simon the high priest.

Hostility from Antiochus VII. [25]When King Antiochus encamped before Dor, he assaulted it continuously both with troops and with the siege engines he had made. He blockaded Trypho by preventing anyone from going in or out. [26]Simon sent to Antiochus' support two thousand elite troops, together with silver and gold and much equipment. [27]But he refused to accept the aid; in fact, he broke all the agreements he had previously made with Simon and became hostile toward him.[n]

[28]He sent Athenobius, one of his Friends, to confer with Simon and say: "You are occupying Joppa and Gazara and the citadel of Jerusalem; these are cities of my kingdom. [29]You have laid waste their territories, done great harm to the land, and taken possession of many districts in my kingdom. [30]Now, therefore, give up the cities you have seized and the tribute money of the districts you control outside the territory of Judea; [31]or instead, pay me five hundred talents of silver for the devastation you have caused and five

15:10 The one hundred and seventy-fourth year: 138 B.C.

15:11 Dor, by the sea: a fortress on the Palestinian coast, fifteen miles south of Carmel.

15:16 Lucius: perhaps Lucius Caecilius Metellus, consul in 142 B.C., or Lucius Calpurnicus Piso, consul in 140–139 B.C. This document pertains to Simon's first years as leader.

15:22 Attalus: Attalus II of Pergamum, reigned 159–138 B.C. **Ariarthes**: Ariarthes V of Cappadocia, reigned 162–130 B.C. **Arsaces**: see note on 14:2.

l: 1 Mc 8:17; 12:16; 14:22, 24. *m:* 1 Mc 14:24. *n:* 1 Mc 15:5–9.

hundred talents more for the tribute money of the cities. If you do not do this, we will come and make war on you."

32 So Athenobius, the king's Friend, came to Jerusalem and on seeing the splendor of Simon's court, the gold and silver plate on the sideboard, and his rich display, he was amazed. When he gave him the king's message, 33 Simon said to him in reply: "It is not foreign land we have taken nor have we seized the property of others, but only our ancestral heritage which for a time had been unjustly held by our enemies. 34 Now that we have the opportunity, we are holding on to the heritage of our ancestors. 35 As for Joppa and Gazara, which you demand, those cities were doing great harm to our people and our country. For these we will give you a hundred talents." Athenobius made no reply, 36 but returned to the king in anger. When he told him of Simon's words, of his splendor, and of all he had seen, the king fell into a violent rage.

Victory over Cendebeus. 37 Trypho had boarded a ship and escaped to Orthosia.* 38 Then the king appointed Cendebeus commander-in-chief of the seacoast, and gave him infantry and cavalry forces. 39 He ordered him to encamp against Judea and to fortify Kedron* and strengthen its gates, so that he could wage war on the people. Meanwhile the king went in pursuit of Trypho. 40 When Cendebeus came to Jamnia, he began to harass the people and to make incursions into Judea, where he took people captive and massacred them. 41 As the king ordered, he fortified Kedron and stationed cavalry and infantry there, so that they could go out and patrol the roads of Judea.

See RG 229–30

CHAPTER 16

1 John then went up from Gazara and told his father Simon what Cendebeus was doing.[o] 2 Simon called his two oldest sons, Judas and John, and said to them: "I and my brothers and my father's house have fought the wars of Israel from our youth until today, and many times we succeeded in saving Israel. 3 I have now grown old, but you, by the mercy of Heaven, have come to maturity. Take my place and my brother's, and go out and fight for our nation; and may the help of Heaven be with you!"

4 John then mustered in the land twenty thousand warriors and cavalry. Setting out against Cendebeus, they spent the night at Modein, 5 rose early, and marched into the plain. There, facing them, was an immense army of foot soldiers and cavalry, and between the two armies was a wadi. 6 John and his people took their position against the enemy. Seeing that his people were afraid to cross the wadi, John crossed first. When his men saw this, they crossed over after him.[p] 7 Then he divided his infantry and put his cavalry in the center, for the enemy's cavalry were very numerous. 8 They blew the trumpets, and Cendebeus and his army were routed; many of them fell wounded, and the rest fled toward the stronghold. 9 It was then that John's brother Judas fell wounded; but John pursued them until Cendebeus reached Kedron, which he had fortified. 10 Some took refuge in the towers on the plain of Azotus, but John set fire to these, and about two thousand of the enemy perished. He then returned to Judea in peace.[q]

Murder of Simon and His Sons. 11 Ptolemy, son of Abubus, had been appointed governor of the plain of Jericho, and he had much silver and gold, 12 being the son-in-law of the high priest. 13 But his heart became proud and he was determined to get control of the country. So he made treacherous plans to do away with Simon and his sons. 14 As Simon was inspecting the cities of the country and providing for their needs, he and his sons Mattathias and Judas went down to Jericho in the one hundred and seventy-seventh year, in the eleventh month* (that is, the month Shebat). 15 The son of Abubus gave them a deceitful welcome in the little strong-

15:37 Orthosia: a port between Tripoli and the Eleutherus River.

15:39 Kedron: a few miles southeast of Jamnia and facing the fortress of Gazara held by John Hyrcanus (13:53; 16:1).

16:14 In the one hundred and seventy-seventh year, in the eleventh month: January–February, 134 B.C., by the Temple calendar.

o: 1 Mc 13:53. *p:* 1 Mc 5:40–43. *q:* 1 Mc 10:84.

hold called Dok* which he had built. He
served them a sumptuous banquet, but he
had his men hidden there. 16Then, when Simon and his sons were drunk, Ptolemy and
his men sprang up, weapons in hand, rushed
upon Simon in the banquet hall, and killed
him, his two sons, and some of his servants.
17By this vicious act of treachery he repaid
good with evil.

18Then Ptolemy wrote a report and sent it
to the king, asking him to send troops to
help him and to turn over to him their country and its cities. 19He sent other men to
Gazara to do away with John. To the army
officers he sent letters inviting them to
come to him so that he might present them
with silver, gold, and gifts. 20He also sent
others to seize Jerusalem and the temple
mount. 21But someone ran ahead and
brought word to John at Gazara that his father and his brothers had perished, and
"Ptolemy has sent men to kill you also."
22On hearing this, John was utterly astounded. When the men came to kill him, he
seized them and put them to death, for he
knew that they sought to kill him.

23* Now the rest of the acts of John, his
wars and the brave deeds he performed, his
rebuilding of the walls, and all his achievements—r 24these are recorded in the chronicle of his high priesthood, from the time that
he succeeded his father as high priest.

16:15 Dok: a fortress built on a cliff three miles northwest of Jericho, near modern Ain Duq.

16:23–24 John Hyrcanus was ruler and high priest from 134 B.C. till his death in 104 B.C. These verses suggest that the book was written, or at least completed, only after he died.

r: 1 Mc 9:22.

See RG 231–34

The Second Book of Maccabees

Although this book, like the preceding one, receives its title from its protagonist, Judas Maccabee (or Maccabeus), it is not a sequel to 1 Maccabees. The two differ in many respects. Whereas the first covers the period from the beginning of the reign of Antiochus IV (175 B.C.) to the accession of John Hyrcanus I (134 B.C.), this book treats of the events in Jewish history from the time of the high priest Onias III and King Seleucus IV (ca. 180 B.C.) to the defeat of Nicanor's army (161 B.C.).

The author of 2 Maccabees states (2:23) that this one-volume work is an abridgment of a five-volume work by Jason of Cyrene; but since this latter has not survived, it is difficult to determine its relationship to the present epitome. One does not know how freely the anonymous epitomizer may have rewritten the original composition or how closely the abridgment follows the wording of the original. Some parts of the text here clearly not derived from Jason's work are the preface (2:19–32), the epilogue (15:37–39), and probably also certain moralizing reflections (e.g., 5:17–20; 6:12–17). It is certain, however, that both works were written in Greek, which explains in part why 2 Maccabees was not included in the canon of the Hebrew Bible.

The book is not without genuine historical value in supplementing 1 Maccabees, and it contains some apparently authentic official documents (11:16–38). Its purpose, whether intended by Jason himself or read into it by the compiler, is to give a theological interpretation to the history of the period. The major concern is the Jerusalem Temple, whose defender is the God of Israel. There is less interest, therefore, in the military exploits of Judas Maccabeus and more in God's marvelous interventions on behalf of the Jews and their Temple. These divine actions direct the course of events, both to punish the sacrilegious and blasphemous pagans and to purify and restore the Temple. The author sometimes effects this purpose by transferring events from their proper chronological order, by giving exaggerated figures for the size of armies and the numbers killed in battle, by placing long, edifying discourses and prayers in the mouths of heroes, and by describing elaborate celestial apparitions (3:24–34; 5:2–4; 10:29–30; 15:11–16). The book is the earliest known source of stories that glorify God's holy martyrs (6:18–7:42; 14:37–46).

Of theological importance are the author's teachings on Israel's sufferings (5:17–20; 6:12–17), the resurrection of the just on the last day

(7:9, 11, 14, 23; 14:46), the intercession of the saints in heaven for people living on earth (15:11–16), and the power of the living to offer prayers and sacrifices for the dead (12:39–46).

The beginning of 2 Maccabees consists of two letters sent by the Jews of Jerusalem to their coreligionists in Egypt. They deal with the observance of the feast commemorating the central event of the book, the purification of the Temple (Hanukkah). It is uncertain whether the author or a later scribe prefixed these letters to the narrative proper. If the author is responsible for their insertion, the book must have been written some time after 124 B.C., the date of the more recent of the two letters. A date of composition in the late second century B.C. is likely.

The main divisions of 2 Maccabees are:

I. Letters to the Jews in Egypt (1:1–2:18)
II. Compiler's Preface (2:19–32)
III. Heliodorus' Attempt to Profane the Temple (3:1–40)
IV. Profanation and Persecution (4:1–7:42)
V. Victories of Judas and Purification of the Temple (8:1–10:9)
VI. Renewed Persecution (10:10–15:36)
VII. Epilogue (15:37–39)

I. Letters to the Jews in Egypt

CHAPTER 1

See RG 231

Letter 1: 124 B.C. [1]The Jews in Jerusalem and in the land of Judea send greetings to their kindred, the Jews in Egypt, and
wish them true peace! [2]May God do good to
you and remember his covenant with his
faithful servants, Abraham, Isaac and Jacob,
[3]give to all of you a heart to worship him and
to do his will wholeheartedly and with a
willing spirit, [4]open your heart to his law
and commandments and grant you peace,
[5]hear your prayers, and be reconciled to you,
and never forsake you in time of adversity.
[6]Even now we are praying for you here.
[7]In the reign of Demetrius,* the one hundred and sixty-ninth year, we Jews wrote to
you during the height of the distress that
overtook us in those years after Jason and
his followers revolted against the holy land
and the kingdom,[a] [8]set fire to the gatehouse
and shed innocent blood. But we prayed to
the Lord, and our prayer was heard;* we offered sacrifices and fine flour; we lighted the
lamps and set out the loaves of bread.[b] [9]We
are now reminding you to celebrate the feast
of Booths in the month of Kislev.* [10]Dated in
the one hundred and eighty-eighth year.*
Letter 2: 164 B.C. The people of Jerusalem and Judea, the senate, and Judas send
greetings and good wishes to Aristobulus,
teacher of King Ptolemy and member of the
family of the anointed priests, and to the
Jews in Egypt. [11]Since we have been saved
by God from grave dangers, we give him
great thanks as befits those who fought
against the king;* [12][c] for it was God who
drove out those who fought against the holy
city. [13]When their leader arrived in Persia
with his seemingly irresistible army, they
were cut to pieces in the temple of the goddess Nanea* through a deceitful stratagem
employed by Nanea's priests. [14]* On the pretext of marrying the goddess, Antiochus

1:7 Demetrius: Demetrius II, king of Syria (145–139, 129–125 B.C.). **The one hundred and sixty-ninth year**: i.e., of the Seleucid era, 143 B.C. Regarding the dates in 1 and 2 Maccabees, see note on 1 Mc 1:10. On the troubles caused by Jason and his revolt against the kingdom, i.e., the rule of the legitimate high priest, see 2 Mc 4:7–22.

1:8 Our prayer was heard: in the victory of the Maccabees.

1:9 Feast of Booths in the month of Kislev: really the feast of the Dedication of the Temple, Hanukkah (2 Mc 10:1–8), celebrated on the twenty-fifth of Kislev (Nov.–Dec.). Its solemnity resembles that of the actual feast of Booths (Lv 23:33–43), celebrated on the fifteenth of Tishri (Sept.–Oct.); cf. 2 Mc 1:18.

1:10 The one hundred and eighty-eighth year: 124 B.C. The date pertains to the preceding, not the following letter. **Senate**: the council of Jewish elders of Jerusalem; cf. 1 Mc 12:6. **King Ptolemy**: Ptolemy VI Philometor, ruler of Egypt from 180 to 145 B.C.; he is mentioned also in 1 Mc 1:18; 10:51–59.

1:11–12 The king: Antiochus IV of Syria, the bitter persecutor of the Jews, who, as leader of the Syrian army that invaded Persia, perished there in 164 B.C.

1:13 Nanea: an oriental goddess comparable to Artemis of the Greeks.

1:14–17 Differing accounts of the death of Antiochus IV are found in 2 Mc 9:1–29 and in 1 Mc 6:1–16 (see also Dn 11:40–45). The writer of this letter had probably heard a distorted rumor of the king's death. This and other indications suggest that the letter was written very soon after Antiochus IV died, perhaps in 164 B.C.

a: 2 Mc 4:7–20. *b:* 1 Mc 4:50–51. *c:* 2 Mc 9:1–29; 1 Mc 6:1–13; Dn 11:40–45.

with his Friends had come to the place to get its great treasures as a dowry. [15]When the priests of Nanea's temple had displayed the treasures and Antiochus with a few attendants had come inside the wall of the temple precincts, the priests locked the temple as soon as he entered. [16]Then they opened a hidden trapdoor in the ceiling, and hurling stones at the leader and his companions, struck them down. They dismembered the bodies, cut off their heads and tossed them to the people outside. [17]Forever blessed be our God, who has thus punished the impious!

[18]* Since we shall be celebrating the purification of the temple on the twenty-fifth day of the month Kislev,[d] we thought it right to inform you, that you too may celebrate the feast of Booths and of the fire that appeared when Nehemiah, the rebuilder of the temple* and the altar, offered sacrifices. [19]For when our ancestors were being led into captivity in Persia,* devout priests at the time took some of the fire from the altar and hid it secretly in the hollow of a dry cistern, making sure that the place would be unknown to anyone. [20]Many years later, when it so pleased God, Nehemiah, commissioned by the king of Persia, sent the descendants of the priests who had hidden the fire to look for it. [21]When they informed us that they could not find any fire, but only a thick liquid, he ordered them to scoop some out and bring it. After the material for the sacrifices had been prepared, Nehemiah ordered the priests to sprinkle the wood and what lay on it with the liquid. [22]This was done, and when at length the sun, which had been clouded over, began to shine, a great fire blazed up, so that everyone marveled. [23]While the sacrifice was being burned, the priests recited a prayer, and all present joined in with them. Jonathan led and the rest responded with Nehemiah.

[24]The prayer was as follows: "Lord, Lord God, creator of all things, awesome and strong, just and merciful, the only king and benefactor, [25]who alone are gracious, just, almighty, and eternal, Israel's savior from all evil, who chose our ancestors and sanctified them: [26]accept this sacrifice on behalf of all your people Israel and guard and sanctify your portion. [27]Gather together our scattered people, free those who are slaves among the Gentiles, look kindly on those who are despised and detested, and let the Gentiles know that you are our God. [28]Punish those who lord it over us and in their arrogance oppress us. [29]Plant your people in your holy place, as Moses said."[e]

[30]Then the priests sang hymns. [31]After the sacrifice was consumed, Nehemiah ordered the rest of the liquid to be poured upon large stones. [32]As soon as this was done, a flame blazed up, but its light was lost in the brilliance coming from the altar. [33]When the event became known and the king of the Persians was told that, in the very place where the exiled priests had hidden the fire, a liquid was found with which Nehemiah and his people had burned the sacrifices, [34]the king, after verifying the fact, fenced the place off and declared it sacred. [35]To those whom the king favored, he distributed many benefits he received. [36]Nehemiah and his companions called the liquid nephthar, meaning purification, but most people named it naphtha.* [f]

CHAPTER 2

See RG 231–33

[1]In the records it will be found that Jeremiah the prophet ordered the deportees to take some of the fire with them as indicated, [2]and that the prophet, in giving them the law, directed the deportees not to forget the commandments of the Lord or be led astray in their thoughts, when seeing the gold and silver idols and their adornments.[g] [3]With other similar words he exhorted them that the law should not depart from their hearts.

[4]* The same document also tells how the

1:18–36 This legendary account of Nehemiah's miraculous fire is incorporated in the letter because of its connection with the Temple and its rededication. **Booths**: see note on v. 9.

1:18 Nehemiah, the rebuilder of the temple: he rebuilt the walls of Jerusalem, but the Temple had been rebuilt by Zerubbabel almost a century before.

1:19 Persia: actually Babylonia, which later became part of the Persian empire.

1:36 By a play on words, the Greek term *naphtha* (petroleum) is assimilated to some Semitic word, perhaps *nephthar*, meaning "loosened."

2:4–5 This legendary account is given for the purpose of explaining why the postexilic Temple was the legitimate

d: 2 Mc 6:7; 10:5; 1 Mc 1:59; 4:59. *e:* 2 Mc 2:18; Ex 15:17; Dt 30:3–5. *f:* 2 Mc 2:18; 10:3; 14:36. *g:* Bar 6:1–72.

prophet, in virtue of an oracle, ordered that
the tent and the ark should accompany him,
and how he went to the very mountain that
Moses climbed to behold God's inheritance.[h] 5When Jeremiah arrived there, he
found a chamber in a cave in which he put
the tent, the ark, and the altar of incense;
then he sealed the entrance. 6Some of those
who followed him came up intending to
mark the path, but they could not find it.
7When Jeremiah heard of this, he reproved
them: "The place is to remain unknown until God gathers his people together again and
shows them mercy. 8Then the Lord will disclose these things, and the glory of the Lord
and the cloud will be seen, just as they appeared in the time of Moses and of Solomon
when he prayed that the place* might be
greatly sanctified."[i]

9It is also related how Solomon in his wisdom offered a sacrifice for the dedication
and the completion of the temple. 10Just as
Moses prayed to the Lord and fire descended
from the sky and consumed the sacrifices, so
also Solomon prayed and fire came down
and consumed the burnt offerings.[j] 11* Moses had said, "Because it had not been eaten,
the purification offering was consumed."[k]
12Solomon also celebrated the feast in the
same way for eight days.

13These same things are also told in the
records and in Nehemiah's memoirs,* as
well as how he founded a library and collected the books about the kings and the
prophets, the books of David, and the royal
letters about votive offerings. 14In like manner Judas also collected for us all the books
that had been scattered because of the war,
and we now have them in our possession.[l]
15If you need them, send messengers to get
them for you.

16As we are about to celebrate the purification, we are writing: you should celebrate
the feast days. 17It is God who has saved all
his people and has restored to all of them
their inheritance, the kingdom, the priesthood, and the sacred rites, 18as he promised
through the law. For we hope in God, that he
will soon have mercy on us and gather us together from everywhere under the heavens
to his holy place, for he has rescued us from
great perils and has purified the place.[m]

II. Compiler's Preface

19This is the story of Judas Maccabeus and
his brothers, of the purification of the great
temple, the dedication of the altar, 20the
campaigns against Antiochus Epiphanes and
his son Eupator,* 21and of the heavenly manifestations accorded to the heroes who
fought bravely for the Jewish people. Few as
they were, they plundered the whole land,
put to flight the barbarian hordes, 22regained
possession of the temple renowned throughout the world, and liberated the city. They re-
established the laws that were in danger of
being abolished, while the Lord favored
them with every kindness. 23All this, detailed by Jason of Cyrene in five volumes,
we will try to condense into a single book.

24For in view of the flood of data, and the
difficulties encountered, given such abundant material, by those who wish to plunge
into accounts of the history, 25we have aimed
to please those who prefer simply to read, to
make it easy for the studious who wish to
commit things to memory, and to be helpful
to all. 26For us who have undertaken the labor of making this digest, the task, far from
being easy, is one of sweat and of sleepless
nights. 27Just so, the preparation of a festive
banquet is no light matter for one who seeks
to give enjoyment to others. Similarly, to
win the gratitude of many we will gladly endure this labor, 28leaving the responsibility
for exact details to the historian, and confining our efforts to presenting only a summary
outline. 29As the architect of a new house

place of worship even without these sacred objects. **The very mountain**: Nebo; cf. Dt 32:49; 34:1.

2:8 The place: the Temple of Jerusalem.

2:11 The statement attributed here to Moses seems to be based on Lv 10:16–20.

2:13 Nehemiah's memoirs: a lost apocryphal work, or perhaps Neh 1–7, 11–13.

2:20 For the account of the campaigns against Antiochus IV Epiphanes, see 4:7–10:9; and for the account of those against his son Antiochus V Eupator, see 10:10–13:26.

h: Dt 32:49; 34:1; Rev 11:19. *i:* Ex 40:34–35; 1 Kgs 8:11. *j:* Lv 9:23–24; 2 Chr 7:1. *k:* Lv 10:16–20. *l:* 1 Mc 1:57. *m:* Dt 30:3–5.

must pay attention to the whole structure, while the one who undertakes the decoration and the frescoes has to be concerned only with what is needed for ornamentation, so I think it is with us.[n] 30To enter into questions and examine them from all sides and to be busy about details is the task of the historian; 31but one who is making an adaptation should be allowed to aim at brevity of expression and to forgo complete treatment of the matter. 32Here, then, let us begin our account without adding to what has already been said; it would be silly to lengthen the preface to the history and then cut short the history itself.

III. Heliodorus' Attempt to Profane the Temple*

CHAPTER 3

See RG 233

Heliodorus' Arrival in Jerusalem. 1While the holy city lived in perfect peace and the laws were strictly observed because of the piety of the high priest Onias* and his hatred of evil,[o] 2the kings themselves honored the place and glorified the temple with the most magnificent gifts. 3Thus Seleucus,* king of Asia, defrayed from his own revenues all the expenses necessary for the liturgy of sacrifice.

4But a certain Simon, of the priestly clan of Bilgah,* who had been appointed superintendent of the temple, had a quarrel with the high priest about the administration of the city market.[p] 5Since he could not prevail against Onias, he went to Apollonius of Tarsus, who at that time was governor of Coelesyria and Phoenicia, 6and reported to him that the treasury in Jerusalem was full of such untold riches that the sum total of the assets was past counting and that since they did not belong to the account of the sacrifices, it would be possible for them to fall under the authority of the king.

7When Apollonius had an audience with the king, he informed him about the riches that had been reported to him. The king chose his chief minister Heliodorus and sent him with instructions to seize those riches. 8So Heliodorus immediately set out on his journey, ostensibly to visit the cities of Coelesyria and Phoenicia, but in reality to carry out the king's purpose.

9When he arrived in Jerusalem and had been graciously received by the high priest of the city, he told him about the information that had been given, and explained the reason for his presence, and he inquired if these things were really true. 10The high priest explained that there were deposits for widows and orphans,[q] 11and some was the property of Hyrcanus, son of Tobias,* a man who occupied a very high position. Contrary to the misrepresentations of the impious Simon, the total amounted only to four hundred talents of silver and two hundred of gold. 12It was utterly unthinkable to defraud those who had placed their trust in the sanctity of the place and in the sacred inviolability of a temple venerated all over the world.

Heliodorus' Plan To Rob the Temple. 13But Heliodorus, because of the orders he had from the king, said that in any case this money must be confiscated for the royal treasury. 14So on the day he had set he went in to take an inventory of the funds. There was no little anguish throughout the city. 15Priests prostrated themselves before the altar in their priestly robes, and called toward heaven for the one who had given the law about deposits to keep the deposits safe for those who had made them.[r] 16Whoever saw the appearance of the high priest was pierced to the heart, for the changed complexion of his face revealed his mental anguish. 17The terror and bodily

3:1–40 This legendary episode about Heliodorus is recounted here for the purpose of stressing the inviolability of the Temple of Jerusalem; its later profanation was interpreted as owing to the sins of the people; cf. 5:17–18.

3:1 Onias: Onias III was high priest from 196 to 175 B.C. and died in 171 B.C. He was the son of Simon, whose praises are sung in Sir 50:1–21.

3:3 Seleucus: Seleucus IV Philopator, who reigned from 187 to 175 B.C.

3:4 Bilgah: a priestly family mentioned in 1 Chr 24:14; Neh 12:5, 18.

3:11 Hyrcanus, son of Tobias: a member of the Tobiad family of Transjordan (Neh 2:10; 6:17–19; 13:4–8). Hyrcanus' father was Joseph, whose mother was the sister of the high priest Onias II.

n: 2 Mc 15:38–39. *o:* 2 Mc 5:19–20; 15:12. *p:* 2 Mc 4:23. *q:* Dt 14:29; 26:12. *r:* Ex 22:6–14.

trembling that had come over the man clearly
showed those who saw him the pain that
lodged in his heart. 18People rushed out of
their houses and crowded together making
common supplication, because the place was
in danger of being profaned. 19Women,
girded with sackcloth below their breasts,
filled the streets. Young women secluded indoors all ran, some to the gates, some to the
walls, others peered through the windows—
20all of them with hands raised toward
heaven, making supplication. 21It was pitiful
to see the populace prostrate everywhere and
the high priest full of dread and anguish.
22While they were imploring the almighty
Lord to keep the deposits safe and secure for
those who had placed them in trust, 23He-
liodorus went on with his plan.

God Protects the Temple. 24But just as Heliodorus was arriving at the treasury with his
bodyguards, the Lord of spirits and all authority produced an apparition so great that
those who had been bold enough to accompany Heliodorus were panic-stricken at
God's power and fainted away in terror.
25There appeared to them a richly ca-
parisoned horse, mounted by a fearsome
rider. Charging furiously, the horse attacked
Heliodorus with its front hooves. The rider
was seen wearing golden armor. 26Then two
other young men, remarkably strong, strikingly handsome, and splendidly attired, appeared before him. Standing on each side of
him, they flogged him unceasingly, inflicting innumerable blows. 27Suddenly he fell to
the ground, enveloped in great darkness. His
men picked him up and laid him on a
stretcher. 28They carried away helpless the
man who a moment before had entered that
treasury under arms with a great retinue and
his whole bodyguard. They clearly recognized the sovereign power of God.

***The Restoration and Testimony of He-
liodorus.*** 29As Heliodorus lay speechless because of God's action and deprived of any
hope of recovery, 30the people praised the
Lord who had marvelously glorified his own
place; and the temple, charged so shortly before with fear and commotion, was filled
with joy and gladness, now that the almighty
Lord had appeared. 31Quickly some of the
companions of Heliodorus begged Onias to
call upon the Most High to spare the life of
one who was about to breathe his last. 32The
high priest, suspecting that the king might
think that Heliodorus had suffered some foul
play at the hands of the Jews, offered a sacrifice for the man's recovery. 33While the
high priest was offering the sacrifice of
atonement, the same young men dressed in
the same clothing again appeared and stood
before Heliodorus. "Be very grateful to the
high priest Onias," they told him. "It is for
his sake that the Lord has spared your life.
34Since you have been scourged by Heaven,
proclaim to all God's great power." When
they had said this, they disappeared.

35After Heliodorus had offered a sacrifice
to the Lord and made most solemn vows to
the one who had spared his life, he bade
Onias farewell, and returned with his soldiers to the king. 36Before all he gave witness to the deeds of the most high God that
he had seen with his own eyes. 37When the
king asked Heliodorus what sort of person
would be suitable to be sent to Jerusalem
next, he answered: 38"If you have an enemy
or one who is plotting against the government, send him there, and you will get him
back with a flogging, if indeed he survives at
all; for there is certainly some divine power
about the place. 39The one whose dwelling is
in heaven watches over that place and protects it, and strikes down and destroys those
who come to harm it." 40This was how the
matter concerning Heliodorus and the
preservation of the treasury turned out.

IV. Profanation and Persecution

CHAPTER 4

See RG 233

Simon Accuses Onias. 1The Simon
mentioned above as the informer about the
funds against his own country slandered
Onias as the one who incited Heliodorus and
instigated the whole miserable affair. 2He
dared to brand as a schemer against the government the man who was the benefactor of
the city, the protector of his compatriots, and
a zealous defender of the laws. 3When Simon's hostility reached such a pitch that
murders were being committed by one of his

henchmen, [4]Onias saw that the opposition was serious and that Apollonius, son of Menestheus, the governor of Coelesyria and Phoenicia, was abetting Simon's wickedness. [5]So he had recourse to the king, not as an accuser of his compatriots, but as one looking to the general and particular good of all the people. [6]He saw that without royal attention it would be impossible to have a peaceful government, and that Simon would not desist from his folly.

Jason as High Priest. [7]But Seleucus died,* and when Antiochus surnamed Epiphanes succeeded him on the throne, Onias' brother Jason obtained the high priesthood by corrupt means:[s] [8]in an interview, he promised the king three hundred and sixty talents of silver, as well as eighty talents from another source of income. [9]Besides this he would undertake to pay a hundred and fifty more, if he was given authority to establish a gymnasium and a youth center* for it and to enroll Jerusalemites as citizens of Antioch.

[10]When Jason received the king's approval and came into office, he immediately initiated his compatriots into the Greek way of life. [11]He set aside the royal concessions granted to the Jews through the mediation of John, father of Eupolemus* (that Eupolemus who would later go on an embassy to the Romans to establish friendship and alliance with them); he set aside the lawful practices and introduced customs contrary to the law.[t] [12][u] With perverse delight he established a gymnasium* at the very foot of the citadel, where he induced the noblest young men to wear the Greek hat. [13]The craze for Hellenism and the adoption of foreign customs reached such a pitch, through the outrageous wickedness of Jason, the renegade and would-be high priest, [14]that the priests no longer cared about the service of the altar. Disdaining the temple and neglecting the sacrifices, they hastened, at the signal for the games, to take part in the unlawful exercises at the arena. [15]What their ancestors had regarded as honors they despised; what the Greeks esteemed as glory they prized highly. [16]For this reason they found themselves in serious trouble: the very people whose manner of life they emulated, and whom they desired to imitate in everything, became their enemies and oppressors. [17]It is no light matter to flout the laws of God, as subsequent events will show.

[18]When the quinquennial games were held at Tyre in the presence of the king, [19]the vile Jason sent representatives of the Antiochians of Jerusalem, to bring three hundred silver drachmas for the sacrifice to Hercules. But the bearers themselves decided that the money should not be spent on a sacrifice, as that was not right, but should be used for some other purpose. [20]So the contribution meant for the sacrifice to Hercules by the sender, was in fact applied to the construction of triremes* by those who brought it.

[21]When Apollonius, son of Menestheus, was sent to Egypt for the coronation of King Philometor,* Antiochus learned from him that the king was opposed to his policies. He took measures for his own security; so after going to Joppa, he proceeded to Jerusalem. [22]There he was received with great pomp by Jason and the people of the city, who escorted him with torchlights and acclamations; following this, he led his army into Phoenicia.

Menelaus as High Priest. [23]Three years later Jason sent Menelaus,* brother of the aforementioned Simon, to deliver the money to the king, and to complete negotiations on

4:7 Seleucus died: he was murdered by Heliodorus. Antiochus Epiphanes was his younger brother. Onias' brother showed his enthusiasm for the Greek way of life (v. 10) by changing his Hebrew name Joshua, or Jesus, to the Greek name Jason.

4:9 Youth center: an educational institution in which young men were trained both in Greek intellectual culture and in physical fitness. **Citizens of Antioch**: honorary citizens of Antioch, a Hellenistic city of the Seleucid Kingdom that had a corporation of such Antiochians, who enjoyed certain political and commercial privileges.

4:11 Eupolemus: one of the two envoys sent to Rome by Judas Maccabeus (1 Mc 8:17).

4:12 Since the **gymnasium**, where the youth exercised naked (Greek *gymnos*), lay in the Tyropoeon Valley to the east of the citadel, it was directly next to the Temple on its eastern side. **The Greek hat**: a wide-brimmed hat, traditional headgear of Hermes, the patron god of athletic contests; it formed part of the distinctive costume of the members of the "youth center."

4:20 Triremes: war vessels with three banks of oars.

4:21 Philometor: Ptolemy VI, king of Egypt, ca. 172 to ca. 145 B.C.

s: 2 Mc 1:7; 1 Mc 1:10. *t:* 1 Mc 8:17. *u:* 1 Mc 1:11–15.

urgent matters. [24]But after his introduction to the king, he flattered him with such an air of authority that he secured the high priesthood for himself, outbidding Jason by three hundred talents of silver. [25]He returned with the royal commission, but with nothing that made him worthy of the high priesthood; he had the temper of a cruel tyrant and the rage of a wild beast. [26]So Jason, who had cheated his own brother and now saw himself cheated by another man, was driven out as a fugitive to the country of the Ammonites. [27]But Menelaus, who obtained the office, paid nothing of the money he had promised to the king, [28]in spite of the demand of Sostratus, the commandant of the citadel, whose duty it was to collect the taxes. For this reason, both were summoned before the king. [29]Menelaus left his brother Lysimachus as his deputy in the high priesthood, while Sostratus left Crates, commander of the Cypriots.[v]

Murder of Onias. [30]While these things were taking place, the people of Tarsus and Mallus* rose in revolt, because their cities had been given as a gift to Antiochis, the king's concubine. [31]So the king hastened off to settle the affair, leaving Andronicus, one of his nobles, as his deputy. [32]Menelaus, for his part, thinking this a good opportunity, stole some gold vessels from the temple and presented them to Andronicus; he had already sold other vessels in Tyre and in the neighboring cities. [33]When Onias had clear evidence, he accused Menelaus publicly, after withdrawing to the inviolable sanctuary at Daphne, near Antioch. [34]Thereupon Menelaus approached Andronicus privately and urged him to seize Onias. So Andronicus went to Onias, treacherously reassuring him by offering his right hand in oath, and persuaded him, in spite of his suspicions, to leave the sanctuary. Then, with no regard for justice, he immediately put him to death.

[35]As a result, not only the Jews, but many people of other nations as well, were indignant and angry over the unjust murder of the man. [36]When the king returned from the region of Cilicia, the Jews of the city,* together with the Greeks who detested the crime, went to see him about the murder of Onias. [37]Antiochus was deeply grieved and full of pity; he wept as he recalled the prudence and noble conduct of the deceased. [38]Inflamed with anger, he immediately stripped Andronicus of his purple robe, tore off his garments, and had him led through the whole city to the very place where he had committed the outrage against Onias; and there he put the murderer to death. Thus the Lord rendered him the punishment he deserved.

More Outrages. [39]Many acts of sacrilege had been committed by Lysimachus in the city* with the connivance of Menelaus. When word spread, the people assembled in protest against Lysimachus, because a large number of gold vessels had been stolen. [40]As the crowds, now thoroughly enraged, began to riot, Lysimachus launched an unjustified attack against them with about three thousand armed men under the leadership of a certain Auranus, a man as advanced in folly as he was in years. [41]Seeing Lysimachus' attack, people picked up stones, pieces of wood or handfuls of the ashes lying there and threw them in wild confusion at Lysimachus and his men. [42]As a result, they wounded many of them and even killed a few, while they put all to flight. The temple robber himself they killed near the treasury.

[43]Charges about this affair were brought against Menelaus. [44]When the king came to Tyre, three men sent by the senate pleaded the case before him. [45]But Menelaus, seeing himself on the losing side, promised Ptolemy, son of Dorymenes, a substantial sum of money if he would win the king over.[w] [46]So Ptolemy took the king aside into a colonnade, as if to get some fresh air, and persuaded him to change his mind. [47]Menelaus, who was the cause of all the trouble, the king acquitted of the charges, while he condemned to death those poor

4:23 Menelaus: Jewish high priest from ca. 172 to his execution in 162 B.C. (13:3–8).

4:30 Mallus: a city of Cilicia (v. 36) in southeastern Asia Minor, about thirty miles east of Tarsus.

4:36 The city: Antioch. But some understand the Greek to mean "each city."

4:39 The city: Jerusalem. Menelaus was still in Syria.

v: 2 Mc 4:39–42. *w*: 2 Mc 8:8; 1 Mc 3:38.

men who would have been declared innocent even if they had pleaded their case before Scythians. [48]Thus, those who had prosecuted the case on behalf of the city, the people, and the sacred vessels, quickly suffered unjust punishment. [49]For this reason, even Tyrians, detesting the crime, provided sumptuously for their burial. [50]But Menelaus, thanks to the greed of those in power, remained in office, where he grew in wickedness, scheming greatly against his fellow citizens.

CHAPTER 5

See RG 233

Jason's Revolt. [1]About this time Antiochus sent his second expedition* into Egypt.[x] [2][y] It then happened that all over the city, for nearly forty days, there appeared horsemen, clothed in garments of a golden weave, charging in midair—companies fully armed with lances and drawn swords; [3]squadrons of cavalry in battle array, charges and countercharges on this side and that, with brandished shields and bristling spears, flights of arrows and flashes of gold ornaments, together with armor of every sort. [4]Therefore all prayed that this vision might be a good omen.

[5]But when a false rumor circulated that Antiochus was dead, Jason* gathered at least a thousand men and suddenly attacked the city. As the defenders on the walls were forced back and the city was finally being taken, Menelaus took refuge in the citadel. [6]For his part, Jason continued the merciless slaughter of his fellow citizens, not realizing that triumph over one's own kindred is the greatest calamity; he thought he was winning a victory over his enemies, not over his own people. [7]Even so, he did not gain control of the government, but in the end received only disgrace for his treachery, and once again took refuge in the country of the Ammonites. [8]At length he met a miserable end. Called to account before Aretas,* ruler of the Arabians, he fled from city to city, hunted by all, hated as an apostate from the laws, abhorred as the executioner of his country and his compatriots. Driven into Egypt, [9]he set out by sea for the Lacedaemonians, among whom he hoped to find protection because of his relations with them. He who had exiled so many from their country perished in exile; [10]and he who had cast out so many to lie unburied went unmourned and without a funeral of any kind, nor any place in the tomb of his ancestors.

Revenge by Antiochus. [11][z]When these happenings were reported to the king, he thought that Judea was in revolt. Raging like a wild animal, he set out from Egypt and took Jerusalem by storm. [12]He ordered his soldiers to cut down without mercy those whom they met and to slay those who took refuge in their houses. [13]There was a massacre of young and old, a killing of women and children, a slaughter of young women and infants. [14]In the space of three days, eighty thousand were lost, forty thousand meeting a violent death, and the same number being sold into slavery.

[15]Not satisfied with this, the king dared to enter the holiest temple in the world; Menelaus, that traitor both to the laws and to his country, served as guide. [16]He laid his impure hands on the sacred vessels and swept up with profane hands the votive offerings made by other kings for the advancement, the glory, and the honor of the place. [17]Antiochus became puffed up in spirit, not realizing that it was because of the sins of the city's inhabitants that the Sovereign Lord was angry for a little while: hence the disregard of the place.[a] [18]If they had not become entangled in so many sins, this man, like that Heliodorus sent by King Seleucus to inspect the treasury, would have been

5:1 Second expedition: the first invasion of Egypt by Antiochus IV in 169 B.C. (1 Mc 1:16–20) is not mentioned in 2 Maccabees, unless the coming of the Syrian army to Palestine (2 Mc 4:21–22) is regarded as the first invasion. The author of 2 Maccabees apparently combines the first pillage of Jerusalem in 169 B.C. after Antiochus' first invasion of Egypt (1 Mc 1:20–28; cf. 2 Mc 5:5–7) with the second pillage of the city two years later (167 B.C.), following the king's second invasion of Egypt in 168 B.C. (1 Mc 1:29–35; cf. 2 Mc 5:24–26).

5:5 Jason: brother of Onias III, claimant of the high priesthood (4:7–10). Later he was supplanted by Menelaus, who drove him into Transjordan (4:26).

5:8 Aretas: King Aretas I of the Nabateans; cf. 1 Mc 5:25.

x: 1 Mc 1:16–19; Dn 11:25–30. *y:* 2 Mc 3:24–26; 10:29–30; 11:8. *z:* 1 Mc 1:20–24. *a:* 2 Mc 6:12–16; 7:16–19, 32–38.

flogged and turned back from his presumptuous act as soon as he approached. 19 The Lord, however, had not chosen the nation for the sake of the place, but the place for the sake of the nation. 20 Therefore, the place itself, having shared in the nation's misfortunes, afterward participated in their good fortune; and what the Almighty had forsaken in wrath was restored in all its glory, once the great Sovereign Lord became reconciled.

21[b] Antiochus carried off eighteen hundred talents from the temple and hurried back to Antioch, thinking in his arrogance that he could make the land navigable and the sea passable on foot, so carried away was he with pride. 22 He left governors to harass the nation: at Jerusalem, Philip, a Phrygian by birth,* and in character more barbarous than the man who appointed him;[c] 23 at Mount Gerizim,* Andronicus; and besides these, Menelaus, who lorded it over his fellow citizens more than the others. Out of hatred for the Jewish citizens, 24[d] the king sent Apollonius,* commander of the Mysians, at the head of an army of twenty-two thousand, with orders to kill all the grown men and sell the women and children into slavery. 25 When this man arrived in Jerusalem, he pretended to be peacefully disposed and waited until the holy day of the sabbath; then, finding the Jews refraining from work, he ordered his men to parade fully armed. 26 All those who came out to watch, he massacred, and running through the city with armed men, he cut down a large number of people.

27 But Judas Maccabeus and about nine others withdrew to the wilderness to avoid sharing in defilement; there he and his companions lived like the animals in the hills, eating what grew wild.[e]

CHAPTER 6

See RG 233

Abolition of Judaism. 1[f] Not long after this the king sent an Athenian senator* to force the Jews to abandon the laws of their ancestors and live no longer by the laws of God, 2 also to profane the temple in Jerusalem and dedicate it to Olympian Zeus,* and the one on Mount Gerizim to Zeus the Host to Strangers, as the local inhabitants were wont to be.[g] 3 This was a harsh and utterly intolerable evil. 4 The Gentiles filled the temple with debauchery and revelry; they amused themselves with prostitutes and had intercourse with women even in the sacred courts. They also brought forbidden things into the temple,[h] 5 so that the altar was covered with abominable offerings prohibited by the laws.

6 No one could keep the sabbath or celebrate the traditional feasts, nor even admit to being a Jew. 7 Moreover, at the monthly celebration of the king's birthday the Jews, from bitter necessity, had to partake of the sacrifices, and when the festival of Dionysus* was celebrated, they were compelled to march in his procession, wearing wreaths of ivy.[i]

8 Following upon a vote of the citizens of Ptolemais, a decree was issued ordering the neighboring Greek cities to adopt the same measures, obliging the Jews to partake of the sacrifices 9 and putting to death those who would not consent to adopt the customs of the Greeks. It was obvious, therefore, that disaster had come upon them. 10 Thus, two women who were arrested for having circumcised their children were publicly paraded about the city with their babies hanging at their breasts and then thrown down from the top of the city wall.[j] 11 Others, who had assembled in nearby caves to observe the seventh day in secret, were betrayed to

5:22 Philip, a Phrygian by birth: the Philip of 2 Mc 6:11 and 8:8, but probably not the same as Philip the regent of 2 Mc 9:29 and 1 Mc 6:14.

5:23 Mount Gerizim: the sacred mountain of the Samaritans at Shechem; cf. 2 Mc 6:2.

5:24 Apollonius: the Mysian commander of 1 Mc 1:29; mentioned also in 2 Mc 3:5; 4:4.

6:1 Athenian senator: or, Geron the Athenian, since *geron* can also be a proper name.

6:2 Olympian Zeus: equated with the Syrian Baal Shamen ("the lord of the heavens"), a term which the Jews mockingly rendered as *shiqqus shomem*, "desolating abomination" (Dn 9:27; 11:31; 12:11; 1 Mc 1:54).

6:7 Dionysus: also called Bacchus, the god of the grape harvest and of wine; ivy was one of his symbols.

b: 1 Mc 1:23–24. *c:* 2 Mc 6:11; 8:8. *d:* 1 Mc 1:29–40. *e:* 2 Mc 8:1; 1 Mc 2:28. *f:* 1 Mc 1:41–63. *g:* 1 Mc 1:46, 54; Dn 9:27; 11:31; 12:11. *h:* Ez 23:36–49; Dn 11:31; Am 2:7. *i:* 1 Mc 1:58–59. *j:* 1 Mc 1:60–61.

Philip and all burned to death. In their respect for the holiness of that day, they refrained from defending themselves.[k]

God's Purpose. [12] Now I urge those who read this book not to be disheartened by these misfortunes, but to consider that these punishments were meant not for the ruin but for the correction of our nation. [13] It is, in fact, a sign of great kindness to punish the impious promptly instead of letting them go for long. [14m] Thus, in dealing with other nations, the Sovereign Lord patiently waits until they reach the full measure of their sins before punishing them; but with us he has decided to deal differently, [15] in order that he may not have to punish us later, when our sins have reached their fullness. [16] Therefore he never withdraws his mercy from us. Although he disciplines us with misfortunes, he does not abandon his own people. [17] Let these words suffice for recalling this truth. Without further ado we must go on with our story.

Martyrdom of Eleazar. [18*] Eleazar, one of the foremost scribes, a man advanced in age and of noble appearance, was being forced to open his mouth to eat pork.[n] [19] But preferring a glorious death to a life of defilement, he went forward of his own accord to the instrument of torture, [20] spitting out the meat as they should do who have the courage to reject food unlawful to taste even for love of life.

[21] Those in charge of that unlawful sacrifice took the man aside, because of their long acquaintance with him, and privately urged him to bring his own provisions that he could legitimately eat, and only to pretend to eat the sacrificial meat prescribed by the king. [22] Thus he would escape death, and be treated kindly because of his old friendship with them. [23] But he made up his mind in a noble manner, worthy of his years, the dignity of his advanced age, the merited distinction of his gray hair, and of the admirable life he had lived from childhood. Above all loyal to the holy laws given by God, he swiftly declared, "Send me to Hades!"

[24] "At our age it would be unbecoming to make such a pretense; many of the young would think the ninety-year-old Eleazar had gone over to an alien religion. [25] If I dissemble to gain a brief moment of life, they would be led astray by me, while I would bring defilement and dishonor on my old age. [26] Even if, for the time being, I avoid human punishment, I shall never, whether alive or dead, escape the hand of the Almighty. [27] Therefore, by bravely giving up life now, I will prove myself worthy of my old age, [28] and I will leave to the young a noble example of how to die willingly and nobly for the revered and holy laws."

He spoke thus, and went immediately to the instrument of torture. [29] Those who shortly before had been kindly disposed, now became hostile toward him because what he had said seemed to them utter madness.[o] [30] When he was about to die under the blows, he groaned, saying: "The Lord in his holy knowledge knows full well that, although I could have escaped death, I am not only enduring terrible pain in my body from this scourging, but also suffering it with joy in my soul because of my devotion to him." [31] This is how he died, leaving in his death a model of nobility and an unforgettable example of virtue not only for the young but for the whole nation.

CHAPTER 7

See RG 233

Martyrdom of a Mother and Her Seven Sons. [1] It also happened that seven brothers with their mother were arrested and tortured with whips and scourges by the king to force them to eat pork in violation of God's law.[p] [2] One of the brothers, speaking for the others, said: "What do you expect to learn by questioning us? We are ready to die rather than transgress the laws of our ancestors."

6:18–7:42 The stories of Eleazar and of the mother and her seven sons, among the earliest models of "martyrology," were understandably popular. Written to encourage God's people in times of persecution, they add gruesome details to the record of tortures, and place long speeches in the mouths of the martyrs.

7:9 The King of the universe will raise us up: here, and in vv. 11, 14, 23, 29, 36, belief in the future resurrection of the body, at least for the just, is clearly stated; cf. also 12:44; 14:46; Dn 12:2.

k: 1 Mc 2:32–38. *l:* 2 Mc 5:17; 7:16–19, 32–38. *m:* Wis 11:9–10; 12:2, 22. *n:* Lv 11:6–8. *o:* Wis 3:1–4; 5:4. *p:* Jer 15:9.

[3]At that the king, in a fury, gave orders to have pans and caldrons heated. [4]These were quickly heated, and he gave the order to cut out the tongue of the one who had spoken for the others, to scalp him and cut off his hands and feet, while the rest of his brothers and his mother looked on. [5]When he was completely maimed but still breathing, the king ordered them to carry him to the fire and fry him. As a cloud of smoke spread from the pan, the brothers and their mother encouraged one another to die nobly, with these words: [6]"The Lord God is looking on and truly has compassion on us, as Moses declared in his song, when he openly bore witness, saying, 'And God will have compassion on his servants.'"[q]

[7]After the first brother had died in this manner, they brought the second to be made sport of. After tearing off the skin and hair of his head, they asked him, "Will you eat the pork rather than have your body tortured limb by limb?" [8]Answering in the language of his ancestors, he said, "Never!" So he in turn suffered the same tortures as the first. [9]With his last breath he said: "You accursed fiend, you are depriving us of this present life, but the King of the universe will raise us up* to live again forever, because we are dying for his laws."[r]

[10]After him the third suffered their cruel sport. He put forth his tongue at once when told to do so, and bravely stretched out his hands, [11]as he spoke these noble words: "It was from Heaven that I received these; for the sake of his laws I disregard them; from him I hope to receive them again." [12]Even the king and his attendants marveled at the young man's spirit, because he regarded his sufferings as nothing.

[13]After he had died, they tortured and maltreated the fourth brother in the same way. [14]When he was near death, he said, "It is my choice to die at the hands of mortals with the hope that God will restore me to life; but for you, there will be no resurrection to life."

[15]They next brought forward the fifth brother and maltreated him. [16]Looking at the king, he said:[s] "Mortal though you are, you have power over human beings, so you do what you please. But do not think that our nation is forsaken by God. [17]Only wait, and you will see how his great power will torment you and your descendants."

[18]After him they brought the sixth brother. When he was about to die, he said: "Have no vain illusions. We suffer these things on our own account, because we have sinned against our God; that is why such shocking things have happened. [19]Do not think, then, that you will go unpunished for having dared to fight against God."

[20]Most admirable and worthy of everlasting remembrance was the mother who, seeing her seven sons perish in a single day, bore it courageously because of her hope in the Lord. [21]Filled with a noble spirit that stirred her womanly reason with manly emotion, she exhorted each of them in the language of their ancestors with these words: [22][t]"I do not know how you came to be in my womb; it was not I who gave you breath and life, nor was it I who arranged the elements you are made of. [23]Therefore, since it is the Creator of the universe who shaped the beginning of humankind and brought about the origin of everything, he, in his mercy, will give you back both breath and life, because you now disregard yourselves for the sake of his law."

[24]Antiochus, suspecting insult in her words, thought he was being ridiculed. As the youngest brother was still alive, the king appealed to him, not with mere words, but with promises on oath, to make him rich and happy if he would abandon his ancestral customs: he would make him his Friend and entrust him with high office. [25]When the youth paid no attention to him at all, the king appealed to the mother, urging her to advise her boy to save his life. [26]After he had urged her for a long time, she agreed to persuade her son. [27]She leaned over close to him and, in derision of the cruel tyrant, said in their native language: "Son, have pity on me, who carried you in my womb for nine months, nursed you for three years, brought you up, educated and sup-

q: Dt 32:36–38. *r:* 2 Mc 12:44; 14:46; Dn 12:1–3. *s:* 2 Mc 5:17; 6:12–16; 7:32. *t:* 2 Mc 7:11, 28; Jb 1:10–12; Ps 139:13–16; Eccl 11:5.

ported you to your present age. [28]I beg you, child, to look at the heavens and the earth and see all that is in them; then you will know that God did not make them out of existing things.* In the same way humankind came into existence. [29]Do not be afraid of this executioner, but be worthy of your brothers and accept death, so that in the time of mercy I may receive you again with your brothers."

[30]She had scarcely finished speaking when the youth said: "What is the delay? I will not obey the king's command. I obey the command of the law given to our ancestors through Moses. [31]But you, who have contrived every kind of evil for the Hebrews, will not escape the hands of God. [32]We, indeed, are suffering because of our sins.[u] [33]Though for a little while our living Lord has been angry, correcting and chastising us, he will again be reconciled with his servants. [34]But you, wretch, most vile of mortals, do not, in your insolence, buoy yourself up with unfounded hopes, as you raise your hand against the children of heaven. [35]You have not yet escaped the judgment of the almighty and all-seeing God. [36]Our brothers, after enduring brief pain, have drunk of never-failing life, under God's covenant. But you, by the judgment of God, shall receive just punishments for your arrogance. [37]Like my brothers, I offer up my body and my life for our ancestral laws, imploring God to show mercy soon to our nation, and by afflictions and blows to make you confess that he alone is God. [38]Through me and my brothers, may there be an end to the wrath of the Almighty that has justly fallen on our whole nation."

[39]At that, the king became enraged and treated him even worse than the others, since he bitterly resented the boy's contempt. [40]Thus he too died undefiled, putting all his trust in the Lord. [41]Last of all, after her sons, the mother was put to death. [42]Enough has been said about the sacrificial meals and the excessive cruelties.

V. Victories of Judas and Purification of the Temple

CHAPTER 8

See RG 233

Resistance from Judas Maccabeus. [1v] Judas Maccabeus and his companions entered the villages secretly, summoned their kindred, and enlisted others who had remained faithful to Judaism. Thus they assembled about six thousand men. [2]They implored the Lord to look kindly upon this people, who were being oppressed by all; to have pity on the sanctuary, which was profaned by renegades; [3]to have mercy on the city, which was being destroyed and was about to be leveled to the ground; to listen to the blood that cried out to him; [4]to remember the criminal slaughter of innocent children and the blasphemies uttered against his name; and to manifest his hatred of evil.

[5w] Once Maccabeus got his men organized, the Gentiles could not withstand him, for the Lord's wrath had now changed to mercy. [6]Coming by surprise upon towns and villages, he set them on fire. He captured strategic positions, and put to flight not a few of the enemy. [7]He preferred the nights as being especially favorable for such attacks. Soon talk of his valor spread everywhere.

*First Victory over Nicanor.** [8]When Philip saw that Judas was gaining ground little by little and that his successful advances were becoming more frequent, he wrote to Ptolemy, governor of Coelesyria and Phoenicia, to come to the aid of the king's interests.[x] [9y] Ptolemy promptly selected Nicanor, son of Patroclus, one of the Chief Friends, and sent him at the head of at least twenty thousand armed men of various nations to wipe out the entire Jewish nation. With him he associated Gorgias, a general, experienced in the art of war.[z] [10]Nicanor planned to raise the two thousand talents of

7:28 God did not make them out of existing things: that is, all things were made solely by God's omnipotent will and creative word; cf. Heb 11:3. This statement has often been taken as a basis for "creation out of nothing" (Latin *creatio ex nihilo*).

8:8–29, 34–35 This account of the campaign of Nicanor and Gorgias against Judas is paralleled, with certain differences, in 1 Mc 3:38–4:24.

u: 2 Mc 5:17; 6:12–16; 7:16–19. *v:* 2 Mc 5:27; 1 Mc 3:10–26. *w:* 1 Mc 3:3–9. *x:* 2 Mc 4:45; 1 Mc 3:38. *y:* 1 Mc 3:38–59. *z:* 1 Mc 7:26.

tribute owed by the king to the Romans* by selling captured Jews into slavery. [11]So he immediately sent word to the coastal cities, inviting them to buy Jewish slaves and promising to deliver ninety slaves for a talent*—little anticipating the punishment that was to fall upon him from the Almighty.

[12]When Judas learned of Nicanor's advance and informed his companions about the approach of the army, [13]those who were fearful and those who lacked faith in God's justice deserted and got away. [14]But the others sold everything they had left, and at the same time entreated the Lord to deliver those whom the ungodly Nicanor had sold before even capturing them. [15]They entreated the Lord to do this, if not for their sake, at least for the sake of the covenants made with their ancestors, and because they themselves invoked his holy and glorious name. [16]Maccabeus assembled his forces, six thousand strong, and exhorted them not to be panic-stricken before the enemy, nor to fear the very large number of Gentiles unjustly attacking them, but to fight nobly. [17]They were to keep before their eyes the lawless outrage perpetrated by the Gentiles against the holy place and the affliction of the humiliated city, as well as the subversion of their ancestral way of life. [18]He said, "They trust in weapons and acts of daring, but we trust in almighty God, who can by a mere nod destroy not only those who attack us but even the whole world." [19]He went on to tell them of the times when help had been given their ancestors: both the time of Sennacherib, when a hundred and eighty-five thousand of his men perished,[a] [20]and the time of the battle in Babylonia against the Galatians,* when only eight thousand Jews fought along with four thousand Macedonians; yet when the Macedonians were hard pressed, the eight thousand, by the help they received from Heaven, destroyed one hundred and twenty thousand and took a great quantity of spoils. [21b] With these words he encouraged them and made them ready to die for their laws and their country.

Then Judas divided his army into four, [22]placing his brothers, Simon, Joseph,* and Jonathan, each over a division, assigning them fifteen hundred men apiece.[c] [23]There was also Eleazar.* After reading to them from the holy book and giving them the watchword, "The help of God," Judas himself took charge of the first division and joined in battle with Nicanor.[d] [24]With the Almighty as their ally, they killed more than nine thousand of the enemy, wounded and disabled the greater part of Nicanor's army, and put all of them to flight. [25]They also seized the money of those who had come to buy them as slaves. When they had pursued the enemy for some time, they were obliged to return by reason of the late hour. [26]It was the day before the sabbath, and for that reason they could not continue the pursuit. [27]They collected the enemy's weapons and stripped them of their spoils, and then observed the sabbath with fervent praise and thanks to the Lord who kept them safe for that day on which he allotted them the beginning of his mercy. [28]After the sabbath, they gave a share of the spoils to those who were tortured and to widows and orphans; the rest they divided among themselves and their children.[e] [29]When this was done, they made supplication in common, imploring the merciful Lord to be completely reconciled with his servants.

Other Victories. [30]They also challenged the forces of Timothy and Bacchides, killed more than twenty thousand of them, and captured some very high fortresses. They di-

8:10 Tribute owed by the king to the Romans: the payment imposed on Antiochus III in 188 B.C. by the treaty of Apamea.

8:11 Ninety slaves for a talent: a low price for so many slaves, thus expressing the opponents' contempt for the Jews.

8:20 Galatians: a mercenary force, defeated by Jews and Macedonians in Babylon. Nothing else is known about this battle.

8:22 Joseph: called John in 1 Mc 2:2; 9:36, 38. This paragraph interrupts the story of Nicanor's defeat, which is resumed in v. 34. The purpose of the author apparently is to group together the defeats suffered by the Syrians on various occasions. Battles against Timothy are recounted in 1 Mc 5:37–44 and 2 Mc 12:10–25; against Bacchides, in 1 Mc 7:8–20.

8:23 Eleazar: this parenthetical reference notes the existence of a fifth brother; cf. 1 Mc 2:5.

a: 2 Mc 15:22; 2 Kgs 19:35–36; 1 Mc 7:41–42; Is 37:36–37. *b:* 1 Mc 4:1–25. *c:* 1 Mc 2:2–5; 5:18, 55–62. *d:* 1 Mc 3:48. *e:* Nm 31:25–47; Dt 26:12–13; 1 Sm 30:21–25.

vided the considerable plunder, allotting half to themselves and the rest to victims of torture, orphans, widows, and the aged. [31]They collected the enemies' weapons and carefully stored them in strategic places; the rest of the spoils they carried to Jerusalem. [32]They also killed the commander of Timothy's forces, a most wicked man, who had done great harm to the Jews. [33]While celebrating the victory in their ancestral city, they burned both those who had set fire to the sacred gates and Callisthenes, who had taken refuge in a little house; so he received the reward his wicked deeds deserved.

[34][f] The thrice-accursed Nicanor, who had brought the thousand slave dealers to buy the Jews, [35]after being humbled through the Lord's help by those whom he had thought of no account, laid aside his fine clothes and fled alone across country like a runaway slave, until he reached Antioch. He was eminently successful in destroying his own army. [36]So he who had promised to provide tribute for the Romans by the capture of the people of Jerusalem proclaimed that the Jews had a champion, and that because they followed the laws laid down by him, they were unharmed.

CHAPTER 9

See RG 233

*Punishment and Death of Antiochus IV.**

[1][g] About that time Antiochus retreated in disgrace from the region of Persia. [2]He had entered the city called Persepolis and attempted to rob the temples and gain control of the city. Thereupon the people had swift recourse to arms, and Antiochus' forces were routed, so that in the end Antiochus was put to flight by the people of that region and forced to beat a shameful retreat. [3]On his arrival in Ecbatana, he learned what had happened to Nicanor and to Timothy's forces. [4]Overcome with anger, he planned to make the Jews suffer for the injury done by those who had put him to flight. Therefore he ordered his charioteer to drive without stopping until he finished the journey. Yet the condemnation of Heaven rode with him, because he said in his arrogance, "I will make Jerusalem the common graveyard of Jews as soon as I arrive there."

[5]So the all-seeing Lord, the God of Israel, struck him down with an incurable and invisible blow; for scarcely had he uttered those words when he was seized with excruciating pains in his bowels and sharp internal torment,[h] [6]a fit punishment for him who had tortured the bowels of others with many barbarous torments. [7]Far from giving up his insolence, he was all the more filled with arrogance. Breathing fire in his rage against the Jews, he gave orders to drive even faster. As a result he hurtled from the speeding chariot, and every part of his body was racked by the violent fall. [8]Thus he who previously, in his superhuman presumption, thought he could command the waves of the sea, and imagined he could weigh the mountaintops in his scales, was now thrown to the ground and had to be carried on a litter, clearly manifesting to all the power of God.[i] [9]The body of this impious man swarmed with worms, and while he was still alive in hideous torments, his flesh rotted off, so that the entire army was sickened by the stench of his corruption.[j] [10]Shortly before, he had thought that he could reach the stars of heaven, and now, no one could endure to transport the man because of this intolerable stench.

[11]At last, broken in spirit, he began to give up his excessive arrogance, and to gain some understanding, under the scourge of God, for he was racked with pain unceasingly. [12]When he could no longer bear his own stench, he said, "It is right to be subject to God, and not to think one's mortal self equal to God."[k] [13]Then this vile man vowed to him who would never again show him mercy, the Sov-

9:1–29 In order to keep together the various accounts of God's punishment of the persecutors of his people, the author places here the stories of Antiochus' illness and death (in actuality the king died about the same time as the purification of the Temple, i.e., 164 B.C.; cf. 1 Mc 4:36–59; 6:1–16; 2 Mc 10:1–8); of Judas' campaigns in Idumea and Transjordan; cf. 1 Mc 5:1–51; 2 Mc 10:14–38; and of the first expedition of Lysias (1 Mc 4:26–35; 2 Mc 11:1–15).

f: 2 Mc 8:23–24; 1 Mc 7:26. *g:* 2 Mc 1:12–17; 1 Mc 6:1–13; Dn 11:40–45. *h:* Acts 12:20–23. *i:* Jb 38:8–11; Ps 65:6–7; Is 40:12. *j:* Jdt 16:17; Sir 7:17; Is 14:11; 66:24; Acts 12:23. *k:* Dn 4:31–34.

ereign Lord, [14]that the holy city, toward which he had been hurrying with the intention of leveling it to the ground and making it a common graveyard, he would now set free; [15]that the Jews, whom he had judged not even worthy of burial, but fit only to be thrown out with their children to be eaten by vultures and wild animals—all of them he would make equal to the Athenians; [16]that he would adorn with the finest offerings the holy temple which he had previously despoiled, restore all the sacred vessels many times over, and provide from his own revenues the expenses required for the sacrifices. [17]Besides all this, he would become a Jew himself and visit every inhabited place to proclaim there the power of God. [18]But since his sufferings were not lessened, for God's just judgment had come upon him, he lost hope for himself and wrote the following letter to the Jews in the form of a supplication. It read thus:

[19]* "To the worthy Jewish citizens, Antiochus, king and general, sends hearty greetings and best wishes for their health and prosperity. [20]If you and your children are well and your affairs are going as you wish, I thank God very much, for my hopes are in heaven. [21]Now that I am ill, I recall with affection your esteem and goodwill. On returning from the regions of Persia, I fell victim to a troublesome illness; so I thought it necessary to form plans for the general security of all. [22]I do not despair about my health, since I have much hope of recovering from my illness. [23]Nevertheless, I know that my father, whenever he went on campaigns in the hinterland, would name his successor, [24]so that, if anything unexpected happened or any unwelcome news came, the people throughout the realm would know to whom the government had been entrusted, and so not be disturbed. [25]I am also bearing in mind that the neighboring rulers, especially those on the borders of our kingdom, are on the watch for opportunities and waiting to see what will happen. I have therefore appointed as king my son Antiochus, whom I have often before entrusted and commended to most of you, when I made hurried visits to the outlying provinces. I have written to him what is written here. [26]Therefore I beg and entreat each of you to remember the general and individual benefits you have received, and to continue to show goodwill toward me and my son. [27]I am confident that, following my policy, he will treat you with equity and kindness in his relations with you."

[28]So this murderer and blasphemer, after extreme sufferings, such as he had inflicted on others, died a miserable death in the mountains of a foreign land. [29]His foster brother* Philip brought the body home; but fearing Antiochus' son, he later withdrew into Egypt, to Ptolemy Philometor.[l]

CHAPTER 10

See RG 233

Purification of the Temple. [1m] When Maccabeus and his companions, under the Lord's leadership, had recovered the temple and the city, [2]they destroyed the altars erected by the foreigners in the marketplace and the sacred shrines. [3]After purifying the temple, they made another altar. Then, with fire struck from flint, they offered sacrifice for the first time in two years,* burned incense, and lighted lamps. They also set out the showbread. [4]When they had done this, they prostrated themselves and begged the Lord that they might never again fall into such misfortunes, and that if they should sin at any time, he might chastise them with moderation and not hand them over to blasphemous and barbarous Gentiles. [5]On the anniversary of the day on which the temple had been profaned by the foreigners, that is, the twenty-fifth of the same month Kislev, the purification of the

9:19–27 Despite the statement in v. 18 this letter is not really a supplication. It is rather a notification to all the king's subjects of the appointment of his son as his successor and a request that they be loyal to the new king. Apparently the same letter, which has every appearance of being authentic, was sent to the various peoples throughout the kingdom, with only a few words of address changed for each group.

9:29 Foster brother: an honorary title conferred by the king on prominent courtiers, whether or not they had been raised with him. Philip tried to seize control of Antioch from the young Antiochus V (1 Mc 6:55–56, 63) and fled to Egypt when he failed.

10:3 Two years: three years according to 1 Mc 1:54 and 4:52.

l: 1 Mc 6:55–56, 63. *m:* 1 Mc 4:36–61.

temple took place. [6]The Jews celebrated joyfully for eight days as on the feast of Booths, remembering how, a little while before, they had spent the feast of Booths living like wild animals in the mountains and in caves. [7]Carrying rods entwined with leaves,* beautiful branches and palms, they sang hymns of grateful praise to him who had successfully brought about the purification of his own place. [8]By public decree and vote they prescribed that the whole Jewish nation should celebrate these days every year. [9]Such was the end of Antiochus surnamed Epiphanes.

VI. Renewed Persecution

Accession of Antiochus V. [10]Now we shall relate what happened under Antiochus Eupator, the son of that godless man, and shall give a summary of the chief evils caused by the wars. [11]When Eupator succeeded to the kingdom, he put a certain Lysias in charge of the government as commander-in-chief of Coelesyria and Phoenicia. [12]Ptolemy, called Macron,* had taken the lead in treating the Jews fairly because of the previous injustice that had been done them, and he endeavored to have peaceful relations with them. [13]As a result, he was accused before Eupator by the King's Friends. In fact, on all sides he heard himself called a traitor for having abandoned Cyprus, which Philometor had entrusted to him, and for having gone over to Antiochus Epiphanes. Since he could not command the respect due to his high office, he ended his life by taking poison.

Victory over the Idumeans.* [14][n]When Gorgias became governor of the region, he employed foreign troops and used every opportunity to attack the Jews. [15]At the same time the Idumeans, who held some strategic strongholds, were harassing the Jews; they welcomed fugitives from Jerusalem and endeavored to continue the war. [16]Maccabeus and his companions, after public prayers asking God to be their ally, moved quickly against the strongholds of the Idumeans. [17]Attacking vigorously, they gained control of the places, drove back all who were fighting on the walls, and cut down those who opposed them, killing no fewer than twenty thousand. [18]When at least nine thousand took refuge in two very strong towers, well equipped to sustain a siege, [19]Maccabeus left Simon and Joseph, along with Zacchaeus and his forces, in sufficient numbers to besiege them, while he himself went off to places where he was more urgently needed. [20]But some of those in Simon's force who were lovers of money let themselves be bribed by some of those in the towers; on receiving seventy thousand drachmas, they allowed a number of them to escape. [21]When Maccabeus was told what had happened, he assembled the rulers of the people and accused those men of having sold their kindred for money by setting their enemies free to fight against them. [22]So he put them to death as traitors, and without delay captured the two towers. [23]As he was successful at arms in all his undertakings, he destroyed more than twenty thousand in the two strongholds.

Victory over Timothy. [24]Timothy, who had previously been defeated by the Jews,* gathered a tremendous force of foreign troops and collected a large number of cavalry from Asia; then he appeared in Judea, ready to conquer it by force. [25]At his approach, Maccabeus and his companions made supplication to God, sprinkling earth upon their heads and girding their loins in sackcloth. [26]Lying prostrate at the foot of the altar, they begged him to be gracious to them, and to be an enemy to their enemies, and a foe to their foes, as the law declares.[o] [27]After the prayer, they took up their weapons and advanced a considerable distance from the city, halting when they were close to the enemy. [28]As soon as dawn broke,* the armies joined bat-

10:7 Rods entwined with leaves: the wreathed wands (*thyrsoi*) carried in processions honoring Dionysus (6:7) were apparently not regarded as distinctively pagan.

10:12 Ptolemy, called Macron: son of Dorymenes (4:45); he supported Antiochus IV in 168 B.C. during his invasion of Cyprus.

10:14–23 Probably the same campaign of Judas against the Idumeans that is mentioned in 1 Mc 5:1–3.

10:24 Timothy, who had previously been defeated by the Jews: as recounted in 8:30–33.

10:28 As soon as dawn broke: the same battle at dawn as in 1 Mc 5:30–34.

n: 1 Mc 5:3–5. *o:* Ex 23:22.

tle, the one having as pledge of success and victory not only their valor but also their reliance on the Lord, and the other taking fury as their leader in the fight.

[29][p] In the midst of the fierce battle, there appeared to the enemy five majestic men from the heavens riding on golden-bridled horses, leading the Jews. [30]They surrounded Maccabeus, and shielding him with their own armor, kept him from being wounded. They shot arrows and hurled thunderbolts at the enemy, who were bewildered and blinded, routed in utter confusion. [31]Twenty thousand five hundred of their foot soldiers and six hundred cavalry were slain.

[32]Timothy, however, fled to a well-fortified stronghold called Gazara, where Chaereas was in command.[q] [33]For four days Maccabeus and his forces eagerly besieged the fortress. [34]Those inside, relying on the strength of the place, kept repeating outrageous blasphemies and uttering abominable words. [35]When the fifth day dawned, twenty young men in the army of Maccabeus, angered over such blasphemies, bravely stormed the wall and with savage fury cut down everyone they encountered. [36]Similarly, others climbed up and swung around on the defenders; they put the towers to the torch, spread the fire and burned the blasphemers alive. Still others broke down the gates and let in the rest of the troops, who took possession of the city. [37]Timothy had hidden in a cistern, but they killed* him, along with his brother Chaereas, and Apollophanes. [38]On completing these exploits, they blessed, with hymns of grateful praise, the Lord who shows great kindness to Israel and grants them victory.

CHAPTER 11

See RG 233

*Defeat of Lysias.** [1][r] Very soon afterward, Lysias, guardian and kinsman of the king and head of the government, being greatly displeased at what had happened, [2]mustered about eighty thousand infantry and all his cavalry and marched against the Jews. His plan was to make their city a Greek settlement; [3]to levy tribute on the temple, as he did on the shrines of the other nations; and to put the high priesthood up for sale every year.[s] [4]He did not take God's power into account at all, but felt exultant confidence in his myriads of foot soldiers, his thousands of cavalry, and his eighty elephants.[t] [5]So he invaded Judea, and when he reached Beth-zur, a fortified place about five stadia* from Jerusalem, launched a strong attack against it.

[6]When Maccabeus and his companions learned that Lysias was besieging the strongholds, they and all the people begged the Lord with lamentations and tears to send a good angel to save Israel.[u] [7]Maccabeus himself was the first to take up arms, and he exhorted the others to join him in risking their lives to help their kindred. Then they resolutely set out together. [8]Suddenly, while they were still near Jerusalem, a horseman appeared at their head, clothed in white garments and brandishing gold weapons.[v] [9]Then all of them together thanked the merciful God, and their hearts were filled with such courage that they were ready to assault not only human beings but even the most savage beasts, or even walls of iron. [10]Now that the Lord had shown mercy toward them, they advanced in battle order with the aid of their heavenly ally. [11]Hurling themselves upon the enemy like lions, they laid low eleven thousand foot soldiers and sixteen hundred cavalry, and put all the rest to flight. [12]Most of those who survived were wounded and disarmed, while Lysias himself escaped only by shameful flight.

Peace Negotiations. [13][w] But Lysias was not a stupid man. He reflected on the defeat he had suffered, and came to realize that the He-

10:37 Timothy . . . they killed: apparently Timothy is still alive in 12:2, 18–25. Perhaps there was more than one Timothy. Or the present passage is not in chronological order. Gazara, v. 32 (Gezer), was not captured by the Jews until much later (cf. 1 Mc 9:50–52; 13:53). See 1 Mc 5:8 for the capture of Jazer.

11:1–12 The defeat of Lysias at Beth-zur probably occurred before the purification of the Temple; cf. 1 Mc 4:26–35.

11:5 Five stadia: one stadium is equal to about six hundred six feet. The actual distance to Beth-zur is about twenty miles.

p: 2 Mc 3:24–26; 5:2–3; 11:8. *q:* 1 Mc 13:43–48. *r:* 1 Mc 4:26–35. *s:* 2 Mc 4:7–8, 23–24. *t:* 1 Mc 3:34. *u:* Ex 23:20. *v:* 2 Mc 3:24–26; 5:2–3; 10:29–30. *w:* 1 Mc 6:57–61.

brews were invincible because the mighty
God was their ally. He therefore sent a message 14 persuading them to settle everything
on just terms, and promising to persuade the
king also, and to induce him to become their
friend. 15 Maccabeus, solicitous for the common good, agreed to all that Lysias proposed;
and the king granted on behalf of the Jews all
the written requests of Maccabeus to Lysias.

16 These are the terms of the letter which
Lysias wrote to the Jews: "Lysias sends
greetings to the Jewish people. 17 John and
Absalom, your envoys, have presented your
signed communication and asked about the
matters contained in it. 18 Whatever had to be
referred to the king I called to his attention,
and the things that were acceptable he has
granted. 19 If you maintain your loyalty to the
government, I will endeavor to further your
interests in the future. 20 On the details of
these matters I have authorized my representatives, as well as your envoys, to confer
with you. 21 Farewell." The one hundred and
forty-eighth year,* the twenty-fourth of Di-
oscorinthius.

22 The king's letter read thus: "King Antiochus sends greetings to his brother Lysias.
23 Now that our father has taken his place
among the gods, we wish the subjects of our
kingdom to be undisturbed in conducting
their own affairs. 24 We have heard that the
Jews do not agree with our father's change
to Greek customs but prefer their own way
of life. They are petitioning us to let them retain their own customs. 25 Since we desire
that this people too should be undisturbed,
our decision is that their temple be restored
to them and that they live in keeping with the
customs of their ancestors. 26 Accordingly,
please send them messengers to give them
our assurances of friendship, so that, when
they learn of our decision, they may have
nothing to worry about but may contentedly
go about their own business."

27 The king's letter to the people was as follows: "King Antiochus sends greetings to the
Jewish senate and to the rest of the Jews. 28 If
you are well, it is what we desire. We too are
in good health. 29 Menelaus has told us of
your wish to return home and attend to your
own affairs. 30 Therefore, those who return by
the thirtieth of Xanthicus will have our assurance of full permission 31 to observe their
dietary and other laws, just as before, and
none of the Jews shall be molested in any
way for faults committed through ignorance.
32 I have also sent Menelaus to reassure you.
33 Farewell." In the one hundred and forty-
eighth year, the fifteenth of Xanthicus.*

34 The Romans also sent them a letter as
follows: "Quintus Memmius and Titus
Manius, legates of the Romans, send greetings to the Jewish people. 35 What Lysias,
kinsman of the king, has granted you, we
also approve. 36 But for the matters that he
decided should be submitted to the king,
send someone to us immediately with your
decisions so that we may present them to
your advantage, for we are on our way to
Antioch. 37 Make haste, then, to send us
those who can inform us of your preference.
38 Farewell." In the one hundred and forty-
eighth year, the fifteenth of Xanthicus.*

CHAPTER 12

See RG
233–34

Incidents at Joppa and Jamnia. 1 After
these agreements were made, Lysias returned to the king, and the Jews went about
their farming. 2 But some of the local governors, Timothy and Apollonius, son of Gennaeus,* as also Hieronymus and Demophon,
to say nothing of Nicanor, the commander of
the Cyprians, would not allow them to live
in peace and quiet.

3 Some people of Joppa also committed
this outrage: they invited the Jews who lived
among them, together with their wives and
children, to embark on boats which they had

11:21 The one hundred and forty-eighth year: 164 B.C. The reading of the name of the month and its position in the calendar are uncertain. The most likely chronological sequence of the four letters is vv. 16–21; vv. 34–38; vv. 27–33; vv. 22–26.

11:33 The date, which is the same as the date of the Romans' letter (v. 38), cannot be correct. The king's letter must be connected with the peace treaty of the one hundred forty-ninth year of the Seleucid era, i.e., 163 B.C. Perhaps the mention of the month of Xanthicus in the body of the letter (v. 30) caused the date of the Romans' letter to be transferred to this one.

11:38 The date is March 12, 164 B.C.

12:2 Apollonius, son of Gennaeus: not the Apollonius who was the son of Menestheus (4:21). **Nicanor**: probably distinct from the Nicanor of 14:2.

provided. There was no hint of enmity toward them. [4]This was done by public vote of the city. When the Jews, wishing to live on friendly terms and not suspecting anything, accepted the invitation, the people of Joppa took them out to sea and drowned at least two hundred of them.

[5]As soon as Judas heard of the barbarous deed perpetrated against his compatriots, he summoned his men; [6]and after calling upon God, the just judge, he marched against the murderers of his kindred. In a night attack he set the harbor on fire, burned the boats, and put to the sword those who had taken refuge there. [7]Because the gates of the town were shut, he withdrew, intending to come back later and wipe out the entire population of Joppa.

[8]On hearing that the people of Jamnia planned in the same way to wipe out the Jews who lived among them, [9]he attacked the Jamnians by night, setting fire to the harbor and the fleet, so that the glow of the flames was visible as far as Jerusalem, thirty miles away.

More Victories by Judas. [10][x] When the Jews had gone about a mile from there* in the march against Timothy, they were attacked by Arabians numbering at least five thousand foot soldiers and five hundred cavalry. [11]After a hard fight, Judas and his companions, with God's help, were victorious. The defeated nomads begged Judas to give pledges of friendship, and they promised to supply the Jews with livestock and to be of service to them in any other way. [12]Realizing that they could indeed be useful in many respects, Judas agreed to make peace with them. After the pledges of friendship had been exchanged, the Arabians withdrew to their tents.

[13]He also attacked a certain city called Caspin, fortified with earthworks and walls and inhabited by a mixed population of Gentiles. [14]Relying on the strength of their walls and their supply of provisions, the besieged treated Judas and his men with contempt, insulting them and even uttering blasphemies and profanity. [15]But Judas and his men invoked the aid of the great Sovereign of the world, who, in the days of Joshua, overthrew Jericho without battering rams or siege engines; then they furiously stormed the walls.[y] [16]Capturing the city by the will of God, they inflicted such indescribable slaughter on it that the adjacent pool, which was about a quarter of a mile wide, seemed to be filled with the blood that flowed into it.

[17][z] When they had gone on some ninety miles, they reached Charax, where there were certain Jews known as Toubians.* [a] [18]But they did not find Timothy in that region, for he had already departed from there without having done anything except to leave behind in one place a very strong garrison. [19]But Dositheus and Sosipater, two of Maccabeus' captains, marched out and destroyed the force of more than ten thousand men that Timothy had left in the stronghold. [20]Meanwhile, Maccabeus divided his army into cohorts, with a commander over each cohort, and went in pursuit of Timothy, who had a force of a hundred and twenty thousand foot soldiers and twenty-five hundred cavalry. [21]When Timothy learned of the approach of Judas, he sent on ahead of him the women and children, as well as the baggage, to a place called Karnion, which was hard to besiege and even hard to reach because of the difficult terrain of that region. [22]But when Judas' first cohort appeared, the enemy was overwhelmed with fear and terror at the manifestation of the all-seeing One. Scattering in every direction, they rushed away in such headlong flight that in many cases they wounded one another, pierced by the points of their own swords. [23]Judas pressed the pursuit vigorously, putting the sinners to the sword and destroying as many as thirty thousand men.

[24]Timothy himself fell into the hands of those under Dositheus and Sosipater; but with great cunning, he begged them to spare his life and let him go, because he had in his power the parents and relatives of many of

12:10 From there: not from Jamnia (vv. 8–9) or Joppa (vv. 3–7), but from a place in Transjordan; vv. 10–26 parallel the account given in 1 Mc 5:9–13, 24–54 of Judas' campaign in northern Transjordan.

12:17 Certain Jews known as Toubians: because they lived "in the land of Tob" (1 Mc 5:13).

x: 1 Mc 5:24–36. *y:* Jos 6:1–21. *z:* 1 Mc 5:37–44. *a:* 1 Mc 5:13.

them, and would show them no consideration. [25]When he had fully confirmed his solemn pledge to restore them unharmed, they let him go for the sake of saving their relatives.

[26][b] Judas then marched to Karnion and the shrine of Atargatis,* where he killed twenty-five thousand people. [27]After the defeat and destruction of these, he moved his army to Ephron, a fortified city inhabited by Lysias and people of many nationalities. Robust young men took up their posts in defense of the walls, from which they fought valiantly; inside were large supplies of war machines and missiles. [28]But the Jews, invoking the Sovereign who powerfully shatters the might of enemies, got possession of the city and slaughtered twenty-five thousand of the people in it.

[29]Then they set out from there and hastened on to Scythopolis,* seventy-five miles from Jerusalem. [30]But when the Jews who lived there testified to the goodwill shown by the Scythopolitans and to their kind treatment even in times of adversity, [31]Judas and his men thanked them and exhorted them to be well disposed to their nation in the future also. Finally they arrived in Jerusalem, shortly before the feast of Weeks.

[32]After this feast, also called Pentecost, they lost no time in marching against Gorgias, governor of Idumea, [33]who opposed them with three thousand foot soldiers and four hundred cavalry. [34]In the ensuing battle, a few of the Jews were slain. [35]A man called Dositheus, a powerful horseman and one of Bacenor's men,* caught hold of Gorgias, grasped his military cloak and dragged him along by brute strength, intending to capture the vile wretch alive, when a Thracian horseman attacked Dositheus and cut off his arm at the shoulder. Then Gorgias fled to Marisa.

[36]After Esdris and his men had been fighting for a long time and were weary, Judas called upon the Lord to show himself their ally and leader in the battle. [37]Then, raising a battle cry in his ancestral language, and with hymns, he charged Gorgias' men when they were not expecting it and put them to flight.

Expiation for the Dead. [38]Judas rallied his army and went to the city of Adullam. As the seventh day was approaching, they purified themselves according to custom and kept the sabbath there. [39]On the following day, since the task had now become urgent, Judas and his companions went to gather up the bodies of the fallen and bury them with their kindred in their ancestral tombs. [40]But under the tunic of each of the dead they found amulets sacred to the idols of Jamnia, which the law forbids the Jews to wear. So it was clear to all that this was why these men had fallen.[c] [41]They all therefore praised the ways of the Lord, the just judge who brings to light the things that are hidden. [42]* Turning to supplication, they prayed that the sinful deed might be fully blotted out. The noble Judas exhorted the people to keep themselves free from sin, for they had seen with their own eyes what had happened because of the sin of those who had fallen.[d] [43]He then took up a collection among all his soldiers, amounting to two thousand silver drachmas, which he sent to Jerusalem to provide for an expiatory sacrifice. In doing this he acted in a very excellent and noble way, inasmuch as he had the resurrection in mind; [44]for if he were not expecting the fallen to rise again, it would have been superfluous and foolish to pray for the dead. [45]But if he did this with a view to the splendid reward that awaits those who had gone to rest in godliness, it was a holy and pious thought. [46]Thus he made atonement for the dead that they might be absolved from their sin.

12:26 Atargatis: a Syrian goddess, represented by the body of a fish, who in Hellenistic times was identified with Astarte and Artemis.

12:29 Scythopolis: the Greek name of the city of Beth-shan; cf. 1 Mc 5:52.

12:35 One of Bacenor's men: certain ancient witnesses to the text have "one of the Toubians"; cf. v. 17.

12:42–45 This is the earliest statement of the doctrine that prayers (v. 42) and sacrifices (v. 43) for the dead are efficacious. Judas probably intended his purification offering to ward off punishment from the living. The author, however, uses the story to demonstrate belief in the resurrection of the just (7:9, 14, 23, 36), and in the possibility of expiation for the sins of otherwise good people who have died. This belief is similar to, but not quite the same as, the Catholic doctrine of purgatory.

b: 1 Mc 5:45–54. *c:* Dt 7:25–26. *d:* Jos 7:1–26.

CHAPTER 13

See RG 233–34

Death of Menelaus. 1[e] In the one hundred and forty-ninth year,* Judas and his men learned that Antiochus Eupator was invading Judea with a large force, 2and that with him was Lysias, his guardian, who was in charge of the government. They led* a Greek army of one hundred and ten thousand foot soldiers, fifty-three hundred cavalry, twenty-two elephants, and three hundred chariots armed with scythes.

3Menelaus also joined them, and with great duplicity kept urging Antiochus on, not for the welfare of his country, but in the hope of being established in office. 4But the King of kings[f] aroused the anger of Antiochus against the scoundrel. When the king was shown by Lysias that Menelaus was to blame for all the trouble, he ordered him to be taken to Beroea* and executed there in the customary local method. 5There is at that place a tower seventy-five feet high, full of ashes,* with a circular rim sloping down steeply on all sides toward the ashes. 6Anyone guilty of sacrilege or notorious for certain other crimes is brought up there and then hurled down to destruction. 7In such a manner was Menelaus, that transgressor of the law, fated to die, deprived even of burial. 8It was altogether just that he who had committed so many sins against the altar with its pure fire and ashes, in ashes should meet his death.

Battle near Modein. 9The king was advancing, his mind full of savage plans for inflicting on the Jews things worse than those they suffered in his father's time. 10When Judas learned of this, he urged the people to call upon the Lord day and night, now more than ever, to help them when they were about to be deprived of their law, their country, and their holy temple; 11and not to allow this people, which had just begun to revive, to be subjected again to blasphemous Gentiles. 12When they had all joined in doing this, and had implored the merciful Lord continuously with weeping and fasting and prostrations for three days, Judas encouraged them and told them to stand ready.

13After a private meeting with the elders, he decided that, before the king's army could invade Judea and take possession of the city, the Jews should march out and settle the matter with God's help. 14Leaving the outcome to the Creator of the world, and exhorting his followers to fight nobly to death for the laws, the temple, the city, the country, and the government, he encamped near Modein. 15Giving his troops the battle cry "God's Victory," he made a night attack on the king's pavilion with a picked force of the bravest young men and killed about two thousand in the camp. He also stabbed the lead elephant and its rider.[g] 16Finally they withdrew in triumph,* having filled the camp with terror and confusion. 17Day was just breaking when this was accomplished with the help and protection of the Lord.

Treaty with Antiochus V. 18[h] The king, having had a taste of the Jews' boldness, tried to take their positions by a stratagem. 19So he marched against Beth-zur, a strong fortress of the Jews; but he was driven back, checked, and defeated. 20Judas sent supplies to the men inside, 21but Rhodocus, of the Jewish army, betrayed military secrets* to the enemy. He was found out, arrested, and imprisoned. 22The king made a second attempt by negotiating with the people of Beth-zur. After giving them his pledge and receiving theirs, he withdrew 23and attacked Judas' men. But he was defeated. Next he heard that Philip, who was left in charge of the government in Antioch, had rebelled. Dismayed, he negotiated with the Jews, submitted to their terms, and swore to observe all their rights. Having come to this agreement, he offered a sacrifice, and honored the

13:1 In the one hundred and forty-ninth year: 163/162 B.C.

13:2 They led: the Greek means literally "each (of them) led," but it is unlikely that the author meant the already immense numbers to be doubled; the numbers are similar to those in 1 Mc 6:30.

13:4 Beroea: the Greek name of Aleppo in Syria.

13:5 Ashes: probably smoldering ashes; the tower resembles the ancient Persian fire towers.

13:16 They withdrew in triumph: according to 1 Mc 6:47 they fled.

13:21 Military secrets: probably about the lack of provisions in the besieged city; cf. 1 Mc 6:49.

---

e: 1 Mc 6:28–54. *f:* 1 Tm 6:15; Rev 17:14; 19:16. *g:* 1 Mc 6:43–46. *h:* 1 Mc 6:48–53.

sanctuary and the place with a generous donation. [24]He received Maccabeus, and left Hegemonides as governor of the territory from Ptolemais to the region of the Gerrhenes.* [25]When he came to Ptolemais, the people of Ptolemais were angered by the peace treaty; in fact they were so indignant that they wanted to annul its provisions. [26]But Lysias took the platform, defended the treaty as well as he could and won them over by persuasion. After calming them and gaining their goodwill, he returned to Antioch. That is the story of the king's attack and withdrawal.

CHAPTER 14

See RG 233–34

[1][i]Three years later,* Judas and his companions learned that Demetrius, son of Seleucus, had sailed into the port of Tripolis with a powerful army and a fleet, [2]and that he had occupied the country, after doing away with Antiochus and his guardian Lysias.

[3]A certain Alcimus, a former high priest,* who had willfully incurred defilement before the time of the revolt, realized that there was no way for him to be safe and regain access to the holy altar. [4]So he went to King Demetrius around the one hundred and fifty-first year and presented him with a gold crown and a palm branch, as well as some of the customary olive branches from the temple. On that day he kept quiet.[j] [5]But he found an opportunity to further his mad scheme when he was invited to the council by Demetrius and questioned about the dispositions and intentions of the Jews. He replied: [6]"Those Jews called Hasideans, led by Judas Maccabeus,* are warmongers, who stir up sedition and keep the kingdom from enjoying peace.[k] [7]For this reason, now that I am deprived of my ancestral dignity, that is to say, the high priesthood, I have come here, [8]first, out of my genuine concern for the king's interests, and second, out of consideration for my own compatriots, since our entire nation is suffering no little affliction from the rash conduct of the people just mentioned. [9]When you have informed yourself in detail on these matters, O king, provide for our country and its hard-pressed people with the same gracious consideration that you show toward all. [10]As long as Judas is around, it is impossible for the government to enjoy peace." [11]When he had said this, the other Friends who were hostile to Judas quickly added fuel to Demetrius' indignation.

Dealings with Nicanor. [12][l]The king immediately chose Nicanor, who had been in command of the elephants, and appointed him governor of Judea. He sent him off [13]with orders to put Judas to death, to disperse his followers, and to set up Alcimus as high priest of the great temple. [14]The Gentiles from Judea, who had fled before Judas, flocked to Nicanor, thinking that the misfortunes and calamities of the Jews would mean prosperity for themselves.

[15][m]When the Jews heard of Nicanor's coming, and that the Gentiles were rallying to him, they sprinkled themselves with earth and prayed to him who established his people forever, and who always comes to the aid of his heritage by manifesting himself. [16]At their leader's command, they set out at once from there and came upon the enemy at the village of Adasa. [17]Judas' brother Simon had engaged Nicanor, but he suffered a slight setback because of the sudden appearance of the enemy.

[18]However, when Nicanor heard of the valor of Judas and his companions, and the great courage with which they fought for their country, he shrank from deciding the issue by bloodshed. [19]So he sent Posidonius, Theodotus and Mattathias to exchange pledges of friendship. [20]After a long discussion of the terms, each leader communicated

13:24 Gerrhenes: probably the inhabitants of Gerar, southeast of Gaza.

14:1 Three years later: actually, Demetrius (I Soter), son of Seleucus (IV), landed at Tripolis in the year 151 of the Seleucid era (1 Mc 14:4), i.e., 162/161 B.C.; cf. 1 Mc 7:1–7.

14:3 Alcimus, a former high priest: he was apparently appointed high priest by Antiochus V after Menelaus was executed, and then deposed for collaborating with the Seleucids.

14:6 Hasideans, led by Judas Maccabeus: according to 1 Mc 2:42 and 7:12–17, the Hasideans were a party separate from the Maccabees.

i: 1 Mc 7:1–7. *j:* 1 Mc 7:5–7, 25. *k:* 1 Mc 2:42; 7:12–17. *l:* 2 Mc 8:9; 1 Mc 3:38; 7:26–27. *m:* 1 Mc 7:26–32.

them to his troops; and when general agreement was expressed, they assented to the treaty. 21A day was set on which the leaders would meet by themselves. From each side a chariot came forward, and thrones were set in place. 22Judas had posted armed men in readiness at strategic points for fear that the enemy might suddenly commit some treachery. But the conference was held in the proper way.

23Nicanor stayed on in Jerusalem, where he did nothing out of place. He disbanded the throngs of people who gathered around him; 24and he always kept Judas in his company, for he felt affection* for the man. 25He urged him to marry and have children; so Judas married and settled into an ordinary life.

Nicanor's Threat Against Judas. 26When Alcimus saw their mutual goodwill, he took the treaty that had been made, went to Demetrius, and said that Nicanor was plotting against the government, for he had appointed Judas, that conspirator against the kingdom, as his successor. 27Stirred up by the villain's slander, the king became enraged. He wrote to Nicanor, stating that he was displeased with the treaty, and ordering him to send Maccabeus at once as a prisoner to Antioch. 28When this message reached Nicanor he was dismayed and troubled at the thought of annulling his agreement with a man who had done no wrong. 29However, there was no way of opposing the king, so he watched for an opportunity to carry out this order by a stratagem. 30But Maccabeus, noticing that Nicanor was more harsh in his dealings with him, and acting with unaccustomed rudeness when they met, concluded that this harshness was not a good sign. So he gathered together not a few of his men, and went into hiding from Nicanor.

31[n]When Nicanor realized that he had been cleverly outwitted by the man, he went to the great and holy temple, at a time when the priests were offering the customary sacrifices, and ordered them to surrender Judas. 32As they declared under oath that they did not know where the man they sought was, 33he stretched out his right arm toward the temple and swore this oath: "If you do not hand Judas over to me as prisoner, I will level this shrine of God to the ground; I will tear down the altar, and erect here a splendid temple to Dionysus."

34With these words he went away. The priests stretched out their hands toward heaven, calling upon the unfailing defender of our nation in these words: 35"Lord of all, though you are in need of nothing, you were pleased to have a temple for your dwelling place among us. 36Therefore, Holy One, Lord of all holiness, preserve forever undefiled this house, which has been so recently purified."[o]

Martyrdom of Razis.* 37A certain Razis, one of the elders of Jerusalem, was denounced to Nicanor as a patriot. A man highly regarded, he was called a father of the Jews because of his goodwill toward them. 38In the days before the revolt, he had been convicted of being a Jew, and had risked body and soul in his ardent zeal for Judaism. 39Nicanor, to show his disdain for the Jews, sent more than five hundred soldiers to arrest him. 40He thought that by arresting that man he would deal the Jews a hard blow.

41But when the troops, on the point of capturing the tower, were forcing the outer gate and calling for fire to set the door ablaze, Razis, now caught on all sides, turned his sword against himself, 42preferring to die nobly* rather than fall into the hands of vile men and suffer outrages unworthy of his noble birth. 43In the excitement of the struggle he failed to strike exactly. So while the troops rushed in through the doors, he gallantly ran up to the top of the wall and courageously threw himself down into the crowd. 44But as they quickly drew back and left an opening, he fell into

14:24 Affection: compare 1 Mc 7:26–32, where there is no hint of this cordial relationship between Nicanor and Judas.

14:37–46 The story of Razis belongs to the "martyrology" class of literature; it is similar to the stories in 6:18–7:42.

14:42 Die nobly: Razis's willingness to die nobly rather than to fall into enemy hands had a precedent in Saul (1 Sm 31:4). Razis took his life because he was convinced that God would restore his body in the resurrection of the dead (see 7:11, 22–23; 14:46).

n: 1 Mc 7:30–38. *o*: 2 Mc 15:34.

the middle of the empty space. 45Still breathing, and inflamed with anger, he got up and ran through the crowd, with blood gushing from his frightful wounds. Then, standing on a steep rock, 46as he lost the last of his blood, he tore out his entrails and flung them with both hands into the crowd, calling upon the Lord of life and of spirit to give these back to him again. Such was the manner of his death.[p]

See RG 233–34

CHAPTER 15

Nicanor's Arrogance. 1When Nicanor learned that Judas and his companions were in the territory of Samaria, he decided he could attack them in complete safety on the day of rest. 2The Jews who were forced to accompany him pleaded, "Do not massacre them so savagely and barbarously, but show respect for the day which the All-seeing has exalted with holiness above all other days." 3At this the thrice-accursed wretch asked if there was a ruler in heaven who prescribed the keeping of the sabbath day.[q] 4They replied, "It is the living Lord, the ruler in heaven, who commands the observance of the sabbath day." 5Then he said, "I, the ruler on earth, command you to take up arms and carry out the king's business." Nevertheless he did not succeed in carrying out his cruel plan.

6In his utter boastfulness and arrogance Nicanor had determined to erect a public victory monument* over Judas and his companions. 7But Maccabeus remained confident, fully convinced that he would receive help from the Lord. 8He urged his men not to fear the attack of the Gentiles, but mindful of the help they had received in the past from Heaven, to expect now the victory that would be given them by the Almighty. 9By encouraging them with words from the law and the prophets,* and by reminding them of the battles they had already won, he filled them with fresh enthusiasm. 10Having stirred up their courage, he gave his orders and pointed out at the same time the perfidy of the Gentiles and their violation of oaths. 11When he had armed each of them, not so much with the security of shield and spear as with the encouragement of noble words, he cheered them all by relating a dream, a kind of waking vision, worthy of belief.

12What he saw was this: Onias, the former high priest,* a noble and good man, modest in bearing, gentle in manner, distinguished in speech, and trained from childhood in all that belongs to excellence, was praying with outstretched arms for the whole Jewish community.[r] 13Then in the same way another man appeared, distinguished by his white hair and dignity, and with an air of wondrous and majestic authority. 14Onias then said of him, "This is a man* who loves his fellow Jews and fervently prays for the people and the holy city—the prophet of God, Jeremiah." 15Stretching out his right hand, Jeremiah presented a gold sword to Judas. As he gave it to him he said, 16"Accept this holy sword as a gift from God; with it you shall shatter your adversaries."

17Encouraged by Judas' words, so noble and capable of instilling valor and stirring young hearts to courage, they determined not merely to march, but to charge gallantly and decide the issue by hand-to-hand combat with the utmost courage, since city, sanctuary and temple were in danger. 18They were not so much concerned about wives and children, or family and relations; their first and foremost fear was for the consecrated sanctuary.[s] 19Those who were left in the city suffered no less an agony, anxious as they were about the battle in the open country. 20Everyone now awaited the decisive moment. The enemy were already drawing near with their troops drawn up in battle line, their beasts placed in strategic

15:6 Public victory monument: a heap of stones covered with the arms and armor of the fallen enemy.

15:9 The law and the prophets: the first of the three parts of the Hebrew Scriptures, called the sacred books (1 Mc 12:9; 2 Mc 2:14).

15:12 Onias, the former high priest: Onias III (3:1–40). Evidently the author believed that departed just persons were in some way alive even before their resurrection.

15:14 A man: regarded by the postexilic Jews as one of the greatest figures in their history; cf. 2:1; Mt 16:14. **Who . . . prays for the people**: Jeremiah's prayer in heaven has been taken in the Roman Catholic tradition as a biblical witness to the intercession of the saints.

p: 2 Mc 7:9–11. *q:* 1 Mc 7:34. *r:* 2 Mc 3:1–40. *s:* 1 Mc 4:36.

positions, and their cavalry stationed on the flanks.

Defeat of Nicanor. [21]Maccabeus, surveying the hosts before him, the variety of weaponry, and the fierceness of their beasts, stretched out his hands toward heaven and called upon the Lord who works wonders; for he knew that it is not weapons but the Lord's decision that brings victory to those who deserve it. [22]Calling upon God, he spoke in this manner: "You, master, sent your angel in the days of King Hezekiah of Judea, and he slew a hundred and eighty-five thousand men of Sennacherib's camp.[t] [23]And now, Sovereign of the heavens, send a good angel to spread fear and trembling ahead of us. [24]By the might of your arm may those be struck down who have blasphemously come against your holy people!" With these words he ended his prayer.

[25][u] Nicanor and his troops advanced to the sound of trumpets and battle songs. [26]But Judas and his troops met the enemy with supplication and prayers. [27]Fighting with their hands and praying to God with their hearts, they laid low at least thirty-five thousand, and rejoiced greatly over this manifestation of God's power. [28]When the battle was over and they were joyfully departing, they discovered Nicanor fallen there in all his armor; [29]so they raised tumultuous shouts in their ancestral language in praise of the divine Sovereign.

[30]Then Judas, that man who was ever in body and soul the chief defender of his fellow citizens, and had maintained from youth his affection for his compatriots, ordered Nicanor's head and right arm up to the shoulder to be cut off and taken to Jerusalem. [31]When he arrived there, he assembled his compatriots, stationed the priests before the altar, and sent for those in the citadel.* [32]He showed them the vile Nicanor's head and the wretched blasphemer's arm that had been boastfully stretched out against the holy dwelling of the Almighty. [33]He cut out the tongue of the godless Nicanor, saying he would feed it piecemeal to the birds and would hang up the other wages of his folly opposite the temple. [34]At this, everyone looked toward heaven and praised the Lord who manifests himself: "Blessed be the one who has preserved undefiled his own place!" [35]Judas hung Nicanor's head and arm on the wall of the citadel, a clear and evident sign to all of the Lord's help.[v] [36]By public vote it was unanimously decreed never to let this day pass unobserved, but to celebrate the thirteenth day of the twelfth month, called Adar in Aramaic, the eve of Mordecai's Day.* [w]

VII. Epilogue

Compiler's Apology. [37]Since Nicanor's doings ended in this way, with the city remaining in the possession of the Hebrews from that time on, I will bring my story to an end here too. [38][x] If it is well written and to the point, that is what I wanted; if it is poorly done and mediocre, that is the best I could do. [39]Just as it is unpleasant to drink wine by itself or just water, whereas wine mixed with water makes a delightful and pleasing drink, so a skillfully composed story delights the ears of those who read the work. Let this, then, be the end.

15:31 Those in the citadel: presumably Jewish soldiers; actually, the citadel was still in the possession of the Syrians (1 Mc 13:50).

15:36 Mordecai's Day: the feast of Purim, celebrated on the fourteenth and fifteenth days of Adar (Est 3:7; 9:20–23; F:10).

t: 2 Mc 8:19; 2 Kgs 19:35–36; 1 Mc 7:41–42; Is 37:36–37. *u:* 1 Mc 7:43. *v:* 1 Sm 31:9–10. *w:* 1 Mc 7:49. *x:* 2 Mc 2:19–32.

See RG 235–36

THE WISDOM BOOKS

"Wisdom" is a convenient umbrella term to designate the Books of Job, Proverbs, Ecclesiastes (Qoheleth), Wisdom, and Sirach (Ecclesiasticus). Two other books are often associated with them: Psalms, a collection of mostly devotional lyrics, and the Song of Songs, a collection of love poems. All are marked by a skillful use of parallelism, or verses of balanced and symmetrical phrases. These works have been classified as wisdom or didactic literature, so called because their general purpose is instruction.

A striking feature of the wisdom books is the absence of references to the promises made to the patriarchs or to Moses, or to Sinai or typical items in Israelite tradition; Sirach (chaps. 44–50) and Wisdom (chaps. 10–19) are the exception. Biblical wisdom literature concentrates on daily human experience: how is life to be lived? In this respect it is comparable to other ancient Near Eastern compositions from Mesopotamia and Egypt that also reflect on the problems of everyday life. The literary style is wide-ranging: aphorisms, numerical sayings, paradoxes, instructions, alphabetical and acrostic poems, lively speeches, and so forth. Wisdom itself is an art: how to deal with various situations and achieve a good life. And it is also a teaching: the lessons garnered from experience were transmitted at various levels, from education in the home all the way to training in the court. Belief in the Lord and acceptance of the prevailing codes of conduct were presupposed; they fed into the training of youths. The task of wisdom is character formation: what is the wise path to follow? The lessons are conveyed by observations that challenge as well as by admonitions that warn. Although the need of discipline is underlined, the general approach is persuasion. The pursuit of wisdom demands more than human industry. Paradoxically, it remains also the gift of God (Prv 2:6). Its religious character is indicated by the steady identification of wisdom and virtue (e.g., Prv 10–15).

But wisdom is far more than a practical guide. The strongest personification in the Bible is Woman Wisdom, and she speaks somewhat mysteriously in divine accents about her origins and identity. Her appeal to humanity is sounded in several books: Prv 8; Sir 24; Wis 7–9; Bar 3:9–4:4. She offers "life" to her followers (Prv 8:35, "whoever finds me finds life"). This image of personified Wisdom is reflected in the Logos poem of Jn 1:1–18 and in Paul's reference to Jesus as "the wisdom of God" (1 Cor 1:24, 30). The bearing of wisdom literature on the New Testament is also exemplified in the sayings and parables of Jesus and in the practical admonitions in the Letter of James.

Each book has a distinctive character. Proverbs consists of long poems dealing with moral conduct (chaps. 1–9), which introduce collections of aphorisms (chaps. 10–29) reflecting on the experiences of life. The Book of Job is a literary presentation of the problem of the suffering of the innocent and god-fearing Job. Psalms, the book of prayer par excellence, derives from varied origins, especially liturgical celebrations; it contains personal cries of agony as well as of praise and thanksgiving. Some betray a wisdom influence (e.g., Ps 37), and the very first Psalm serves as an invitation to learn about the ways of the just and wicked in the rest of the psalter. Ecclesiastes examines the hard questions of life, and has become famous for the expressive phrase "vanity of vanities." The Song of Songs is a collection of poems that give meaning to human and divine love (Sg 8:6; Prv 30:18–19). Ben Sira is the only author who identifies himself (Sir 50:27), and circa 200 B.C. he writes a compendium of Jewish wisdom and creation theology. The Wisdom of Solomon was written in Greek against a Hellenistic background, affirming human immortality in terms of a continuing relationship with God. Except for Psalms (of which almost half are attributed to David), Job, and Sirach, the books are attributed to Solomon, but he is not the author. The Solomonic claim is doubtless due to his fame as a wise man, according to 1 Kgs 5:9–14; 10:1–10. Who were the sages? Some were found in ordinary families (father, mother, Prv 1:8; 10:1); others were scribes at court. All contributed, both men (the counselors of Absalom, 2 Sm 16–17; the men of King Hezekiah, Prv 25:1) and also women (the "wise woman" of Abel Beth-maacah, 2 Sm 20:16). The wisdom literature is predominantly a postexilic composition, but the dating is only approximate.

In Jewish tradition, *Megillot* (Scrolls) came to be the accepted term for the five books of Ruth, Song of Songs, Ecclesiastes, Lamentations, and Esther. In the Protestant tradition, Sirach and Wisdom are classified as apocrypha and not printed as a part of Scripture. The Orthodox tradition does accept them, along with other works, such as 3–4 Maccabees and the Prayer of Manasseh.

See RG 236–43

The Book of Job

The Book of Job, named after its protagonist (apparently not an Israelite; cf. Ez 14:14, 20), is an exquisite dramatic treatment of the problem of the suffering of the innocent. The contents of the book, together with its artistic structure and elegant style, place it among the literary masterpieces of all time. This is a literary composition, and not a transcript of historical events and conversations.

The prologue (chaps. 1–2) provides the setting for Job's testing. When challenged by the satan's questioning of Job's sincerity, the Lord gives leave for a series of catastrophes to afflict Job. Three friends come to console him. Job breaks out in complaint (chap. 3), and a cycle of speeches begins. Job's friends insist that his plight can only be a punishment for personal wrongdoing and an invitation from God to repent. Job rejects their inadequate explanation and challenges God to respond (chaps. 3–31). A young bystander, Elihu, now delivers four speeches in support of the views of the three friends (chaps. 32–37). In response to Job's plea that he be allowed to see God and hear directly the reason for his suffering, the Lord answers (38:1–42:6), not by explaining divine justice, but by cataloguing the wonders of creation. Job is apparently content with this, and, in an epilogue (42:7–17), the Lord restores Job's fortune.

The author or authors of the book are unknown; it was probably composed some time between the seventh and fifth centuries B.C. Its literary pattern, with speeches, prologue and epilogue disposed according to a studied plan, indicates that the purpose of the writing is didactic. But the lessons that the book teaches are not transparent, and different interpretations of the divine speeches and of the final chapter are possible. The Book of Job does not definitively answer the problem of the suffering of the innocent, but challenges readers to come to their own understanding.

The Book of Job can be divided as follows:

I. Prologue (1:1–2:13)
II. First Cycle of Speeches (3:1–14:22)
III. Second Cycle of Speeches (15:1–21:34)
IV. Third Cycle of Speeches (22:1–27:21)
V. The Poem on Wisdom (28:1–28)
VI. Job's Final Summary of His Cause (29:1–31:37)
VII. Elihu's Speeches (32:1–37:24)
VIII. The Lord and Job Meet (38:1–42:6)
IX. Epilogue (42:7–17)

I. Prologue

CHAPTER 1

See RG 236–43

Job's Piety. [1]In the land of Uz* there was a blameless and upright man named Job,[a] who feared God and avoided evil. [2]Seven sons and three daughters were born to him; [3]and he had seven thousand sheep, three thousand camels, five hundred yoke of oxen, five hundred she-donkeys, and a very large household, so that he was greater than anyone in the East.* [4]His sons used to take turns giving feasts, sending invitations to their three sisters to eat and drink with them. [5]And when each feast had run its course, Job would send for them and sanctify them, rising early and offering sacrifices for every one of them. For Job said, "It may be that my children have sinned and cursed* God in their hearts." Job did this habitually.

The Interview Between the Lord and the Satan. [6][b] One day, when the sons of God* came to present themselves before the LORD, the satan also came among them.[c] [7]The LORD said to the satan, "Where have you been?" Then the satan answered the LORD and said,[d] "Roaming the earth and patrolling it." [8]The LORD said to the satan, "Have you noticed my servant Job? There is no one on earth like him, blameless and upright, fearing God and avoiding evil." [9]The satan answered the LORD and said, "Is it for nothing that Job is God-fearing? [10]Have you not surrounded him and his family and all that he has with your protection? You have blessed the work of his hands, and his livestock are spread over the land. [11][e] But now put forth your hand and touch all that he has, and surely he will curse you to your face." [12]The LORD said to the satan, "Very well, all that he has is in your power; only do not lay a hand on him." So the satan went forth from the presence of the LORD.

The First Trial. [13]One day, while his sons and daughters were eating and drinking wine in the house of their eldest brother, [14]a messenger came to Job and said, "The oxen were plowing and the donkeys grazing beside them, [15]and the Sabeans* carried them off in a raid. They put the servants to the sword, and I alone have escaped to tell you." [16]He was still speaking when another came and said, "God's fire has fallen from heaven and struck the sheep and the servants and consumed them; I alone have escaped to tell you." [17]He was still speaking when another came and said, "The Chaldeans* formed three columns, seized the camels, carried them off, and put the servants to the sword; I alone have escaped to tell you." [18]He was still speaking when another came and said, "Your sons and daughters were eating and drinking wine in the house of their eldest brother, [19]and suddenly a great wind came from across the desert and smashed the four corners of the house. It fell upon the young people and they are dead; I alone have escaped to tell you."

Job's Reaction. [20]Then Job arose and tore his cloak and cut off his hair. He fell to the ground and worshiped. [21]He said,

"Naked I came forth from my mother's
  womb,[f]
 and naked shall I go back there.*
The LORD gave and the LORD has taken
  away;
 blessed be the name of the LORD!"

1:1 Uz: somewhere in Edom or Arabia; see Lam 4:21. **Job**: the name probably means "Where is the (divine) father?" In Hebrew it is almost a homonym with the word for "enemy" (see note on 13:24; cf. 33:10).

1:3 The East: that is, east of Palestine.

1:5 Cursed: lit., "blessed." So also in v. 11; 2:5, 9.

1:6 Sons of God: members of the divine council; see Gn 6:1–4; Dt 32:8; Ps 82:1. **The satan**: lit., "adversary" (as in 1 Kgs 11:14). Here a member of the heavenly court, "the accuser" (Zec 3:1). In later biblical traditions this character will be developed as the devil (Gk. *diabolos*, "adversary").

1:15 Sabeans: from southern Arabia.

1:17 Chaldeans: from southern Mesopotamia; in the mid-first millennium B.C., synonymous with "Babylonians."

1:21 Go back there: to the earth; cf. Gn 2:7; see note on Sir 40:1.

2:4 Skin for skin: a proverbial expression derived perhaps from bartering; the precise meaning is unclear.

2:9 Curse God and die: the presupposition is that such blasphemy would be met with immediate death.

2:11 Teman: in Edom (see Gn 36:9–11). The Temanites (Jer 49:7; cf. Ob 8) enjoyed a reputation for wisdom. **Shuh** and **Naamath**: locations unknown.

a: Jb 2:3. *b:* Jb 2:1–3. *c:* Gn 6:2, 4; Zec 3:1; Lk 22:31; Rev 12:9. *d:* 1 Pt 5:8. *e:* Jb 2:5. *f:* Eccl 5:14; 1 Tm 6:7.

[22]In all this Job did not sin,[g] nor did he charge God with wrong.

CHAPTER 2

See RG 236–43

The Second Interview. [1]One day, when the sons of God[h] came to present themselves before the LORD, the satan also came with them. [2]The LORD said to the satan, "Where have you been?" Then the satan answered the LORD and said, "Roaming the earth and patrolling it." [3]The LORD said to the satan, "Have you noticed my servant Job? There is no one on earth like him, blameless and upright, fearing God and avoiding evil.[i] He still holds fast to his innocence although you incited me against him to ruin him for nothing." [4]The satan answered the LORD and said, "Skin for skin!* All that a man has he will give for his life. [5][j] But put forth your hand and touch his bone and his flesh. Then surely he will curse you to your face." [6]And the LORD said to the satan, "He is in your power; only spare his life."

The Second Trial. [7]So the satan went forth from the presence of the LORD and struck Job with severe boils from the soles of his feet to the crown of his head.

Job's Reaction. [8]He took a potsherd to scrape himself, as he sat among the ashes. [9]Then his wife said to him,[k] "Are you still holding to your innocence? Curse God and die!"* [10]But he said to her, "You speak as foolish women do. We accept good things from God; should we not accept evil?" Through all this, Job did not sin in what he said.[l]

Job's Three Friends. [11]Now when three of Job's friends heard of all the misfortune that had come upon him, they set out each one from his own place: Eliphaz from Teman,* Bildad from Shuh, and Zophar from Naamath. They met and journeyed together to give him sympathy and comfort. [12]But when, at a distance, they lifted up their eyes and did not recognize him, they began to weep aloud; they tore their cloaks and threw dust into the air over their heads. [13]Then they sat down upon the ground with him seven days and seven nights, but none of them spoke a word to him; for they saw how great was his suffering.

II. First Cycle of Speeches

CHAPTER 3

See RG 236–43

Job's Complaint. [1]After this, Job opened his mouth and cursed his day.* [2]Job spoke out and said:

[3] Perish the day on which I was born,[m]
the night when they said, "The child is a boy!"
[4] May that day be darkness:
may God* above not care for it,
may light not shine upon it!
[5] May darkness and gloom claim it,
clouds settle upon it,
blackness of day* affright it!
[6] May obscurity seize that night;
may it not be counted among the days of the year,
nor enter into the number of the months!
[7] May that night be barren;
let no joyful outcry greet it!
[8] Let them curse it who curse the Sea,
those skilled at disturbing Leviathan!*
[9] May the stars of its twilight be darkened;
may it look for daylight, but have none,
nor gaze on the eyes of the dawn,
[10] Because it did not keep shut the doors of the womb
to shield my eyes from trouble!
[11] Why did I not die at birth,[n]
come forth from the womb and expire?
[12] Why did knees receive me,
or breasts nurse me?
[13] For then I should have lain down and been tranquil;

3:1 His day: that is, the day of his birth.

3:4 God: in Heb. *'Eloah*, another name for the divinity, used frequently in Job.

3:5 Blackness of day: that is, an eclipse.

3:8 Leviathan: a mythological sea monster symbolizing primeval chaos. It is parallel to Sea, which was the opponent of Baal in the Ugaritic legends. Cf. 9:13; 26:13; 40:25–41:26; Ps 74:13–14; 104:26; Is 27:1.

g: Jb 2:10; Jas 5:11. *h:* Jb 1:6. *i:* Jb 1:1. *j:* Jb 1:11. *k:* Jb 19:17. *l:* Jb 1:22; Sir 2:4. *m:* Jer 20:14. *n:* Jb 10:18–19.

had I slept, I should then have been at
rest
14 With kings and counselors of the earth
who rebuilt what were ruins
15 Or with princes who had gold
and filled their houses with silver.
16 Or why was I not buried away like a
stillborn child,
like babies that have never seen the
light?
17 There* the wicked cease from troubling,
there the weary are at rest.
18 The captives are at ease together,
and hear no overseer's voice.
19 Small and great are there;
the servant is free from the master.
20 Why is light given to the toilers,
life to the bitter in spirit?
21 They wait for death and it does not come;
they search for it more than for hidden
treasures.
22 They rejoice in it exultingly,
and are glad when they find the grave:
23 A man whose path is hidden from him,
one whom God has hemmed in!*
24 For to me sighing comes more readily
than food;
my groans well forth like water.
25 For what I feared overtakes me;
what I dreaded comes upon me.
26 I have no peace nor ease;
I have no rest, for trouble has come!

CHAPTER 4

See RG 236–43

Eliphaz's First Speech. 1 Then Eliphaz
the Temanite answered and said:

2 If someone attempts a word with you,
would you mind?
How can anyone refrain from
speaking?
3 Look, you have instructed many,
and made firm their feeble hands.
4 Your words have upheld the stumbler;
you have strengthened faltering knees.
5 But now that it comes to you, you are
impatient;
when it touches you, you are
dismayed.
6 Is not your piety a source of confidence,
and your integrity of life your hope?
7 Reflect now, what innocent person
perishes?[o]
Where are the upright destroyed?
8 As I see it, those who plow mischief
and sow trouble will reap them.
9 By the breath of God they perish,[p]
and by the blast of his wrath they are
consumed.
10 Though the lion* roars, though the king
of beasts cries out,
yet the teeth of the young lions are
broken;
11 The old lion perishes for lack of prey,
and the cubs of the lioness are
scattered.
12 A word was stealthily brought to me,*
my ear caught a whisper of it.
13 In my thoughts during visions of the
night,[q]
when deep sleep falls on mortals,
14 Fear came upon me, and shuddering,
that terrified me to the bone.
15 Then a spirit passed before me,
and the hair of my body stood on end.
16 It paused, but its likeness I could not
recognize;
a figure was before my eyes,
in silence I heard a voice:[r]
17 "Can anyone be more in the right than
God?[s]
Can mortals be more blameless than
their Maker?
18 Look, he puts no trust in his servants,[t]
and even with his messengers he finds
fault.
19 How much more with those who dwell in
houses of clay,

3:17 There: in death.

3:23 Hemmed in: contrast the same verb as used in 1:10.

4:10 The lion: used figuratively here for the violent, rapacious sinner who cannot prevail against God.

4:12–21 A dramatic presentation of the idea of human nothingness in contrast to God's greatness (v. 17). The message of the "private revelation" that stirs Eliphaz so deeply is in reality expressed countless times in the Bible. The statements of the friends are often "truths" that are insensitive or irrelevant to Job's questioning.

o: Ps 37:25. *p:* Ps 18:16; Is 11:4; 2 Thes 2:8. *q:* Jb 33:15. *r:* 1 Kgs 19:12. *s:* Jb 9:2; 15:14–16; 25:4; Ps 130:3; 143:2. *t:* Jb 15:15; 2 Pt 2:4; Jude 6.

whose foundation is in the dust,
who are crushed more easily than a moth!
20 Morning or evening they may be shattered;
unnoticed, they perish forever.
21 The pegs of their tent are plucked up;
they die without knowing wisdom."

See RG 236–43

CHAPTER 5

1 Call now! Will anyone respond to you?
To which of the holy ones* will you turn?
2 Surely impatience kills the fool
and indignation slays the simpleton.
3 I have seen a fool spreading his roots,[u]
but I cursed his household suddenly:
4 May his children be far from safety;
may they be crushed at the gate*
without a rescuer.
5 What they have reaped may the hungry eat up,
or God take away by blight,
or the thirsty swallow their substance.
6 For not from dust does mischief come,
nor from the soil does trouble sprout.
7 Human beings beget mischief
as sparks* fly upward.
8 In your place, I would appeal to God,
and to God I would state my plea.
9 * He does things great and unsearchable,
things marvelous and innumerable.
10 He gives rain upon the earth
and sends water upon the fields;
11 [v] He sets up the lowly on high,
and those who mourn are raised to safety.
12 He frustrates the plans of the cunning,
so that their hands achieve no success;
13 He catches the wise in their own ruses,[w]
and the designs of the crafty are routed.
14 They meet with darkness in the daytime,
at noonday they grope as though it were night.
15 But he saves the poor from the sword of their mouth,*
from the hand of the mighty.
16 Thus the needy have hope,
and iniquity closes its mouth.
17 Happy the one whom God reproves!
The Almighty's* discipline do not reject.
18 For he wounds, but he binds up;[x]
he strikes, but his hands give healing.
19 Out of six troubles he will deliver you,
and at the seventh* no evil shall touch you.
20 In famine he will deliver you from death,
and in war from the power of the sword;
21 From the scourge of the tongue you shall be hidden,
and you shall not fear approaching ruin.
22 At ruin and want you shall laugh;
the beasts of the earth, do not fear.
23 With the stones of the field shall your covenant be,
and the wild beasts shall be at peace with you.
24 And you shall know that your tent is secure;
taking stock of your household, you shall miss nothing.
25 You shall know that your descendants are many,
and your offspring like the grass of the earth.
26 You shall approach the grave in full vigor,
as a shock of grain comes in at its season.
27 See, this we have searched out; so it is!
This we have heard, and you should know.

5:1 Holy ones: members of the heavenly court; cf. 1:6 and note. They were viewed as heavenly intercessors.

5:4 At the gate: of the city, where justice was administered.

5:7 Sparks: in Hebrew, "sons of resheph," which the ancient versions took as the name of a bird. Resheph was an underworld deity of plague, but the word also means "flames" in Sg 8:6.

5:9 Perhaps to be omitted here; it is a duplicate of 9:10.

5:15 From the sword of their mouth: the Hebrew is obscure.

5:17 Almighty: standard translation of Heb. *Shaddai*.

5:19 Six . . . the seventh: proverbial expression for any large number; cf. Prv 24:16; Lk 17:4.

u: Ps 37:35–36. *v:* 1 Sm 2:7–8; Ps 113:7; Lk 1:52. *w:* 1 Cor 3:19. *x:* Hos 6:1–2.

See RG 236–43

CHAPTER 6

Job's First Reply. 1 Then Job answered and said:

2 Ah, could my anguish but be measured
and my calamity laid with it in the scales,
3 They would now outweigh the sands of the sea!
Because of this I speak without restraint.
4 For the arrows of the Almighty are in me,[y]
and my spirit drinks in their poison;
the terrors of God are arrayed against me.
5 Does the wild donkey bray when it has grass?*
Does the ox low over its fodder?
6 Can anything insipid be eaten without salt?
Is there flavor in the white of an egg?
7 I refuse to touch them;
they are like loathsome food to me.
8 Oh, that I might have my request,
and that God would grant what I long for:
9 Even that God would decide to crush me,
that he would put forth his hand and cut me off!
10 Then I should still have consolation
and could exult through unremitting pain,
because I have not transgressed the commands of the Holy One.
11 What strength have I that I should endure,
and what is my limit that I should be patient?
12 Have I the strength of stones,
or is my flesh of bronze?
13 Have I no helper,[z]
and has my good sense deserted me?
14 A friend owes kindness to one in despair,
though he has forsaken the fear of the Almighty.
15 My companions are undependable as a wadi,
as watercourses that run dry in the wadies;
16 Though they may be black with ice,
and with snow heaped upon them,
17 Yet once they flow, they cease to be;
in the heat, they disappear from their place.
18 Caravans wander from their routes;
they go into the wasteland and perish.
19 The caravans of Tema* search,
the companies of Sheba have hopes;
20 They are disappointed, though they were confident;
they come there and are frustrated.
21 It is thus that you have now become for me;*
you see a terrifying thing and are afraid.
22 Have I said, "Give me something,
make a bribe on my behalf from your possessions"?
23 Or "Deliver me from the hand of the enemy,
redeem me from oppressors"?
24 Teach me, and I will be silent;
make me understand how I have erred.
25 How painful honest words can be;
yet how unconvincing is your argument!
26 Do you consider your words as proof,
but the sayings of a desperate man as wind?
27 You would even cast lots for the orphan,
and would barter over your friend!
28 Come, now, give me your attention;
surely I will not lie to your face.
29 Think it over; let there be no injustice.
Think it over; I still am right.
30 Is there insincerity on my tongue,
or cannot my taste discern falsehood?

6:5–6 Job would not complain if his life were as pleasant to him as fodder to a hungry animal; but his life is as disagreeable as insipid food. **White of an egg**: thus the obscure Hebrew has been understood in Jewish tradition; some render it "mallow juice."

6:19 Tema: in northwest Arabia. **Sheba**: home of the Sabeans; see note on 1:15.

6:21 It is only at this point that the previous lines (vv. 1–20) are clearly directed to the three friends. The style of replying in these chapters (3–31) is often indirect. Job and the friends become mouthpieces through which the author presents current views on divine retribution in dramatic fashion. In chap. 7, Job will not even speak directly to the friends.

y: Ps 88:17. *z:* Jb 19:14–15.

CHAPTER 7

See RG 236–43

1[a] Is not life on earth a drudgery,*
its days like those of a hireling?
2 Like a slave who longs for the shade,
a hireling who waits for wages,
3 So I have been assigned months of futility,
and troubled nights have been counted off for me.
4 When I lie down I say, "When shall I arise?"
then the night drags on;
I am filled with restlessness until the dawn.
5 My flesh is clothed with worms and scabs;[b]
my skin cracks and festers;
6 My days are swifter than a weaver's shuttle;
they come to an end without hope.
7 Remember that my life is like the wind;[c]
my eye will not see happiness again.
8 The eye that now sees me shall no more behold me;
when your eye is on me, I shall be gone.
9 As a cloud dissolves and vanishes,[d]
so whoever goes down to Sheol shall not come up.
10 They shall not return home again;
their place shall know them no more.
11 My own utterance I will not restrain;
I will speak in the anguish of my spirit;
I will complain in the bitterness of my soul.
12 * Am I the Sea, or the dragon,
that you place a watch over me?*
13 When I say, "My bed shall comfort me,
my couch shall ease my complaint,"
14 Then you frighten me with dreams
and terrify me with visions,
15 So that I should prefer strangulation
and death rather than my existence.*
16 I waste away: I will not live forever;[e]
let me alone, for my days are but a breath.
17 * What are human beings, that you make much of them,
or pay them any heed?
18 You observe them every morning[f]
and try them at every moment!
19 How long before you look away from me,
and let me alone till I swallow my spit?
20 If I sin, what do I do to you,
O watcher of mortals?
Why have you made me your target?
Why should I be a burden for you?
21 Why do you not pardon my offense,
or take away my guilt?
For soon I shall lie down in the dust;
and should you seek me I shall be gone.

CHAPTER 8

See RG 236–43

Bildad's First Speech. 1 Bildad the Shuhite answered and said:

2 How long will you utter such things?
The words from your mouth are a mighty wind!
3 Does God pervert judgment,[g]
does the Almighty pervert justice?
4 If your children have sinned against him
and he has left them in the grip of their guilt,
5 Still, if you yourself have recourse to God
and make supplication to the Almighty,
6 Should you be blameless and upright,
surely now he will rouse himself for you
and restore your rightful home.
7 Though your beginning was small,

7:1 Drudgery: taken by some to refer to military service; cf. also 14:14.

7:12–21 Job now speaks not to his friends (who never speak to God), but to God. He does this frequently; cf. 9:28; 10:2–22; 13:20–28; 14:13–22.

7:12 An allusion to the personification of primeval chaos as a monstrous ocean vanquished by God; see note on 3:8.

7:15 Existence: lit., bones; the Hebrew is unclear.

7:17–18 An ironic allusion to Ps 8:5.

a: Jb 14:14. *b:* Jb 2:7–8. *c:* Ps 144:4. *d:* Jb 10:21; 14:10–12; 2 Sm 12:23; 14:14; Wis 2:1. *e:* Jb 14:1–2, 5. *f:* Ps 17:3. *g:* Jb 34:10–12.

your future will flourish indeed.
8 Inquire of the former generations,
pay attention to the experience of their ancestors—[h]
9 As we are but of yesterday and have no knowledge,
because our days on earth are but a shadow—[i]
10 Will they not teach you and tell you
and utter their words of understanding?
11 * Can the papyrus grow up without mire?
Can the reed grass flourish without water?
12 While it is yet green and uncut,
it withers quicker than any grass.
13 So is the end of everyone who forgets God,
and so shall the hope of the godless perish.
14 His confidence is but a gossamer thread,
his trust is a spider's house.
15 He shall lean upon his house, but it shall not stand;
he shall cling to it, but it shall not endure.
16 He thrives in full sun,
and over his garden his shoots go forth;
17 About a heap of stones his roots are entwined;
among the rocks he takes hold.
18 Yet if one tears him from his place,
it will disown him: "I have never seen you!"
19 There he lies rotting beside the road,
and out of the soil another sprouts.
20 Behold, God will not cast away the upright;
neither will he take the hand of the wicked.
21 Once more will he fill your mouth with laughter
and your lips with rejoicing.
22 Those who hate you shall be clothed with shame,
and the tent of the wicked shall be no more.

CHAPTER 9

See RG 236–43

Job's Second Reply. 1 Then Job answered and said:

2 I know well that it is so;
but how can anyone be in the right before God?
3 Should one wish to contend with him,*
he could not answer him once in a thousand times.
4 God is wise in heart and mighty in strength;
who has withstood him and remained whole?
5 He removes the mountains before they know it;
he overturns them in his anger.
6 He shakes the earth out of its place,[j]
and the pillars beneath it tremble.
7 He commands the sun, and it does not rise;
he seals up the stars.
8 He alone stretches out the heavens[k]
and treads upon the back of the sea.
9 He made the Bear and Orion,
the Pleiades and the constellations of the south;
10 He does things great and unsearchable,
things marvelous and innumerable.
11 Should he come near me, I do not see him;
should he pass by, I am not aware of him;
12 Should he seize me forcibly, who can resist?
Who can say to him, "What are you doing?"
13 He is God and he does not relent;
the helpers of Rahab* bow beneath him.
14 How then could I give him any answer,
or choose out arguments against him!

8:11–13 As marsh plants need water, so human beings need God. These verses may be a quotation from the teaching of the ancestors; cf. v. 10.

9:3 Job begins to explore the possibility of challenging God in a lawsuit, a theme that will recur (10:2), but he knows the odds are against him (vv. 12–20).

9:13 Rahab: another name for the primeval sea-monster; see notes on 3:8 and Ps 89:11; cf. Jb 7:12; 26:12.

h: Dt 4:32; 32:7. *i:* Jb 14:2; Ps 102:12; 109:23; 144:4; Wis 2:5. *j:* Jb 26:11. *k:* Ps 104:2; Is 40:22.

15 Even though I were right, I could not answer,[l]
but should rather beg for what was due me.
16 If I appealed to him and he answered me,
I could not believe that he would listen to me;
17 With a storm he might overwhelm me,
and multiply my wounds for nothing;
18 He would not allow me to draw breath,
but might fill me with bitter griefs.
19 If it be a question of strength, he is mighty;
or of judgment, who will call him to account?
20 Though I were right, my own mouth might condemn me;[m]
were I innocent, it might put me in the wrong.
21 I am innocent, but I cannot know it;
I despise my life.
22 It is all one! therefore I say:
Both the innocent and the wicked he destroys.[n]
23 When the scourge slays suddenly,
he scoffs at the despair of the innocent.
24 The earth is given into the hands of the wicked;
he covers the faces of its judges.
If it is not he, who then is it?
25 My days are swifter than a runner,
they flee away; they see no happiness;[o]
26 They shoot by like skiffs of reed,
like an eagle swooping upon its prey.
27 If I say: I will forget my complaining,
I will lay aside my sadness and be of good cheer,
28 Then I am in dread of all my pains;
I know that you* will not hold me innocent.
29 It is I who will be accounted guilty;
why then should I strive in vain?
30 If I should wash myself with soap
and cleanse my hands with lye,
31 Yet you would plunge me in the ditch,
so that my garments would abhor me.
32 For he is not a man like myself, that I should answer him,
that we should come together in judgment.
33 Would that there were an arbiter between us,
who could lay his hand upon us both
34 and withdraw his rod from me,
So that his terrors did not frighten me;
35 that I might speak without being afraid of him.
Since this is not the case with me,
10:1 * I loathe my life.[p]

CHAPTER 10

See RG 236–43

I will give myself up to complaint;
I will speak from the bitterness of my soul.
2 I will say to God: Do not put me in the wrong!
Let me know why you oppose me.
3 * Is it a pleasure for you to oppress,
to spurn the work of your hands,
and shine on the plan of the wicked?
4 Have you eyes of flesh?
Do you see as mortals see?
5 Are your days like the days of a mortal,[q]
and are your years like a human lifetime,
6 That you seek for guilt in me
and search after my sins,
7 Even though you know that I am not wicked,[r]
and that none can deliver me out of your hand?
8 Your hands have formed me and fashioned me;
will you then turn and destroy me?
9 Oh, remember that you fashioned me from clay![s]
Will you then bring me down to dust again?
10 Did you not pour me out like milk,
and thicken me like cheese?
11 With skin and flesh you clothed me,
with bones and sinews knit me together.

9:28–31 You: refers to God.

10:1 I loathe my life: these words complete the thought of 9:35.

10:3–12 These lines are a delicate mixture of sarcasm and prayer; Job "reminds" God, challenging the divine providence. Note the piteous tone of the final request in vv. 20–22.

l: Jb 10:15. *m:* Jb 15:6. *n:* Eccl 9:2. *o:* Jb 7:6. *p:* Jb 9:21. *q:* Jb 36:26. *r:* Jb 2:3, 9; Dt 32:39; Wis 16:15. *s:* Jb 4:19; 33:6; Gn 2:7; 3:19; Ps 146:4.

12 Life and love you granted me,
and your providence has preserved my spirit.
13 Yet these things you have hidden in your heart;
I know they are your purpose:
14 If I should sin, you would keep a watch on me,
and from my guilt you would not absolve me.
15 If I should be wicked, alas for me!
even if righteous, I dare not hold up my head,
sated with shame, drenched in affliction!
16 Should it lift up, you hunt me like a lion:
repeatedly you show your wondrous power against me,
17 You renew your attack* upon me
and multiply your harassment of me;
in waves your troops come against me.
18 Why then did you bring me forth from the womb?[t]
I should have died and no eye have seen me.
19 I should be as though I had never lived;
I should have been taken from the womb to the grave.
20 Are not my days few? Stop!
Let me alone, that I may recover a little
21 Before I go whence I shall not return,[u]
to the land of darkness and of gloom,
22 The dark, disordered land
where darkness is the only light.

CHAPTER 11

See RG 236–43

Zophar's First Speech. 1 And Zophar the Naamathite answered and said:

2 Should not many words be answered,
or must the garrulous man necessarily be right?
3 Shall your babblings keep others silent,
and shall you deride and no one give rebuke?
4 Shall you say: "My teaching is pure,
and I am clean in your sight"?
5 But oh, that God would speak,*
and open his lips against you,
6 And tell you the secrets of wisdom,
for good sense has two sides;
So you might learn that God
overlooks some of your sinfulness.
7 Can you find out the depths of God?[v]
or find out the perfection of the Almighty?
8 It is higher than the heavens; what can you do?
It is deeper than Sheol; what can you know?
9 It is longer than the earth in measure,
and broader than the sea.
10 If he should seize and imprison
or call to judgment, who then could turn him back?
11 For he knows the worthless
and sees iniquity; will he then ignore it?
12 An empty head will gain understanding,
when a colt of a wild jackass[w] is born human.*
13 If you set your heart aright
and stretch out your hands toward him,
14 If iniquity is in your hand, remove it,
and do not let injustice dwell in your tent,
15 Surely then you may lift up your face in innocence;
you may stand firm and unafraid.
16 For then you shall forget your misery,
like water that has ebbed away you shall regard it.
17 Then your life shall be brighter than the noonday;
its gloom shall become like the morning,
18 And you shall be secure, because there is hope;
you shall look round you and lie down in safety;[x]
19 you shall lie down and no one will disturb you.
Many shall entreat your favor,

10:17 Attack: or "witnesses," continuing the metaphor of lawsuit used in these chapters.

11:5 This is another of many ironies (e.g., cf. 11:16–19) that occur throughout the book. Zophar does not know that God will speak (chaps. 38–42), but contrary to what he thinks.

t: Jb 3:3, 11. *u:* Jb 7:9–10; 16:22. *v:* Rom 11:33. *w:* Jb 39:5–8. *x:* Lv 26:6; Ps 4:9.

20 but the wicked, looking on, shall be
consumed with envy.
Escape shall be cut off from them,
their only hope their last breath.

See RG 236–43

CHAPTER 12

Job's Third Reply. 1* Then Job answered and said:

2 No doubt you are the people
with whom wisdom shall die!
3 But I have intelligence as well as you;[y]
I do not fall short of you;
for who does not know such things as these?
4 I have become the sport of my neighbors:*
"The one whom God answers when he calls upon him,
The just, the perfect man," is a laughingstock;[z]
5 The undisturbed esteem my downfall a disgrace
such as awaits unsteady feet;
6 Yet the tents of robbers are prosperous,
and those who provoke God are secure,
whom God has in his power.*
7 But now ask the beasts to teach you,
the birds of the air to tell you;
8 Or speak to the earth to instruct you,
and the fish of the sea to inform you.
9 Which of all these does not know
that the hand of God has done this?
10 In his hand is the soul of every living thing,[a]
and the life breath of all mortal flesh.
11 Does not the ear judge words
as the mouth tastes food?[b]
12 So with old age is wisdom,[c]
and with length of days understanding.
13 With him are wisdom and might;
his are counsel and understanding.
14 If he knocks a thing down, there is no rebuilding;[d]
if he imprisons, there is no release.
15 He holds back the waters and there is drought;[e]
he sends them forth and they overwhelm the land.
16 With him are strength and prudence;
the misled and the misleaders are his.
17 He sends counselors away barefoot,
makes fools of judges.
18 He loosens the belt of kings,
ties a waistcloth on their loins.*
19 He sends priests away barefoot,
leads the powerful astray.
20 He silences the trusted adviser,
takes discretion from the elders.
21 He pours shame on nobles,[f]
the waistband of the strong he loosens.
22 He uncovers deep things from the darkness,
brings the gloom into the light.
23 He makes nations great and destroys them,
spreads peoples abroad and abandons them.
24 He takes understanding from the leaders of the land,
makes them wander in a pathless desert.
25 They grope in the darkness without light;
he makes them wander like drunkards.

CHAPTER 13

1 All this my eye has seen; See RG 236–43
my ear has heard and perceived it.
2 What you know, I also know;[g]
I do not fall short of you.
3 But I would speak with the Almighty;[h]
I want to argue with God.

11:12 A colt . . . is born human: the Hebrew is obscure. As translated, it seems to be a proverb referring to an impossible event.

12:1 Job begins his third and longest speech to the friends with sarcasm, and eventually he accuses them of falsehood (13:4–11). The dialogue between them becomes increasingly sharp. With the appeal to learning from beasts and birds (12:7), Job launches into what seems to be a bitter parody of the power of God.

12:4–5 The Hebrew is somewhat obscure, but the general sense is that the wicked mock the pious when the latter appear to be abandoned by God; cf. Ps 22:7–9; Mt 27:39–43.

12:6 Whom God has in his power: the Hebrew is obscure. The line may be a scribal error; some of the phrases occur in vv. 9, 10.

12:18 He reduces kings to the condition of slaves, who wear only a cloth wrapped about the waist.

y: Jb 13:2; 15:9. *z:* Jb 21:3; 30:1. *a:* Acts 17:28. *b:* Jb 34:3. *c:* Jb 32:7. *d:* Jer 1:10; Rev 3:7. *e:* Gn 7:11–24. *f:* Ps 107:40. *g:* Jb 12:3; 15:9. *h:* Jb 23:4.

4 But you gloss over falsehoods,
you are worthless physicians, every one of you!
5 Oh, that you would be altogether silent;
that for you would be wisdom!
6 Hear now my argument
and listen to the accusations from my lips.
7 Is it for God that you speak falsehood?
Is it for him that you utter deceit?
8 Is it for him that you show partiality?
Do you make accusations on behalf of God?
9 Will it be well when he shall search you out?
Can you deceive him as you do a mere human being?
10 He will openly rebuke you
if in secret you show partiality.
11 Surely his majesty will frighten you
and dread of him fall upon you.
12 Your reminders are ashy maxims,
your fabrications mounds of clay.
13 Be silent! Let me alone that I may speak,
no matter what happens to me.
14 I will carry my flesh between my teeth,
and take my life in my hand.*
15 Slay me though he might,[i] I will wait for him;*
I will defend my conduct before him.
16 This shall be my salvation:
no impious man can come into his presence.
17 Pay close attention to my speech,
give my statement a hearing.
18 Behold, I have prepared my case,[j]
I know that I am in the right.
19 If anyone can make a case against me,
then I shall be silent and expire.
20 Two things only do not use against me,*
then from your presence I need not hide:
21 Withdraw your hand far from me,
do not let the terror of you frighten me.
22 Then call me, and I will respond;
or let me speak first, and answer me.
23 What are my faults and my sins?
My misdeed, my sin make known to me!
24 Why do you hide your face
and consider me your enemy?* [k]
25 Will you harass a wind-driven leaf
or pursue a withered straw?
26 For you draw up bitter indictments against me,
and punish in me the faults of my youth.
27 You put my feet in the stocks;
you watch all my paths
and trace out all my footsteps,
28 Though I wear out like a leather bottle,
like a garment the moth has consumed.

CHAPTER 14

See RG 236–43

1 Man born of woman
is short-lived and full of trouble,* [l]
2 Like a flower that springs up and fades,[m]
swift as a shadow that does not abide.
3 Upon such a one will you set your eyes,
bringing me into judgment before you?
4 Can anyone make the unclean clean?[n]
No one can.
5 Since his days are determined—
you know the number of his months;
you have fixed the limit which he cannot pass—
6 Look away from him and let him be,
while, like a hireling, he completes his day.

13:14 The second half of the verse is a common biblical expression for risking one's life; cf. Jgs 12:3; 1 Sm 19:5; 28:21; Ps 119:109; the first half of the verse must have a similar meaning. Job is so confident of his innocence that he is willing to risk his life by going to judgment with God.

13:15 Many translations adopt the Ketib reading, "I have no hope."

13:20 In 13:20–14:22, Job directs his address to God; cf. 7:8–21; 9:28–10:22. His three friends never do this.

13:24 The Hebrew word for "enemy" (*'oyeb*) is very close to the Hebrew form of Job's name (*'iyyob*). The play on the word implies that God has confused the two.

14:1 The sorrowful lament of Job is that God should relent in view of the limited life of human beings. When compared to plant life, which dies but can revive, the death of human beings is final. Job's wild and "unthinkable" wish in vv. 13–17 is a bold stroke of imagination and desire: if only in Sheol he were protected till God would remember him! Were he to live again (v. 14), things would be different, but alas, God destroys "the hope of mortals" (v. 19).

i: Jb 27:5. *j:* Jb 33:9. *k:* Jb 19:11; 33:10. *l:* Jb 10:20; 15:14; Ps 39:5–6; 89:46; Wis 2:1. *m:* Jb 8:9; Ps 90:6; 102:12; 103:15; 109:23; 144:4; Is 40:6–7; Jas 1:10. *n:* Ps 51:4, 7.

7 For a tree there is hope;
if it is cut down, it will sprout again,
its tender shoots will not cease.
8 Even though its root grow old in the earth
and its stump die in the dust,
9 Yet at the first whiff of water it sprouts
and puts forth branches like a young plant.
10 But when a man dies, all vigor leaves him;[o]
when a mortal expires, where then is he?
11 As when the waters of a lake fail,
or a stream shrivels and dries up,
12 So mortals lie down, never to rise.
Until the heavens are no more, they shall not awake,
nor be roused out of their sleep.[p]
13 Oh, that you would hide me in Sheol,
shelter me till your wrath is past,
fix a time to remember me!
14 If a man were to die, and live again,
all the days of my drudgery I would wait[q]
for my relief to come.
15 You would call, and I would answer you;
you would long for the work of your hands.
16 Surely then you would count my steps,[r]
and not keep watch for sin in me.
17 My misdeeds would be sealed up in a pouch,*
and you would cover over my guilt.
18 Mountains fall and crumble,
rocks move from their place,
19 And water wears away stone,
and floods wash away the soil of the land—
so you destroy the hope of mortals!
20 You prevail once for all against them and they pass on;
you dismiss them with changed appearance.
21 If their children are honored, they are not aware of it;
or if disgraced, they do not know about them.
22 Only for themselves, their pain;
only for themselves, their mourning.

III. Second Cycle of Speeches

CHAPTER 15

See RG 236–43

Second Speech of Eliphaz. 1* Then Eliphaz the Temanite answered and said:

2 Does a wise man answer with windy opinions,
or puff himself up with the east wind?
3 Does he argue in speech that does not avail,
and in words that are to no profit?
4 You in fact do away with piety,
you lessen devotion toward God,
5 Because your wickedness instructs your mouth,
and you choose to speak like the crafty.
6 Your own mouth condemns you, not I;[s]
your own lips refute you.
7 Were you the first to be born?
Were you brought forth before the hills?
8 Do you listen in on God's council[t]
and restrict wisdom to yourself?
9 What do you know that we do not know,[u]
or understand that we do not?
10 There are gray-haired old men among us,
more advanced in years than your father.
11 Are the consolations of God not enough for you,
and speech that deals gently with you?
12 Why does your heart carry you away,
and why do your eyes flash,
13 So that you turn your anger against God
and let such words escape your mouth!
14 How can any mortal be blameless,[v]
anyone born of woman be righteous?[w]
15 If in his holy ones God places no confidence,[x]

14:17 Sealed up in a pouch: hidden away and forgotten.

15:1 The tone of Eliphaz's speech is now much rougher. In vv. 7–9 he ridicules Job's knowledge with a sarcastic question about whether he was a member of the divine council before creation and thus had unique wisdom (according to Prv 8:22–31, only Woman Wisdom existed before creation). Verses 20–35 are a typical description of the fate of the wicked.

o: Jb 20:7. *p:* Jb 7:10. *q:* Jb 7:1. *r:* Jb 31:4; 34:21. *s:* Jb 9:20. *t:* Jb 11:7; Wis 9:13; Jer 23:18; Rom 11:34; 1 Cor 2:11, 16. *u:* Jb 12:3; 13:2. *v:* Jb 25:4–6. *w:* Jb 14:4. *x:* Jb 4:18–19.

and if the heavens are not without
blame in his sight,
16 How much less so is the abominable and
corrupt:
people who drink in iniquity like
water!
17 I will show you, if you listen to me;
what I have seen I will tell—
18 What the wise relate
and have not contradicted since the
days of their ancestors,
19 To whom alone the land was given,
when no foreigner moved among
them:
20 The wicked is in torment all his days,
and limited years are in store for the
ruthless;
21 The sound of terrors is in his ears;
when all is prosperous, a spoiler
comes upon him.
22 He despairs of escaping the darkness,
and looks ever for the sword;
23 A wanderer, food for vultures,
he knows destruction is imminent.
24 A day of darkness fills him with dread;
distress and anguish overpower him,
like a king expecting an attack.
25 Because he has stretched out his hand
against God
and arrogantly challenged the
Almighty,
26 Rushing defiantly against him,
with the stout bosses of his shields.
27 Although he has covered his face with
his crassness,
padded his loins with blubber,
28 He shall dwell in ruined cities,
in houses that are deserted,
crumbling into rubble.
29 He shall not be rich, his possessions shall
not endure;
his property shall not spread over the
land.
30 A flame shall sear his early growth,
and with the wind his blossoms shall
disappear.
31 Let him not trust in his height, misled,
even though his height be like the
palm tree.*
32 He shall wither before his time,
his branches no longer green.
33 He shall be like a vine that sheds its
grapes unripened,
like an olive tree casting off its
blossom.
34 For the breed of the impious shall be
sterile,[y]
and fire shall consume the tents of
extortioners.
35 They conceive malice, bring forth
deceit,[z]
give birth to fraud.*

CHAPTER 16

See RG 236–43

Job's Fourth Reply. 1 Then Job answered and said:

2 I have heard this sort of thing many
times.[a]
Troublesome comforters, all of you!
3 Is there no end to windy words?
What sickness makes you rattle on?
4 I also could talk as you do,
were you in my place.
I could declaim over you,
or wag my head at you;
5 I could strengthen you with talk,
with mere chatter give relief.
6 If I speak, my pain is not relieved;
if I stop speaking, nothing changes.
7 But now he has exhausted me;
you have stunned all my companions.
8 You* have shriveled me up; it is a witness,
my gauntness rises up to testify against
me;
9 His wrath tears and assails me,
he gnashes his teeth against me;
My enemy looks daggers at me.
10 They gape at me with their mouths;
They strike me on the cheek with insults;
they are all enlisted against me.
11 God has given me over to the impious;
into the hands of the wicked he has
cast me.

15:31 The translation is uncertain.
15:35 The plans of the wicked yield nothing but futile results. Cf. Ps 7:15; Is 59:4.
16:8 You: God. Job then describes in vv. 9–17 the savage treatment that he has received from God.

y: Wis 3:11, 18. *z:* Ps 7:15; Is 59:4. *a:* Jb 12:3.

12 I was in peace, but he dislodged me,
seized me by the neck, dashed me to pieces.
He has set me up for a target;
13 his arrows strike me from all directions.
He pierces my sides without mercy,
pours out my gall upon the ground.
14 He pierces me, thrust upon thrust,
rushes at me like a warrior.
15 I have sewn sackcloth on my skin,
laid my horn low in the dust.
16 My face is inflamed with weeping,
darkness covers my eyes,
17 Although my hands are free from violence,
and my prayer sincere.
18 O earth, do not cover my blood,
nor let my outcry come to rest!*
19 Even now my witness* is in heaven,
my advocate is on high.
20 My friends it is who wrong me;
before God my eyes shed tears,
21 That justice may be done for a mortal with God:
as for a man with his neighbor.
22 For my years are numbered,
and I go the road of no return.

CHAPTER 17

See RG 236–43

1 My spirit is broken, my days finished,
my burial at hand.
2 Surely mockers surround me,
at their provocation, my eyes grow dim.
3 Put up a pledge for me with you:*
who is there to give surety for me?
4 You darken their minds to knowledge;
therefore you will not exalt them.
5 For a share of property he informs on friends,
while the eyes of his children grow dim.
6 I am made a byword of the people;[b]
I am one at whom people spit.
7 My eyes are blind with anguish,
and my whole frame is like a shadow.
8 The upright are astonished at this,
the innocent aroused against the wicked.
9 The righteous holds to his way,
the one with clean hands increases in strength.
10 But turn now, and come on again;
I do not find a wise man among you!
11 My days pass by, my plans are at an end,
the yearning of my heart.
12 They would change the night into day;
where there is darkness they talk of approaching light.
13 * If my only hope is dwelling in Sheol,
and spreading my couch in darkness,
14 If I am to say to the pit, "You are my father,"
and to the worm "my mother," "my sister,"
15 Where then is my hope,
my happiness, who can see it?
16 Will they descend with me into Sheol?
Shall we go down together into the dust?

CHAPTER 18

See RG 236–43

Bildad's Second Speech. 1 Then Bildad the Shuhite answered and said:

2 When will you put an end to words?
Reflect, and then we can have discussion.
3 Why are we accounted like beasts,
equal to them in your sight?
4 You who tear yourself in your anger—
shall the earth be neglected on your account
or the rock be moved out of its place?
5 Truly, the light of the wicked is extinguished;
the flame of his fire casts no light.
6 In his tent light is darkness;
the lamp above him goes out.[c]
7 His vigorous steps are hemmed in,

16:18 As the exposed blood of those who were unjustly slain cries to heaven for vengeance (Gn 4:10; Ez 24:6–9), so Job's sufferings demand redress.

16:19 Witness: refers perhaps to God (is Job appealing to God against God?), or to a mediator (cf. 9:33), or to a personification of Job's prayer.

17:3 Addressed to God; v. 10 to Job's friends.

b: Jb 30:9. *c:* Jb 21:17; Prv 13:9; 24:20.

his own counsel casts him down.
8 A net catches him by the feet,
he wanders into a pitfall.
9 A trap seizes him by the heel,
a snare lays hold of him.
10 A noose is hidden for him on the ground,
a netting for him on the path.
11 On every side terrors frighten him;[d]
they harry him at each step.
12 His strength is famished,
disaster is ready at his side,
13 His skin is eaten to the limbs,
the firstborn of Death* eats his limbs.
14 He is plucked from the security of his tent;
and marched off to the king of terrors.*
15 Fire lodges in his tent,
over his abode brimstone is scattered.
16 Below, his roots dry up,
and above, his branches wither.
17 His memory perishes from the earth,[e]
and he has no name in the countryside.
18 He is driven from light into darkness,
and banished from the world.
19 He has neither offshoot nor offspring among his people,
no survivor where once he dwelt.
20 Those who come after shall be appalled at his fate;
those who went before are seized with horror.
21 So is it then with the dwelling of the impious;
such is the place of the one who does not know God!

CHAPTER 19

See RG 236–43

Job's Fifth Reply. 1* Then Job answered and said:

2 How long will you afflict my spirit,
grind me down with words?
3 These ten times you have humiliated me,
have assailed me without shame!
4 Even if it were true that I am at fault,
my fault would remain with me;
5 If truly you exalt yourselves at my expense,
and use my shame as an argument against me,
6 Know then that it is God who has dealt unfairly with me,
and compassed me round with his net.
7 If I cry out "Violence!" I am not answered.[f]
I shout for help, but there is no justice.
8 He has barred my way and I cannot pass;
veiled my path in darkness;
9 He has stripped me of my glory,
taken the diadem from my brow.
10 He breaks me down on every side, and I am gone;
he has uprooted my hope like a tree.
11 He has kindled his wrath against me;
he counts me one of his enemies.[g]
12 His troops advance as one;
they build up their road to attack me,
encamp around my tent.
13 My family has withdrawn from me,[h]
my friends are wholly estranged.
14 My relatives and companions neglect me,
my guests have forgotten me.
15 Even my maidservants consider me a stranger;
I am a foreigner in their sight.
16 I call my servant, but he gives no answer,
though I plead aloud with him.
17 My breath is abhorrent to my wife;[i]
I am loathsome to my very children.
18 Even young children despise me;
when I appear, they speak against me.
19 All my intimate friends hold me in horror;
those whom I loved have turned against me![j]
20 My bones cling to my skin,
and I have escaped by the skin of my teeth.*

17:13–16 Job elaborates another of the vivid descriptions of "life" in Sheol; cf. 3:13–23; 10:21–22.

18:13 Firstborn of Death: that is, disease, plague.

18:14 The king of terrors: of Sheol, of Death (cf. the "terrors" in v. 11). However, the Hebrew of this verse is obscure.

19:1 Job continues railing against his friends (vv. 2–5), and describing God's savage attack in words reminiscent of 16:9–17.

19:20 Skin of my teeth: although the metaphor is not clear, this has become a proverbial expression for a narrow escape. It does not fit Job's situation here.

d: Jb 15:20–24; 27:20. *e:* Ps 34:17; Prv 2:22; 10:7. *f:* Jb 30:20. *g:* Jb 13:24; 33:10. *h:* Jb 6:13. *i:* Jb 2:9. *j:* Sir 6:8.

21 Pity me, pity me, you my friends,
for the hand of God has struck me!
22 Why do you pursue me like God,
and prey insatiably upon me?
23 Oh, would that my words were written down![k]
Would that they were inscribed in a record:*
24 That with an iron chisel and with lead
they were cut in the rock forever!
25 As for me, I know that my vindicator lives,*
and that he will at last stand forth upon the dust.[l]
26 This will happen when my skin has been stripped off,
and from my flesh I will see God:
27 I will see for myself,
my own eyes, not another's, will behold him:
my inmost being is consumed with longing.
28 But you who say, "How shall we persecute him,
seeing that the root of the matter is found in him?"
29 Be afraid of the sword for yourselves,
for your anger is a crime deserving the sword;
that you may know that there is a judgment.

CHAPTER 20

See RG 236–43

Zophar's Second Speech. 1 Then Zophar the Naamathite answered and said:

2 So now my thoughts provide an answer for me,
because of the feelings within me.
3 A rebuke that puts me to shame I hear,
and from my understanding a spirit gives me a reply.
4 Do you not know this: from of old,
since human beings were placed upon the earth,
5 The triumph of the wicked is short
and the joy of the impious but for a moment?[m]
6 Though his pride mount up to the heavens
and his head reach to the clouds,
7 Yet he perishes forever like the dung he uses for fuel,
and onlookers say, "Where is he?"[n]
8 Like a dream he takes flight and cannot be found;
he fades away like a vision of the night.
9 The eye which saw him does so no more;
nor shall his dwelling again behold him.
10 His sons will restore to the poor,
and his hands will yield up his riches.[o]
11 Though his bones are full of youthful vigor,
it shall lie with him in the dust.
12 Though wickedness is sweet in his mouth,
and he hides it under his tongue,
13 Though he retains it and will not let it go
but keeps it still within his mouth,
14 Yet in his stomach the food shall turn;
it shall be venom of asps inside him.
15 The riches he swallowed he shall vomit up;
God shall make his belly disgorge them.
16 The poison of asps he shall drink in;
the viper's fangs shall slay him.
17 He shall see no streams of oil,*
no torrents of honey or milk.
18 He shall give back his gains, never used;
like his profit from trade, never enjoyed.
19 Because he has oppressed and neglected the poor,

19:23–24 What Job is about to say is so important that he wants it recorded in a permanent manner.

19:25–27 The meaning of this passage is obscure because the original text has been poorly preserved and the ancient versions do not agree among themselves. Job asserts three times that he shall see a future vindicator (Hebrew *goel*), but he leaves the time and manner of this vindication undefined. The Vulgate translation has Job indicating a belief in resurrection after death, but the Hebrew and the other ancient versions are less specific.

20:17 Oil: olive oil, one of the main agricultural products of ancient Palestine, a land proverbially rich in honey and milk; see Ex 3:8; etc.

k: Jb 31:35. *l:* Phil 3:20; Ti 2:13. *m:* Jb 21:13; Ps 37:35–36. *n:* Jb 14:10; Ps 37:10, 36. *o:* Jb 27:14.

and stolen a house he did not build;
20 For he has known no quiet in his greed,
in his treasure he cannot save himself.[p]
21 None of his survivors will consume it,
therefore his prosperity shall not endure.
22 [q] When he has more than enough,
distress shall be his,
every sort of trouble shall come upon him.
23 When he has filled his belly,
God shall send against him the fury of his wrath
and rain down his missiles upon him.
24 Should he escape an iron weapon,
a bronze bow shall pierce him through;
25 The dart shall come out of his back,
a shining point out of his gall-bladder:
terrors fall upon him.
26 Complete darkness is in store for his treasured ones;
a fire unfanned shall consume him;[r]
any survivor in his tent shall be destroyed.
27 The heavens shall reveal his guilt,
and the earth rise up against him.
28 The flood shall sweep away his house,
torrents in the day of God's anger.
29 This is the portion of the wicked,
the heritage appointed him by God.* [s]

CHAPTER 21

See RG 236–43

Job's Sixth Reply. 1 Then Job answered and said:

2 At least listen to my words,[t]
and let that be the consolation you offer.
3 Bear with me while I speak;
and after I have spoken, you can mock!
4 Is my complaint toward any human being?
Why should I not be impatient?
5 Look at me and be appalled,
put your hands over your mouths.
6 When I think of it, I am dismayed,
and shuddering seizes my flesh.
7 * Why do the wicked keep on living,
grow old, become mighty in power?[u]
8 Their progeny is secure in their sight;
their offspring are before their eyes.
9 Their homes are safe, without fear,
and the rod of God is not upon them.
10 Their bulls breed without fail;
their cows calve and do not miscarry.
11 They let their young run free like sheep,
their children skip about.
12 They sing along with drum and lyre,
and make merry to the sound of the pipe.
13 They live out their days in prosperity,
and tranquilly go down to Sheol.[v]
14 Yet they say to God, "Depart from us,[w]
for we have no desire to know your ways!
15 What is the Almighty that we should serve him?
And what do we gain by praying to him?"[x]
16 Their happiness is not in their own hands.
The designs of the wicked are far from me![y]
17 How often is the lamp of the wicked put out?
How often does destruction come upon them,
the portion God allots in his anger?
18 Let them be like straw before the wind,
like chaff the storm carries away!
19 "God is storing up the man's misery for his children"?—
let him requite the man himself so that he knows it!
20 Let his own eyes behold his calamity,
and the wrath of the Almighty let him drink!
21 For what interest has he in his family after him,

20:29 Zophar ends his lecture in the style of Bildad (cf. 18:19) with a summary appraisal of what he has been saying about the fate of the wicked.

21:7 In vv. 7–29 Job launches into a realistic description of the fate of the wicked, contrary to the claims made by the friends.

p: Eccl 5:9; Lk 12:20. *q:* Jb 15:20–35. *r:* Dt 32:22. *s:* Jb 27:13. *t:* Jb 13:17. *u:* Jb 12:6; Ps 37:35; 73:3; Eccl 8:14; Jer 12:1–2; Mal 3:14–15. *v:* Jb 34:20. *w:* Jb 22:17. *x:* Mal 3:14. *y:* Jb 22:18.

when the number of his months is
finished?
22 Can anyone teach God knowledge,
seeing that he judges those on high?*
23 One dies in his full vigor,
wholly at ease and content;
24 His figure is full and nourished,
his bones are moist with marrow.
25 Another dies with a bitter spirit,
never having tasted happiness.
26 Alike they lie down in the dust,
and worms cover them both.
27 See, I know your thoughts,
and the arguments you plot against me.
28 For you say, "Where is the house of the
great,
and where the dwelling place of the
wicked?"
29 Have you not asked the wayfarers
and do you not acknowledge the
witness they give?
30 On the day of calamity the evil man is
spared,
on the day that wrath is released.
31 Who will charge him to his face about his
conduct,
and for what he has done who will
repay him?
32 He is carried to the grave
and at his tomb they keep watch.
33 Sweet to him are the clods of the valley.
All humankind will follow after him,
and countless others before him.
34 How empty the consolation you offer
me!
Your arguments remain a fraud.

IV. Third Cycle of Speeches*

CHAPTER 22

See RG 236–43

Eliphaz's Third Speech. 1 Then Eliphaz the Temanite answered and said:

2 Can a man be profitable to God?[z]
Can a wise man be profitable to him?
3 Does it please the Almighty that you are
just?[a]
Does he gain if your ways are perfect?*
4 Is it because of your piety that he
reproves you—
that he enters into judgment with you?
5 Is not your wickedness great,
your iniquity endless?
6 You keep your relatives' goods in pledge
unjustly,*
leave them stripped naked of their
clothing.[b]
7 To the thirsty you give no water to drink,
and from the hungry you withhold
bread;
8 As if the land belonged to the powerful,
and only the privileged could dwell in
it!
9 You sent widows away empty-handed,
and the resources of orphans are
destroyed.[c]
10 Therefore snares are round about you,[d]
sudden terror makes you panic,
11 Or darkness—you cannot see!
A deluge of waters covers you.
12 Does not God, in the heights of the
heavens,[e]
behold the top of the stars, high though
they are?
13 Yet you say, "What does God know?[f]
Can he judge through the thick
darkness?
14 Clouds hide him so that he cannot see
as he walks around the circuit of the
heavens!"
15 Do you indeed keep to the ancient way
trodden by the worthless?
16 They were snatched before their time;
their foundations a river swept away.
17 They said to God, "Let us alone!"

21:22 Those on high: the heavenly beings; cf. 1:6; Ps 82:1–8.

22:1–27:23 The traditional three cycles of speeches breaks down in chaps. 22–27, because Zophar does not appear. This may be interpreted as a sign that the three friends see no point in further dialogue, or that Job's replies have reduced them to silence, or that there has been a mistake in the transmission of the text (hence various transferrals of verses have been proposed to include Zophar, but without any textual evidence).

22:3 Another irony: God will "gain," because he will have been proved right in his claim to the satan that Job is "perfect."

22:6–9 This criticism of Job by Eliphaz is untrue (cf. 31:19), but he is driven to it by his belief that God always acts justly, even when he causes someone to suffer; suffering is due to wrongdoing (cf. v. 29).

z: Jb 9:2. *a:* Jb 35:7. *b:* Jb 24:3; Dt 24:6, 17; Ez 18:12, 16. *c:* Jb 29:12–13; Dt 24:17; 27:19. *d:* Jb 18:8–10. *e:* Jb 11:8. *f:* Ps 10:11; 73:11; 94:7; Is 29:15; Ez 8:12; 9:9.

and, "What can the Almighty do to us?"
18 Yet he had filled their houses with good
things.
The designs of the wicked are far from
me!* [g]
19 The just look on and are glad,
and the innocent deride them:* [h]
20 "Truly our enemies are destroyed,
and what was left to them, fire has
consumed!"
21 Settle with him and have peace.
That way good shall come to you:
22 Receive instruction from his mouth,
and place his words in your heart.
23 If you return to the Almighty, you will be
restored;
if you put iniquity far from your tent,
24 And treat raw gold as dust,
the fine gold of Ophir* as pebbles in
the wadi,
25 Then the Almighty himself shall be your
gold
and your sparkling silver.
26 For then you shall delight in the
Almighty,
you shall lift up your face toward God.
27 Entreat him and he will hear you,[i]
and your vows you shall fulfill.
28 What you decide shall succeed for you,
and upon your ways light shall shine.
29 For when they are brought low, you will
say, "It is pride!"
But downcast eyes he saves.[j]
30 He will deliver whoever is innocent;
you shall be delivered if your hands
are clean.[k]

See RG 236–43

CHAPTER 23

Job's Seventh Reply. 1 Then Job answered and said:

2 Today especially my complaint is bitter,
his hand is heavy upon me in my
groanings.
3 Would that I knew how to find him,
that I might come to his dwelling!
4 I would set out my case before him,
fill my mouth with arguments;
5 I would learn the words he would answer
me,
understand what he would say to me.
6 Would he contend against me with his
great power?
No, he himself would heed me!
7 There an upright man might argue with
him,
and I would once and for all be
delivered from my judge.
8 But if I go east, he is not there;*
or west, I cannot perceive him;
9 The north enfolds him, and I cannot
catch sight of him;
The south hides him, and I cannot see
him.
10 Yet he knows my way;
if he tested me, I should come forth
like gold.[l]
11 My foot has always walked in his steps;
I have kept his way and not turned
aside.
12 From the commands of his lips I have not
departed;
the words of his mouth I have
treasured in my heart.
13 But once he decides, who can contradict
him?
What he desires, that he does.[m]
14 For he will carry out what is appointed
for me,
and many such things he has in store.
15 Therefore I am terrified before him;
when I take thought, I dread him.
16 For it is God who has made my heart
faint,
the Almighty who has terrified me.
17 Yes, would that I had vanished in
darkness,
hidden by the thick gloom before me.

22:18 The second part of the verse repeats 21:16.

22:19 Them: the wicked. Eliphaz obviously thinks that the just can be pleased by God's punishment of the wicked. Such pleasure at the downfall of the wicked is expressed elsewhere, e.g., Ps 58:11; 63:12.

22:24 Ophir: see note on Ps 45:10.

23:8 Job's confident desire to confront God (vv. 2–7, contrary to his fears in 9:14–20 and 13:21–27) gives way to his dark night: God's absence (vv. 8–9), which also terrifies (vv. 13–17).

g: Jb 21:16. *h:* Ps 107:42. *i:* Jb 33:26. *j:* Ps 138:6; Prv 29:23; Mt 23:12; Lk 1:52; Jas 4:10; 1 Pt 5:5. *k:* Jb 17:9; Ps 18:21, 25; 24:4. *l:* Ps 66:10; Prv 17:3; Mal 3:3; 1 Pt 1:7. *m:* Jb 42:2; Ps 115:3; 135:6.

CHAPTER 24

See RG 236–43

1 Why are times not set by the Almighty,
and why do his friends not see his days?*
2 People remove landmarks;
they steal herds and pasture them.
3 The donkeys of orphans they drive away;
they take the widow's ox for a pledge.
4 They force the needy off the road;
all the poor of the land are driven into hiding.
5 Like wild donkeys in the wilderness,
they go forth to their task of seeking prey;
the steppe provides food for their young;
6 They harvest fodder in the field,
and glean in the vineyard of the wicked.
7 They pass the night naked, without clothing;
they have no covering against the cold;
8 They are drenched with rain from the mountains,
and for want of shelter they cling to the rock.
9 Orphans are snatched from the breast,
infants of the needy are taken in pledge.*
10 They go about naked, without clothing,
and famished, they carry the sheaves.*
11 Between the rows they press out the oil;
they tread the wine presses, yet are thirsty.
12 In the city the dying groan,
and the souls of the wounded cry out.
Yet God does not treat it as a disgrace!
13 They are rebels against the light:[n]
they do not recognize its ways;
they do not stay in its paths.
14 When there is no light the murderer rises,
to kill the poor and needy;
in the night he acts like a thief.
15 The eye of the adulterer watches for the twilight;[o]
he says, "No eye will see me."
He puts a mask over his face;
16 in the dark he breaks into houses;
By day they shut themselves in;
they do not know the light.
17 Indeed, for all of them morning is deep darkness;
then they recognize the terrors of deep darkness.
18 He is swift on the surface of the water:*
their portion in the land is accursed,
they do not turn aside by way of the vineyards.
19 Drought and heat snatch away the snow waters,
Sheol, those who have sinned.
20 May the womb forget him,
may the worm find him sweet,
may he no longer be remembered;
And may wickedness be broken like a tree.
21 May his companion be barren, unable to give birth,
may his widow not prosper!
22 He* sustains the mighty by his strength,
to him who rises without assurance of his life
23 he gives safety and support,
and his eyes are on their ways.
24 They are exalted for a while, and then are no more;
laid low, like everyone else they are gathered up;
like ears of grain they shrivel.
25 If this be not so, who can make me a liar,
and reduce my words to nothing?

CHAPTER 25

See RG 236–43

Bildad's Third Speech. 1* Then Bildad the Shuhite answered and said:

24:1 After his failure to find God, Job takes up the question: Why does God not favor his friends by the speedy punishment of his enemies?

24:9 This verse continues the description of the plight of the poor in vv. 2–4, and may belong there.

24:10 This verse is a variant of v. 7, and may be an erroneous scribal repetition.

24:18–24 These verses are inconsistent with Job's views elsewhere. Moreover, they are in general poorly preserved, and in some cases obscure.

24:22 He: God.

25:1 At this point any structure in the dialogues disappears. Bildad's speech is very short, and there follow two speeches attributed to Job, with significantly different introductions in 27:1 and 29:1, and with no intervening third speech of Zophar.

n: Jn 3:19–20. *o:* Prv 7:9–10.

2 Dominion and dread are his
who brings about harmony in his
heavens.
3 Is there any numbering of his troops?*
Yet on which of them does his light
not rise?
4 How can anyone be in the right against
God,[p]
or how can any born of woman be
innocent?
5 Even the moon is not bright
and the stars are not clean in his eyes.
6 How much less a human being, who is
but a worm,
a mortal, who is only a maggot?[q]

CHAPTER 26

See RG 236–43

Job's Reply. 1 Then Job answered and said:*

2 What help you give to the powerless,
what strength to the feeble arm!
3 How you give counsel to one without
wisdom;
how profuse is the advice you offer!
4 With whose help have you uttered those
words,
whose breath comes forth from you?[r]
5 The shades* beneath writhe in terror,[s]
the waters, and their inhabitants.
6 Naked before him is Sheol,*
and Abaddon has no covering.[t]
7 He stretches out Zaphon* over the void,
and suspends the earth over nothing at
all;
8 He binds up the waters in his clouds,
yet the cloud is not split by their
weight;
9 He holds back the appearance of the full
moon
by spreading his clouds before it.
10 He has marked out a circle* on the
surface of the deep[u]
as the boundary of light and darkness.
11 The pillars of the heavens tremble
and are stunned at his thunderous
rebuke;[v]
12 By his power he stilled Sea,
by his skill he crushed Rahab;*
13 By his wind the heavens were made clear,
his hand pierced the fleeing serpent.* [w]
14 Lo, these are but the outlines of his ways,
and what a whisper of a word we hear
of him:
Who can comprehend the thunder of
his power?

CHAPTER 27

See RG 236–43

Job's Reply. 1 Job took up his theme again and said:

2 As God lives,* who takes away my right,[x]
the Almighty, who has made my life
bitter,
3 So long as I still have life breath in me,
the breath of God in my nostrils,
4 My lips shall not speak falsehood,
nor my tongue utter deceit!
5 Far be it from me to account you right;
till I die I will not renounce my
innocence.[y]
6 My justice I maintain and I will not
relinquish it;
my heart does not reproach me for any
of my days.
7 * Let my enemy be as the wicked

25:3 His troops: the heavenly host, or army, the stars (cf. Jgs 5:20), later understood as angels.

26:1–14 Perhaps to be read as Job's reply to Bildad's short speech.

26:5 Shades: the dead in Sheol, the nether world; cf. Ps 88:11; Is 26:14.

26:6 Sheol: cf. note on Ps 6:6. **Abaddon**: Hebrew for "(place of) destruction," a synonym for nether world; cf. Jb 28:22; Rev 9:11.

26:7 Zaphon: lit., "the north," used here as a synonym for the firmament, the heavens; cf. Is 14:13.

26:10 Circle: the horizon of the ocean which serves as the boundary for the activity of light and darkness; cf. Prv 8:27.

26:12 Rahab: another name for the primeval sea-monster; see notes on Jb 3:8 and Ps 89:11; cf. also Jb 7:12; 9:13.

26:13 The fleeing serpent: the same term occurs in Is 27:1 in apposition to Leviathan; see note on Jb 3:8.

27:2–6 As God lives . . . far be it: Job affirms two oaths about his innocence by the very God whom he has accused of violating his right. Such is the paradoxical situation of a tortured person who cannot give the lie to his personal justice, but also refuses to renounce God. He dares God to be "just" as he, Job, understands this.

27:7–23 These verses are inconsistent with Job's views elsewhere, and may be part of a missing speech of Zophar; cf. notes on 24:18–24 and 25:1. Or possibly they are an

p: Jb 4:17; 9:2; 35:2. *q:* Jb 4:19; 15:16. *r:* Gn 2:7. *s:* Prv 9:18. *t:* Ps 139:7–12. *u:* Jb 38:8–11; Prv 8:29. *v:* Jb 9:6; Ps 18:16; 104:7. *w:* Is 27:1. *x:* Jb 34:5. *y:* Jb 2:3, 9; 13:15; 33:9.

and my adversary as the unjust!
8 For what hope has the impious when he
is cut off,
when God requires his life?
9 Will God then listen to his cry
when distress comes upon him,
10 If he delights in the Almighty
and calls upon God constantly?
11 I will teach you what is in God's hand,
and the way of the Almighty I will not
conceal.
12 Look, you yourselves have all seen it;
why do you spend yourselves in empty
words!
13 This is the portion of the wicked with
God,
the heritage oppressors receive from
the Almighty:[z]
14 Though his children be many, the sword
awaits them.
His descendants shall want for bread.
15 His survivors shall be buried in death;
their widows shall not weep.
16 Though he heap up silver like dust
and store away mounds of clothing,
17 What he has stored the righteous shall
wear,
and the innocent shall divide the
silver.
18 He builds his house as of cobwebs,
or like a booth put up by a watchman.
19 He lies down a rich man, one last time;
he opens his eyes—nothing is there.[a]
20 Terrors flood over him like water,
at night the tempest carries him off.
21 The east wind seizes him and he is
gone;
it sweeps him from his place;
22 It hurls itself at him without pity,
as he tries to flee from its power.
23 It claps its hands at him,
and whistles at him from its place.

V. The Poem on Wisdom*

CHAPTER 28

See RG 236–43

Where Is Wisdom to be Found?

1 There is indeed a mine for silver,*
and a place for refining gold.
2 Iron is taken from the earth,
and copper smelted out of stone.
3 * He sets a boundary for the darkness;
the farthest confines he explores.
4 He breaks open a shaft far from habitation,
unknown to human feet;
suspended, far from people, they sway.
5 The earth, though out of it comes forth
bread,
is in fiery upheaval underneath.
6 Its stones are the source of lapis lazuli,
and there is gold in its dust.
7 The path no bird of prey knows,
nor has the hawk's eye seen it.
8 The proud beasts have not trodden it,
nor has the lion gone that way.
9 He sets his hand to the flinty rock,
and overturns the mountains at their
root.
10 He splits channels in the rocks;
his eyes behold all that is precious.
11 He dams up the sources of the streams,
and brings hidden things to light.
12 As for wisdom—where can she be
found?
Where is the place of understanding?[b]
13 Mortals do not know her path,
nor is she to be found in the land of the
living.
14 The Deep says, "She is not in me";
and the Sea says, "She is not with me."
15 Solid gold cannot purchase her,
nor can her price be paid with silver.[c]
16 She cannot be bought with gold of
Ophir,*
with precious onyx or lapis lazuli,

ironic description of the fate of the three friends.

28:1–28 This chapter contains a beautifully vivid description of that Wisdom which is beyond the attainment of creatures and known only to God. The pronouns referring to Wisdom may be translated as either feminine or neuter; in view of Wisdom's role as God's companion and partner in creation (see Prv 8:22–30; Sir 24:1–21; Wis 9:9; Bar 3:9–4:4), the feminine is used here. There is no consensus about the authorship of this poem; it may originally have been an independent composition incorporated into the Book of Job.

28:3–4 The subject of the verbs in these verses has no clear antecedent; the context of vv. 2–6 suggests miners. The Hebrew of v. 4 is especially difficult. The general sense of vv. 1–11 is that one can find minerals in the earth; in contrast, where is Wisdom to be found (vv. 12, 20)?

28:16 Ophir: cf. note on Ps 45:10.

z: Jb 20:4–29. *a:* Ps 49:18; 76:6. *b:* Eccl 7:24–25; Bar 3:14–15, 29–33. *c:* Prv 3:14; 8:10–11, 19; 16:16; Wis 7:7–11.

17 Gold or crystal cannot equal her,
nor can golden vessels be exchanged for her.
18 Neither coral nor crystal should be thought of;
the value of wisdom surpasses pearls.
19 Ethiopian topaz does not equal her,
nor can she be weighed out for pure gold.
20 As for wisdom, where does she come from?
Where is the place of understanding?
21 She is hidden from the eyes of every living thing;
even from the birds of the air she is concealed.
22 Abaddon* and Death say,
"Only by rumor have we heard of her."
23 * But God understands the way to her;[d]
it is he who knows her place.[e]
24 For he beholds the ends of the earth
and sees all that is under the heavens.
25 When he weighed out the wind,
and measured out the waters;
26 When he made a rule for the rain
and a path for the thunderbolts,[f]
27 Then he saw wisdom and appraised her,
established her, and searched her out.
28 * And to mortals he said:
See: the fear of the Lord is wisdom;
and avoiding evil is understanding.[g]

VI. Job's Final Summary of His Cause

CHAPTER 29

See RG 236–43

1* Job took up his theme again and said:

2 Oh, that I were as in the months past,
as in the days when God watched over me:[h]
3 While he kept his lamp shining above my head,
and by his light I walked through darkness;
4 As I was in my flourishing days,
when God sheltered my tent;
5 When the Almighty was still with me,
and my children were round about me;
6 When my footsteps were bathed in cream,
and the rock flowed with streams of oil.*
7 Whenever I went out to the gate of the city
and took my seat in the square,
8 The young men saw me and withdrew,
and the elders rose up and stood;
9 Officials refrained from speaking
and covered their mouths with their hands;[i]
10 The voice of the princes was silenced,
and their tongues stuck to the roofs of their mouths.
11 The ear that heard blessed me;
the eye that saw acclaimed me.
12 For I rescued the poor who cried out for help,
the orphans, and the unassisted;
13 The blessing of those in extremity came upon me,
and the heart of the widow I made joyful.
14 I wore my righteousness like a garment;
justice was my robe and my turban.
15 I was eyes to the blind,
and feet to the lame was I.
16 I was a father to the poor;
the complaint of the stranger I pursued,
17 And I broke the jaws of the wicked man;
from his teeth I forced the prey.
18 I said: "In my own nest I shall grow old;
I shall multiply years like the phoenix.*

28:22 Abaddon: cf. note on Jb 26:6.

28:23–27 In reply to the question of vv. 12, 20, these verses indicate that the creator (vv. 24–26) knows the "place" of wisdom and even "established" her, but the specifics are not given. For further development of this theme, cf. Sir 1:1–10 and Bar 3:9–4:4.

28:28 This verse may be a later addition expressing a commonplace of the wisdom tradition; see cross-references. The addition seems to tie the poem in with the description of Job as fearing God and avoiding evil (1:1, 8; 2:3).

29:1 This chapter begins Job's soliloquy, which will end in 31:40. He describes in florid and exaggerated terms his former lifestyle with all its blessings, a deliberate contrast to his current plight, which will be further described in chap. 30.

29:6 Hyperbole to express abundance; see note on 20:17.

29:18 Phoenix: a legendary bird which, after several cen-

d: Prv 8:22–31. *e:* Prv 2:6; Sir 1:1; Jas 1:5. *f:* Jb 38:25; Prv 3:20. *g:* Ps 111:10; Prv 1:7; 9:10; Sir 1:13–21. *h:* Jb 1:10. *i:* Wis 8:10–12.

[19] My root is spread out to the waters;
the dew rests by night on my branches.
[20] My glory is fresh within me,
and my bow is renewed in my hand!"
[21] For me they listened and waited;
they were silent for my counsel.
[22] Once I spoke, they said no more,
but received my pronouncement drop by drop.
[23] They waited for me as for the rain;
they drank in my words like the spring rains.
[24] When I smiled on them they could not believe it;
they would not let the light of my face be dimmed.
[25] I decided their course and sat at their head,
I lived like a king among the troops,
like one who comforts mourners.

CHAPTER 30

See RG 236–43

[1] But now they hold me in derision
who are younger than I,[j]
Whose fathers I should have disdained
to rank with the dogs of my flock.
[2] Such strength as they had meant nothing to me;
their vigor had perished.
[3] In want and emaciating hunger[k]
they fled to the parched lands:
to the desolate wasteland by night.
[4] They plucked saltwort* and shrubs;
the roots of the broom plant were their food.
[5] They were banished from the community,
with an outcry like that against a thief—
[6] To dwell on the slopes of the wadies,
in caves of sand and stone;
[7] Among the bushes they brayed;
under the nettles they huddled together.
[8] Irresponsible, of no account,
they were driven out of the land.
[9] Yet now they sing of me in mockery;
I have become a byword among them.[l]
[10] They abhor me, they stand aloof,
they do not hesitate to spit in my face!
[11] * Because he has loosened my bowstring
and afflicted me,
they have thrown off restraint in my presence.
[12] On my right the young rabble rise up;
they trip my feet,
they build their approaches for my ruin.
[13] They tear up my path,
they promote my ruin,
no helper is there against them.
[14] As through a wide breach they advance;
amid the uproar they come on in waves;
[15] terrors roll over me.
My dignity is driven off like the wind,
and my well-being vanishes like a cloud.
[16] And now my life ebbs away from me,
days of affliction have taken hold of me.
[17] * At night he pierces my bones,
my sinews have no rest.
[18] With great difficulty I change my clothes,
the collar of my tunic fits around my waist.
[19] He has cast me into the mire;
I have become like dust and ashes.
[20] I cry to you, but you do not answer me;[m]
I stand, but you take no notice.
[21] You have turned into my tormentor,
and with your strong hand you attack me.
[22] You raise me up and drive me before the wind;
I am tossed about by the tempest.
[23] Indeed I know that you will return me to death

turies of life, consumed itself in fire, then rose from its ashes in youthful freshness.

30:4 Saltwort: found in salt marshes and very sour to the taste; eaten by the extremely poor as a cooked vegetable. **Broom plant**: the juniper or brushwood; cf. Ps 120:4; a figure of bitterness and poverty, because of its bitter-tasting roots which are practically inedible.

30:11 God is the subject of the verbs. **Loosened my bowstring**: i.e., disarmed and disabled me.

30:17–23 Job here refers to God's harsh treatment of him. Cf. 16:9–17; 19:6–12.

j: Jb 12:4; 19:18. *k:* Jb 24:5–6. *l:* Jb 17:6. *m:* Jb 19:7.

to the house destined for everyone
alive.[n]
24 Yet should not a hand be held out
to help a wretched person in distress?
25 Did I not weep for the hardships of
others;
was not my soul grieved for the poor?[o]
26 Yet when I looked for good, evil came;
when I expected light, darkness came.
27 My inward parts seethe and will not be
stilled;
days of affliction have overtaken me.
28 I go about in gloom, without the sun;
I rise in the assembly and cry for help.
29 I have become a brother to jackals,
a companion to ostriches.
30 My blackened skin falls away from me;
my very frame is scorched by the heat.
31 My lyre is tuned to mourning,
and my reed pipe to sounds of
weeping.

CHAPTER 31

See RG 236–43

1 I made a covenant with my eyes
not to gaze upon a virgin.
2 What portion comes from God above,
what heritage from the Almighty on
high?
3 Is it not calamity for the unrighteous,
and woe for evildoers?
4 Does he not see my ways,
and number all my steps?[p]
5 If I have walked in falsehood*
and my foot has hastened to deceit,
6 Let God weigh me in the scales of
justice;
thus will he know my innocence![q]
7 If my steps have turned out of the way,
and my heart has followed my eyes,
or any stain clings to my hands,
8 Then may I sow, but another eat,
and may my produce be rooted up!
9 If my heart has been enticed toward a
woman,
and I have lain in wait at my
neighbor's door;
10 Then may my wife grind for another,
and may others kneel over her!
11 For that would be heinous,
a crime to be condemned,[r]
12 A fire that would consume down to
Abaddon*
till it uprooted all my crops.[s]
13 Had I refused justice to my manservant
or to my maidservant, when they had a
complaint against me,
14 What then should I do when God rises
up?
What could I answer when he
demands an account?
15 Did not he who made me in the belly
make him?
Did not the same One fashion us in the
womb?
16 If I have denied anything that the poor
desired,[t]
or allowed the eyes of the widow to
languish
17 While I ate my portion alone,
with no share in it for the fatherless,
18 Though like a father he* has reared me
from my youth,
guiding me even from my mother's
womb—
19 If I have seen a wanderer without
clothing,
or a poor man without covering,
20 Whose limbs have not blessed me
when warmed with the fleece of my
sheep;
21 If I have raised my hand against the
innocent
because I saw that I had supporters at
the gate—*
22 Then may my arm fall from the shoulder,
my forearm be broken at the elbow!
23 For I dread calamity from God,
and his majesty will overpower me.

31:5–34 In a series of purificatory oaths, Job protests his innocence.
31:12 Abaddon: see note on 26:6.
31:18 He: presumably God.
31:21 Gate: cf. notes on 5:4; Ru 4:1.

n: Heb 9:27. *o:* Jb 29:12–16. *p:* Jb 14:16; 34:21; Ps 139:3; Prv 5:21. *q:* Jb 23:10. *r:* Ex 20:14; Lv 20:10; Dt 22:22. *s:* Sir 9:8–9. *t:* Jb 29:12–16.

24 Had I put my trust in gold
or called fine gold my security;
25 Or had I rejoiced that my wealth was great,
or that my hand had acquired abundance—
26 Had I looked upon the light* as it shone,[u]
or the moon in the splendor of its progress,
27 And had my heart been secretly enticed
to blow them a kiss with my hand,
28 This too would be a crime for condemnation,
for I should have denied God above.[v]
29 Had I rejoiced at the destruction of my enemy
or exulted when evil came upon him,[w]
30 Even though I had not allowed my mouth to sin
by invoking a curse against his life—
31 Had not the men of my tent exclaimed,
"Who has not been filled with his meat!"*
32 No stranger lodged in the street,
for I opened my door to wayfarers—
33 * Had I, all too human, hidden my sins
and buried my guilt in my bosom
34 Because I feared the great multitude
and the scorn of the clans terrified me—
then I should have remained silent,
and not come out of doors!
35 * Oh, that I had one to hear my case:
here is my signature:* let the Almighty answer me!
Let my accuser write out his indictment![x]
36 Surely, I should wear it on my shoulder*
or put it on me like a diadem;
37 Of all my steps I should give him an account;
like a prince* I should present myself before him.
38 If my land has cried out against me
till its furrows wept together;
39 If I have eaten its strength without payment
and grieved the hearts of its tenants;
40 Then let the thorns grow instead of wheat
and stinkweed instead of barley!

The words of Job are ended.

VII. Elihu's Speeches

CHAPTER 32

See RG 236–43

1 Then the three men ceased to answer
Job, because in his own eyes he was in the
right.[y] 2[z] But the anger of Elihu,* son of
Barachel the Buzite, of the clan of Ram, was
kindled. He was angry with Job for considering himself rather than God to be in the
right. 3[a] He was angry also with the three
friends because they had not found a good
answer and had not condemned Job. 4 But
since these men were older than he, Elihu
bided his time before addressing Job.
5 When, however, Elihu saw that there was
no reply in the mouths of the three men, his
wrath was inflamed. 6 So Elihu, son of
Barachel the Buzite, answered and said:

I am young and you are very old;
therefore I held back and was afraid
to declare to you my knowledge.
7 I thought, days should speak,

31:26–28 Light: of the sun. Job never sinned by worshiping the sun or the moon. **Blow them a kiss**: an act of idolatrous worship.

31:31 The members of his extended family will testify to his hospitality.

31:33–34 Job's present protest is made, not in spite of hidden sins which he had been unwilling to disclose, but out of genuine innocence. **All too human**: can also be translated "like Adam."

31:35–37 This concluding bravado fits better after v. 40a.

31:35 My signature: lit., "*tau*," the last letter of the Hebrew alphabet, shaped like a cross. Job issues a subpoena to God, and challenges him to follow proper legal procedure as well.

31:36 On my shoulder: i.e., boldly, proudly.

31:37 Like a prince: not as a frightened criminal.

32:2 Elihu means "My God is he." This speaker was from Buz, which, according to Jer 25:23, was near Tema and Dedan. A young man, he impetuously and impatiently upbraids Job for his boldness toward God, and the three friends for not successfully answering Job. He undertakes to defend God's absolute justice and to explain more clearly why there is suffering. While fundamentally his position is the same as that of the three friends, he locates the place of suffering in the divine plan. Because Elihu's four speeches (32:6–33:33; 34:2–37; 35:2–16; 36:2–37:24) repeat the substance of the earlier arguments of the three friends and also anticipate the content of the divine speeches (chaps. 39–41), many scholars consider them a later addition to the book.

u: Dt 4:19. *v:* Dt 17:2–7. *w:* Prv 24:17. *x:* Jb 19:23; 23:3–7. *y:* Jb 33:9. *z:* Jb 13:18; 27:6; 34:5; 35:2. *a:* Jb 22:5.

and many years teach wisdom![b]
8 But there is a spirit in human beings,[c]
the breath of the Almighty, that gives them understanding.
9 It is not those of many days who are wise,
nor the aged who understand the right.
10 Therefore I say, listen to me;
I also will declare my knowledge!
11 Behold, I have waited for your words,
have given ear to your arguments,
as you searched out what to say.
12 Yes, I followed you attentively:
And look, none of you has convicted Job,
not one could refute his statements.
13 So do not say, "We have met wisdom;*
God can vanquish him but no mortal!"
14 For had he addressed his words to me,
I would not then have answered him with your words.
15 They are dismayed, they make no more reply;
words fail them.
16 Must I wait? Now that they speak no more,
and have ceased to make reply,
17 I too will speak my part;
I also will declare my knowledge!
18 For I am full of words;
the spirit within me compels me.
19 My belly is like unopened wine,
like wineskins ready to burst.
20 Let me speak and obtain relief;
let me open my lips, and reply.
21 I would not be partial to anyone,
nor give flattering titles to any.
22 For I know nothing of flattery;
if I did, my Maker would soon take me away.

CHAPTER 33

See RG 236–43

1 Therefore, O Job, hear my discourse;
listen to all my words.
2 Behold, now I open my mouth;
my tongue and voice form words.
3 I will state directly what is in my mind,
my lips shall speak knowledge clearly;
4 For the spirit of God made me,
the breath of the Almighty keeps me alive.[d]
5 If you are able, refute me;
draw up your arguments and take your stand.
6 Look, I am like you before God,
I too was pinched from clay.* [e]
7 Therefore fear of me should not dismay you,
nor should I weigh heavily upon you.
8 But you have said in my hearing,
as I listened to the sound of your words:
9 "I am clean, without transgression;
I am innocent, there is no guilt in me.[f]
10 Yet he invents pretexts against me
and counts me as an enemy.* [g]
11 He puts my feet in the stocks,
watches all my paths!"[h]
12 In this you are not just, let me tell you;
for God is greater than mortals.
13 Why, then, do you make complaint against him
that he gives no reply to their words?[i]
14 For God does speak, once,
even twice, though you do not see it:*
15 In a dream, in a vision of the night,
when deep sleep falls upon mortals
as they slumber in their beds.
16 It is then he opens their ears
and with a warning, terrifies them,
17 By turning mortals from acting
and keeping pride away from a man,
18 He holds his soul from the pit,
his life from passing to the grave.
19 Or he is chastened on a bed of pain,
suffering continually in his bones,
20 So that to his appetite food is repulsive,
his throat rejects the choicest nourishment.[j]

32:13 Met wisdom: in Job's arguments.

33:6 Pinched from clay: a reference to the tradition that human beings were made from clay; cf. Gn 2:7; Jb 10:9; Is 64:7.

33:10 Enemy: see note on 1:1; cf. 13:24.

33:14 Elihu asserts that God speaks through warning in dream and also through pain. However, his presupposition is that the restored person admits sinfulness (v. 27). This of course is not relevant to Job's situation.

b: Jb 12:12. *c:* Jb 33:4. *d:* Jb 32:8. *e:* Jb 31:15. *f:* Jb 10:7; 13:18; 27:5–6; 29:14; 32:1; 34:5. *g:* Jb 13:24; 19:11. *h:* Jb 13:27; 31:4. *i:* Jb 31:35. *j:* Jb 6:7.

21 His flesh is wasted, it cannot be seen;
bones, once invisible, appear;
22 His soul draws near to the pit,
his life to the place of the dead.
23 If then there be a divine messenger,*
a mediator, one out of a thousand,
to show him what is right,
24 He will take pity on him and say,
"Deliver him from going down to the pit;
I have found him a ransom."
25 Then his flesh shall become soft as a boy's;
he shall be again as in the days of his youth.
26 He shall pray and God will favor him;
he shall see God's face with rejoicing;[k]
for he restores a person's righteousness.
27 He shall sing before all and say,
"I sinned and did wrong,
yet I was not punished accordingly.
28 He delivered me from passing to the pit,
and my life sees light."
29 See, all these things God does,
two, even three times, for a man,
30 Bringing back his soul from the pit
to the light, in the light of the living.
31 Be attentive, Job, listen to me!
Be silent and I will speak.
32 If you have anything to say, then answer me.
Speak out! I should like to see you justified.
33 If not, then you listen to me;
be silent, and I will teach you wisdom.

See RG 236–43

CHAPTER 34

1 Then Elihu answered and said:*

2 Hear my discourse, you that are wise;
you that have knowledge, listen to me!
3 For the ear tests words,
as the palate tastes food.[l]
4 Let us choose what is right;
let us determine among ourselves what is good.
5 For Job has said, "I am innocent,
but God has taken away what is my right.[m]
6 I declare the judgment on me to be a lie;
my arrow-wound is incurable, sinless though I am."[n]
7 What man is like Job?
He drinks in blasphemies like water,
8 Keeps company with evildoers
and goes along with the wicked,
9 When he says, "There is no profit
in pleasing God."[o]
10 Therefore, you that have understanding, hear me:
far be it from God to do wickedness;
far from the Almighty to do wrong![p]
11 Rather, he requites mortals for their conduct,
and brings home to them their way of life.[q]
12 Surely, God cannot act wickedly,
the Almighty cannot pervert justice.[r]
13 Who gave him charge over the earth,
or who set all the world in its place?[s]
14 If he were to set his mind to it,
gather to himself his spirit and breath,
15 All flesh would perish together,
and mortals return to dust.[t]
16 Now you*—understand, hear this!
Listen to the words I speak!
17 Can an enemy of justice be in control,
will you condemn the supreme Just One,
18 Who says to a king, "You are worthless!"
and to nobles, "You are wicked!"
19 Who neither favors the person of princes,
nor respects the rich more than the poor?
For they are all the work of his hands;[u]
20 in a moment they die, even at midnight.[v]

33:23 Divine messenger: or "angel," one of the thousands who serve as mediators.
34:1 Elihu replies, although no one else has spoken. This connective phrase (see also 35:1 and 36:1) may indicate that these speeches of Elihu are a secondary addition to the book (see note on 32:2).
34:16 Now you: Elihu turns to Job and addresses him directly.

k: Jb 22:26–29. *l:* Jb 12:11. *m:* Jb 33:9–10. *n:* Jb 9:20. *o:* Jb 9:22–23, 30–31; 21:15; 35:3. *p:* Jb 36:23. *q:* Ps 62:13; Prv 24:12; Mt 16:27; Rom 2:6; 2 Cor 5:10; Rev 22:12. *r:* Jb 8:3. *s:* Jb 38:4–7. *t:* Jb 10:9. *u:* Dt 10:17; 2 Chr 19:7; Wis 6:7; Acts 10:34; Rom 2:11; Eph 6:9; Col 3:25; 1 Pt 1:17. *v:* Jb 21:13.

People are shaken, and pass away,
the powerful are removed without
lifting a hand;
21 For his eyes are upon our ways,
and all our steps he sees.
22 There is no darkness so dense
that evildoers can hide in it.
23 For no one has God set a time
to come before him in judgment.
24 Without inquiry he shatters the mighty,[w]
and appoints others in their place,
25 Thus he discerns their works;
overnight they are crushed.
26 * Where the wicked are, he strikes them,
in a place where all can see,
27 Because they turned away from him
and did not understand his ways at all:
28 And made the cry of the poor reach him,
so that he heard the cry of the
afflicted.
29 If he is silent, who then can condemn?
If he hides his face, who then can
behold him,
whether nation or individual?
30 Let an impious man not rule,
nor those who ensnare their people.
31 Should anyone say to God,
"I accept my punishment; I will offend
no more;
32 What I cannot see, teach me:
if I have done wrong, I will do so no
more,"
33 Would you then say that God must
punish,
when you are disdainful?
It is you who must choose, not I;
speak, therefore, what you know.
34 Those who understand will say to me,
all the wise who hear my views:
35 "Job speaks without knowledge,
his words make no sense.[x]
36 Let Job be tested to the limit,
since his answers are those of the
impious;
37 For he is adding rebellion to his sin
by brushing off our arguments
and addressing many words to God."

CHAPTER 35

See RG 236–43

1* Then Elihu answered and said:

2 Do you think it right to say,
"I am in the right, not God"?[y]
3 When you ask what it profits you,
"What advantage do I have from not
sinning?"[z]
4 I have words for a reply to you*
and your friends as well.
5 Look up to the skies and see;
behold the heavens high above you.
6 If you sin, what do you do to God?
Even if your offenses are many, how
do you affect him?
7 If you are righteous, what do you give
him,
or what does he receive from your
hand?[a]
8 Your wickedness affects only someone
like yourself,
and your justice, only a fellow human
being.
9 In great oppression people cry out;
they call for help because of the power
of the great,
10 No one says, "Where is God, my Maker,
who gives songs in the night,
11 Teaches us more than the beasts of the
earth,
and makes us wiser than the birds of
the heavens?"
12 Though thus they cry out, he does not
answer
because of the pride of the wicked.
13 But it is idle to say God does not hear
or that the Almighty does not take
notice.
14 Even though you say, "You take no
notice of it,"*

34:26, 29–30 The extant Hebrew text of these verses is obscure.

35:1 See note on 34:1.

35:4 A reply to you: Elihu refers to Job's statement that the innocent suffer as much as the wicked, and especially to Eliphaz's words in 22:2–3.

35:14–15 The text here is uncertain. It seems to indicate that Job should have realized God's indifference is only apparent, and that, because he has not done so, God will punish him.

w: Ps 2:9. *x*: Jb 35:16; 38:2; 42:3. *y*: Jb 32:2. *z*: Jb 34:9. *a*: Jb 22:3; 41:2; Lk 17:10; Rom 11:35.

the case is before him; with trembling
wait upon him.
15 But now that you have done otherwise,
God's anger punishes,
nor does he show much concern over a
life.
16 Yet Job to no purpose opens his mouth,
multiplying words without
knowledge.[b]

CHAPTER 36

See RG 236–43

1 Elihu continued and said:

2 Wait a little and I will instruct you,
for there are still words to be said for
God.
3 I will assemble arguments from afar,
and for my maker I will establish what
is right.
4 For indeed, my words are not a lie;
one perfect in knowledge is before
you.
5 Look, God is great, not disdainful;
his strength of purpose is great.
He does not preserve the life of the
wicked.
6 He establishes the right of the poor;[c]
he does not divert his eyes from the
just
7 But he seats them upon thrones
with kings, exalted forever.[d]
8 If they are bound with fetters,
held fast by bonds of affliction,
9 He lets them know what they have done,
and how arrogant are their sins.
10 He opens their ears to correction
and tells them to turn back from evil.
11 If they listen and serve him,
they spend their days in prosperity,
their years in happiness.
12 But if they do not listen, they pass to the
grave,
they perish for lack of knowledge.
13 The impious in heart lay up anger;
they do not cry for help when he binds
them;
14 They will die young—
their life* among the reprobate.
15 But he saves the afflicted through their
affliction,
and opens their ears through
oppression.
16 * He entices you from distress,
to a broad place without constraint;
what rests on your table is rich food.
17 Though you are full of the judgment of
the wicked,
judgment and justice will be
maintained.
18 Let not anger at abundance entice you,
nor great bribery lead you astray.
19 Will your wealth equip you against
distress,
or all your exertions of strength?
20 Do not long for the night,
when peoples vanish in their place.
21 Be careful; do not turn to evil;
for this you have preferred to
affliction.
22 * Look, God is exalted in his power.
What teacher is there like him?
23 Who prescribes for him his way?
Who says, "You have done wrong"?[e]
24 Remember, you should extol his work,
which people have praised in song.
25 All humankind beholds it;
everyone views it from afar.
26 See, God is great beyond our knowledge,
the number of his years past searching
out.
27 He holds in check the waterdrops
that filter in rain from his flood,
28 Till the clouds flow with them
and they rain down on all humankind.
29 * Can anyone understand the spreading
clouds,
the thunderings from his tent?
30 Look, he spreads his light over it,

36:14 Life: a miserable life before death or a shadowy existence in Sheol. **Reprobate**: cf. Dt 23:18–19.

36:16–20 The Hebrew text here is obscure. Although each verse makes some sense, they do not constitute a logical sequence.

36:22–25 These verses serve as an introduction to the hymn about the divine marvels, 36:26–37:24, which in some respects anticipates the tone and content of the Lord's speeches in chaps. 38–41.

36:29–31 The translation of these verses is uncertain.

b: Jb 34:35; 38:2; 42:3. *c:* Ps 72:4, 12–13. *d:* Ps 113:7–8. *e:* Jb 34:10; Is 40:13.

it covers the roots of the sea.
31 For by these he judges the nations,
and gives food in abundance.
32 In his hands he holds the lightning,
and he commands it to strike the mark.
33 His thunder announces him
and incites the fury of the storm.

CHAPTER 37

See RG 236–43

1 At this my heart trembles
and leaps out of its place.
2 Listen to his angry voice*
and the rumble that comes forth from his mouth!
3 Everywhere under the heavens he sends it,
with his light, to the ends of the earth.
4 Again his voice roars,
his majestic voice thunders;
he does not restrain them when his voice is heard.
5 God thunders forth marvels with his voice;
he does great things beyond our knowing.
6 He says to the snow, "Fall to the earth";
likewise to his heavy, drenching rain.
7 He shuts up all humankind indoors,
so that all people may know his work.
8 The wild beasts take to cover
and remain quiet in their dens.
9 Out of its chamber the tempest comes forth;
from the north winds, the cold.
10 With his breath God brings the frost,
and the broad waters congeal.[f]
11 The clouds too are laden with moisture,
the storm-cloud scatters its light.
12 * He it is who changes their rounds,
according to his plans,
to do all that he commands them
across the inhabited world.
13 Whether for punishment or mercy,
he makes it happen.
14 Listen to this, Job!
Stand and consider the marvels of God!
15 Do you know how God lays his command upon them,
and makes the light shine forth from his clouds?
16 Do you know how the clouds are banked,
the marvels of him who is perfect in knowledge?
17 You, who swelter in your clothes
when calm lies over the land from the south,
18 Can you with him spread out the firmament of the skies,
hard as a molten mirror?*
19 Teach us then what we shall say to him;
we cannot, for the darkness, make our plea.
20 Will he be told about it when I speak?
Can anyone talk when he is being destroyed?
21 Rather, it is as the light that cannot be seen
while it is obscured by the clouds,
till the wind comes by and sweeps them away.*
22 From Zaphon* the golden splendor comes,
surrounding God's awesome majesty!
23 The Almighty! We cannot find him,
preeminent in power and judgment,
abundant in justice, who never oppresses.
24 Therefore people fear him;
none can see him, however wise their hearts.*

VIII. The Lord and Job Meet

CHAPTER 38

See RG 236–43

1 Then the LORD* answered Job out of the storm and said:

37:2 Voice: the thunder.

37:12–13 The translation of these verses is uncertain.

37:18 The firmament . . . mirror: the ancients thought of the sky as a ceiling above which were the "upper waters" (cf. Gn 1:6–7; 7:11); when this ceiling became as hard as metal, the usual rain failed to fall on the earth (cf. Lv 26:19; Dt 28:23).

37:21 Elihu argues that even though God seems not to know our circumstances, he does know them, just as surely as the sun shines behind the clouds.

37:22 Zaphon: the mythical mountain of the gods; cf. note on 26:7.

37:24 The concluding remark of Elihu is ironic in view of the appearance of the Lord in the next chapter and Job's claim in 42:5.

38:1 Now the Lord enters the debate and addresses two discourses (chaps. 38–39 and 40–41) to Job, speaking of di-

f: Ps 147:17.

2 Who is this who darkens counsel
with words of ignorance?
3 Gird up your loins* now, like a man;
I will question you, and you tell me the answers![g]
4 Where were you when I founded the earth?
Tell me, if you have understanding.
5 Who determined its size? Surely you know?
Who stretched out the measuring line for it?
6 Into what were its pedestals sunk,
and who laid its cornerstone,
7 While the morning stars sang together
and all the sons of God* shouted for joy?
8 Who shut within doors the sea,
when it burst forth from the womb,[h]
9 When I made the clouds its garment
and thick darkness its swaddling bands?
10 When I set limits for it
and fastened the bar of its door,
11 And said: Thus far shall you come but no farther,
and here shall your proud waves stop?
12 Have you ever in your lifetime commanded the morning
and shown the dawn its place
13 For taking hold of the ends of the earth,
till the wicked are shaken from it?
14 The earth is changed as clay by the seal,
and dyed like a garment;
15 But from the wicked their light is withheld,
and the arm of pride is shattered.
16 Have you entered into the sources of the sea,
or walked about on the bottom of the deep?
17 Have the gates of death been shown to you,
or have you seen the gates of darkness?
18 Have you comprehended the breadth of the earth?
Tell me, if you know it all.
19 What is the way to the dwelling of light,
and darkness—where is its place?
20 That you may take it to its territory
and know the paths to its home?
21 You know, because you were born then,
and the number of your days is great!*
22 Have you entered the storehouses of the snow,
and seen the storehouses of the hail
23 Which I have reserved for times of distress,
for a day of war and battle?[i]
24 What is the way to the parting of the winds,
where the east wind spreads over the earth?
25 Who has laid out a channel for the downpour
and a path for the thunderstorm
26 To bring rain to uninhabited land,
the unpeopled wilderness;
27 To drench the desolate wasteland
till the desert blooms with verdure?
28 Has the rain a father?
Who has begotten the drops of dew?
29 Out of whose womb comes the ice,
and who gives the hoarfrost its birth in the skies,
30 When the waters lie covered as though with stone
that holds captive the surface of the deep?
31 Have you tied cords to the Pleiades,*
or loosened the bonds of Orion?
32 Can you bring forth the Mazzaroth in their season,
or guide the Bear with her children?
33 Do you know the ordinances of the heavens;
can you put into effect their plan on the earth?

vine wisdom and power. Such things are altogether beyond the capacity of Job. **Out of the storm**: frequently the background of the appearances of the Lord in the Old Testament; cf. Ps 18; 50; Na 1:3; Hb 3:2–15.

38:3 Gird up your loins: prepare for combat—figuratively, be ready to defend yourself in debate.

38:7 Sons of God: see note on 1:6.

38:21 Ironic, but not a harsh rebuke.

38:31–32 Pleiades . . . Orion . . . Bear: cf. 9:9. **Mazzaroth**: it is uncertain what astronomical group is meant by this Hebrew word; perhaps a southern constellation.

g: Jb 40:2. *h:* Gn 1:9. *i:* Jos 10:11; Sir 46:5.

34 Can you raise your voice to the clouds,
for them to cover you with a deluge of waters?
35 Can you send forth the lightnings on their way,
so that they say to you, "Here we are"?
36 Who gives wisdom to the ibis,
and gives the rooster* understanding?
37 Who counts the clouds with wisdom?
Who tilts the water jars of heaven
38 So that the dust of earth is fused into a mass
and its clods stick together?
39 Do you hunt the prey for the lion
or appease the hunger of young lions,
40 While they crouch in their dens,
or lie in ambush in the thicket?
41 Who provides nourishment for the raven
when its young cry out to God,[j]
wandering about without food?

CHAPTER 39

See RG 236–43

1 Do you know when mountain goats are born,
or watch for the birth pangs of deer,
2 Number the months that they must fulfill,
or know when they give birth,
3 When they crouch down and drop their young,
when they deliver their progeny?
4 Their offspring thrive and grow in the open,
they leave and do not return.
5 Who has given the wild donkey his freedom,
and who has loosed the wild ass from bonds?
6 I have made the wilderness his home
and the salt flats his dwelling.
7 He scoffs at the uproar of the city,
hears no shouts of a driver.
8 He ranges the mountains for pasture,
and seeks out every patch of green.
9 Will the wild ox consent to serve you,
or pass the nights at your manger?
10 Will you bind the wild ox with a rope in the furrow,
and will he plow the valleys after you?
11 Will you depend on him for his great strength
and leave to him the fruits of your toil?
12 Can you rely on him to bring in your grain
and gather in the yield of your threshing floor?
13 The wings of the ostrich* flap away;
her plumage is lacking in feathers.
14 When she abandons her eggs on the ground*
and lets them warm in the sand,
15 She forgets that a foot may crush them,
that the wild beasts may trample them;
16 She cruelly disowns her young
and her labor is useless; she has no fear.
17 For God has withheld wisdom from her
and given her no share in understanding.
18 Yet when she spreads her wings high,
she laughs at a horse and rider.
19 Do you give the horse his strength,*
and clothe his neck with a mane?
20 Do you make him quiver like a locust,
while his thunderous snorting spreads terror?
21 He paws the valley, he rejoices in his strength,
and charges into battle.
22 He laughs at fear and cannot be terrified;
he does not retreat from the sword.
23 Around him rattles the quiver,
flashes the spear and the javelin.
24 Frenzied and trembling he devours the ground;
he does not hold back at the sound of the trumpet;
25 at the trumpet's call he cries, "Aha!"
Even from afar he scents the battle,
the roar of the officers and the shouting.
26 Is it by your understanding that the hawk soars,
that he spreads his wings toward the south?

38:36 Ibis . . . rooster: the translation is uncertain.

39:13 The wings of the ostrich cannot raise her from the ground, but they help her to run swiftly.

39:14–16 People thought that, because the ostrich laid her eggs on the sand, she was thereby cruelly abandoning them; cf. Lam 4:3.

39:19–25 A classic description of a war horse.

j: Ps 147:9.

27 Does the eagle fly up at your command
to build his nest up high?
28 On a cliff he dwells and spends the night,
on the spur of cliff or fortress.
29 From there he watches for his food;
his eyes behold it afar off.
30 His young ones greedily drink blood;
where the slain are, there is he.[k]

CHAPTER 40

See RG 236–43

1 The LORD then answered Job and
said:

2 Will one who argues with the Almighty
be corrected?
Let him who would instruct God give
answer![l]

3 Then Job answered the LORD and said:

4 * Look, I am of little account; what can I
answer you?
I put my hand over my mouth.
5 I have spoken once, I will not reply;
twice, but I will do so no more.

6 Then the LORD answered Job out of the
storm and said:

7 Gird up your loins now, like a man.
I will question you, and you tell me the
answers!
8 * Would you refuse to acknowledge my
right?
Would you condemn me that you may
be justified?
9 Have you an arm like that of God,
or can you thunder with a voice like his?
10 Adorn yourself with grandeur and
majesty,
and clothe yourself with glory and
splendor.
11 Let loose the fury of your wrath;
look at everyone who is proud and
bring them down.
12 Look at everyone who is proud, and
humble them.
Tear down the wicked in their place,
13 bury them in the dust together;
in the hidden world imprison them.
14 Then will I too praise you,
for your own right hand can save you.
15 Look at Behemoth,* whom I made along
with you,
who feeds on grass like an ox.
16 See the strength in his loins,
the power in the sinews of his belly.
17 He carries his tail like a cedar;
the sinews of his thighs are like cables.
18 His bones are like tubes of bronze;
his limbs are like iron rods.
19 He is the first of God's ways,
only his maker can approach him with
a sword.
20 For the mountains bring him produce,
and all wild animals make sport there.
21 Under lotus trees he lies,
in coverts of the reedy swamp.
22 The lotus trees cover him with their
shade;
all about him are the poplars in the
wadi.
23 If the river grows violent, he is not
disturbed;
he is tranquil though the Jordan surges
about his mouth.
24 Who can capture him by his eyes,
or pierce his nose* with a trap?
25 Can you lead Leviathan* about with a
hook,
or tie down his tongue with a rope?
26 Can you put a ring into his nose,
or pierce through his cheek with a
gaff?
27 Will he then plead with you, time after
time,
or address you with tender words?
28 Will he make a covenant with you

40:4–5 Job's first reaction is humble, but also seemingly cautious.

40:8–14 The issue is joined in these verses, and the Lord seems to challenge Job to play God and to bring down the proud and wicked.

40:15 Behemoth: a primeval monster of chaos; identified by some scholars as the hippopotamus, on which the description of Behemoth is partially based. The point of the Behemoth-Leviathan passages is that only the Lord, not Job, can control the cosmic evil which these forces symbolize.

40:24 Eyes . . . nose: the only exposed parts of the submerged beast.

40:25 Leviathan: although identified by some scholars as the crocodile, it is more likely another chaos monster; see note on 3:8.

k: Mt 24:28; Lk 17:37. *l:* Jb 38:3.

that you may have him as a slave
forever?
29 Can you play with him, as with a bird?
Can you tie him up for your little
girls?
30 Will the traders bargain for him?
Will the merchants* divide him up?
31 Can you fill his hide with barbs,
or his head with fish spears?
32 Once you but lay a hand upon him,
no need to recall any other conflict!

CHAPTER 41

See RG 236–43

1 Whoever might vainly hope to do so
need only see him to be overthrown.
2 No one is fierce enough to arouse him;
who then dares stand before me?
3 Whoever has assailed me, I will pay
back—
Everything under the heavens is mine.
4 I need hardly mention his limbs,
his strength, and the fitness of his
equipment.
5 Who can strip off his outer garment,
or penetrate his double armor?
6 Who can force open the doors of his face,
close to his terrible teeth?
7 Rows of scales are on his back,
tightly sealed together;
8 They are fitted so close to each other
that no air can come between them;
9 So joined to one another
that they hold fast and cannot be
parted.
10 When he sneezes, light flashes forth;
his eyes are like the eyelids of the
dawn.
11 Out of his mouth go forth torches;
sparks of fire leap forth.
12 From his nostrils comes smoke
as from a seething pot or bowl.
13 His breath sets coals afire;
a flame comes from his mouth.
14 Strength abides in his neck,
and power leaps before him.
15 The folds of his flesh stick together,
it is cast over him and immovable.
16 His heart is cast as hard as stone;
cast as the lower millstone.
17 When he rises up, the gods are afraid;
when he crashes down, they fall back.
18 Should a sword reach him, it will not
avail;
nor will spear, dart, or javelin.
19 He regards iron as chaff,
and bronze as rotten wood.
20 No arrow will put him to flight;
slingstones used against him are but
straw.
21 Clubs he regards as straw;
he laughs at the crash of the spear.
22 Under him are sharp pottery fragments,
spreading a threshing sledge upon the
mire.
23 He makes the depths boil like a pot;
he makes the sea like a perfume
bottle.
24 Behind him he leaves a shining path;
you would think the deep had white
hair.
25 Upon the earth there is none like him,
he was made fearless.
26 He looks over all who are haughty,
he is king over all proud beasts.

CHAPTER 42

See RG 236–43

1 Then Job answered the LORD and
said:
2 I know that you can do all things,*
and that no purpose of yours can be
hindered.
3 "Who is this who obscures counsel with
ignorance?"
I have spoken but did not understand;
things too marvelous for me, which I
did not know.[m]
4 "Listen, and I will speak;
I will question you, and you tell me the
answers."
5 By hearsay I had heard of you,
but now my eye has seen you.*

40:30 Merchants: lit., "Canaanites," whose reputation for trading was so widespread that their name came to be used for merchants; cf. Prv 31:24.

42:2–4 In his final speech, Job quotes God's own words (see 38:2–3; 40:7).

42:5 In 19:25–27 Job had affirmed a hope to "see" (three times) his vindicator. Now he has seen the Lord about whom he had heard so much.

m: Jb 34:35; 35:16; 38:2; Ps 131:1; Prv 30:18.

[6] Therefore I disown what I have said,
and repent in dust and ashes.*

IX. Epilogue

Job's Restoration. [7]And after the LORD had
spoken these words to Job, the LORD said to
Eliphaz the Temanite, "My anger blazes
against you and your two friends!* You have
not spoken rightly concerning me, as has my
servant Job. [8]So now take seven bulls and
seven rams, and go to my servant Job, and
sacrifice a burnt offering for yourselves, and
let my servant Job pray for you.* To him I
will show favor, and not punish your folly,
for you have not spoken rightly concerning
me, as has my servant Job." [9]Then Eliphaz
the Temanite, and Bildad the Shuhite, and
Zophar the Naamathite, went and did as the
LORD had commanded them. The LORD
showed favor to Job.

[10]The LORD also restored the prosperity of
Job, after he had prayed for his friends; the
LORD even gave to Job twice* as much as he
had before. [11]Then all his brothers and sisters
came to him, and all his former acquaintances,
and they dined with him in his house. They
consoled and comforted him for all the evil the
LORD had brought upon him, and each one
gave him a piece of money* and a gold ring.

[12][n] Thus the LORD blessed the later days
of Job more than his earlier ones. Now he
had fourteen thousand sheep, six thousand
camels, a thousand yoke of oxen, and a
thousand she-donkeys. [13]He also had seven
sons and three daughters: [14]the first daughter
he called Jemimah, the second Keziah, and
the third Keren-happuch.* [15]In all the land
no other women were as beautiful as the
daughters of Job; and their father gave them
an inheritance* among their brothers.

[16]After this, Job lived a hundred and forty
years; and he saw his children, his grandchildren, and even his great-grandchildren.[o]
[17]Then Job died, old and full of years.

42:6 A difficult verse. Some doubt, in view of God's commendation in v. 7, that Job does in fact express repentance, and alternative translations are often given. Along with v. 5, it describes a change in Job, which the encounter with the Lord has brought about. **Dust and ashes**: an ambiguous phrase. It can refer to the human condition (cf. Gn 18:27; Jb 30:19) or to Job's ash heap (2:8).

42:7 The three friends of Job (Elihu is ignored in the epilogue) are criticized by the Lord because they had "not spoken rightly" (vv. 7–8).

42:8 An ironic touch: Job becomes the intercessor for his friends.

42:10 Twice: this is the fine for damage inflicted upon another; cf. Ex 22:3. The Lord pays up!

42:11 A piece of money: lit., *qesitah*, value unknown; also used in Gn 33:19; Jos 24:32. **Gold ring**: for the nose or ear.

42:14 Job's daughters had names symbolic of their charms: **Jemimah**, dove; **Keziah**, precious perfume (cf. Ps 45:9); **Keren-happuch**, cosmetic jar—more precisely, a container for a black powder used like modern mascara.

42:15 Ordinarily daughters did not inherit property unless there were no sons; cf. Nm 27:1–11.

n: Jb 1:3. *o:* Jb 5:25–26.

See RG 243–54

The Book of Psalms

The Hebrew Psalter numbers 150 songs. The corresponding number in the Septuagint differs because of a different division of certain Psalms. Hence the numbering in the Greek Psalter (which was followed by the Latin Vulgate) is usually one digit behind the Hebrew. In the New American Bible the numbering of the verses follows the Hebrew numbering; many of the traditional English translations are often a verse number behind the Hebrew because they do not count the superscriptions as a verse.

The superscriptions derive from pre-Christian Jewish tradition, and they contain technical terms, many of them apparently liturgical, which are no longer known to us. Seventy-three Psalms are attributed to David, but there is no sure way of dating any Psalm. Some are preexilic (before 587), and others are postexilic (after 539), but not as late as the Maccabean period (ca. 165). The Psalms are the product of many individual collections (e.g., Songs of Ascents, Ps 120–134), which were eventually combined into the present work in which one can detect five "books," because of the doxologies which occur at 41:14; 72:18–19; 89:53; 106:48.

Two important features of the Psalms deserve special notice. First, the majority were composed originally precisely for liturgical worship. This is shown by the frequent indication of liturgical leaders interacting with the community (e.g., Ps 118:1–4). Secondly, they follow certain distinct patterns or literary forms. Thus, the hymn is a song of praise, in which a community is urged joyfully to sing out the praise of God. Various reasons are given for this praise (often introduced by "for" or "because"): the divine work of creation and sustenance (Ps 135:1–12; 136). Some of the hymns have received a more specific classification, based on content. The "Songs of Zion" are so called because they exalt Zion, the city in which God dwells among the people (Ps 47; 96–99). Characteristic of the songs of praise is the joyful summons to get involved in the activity; Ps 104 is an exception to this, although it remains universal in its thrust.

Another type of Psalm is similar to the hymn: the thanksgiving Psalm. This too is a song of praise acknowledging the Lord as the rescuer of the psalmist from a desperate situation. Very often the psalmist will give a flashback, recounting the past distress, and the plea that was uttered (Ps 30; 116). The setting for such prayers seems to have been the offering of a *todah* (a "praise" sacrifice) with friends in the Temple.

There are more Psalms of lament than of any other type. They may be individual (e.g., Ps 3–7; 22) or communal (e.g., Ps 44). Although they usually begin with a cry for help, they develop in various ways. The description of the distress is couched in the broad imagery typical of the Bible (one is in Sheol, the Pit, or is afflicted by enemies or wild beasts, etc.)—in such a way that one cannot pinpoint the exact nature of the psalmist's plight. However, Ps 51 (cf. also Ps 130) seems to refer clearly to deliverance from sin. Several laments end on a note of certainty that the Lord has heard the prayer (cf. Ps 7, but contrast Ps 88), and the Psalter has been characterized as a movement from lament to praise. If this is somewhat of an exaggeration, it serves at least to emphasize the frequent expressions of trust which characterize the lament. In some cases it would seem as if the theme of trust has been lifted out to form a literary type all its own; cf. Ps 23, 62, 91. Among the communal laments can be counted Ps 74 and 79. They complain to the Lord about some national disaster, and try to motivate God to intervene in favor of the suffering people.

Other Psalms are clearly classified on account of content, and they may be in themselves laments or Psalms of thanksgiving. Among the "royal" Psalms that deal directly with the currently reigning king, are Ps 20, 21, and 72. Many of the royal Psalms were given a messianic interpretation by Christians. In Jewish tradition they were preserved, even after kingship had disappeared, because they were read in the light of the Davidic covenant reported in 2 Sm 7. Certain Psalms are called wisdom Psalms because they seem to betray the influence of the concerns of the ages (cf. Ps 37, 49), but there is no general agreement as to the number of these prayers. Somewhat related to the wisdom Psalms are the "torah" Psalms, in which the torah (instruction or law) of the Lord is glorified (Ps 1; 19:8–14; 119). Ps 78, 105, 106 can be considered as "historical" Psalms. Although the majority of the Psalms have a liturgical setting, there are certain prayers that may be termed "liturgies," so clearly does their structure reflect a liturgical incident (e.g., Ps 15, 24).

It is obvious that not all of the Psalms can be pigeon-holed into neat classifications, but even a brief sketch of these types help us to catch the structure and spirit of the Psalms we read. It has been rightly said that the Psalms are "a school of prayer." They not only provide us with models to follow, but inspire us to voice our own deepest feelings and aspirations.

First Book—Psalms 1–41

PSALM 1*

True Happiness in God's Law

See RG 245–46

I

[1] Blessed is the man who does not walk
in the counsel of the wicked,
Nor stand in the way* of sinners,
nor sit in company with scoffers.[a]

Psalm 1 A preface to the whole Book of Psalms, contrasting with striking similes the destiny of the good and the wicked. The Psalm views life as activity, as choosing either the good or the bad. Each "way" brings its inevitable consequences. The wise through their good actions will experience rootedness and life, and the wicked, rootlessness and death.

1:1 The way: a common biblical term for manner of living or moral conduct (Ps 32:8; 101:2, 6; Prv 2:20; 1 Kgs 8:36).

a: Ps 26:4–5; 40:5.

The Structure of the Book of Psalms

PSALMS IS DIVIDED into five "books," each of which ends with a verse or song of praise (a doxology).

Book 1, Psalms 1–41	Doxology is 41:14
Book 2, Psalms 42–72	Doxology is 72:18–19
Book 3, Psalms 73–89	Doxology is 89:53
Book 4, Psalms 90–106	Doxology is 106:48
Book 5, Psalms 107–150	Doxology is Psalm 150

Books 1, 4, and 5 tend to use "LORD" ("Yahweh") as the name of God; books 2 and 3 use "God" ("Elohim"). This indicates that there may have been two centers of collection for Psalms, and in one case—Psalms 14 and 53—we have a nearly identical Psalm with the different names for God.

2 Rather, the law of the LORD* is his joy;
and on his law he meditates day and night.[b]
3 He is like a tree[c]
planted near streams of water,
that yields its fruit in season;
Its leaves never wither;
whatever he does prospers.

II

4 But not so are the wicked,* not so!
They are like chaff driven by the wind.[d]
5 Therefore the wicked will not arise at the judgment,
nor will sinners in the assembly of the just.
6 Because the LORD knows the way of the just,[e]
but the way of the wicked leads to ruin.

See RG 245, 250, 251

PSALM 2*
A Psalm for a Royal Coronation

1 Why do the nations protest
and the peoples conspire in vain?[f]
2 Kings on earth rise up
and princes plot together
against the LORD and against his anointed one:*[g]
3 "Let us break their shackles
and cast off their chains from us!"[h]
4 The one enthroned in heaven laughs;
the Lord derides them,[i]
5 Then he speaks to them in his anger,
in his wrath he terrifies them:
6 "I myself have installed my king
on Zion, my holy mountain."
7 I will proclaim the decree of the LORD,
he said to me, "You are my son;
today I have begotten you.[j]
8 Ask it of me,
and I will give you the nations as your inheritance,
and, as your possession, the ends of the earth.
9 With an iron rod you will shepherd them,
like a potter's vessel you will shatter them."[k]
10 And now, kings, give heed;
take warning, judges on earth.
11 Serve the LORD with fear;

1:2 The law of the LORD: either the Torah, the first five books of the Bible, or, more probably, divine teaching or instruction.

1:4 The wicked: those who by their actions distance themselves from God's life-giving presence.

Psalm 2 A royal Psalm. To rebellious kings (Ps 2:1–3) God responds vigorously (Ps 2:4–6). A speaker proclaims the divine decree (in the legal adoption language of the day), making the Israelite king the earthly representative of God (Ps 2:7–9) and warning kings to obey (Ps 2:10–11). The Psalm has a messianic meaning for the Church; the New Testament understands it of Christ (Acts 4:25–27; 13:33; Heb 1:5).

2:2 Anointed: in Hebrew *mashiah*, "anointed"; in Greek *christos*, whence English Messiah and Christ. In Israel kings (Jgs 9:8; 1 Sm 9:16; 16:12–13) and high priests (Lv 8:12; Nm 3:3) received the power of their office through anointing.

b: Jos 1:8; Ps 119; Sir 39:1. *c:* Ps 52:10; 92:13–15; Jer 17:8. *d:* Ps 35:5; 83:14–16; Jb 21:18. *e:* Ps 37:18. *f:* Rev 11:18. *g:* Ps 83:6. *h:* Ps 149:8. *i:* Ps 37:13; 59:9; Wis 4:18. *j:* Ps 89:27; 110:2–3; Is 49:1. *k:* Rev 2:27; 12:5; 19:15.

exult with trembling,
Accept correction
lest he become angry and you perish along the way
when his anger suddenly blazes up.[l]
Blessed are all who take refuge in him!

PSALM 3*

See RG 244

Threatened but Trusting

1 A psalm of David, when he fled from his son Absalom.*[m]

I

2 How many are my foes, LORD!
How many rise against me!
3 *How many say of me,
"There is no salvation for him in God."[n] *Selah*
4 But you, LORD, are a shield around me;
my glory, you keep my head high.[o]

II

5 With my own voice I will call out to the LORD,
and he will answer me from his holy mountain. *Selah*
6 I lie down and I fall asleep,
[and] I will wake up, for the LORD sustains me.[p]
7 I do not fear, then, thousands of people
arrayed against me on every side.

III

8 Arise, LORD! Save me, my God!
For you strike the cheekbone of all my foes;
you break the teeth of the wicked.[q]
9 Salvation is from the LORD!
May your blessing be upon your people![r] *Selah*

PSALM 4*

See RG 244

Trust in God

1 For the leader;* with stringed instruments. A psalm of David.

I

2 Answer me when I call, my saving God.
When troubles hem me in, set me free;
take pity on me, hear my prayer.[s]

II

3 How long, O people, will you be hard of heart?
Why do you love what is worthless, chase after lies?*[t] *Selah*
4 Know that the LORD works wonders for his faithful one;
the LORD hears when I call out to him.
5 Tremble* and sin no more;
weep bitterly* within your hearts,
wail upon your beds,[u]
6 Offer fitting sacrifices
and trust in the LORD.[v]

III

7 Many say, "May we see better times!
LORD, show us the light of your face!"[w] *Selah*
8 But you have given my heart more joy
than they have when grain and wine abound.
9 [x]*In peace I will lie down and fall asleep,
for you alone, LORD, make me secure.

Psalm 3 An individual lament complaining of enemies who deny that God will come to the rescue (Ps 3:2–3). Despite such taunts the psalmist hopes for God's protection even in sleep (Ps 3:4–7). The Psalm prays for an end to the enemies' power to speak maliciously (Ps 3:8) and closes peacefully with an expression of trust (Ps 3:9).

3:1 The superscription, added later, relates the Psalm to an incident in the life of David.

3:3, 3:5, 3:9 Selah: the term is generally considered a direction to the cantor or musicians but its exact meaning is not known. It occurs 71 times in 39 Psalms.

Psalm 4 An individual lament emphasizing trust in God. The petition is based upon the psalmist's vivid experience of God as savior (Ps 4:2). That experience of God is the basis for the warning to the wicked: revere God who intervenes on the side of the faithful (Ps 4:3–6). The faithful psalmist exemplifies the blessings given to the just (Ps 4:7–8).

4:1 For the leader: many Psalm headings contain this rubric. Its exact meaning is unknown but may signify that such Psalms once stood together in a collection of "the choirmaster," cf. 1 Chr 15:21.

4:3 Love what is worthless . . . lies: these expressions probably refer to false gods worshiped by those the psalmist is addressing.

4:5 Tremble: be moved deeply with fear for failing to worship the true God. The Greek translation understood the emotion to be anger, and it is so cited in Eph 4:26. **Weep bitterly . . . wail**: weeping within one's heart and wailing upon one's bed denote sincere repentance because these actions are not done in public or with the community but in the privacy of one's heart and one's home. The same idiom is found in Hos 7:14.

4:9 In peace I will . . . fall asleep: the last verse repeats

l: Ps 34:9; 146:5; Prv 16:20. *m:* 2 Sm 15:13ff. *n:* Ps 71:11. *o:* Ps 7:11; 18:3; 62:7–8; Dt 33:29; Is 60:19. *p:* Ps 4:9; Prv 3:24. *q:* Ps 58:7. *r:* Ps 28:9; Jon 2:10. *s:* Ps 118:5. *t:* Ps 62:4. *u:* Eph 4:26. *v:* Ps 51:19. *w:* Ps 31:17; 44:4; 67:1; 80:4; Jb 13:24; Nm 6:25; Dn 9:17. *x:* Ps 3:6.

See RG 244

PSALM 5*

Prayer for Divine Help

[1]For the leader; with wind instruments.
A psalm of David.

I

2 Give ear to my words, O LORD;
understand my sighing.[y]
3 Attend to the sound of my cry,
my king and my God!
For to you I will pray, LORD;
4 in the morning you will hear my voice;
in the morning I will plead before you
and wait.[z]

II

5 You are not a god who delights in evil;
no wicked person finds refuge with
you;
6 the arrogant cannot stand before your
eyes.
You hate all who do evil;
7 you destroy those who speak falsely.[a]
A bloody and fraudulent man
the LORD abhors.

III

8 But I, through the abundance of your
mercy,*
will enter into your house.
I will bow down toward your holy
sanctuary
out of fear of you.[b]
9 LORD, guide me in your justice because
of my foes;
make straight your way before me.[c]

IV

10 For there is no sincerity in their mouth;
their heart is corrupt.
Their throat* is an open grave;[d]
on their tongue are subtle lies.
11 Declare them guilty, God;
make them fall by their own devices.[e]
Drive them out for their many sins;
for they have rebelled against you.

V

12 Then all who trust in you will be glad
and forever shout for joy.[f]
You will protect them and those will
rejoice in you
who love your name.
13 For you, LORD, bless the just one;
you surround him with favor like a
shield.

PSALM 6*

See RG 244

Prayer in Distress

[1]For the leader; with stringed instruments,
"upon the eighth."*
A psalm of David.

I

2 Do not reprove me in your anger, LORD,
nor punish me in your wrath.[g]
3 Have pity on me, LORD, for I am weak;
heal me, LORD, for my bones are
shuddering.[h]
4 My soul too is shuddering greatly—
and you, LORD, how long . . . ?*[i]
5 Turn back, LORD, rescue my soul;
save me because of your mercy.

two themes in the Psalm. One is the security of one who trusts in the true God; the other is the interior peace of those who sincerely repent ("on [their] beds"), whose sleep is not disturbed by a guilty conscience.

Psalm 5 A lament contrasting the security of the house of God (Ps 5:8–9, 12–13) with the danger of the company of evildoers (Ps 5:5–7, 10–11). The psalmist therefore prays that God will hear (Ps 5:2–4) and grant the protection and joy of the Temple.

5:8 Mercy: used to translate the Hebrew word, *hesed*. This term speaks to a relationship between persons. It is manifested in concrete actions to persons with some need or desire. The one who offers *hesed* has the ability to respond to that need of the other person. Other possible ways to translate *hesed* include "steadfast love" and "loving kindness."

5:10 Their throat: their speech brings harm to their hearers (cf. Jer 5:16). The verse mentions four parts of the body, each a source of evil to the innocent.

Psalm 6 The first of the seven Penitential Psalms (Ps 6, 32, 38, 51, 102, 130, 143), a designation dating from the seventh century A.D. for Psalms suitable to express repentance. The psalmist does not, as in many laments, claim to be innocent but appeals to God's mercy (Ps 6:5). Sin here, as often in the Bible, is both the sinful act and its injurious consequences; here it is physical sickness (Ps 6:3–4, 7–8) and the attacks of enemies (Ps 6:8, 9, 11). The psalmist prays that the effects of personal and social sin be taken away.

6:1 Upon the eighth: apparently a musical notation, now lost.

6:4 How long?: elliptical for "How long will it be before you answer my prayer?" cf. Ps 13:2–3.

y: Ps 86:6; 130:1–2. *z:* Wis 16:28. *a:* Ps 101:7; Wis 14:9; Heb 1:13. *b:* Ps 138:2; Jon 2:5. *c:* Ps 23:3; Prv 4:11; Is 26:7. *d:* Rom 3:13. *e:* Ps 141:10. *f:* Ps 64:11. *g:* Ps 38:2. *h:* Jer 17:14–15. *i:* Ps 13:2–3; 74:10; 89:47.

6 For in death there is no remembrance of
you.
Who praises you in Sheol?*[j]
II
7 I am wearied with sighing;
all night long I drench my bed with
tears;
I soak my couch with weeping.
8 My eyes are dimmed with sorrow,
worn out because of all my foes.[k]
III
9 Away from me, all who do evil![l]
The LORD has heard the sound of my
weeping.
10 The LORD has heard my plea;
the LORD will receive my prayer.
11 My foes will all be disgraced and will
shudder greatly;
they will turn back in sudden
disgrace.[m]

See RG 244

PSALM 7*

God the Vindicator

1 A plaintive song of David, which he sang to the LORD concerning Cush, the Benjaminite.

I
2 LORD my God, in you I trusted;
save me; rescue me from all who
pursue me,[n]
3 Lest someone maul me like a lion,
tear my soul apart with no one to
deliver.
II
4 LORD my God, if I have done this,*
if there is guilt on my hands,
5 If I have maltreated someone treating me
equitably—
or even despoiled my oppressor
without cause—
6 Then let my enemy pursue and overtake
my soul,
trample my life to the ground,
and lay my honor in the dust.[o] *Selah*
III
7 Rise up, LORD, in your anger;
be aroused against the outrages of my
oppressors.[p]
Stir up the justice, my God, you have
commanded.
8 Have the assembly of the peoples gather
about you;
and return on high above them,
9 the LORD will pass judgment on the
peoples.
Judge me, LORD, according to my
righteousness,
and my integrity.
10 Let the malice of the wicked end.
Uphold the just one,
O just God,[q]
who tries hearts and minds.
IV
11 God is a shield above me
saving the upright of heart.[r]
12 God is a just judge, powerful and
patient,*
not exercising anger every day.
13 If one does not repent,
God sharpens his sword,
strings and readies the bow,[s]
14 Prepares his deadly shafts,
makes arrows blazing thunderbolts.[t]
V
15 Consider how one conceives iniquity;
is pregnant with mischief,
and gives birth to deception.[u]
16 He digs a hole and bores it deep,
but he falls into the pit he has made.[v]

6:6 A motive for God to preserve the psalmist from death: in the shadowy world of the dead no one offers you praise. Sheol is the biblical term for the underworld where the insubstantial souls of dead human beings dwelt. It was similar to the Hades of Greek and Latin literature. In the second century B.C., biblical books begin to speak positively of life with God after death (Dn 12:1–3; Wis 3).

Psalm 7 An individual lament. The psalmist flees to God's presence in the sanctuary for justice and protection (Ps 7:2–3) and takes an oath that only the innocent can swear (Ps 7:4–6). The innocent psalmist can thus hope for the just God's protection (Ps 7:7–14) and be confident that the actions of the wicked will come back upon their own heads (Ps 7:15–17). The justice of God leads the psalmist to praise (Ps 7:18).

7:4 Have done this: in the accusation the enemies have made against the psalmist.

7:12 Powerful and patient: the inclusion of these words is drawn from the Septuagint tradition concerning this verse.

j: Ps 30:10; 88:11; 115:17; Is 38:18. *k:* Ps 31:10; 38:11; 40:13. *l:* Ps 119:115; Mt 7:23; Lk 13:27. *m:* Ps 35:4, 26; 40:15; 71:13. *n:* Ps 6:5; 22:21. *o:* Ps 143:3. *p:* Ps 9:4; 19:20. *q:* Ps 17:3; 26:2; 35:24; 43:1; 139:23; Jer 17:10; 20:12. *r:* Ps 3:4. *s:* Ps 11:2. *t:* Is 50:11. *u:* Jb 15:35; Is 59:4. *v:* Ps 9:16; 35:8; 57:7; Prv 26:27; Eccl 10:8; Sir 27:26.

17 His malice turns back upon his head;
his violence falls on his own skull.

VI

18 I will thank the LORD in accordance with his justice;
I will sing the name of the LORD Most High.[w]

PSALM 8*

See RG 244, 249

Divine Majesty and Human Dignity

1 For the leader; "upon the *gittith*."* A psalm of David.

2 O LORD, our Lord,
how awesome is your name through all the earth!

I will sing of your majesty above the heavens
3 with the mouths of babes[x] and infants.*
You have established a bulwark* against your foes,
to silence enemy and avenger.*

4 When I see your heavens, the work of your fingers,
the moon and stars that you set in place—
5 *What is man that you are mindful of him,[y]
and a son of man that you care for him?[z]
6 Yet you have made him little less than a god,*
crowned him with glory and honor.
7 You have given him rule over the works of your hands,[a]
put all things at his feet:
8 All sheep and oxen,
even the beasts of the field,
9 The birds of the air, the fish of the sea,
and whatever swims the paths of the seas.

10 O LORD, our Lord,
how awesome is your name through all the earth!

PSALM 9*

See RG 245

Thanksgiving for Victory and Prayer for Justice

1 For the leader; according to *Muth Labben*.* A psalm of David.

I

2 I will praise you, LORD, with all my heart;
I will declare all your wondrous deeds.
3 I will delight and rejoice in you;
I will sing hymns to your name, Most High.
4 When my enemies turn back,
they stumble and perish before you.

II

5 For you upheld my right and my cause,
seated on your throne, judging justly.

Psalm 8 While marvelling at the limitless grandeur of God (Ps 8:2–3), the psalmist is struck first by the smallness of human beings in creation (Ps 8:4–5), and then by the royal dignity and power that God has graciously bestowed upon them (Ps 8:6–9).

8:1 Upon the gittith: probably the title of the melody to which the Psalm was to be sung or a musical instrument.

8:3 With the mouths of babes and infants: the psalmist realizes that his attempts to praise such an awesome God are hopelessly inadequate and amount to little more than the sounds made by infants. **Established a bulwark**: an allusion to lost myth telling how God built a fortress for himself in the heavens in primordial times in his battle with the powers of chaos. This "bulwark" is the firmament. **Enemy and avenger**: probably cosmic enemies. The primeval powers of watery chaos are often personified in poetic texts (Ps 74:13–14; 89:11; Jb 9:13; 26:12–13; Is 51:9).

8:5 Man . . . a son of man: the emphasis is on the fragility and mortality of human beings to whom God has given great dignity.

8:6 Little less than a god: Hebrew *'elohim*, the ordinary word for "God" or "the gods" or members of the heavenly court. The Greek version translated *'elohim* by "angel, messenger"; several ancient and modern versions so translate. The meaning seems to be that God created human beings almost at the level of the beings in the heavenly world. Heb 2:9, translating "for a little while," finds the eminent fulfillment of this verse in Jesus Christ, who was humbled before being glorified, cf. also 1 Cor 15:27 where St. Paul applies to Christ the closing words of Ps 8:7.

Psalms 9–10 Ps 9 and Ps 10 in the Hebrew text have been transmitted as separate poems but they actually form a single acrostic poem and are so transmitted in the Greek and Latin tradition. Each verse of the two Psalms begins with a successive letter of the Hebrew alphabet (though several letters have no corresponding stanza). The Psalm states loosely connected themes: the rescue of the helpless poor from their enemies, God's worldwide judgment and rule over the nations, the psalmist's own concern for rescue (Ps 9:14–15).

9:1 Muth Labben: probably the melodic accompaniment of the Psalm, now lost.

---

w: Ps 18:50; 30:5; 135:3; 146:2. *x:* Mt 21:16; Wis 10:21. *y:* Ps 144:3; Jb 7:17. *z:* Heb 2:6ff. *a:* Gn 1:26, 28; Wis 9:2; 1 Cor 15:27.

6 You rebuked the nations, you destroyed
the wicked;
their name you blotted out for all time.[b]
7 The enemies have been ruined forever;
you destroyed their cities;
their memory has perished.

III

8 The LORD rules forever,
has set up his throne for judgment.
9 It is he who judges the world with justice,[c]
who judges the peoples with fairness.
10 The LORD is a stronghold for the
oppressed,
a stronghold in times of trouble.[d]
11 Those who know your name trust in you;
you never forsake those who seek you,
LORD.

IV

12 Sing hymns to the LORD enthroned on
Zion;
proclaim his deeds among the nations!
13 For the avenger of bloodshed remembers,
does not forget the cry of the afflicted.[e]

V

14 Be gracious to me, LORD;
see how my foes afflict me!
You alone can raise me from the gates
of death.[f]
15 Then I will declare all your praises,
sing joyously of your salvation
in the gates of daughter Zion.*

VI

16 The nations fall into the pit they dig;
in the snare they hide, their own foot is
caught.
17 *The LORD is revealed in making
judgments:
by the deeds they do the wicked are
trapped.[g] *Higgaion. Selah**

VII

18 To Sheol the wicked will depart,
all the nations that forget God.
19 For the needy will never be forgotten,
nor will the hope of the afflicted ever
fade.[h]
20 Arise, LORD, let no mortal prevail;
let the nations be judged in your
presence.
21 Strike them with terror, LORD;
show the nations they are only human.
Selah

PSALM 10

I

See RG 245

1 Why, LORD, do you stand afar
and pay no heed in times of trouble?
2 Arrogant scoundrels pursue the poor;
they trap them by their cunning
schemes.[i]

II

3 The wicked even boast of their greed;
these robbers curse and scorn the
LORD.[j]
4 In their insolence the wicked boast:
"God does not care; there is no God."[k]
5 Yet their affairs always succeed;
they ignore your judgment on high;
they sneer at all who oppose them.
6 They say in their hearts, "We will never
fall;
never will we see misfortune."
7 Their mouths are full of oaths, violence,
and lies;
discord and evil are under their tongues.[l]
8 They wait in ambush near towns;
their eyes watch for the helpless
to murder the innocent in secret.[m]
9 They lurk in ambush like lions in a thicket,
hide there to trap the poor,
snare them and close the net.[n]
10 The helpless are crushed, laid low;
they fall into the power of the wicked,
11 Who say in their hearts, "God has
forgotten,
shows no concern, never bothers to
look."[o]

9:15 Daughter Zion: an ancient Near Eastern city could sometimes be personified as a woman or a queen, the spouse of the god of the city.

9:17 The LORD is revealed in making judgments: God has so made the universe that the wicked are punished by the very actions they perform. **Selah**: see note on Ps 3:3.

b: Jb 18:17. *c:* Ps 96:10; 98:9. *d:* Ps 37:39; Is 25:4. *e:* Jb 16:18. *f:* Wis 16:13. *g:* Ps 35:8; Sir 27:26. *h:* Prv 23:18. *i:* Is 32:7. *j:* Ps 36:2. *k:* Ps 14:1; Jb 22:13; Is 29:15; Jer 5:12; Zep 1:12. *l:* Is 32:7; Rom 3:14. *m:* Ps 11:2; Jb 24:14. *n:* Ps 17:12; Prv 1:11; Jer 5:26. *o:* Ps 44:25; 64:6; 73:11; 94:7; Ez 9:9.

III

12 Rise up, LORD! God, lift up your hand!
Do not forget the poor!
13 Why should the wicked scorn God,
say in their hearts, "God does not care"?
14 But you do see;
you take note of misery and sorrow;[p]
you take the matter in hand.
To you the helpless can entrust their cause;
you are the defender of orphans.[q]
15 Break the arm of the wicked and depraved;
make them account for their crimes;
let none of them survive.

IV

16 The LORD is king forever;[r]
the nations have vanished from his land.
17 You listen, LORD, to the needs of the poor;
you strengthen their heart and incline your ear.
18 You win justice for the orphaned and oppressed;[s]
no one on earth will cause terror again.

PSALM 11*

See RG 245

Confidence in the Presence of God

1 For the leader. Of David.

I

In the LORD I take refuge;
how can you say to me,
"Flee like a bird to the mountains![t]
2 See how the wicked string their bows,
fit their arrows to the string
to shoot from the shadows at the upright of heart.[u]
3 *If foundations are destroyed,
what can the just one do?"

II

4 The LORD is in his holy temple;
the LORD's throne is in heaven.[v]
God's eyes keep careful watch;
they test the children of Adam.
5 The LORD tests the righteous and the wicked,
hates those who love violence,
6 And rains upon the wicked
fiery coals and brimstone,
a scorching wind their allotted cup.*[w]
7 The LORD is just and loves just deeds;
the upright will see his face.

PSALM 12*

See RG 244

Prayer Against Evil Tongues

1 For the leader; "upon the eighth." A psalm of David.

I

2 Help, LORD, for no one loyal remains;
the faithful have vanished from the children of men.[x]
3 They tell lies to one another,
speak with deceiving lips and a double heart.[y]

II

4 May the LORD cut off all deceiving lips,
and every boastful tongue,
5 Those who say, "By our tongues we prevail;
when our lips speak, who can lord it over us?"[z]

III

6 "Because they rob the weak, and the needy groan,
I will now arise," says the LORD;
"I will grant safety to whoever longs for it."[a]

IV

7 The promises of the LORD are sure,
silver refined in a crucible,*

Psalm 11 A song of trust. Though friends counsel flight to the mountain country (a traditional hideout) to escape trouble (Ps 11:1–3), the innocent psalmist reaffirms confidence in God, who protects those who seek asylum in the Temple (Ps 11:4–7).

11:3 Foundations: usually understood of public order, cf. Ps 82:5.

11:6 Their allotted cup: the cup that God gives people to drink is a common figure for their destiny, cf. Ps 16:5; 75:9; Mt 20:22; 26:39; Rev 14:10.

Psalm 12 A lament. The psalmist, thrown into a world where lying and violent people persecute the just (Ps 12:2–3), prays that the wicked be punished (Ps 12:4–5). The prayer is not simply for vengeance but arises from a desire to see God's justice appear on earth. Ps 12:6 preserves the word of assurance spoken by the priest to the lamenter; it is not usually transmitted in such Psalms. In Ps 12:7–8 the psalmist affirms the intention to live by the word of assurance.

12:7 A crucible: lit., "in a crucible in the ground." The crucible was placed in the ground for support.

p: Ps 31:8; 56:9; 2 Kgs 20:5; Is 25:8; Rev 7:17. *q:* Ex 22:21–22. *r:* Ps 145:13; Jer 10:10. *s:* Dt 10:18. *t:* Ps 55:7; 91:4. *u:* Ps 7:13; 37:14; 57:5; 64:4. *v:* Ps 14:2; 102:20; Hab 2:20; Dt 26:15; Is 66:1; Mt 5:34. *w:* Ps 120:4; 140:11; Prv 16:27; Ez 38:22; Rev 8:5; 20:10. *x:* Ps 14:3; 116:11; Is 59:15; Mi 7:2. *y:* Ps 28:3; 55:22; Is 59:3–4; Jer 9:7. *z:* Sir 5:3. *a:* Is 33:10.

silver purified seven times.[b]
8 You, O LORD, protect us always;
preserve us from this generation.
9 On every side the wicked roam;
the shameless are extolled by the
children of men.

See RG 244

PSALM 13*

Prayer for Help

1 For the leader. A psalm of David.

I

2 How long, LORD? Will you utterly forget
me?
How long will you hide your face
from me?[c]
3 How long must I carry sorrow in my soul,
grief in my heart day after day?
How long will my enemy triumph over
me?

II

4 Look upon me, answer me, LORD, my
God!
Give light to my eyes lest I sleep in
death,
5 Lest my enemy say, "I have prevailed,"
lest my foes rejoice at my downfall.[d]

III

6 But I trust in your mercy.
Grant my heart joy in your salvation,
I will sing to the LORD,
for he has dealt bountifully with me![e]

See RG 244, 250

PSALM 14*

A Lament over Widespread Corruption

1 For the leader. Of David.

I

The fool says in his heart,
"There is no God."
Their deeds are loathsome and corrupt;
not one does what is good.[f]
2 The LORD looks down from heaven
upon the children of men,[g]
To see if even one is wise,
if even one seeks God.[h]
3 All have gone astray;
all alike are perverse.
Not one does what is good,
not even one.[i]

II

4 Will these evildoers never learn?
They devour my people as they devour
bread;[j]
they do not call upon the LORD.[k]
5 They have good reason, then, to fear;
God is with the company of the just.
6 They would crush the hopes of the poor,
but the poor have the LORD as their
refuge.

III

7 [l]Oh, that from Zion might come
the salvation of Israel!
Jacob would rejoice, and Israel be glad
when the LORD restores his people!*

PSALM 15*

See RG 246

The Righteous Israelite

1 [m]A psalm of David.

I

LORD, who may abide in your tent?*
Who may dwell on your holy
mountain?*

II

2 Whoever walks without blame,[n]
doing what is right,
speaking truth from the heart;
3 Who does not slander with his tongue,
does no harm to a friend,

Psalm 13 A typical lament, in which the psalmist feels forgotten by God (Ps 13:2–3)—note the force of the repetition of "How long." The references to enemies may suggest some have wished evil on the psalmist. The heartfelt prayer (Ps 13:4–5) passes on a statement of trust (Ps 13:6a), intended to reinforce the prayer, and a vow to thank God when deliverance has come (Ps 13:6b).

Psalm 14 The lament (duplicated in Ps 53) depicts the world as consisting of two types of people: "the fool" (equals the wicked, Ps 14:1–3) and "the company of the just" (Ps 14:4–6; also called "my people," and "the poor"). The wicked persecute the just, but the Psalm expresses the hope that God will punish the wicked and reward the good.

14:7 Jacob . . . Israel . . . his people: the righteous poor are identified with God's people.

Psalm 15 The Psalm records a liturgical scrutiny at the entrance to the Temple court (cf. Ps 24:3–6; Is 33:14b–16). The Israelite wishing to be admitted had to ask the Temple official what conduct was appropriate to God's precincts. Note the emphasis on virtues relating to one's neighbor.

15:1 Your tent: the Temple could be referred to as "tent" (Ps 61:5; Is 33:20), a reference to the tent of the wilderness

b: Ps 18:31; 19:8; Prv 30:5. *c:* Ps 6:4; 44:25; 77:8; 79:5; 89:47; 94:3; Lam 5:20. *d:* Ps 38:17. *e:* Ps 116:7. *f:* Ps 10:4; 36:2; Is 32:6; Jer 5:12. *g:* Rom 3:11–12. *h:* Ps 11:4; 102:20. *i:* Ps 12:1. *j:* Ps 27:2; Is 9:11. *k:* Ps 79:6. *l:* Ps 85:2. *m:* Is 56:7. *n:* Ps 119:1.

never defames a neighbor;
4 Who disdains the wicked,
but honors those who fear the LORD;
Who keeps an oath despite the cost,
5 lends no money at interest,*
accepts no bribe against the innocent.[o]

III

Whoever acts like this
shall never be shaken.

See RG 245

PSALM 16*

God the Supreme Good

1[p]A *miktam** of David.

I

Keep me safe, O God;
in you I take refuge.
2 I say to the LORD,
you are my Lord,
you are my only good.
3 As for the holy ones who are in the land,
they are noble,
in whom is all my delight.
4 *They multiply their sorrows
who court other gods.
Blood libations to them I will not pour out,
nor will I take their names upon my lips.
5 LORD, my allotted portion and my cup,
you have made my destiny secure.[q]
6 *Pleasant places were measured out for me;
fair to me indeed is my inheritance.

II

7 I bless the LORD who counsels me;
even at night my heart exhorts me.
8 I keep the LORD always before me;
with him at my right hand, I shall never be shaken.[r]
9 Therefore my heart is glad, my soul rejoices;
my body also dwells secure,
10 For you will not abandon my soul to Sheol,
nor let your devout one see the pit.*[s]
11 You will show me the path to life,
abounding joy in your presence,
the delights at your right hand forever.

PSALM 17*

See RG 244

Prayer for Rescue from Persecutors

1A prayer of David.

I

Hear, LORD, my plea for justice;
pay heed to my cry;
Listen to my prayer
from lips without guile.
2 From you let my vindication come;
your eyes see what is right.
3 You have tested my heart,
searched it in the night.[t]
You have tried me by fire,
but find no malice in me.
My mouth has not transgressed
4 as others often do.
As your lips have instructed me,

period and the tent of David (2 Sm 6:17; 7:2), predecessors of the Temple. **Holy mountain**: a venerable designation of the divine abode (Ps 2:6; 3:5; 43:3; 48:2, etc.).

15:5 Lends no money at interest: lending money in the Old Testament was often seen as assistance to the poor in their distress, not as an investment; making money off the poor by charging interest was thus forbidden (Ex 22:24; Lv 25:36–37; Dt 23:20).

Psalm 16 In the first section, the psalmist rejects the futile worship of false gods (Ps 16:2–5), preferring Israel's God (Ps 16:1), the giver of the land (Ps 16:6). The second section reflects on the wise and life-giving presence of God (Ps 16:7–11).

16:1 Miktam: a term occurring six times in Psalm superscriptions, always with "David." Its meaning is unknown.

16:4 Take their names: to use the gods' names in oaths and hence to affirm them as one's own gods.

16:6 Pleasant places were measured out for me: the psalmist is pleased with the plot of land measured out to the family, which was to be passed on to succeeding generations ("my inheritance").

16:10 Nor let your devout one see the pit: Hebrew *shahath* means here the pit, a synonym for Sheol, the underworld. The Greek translation derives the word here and elsewhere from the verb *shahath*, "to be corrupt." On the basis of the Greek, Acts 2:25–32; 13:35–37 apply the verse to Christ's resurrection, "Nor will you suffer your holy one to see corruption."

Psalm 17 A lament of an individual unjustly attacked. Confident of being found innocent, the psalmist cries out for God's just judgment (Ps 17:1–5) and requests divine help against enemies (Ps 17:6–9a). Those ravenous lions (Ps 17:9b–12) should be punished (Ps 17:13–14). The Psalm ends with a serene statement of praise (Ps 17:15). The Hebrew text of Ps 17:3–4, 14 is uncertain.

o: Ex 22:24; 23:8. *p:* Ps 25:20. *q:* Ps 23:5; 73:26; Nm 18:20; Lam 3:24. *r:* Ps 73:23; 121:5, 8–12; Acts 2:25–28. *s:* Ps 28:1; 30:4; 49:16; 86:13; Jon 2:7; Acts 13:35. *t:* Ps 26:2; 139:23.

I have kept from the way of the lawless.
5 My steps have kept to your paths;
my feet have not faltered.[u]

II

6 I call upon you; answer me, O God.
Turn your ear to me; hear my speech.
7 Show your wonderful mercy,
you who deliver with your right arm
those who seek refuge from their foes.
8 *Keep me as the apple of your eye;
hide me in the shadow of your wings
9 from the wicked who despoil me.[v]

III

My ravenous enemies press upon me;[w]
10 *they close their hearts,
they fill their mouths with proud
roaring.
11 Their steps even now encircle me;
they watch closely, keeping low to the
ground,
12 Like lions eager for prey,
like a young lion lurking in ambush.
13 Rise, O LORD, confront and cast them
down;
rescue my soul from the wicked.
14 Slay them with your sword;
with your hand, LORD, slay them;
snatch them from the world in their
prime.
Their bellies are being filled with your
friends;
their children are satisfied too,
for they share what is left with their
young.
15 I am just—let me see your face;
when I awake, let me be filled with
your presence.[x]

PSALM 18*

See RG 245

A King's Thanksgiving for Victory

1 For the leader. Of David, the servant of the LORD, who sang to the LORD the words of this song after the LORD had rescued him from the clutches of all his enemies and from the hand of Saul. 2 He said:[y]

I

I love you, LORD, my strength,
3 LORD, my rock, my fortress, my
deliverer,
My God, my rock of refuge,
my shield, my saving horn,* my
stronghold![z]
4 Praised be the LORD, I exclaim!
I have been delivered from my
enemies.

II

5 The cords of death encompassed me;
the torrents of destruction terrified me.
6 The cords* of Sheol encircled me;
the snares of death lay in wait for me.[a]
7 In my distress I called out: LORD!
I cried out to my God.[b]
From his temple he heard my voice;
my cry to him reached his ears.
8 *The earth rocked and shook;
the foundations of the mountains
trembled;
they shook as his wrath flared up.[c]
9 Smoke rose from his nostrils,
a devouring fire from his mouth;
it kindled coals into flame.
10 He parted the heavens and came down,
a dark cloud under his feet.[d]

17:8 Apple of your eye . . . shadow of your wings: images of God's special care, cf. Dt 32:10; Prv 7:2; Is 49:2.

17:10–12, 14 An extended metaphor: the enemies are lions.

Psalm 18 A royal thanksgiving for a military victory, duplicated in 2 Sm 22. Thanksgiving Psalms are in essence reports of divine rescue. The Psalm has two parallel reports of rescue, the first told from a heavenly perspective (Ps 18:5–20), and the second from an earthly perspective (Ps 18:36–46). The first report adapts old mythic language of a cosmic battle between sea and rainstorm in order to depict God's rescue of the Israelite king from his enemies. Each report has a short hymnic introduction (Ps 18:2–4, 32–36) and conclusion (Ps 18:21–31, 47–50).

18:3 My saving horn: my strong savior. The horn referred to is the weapon of a bull and the symbol of fertility, cf. 1 Sm 2:10; Ps 132:17; Lk 1:69.

18:6 Cords: hunting imagery, the cords of a snare.

18:8–16 God appears in the storm, which in Palestine comes from the west. The introduction to the theophany (Ps 18:8–9) is probably a description of a violent, hot, and dry east-wind storm. In the fall transition period from the rainless summer to the rainy winter such storms regularly precede the rains, cf. Ex 14:21–22.

---

u: Ps 18:36; Jb 23:11–12. *v:* Ps 10:9; 22:14, 22; 35:17; 58:7; Jb 4:10–11. *w:* Ps 36:8; 57:2; 61:5; 63:8; 91:4; Dt 32:10; Ru 2:12; Zec 2:12; Mt 23:37. *x:* Ps 4:7; 31:17; 67:2; 80:4; Nm 6:25; Dn 9:17. *y:* 2 Sm 22:2–51. *z:* Ps 3:4; 31:3–4; 42:10; Gn 49:24; Dt 32:4. *a:* Ps 88:8; 93:3–4; 116:3–4. *b:* Jon 2:3. *c:* Ps 97:3–4; 99:1; Jgs 5:4–5; Is 64:1; Heb 3:9–11. *d:* Ps 104:3; 144:5; Is 63:19.

11 Mounted on a cherub* he flew,
borne along on the wings of the wind.
12 He made darkness his cloak around him;
his canopy, water-darkened
stormclouds.
13 From the gleam before him, his clouds
passed,
hail and coals of fire.[e]
14 The LORD thundered from heaven;
the Most High made his voice
resound.[f]
15 He let fly his arrows* and scattered them;
shot his lightning bolts and dispersed
them.[g]
16 Then the bed of the sea appeared;
the world's foundations lay bare,[h]
At your rebuke, O LORD,
at the storming breath of your nostrils.
17 He reached down from on high and
seized me;
drew me out of the deep waters.[i]
18 He rescued me from my mighty enemy,
from foes too powerful for me.
19 They attacked me on my day of distress,
but the LORD was my support.
20 He set me free in the open;
he rescued me because he loves me.

III

21 The LORD acknowledged my
righteousness,
rewarded my clean hands.[j]
22 For I kept the ways of the LORD;
I was not disloyal to my God.
23 For his laws were all before me,
his decrees I did not cast aside.
24 I was honest toward him;
I was on guard against sin.
25 So the LORD rewarded my righteousness,
the cleanness of my hands in his sight.
26 Toward the faithful you are faithful;
to the honest man you are honest;[k]
27 Toward the pure, you are pure;
but to the perverse you are devious.
28 For humble people you save;
haughty eyes you bring low.[l]
29 For you, LORD, give light to my lamp;
my God brightens my darkness.[m]
30 With you I can rush an armed band,
with my God to help I can leap a wall.
31 God's way is unerring;
the LORD's promise is refined;
he is a shield for all who take refuge in
him.[n]

IV

32 Truly, who is God except the LORD?
Who but our God is the rock?[o]
33 This God who girded me with might,
kept my way unerring,
34 Who made my feet like a deer's,
and set me on the heights,[p]
35 Who trained my hands for war,
my arms to string a bow of bronze.*[q]

V

36 You have given me your saving shield;
your right hand has upheld me;
your favor made me great.
37 You made room for my steps beneath
me;
my ankles never twisted.[r]
38 I pursued my enemies and overtook
them;
I did not turn back till I destroyed
them.
39 I decimated them; they could not rise;
they fell at my feet.
40 You girded me with valor for war,
subjugated my opponents beneath me.
41 You made my foes expose their necks to
me;
those who hated me I silenced.
42 They cried for help, but no one saved
them;
cried to the LORD but received no
answer.
43 I ground them to dust before the wind;
I left them like mud in the streets.
44 You rescued me from the strife of
peoples;

18:11 Cherub: a winged creature, derived from myth, in the service of the deity (Gn 3:24; Ex 25:18–20; 37:6–9). Cherubim were the throne bearers of the deity (Ps 80:2; 99:1; 1 Kgs 6:23–28; 8:6–8).

18:15 Arrows: lightning.

18:35 Bow of bronze: hyperbole for a bow difficult to bend and therefore capable of propelling an arrow with great force.

e: Ex 13:21; 19:16. *f:* Ps 29; 77:19; Ex 19:19; Jb 37:3–4. *g:* Ps 144:6; Wis 5:21. *h:* Ps 77:17; Zec 9:14. *i:* Ps 144:7. *j:* Ps 26; 1 Sm 26:23. *k:* Ps 125:4. *l:* Jb 22:29; Prv 3:34. *m:* Ps 27:1; 36:10; 43:3; 119:105; Jb 29:3; Mi 7:8. *n:* Ps 12:6; 77:13; Prv 30:5. *o:* Is 44:8; 45:21. *p:* Heb 3:19. *q:* Ps 144:1. *r:* Ps 17:5.

you made me head over nations.
A people I had not known served me;
45 as soon as they heard of me they obeyed.
Foreigners submitted before me;
46 foreigners cringed;
they came cowering from their dungeons.[s]

VI

47 The LORD lives! Blessed be my rock![t]
Exalted be God, my savior!
48 O God who granted me vengeance,
made peoples subject to me,[u]
49 and saved me from my enemies,
Truly you have elevated me above my opponents,
from a man of lawlessness you have rescued me.
50 Thus I will praise you, LORD, among the nations;
I will sing praises to your name.[v]
51 You have given great victories to your king,
and shown mercy to his anointed,
to David and his posterity forever.[w]

See RG 244

PSALM 19*

God's Glory in the Heavens and in the Law

1 For the leader. A psalm of David.

I

2 The heavens declare the glory of God;
the firmament proclaims the works of his hands.[x]
3 Day unto day pours forth speech;
night unto night whispers knowledge.
4 *There is no speech, no words;
their voice is not heard;
5 A report goes forth through all the earth,
their messages, to the ends of the world.
He has pitched in them a tent for the sun;*
6 it comes forth like a bridegroom from his canopy,
and like a hero joyfully runs its course.
7 From one end of the heavens it comes forth;
its course runs through to the other;
nothing escapes its heat.

II

8 The law of the LORD is perfect,
refreshing the soul.
The decree of the LORD is trustworthy,
giving wisdom to the simple.[y]
9 The precepts of the LORD are right,
rejoicing the heart.
The command of the LORD is clear,
enlightening the eye.
10 The fear of the LORD is pure,
enduring forever.
The statutes of the LORD are true,
all of them just;
11 More desirable than gold,
than a hoard of purest gold,
Sweeter also than honey
or drippings from the comb.[z]
12 By them your servant is warned;*
obeying them brings much reward.

III

13 Who can detect trespasses?
Cleanse me from my inadvertent sins.
14 Also from arrogant ones restrain your servant;
let them never control me.
Then shall I be blameless,
innocent of grave sin.
15 Let the words of my mouth be acceptable,
the thoughts of my heart before you,
LORD, my rock and my redeemer.

Psalm 19 The heavenly elements of the world, now beautifully arranged, bespeak the power and wisdom of their creator (Ps 19:2–7). The creator's wisdom is available to human beings in the law (Ps 19:8–11), toward which the psalmist prays to be open (Ps 19:12–14). The themes of light and speech unify the poem.

19:4 No speech, no words: the regular functioning of the heavens and the alternation of day and night inform human beings without words of the creator's power and wisdom.

19:5 The sun: in other religious literature the sun is a judge and lawgiver since it sees all in its daily course; Ps 19:5b–7 form a transition to the law in Ps 19:8–11. The six synonyms for God's revelation (Ps 19:8–11) are applied to the sun in comparable literature.

19:12 Warned: the Hebrew verb means both to shine and to warn, cf. Dn 12:3.

s: Mi 7:17. *t:* Ps 144:1. *u:* Ps 144:2. *v:* Ps 7:18; 30:5; 57:9; 135:3; 146:2; Rom 15:9. *w:* Ps 89:28–37; 144:10; 1 Sm 2:10. *x:* Ps 8:1; 50:6; 97:6. *y:* Ps 12:7; 119. *z:* Sir 24:19.

See RG 245

PSALM 20*

Prayer for the King in Time of War

[1]For the leader. A psalm of David.

I

[2] The LORD answer you in time of distress;
the name of the God of Jacob defend you!
[3] May he send you help from the sanctuary,
from Zion be your support.[a]
[4] May he remember* your every offering,
graciously accept your burnt offering, *Selah*
[5] Grant what is in your heart,
fulfill your every plan.
[6] May we shout for joy at your victory,*
raise the banners in the name of our God.
The LORD grant your every petition!

II

[7] Now I know the LORD gives victory
to his anointed.[b]
He will answer him from the holy heavens
with a strong arm that brings victory.
[8] Some rely on chariots, others on horses,
but we on the name of the LORD our God.[c]
[9] They collapse and fall,
but we stand strong and firm.[d]
[10] LORD, grant victory to the king;
answer when we call upon you.

See RG 245

PSALM 21*

Thanksgiving and Assurances for the King

[1]For the leader. A psalm of David.

I

[2] LORD, the king finds joy in your power;[e]
in your victory how greatly he rejoices!
[3] You have granted him his heart's desire;
you did not refuse the request of his lips. *Selah*
[4] For you welcomed him with goodly blessings;
you placed on his head a crown of pure gold.
[5] He asked life of you;
you gave it to him,
length of days forever.[f]
[6] Great is his glory in your victory;
majesty and splendor you confer upon him.
[7] You make him the pattern of blessings forever,
you gladden him with the joy of your face.
[8] For the king trusts in the LORD,
stands firm through the mercy of the Most High.

II

[9] Your hand will find all your enemies;
your right hand will find your foes!
[10] At the time of your coming
you will make them a fiery furnace.
Then the LORD in his anger will consume them,
devour them with fire.
[11] Even their descendants you will wipe out from the earth,
their offspring from the human race.
[12] Though they intend evil against you,
devising plots, they will not succeed,
[13] For you will put them to flight;
you will aim at their faces with your bow.

III

[14] Arise, LORD, in your power![g]
We will sing and chant the praise of your might.

Psalm 20 The people pray for the king before battle. The people ask for divine help (Ps 20:2–6) and express confidence that such help will be given (Ps 20:7–10). A solemn assurance of divine help may well have been given between the two sections in the liturgy, something like the promises of Ps 12:6; 21:9–13. The final verse (Ps 20:10) echoes the opening verse.

20:4 Remember: God's remembering implies readiness to act, cf. Gn 8:1; Ex 2:24.

20:6 Victory: the Hebrew root is often translated "salvation," "to save," but in military contexts it can have the specific meaning of "victory."

Psalm 21 The first part of this royal Psalm is a thanksgiving (Ps 21:2–8), and the second is a promise that the king will triumph over his enemies (Ps 21:9–13). The king's confident prayer (Ps 21:3–5) and trust in God (Ps 21:8) enable him to receive the divine gifts of vitality, peace, and military success. Ps 21:14 reprises Ps 21:2. When kings ceased in Israel after the sixth century B.C., the Psalm was sung of a future Davidic king.

---

a: Ps 128:5; 134:3. *b:* Ps 18:51; 144:10; 1 Sm 2:10. *c:* Ps 147:10–11; 2 Chr 14:10; Prv 21:31; 1 Sm 17:45; Is 31:1; 36:9. *d:* Is 40:30. *e:* Ps 63:12. *f:* 1 Kgs 3:14. *g:* Nm 10:35.

See RG 245, 251

PSALM 22*

The Prayer of an Innocent Person

1 For the leader; according to "The deer of the dawn."* A psalm of David.

I

2 My God, my God, why have you
abandoned me?
Why so far from my call for help,
from my cries of anguish?[h]
3 My God, I call by day, but you do not
answer;
by night, but I have no relief.[i]
4 Yet you are enthroned as the Holy One;
you are the glory of Israel.[j]
5 In you our fathers trusted;
they trusted and you rescued them.
6 To you they cried out and they escaped;
in you they trusted and were not
disappointed.[k]
7 *But I am a worm, not a man,
scorned by men, despised by the
people.[l]
8 All who see me mock me;
they curl their lips and jeer;
they shake their heads at me:[m]
9 "He relied on the LORD—let him deliver
him;
if he loves him, let him rescue him."[n]
10 For you drew me forth from the womb,
made me safe at my mother's breasts.
11 Upon you I was thrust from the womb;
since my mother bore me you are my
God.[o]
12 Do not stay far from me,
for trouble is near,
and there is no one to help.[p]

II

13 Many bulls* surround me;
fierce bulls of Bashan* encircle me.
14 They open their mouths against me,
lions that rend and roar.[q]
15 Like water my life drains away;
all my bones are disjointed.
My heart has become like wax,
it melts away within me.
16 As dry as a potsherd is my throat;
my tongue cleaves to my palate;
you lay me in the dust of death.*
17 Dogs surround me;
a pack of evildoers closes in on me.
They have pierced my hands and my
feet
18 I can count all my bones.[r]
They stare at me and gloat;
19 they divide my garments among
them;
for my clothing they cast lots.[s]
20 But you, LORD, do not stay far off;
my strength, come quickly to help me.
21 Deliver my soul from the sword,
my life from the grip of the dog.
22 Save me from the lion's mouth,
my poor life from the horns of wild
bulls.[t]

III

23 Then I will proclaim your name to my
brethren;
in the assembly I will praise you:*[u]

Psalm 22 A lament unusual in structure and in intensity of feeling. The psalmist's present distress is contrasted with God's past mercy in Ps 22:2–12. In Ps 22:13–22 enemies surround the psalmist. The last third is an invitation to praise God (Ps 22:23–27), becoming a universal chorus of praise (Ps 22:28–31). The Psalm is important in the New Testament. Its opening words occur on the lips of the crucified Jesus (Mk 15:34; Mt 27:46), and several other verses are quoted, or at least alluded to, in the accounts of Jesus' passion (Mt 27:35, 43; Jn 19:24).

22:1 The deer of the dawn: apparently the title of the melody.

22:7 I am a worm, not a man: the psalmist's sense of isolation and dehumanization, an important motif of Ps 22, is vividly portrayed here.

22:13–14 Bulls: the enemies of the psalmist are also portrayed in less-than-human form, as wild animals (cf. Ps 22:17, 21–22). **Bashan**: a grazing land northeast of the Sea of Galilee, famed for its cattle, cf. Dt 32:14; Ez 39:18; Am 4:1.

22:16 The dust of death: the netherworld, the domain of the dead.

22:23 In the assembly I will praise you: the person who offered a thanksgiving sacrifice in the Temple recounted to the other worshipers the favor received from God and invited them to share in the sacrificial banquet. The final section (Ps 22:24–32) may be a summary or a citation of the psalmist's poem of praise.

h: Is 49:14; 54:7; Mt 27:46; Mk 15:34. *i:* Sir 2:10. *j:* Is 6:3. *k:* Ps 25:3; Is 49:23; Dn 3:40. *l:* Is 53:3. *m:* Ps 109:25; Mt 27:39; Mk 15:29; Lk 23:35. *n:* Ps 71:11; Wis 2:18–20; Mt 27:43. *o:* Ps 71:6; Is 44:2; 46:3. *p:* Ps 35:22; 38:22; 71:12. *q:* Ps 17:12; Jb 4:10; 1 Pt 5:8. *r:* Ps 109:24. *s:* Mt 27:35; Mk 15:24; Lk 23:34; Jn 19:24. *t:* Ps 7:2–3; 17:12; 35:17; 57:5; 58:7; 2 Tm 4:17. *u:* Ps 26:12; 35:18; 40:10; 109:30; 149:1; 2 Sm 22:50; Heb 2:12.

24 "You who fear the LORD, give praise!
All descendants of Jacob, give honor;
show reverence, all descendants of Israel!
25 For he has not spurned or disdained
the misery of this poor wretch,
Did not turn away* from me,
but heard me when I cried out.
26 I will offer praise in the great assembly;
my vows I will fulfill before those who fear him.
27 The poor* will eat their fill;
those who seek the LORD will offer praise.
May your hearts enjoy life forever!"[v]

IV

28 All the ends of the earth
will remember and turn to the LORD;
All the families of nations
will bow low before him.[w]
29 For kingship belongs to the LORD,
the ruler over the nations.[x]
30 *All who sleep in the earth
will bow low before God;
All who have gone down into the dust
will kneel in homage.
31 And I will live for the LORD;
my descendants will serve you.
32 The generation to come will be told of the Lord,
that they may proclaim to a people yet unborn
the deliverance you have brought.[y]

PSALM 23*

The Lord, Shepherd and Host

See RG 245, 249

1 A psalm of David.

I

The LORD is my shepherd;*
there is nothing I lack.[z]
2 In green pastures he makes me lie down;
to still waters he leads me;
3 [a]he restores my soul.
He guides me along right paths*
for the sake of his name.
4 Even though I walk through the valley of the shadow of death,[b]
I will fear no evil, for you are with me;
your rod and your staff comfort me.

II

5 *You set a table before me
in front of my enemies;*
You anoint my head with oil;*[c]
my cup overflows.[d]
6 Indeed, goodness and mercy* will pursue me
all the days of my life;
I will dwell in the house of the LORD[e]
for endless days.

PSALM 24*

See RG 246

The Glory of God in Procession to Zion

1 A psalm of David.

I

The earth is the LORD's and all it holds,[f]
the world and those who dwell in it.

22:25 Turn away: lit., "hides his face from me," an important metaphor for God withdrawing from someone, e.g., Mi 3:4; Is 8:17; Ps 27:9; 69:18; 88:15.

22:27 The poor: originally the poor, who were dependent on God; the term (*'anawim*) came to include the religious sense of "humble, pious, devout."

22:30 Hebrew unclear. The translation assumes that all on earth (Ps 22:27–28) and under the earth (Ps 22:29) will worship God.

Psalm 23 God's loving care for the psalmist is portrayed under the figures of a shepherd for the flock (Ps 23:1–4) and a host's generosity toward a guest (Ps 23:5–6). The imagery of both sections is drawn from traditions of the exodus (Is 40:11; 49:10; Jer 31:10).

23:1 My shepherd: God as good shepherd is common in both the Old Testament and the New Testament (Ez 34:11–16; Jn 10:11–18).

23:3 Right paths: connotes "right way" and "way of righteousness."

23:5 You set a table before me: this expression occurs in an exodus context in Ps 78:19. **In front of my enemies**: my enemies see that I am God's friend and guest. **Oil**: a perfumed ointment made from olive oil, used especially at banquets (Ps 104:15; Mt 26:7; Lk 7:37, 46; Jn 12:2).

23:6 Goodness and mercy: the blessings of God's covenant with Israel.

Psalm 24 The Psalm apparently accompanied a ceremony of the entry of God (invisibly enthroned upon the ark), followed by the people, into the Temple. The Temple commemorated the creation of the world (Ps 24:1–2). The people had to affirm their fidelity before being admitted into the sanctuary (Ps 24:3–6; cf. Ps 15). A choir identifies the approaching God and invites the very Temple gates to bow down in obeisance (Ps 24:7–10).

v: Ps 23:5; 69:33. *w:* Ps 86:9; Tb 13:11; Is 45:22; 52:10; Zec 14:16. *x:* Ps 103:19; Ob 21; Zec 14:9. *y:* Ps 48:14–15; 71:18; 78:6; 102:19; Is 53:10. *z:* Ps 80:2; 95:7; 100:3; Dt 2:7. *a:* Prv 4:11. *b:* Jb 10:21–22; Is 50:10. *c:* Ps 92:11. *d:* Ps 16:5. *e:* Ps 27:4. *f:* Ps 50:12; 89:12; Dt 10:14; 1 Cor 10:26.

2 For he founded it on the seas,
established it over the rivers.[g]

II

3 Who may go up the mountain of the LORD?[h]
Who can stand in his holy place?
4 *"The clean of hand and pure of heart,
who has not given his soul to useless things,
what is vain.
5 He will receive blessings from the LORD,
and justice from his saving God.
6 Such is the generation that seeks him,
that seeks the face of the God of Jacob." *Selah*

III

7 Lift up your heads, O gates;*
be lifted, you ancient portals,
that the king of glory may enter.[i]
8 Who is this king of glory?
The LORD, strong and mighty,
the LORD, mighty in war.
9 Lift up your heads, O gates;
rise up, you ancient portals,
that the king of glory may enter.
10 Who is this king of glory?
The LORD of hosts, he is the king of glory. *Selah*

PSALM 25*

See RG 244, 245

Confident Prayer for Forgiveness and Guidance

1 Of David.

I

To you, O LORD, I lift up my soul,
2 [j]my God, in you I trust;
do not let me be disgraced;[k]
do not let my enemies gloat over me.
3 No one is disgraced who waits for you,[l]
but only those who are treacherous without cause.
4 Make known to me your ways, LORD;
teach me your paths.[m]
5 Guide me by your fidelity and teach me,
for you are God my savior,
for you I wait all the day long.
6 Remember your compassion and your mercy, O LORD,
for they are ages old.[n]
7 Remember no more the sins of my youth;[o]
remember me according to your mercy,
because of your goodness, LORD.

II

8 Good and upright is the LORD,
therefore he shows sinners the way,
9 He guides the humble in righteousness,
and teaches the humble his way.
10 All the paths of the LORD are mercy and truth
toward those who honor his covenant and decrees.
11 For the sake of your name, LORD,
pardon my guilt, though it is great.
12 Who is the one who fears the LORD?
God shows him the way he should choose.[p]
13 He will abide in prosperity,
and his descendants will inherit the land.[q]
14 The counsel of the LORD belongs to those who fear him;
and his covenant instructs them.
15 My eyes are ever upon the LORD,
who frees my feet from the snare.[r]

III

16 Look upon me, have pity on me,
for I am alone and afflicted.[s]
17 Relieve the troubles of my heart;
bring me out of my distress.
18 Look upon my affliction and suffering;
take away all my sins.
19 See how many are my enemies,

24:4–5 Lit., "the one whose hands are clean." The singular is used for the entire class of worshipers.

24:7, 9 Lift up your heads, O gates . . . you ancient portals: the literal meaning would involve disassembly of the gates, since the portcullis (a gate that moves up and down) was unknown in the ancient world. Extra-biblical parallels might also suggest a full personification of the circle of gate towers: they are like a council of elders, bowed down and anxious, awaiting the return of the army and the great warrior gone to battle.

Psalm 25 A lament. Each verse begins with a successive letter of the Hebrew alphabet. Such acrostic Psalms are often a series of statements only loosely connected. The psalmist mixes ardent pleas (Ps 25:1–2, 16–22) with expressions of confidence in God who forgives and guides.

g: Ps 136:6; Is 42:5. *h:* Ps 15:1. *i:* Ps 118:19–20. *j:* Ps 86:4; 143:8. *k:* Ps 71:1. *l:* Ps 22:6; Is 49:23; Dn 3:40. *m:* Ps 27:11; 86:11; 119:12, 35; 143:8, 10. *n:* Sir 51:8. *o:* Jb 13:26; Is 64:8. *p:* Prv 19:23. *q:* Ps 37:9, 29. *r:* Ps 123:1, 2; 141:8. *s:* Ps 86:16; 119:132.

see how fiercely they hate me.
20 Preserve my soul and rescue me;
do not let me be disgraced, for in you I seek refuge.
21 Let integrity and uprightness preserve me;
I wait for you, O LORD.
22 *Redeem Israel, O God,
from all its distress!

See RG 244

PSALM 26*

Prayer of Innocence

1 Of David.

I

Judge me, LORD!
For I have walked in my integrity.[t]
In the LORD I trust;
I do not falter.
2 Examine me, Lord, and test me;
search my heart and mind.[u]
3 Your mercy is before my eyes;
I walk guided by your faithfulness.[v]

II

4 I do not sit with worthless men,
nor with hypocrites do I mingle.
5 I hate an evil assembly;
with the wicked I do not sit.
6 I will wash my hands* in innocence[w]
so that I may process around your altar, Lord,
7 To hear the sound of thanksgiving,
and recount all your wondrous deeds.
8 Lord, I love the refuge of your house,
the site of the dwelling-place of your glory.[x]

III

9 Do not take me away with sinners,
nor my life with the men of blood,[y]
10 In whose hands there is a plot,
their right hands full of bribery.
11 But I walk in my integrity;[z]
redeem me, be gracious to me![a]
12 My foot stands on level ground;*
in assemblies I will bless the LORD.[b]

See RG 244

PSALM 27*

Trust in God

1 [c]Of David.

A

I

The LORD is my light and my salvation;
whom should I fear?
The LORD is my life's refuge;
of whom should I be afraid?
2 When evildoers come at me
to devour my flesh,*[d]
These my enemies and foes
themselves stumble and fall.
3 Though an army encamp against me,
my heart does not fear;
Though war be waged against me,
even then do I trust.

II

4 One thing I ask of the LORD;
this I seek:
To dwell in the LORD's house
all the days of my life,
To gaze on the LORD's beauty,
to visit his temple.[e]
5 For God will hide me in his shelter
in time of trouble,[f]
He will conceal me in the cover of his tent;

25:22 A final verse beginning with the Hebrew letter *pe* is added to the normal 22-letter alphabet. Thus the letters *aleph*, *lamed*, and *pe* open the first, middle (Ps 25:11), and last lines of the Psalm. Together, they spell *aleph*, the first letter of the alphabet, from a Hebrew root that means "to learn."

Psalm 26 Like a priest washing before approaching the altar (Ex 30:17–21), the psalmist seeks God's protection upon entering the Temple. Ps 26:1–3, matched by Ps 26:11–12, remind God of past integrity while asking for purification; Ps 26:4–5, matched by Ps 26:9–10, pray for inclusion among the just; Ps 26:6–8, the center of the poem, express the joy in God at the heart of all ritual.

26:6 I will wash my hands: the washing of hands was a liturgical act (Ex 30:19, 21; 40:31–32), symbolic of inner as well as outer cleanness, cf. Is 1:16.

26:12 On level ground: in safety, where there is no danger of tripping and falling. **In assemblies**: at the Temple. Having walked around the altar, the symbol of God's presence, the psalmist blesses God.

Psalm 27 Tradition has handed down the two sections of the Psalm (Ps 27:1–6; 7–14) as one Psalm, though each part could be understood as complete in itself. Asserting boundless hope that God will bring rescue (Ps 27:1–3), the psalmist longs for the presence of God in the Temple, protection from all enemies (Ps 27:4–6). In part B there is a clear shift in tone (Ps 27:7–12); the climax of the poem comes with "I believe" (Ps 27:13), echoing "I trust" (Ps 27:3).

27:2 To devour my flesh: the psalmist's enemies are rapacious beasts (Ps 7:3; 17:12; 22:14, 17).

t: Ps 7:9. *u:* Ps 17:3; 139:23. *v:* Ps 86:11. *w:* Ps 73:13. *x:* Ps 29:9; 63:3; Ex 24:16; 25:8. *y:* Ps 28:3. *z:* Ps 101:6. *a:* Ps 25:16. *b:* Ps 22:23; 35:18; 149:1. *c:* Ps 18:29; 36:10; 43:3; Is 10:17; Mi 7:8. *d:* Ps 14:4. *e:* Ps 23:6; 61:5. *f:* Ps 31:21.

and set me high upon a rock.
6 Even now my head is held high
above my enemies on every side!
I will offer in his tent
sacrifices with shouts of joy;
I will sing and chant praise to the
LORD.

B

I

7 Hear my voice, LORD, when I call;
have mercy on me and answer me.
8 "Come," says my heart, "seek his face";*
your face, LORD, do I seek![g]
9 Do not hide your face from me;
do not repel your servant in anger.
You are my salvation; do not cast me off;
do not forsake me, God my savior!
10 Even if my father and mother forsake me,
the LORD will take me in.[h]

II

11 LORD, show me your way;
lead me on a level path
because of my enemies.[i]
12 Do not abandon me to the desire of my
foes;
malicious and lying witnesses have
risen against me.
13 I believe I shall see the LORD's goodness
in the land of the living.*[j]
14 Wait for the LORD, take courage;
be stouthearted, wait for the LORD!

See RG 244

PSALM 28*

Petition and Thanksgiving

1 Of David.

I

To you, LORD, I call;
my Rock, do not be deaf to me,[k]
Do not be silent toward me,
so that I join those who go down to the
pit.[l]
2 Hear the sound of my pleading when I
cry to you for help
when I lift up my hands toward your
holy place.*[m]
3 Do not drag me off with the wicked,
with those who do wrong,[n]
Who speak peace to their neighbors
though evil is in their hearts.[o]
4 Repay them for their deeds,
for the evil that they do.
For the work of their hands repay them;
give them what they deserve.[p]
5 Because they do not understand the
LORD's works,
the work of his hands,[q]
He will tear them down,
never to rebuild them.

II

6 *Blessed be the LORD,
who has heard the sound of my pleading.
7 The LORD is my strength and my shield,
in whom my heart trusts.
I am helped, so my heart rejoices;
with my song I praise him.

III

8 * LORD, you are a strength for your people,
the saving refuge of your anointed.
9 Save your people, bless your inheritance;
pasture and carry them forever!

PSALM 29*

See RG 244, 250

The Lord of Majesty Acclaimed as King of the World

1 A psalm of David.

I

Give to the LORD, you sons of God,*
give to the LORD glory and might;

27:8 Seek his face: to commune with God in the Temple. The idiom is derived from the practice of journeying to sacred places, cf. Hos 5:15; 2 Sm 21:1; Ps 24:6.

27:13 In the land of the living: or "in the land of life," an epithet of the Jerusalem Temple (Ps 52:7; 116:9; Is 38:11), where the faithful had access to the life-giving presence of God.

Psalm 28 A lament asking that the psalmist, who has taken refuge in the Temple (Ps 28:2), not be punished with the wicked, who are headed inevitably toward destruction (Ps 28:1, 3–5). The statement of praise is exceptionally lengthy and vigorous (Ps 28:6–7). The Psalm ends with a prayer (Ps 28:8–9).

28:2 Your holy place: the innermost part of the Temple, the holy of holies, containing the ark, cf. 1 Kgs 6:16, 19–23; 8:6–8.

28:6 The psalmist shifts to fervent thanksgiving, probably responding to a priestly or prophetic oracle in Ps 28:5cd (not usually transmitted) assuring the worshiper that the prayer has been heard.

28:8 Your people . . . your anointed: salvation is more than individual, affecting all the people and their God-given leader.

Psalm 29 The hymn invites the members of the heavenly court to acknowledge God's supremacy by ascribing glory

g: Ps 24:6; Hos 5:15. *h:* Is 49:15. *i:* Ps 25:4; 86:11. *j:* Ps 116:9; Is 38:11. *k:* Ps 18:2. *l:* Ps 30:4; 88:5; 143:7; Prv 1:12. *m:* Ps 134:2. *n:* Ps 26:9. *o:* Ps 12:2; 55:22; 62:5; Prv 26:24–28. *p:* 2 Sm 3:39. *q:* Is 5:12.

[2] Give to the LORD the glory due his name.
Bow down before the LORD's holy splendor![r]

II

[3] The voice of the LORD* is over the waters;
the God of glory thunders,
the LORD, over the mighty waters.
[4] The voice of the LORD is power;
the voice of the LORD is splendor.[s]
[5] The voice of the LORD cracks the cedars;
the LORD splinters the cedars of Lebanon,
[6] Makes Lebanon leap like a calf,
and Sirion* like a young bull.
[7] The voice of the LORD strikes with fiery flame;
[8] the voice of the LORD shakes the desert;
the LORD shakes the desert of Kadesh.
[9] *The voice of the LORD makes the deer dance
and strips the forests bare.
All in his Temple say, "Glory!"

III

[10] The LORD sits enthroned above the flood![*t]
The LORD reigns as king forever!
[11] May the LORD give might to his people;*
may the LORD bless his people with peace![u]

PSALM 30*

See RG 245

Thanksgiving for Deliverance

[1] A psalm. A song for the dedication of the Temple.* Of David.

I

[2] I praise you, LORD, for you raised me up
and did not let my enemies rejoice over me.
[3] O LORD, my God,
I cried out to you for help and you healed* me.
[4] LORD, you brought my soul up from Sheol;
you let me live, from going down to the pit.[*v]

II

[5] Sing praise to the LORD, you faithful;
give thanks to his holy memory.
[6] For his anger lasts but a moment;
his favor a lifetime.
At dusk weeping comes for the night;
but at dawn there is rejoicing.

III

[7] Complacent,* I once said,
"I shall never be shaken."
[8] LORD, you showed me favor,
established for me mountains of virtue.
But when you hid your face
I was struck with terror.[w]
[9] To you, LORD, I cried out;
with the Lord I pleaded for mercy:
[10] *"What gain is there from my lifeblood,

and might to God alone (Ps 29:1–2a, 9b). Divine glory and might are dramatically visible in the storm (Ps 29:3–9a). The storm apparently comes from the Mediterranean onto the coast of Syria-Palestine and then moves inland. In Ps 29:10 the divine beings acclaim God's eternal kingship. The Psalm concludes with a prayer that God will impart the power just displayed to the Israelite king and through the king to Israel.

29:1 Sons of God: members of the heavenly court who served Israel's God in a variety of capacities.

29:3 The voice of the LORD: the sevenfold repetition of the phrase imitates the sound of crashing thunder and may allude to God's primordial slaying of Leviathan, the seven-headed sea monster of Canaanite mythology.

29:6 Sirion: the Phoenician name for Mount Hermon, cf. Dt 3:9.

29:9b–10 Having witnessed God's supreme power (Ps 29:3–9a), the gods acknowledge the glory that befits the king of the divine and human world.

29:10 The flood: God defeated the primordial waters and made them part of the universe, cf. Ps 89:10–13; 93:3–4.

29:11 His people: God's people, Israel.

Psalm 30 An individual thanksgiving in four parts: praise and thanks for deliverance and restoration (Ps 30:2–4); an invitation to others to join in (Ps 30:5–6); a flashback to the time before deliverance (Ps 30:7–11); a return to praise and thanks (Ps 30:12). Two sets of images recur: 1) going down, death, silence; 2) coming up, life, praising. God has delivered the psalmist from one state to the other.

30:1 For the dedication of the Temple: a later adaptation of the Psalm to celebrate the purification of the Temple in 164 B.C. during the Maccabean Revolt.

30:3 Healed: for God as healer, see also Ps 103:3; 107:20; Hos 6:1; 7:1; 11:3; 14:5.

30:4 Sheol . . . pit: the shadowy underworld residence of the spirits of the dead, here a metaphor for near-death.

30:7 Complacent: untroubled existence is often seen as a source of temptation to forget God, cf. Dt 8:10–18; Hos 13:6; Prv 30:9.

30:10 In the stillness of Sheol no one gives you praise; let me live and be among your worshipers, cf. Ps 6:6; 88:11–13; 115:17; Is 38:18.

r: Ps 68:35; 96:7–9. *s:* Ps 46:7; 77:18–19; Jb 37:4; Is 30:30. *t:* Bar 3:3. *u:* Ps 68:36. *v:* Ps 28:1; Jon 2:7. *w:* Ps 104:29.

from my going down to the grave?
Does dust give you thanks
or declare your faithfulness?
11 Hear, O LORD, have mercy on me;
LORD, be my helper."

IV

12 You changed my mourning into dancing;
you took off my sackcloth
and clothed me with gladness.[x]
13 So that my glory may praise you
and not be silent.
O LORD, my God,
forever will I give you thanks.

PSALM 31*

See RG 244

Prayer in Distress and Thanksgiving for Escape

1 For the leader. A psalm of David.

I

2 In you, LORD, I take refuge;[y]
let me never be put to shame.
In your righteousness deliver me;
3 incline your ear to me;
make haste to rescue me!
Be my rock of refuge,
a stronghold to save me.
4 For you are my rock and my fortress;[z]
for your name's sake lead me and guide me.
5 Free me from the net they have set for me,
for you are my refuge.
6 *Into your hands I commend my spirit;[a]
you will redeem me, LORD, God of truth.
7 You hate those who serve worthless idols,
but I trust in the LORD.
8 I will rejoice and be glad in your mercy,
once you have seen my misery,
[and] gotten to know the distress of my soul.[b]
9 You will not abandon me into enemy hands,
but will set my feet in a free and open space.

II

10 Be gracious to me, LORD, for I am in distress;
affliction is wearing down my eyes,
my throat and my insides.
11 My life is worn out by sorrow,
and my years by sighing.
My strength fails in my affliction;
my bones are wearing down.[c]
12 To all my foes I am a thing of scorn,
and especially to my neighbors
a horror to my friends.
When they see me in public,
they quickly shy away.[d]
13 I am forgotten, out of mind like the dead;
I am like a worn-out tool.*
14 I hear the whispers of the crowd;
terrors are all around me.*
They conspire together against me;
they plot to take my life.
15 But I trust in you, LORD;
I say, "You are my God."[e]
16 My destiny is in your hands;
rescue me from my enemies,
from the hands of my pursuers.
17 Let your face shine on your servant;[f]
save me in your mercy.
18 Do not let me be put to shame,
for I have called to you, LORD.
Put the wicked to shame;
reduce them to silence in Sheol.
19 Strike dumb their lying lips,
which speak arrogantly against the righteous
in contempt and scorn.[g]

III

20 How great is your goodness, Lord,
stored up for those who fear you.

Psalm 31 A lament (Ps 31:2–19) with a strong emphasis on trust (Ps 31:4, 6, 15–16), ending with an anticipatory thanksgiving (Ps 31:20–24). As is usual in laments, the affliction is couched in general terms. The psalmist feels overwhelmed by evil people but trusts in the "God of truth" (Ps 31:6).

31:6 Into your hands I commend my spirit: in Lk 23:46 Jesus breathes his last with this Psalm verse. Stephen in Acts 7:59 alludes to these words as he is attacked by enemies. The verse is used as an antiphon in the Divine Office at Compline, the last prayer of the day.

31:13 Like a worn-out tool: a common comparison for something ruined and useless, cf. Is 30:14; Jer 19:11; 22:28.

31:14 Terrors are all around me: a cry used in inescapable danger, cf. Jer 6:25; 20:10; 46:5; 49:29.

x: Is 61:3; Jer 31:13. *y*: Ps 71:1–3. *z*: Ps 18:2. *a*: Lk 23:46; Acts 7:59. *b*: Ps 10:14. *c*: Ps 32:3; 38:10–11. *d*: Jb 19:13–19. *e*: Ps 140:7; Is 25:1. *f*: Ps 67:1; Nm 6:24. *g*: Ps 12:4.

You display it for those who trust you,
in the sight of the children of Adam.
21 You hide them in the shelter of your presence,
safe from scheming enemies.
You conceal them in your tent,
away from the strife of tongues.[h]
22 Blessed be the LORD,
marvelously he showed to me
his mercy in a fortified city.
23 Though I had said in my alarm,
"I am cut off from your eyes."[i]
Yet you heard my voice, my cry for mercy,
when I pleaded with you for help.
24 Love the LORD, all you who are faithful to him.
The LORD protects the loyal,
but repays the arrogant in full.
25 Be strong and take heart,
all who hope in the LORD.

PSALM 32*

See RG 245

Remission of Sin

1 [j]Of David. A *maskil*.

I

Blessed is the one whose fault is removed,
whose sin is forgiven.
2 Blessed is the man to whom the LORD imputes no guilt,
in whose spirit is no deceit.

II

3 Because I kept silent,* my bones wasted away;
I groaned all day long.[k]
4 For day and night your hand was heavy upon me;
my strength withered as in dry summer heat. *Selah*
5 Then I declared my sin to you;
my guilt I did not hide.[l]
I said, "I confess my transgression to the LORD,"
and you took away the guilt of my sin. *Selah*
6 Therefore every loyal person should pray to you
in time of distress.
Though flood waters* threaten,
they will never reach him.[m]
7 You are my shelter; you guard me from distress;
with joyful shouts of deliverance you surround me. *Selah*

III

8 I will instruct you and show you the way you should walk,
give you counsel with my eye upon you.
9 Do not be like a horse or mule, without understanding;
with bit and bridle their temper is curbed,
else they will not come to you.

IV

10 Many are the sorrows of the wicked one,
but mercy surrounds the one who trusts in the LORD.
11 Be glad in the LORD and rejoice, you righteous;
exult, all you upright of heart.[n]

PSALM 33*

See RG 244

Praise of God's Power and Providence

I

1 Rejoice, you righteous, in the LORD;
praise from the upright is fitting.[o]
2 Give thanks to the LORD on the harp;
on the ten-stringed lyre offer praise.[p]

Psalm 32 An individual thanksgiving and the second of the seven Penitential Psalms (cf. Ps 6). The opening declaration—the forgiven are blessed (Ps 32:1–2)—arises from the psalmist's own experience. At one time the psalmist was stubborn and closed, a victim of sin's power (Ps 32:3–4), and then became open to the forgiving God (Ps 32:5–7). Sin here, as often in the Bible, is not only the personal act of rebellion against God but also the consequences of that act—frustration and waning of vitality. Having been rescued, the psalmist can teach others the joys of justice and the folly of sin (Ps 32:8–11).

32:3 I kept silent: did not confess the sin before God.

32:6 Flood waters: the untamed waters surrounding the earth, a metaphor for danger.

Psalm 33 A hymn in which the just are invited (Ps 33:1–3) to praise God, who by a mere word (Ps 33:4–5) created the three-tiered universe of the heavens, the cosmic waters, and the earth (Ps 33:6–9). Human words, in contrast, effect nothing (Ps 33:10–11). The greatness of human beings consists in God's choosing them as a special people and their faithful response (Ps 33:12–22).

h: Ps 27:5. *i:* Jon 2:5. *j:* Is 1:18; Ps 65:3; Rom 4:7–8. *k:* Ps 31:11. *l:* Ps 38:19; 51:5. *m:* Ps 18:5. *n:* Ps 33:1. *o:* Ps 32:11; 147:1. *p:* Ps 92:4; 144:9.

3 Sing to him a new song;
skillfully play with joyful chant.
4 For the LORD's word is upright;
all his works are trustworthy.
5 He loves justice and right.
The earth is full of the mercy of the
LORD.[q]

II

6 By the LORD's word the heavens were
made;
by the breath of his mouth all their
host.*[r]
7 *He gathered the waters of the sea as a
mound;
he sets the deep into storage vaults.[s]

III

8 Let all the earth fear the LORD;
let all who dwell in the world show
him reverence.
9 For he spoke, and it came to be,
commanded, and it stood in place.[t]
10 The LORD foils the plan of nations,
frustrates the designs of peoples.
11 But the plan of the LORD stands forever,
the designs of his heart through all
generations.[u]
12 Blessed is the nation whose God is the
LORD,
the people chosen as his inheritance.[v]

IV

13 From heaven the LORD looks down
and observes the children of Adam,[w]
14 From his dwelling place he surveys
all who dwell on earth.
15 The One who fashioned together their
hearts
is the One who knows all their works.

V

16 A king is not saved by a great army,
nor a warrior delivered by great
strength.
17 Useless is the horse for safety;
despite its great strength, it cannot be
saved.
18 Behold, the eye of the LORD is upon
those who fear him,
upon those who count on his mercy,
19 To deliver their soul from death,
and to keep them alive through
famine.

VI

20 Our soul waits for the LORD,
he is our help and shield.[x]
21 For in him our hearts rejoice;
in his holy name we trust.
22 May your mercy, LORD, be upon us;
as we put our hope in you.

PSALM 34*

See RG 245–46

Thanksgiving to God Who Delivers the Just

1 Of David, when he feigned madness before Abimelech,* who drove him out and he went away.

I

2 I will bless the LORD at all times;
his praise shall be always in my
mouth.[y]
3 My soul will glory in the LORD;
let the poor hear and be glad.
4 Magnify the LORD with me;
and let us exalt his name together.

II

5 I sought the LORD, and he answered me,
delivered me from all my fears.
6 Look to him and be radiant,
and your faces may not blush for
shame.
7 This poor one cried out and the LORD
heard,
and from all his distress he saved him.
8 The angel of the LORD encamps
around those who fear him, and he
saves them.[z]

33:6 All their host: the stars of the sky are commonly viewed as a vast army, e.g., Neh 9:6; Is 40:26; 45:12; Jer 33:22.

33:7 The waters . . . as a mound: ancients sometimes attributed the power keeping the seas from overwhelming land to a primordial victory of the storm-god over personified Sea.

Psalm 34 A thanksgiving in acrostic form, each line beginning with a successive letter of the Hebrew alphabet. In this Psalm one letter is missing and two are in reverse order. The psalmist, fresh from the experience of being rescued (Ps 34:5, 7), can teach the "poor," those who are defenseless, to trust in God alone (Ps 34:4, 12). God will make them powerful (Ps 34:5–11) and give them protection (Ps 34:12–22).

34:1 Abimelech: a scribal error for Achish. In 1 Sm 21:13–16, David feigned madness before Achish, not Abimelech.

q: Ps 119:64. *r:* Gn 2:1. *s:* Ps 78:13; Gn 1:9–10; Ex 15:8; Jos 3:16. *t:* Ps 148:5; Gn 1:3f; Jdt 16:14. *u:* Prv 19:21; Is 40:8. *v:* Ps 144:15; Ex 19:6; Dt 7:6. *w:* Jb 34:21; Sir 15:19; Jer 16:17; 32:19. *x:* Ps 115:9. *y:* Ps 145:2. *z:* Ex 14:19.

9 Taste and see that the LORD is good;
blessed is the stalwart one who takes refuge in him.[a]
10 Fear the LORD, you his holy ones;
nothing is lacking to those who fear him.[b]
11 The rich grow poor and go hungry,
but those who seek the LORD lack no good thing.

III

12 Come, children,* listen to me;[c]
I will teach you fear of the LORD.
13 Who is the man who delights in life,[d]
who loves to see the good days?
14 Keep your tongue from evil,
your lips from speaking lies.
15 Turn from evil and do good;[e]
seek peace and pursue it.
16 The eyes of the LORD are directed toward the righteous[f]
and his ears toward their cry.
17 The LORD's face is against evildoers
to wipe out their memory from the earth.
18 The righteous cry out, the LORD hears
and he rescues them from all their afflictions.
19 The LORD is close to the brokenhearted,
saves those whose spirit is crushed.
20 Many are the troubles of the righteous,
but the LORD delivers him from them all.
21 He watches over all his bones;
not one of them shall be broken.[g]
22 Evil will slay the wicked;
those who hate the righteous are condemned.
23 The LORD is the redeemer of the souls of his servants;
and none are condemned who take refuge in him.

PSALM 35*

See RG 244

Prayer for Help Against Unjust Enemies

1 Of David.

I

*Oppose, O LORD, those who oppose me;
war upon those who make war upon me.
2 Take up the shield and buckler;
rise up in my defense.
3 Brandish lance and battle-ax
against my pursuers.
Say to my soul,
"I am your salvation."
4 Let those who seek my life
be put to shame and disgrace.
Let those who plot evil against me[h]
be turned back and confounded.
5 Make them like chaff before the wind,[i]
with the angel of the LORD driving them on.
6 Make their way slippery and dark,
with the angel of the LORD pursuing them.

II

7 Without cause they set their snare for me;
without cause they dug a pit for me.
8 Let ruin overtake them unawares;
let the snare they have set catch them;
let them fall into the pit they have dug.[j]
9 Then I will rejoice in the LORD,
exult in God's salvation.
10 My very bones shall say,
"O LORD, who is like you,[k]
Who rescue the afflicted from the powerful,
the afflicted and needy from the despoiler?"

III

11 Malicious witnesses rise up,

34:12 Children: the customary term for students in wisdom literature.

Psalm 35 A lament of a person betrayed by friends. The psalmist prays that the evildoers be publicly exposed as unjust (Ps 35:1–8), and gives thanks in anticipation of vindication (Ps 35:9–10). Old friends are the enemies (Ps 35:11–16). May their punishment come quickly (Ps 35:17–21)! The last part (Ps 35:22–26) echoes the opening in praying for the destruction of the psalmist's persecutors. The Psalm may appear vindictive, but one must keep in mind that the psalmist is praying for public redress now of a public injustice. There is at this time no belief in an afterlife in which justice will be redressed.

35:1–6 The mixture of judicial, martial, and hunting images shows that the language is figurative. The actual injustice is false accusation of serious crimes (Ps 35:11, 15, 20–21). The psalmist seeks lost honor through a trial before God.

a: Ps 2:12. *b:* Prv 3:7. *c:* Prv 1:8; 4:1. *d:* 1 Pt 3:10–12. *e:* Ps 37:27. *f:* Ps 33:18. *g:* Jn 19:36. *h:* Ps 40:15; 71:13. *i:* Ps 1:4; 83:14; Jb 21:18. *j:* Ps 7:16; 9:16; 57:7; Prv 26:27; Eccl 10:8; Sir 27:26. *k:* Ps 86:8; 89:7, 9; Ex 15:11.

accuse me of things I do not know.
12 They repay me evil for good;
my soul is desolate.[l]
13 *Yet I, when they were ill, put on sackcloth,
afflicted myself with fasting,
sobbed my prayers upon my bosom.
14 I went about in grief as for my brother,
bent in mourning as for my mother.
15 Yet when I stumbled they gathered with glee,
gathered against me and I did not know it.
They slandered me without ceasing;
16 without respect they mocked me,
gnashed their teeth against me.

IV

17 O Lord, how long will you look on?
Restore my soul from their destruction,
my very life from lions![m]
18 Then I will thank you in the great assembly;
I will praise you before the mighty throng.[n]
19 Do not let lying foes rejoice over me,
my undeserved enemies wink knowingly.[o]
20 They speak no words of peace,
but against the quiet in the land
they fashion deceitful speech.[p]
21 They open wide their mouths against me.
They say, "Aha! Good!
Our eyes have seen it!"[q]
22 You see this, LORD; do not be silent;[r]
Lord, do not withdraw from me.
23 Awake, be vigilant in my defense,
in my cause, my God and my Lord.
24 Defend me because you are just, LORD;
my God, do not let them rejoice over me.
25 Do not let them say in their hearts,
"Aha! Our soul!"*
Do not let them say,
"We have devoured that one!"
26 Put to shame and confound
all who relish my misfortune.
Clothe with shame and disgrace
those who lord it over me.
27 But let those who favor my just cause
shout for joy and be glad.
May they ever say, "Exalted be the LORD
who delights in the peace of his loyal servant."
28 Then my tongue shall recount your justice,
declare your praise, all the day long.[s]

PSALM 36*

See RG 244, 249

Human Wickedness and Divine Providence

1 For the leader. Of David, the servant of the LORD.

I

2 Sin directs the heart of the wicked man;
his eyes are closed to the fear of God.[t]
3 For he lives with the delusion:
his guilt will not be known and hated.*
4 Empty and false are the words of his mouth;
he has ceased to be wise and do good.
5 On his bed he hatches plots;
he sets out on a wicked way;
he does not reject evil.[u]

II

6 *LORD, your mercy reaches to heaven;
your fidelity, to the clouds.[v]
7 Your justice is like the highest mountains;
your judgments, like the mighty deep;
human being and beast you sustain, LORD.
8 How precious is your mercy, O God!
The children of Adam take refuge in the shadow of your wings.*[w]

35:13, 15–17 The Hebrew is obscure.

35:25 Aha! Our soul!: an ancient idiomatic expression meaning that we have attained what we wanted.

Psalm 36 A Psalm with elements of wisdom (Ps 36:2–5), the hymn (Ps 36:6–10), and the lament (Ps 36:11–13). The rule of sin over the wicked (Ps 36:2–5) is contrasted with the rule of divine love and mercy over God's friends (Ps 36:6–10). The Psalm ends with a prayer that God's guidance never cease (Ps 36:11–12).

36:3 Hated: punished by God.

36:6–7 God actively controls the entire world.

36:8 The shadow of your wings: metaphor for divine protection. It probably refers to the winged cherubim in the holy of holies in the Temple, cf. 1 Kgs 6:23–28, 32; 2 Chr 3:10–13; Ez 1:4–9.

l: Ps 27:12; 38:20–21; 109:5; Jer 18:20. *m:* Ps 17:12; 22:22; 58:7. *n:* Ps 22:23; 26:12; 35:18; 40:10; 149:1. *o:* Ps 38:17. *p:* Ps 120:6–7. *q:* Ps 40:16; Lam 2:16. *r:* Ps 22:12; 38:21; 109:1. *s:* Ps 71:15–16. *t:* Rom 3:18. *u:* Mi 2:1. *v:* Ps 57:11; 71:19. *w:* Ps 17:8.

9 They feast on the rich food of your
house;
from your delightful stream[x] you give
them drink.
10 For with you is the fountain of life,[y]
and in your light we see light.[z]
11 Show mercy on those who know you,
your just defense to the upright of
heart.
12 Do not let the foot of the proud overtake
me,
nor the hand of the wicked disturb me.
13 There make the evildoers fall;
thrust them down, unable to rise.

See RG 245–46, 251

PSALM 37*

The Fate of Sinners and the Reward of the Just

1 Of David.

ALEPH
Do not be provoked by evildoers;
do not envy those who do wrong.[a]
2 Like grass they wither quickly;
like green plants they wilt away.[b]
BETH
3 Trust in the LORD and do good
that you may dwell in the land* and
live secure.[c]
4 Find your delight in the LORD
who will give you your heart's desire.[d]
GIMEL
5 Commit your way to the LORD;
trust in him and he will act[e]
6 And make your righteousness shine like
the dawn,
your justice like noonday.[f]
DALETH
7 Be still before the LORD;
wait for him.
Do not be provoked by the prosperous,
nor by malicious schemers.
HE
8 Refrain from anger; abandon wrath;
do not be provoked; it brings only
harm.
9 Those who do evil will be cut off,
but those who wait for the LORD will
inherit the earth.[g]
WAW
10 Wait a little, and the wicked will be no
more;
look for them and they will not be
there.
11 But the poor will inherit the earth,[h]
will delight in great prosperity.
ZAYIN
12 The wicked plot against the righteous
and gnash their teeth at them;
13 But my Lord laughs at them,[i]
because he sees that their day is
coming.
HETH
14 The wicked unsheath their swords;
they string their bows
To fell the poor and oppressed,
to slaughter those whose way is
upright.[j]
15 Their swords will pierce their own
hearts;
their bows will be broken.
TETH
16 Better the meagerness of the righteous
one
than the plenty of the wicked.[k]
17 The arms of the wicked will be broken,
while the LORD will sustain the
righteous.
YODH
18 The LORD knows the days of the
blameless;

Psalm 37 The Psalm responds to the problem of evil, which the Old Testament often expresses as a question: why do the wicked prosper and the good suffer? The Psalm answers that the situation is only temporary. God will reverse things, rewarding the good and punishing the wicked here on earth. The perspective is concrete and earthbound: people's very actions place them among the ranks of the good or wicked. Each group or "way" has its own inherent dynamism—eventual frustration for the wicked, eventual reward for the just. The Psalm is an acrostic, i.e., each section begins with a successive letter of the Hebrew alphabet. Each section has its own imagery and logic.

37:3 The land: the promised land, Israel, which became for later interpreters a type or figure of heaven, cf. Heb 11:9–10, 13–16. The New Testament Beatitudes (Mt 5:3–12; Lk 6:20–26) have been influenced by the Psalm, especially their total reversal of the present and their interpretation of the happy future as possession of the land.

x: Gn 2:8, 10. *y:* Is 55:1; Jn 4:14. *z:* Ps 80:4, 8, 20. *a:* Prv 3:31; 23:17; 24:1, 19. *b:* Ps 90:5–6; 102:12; 103:15–16; Jb 14:2; Is 40:7. *c:* Ps 128:2. *d:* Prv 10:24. *e:* Ps 55:23; Prv 3:5; 16:3. *f:* Wis 5:6; Is 58:10. *g:* Ps 25:13; Prv 2:21; Is 57:13. *h:* Mt 5:4. *i:* Ps 2:4; 59:9; Wis 4:18. *j:* Ps 11:2; 57:5; 64:4. *k:* Prv 15:16; 16:8.

their heritage lasts forever.
19 They will not be ashamed when times are bad;
in days of famine they will be satisfied.
KAPH
20 The wicked perish,
enemies of the LORD;
They shall be consumed like fattened lambs;
like smoke they disappear.[l]
LAMEDH
21 The wicked one borrows but does not repay;
the righteous one is generous and gives.
22 For those blessed by the Lord will inherit the earth,
but those accursed will be cut off.
MEM
23 The valiant one whose steps are guided by the LORD,
who will delight in his way,[m]
24 May stumble, but he will never fall,
for the LORD holds his hand.
NUN
25 Neither in my youth, nor now in old age
have I seen the righteous one abandoned[n]
or his offspring begging for bread.
26 All day long he is gracious and lends,
and his offspring become a blessing.
SAMEKH
27 Turn from evil and do good,
that you may be settled forever.[o]
28 For the LORD loves justice
and does not abandon the faithful.
AYIN
When the unjust are destroyed,
and the offspring of the wicked cut off,
29 The righteous will inherit the earth
and dwell in it forever.[p]
PE
30 The mouth of the righteous utters wisdom;[q]
his tongue speaks what is right.
31 God's teaching is in his heart;[r]
his steps do not falter.
SADHE
32 The wicked spies on the righteous
and seeks to kill him.
33 But the LORD does not abandon him in his power,
nor let him be condemned when tried.
QOPH
34 Wait eagerly for the LORD,
and keep his way;[s]
He will raise you up to inherit the earth;
you will see when the wicked are cut off.
RESH
35 I have seen a ruthless scoundrel,
spreading out like a green cedar.[t]
36 When I passed by again, he was gone;
though I searched, he could not be found.
SHIN
37 Observe the person of integrity and mark the upright;
Because there is a future for a man of peace.[u]
38 Sinners will be destroyed together;
the future of the wicked will be cut off.
TAW
39 The salvation of the righteous is from the LORD,
their refuge in a time of distress.[v]
40 The LORD helps and rescues them,
rescues and saves them from the wicked,
because they take refuge in him.

PSALM 38*

See RG 244

Prayer of an Afflicted Sinner

1 A psalm of David. For remembrance.

I

2 LORD, do not punish me in your anger;
in your wrath do not chastise me![w]
3 Your arrows have sunk deep in me;[x]
your hand has come down upon me.

Psalm 38 In this lament, one of the Penitential Psalms (cf. Ps 6), the psalmist acknowledges the sin that has brought physical and mental sickness and social ostracism. There is no one to turn to for help; only God can undo the past and restore the psalmist.

l: Wis 5:14. *m:* Prv 20:24. *n:* Jb 4:7; Sir 2:10. *o:* Ps 34:14–15; Am 5:14. *p:* Ps 25:13; Prv 2:21; Is 57:13. *q:* Prv 10:31. *r:* Ps 40:9; Dt 6:6; Is 51:7; Jer 31:33. *s:* Ps 31:24. *t:* Ps 92:8–9; Is 2:13; Ez 31:10–11. *u:* Prv 23:18; 24:14. *v:* Ps 9:10; Is 25:4. *w:* Ps 6:2. *x:* Jb 6:4; Lam 3:12; Ps 31:11; 64:7.

4 There is no wholesomeness in my flesh
because of your anger;
there is no health in my bones because
of my sin.[y]
5 My iniquities overwhelm me,
a burden too heavy for me.[z]

II

6 Foul and festering are my sores
because of my folly.
7 I am stooped and deeply bowed;[a]
every day I go about mourning.
8 My loins burn with fever;
there is no wholesomeness in my
flesh.
9 I am numb and utterly crushed;
I wail with anguish of heart.[b]
10 My Lord, my deepest yearning is before
you;
my groaning is not hidden from you.
11 My heart shudders, my strength forsakes
me;
the very light of my eyes has failed.[c]
12 Friends and companions shun my
disease;
my neighbors stand far off.
13 Those who seek my life lay snares for
me;
they seek my misfortune, they speak
of ruin;
they plot treachery every day.

III

14 But I am like the deaf, hearing nothing,
like the mute, I do not open my mouth,
15 I am even like someone who does not
hear,
who has no answer ready.
16 LORD, it is for you that I wait;
O Lord, my God, you respond.[d]
17 For I have said that they would gloat
over me,
exult over me if I stumble.

IV

18 I am very near to falling;
my wounds are with me always.
19 I acknowledge my guilt
and grieve over my sin.[e]
20 My enemies live and grow strong,
those who hate me grow numerous
fraudulently,
21 Repaying me evil for good,
accusing me for pursuing good.[f]
22 Do not forsake me, O LORD;
my God, be not far from me![g]
23 Come quickly to help me,[h]
my Lord and my salvation!

PSALM 39*

See RG 244, 250

The Vanity of Life

1 For the leader, for Jeduthun.[i]
A psalm of David.

I

2 I said, "I will watch my ways,
lest I sin with my tongue;
I will keep a muzzle on my mouth."
3 Mute and silent before the wicked,
I refrain from good things.
But my sorrow increases;
4 my heart smolders within me.[j]
In my sighing a fire blazes up,
and I break into speech:

II

5 LORD, let me know my end, the number
of my days,
that I may learn how frail I am.
6 To be sure, you establish the expanse of
my days;
indeed, my life is as nothing before
you.
Every man is but a breath.[k] *Selah*

III

7 Man goes about as a mere phantom;
they hurry about, although in vain;
he heaps up stores without knowing
for whom.
8 And now, LORD, for what do I wait?
You are my only hope.
9 From all my sins deliver me;
let me not be the taunt of fools.

Psalm 39 The lament of a mortally ill person who at first had resolved to remain silently submissive (Ps 39:2–4). But the grief was too much and now the psalmist laments the brevity and vanity of life (Ps 39:5–7), yet remaining hopeful (Ps 39:8–10). The psalmist continues to express both acceptance of the illness and hope for healing in Ps 39:11–13.

y: Is 1:5–6. *z:* Ps 40:13; Ezr 9:6. *a:* Ps 35:14. *b:* Ps 102:4–6. *c:* Ps 6:8; 31:10. *d:* Ps 13:4. *e:* Ps 32:5; 51:5. *f:* Ps 109:5. *g:* Ps 22:2, 12, 20; 35:22. *h:* Ps 40:14. *i:* 1 Chr 16:41; Ps 62:1; 77:1. *j:* Jer 20:9. *k:* Ps 62:10; 90:9–10; 144:4; Jb 7:6, 16; 14:1, 5; Eccl 6:12; Wis 2:5.

10 I am silent and do not open my mouth
because you are the one who did this.
11 Take your plague away from me;
I am ravaged by the touch of your hand.
12 You chastise man with rebukes for sin;
like a moth you consume his treasures.
Every man is but a breath. *Selah*
13 Listen to my prayer, LORD, hear my cry;
do not be deaf to my weeping!
For I am with you like a foreigner,
a refugee, like my ancestors.[l]
14 Turn your gaze from me, that I may smile
before I depart to be no more.

See RG 244

PSALM 40*

Gratitude and Prayer for Help

1 For the leader. A psalm of David.

A

2 Surely, I wait for the LORD;
who bends down to me and hears my cry,[m]
3 Draws me up from the pit of destruction,
out of the muddy clay,[n]
Sets my feet upon rock,
steadies my steps,
4 And puts a new song* in my mouth,[o]
a hymn to our God.
Many shall look on in fear
and they shall trust in the LORD.
5 Blessed the man who sets
his security in the LORD,
who turns not to the arrogant
or to those who stray after falsehood.[p]
6 You, yes you, O LORD, my God,
have done many wondrous deeds!
And in your plans for us
there is none to equal you.[q]
Should I wish to declare or tell them,
too many are they to recount.[r]
7 *Sacrifice and offering you do not want;[s]
you opened my ears.
Holocaust and sin-offering you do not request;
8 so I said, "See; I come
with an inscribed scroll written upon me.
9 I delight to do your will, my God;
your law is in my inner being!"[t]
10 When I sing of your righteousness
in a great assembly,
See, I do not restrain my lips;
as you, LORD, know.[u]
11 I do not conceal your righteousness
within my heart;
I speak of your loyalty and your salvation.
I do not hide your mercy or faithfulness
from a great assembly.
12 LORD, may you not withhold
your compassion from me;
May your mercy and your faithfulness
continually protect me.[v]

B

13 But evils surround me
until they cannot be counted.
My sins overtake me,
so that I can no longer see.
They are more numerous than the hairs of my head;
my courage fails me.[w]
14 LORD, graciously rescue me![x]
Come quickly to help me, LORD!
15 May those who seek to destroy my life
be shamed and confounded.
Turn back in disgrace
those who desire my ruin.[y]
16 Let those who say to me "Aha!"[z]
Be made desolate on account of their shame.

Psalm 40 A thanksgiving (Ps 40:2–13) has been combined with a lament (Ps 40:14–17) that appears also in Ps 70. The psalmist describes the rescue in spatial terms—being raised up from the swampy underworld to firm earth where one can praise God (Ps 40:2–4). All who trust God will experience like protection (Ps 40:5–6)! The Psalm stipulates the precise mode of thanksgiving: not animal sacrifice but open and enthusiastic proclamation of the salvation just experienced (Ps 40:7–11). A prayer for protection concludes (Ps 40:12–17).

40:4 A new song: a song in response to the new action of God (cf. Ps 33:3; 96:1; 144:9; 149:1; Is 42:10). Giving thanks is not purely a human response but is itself a divine gift.

40:7–9 Obedience is better than sacrifice (cf. 1 Sm 15:22; Is 1:10–20; Hos 6:6; Am 5:22–25; Mi 6:6–8; Acts 7:42–43 [quoting Am 5:25–26]). Heb 10:5–9 quotes the somewhat different Greek version and interprets it as Christ's self-oblation.

l: Ps 119:19; Gn 23:4; Heb 11:13; 1 Pt 2:11. *m:* Lam 3:25. *n:* Ps 28:1; 30:4; 69:3, 15–16; 88:5; Prv 1:12; Jon 2:7. *o:* Ps 33:3. *p:* Ps 1:1; Prv 16:20; Jer 17:7. *q:* Ps 35:10. *r:* Ps 71:15; 139:17–18. *s:* Heb 10:5–7; Ps 51:18–19; Am 5:22; Hos 6:6; Is 1:11–15. *t:* Ps 37:31. *u:* Ps 22:23; 26:12; 35:18; 149:1. *v:* Ps 89:34. *w:* Ps 38:5, 11; Ezr 9:6. *x:* Ps 70:2–6; 71:12. *y:* Ps 35:4, 26. *z:* Ps 35:21, 25.

17 While those who seek you
rejoice and be glad in you.
May those who long for your salvation
always say, "The LORD is great."[a]
18 Though I am afflicted and poor,
my Lord keeps me in mind.
You are my help and deliverer;
my God, do not delay!

PSALM 41*

See RG 245, 250

Thanksgiving After Sickness

1 For the leader. A psalm of David.

I

2 Blessed the one concerned for the poor;*
on a day of misfortune, the LORD
delivers him.[b]
3 The LORD keeps and preserves him,
makes him blessed in the land,
and does not betray him to his
enemies.
4 The LORD sustains him on his sickbed,
you turn down his bedding whenever
he is ill.*

II

5 Even I have said, "LORD, take note of
me;
heal me, although I have sinned
against you.
6 My enemies say bad things against me:
'When will he die and his name be
forgotten?'
7 When someone comes to visit me, he
speaks without sincerity.
His heart stores up malice;
when he leaves, he gossips.[c]
8 All those who hate me whisper together
against me;
they imagine the worst about me:
9 'He has had ruin poured over him;
that one lying down will never rise
again.'
10 *Even my trusted friend,
who ate my bread,
has raised his heel against me.[d]

III

11 "But you, LORD, take note of me to raise
me up
that I may repay them."*
12 By this I will know you are pleased with
me,
that my enemy no longer shouts in
triumph over me.
13 In my integrity may you support me
and let me stand in your presence
forever.
14 *Blessed be the LORD, the God of Israel,
from all eternity and forever.
Amen. Amen.[e]

Second Book—Psalms 42–72

PSALM 42*

See RG 244

Longing for God's Presence in the Temple

1 For the leader. A *maskil* of the Korahites.*

I

2 As the deer longs for streams of water,[f]
so my soul longs for you, O God.
3 My soul thirsts for God, the living God.

Psalm 41 A thanksgiving for rescue from illness (Ps 41:4, 5, 9). Many people, even friends, have interpreted the illness as a divine punishment for sin and have ostracized the psalmist (Ps 41:5–11). The healing shows the return of God's favor and rebukes the psalmist's detractors (Ps 41:12–13).

41:2 Blessed the one concerned for the poor: cf. Ps 32:1–2; 34:9; 40:5; 65:5. The psalmist's statement about God's love of the poor is based on the experience of being rescued (Ps 41:1–3).

41:4 You turn down his bedding whenever he is ill: the Hebrew is obscure. It suggests ongoing attentive care of the one who is sick.

41:10 Even my trusted friend . . . has raised his heel against me: Jn 13:18 cites this verse to characterize Judas as a false friend. **Raised his heel against me**: an interpretation of the unclear Hebrew, "made great the heel against me."

41:11 That I may repay them: the healing itself is an act of judgment through which God decides for the psalmist and against the false friends. The prayer is not necessarily for strength to punish enemies.

41:14 The doxology, not part of the Psalm, marks the end of the first of the five books of the Psalter, cf. Ps 72:18–20; 89:53; 106:48.

Psalms 42–43 Ps 42–43 form a single lament of three sections, each section ending in an identical refrain (Ps 42:6, 12; 43:5). The psalmist is far from Jerusalem, and longs for the divine presence that Israel experienced in the Temple liturgy. Despite sadness, the psalmist hopes once again to join the worshiping crowds.

42:1 The Korahites: a major guild of Temple singers (2 Chr 20:19) whose name appears in the superscriptions of Ps 42; 44–49; 84–85; 87–88.

a: Ps 35:27. *b:* Tb 4:7–11. *c:* Ps 31:12; 38:12–13; 88:8; Jb 19:13–19; Jer 20:10. *d:* Ps 55:14–15; Jn 13:18. *e:* Neh 9:5. *f:* Ps 63:2; 84:3; 143:6; Is 26:9.

When can I enter and see the face of
God?*[g]
4 My tears have been my bread day and
night,[h]
as they ask me every day, "Where is
your God?"[i]
5 Those times I recall
as I pour out my soul,[j]
When I would cross over to the shrine of
the Mighty One,*
to the house of God,
Amid loud cries of thanksgiving,
with the multitude keeping festival.[k]
6 Why are you downcast, my soul;
why do you groan within me?
Wait for God, for I shall again praise
him,
my savior and my God.

II

7 My soul is downcast within me;
therefore I remember you
From the land of the Jordan* and
Hermon,
from Mount Mizar,[l]
8 *Deep calls to deep
in the roar of your torrents,
and all your waves and breakers
sweep over me.[m]
9 By day may the LORD send his mercy,
and by night may his righteousness be
with me!
I will pray* to the God of my life,
10 I will say to God, my rock:
"Why do you forget me?[n]
Why must I go about mourning
with the enemy oppressing me?"
11 It shatters my bones, when my
adversaries reproach me,
when they say to me every day:
"Where is your God?"
12 Why are you downcast, my soul,
why do you groan within me?
Wait for God, for I shall again praise
him,
my savior and my God.

PSALM 43

1 Grant me justice, O God;
defend me from a faithless people;
from the deceitful and unjust rescue
me.[o]
2 You, O God, are my strength.
Why then do you spurn me?
Why must I go about mourning,
with the enemy oppressing me?
3 [p]Send your light and your fidelity,*
that they may be my guide;[q]
Let them bring me to your holy
mountain,
to the place of your dwelling,
4 That I may come to the altar of God,
to God, my joy, my delight.
Then I will praise you with the harp,
O God, my God.
5 Why are you downcast, my soul?
Why do you groan within me?
Wait for God, for I shall again praise him,
my savior and my God.

PSALM 44*

See RG 244, 247

God's Past Favor and Israel's Present Need

1 For the leader. A *maskil* of the Korahites.

I

2 O God, we have heard with our own ears;
our ancestors have told us[r]

42:3 See the face of God: "face" designates a personal presence (Gn 33:10; Ex 10:28–29; 2 Sm 17:11). The expressions "see God/God's face" occur elsewhere (Ps 11:7; 17:15; cf. Ex 24:10; 33:7–11; Jb 33:26) for the presence of God in the Temple.

42:5 The shrine of the Mighty One: this reading follows the tradition of the Septuagint and the Vulgate.

42:7 From the land of the Jordan: the sources of the Jordan are in the foothills of Mount Hermon in present-day southern Lebanon. Mount Mizar is presumed to be a mountain in the same range.

42:8 Deep calls to deep: to the psalmist, the waters arising in the north are overwhelming and far from God's presence, like the waters of chaos (Ps 18:5; 69:2–3, 15; Jon 2:3–6).

42:9–10 I will pray . . . I will say: in the midst of his depression the psalmist turns to prayer. Despite his situation he trusts the Lord to deliver him from his sorrow so that he may enter the Temple precincts and praise him once again (Ps 43:3–4, 5b).

43:3 Your light and your fidelity: a pair of divine attributes personified as guides for the pilgrimage. As in Ps 42:9 the psalmist prays that these divine attributes lead him back to Jerusalem and ultimately to God's presence in the Temple.

Psalm 44 In this lament the community reminds God of past favors which it has always acknowledged (Ps 44:2–9). But now God has abandoned Israel to defeat and humiliation

g: Ps 27:4. *h:* Ps 80:6; 102:10. *i:* Ps 79:10; Jl 2:17. *j:* Lam 3:20. *k:* Ps 122:5. *l:* Ps 43:3. *m:* Ps 18:5; 32:6; 69:2; 88:8; Jon 2:4. *n:* Ps 18:2; 31:3–4. *o:* Ps 119:154. *p:* Ps 18:29; 27:1; 36:10; Mi 7:8. *q:* Ps 122:1. *r:* Ps 78:3.

The deeds you did in their days,
with your own hand in days of old:
3 You rooted out nations to plant them,[s]
crushed peoples and expelled them.
4 Not with their own swords did they conquer the land,[t]
nor did their own arms bring victory;
It was your right hand, your own arm,
the light of your face for you favored them.[u]
5 You are my king and my God,[v]
who bestows victories on Jacob.
6 Through you we batter our foes;
through your name we trample our adversaries.
7 Not in my bow do I trust,
nor does my sword bring me victory.
8 You have brought us victory over our enemies,
shamed those who hate us.
9 In God we have boasted all the day long;
your name we will praise forever.*Selah*

II

10 [w]But now you have rejected and disgraced us;
you do not march out with our armies.[x]
11 You make us retreat* before the foe;
those who hate us plunder us at will.[y]
12 You hand us over like sheep to be slaughtered,
scatter us among the nations.[z]
13 You sell your people for nothing;
you make no profit from their sale.[a]
14 You make us the reproach of our neighbors,[b]
the mockery and scorn of those around us.
15 You make us a byword among the nations;
the peoples shake their heads at us.
16 All day long my disgrace is before me;
shame has covered my face
17 At the sound of those who taunt and revile,
at the sight of the enemy and avenger.

III

18 All this has come upon us,
though we have not forgotten you,
nor been disloyal to your covenant.
19 *Our hearts have not turned back,
nor have our steps strayed from your path.
20 Yet you have left us crushed,
desolate in a place of jackals;*[c]
you have covered us with a shadow of death.
21 If we had forgotten the name of our God,
stretched out our hands to another god,
22 Would not God have discovered this,
God who knows the secrets of the heart?
23 For you we are slain all the day long,
considered only as sheep to be slaughtered.[d]

IV

24 Awake! Why do you sleep, O Lord?
Rise up! Do not reject us forever![e]
25 Why do you hide your face;[f]
why forget our pain and misery?
26 For our soul has been humiliated in the dust;[g]
our belly is pressed to the earth.
27 Rise up, help us!
Redeem us in your mercy.

PSALM 45*

See RG 245

Song for a Royal Wedding

1 For the leader; according to "Lilies."
A *maskil* of the Korahites. A love song.

I

2 My heart is stirred by a noble theme,
as I sing my ode to the king.

(Ps 44:10–17), though the people are not conscious of any sin against the covenant (Ps 44:18–23). They struggle with being God's special people amid divine silence; yet they continue to pray (Ps 44:24–26).

44:11 You make us retreat: the corollary of Ps 44:3. Defeat, like victory, is God's doing; neither Israel nor its enemies can claim credit (Ps 44:23).

44:19 Our hearts have not turned back: Israel's defeat was not caused by its lack of fidelity.

44:20 A place of jackals: following Israel's defeat and exile (Ps 44:11–12), the land lies desolate, inhabited only by jackals, cf. Is 13:22; Jer 9:10; 10:22. Others take *tannim* as "sea monster" (cf. Ez 29:3; 32:2) and render: "you crushed us as you did the sea monster."

Psalm 45 A song for the Davidic king's marriage to a foreign princess from Tyre in Phoenicia. The court poet sings (Ps 45:2, 18) of God's choice of the king (Ps 45:3, 8), of his role

s: Ps 78:55; 80:9f. *t:* Dt 8:17f; Jos 24:12. *u:* Ps 4:7; 31:17; 67:2; 80:4; Nm 6:25; Dn 9:17. *v:* Ps 145:1. *w:* Ps 89:39–52. *x:* Ps 60:12. *y:* Lv 26:17; Dt 28:25. *z:* Lv 26:33; Dt 28:64. *a:* Dt 32:30; Is 52:3. *b:* Ps 79:4; 80:7; 123:3–4; Jb 12:4; Dn 9:16. *c:* Jer 9:10. *d:* Rom 8:36. *e:* Ps 10:1; 74:1; 77:8; 79:5; 83:2. *f:* Ps 10:11; 89:47; Jb 13:24. *g:* Ps 119:25.

My tongue is the pen of a nimble
scribe.
II
3 You are the most handsome of men;
fair speech has graced your lips,
for God has blessed you forever.[h]
4 Gird your sword upon your hip, mighty
warrior!
In splendor and majesty ride on
triumphant![i]
5 In the cause of truth, meekness, and justice
may your right hand show your
wondrous deeds.
6 Your arrows are sharp;
peoples will cower at your feet;
the king's enemies will lose heart.
7 Your throne, O God,* stands forever;[j]
your royal scepter is a scepter for
justice.
8 You love justice and hate wrongdoing;
therefore God, your God, has anointed
you
with the oil of gladness above your
fellow kings.
9 With myrrh, aloes, and cassia
your robes are fragrant.
From ivory-paneled palaces*
stringed instruments bring you joy.
10 Daughters of kings are your lovely wives;
a princess arrayed in Ophir's gold*
comes to stand at your right hand.
III
11 Listen, my daughter, and understand;
pay me careful heed.
Forget your people and your father's
house,*
12 that the king might desire your beauty.
He is your lord;
13 [k]honor him, daughter of Tyre.
Then the richest of the people
will seek your favor with gifts.
14 All glorious is the king's daughter as she
enters,[l]
her raiment threaded with gold;
15 In embroidered apparel she is led to the
king.
The maids of her train are presented to
the king.
16 They are led in with glad and joyous
acclaim;
they enter the palace of the king.
IV
17 The throne of your fathers your sons will
have;
you shall make them princes through
all the land.[m]
18 I will make your name renowned through
all generations;
thus nations shall praise you forever.[n]

PSALM 46*

See RG 245

God, the Protector of Zion

1 For the leader. A song of the Korahites.
According to *alamoth*.*

I
2 God is our refuge and our strength,
an ever-present help in distress.[o]
3 *Thus we do not fear, though earth be
shaken
and mountains quake to the depths of
the sea,
4 Though its waters rage and foam

in establishing divine rule (Ps 45:4–8), and of his splendor as he waits for his bride (Ps 45:9–10). The woman is to forget her own house when she becomes wife to the king (Ps 45:11–13). Her majestic beauty today is a sign of the future prosperity of the royal house (Ps 45:14–17). The Psalm was retained in the collection when there was no reigning king, and came to be applied to the king who was to come, the messiah.

45:7 O God: the king, in courtly language, is called "god," i.e., more than human, representing God to the people. Heb 1:8–9 applies Ps 45:7–8 to Christ.

45:9 Ivory-paneled palaces: lit., "palaces of ivory." Ivory paneling and furniture decoration have been found in Samaria and other ancient Near Eastern cities, cf. Am 3:15.

45:10 Ophir's gold: uncertain location, possibly a region on the coast of southern Arabia or eastern Africa, famous for its gold, cf. 1 Kgs 9:28; 10:11; Jb 22:24.

45:11 Forget your people and your father's house: the bride should no longer consider herself a daughter of her father's house, but the wife of the king—the queen.

Psalm 46 A song of confidence in God's protection of Zion with close parallels to Ps 48. The dominant note in Ps 46 is sounded by the refrain, The LORD of hosts is with us (Ps 46:8, 12). The first strophe (Ps 46:2–4) sings of the security of God's presence even in utter chaos; the second (Ps 46:5–8), of divine protection of the city from its enemies; the third (Ps 46:9–11), of God's imposition of imperial peace.

46:1 Alamoth: the melody of the Psalm, now lost.

46:3–4 Figurative ancient Near Eastern language to describe social and political upheavals.

h: Sg 5:10–16. *i:* Ps 21:5. *j:* Heb 1:8–9. *k:* Ps 72:10–11; Is 60:5f. *l:* Ez 16:10–13. *m:* Gn 17:6. *n:* Is 60:15. *o:* Ps 48:4; Is 33:2.

and mountains totter at its surging.[p]
Selah

II

5 *Streams of the river gladden the city of God,
the holy dwelling of the Most High.[q]
6 God is in its midst; it shall not be shaken;
God will help it at break of day.[r]
7 Though nations rage and kingdoms totter,
he utters his voice and the earth melts.[s]
8 *The LORD of hosts is with us;
our stronghold is the God of Jacob.
Selah

III

9 Come and see the works of the LORD,
who has done fearsome deeds on earth;[t]
10 Who stops wars to the ends of the earth,
breaks the bow, splinters the spear,
and burns the shields with fire;[u]
11 [v]"Be still and know that I am God!
I am exalted among the nations,
exalted on the earth."
12 The LORD of hosts is with us;
our stronghold is the God of Jacob.
Selah

PSALM 47*

See RG 245, 249

The Ruler of All the Nations

1 For the leader. A psalm of the Korahites.

I

2 All you peoples, clap your hands;
shout to God with joyful cries.[w]
3 For the LORD, the Most High, is to be feared,
the great king over all the earth,[x]
4 Who made people subject to us,
nations under our feet,[y]
5 *Who chose our heritage for us,
the glory of Jacob, whom he loves.[z]
Selah

II

6 *God has gone up with a shout;
the LORD, amid trumpet blasts.[a]
7 Sing praise to God, sing praise;
sing praise to our king, sing praise.

III

8 For God is king over all the earth;[b]
sing hymns of praise.
9 God rules over the nations;
God sits upon his holy throne.
10 The princes of the peoples assemble
with the people of the God of Abraham.
For the shields of the earth belong to God,
highly exalted.[c]

PSALM 48*

See RG 245

The Splendor of the Invincible City

1 A psalm of the Korahites.* A song.

I

2 Great is the LORD and highly praised
in the city of our God:[d]
His holy mountain,
3 fairest of heights,
the joy of all the earth,[e]
Mount Zion, the heights of Zaphon,*[f]
the city of the great king.

46:5 Jerusalem is not situated on a river. This description derives from mythological descriptions of the divine abode and symbolizes the divine presence as the source of all life (cf. Is 33:21; Ez 47:1–12; Jl 4:18; Zec 14:8; Rev 22:1–2).

46:8 The first line of the refrain is similar in structure and meaning to Isaiah's name for the royal child, Emmanuel, With us is God (Is 7:14; 8:8, 10).

Psalm 47 A hymn calling on the nations to acknowledge the universal rule of Israel's God (Ps 47:2–5) who is enthroned as king over Israel and the nations (Ps 47:6–9).

47:5 Our heritage . . . the glory: the land of Israel (cf. Is 58:14), which God has given Israel in an act of sovereignty.

47:6 God has gone up: Christian liturgical tradition has applied the verse to the Ascension of Christ.

Psalm 48 A Zion hymn, praising the holy city as the invincible dwelling place of God. Unconquerable, it is an apt symbol of God who has defeated all enemies. After seven epithets describing the city (Ps 48:2–3), the Psalm describes the victory by the Divine Warrior over hostile kings (Ps 48:4–8). The second half proclaims the dominion of the God of Zion over all the earth (Ps 48:9–12) and invites pilgrims to announce that God is eternally invincible like Zion itself (Ps 48:13–14).

48:1 Korahites: see note on Ps 42:1.

48:3 The heights of Zaphon: the mountain abode of the Canaanite storm-god Baal in comparable texts. To speak of Zion as if it were Zaphon was to claim for Israel's God what Canaanites claimed for Baal. Though topographically speaking Zion is only a hill, viewed religiously it towers over other mountains as the home of the supreme God (cf. Ps 68:16–17).

p: Ps 93:3–4; Jb 9:5–6; Is 24:18–20; 54:10. *q:* Ps 48:2–3; 76:3. *r:* Is 7:14. *s:* Ps 2:1–5; 48:5–8; 76:7–9; Is 17:12–14. *t:* Ps 48:9–10. *u:* Ps 76:4. *v:* Ps 48:11. *w:* Ps 89:16; Zep 3:14. *x:* Ps 95:3; Ex 15:18; Is 24:23; 52:7. *y:* Ps 2:8. *z:* Is 58:14. *a:* Ps 24:8, 10; 68:18–19; 98:6. *b:* Ps 72:11; 93:1; 96:10; 97:1; 99:1; Jer 10:7. *c:* Ps 89:19; Ex 3:6; Is 2:2–4. *d:* Ps 96:4; 145:3. *e:* Ps 50:2; Lam 2:15. *f:* Is 14:13.

II

4 God is in its citadel,
renowned as a stronghold.
5 See! The kings assembled,
together they advanced.
6 *When they looked they were astounded;
terrified, they were put to flight![g]
7 Trembling seized them there,
anguish, like a woman's labor,[h]
8 As when the east wind wrecks
the ships of Tarshish!*

III

9 *What we had heard we have now seen
in the city of the LORD of hosts,
In the city of our God,
which God establishes forever. *Selah*
10 We ponder, O God, your mercy
within your temple
11 Like your name, O God,
so is your praise to the ends of the
earth.[i]
Your right hand is fully victorious.
12 Mount Zion is glad!
The daughters of Judah rejoice
because of your judgments![j]

IV

13 Go about Zion, walk all around it,
note the number of its towers.
14 Consider the ramparts, examine its
citadels,
that you may tell future generations:[k]
15 That this is God,
our God for ever and ever.*
He will lead us until death.

PSALM 49*

See RG 245, 251

Confidence in God Rather than in Riches

1 For the leader. A psalm of the Korahites.*
2 Hear this, all you peoples!
Give ear, all who inhabit the world,
3 You of lowly birth or high estate,
rich and poor together.
4 My mouth shall speak words of wisdom,
my heart shall offer insights.[l]
5 I will turn my ear to a riddle,*
expound my question on a lyre.

I

6 Why should I fear in evil days,
with the iniquity of my assailants
surrounding me,
7 Of those who trust in their wealth
and boast of their abundant riches?[m]
8 *No man can ransom even a brother,
or pay to God his own ransom.[n]
9 The redemption of his soul is costly;
and he will pass away forever.
10 Will he live on forever, then,
and never see the Pit of Corruption?
11 Indeed, he will see that the wise die,
and the fool will perish together with
the senseless,[o]
and they leave their wealth to others.[p]
12 Their tombs are their homes forever,
their dwellings through all
generations,
"They named countries after
themselves"

48:6 When they looked: the kings are stunned by the sight of Zion, touched by divine splendor. The language is that of holy war, in which the enemy panics and flees at the sight of divine glory.

48:8 The ships of Tarshish: large ships, named after the distant land or port of Tarshish, probably ancient Tartessus in southern Spain, although other identifications have been proposed, cf. Is 2:16; 60:9; Jon 1:3.

48:9 What we had heard we have now seen: the glorious things that new pilgrims had heard about the holy city—its beauty and awesomeness—they now see with their own eyes. The seeing here contrasts with the seeing of the hostile kings in Ps 48:6.

48:15 Our God for ever and ever: Israel's God is like Zion in being eternal and invincible. The holy city is therefore a kind of "sacrament" of God.

Psalm 49 The Psalm affirms confidence in God (cf. Ps 23; 27:1–6; 62) in the face of the apparent good fortune of the unjust rich, cf. Ps 37; 73. Reliance on wealth is misplaced (Ps 49:8–10) for it is of no avail in the face of death (Ps 49:18–20). After inviting all to listen to this axiom of faith (Ps 49:2–5), the psalmist depicts the self-delusion of the ungodly (Ps 49:6–13), whose destiny is to die like ignorant beasts (Ps 49:13, 18; cf. Prv 7:21–23). Their wealth should occasion no alarm, for they will come to nought, whereas God will save the just (Ps 49:14–20).

49:1 Korahites: see note on Ps 42:1.

49:5 Riddle: the psalmist's personal solution to the perennial biblical problem of the prosperity of the wicked. **Question**: parallel in meaning to problem; in wisdom literature it means the mysterious way of how the world works.

49:8 No man can ransom even a brother: an axiom. For the practice of redemption, cf. Jb 6:21–23. A play on the first Hebrew word of Ps 49:8, 16 relates the two verses.

g: Jgs 5:19. *h:* Ex 15:14; Jer 4:31. *i:* Mal 1:11. *j:* Ps 97:8. *k:* Ps 22:31–32; 71:18. *l:* Ps 78:2; Mt 13:35. *m:* Jb 31:24. *n:* Prv 10:15; 11:4; Ez 7:19; Mt 16:26. *o:* Eccl 2:16. *p:* Ps 39:7; Sir 11:18–19.

13 —but man does not abide in splendor.
He is like the beasts—they perish.[q]

II

14 This is the way of those who trust in themselves,
and the end of those who take pleasure in their own mouth. *Selah*
15 Like a herd of sheep they will be put into Sheol,
and Death will shepherd them.
Straight to the grave they descend,
where their form will waste away,
Sheol will be their palace.
16 But God will redeem my life,
will take me* from the hand of Sheol.[r] *Selah*
17 Do not fear when a man becomes rich,
when the wealth of his house grows great.
18 At his death he will not take along anything,
his glory will not go down after him.[s]
19 During his life his soul uttered blessings;
"They will praise you, for you do well for yourself."
20 But he will join the company of his fathers,
never again to see the light.[t]
21 In his prime, man does not understand.
He is like the beasts—they perish.

See RG 246

PSALM 50*

The Acceptable Sacrifice

1 A psalm of Asaph.

I

The God of gods, the LORD,
has spoken and summoned the earth
from the rising of the sun to its setting.[u]
2 From Zion, the perfection of beauty,
God shines forth.[v]
3 Our God comes and will not be silent!
Devouring fire precedes him,
it rages strongly around him.[w]
4 He calls to the heavens above
and to the earth to judge his people:
5 "Gather my loyal ones to me,
those who made a covenant with me by sacrifice."
6 The heavens proclaim his righteousness,
for God himself is the judge.[x] *Selah*

II

7 "Listen, my people, I will speak;
Israel, I will testify against you;
God, your God, am I.
8 Not for your sacrifices do I rebuke you,
your burnt offerings are always before me.
9 I will not take a bullock from your house,
or he-goats from your folds.[y]
10 For every animal of the forest is mine,
beasts by the thousands on my mountains.
11 I know every bird in the heights;
whatever moves in the wild is mine.
12 Were I hungry, I would not tell you,
for mine is the world and all that fills it.[z]
13 Do I eat the flesh of bulls
or drink the blood of he-goats?
14 Offer praise as your sacrifice to God;[a]
fulfill your vows to the Most High.
15 Then call on me on the day of distress;[b]
I will rescue you, and you shall honor me."

III

16 But to the wicked God says:
"Why do you recite my commandments
and profess my covenant with your mouth?
17 You hate discipline;
you cast my words behind you!
18 If you see a thief, you run with him;
with adulterers you throw in your lot.
19 You give your mouth free rein for evil;
you yoke your tongue to deceit.

49:16 Will take me: the same Hebrew verb is used of God "taking up" a favored servant: Enoch in Gn 5:24; Elijah in 2 Kgs 2:11–12; the righteous person in Ps 73:24. The verse apparently states the hope that God will rescue the faithful psalmist in the same manner.

Psalm 50 A covenant lawsuit stating that the sacrifice God really wants is the sacrifice of praise accompanied by genuine obedience (cf. Mi 6:1–8). It begins with a theophany and the summoning of the court (Ps 50:1–6). Then in direct address God explains what is required of the faithful (Ps 50:7–15), rebukes the hypocritical worshiper (Ps 50:16–21), and concludes with a threat and a promise (Ps 50:22–23; cf. Is 1:19–20).

q: Eccl 3:18–21. *r:* Ps 16:10; 86:13; 103:4; 116:8. *s:* Sir 11:18–19; Eccl 5:15; 1 Tm 6:7. *t:* Jb 10:21–22. *u:* Dt 10:17; Jos 22:22. *v:* Ps 48:2. *w:* Ps 97:3; Dn 7:10. *x:* Ps 19:2; 97:6. *y:* Ps 69:32; Am 5:21–22. *z:* Ps 24:1; 89:12; Dt 10:14; 1 Cor 10:26. *a:* Heb 13:15. *b:* Ps 77:3.

20 You sit and speak against your brother,
slandering your mother's son.
21 When you do these things should I be silent?
Do you think that I am like you?
I accuse you, I lay out the matter before your eyes.

IV

22 "Now understand this, you who forget God,
lest I start ripping apart and there be no rescuer.
23 Those who offer praise as a sacrifice honor me;
I will let him whose way is steadfast
look upon the salvation of God."[c]

See RG 244

PSALM 51*

The Miserere: Prayer of Repentance

1 For the leader. A psalm of David, 2 when Nathan the prophet came to him after he had gone in to Bathsheba.[d]

I

3 Have mercy on me, God, in accord with your merciful love;
in your abundant compassion blot out my transgressions.
4 Thoroughly wash away my guilt;
and from my sin cleanse me.
5 For I know my transgressions;
my sin is always before me.[e]
6 Against you, you alone have I sinned;
I have done what is evil in your eyes
So that you are just in your word,
and without reproach in your judgment.[f]
7 Behold, I was born in guilt,
in sin my mother conceived me.*[g]
8 Behold, you desire true sincerity;
and secretly you teach me wisdom.
9 Cleanse me with hyssop,* that I may be pure;
wash me, and I will be whiter than snow.[h]
10 You will let me hear gladness and joy;
the bones you have crushed will rejoice.

II

11 Turn away your face from my sins;
blot out all my iniquities.
12 A clean heart create for me, God;
renew within me a steadfast spirit.[i]
13 Do not drive me from before your face,
nor take from me your holy spirit.[j]
14 Restore to me the gladness of your salvation;
uphold me with a willing spirit.
15 I will teach the wicked your ways,
that sinners may return to you.
16 Rescue me from violent bloodshed, God, my saving God,
and my tongue will sing joyfully of your justice.[k]
17 Lord, you will open my lips;
and my mouth will proclaim your praise.
18 For you do not desire sacrifice* or I would give it;
a burnt offering you would not accept.[l]

Psalm 51 A lament, the most famous of the seven Penitential Psalms, prays for the removal of the personal and social disorders that sin has brought. The poem has two parts of approximately equal length: Ps 51:3–10 and Ps 51:11–19, and a conclusion in Ps 51:20–21. The two parts interlock by repetition of "blot out" in the first verse of each section (Ps 51:3, 11), of "wash (away)" just after the first verse of each section (Ps 51:4) and just before the last verse (Ps 51:9) of the first section, and of "heart," "God," and "spirit" in Ps 51:12, 19. The first part (Ps 51:3–10) asks deliverance from sin, not just a past act but its emotional, physical, and social consequences. The second part (Ps 51:11–19) seeks something more profound than wiping the slate clean: nearness to God, living by the spirit of God (Ps 51:12–13), like the relation between God and people described in Jer 31:33–34. Nearness to God brings joy and the authority to teach sinners (Ps 51:15–16). Such proclamation is better than offering sacrifice (Ps 51:17–19). The last two verses express the hope that God's good will toward those who are cleansed and contrite will prompt him to look favorably on the acts of worship offered in the Jerusalem Temple (Ps 51:19 [20–21]).

51:7 In sin my mother conceived me: lit., "In iniquity was I conceived," an instance of hyperbole: at no time was the psalmist ever without sin, cf. Ps 88:15, "I am mortally afflicted since youth," i.e., I have always been afflicted. The verse does not imply that the sexual act of conception is sinful.

51:9 Hyssop: a small bush whose many woody twigs make a natural sprinkler. It was prescribed in the Mosaic law as an instrument for sprinkling sacrificial blood or lustral water for cleansing, cf. Ex 12:22; Lv 14:4; Nm 19:18.

51:18 For you do not desire sacrifice: the mere offering

c: Ps 91:16. *d:* 2 Sm 12. *e:* Ps 32:5; 38:19; Is 59:12. *f:* Rom 3:4. *g:* Jb 14:4. *h:* Jb 9:30; Is 1:18; Ez 36:25. *i:* Ez 11:19. *j:* Wis 1:5; 9:17; Is 63:11; Hg 2:5; Rom 8:9. *k:* Ps 30:10. *l:* Ps 40:7; 50:8; Am 5:21–22; Hos 6:6; Is 1:11–15; Heb 10:5–7.

19 My sacrifice, O God, is a contrite spirit;
a contrite, humbled heart, O God, you will not scorn.

III

20 *Treat Zion kindly according to your good will;
build up the walls of Jerusalem.[m]
21 Then you will desire the sacrifices of the just,
burnt offering and whole offerings;
then they will offer up young bulls on your altar.

See RG 244

PSALM 52*

The Deceitful Tongue

1 For the leader. A *maskil* of David, 2 when Doeg the Edomite entered and reported to Saul, saying to him: "David has entered the house of Ahimelech."[n]

I

3 Why do you glory in what is evil, you who are mighty by the mercy of God?
All day long
4 you are thinking up intrigues;
your tongue is like a sharpened razor,
you worker of deceit.[o]
5 You love evil more than good,
lying rather than saying what is right.[p]
Selah
6 You love all the words that create confusion,
you deceitful tongue.[q]

II

7 God too will strike you down forever,
he will lay hold of you and pluck you from your tent,
uproot you from the land of the living.[r]
Selah
8 The righteous will see and they will fear;
but they will laugh at him:[s]
9 "Behold the man! He did not take God as his refuge,
but he trusted in the abundance of his wealth,
and grew powerful through his wickedness."[t]

III

10 But I, like an olive tree* flourishing in the house of God,[u]
I trust in God's mercy forever and ever.
11 I will thank you forever
for what you have done.
I will put my hope in your name—for it is good,[v]
—in the presence of those devoted to you.

PSALM 53*

See RG 244

A Lament over Widespread Corruption

1 For the leader; according to *Mahalath*. A *maskil* of David.

I

2 The fool says in his heart,[w]
"There is no God."[x]
They act corruptly and practice injustice;
there is none that does good.
3 God looks out from the heavens
upon the children of Adam,[y]
To see if there is a discerning person[z]
who is seeking God.
4 All have gone astray;
each one is altogether perverse.
There is not one who does what is good, not even one.[a]

II

5 [b]Do they not know better, those who do evil,
who feed upon my people as they feed upon bread?[c]

of the ritual sacrifice apart from good dispositions is not acceptable to God, cf. Ps 50.

51:20–21 Most scholars think that these verses were added to the Psalm some time after the destruction of the Temple in 587 B.C. The verses assume that the rebuilt Temple will be an ideal site for national reconciliation.

Psalm 52 A condemnation of the powerful and arrogant (Ps 52:3–6), who bring down upon themselves God's judgment (Ps 52:7). The just, those who trust in God alone, are gladdened and strengthened by the downfall of their traditional enemies (Ps 52:8–9).

52:10 Like an olive tree: the righteous will flourish in the house of God like a well-watered olive tree, cf. Ps 92:14; 128:3.

Psalm 53 A lament of an individual, duplicated in Ps 14, except that "God" is used for "the LORD," and Ps 53:6 is different, cf. Ps 14.

m: Jer 31:4; Ez 36:33. *n:* 1 Sm 21:8; 22:6ff. *o:* Ps 12:3; 59:8; 120:2–3; Sir 51:3. *p:* Jer 4:22; Jn 3:19–20. *q:* Jer 9:4. *r:* Ps 27:13; 28:5; 56:14; Jb 18:14; Prv 2:22; Is 38:11. *s:* Ps 44:14; 64:9. *t:* Jb 31:24; Prv 11:28. *u:* Ps 1:3; 92:12–14; Jer 11:16; 17:8. *v:* Ps 22:23; 26:12; 35:18; 149:1. *w:* Ps 14:1–5a. *x:* Ps 10:4; 36:2; Is 32:6; Jer 5:12. *y:* Rom 3:11–12. *z:* Ps 11:4; 102:20. *a:* Ps 12:2. *b:* Ps 79:6. *c:* Ps 27:2; Is 9:11.

Have they not called upon God?
6 They are going to fear his name with great fear,
though they had not feared it before.
For God will scatter the bones
of those encamped against you.
They will surely be put to shame,
for God has rejected them.

III

7 Who will bring forth from Zion
the salvation of Israel?
When God reverses the captivity of his people
Jacob will rejoice and Israel will be glad.[d]

See RG 244

PSALM 54*

Confident Prayer in Great Peril

1 For the leader. On stringed instruments. A *maskil* of David, 2 when the Ziphites came and said to Saul, "David is hiding among us."[e]

I

3 O God, by your name* save me.
By your strength defend my cause.
4 O God, hear my prayer.
Listen to the words of my mouth.
5 Strangers have risen against me;
the ruthless seek my life;
they do not keep God before them.[f]
Selah

II

6 God is present as my helper;[g]
the Lord sustains my life.
7 Turn back the evil upon my foes;
in your faithfulness, destroy them.[h]
8 Then I will offer you generous sacrifice
and give thanks to your name, LORD,
for it is good.
9 Because it has rescued me from every trouble,
and my eyes look down on my foes.[i]

PSALM 55*

See RG 244

A Lament over Betrayal

1 For the leader. On stringed instruments. A *maskil* of David.

I

2 Listen, God, to my prayer;[j]
do not hide from my pleading;
3 hear me and give answer.
I rock with grief; I groan
4 at the uproar of the enemy,
the clamor of the wicked.
They heap trouble upon me,
savagely accuse me.
5 My heart pounds within me;
death's terrors fall upon me.
6 Fear and trembling overwhelm me;
shuddering sweeps over me.
7 I say, "If only I had wings like a dove
that I might fly away and find rest.[k]
8 Far away I would flee;
I would stay in the desert.[l] 9 I would
soon find a shelter *Selah*
from the raging wind and storm."

II

10 Lord, check and confuse their tongues.
For I see violence and strife in the city
11 making rounds on its walls day and night.
Within are mischief and trouble;
12 treachery is in its midst;
oppression and fraud never leave its streets.[m]

Psalm 54 A lament in which the person under attack calls directly upon God for help (Ps 54:3–5). Refusing to despair, the psalmist hopes in God, who is active in history and just (Ps 54:6–7). The Psalm ends with a serene promise to return thanks (Ps 54:8–9).

54:3 By your name: one is present in one's name, hence God as revealed to human beings.

Psalm 55 The psalmist, betrayed by intimate friends (Ps 55:14–15, 20–21), prays that God punish those oath breakers and thus be acknowledged as the protector of the wronged. The sufferings of the psalmist include both ostracism (Ps 55:4) and mental turmoil (Ps 55:5–6), culminating in the wish to flee society (Ps 55:7–9). The wish for a sudden death for one's enemies (Ps 55:16) occurs elsewhere in the Psalms; an example of such a death is the earth opening under the wicked Dathan and Abiram (Nm 16:31–32). The psalmist, confident of vindication, exhorts others to a like trust in the God of justice (Ps 55:23). The Psalm is not so much for personal vengeance as for a public vindication of God's righteousness now. There was no belief in an afterlife where such vindication could take place.

d: Ps 85:2. *e:* 1 Sm 23:19; 26:1. *f:* Ps 86:14. *g:* Ps 118:7. *h:* Ps 143:12. *i:* Ps 59:11; 91:8; 92:12. *j:* Ps 5:2–3; 86:6; 130:1–2; Lam 3:56; Jon 2:3. *k:* Ps 11:1. *l:* Jer 9:1; Rev 12:6. *m:* Jer 5:1; 6:6; Ez 22:2; Heb 1:3; Zep 3:1.

[13] For it is not an enemy that reviled me—
that I could bear—
Not a foe who viewed me with
contempt,
from that I could hide.
[14] But it was you, my other self,
my comrade and friend,[n]
[15] You, whose company I enjoyed,
at whose side I walked
in the house of God.

III

[16] Let death take them;
let them go down alive to Sheol,[o]
for evil is in their homes and bellies.
[17] But I will call upon God,
and the LORD will save me.
[18] At dusk, dawn, and noon
I will grieve and complain,
and my prayer will be heard.[p]
[19] He will redeem my soul in peace
from those who war against me,
though there are many who
oppose me.
[20] God, who sits enthroned forever,[q]
will hear me and afflict them. *Selah*
For they will not mend their ways;
they have no fear of God.
[21] He stretched out his hand at his friends
and broke his covenant.
[22] Softer than butter is his speech,
but war is in his heart.
Smoother than oil are his words,
but they are unsheathed swords.[r]
[23] Cast your care upon the LORD,
who will give you support.
He will never allow
the righteous to stumble.[s]
[24] But you, God, will bring them down
to the pit of destruction.[t]
These bloodthirsty liars
will not live half their days,
but I put my trust in you.[u]

PSALM 56*

See RG 244

Trust in God

[1]For the director. According to *Yonath elem rehoqim*.* A *miktam* of David, when the Philistines seized him at Gath.[v]

I

[2] Have mercy on me, God,
for I am treated harshly;
attackers press me all the day.
[3] My foes treat me harshly all the day;
yes, many are my attackers.
O Most High, [4]when I am afraid,
in you I place my trust.
[5] I praise the word of God;
I trust in God, I do not fear.[w]
What can mere flesh do to me?[x]

II

[6] All the day they foil my plans;
their every thought is of evil against
me.
[7] They hide together in ambush;
they watch my every step;
they lie in wait for my life.[y]
[8] They are evil; watch them, God!
Cast the nations down in your anger!
[9] My wanderings you have noted;
are my tears not stored in your flask,*
recorded in your book?[z]
[10] My foes turn back when I call on you.
This I know: God is on my side.
[11] I praise the word of God,
I praise the word of the LORD.
[12] In God I trust, I do not fear.
What can man do to me?

III

[13] I have made vows to you, God;
with offerings I will fulfill them,[a]
[14] For you have snatched me from death,
kept my feet from stumbling,
That I may walk before God
in the light of the living.

Psalm 56 Beset physically (Ps 56:2–3) and psychologically (Ps 56:6–7), the psalmist maintains a firm confidence in God (Ps 56:5, 9–10). Nothing will prevent the psalmist from keeping the vow to give thanks for God's gift of life (Ps 56:13). A refrain (Ps 56:5, 11–12) divides the Psalm in two equal parts.

56:1 Yonath elem rehoqim: Hebrew words probably designating the melody to which the Psalm was to be sung.

56:9 Are my tears not stored in your flask: a unique saying in the Old Testament. The context suggests that the tears are saved because they are precious; God puts a high value on each of the psalmist's troubles.

n: Ps 41:10; Jer 9:3; Mt 26:21–24 par. *o:* Ps 49:15; Nm 16:33; Prv 1:2; Is 5:14. *p:* Dn 6:11. *q:* Ps 29:10; 93:2; Bar 3:3. *r:* Ps 12:3; 28:3; 57:5; 62:5; 64:4; Prv 26:24–28; Jer 9:7. *s:* Ps 37:5; Prv 3:5; 16:3; 1 Pt 5:7. *t:* Ps 28:1; 30:4; 40:3; 88:5; 143:7; Prv 1:12; Jon 2:7. *u:* Ps 25:2; 56:4; 130:5. *v:* 1 Sm 21:10. *w:* Ps 130:5. *x:* Ps 118:6; Heb 13:6. *y:* Ps 140:5–6. *z:* Ps 10:14; 2 Kgs 20:5; Is 25:8; Rev 7:17. *a:* Nm 30:3.

PSALM 57*

See RG 244

Confident Prayer for Deliverance

1 For the director. Do not destroy.* A *miktam* of David, when he fled from Saul into a cave.[b]

I

2 Have mercy on me, God,
have mercy on me.
In you I seek refuge.
In the shadow of your wings* I seek refuge
till harm pass by.[c]
3 I call to God Most High,
to God who provides for me.
4 May God send help from heaven to save me,
shame those who trample upon me.
May God send fidelity and mercy. *Selah*
5 I must lie down in the midst of lions
hungry for human prey.[d]
Their teeth are spears and arrows;
their tongue, a sharpened sword.[e]
6 Be exalted over the heavens, God;
may your glory appear above all the earth.[f]

II

7 They have set a trap for my feet;
my soul is bowed down;
They have dug a pit before me.
May they fall into it themselves![g] *Selah*
8 My heart is steadfast, God,
my heart is steadfast.
I will sing and chant praise.[h]
9 Awake, my soul;
awake, lyre and harp!
I will wake the dawn.*[i]
10 I will praise you among the peoples, Lord;
I will chant your praise among the nations.[j]
11 For your mercy towers to the heavens;
your faithfulness reaches to the skies.[k]
12 Exalt yourself over the heavens, God;
may your glory appear above all the earth.

PSALM 58*

See RG 244

The Dethroning of Unjust Rulers

1 For the leader. Do not destroy.* A *miktam* of David.

I

2 Do you indeed pronounce justice, O gods;*
do you judge fairly you children of Adam?[l]
3 No, you freely engage in crime;
your hands dispense violence to the earth.

II

4 The wicked have been corrupt since birth;
liars from the womb, they have gone astray.
5 *Their venom is like the venom of a snake,
like that of a serpent stopping its ears,[m]

Psalm 57 Each of the two equal strophes contains a prayer for rescue from enemies, accompanied by joyful trust in God (Ps 57:2–5, 7–11). The refrain prays that God be manifested as saving (Ps 57:6, 12). Ps 108 is nearly identical to part of this Psalm (cf. Ps 57:8–11, Ps 108:2–6).

57:1 Do not destroy: probably the title of the melody to which the Psalm was to be sung.

57:2 The shadow of your wings: probably refers to the wings of the cherubim (powerful winged animals) whose wings spread over the ark in the inner chamber of the Temple (1 Kgs 6:23–28).

57:9 I will wake the dawn: by a bold figure the psalmist imagines the sound of music and singing will waken a new day.

Psalm 58 A lament expressing trust in God's power to dethrone all powers obstructing divine rule of the world. First condemned are "the gods," the powers that were popularly imagined to control human destinies (Ps 58:2–3), then "the wicked," the human instruments of these forces (Ps 58:4–6). The psalmist prays God to prevent them from harming the just (Ps 58:7–10). The manifestation of justice will gladden the just; they will see that their God is with them (Ps 58:11). The Psalm is less concerned with personal vengeance than with public vindication of God's justice now.

58:1 Do not destroy: probably the title of the melody to which the Psalm was to be sung.

58:2 Gods: the Bible sometimes understands pagan gods to be lesser divine beings who are assigned by Israel's God to rule the foreign nations. Here they are accused of injustice, permitting the human judges under their patronage to abuse the righteous, cf. Ps 82.

58:5–6 The image is that of a poisonous snake that is controlled by the voice or piping of its trainer.

b: 1 Sm 22:1. *c:* Ps 17:8; 36:8. *d:* Ps 17:11–12; 22:22; 58:7. *e:* Ps 11:2; 64:4. *f:* Ps 72:19; Nm 14:21. *g:* Ps 7:15; 9:16–17; 140:5–6. *h:* Ps 108:2. *i:* Jb 38:12. *j:* Ps 9:12; 18:50. *k:* Ps 36:6; 71:19. *l:* Ps 82:2; Dt 16:19. *m:* Ps 64:4; 140:3; Rom 3:13.

6 So as not to hear the voice of the charmer
or the enchanter with cunning spells.

III

7 O God, smash the teeth in their mouths;
break the fangs of these lions, LORD![n]
8 Make them vanish like water flowing away;[o]
trodden down, let them wither like grass.[p]
9 Let them dissolve like a snail that oozes away,*
like an untimely birth that never sees the sun.[q]
10 Suddenly, like brambles or thistles,
have the whirlwind snatch them away.[r]
11 Then the just shall rejoice to see the vengeance
and bathe their feet in the blood of the wicked.[s]
12 Then people will say:
"Truly there is a reward for the just;
there is a God who is judge on earth!"

PSALM 59*

See RG 244

Complaint Against Bloodthirsty Enemies

1 For the director. Do not destroy.* A *miktam* of David, when Saul sent people to watch his house and kill him.[t]

I

2 Rescue me from my enemies, my God;
lift me out of reach of my foes.
3 Deliver me from evildoers;
from the bloodthirsty save me.
4 They have set an ambush for my life;
the powerful conspire against me.
For no offense or misdeed of mine, LORD,
5 for no fault they hurry to take up arms.
Come near and see my plight!
6 You, LORD God of hosts, are the God of Israel!
Awake! Punish all the nations.
Have no mercy on these worthless traitors. *Selah*
7 Each evening they return,
growling like dogs, prowling the city.[u]
8 Their mouths pour out insult;
sharp words are on their lips.
They say: "Who is there to hear?"*
9 But you, LORD, laugh at them;
you deride all the nations.[v]
10 My strength, for you I watch;
you, God, are my fortress,
11 my loving God.

II

May God go before me,
and show me my fallen foes.
12 Slay them, God,
lest they deceive my people.
Shake them by your power;
Lord, our shield, bring them down.
13 For the sinful words of their mouths and lips
let them be caught in their pride.
For the lies they have told under oath[w]
14 destroy them in anger,
destroy till they are no more.
Then people will know God rules over Jacob,
yes, even to the ends of the earth.[x] *Selah*
15 Each evening they return,
growling like dogs, prowling the city.
16 They roam about as scavengers;
if they are not filled, they howl.

III

17 But I shall sing of your strength,
extol your mercy at dawn,
For you are my fortress,
my refuge in time of trouble.
18 My strength, your praise I will sing;
you, God, are my fortress, my loving God.

58:9 A snail that oozes away: empty shells suggested to ancients that snails melted away as they left a slimy trail.

Psalm 59 A lament in two parts (Ps 59:2–9, 11b–17), each ending in a refrain (Ps 59:10, 18). Both parts alternate prayer for vindication (Ps 59:2–3, 4b–5, 11b–14) with vivid depictions of the psalmist's enemies (Ps 59:4–5a, 7–8, 15–16). The near curse in Ps 59:12–13 is not a crude desire for revenge but a wish that God's just rule over human affairs be recognized now.

59:1 Do not destroy: probably the title of the melody to which the Psalm was to be sung.

59:8 Who is there to hear?: a sample of the enemies' godless reflection. The answer is that God hears their blasphemies.

n: Ps 3:7. *o:* Wis 16:29. *p:* Ps 37:2. *q:* Jb 3:16. *r:* Jb 21:18; Hos 13:3; Na 1:10. *s:* Ps 68:24; Is 63:1–6. *t:* 1 Sm 19:11. *u:* Ps 55:11. *v:* Ps 2:4; 37:13; Wis 4:18. *w:* Prv 12:13; 18:7. *x:* Ps 83:18–19; Ez 5:13.

See RG 244, 252

PSALM 60*
Lament After Defeat in Battle

1 For the leader; according to "The Lily of. . . . " A *miktam* of David (for teaching),
2 when he fought against Aram-Naharaim and Aram-Zobah; and Joab, coming back, killed twelve thousand Edomites in the Valley of Salt.[y]

I

3 O God, you rejected us, broke our defenses;
you were angry but now revive us.
4 You rocked the earth, split it open;[z]
repair the cracks for it totters.
5 You made your people go through hardship,
made us stagger from the wine you gave us.[a]
6 Raise up a banner for those who revere you,
a refuge for them out of bow shot.
Selah
7 *Help with your right hand and answer us
that your loved ones may escape.

II

8 *In the sanctuary God promised:
"I will exult, will apportion Shechem;
the valley of Succoth* I will measure out.
9 Gilead is mine, mine is Manasseh;
Ephraim is the helmet for my head,
Judah, my own scepter.*
10 *Moab is my washbowl;
upon Edom I cast my sandal.*[b]
I will triumph over Philistia."

III

11 Who will bring me to the fortified city?*
Who will lead me into Edom?
12 Was it not you who rejected us, God?
Do you no longer march with our armies?[c]
13 Give us aid against the foe;
worthless is human help.
14 We will triumph with the help of God,
who will trample down our foes.

See RG 244

PSALM 61*
Prayer of the King in Time of Danger

1 For the leader; with stringed instruments. Of David.

I

2 Hear my cry, O God,
listen to my prayer!
3 From the ends of the earth* I call;
my heart grows faint.
Raise me up, set me on a rock,
4 for you are my refuge,
a tower of strength against the foe.[d]
5 Let me dwell in your tent forever,
take refuge in the shelter of your wings.[e]
Selah

II

6 For you, O God, have heard my vows,
you have granted me the heritage of those who revere your name.
7 Add days to the life of the king;
may his years be as from generation to generation;[f]
8 [g]May he reign before God forever;
send your love and fidelity* to preserve him—[h]

Psalm 60 The community complains that God has let the enemy win the battle (Ps 60:3–5) and asks for an assurance of victory (Ps 60:6–7). In the oracle God affirms ownership of the land; the invasion of other nations is not permanent and will be reversed ultimately (Ps 60:8–10). With renewed confidence, the community resolves to fight again (Ps 60:11). The opening lament is picked up again (Ps 60:12), but this time with new awareness of God's power and human limitation.

60:7–12 These verses occur again as the second half of Ps 108.

60:8 I will . . . apportion . . . measure out: God lays claim to these places. **The valley of Succoth**: probably the lower stretch of the Jabbok valley.

60:9 Judah, my own scepter: an allusion to the Testament of Jacob, Gn 49:10.

60:10 Moab is my washbowl: Moab borders the Dead Sea, hence a metaphor for the country. **Upon Edom I cast my sandal**: an ancient legal gesture of taking possession of land.

60:11 The fortified city: perhaps Bozrah, the fortified capital of Edom, cf. Is 34:6; 63:1; Am 1:12.

Psalm 61 A lament of the king who feels himself at the brink of death (Ps 61:3) and cries out for the strong and saving presence of God (Ps 61:3b–5). The king cites the prayer being made for him (Ps 61:7–8), and promises to give thanks to God.

61:3 Ends of the earth: "earth" being taken in its occasional meaning "the underworld," cf. Jon 2:3.

61:8 Send your love and fidelity: as in Ps 43:3 the

y: 2 Sm 8:2, 3, 13; 1 Chr 18:2, 3, 12. *z:* Ps 75:4; Is 24:19. *a:* Ps 75:9; Is 51:17, 21–22; Jer 25:15. *b:* Ru 4:7–8. *c:* Ps 44:10. *d:* Ps 46:2. *e:* Ps 17:8; 36:8; 57:2. *f:* Ps 21:5. *g:* Ps 72:5; 89:5, 30, 37. *h:* Ps 85:11; 89:15, 25; Prv 20:28.

9 I will duly sing to your name forever,
fulfill my vows day after day.

PSALM 62*

See RG 245

Trust in God Alone

1 For the leader; *'al Jeduthun*.* A psalm of David.

I

2 My soul rests in God alone,[i]
from whom comes my salvation.
3 God alone is my rock and salvation,
my fortress; I shall never fall.
4 How long will you set yourself against a man?
You shall all be destroyed,
Like a sagging wall
or a tumbled down fence!
5 Even highly placed people
plot to overthrow him.
They delight in lies;
they bless with their mouths,
but inwardly they curse.[j] *Selah*

II

6 My soul, be at rest in God alone,
from whom comes my hope.
7 God alone is my rock and my salvation,
my fortress; I shall not fall.
8 My deliverance and honor are with God,[k]
my strong rock;
my refuge is with God.
9 Trust God at all times, my people!
Pour out your hearts to God our refuge! *Selah*

III

10 Mortals are a mere breath,
the sons of man but an illusion;[l]
On a balance they rise;*
together they weigh nothing.
11 Do not trust in extortion;
in plunder put no empty hope.
On wealth that increases,
do not set your heart.[m]
12 *One thing God has said;
two things I have heard:[n]
Strength belongs to God;
13 so too, my Lord, does mercy,
For you repay each man
according to his deeds.[o]

PSALM 63*

See RG 244

Ardent Longing for God

1 A psalm of David, when he was in the wilderness of Judah.[p]

I

2 O God, you are my God—
it is you I seek!
For you my body yearns;
for you my soul thirsts,
In a land parched, lifeless,
and without water.[q]
3 I look to you in the sanctuary
to see your power and glory.
4 For your love is better than life;*
my lips shall ever praise you!

II

5 I will bless you as long as I live;
I will lift up my hands, calling on your name.
6 My soul shall be sated as with choice food,
with joyous lips my mouth shall praise you!
7 I think of you upon my bed,
I remember you through the watches of the night

psalmist asks God to send these two divine attributes like angels to protect the king.

Psalm 62 A song of trust displaying serenity from experiencing God's power (the refrains of Ps 62:2–3 and Ps 62:6–7) and anger toward unjust enemies (Ps 62:4–5). From the experience of being rescued, the psalmist can teach others to trust in God (Ps 62:9–12).

62:1 'Al Jeduthun: apparently the Hebrew name for the melody.

62:10 On a balance they rise: precious objects were weighed by balancing two pans suspended from a beam. The lighter pan rises.

62:12 One thing . . . two things: parallelism of numbers for the sake of variation, a common device in Semitic poetry. One should not literally add up the numbers, cf. Am 1:3; Prv 6:16–19; 30:15, 18, 21.

Psalm 63 A Psalm expressing the intimate relationship between God and the worshiper. Separated from God (Ps 63:2), the psalmist longs for the divine life given in the Temple (Ps 63:3–6), which is based on a close relationship with God (Ps 63:7–9). May all my enemies be destroyed and God's true worshipers continue in giving praise (Ps 63:10–11)!

63:4 For your love is better than life: only here in the Old Testament is anything prized above life—in this case God's love.

i: Ps 18:3; 31:3–4; 42:10; 118:8; 146:3. *j:* Ps 12:3; 28:3; 55:22; Prv 26:24–25. *k:* Ps 3:3; Is 26:4; 60:19. *l:* Ps 39:6–7; 144:4; Jb 7:16; Wis 2:5. *m:* Jb 31:25; Eccl 5:9; Jer 17:11; Mt 6:19–21, 24. *n:* Jb 40:5. *o:* Ps 28:4; 31:24; 2 Sm 3:39; Jb 34:11; Jer 17:10; Mt 16:27; Rom 2:6; 2 Tm 4:14. *p:* 1 Sm 24. *q:* Ps 42:2; 143:6; Is 26:9.

8 You indeed are my savior,
and in the shadow of your wings I
shout for joy.[r]
9 My soul clings fast to you;
your right hand upholds me.

III

10 But those who seek my life will come to
ruin;
they shall go down to the depths of the
netherworld!
11 Those who would hand over my life to
the sword shall
become the prey of jackals!
12 But the king shall rejoice in God;
all who swear by the Lord* shall exult,
but the mouths of liars will be shut![s]

PSALM 64*

See RG 244

Treacherous Conspirators Punished by God

1 For the leader. A psalm of David.

I

2 O God, hear my anguished voice;
from a dreadful foe protect my life.
3 Hide me from the malicious crowd,
the mob of evildoers.
4 They sharpen their tongues like swords,
bend their bows of poison words.[t]
5 They shoot at the innocent from ambush,
they shoot him in a moment and do not
fear.
6 They resolve on their wicked plan;
they conspire to set snares;
they say: "Who will see us?"
7 They devise wicked schemes,
conceal the schemes they devise;
the designs of their hearts are hidden.[u]

II

8 God shoots an arrow at them;
in a moment they are struck down.[v]
9 They are brought down by their own
tongues;
all who see them flee.[w]
10 Every person fears and proclaims God's
actions,
they ponder his deeds.
11 The righteous rejoices and takes refuge
in the LORD;
all the upright give praise.[x]

PSALM 65*

See RG 245, 250

Thanksgiving for God's Blessings

1 For the leader. A psalm of David. A song.

I

2 To you we owe our hymn of praise,
O God on Zion;
To you our vows* must be fulfilled,
3 *you who hear our prayers.
To you all flesh must come[y]
4 with its burden of wicked deeds.
We are overcome by our sins;
only you can pardon them.[z]
5 Blessed the one whom you will choose
and bring
to dwell in your courts.
May we be filled with the good things of
your house,
your holy temple!

II

6 You answer us with awesome deeds* of
justice,
O God our savior,
The hope of all the ends of the earth
and of those far off across the sea.[a]
7 You are robed in power,
you set up the mountains by your
might.

63:12 All who swear by the Lord: to swear by a particular god meant that one was a worshiper of that god (Is 45:23; 48:1; Zep 1:5).

Psalm 64 A lament of a person overwhelmed by the malice of the wicked who are depicted in the Psalms as the enemies of the righteous (Ps 64:2–7). When people see God bringing upon the wicked the evil they intended against others, they will know who is the true ruler of the world (Ps 64:8–10). The final verse is a vow of praise (Ps 64:11).

Psalm 65 The community, aware of its unworthiness (Ps 65:3–4), gives thanks for divine bounty (Ps 65:5), a bounty resulting from God's creation victory (Ps 65:6–9). At God's touch the earth comes alive with vegetation and flocks (Ps 65:10–13).

65:2 Vows: the Israelites were accustomed to promising sacrifices in the Temple if their prayers were heard.

65:3 To you all flesh must come: all must have recourse to God's mercy.

65:6 Awesome deeds: the acts of creating—installing mountains, taming seas, restraining nations (Ps 65:7–8)—that are visible worldwide (Ps 65:6, 9).

r: Ps 17:8; 36:8. *s:* Ps 107:42. *t:* Ps 11:2; 37:14; 55:22; 57:5. *u:* Ps 140:3; Prv 6:14. *v:* Ps 7:13–14; 38:3; Dt 32:42. *w:* Ps 5:11; 44:14; 52:6. *x:* Ps 36:8; 57:2. *y:* Is 66:23. *z:* Ps 32:1–2; 78:38; Is 1:18. *a:* Is 66:19.

8 You still the roaring of the seas,[b]
the roaring of their waves,
the tumult of the peoples.[c]
9 Distant peoples stand in awe of your
marvels;
the places of morning and evening you
make resound with joy.
10 *You visit the earth and water it,
make it abundantly fertile.[d]
God's stream* is filled with water;
you supply their grain.
Thus do you prepare it:
11 you drench its plowed furrows,
and level its ridges.
With showers you keep it soft,
blessing its young sprouts.
12 You adorn the year with your bounty;
your paths* drip with fruitful rain.
13 The meadows of the wilderness also drip;
the hills are robed with joy.
14 The pastures are clothed with flocks,
the valleys blanketed with grain;
they cheer and sing for joy.[e]

PSALM 66*

See RG 245, 249

Praise of God, Israel's Deliverer

1 For the leader. A song; a psalm.

I

2 Shout joyfully to God, all the earth;
sing of his glorious name;
give him glorious praise.[f]
3 Say to God: "How awesome your deeds!
Before your great strength your
enemies cringe.
4 All the earth falls in worship before you;[g]
they sing of you, sing of your name!"
Selah

II

5 *Come and see the works of God,
awesome in deeds before the children
of Adam.
6 He changed the sea to dry land;
through the river they passed on foot.[h]
There we rejoiced in him,
7 who rules by his might forever,
His eyes are fixed upon the nations.
Let no rebel rise to challenge! *Selah*
8 Bless our God, you peoples;
loudly sound his praise,
9 Who has kept us alive
and not allowed our feet to slip.[i]
10 You tested us, O God,
tried us as silver tried by fire.[j]
11 You led us into a snare;
you bound us at the waist as captives.
12 *You let captors set foot on our neck;
we went through fire and water;
then you led us out to freedom.[k]

III

13 I will bring burnt offerings* to your
house;
to you I will fulfill my vows,
14 Which my lips pronounced
and my mouth spoke in my distress.
15 Burnt offerings of fatlings I will offer
you
and sacrificial smoke of rams;
I will sacrifice oxen and goats. *Selah*
16 Come and hear, all you who fear God,
while I recount what has been done
for me.

65:10–14 Apparently a description of the agricultural year, beginning with the first fall rains that soften the hard sun-baked soil (Ps 65:9–10).

65:10 God's stream: the fertile waters of the earth derive from God's fertile waters in the heavenly world.

65:12 Paths: probably the tracks of God's storm chariot dropping rain upon earth.

Psalm 66 In the first part (Ps 66:1–12), the community praises God for powerful acts for Israel, both in the past (the exodus from Egypt and the entry into the land [Ps 66:6]) and in the present (deliverance from a recent but unspecified calamity [Ps 66:8–12]). In the second part (Ps 66:13–20), an individual from the rescued community fulfills a vow to offer a sacrifice of thanksgiving. As often in thanksgivings, the rescued person steps forward to teach the community what God has done (Ps 66:16–20).

66:5–6 cf. the events described in Ex 14:1–15, 21; Jos 3:11–4:24 and Ps 114.

66:12 You let captors set foot on our neck: lit., "you let men mount our heads." Conquerors placed their feet on the neck of their enemies as a sign of complete defeat, cf. Jos 10:24. A ceremonial footstool of the Egyptian king Tutankhamen portrays bound and prostrate bodies of enemies ready for the king's feet on their heads, and one of Tutankhamen's ceremonial chariots depicts the king as a sphinx standing with paw atop the neck of an enemy.

66:13 Burnt offerings: cf. Lv 1:3–13; 6:1–4; 22:17–20.

b: Ps 89:10; 107:29; Jb 38:11; Mt 8:26. *c:* Is 17:12. *d:* Lv 26:4; Is 30:23, 25; Jl 2:22–23. *e:* Is 44:23. *f:* Ps 65:14; Is 44:23. *g:* Ps 18:45; Mi 7:17. *h:* Ps 74:15; 114:3; Ex 14:21f; Jos 3:14ff; Is 44:27; 50:2. *i:* Ps 91:12; 121:3; 1 Sm 2:9; Prv 3:23. *j:* Is 48:10. *k:* Is 43:2.

17 I called to him with my mouth;
praise was upon my tongue.
18 Had I cherished evil in my heart,
the Lord would not have heard.
19 But God did hear
and listened to my voice in prayer.
20 Blessed be God, who did not reject my prayer
and refuse his mercy.

PSALM 67*

See RG 245

Harvest Thanks and Petition

1 For the leader; with stringed instruments. A psalm; a song.

I

2 May God be gracious to us* and bless us;
may his face shine upon us.[l] *Selah*
3 So shall your way be known upon the earth,
your victory among all the nations.[m]
4 May the peoples praise you, God;
may all the peoples praise you!

II

5 May the nations be glad and rejoice;
for you judge the peoples with fairness,
you guide the nations upon the earth.[n] *Selah*
6 May the peoples praise you, God;
may all the peoples praise you!

III

7 The earth has yielded its harvest;
God, our God, blesses us.[o]
8 May God bless us still;
that the ends of the earth may revere him.

PSALM 68*

See RG 245, 250

The Exodus and Conquest, Pledge of Future Help

1 For the leader. A psalm of David; a song.

I

2 *May God arise;
may his enemies be scattered;
may those who hate him flee before him.[p]
3 As the smoke is dispersed, disperse them;
as wax is melted by fire,
so may the wicked perish before God.[q]
4 Then the just will be glad;
they will rejoice before God;
they will celebrate with great joy.

II

5 Sing to God, praise his name;
exalt the rider of the clouds.*
Rejoice before him
whose name is the LORD.[r]
6 Father of the fatherless, defender of widows[s]—
God in his holy abode,
7 God gives a home to the forsaken,
who leads prisoners out to prosperity,
while rebels live in the desert.*

Psalm 67 A petition for a bountiful harvest (Ps 67:7), made in the awareness that Israel's prosperity will persuade the nations to worship its God.

67:2 May God be gracious to us: the people's petition echoes the blessing pronounced upon them by the priests, cf. Nm 6:22–27.

Psalm 68 The Psalm is extremely difficult because the Hebrew text is badly preserved and the ceremony that it describes is uncertain. The translation assumes the Psalm accompanied the early autumn Feast of Tabernacles (Sukkoth), which included a procession of the tribes (Ps 68:25–28). Israel was being oppressed by a foreign power, perhaps Egypt (Ps 68:31–32)—unless Egypt stands for any oppressor. The Psalm may have been composed from segments of ancient poems, which would explain why the transitions are implied rather than explicitly stated. At any rate, Ps 68:2 is based on Nm 10:35–36, and Ps 68:8–9 are derived from Jgs 5:4–5. The argument develops in nine stanzas (each of three to five poetic lines): 1. confidence that God will destroy Israel's enemies (Ps 68:2–4); 2. call to praise God as savior (Ps 68:5–7); 3. God's initial rescue of Israel from Egypt (Ps 68:8), the Sinai encounter (Ps 68:9), and the settlement in Canaan (Ps 68:10–11); 4. the defeat of the Canaanite kings (Ps 68:12–15); 5. the taking of Jerusalem, where Israel's God will rule the world (Ps 68:16–19); 6. praise for God's past help and for the future interventions that will be modeled on the ancient exodus-conquest (Ps 68:20–24); 7. procession at the Feast of Tabernacles (Ps 68:25–28); 8. prayer that the defeated enemies bring tribute to the Temple (Ps 68:29–32); 9. invitation for all kingdoms to praise Israel's God (Ps 68:33–35).

68:2 The opening line alluding to Nm 10:35 makes clear that God's assistance in the period of the exodus and conquest is the model and assurance of all future divine help.

68:5 Exalt the rider of the clouds: God's intervention is in the imagery of Canaanite myth in which the storm-god mounted the storm clouds to ride to battle. Such theophanies occur throughout the Psalm: Ps 68:2–3, 8–10, 12–15, 18–19, 22–24, 29–32, 34–35. See Dt 33:26; Ps 18:8–16; Is 19:1.

68:7 While rebels live in the desert: rebels must live in

l: Ps 4:7; 31:17; 44:4; 80:4; Dn 9:17. *m:* Jer 33:9. *n:* Ps 98:9. *o:* Ps 85:13; Lv 26:4; Ez 34:27; Hos 2:23–24. *p:* Nm 10:35. *q:* Ps 97:5; Jdt 16:15; Wis 5:14; Mi 1:4. *r:* Ps 18:10; 104:3; Dt 33:26; Is 19:1. *s:* Ps 103:6; 146:7, 9; Ex 22:20–22; Bar 6:37.

III

8 God, when you went forth before your
people,[t]
when you marched through the desert,
Selah
9 The earth quaked, the heavens poured,
before God, the One of Sinai,
before God, the God of Israel.
10 You poured abundant rains, God,
your inheritance was weak and you
repaired it.
11 Your creatures dwelt in it;
you will establish it in your goodness
for the poor, O God.

IV

12 The Lord announced:
"Those bringing news are a great Army.
13 The kings of the armies are in
desperate flight.[u]
Every household will share the spoil,
14 though you lie down among the
sheepfolds,[v]
you shall be covered with silver as the
wings of a dove,
her feathers bright as fine gold."
15 When the Almighty routs the kings there,
it will be as when snow fell on
Zalmon.*

V

16 You mountain of God, mountain of
Bashan,
you rugged mountain, mountain of
Bashan,
17 You rugged mountains, why look with
envy
at the mountain* where God has
chosen to dwell,
where the LORD resides forever?[w]
18 God's chariots were myriad, thousands
upon thousands;
from Sinai the Lord entered the holy
place.
19 You went up to its lofty height;
you took captives, received slaves as
tribute,[x]
even rebels, for the LORD God to dwell.

VI

20 Blessed be the Lord day by day,
God, our salvation, who carries us.[y]
Selah
21 Our God is a God who saves;
escape from death is the LORD God's.
22 God will crush the heads of his enemies,
the hairy scalp of the one who walks in
sin.[z]
23 The Lord has said:
"Even from Bashan I will fetch them,
fetch them even from the depths of the
sea.*
24 You will wash your feet in your enemy's
blood;
the tongues of your dogs will lap it up."[a]

VII

25 *Your procession comes into view, O God,
your procession into the holy place,
my God and king.
26 The singers go first, the harpists follow;
in their midst girls sound the timbrels.[b]
27 In your choirs, bless God;
LORD, Israel's fountain.
28 In the lead is Benjamin, few in number;
there the princes of Judah, a large
throng,
the princes of Zebulun, the princes of
Naphtali, too.[c]

VIII

29 Summon again, O God, your power,
the divine power you once showed
for us,
30 From your temple on behalf of Jerusalem,
that kings may bring you tribute.
31 Roar at the wild beast of the reeds,*
the herd of mighty bulls, the calves of
the peoples;

the arid desert, whereas God's people will live in the well-watered land (Ps 68:8–11).

68:15 Zalmon: generally taken as the name of a mountain where snow is visible in winter, perhaps to be located in the Golan Heights or in the mountains of Bashan or Hauran east of the Sea of Galilee.

68:17 The mountain: Mount Zion, the site of the Temple.

68:23 Even from Bashan . . . from the depths of the sea: the heights and the depths, the farthest places where enemies might flee.

68:25–28 Your procession: the procession renews God's original taking up of residence on Zion, described in Ps 68:16–19.

68:31 The wild beast of the reeds: probably the Nile crocodile, a symbol for Egypt; see Ps 68:32 and Ez 29:2–5.

t: Ps 44:10; 114:4, 7; Jgs 5:4–5; Heb 12:26. *u:* Jgs 5:19, 22. *v:* Jgs 5:16. *w:* Ps 132:13–14; Ez 43:7. *x:* Ps 47:8; Eph 4:8–10. *y:* Ps 34:2; 145:2; Is 46:3–4; 63:9. *z:* Dt 32:42. *a:* Ps 58:11; 1 Kgs 21:19; 22:38; Is 63:1–6. *b:* Ps 81:2–3; 87:7; 149:3; 150:3–5; 2 Sm 6:5. *c:* Is 8:23.

trampling those who lust after silver
scatter the peoples that delight in war.
32 Let bronze be brought from Egypt,[d]
Ethiopia hurry its hands to God.[e]

IX

33 You kingdoms of the earth, sing to God;[f]
chant the praises of the Lord, *Selah*
34 Who rides the heights of the ancient heavens,
Who sends forth his voice as a mighty voice?
35 Confess the power of God,
whose majesty protects Israel,
whose power is in the sky.
36 Awesome is God in his holy place,
the God of Israel,
who gives power and strength to his people.[g]
Blessed be God!

PSALM 69*

See RG 244, 251

A Cry of Anguish in Great Distress

1 For the leader; according to "Lilies."*
Of David.

I

2 Save me, God,
for the waters* have reached my neck.[h]
3 I have sunk into the mire of the deep,
where there is no foothold.
I have gone down to the watery depths;
the flood overwhelms me.[i]
4 I am weary with crying out;
my throat is parched.
My eyes fail,
from looking for my God.[j]
5 More numerous than the hairs of my head
are those who hate me without cause.[k]
Those who would destroy me are mighty,
my enemies without reason.
Must I now restore
what I did not steal?*

II

6 God, you know my folly;
my faults are not hidden from you.
7 Let those who wait in hope for you,
LORD of hosts,
not be shamed because of me.
Let those who seek you, God of Israel,[l]
not be disgraced because of me.
8 For it is on your account I bear insult,
that disgrace covers my face.[m]
9 I have become an outcast to my kindred,
a stranger to my mother's children.[n]
10 Because zeal for your house has consumed me,*
I am scorned by those who scorn you.*[o]
11 When I humbled my spirit with fasting,[p]
this led only to scorn.
12 When I clothed myself in sackcloth;
I became a byword for them.
13 Those who sit in the gate gossip about me;
drunkards make me the butt of songs.

III

14 But I will pray to you, LORD,
at a favorable time.
God, in your abundant kindness,
answer me
with your sure deliverance.[q]
15 Rescue me from the mire,[r]
and do not let me sink.
Rescue me from those who hate me

Psalm 69 A lament complaining of suffering in language both metaphorical (Ps 69:2–3, 15–16, the waters of chaos) and literal (Ps 69:4, 5, 9, 11–13, exhaustion, alienation from family and community, false accusation). In the second part the psalmist prays with special emphasis that the enemies be punished for all to see (Ps 69:23–29). Despite the pain, the psalmist does not lose hope that all be set right, and promises public praise (Ps 69:30–36). The Psalm, which depicts the suffering of the innocent just person vividly, is cited often by the New Testament especially in the passion accounts, e.g., Ps 69:5 in Jn 15:25; Ps 69:22 in Mk 15:23, 36 and parallels and in Jn 19:29. The Psalm prays not so much for personal vengeance as for public vindication of God's justice. There was, at this time, no belief in an afterlife where such vindication could take place. Redress had to take place now, in the sight of all.

69:1 "Lilies": apparently the name of the melody.

69:2 Waters: the waters of chaos from which God created the world are a common metaphor for extreme distress, cf. Ps 18:5; 42:8; 88:8; Jon 2:3–6.

69:5 What I did not steal: the psalmist, falsely accused of theft, is being forced to make restitution.

69:10 Zeal for your house has consumed me: the psalmist's commitment to God's cause brings only opposition, cf. Jn 2:17. **I am scorned by those who scorn you**: Rom 15:3 uses the verse as an example of Jesus' unselfishness.

d: Ez 29:2ff. *e:* Is 18:7; 45:14. *f:* Ps 138:4. *g:* Ps 28:8; 29:11. *h:* Ps 18:5; 93:3–4; Jb 22:11. *i:* Ps 40:2; 124:4–5. *j:* Ps 25:15; 119:82; 123:2; 141:8; Is 38:14. *k:* Ps 40:13; Lam 3:52; Jn 15:25. *l:* Ps 40:17. *m:* Jer 15:15. *n:* Jb 19:13–15. *o:* Ps 119:139; Jn 2:17; Rom 15:3. *p:* Ps 109:24–25; Jb 30:9; Lam 3:14. *q:* Is 49:8. *r:* Ps 28:1; 30:4; 32:6; 40:3; 88:5; Prv 1:12.

and from the watery depths.
16 Do not let the flood waters
overwhelm me,
nor the deep swallow me,
nor the pit close its mouth over me.
17 Answer me, LORD, in your generous
love;
in your great mercy turn to me.
18 Do not hide your face from your servant;
hasten to answer me, for I am in
distress.[s]
19 Come and redeem my life;
because of my enemies ransom me.
20 You know my reproach, my shame, my
disgrace;
before you stand all my foes.
21 Insult has broken my heart, and I
despair;
I looked for compassion, but there was
none,[t]
for comforters, but found none.
22 Instead they gave me poison for my
food;
and for my thirst they gave me
vinegar.[u]

IV

23 May their own table be a snare for them,
and their communion offerings a trap.[v]
24 Make their eyes so dim they cannot see;
keep their backs ever feeble.
25 Pour out your wrath upon them;
let the fury of your anger overtake
them.
26 Make their camp desolate,
with none to dwell in their tents.[w]
27 For they pursued the one you struck,
added to the pain of the one you
wounded.
28 Heap punishment upon their punishment;
let them gain from you no vindication.
29 May they be blotted from the book of
life;
not registered among the just![x]

V

30 But here I am miserable and in pain;
let your saving help protect me, God,
31 *That I may praise God's name in song
and glorify it with thanksgiving.
32 That will please the LORD more than
oxen,
more than bulls with horns and hooves:[y]
33 "See, you lowly ones, and be glad;
you who seek God, take heart![z]
34 For the LORD hears the poor,
and does not spurn those in bondage.
35 Let the heaven and the earth praise him,
the seas and whatever moves in them!"

VI

36 For God will rescue Zion,
and rebuild the cities of Judah.[a]
They will dwell there and possess it;
37 the descendants of God's servants will
inherit it;
those who love God's name will dwell
in it.[b]

PSALM 70*

See RG 244

Prayer for Divine Help

1 For the leader; of David. For remembrance.

2 Graciously rescue me, God![c]
Come quickly to help me, LORD![d]
3 Let those who seek my life
be confused and put to shame.[e]
Let those who desire my ruin
turn back in disgrace.
4 Let those who say "Aha!"[f]
turn back in their shame.
5 But may all who seek you
rejoice and be glad in you,
Those who long for your help
always say, "God be glorified!"[g]
6 I am miserable and poor.
God, come to me quickly!
You are my help and deliverer.
LORD, do not delay!

69:31 That I may praise God's name in song: the actual song is cited in Ps 69:33–35, the word "praise" in Ps 69:35 referring back to "praise" in Ps 69:31.

Psalm 70 A lament of a poor and afflicted person (Ps 70:6) who has no resource except God, and who cries out to be saved from the enemy. The Psalm is almost identical to Ps 40:14–17.

s: Ps 102:3; 143:7. *t:* Lam 1:2. *u:* Lam 3:15; Mt 27:34, 48; Mk 15:23. *v:* Rom 11:9–10. *w:* Acts 1:20. *x:* Ps 139:16; Ex 32:32; Is 4:3; Dn 12:1; Mal 3:16; Rev 3:5. *y:* Ps 40:7; 50:8–9, 14; 51:18; Is 1:11–15; Hos 6:6; Am 5:21–22; Heb 10:5–8. *z:* Ps 22:27; 35:27; 70:5. *a:* Is 44:26; Ez 36:10. *b:* Ps 102:29; Is 65:9. *c:* Ps 40:14–18. *d:* Ps 71:12. *e:* Ps 35:4, 26. *f:* Ps 35:21, 25. *g:* Ps 35:27.

See RG 244

PSALM 71*

Prayer in Time of Old Age

I

[1] In you, LORD, I take refuge;[h]
let me never be put to shame.[i]
[2] In your justice rescue and deliver me;
listen to me and save me!
[3] Be my rock of refuge,
my stronghold to give me safety;
for you are my rock and fortress.[j]
[4] My God, rescue me from the hand of the wicked,
from the clutches of the evil and violent.[k]
[5] You are my hope, Lord;
my trust, GOD, from my youth.
[6] On you I have depended since birth;
from my mother's womb you are my strength;[l]
my hope in you never wavers.
[7] *I have become a portent to many,
but you are my strong refuge!
[8] My mouth shall be filled with your praise,
shall sing your glory every day.

II

[9] Do not cast me aside in my old age;
as my strength fails, do not forsake me.
[10] For my enemies speak against me;
they watch and plot against me.[m]
[11] They say, "God has abandoned him.
Pursue, and seize him!
No one will come to the rescue!"
[12] God, be not far from me;
my God, hasten to help me.[n]
[13] Bring to a shameful end
those who attack me;
Cover with contempt and scorn
those who seek my ruin.[o]
[14] I will always hope in you
and add to all your praise.
[15] My mouth shall proclaim your just deeds,
day after day your acts of deliverance,
though I cannot number them all.[p]
[16] I will speak of the mighty works of the Lord;
O GOD, I will tell of your singular justice.

III

[17] God, you have taught me from my youth;
to this day I proclaim your wondrous deeds.
[18] Now that I am old and gray,[q]
do not forsake me, God,
That I may proclaim your might
to all generations yet to come,[r]
Your power [19] and justice, God,
to the highest heaven.
You have done great things;[s]
O God, who is your equal?[t]
[20] Whatever bitter afflictions you sent me,
you would turn and revive me.
From the watery depths of the earth
once more raise me up.
[21] Restore my honor;
turn and comfort me,
[22] That I may praise you with the lyre
for your faithfulness, my God,
And sing to you with the harp,
O Holy One of Israel!
[23] My lips will shout for joy as I sing your praise;
my soul, too, which you have redeemed.
[24] Yes, my tongue shall recount
your justice day by day.
For those who sought my ruin
have been shamed and disgraced.

PSALM 72*

See RG 245

A Prayer for the King

[1] Of Solomon.[u]

I

[2] O God, give your judgment to the king;

Psalm 71 A lament of an old person (Ps 71:9, 18) whose afflictions are interpreted by enemies as a divine judgment (Ps 71:11). The first part of the Psalm pleads for help (Ps 71:1–4) on the basis of a hope learned from a lifetime's experience of God; the second part describes the menace (Ps 71:9–13) yet remains buoyant (Ps 71:14–16); the third develops the theme of hope and praise.

71:7 A portent to many: the afflictions of the sufferer are taken as a manifestation of God's anger, cf. Dt 28:46; Ps 31:12.

Psalm 72 A royal Psalm in which the Israelite king, as the representative of God, is the instrument of divine justice (Ps 72:1–4, 12–14) and blessing (Ps 72:5–7, 15–17) for the whole world. The king is human, giving only what he has received

h: Ps 31:2–4. *i:* Ps 25:2. *j:* Ps 18:3. *k:* Ps 140:2. *l:* Ps 22:11. *m:* Ps 3:2; 22:8. *n:* Ps 22:20. *o:* Ps 35:4; 40:15; 70:3. *p:* Ps 35:28. *q:* Is 46:3–4. *r:* Ps 22:31–32; 48:14–15; 145:4. *s:* Ps 72:18. *t:* Ps 86:8. *u:* Ps 99:4; Jer 23:5.

your justice to the king's son;*
That he may govern your people with justice,
your oppressed with right judgment,[v]
3 That the mountains may yield their bounty for the people,
and the hills great abundance,[w]
4 That he may defend the oppressed among the people,
save the children of the poor and crush the oppressor.

II

5 May they fear you with the sun,
and before the moon, through all generations.[x]
6 May he be like rain coming down upon the fields,
like showers watering the earth,[y]
7 That abundance may flourish in his days,
great bounty, till the moon be no more.

III

8 *May he rule from sea to sea,
from the river to the ends of the earth.[z]
9 May his foes kneel before him,
his enemies lick the dust.[a]
10 May the kings of Tarshish and the islands* bring tribute,
the kings of Sheba and Seba offer gifts.[b]
11 May all kings bow before him,
all nations serve him.[c]
12 For he rescues the poor when they cry out,
the oppressed who have no one to help.
13 He shows pity to the needy and the poor[d]
and saves the lives of the poor.
14 From extortion and violence he redeems them,
for precious is their blood* in his sight.

IV

15 Long may he live, receiving gold from Sheba,
prayed for without cease, blessed day by day.
16 *May wheat abound in the land,
flourish even on the mountain heights.
May his fruit be like that of Lebanon,
and flourish in the city like the grasses of the land.[e]
17 May his name be forever;
as long as the sun, may his name endure.[f]
May the tribes of the earth give blessings with his name;*
may all the nations regard him as favored.[g]
18 *Blessed be the LORD God, the God of Israel,
who alone does wonderful deeds.[h]
19 Blessed be his glorious name forever;
may he fill all the earth with his glory.[i]
Amen and amen.

20 The end of the psalms of David, son of Jesse.

Third Book—Psalms 73–89

PSALM 73*

See RG 245

The Trial of the Just

1 A psalm of Asaph.

How good God is to the upright,
to those who are pure of heart!

from God. Hence intercession must be made for him. The extravagant language is typical of oriental royal courts.

72:2 The king . . . the king's son: the crown prince is the king's son; the prayer envisages the dynasty.

72:8 From sea to sea . . . the ends of the earth: the boundaries of the civilized world known at the time: from the Mediterranean Sea (the western sea) to the Persian Gulf (the eastern sea), and from the Euphrates (the river) to the islands and lands of southwestern Europe, "the ends of the earth." The words may also have a mythic nuance—the earth surrounded by cosmic waters, hence everywhere.

72:10 Tarshish and the islands: the far west (Ps 48:6); Arabia and Seba: the far south (1 Kgs 10:1).

72:14 Their blood: cf. Ps 116:15.

72:16 The translation of the difficult Hebrew is tentative.

72:17 May the tribes of the earth give blessings with his name: an echo of the promise to the ancestors (Gn 12:3; 26:4; 28:14), suggesting that the monarchy in Israel fulfilled the promise to Abraham, Isaac, and Jacob.

72:18–19 A doxology marking the end of Book II of the Psalter.

Psalm 73 The opening verse of this probing poem (cf. Ps 37; 49) is actually the psalmist's hard-won conclusion from personal experience: God is just and good! The psalmist describes near loss of faith (Ps 73:2–3), occasioned by observing the wicked who blasphemed God with seeming impunity (Ps 73:4–12). Feeling abandoned despite personal righteousness, the psalmist

v: Prv 31:8–9. *w:* Is 52:7; 55:12. *x:* Ps 89:37–38; Jer 31:35. *y:* Dt 32:2; Is 45:8; Hos 6:3. *z:* Dt 11:24; Zec 9:10. *a:* Is 49:23; Mi 7:17. *b:* Ps 68:30; Is 60:5–6; 1 Kgs 10:1ff. *c:* Ps 47:8. *d:* Prv 31:9. *e:* Is 27:6; Hos 14:6–8; Am 9:13. *f:* Ps 21:7. *g:* Gn 12:3; 22:18; 26:4; Zec 8:13. *h:* Ps 41:14; 89:53; 106:48; 136:4. *i:* Ps 57:5; Nm 14:21.

I

2 But, as for me, my feet had almost
stumbled;
my steps had nearly slipped,
3 Because I was envious of the arrogant
when I saw the prosperity of the
wicked.[j]
4 For they suffer no pain;
their bodies are healthy and sleek.
5 They are free of the burdens of life;
they are not afflicted like others.
6 Thus pride adorns them as a necklace;
violence clothes them as a robe.
7 Out of such blindness comes sin;
evil thoughts flood their hearts.[k]
8 They scoff and spout their malice;
from on high they utter threats.[l]
9 *They set their mouths against the
heavens,
their tongues roam the earth.
10 *So my people turn to them
and drink deeply of their words.
11 They say, "Does God really know?"
"Does the Most High have any
knowledge?"[m]
12 Such, then, are the wicked,
always carefree, increasing their
wealth.

II

13 Is it in vain that I have kept my heart pure,
washed my hands in innocence?[n]
14 For I am afflicted day after day,
chastised every morning.
15 Had I thought, "I will speak as they do,"
I would have betrayed this generation
of your children.
16 Though I tried to understand all this,
it was too difficult for me,
17 Till I entered the sanctuary of God
and came to understand their end.*

III

18 You set them, indeed, on a slippery road;
you hurl them down to ruin.
19 How suddenly they are devastated;
utterly undone by disaster!
20 They are like a dream after waking, Lord,
dismissed like shadows when you
arise.[o]

IV

21 Since my heart was embittered
and my soul deeply wounded,
22 I was stupid and could not understand;
I was like a brute beast in your presence.
23 Yet I am always with you;
you take hold of my right hand.[p]
24 With your counsel you guide me,
and at the end receive me with honor.*
25 Whom else have I in the heavens?
None beside you delights me on earth.
26 Though my flesh and my heart fail,
God is the rock of my heart, my
portion forever.
27 But those who are far from you perish;
you destroy those unfaithful to you.
28 As for me, to be near God is my good,
to make the Lord GOD my refuge.
I shall declare all your works
in the gates of daughter Zion.*

PSALM 74*

See RG 244, 247

Prayer at the Destruction of the Temple

1 A *maskil* of Asaph.

I

Why, God, have you cast us off
forever?*[q]

could not bear the injustice until an experience of God's nearness in the Temple made clear how deluded the wicked were. Their sudden destruction shows their impermanence (Ps 73:13–20). The just can thus be confident, for, as the psalmist now knows, their security is from God (Ps 73:1, 23–28).

73:9 They set their mouths against the heavens: in an image probably derived from mythic stories of half-divine giants, the monstrous speech of the wicked is likened to enormous jaws gaping wide, devouring everything in sight.

73:10 The Hebrew is obscure.

73:17 And came to understand their end: the psalmist receives a double revelation in the Temple: 1) the end of the wicked comes unexpectedly (Ps 73:18–20); 2) God is with me.

73:24 And at the end receive me with honor: a perhaps deliberately enigmatic verse. It is understood by some commentators as reception into heavenly glory, hence the traditional translation, "receive me into glory." The Hebrew verb can indeed refer to mysterious divine elevation of a righteous person into God's domain: Enoch in Gn 5:24; Elijah in 2 Kgs 2:11–12; the righteous psalmist in Ps 49:16. Personal resurrection in the Old Testament, however, is clearly attested only in the second century B.C. The verse is perhaps best left unspecified as a reference to God's nearness and protection.

73:28 In the gates of daughter Zion: this reading follows the tradition of the Septuagint and Vulgate.

Psalm 74 A communal lament sung when the enemy in-

j: Ps 37:1; Jb 21:13. *k:* Jb 15:27. *l:* Ps 17:10. *m:* Ps 10:11; Jb 22:13. *n:* Ps 26:6; Mal 3:14. *o:* Jb 20:8. *p:* Ps 121:5. *q:* Ps 10:1; 44:24; 77:8.

Why does your anger burn against the
sheep of your pasture?[r]
2 Remember your people, whom you
acquired of old,
the tribe you redeemed as your own
heritage,
Mount Zion where you dwell.[s]
3 Direct your steps toward the utter
destruction,
everything the enemy laid waste in the
sanctuary.
4 Your foes roared triumphantly in the
place of your assembly;
they set up their own tokens of victory.
5 They hacked away like a forester
gathering boughs,
swinging his ax in a thicket of trees.
6 They smashed all its engraved work,
struck it with ax and pick.
7 They set your sanctuary on fire,
profaned your name's abode by razing
it to the ground.[t]
8 They said in their hearts, "We will
destroy them all!
Burn all the assembly-places of God in
the land!"
9 *Even so we have seen no signs for us,
there is no prophet any more,[u]
no one among us who knows for how
long.
10 How long, O God, will the enemy jeer?[v]
Will the enemy revile your name
forever?
11 Why draw back your hand,
why hold back your right hand within
your bosom?*

II

12 *Yet you, God, are my king from of old,
winning victories throughout the
earth.
13 You stirred up the sea by your might;[w]
you smashed the heads of the dragons
on the waters.[x]
14 You crushed the heads of Leviathan,[y]
gave him as food to the sharks.
15 You opened up springs and torrents,
brought dry land out of the primeval
waters.*
16 Yours the day and yours the night too;
you set the moon and sun in place.
17 You fixed all the limits of the earth;
summer and winter you made.[z]
18 Remember how the enemy has jeered,
LORD,
how a foolish people has reviled your
name.
19 Do not surrender to wild animals those
who praise you;
do not forget forever the life of your
afflicted.
20 Look to your covenant,
for the recesses of the land
are full of the haunts of violence.
21 Let not the oppressed turn back in
shame;
may the poor and needy praise your
name.
22 Arise, God, defend your cause;
remember the constant jeering of the
fools.
23 Do not forget the clamor of your foes,
the unceasing uproar of your enemies.

vaded the Temple; it would be especially appropriate at the destruction of Jerusalem in 587 B.C. Israel's God is urged to look upon the ruined sanctuary and remember the congregation who worshiped there (Ps 74:1–11). People and sanctuary are bound together; an attack on Zion is an attack on Israel. In the second half of the poem, the community brings before God the story of their origins—their creation (Ps 74:12–17)—in order to move God to reenact that deed of creation now. Will God allow a lesser power to destroy the divine project (Ps 74:18–23)?

74:1 Forever: the word implies that the disaster is already of long duration, cf. Ps 74:9 and note.

74:9 Even so we have seen no signs . . . : ancients often asked prophets to say for how long a divine punishment was to last, cf. 2 Sm 24:13. Here no prophet has arisen to indicate the duration.

74:11 Why hold back . . . within your bosom: i.e., idle beneath your cloak.

74:12–17 Comparable Canaanite literature describes the storm-god's victory over all-encompassing Sea and its allies (dragons and Leviathan) and the subsequent peaceful arrangement of the universe, sometimes through the placement of paired cosmic elements (day and night, sun and moon), cf. Ps 89:12–13. The Psalm apparently equates the enemies attacking the Temple with the destructive cosmic forces already tamed by God. Why then are those forces now raging untamed against your own people?

74:15 Waters: lit., "rivers" (cf. Ps 24:7; Isa 50:2) upon which, or from which, in primordial times the earth is created.

r: Ps 80:5. *s:* Ps 68:17; 132:13; Ex 15:17; Jer 10:16; 51:19. *t:* Ps 79:1; Is 64:10. *u:* Lam 2:9. *v:* Ps 89:47. *w:* Ps 89:10. *x:* Is 51:9–10. *y:* Jb 3:8; 40:25; Is 27:1. *z:* Gn 1.

PSALM 75*

See RG 245, 250

God the Judge of the World

1 For the leader. Do not destroy! A psalm of Asaph; a song.

I

2 We thank you, God, we give thanks;
we call upon your name,
we declare your wonderful deeds.
[You said:]*
3 "I will choose the time;
I will judge fairly.
4 Though the earth and all its inhabitants quake,
I make steady its pillars."[a] *Selah*

II

5 So I say to the boastful: "Do not boast!"[b]
to the wicked: "Do not raise your horns!*
6 Do not raise your horns against heaven!
Do not speak with a stiff neck!"[c]
7 For judgment comes not from east or from west,
not from the wilderness or the mountains,[d]
8 But from God who decides,
who brings some low and raises others high.[e]
9 Yes, a cup* is in the LORD's hand,
foaming wine, fully spiced.*
When God pours it out,
they will drain it even to the dregs;
all the wicked of the earth will drink.[f]
10 But I will rejoice forever;
I will sing praise to the God of Jacob,
11 [g][Who has said:]
"I will cut off all the horns of the wicked,
but the horns of the righteous will be exalted."

PSALM 76*

See RG 245, 249

God Defends Zion

1 For the leader; a psalm with stringed instruments. A song of Asaph.

I

2 Renowned in Judah is God,[h]
whose name is great in Israel.
3 On Salem* is God's tent, his shelter on Zion.
4 There the flashing arrows were shattered,
shield, sword, and weapons of war.[i] *Selah*

II

5 Terrible and awesome are you,
stronger than the ancient mountains.*
6 Despoiled are the stouthearted;
they sank into sleep;
the hands of all the men of valor have failed.[j]
7 At your roar, O God of Jacob,
chariot and steed lay still.
8 You, terrible are you;
who can stand before you and your great anger?[k]
9 From the heavens you pronounced sentence;
the earth was terrified and reduced to silence,
10 When you arose, O God, for judgment
to save the afflicted of the land. *Selah*
11 Surely the wrath of man will give you thanks;

Psalm 75 The psalmist gives thanks and rejoices (Ps 75:2, 10) for the direct intervention of God, which is promised in two oracles (Ps 75:3–4, 11). Expecting that divine intervention, the psalmist warns evildoers to repent (Ps 75:5–9).

75:2 You said: supplied for clarity here and in Ps 75:11. The translation assumes in both places that the psalmist is citing an oracle of God.

75:5 Do not raise your horns!: the horn is the symbol of strength; to raise one's horn is to exalt one's own power as Ps 75:5 explains.

75:9 A cup: "the cup of God's wrath" is the punishment inflicted on the wicked, cf. Is 51:17; Jer 25:15–29; 49:12; Eze 23:31–33. **Spiced**: lit., "a mixed drink"; spices or drugs were added to wine, cf. Prv 9:2, 5.

Psalm 76 A song glorifying Zion, the mountain of Jerusalem where God destroyed Israel's enemies. Zion is thus the appropriate site to celebrate the victory (Ps 76:3–4), a victory described in parallel scenes (Ps 76:5–7, 8–11). Israel is invited to worship its powerful patron deity (Ps 76:12).

76:3 Salem: an ancient name for Jerusalem, used here perhaps on account of its allusion to the Hebrew word for peace, *shalom*, cf. Gn 14:18; Heb 7:1–3.

76:5 Ancient mountains: conjectural translation of a difficult Hebrew phrase on the basis of Gn 49:26. The mountains are part of the structure of the universe (Ps 89:12–13).

---

a: Ps 46:3; 60:4; 93:1; 96:10; 104:5; 1 Sm 2:8; Is 24:19. *b:* 1 Sm 2:3; Zec 2:1–4. *c:* Jb 15:25. *d:* Mt 24:23–27. *e:* Jb 5:11; 1 Sm 2:7. *f:* Ps 60:5; Jb 21:20; Is 51:17, 21–22; Jer 25:15ff; Hab 2:16. *g:* Ps 92:11. *h:* Heb 3:2. *i:* Ps 46:10; 122:6–9. *j:* 2 Kgs 19:35; Jer 51:39; Na 3:18. *k:* Dt 7:21; 1 Sm 6:20; Na 1:6; Mal 3:2.

the remnant of your furor will keep
your feast.

III

12 Make and keep vows to the LORD your
God.[l]
May all around him bring gifts to the
one to be feared,
13 Who checks the spirit of princes,
who is fearful to the kings of earth.

See RG 244

PSALM 77*

Confidence in God During National Distress

1 For the leader; According to *Jeduthun*.
A psalm of Asaph.

I

2 I cry aloud to God,
I cry to God to hear me.
3 On the day of my distress I seek the Lord;
by night my hands are stretched out
unceasingly;[m]
I refuse to be consoled.
4 When I think of God, I groan;
as I meditate, my spirit grows faint.[n]
Selah
5 You have kept me from closing my eyes
in sleep;
I am troubled and cannot speak.
6 I consider the days of old;
the years long past 7 I remember.[o]
At night I ponder in my heart;
and as I meditate, my spirit probes:
8 "Will the Lord reject us forever,[p]
never again show favor?
9 Has God's mercy ceased forever?
The promise to go unfulfilled for
future ages?
10 Has God forgotten how to show mercy,
in anger withheld his compassion?"
Selah
11 * I conclude: "My sorrow is this,
the right hand of the Most High has
abandoned us."[q]

II

12 *I will recall the deeds of the LORD;
yes, recall your wonders of old.[r]
13 I will ponder all your works;
on your exploits I will meditate.
14 Your way, God, is holy;
what god is as great as our God?[s]
15 You are the God who does wonders;
among the peoples you have revealed
your might.[t]
16 With your mighty arm you redeemed
your people,
the children of Jacob and Joseph.[u]
Selah
17 The waters saw you, God;
the waters saw you and lashed about,
even the deeps of the sea* trembled.[v]
18 The clouds poured down their rains;
the thunderheads rumbled;
your arrows flashed back and forth.[w]
19 The thunder of your chariot wheels
resounded;
your lightning lit up the world;
the earth trembled and quaked.[x]
20 Through the sea was your way;
your path, through the mighty waters,
though your footsteps were unseen.[y]
21 You led your people like a flock
by the hand of Moses and Aaron.[z]

PSALM 78*

See RG 246

A New Beginning in Zion and David

1 A *maskil* of Asaph.

I

Attend, my people, to my teaching;
listen to the words of my mouth.

Psalm 77 A community lament in which the speaker ("I") describes the anguish of Israel at God's silence when its very existence is at stake (Ps 77:2–11). In response the speaker recites the story of how God brought the people into existence (Ps 77:12–20). The question is thus posed to God: Will you allow the people you created to be destroyed?

77:11 I conclude: lit., "I said." The psalmist, after pondering the present distress and God's promises to Israel, has decided that God has forgotten the people.

77:12 I will recall: the verb sometimes means to make present the great deeds of Israel's past by reciting them, cf. Ps 78:42; 105:5; 106:7.

77:17 The deeps of the sea: Heb. *tehom*; the same word is used in Gn 1:2, where it alludes to the primeval seas which in ancient Semitic cosmography are tamed by God in creation, cf. Ps 74:12–17; 89:12–13 and notes.

Psalm 78 A recital of history to show that past generations

l: Nm 30:3. *m:* Ps 50:15; 88:2. *n:* Jon 2:8. *o:* Ps 143:5; Dt 32:7. *p:* Ps 13:2; 44:24; 74:1; 80:5; 89:47; Lam 3:31. *q:* Ps 17:7; 18:36; Ex 15:6, 12. *r:* Ps 143:5. *s:* Ps 18:31; Ex 15:11. *t:* Ps 86:10; 89:6. *u:* Gn 46:26–27; Neh 1:10. *v:* Ps 18:16; 114:3; Na 1:4. *w:* Ps 18:14–15; 29; 144:6; Jb 37:3–4; Wis 5:21; Hab 3:10–11; Zec 9:14. *x:* Ps 18:8; 97:4; 99:1; Ex 19:16; Jgs 5:4–5. *y:* Neh 9:11; Wis 14:3; Is 51:10; Hab 3:15. *z:* Ps 78:52; Is 63:11–14; Hos 12:14; Mi 6:4.

2 I will open my mouth in a parable,*
unfold the puzzling events of the past.[a]
3 What we have heard and know;
things our ancestors have recounted to us.[b]
4 We do not keep them from our children;
we recount them to the next generation,
The praiseworthy deeds of the LORD and his strength,
the wonders that he performed.[c]
5 God made a decree in Jacob,
established a law in Israel:[d]
Which he commanded our ancestors,
they were to teach their children;
6 That the next generation might come to know,
children yet to be born.[e]
In turn they were to recount them to their children,
7 that they too might put their confidence in God,
And not forget God's deeds,
but keep his commandments.
8 They were not to be like their ancestors,
a rebellious and defiant generation,[f]
A generation whose heart was not constant,[g]
and whose spirit was not faithful to God.
9 The ranks of Ephraimite archers,*
retreated on the day of battle.
10 They did not keep God's covenant;
they refused to walk according to his law.
11 They forgot his deeds,
the wonders that he had shown them.

II

A

12 In the sight of their ancestors God did wonders,
in the land of Egypt, the plain of Zoan.*[h]
13 He split the sea and led them across,[i]
making the waters stand like walls.[j]
14 He led them with a cloud by day,
all night with the light of fire.[k]
15 He split rocks in the desert,
gave water to drink, abundant as the deeps of the sea.[l]
16 He made streams flow from crags,
caused rivers of water to flow down.

B

17 But they went on sinning against him,
rebelling against the Most High in the desert.[m]
18 They tested God in their hearts,
demanding the food they craved.[n]
19 They spoke against God, and said,
"Can God spread a table in the wilderness?[o]
20 True, when he struck the rock,
water gushed forth,
the wadies flooded.
But can he also give bread,
or provide meat to his people?"

C

21 The LORD heard and grew angry;[p]
fire blazed up against Jacob;
anger flared up against Israel.

did not respond to God's gracious deeds and were punished by God making the gift into a punishment. Will Israel fail to appreciate God's act—the choosing of Zion and of David? The tripartite introduction invites Israel to learn the lessons hidden in its traditions (Ps 78:1–4, 5–7, 8–11); each section ends with the mention of God's acts. There are two distinct narratives of approximately equal length: the wilderness events (Ps 78:12–39) and the movement from Egypt to Canaan (Ps 78:40–72). The structure of both is parallel: gracious act (Ps 78:12–16, 40–55), rebellion (Ps 78:17–20, 56–58), divine punishment (Ps 78:21–31, 59–64), God's readiness to forgive and begin anew (Ps 78:32–39, 65–72). While the Psalm has been thought to reflect the reunification program of either King Hezekiah (late eighth century) or King Josiah (late seventh century) in that the Northern Kingdom (Ephraim, Joseph) is especially invited to accept Zion and the Davidic king, a postexilic setting is also possible. Notable is the inclusion of the David-Zion tradition into the history of Israel recounted in the sources of the Pentateuch.

78:2 Parable: Hebrew *mashal* literally refers to some sort of relationship of comparison and can signify a story whose didactic potential becomes clear in the telling, as here in the retrospective examination of the history of Israel. Mt 13:35 cites the verse to explain Jesus' use of parables.

78:9 Ephraimite archers: Ephraim was the most important tribe of the Northern Kingdom. Its military defeat (here unspecified) demonstrates its infidelity to God, who otherwise would have protected it.

78:12, 43 Zoan: a city on the arm of the Nile, a former capital of Egypt.

a: Ps 49:5; Mt 13:35. *b:* Ps 44:2. *c:* Ex 10:2; Dt 4:9; Jb 8:8. *d:* Ps 147:19; Dt 33:4. *e:* Ps 22:31–32; Dt 4:9; 6:7. *f:* Dt 31:27; 32:5. *g:* Ps 95:10. *h:* Ps 106:7. *i:* Ps 136:13; Ex 14–15. *j:* Ex 14:22; 15:8. *k:* Ps 105:39; Ex 13:21; Wis 18:3. *l:* Ps 105:41; 114:8; Ex 17:1–7; Nm 20:2–13; Dt 8:15; Wis 11:4; Is 48:21. *m:* Dt 9:7; Ez 20:13. *n:* Ps 106:14; Ex 16:2–36. *o:* Ps 23:5. *p:* Nm 11; Dt 32:22.

22 For they did not believe in God,
did not trust in his saving power.
23 *So he commanded the clouds above;
and opened the doors of heaven.
24 God rained manna upon them for food;
grain from heaven he gave them.[q]
25 Man ate the bread of the angels;*
food he sent in abundance.
26 He stirred up the east wind in the skies;
by his might God brought on the south wind.
27 He rained meat upon them like dust,
winged fowl like the sands of the sea,
28 They fell down in the midst of their camp,
all round their dwellings.
29 They ate and were well filled;
he gave them what they had craved.
30 But while they still wanted more,
and the food was still in their mouths,
31 God's anger flared up against them,
and he made a slaughter of their strongest,
laying low the youth of Israel.[r]
32 In spite of all this they went on sinning,
they did not believe in his wonders.

D

33 God ended their days abruptly,
their years in sudden death.
34 When he slew them, they began to seek him;
they again looked for God.[s]
35 They remembered* that God was their rock,
God Most High, their redeemer.
36 But they deceived him with their mouths,
lied to him with their tongues.
37 Their hearts were not constant toward him;
they were not faithful to his covenant.[t]
38 *But God being compassionate forgave their sin;
he did not utterly destroy them.
Time and again he turned back his anger,
unwilling to unleash all his rage.[u]
39 He remembered that they were flesh,
a breath that passes on and does not return.

III

A

40 How often they rebelled against God in the wilderness,
grieved him in the wasteland.
41 Again and again they tested God,
provoked the Holy One of Israel.
42 They did not remember his power,
the day he redeemed them from the foe,[v]
43 *When he performed his signs in Egypt,
his wonders in the plain of Zoan.[w]
44 God turned their rivers to blood;
their streams they could not drink.
45 He sent swarms of insects that devoured them,[x]
frogs that destroyed them.
46 He gave their harvest to the caterpillar,
the fruits of their labor to the locust.
47 He killed their vines with hail,[y]
their sycamores with frost.
48 He exposed their cattle to plague,
their flocks to pestilence.[z]
49 He let loose against them the heat of his anger,
wrath, fury, and distress,
a band of deadly messengers.
50 He cleared a path for his anger;
he did not spare them from death,
but delivered their animals to the plague.
51 He struck all the firstborn of Egypt,[a]

78:23–31 On the manna and the quail, see Ex 16 and Nm 11. Unlike Ex 16, here both manna and quail are instruments of punishment, showing that a divine gift can become deadly because of Israel's apostasy.

78:25 Bread of the angels: the translation "angels" comports with the supernatural origin of the manna, though the Hebrew *lechem 'abbirim* is more literally translated as "bread of the strong ones" or "bread of the mighty." In the context of the manna event, this phrase cannot possibly mean the Israelites or any human being.

78:35 Remembered: invoked God publicly in worship. Their words were insincere (Ps 78:36).

78:38 God is always ready to forgive and begin anew, as in choosing Zion and David (Ps 78:65–72).

78:43–55 Ex 7–12 records ten plagues. Here there are six divine attacks upon Egypt; the seventh climactic act is God's bringing Israel to the holy land.

q: Ps 105:40; Ex 16:4, 14; Dt 8:3; Wis 16:20; Jn 6:31. *r:* Nm 14:29. *s:* Dt 32:15, 18; Is 26:16. *t:* Ps 95:10; Is 29:13. *u:* Ps 85:4; Ex 32:14; Is 48:9; Ez 20:22. *v:* Ps 106:21. *w:* Ps 105:27–36; 135:9; Ex 7:14–11:10; 12:29–36; Wis 16–18. *x:* Ex 8:17. *y:* Wis 16:16. *z:* Ex 9:3. *a:* Ps 105:36; 136:10; Ex 12:29.

the first fruits of their vigor in the tents
of Ham.
52 Then God led forth his people like sheep,
guided them like a flock through the
wilderness.[b]
53 He led them on secure and unafraid,
while the sea enveloped their
enemies.[c]
54 And he brought them to his holy
mountain,
the hill his right hand had won.[d]
55 He drove out the nations before them,
allotted them as their inherited portion,
and settled in their tents the tribes of
Israel.

B

56 But they tested and rebelled against God
Most High,
his decrees they did not observe.
57 They turned disloyal, faithless like their
ancestors;
they proved false like a slack bow.
58 They enraged him with their high places,
and with their idols provoked him* to
jealous anger.[e]

C

59 God heard and grew angry;
he rejected Israel completely.
60 He forsook the shrine at Shiloh,*[f]
the tent he set up among human beings.
61 He gave up his might into captivity,
his glorious ark into the hands of the
foe.[g]
62 God delivered his people to the sword;
he was enraged against his heritage.
63 Fire consumed their young men;
their young women heard no wedding
songs.[h]
64 Their priests fell by the sword;
their widows made no lamentation.

D

65 Then the Lord awoke as from sleep,
like a warrior shouting from the effects
of wine.
66 He put his foes to flight;
everlasting shame he dealt them.
67 He rejected the tent of Joseph,
chose not the tribe of Ephraim.
68 *God chose the tribe of Judah,
Mount Zion which he loved.[i]
69 He built his shrine like the heavens,
like the earth which he founded forever.
70 He chose David his servant,
took him from the sheepfolds.[j]
71 From tending ewes God brought him,
to shepherd Jacob, his people,
Israel, his heritage.[k]
72 He shepherded them with a pure heart;
with skilled hands he guided them.

PSALM 79*

See RG 244

A Prayer for Jerusalem

1 A psalm of Asaph.

I

O God, the nations have invaded your
inheritance;
they have defiled your holy temple;
they have laid Jerusalem in ruins.[l]
2 They have left the corpses of your servants
as food for the birds of the sky,
the flesh of those devoted to you for
the beasts of the earth.[m]
3 They have poured out their blood like
water
all around Jerusalem,
and no one is left to do the burying.[n]
4 We have become the reproach of our
neighbors,
the scorn and derision of those
around us.[o]

78:58 Provoked him: lit., "made him jealous."

78:60 Shiloh: an important shrine in the north prior to Jerusalem. Despite its holy status, it was destroyed (Ps 78:60–64; cf. Jer 7:12, 14).

78:68, 70 God's ultimate offer of mercy to the sinful, helpless people is Zion and the Davidic king.

Psalm 79 A communal lament complaining that the nations have defiled the Temple and murdered the holy people, leaving their corpses unburied (Ps 79:1–4). The occasion is probably the destruction of Jerusalem by the Babylonian army in 587 B.C. The people ask how long the withdrawal of divine favor will last (Ps 79:5), pray for action now (Ps 79:6–7), and admit that their own sins have brought about the catastrophe (Ps 79:8–9). They seek to persuade God to act for reasons of honor: the nations who do not call upon the Name are running amok (Ps 79:6); the divine honor is compromised (Ps 79:1, 10, 12); God's own servants suffer (Ps 79:2–4, 11).

b: Ps 77:21. *c:* Ex 14:26–28. *d:* Ex 15:17. *e:* Dt 32:16, 21. *f:* Jos 18:1; 1 Sm 1:3; Jer 7:12; 26:6. *g:* 1 Sm 4:11, 22. *h:* Dt 32:25; Jer 7:34. *i:* Ps 48:2; 50:2; Lam 2:15. *j:* Ps 89:21; Ez 34:23; 37:24; 2 Chr 6:6. *k:* 1 Sm 16:11–13; 2 Sm 7:8. *l:* 2 Kgs 25:9–10; Lam 1:10. *m:* Jer 7:33. *n:* 1 Mc 7:17; Jer 14:16. *o:* Ps 44:14; 80:7; 123:3–4; Jb 12:4; Dn 9:16; Zep 2:8.

II

5 How long, LORD? Will you be angry
forever?
Will your jealous anger keep burning
like fire?[p]
6 Pour out your wrath on nations that do
not recognize you,
on kingdoms that do not call on your
name,[q]
7 For they have devoured Jacob,
laid waste his dwelling place.
8 Do not remember against us the
iniquities of our forefathers;
let your compassion move quickly
ahead of us,
for we have been brought very low.[r]

III

9 Help us, God our savior,
on account of the glory of your name.
Deliver us, pardon our sins
for your name's sake.[s]
10 Why should the nations say,
"Where is their God?"[t]
Before our eyes make known to the
nations
that you avenge the blood of your
servants which has been poured
out.[u]

IV

11 Let the groaning of the imprisoned come
in before you;
in accord with the greatness of your
arm
preserve those doomed to die.[v]
12 Turn back sevenfold into the bosom of
our neighbors
the insult with which they insulted
you, Lord.[w]
13 Then we, your people, the sheep of your
pasture,
will give thanks to you forever;
from generation to generation
we will recount your praise.

PSALM 80*

See RG 244, 247

Prayer to Restore God's Vineyard

1 For the leader; according to "Lilies."
*Edutb.** A psalm of Asaph.

I

2 O Shepherd of Israel, lend an ear,
you who guide Joseph like a flock!
Seated upon the cherubim, shine forth[x]
3 upon Ephraim, Benjamin, and
Manasseh.
Stir up your power, and come to save us.
4 [y]O God, restore us;
light up your face and we shall be
saved.

II

5 LORD of hosts,
how long will you smolder in anger
while your people pray?[z]
6 You have fed them the bread of tears,
made them drink tears in great
measure.*[a]
7 You have left us to be fought over by our
neighbors;
our enemies deride us.[b]
8 O God of hosts, restore us;
light up your face and we shall be
saved.

III

9 You brought a vine* out of Egypt;
you drove out nations and planted it.
10 You cleared out what was before it;
it took deep root and filled the land.
11 The mountains were covered by its
shadow,
the cedars of God by its branches.
12 It sent out its boughs as far as the sea,*
its shoots as far as the river.*

Psalm 80 A community lament in time of military defeat. Using the familiar image of Israel as a vineyard, the people complain that God has broken down the wall protecting the once splendid vine brought from Egypt (Ps 80:9–14). They pray that God will again turn to them and use the Davidic king to lead them to victory (Ps 80:15–19).

80:1 Lilies . . . . Eduth: the first term is probably the title of the melody to which the Psalm was to be sung; the second is unexplained.

80:6 Both the Septuagint and the Vulgate translate this verse in the first person, i.e., "You have fed us the bread of tears."

80:9 A vine: a frequent metaphor for Israel, cf. Is 5:1–7; 27:2–5; Jer 2:21; Hos 10:1; Mt 21:33.

80:12 The sea: the Mediterranean. **The river**: the Euphrates.

p: Ps 13:2; 44:24; 89:47; Dt 4:24. *q:* Ps 14:4; Jer 10:25. *r:* Ps 142:7. *s:* Ez 20:44; 36:22. *t:* Ps 42:4; 115:2; Jl 2:17. *u:* Jl 4:21. *v:* Ps 102:21. *w:* Ps 89:51–52. *x:* Ps 23:1–3; 95:7; 100:3; Gn 48:15; Ex 25:22; 1 Sm 4:4; 2 Sm 6:2; Mi 7:14. *y:* Ps 4:7; 31:17; 67:2; 85:5; Nm 6:25; Dn 9:17. *z:* Ps 13:2; 44:24; 74:1; 79:5; 89:47; Dt 4:24. *a:* Ps 42:4; 102:10. *b:* Ps 44:14; 79:4; 123:3–4; Jb 12:4; Dn 9:16; Zep 2:8.

13 Why have you broken down its walls,
so that all who pass along the way
pluck its fruit?[c]
14 The boar from the forest strips the vine;
the beast of the field feeds upon it.[d]
15 Turn back again, God of hosts;
look down from heaven and see;
Visit this vine,
16 the stock your right hand has planted,
and the son* whom you made strong
for yourself.
17 Those who would burn or cut it down—
may they perish at your rebuke.
18 May your hand be with the man on your
right,*
with the son of man whom you made
strong for yourself.
19 Then we will not withdraw from you;
revive us, and we will call on your
name.
20 LORD God of hosts, restore us;
light up your face and we shall be
saved.

See RG 246

PSALM 81*

An Admonition to Fidelity

1 For the leader; "upon the *gittith*."*
Of Asaph.

I

2 Sing joyfully to God our strength;[e]
raise loud shouts to the God of Jacob!
3 Take up a melody, sound the timbrel,
the pleasant lyre with a harp.
4 *Blow the shofar at the new moon,
at the full moon, on our solemn feast.[f]
5 For this is a law for Israel,
an edict of the God of Jacob,[g]
6 He made it a decree for Joseph
when he came out of the land of
Egypt.

II

7 *I heard a tongue I did not know:
"I removed his shoulder from the
burden;*
his hands moved away from the
basket.*[h]
8 In distress you called and I rescued you;
I answered you in secret with thunder;
At the waters of Meribah* I tested you:[i]
9 'Listen, my people, I will testify
against you *Selah*
If only you will listen to me, Israel![j]
10 There shall be no foreign god among
you;*[k]
you shall not bow down to an alien
god.
11 'I am the LORD your God,
who brought you up from the land of
Egypt.
Open wide your mouth that I may fill
it.'
12 But my people did not listen to my
words;
Israel would not submit to me.
13 So I thrust them away to the hardness of
their heart;
'Let them walk in their own
machinations.'[l]
14 O that my people would listen to me,
that Israel would walk in my ways,[m]

cf. Gn 15:18; 1 Kgs 5:1. The terms may also have a mythic nuance—the seas that surround the earth; sea and river are sometimes paralleled in poetry.

80:16 The Vulgate and Septuagint use "son of man."

80:18 The man on your right: the Davidic king who will lead the army in battle.

Psalm 81 At a pilgrimage feast, probably harvest in the fall, the people assemble in the Temple in accord with the Sinai ordinances (Ps 81:2–6). They hear a divine word (mediated by a Temple speaker) telling how God rescued them from slavery in Egypt (Ps 81:7–9), gave them the fundamental commandment of fidelity (Ps 81:9–11), which would bring punishment if they refused to obey (Ps 81:12–13). But if Israel repents, God will be with them once again, bestowing protection and fertility (Ps 81:14–16).

81:1 Upon the gittith: probably the title of the melody to which the Psalm was to be sung or a musical instrument.

81:4 New moon . . . full moon: the pilgrimage feast of harvest began with a great assembly (Lv 23:24; Nm 29:1), used the new moon as a sign (Nm 29:6), and included trumpets (Lv 23:24).

81:7 I heard a tongue I did not know: a Temple official speaks the word of God (Ps 81:5b–16), which is authoritative and unlike merely human words (cf. Nm 24:4, 16).

81:7 I removed his shoulder from the burden: A reference to the liberation of Israel from slavery in Egypt. **The basket**: for carrying clay to make bricks, cf. Ex 1:14.

81:8 Meribah: place of rebellion in the wilderness; cf. Ex 17:7; Nm 20:13.

81:10 There shall be no foreign god among you: as in Ps 50 and 95, Israel is challenged to obey the first commandment.

c: Ps 89:41. *d:* Hos 2:14. *e:* Ps 43:4; 68:26; 149:3; 150:3–4; Jdt 16:1. *f:* Lv 23:24; Nm 29:1. *g:* Ex 23:14ff. *h:* Ex 1:14; 6:6. *i:* Ps 95:8; Ex 2:23ff; 17:7; 19:16; Nm 20:13; 27:14. *j:* Ex 1:14; 6:6. *k:* Ex 20:2–6; Dt 5:6–10. *l:* Jer 3:17; 7:24. *m:* Is 48:18.

15 In a moment I would humble their foes,
and turn back my hand against their oppressors.[n]
16 Those who hate the LORD will try flattering him,
but their fate is fixed forever.
17 But Israel I will feed with the finest wheat,
I will satisfy them with honey from the rock."[o]

See RG 246

PSALM 82*

The Downfall of Unjust Gods

1 A psalm of Asaph.

I

God takes a stand in the divine council,
gives judgment in the midst of the gods.[p]
2 "How long will you judge unjustly
and favor the cause of the wicked?[q] *Selah*
3 "Defend the lowly and fatherless;
render justice to the afflicted and needy.
4 Rescue the lowly and poor;
deliver them from the hand of the wicked."[r]

II

5 *The gods neither know nor understand,
wandering about in darkness,
and all the world's foundations shake.
6 I declare: "Gods though you be,*[s]
offspring of the Most High all of you,
7 Yet like any mortal you shall die;
like any prince you shall fall."
8 Arise, O God, judge the earth,*
for yours are all the nations.

PSALM 83*

See RG 244, 246

Prayer Against a Hostile Alliance

1 A song; a psalm of Asaph.

I

2 God, do not be silent;
God, do not be deaf or remain unmoved![t]
3 See how your enemies rage;
your foes proudly raise their heads.
4 They conspire against your people,
plot against those you protect.[u]
5 They say, "Come, let us wipe them out as a nation;
let Israel's name be remembered no more!"
6 They scheme with one mind,
they have entered into a covenant against you:[v]
7 *The tents of Edom and the Ishmaelites,
of Moab and the Hagrites,[w]
8 Gebal, Ammon, and Amalek,[x]
Philistia and the inhabitants of Tyre.[y]
9 Assyria, too, in league with them,
backs the descendants of Lot. *Selah*

II

10 *Deal with them as with Midian;
as with Sisera and Jabin at the wadi Kishon,[z]

ment of fidelity to God after the proclamation of the exodus.

Psalm 82 As in Ps 58, the pagan gods are seen as subordinate divine beings to whom Israel's God had delegated oversight of the foreign countries in the beginning (Dt 32:8–9). Now God arises in the heavenly assembly (Ps 82:1) to rebuke the unjust "gods" (Ps 82:2–4), who are stripped of divine status and reduced in rank to mortals (Ps 82:5–7). They are accused of misruling the earth by not upholding the poor. A short prayer for universal justice concludes the Psalm (Ps 82:8).

82:5 The gods are blind and unable to declare what is right. Their misrule shakes earth's foundations (cf. Ps 11:3; 75:4), which God made firm in creation (Ps 96:10).

82:6 I declare: "Gods though you be": in Jn 10:34 Jesus uses the verse to prove that those to whom the word of God is addressed can fittingly be called "gods."

82:8 Judge the earth: according to Dt 32:8–9, Israel's God had originally assigned jurisdiction over the foreign nations to the subordinate deities, keeping Israel as a personal possession. Now God will directly take over the rulership of the whole world.

Psalm 83 The community lament complains to God of the nations' attempts to wipe out the name of Israel (Ps 83:1–8). The psalmist sees all Israel's enemies throughout its history united in a conspiracy (Ps 83:2–8). May God destroy the current crop of enemies as the enemies of old were destroyed (Ps 83:9–12), and may they be pursued until they acknowledge the name of Israel's God (Ps 83:13–18).

83:7–9 Apart from the Assyrians, all the nations listed here were neighbors of Israel. The Hagrites are a tribe of the desert regions east of Ammon and Moab (1 Chr 5:10, 19–22). Gebal is the Phoenician city of Byblos or perhaps a mountain region south of the Dead Sea. The descendants of Lot are Moab and Edom (Gn 19:36–38 and Dt 2:9). These nations were never united against Israel in the same period; the Psalm has lumped them all together.

83:10–13 For the historical events, see Jgs 4–8.

---

n: Lv 26:7–8. *o:* Ps 147:14; Dt 32:13–14. *p:* Is 3:13–14. *q:* Ps 58:2. *r:* Dt 1:17. *s:* 2 Pt 1:4. *t:* Ps 10:1; 44:24; 109:1. *u:* Jer 11:9. *v:* Ps 2:2. *w:* Nm 20:23; 1 Chr 5:10, 19. *x:* Ex 17:8. *y:* Jos 13:2. *z:* Ex 2:15; Is 9:3; 10:26.

11 Those destroyed at Endor,
who became dung for the ground.[a]
12 Make their nobles like Oreb and Zeeb,
all their princes like Zebah and Zalmunna,
13 Who made a plan together,
"Let us take for ourselves the pastures of God."
14 My God, make them like tumbleweed,
into chaff flying before the wind.[b]
15 As a fire raging through a forest,
a flame setting mountains ablaze,[c]
16 Pursue them with your tempest;
terrify them with your storm-wind.
17 Cover their faces with shame,
till they seek your name,* LORD.
18 Let them be ashamed and terrified forever;
let them perish in disgrace.
19 Let them know that your name is LORD,
you alone are the Most High over all the earth.[d]

PSALM 84*

See RG 245

Prayer of a Pilgrim to Jerusalem

1 For the leader; "upon the *gittith*." A psalm of the Korahites.

I

2 How lovely your dwelling,
O LORD of hosts![e]
3 My soul yearns and pines
for the courts of the LORD.[f]
My heart and flesh cry out
for the living God.
4 *As the sparrow finds a home
and the swallow a nest to settle her young,
My home is by your altars,
LORD of hosts, my king and my God![g]
5 Blessed are those who dwell in your house!
They never cease to praise you. *Selah*

II

6 Blessed the man who finds refuge in you,
in their hearts are pilgrim roads.
7 As they pass through the Baca valley,*
they find spring water to drink.
The early rain covers it with blessings.
8 They will go from strength to strength*
and see the God of gods on Zion.

III

9 LORD God of hosts, hear my prayer;
listen, God of Jacob. *Selah*
10 *O God, watch over our shield;
look upon the face of your anointed.[h]

IV

11 Better one day in your courts
than a thousand elsewhere.
Better the threshold of the house of my God
than a home in the tents of the wicked.
12 For a sun and shield is the LORD God,
bestowing all grace and glory.
The LORD withholds no good thing
from those who walk without reproach.
13 O LORD of hosts,
blessed the man who trusts in you!

PSALM 85*

See RG 244, 250

Prayer for Divine Favor

1 For the leader. A psalm of the Korahites.

I

2 You once favored, LORD, your land,
restored the captives of Jacob.[i]

83:17 Seek your name: a variant of the more typical phrase "to seek the face of God" (Ps 24:6; 27:8; 105:4). Seeking the face of God refers to the worshiper having recourse to a temple or sanctuary where in non-Jewish contexts a statue embodies the physical presence of the Deity. In Israel's aniconic tradition no visible image or statue can represent God. This understanding is conveyed here concretely by use of the term "your name" rather than the more typical "your face."

Psalm 84 Israelites celebrated three pilgrimage feasts in Jerusalem annually. The Psalm expresses the sentiments of the pilgrims eager to enjoy the divine presence.

84:4 The desire of a restless bird for a secure home is an image of the desire of a pilgrim for the secure house of God, cf. Ps 42:2–3, where the image for the desire of the pilgrim is the thirst of the deer for water.

84:7 Baca valley: Hebrew obscure; probably a valley on the way to Jerusalem.

84:8 Strength to strength: pass through outer and inner wall.

84:10 Our shield . . . your anointed: the king had a role in the liturgical celebration. For the king as shield, cf. Ps 89:19.

Psalm 85 A national lament reminding God of past favors and forgiveness (Ps 85:2–4) and begging for forgiveness and grace now (Ps 85:5–8). A speaker represents the people who wait humbly with open hearts (Ps 85:9–10): God will be ac-

a: Jer 8:2. *b:* Ps 1:4; 35:5; 58:10; Is 5:24; 10:17; 17:13; 29:5; Ez 21:3. *c:* Ps 50:3. *d:* Ps 97:9; Dt 4:39; Dn 3:45. *e:* Ps 43:3–4; 122:1. *f:* Ps 42:2–3; 63:2–3; 143:6; Is 26:9. *g:* Ps 5:3. *h:* Ps 89:19. *i:* Ps 14:7; 126:4.

3 You forgave the guilt of your people,
pardoned all their sins. *Selah*
4 You withdrew all your wrath,
turned back from your burning anger.[j]

II

5 Restore us, God of our salvation;
let go of your displeasure with us.[k]
6 Will you be angry with us forever,
prolong your anger for all generations?[l]
7 Certainly you will again restore our life,
that your people may rejoice in you.
8 Show us, LORD, your mercy;
grant us your salvation.

III

9 *I will listen for what God, the LORD, has to say;
surely he will speak of peace
To his people and to his faithful.
May they not turn to foolishness!
10 Near indeed is his salvation for those who fear him;
glory will dwell in our land.
11 *Love and truth will meet;
justice and peace will kiss.[m]
12 Truth will spring from the earth;
justice will look down from heaven.[n]
13 Yes, the LORD will grant his bounty;
our land will yield its produce.[o]
14 Justice will march before him,
and make a way for his footsteps.

See RG 244, 250

PSALM 86*

Prayer in Time of Distress

1 A prayer of David.

I

Incline your ear, LORD, and answer me,
for I am poor and oppressed.
2 Preserve my life, for I am devoted;
save your servant who trusts in you.
You are my God; 3 be gracious to me, Lord;
to you I call all the day.
4 Gladden the soul of your servant;
to you, Lord, I lift up my soul.[p]
5 Lord, you are good and forgiving,
most merciful to all who call on you.[q]
6 LORD, hear my prayer;
listen to my cry for help.[r]
7 On the day of my distress I call to you,
for you will answer me.

II

8 None among the gods can equal you, O Lord;
nor can their deeds compare to yours.[s]
9 All the nations you have made shall come
to bow before you, Lord,
and give honor to your name.[t]
10 For you are great and do wondrous deeds;
and you alone are God.

III

11 Teach me, LORD, your way
that I may walk in your truth,[u]
single-hearted and revering your name.
12 I will praise you with all my heart,
glorify your name forever, Lord my God.
13 Your mercy to me is great;
you have rescued me from the depths of Sheol.[v]
14 O God, the arrogant have risen against me;
a ruthless band has sought my life;
to you they pay no heed.
15 But you, Lord, are a compassionate and gracious God,
slow to anger, abounding in mercy and truth.[w]
16 Turn to me, be gracious to me;
give your strength to your servant;
save the son of your handmaid.[x]
17 Give me a sign of your favor:
make my enemies see, to their confusion,
that you, LORD, help and comfort me.

tive on their behalf (Ps 85:11–13). The situation suggests the conditions of Judea during the early postexilic period, the fifth century B.C.; the thoughts are similar to those of postexilic prophets (Hg 1:5–11; 2:6–9).

85:9 The prophet listens to God's revelation, cf. Heb 2:1.

85:11–13 Divine activity is personified as pairs of virtues.

Psalm 86 An individual lament. The psalmist, "poor and oppressed" (Ps 86:1), "devoted" (Ps 86:2), "your servant" (Ps 86:2, 4, 16), "rescued . . . from the depths of Sheol" (Ps 86:13), attacked by the ruthless (Ps 86:14), desires only God's protection (Ps 86:1–7, 11–17).

j: Ps 78:38; Ex 32:14; Is 48:9. *k:* Ps 80:4. *l:* Ps 79:5; 89:47. *m:* Ps 89:15; 97:2. *n:* Is 45:8. *o:* Ps 67:7; Lv 26:4; Ez 34:27; Hos 2:23–24; Zec 8:12. *p:* Ps 25:1; 143:8. *q:* Jl 2:13. *r:* Ps 5:2; 130:1–2. *s:* Ps 35:10; 89:9; Ex 15:11; Dt 3:24; Jer 10:6. *t:* Ps 22:28; Zec 14:16; Rev 15:4. *u:* Ps 25:4; 26:3; 27:11; 119:12, 35; 143:8, 10. *v:* Ps 30:4; 40:3; Jon 2:7. *w:* Ps 103:8; 130:7; 145:8; Ex 34:6. *x:* Ps 25:16; 116:16; Wis 9:5.

See RG 245

PSALM 87*

Zion the True Birthplace

1 [y]A psalm of the Korahites. A song.

I

His foundation is on holy mountains,
2 The LORD loves the gates* of Zion
more than any dwelling in Jacob.
3 Glorious things are said of you,
O city of God! *Selah*

II

4 Rahab and Babylon I count
among those who know me.
See, Philistia and Tyre, with Ethiopia,
"This one was born there."
5 *And of Zion it will be said:
"Each one was born in it."[z]
The Most High will establish it;[a]
6 the LORD notes in the register of the peoples:
"This one was born there."[b] *Selah*
7 So singers and dancers:
"All my springs are in you."[c]

See RG 244

PSALM 88*

A Despairing Lament

1 A song; a psalm of the Korahites. For the leader; according to *Mahalath*. For singing; a *maskil* of Heman the Ezrahite.

I

2 LORD, the God of my salvation, I call out by day;
at night I cry aloud in your presence.[d]
3 Let my prayer come before you;
incline your ear to my cry.[e]
4 *For my soul is filled with troubles;[f]
my life draws near to Sheol.
5 I am reckoned with those who go down to the pit;
I am like a warrior without strength.
6 My couch is among the dead,
like the slain who lie in the grave.
You remember them no more;
they are cut off from your influence.
7 You plunge me into the bottom of the pit,
into the darkness of the abyss.
8 Your wrath lies heavy upon me;
all your waves crash over me.[g] *Selah*

II

9 Because of you my acquaintances shun me;
you make me loathsome to them;[h]
Caged in, I cannot escape;
10 my eyes grow dim from trouble.
All day I call on you, LORD;
I stretch out my hands to you.
11 *Do you work wonders for the dead?
Do the shades arise and praise you?[i] *Selah*

III

12 Is your mercy proclaimed in the grave,
your faithfulness among those who have perished?*
13 Are your marvels declared in the darkness,
your righteous deeds in the land of oblivion?

IV

14 But I cry out to you, LORD;
in the morning my prayer comes before you.
15 Why do you reject my soul, LORD,
and hide your face from me?
16 I have been mortally afflicted since youth;
I have borne your terrors and I am made numb.
17 Your wrath has swept over me;
your terrors have destroyed me.[j]
18 All day they surge round like a flood;
from every side they encircle me.

Psalm 87 A song of Zion, like Ps 46; 48; 76; 132.

87:2 The gates: the city itself, a common Hebrew idiom.

87:5–6 The bond between the exile and the holy city was so strong as to override the exile's citizenship of lesser cities.

Psalm 88 A lament in which the psalmist prays for rescue from the alienation of approaching death. Each of the three stanzas begins with a call to God (Ps 88:2, 10, 14) and complains of the death that separates one from God. The tone is persistently grim.

88:4–8 In imagination the psalmist already experiences the alienation of Sheol.

88:11–13 The psalmist seeks to persuade God to act out of concern for divine honor: the shades give you no worship, so keep me alive to offer you praise.

88:12 Perished: lit., "Abaddon," the deepest part of Sheol.

y: Ps 76:2–3; 78:68–69. *z:* Gal 4:26. *a:* Ps 48:9. *b:* Is 4:3. *c:* Ps 68:26; 149:3. *d:* Ps 77:3. *e:* Ps 119:170. *f:* Ps 28:1; 30:4; 40:3; 86:13; 143:7; Nm 16:33; Jb 17:1; Jon 2:7. *g:* Ps 18:5; 32:6; 42:8; 69:2; Jon 2:4. *h:* Ps 38:12; 79:4; 80:7; 123:3–4; 142:8; Jb 12:4; 19:13; Lam 3:7; Dn 9:16. *i:* Ps 6:6; 30:10; 38:18; 115:17. *j:* Jb 6:4; 20:25.

19 Because of you friend and neighbor shun
me;[k]
my only friend is darkness.

See RG 244, 250

PSALM 89*

A Lament over God's Promise to David

1 A *maskil* of Ethan the Ezrahite.

A

I

2 I will sing of your mercy forever, LORD[l]
proclaim your faithfulness through all
ages.
3 *For I said, "My mercy is established
forever;
my faithfulness will stand as long as
the heavens.
4 I have made a covenant with my chosen
one;
I have sworn to David my servant:
5 I will make your dynasty stand forever
and establish your throne through all
ages."[m] *Selah*

II

6 The heavens praise your marvels, LORD,
your loyalty in the assembly of the
holy ones.[n]
7 Who in the skies ranks with the LORD?
Who is like the LORD among the sons
of the gods?*[o]
8 A God dreaded in the council of the holy
ones,
greater and more awesome than all
those around him!
9 LORD, God of hosts, who is like you?
Mighty LORD, your faithfulness
surrounds you.
10 You rule the raging sea;[p]
you still its swelling waves.
11 You crush Rahab* with a mortal blow;
with your strong arm you scatter your
foes.
12 Yours are the heavens, yours the earth;
you founded the world and everything
in it.[q]
13 *Zaphon and Amanus you created;
Tabor and Hermon rejoice in your
name.
14 You have a mighty arm.
Your hand is strong; your right hand is
ever exalted.
15 Justice and judgment are the foundation
of your throne;
mercy and faithfulness march before
you.[r]
16 Blessed the people who know the war cry,
who walk in the radiance of your face,
LORD.
17 In your name they sing joyfully all the
day;
they rejoice in your righteousness.[s]
18 You are their majestic strength;
by your favor our horn* is exalted.[t]
19 Truly the LORD is our shield,
the Holy One of Israel, our king![u]

III

20 Then you spoke in vision;[v]
to your faithful ones you said:
"I have set a leader over the warriors;
I have raised up a chosen one from the
people.

Psalm 89 The community laments the defeat of the Davidic king, to whom God promised kingship as enduring as the heavens (Ps 89:2–5). The Psalm narrates how God became king of the divine beings (Ps 89:6–9) and how the Davidic king became king of earthly kings (Ps 89:20–38). Since the defeat of the king calls into question God's promise, the community ardently prays God to be faithful to the original promise to David (Ps 89:39–52).

89:3–5 David's dynasty is to be as long-lasting as the heavens, a statement reinforced by using the same verbs (establish, stand) both of the divine love and loyalty and of the Davidic dynasty and throne, cf. Ps 89:29–30.

89:7 The sons of the gods: "the holy ones" and "courtiers" of Ps 89:6, 8. These heavenly spirits are members of God's court.

89:11 Rahab: a mythological sea monster whose name is used in the Bible mainly as a personification of primeval chaos, cf. Jb 9:13; 26:12; Ps 74:13–14; Is 51:9.

89:13 Zaphon and Amanus: two sacred mountains in northern Syria which came to designate the directions of north and south. **Tabor**: a high hill in the valley of Jezreel in northern Israel. **Hermon**: a mountain in Lebanon, forming the southern spur of the Anti-Lebanon range.

89:18, 25 Horn: a concrete noun for an abstract quality; horn is a symbol of strength.

k: Jb 19:13. *l:* Is 63:7. *m:* Ps 61:7–8; 132:11; 2 Sm 7:8–16. *n:* Ps 29:1; 82:1; Jb 1:6; 5:1. *o:* Ps 35:10; 86:8; 113:5; Ex 15:11; Jer 10:6. *p:* Ps 65:8; 74:13–15; 107:29; Jb 7:12; Is 51:9–10. *q:* Ps 24:1–2; 50:12; Dt 10:14; 1 Cor 10:26. *r:* Ps 85:11–12; 97:2. *s:* Ps 47:2; Zep 3:14. *t:* Ps 112:9; 148:14. *u:* Ps 47:9; 96:10; 97:1; 99:1; Is 6:3. *v:* Ps 78:70; 132:11–12; 2 Sm 7:4, 8–16; 1 Chr 17:3, 7–14; Is 42:1; Acts 13:22.

21 I have chosen David, my servant;
with my holy oil I have anointed him.
22 My hand will be with him;[w]
my arm will make him strong.
23 No enemy shall outwit him,
nor shall the wicked defeat him.
24 I will crush his foes before him,
strike down those who hate him.
25 My faithfulness and mercy will be with him;
through my name his horn will be exalted.
26 *I will set his hand upon the sea,
his right hand upon the rivers.
27 He shall cry to me, 'You are my father,[x]
my God, the Rock of my salvation!'
28 I myself make him the firstborn,
Most High* over the kings of the earth.
29 Forever I will maintain my mercy for him;[y]
my covenant with him stands firm.
30 I will establish his dynasty forever,
his throne as the days of the heavens.
31 If his descendants forsake my teaching,[z]
do not follow my decrees,
32 If they fail to observe my statutes,
do not keep my commandments,
33 I will punish their crime with a rod
and their guilt with blows.
34 But I will not take my mercy from him,
nor will I betray my bond of faithfulness.[a]
35 I will not violate my covenant;
the promise of my lips I will not alter.[b]
36 By my holiness I swore once for all:[c]
I will never be false to David.
37 *His dynasty will continue forever,[d]
his throne, like the sun before me.
38 Like the moon it will stand eternal,
forever firm like the sky!" *Selah*

B
IV

39 But now you have rejected and spurned,[e]
been enraged at your anointed.
40 You renounced the covenant with your servant,
defiled his crown in the dust.
41 You broke down all city walls,[f]
left his strongholds in ruins.
42 All who pass through seize plunder;
his neighbors deride him.
43 You have exalted the right hand of his foes,
have gladdened all his enemies.[g]
44 You turned back his sharp sword,
did not support him in battle.
45 You brought to an end his splendor,
hurled his throne to the ground.
46 You cut short the days of his youth,
covered him with shame. *Selah*

V

47 How long, LORD? Will you hide forever?
Must your wrath smolder like fire?[h]
48 Remember how brief life is,
how frail the sons of man you have created![i]
49 What is man, that he should live and not see death?
Who can deliver his soul from the power of Sheol?[j] *Selah*

VI

50 Where are your former mercies, Lord,
that you swore to David in your faithfulness?
51 Remember, Lord, the insults to your servants,
how I have borne in my bosom the slander of the nations.[k]
52 Your enemies, LORD, insult;
they insult each step of your anointed.
53 *Blessed be the LORD forever! Amen and amen![l]

89:26 The sea . . . the rivers: geographically the limits of the Davidic empire (the Mediterranean and the Euphrates); mythologically, the traditional forces of chaos. See note on Ps 89:11.

89:28 Most High: a divine title, which is here extended to David as God's own king, cf. Ps 2:7–9; Is 9:5. As God rules over the members of the heavenly council (Ps 89:6–9), so David, God's surrogate, rules over earthly kings.

89:37–38 Like the sun before me . . . like the sky: as enduring as the heavenly lights, cf. Ps 89:2–5 and Ps 72:5, 17.

89:53 The doxology at the end of the third book of the Psalms; it is not part of Ps 89.

w: 1 Sm 2:9–10. *x:* Ps 2:7; 110:2–3; 2 Sm 7:9, 14; Col 1:15, 18; Rev 1:5. *y:* Ps 18:51; 61:8; 144:10; 2 Sm 7:11; Is 55:3. *z:* Lv 26:14–33. *a:* Ps 40:12; Sir 47:22. *b:* Jer 33:20–21. *c:* Am 4:2. *d:* Ps 61:8; 72:5; Sir 43:6. *e:* Ps 44:10–25. *f:* Ps 80:13–14. *g:* Lam 1:5. *h:* Ps 13:2; 44:25; 74:10; 79:5; Dt 4:24. *i:* Ps 39:5–6; 62:10; 90:9–10; 144:4; Jb 7:6, 16; 14:1, 5; Eccl 6:12; Wis 2:5. *j:* Ps 90:3. *k:* Ps 79:12. *l:* Ps 41:14; 72:18; 106:48.

Fourth Book—Psalms 90–106

PSALM 90*

See RG 244, 247

God's Eternity and Human Frailty

1 A prayer of Moses, the man of God.

I

Lord, you have been our refuge
through all generations.
2 Before the mountains were born,
the earth and the world brought forth,
from eternity to eternity you are God.[m]
3 You turn humanity back into dust,*
saying, "Return, you children of Adam!"[n]
4 A thousand years in your eyes
are merely a day gone by,[o]
Before a watch passes in the night,
5 *you wash them away;[p]
They sleep,
and in the morning they sprout again like an herb.
6 In the morning it blooms only to pass away;
in the evening it is wilted and withered.*[q]

II

7 Truly we are consumed by your anger,
filled with terror by your wrath.
8 You have kept our faults before you,
our hidden sins in the light of your face.[r]
9 Our life ebbs away under your wrath;[s]
our years end like a sigh.
10 Seventy is the sum of our years,
or eighty, if we are strong;
Most of them are toil and sorrow;
they pass quickly, and we are gone.
11 Who comprehends the strength of your anger?
Your wrath matches the fear it inspires.
12 Teach us to count our days aright,
that we may gain wisdom of heart.

III

13 Relent, O LORD! How long?
Have pity on your servants!
14 Fill us at daybreak with your mercy,[t]
that all our days we may sing for joy.
15 Make us glad as many days as you humbled us,
for as many years as we have seen trouble.[u]
16 Show your deeds to your servants,
your glory to their children.
17 May the favor of the Lord our God be ours.[v]
Prosper the work of our hands!
Prosper the work of our hands!

PSALM 91*

See RG 245

Security Under God's Protection

I

1 You who dwell in the shelter of the Most High,*
who abide in the shade of the Almighty,*
2 Say to the LORD, "My refuge and fortress,

Psalm 90 A communal lament that describes only in general terms the cause of the community's distress. After confidently invoking God (Ps 90:1), the Psalm turns to a complaint contrasting God's eternity with the brevity of human life (Ps 90:2–6) and sees in human suffering the punishment for sin (Ps 90:7–12). The Psalm concludes with a plea for God's intervention (Ps 90:13–17).

90:3 Dust: one word of God is enough to return mortals to the dust from which they were created. Human beings were created from earth in Gn 2:7; 3:19.

90:5 You wash them away: the Hebrew of Ps 90:4–5 is unclear.

90:6 It is wilted and withered: the transitory nature of the grass under the scorching sun was proverbial, cf. Ps 129:6; Is 40:6–8.

Psalm 91 A prayer of someone who has taken refuge in the Lord, possibly within the Temple (Ps 91:1–2). The psalmist is confident that God's presence will protect the people in every dangerous situation (Ps 91:3–13). The final verses are an oracle of salvation promising salvation to those who trust in God (Ps 91:14–16).

91:1 The shelter of the Most High: basically "hiding place" but in the Psalms a designation for the protected Temple precincts, cf. Ps 27:5; 31:21; 61:5. **The shade of the Almighty**: lit., "the shadow of the wings of the Almighty," cf. Ps 17:8; 36:8; 57:2; 63:8. Ps 91:4 makes clear that the shadow is an image of the safety afforded by the outstretched wings of the cherubim in the holy of holies.

m: Ps 48:15; 55:20; 93:2; 102:13; Heb 1:12. *n:* Ps 103:14; 104:29; 146:4; Gn 3:19; 1 Mc 2:63; Jb 34:14–15; Eccl 3:20; 12:7; Sir 40:11. *o:* 2 Pt 3:8. *p:* Ps 89:48. *q:* Ps 37:2; 102:11; 103:15–16; Jb 14:1–2; Is 40:6–8. *r:* Ps 109:14–15; Hos 7:2. *s:* Ps 39:5–7; 62:10; 102:24–25; 144:4; Gn 6:3; Jb 7:6, 16; 14:5; Prv 10:27; Eccl 6:12; Wis 2:5; Sir 18:8; Is 65:20. *t:* Ps 17:15. *u:* Nm 14:34; Jer 31:13. *v:* Ps 33:22.

my God in whom I trust."[w]
3 He will rescue you from the fowler's snare,
from the destroying plague,
4 He will shelter you with his pinions,
and under his wings you may take refuge;[x]
his faithfulness is a protecting shield.
5 You shall not fear the terror of the night
nor the arrow that flies by day,[y]
6 Nor the pestilence that roams in darkness,
nor the plague that ravages at noon.[z]
7 Though a thousand fall at your side,
ten thousand at your right hand,
near you it shall not come.
8 You need simply watch;
the punishment of the wicked you will see.[a]
9 Because you have the LORD for your refuge
and have made the Most High your stronghold,
10 No evil shall befall you,
no affliction come near your tent.[b]
11 *For he commands his angels with regard to you,[c]
to guard you wherever you go.[d]
12 With their hands they shall support you,
lest you strike your foot against a stone.[e]
13 You can tread upon the asp and the viper,
trample the lion and the dragon.[f]

II

14 Because he clings to me I will deliver him;
because he knows my name I will set him on high.[g]
15 He will call upon me and I will answer;[h]
I will be with him in distress;[i]
I will deliver him and give him honor.
16 With length of days I will satisfy him,
and fill him with my saving power.[j]

PSALM 92*

A Hymn of Thanksgiving for God's Fidelity

See RG 245

1 A psalm. A sabbath song.

I

2 It is good to give thanks to the LORD,
to sing praise to your name, Most High,[k]
3 To proclaim your love at daybreak,
your faithfulness in the night,
4 With the ten-stringed harp,
with melody upon the lyre.[l]
5 For you make me jubilant, LORD, by your deeds;
at the works of your hands I shout for joy.

II

6 How great are your works, LORD![m]
How profound your designs!
7 A senseless person cannot know this;
a fool cannot comprehend.
8 Though the wicked flourish like grass[n]
and all sinners thrive,
They are destined for eternal destruction;
9 but you, LORD, are forever on high.
10 Indeed your enemies, LORD,
indeed your enemies shall perish;
all sinners shall be scattered.[o]

III

11 You have given me the strength of a wild ox;[p]
you have poured rich oil upon me.[q]
12 My eyes look with glee on my wicked enemies;
my ears shall hear what happens to my wicked foes.[r]
13 The just shall flourish like the palm tree,
shall grow like a cedar of Lebanon.[s]
14 *Planted in the house of the LORD,
they shall flourish in the courts of our God.

91:11–12 The words are cited in Lk 4:10–11; Mt 4:6, as Satan tempts Jesus in the desert.

Psalm 92 A hymn of praise and thanks for God's faithful deeds (Ps 92:2–5). The wicked, deluded by their prosperity (Ps 92:6–9), are punished (Ps 92:10), whereas the psalmist has already experienced God's protection (Ps 92:11–15).

92:14 Planted: the just are likened to trees growing in the sacred precincts of the Temple, which is often seen as the source of life and fertility because of God's presence, cf. Ps 36:9, 10; Ez 47:1–12.

w: Ps 18:3; 31:3–4; 42:10; 142:6; 2 Sm 22:3. *x:* Ps 17:8; 36:8; 57:2; 63:8; Dt 32:11; Ru 2:12; Mt 23:37. *y:* Prv 3:25; Sg 3:8. *z:* Dt 32:24. *a:* Ps 92:12. *b:* Prv 12:21; Dt 7:15. *c:* Mt 4:6; Lk 4:10f. *d:* Heb 1:14. *e:* Ps 121:3; Prv 3:23. *f:* Is 11:8; Lk 10:19. *g:* Ps 9:11; 119:132. *h:* Jer 33:3; Zec 13:9. *i:* Is 43:2. *j:* Prv 3:2. *k:* Ps 33:1; 147:1. *l:* Ps 33:2; 144:9. *m:* Ps 131:1; 139:6, 17; Wis 13:1; 17:1. *n:* Ps 37:35. *o:* Ps 68:1–2; 125:5. *p:* Ps 75:11; Dt 33:17. *q:* Ps 23:5. *r:* Ps 91:8. *s:* Ps 1:3; 52:10; Jer 17:8.

15 They shall bear fruit even in old age,
they will stay fresh and green,
16 To proclaim: "The LORD is just;
my rock, in whom there is no wrong."[t]

PSALM 93*

See RG 245

God Is a Mighty King

1 The LORD is king,* robed with majesty;
the LORD is robed, girded with might.[u]
The world will surely stand in place,
never to be moved.[v]
2 Your throne stands firm from of old;
you are from everlasting.[w]
3 *The flood has raised up, LORD;
the flood has raised up its roar;
the flood has raised its pounding waves.
4 More powerful than the roar of many
waters,
more powerful than the breakers of the
sea,
powerful in the heavens is the LORD.
5 Your decrees are firmly established;
holiness befits your house, LORD,
for all the length of days.

PSALM 94*

See RG 244–45

A Prayer for Deliverance from the Wicked

I

1 LORD, avenging God,
avenging God, shine forth![x]
2 Rise up, O judge of the earth;
give the proud what they deserve![y]

II

3 How long, LORD, shall the wicked,
how long shall the wicked glory?[z]
4 How long will they mouth haughty
speeches,
go on boasting, all these evildoers?[a]
5 They crush your people, LORD,
torment your very own.
6 They kill the widow and alien;
the orphan they murder.[b]
7 They say, "The LORD does not see;
the God of Jacob takes no notice."[c]

III

8 Understand, you stupid people!
You fools, when will you be wise?[d]
9 Does the one who shaped the ear not hear?
The one who formed the eye not see?[e]
10 Does the one who guides nations not
rebuke?
The one who teaches man not have
knowledge?
11 The LORD knows the plans of man;
they are like a fleeting breath.[f]

IV

12 Blessed the one whom you guide, LORD,[g]
whom you teach by your instruction,
13 To give rest from evil days,
while a pit is being dug for the wicked.
14 For the LORD will not forsake his people,
nor abandon his inheritance.[h]
15 Judgment shall again be just,
and all the upright of heart will
follow it.

V

16 Who will rise up for me against the
wicked?
Who will stand up for me against
evildoers?
17 If the LORD were not my help,

Psalm 93 A hymn celebrating the kingship of God, who created the world (Ps 93:1–2) by defeating the sea (Ps 93:3–4). In the ancient myth that is alluded to here, Sea completely covered the land, making it impossible for the human community to live. Sea, or Flood, roars in anger against God, who is personified in the storm. God's utterances or decrees are given authority by the victory over Sea (Ps 93:5).

93:1 The LORD is king: lit., "the LORD reigns." This Psalm, and Ps 47; 96–99, are sometimes called enthronement Psalms. They may have been used in a special liturgy during which God's ascent to the throne was ritually reenacted. They have also been interpreted eschatologically, pointing to the coming of God as king at the end-time.

93:3 The flood: the primordial sea was tamed by God in the act of creation. It is a figure of chaos and rebellion, cf. Ps 46:4.

Psalm 94 A lament of an individual who is threatened by wicked people. The danger affects the whole community. Calling upon God as judge (Ps 94:1–2), the Psalm complains about oppression of the holy community by people within (Ps 94:3–7). Bold declarations of faith follow: denunciation of evildoers (Ps 94:8–11) and assurance to the just (Ps 94:12–15). The Psalm continues with further lament (Ps 94:16–19) and ends with strong confidence in God's response (Ps 94:20–23).

---

t: Dt 32:4. *u:* Ps 47:8; 96:10; 97:1; 99:1. *v:* Ps 75:2–3; 104:5. *w:* Ps 55:20; 90:2; 102:13; Heb 1:12. *x:* Na 1:2. *y:* Jer 51:56; Lam 3:64. *z:* Ps 13:2; 75:5; Jer 12:1. *a:* Ps 73; Mal 2:17; 3:14. *b:* Ex 22:21–22; Dt 24:17–22. *c:* Ps 10:11; 64:6; 73:11; Jb 22:13–14; Ez 9:9. *d:* Prv 1:22; 8:5. *e:* Ex 4:11; Prv 20:12. *f:* Ps 33:15; 1 Cor 3:20. *g:* Ps 119:71; Jb 5:17. *h:* 1 Sm 12:22; Sir 47:22.

I would long have been silent in the
grave.[i]
18 When I say, "My foot is slipping,"
your mercy, LORD, holds me up.[j]
19 When cares increase within me,
your comfort gives me joy.

VI

20 Can unjust judges be your allies,
those who create burdens by decree,
21 Those who conspire against the just
and condemn the innocent to death?
22 No, the LORD is my secure height,
my God, my rock of refuge,
23 [k]Who will turn back their evil upon them[l]
and destroy them for their wickedness.
Surely the LORD our God will destroy
them!

PSALM 95*

See RG 246

A Call to Praise and Obedience

I

1 Come, let us sing joyfully to the LORD;
cry out to the rock of our salvation.[m]
2 Let us come before him with a song of
praise,
joyfully sing out our psalms.
3 For the LORD is the great God,
the great king over all gods,[n]
4 Whose hand holds the depths of the
earth;
who owns the tops of the mountains.
5 The sea and dry land belong to God,
who made them, formed them by
hand.[o]

II

6 Enter, let us bow down in worship;
let us kneel before the LORD who
made us.
7 For he is our God,
we are the people he shepherds,
the sheep in his hands.[p]

III

Oh, that today you would hear his voice:[q]
8 Do not harden your hearts as at
Meribah,
as on the day of Massah in the desert.*
9 There your ancestors tested me;
they tried me though they had seen my
works.[r]
10 Forty years I loathed that generation;
I said: "This people's heart goes astray;
they do not know my ways."[s]
11 Therefore I swore in my anger:
"They shall never enter my rest."*

PSALM 96*

See RG 245, 248, 250

God of the Universe

I

1 Sing to the LORD a new song;[t]
sing to the LORD, all the earth.
2 Sing to the LORD, bless his name;
proclaim his salvation day after day.
3 Tell his glory among the nations;
among all peoples, his marvelous
deeds.[u]

II

4 *For great is the LORD and highly to be
praised,
to be feared above all gods.[v]
5 For the gods of the nations are idols,
but the LORD made the heavens.[w]
6 Splendor and power go before him;
power and grandeur are in his holy
place.

III

7 Give to the LORD, you families of
nations,
give to the LORD glory and might;

Psalm 95 Twice the Psalm calls the people to praise and worship God (Ps 95:1–2, 6), the king of all creatures (Ps 95:3–5) and shepherd of the flock (Ps 95:7a, 7b). The last strophe warns the people to be more faithful than were their ancestors in the journey to the promised land (Ps 95:7c–11). This invitation to praise God regularly opens the Church's official prayer, the Liturgy of the Hours.

95:8 Meribah: lit., "contention"; the place where the Israelites quarreled with God. **Massah**: "testing," the place where they put God to the trial, cf. Ex 17:7; Nm 20:13.

95:11 My rest: the promised land as in Dt 12:9. Heb 4 applies the verse to the eternal rest of heaven.

Psalm 96 A hymn inviting all humanity to praise the glories of Israel's God (Ps 96:1–3), who is the sole God (Ps 96:4–6). To the just ruler of all belongs worship (Ps 96:7–10); even inanimate creation is to offer praise (Ps 96:11–13). This Psalm has numerous verbal and thematic contacts with Is 40–55, as does Ps 98. Another version of the Psalm is 1 Chr 16:23–33.

96:4 For references to other gods, see comments on Ps 58 and 82.

i: Ps 6:6; 115:17. *j:* Ps 145:14. *k:* Ps 7:16; 9:16; 35:8; 57:7; Prv 26:27; Eccl 10:8; Sir 27:26. *l:* Ps 107:42. *m:* Dt 32:15. *n:* Ps 47:2; 135:5. *o:* Ps 24:1–2. *p:* Ps 81:8; 106:32; Heb 3:7–11, 15; 4:3, 5, 7. *q:* Ps 23:1–3; 100:3; Mi 7:14. *r:* Nm 14:22; 20:2–13; Dt 6:16; 33:8. *s:* Ps 78:8; Nm 14:34; Dt 32:5. *t:* Ps 98:1; Is 42:10. *u:* Ps 98:4; 105:1. *v:* Ps 48:2; 95:3; 145:3. *w:* Ps 97:7; 115:4–8; Is 40:17; 1 Cor 8:4.

8 give to the LORD the glory due his
name![x]
Bring gifts and enter his courts;
9 bow down to the LORD, splendid in
holiness.
Tremble before him, all the earth;
10 [y]declare among the nations: The LORD
is king.
The world will surely stand fast, never to
be shaken.
He rules the peoples with fairness.

IV

11 Let the heavens be glad and the earth
rejoice;
let the sea and what fills it resound;[z]
12 let the plains be joyful and all that is in
them.
Then let all the trees of the forest rejoice
13 before the LORD who comes,
who comes to govern the earth,[a]
To govern the world with justice
and the peoples with faithfulness.

See RG 245

PSALM 97*

The Divine Ruler of All

I

1 The LORD is king; let the earth
rejoice;
let the many islands be glad.[b]
2 Cloud and darkness surround him;
justice and right are the foundation of
his throne.[c]
3 Fire goes before him,
consuming his foes on every side.
4 His lightning illumines the world;
the earth sees and trembles.[d]
5 The mountains melt like wax before the
LORD,
before the Lord of all the earth.[e]
6 The heavens proclaim his justice;
all peoples see his glory.[f]

II

7 All who serve idols are put to shame,
who glory in worthless things;
all gods* bow down before him.[g]
8 Zion hears and is glad,
and the daughters of Judah rejoice
because of your judgments, O LORD.[h]
9 For you, LORD, are the Most High over
all the earth,[i]
exalted far above all gods.
10 You who love the LORD, hate evil,
he protects the souls of the faithful,[j]
rescues them from the hand of the
wicked.
11 Light dawns for the just,
and gladness for the honest of heart.[k]
12 Rejoice in the LORD, you just,
and give thanks at the remembrance of
his holiness.[l]

PSALM 98*

See RG 245, 248

The Coming of God

1 A psalm.

I

Sing a new song to the LORD,
for he has done marvelous deeds.[m]
His right hand and holy arm
have won the victory.*[n]
2 The LORD has made his victory
known;
has revealed his triumph in the sight of
the nations,
3 He has remembered his mercy and
faithfulness
toward the house of Israel.
All the ends of the earth have seen
the victory of our God.

Psalm 97 The hymn begins with God appearing in a storm, a traditional picture of some ancient Near Eastern gods (Ps 97:1–6); cf. Ps 18:8–16; Mi 1:3–4; Heb 3:3–15. Israel rejoices in the overthrowing of idol worshipers and their gods (Ps 97:7–9) and the rewarding of the faithful righteous (Ps 97:10–12).

97:7 All gods: divine beings thoroughly subordinate to Israel's God. The Greek translates "angels," an interpretation adopted by Heb 1:6.

Psalm 98 A hymn, similar to Ps 96, extolling God for Israel's victory (Ps 98:1–3). All nations (Ps 98:4–6) and even inanimate nature (Ps 98:7–8) are summoned to welcome God's coming to rule over the world (Ps 98:9).

98:1 Marvelous deeds . . . victory: the conquest of all threats to the peaceful existence of Israel, depicted in the Psalms variously as a cosmic force such as sea, or nations bent on Israel's destruction, or evildoers seemingly triumphant. **His right hand and holy arm**: God is pictured as a powerful warrior.

x: Ps 29:2. *y:* Ps 75:4; 93:1. *z:* Ps 98:7. *a:* Ps 98:9. *b:* Ps 75:4; 93:1; 96:10. *c:* Ps 85:11; 89:15; Ex 19:6; Dt 4:11; 5:22; 1 Kgs 8:12. *d:* Ps 18:8; 50:3; 77:18; 99:1; Jgs 5:4–5. *e:* Jdt 16:15; Mi 1:4. *f:* Ps 50:6. *g:* Ps 96:5. *h:* Ps 48:12. *i:* Ps 83:19. *j:* Ps 121:7. *k:* Ps 112:4. *l:* Ps 30:5. *m:* Ps 96:1; Is 42:10. *n:* Is 59:16; 63:5.

II

4 Shout with joy to the LORD, all the earth;
break into song; sing praise.
5 Sing praise to the LORD with the lyre,
with the lyre and melodious song.
6 With trumpets and the sound of the horn
shout with joy to the King, the LORD.[o]

III

7 Let the sea and what fills it resound,[p]
the world and those who dwell there.
8 Let the rivers clap their hands,
the mountains shout with them for joy,[q]
9 [r]Before the LORD who comes,
who comes to govern the earth,[s]
To govern the world with justice
and the peoples with fairness.

PSALM 99*

See RG 245

The Holy King

I

1 The LORD is king, the peoples tremble;
he is enthroned on the cherubim,* the
earth quakes.[t]
2 Great is the LORD in Zion,
exalted above all the peoples.
3 Let them praise your great and awesome
name:
Holy is he![u]

II

4 O mighty king, lover of justice,
you have established fairness;
you have created just rule in Jacob.[v]
5 Exalt the LORD, our God;
bow down before his footstool;*[w]
holy is he!

III

6 Moses and Aaron were among his
priests,
Samuel among those who called on his
name;
they called on the LORD, and he
answered them.[x]
7 From the pillar of cloud he spoke to them;
they kept his decrees, the law he had
given them.[y]
8 O LORD, our God, you answered them;
you were a forgiving God to them,
though you punished their offenses.[z]
9 Exalt the LORD, our God;
bow down before his holy mountain;
holy is the LORD, our God.

PSALM 100*

See RG 244

Processional Hymn

1 A psalm of thanksgiving.

Shout joyfully to the LORD, all you lands;
2 serve the LORD with gladness;
come before him with joyful song.
3 *Know that the LORD is God,
he made us, we belong to him,
we are his people, the flock he
shepherds.[a]
4 Enter his gates with thanksgiving,
his courts with praise.
Give thanks to him, bless his name;[b]
5 good indeed is the LORD,
His mercy endures forever,
his faithfulness lasts through every
generation.

PSALM 101*

See RG 245

Norm of Life for Rulers

1 A psalm of David.

I

I sing of mercy and justice;

Psalm 99 A hymn to God as the king whose grandeur is most clearly seen on Mount Zion (Ps 99:2) and in the laws given to Israel (Ps 99:4). Israel is special because of God's word of justice, which was mediated by the revered speakers, Moses, Aaron, and Samuel (Ps 99:6–8). The poem is structured by the threefold statement that God is holy (Ps 99:3, 5, 9) and by the twice-repeated command to praise (Ps 99:5, 9).

99:1 Enthroned on the cherubim: cherubim were composite beings with animal and human features, common in ancient Near Eastern art. Two cherubim were placed on the ark (or box) of the covenant in the holy of holies. Upon them God was believed to dwell invisibly, cf. Ex 25:20–22; 1 Sm 4:4; 2 Sm 6:2; Ps 80:2.

99:5 Footstool: a reference to the ark, cf. 1 Chr 28:2; Ps 132:7.

Psalm 100 A hymn inviting the people to enter the Temple courts with thank offerings for the God who created them.

100:3 Although the people call on all the nations of the world to join in their hymn, they are conscious of being the chosen people of God.

Psalm 101 The king, grateful at being God's chosen (Ps 101:1), promises to be a ruler after God's own heart (Ps 101:2–3), allowing into the royal service only the God-fearing (Ps 101:3–8).

o: Ps 47:6–7. *p:* Ps 96:11. *q:* Is 44:23; 55:12. *r:* Ps 96:13. *s:* Ps 67:5. *t:* Ps 18:8–11; 80:2; 93:1; Ex 25:22; 1 Sm 4:4; 2 Sm 6:2. *u:* Is 6:3. *v:* Ps 72:1; Jer 23:5. *w:* Ps 132:7. *x:* Jer 15:1. *y:* Ex 33:9; Nm 12:5. *z:* Ex 32:11; Nm 20:12. *a:* Ps 23:1; 95:7; Mi 7:14; Is 64:7. *b:* Ps 106:1; 107:1; 118:1; 136:1; 138:8; Jer 33:11.

to you, LORD, I sing praise.
2 I study the way of integrity;[c]
when will you come to me?
I act with integrity of heart
within my household.*[d]
3 I do not allow into my presence anything
base.
I hate wrongdoing;
I will have no part of it.[e]
4 May the devious heart keep far from me;
the wicked I will not acknowledge.
5 Whoever slanders a neighbor in secret
I will reduce to silence.[f]
Haughty eyes and arrogant hearts[g]
I cannot endure.

II

6 I look to the faithful of the land*
to sit at my side.
Whoever follows the way of integrity[h]
is the one to enter my service.
7 No one who practices deceit
can remain within my house.
No one who speaks falsely
can last in my presence.[i]
8 *Morning after morning I clear all the
wicked from the land,
to rid the city of the LORD of all doers
of evil.

See RG 244

PSALM 102*

Prayer in Time of Distress

1 The prayer of one afflicted and wasting away whose anguish is poured out before the LORD.

I

2 LORD, hear my prayer;
let my cry come to you.
3 Do not hide your face from me
in the day of my distress.[j]
Turn your ear to me;
when I call, answer me quickly.
4 For my days vanish like smoke;[k]
my bones burn away as in a furnace.
5 My heart is withered, dried up like grass,
too wasted to eat my food.
6 From my loud groaning
I become just skin and bones.
7 I am like a desert owl,
like an owl among the ruins.
8 I lie awake and moan,
like a lone sparrow on the roof.
9 All day long my enemies taunt me;
in their rage, they make my name a
curse.*
10 I eat ashes like bread,
mingle my drink with tears.[l]
11 Because of your furious wrath,
you lifted me up just to cast me down.
12 [m]My days are like a lengthening
shadow;[n]
I wither like the grass.

II

13 But you, LORD, are enthroned forever;
your renown is for all generations.[o]
14 You will again show mercy to Zion;
now is the time for pity;
the appointed time has come.
15 Its stones are dear to your servants;
its dust moves them to pity.
16 The nations shall fear your name, LORD,
all the kings of the earth, your glory,[p]
17 Once the LORD has rebuilt Zion
and appeared in glory,
18 Heeding the plea of the lowly,
not scorning their prayer.
19 Let this be written for the next
generation,
for a people not yet born,

101:2 Within my household: the king promises to make his own household, i.e., the royal court, a model for Israel, banning all officials who abuse their power.

101:6 I look to the faithful of the land: the king seeks companions only among those faithful to God.

101:8 Morning after morning: the morning is the normal time for the administration of justice (2 Sm 15:2; Jer 21:12) and for the arrival of divine aid (Ps 59:17; 143:8; Is 33:2). **I clear all the wicked from the land**: the king, as God's servant, is responsible for seeing that divine justice is carried out.

Psalm 102 A lament, one of the Penitential Psalms. The psalmist, experiencing psychological and bodily disintegration (Ps 102:4–12), cries out to God (Ps 102:1–3). In the Temple precincts where God has promised to be present, the psalmist recalls God's venerable promises to save the poor (Ps 102:13–23). The final part (Ps 102:24–28) restates the original complaint and prayer, and emphasizes God's eternity.

102:9 They make my name a curse: enemies use the psalmist's name in phrases such as, "May you be as wretched as this person!"

c: Ps 26:11; Is 33:15. *d:* 1 Kgs 9:4. *e:* Prv 11:20. *f:* Prv 17:20; 30:10. *g:* Prv 21:4. *h:* Ps 26:11; Prv 20:7. *i:* Ps 5:5; Prv 25:5. *j:* Ps 69:18; 143:7. *k:* Ps 38:7–9. *l:* Ps 42:4; 80:6. *m:* Ps 109:23; 144:4; Jb 8:9; 14:2; Eccl 6:12; Wis 2:5. *n:* Ps 90:5–6. *o:* Ps 55:20; 90:2; 93:2; 135:13; 145:13; Lam 5:19; Heb 1:12. *p:* Is 59:19; 66:18.

that they may praise the LORD:[q]
20 *"The LORD looked down from the holy heights,
viewed the earth from heaven,[r]
21 To attend to the groaning of the prisoners,
to release those doomed to die."[s]
22 Then the LORD's name will be declared on Zion,
his praise in Jerusalem,
23 When peoples and kingdoms gather
to serve the LORD.[t]

III

24 He has shattered my strength in mid-course,
has cut short my days.
25 I plead, O my God,
do not take me in the midst of my days.*[u]
Your years last through all generations.
26 Of old you laid the earth's foundations;[v]
the heavens are the work of your hands.
27 They perish, but you remain;
they all wear out like a garment;
Like clothing you change them and they are changed,
28 but you are the same, your years have no end.
29 May the children of your servants live on;
may their descendants live in your presence.[w]

PSALM 103*

See RG 244, 250

Praise of Divine Goodness

1 Of David.

I

Bless the LORD, my soul;
all my being, bless his holy name!
2 Bless the LORD, my soul;
and do not forget all his gifts,
3 Who pardons all your sins,
and heals all your ills,
4 Who redeems your life from the pit,[x]
and crowns you with mercy and compassion,
5 Who fills your days with good things,
so your youth is renewed like the eagle's.*

II

6 The LORD does righteous deeds,
brings justice to all the oppressed.[y]
7 He made known his ways to Moses,
to the Israelites his deeds.
8 Merciful and gracious is the LORD,
slow to anger, abounding in mercy.[z]
9 He will not always accuse,
and nurses no lasting anger;
10 He has not dealt with us as our sins merit,
nor requited us as our wrongs deserve.

III

11 For as the heavens tower over the earth,
so his mercy towers over those who fear him.[a]
12 As far as the east is from the west,
so far has he removed our sins from us.
13 As a father has compassion on his children,
so the LORD has compassion on those who fear him.
14 For he knows how we are formed,
remembers that we are dust.[b]
15 As for man, his days are like the grass;
he blossoms like a flower in the field.[c]
16 A wind sweeps over it and it is gone;
its place knows it no more.
17 But the LORD's mercy is from age to age,
toward those who fear him.
His salvation is for the children's children
18 of those who keep his covenant,
and remember to carry out his precepts.

102:20–23 Both Ps 102:20–21 and Ps 102:22–23 depend on Ps 102:19.

102:25 In the midst of my days: when the normal span of life is but half completed, cf. Is 38:10; Jer 17:11.

Psalm 103 The speaker in this hymn begins by praising God for personal benefits (Ps 103:1–5), then moves on to God's mercy toward all the people (Ps 103:6–18). Even sin cannot destroy that mercy (Ps 103:11–13), for the eternal God is well aware of the people's human fragility (Ps 103:14–18). The psalmist invites the heavenly beings to join in praise (Ps 103:19–22).

103:5 Your youth is renewed like the eagle's: because of the eagle's long life it was a symbol of perennial youth and vigor, cf. Is 40:31.

q: Ps 22:31–32. *r:* Ps 11:4; 14:2. *s:* Ps 79:11. *t:* Is 60:3–4; Zec 2:15; 8:22. *u:* Ps 39:5; 90:10; Jb 14:5. *v:* Heb 1:10–12. *w:* Ps 69:36–37. *x:* Ps 28:1; 30:4; 40:3; 69:16; 88:5; 143:7; Prv 1:12; Jon 2:7. *y:* Ps 146:6–7. *z:* Ps 86:15; 145:8; Ex 34:6–7; Nm 14:18; Jer 3:12; Jl 2:13; Jon 4:2. *a:* Is 55:9. *b:* Ps 90:3. *c:* Ps 37:2; 90:5–6; Is 40:7.

IV

19 The LORD has set his throne in heaven;
his dominion extends over all.
20 Bless the LORD, all you his angels,[d]
mighty in strength, acting at his behest,
obedient to his command.
21 Bless the LORD, all you his hosts,
his ministers who carry out his will.
22 Bless the LORD, all his creatures,
everywhere in his domain.
Bless the LORD, my soul!

PSALM 104*

See RG 244, 250

Praise of God the Creator

I

1 Bless the LORD, my soul!
LORD, my God, you are great indeed!
You are clothed with majesty and splendor,
2 robed in light as with a cloak.
You spread out the heavens like a tent;[e]
3 setting the beams of your chambers upon the waters.*
You make the clouds your chariot;
traveling on the wings of the wind.
4 You make the winds your messengers;
flaming fire, your ministers.[f]

II

5 *You fixed the earth on its foundation,
so it can never be shaken.
6 The deeps covered it like a garment;
above the mountains stood the waters.
7 At your rebuke they took flight;
at the sound of your thunder they fled.[g]
8 They rushed up the mountains, down the valleys
to the place you had fixed for them.
9 You set a limit they cannot pass;
never again will they cover the earth.[h]

III

10 You made springs flow in wadies
that wind among the mountains.
11 They give drink to every beast of the field;[i]
here wild asses quench their thirst.
12 Beside them the birds of heaven nest;
among the branches they sing.
13 You water the mountains from your chambers;
from the fruit of your labor the earth abounds.
14 You make the grass grow for the cattle
and plants for people's work
to bring forth food from the earth,
15 wine to gladden their hearts,
oil to make their faces shine,
and bread to sustain the human heart.
16 *The trees of the LORD drink their fill,
the cedars of Lebanon, which you planted.
17 There the birds build their nests;
the stork in the junipers, its home.[j]
18 The high mountains are for wild goats;
the rocky cliffs, a refuge for badgers.

IV

19 You made the moon to mark the seasons,[k]
the sun that knows the hour of its setting.
20 You bring darkness and night falls,
then all the animals of the forest wander about.
21 Young lions roar for prey;
they seek their food from God.[l]
22 When the sun rises, they steal away
and settle down in their dens.
23 People go out to their work,
to their labor till evening falls.

V

24 How varied are your works, LORD!
In wisdom you have made them all;

Psalm 104 A hymn praising God who easily and skillfully made rampaging waters and primordial night into a world vibrant with life. The psalmist describes God's splendor in the heavens (Ps 104:1–4), how the chaotic waters were tamed to fertilize and feed the world (Ps 104:5–18), and how primordial night was made into a gentle time of refreshment (Ps 104:19–23). The picture is like Gn 1:1–2: a dark and watery chaos is made dry and lighted so that creatures might live. The psalmist reacts to the beauty of creation with awe (Ps 104:24–34). May sin not deface God's work (Ps 104:35)!

104:3 Your chambers upon the waters: God's heavenly dwelling above the upper waters of the sky, cf. Gn 1:6–7; Ps 29:10.

104:5–9 God places the gigantic disk of the earth securely on its foundation and then, as a warrior, chases away the enveloping waters and confines them under, above, and around the earth.

104:16–18 Even the exotic flora and fauna of the high mountains of the Lebanon range receive adequate water.

d: Ps 148:2; Dn 3:58. *e:* Prv 8:27–28; Jb 9:8; Is 40:22; Gn 1:6–7; Am 9:6. *f:* Heb 1:7. *g:* Ps 29:3. *h:* Jer 5:22; Gn 9:11–15. *i:* Ps 147:8–9. *j:* Ez 31:6. *k:* Sir 43:6. *l:* Jb 38:39.

the earth is full of your creatures.[m]
25 There is the sea, great and wide!
It teems with countless beings,
living things both large and small.[n]
26 There ships ply their course
and Leviathan,* whom you formed to play with.[o]

VI

27 All of these look to you
to give them food in due time.[p]
28 When you give it to them, they gather;
when you open your hand, they are well filled.
29 *When you hide your face, they panic.
Take away their breath, they perish
and return to the dust.[q]
30 Send forth your spirit, they are created
and you renew the face of the earth.

VII

31 May the glory of the LORD endure forever;
may the LORD be glad in his works!
32 Who looks at the earth and it trembles,
touches the mountains and they smoke![r]
33 I will sing to the LORD all my life;
I will sing praise to my God while I live.[s]
34 May my meditation be pleasing to him;
I will rejoice in the LORD.
35 May sinners vanish from the earth,
and the wicked be no more.
Bless the LORD, my soul! Hallelujah!*

PSALM 105*

See RG 246, 247

God's Fidelity to the Promise

I

1 Give thanks to the LORD, invoke his name;[t]
make known among the peoples his deeds![u]
2 Sing praise to him, play music;
proclaim all his wondrous deeds!
3 Glory in his holy name;
let hearts that seek the LORD rejoice!
4 Seek out the LORD and his might;
constantly seek his face.[v]
5 Recall the wondrous deeds he has done,
his wonders and words of judgment,
6 You descendants of Abraham his servant,
offspring of Jacob the chosen one!

II

7 He the LORD, is our God
whose judgments reach through all the earth.
8 He remembers forever his covenant,
the word he commanded for a thousand generations,
9 Which he made with Abraham,
and swore to Isaac,[w]
10 And ratified in a statute for Jacob,
an everlasting covenant for Israel:
11 "To you I give the land of Canaan,
your own allotted inheritance."[x]

III

12 When they were few in number,[y]
a handful, and strangers there,
13 Wandering from nation to nation,
from one kingdom to another people,
14 He let no one oppress them;
for their sake he rebuked kings:*
15 *"Do not touch my anointed ones,
to my prophets do no harm."

IV

16 Then he called down a famine on the land,

104:26 Leviathan: a sea monster symbolizing primeval chaos, cf. Ps 74:14; Is 27:1; Jb 40:25. God does not destroy chaos but makes it part of the created order.

104:29–30 On one level, the spirit (or wind) of God is the fall and winter rains that provide food for all creatures. On another, it is the breath (or spirit) of God that makes beings live.

104:35 Hallelujah: a frequent word in the last third of the Psalter. The word combines the plural imperative of praise (*hallelu*) with an abbreviated form of the divine name Yah(weh).

Psalm 105 A hymn to God who promised the land of Canaan to the holy people, cf. Ps 78; 106; 136. Israel is invited to praise and seek the presence of God (Ps 105:1–6), who is faithful to the promise of land to the ancestors (Ps 105:7–11). In every phase of the national story—the ancestors in the land of Canaan (Ps 105:12–15), Joseph in Egypt (Ps 105:16–22), Israel in Egypt (Ps 105:23–38), Israel in the desert on the way to Canaan (Ps 105:39–45)—God remained faithful, reiterating the promise of the land to successive servants.

105:14 Kings: Pharaoh and Abimelech of Gerar, cf. Gn 12:17; 20:6–7.

105:15 My anointed ones . . . my prophets: the patriarchs Abraham, Isaac, and Jacob, who were "anointed" in the sense of being consecrated and recipients of God's revelation.

m: Ps 92:6; Sir 39:16. *n:* Sir 43:26. *o:* Jb 3:8; 40:25, 29. *p:* Ps 136:25; 145:15–16. *q:* Ps 90:3; Jb 34:14–15; Eccl 3:20. *r:* Ps 144:5. *s:* Ps 146:2. *t:* 1 Chr 16:8–22. *u:* Ps 18:50; 96:3; 145:5; Is 12:4–5. *v:* Ps 24:6; 27:8. *w:* Gn 15:1ff; 26:3. *x:* Gn 12:7; 15:18. *y:* Dt 4:27; 26:5.

destroyed the grain that sustained
them.*[z]
17 He had sent a man ahead of them,
Joseph, sold as a slave.[a]
18 They shackled his feet with chains;
collared his neck in iron,[b]
19 Till his prediction came to pass,
and the word of the LORD proved him
true.[c]
20 The king sent and released him;
the ruler of peoples set him free.[d]
21 He made him lord over his household,
ruler over all his possessions,[e]
22 To instruct his princes as he desired,
to teach his elders wisdom.

V

23 Then Israel entered Egypt;[f]
Jacob sojourned in the land of Ham.*
24 God greatly increased his people,
made them more numerous than their
foes.[g]
25 He turned their hearts to hate his people,
to treat his servants deceitfully.[h]
26 He sent his servant Moses,
and Aaron whom he had chosen.[i]
27 *They worked his signs in Egypt[j]
and wonders in the land of Ham.
28 He sent darkness and it grew dark,
but they rebelled against his word.
29 He turned their waters into blood
and killed their fish.
30 Their land swarmed with frogs,
even the chambers of their kings.
31 He spoke and there came swarms of flies,
gnats through all their country.
32 For rain he gave them hail,
flashes of lightning throughout their
land.
33 He struck down their vines and fig trees,
shattered the trees of their country.
34 He spoke and the locusts came,
grasshoppers without number.[k]
35 They devoured every plant in the land;
they devoured the crops of their fields.
36 He struck down every firstborn in the
land,
the first fruits of all their vigor.
37 He brought his people out,
laden with silver and gold;[l]
no one among the tribes stumbled.
38 Egypt rejoiced when they left,
for fear had seized them.

VI

39 He spread a cloud out as a cover,
and made a fire to light up the night.[m]
40 They asked and he brought them quail;
with bread from heaven he filled
them.[n]
41 He split the rock and water gushed forth;
it flowed through the desert like a river.[o]
42 For he remembered his sacred promise
to Abraham his servant.
43 He brought his people out with joy,
his chosen ones with shouts of
triumph.
44 He gave them the lands of the nations,
they took possession of the wealth of
the peoples,[p]
45 That they might keep his statutes
and observe his teachings.[q]
Hallelujah!

PSALM 106*

See RG 244, 247

Israel's Confession of Sin

1 Hallelujah!

A

Give thanks to the LORD, who is good,
whose mercy endures forever.[r]

105:16 The grain that sustained them: lit., every "staff of bread."

105:23, 27 The land of Ham: a synonym for Egypt, cf. Gn 10:6.

105:27–38 This Psalm and Ps 78:43–51 have an account of the plagues differing in number or in order from Ex 7:14–12:30. Several versions of the exodus story were current.

Psalm 106 Israel is invited to praise the God whose mercy has always tempered judgment of Israel (Ps 106:1–3). The speaker, on behalf of all, seeks solidarity with the people, who can always count on God's fidelity despite their sin (Ps 106:4–5). Confident of God's mercy, the speaker invites national repentance (Ps 106:6) by reciting from Israel's history eight instances of sin, judgment, and forgiveness. The sins are the rebellion at the Red Sea (Ps 106:6–12; see Ex 14–15), the craving for meat in the desert (Ps 106:13–15; see Nm 11), the challenge to Moses' authority (Ps 106:16–18; see Nm 16), the golden calf episode (Ps 106:19–23; see Ex 32–34), the refusal to take Canaan by the southern route (Ps 106:24–27; see Nm

z: Gn 41:54, 57. a: Gn 37:28, 36; 45:5. b: Gn 39:20. c: Gn 40–41. d: Gn 41:14. e: Gn 41:41–44. f: Gn 46:1–47:12; Acts 7:15. g: Ex 1:7; Acts 7:17. h: Ex 1:8–14. i: Ex 3:10; 4:27. j: Ps 78:43–51; Ex 7–12. k: Jl 1:4. l: Ex 12:33–36. m: Ps 78:14; Ex 13:21–22; Wis 18:3. n: Ps 78:24–28; Ex 16:13–15; Nm 11:31ff; Wis 16:20. o: Ps 78:15–16; Ex 17:1–7; Nm 20:11. p: Dt 4:37–40. q: Dt 6:20–25; 7:8–11. r: Ps 100:5; 107:1; 1 Chr 16:34; Jer 33:11; Dn 3:89.

2 Who can recount the mighty deeds of the LORD,
proclaim in full God's praise?
3 Blessed those who do what is right,
whose deeds are always just.[s]
4 Remember me, LORD, as you favor your people;
come to me with your saving help,[t]
5 That I may see the prosperity of your chosen ones,
rejoice in the joy of your people,
and glory with your heritage.

B

6 We have sinned like our ancestors;[u]
we have done wrong and are guilty.

I

7 Our ancestors in Egypt
did not attend to your wonders.
They did not remember your manifold mercy;
they defied the Most High at the Red Sea.
8 Yet he saved them for his name's sake
to make his power known.[v]
9 He roared at the Red Sea and it dried up.
He led them through the deep as through a desert.[w]
10 He rescued them from hostile hands,
freed them from the power of the enemy.
11 The waters covered their oppressors;
not one of them survived.
12 Then they believed his words
and sang his praise.[x]

II

13 But they soon forgot all he had done;
they had no patience for his plan.
14 In the desert they gave in to their cravings,
tempted God in the wasteland.[y]
15 So he gave them what they asked
and sent a wasting disease against them.[z]

III

16 In the camp they challenged Moses[a]
and Aaron, the holy one of the LORD.
17 The earth opened and swallowed Dathan,
it closed on the followers of Abiram.
18 Against their company the fire blazed;
flames consumed the wicked.

IV

19 At Horeb they fashioned a calf,[b]
worshiped a metal statue.
20 They exchanged their glory*
for the image of a grass-eating bull.
21 They forgot the God who had saved them,
who had done great deeds in Egypt,[c]
22 Amazing deeds in the land of Ham,
fearsome deeds at the Red Sea.
23 He would have decreed their destruction,
had not Moses, his chosen one,
Withstood him in the breach*
to turn back his destroying anger.[d]

V

24 Next they despised the beautiful land;[e]
they did not believe the promise.
25 In their tents they complained;
they did not heed the voice of the LORD.
26 So with raised hand he swore
he would destroy them in the desert,
27 And scatter their descendants among the nations,
disperse them in foreign lands.

VI

28 They joined in the rites of Baal of Peor,[f]
ate food sacrificed to the dead.
29 They provoked him by their actions,
and a plague broke out among them.
30 Then Phinehas rose to intervene,
and the plague was brought to a halt.
31 This was counted for him as a righteous deed
for all generations to come.

13–14 and Dt 1–2), the rebellion at Baal-Peor (Ps 106:28–31; see Nm 25:1–10), the anger of Moses (Ps 106:32–33; see Nm 20:1–13), and mingling with the nations (Ps 106:34–47). The last, as suggested by its length and generalized language, may be the sin that invites the repentance of the present generation. The text gives the site of each sin: Egypt (Ps 106:7), the desert (Ps 106:14), the camp (Ps 106:16), Horeb (Ps 106:19), in their tents (Ps 106:25), Baal-Peor (Ps 106:28), the waters of Meribah (Ps 106:32), Canaan (Ps 106:38).

106:20 Their glory: meant as a reference to God.

106:23 Withstood him in the breach: the image is that of Moses standing in a narrow break made in the wall to keep anyone from entering.

s: Is 56:1–2. *t:* Ps 25:7; Neh 5:19. *u:* Ps 78:11–17; Ex 14:11; Lv 26:40; 1 Kgs 8:47; Bar 2:12; Dn 9:5. *v:* Ez 36:20–22. *w:* Ex 14:21–31; Is 50:2; 63:11–14; Na 1:4. *x:* Ex 15:1–21. *y:* Ps 78:18; Ex 15:24; 16:3; Nm 11:1–6. *z:* Ps 78:26–31; Nm 11:33. *a:* Nm 16; Dt 11:6; Is 26:11. *b:* Ex 32; Dt 9:8–21; Jer 2:11; Acts 7:41; Rom 1:23. *c:* Ps 78:42–58; Dt 32:18; Jer 2:32. *d:* Ex 32:11; Dt 9:25; Ez 22:30. *e:* Lv 26:33; Nm 14; Dt 1:25–36; Ez 20:15, 23. *f:* Nm 25; Dt 26:14; Sir 45:23–24.

VII

32 At the waters of Meribah they angered
God,[g]
and Moses suffered because of them.*
33 They so embittered his spirit
that rash words crossed his lips.

VIII

34 They did not destroy the peoples
as the LORD had commanded them,[h]
35 But mingled with the nations
and imitated their ways.[i]
36 They served their idols
and were ensnared by them.[j]
37 They sacrificed to demons*
their own sons and daughters,
38 Shedding innocent blood,
the blood of their own sons and
daughters,
Whom they sacrificed to the idols of
Canaan,
desecrating the land with bloodshed.
39 They defiled themselves by their actions,
became adulterers by their conduct.
40 So the LORD grew angry with his people,
abhorred his own heritage.
41 He handed them over to the nations,
and their adversaries ruled over them.[k]
42 Their enemies oppressed them,
kept them under subjection.
43 Many times did he rescue them,
but they kept rebelling and scheming
and were brought low by their own
guilt.[l]
44 Still God had regard for their affliction
when he heard their wailing.
45 For their sake he remembered his covenant
and relented in his abundant mercy,[m]
46 Winning for them compassion
from all who held them captive.

C

47 Save us, LORD, our God;
gather us from among the nations
That we may give thanks to your holy
name
and glory in praising you.[n]
48 *Blessed be the LORD, the God of Israel,
from everlasting to everlasting!
Let all the people say, Amen![o]
Hallelujah!

Fifth Book—Psalms 107–150

PSALM 107*

See RG 244

*God the Savior of
Those in Distress*

1 "Give thanks to the LORD for he is good,
his mercy endures forever!"[p]
2 Let that be the prayer of the LORD's
redeemed,
those redeemed from the hand of the
foe,[q]
3 Those gathered from foreign lands,
from east and west, from north and
south.[r]

I

4 Some had lost their way in a barren desert;
found no path toward a city to live in.
5 They were hungry and thirsty;
their life was ebbing away.[s]
6 In their distress they cried to the LORD,
who rescued them in their peril,
7 [t]Guided them by a direct path
so they reached a city to live in.[u]
8 Let them thank the LORD for his mercy,
such wondrous deeds for the children
of Adam.
9 For he satisfied the thirsty,
filled the hungry with good things.[v]

106:32 Moses suffered because of them: Moses was not allowed to enter the promised land because of his rash words (Nm 20:12). According to Dt 1:37, Moses was not allowed to cross because of the people's sin, not his own.

106:37 Demons: Hebrew *shedim* occurs in parallelism with "gods" in an important inscription from Transjordan and hence can also be translated "the gods."

106:48 A doxology ending Book IV of the Psalter. It is not part of the Psalm.

Psalm 107 A hymn inviting those who have been rescued by God to give praise (Ps 107:1–3). Four archetypal divine rescues are described, each ending in thanksgiving: from the sterile desert (Ps 107:4–9), from imprisonment in gloom (Ps 107:10–16), from mortal illness (Ps 107:17–22), and from the angry sea (Ps 107:23–32). The number four connotes totality, all the possible varieties of rescue. The same saving activity of God is shown in Israel's history (Ps 107:33–41); whenever the people were endangered God rescued them. The last verses invite people to ponder the persistent saving acts of God (Ps 107:42–43).

g: Ps 95:8–9; Ex 17:1–7; Nm 20:2–13; Dt 6:16; 33:8. *h:* Dt 7:1; Jgs 2:1–5. *i:* Lv 18:3; Jgs 1:27–35; 3:5. *j:* Lv 18:21; Nm 35:33; Dt 32:17; Jgs 2:11–13, 17, 19; 2 Kgs 16:3; Bar 4:7; 1 Cor 10:20. *k:* Jgs 2:14–23. *l:* Is 63:7–9. *m:* Lv 26:42. *n:* 1 Chr 16:35. *o:* Ps 41:14; 72:18; 89:53; 1 Chr 16:36; Neh 9:5. *p:* Ps 100:4–5; 106:1; Jer 33:11. *q:* Is 63:12. *r:* Is 43:5–6; 49:12; Zec 8:7. *s:* Dt 8:15; 32:10; Is 49:10. *t:* Is 35:8; 40:3; 43:19. *u:* Dt 6:10. *v:* Lk 1:53.

II

10 Some lived in darkness and gloom,
imprisoned in misery and chains.
11 Because they rebelled against God's word,
and scorned the counsel of the Most High,[w]
12 He humbled their hearts through hardship;
they stumbled with no one to help.[x]
13 In their distress they cried to the LORD,
who saved them in their peril;
14 He brought them forth from darkness and the shadow of death
and broke their chains asunder.[y]
15 Let them thank the LORD for his mercy,
such wondrous deeds for the children of Adam.
16 For he broke down the gates of bronze
and snapped the bars of iron.

III

17 Some fell sick from their wicked ways,
afflicted because of their sins.
18 They loathed all manner of food;[z]
they were at the gates of death.
19 In their distress they cried to the LORD,
who saved them in their peril,
20 Sent forth his word to heal them,[a]
and snatched them from the grave.
21 Let them thank the LORD for his mercy,
such wondrous deeds for the children of Adam.
22 Let them offer a sacrifice in thanks,
recount his works with shouts of joy.

IV

23 Some went off to sea in ships,
plied their trade on the deep waters.[b]
24 They saw the works of the LORD,
the wonders of God in the deep.
25 He commanded and roused a storm wind;
it tossed the waves on high.[c]
26 They rose up to the heavens, sank to the depths;
their hearts trembled at the danger.
27 They reeled, staggered like drunkards;
their skill was of no avail.[d]
28 In their distress they cried to the LORD,
who brought them out of their peril;
29 He hushed the storm to silence,
the waves of the sea were stilled.[e]
30 They rejoiced that the sea grew calm,
that God brought them to the harbor they longed for.
31 Let them thank the LORD for his mercy,
such wondrous deeds for the children of Adam.
32 Let them extol him in the assembly of the people,
and praise him in the council of the elders.

V

33 *God changed rivers into desert,
springs of water into thirsty ground,[f]
34 Fruitful land into a salty waste,
because of the wickedness of its people.[g]
35 He changed the desert into pools of water,
arid land into springs of water,[h]
36 And settled the hungry there;
they built a city to live in.[i]
37 They sowed fields and planted vineyards,
brought in an abundant harvest.[j]
38 [k]God blessed them, and they increased greatly,
and their livestock did not decrease.[l]
39 But he poured out contempt on princes,
made them wander trackless wastes,
40 Where they were diminished and brought low
through misery and cruel oppression.
41 While he released the poor man from affliction,
and increased their families like flocks.[m]
42 The upright saw this and rejoiced;[n]
all wickedness shut its mouth.
43 Whoever is wise will take note of these things,[o]
and ponder the merciful deeds of the LORD.

107:33–41 God destroyed Sodom and Gomorrah in Gn 18–19, which the Psalm sees as the destruction of the wicked inhabitants of Canaan to prepare the way for Israel (Ps 107:33–34). God then led Israel through the desert to give them a fertile land (Ps 107:35–38) and protected them from every danger (Ps 107:39–41).

w: Is 42:7, 22; Jb 36:8–9; Prv 1:25. *x:* Ps 106:43. *y:* Is 42:7; 49:9; 51:14. *z:* Jb 6:6–7; 33:20. *a:* Ps 147:15; Wis 16:12; Is 55:11; Mt 8:8. *b:* Sir 43:25. *c:* Jon 1:4. *d:* Is 29:9. *e:* Ps 65:8; 89:10; Mt 8:26 par. *f:* Is 35:7; 42:15; 50:2. *g:* Gn 19:23–28; Dt 29:22; Sir 39:23. *h:* Ps 114:8; Is 41:8. *i:* Ez 36:35. *j:* Is 65:21; Jer 31:5. *k:* Jb 12:23–25. *l:* Dt 7:13–14. *m:* Ps 113:7. *n:* Ps 58:11; 63:12. *o:* Hos 14:10.

See RG 246

PSALM 108*

Prayer for Victory

1 A song; a psalm of David.

I

2 My heart is steadfast, God;[p]
my heart is steadfast.
Let me sing and chant praise.
3 Awake, lyre and harp!
I will wake the dawn.[q]
4 I will praise you among the peoples, LORD;
I will chant your praise among the nations.[r]
5 For your mercy is greater than the heavens;
your faithfulness, to the skies.[s]

II

6 Appear on high over the heavens, God;
your glory above all the earth.
7 Help with your right hand and answer us
that your loved ones may escape.

8 God speaks in his holiness:*[t]
"I will exult, I will apportion Shechem;
the valley of Succoth I will measure out.
9 Gilead is mine, mine is Manasseh;
Ephraim is the helmet for my head,
Judah, my scepter.
10 Moab is my washbowl;
upon Edom I cast my sandal;[u]
I will shout in triumph over Philistia."
11 Who will bring me to the fortified city?
Who will lead me into Edom?
12 Was it not you who rejected us, God?
Do you no longer march with our armies?[v]
13 Give us aid against the foe;
worthless is human help.
14 We will triumph with the help of God,
who will trample down our foes.

PSALM 109*

See RG 244

Prayer of a Person Falsely Accused

1 For the leader. A psalm of David.

I

2 O God, whom I praise, do not be silent,[w]
for wicked and treacherous mouths attack me.
They speak against me with lying tongues;
3 with hateful words they surround me,
attacking me without cause.
4 In return for my love they slander me,
even though I prayed for them.
5 They repay me evil for good,
hatred for my love.[x]

II

6 Appoint an evil one over him,
an accuser* to stand at his right hand,
7 That he may be judged and found guilty,
that his plea may be in vain.
8 May his days be few;
may another take his office.[y]
9 May his children be fatherless,
his wife, a widow.[z]
10 May his children wander and beg,
driven from their hovels.
11 May the usurer snare all he owns,
strangers plunder all he earns.
12 May no one treat him with mercy
or pity his fatherless children.
13 May his posterity be destroyed,[a]
their name rooted out in the next generation.

Psalm 108 A prayer compiled from two other Psalms: Ps 108:2–6 are virtually the same as Ps 57:8–12; Ps 108:7–14 are the same as Ps 60:7–14. An old promise of salvation (Ps 108:8–10) is combined with a confident assurance (Ps 108:2–6, 13) and petition (Ps 108:7, 12–13).

108:8 Holiness: may also be translated as "sanctuary" or as referring to God's heavenly abode.

Psalm 109 A lament notable for the length and vehemence of its prayer against evildoers (Ps 109:6–20); the cry to God (Ps 109:1) and the complaint (Ps 109:22–25) are brief in comparison. The psalmist is apparently the victim of a slander campaign, potentially devastating in a society where reputation and honor are paramount. In the emotional perspective of the Psalm, there are only two types of people: the wicked and their poor victims. The psalmist is a poor victim (Ps 109:22, 31) and by that fact a friend of God and enemy of the wicked. The psalmist seeks vindication not on the basis of personal virtue but because of God's promise to protect the poor.

109:6 An accuser: Hebrew *satan*, a word occurring in Job 1–2 and Zec 3:1–2. In the latter passage Satan stands at the right hand of the high priest to bring false accusations against him before God. Here the accuser is human.

p: Ps 57:8–12. *q:* Jb 38:12. *r:* Ps 9:12; 18:50; 148:13. *s:* Ps 36:6; 71:19. *t:* Ps 60:8–14. *u:* Ru 4:7–8. *v:* Ps 44:10. *w:* Ps 35:22; 83:1. *x:* Ps 35:12; 38:21; Prv 17:13; Jer 18:20. *y:* Acts 1:20. *z:* Ex 22:23; Jer 18:21. *a:* Ps 21:11; Prv 10:7.

14 May his fathers' guilt be mentioned to
the LORD;
his mother's sin not rooted out.[b]
15 May their guilt be always before the
LORD,[c]
till their memory is banished from the
earth,[d]
16 For he did not remember to show mercy,
but hounded the wretched poor
and brought death to the brokenhearted.
17 He loved cursing; may it come upon him;
he hated blessing; may none come to
him.
18 May cursing clothe him like a robe;
may it enter his belly like water,
his bones like oil.
19 May it be near as the clothes he wears,
as the belt always around him.
20 *May this be the reward for my accusers
from the LORD,
for those speaking evil against me.

III

21 But you, LORD, are my Lord,
deal kindly with me for your name's
sake;
in your great mercy rescue me.
22 For I am poor and needy;
my heart is pierced within me.
23 Like a lengthening shadow I am gone,
I am shaken off like the locust.
24 My knees totter from fasting;[e]
my flesh has wasted away.
25 I have become a mockery to them;
when they see me, they shake their
heads.
26 Help me, LORD, my God;
save me in your mercy.
27 Make them know this is your hand,
that you, LORD, have done this.
28 Though they curse, may you bless;
arise, shame them, that your servant
may rejoice.
29 Clothe my accusers with disgrace;
make them wear their shame like a
mantle.
30 I will give fervent thanks to the LORD;
before a crowd I will praise him.[f]
31 For he stands at the right hand of the
poor
to save him from those who pass
judgment on him.

PSALM 110*

See RG 245, 251

God Appoints the King both King and Priest

1 A psalm of David.

The LORD says to my lord:*
"Sit at my right hand,
while I make your enemies your
footstool."*[g]
2 The scepter of your might:
the LORD extends your strong scepter
from Zion.
Have dominion over your enemies!
3 Yours is princely power from the day of
your birth.
In holy splendor before the daystar,
like dew I begot you.[h]
4 The LORD has sworn and will not waver:
"You are a priest forever in the manner
of Melchizedek."*[i]
5 At your right hand is the Lord,
who crushes kings on the day of his
wrath,[j]
6 Who judges nations, heaps up corpses,
crushes heads across the wide earth,

109:20 May this be the reward . . . from the LORD: the psalmist prays that God ratify the curses of Ps 109:6–19 and bring them upon the wicked.

Psalm 110 A royal Psalm in which a court singer recites three oracles in which God assures the king that his enemies are conquered (Ps 110:1–2), makes the king "son" in traditional adoption language (Ps 110:3), gives priestly status to the king and promises to be with him in future military ventures (Ps 110:4–7).

110:1 The LORD says to my lord: a polite form of address of an inferior to a superior, cf. 1 Sm 25:25; 2 Sm 1:10. The court singer refers to the king. Jesus in the synoptic gospels (Mt 22:41–46 and parallels) takes the psalmist to be David and hence "my lord" refers to the messiah, who must be someone greater than David. **Your footstool**: in ancient times victorious kings put their feet on the prostrate bodies of their enemies.

110:4 Melchizedek: Melchizedek was the ancient king of Salem (Jerusalem) who blessed Abraham (Gn 14:18–20); like other kings of the time he performed priestly functions. Heb 7 sees in Melchizedek a type of Christ.

b: Ex 20:5. *c:* Ps 90:8. *d:* Ps 34:16. *e:* Ps 69:11–13. *f:* Ps 111:1. *g:* Mt 22:44; Acts 2:34–35; 1 Cor 15:25; Heb 1:13; 8:1; 10:12–13; 1 Pt 3:22. *h:* Ps 2:7; 89:27; Is 49:1. *i:* Ps 89:35; 132:11; Gn 14:18; Heb 5:6; 7:21. *j:* Ps 2:9; Rev 2:27; 12:5; 19:15.

7 *Who drinks from the brook by the
wayside
and thus holds high his head.[k]

See RG 244, 246

PSALM 111*

Praise of God for Goodness to Israel

1 Hallelujah!

I will praise the LORD with all my heart[l]
in the assembled congregation of the
upright.*
2 Great are the works of the LORD,
studied by all who delight in them.
3 Majestic and glorious is his work,
his righteousness endures forever.
4 He won renown for his wondrous deeds;
gracious and merciful is the LORD.[m]
5 He gives food to those who fear him,*
he remembers his covenant forever.
6 He showed his powerful deeds to his
people,
giving them the inheritance of the
nations.
7 The works of his hands are true and
just,
reliable all his decrees,
8 Established forever and ever,
to be observed with truth and equity.
9 He sent release to his people,
decreed his covenant forever;
holy and fearsome is his name.
10 *The fear of the LORD is the beginning of
wisdom;[n]
prudent are all who practice it.
His praise endures forever.

PSALM 112*

See RG 245–46

The Blessings of the Just

1 Hallelujah!

Blessed the man who fears the LORD,
who greatly delights in his
commands.[o]
2 His descendants shall be mighty in the
land,
a generation of the upright will be
blessed.
3 Wealth and riches shall be in his house;
his righteousness* shall endure forever.
4 Light shines through the darkness for the
upright;[p]
gracious, compassionate, and
righteous.
5 It is good for the man gracious in
lending,
who conducts his affairs with justice.
6 For he shall never be shaken;
the righteous shall be remembered
forever.[q]
7 He shall not fear an ill report;
his heart is steadfast, trusting the
LORD.
8 His heart is tranquil, without fear,
till at last he looks down on his foes.
9 Lavishly he gives to the poor;
his righteousness shall endure forever;[r]
his horn* shall be exalted in honor.
10 The wicked sees and is angry;
gnashes his teeth and wastes away;
the desire of the wicked come to
nothing.

110:7 Who drinks from the brook by the wayside: the meaning is uncertain. Some see an allusion to a rite of royal consecration at the Gihon spring (cf. 1 Kgs 1:33, 38). Others find here an image of the divine warrior (or king) pursuing enemies so relentlessly that he does not stop long enough to eat and drink.

Psalm 111 A Temple singer (Ps 111:1) tells how God is revealed in Israel's history (Ps 111:2–10). The deeds reveal God's very self, powerful, merciful, faithful. The poem is an acrostic, each verse beginning with a successive letter of the Hebrew alphabet.

111:1 In the assembled congregation of the upright: in the Temple, cf. Ps 149:1.

111:5 Food to those who fear him: probably a reference to the manna in the desert, which elsewhere is seen as a type of the Eucharist, cf. Jn 6:31–33, 49–51.

111:10 The fear of the LORD: reverence for God.

Psalm 112 An acrostic poem detailing the blessings received by those who remain close to God by obedience to the commandments. Among their blessings are children (Ps 112:2), wealth that enables them to be magnanimous (Ps 112:3, 5, 9), and virtue by which they encourage others (Ps 112:4). The just person is an affront to the wicked, whose hopes remain unfulfilled (Ps 112:10). The logic resembles Ps 1; 111.

112:3 Righteousness: in the Second Temple period the word acquired the nuance of liberality and almsgiving, cf. Sir 3:30; 7:10; Mt 6:1–4.

112:9 His horn: the symbol for vitality and honor.

k: Ps 3:4. *l:* Ps 138:1. *m:* Ps 103:8; 112:4. *n:* Prv 1:7; 9:10; Sir 1:16. *o:* Ps 1:1–2; 119:1–2; 128:1. *p:* Ps 37:6; 97:11; Prv 13:9; Is 58:10. *q:* Prv 10:7; Wis 8:13. *r:* Prv 22:9; 2 Cor 9:9.

See RG 244

PSALM 113*

Praise of God's Care for the Poor

1 Hallelujah!

I

Praise, you servants of the LORD,
praise the name of the LORD.[s]
2 Blessed be the name of the LORD
both now and forever.
3 From the rising of the sun to its setting[t]
let the name of the LORD be praised.

II

4 High above all nations is the LORD;
above the heavens his glory.[u]
5 Who is like the LORD our God,
enthroned on high,
6 [v]looking down on heaven and earth?
7 He raises the needy from the dust,
lifts the poor from the ash heap,[w]
8 Seats them with princes,
the princes of the people,
9 Gives the childless wife a home,
the joyful mother of children.[x]
Hallelujah!

See RG 244, 247, 250

PSALM 114*

The Lord's Wonders at the Exodus

1 When Israel came forth from Egypt,
the house of Jacob from an alien people,
2 Judah became God's sanctuary,
Israel, God's domain.[y]
3 *The sea saw and fled;
the Jordan turned back.[z]
4 The mountains skipped like rams;
the hills, like lambs.[a]
5 Why was it, sea, that you fled?
Jordan, that you turned back?
6 Mountains, that you skipped like rams?
You hills, like lambs?
7 Tremble, earth, before the Lord,[b]
before the God of Jacob,
8 *Who turned the rock into pools of water,
flint into a flowing spring.[c]

PSALM 115*

See RG 245

The Greatness of the True God

I

1 Not to us, LORD, not to us
but to your name give glory
because of your mercy and
faithfulness.[d]
2 Why should the nations say,
"Where is their God?"*[e]
3 Our God is in heaven
and does whatever he wills.[f]

II

4 Their idols are silver and gold,[g]
the work of human hands.[h]
5 They have mouths but do not speak,
eyes but do not see.
6 They have ears but do not hear,
noses but do not smell.
7 They have hands but do not feel,
feet but do not walk;

Psalm 113 A hymn exhorting the congregation to praise God's name, i.e., the way in which God is present in the world; the name is mentioned three times in Ps 113:1–3. The divine name is especially honored in the Temple (Ps 113:1) but its recognition is not limited by time (Ps 113:2) and space (Ps 113:3), for God is everywhere active (Ps 113:4–5) especially in rescuing the lowly faithful (Ps 113:7–9).

Psalm 114 A hymn celebrating Israel's escape from Egypt, journey through the wilderness, and entry into the promised land, and the miracles of nature that bore witness to God's presence in their midst. In the perspective of the Psalm, the people proceed directly from Egypt into the promised land (Ps 114:1–2). Sea and Jordan, which stood like soldiers barring the people from their land, flee before the mighty God as the earth recoils from the battle (Ps 114:3–4). The poet taunts the natural elements as one taunts defeated enemies (Ps 114:5–6).

114:3–4 Pairs of cosmic elements such as sea and rivers, mountains and hills, are sometimes mentioned in creation accounts. Personified here as warriors, the pairs tremble in fear before the Divine Warrior. The quaking also recalls the divine appearance in the storm at Sinai (Ex 19:16–19) and elsewhere (Jgs 5:4–5; Ps 18:7–15).

114:8 The miracles of giving drink to the people in the arid desert, cf. Ex 17:1–7; Is 41:17–18.

Psalm 115 A response to the enemy taunt, "Where is your God?" This hymn to the glory of Israel's God (Ps 115:1–3) ridicules the lifeless idols of the nations (Ps 115:4–8), expresses in a litany the trust of the various classes of the people in God (Ps 115:9–11), invokes God's blessing on them as they invoke the divine name (Ps 115:12–15), and concludes as it began with praise of God. Ps 135:15–18 similarly mocks the Gentile gods and has a similar litany and hymn (Ps 135:19–21).

115:2 Where is their God?: implies that God cannot help them.

---

s: Ps 135:1. *t:* Mal 1:11. *u:* Ps 148:13. *v:* Ps 89:7–9. *w:* Ps 107:41; 1 Sm 2:7–8. *x:* 1 Sm 2:5; Is 54:1. *y:* Ex 19:6. *z:* Ps 66:6; 74:15; Ex 14:21f; Jos 3:14ff. *a:* Ps 29:6; Wis 19:9. *b:* Ps 68:9. *c:* Ex 17:6; Nm 20:11. *d:* Ez 36:22–23. *e:* Ps 79:10. *f:* Ps 135:6. *g:* Ps 135:15–19; Wis 15:15–16; Is 44:9f; Jer 10:1–5. *h:* Is 40:19.

they produce no sound from their
throats.
8 Their makers will be like them,
and anyone who trusts in them.

III

9 *The house of Israel trusts in the LORD,[i]
who is their help and shield.[j]
10 The house of Aaron trusts in the LORD,
who is their help and shield.
11 Those who fear the LORD trust in the LORD,
who is their help and shield.
12 The LORD remembers us and will bless us,
will bless the house of Israel,
will bless the house of Aaron,
13 Will bless those who fear the LORD,
small and great alike.
14 May the LORD increase your number,
yours and your descendants.
15 May you be blessed by the LORD,
maker of heaven and earth.
16 *The heavens belong to the LORD,
but he has given the earth to the
children of Adam.[k]
17 *The dead do not praise the LORD,
not all those go down into silence.[l]
18 It is we who bless the LORD,
both now and forever.
Hallelujah!

See RG 245

PSALM 116*

Thanksgiving to God Who Saves from Death

I

1 I love the LORD, who listened
to my voice in supplication,
2 Who turned an ear to me
on the day I called.
3 I was caught by the cords of death;*[m]
the snares of Sheol had seized me;
I felt agony and dread.
4 Then I called on the name of the LORD,
"O LORD, save my life!"

II

5 Gracious is the LORD and righteous;
yes, our God is merciful.[n]
6 The LORD protects the simple;
I was helpless, but he saved me.
7 Return, my soul, to your rest;
the LORD has been very good to you.[o]
8 For my soul has been freed from death,
my eyes from tears, my feet from
stumbling.[p]
9 I shall walk before the LORD
in the land of the living.*[q]

III

10 *I kept faith, even when I said,
"I am greatly afflicted!"[r]
11 I said in my alarm,
"All men are liars!"[s]
12 How can I repay the LORD
for all the great good done for me?
13 I will raise the cup of salvation*
and call on the name of the LORD.
14 I will pay my vows to the LORD
in the presence of all his people.
15 *Dear in the eyes of the LORD
is the death of his devoted.[t]
16 LORD, I am your servant,
your servant, the child of your
maidservant;[u]

115:9–11 The house of Israel . . . the house of Aaron . . . those who fear the LORD: the laity of Israelite birth, the priests, and the converts to Judaism, cf. Ps 118:2–4; 135:19–21. In the New Testament likewise "those who fear the Lord" means converts to Judaism (cf. Acts 10:2, 22, 35; 13:16, 26).

115:16 The heavens: the Septuagint reads here "the heaven of heavens" or "the highest heavens," i.e., above the firmament. See note on Ps 148:4.

115:17 See note on Ps 6:5.

Psalm 116 A thanksgiving in which the psalmist responds to divine rescue from mortal danger (Ps 116:3–4) and from near despair (Ps 116:10–11) with vows and Temple sacrifices (Ps 116:13–14, 17–19). The Greek and Latin versions divide the Psalm into two parts: Ps 116:1–9 and Ps 116:10–19, corresponding to its two major divisions.

116:3 The cords of death: death is personified here; it attempts to capture the psalmist with snares and nets, cf. Ps 18:6.

116:9 The land of the living: the phrase elsewhere is an epithet of the Jerusalem Temple (cf. Ps 27:13; 52:5; Is 38:11). Hence the psalmist probably refers to being present to God in the Temple.

116:10 I kept faith, even when I said: even in the days of despair, the psalmist did not lose all hope.

116:13 The cup of salvation: probably the libation of wine poured out in gratitude for rescue, cf. Ex 25:29; Nm 15:5, 7, 10.

116:15 Dear in the eyes of the LORD: the meaning is that the death of God's faithful is grievous to God, not that God is pleased with the death, cf. Ps 72:14. In Wis 3:5–6, God accepts the death of the righteous as a sacrificial burnt offering.

i: Ps 118:2–4. *j:* Ps 33:20. *k:* Gn 1:28. *l:* Ps 6:6; 88:11ff; Sir 17:22f; Is 38:18. *m:* Ps 18:5; Jon 2:3. *n:* Ex 34:6. *o:* Ps 13:6. *p:* Ps 56:14; Is 25:8; Rev 21:4. *q:* Ps 27:13; 56:14; Is 38:11. *r:* 2 Cor 4:13. *s:* Ps 12:2. *t:* Ps 72:14; Is 43:4. *u:* Ps 86:16; 143:12; Wis 9:5.

you have loosed my bonds.
17 I will offer a sacrifice of praise
and call on the name of the LORD.[v]
18 I will pay my vows to the LORD[w]
in the presence of all his people,
19 In the courts of the house of the LORD,
in your midst, O Jerusalem.
Hallelujah!

See RG 244, 250

PSALM 117*

The Nations Called To Praise

1 Praise the LORD, all you nations!
Extol him, all you peoples![x]
2 His mercy for us is strong;
the faithfulness of the LORD is forever.
Hallelujah!

See RG 245, 252

PSALM 118*

Hymn of Thanksgiving

I

1 Give thanks to the LORD, for he is good,[y]
his mercy endures forever.
2 Let Israel say:
his mercy endures forever.
3 Let the house of Aaron say,
his mercy endures forever.
4 Let those who fear the LORD say,[z]
his mercy endures forever.

II

5 In danger I called on the LORD;
the LORD answered me and set me
free.
6 The LORD is with me; I am not afraid;
what can mortals do against me?[a]
7 The LORD is with me as my helper;
I shall look in triumph on my foes.
8 Better to take refuge in the LORD[b]
than to put one's trust in mortals.
9 Better to take refuge in the LORD
than to put one's trust in princes.

III

10 All the nations surrounded me;
in the LORD's name I cut them off.
11 They surrounded me on every side;
in the LORD's name I cut them off.
12 They surrounded me like bees;[c]
they burned up like fire among thorns;
in the LORD's name I cut them off.
13 I was hard pressed and falling,
but the LORD came to my help.[d]
14 The LORD, my strength and might,
has become my savior.[e]

IV

15 The joyful shout of deliverance
is heard in the tents of the righteous:
"The LORD's right hand works valiantly;
16 the LORD's right hand is raised;
the LORD's right hand works
valiantly."
17 I shall not die but live
and declare the deeds of the LORD.
18 The LORD chastised me harshly,
but did not hand me over to death.

V

19 Open the gates of righteousness;
I will enter and thank the LORD.[f]
20 This is the LORD's own gate,
through it the righteous enter.
21 I thank you for you answered me;
you have been my savior.
22 *The stone the builders rejected
has become the cornerstone.[g]
23 By the LORD has this been done;
it is wonderful in our eyes.

Psalm 117 This shortest of hymns calls on the nations to acknowledge God's supremacy. The supremacy of Israel's God has been demonstrated to them by the people's secure existence, which is owed entirely to God's gracious fidelity.

Psalm 118 A thanksgiving liturgy accompanying a procession of the king and the people into the Temple precincts. After an invocation in the form of a litany (Ps 118:1–4), the psalmist (very likely speaking in the name of the community) describes how the people confidently implored God's help (Ps 118:5–9) when hostile peoples threatened its life (Ps 118:10–14); vividly God's rescue is recounted (Ps 118:15–18). Then follows a possible dialogue at the Temple gates between the priests and the psalmist as the latter enters to offer the thanksgiving sacrifice (Ps 118:19–25). Finally, the priests impart their blessing (Ps 118:26–27), and the psalmist sings in gratitude (Ps 118:28–29).

118:22 The stone the builders rejected: a proverb: what is insignificant to human beings has become great through divine election. The "stone" may originally have meant the foundation stone or capstone of the Temple. The New Testament interpreted the verse as referring to the death and resurrection of Christ (Mt 21:42; Acts 4:11; cf. Is 28:16 and Rom 9:33; 1 Pt 2:7).

118:25 Grant salvation: the Hebrew for this cry has come into English as "Hosanna." This cry and the words in Ps 118:26 were used in the gospels to welcome Jesus entering the Temple on Palm Sunday (Mk 11:9–10).

v: Lv 7:12ff. *w:* Jon 2:10. *x:* Rom 15:11. *y:* Ps 100:5; 136:1f. *z:* Ps 115:9–11. *a:* Ps 27:1; Heb 13:6. *b:* Ps 146:3. *c:* Dt 1:44. *d:* Ps 129:1–2. *e:* Ex 15:2; Is 12:2. *f:* Is 26:2. *g:* Mt 21:42; Lk 20:17; Acts 4:11; Rom 9:33; 1 Pt 2:7.

24 This is the day the LORD has made;
let us rejoice in it and be glad.
25 LORD, grant salvation!*
LORD, grant good fortune!
VI
26 Blessed is he
who comes in the name of the LORD.[h]
We bless you from the house of the LORD.
27 The LORD is God and has
enlightened us.
Join in procession with leafy branches
up to the horns of the altar.
VII
28 You are my God, I give you thanks;
my God, I offer you praise.
29 Give thanks to the LORD, for he is good,
his mercy endures forever.

See RG 245–46

PSALM 119*

A Prayer to God, the Lawgiver

ALEPH
1 Blessed those whose way is blameless,
who walk by the law of the LORD.[i]
2 Blessed those who keep his
testimonies,
who seek him with all their heart.[j]
3 They do no wrong;
they walk in his ways.
4 You have given them the command
to observe your precepts with care.
5 May my ways be firm
in the observance of your statutes!
6 Then I will not be ashamed
to ponder all your commandments.
7 I will praise you with sincere heart
as I study your righteous judgments.
8 I will observe your statutes;
do not leave me all alone.

BETH
9 How can the young keep his way without
fault?
Only by observing your words.
10 With all my heart I seek you;
do not let me stray from your
commandments.
11 In my heart I treasure your promise,
that I may not sin against you.
12 Blessed are you, O LORD;
teach me your statutes.[k]
13 With my lips I recite
all the judgments you have spoken.
14 I find joy in the way of your testimonies
more than in all riches.
15 I will ponder your precepts
and consider your paths.
16 In your statutes I take delight;
I will never forget your word.

GIMEL
17 Be kind to your servant that I may live,
that I may keep your word.
18 Open my eyes to see clearly
the wonders of your law.
19 I am a sojourner in the land;*[l]
do not hide your commandments from
me.
20 At all times my soul is stirred
with longing for your judgments.
21 With a curse you rebuke the proud
who stray from your commandments.
22 Free me from disgrace and contempt,
for I keep your testimonies.
23 Though princes meet and talk against me,
your servant meditates on your
statutes.
24 Your testimonies are my delight;
they are my counselors.

Psalm 119 This Psalm, the longest by far in the Psalter, praises God for giving such splendid laws and instruction for people to live by. The author glorifies and thanks God for the Torah, prays for protection from sinners enraged by others' fidelity to the law, laments the cost of obedience, delights in the law's consolations, begs for wisdom to understand the precepts, and asks for the rewards of keeping them. Several expected elements do not appear in the Psalm: Mount Sinai with its story of God's revelation and gift to Israel of instruction and commandments, the Temple and other institutions related to revelation and laws (frequent in other Psalms). The Psalm is fascinated with God's word directing and guiding human life. The poem is an acrostic; its twenty-two stanzas (of eight verses each) are in the order of the Hebrew alphabet. Each of the eight verses within a stanza begins with the same letter. Each verse contains one word for "instruction." The translation here given attempts to translate each Hebrew word for "instruction" with the same English word. There are, however, nine words for "instruction," not eight, so the principle of a different word for "instruction" in each verse cannot be maintained with perfect consistency. The nine words for "instruction" in the translation are: law, statute, commandment, precept, testimony, word, judgment, way, and promise.

119:19 A sojourner in the land: like someone without the legal protection of a native inhabitant, the psalmist has a special need for the guidance of God's teaching.

h: Mt 21:9; 23:39. *i:* Ps 1:1–2; 15:2; 112:1. *j:* Dt 4:29. *k:* Ps 25:4; 27:11; 86:11; 143:8, 10. *l:* Ps 39:13.

DALETH

25 My soul clings to the dust;[m]
give me life in accord with your word.
26 I disclosed my ways and you
answered me;
teach me your statutes.
27 Make me understand the way of your
precepts;
I will ponder your wondrous deeds.
28 My soul is depressed;
lift me up acccording to your word.
29 Lead me from the way of deceit;
favor me with your law.
30 The way of loyalty I have chosen;
I have kept your judgments.
31 I cling to your testimonies, LORD;
do not let me come to shame.
32 I will run the way of your commandments,
for you will broaden my heart.

HE

33 LORD, teach me the way of your statutes;
I shall keep them with care.[n]
34 Give me understanding to keep your law,
to observe it with all my heart.
35 Lead me in the path of your
commandments,[o]
for that is my delight.
36 Direct my heart toward your testimonies
and away from gain.
37 Avert my eyes from what is worthless;
by your way give me life.
38 For your servant, fulfill your promise
made to those who fear you.
39 Turn away from me the taunts I dread,
for your judgments are good.
40 See how I long for your precepts;
in your righteousness give me life.

WAW

41 Let your mercy come to me, LORD,
salvation in accord with your promise.
42 Let me answer my taunters with a word,
for I trust in your word.
43 Do not take the word of truth from my
mouth,
for in your judgments is my hope.
44 I will keep your law always,
for all time and forever.
45 I will walk freely in an open space
because I cherish your precepts.
46 I will speak openly of your testimonies
without fear even before kings.
47 I delight in your commandments,
which I dearly love.
48 *I lift up my hands to your
commandments;
I study your statutes, which I love.

ZAYIN

49 Remember your word to your servant
by which you give me hope.
50 This is my comfort in affliction,
your promise that gives me life.
51 Though the arrogant utterly scorn me,
I do not turn from your law.
52 When I recite your judgments of old
I am comforted, LORD.
53 Rage seizes me because of the wicked;
they forsake your law.
54 Your statutes become my songs
wherever I make my home.
55 Even at night I remember your name
in observance of your law, LORD.
56 This is my good fortune,
for I have kept your precepts.

HETH

57 My portion is the LORD;
I promise to observe your words.
58 I entreat you with all my heart:
have mercy on me in accord with your
promise.
59 I have examined my ways
and turned my steps to your
testimonies.
60 I am prompt, I do not hesitate
in observing your commandments.
61 Though the snares of the wicked
surround me,
your law I do not forget.
62 At midnight I rise to praise you
because of your righteous judgments.
63 I am the friend of all who fear you,
of all who observe your precepts.
64 The earth, LORD, is filled with your
mercy;[p]
teach me your statutes.

119:48 I lift up my hands to your commandments: to lift up the hands was an ancient gesture of reverence to God. Here the picture is applied to God's law.

m: Ps 44:26. *n:* Ps 19:12. *o:* Ps 25:4; 27:11; 86:11; 143:8, 10. *p:* Ps 33:5.

TETH

65 You have treated your servant well,
according to your word, O LORD.
66 Teach me wisdom and knowledge,
for in your commandments I trust.
67 Before I was afflicted I went astray,
but now I hold to your promise.
68 You are good and do what is good;
teach me your statutes.
69 The arrogant smear me with lies,
but I keep your precepts with all my heart.
70 Their hearts are gross and fat;[q]
as for me, your law is my delight.
71 It was good for me to be afflicted,
in order to learn your statutes.
72 The law of your mouth is more precious to me
than heaps of silver and gold.

YODH

73 Your hands made me and fashioned me;
give me understanding to learn your commandments.
74 Those who fear you rejoice to see me,
because I hope in your word.
75 I know, LORD, that your judgments are righteous;
though you afflict me, you are faithful.
76 May your mercy comfort me
in accord with your promise to your servant.
77 Show me compassion that I may live,
for your law is my delight.
78 Shame the proud for leading me astray with falsehood,
that I may study your testimonies.
79 Let those who fear you turn to me,
those who acknowledge your testimonies.
80 May I be wholehearted toward your statutes,
that I may not be put to shame.

KAPH

81 My soul longs for your salvation;
I put my hope in your word.[r]
82 My eyes long to see your promise.[s]
When will you comfort me?
83 I am like a wineskin shriveled by smoke,[t]
but I have not forgotten your statutes.
84 How long can your servant survive?
When will your judgment doom my foes?
85 The arrogant have dug pits for me;
defying your law.
86 All your commandments are steadfast.
Help me! I am pursued without cause.
87 They have almost put an end to me on earth,
but I do not forsake your precepts.
88 In your mercy give me life,
to observe the testimonies of your mouth.

LAMEDH

89 *Your word, LORD, stands forever;[u]
it is firm as the heavens.
90 Through all generations your truth endures;
fixed to stand firm like the earth.
91 By your judgments they stand firm to this day,
for all things are your servants.
92 Had your law not been my delight,
I would have perished in my affliction.
93 I will never forget your precepts;
through them you give me life.
94 I am yours; save me,
for I cherish your precepts.
95 The wicked hope to destroy me,
but I seek to understand your testimonies.
96 I have seen the limits of all perfection,
but your commandment is without bounds.

MEM

97 How I love your law, Lord!*
I study it all day long.
98 Your commandment makes me wiser than my foes,
as it is forever with me.
99 I have more insight than all my teachers,
because I ponder your testimonies.
100 I have more understanding than my elders,
because I keep your precepts.[v]

119:89–91 God's word creates the world, which manifests that word by its permanence and reliability.
119:97 Lord: the inclusion of "Lord" follows the tradition of the Septuagint and the Vulgate.

q: Ps 17:10; 73:7; Jb 15:27. *r:* Ps 130:6. *s:* Ps 25:15; 123:1–2; 141:8. *t:* Jb 30:30. *u:* Is 40:8. *v:* Jb 32:6; Wis 4:8–9.

101 I keep my steps from every evil path,
that I may observe your word.
102 From your judgments I do not turn,
for you have instructed me.
103 How sweet to my tongue is your promise,
sweeter than honey to my mouth![w]
104 Through your precepts I gain understanding;
therefore I hate all false ways.

NUN

105 Your word is a lamp for my feet,
a light for my path.[x]
106 I make a solemn vow
to observe your righteous judgments.
107 I am very much afflicted, LORD;
give me life in accord with your word.
108 Accept my freely offered praise;[y]
LORD, teach me your judgments.
109 My life is always at risk,
but I do not forget your law.
110 The wicked have set snares for me,
but from your precepts I do not stray.
111 Your testimonies are my heritage forever;
they are the joy of my heart.
112 My heart is set on fulfilling your statutes;
they are my reward forever.

SAMEKH

113 I hate every hypocrite;
your law I love.
114 You are my refuge and shield;
in your word I hope.
115 Depart from me, you wicked,[z]
that I may keep the commandments of my God.
116 Sustain me by your promise that I may live;
do not disappoint me in my hope.
117 Strengthen me that I may be safe,
ever to contemplate your statutes.
118 You reject all who stray from your statutes,
for vain is their deceit.
119 Like dross you regard all the wicked on earth;
therefore I love your testimonies.
120 My flesh shudders with dread of you;
I fear your judgments.

AYIN

121 I have fulfilled your righteous judgment;
do not abandon me to my oppressors.
122 Guarantee your servant's welfare;
do not let the arrogant oppress me.
123 My eyes long to see your salvation
and the promise of your righteousness.
124 Act with mercy toward your servant;
teach me your statutes.
125 I am your servant; give me discernment
that I may know your testimonies.
126 It is time for the LORD to act;
they have disobeyed your law.
127 Truly I love your commandments
more than gold, more than the finest gold.
128 Thus, I follow all your precepts;
every wrong way I hate.

PE

129 Wonderful are your testimonies;
therefore I keep them.
130 The revelation of your words sheds light,
gives understanding to the simple.
131 I sigh with open mouth,
yearning for your commandments.
132 Turn to me and be gracious,[a]
according to your judgment for those who love your name.
133 Steady my feet in accord with your promise;
do not let iniquity lead me.
134 Free me from human oppression,
that I may observe your precepts.
135 Let your face shine upon your servant;
teach me your statutes.
136 My eyes shed streams of tears
because your law is not observed.

SADHE

137 You are righteous, LORD,
and just are your judgments.[b]
138 You have given your testimonies in righteousness
and in surpassing faithfulness.
139 I am consumed with rage,
because my foes forget your words.
140 Your servant loves your promise;
it has been proved by fire.
141 Though belittled and despised,
I do not forget your precepts.
142 Your justice is forever right,
your law true.

---

w: Ps 19:11. *x:* Ps 18:29; Prv 6:23. *y:* Ps 50:14, 23; Heb 13:15. *z:* Ps 6:9; 139:19; Jb 21:14. *a:* Ps 25:16; 86:16. *b:* Tb 3:2.

143 Though distress and anguish come
upon me,
your commandments are my delight.
144 Your testimonies are forever righteous;
give me understanding that I may live.
145 I call with all my heart, O LORD;
answer me that I may keep your
statutes.
146 I call to you to save me
that I may observe your testimonies.
147 I rise before dawn and cry out;
I put my hope in your words.
148 My eyes greet the night watches
as I meditate on your promise.[c]
149 Hear my voice in your mercy, O LORD;
by your judgment give me life.
150 Malicious persecutors draw near me;
they are far from your law.
151 You are near, O LORD;
reliable are all your commandments.
152 Long have I known from your
testimonies
that you have established them forever.

RESH

153 Look at my affliction and rescue me,
for I have not forgotten your law.
154 Take up my cause and redeem me;[d]
for the sake of your promise give me
life.
155 Salvation is far from sinners
because they do not cherish your
statutes.
156 Your compassion is great, O LORD;
in accord with your judgments, give
me life.
157 Though my persecutors and foes are many,
I do not turn from your testimonies.
158 I view the faithless with loathing[e]
because they do not heed your
promise.
159 See how I love your precepts, LORD;
in your mercy give me life.
160 Your every word is enduring;
all your righteous judgments are
forever.

SHIN

161 Princes persecute me without reason,
but my heart reveres only your word.
162 I rejoice at your promise,
as one who has found rich spoil.
163 Falsehood I hate and abhor;
your law I love.
164 Seven times a day I praise you
because your judgments are righteous.
165 Lovers of your law have much peace;[f]
for them there is no stumbling block.
166 I look for your salvation, LORD,
and I fulfill your commandments.
167 I observe your testimonies;
I love them very much.
168 I observe your precepts and testimonies;
all my ways are before you.

TAW

169 Let my cry come before you, LORD;[g]
in keeping with your word, give me
understanding.
170 Let my prayer come before you;
rescue me according to your promise.
171 May my lips pour forth your praise,
because you teach me your statutes.
172 May my tongue sing of your promise,
for all your commandments are
righteous.
173 Keep your hand ready to help me,
for I have chosen your precepts.
174 I long for your salvation, LORD;
your law is my delight.
175 Let my soul live to praise you;
may your judgments give me help.
176 I have wandered like a lost sheep;
seek out your servant,
for I do not forget your
commandments.[h]

PSALM 120*

See RG 244

Prayer of a Returned Exile

1 A song of ascents.*

The LORD answered me
when I called in my distress:[i]

Psalm 120 A thanksgiving, reporting divine rescue (Ps 120:1) yet with fervent prayer for further protection against lying attackers (Ps 120:2–4). The psalmist is acutely conscious of living away from God's own land where divine peace prevails (Ps 120:5–7).

120:1 A song of ascents: Ps 120–134 all begin with this superscription. Most probably these fifteen Psalms once formed a collection of Psalms sung when pilgrims went to Jerusalem, since one "ascended" to Jerusalem (1 Kgs 12:28; Ps

c: Ps 63:7; 77:7. *d:* Ps 43:1. *e:* Ps 139:22. *f:* Ps 72:7. *g:* Ps 88:3. *h:* Is 53:6; Jer 50:6; Lk 15:1–7. *i:* Jon 2:3.

[2] LORD, deliver my soul from lying lips,
from a treacherous tongue.[j]

[3] What will he inflict on you,
O treacherous tongue,
and what more besides?*

[4] A warrior's arrows
sharpened with coals of brush wood!*[k]

[5] *Alas, I am a foreigner in Meshech,
I live among the tents of Kedar!

[6] Too long do I live
among those who hate peace.

[7] When I speak of peace,
they are for war.[l]

See RG 245, 250

PSALM 121*

The Lord My Guardian

[1] A song of ascents.

I raise my eyes toward the mountains.*
From whence shall come my help?[m]

[2] My help comes from the LORD,
the maker of heaven and earth.[n]

[3] He will not allow your foot to slip;[o]
or your guardian to sleep.

[4] Behold, the guardian of Israel
never slumbers nor sleeps.

[5] *The LORD is your guardian;
the LORD is your shade
at your right hand.[p]

[6] By day the sun will not strike you,
nor the moon by night.[q]

[7] The LORD will guard you from all evil;
he will guard your soul.[r]

[8] The LORD will guard your coming and going
both now and forever.[s]

See RG 245

PSALM 122*

A Pilgrim's Prayer for Jerusalem

[1] A song of ascents. Of David.

I

I rejoiced when they said to me,
"Let us go to the house of the LORD."[t]

[2] And now our feet are standing
within your gates, Jerusalem.

[3] Jerusalem, built as a city,
walled round about.*[u]

[4] There the tribes go up,
the tribes of the LORD,
As it was decreed for Israel,
to give thanks to the name of the LORD.[v]

24:3; 122:4; Lk 2:42) or to the house of God or to an altar (1 Kgs 12:33; 2 Kgs 23:2; Ps 24:3). Less probable is the explanation that these Psalms were sung by the exiles when they "ascended" to Jerusalem from Babylonia (cf. Ezr 7:9). The idea, found in the Mishnah, that the fifteen steps on which the Levites sang corresponded to these fifteen Psalms (Middot 2:5) must underlie the Vulgate translation *canticum graduum*, "song of the steps" or "gradual song."

120:3 More besides: a common curse formula in Hebrew was "May the Lord do such and such evils to you [the evils being specified], and add still more to them," cf. 1 Sm 3:17; 14:44; 25:22. Here the psalmist is at a loss for a suitable malediction.

120:4 Coals of brush wood: coals made from the stalk of the broom plant burn with intense heat. The psalmist thinks of lighted coals cast at his enemies.

120:5 Meshech was in the far north (Gn 10:2) and Kedar was a tribe of the north Arabian desert (Gn 25:13). The psalmist may be thinking generally of all aliens living among inhospitable peoples.

Psalm 121 A blessing given to someone embarking on a dangerous journey whether a soldier going on a campaign or a pilgrim returning home from the Temple. People look anxiously at the wooded hills. Will God protect them on their journey (Ps 121:1)? The speaker declares that God is not confined to a place or a time (Ps 121:2), that every step is guarded (Ps 121:3–4); night and day (Ps 121:5–6) God watches over their every movement (Ps 121:7–8).

121:1 The mountains: possibly Mount Zion, the site of the Temple and hence of safety, but more probably mountains as a place of dangers, causing anxiety to the psalmist.

121:5–6 The image of shade, a symbol of protection, is apt: God as shade protects from the harmful effects that ancients believed were caused by the sun and moon.

Psalm 122 A song of Zion, sung by pilgrims obeying the law to visit Jerusalem three times on a journey. The singer anticipates joining the procession into the city (Ps 122:1–3). Jerusalem is a place of encounter, where the people praise God (Ps 122:4) and hear the divine justice mediated by the king (Ps 122:5). The very buildings bespeak God's power (cf. Ps 48:13–15). May the grace of this place transform the people's lives (Ps 122:6–9)!

122:3 Walled round about: lit., "which is joined to it," probably referring both to the density of the buildings and to the dense population.

Psalm 123 A lament that begins as a prayer of an individual (Ps 123:1), who expresses by a touching comparison exemplary confidence in God (Ps 123:2). The Psalm ends in prayer that God relieve the people's humiliation at the hands of the arrogant (Ps 123:3–4).

j: Ps 12:3–5; Sir 51:3. *k:* Ps 11:6; 140:11; Prv 16:27. *l:* Ps 35:20; 140:3–4. *m:* Jer 3:23. *n:* Ps 124:8; 146:6. *o:* Ps 66:9; 91:12; 1 Sm 2:9; Prv 3:23. *p:* Ps 16:8; 73:23. *q:* Wis 18:3; Is 25:4; 49:10. *r:* Ps 97:10. *s:* Dt 28:6. *t:* Ps 43:3–4; 84:2–5. *u:* Ps 48:13–14. *v:* Dt 16:16.

5 There are the thrones of justice,
the thrones of the house of David.

II

6 For the peace of Jerusalem pray:
"May those who love you prosper!
7 May peace be within your ramparts,
prosperity within your towers."[w]
8 For the sake of my brothers and friends I say,
"Peace be with you."[x]
9 For the sake of the house of the LORD, our God,
I pray for your good.

See RG 244

PSALM 123*

Reliance on the Lord

1 A song of ascents.

To you I raise my eyes,
to you enthroned in heaven.[y]
2 Yes, like the eyes of servants
on the hand of their masters,
Like the eyes of a maid
on the hand of her mistress,
So our eyes are on the LORD our God,
till we are shown favor.
3 Show us favor, LORD, show us favor,
for we have our fill of contempt.[z]
4 Our souls are more than sated
with mockery from the insolent,
with contempt from the arrogant.

See RG 245

PSALM 124*

God, the Rescuer of the People

1 A song of ascents. Of David.

Had not the LORD been with us,
let Israel say,[a]
2 Had not the LORD been with us,
when people rose against us,
3 Then they would have swallowed us alive,[b]
for their fury blazed against us.
4 Then the waters would have engulfed us,
the torrent overwhelmed us;[c]
5 then seething water would have drowned us.
6 Blessed is the LORD, who did not leave us
to be torn by their teeth.
7 We escaped with our lives like a bird
from the fowler's snare;
the snare was broken,
and we escaped.
8 *Our help is in the name of the LORD,
the maker of heaven and earth.[d]

PSALM 125*

See RG 245

Israel's Protector

1 A song of ascents.

Those trusting in the LORD are like Mount Zion,
unshakable, forever enduring.[e]
2 As mountains surround Jerusalem,
the LORD surrounds his people
both now and forever.[f]
3 The scepter of the wicked will not prevail
in the land allotted to the just,*
Lest the just themselves
turn their hands to evil.

4 Do good, LORD, to the good,
to those who are upright of heart.[g]
5 But those who turn aside to crooked ways
may the LORD send down with the evildoers.[h]
Peace upon Israel![i]

Psalm 124 A thanksgiving which teaches that Israel's very existence is owed to God who rescues them. In the first part Israel's enemies are compared to the mythic sea dragon (Ps 124:2b–3a; cf. Jer 51:34) and Flood (Ps 124:3b–5; cf. Is 51:9–10). The Psalm heightens the malice of human enemies by linking them to the primordial enemies of God's creation. Israel is a bird freed from the trapper's snare (Ps 124:6–8)—freed originally from Pharaoh and now from the current danger.

124:8 Our help is in the name: for the idiom, see Ex 18:4.

Psalm 125 In response to exilic anxieties about the ancient promises of restoration, the Psalm expresses confidence that God will surround the people as the mountains surround Zion (Ps 125:1–2). The just will not be contaminated by the wicked (Ps 125:3). May God judge between the two groups (Ps 125:4–5).

125:3 The land allotted to the just: lit., "the lot of the righteous." The promised land was divided among the tribes of Israel by lot (Nm 26:55; Jos 18). The righteous are the members of the people who are obedient to God. If the domination of the wicked were to continue in the land, even the just would be infected by their evil attitudes.

w: Ps 128:5. *x:* Jn 20:19ff. *y:* Ps 25:15; 119:82; 141:8. *z:* Ps 44:13–14; Jb 12:4. *a:* Ps 129:1. *b:* Prv 1:12. *c:* Ps 18:5; 69:2. *d:* Ps 121:2; 146:6. *e:* Prv 10:25. *f:* Dt 32:11. *g:* Ps 18:25ff. *h:* Prv 3:32. *i:* Ps 128:6.

See RG 244

PSALM 126*

The Reversal of Zion's Fortunes

1 A song of ascents.

I

When the LORD restored the captives of
Zion,[j]
we thought we were dreaming.
2 Then our mouths were filled with
laughter;
our tongues sang for joy.[k]
Then it was said among the nations,
"The LORD had done great things for
them."
3 The LORD has done great things for us;
Oh, how happy we were!
4 Restore our captives, LORD,
like the dry stream beds of the
Negeb.*

II

5 Those who sow in tears
will reap with cries of joy.[l]
6 Those who go forth weeping,
carrying sacks of seed,
Will return with cries of joy,
carrying their bundled sheaves.

See RG 245

PSALM 127*

The Need of God's Blessing

1 A song of ascents. Of Solomon.

I

Unless the LORD build the house,
they labor in vain who build.
Unless the LORD guard the city,
in vain does the guard keep watch.
2 It is vain for you to rise early
and put off your rest at night,
To eat bread earned by hard toil—
all this God gives to his beloved in
sleep.[m]

II

3 Certainly sons are a gift from the LORD,
the fruit of the womb, a reward.[n]
4 Like arrows in the hand of a warrior
are the sons born in one's youth.
5 Blessed is the man who has filled his
quiver with them.
He will never be shamed
for he will destroy his foes at the
gate.*

PSALM 128*

See RG 245

The Blessed Home of the Just

1 A song of ascents.

I

Blessed are all who fear the LORD,
and who walk in his ways.[o]
2 What your hands provide you will
enjoy;
you will be blessed and prosper:[p]
3 Your wife will be like a fruitful vine
within your home,
Your children like young olive plants
around your table.[q]
4 Just so will the man be blessed
who fears the LORD.

II

5 May the LORD bless you from Zion;
may you see Jerusalem's prosperity
all the days of your life,[r]
6 and live to see your children's
children.[s]
Peace upon Israel![t]

Psalm 126 A lament probably sung shortly after Israel's return from exile. The people rejoice that they are in Zion (Ps 126:1–3) but mere presence in the holy city is not enough; they must pray for the prosperity and the fertility of the land (Ps 126:4). The last verses are probably an oracle of promise: the painful work of sowing will be crowned with life (Ps 126:5–6).

126:4 Like the dry stream beds of the Negeb: the psalmist prays for rain in such abundance that the dry riverbeds will run.

Psalm 127 The Psalm puts together two proverbs (Ps 127:1–2, 3–5) on God establishing "houses" or families. The prosperity of human groups is not the work of human beings but the gift of God.

127:5 At the gate: the reference is not to enemies besieging the walls of a city but to adversaries in litigation. Law courts functioned in the open area near the main city gate. The more adult sons a man had, the more forceful he would appear in disputes, cf. Prv 31:23.

Psalm 128 A statement that the ever-reliable God will bless the reverent (Ps 128:1). God's blessing is concrete: satisfaction and prosperity, a fertile spouse and abundant children (Ps 128:2–4). The perspective is that of the adult male, ordinarily the ruler and representative of the household to the community. The last verses extend the blessing to all the people for generations to come (Ps 128:5–6).

j: Ps 14:7. *k:* Jb 8:21. *l:* Bar 4:23; Is 65:19. *m:* Eccl 2:24. *n:* Ps 115:14; 128:3; Dt 28:11; Prv 17:6. *o:* Ps 112:1. *p:* Ps 112:3. *q:* Ps 144:12; Jb 29:5. *r:* Ps 20:3; 134:3. *s:* Jb 42:16; Prv 17:6. *t:* Ps 125:5.

PSALM 129*

See RG 245

Against Israel's Enemies

[1] A song of ascents.

I

Viciously have they attacked me from
my youth,
let Israel say now.[u]
[2] Viciously have they attacked me from
my youth,[v]
yet they have not prevailed
against me.
[3] Upon my back the plowers plowed,
as they traced their long furrows.[w]
[4] But the just LORD cut me free
from the ropes of the wicked.*

II

[5] May they recoil in disgrace,
all who hate Zion.
[6] May they be like grass on the rooftops*[x]
withered in early growth,
[7] Never to fill the reaper's hands,
nor the arms of the binders of
sheaves,
[8] And with none passing by to call out:
"The blessing of the LORD be upon
you!*
We bless you in the name of the
LORD!"[y]

PSALM 130*

See RG 244

Prayer for Pardon and Mercy

[1] A song of ascents.

I

Out of the depths* I call to you, LORD;
[2] Lord, hear my cry!
May your ears be attentive
to my cry for mercy.[z]
[3] If you, LORD, keep account of sins,
Lord, who can stand?[a]
[4] But with you is forgiveness
and so you are revered.*

II

[5] I wait for the LORD,
my soul waits
and I hope for his word.[b]
[6] My soul looks for the Lord
more than sentinels for
daybreak.[c]
More than sentinels for daybreak,
[7] let Israel hope in the LORD,
For with the LORD is mercy,
with him is plenteous
redemption,[d]
[8] And he will redeem Israel
from all its sins.[e]

PSALM 131*

See RG 245

Humble Trust in God

[1] A song of ascents. Of David.

LORD, my heart is not proud;
nor are my eyes haughty.
I do not busy myself with great
matters,
with things too sublime for me.[f]
[2] Rather, I have stilled my soul,
Like a weaned child to its mother,
weaned is my soul.[g]
[3] Israel, hope in the LORD,
now and forever.

Psalm 129 A Psalm giving thanks for God's many rescues of Israel over the long course of their history (Ps 129:1–4); the people pray that their oppressors never know the joy of harvest (Ps 129:5–8).

129:4 The ropes of the wicked: usually understood as the rope for yoking animals to the plow. If it is severed, the plowing (cf. Ps 129:3) comes to a halt.

129:6 Like grass on the rooftops: after the spring rains, grass would sprout from the coat of mud with which the flat roofs of simple houses were covered, but when the dry summer began there was no moisture in the thin roof-covering to sustain the grass.

129:8 The blessing of the LORD be upon you: harvesters greeted one another with such blessings, cf. Ru 2:4.

Psalm 130 This lament, a Penitential Psalm, is the *De profundis* used in liturgical prayers for the faithful departed. In deep sorrow the psalmist cries to God (Ps 130:1–2), asking for mercy (Ps 130:3–4). The psalmist's trust (Ps 130:5–6) becomes a model for the people (Ps 130:7–8).

130:1 The depths: Sheol here is a metaphor of total misery. Deep anguish makes the psalmist feel "like those descending to the pit" (Ps 143:7).

130:4 And so you are revered: the experience of God's mercy leads one to a greater sense of God.

Psalm 131 A song of trust, in which the psalmist gives up self-sufficiency (Ps 131:1), like a babe enjoying the comfort of its mother's lap (Ps 131:2), thus providing a model for Israel's faith (Ps 131:3).

u: Ps 124:1. *v:* Ps 118:13. *w:* Is 51:23. *x:* Is 37:27. *y:* Ps 118:26. *z:* Ps 5:2–3; 55:2–3; 86:6; Lam 3:55–56; Jon 2:3. *a:* Na 1:6. *b:* Ps 119:81. *c:* Is 21:11; 26:9. *d:* Ps 86:15; 100:5; 103:8. *e:* Ps 25:22; Mt 1:21. *f:* Ps 139:6. *g:* Is 66:12–13.

PSALM 132*

See RG 245, 260

The Covenant Between David and God

[1] A song of ascents.

I

Remember, O LORD, for David
all his hardships;
[2] How he swore an oath to the LORD,
vowed to the Mighty One of Jacob:*
[3] "I will not enter the house where I live,[h]
nor lie on the couch where I sleep;
[4] I will give my eyes no sleep,
my eyelids no rest,
[5] Till I find a place for the LORD,
a dwelling for the Mighty One of Jacob."
[6] "We have heard of it in Ephrathah;*
we have found it in the fields of Jaar.*
[7] Let us enter his dwelling;
let us worship at his footstool."[i]
[8] "Arise, LORD, come to your resting place,[j]
you and your mighty ark.
[9] Your priests will be clothed with justice;
your devout will shout for joy."
[10] For the sake of David your servant,
do not reject your anointed.

II

[11] The LORD swore an oath to David in truth,
he will never turn back from it:[k]
"Your own offspring[l] I will set upon your throne.
[12] If your sons observe my covenant,
and my decrees I shall teach them,
Their sons, in turn,
shall sit forever on your throne."
[13] Yes, the LORD has chosen Zion,
desired it for a dwelling:
[14] "This is my resting place forever;
here I will dwell, for I desire it.
[15] I will bless Zion with provisions;
its poor I will fill with bread.
[16] I will clothe its priests with salvation;
its devout shall shout for joy.[m]
[17] There I will make a horn sprout for David;*[n]
I will set a lamp for my anointed.
[18] His foes I will clothe with shame,
but on him his crown shall shine."

PSALM 133*

See RG 246

A Vision of a Blessed Community

[1] A song of ascents. Of David.

How good and how pleasant it is,
when brothers* dwell together as one!
[2] Like fine oil on the head,*[o]
running down upon the beard,
Upon the beard of Aaron,
upon the collar of his robe.
[3] Like dew* of Hermon* coming down
upon the mountains of Zion.[p]

Psalm 132 A song for a liturgical ceremony in which the ark, the throne of Israel's God, was carried in procession to the Temple. The singer asks that David's care for the proper housing of the ark be regarded with favor (Ps 132:1–5), and tells how it was brought to Jerusalem (Ps 132:6–10). There follows God's promise of favor to the Davidic dynasty (Ps 132:11–12) and to Zion (Ps 132:13–17). The transfer of the ark to the tent in Jerusalem is described in 2 Sm 6.

132:2, 132:5 Mighty One of Jacob: one of the titles of Israel's God, cf. Gn 49:24; Is 49:26; 60:16.

132:6 Ephrathah: the homeland of David, cf. Ru 4:11. **The fields of Jaar**: poetic for Kiriath-jearim, a town west of Jerusalem, where the ark remained for several generations, cf. 1 Sm 7:1–2; 2 Sm 6:2; 1 Chr 13:5–6.

132:17 A horn sprout for David: the image of the horn, a symbol of strength, is combined with that of a "sprout," a term used for the Davidic descendant (cf. Jer 23:5; 33:15; Zec 3:8; 6:12). Early Christians referred the latter designation to Christ as son of David (Lk 1:69).

Psalm 133 A benediction over a peaceful community, most probably the people Israel, but appropriate too for Israelite families (Ps 133:1). The history of Israel, whether of its ancestors in the Book of Genesis or of later periods, was a history of distinct groups struggling to live in unity. Here that unity is declared blessed, like the holy oils upon the priest Aaron or the dew of the rainless summer that waters the crops (Ps 133:2–3).

133:1 Brothers: in biblical Hebrew this word includes both the male and female members of a group united by blood relationships or by shared experiences and values. In this Psalm, the term could be applied most appropriately to the people of Israel, those privileged by God to be his chosen children.

133:2 Oil on the head: oil was used at the consecration of the high priest (Ex 30:22–33).

133:3 Dew: dew was an important source of moisture in the dry climate (Gn 27:28; Hos 14:6). **Hermon**: the majestic snow-capped mountain visible in the north of Palestine.

---

h: 2 Sm 7; 1 Chr 28:2. *i:* Ps 99:5. *j:* Ps 2:2; 89:21; 95:11; Nm 10:35; 2 Chr 6:41–42; Sir 24:7. *k:* Ps 68:17; 1 Kgs 8:13; Sir 24:7. *l:* Ps 110:4; 2 Sm 7:12. *m:* 2 Chr 6:41; Is 61:10. *n:* Is 11:1; Jer 33:15; Ez 29:21; Zec 3:8; Lk 1:69. *o:* Ex 30:25, 30. *p:* Hos 14:6.

There the LORD has decreed a blessing,
life for evermore![q]

See RG 246

PSALM 134*

Exhortation to the Night Watch to Bless God

1 A song of ascents.

O come, bless the LORD,
all you servants of the LORD*
You who stand in the house of the LORD
throughout the nights.[r]
2 Lift up your hands toward the sanctuary,[s]
and bless the LORD.
3 May the LORD bless you from Zion,
the Maker of heaven and earth.[t]

See RG 244, 247

PSALM 135*

Praise of God, the Ruler and Benefactor of Israel

1 Hallelujah!

I

Praise the name of the LORD!
Praise, you servants of the LORD,[u]
2 Who stand in the house of the LORD,
in the courts of the house of our God![v]
3 Praise the LORD, for the LORD is good!
Sing to his name, for it brings joy!
4 *For the LORD has chosen Jacob for himself,
Israel as his treasured possession.[w]

II

5 For I know that the LORD is great,
that our Lord is greater than all gods.[x]
6 Whatever the LORD desires
he does in heaven and on earth,
in the seas and all the depths.[y]
7 It is he who raises storm clouds from the end of the earth,
makes lightning for the rain,
and brings forth wind from his storehouse.[z]

III

8 He struck down Egypt's firstborn,[a]
of human being and beast alike,
9 And sent signs and wonders against you, Egypt,
against Pharaoh and all his servants.
10 It is he who struck down many nations,[b]
and slew mighty kings—
11 Sihon, king of the Amorites,
and Og, king of Bashan,
all the kings of Canaan—
12 And made their land a heritage,
a heritage for Israel his people.
13 O LORD, your name is forever,
your renown, from generation to generation![c]
14 For the LORD defends his people,
shows mercy to his servants.[d]

IV

15 The idols of the nations are silver and gold,[e]
the work of human hands.
16 They have mouths but do not speak;
they have eyes but do not see;
17 They have ears but do not hear;
nor is there breath in their mouths.
18 Their makers will become like them,
and anyone who trusts in them.

V

19 House of Israel, bless the LORD![f]
House of Aaron, bless the LORD!
20 House of Levi, bless the LORD!
You who fear the LORD, bless the LORD!
21 Blessed be the LORD from Zion,
who dwells in Jerusalem!
Hallelujah!

Psalm 134 A brief liturgy exhorting all those who serve in the Jerusalem Temple during the night (cf. Is 30:29) to praise God with words and gestures. Although he is the Creator of the whole universe, God's blessings emanate in a unique way from Zion, the city of Jerusalem.

134:1 Servants of the LORD: priests and Levites, cf. Dt 10:8; Ps 113:1; 135:1; Dn 3:85.

Psalm 135 The hymn begins and ends with an invitation to praise God (Ps 135:1–3, 19–20) for the great act of choosing Israel (Ps 135:4). The story of Israel's emergence as a people is told in Ps 135:5–14; God created and redeemed the people, easily conquering all opposition. God's defeat of hostile powers means that the powers themselves and their images are useless (Ps 135:15–18). The last three verses appear also in Ps 115:4–8.

135:4 Though all nations are God's, Israel has a special status as God's "treasured" people: Ex 19:5; Dt 7:6; 14:2; 26:18; Mal 3:17.

q: Dt 28:8; 30:20. *r:* Ps 135:1–2; 1 Chr 9:33. *s:* Ps 28:2; 141:2. *t:* Ps 20:3; 128:5; Nm 6:24. *u:* Ps 113:1. *v:* Ps 134:1. *w:* Ps 33:12; 144:15; Ex 19:6; Dt 7:6. *x:* Ps 95:3; Ex 18:11. *y:* Ps 115:3. *z:* Ps 148:8; Jer 10:13; 51:16; Jb 37:9. *a:* Ps 78:51; 105:27, 36; 136:10; Ex 12:29. *b:* Ps 136:17–22; Nm 21:21–35; Dt 2:24–3:17. *c:* Ps 102:13; Ex 3:15. *d:* Dt 32:36. *e:* Ps 115:4–6, 8. *f:* Ps 118:2–4.

PSALM 136*

See RG 244

Hymn of Thanksgiving for God's Everlasting Mercy

I

1 Praise the LORD, for he is good;[g]
for his mercy endures forever;
2 Praise the God of gods;
for his mercy endures forever;
3 Praise the Lord of lords;
for his mercy endures forever;

II

4 Who alone has done great wonders,[h]
for his mercy endures forever;
5 Who skillfully made the heavens,[i]
for his mercy endures forever;
6 Who spread the earth upon the waters,[j]
for his mercy endures forever;
7 Who made the great lights,
for his mercy endures forever;
8 The sun to rule the day,
for his mercy endures forever;
9 The moon and stars to rule the night,[k]
for his mercy endures forever;

III

10 Who struck down the firstborn of Egypt,[l]
for his mercy endures forever;
11 And led Israel from their midst,
for his mercy endures forever;
12 With mighty hand and outstretched arm,[m]
for his mercy endures forever;
13 Who split in two the Red Sea,
for his mercy endures forever;
14 And led Israel through its midst,
for his mercy endures forever;
15 But swept Pharaoh and his army into the Red Sea,[n]
for his mercy endures forever;
16 Who led the people through the desert,[o]
for his mercy endures forever;

IV

17 Who struck down great kings,[p]
for his mercy endures forever;
18 Slew powerful kings,
for his mercy endures forever;
19 Sihon, king of the Amorites,
for his mercy endures forever;
20 Og, king of Bashan,
for his mercy endures forever;
21 And made their lands a heritage,
for his mercy endures forever;
22 *A heritage for Israel, his servant,
for his mercy endures forever.

V

23 The Lord remembered us in our low estate,
for his mercy endures forever;
24 Freed us from our foes,
for his mercy endures forever;
25 And gives bread to all flesh,
for his mercy endures forever.

VI

26 Praise the God of heaven,
for his mercy endures forever.

PSALM 137*

See RG 244

Sorrow and Hope in Exile

I

1 By the rivers of Babylon
there we sat weeping
when we remembered Zion.[q]
2 On the poplars in its midst
we hung up our harps.[r]
3 For there our captors asked us
for the words of a song;
Our tormentors, for joy:
"Sing for us a song of Zion!"
4 But how could we sing a song of the LORD
in a foreign land?

Psalm 136 The hymn praises Israel's God ("the God of gods," Ps 136:2), who has created the world in which Israel lives. The refrain occurring after every line suggests that a speaker and chorus sang the Psalm in antiphonal fashion. A single act of God is described in Ps 136:4–25. God arranges the heavens and the earth as the environment for human community, and then creates the community by freeing them and giving them land. In the final section (Ps 136:23–25) God, who created the people and gave them land, continues to protect and nurture them.

136:22 A heritage for Israel: the land was given to Israel by God to be handed on to future generations.

Psalm 137 A singer refuses to sing the people's sacred songs in an alien land despite demands from Babylonian captors (Ps 137:1–4). The singer swears an oath by what is most dear to a musician—hands and tongue—to exalt Jerusalem always (Ps 137:5–6). The Psalm ends with a prayer that the old enemies of Jerusalem, Edom and Babylon, be destroyed (Ps 137:7–9).

g: Ps 100:5; 118:1. *h:* Ps 72:18. *i:* Gn 1:9–19. *j:* Ps 24:2. *k:* Jer 31:35. *l:* Ex 12:29, 51; 14:22, 27; 15:22; Ps 78:51–52; 135:8. *m:* Dt 4:34. *n:* Ex 14:21f. *o:* Dt 8:2, 15. *p:* Ps 135:10–12. *q:* Ez 3:15; Lam 3:48. *r:* Is 24:8; Lam 5:14.

II

5 If I forget you, Jerusalem,
may my right hand forget.[s]
6 May my tongue stick to my palate
if I do not remember you,
If I do not exalt Jerusalem
beyond all my delights.

III

7 Remember, LORD, against Edom
that day at Jerusalem.
They said: "Level it, level it
down to its foundations!"[t]
8 Desolate Daughter Babylon, you shall be
destroyed,
blessed the one who pays you back
what you have done us![u]
9 *Blessed the one who seizes your children
and smashes them against the rock.[v]

PSALM 138*

See RG 245, 246

Hymn of a Grateful Heart

1 Of David.

I

I thank you, Lord, with all my heart;[w]
in the presence of the angels* to you I
sing.
2 I bow low toward your holy temple;
I praise your name for your mercy and
faithfulness.
For you have exalted over all
your name and your promise.
3 On the day I cried out, you answered;
you strengthened my spirit.

II

4 All the kings of earth will praise you,
LORD,
when they hear the words of your
mouth.
5 They will sing of the ways of the LORD:
"How great is the glory of the LORD!"
6 The LORD is on high, but cares for the
lowly[x]
and knows the proud from afar.
7 Though I walk in the midst of dangers,
you guard my life when my enemies
rage.
You stretch out your hand;
your right hand saves me.
8 The LORD is with me to the end.
LORD, your mercy endures forever.
Never forsake the work of your hands!

PSALM 139*

See RG 250

The All-knowing and Ever-present God

1 For the leader. A psalm of David.

I

LORD, you have probed me, you know me:
2 you know when I sit and stand;*[y]
you understand my thoughts from afar.
3 You sift through my travels and my rest;
with all my ways you are familiar.
4 Even before a word is on my tongue,
LORD, you know it all.
5 Behind and before you encircle me
and rest your hand upon me.
6 Such knowledge is too wonderful for me,
far too lofty for me to reach.[z]

7 Where can I go from your spirit?
From your presence, where can I flee?
8 If I ascend to the heavens, you are there;
if I lie down in Sheol, there you are.[a]
9 If I take the wings of dawn*
and dwell beyond the sea,*
10 Even there your hand guides me,

137:9 Blessed the one who seizes your children and smashes them against the rock: the children represent the future generations, and so must be destroyed if the enemy is truly to be eradicated.

Psalm 138 A thanksgiving to God, who came to the rescue of the psalmist. Divine rescue was not the result of the psalmist's virtues but of God's loving fidelity (Ps 138:1–3). The act is not a private transaction but a public act that stirs the surrounding nations to praise God's greatness and care for the people (Ps 138:4–6). The psalmist, having experienced salvation, trusts that God will always be there in moments of danger (Ps 138:7–8).

138:1 In the presence of the angels: heavenly beings who were completely subordinate to Israel's God. The earthly Temple represents the heavenly palace of God.

Psalm 139 A hymnic meditation on God's omnipresence and omniscience. The psalmist is keenly aware of God's all-knowing gaze (Ps 139:1–6), of God's presence in every part of the universe (Ps 139:7–12), and of God's control over the psalmist's very self (Ps 139:13–16). Summing up Ps 139:1–16, 17–18 express wonder. There is only one place hostile to God's rule—wicked people. The psalmist prays to be removed from their company (Ps 139:19–24).

139:2 When I sit and stand: in all my physical movement.

139:9 Take the wings of dawn: go to the extremities of the

s: Jer 51:50. *t:* Jer 49:7; Lam 4:21–22; Ez 25:12–14. *u:* Is 47:1–3; Jer 50–51. *v:* Hos 14:1. *w:* Ps 9:1. *x:* Lk 1:51–52. *y:* 2 Kgs 19:27; Jb 12:3. *z:* Ps 131:1. *a:* Jb 23:8–9; Jer 23:23–24.

your right hand holds me fast.
11 If I say, "Surely darkness shall hide me,
and night shall be my light"*—
12 Darkness is not dark for you,
and night shines as the day.
Darkness and light are but one.[b]

II

13 You formed my inmost being;
you knit me in my mother's womb.[c]
14 I praise you, because I am wonderfully made;
wonderful are your works!
My very self you know.
15 My bones are not hidden from you,
When I was being made in secret,
fashioned in the depths of the earth.*
16 Your eyes saw me unformed;
in your book all are written down;[d]
my days were shaped, before one came to be.

III

17 How precious to me are your designs, O God;
how vast the sum of them!
18 Were I to count them, they would outnumber the sands;
when I complete them, still you are with me.[e]
19 When you would destroy the wicked, O God,
the bloodthirsty depart from me![f]
20 Your foes who conspire a plot against you
are exalted in vain.

IV

21 Do I not hate, LORD, those who hate you?
Those who rise against you, do I not loathe?[g]
22 With fierce hatred I hate them,
enemies I count as my own.
23 Probe me, God, know my heart;
try me, know my thoughts.[h]
24 See if there is a wicked path in me;
lead me along an ancient path.*

PSALM 140*

See RG 244

Prayer for Deliverance from the Wicked

1 For the leader. A psalm of David.

I

2 Deliver me, LORD, from the wicked;
preserve me from the violent,[i]
3 From those who plan evil in their hearts,
who stir up conflicts every day,
4 *Who sharpen their tongue like a serpent,
venom of asps upon their lips.[j] *Selah*

II

5 Keep me, LORD, from the clutches of the wicked;
preserve me from the violent,
who plot to trip me up.[k]
6 *The arrogant have set a trap for me;
they have spread out ropes for a net,
laid snares for me by the wayside. *Selah*
7 I say to the LORD: You are my God;[l]
listen, LORD, to the words of my pleas.
8 LORD, my master, my strong deliverer,
you cover my head on the day of armed conflict.
9 LORD, do not grant the desires of the wicked one;
do not let his plot succeed. *Selah*

III

10 Those who surround me raise their heads;
may the mischief they threaten overwhelm them.
11 Drop burning coals upon them;[m]

east. **Beyond the sea**: uttermost bounds of the west; the sea is the Mediterranean.

139:11 Night shall be my light: night to me is what day is to others.

139:15 The depths of the earth: figurative language for the womb, stressing the hidden and mysterious operations that occur there.

139:24 Lead me along an ancient path: the manner of living of our ancestors, who were faithful to God's will, cf. Jer 6:16.

Psalm 140 A lament seeking rescue from violent and treacherous foes (Ps 140:2–6). The psalmist remains trusting (Ps 140:7–8), vigorously praying that the plans of the wicked recoil upon themselves (Ps 140:9–12). A serene statement of praise ends the Psalm (Ps 140:13). The psalmist is content to be known as one of "the needy," "the poor," "the just," "the upright" (Ps 140:13), a class of people expecting divine protection.

140:4 Similar metaphors for a wicked tongue are used in Ps 52:2; 55:20; 58:3.

140:6 Have set a trap . . . have spread out ropes for a net: the same figure, of hunters setting traps, occurs in Ps 9:16; 31:5; 35:7; 64:6, cf. Mt 22:15; Lk 11:54.

b: Jb 12:22. *c:* Wis 7:1; Eccl 11:5; Jb 1:21. *d:* Mal 3:16. *e:* Jb 11:7. *f:* Jb 21:14. *g:* Ps 119:158. *h:* Ps 17:3; 26:2. *i:* Ps 71:4. *j:* Ps 64:4; Rom 3:13. *k:* Jer 18:22; Ps 56:7; 57:7. *l:* Ps 31:15. *m:* Ps 11:6; 120:4; Gn 19:24.

cast them into the watery pit never
more to rise.
12 Slanderers will not survive on earth;
evil will hunt down the man of
violence to overthrow him.
13 For I know the LORD will take up the
cause of the needy,
justice for the poor.
14 Then the righteous will give thanks to
your name;
the upright will dwell in your presence.[n]

See RG 244

PSALM 141*

Prayer for Deliverance from the Wicked

1 A psalm of David.

LORD, I call to you; hasten to me;
listen to my plea when I call.
2 Let my prayer be incense* before you;
my uplifted hands* an evening offering.[o]
3 Set a guard, LORD, before my mouth,
keep watch over the door of my lips.[p]
4 Do not let my heart incline to evil,
to perform deeds in wickedness.
On the delicacies of evildoers
let me not feast.
5 *Let a righteous person strike me; it is
mercy if he reproves me.
Do not withhold oil from my head[q]
while my prayer opposes their evil
deeds.
6 May their leaders be cast over the cliff,
so that they hear that my speeches are
pleasing.
7 Like the plowing and breaking up of the
earth,
our bones are strewn at the mouth of
Sheol.
8 For my eyes are upon you, O LORD, my
Lord;[r]
in you I take refuge; do not take away
my soul.
9 Guard me from the trap they have set
for me,
from the snares of evildoers.[s]
10 Let the wicked fall into their own nets,
while only I pass over them safely.

PSALM 142*

See RG 244

A Prayer in Time of Trouble

1 A *maskil* of David, when he was in the
cave.* A prayer.

2 With my own voice I cry to the LORD;
with my own voice I beseech the
LORD.
3 Before him I pour out my complaint,
tell of my distress in front of him.
4 When my spirit is faint within me,[t]
you know my path.[u]
As I go along this path,
they have hidden a trap for me.[v]
5 I look to my right hand to see[w]
that there is no one willing to
acknowledge me.
My escape has perished;
no one cares for me.
6 I cry out to you, LORD,
I say, You are my refuge,[x]
my portion in the land of the living.[y]
7 Listen to my cry for help,
for I am brought very low.[z]
Rescue me from my pursuers,
for they are too strong for me.
8 Lead my soul from prison,
that I may give thanks to your name.
Then the righteous shall gather around me*
because you have been good to me.

Psalm 141 A lament of an individual (Ps 141:1–2) who is keenly aware that only the righteous can worship God properly and who therefore prays to be protected from the doomed wicked (Ps 141:3–10).

141:2 Incense: lit., "smoke," i.e., the fragrant fumes arising from the altar at the burning of sacrificial animals or of aromatic spices; also used in Rev 5:8 as a symbol of prayer. **My uplifted hands**: the gesture of supplication, cf. Ps 28:2; 63:5; 88:10; 119:48; 134:2; 143:6.

141:5–7 The Hebrew text is obscure.

Psalm 142 In this lament imploring God for help (Ps 142:2–4), the psalmist tells how enemies have set a trap (Ps 142:4–5), and prays for rescue (Ps 142:6–8). The speaker feels utterly alone (Ps 142:5), exhausted (Ps 142:7), and may even be imprisoned (Ps 142:7). Prison is possibly a metaphor for general distress. The last two verses are the vow of praise, made after receiving an assurance of divine help (Ps 142:7).

142:1 In the cave: cf. 1 Sm 22:1; 24:1–3; Ps 57:1.

142:8 Then the righteous shall gather around me: in the Temple, when the psalmist offers a thanksgiving sacrifice.

n: Ps 11:7; 16:11; 17:15. *o:* Ps 134:2; Ex 30:8. *p:* Sir 22:27. *q:* Prv 9:8; 25:12. *r:* Ps 25:15; 123:1–2. *s:* Ps 142:4. *t:* Ps 143:4. *u:* Ps 139:24. *v:* Ps 141:9. *w:* Ps 16:8; 73:23; 121:5. *x:* Ps 91:2, 9. *y:* Ps 16:5; 27:13; 116:9; Is 38:11. *z:* Ps 79:8.

PSALM 143*

See RG 244

A Prayer in Distress

1 A psalm of David.

LORD, hear my prayer;
in your faithfulness listen to my pleading;
answer me in your righteousness.
2 Do not enter into judgment with your servant;
before you no one can be just.[a]
3 The enemy has pursued my soul;
he has crushed my life to the ground.[b]
He has made me dwell in darkness
like those long dead.[c]
4 My spirit is faint within me;
my heart despairs.[d]
5 I remember the days of old;
I ponder all your deeds;
the works of your hands I recall.[e]
6 I stretch out my hands toward you,
my soul to you like a parched land.[f]
Selah
7 Hasten to answer me, LORD;
for my spirit fails me.
Do not hide your face from me,
lest I become like those descending to the pit.[g]
8 In the morning let me hear of your mercy,
for in you I trust.
Show me the path I should walk,
for I entrust my life to you.[h]
9 Rescue me, LORD, from my foes,
for I seek refuge in you.
10 Teach me to do your will,
for you are my God.
May your kind spirit guide me
on ground that is level.
11 For your name's sake, LORD, give me life;
in your righteousness lead my soul out of distress.
12 In your mercy put an end to my foes;
all those who are oppressing my soul,
for I am your servant.[i]

PSALM 144*

See RG 245, 250

A Prayer for Victory and Prosperity

1 Of David.

I

*Blessed be the LORD, my rock,
who trains my hands for battle,
my fingers for war;
2 My safeguard and my fortress,
my stronghold, my deliverer,
My shield, in whom I take refuge,
who subdues peoples under me.

II

3 *LORD, what is man that you take notice of him;
the son of man, that you think of him?[j]
4 *Man is but a breath,
his days are like a passing shadow.[k]
5 *LORD, incline your heavens and come down;
touch the mountains and make them smoke.[l]
6 Flash forth lightning and scatter my foes;
shoot your arrows and rout them.

Psalm 143 One of the Church's seven Penitential Psalms, this lament is a prayer to be freed from death-dealing enemies. The psalmist addresses God, aware that there is no equality between God and human beings; salvation is a gift (Ps 143:1–2). Victimized by evil people (Ps 143:3–4), the psalmist recites ("remembers") God's past actions on behalf of the innocent (Ps 143:5–6). The Psalm continues with fervent prayer (Ps 143:7–9) and a strong desire for guidance and protection (Ps 143:10–12).

Psalm 144 The Psalm may reflect a ceremony in which the king, as leader of the army, asked God's help (Ps 144:1–8). In Ps 144:9 the poem shifts abruptly from pleading to thanksgiving, and (except for Ps 144:11) shifts again to prayer for the people. The first section (Ps 144:1–2) is a prayer of thanks for victory; the second (Ps 144:3–7a), a humble acknowledgment of human nothingness and a supplication that God show forth saving power; the third (Ps 144:9–11), a promise of future thanksgiving; the fourth (Ps 144:12–15), a wish for prosperity and peace. A prayer for deliverance from treacherous foes serves as a refrain after the second and third sections (Ps 144:7b–8, 11). Except for its final section, the Psalm is made up almost entirely of verses from other Psalms.

144:1–2 Composed of phrases from Ps 18:3, 35, 47–48.

144:3 Similar to Ps 8:4.

144:4 Composed of phrases from Ps 39:6; 102:12.

144:5–7 Adapted in large part from Ps 18:10, 15, 17; 104:32.

a: Eccl 7:20; Jb 4:17; Rom 3:20. *b:* Ps 7:6. *c:* Lam 3:6. *d:* Ps 142:4; Jb 17:1. *e:* Ps 77:6, 12. *f:* Ps 42:2; 63:2. *g:* Ps 28:1; 30:4; 88:5; Prv 1:12. *h:* Ps 25:4; 27:11; 86:11; 119:12, 35. *i:* Ps 116:16. *j:* Jb 7:17. *k:* Ps 62:10; 90:9–10; Jb 7:16; Eccl 6:12; Wis 2:5. *l:* Is 63:19.

7 Reach out your hand from on high;
deliver me from the many waters;
rescue me from the hands of foreign
foes.
8 Their mouths speak untruth;
their right hands are raised in lying
oaths.*
9 O God, a new song I will sing to you;
on a ten-stringed lyre I will play for
you.[m]
10 You give victory to kings;
you delivered David your servant.[n]
From the menacing sword 11 deliver me;
rescue me from the hands of foreign
foes.
Their mouths speak untruth;
their right hands are raised in lying
oaths.

III

12 May our sons be like plants[o]
well nurtured from their youth,
Our daughters, like carved columns,
shapely as those of the temple.
13 May our barns be full
with every kind of store.
May our sheep increase by thousands,
by tens of thousands in our fields;
may our oxen be well fattened.
14 May there be no breach in the walls,
no exile, no outcry in our streets.[p]
15 Blessed the people so fortunate;
blessed the people whose God is the
LORD.[q]

See RG 244, 246

PSALM 145*

The Greatness and Goodness of God

1 Praise. Of David.

I will extol you, my God and king;
I will bless your name forever and
ever.
2 Every day I will bless you;
I will praise your name forever and
ever.[r]
3 Great is the LORD and worthy of much
praise,[s]
whose grandeur is beyond
understanding.
4 One generation praises your deeds to the
next
and proclaims your mighty works.[t]
5 They speak of the splendor of your
majestic glory,
tell of your wonderful deeds.[u]
6 They speak of the power of your
awesome acts
and recount your great deeds.[v]
7 They celebrate your abounding goodness
and joyfully sing of your justice.
8 The LORD is gracious and merciful,
slow to anger and abounding in
mercy.[w]
9 The LORD is good to all,
compassionate toward all your works.[x]
10 All your works give you thanks, LORD
and your faithful bless you.[y]
11 They speak of the glory of your reign
and tell of your mighty works,
12 Making known to the sons of men your
mighty acts,
the majestic glory of your rule.
13 Your reign is a reign for all ages,
your dominion for all generations.[z]
The LORD is trustworthy in all his words,
and loving in all his works.
14 The LORD supports all who are falling
and raises up all who are bowed
down.[a]
15 The eyes of all look hopefully to you;
you give them their food in due
season.[b]
16 You open wide your hand
and satisfy the desire of every living
thing.
17 The LORD is just in all his ways,

144:8b, 11b Their right hands are raised in lying oaths: the psalmist's enemies give false testimony.

Psalm 145 A hymn in acrostic form; every verse begins with a successive letter of the Hebrew alphabet. Acrostic poems usually do not develop ideas but consist rather of loosely connected statements. The singer invites all to praise God (Ps 145:1–3, 21). The "works of God" make God present and invite human praise (Ps 145:4–7); they climax in a confession (Ps 145:8–9). God's mighty acts show forth divine kingship (Ps 145:10–20), a major theme in the literature of early Judaism and in Christianity.

m: Ps 33:2–3. *n:* Ps 18:51. *o:* Ps 128:3. *p:* Is 65:19. *q:* Ps 33:12. *r:* Ps 34:2. *s:* Ps 48:2; 95:3; 96:4; Jb 36:26. *t:* Ps 22:31–32; 48:14–15; 71:18; 78:4; Ex 10:2; Dt 4:9. *u:* Ps 96:3; 105:2. *v:* Ps 66:3. *w:* Ps 86:5, 15; 103:8; Ex 34:6; Sir 2:11. *x:* Ps 103:13; Wis 11:24. *y:* Dn 3:57. *z:* Ps 10:16; 102:13; 146:10; Lam 5:19; Dn 3:33; Rev 11:15. *a:* Ps 94:18; 146:8. *b:* Ps 136:25; 104:27–28; Mt 6:25–26.

merciful in all his works.[c]
18 The LORD is near to all who call upon him,
to all who call upon him in truth.[d]
19 He fulfills the desire of those who fear him;
he hears their cry and saves them.[e]
20 The LORD watches over all who love him,
but all the wicked he destroys.[f]
21 My mouth will speak the praises of the LORD;
all flesh will bless his holy name forever and ever.

See RG 244

PSALM 146*

Trust in God the Creator and Redeemer

1 Hallelujah!
2 Praise the LORD, my soul;
I will praise the LORD all my life,
sing praise to my God while I live.[g]

I

3 Put no trust in princes,
in children of Adam powerless to save.[h]
4 Who breathing his last, returns to the earth;
that day all his planning comes to nothing.[i]

II

5 Blessed the one whose help is the God of Jacob,
whose hope is in the LORD, his God,
6 The maker of heaven and earth,
the seas and all that is in them,[j]
Who keeps faith forever,
7 secures justice for the oppressed,[k]
who gives bread to the hungry.
The LORD sets prisoners free;[l]
8 the LORD gives sight to the blind.
The LORD raises up those who are bowed down;[m]
the LORD loves the righteous.
9 The LORD protects the resident alien,
comes to the aid of the orphan and the widow,[n]
but thwarts the way of the wicked.
10 The LORD shall reign forever,
your God, Zion, through all generations![o]
Hallelujah!

See RG 244, 250

PSALM 147*

God's Word Restores Jerusalem

1 Hallelujah!

I

How good to sing praise to our God;
how pleasant to give fitting praise.[p]
2 The LORD rebuilds Jerusalem,
and gathers the dispersed of Israel,[q]
3 Healing the brokenhearted,
and binding up their wounds.[r]
4 He numbers the stars,
and gives to all of them their names.[s]
5 Great is our Lord, vast in power,
with wisdom beyond measure.[t]
6 The LORD gives aid to the poor,
but casts the wicked to the ground.[u]

II

7 Sing to the LORD with thanksgiving;
with the lyre make music to our God,[v]
8 *Who covers the heavens with clouds,
provides rain for the earth,
makes grass sprout on the mountains,[w]
9 Who gives animals their food
and young ravens what they cry for.[x]
10 *He takes no delight in the strength of horses,

Psalm 146 A hymn of someone who has learned there is no other source of strength except the merciful God. Only God, not mortal human beings (Ps 146:3–4), can help vulnerable and oppressed people (Ps 146:5–9). The first of the five hymns that conclude the Psalter.

Psalm 147 The hymn is divided into three sections by the calls to praise in Ps 147:1, 7, 12. The first section praises the powerful creator who restores exiled Judah (Ps 147:1–6); the second section, the creator who provides food to animals and human beings; the third and climactic section exhorts the holy city to recognize it has been re-created and made the place of disclosure for God's word, a word as life-giving as water.

147:8–9 God clothes the fields and feeds the birds, cf. Mt 6:26, 30.

147:10–11 Acknowledging one's dependence upon God rather than claiming self-sufficiency pleases God, cf. Ps 20:8; 33:16–19.

---

c: Dt 32:4. *d:* Dt 4:7; Is 55:6; 58:9. *e:* Ps 34:18. *f:* Jgs 5:31. *g:* Ps 103:1; 104:33. *h:* Ps 118:8–9. *i:* Ps 90:3; 104:29; 1 Mc 2:63; Jb 34:14–15; Eccl 3:20; 12:7; Sir 40:11; Is 2:22. *j:* Ps 121:2; 124:8; Ex 20:11; Acts 14:15; Rev 14:7. *k:* Ps 103:6. *l:* Ps 68:7; Is 49:9; 61:1. *m:* Ps 145:14. *n:* Ps 68:6; Dt 10:18. *o:* Ps 145:13; Lam 5:19. *p:* Ps 33:1; 92:2. *q:* Is 11:12; 56:8; Jer 31:10. *r:* Jb 5:18; Is 30:26; 61:1; Jer 33:6. *s:* Is 40:26. *t:* Jdt 16:13; Jer 51:15. *u:* Ps 146:9; 1 Sm 2:7–8. *v:* Ps 71:22. *w:* Ps 104:13f; Jb 5:10; Jer 14:22; Jl 2:23. *x:* Jb 38:41; Mt 6:26.

no pleasure in the runner's stride.[y]
11 Rather the LORD takes pleasure in those who fear him,
those who put their hope in his mercy.

III

12 Glorify the LORD, Jerusalem;
Zion, offer praise to your God,
13 For he has strengthened the bars of your gates,
blessed your children within you.[z]
14 He brings peace to your borders,
and satisfies you with finest wheat.[a]
15 *He sends his command to earth;
his word runs swiftly![b]
16 Thus he makes the snow like wool,
and spreads the frost like ash;[c]
17 He disperses hail like crumbs.
Who can withstand his cold?
18 Yet when again he issues his command, it melts them;
he raises his winds and the waters flow.
19 He proclaims his word to Jacob,
his statutes and laws to Israel.[d]
20 He has not done this for any other nation;
of such laws they know nothing.
Hallelujah!

PSALM 148*

See RG 244, 250

All Creation Summoned To Praise

1 Hallelujah!

I

Praise the LORD from the heavens;
praise him in the heights.
2 Praise him, all you his angels;
give praise, all you his hosts.[e]
3 Praise him, sun and moon;
praise him, all shining stars.
4 Praise him, highest heavens,*
you waters above the heavens.
5 Let them all praise the LORD's name;
for he commanded and they were created,[f]
6 Assigned them their station forever,
set an order that will never change.

II

7 Praise the LORD from the earth,
you sea monsters and all the deeps of the sea;[g]
8 Lightning and hail, snow and thick clouds,
storm wind that fulfills his command;
9 Mountains and all hills,
fruit trees and all cedars;[h]
10 Animals wild and tame,
creatures that crawl and birds that fly;[i]
11 Kings of the earth and all peoples,
princes and all who govern on earth;
12 Young men and women too,
old and young alike.
13 Let them all praise the LORD's name,
for his name alone is exalted,
His majesty above earth and heaven.[j]
14 *He has lifted high the horn of his people;
to the praise of all his faithful,
the Israelites, the people near to him.
Hallelujah!

PSALM 149*

See RG 244

Praise God with Song and Sword

1 Hallelujah!

Sing to the LORD a new song,
his praise in the assembly of the faithful.[k]
2 Let Israel be glad in its maker,
the people of Zion rejoice in their king.

147:15–19 God speaks through the thunder of nature and the word of revealed law, cf. Is 55:10–11. The weather phenomena are well known in Jerusalem: a blizzard of snow and hail followed by a thunderstorm that melts the ice.

Psalm 148 A hymn inviting the beings of heaven (Ps 148:1–6) and of earth (Ps 148:7–14) to praise God. The hymn does not distinguish between inanimate and animate (and rational) nature.

148:4 Highest heavens: lit., "the heavens of the heavens," i.e., the space above the firmament, where the "upper waters" are stored, cf. Gn 1:6–7; Dt 10:14; 1 Kgs 8:27; Ps 104:3, 13.

148:14 Has lifted high the horn of his people: the horn symbolizes strength, the concrete noun for the abstract. Of all peoples, God has chosen Israel to return praise and thanks in a special way.

Psalm 149 A hymn inviting the people of Israel to celebrate their God in song and festive dance (Ps 149:1–3, 5) because God has chosen them and given them victory (Ps 149:4). The exodus and conquest are the defining acts of Israel; the people must be ready to do again those acts in the future at the divine command (Ps 149:6–9).

y: Ps 20:8; 33:16–18. *z:* Ps 48:14. *a:* Ps 81:17. *b:* Ps 33:9. *c:* Jb 6:16; 37:10; 38:22. *d:* Ps 78:5; Bar 3:37; Dt 4:7–8. *e:* Ps 103:20f; Dn 3:58–63. *f:* Ps 33:9; Gn 1:3f; Jdt 16:14. *g:* Ps 135:6; Gn 1:21. *h:* Is 44:23. *i:* Ps 30:5; Gn 1:21, 24f; Dt 4:7. *j:* Ps 30:5; Dt 4:7. *k:* Ps 22:23; 26:12; 35:18; 40:10; Jdt 16:1.

3 Let them praise his name in dance,
make music with tambourine and lyre.*[l]
4 For the LORD takes delight in his people,
honors the poor with victory.
5 Let the faithful rejoice in their glory,
cry out for joy on their couches,*
6 With the praise of God in their mouths,
and a two-edged sword in their hands,[m]
7 To bring retribution on the nations,
punishment on the peoples,[n]
8 To bind their kings in shackles,
their nobles in chains of iron,
9 To execute the judgments decreed for them—
such is the glory* of all God's faithful.
Hallelujah!

PSALM 150*

See RG 244

Final Doxology

1 Hallelujah!

Praise God in his holy sanctuary;*[o]
give praise in the mighty dome of heaven.
2 Give praise for his mighty deeds,[p]
praise him for his great majesty.
3 Give praise with blasts upon the horn,[q]
praise him with harp and lyre.
4 Give praise with tambourines and dance,
praise him with strings and pipes.[r]
5 Give praise with crashing cymbals,
praise him with sounding cymbals.
6 Let everything that has breath
give praise to the LORD![s]
Hallelujah!

149:3 Make music with tambourine and lyre: the verse recalls the great exodus hymn of Ex 15:20.

149:5 On their couches: the people reclined to banquet.

149:9 The glory: what brings honor to the people is their readiness to carry out the divine will, here conceived as punishing injustice done by the nations.

Psalm 150 The Psalm is a closing doxology both for the fifth book of the Psalms (Ps 107–149) and for the Psalter as a whole. Temple musicians and dancers are called to lead all beings on earth and in heaven in praise of God. The Psalm proclaims to whom praise shall be given, and where (Ps 150:1); what praise shall be given, and why (Ps 150:2); how praise shall be given (Ps 150:3–5), and by whom (Ps 150:6).

150:1 His holy sanctuary: God's Temple on earth. **The mighty dome of heaven**: lit., "[God's] strong vault"; heaven is here imagined as a giant plate separating the inhabited world from the waters of the heavens.

l: Ps 68:26; 81:2–3; 87:7; 150:3–4. *m:* Neh 4:10–12; 2 Mc 15:27. *n:* Wis 3:8. *o:* Dn 3:53. *p:* Dt 3:24. *q:* Ps 81:3–4; 149:3; 2 Sm 6:5; 1 Chr 13:8; 16:5, 42; 2 Chr 5:12–13; 7:6. *r:* Ps 68:26; Ex 15:20. *s:* Rev 5:13.

See RG 254, 262

The Book of Proverbs

Proverbs is an anthology of collections of sayings and instructions. Many of the sayings and perhaps some instructions were composed in the monarchic period (late eleventh to the early sixth centuries). Editing of the whole book was done in the early postexilic period, in the view of most scholars; at that time chaps. 1–9 would have been added as the introduction. Whether the material originated among royal scribes (as 25:1 seems to suggest) imitating common literary genres, or whether it arose among tribal elders inculcating traditional ways, is disputed. The origin of the material, however, need not be imagined in an either/or scenario. Folk wisdom and observations could surely have been elaborated and re-expressed by learned scribes: "What oft was thought but ne'er so well expressed" (Alexander Pope). There can be no doubt, however, that Proverbs is sophisticated literature by talented writers, winning readers with its compelling portrait of wisdom and inviting them to see life afresh, "wisely," through its wit, originality, and shrewd observation.

The primary purpose of the book is to teach wisdom, not only to the young and inexperienced (1:2–4) but also to the advanced (1:5–6). Wisdom in the ancient Near East was not theoretical knowledge but practical expertise. Jewelers who cut precious stones were wise; kings who made their dominion peaceful and prosperous were wise. One could be wise in daily life, too, in knowing how to live successfully (having a prosperous household and living a long and healthy life) and without trouble in God's universe. Ultimately wisdom, or "sound guidance" (1:5), aims at the formation of character.

In the ancient Near East, people assumed that wisdom belonged to the gods, who were wise by reason of their divinity; human beings needed to have wisdom *granted* them by the gods. Creation accounts of neighboring cultures depict creation in two stages. In the first stage, human beings lived an animal-like existence, without clothes, writing, or kingship (proper governance). Over time, the gods came to realize that such a low grade of existence made the human race inadequate as their servants, so they endowed the race with "wisdom," which consisted of culture (e.g., kingship) and crafts (e.g., knowledge of farming, ability to weave). Such wisdom elevated the race to a "human" level and made them effective servants of the gods. Furthermore, divine wisdom was *mediated* to human beings through earthly institutions—the king, scribes (who produced wise writings), and heads of families (fathers, sometimes mothers). These traditional mediators appear in Proverbs: the book is credited to King Solomon, and kings are respectfully mentioned as pillars of society (e.g., 16:12–15); *writings* are a source of wisdom (1:1–7); the father instructing his son is the major paradigm of teaching. Proverbs differs, however, from other wisdom books in concentrating on wisdom itself, treating it as a virtually independent entity and personifying it as an attractive woman. Other books urge readers to perform wise acts, but Proverbs urges them to seek wisdom itself and portrays wisdom as a woman seeking human beings as disciples and companions.

Chapters 1–9 introduce the book, drawing attention to wisdom itself and its inherent value rather than exhorting to particular wise actions. The chapters personify wisdom as a woman and draw an extended analogy between finding a wife, or founding and maintaining a house(hold), and finding wisdom. The collections following chap. 9 consist largely of independent, two-line sayings, yielding their often indirect or paradoxical meaning only to readers willing to ponder them. To reflect on the sayings is perhaps what chaps. 1–9 mean by living with Wisdom and dwelling in her house.

The Book of Proverbs can make an important contribution to Christians and Jews today. First, it places the pursuit of wisdom over the performance of individual wise acts. To seek wisdom above all things is a fundamental option and a way of life. Second, it portrays the quest as filled with obstacles. There are men and women who offer a substitute for the real thing; discernment is required. Third, the book teaches that acquiring wisdom is both a human task and a divine gift. One can make oneself ready to receive by discipline, but one cannot take so divine a gift. Fourth, wisdom is in the world but it is not obvious to people entirely caught up with daily activities. The instructions and the aphorisms of the book can free the mind to see new things. Christians will see in personified Wisdom aspects of Jesus Christ, who they believe is divine wisdom sent to give human beings true and full life. Yet there is a universal dimension to Proverbs, for in its attention to human experience it creates a link to all people of good will.

The genres and themes of Proverbs continued on in Sirach, Wisdom of Solomon, and the later *Pirqe Abot* (The Sayings of the Fathers), a treatise in the Mishnah, which became the object of commentary in *Abot de Rabbi Nathan*. The New Testament saw Jesus as a wisdom teacher and employed the tradition of personified wisdom of chaps. 2 and 8 to express his incarnation. The Letter of James is an instruction resembling those in Proverbs. Wisdom traditions influenced the Gospels of Matthew and Luke through a common source (see, e.g., Mt 11:25–27 and Lk 10:21–22, which seem to derive their father-son language, at least in part, from the parental language of Proverbs). The Gospel of John regards Jesus as incarnate wisdom descended from on high to offer human beings life and truth and make disciples of them, a view largely reflected in Proverbs 1–9. In later Judaism, Hebrew ethical wills, in which parents hand on to their children their wisdom, borrowed from the genre of instruction.

The original audience of the instructions and sayings seems to have been male. The father addresses his son, marriage is finding a wife, success often is serving the king or farming effectively. The book itself, however, expands the traditional audience of youths (1:4) to include older, more experienced, people (1:5). It broadens the father-son language by mentioning the mother, and incorporates sayings on human experience generally. The father teaching his son becomes a model for anyone teaching a way of life to another person. The canonical process furthered such inclusiveness, for Proverbs was made part of the Bible that addresses *all* Israel.

The Book of Proverbs has nine sections:

I. Title and Introduction (1:1–7)
II. Instructions of Parents and of Woman Wisdom (1:8–9:18)
III. First Solomonic Collection of Sayings (10:1–22:16)
IV. Sayings of the Wise (22:17–24:22)
V. Further Sayings of the Wise (24:23–34)
VI. Second Solomonic Collection, Collected under King Hezekiah (25:1–29:27)
VII. Sayings of Agur and Others (30:1–33)
VIII. Sayings of King Lemuel (31:1–9)
IX. Poem on the Woman of Worth (31:10–31)

Part II is judged by many scholars to contain ten instructions (1:8–19; chap. 2; 3:1–12, 21–35; 4:1–9, 10–19, 20–27; chap. 5; 6:20–35; chap. 7), three wisdom poems (1:20–33; chap. 8; 9:1–6 + 11, 13–18), and two interludes (3:13–20; 6:1–19).

I. Title and Introduction

CHAPTER 1

See RG 254–61

*Purpose of the Proverbs of Solomon**

1 The proverbs* of Solomon,[a] the son of David,
king of Israel:
2 That people may know wisdom and discipline,*
may understand intelligent sayings;
3 May receive instruction in wise conduct,
in what is right, just and fair;
4 That resourcefulness may be imparted to the naive,*
knowledge and discretion to the young.
5 The wise by hearing them will advance in learning,
the intelligent will gain sound guidance,
6 To comprehend proverb and byword,
the words of the wise and their riddles.
7 Fear of the LORD* is the beginning of knowledge;[b]
fools despise wisdom and discipline.

II. Instructions of Parents and of Woman Wisdom

*The Path of the Wicked: Greed and Violence**

8 Hear, my son, your father's instruction,
and reject not your mother's teaching;
9 A graceful diadem will they be for your head;
a pendant for your neck.
10 My son, should sinners entice you,
11 do not go if they say, "Come along with us!
Let us lie in wait for blood,
unprovoked, let us trap the innocent;
12 Let us swallow them alive, like Sheol,
whole, like those who go down to the pit!
13 All kinds of precious wealth shall we gain,
we shall fill our houses with booty;
14 Cast in your lot with us,
we shall all have one purse!"
15 My son, do not walk in the way with them,
hold back your foot from their path!
16 [For their feet run to evil,
they hasten to shed blood.[c]]

1:1–7 The prologue explains the purpose of the book. The book has a sapiential, ethical, and religious dimension: to bring the inexperienced to knowledge and right conduct, to increase the facility of those already wise for interpreting proverbs, parables and riddles, and to encourage the fulfillment of one's duties to God.

1:1 Proverbs: the Hebrew word *mashal* is broader than English "proverb," embracing the instructions of chaps. 1–9 and the sayings, observations, and comparisons of chaps. 10–31.

1:2 Discipline: education or formation which dispels ignorance and corrects vice. Note the reprise of v. 2a in v. 7b.

1:4 Naive: immature, inexperienced, sometimes the young, hence easily influenced for good or evil.

1:7 Fear of the LORD: primarily a disposition rather than the emotion of fear; reverential awe and respect toward God combined with obedience to God's will.

1:8–19 A parental warning to a young person leaving home, for them to avoid the company of the greedy and violent. Two ways lie before the hearer, a way that leads to death and a way that leads to life. The trap which the wicked set for the innocent (v. 11) in the end takes away the lives of the wicked themselves (v. 19). This theme will recur especially in chaps. 1–9. A second theme introduced here is that of founding (or managing) a household and choosing a spouse. A third theme is the human obstacles to attaining wisdom. Here (and in 2:12–15 and 4:10–19), the obstacle is men (always in the plural); in 2:16–19; 5:1–6; 6:20–35; chap. 7; 9:13–18, the obstacle to the quest is the "foreign" woman (always in the singular).

a: Prv 10:1; 25:1; 1 Kgs 4:32. *b:* Prv 9:10; Jb 28:28; Ps 111:10; Sir 1:16. *c:* Is 59:7.

17 In vain a net is spread*
right under the eyes of any bird—
18 They lie in wait for their own blood,
they set a trap for their own lives.
19 This is the way of everyone greedy for loot:
it takes away their lives.

*Wisdom in Person Gives a Warning**

20 Wisdom cries aloud in the street,
in the open squares she raises her voice;[d]
21 Down the crowded ways she calls out,
at the city gates she utters her words:
22 * "How long, you naive ones, will you love naivete,
23 How long will you turn away at my reproof?
[The arrogant delight in their arrogance,
and fools hate knowledge.]
Lo! I will pour out to you my spirit,
I will acquaint you with my words:
24 'Because I called and you refused,
extended my hand and no one took notice;[e]
25 Because you disdained all my counsel,
and my reproof you ignored—
26 I, in my turn, will laugh at your doom;
will mock when terror overtakes you;
27 When terror comes upon you like a storm,
and your doom approaches like a whirlwind;
when distress and anguish befall you.'
28 Then they will call me, but I will not answer;
they will seek me, but will not find me,
29 Because they hated knowledge,
and the fear of the LORD they did not choose.
30 They ignored my counsel,
they spurned all my reproof;
31 Well, then, they shall eat the fruit* of their own way,
and with their own devices be glutted.
32 For the straying of the naive kills them,
the smugness of fools destroys them.
33 But whoever obeys me dwells in security,
in peace, without fear of harm."[f]

CHAPTER 2

See RG 254–62

*The Blessings of Wisdom**

1 My son, if you receive my words
and treasure my commands,
2 Turning your ear to wisdom,*
inclining your heart to understanding;
3 Yes, if you call for intelligence,
and to understanding raise your voice;
4 If you seek her like silver,
and like hidden treasures search her out,

1:17 A difficult verse. The most probable interpretation is that no fowler lifts up the net so the bird can see it. The verse might be paraphrased: God does not let those who walk on evil paths see the net that will entrap them. The passive construction ("a net is spread") is sometimes used to express divine activity. Verse 16 is a later attempt to add clarity. It is a quotation from Is 59:7 and is not in the best Greek manuscripts.

1:20–33 Wisdom is personified as in chaps. 8 and 9:1–6. With divine authority she proclaims the moral order, threatening to leave to their own devices those who disregard her invitation. All three speeches of Woman Wisdom have common features: a setting in city streets; an audience of simple or naive people; a competing appeal (chap. 7 is the competing appeal for chap. 8); an invitation to a relationship that brings long life, riches, repute.

The structure of the speeches is: A: setting (vv. 20–21); B: Wisdom's withdrawal, rebuke and announcement (vv. 22–23); reason and rejection I (vv. 24–27); reason and rejection II (vv. 28–31); summary (v. 32); C: the effects of Wisdom's presence (v. 33). Wisdom's opening speech is an extended threat ending with a brief invitation (v. 33). Her second speech is an extended invitation ending with a brief threat (8:36). The surprisingly abrupt and harsh tone of her speech is perhaps to be explained as a response to the arrogant words of the men in the previous scene (1:8–19).

1:22–23 There is textual confusion. Verse 22bc (in the third person) is an addition, interrupting vv. 22a and 23a (in the second person). The addition has been put in brackets, to separate it from the original poem. The original verses do not ask for a change of heart but begin to detail the consequences of disobedience to Wisdom.

1:31 Eat the fruit: sinners are punished by the consequences of their sins. Wisdom's voice echoes that of the parents in vv. 8–19. The parents mediate wisdom in vv. 8–19, but here Wisdom herself speaks.

2:1–22 Chapter 2 is a single poem, an acrostic of twenty-two lines, the number of consonants in the Hebrew alphabet. In vv. 1–11, the letter *aleph*, the first letter of the alphabet, predominates, and in vv. 12–22, the letter *lamed*, the first letter of the second half of the alphabet. A single structure runs through the whole: if (*aleph*) you search . . . then (*aleph*) the Lord/Wisdom will grant . . . saving (*lamed*) you from the wicked man/woman . . . thus (*lamed*) you can walk in the safe way . . .

2:2–3 Wisdom . . . understanding . . . intelligence: various names or aspects of the same gift.

d: Prv 8:1–3; 9:3. *e:* Is 65:2, 12; 66:4; Jer 7:13. *f:* Prv 8:33–34.

5 Then will you understand the fear of the LORD;
the knowledge of God you will find;
6 For the LORD gives wisdom,
from his mouth come knowledge and understanding;[g]
7 He has success in store for the upright,
is the shield of those who walk honestly,
8 Guarding the paths of justice,
protecting the way of his faithful ones,
9 Then you will understand what is right and just,
what is fair, every good path;
10 For wisdom will enter your heart,
knowledge will be at home in your soul,
11 Discretion will watch over you,
understanding will guard you;
12 * Saving you from the way of the wicked,
from those whose speech is perverse.
13 From those who have left the straight paths
to walk in the ways of darkness,
14 Who delight in doing evil
and celebrate perversity;
15 Whose ways are crooked,
whose paths are devious;
16 * Saving you from a stranger,
from a foreign woman with her smooth words,[h]
17 One who forsakes the companion of her youth
and forgets the covenant of her God;
18 For her path sinks down to death,
and her footsteps lead to the shades.* [i]
19 None who enter there come back,
or gain the paths of life.
20 Thus you may walk in the way of the good,
and keep to the paths of the just.
21 * For the upright will dwell in the land,[j]
people of integrity will remain in it;
22 But the wicked will be cut off from the land,
the faithless will be rooted out of it.

CHAPTER 3

See RG 254–62

*Confidence in God Leads to Prosperity**

1 My son, do not forget* my teaching,
take to heart my commands;
2 For many days, and years of life,[k]
and peace, will they bring you.
3 Do not let love and fidelity forsake you;
bind them around your neck;
write them on the tablet of your heart.
4 Then will you win favor and esteem
before God and human beings.
5 Trust in the LORD with all your heart,
on your own intelligence do not rely;

2:12–15 As in 1:8–19, there is an obstacle to the quest for wisdom—deceitful and violent men. Cf. also 4:10–19. They offer a way of life that is opposed to the way of wisdom.

2:16–19 A second obstacle and counter-figure to Wisdom, personified as an attractive woman, is the "stranger," or "foreigner," from outside the territory or kinship group, hence inappropriate as a marriage partner. In Proverbs she comes to be identified with Woman Folly, whose deceitful words promise life but lead to death. Woman Folly appears also in chap. 5, 6:20–35, chap. 7 and 9:13–18. **Covenant**: refers to the vow uttered with divine sanction at the woman's previous marriage, as the parallel verse suggests. She is already married and relations with her would be adulterous.

2:18 Shades: the inhabitants of Sheol.

2:21–22 Verses 21–22 echo the ending of Wisdom's speech in 1:32–33, in which refusing Wisdom's invitation meant death and obedience to her meant life. The same set of ideas is found in Ps 37 (especially vv. 3, 9, 11, 22, 29, 34, and 38): to live on (or inherit) the land and to be uprooted from the land are expressions of divine recompense.

3:1–12 The instruction consists of a series of six four-line exhortations in which the second line of each exhortation mentions a reward or benefit. In the first five exhortations, the teacher promises a reward: long life, a good name, divine protection, health, abundant crops. The last exhortation, vv. 11–12, departs from the command-reward scheme, implying that being a disciple of the Lord does not guarantee unalloyed bliss: one must allow God freedom to "reprove" or educate. The process of education is like that described in chap. 2: the father first invites his son (or disciple) to memorize his teaching (v. 1), then to enter upon a relationship of trust with him (v. 3), and finally to place his trust in God, who takes up the parental task of education (v. 5). Education begun by the parent is brought to full completion by God.

3:1 Do not forget: this word and several others in the section such as "teaching," "commands," "years of life," and the custom of affixing written teaching to one's body, occur also in Deuteronomy. This vocabulary suggests that Proverbs and Deuteronomy had a common origin in the scribal class of Jerusalem. This section (and vv. 21–34) subtly elaborates Dt 6:5–9, "You shall love the LORD with all your heart (v. 5) . . . Take to heart these words (v. 1) . . . Recite them when you are at home and when you are away (v. 23) . . . when you lie down (v. 24) . . . Bind them (v. 3) on your arm as a sign and let them be a pendant on your forehead" (v. 21).

g: Jb 32:8; Wis 7:25; Sir 1:1; Jas 1:5. *h:* Prv 5:3, 20; 6:24; 7:5; 22:14. *i:* Prv 5:5; 7:27. *j:* Prv 10:7, 30; Jb 18:17; Ps 21:9–13; 37:22, 28. *k:* Prv 4:10; 9:11; 10:27.

6 In all your ways be mindful of him,
and he will make straight your paths.
7 Do not be wise in your own eyes,[l]
fear the LORD and turn away from evil;
8 This will mean health for your flesh
and vigor for your bones.
9 Honor the LORD with your wealth,
with first fruits of all your produce;[m]
10 Then will your barns be filled with
plenty,
with new wine your vats will overflow.
11 The discipline of the LORD, my son, do
not spurn;[n]
do not disdain his reproof;
12 * For whom the LORD loves he reproves,
as a father, the son he favors.[o]

*The Benefits of Finding Wisdom**

13 Happy the one who finds wisdom,
the one who gains understanding![p]
14 Her profit is better than profit in silver,
and better than gold is her revenue;
15 She is more precious than corals,
and no treasure of yours can compare
with her.[q]
16 Long life is in her right hand,
in her left are riches and honor;
17 Her ways are pleasant ways,
and all her paths are peace;
18 She is a tree of life* to those who grasp
her,
and those who hold her fast are happy.[r]
19 The LORD by wisdom founded the earth,
established the heavens by
understanding;
20 By his knowledge the depths* are split,
and the clouds drop down dew.

*Justice Toward One's Neighbor Brings Blessing**

21 My son, do not let these slip from your
sight:
hold to deliberation and planning;
22 So will they be life to your soul,*
and an adornment for your neck.
23 Then you may go your way securely;
your foot will never stumble;
24 When you lie down, you will not be afraid,
when you rest, your sleep will be sweet.
25 Do not be afraid of sudden terror,

3:12 One might be tempted to judge the quality of one's relationship to God by one's prosperity. It is an inadequate criterion, for God as a teacher might go counter to student expectations. The discipline of God can involve suffering.

3:13–20 An encomium of Wisdom through the listing of her benefits to the human race and the depiction of her role in creation. Wisdom, or understanding, is more valuable than silver and gold. Its fruit is long life, riches, honor and happiness (vv. 13–18). Even the creation of the universe and its adornment (Gn 1) were not done without wisdom (vv. 19–20). The praise of Wisdom foreshadows the praise of a noble wife in the final poem (31:10–31), even to the singling out of the hands extended in a helpful way toward human beings.

3:18 A tree of life: in the Old Testament this phrase occurs only in Proverbs (11:30; 13:12; 15:4) and Genesis (2:9; 3:22, 24). The origins of the concept are obscure; there is no explicit mention of it in ancient Near Eastern literature, though on ancient seals trees are sometimes identified as trees of life. When the man and the woman were expelled from the garden, the tree of life was put off limits to them, lest they "eat of it and live forever" (Gn 3:22). The quest for wisdom gives access to the previously sequestered tree of life. The tree of life is mentioned also in the apocryphal work 1 Enoch 25:4–5. Rev 2 and 22 mention the tree of life as a source of eternal life.

3:20 Depths: for the Hebrews, the depths enclosed the great subterranean waters; the rain and dew descended from the waters above the firmament; cf. Gn 1:6–10; Jb 26:8, 12; Ps 18:15; 24:2. The cosmogony provides the reason why Wisdom offers such benefits to human beings: the world was created in wisdom so that all who live in accord with wisdom live in tune with the universe.

3:21–35 As in other instructions, the father in vv. 21–26 urges the son to seek wisdom, which in this case means practicing the virtues of "deliberation and planning," a specification of wisdom. Practicing these virtues brings protection from violence (vv. 22–26) and friendship with God (vv. 32–35). The language is like Ps 91.

Verses 27–35 are arranged according to a clear order. Serving God requires serving one's neighbor through kindness (vv. 27–28), maintaining peace with the good (vv. 29–31), having no envy of the wicked (v. 31), because the Lord's friendship and kindness are with the just, not with the wicked. Matching the six exhortations of vv. 1–12, vv. 27–34 contain six prohibitions. The righteous/wicked contrast is progressively developed: in contrast to the wicked, the righteous are in God's inner circle, their houses are blessed, they deal with a merciful God, and obtain honor.

3:22 Your soul: Heb. *nephesh* means "throat, esophagus; life; soul." The meanings are connected. The throat area is the moist, breathing center of the body, which stands for life and for self. The figure of speech is called metonymy, in which one word is substituted for another on the basis of a causal relation, e.g., eye for sight, arm for power, or, as here, "throat area" for life. Proverbs sometimes plays on this concrete meaning of life (e.g., 21:23).

l: Rom 11:25; 12:16. *m:* Ex 34:26; Lv 27:30; Dt 26:2; Sir 7:31; 35:7. *n:* Heb 12:5–6. *o:* Jdt 8:27; Rev 3:19. *p:* Prv 8:34–35. *q:* Prv 8:11, 19; Wis 7:8–11. *r:* Prv 4:13; 8:35; 11:30; Gn 2:9; 3:22.

of the ruin of the wicked when it
comes;
26 For the LORD will be your confidence,
and will keep your foot from the snare.
27 Do not withhold any goods from the
owner
when it is in your power to act.
28 Say not to your neighbor, "Go, come
back tomorrow,
and I will give it to you," when all the
while you have it.
29 Do not plot evil against your neighbors,
when they live at peace with you.
30 Do not contend with someone without
cause,
with one who has done you no harm.
31 Do not envy the violent
and choose none of their ways:[s]
32 To the LORD the devious are an
abomination,
but the upright are close to him.
33 The curse of the LORD is on the house of
the wicked,
but the dwelling of the just he blesses;
34 Those who scoff, he scoffs at,[t]
but the lowly he favors.
35 The wise will possess glory,
but fools will bear shame.

CHAPTER 4

See RG 254–62

*The Teacher as Model Disciple**

1 Hear, O children, a father's instruction,
be attentive, that you may gain
understanding!
2 Yes, excellent advice I give you;
my teaching do not forsake.
3 When I was my father's child,
tender, the darling of my mother,
4 He taught me and said to me:
"Let your heart hold fast my words:[u]
keep my commands, and live!
5 Get wisdom,* get understanding!
Do not forget or turn aside from the
words of my mouth.
6 Do not forsake her, and she will preserve
you;
love her, and she will safeguard you;
7 The beginning of wisdom is: get wisdom;
whatever else you get, get
understanding.
8 Extol her, and she will exalt you;
she will bring you honors if you
embrace her;
9 She will put on your head a graceful
diadem;
a glorious crown will she bestow on
you."

*The Two Ways**

10 Hear, my son, and receive my words,
and the years of your life shall be many.[v]
11 On the way of wisdom I direct you,
I lead you on straight paths.
12 When you walk, your step will not be
impeded,
and should you run, you will not
stumble.
13 Hold fast to instruction, never let it go;

4:1–9 The teacher draws a parallel between his teaching the disciples now and his father's teaching him in his youth (vv. 3–4): what my father taught me about wisdom is what I am teaching you. The poem implies that the teacher has acquired wisdom and has in fact been protected and honored as his father promised long ago. Thus the teacher has the authority of someone who has been under wisdom's sway since earliest youth.

There are two sections, a call for attention and introduction of the speaker (vv. 1–3) and the father's quoting of his own father's teaching (vv. 4–9). Beginning with v. 5, the father's words are no longer quoted, wisdom herself becoming the active agent; she becomes the subject, not the object, of the verbs. Three Hebrew verbs are repeated in the two parts, "to forsake" in vv. 2 and 6, "to keep/guard" in vv. 4 and 6, and "to give/bestow" in vv. 2 and 9. Each verb in its first appearance has the father's words as its object; in its second appearance each verb has wisdom as its subject or object. The teaching process is like that in 2:1–22 and 3:1–12: heeding the words of one's parent puts one in touch with wisdom, who completes the process and bestows her gifts.

4:5, 7 Get wisdom: the same Hebrew word "to get" can mean to acquire merchandise and to acquire a wife (18:22; 31:10); both meanings are in keeping with Proverbs' metaphors of acquiring wisdom over gold and silver and of acquiring wisdom as a personified woman, a wife.

4:10–19 A central metaphor of the poem is "the way." The way of wisdom leads directly to life (vv. 10–13); it is a light that grows brighter (v. 18). The wise are bound to shun (vv. 14–17) the dark and violent path of the wicked (v. 19). Singleness of purpose and right conduct proceed from the heart of the wise as from the source of life (vv. 23–26), saving them from destruction on evil paths (4:27; 5:21–23). As in 1:8–19 and 2:12–15, the obstacles to the quest are men and their way. Elsewhere in chaps. 1–9, the obstacle is the foreign woman (2:16–19; chap. 5; 6:20–35; chap. 7; 9:13–18).

s: Prv 23:17; 24:1, 19; Ps 37:1. *t:* Prv 1:26. *u:* Dt 6:1–6. *v:* Prv 3:2.

Hebrew Poetry

MOST READERS NOTICE a particular feature of Hebrew poetry, and one that is particularly prevalent in the Book of Proverbs. This is the use of "parallelism," or the statement of an idea in two (or more) different ways.

Parallelism can be simple, as in Proverbs 3:12:

For whom the LORD loves he reproves,
and he chastises the son he favors.

Here the idea is simply restated in different words. A second type of parallelism is the antithesis, as in Proverbs 2:21-22:

For the upright will dwell in the land,
the honest will remain in it;
But the wicked will be cut off from the land,
the faithless will be rooted out of it.

The ideas in the first verse are echoed as negatives in the second.

Finally, the restatement of the idea may serve to advance the thought in some way. Proverbs 4:1 says:

Hear, O children, a father's instruction,
be attentive, that you may gain understanding!

The exhortation to hear is explained in the second line: "you will benefit from paying attention."

Parallelism seems to have served several functions. It allowed Hebrew poetry to be very terse; if the idea was obscure the first time it was stated, perhaps the second time would make things clearer. In addition, it was a substitute for grammatical links between different parts of a line. Hebrew poetry tends to avoid subordinate clauses, connectives (such as "so that"), and other means of leading the reader on from one line to the next. Instead, the lines seem almost detached from one another. But the parallel structure serves to link lines together, and sometimes leads on to larger units as well. In this way, parallelism unites the structure and the content of much Hebrew poetry.

keep it, for it is your life.
14 * The path of the wicked do not enter,
nor walk in the way of the evil;
15 Shun it, do not cross it,
turn aside from it, pass on.
16 For they cannot rest unless they have done evil;
if they do not trip anyone they lose sleep.
17 For they eat the bread of wickedness
and drink the wine of violence.
18 But the path of the just is like shining light,
that grows in brilliance till perfect day.*
19 The way of the wicked is like darkness;
they do not know on what they stumble.

*With Your Whole Being Heed My Words and Live**

20 My son, to my words be attentive,
to my sayings incline your ear;
21 Let them not slip from your sight,
keep them within your heart;

4:14–15 One is always free to choose. The righteous may choose to leave their path to walk on the wicked path and the wicked may choose the righteous path.

4:18 Till perfect day: lit., "till the day is established"; this may refer to full daylight or to noonday.

4:20–27 Acquiring wisdom brings life and health. The

22 For they are life to those who find them,[w]
bringing health to one's whole being.
23 With all vigilance guard your heart,
for in it are the sources of life.
24 * Dishonest mouth put away from you,
deceitful lips put far from you.
25 Let your eyes look straight ahead
and your gaze be focused forward.
26 Survey the path for your feet,
and all your ways will be sure.
27 Turn neither to right nor to left,
keep your foot far from evil.

CHAPTER 5

See RG 254–62

*Warning Against Adultery**

1 My son, to my wisdom be attentive,
to understanding incline your ear,
2 That you may act discreetly,
and your lips guard what you know.
3 Indeed, the lips of the stranger drip honey,*
and her mouth is smoother than oil;
4 But in the end she is as bitter as
wormwood,
as sharp as a two-edged sword.
5 Her feet go down to death,
her steps reach Sheol;[y]
6 Her paths ramble, you know not where,
lest you see before you the road to life.
7 So now, children, listen to me,
do not stray from the words of my
mouth.
8 Keep your way far from her,[z]
do not go near the door of her house,
9 Lest you give your honor* to others,[a]
and your years to a merciless one;
10 Lest outsiders take their fill of your wealth,
and your hard-won earnings go to
another's house;
11 And you groan in the end,
when your flesh and your body are
consumed;
12 And you say, "Oh, why did I hate
instruction,
and my heart spurn reproof!
13 Why did I not listen to the voice of my
teachers,
incline my ear to my instructors!
14 I am all but ruined,
in the midst of the public assembly!"
15 Drink water* from your own cistern,
running water from your own well.
16 Should your water sources be dispersed
abroad,
streams of water in the streets?
17 Let them be yours alone,
not shared with outsiders;
18 Let your fountain be blessed and have
joy of the wife of your youth,
19 your lovely hind, your graceful doe.*

learning process involves two stages: (1) hearing the teacher's words and treasuring them in the heart; (2) speaking and acting in accord with the wisdom that one has stored in one's heart. Seven organs of the body are mentioned: ear, eyes, heart, mouth, lips, eyelids ("gaze," v. 25), feet. Each of the organs is to be strained to its limit as the disciple puts wisdom into practice. The physical organ stands for the faculty, e.g., the eye for sight, the foot for movement. The figure of speech is called metonymy; one word is substituted for another on the basis of a causal relation.

4:24–27 In vv. 20–21 the faculties of hearing (ear) and seeing (eye) take in the teaching and the heart stores and ponders it, so in the second half of the poem, vv. 24–27, the faculties of speech, sight, and walking enable the disciple to put the teaching into practice.

5:1–23 This is the first of three poems on the forbidden woman, the "stranger" outside the social boundaries (cf. 2:16–19); the other two are 6:20–35 and chap. 7. Understanding and discretion are necessary to avoid adultery, which leads astray and begets bitterness, bloodshed, and death (vv. 1–6). It destroys honor, wastes the years of life, despoils hard-earned wealth, and brings remorse in the end (vv. 7–14). Conjugal fidelity and love bring happiness and security (vv. 15–20). Cf. 6:20–7:27. The structure of the poem consists of a two-line introduction; part one consists of three stanzas of four lines each warning of the forbidden woman's effect on her lovers (vv. 3–14); part two consists of a stanza of twelve lines exhorting the disciple to marital fidelity (vv. 15–20); and a final stanza of six lines on the perils of the woman (vv. 21–23).

5:3 A metaphorical level is established in the opening description of the forbidden woman: her lips drip honey and her feet lead to death. By her lies, she leads people away from the wisdom that gives life.

5:9 Honor: the words "life" and "wealth" have also been read in this place. **A merciless one**: the offended husband; cf. 6:34–35.

5:15–16 Water: water may have an erotic meaning as in Sg 4:15, "[You are] a garden fountain, a well of living water." Eating and drinking can be metaphors expressing the mutuality of love. The wife is the opposite of the adulterous woman; she is not an outsider, not unfeeling, not a destroyer of her husband's self and goods. The best defense against adultery is appreciating and loving one's spouse. The best defense against folly is to appreciate and love wisdom.

w: Prv 8:35. *x:* Prv 7:5. *y:* Prv 2:18; 7:27. *z:* Prv 7:25. *a:* Sir 9:6.

Of whose love you will ever have your fill,
and by her ardor always be intoxicated.
20 Why then, my son, should you be intoxicated with a stranger,
and embrace another woman?
21 Indeed, the ways of each person are plain to the LORD's sight;
all their paths he surveys;[b]
22 By their own iniquities the wicked will be caught,
in the meshes of their own sin they will be held fast;
23 They will die from lack of discipline,
lost because of their great folly.

CHAPTER 6

*Miscellaneous Proverbs**

See RG 254–62

Against Going Surety for One's Neighbor

1 * My son, if you have become surety to your neighbor,[c]
given your hand in pledge to another,
2 You have been snared by the utterance of your lips,
caught by the words of your mouth;
3 So do this, my son, to free yourself,
since you have fallen into your neighbor's power:
Go, hurry, rouse your neighbor!
4 Give no sleep to your eyes,
nor slumber to your eyelids;
5 Free yourself like a gazelle from the hunter,
or like a bird from the hand of the fowler.

The Ant and the Sluggard at Harvest

6 * Go to the ant,[d] O sluggard,
study her ways and learn wisdom;
7 For though she has no chief,
no commander or ruler,
8 She procures her food in the summer,
stores up her provisions in the harvest.
9 How long, O sluggard, will you lie there?
when will you rise from your sleep?
10 A little sleep, a little slumber,
a little folding of the arms to rest—*
11 Then poverty will come upon you like a robber,
and want like a brigand.

The Scoundrel

12 * Scoundrels, villains, are they
who deal in crooked talk.
13 Shifty of eye,

5:19 Lovely hind . . . graceful doe: ancient Near Eastern symbols of feminine beauty and charm; cf. Sg 2:7, 9, 17.

6:1–19 Four independent pieces akin to those in 30:1–5, 6–11, 12–15, and 16–19. Some judge the verses to be an ancient addition, but the fact that the pieces differ from the other material in chaps. 1–9 is not a strong argument against their originality. Ancient anthologies did not always have the symmetry of modern collections. An editor may have placed the four pieces in the midst of the three poems on the forbidden woman to shed light on some of their themes. Verses 1–5 warn against getting trapped by one's words to another person (the Hebrew word for "another" is the same used for the forbidden woman); vv. 6–11 proposes the ant as a model of forethought and diligence; vv. 12–15 describes the reprobate who bears some similarity to the seductive woman, especially as portrayed in chap. 7; vv. 16–19 depicts the typical enemy of God, underscoring the person's destructive words.

6:1–5 Unlike other instructions that begin with "my son," this instruction does not urge the hearer to store up the father's words as a means to wisdom, but only to avoid one practice—going surety for one's neighbor. The warning is intensified by repetition of "neighbor" and "free yourself," the mention of bodily organs, and the imagery of hunting. **Given your hand in pledge**: lit., "struck your hands"; this was probably the legal method for closing a contract. To become surety meant intervening in favor of the insolvent debtor and assuming responsibility for the payment of the debt, either by obtaining it from the debtor or substituting oneself. Proverbs is strongly opposed to the practice (11:15; 17:18; 20:16; 22:26–27; 27:13) apparently because of the danger it poses to the freedom of the one providing surety.

6:6–11 The sluggard or lazybones is a type in Proverbs, like the righteous and the wicked. Sometimes the opposite type to the sluggard is the diligent person. Other extended passages on the sluggard are 24:30–34 and 26:13–16. The malice of the type is not low physical energy but the refusal to act. To describe human types, Proverbs often uses comparisons from the animal world, e.g., 27:8 (bird); 28:1, 15 (lion); 30:18–19 (eagle, snake); 30:24–28 (ant, badger, locust, lizard).

6:10 This verse may be regarded as the sluggard's reply or as a continuation of the remonstrance.

6:12–15 Proverbs uses types to make the point that certain ways of acting have inherent consequences. The typifying intensifies the picture. All the physical organs—mouth, eyes, feet, fingers—are at the service of evil. Cf. Rom 6:12–13: "Therefore, sin must not reign over your mortal bodies so that you obey their desires. And do not present the parts of your bodies to sin as weapons for wickedness, but present your-

b: Jb 14:16; 31:4; 34:21. *c:* Prv 11:15; 22:26; Sir 8:13; 29:19. *d:* Prv 30:25.

feet ever moving,
pointing with fingers,
14 They have perversity in their hearts,
always plotting evil,
sowing discord.
15 Therefore their doom comes suddenly;
in an instant they are crushed beyond cure.

What the Lord Rejects

16 There are six things the LORD hates,
yes, seven* are an abomination to him;
17 * Haughty eyes, a lying tongue,
hands that shed innocent blood,
18 A heart that plots wicked schemes,
feet that are quick to run to evil,
19 The false witness who utters lies,
and the one who sows discord among kindred.

*Warning Against Adultery**

20 Observe, my son, your father's command,
and do not reject your mother's teaching;
21 Keep them fastened over your heart always,
tie them around your neck.
22 When you lie down they* will watch over you,
when you wake, they will share your concerns;
wherever you turn, they will guide you.
23 For the command is a lamp, and the teaching a light,
and a way to life are the reproofs that discipline,
24 Keeping you from another's wife,
from the smooth tongue of the foreign woman.[e]
25 Do not lust in your heart after her beauty,
do not let her captivate you with her glance![f]
26 For the price of a harlot
may be scarcely a loaf of bread,
But a married woman
is a trap for your precious life.
27 * Can a man take embers into his bosom,
and his garments not be burned?
28 Or can a man walk on live coals,
and his feet not be scorched?
29 So with him who sleeps with another's wife—
none who touches her shall go unpunished.[g]
30 Thieves are not despised
if out of hunger they steal to satisfy their appetite.
31 Yet if caught they must pay back sevenfold,
yield up all the wealth of their house.
32 But those who commit adultery have no sense;

selves to God as raised from the dead to life and the parts of your bodies to God as weapons of righteousness."

6:16 Six . . . seven: this literary pattern (n, n + 1) occurs frequently; cf., e.g., Am 1–2; Prv 30:18–19.

6:17–19 The seven vices, symbolized for the most part by bodily organs, are pride, lying, murder, intrigue, readiness to do evil, false witness, and the stirring up of discord.

6:20–35 The second of three instructions on adultery (5:1–23; 6:20–35; and chap. 7). The instructions assume that wisdom will protect one from adultery and its consequences: loss of property and danger to one's person. In this poem, the father and the mother urge their son to keep their teaching constantly before his eyes. The teaching will light his way and make it a path to life (v. 23). The teaching will preserve him from the adulterous woman who is far more dangerous than a prostitute. Prostitutes may cost one money, but having an affair with someone else's wife puts one in grave danger. The poem bluntly urges self-interest as a motive to refrain from adultery.

The poem has three parts. I (vv. 20–24, ten lines), in which v. 23 repeats "command" and "teaching" of v. 20 and "keeping" in v. 24 completes the fixed pair initiated by "observe" in v. 20; II (vv. 25–29, ten lines) is a self-contained argument comparing the costs of a liaison with a prostitute and a married woman; III (vv. 30–35, twelve lines) draws conclusions from the comparison of adultery with theft: the latter involves property only but adultery destroys one's name and very self. The best protection against such a woman is heeding parental instruction, which is to be kept vividly before one's eyes like a written tablet.

6:22 They: Heb. has "she." If this verse is not out of place, then the antecedent of "she" is command (v. 20), or perhaps wisdom.

6:27–29 There is a play on three words of similar sound, *'îsh*, "man," *'ishshâ*, "woman," and *'ēsh*, "fire, embers." The question, "Can a man (*'îsh*) take embers (*'ēsh*) into his bosom / and his garments not be burned?", has a double meaning. "Into his bosom" has an erotic meaning as in the phrase "wife of one's bosom" (Dt 13:6; 28:54; Sir 9:1). Hence one will destroy one's garments, which symbolize one's public position, by taking fire/another's wife into one's bosom.

e: Prv 2:16; 7:5. *f:* Ex 20:17; Dt 5:21; Sir 9:8; 25:20; Mt 5:28. *g:* Sir 9:9.

those who do it destroy themselves.
33 * They will be beaten and disgraced,
and their shame will not be wiped away;
34 For passion enrages the husband,
he will have no pity on the day of vengeance;
35 He will not consider any restitution,
nor be satisfied by your many bribes.

See RG 254–62

CHAPTER 7

*The Seduction**

1 * My son, keep my words,
and treasure my commands.
2 Keep my commands and live,*
and my teaching as the apple of your eye;
3 Bind them on your fingers,
write them on the tablet of your heart.[h]
4 Say to Wisdom, "You are my sister!"*
Call Understanding, "Friend!"
5 That they may keep you from a stranger,
from the foreign woman with her smooth words.[i]
6 For at the window of my house,
through my lattice I looked out*
7 And I saw among the naive,
I observed among the young men,
a youth with no sense,
8 Crossing the street near the corner,
then walking toward her house,
9 In the twilight, at dusk of day,
in the very dark of night.
10 Then the woman comes to meet him,
dressed like a harlot, with secret designs.
11 She is raucous and unruly,
her feet cannot stay at home;
12 Now she is in the streets, now in the open squares,
lurking in ambush at every corner.
13 Then she grabs him, kisses him,
and with an impudent look says to him:
14 "I owed peace offerings,
and today I have fulfilled my vows;
15 So I came out to meet you,
to look for you, and I have found you!
16 With coverlets I have spread my couch,
with brocaded cloths of Egyptian linen;
17 I have sprinkled my bed* with myrrh,
with aloes, and with cinnamon.
18 Come, let us drink our fill of love,
until morning, let us feast on love!
19 For my husband is not at home,*
he has gone on a long journey;

6:33–35 The nature of the husband's vengeance is disputed, some believing it is simply a physical beating whereas others hold it is public and involves the death penalty because Lv 20:20 and Dt 22:22 demand the death penalty.

7:1–27 The third and climactic instruction on adultery and seduction is an example story, of the same type as the example story in 24:30–34. By its negative portrayal of the deceitful woman, who speaks in the night to a lone youth, it serves as a foil to trustworthy Wisdom in chap. 8, who speaks in broad daylight to all who pass in the street.

As in 6:20–24, the father warns his son to keep his teaching to protect him from the dangerous forbidden woman. The father's language in 7:4 ("Say to Wisdom, 'You are my sister,' and call Understanding 'Friend' ") sets this admonition apart, however; it is the language of courtship and love. If the son makes Woman Wisdom his companion and lover, she will protect him from the other woman. As in chap. 5, loving the right woman protects the man from the wrong woman.

As motivation, the father in vv. 6–23 tells his son of an incident he once observed while looking out his window—a young man went to the bed of an adulterous woman and wound up dead. As in chap. 5, the realistic details—the purposeful woman, the silent youth, the vow, the perfumed bed—have a metaphorical level. Ultimately the story is about two different kinds of love.

7:1–3 Verses 1–3 are artistically constructed. "Keep" in v. 1a recurs in v. 2a; "commands" in v. 1b recurs in v. 2a; the imperative verb "live" occurs in the very center of the three lines; v. 3, on preserving the teaching upon one's very person, matches vv. 1–2, on preserving the teaching internally by memorizing it.

7:2 Live: here as elsewhere (Gn 20:7; 42:18; 2 Kgs 18:32; Jer 27:12, 17; Ez 18:32), the imperative ("Live!") is uttered against the danger of death, e.g., "Do such and such and you will live (=survive the danger); why should you die?"

7:4 You are my sister: "sister" and "brother" are examples of love language in the ancient Near East, occurring in Egyptian love poetry and Mesopotamian marriage songs. In Sg 4:9, 10, 12; 5:1, the man calls the woman, "my sister, my bride." Intimate friendship with Woman Wisdom saves one from false and dangerous relationships.

7:6–7 I looked out . . . I saw . . .: the perspective is unusual. The narrator looks through a window upon the drama in the street.

7:17 Bed: a bed can designate a place of burial in Is 57:2; Ez 32:25; 2 Chr 16:14. **Myrrh . . . aloes**: the spices could be used for funerals as for weddings (Jn 19:39). It is possible that the language is ambivalent, speaking of death as it seems to speak of life. As the woman offers the youth a nuptial feast, she is in reality describing his funerary feast.

7:19–20 For my husband is not at home: the woman is calculating. She knows exactly how long her husband will be gone.

h: Dt 6:8. *i:* Prv 2:16; 6:24.

20 A bag of money he took with him,
he will not return home till the full moon."
21 She wins him over by repeated urging,
with her smooth lips she leads him astray.* [j]
22 He follows her impulsively,
like an ox that goes to slaughter;
Like a stag that bounds toward the net,
23 till an arrow pierces its liver;
Like a bird that rushes into a snare,
unaware that his life is at stake.
24 So now, children, listen to me,*
be attentive to the words of my mouth!
25 Do not let your heart turn to her ways,
do not go astray in her paths;
26 For many are those she has struck down dead,
numerous, those she has slain.
27 Her house is a highway to Sheol,
leading down into the chambers of death.[k]

CHAPTER 8

See RG 254–62

*The Discourse of Wisdom**

1 Does not Wisdom call,
and Understanding raise her voice?[l]
2 On the top of the heights along the road,
at the crossroads she takes her stand;
3 By the gates at the approaches of the city,
in the entryways she cries aloud:
4 "To you, O people, I call;
my appeal is to you mortals.
5 You naive ones, gain prudence,
you fools,* gain sense.
6 Listen! for noble things I speak;
my lips proclaim honest words.
7 * Indeed, my mouth utters truth,
and my lips abhor wickedness.
8 All the words of my mouth are sincere,
none of them wily or crooked;
9 All of them are straightforward to the intelligent,
and right to those who attain knowledge.
10 Take my instruction instead of silver,
and knowledge rather than choice gold.
11 [For Wisdom is better than corals,
and no treasures can compare with her.[m]]
12 I, Wisdom, dwell with prudence,
and useful knowledge I have.
13 [The fear of the LORD is hatred of evil;]
Pride, arrogance, the evil way,
and the perverse mouth I hate.[n]
14 Mine are counsel and advice;
Mine is strength; I am understanding.*
15 By me kings reign,
and rulers enact justice;

7:21 The verbs "to win over" (lit., "to lead astray") and "to lead off" can be used of leading animals such as a donkey (Nm 22:23) or sheep (Jer 23:2 and 50:17). The animal imagery continues as the youth is compared to an ox, a fallow deer, and a bird in the moment they are slaughtered. None of the animals are aware of their impending death.

7:24–27 The father addresses "children," a larger audience than his own son; the story is typical, intended for others as an example. The story is a foil to the speech of the other woman in chap. 8.

8:1–36 Chapter 8 is Wisdom's longest speech in the book. Wisdom is here personified as in 1:20–33. She exalts her grandeur and origin, and invites all (vv. 1–11) to be attentive to her salutary influence in human society (vv. 12–21), for she was privileged to be present at the creation of the world (vv. 22–31). Finally, she promises life and the favor of God to those who are devoted to her, death to those who reject her.

The poem has four sections, each (except the fourth) with two parts of five lines each:

I.	A. vv. 1–5	B. vv. 6–10
II.	A. vv. 12–16	B. vv. 17–21
III.	A. vv. 22–26	B. vv. 27–31
IV.	vv. 32–36	

Within chaps. 1–9, chap. 8 is the companion piece to Wisdom's first speech in 1:20–33. There she spoke harshly, giving a promise only in the last line; here she speaks invitingly, giving a threat only in the last line.

Chapter 8 is the best-known chapter in Proverbs and has profoundly influenced Jewish and Christian thought. The most explicit and lengthy biblical comment is in Sir 24; it too has thirty-five lines in seven five-line stanzas and develops the theme of Wisdom's intimacy with God and desire to be with human beings. The Gospel of John portrays Jesus in the language of wisdom in Proverbs: Jesus, like Wisdom, calls out to people to listen to him, promises to tell them the truth, seeks disciples, invites them to a banquet, and gives them life. Writers in the patristic period used the language of pre-existent wisdom to express the idea of the pre-existent Word with God.

8:5 Naive ones . . . fools: see note on 1:4.

8:7–8 The truth and sincerity of wisdom are absolute because they are of divine origin. They can neither deceive nor tolerate deception. The intelligent understand and accept this. "Straight" and "crooked" in Hebrew and English are metaphors for true, trustworthy and false, deceitful.

8:14 What is here predicated of Wisdom is elsewhere attributed to God (Jb 12:13–16).

---

j: Prv 5:3; 6:24. *k:* Prv 2:18–19; 5:5. *l:* Prv 1:20–21; 9:3. *m:* Prv 3:15; Wis 7:8. *n:* Prv 6:16–17; 16:5.

16 By me princes govern,
and nobles, all the judges of the earth.
17 Those who love me I also love,
and those who seek me find me.
18 With me are riches and honor,[o]
wealth that endures, and righteousness.
19 My fruit is better than gold, even pure
gold,
and my yield than choice silver.[p]
20 On the way of righteousness I walk,
along the paths of justice,
21 Granting wealth to those who love me,
and filling their treasuries.

22 * "The LORD begot me, the beginning of
his works,
the forerunner of his deeds of long ago;[q]
23 From of old I was formed,*
at the first, before the earth.[r]
24 * When there were no deeps I was
brought forth,
when there were no fountains or
springs of water;
25 Before the mountains were settled into
place,
before the hills, I was brought forth;
26 When the earth and the fields were not
yet made,
nor the first clods of the world.
27 When he established the heavens, there
was I,[s]
when he marked out the vault over the
face of the deep;
28 When he made firm the skies above,
when he fixed fast the springs of the
deep;
29 When he set for the sea its limit,
so that the waters should not transgress
his command;
When he fixed the foundations of earth,
30 then was I beside him as artisan;* [t]
I was his delight day by day,
playing before him all the while,
31 Playing over the whole of his earth,
having my delight with human beings.
32 * Now, children, listen to me;
happy are they who keep my ways.
33 Listen to instruction and grow wise,
do not reject it!
34 Happy the one who listens to me,
attending daily at my gates,
keeping watch at my doorposts;
35 For whoever finds me finds life,[u]
and wins favor from the LORD;
36 But those who pass me by do violence to
themselves;
all who hate me love death."

CHAPTER 9

See RG 254–62

*The Two Women Invite Passersby to Their Banquets**

Woman Wisdom Issues Her Invitation

1 Wisdom has built her house,*
she has set up her seven columns;
2 She has prepared her meat, mixed her
wine,
yes, she has spread her table.

8:22–31 Wisdom is of divine origin. She is represented as existing before all things (vv. 22–26), when God planned and created the universe, adorning it with beauty and variety, and establishing its wonderful order (vv. 27–30). The purpose of the two cosmogonies (vv. 22–26 and 27–31) is to ground Wisdom's claims. The first cosmogony emphasizes that she was born before all else (and so deserving of honor) and the second underscores that she was with the Lord during the creation of the universe. The pre-existence of Woman Wisdom with God is developed in Sir 24 and in New Testament hymns to Christ, especially in Jn 1 and Col 1:15–20.

8:23 Formed: since the other verbs of the origin of Wisdom in these verses describe birth, it is likely that the somewhat uncertain verb is to be understood of birth as in Ps 139:13.

8:24–26 Perhaps the formless mass from which God created the heavens and the earth; cf. Gn 1:1–2; 2:4–6.

8:30 Artisan: the translation of the Hebrew word *'āmôn* has been controverted since antiquity. There have been three main opinions: (1) artisan; (2) trustworthy (friend); (3) ward, nursling. The most likely explanation is that *'āmôn* is artisan, related to Akkadian *ummānu*, legendary sages and heroes who brought divine gifts and culture to the human race. **I was his delight**: the chiastic or ABBA structure of vv. 30–31 unifies the four lines and underscores the analogy between Woman Wisdom's intimate relation to the Lord and her intimate relation to human beings, i.e., "delight" + "playing" parallels "playing" + "delight." She is God's friend and intimate and invites human beings to a similar relationship to God through her.

8:32–36 The final appeal of Woman Wisdom to her disciples is similar to the appeal of the father in 7:24–27.

9:1–6, 13–18 Wisdom and folly are represented as women, each inviting people to her banquet. Wisdom's banquet symbolizes joy and closeness to God. Unstable and senseless Folly furnishes stolen bread and water of deceit and vice that bring death to her guests. The opposition between wisdom and folly was stated at the beginning of chaps. 1–9 (folly in

o: Prv 3:16. *p:* Prv 3:14. *q:* Wis 9:9; Sir 1:1; 24:9. *r:* Sir 1:4. *s:* Prv 3:19; Sir 24:4–5. *t:* Wis 9:9. *u:* Prv 3:13–18; 4:22.

3 She has sent out her maidservants; she
calls*
from the heights out over the city:[v]
4 "Let whoever is naive turn in here;
to any who lack sense I say,
5 Come, eat of my food,
and drink of the wine I have mixed!
6 Forsake foolishness that you may live;*
advance in the way of understanding."

Miscellaneous Aphorisms

7 Whoever corrects the arrogant earns
insults;
and whoever reproves the wicked
incurs opprobrium.
8 Do not reprove the arrogant, lest they
hate you;
reprove the wise, and they will love
you.[w]
9 Instruct the wise, and they become still
wiser;
teach the just, and they advance in
learning.
10 The beginning of wisdom is fear of the
LORD,
and knowledge of the Holy One is
understanding.[x]
11 For by me your days will be multiplied
and the years of your life increased.[y]
12 If you are wise, wisdom is to your
advantage;
if you are arrogant, you alone shall
bear it.

Woman Folly Issues Her Invitation

13 * Woman Folly is raucous,[z]
utterly foolish; she knows nothing.
14 She sits at the door of her house
upon a seat on the city heights,
15 Calling to passersby
as they go on their way straight
ahead:
16 "Let those who are naive turn in here,
to those who lack sense I say,
17 Stolen water is sweet,
and bread taken secretly is pleasing!"*
18 Little do they know that the shades are
there,
that her guests are in the depths of
Sheol!*

1:8–19 and wisdom in 1:20–33) and is maintained throughout, down to this last chapter.

In comparable literature, gods might celebrate their sovereign by building a palace and inviting the other gods to come to a banquet and celebrate with them. Presumably, Woman Wisdom is celebrating her grandeur (just described in chap. 8); her grand house is a symbol of her status as the Lord's friend. In order to enter the sacred building and take part in the banquet ("eat of my food"), guests must leave aside their old ways ("forsake foolishness").

Verses 7–12 are unrelated to the two invitations to the banquet. They appear to be based on chap. 1, especially on 1:1–7, 22. The Greek version has added a number of verses after v. 12 and v. 18. In the confusion, 9:11 seems to have been displaced from its original position after 9:6. It has been restored to its original place in the text.

9:1 House: house has a symbolic meaning. Woman Wisdom encourages marital fidelity (2:16–19; 5; 6:20–35; 7), which builds up a household (cf. chap. 5). Some scholars propose that an actual seven-pillared house is referred to, but so far none have been unearthed by archaeologists. Seven may simply connote completeness—a great house.

Some scholars see a connection between the woman's house here and the woman's house in the final poem (31:10–31). In chap. 9, she invites the young man to enter her house and feast, i.e., to marry her. Chapter 31 shows what happens to the man who marries her; he has a house and enjoys "life" understood as consisting of a suitable wife, children, wealth, and honor.

9:3 She calls: i.e., invites; this is done indirectly through her maidservants, but the text could also mean that Wisdom herself publicly proclaims her invitation.

9:6 That you may live: life in Proverbs is this-worldly, consisting in fearing God or doing one's duty toward God, enjoying health and long life, possessing wealth, good reputation, and a family. Such a life cannot be attained without God's help. Hence Wisdom speaks not of life simply but of life with her; the guest is to live in Wisdom's house.

9:13–18 Woman Folly is the mirror image of Woman Wisdom. Both make identical invitations but only one of the offers is trustworthy. Their hearers must discern which is the true offer. She is depicted with traits of the adulterous woman in 2:16–19; chap. 5; 6:20–35; chap. 7. Woman Folly is restless (cf. 7:11), her path leads to the underworld (2:18; 5:5; 7:27), and she is ignorant (5:6). In this final scene, she appears in single combat with her great nemesis, Woman Wisdom. Though the invitations of the two women appear at first hearing to be the same, they differ profoundly. Wisdom demands that her guests reject their ignorance, whereas Woman Folly trades on their ignorance.

9:17 "Stolen water" seems to refer to adultery, for "water" in 5:15–17 refers to the wife's sexuality; "stolen" refers to stealing the sexuality belonging to another's household. "Secret" evokes the furtive meeting of the wife and the youth in chap. 7.

9:18 The banquet chamber of Folly is a tomb from which no one who enters it is released; cf. 7:27. **Shades**: the Rephaim, the inhabitants of the underworld.

v: Prv 8:1–2. *w:* Sir 10:27. *x:* Prv 1:7; Jb 28:28; Ps 111:10; Sir 1:16. *y:* Prv 3:2; 16:4, 10; 10:27. *z:* Prv 7:7–27.

III. First Solomonic Collection of Sayings*

CHAPTER 10

See RG 254–62

1 The Proverbs of Solomon:
A wise son gives his father joy,
but a foolish son is a grief to his mother.* a
2 Ill-gotten treasures profit nothing,
but justice saves from death.* b
3 The LORD does not let the just go hungry,
but the craving of the wicked he thwarts.*
4 The slack hand impoverishes,
but the busy hand brings riches.c
5 A son who gathers in summer is a credit;
a son who slumbers during harvest, a disgrace.
6 Blessings are for the head of the just;
but the mouth of the wicked conceals violence.*
7 The memory of the just serves as blessing,
but the name of the wicked will rot.*
8 A wise heart accepts commands,
but a babbling fool will be overthrown.*
9 Whoever walks honestly walks securely,
but one whose ways are crooked will fare badly.
10 One who winks at a fault causes trouble,
but one who frankly reproves promotes peace.
11 The mouth of the just is a fountain of life,
but the mouth of the wicked conceals violence.
12 Hatred stirs up disputes,
d but love covers all offenses.*
13 On the lips of the intelligent is found wisdom,
but a rod for the back of one without sense.*
14 The wise store up knowledge,
but the mouth of a fool is imminent ruin.
15 The wealth of the rich is their strong city;
the ruin of the poor is their poverty.*
16 The labor of the just leads to life,
the gains of the wicked, to futility.* e

10:1–22:16 The Proverbs of Solomon are a collection of three hundred and seventy-five proverbs on a wide variety of subjects. No overall arrangement is discernible, but there are many clusters of sayings related by vocabulary and theme. One thread running through the whole is the relationship of the "son," the disciple, to the parents, and its effect upon the house(hold). In chaps. 10–14 almost all the proverbs are antithetical; "the righteous" and "the wicked" (ethical), "the wise" and "the foolish" (sapiential), and "the devout, the pious" and "the irreverent" (religious). Chapters 15–22 have fewer sharp antitheses. The sayings are generally witty, often indirect, and are rich in irony and paradox.

10:1 The opening saying ties the whole collection to the first section, for "son," "father," and "mother" evoke the opening line of the first instruction, "Hear, my son, your father's instruction, and reject not your mother's teaching." The son is the subject of parental exhortation throughout chaps. 1–9. This is the first of many sayings on domestic happiness or unhappiness, between parents and children (e.g., 15:20; 17:21) and between husband and wife (e.g., 12:4; 14:1). Founding or maintaining a household is an important metaphor in the book.

Adult children represented the family (headed by the oldest married male) to the outside world. Foolishness, i.e., malicious ignorance, brought dishonor to the parents and the family.

10:2 Death: untimely, premature, or sorrowful. The word "death" can have other overtones (see Wis 1:15).

10:3 The last of the three introductory sayings in the collection, which emphasize, respectively, the sapiential (v. 1), ethical (v. 2), and religious (v. 3) dimensions of wisdom. In this saying, God will not allow the appetite of the righteous to go unfulfilled. The appetite of hunger is singled out; it stands for all the appetites.

10:6 This saying, like several others in the chapter, plays on the different senses of the verb "to cover." As in English, "to cover" can mean to fill (as in Is 60:2) and to conceal (as in Jb 16:18). Colon B can be read either "violence *fills* the mouth (= head) of the wicked" or "the mouth of the wicked *conceals* violence." The ambiguity is intentional; the proverb is meant to be read both ways.

10:7 The name of the righteous continues to be used after their death in blessings such as "May you be as blessed as Abraham," but the wicked, being enemies of God, do not live on in anyone's memory. Their names rot with their bodies.

10:8 The wise take in instruction from their teachers but those who expel or pour out folly through their words will themselves be expelled.

10:12 Love covers all offenses: a favorite maxim in the New Testament; cf. 1 Cor 13:7; Jas 5:20; 1 Pt 4:8. Cf. also Prv 17:9.

10:13 An unusual juxtaposition of "lips" and "back." Those who have no wisdom on their lips (words) are fated to feel a punishing rod on their back.

10:15 An observation rather than a moral evaluation of wealth and poverty; but cf. 18:10–11.

10:16 Wages are a metaphor for reward and punishment. The Hebrew word does not mean "sin" here but falling short,

a: Prv 1:1; 15:20; 17:25; 19:13; 25:1; 29:15. *b:* Prv 11:4, 6. *c:* Prv 6:11; 12:24; 13:4; 20:13; 28:19. *d:* 1 Cor 13:4–7; 1 Pt 4:8. *e:* Prv 11:18–19.

[17] Whoever follows instruction is in the path to life,
but whoever disregards reproof goes astray.[f]
[18] Whoever conceals hatred has lying lips,
and whoever spreads slander is a fool.
[19] Where words are many, sin is not wanting;
but those who restrain their lips do well.[g]
[20] Choice silver is the tongue of the just;
the heart of the wicked is of little worth.
[21] The lips of the just nourish many,
but fools die for want of sense.*
[22] It is the LORD's blessing that brings wealth,[h]
and no effort can substitute for it.*
[23] Crime is the entertainment of the fool;
but wisdom is for the person of understanding.
[24] What the wicked fear will befall them,
but the desire of the just will be granted.
[25] When the tempest passes, the wicked are no more;
but the just are established forever.
[26] As vinegar to the teeth, and smoke to the eyes,
are sluggards to those who send them.
[27] Fear of the LORD prolongs life,
but the years of the wicked are cut short.[i]
[28] The hope of the just brings joy,
but the expectation of the wicked perishes.*
[29] The LORD is a stronghold to those who walk honestly,
downfall for evildoers.
[30] The just will never be disturbed,
but the wicked will not abide in the land.
[31] The mouth of the just yields wisdom,
but the perverse tongue will be cut off.
[32] The lips of the just know favor,
but the mouth of the wicked, perversion.*

CHAPTER 11

See RG 254–62

[1] False scales are an abomination to the LORD,
but an honest weight, his delight.* [j]
[2] When pride comes, disgrace comes;
but with the humble is wisdom.*
[3] The honesty of the upright guides them;
the faithless are ruined by their duplicity.
[4] Wealth is useless on a day of wrath,* [k]
but justice saves from death.
[5] The justice of the honest makes their way straight,
but by their wickedness the wicked fall.* [l]
[6] The justice of the upright saves them,
but the faithless are caught in their own intrigue.
[7] When a person dies, hope is destroyed;[m]
expectation pinned on wealth is destroyed.*
[8] The just are rescued from a tight spot,

a meaning that is frequent in Proverbs. Cf. Rom 6:1: "But what profit did you get then from the things of which you are now ashamed? For the end of those things is death."

10:21 The wise by their words maintain others in life whereas the foolish cannot keep themselves from sin that leads to premature death.

10:22 Human industry is futile without divine approval; cf. Ps 127:1–2; Mt 6:25–34.

10:28 The thought is elliptical. Joy comes from fulfillment of one's plans, which the righteous can count on. The opposite of joy thus is not sadness but unfulfillment ("perishes").

10:32 The word used for "favor" is favor shown by an authority (God or the king), not favor shown by a peer. A righteous person's words create a climate of favor and acceptance, whereas crooked words will not gain acceptance. In Hebrew as in English, straight and crooked are metaphors for good and wicked.

11:1 The word pair "abomination" and "delight" (= acceptable) to God is common in Proverbs. Originally the language of ritual, the words came to be applied to whatever pleases or displeases God (cf. also 11:20). False weights were a constant problem even though weights were standardized. Cf. 20:23; Hos 12:8; Am 8:5.

11:2 Disgrace is the very opposite of what the proud so ardently want. Those who do not demand their due receive wisdom.

11:4 Cf. note on 10:2. A day of wrath is an unforeseen disaster (even death). Only one's relationship to God, which makes one righteous, is of any help on such a day.

11:5 In Hebrew as in English, "way" means the course of one's life; similarly, "straight" and "crooked" are metaphors for morally straightforward and for bad, deviant, perverted.

11:7 An ancient scribe added "wicked" to person in colon A, for the statement that hope ends at death seemed to deny life after death. The saying, however, is not concerned with life after death but with the fact that in the face of death all

f: Prv 15:10. *g:* Prv 17:27; Sir 20:17; Jas 1:19. *h:* Sir 11:22. *i:* Prv 3:2; 4:10; 9:11; 14:27. *j:* Prv 16:11; 20:10; Lv 19:35–36. *k:* Prv 10:2. *l:* Prv 28:18. *m:* Prv 10:28; Wis 3:18.

but the wicked fall into it instead.
9 By a word the impious ruin their
neighbors,[n]
but through their knowledge the just
are rescued.*
10 When the just prosper, the city rejoices;[o]
when the wicked perish, there is
jubilation.
11 Through the blessing of the upright the
city is exalted,
but through the mouth of the wicked it
is overthrown.
12 Whoever reviles a neighbor lacks sense,
but the intelligent keep silent.
13 One who slanders reveals secrets,[p]
but a trustworthy person keeps a
confidence.
14 For lack of guidance a people falls;
security lies in many counselors.[q]
15 Harm will come to anyone going surety
for another,[r]
but whoever hates giving pledges is
secure.*
16 A gracious woman gains esteem,
and ruthless men gain wealth.*
17 Kindly people benefit themselves,
but the merciless harm themselves.
18 The wicked make empty profits,
but those who sow justice have a sure
reward.[s]
19 Justice leads toward life,
but pursuit of evil, toward death.
20 The crooked in heart are an abomination
to the LORD,
but those who walk blamelessly are his
delight.*
21 Be assured, the wicked shall not go
unpunished,
but the offspring of the just shall
escape.
22 Like a golden ring in a swine's snout
is a beautiful woman without
judgment.*
23 The desire of the just ends only in good;
the expectation of the wicked is wrath.
24 One person is lavish yet grows still
richer;
another is too sparing, yet is the
poorer.*
25 Whoever confers benefits will be amply
enriched,
and whoever refreshes others will be
refreshed.
26 Whoever hoards grain, the people curse,
but blessings are on the head of one
who distributes it!
27 Those who seek the good seek favor,
but those who pursue evil will have
evil come upon them.*
28 Those who trust in their riches will fall,
but like green leaves the just will
flourish.[t]
29 Those who trouble their household
inherit the wind,
and fools become slaves to the wise of
heart.
30 The fruit of justice is a tree of life,
and one who takes lives is a sage.*

hopes based on one's own resources are vain. The aphorism is the climax of the preceding six verses; human resources cannot overcome mortality (cf. Ps 49:13).

11:9 What the wicked express harms others; what the righteous leave unsaid protects. Verses 9–14 are related in theme: the effect of good and bad people, especially their words, on their community.

11:15 Proverbs is opposed to providing surety for another's loan (see note on 6:1–5) and expresses this view throughout the book.

11:16 Wealth and esteem are good things in Proverbs, but the means for acquiring them are flawed. As precious gifts, they must be granted, not taken. The esteem of others that depends on beauty is as fleeting as beauty itself (cf. 31:30) and the wealth acquired by aggressive behavior lasts only as long as one has physical strength.

11:20 The terminology of ritual (acceptable and unacceptable sacrifice, "abomination" and "delight") is applied to human conduct as in v. 1. The whole of human life is under divine scrutiny, not just ritual.

11:22 Ear and nose rings were common jewelry for women. A humorous saying on the priority of wisdom over beauty in choosing a wife.

11:24 A paradox: spending leads to more wealth.

11:27 The saying is about seeking one thing and finding another. Striving for good leads to acceptance by God; seeking evil means only that trouble will come. The same Hebrew word means evil and trouble.

11:30 Most translations emend Hebrew "wise person" in colon B on the basis of the Greek and Syriac translations to "violence" (similar in spelling), because the verb "to take a life" is a Hebrew idiom for "to kill" (as also in English). The emendation is unnecessary, however, for the saying deliberately plays on the odd meaning: the one who takes lives is not the violent but the wise person, for the wise have a profound influence upon life. There is a similar wordplay in 29:10.

n: Prv 29:5. *o:* Prv 28:12; 29:2. *p:* Prv 20:19. *q:* Prv 15:22; 20:18; 24:6. *r:* Prv 6:1–2. *s:* Prv 10:16. *t:* Ps 52:9–10.

31 If the just are recompensed on the earth,
how much more the wicked and the sinner!* [u]

CHAPTER 12

See RG 254–62

1 Whoever loves discipline loves knowledge,
but whoever hates reproof is stupid.* [v]
2 A good person wins favor from the LORD,
but the schemer he condemns.*
3 No one is made secure by wickedness,
but the root of the just will never be disturbed.*
4 A woman of worth is the crown of her husband,[w]
but a disgraceful one is like rot in his bones.*
5 The plans of the just are right;
the designs of the wicked are deceit.*
6 The words of the wicked are a deadly ambush,
but the speech of the upright saves them.*
7 Overthrow the wicked and they are no more,
but the house of the just stands firm.
8 For their good sense people are praised,
but the perverse of heart are despised.*
9 Better to be slighted and have a servant
than put on airs and lack bread.[x]
10 The just take care of their livestock,
but the compassion of the wicked is cruel.*
11 Those who till their own land have food in plenty,
but those who engage in idle pursuits lack sense.* [y]
12 A wicked person desires the catch of evil people,
but the root of the righteous will bear fruit.*
13 By the sin of their lips the wicked are ensnared,
but the just escape from a tight spot.
14 From the fruit of their mouths people have their fill of good,[z]
and the works of their hands come back upon them.*
15 The way of fools is right in their own eyes,
but those who listen to advice are the wise.
16 Fools immediately show their anger,
but the shrewd conceal contempt.
17 Whoever speaks honestly testifies truly,
but the deceitful make lying witnesses.* [a]

11:31 The saying is not about life after death; "on the earth" means life in the present world. The meaning is that divine judgment is exercised on all human action, even the best. The thought should strike terror into the hearts of habitual wrongdoers.

12:1 Discipline in Proverbs is both doctrine and training. The path to wisdom includes obedience to teachers and parents, acceptance of the community's traditions.

12:2 The antithesis is between the good person who, by reason of that goodness, already has divine acceptance, and the wicked person who, despite great effort, gains only condemnation.

12:3 Human beings are described as "made secure" in Jb 21:8; Ps 101:7; 102:29. "Root" in the context means enduring to succeeding generations, as in Mal 3:19 and Jb 8:17.

12:4 In Proverbs a crown is the result and sign of wise conduct. A good wife is a public sign of the husband's shrewd judgment and divine blessing (crown), whereas a bad wife brings him inner pain (rot in the bones).

12:5 The opposite of "just" is not injustice but "deceit." The wicked will be deceived in their plans in the sense that their planning will not succeed.

12:6 Words are a favorite theme of Proverbs. The words of the wicked effect harm to others whereas the words of the righteous protect themselves.

12:8 The heart, the seat of intelligence, will eventually be revealed in the actions that people do, either for praise or for blame.

12:10 The righteous are sympathetically aware of the needs of their livestock and prosper from their herd's good health. The wicked will pay the price for their self-centeredness and cruelty.

12:11 The second line clarifies the first: idleness will give one plenty of nothing. "Lacking sense" is a common phrase for fools.

12:12 A difficult, possibly corrupt saying, but there is no good alternative to the Hebrew text. The wicked desire what the malevolent have captured or killed, but their actions will go for naught because they invite punishment. The righteous, on the other hand, will bear fruit.

12:14 The saying contrasts words and deeds. "Fruit" here is not what one normally eats, as in 1:31; 8:19; 31:16, 31, but the consequences of one's actions. In the second line the things that issue from one's hands (one's deeds) come back to one in recompense or punishment. Prv 13:2a and 18:20 are variants. Cf. Mt 7:17; Gal 6:8.

12:17 What is the rule of thumb for judging legal testimony? Look to the ordinary conduct and daily speech of a witness.

u: 1 Pt 4:18. *v:* Prv 15:5, 10; Sir 21:6. *w:* Prv 31:10; Sir 21:1, 16. *x:* Sir 10:26. *y:* Prv 28:19; Sir 20:27. *z:* Prv 13:2; 18:20. *a:* Prv 14:5.

18 The babble of some people is like sword
thrusts,
but the tongue of the wise is healing.
19 Truthful lips endure forever,
the lying tongue, for only a moment.*
20 Deceit is in the heart of those who plot
evil,
but those who counsel peace have joy.
21 No harm befalls the just,
but the wicked are overwhelmed with
misfortune.
22 Lying lips are an abomination to the
LORD,[b]
but those who are truthful, his delight.
23 The shrewd conceal knowledge,
but the hearts of fools proclaim folly.*
24 The diligent hand will govern,
but sloth makes for forced labor.[c]
25 Worry weighs down the heart,
but a kind word gives it joy.[d]
26 The just act as guides to their neighbors,
but the way of the wicked leads them
astray.
27 Sloth does not catch its prey,
but the wealth of the diligent is
splendid.
28 In the path of justice is life,
but the way of abomination leads to
death.

CHAPTER 13

See RG 254–62

1 A wise son loves correction,
but the scoffer heeds no rebuke.*
2 From the fruit of the mouth one enjoys
good things,[e]
but from the throat of the treacherous
comes violence.*
3 Those who guard their mouths preserve
themselves;*
those who open wide their lips bring
ruin.[f]
4 The appetite of the sluggard craves but
has nothing,
but the appetite of the diligent is
amply satisfied.
5 The just hate deceitful words,
but the wicked are odious and
disgraceful.
6 Justice guards one who walks honestly,
but sin leads the wicked astray.[g]
7 One acts rich but has nothing;
another acts poor but has great
wealth.*
8 People's riches serve as ransom for their
lives,
but the poor do not even hear a threat.*
9 The light of the just gives joy,
but the lamp* of the wicked goes out.[h]
10 The stupid sow discord by their
insolence,
but wisdom is with those who take
counsel.
11 Wealth won quickly dwindles away,
but gathered little by little, it grows.[i]
12 Hope deferred makes the heart sick,
but a wish fulfilled is a tree of life.*

12:19 The saying has a double meaning: lies are quickly found out whereas truthful statements endure; truth-tellers, being favored by God, live long lives, whereas liars invite punishment.

12:23 "Knowledge" here is "what one knows, has in one's heart," not knowledge in general. Fools reveal all they have stored in their heart and it naturally turns out to be folly. Revealing and concealing are constant themes in Proverbs.

13:1 Another in the series on the household, this one on the relation of parents and children. See under 10:1. The scoffer in Proverbs condemns discipline and thus can never become wise. Wise adult children advertise to the community what they received from their parents, for children become wise through a dialectical process involving the parents. A foolish adult child witnesses to foolish parents.

13:2 One's mouth normally eats food from outside, but in the moral life, things are reversed: one eats from the fruit of one's mouth, i.e., one experiences the consequences of one's own actions. Since the mouth of the treacherous is filled with violence, one must assume that they will some day endure violence.

13:3 Preserve themselves: in Hebrew, literally to preserve the throat area, the moist breathing center of one's body, thus "life," "soul," or "self." There is wordplay: if you guard your mouth (= words) you guard your "soul." Fools, on the other hand, do not guard but open their lips and disaster strikes. A near duplicate is 21:23.

13:7 Appearances can be deceiving; possessions do not always reveal the true state of a person.

13:8 Related to v. 7. Possessions enable the wealthy to pay ransom but the poor are "protected" by lack of possessions: they never hear the threat of the pursuer. Cf. the use of the word "threat" in Is 30:17.

13:9 Light . . . lamp: symbols of life and prosperity; cf. 4:18–19.

13:12 "Tree of life" occurs in Gn 2–3, Prv 3:18; 11:30; 13:12; 15:4, and Rev 2:7; 22:2, 14, 19. It provides food and healing.

b: Prv 6:17. *c:* Prv 10:4; 13:4. *d:* Prv 15:13; 17:22. *e:* Prv 12:14; 18:20. *f:* Prv 18:7; 21:23. *g:* Prv 11:3, 5–6. *h:* Prv 24:20. *i:* Prv 28:20, 22.

13 Whoever despises the word must pay
for it,*
but whoever reveres the command will
be rewarded.
14 The teaching of the wise is a fountain of
life,
turning one from the snares of death.
15 Good sense brings favor,
but the way of the faithless is their
ruin.*
16 The shrewd always act prudently
but the foolish parade folly.*
17 A wicked messenger brings on disaster,
but a trustworthy envoy is a healing
remedy.
18 Poverty and shame befall those who let
go of discipline,
but those who hold on to reproof
receive honor.*
19 Desire fulfilled delights the soul,
but turning from evil is an
abomination to fools.
20 Walk with the wise and you become
wise,
but the companion of fools fares
badly.[j]
21 Misfortune pursues sinners,
but the just shall be recompensed with
good.
22 The good leave an inheritance to their
children's children,
but the wealth of the sinner is stored
up for the just.
23 The tillage of the poor yields abundant
food,
but possessions are swept away for
lack of justice.*
24 Whoever spares the rod hates the child,
but whoever loves will apply
discipline.[k]
25 When the just eat, their hunger is
appeased;
but the belly of the wicked suffers want.

CHAPTER 14

See RG 254–62

1 Wisdom builds her house,
but Folly tears hers down with
her own hands.*
2 Those who walk uprightly fear the LORD,
but those who are devious in their
ways spurn him.
3 In the mouth of the fool is a rod for pride,
but the lips of the wise preserve them.
4 Where there are no oxen, the crib is clean;
but abundant crops come through the
strength of the bull.*
5 A trustworthy witness does not lie,
but one who spouts lies makes a lying
witness.*[l]
6 The scoffer seeks wisdom in vain,
but knowledge is easy for the
intelligent.
7 Go from the face of the fool;
you get no knowledge from such lips.
8 The wisdom of the shrewd enlightens
their way,
but the folly of fools is deceit.*
9 The wicked scorn a guilt offering,
but the upright find acceptance.
10 The heart knows its own bitterness,

13:13 Must pay for it: lit., "is pledge to it," i.e., just as one who has pledged or provided surety for another's loan is obligated to that pledge, so one is not free of a command until one performs it.

13:15 As the behavior of the wise wins them favor that increases their prosperity, like Abigail with David in 1 Sm 25, so the way (= conduct) of the faithless ruins their lives.

13:16 Like 12:23 and 15:2, 3, the saying is about revealing and concealing. The wise reveal their wisdom in their actions whereas fools "parade," spread out their folly for all to see. The verb is used of vendors spreading their wares and of birds spreading their wings.

13:18 The saying plays on letting go and holding on. Wisdom consists in not rejecting discipline and being open to the comments of others, even if they are reproving comments.

13:23 An observation on the poor. The lands of the poor are as fertile as anyone's, for nature does not discriminate against them. Their problem is lack of justice, which puts their harvest at risk from unscrupulous human beings.

14:1 The relationship between Wisdom, personified as a woman, and building a house is a constant theme. As elsewhere, the book here warns against the wrong woman and praises the right woman.

14:4 If one has no animals, one does not have the burden of keeping the crib full, but without them one will have no crops to fill the barn. Colon B reverses the sense of colon A and also reverses the consonants of *bar* ("clean") to *rab* ("abundant").

14:5 On discerning the truthfulness of witnesses; see 12:17.

14:8 Wisdom enables the shrewd to know their path is right but folly leads fools on the wrong path ("deceit"), which calls down retribution.

j: Sir 6:34; 8:8, 17. *k:* Prv 19:18; 22:15; 23:13–14; 29:15; Sir 30:1, 8–13. *l:* Prv 12:17.

and its joy no stranger shares.*
11 The house of the wicked will be destroyed,
but the tent of the upright will flourish.* [m]
12 Sometimes a way seems right,
but the end of it leads to death![n]
13 Even in laughter the heart may be sad,
and the end of joy may be sorrow.
14 From their own ways turncoats are sated,
from their own actions, the loyal.
15 The naive believe everything,
but the shrewd watch their steps.*
16 The wise person is cautious and turns from evil;
the fool is reckless and gets embroiled.
17 The quick-tempered make fools of themselves,
and schemers are hated.
18 The simple have folly as an adornment,
but the shrewd wear knowledge as a crown.*
19 The malicious bow down before the good,
and the wicked, at the gates of the just.
20 Even by their neighbors the poor are despised,
but a rich person's friends are many.[o]
21 Whoever despises the hungry comes up short,
but happy the one who is kind to the poor!*
22 Do not those who plan evil go astray?
But those who plan good win steadfast loyalty.
23 In all labor there is profit,
but mere talk tends only to loss.
24 The crown of the wise is wealth;
the diadem of fools is folly.
25 The truthful witness saves lives,
but whoever utters lies is a betrayer.
26 The fear of the LORD is a strong defense,
a refuge even for one's children.
27 The fear of the LORD is a fountain of life,
turning one from the snares of death.
28 A multitude of subjects is the glory of the king;
but if his people are few, a prince is ruined.
29 Long-suffering results in great wisdom;
a short temper raises folly high.* [p]
30 A tranquil mind gives life to the body,
but jealousy rots the bones.
31 Those who oppress the poor revile their Maker,
but those who are kind to the needy honor him.[q]
32 The wicked are overthrown by their wickedness,
but the just find a refuge in their integrity.
33 Wisdom can remain silent in the discerning heart,
but among fools she must make herself known.* [r]
34 Justice exalts a nation,
but sin is a people's disgrace.*
35 The king favors the skillful servant,
but the shameless one incurs his wrath.

CHAPTER 15

See RG 254–62

1 * A mild answer turns back wrath,[s]
but a harsh word stirs up anger.*

14:10 The heart in Proverbs is where a person's sense impressions are stored and reflected upon. It is thus one's most personal and individual part. One's sorrows and joys (= the full range of emotions) cannot be shared fully with another. Verse 13 expresses the same individuality of the human person.

14:11 The traditional fixed pair "house" and "tent" is used to express the paradox that a house can be less secure than a tent if there is no justice.

14:15 The naive gullibly rely on others' words whereas the shrewd watch their own steps.

14:18 The inner quality of a person, simple or wise, will eventually be revealed.

14:21 The paradox is that anyone who spurns the hungry will lack something, but anyone who shows mercy (presumably by giving to the poor) will gain prosperity.

14:29 A series of puns on short and long; lit., "long of nostrils (idiom for "patient"), large in wisdom, / short in breath (idiom for "impatient"), makes folly tall."

14:33 Wisdom can remain silent in a wise person as a welcome friend. But it must speak out among fools, for the dissonance is so strong.

14:34 The rare noun "disgrace" occurs elsewhere only in Lv 20:17. In measuring the greatness of a nation, one is tempted to consider territory, wealth, history, but the most important criterion is its relationship to God ("justice").

15:1–7 These verses form a section beginning and ending with the topic of words.

15:1 Paradoxically, where words are concerned soft is powerful and hard is ineffective.

m: Prv 3:33; 12:7; 15:25. *n:* Prv 16:25. *o:* Prv 19:4, 7; Sir 6:8, 12. *p:* Prv 16:32; 19:11; Jas 1:19. *q:* Prv 17:5. *r:* Prv 1:22; 8:1. *s:* Prv 25:15; Sir 6:5.

2 The tongue of the wise pours out
knowledge,
but the mouth of fools spews folly.
3 The eyes of the LORD are in every place,
keeping watch on the evil and the
good.
4 A soothing tongue is a tree of life,
but a perverse one breaks the spirit.
5 The fool spurns a father's instruction,
but whoever heeds reproof is
prudent.* [t]
6 In the house of the just there are ample
resources,
but the harvest of the wicked is in
peril.
7 The lips of the wise spread knowledge,
but the heart of fools is not steadfast.*
8 The sacrifice of the wicked is an
abomination to the LORD,[u]
but the prayer of the upright is his
delight.
9 The way of the wicked is an abomination
to the LORD,
but he loves one who pursues justice.[v]
10 Discipline seems bad to those going
astray;
one who hates reproof will die.*
11 Sheol and Abaddon* lie open before the
LORD;
how much more the hearts of mortals!
12 Scoffers do not love reproof;
to the wise they will not go.
13 A glad heart lights up the face,
but an anguished heart breaks the
spirit.[w]
14 The discerning heart seeks knowledge,
but the mouth of fools feeds on folly.*
15 All the days of the poor are evil,
but a good heart is a continual feast.*
16 * Better a little with fear of the LORD
than a great fortune with anxiety.
17 Better a dish of herbs where love is
than a fatted ox and hatred with it.
18 The ill-tempered stir up strife,[x]
but the patient settle disputes.
19 The way of the sluggard is like a thorn
hedge,
but the path of the diligent is a
highway.
20 A wise son gives his father joy,
but a fool despises his mother.[y]
21 Folly is joy* to the senseless,
but the person of understanding goes
the straight way.
22 Plans fail when there is no counsel,
but they succeed when advisers are
many.* [z]
23 One has joy from an apt response;
a word in season, how good it is!* [a]
24 The path of life leads upward for the
prudent,
turning them from Sheol below.*
25 The LORD pulls down the house of the
proud,
but preserves intact the widow's
landmark.
26 The schemes of the wicked are an
abomination to the LORD,[b]
but gracious words are pure.*
27 The greedy tear down their own house,

15:5 One becomes wise by keeping and foolish by rejecting. One must accept the tradition of the community.

15:7 "Lips" and "heart" are a fixed pair, in Proverbs signifying, respectively, expression and source. The wise disseminate what they have in their heart, but the wicked are unsound even in the source of their words, their hearts.

15:10 Discipline, always a good thing in Proverbs, seems bad to those deliberately wandering from justice.

15:11 Sheol and Abaddon: terms for the abode of the dead, signifying the profound obscurity which is open nevertheless to the sight and power of God; cf. 27:20.

15:14 The contrasts include heart (organ of reflection) and mouth (organ of expression), and the wise and fools. One type feeds its mind with wisdom and the other feeds its face with folly.

15:15 Good heart does not refer to good intentions but to an instructed mind. Wisdom makes poverty not only bearable but even joyful like the joy of feast days.

15:16–17 The sages favor wealth over poverty—but not at any price; cf. Ps 37:16.

15:21 The word "joy" occurs in the first line of vv. 20, 21, and 23. The state of folly is joy to a fool but the wise person is totally absorbed in keeping on the right or straight road.

15:22 Failure to consult makes it likely a plan will not succeed. The point is nicely made by contrasting the singular number in the first line ("no counsel") with the plural number in the second line ("many advisors").

15:23 Conversation is the art of saying the right thing at the right time. It gives pleasure to speaker and hearer alike.

15:24 Death is personified as Sheol, the underworld. "Up" and "down" in Hebrew as in English are metaphors for success and failure (see Dt 28:43). One who stays on the path of life need not fear the punishment that stalks sinners.

15:26 "Pure" here means acceptable. The language of rit-

t: Prv 12:1; 13:18. *u:* Prv 21:27; Eccl 4:17; Is 1:11–15. *v:* Prv 11:20; 21:21. *w:* Prv 12:25; 17:22; Sir 30:22. *x:* Prv 6:21; 29:22; Sir 28:11. *y:* Prv 10:1; 29:3. *z:* Prv 11:14. *a:* Prv 25:11; Sir 20:6. *b:* Prv 6:18.

but those who hate bribes will live.*
28 The heart of the just ponders a response,
but the mouth of the wicked spews evil.
29 The LORD is far from the wicked,
but hears the prayer of the just.
30 A cheerful glance brings joy to the heart;
good news invigorates the bones.
31 The ear that listens to salutary reproof[c]
is at home among the wise.*
32 Those who disregard discipline hate themselves,
but those who heed reproof acquire understanding.
33 The fear of the LORD is training for wisdom,
and humility goes before honors.[d]

See RG 254–62

CHAPTER 16

1 Plans are made in human hearts,
but from the LORD comes the tongue's response.*
2 All one's ways are pure* in one's own eyes,
but the measurer of motives is the LORD.[e]
3 Entrust your works to the LORD,
and your plans will succeed.
4 The LORD has made everything for a purpose,
even the wicked for the evil day.*
5 Every proud heart* is an abomination to the LORD;[f]
be assured that none will go unpunished.
6 By steadfast loyalty guilt is expiated,
and by the fear of the LORD evil is avoided.*
7 When the LORD is pleased with someone's ways,
he makes even enemies be at peace with them.
8 Better a little with justice,
than a large income with injustice.
9 The human heart plans the way,
but the LORD directs the steps.* [g]
10 An oracle is upon the king's lips,
no judgment of his mouth is false.*
11 Balance and scales belong to the LORD;
every weight in the sack is his concern.[h]
12 Wrongdoing is an abomination to kings,
for by justice the throne endures.[i]
13 The king takes delight in honest lips,
and whoever speaks what is right he loves.[j]
14 The king's wrath is a messenger of death,[k]
but a wise person can pacify it.
15 A king's smile means life,
and his favor is like a rain cloud in spring.*
16 How much better to get wisdom than gold!
To get understanding is preferable to silver.* [l]

ual (acceptable or pure) is applied to ordinary human actions. "Gracious words" are words that bring peace to the neighbor.

15:27 The same lesson as the opening scene of Proverbs (1:8–19): one cannot build a house by unjust gain. Injustice will come back upon a house so built.

15:31 To become wise, one must hear and integrate perspectives contrary to one's own, which means accepting "reproof." Wisdom does not isolate one but places one in the company of the wise.

16:1 Words, like actions, often produce results different from those which were planned, and this comes under the agency of God.

16:2 "Pure" in a moral sense for human action is found only in Job and Proverbs. As in v. 1, the contrast is between human intent and divine assessment.

16:4 Even the wicked do not lie outside God's plan.

16:5 Proud heart: lit., "high of heart." To forget one is a fallible human being is so basic an error that one cannot escape exposure and punishment.

16:6 As v. 5 used the language of worship to express what is acceptable or not to God, so this saying uses similar language to declare that lovingly loyal conduct undoes the effects of sin.

16:9 As in vv. 1–3, the antithesis is between human plans and divine disposal. The saying uses the familiar metaphor of path for the course of life.

16:10 Six sayings on the king and his divine authority begin here, following the series of sayings about the Lord's governance in 15:33–16:9, in which "LORD" was mentioned nine times.

16:15 The last of six sayings about the king. In the previous verse, royal wrath means death; in this verse royal favor means life. It is significant that royal favor is compared to something not under human control—the clouds preceding the spring rains.

16:16 The point of comparison is the superiority of the pursuit of wisdom and gold, not the relative merits of wealth and wisdom.

c: Prv 25:12. *d:* Prv 1:7; 19:12; Sir 1:24. *e:* Prv 21:2. *f:* Prv 6:16–17; 8:13. *g:* Prv 19:21; 20:24; Jer 10:23. *h:* Prv 11:1. *i:* Prv 25:5. *j:* Prv 14:35; 22:11. *k:* Prv 19:12; 20:2. *l:* Prv 8:10–11.

17 The path of the upright leads away from
misfortune;
those who attend to their way guard
their lives.*
18 Pride goes before disaster,
and a haughty spirit before a fall.
19 It is better to be humble with the poor
than to share plunder with the proud.[m]
20 Whoever ponders a matter will be
successful;
happy the one who trusts in the LORD!
21 The wise of heart is esteemed for
discernment,
and pleasing speech gains a reputation
for learning.
22 Good sense is a fountain of life to those
who have it,
but folly is the training of fools.
23 The heart of the wise makes for eloquent
speech,
and increases the learning on their lips.
24 Pleasing words are a honeycomb,
sweet to the taste and invigorating to
the bones.
25 Sometimes a way seems right,
but the end of it leads to death![n]
26 The appetite of workers works for them,
for their mouths urge them on.* [o]
27 Scoundrels are a furnace of evil,
and their lips are like a scorching fire.
28 Perverse speech sows discord,
and talebearing separates bosom
friends.[p]
29 The violent deceive their neighbors,
and lead them into a way that is not
good.
30 Whoever winks an eye plans perversity;
whoever purses the lips does evil.*
31 Gray hair is a crown of glory;[q]
it is gained by a life that is just.
32 The patient are better than warriors,
and those who rule their temper, better
than the conqueror of a city.[r]
33 Into the bag the lot is cast,
but from the LORD comes every
decision.*

CHAPTER 17

See RG 254–62

1 Better a dry crust with quiet
than a house full of feasting with
strife.*
2 A wise servant will rule over an
unworthy son,
and will share the inheritance of the
children.*
3 The crucible for silver, and the furnace
for gold,
but the tester of hearts is the LORD.
4 The evildoer gives heed to wicked lips,
the liar, to a mischievous tongue.
5 Whoever mocks the poor reviles their
Maker;
whoever rejoices in their misfortune
will not go unpunished.[s]
6 Children's children are the crown of the
elderly,
and the glory of children is their
parentage.
7 Fine words ill fit a fool;
how much more lying lips, a noble!
8 A bribe seems a charm to its user;
at every turn it brings success.*
9 Whoever overlooks an offense fosters
friendship,
but whoever gossips about it separates
friends.*

16:17 In the metaphor of the two ways, the way of the righteous is protected and the way of the wicked is unprotected. Since the path of the righteous leads therefore away from trouble, one's task is to stay on it, to "attend to" it.

16:26 The adage puzzled ancient and modern commentators. The meaning seems to state the paradox that a person does not toil to feed the gullet but that the gullet itself "toils" in the sense that it forces the person to work. As often in Proverbs, the sense organ stands for the faculty by metonymy. Cf. Eccl 6:7.

16:30 A restless or twitching eye or lip betrays the condition of the heart (cf. 6:13).

16:33 Dice were given meanings of "yes" or "no" and then cast for their answer. What came out was the decision. Here the saying interprets the sequence of actions: a human being puts the dice in the bag but what emerges from the bag is the Lord's decision.

17:1 A "better than" saying, stating the circumstances when a dry crust is better than a banquet. Peace and fellowship give joy to a meal, not the richness of the food. For a similar thought, see 15:16 and 16:8.

17:2 Ability is esteemed more highly than ties of blood.

17:8 An observation on the effect of the bribe upon the bribe-giver: it gives an intoxicating feeling of power ("seems"). In v. 23 the evil effects of a bribe are noted.

17:9 A paradox. One finds (love, friend) by concealing (an offense), one loses (a friend) by revealing (a secret). In 10:12

m: Prv 11:2. *n:* Prv 14:12. *o:* Prv 10:4. *p:* Prv 6:14, 19; 17:9; 26:22; Sir 28:15. *q:* Prv 20:29. *r:* Prv 14:29. *s:* Prv 14:31.

10 A single reprimand does more for a
discerning person
than a hundred lashes for a fool.*
11 The wicked pursue only rebellion,
and a merciless messenger is sent
against them.*
12 Face a bear robbed of her cubs,
but never fools in their folly!*
13 If you return evil for good,
evil will not depart from your house.* [t]
14 The start of strife is like the opening of a
dam;
check a quarrel before it bursts forth!
15 Whoever acquits the wicked,[u] whoever
condemns the just—
both are an abomination to the LORD.
16 Of what use is money in the hands of
fools
when they have no heart to acquire
wisdom?*
17 A friend is a friend at all times,
and a brother is born for the time of
adversity.[v]
18 Those without sense give their hands in
pledge,
becoming surety for their neighbors.[w]
19 Those who love an offense love a fight;[x]
those who build their gate high* court
disaster.
20 The perverse in heart come to no good,
and the double-tongued fall into
trouble.*
21 Whoever conceives a fool has grief;
the father of a numskull has no joy.
22 A joyful heart is the health of the body,
but a depressed spirit dries up the
bones.[y]
23 A guilty person takes out a bribe from the
pocket,
thus perverting the course of justice.*
24 On the countenance of a discerning
person is wisdom,[z]
but the eyes of a fool are on the ends
of the earth.*
25 A foolish son is vexation to his father,
and bitter sorrow to her who bore him.[a]
26 It is wrong to fine an innocent person,
but beyond reason to scourge nobles.
27 Those who spare their words are truly
knowledgeable,
and those who are discreet are
intelligent.[b]
28 Even fools, keeping silent, are
considered wise;
if they keep their lips closed,
intelligent.*

CHAPTER 18

See RG 254–62

1 One who is alienated seeks a
pretext,
with all persistence picks a quarrel.
2 Fools take no delight in understanding,
but only in displaying what they
think.*
3 With wickedness comes contempt,
and with disgrace, scorn.
4 The words of one's mouth are deep
waters,

love also covers over a multitude of offenses.

17:10 A wonderful comment on the openness and sensitivity of the wise and the foolish. One type learns from a single word and for the other one hundred blows are not enough.

17:11 The irony is that such people will meet up with what they so energetically pursue—in the form of an unrelenting emissary sent to them.

17:12 Humorous hyperbole. An outraged dangerous beast poses less danger than a fool.

17:13 The paradox is that to pay out evil for good means that the evil will never leave one's own house.

17:16 The exhortation to acquire or purchase wisdom is common in Proverbs. Fools misunderstand the metaphor, assuming they can buy it with money. Their very misunderstanding shows they have no "heart" = mind, understanding. Money in the hand is no good without such a "heart" to store it in.

17:19 Build their gate high: a symbol of arrogance.

17:20 The saying employs the familiar metaphors of walking = conducting oneself ("fall into trouble"), and of straight and crooked = right and wrong ("perverse," "double-tongued").

17:23 A sharp look at the sly withdrawing of a bribe from the pocket and a blunt judgment on its significance.

17:24 Wisdom is visible on the countenance (i.e., mouth, lips, tongue) of the wise person; its ultimate source is the heart. Fools have no such source of wisdom within them, a point that is nicely made by referring to the eye of the fool, roving over the landscape.

17:28 Related to v. 27. Words provide a glimpse into the heart. In the unlikely event that fools, who usually pour out words (15:2), were to say nothing, people would not be able to see their folly and would presume them intelligent. Alas, the saying is contrary to fact.

18:2 One grows in wisdom by listening to others, but fools take delight in expounding the contents of their minds.

t: Mt 5:39; Rom 12:17; 1 Thes 5:15; 1 Pt 3:9. *u:* Prv 24:24; Is 5:23. *v:* Prv 18:24. *w:* Prv 6:1–2; 11:15. *x:* Prv 15:18. *y:* Prv 12:25; 15:13. *z:* Eccl 8:1. *a:* Prv 10:1; 29:15. *b:* Prv 10:19; Sir 1:21; Jas 1:19.

the spring of wisdom, a running
brook.* [c]
5 It is not good to favor the guilty,
nor to reject the claim of the just.[d]
6 The lips of fools walk into a fight,
and their mouths are asking for a
beating.*
7 The mouths of fools are their ruin;
their lips are a deadly snare.[e]
8 The words of a talebearer are like dainty
morsels:
they sink into one's inmost being.[f]
9 Those slack in their work
are kin to the destroyer.
10 * The name of the LORD is a strong
tower;
the just run to it and are safe.
11 The wealth of the rich is their strong city;[g]
they fancy it a high wall.
12 Before disaster the heart is haughty,[h]
but before honor is humility.
13 Whoever answers before listening,[i]
theirs is folly and shame.*
14 One's spirit supports one when ill,
but a broken spirit who can bear?*
15 The heart of the intelligent acquires
knowledge,
and the ear of the wise seeks
knowledge.*
16 Gifts clear the way for people,
winning access to the great.[j]
17 Those who plead the case first seem to be
in the right;
then the opponent comes and cross-
examines them.*
18 The lot puts an end to disputes,
and decides a controversy between the
mighty.*
19 A brother offended is more unyielding
than a stronghold;
such strife is more daunting than castle
gates.*
20 With the fruit of one's mouth one's belly
is filled,
with the produce of one's lips one is
sated.* [k]
21 Death and life are in the power of the
tongue;[l]
those who choose one shall eat its
fruit.*
22 To find a wife is to find happiness,
a favor granted by the LORD.[m]
23 The poor implore,
but the rich answer harshly.
24 There are friends who bring ruin,
but there are true friends more loyal
than a brother.[n]

CHAPTER 19

See RG 254–62

1 Better to be poor and walk in
integrity
than rich and crooked in one's ways.[o]

18:4 Words express a person's thoughts ("deep waters"), which in turn become accessible to others. Cf. 20:5a.

18:6 The bold personification of lips and mouth is similar to Ps 73:9, "They set their mouths against the heavens, their tongues roam the earth." Careless words can lead one into serious trouble.

18:10–11 Contrast this judgment with the observation in 10:15.

18:13 To speak without first listening is characteristic of a fool; cf. 10:14; Sir 11:8.

18:14 The paradox is that something as slight as a column of air offers protection against the encroachment of death. If it is stilled, nothing, no matter how powerful, can substitute for it.

18:15 "Knowledge" here refers to what one knows, not knowledge in itself. The mind acquires and stores it, the ear strains toward it.

18:17 A persuasive speech in court can easily make one forget there is another side to the question. When the other party speaks, people realize they made a premature judgment. The experience at court is a lesson for daily life: there are two sides to every question.

18:18 See note on 16:33.

18:19 The Greek version, followed by several ancient versions, has the opposite meaning: "A brother helped by a brother is like a strong and lofty city; it is strong like a well-founded palace." The Greek is secondary as is shown by the need to supply the phrase "by a brother"; further, the parallelism is inadequate. The Hebrew is to be preferred.

18:20 Fruit from the earth is our ordinary sustenance, but "the fruit of one's lips," i.e., our words, also affect our well-being. If our words and our deeds are right, then we are blessed, our "belly is filled."

18:21 This enigmatic saying has provoked many interpretations, e.g., judicious speech brings a reward; those who love the tongue in the sense of rattling on must face the consequences of their loquacity. This translation interprets the verb "love" in colon B in its occasional sense of "choose" (e.g., 12:1; 20:13; Dt 4:37) and interprets its pronominal object as referring to both death and life in colon A. Death and life are set before every person (cf. Dt 30:15–20) and we have the

c: Prv 20:5; Jn 7:38. *d:* Prv 24:23; 28:21. *e:* Prv 10:14; 12:13; 13:3; Eccl 10:12. *f:* Prv 26:22. *g:* Prv 10:15. *h:* Prv 11:2; 16:18; Sir 10:15. *i:* Sir 11:8. *j:* Prv 21:14. *k:* Prv 12:14; 13:2. *l:* Sir 37:18. *m:* Prv 12:4; 19:14; Sir 7:26. *n:* Prv 17:17. *o:* Prv 28:6.

[2] Desire without knowledge is not good;
and whoever acts hastily, blunders.*
[3] Their own folly leads people astray;
in their hearts they rage against the LORD.*
[4] Wealth adds many friends,
but the poor are left friendless.[p]
[5] The false witness will not go unpunished,
and whoever utters lies will not escape.* [q]
[6] Many curry favor with a noble;
everybody is a friend of a gift giver.
[7] All the kin of the poor despise them;
how much more do their friends shun them!*
[8] Those who gain sense truly love themselves;
those who preserve understanding will find success.*
[9] The false witness will not go unpunished,
and whoever utters lies will perish.
[10] Luxury is not befitting a fool;
much less should a slave rule over princes.
[11] It is good sense to be slow to anger,
and an honor to overlook an offense.*
[12] The king's wrath is like the roar of a lion,
but his favor, like dew on the grass.* [r]
[13] The foolish son is ruin to his father,[s]
and a quarrelsome wife is water constantly dripping.*
[14] Home and possessions are an inheritance from parents,
but a prudent wife is from the LORD.[t]
[15] Laziness brings on deep sleep,
and the sluggard goes hungry.[u]
[16] Those who keep commands keep their lives,
but those who despise these ways will die.[v]
[17] Whoever cares for the poor lends to the LORD,[w]
who will pay back the sum in full.
[18] Discipline your son, for there is hope;
but do not be intent on his death.* [x]
[19] A wrathful person bears the penalty;
after one rescue, you will have it to do again.
[20] Listen to counsel and receive instruction,
that you may eventually become wise.
[21] Many are the plans of the human heart,
but it is the decision of the LORD that endures.[y]
[22] What is desired of a person is fidelity;
rather be poor than a liar.*
[23] The fear of the LORD leads to life;
one eats and sleeps free from any harm.
[24] The sluggard buries a hand in the dish;
not even lifting it to the mouth.[z]
[25] Beat a scoffer and the naive learn a lesson;
rebuke the intelligent and they gain knowledge.[a]
[26] Whoever mistreats a father or drives away a mother,
is a shameless and disgraceful child.* [b]

power to choose either one by the quality of our deeds. Words (= "the tongue") are regarded here as the defining actions of human beings.

19:2 When not guided by wisdom, appetite—or desire—is not good. "Running feet" (so the Hebrew) miss the mark, i.e., do not reach their destination.

19:3 One's own folly destroys one's life. It is an indication of that folly that one blames God rather than oneself.

19:5 The punishment fits the crime: those who abuse the legal system will be punished by the same system. They will not be acquitted.

19:7 Closely related to vv. 4 and 6. An observation, not without sympathy, on the social isolation of poor people.

19:8 Wisdom benefits the one who practices it.

19:11 The paradox is that one obtains one thing by giving up another.

19:12 An observation on the exercise of royal power. Both images suggest royal attitudes are beyond human control. Colon A is a variant of 20:2a and colon B of 16:15b.

19:13 One of many sayings about domestic happiness. The perspective is male; the two greatest pains to a father is a malicious son and an unsuitable wife. The immediately following saying is on the noble wife, perhaps to make a positive statement about women.

19:18 The pain of disciplining the young cannot be compared with the danger no discipline may bring. The chief reason for disciplining the young is their capacity to change; excluded thereby are revenge and punishment.

19:22 The proverb has been read in two ways: (1) "Desire (greed) is a shame to a person," which assumes the rare Hebrew word for "shame" is being used; (2) "What is desired in a person is fidelity." The second interpretation is preferable. The context may be the court: better to forego money (a bribe) than perjure oneself.

19:26 Children who disgrace the family equivalently plunder their father's wealth and expel their mother from the home.

p: Prv 14:20; Sir 13:20–23. *q:* Dt 19:16–20; Dn 13:61. *r:* Prv 20:2. *s:* Prv 10:1; 17:25. *t:* Prv 18:22. *u:* Prv 6:9–10. *v:* Prv 13:13; 16:17. *w:* Prv 14:21; 22:9; 28:27. *x:* Prv 13:24; 23:13–14. *y:* Prv 16:9. *z:* Prv 26:15. *a:* Prv 17:10; 21:11. *b:* Sir 3:16.

27 My son, stop attending to correction;
start straying from words of knowledge.*
28 An unprincipled witness scoffs at justice,
and the mouth of the wicked pours out iniquity.
29 Rods are prepared for scoffers,
and blows for the backs of fools.[c]

CHAPTER 20

See RG 254–62

1 Wine is arrogant, strong drink is riotous;
none who are intoxicated by them are wise.* [d]
2 The terror of a king is like the roar of a lion;[e]
those who incur his anger forfeit their lives.
3 A person gains honor by avoiding strife,
while every fool starts a quarrel.*
4 In seedtime sluggards do not plow;
when they look for the harvest, it is not there.
5 The intention of the human heart is deep water,
but the intelligent draw it forth.* [f]
6 Many say, "My loyal friend,"
but who can find someone worthy of trust?
7 The just walk in integrity;
happy are their children after them!
8 A king seated on the throne of judgment
dispels all evil with his glance.*
9 Who can say, "I have made my heart clean,[g]
I am cleansed of my sin"?*
10 Varying weights, varying measures,
are both an abomination to the LORD.[h]
11 In their actions even children can playact
though their deeds be blameless and right.*
12 The ear that hears, the eye that sees—
the LORD has made them both.*
13 Do not love sleep lest you be reduced to poverty;
keep your eyes open, have your fill of food.
14 "Bad, bad!" says the buyer,
then goes away only to boast.*
15 One can put on gold and abundant jewels,
but wise lips are the most precious ornament.*
16 Take the garment of the one who became surety for a stranger;[i]
if for foreigners, exact the pledge!*
17 Bread earned by deceit is sweet,
but afterward the mouth is filled with gravel.
18 Plans made with advice succeed;
with wise direction wage your war.
19 A slanderer reveals secrets;
so have nothing to do with a babbler!
20 Those who curse father or mother—
their lamp will go out* in the dead of night.[j]

19:27 The meaning was disputed even in antiquity. The interpretation that most respects the syntax is to take it as ironic advice as in 22:6: to stop (listening) is to go (wandering).

20:1 The cause stands for its effect (wine, drunken behavior). In Proverbs wine is a sign of prosperity and a symbol of feasting (3:10; 4:17; 9:2, 5) but also a potential threat to wisdom as in 20:1; 21:17; 23:29–35.

20:3 The honor that one might seek to gain from fighting comes of itself to the person who refrains from fighting.

20:5 The heart is where human plans are made and stored; they remain "deep water" until words reveal them to others. The wise know how to draw up those waters, i.e., express them. Cf. 18:4.

20:8 The royal throne is established in justice and the king is the agent of that justice.

20:9 A claim to sinlessness can be merely self-deception; see 16:2; cf. also 15:11.

20:11 The verb in colon A can mean either "to make oneself known" or "to play another person" (as in Gn 42:7 and 1 Kgs 14:5, 6). The second meaning makes a better parallel to colon B. The meaning is that if a child can playact, an adult can do so even more. Actions do not always reveal character.

20:12 Human judgments are not ultimate; the Lord expects proper use of these faculties.

20:14 Bartering invites playacting and masking one's true intent. The truth of words depends on their context.

20:15 Wisdom is said to be preferable to gold in 3:14; 8:10, 19; 16:16. Colon B suggests that the gold and jewelry here are ornaments for the face (cf. Gn 24:53; Ex 3:22; Is 61:10). Wise lips are the most beautiful adornment, for they display the wisdom of the heart.

20:16 The text is not clear. See 27:13. Caution in becoming surety is always advised (cf. 6:1–3), and it is especially advisable with strangers.

20:20 Their lamp will go out: misfortune, even death, awaits them; cf. 13:9; Ex 21:17.

c: Prv 26:3. *d:* Prv 23:29–35. *e:* Prv 19:12. *f:* Prv 18:4. *g:* 1 Kgs 8:46; 2 Chr 6:36; Eccl 7:20; 1 Jn 1:8. *h:* Prv 11:1; 20:23. *i:* Prv 27:13. *j:* Prv 30:11, 17; Ex 21:17; Lv 20:9; Mt 15:4.

21 Possessions greedily guarded at the outset
will not be blessed in the end.*
22 Do not say, "I will repay evil!"
Wait for the LORD, who will help you.* [k]
23 Varying weights are an abomination to the LORD,
and false scales are not good.[l]
24 Our steps are from the LORD;[m]
how, then, can mortals understand their way?*
25 It is a trap to pledge rashly a sacred gift,
and after a vow, then to reflect.*
26 A wise king winnows the wicked,
and threshes them under the cartwheel.*
27 A lamp from the LORD is human life-breath;
it searches through the inmost being.*
28 His steadfast loyalty safeguards the king,
and he upholds his throne by justice.[n]
29 The glory of the young is their strength,
and the dignity of the old is gray hair.[o]
30 Evil is cleansed away by bloody lashes,
and a scourging to the inmost being.

CHAPTER 21

See RG 254-62

1 A king's heart is channeled water in the hand of the LORD;
God directs it where he pleases.*
2 All your ways may be straight in your own eyes,
but it is the LORD who weighs hearts.[p]
3 To do what is right and just[q]
is more acceptable to the LORD than sacrifice.*
4 Haughty eyes and a proud heart—
the lamp of the wicked will fail.*
5 The plans of the diligent end in profit,
but those of the hasty end in loss.*
6 Trying to get rich by lying
is chasing a bubble over deadly snares.
7 The violence of the wicked will sweep them away,
because they refuse to do what is right.
8 One's path may be winding and unfamiliar,
but one's conduct is blameless and right.*
9 It is better to dwell in a corner of the housetop
than in a mansion with a quarrelsome woman.* [r]
10 The soul of the wicked desires evil;
their neighbor finds no pity in their eyes.
11 When scoffers are punished the naive become wise;
when the wise succeed, they gain knowledge.[s]
12 The Righteous One appraises the house of the wicked,

20:21 By definition, an inheritance is not gained by one's own efforts but is received as a gift. If, when one first receives the inheritance, one drives everyone away, one treats it as if one acquired it by one's own efforts. In an agricultural society, an inheritance would often be a field that would require God's blessing to be fertile.

20:22 Appointing oneself an agent of divine retribution is dangerous. Better to wait for God to effect justice. Cf. 24:17–18.

20:24 An indication of the Lord's inscrutable providence; cf. Jer 10:23; see Prv 21:2; cf. also 14:12.

20:25 This verse cautions against making vows without proper reflection; cf. Dt 23:22–25; Eccl 5:4–5.

20:26 The king is responsible for effecting justice. Judgment is portrayed in agricultural imagery—exposing grain to a current of air so that the chaff is blown away, and passing a wheel over the cereal to break the husk. Winnowing as image for judgment is found throughout the Bible.

20:27 A parallel is drawn between the life-breath that is God's gift (Jb 32:8; 33:2) coursing through the human body (Is 2:22) and the lamp of God, which can be a symbol of divine scrutiny. In Zep 1:12, God declares, "And in that day I will search through Jerusalem with lamps."

21:1 "Channeled water" in Is 32:2 and Prv 5:16 is water that fertilizes arid land. It takes great skill to direct water, whether it be water to fertilize fields or cosmic floods harnessed at creation, for water is powerful and seems to have a mind of its own. It also requires great skill to direct the heart of a king, for it is inscrutable and beyond ordinary human control.

21:3 External rites or sacrifices do not please God unless accompanied by internal worship and right moral conduct; cf. 15:8; 21:27; Is 1:11–15; Am 5:22; Mal 1:12.

21:4 Heart and eyes depict, respectively, the inner and the outer person. "Haughty eyes" peering out from a "proud heart" show a thoroughly arrogant person. How can such a person flourish! Their lamp, which signifies life, will go out.

21:5 The antitheses are diligent and impetuous. The metaphor characterizing each type is taken from the world of commerce. Planning is important; bustle leads to waste.

21:8 One cannot always read others' hearts from their behavior. Unconventional conduct need not indicate evil motives.

21:9 In Proverbs, two great obstacles to a happy household are foolish children and quarrelsome spouses. The nagging wife is also mentioned in 19:13 and 27:15; 25:24 is a duplicate.

k: Prv 24:29; Sir 28:1; Mt 5:39; Rom 12:17, 19; 1 Thes 5:15; 1 Pt 3:9. *l:* Prv 11:1; 20:10. *m:* Prv 16:9. *n:* Prv 16:12. *o:* Prv 16:31. *p:* Prv 16:2. *q:* 1 Sm 15:22; Hos 6:6. *r:* Prv 21:19; 25:24; 27:15; Sir 25:23. *s:* Prv 19:25.

bringing down the wicked to ruin.*
13 Those who shut their ears to the cry of the poor
will themselves call out and not be answered.
14 A secret gift allays anger,
and a present concealed, violent wrath.*
15 When justice is done it is a joy for the just,
downfall for evildoers.* [t]
16 Whoever strays from the way of good sense
will abide in the assembly of the shades.*
17 The lover of pleasure will suffer want;
the lover of wine and perfume will never be rich.
18 The wicked serve as ransom for the just,
and the faithless for the upright.* [u]
19 It is better to dwell in a wilderness
than with a quarrelsome wife and trouble.
20 Precious treasure and oil are in the house of the wise,
but the fool consumes them.
21 Whoever pursues justice and kindness
will find life and honor.*
22 The wise person storms the city of the mighty,
and overthrows the stronghold in which they trust.
23 Those who guard mouth and tongue
guard themselves* from trouble.[v]
24 Proud, boastful—scoffer is the name:
those who act with overbearing pride.
25 The desire of sluggards will slay them,
for their hands refuse to work.*
26 Some are consumed with avarice all the day,
but the just give unsparingly.
27 The sacrifice of the wicked is an abomination,
the more so when they offer it with bad intent.[w]
28 The false witness will perish,[x]
but one who listens will give lasting testimony.
29 The face of the wicked hardens,
but the upright maintains a straight course.*
30 No wisdom, no understanding,
no counsel prevail against the LORD.
31 The horse is equipped for the day of battle,
but victory is the LORD's.

CHAPTER 22

See RG 254–62

1 A good name is more desirable
than great riches,
and high esteem, than gold and silver.* [y]
2 Rich and poor have a common bond:
the LORD is the maker of them all.[z]

21:12 It is difficult to ascertain the subject of the saying. Some hold it is the Lord, the "Righteous One," who is normally the executor of justice in Proverbs. Others believe it is the just person who is the agent of divine justice. "Righteous One" is a title for God in Is 24:16. The best argument for making God the subject of the verb is that elsewhere in Proverbs righteous human beings never do anything to the wicked; only God does.

21:14 Proverbs offers several remedies for anger—a soft word (15:1), patience, and a bribe. The last remedy implies a certain disdain for the disordered passion of anger, for it can be so easily assuaged by a discreetly offered "gift."

21:15 The second line is a duplicate of 10:29b.

21:16 Assembly of the shades: those who dwell in Sheol.

21:18 In this bold paradox, the ransom that protects the righteous is the wicked person who attracts, like a lightning rod, the divine wrath that might have been directed at the righteous.

21:21 The paradox is that one comes upon something other than what one pursued. The way to (long and healthy) life and honor is the vigorous pursuit of virtue.

21:23 Themselves: see note on 13:3. To guard your "self" (lit., "throat," the moist and breathing center of the body, by metonymy, "life"), you must guard your tongue. Speech in Proverbs is the quintessential human activity and often has a meaning broader than speech alone; it can stand for all human activity. Acting rightly is the best way to protect yourself from evil.

21:25 Desire, or appetite, is the impulse toward food and drink (see Ps 42:3) which spurs animals and human beings into action. But sluggards cannot lift hand to mouth; they bury their hand in the dish (19:24), and so their appetite is thwarted.

21:29 The wicked cannot deter the righteous from walking the straight path, i.e., from practicing virtue.

22:1 "Good name" (Heb. *shem*) and "high esteem" (Heb. *chen*) are declared to be of more value than great riches. Human beings belong to a community and without the acceptance of that community, which is built on esteem and trust, human life is grievously damaged. Riches are less essential to the human spirit.

---

t: Prv 10:29. *u:* Prv 11:8. *v:* Prv 13:3. *w:* Prv 15:8; Sir 34:21–23. *x:* Prv 19:5, 9. *y:* Eccl 7:1. *z:* Prv 29:13.

[3] The astute see an evil and hide,
while the naive continue on and pay the penalty.* [a]
[4] The result of humility and fear of the LORD
is riches, honor and life.*
[5] Thorns and snares are on the path of the crooked;
those who would safeguard their lives will avoid them.
[6] Train the young in the way they should go;
even when old, they will not swerve from it.*
[7] The rich rule over the poor,
and the borrower is the slave of the lender.*
[8] Those who sow iniquity reap calamity,[b]
and the rod used in anger will fail.*
[9] The generous will be blessed,
for they share their food with the poor.
[10] Expel the arrogant and discord goes too;
strife and insult cease.
[11] The LORD loves the pure of heart;[c]
the person of winning speech has a king for a friend.
[12] The eyes of the LORD watch over the knowledgeable,
but he defeats the projects of the faithless.
[13] The sluggard says, "A lion is outside;[d]
I might be slain in the street."*
[14] The mouth of the foreign woman is a deep pit;[e]
whoever incurs the LORD's anger will fall into it.
[15] Folly is bound to the heart of a youth,
but the rod of discipline will drive it out.*
[16] Oppressing the poor for enrichment,
giving to the rich: both are sheer loss.*

IV. Sayings of the Wise*

[17] The Words of the Wise:*
Incline your ear, and hear my words,[f]

22:3 The wise see dangers before they are engulfed by them whereas fools, through dullness or boldness, march right on.

22:4 Humiliation can be an occasion for knowing one's place in God's world. Such knowledge is part of fear (or revering) of the Lord. Revering the Lord brings the blessings of wealth, honor, and long life. The saying is perhaps meant to counter the view that humiliation is an unmixed evil; something good can come of it.

22:6 One of the few exhortations in the collection (cf. 14:7; 16:3; 19:18, 20). "Way" in the first colon has been taken in two different senses: (1) the morally right way, "according to the way one ought to go"; (2) personal aptitude, i.e., the manner of life for which one is destined, as "the way of Egypt" (Is 10:24). Neither interpretation, however, accounts for the pronoun in the Hebrew phrase, lit., "his own way." The most natural solution is to take the whole as ironic advice (like 19:27): yes, go ahead and let the young do exactly what they want; they will become self-willed adults.

22:7 An observation on money and power. One who borrows becomes poor in the sense of indebted, a slave to the lender.

22:8 Agricultural metaphors express the failure of malicious actions. In the first line, bad actions are seeds yielding trouble. In the second line, "the rod" is a flail used to beat grains as in Is 28:27.

22:13 To avoid the effort required for action, the sluggard exaggerates the difficulties that must be overcome.

22:15 Folly is attached to children as the husk is attached to the grain. "Rod" here, as in v. 8, seems to be the flail. Discipline is the process of winnowing away the folly.

22:16 A difficult saying. One possibility is to take it as a seemingly neutral observation on the plight of the poor: taking money from the poor is relatively easy for the powerful but it is dangerous as the poor have the Lord as their defender (24:22–23), who will punish their oppressors. Giving to the rich, perhaps to win their favor by presents and bribes, is equally a waste of money, for the rich will always do what they please in any case.

22:17–24:22 This collection consists of an introduction (22:17–21) urging openness and stating the purpose of the Words and diverse admonitions, aphorisms, and counsels. It is written with faith in the Lord, shrewdness, and a satirical eye. The first part seems aimed at young people intent on a career (22:22–23:11); the second is taken up with the concerns of youth (23:12–35); the third part is interested in the ultimate fate of the good and the wicked (24:1–22). The whole can be described as a guidebook of professional ethics. The aim is to inculcate trust in the Lord and to help readers avoid trouble and advance their careers by living according to wisdom. Its outlook is very practical: avoid bad companions because in time you will take on some of their qualities; do not post bond for others because you yourself will be encumbered; do not promote yourself too aggressively because such promotion is self-defeating; do not abuse sex or alcohol because they will harm you; do not emulate your peers if they are wicked (23:14; 24:1, 19) because such people have no future. Rather, trust the vocation of a sage (22:29–23:9).

The Egyptian *Instructions of Amenemope* (written ca. 1100 B.C.) was discovered in 1923. Scholars immediately recognized it as a source of Prv 22:17–23:11. The Egyptian work has thirty chapters (cf. Prv 22:20); its preface resembled Prv 22:17–21; its first two admonitions matched the first two in Proverbs (Prv 22:22–25). There are many other resemblances as well, some of which are pointed out in the notes. The instruction of a father to his son (or an administrator to his successor) was a well-known genre in Egypt; seventeen works

a: Prv 27:12. *b:* Jb 4:8; Sir 7:3; Hos 8:7. *c:* Mt 5:8. *d:* Prv 26:13. *e:* Prv 23:27. *f:* Prv 5:1.

and let your mind attend to my
teaching;
18 For it will be well if you hold them
within you,
if they all are ready on your lips.
19 That your trust may be in the LORD,
I make them known to you today—
yes, to you.
20 Have I not written for you thirty sayings,
containing counsels and knowledge,
21 To teach you truly
how to give a dependable report to one
who sends you?
22 Do not rob the poor because they are
poor,
nor crush the needy at the gate;*
23 For the LORD will defend their cause,[g]
and will plunder those who plunder
them.
24 Do not be friendly with hotheads,
nor associate with the wrathful,
25 Lest you learn their ways,
and become ensnared.
26 Do not be one of those who give their
hand in pledge,
those who become surety for debts;[h]
27 For if you are unable to pay,
your bed will be taken from under you.*
28 Do not remove the ancient landmark*
that your ancestors set up.[i]
29 Do you see those skilled at their work?
They will stand in the presence of kings,
but not in the presence of the obscure.

CHAPTER 23

See RG 254–62

1 * When you sit down to dine with
a ruler,
mark well the one who is before you;
2 Stick the knife in your gullet*
if you have a ravenous appetite.
3 Do not desire his delicacies;
it is food that deceives.
4 Do not wear yourself out to gain wealth,
cease to be worried about it;
5 When your glance flits to it, it is gone!
For assuredly it grows wings,
like the eagle that flies toward heaven.*
6 * Do not take food with unwilling hosts,
and do not desire their delicacies;
7 For like something stuck in the throat is
that food.
"Eat and drink," they say to you,

are extant, spanning the period from 2500 B.C. to the first century A.D. The instructions aimed to help a young person live a happy and prosperous life and avoid mistakes that cause difficulties. They make concrete and pragmatic suggestions rather than hold up abstract ideals. Pragmatic though they were, the instructions were religious; they assumed that the gods implanted an order in the world (Egyptian *maat*), which is found both in nature and in the human world. *Amenemope* represents a stage in the development of the Egyptian genre, displaying a new inwardness and quest for serenity while still assuming that the practice of virtue brings worldly success. Proverbs borrows from the Egyptian work with great freedom: it does not, for example, import as such the Egyptian concept of order; it engages the reader with its characteristic wit, irony, and paradox (e.g., 22:26–27; 23:1–3).

22:17–23:35 The maxims warn against: robbing the poor and defenseless (22:22–23), anger (22:24–25), giving surety for debts (22:26–27), advancing oneself by socializing with rulers (23:1–2), anxiety for riches (23:4–5), forcing oneself on a grudging host (23:6–8), intemperance in food and drink (23:19–21, 29–35), and adultery (23:26–28). They exhort to: careful workmanship (22:29), respect for the rights of orphans (23:10–11), correction of the young (23:13–14), filial piety (23:15–16, 22–25), and fear of the Lord (23:17–18).

22:22 At the gate: of the city, where justice was administered and public affairs discussed; cf. Ru 4:1. Cf. also Ps 69:13; 127:5; Prv 24:7; 31:23, 31. The Lord will personally avenge those who have no one to defend them.

22:27 Providing surety for a debtor puts one in danger of having the very basics of one's life suddenly seized.

22:28 Landmark: marks the boundary of property. To remove it is the equivalent of stealing land. A similar warning is contained in 23:10.

23:1–9 Four admonitions for someone aspiring to be a sage: be careful about advancing your career by socializing with the great (vv. 1–3); avoid greed (vv. 4–5); do not force yourself on an unwilling host (vv. 6–8); do not waste your wisdom on those who cannot profit from it (v. 9).

23:2 Stick the knife in your gullet: a metaphor for self-restraint. The usual translation, "Put a knife to your throat," is misleading, for in English it is a death threat. The exhortation is humorously exaggerated: stick the table-knife in your own gullet rather than take too much food. It assumes that the young courtier is unused to opulent banquets and will be tempted to overindulgence.

23:5 The frustration of covetous intent and elusiveness of wealth are portrayed by the sudden flight of an eagle. *Amenemope*, chap. 7, has a similar statement: "Do not set your heart on wealth. There is no ignoring Fate and Destiny; / Do not let your heart go straying." Proverbs imagines covetous intent as a flight of the eyes, whereas *Amenemope* imagines it as a straying of the heart.

23:6–8 Some humorous advice on not trading on the courtesy of unwilling hosts who, for convention's sake, use the language of welcome. *Amenemope*, chap. 11, gives similar advice: "Do not intrude on a man in his house, / Enter when you have been called; / He may say 'Welcome' with his

g: Prv 23:11. *h:* Prv 6:1–2; 11:15; 17:18. *i:* Prv 23:10; Dt 19:14; 27:17.

but their hearts are not with you;
8 The little you have eaten you will vomit up,
and you will have wasted your
agreeable words.
9 Do not speak in the hearing of fools;
they will despise the wisdom of your
words.[j]
10 Do not remove the ancient landmark,[k]
nor invade the fields of the fatherless;*
11 For their redeemer is strong;
he will defend their cause against you.[l]
12 Apply your heart to instruction,
and your ear to words of knowledge.
13 * Do not withhold discipline from youths;
if you beat them with the rod, they will
not die.[m]
14 Beat them with the rod,[n]
and you will save them from Sheol.
15 My son, if your heart is wise,
my heart also will rejoice;
16 And my inmost being will exult,
when your lips speak what is right.
17 Do not let your heart envy sinners,[o]
but only those who always fear the
LORD;*
18 For you will surely have a future,
and your hope will not be cut off.[p]
19 Hear, my son, and be wise,
and guide your heart in the right way.
20 Do not join with wine bibbers,
nor with those who glut themselves on
meat.
21 For drunkards and gluttons come to
poverty,
and lazing about clothes one in rags.
22 * Listen to your father who begot you,
do not despise your mother when she
is old.
23 Buy truth and do not sell:
wisdom, instruction, understanding!
24 The father of a just person will exult
greatly;
whoever begets a wise son will rejoice
in him.[q]
25 Let your father and mother rejoice;
let her who bore you exult.
26 * My son, give me your heart,
and let your eyes keep to my ways,
27 For the harlot is a deep pit,
and the foreign woman a narrow well;
28 Yes, she lies in wait like a robber,[r]
and increases the number of the
faithless.
29 * Who scream? Who shout?
Who have strife? Who have anxiety?
Who have wounds for nothing?
Who have bleary eyes?
30 Whoever linger long over wine,
whoever go around quaffing wine.[s]
31 Do not look on the wine when it is red,
when it sparkles in the cup.
It goes down smoothly,
32 but in the end it bites like a serpent,
and stings like an adder.
33 Your eyes behold strange sights,
and your heart utters incoherent
things;
34 You are like one sleeping on the high seas,

mouth, / Yet deride you in his thoughts." "Unwilling," lit., "evil of eye," is usually translated "stingy," but the context suggests unwilling. In v. 8, the unwanted guest vomits up the food, thus destroying the desired good impression. Proverbs regards the uninvited banqueters as thieves who will suffer the consequences of their theft. *Amenemope*, chap. 11, is relevant: "Do not covet a poor man's goods, . . . A poor man's goods are a block in the throat, / It makes the gullet vomit."

23:10 In Israel ownership of property and other legal rights were vested mainly in the father as head of the family; thus the widow and fatherless child were vulnerable, left prey to those who would exploit them.

23:13–14 The young will not die from instructional blows but from their absence, for (premature) death results from uncorrected folly. The sardonic humor means the exhortation is not to be taken literally, as an argument for corporal punishment. The next verses (vv. 15–16) are exceedingly tender toward the young.

23:17 Those whom one admires or associates with exercise enormous influence. Do not join the wicked, who are a doomed group. The warning is repeated in 24:1–2, 19–20.

23:22–23 Father and mother are associated with truth and wisdom. One should no more rid oneself of truth and wisdom than rid oneself of one's parents, who are their source.

23:26–28 The exhortation is a condensed version of chap. 7 with its emotional appeal to "my son" to avoid the forbidden woman (7:1–5), her traps (7:21–23), and her intent to add the youth to her list of victims (7:24–27). As in 23:15, 19, 22, a trustful and affectionate relationship between student and teacher is the basis of teaching. The danger of the woman is expressed in imagery that has sexual overtones (cf. 22:14).

23:29–35 A vivid description of the evil effects, physical and psychological, of drunkenness. The emphasis is on the unwise behavior, the folly, caused by alcohol. Cf. 20:1.

j: Prv 9:7. *k:* Prv 22:28. *l:* Prv 22:23. *m:* Prv 13:24; 19:18; Sir 30:1. *n:* Prv 29:15, 17. *o:* Prv 3:31; 24:1, 19. *p:* Prv 24:14. *q:* Prv 10:1. *r:* Prv 7:10–27. *s:* Prv 20:1; Sir 19:2; Hos 4:11.

sprawled at the top of the mast.
35 "They struck me, but it did not pain me;
they beat me, but I did not feel it.
When can I get up,
when can I go out and get more?"*

CHAPTER 24

See RG 254–62

1* Do not envy the wicked,
nor desire to be with them;[t]
2 For their hearts plot violence,
and their lips speak of foul play.
3 By wisdom a house is built,
by understanding it is established;
4 And by knowledge its rooms are filled
with every precious and pleasing possession.
5 The wise are more powerful than the strong,
and the learned, than the mighty,[u]
6 For by strategy war is waged,
and victory depends on many counselors.[v]
7 * Wise words are beyond fools' reach,[w]
in the assembly they do not open their mouth;
8 As they calculate how to do evil,
people brand them troublemakers.
9 The scheme of a fool gains no acceptance,
the scoffer is an abomination to the community.
10 * Did you fail in a day of adversity,
did your strength fall short?
11 Did you fail to rescue those who were being dragged off to death,*
those tottering, those near death,
12 because you said, "We didn't know about it"?
Surely, the Searcher of hearts knows
and will repay all according to their deeds.[x]
13 * If you eat honey, my son, because it is good,
if pure honey is sweet to your taste,
14 Such, you must know, is wisdom to your soul.
If you find it, you will have a future,
and your hope will not be cut off.[y]
15 * Do not lie in wait at the abode of the just,
do not ravage their dwelling places;
16 Though the just fall seven times, they rise again,
but the wicked stumble from only one mishap.
17 * Do not rejoice when your enemies fall,
and when they stumble, do not let your heart exult,
18 Lest the LORD see it, be displeased with you,
and withdraw his wrath from your enemies.
19 Do not be provoked at evildoers,
do not envy the wicked;
20 For the evil have no future,
the lamp of the wicked will be put out.[z]
21 My son, fear the LORD and the king;
have nothing to do with those who hate them;
22 For disaster will issue suddenly,
and calamity from them both, who knows when?

23:35 Drunkards become insensible to bodily and moral harm. Their one desire is to indulge again.

24:1–22 A new section (24:1–14)—on the fates of the wicked and foolish—begins with a warning not to take the foolish as role models. The same admonition is repeated in 23:17–18 and 24:19–20. In 24:1, the verb means "to be jealous, zealous; to emulate." The motive stated in the other passages—the wicked have no future—is indirectly stated here.

24:7–9 The verses are unclear; most scholars take them as two or even three single sayings, but, taken singly, the verses are banal. They are best taken as a single statement. Just as vv. 3–6 described the advantages of wisdom, so vv. 7–9 describe the disadvantages of its opposite, folly: it alienates one from the community (v. 7), for fools become notorious (v. 8), dooming their plans and ostracizing themselves.

24:10–12 Excuses for not coming to the aid of one's neighbor in serious trouble do not suffice before God, who sees through self-serving excuses.

24:11 Rescue . . . death: perhaps refers to the legal rescue of those unjustly condemned to death.

24:13–14 God's word is sometimes said to be sweeter than honey, e.g., Ps 119:101–103. Cf. also Ps 19:11; Prv 16:24; Ez 3:3; Sir 24:19–22.

24:15–16 The just will overcome every misfortune that oppresses them. *Seven times* is an indefinite number.

24:17–18 The admonition is linked to the previous by the words "fall" and "stumble." Premature public celebration of the downfall of enemies equivalently preempts the retribution that belongs to God.

t: Prv 3:31; 23:17; Ps 37:1. *u:* Prv 21:22. *v:* Prv 20:18. *w:* Sir 6:21. *x:* Ps 62:13; Sir 16:12; Mt 16:27; Rom 2:6. *y:* Prv 23:18. *z:* Prv 13:9.

V. Further Sayings of the Wise*

23 These also are Words of the Wise:
To show partiality in judgment is not good.[a]
24 Whoever says to the guilty party, "You are innocent,"
will be cursed by nations, scorned by peoples;
25 But those who render just verdicts will fare well,
and on them will come the blessing of prosperity.
26 An honest reply—
a kiss on the lips.*
27 Complete your outdoor tasks,
and arrange your work in the field;
afterward you can build your house.*
28 Do not testify falsely against your neighbor[b]
and so deceive with your lips.
29 Do not say, "As they did to me, so will I do to them;[c]
I will repay them according to their deeds."*
30 * I passed by the field of a sluggard,
by the vineyard of one with no sense;
31 It was all overgrown with thistles;
its surface was covered with nettles,
and its stone wall broken down.
32 As I gazed at it, I reflected;
I saw and learned a lesson:
33 A little sleep, a little slumber,[d]
a little folding of the arms to rest—
34 Then poverty will come upon you like a robber,
and want like a brigand.

VI. Second Solomonic Collection, Collected under King Hezekiah*

CHAPTER 25

See RG 254–62

1 These also are proverbs of Solomon.[e] The servants of Hezekiah,* king of Judah, transmitted them.

2 * It is the glory of God to conceal a matter,
and the glory of kings to fathom a matter.*
3 Like the heavens in height, and the earth in depth,

24:23–34 A little collection between the thirty sayings of 22:17–24:22 and the Hezekiah collection in chaps. 25–29. Its title (v. 23) suggests that editors took it as an appendix. At this point, the Greek edition of Proverbs begins to arrange the later sections of the book in a different order than the Hebrew edition.

An editor has arranged originally separate sayings into two parallel groups.

	I.	II.
Conduct in court:	Judges (vv. 24–25)	Witnesses (v. 28)
Speaking, thinking:	Good speech (v. 26)	Bad speech (v. 29)
Wisdom in work:	Positive (v. 27)	Negative (vv. 30–34)

24:26 The kiss is a gesture of respect and affection. The greatest sign of affection and respect for another is to tell that person the truth.

24:27 House: can refer to both the building and the family (cf. 2 Sm 7). In the context established by the placement noted above under 24:23, the saying means that neglect of one's field is a sign that one is not building the house properly. In an agricultural society especially, the concept of household includes fields for animals and crops. On the metaphorical level, one must lay a careful preparation before embarking on a great project. This verse is sometimes interpreted as advocating careful and practical preparation for marriage.

24:29 Retribution is a long and complex process that belongs to the Lord, not to individuals. Cf. vv. 12d, 17–18.

24:30–34 Neglect of one's fields through laziness ruins all plans to build a house (v. 27). This vignette is a teaching story, like those in 7:1–27; Ps 37:35–36.

25:1–29:27 Chaps. 25–29 make up the fifth collection in the book, and the third longest. King Hezekiah reigned in Judah in 715–687 B.C. According to 2 Kgs 18–20 and 2 Chr 29–32, he initiated political and religious reforms after the destruction of the Northern Kingdom in 722 B.C. Such reforms probably included copying and editing sacred literature such as Proverbs. Prv 25:1 is an important piece of evidence about the composition of the book, suggesting this collection was added to an already-existing collection also attributed to Solomon. The older collection is probably 10:1–22:16 (or part of it). By the end of the eighth century B.C., therefore, there existed in Israel two large collections of aphorisms.

Chap. 25 has two general themes: (1) social hierarchy, rank, or position; (2) social conflict and its resolution.

25:1 The servants of Hezekiah: presumably scribes at the court of Hezekiah. **Transmitted**: lit., "to move, transfer from," hence "to collect," and perhaps also to arrange and compose.

25:2–7 The topic is the king—who he is (vv. 2–3) and how one is to behave in his presence (vv. 4–7).

25:2 God and king were closely related in the ancient world and in the Bible. The king had a special responsibility for divine justice. Hence, God would give him special wisdom to search it out.

a: Prv 18:5; 28:21; Lv 19:15; Dt 1:17; 16:19. *b:* Prv 19:5; 25:18. *c:* Prv 20:22. *d:* Prv 6:10–11. *e:* Prv 1:1.

the heart of kings is unfathomable.
4 * Remove the dross from silver,
and it comes forth perfectly purified;
5 Remove the wicked from the presence of the king,
and his throne is made firm through justice.
6 * Claim no honor in the king's presence,
nor occupy the place of superiors;
7 For it is better to be told, "Come up closer!"
than to be humbled before the prince.[f]
8 What your eyes have seen
do not bring forth too quickly against an opponent;
For what will you do later on
when your neighbor puts you to shame?
9 * Argue your own case with your neighbor,
but the secrets of others do not disclose;
10 Lest, hearing it, they reproach you,
and your ill repute never ceases.
11 Golden apples in silver settings
are words spoken at the proper time.
12 A golden earring or a necklace of fine gold—
one who gives wise reproof to a listening ear.
13 Like the coolness of snow in the heat of the harvest
are faithful messengers for those who send them,
lifting the spirits of their masters.
14 Clouds and wind but no rain—
the one who boasts of a gift not given.
15 By patience is a ruler persuaded,[g]
and a soft tongue can break a bone.
16 * If you find honey, eat only what you need,
lest you have your fill and vomit it up.
17 Let your foot be seldom in your neighbors' house,
lest they have their fill of you—and hate you.
18 A club, sword, or sharp arrow—
the one who bears false witness against a neighbor.[h]
19 A bad tooth or an unsteady foot—
a trust betrayed in time of trouble.*
20 Like the removal of clothes on a cold day, or vinegar on soda,
is the one who sings to a troubled heart.
21 * If your enemies are hungry, give them food to eat,
if thirsty, give something to drink;[i]
22 For live coals you will heap on their heads,
and the LORD will vindicate you.
23 The north wind brings rain,
and a backbiting tongue, angry looks.
24 It is better to dwell in a corner of the housetop
than in a mansion with a quarrelsome wife.* [j]
25 Cool water to one faint from thirst
is good news from a far country.
26 A trampled fountain or a polluted spring—*

25:4–5 Wisdom involves virtue as well as knowledge. As in Ps 101 the king cannot tolerate any wickedness in the royal service.

25:6–7 An admonition with a practical motive for putting the teaching into practice. Pragmatic shrewdness suggests that we not promote ourselves but let others do it for us. See Lk 14:7–11.

25:9–10 Another admonition on the use of law courts to settle personal disputes. Speak privately with your opponent lest others' personal business become public and they resent you.

25:16–17 The two admonitions are complementary, expressing nicely the need to restrain the inclination for delightful things, whether for honey or friendship.

25:19 "A time of trouble" defeats all plans (cf. 10:2; 11:4). At such times human resources alone are like a tooth that falls out as one bites or a foot that goes suddenly lame.

25:21–22 A memorable statement of humanity and moderation; such sentiments could be occasionally found even outside the Bible, e.g., "It is better to bless someone than to do harm to one who has insulted you" (Egyptian *Papyrus Insinger*). Cf. Ex 23:4 and Lv 19:17–18. Human beings should not take it upon themselves to exact vengeance, leaving it rather in God's hands. This saying has in view an enemy's vulnerability in time of need, in this case extreme hunger and thirst; such a need should not be an occasion for revenge. The motive for restraining oneself is to allow God's justice to take its own course, as in 20:22 and 24:17–19. **Live coals**: either remorse and embarrassment for the harm done, or increased punishment for refusing reconciliation. Cf. Mt 5:44. Rom 12:20 cites the Greek version and interprets it, "Do not be overcome by evil but overcome evil with good."

25:24 A humorous saying about domestic unhappiness: better to live alone outdoors than indoors with an angry spouse. Prv 21:9 is identical and 21:19 is similar in thought.

25:26 "Spring" is a common metaphor for source. The righteous should be a source of life for others. When they fail, it is as if a spring became foul and its water undrinkable. It is

f: Lk 14:8–10. *g:* Prv 15:1, 4. *h:* Ex 20:16. *i:* Rom 12:20. *j:* Prv 21:9.

a just person fallen before the wicked.
27 To eat too much honey is not good;
nor to seek honor after honor.*
28 A city breached and left defenseless
are those who do not control their temper.

CHAPTER 26*

See RG 254–62

1 Like snow in summer, like rain in harvest,
honor for a fool is out of place.*
2 Like the sparrow in its flitting, like the swallow in its flight,
a curse uncalled-for never lands.*
3 The whip for the horse, the bridle for the ass,
and the rod for the back of fools.[k]
4 * Do not answer fools according to their folly,
lest you too become like them.
5 Answer fools according to their folly,
lest they become wise in their own eyes.
6 Those who send messages by a fool
cut off their feet; they drink down violence.
7 * A proverb in the mouth of a fool
hangs limp, like crippled legs.
8 Giving honor to a fool
is like entangling a stone in the sling.
9 A thorn stuck in the hand of a drunkard
is a proverb in the mouth of fools.
10 An archer wounding all who pass by
is anyone who hires a drunken fool.
11 As dogs return to their vomit,
so fools repeat their folly.[l]
12 You see those who are wise in their own eyes?
There is more hope for fools than for them.
13 * The sluggard says, "There is a lion in the street,
a lion in the middle of the square!"[m]
14 The door turns on its hinges
and sluggards, on their beds.
15 The sluggard buries a hand in the dish,
too weary to lift it to the mouth.[n]
16 In their own eyes sluggards are wiser
than seven who answer with good judgment.
17 Whoever meddles in the quarrel of another
is one who grabs a passing dog by the ears.
18 Like a crazed archer
scattering firebrands and deadly arrows,
19 Such are those who deceive their neighbor,
and then say, "I was only joking."
20 * Without wood the fire dies out;
without a talebearer strife subsides.
21 Charcoal for coals, wood for fire—
such are the quarrelsome, enkindling strife.[o]
22 The words of a talebearer are like dainty morsels:
they sink into one's inmost being.* [p]

not clear whether the righteous person yielded to a scoundrel out of cowardice or was simply defeated by evil. The latter seems more likely, for other proverbs say the just person will never "fall" (lit., "be moved," 10:30; 12:3). The fall, even temporary, of a righteous person is a loss of life for others.

25:27 Nor . . . honor: the text is uncertain.

26:1–28 Concrete images describe the vices of fools (vv. 1–12), of sluggards (vv. 13–16), of meddlers (vv. 17–19), of talebearers (vv. 20–22), and of flatterers (vv. 23–28).

26:1 There is no fit ("out of place") between weather and agricultural season.

26:2 The point is the similarity of actions: a hovering bird that never lands, a groundless curse that never "lands." It hangs in the air posing no threat to anyone.

26:4–5 There is no contradiction between these two proverbs. In their answers, the wise must protect their own interests against fools. Or perhaps the juxtaposition of the two proverbs suggests that no single proverb can resolve every problem in life.

26:7–9 Fools either abuse or are unable to use whatever knowledge they have. **A thorn**: a proverb is "words spoken at the proper time" (25:11). Fools have no sense of the right time; their statements are like thorns that fasten on clothing randomly.

26:13–16 Each verse mentions the sluggard, whom Proverbs regards with derision. The criticism is not against low energy but failure to act and take responsibility. Proverbs' ideal is the active person who uses heart, lips, hands, feet to keep to the good path. The verses are examples of the sardonic humor of the book.

26:20–22 The three proverbs have a common theme—the destructive power of slanderous words. Certain words are repeated: wood and fire, talebearer.

26:22 Malicious gossip is compared to delicious food that is swallowed and lodges in the deepest recesses of one's body. Negative comments are seldom forgotten. Prv 18:8 is a duplicate.

k: Prv 19:29; Sir 33:25. *l:* 2 Pt 2:22. *m:* Prv 22:13. *n:* Prv 19:24. *o:* Prv 15:18; 29:22. *p:* Prv 18:8.

23 Like a glazed finish on earthenware
are smooth lips and a wicked heart.*
24 With their lips enemies pretend,
but inwardly they maintain deceit;
25 When they speak graciously, do not trust
them,[q]
for seven abominations* are in their
hearts.
26 Hatred can be concealed by pretense,
but malice will be revealed in the
assembly.*
27 Whoever digs a pit falls into it;
and a stone comes back upon the one
who rolls it.[r]
28 The lying tongue is its owner's enemy,
and the flattering mouth works ruin.

CHAPTER 27

See RG 254–62

1 Do not boast about tomorrow,
for you do not know what any day
may bring forth.
2 Let another praise you, not your own
mouth;
a stranger, not your own lips.
3 Stone is heavy, and sand a burden,
but a fool's provocation is heavier than
both.[s]
4 Anger is cruel, and wrath overwhelming,
but before jealousy who can stand?*
5 * Better is an open rebuke
than a love that remains hidden.
6 Trustworthy are the blows of a friend,
dangerous, the kisses of an enemy.*
7 One who is full spurns honey;
but to the hungry, any bitter thing is
sweet.
8 Like a bird far from the nest
so is anyone far from home.*
9 Perfume and incense bring joy to the
heart,
but by grief the soul is torn asunder.
10 Do not give up your own friend and your
father's friend;
do not resort to the house of your
kindred when trouble strikes.
Better a neighbor near than kin far away.*
11 Be wise, my son, and bring joy to my
heart,
so that I can answer whoever taunts me.*
12 The astute see an evil and hide;
the naive continue on and pay the
penalty.[t]
13 Take the garment of the one who became
surety for a stranger;[u]
if for a foreign woman, exact the
pledge!*
14 Those who greet their neighbor with a
loud voice* in the early morning,
a curse can be laid to their charge.
15 For a persistent leak on a rainy day
the match is a quarrelsome wife;[v]
16 Whoever would hide her hides a
stormwind
and cannot tell north from south.
17 Iron is sharpened by iron;
one person sharpens another.*

26:23 Heart = what is within, and lips (words) = what is expressed, are compared to an earthenware jar covered with glaze.

26:25 Seven abominations: many evil intentions.

26:26 Hate may be concealed for a time, but it will eventually issue in a deed and become known in the public assembly. There is a play on words: the consonants of the word "hatred" (*ś'n*) are literally concealed in the word "pretense" (*mś'n*).

27:4 Anger generally subsides with time but jealousy coolly calculates and plots revenge.

27:5–6 Verses 5 and 6 are concerned with true friendship. "Better than" sayings often declare one thing superior to another in view of some value, e.g., 15:17, vegetables are better than meat in view of a milieu of love. In v. 5, a rebuke is better than an act of affection in view of discipline that imparts wisdom.

27:6 The present translation is conjectural. The meaning seems to be that a friend's rebuke can be life-giving and an enemy's kiss can be deadly (like the kiss of Judas in Mt 26:48).

27:8 The bird symbolizes vulnerability as it flees before danger as in Is 10:14; 16:2; and Ps 11:1. For the importance of place in human life, see Jb 20:8–9. People are defined by their place, but, tragically, war, poverty, or illness can force them from it.

27:10 The adage is about the difference between friends and kin in a crisis. Two admonitions are grounded in one maxim (colon C). The same Hebrew word means both "one who is near" and "friend." The whole proverb urges the reader to cultivate old family friends and neighbors and not to rely exclusively on kin in times of trouble, for kin may not be there for us.

27:11 A father's command to a son to be wise, another way of saying that sons or daughters bring joy or shame to their parents.

27:13 See note on 20:16.

27:14 One interpretation takes the proverb as humorous and the other takes it as serious: (1) an overly loud and ill-timed greeting (lit., "blessing") invites the response of a curse rather than a "blessing" (greeting); (2) the loud voice suggests hypocrisy in the greeting.

27:17 Iron sharpens the "face" (*panim* = surface, edge) of iron, and a human being sharpens the "face" (*panim* = face,

q: Sir 12:10; 27:33. *r:* Eccl 10:8; Sir 27:25–26. *s:* Sir 22:14–15. *t:* Prv 22:3. *u:* Prv 20:16. *v:* Prv 21:9; 25:24.

18 Those who tend a fig tree eat its fruit;
so those attentive to their master will be honored.
19 As face mirrors face in water,
so the heart reflects the person.
20 Sheol and Abaddon can never be satisfied;[w]
so the eyes of mortals can never be satisfied.*
21 The crucible for silver, the furnace for gold,
so you must assay the praise you receive.
22 Though you pound fools with a pestle,
their folly never leaves them.
23 * Take good care of your flocks,
give careful attention to your herds;
24 For wealth does not last forever,
nor even a crown from age to age.
25 When the grass comes up and the new growth appears,
and the mountain greens are gathered in,
26 The lambs will provide you with clothing,
and the goats, the price of a field,
27 And there will be ample goat's milk for your food,
food for your house, sustenance for your maidens.

CHAPTER 28

See RG 254–62

1 The wicked flee though none pursue;
but the just, like a lion, are confident.
2 If a land is rebellious, its princes will be many;
but with an intelligent and wise ruler there is stability.*
3 One who is poor and extorts from the lowly
is a devastating rain that leaves no food.*
4 Those who abandon instruction* praise the wicked,
but those who keep instruction oppose them.
5 The evil understand nothing of justice,*
but those who seek the LORD understand everything.
6 Better to be poor and walk in integrity
than rich and crooked in one's ways.[x]
7 Whoever heeds instruction is a wise son,
but whoever joins with wastrels disgraces his father.
8 Whoever amasses wealth by interest and overcharge*
gathers it for the one who is kind to the poor.
9 Those who turn their ears from hearing instruction,[y]
even their prayer is an abomination.
10 Those who mislead the upright into an evil way
will themselves fall into their own pit,
but the blameless will attain prosperity.
11 The rich are wise in their own eyes,
but the poor who are intelligent see through them.
12 When the just triumph, there is great glory;
but when the wicked prevail, people hide.*

words) of another. Human beings learn from each other and grow in wisdom by conversing.

27:20 Sheol, the underworld abode of the dead, is personified as a force that is never satisfied and always desires more. Cf. Is 5:14 and Hos 13:14. The saying is applicable to modern consumerism.

27:23–27 A little treatise on farming in the form of admonitions. It proposes the advantages of field and flock over other forms of wealth. Herds are the most productive wealth, for their value does not diminish; they are a source of money, clothing, and food. The thought is conservative and traditional but the development is vivid and concrete.

28:2 The first line expresses the paradox that rebellion, far from doing away with rulers, actually multiplies them. The second line is corrupt.

28:3 The reference may be to tax farmers who collected taxes and took a commission. The collectors' lack of wealth was the cause of their oppression of poor farmers. They are like a rain too violent to allow crops to grow.

28:4 Instruction: *torah*; the word is used both for the teaching of the wise and the law of Moses.

28:5 Understanding nothing of justice plays on the twofold sense of justice as righteousness and as punishment that comes on the wicked. On the other hand, **those who seek the LORD understand everything**, i.e., that the Lord punishes the wicked and rewards the righteous (themselves).

28:8 Interest and overcharge were strictly forbidden in the old law among Israelites because it was presumed that the borrower was in distress; cf. Ex 22:25; Lv 25:35–37; Dt 23:20; Ps 15:5; Ez 18:8. Divine providence will take the offender's wealth; cf. Eccl 2:26.

28:12 People react in opposite ways to the triumph of good

w: Prv 30:16; Eccl 4:8. *x:* Prv 19:1. *y:* Prv 15:8; 21:27.

13 Those who conceal their sins do not
prosper,
but those who confess and forsake
them obtain mercy.*
14 Happy those who always fear;*
but those who harden their hearts fall
into evil.
15 A roaring lion or a ravenous bear
is a wicked ruler over a poor people.
16 The less prudent the rulers, the more
oppressive their deeds.
Those who hate ill-gotten gain prolong
their days.
17 Though a person burdened with blood
guilt is in flight even to the grave,
let no one offer support.
18 Whoever walks blamelessly is safe,
but one whose ways are crooked falls
into a pit.
19 Those who cultivate their land will have
plenty of food,
but those who engage in idle pursuits
will have plenty of want.[z]
20 The trustworthy will be richly blessed;
but whoever hastens to be rich will not
go unpunished.[a]
21 To show partiality is never good:[b]
for even a morsel of bread one may do
wrong.*
22 Misers hurry toward wealth,
not knowing that want is coming
toward them.*
23 Whoever rebukes another wins more favor
than one who flatters with the tongue.
24 Whoever defrauds father or mother and
says, "It is no sin,"[c]
is a partner to a brigand.
25 The greedy person stirs up strife,
but the one who trusts in the LORD will
prosper.
26 Those who trust in themselves are fools,
but those who walk in wisdom are
safe.
27 Those who give to the poor have no
lack,[d]
but those who avert their eyes, many
curses.
28 When the wicked prevail, people hide;
but at their fall the just abound.[e]

CHAPTER 29

See RG 254–62

1 Those stiff-necked in the face of
reproof
in an instant will be shattered beyond
cure.*
2 When the just flourish, the people
rejoice;
but when the wicked rule, the people
groan.*[f]
3 Whoever loves wisdom gives joy to his
father,
but whoever consorts with harlots
squanders his wealth.
4 By justice a king builds up the land;
but one who raises taxes tears it
down.*
5 Those who speak flattery to their
neighbor
cast a net at their feet.*
6 The sin of the wicked is a trap,
but the just run along joyfully.[g]
7 The just care for the cause of the poor;

and evil. To the triumph of good, they react by public display, public celebration, and to the triumph of evil, by hiding.

28:13 Concealing the faults of another is a good thing in Proverbs (17:9), but concealing one's own sins is not. Ps 32:1–5 expresses the anguish caused by concealing one's sins rather than bringing them to light so they can be healed by God.

28:14 Fear is a different verb than in the phrase "to fear (or revere) the Lord." In its only other biblical occurrence (Is 51:13), the verb means to dread an oppressor. The saying states a paradox: those who fear in the sense of being cautious are declared happy, whereas those who are fearless will fall into traps they did not "fear." In short, there is good fear and bad fear.

28:21 Cf. 24:23. Verse 21b warns that even in a light matter one must remain impartial.

28:22 "Bad of eye" is the Hebrew idiom for miserly. Misers fail to see that poverty is hurrying toward them because of their wrong attitude toward wealth. Because misers are "bad of eye," they do not see the danger.

29:1 The idiom "to stiffen one's neck" occurs in a context of not heeding a message in Dt 10:16 and 2 Kgs 17:14. To stiffen one's neck in this sense risks having it broken, as in 1 Sm 4:18.

29:2 Popular response to a just or unjust ruler is expressed in sound—shouts of joy or groans of anguish. "Rejoice" can mean to express one's joy, i.e., joyous shouts.

29:4 In Hebrew as in English high and low are metaphors for prosperity and depression. A king who is just "causes the land to stand up," i.e., to be prosperous, and one who makes taxes high brings a country low.

29:5 When one addresses deceptive words to someone's face, one equivalently throws a net at their feet to snare them.

z: Prv 12:11. *a:* Prv 13:11. *b:* Prv 24:23. *c:* Mk 7:11–13. *d:* Prv 19:17; Sir 4:3–8. *e:* Prv 28:12. *f:* Prv 11:10; 28:12, 28. *g:* Prv 12:13.

the wicked do not understand such
care.*
8 Scoffers enflame the city,
but the wise calm the fury.[h]
9 If a wise person disputes with a fool,
there is railing and ridicule but no
resolution.
10 The bloodthirsty hate the blameless,
but the upright seek his life.*
11 Fools give vent to all their anger;
but the wise, biding their time,
control it.[i]
12 If rulers listen to lying words,
their servants all become wicked.
13 The poor and the oppressor meet:[j]
the LORD gives light to the eyes of
both.
14 If a king is honestly for the rights of the
poor,
his throne stands firm forever.[k]
15 The rod of correction gives wisdom,
but uncontrolled youths disgrace their
mothers.[l]
16 When the wicked increase, crime
increases;
but the just will behold their
downfall.*
17 Discipline your children, and they will
bring you comfort,
and give delight to your soul.
18 Without a vision the people lose
restraint;
but happy is the one who follows
instruction.*
19 Not by words alone can servants be
trained;[m]
for they understand but do not
respond.*
20 Do you see someone hasty in speech?[n]
There is more hope for a fool!
21 If servants are pampered from childhood
they will turn out to be stubborn.
22 The ill-tempered stir up strife,
and the hotheaded cause many sins.[o]
23 Haughtiness brings humiliation,
but the humble of spirit acquire honor.* [p]
24 Partners of a thief hate themselves;*
they hear the imprecation but do not
testify.
25 Fear of others becomes a snare,
but the one who trusts in the LORD is
safe.
26 Many curry favor with a ruler,
but it is from the LORD that one
receives justice.
27 An abomination to the just, the evildoer;
an abomination to the wicked, one
whose way is straight.

VII. Sayings of Agur and Others

CHAPTER 30

See RG 254–62

1* The words of Agur, son of Jakeh
the Massaite:

29:7 As in 12:10 (on care for animals), the righteous care for those who are without a voice and often treated like animals. Colon B has a double meaning: the wicked have no such knowledge (care for the poor) and they have no knowledge (wisdom), for they are fools.

29:10 An enigmatic saying in that "seek one's life" is a common idiom for killing. The saying probably plays on the idiom, interpreting "to seek the life of another" not as killing but as caring for another (as in 11:30).

29:16 When the wicked grow numerous they sow the seeds of their own destruction, for there is a corresponding increase in offenses calling down divine retribution.

29:18 This much-cited proverb has been interpreted in several different ways. "Vision" and "instruction" mean authoritative guidance for the community. People are demoralized without credible leadership, but any individual heeding traditional instruction can still find happiness. As in 15:15 wisdom enables an individual to surmount days of trouble.

29:19 The give and take of reproving is not possible for servants or slaves. Ancient custom dictated silent acquiescence for them. There is no open and free dialogue, which is part of ancient discipline.

29:23 One's prideful height brings one down and one's lowly state brings glory.

29:24 **Hate themselves**: because they not only incur guilt as accomplices but, by their silence, bring down on themselves the curse invoked on the unknown guilty partner. Such a case is envisioned in Lv 5:1. After a theft, a public proclamation was made, enforced by a curse. No one in a town or city could avoid hearing it. The curse hung over the accomplice. By doing nothing, neither directly stealing nor confessing, accomplices put themselves in serious danger.

30:1–6 Scholars are divided on the original literary unit. Is it vv. 1–3, 1–4, 1–5, or 1–6? The unit is probably vv. 1–6, for a single contrast dominates: human fragility (and ignorance) and divine power (and knowledge). A similar contrast is found in Jb 28; Ps 73; Is 49:1–4. The language of self-abasement is hyperbolic; cf. 2 Sm 9:8; Ps 73:21–22; Jb 25:4–6. **Agur**: an unknown person. **Massaite**: from Massa in north-

h: Prv 11:11. *i:* Prv 12:16; 25:28; Sir 21:26. *j:* Prv 22:2. *k:* Prv 16:12; 20:28; 25:5. *l:* Prv 13:24; 22:15; 23:13–14; Sir 22:6; 30:1. *m:* Sir 33:25–30. *n:* Sir 9:18; Prv 26:12. *o:* Prv 15:18; 22:24. *p:* Prv 11:2; 16:18; 18:12.

The pronouncement of mortal man: "I
am weary, O God;
I am weary, O God, and I am
exhausted.
2 I am more brute than human being,
without even human intelligence;
3 * Neither have I learned wisdom,
nor have I the knowledge of the Holy
One.
4 Who has gone up to heaven and come
down again—
who has cupped the wind in the
hollow of the hand?
Who has bound up the waters in a
cloak—
who has established all the ends of the
earth?
What is that person's name, or the name
of his son?"*

5 * Every word of God is tested;[q]
he is a shield to those who take refuge
in him.
6 Add nothing to his words,[r]
lest he reprimand you, and you be
proved a liar.

7 * Two things I ask of you,
do not deny them to me before I die:
8 Put falsehood and lying far from me,
give me neither poverty nor riches;
provide me only with the food I need;
9 Lest, being full, I deny you,
saying, "Who is the LORD?"
Or, being in want, I steal,
and profane the name of my God.
10 Do not criticize servants to their master,
lest they curse you, and you have to
pay the penalty.
11 * There are some who curse their fathers,
and do not bless their mothers.[s]
12 There are some pure in their own eyes,
yet not cleansed of their filth.
13 There are some—how haughty their
eyes!
how overbearing their glance!
14 There are some—their teeth are swords,
their teeth are knives,
Devouring the needy from the earth,
and the poor from the human race.
15 * The leech has two daughters:
"Give," and "Give."
Three things never get their fill,
four never say, "Enough!"
16 Sheol, a barren womb,[t]
land that never gets its fill of water,
and fire, which never says, "Enough!"
17 The eye that mocks a father,
or scorns the homage due a mother,
Will be plucked out by brook ravens;
devoured by a brood of vultures.
18 * Three things are too wonderful for me,
yes, four I cannot understand:
19 The way of an eagle in the sky,
the way of a serpent upon a rock,
The way of a ship on the high seas,
and the way of a man with a woman.

ern Arabia, elsewhere referred to as an encampment of the Ishmaelites (Gn 25:14). But Heb. *massa* may not be intended as a place name; it might signify "an oracle," "a prophecy," as in Is 15:1; 17:1; etc.

30:3–4 Agur denies he has secret heavenly knowledge. The purpose of the denial is to underline that God directly gives wisdom to those whose conduct pleases him.

30:4 The Hebrew text has the phrase "do you know?" at the end of v. 4, which is supported by the versions. The phrase, however, does not appear in the important Greek manuscripts Vaticanus and Sinaiticus and spoils the sense, for Agur, not God, is the questioner. The phrase seems to be an addition to the Hebrew text, borrowed from Job 38:5, where it also follows a cosmic question.

30:5–6 Verse 5, like the confession of the king in Ps 18:31 (and its parallel, 2 Sm 22:31), expresses total confidence in the one who rescues from death. Agur has refused a word from any other except God and makes an act of trust in God.

30:7–9 A prayer against lying words and for sufficiency of goods, lest reaction to riches or destitution lead to offenses against God.

30:11–14 Perverted people are here classified as unfilial (v. 11), self-righteous (v. 12), proud (v. 13) and rapacious (v. 14).

30:15–16 Here begins a series of numerical sayings; the pattern is n, n + 1. The slight variation in number (two and three, three and four) is an example of parallelism applied to numbers. The poetic technique is attested even outside the Bible. **Two daughters: "Give," and "Give"**: the text is obscure; as the leech (a bloodsucking worm) is insatiable in its desire for blood (v. 15), so are the nether world for victims, the barren womb for offspring, the earth for water, and fire for fuel (v. 16). **Sheol**: here not so much the place of the dead as a force (death) that eventually draws all the living into it; cf. 27:20; Is 5:14; Hb 2:5. **Land . . . fire**: land (especially the dry land of Palestine) always absorbs more water; fire always requires more fuel.

30:18–19 The soaring flight of the eagle, the mysterious movement upon a rock of the serpent which has no feet, the path of the ship through the trackless deep, and the marvelous attraction between the sexes; there is a mysterious way common to them all.

q: Ps 12:7; 18:31. *r:* Dt 4:2; 13:1. *s:* Prv 20:20. *t:* Prv 27:20.

20 This is the way of an adulterous woman:
she eats, wipes her mouth,
and says, "I have done no wrong."*
21 * Under three things the earth trembles,
yes, under four it cannot bear up:
22 Under a slave who becomes king,
and a fool who is glutted with food;[u]
23 Under an unloved woman who is wed,
and a maidservant who displaces her mistress.
24 * Four things are among the smallest on the earth,
and yet are exceedingly wise:
25 Ants—a species not strong,
yet they store up their food in the summer;
26 Badgers—a species not mighty,
yet they make their home in the crags;
27 Locusts—they have no king,
yet they march forth in formation;
28 Lizards—you can catch them with your hands,
yet they find their way into kings' palaces.
29 * Three things are stately in their stride,
yes, four are stately in their carriage:
30 The lion, mightiest of beasts,
retreats before nothing;
31 The strutting cock, and the he-goat,
and the king at the head of his people.
32 * If you have foolishly been proud
or presumptuous—put your hand on your mouth;
33 For as the churning of milk produces curds,
and the pressing of the nose produces blood,
the churning of anger produces strife.

VIII. Sayings of King Lemuel*

CHAPTER 31

See RG 254–62

1 The words of Lemuel, king of Massa,* the instruction his mother taught him:

2 What are you doing, my son!*
what are you doing, son of my womb;
what are you doing, son of my vows!
3 Do not give your vigor to women,
or your strength* to those who ruin kings.
4 It is not for kings, Lemuel,
not for kings to drink wine;
strong drink is not for princes,
5 Lest in drinking they forget what has been decreed,
and violate the rights of any who are in need.
6 Give strong drink to anyone who is perishing,
and wine to the embittered;

30:20 This verse portrays the indifference of an adulterous woman who casually dismisses her guilt because it cannot be traced.

30:21–23 Shaking heavens are part of general cosmic upheaval in Is 14:16; Jl 2:10; Am 8:8; Jb 9:6. Disturbances in nature mirror the disturbance of unworthy people attaining what they do not deserve. **Glutted with food**: someone unworthy ends up with the fulfillment that befits a wise person. **Unloved woman**: an older woman who, contrary to expectation, finds a husband.

30:24–28 The creatures may be small, but they are wise in knowing how to govern themselves—the definition of wisdom. **Badgers**: the rock badger is able to live on rocky heights that provide security from its enemies. **Locusts**: though vulnerable individually their huge swarms are impossible to deflect.

30:29–31 Four beings with an imperiousness visible in their walk. Only the lion is described in detail; the reader is expected to transpose its qualities to the others.

30:32–33 The same Hebrew verb, "to churn, shake," is applied to milk, the nose (sometimes a symbol of anger), and wrath. In each case something is eventually produced by the constant agitation. The wise make peace and avoid strife, for strife eventually harms those who provoke it.

31:1–9 Though mothers are sources of wisdom in Proverbs (1:8; 6:20), the mother of Lemuel is special in being queen mother, which was an important position in the palace. Queen mothers played an important role in ancient palace life because of their longevity, knowledge of palace politics, and loyalty to their sons; they were in a good position to offer him sound counsel. The language of the poem contains Aramaisms, a sign of its non-Israelite origin.

The first section, vv. 3–5, warns against abuse of sex and alcohol (wine, strong drink) lest the king *forget* the *poor*. The second section, vv. 6–9, urges the use of alcohol (strong drink, wine) so that the downtrodden *poor* can *forget* their poverty. The real subject of the poem is justice for the poor.

31:1 Massa: see note on 30:1–6.

31:2 My son: in the Septuagint, "my son, my firstborn."

31:3 The Hebrew word here translated "strength" normally means "ways," but the context and a cognate language support "authority" or "strength" here.

u: Prv 19:10; Eccl 10:6–7.

7 When they drink, they will forget their
misery,
and think no more of their troubles.
8 Open your mouth in behalf of the mute,
and for the rights of the destitute;
9 Open your mouth, judge justly,
defend the needy and the poor!

IX. Poem on the Woman of Worth*

10 Who can find* a woman of worth?[v]
Far beyond jewels is her value.
11 Her husband trusts her judgment;
he does not lack income.
12 She brings him profit, not loss,*
all the days of her life.
13 She seeks out wool and flax
and weaves with skillful hands.
14 Like a merchant fleet,*
she secures her provisions from afar.
15 She rises while it is still night,
and distributes food to her household,
a portion to her maidservants.
16 She picks out a field and acquires it;
from her earnings she plants a vineyard.
17 She girds herself with strength;
she exerts her arms with vigor.*
18 She enjoys the profit from her dealings;
her lamp is never extinguished at night.*
19 She puts her hands to the distaff,
and her fingers ply the spindle.*
20 She reaches out her hands to the poor,
and extends her arms to the needy.
21 She is not concerned for her household
when it snows—
all her charges are doubly clothed.
22 She makes her own coverlets;
fine linen and purple are her clothing.
23 Her husband is prominent at the city gates
as he sits with the elders of the land.*
24 She makes garments and sells them,
and stocks the merchants with belts.
25 She is clothed with strength and dignity,
and laughs at the days to come.*
26 She opens her mouth in wisdom;
kindly instruction is on her tongue.
27 She watches over* the affairs of her
household,
and does not eat the bread of idleness.
28 Her children rise up and call her blessed;
her husband, too, praises her:
29 "Many are the women of proven worth,
but you have excelled them all."
30 Charm is deceptive and beauty fleeting;
the woman who fears the LORD is to be
praised.*
31 Acclaim her for the work of her hands,
and let her deeds praise her at the city
gates.

31:10–31 An acrostic poem of twenty-two lines; each line begins with a successive letter of the Hebrew alphabet. As with many other acrostic poems in the Bible, the unity of the poem is largely extrinsic, coming not from the narrative logic but from the familiar sequence of letters. The topic is the ideal woman described through her activity as a wife. Some have suggested that the traditional hymn extolling the great deeds of a warrior has been transposed to extol a heroic wife; the focus is on her exploits. She runs a household distinguished by abundant food and clothing for all within, by its trade (import of raw materials and export of finished products), and by the renown of its head, her husband, in the community. At v. 28, the voice is no longer that of the narrator but of her children and husband as they praise her. The purpose of the poem has been interpreted variously: an encomium to offset the sometimes negative portrayal of women in the book, or, more symbolically (and more likely), a portrait of a household ruled by Woman Wisdom and a disciple of Woman Wisdom, i.e., he now has a worthy wife and children, a great household, renown in the community.

31:10 Who can find . . . ?: in 20:6 and Eccl 8:1 the question implies that finding such a person is well-nigh impossible.

31:12 Profit, not loss: a commercial metaphor.

31:14 Like a merchant fleet: she has her eye on the far horizon, like the ship of a merchant ready to bring supplies into her larder. It is the only simile ("like") in the poem.

31:17 The metaphor of clothing oneself is used to show the woman's readiness. One can gird on weapons of war and might and splendor (Ps 69:7; Is 52:9).

31:18 Her lamp is never extinguished at night: indicates abundance of productive work and its accompanying prosperity; cf. 20:20; Jb 18:6.

31:19 The wife weaves linen cloth from flax and wool from fleece, which she cultivated according to v. 13. **Distaff**: staff for holding the flax, tow, or wool, which in spinning was drawn out and twisted into yarn or thread by the spindle or round stick.

31:23 The husband is mentioned for the first time since vv. 10–12 but as "her husband." He will not be mentioned again until v. 28, where he praises her.

31:25 Laughs at the days to come: anticipates the future with joy, free of anxiety.

31:27 Watches over: Hebrew *sopiyyâ*, perhaps a pun on the Greek *sophia* (= wisdom). **Bread of idleness**: she does not eat from the table of others but from her own labors.

31:30 The true charm of this woman is her religious spirit, for she fears the Lord; cf. note on 1:7.

v: Prv 12:4; Sir 26:1–4, 13–18.

See RG 261–67

The Book of Ecclesiastes

The Hebrew name of this book and of its author, Qoheleth, is actually a title, and it perhaps means "assembler" (of students, listeners) or "collector" (of wisdom sayings). The book's more common name, Ecclesiastes, is an approximate translation into Greek of this Hebrew word. The book comprises an extended reflective essay employing autobiographical narrative, proverbs, parables, and allegories. An almost unrelenting skepticism characterizes the tone or outlook. The issues with which the author deals and the questions he raises are aimed at those who would claim any absolute values in this life, including possessions, fame, success, or pleasure. Wisdom itself is challenged, but folly is condemned.

The refrain which begins and ends the book, "Vanity of vanities" (1:1; 12:8), recurs at key points throughout. The Hebrew word, *hebel* ("vanity"), has the sense of "emptiness, futility, absurdity": "I have seen all things that are done under the sun, and behold, all is vanity and a chase after wind" (1:14; 2:11, 17, 26; etc.). Everything in human life is subject to change, to qualification, to loss: "What profit have we from all the toil which we toil at under the sun?" (1:3). The answer is in the negative: No absolute profit or gain is possible. Even if some temporary profit or gain is achieved, it will ultimately be cancelled out by death, the great leveller (2:14–15; 3:19–20). Wisdom has some advantage over foolishness, but even wisdom's advantage is only a temporary and qualified one.

Many would locate Ecclesiastes in the third century B.C., when Judea was under the oppressive domination of Hellenistic kings from Egypt. These kings were highly efficient in their ruthless exploitation of the land and people (4:1; 5:7). The average Jew would have felt a sense of powerlessness and inability to change things for the better. For Qoheleth, God seems remote and uncommunicative, and we cannot hope to understand, much less influence, God's activity in the world (3:11; 8:16–17).

The book's honest and blunt appraisal of the human condition provides a healthy corrective to the occasionally excessive self-assurance of other wisdom writers. Its radical skepticism is somewhat tempered by the resigned conclusions to rejoice in whatever gifts God may give (2:24; 3:12–13, 22; 5:17–18; 8:15; 9:7–9; 11:9).

The Book of Ecclesiastes is divided as follows:

I. Qoheleth's Investigation of Life (1:12–6:9)
II. Qoheleth's Conclusions (6:10–12:14)
  A. No One Can Find Out the Best Way of Acting (7:1–8:17)
  B. No One Knows the Future (9:1–12:14)

CHAPTER 1

See RG 261–67

1 The words of David's son, Qoheleth, king in Jerusalem:* [a]

2 Vanity of vanities,* says Qoheleth,
vanity of vanities! All things are vanity![b]

Vanity of Human Toil

3 What profit have we from all the toil
which we toil at under the sun?* [c]
4 One generation departs and another
generation comes,
but the world forever stays.
5 The sun rises and the sun sets;
then it presses on to the place where it
rises.
6 Shifting south, then north,
back and forth shifts the wind,
constantly shifting its course.
7 All rivers flow to the sea,
yet never does the sea become full.
To the place where they flow,
the rivers continue to flow.

1:1 David's son . . . king in Jerusalem: the intent of the author is to identify himself with Solomon. This is a literary device, by which the author hopes to commend his work to the public under the name of Israel's most famous sage (see 1 Kgs 5:9–14).

1:2 Vanity of vanities: a Hebrew superlative expressing the supreme degree of futility and emptiness.

1:3 Under the sun: used throughout this book to signify "on the earth."

a: Eccl 1:12; 12:9–10. *b*: Eccl 12:8. *c*: Eccl 2:11, 22; 3:9; 5:15.

8 All things are wearisome,*
too wearisome for words.
The eye is not satisfied by seeing
nor has the ear enough of hearing.[d]

9 What has been, that will be; what has
been done, that will be done. Nothing is new
under the sun![e] 10 Even the thing of which we
say, "See, this is new!" has already existed in
the ages that preceded us.[f] 11 There is no remembrance of past generations;[g] nor will future generations be remembered by those
who come after them.*

I. Qoheleth's Investigation of Life

Twofold Introduction. 12 I, Qoheleth, was
king over Israel in Jerusalem, 13 and I applied
my mind to search and investigate in wisdom all things that are done under the sun.[h]

A bad business God has given
to human beings to be busied with.

14 I have seen all things that are done under the sun, and behold, all is vanity and a
chase after wind.* [i]

15 What is crooked cannot be made straight,
and you cannot count what is not
there.*

16[j] Though I said to myself, "See, I have
greatly increased my wisdom beyond all
who were before me in Jerusalem, and my
mind has broad experience of wisdom and
knowledge," 17 yet when I applied my mind
to know wisdom and knowledge, madness
and folly, I learned that this also is a chase
after wind.[k]

18 For in much wisdom there is much sorrow;
whoever increases knowledge
increases grief.*

CHAPTER 2

See RG 261–67

Study of Pleasure-seeking. 1 I said in
my heart,* "Come, now, let me try you with
pleasure and the enjoyment of good things."
See, this too was vanity. 2 Of laughter I said:
"Mad!" and of mirth: "What good does this
do?" 3 Guided by wisdom,* I probed with my
mind how to beguile my senses with wine
and take up folly, until I should understand
what is good for human beings to do under
the heavens during the limited days of their
lives.

4 I undertook great works; I built myself
houses and planted vineyards; 5 I made gardens and parks, and in them set out fruit trees
of all sorts. 6 And I constructed for myself
reservoirs to water a flourishing woodland.
7 I acquired male and female slaves, and had
slaves who were born in my house. I also
owned vast herds of cattle and flocks of
sheep, more than all who had been before
me in Jerusalem. 8 I amassed for myself silver and gold, and the treasures of kings and
provinces. I provided for myself male and
female singers and delights of men, many
women.* 9 I accumulated much more than all
others before me in Jerusalem; my wisdom,
too, stayed with me. 10 Nothing that my eyes

1:8 All things are wearisome: or, "All speech is wearisome."

1:11 Movement in nature and human activity appears to result in change and progress. The author argues that this change and progress are an illusion: "Nothing is new under the sun."

1:14 A chase after wind: an image of futile activity, like an attempt to corral the winds; cf. Hos 12:2. The ancient versions understood "affliction, dissipation of the spirit." This phrase concludes sections of the text as far as 6:9.

1:15 You cannot count what is not there: perhaps originally a commercial metaphor alluding to loss or deficit in the accounts ledger.

1:18 Sorrow . . . grief: these terms refer not just to a store of knowledge or to psychological or emotional pain. Corporal punishment, sometimes quite harsh, was also employed frequently by parents and teachers.

2:1–11 The author here assumes the role of Solomon who, as king, would have had the wealth and resources at his disposal to acquire wisdom and engage in pleasurable pursuits. Verses 4–8 in particular, with their description of abundant wealth and physical gratifications, parallel the descriptions in 1 Kgs 4–11 of the extravagances of Solomon's reign.

2:3 Guided by wisdom: using all the means money can buy, the author sets out on a deliberate search to discover if pleasure constitutes true happiness.

2:8 Many women: the final phrase of this verse is difficult to translate. One word, *shiddah*, which appears here in both singular and plural, is found nowhere else in the Hebrew Bible. A suggested meaning is "woman" or "concubine," as it is interpreted here: "many women." The rest of the section (2:1–12) seems to be a description of Solomon's kingdom, and the "many women" would represent his huge harem (1 Kgs 11:1–3). In rabbinic Hebrew the word comes to mean "chest" or "coffer."

d: Eccl 4:8; 5:9–11. *e:* Eccl 3:15; 6:10. *f:* Eccl 3:15. *g:* Eccl 2:16. *h:* Eccl 8:9. *i:* Eccl 2:11, 17. *j:* Eccl 2:9. *k:* Eccl 1:3; 8:16.

desired did I deny them, nor did I deprive myself of any joy; rather, my heart rejoiced in the fruit of all my toil. This was my share for all my toil. [11][l] But when I turned to all the works that my hands had wrought, and to the fruit of the toil for which I had toiled so much, see! all was vanity and a chase after wind. There is no profit under the sun. [12]What about one who succeeds a king? He can do only what has already been done.*

Study of Wisdom and Folly. I went on to the consideration of wisdom, madness and folly. [13]And I saw that wisdom has as much profit over folly as light has over darkness.

[14] Wise people have eyes in their heads,
but fools walk in darkness.

Yet I knew that the same lot befalls both.* [m] [15]So I said in my heart, if the fool's lot is to befall me also, why should I be wise? Where is the profit? And in my heart I decided that this too is vanity. [16][n] The wise person will have no more abiding remembrance than the fool; for in days to come both will have been forgotten. How is it that the wise person dies* like the fool! [17]Therefore I detested life, since for me the work that is done under the sun is bad; for all is vanity and a chase after wind.

Study of the Fruits of Toil

To Others the Profits. [18]And I detested all the fruits of my toil under the sun, because I must leave them to the one who is to come after me. [19]And who knows whether that one will be wise or a fool? Yet that one will take control of all the fruits of my toil and wisdom under the sun. This also is vanity. [20]So my heart turned to despair over all the fruits of my toil under the sun. [21]For here is one who has toiled with wisdom and knowledge and skill, and that one's legacy must be left to another who has not toiled for it. This also is vanity and a great evil. [22][o] For what profit comes to mortals from all the toil and anxiety of heart with which they toil under the sun? [23]Every day sorrow and grief are their occupation; even at night their hearts are not at rest. This also is vanity.

[24]* [p] There is nothing better for mortals than to eat and drink and provide themselves with good things from their toil. Even this, I saw, is from the hand of God. [25]For who can eat or drink apart from God? [26]* [q] For to the one who pleases God, he gives wisdom and knowledge and joy; but to the one who displeases, God gives the task of gathering possessions for the one who pleases God. This also is vanity and a chase after wind.

CHAPTER 3

See RG 261–67

No One Can Determine the Right Time To Act

[1] * There is an appointed time for everything,
and a time for every affair under the heavens.
[2] A time to give birth, and a time to die;
a time to plant, and a time to uproot the plant.
[3] A time to kill, and a time to heal;
a time to tear down, and a time to build.
[4] A time to weep, and a time to laugh;
a time to mourn, and a time to dance.
[5] A time to scatter stones, and a time to gather them;

2:12 What . . . been done: the verse is difficult and elliptical. The words "He can do only" have been added for clarity. The two halves of the verse have been reversed. The author argues that it is useless to repeat the royal experiment described in vv. 1–11. The results would only be the same.

2:14 Yet I knew . . . befalls both: the author quotes a traditional saying upholding the advantages of wisdom, but then qualifies it. Nothing, not even wisdom itself, can give someone absolute control over their destiny and therefore guarantee any advantage.

2:16 The wise person dies: death, until now only alluded to (vv. 14–15), takes center stage and will constantly appear in the author's reflections through the remainder of the book.

2:24–26 The author is not advocating unrestrained indulgence. Rather he counsels acceptance of the good things God chooses to give. This is the first of seven similar conclusions that Qoheleth provides; see 3:12–13, 22; 5:17–18; 8:15; 9:7–9; 11:9.

2:26 According to 7:15 and 9:1–3, God does not make an objective, evidential, moral distinction between saint and sinner. God "gives" as God pleases.

3:1–8 The fourteen pairs of opposites describe various human activities. The poem affirms that God has determined the appropriate moment or "time" for each. Human beings cannot know that moment; further, the wider course of events and purposes fixed by God are beyond them as well.

l: Eccl 1:3, 17; Sir 44:9. *m:* Eccl 9:2–3. *n:* Eccl 1:11; Wis 2:4. *o:* Eccl 1:3. *p:* Eccl 3:12–13, 22; 5:17–19; 8:15. *q:* Eccl 7:26; Prv 13:22.

a time to embrace, and a time to be far
from embraces.
[6] A time to seek, and a time to lose;
a time to keep, and a time to cast away.
[7] A time to rend, and a time to sew;
a time to be silent, and a time to speak.
[8] A time to love, and a time to hate;
a time of war, and a time of peace.

[9r] What profit have workers from their
toil? [10]I have seen the business that God has
given to mortals to be busied about. [11s] God
has made everything appropriate to its time,
but has put the timeless[*] into their hearts so
they cannot find out, from beginning to end,
the work which God has done. [12t] I recognized that there is nothing better than to rejoice and to do well during life. [13]Moreover,
that all can eat and drink and enjoy the good
of all their toil—this is a gift of God. [14]I recognized that whatever God does will endure
forever; there is no adding to it, or taking
from it. Thus has God done that he may be
revered. [15*][u] What now is has already been;
what is to be, already is: God retrieves what
has gone by.

The Problem of Retribution. [16v] And still
under the sun in the judgment place I saw
wickedness, and wickedness also in the seat
of justice. [17w] I said in my heart, both the just
and the wicked God will judge, since a time
is set for every affair and for every work.[*] [18]I
said in my heart: As for human beings, it is
God's way of testing them and of showing
that they are in themselves like beasts. [19]For
the lot of mortals and the lot of beasts is the
same lot: The one dies as well as the other.
Both have the same life breath. Human beings have no advantage over beasts, but all is
vanity. [20x] Both go to the same place; both
were made from the dust, and to the dust
they both return. [21]Who knows[*] if the life
breath of mortals goes upward and the life
breath of beasts goes earthward? [22y] And I
saw that there is nothing better for mortals
than to rejoice in their work; for this is their
lot. Who will let them see what is to come
after them?[z]

CHAPTER 4

See RG 261–67

Vanity of Toil. [1] Again I saw all the oppressions that take place under the sun: the
tears of the victims with none to comfort[*]
them! From the hand of their oppressors
comes violence, and there is none to comfort
them![a] [2]And those now dead, I declared
more fortunate in death than are the living to
be still alive.[b] [3]And better off than both is the
yet unborn, who has not seen the wicked
work that is done under the sun. [4]Then I saw
that all toil and skillful work is the rivalry of
one person with another. This also is vanity
and a chase after wind.

[5] "Fools fold their arms
and consume their own flesh"—[*]
[6] Better is one handful with tranquility
than two with toil and a chase after
wind!

Companions and Successors. [7]Again I
saw this vanity under the sun: [8]those all
alone with no companion, with neither child
nor sibling—with no end to all their toil, and
no satisfaction from riches. For whom do I
toil and deprive myself of good things? This
also is vanity and a bad business. [9]Two are

3:11 The timeless: others translate "eternity," "the world," or "darkness." The author credits God with keeping human beings ignorant about God's "work"—present and future.

3:15 The verse is difficult. Literally it reads "and God seeks out what was pursued." It appears to be a variation of the theme in 1:9, "There is nothing new under the sun."

3:17 A time is set . . . work: another possible reading would see this verse referring to a judgment in or after death: "a time for every affair and for every work *there*" (that is, in death or in Sheol).

3:21 Who knows: the author presumes a negative answer: "No one knows." In place of speculation on impossible questions, the author counsels enjoyment of what is possible (cf. v. 22; but see also 2:10–11).

4:1 Oppressions . . . victims . . . none to comfort: the author obviously feels deeply about the plight of the oppressed, but he seems to feel powerless to do anything. The repetition of "none to comfort" is purposeful, and emphatic.

4:5 Consume their own flesh: an enigmatic statement. In the context of vv. 4 and 6 it seems to warn that those who refuse to work for the necessities of life will suffer hunger and impair their bodily health. But the verse could also be intended for the industrious: Even the lazy may manage to have "their own flesh," that is, have sufficient food to eat.

r: Eccl 1:3. *s:* Eccl 8:17; 11:5. *t:* Eccl 2:24. *u:* Eccl 1:9. *v:* Eccl 4:1. *w:* Eccl 8:6a; 11:9; 12:14. *x:* Eccl 12:7; Gn 3:19; Sir 17:2. *y:* Eccl 3:12–13; 5:17–18. *z:* Eccl 8:7; 10:14. *a:* Eccl 3:16; 5:7; 9:4–5. *b:* Eccl 6:3–5.

better than one: They get a good wage for their toil. [10]If the one falls, the other will help the fallen one. But woe to the solitary person! If that one should fall, there is no other to help. [11]So also, if two sleep together, they keep each other warm. How can one alone keep warm? [12]Where one alone may be overcome, two together can resist. A three-ply cord* is not easily broken.

[13*] Better is a poor but wise youth than an old but foolish king who no longer knows caution; [14]for from a prison house he came forth to reign; despite his kingship he was born poor. [15]I saw all the living, those who move about under the sun, with the second youth who will succeed him.* [16]There is no end to all this people, to all who were before them; yet the later generations will not have joy in him. This also is vanity and a chase after wind.

Vanity of Many Words. [17c] Guard your step when you go to the house of God.* Draw near for obedience, rather than for the fools' offering of sacrifice; for they know not how to keep from doing evil.

CHAPTER 5

See RG 261–67

[1*] Be not hasty in your utterance and let not your heart be quick to utter a promise in God's presence. God is in heaven and you are on earth; therefore let your words be few.[d]

[2] As dreams come along with many cares,
so a fool's voice along with a
multitude of words.

[3e] When you make a vow to God, delay not its fulfillment. For God has no pleasure in fools; fulfill what you have vowed. [4]It is better not to make a vow than make it and not fulfill it. [5]Let not your utterances make you guilty, and say not before his representative, "It was a mistake." Why should God be angered by your words and destroy the works of your hands? [6f] Despite many dreams, futilities, and a multitude of words, fear God!

Gain and Loss of Goods. [7g] If you see oppression of the poor, and violation of rights and justice in the realm, do not be astonished by the fact, for the high official has another higher than he watching him and above these are others higher still—. [8]But profitable for a land in such circumstances is a king concerned about cultivation.*

[9h] The covetous are never satisfied with money, nor lovers of wealth with their gain; so this too is vanity. [10]Where there are great riches, there are also many to devour them. Of what use are they to the owner except as a feast for the eyes alone? [11]Sleep is sweet to the laborer, whether there is little or much to eat; but the abundance of the rich allows them no sleep.

[12]This is a grievous evil which I have seen under the sun: riches hoarded by their owners to their own hurt. [13]Should the riches be lost through some misfortune, they may have offspring when they have no means. [14i] As they came forth from their mother's womb, so again shall they return, naked as they came, having nothing from their toil to bring with them. [15]This too is a grievous evil, that they go just as they came. What then does it profit them to toil for the wind? [16]All their days they eat in gloom with great vexation, sickness and resentment.

[17j] Here is what I see as good: It is appro-

4:12 A three-ply cord: an ancient proverb known centuries before biblical times. The progression ("two together . . . three-ply") seems to imply, "If two are good, three are even better."

4:13–16 This passage deals with kingship and succession, but is obscure.

4:15 The king is no sooner dead than the people transfer their allegiance to his successor.

4:17 The house of God: the Temple in Jerusalem. **Obedience . . . sacrifice**: the Temple was the place not only for sacrifice but also for instruction in the Law. Sacrifice without obedience was unacceptable; cf. 1 Sm 15:22; Hos 6:6.

5:1–6 Further counsels on prudence and circumspection in fulfilling one's religious obligations. It is not the multitude of words but one's sincerity that counts in the acknowledgment of God's sovereignty (v. 1), especially through obedience (4:17) and reverence (v. 6).

5:8 A king concerned about cultivation: the Hebrew text is ambiguous and obscure. The author does not criticize the oppression he describes in v. 7. Now perhaps he expresses the hope that the king would use his power to upbuild agriculture in order to alleviate the hunger and suffering of the poor and oppressed.

c: 1 Sm 15:22; Ps 40:7–9; Prv 15:8; 21:3; Hos 6:6. *d:* Ps 115:3, 16; Mt 6:7; Jas 1:19. *e:* Nm 30:3; Dt 23:22–24; Prv 20:25; Sir 18:22–23. *f:* Eccl 3:14. *g:* Eccl 3:16; 4:1. *h:* Eccl 4:8; Prv 28:22. *i:* Jb 1:21; 1 Tm 6:7. *j:* Eccl 2:24.

priate to eat and drink and prosper from all
the toil one toils at under the sun during the
limited days of life God gives us; for this is
our lot. 18 Those to whom God gives riches
and property, and grants power to partake of
them, so that they receive their lot and find
joy in the fruits of their toil: This is a gift
from God. 19 For they will hardly dwell on
the shortness of life, because God lets them
busy themselves with the joy of their heart.*

See RG 261–67

CHAPTER 6

Limited Worth of Enjoyment. 1 There
is another evil I have seen under the sun, and
it weighs heavily upon humankind: 2[k] There
is one to whom God gives riches and property and honor, and who lacks nothing the
heart could desire; yet God does not grant
the power to partake of them, but a stranger
devours them. This is vanity and a dire
plague. 3 Should one have a hundred children
and live many years, no matter to what great
age, still if one has not the full benefit of
those goods, I proclaim that the child born
dead, even if left unburied, is more fortunate.* 4[l] Though it came in vain and goes
into darkness and its name is enveloped in
darkness, 5 though it has not seen the sun or
known anything, yet the dead child has more
peace. 6 Should such a one live twice a thousand years and not enjoy those goods, do not
both go to the same place?*

7 All human toil is for the mouth,* yet the
appetite is never satisfied. 8 What profit have
the wise compared to fools, or what profit
have the lowly in knowing how to conduct
themselves in life? 9 "What the eyes see is
better than what the desires wander after."*
This also is vanity and a chase after wind.

II. Qoheleth's Conclusions

10 Whatever is, was long ago given its name,
and human nature is known; mortals cannot
contend in judgment with One who is
stronger.* 11 For the more words, the more
vanity; what profit is there for anyone?
12[m] For who knows what is good for mortals
in life, the limited days of their vain life, spent
like a shadow? Because who can tell them
what will come afterward under the sun?[n]

A. No One Can Find Out the Best Way of Acting

CHAPTER 7

See RG 261–67

Critique of Sages on the Day of Adversity

1 A good name is better than good
ointment,*
and the day of death than the day of
birth.[o]
2 It is better to go to the house of mourning
than to the house of feasting,
For that is the end of every mortal,
and the living should take it to heart.[p]
3 Sorrow is better than laughter;
when the face is sad, the heart grows
wise.
4 The heart of the wise is in the house of
mourning,
but the heart of fools is in the house of
merriment.
5 It is better to listen to the rebuke of the
wise
than to listen to the song of fools;
6 For as the crackling of thorns under a
pot,
so is the fool's laughter.

5:19 The joys of life, though temporary and never assured, keep one from dwelling on the ills which afflict humanity.

6:3 Even a large family and exceptionally long life cannot compensate for the absence of good things and the joy which they bring.

6:6 Same place: the grave; cf. 3:20; 12:7.

6:7 The mouth: symbolic of human desires.

6:9 Compare the English proverb, "A bird in the hand is worth two in the bush." However, it could also mean, "The seeing of the eyes is better than the wandering of the desire," with the emphasis on the actions of seeing and desiring. Seeing is a way of possessing whereas desire, by definition, can remain frustrated and unfulfilled.

6:10–11 One who is stronger is, of course, God. **The more vanity**: contending with God is futile.

7:1 Ointment: a good name can be affirmed only with death, when one is normally anointed. The author dialogues in this section (vv. 1–14) with traditional wisdom, alternately affirming or countering its assertions. The real value of traditional wisdom lies in its ability to provoke one to thought and reflection, and not to absolve one from such activity.

k: Eccl 2:18–19. *l:* Eccl 4:2–3; Jb 3:11, 16. *m:* Jb 8:9; 14:2; Ps 102:12. *n:* Eccl 3:22; 8:7. *o:* Eccl 4:2; Prv 22:1. *p:* Eccl 12:1.

This also is vanity.
7 Extortion can make a fool out of the
wise,
and a bribe corrupts the heart.
8 Better is the end of a thing than its
beginning;
better is a patient spirit than a lofty one.
9 Do not let anger upset your spirit,
for anger lodges in the bosom of a fool.

10 Do not say: How is it that former times
were better than these? For it is not out of
wisdom that you ask about this.
11 Wisdom is as good as an inheritance
and profitable to those who see the sun.

12* For the protection of wisdom is as the
protection of money; and knowledge is profitable because wisdom gives life to those
who possess it.
13 Consider the work of God. Who can
make straight what God has made crooked?[q]
14 On a good day enjoy good things, and on
an evil day consider: Both the one and the
other God has made, so that no one may find
the least fault with him.

Critique of Sages on Justice and Wicked-ness.
15* I have seen all manner of things in
my vain days: the just perishing in their justice, and the wicked living long in their
wickedness. 16 "Be not just to excess, and be
not overwise. Why work your own ruin?
17 Be not wicked to excess, and be not foolish. Why should you die before your time?"
18 It is good to hold to this rule, and not to let
that one go; but the one who fears God will
succeed with both.
19 Wisdom is a better defense for the wise
than ten princes in the city, 20[r] yet there is no
one on earth so just as to do good and never
sin. 21 Do not give your heart to every word
that is spoken; you may hear your servant
cursing you, 22 for your heart knows that you
have many times cursed others.
23 All these things I probed in wisdom. I
said, "I will acquire wisdom"; but it was far
beyond me. 24 What exists is far-reaching; it
is deep, very deep:* Who can find it out?
25*[s] I turned my heart toward knowledge; I
sought and pursued wisdom and its design,
and I recognized that wickedness is foolishness and folly is madness.

Critique of Advice on Women. 26[t] More
bitter than death I find the woman* who is a
hunter's trap, whose heart is a snare, whose
hands are prison bonds. The one who pleases
God will be delivered from her, but the one
who displeases will be entrapped by her.
27 See, this have I found, says Qoheleth,
adding one to one to find the sum. 28 What
my soul still seeks and has yet to find is this:
"One man out of a thousand have I found,
but a woman among them all I have not
found." 29 But this alone I have found: God
made humankind honest, but they have pursued many designs.

CHAPTER 8

See RG 261–67

Critique of Advice To Heed Authority

1 * Who is like the wise person,
and who knows the explanation of
things?
Wisdom illumines the face
and transforms a grim countenance.

2 Observe the command of the king, in
view of your oath to God. 3 Be not hasty to

7:12 St. Jerome's translation of v. 12b gives an edge to wisdom over money: "But learning and wisdom excel in this, that they bestow life on the one who possesses them."

7:15–24 The author continues both to affirm and to counter traditional wisdom. He affirms a certain validity to wisdom, but challenges complacency and mindless optimism. His sense of life's uncertainty and insecurity finds expression, for example, in the irony evident when v. 16 is read in the light of vv. 20–24: How can one be "excessively" just or wise, when justice and wisdom may be out of reach to begin with? The only sure thing is to "fear God" (v. 18).

7:24 Far-reaching . . . deep: the spatial metaphor here emphasizes wisdom's inaccessibility, a frequent theme in wisdom literature; cf. Jb 28; Prv 30:1–4; Sir 24:28–29; Bar 3:14–23.

7:25–29 The emphasis is on the devious designs of human beings in general, reflecting the viewpoint of Genesis.

7:26 More bitter than death . . . the woman: warnings against the scheming, adulterous woman are common in ancient wisdom (e.g., Prv 2:16–19, etc.).

8:1–4 The author continues to quote traditional wisdom but then to counter and qualify it. He concedes wisdom's advantages (v. 1), but then describes the subservience and sometimes demeaning demands required of the sage in the court of the king (vv. 2–4).

q: Eccl 1:15. *r:* Jb 9:2; 1 Kgs 8:46; Rom 3:23. *s:* Eccl 1:17. *t:* Prv 5:4.

withdraw from the king; do not persist in an unpleasant situation, for he does whatever he pleases. [4]His word is sovereign, and who can say to him, "What are you doing?"

[5*u] "Whoever observes a command knows no harm, and the wise heart knows times and judgments." [6v] Yes, there is a time and a judgment for everything. But it is a great evil for mortals [7w] that they are ignorant of what is to come; for who will make known to them how it will be? [8]No one is master of the breath of life so as to retain it, and none has mastery of the day of death. There is no exemption in wartime, nor does wickedness deliver those who practice it. [9]All these things I saw and I applied my heart to every work that is done under the sun, while one person tyrannizes over another for harm.

The Problem of Retribution. [10]Meanwhile I saw the wicked buried. They would come and go from the holy place. But those were forgotten in the city who had acted justly. This also is vanity.* [11]Because the sentence against an evil deed is not promptly executed, the human heart is filled with the desire to commit evil— [12*] because the sinner does evil a hundred times and survives. Though indeed I know that it shall be well with those who fear God, for their reverence toward him; [13]and that it shall not be well with the wicked, who shall not prolong their shadowy days, for their lack of reverence toward God.

[14]This is a vanity that occurs on earth: There are those who are just but are treated as though they had done evil, and those who are wicked but are treated as though they had done justly. This, too, I say is vanity. [15x] Therefore I praised joy, because there is nothing better for mortals under the sun than to eat and to drink and to be joyful; this will accompany them in their toil through the limited days of life God gives them under the sun.

[16]I applied my heart to know wisdom and to see the business that is done on earth, though neither by day nor by night do one's eyes see sleep, [17y] and I saw all the work of God: No mortal can find out the work that is done under the sun. However much mortals may toil in searching, no one finds it out; and even if the wise claim to know, they are unable to find it out.

B. No One Knows the Future

CHAPTER 9

See RG 261–67

[1]All this I have kept in my heart and all this I examined: The just, the wise, and their deeds are in the hand of God. Love from hatred* mortals cannot tell; both are before them. [2z] Everything is the same for everybody: the same lot for the just and the wicked, for the good, for the clean and the unclean, for the one who offers sacrifice and the one who does not. As it is for the good, so it is for the sinner; as it is for the one who takes an oath, so it is for the one who fears an oath. [3]Among all the things that are done under the sun, this is the worst, that there is one lot for all. Hence the hearts of human beings are filled with evil, and madness is in their hearts during life; and afterward—to the dead!

[4]For whoever is chosen among all the living has hope: "A live dog* is better off than a dead lion." [5a] For the living know that they are

8:5–9 The wise exhibit keen insight about human nature and the course of events (vv. 5–6a). Yet their knowledge and wisdom confront certain limits, such as the mystery of evil and the time and inevitability of death (vv. 6b–9).

8:10 This difficult verse seems to contrast the wicked, who die enjoying a good reputation as pious individuals, and the just, who are quietly forgotten.

8:12–17 The author admits that traditional wisdom affirms the long life and success of the just and the short unhappy life of the wicked (vv. 12b–13). But he points out clear exceptions: the wicked who live long, and the just who suffer for no apparent reason (v. 14). His puzzlement and frustration prompt a twofold response: acceptance of whatever joy God chooses to give each day, and honest acknowledgment that no one can discover "the work of God" (cf. 3:11; 7:13; 11:5).

9:1–3 Love from hatred . . . everything is the same: God seems to bestow divine favor or disfavor (love or hatred) indiscriminately on the just and wicked alike. More ominously, the arbitrariness and inevitability of death and adversity confront every human being, whether good or bad.

9:4–6 A live dog . . . no further recompense: human reason and experience persuaded Qoheleth that death with its fi-

u: Prv 19:16. *v:* Eccl 3:17; 9:12. *w:* Eccl 3:22; 6:12; 10:14. *x:* Eccl 2:24; 3:22; 5:17–18; 9:7. *y:* Eccl 3:11. *z:* Eccl 2:14; 3:15. *a:* Eccl 1:11; 2:16.

to die, but the dead no longer know anything.
There is no further recompense for them, because all memory of them is lost. 6 For them,
love and hatred and rivalry have long since
perished. Never again will they have part in
anything that is done under the sun.

7[b] Go, eat your bread* with joy and drink
your wine with a merry heart, because it is
now that God favors your works. 8 At all
times let your garments be white, and spare
not the perfume for your head. 9 Enjoy life
with the wife you love, all the days of the
vain life granted you under the sun. This is
your lot in life, for the toil of your labors under the sun. 10 Anything you can turn your
hand to, do with what power you have; for
there will be no work, no planning, no
knowledge, no wisdom in Sheol where you
are going.

The Time of Misfortune Is Not Known.
11 Again I saw under the sun that the race is
not won by the swift, nor the battle by the
valiant, nor a livelihood by the wise, nor
riches by the shrewd, nor favor by the experts; for a time of misfortune comes to all
alike. 12 Human beings no more know their
own time than fish taken in the fatal net or
birds trapped in the snare; like these, mortals
are caught when an evil time suddenly falls
upon them.

The Uncertain Future and the Sages. 13 On
the other hand I saw this wise deed under the
sun, which I thought magnificent. 14 Against
a small city with few inhabitants advanced a
mighty king, who surrounded it and threw
up great siegeworks about it. 15 But in the
city lived a man who, though poor, was wise,
and he delivered it through his wisdom. Yet
no one remembered this poor man.
16[c] Though I had said, "Wisdom is better
than force," yet the wisdom of the poor man
is despised and his words go unheeded.

17 The quiet words of the wise are better heeded
than the shout of a ruler of fools.
18 Wisdom is better than weapons of war,
but one bungler destroys much good.

CHAPTER 10

See RG 261–67

1 Dead flies corrupt and spoil the perfumer's oil;
more weighty than wisdom or wealth is a little folly!*
2 The wise heart turns to the right;
the foolish heart to the left.*

3 Even when walking in the street the fool,
lacking understanding, calls everyone a
fool.*
4 Should the anger of a ruler burst upon
you, do not yield your place; for calmness*
abates great offenses.
5 I have seen under the sun another evil,
like a mistake that proceeds from a tyrant: 6 a
fool put in high position, while the great and
the rich sit in lowly places. 7 I have seen
slaves on horseback, while princes* went on
foot like slaves.

8 Whoever digs a pit may fall into it,[d]
and whoever breaks through a wall, a snake may bite.
9 Whoever quarries stones may be hurt by them,

nality and annihilating power cruelly negates the supreme value—life, and with it, all possibilities (cf. v. 10). Faith in eternal life has its foundation only in hope and trust in God's promise and in God's love.

9:7–10 Go, eat your bread . . . enjoy life: the author confesses his inability to imprison God in a fixed and predictable way of acting. Thus he ponders a practical and pragmatic solution: Seize whatever opportunity one has to find joy, if God grants it.

10:1 Dead flies . . . a little folly: wisdom is vulnerable to even the smallest amount of folly. The collection of proverbs and sayings in chaps. 10 and 11 demonstrates the author's sharp insight and strengthens his credentials as a sage. It thus adds weight to his critique of the wisdom tradition's tendencies to self-assurance and naive optimism.

10:2 Right . . . left: the right hand is identified with power, moral goodness, favor; the left hand with ineptness and bad luck.

10:3 Calls everyone a fool: or, "tells everyone that he (himself) is a fool."

10:4 Calmness: a frequent motif of wisdom; silence and reserve characterize the wise, while boisterousness and impetuosity identify the fool.

10:6–7 A fool . . . the rich . . . slaves . . . princes: another wisdom motif: astonishment at the reversal of the usual order in the world and in human affairs.

10:8–9 A pit . . . a wall . . . stones . . . wood: popular sayings reflecting the need for caution and alertness against the unexpected. Snakes could find a home in the stone walls of ancient Palestine; cf. Am 5:19.

b: Eccl 2:24; 8:15; 11:9. *c:* Prv 24:5. *d:* Prv 26:27; Ps 7:16; Sir 27:29.

and whoever chops wood* is in danger
from it.

10 If the ax becomes dull, and the blade is not sharpened, then effort must be increased. But the advantage of wisdom is success.

11 If the snake bites before it is charmed,
then there is no advantage in a charmer.*
12 Words from the mouth of the wise win
favor,
but the lips of fools consume them.
13 [e] The beginning of their words is folly,
and the end of their talk is utter
madness;
14 yet fools multiply words.
No one knows what is to come,
for who can tell anyone what will be?[f]
15 The toil of fools wearies them,
so they do not know even the way to
town.

No One Knows What Evil Will Come

16 Woe to you, O land, whose king is a
youth,*
and whose princes feast in the morning!
17 Happy are you, O land, whose king is of
noble birth,
and whose princes dine at the right
time—
for vigor* and not in drinking bouts.
18 Because of laziness, the rafters sag;
when hands are slack, the house leaks.
19 A feast is made for merriment
and wine gives joy to the living,
but money answers* for everything.
20 Even in your thoughts do not curse the
king,
nor in the privacy of your bedroom
curse the rich;
For the birds of the air may carry your
voice,
a winged creature* may tell what you
say.

CHAPTER 11

See RG 261–67

1 * Send forth your bread upon the
face of the waters;
after a long time you may find it
again.
2 Make seven, or even eight portions;
you know not what misfortune may
come upon the earth.

No One Knows What Good Will Come

3 * When the clouds are full,
they pour out rain upon the earth.
Whether a tree falls to the south or to the
north,
wherever it falls, there shall it lie.
4 One who pays heed to the wind will
never sow,
and one who watches the clouds will
never reap.
5 Just as you do not know how the life
breath
enters the human frame in the
mother's womb,
So you do not know the work of God,
who is working in everything.[g]
6 In the morning sow your seed,
and at evening do not let your hand be
idle:
For you do not know which of the two
will be successful,

10:10–11 Ax . . . success . . . snake . . . charmer: possession of the proper skill (a form of "wisdom") can ensure success, as in the case of a sharpened ax; but one must use it before it is too late (v. 11). Cf. Sir 12:13.

10:16 A youth: thus too young and inexperienced to govern effectively. **Feast in the morning**: either concluding a whole night of revelry or beginning a new round of merry-making.

10:17 For vigor: or, "with self-control, restraint."

10:19 Money answers: a stark reminder that such a life requires money. It could also be an affirmation of the power of wealth: "Money conquers all."

10:20 Birds of the air . . . winged creature: a common motif in ancient literature, and a vivid reminder of the need for caution in dealing with the rich and powerful.

11:1–2 These two sayings can be understood against a commercial background. They acknowledge the uncertainty and risk such activity involves. At the same time they encourage action and a spirit of adventure. The first (v. 1) speaks of trade and overseas investment: Export your grain ("bread") to foreign markets and you may be surprised at the substantial profits. The second (v. 2) encourages diversification of investment (seven, or even eight shipments of grain) to insure against heavy losses.

11:3–6 Verses 3, 4, and 6 expand on the theme of uncertainty and human inability to assess accurately every situation. Verse 4, however, comments on the disadvantages of too much caution: Only those willing to risk will enjoy success. But only the Creator knows the mystery of the "work of God" (v. 5).

e: Eccl 5:2; 6:11. *f:* Eccl 3:22; 6:12; 10:14. *g:* Eccl 3:11; 7:13; 8:17.

or whether both alike will turn out
well.

Poem on Youth and Old Age. [7]* Light is
sweet! and it is pleasant for the eyes to see
the sun. [8]However many years mortals may
live, let them, as they enjoy them all, remember that the days of darkness will be
many. All that is to come is vanity.

[9] Rejoice, O youth, while you are young
and let your heart be glad in the days
of your youth.
Follow the ways of your heart,
the vision of your eyes;
Yet understand regarding all this
that God will bring you to judgment.
[10] Banish misery from your heart
and remove pain from your body,
for youth and black hair are
fleeting.*

CHAPTER 12

See RG 261–67

[1]* Remember your Creator in the
days of your youth,
before the evil days come
And the years approach of which you
will say,
"I have no pleasure in them";
[2] Before the sun is darkened
and the light and the moon and the
stars
and the clouds return after the rain;
[3] * When the guardians of the house
tremble,
and the strong men are bent;
When the women who grind are idle
because they are few,
and those who look through the
windows grow blind;
[4] When the doors to the street are shut,
and the sound of the mill is low;
When one rises at the call of a bird,
and all the daughters of song are quiet;
[5] When one is afraid of heights,
and perils in the street;
When the almond tree blooms,
and the locust grows sluggish
and the caper berry is without effect,
Because mortals go to their lasting home,
and mourners go about the streets;
[6] * Before the silver cord is snapped
and the golden bowl is broken,
And the pitcher is shattered at the spring,
and the pulley is broken at the well,
[7] And the dust returns to the earth as it
once was,
and the life breath returns to God who
gave it.* [h]
[8] Vanity of vanities, says Qoheleth,
all things are vanity![i]

Epilogue. [9]* Besides being wise, Qoheleth
taught the people knowledge, and weighed,
scrutinized and arranged many proverbs.
[10]Qoheleth sought to find appropriate sayings, and to write down true sayings with
precision. [11]The sayings of the wise are like
goads; like fixed spikes are the collected
sayings given by one shepherd.* [12j] As to
more than these,* my son, beware. Of the
making of many books there is no end, and

11:7–10 The concluding part of the book opens with a final bittersweet homage to life and an enthusiastic encouragement to rejoice in its gifts while they are within grasp.

11:10 Fleeting: lit., "vanity."

12:1–7 The homage to life of 11:7–10 is deliberately balanced by the sombre yet shimmering radiance of this poem on old age and death. The poem's enigmatic imagery has often been interpreted allegorically, especially in vv. 3–5. Above all it seeks to evoke an atmosphere as well as an attitude toward death and old age.

12:3–5 An allegorical reading of these verses sees references to the human body—"guardians": the arms; "strong men": the legs; "women who grind": the teeth; "those who look": the eyes; "the doors": the lips; "daughters of song": the voice; "the almond tree blooms": resembling the white hair of old age; "the locust . . . sluggish": the stiffness in movement of the aged; "the caper berry": a stimulant for appetite.

12:6 The golden bowl suspended by the silver cord is a symbol of life; the snapping of the cord and the breaking of the bowl, a symbol of death. **The pitcher . . . the pulley**: another pair of metaphors for life and its ending.

12:7 Death is portrayed in terms of the description of creation in Gn 2:7; the body corrupts in the grave, and the life breath (lit., "spirit"), or gift of life, returns to God who had breathed upon what he had formed.

12:9 A disciple briefly describes and praises the master's skill and reputation as a sage.

12:11 One shepherd: perhaps referring to the book's author, who gathers or "shepherds" together its contents. God could also be "the one shepherd," the ultimate depository and source of true wisdom.

12:12 As to more than these: the words seem to refer to the writings of Ecclesiastes and other sages. They are adequate and sufficient; any more involves exhaustive labor.

h: Eccl 3:20–21; Jb 34:14–15. *i:* Eccl 1:2. *j:* Eccl 1:18.

in much study there is weariness for the flesh.

13* k The last word, when all is heard: Fear God and keep his commandments, for this concerns all humankind; 14 l because God will bring to judgment every work, with all its hidden qualities, whether good or bad.

12:13–14 These words reaffirm traditional wisdom doctrine such as fear of God and faithful obedience, perhaps lest some of the more extreme statements of the author be misunderstood. Although the epilogue has been interpreted as a criticism of the book's author, it is really a summary that betrays the unruffled spirit of later sages, who were not shocked by Qoheleth's statements. They honored him as a *hakam* or sage (v. 9), even as they preserved his statements about the futility of life (v. 8), and the mystery of divine judgment (8:17; 11:5).

k: Eccl 5:6. *l:* Eccl 11:9.

See RG 267–71

The Song of Songs

The Song of Songs (or Canticle of Canticles) is an exquisite collection of love lyrics, arranged to tell a dramatic tale of mutual desire and courtship. It presents an inspired portrayal of ideal human love, a resounding affirmation of the goodness of human sexuality that is applicable to the sacredness and the depth of married union.

Although the poem is attributed to Solomon in the traditional title (1:1), the language and style of the work, among other considerations, suggest a time after the end of the Babylonian exile (538 B.C.) when an unknown poet collected extant love poems, perhaps composing new material, and arranged the whole into the masterpiece we have before us. Some scholars argue the possibility of female authorship for at least portions of the Song.

The structure of the Song is difficult to analyze; this translation regards it as a lyric dialogue, with dramatic movement and interest. In both form and content, sections of the Song bear great similarity to the secular love songs of ancient Egypt and the "Sacred Marriage" cult songs of Mesopotamia which celebrate the union between divine partners.

While the lovers in the Song are clearly human figures, both Jewish and Christian traditions across the centuries have adopted "allegorical" interpretations. The Song is seen as a beautiful picture of the ideal Israel, the chosen people whom the Lord leads by degrees to a greater understanding and closer union in the bond of perfect love. Such readings of the Song build on Israel's covenant tradition. Isaiah (Is 5:1–7; 54:4–8; 62:5), Jeremiah (Jer 2:2, 3, 32), and Ezekiel (Ez 16; 23) all characterize the covenant between the Lord and Israel as a marriage. Hosea the prophet sees the idolatry of Israel in the adultery of Gomer (Hos 1–3). He also represents the Lord speaking to Israel's heart (Hos 2:16) and changing her into a new spiritual people, purified by the Babylonian captivity and betrothed anew to her divine Lover "in justice and uprightness, in love and mercy" (Hos 2:21). Similar imagery has also been used frequently in Jewish mystical texts. The Song offers a welcome corrective to negative applications of the theological metaphor of the marriage/covenant in some prophetic texts. It frequently proclaims a joyous reciprocity between the lovers and highlights the active role of the female partner, now a pure figure to be cherished rather than an adulterous woman to be punished and abused. See also Is 62:3–5.

Christian tradition has followed Israel's example in using marriage as an image for the relationship with God. This image is found extensively in the New Testament (Mt 9:15; 25:1–13; Jn 3:29; 2 Cor 11:2; Eph 5:23–32; Rev 19:7–9; 21:9–11). Thus the Song has been read as a sublime portrayal and praise of this mutual love of the Lord and his people. Christian writers have interpreted the Song in terms of the union between Christ and the Church and of the union between Christ and the individual soul, particularly in the writings of Origen and St. Bernard.

CHAPTER 1

See RG 267–71

1 The Song of Songs,* which is Solomon's.

The Woman Speaks of Her Lover

W 2 * [a] Let him kiss me with kisses of his
mouth,
for your love is better than wine,*
3 better than the fragrance of your
perfumes.*
Your name is a flowing perfume—
therefore young women love you.
4 [b] Draw me after you! Let us run!*
The king has brought me to his bed
chambers.
Let us exult and rejoice in you;
let us celebrate your love: it is
beyond wine!
Rightly do they love you!

Love's Boast

W 5 I am black and beautiful,
Daughters of Jerusalem*—
Like the tents of Qedar,
like the curtains of Solomon.
6 Do not stare at me because I am so
black,*
because the sun has burned me.
The sons of my mother were angry
with me;
they charged me with the care of the
vineyards:
my own vineyard I did not take
care of.

Love's Inquiry

W 7 Tell me, you whom my soul loves,
where you shepherd,* where you
give rest at midday.
Why should I be like one wandering
after the flocks of your companions?
M 8 If you do not know,
most beautiful among women,
Follow the tracks of the flock
and pasture your lambs*
near the shepherds' tents.

Love's Vision

M 9 To a mare among Pharaoh's chariotry*
I compare you, my friend:
10 Your cheeks lovely in pendants,
your neck in jewels.
11 We will make pendants of gold for
you,
and ornaments of silver.

1:1 Song of Songs: in Hebrew and Aramaic the idiom "the X of Xs" denotes the superlative (e.g., "king of kings" = "the highest king"; cf. Dt 10:17; Eccl 1:2; 12:8; Ezr 7:12; Dn 2:37). The ascription of authorship to Solomon is traditional. The heading may also mean "for Solomon" or "about Solomon."

1:2–8:14 This translation augments the canonical text of the Song with the letters *W*, *M*, and *D*, placed in the margin, to indicate which of the characters in the Song is speaking: the woman, the man, or the "Daughters of Jerusalem." This interpretive gloss follows an early Christian scribal practice, attested in some Septuagint manuscripts from the first half of the first millennium A.D.

1:2–7 The woman and her female chorus address the man, here viewed as king and shepherd (both are familiar metaphors for God; cf. Ps 23:1; Is 40:11; Jn 10:1–16). There is a wordplay between "kiss" (Hebrew *nashaq*) and "drink" (*shaqah*), anticipating 8:1–2. The change from third person ("let him kiss . . . ") to second person (" . . . for your love . . . ") is not uncommon in the Song and elsewhere (1:4; 2:4; etc.; Ps 23:1–3, 4–5, 6; etc.) and reflects the woman's move from interior monologue to direct address to her partner.

1:3 Your perfumes: *shemen* (perfume) is a play on *shem* (name).

1:4 Another change, but from second to third person (cf. 1:2). The "king" metaphor recurs in 1:12; 3:5–11; 7:6. **Let us exult**: perhaps she is addressing young women, calling on them to join in the praise of her lover.

1:5 Daughters of Jerusalem: the woman contrasts herself with the elite city women, who act as her female "chorus" (5:9; 6:1). **Qedar**: a Syrian desert region whose name suggests darkness; tents were often made of black goat hair. **Curtains**: tent coverings, or tapestries. **Solomon**: it could also be read Salma, a region close to Qedar.

1:6 So black: tanned from working outdoors in her brothers' vineyards, unlike the city women she addresses. **My own vineyard**: perhaps the woman herself; see 8:8–10 for her relationship to her brothers.

1:7 Shepherd: a common metaphor for kings. Here and elsewhere in the Song (3:1; 5:8; 6:1), the woman expresses her desire to be in the company of her lover. The search for the lover and her failure to find him create a degree of tension. Only at the end (8:5–14) do the lovers finally possess each other.

1:8 Pasture your lambs: both the woman and the man act as shepherds in the Song.

1:9–11 The man compares the woman's beauty to the rich adornment of the royal chariot of Pharaoh. **My friend**: a special feminine form of the word "friend," appearing only in the Song (1:15; 2:2, 10, 13; 4:1, 7; 5:2; 6:4) and used to express endearment and equality in love. Cf. Hos 3:1 for the use of the masculine form of the term in a context with sexual overtones.

a: Sg 4:10. *b:* Sg 4:10.

How Near Is Love!

W 12 While the king was upon his couch,
my spikenard* gave forth its fragrance.
13 My lover* is to me a sachet of myrrh;
between my breasts he lies.
14 My lover is to me a cluster of henna*
from the vineyards of En-gedi.

M 15 *c* How beautiful you are, my friend,
how beautiful! your eyes are doves!*

W 16 How beautiful you are, my lover—
handsome indeed!
Verdant indeed is our couch;*
17 the beams of our house are cedars,
our rafters, cypresses.

CHAPTER 2

See RG 267–71

W 1 I am a flower of Sharon,*
a lily of the valleys.

M 2 Like a lily among thorns,
so is my friend among women.

W 3 Like an apple tree among the trees of the woods,
so is my lover among men.
In his shadow* I delight to sit,
and his fruit is sweet to my taste.
4 *d* He brought me to the banquet hall*
and his glance at me signaled love.
5 *e* Strengthen me with raisin cakes,*
refresh me with apples,
for I am sick with love.
6 *f* His left hand is under my head
and his right arm embraces me.
7 *g* I adjure you, Daughters of Jerusalem,*
by the gazelles and the does of the field,
Do not awaken, or stir up love
until it is ready.

Her Lover's Visit Remembered

W 8 The sound of my lover! here he comes*
springing across the mountains,
leaping across the hills.
9 My lover is like a gazelle*
or a young stag.
See! He is standing behind our wall,
gazing through the windows,
peering through the lattices.
10 My lover speaks and says to me,

M "Arise, my friend, my beautiful one,
and come!
11 For see, the winter is past,
the rains are over and gone.
12 The flowers appear on the earth,
the time of pruning the vines has come,
and the song of the turtledove is heard in our land.
13 The fig tree puts forth its figs,
and the vines, in bloom, give forth fragrance.
Arise, my friend, my beautiful one,
and come!

1:12 Spikenard: a precious perfumed ointment from India; in 4:13–14, a metaphor for the woman herself.

1:13 My lover: the woman's favorite term for her partner (used 27 times). **Myrrh**: an aromatic resin of balsam or roses used in cosmetics, incense, and medicines.

1:14 Henna: a plant which bears white scented flowers, used in cosmetics and medicines. **En-gedi**: a Judean desert oasis overlooking the Dead Sea.

1:15 Doves: doves are pictured in the ancient world as messengers of love.

1:16–17 Continuing the royal metaphor, the meeting place of the lovers, a shepherd's hut of green branches, becomes a palace with beams of cedar and rafters of cypress when adorned with their love.

2:1 Flower of Sharon: probably the narcissus, which grows in the fertile Plain of Sharon lying between Mount Carmel and Jaffa on the Mediterranean coast. **Lily**: the lotus plant.

2:3 Shadow: suggestive of protection (cf. Jgs 9:15; Ez 17:23; Ps 17:8; 121:5) and, here, of the woman's joy in the presence of her lover.

2:4–6 The banquet hall: the sweet things of the table, the embrace of the woman and man, express the richness of their affection and the intimacy of their love.

2:5 Raisin cakes: perhaps pastries used in the worship of the fertility goddess (cf. Hos 3:1; Jer 7:18; 44:19). **Apples**: this is the common translation of a fruit that cannot be identified (cf. 2:3; 8:5); it appears frequently in Sumerian love poetry associated with the worship of the goddess Inanna. **Sick**: love-sickness is a popular motif in ancient love poetry.

2:7 Cf. 3:5; 5:8; 8:4. **By the gazelles and the does**: perhaps a mitigated invocation of the divinity based on the assonance in Hebrew of the names of these animals with terms for God.

2:8–13 In this sudden change of scene, the woman describes a rendezvous and pictures her lover hastening toward her dwelling until his voice is heard calling her to him.

2:9 Gazelle: a frequent motif in ancient poems from Mesopotamia.

c: Sg 4:1, 7. *d:* Sg 1:4. *e:* Sg 5:8. *f:* Sg 8:3. *g:* Sg 3:5; 8:4.

14 My dove in the clefts of the rock,*
in the secret recesses of the cliff,
Let me see your face,
let me hear your voice,
For your voice is sweet,
and your face is lovely."
W 15 Catch us the foxes,* the little foxes
that damage the vineyards; for our vineyards are in bloom!
16 [h] My lover belongs to me and I to him;
he feeds among the lilies.
17 [i] Until the day grows cool* and the shadows flee,
roam, my lover,
Like a gazelle or a young stag
upon the rugged mountains.

CHAPTER 3

See RG 267–71

Loss and Discovery

W 1 [j] On my bed at night I sought him*
whom my soul loves—
I sought him but I did not find him.
2 "Let me rise then and go about the city,*
through the streets and squares;
Let me seek him whom my soul loves."
I sought him but I did not find him.
3 The watchmen found me,
as they made their rounds in the city:
"Him whom my soul loves—have you seen him?"
4 [k] Hardly had I left them
when I found him whom my soul loves.*
I held him and would not let him go
until I had brought him to my mother's house,
to the chamber of her who conceived me.
5 [l] I adjure you, Daughters of Jerusalem,
by the gazelles and the does of the field,
Do not awaken or stir up love
until it is ready.

Solomon's Wedding Procession

D 6 [m] Who is this coming up from the desert,*
like columns of smoke
Perfumed with myrrh and frankincense,
with all kinds of exotic powders?
7 See! it is the litter of Solomon;
sixty valiant men surround it,
of the valiant men of Israel:
8 All of them expert with the sword,
skilled in battle,
Each with his sword at his side
against the terrors* of the night.
9 King Solomon made himself an enclosed litter
of wood from Lebanon.
10 He made its columns of silver,
its roof of gold,
Its seat of purple cloth,
its interior lovingly fitted.*
Daughters of Jerusalem, 11 go out
and look upon King Solomon
In the crown with which his mother has crowned him
on the day of his marriage,
on the day of the joy of his heart.

2:14 The woman is addressed as though she were a dove in a mountain cleft out of sight and reach.

2:15 A snatch of song in answer to the request of 2:14; cf. 8:13–14. **Foxes**: they threaten to disturb the security of vineyards. The vineyards are women sought after by young lovers, i.e., foxes.

2:17 Grows cool: in the evening when the sun is going down. Cf. Gn 3:8. **Rugged**: Hebrew obscure; some interpret it as a geographical name; others, in the sense of spices (cf. 8:14); still others, of sacrifice (Gn 15:10); the image probably refers here to the woman herself.

3:1–5 See the parallel in 5:2–8.

3:2 The motif of seeking/finding here and elsewhere is used by later Christian and Jewish mystics to speak of the soul's search for the divine.

3:4 Whom my soul loves: the fourfold repetition of this phrase in vv. 1–4 highlights the depth of the woman's emotion and desire. **Mother's house**: cf. 8:2; a place of safety and intimacy, one which implicitly signifies approval of the lovers' relationship.

3:6–11 This may be an independent poem. In context it portrays the lover as King Solomon, escorted by sixty armed men, coming in royal procession to meet a bride.

3:8 Terrors: cf. Ps 91:5; perhaps bandits lying in wait, unidentified dangers lurking in darkness.

3:10 Lovingly fitted: translation uncertain. The phrase "Daughters of Jerusalem" is read here with the following verse.

h: Sg 6:3; 7:10. *i:* Sg 4:6; 8:14. *j:* Sg 5:2–8. *k:* Sg 8:2. *l:* Sg 2:7; 8:4. *m:* Sg 6:10; 8:5.

CHAPTER 4

See RG 267–71

The Beauty of the Woman

M 1 [n,o] How beautiful you are, my friend,
how beautiful you are!
Your eyes are doves
behind your veil.
Your hair is like a flock of goats
streaming down Mount Gilead.*
2 Your teeth* are like a flock of ewes to
be shorn,
that come up from the washing,
All of them big with twins,
none of them barren.
3 Like a scarlet strand, your lips,
and your mouth—lovely!
Like pomegranate* halves, your
cheeks
behind your veil.
4 [p] Like a tower of David, your neck,
built in courses,
A thousand shields hanging upon it,
all the armor of warriors.*
5 [q] Your breasts are like two fawns,
twins of a gazelle
feeding among the lilies.
6 [r] Until the day grows cool
and the shadows flee,
I shall go to the mountain of myrrh,
to the hill of frankincense.*
7 You are beautiful in every way, my
friend,
there is no flaw in you!*
8 With me from Lebanon, my bride!
With me from Lebanon, come!
Descend from the peak of Amana,
from the peak of Senir and Hermon,*
From the lairs of lions,
from the leopards' heights.
9 [s] You have ravished my heart, my
sister,* my bride;
you have ravished my heart with
one glance of your eyes,
with one bead of your necklace.
10 [t] How beautiful is your love,
my sister, my bride,
How much better is your love than
wine,
and the fragrance of your perfumes
than any spice!
11 Your lips drip honey,* my bride,
honey and milk are under your
tongue;
And the fragrance of your garments
is like the fragrance of Lebanon.

The Lover's Garden

M 12 [u] A garden enclosed, my sister, my
bride,
a garden enclosed, a fountain sealed!*
13 Your branches are a grove of
pomegranates,
with fruits of choicest yield:
Henna with spikenard,
14 spikenard and saffron,
Sweet cane and cinnamon,
with all kinds of frankincense;
Myrrh and aloes,
with all the finest spices;*
15 A garden fountain, a well of living
water,
streams flowing from Lebanon.
16 Awake,* north wind!
Come, south wind!

4:1 This section (vv. 1–7) begins a *wasf*, a traditional poetic form describing the physical attributes of one's partner in terms of the natural world (cf. 5:10–16; 6:5b–7; 7:1–7). **Veil**: women of the region customarily veiled their faces for some occasions (cf. 4:3; 6:7; Gn 24:65–67; 38:14–19).

4:2 Teeth: praised for whiteness and evenness.

4:3 Pomegranate: a fruit with a firm skin and deep red color. The woman's cheek (or perhaps her brow) is compared, in roundness and tint, to a half-pomegranate.

4:4 The ornaments about her neck are compared to the trophies and armaments on the city walls. Cf. 1 Kgs 10:10; 14:26–28; Ez 27:10.

4:6 Mountain of myrrh . . . hill of frankincense: spoken figuratively of the woman; cf. 8:14.

4:7 Cf. the description of the church in Eph 5:27.

4:8 Amana . . . Senir and Hermon: these rugged heights symbolize obstacles that would separate the lovers; cf. 2:14.

4:9 Sister: a term of endearment; brother-sister language forms part of the conventional language of love used in this canticle, the Book of Tobit, and elsewhere in poetry from Egypt, Mesopotamia, and Syro-Palestine.

4:11 Honey: sweet words (cf. Prv 5:3) or perhaps kisses (1:2–3). **Honey and milk**: familiar descriptions for the fertile promised land (Ex 3:8, 17; Lv 20:24; Nm 13:27; Dt 6:3).

4:12 Garden enclosed . . . fountain sealed: reserved for the lover alone. Cf. Prv 5:15–19 for similar images used to describe fruitful, committed relationship.

4:14 These plants are all known for their sweet fragrance.

4:16 Awake: the same verb is used of love in 3:5. The

n: Sg 6:5–7. *o:* Sg 1:15. *p:* Sg 7:5. *q:* Sg 7:4. *r:* Sg 2:17. *s:* Sg 6:5. *t:* Sg 1:2–3. *u:* Sg 6:2, 11.

Blow upon my garden
that its perfumes may spread abroad.
W Let my lover come to his garden
and eat its fruits of choicest yield.

CHAPTER 5

See RG 267–71

M 1 [v] I have come to my garden, my sister, my bride;
I gather my myrrh with my spices,
I eat my honeycomb with my honey,
I drink my wine with my milk.
D? Eat, friends; drink!
Drink deeply, lovers!*

A Fruitless Search

W 2 [w] I was sleeping, but my heart was awake.*
The sound of my lover knocking!
"Open to me, my sister, my friend,
my dove, my perfect one!
For my head is wet with dew,
my hair, with the moisture of the night."
3 I have taken off my robe,*
am I then to put it on?
I have bathed my feet,
am I then to soil them?
4 My lover put his hand in through the opening:
my innermost being* trembled because of him.
5 I rose to open for my lover,
my hands dripping myrrh:
My fingers, flowing myrrh
upon the handles of the lock.
6 I opened for my lover—
but my lover had turned and gone!
At his leaving, my soul sank.
I sought him, but I did not find him;
I called out after him, but he did not answer me.*
7 The watchmen* found me,
as they made their rounds in the city;
They beat me, they wounded me,
they tore off my mantle,
the watchmen of the walls.
8 [x] I adjure you, Daughters of Jerusalem,
if you find my lover
What shall you tell him?
that I am sick with love.

The Lost Lover Described

D 9 How does your lover differ from any other lover,
most beautiful among women?
How does your lover differ from any other,
that you adjure us so?
W 10 My lover is radiant and ruddy;*
outstanding among thousands.
11 His head is gold, pure gold,
his hair like palm fronds,
as black as a raven.
12 His eyes are like doves
beside streams of water,
Bathing in milk,
sitting* by brimming pools.
13 His cheeks are like beds of spices
yielding aromatic scents;
his lips are lilies
that drip flowing myrrh.
14 His arms are rods of gold
adorned with gems;
His loins, a work of ivory
covered with sapphires.
15 His legs, pillars of alabaster,
resting on golden pedestals.

woman may be the speaker of 16a, as it is she who issues the invitation of 16b. **His garden**: the woman herself.

5:1 Eat . . . lovers: the translation and meaning are uncertain.

5:2–8 An experience of anticipation and loss similar to that in 3:1–5. The lover's abrupt appearance resembles that in 2:8–9.

5:3 Robe: knee-length undergarment worn by men and women. **Am I then . . . ?**: the woman's refusal is a form of gentle teasing; that she does not really reject her lover is shown by her actions in vv. 5–6. See 1:7–8; 2:14–15, for other teasing interchanges.

5:4 My innermost being: lit., "innards." In Gn 25:23, Is 49:1; Ps 71:6, the word appears to carry the meaning of "womb."

5:6 The motif of the locked-out lover is common in classical Greek and Latin poetry.

5:7 The watchmen: they do not know the reason for the woman's appearance in the city streets; cf. 3:2–4.

5:10–11 In answer to the question of 5:9 the woman sings her lover's praises (vv. 10–16). **Ruddy**: also used of David (1 Sm 16:12; 17:42). **Gold**: indicates how precious the lover is. **Palm fronds**: his thick, luxuriant growth of hair.

5:12 Sitting . . . : the translation of this line is uncertain; it may continue the metaphor of the lover's eyes, or refer to another part of his anatomy (e.g., teeth) which has been omitted from the text.

v: Sg 6:2. *w:* Sg 3:1–2. *x:* Sg 2:7; 8:4.

His appearance, like the Lebanon,
imposing as the cedars.
16 His mouth is sweetness itself;
he is delightful in every way.
Such is my lover, and such my friend,
Daughters of Jerusalem!

See RG 267–71

CHAPTER 6

The Lost Lover Found

D 1 Where has your lover gone,
most beautiful among women?
Where has your lover withdrawn
that we may seek him with you?*
W 2 [y] My lover has come down to his
garden,*
to the beds of spices,
To feed in the gardens
and to gather lilies.
3 [z] I belong to my lover, and my lover
belongs to me;
he feeds among the lilies.

The Beauty of the Woman

M 4 Beautiful as Tirzah are you, my
friend;*
fair as Jerusalem,
fearsome as celestial visions!
5 [a] Turn your eyes away from me,
for they stir me up.
Your hair is like a flock of goats
streaming down from Gilead.
6 [b] Your teeth are like a flock of ewes
that come up from the washing,
All of them big with twins,
none of them barren.
7 Like pomegranate halves,
your cheeks behind your veil.
8 Sixty are the queens, eighty the
concubines,
and young women without
number—
9 One alone* is my dove, my perfect
one,
her mother's special one,
favorite of the one who bore her.
Daughters see her and call her happy,
queens and concubines, and they
praise her:
10 [c] "Who* is this that comes forth like
the dawn,
beautiful as the white moon, pure as
the blazing sun,
fearsome as celestial visions?"

Love's Meeting

W 11 [d] To the walnut grove* I went down,
to see the young growth of the
valley;
To see if the vines were in bloom,
if the pomegranates had blossomed.
12 Before I knew it, my desire had made
me
the blessed one of the prince's
people.*

CHAPTER 7

See RG 267–71

The Beauty of the Beloved

D? 1 Turn, turn, O Shulammite!*
turn, turn that we may gaze upon
you!

6:1 The Daughters of Jerusalem are won by this description of the lover and offer their aid in seeking him (cf. 5:6, 9).

6:2–3 The woman implies here that she had never really lost her lover, for he has come down to his garden (cf. 2:16; 4:5). **Feed . . . lilies**: the imagery here evokes both a shepherd pasturing his flocks and erotic play between the lovers (2:16; 4:5, 12, 16).

6:4–9 The man again celebrates the woman's beauty. **Tirzah**: probably meaning "pleasant"; it was the early capital of the Northern Kingdom of Israel (1 Kgs 16). **Celestial visions**: the meaning is uncertain. Military images may be implied here, i.e., the "heavenly hosts" who fight along with God on Israel's behalf (cf. Jgs 5:20), or perhaps a reference to the awesome goddesses of the region who combined aspects of both fertility and war.

6:9 One alone: the incomparability of the woman is a favorite motif in love poetry.

6:10 "Who . . . ": the speakers may be the women of vv. 8–9. **Moon . . . sun**: lit., "the white" and "the hot," respectively (cf. Is 24:23; 30:26). **Fearsome**: see note on 6:4–9.

6:11 Walnut grove: also a site of activity in a wedding hymn of the Syrian moon goddess Nikkal (cf. the woman compared to the moon in v. 10).

6:12 The text is obscure in Hebrew and in the ancient versions. The Vulgate reads: "I did not know; my soul disturbed me because of the chariots of Aminadab." Based on a parallel in Jgs 5:24, "chariots" is here emended to "blessed one."

7:1 Shulammite: the woman is so designated because she is considered to be from Shulam (or Shunem) in the plain of Esdraelon (cf. 1 Kgs 1:3), or because the name may mean "the peaceful one," and thus recall the name of Solomon. **Turn**: she is asked to face the speaker(s). **How . . .** : she refuses to be regarded as a spectacle ("the dance of the two

y: Sg 4:12; 5:1. *z:* Sg 2:16; 7:11. *a:* Sg 4:9. *b:* Sg 4:1–3. *c:* Sg 3:6; 8:5. *d:* Sg 4:12–5:1; 7:13.

W How can you gaze upon the
Shulammite
as at the dance of the two camps?
M 2 How beautiful are your feet in
sandals,*
O noble daughter!
Your curving thighs like jewels,
the product of skilled hands.
3 Your valley,* a round bowl
that should never lack mixed wine.
Your belly, a mound of wheat,
encircled with lilies.
4 [e] Your breasts are like two fawns,
twins of a gazelle.
5 [f] Your neck like a tower of ivory;
your eyes, pools in Heshbon
by the gate of Bath-rabbim.
Your nose like the tower of Lebanon
that looks toward Damascus.*
6 Your head rises upon you like
Carmel;*
your hair is like purple;
a king is caught in its locks.

Love's Desires

7 How beautiful you are, how fair,
my love, daughter of delights!
8 Your very form resembles a date-
palm,*
and your breasts, clusters.
9 I thought, "Let me climb the date-
palm!
Let me take hold of its branches!
Let your breasts be like clusters of the
vine
and the fragrance of your breath like
apples,
10 And your mouth like the best wine—
W that flows down smoothly for my
lover,
gliding* over my lips and teeth.
11 [g] I belong to my lover,*
his yearning is for me.
12 Come, my lover! Let us go out to the
fields,
let us pass the night among the
henna.
13 [h] Let us go early to the vineyards, and
see
if the vines are in bloom,
If the buds have opened,
if the pomegranates have
blossomed;
There will I give you my love.
14 The mandrakes* give forth fragrance,
and over our doors are all choice
fruits;
Fruits both fresh and dried, my lover,
have I kept in store for you.

CHAPTER 8

See RG 267–71

1 Would that you were a brother
to me,
nursed at my mother's breasts!
If I met you out of doors, I would kiss
you
and none would despise me.
2 [i] I would lead you, bring you to my
mother's house,
where you would teach me,
Where I would give you to drink
spiced wine, my pomegranate*
juice.
3 [j] His left hand is under my head,

camps" is unknown). Some interpret the episode as an invitation to her to dance.

7:2–6 Another description of the woman's charms. **Sandals**: the woman's sandaled foot was apparently considered quite seductive (Jdt 16:9). **Noble**: a possible connection to the enigmatic "prince" of 6:12. **Curving . . . jewels**: the meaning of these Hebrew words is not certain. Wine and wheat suggest fertility.

7:3 Valley: lit., navel; a discreet allusion to her sex.

7:5 The comparison emphasizes the stateliness of her neck, and the clarity of her eyes. **Bath-rabbim**: a proper name which occurs only here; there was a city of Rabbah northeast of Heshbon in Transjordan. Cf. Jer 49:3.

7:6 Carmel: a prominent set of cliffs overlooking the Mediterranean.

7:8–9 Date-palm: a figure of stateliness. The lover is eager to enjoy the possession of his beloved.

7:10 Gliding: the beloved interrupts her partner's compliment by referring to the intoxication of their union. The translation rests on an emendation of the enigmatic "the lips of the sleepers."

7:11–14 The woman's answer assures him of her love, and invites him to return with her to the rural delights associated with their love (cf. also 6:11–12). **Yearning**: used only here and in Gn 3:16; 4:7. The dependency and subordination of woman to man presented as a consequence of sin in the Genesis story is here transcended in the mutuality of true love.

7:14 Mandrakes: herbs believed to have power to arouse love and promote fertility; cf. Gn 30:14–16.

8:2 Wine . . . pomegranate: sexual connotations are im-

e: Sg 4:5. *f:* Sg 4:4. *g:* Sg 2:16; 6:3. *h:* Sg 6:11. *i:* Sg 3:4. *j:* Sg 2:6.

and his right arm embraces me.
4 [k] I adjure you, Daughters of Jerusalem,
do not awaken or stir up love
until it is ready!

The Return from the Desert

D? 5 [l] Who is this coming up from the desert,
leaning upon her lover?
W Beneath the apple tree I awakened you;*
there your mother conceived you;
there she who bore you conceived.

True Love

6 Set me as a seal* upon your heart,
as a seal upon your arm;
For Love is strong as Death,
longing is fierce as Sheol.
Its arrows are arrows of fire,
flames of the divine.
7 [m] Deep waters* cannot quench love,
nor rivers sweep it away.
Were one to offer all the wealth of his house for love,
he would be utterly despised.

An Answer to the Brothers

W 8 "We have a little sister;*
she has no breasts as yet.
What shall we do for our sister
on the day she is spoken for?
9 If she is a wall,
we will build upon her a silver turret;
But if she is a door,
we will board her up with cedar planks."
10 I am a wall,*
and my breasts are like towers.
I became in his eyes
as one who brings peace.

A Boast

M? 11 Solomon had a vineyard at Baal-hamon;*
he gave over the vineyard to caretakers.
For its fruit one would have to pay
a thousand silver pieces.
12 My vineyard is at my own disposal;
the thousand pieces are for you, Solomon,
and two hundred for the caretakers of its fruit.

The Lovers' Yearnings

M 13 You who dwell in the gardens,*
my companions are listening for your voice—
let me hear it!
W 14 [n] Swiftly, my lover,
be like a gazelle or a young stag
upon the mountains of spices.

plied, since the root "drink" (*shaqah*) is a wordplay on "kiss" (*nashaq*) in v. 1; cf. 1:2.

8:5 Awakened you: the speakers in this verse are difficult to identify. Someone (the poet? Daughters?) hails the couple in v. 5a. According to the Masoretic vocalization, the woman is the speaker in v. 5b.

8:6 Seal: this could be worn bound to the arm, as here, or suspended at the neck, or as a ring (Jer 22:24). It was used for identification and signatures. **Strong . . . fierce**: in human experience, Death and Sheol are inevitable, unrelenting; in the end they always triumph. Love, which is just as certain of its victory, matches its strength against the natural enemies of life; waters cannot extinguish it nor floods carry it away. It is more priceless than all riches. **Flames of the divine**: the Hebrew is difficult: the short form (-Yah) of the divine name Yhwh found here may associate love with the Lord, or it may be acting as a superlative—i.e., god-sized flames.

8:7 Deep waters: often used to designate chaos (Ps 93:4; 144:7; Is 17:12–13; Hb 3:15). The fires of love cannot be extinguished, even by waters of chaos. **Wealth**: love cannot be bought.

8:8–9 The woman quotes the course of action her elder brothers had decided on. While she is yet immature, they will shelter her in view of eventual marriage. **Wall . . . door**: if she is virtuous, she will be honored; if she is not, she will be kept under strict vigilance. **Silver turret**: a precious ornament.

8:10 In reply to the officious and meddling attitude of the brothers, she answers with their terms: she is mature ("wall," "towers"). **Brings peace**: or, "finds peace."

8:11–12 These enigmatic verses have been variously interpreted, depending on who is taken to be the speaker. In v. 11, if the woman, she boasts that she is a vineyard of great value. If the man, he boasts over his possession of her.

8:13–14 As in 2:14, her lover asks for a word or a song and she replies in words similar to those found in 2:17.

k: Sg 2:7; 3:5. *l:* Sg 3:6; 6:10. *m:* Prv 6:31. *n:* Sg 2:9, 17; 4:6.

See RG 272–76

The Book of Wisdom

The Book of Wisdom was written about fifty years before the coming of Christ. Its author, whose name is not known to us, was probably a member of the Jewish community at Alexandria, in Egypt. He wrote in Greek, in a style patterned on that of Hebrew verse. At times he speaks in the person of Solomon, placing his teachings on the lips of the wise king of Hebrew tradition in order to emphasize their value. His profound knowledge of the earlier Old Testament writings is reflected in almost every line of the book, and marks him, like Ben Sira, as an outstanding representative of religious devotion and learning among the sages of postexilic Judaism.

The primary purpose of the author was the edification of his co-religionists in a time when they had experienced suffering and oppression, in part at least at the hands of apostate fellow Jews. To convey his message he made use of the most popular religious themes of his time, namely the splendor and worth of divine wisdom (6:22–11:1), the glorious events of the exodus (11:2–16; 12:23–27; 15:18–19:22), God's mercy (11:17–12:22), the folly of idolatry (13:1–15:17), and the manner in which God's justice operates in rewarding or punishing the individual (1:1–6:21). The first ten chapters in particular provide background for the teaching of Jesus and for some New Testament theology about Jesus. Many passages from this section of the book, notably 3:1–8, are used by the church in the liturgy.

The principal divisions of the Book of Wisdom are:

I. The Reward of Righteousness (1:1–6:21).
II. Praise of Wisdom by Solomon (6:22–11:1).
III. Special Providence of God During the Exodus (11:2–16; 12:23–27; 15:18–19:22) with digressions on God's mercy (11:17–12:22) and on the folly and shame of idolatry (13:1–15:17).

I. The Reward of Righteousness*

CHAPTER 1

See RG 273–74

Exhortation to Righteousness, the Key to Life

1 Love righteousness,* you who judge the earth;[a]
think of the LORD in goodness,
and seek him in integrity of heart;[b]
2 Because he is found by those who do not test him,
and manifests himself to those who do not disbelieve him.[c]
3 For perverse counsels separate people from God,
and his power, put to the proof, rebukes the foolhardy;[d]
4 * Because into a soul that plots evil wisdom does not enter,
nor does she dwell in a body under debt of sin.[e]
5 For the holy spirit of discipline* flees deceit
and withdraws from senseless counsels
and is rebuked when unrighteousness occurs.[f]

6 For wisdom is a kindly spirit,
yet she does not acquit blasphemous lips;

1:1–6:21 The reward is the gift of immortality, to the righteous (1:15; 3:1–3), but not to the wicked (5:1–13). Contrasts between these two groups dominate chaps. 1–5. The philosophy of the wicked and their persecution of the righteous are dramatically presented in 1:16–2:24. New light is shed on the suffering of the righteous (3:1–9), childlessness (3:13–15), and premature death (4:7–16)—in contrast to the fate of the wicked (3:10–12, 16–19; 4:3–6, 17–20).

1:1 Righteousness: not merely the cardinal virtue of justice (cf. 8:7), but the universal moral quality which is the application of wisdom to moral conduct. **You who judge**: "judges" and "kings" (cf. 6:1) are addressed in accordance with the literary customs of the times and with the putative Solomonic authorship, but the real audience is the Jewish community.

1:4 In these verses personified Wisdom is identified with the spirit of the Lord; so also in 9:17.

1:5 Discipline: here and elsewhere, another name for Wisdom.

a: 1 Chr 29:17; Ps 2:10; Is 26:9. *b:* Sir 1:25. *c:* 1 Chr 28:9. *d:* Is 59:2. *e:* Sir 15:7–8; Rom 7:14. *f:* Is 63:10.

Because God is the witness of the inmost
self[g]
and the sure observer of the heart
and the listener to the tongue.[h]
7 For the spirit of the LORD fills the world,[i]
is all-embracing, and knows whatever
is said.
8 Therefore those who utter wicked things
will not go unnoticed,
nor will chastising condemnation pass
them by.[j]
9 For the devices of the wicked shall be
scrutinized,
and the sound of their words shall
reach the LORD,
for the chastisement of their
transgressions;
10 Because a jealous ear hearkens to
everything,[k]
and discordant grumblings are not
secret.
11 Therefore guard against profitless
grumbling,
and from calumny* withhold your
tongues;
For a stealthy utterance will not go
unpunished,
and a lying mouth destroys the soul.

12 Do not court death* by your erring way
of life,
nor draw to yourselves destruction by
the works of your hands.
13 Because God did not make death,[l]
nor does he rejoice in the destruction
of the living.
14 For he fashioned all things that they
might have being,
and the creatures of the world are
wholesome;
There is not a destructive drug among them
nor any domain of Hades* on earth,
15 For righteousness is undying.* [m]

The Wicked Reject Immortality and Righteousness Alike

16 It was the wicked who with hands and
words invited death,
considered it a friend, and pined for it,
and made a covenant with it,
Because they deserve to be allied with it.[n]

CHAPTER 2

See RG 273–74

1 For, not thinking rightly, they
said among themselves:*
"Brief and troubled is our lifetime;[o]
there is no remedy for our dying,
nor is anyone known to have come
back from Hades.
2 For by mere chance were we born,
and hereafter we shall be as though we
had not been;
Because the breath in our nostrils is
smoke,
and reason a spark from the beating of
our hearts,
3 And when this is quenched, our body
will be ashes
and our spirit will be poured abroad
like empty air.[p]
4 Even our name will be forgotten in time,
and no one will recall our deeds.
So our life will pass away like the traces
of a cloud,
and will be dispersed like a mist
Pursued by the sun's rays
and overpowered by its heat.
5 For our lifetime is the passing of a shadow;
and our dying cannot be deferred
because it is fixed with a seal; and no
one returns.[q]
6 Come, therefore, let us enjoy the good
things that are here,
and make use of creation with youthful
zest.[r]
7 Let us have our fill of costly wine and
perfumes,

1:11 Calumny: speech against God and divine providence is meant.

1:12 Death: as will become clear, the author is not speaking of physical death but of spiritual death, the eternal separation from God.

1:14 Hades: the Greek term for the Hebrew Sheol, the dwelling place of the dead.

1:15 Undying: immortality is not seen as an innate quality of the soul but as a gift of God to the righteous.

2:1–20 In this speech the wicked deny survival after death and indeed invite death by their evil deeds.

g: Jer 17:10. *h:* Jer 23:24–25. *i:* Wis 12:1. *j:* Prv 19:5. *k:* Nm 14:27–28. *l:* Ez 18:32; 33:11; 2 Pt 3:9. *m:* Is 51:6–8. *n:* Is 28:15. *o:* Jb 14:1; 7:9. *p:* Jb 7:9; Jas 4:14. *q:* Ps 144:4. *r:* Is 22:13; 1 Cor 15:32.

and let no springtime blossom pass us by;
8 let us crown ourselves with rosebuds before they wither.
9 Let no meadow be free from our wantonness;
everywhere let us leave tokens of our merriment,
for this is our portion, and this our lot.[s]
10 Let us oppress the righteous poor;
let us neither spare the widow
nor revere the aged for hair grown white with time.[t]
11 But let our strength be our norm of righteousness;
for weakness proves itself useless.

12 * Let us lie in wait for the righteous one, because he is annoying to us;
he opposes our actions,
Reproaches us for transgressions of the law*
and charges us with violations of our training.[u]
13 He professes to have knowledge of God
and styles himself a child of the LORD.[v]
14 To us he is the censure of our thoughts;
merely to see him is a hardship for us,[w]
15 Because his life is not like that of others,
and different are his ways.
16 He judges us debased;
he holds aloof from our paths as from things impure.
He calls blest the destiny of the righteous
and boasts that God is his Father.[x]
17 Let us see whether his words be true;
let us find out what will happen to him in the end.[y]
18 For if the righteous one is the son of God, God will help him
and deliver him from the hand of his foes.[z]
19 With violence and torture let us put him to the test
that we may have proof of his gentleness
and try his patience.
20 Let us condemn him to a shameful death;
for according to his own words, God will take care of him."[a]

21 These were their thoughts, but they erred;
for their wickedness blinded them,[b]
22 * And they did not know the hidden counsels of God;
neither did they count on a recompense for holiness
nor discern the innocent souls' reward.[c]
23 For God formed us to be imperishable;
the image of his own nature he made us.[d]
24 But by the envy* of the devil, death entered the world,
and they who are allied with him experience it.[e]

CHAPTER 3

See RG 273–74

*The Hidden Counsels of God** *A. On Suffering**

1 The souls of the righteous are in the hand of God,[f]
and no torment shall touch them.
2 They seemed, in the view of the foolish, to be dead;
and their passing away was thought an affliction

2:12–5:23 From 2:12 to 5:23 the author draws heavily on Is 52–62, setting forth his teaching in a series of characters or types taken from Isaiah and embellished with additional details from other texts. The description of the "righteous one" in 2:12–20 seems to undergird the New Testament passion narrative.

2:12 Law: the law of Moses; "training" has the same meaning.

2:22 This verse announces the subject of the next section.

2:24 Envy: perhaps because Adam was in the image of God or because Adam had control over all creation. **Devil**: the first biblical text to equate the serpent of Gn 3 with the devil.

3:1–4:19 The central section of chaps. 1–6. The author begins by stating that immortality is the reward of the righteous, and then in the light of that belief comments on three points of the traditional discussion of the problem of retribution (suffering, childlessness, early death) each of which was often seen as a divine punishment.

3:1–12 The author affirms that, for the righteous, sufferings are not punishments but purification and opportunities to show fidelity, whereas for the wicked suffering is truly a punishment.

s: Jer 13:25. *t:* Ex 22:21–23; Lv 19:32. *u:* Hos 8:1. *v:* Mt 27:43; Jn 8:55; 10:36–39. *w:* Mt 9:4. *x:* Jer 6:30. *y:* Gn 37:20. *z:* Ps 22:9; Is 42:1; Mt 27:43; Jn 5:18. *a:* Jas 5:6. *b:* Rom 1:21. *c:* Ps 18:24–25; Prv 11:18; Mt 11:25. *d:* Gn 1:26–27; Is 54:16 LXX. *e:* Gn 3:1–24; Rom 5:12. *f:* Jb 12:10.

3 and their going forth from us, utter destruction.
But they are in peace.[g]
4 For if to others, indeed, they seem punished,
yet is their hope full of immortality;
5 Chastised a little, they shall be greatly blessed,
because God tried them
and found them worthy of himself.[h]
6 As gold in the furnace, he proved them,
and as sacrificial offerings* he took them to himself.[i]
7 In the time of their judgment* they shall shine
and dart about as sparks through stubble;[j]
8 They shall judge nations and rule over peoples,
and the LORD shall be their King forever.[k]
9 Those who trust in him shall understand truth,
and the faithful shall abide with him in love:
Because grace and mercy are with his holy ones,[l]
and his care is with the elect.
10 But the wicked shall receive a punishment to match their thoughts,*
since they neglected righteousness and forsook the LORD.
11 For those who despise wisdom and instruction are doomed.[m]
Vain is their hope, fruitless their labors,
and worthless their works.[n]
12 Their wives are foolish and their children wicked,
accursed their brood.[o]

*B. On Childlessness**

13 Yes, blessed is she who, childless and undefiled,
never knew transgression of the marriage bed;
for she shall bear fruit at the judgment of souls.*
14 So also the eunuch whose hand wrought no misdeed,
who held no wicked thoughts against the LORD—
For he shall be given fidelity's choice reward*
and a more gratifying heritage in the LORD's temple.[p]
15 For the fruit of noble struggles is a glorious one;
and unfailing is the root of understanding.*[q]
16 But the children of adulterers* will remain without issue,
and the progeny of an unlawful bed will disappear.[r]
17 For should they attain long life, they will be held in no esteem,
and dishonored will their old age be in the end;
18 Should they die abruptly, they will have no hope
nor comfort in the day of scrutiny;
19 for dire is the end of the wicked generation.[s]

CHAPTER 4

See RG 273–74

1 Better is childlessness with virtue;
for immortal is the memory of virtue,
acknowledged both by God and human beings.[t]
2 When it is present people imitate it,

3:6 Offerings: the image is that of the burnt offering, in which the victim is completely consumed by fire.

3:7 Judgment: the Greek *episkopē* is God's loving judgment of those who have been faithful to him; the same word is used in 14:11 for the punishment of the wicked at God's judgment. Cf. also v. 13.

3:10 To match their thoughts: a fate as empty as that which they describe in 2:1–5.

3:13–4:6 The true fruit of life is not children but virtue which leads to immortality. The many children of the wicked will be a disappointing fruit.

3:13 See vv. 7–9.

3:14 Fidelity's choice reward: cf. Is 56:1–8. **More gratifying**: better than sons and daughters; cf. Is 56:5.

3:15 Root of understanding: the root that is understanding (wisdom).

3:16 Adulterers: understood here as a type of sinners in general; cf. Is 57:3–5.

g: Is 57:2. *h:* Tb 12:13; 2 Cor 4:17; 1 Pt 1:6–7. *i:* Ps 51:19; Prv 17:3; Sir 2:5; Is 48:10. *j:* Dn 12:3; Ob 18; Mal 3:3; Mt 13:43. *k:* Wis 8:14; Prv 8:16; Dn 7:22; 1 Cor 6:2; Rev 20:4. *l:* Wis 4:15; Jb 10:12; Jn 15:10. *m:* Prv 1:7. *n:* Sir 41:8. *o:* Dt 28:18. *p:* Is 56:2–5. *q:* Sir 1:18. *r:* 2 Sm 12:14. *s:* Ps 34:22. *t:* Prv 3:3–4; Sir 16:1–3.

and they long for it when it is gone;
Forever it marches crowned in triumph,
victorious in unsullied deeds of valor.
3 But the numerous progeny of the wicked
shall be of no avail;
their spurious offshoots shall not strike
deep root
nor take firm hold.[u]
4 For even though their branches flourish
for a time,
they are unsteady and shall be rocked
by the wind
and, by the violence of the winds,
uprooted;[v]
5 Their twigs shall be broken off untimely,
their fruit useless, unripe for eating,
fit for nothing.
6 For children born of lawless unions
give evidence of the wickedness of
their parents, when they are
examined.

*C. On Early Death**

7 But the righteous one, though he die
early, shall be at rest.[w]
8 For the age that is honorable comes not
with the passing of time,[x]
nor can it be measured in terms of
years.
9 Rather, understanding passes for gray
hair,
and an unsullied life is the attainment
of old age.
10 * The one who pleased God was loved,[y]
living among sinners, was
transported—
11 Snatched away, lest wickedness pervert
his mind
or deceit beguile his soul;[z]
12 For the witchery of paltry things
obscures what is right
and the whirl of desire transforms the
innocent mind.[a]
13 Having become perfect in a short while,
he reached the fullness of a long
career;
14 for his soul was pleasing to the LORD,
therefore he sped him out of the midst
of wickedness.[b]
But the people saw and did not
understand,
nor did they take that consideration
into account.*
16 Yes, the righteous one who has died will
condemn
the sinful who live;
And youth, swiftly completed, will
condemn
the many years of the unrighteous who
have grown old.[c]
17 For they will see the death of the wise
one
and will not understand what the LORD
intended,
or why he kept him safe.
18 They will see, and hold him in
contempt;
but the LORD will laugh them to
scorn.[d]
19 And they shall afterward become
dishonored corpses[e]
and an unceasing mockery among the
dead.
For he shall strike them down speechless
and prostrate[f]
and rock them to their foundations;
They shall be utterly laid waste
and shall be in grief
and their memory shall perish.

The Judgment of the Wicked

20 Fearful shall they come, at the counting
up of their sins,
and their lawless deeds shall convict
them to their face.

4:7–19 Early death is not a punishment for the righteous because genuine old age is the attainment of perfection and early death is a preservation from corruption. The old age and death of the wicked, however, will not be honorable.

4:10–11 There are allusions here to Enoch (Gn 5:21–24), who was young by patriarchal standards, and to Lot (Gn 19:10–11; 2 Pt 2:7–8). Cf. also Is 57:1–2.

4:14 Verse 15 is omitted because it repeats the last two lines of 3:9.

u: Sir 23:25. *v:* Sir 40:15; Is 40:24. *w:* Wis 3:3. *x:* Jb 12:12; 32:9; Sir 25:4–6. *y:* Gn 5:24; Sir 44:16; Heb 11:5. *z:* Is 57:1–2. *a:* Wis 2:21; Dn 13:9. *b:* Gn 19:22, 29; 2 Pt 2:7. *c:* Mt 12:41–42. *d:* Ps 37:13. *e:* Neh 1:10 LXX; Ps 18:8; Is 14:19; Jer 23:39–40. *f:* 2 Mc 3:29.

See RG 273–74

CHAPTER 5

1* Then shall the righteous one with great assurance confront[g]
his oppressors who set at nought his labors.[h]
2 Seeing this, the wicked shall be shaken with dreadful fear,
and be amazed at the unexpected salvation.
3 They shall say among themselves, rueful
and groaning through anguish of spirit:

"This is the one whom once we held as a laughingstock
and as a type for mockery,
4 fools that we were!
His life we accounted madness,
and death dishonored.
5 See how he is accounted among the heavenly beings;*
how his lot is with the holy ones![i]
6 We, then, have strayed from the way of truth,[j]
and the light of righteousness did not shine for us,
and the sun did not rise for us.[k]
7 We were entangled in the thorns of mischief and of ruin;
we journeyed through trackless deserts,
but the way of the LORD we never knew.
8 What did our pride avail us?
What have wealth and its boastfulness afforded us?[l]
9 All of them passed like a shadow
and like a fleeting rumor;[m]
10 Like a ship traversing the heaving water:
when it has passed, no trace can be found,
no path of its keel in the waves.
11 Or like a bird flying through the air;
no evidence of its course is to be found—
But the fluid air, lashed by the beating of pinions,
and cleft by the rushing force
Of speeding wings, is traversed;
and afterward no mark of passage can be found in it.
12 Or as, when an arrow has been shot at a mark,
the parted air straightway flows together again
so that none discerns the way it went—
13 Even so, once born, we abruptly came to nought
and held no sign of virtue to display,
but were consumed in our wickedness."[n]

14 * Yes, the hope of the wicked is like chaff borne by the wind,
and like fine, storm-driven snow;
Like smoke scattered by the wind,
and like the passing memory of the nomad camping for a single day.[o]
15 But the righteous live forever,
and in the LORD is their recompense,
and the thought of them is with the Most High.[p]
16 Therefore shall they receive the splendid crown,
the beautiful diadem, from the hand of the LORD,
For he will shelter them with his right hand,
and protect them with his arm.[q]
17 He shall take his zeal for armor[r]
and arm creation to requite the enemy,
18 Shall put on righteousness for a breastplate,
wear sure judgment for a helmet,
19 Shall take invincible holiness for a shield,[s]
20 and sharpen his sudden anger for a sword.

5:1–13 In contrast to their speech in chap. 2 the wicked now regret their assessment of life and righteousness.

5:5 Heavenly beings: lit., "sons of God." These are the holy ones, members of the heavenly court, among whom the righteous are to be found. A bodily resurrection does not seem to be envisioned.

5:14–23 A picture of the reward of the righteous which develops into an apocalyptic description of the divine warrior's destruction of evil. The author utilizes Is 59–62.

g: 2 Thes 1:6–7. *h:* Col 2:15. *i:* Acts 26:18; Col 1:12. *j:* Prv 4:18–19; Jn 12:35. *k:* Prv 22:5; Is 59:6–14. *l:* Ps 49:7; Prv 10:2. *m:* 1 Chr 20:15; Jb 9:25–26 LXX; Ps 144:4. *n:* Ez 33:10. *o:* Jb 21:18; Ps 1:4; 37:20; Is 17:13. *p:* Is 62:11; Ez 18:9. *q:* Ex 33:22; Is 62:3; 2 Tm 4:8; 1 Pt 5:4. *r:* Is 59:17. *s:* Dt 32:40–43.

The universe will war with him against
the foolhardy;
21 Well-aimed bolts of lightning will go forth
and from the clouds will leap to the
mark as from a well-drawn bow;[t]
22 and as from a sling, wrathful
hailstones shall be hurled.
The waters of the sea will be enraged
and flooding rivers will overwhelm
them;[u]
23 A mighty wind will confront them
and winnow them like a tempest;
Thus lawlessness will lay waste the
whole earth
and evildoing overturn the thrones of
the mighty.[v]

CHAPTER 6

See RG 274–75

*Exhortation to Seek Wisdom**

1 Hear, therefore, kings, and understand;[w]
learn, you magistrates* of the earth's
expanse!
2 Give ear, you who have power over
multitudes
and lord it over throngs of peoples!
3 Because authority was given you by the
Lord
and sovereignty by the Most High,
who shall probe your works and
scrutinize your counsels![x]
4 Because, though you were ministers of
his kingdom, you did not judge
rightly,
and did not keep the law,*
nor walk according to the will of God,
5 Terribly and swiftly he shall come
against you,
because severe judgment awaits the
exalted—
6 For the lowly may be pardoned out of
mercy[y]
but the mighty shall be mightily put to
the test.
7 For the Ruler of all shows no partiality,
nor does he fear greatness,[z]
Because he himself made the great as
well as the small,
and provides for all alike;
8 but for those in power a rigorous
scrutiny impends.

9 To you, therefore, O princes, are my
words addressed[a]
that you may learn wisdom and that
you may not fall away.
10 For those who keep the holy precepts
hallowed will be found holy,
and those learned in them will have
ready a response.*
11 Desire therefore my words;
long for them and you will be
instructed.
12 Resplendent and unfading is Wisdom,
and she is readily perceived by those
who love her,
and found by those who seek her.[b]
13 She hastens to make herself known to
those who desire her;[c]
14 one who watches for her at dawn will
not be disappointed,
for she will be found sitting at the
gate.
15 For setting your heart on her is the
perfection of prudence,
and whoever keeps vigil for her is
quickly free from care;
16 Because she makes her rounds, seeking
those worthy of her,
and graciously appears to them on the
way,
and goes to meet them with full
attention.[d]

6:1–21 The first part of the book closes with an exhortation comparable to 1:1–15, and it leads into "Solomon's" personal comments on wisdom in chaps. 7–9.

6:1 Kings . . . magistrates: note the inclusion with v. 21 ("kings"). The address to earthly powers is in accord with the opening (1:1), but the true audience remains the Jewish community.

6:4 Law: that of Moses; cf. 2:12; 6:10.

6:10 Response: a suitable plea before the great Judge. Cf. Prv 22:21; Jb 31:14; Hb 2:1; Sir 8:9.

---

t: Hb 3:9–11. *u:* Dt 11:4. *v:* Wis 11:20; Sir 10:13–14. *w:* Wis 1:1; Ps 2:10; Sir 33:19; Mi 3:1, 9. *x:* 2 Chr 36:23; Prv 8:15–16; Jn 19:11; Rom 13:1. *y:* Lk 12:48. *z:* Dt 1:17; Prv 22:2. *a:* Dt 4:10; Ps 2:12; Sir 32:14; 1 Jn 3:7. *b:* Wis 7:10; Prv 8:17; Jer 29:13. *c:* Prv 8:3, 17, 34. *d:* Prv 8:20–21; Sir 15:1–5.

17 * For the first step toward Wisdom is an
earnest desire for discipline;[e]
18 then, care for discipline is love of her;
love means the keeping of her laws;
To observe her laws is the basis for
incorruptibility;
19 and incorruptibility makes one close to
God;
20 thus the desire for Wisdom leads to a
kingdom.
21 If, then, you find pleasure in throne and
scepter, you princes of peoples,
honor Wisdom, that you may reign as
kings forever.

II. Praise of Wisdom by Solomon*

Introduction

22 Now what wisdom is, and how she came
to be I shall proclaim;
and I shall conceal no secrets from you,
But from the very beginning I shall
search out
and bring to light knowledge of her;
I shall not diverge from the truth.[f]
23 Neither shall I admit consuming jealousy
to my company,
because that can have no fellowship
with Wisdom.[g]
24 A multitude of the wise is the safety of
the world,
and a prudent king, the stability of the
people;[h]
25 so take instruction from my words, to
your profit.

CHAPTER 7

See RG 274–75

Solomon Is Like All Others

1 I too am a mortal, the same as all the
rest,[i]
and a descendant of the first one
formed of earth.*
And in my mother's womb I was molded
into flesh
2 in a ten-month period*—body and
blood,
from the seed of a man, and the
pleasure that accompanies
marriage.
3 And I too, when born, inhaled the
common air,
and fell upon the kindred earth;
wailing, I uttered that first sound
common to all.
4 In swaddling clothes and with constant
care I was nurtured.
5 For no king has any different origin or
birth;
6 one is the entry into life for all,
and in one same way they leave it.[j]

Solomon Prayed and Wisdom and Riches Came to Him

7 Therefore I prayed, and prudence was
given me;
I pleaded and the spirit of Wisdom
came to me.[k]
8 I preferred her to scepter and throne,[l]
And deemed riches nothing in
comparison with her,
9 nor did I liken any priceless gem to
her;
Because all gold, in view of her, is a bit
of sand,
and before her, silver is to be
accounted mire.
10 Beyond health and beauty I loved her,
And I chose to have her rather than the
light,
because her radiance never
ceases.[m]
11 Yet all good things together came to me
with her,[n]
and countless riches at her hands;

6:17–20 This type of reasoning approximates the rhetorical sorites, a series of statements in which the predicate of each becomes the subject of the next. Cf. Rom 5:3–5.

6:22–9:18 In these verses the author identifies with Solomon (without mentioning that name anywhere), and praises the beauty of Wisdom, describing how he sought her out. Thus the readers of the book can find a model in their search for Wisdom.

7:1 First one formed of earth: Adam. The author omits throughout the book the proper names of the characters in sacred history of whom he speaks; see especially chap. 10.

7:2 In a ten-month period: ten lunar months.

e: Ps 2:10–12; Prv 4:4–9; 7:1–4; 8:15–16; Dn 7:27; Jn 14:15, 21; 1 Jn 5:3. *f:* Tb 12:7, 11; Mt 13:11; Jn 15:15. *g:* Wis 7:13; Jas 3:14–15. *h:* Prv 11:14; 24:6; 29:4; Sir 10:1–5. *i:* Wis 10:1; Gn 2:7; Jb 10:9–12; 33:6; 1 Cor 15:47–49. *j:* Jb 1:21; Lk 2:12; 1 Tm 6:7–8. *k:* 1 Kgs 3:5–15; Prv 2:3–11. *l:* Wis 8:5; 1 Kgs 10:21; Jb 28:15–19; Prv 3:14–16; 8:10, 18–19. *m:* Prv 6:23. *n:* Prv 8:21.

12 I rejoiced in them all, because Wisdom is
their leader,
though I had not known that she is
their mother.* [o]

Solomon Prays for Help to Speak Worthily of Wisdom

13 Sincerely I learned about her, and
ungrudgingly do I share—
her riches I do not hide away;[p]
14 For she is an unfailing treasure;
those who gain this treasure win the
friendship of God,
being commended by the gifts that
come from her discipline.*
15 Now God grant I speak suitably
and value these endowments at their
worth:
For he is the guide of Wisdom
and the director of the wise.
16 For both we and our words are in his
hand,
as well as all prudence and knowledge
of crafts.[q]
17 * For he gave me sound knowledge of
what exists,
that I might know the structure of the
universe and the force of its
elements,
18 The beginning and the end and the
midpoint of times,
the changes in the sun's course and the
variations of the seasons,
19 Cycles of years, positions of stars,
20 natures of living things, tempers of
beasts,
Powers of the winds and thoughts of
human beings,
uses of plants and virtues of roots—
21 Whatever is hidden or plain I learned,
22 for Wisdom, the artisan of all, taught
me.[r]

Nature and Incomparable Dignity of Wisdom

* For in her is a spirit
intelligent, holy, unique,
Manifold, subtle, agile,
clear, unstained, certain,
Never harmful, loving the good, keen,[s]
23 unhampered, beneficent, kindly,
Firm, secure, tranquil,
all-powerful, all-seeing,
And pervading all spirits,
though they be intelligent, pure and
very subtle.
24 For Wisdom is mobile beyond all
motion,
and she penetrates and pervades all
things by reason of her purity.[t]
25 * For she is a breath of the might of God
and a pure emanation of the glory of
the Almighty;
therefore nothing defiled can enter into
her.
26 For she is the reflection of eternal light,
the spotless mirror of the power of
God,
the image of his goodness.[u]
27 Although she is one, she can do all
things,
and she renews everything while
herself perduring;
Passing into holy souls from age to age,
she produces friends of God and
prophets.[v]
28 For God loves nothing so much as the
one who dwells with Wisdom.
29 For she is fairer than the sun[w]
and surpasses every constellation of
the stars.
Compared to light, she is found more
radiant;
30 though night supplants light,

7:12 Mother: lit., "she who begets." Although Wisdom herself is begotten of God (Prv 8:22–24), she is here the one who brings into being.

7:14 Discipline: cf. note on 1:5.

7:17–22a Wisdom teaches not only righteousness and friendship with God but also sound knowledge of the world, the universe, plants, animals and human beings. See also 1 Kgs 5:9–14; these specialties reflect Hellenistic culture.

7:22b–23 The twenty-one (7 × 3) attributes of the spirit in Wisdom reflect the influence of contemporary philosophy, especially the Stoa, but the personification rests also on Prv 8:22–31 and Sir 24.

7:25–26 Five strong metaphors underline the origins and closeness of Wisdom with God. See the use of this language in Heb 1:3; Col 1:15.

o: Prv 8:14–15. *p:* Wis 6:23. *q:* Wis 3:1. *r:* Wis 14:2; Prv 8:30. *s:* Heb 4:12–13; Jas 3:17. *t:* Wis 8:1. *u:* 2 Cor 4:4; Col 1:15; Heb 1:3. *v:* Ex 33:11; Jb 42:2; Ps 104:29; Jl 3:1. *w:* Sg 6:3, 9.

wickedness does not prevail over
Wisdom.

CHAPTER 8

See RG 274–75

1 Indeed, she spans the world from
end to end mightily
and governs all things well.[x]

Wisdom, the Source of Blessings

2 Her I loved and sought after from my
youth;
I sought to take her for my bride*
and was enamored of her beauty.[y]
3 She adds to nobility the splendor of
companionship with God;
even the Ruler of all loved her.
4 For she leads into the understanding of
God,
and chooses his works.[z]
5 If riches are desirable in life,
what is richer than Wisdom, who
produces all things?[a]
6 And if prudence is at work,[b]
who in the world is a better artisan
than she?
7 Or if one loves righteousness,
whose works are virtues,
She teaches moderation and
prudence,
righteousness and fortitude,*
and nothing in life is more useful than
these.
8 Or again, if one yearns for wide
experience,
she knows the things of old, and infers
the things to come.
She understands the turns of phrases and
the solutions of riddles;
signs and wonders she knows in
advance
and the outcome of times and
ages.[c]

Wisdom as Solomon's Counselor and Comfort

9 So I determined to take her to live with
me,
knowing that she would be my
counselor while all was well,
and my comfort in care and grief.
10 Because of her I have glory among the
multitudes,[d]
and esteem from the elders, though I
am but a youth.
11 I shall become keen in judgment,
and shall be a marvel before rulers.
12 They will wait while I am silent and
listen when I speak;
and when I shall speak the more,
they will put their hands upon their
mouths.*
13 Because of her I shall have immortality
and leave to those after me an
everlasting memory.[e]
14 I shall govern peoples, and nations will
be my subjects—[f]
15 tyrannical princes, hearing of me, will
be afraid;
in the assembly I shall appear noble,
and in war courageous.
16 Entering my house, I shall take my
repose beside her;
For association with her involves no
bitterness
and living with her no grief,
but rather joy and gladness.[g]

Wisdom is a Gift of God

17 Reflecting on these things,
and considering in my heart
That immortality lies in kinship with
Wisdom,[h]
18 great delight in love of her,
and unfailing riches in the works of
her hands;

8:2 I loved . . . my bride: the erotic quality in the pursuit of and living with Woman Wisdom, who is the Lord's consort (9:4) and loved by him, continues throughout this chapter (vv. 16, 18). It is reflected already in Prv 4:5–9; 7:4–5. See also Sir 15:2–5; 51:13–21.

8:7 Moderation . . . fortitude: known also as the cardinal virtues, and recognized in Greek philosophy (Plato).

8:12 Hands upon their mouths: a sign of respect for unanswerable wisdom; cf. Jb 40:4.

x: Wis 7:24; 15:1. *y:* Prv 5:13–18; 8:17. *z:* Prv 8:27–31. *a:* Prv 8:18–19. *b:* Prv 8:14–15. *c:* Prv 1:6; Sir 39:1–3; 42:19–20; Dn 2:21. *d:* 1 Kgs 3:28; Jb 29:8–10, 21–22. *e:* Sir 15:6; 41:12–13; Is 56:5. *f:* Wis 3:8; Ps 18:48; 47:4. *g:* Prv 29:6; Sir 15:6; Bar 3:38. *h:* Prv 3:18.

And that in associating with her there is prudence,
and fair renown in sharing her discourses,
I went about seeking to take her for my own.
19 * Now, I was a well-favored child,
and I came by a noble nature;
20 or rather, being noble, I attained an unblemished body.
21 And knowing that I could not otherwise possess her unless God gave it—
and this, too, was prudence, to know whose gift she is—
I went to the LORD and besought him,[i]
and said with all my heart:

CHAPTER 9

See RG 274–75

*Solomon's Prayer**

1 * God of my ancestors, Lord of mercy,[j]
you who have made all things by your word[k]
2 And in your wisdom have established humankind
to rule the creatures produced by you,[l]
3 And to govern the world in holiness and righteousness,
and to render judgment in integrity of heart:[m]
4 Give me Wisdom, the consort at your throne,
and do not reject me from among your children;[n]
5 For I am your servant, the child of your maidservant,
a man weak and short-lived
and lacking in comprehension of judgment and of laws.[o]
6 Indeed, though one be perfect among mortals,
if Wisdom, who comes from you, be lacking,
that one will count for nothing.[p]
7 You have chosen me king over your people
and magistrate over your sons and daughters.[q]
8 You have bid me build a temple on your holy mountain
and an altar in the city that is your dwelling place,
a copy of the holy tabernacle which you had established from of old.[r]
9 Now with you is Wisdom, who knows your works
and was present when you made the world;
Who understands what is pleasing in your eyes
and what is conformable with your commands.[s]
10 Send her forth from your holy heavens
and from your glorious throne dispatch her
That she may be with me and work with me,
that I may know what is pleasing to you.[t]
11 For she knows and understands all things,
and will guide me prudently in my affairs
and safeguard me by her glory;[u]
12 Thus my deeds will be acceptable,
and I will judge your people justly
and be worthy of my father's throne.[v]
13 For who knows God's counsel,
or who can conceive what the Lord intends?[w]
14 For the deliberations of mortals are timid,

8:19–20 Here the author mentions first bodily, then spiritual, excellence. To make it plain that the latter is the governing factor in the harmonious development of the human person, he then reverses the order. The Platonic doctrine of the pre-existence of the soul is often read into these lines, but such an anthropology does not seem to be the intent of the author (cf. 7:1–6). Verse 20 appears to rule out any misunderstanding of v. 19. Verse 21 emphasizes that he did not bring talent to his "birth"; his wisdom is the gift of God.

9:1–18 The author presents his version of Solomon's prayer (1 Kgs 3:6–9; 2 Chr 1:8–10).

9:1–2 The author identifies Wisdom with the word of God just as he again identifies Wisdom with the spirit of God in v. 17. All three are alternate ways of expressing God's activity in relationship with the world and its inhabitants.

i: 1 Kgs 3:9; 1 Kgs 5:9; Prv 2:6; Jas 1:5. *j:* Ps 86:15. *k:* Gn 1; Ps 33:6; Prv 3:19; Jer 10:12; Jn 1:3, 10. *l:* Ps 8:7–9; Sir 17:3–4. *m:* 1 Kgs 3:6; 9:4–5; Ps 9:8–9. *n:* 2 Chr 1:10. *o:* 1 Kgs 3:7; Ps 116:16. *p:* Wis 3:17; 1 Kgs 11:4; 1 Cor 3:18–21. *q:* 1 Chr 28:5. *r:* Ex 25:8–9; 2 Sm 7:13; 1 Chr 28:5; 2 Chr 6:1–2; 7:7; Tb 1:4; Ps 15:1; 48:2–3. *s:* Dt 6:17–18; Prv 8:22–31; Jn 1:1–3, 10. *t:* Wis 18:15; Mt 5:34; Jn 3:17; 20:21. *u:* Wis 8:8. *v:* 1 Kgs 3:6–9. *w:* Is 40:13; Bar 3:31.

and uncertain our plans.
15 * For the corruptible body burdens the soul
and the earthly tent weighs down the mind with its many concerns.[x]
16 Scarcely can we guess the things on earth,
and only with difficulty grasp what is at hand;
but things in heaven, who can search them out?[y]
17 Or who can know your counsel, unless you give Wisdom
and send your holy spirit from on high?[z]
18 * Thus were the paths of those on earth made straight,
and people learned what pleases you,
and were saved by Wisdom.[a]

See RG 274–75

CHAPTER 10*

Wisdom Preserves Her Followers

1 She preserved the first-formed father* of the world[b]
when he alone had been created;[c]
And she raised him up from his fall,
2 and gave him power to rule all things.[d]
3 But when an unrighteous man* withdrew from her in his anger,
he perished through his fratricidal wrath.[e]
4 When on his account the earth was flooded, Wisdom again saved it,
piloting the righteous man* on frailest wood.[f]
5 She, when the nations were sunk in universal wickedness,
knew the righteous man,* kept him blameless before God,
and preserved him resolute against pity for his child.[g]
6 She rescued a righteous man* from among the wicked who were being destroyed,[h]
when he fled as fire descended upon the Pentapolis—
7 Where as a testimony to its wickedness,
even yet there remain a smoking desert,
Plants bearing fruit that never ripens,
and the tomb of a disbelieving soul,* a standing pillar of salt.[i]
8 For those who forsook Wisdom
not only were deprived of knowledge of the good,
But also left the world a memorial of their folly,
so that they could not even be hidden in their fall.
9 But Wisdom rescued from tribulations
those who served her.[j]
10 She, when a righteous man* fled from his brother's anger,[k]
guided him in right ways,
Showed him the kingdom of God
and gave him knowledge of holy things;
She prospered him in his labors
and made abundant the fruit of his works,
11 Stood by him against the greed of his defrauders,
and enriched him;[l]
12 She preserved him from foes,
and secured him against ambush,
And she gave him the prize for his hard struggle
that he might know that devotion to God* is mightier than all else.[m]

9:15–17 Although the expressions in v. 15 draw on the language of Plato concerning the human condition, the conclusion is very biblical: God remains a mystery (Jb 38–39; Eccl 8:17; Is 40:12–14; Rom 11:33–34). The plight of humankind is clearly one of ignorance, unless the "holy spirit" is sent from God.

9:18 An announcement of the next section.

10:1–21 This chapter prepares for the following section (Wis 11:2–19:22) on the history of Israel in the exodus, by reviewing the dealings of Wisdom with the patriarchs. It has a parallel in Sir 44–50; cf. also Wis 18:9.

10:1–2 Adam.

10:3 Cain.

10:4 Noah.

10:5 Abraham.

10:6 Lot. **Pentapolis**: the five cities, including Sodom; cf. Gn 14:2.

10:7 Disbelieving soul: Lot's wife; cf. Gn 19:26.

10:10–12 Jacob.

10:12 Devotion to God: in the Greek this signifies "piety"

x: Jb 4:19. *y:* Sir 1:3; Jn 3:12. *z:* Jn 14:26. *a:* Wis 10:9; Prv 28:26. *b:* Heb 11:17–27. *c:* Wis 7:1. *d:* Gn 1:28. *e:* Gn 4:1–16. *f:* Wis 14:5–6; Gn 6:5–9. *g:* Gn 22:7–10. *h:* Gn 18:22–33; 19:15–25; 2 Pt 2:6–7. *i:* Gn 19:26; Lk 17:32. *j:* Wis 16:8. *k:* Gn 27:43–45; 28:12–15. *l:* Gn 30:29–30; 31:5–12. *m:* Gn 32:24–29; 1 Tm 4:8.

13 She did not abandon a righteous man*
when he was sold,[n]
but rescued him from sin.[o]
14 She went down with him into the dungeon,
and did not desert him in his bonds,
Until she brought him the scepter of royalty
and authority over his oppressors,
Proved false those who had defamed him,
and gave him eternal glory.

15 The holy people and their blameless descendants—it was she
who rescued them from the nation that oppressed them.[p]
16 She entered the soul of the Lord's servant,*
and withstood fearsome kings with signs and wonders;[q]
17 she gave the holy ones the reward of their labors,[r]
Conducted them by a wondrous road,
became a shelter for them by day
a starry flame by night.
18 She took them across the Red Sea
and brought them through the deep waters.
19 Their enemies she overwhelmed,
and churned them up* from the bottom of the depths.
20 Therefore the righteous despoiled the wicked;
and they sang of your holy name, Lord,
and praised in unison your conquering hand,[s]
21 Because Wisdom opened the mouths of the mute,
and gave ready speech to infants.[t]

CHAPTER 11

See RG 275–76

1 She prospered their affairs through the holy prophet.[u]

III. Special Providence of God During the Exodus*

Introduction

2 They journeyed through the uninhabited desert,
and in lonely places they pitched their tents;[v]
3 they withstood enemies and warded off their foes.[w]
4 When they thirsted, they called upon you,
and water was given them from the sheer rock,
a quenching of their thirst from the hard stone.
5 For by the things through which their foes were punished
they in their need were benefited.[x]

First Example: Water Punishes the Egyptians and Benefits the Israelites

6 Instead of a river's* perennial source,
troubled with impure blood[y]
7 as a rebuke to the decree for the slaying of infants,
You gave them abundant water beyond their hope,
8 after you had shown by the thirst they experienced
how you punished their adversaries.
9 For when they had been tried, though only mildly chastised,[z]
they recognized how the wicked,
condemned in anger, were being tormented.

or "religion," and is the equivalent of the Hebrew "fear of the Lord"; cf. Prv 1:7.

10:13–14 Joseph.

10:16 Moses.

10:19 Churned them up: casting their bodies on the shore.

11:2–19:22 Few verses in chaps. 11–19 can be fully understood without consulting the passages in the Pentateuch which are indicated in the cross-references. The theme of this part of the book is expressed in v. 5 and is illustrated in the following chapters by five examples drawn from Exodus events.

11:6–8 River: the Nile; the contrast is between the first plague of Egypt (Ex 7:17–24) and the water drawn from the rock in Horeb (Ex 17:5–7; Nm 20:8–11).

n: Gn 37–45. *o:* Gn 39:7–10. *p:* Ex 3:9; 14:30; 19:6. *q:* Wis 1:4; 7:27; Ex 4:10; Ps 76:13. *r:* Wis 14:3; 19:7; Ex 13:21–22; Ex 14–15; Ps 77:20–21; 78:13, 53; Is 4:5–6. *s:* Ex 12:35–36; 15:1–21. *t:* Ex 4:10–15; Ps 8:3; Mt 11:25. *u:* Dt 2:7; Hos 12:14. *v:* Ex 17:2–6; Nm 20:1–13; Ps 63:2; 107:4–7; Jer 2:6. *w:* Ex 17:8–16; Nm 21:1–3, 21–35; 31:1–12; Ps 118:10–12. *x:* Wis 16:1–2. *y:* Wis 18:5; Ex 1:22; 7:17–24. *z:* Wis 3:5; 16:3–4; Dt 8:2–5; 2 Mc 6:12–16; Ps 6:2; Prv 3:12.

10 You tested your own people,
admonishing them as a father;
but as a stern king you probed and
condemned the wicked.
11 Those near and far were equally afflicted:[a]
12 for a twofold grief* took hold of them[b]
and a groaning at the remembrance of
the ones who had departed.
13 For when they heard that the cause of
their own torments
was a benefit to these others, they
recognized the Lord.
14 For though they had mocked and rejected
him who had been cast out and
abandoned long ago,
in the final outcome, they marveled at
him,
since their thirst proved unlike that of
the righteous.[c]

Second Example: Animals Punish the Egyptians and Benefit the Israelites

15 In return for their senseless, wicked
thoughts,
which misled them into worshiping
dumb* serpents and worthless
insects,
You sent upon them swarms of dumb
creatures for vengeance;[d]
16 that they might recognize that one is
punished by the very things
through which one sins.[e]

Digression on God's Mercy

17 For not without means was your
almighty hand,[f]
that had fashioned the universe from
formless matter,*
to send upon them many bears or
fierce lions,
18 Or newly created, wrathful, unknown
beasts
breathing forth fiery breath,
Or pouring out roaring smoke,
or flashing terrible sparks from their
eyes.
19 Not only could these attack and
completely destroy them;
even their frightful appearance itself
could slay.
20 Even without these, they could have been
killed at a single blast,
pursued by justice
and winnowed by your mighty spirit.
But you have disposed all things by
measure and number and
weight.[g]
21 For great strength is always present with
you;
who can resist the might of your
arm?[h]
22 Indeed, before you the whole universe is
like a grain from a balance,*
or a drop of morning dew come down
upon the earth.[i]
23 * But you have mercy on all, because you
can do all things;
and you overlook sins for the sake of
repentance.[j]
24 For you love all things that are
and loathe nothing that you have
made;
for you would not fashion what you
hate.[k]
25 How could a thing remain, unless you
willed it;
or be preserved, had it not been called
forth by you?[l]
26 But you spare all things, because they are
yours,
O Ruler and Lover of souls,[m]
12:1 for your imperishable spirit is in all
things![n]

11:12 Twofold grief: the double distress described in vv. 13–14.

11:15 Dumb: that is, irrational.

11:17 Formless matter: a Greek philosophical concept is used to interpret the chaos of Gn 1:2.

11:22 Grain from a balance: a tiny particle used for weighing on sensitive scales.

11:23 The combination of divine mercy and power is an unusual paradox, but cf. 12:15–18; Ps 62:12–13; Sir 2:18. The main emphasis is on a creating that is motivated by love; the divine "imperishable spirit" (either Wisdom as in 1:4, 7, or perhaps the breath of life as in Gn 2:7) is in everything (12:1).

---

a: Ps 6:2. *b:* Wis 16:8; Ex 14:4, 18. *c:* Ex 2:3. *d:* Wis 12:23–24; 15:18–16:1; Ex 7:26–8:11. *e:* Wis 12:23, 27; Ex 10:16; Prv 1:31–32; 26:27. *f:* Wis 12:8–9; 16:1, 5; Gn 1:1–2; Dt 32:24; 2 Kgs 17:25–26; Hos 13:4–8. *g:* Jb 4:9. *h:* Wis 12:12; 2 Chr 20:6. *i:* Hos 13:3. *j:* Wis 12:10; Dt 9:27; Acts 17:30; Rom 2:4; 11:32; 2 Pt 3:9. *k:* Ps 145:9. *l:* Is 41:4. *m:* Wis 12:16; Is 63:9. *n:* Wis 1:7.

See RG 275–76

CHAPTER 12

2 Therefore you rebuke offenders little by little,
warn them, and remind them of the sins they are committing,
that they may abandon their wickedness and believe in you, Lord!

3 For truly, the ancient inhabitants of your holy land,[o]
4 whom you hated for deeds most odious—
works of sorcery and impious sacrifices;
5 These merciless murderers of children,
devourers of human flesh,*
and initiates engaged in a blood ritual,
6 and parents who took with their own hands defenseless lives,[p]
You willed to destroy by the hands of our ancestors,
7 that the land that is dearest of all to you
might receive a worthy colony of God's servants.[q]
8 But even these you spared, since they were but mortals
and sent wasps as forerunners of your army
that they might exterminate them by degrees.[r]
9 Not that you were without power to have the wicked vanquished in battle by the righteous,
or wiped out at once by terrible beasts or by one decisive word;[s]
10 But condemning them by degrees, you gave them space for repentance.
You were not unaware that their origins were wicked
and their malice ingrained,[t]
And that their dispositions would never change;
11 for they were a people accursed from the beginning.
Neither out of fear for anyone
did you grant release from their sins.[u]
12 For who can say to you, "What have you done?"
or who can oppose your decree?
Or when peoples perish, who can challenge you, their maker;
or who can come into your presence to vindicate the unrighteous?[v]
13 For neither is there any god besides you who have the care of all,
that you need show you have not unjustly condemned;[w]
14 Nor can any king or prince confront you on behalf of those you have punished.[x]
15 But as you are righteous, you govern all things righteously;
you regard it as unworthy of your power
to punish one who has incurred no blame.[y]
16 For your might is the source of righteousness;
your mastery over all things makes you lenient to all.[z]
17 For you show your might when the perfection of your power is disbelieved;
and in those who know you, you rebuke insolence.* [a]
18 But though you are master of might, you judge with clemency,
and with much lenience you govern us;
for power, whenever you will, attends you.

19 You taught your people, by these deeds,[b]
that those who are righteous must be kind;
And you gave your children reason to hope

12:5 The horrible crimes here attributed to the Canaanites (cf. also 14:23) were not unheard of in the ancient world.
12:17 The brunt of divine anger and justice is borne by those who know God but defy divine authority and might. Cf. 1:2; 15:2, but also 12:27; 18:13.

o: Wis 14:23; Dt 18:9–12; Ps 5:6; 106:28, 34–39; Jer 19:4–5; Ez 16:3, 20–21, 36. *p:* Nm 33:52. *q:* Dt 11:12. *r:* Ex 23:28–30; Dt 7:17–24. *s:* Wis 11:18; 18:15; Nm 16:21. *t:* Wis 11:23; Ps 55:20; Sir 16:9. *u:* Gn 9:25. *v:* 2 Sm 16:10; Eccl 8:4; Sir 46:19; Is 45:9; Dn 4:32; Rom 9:19–21. *w:* Wis 6:7; Dt 3:24; 32:39; Is 44:6, 8. *x:* Jer 49:19; 50:44. *y:* Gn 18:23–32; Dt 32:4. *z:* Wis 2:11; 11:26; Ps 103:19. *a:* Wis 15:2–3; Ex 9:16. *b:* Wis 11:23; Sir 17:24.

that you would allow them to repent
for their sins.
20 For these were enemies of your servants,
doomed to death;
yet, while you punished them with
such solicitude and indulgence,
granting time and opportunity to
abandon wickedness,
21 With what exactitude you judged your
children,
to whose ancestors you gave the sworn
covenants of goodly promises![c]
22 Therefore to give us a lesson you punish
our enemies with measured
deliberation
so that we may think earnestly of your
goodness when we judge,
and, when being judged, we may look
for mercy.

Second Example Resumed

23 Hence those unrighteous who lived a life
of folly,
you tormented through their own
abominations.[d]
24 For they went far astray in the paths of
error,
taking for gods the worthless and
disgusting among beasts,
being deceived like senseless infants.[e]
25 Therefore as though upon unreasoning
children,
you sent your judgment on them as a
mockery;[f]
26 But they who took no heed of a
punishment which was but child's
play
were to experience a condemnation
worthy of God.
27 For by the things through which they
suffered distress,
being tortured by the very things they
deemed gods,
They saw and recognized the true God
whom formerly they had refused
to know;
with this, their final condemnation*
came upon them.[g]

CHAPTER 13

See RG 275–76

Digression on False Worship
*A. Nature Worship**

1 Foolish by nature were all who were in
ignorance of God,
and who from the good things seen did
not succeed in knowing the one
who is,*
and from studying the works did not
discern the artisan;[h]
2 Instead either fire, or wind, or the swift
air,
or the circuit of the stars, or the mighty
water,
or the luminaries of heaven, the
governors* of the world, they
considered gods.[i]
3 Now if out of joy in their beauty they
thought them gods,
let them know how far more excellent
is the Lord than these;
for the original source of beauty
fashioned them.[j]
4 Or if they were struck by their might and
energy,
let them realize from these things how
much more powerful is the one
who made them.[k]
5 For from the greatness and the beauty of
created things
their original author, by analogy, is
seen.
6 But yet, for these the blame is less;*

12:27 Condemnation: the death of Egyptian firstborn and the destruction of their army in the sea.

13:1–9 The author holds a relatively benign view of the efforts of the philosophers to come to know God from various natural phenomena. This is not a question of proving the existence of God in scholastic style. The author thinks that the beauty and might of the world should have pointed by analogy (v. 5) to the Maker. Instead, those "in ignorance of God" remained fixed on the elements (v. 2, three named, along with the stars). His Greek counterparts are not totally blameless; they should have gone further and acknowledged the creator of nature's wonders (vv. 4–5). Cf. Rom 1:18–23; Acts 17:27–28.

13:1 One who is: this follows the Greek translation of the sacred name for God in Hebrew; cf. Ex 3:14.

13:2 Governors: the sun and moon (cf. Gn 1:16).

13:6 The blame is less: the greater blame is incurred by those mentioned in v. 10; 15:14–16.

c: Wis 18:22; Gn 50:24; Dt 7:6–14; Ps 105:8–11. *d:* Wis 11:16; 16:1. *e:* Dt 11:28; Jer 5:28; Rom 1:23. *f:* Jer 4:22. *g:* Wis 16:16; Ex 14:4, 28. *h:* Acts 14:17; Eph 4:17–19. *i:* Gn 1:14–19; Dt 4:19; Jb 31:26–28. *j:* Ps 8:4. *k:* Jer 10:2; Bar 6:39.

For they have gone astray perhaps,
though they seek God and wish to find him.
7 For they search busily among his works,
but are distracted by what they see,
because the things seen are fair.
8 But again, not even these are pardonable.
9 For if they so far succeeded in knowledge
that they could speculate about the world,
how did they not more quickly find its Lord?

*B. Idolatry**

10 But wretched are they, and in dead things are their hopes,
who termed gods things made by human hands:
Gold and silver, the product of art, and images of beasts,
or useless stone, the work of an ancient hand.[l]

The Carpenter and Wooden Idols

11 A carpenter may cut down a suitable tree[m]
and skillfully scrape off all its bark,
And deftly plying his art
produce something fit for daily use,[n]
12 And use the scraps from his handiwork
in preparing his food, and have his fill;
13 Then the good-for-nothing refuse from these remnants,
crooked wood grown full of knots,
he takes and carves to occupy his spare time.[o]
This wood he models with mindless skill,
and patterns it on the image of a human being
14 or makes it resemble some worthless beast.
When he has daubed it with red and crimsoned its surface with red stain,
and daubed over every blemish in it,[p]
15 He makes a fitting shrine for it
and puts it on the wall, fastening it with a nail.[q]
16 Thus he provides for it lest it fall down,
knowing that it cannot help itself;
for, truly, it is an image and needs help.[r]
17 But when he prays about his goods or marriage or children,[s]
he is not ashamed to address the thing without a soul.
For vigor he invokes the powerless;
18 for life he entreats the dead;
For aid he beseeches the wholly incompetent;
for travel, something that cannot even walk;
19 For profit in business and success with his hands
he asks power of a thing with hands utterly powerless.

CHAPTER 14

See RG 275–76

1 Again, one preparing for a voyage
and about to traverse the wild waves
cries out to wood more unsound than the boat that bears him.[t]
2 For the urge for profits devised this latter,
and Wisdom the artisan produced it.

3 * But your providence, O Father! guides it,
for you have furnished even in the sea a road,
and through the waves a steady path,[u]
4 Showing that you can save from any danger,
so that even one without skill may embark.[v]
5 But you will that the products of your Wisdom be not idle;

13:10–19 The second digression is an example of the polemic against idolatry (cf. Is 44:9–20; Jer 10:3–9; Ps 135:15–18). Whether the idols be of wood or clay, they were made by human beings and have become the source of evil.

14:3–6 The wooden ship mentioned in vv. 1–2 prompts a short meditation on the providence of God, who in fact has watched over boats in their dangerous courses. The wood as described in v. 7 became a favorite patristic type for the wood of the cross.

l: Wis 3:11; 15:5, 17; Dt 4:25–28; 7:25; 27:15; Ps 115:4; Hos 14:4; Acts 17:29. *m:* Is 44:9–20. *n:* Wis 15:7; Bar 6:58. *o:* Dt 4:16. *p:* Jer 10:9. *q:* Is 40:20; 41:7; 44:13. *r:* 1 Sm 5:3–5; Bar 6:57. *s:* Wis 15:15. *t:* Is 46:7. *u:* Ps 107:23–30; Is 43:16. *v:* Wis 16:8.

therefore people trust their lives even
to most frail wood,
and were safe crossing the waves on a
raft.[w]
6 For of old, when the proud giants were
being destroyed,
the hope of the universe, who took
refuge on a raft,*
left to the world a future for the human
family, under the guidance of
your hand.
7 For blest is the wood through which
righteousness comes about;
8 but the handmade idol is accursed, and
its maker as well:
he for having produced it, and the
corruptible thing, because it was
termed a god.[x]
9 Equally odious to God are the evildoer
and the evil deed;
10 and the thing made will be punished
with its maker.
11 Therefore upon even the idols of the
nations shall a judgment come,
since they became abominable among
God's works,
Snares for human souls
and a trap for the feet of the senseless.[y]

The Origin and Evils of Idolatry

12 For the source of wantonness is the
devising of idols;
and their invention, a corruption of life.[z]
13 For in the beginning they were not,
nor can they ever continue;[a]
14 for from human emptiness they came
into the world,
and therefore a sudden end is devised
for them.
15 * For a father, afflicted with untimely
mourning,
made an image of the child so quickly
taken from him,
And now honored as a god what once
was dead
and handed down to his household
mysteries and sacrifices.
16 Then, in the course of time, the impious
practice gained strength and was
observed as law,
and graven things were worshiped by
royal decrees.[b]
17 People who lived so far away that they
could not honor him in his presence
copied the appearance of the distant
king
And made a public image of him they
wished to honor,
out of zeal to flatter the absent one as
though present.
18 And to promote this observance among
those to whom it was strange,
the artisan's ambition provided a
stimulus.
19 For he, perhaps in his determination to
please the ruler,
labored over the likeness* to the best
of his skill;[c]
20 And the masses, drawn by the charm of
the workmanship,
soon took as an object of worship the
one who shortly before was
honored as a human being.[d]
21 And this became a snare for the world,
that people enslaved to either grief or
tyranny
conferred the incommunicable Name
on stones and wood.
22 Then it was not enough for them to err in
their knowledge of God;[e]
but even though they live in a great
war resulting from ignorance,
they call such evils peace.[f]
23 For while they practice either child
sacrifices or occult mysteries,
or frenzied carousing in exotic rites,[g]

14:6 Noah.
14:15–21 The author develops two examples of idolatry: cult of the dead, and cult of the king.
14:19 Likeness: he made this more flattering than the reality.

w: Wis 10:4. *x:* Rom 1:23. *y:* Wis 3:7; Nm 33:4; Jos 23:13; Ps 115:4; Jer 6:15; 10:15; 46:25; Hos 9:15. *z:* Rom 1:23–32. *a:* Is 2:18. *b:* 1 Mc 1:47–50; Dn 3:4–7. *c:* Is 44:12–13 LXX. *d:* Wis 15:4. *e:* Jer 2:20; 3:1–25; Hos 4:1–2, 9–19; Rom 1:26–31; Gal 5:19–21; 1 Tm 1:9–10. *f:* Jer 6:14; Ez 13:10. *g:* Wis 12:4–5; 14:15; Is 57:5.

24 They no longer respect either lives or
purity of marriage;
but they either waylay and kill each
other, or aggrieve each other by
adultery.
25 And all is confusion—blood and murder,
theft and guile,[h]
corruption, faithlessness, turmoil,
perjury,
26 Disturbance of good people, neglect of
gratitude,
besmirching of souls, unnatural lust,
disorder in marriage, adultery and
shamelessness.
27 For the worship of infamous idols
is the reason and source and extreme
of all evil.[i]
28 For they either go mad with enjoyment,
or prophesy lies,
or live lawlessly or lightly perjure
themselves.[j]
29 For as their trust is in lifeless idols,
they expect no harm when they have
sworn falsely.
30 But on both counts justice shall overtake
them:
because they thought perversely of
God by devoting themselves to
idols,[k]
and because they deliberately swore
false oaths, despising piety.*
31 For it is not the might of those by whom
they swear,
but the just retribution of sinners,
that ever follows upon the
transgression of the wicked.*

CHAPTER 15

See RG 275–76

1 * But you, our God, are good and
true,
slow to anger, and governing all with
mercy.[l]
2 For even if we sin, we are yours, and
know your might;
but we will not sin, knowing that we
belong to you.[m]
3 For to know you well is complete
righteousness,
and to know your might is the root of
immortality.[n]
4 For the evil creation of human fancy did
not deceive us,
nor the fruitless labor of painters,[o]
A form smeared with varied colors,
5 the sight of which arouses yearning in
a fool,
till he longs for the inanimate form of
a dead image.
6 Lovers of evil things, and worthy of such
hopes
are they who make them and long for
them and worship them.[p]

The Potter's Clay Idols

7 For the potter, laboriously working the
soft earth,
molds for our service each single
article:
He fashions out of the same clay
both the vessels that serve for clean
purposes
and their opposites, all alike;
As to what shall be the use of each vessel
of either class
the worker in clay is the judge.[q]
8 * With misspent toil he molds a
meaningless god from the
selfsame clay,
though he himself shortly before was
made from the earth,
And is soon to go whence he was taken,
when the life that was lent him is
demanded back.[r]
9 But his concern is not that he is to die
nor that his span of life is brief;

14:30 Piety: the sanctity of oaths.

14:31 Perjury is a form of deceit which calls for punishment even though it be practiced in the name of a lifeless idol.

15:1–3 As often before (11:26; 12:2; 14:3–6), the author addresses God directly, so that chaps. 11–19 can be conceived as a more or less continuous prayer (cf. 11:7 and 19:22). This is the living God who is in stark contrast to the deadness of the idols that have been discussed. The merciful God (cf. Ex 34:6) is the source of immortality (1:15) for the community.

15:8–9 The author matches the irony of his words about the carpenter in 13:15–19 with this description of the potter's vain work.

h: Jer 7:8–9; 22:17. *i:* Ex 23:13. *j:* Jer 5:31; 29:26. *k:* Wis 1:1, 8; 11:20; Jer 5:2, 7. *l:* Ex 34:6–7; Ps 86:5, 15; 145:8, 9, 14. *m:* Jb 10:14–15 LXX. *n:* Wis 3:15; Jn 17:3. *o:* Wis 13:14. *p:* Ps 115:8. *q:* Wis 13:11; Jer 18:3–4; Rom 9:21; 2 Tm 2:20–21. *r:* Gn 3:19; Eccl 12:7.

Rather, he vies with goldsmiths and silversmiths
and emulates molders of bronze,
and takes pride in fashioning counterfeits.[s]
10 Ashes his heart is!* more worthless than earth is his hope,[t]
more ignoble than clay his life;
11 Because he knew not the one who fashioned him,
and breathed into him a quickening soul,
and infused a vital spirit.[u]
12 Instead, he esteemed our life a mere game,
and our span of life a holiday for gain;
"For one must," says he, "make a profit in every way, be it even from evil."[v]
13 For more than anyone else he knows that he is sinning,
when out of earthen stuff he creates fragile vessels and idols alike.
14 But most stupid of all and worse than senseless in mind,
are the enemies of your people who enslaved them.[w]
15 For they esteemed all the idols of the nations as gods,
which cannot use their eyes to see,
nor nostrils to breathe the air,
Nor ears to hear,
nor fingers on their hands for feeling;
even their feet are useless to walk with.[x]
16 For it was a mere human being who made them;[y]
one living on borrowed breath who fashioned them.
For no one is able to fashion a god like himself;
17 he is mortal, and what he makes with lawless hands is dead.
For he is better than the things he worships;
he at least lives, but never his idols.

Second Example Resumed

18 * Besides, they worship the most loathsome beasts—[z]
as regards stupidity, these are worse than the rest,*
19 For beasts are neither good-looking nor desirable;
they have escaped both the approval of God and his blessing.[a]

CHAPTER 16

See RG 275–76

1 Therefore they* were fittingly punished by similar creatures,
and were tormented by a swarm of insects.[b]
2 Instead of this punishment, you benefited your people
with a novel dish, the delight they craved,
by providing quail for their food,[c]
3 So that those others, when they desired food,
should lose their appetite even for necessities,
since the creatures sent to plague them were so loathsome,
While these, after a brief period of privation,
partook of a novel dish.[d]
4 For inexorable want had to come upon those oppressors;
but these needed only to be shown how their enemies were being tormented.[e]
5 For when the dire venom of beasts came upon them[f]
and they were dying from the bite of crooked serpents,

15:10 Ashes his heart is!: the words of this cry are taken from Is 44:20 (the Septuagint).

15:18–19 The author here returns (11:15; 12:23–27) to the main theme of chaps. 11–19, which was interrupted by the digression of 13:1–15:17.

15:18 Worse than the rest: this may mean that the creatures worshiped by the Egyptians (e.g., crocodiles, serpents, scarabs, etc.) were less intelligent than the general run of beasts.

16:1 They: the Egyptian idolaters, who are punished according to the principle laid down in 11:5, 15–16.

s: Bar 6:46. *t:* Jb 13:12 LXX. *u:* Gn 2:7; Zec 12:1. *v:* Jas 4:13–14. *w:* Ex 1:13. *x:* Wis 14:11; Dt 4:28; Ps 115:4–7; 135:15–18. *y:* Wis 13:10. *z:* Wis 11:15; 12:24. *a:* Gn 1:25; 3:14. *b:* Wis 11:15–16; 12:23, 27; Ex 7:27; 8:12, 17. *c:* Wis 11:13; 19:11–12; Ex 16:13; Nm 11:31–32; Ps 105:40. *d:* Wis 11:15; Ex 8:10; 16:3. *e:* Wis 11:8–9. *f:* Nm 21:4–9; Dt 32:24; Jer 8:17 LXX.

your anger endured not to the end.
6 But as a warning, for a short time they were terrorized,
though they had a sign* of salvation, to remind them of the precept of your law.
7 For the one who turned toward it was saved,
not by what was seen,
but by you, the savior of all.
8 By this also you convinced our foes
that you are the one who delivers from all evil.[g]
9 For the bites of locusts and of flies slew them,
and no remedy was found to save their lives
because they deserved to be punished by such means;[h]
10 But not even the fangs of poisonous reptiles overcame your children,
for your mercy came forth and healed them.[i]
11 For as a reminder of your injunctions, they were stung,
and swiftly they were saved,
Lest they should fall into deep forgetfulness
and become unresponsive to your beneficence.[j]
12 For indeed, neither herb nor application cured them,
but your all-healing word, O LORD![k]
13 * For you have dominion over life and death;[l]
you lead down to the gates of Hades and lead back.
14 Human beings, however, may kill another with malice,
but they cannot bring back the departed spirit,
or release the soul that death has confined.
15 Your hand no one can escape.

Third Example: A Rain of Manna for Israel Instead of the Plague of Storms

16 For the wicked who refused to know you were punished by the might of your arm,
Were pursued by unusual rains and hailstorms and unremitting downpours,
and were consumed by fire.[m]
17 For against all expectation, in water which quenches everything,
the fire grew more active;
For the universe fights on behalf of the righteous.[n]
18 Then the flame was tempered[o]
so that the beasts that were sent upon the wicked might not be burnt up,
but that these might see and know that they were struck by the judgment of God;
19 And again, even in the water, fire blazed beyond its strength
so as to consume the produce of the wicked land.
20 Instead of this, you nourished your people with food of angels*
and furnished them bread from heaven, ready to hand, untoiled-for,
endowed with all delights and conforming to every taste.[p]
21 For this substance of yours revealed your sweetness toward your children,
and serving the desire of the one who received it,

16:6 Sign: the brazen serpent, as related in Numbers 21, but the author deliberately avoids any misunderstanding by addressing the Lord as responsible for the healing, since he is "the savior of all" (v. 7; see also vv. 12 and 26 for the role of the "word" of God).

16:13–14 The author recognizes the power of the Lord over life and death, as expressed in 1 Sm 2:6; Tb 13:2. The traditional imagery of Sheol (gates and confinement) colors the passage.

16:20 Food of angels: the famous phrase (cf. the hymn "Panis Angelicus") is taken from Ps 78:24 as rendered by the Septuagint. The "bread from heaven" (cf. Ex 16:4; Ps 105:40) with its marvelous "sweetness" becomes a type of the "bread come down from heaven" in Jn 6:32–51, and plays a large role in later Christian devotion.

g: Gn 48:16; 2 Mc 1:24–25. *h:* Ex 8:16–28; 10:4–19; Ps 78:45–46; 105:31, 34; Rev 9:1–11. *i:* Dt 32:33. *j:* Ps 78:11. *k:* Ex 15:26. *l:* Dt 32:39; 1 Sm 2:6; Tb 13:2; 2 Mc 6:26; 7:23; Ps 78:34, 39; Eccl 8:8; Dn 5:19. *m:* Wis 11:21; 12:27; Ex 5:2; 9:29–34. *n:* Wis 10:20; 19:20; Ex 9:23–28; 2 Mc 8:36; 14:34. *o:* Wis 19:20–21. *p:* Ex 16:4; Nm 11:8; Ps 78:24–25; Jn 6:31.

was changed to whatever flavor each
one wished.[q]
22 Yet snow and ice* withstood fire and
were not melted,
so that they might know that their
enemies' fruits
Were consumed by a fire that blazed in
the hail
and flashed lightning in the rain.[r]

23 But this fire, again, in order that the
righteous might be nourished,
forgot even its proper strength;[s]
24 For your creation, serving you, its
maker,
grows tense for punishment against
the wicked,
but is relaxed in benefit for those who
trust in you.[t]
25 Therefore at that very time, transformed
in all sorts of ways,
it was serving your all-nourishing
bounty
according to what they needed and
desired;
26 That your children whom you loved
might learn, O LORD,
that it is not the various kinds of fruits
that nourish,
but your word that preserves those
who believe you![u]
27 For what was not destroyed by fire,
melted when merely warmed by a
momentary sunbeam;[v]
28 To make known that one must give you
thanks before sunrise,
and turn to you at daybreak.[w]
29 For the hope of the ungrateful melts
like a wintry frost
and runs off like useless
water.[x]

CHAPTER 17

See RG 275–76

*Fourth Example: Darkness Afflicts the Egyptians, While the Israelites Have Light**

1 For great are your judgments, and hard to
describe;
therefore the unruly souls went astray.[y]
2 For when the lawless thought to enslave
the holy nation,
they themselves lay shackled with
darkness, fettered by the long
night,
confined beneath their own roofs as
exiles from the eternal
providence.[z]
3 For they, who supposed their secret sins
were hid[a]
under the dark veil of oblivion,
Were scattered in fearful trembling,
terrified by apparitions.
4 For not even their inner chambers kept
them unafraid,
for crashing sounds on all sides
terrified them,
and mute phantoms with somber looks
appeared.
5 No fire had force enough to give light,
nor did the flaming brilliance of the
stars
succeed in lighting up that gloomy
night.[b]
6 But only intermittent, fearful fires
flashed through upon them;
And in their terror they thought
beholding these was worse
than the times when that sight was no
longer to be seen.[c]
7 And mockeries of their magic art* failed,
and there was a humiliating refutation
of their vaunted shrewdness.[d]

16:22 Snow and ice: the manna; cf. v. 27; 19:21.

17:1–18:4 The description of the darkness of the ninth plague is a very creative development of Ex 10:21–29. It betrays a wide knowledge of contemporary thought. For the first and only time in the Septuagint the Greek word for "conscience" occurs, in 17:11. There is no Hebrew word that is equivalent; the idea is expressed indirectly. The horrendous darkness is illumined by "fires" (v. 6), i.e., lightnings that only contributed to the terror.

17:7 Magic art: the Egyptian magicians who were successful at first (Ex 7:11, 22) and then failed (Ex 8:14; 9:11) are now powerless against the darkness and the phantoms and are totally discredited.

q: Ps 34:9. *r:* Ex 9:25–31; 10:12; Ps 148:8. *s:* Wis 19:21. *t:* Wis 5:17, 20; 19:6; Sir 39:25–27. *u:* Dt 8:3; Mt 4:4. *v:* Ex 16:21. *w:* Ps 57:9–10; 92:3. *x:* Wis 5:14; 2 Sm 14:14. *y:* Ex 6:6 LXX. *z:* Wis 18:4; Ex 1:13–14; 9:6; 10:21–23. *a:* Wis 1:7–8; 10:8; 18:17. *b:* Wis 10:17; Jer 23:24 LXX. *c:* Ex 9:23–24. *d:* Wis 12:25–26; Ex 7:11–12, 22; 8:3; 9:11; 10:2.

8 For they who undertook to banish fears
and terrors from the sick soul
themselves sickened with ridiculous
fear.
9 For even though no monstrous thing
frightened them,
they shook at the passing of insects
and the hissing of reptiles,[e]
10 And perished trembling,
reluctant to face even the air that they
could nowhere escape.
11 For wickedness, of its nature cowardly,
testifies in its own condemnation,
and because of a distressed
conscience, always magnifies
misfortunes.[f]
12 For fear is nought but the surrender of
the helps that come from reason;
13 and the more one's expectation is of
itself uncertain,
the more one makes of not knowing
the cause that brings on torment.
14 So they, during that night, powerless
though it was,
since it had come upon them from the
recesses of a powerless* Hades,
while all sleeping the same sleep,
15 Were partly smitten by fearsome
apparitions
and partly stricken by their souls'
surrender;
for fear overwhelmed them, sudden
and unexpected.[g]
16 Thus, then, whoever was there fell
into that prison without bars and was
kept confined.[h]
17 For whether one was a farmer, or a
shepherd,
or a worker at tasks in the wasteland,
Taken unawares, each served out the
inescapable sentence;
18 for all were bound by the one bond of
darkness.[i]
And were it only the whistling wind,
or the melodious song of birds in the
spreading branches,
Or the steady sound of rushing water,
19 or the rude crash of overthrown rocks,
Or the unseen gallop of bounding animals,
or the roaring cry of the fiercest beasts,
Or an echo resounding from the hollow
of the hills—
these sounds, inspiring terror,
paralyzed them.
20 For the whole world shone with brilliant
light[j]
and continued its works without
interruption;
21 But over them alone was spread
oppressive night,
an image of the darkness* that was
about to come upon them.
Yet they were more a burden to
themselves than was the darkness.

CHAPTER 18

See RG 275–76

1 But your holy ones had very great
light;
And those others, who heard their voices
but did not see their forms,
counted them blest for not having
suffered;
2 And because they who formerly had been
wronged did not harm them, they
thanked them,
and because of the difference between
them,* pleaded with them.
3 Instead of this, you furnished the flaming
pillar,
a guide on the unknown way,
and the mild sun for an honorable
migration.[k]
4 * For they deserved to be deprived of
light and imprisoned by darkness,
they had kept your children confined,
through whom the imperishable light
of the law was to be given to the
world.[l]

17:14 Powerless: Hades (or Sheol), i.e., the nether world, is often portrayed in the Old Testament as a hostile power, since all must die (Ps 49:8–13), but it has no power against God.

17:21 Darkness: of Hades or Sheol; see note on 16:13–14.

18:2 The difference between them: God's distinctive manner of treating the Israelites and the Egyptians according to their respective deeds. **Pleaded**: perhaps, for their departure.

18:4 The discussion of physical light climaxes with a reference to the "imperishable light" of the torah.

e: Wis 16:1; Jer 26:22 LXX. *f:* Wis 4:6; 10:7; Rom 2:15. *g:* Ex 11:9–10. *h:* Wis 18:4; Ex 10:23. *i:* Lv 26:36. *j:* Ex 10:23; Is 9:1; 60:1–3; 2 Pt 2:17. *k:* Ex 13:21. *l:* Wis 17:2; Ps 119:105; Is 2:3, 5.

Fifth Example: Death of the Egyptian Firstborn; the Israelites Are Spared

5 When they determined to put to death the infants of the holy ones,
and when a single boy* had been cast forth and then saved,
As a reproof you carried off a multitude of their children
and made them perish all at once in the mighty water.[m]
6 That night was known beforehand to our ancestors,
so that, with sure knowledge of the oaths in which they put their faith, they might have courage.[n]
7 The expectation of your people
was the salvation of the righteous and the destruction of their foes.[o]
8 For by the same means with which you punished our adversaries,
you glorified us whom you had summoned.[p]
9 For in secret the holy children of the good were offering sacrifice
and carried out with one mind the divine institution,*
So that your holy ones should share alike the same blessings and dangers,
once they had sung the ancestral hymns of praise.[q]
10 But the discordant cry of their enemies echoed back,
and the piteous wail of mourning for children was borne to them.[r]
11 And the slave was smitten with the same retribution as the master;
even the commoner suffered the same as the king.[s]
12 And all alike by one common form of death
had countless dead;
For the living were not even sufficient for the burial,
since at a single instant their most valued offspring had been destroyed.[t]
13 For though they disbelieved at every turn on account of sorceries,
at the destruction of the firstborn they acknowledged that this people* was God's son.[u]
14 * For when peaceful stillness encompassed everything
and the night in its swift course was half spent,
15 Your all-powerful word from heaven's royal throne
leapt into the doomed land,[v]
16 a fierce warrior bearing the sharp sword of your inexorable decree,
And alighted, and filled every place with death,
and touched heaven, while standing upon the earth.[w]
17 Then, at once, visions in horrible dreams perturbed them[x]
and unexpected fears assailed them;
18 And cast half-dead, one here, another there,
they revealed why they were dying.
19 For the dreams that disturbed them had proclaimed this beforehand,
lest they perish unaware of why they endured such evil.
20 The trial of death touched even the righteous,
and in the desert a plague struck the multitude;
Yet not for long did the anger last.[y]
21 For the blameless man* hastened to be their champion,
bearing the weapon of his special office,
prayer and the propitiation of incense;
He withstood the wrath and put a stop to the calamity,

18:5 Single boy: Moses.

18:9 Divine institution: the Passover. **Ancestral hymns of praise**: possibly the Hallel psalms, the psalms sung at the end of the Passover meal; cf. Mt 26:30; Mk 14:26.

18:13 People: the Israelites (cf. Ex 4:22).

18:14–16 These verses attribute to the personified "word" the actions of the Lord mentioned in Ex 12:13–17 (note the role of the "destroyer" in Ex 12:23 and compare Wis 18:22, 25).

18:21 Blameless man: Aaron, acting according to his office of high priest and intercessor (cf. Nm 17:9–15; Ex 28:15–21, 31–38).

m: Wis 11:7, 14; Ex 1:16, 22; 2:3, 6–10; 15:10; Neh 9:11. *n:* Wis 12:21; Ex 6:8; 13:5. *o:* Ex 14:13. *p:* Wis 19:22; Ex 3:18; Is 43:3–4. *q:* Ex 12:21–28; Sir 44–50. *r:* Ex 12:30; Jer 9:17, 19. *s:* Ex 11:5; 12:29. *t:* Nm 33:4. *u:* Wis 17:7; Ex 4:22–23; 12:12, 29; 13:2, 13, 15. *v:* Wis 9:10; Ex 15:3. *w:* 1 Chr 21:16; Heb 4:12; Rev 1:16. *x:* Wis 17:3–4. *y:* Wis 16:5; Nm 17:9–15.

showing that he was your servant.
22 He overcame the bitterness
not by bodily strength, not by force of arms;
But by word he overcame the smiter,*
recalling the sworn covenants with their ancestors.[z]
23 For when corpses had already fallen one on another in heaps,
he stood in the midst and checked the anger,
and cut off its way to the living.[a]
24 For on his full-length robe was the whole world,
and ancestral glories were carved on the four rows of stones,
and your grandeur* was on the crown upon his head.[b]
25 To these the destroyer yielded, these he feared;
for this sole trial of anger sufficed.[c]

CHAPTER 19

See RG 275–76

1 But merciless wrath assailed the wicked until the end,
for God knew beforehand what they were yet to do:[d]
2 That though they themselves had agreed to the departure
and had anxiously sent them on their way,
they would regret it and pursue them.[e]
3 For while they were still engaged in funeral rites
and mourning at the burials of the dead,
They adopted another senseless plan:
those whom they had driven out with entreaties
they now pursued as fugitives.[f]
4 For a compulsion appropriate to this ending drew them on,
and made them forget what had befallen them,
That they might complete the torments of their punishment,
5 and your people might experience a glorious* journey
while those others met an extraordinary death.
6 * For all creation, in its several kinds,
was being made over anew,
serving your commands, that your children might be preserved unharmed.[g]
7 The cloud overshadowed their camp;
and out of what had been water, dry land was seen emerging:
Out of the Red Sea an unimpeded road,
and a grassy plain out of the mighty flood.[h]
8 Over this crossed the whole nation sheltered by your hand,
and they beheld stupendous wonders.
9 For they ranged about like horses,
and leapt like lambs,
praising you, LORD, their deliverer.[i]
10 For they were still mindful of what had happened in their sojourn:
how instead of the young of animals the land brought forth gnats,
and instead of fishes the river swarmed with countless frogs.[j]
11 And later they saw also a new kind of bird[k]
when, prompted by desire, they asked for pleasant foods;
12 For to appease them quail came to them from the sea.
13 And the punishments came upon the sinners
not without forewarnings from the violence of the thunderbolts.
For they justly suffered for their own misdeeds,
since they treated their guests with the more grievous* hatred.[l]

18:22 Smiter: the destroying angel; cf. v. 25.

18:24 Glories . . . grandeur: the name of God and the names of the tribes were inscribed on the high priest's apparel.

19:5 Glorious: more precisely, "wondrous," but the word reflects "glorified" in 18:8 and 19:22.

19:6 The cooperation of creation in Israel's deliverance (vv. 7–12) under the direction of the Lord is a favorite theme; cf. 16:24–25.

19:13 More grievous: than that of the people of Sodom (Gn 19) with whom the Egyptians are compared.

z: Wis 12:21; Ex 32:12–13; Ps 20:8. *a:* Nm 14:29–30. *b:* Ex 28:15–21, 31–38; Sir 45:8–12; 50:11. *c:* 1 Chr 21:15. *d:* Ex 14:4. *e:* Ex 12:33; 14:5, 8. *f:* Wis 18:10, 12; Ex 12:30–36. *g:* Wis 5:17; 16:24. *h:* Ex 14:21–29. *i:* Wis 10:20; 16:8; Ex 15:1–18; Ps 114:4–6. *j:* Ex 7:27–8:3; 8:12–15; Ps 105:30–31. *k:* Wis 16:2; Ps 78:18. *l:* 2 Mc 7:18, 32.

[14] For those others* did not receive
unfamiliar visitors,[m]
but these were enslaving beneficent
guests.
[15] And not that only; but what punishment
was to be theirs*
since they received strangers
unwillingly!
[16] Yet these,* after welcoming them with
festivities,
oppressed with awful toils
those who had shared with them the
same rights.[n]
[17] And they were struck with blindness,*
as those others had been at the doors
of the righteous man—
When, surrounded by yawning darkness,
each sought the entrance of his own
door.[o]

[18] For the elements, in ever-changing
harmony,
like strings of the harp, produce new
melody,
while the flow of music steadily
persists.
And this can be perceived exactly from a
review of what took place.
[19] For land creatures were changed into
water creatures,
and those that swam went over on
land.
[20] Fire in water maintained its own strength,[p]
and water forgot its quenching nature;
[21] Flames, by contrast, neither consumed
the flesh
of the perishable animals that went
about in them,
nor melted the icelike, quick-melting
kind of ambrosial food.
[22] For every way, LORD! you magnified and
glorified your people;
unfailing, you stood by them in every
time and circumstance.[q]

19:14 Others: the people of Sodom refused to receive strangers. **Beneficent**: because of the services rendered by Joseph.
19:15 Theirs: the people of Sodom.
19:16 These: the Egyptians.
19:17 Blindness: the plague of darkness. **Righteous man**: Lot (Gn 19:11).

m: Gn 15:13; Ex 2:22. *n:* Gn 45:17–20; 47:4–6; Ex 1:11. *o:* Wis 17:2; Gn 19:11. *p:* Wis 16:17–19, 22–23, 27. *q:* Wis 18:8; Lv 26:44; Ps 126:3.

See RG 276–79

The Wisdom of Ben Sira (Ecclesiasticus)

The Wisdom of Ben Sira derives its title from the author, "Yeshua [Jesus], son of Eleazar, son of Sira" (50:27). This seems to be the earliest title of the book. The designation "Liber Ecclesiasticus," meaning "Church Book," appended to some Greek and Latin manuscripts, is perhaps due to the extensive use the church made of this book in presenting moral teaching to catechumens and to the faithful. The title "Sirach" comes from the Greek form of the author's name.

The author, a sage who lived in Jerusalem, was thoroughly imbued with love for the wisdom tradition, and also for the law, priesthood, Temple, and divine worship. As a wise and experienced observer of life he addressed himself to his contemporaries with the motive of helping them to maintain religious faith and integrity through study of the books sacred to the Jewish tradition.

The book contains numerous well-crafted maxims, grouped by affinity, and dealing with a variety of subjects such as the individual, the family, and the community in their relations with one another and with God. It treats of friendship, education, poverty and wealth, laws, religious worship, and many other matters that reflect the religious and social customs of the time.

Written in Hebrew in the early years of the second century B.C., the book was finished by ca. 175. The text was translated into Greek by the author's grandson after 117 B.C. He also wrote a foreword which contains valuable information about the book, its author, and himself as translator. Until the close of the nineteenth century the Wisdom of Ben Sira was known to Christians in translations, of which the Greek rendering was the most important. From it the Latin version was made. Between 1896 and 1900, again in 1931, and several times since 1956, incomplete manuscripts were discovered, so that more than two thirds of the book in Hebrew is available; these Hebrew texts agree substantially with the Greek. One such text, from Masada, is pre-Christian in date. The New American Bible provides a critical translation based on the evidence of all the ancient texts.

Though not included in the Jewish Bible after the first century A.D., nor, therefore, accepted by Protestants, the Wisdom of Ben Sira has been recognized by the Catholic Church as inspired and canonical. The Foreword, though not properly part of the book, is always included with it because of its antiquity and importance.

The contents of the Wisdom of Ben Sira are of a discursive nature, not easily divided into separate parts. Chapters 1–43 deal largely with moral instruction; 44:1–50:24 contain a eulogy of the heroes of Israel. There are two appendixes in which the author expresses his gratitude to God (51:1–12), and invites the unschooled to acquire true wisdom (51:13–30).

FOREWORD

Inasmuch as many and great truths have been given to us through the Law, the prophets, and the authors who followed them,* for which the instruction and wisdom of Israel merit praise, it is the duty of those who read the scriptures not only to become knowledgeable themselves but also to use their love of learning in speech and in writing to help others less familiar. So my grandfather Jesus, who had long devoted himself to the study of the law, the prophets, and the rest of the books of our ancestors, and had acquired great familiarity with them, was moved to write something himself regarding instruction and wisdom. He did this so that those who love learning might, by accepting what he had written, make even greater progress in living according to the Law.

You are invited therefore to read it with good will and attention, with indulgence for any failure on our part, despite earnest efforts, in the interpretation of particular passages. For words spoken originally in Hebrew do not have the same effect when they are translated into another language. That is true not only of this book but of the Law itself, the prophecies, and the rest of the books, which differ no little when they are read in the original.

I arrived in Egypt in the thirty-eighth year of the reign of King Euergetes, and while there, I had access to no little learning. I therefore considered it my duty to devote some diligence and industry to the translation of this book. During this time I applied my skill for many sleepless hours to complete the book and publish it for those living abroad who wish to acquire learning and are disposed to live their lives according to the Law.

The Wisdom of Ben Sira

CHAPTER 1

See RG 276–79

*God's Gift of Wisdom**

1 All wisdom* is from the Lord
and remains with him forever.[a]
2 The sands of the sea, the drops of rain,
the days of eternity—who can count them?
3 Heaven's height, earth's extent,
the abyss and wisdom—who can explore them?
4 Before all other things wisdom was created;
and prudent understanding, from eternity.†

Foreword The Law, the prophets, and the authors who followed them: an indication of the eventual tripartite division of the Hebrew Scriptures: Law (*torah*), Prophets (*nebi'im*), and Writings (*ketubim*), shortened in the acronym Tanak. **Thirty-eighth . . . Euergetes**: 132 B.C. The reference is to Ptolemy VII, Physkon Euergetes II (170–163; 145–117 B.C.).

1:1–10 This brief poem serves as an introduction to the book. The Lord is the source and preserver of all wisdom, which he pours out upon all. See Jb 28:20–28; Prv 2:6; 8:22–31; Wis 7:25–27.

1:1 Wisdom: throughout the book Ben Sira describes in great detail just what wisdom is: sometimes divine (1:6, 8), sometimes a synonym for God's law (24:22–23). Ben Sira makes clear that all wisdom comes from God.

† Other ancient texts read as v. 5:

The wellspring of wisdom is the word of God in the heights,
and its runlets are the ageless commandments.

a: 1 Kgs 3:9.

6 The root of wisdom—to whom has it
been revealed?
Her subtleties—who knows them?† [b]
8 * There is but one, wise and truly
awesome,
seated upon his throne—the Lord.
9 It is he who created her,
saw her and measured her,[c]
Poured her forth upon all his works,
10 upon every living thing according to
his bounty,
lavished her upon those who love him.

*Fear of the Lord Is Wisdom**

11 The fear of the Lord* is glory and
exultation,
gladness and a festive crown.
12 The fear of the Lord rejoices the heart,
giving gladness, joy, and long life.†
13 Those who fear the Lord will be happy at
the end,
even on the day of death they will be
blessed.
14 The beginning of wisdom is to fear the
Lord;
she is created with the faithful in the
womb.[d]
15 With the godly she was created from of
old,
and with their descendants she will
keep faith.
16 The fullness of wisdom is to fear the
Lord;
she inebriates them with her fruits.[e]
17 Their entire house she fills with choice
foods,
their granaries with her produce.
18 The crown of wisdom is the fear of the
Lord,
flowering with peace and perfect
health.†
19 Knowledge and full understanding she
rains down;
she heightens the glory of those who
possess her.
20 The root of wisdom is to fear the Lord;
her branches are long life.
21 The fear of the Lord drives away sins;
where it abides it turns back all anger.
22 Unjust anger can never be justified;
anger pulls a person to utter ruin.
23 * Until the right time, the patient remain
calm,
then cheerfulness comes back to them.
24 Until the right time they hold back their
words;
then the lips of many will tell of their
good sense.
25 Among wisdom's treasures is the model
for knowledge;
but godliness is an abomination to the
sinner.
26 If you desire wisdom, keep the
commandments,
and the Lord will bestow her upon
you;
27 For the fear of the Lord is wisdom and
discipline;
faithfulness and humility are his
delight.
28 Do not disobey the fear of the Lord,*
do not approach it with duplicity of
heart.[f]

† Other ancient texts read as v. 7:
An understanding of wisdom—to whom has this been disclosed;
her resourcefulness, who has known?

1:8–10 In contrast to Jb 28, wisdom is not only with God, but given to all, especially Israel; see Bar 3:9; 4:4.

1:11–30 This is one of several poems of 22 bicola, or poetic lines, corresponding to the number of letters in the Hebrew alphabet. Ben Sira uses the expression "fear of the Lord" twelve times and the noun "wisdom" seven times to emphasize the connection between the two ideas. He describes the blessings that come to those who fear the Lord, i.e., those who practice true religion by loving and serving God and keeping the Law (2:7–10, 15–17; 4:11–16; see Dt 6:1–5, 24). Such blessings recur throughout the book.

1:11 Fear of the Lord: Ben Sira identifies wisdom with the fear of the Lord (vv. 26–27).

† Other ancient texts read as v. 12cd:
Fear of the Lord is the Lord's gift;
also for love he makes firm paths.

† Other ancient texts read as v. 18cd:
Both are gifts of God toward peace;
splendor opens out for those who love him.

1:23–24 Ben Sira pays close attention to *kaîros*, the right time, occurring some sixty times in his book.

1:28–30 Attempting to serve the Lord with duplicity of heart is hypocrisy and self-exaltation, deserving of public disgrace.

b: Bar 3:15; Jb 28:10, 20. *c:* Jb 28:27. *d:* Jb 28:28; Ps 111:10; Prv 1:7; 9:10. *e:* Eccl 12:13. *f:* Jas 1:8; 2:8.

29 Do not be a hypocrite before others;
over your lips keep watch.
30 Do not exalt yourself lest you fall
and bring dishonor upon yourself;
For then the Lord will reveal your secrets
and cast you down in the midst of the assembly.
Because you did not approach the fear of the Lord,
and your heart was full of deceit.

CHAPTER 2

See RG 276–79

Trust in God

1 My child, when you come to serve the Lord,*
prepare yourself for trials.[g]
2 Be sincere of heart and steadfast,
and do not be impetuous in time of adversity.
3 Cling to him, do not leave him,
that you may prosper in your last days.
4 Accept whatever happens to you;
in periods of humiliation be patient.
5 For in fire gold is tested,
and the chosen, in the crucible of humiliation.[h]
6 Trust in God, and he will help you;
make your ways straight and hope in him.

7 You that fear the Lord, wait for his mercy,
do not stray lest you fall.
8 You that fear the Lord, trust in him,
and your reward will not be lost.
9 You that fear the LORD, hope for good things,
for lasting joy and mercy.
10 Consider the generations long past and see:
has anyone trusted in the Lord and been disappointed?
Has anyone persevered in his fear and been forsaken?
has anyone called upon him and been ignored?[i]
11 For the Lord is compassionate and merciful;
forgives sins and saves in time of trouble.

12 Woe to timid hearts and drooping hands,*
to the sinner who walks a double path!
13 Woe to the faint of heart! For they do not trust,
and therefore have no shelter!
14 Woe to you that have lost hope!
what will you do at the Lord's visitation?
15 Those who fear the Lord do not disobey his words;
those who love him keep his ways.[j]
16 Those who fear the Lord seek to please him;
those who love him are filled with his law.
17 Those who fear the Lord prepare their hearts
and humble themselves before him.

18 Let us fall into the hands of the Lord
and not into the hands of mortals,
For equal to his majesty is his mercy;
and equal to his name are his works.[k]

CHAPTER 3

See RG 276–79

*Responsibilities to Parents**

1 Children, listen to me, your father;
act accordingly, that you may be safe.
2 For the Lord sets a father in honor over his children

2:1–11 Serving the Lord is not without its trials (v. 1); but no matter what happens, the genuine believer will remain sincere, steadfast, and faithful (vv. 2–3). Misfortune and humiliation are means of purification to prove one's worth (vv. 4–5). Ben Sira believed that patience and unwavering trust in God are ultimately rewarded with the benefits of God's mercy and of lasting joy (vv. 6–11).

2:12–18 A stern warning to those who compromise their faith in time of affliction; they fail in courage and trust and therefore have no security (vv. 12–14). But those who fear the Lord through obedience, reverence, love, and humility find his "mercy equal to his majesty" (vv. 15–18).

3:1–16 Besides the virtues that must characterize our conduct toward God, special duties are enjoined, such as honor and respect toward parents, with corresponding blessings (vv. 1–9). By showing such respect especially to old and infirm parents (vv. 10–13), the sins of children are pardoned (vv. 14–15). Failure to honor father and mother is blasphemy and merits a curse from God (v. 16). Cf. Ex 20:12; Eph 6:2–3.

g: 2 Tm 3:10–12. *h:* Prv 17:3; Wis 3:6; Is 48:10; 1 Pt 1:7. *i:* Ps 31:2; 145:18–20. *j:* Jn 14:23. *k:* Sir 17:29.

and confirms a mother's authority over
her sons.
3 Those who honor their father atone for
sins;
4 they store up riches who respect their
mother.
5 Those who honor their father will have
joy in their own children,
and when they pray they are heard.
6 Those who respect their father will live a
long life;
those who obey the Lord honor their
mother.
7 Those who fear the Lord honor their
father,
and serve their parents as masters.
8 In word and deed honor your father,
that all blessings may come to you.[l]
9 A father's blessing gives a person firm
roots,
but a mother's curse uproots the
growing plant.[m]
10 Do not glory in your father's disgrace,
for that is no glory to you!
11 A father's glory is glory also for oneself;
they multiply sin who demean their
mother.[n]

12 My son, be steadfast in honoring your
father;
do not grieve him as long as he lives.[o]
13 Even if his mind fails, be considerate of
him;
do not revile him because you are in
your prime.
14 Kindness to a father will not be forgotten;
it will serve as a sin offering—it will
take lasting root.
15 In time of trouble it will be recalled to
your advantage,
like warmth upon frost it will melt
away your sins.
16 Those who neglect their father are like
blasphemers;
those who provoke their mother are
accursed by their Creator.[p]

*Humility**

17 My son, conduct your affairs with
humility,
and you will be loved more than a
giver of gifts.
18 Humble yourself the more, the greater
you are,
and you will find mercy in the sight of
God.[†] [q]
20 For great is the power of the Lord;
by the humble he is glorified.
21 What is too sublime for you, do not seek;
do not reach into things that are hidden
from you.[r]
22 What is committed to you, pay heed to;
what is hidden is not your concern.
23 In matters that are beyond you do not
meddle,
when you have been shown more than
you can understand.
24 Indeed, many are the conceits of human
beings;
evil imaginations lead them astray.

*Docility**

25 Without the pupil of the eye, light is
missing;
without knowledge, wisdom is
missing.
26 A stubborn heart will fare badly in the
end;
those who love danger will perish in it.
27 A stubborn heart will have many a hurt;
adding sin to sin is madness.
28 When the proud are afflicted, there is no
cure;
for they are offshoots of an evil plant.[s]
29 The mind of the wise appreciates
proverbs,
and the ear that listens to wisdom
rejoices.

3:17–24 Humility gives you a true estimate of yourself (vv. 17–20; cf. 10:28), so that you will do what should be done, and avoid what is beyond your understanding and strength (vv. 21–23). Intellectual pride, however, leads you astray (v. 24). Ben Sira is perhaps warning his students against the perils of Greek philosophy.

† Other ancient texts read as v. 19:
Many are lofty and famous,
but to the humble he reveals his plan.

3:25–29 The antidote for stubbornness is to be found in the search for knowledge and wisdom.

l: Ex 20:12; Dt 5:16; Mt 15:4; 19:19; Mk 7:10; 10:19; Lk 18:20; Eph 6:2–3. *m:* Gn 27:27–29; 49:2–27. *n:* Prv 17:6. *o:* Prv 23:22. *p:* Prv 19:26; 30:11, 14, 17. *q:* Mt 23:12; Lk 1:52; 14:11; 18:14. *r:* Ps 131:1. *s:* Dt 32:32; Wis 12:10.

Alms for the Poor

30 As water quenches a flaming fire,
so almsgiving atones for sins.[t]
31 The kindness people have done crosses
their paths later on;
should they stumble, they will find
support.

CHAPTER 4

See RG 276–79

1 My child, do not mock the life of
the poor;
do not keep needy eyes* waiting.[u]
2 Do not grieve the hungry,
nor anger the needy.
3 Do not aggravate a heart already angry,
nor delay giving to the needy.
4 A beggar's request do not reject;
do not turn your face away from the
poor.
5 From the needy do not turn your eyes;
do not give them reason to curse
you.
6 If in their pain they cry out bitterly,
their Rock will hear the sound of their
cry.

Social Conduct

7 Endear yourself to the assembly;
before the city's ruler bow your
head.
8 Give a hearing to the poor,
and return their greeting with
deference;
9 Deliver the oppressed from their
oppressors;[v]
right judgment should not be
repugnant to you.
10 Be like a father to orphans,
and take the place of a husband to
widows.
Then God will call you his child,
and he will be merciful to you and
deliver you from the pit.

*The Rewards of Wisdom**

11 Wisdom teaches her children
and admonishes all who can
understand her.
12 Those who love her love life;
those who seek her out win the LORD's
favor.
13 Those who hold her fast will attain glory,
and they shall abide in the blessing of
the LORD.
14 Those who serve her serve the Holy One;
those who love her the Lord loves.[w]
15 "Whoever obeys me will judge nations;
whoever listens to me will dwell in my
inmost chambers.
16 If they remain faithful, they will
possess me;
their descendants too will inherit me.
17 "I will walk with them in disguise,
and at first I will test them with trials.
Fear and dread I will bring upon them
and I will discipline them with my
constraints.
When their hearts are fully with me,
18 then I will set them again on the
straight path
and reveal my secrets to them.
19 But if they turn away from me, I will
abandon them
and deliver them over to robbers."

*Sincerity and Justice**

20 My son, watch for the right time; fear
what is evil;
do not bring shame upon yourself.
21 There is a shame heavy with guilt,
and a shame that brings glory and
respect.
22 Show no favoritism to your own
discredit;
let no one intimidate you to your own
downfall.

4:1 Needy eyes: when the poor look for help; cf. 18:18.

4:11–19 The Hebrew text in vv. 15–19 presents wisdom speaking in the first person, as in chap. 24. The precious fruits of wisdom—life, favor, glory, blessings, God's love—arouse desire for her (vv. 11–14). Her disciples are like ministers (v. 14) and judges (v. 15), whose descendants have her for their heritage (v. 16). They enjoy happiness and learn her secrets after surviving her tests (vv. 17–18). Those who fail her are abandoned to destruction (v. 19).

4:20–31 The student of wisdom is warned about interior trials of discipline and external dangers to sincerity and justice, namely evil, human respect (vv. 20–22), compromise of liberty in speech and action (vv. 23–25), false shame (v. 26). The student must fight for the truth (vv. 25, 28), avoiding cynicism and laziness (v. 29), and inconsistency (v. 30).

t: Sir 7:32–36; 29:8–13; Dt 15:7–11; Tb 12:9; Dn 4:24. *u:* Tb 4:7–11. *v:* Jb 29:12, 17. *w:* Wis 7:28.

23 Do not refrain from speaking at the proper time,
and do not hide your wisdom;
24 For wisdom becomes known through speech,
and knowledge through the tongue's response.

25 Never speak against the truth,
but of your own ignorance be ashamed.
26 Do not be ashamed to acknowledge your sins,
and do not struggle against a rushing stream.
27 Do not abase yourself before a fool;
do not refuse to do so before rulers.
28 Even to the death, fight for what is right,
and the LORD will do battle for you.

29 Do not be haughty in your speech,
or lazy and slack in your deeds.
30 Do not be like a lion at home,
or sly and suspicious with your servants.
31 Do not let your hand be open to receive,
but clenched when it is time to give.

CHAPTER 5

See RG 276–79

*Against Presumption**

1 Do not rely on your wealth,
or say, "I have the power."[x]
2 Do not rely on your strength
in following the desires of your heart.
3 Do not say, "Who can prevail against me?"
for the LORD will exact punishment.
4 Do not say, "I have sinned, yet what has happened to me?"
for the LORD is slow to anger!
5 Do not be so confident of forgiveness
that you add sin upon sin.
6 Do not say, "His mercy is great;
my many sins he will forgive."
For mercy and anger alike are with him;
his wrath comes to rest on the wicked.
7 Do not delay turning back to the LORD,
do not put it off day after day.
For suddenly his wrath will come forth;
at the time of vengeance, you will perish.
8 Do not rely on deceitful wealth,
for it will be no help on the day of wrath.[y]

*Use and Abuse of the Tongue**

9 Do not winnow in every wind,
nor walk in every path.*
10 Be steadfast regarding your knowledge,
and let your speech be consistent.
11 Be swift to hear,
but slow to answer.[z]
12 If you can, answer your neighbor;
if not, place your hand over your mouth!
13 Honor and dishonor through speaking!
The tongue can be your downfall.
14 Do not be called double-tongued;
and with your tongue do not slander a neighbor.
For shame has been created for the thief,
and sore disgrace for the double-tongued.
15 In little or in much, do not act corruptly;

CHAPTER 6

See RG 276–79

1 Do not be a foe instead of a friend.
A bad name, disgrace, and dishonor you will inherit.
Thus the wicked, the double-tongued!*

Unruly Passions

2 Do not fall into the grip of your passion,[a]
lest like fire it consume your strength.
3 It will eat your leaves and destroy your fruits,
and you will be left like a dry tree.
4 For fierce passion destroys its owner
and makes him the sport of his enemies.

5:1–8 The vices of the rich are pride and independence (vv. 1–2), presumption (v. 3), false security (vv. 4–6), and impenitence (v. 7), which cannot escape the divine wrath (vv. 7–8). Cf. Prv 18:23; 19:1; 28:6.

5:9–6:1 Proper use of the tongue requires constancy in speech (v. 10), prudence (vv. 11–12), good judgment (v. 13), charity (5:15; 6:1); detraction, calumny (v. 14), and double-talk bring shame and disgrace (5:14; 6:1).

5:9 The metaphors indicate careless behavior.

6:1 Thus . . . double-tongued!: people will say this against those disgraced by lying and double-talk.

x: Sir 11:24; Prv 27:1; Lk 12:19; 1 Tm 6:17. *y:* Prv 10:2; 11:4, 28; Ps 52:9. *z:* Prv 29:20; Eccl 5:1; Jas 1:19. *a:* Sir 9:8; 23:16; 25:21; 41:20, 22; Jb 31:12.

*True Friendship**

[5] Pleasant speech multiplies friends,
and gracious lips, friendly greetings.
[6] Let those who are friendly to you be many,
but one in a thousand your confidant.
[7] When you gain friends, gain them through testing,[b]
and do not be quick to trust them.
[8] For there are friends when it suits them,
but they will not be around in time of trouble.
[9] Another is a friend who turns into an enemy,
and tells of the quarrel to your disgrace.
[10] Others are friends, table companions,
but they cannot be found in time of affliction.
[11] When things go well, they are your other self,
and lord it over your servants.
[12] If disaster comes upon you, they turn against you
and hide themselves.
[13] Stay away from your enemies,
and be on guard with your friends.
[14] Faithful friends are a sturdy shelter;
whoever finds one finds a treasure.
[15] Faithful friends are beyond price,
no amount can balance their worth.
[16] Faithful friends are life-saving medicine;
those who fear God will find them.
[17] Those who fear the Lord enjoy stable friendship,
for as they are, so will their neighbors be.

*Blessings of Wisdom**

[18] My child, from your youth choose discipline;
and when you have gray hair you will find wisdom.
[19] As though plowing and sowing, draw close to her;
then wait for her bountiful crops.
For in cultivating her you will work but little,
and soon you will eat her fruit.
[20] She is rough ground to the fool!
The stupid cannot abide her.
[21] She will be like a burdensome stone to them,
and they will not delay in casting her aside.
[22] For discipline* is like her name,
she is not accessible to many.
[23] Listen, my child, and take my advice;
do not refuse my counsel.
[24] Put your feet into her fetters,
and your neck under her yoke.
[25] Bend your shoulders and carry her
and do not be irked at her bonds.
[26] With all your soul draw close to her;
and with all your strength keep her ways.
[27] Inquire and search, seek and find;
when you get hold of her, do not let her go.
[28] Thus at last you will find rest in her,
and she will become your joy.
[29] Her fetters will be a place of strength;
her snare, a robe of spun gold.
[30] Her yoke will be a gold ornament;[c]
her bonds, a purple cord.
[31] You will wear her as a robe of glory,
and bear her as a splendid crown.
[32] If you wish, my son, you can be wise;
if you apply yourself, you can be shrewd.
[33] If you are willing to listen, you can learn;
if you pay attention, you can be instructed.

6:5–17 One of several poems Ben Sira wrote on friendship; see also 9:10–16; 12:8–18; 13:1–23; 19:13–17; 22:19–26; 27:16–21. True friends are discerned not by prosperity (v. 11), but through the trials of adversity: distress, quarrels (v. 9), sorrow (v. 10) and misfortune (v. 12). Such friends are rare, a gift from God (vv. 14–17).

6:18–37 The various figures in each of the eight stanzas urge the search for wisdom through patience (vv. 18–19), persistence (vv. 20–22), docility and perseverance (vv. 23–28). Wisdom bestows rich rewards (vv. 29–31) on those who apply themselves and learn from the wise (vv. 32–36). Although one must strive for wisdom, it is God who grants it (v. 37). Cf. 4:11–19.

6:22 Discipline: *musar* (in the sense of wisdom) is a perfect homonym for *musar*, "removed, withdrawn"; thus the path of discipline is not accessible to many.

b: Sir 12:8–9; 37:1–5; Prv 19:4. *c:* Is 62:3.

34 Stand in the company of the elders;
stay close to whoever is wise.
35 Be eager to hear every discourse;
let no insightful saying escape you.[d]
36 If you see the intelligent, seek them out;
let your feet wear away their doorsteps!

37 Reflect on the law of the Most High,
and let his commandments be your constant study.
Then he will enlighten your mind,
and make you wise as you desire.[e]

See RG 276–79

CHAPTER 7

*Conduct Toward God and Neighbor**

1 Do no evil, and evil will not overtake you;*
2 avoid wickedness, and it will turn away from you.
3 Do not sow in the furrows of injustice,
lest you harvest it sevenfold.[f]
4 Do not seek from God authority
or from the king a place of honor.
5 Do not parade your righteousness before the LORD,
and before the king do not flaunt your wisdom.[g]
6 Do not seek to become a judge
if you do not have the strength to root out crime,
Lest you show fear in the presence of the prominent
and mar your integrity.
7 Do not be guilty of any evil before the city court
or disgrace yourself before the assembly.
8 Do not plot to repeat a sin;
even for one, you will not go unpunished.
9 Do not say, "He will appreciate my many gifts;
the Most High God will accept my offerings."[h]
10 Do not be impatient in prayer
or neglect almsgiving.
11 Do not ridicule the embittered;
Remember: there is One who exalts and humbles.*
12 Do not plot mischief against your relative
or against your friend and companion.
13 Refuse to tell lie after lie,
for it never results in good.
14 Do not babble in the assembly of the elders
or repeat the words of your prayer.* [i]
15 Do not hate hard work;
work was assigned by God.[j]
16 Do not esteem yourself more than your compatriots;
remember, his wrath will not delay.
17 More and more, humble your pride;
what awaits mortals is worms.* [k]

*Duties of Family Life, Religion and Charity**

18 Do not barter a friend for money,
or a true brother for the gold of Ophir.*
19 Do not reject a sensible wife;
a gracious wife is more precious than pearls.
20 Do not mistreat a servant who works faithfully,
or laborers who devote themselves to their task.[l]
21 Love wise servants as yourself;
do not refuse them freedom.*

7:1–17 In the conduct of social relations wisdom forbids evil and injustice (vv. 1–3), pride (vv. 5, 15–17), ambition and partiality (vv. 4, 6), public disorder (v. 7), presumption and impatience toward God (vv. 9–10), ridicule (v. 11), mischief and deceit toward one's neighbor (vv. 8, 12–13). See the several wisdom poems in Prv 1–9.

7:1 There is a play on "evil" which means both moral wrong and material calamity.

7:11 One who exalts and humbles: God; cf. 1 Sm 2:7; Ps 75:8; Lk 1:52.

7:14 Repeat . . . prayer: brevity of speech is a wisdom ideal; toward superiors and God it is a sign of respect; cf. Eccl 5:1; Mt 6:7.

7:17 Worms: i.e., corruption; the Septuagint adds "fire."

7:18–36 Respect and appreciation, justice and kindness should characterize relations toward members of the household (vv. 18–28), God and the priests (vv. 29–31), the poor and afflicted, the living and the dead (vv. 32–35).

7:18 Ophir: the port, at present unidentified, to which the ships of Solomon sailed and from which they brought back gold and silver; cf. note on Ps 45:10.

7:21 After six years of service a Hebrew slave was entitled to freedom; cf. Ex 21:2; Dt 15:12–15.

d: Sir 8:8–9. *e:* Ps 1:2. *f:* Jb 4:8; Prv 22:8; Hos 8:7. *g:* Jb 9:2; Ps 143:2; Prv 25:6; 1 Cor 4:4. *h:* Sir 34:21–24; 35:14–15. *i:* Sir 32:7–10; Mt 6:7. *j:* Gn 2:15; 3:17. *k:* Sir 10:11; Jb 17:14; Is 66:24. *l:* Lv 19:13; Dt 24:14–15; Jas 5:4.

22 Do you have livestock? Look after them;
if they are dependable, keep them.
23 Do you have sons? Correct them
and cure their stubbornness* in their early youth.[m]
24 Do you have daughters? Keep them chaste,
and do not be indulgent to them.[n]
25 Give your daughter in marriage, and a worry comes to an end;
but give her to a sensible man.
26 Do you have a wife? Do not mistreat her,
but do not trust the wife you hate.
27 With your whole heart honor your father;
your mother's birth pangs do not forget.[o]
28 Remember, of these parents you were born;
what can you give them for all they gave you?
29 With all your soul fear God
and revere his priests.
30 With all your strength love your Maker
and do not neglect his ministers.
31 Honor God and respect the priest;
give him his portion as you have been commanded:[p]
First fruits and contributions,
his portion of victims and holy offerings.*

32 To the poor also extend your hand,
that your blessing may be complete.
33 Give your gift to all the living,
and do not withhold your kindness from the dead.*
34 Do not avoid those who weep,
but mourn with those who mourn.[q]
35 Do not hesitate to visit the sick,
because for such things you will be loved.[r]

36 In whatever you do, remember your last days,
and you will never sin.*

CHAPTER 8

See RG 276–79

*Prudence in Dealing with Others**

1 Do not contend with the mighty,
lest you fall into their power.
2 Do not quarrel with the rich,
lest they pay out the price of your downfall.
For gold has unsettled many,
and wealth perverts the character of princes.[s]

3 Do not quarrel with loud-mouths,
or heap wood upon their fire.* [t]
4 Do not associate with the senseless,
lest your ancestors be insulted.

5 Do not reproach one who turns away from sin;[u]
remember, we all are guilty.*
6 Do not insult one who is old,
for some of us will also grow old.
7 Do not rejoice when someone dies;
remember, we are all to be gathered in.

8 Do not neglect the discourse of the wise,[v]
but busy yourself with their proverbs;
For in this way you will acquire the training
to stand in the presence of princes.
9 Do not reject the tradition of the elders
which they have heard from their ancestors;

7:23 Cure their stubbornness: keep them from rebellious pride; so with the Greek. Cf. 30:1–13. The Hebrew text, probably not original here, reads: "Choose wives for them while they are young."

7:31 First fruits . . . holy offerings: cf. Ex 29:27; Lv 7:31–34; Nm 18:8–20; Dt 18:1–5.

7:33 This seems to refer to the observances ordained toward the dead, that is, proper mourning and burial. Cf. 2 Sm 21:12–14; Tb 1:17–18; 12:12.

7:36 Never sin: because the last days of the sinner, it was presumed, would be troubled.

8:1–19 The prudent will be circumspect, avoiding conflict with the powerful, the rich and insolent, the impious, the irascible, and judges (vv. 1–3, 10–12, 14, 16). They will not associate with the undisciplined (v. 4) or the ruthless (v. 15), with fools or strangers (vv. 17–19), but with the wise and the elders of the people (vv. 8–9). Caution is a recurring theme in Ben Sira.

8:3 One should avoid increasing the ire of those who are hotheaded; cf. vv. 10, 16.

8:5 We all are guilty: cf. 1 Kgs 8:46; 2 Chr 6:36; Jb 25:4; Eccl 7:20; Rom 3:9–10; 5:12; 1 Jn 1:8.

m: Sir 30:1–13; Prv 13:24; 19:18; 23:13–14; 29:15, 17. *n:* Sir 42:9–12. *o:* Sir 3:1–16; Ex 20:12; Dt 5:16; Tb 4:3–4; Prv 23:22. *p:* Lv 7:31; Nm 18:18. *q:* Rom 12:15. *r:* Mt 25:36. *s:* Sir 31:5–6; Dt 16:19. *t:* Prv 26:20–21. *u:* 1 Kgs 8:46; 1 Jn 1:8. *v:* Sir 6:34–36.

For from it you will learn
how to answer when the need arises.

10 Do not kindle the coals of sinners,
lest you be burned in their flaming fire.
11 Do not give ground before scoundrels;
it will set them in ambush against you.*
12 Do not lend to one more powerful than yourself;
or if you lend, count it as lost.[w]
13 Do not give collateral beyond your means;
consider any collateral a debt you must pay.
14 Do not go to court against a judge,
for the case will be settled in his favor.
15 Do not travel with the ruthless
lest they weigh you down with calamity;
For they will only go their own way,
and through their folly you will also perish.
16 Do not defy the quick-tempered,
or ride with them through the desert.
For bloodshed is nothing to them;
when there is no one to help, they will destroy you.
17 Do not take counsel with simpletons,
for they cannot keep a confidence.
18 Before a stranger do nothing that should be kept secret,
for you do not know what it will produce later on.*[x]
19 Open your heart to no one,
do not banish your happiness.

CHAPTER 9

See RG 276–79

*Advice Concerning Women**

1 Do not be jealous of the wife of your bosom,
lest you teach her to do evil against you.*
2 Do not give a woman power over you
to trample on your dignity.[y]
3 Do not go near a strange woman,
lest you fall into her snares.
4 Do not dally with a singer,
lest you be captivated by her charms.
5 Do not entertain any thoughts about a virgin,
lest you be enmeshed in damages for her.*
6 Do not give yourself to a prostitute
lest you lose your inheritance.[z]
7 Do not look around the streets of the city
or wander through its squares.
8 Avert your eyes from a shapely woman;
do not gaze upon beauty that is not yours;
Through woman's beauty many have been ruined,
for love of it burns like fire.[a]
9 Never recline at table with a married woman,
or drink intoxicants with her,
Lest your heart be drawn to her
and you go down in blood* to the grave.

*Choice of Friends**

10 Do not abandon old friends;
new ones cannot equal them.
A new friend is like new wine—
when it has aged, you drink it with pleasure.
11 Do not envy the wicked
for you do not know when their day will come.
12 Do not delight in the pleasures of the ungodly;
remember, they will not die unpunished.

8:11 Giving in to the wicked only encourages them to take advantage.

8:18 To keep a secret, or a confidence, is a major concern of Ben Sira; cf. 1:30; 22:22; 27:16–21; 37:10; 42:1.

9:1–9 Ben Sira writes about women only from the androcentric viewpoint of his culture. Cf. 25:13–26:27.

9:1 Jealousy may lead to suspicion and may prompt a wife to those actions her husband fears.

9:5 Cf. Ex 22:15–16; Dt 22:28–29; Jb 31:1. Cf. note on Ex 22:16.

9:9 In blood: perhaps refers to blood revenge; cf. Lv 20:10.

9:10–16 The second of Ben Sira's poems on friendship; cf. note on 6:5–17. In choosing friends, adherence to the law of the Lord should serve as a guide (v. 15). Associate with true friends (v. 10), with the righteous and the learned (vv. 14–16); avoid the company of the mighty and of sinners (vv. 11–13). Cf. 8:1–19.

w: Sir 29:4–7; Prv 17:18. *x:* Prv 25:9–10. *y:* Sir 25:21. *z:* Prv 5:1–14; 6:24; 29:3. *a:* Sir 25:20; 41:21; Prv 6:25–29.

13 Keep away from those who have power to kill,
and you will not be filled with the dread of death.
But if you come near them, do not offend them,
lest they take away your life.
Know that you are stepping among snares
and walking over a net.
14 As best you can, answer your neighbor,
and associate with the wise.
15 With the learned exchange ideas;
and let all your conversation be about the law of the Most High.
16 Take the righteous for your table companions;
and let your glory be in the fear of God.

*Concerning Rulers**

17 Work by skilled hands will earn praise;
but the people's leader is proved wise by his words.
18 Loud mouths are feared in their city,
and whoever is reckless in speech is hated.

CHAPTER 10

See RG 276–79

1 A wise magistrate gives stability to his people,
and government by the intelligent is well ordered.[b]
2 As the people's judge, so the officials;[c]
as the head of a city, so the inhabitants.
3 A reckless king destroys his people,
but a city grows through the intelligence of its princes.[d]
4 Sovereignty over the earth is in the hand of God,
who appoints the right person for the right time.
5 Sovereignty over everyone is in the hand of God,
who imparts his majesty to the ruler.

The Sin of Pride

6 No matter what the wrong, never harm your neighbor
or go the way of arrogance.[e]
7 Odious to the Lord and to mortals is pride,
and for both oppression is a crime.
8 Sovereignty is transferred from one people to another
because of the lawlessness of the proud.
9 Why are dust and ashes proud?*
Even during life the body decays.
10 A slight illness—the doctor jests;
a king today—tomorrow he is dead.
11 When a people die,
they inherit corruption and worms,
gnats and maggots.[f]

12 The beginning of pride is stubbornness
in withdrawing the heart from one's Maker.
13 For sin is a reservoir of insolence,
a source which runs over with vice;
Because of it God sends unheard-of afflictions
and strikes people with utter ruin.[g]
14 God overturns the thrones of the proud
and enthrones the lowly in their place.
15 God plucks up the roots of the proud,
and plants the lowly in their place.
16 The Lord lays waste the lands of the nations,
and destroys them to the very foundations of the earth.
17 He removes them from the earth,
destroying them,
erasing their memory from the world.
18 Insolence does not befit mortals,
nor impudent anger those born of women.

*True Glory**

19 Whose offspring can be honorable?
Human offspring.

9:17–10:5 Public office as conducted justly or unjustly benefits or destroys the people, according to the axiom, "as the prince, so the people." God, however, has sovereignty over both.

10:9–10 The general implication is that a slight illness today may be followed by death tomorrow. The uncertainty of life leaves no room for pride.

10:19–11:6 Genuine honor comes not from one's place in society but from fear of the Lord and a true estimate of oneself. The Lord exalts the lowly and oppressed; transgressors of the commandment merit dishonor and disgrace.

b: Prv 29:4; Wis 6:24. *c:* Ez 16:44; Prv 29:12. *d:* Prv 29:4–8. *e:* Lv 19:18. *f:* Sir 7:17; Jb 17:14; Is 66:24. *g:* Prv 11:2; 16:18; 18:12.

Those who fear the LORD are
honorable offspring.
Whose offspring can be disgraceful?
Human offspring.
Those who transgress the
commandment are disgraceful
offspring.
20 Among relatives their leader is
honored;
but whoever fears God is honored
among God's people.†
22 Resident alien, stranger, foreigner,
pauper—
their glory is the fear of the LORD.
23 It is not right to despise anyone wise but
poor,
nor proper to honor the lawless.[h]
24 The prince, the ruler, the judge are in
honor;
but none is greater than the one who
fears God.
25 When the free serve a wise slave,
the wise will not complain.[i]
26 Do not flaunt your wisdom in managing
your affairs,
or boast in your time of need.
27 Better the worker who has goods in
plenty
than the boaster who has no food.[j]
28 My son, with humility have self-esteem;
and give yourself the esteem you
deserve.
29 Who will acquit those who condemn
themselves?
Who will honor those who disgrace
themselves?
30 The poor are honored for their wisdom;
the rich are honored for their wealth.
31 Honored in poverty, how much more so
in wealth!
Disgraced in wealth, in poverty how
much the more!

CHAPTER 11

See RG 276–79

1 The wisdom of the poor lifts their
head high
and sets them among princes.
2 Do not praise anyone for good looks;
or despise anyone because of
appearance.
3 The bee is least among winged creatures,
but it reaps the choicest of harvests.
4 Do not mock the one who wears only a
loin-cloth,
or scoff at a person's bitter day.
For strange are the deeds of the LORD,
hidden from mortals his work.*
5 Many are the oppressed who rise to the
throne;
some that none would consider wear a
crown.*
6 Many are the exalted who fall into utter
disgrace,
many the honored who are given into
the power of the few.

*Moderation and Patience**

7 Before investigating, do not find fault;
examine first, then criticize.
8 Before listening, do not say a word,
interrupt no one in the midst of
speaking.[k]
9 Do not dispute about what is not your
concern;
in the quarrels of the arrogant do not
take part.
10 My son, why increase your anxiety,
since whoever is greedy for wealth
will not be blameless?
Even if you chase after it, you will never
overtake it;
and by fleeing you will not escape.
11 One may work and struggle and drive,
and fall short all the same.[l]
12 Others go their way broken-down drifters,

† Other ancient texts read as v. 21:
The beginning of acceptance is the fear of the Lord;
the beginning of rejection, effrontery and pride.

11:4 The implication is similar to Eccl 7:13; 8:17: the mysterious work of God.

11:5 Cf. 1 Sm 2:8; Ps 75:8; 105:17–22; Lk 1:52.

11:7–28 Discretion should regulate conduct toward others (vv. 7–9); as regards personal interests, one should avoid solicitude for the passing external benefits of life and property (vv. 10–14, 18–19, 21, 23–25) and cultivate the lasting inward gifts of wisdom, virtue (vv. 20, 22), and patience (vv. 25–28).

h: Jas 2:1–4. *i:* Prv 17:2. *j:* Prv 12:9. *k:* Prv 18:13. *l:* Ps 127:2; Eccl 4:8.

with little strength and great misery—
Yet the eye of the LORD looks favorably upon them,
shaking them free of the stinking mire.
13 He lifts up their heads and exalts them
to the amazement of the many.

14 * Good and evil, life and death,[m]
poverty and riches—all are from the LORD.†
17 The Lord's gift remains with the devout;
his favor brings lasting success.
18 Some become rich through a miser's life,
and this is their allotted reward:
19 When they say: "I have found rest,[n]
now I will feast on my goods,"
They do not know how long it will be
till they die and leave them to others.*

20 My child, stand by your agreement and attend to it,
grow old while doing your work.
21 Do not marvel at the works of a sinner,
but trust in the LORD and wait for his light;
For it is easy in the eyes of the LORD
suddenly, in an instant, to make the poor rich.

22 God's blessing is the lot of the righteous,
and in due time their hope bears fruit.
23 Do not say: "What do I need?
What further benefits can be mine?"
24 Do not say: "I am self-sufficient.
What harm can come to me now?"
25 The day of prosperity makes one forget adversity;
the day of adversity makes one forget prosperity.[o]
26 For it is easy for the Lord on the day of death*
to repay mortals according to their conduct.
27 A time of affliction brings forgetfulness of past delights;
at the end of life one's deeds are revealed.
28 Call none happy before death,
for how they end, they are known.

Care in Choosing Friends

29 Not everyone should be brought into your house,
for many are the snares of the crafty.
30 Like a decoy partridge in a cage, so is the heart of the proud,
and like a spy they will pick out the weak spots.
31 For they lie in wait to turn good into evil,
and to praiseworthy deeds they attach blame.
32 One spark kindles many coals;
a sinner lies in wait for blood.
33 Beware of scoundrels, for they breed only evil,
and they may give you a lasting stain.
34 Admit strangers into your home, and they will stir up trouble
and make you a stranger to your own family.

CHAPTER 12

See RG 276–79

1 If you do good, know for whom you are doing it,*
and your kindness will have its effect.
2 Do good to the righteous and reward will be yours,
if not from them, from the LORD.[p]
3 No good comes to those who give comfort to the wicked,
nor is it an act of mercy that they do.
4 Give to the good but refuse the sinner;
5 refresh the downtrodden but give nothing to the proud.
No arms for combat should you give them,

11:14 In mysterious ways God ultimately governs the lives of men and women.

† Other ancient texts read as vv. 15–16:
15 Wisdom and understanding and knowledge of the Law,
love and virtuous paths, are from the Lord.
16 Error and darkness were formed with sinners from their birth,
and evil grows old with those who exult in evil.

11:19 Cf. the parable of the rich man, Lk 12:16–21.

11:26–28 Ben Sira thought that divine retribution took place only in the present life, and even at the end of life; cf. 9:12; 14:16–17.

12:1 The import of this verse is brought out in vv. 4–5.

m: Jb 1:21; 2:10. *n:* Eccl 4:8; 6:2; Lk 12:19. *o:* Sir 18:24–25. *p:* Dt 14:29.

lest they use these against you;
Twofold evil you will obtain for every
good deed you do for them.
6 For God also hates sinners,
and takes vengeance on evildoers.*
8 In prosperity we cannot know our friends;*
in adversity an enemy will not remain
concealed.[q]
9 When one is successful even an enemy is
friendly;
but in adversity even a friend
disappears.[r]
10 Never trust your enemies,
for their wickedness is like corrosion
in bronze.
11 Even though they act deferentially and
peaceably toward you,
take care to be on your guard against
them.[s]
Treat them as those who reveal secrets,*
and be certain that in the end there will
still be envy.
12 Do not let them stand near you,
lest they push you aside and take your
place.
Do not let them sit at your right hand,
or they will demand your seat,
And in the end you will appreciate my
advice,
when you groan with regret, as I
warned.
13 Who pities a snake charmer when he is
bitten,*
or anyone who goes near a wild beast?
14 So it is with the companion of the proud,
who is involved in their sins:
15 While you stand firm, they make no
move;
but if you slip, they cannot hold back.
16 With their lips enemies speak sweetly,
but in their heart they scheme to
plunge you into the abyss.
Though enemies have tears in their eyes,
given the chance, they will never have
enough of your blood.[t]
17 If evil comes upon you, you will find
them at hand;
pretending to help, they will trip you up,
18 Then they will shake their heads and clap
their hands
and hiss repeatedly, and show their
true faces.

CHAPTER 13

See RG 276–79

*Caution Regarding Associates**

1 Touch pitch and you blacken your hand;
associate with scoundrels and you
learn their ways.
2 Do not lift a weight too heavy for you,
or associate with anyone wealthier
than you.
How can the clay pot go with the metal
cauldron?
When they knock together, the pot will
be smashed:
3 The rich do wrong and boast of it,
while the poor are wronged and beg
forgiveness.
4 As long as the rich can use you they will
enslave you,
but when you are down and out they
will abandon you.
5 As long as you have anything they will
live with you,
but they will drain you dry without
remorse.
6 When they need you they will deceive
you
and smile at you and raise your hopes;
they will speak kindly to you and say,
"What do you need?"
7 They will embarrass you at their dinner
parties,
and finally laugh at you.
Afterwards, when they see you, they will
pass you by,
and shake their heads at you.

12:6 Verse 7 is a variant of verse 4 and is omitted.

12:8–18 Adversity distinguishes friends from enemies; to trust the latter or permit them intimacy is to invite disaster. Cf. note on 6:5–17.

12:11 Ben Sira has harsh words for those who reveal secrets; see also 8:18; 27:16–21; 42:1; Prv 11:13; 20:19.

12:13 For v. 13a, see especially Eccl 10:11.

13:1–14:2 By means of various images, most of them unfavorable to the rich, Ben Sira indicates the practical impossibility of genuine and sincere companionship between the poor and the rich. He lays down a principle of associating with equals (13:6–19).

q: Prv 17:17. *r:* Prv 19:4–7. *s:* Prv 26:24–26. *t:* Jer 9:7.

8 Be on guard: do not act too boldly;
do not be like those who lack sense.
9 When the influential draw near, keep your distance;
then they will urge you all the more.
10 Do not draw too close, lest you be rebuffed,
but do not keep too far away lest you be regarded as an enemy.
11 Do not venture to be free with them,
do not trust their many words;
For by prolonged talk they will test you,
and though smiling they will probe you.
12 Mercilessly they will make you a laughingstock,
and will not refrain from injury or chains.
13 Be on your guard and take care
never to accompany lawless people.†
15 Every living thing loves its own kind,
and we all love someone like ourselves.
16 Every living being keeps close to its own kind;
and people associate with their own kind.
17 Is a wolf ever allied with a lamb?
So the sinner with the righteous.[u]
18 Can there be peace between the hyena and the dog?
Or peace between the rich and the poor?*
19 Wild donkeys of the desert are lion's prey;
likewise the poor are feeding grounds for the rich.
20 Humility is an abomination to the proud;
and the poor are an abomination to the rich.
21 When the rich stumble they are supported by friends;
when the poor trip they are pushed down by friends.
22 When the rich speak they have many supporters;
though what they say is repugnant, it wins approval.
When the poor speak people say, "Come, come, speak up!"
though they are talking sense, they get no hearing.
23 When the rich speak all are silent,
their wisdom people extol to the clouds.
When the poor speak people say: "Who is that?"
If they stumble, people knock them down.[v]
24 Wealth is good where there is no sin;*
but poverty is evil by the standards of the proud.
25 The heart changes one's face,
either for good or for evil.[w]
26 The sign of a good heart is a radiant face;
withdrawn and perplexed is the toiling schemer.

CHAPTER 14

See RG 276–79

1 * Happy those whose mouth causes them no grief,
those who are not stung by remorse for sin.[x]
2 Happy are those whose conscience does not reproach them,
those who have not lost hope.

The Use of Wealth

3 Wealth is not appropriate for the mean-spirited;*
to misers, what use is gold?

† Other ancient texts read as v. 14:
If you hear these things in your sleep, wake up!
With your whole life, love the Lord
and call on him for your salvation.

13:18 The hostility between the dogs which guard the flocks (Jb 30:1) and the rapacious hyenas (Jer 12:9) is proverbial in Palestine.

13:24 Ben Sira allows that the rich can be virtuous—but with difficulty; cf. 31:1–11.

14:1–2 A clear conscience, the result of honoring personal commitments and responsibilities, brings contentment and peace.

14:3–10 Ben Sira offers a case study about the miserable life of the "small-hearted" (Heb. *leb qatan*) to verify vv. 1–2. They are evil because they do not use their wealth properly to benefit themselves or others. While they are never satisfied that they have enough, they ignore their own needs and hospitality itself, feeding on the generosity of others, in order to protect their own resources. Ironically, after their death, strangers, with no obligation to keep their memory alive, enjoy their wealth.

u: 2 Cor 6:14–17. *v:* Prv 14:20; 19:4, 7. *w:* Prv 15:13. *x:* Sir 5:13–14; 19:16; 25:8; Jas 1:26; 3:2.

4 What they deny themselves they collect
for someone else,
and strangers will live sumptuously on
their possessions.[y]
5 To whom will they be generous that are
stingy with themselves
and do not enjoy what is their own?
6 None are worse than those who are
stingy with themselves;
they punish their own avarice.
7 If ever they do good, it is by mistake;
in the end they reveal their meanness.
8 Misers are evil people,
they turn away and disregard others.
9 The greedy see their share as not enough;
greedy injustice dries up the soul.
10 The eye of the miserly is rapacious for
food,
but there is none of it on their own
table.

11 * My son, if you have the means, treat
yourself well,
and enjoy life as best you can.[z]
12 Remember that death does not delay,
and you have not been told the grave's
appointed time.
13 Before you die, be good to your friends;
give them a share in what you possess.[a]
14 Do not deprive yourself of good things
now
or let a choice portion escape you.
15 Will you not leave your riches to others,
and your earnings to be divided by lot?
16 Give and take, treat yourself well,
for in Sheol there are no joys to seek.
17 All flesh grows old like a garment;
the age-old law is: everyone must die.[b]
18 As with the leaves growing on a
luxuriant tree—
one falls off and another sprouts—
So with the generations of flesh and
blood:
one dies and another flourishes.[c]
19 All human deeds surely perish;
the works they do follow after them.

*The Search for Wisdom and Her Blessings**

20 Happy those who meditate on Wisdom,
and fix their gaze on knowledge;[d]
21 Who ponder her ways in their heart,
and understand her paths;
22 Who pursue her like a scout,
and watch at her entry way;
23 Who peep through her windows,
and listen at her doors;
24 Who encamp near her house
and fasten their tent pegs next to her
walls;
25 Who pitch their tent beside her,
and dwell in a good place;*
26 * Who build their nest in her leaves,
and lodge in her branches;
27 Who take refuge from the heat in her
shade
and dwell in her home.

CHAPTER 15

See RG 276–79

1 Whoever fears the LORD will do
this;
whoever is practiced in the Law will
come to Wisdom.
2 She will meet him like a mother;
like a young bride she will receive
him,
3 * She will feed him with the bread of
learning,
and give him the water of
understanding to drink.[e]
4 He will lean upon her and not fall;

14:11–19 Three realities govern Ben Sira's attitude toward a proper use of wealth: the inevitability and uncertainty of death, the ephemeral nature of human accomplishments, the lack of reward or punishment after death. He advises generous enjoyment of God's gift of wealth before death.

14:20–15:10 This poem charts the growing intimacy between those seeking Wisdom and Wisdom herself. They move from static reflection to playful pursuit, from camping outside the walls of her house to nesting inside her leafy shade. Ben Sira portrays Wisdom as both mother and bride, a feminine figure who is the fullness of womanhood according to his androcentric society.

14:25 In a good place: i.e., where Wisdom dwells.

14:26–27 The shift in imagery creates a more intimate relationship. Those seeking Wisdom dwell within her as a bird nests within a leafy tree.

15:3–6 In this role reversal Woman Wisdom teaches, nourishes, supports, and protects the vulnerable man. For similar imagery cf. Prv 8:4–21, 34–35; 9:1–5; 31:10–31.

y: Eccl 2:18–19; 6:2. *z:* Eccl 5:17–19. *a:* Prv 3:27–28; Tb 4:7. *b:* Ps 103:14–16; Jb 14:1–2; Is 40:6; Jas 1:10; 1 Pt 1:24. *c:* Eccl 1:4. *d:* Ps 1:2. *e:* Jn 4:10; 6:31–33.

he will trust in her and not be put to shame.
5 She will exalt him above his neighbors,
and in the assembly she will make him eloquent.
6 Joy and gladness he will find,
and an everlasting name he will inherit.[f]
7 The worthless will not attain her,
and the haughty will not behold her.
8 She is far from the impious;
liars never think of her.
9 * Praise is unseemly on the lips of sinners,
for it has not been allotted to them by God.
10 But praise is uttered by the mouth of the wise,
and its rightful owner teaches it.

*Free Will**

11 Do not say: "It was God's doing that I fell away,"
for what he hates he does not do.
12 Do not say: "He himself has led me astray,"
for he has no need of the wicked.[g]
13 Abominable wickedness the LORD hates
and he does not let it happen to those who fear him.
14 God in the beginning created human beings
and made them subject to their own free choice.[h]
15 If you choose, you can keep the commandments;
loyalty is doing the will of God.
16 Set before you are fire and water;
to whatever you choose, stretch out your hand.
17 Before everyone are life and death,
whichever they choose will be given them.[i]
18 Immense is the wisdom of the LORD;
mighty in power, he sees all things.
19 The eyes of God behold his works,
and he understands every human deed.[j]
20 He never commands anyone to sin,
nor shows leniency toward deceivers.*

CHAPTER 16

See RG 276–79

*God's Punishment of Sinners**

1 Do not yearn for worthless children,
or rejoice in wicked offspring.
2 Even if they be many, do not rejoice in them
if they do not have fear of the LORD.
3 Do not count on long life for them,[k]
or have any hope for their future.
For one can be better than a thousand;
rather die childless than have impious children!
4 Through one wise person a city can be peopled;
but through a clan of rebels it becomes desolate.
5 Many such things my eye has seen,
and even more than these my ear has heard.
6 Against a sinful band fire is kindled,[l]
upon a godless people wrath blazes.*
7 He did not forgive the princes of old*
who rebelled long ago in their might.[m]
8 He did not spare the neighbors of Lot,* [n]

15:9–10 There is an intimate association between wisdom and praise of the Lord.

15:11–20 Here Ben Sira links freedom of the will with human responsibility. God, who sees everything, is neither the cause nor the occasion of sin. We have the power to choose our behavior and we are responsible for both the good and the evil we do (vv. 15–17).

15:20 Deceivers: those who hold the Lord responsible for their sins.

16:1–23 One child who does God's will is a greater blessing than many sinful offspring (vv. 1–4), for history and experience show that God punishes sin (vv. 5–10). God judges everyone according to their deeds (vv. 11–14); no one can hide from God or escape retribution at his hand (vv. 17–23).

16:6 For Korah and his band (v. 6a), see 45:18–19; Nm 16:1–35; Ps 106:18; for the disgruntled Israelites (v. 6b), Ps 78:21–22.

16:7 The princes of old: e.g., the mighty destroyed in the flood (Gn 6:1–4; Wis 14:6; Bar 3:26–28), as well as the king of Babylon (Is 14:4–21) and Nebuchadnezzar (Dn 4:7–30).

16:8 Neighbors of Lot: the people of Sodom and Gomorrah, condemned elsewhere for their sexual violence (Gn 19:24–25) and failure at hospitality (Ez 16:49–50).

f: Sir 6:28–33. *g:* Jas 1:13. *h:* Gn 1:27. *i:* Dt 30:15–20. *j:* Ps 33:18; 34:16; Heb 4:13. *k:* Wis 4:1–2. *l:* Sir 21:9. *m:* Gn 6:4; Wis 14:6; Bar 3:26–28. *n:* Gn 19:24–25.

abominable in their pride.
9 He did not spare the doomed people,*
dispossessed because of their sin;
10 Nor the six hundred thousand foot
soldiers,* [o]
sent to their graves for the arrogance
of their hearts.
11 Had there been but one stiff-necked*
person,
it would be a wonder had he gone
unpunished.
For mercy and anger alike are with him;
he remits and forgives, but also pours
out wrath.
12 Great as his mercy is his punishment;
he judges people, each according to
their deeds.
13 Criminals do not escape with their
plunder;
the hope of the righteous, God never
leaves unfulfilled.
14 Whoever does good has a reward;
each receives according to their
deeds.†
17 Do not say: "I am hidden from God;
and on high who remembers me?
Among so many people I am unknown;
what am I in the world of spirits?
18 Look, the heavens and the highest
heavens,
the abyss and the earth tremble at his
visitation.
19 The roots of the mountains and the
earth's foundations—
at his mere glance they quiver and
quake.
20 Of me, therefore, he will take no notice;
with my ways who will be concerned?
21 If I sin, no eye will see me;
if all in secret I act deceitfully, who is
to know?[p]
22 Who tells him about just deeds?
What can I expect for doing my duty?"
23 Such the thoughts of the senseless;
only the foolish entertain them.

*Divine Wisdom Seen in Creation**

24 Listen to me, my son, and take my
advice,
and apply your mind to my words,
25 While I pour out my spirit by measure
and impart knowledge with care.
26 When at the first God created his works
and, as he made them, assigned their
tasks,[q]
27 He arranged for all time what they were
to do,
their domains from generation to
generation.
They were not to go hungry or grow
weary,
or ever cease from their tasks.
28 Never does a single one crowd its
neighbor,
or do any ever disobey his word.
29 Then the Lord looked upon the earth,
and filled it with his blessings.[r]
30 Its surface he covered with every kind of
living creature
which must return into it again.

CHAPTER 17

See RG 276–79

Creation of Human Beings

1 The Lord created human beings from the
earth,
and makes them return to earth again.[s]
2 A limited number of days he gave them,[t]

16:9 Doomed people: the Canaanite tribes whose aberrant religious practices, at least in Israelite opinion, caused their downfall: Ex 23:23–24, 27–33; 33:2; 34:11–16; Dt 7:1–2; Wis 12:3–7.

16:10 Six hundred thousand foot soldiers: the number given for those rescued by Moses, who murmured against the Lord in the wilderness and died there: 46:1, 7–8; Nm 11:20; 14:1–12, 22–24, 29, 36–38; 26:65; Dt 1:35–38.

16:11 Stiff-necked: sinful Israelites; cf. Ex 32:9; 33:3, 5. Not even one Israelite would have gone unpunished for insolence or pride.

† Other ancient texts read as vv. 15–16:

15 The LORD hardened the heart of Pharaoh so that he
did not recognize him
whose acts were manifest under the heavens;
16 His mercy was seen by all his creatures,
and his light and his darkness he apportioned to
humankind.

16:24–17:23 In harmony with Gn 1–2, the author describes God's wisdom in creating the universe and everything in it (vv. 24–30), endowing human beings with a moral nature, with wisdom, knowledge, and freedom of will (cf. 15:14) according to his own image (17:1–3, 7). Now they can govern the earth (vv. 3–4), praise God's name (vv. 9–10), obey his law (vv. 11–14), and render to him an account of their deeds (v. 23). Cf. Ps 19; 104.

o: Nm 14:29. *p:* Sir 23:18–20. *q:* Gn 1:3–30. *r:* Gn 1:11–31. *s:* Gn 2:7; 3:19. *t:* Gn 1:26–28; Ps 8:4–9.

but granted them authority over
everything on earth.
3 He endowed them with strength like his
own,
and made them in his image.
4 He put fear of them in all flesh,
and gave them dominion over beasts
and birds.†
6 Discernment, tongues, and eyes,
ears, and a mind for thinking he gave
them.
7 With knowledge and understanding he
filled them;
good and evil he showed them.
8 He put fear of him into their hearts
to show them the grandeur of his
works,
9 That they might describe the wonders of
his deeds
10 and praise his holy name.
11 He set before them knowledge,
and allotted to them the law of life.
12 An everlasting covenant he made with
them,
and his commandments* he revealed to
them.
13 His majestic glory their eyes beheld,
his glorious voice their ears heard.
14 He said to them, "Avoid all evil";
to each of them he gave precepts about
their neighbor.
15 Their ways are ever known to him,
they cannot be hidden from his eyes.†
17 Over every nation he appointed a ruler,*
but Israel is the Lord's own portion.† [u]
19 All their works are clear as the sun to him,
and his eyes are ever upon their ways.
20 Their iniquities cannot be hidden from
him;
all their sins are before the Lord.†
22 Human goodness is like a signet ring
with God,
and virtue he keeps like the apple of
his eye.
23 Later he will rise up and repay them,
requiting each one as they deserve.[v]

*Appeal for a Return to God**

24 But to the penitent he provides a way
back
and encourages those who are losing
hope!
25 Turn back to the Lord and give up your
sins,
pray before him and make your
offenses few.
26 Turn again to the Most High and away
from iniquity,
and hate intensely what he loathes.
27 * Who in Sheol can glorify the Most
High[w]
in place of the living who offer their
praise?
28 The dead can no more give praise than
those who have never lived;
they who are alive and well glorify the
Lord.
29 How great is the mercy of the Lord,
and his forgiveness for those who
return to him!

† Other ancient texts read as v. 5:
They received the use of the Lord's five faculties;
of mind, the sixth, he granted them a share,
as also of speech, the seventh, the interpreter of his actions.

17:12 An everlasting covenant . . . his commandments: God made several covenants, e.g., Gn 9:8–17; 15:17–21; 17:1–22, entered into with humankind, especially on Mount Sinai, where the people saw God's glory and heard his voice (v. 13; cf. Ex 19:16–24:18).

† Other ancient texts read as v. 16:
Their ways are directed toward evils from their youth,
and they are unable to make their hearts flesh rather than stone.

17:17 Ruler: this may refer to civil officials or to heavenly beings placed over nations as guardians; see note on Dt 32:8, and the cross-references.

† Other ancient texts read as v. 18:
Israel, as his firstborn, he cares for with chastisement;
the light of his love he shares with him without neglect.

† Other ancient texts read as v. 21:
But the Lord, being good and knowing how they are formed,
neither neglected them nor ceased to spare them.

17:24–32 Ben Sira opens this poem with a prophetic summons to repent, urging sinners to give up their sins and to pray for forgiveness (vv. 24–26, 29). Ben Sira reflects the belief of his day that there was no life after death (vv. 27–28, 30; see note on 11:26–28). Cf. Ez 18:23, 30–32; 33:11–16. See note on Ps 6:6.

17:27–28 True life consists in praise of God; this is not possible in Sheol.

u: Ex 19:5; Dt 4:19–20; 32:8–9; Dn 10:13–21; 12:1. *v:* Ps 7:17; Jl 4:4, 7; Jer 23:19; Ez 22:31. *w:* Ps 6:6; 88:4–7; 115:17; Is 38:18.

30 For not everything is within human reach,
since human beings are not immortal.
31 Is anything brighter than the sun? Yet it can be eclipsed.
How worthless* then the thoughts of flesh and blood!
32 God holds accountable the hosts of highest heaven,
while all mortals are dust and ashes.

CHAPTER 18

See RG 276–79

*The Divine Power and Mercy**

1 He who lives forever created the whole universe;
2 the LORD alone is just.†
4 To whom has he given power to describe his works,
and who can search out his mighty deeds?
5 Who can measure his majestic power,
or fully recount his mercies?
6 No one can lessen, increase,
or fathom the wonders of the Lord.
7 When mortals finish, they are only beginning,
and when they stop they are still bewildered.
8 What are mortals? What are they worth?
What is good in them, and what is evil?
9 The number of their days seems great
if it reaches a hundred years.[x]
10 Like a drop of water from the sea and a grain of sand,
so are these few years among the days of eternity.
11 That is why the Lord is patient with them
and pours out his mercy on them.
12 He sees and understands that their death is wretched,
and so he forgives them all the more.
13 Their compassion is for their neighbor,
but the Lord's compassion reaches all flesh,
Reproving, admonishing, teaching,
and turning them back, as a shepherd his flock.[y]
14 He has compassion on those who accept his discipline,
who are eager for his precepts.

The Need for Prudence

15 My child, add no reproach to your charity,*
or spoil any gift by harsh words.
16 Does not the dew give relief from the scorching heat?
So a word can be better than a gift.
17 Indeed does not a word count more than a good gift?
But both are offered by a kind person.
18 The fool is ungracious and abusive,
and a grudging gift makes the eyes smart.[z]

19 Before you speak, learn;
before you get sick, prepare the cure.
20 Before you are judged, examine yourself,
and at the time of scrutiny you will have forgiveness.
21 Before you fall ill, humble yourself;
and when you have sinned, show repentance.*
Do not delay forsaking your sins;
do not neglect to do so until you are in distress.
22 Let nothing prevent the prompt payment of your vows;
do not wait until death to fulfill them.[a]
23 Before making a vow prepare yourself;

17:31 Worthless: cf. Gn 6:5. Though moral fault is not excluded, the thought here is the inability to understand the designs of God. Cf. Wis 9:14–18.

18:1–14 Not only are God's justice and power beyond human understanding (vv. 1–7), his mercy also is boundless and surpasses all human compassion (vv. 8–14); he pities human frailty and mortality.

† Other ancient texts read as v. 3:

He controls the world within the span of his hand,
and everything obeys his will;
For he in his might is the King of all,
separating what is holy among them from what is profane.

18:15–27 The practice of charity, especially almsgiving, is an art which avoids every offense to another (vv. 15–18). Prudence directs the changing circumstances of daily life in view of the time of scrutiny (i.e., the day of reckoning, or death, v. 24).

18:21 Sickness was often viewed as a punishment for sin; hence, the need for repentance. Cf. 38:9–10; Jb 15:20–24.

x: Ps 90:10. *y:* Ps 23:1–4; Is 40:11; 49:9–10; Jn 10:11–16; Heb 13:20–21; Rev 7:17. *z:* Sir 20:14–15. *a:* Nm 30:3; Dt 23:22; Ps 50:14; Prv 20:25; Eccl 5:4.

do not be like one who puts the Lord
to the test.
24 Think of wrath on the day of death,
the time of vengeance when he will
hide his face.[b]
25 Think of the time of hunger in the time of
plenty,
poverty and need in the day of
wealth.[c]
26 Between morning and evening there is a
change of time;
before the Lord all things are fleeting.

27 The wise are discreet in all things;
where sin is rife they keep themselves
from wrongdoing.
28 Every wise person teaches wisdom,*
and those who know her declare her
praise;
29 Those skilled in words become wise
themselves,
and pour forth apt proverbs.

*Self-Control**

30 Do not let your passions be your guide,[d]
but keep your desires in check.
31 If you allow yourself to satisfy your
passions,
they will make you the laughingstock
of your enemies.
32 Take no pleasure in too much luxury
which brings on poverty redoubled.
33 Do not become a glutton and a drunkard
with nothing in your purse.

CHAPTER 19

See RG 276–79

1 Whoever does this grows no richer;
those who waste the little they have
will be stripped bare.
2 Wine and women make the heart lustful,
and the companion of prostitutes
becomes reckless.[e]
3 Rottenness and worms will possess
him,
and the reckless will be snatched
away.[f]
4 Whoever trusts others too quickly has a
shallow mind,
and those who sin wrong themselves.

*The Proper Use of Speech**

5 Whoever gloats over evil will be
destroyed,
6 and whoever repeats gossip has no
sense.
7 Never repeat gossip,
and no one will reproach you.[g]
8 Tell nothing to friend or foe;
and unless it be a sin for you, do not
reveal a thing.[h]
9 For someone may have heard you and
watched you,
and in time come to hate you.
10 Let anything you hear die with you;
never fear, it will not make you burst!
11 Having heard something, the fool goes
into labor,
like a woman giving birth to a child.
12 Like an arrow stuck in a fool's thigh,
so is gossip in the belly of a fool.
13 Admonish your friend—he may not have
done it;
and if he did, that he may not do it
again.[i]
14 Admonish your neighbor—he may not
have said it;
and if he did, that he may not say it
again.
15 Admonish your friend—often it may be
slander;
do not believe every story.
16 Then, too, a person can slip and not
mean it;
who has not sinned with his tongue?[j]

18:28–29 A general statement on the teaching of wisdom, serving either as a conclusion to the preceding section or as an introduction to the following one.

18:30–19:4 Inordinate gratification of the senses makes people unreasonable, slaves of passion, the laughingstock of their enemies, and it leads to an untimely death.

19:5–17 An excellent commentary on bearing false witness (Ex 20:16; Dt 5:20). Ben Sira speaks harshly about calumny, rash judgment, and detraction (vv. 5–7), and urges discreet silence (vv. 8–12). Justice requires that an accused neighbor be given a hearing, and charity urges fraternal correction; both together fulfill the law of the Most High (vv. 13–17); cf. Mt 7:1–2; 18:15–16.

b: Sir 7:16. *c:* Sir 11:25–27. *d:* Rom 6:12; 13:14; 2 Tm 2:22; Jas 1:14–15. *e:* Prv 20:1; 23:20–28. *f:* Gal 6:8. *g:* Prv 25:10. *h:* Sir 8:18–19. *i:* Lv 19:17; Mt 18:15; Lk 17:3. *j:* Sir 14:1; Jas 3:2.

17 Admonish your neighbor before you
break with him;
and give due place to the Law of the
Most High.† [k]

*How to Recognize True Wisdom**

20 All wisdom is fear of the LORD;
and in all wisdom, the observance of
the Law.† [l]
22 The knowledge of wickedness is not
wisdom,
nor is there prudence in the counsel of
sinners.
23 There is a shrewdness that is detestable,
while the fool may be free from sin.
24 Better are the God-fearing who have
little understanding
than those of great intelligence who
violate the Law.
25 There is a shrewdness keen but
dishonest,
and there are those who are duplicitous
to win a judgment.
26 There is the villain bowed in grief,
but full of deceit within.
27 He hides his face and pretends not to
hear,
but when not observed, he will take
advantage of you:
28 Even if his lack of strength keeps him
from sinning,
when he finds the right time he will do
harm.
29 People are known by their appearance;
the sensible are recognized as such
when first met.
30 One's attire, hearty laughter, and gait
proclaim him for what he is.

CHAPTER 20

See RG 276–79

Conduct of the Wise and the Foolish

1 There is an admonition that is untimely,*
but the silent person is the wise one.
2 It is much better to admonish than to lose
one's temper;
3 one who admits a fault will be kept
from disgrace.
4 Like a eunuch lusting to violate a young
woman
is the one who does right under
compulsion.*
5 One is silent and is thought wise;
another, for being talkative, is disliked.
6 One is silent, having nothing to say;
another is silent, biding his time.[m]
7 The wise remain silent till the right time
comes,
but a boasting fool misses the proper
time.
8 Whoever talks too much is detested;
whoever pretends to authority is hated.
9 There is the misfortune that brings
success;*
and there is the gain that turns into
loss.
10 There is the gift that profits you nothing,
and there is the gift that must be paid
back double.
11 There is the loss for the sake of glory,
and there is the one who rises above
humble circumstances.
12 There is one who buys much for little,
but pays for it seven times over.
13 The wise make themselves beloved by a
few words,

† Other ancient texts read as vv. 18–19:
18 Fear of the Lord is the beginning of acceptance;
and wisdom from him obtains love.
19 Knowledge of the Lord's commandments is life-giving instruction;
those who do what pleases him will harvest the fruit of the tree of immortality.

19:20–30 True wisdom is contrasted with a dishonest shrewdness.

† Other ancient texts read as v. 21:
The slave who says to his master, "What pleases you I will not do"—
even if he does it later, provokes the one who feeds him.

20:1–8 The wise know the proper times for speech and silence, that is, the occasions when the most benefit can be gained from them. On the ambiguity of silences, see Prv 17:27–28.

20:4 Force can prevent an external act of sin or compel a good deed, but it does not eliminate the internal sin or desire of wrongdoing.

20:9–17 In a series of paradoxes the author indicates how much true and lasting values differ from apparent ones.

k: Lv 19:17. *l:* Sir 1:1, 12, 14; Jb 28:28; Ps 111:10; Prv 1:7; 9:10. *m:* Prv 17:27–28.

but the courtesies of fools are wasted.
14 A gift from a fool will do you no good,
for in his eyes this one gift is equal to many.
15 He gives little, criticizes often,
and opens his mouth like a town crier.
He lends today and asks for it tomorrow;
such a person is hateful.
16 A fool says, "I have no friends
nor thanks for my generosity."
Those who eat his bread have a mocking tongue.
17 How many will ridicule him, and how often!
18 A slip on the floor is better than a slip of the tongue;*
in like manner the downfall of the wicked comes quickly.
19 A coarse person, an untimely story;
the ignorant are always ready to offer it.
20 A proverb spoken by a fool is unwelcome,
for he does not tell it at the proper time.
21 There is a person whose poverty prevents him from sinning,
but when he takes his rest he has no regrets.
22 There is a person who is destroyed through shame,
and ruined by foolish posturing.
23 There is one who promises a friend out of shame,
and so makes an enemy needlessly.
24 A lie is a foul blot in a person,
yet it is always on the lips of the ignorant.
25 A thief is better than an inveterate liar,
yet both will suffer ruin.
26 A liar's way leads to dishonor,
and his shame remains ever with him.
27 The wise gain promotion with few words,*
the prudent please the great.
28 Those who work the land have abundant crops,
and those who please the great are pardoned their faults.
29 Favors and gifts blind the eyes;
like a muzzle over the mouth they silence reproofs.[n]
30 Hidden wisdom and unseen treasure—
what value has either?
31 Better are those who hide their folly
than those who hide their wisdom.†

CHAPTER 21

See RG 276–79

*Dangers from Sin**

1 My child, if you have sinned, do so no more,
and for your past sins pray to be forgiven.
2 Flee from sin as from a serpent
that will bite you if you go near it;
Its teeth, lion's teeth,
destroying human lives.
3 All lawlessness is like a two-edged sword;
when it cuts, there is no healing.[o]
4 Panic and pride wipe out wealth;
so too the house of the proud is uprooted.
5 Prayer from the lips of the poor is heard at once,
and justice is quickly granted them.
6 Whoever hates correction walks the sinner's path,[p]
but whoever fears the Lord repents in his heart.
7 Glib speakers are widely known,

20:18–26 The ill-timed speech brings disaster (vv. 18–20); human respect may lead to rash promises and enmity (vv. 22–23); lies bring dishonor and lasting disgrace (vv. 24–26).

20:27–31 Through prudent speech the wise gain honor and esteem among the great (vv. 27–28). They must beware, however, of accepting bribes, lest they share in evil through silence when they should reprove (vv. 29–31).

† Other ancient texts read as v. 32:
It is better to await the inevitable while serving the Lord
than to be the ungoverned helmsman for the careening of one's life.

21:1–10 Under various figures, the consequences of sin are described as destructive of wealth, and even of life, deserving of death (vv. 2–4, 6a, 8–10). Fear of the Lord motivates repentance (vv. 5, 6b).

n: Ex 23:8; Dt 16:19. *o:* Prv 5:4. *p:* Prv 12:1.

but when they slip the sensible
perceive it.
8 Those who build their houses with
someone else's money
are like those who collect stones for
their funeral mounds.
9 A band of criminals is like a bundle of
tow;
they will end in a flaming fire.[q]
10 The path of sinners is smooth stones,
but its end is the pit of Sheol.*

*The Wise and Foolish: A Contrast**

11 Those who keep the Law control their
thoughts;
perfect fear of the Lord is wisdom.
12 One who is not clever can never be
taught,
but there is a cleverness filled with
bitterness.
13 The knowledge of the wise wells up like
a flood,
and their counsel like a living spring.[r]
14 A fool's mind is like a broken jar:
it cannot hold any knowledge at all.

15 When the intelligent hear a wise saying,
they praise it and add to it.
The wanton hear it with distaste
and cast it behind their back.

16 A fool's chatter is like a load on a
journey,
but delight is to be found on the lips of
the intelligent.
17 The views of the prudent are sought in an
assembly,
and their words are taken to heart.
18 Like a house in ruins is wisdom to a fool;
to the stupid, knowledge is
incomprehensible chatter.
19 To the senseless, education is fetters on
the feet,
like manacles on the right hand.
20 Fools raise their voice in laughter,
but the prudent at most smile quietly.[s]
21 Like a gold ornament is education to the
wise,
like a bracelet on the right arm.

22 A fool steps boldly into a house,
while the well-bred are slow to make
an entrance.[t]
23 A boor peeps through the doorway of a
house,
but the educated stay outside.
24 It is rude for one to listen at a door;
the discreet person would be
overwhelmed by the disgrace.

25 The lips of the arrogant talk of what is
not their concern,
but the discreet carefully weigh their
words.
26 The mind of fools is in their mouths,
but the mouth of the wise is in their
mind.*
27 When the godless curse their adversary,*
they really curse themselves.
28 Slanderers sully themselves,
and are hated by their neighbors.

CHAPTER 22

See RG 276–79

On Laziness and Foolishness

1 * The sluggard is like a filthy stone;*
everyone hisses at his disgrace.
2 The sluggard is like a lump of dung;

21:10 The path of sinners . . . Sheol: Ben Sira refers to the death that awaits unrepentant sinners; see notes on 11:26–28; 17:24–32.

21:11–28 The mind of the wise is a fountain of knowledge (vv. 13, 15); their will is trained to keep the Law (v. 11); their words are gracious, valued, carefully weighed, sincere (vv. 16–17, 25–26); their conduct is respectful, cultured and restrained (vv. 20, 22–24). The mind of the foolish is devoid of knowledge and impenetrable to it (vv. 12, 14, 18–19); their will rejects it (v. 15); their talk is burdensome (v. 16), their laughter unrestrained (v. 20), their conversation shallow and meddlesome (vv. 25–26); their conduct is bold and rude (vv. 22–24); their abuse of others redounds on themselves (vv. 27–28).

21:26 A clever play on words.

21:27 Curse their adversary: the curse of the godless often recoils on their own head; cf. Gn 27:29; Nm 24:9.

22:1–15 To Ben Sira, a lazy person and an unruly child are a cause of shame and disgrace; everyone wishes to be rid of them (vv. 1–5). Speaking with a wicked fool is as senseless as talking with someone who is asleep or dead (v. 10). The fool is an intolerable burden that merits a lifetime of mourning (v. 12). Seven days was the usual mourning period. Cf. Gn 50:10; Jdt 16:24.

22:1 Stone: used then and even today for wiping oneself after a bowel movement.

---

q: Sir 16:6; Ps 21:10. *r:* Prv 13:14; 16:22; 18:4. *s:* Eccl 7:6. *t:* Prv 25:17.

whoever touches it shakes it off the
hands.
3 An undisciplined child is a disgrace to its
father;
if it be a daughter, she brings him to
poverty.[u]
4 A thoughtful daughter obtains a husband
of her own;
a shameless one is her father's grief.
5 A hussy shames her father and her
husband;
she is despised by both.
6 Like music at the time of mourning is ill-
timed talk,*
but lashes and discipline are at all
times wisdom.†
9 Teaching a fool is like gluing a broken
pot,[v]
or rousing another from deep sleep.
10 Whoever talks with a fool talks to
someone asleep;
when it is over, he says, "What was
that?"
11 Weep over the dead, for their light has
gone out;
weep over the fool, for sense has left
him.
Weep but less bitterly over the dead, for
they are at rest;
worse than death is the life of a fool.
12 Mourning for the dead, seven days—[w]
but for the wicked fool, a whole
lifetime.
13 Do not talk much with the stupid,
or visit the unintelligent.
Beware of them lest you have trouble
and be spattered when they shake
themselves off.
Avoid them and you will find rest
and not be wearied by their lack of
sense.
14 What is heavier than lead?
What is its name but "Fool"?
15 Sand, salt, and an iron weight
are easier to bear than the stupid
person.[x]
16 A wooden beam firmly bonded into a
building*
is not loosened by an earthquake;
So the mind firmly resolved after careful
deliberation
will not be afraid at any time.
17 The mind solidly backed by intelligent
thought
is like a stucco decoration on a smooth
wall.
18 Small stones lying on an open height
will not remain when the wind blows;
So a timid mind based on foolish plans
cannot stand up to fear of any kind.

*The Preservation of Friendship**

19 Whoever jabs the eye brings tears;
whoever pierces the heart bares its
feelings.
20 Whoever throws a stone at birds drives
them away;
whoever insults a friend breaks up the
friendship.
21 Should you draw a sword against a
friend,
do not despair, for it can be undone.
22 Should you open your mouth against a
friend,
do not worry, for you can be
reconciled.
But a contemptuous insult, a confidence
broken,
or a treacherous attack will drive any
friend away.

22:6 As a joyful song is out of place among mourners so a rebuke may be insufficient when corporal punishment is called for.

† Other ancient texts read as vv. 7–8:

[7] Children whose upbringing leads to a wholesome life
veil over the lowly origins of their parents.

[8] Children whose pride is in scornful misconduct
besmirch the nobility of their own family.

22:16–18 A prudent mind firmly resolved is undisturbed by violent and conflicting thoughts, whereas a foolish person is tossed about by the winds of fear, like small stones whipped about by high winds.

22:19–26 Disputes and violence weaken friendship, and disloyalty and abuse of confidence destroy it utterly (vv. 19–22, 24, 26); but kindness to a poor person in time of poverty and adversity builds up friendship and merits a share in his prosperity and inheritance (vv. 23, 25).

u: Prv 10:1; 17:21, 25; 19:13. *v:* Prv 23:9. *w:* Gn 50:10; Jdt 16:24. *x:* Prv 27:3.

23 Win your neighbor's trust while he is poor,
so that you may rejoice with him in his prosperity.
In time of trouble remain true to him,
so that you may share in his inheritance when it comes.
24 The billowing smoke of a furnace precedes the fire,
so insults precede bloodshed.
25 I am not ashamed to shelter a friend,
and I will not hide from him.
26 But if harm should come to me because of him,
all who hear of it will beware of him.

*Prayer**

27 Who will set a guard over my mouth,
an effective seal on my lips,
That I may not fail through them,
and my tongue may not destroy me?[y]

CHAPTER 23

See RG 276–79

1 Lord, Father and Master of my life,*
do not abandon me to their designs,
do not let me fall because of them!
2 Who will apply the lash to my thoughts,
and to my mind the rod of discipline,
That my failings may not be spared
or the sins of my heart overlooked?
3 Otherwise my failings may increase,
and my sins be multiplied;
And I fall before my adversaries,
and my enemy rejoice over me?
4 Lord, Father and God of my life,
do not give me haughty eyes;
5 remove evil desire from my heart.
6 Let neither gluttony nor lust overcome me;
do not give me up to shameless desires.[z]

*Proper Use of the Tongue**

7 Listen, my children, to instruction concerning the mouth,
for whoever keeps it will not be ensnared.
8 Through the lips the sinner is caught;
by them the reviler and the arrogant are tripped up.
9 Do not accustom your mouth to oaths,
or habitually utter the Holy Name.[a]
10 Just as a servant constantly under scrutiny
will not be without bruises,
So one who swears continually by the Holy Name
will never remain free from sin.
11 Those who swear many oaths heap up offenses;
and the scourge will never be far from their houses.
If they swear in error, guilt is incurred;
if they neglect their obligation, the sin is doubly great.[b]
If they swear without reason they cannot be declared innocent,
for their households will be filled with calamities.
12 There are words comparable to death;
may they never be heard in the inheritance of Jacob.
To the devout all such words are foreign;
they do not wallow in sin.
13 Do not accustom your mouth to coarse talk,
for it involves sinful speech.
14 Keep your father and mother in mind
when you sit among the mighty,[c]
Lest you forget yourself in their presence
and disgrace your upbringing.
Then you will wish you had never been born
and will curse the day of your birth.
15 Those accustomed to using abusive language
will never acquire discipline as long as they live.

22:27–23:6 Ben Sira implores the divine assistance to preserve him through stern discipline from sins of the tongue (22:27; 23:1), from ignorance of mind and weakness of will (vv. 2–3), and from inclinations of the senses and the flesh, lest he fall into the hands of his enemies or become a prey of shameful desires (vv. 4–6).

23:1–6 Lord, Father and Master of my life: these words express the tender personal relationship Ben Sira experiences with God, and introduce his prayer for divine assistance and providence in avoiding sins of pride and lust.

23:7–15 A warning against sins of the tongue through misuse of the sacred Name, against thoughtless swearing (vv. 7–11), blasphemy (v. 12), coarse talk (vv. 13–14), and abusive language (v. 15).

y: Ps 141:3. *z:* Rom 13:13. *a:* Ex 20:7; Lv 19:12; 24:16; Dt 5:11; Mt 5:33–37; Jas 5:12. *b:* Lv 5:4–10. *c:* Sir 7:27; Ex 20:12; Dt 5:16.

*Sins of the Flesh**

16 Two types of people multiply sins,
and a third* draws down wrath:
Burning passion is like a blazing fire,
not to be quenched till it burns itself out;
One unchaste with his kindred
never stops until fire breaks forth.
17 To the unchaste all bread is sweet;
he is never through till he dies.[d]

18 The man who dishonors his marriage bed
says to himself, "Who can see me?
Darkness surrounds me, walls hide me,
no one sees me. Who can stop me from sinning?"[e]
He is not mindful of the Most High,
19 fearing only human eyes.
He does not realize that the eyes of the Lord,
ten thousand times brighter than the sun,
Observe every step taken
and peer into hidden corners.
20 The one who knows all things before they exist
still knows them all after they are made.
21 Such a man will be denounced in the streets of the city;[f]
and where he least suspects it, he will be apprehended.

22 So it is with the woman unfaithful to her husband,
who offers him an heir by another man.
23 First of all, she has disobeyed the law of the Most High;
second, she has wronged her husband;
Third, through her wanton adultery
she has brought forth children by another man.
24 Such a woman will be dragged before the assembly,*
and her punishment will extend to her children.
25 Her children will not take root;
her branches will not bring forth fruit.
26 She will leave behind an accursed memory;
her disgrace will never be blotted out.

27 Thus all who dwell on the earth shall know,
all who remain in the world shall understand,
That nothing is better than the fear of the Lord,
nothing sweeter than obeying the commandments of the Lord.[g] †

CHAPTER 24

See RG 276–79

Praise of Wisdom

1 Wisdom sings her own praises,*
among her own people she proclaims her glory.
2 In the assembly of the Most High she opens her mouth,
in the presence of his host she tells of her glory:

3 "From the mouth of the Most High I came forth,[h]
and covered the earth like a mist.
4 In the heights of heaven I dwelt,
and my throne was in a pillar of cloud.
5 The vault of heaven I compassed alone,
and walked through the deep abyss.
6 Over waves of the sea, over all the land,
over every people and nation I held sway.

23:16–27 Ben Sira treats sexual sins and their consequences. Lust destroys its victims (vv. 16–17, 22–26). A false sense of security aggravates the adulterer's inevitable fate (vv. 18–21).

23:16 Two types . . . a third: a numerical proverb, as in 25:1–2, 7–11; 26:5–6, 28; 50:25–26; Prv 6:16–19; 30:15b–16, 18–19, 21–23, 29–31. Ben Sira condemns three kinds of sexual sin: incest (v. 16), fornication (v. 17), and adultery (vv. 18–26).

23:24–25 The judgment of the assembly determined the illegitimacy of children born of adultery or incest and excluded them from the "community of the Lord" (Dt 23:3). Cf. Wis 3:16–19; 4:3–6.

† Other ancient texts read as v. 28:
It is a great glory to follow after God,
and for you to be received by him is length of days.

24:1–29 Wisdom speaks in the first person, describing her origin, her dwelling place in Israel, and the reward she gives her followers. As in Proverbs 8, Wisdom is personified as coming from God, yet distinct from him. This description is reflected in the Johannine *logos*, or Word (Jn 1:1–14). It is used extensively in the Roman liturgy.

d: Prv 9:17. *e:* Jb 24:15; Prv 15:3, 11; 17:3; 24:12; Is 29:15; Ez 8:12. *f:* Lv 18:20; 20:10; Dt 22:21–22. *g:* Sir 1:11–30; Prv 3:1–2. *h:* Sir 1:1–4; Prv 2:6; 8:22–36; Wis 7:24–25.

7 Among all these I sought a resting place.
In whose inheritance should I abide?

8 "Then the Creator of all gave me his command,
and my Creator chose the spot for my tent.
He said, 'In Jacob make your dwelling,
in Israel your inheritance.'
9 Before all ages, from the beginning, he created me,
and through all ages I shall not cease to be.
10 In the holy tent I ministered before him,
and so I was established in Zion.
11 In the city he loves as he loves me, he gave me rest;
in Jerusalem, my domain.
12 I struck root among the glorious people,
in the portion of the Lord, his heritage.

13 "Like a cedar in Lebanon I grew tall,
like a cypress on Mount Hermon;
14 I grew tall like a palm tree in Engedi,
like rosebushes in Jericho;
Like a fair olive tree in the field,
like a plane tree beside water I grew tall.
15 Like cinnamon and fragrant cane,
like precious myrrh I gave forth perfume;
Like galbanum and onycha and mastic,[i]
like the odor of incense in the holy tent.*

16 "I spread out my branches like a terebinth,
my branches so glorious and so graceful.
17 I bud forth delights like a vine;
my blossoms are glorious and rich fruit.†
19 Come to me, all who desire me,
and be filled with my fruits.*
20 You will remember me as sweeter than honey,
better to have than the honeycomb.
21 Those who eat of me will hunger still,*
those who drink of me will thirst for more.[j]
22 Whoever obeys me will not be put to shame,
and those who serve me will never go astray."

23 All this is the book of the covenant of the Most High God,[k]
the Law which Moses commanded us*
as a heritage for the community of Jacob.†
25 It overflows, like the Pishon, with wisdom,[l]
and like the Tigris at the time of first fruits.
26 It runs over, like the Euphrates, with understanding,
and like the Jordan at harvest time.
27 It floods like the Nile with instruction,
like the Gihon* at vintage time.
28 The first human being never finished comprehending wisdom,
nor will the last succeed in fathoming her.
29 For deeper than the sea are her thoughts,
and her counsels, than the great abyss.
30 Now I, like a stream from a river,*
and like water channeling into a garden—
31 I said, "I will water my plants,

24:15 These substances, associated with worship, are mentioned in Ex 30:23–28, 34–35 as the ingredients of the anointing oil and the sacred incense. Israel was a priestly nation (Ex 19:6; Is 61:6).

† Other ancient texts read as v. 18:
I am the mother of fair love, of reverence,
of knowledge, and of holy hope;
To all my children I give
to be everlasting: to those named by Him.

24:19 Mt 11:28–30 contains a similar invitation.

24:21 The paradox of wisdom is that, far from being satiated, those who partake of her will always desire more.

24:23 Ben Sira now identifies Wisdom and the law of Moses; see also Bar 4:1.

† Other ancient texts read as v. 24:
Do not grow weary of striving with the Lord's help,
but cling to him that he may reinforce you.
The Lord Almighty alone is God,
and apart from him there is no savior.

24:27 Gihon: understood by some to have been a name for the Nile; cf. Gn 2:13.

24:30–33 Ben Sira again speaks about himself. He had at first drawn a small portion of the water of wisdom for his own private benefit, but finding it so useful, he soon began to let others share in this boon by teaching them the lessons of wisdom.

i: Ex 30:23–28, 34–35. *j:* Is 55:1; Jn 4:10–14; 6:35. *k:* Ex 24:7. *l:* Gn 2:11–14.

I will drench my flower beds."
Then suddenly this stream of mine
became a river,
and this river of mine became a sea.
32 Again I will make my teachings shine
forth like the dawn;
I will spread their brightness afar off.
33 Again I will pour out instruction like
prophecy
and bestow it on generations yet to
come.

See RG 276–79

CHAPTER 25

Those Who Are Worthy of Praise

1 * With three things I am delighted,
for they are pleasing to the Lord and to
human beings:
Harmony among relatives, friendship
among neighbors,
and a wife and a husband living
happily together.
2 Three kinds of people I hate,
and I loathe their manner of life:
A proud pauper, a rich liar,
and a lecherous old fool.
3 In your youth you did not gather.
How will you find anything in your
old age?
4 How appropriate is sound judgment in
the gray-haired,
and good counsel in the elderly!
5 How appropriate is wisdom in the aged,
understanding and counsel in the
venerable!
6 The crown of the elderly, wide
experience;
their glory, the fear of the Lord.
7 There are nine who come to mind as
blessed,
a tenth whom my tongue proclaims:*
The man who finds joy in his children,
and the one who lives to see the
downfall of his enemies.
8 Happy the man who lives with a sensible
woman,
and the one who does not plow with an
ox and a donkey combined.*
Happy the one who does not sin with the
tongue,
who does not serve an inferior.
9 Happy the one who finds a friend,
who speaks to attentive ears.
10 How great is the one who finds wisdom,
but none is greater than the one who
fears the Lord.
11 Fear of the Lord surpasses all else.
To whom can we compare the one who
has it?†

*Wicked and Virtuous Women**

13 Any wound, but not a wound of the heart!
Any wickedness, but not the
wickedness of a woman!
14 Any suffering, but not suffering from
one's foes!
Any vengeance, but not the vengeance
of one's enemies!
15 There is no poison worse than that of a
serpent,
no venom greater than that of a
woman.
16 I would rather live with a dragon or a
lion
than live with a wicked woman.[m]
17 A woman's wicked disposition changes
her appearance,
and makes her face as dark as a bear.
18 When her husband sits among his
neighbors,
a bitter sigh escapes him unawares.
19 There is hardly an evil like that in a
woman;
may she fall to the lot of the sinner!

dom. Like the words of the prophets, Ben Sira's instruction is valuable for all generations (v. 33). The comparison to prophecy is bold and unique.

25:1–2 A numerical saying in threes.

25:7–11 A numerical proverb (9 + 1), in which the tenth element, "the one who fears the Lord," is the most important.

25:8 An ox and a donkey combined: the reference is to a man married to two incompatible women (cf. 37:11a); the imagery derives from Dt 22:10.

† Other ancient texts read as v. 12:
Fear of the Lord is the beginning of loving him,
and fidelity is the beginning of clinging to him.

25:13–26 The harsh statements Ben Sira makes about women reflect the kind of instruction young Jewish males were exposed to in the early second century B.C. His patriarchal perspective is as unfair as it is one-sided.

m: Prv 21:9, 19; 25:24; 27:15.

[20] Like a sandy hill to aged feet
is a garrulous wife to a quiet husband.
[21] Do not be enticed by a woman's beauty,
or be greedy for her wealth.
[22] Harsh is the slavery and great the shame
when a wife supports her husband.

[23] Depressed mind, gloomy face,
and a wounded heart—a wicked woman.
Drooping hands and quaking knees,
any wife who does not make her husband happy.
[24] With a woman sin had a beginning,
and because of her we all die.*
[25] Allow water no outlet,
and no boldness of speech to a wicked woman.
[26] If she does not go along as you direct,
cut her away from you.

CHAPTER 26

See RG 276–79

[1] Happy the husband of a good wife;*
the number of his days will be doubled.[n]
[2] A loyal wife brings joy to her husband,
and he will finish his years in peace.
[3] A good wife is a generous gift
bestowed upon him who fears the Lord.[o]
[4] Whether rich or poor, his heart is content,
a smile ever on his face.

[5] There are three things I dread,
and a fourth which terrifies me:
Public slander, the gathering of a mob,
and false accusation—all harder to bear than death.
[6] A wife jealous of another wife is
heartache and mourning;*
everyone feels the lash of her tongue.

[7] A wicked wife is a chafing yoke;
taking hold of her is like grasping a scorpion.
[8] A drunken wife arouses great anger,
for she does not hide her shame.
[9] By her haughty stare and her eyelids
an unchaste wife can be recognized.

[10] Keep a strict watch over an unruly wife,
lest, finding an opportunity, she use it;[p]
[11] Watch out for her impudent eye,
and do not be surprised if she betrays you:
[12] As a thirsty traveler opens his mouth
and drinks from any water nearby,
So she sits down before every tent peg
and opens her quiver for every arrow.

[13] A gracious wife delights her husband;
her thoughtfulness puts flesh on his bones.
[14] A silent wife is a gift from the Lord;
nothing is worth more than her self-discipline.
[15] A modest wife is a supreme blessing;
no scales can weigh the worth of her chastity.
[16] The sun rising in the Lord's heavens—
the beauty of a good wife in her well-ordered home.
[17] The light which shines above the holy lampstand—*
a beautiful face on a stately figure.
[18] Golden columns on silver bases—
so her shapely legs and steady feet.†

25:24 Ben Sira refers to the story of the first sin in Gn 3:1–6. Cf. 2 Cor 11:3 and 1 Tm 2:14. St. Paul, however, singles out Adam; cf. Rom 5:12–19; 1 Cor 15:22.

26:1–4, 13–18 A good wife is as a gift from God, bringing joy and peace, happiness and contentment to her husband (vv. 1–4) through her thoughtfulness, reserve, modesty and chastity, beauty, grace, and virtue (vv. 13–18).

26:6–12 A repetition of the thought expressed in 25:13–26.

26:17–18 The lampstand and the columns were located in the holy place of the ancient tabernacle (Ex 25:31–40; 26:32).

† Other ancient texts read as vv. 19–27:
[19] My child, keep intact the bloom of your youth,
and do not give your strength to strangers.
[20] Seek out a fertile field from all the land,
and sow it with your own seed, confident in your fine stock.
[21] So shall your offspring prosper,
and grow great, confident in their good descent.
[22] A woman for hire is regarded as spittle,
but a married woman is a deadly snare for her lovers.
[23] A godless wife will be given to the lawless man as his portion,
but a godly wife will be given to the man who fears the Lord.
[24] A shameless woman wears out reproach,

n: Sir 25:8; Prv 18:22. *o:* Sir 36:27–29. *p:* Sir 42:11.

Dangers to Integrity and Friendship

28 * Two things bring grief to my heart,
and a third arouses my anger:
The wealthy reduced to want,
the intelligent held in contempt,
And those who pass from righteousness
to sin—
the Lord prepares them for the sword.[q]

29 A merchant can hardly keep from
wrongdoing,
nor can a shopkeeper stay free from sin;

CHAPTER 27

See RG 276–79

1 For the sake of profit many sin,
and the struggle for wealth blinds the
eyes.[r]
2 A stake will be driven between fitted
stones—
sin will be wedged in between buying
and selling.
3 Unless one holds fast to the fear of the
Lord,
with sudden swiftness will one's house
be thrown down.

4 When a sieve is shaken, the husks appear;
so do people's faults when they
speak.*
5 The furnace tests the potter's vessels;
the test of a person is in conversation.[s]
6 The fruit of a tree shows the care it has
had;
so speech discloses the bent of a
person's heart.[t]
7 Praise no one before he speaks,
for it is then that people are tested.

8 If you strive after justice, you will
attain it,
and wear it like a splendid robe.
9 Birds nest with their own kind,
and honesty comes to those who work
at it.
10 A lion lies in wait for prey,
so does sin for evildoers.

11 The conversation of the godly is always
wisdom,
but the fool changes like the moon.
12 Limit the time you spend among the
stupid,
but frequent the company of the
thoughtful.
13 The conversation of fools is offensive,
and their laughter is wanton sin.
14 Their oath-filled talk makes the hair
stand on end,
and their brawls make one stop the
ears.
15 The wrangling of the proud ends in
bloodshed,
and their cursing is painful to hear.[u]

16 Whoever betrays a secret destroys
confidence,*
and will never find a congenial friend.[v]
17 Cherish your friend, keep faith with him;
but if you betray his secrets, do not go
after him;
18 For as one might kill another,

but a virtuous daughter will be modest even before
her husband.
25 A headstrong wife is regarded as a bitch,
but the one with a sense of shame fears the Lord.
26 The wife who honors her husband will seem wise to
everyone,
but if she dishonors him in her pride, she will be
known to everyone as ungodly.
Happy is the husband of a good wife,
for the number of his years will be doubled.
27 A loud-mouthed and garrulous wife will be regarded
as a trumpet sounding the charge,
And every person who lives like this
will spend his life in the anarchy of war.

26:28–27:15 From proper conduct in family life, Ben Sira proceeds to social morality, warning especially against injustice in business (26:29–27:3), and perversity of speech in daily life (27:4–7). The pursuit of justice in these matters is all the more meritorious as it is difficult (27:8–10). The discourses of the godly are marked with wisdom, but the conversations of the wicked with offense, swearing, cursing, quarrels, and even bloodshed (27:11–15).

27:4–7, 11–15 The importance of effective speech is a favorite wisdom topic; e.g., cf. 20:1–8, 18–20; 22:27–23:15.

27:16–28:11 Betrayal of confidence through indiscretion destroys friendship and does irreparable harm (27:16–21); cf. 22:22. False friendship based on hypocrisy and deceit is hateful to Ben Sira and, he adds, to God as well (27:22–24); it soon becomes a victim of its own treachery (27:25–27). The same fate awaits the malicious and vengeful (27:28–28:1). They can obtain mercy and forgiveness only by first forgiving their neighbor, being mindful of death and of the commandments of the Most High (28:2–7). And they must avoid quarrels and strife (28:8–11).

q: Ez 18:24–29. *r:* Sir 7:18; 31:5–6; Prv 30:7–9. *s:* 1 Pt 1:7. *t:* Mt 7:20. *u:* Sir 23:8–15. *v:* Prv 11:13; 20:19.

you have killed your neighbor's
friendship.
19 Like a bird released from your hand,
you have let your friend go and cannot
recapture him.
20 Do not go after him, for he is far away,
and has escaped like a gazelle from a
snare.
21 For a wound can be bandaged, and an
insult forgiven,
but whoever betrays secrets does
hopeless damage.[w]

Malice, Anger and Vengeance

22 Whoever has shifty eyes plots mischief
and those who know him will keep
their distance;
23 In your presence he uses honeyed talk,
and admires your words,
But later he changes his tone
and twists the words to your ruin.[x]
24 I have hated many things but not as much
as him,
and the Lord hates him as well.[y]
25 A stone falls back on the head of the one
who throws it high,[z]
and a treacherous blow causes many
wounds.
26 Whoever digs a pit falls into it,
and whoever lays a snare is caught in it.*
27 The evil anyone does will recoil on him
without knowing how it came upon him.
28 Mockery and abuse will befall the
arrogant,
and vengeance lies in wait for them
like a lion.
29 Those who rejoice in the downfall of the
godly will be caught in a snare,
and pain will consume them before
they die.
30 Wrath and anger, these also are
abominations,
yet a sinner holds on to them.

CHAPTER 28

See RG 276–79

1 The vengeful will face the Lord's
vengeance;
indeed he remembers their sins in
detail.[a]
2 Forgive your neighbor the wrong done to
you;
then when you pray, your own sins
will be forgiven.[b]
3 Does anyone nourish anger against another
and expect healing from the LORD?[c]
4 Can one refuse mercy to a sinner like
oneself,
yet seek pardon for one's own sins?
5 If a mere mortal cherishes wrath,
who will forgive his sins?
6 Remember your last days and set enmity
aside;
remember death and decay, and cease
from sin![d]
7 Remember the commandments and do
not be angry with your neighbor;
remember the covenant of the Most
High, and overlook faults.
8 Avoid strife and your sins will be fewer,
for the hot-tempered kindle strife;
9 The sinner disrupts friendships
and sows discord among those who are
at peace.[e]
10 The more the wood, the greater the fire,[f]
the more the cruelty, the fiercer the strife;
The greater the strength, the sterner the
anger,
the greater the wealth, the greater the
wrath.
11 Pitch and resin make fire flare up,
and a hasty quarrel provokes bloodshed.

*The Evil Tongue**

12 If you blow on a spark, it turns into flame,
if you spit on it, it dies out;

27:26 This expresses a popular idea of act and consequence; an evil (or good) deed is repaid by an evil (or good) result. The frequent metaphor is the digging of a hole for another to fall into; cf. Prv 26:27; Ps 7:14; 9:16; Eccl 10:8.

28:12–26 Further treatment of sins of the tongue and the havoc that results; cf. 5:9–6:1; 19:5–17; 20:18–26; 23:7–15. Gossips and the double-tongued destroy domestic peace (vv. 12–16). The whip, the sword, chains, even Sheol, are not so cruel as the suffering inflicted by an evil tongue (vv. 17–21). Not the godly but those who forsake the Lord are victims of their evil tongues (vv. 22–23). Therefore, guard your mouth

w: Sir 22:20. *x:* Prv 26:24–28. *y:* Prv 6:16–19. *z:* Ps 7:16–17; Prv 26:27; Eccl 10:8. *a:* Dt 32:35; Rom 12:19. *b:* Mt 6:14. *c:* Mt 18:23–35. *d:* Sir 7:36; 38:20. *e:* Prv 15:18. *f:* Prv 26:20–21.

yet both you do with your mouth!
13 Cursed be gossips and the double-tongued,
for they destroy the peace of many.[g]
14 A meddlesome tongue subverts many,
and makes them refugees among peoples.
It destroys strong cities,
and overthrows the houses of the great.
15 A meddlesome tongue drives virtuous women from their homes,
and robs them of the fruit of their toil.
16 Whoever heed it will find no rest,
nor will they dwell in peace.
17 A blow from a whip raises a welt,
but a blow from the tongue will break bones.
18 Many have fallen by the edge of the sword,
but not as many as by the tongue.[h]
19 Happy the one who is sheltered from it,
and has not endured its wrath;
Who has not borne its yoke
nor been bound with its chains.
20 For its yoke is a yoke of iron,
and its chains are chains of bronze;
21 The death it inflicts is an evil death,
even Sheol is preferable to it.
22 It will have no power over the godly,
nor will they be burned in its flame.
23 But those who forsake the Lord will fall victim to it,
as it burns among them unquenchably;
It will hurl itself against them like a lion,
and like a leopard, it will tear them to pieces.
24 As you fence in your property with thorns,
so make a door and a bolt for your mouth.[i]
25 As you lock up your silver and gold,
so make balances and scales for your words.
26 Take care not to slip by your tongue
and fall victim to one lying in ambush.

CHAPTER 29

See RG 276–79

*Loans, Alms and Surety**

1 The merciful lend to their neighbor,
by holding out a helping hand, they keep the commandments.[j]
2 Lend to your neighbor in his time of need,
and pay back your neighbor in time.[k]
3 Keep your promise and be honest with him,
and at all times you will find what you need.
4 Many borrowers ask for a loan
and cause trouble for those who help them.
5 Till he gets a loan, he kisses the lender's hand
and speaks softly of his creditor's money,
But at time of payment, delays,
makes excuses, and finds fault with the timing.
6 If he can pay, the lender will recover barely half,
and will consider that a windfall.
If he cannot pay, the lender is cheated of his money
and acquires an enemy at no extra charge;
With curses and insults the borrower will repay,
and instead of honor will repay with abuse.
7 Many refuse to lend, not out of meanness,
but from fear of being cheated needlessly.
8 But with those in humble circumstances be patient;
do not keep them waiting for your alms.

and tongue as you would guard treasure against an enemy (vv. 24–26).

29:1–20 Some practical maxims concerning the use of wealth. Give to the poor (vv. 8–9), lend to a needy neighbor, but repay when a loan falls due lest the lender's burden be increased (vv. 1–5) and his kindness abused (vv. 6–7); through charity build up defense against evil (vv. 10–13). Help your neighbor according to your means, but take care not to fall (v. 20), for the shameless play false and bring their protectors and themselves to misfortune and ruin (vv. 14–19).

g: Sir 5:13–6:1. *h:* Jas 3:5–12. *i:* Sir 22:27; Ps 141:3. *j:* Dt 15:8; Ps 112:5; Prv 19:17. *k:* Ex 22:24–26; Lv 25:36; Mt 5:42.

9 Because of the commandment, help the poor,
and in their need, do not send them away empty-handed.[l]
10 Lose your money for relative or friend;
do not hide it under a stone to rot.
11 Dispose of your treasure according to the commandments of the Most High,
and that will profit you more than the gold.[m]
12 * Store up almsgiving in your treasury,
and it will save you from every evil.
13 Better than a mighty shield and a sturdy spear
it will fight for you against the enemy.

14 * A good person will be surety for a neighbor,
but whoever has lost a sense of shame will fail him.[n]
15 Do not forget the kindness of your backer,
for he has given his very life for you.
16 A sinner will turn the favor of a pledge into misfortune,
17 and the ungrateful will abandon his rescuer.
18 Going surety has ruined many who were prosperous
and tossed them about like waves of the sea;[o]
It has exiled the prominent
and sent them wandering through foreign lands.
19 The sinner will come to grief through surety,
and whoever undertakes too much will fall into lawsuits.
20 Help your neighbor according to your means,
but take care lest you fall yourself.

*Frugality and Its Rewards**

21 Life's prime needs are water, bread, and clothing,
and also a house for decent privacy.[p]
22 Better is the life of the poor under the shadow of their own roof
than sumptuous banquets among strangers.[q]
23 Whether little or much, be content with what you have:
then you will hear no reproach as a parasite.
24 It is a miserable life to go from house to house,
for where you are a guest you dare not open your mouth.
25 You will entertain and provide drink without being thanked;
besides, you will hear these bitter words:
26 "Come here, you parasite, set the table,
let me eat the food you have there!
27 Go away, you parasite, for one more worthy;
for my relative's visit I need the room!"
28 Painful things to a sensitive person
are rebuke as a parasite and insults from creditors.

CHAPTER 30

See RG 276–79

*The Training of Children**

1 Whoever loves a son will chastise him often,
that he may be his joy when he grows up.[r]
2 Whoever disciplines a son will benefit from him,
and boast of him among acquaintances.
3 Whoever educates a son will make his enemy jealous,

29:12–13 In Ben Sira's day, almsgiving and righteousness were practically identified.

29:14–17 Ben Sira is more lenient on going surety than earlier sages; cf. Prv 6:1–5.

29:21–28 Those who provide their own basic needs of food, clothing and dwelling, and are content with what they have, preserve their freedom and self-respect (vv. 21–23). But if they live as guests, even among the rich, they expose themselves to insult and rebuke (vv. 24–28).

30:1–13 Sound discipline (which would include physical beating) and careful education of children correct self-indulgence and stubbornness, prevent remorse and humiliation, and bring to parents lasting joy and delight, prestige among friends, jealousy of enemies, perpetuation and vindication of themselves through their offspring (vv. 1–6). Lack of discipline and overindulgence of children bring sorrow and disappointment, terror and grief (vv. 7–13).

l: Sir 4:1–6; Lv 19:9–10; 23:22. *m:* Sir 17:22–23; Tb 4:7–11. *n:* Sir 8:13. *o:* Prv 6:1–2; 11:15. *p:* Sir 39:26. *q:* Sir 40:29. *r:* Prv 13:24; 19:18; 22:15; 23:13; 29:15; Heb 12:7.

and rejoice in him among his friends.
4 At the father's death, he will seem not dead,
for he leaves after him one like himself,
5 Whom he looked upon through life with joy,
and in death, without regret.
6 Against his enemies he has left an avenger,
and one to repay his friends with kindness.

7 Whoever spoils a son will have wounds to bandage,
and will suffer heartache at every cry.
8 An untamed horse turns out stubborn;
and a son left to himself grows up unruly.
9 Pamper a child and he will be a terror for you,
indulge him, and he will bring you grief.
10 Do not laugh with him lest you share sorrow with him,
and in the end you will gnash your teeth.
11 Do not give him his own way in his youth,
and do not ignore his follies.
12 Bow down his head in his youth,
beat his sides while he is still young,
Lest he become stubborn and disobey you,
and leave you disconsolate.[s]
13 Discipline your son and make heavy his yoke,
lest you be offended by his shamelessness.

*Health and Cheerfulness**

14 Better the poor in vigorous health
than the rich with bodily ills.
15 I would rather have bodily health than any gold,
and contentment of spirit than pearls.
16 No riches are greater than a healthy body;
and no happiness than a joyful heart.
17 Better is death than a wretched life,[t]
everlasting sleep than constant illness.
18 Good things set before one who cannot eat
are like food offerings placed before a tomb.* [u]
19 What good is an offering to an idol
that can neither eat nor smell?
So it is with the one being punished by the Lord,
20 who groans at what his eyes behold.
21 Do not give in to sadness,
or torment yourself deliberately.[v]
22 Gladness of heart is the very life of a person,
and cheerfulness prolongs his days.
23 Distract yourself and renew your courage,
drive resentment far away from you;
For grief has killed many,[w]
and nothing is to be gained from resentment.
24 Envy and anger shorten one's days,
and anxiety brings on premature old age.
25 Those who are cheerful and merry at table
benefit from their food.* [x]

CHAPTER 31

See RG 276–79

*The Proper Attitude Toward Riches**

1 Wakefulness over wealth wastes away the flesh,
and anxiety over it drives away sleep.

30:14–25 Health of mind and body and joy of heart Ben Sira judges to be more precious than wealth (vv. 14–16), whereas bitterness, constant illness, and affliction are more difficult to bear than death (vv. 17–20). Sadness, resentment, anxiety, envy, and anger shorten days; they should be dispelled by cheerfulness and gladness of heart, which help to prolong one's days (vv. 21–25).

30:18 The saying ridicules the practice of putting food and drink on the tombs of the dead.

30:25(27) Because of the dislocation of the Greek text, the numbering of this verse follows Ziegler's edition. There are no verses 25–26.

31:1–11 Solicitude for acquiring wealth and anxiety over preserving it disturb repose and easily lead to sin and ruin (vv. 1–7). Cf. Mt 6:25–34. The rich who have not sinned or been seduced by wealth are worthy of highest praise (vv. 8–11).

s: Sir 7:23; Prv 23:14. *t:* Sir 41:2. *u:* Tb 4:17. *v:* Prv 12:25; 15:13; 17:22. *w:* Sir 38:18–19. *x:* Prv 15:15.

2 Wakeful anxiety banishes slumber;
more than a serious illness it disturbs repose.
3 The rich labor to pile up wealth,
and if they rest, it is to enjoy pleasure;
4 The poor labor for a meager living,
and if they ever rest, they become needy.
5 The lover of gold will not be free from sin;
whoever pursues money will be led astray by it.
6 Many have come to ruin for the sake of gold,
yet destruction lay before their very eyes;[y]
7 It is a stumbling block for fools;
any simpleton will be ensnared by it.
8 Happy the rich person found without fault,
who does not turn aside after wealth.[z]
9 Who is he, that we may praise him?
For he has done wonders among his people.
10 Who has been tested by gold and been found perfect?
Let it be for him his glory;
Who could have sinned but did not,
and could have done evil but did not?
11 So his good fortune is secure,
and the assembly will recount his praises.[a]

*Table Etiquette**

12 Are you seated at the table of the great?
Bring to it no greedy gullet,
Nor say, "How much food there is here!"
13 Remember that the greedy eye is evil.
What has been created more greedy than the eye?
Therefore, it weeps for any cause.[b]
15 Recognize that your neighbor feels as you do,
and keep in mind everything you dislike.
14 Toward what he looks at, do not put out a hand;
nor reach for the same dish when he does.
16 Eat, like anyone else, what is set before you,
but do not eat greedily, lest you be despised.
17 Be the first to stop, as befits good manners;
and do not gorge yourself, lest you give offense.[c]
18 If there are many with you at table,
do not be the first to stretch out your hand.
19 Does not a little suffice for a well-bred person?
When he lies down, he does not wheeze.[d]
20 Moderate eating ensures sound slumber
and a clear mind on rising the next day.
The distress of sleeplessness and of nausea
and colic are with the glutton!
21 Should you have eaten too much,
get up to vomit* and you will have relief.
22 Listen to me, my child, and do not scorn me;
later you will find my advice good.
In whatever you do, be moderate,
and no sickness will befall you.
23 People bless one who is generous with food,
and this testimony to his goodness is lasting.[e]
24 The city complains about one who is stingy with food,
and this testimony to his stinginess is lasting.

31:12–32:13 Whoever observes etiquette at table avoids greed and selfishness (31:12–13), is considerate of a neighbor's likes and dislikes and is generous toward him (31:15, 14, 23, 24), observes proper manners (31:16–18), is moderate in eating and drinking (31:19–20, 25–30). A good host is solicitous for the guests (32:1–2), provides conversation and diversion (32:3–6), is modest in speech (32:7, 8, 10), is respectful of elders (32:9), polite in comportment and grateful to God for his favors (32:11–13).

31:21 Get up to vomit: the practice of induced vomiting, well-known among Romans, and less well-known among the Jews, seems to be referred to here.

y: Sir 8:2. *z:* Sir 5:1, 8. *a:* Prv 29:14. *b:* Prv 23:1–2. *c:* Sir 37:27–31. *d:* Eccl 5:11. *e:* Prv 22:9.

[25] Let not wine be the proof of your strength,
for wine has been the ruin of many.
[26] As the furnace tests the work of the smith,
so does wine the hearts of the insolent.
[27] Wine is very life to anyone,
if taken in moderation.
Does anyone really live who lacks the wine
which from the beginning was created for joy?[f]
[28] Joy of heart, good cheer, and delight
is wine enough, drunk at the proper time.
[29] Headache, bitterness, and disgrace
is wine drunk amid anger and strife.
[30] Wine in excess is a snare for the fool;
it lessens strength and multiplies wounds.
[31] Do not wrangle with your neighbor when wine is served,
nor despise him while he is having a good time;
Say no harsh words to him
nor distress him by making demands.

CHAPTER 32

See RG 276–79

[1] If you are chosen to preside at a dinner, do not be puffed up,
but with the guests be as one of them;
Take care of them first and then sit down;
[2] see to their needs, and then take your place,
To share in their joy
and receive a wreath for a job well done.
[3] You who are older, it is your right to speak,
but temper your knowledge and do not interrupt the singing.
[4] Where there is entertainment, do not pour out discourse,
and do not display your wisdom at the wrong time.
[5] Like a seal of carnelian in a setting of gold:
a concert of music at a banquet of wine.
[6] A seal of emerald in a work of gold:
the melody of music with delicious wine.
[7] Speak, young man, only when necessary,[g]
when they have asked you more than once.
[8] Be brief, say much in few words;
be knowledgeable and yet quiet.
[9] When among elders do not be forward,
and with officials do not be too insistent.
[10] The lightning that flashes before a hailstorm:
the esteem that shines on modesty.
[11] Leave in good time and do not be the last;
go home quickly without delay.
[12] There enjoy doing as you wish,
but do not sin through words of pride.
[13] Above all, bless your Maker,
who showers his favors upon you.

The Providence of God

[14] Whoever seeks God must accept discipline;*
and whoever resorts to him obtains an answer.[h]
[15] Whoever seeks the law will master it,
but the hypocrite will be ensnared by it.[i]
[16] Whoever fears the LORD will understand what is right,
and out of obscurity he will draw forth a course of action.[j]
[17] The lawless turn aside warnings
and distort the law to suit their purpose.[k]
[18] The sensible will not neglect direction;
the proud and insolent are deterred by no fear.
[19] Do nothing without deliberation;
then once you have acted, have no regrets.[l]
[20] Do not go on a way set with snares,

32:14–33:4 God is shown to reveal himself through the discipline of his law, a clear and safe plan of life for the pious. Direction and deliberation are aids in following it (32:14–16, 18–24; 33:1, 3–4). Sinners and hypocrites, hating the law or distorting it, fail in wisdom and are devoid of security (32:15b, 17, 18b; 33:2).

f: Ps 104:15; 1 Tm 5:23. *g:* Sir 7:14. *h:* Sir 4:13. *i:* Sir 2:16. *j:* Ps 37:6. *k:* Sir 21:6; Prv 12:1. *l:* Sir 37:16; Tb 4:18.

and do not stumble on the same thing
twice.
21 Do not trust the road, because of bandits;
22 be careful on your paths.
23 Whatever you do, be on your guard,
for whoever does so keeps the
commandments.
24 Whoever keeps the law preserves himself;
and whoever trusts in the LORD shall
not be put to shame.

CHAPTER 33

See RG 276–79

1 No evil can harm the one who fears
the LORD;
through trials, again and again he is
rescued.[m]
2 Whoever hates the law is without wisdom,
and is tossed about like a boat in a
storm.
3 The prudent trust in the word of the
LORD,
and the law is dependable for them as
a divine oracle.*
4 Prepare your words and then you will be
listened to;
draw upon your training, and give
your answer.
5 Like the wheel of a cart is the mind of a
fool,
and his thoughts like a turning axle.
6 A mocking friend is like a stallion
that neighs, no matter who the rider
may be.
7 * Why is one day more important than
another,
when the same sun lights up every day
of the year?
8 By the LORD's knowledge they are kept
distinct;
and he designates the seasons and
feasts.[n]
9 Some he exalts and sanctifies,
and others he lists as ordinary days.[o]
10 Likewise, all people are of clay,
and from earth humankind was formed;[p]
11 In the fullness of his knowledge the Lord
distinguished them,
and he designated their different ways.
12 Some he blessed and exalted,
and some he sanctified and drew to
himself.
Others he cursed and brought low,
and expelled them from their place.
13 Like clay in the hands of a potter,
to be molded according to his
pleasure,
So are people in the hands of their
Maker,
to be dealt with as he decides.[q]
14 As evil contrasts with good, and death
with life,
so are sinners in contrast with the
godly.[r]
15 See now all the works of the Most High:
they come in pairs, one the opposite of
the other.

16 Now I am the last to keep vigil,*
like a gleaner following the grape-
pickers;
17 Since by the Lord's blessing I have made
progress
till like a grape-picker I have filled my
wine press,
18 Consider that not for myself only have I
labored,
but for all who seek instruction.

*Property and Servants**

19 Listen to me, leaders of the people;
rulers of the congregation, pay heed![s]
20a Let neither son nor wife, neither brother
nor friend,

33:3 Oracle: as the answer given through the Urim and Thummim to the high priest is true, so the law proves itself true to those who obey it. Cf. Ex 28:30; Nm 27:21.

33:7–15 An important doctrine of Ben Sira is his view of the polarities in creation and history; cf. v. 15; 42:24. Contrasts observable in the physical universe as well as in the moral order serve the purposes of divine wisdom (vv. 5–9). All creatures are like clay in the hands of their Maker—the fool and the wise, the sinner and the just (vv. 10–15). This does not imply that some are created to be sinners: God is not the author of wickedness. Divine determinism and human freedom are a mysterious mix.

33:16–18 Ben Sira refers to himself as the most recent of the biblical writers who have endeavored to present true wisdom to their readers.

33:19–33 Public officials should reject every influence

m: Ps 91:10–13; Mt 4:6; Lk 4:10–11. *n:* Gn 1:14. *o:* Ex 20:11; Dt 5:13–14. *p:* Gn 2:7. *q:* Wis 15:7; Jer 18:1–6; Rom 9:20–21. *r:* Sir 42:25. *s:* Wis 6:1–2.

have power over you as long as you
live.
21 While breath of life is still in you,
let no one take your place.
20b Do not give your wealth to another,
lest you must plead for support
yourself.
22 Far better that your children plead with
you
than that you should look for a
handout from them.
23 Keep control over all your affairs;
bring no stain on your honor.
24 When your few days reach their limit,
at the time of death distribute your
inheritance.

25 Fodder and whip and loads for a donkey;
food, correction and work for a slave.
26 Make a slave work, and he will look for
rest;
let his hands be idle and he will seek to
be free.[t]
27 The yoke and harness will bow the neck;
and for a wicked slave, punishment in
the stocks.
28 Force him to work that he be not idle,
29 for idleness teaches much mischief.
30 Put him to work, as is fitting for him;
and if he does not obey, load him with
chains.
But never lord it over any human being,
and do nothing unjust.
31 If you have but one slave, treat him like
yourself,
for you have acquired him with your
life's blood;
If you have but one slave, deal with him
as a brother,
for you need him as you need your
life.[u]
32 If you mistreat him and he runs away,
33 in what direction will you look for
him?

CHAPTER 34

See RG 276–79

*Trust in the Lord and Not in Dreams**

1 Empty and false are the hopes of the
senseless,
and dreams give wings to fools.
2 Like one grasping at shadows or chasing
the wind,
so anyone who believes in dreams.
3 What is seen in dreams is a reflection,
the likeness of a face looking at itself.
4 How can the unclean produce what is
clean?
How can the false produce what is
true?[v]
5 Divination, omens, and dreams are
unreal;
what you already expect, the mind
fantasizes.
6 Unless they are specially sent by the
Most High,
do not fix your heart on them.
7 For dreams have led many astray,
and those who put their hope in them
have perished.
8 Without such deceptions the Law will be
fulfilled,
and in the mouth of the faithful is
complete wisdom.

9 A much-traveled person knows many
things;
and one with much experience speaks
sense.
10 An inexperienced person knows little,
11 whereas with travel one adds to
resourcefulness.
12 I have seen much in my travels,
and learned more than I could ever
say.
13 Often I was in danger of death,
but by these experiences I was
saved.

that would restrict their freedom in the management of their affairs. They must make their own household subservient to them rather than be subservient to it (vv. 19–24). Slaves are to be given food and work and correction but never to be treated unjustly (vv. 25–30). Great care should be taken of good slaves (vv. 31–33).

34:1–20 Confidence placed in dreams, divinations, and omens is false because these are devoid of reality (vv. 1–8). True confidence is founded on knowledge and experience (vv. 9–13), and above all on the fear of the Lord, with its accompanying blessings of divine assistance and protection (vv. 14–20).

t: Prv 29:19. *u:* Sir 7:20–21. *v:* Jb 14:4.

14 Living is the spirit of those who fear the Lord,
15 for their hope is in their savior.
16 Whoever fear the Lord are afraid of nothing
and are never discouraged, for he is their hope.[w]
17 Happy the soul that fears the Lord!
18 In whom does he trust, and who is his support?
19 The eyes of the Lord are upon those who love him;
he is their mighty shield and strong support,
A shelter from the heat, a shade from the noonday sun,
a guard against stumbling, a help against falling.[x]
20 He lifts up spirits, brings a sparkle to the eyes,
gives health and life and blessing.

*True Worship of God**

21 Ill-gotten goods offered in sacrifice are tainted.
22 Presents from the lawless do not win God's favor.[y]
23 The Most High is not pleased with the gifts of the godless,
nor for their many sacrifices does he forgive their sins.
24 One who slays a son in his father's presence—
whoever offers sacrifice from the holdings of the poor.
25 The bread of charity is life itself for the needy;[z]
whoever withholds it is a murderer.
26 To take away a neighbor's living is to commit murder;
27 to deny a laborer wages is to shed blood.
28 If one builds up and another tears down,
what do they gain but trouble?
29 If one prays and another curses,
whose voice will God hear?
30 If one again touches a corpse after bathing,
what does he gain by the purification?[a]
31 So one who fasts for sins,
but goes and commits them again:
Who will hear his prayer,
what is gained by mortification?

CHAPTER 35*

See RG 276–79

1 To keep the law is to make many offerings;[b]
2 whoever observes the commandments sacrifices a peace offering.
3 By works of charity one offers fine flour,*
4 and one who gives alms presents a sacrifice of praise.
5 To refrain from evil pleases the Lord,
and to avoid injustice is atonement.
6 Do not appear before the Lord empty-handed,
7 for all that you offer is in fulfillment of the precepts.[c]
8 The offering of the just enriches the altar:
a sweet odor before the Most High.
9 The sacrifice of the just is accepted,
never to be forgotten.
10 With a generous spirit pay homage to the Lord,
and do not spare your freewill gifts.[d]
11 With each contribution show a cheerful countenance,
and pay your tithes in a spirit of joy.[e]

34:21–31 To be acts of true religion, sacrifice and penance must be accompanied by the proper moral dispositions. To offer to God goods taken from the poor (vv. 21–27), or to practice penance without interior reform, is a mockery, worthless in the sight of God (vv. 28–31). Cf. Mt 15:4–7; Mk 7:9–13.

35:1–26 Keeping the commandments of the law and avoiding injustice constitute sacrifice pleasing and acceptable to God (vv. 1–5). Offerings also should be made to him, cheerfully and generously; these he repays sevenfold (vv. 6–13). Extortion from widows and orphans is injustice, and God will hear their cries (vv. 14–22a). Punishing the proud and the merciless and coming to the aid of the distressed, he requites everyone according to their deeds (vv. 22b–26).

35:3 Fine flour, together with oil and frankincense, was a prescribed offering to God; cf. Lv 2:1–3.

w: Ps 23:4; 112:7–8; Prv 3:23–24; 28:1. *x:* Ps 33:18–19; 34:16. *y:* Sir 35:14–15; Prv 21:27. *z:* Lv 19:13; Dt 24:14–15; Tb 4:14. *a:* Nm 19:11–12; Prv 26:11; 2 Pt 2:22. *b:* 1 Sm 15:22; Ps 51:18–19; Is 1:11–18; Hos 6:6; Am 5:21–24. *c:* Ex 23:15; 34:20; Dt 16:16. *d:* Sir 7:31. *e:* Dt 14:22; 2 Cor 9:7.

12 Give to the Most High as he has given to
you,
generously, according to your means.
13 For he is a God who always repays
and will give back to you sevenfold.[f]

14 But offer no bribes; these he does not
accept!
15 Do not trust in sacrifice of the fruits of
extortion,[g]
For he is a God of justice,
who shows no partiality.[h]
16 He shows no partiality to the weak
but hears the grievance of the
oppressed.*
17 He does not forsake the cry of the orphan,[i]
nor the widow when she pours out her
complaint.
18 Do not the tears that stream down her
cheek
19 cry out against the one that causes
them to fall?
20 Those who serve God to please him are
accepted;
their petition reaches the clouds.
21 The prayer of the lowly pierces the
clouds;
it does not rest till it reaches its goal;
Nor will it withdraw till the Most High
responds,
22 judges justly and affirms the right.[j]

God indeed will not delay,
and like a warrior, will not be still[k]
Till he breaks the backs of the merciless
23 and wreaks vengeance upon the nations;
Till he destroys the scepter of the proud,
and cuts off the staff of the wicked;
24 Till he requites everyone according to
their deeds,
and repays them according to their
thoughts;
25 Till he defends the cause of his people,
and makes them glad by his salvation.
26 Welcome is his mercy in time of distress
as rain clouds in time of drought.

CHAPTER 36

See RG 276–79

*A Prayer for God's People**

1 Come to our aid, O God of the universe,
2 and put all the nations in dread of you!
3 Raise your hand against the foreign
people,
that they may see your mighty deeds.
4 As you have used us to show them your
holiness,*
so now use them to show us your
glory.
5 Thus they will know, as we know,
that there is no God but you.

6 Give new signs and work new wonders;
7 show forth the splendor of your right
hand and arm.
8 Rouse your anger, pour out wrath;
9 humble the enemy, scatter the foe.[l]
10 Hasten the ending, appoint the time,
and let people proclaim your mighty
deeds.
11 Let raging fire consume the fugitive,
and your people's oppressors meet
destruction.
12 Crush the heads of the hostile rulers
who say, "There is no one besides me."

13 Gather all the tribes of Jacob,*
16 that they may inherit the land as in
days of old.
17 Show mercy to the people called by your
name:
Israel, whom you named your
firstborn.[m]
18 Take pity on your holy city:
Jerusalem, your dwelling place.[n]

35:16 Cf. Lv 19:15; Dt 1:17. The divine impartiality is paradoxical, for it is tilted toward the poor.

36:1–22 A prayer that God hasten the day for the gathering of the tribes of Israel, and Zion once more be filled with the divine glory. All the earth will then know that the Lord is the eternal God.

36:4 Show . . . holiness: this cultic language is used to indicate God's liberation of his people; cf. Ez 20:41; 28:25.

36:13 This verse marks the end of a major dislocation in the Greek text of Sirach (which is followed here) at the head of chap. 33. The verse numbers 1–13 come from the placement of these verses in Greek. Verse 13 here is the first half of a bicolon, the matching half of which is numbered in the Greek 36:16b. Thus although the numbering for vv. 14–15 is not used, none of the text is missing.

f: Prv 19:17; Mt 25:34–40. *g:* Sir 34:21–23; Prv 15:8; 21:27. *h:* Dt 10:17; 2 Chr 19:7; Jb 34:19; Wis 6:7; Acts 10:34; Rom 2:11; Gal 2:6; 1 Pt 1:17. *i:* Ex 22:22. *j:* Lk 18:7. *k:* Is 42:13–16; 2 Pt 3:9. *l:* Ps 79:6; Jer 10:25. *m:* Ex 4:22. *n:* 2 Chr 6:41; Ps 132:8, 14; Is 2:1–3; Mi 4:1–3.

19 Fill Zion with your majesty,
your temple with your glory.
20 Give evidence of your deeds of old;
fulfill the prophecies spoken in your name.
21 Reward those who have hoped in you,
and let your prophets be proved true.
22 Hear the prayer of your servants,
according to your good will toward your people.
Thus all the ends of the earth will know
that you are the eternal God.

*Choice of Associates**

23 The throat can swallow any food,
yet some foods are more agreeable than others.
24 The palate tests delicacies put forward as gifts,
so does a keen mind test deceitful tidbits.
25 One with a tortuous heart brings about grief,
but an experienced person can turn the tables on him.
26 A woman will accept any man as husband,
but one woman will be preferable to another.
27 A woman's beauty makes her husband's face light up,
for it surpasses all else that delights the eye.[o]
28 And if, besides, her speech is soothing,
her husband's lot is beyond that of mortal men.
29 A wife is her husband's richest treasure,
a help like himself and a staunch support.[p]
30 A vineyard with no hedge will be overrun;
and a man with no wife becomes a homeless wanderer.
31 Who will trust an armed band
that shifts from city to city?
Or a man who has no nest,
who lodges wherever night overtakes him?[q]

CHAPTER 37

See RG 276–79

1 Every friend declares friendship,
but there are friends who are friends in name only.[r]
2 Is it not a sorrow unto death
when your other self becomes your enemy?
3 "Alas, my companion! Why were you created
to fill the earth with deceit?"
4 A harmful friend will look to your table,
but in time of trouble he stands aloof.
5 A good friend will fight with you against the foe,
and against your enemies he will hold up your shield.
6 Do not forget your comrade during the battle,
and do not neglect him when you distribute your spoils.

7 Every counselor points out a way,
but some counsel ways of their own.
8 Watch out when one offers advice;
find out first of all what he wants.
For he also may be thinking of himself—
Why should the opportunity fall to him?
9 He may tell you how good your way will be,
and then stand by to see you impoverished.
10 Seek no advice from your father-in-law,
and from one who is envious of you, keep your intentions hidden.
11 Seek no advice from a woman about her rival,
from a coward about war,
from a merchant about business,

36:23–37:15 In the choice of wife, friend, or associate, experience is a discerner of character (36:23–26). Beauty and soothing speech make a woman desirable as wife (36:27–28). The good wife becomes her husband's richest treasure, his help in establishing his household (36:29–31). Good friends fight for comrades and share the spoils with them (37:5–6); false friends deceive and abandon in time of need (37:1–4). A true counselor and associate should be sought among those who keep the commandments, not among those who break them and seek their own advantage (37:7–12). In all things one should pray to God for light and follow conscience (37:13–15).

o: Sir 26:13–18; Prv 12:4; 18:22; 19:14. *p:* Gn 2:18. *q:* Prv 27:8. *r:* Sir 6:7–17.

from a buyer about value,
from a miser about generosity,
from a cruel person about well-being,
from a worthless worker about his work,
from a seasonal laborer about the harvest,
from an idle slave about a great task—
pay no attention to any advice they give.

12 Instead, associate with a religious person,
who you know keeps the commandments;
Who is like-minded with yourself
and will grieve for you if you fall.
13 Then, too, heed your own heart's counsel;
for there is nothing you can depend on more.
14 The heart can reveal your situation
better than seven sentinels on a tower.
15 Then with all this, pray to God
to make your steps firm in the true path.

Wisdom and Temperance

16 A word is the source of every deed;*
a thought, of every act.[s]
17 The root of all conduct is the heart;
18 four branches it shoots forth:
Good and evil, death and life,
and their absolute mistress is the tongue.[t]
19 One may be wise and benefit many,
yet appear foolish to himself.
20 One may be wise, but if his words are rejected,
he will be deprived of all enjoyment.*
22 When one is wise to his own advantage,
the fruits of knowledge are seen in his own person.
23 When one is wise to the advantage of people,
the fruits of knowledge are lasting.[u]
24 One wise for himself has full enjoyment,
and all who see him praise him.
25 The days of one's life are numbered,
but the life of Israel, days without number.
26 One wise among the people wins a heritage of glory,
and his name lives on and on.[v]

27 My son, while you are well, govern your appetite,*
and see that you do not allow it what is bad for you.
28 For not everything is good for everyone,
nor is everything suited to every taste.[w]
29 Do not go to excess with any enjoyment,[x]
neither become a glutton for choice foods;
30 For sickness comes with overeating,
and gluttony brings on nausea.
31 Through lack of self-control many have died,
but the abstemious one prolongs life.

CHAPTER 38

See RG 276–79

Sickness and Death

1 Make friends with the doctor, for he is essential to you;*
God has also established him in his profession.
2 From God the doctor has wisdom,
and from the king he receives sustenance.
3 Knowledge makes the doctor distinguished,
and gives access to those in authority.
4 God makes the earth yield healing herbs
which the prudent should not neglect;
5 Was not the water sweetened by a twig,
so that all might learn his power?[y]
6 He endows people with knowledge,

37:16–26 Thoughts determine action. Wisdom is the source of good and life; folly, of evil and death (vv. 16–18). If the fruits of a person's wisdom benefit himself, he may be praised in his own lifetime; if they benefit others, the praise endures after him, in their lives (vv. 19–26).

37:20 Verse 21 appears only in Greek, but not in the Hebrew, which is the basis for the translation here.

37:27–31 Temperance and self-control should govern appetite for food, which is intended not to destroy but to preserve life.

38:1–15 The profession of medicine comes from God, who makes the earth yield healing herbs and gives the physician knowledge of their power (vv. 1–8). In illness the sick should cleanse their soul from sin and petition God for help through an offering of sacrifice; the physician, too, does well to invoke God that he may understand the illness and apply the proper remedy (vv. 9–14). The sinner, in contrast, defies both his Maker and the doctor (v. 15).

s: Sir 32:19. *t:* Prv 18:21. *u:* Sir 39:10–11. *v:* Sir 39:9; 44:13–16. *w:* 1 Cor 6:12; 10:23. *x:* Sir 31:13, 16–21. *y:* Ex 15:25.

to glory in his mighty works,
7 Through which the doctor eases pain,
8 and the druggist prepares his medicines.
Thus God's work continues without cease
in its efficacy on the surface of the earth.

9 My son, when you are ill, do not delay,
but pray to God, for it is he who heals.[z]
10 Flee wickedness and purify your hands;
cleanse your heart of every sin.
11 Offer your sweet-smelling oblation and memorial,
a generous offering according to your means.[a]
12 Then give the doctor his place
lest he leave; you need him too,
13 For there are times when recovery is in his hands.
14 He too prays to God
That his diagnosis may be correct
and his treatment bring about a cure.
15 Whoever is a sinner before his Maker
will be defiant toward the doctor.

16 My son, shed tears for one who is dead*
with wailing and bitter lament;
As is only proper, prepare the body,
and do not absent yourself from the burial.
17 Weeping bitterly, mourning fully,
pay your tribute of sorrow, as deserved:
A day or two, to prevent gossip;
then compose yourself after your grief.
18 For grief can bring on death,
and heartache can sap one's strength.[b]
19 When a person is carried away, sorrow is over;
and the life of the poor one is grievous to the heart.
20 Do not turn your thoughts to him again;
cease to recall him; think rather of the end.[c]
21 Do not recall him, for there is no hope of his return;
you do him no good, and you harm yourself.[d]
22 Remember that his fate will also be yours;
for him it was yesterday, for you today.[e]
23 With the dead at rest, let memory cease;
be consoled, once the spirit has gone.

*Vocations of the Skilled Worker and the Scribe**

24 The scribe's wisdom increases wisdom;
whoever is free from toil can become wise.
25 How can one become learned who guides the plow,
and thrills in wielding the goad like a lance,
Who guides the ox and urges on the bullock,
and whose every concern is for cattle?
26 His concern is to plow furrows,
and he is careful to fatten the livestock.

27 So with every engraver and designer
who, laboring night and day,
Fashions carved seals,
and whose concern is to vary the pattern.
His determination is to produce a lifelike impression,
and he is careful to finish the work.

28 So too the smith sitting by the anvil,
intent on the iron he forges.
The flame from the fire sears his flesh,
yet he toils away in the furnace heat.
The clang of the hammer deafens his ears;
his eyes are on the object he is shaping.

38:16–23 A period of mourning for the deceased and care for their burial are proper (vv. 16–17). But grief should not be excessive, for it cannot help the dead, who will not return, and may do harm to the living. The mourner should be realistic (vv. 18–23).

38:24–39:11 Ben Sira has a balanced view of the various vocations of skilled laborers—the farmer, engraver, smith and potter—but the profession of scribe is more excellent (38:24–34). He studies and meditates on the law of the Most High, seeks him in prayer of thanksgiving, petition and repentance for sin (39:1, 5, 7), explores the wisdom of the past and present, travels abroad to observe the conduct of many peoples, and attends rulers and great men. Through the spirit of understanding granted by God, he will show forth his wisdom to the glory of God's law, gaining renown for generations to come (39:2–4, 6–11).

z: Is 38:1–3. *a:* Lv 2:1–3. *b:* Prv 12:25; 15:13; 17:22. *c:* Sir 7:36; 18:24; 30:21. *d:* 2 Sm 12:23; Wis 2:1. *e:* Jas 4:13–15.

His determination is to finish the work,
and he is careful to perfect it in detail.

29 So also the potter sitting at his labor,
revolving the wheel with his feet.
He is always concerned for his products,
and turns them out in quantity.
30 With his hands he molds the clay,
and with his feet softens it.
His determination is to complete the glazing,
and he is careful to fire the kiln.

31 All these are skilled with their hands,
each one an expert at his own work;
32 Without them no city could be lived in,
and wherever they stay, they do not go hungry.
But they are not sought out for the council of the people,
33 nor are they prominent in the assembly.
They do not sit on the judge's bench,
nor can they understand law and justice.
They cannot expound discipline or judgment,
nor are they found among the rulers.
34 Yet they maintain the fabric of the world,
and their concern is for exercise of their skill.

CHAPTER 39

See RG 276–79

How different the person who devotes himself
to the study of the law of the Most High!
1 He explores the wisdom of all the ancients
and is occupied with the prophecies;
2 He preserves the discourses of the famous,
and goes to the heart of involved sayings;
3 He seeks out the hidden meaning of proverbs,
and is busied with the enigmas found in parables.
4 He is in attendance on the great,
and appears before rulers.
He travels among the peoples of foreign lands
to test what is good and evil among people.
5 His care is to rise early
to seek the Lord his Maker,
to petition the Most High,
To open his mouth in prayer,
to ask pardon for his sins.
6 If it pleases the Lord Almighty,
he will be filled with the spirit of understanding;
He will pour forth his words of wisdom
and in prayer give praise to the Lord.
7 He will direct his knowledge and his counsel,
as he meditates upon God's mysteries.
8 He will show the wisdom of what he has learned
and glory in the Law of the Lord's covenant.

9 Many will praise his understanding;
his name can never be blotted out;
Unfading will be his memory,
through all generations his name will live;[f]
10 Peoples will speak of his wisdom,
and the assembly will declare his praise.
11 While he lives he is one out of a thousand,
and when he dies he leaves a good name.

Praise of God the Creator[*]

12 Once more I will set forth my theme
to shine like the moon in its fullness!
13 Listen to me, my faithful children: open up your petals,
like roses planted near running waters;
14 Send up the sweet odor of incense,
break forth in blossoms like the lily.

39:12–35 Ben Sira invites his disciples to join him in joyfully proclaiming his favorite theme: The works of God are all good; God supplies for every need in its own time (vv. 12–16, 32–35). The sage describes God's omniscience, supreme power and wisdom, whereby all created things, good in themselves, are ever present to him, obey him, and fulfill their intended purpose (vv. 17–21), bringing blessing to the virtuous, but evil and punishment to the wicked who misuse them (vv. 22–31). Cf. similar hymns of praise, 36:1–22; 42:15–43:33.

f: Sir 37:26; 44:14.

Raise your voices in a chorus of praise;
bless the Lord for all his works!
15 Proclaim the greatness of his name,
loudly sing his praises,
With music on the harp and all stringed instruments;
sing out with joy as you proclaim:
16 The works of God are all of them good;
he supplies for every need in its own time.[g]
17 At his word the waters become still as in a flask;
he had but to speak and the reservoirs were made.[h]
18 He has but to command and his will is done;
nothing can limit his saving action.
19 The works of all humankind are present to him;
nothing is hidden from his eyes.[i]
20 His gaze spans all the ages:
is there any limit to his saving action?
To him, nothing is small or insignificant,
and nothing too wonderful or hard for him.
21 No cause then to say: "What is the purpose of this?"
Everything is chosen to satisfy a need.
22 His blessing overflows like the Nile;
like the Euphrates it enriches the surface of the earth.
23 Even so, his wrath dispossesses the nations
and turns fertile land into a salt marsh.[j]
24 For the virtuous his paths are level,
to the haughty they are clogged with stones.
25 Good things for the good he provided from the beginning,
but for the wicked good things and bad.
26 Chief of all needs for human life
are water and fire, iron and salt,
The heart of the wheat, milk and honey,
the blood of the grape, and oil, and clothing.[k]
27 For the good all these are good,
but for the wicked they turn out evil.
28 There are stormwinds created to punish;
in their fury they can dislodge mountains.
In a time of destruction they hurl their force
and calm the anger of their Maker.
29 Fire and hail, famine and disease:
these too were created for punishment.
30 Ravenous beasts, scorpions, vipers,
and the avenging sword to exterminate the wicked:
All these were created to meet a need,
and are kept in his storehouse for the proper time.
31 When he commands them, they rejoice,
in their assigned tasks they do not disobey his command.
32 That is why from the first I took my stand,
and wrote down as my theme:
33 The works of God are all of them good;
he supplies for every need in its own time.[l]
34 There is no cause then to say: "This is not as good as that";
for each shows its worth at the proper time.
35 So now with full heart and voice proclaim
and bless his name!

CHAPTER 40

See RG 276–79

Joys and Miseries of Life

1 A great anxiety has God allotted,*
and a heavy yoke, to the children of Adam,[m]
From the day they leave their mother's womb
until the day they return to the mother of all the living.*

40:1–17 The former idyllic description of the universe is contrasted with the picture of the evils afflicting humanity. Every person, high or low, is burdened from birth to death with fears, anxieties, and troubles, by day and often by night, the time appointed for rest (vv. 1–7). For sinners, the suffering is much greater (vv. 8–10). What they gained by violence and injustice is quickly destroyed; but righteousness will prevail (vv. 14–17).

40:1 Mother of all the living: the earth from which human beings were taken. Cf. Gn 2:7; 3:19–20; Jb 1:21; Ps 139:15.

g: Sir 39:33; Gn 1:29–31; Eccl 3:11. *h:* Gn 1:6–10; Ex 14:21–22; Jos 3:15–16. *i:* Sir 15:18–19; 42:18–20. *j:* Gn 13:10; 19:24–28; Dt 29:22; Jos 1:2–6; Ps 107:34; Wis 10:7. *k:* Sir 29:21. *l:* Sir 39:16; Gn 1:29–31; Eccl 3:11. *m:* Gn 3:17–19; Jb 7:1; 14:1–2; Eccl 2:23.

2 Troubled thoughts and fear of heart are theirs
and anxious foreboding until death.
3 Whether one sits on a lofty throne
or grovels in dust and ashes,
4 Whether one wears a splendid crown
or is clothed in the coarsest of garments—
5 There is wrath and envy, trouble and dread,
terror of death, fury and strife.
Even when one lies on his bed to rest,
his cares disturb his sleep at night.
6 So short is his rest it seems like none,
till in his dreams he struggles as he did by day,
Troubled by the visions of his mind,
like a fugitive fleeing from the pursuer.
7 As he reaches safety, he wakes up,
astonished that there was nothing to fear.
8 To all flesh, human being and beast,
but for sinners seven times more,
9 Come plague and bloodshed, fiery heat and drought,
plunder and ruin, famine and death.[n]
10 For the wicked evil was created,
and because of them destruction hastens.
11 All that is of earth returns to earth,
and what is from above returns above.*
12 All that comes from bribes or injustice will be wiped out,
but loyalty remains forever.
13 Wealth from injustice is like a flooding wadi,
like a mighty stream with lightning and thunder,
14 Which, in its rising, rolls along the stones,
but suddenly, once and for all, comes to an end.[o]
15 The offshoot of violence will not flourish,
for the root of the godless is on sheer rock.
16 They are like reeds on riverbanks,
withered before all other plants;
17 But goodness, like eternity, will never be cut off,
and righteousness endures forever.

18 Wealth or wages can make life sweet,*
but better than either, finding a treasure.
19 A child or a city will preserve one's name,
but better than either, finding wisdom.
Cattle and orchards make a person flourish;
but better than either, a devoted wife.[p]
20 Wine and strong drink delight the soul,
but better than either, love of friends.[q]
21 Flute and harp offer sweet melody,
but better than either, a pure tongue.
22 Grace and beauty delight the eye,
but better than either, the produce of the field.
23 A friend and a neighbor are timely guides,
but better than either, a sensible wife.
24 Relatives and helpers for times of stress;
but better than either, charity that rescues.
25 Gold and silver make one's way secure,
but better than either, sound judgment.
26 Wealth and vigor make the heart exult,
but better than either, fear of God.
In the fear of the Lord there is no want;
whoever has it need seek no other support.
27 The fear of God is a paradise of blessings;
its canopy is over all that is glorious.[r]

28 My son, do not live the life of a beggar;*
better to die than to beg.
29 When one has to look to a stranger's table,

40:11 All that is of earth . . . returns above: a reference to bodily mortality and to the divine origin of life. Cf. 41:10; Gn 2:7; 3:19; Jb 34:14–15; Ps 104:29–30; 146:4; Eccl 12:7. The Greek and the Latin render the second half of the verse: "all waters shall return to the sea."

40:18–27 Of the many treasures making life sweet, such as children, friends, music, vigor, the best are called true married love, wisdom, and above all, fear of God; cf. 25:6–11.

40:28–30 Among the Jews, begging was considered degrading to human dignity; it was agreeable only to the shameless, who had lost their sense of honor. Cf. 29:22–23.

n: Sir 39:28–31. *o:* Sir 23:25–26; Wis 4:3–6. *p:* Prv 18:22; 19:14. *q:* Ps 104:15. *r:* Is 4:5–6.

life is not worth living.
The delicacies offered bring revulsion of spirit,
and to the intelligent, inward torture.[s]
30 In the mouth of the shameless begging is sweet,
but within him it burns like fire.

CHAPTER 41

See RG 276–79

1 O death! How bitter is the thought of you[*]
for the one at peace in his home,
For the one who is serene and always successful,
who can still enjoy life's pleasures.
2 O death! How welcome is your sentence
to the weak, failing in strength,
Stumbling and tripping on everything,
with sight gone and hope lost.[t]
3 Do not fear death's decree for you;
remember, it embraces those before you and those to come.[u]
4 This decree for all flesh is from God;
why then should you reject a law of the Most High?
Whether one has lived a thousand years,
a hundred, or ten,
in Sheol there are no arguments about life.

5 The children of sinners are a reprobate line,[v]
and witless offspring are in the homes of the wicked.
6 The inheritance of children of sinners will perish,
and on their offspring will be perpetual disgrace.
7 Children curse their wicked father,
for they suffer disgrace because of him.
8 Woe to you, O wicked people,
who forsake the Law of the Most High.
9 If you have children, calamity will be theirs;
and if you beget them, it will be only for groaning.
When you stumble, there is lasting joy;
and when you die, you become a curse.
10 All that is nought returns to nought,
so too the godless—from void to void.[w]

11 The human body is a fleeting thing,
but a virtuous name will never be annihilated.[x]
12 Have respect for your name, for it will stand by you
more than thousands of precious treasures.[y]
13 The good things of life last a number of days,
but a good name, for days without number.

True and False Shame[*]

14b Hidden wisdom and concealed treasure,
of what value is either?
15 Better is the person who hides his folly
than the one who hides his wisdom.
14a My children, listen to instruction about shame;
16a judge of disgrace according to my rules,
16b Not every kind of shame is shameful,
nor is every kind of disgrace to be recognized.
17 Before father and mother be ashamed of immorality,
before prince and ruler, of falsehood;
18 Before master and mistress, of deceit;
before the public assembly, of crime;
Before associate and friend, of disloyalty,
19 and in the place where you settle, of theft.
Be ashamed of breaking an oath or a covenant,

41:1–13 Whether death seems bitter to one who enjoys peace, success, and pleasure, or welcome to one who is weak and in despair, it comes to all and must be accepted as the will of God (vv. 1–4). The human body passes away (v. 11). Sinners as well as their offspring pass away as if they had never been (vv. 5–10). Only the good name of the virtuous endures (vv. 11–13).

41:14–42:8 Ben Sira illustrates the subject of true and false shame with numerous and detailed examples of wrongdoing (41:14–22) and virtue (42:1–8), following the norm of the commandments.

s: Sir 29:24. *t:* Sir 30:17. *u:* Sir 38:20–22. *v:* Sir 3:9–11; Wis 3:16–19. *w:* Sir 40:11; Wis 4:19. *x:* Prv 10:7. *y:* Prv 22:1; Eccl 7:1.

and of stretching your elbow at dinner;
Of refusing to give when asked,
21 of rebuffing your own relatives;
Of defrauding another of his appointed share,
20a of failing to return a greeting;
21c Of gazing at a man's wife,
20b of entertaining thoughts about another woman;[z]
22 Of trifling with a servant girl you have,
of violating her bed;
Of using harsh words with friends,
of following up your gifts with insults;[a]

CHAPTER 42

See RG 276–79

1 Of repeating what you hear,
of betraying any secret.[b]
Be ashamed of the right things,
and you will find favor in the sight of all.

But of these things do not be ashamed,
lest you sin to save face:[c]
2 Of the Law of the Most High and his precepts,
or of justice that acquits the ungodly;
3 Of sharing the expenses of a business or a journey,
of dividing an inheritance or property;
4 Of accuracy of scales and balances,
of tested measures and weights;[d]
Of acquiring much or little,
5 of bargaining in dealing with a merchant;
Of constant training of children,
of beating the sides of a wicked servant;[e]
6 Of a seal to keep a foolish wife at home,
of a key where there are many hands;
7 Of numbering every deposit,
of recording all that is taken in and given out;
8 Of chastisement for the silly and the foolish,
for the aged and infirm answering for wanton conduct.
Thus you will be truly refined
and recognized by all as discreet.

*A Father's Care for His Daughter**

9 A daughter is a treasure that keeps her father wakeful,
and worry over her drives away sleep:[f]
Lest in her youth she remain unmarried,
or when she is married, lest she be childless;
10 While unmarried, lest she be defiled,
or in her husband's house, lest she prove unfaithful;
Lest she become pregnant in her father's house,
or be sterile in that of her husband.
11 My son, keep a close watch on your daughter,
lest she make you a laughingstock for your enemies,
A byword in the city and the assembly of the people,
an object of derision in public gatherings.[g]
See that there is no lattice in her room,
or spot that overlooks the approaches to the house.
12 Do not let her reveal her beauty to any male,[h]
or spend her time with married women;
13 For just as moths come from garments,
so a woman's wickedness comes from a woman.
14 Better a man's harshness than a woman's indulgence,
a frightened daughter than any disgrace.

42:9–14 Ben Sira considers a daughter to be a source of anxiety to her father, lest she fail to marry, or be defiled, or lest, marrying, she be childless, prove unfaithful, or find herself sterile (vv. 9–10). He is advised to keep a close watch on her and on her companions, lest he suffer on her account among the people (vv. 11–12). The exhortations, which take into account only a father's concern, are quite unflattering to young women. The concluding statements (vv. 13–14) show the limitations of Ben Sira's perspective in the male-oriented society of his day.

z: Sir 9:8; Mt 5:28. *a:* Sir 18:15; 20:14. *b:* Sir 27:16. *c:* Prv 24:23; Jas 2:1. *d:* Lv 19:35; Prv 11:1; 16:11; 20:10. *e:* Sir 30:1–13; 33:25–33. *f:* Sir 7:24–25. *g:* Dt 22:20–21. *h:* Sir 9:1–9.

*The Works of God in Nature**

[15] Now will I recall God's works;
what I have seen, I will describe.
By the LORD's word his works were brought into being;
he accepts the one who does his will.[i]
[16] As the shining sun is clear to all,
so the glory of the LORD fills all his works;
[17] Yet even God's holy ones must fail
in recounting the wonders of the LORD,
Though God has given his hosts the strength
to stand firm before his glory.
[18] He searches out the abyss and penetrates the heart;
their secrets he understands.
For the Most High possesses all knowledge,
and sees from of old the things that are to come.
[19] He makes known the past and the future,
and reveals the deepest secrets.
[20] He lacks no understanding;
no single thing escapes him.[j]
[21] He regulates the mighty deeds of his wisdom;
he is from all eternity one and the same,
With nothing added, nothing taken away;
no need of a counselor for him![k]
[22] How beautiful are all his works,
delightful to gaze upon and a joy to behold!
[23] Everything lives and abides forever;
and to meet each need all things are preserved.
[24] All of them differ, one from another,
yet none of them has he made in vain;
[25] For each in turn, as it comes, is good;
can one ever see enough of their splendor?[l]

CHAPTER 43

See RG 276–79

[1] The beauty of the celestial height
and the pure firmament,[m]
heaven itself manifests its glory.
[2] The sun at its rising shines at its fullest,
a wonderful instrument, the work of the Most High!
[3] At noon it scorches the earth,
and who can bear its fiery heat?
[4] Like a blazing furnace of solid metal,
the sun's rays set the mountains aflame;
Its fiery tongue consumes the world;
the eyes are burned by its fire.
[5] Great indeed is the LORD who made it,
at whose orders it urges on its steeds.
[6] It is the moon that marks the changing seasons,
governing the times, their lasting sign.[n]
[7] By it we know the sacred seasons and pilgrimage feasts,
a light which wanes in its course:
[8] The new moon like its name* renews itself;
how wondrous it is when it changes:
A military signal for the waterskins on high,
it paves the firmament with its brilliance,
[9] The beauty of the heavens and the glory of the stars,
a shining ornament in the heights of God.[o]
[10] By the LORD's command the moon keeps its appointed place,
and does not fade as the stars keep watch.
[11] Behold the rainbow! Then bless its Maker,
for majestic indeed is its splendor;[p]
[12] It spans the heavens with its glory,
the hand of God has stretched it out in power.

42:15–43:33 These verses comprise another hymn; cf. 16:24–18:14. In them Ben Sira contemplates God's power, beauty, and goodness as manifested in the mighty work of creating and preserving the universe (42:15–17, 22–25; 43:1–26), his omniscience (42:18–20), perfect wisdom and eternity (42:21). The conclusion is a fervent hymn of praise (43:27–31).

43:8 Like its name: there is a play in the Hebrew text on the words for moon and renewal. **Waterskins**: clouds as source of rain.

i: Ps 77:12–13. *j:* Sir 39:19; Wis 1:6–9. *k:* Wis 9:13; Is 40:13; Rom 11:34; 1 Cor 2:11. *l:* Sir 33:15. *m:* Ps 19:2–5. *n:* Lv 23:5; Nm 28:11–14; Ps 81:4–6. *o:* Ps 8:4. *p:* Gn 9:13.

[13] His rebuke marks out the path for the
hail,
and makes the flashes of his judgment
shine forth.
[14] For his own purposes he opens the
storehouse
and makes the rain clouds fly like
vultures.
[15] His might gives the clouds their strength,
and breaks off the hailstones.
[16] The thunder of his voice makes the earth
writhe;
by his power he shakes the mountains.
[17] A word from him drives on the south
wind,
whirlwind, hurricane, and stormwind.
He makes the snow fly like birds;
it settles down like swarms of locusts.
[18] Its shining whiteness blinds the eyes,
the mind marvels at its steady fall.
[19] He scatters frost like salt;
it shines like blossoms on the
thornbush.
[20] He sends cold northern blasts
that harden the ponds like solid
ground,
Spreads a crust over every body of water,
and clothes each pool with a coat of
armor.
[21] When mountain growth is scorched by
heat,
and flowering plains as by fire,
[22] The dripping clouds restore them all,
and the scattered dew enriches the
parched land.
[23] His is the plan that calms the deep,
and plants the islands in the sea.
[24] Those who go down to the sea recount its
extent,
and when we hear them we are
thunderstruck;[q]
[25] In it are his creatures, stupendous,
amazing,
all kinds of life, and the monsters of
the deep.
[26] For him each messenger succeeds,
and at his bidding accomplishes his
will.[r]
[27] More than this we need not add;
let the last word be, he is the all!*
[28] Let us praise him the more, since we
cannot fathom him,
for greater is he than all his works;
[29] Awesome indeed is the LORD,
and wonderful his power.
[30] Lift up your voices to glorify the LORD
as much as you can, for there is still
more.
Extol him with renewed strength,
do not grow weary, for you cannot
fathom him.
[31] For who has seen him and can describe
him?
Who can praise him as he is?[s]
[32] Beyond these, many things lie hidden;
only a few of his works have I seen.
[33] It is the LORD who has made all things;
to those who fear him he gives
wisdom.[t]

CHAPTER 44

See RG 276–79

*Praise of Israel's Great Ancestors**

[1] I will now praise the godly,
our ancestors, in their own time,*
[2] The abounding glory of the Most High's
portion,
his own part, since the days of old.[u]
[3] Subduers of the land in kingly fashion,
renowned for their might,
Counselors in their prudence,
seers of all things in prophecy,[v]
[4] Resolute princes of the flock,
lawgivers and their rules,
Sages skilled in composition,

43:27 The all: the perfections reflected in creation are found in a transcendent way in God, who alone is their source.

44:1–50:24 As in the previous section God's glory shone forth in the works of nature, so in these chapters it is revealed through the history of God's people as seen in the lives of their ancestors, prophets, priests, and rulers. The example of these great people, whose virtues are recalled here, constitutes a high point of Ben Sira's teaching.

44:1–15 The reader is here introduced to those people of Israel, later mentioned by name, who through various achievements and beneficial social activities have acquired great renown (vv. 1–8, 14–15); and also to those who, though forgotten, endure through the fruit of their virtues and through their families because of God's covenant with them (vv. 9–15).

q: Ps 104:25–26. *r:* Ps 33:6. *s:* Ps 106:2. *t:* Sir 1:10. *u:* Dt 32:8–9. *v:* Sir 39:1.

authors of sharp proverbs,
5 Composers of melodious psalms,
writers of lyric poems;
6 Stalwart, solidly established,
at peace in their own estates—
7 All these were glorious in their time,
illustrious in their day.
8 Some of them left behind a name
so that people recount their praises.
9 Of others no memory remains,
for when they perished, they perished,
As if they had never lived,
they and their children after them.
10 Yet these also were godly;
their virtues have not been forgotten.
11 Their wealth remains in their families,
their heritage with their descendants.
12 Through God's covenant their family endures,
and their offspring for their sake.
13 And for all time their progeny will endure,
their glory will never be blotted out;
14 Their bodies are buried in peace,
but their name lives on and on.[w]
15 At gatherings their wisdom is retold,
and the assembly proclaims their praises.

The Early Ancestors

16 [ENOCH* walked with the LORD and was taken,[x]
that succeeding generations might learn by his example.]
17 NOAH, found just and perfect,
renewed the race in the time of devastation.[y]
Because of his worth there were survivors,
and with a sign to him the deluge ended.
18 A lasting covenant was made with him,
that never again would all flesh be destroyed.
19 ABRAHAM, father of many peoples,
kept his glory without stain:[z]
20 He observed the Most High's command,
and entered into a covenant with him;
In his own flesh he incised the ordinance,*
and when tested was found loyal.[a]
21 For this reason, God promised him with an oath
to bless the nations through his descendants,
To make him numerous as grains of dust,
and to exalt his posterity like the stars,
Giving them an inheritance from sea to sea,
and from the River* to the ends of the earth.

22 For ISAAC, too, he renewed the same promise
because of Abraham, his father.
The covenant with all his forebears was confirmed,
23 and the blessing rested upon the head of ISRAEL.[b]
God acknowledged him as the firstborn,
and gave him his inheritance.
He fixed the boundaries for his tribes
and their division into twelve.

CHAPTER 45

See RG 276–79

Praise of Moses, Aaron, and Phinehas

1 From him came the man*
who would win the favor of all the living:[c]
Dear to God and human beings,
MOSES, whose memory is a blessing.

44:16 Enoch: because of his friendship with God and his unusual disappearance from the earth, this prophet's renown was great among the chosen people, particularly in the two centuries just before the coming of Christ; cf. Gn 5:21–24; Heb 11:5. The present verse is an expansion of the original text; cf. 49:14.

44:20 In his own flesh . . . ordinance: the covenant of circumcision; cf. Gn 17:10–14. **And when tested . . . loyal**: Abraham's willingness to sacrifice his son Isaac at the Lord's command; cf. Gn 22:1–12.

44:21 The River: the Euphrates; cf. Gn 2:14.

44:23(end)–45:5 Moses manifested God's power through marvels (vv. 1–3), God's authority through the commandments and the Law (v. 5), and God's mercy through the intimacy granted him by the Lord for his own faithfulness and meekness (v. 4).

w: Wis 3:2–3. *x:* Sir 49:14; Gn 5:18–24; Heb 11:5. *y:* Gn 6:8–9:29; Heb 11:7. *z:* Gn 12:1–25:10; Rom 4:3; Gal 3:6; Heb 11:8–19; Jas 2:23. *a:* Gn 17:10–14; 22:1–12. *b:* Gn 26:3–5, 24; 27:28–29; 28:13–15. *c:* Ex 2:2; 11:3; 33:11; Nm 12:7.

2 God made him like the angels in honor,
and strengthened him with fearful powers.[d]
3 At his words God performed signs
and sustained him in the king's presence.
He gave him the commandments for his people,
and revealed to him his glory.[e]
4 Because of his trustworthiness and meekness
God selected him from all flesh;[f]
5 He let him hear his voice,
and led him into the cloud,
Where he handed over the commandments,
the law of life and understanding,*
That he might teach his precepts to Jacob,
his judgments and decrees to Israel.

6 He also raised up, like Moses in holiness,*
his brother AARON, of the tribe of Levi.[g]
7 He made his office perpetual
and bestowed on him priesthood for his people;
He established him in honor
and crowned him with lofty majesty.
8 He clothed him in splendid garments,
and adorned him with glorious vestments:
Breeches, tunic, and robe
9 with pomegranates at the hem
And a rustle of bells round about,
whose pleasing sound at each step
Would make him heard within the sanctuary,
a reminder for the people;
10 The sacred vestments of gold, violet,
and crimson, worked with embroidery;
The breastpiece for decision, the ephod and cincture
11 with scarlet yarn, the work of the weaver;
Precious stones with seal engravings
in golden settings, the work of the jeweler,
To commemorate in incised letters
each of the tribes of Israel;
12 On his turban a diadem of gold,
its plate engraved with the sacred inscription—
Majestic, glorious, renowned for splendor,
a delight to the eyes, supremely beautiful.
13 Before him, no one had been adorned with these,
nor may they ever be worn by any other
Except his sons and them alone,
generation after generation, for all time.
14 His grain offering is wholly burnt
as an established offering twice each day;
15 For Moses ordained him
and anointed him with the holy oil,
In a lasting covenant with him and his family,
as permanent as the heavens,
That he should serve God in the priesthood
and bless the people in his name.
16 He chose him from all the living
to sacrifice burnt offerings and choice portions,
To burn incense, sweet odor as a memorial,
and to atone for the people of Israel.
17 He gave to him the laws,
and authority to prescribe and to judge:
To teach precepts to the people,
and judgments to the Israelites.

45:5 On God's intimacy with Moses, see Ex 33:11; Nm 12:8; Dt 34:10.

45:6–25 Ben Sira here expresses his reverence and esteem for the priesthood of the old covenant. He recalls God's choice of Aaron and his sons for this sublime office (vv. 6–7), and describes in detail the beauty of the high priest's vestments (vv. 8–13). He relates the ordination of Aaron at the hands of Moses (v. 15), and describes the priestly functions, namely, offering sacrifice to God (v. 16), and blessing (v. 15), teaching, governing, and judging the people (v. 17); the inheritance of the high priest (vv. 20–22); the punishment of those who were jealous of Aaron (vv. 18–19); and the confirmation of the covenant of the priesthood with Aaron's descendants through Phinehas (vv. 23–25).

d: Ex 7–Dt 34. *e:* Ex 7:1–7; 20:2–17; Dt 5:6–21. *f:* Nm 12:3, 7. *g:* Ex 28–29; Wis 18:24.

18 Strangers rose in anger against him,
grew jealous of him in the desert—
The followers of Dathan and Abiram,
and the band of Korah in their defiance.[h]
19 When the LORD saw this he became angry,
and destroyed them in his burning
wrath.
He brought against them a marvel,
and consumed them in flaming fire.
20 Then he increased the glory of Aaron[i]
and bestowed upon him his
inheritance:
The sacred offerings he allotted to him,
with the showbread* as his portion;
21 The oblations of the LORD are his food,
a gift to him and his descendants.
22 But he holds no land among the people
nor shares with them their heritage;
For the LORD himself is his portion and
inheritance
among the Israelites.
23 PHINEHAS too, the son of Eleazar,
was the courageous third of his line
When, zealous for the God of all,
he met the crisis of his people[j]
And, at the prompting of his noble heart,
atoned for the children of Israel.
24 Therefore, on him also God conferred the
right,
in a covenant of friendship, to provide
for the sanctuary,
So that he and his descendants
should possess the high priesthood
forever.
25 For even his covenant with David,
the son of Jesse of the tribe of Judah,
Was an individual heritage through one
son alone;[k]
but the heritage of Aaron is for all his
descendants.
So now bless* the LORD
who has crowned you with glory!
26 May he grant you wisdom of heart
to govern his people in justice,
Lest the benefits you confer should be
forgotten,
or your authority, throughout all time.

CHAPTER 46

See RG 276–79

Joshua, Caleb, the Judges, and Samuel

1 Valiant warrior was JOSHUA,* son of Nun,
aide to Moses in the prophetic office,
Formed to be, as his name implies,
the great savior of God's chosen ones,
To punish the enemy
and to give to Israel their heritage.[l]
2 What glory was his when he raised his
hand,
to brandish his sword against the city![m]
3 Who could withstand him
when he fought the battles of the
LORD?*
4 Was it not by that same hand the sun
stopped,
so that one day became two?[n]
5 He called upon the Most High God
when his enemies beset him on all
sides,
And God Most High answered him
with hailstones of tremendous power,
6 That rained down upon the hostile army
till on the slope he destroyed the foe;
That all the doomed nations might know
the LORD was watching over his
people's battles.
He was indeed a devoted follower of God
7 and showed himself loyal in Moses'
lifetime.
He and CALEB,* son of Jephunneh,
when they opposed the rebel assembly,
Averted God's anger from the people
and suppressed the wicked complaint.[o]
8 Because of this, these two alone were
spared

45:20 Showbread: cf. note on Ex 25:29–30.

45:25–26 So now bless: Ben Sira addresses the whole line of high priests, especially Simon II; cf. 50:1.

46:1–6 Joshua: whose name means "the Lord is savior" (v. 1), was the instrument through which God delivered his people in marvelous ways (vv. 2–6) by destroying their enemies, whose land he gave to the Israelites as a heritage (v. 1).

46:3 The battles of the Lord: cf. Jos 6–11.

46:7–10 Caleb: with Joshua he advised Moses to enter Canaan, despite the counsel of their companion scouts and the rebellion of the people. He led the next generation of Israelites into the promised land. He received a portion of land which he himself had conquered; cf. Jos 15:13–14.

h: Nm 16:1–35. *i:* Nm 18:11–24; Dt 10:9. *j:* Nm 25:7–13; 1 Mc 2:26, 54; Ps 106:30–31. *k:* 2 Sm 7:12–16. *l:* Ex 17:9; Nm 27:18–23; Dt 34:9; Jos 1:1–9. *m:* Jos 8:18–19. *n:* Jos 10:12–13. *o:* Nm 13:30; 14:1–3.

from the six hundred thousand infantry,
To lead the people into their heritage,
the land flowing with milk and honey.[p]
9 The strength God gave to Caleb
remained with him even in old age
Till he won his way onto the summits of the land;
his family too received a heritage,[q]
10 That all the offspring of Jacob might know
how good it is to be a devoted follower of the LORD.

11 The JUDGES,* each one of them,
whose hearts were not deceived,
Who did not abandon God—
may their memory be ever blessed![r]
12 May their bones flourish with new life where they lie,
and their names receive fresh luster in their children!
13 Beloved of his people, dear to his Maker,
pledged in a vow from his mother's womb,
As one consecrated to the LORD in the prophetic office,
was SAMUEL, the judge who offered sacrifice.
At God's word he established the kingdom
and anointed princes to rule the people.[s]
14 By the law of the LORD he judged the congregation,
and visited the encampments of Jacob.
15 As a trustworthy prophet he was sought out
and his words proved him to be a true seer.
16 He, too, called upon the mighty Lord
when his enemies pressed him on every side,
and offered up a suckling lamb.[t]
17 Then the LORD thundered from heaven,
and the tremendous roar of his voice was heard.[u]
18 He brought low the rulers of the enemy
and destroyed all the lords of the Philistines.
19 When Samuel neared the end of life,
he testified before the LORD and his anointed prince,
"No bribe or secret gift have I taken from anyone!"
and no one could accuse him.[v]
20 Even after death his guidance was sought;
he made known to the king his fate.
From the grave he spoke in prophecy
to put an end to wickedness.[w]

CHAPTER 47

Nathan, David, and Solomon

See RG 276–79

1 After him came NATHAN*
who served in David's presence.[x]
2 Like the choice fat of sacred offerings,
so was DAVID in Israel.[y]
3 He played with lions as though they were young goats,
and with bears, like lambs of the flock.[z]
4 As a youth he struck down the giant
and wiped out the people's disgrace;
His hand let fly the slingstone
that shattered the pride of Goliath.[a]
5 For he had called upon the Most High God,
who gave strength to his right arm
To defeat the skilled warrior
and establish the might of his people.
6 Therefore the women sang his praises
and honored him for "the tens of thousands."
When he received the royal crown, he battled[b]
7 and subdued the enemy on every side.
He campaigned against the hostile Philistines

46:11–20 Of the judges praised and blessed for their fidelity to God in opposing idolatry, Samuel was the greatest (vv. 11–13, 19). He was judge, prophet, and priest. Through his sacrificial offering he obtained victory over the Philistines. He established the kingdom, anointed kings (vv. 13–18), and even after his death foretold the king's fate (v. 20).

47:1–11 An idealized portrait of David; cf. 1 Chronicles.

p: Nm 14:22–38. *q:* Jos 14:6–13; 15:13. *r:* Jgs 1:1–16:31. *s:* 1 Sm 1:10–20; 8:4–10:1; 16:12–13. *t:* 1 Sm 7:9. *u:* 1 Sm 7:10–13. *v:* 1 Sm 12:3. *w:* 1 Sm 28:14–19. *x:* 2 Sm 7:2–17. *y:* 1 Sm 16:11–13. *z:* 1 Sm 17:34–36. *a:* 1 Sm 17:49. *b:* 1 Sm 18:7.

and shattered their power till our own day.[c]

8 With his every deed he offered thanks
to God Most High, in words of praise.
With his whole heart he loved his Maker
9 and daily had his praises sung;
10 He added beauty to the feasts
and solemnized the seasons of each year
9b With string music before the altar,
providing sweet melody for the psalms[d]
10b So that when the Holy Name was praised,
before daybreak the sanctuary would resound.
11 The LORD forgave him his sins
and exalted his strength forever;
He conferred on him the rights of royalty
and established his throne in Israel.[e]
12 Because of his merits he had as successor*
a wise son, who lived in security:[f]
13 SOLOMON reigned during an era of peace,
for God brought rest to all his borders.
He built a house to the name of God,
and established a lasting sanctuary.[g]
14 How wise you were when you were young,
overflowing with instruction, like the Nile in flood![h]
15 Your understanding covered the whole earth,
and, like a sea, filled it with knowledge.
16 Your fame reached distant coasts,
and you were beloved for your peaceful reign.
17 With song and proverb and riddle,
and with your answers, you astounded the nations.
18 You were called by that glorious name
which was conferred upon Israel.*
Gold you gathered like so much iron;
you heaped up silver as though it were lead.
19 But you abandoned yourself to women
and gave them dominion over your body.[i]
20 You brought a stain upon your glory,
shame upon your marriage bed,
Wrath upon your descendants,
and groaning upon your deathbed.
21 Thus two governments came into being,
when in Ephraim kingship was usurped.[j]
22 But God does not withdraw his mercy,
nor permit even one of his promises to fail.
He does not uproot the posterity of the chosen,
nor destroy the offspring of his friends.
So he gave to Jacob a remnant,
to David a root from his own family.[k]

Rehoboam and Jeroboam

23 Solomon finally slept with his ancestors,
and left behind him one of his sons,
Broad* in folly, narrow in sense,
whose policy made the people rebel.
Then arose the one who should not be remembered,
the sinner who led Israel into sin,[l]
Who brought ruin to Ephraim
24 and caused them to be exiled from their land.

Elijah and Elisha

25 Their sinfulness grew more and more,
and they gave themselves to every evil*

CHAPTER 48

See RG 276–79

1 Until like fire a prophet appeared,
his words a flaming furnace.[m]

47:12–24 The standard view of Solomon is echoed by Ben Sira, but he affirms the divine promise (v. 22) to David's line.

47:18 Cf. 2 Sm 12:25, where Solomon is called Jedidiah, "beloved of the Lord." A similar term is used of Israel in Jer 11:15.

47:23 Broad: the name Rehoboam means "the people is broad, or expansive," that is, widespread. **The sinner**: Jeroboam; cf. 1 Kgs 12:1, 20, 26–32.

47:25–48:11 The prophetic ministry of Elijah amid widespread idolatry is here described as a judgment by fire (48:1). Through his preaching, marvels, and acts of vengeance against God's enemies, he succeeded for a time in restoring faith in and worship of the Lord (vv. 2–8). His mysterious departure from this life gave rise to the belief that he did not die but would return before the day of the Lord. Cf. Mal 3:23–24; Mt 17:9–13.

c: 2 Sm 5:6–25. *d:* 1 Chr 16:4–37; 23:5; 25:1–7. *e:* 2 Sm 12:13; 7:12–16. *f:* 1 Kgs 2:12. *g:* 1 Kgs 5:1, 5; 6:2–38. *h:* 1 Kgs 5:9–14; 10:14–29. *i:* 1 Kgs 11:1–10. *j:* 1 Kgs 12:1–25. *k:* 2 Sm 7:15; Ps 89:34–38. *l:* 1 Kgs 11:43; 12:13, 21; 13:34; 2 Kgs 17:6–22. *m:* 1 Kgs 17:1.

[2] The staff of life, their bread, he shattered,
and in his zeal he made them few in number.
[3] By God's word he shut up the heavens
and three times brought down fire.[n]
[4] How awesome are you, ELIJAH!
Whose glory is equal to yours?
[5] You brought a dead body back to life
from Sheol, by the will of the LORD.[o]
[6] You sent kings down to destruction,
and nobles, from their beds of sickness.[p]
[7] You heard threats at Sinai,
at Horeb avenging judgments.[q]
[8] You anointed the agent of these punishments,
the prophet to succeed in your place.[r]
[9] You were taken aloft in a whirlwind,
in a chariot with fiery horses.[s]
[10] You are destined, it is written, in time to come
to put an end to wrath before the day of the LORD,
To turn back the hearts of parents toward their children,
and to re-establish the tribes of Israel.[t]
[11] Blessed is the one who shall have seen you before he dies!*

[12] When Elijah was enveloped in the whirlwind,
ELISHA was filled with his spirit;*
He worked twice as many marvels,[u]
and every utterance of his mouth was wonderful.
During his lifetime he feared no one,
nor was anyone able to intimidate his will.
[13] Nothing was beyond his power;[v]
and from where he lay buried, his body prophesied.*
[14] In life he performed wonders,
and after death, marvelous deeds.
[15] Despite all this the people did not repent,
nor did they give up their sins,
Until they were uprooted from their land
and scattered all over the earth.

Judah

But Judah remained, a tiny people,
with its ruler from the house of David.[w]
[16] Some of them did what was right,
but others were extremely sinful.

*Hezekiah and Isaiah**

[17] HEZEKIAH fortified his city
and had water brought into it;[x]
With bronze tools he cut through the rocks
and dammed up a mountain site for water.*
[18] During his reign Sennacherib led an invasion
and sent his adjutant;
He shook his fist at Zion
and blasphemed God in his pride.[y]
[19] The people's hearts melted within them,
and they were in anguish like that of childbirth.
[20] But they called upon the Most High God
and lifted up their hands to him;
He heard the prayer they uttered,
and saved them through ISAIAH.[z]
[21] God struck the camp of the Assyrians
and routed them with a plague.[a]
[22] For Hezekiah did what was right
and held fast to the paths of David,

48:11 Verse 11b is not extant in the Hebrew; it is represented in the Greek tradition by "for we too shall certainly live." But this can hardly be the original reading.

48:12–16 Elisha continued Elijah's work (vv. 12–14), but the obstinacy of the people eventually brought on the destruction of the kingdom of Israel and the dispersion of its subjects. Judah, however, survived under the rule of Davidic kings, both good and bad (vv. 15–16).

48:13 The reference in v. 13b seems to be to 2 Kgs 13:21 where it is related that a dead man, thrown into Elisha's grave, came back to life.

48:17–25 The fidelity of King Hezekiah (vv. 17, 22), the zeal of the prophet Isaiah, and the prayer of the people (v. 20) were effective. The Assyrian oppressors under Sennacherib withdrew (vv. 18–19, 21). The king's life was prolonged. The people were consoled by Isaiah's words about the future (vv. 23–25); the "consolations" refer to Is 40–66.

48:17 The reference is to the famous Siloam tunnel in present-day Jerusalem.

n: 2 Kgs 1:9–14. *o:* 1 Kgs 17:17–23. *p:* 1 Kgs 21:19; 2 Kgs 1:17. *q:* 1 Kgs 19:8–15. *r:* 1 Kgs 19:16–17. *s:* 2 Kgs 2:11. *t:* Mal 3:23–24; Mt 17:10. *u:* 2 Kgs 2:9–12. *v:* 2 Kgs 13:21. *w:* 2 Kgs 15:29; 18:11–12. *x:* 2 Kgs 20:20; 2 Chr 32:30. *y:* 2 Kgs 18:13–37; Is 36:1–22. *z:* 2 Kgs 19:20. *a:* 2 Kgs 19:35; Is 37:36.

As ordered by the illustrious prophet
Isaiah, who saw truth in visions.
23 In his lifetime he turned back the sun
and prolonged the life of the king.[b]
24 By his powerful spirit he looked into the future[c]
and consoled the mourners of Zion;
25 He foretold what would happen till the end of time,
hidden things yet to be fulfilled.

See RG 276–79

CHAPTER 49

*Josiah and the Prophets**

1 The name JOSIAH is like blended incense,
made lasting by a skilled perfumer.[d]
Precious is his memory, like honey to the taste,
like music at a banquet.
2 For he grieved over our betrayals,
and destroyed the abominable idols.
3 He kept his heart fixed on God,
and in times of lawlessness practiced virtue.
4 Except for David, Hezekiah, and Josiah,
they all were wicked;
They abandoned the Law of the Most High,
these kings of Judah, right to the very end.
5 So he gave over their power to others,
their glory to a foreign nation
6 Who burned the holy city
and left its streets desolate,
7 As foretold by JEREMIAH.[e] They mistreated him
who even in the womb had been made a prophet,
To root out, pull down, and destroy,
and then to build and to plant.[f]
8 EZEKIEL beheld a vision
and described the different creatures of the chariot;[g]
9 He also referred to JOB,
who always persevered in the right path.[h]
10 Then, too, the TWELVE PROPHETS—
may their bones flourish with new life where they lie!—
They gave new strength to Jacob
and saved him with steadfast hope.

The Heroes After the Exile

11 How to extol ZERUBBABEL?*
He was like a signet ring on the right hand,[i]
12 And JESHUA, Jozadak's son?
In their time they rebuilt the altar
And erected the holy temple,
destined for everlasting glory.
13 Exalted be the memory of NEHEMIAH!
He rebuilt our ruined walls,
Restored our shattered defenses,
and set up gates and bars.[j]

The Earliest Patriarchs

14 Few on earth have been created like ENOCH;*
he also was taken up bodily.[k]
15 Was ever a man born like JOSEPH?
Even his dead body was provided for.[l]
16 Glorious, too, were SHEM and SETH and ENOSH;
but beyond that of any living being
was the splendor of ADAM.[m]

CHAPTER 50

See RG 276–79

Simeon, Son of Jochanan

1 Greatest of his family, the glory of his people,
was SIMEON the priest, son of Jochanan,*

49:1–10 Ben Sira's praise of King Josiah (vv. 1–3) and of the prophets Jeremiah and Ezekiel and the minor prophets (vv. 7–10) derives from their spirit of fidelity to the Lord and his Law (vv. 4–6, 10).

49:11–13 The rebuilding of the Temple and the repair of the walls of the Holy City led to a restoration of religious worship and civil authority.

49:14–16 The patriarchs here mentioned were glorious because of their spirit of religion, i.e., their profound reverence for God and obedience to him. **The splendor of Adam**: suggests his direct origin from God (Gn 1:26–27; 2:7).

50:1–21 Son of Jochanan: Simeon II, in whose time as high priest (219–196 B.C.) great works were accomplished for the benefit of public worship and welfare (vv. 1–4). Ben Sira, a contemporary, describes detailed liturgical action, perhaps pertaining to the Day of Atonement (Yom Kippur, cf. Lv 16).

b: 2 Kgs 20:11; Is 38:8. *c:* 2 Kgs 20:17; Is 40:1–11; 42:9; 46:10; 48:6; 61:2–3. *d:* 2 Kgs 22:1–2, 10–13, 19; 23:4–15, 19–20, 24; 2 Chr 34:1–7. *e:* 2 Kgs 25:9; 2 Chr 36:19. *f:* Jer 1:5, 10. *g:* Ez 1:4–21. *h:* Ez 14:14, 20. *i:* Ezr 3:2; Hg 1:12; Zec 3:1. *j:* Neh 1:1–3:32. *k:* Sir 44:16; Gn 5:18–24. *l:* Gn 37; 39–50; Ex 13:19; Jos 24:32. *m:* Gn 1:26–30; 2:7; 4:25–26.

In whose time the house of God was renovated,
in whose days the temple was reinforced.
2 In his time also the retaining wall was built
with powerful turrets for the temple precincts.
3 In his time the reservoir was dug,
a pool as vast as the sea.
4 He protected the people against brigands
and strengthened the city against the enemy.
5 How splendid he was as he looked out from the tent,
as he came from behind the veil!
6 Like a star shining among the clouds,
like the full moon at the festal season;
7 Like sun shining upon the temple of the King,
like a rainbow appearing in the cloudy sky;
8 Like blossoms on the branches in springtime,
like a lily by running waters;
Like a green shoot on Lebanon in summer,
9 like the fire of incense at sacrifice;
Like a vessel of hammered gold,
studded with all kinds of precious stones;
10 Like a luxuriant olive tree heavy with fruit,
a plant with branches abounding in oil;
11 Wearing his glorious robes,
and vested in sublime magnificence,[n]
As he ascended the glorious altar
and lent majesty to the court of the sanctuary.
12 When he received the portions from the priests
while he stood before the sacrificial wood,
His sons stood round him like a garland,
like young cedars on Lebanon;
And like poplars by the brook they surrounded him,
13 all the sons of Aaron in their glory,
With the offerings to the LORD in their hands,
in the presence of the whole assembly of Israel.
14 Once he had completed the service at the altar
and arranged the sacrificial hearth for the Most High,
15 And had stretched forth his hand for the cup,
to offer blood of the grape,
And poured it out at the foot of the altar,
a sweet-smelling odor to God the Most High,[o]
16 Then the sons of Aaron would sound a blast,
the priests, on their trumpets of beaten metal;
A blast to resound mightily
as a reminder before the Most High.[p]
17 All the people with one accord
would fall with face to the ground
In adoration before the Most High,
before the Holy One of Israel.
18 Then hymns would re-echo,
and over the throng sweet strains of praise resound.
19 All the people of the land would shout for joy,
praying to the Merciful One,
As the high priest completed the service at the altar
by presenting to God the fitting sacrifice.
20 Then coming down he would raise his hands
over all the congregation of Israel;
The blessing of the LORD would be upon his lips,
the name of the LORD would be his glory.[q]
21 The people would again fall down
to receive the blessing of the Most High.
22 And now, bless the God of all,*
who has done wonders on earth;

50:22–24 Ben Sira urges the reader to praise and bless God for his wondrous works and then invokes a blessing on all that they may enjoy peace and gladness of heart and the abiding goodness of the Most High.

n: Sir 45:8–13; Ex 28:2–43; 39:1–31. *o:* Nm 15:5; 28:7. *p:* Nm 10:10. *q:* Nm 6:23–27.

Who fosters growth from the womb,
fashioning it according to his will!
23 May he grant you a wise heart
and abide with you in peace;
24 May his goodness toward Simeon last forever;
may he fulfill for him the covenant with Phinehas
So that it may not be abrogated for him
or his descendants while the heavens last.

Epilogue

25 My whole being loathes two nations,
the third is not even a people:*
26 The inhabitants of Seir* and Philistia,
and the foolish people who dwell in Shechem.[r]
27 Wise instruction, appropriate proverbs,*
I have written in this book—
I, Yeshua Ben Eleazar Ben Sira—
as they poured forth from my heart's understanding.
28 Happy those who meditate upon these things;
wise those who take them to heart!
29 If they put them into practice, they can cope with anything,
for the fear of the LORD is their lamp.

CHAPTER 51

See RG 276–79

A Prayer of Thanksgiving

1 I give you thanks, LORD and King,*
I praise you, God my savior!
I declare your name, refuge of my life,[s]
2 because you have ransomed my life from death;
You held back my body from the pit,
and delivered my foot from the power of Sheol.[t]

You have preserved me from the scourge of the slanderous tongue,
and from the lips of those who went over to falsehood.
You were with me against those who rise up against me;
3 You have rescued me according to your abundant mercy[u]
From the snare of those who look for my downfall,
and from the power of those who seek my life.

From many dangers you have saved me,
4 from flames that beset me on every side,[v]
From the midst of fire till there was not a whiff of it,*
5 from the deep belly of Sheol,
From deceiving lips and painters of lies,
6 from the arrows of a treacherous tongue.

I was at the point of death,
my life was nearing the depths of Sheol;[w]
7 I turned every way, but there was no one to help;
I looked for support but there was none.[x]
8 Then I remembered the mercies of the LORD,
his acts of kindness through ages past;
For he saves those who take refuge in him,
and rescues them from every evil.
9 So I raised my voice from the grave;
from the gates of Sheol I cried for help.
10 I called out: LORD, you are my Father,
my champion, my savior!
Do not abandon me in time of trouble,
in the midst of storms and dangers.[y]
11 I will always praise your name
and remember you in prayer!

Then the LORD heard my voice,
and listened to my appeal.

50:25 Not even a people: the Samaritans.

50:26 Seir: Mount Seir in the territory of the Edomites. **Shechem**: a city in Samaria.

50:27 This colophon may have been the original ending of the book. It is unusual for a biblical writer to append his name.

51:1–30 This chapter contains two appendixes: a prayer (vv. 1–12) and an autobiographical poem praising wisdom (vv. 13–30).

51:4 So complete is the deliverance from fire that even the smell of smoke cannot be detected. Cf. Dn 3:27.

r: 2 Kgs 17:24; Jn 4:9. *s:* Ps 138:1. *t:* Ps 91:3. *u:* Ps 56:10–12; 124:2. *v:* Ps 66:12. *w:* Ps 88:4; 94:17. *x:* Ps 22:12; 142:5. *y:* Ps 89:27; 95:1.

12 He saved me from every evil
and preserved me in time of trouble.
For this reason I thank and praise him;
I bless the name of the LORD.*

Ben Sira's Pursuit of Wisdom

13 * When I was young and innocent,
I sought wisdom.[z]
14 She came to me in her beauty,
and until the end I will cultivate her.

15 As the blossoms yielded to ripening grapes,
the heart's joy,
My feet kept to the level path
because from earliest youth I was familiar with her.

16 In the short time I paid heed,
I met with great instruction.
17 Since in this way I have profited,
I will give my Teacher grateful praise.

18 I resolved to tread her paths;
I have been jealous for the good and will not turn back.
19 I burned with desire for her,
never relenting.
I became preoccupied with her,
never weary of extolling her.

I spread out my hands to the heavens
and I came to know her secrets.
20 For her I purified my hands;
in cleanness I attained to her.

At first acquaintance with her, I gained understanding
such that I will never forsake her.[a]
21 My whole being was stirred to seek her;
therefore I have made her my prize possession.
22 The LORD has rewarded me with lips,
with a tongue for praising him.

23 Come aside to me, you untutored,
and take up lodging in the house of instruction;* [b]
24 How long will you deprive yourself of wisdom's food,
how long endure such bitter thirst?
25 I open my mouth and speak of her:
gain wisdom for yourselves at no cost.[c]

26 Take her yoke upon your neck;
that your mind may receive her teaching.

51:12 After this verse the Hebrew text gives the litany of praise contained below. It is similar to Ps 136. Though not found in any versions, and therefore of doubtful authenticity, the litany seems from internal evidence to go back to the time of Ben Sira.

Give praise to the LORD, for he is good, for God's love endures forever;
Give praise to the God of glory, for God's love endures forever;
Give praise to the Guardian of Israel, for God's love endures forever;
Give praise to the creator of all things, for God's love endures forever;
Give praise to the redeemer of Israel, for God's love endures forever;
Give praise to God who gathers the dispersed of Israel, for God's love endures forever;
Give praise to God who builds the city and sanctuary, for God's love endures forever;
Give praise to God who makes a horn sprout forth for the house of David, for God's love endures forever;
Give praise to God who has chosen the sons of Zadok as priests, for God's love endures forever;
Give praise to the Shield of Abraham, for God's love endures forever;
Give praise to the Rock of Isaac, for God's love endures forever;
Give praise to the Mighty One of Jacob, for God's love endures forever;
Give praise to God who has chosen Zion, for God's love endures forever;
Give praise to the King, the king of kings, for God's love endures forever.
He has lifted up the horn of his people! Let this be his praise from all the faithful,
From Israel, the people near to him. Hallelujah! (Cf. Ps 148:14.)

51:13–30 A Hebrew manuscript from Qumran demonstrates the acrostic style of vv. 13–20. This is an elegant twenty-three-line alphabetic acrostic hymn that describes Ben Sira's relationship to wisdom: (a) his approach to wisdom through prayer, persistent study, and instruction (vv. 13–17); (b) his purification from sin, his enlightenment, and ardent desire to possess wisdom (vv. 18–22). Ben Sira concludes with an urgent invitation to his students to receive instruction in wisdom from him, and to live by it, because wisdom gives herself to those who seek her (vv. 23–26); and for their labor, God will reward them in his own time (vv. 27–30). Cf. Mt 11:28; Eccl 12:14.

51:23 House of instruction: this may be a metaphor for Ben Sira's teaching.

z: Sir 34:9–13; Prv 8:17. *a:* Prv 4:6. *b:* Prv 8:5. *c:* Sir 6:19; Is 55:1–3.

For she is close to those who seek her,
and the one who is in earnest finds her.[d]
27 See for yourselves! I have labored only a little,
but have found much.
28 Acquire but a little instruction,
and you will win silver and gold through her.
29 May your soul rejoice in God's mercy;
do not be ashamed to give him praise.
30 Work at your tasks in due season,
and in his own time God will give you your reward.[e]

d: Sir 6:26–28. *e:* Sir 2:8; Jb 34:11; Jn 9:4.

See RG
280–370

THE PROPHETIC BOOKS

The prophetic books bear the names of the four major and twelve minor prophets, in addition to Lamentations and Baruch. The terms "major" and "minor" refer to the length of the respective compositions and not to their relative importance. Jonah is a story about a prophet rather than a collection of prophetic pronouncements. In the Hebrew Bible, Lamentations and Daniel are listed among the Writings (Hagiographa), not among the prophetic books. The former contains a series of laments over the destruction of Jerusalem by the Babylonians. The latter is considered to be a prophetic book, though it consists of a collection of six edifying diaspora tales (chaps. 1–6) and four apocalyptic visions about the end time (chaps. 7–12). Baruch is not included in the Hebrew canon, but is in the Septuagint or Old Greek version of the Bible, and the Church has from the beginning acknowledged its sacred and inspired character.

The prophetic books contain a deposit of prophetic preaching, and several of them in addition are filled out with narrative about prophets (e.g., Is 7; 36–39; Jer 26–29; 36–45; Am 7:10–17). In ancient Israel a prophet was understood to be an intermediary between God and the community, someone called to proclaim the word of God. Prophets received such communications through various means, including visions and dreams, often in a state of transformed consciousness, and transmitted them to the people as God's messengers through oracular utterances, sermons, writings, and symbolic actions.

It would be misleading to think of these works as books in our sense of the term. While some prophecies originated as written material, prophetic activity more commonly took the form of public speaking. Prophetic discourse addressed to different audiences in different situations would, typically, be committed first to memory, then to writing, often by the prophet's followers, sometimes by the prophet himself (e.g., Is 8:1–4, 16; Jer 36:1–2; Hb 2:2). Small compilations of such pronouncements and discourses would be put together, arranged according to subject matter (e.g., pronouncements against foreign nations), audience (e.g., Jeremiah to King Zedekiah, Jer 21:1–24:10), chronological sequence (e.g., in Ezekiel generally), or by verbal association (e.g., catchwords). These units would be circulated, edited, expanded and interpreted as the need arose to bring out the contemporary relevance of older prophecies, and eventually integrated into larger collections. The titles would have been added at a later date, in some instances centuries after the time of the prophet in question.

The office of the prophet came about as the result of a direct call from God. Unlike that of the priest, the prophetic function was not hereditary and did not correspond to a fixed office. In Israel as elsewhere in the ancient Near East and Levant, there were, however, prophets (*nebî'îm* in Hebrew) who were employed in temples and at royal courts, and some of the canonical prophets may have started out as "professionals" of this kind. Prophecy also differed from priesthood in ancient Israel in that there were both male and female prophets. Though none of the prophetic books is named for a female prophet, Miriam (Ex 15:20) and Deborah (Jgs 4:4) played important roles at the beginning of Israel's history and Huldah (2 Kgs 22:14) toward the end. The Bible gives great importance to the call or commissioning of the prophet, which was often accompanied by visionary or other extraordinary experiences (e.g., Jer 23:21–22; Ez 1–2). In these accounts the prophetic intermediary can be represented as a messenger commissioned by the Lord as king (e.g., Micaiah in 1 Kgs 22:19–23, and Isaiah in Is 6:1–13), and therefore prophetic speech is often introduced with the form used in the delivery of a message: "thus says the Lord" or some similar formula. Sometimes the prophetic calling could be expected to involve struggle, persecution, and suffering.

While prophetic messages sometimes bore on the future, their primary concern was with contemporary events in the public sphere of social life and politics, national and international. They focus on public morality, the treatment of the poor and disadvantaged, and the abuse of power, especially of the judicial system. They pass judgment in the strongest terms on the moral conduct of rulers and the ruling class, in the belief that a society that does not practice justice and righteousness will not survive. With equal rigor, they also condemn a religious formalism that would legitimate such a society (e.g., Is 1:10–17; Jer 7:1–15; Am 5:21–24). They view international affairs, the rise and fall of the great empires, in the light of their own passionate belief in the God of Israel and the destiny of Israel. The prophets never take political and military power as absolutes. They do not preach a new morality. They are radicals only in the sense of a radical commitment to and interpretation of the religious, legal, and moral traditions inherited from Israel's past.

Prophetic speech is not, however, confined to judgment and condemnation. The prophets also exhort, cajole, encourage; they announce salvation and a good prognosis for the future. Sometimes present realities and situations shade off into, or are taken up into, a panorama of a more distant future. In many instances, too, prophetic pronouncements are developed by a cumulative and incremental editorial process into a more inclusive and total vision of a final salvation and a final judgment, with or without the presence of a messianic figure. This process is particularly evident throughout the Book of Isaiah, and played an important part in the self-understanding of early Christian churches and their interpretation of the person and mission of Jesus. For early Christianity, therefore, prophetic texts were used to describe the new reality of Christ and the church (e.g., Mt 1:23; Acts 2:14–21; Gal 4:27).

The Book of Isaiah

See RG 280–95

Isaiah, one of the greatest of the prophets, appeared at a critical moment in Israel's history. The Northern Kingdom collapsed, under the hammer-like blows of Assyria, in 722/721 B.C., and in 701 Jerusalem itself saw the army of Sennacherib drawn up before its walls. In the year that Uzziah, king of Judah, died (742), Isaiah received his call to the prophetic office in the Temple of Jerusalem. Close attention should be given to chap. 6, where this divine summons to be the ambassador of the Most High is circumstantially described.

The vision of the Lord enthroned in glory stamps an indelible character on Isaiah's ministry and provides a key to the understanding of his message. The majesty, holiness and glory of the Lord took possession of his spirit and, at the same time, he gained a new awareness of human pettiness and sinfulness. The enormous abyss between God's sovereign holiness and human sinfulness overwhelmed the prophet. Only the purifying coal of the seraphim could cleanse his lips and prepare him for acceptance of the call: "Here I am, send me!"

The ministry of Isaiah extended from the death of Uzziah in 742 B.C. to Sennacherib's siege of Jerusalem in 701 B.C., and it may have continued even longer, until after the death of Hezekiah in 687 B.C. Later legend (the Martyrdom and Ascension of Isaiah) claims that Hezekiah's son, Manasseh, executed Isaiah by having him sawed in two; cf. Heb 11:37. During this long ministry, the prophet returned again and again to the same themes, and there are indications that he may have sometimes re-edited his older prophecies to fit new occasions. There is no evidence that the present arrangement of the oracles in the book reflects a chronological order. Indeed, it appears that there were originally separate smaller collections of oracles (note especially chaps. 6–12), each with its own logic for ordering, that were preserved fairly intact as blocks when the material was finally put together as a single literary work.

Isaiah's oracles cluster around several key historical events of the late eighth century: the Syro-Ephraimite War (735–732 B.C.), the accession of Hezekiah (715 B.C.), the revolt of Ashdod (714–711 B.C.), the death of Sargon (705 B.C.), and the revolt against Sennacherib (705–701 B.C.). In 738 B.C., with the Assyrian defeat of Calno/Calneh (Is 10:9; Am 6:2), the anti-Assyrian league, of which Judah may have been the ringleader, collapsed, and both Israel and the Arameans of Damascus paid tribute to Assyria. By 735 B.C., however, Rezin of Damascus had created a new anti-Assyrian league, and when Ahaz refused to join, the league attempted to remove Ahaz from the throne of Judah. The resulting Syro-Ephraimite War was the original occasion for many of Isaiah's oracles (cf. chaps. 7–8), in which he tried to reassure Ahaz of God's protection and dissuade him from seeking protection by an alliance with Assyria. Ahaz refused Isaiah's message, however.

When Hezekiah came to the throne in 715 B.C., Isaiah appears to have put great hopes in this new scion of David, and he undoubtedly supported the religious reform that Hezekiah undertook. But the old intrigues began again, and the king was sorely tempted to join with neighboring states in an alliance sponsored by Egypt against Assyria. Isaiah succeeded in keeping Hezekiah out of Ashdod's abortive revolt against Assyria, but when Sargon died in 705 B.C., with both Egypt and Babylon encouraging revolt, Hezekiah was won over to the pro-Egyptian party. Isaiah denounced this "covenant with death" (28:15, 18), and again summoned Judah to faith in the Lord as the only hope. But it was too late; the revolt had already begun. Assyria acted quickly and its army, after ravaging Judah, laid siege to Jerusalem (701). "I shut up Hezekiah like a bird in his cage," boasts the famous inscription of Sennacherib. The city was spared but at the cost of paying a huge indemnity to Assyria. Isaiah may have lived and prophesied for another dozen years after 701. There is material in the book that may plausibly be associated with Sennacherib's campaign against Babylon and its Arabian allies in 694–689 B.C.

For Isaiah, the vision of God's majesty was so overwhelming that military and political power faded into insignificance. He constantly called his people back to a reliance on God's promises and away from vain attempts to find security in human plans and intrigues. This vision also led him to insist on the ethical behavior that was required of human beings who wished to live in the presence of such a holy God. Isaiah couched this message in oracles of singular poetic beauty and power, oracles in which surprising shifts in syntax, audacious puns, and double- or triple-entendre are a constant feature.

The complete Book of Isaiah is an anthology of poems composed chiefly by the great prophet, but also by disciples, some of whom came many years after Isaiah. In 1–39 most of the oracles come from Isaiah and reflect the situation in eighth-century Judah. Sections such as the Apocalypse of Isaiah (24–27), the oracles against Babylon (13–14), and probably the poems of 34–35 were written by followers deeply influenced by the prophet, in some cases reusing earlier Isaianic material; cf., e.g., 27:2–8 with 5:1–7.

Chapters 40–55 (Second Isaiah, or Deutero-Isaiah) are generally attributed to an anonymous poet who prophesied toward the end of the Babylonian exile. From this section come the great oracles known as the Servant Songs, which are reflected in the New Testament understanding of the passion and glorification of Christ. Chapters 56–66 (Third Isaiah, or Trito-Isaiah) contain oracles from the postexilic period and were composed by writers imbued with the spirit of Isaiah who continued his work.

The principal divisions of the Book of Isaiah are the following:

I. Isaiah 1–39
- A. Indictment of Israel and Judah (1:1–5:30)
- B. The Book of Emmanuel (6:1–12:6)
- C. Oracles Against the Foreign Nations (13:1–23:18)
- D. Apocalypse of Isaiah (24:1–27:13)
- E. The Lord Alone, Israel's and Judah's Salvation (28:1–33:24)
- F. The Lord, Zion's Avenger (34:1–35:10)
- G. Historical Appendix (36:1–39:8)

II. Isaiah 40–55
A. The Lord's Glory in Israel's Liberation (40:1–48:22)
B. Expiation of Sin, Spiritual Liberation of Israel (49:1–55:13)
III. Isaiah 56–66

I. Isaiah 1—39

A. Indictment of Israel and Judah

CHAPTER 1

See RG 280–95

1* The vision which Isaiah, son of
Amoz, saw concerning Judah and Jerusalem
in the days of Uzziah, Jotham, Ahaz and
Hezekiah, kings of Judah.

Accusation and Appeal

2 * Hear, O heavens, and listen, O earth,
for the LORD speaks:
Sons have I raised and reared,
but they have rebelled against me![a]
3 An ox knows its owner,
and an ass,* its master's manger;
But Israel does not know,
my people has not understood.[b]
4 Ah!* Sinful nation, people laden with
wickedness,
evil offspring, corrupt children!
They have forsaken the LORD,
spurned the Holy One of Israel,
apostatized,[c]
5 Why* would you yet be struck,
that you continue to rebel?
The whole head is sick,
the whole heart faint.
6 From the sole of the foot to the head
there is no sound spot in it;
Just bruise and welt and oozing wound,
not drained, or bandaged,
or eased with salve.
7 Your country is waste,
your cities burnt with fire;
Your land—before your eyes
strangers devour it,
a waste, like the devastation of
Sodom.* [d]
8 And daughter Zion* is left
like a hut in a vineyard,
Like a shed in a melon patch,
like a city blockaded.
9 If the LORD of hosts* had not
left us a small remnant,
We would have become as Sodom,
would have resembled Gomorrah.[e]

10 * Hear the word of the LORD,
princes of Sodom!

1:1 The title, or inscription, of the book is an editorial addition to identify the prophet and the circumstances of his ministry. **Isaiah**: meaning "the salvation of the Lord," or "the Lord is salvation." **Amoz**: not Amos the prophet. **Judah**: the Southern Kingdom of the tribes of Judah and Benjamin. **Uzziah**: also called Azariah; cf. 2 Kgs 15:1; 2 Chr 26:1.

1:2–31 This chapter is widely considered to be a collection of oracles from various periods in Isaiah's ministry, chosen by the editor as a compendium of his most characteristic teachings.

1:3 Ox . . . ass: Isaiah uses animals proverbial for their stupidity and stubbornness to underline Israel's failure to respond to God. **Israel**: a term Isaiah (and other prophets) frequently applies to Judah, especially after the fall of the Northern Kingdom (which Isaiah normally calls Ephraim, as in 7:2, 9, 17; 9:8), but sometimes applies to the entire chosen people, as in 8:14.

1:4 Ah: see note on 5:8–24. **Holy One of Israel**: a title used frequently in the Book of Isaiah, rarely elsewhere in the Old Testament (see 5:19, 24; 10:20; 12:6; 17:7; 29:19; 30:11, 12, 15; 31:1; 37:23; 41:14, 16, 20; 43:3, 14; 45:11; 47:4; 48:17; 49:7; 54:5; 55:5; 60:9, 14).

1:5–6 The Hebrew expression translated "Why?" may also be translated "Where?" The ambiguity is probably intentional: "Why, O Israel, would you still be beaten, and where on your bruised body do you want the next blow?" The bruised body is a metaphor for the historical disaster that has overtaken Israel (see v. 7) because of its sins.

1:7 Sodom: Sodom and Gomorrah (see vv. 9–10; cf. Gn 19) were proverbial as wicked cities completely overthrown and destroyed by God. Judah, more fortunate, survives at least as a remnant. The devastation of the land and the isolation of Jerusalem suggest the time of Sennacherib's invasion of 701.

1:8 Daughter Zion: Jerusalem, as isolated as a little hut erected in a field for the shelter of watchmen and laborers.

1:9 LORD of hosts: God, who is the Creator and Ruler of the armies of Israel, the angels, stars, etc.

1:10–17 A powerful indictment of the religious hypocrisy of rulers and others who neglect just judgment and oppress the weaker members, yet believe they can please God with sacrifices and other external forms of worship. The long list of observances suggests the Lord's tedium with such attempts. **Sodom . . . Gomorrah**: the names are picked up from v. 9, but now to emphasize their wickedness rather than the good fortune of escaping total destruction.

a: Dt 32:1, 5–6, 18. *b:* Jer 8:7; Lk 2:12. *c:* Is 5:24; Dt 32:15. *d:* Is 13:19; Dt 29:22; Jer 49:18; 50:40; Am 4:11. *e:* Rom 9:29.

Listen to the instruction of our God,
people of Gomorrah!
11 What do I care for the multitude of your sacrifices?
says the LORD.
I have had enough of whole-burnt rams
and fat of fatlings;
In the blood of calves, lambs, and goats
I find no pleasure.[f]
12 When you come to appear before me,
who asks these things of you?
13 Trample my courts no more!
To bring offerings is useless;
incense is an abomination to me.
New moon and sabbath, calling assemblies—
festive convocations with wickedness—
these I cannot bear.[g]
14 Your new moons and festivals I detest;[h]
they weigh me down, I tire of the load.
15 When you spread out your hands,
I will close my eyes to you;
Though you pray the more,
I will not listen.
Your hands are full of blood!* [i]
16 Wash yourselves clean!
Put away your misdeeds from before my eyes;
cease doing evil;
17 learn to do good.
Make justice your aim: redress the wronged,
hear the orphan's plea, defend the widow.[j]
18 Come now, let us set things right,*
says the LORD:
Though your sins be like scarlet,
they may become white as snow;
Though they be red like crimson,
they may become white as wool.[k]
19 If you are willing, and obey,
you shall eat the good things of the land;
20 But if you refuse and resist,
you shall be eaten by the sword:
for the mouth of the LORD has spoken!

The Purification of Jerusalem

21 How she has become a prostitute,
the faithful city,* so upright!
Justice used to lodge within her,
but now, murderers.[l]
22 Your silver is turned to dross,
your wine is mixed with water.
23 Your princes are rebels
and comrades of thieves;
Each one of them loves a bribe
and looks for gifts.
The fatherless they do not defend,
the widow's plea does not reach them.[m]
24 Now, therefore, says the Lord,
the LORD of hosts, the Mighty One of Israel:
Ah! I will take vengeance on my foes
and fully repay my enemies![n]
25 I will turn my hand against you,
and refine your dross in the furnace,
removing all your alloy.
26 I will restore your judges* as at first,
and your counselors as in the beginning;
After that you shall be called
city of justice, faithful city.[o]

1:15–16 Hands . . . blood: oppression of the poor is likened to violence that bloodies the hands, which explains why the hands spread out in prayer (v. 15) are not regarded by the Lord. This climax of the accusations is followed by positive admonitions for reversing the evil situation.

1:18–20 Let us set things right: the Hebrew word refers to the arbitration of legal disputes (Jb 23:7). God offers to settle his case with Israel on the basis of the change of behavior demanded above. For Israel it is a life or death choice; life in conformity with God's will or death for continued disobedience.

1:21–28 Faithful city: the phrase, found in v. 21 and v. 28, forms an *inclusio* which marks off the passage and also suggests three chronological periods: the city's former ideal state, its present wicked condition (described in vv. 21b–23), and the future ideal conditions intended by God. This will be brought about by a purging judgment directed primarily against the leaders ("judges . . . counselors").

1:26 Judges: the reference must be to royal judges appointed by David and his successors, not to the tribal judges of the Book of Judges, since the "beginning" of Jerusalem as an Israelite city dates only to the time of David. The Davidic era is idealized here; obtaining justice in the historical Jerusalem of David's time was more problematic (see 2 Sm 15:1–6).

---

f: Ps 50:8–13; Sir 34:23; Mi 6:7. *g*: Prv 15:8; Jer 6:20. *h*: Am 5:21–24. *i*: Prv 1:28; Sir 34:25–31. *j*: Ex 23:6; Dt 24:17; Sir 4:9–10; Jer 22:3; Ez 22:7; Am 5:14–15; Zec 7:9–10. *k*: Ps 51:9. *l*: Jer 3:8; Hos 2:7. *m*: Ex 23:8; Dt 16:19. *n*: Dt 32:41. *o*: Jer 33:7–11; Zec 8:8.

27 * Zion shall be redeemed by justice,
and her repentant ones by righteousness.
28 Rebels and sinners together shall be crushed,
those who desert the LORD shall be consumed.

Judgment on the Sacred Groves

29 * You shall be ashamed of the terebinths which you desired,
and blush on account of the gardens which you chose.
30 You shall become like a terebinth whose leaves wither,
like a garden that has no water.
31 The strong tree shall turn to tinder,
and the one who tends it shall become a spark;
Both of them shall burn together,
and there shall be none to quench them.

CHAPTER 2

See RG 280–95

1* This is what Isaiah, son of Amoz, saw concerning Judah and Jerusalem.

Zion, the Royal City of God

2 * In days to come,
The mountain of the LORD's house
shall be established as the highest mountain
and raised above the hills.
All nations shall stream toward it.[p]
3 Many peoples shall come and say:
"Come, let us go up to the LORD's mountain,
to the house of the God of Jacob,
That he may instruct us in his ways,
and we may walk in his paths."[q]
For from Zion shall go forth instruction,
and the word of the LORD from Jerusalem.
4 * He shall judge between the nations,
and set terms for many peoples.
They shall beat their swords into plowshares
and their spears into pruning hooks;[r]
One nation shall not raise the sword against another,
nor shall they train for war again.[s]
5 * House of Jacob, come,
let us walk in the light of the LORD!

The Lord's Day of Judgment on Pride

6 You have abandoned your people,
the house of Jacob!
Because they are filled with diviners,
and soothsayers, like the Philistines;

1:27–28 These verses expand the oracle that originally ended at v. 26. The expansion correctly interprets the preceding text as proclaiming a purifying judgment on Zion in which the righteous are saved while the wicked perish. The meaning of "by justice" and "by righteousness" is ambiguous. Do these terms refer to God's judgment or to the justice and righteousness of Zion's surviving inhabitants? Is 33:14–16 suggests the latter interpretation.

1:29–31 These verses were secondarily inserted here on the catchword principle; like v. 28 they pronounce judgment on certain parties "together" (v. 31). The terebinths and gardens refer to the sacred groves or asherahs that functioned as idolatrous cultic symbols at the popular shrines or high places (1 Kgs 14:23; 2 Kgs 17:10). Hezekiah cut down these groves during his reform (2 Kgs 18:4); they were a religious issue during Isaiah's ministry (cf. Is 17:7–11). Isaiah threatens those who cultivate these symbols with the same fate that befalls trees when deprived of water.

2:1 This editorial heading probably introduced the collection of chaps. 2–12, to which chap. 1 with its introduction was added later (see note on 1:2–31).

2:2–22 These verses contain two very important oracles, one on the pilgrimage of nations to Mount Zion (vv. 2–4—completed with an invitation to the "house of Jacob," v. 5), the other on the day of the Lord (see note on Am 5:18), which was probably composed from at least two earlier pieces. Whereas vv. 6–8 indict Judah for trust in superstitious practices and human resources rather than in the Lord, the following verses are directed against humankind in general and emphasize the effect of the "day of the Lord," the humbling of human pride. This may be taken as a precondition for the glorious vision of vv. 2–4. This vision of Zion's glorious future, which is also found in a slightly variant form in Mi 4:1–4, is rooted in the early Zion tradition, cultivated in the royal cult in Jerusalem. It celebrated God's choice of Jerusalem as the divine dwelling place, along with God's choice of the Davidic dynasty (Ps 68:16–17; 78:67–72; 132:13–18). **Highest mountain**: the Zion tradition followed earlier mythological conceptions that associate the abode of deities with very high mountains (Ps 48:2–3). The lifting of Mount Zion is a metaphor for universal recognition of the Lord's authority.

2:4 Once the nations acknowledge God as sovereign, they go up to Jerusalem to settle their disputes, rather than having recourse to war.

2:5 This verse is added as a conclusion to vv. 2–4; cf. Mi 4:4–5, where a quite different conclusion is provided for the parallel version of this oracle.

p: Mi 4:1–4. *q:* Is 56:7; 2 Kgs 17:26–28; Jer 31:6–14; Zec 8:20–23. *r:* Jl 4:10. *s:* Is 9:7; 11:4; Ps 46:10; Zec 9:10.

with foreigners they clasp hands.[t]
7 Their land is full of silver and gold,
there is no end to their treasures;
Their land is full of horses,
there is no end to their chariots.
8 Their land is full of idols;
they bow down to the works of their hands,
what their fingers have made.[u]
9 So all shall be abased,
each one brought low.*
Do not pardon them!
10 Get behind the rocks,
hide in the dust,
From the terror of the LORD
and the splendor of his majesty!
11 The eyes of human pride shall be lowered,
the arrogance of mortals shall be abased,
and the LORD alone will be exalted, on that day.*
12 For the LORD of hosts will have his day
against all that is proud and arrogant,
against all that is high, and it will be brought low;
13 Yes, against all the cedars of Lebanon*
and against all the oaks of Bashan,
14 Against all the lofty mountains
and all the high hills,
15 Against every lofty tower
and every fortified wall,
16 Against all the ships of Tarshish
and all stately vessels.
17 Then human pride shall be abased,
the arrogance of mortals brought low,
And the LORD alone will be exalted on that day.
18 The idols will vanish completely.
19 People will go into caves in the rocks
and into holes in the earth,
At the terror of the LORD
and the splendor of his majesty,
as he rises to overawe the earth.
20 On that day people shall throw to moles and bats
their idols of silver and their idols of gold
which they made for themselves to worship.
21 And they shall go into caverns in the rocks
and into crevices in the cliffs,
At the terror of the LORD
and the splendor of his majesty,
as he rises to overawe the earth.
22 * As for you, stop worrying about mortals,
in whose nostrils is but a breath;
for of what worth are they?

CHAPTER 3

See RG 280–95

Judgment on Jerusalem and Judah

1 * The Lord, the LORD of hosts,
will take away from Jerusalem and from Judah
Support and staff—
all support of bread,
all support of water:[v]
2 Hero and warrior,
judge and prophet, diviner and elder,
3 The captain of fifty and the nobleman,
counselor, skilled magician, and expert charmer.
4 I will place boys as their princes;
the fickle will govern them,[w]
5 And the people will oppress one another,
yes, each one the neighbor.
The child will be insolent toward the elder,
and the base toward the honorable.[x]

2:9 Bowing down to idols will not bring deliverance to Israel, but rather total abasement. **Do not pardon them**: this line is so abrupt that it is almost certainly an intrusion in the text.

2:11 That day: i.e., the day of the Lord; cf. note on Am 5:18.

2:13 Lebanon: Mount Lebanon in Syria, famed for its cedars. **Bashan**: the fertile uplands east of the Sea of Galilee.

2:22 The meaning of this verse, certainly a later addition, is not clear. It is not addressed to God but to a plural subject.

3:1–12 These verses suggest deportation, with resulting social upheaval, and thus may date to sometime after Ahaz submitted as vassal to Assyria. The deportation practiced by Assyria, as later by Babylon, exiled the leading elements of society, such as those named in vv. 2–3; cf. 2 Kgs 24:12, 14–16 for a similar list of those exiled by the Babylonians. Denuding society of its leaders opens the way to near anarchy and a situation in which leadership is seized by or thrust upon those unqualified for it (vv. 5–7). The situation has been provoked by sinfully inept leadership (vv. 4, 8–9, 12). Some suggest that vv. 4 and 12 refer to Ahaz, who may have come to the throne at an early age. Verses 10–11 form a wisdom couplet that was inserted later.

t: Is 10:32. *u:* Is 17:7–8; 31:1–3. *v:* Lv 26:26; Ez 4:16. *w:* Eccl 10:16. *x:* Mi 7:5–6.

[6] When anyone seizes a brother
in their father's house, saying,
"You have clothes! Be our ruler,
and take in hand this ruin!"—
[7] He will cry out in that day:
"I cannot be a healer,[y]
when there is neither bread nor
clothing in my own house!
You will not make me a ruler of the
people!"
[8] Jerusalem has stumbled, Judah has fallen;
for their speech and deeds affront the
LORD,
a provocation in the sight of his majesty.
[9] Their very look bears witness against
them;[z]
they boast of their sin like Sodom,[a]
They do not hide it.
Woe to them!
They deal out evil to themselves.
[10] Happy the just, for it will go well with
them,
the fruit of their works they will eat.
[11] Woe to the wicked! It will go ill with them,
with the work of their hands they will
be repaid.
[12] My people—infants oppress them,
women rule over them!
My people, your leaders deceive you,[b]
they confuse the paths you should
follow.

[13] * The LORD rises to accuse,
stands to try his people.
[14] The Lord enters into judgment
with the people's elders and princes:
You, you who have devoured the vineyard;
the loot wrested from the poor is in
your houses.
[15] What do you mean by crushing my people,
and grinding down the faces of the
poor?
says the Lord, the GOD of hosts.

*The Haughty Women of Zion**

[16] The LORD said:[c]
Because the daughters of Zion are
haughty,
and walk with necks outstretched,
Ogling and mincing as they go,
their anklets tinkling with every step,
[17] The Lord shall cover the scalps of Zion's
daughters with scabs,
and the LORD shall lay bare their
heads.* [d]

[18]* On that day the LORD will do away with
the finery of the anklets, sunbursts, and crescents; [19]the pendants, bracelets, and veils;
[20]the headdresses, bangles, cinctures, perfume boxes, and amulets; [21]the signet rings,
and the nose rings; [22]the court dresses,
wraps, cloaks, and purses; [23]the lace gowns,
linen tunics, turbans, and shawls.

[24] Instead of perfume there will be stench,
instead of a girdle, a rope,
And instead of elaborate coiffure,
baldness;
instead of a rich gown, a sackcloth
skirt.
Then, instead of beauty, shame.
[25] Your men will fall by the sword,
and your champions,* in war;[e]
[26] Her gates will lament and mourn,
as the city sits desolate on the ground.[f]

CHAPTER 4

See RG 280–95

[1] Seven women will take hold of
one man*
on that day, saying:

3:13–15 The princes and the elders, here accused of despoiling the poor, are the very ones who should be their defenders. **Loot**: by the Hebrew term (*gazela*) Isaiah conveys the idea of violent seizure, though 10:1–4 suggests the poor could be plundered by legal means.

3:16–4:1 Here and again in 32:9–14 Isaiah condemns the women of the ruling class for their part in Jerusalem's plight.

3:17 A shaven head is a mark of social disgrace; cf. Nm 5:18.

3:18–23 The long list of women's apparel in these verses suggests luxury and vanity; it contains a number of rare words, and the precise meaning of many of the terms is uncertain.

3:25 Your men . . . your champions: the second person feminine singular pronoun here shows that the prophet has shifted his attention from the women of Zion to the personified city of Zion.

4:1 Seven women . . . one man: deportation (cf. note on 3:1–12) would result in a disproportion of the sexes and leave the female population without enough male partners. The women are willing to marry, not for support, but to avoid disgrace.

y: Is 1:6. *z:* Jer 3:3. *a:* Is 1:10. *b:* Mi 3:5. *c:* Is 32:9–14; Ez 16:50; Am 4:1–3. *d:* Jer 13:26; Ez 16:37. *e:* Hos 14:1. *f:* Is 47:1; Lam 2:10.

"We will eat our own food
and wear our own clothing;
Only let your name be given us,
put an end to our disgrace!"

Jerusalem Purified

2 * On that day,
The branch* of the LORD will be beauty and glory,
and the fruit of the land will be honor and splendor
for the survivors of Israel.
3 Everyone who remains in Zion,
everyone left in Jerusalem
Will be called holy:
everyone inscribed for life* in Jerusalem.[g]
4 When the Lord washes away
the filth of the daughters of Zion,
And purges Jerusalem's blood from her midst
with a blast of judgment, a searing blast,[h]
5 Then will the LORD create,
over the whole site of Mount Zion
and over her place of assembly,
A smoking cloud by day
and a light of flaming fire by night.[i]
6 For over all, his glory will be shelter and protection:
shade from the parching heat of day,
refuge and cover from storm and rain.[j]

CHAPTER 5

See RG 280–95

*The Song of the Vineyard**

1 Now let me sing of my friend,
my beloved's song about his vineyard.
My friend had a vineyard
on a fertile hillside;
2 He spaded it, cleared it of stones,
and planted the choicest vines;
Within it he built a watchtower,
and hewed out a wine press.
Then he waited for the crop of grapes,
but it yielded rotten grapes.[k]
3 Now, inhabitants of Jerusalem, people of Judah,
judge between me and my vineyard:
4 What more could be done for my vineyard
that I did not do?[l]
Why, when I waited for the crop of grapes,
did it yield rotten grapes?
5 Now, I will let you know
what I am going to do to my vineyard:
Take away its hedge, give it to grazing,
break through its wall, let it be trampled!*
6 Yes, I will make it a ruin:
it shall not be pruned or hoed,
but will be overgrown with thorns and briers;
I will command the clouds
not to rain upon it.
7 The vineyard of the LORD of hosts is the house of Israel,
the people of Judah, his cherished plant;
He waited for judgment, but see, bloodshed!
for justice, but hark, the outcry!*

*Oracles of Reproach**

8 * Ah! Those who join house to house,
who connect field with field,

4:2–6 Usually judged a later addition to the oracles of Isaiah. It relieves the threatening tone of the surrounding chaps. 3 and 5.

4:2 Branch: the term (Heb. *semah*) that is sometimes used of the ideal Davidic king of the future (cf. Jer 23:5; 33:15; Zec 3:8; 6:12). However, the parallel "fruit of the land" does not favor that usage here.

4:3 Inscribed for life: in God's list of the elect; cf. Ex 32:32.

5:1–7 Vineyard: although the term is sometimes used in an erotic context (Sg 1:6; 8:12), "vineyard" or "vine" is used more frequently as a metaphor for God's people (27:2; Ps 80:9, 14, 15; Jer 2:21; 12:10; Ez 17:7; Hos 10:1; Na 2:2). The terms translated "friend" (*yadid*) and "beloved" (*dod*) suggest the Lord's favor (Dt 33:12; 2 Sm 12:25; Ps 127:2) and familial background rather than introducing the piece as a "love song," as is sometimes suggested. The prophet disguises the real theme (the people's infidelity) so that the hearers will participate in the unfavorable judgment called for (vv. 3–4). Cf. the reversal of this parable in 27:2–6.

5:5–6 Trampled . . . thorns and briers: this judgment is echoed in the description of the devastated land in 7:23–25.

5:7 Judgment . . . bloodshed . . . justice . . . outcry: in Hebrew there is an impressive play on words: *mishpat* parallels *mispah*, *sedaqah* parallels *se'aqah*. See also the threefold "waited for" in vv. 2, 4, 7.

5:8–24 These verses contain a series of short oracles introduced by the Hebrew particle *hoy* ("Ah!"), an emphatic exclamation, sometimes translated "Woe!"

5:8–10 An oracle against land-grabbers (v. 8); they will be impoverished instead of enriched (vv. 9–10).

g: Is 6:13; Ob 17; Mal 3:16. *h:* Is 1:21–28. *i:* Ex 13:21. *j:* Is 32:1–2. *k:* Dt 32:32. *l:* Mi 6:3–5.

Until no space remains, and you alone
dwell
in the midst of the land![m]
9 In my hearing the LORD of hosts has
sworn:[n]
Many houses shall be in ruins,
houses large and fine, with nobody
living there.[o]
10 Ten acres of vineyard
shall yield but one bath,*
And a homer of seed
shall yield but an ephah.
11 * Ah! Those who rise early in the
morning
in pursuit of strong drink,
lingering late
inflamed by wine,
12 Banqueting on wine with harp and lyre,
timbrel and flute,[p]
But the deed of the LORD they do not
regard,
the work of his hands they do not
see![q]
13 Therefore my people go into exile
for lack of understanding,[r]
Its nobles starving,
its masses parched with thirst.
14 Therefore Sheol enlarges its throat
and opens its mouth beyond
measure;[s]
Down into it go nobility and masses,
tumult and revelry.
15 All shall be abased, each one brought
low,
and the eyes of the haughty lowered,[t]
16 But the LORD of hosts shall be exalted by
judgment,
by justice the Holy God shown
holy.[u]
17 Lambs shall graze as at pasture,
young goats shall eat in the ruins of
the rich.
18 Ah! Those who tug at guilt with cords of
perversity,
and at sin as if with cart ropes!
19 * Who say, "Let him make haste,
let him speed his work, that we may
see it;
On with the plan of the Holy One of
Israel!
let it come to pass, that we may
know it!"[v]
20 Ah! Those who call evil good, and good
evil,
who change darkness to light, and
light into darkness,
who change bitter to sweet, and sweet
into bitter![w]
21 Ah! Those who are wise in their own
eyes,
prudent in their own view![x]
22 Ah! Those who are champions at
drinking wine,
masters at mixing drink!
23 Those who acquit the guilty for bribes,
and deprive the innocent of justice![y]
24 Therefore, as the tongue of fire licks up
stubble,
as dry grass shrivels in the flame,
Their root shall rot
and their blossom scatter like dust;
For they have rejected the instruction of
the LORD of hosts,
and scorned the word of the Holy One
of Israel.
25 * Therefore the wrath of the LORD blazes
against his people,

5:10 Ten acres: a field with ten times the surface area a yoke of oxen could plow in one day. **Bath**: a liquid measure equal to about twelve gallons. **Homer**: a dry measure equal to what a donkey can carry, calculated to be about ten bushels. **Ephah**: a dry measure of about one bushel. So small a harvest is the fruit of the land-grabbers' greed.

5:11–13 An oracle against debauchery and indifference. **Strong drink**: the Hebrew word *shekar* means either beer or a type of wine, perhaps date wine, not distilled liquor.

5:19 An indication that some, presumably of the ruling class, scoff at Isaiah's teaching on the Lord's "plan" and "work" (cf. v. 12; 14:26–27; 28:9–14; 30:10–11).

5:25–30 These verses do not suit their present context. Apparently v. 25 was originally the conclusion of the poem of 9:7–20 directed against the Northern Kingdom; cf. the refrain that occurs here and in 9:11, 16, and 20. Verses 26–30 look to an invasion by Assyria and might originally have come immediately after the poem of 9:1–20 plus 5:25. The insertion of chaps. 6–8 may have occasioned the dislocation, as well as that of 10:1–4a, which may have originally belonged with the "reproach" oracles of 5:8–23.

m: Mi 2:1–3. *n:* Is 22:14. *o:* Is 6:12. *p:* Is 5:22; Am 6:1–7. *q:* Is 5:19; 10:12; 14:24–27; 19:12, 17; 23:9; 28:21; 30:1. *r:* Hos 4:6. *s:* Hb 2:5. *t:* Is 2:9, 11, 17. *u:* Is 1:27. *v:* Jer 17:15; 2 Pt 3:3–4. *w:* Is 32:4–5. *x:* Prv 3:7; 26:12; Rom 11:25; 12:16. *y:* Ex 23:8; Prv 17:15.

he stretches out his hand to strike
them;
The mountains quake,[z]
their corpses shall be like refuse in the
streets.
For all this, his wrath is not turned back,
his hand is still outstretched.

Invasion*

26 He will raise a signal to a far-off nation,
and whistle for it from the ends of the
earth.[a]
Then speedily and promptly they will
come.
27 None among them is weary, none
stumbles,
none will slumber, none will sleep.
None with waist belt loose,
none with sandal thong broken.
28 Their arrows are sharp,
and all their bows are bent,
The hooves of their horses like flint,
and their chariot wheels like the
whirlwind.
29 They roar like the lion,
like young lions, they roar;
They growl and seize the prey,
they carry it off and none can rescue.
30 They will growl over it, on that day,
like the growling of the sea,
Look to the land—
darkness closing in,
the light dark with clouds![b]

B. The Book of Emmanuel

CHAPTER 6

See RG 280–95

The Sending of Isaiah. [1]In the year
King Uzziah died,* I saw the Lord seated on
a high and lofty throne,[c] with the train of his
garment filling the temple. [2]Seraphim* were
stationed above; each of them had six wings:
with two they covered their faces, with two
they covered their feet, and with two they
hovered.[d] [3]One cried out to the other:

"Holy, holy, holy* is the LORD of hosts!
All the earth is filled with his glory!"

[4]At the sound of that cry, the frame of the
door shook and the house was filled with
smoke.* [e]

[5]Then I said, "Woe is me, I am doomed!*
For I am a man of unclean lips, living among
a people of unclean lips,[f] and my eyes have
seen the King, the LORD of hosts!" [6]Then
one of the seraphim flew to me, holding an
ember which he had taken with tongs from
the altar.

[7]He touched my mouth with it. "See," he
said, "now that this has touched your lips,*
your wickedness is removed, your sin
purged."[g]

[8]Then I heard the voice of the Lord saying, "Whom shall I send? Who will go for
us?" "Here I am," I said; "send me!" [9]* And
he replied: Go and say to this people:

5:26–30 This oracle threatens a future judgment, an invasion of the Assyrian army, God's instrument for punishing Judah (10:5, 15).

6:1 In the year King Uzziah died: probably 742 B.C., although the chronology of this period is disputed. **A high and lofty throne**: within the holy of holies of the Jerusalem Temple stood two cherubim, or winged sphinxes, whose outstretched wings served as the divine throne (1 Kgs 6:23–28; Ez 1:4–28; 10:1, 20). The ark of the covenant was God's footstool (Ps 132:7–8; 1 Chr 28:2), placed under the cherubim (1 Kgs 8:6–7). **Temple**: the holy place, just in front of the holy of holies.

6:2 Seraphim: the plural of *saraph* ("to burn"), a term used to designate the "fiery" serpents of the wilderness (Nm 21:8; Dt 8:15), and to refer to "winged" serpents (Is 14:29; 30:6). Here, however, it is used adjectivally of the cherubim, who are not serpent-like, as seen in the fact that they have faces and sexual parts ("feet"). See the adaptation of these figures by Ezekiel (Ez 1:10–12; 10:4–15).

6:3 Holy, holy, holy: these words have been used in Christian liturgy from the earliest times.

6:4 Smoke: reminiscent of the clouds which indicated God's presence at Mount Sinai (Ex 19:16–19; Dt 4:11) and which filled the tabernacle (Ex 40:34–38) and the Temple (1 Kgs 8:10–11) at their dedication.

6:5 Doomed: there are two roots from which the verb here could be derived; one means "to perish, be doomed," the other "to become silent," and given Isaiah's delight in puns and double entendre, he probably intended to sound both notes. "I am doomed!" is suggested by the popular belief that to see God would lead to one's death; cf. Gn 32:31; Ex 33:20; Jgs 13:22. "I am struck silent!" is suggested by the emphasis on the lips in vv. 5–6, and such silence is attested elsewhere as the appropriate response to the vision of the Lord in the Temple (Hb 2:20).

6:7 Touched your lips: Isaiah is thus symbolically purified of sin in preparation for his mission as God's prophet.

6:9–10 Isaiah's words give evidence that he attempted in every way, through admonition, threat, and promise, to bring

z: Am 1:1; Zec 14:5; cf. Is 9:18a. *a:* Is 7:18; 11:12; Jer 4:6; 50:2. *b:* Is 8:22. *c:* 1 Kgs 22:19–23; Jn 12:41. *d:* Rev 4:8. *e:* Rev 15:8. *f:* Is 29:13; Mt 15:1–11; Mk 7:1–13; Col 2:20–23. *g:* Jer 1:9; Dn 10:16.

Listen carefully, but do not understand!
Look intently, but do not perceive![h]
10 Make the heart of this people sluggish,
dull their ears and close their eyes;
Lest they see with their eyes, and hear
with their ears,
and their heart understand,
and they turn and be healed.[i]

11 "How long, O Lord?" I asked. And he
replied:
* Until the cities are desolate,
without inhabitants,
Houses, without people,
and the land is a desolate waste.
12 Until the LORD sends the people far
away,
and great is the desolation in the midst
of the land.
13 If there remain a tenth part in it,
then this in turn shall be laid waste;
As with a terebinth or an oak
whose trunk remains when its leaves
have fallen.* [j]
Holy offspring is the trunk.

See RG 280–95

CHAPTER 7

*The Syro-Ephraimite War**

Crisis in Judah. 1 In the days of Ahaz,* king of
Judah, son of Jotham, son of Uzziah, Rezin,
king of Aram, and Pekah, king of Israel, son
of Remaliah, went up to attack Jerusalem, but
they were not able to conquer it.[k] 2 When word
came to the house of David that Aram had allied itself with Ephraim, the heart of the king
and heart of the people trembled, as the trees
of the forest tremble in the wind.

3 Then the LORD said to Isaiah: Go out to
meet Ahaz, you and your son Shear-jashub,*
at the end of the conduit of the upper pool,
on the highway to the fuller's field, 4 and say
to him: Take care you remain calm and do
not fear; do not let your courage fail before
these two stumps of smoldering brands,[l] the
blazing anger of Rezin and the Arameans
and of the son of Remaliah— 5 because
Aram, with Ephraim and the son of Remaliah, has planned* evil against you. They say,
6 "Let us go up against Judah, tear it apart,
make it our own by force, and appoint the
son of Tabeel* king there."

7 Thus says the Lord GOD:
It shall not stand, it shall not be![m]
8 * The head of Aram is Damascus,
and the head of Damascus is Rezin;
9 The head of Ephraim is Samaria,
and the head of Samaria is the son of
Remaliah.
Within sixty-five years,

the people to conversion (cf. 1:18–20), so it is unlikely that this charge to "harden" is to be understood as Isaiah's task; more probably it reflects the refusal of the people, more particularly the leaders, who were supposed to "see," "hear," and "understand," a refusal which would then lead to a disastrous outcome (vv. 11–12).

6:11–12 The desolation described would be the result of the sort of deportation practiced by the Assyrians and later by the Babylonians. Isaiah seems to expect this as an eventual consequence of Judah's submission as vassal to the Assyrians; cf. 3:1–3; 5:13.

6:13 When its leaves have fallen: the meaning of the Hebrew is uncertain, and the text may be corrupt. **Holy offspring**: part of the phrase is missing from the Septuagint and may be a later addition; it provides a basis for hope for the future.

7:1–8:18 These verses (often termed Isaiah's "Memoirs") contain a series of oracles and narratives (some in first person), all closely related to the Syro-Ephraimite war of 735–732 B.C. Several passages feature three children whose symbolic names refer to the Lord's purposes: Shear-jashub (7:3), Emmanuel (7:10–17; 8:8–10), and Maher-shalal-hash-baz (8:1–4). Judah and its Davidic dynasty should trust God's promises and not fear the combined armies of Israel and Syria; within a very short time these two enemy states will be destroyed, and David's dynasty will continue.

7:1 Days of Ahaz: who ruled from 735 to 715 B.C. This attack against Jerusalem by the kings of Aram (Syria) and Israel in 735 B.C. was occasioned by the refusal of Ahaz to enter with them into an anti-Assyrian alliance; cf. 2 Kgs 16.

7:3 Shear-jashub: this name means "a remnant will return" (cf. 10:20–22).

7:5 Planned: the plans of those who plot against Ahaz shall not be accomplished (v. 7). What the Lord plans will unfailingly come to pass, whereas human plans contrary to those of the Lord are doomed to frustration; cf. 8:10; 14:24–27; 19:11–14; 29:15; 30:1. See further the note on 14:24–27.

7:6 Son of Tabeel: a puppet of Jerusalem's enemies. His appointment would interrupt the lawful succession from David.

7:8–9 God had chosen and made a commitment to David's dynasty and his capital city Jerusalem, not to Rezin and his capital Damascus, nor to the son of Remaliah and his capital Samaria (2 Sm 7:12–16; Ps 2:6; 78:68–72; 132:11–18). **Within sixty-five years . . . nation**: this text occurs at the end of v. 8 in the Hebrew. Ahaz would not have been reassured by so distant a promise; the phrase is probably a later addition.

---

h: Mt 13:10–17; Mk 4:10–12; Lk 8:9–10; Acts 28:25–28. *i:* Jer 5:21; Jn 12:40. *j:* Is 10:22. *k:* 2 Kgs 16:5; 2 Chr 28:5–15. *l:* Is 8:12; 30:15. *m:* Is 8:10; Ps 33:10.

Ephraim shall be crushed, no longer a nation.
Unless your faith is firm,
you shall not be firm![n]

Emmanuel. [10]Again the LORD spoke to Ahaz: [11]Ask for a sign from the LORD, your God; let it be deep as Sheol, or high as the sky!* [12]But Ahaz answered, "I will not ask! I will not tempt the LORD!"* [13]Then he said: Listen, house of David! Is it not enough that you weary human beings? Must you also weary my God? [14]Therefore the Lord himself will give you a sign;* the young woman, pregnant and about to bear a son, shall name him Emmanuel. [15]Curds and honey* he will eat so that he may learn to reject evil and choose good; [16]for before the child learns to reject evil and choose good, the land of those two kings whom you dread shall be deserted.

[17]The LORD shall bring upon you and your people and your father's house such days as have not come since Ephraim seceded* from Judah (the king of Assyria). [18]On that day

The LORD shall whistle
for the fly in the farthest streams of Egypt,
and for the bee in the land of Assyria.[o]
19 All of them shall come and settle
in the steep ravines and in the rocky clefts,
on all thornbushes and in all pastures.

[20]* On that day the Lord shall shave with the razor hired from across the River (the king of Assyria) the head, and the hair of the feet; it shall also shave off the beard.[p]

[21]On that day a man shall keep alive a young cow or a couple of sheep, [22]and from their abundant yield of milk he shall eat curds; curds and honey shall be the food of all who are left in the land. [23]* On that day every place where there were a thousand vines worth a thousand pieces of silver shall become briers and thorns. [24]One shall have to go there with bow and arrows, for all the country shall be briers and thorns.[q] [25]But as for all the hills which were hoed with a mattock, for fear of briers and thorns you will not go there; they shall become a place for cattle to roam and sheep to trample.[r]

CHAPTER 8

See RG 280–95

A Son of Isaiah. [1]The LORD said to me: Take a large tablet, and inscribe on it with an ordinary stylus,* "belonging to Maher-shalal-hash-baz,"[s] [2]and call reliable witnesses* for me, Uriah the priest, and Zechariah, son of Jeberechiah.

[3]Then I went to the prophetess and she conceived and bore a son. The LORD said to me: Name him Maher-shalal-hash-baz, [4]for before the child learns to say, "My father, my mother," the wealth of Damascus and the

7:11 Deep . . . sky: an extraordinary or miraculous sign that would prove God's firm will to save the royal house of David from its oppressors.

7:12 Tempt the LORD: Ahaz prefers to depend upon the might of Assyria rather than the might of God.

7:14 Isaiah's sign seeks to reassure Ahaz that he need not fear the invading armies of Syria and Israel in the light of God's promise to David (2 Sm 7:12–16). The oracle follows a traditional announcement formula by which the birth and sometimes naming of a child is promised to particular individuals (Gn 16:11; Jgs 13:3). **The young woman**: Hebrew *'almah* designates a young woman of marriageable age without specific reference to virginity. The Septuagint translated the Hebrew term as *parthenos*, which normally does mean virgin, and this translation underlies Mt 1:23. **Emmanuel**: the name means "with us is God." Since for the Christian the incarnation is the ultimate expression of God's willingness to "be with us," it is understandable that this text was interpreted to refer to the birth of Christ.

7:15–16 Curds and honey: the only diet available to those who are left after the devastation of the land; cf. vv. 21–25.

7:17 Such days as have not come since Ephraim seceded: the days of the kingdom prior to the secession of Ephraim and the other northern tribes (1 Kgs 12). **The king of Assyria**: the final comment appears to be a later editorial gloss indicating days worse than any since the secession.

7:20 God will use the Assyrians from across the River (the Euphrates) as his instrument ("razor") to inflict disgrace and suffering upon his people. Ahaz paid tribute to the Assyrian king Tiglath-pileser III, who decimated Syria and Israel in his campaigns of 734–732 B.C. (cf. 2 Kgs 16:7–9). **The feet**: euphemism for sexual parts; cf. Is 6:2.

7:23–25 Cf. note on 5:5–6.

8:1 Ordinary stylus: lit., "stylus of men." **Maher-shalal-hash-baz**: a symbolic name to be given to another son of Isaiah (v. 3); it means "quick spoils; speedy plunder," and describes what the Assyrians will do to Syria and Israel.

8:2 Reliable witnesses: who would testify that Isaiah had indeed prophesied the future destruction. **Uriah the priest**: cf. 2 Kgs 16:10.

n: 2 Chr 20:20. *o:* Is 5:26. *p:* Is 3:24; 2 Sm 10:4–6; Ez 5:1. *q:* Is 32:13. *r:* Is 5:5; 32:14. *s:* Is 10:6.

spoils of Samaria shall be carried off by the king of Assyria.

The Choice: The Lord or Assyria. 5 Again the LORD spoke to me:

6 Because this people* has rejected
the waters of Shiloah that flow gently,
And melts with fear at the display of
Rezin and Remaliah's son,
7 Therefore the Lord is bringing up against them
the waters of the River, great and mighty,
the king of Assyria and all his glory.
It shall rise above all its channels,
and overflow all its banks.
8 It shall roll on into Judah,
it shall rage and pass on—
up to the neck it shall reach.[t]
But his outspread wings will fill
the width of your land, Emmanuel!
9 Band together, O peoples, but be shattered!
Give ear, all you distant lands!
Arm yourselves, but be shattered! Arm yourselves, but be shattered!
10 Form a plan, it shall be thwarted;
make a resolve, it shall not be carried out,
for "With us is God!"* [u]

Disciples of Isaiah. 11 For thus said the LORD—his hand strong upon me—warning me not to walk in the way of this people:

12 * Do not call conspiracy what this people calls conspiracy,
nor fear what they fear, nor feel dread.
13 But conspire with the LORD of hosts;
he shall be your fear, he shall be your dread.[v]
14 He shall be a snare,
a stone for injury,
A rock for stumbling
to both the houses of Israel,
A trap and a snare
to those who dwell in Jerusalem;[w]
15 And many among them shall stumble;
fallen and broken;
snared and captured.[x]

16 Bind up my testimony, seal the instruction
with my disciples.* 17 I will trust in the LORD,
who is hiding his face from the house of Jacob; yes, I will wait for him. 18 Here am I and
the children whom the LORD has given me: we
are signs* and portents in Israel from the LORD
of hosts, who dwells on Mount Zion.[y]
19 And when they say to you, "Inquire of
ghosts and soothsayers who chirp and mutter;* [z] should not a people inquire of their
gods, consulting the dead on behalf of the
living, 20 for instruction and testimony?"
Surely, those who speak like this are the
ones for whom there is no dawn.*

21 He will pass through it hard-pressed and hungry,
and when hungry, shall become enraged,
and curse king and gods.
He will look upward,
22 and will gaze at the earth,
But will see only distress and darkness,
oppressive gloom,
murky, without light.*

8:6–8 This people: Judah. **Waters of Shiloah**: the stream that flows from the Gihon spring into the pool of Shiloah in Jerusalem and provides a sure supply in time of siege; here it symbolizes the divine protection which Judah has rejected by seeking Assyrian support, symbolized by "the River" (i.e., the Euphrates). Ultimately Assyrian power will devastate Judah. **His outspread wings**: the Lord's wings, a recurring symbol for divine protection (Ps 17:8; 36:8; 57:2; 61:5; 91:4; Ru 2:12). Some understand the image to refer to the sides of the flooding river, but this use of the Hebrew word for "wings" is unparalleled elsewhere in classical Hebrew.

8:10 The plan of Israel's enemies will be thwarted because, as the name "Emmanuel" signifies, "with us is God."

8:12–14 Because Isaiah and his followers resisted the official policy of seeking help from Assyria they were labeled "conspirators"; Isaiah uses the term to express what is really the case, cooperating with the Lord.

8:16 Bind . . . seal . . . with my disciples: because the prophet's message was not well received at the time, he wanted to preserve it until the future had vindicated him as God's true prophet (cf. 30:8–9).

8:18 Signs: in the meantime, while awaiting the vindication of his message, Isaiah and his children with their symbolic names stood as a reminder of God's message to Israel.

8:19 Chirp and mutter: a mocking reference to necromancers.

8:20 Surely . . . no dawn: reliance on necromancy brings futility.

8:22 Oppressive gloom . . . without light: the meaning of the Hebrew here is quite uncertain.

t: Is 30:28. *u:* Is 7:7; 17:12–14. *v:* Is 29:23; 1 Pt 3:14–15. *w:* Lk 2:34; Rom 9:32–33; 1 Pt 2:7–8. *x:* Mt 21:44. *y:* Is 2:2–5; 4:5; 11:9; 14:32; 28:16; 31:9; 33:5. *z:* Is 29:4.

The Promise of Salvation Under a New Davidic King. * 23 There is no gloom where there had been distress. Where once he degraded the land of Zebulun and the land of Naphtali, now he has glorified the way of the Sea, the land across the Jordan, Galilee of the Nations.*

CHAPTER 9

See RG 280–95

1 The people who walked in darkness
have seen a great light;
Upon those who lived in a land of gloom
a light has shone.[a]
2 You have brought them abundant joy
and great rejoicing;
They rejoice before you as people rejoice
at harvest,
as they exult when dividing the
spoils.
3 For the yoke that burdened them,
the pole on their shoulder,
The rod of their taskmaster,
you have smashed, as on the day of
Midian.* [b]
4 For every boot that tramped in battle,
every cloak rolled in blood,
will be burned as fuel for fire.[c]
5 For a child* is born to us, a son is given
to us;
upon his shoulder dominion rests.
They name him Wonder-Counselor,
God-Hero,[d]
Father-Forever, Prince of Peace.
6 His dominion is vast
and forever peaceful,
Upon David's throne, and over his
kingdom,
which he confirms and sustains
By judgment and justice,
both now and forever.[e]
The zeal of the LORD of hosts will do
this!

Judgment on the Northern Kingdom*

7 The Lord has sent a word against Jacob,
and it falls upon Israel;
8 And all the people know it—
Ephraim and those who dwell in
Samaria—
those who say in arrogance and pride
of heart,
9 "Bricks have fallen,
but we will rebuild with cut stone;
Sycamores have been felled,
but we will replace them with cedars."[f]
10 So the LORD raises up their foes against
them
and stirs up their enemies to action—
11 Aram* from the east and the Philistines
from the west—

8:23–9:6 The meaning of 8:23 is somewhat uncertain, for example, whether the expressions translated "once" and "now" refer to times or to individuals, and also whether the verbs speak of degrading and glorifying the territories. If this traditional translation is correct, the passage would seem to promise the former Northern Kingdom of Israel deliverance from the Assyrians and might relate to Hezekiah's program of trying to reincorporate the northern territories into the kingdom of Judah and thus restore the boundaries of the country as it was under David.

8:23 The territories mentioned in this verse are those which the Assyrian king Tiglath-pileser III took from Israel and incorporated into the Assyrian provincial system as a result of the Syro-Ephraimite War of 735–732 B.C. (2 Kgs 15:29). **Zebulun . . . Naphtali**: regions of the former Northern Kingdom of Israel. **The way of the Sea**: the area along the Mediterranean coast south of Mount Carmel which became the Assyrian province of Dor. **Land across the Jordan**: the province of Gilead east of the Jordan. **Galilee of the Nations**: the territory north of Mount Carmel which was incorporated in the Assyrian province of Megiddo. Galilee apparently had a large non-Israelite population. Mt 4:15–16 cites this verse in the context of the beginning of Jesus' public mission in Galilee.

9:3 Day of Midian: when God used the judge Gideon to deliver these northern territories from Midianite oppression (Jgs 6–7).

9:5 A child: perhaps to be identified with the Emmanuel of 7:14 and 8:8; cf. 11:1–2, 9. This verse may reflect a coronation rather than a birth. **Upon his shoulder**: the reference may be to a particular act in the ritual in which a symbol of the king's authority was placed on his shoulder (cf. 2 Kgs 11:12; Is 22:22).

9:7–20 + 5:25–30 These verses describe a series of judgments God sent against the Northern Kingdom of Israel because of its sins. Despite the judgments, however, Israel continued to rebel, and God's anger remained unabated, as the recurring refrain emphasizes (9:11, 16, 20). The refrain ties Is 9:7–20 together as a unit, but 9:20 is far too abrupt to be the original conclusion to the oracle. With its series of past judgments and repeated refrain, the oracle resembles Am 4:6–12; by analogy with that model one expects a conclusion in which the prophet turns from the narration of past judgments to the announcement of a future judgment. Is 5:25–30 fits the pattern found in 9:7–20 and provides a suitable and possibly original conclusion for the whole oracle.

9:11 Aram: the Syrian kingdom, with its capital at Damascus.

a: Mt 4:15–16. *b:* Is 10:26; Jgs 7:22–25. *c:* Ps 46:10. *d:* Is 10:21. *e:* Jer 23:5; Lk 1:32–33. *f:* Mal 1:4.

they devour Israel with open mouth.
For all this, his wrath is not turned back,
and his hand is still outstretched!
12 The people do not turn back to the one who struck them,
nor do they seek the LORD of hosts.
13 So the LORD cuts off from Israel head and tail,
palm branch and reed in one day.[g]
14 (The elder and the noble are the head,
the prophet who teaches falsehood is the tail.)[h]
15 Those who lead this people lead them astray,
and those who are led are swallowed up.[i]
16 That is why the Lord does not spare their young men,
and their orphans and widows he does not pity;
For they are totally impious and wicked,
and every mouth speaks folly.
For all this, his wrath is not turned back,
his hand is still outstretched!
17 For wickedness burns like fire,
devouring brier and thorn;
It kindles the forest thickets,
which go up in columns of smoke.[j]
18 At the wrath of the LORD of hosts the land quakes,
and the people are like fuel for fire;
no one spares his brother.[k]
19 They hack on the right, but remain hungry;
they devour on the left, but are not filled.
Each devours the flesh of the neighbor;
20 Manasseh devours Ephraim,* and Ephraim Manasseh,
together they turn on Judah.
For all this, his wrath is not turned back,
his hand is still outstretched!

CHAPTER 10

See RG 280–95

Perversion of Justice

1 * Ah! Those who enact unjust statutes,
who write oppressive decrees,[l]
2 Depriving the needy of judgment,
robbing my people's poor of justice,
Making widows their plunder,
and orphans their prey![m]
3 What will you do on the day of punishment,
when the storm comes from afar?
To whom will you flee for help?
Where will you leave your wealth,
4 Lest it sink beneath the captive
or fall beneath the slain?
For all this, his wrath is not turned back,
his hand is still outstretched!*

Judgment on Assyria

5 * Ah! Assyria, the rod of my wrath,
the staff I wield in anger.[n]
6 Against an impious nation* I send him,
and against a people under my wrath I order him
To seize plunder, carry off loot,
and to trample them like the mud of the street.
7 But this is not what he intends,
nor does he have this in mind;
Rather, it is in his heart to destroy,
to make an end of not a few nations.
8 For he says, "Are not my commanders all kings?"
9 * "Is not Calno like Carchemish,
Or Hamath like Arpad,
or Samaria like Damascus?

9:20 Manasseh . . . Ephraim: two of the leading tribes of the Northern Kingdom. The reference is to the civil wars that marked the final decades of the Northern Kingdom (2 Kgs 15:10, 14–16, 25; cf. Hos 7:3–7).

10:1–4 This is another *hoy*-oracle; cf. note on 5:8–24. It may originally have been part of the collection at 5:8–24.

10:4 For all this . . . outstretched!: this refrain appears to be out of place here; cf. 9:11, 16, 20.

10:5–34 These verses contain a series of oracles directed against Assyria. Verses 5–15 portray Assyria as simply the rod God uses to punish Israel, though Assyria does not realize this. The original conclusion to this unit may be the judgment found in vv. 24–27a, which continues the imagery and motifs found in vv. 5–15. Verses 16–23, because of the quite different imagery and motifs, may originally have been an insertion directed against Aram and Israel at the time of the Syro-Ephraimite War.

10:6 Impious nation: Judah. It was God's intention to use Assyria merely to punish, not to destroy, the nation.

10:9–10 The cities mentioned were all cities captured,

g: Is 19:15; Dt 28:13, 44. *h:* Is 28:7. *i:* Is 3:12. *j:* Is 5:24; 33:11–12. *k:* Is 3:5. *l:* Jer 8:8. *m:* Is 1:23; 3:14–15. *n:* Jer 51:20–23.

10 Just as my hand reached out to idolatrous
kingdoms
that had more images than Jerusalem
and Samaria—
11 Just as I treated Samaria and her idols,
shall I not do to Jerusalem and her
graven images?"

12 But when the LORD has brought to an end all his work on Mount Zion and in Jerusalem,

I will punish the utterance
of the king of Assyria's proud heart,
and the boastfulness of his haughty
eyes.
13 For he says:
"By my own power I have done it,
and by my wisdom, for I am shrewd.
I have moved the boundaries of peoples,
their treasures I have pillaged,
and, like a mighty one, I have brought
down the enthroned.
14 My hand has seized, like a nest,
the wealth of nations.
As one takes eggs left alone,
so I took in all the earth;
No one fluttered a wing,
or opened a mouth, or chirped!"
15 Will the ax boast against the one who
hews with it?
Will the saw exalt itself above the one
who wields it?
As if a rod could sway the one who lifts
it,
or a staff could lift the one who is not
wood!
16 Therefore the Lord, the LORD of hosts,
will send leanness among his fat ones,*
And under his glory there will be a
kindling
like the kindling of fire.[o]
17 The Light of Israel will become a fire,
the Holy One, a flame,
That burns and consumes its briers
and its thorns in a single day.[p]
18 And the glory of its forests and orchards
will be consumed, soul and body,
and it will be like a sick man who
wastes away.
19 And the remnant of the trees in his forest
will be so few,
that any child can record them.
20 On that day
The remnant of Israel,
the survivors of the house of Jacob,
will no more lean upon the one who
struck them;
But they will lean upon the LORD,
the Holy One of Israel, in truth.
21 A remnant will return,* the remnant of
Jacob,
to the mighty God.
22 Though your people, O Israel,
were like the sand of the sea,[q]
Only a remnant of them will return;
their destruction is decreed,
as overflowing justice demands.[r]

23 For the Lord, the GOD of hosts, is about to carry out the destruction decreed in the midst of the whole land.[s]

24* Therefore thus says the Lord, the GOD of hosts: My people, who dwell in Zion, do not fear the Assyrian, though he strikes you with a rod, and raises his staff against you as did the Egyptians.
25 For just a brief moment more, and my wrath shall be over, and my anger shall be set for their destruction.
26 Then the LORD of hosts will raise against them a scourge such as struck Midian at the rock of Oreb;[t] and he will raise his staff over the sea as he did in Egypt.[u]
27 On that day,

His burden shall be taken from your
shoulder,
and his yoke shattered from your
neck.[v]

some more than once, by the Assyrians in the eighth century B.C. Verse 9 suggests a certain historical order in the fall of these cities, and v. 10 suggests that all of them had fallen before Samaria (cf. Am 6:2). That implies that one should think primarily of events during the reign of Tiglath-pileser III (745–727).

10:16 His fat ones: the strong men of the enemy army.

10:21 A remnant will return: in Hebrew, *shear-jashub*, an allusion to the name of Isaiah's son, Shear-jashub; cf. 7:3.

10:24 This verse with its reference to Assyria's rod may introduce the original conclusion to vv. 5–15.

10:27b–32 A poetic description of the march of an enemy

o: Is 17:4. *p:* Is 9:17–18; 30:27–33; 31:9; 33:14. *q:* Hos 2:1; Rom 9:27–28. *r:* Is 28:16–18. *s:* Is 28:22. *t:* Is 9:3; Jgs 7:25. *u:* Ex 14:16. *v:* Is 9:3.

*The March of an Enemy Army**

He has come up from Rimmon,
28 he has reached Aiath, passed through Migron,
at Michmash he has stored his supplies.
29 He has crossed the ravine,
at Geba he has camped for the night.
Ramah trembles,
Gibeah of Saul has fled.
30 Cry and shriek, Bath-Gallim!
Hearken, Laishah! Answer her, Anathoth!
31 Madmenah is in flight,
the inhabitants of Gebim seek refuge.
32 Even today he will halt at Nob,
he will shake his fist at the mount of daughter Zion,
the hill of Jerusalem!
33 * Now the Lord, the LORD of hosts,
is about to lop off the boughs with terrible violence;
The tall of stature shall be felled,
and the lofty ones shall be brought low;
34 He shall hack down the forest thickets with an ax,
and Lebanon in its splendor shall fall.

See RG 280–95

CHAPTER 11*

*The Ideal Davidic King**

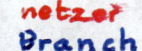

1 But a shoot shall sprout from the stump* of Jesse,
and from his roots a bud shall blossom.[w]
2 * The spirit of the LORD shall rest upon him:[x]
a spirit of wisdom and of understanding,
A spirit of counsel and of strength,
a spirit of knowledge and of fear of the LORD,
3 and his delight shall be the fear of the LORD.
Not by appearance shall he judge,
nor by hearsay shall he decide,
4 But he shall judge the poor with justice,
and decide fairly for the land's afflicted.[y]
He shall strike the ruthless with the rod of his mouth,
and with the breath of his lips he shall slay the wicked.[z]
5 Justice shall be the band around his waist,
and faithfulness a belt upon his hips.[a]
6 * Then the wolf shall be a guest of the lamb,
and the leopard shall lie down with the young goat;
The calf and the young lion shall browse together,
with a little child to guide them.[b]
7 The cow and the bear shall graze,
together their young shall lie down;
the lion shall eat hay like the ox.[c]

army from the north, advancing south to the very gates of Jerusalem, where the enemy waves his hand in a gesture of derision against the city. Though Sennacherib's troops took a different route, advancing down the coast and then approaching Jerusalem from the southeast, the arrogant attitude toward God's chosen city was the same. **Aiath**: the Ai of Jos 7:22–8:29. **Migron**: modern Makrun north of Michmash. **The ravine**: the deep valley between Michmash and Geba (cf. 1 Sm 14:1–5). **Ramah . . . Gibeah . . . Bath-Gallim . . . Laishah . . . Anathoth . . . Madmenah . . . Gebim**: cities north of Jerusalem threatened by the sudden appearance of this enemy army. **Nob**: probably to be identified with the present Mount Scopus from where one has a clear view of Jerusalem.

10:33–34 Just when the enemy is about to capture Jerusalem, God intervenes and destroys the hostile army. Cf. 29:1–8; 31:4–9.

11:1–16 Isaiah 11 contains a prophecy of the rise of a new Davidic king who will embody the ancient ideal of Davidic kingship (vv. 1–9), an elaboration of that prophecy in a further description of that king's rule (v. 10), and a prophecy of God's deliverance of the chosen people from exile and cessation of enmities (vv. 11–16).

11:1–9 (10) Here Isaiah looks forward to a new Davidide who will realize the ancient ideals (see Ps 72). The oracle does not seem to have a particular historical person in mind.

11:1 Shoot . . . stump: the imagery suggests the bankruptcy of the monarchy as embodied in the historical kings, along with the need for a new beginning, to spring from the very origin from which David and his dynasty arose. **Jesse**: David's father (cf. 1 Sm 16:1–13).

11:2–3 The source of the traditional names of the gifts of the Holy Spirit. The Septuagint and the Vulgate read "piety" for "fear of the Lord" in its first occurrence, thus listing seven gifts.

11:6–9 This picture of the idyllic harmony of paradise is a dramatic symbol of universal peace and justice under the rule of the new Davidic king. The peace and harmony even among carnivores and their natural prey in this description suggest a paradisiac aspect of the reign of the new king.

w: Is 4:2; 53:2; Jer 23:5–6; 33:14–16; Zec 3:8; 6:12; Rev 22:16. *x:* Is 42:1; 1 Sm 16:13; Mt 3:16; Mk 1:10; Jn 1:32. *y:* Ps 72:2, 4; 98:9. *z:* 2 Thes 2:8; Rev 2:16. *a:* Eph 6:14. *b:* Hos 2:20. *c:* Is 65:25.

8 The baby shall play by the viper's den,
and the child lay his hand on the
adder's lair.
9 They shall not harm or destroy on all my
holy mountain;
for the earth shall be filled with
knowledge of the LORD,
as water covers the sea.

*Restoration**

10 On that day,
The root of Jesse,
set up as a signal for the peoples—
Him the nations will seek out;
his dwelling shall be glorious.[d]
11 On that day,
The Lord shall again take it in hand
to reclaim the remnant of his people
that is left from Assyria and Egypt,
Pathros, Ethiopia, and Elam,
Shinar, Hamath, and the isles of the
sea.[e]
12 He shall raise a signal to the nations[f]
and gather the outcasts of Israel;
The dispersed of Judah he shall assemble
from the four corners of the earth.
13 The envy of Ephraim shall pass away,
and those hostile to Judah shall be cut
off;
Ephraim shall not envy Judah,
and Judah shall not be hostile to
Ephraim;
14 But they shall swoop down on the
foothills
of the Philistines to the west,
together they shall plunder the people
of the east;*
Edom and Moab shall be their
possessions,
and the Ammonites their subjects.
15 The LORD shall dry up the tongue* of the
Sea of Egypt,
and wave his hand over the Euphrates
with his fierce wind,
And divide it into seven streamlets,
so that it can be crossed in sandals.[g]
16 There shall be a highway for the remnant
of his people
that is left from Assyria,
As there was for Israel
when it came up from the land of
Egypt.[h]

CHAPTER 12

See RG 280–95

*Song of Thanksgiving**

1 On that day, you will say:
I give you thanks, O LORD;
though you have been angry with me,
your anger has abated, and you have
consoled me.
2 God indeed is my salvation;
I am confident and unafraid.
For the LORD is my strength and my
might,
and he has been my salvation.[i]
3 With joy you will draw water
from the fountains of salvation,[j]
4 And you will say on that day:
give thanks to the LORD, acclaim his
name;
Among the nations make known his
deeds,
proclaim how exalted is his name.[k]
5 Sing praise to the LORD for he has done
glorious things;
let this be known throughout all the
earth.[l]
6 Shout with exultation, City of Zion,
for great in your midst
is the Holy One of Israel![m]

11:10–16 This passage, with its reference to God's people in widely scattered lands, is probably from a much later period. God will restore them to their own land. The reconciliation of Ephraim (i.e., the Northern Kingdom) and Judah reverses what Isaiah saw as a disastrous event of the past (cf. 7:17). God's action is likened to a new exodus, analogous to the time God first acquired Israel in bringing them out of the land of Egypt. **Pathros**: upper Egypt. **Elam**: east of Babylonia. **Shinar**: Babylonia. **Hamath**: on the Orontes River in Syria. **Isles**: or coastlands, in the Mediterranean.

11:14 People of the east: tribes in the Arabian Desert (cf. Jgs 6:3, 33; 7:12).

11:15 Tongue: perhaps to be identified with the Gulf of Suez.

12:1–6 Israel's thanksgiving to the Lord, expressed in language like that of the Psalms.

d: Is 2:2–4; Rom 15:12. *e:* Ex 3:20; Jer 23:7–8; 31:1–22; Zec 10:10. *f:* Is 18:3. *g:* Zec 10:11; Rev 16:12. *h:* Is 51:10; Ex 14:29. *i:* Ex 15:2; Ps 118:14. *j:* Jgs 5:11; Jer 2:13; Jn 4:10, 14. *k:* Ps 105:1; 148:13. *l:* Is 11:9; Ex 15:1. *m:* Is 52:8–9; 54:1; Zep 3:14–15.

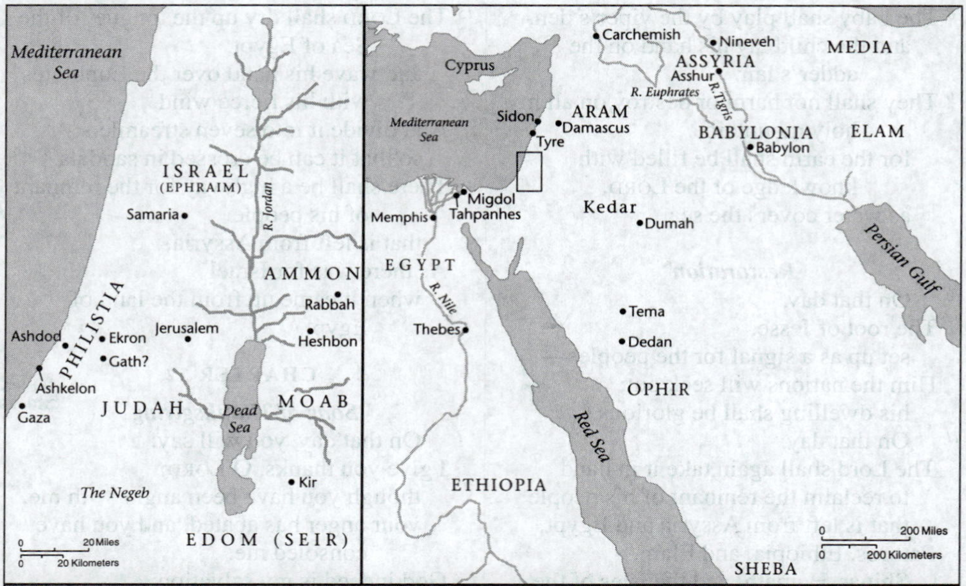

Places Mentioned in the Oracles against the Nations

C. Oracles Against the Foreign Nations*

CHAPTER 13

See RG 280–95

*Babylon.** [1] An oracle* concerning Babylon; a vision of Isaiah, son of Amoz.

[2] Upon the bare mountains set up a signal;
cry out to them,*
Beckon for them to enter
the gates of the nobles.[n]
[3] I have commanded my consecrated
ones,*
I have summoned my warriors,
eager and bold to carry out my anger.[o]
[4] Listen! the rumble on the mountains:
that of an immense throng!
Listen! the noise of kingdoms, nations
assembled!
The LORD of hosts is mustering
an army for battle.[p]
[5] They come from a far-off country,
and from the end of the heavens,
The LORD and the instruments of his
wrath,
to destroy all the land.
[6] Howl, for the day of the LORD* is near;
as destruction from the Almighty it
comes.[q]

13:1–23:18 These chapters, which probably existed at one time as an independent collection, consist primarily of oracles from various sources against foreign nations. While some of the material is Isaianic, in many cases it has been reworked by later editors or writers.

13:1–22 Although attributed to Isaiah (v. 1), this oracle does not reflect conditions of Isaiah's time. Babylon did not achieve imperial status until a century later, after its victory over Assyria in 609 B.C. The mention of the Medes (v. 17) rather than Persia suggests a date prior to 550 B.C., when the Median empire of Astyages fell to Cyrus the Persian. Tension is created in that the attackers are not named until v. 17 and the foe to be attacked until v. 19.

13:1 Oracle: Heb. *massa'*; used eight more times in this collection.

13:2 To them: the Medes (v. 17), who are being summoned to destroy Babylon. **Gates of the nobles**: the reference is apparently to the gates of Babylon and involves a wordplay on the city name (Babylon = *bab ilani*, "gate of the gods").

13:3 Consecrated ones: in the sense that they will wage a "holy war" and carry out God's plan.

13:6–8 Day of the LORD: described often in prophetic writings, it generally signified the coming of the Lord in

n: Is 5:26; Jer 50:2. *o:* Jl 4:9. *p:* Jer 50:9. *q:* Is 2:12–21; Jer 46:10; Am 5:18–20; Jl 1:15; Zep 1:7; Rev 6:17.

7 Therefore all hands fall helpless,[r]
every human heart melts,
8 and they are terrified,
Pangs and sorrows take hold of them,
like a woman in labor they writhe;
They look aghast at each other,
their faces aflame.[s]
9 Indeed, the day of the LORD comes,
cruel, with wrath and burning anger;
To lay waste the land
and destroy the sinners within it![t]
10 The stars of the heavens and their
constellations
will send forth no light;
The sun will be dark at its rising,
and the moon will not give its light.[u]
11 Thus I will punish the world for its evil
and the wicked for their guilt.
I will put an end to the pride of the
arrogant,
the insolence of tyrants I will humble.[v]
12 I will make mortals more rare than pure
gold,
human beings, than the gold of Ophir.* [w]
13 For this I will make the heavens tremble
and the earth shall be shaken from its
place,
At the wrath of the LORD of hosts
on the day of his burning anger.[x]
14 Like a hunted gazelle,
or a flock that no one gathers,
They shall turn each to their own people
and flee each to their own land.[y]
15 Everyone who is taken shall be run
through;
and everyone who is caught shall fall
by the sword.
16 Their infants shall be dashed to pieces in
their sight;
their houses shall be plundered
and their wives ravished.[z]
17 I am stirring up against them the Medes,
who think nothing of silver
and take no delight in gold.[a]
18 With their bows they shall shatter the
young men,
And the fruit of the womb they shall not
spare,
nor shall their eye take pity on
children.
19 And Babylon, the jewel of kingdoms,
the glory and pride of the Chaldeans,
Shall become like Sodom and Gomorrah,
overthrown by God.[b]
20 It shall never be inhabited,
nor dwelt in, from age to age;
Arabians shall not pitch their tents there,
nor shepherds rest their flocks there.[c]
21 But desert demons shall rest there
and owls shall fill the houses;
There ostriches shall dwell,
and satyrs* shall dance.[d]
22 Wild dogs shall dwell in its castles,
and jackals in its luxurious palaces.
Its time is near at hand
and its days shall not be prolonged.[e]

CHAPTER 14

See RG 280–95

Restoration of Israel. 1 But the LORD
will take pity on Jacob and again choose Israel, and will settle them on their own land;
foreigners will join them and attach themselves to the house of Jacob.[f] 2 The nations
will take them and bring them to their place,
and the house of Israel will possess them* as
male and female slaves on the Lord's land;
they will take captive their captors and rule
over their oppressors.[g]

Downfall of the King of Babylon. 3 On the
day when the LORD gives you rest from your
sorrow and turmoil, from the hard service
with which you served,[h] 4 you will take up

power and majesty to destroy his enemies. The figures used convey the idea of horror and destruction (Am 5:18–20). **The Almighty**: Heb. *shaddai*; there is a play on words between destruction (*shod*) and Shaddai, a title for God traditionally rendered as "the Almighty" (cf. Gn 17:1; Ex 6:3).

13:12 Ophir: cf. note on Ps 45:10.

13:21 Satyrs: in the popular mind, demons of goatlike form dwelling in ruins, symbols of immorality; cf. Lv 17:7; Is 34:14.

14:2 Possess them: Israel will make slaves of the nations who escort it back to its land.

r: Jer 6:24; Ez 7:17. *s:* Is 21:3; Ps 48:7; Mi 4:9. *t:* Jer 4:7; 18:16; Mal 3:19. *u:* Is 24:23; Jer 4:23; Zep 1:15; Mt 24:29. *v:* Is 2:17; Jer 50:32. *w:* 1 Kgs 9:28; Jb 22:24. *x:* Hg 2:6; Lam 1:12. *y:* 1 Kgs 22:17; Jer 50:16; 51:9. *z:* 2 Kgs 8:12; Ps 137:9; Na 3:10. *a:* Is 21:2; Jer 51:11, 28. *b:* Dt 29:22; Is 1:7; Jer 49:18; 50:40; Am 4:11. *c:* Jer 51:62. *d:* Is 34:13–14; 35:7. *e:* Ez 32:23. *f:* Is 56:3; 60:4; Ps 102:14; Jer 24:6; Zec 1:17. *g:* Is 49:22–23; 60:14; 66:20. *h:* Ex 33:14; Jos 1:13; Jer 30:10.

this taunt-song* against the king of Babylon:[i]

How the oppressor has come to an end!
how the turmoil has ended!
5 The LORD has broken the rod of the wicked,
the staff of the tyrants[j]
6 That struck the peoples in wrath
with relentless blows;
That ruled the nations in anger,
with boundless persecution.[k]
7 The whole earth rests peacefully,
song breaks forth;
8 The very cypresses rejoice over you,
the cedars of Lebanon:
"Now that you are laid to rest,
no one comes to cut us down."[l]
9 Below, Sheol is all astir
preparing for your coming;
Awakening the shades to greet you,
all the leaders of the earth;
Making all the kings of the nations
rise from their thrones.
10 All of them speak out
and say to you,
"You too have become weak like us,
you are just like us!
11 Down to Sheol your pomp is brought,
the sound of your harps.
Maggots are the couch beneath you,
worms your blanket."[m]
12 How you have fallen from the heavens,
O Morning Star,* son of the dawn!
How you have been cut down to the earth,
you who conquered nations![n]
13 In your heart you said:
"I will scale the heavens;
Above the stars of God*
I will set up my throne;
I will take my seat on the Mount of Assembly,
on the heights of Zaphon.[o]
14 I will ascend above the tops of the clouds;
I will be like the Most High!"[p]
15 No! Down to Sheol you will be brought
to the depths of the pit![q]
16 When they see you they will stare,
pondering over you:
"Is this the man who made the earth tremble,
who shook kingdoms?
17 Who made the world a wilderness,
razed its cities,
and gave captives no release?"
18 All the kings of the nations lie in glory,
each in his own tomb;[r]
19 But you are cast forth without burial,
like loathsome carrion,
Covered with the slain, with those struck by the sword,
a trampled corpse,
Going down to the very stones of the pit.[s]
20 You will never be together with them in the grave,
For you have ruined your land,
you have slain your people!
Let him never be named,
that offshoot of evil!
21 Make ready to slaughter his sons
for the guilt of their fathers;[t]
Lest they rise and possess the earth,

14:4–21 This taunt-song, a satirical funeral lament, is a beautiful example of classical Hebrew poetry. According to the prose introduction and the prosaic conclusion (vv. 22–23), it is directed against the king of Babylon, though Babylon is mentioned nowhere in the song itself. If the reference to Babylon is accurate, the piece was composed long after the time of Isaiah, for Babylon was not a threat to Judah in the eighth century. Some have argued that Isaiah wrote it at the death of an Assyrian king and the references to Babylon were made by a later editor, but this is far from certain.

14:12 Morning Star: term addressed to the king of Babylon. The Vulgate translates as "Lucifer," a name applied by the church Fathers to Satan. **Son of the dawn**: Heb., *ben shahar*, may reflect the name of a pagan deity.

14:13–15 God: not Elohim, the common word for God, but El, the name of the head of the pantheon in Canaanite mythology, a god who was early identified with the Lord in Israelite thought. **Mount of Assembly**: mountain where the council of the gods met, according to Canaanite mythology. **Zaphon**: the sacred mountain of Baal, originally the Jebel el-Aqra north of Ugarit, but other mountains have been identified with it, including Mount Zion in Jerusalem (Ps 48:3). The attempt to usurp the place of God (v. 14), coupled with the dramatic reversal ("above the stars of God" to "the depths of the pit") occasioned the interpretation that saw here the rebellion and fall of Satan.

i: Hb 2:6. *j:* Is 10:24–27. *k:* Is 10:5–7. *l:* Is 37:24; 44:23; 55:12; Ez 31:16. *m:* Sir 10:11. *n:* Jb 14:10. *o:* Jer 51:53; Am 9:2. *p:* Ez 28:2; Zep 2:15; 2 Thes 2:4. *q:* Ez 28:8–9; 32:23; Mt 11:23; Acts 12:23. *r:* Jb 3:14–15. *s:* Is 66:24. *t:* Ex 20:5; Mt 23:35.

and fill the breadth of the world with
cities.*

22 I will rise up against them, says the
LORD of hosts, and cut off from Babylon
name and remnant, progeny and offspring,
says the LORD.[u] 23 I will make it a haunt of
hoot owls and a marshland; I will sweep it
with the broom of destruction, oracle of the
LORD of hosts.

*God's Plan for Assyria**

24 The LORD of hosts has sworn:
As I have resolved,
so shall it be;
As I have planned,
so shall it stand:
25 To break the Assyrian in my land
and trample him on my mountains;
Then his yoke shall be removed from
them,
and his burden from their shoulder.[v]
26 This is the plan proposed for the whole
earth,
and this the hand outstretched over all
the nations.*
27 The LORD of hosts has planned;
who can thwart him?
His hand is stretched out;
who can turn it back?[w]

Philistia.* 28 In the year that King Ahaz
died,* there came this oracle:

29 * Do not rejoice, Philistia, not one of you,
that the rod which struck you is broken;
For out of the serpent's root shall come
an adder,
its offspring shall be a flying saraph.
30 In my pastures the poor shall graze,
and the needy lie down in safety;
But I will kill your root with famine
that shall slay even your remnant.
31 Howl, O gate; cry out, O city!
Philistia, all of you melts away!
For there comes a smoke from the north,*
without a straggler in its ranks.
32 What will one answer the messengers of
the nations?*
"The LORD has established Zion,
and in her the afflicted of his people
find refuge."

CHAPTER 15

See RG 280–95

*Moab**

1 Oracle on Moab:
Laid waste in a night,
Ar of Moab is destroyed;
Laid waste in a night,
Kir of Moab is destroyed.
2 Daughter Dibon has gone up
to the high places to weep;
Over Nebo and over Medeba
Moab is wailing.
Every head is shaved,
every beard sheared off.* [x]

14:21 Cities: if the text is correct, it presumably refers to cities as expressions of human pride, authority, and oppression (cf. Gn 11:1–9; Na 3:1–4).

14:24–27 The motif of God's plan or work is a recurring thread running through Isaiah's oracles. The plans of Judah's enemies will not come to pass (7:5–7; 8:9–10; 10:7), but God's plan for his work of disciplining his own people (5:12, 19; 28:21), and then for punishing the foreign agents God used to administer that discipline (10:12) will come to pass.

14:26 Hand outstretched over all the nations: as it was once outstretched over Israel (9:11, 16, 20; 5:25).

14:28–31 This oracle seems to reflect the political situation soon after the death of Ahaz in 715 B.C., when Ashdod and the other Philistine cities were trying to create a united front to rebel against Assyria. Ahaz had refused to join the rebels in 735 B.C. and remained loyal to Assyria during the rest of his reign, but the Philistines may have had higher hopes for his son Hezekiah. Judah, however, did not join in Ashdod's disastrous revolt in 713–711 B.C. (cf. 20:1).

14:28 The year that King Ahaz died: 715 B.C.

14:29 The occasion for this oracle is usually taken to be the death of an Assyrian king; the Philistines were vassals of Assyria, whereas no victories of Ahaz over the Philistines are recorded. The chronological notice (*in the year that King Ahaz died*) may be incorrect, for no Assyrian king died around 715, the date usually assigned for the death of Ahaz. **Flying saraph**: a winged cobra, often portrayed in Egyptian art and on Israelite seals. The Hebrew *saraph* means "to burn" and perhaps is applied to the cobra because of the burning sensation of its bite.

14:31 Smoke from the north: the dust raised from the approach of the Assyrian army.

14:32 Messengers of the nations: envoys from Philistia, and from Egypt and Ethiopia, the real powers behind the Philistine revolt (20:1–6; cf. 18:1–2).

15:1–16:14 Both the historical situation reflected in this oracle against Moab and the date of composition are uncertain. Variants of the same poem are found in Jer 48, and there are connections with Nm 21:27–30 as well.

15:2 Shaved . . . sheared off: traditional signs of grief.

u: Jer 51:62; Jb 18:19. *v:* Is 9:3; 10:27a. *w:* Is 23:8–9; Jb 40:8; Jer 4:28. *x:* Jer 48:37; Ez 7:18; Am 8:10.

3 In the streets they wear sackcloth,
and on the rooftops;
In the squares
everyone wails, streaming with tears.[y]
4 Heshbon and Elealeh cry out,
they are heard as far as Jahaz.
At this the loins of Moab tremble,
his soul quivers within him;[z]
5 My heart cries out for Moab,
his fugitives reach Zoar,
Eglath-shelishiyah:
The ascent of Luhith
they ascend weeping;
On the way to Horonaim
they utter rending cries;[a]
6 The waters of Nimrim
have become a waste,
The grass is withered,
new growth is gone,
nothing is green.
7 So now whatever they have acquired or stored away
they carry across the Wadi of the Poplars.
8 The cry has gone round
the territory of Moab;
As far as Eglaim his wailing,
even at Beer-elim his wailing.
9 * The waters of Dimon are filled with blood,
but I will bring still more upon Dimon:
Lions for those who are fleeing from Moab
and for those who remain in the land!

CHAPTER 16

See RG 280–95

1 Send them forth,* hugging the earth like reptiles,
from Sela across the desert,
to the mount of daughter Zion.
2 Like flushed birds,
like scattered nestlings,
Are the daughters of Moab
at the fords of the Arnon.* [b]
3 * Offer counsel, take their part;
at high noon make your shade like the night;
Hide the outcasts,
do not betray the fugitives.
4 Let the outcasts of Moab live with you,
be their shelter from the destroyer.
When there is an end to the oppressor,
when destruction has ceased,
and the marauders have vanished from the land,
5 A throne shall be set up in mercy,
and on it shall sit in fidelity,
in David's tent,
A judge upholding right,
prompt to do justice.[c]
6 We have heard of the pride of Moab,
how very proud he is,
Of his haughtiness, pride, and arrogance
that his empty words do not match.[d]
7 * Therefore let Moab wail,
let everyone wail for Moab;
For the raisin cakes* of Kir-hareseth
let them sigh, stricken with grief.
8 The terraced slopes of Heshbon languish,
the vines of Sibmah,
Whose clusters once overpowered
the lords of nations,
Reaching as far as Jazer
winding through the wilderness,*
Whose branches spread forth,
crossing over the sea.
9 Therefore I weep with Jazer
for the vines of Sibmah;
I drench you with my tears,
Heshbon and Elealeh;

15:9 There is a play on words between "Dimon" and *dam*, the Hebrew word for blood.

16:1 Send them forth: the Hebrew text is disturbed; it could also be understood to refer to tribute (a lamb) sent from Moab to Zion, presumably to encourage the king to receive the Moabite refugees.

16:2 The Arnon: principal river of Moab.

16:3–5 Directed to Jerusalem, which should receive the suffering Moabites with mercy, as befits the city of David's family, who were partly descended from Ruth the Moabite; and cf. 1 Sm 22:3–4. This would be a gracious act on Judah's part, since its relations with Moab were strained at best.

16:7–14 Moab had been prosperous; now it has become a desert.

16:7 Raisin cakes: masses of dried compressed grapes used as food (cf. 2 Sm 6:19; 1 Chr 16:3; Sg 2:5), and also in the worship of other gods (Hos 3:1).

16:8 Wilderness: i.e., eastward. **Sea**: i.e., westward.

y: Is 22:12; Jer 48:38. *z:* Jer 48:34. *a:* Jer 48:5, 34. *b:* Nm 21:13. *c:* Is 9:6; 11:3–4; 32:1; Jer 23:5; Ps 89:14; Prv 20:28. *d:* Jer 48:29–30.

For on your summer fruits and harvests
the battle cry* has fallen.[e]
10 From the orchards are taken away
joy and gladness,
In the vineyards there is no singing,
no shout of joy;
In the wine presses no one treads grapes,
the vintage shout is stilled.[f]
11 Therefore for Moab
my heart moans like a lyre,
my inmost being for Kir-hareseth.[g]
12 * When Moab wears himself out on the
high places,
and enters his sanctuary to pray,
it shall avail him nothing.[h]

13* That is the word the LORD spoke
against Moab in times past. 14But now the
LORD speaks: In three years, like the years of
a hired laborer, the glory of Moab shall be
empty despite all its great multitude; and the
remnant shall be very small and weak.[i]

See RG 280–95

CHAPTER 17

Damascus

1 Oracle on Damascus:*
See, Damascus shall cease to be a city
and become a pile of ruins;[j]
2 Her cities shall be forever abandoned,
for flocks to lie in undisturbed.
3 The fortress shall vanish from Ephraim*
and dominion from Damascus;
The remnant of Aram shall become like
the glory
of the Israelites—
oracle of the LORD of hosts.
4 On that day
The glory of Jacob shall fade,
and his full body shall grow thin.[k]
5 Like the reaper's mere armful of stalks,
when he gathers the standing grain;
Or as when one gleans the ears
in the Valley of Rephaim.*
6 * Only gleanings shall be left in it,
as when an olive tree has been beaten—
Two or three olives at the very top,
four or five on its most fruitful
branches—
oracle of the LORD, the God of Israel.[l]
7 On that day people shall turn to their
maker,
their eyes shall look to the Holy One
of Israel.[m]
8 They shall not turn to the altars, the work
of their hands,
nor shall they look to what their
fingers have made:
the asherahs* or the incense stands.
9 On that day his strong cities shall be
like those abandoned by the Hivites
and Amorites
When faced with the Israelites;
and there shall be desolation.[n]
10 Truly, you have forgotten the God who
saves you,
the Rock, your refuge, you have not
remembered.[o]
Therefore, though you plant plants for
the Pleasant One,*
and set out cuttings for a foreign one,[p]

16:9–10 Battle cry . . . shout of joy: the same Hebrew word (*hedad*), which normally refers to the joyful shout of those treading the grapes (cf. Jer 25:30), here is used both for the triumphant shout of the enemy (v. 9) and for the vintagers' shout, which has ceased.

16:12 In vain do the Moabites appeal to their god Chemosh.

16:13–14 A prose application of the preceding poetic oracle against Moab (15:1–16:12); cf. Jer 4:8. **Like the years of a hired laborer**: the fixed period of time for which the hired laborer contracted his services; cf. Is 21:16.

17:1 Damascus: capital of Aram or Syria, conquered by Tiglath-pileser III at the end of the Syro-Ephraimite War in 732 B.C.

17:3 Ephraim: Israel, leagued with Aram against Judah in the Syro-Ephraimite War. Assyria ravaged and captured most of Israelite territory in 734–733 B.C. **Like the glory of the Israelites**: the remnant of Aram will be no more impressive than the pitiful remnant of the Northern Kingdom.

17:5 Valley of Rephaim: a fertile plain just to the southwest of Jerusalem (cf. Jos 15:8; 2 Sm 5:18). Since it was near a large population center, the fields there would be thoroughly gleaned by the poor after the harvest, leaving very few ears of grain.

17:6 Olives not easily picked by hand were knocked from the tree by means of a long stick; cf. 24:13.

17:8 Asherahs: see note on Ex 34:13. **Incense stands**: small altars on which incense was burned; cf. Is 27:9; Lv 26:30.

17:10 The Pleasant One: an epithet for a foreign god of fertility, probably Adonis, in whose honor saplings were planted.

17:12 Many peoples: the hordes that accompanied the in-

e: Is 15:5; Jer 48:32. *f:* Is 24:8. *g:* Is 15:5; Jer 48:36. *h:* Jer 48:13. *i:* Dt 15:18. *j:* 2 Kgs 16:9; Jer 49:23; Am 1:3; Zec 9:1. *k:* Is 10:16. *l:* Is 24:13. *m:* Is 5:12. *n:* Is 27:10. *o:* Ps 106:13, 21; Jer 2:32; Hos 8:14. *p:* Is 1:29–31.

11 Though you make them grow the day
you plant them
and make them blossom the morning
you set them out,
The harvest shall disappear on a day of
sickness
and incurable pain.
12 Ah! the roaring of many peoples—*
a roar like the roar of the seas!
The thundering of nations—
thunder like the thundering of mighty
waters![q]
13 * But God shall rebuke them,
and they shall flee far away,
Driven like chaff on the mountains
before a wind,
like tumbleweed before a storm.[r]
14 At evening, there is terror,
but before morning, they are gone!
Such is the portion of those who despoil us,
the lot of those who plunder us.[s]

CHAPTER 18

See RG 280–95

Ethiopia

1 Ah! Land of buzzing insects,*
beyond the rivers of Ethiopia,[t]
2 Sending ambassadors by sea,
in papyrus boats on the waters!
Go, swift messengers,
to a nation tall and bronzed,
To a people dreaded near and far,
a nation strong and conquering,
whose land is washed by rivers.[u]
3 * All you who inhabit the world,
who dwell on earth,
When the signal is raised on the
mountain, look!
When the trumpet blows, listen!
4 For thus says the LORD to me:
I will be quiet, looking on from where
I dwell,[v]
Like the shimmering heat in sunshine,
like a cloud of dew at harvest time.
5 Before the vintage, when the flowering
has ended,
and the blooms are succeeded by
ripening grapes,
Then comes the cutting of branches with
pruning hooks,
and the discarding of the lopped-off
shoots.
6 They shall all be left to the mountain
vultures
and to the beasts of the earth;
The vultures shall summer on them,
all the beasts of the earth shall winter
on them.

7 Then will gifts be brought to the LORD of
hosts—to the place of the name of the LORD
of hosts, Mount Zion—from a people tall
and bronzed, from a people dreaded near
and far, a nation strong and conquering,
whose land is washed by rivers.[w]

CHAPTER 19

See RG 280–95

Egypt

1 Oracle on Egypt:
See, the LORD is riding on a swift cloud
on his way to Egypt;
The idols of Egypt tremble before him,
the hearts of the Egyptians melt within
them.[x]
2 I will stir up Egypt against Egypt:
brother will war against brother,
Neighbor against neighbor,
city against city, kingdom against
kingdom.
3 The courage of the Egyptians shall ebb
away within them,
and I will bring their counsel to
nought;

vading Assyrians, whom God repels just as he vanquished the primeval waters of chaos; see notes on Jb 3:8; 7:12; Ps 89:11.

17:13–14 The passage seems to evoke the motif of invincibility, part of the early Zion tradition that Jerusalem could not be conquered because God protected it (Ps 48:1–8).

18:1–2 Land of buzzing insects: the region of the Upper Nile where these multiplied with great rapidity. **Ethiopia**: in Hebrew, *Kush*. The center of this ancient kingdom corresponds geographically to the modern Sudan, Roman Nubia. **Papyrus boats**: light and serviceable vessels made of bundles of papyrus stalks and sealed with pitch. Egypt, ruled by a dynasty from Ethiopia, had invited Judah to join a coalition against Assyria, but Isaiah told the ambassadors to return to their own people.

18:3–6 A more general address but probably relating to the same topic. The Lord will not act at once, but later there will be a "harvest" of terrible destruction, probably directed against Assyria (cf. 14:24–27).

q: Ps 46:3–7; 93:3–4. *r:* Ps 76:7; 83:14. *s:* Is 29:8. *t:* Zep 3:10. *u:* Is 18:7. *v:* Is 8:18; 18:7; 2 Chr 6:30; Ps 33:14. *w:* Is 45:14; Ps 68:30; Zep 3:10; Mal 1:11. *x:* Is 13:7.

They shall consult idols and charmers,
ghosts and clairvoyants.[y]
4 I will deliver Egypt
into the power of a cruel master,
A harsh king* who shall rule over them—
oracle of the Lord, the LORD of hosts.[z]
5 The waters shall be drained from the sea,
the river shall parch and dry up;[a]
6 Its streams shall become foul,
and the canals of Egypt shall dwindle
and parch.[b]
Reeds and rushes shall wither away,
7 and bulrushes on the bank of the Nile;[c]
All the sown land along the Nile
shall dry up and blow away, and be no
more.
8 The fishermen shall mourn and lament,
all who cast hook in the Nile;
Those who spread their nets in the water
shall pine away.
9 The linen-workers shall be disappointed,
the combers and weavers shall turn
pale;[d]
10 The spinners shall be crushed,
all the hired laborers shall be
despondent.
11 Utter fools are the princes of Zoan!*
the wisest of Pharaoh's advisers give
stupid counsel.
How can you say to Pharaoh,
"I am a descendant of wise men, of
ancient kings"?
12 Where then are your wise men?
Let them tell you and make known
What the LORD of hosts has planned
against Egypt.[e]
13 The princes of Zoan have become fools,
the princes of Memphis have been
deceived.
The chiefs of its tribes
have led Egypt astray.[f]
14 The LORD has prepared among them
a spirit of dizziness,
And they have made Egypt stagger in
whatever she does,
as a drunkard staggers in his vomit.[g]
15 Egypt shall accomplish nothing—
neither head nor tail, palm branch nor
reed,* shall accomplish anything.

16 On that day the Egyptians shall be like
women, trembling with fear, because of the
LORD of hosts shaking his fist at them.[h]
17 And the land of Judah shall be a terror to
the Egyptians. Every time they think of Judah, they shall stand in dread because of the
plan the LORD of hosts has in mind for them.
18 On that day there shall be five cities* in
the land of Egypt that speak the language of
Canaan and swear by the LORD of hosts; one
shall be called "City of the Sun."
19 On that day there shall be an altar to the
LORD at the center of Egypt, and a sacred pillar to the LORD near its boundary.
20 This will
be a sign and witness to the LORD of hosts in
the land of Egypt, so that when they cry out
to the LORD because of their oppressors, he
will send them a savior to defend and deliver
them.[i]
21 The LORD shall make himself
known to Egypt, and the Egyptians shall
know the LORD in that day; they shall offer
sacrifices and oblations, make vows to the
LORD and fulfill them.[j]
22 Although the LORD
shall smite Egypt severely, he shall heal
them; they shall turn to the LORD and he
shall be moved by their entreaty and heal
them.[k]
23 On that day there shall be a highway
from Egypt to Assyria; the Assyrians shall
enter Egypt, and the Egyptians enter Assyria, and the Egyptians shall worship with
the Assyrians.
24 On that day Israel shall be a third party
with Egypt and Assyria, a blessing in the
midst of the earth,[l]
25 when the LORD of hosts
gives this blessing: "Blessed be my people

19:4 Cruel master . . . harsh king: possibly the Nubian (Ethiopian) Shabaka who gained control of all of Egypt around 712 B.C.

19:11, 13 Zoan, later known as Tanis, and **Memphis** (Hebrew *Noph*) were key cities in the Nile Delta.

19:15 Head . . . reed: the leaders and the people; cf. 9:13–14.

19:18 Five cities: colonies of Jews living together and speaking their native language; cf. Jer 43. **City of the Sun**: the meaning is uncertain, but the reference seems to be to the city known later as Heliopolis.

y: Is 8:19; 44:25; Lv 19:31. *z:* Ez 29:19; 30:10. *a:* Jer 51:36; Ez 30:12; 32:2. *b:* 2 Kgs 19:24. *c:* Jb 8:11. *d:* Ez 27:7. *e:* Is 14:26; 41:22–23. *f:* Jer 2:16; Hos 9:6. *g:* Is 28:7; Jer 48:26. *h:* Na 3:13. *i:* Ex 2:23; Jgs 2:18. *j:* Zec 14:16, 18. *k:* Hos 6:1. *l:* Gn 12:2; Zec 8:13.

Egypt, and the work of my hands Assyria,
and my heritage, Israel."

CHAPTER 20

See RG 280–95

*Isaiah's Warning Against Trust in
Egypt and Ethiopia.* 1 In the year the general
sent by Sargon, king of Assyria, came to
Ashdod,* fought against it, and captured it—
2* at that time the LORD had spoken through
Isaiah, the son of Amoz: Go and take off the
sackcloth from your waist, and remove the
sandals from your feet. This he did, walking
naked and barefoot.[m] 3 Then the LORD said:
Just as my servant Isaiah has gone naked and
barefoot for three years as a sign and portent
against Egypt and Ethiopia,[n] 4 so shall the
king of Assyria lead away captives from
Egypt, and exiles from Ethiopia, young and
old, naked and barefoot, with buttocks uncovered, the shame of Egypt.[o] 5 They shall be
dismayed and ashamed because of Ethiopia,
their hope, and because of Egypt, their
boast.[p] 6 The inhabitants of this coastland
shall say on that day, "See what has happened to those we hoped in, to whom we fled
for help and deliverance from the king of
Assyria! What escape is there for us now?"[q]

CHAPTER 21

See RG 280–95

*Fall of Babylon**

1 Oracle on the wastelands by the sea:*
Like whirlwinds sweeping through the
Negeb,
it comes from the desert,
from the fearful land.[r]
2 A harsh vision has been announced to me:
"The traitor betrays,
the despoiler spoils.[s]
Go up, O Elam; besiege, O Media;*
put an end to all its groaning!"[t]
3 Therefore my loins are filled with
anguish,
pangs have seized me like those of a
woman in labor;
I am too bewildered to hear,
too dismayed to look.[u]
4 My mind reels,
shuddering assails me;
The twilight I yearned for
he has turned into dread.[v]
5 They set the table,
spread out the rugs;
they eat, they drink.* [w]
Rise up, O princes,
oil the shield!
6 For thus my Lord said to me:
Go, station a watchman,
let him tell what he sees.
7 If he sees a chariot,
a pair of horses,
Someone riding a donkey,
someone riding a camel,
Then let him pay heed,
very close heed.
8 Then the watchman cried,
"On the watchtower, my Lord,
I stand constantly by day;
And I stay at my post
through all the watches of the night.[x]
9 Here he comes—
a single chariot,
a pair of horses—
He calls out and says,
'Fallen, fallen is Babylon!

20:1 Ashdod: a city of Philistia. In 713 B.C., Azuri, the king of Ashdod was deposed by Sargon for plotting rebellion, but the citizens of Ashdod rejected the ruler installed by the Assyrian king and followed a certain Yamani, who in 712 B.C., with the protection of Egypt, attempted to draw Edom, Moab, and Judah into a coalition against Assyria. In 711 B.C., Sargon's general marched against Ashdod, and Yamani fled to Ethiopia. Ashdod was captured, and a short time later Ethiopia handed Yamani over to the Assyrians for punishment.

20:2–6 Isaiah's nakedness is a symbolic act to convey the message that Assyria would lead the Egyptians and Ethiopians away as captives. The Judeans and their allies would then realize the folly of having trusted in them. The purpose of the oracle was to dissuade Hezekiah, the Judean king, from being drawn into Ashdod's anti-Assyrian coalition (14:28–32).

21:1–10 This oracle against Babylon is probably to be dated to the period just before the fall of Babylon to the Persians in 539 B.C. (v. 9).

21:1 Wastelands by the sea: Babylonia. **Negeb**: the wilderness south of Judah.

21:2 Elam . . . Media: nations which, under the leadership of Cyrus, captured Babylon in 539 B.C. **End to all its groaning**: those who were captive of Babylon will be freed.

21:5 Babylon is destroyed while its leaders are feasting; cf. Dn 5. **Oil the shield**: shields were oiled and greased so as to divert blows more easily; cf. 2 Sm 1:21.

m: 1 Sm 19:24. *n:* Is 8:18. *o:* 2 Sm 10:4. *p:* Is 30:3, 5. *q:* Is 31:3; 36:6. *r:* Is 30:6; Dt 1:19; Jer 2:6. *s:* Is 24:16; 33:1. *t:* Is 13:17; Jer 49:34. *u:* Is 16:11; Ps 38:8. *v:* Dt 28:67. *w:* Dn 5:5. *x:* Hb 2:1.

All the images of her gods
are smashed to the ground!' "[y]
10 To you, who have been threshed,
beaten on my threshing floor,
What I have heard
from the LORD of hosts,
The God of Israel,
I have announced to you.[z]

Dumah

11 Oracle on Dumah:*
They call to me from Seir,
"Watchman, how much longer the night?
Watchman, how much longer the night?"
12 The watchman replies,
"Morning has come, and again night.
If you will ask, ask; come back again."

In the Steppe

13 Oracle: in the steppe:*
In the thicket in the steppe you will spend the night,
caravans of Dedanites.
14 Meet the thirsty, bring them water,
inhabitants of the land of Tema,
greet the fugitives with bread.[a]
15 For they have fled from the sword,
from the drawn sword;
From the taut bow,
from the thick of battle.

16 For thus the Lord has said to me: In another
year, like the years of a hired laborer,* all the
glory of Kedar shall come to an end. 17 Few of
Kedar's stalwart archers shall remain, for the
LORD, the God of Israel, has spoken.

CHAPTER 22

See RG 280–95

The Valley of Vision

1 Oracle on the Valley of Vision:* [b]
What is the matter with you now, that you have gone up,
all of you, to the housetops,
2 * You who were full of noise,
tumultuous city,
exultant town?[c]
Your slain are not slain with the sword,
nor killed in battle.
3 All your leaders fled away together,
they were captured without use of bow;
All who were found were captured together,
though they had fled afar off.
4 That is why I say: Turn away from me,
let me weep bitterly;
Do not try to comfort me
for the ruin of the daughter of my people.[d]
5 It is a day of panic, rout and confusion,
from the Lord, the GOD of hosts, in the Valley of Vision*
Walls crash;
a cry for help to the mountains.
6 Elam takes up the quiver,

21:11–12 Dumah: an oasis in north Arabia (cf. Gn 25:14 and 1 Chr 1:30), may be identified with the north Arabian Adummatu mentioned in Assyrian records of Sennacherib's campaign against north Arabia. **Seir**: a site in Edom. The Edomites ask the prophet how much longer they must suffer ("the night" of suffering); he answers ambiguously: "Liberation ("morning") and further suffering ("night")," but perhaps they will later receive a more encouraging answer ("ask; come back again").

21:13–14 In the steppe: the north Arabian steppe where the oases referred to were located. **Dedanites**: a north Arabian tribe associated with the oasis of Tema; cf. Gn 10:7; 25:3; Jer 25:23.

21:16 Year . . . of a hired laborer: see note on 16:13–14. **Kedar**: a nomadic tribe in Arabia; cf. 42:11; 60:7; Ps 120:5.

22:1–14 The title "oracle on the valley of vision," like the other oracle headings in chaps. 13–23, was supplied by an editor and is taken from v. 5. In all probability it relates to the events of 701, the lifting of Sennacherib's siege of Jerusalem. The death of the Assyrian king Sargon II in 705 occasioned the revolt of many of the vassal nations subject to Assyria, a revolt in which Hezekiah joined, over Isaiah's bitter opposition. The biblical and other data concerning the outcome of this adventure are conflicting and confusing. While 2 Kgs 19 (Is 37) tells of a miraculous deliverance of the city after the siege had been renewed, Assyrian documents and 2 Kgs 18:13–16 report that Sennacherib, Sargon II's successor, devastated Judah (the destruction of 46 cities is mentioned in Assyrian records); Hezekiah had to surrender and paid Sennacherib a heavy indemnity, taken from the Temple treasury and adornments. The inhabitants of Jerusalem apparently took the lifting of the siege as occasion for great rejoicing, a response that Isaiah condemns. They should be mourning the dead and learning that their confidence in allies rather than in the Lord leads to disaster.

22:2–3 The retreat of Judah's soldiers is a further reason that rejoicing is not in order.

22:5 Valley of Vision: frequently identified as the Hinnom Valley, west of Jerusalem.

y: Is 46:1; Jer 50:2; 51:8; Rev 14:8; 18:2. *z:* Is 51:23; Jer 51:33; Mi 4:13; Hb 3:12. *a:* Jb 6:19. *b:* Is 21:2. *c:* Is 32:13. *d:* Jer 6:26; 9:1; 14:17.

Aram mounts the horses
and Kir* uncovers the shields.
7 Your choice valleys are filled with chariots,
horses are posted at the gates—
8 and shelter over Judah is removed.*

On that day you looked to the weapons in
the House of the Forest; 9* you saw that the
breaches in the City of David were many;
you collected the water of the lower pool.
10 You numbered the houses of Jerusalem,
tearing some down to strengthen the wall;
11 you made a reservoir between the two
walls for the water of the old pool. But you
did not look to the city's Maker, nor consider
the one who fashioned it long ago.

12 On that day the Lord,
the GOD of hosts, called
For weeping and mourning,
for shaving the head and wearing sackcloth.
13 But look! instead, there was celebration and joy,
slaughtering cattle and butchering sheep,
Eating meat and drinking wine:
"Eat and drink, for tomorrow we die!"[e]

14 This message was revealed in my hearing
from the LORD of hosts:

This iniquity will not be forgiven you
until you die,
says the Lord, the GOD of hosts.

Shebna and Eliakim

15 Thus says the Lord, the GOD of hosts:
Up, go to that official,
Shebna,* master of the palace,
16 * "What have you here? Whom have you here,
that you have hewn for yourself a tomb here,
Hewing a tomb on high,
carving a resting place in the rock?"
17 The LORD shall hurl you down headlong, mortal man!
He shall grip you firmly,
18 And roll you up and toss you like a ball
into a broad land.
There you will die, there with the chariots you glory in,
you disgrace to your master's house!
19 I will thrust you from your office
and pull you down from your station.
20 On that day I will summon my servant
Eliakim,* son of Hilkiah;[f]
21 I will clothe him with your robe,
gird him with your sash,
confer on him your authority.
He shall be a father to the inhabitants of Jerusalem,
and to the house of Judah.[g]
22 I will place the key* of the House of David on his shoulder;
what he opens, no one will shut,
what he shuts, no one will open.[h]
23 I will fix him as a peg in a firm place,
a seat of honor for his ancestral house;
24 On him shall hang all the glory of his ancestral house:*
descendants and offspring,
all the little dishes, from bowls to jugs.

22:6 Elam . . . Kir: the Assyrian forces presumably included auxiliary troops from various places.

22:8 Shelter over Judah is removed: the reference is obscure; it has been suggested that Judah's protection was Jerusalem itself, and with the fall of the city the country was exposed. **House of the Forest**: an armory built by Solomon; its columns of wood suggested the trees of a forest; cf. 1 Kgs 7:2; 10:17.

22:9–11 Frenetic efforts made to fortify the city before the impending siege; cf. 2 Kgs 20:20; 2 Chr 32:3–4, 30. Some suggest that the description of these preparations comes from the time of Nebuchadnezzar's assault on Jerusalem in 588. **You did not look to the city's Maker**: Isaiah here makes the crucial point. Jerusalem's safety lay not in military forces nor in alliances with other nations nor in playing power politics but in the Lord, here presented as the creator and founder of the city. Isaiah may be alluding to the belief that the city was inviolable.

22:15 Shebna: by the time of the siege of Jerusalem in 36:3, Shebna, the scribe, no longer held the office of master of the palace.

22:16 What is probably Shebna's inscribed tomb has been discovered in the village of Silwan on the eastern slope of Jerusalem.

22:20 Eliakim: by the time of the events described in 36:3, Eliakim had replaced Shebna as master of the palace.

22:22 Key: symbol of authority; cf. Mt 16:19; Rev 3:7.

22:24–25 Apparently Eliakim proved to be a disappointment, so an oracle of judgment was added to the originally positive oracle to Eliakim.

e: Is 56:12; Wis 2:6; 1 Cor 15:32. *f:* 2 Kgs 18:18, 37. *g:* Jb 29:16. *h:* Rev 3:7.

25On that day, says the LORD of hosts, the
peg fixed in a firm place shall give way,
break off and fall, and the weight that hung
on it shall be done away with; for the LORD
has spoken.

See RG 280–95

CHAPTER 23

Tyre and Sidon

1 * Oracle on Tyre:
Wail, ships of Tarshish,
for your port is destroyed;
From the land of the Kittim*
the news reaches them.[i]
2 Silence! you who dwell on the coast,
you merchants of Sidon,
Whose messengers crossed the sea
3 over the deep waters,
Whose revenue was the grain of Shihor,*
the harvest of the Nile,
you who were the merchant among the
nations.[j]
4 Be ashamed, Sidon, fortress on the sea,
for the sea* has spoken,
"I have not been in labor, nor given birth,
nor raised young men,
nor reared young women."
5 When the report reaches Egypt
they shall be in anguish at the report
about Tyre.
6 Pass over to Tarshish,*
wail, you who dwell on the coast!
7 Is this your exultant city,
whose origin is from old,
Whose feet have taken her
to dwell in distant lands?
8 Who has planned such a thing
against Tyre, the bestower of crowns,
Whose merchants are princes,
whose traders are the earth's honored
men?
9 The LORD of hosts has planned it,
to disgrace the height of all beauty,
to degrade all the honored of the earth.[k]
10 Cross to your own land,
ship of Tarshish;
the harbor is no more.
11 His hand he stretches out over the sea,
he shakes kingdoms;
The LORD commanded the destruction
of Canaan's strongholds:* [l]
12 Crushed, you shall exult no more,
virgin daughter Sidon.
Arise, pass over to the Kittim,
even there you shall find no rest.[m]
13 * Look at the land of the Chaldeans,
the people that has ceased to be.
Assyria founded it for ships,
raised its towers,
Only to tear down its palaces,
and turn it into a ruin.[n]
14 Lament, ships of Tarshish,
for your stronghold is destroyed.

15On that day, Tyre shall be forgotten for
seventy years,* the lifetime of one king. At
the end of seventy years, the song about the
prostitute will be Tyre's song:

16 Take a harp, go about the city,
forgotten prostitute;
Pluck the strings skillfully, sing many
songs,
that you may be remembered.

17At the end of the seventy years the LORD
shall visit Tyre. She shall return to her hire and
serve as prostitute* with all the world's king-

23:1–17 This oracle, a satire directed against the Phoenician cities of Tyre and Sidon, is perhaps to be situated at the time of Sennacherib's campaign against the Phoenican cities in 701 B.C, following his subjugation of their Babylonian allies in 703 B.C.

23:1 Kittim: Cyprus. The Hebrew word is derived from the term for the well-known city of Cyprus, Kition. In later centuries the term Kittim is used for the Greeks, the Romans, and other distant peoples.

23:3 Shihor: a synonym for the Nile.

23:4 The sea: here personified, it brings to distant coasts the news that Sidon must disown her children; her people are dispersed.

23:6–7 Tarshish: perhaps Tartessus in Spain. **Distant lands**: the reference is to the far-flung colonies established by the Phoenicians throughout the Mediterranean, including North Africa, Spain, and Sardinia. Oceangoing vessels were therefore called Tarshish ships.

23:11 Canaan's strongholds: the fortresses of Phoenicia.

23:13 The reference here seems to be to Assyria's subjugation of Babylon in 703 B.C., which left the coastal cities of Phoenicia as well as Judah open to Sennacherib's invasion in 701 B.C. **Founded it ... its palaces ... turn it**: the city of Babylon.

23:15 Seventy years: a conventional expression for a long period of time; cf. Jer 25:11 and 29:10.

23:17–18 Her hire ... prostitute: the international trade

i: Jer 25:22; Ez 26; Am 1:9; Zec 9:2, 4. *j:* Ez 27:3. *k:* Is 14:24–27; 22:11; Ez 28:7. *l:* Is 14:27; Ps 65:8. *m:* Ez 28:21–22. *n:* Is 13:21; 34:14; Jer 50:39.

doms on the face of the earth.[o] 18But her merchandise and her hire shall be sacred to the LORD. It shall not be stored up or laid away; instead, her merchandise shall belong to those who dwell before the LORD, to eat their fill and clothe themselves in choice attire.

D. Apocalypse of Isaiah*

CHAPTER 24

See RG 280–95

Judgment upon the World and the Lord's Enthronement on Mount Zion*

1 See! The LORD is about to empty the
earth and lay it waste;
he will twist its surface,
and scatter its inhabitants:[p]
2 People and priest shall fare alike:
servant and master,
Maid and mistress,
buyer and seller,
Lender and borrower,
creditor and debtor.[q]
3 The earth shall be utterly laid waste,
utterly stripped,
for the LORD has decreed this word.
4 The earth mourns and fades,
the world languishes and fades;
both heaven and earth languish.[r]
5 The earth is polluted because of its
inhabitants,
for they have transgressed laws,
violated statutes,
broken the ancient covenant.* [s]
6 Therefore a curse devours the earth,
and its inhabitants pay for their guilt;
Therefore they who dwell on earth have
dwindled,
and only a few are left.[t]
7 The new wine mourns, the vine
languishes,
all the merry-hearted groan.[u]
8 Stilled are the cheerful timbrels,
ended the shouts of the jubilant,
stilled the cheerful harp.[v]
9 They no longer drink wine and sing;
strong brew is bitter to those who
drink it.[w]
10 Broken down is the city of chaos,*
every house is shut against entry.[x]
11 In the streets they cry out for lack of wine;
all joy has grown dim,
cheer is exiled from the land.[y]
12 In the city nothing remains but
desolation,
gates battered into ruins.
13 For thus it shall be in the midst of the
earth,
among the peoples,
As when an olive tree has been beaten,
as with a gleaning when the vintage is
done.[z]
14 These* shall lift up their voice,
they shall sing for joy in the majesty of
the LORD,
they shall shout from the western sea:
15 "Therefore, in the east
give glory to the LORD!
In the coastlands of the sea,
to the name of the LORD, the God of
Israel!"[a]
16 From the end of the earth we hear songs:
"Splendor to the Just One!"
But I said, "I am wasted, wasted away.
Woe is me! The traitors betray;

engaged in by Tyre will become a source of wealth to God's people (cf. 45:14; 60:4–14; Zec 14:14).

24:1–27:13 Although it has become traditional to call these chapters "Apocalypse of Isaiah," and although they do contain some apocalyptic traits, many others are lacking, so that the title is imprecise as a designation. These chapters are not a unified composition and their growth into their present form was a long, complicated process. They echo many themes from chaps. 13–23, "Oracles Against the Foreign Nations," as well as from earlier parts of Isaiah (e.g., the reversal of the "vineyard song," 5:1–7, in 27:2–5). Of particular interest is an unnamed city (24:10–13; 25:2; 26:5–6; 27:10–11), a wicked city, doomed to destruction; to the extent that it is identifiable, it may be Babylon, but more generally it symbolizes all forces hostile to God. And it stands in contrast to another city, also unnamed but no doubt to be identified with Jerusalem (26:1–2).

24:1–23 The world is about to be shaken by a devastating judgment that will overthrow both the human and divine enemies of the Lord, who will then reign in glory over his people on Mount Zion.

24:5 Ancient covenant: God's commandments to all humankind (cf. Gn 9:4–6).

24:10 City of chaos: a godless city which appears several times in chaps. 24–27; see note on 24:1–27:13.

24:14 These: the saved.

o: Rev 17:5; 18:3, 11, 13. *p:* Is 13:9; Na 2:3, 11. *q:* Hos 4:9. *r:* Is 33:9. *s:* Nm 35:33; Hos 4:2–3. *t:* Lv 26:15–16. *u:* Jl 1:10–12. *v:* Jer 7:34; Hos 2:13. *w:* Am 6:5–7. *x:* Is 25:2. *y:* Jer 48:33; Lam 5:14–15. *z:* Is 17:6; Mi 7:1. *a:* Is 42:10, 12; Zep 2:11.

with treachery have the traitors
betrayed![b]
17 Terror, pit, and trap
for you, inhabitant of the earth![c]
18 One who flees at the sound of terror
will fall into the pit;
One who climbs out of the pit
will be caught in the trap.
For the windows on high are open
and the foundations of the earth
shake.[d]
19 The earth will burst asunder,
the earth will be shaken apart,
the earth will be convulsed.
20 The earth will reel like a drunkard,
sway like a hut;
Its rebellion will weigh it down;
it will fall, never to rise again."[e]
21 On that day the LORD will punish
the host of the heavens* in the
heavens,
and the kings of the earth on the earth.
22 They will be gathered together
like prisoners into a pit;
They will be shut up in a dungeon,
and after many days they will be
punished.[f]
23 Then the moon will blush
and the sun be ashamed,[g]
For the LORD of hosts will reign
on Mount Zion and in Jerusalem,
glorious in the sight of the elders.* [h]

CHAPTER 25

See RG 280–95

*Praise for God's Deliverance and the Celebration in Zion**

1 O LORD, you are my God,
I extol you, I praise your name;
For you have carried out your wonderful
plans of old,
faithful and true.[i]
2 For you have made the city a heap,
the fortified city a ruin,
The castle of the insolent, a city no more,
not ever to be rebuilt.[j]
3 Therefore a strong people will honor
you,
ruthless nations will fear you.
4 For you have been a refuge to the poor,
a refuge to the needy in their distress;
Shelter from the rain,
shade from the heat.[k]
When the blast of the ruthless was like a
winter rain,
5 the roar of strangers like heat in the
desert,
You subdued the heat with the shade of a
cloud,
the rain of the tyrants was vanquished.
6 On this mountain* the LORD of hosts
will provide for all peoples
A feast of rich food and choice wines,
juicy, rich food and pure, choice
wines.
7 On this mountain he will destroy
the veil that veils all peoples,
The web that is woven over all nations.
8 He will destroy death forever.
The Lord GOD will wipe away
the tears from all faces;
The reproach of his people he will
remove
from the whole earth; for the LORD has
spoken.[l]
9 On that day it will be said:
"Indeed, this is our God; we looked to
him, and he saved us!
This is the LORD to whom we looked;
let us rejoice and be glad that he has
saved us!"[m]

*Judgment on Moab**

10 For the hand of the LORD will rest on this
mountain,
but Moab will be trodden down
as straw is trodden down in the mire.[n]

24:21 Host of the heavens: the stars, which were often regarded as gods; cf. Dt 4:19; Jer 8:2.

24:23 The elders: the tradition in Ex 24:9–11 suggests that this refers to the people of God who are to share in the banquet on Mount Zion (Is 25:6–8).

25:1–9 These verses praise God for carrying out his plan to destroy the enemy and to save the poor of his people in Zion (14:32), and they announce the victory banquet to be celebrated in the Lord's city.

25:6 This mountain: i.e., Jerusalem's mountain, Zion.

25:10–12 Moab: one of Israel's bitterest enemies.

b: Is 21:2; 33:1. *c:* Jer 48:43. *d:* Gn 7:11; Am 5:19. *e:* Am 5:2. *f:* 2 Pt 2:4; Jude 6. *g:* Is 13:10; Jl 3:3–4; 4:15. *h:* Is 4:5; 60:1–3; Ex 24:9–11; Mi 4:7; Rev 19:4–6. *i:* Is 12:1, 4; 22:11; 28:29; 37:26. *j:* Is 17:1; Jer 51:37. *k:* Is 14:32; 32:2; Na 1:7. *l:* Is 60:1, 3; 1 Cor 15:53–55; Rev 7:17; 21:4. *m:* Is 30:18–19. *n:* Zep 2:9–10.

11 He will spread out his hands in its midst,
as a swimmer spreads out his hands to swim;
His pride will be brought low
despite his strokes.[o]
12 The high-walled fortress he will raze,
bringing it low, leveling it to the ground, to the very dust.[p]

CHAPTER 26

See RG 280–95

Judah's Praise and Prayer for Deliverance.* 1 On that day this song shall be sung in the land of Judah:

"A strong city* have we;
he sets up victory as our walls and ramparts.[q]
2 Open up the gates
that a righteous nation may enter,
one that keeps faith.[r]
3 With firm purpose you maintain peace;
in peace, because of our trust in you."[s]
4 Trust in the LORD forever!
For the LORD is an eternal Rock.[t]
5 He humbles those who dwell on high,
the lofty city he brings down,
Brings it down to the ground,
levels it to the dust.[u]
6 The feet of the needy trample on it—
the feet of the poor.
7 The way of the just is smooth;
the path of the just you make level.[v]
8 The course of your judgments, LORD, we await;
your name and your memory are the desire of our souls.
9 My soul yearns for you at night,
yes, my spirit within me seeks you at dawn;
When your judgment comes upon the earth,
the world's inhabitants learn justice.[w]
10 The wicked, when spared, do not learn justice;
in an upright land they act perversely,
and do not see the majesty of the LORD.[x]
11 LORD, your hand is raised high,
but they do not perceive it;
Let them be put to shame when they see your zeal for your people:
let the fire prepared for your enemies consume them.[y]
12 LORD, you will decree peace for us,
for you have accomplished all we have done.[z]
13 LORD, our God, lords other than you have ruled us;
only because of you can we call upon your name.
14 Dead they are, they cannot live,
shades that cannot rise;
Indeed, you have punished and destroyed them,
and wiped out all memory of them.
15 You have increased the nation, LORD,
you have increased the nation, have added to your glory,
you have extended far all the boundaries of the land.[a]
16 LORD, oppressed by your punishment,
we cried out in anguish under your discipline.[b]
17 As a woman about to give birth
writhes and cries out in pain,
so were we before you, LORD.[c]
18 We conceived and writhed in pain,
giving birth only to wind;
Salvation we have not achieved for the earth,
no inhabitants for the world were born.[d]
19 * But your dead shall live, their corpses shall rise!
Awake and sing, you who lie in the dust!

26:1–19 This text is a mixture of praise for the salvation that will take place, a confession of Judah's inability to achieve deliverance on its own, and earnest prayer that God may quickly bring about the longed-for salvation.

26:1 Strong city: Jerusalem, the antithesis of the "city of chaos" (24:10); see note on 24:1–27:13.

26:19 This verse refers not to resurrection of the dead, but to the restoration of the people; cf. Ez 37. The population of Judah was radically reduced by the slaughter and deportations that the historical disasters of the late eighth and seventh centuries B.C. brought upon the country. In this context, a major concern for the future was for an increase in the population, a rebirth of the nation's life.

o: Is 16:6–7, 14. *p:* Is 26:5. *q:* Is 60:18. *r:* Ps 118:19–20. *s:* Is 32:17–18; Ps 112:7. *t:* Is 17:10; 30:29; Ps 62:8. *u:* Is 25:11–12; 32:19. *v:* Ps 23:3–4; Prv 11:3, 5. *w:* Ps 63:2. *x:* Is 5:12; Eccl 8:11. *y:* Is 9:6; 30:27; 37:32. *z:* Jer 29:11; Phil 2:13. *a:* Is 54:2–3. *b:* Hos 5:15. *c:* Mi 4:10. *d:* Is 37:3.

For your dew is a dew of light,
and you cause the land of shades to give birth.[e]

*The Lord's Response**

20 Go, my people, enter your chambers,
and close the doors behind you;
Hide yourselves for a brief moment,
until the wrath is past.[f]
21 See, the LORD goes forth from his place,
to punish the wickedness of the earth's inhabitants;
The earth will reveal the blood shed upon it,
and no longer conceal the slain.[g]

See RG 280–95

CHAPTER 27

The Judgment and Deliverance of Israel

1 On that day,
The LORD will punish with his sword
that is cruel, great, and strong,
Leviathan the fleeing serpent,
Leviathan the coiled serpent;
he will slay the dragon* in the sea.[h]

2 * On that day—
The pleasant vineyard, sing about it![i]
3 I, the LORD, am its keeper,
I water it every moment;
Lest anyone harm it,
night and day I guard it.[j]
4 I am not angry.
But if I were to find briers and thorns,
In battle I would march against it;
I would burn it all.[k]
5 But if it holds fast to my refuge,
it shall have peace with me;[l]
it shall have peace with me.
6 In days to come Jacob shall take root,
Israel shall sprout and blossom,
covering all the world with fruit.[m]
7 *Was he smitten as his smiter was smitten?
Was he slain as his slayer was slain?
8 Driving out and expelling, he struggled against it,
carrying it off with his cruel wind on a day of storm.[n]
9 This, then, shall be the expiation of Jacob's guilt,
this the result of removing his sin:
He shall pulverize all the stones of the altars
like pieces of chalk;
no asherahs or incense altars shall stand.
10 For the fortified city shall be desolate,
an abandoned pasture, a forsaken wilderness;
There calves shall graze, there they shall lie down,
and consume its branches.
11 When its boughs wither, they shall be broken off;
and women shall come to kindle fires with them.
For this is not an understanding people;
therefore their maker shall not spare them;
their creator shall not be gracious to them.[o]
12 On that day,
The LORD shall beat out grain
from the channel of the Euphrates to the Wadi of Egypt,
and you shall be gleaned* one by one,
children of Israel.

26:20–21 The time of wrath for Judah would soon be over, and the just punishment of its enemies would begin (cf. Hb 2:1–3).

27:1 Leviathan . . . dragon: the description of Leviathan is almost identical to a passage from a much earlier Ugaritic text. The sea dragon became a symbol of the forces of evil which God vanquishes even as he overcame primeval chaos; cf. notes on 30:7; 51:9–10; Jb 3:8; 7:12; no power can challenge God. Leviathan is even spoken of playfully in Ps 104:26.

27:2–5 This passage mitigates the harsh words on Israel as the Lord's vineyard in 5:1–7; here is given the rain there withheld, though Israel's welfare is still made dependent on fidelity.

27:7–9 Israel was not treated as sternly as were its enemies whom God used to punish it. God did, however, drive Israel from its land, and if it wants to make peace with God, it must change its former cultic practices, destroying its altars and sacred groves (cf. 17:7–11).

27:12 Gleaned: God will harvest his people who have been scattered from Assyria to Egypt. Note the same language of gleaning to describe the remnant of the Northern Kingdom in 17:5–6.

e: Ez 37:5–14; Dn 12:2; Hos 6:2. *f*: Is 10:25. *g*: Gn 4:10; Jb 16:18; Ps 106:38; Mi 1:3. *h*: Jb 40:25–32; Ps 74:12–14; Ez 32:2. *i*: Is 5:1; Am 5:11. *j*: Is 5:2–7. *k*: Is 10:17. *l*: Jb 22:21. *m*: Is 37:31–32; Hos 14:5–6. *n*: Jer 18:17. *o*: Is 1:3; 5:13; Jer 4:22.

13 On that day,*
A great trumpet shall blow,
and the lost in the land of Assyria
and the outcasts in the land of Egypt
Shall come and worship the LORD
on the holy mountain, in Jerusalem.[p]

E. The Lord Alone, Israel's and Judah's Salvation

CHAPTER 28

See RG 280–95

*The Fate of Samaria**

1 Ah! majestic garland
of the drunkards of Ephraim,*
Fading blooms of his glorious beauty,
at the head of the fertile valley,
upon those stupefied with wine.[q]
2 See, the LORD has a strong one, a mighty one,*
who, like an onslaught of hail, a destructive storm,
Like a flood of water, great and overflowing,
levels to the ground with violence;[r]
3 With feet that will trample
the majestic garland of the drunkards of Ephraim.
4 The fading blooms of his glorious beauty
at the head of the fertile valley
Will be like an early fig before summer:
whoever sees it,
swallows it as soon as it is in hand.[s]
5 On that day the LORD of hosts
will be a glorious crown
And a brilliant diadem
for the remnant of his people,
6 A spirit of judgment
for the one who sits in judgment,
And strength for those
who turn back the battle at the gate.

Against Judah

7 But these also stagger from wine
and stumble from strong drink:
Priest and prophet stagger from strong drink,
overpowered by wine;
They are confused by strong drink,
they stagger in their visions,
they totter when giving judgment.[t]
8 Yes, all the tables
are covered with vomit,
with filth, and no place left clean.
9 * "To whom would he impart knowledge?
To whom would he convey the message?
To those just weaned from milk,
those weaned from the breast?
10 For he says,
'Command on command, command on command,
rule on rule, rule on rule,
here a little, there a little!' "
11 * Yes, with stammering lips and in a strange language
he will speak to this people,[u]
12 to whom he said:
"This is the resting place,
give rest to the weary;
And this is the place of repose"—
but they refused to hear.[v]
13 So for them the word of the LORD shall be:
"Command on command, command on command,
Rule on rule, rule on rule,
here a little, there a little!"

27:13 The remnant of Israel will return to Jerusalem for worship; cf. 11:10–16.

28:1–6 These verses once constituted an independent oracle against the Northern Kingdom, probably originally spoken during the time between its overthrow by Assyria in 732 and its destruction in 722/721. Isaiah has reused them as an introduction to his oracle against Judah (vv. 7–22), because the leaders of Judah were guilty of the same excesses that had once marked Ephraim's leadership.

28:1 Ephraim: the Northern Kingdom. Its capital, Samaria, was built upon a hill, suggestive of a majestic garland adorning a human head. The characterization of the leadership of Ephraim as drunken underscores its inattention to justice and good government (cf. 5:11–13; Am 6:1–6).

28:2 A strong one, a mighty one: Assyria (cf. 8:7–8).

28:9–10 The words of those who ridicule Isaiah. The Hebrew of v. 10, by its very sound, conveys the idea of mocking imitation of what the prophet says, as though he spoke like a stammering child: "sau lasau, sau lasau, kau lakau, kau lakau, ze'er sham, ze'er sham." But in v. 13 God repeats these words in deadly earnest, putting them in the mouth of the victorious Assyrian army.

28:11 God will answer the mockers and defend Isaiah. **Strange language**: spoken by the invading army.

p: Is 11:11–16. *q:* Hos 7:5; Am 6:1–6. *r:* Is 25:4–5; 28:17–18; 30:30. *s:* Is 17:6; Na 3:12. *t:* Is 5:11–12; Mi 2:11. *u:* Jer 5:15; 1 Cor 14:21; Dt 28:49; Bar 4:15. *v:* Is 30:9.

So that when they walk, they shall
stumble backward,
broken, ensnared, and captured.[w]
14 Therefore, hear the word of the LORD,
you scoffers,
who rule* this people in Jerusalem:[x]
15 You have declared, "We have made a
covenant with death,
with Sheol* we have made a pact;
When the raging flood passes through,
it will not reach us;
For we have made lies our refuge,
and in falsehood we have found a
hiding place,"—[y]
16 Therefore, thus says the Lord GOD:
See, I am laying a stone in Zion,*
a stone that has been tested,
A precious cornerstone as a sure
foundation;
whoever puts faith in it will not
waver.[z]
17 I will make judgment a measuring line,
and justice a level.—*
Hail shall sweep away the refuge of lies,
and waters shall flood the hiding place.
18 Your covenant with death shall be
canceled
and your pact with Sheol shall not
stand.
When the raging flood passes through,
you shall be beaten down by it.[a]
19 Whenever it passes, it shall seize you;
morning after morning it shall pass,
by day and by night.
Sheer terror
to impart the message!
20 For the bed shall be too short to stretch
out in,
and the cover too narrow to wrap in.
21 For the LORD shall rise up as on Mount
Perazim,
bestir himself as in the Valley of
Gibeon,*
To carry out his work—strange his work!
to perform his deed—alien his deed!
22 Now, cease scoffing,
lest your bonds be tightened,
For I have heard a decree of destruction
from the Lord, the GOD of hosts,
for the whole land.[b]

The Parable of the Farmer

23 * Give ear and hear my voice,
pay attention and hear my word:
24 Is the plowman forever plowing in order
to sow,
always loosening and harrowing the
field?
25 When he has leveled the surface,
does he not scatter caraway and sow
cumin,*
Put in wheat and barley,
with spelt as its border?
26 His God has taught him this rule,
he has instructed him.
27 For caraway is not threshed with a sledge,
nor does a cartwheel roll over cumin.
But caraway is beaten out with a staff,

28:14 Who rule: there is a play on words; the same expression could also mean, "Proverb makers," that is, scoffers of this people.

28:15, 18 A covenant with death, with Sheol: an alliance with foreign powers, such as Egypt and Babylon. **Have made lies . . . a hiding place**: this confidence in human aid will prove to be false and deceitful, incapable of averting the dreaded disaster. **Raging flood**: the Assyrian invasion; cf. 8:7–8.

28:16 A stone in Zion: the true and sure foundation of salvation, i.e., the presence of God, who had chosen and founded Zion as his city (Ps 78:68–69; Is 14:32) and had chosen the Davidic dynasty to rule over his people (Ps 78:70–72; Is 9:1–6; 11:1–10). **Cornerstone**: the assurance of salvation, rejected by the people of Judah in the prophet's time, is picked up in Ps 118:22 and later applied to Christ; cf. Mt 21:42; Lk 20:17; Acts 4:11; Rom 9:33; 1 Pt 2:7. Chapters 28–31 alternate between threats of the danger of rebelling against Assyria (with implied trust in Egypt) with assurances of the power and protection of the Lord.

28:17 Line . . . level: instruments used in constructing a building, to keep it true. They are used metaphorically here to refer to the qualities that Zion, the city of God, must manifest, judgment and justice, not bloodshed (Mi 3:10), nor deceit and violence, which would result in a bulging unstable wall doomed to destruction (Is 30:12–14). Cf. 1 Cor 3:10–17.

28:21 Mount Perazim . . . Valley of Gibeon: where David defeated the Philistines; cf. 2 Sm 5:20, 25; 1 Chr 14:11, 16. God's new work will be strange, because instead of fighting for Judah as the Lord did in David's time, God will now fight against Jerusalem (see 29:1–4).

28:23–29 The practical variation of the farmer's work reflects the way God deals with his people, wisely adapted to circumstances; he does not altogether crush them in their weakness.

28:25 Caraway . . . cumin: herbs used in seasoning food. **Spelt**: a variety of wheat.

w: Is 8:15. *x:* Is 3:1–4; 5:18–21. *y:* Wis 1:16; Jer 5:12. *z:* Ps 118:22; Mt 21:42; Acts 4:11; Rom 9:33; 1 Pt 2:6. *a:* Is 28:2–3. *b:* Is 5:18–19; 10:23.

and cumin with a rod.
28 Grain is crushed for bread, but not forever;
though he thresh it thoroughly,
and drive his cartwheel and horses
over it,
he does not pulverize it.
29 This too comes from the LORD of hosts;
wonderful is his counsel and great his
wisdom.[c]

See RG 280–95

CHAPTER 29

Judgment and Deliverance of Jerusalem

1 Ah! Ariel, Ariel,*
city where David encamped!
Let year follow year,
and feast follow feast,[d]
2 But I will bring distress upon Ariel,
and there will be mourning and
moaning.
You shall be to me like Ariel:[e]
3 I will encamp like David against you;
I will circle you with outposts
and set up siege works against you.[f]
4 You shall speak from beneath the earth,
and from the dust below, your words
shall come.
Your voice shall be that of a ghost from
the earth,
and your words shall whisper from the
dust.[g]
5 The horde of your arrogant shall be like
fine dust,
a horde of tyrants like flying chaff.[h]
Then suddenly, in an instant,
6 you shall be visited by the LORD of
hosts,
With thunder, earthquake, and great noise,
whirlwind, storm, and the flame of
consuming fire.[i]
7 * Then like a dream,
a vision of the night,
Shall be the horde of all the nations
who make war against Ariel:
All the outposts, the siege works
against it,
all who distress it.
8 As when a hungry man dreams he is
eating
and awakens with an empty stomach,
Or when a thirsty man dreams he is
drinking
and awakens faint, his throat parched,
So shall the horde of all the nations be,
who make war against Mount Zion.

Blindness and Perversity

9 * Stupefy yourselves and stay stupid;
blind yourselves and stay blind!
You who are drunk, but not from wine,
who stagger, but not from strong drink![j]
10 For the LORD has poured out on you
a spirit of deep sleep.
He has shut your eyes (the prophets)
and covered your heads (the seers).* [k]

11 For you the vision of all this has become
like the words of a sealed scroll. When it is
handed to one who can read, with the request,
"Read this," the reply is, "I cannot, because it
is sealed." 12 When the scroll is handed to one
who cannot read, with the request, "Read
this," the reply is, "I cannot read."

13 The Lord said:
Since this people draws near with words
only
and honors me with their lips alone,
though their hearts are far from me,
And fear of me has become
mere precept of human teaching,[l]

29:1–2 Ariel: a poetic name for Jerusalem. It has been variously interpreted to mean "lion of God," "altar hearth of God" (Ez 43:15–16), "city of God," or "foundation of God." In v. 2 the term refers to "altar hearth," i.e., a place of burning for its people (cf. 30:33; 31:9). God will attack Jerusalem, as David did long ago.

29:7–8 Just when the attackers think their capture of Jerusalem is certain, the Lord will snatch victory from their hands and save the city. The sudden shift from the Lord's attack on the city to its deliverance by him is surprising and unexplained; it may reflect the account related in 37:36.

29:9–16 Despite their show of piety, Judah's leaders refused to accept the prophet's words of assurance. They rejected prophetic advice (cf. 30:10–11), did not consult the prophetic oracle in forming their political plans (30:1–2; 31:1), and tried to hide their plans even from God's prophet (v. 15), who, they thought, simply did not understand military and political reality.

29:10 Prophets . . . seers: interpretive glosses.

c: Rom 11:33. *d:* 2 Sm 5:6–9. *e:* Is 33:7. *f:* 2 Kgs 25:1; Ez 4:2. *g:* Is 8:19; 1 Sm 28:14. *h:* Is 17:13; Ps 18:43; Jb 21:18. *i:* Is 30:27, 30. *j:* Is 19:14; 28:7–8. *k:* Is 6:10; Rom 11:8. *l:* Ez 33:31; Mt 15:8–9; Mk 7:6–7.

14 Therefore I will again deal with this people
in surprising and wondrous fashion:
The wisdom of the wise shall perish,
the prudence of the prudent shall
vanish.[m]
15 Ah! You who would hide a plan
too deep for the LORD!
Who work in the dark, saying,
"Who sees us, who knows us?"[n]
16 Your perversity is as though the potter
were taken to be the clay:
As though what is made should say of its
maker,
"He did not make me!"
Or the vessel should say of the potter,
"He does not understand."[o]

*Redemption**

17 Surely, in a very little while,
Lebanon shall be changed into an
orchard,
and the orchard be considered a forest![p]
18 On that day the deaf shall hear
the words of a scroll;
And out of gloom and darkness,
the eyes of the blind shall see.[q]
19 The lowly shall again find joy in the LORD,
the poorest rejoice in the Holy One of
Israel.[r]
20 For the tyrant shall be no more,
the scoffer shall cease to be;
All who are ready for evil shall be cut off,[s]
21 those who condemn with a mere word,
Who ensnare the defender at the gate,
and leave the just with an empty claim.[t]
22 Therefore thus says the LORD,
the God of the house of Jacob,
who redeemed Abraham:*
No longer shall Jacob be ashamed,
no longer shall his face grow pale.[u]
23 For when his children see
the work of my hands in his midst,
They shall sanctify my name;
they shall sanctify the Holy One of
Jacob,
be in awe of the God of Israel.[v]
24 Those who err in spirit shall acquire
understanding,
those who find fault shall receive
instruction.

CHAPTER 30

See RG 280–95

*Oracle on the Futility of an Alliance with Egypt**

1 Ah! Rebellious children,
oracle of the LORD,
Who carry out a plan that is not mine,
who make an alliance* I did not inspire,
thus adding sin upon sin;[w]
2 They go down to Egypt,
without asking my counsel,*
To seek strength in Pharaoh's protection
and take refuge in Egypt's shadow.[x]
3 Pharaoh's protection shall become your
shame,
refuge in Egypt's shadow your
disgrace.[y]
4 When his princes are at Zoan
and his messengers reach Hanes,[z]
5 All shall be ashamed
of a people that gain them nothing,
Neither help nor benefit,
but only shame and reproach.[a]
6 Oracle on the Beasts of the Negeb.
Through the distressed and troubled land*
of the lioness and roaring lion,

29:17–24 The prophet presents the positive aspects of God's plan in terms of a series of reversals: an end to pride, ignorance, and injustice. Cf. 32:3–5.

29:22 Who redeemed Abraham: perhaps by revealing himself and delivering Abraham from idolatrous worship; cf. Gn 12:1–3; 17:1; Jos 24:2–3.

30:1–17 Several independent oracles against making an alliance with Egypt have been strung together in this chapter: vv. 1–5, vv. 6–7, and vv. 8–17. That these were originally separate oracles is indicated by the fact that the oracle in vv. 6–7 is still introduced by its own heading: Oracle on the Beasts of the Negeb.

30:1 Make an alliance: lit., "pour out a libation," namely, as part of the ritual of treaty making.

30:2 Without asking my counsel: it was a practice to consult God through the prophets or through the priestly oracle before making a major political decision (1 Sm 23:1–12; 1 Kgs 22:5), but Judah's leadership, in its concern for security, was apparently trying to keep its plan for a treaty with Egypt secret even from the prophets, thus implicitly from God (29:15).

30:6 Distressed . . . land: the wilderness between Judah and Egypt, through which Judahite messengers had to pass, carrying their tribute to Egypt to buy assistance in the struggle against Assyria. **Flying saraph**: see notes on 6:2; 14:29.

m: Jer 49:7; 1 Cor 1:19. *n:* Is 30:1–2; 31:1; Ez 8:12; Jn 3:19–20. *o:* Is 45:9; Jer 18:6; Rom 9:20. *p:* Is 32:15. *q:* Is 35:5; 42:6–7. *r:* Is 61:1–2. *s:* Is 28:22. *t:* Is 5:23; 10:1–2; Am 5:10, 12. *u:* Is 45:17. *v:* Is 8:12–13. *w:* Is 1:4; 5:21; 28:15; 29:15. *x:* Is 31:1; 36:6. *y:* Is 20:5; Jer 2:36–37. *z:* Is 19:11. *a:* Is 36:6.

of the viper and flying saraph,
They carry their riches on the backs of donkeys
and their treasures on the humps of camels
To a people good for nothing,
7 to Egypt whose help is futile and vain.
Therefore I call her
"Rahab* Sit-still."
8 * Now come, write it on a tablet they can keep,
inscribe it on a scroll;
That in time to come it may be
an eternal witness.[b]
9 For this is a rebellious people,
deceitful children,
Children who refuse
to listen to the instruction of the LORD;[c]
10 Who say to the seers, "Do not see";
to the prophets,* "Do not prophesy truth for us;
speak smooth things to us, see visions that deceive![d]
11 Turn aside from the way! Get out of the path!
Let us hear no more
of the Holy One of Israel!"[e]
12 Therefore, thus says the Holy One of Israel:
Because you reject this word,
And put your trust in oppression and deceit,
and depend on them,[f]
13 This iniquity of yours shall be
like a descending rift
Bulging out in a high wall
whose crash comes suddenly, in an instant,[g]
14 Crashing like a potter's jar
smashed beyond rescue,
And among its fragments cannot be found
a sherd to scoop fire from the hearth
or dip water from the cistern.[h]
15 For thus said the Lord GOD,
the Holy One of Israel:
By waiting and by calm you shall be saved,
in quiet and in trust shall be your strength.
But this you did not will.[i]
16 "No," you said,
"Upon horses we will flee."
Very well, you shall flee!
"Upon swift steeds we will ride."
Very well, swift shall be your pursuers![j]
17 A thousand shall tremble at the threat of one—
if five threaten, you shall flee.
You will then be left like a flagstaff on a mountaintop,
like a flag on a hill.[k]

Zion's Future Deliverance

18 Truly, the LORD is waiting to be gracious to you,
truly, he shall rise to show you mercy;
For the LORD is a God of justice:
happy are all who wait for him![l]
19 Yes, people of Zion, dwelling in Jerusalem,
you shall no longer weep;
He will be most gracious to you when you cry out;
as soon as he hears he will answer you.[m]
20 The Lord will give you bread in adversity
and water in affliction.
No longer will your Teacher* hide himself,
but with your own eyes you shall see your Teacher,[n]

30:7 Here as elsewhere (cf. Ps 87:4) Egypt is compared to Rahab, the raging, destructive sea monster (cf. Is 51:9; Jb 26:12; Ps 89:11); yet Egypt, when asked for aid by Judah, becomes silent and "sits still."

30:8 Isaiah will write down his condemnation of the foolish policy pursued so that the truth of his warning of its dire consequences (vv. 12–17) may afterward be recognized.

30:10 Seers . . . prophets: the two terms are synonyms for prophetic figures such as Isaiah (1:1; 2:1; 6:1, 5). There is wordplay between the nouns and their cognate verbs, both of which mean "to see." The authorities are depicted as forbidding prophets to contradict their secret political and military policies.

30:20 Teacher: God, who in the past made the people blind and deaf through the prophetic message (6:9–10) and who in his anger hid his face from the house of Jacob (8:17),

b: Is 8:1, 16; Jer 36:2; Hb 2:2. *c:* Is 1:4; 28:12; Jer 7:28. *d:* Is 29:10; Jer 5:31; 11:21; Am 2:12. *e:* Jb 21:14–15. *f:* Is 28:15; Ps 62:11. *g:* Is 28:17; Ez 13:14. *h:* Jer 19:11. *i:* Is 7:4; 8:6; 28:12. *j:* Is 31:3. *k:* Is 11:10; Dt 32:30. *l:* Ex 34:6; Ps 34:9; Jer 17:7. *m:* Is 25:8; 58:9; 65:24. *n:* Is 6:9–10; 8:17; 29:18.

21 And your ears shall hear a word behind
you:
"This is the way; walk in it,"
when you would turn to the right or
the left.
22 You shall defile your silver-plated idols
and your gold-covered images;
You shall throw them away like filthy
rags,
you shall say, "Get out!"[o]
23 He will give rain for the seed
you sow in the ground,
And the bread that the soil produces
will be rich and abundant.
On that day your cattle will graze
in broad meadows;[p]
24 The oxen and the donkeys that till the
ground
will eat silage tossed to them
with shovel and pitchfork.
25 Upon every high mountain and lofty hill
there will be streams of running water.
On the day of the great slaughter,
when the towers fall,
26 The light of the moon will be like the
light of the sun,
and the light of the sun will be seven
times greater,
like the light of seven days,
On the day the LORD binds up the
wounds of his people
and heals the bruises left by his blows.[q]

*Divine Judgment on Assyria**

27 See, the name of the LORD is coming
from afar,
burning with anger, heavy with threat,
His lips filled with fury,
tongue like a consuming fire,[r]
28 Breath like an overflowing torrent
that reaches up to the neck!
He will winnow the nations with a
destructive winnowing
and bridle the jaws of the peoples to
send them astray.[s]
29 For you, there will be singing
as on a night when a feast is observed,
And joy of heart
as when one marches along with a
flute
Going to the mountain of the LORD,
to the Rock of Israel.
30 The LORD will make his glorious voice
heard,
and reveal his arm coming down
In raging fury and flame of consuming
fire,
in tempest, and rainstorm, and hail.[t]
31 For at the voice of the LORD, Assyria will
be shattered,
as he strikes with the rod;
32 And every sweep of the rod of his
punishment,
which the LORD will bring down on
him,
Will be accompanied by timbrels and
lyres,
while he wages war against him.[u]
33 For his tophet* has long been ready,
truly it is prepared for the king;
His firepit made both deep and wide,
with fire and firewood in abundance,
And the breath of the LORD, like a stream
of sulfur,
setting it afire.[v]

CHAPTER 31

See RG 280–95

Against the Egyptian Alliance

1 Ah! Those who go down to Egypt for
help,
who rely on horses;
Who put their trust in chariots because of
their number,
and in horsemen because of their
combined power,
But look not to the Holy One of Israel

shall in the future help them to understand his teaching clearly (cf. Jer 31:34).

30:27–33 God's punishment of Assyria. **The name of the LORD**: here, God himself; cf. Ps 20:2.

30:33 Tophet: a site, near Jerusalem, where children were sacrificed by fire to Molech (2 Kgs 23:10), and where, probably, Ahaz sacrificed his son (2 Kgs 16:3). Here, Isaiah speaks of "his tophet," the site prepared for burning up the king of Assyria. **King**: there seems to be a play on words between the Heb. word for king (*melek*) and the name Molech. This defeat of Assyria becomes the occasion for Israel's festal rejoicing (v. 32).

o: Is 2:20; 27:9; 31:7. *p:* Lv 26:3–5. *q:* Is 1:6; Jer 30:17; Hos 6:1. *r:* Is 10:17; 29:6. *s:* Is 8:7–8; 37:29. *t:* Is 10:17; 28:2; 29:6. *u:* Is 10:24–26; 14:24–27. *v:* Gn 19:24; Ez 38:22.

nor seek the LORD!* [w]
[2] Yet he too is wise and will bring disaster;
he will not turn from his threats.
He will rise up against the house of the wicked
and against those who help evildoers.[x]
[3] The Egyptians are human beings, not God,
their horses flesh, not spirit;
When the LORD stretches forth his hand,
the helper shall stumble, the one helped shall fall,
and both of them shall perish together.[y]
[4] For thus says the LORD to me:
As a lion or its young
growling over the prey,
With a band of shepherds
assembled against it,
Is neither dismayed by their shouts
nor cowed by their noise,
So shall the LORD of hosts come down
to wage war upon Mount Zion, upon its height.[z]
[5] Like hovering birds, so the LORD of hosts
shall shield Jerusalem,
To shield and deliver,
to spare and rescue.[a]

[6]Return, O Israelites, to him whom you
have utterly deserted.[b] [7]On that day each one
of you shall reject his idols of silver and
gold, which your hands have made.[c]

[8] Assyria shall fall by a sword, not wielded by human being,
no mortal sword shall devour him;
He shall flee before the sword,
and his young men shall be impressed as laborers.[d]
[9] He shall rush past his crag* in panic,
and his princes desert the standard in terror,
Says the LORD who has a fire in Zion
and a furnace in Jerusalem.[e]

CHAPTER 32

See RG 280–95

The Kingdom of Justice

[1] See, a king will reign justly
and princes will rule rightly.[f]
[2] Each of them will be like a shelter from the wind,
a refuge from the rain.
They will be like streams of water in a dry country,
like the shade of a great rock in a parched land.[g]
[3] The eyes of those who see will not be closed;
the ears of those who hear will be attentive.[h]
[4] The hasty of heart shall take thought to know,
and tongues of stutterers shall speak readily and clearly.
[5] No more will the fool be called noble,
nor the deceiver be considered honorable.[i]
[6] For the fool speaks folly,
his heart plans evil:
Godless actions,
perverse speech against the LORD,
Letting the hungry go empty
and the thirsty without drink.[j]
[7] The deceits of the deceiver are evil,
he plans devious schemes:
To ruin the poor with lies,
and the needy when they plead their case.[k]
[8] But the noble plan noble deeds,
and in noble deeds they persist.

The Women of Jerusalem

[9] You women so complacent, rise up and hear my voice,
daughters so confident, give heed to my words.[l]
[10] In a little more than a year

31:1 Seek the LORD: a technical expression for seeking a prophetic or priestly oracle, similar to the expression "asking my counsel" in 30:2. The prophet complains that Judah has decided on its policy of alliance with Egypt without first consulting the Lord.

31:9 Crag: the king as the rallying point of the princes. **Panic**: terror is an element of Israel's holy war tradition, in which defeat of the enemy is accomplished by the Lord rather than by human means (cf. v. 8).

w: Is 5:12, 24; 18:2; 22:11; 29:15; 30:2; 36:6. *x:* Is 28:21. *y:* Ps 146:3–5. *z:* Hos 5:14; Am 1:2; 3:8, 12. *a:* Is 37:35; Dt 32:11; Ps 91:4. *b:* Is 1:2–4; Jer 3:12. *c:* Is 2:20; 30:22. *d:* Is 27:1; 34:5–6; 37:36. *e:* Is 30:17, 33. *f:* Is 9:6; 11:4; 16:5; Ps 72:1–4; Jer 23:5–6. *g:* Is 4:6; 16:4; 25:4. *h:* Is 6:10; 29:18; 35:5. *i:* Is 5:20. *j:* Prv 15:2. *k:* Is 29:20–21; Mi 2:1. *l:* Is 3:16–24; Am 6:1.

your confidence will be shaken;
For the vintage will fail,
no fruit harvest will come in.[m]
11 Tremble, you who are so complacent!
Shudder, you who are so confident!
Strip yourselves bare,
with only a loincloth for cover.[n]
12 Beat your breasts
for the pleasant fields,
for the fruitful vine;[o]
13 For the soil of my people,
overgrown with thorns and briers;
For all the joyful houses,
the exultant city.[p]
14 The castle* will be forsaken,
the noisy city deserted;
Citadel and tower will become wasteland
forever,
the joy of wild donkeys, the pasture of
flocks;[q]
15 * Until the spirit from on high
is poured out on us.
And the wilderness becomes a garden
land
and the garden land seems as common
as forest.[r]
16 Then judgment will dwell in the
wilderness
and justice abide in the garden land.
17 The work of justice will be peace;
the effect of justice, calm and security
forever.[s]
18 My people will live in peaceful country,
in secure dwellings and quiet resting
places.[t]
19 And the forest will come down
completely,
the city will be utterly laid low.* [u]
20 Happy are you who sow beside every
stream,
and let the ox and the donkey go
freely![v]

CHAPTER 33

See RG 280–95

*Overthrow of Assyria**

1 Ah! You destroyer never destroyed,
betrayer never betrayed!
When you have finished destroying, you
will be destroyed;
when you have stopped betraying, you
will be betrayed.[w]
2 LORD, be gracious to us; for you we wait.
Be our strength every morning,
our salvation in time of trouble![x]
3 At the roaring sound, peoples flee;
when you rise in your majesty, nations
are scattered.[y]
4 Spoil is gathered up as caterpillars gather,
an onrush like the rush of locusts.[z]
5 The LORD is exalted, enthroned on high;
he fills Zion with right and justice.[a]
6 That which makes her seasons certain,
her wealth, salvation, wisdom, and
knowledge,
is the fear of the LORD, her treasure.[b]
7 See, the men of Ariel cry out in the
streets,
the messengers of Shalem* weep
bitterly.
8 The highways are desolate,
travelers have quit the paths,
Covenants are broken, witnesses spurned;
yet no one gives it a thought.[c]
9 The country languishes in mourning,
Lebanon withers with shame;
Sharon* is like the Arabah,
Bashan and Carmel are stripped bare.[d]
10 Now I will rise up, says the LORD,
now exalt myself,
now lift myself up.[e]

32:14 The castle: the fortified royal palace in Jerusalem. **Citadel**: Ophel, the fortified hill, with its stronghold called "the great projecting tower" (Neh 3:27).

32:15–18, 20 Extraordinary peace and prosperity will come to Israel under just rulers.

32:19 Probably from a different context, perhaps after v. 14a.

33:1–24 After an introductory address to Assyria (v. 1), there follows a prayer on behalf of Jerusalem which recalls what God had done in the past (vv. 2–6) and a description of the present situation (vv. 7–9). In response, the Lord announces a judgment on Assyria (vv. 10–12) that will lead to the purification of Jerusalem's inhabitants (vv. 13–16). The text ends with an idealized portrait of the redeemed Jerusalem of the future (vv. 17–24).

m: Zep 1:13. *n:* Is 20:2; Jer 4:8; Mi 1:8. *o:* Is 16:9. *p:* Is 5:6; 7:23–25; 22:2; 34:13. *q:* Is 7:25; 24:10–11. *r:* Is 44:3; Ps 104:30; Ez 37:9–10; Jl 3:1–2. *s:* Is 9:6; 30:15; 33:15–16; Ps 72:2–3, 7; Jas 3:18. *t:* Jer 23:6; Mi 4:4. *u:* Is 10:33–34; 26:5. *v:* Is 7:25; 30:18, 23. *w:* Is 10:12; 16:4; 21:2; 24:16. *x:* Is 25:9; 30:18–19. *y:* Is 17:13; Nm 10:35; Ps 68:2. *z:* Is 9:2; 33:23. *a:* Is 1:26–27; 2:11, 17; 32:1; 33:16. *b:* Is 11:2; 13:22; 60:22. *c:* Is 24:5; Jgs 5:6. *d:* Na 1:4. *e:* Ps 12:6; Zep 3:8.

11 You conceive dry grass, bring forth
stubble;
my spirit shall consume you like fire.
12 The peoples shall be burned to lime,
thorns cut down to burn in fire.[f]
13 Hear, you who are far off, what I have
done;
you who are near, acknowledge my
might.
14 In Zion sinners are in dread,
trembling grips the impious:
"Who of us can live with consuming fire?
who of us can live with everlasting
flames?"[g]
15 Whoever walks righteously and speaks
honestly,
who spurns what is gained by
oppression,
Who waves off contact with a bribe,
who stops his ears so as not to hear of
bloodshed,
who closes his eyes so as not to look
on evil—[h]
16 That one shall dwell on the heights,
with fortresses of rock for stronghold,
food and drink in steady supply.
17 Your eyes will see a king* in his
splendor,
they will look upon a vast land.[i]
18 Your mind will dwell on the terror:
"Where is the one who counted, where
the one who weighed?
Where the one who counted the
towers?"[j]
19 You shall no longer see a defiant people,
a people of speech too obscure to
comprehend,
stammering in a tongue not
understood.[k]
20 Look to Zion, the city of our festivals;
your eyes shall see Jerusalem
as a quiet abode, a tent not to be struck,
Whose pegs will never be pulled up,
nor any of its ropes severed.[l]
21 Indeed the LORD in majesty will be there
for us
a place of rivers and wide streams
on which no galley may go,
where no majestic ship* may pass.[m]
22 For the LORD is our judge,
the LORD is our lawgiver,
the LORD is our king;
he it is who will save us.
23 The rigging hangs slack;
it cannot hold the mast in place,
nor keep the sail spread out.
Then the blind will divide great spoils
and the lame will carry off the loot.[n]
24 No one who dwells there will say, "I am
sick";
the people who live there will be
forgiven their guilt.[o]

F. The Lord, Zion's Avenger*

CHAPTER 34

See RG 280–95

Judgment upon Edom

1 Come near, nations, and listen;
be attentive, you peoples!
Let the earth and what fills it listen,
the world and all it produces.[p]
2 The LORD is angry with all the nations,
enraged against all their host;
He has placed them under the ban,
given them up to slaughter.[q]
3 Their slain shall be cast out,
their corpses shall send up a stench;
the mountains shall run with their
blood,[r]
4 All the host of heaven shall rot;

33:7 Ariel . . . Shalem: Jerusalem; cf. 29:1; Gn 14:18; Ps 76:3. There is a play on words between "Shalem," the city name, and *shalom*, Heb. for "peace."

33:9 Sharon: the fertile plain near the Mediterranean.

33:17 King: either the ideal Davidic king or God; cf. v. 22.

33:21–23 Galley . . . majestic ship: of a foreign oppressor. Though the broad streams of the future Jerusalem will make it accessible by boat, no foreign invader will succeed in a naval attack on the city, for the Lord will protect it, the enemy fleet will be disabled, and even the weakest inhabitants will gather much plunder from the defeated enemy.

34:1–35:10 These two chapters form a small collection which looks forward to the vindication of Zion, first by defeat of its enemies (chap. 34), then by its restoration (chap. 35). They are generally judged to be later than the time of Isaiah (eighth century), perhaps during the Babylonian exile or thereafter; they are strongly influenced by Deutero-Isaiah (sixth century). In places they reflect themes from other parts of the Isaian collection.

f: Is 10:17. *g:* Is 30:27, 30, 32; 31:9. *h:* Ps 15:2–6; 24:4–5. *i:* Is 26:15. *j:* Ps 48:13–14. *k:* Is 28:11. *l:* Is 32:18; Ps 46:6; 122:1–4. *m:* Ez 47:1–12; Ps 46:5; 48:7. *n:* 2 Sm 8:6–7. *o:* Mi 7:18–19. *p:* Mi 1:2. *q:* Is 24:21. *r:* Ez 32:4, 6.

the heavens shall be rolled up like a
scroll.
All their host shall wither away,
as the leaf wilts on the vine,
or as the fig withers on the tree.[s]
5 When my sword has drunk its fill in the
heavens,
it shall come down upon Edom for
judgment,
upon a people under my ban.[t]
6 The LORD has a sword sated with blood,
greasy with fat,
With the blood of lambs and goats,
with the fat of rams' kidneys;
For the LORD has a sacrifice in Bozrah,
a great slaughter in the land of Edom.[u]
7 Wild oxen shall be struck down with
fatlings,
and bullocks with bulls;
Their land shall be soaked with blood,
and their soil greasy with fat.
8 * For the LORD has a day of vengeance,
a year of requital for the cause of Zion.[v]
9 Edom's streams shall be changed into
pitch,
its soil into sulfur,
and its land shall become burning pitch;
10 Night and day it shall not be quenched,
its smoke shall rise forever.
From generation to generation it shall lie
waste,
never again shall anyone pass through
it.[w]
11 But the desert owl and hoot owl shall
possess it,
the screech owl and raven shall dwell
in it.
The LORD will stretch over it the
measuring line of chaos,
the plumb line of confusion.* [x]
12 Its nobles shall be no more,
nor shall kings be proclaimed there;
all its princes are gone.[y]
13 Its castles shall be overgrown with thorns,
its fortresses with thistles and briers.
It shall become an abode for jackals,
a haunt for ostriches.[z]
14 Wildcats shall meet with desert beasts,
satyrs* shall call to one another;
There shall the lilith repose,
and find for herself a place to rest.
15 There the hoot owl shall nest and lay eggs,
hatch them out and gather them in her
shadow;
There shall the kites assemble,
each with its mate.
16 Search through the book of the LORD*
and read:
not one of these shall be lacking,
For the mouth of the LORD has ordered it,
and his spirit gathers them there.
17 It is he who casts the lot for them;
his hand measures off* their portions;
They shall possess it forever,
and dwell in it from generation to
generation.[a]

CHAPTER 35

See RG 280–95

*Israel's Deliverance**

1 The wilderness and the parched land will
exult;
the Arabah will rejoice and bloom;[b]
2 Like the crocus it shall bloom abundantly,
and rejoice with joyful song.

34:8–17 The extreme hostility against Edom in this passage is reflected in a number of other prophetic texts from the seventh and sixth centuries B.C. (cf. e.g., 63:1–6; Jer 49:7–22; Ez 25:12–14). The animus was probably prompted by Edomite infiltration of the southern territories of Judah, especially after the Babylonian conquest of Judah.

34:11 Chaos . . . confusion: *tohu . . . bohu* in Hebrew, the terms used to describe the primeval chaos in Gn 1:2.

34:14 Satyrs: see note on 13:21. **The lilith**: a female demon thought to roam about the desert.

34:16 Book of the LORD: a list of God's creatures; cf. Ex 32:32–33; Ps 69:29, "the book of the living"; Ps 139:16, "your book."

34:17 Casts the lot . . . measures off: an ironic reference to how land might be distributed to new possessors (cf. Jos 14–21; Mi 2:5).

35:1–10 This chapter contains a number of themes similar to those in Deutero-Isaiah (chaps. 40–55), for example, the blossoming of the wilderness (vv. 1–2; cf. 41:18–19), which is now well-irrigated (v. 7; cf. 43:19–20); sight to the blind (vv. 5–6; cf. 42:7, 16); a highway in the wilderness (v. 8; cf. 41:3); and the return of the redeemed/ransomed to Zion (vv. 9–10; cf. 51:11). Nevertheless, it forms a unit with chap. 34 (see note on 34:1–35:10) and reflects, along with that chapter, themes found in chaps. 1–33.

s: Is 13:10; 24:23; Ez 32:7; Jl 3:3–4; Mt 24:29; 2 Pt 3:10; Rev 6:12–14. *t:* Jer 46:10. *u:* Is 63:1; Lv 3:4; 2 Sm 1:22; Jer 49:12–13; Zep 1:7. *v:* Is 13:9; 63:4. *w:* Mal 1:4; Rev 14:11; 18:18. *x:* Is 14:23; 28:17; 2 Kgs 21:13; Zep 2:14. *y:* Ob 18. *z:* Is 13:21; Hos 9:6. *a:* Jos 18:10; Ps 78:55. *b:* Is 41:18–19; 55:12–13.

The glory of Lebanon will be given to it,
the splendor of Carmel and Sharon;
They will see the glory of the LORD,
the splendor of our God.[c]
3 Strengthen hands that are feeble,
make firm knees that are weak,[d]
4 Say to the fearful of heart:
Be strong, do not fear!
Here is your God,
he comes with vindication;
With divine recompense
he comes to save you.[e]
5 Then the eyes of the blind shall see,
and the ears of the deaf be opened;[f]
6 Then the lame shall leap like a stag,
and the mute tongue sing for joy.
For waters will burst forth in the
wilderness,
and streams in the Arabah.[g]
7 The burning sands will become pools,
and the thirsty ground, springs of water;
The abode where jackals crouch
will be a marsh for the reed and
papyrus.
8 A highway will be there,
called the holy way;
No one unclean may pass over it,
but it will be for his people;
no traveler, not even fools, shall go
astray on it.[h]
9 No lion shall be there,
nor any beast of prey approach,
nor be found.
But there the redeemed shall walk,[i]
10 And the ransomed of the LORD shall
return,
and enter Zion singing,
crowned with everlasting joy;
They meet with joy and gladness,
sorrow and mourning flee away.[j]

G. Historical Appendix*

CHAPTER 36

See RG 280–95

Invasion of Sennacherib. 1 In the fourteenth year of King Hezekiah, Sennacherib,
king of Assyria, went up against all the fortified cities of Judah and captured them.* [k]
2 From Lachish the king of Assyria sent his
commander with a great army to King Hezekiah in Jerusalem. When he stopped at the
conduit of the upper pool, on the highway of
the fuller's field, 3 there came out to him the
master of the palace, Eliakim, son of Hilkiah, and Shebna the scribe, and the chancellor, Joah, son of Asaph. 4 The commander
said to them, "Tell Hezekiah: Thus says the
great king, the king of Assyria: On what do
you base this trust of yours? 5 Do you think
mere words substitute for strategy and might
in war? In whom, then, do you place your
trust, that you rebel against me? 6 Do you
trust in Egypt, that broken reed of a staff
which pierces the hand of anyone who leans
on it? That is what Pharaoh, king of Egypt,
is to all who trust in him.[l] 7 Or do you say to
me: It is in the LORD, our God, we trust? Is it
not he whose high places and altars Hezekiah has removed,* commanding Judah and
Jerusalem, 'Worship before this altar'?[m]

8 "Now, make a wager with my lord, the
king of Assyria: I will give you two thousand horses, if you are able to put riders on
them. 9 How then can you turn back even a
captain, one of the least servants of my lord,
trusting, as you do, in Egypt for chariots and
horses? 10 Did I come up to destroy this land
without the LORD? The LORD himself said to
me, Go up and destroy that land!"[n]

11 Then Eliakim and Shebna and Joah said

36:1–39:8 Except for 38:9–20 (Hezekiah's prayer of thanksgiving), this historical appendix describing the siege, etc., is paralleled in 2 Kgs 18:13–20:19, which, however, has certain details proper to itself. The events are also reflected in the cuneiform inscriptions of Sennacherib.

36:1 The occasion for this Assyrian attack was Hezekiah's attempt to reject Judah's status as vassal to Assyria, relying on help from Egypt, a course of action condemned by Isaiah (see notes on 28:15, 18; 28:16; 29:7–8; 30:1–17; etc.). 2 Kgs 19:14–16 reports that Hezekiah surrendered to the Assyrians and paid the tribute imposed on him—a report omitted in the Isaiah text.

36:7 The Assyrians assert that Hezekiah's removal of the high places and altars (unofficial sanctuaries) was taken by the Lord as an insult. They declare to Jerusalem's emissaries that the city therefore no longer has a right to the Lord's protection and that they are the ones who truly carry out his will (cf. v. 10).

c: Is 40:5; 60:13. *d:* Is 40:29–30; Jb 4:3–4; Heb 12:12. *e:* Is 41:10; Zec 8:13. *f:* Is 29:18; 32:3. *g:* Is 32:3–4; 41:18; 43:19–20; 44:3; Mt 11:5. *h:* Is 11:16; 43:19; 49:11. *i:* Is 62:10; Lv 26:6. *j:* Is 51:11. *k:* 2 Kgs 18:13; 2 Chr 32:1. *l:* Is 30:2–3, 7. *m:* 2 Kgs 18:4. *n:* Is 10:5–6.

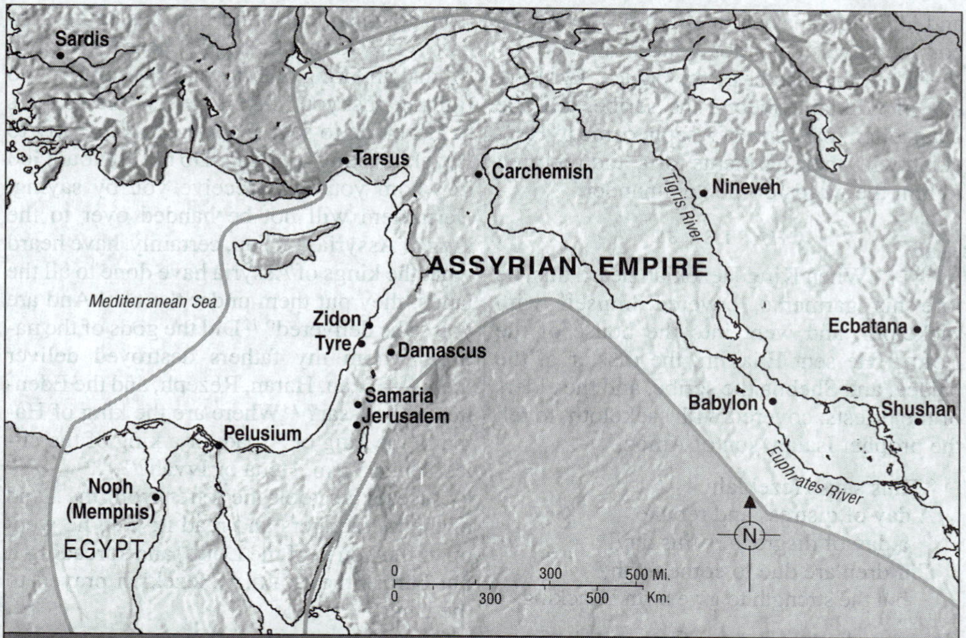

The Assyrian Empire

to the commander, “Please speak to your
servants in Aramaic; we understand it. Do
not speak to us in the language of Judah
within earshot of the people who are on the
wall.”*
[12]But the commander replied, “Was it to
your lord and to you that my lord sent me to
speak these words? Was it not rather to those
sitting on the wall, who, with you, will have
to eat their own excrement and drink their
own urine?” [13]Then the commander stepped
forward and cried out in a loud voice in the
language of Judah, “Listen to the words of
the great king, the king of Assyria. [14]Thus
says the king: Do not let Hezekiah deceive
you, for he cannot rescue you. [15]And do not
let Hezekiah induce you to trust in the LORD,
saying, ‘The LORD will surely rescue us, and
this city will not be handed over to the king
of Assyria.’ [16]Do not listen to Hezekiah, for
thus says the king of Assyria:

Make peace with me
and surrender to me!
Eat, each of you, from your vine,
each from your own fig tree.
Drink water, each from your own well,[o]
17 until I arrive and take you
to a land like your own,
A land of grain and wine,
a land of bread and vineyards.

[18]Do not let Hezekiah seduce you by saying,
‘The LORD will rescue us.’ Has any of the
gods of the nations rescued his land from the
power of the king of Assyria?[p] [19]Where are
the gods of Hamath and Arpad? Where are
the gods of Sepharvaim? Where are the gods
of Samaria? Have they saved Samaria from
my power?[q] [20]Who among all the gods of
these lands ever rescued their land from my
power, that the LORD should save Jerusalem
from my power?” [21]But they remained silent

36:11 The emissaries of King Hezekiah ask that the conversation be carried on in Aramaic, not in Hebrew, for they fear the effect of the Assyrian claims upon the morale of the people.

o: 1 Kgs 5:5; Zec 3:10. *p:* Is 37:11. *q:* Is 10:9; 37:13.

and did not answer at all, for the king's command was, "Do not answer him."

22 Then the master of the palace, Eliakim, son of Hilkiah, Shebna the scribe, and the chancellor Joah, son of Asaph, came to Hezekiah with their garments torn, and reported to him the words of the commander.

CHAPTER 37

See RG 280–95

1* When King Hezekiah heard this, he tore his garments, covered himself with sackcloth, and went into the house of the LORD. 2 He sent Eliakim, the master of the palace, and Shebna the scribe, and the elders of the priests, covered with sackcloth, to tell the prophet Isaiah, son of Amoz,

3 "Thus says Hezekiah:
A day of distress and rebuke,
a day of disgrace is this day!
Children are due to come forth,
but the strength to give birth is lacking.*[r]

4 Perhaps the LORD, your God, will hear the words of the commander, whom his lord, the king of Assyria, sent to taunt the living God, and will rebuke him for the words which the LORD, your God, has heard. So lift up a prayer for the remnant that is here."

5 When the servants of King Hezekiah had come to Isaiah, 6 he said to them: "Tell this to your lord: Thus says the LORD: Do not be frightened by the words you have heard, by which the deputies of the king of Assyria have blasphemed me.[s]

7 I am putting in him such a spirit
that when he hears a report
he will return to his land.
I will make him fall by the sword in
his land."

8 When the commander, on his return, heard that the king of Assyria had withdrawn from Lachish, he found him besieging Libnah. 9 The king of Assyria heard a report: "Tirhakah,* king of Ethiopia, has come out to fight against you." Again he sent messengers to Hezekiah to say: 10 "Thus shall you say to Hezekiah, king of Judah: Do not let your God in whom you trust deceive you by saying, 'Jerusalem will not be handed over to the king of Assyria.'[t] 11 You, certainly, have heard what the kings of Assyria have done to all the lands: they put them under the ban! And are you to be delivered? 12 Did the gods of the nations whom my fathers destroyed deliver them—Gozan, Haran, Rezeph, and the Edenites in Telassar? 13 Where are the king of Hamath, the king of Arpad, or a king of the cities Sepharvaim, Hena or Ivvah?"

14 Hezekiah took the letter from the hand of the messengers and read it; then he went up to the house of the LORD, and spreading it out before the LORD, 15 Hezekiah prayed to the LORD:

16 "LORD of hosts, God of Israel,
enthroned on the cherubim!
You alone are God
over all the kingdoms of the earth.
It is you who made
the heavens and the earth.*
17 Incline your ear, LORD, and listen!
open your eyes, LORD, and see!
Hear all the words Sennacherib has sent
to taunt the living God.
18 Truly, O LORD,
the kings of Assyria have laid waste
the nations and their lands.
19 They gave their gods to the fire
—they were not gods at all,
but the work of human hands—
Wood and stone, they destroyed them.[u]
20 Therefore, LORD, our God,
save us from this man's power,

37:1–35 There appear to be parallel accounts of Hezekiah's appeal and the response received (vv. 1–7 and vv. 14–35): in each, Hezekiah goes to the Temple, refers to the Assyrian boasts (found in 36:15–20; 37:10–14), and receives a favorable response from Isaiah.

37:3 A proverbial expression. In the Bible the pangs of childbirth often typify extreme anguish; cf. 13:8; Jer 6:24; Mi 4:9–10. In this instance there is reference to the desperate situation of Hezekiah from which he would scarcely be able to free himself.

37:9 Tirhakah: may have been general of the Egyptian army in 701 B.C.; later he became Pharaoh, one of the Ethiopian dynasty of Egyptian kings (ca. 690–664 B.C.). Many consider that this account in Isaiah combines features of two originally distinct sieges of Jerusalem by Sennacherib.

37:16 In contrast to the empty boasting of the Assyrians, Hezekiah proclaims the Lord as "God over all the kingdoms of the earth."

r: Is 26:18. *s:* Is 7:4; 10:24. *t:* Is 36:14. *u:* Jer 16:20.

That all the kingdoms of the earth may
know
that you alone, LORD, are God."

21* Then Isaiah, son of Amoz, sent this
message to Hezekiah: "Thus says the LORD,
the God of Israel, to whom you have prayed
concerning Sennacherib, king of Assyria: I
have listened! 22 This is the word the LORD
has spoken concerning him:[v]

She despises you, laughs you to scorn,
the virgin daughter Zion;
Behind you she wags her head,
daughter Jerusalem.
23 Whom have you insulted and blasphemed,
at whom have you raised your voice
And lifted up your eyes on high?
At the Holy One of Israel![w]
24 Through the mouths of your messengers
you have insulted the Lord when you
said:
'With my many chariots I went up
to the tops of the peaks,
to the recesses of Lebanon,
To cut down its lofty cedars,
its choice cypresses;
I reached the farthest shelter,
the forest ranges.
25 I myself dug wells
and drank foreign water;
Drying up all the rivers of Egypt
beneath the soles of my feet.'
26 Have you not heard?
A long time ago I prepared it,
from days of old I planned it,
Now I have brought it about:
You are here to reduce
fortified cities to heaps of ruins,[x]
27 Their people powerless,
dismayed and distraught,
They are plants of the field,
green growth,
thatch on the rooftops,
Grain scorched by the east wind.
28 I know when you stand or sit,
when you come or go,
and how you rage against me.
29 Because you rage against me
and your smugness has reached my
ears,
I will put my hook in your nose
and my bit in your mouth,
And make you leave by the way you
came.[y]
30 This shall be a sign* for you:
This year you shall eat the aftergrowth,
next year, what grows of itself;
But in the third year, sow and reap,
plant vineyards and eat their fruit!
31 The remaining survivors of the house of
Judah
shall again strike root below
and bear fruit above.[z]
32 For out of Jerusalem shall come a remnant,
and from Mount Zion, survivors.
The zeal of the LORD of hosts shall do
this.[a]

33 Therefore, thus says the LORD about the
king of Assyria:

He shall not come as far as this city,
nor shoot there an arrow,
nor confront it with a shield,
Nor cast up a siege-work against it.
34 By the way he came he shall leave,
never coming as far as this city,
oracle of the LORD.
35 I will shield and save this city
for my own sake and the sake of David
my servant."[b]

36 Then the angel of the LORD went forth
and struck down one hundred and eighty-
five thousand in the Assyrian camp. Early
the next morning, there they were, all those
corpses, dead!* [c]
37 So Sennacherib, the king
of Assyria, broke camp, departed, returned
home, and stayed in Nineveh.

37:21–37 The reversal of Isaiah's attitude toward Hezekiah's revolt (see note on 36:1) and a wonderful deliverance after Hezekiah had already submitted and paid tribute raise questions difficult to answer. See note on 22:1–14. Some have postulated that chaps. 36–37 combine accounts of two different Assyrian invasions.

37:30 A sign: sets a time limit. After two years the normal conditions of life will be resumed. See the similar use of time limits as signs in 7:15–16; 8:4; 16:14; and 21:16. **You**: Hezekiah.

37:36 The destruction of Sennacherib's army is also recorded by Herodotus, a Greek historian of the fifth century B.C. It was possibly owing to a plague, which the author interprets as God's activity.

v: 2 Kgs 19:21. *w:* Is 10:12. *x:* Is 10:6, 15. *y:* Is 30:28. *z:* Is 27:6. *a:* Is 9:6. *b:* Is 31:5; 1 Kgs 15:4. *c:* Is 10:12; 17:14.

38 When he was worshiping in the temple
of his god Nisroch, his sons Adrammelech
and Sharezer struck him down with the
sword and fled into the land of Ararat.* His
son Esarhaddon reigned in his place.

See RG 280–95

CHAPTER 38

Sickness and Recovery of Hezekiah.
1* In those days,* when Hezekiah was mortally ill, the prophet Isaiah, son of Amoz,
came and said to him: "Thus says the LORD:
Put your house in order, for you are about to
die; you shall not recover."[d] 2 Hezekiah
turned his face to the wall and prayed to the
LORD:
3 "Ah, LORD, remember how faithfully
and wholeheartedly I conducted myself in
your presence, doing what was good in your
sight!" And Hezekiah wept bitterly.[e]
4 Then the word of the LORD came to Isaiah: 5 Go, tell Hezekiah:* Thus says the
LORD, the God of your father David: I have
heard your prayer; I have seen your tears.
Now I will add fifteen years to your life. 6 I
will rescue you and this city from the hand
of the king of Assyria; I will be a shield to
this city.[f]
7 This will be the sign for you from the
LORD that the LORD will carry out the word
he has spoken: 8 See, I will make the shadow
cast by the sun on the stairway to the terrace
of Ahaz* go back the ten steps it has advanced. So the sun came back the ten steps it
had advanced.[g]
Hezekiah's Hymn of Thanksgiving. 9 The
song of Hezekiah, king of Judah, after he
had been sick and had recovered from his illness:

10 In the noontime of life* I said,
I must depart!
To the gates of Sheol I have been
consigned
for the rest of my years.[h]
11 I said, I shall see the LORD* no more
in the land of the living.
Nor look on any mortals
among those who dwell in the world.
12 My dwelling, like a shepherd's tent,
is struck down and borne away
from me;
You have folded up my life, like a weaver
who severs me from the last thread.*[i]
From morning to night you make an end
of me;
13 I cry out even until the dawn.
Like a lion he breaks all my bones;
from morning to night you make an
end of me.[j]
14 Like a swallow I chirp;
I moan like a dove.
My eyes grow weary looking heavenward:
Lord, I am overwhelmed; go security
for me!
15 * What am I to say or tell him?
He is the one who has done it!
All my sleep has fled,
because of the bitterness of my soul.
16 Those live whom the LORD protects;
yours is the life of my spirit.
You have given me health and restored
my life!
17 Peace in place of bitterness!
You have preserved my life
from the pit of destruction;
Behind your back
you cast all my sins.*

37:38 The violent death of Sennacherib (681 B.C.) is also mentioned in non-biblical sources. It occurred twenty years after his invasion of Judah. **Ararat**: the land of Urartu in the mountains north of Assyria.

38:1–39:8 The events of this section—sickness and recovery of Hezekiah, embassy of Merodach-baladan—anticipate the rise of Babylon (chaps. 40–66). They occurred prior to the events of 36:1–37:38, which point back to Assyria (1:1–35:10).

38:1 In those days: before the siege of Jerusalem in 701 B.C.

38:5 Since Hezekiah died in 687 B.C., his sickness may have occurred in 702 B.C., that is, fifteen years before.

38:8 Stairway to the terrace of Ahaz: this interpretation is based on a reading of the Hebrew text revised according to the Dead Sea Scroll of Isaiah; cf. 2 Kgs 23:12. Many translate the phrase as "steps of Ahaz" and understand this as referring to a sundial.

38:10 In the noontime of life: long before the end of a full span of life; cf. Ps 55:24; 102:25.

38:11 See the LORD: go to the Temple and take part in its service.

38:12 These two metaphors emphasize the suddenness and finality of death.

38:15–16 The Hebrew text is very problematic and its meaning uncertain.

38:17 Behind your back you cast all my sins: figurative language to express the divine forgiveness of sins, as if God no longer saw or cared about them.

d: 2 Kgs 20:1. *e:* 2 Kgs 18:5–6. *f:* Is 37:35. *g:* 2 Kgs 20:9–11. *h:* Jb 17:11–13; Ps 102:25. *i:* Jb 7:6. *j:* Jb 23:14.

18 * For it is not Sheol that gives you thanks,
nor death that praises you;
Neither do those who go down into the pit
await your kindness.[k]
19 The living, the living give you thanks,
as I do today.
Parents declare to their children,
O God, your faithfulness.
20 The LORD is there to save us.
We shall play our music
In the house of the LORD
all the days of our life.

21* Then Isaiah said, "Bring a poultice of
figs and apply it to the boil for his recovery."
22 Hezekiah asked, "What is the sign that I
shall go up to the house of the LORD?"

See RG 280–95

CHAPTER 39

Embassy from Merodach-baladan. 1 At
that time Merodach-baladan,* son of Baladan, king of Babylon, sent letters and gifts to
Hezekiah, when he heard that he had been
sick and had recovered.[l] 2 Hezekiah was
pleased at their coming, and then showed the
messengers his treasury, the silver and gold,
the spices and perfumed oil, his whole armory, and everything in his storerooms; there
was nothing in his house or in all his realm
that Hezekiah did not show them.[m]
3 Then Isaiah the prophet came to King
Hezekiah and asked him, "What did these
men say to you? Where did they come
from?" Hezekiah replied, "They came to me
from a distant land, from Babylon." 4 He
asked, "What did they see in your house?"
Hezekiah answered, "They saw everything
in my house. There is nothing in my storerooms that I did not show them." 5 Then Isaiah said to Hezekiah, "Hear the word of the
LORD of hosts: 6 The time is coming when all
that is in your house, everything that your
ancestors have stored up until this day, shall
be carried off to Babylon;* nothing shall be
left, says the LORD.[n] 7 Some of your own descendants, your progeny, shall be taken and
made attendants in the palace of the king of
Babylon."[o] 8 Hezekiah replied to Isaiah,
"The word of the LORD which you have spoken is good."* For he thought, "There will be
peace and stability in my lifetime."

II. Isaiah 40—55*

A. The Lord's Glory in Israel's Liberation

CHAPTER 40

See RG 280–95

Promise of Salvation

1 * Comfort, give comfort to my people,
says your God.

38:18–19 See note on Ps 6:6.

38:21–22 These verses are clearly out of place. Logically they should come after v. 6, as they do in the parallel account in 2 Kgs 20, but the two accounts are not identical, and it appears that the version in Isaiah is abbreviated from that in Kings. If that is so, Is 38:21–22 would be a secondary addition from Kings, inserted by a later reader who thought the account incomplete.

39:1 Merodach-baladan: twice king of Babylon, probably from 721 to 710 B.C., and again for nine months, in 704–703. This visit of his messengers, certainly before 701, was in reality a political one. Babylon hoped to lead an anti-Assyrian confederation composed of neighboring states and wanted Judah to join.

39:6 Because Judah preferred to follow a pro-Babylonian policy, instead of trusting in the Lord, it would later be exiled to Babylon.

39:8 Hezekiah was relieved that the disaster would not occur in his lifetime.

40:1–55:13 Chapters 40–55 are usually designated Second Isaiah (or Deutero-Isaiah) and are believed to have been written by an anonymous prophet toward the end of the Babylonian exile. Isaiah, who is named frequently in chaps. 1–39, does not appear here; the Assyrians, the great threat during the eighth century, hardly appear; the Judeans are in Babylon, having been taken there by the victorious Babylonians; Cyrus, the Persian king, is named; he will defeat Babylon and release the captives. Second Isaiah, who sees this not as a happy circumstance but as part of God's age-old plan, exhorts the Judeans to resist the temptations of Babylonian religion and stirs up hopes of an imminent return to Judah, where the Lord will again be acknowledged as King (52:7). Because the prophet proclaimed the triumph of Persia over Babylon, his message would have been considered seditious, and it is very likely for this reason that the collection would have circulated anonymously. At some point it was appended to Is 1–39 and consequently was long considered the work of Isaiah of Jerusalem of the eighth century. But the fact that it is addressed to Judean exiles in Babylon indicates a sixth-century date. Nevertheless, this eloquent prophet in many ways works within the tradition of Isaiah and develops themes found in the earlier chapters, such as the holiness of the Lord (cf. note on 1:4) and his lordship of history. Second Isaiah also develops other

k: Ps 6:6; 88:11–13. *l:* 2 Kgs 20:12. *m:* 2 Chr 32:25–31. *n:* 2 Kgs 24:13; 25:13–17. *o:* Dn 1:3–19.

2 Speak to the heart of Jerusalem, and
proclaim to her
that her service* has ended,
that her guilt is expiated,
That she has received from the hand of
the LORD
double for all her sins.[p]

3 A voice proclaims:*
In the wilderness prepare the way of the
LORD!
Make straight in the wasteland a
highway for our God![q]
4 Every valley shall be lifted up,
every mountain and hill made low;
The rugged land shall be a plain,
the rough country, a broad valley.
5 Then the glory of the LORD shall be
revealed,
and all flesh shall see it together;
for the mouth of the LORD has spoken.

6 A voice says, "Proclaim!"
I answer, "What shall I proclaim?"
"All flesh is grass,
and all their loyalty like the flower of
the field.[r]
7 The grass withers, the flower wilts,
when the breath of the LORD blows
upon it."
"Yes, the people is grass!
8 The grass withers, the flower wilts,
but the word of our God stands forever."

9 Go up onto a high mountain,
Zion, herald of good news!*
Cry out at the top of your voice,
Jerusalem, herald of good news!
Cry out, do not fear!
Say to the cities of Judah:
Here is your God!
10 Here comes with power
the Lord GOD,
who rules by his strong arm;
Here is his reward with him,
his recompense before him.
11 Like a shepherd he feeds his flock;
in his arms he gathers the lambs,
Carrying them in his bosom,
leading the ewes with care.[s]

Power of God and the Vanity of Idols

12 Who has measured with his palm the
waters,
marked off the heavens with a span,
held in his fingers the dust of the earth,
weighed the mountains in scales
and the hills in a balance?*
13 Who has directed the spirit of the LORD,
or instructed him as his counselor?[t]
14 Whom did he consult to gain knowledge?
Who taught him the path of judgment,
or showed him the way of
understanding?

15 See, the nations count as a drop in the
bucket,
as a wisp of cloud on the scales;
the coastlands weigh no more than a
speck.*
16 Lebanon would not suffice for fuel,*
nor its animals be enough for burnt
offerings.

Old Testament themes, such as the Lord as Israel's redeemer or deliverer (cf. Ex 3:8; 6:6; 15:13; 18:8).

40:1 The "voices" of vv. 3, 6 are members of the heavenly court addressing the prophet; then v. 1 can be understood as the Lord addressing them. It is also possible to translate, with the Vulgate, "Comfort, give comfort, O my people" (i.e., the exiles are called to comfort Jerusalem). The juxtaposition of "my people" and "your God" recalls the covenant formulary.

40:2 Service: servitude (cf. Jb 7:1) and exile.

40:3–5 A description of the return of the exiles from Babylon to Jerusalem (Zion). The language used here figuratively describes the way the exiles will take. The Lord leads them, so their way lies straight across the wilderness rather than along the well-watered routes usually followed from Mesopotamia to Israel. Mt 3:3 and gospel parallels adapt these verses to the witness of John the Baptizer to Jesus.

40:9 Herald of good news: i.e., of the imminent restoration of the people to their land. This theme of the proclamation of the good news occurs elsewhere in Second Isaiah; cf. also 41:27; 52:7.

40:12 The implicit answer is "the hand of the LORD" (v. 2). **Waters . . . heavens . . . earth**: together form the universe; cf. Gn 1:1–2. **Span**: the distance between the extended little finger and the thumb. **Fingers**: lit., "three fingers" (i.e., thumb, index, and middle).

40:15 Drop . . . wisp of cloud . . . a speck: the smallest constituent parts of the cosmic waters, heavens, and earth mentioned in v. 12.

40:16 Lebanon . . . fuel: the famed cedars would not be enough to keep the fires of sacrifice burning.

p: Is 50:21. *q:* Mt 3:3; Mk 1:3; Lk 2:27; Jn 1:23. *r:* Jb 8:12; 14:2; Ps 37:2; Sir 14:18; Jas 1:10; 1 Pt 1:24. *s:* Is 49:9–10; 63:11; Ez 34:23; 37:24; Jn 10:11. *t:* Wis 9:13; Rom 11:34; 1 Cor 2:16; Jb 38:1–11.

17 Before him all the nations are as nought,
as nothing and void he counts them.

18 To whom can you liken God?[u]
With what likeness can you confront him?
19 An idol? An artisan casts it,
the smith plates it with gold,
fits it with silver chains.* [v]
20 Is mulberry wood the offering?
A skilled artisan picks out
a wood that will not rot,
Seeks to set up for himself
an idol that will not totter.[w]

21 Do you not know? Have you not heard?
Was it not told you from the beginning?
Have you not understood from the founding of the earth?
22 The one who is enthroned above the vault of the earth,
its inhabitants like grasshoppers,
Who stretches out the heavens like a veil
and spreads them out like a tent to dwell in,[x]
23 Who brings princes to nought
and makes the rulers of the earth as nothing.
24 Scarcely are they planted, scarcely sown,
scarcely their stem rooted in the earth,
When he breathes upon them and they wither,
and the stormwind carries them away like straw.

25 To whom can you liken me as an equal?
says the Holy One.
26 Lift up your eyes on high
and see who created* these:
He leads out their army and numbers them,
calling them all by name.
By his great might and the strength of his power
not one of them is missing![y]
27 Why, O Jacob, do you say,*
and declare, O Israel,
"My way is hidden from the LORD,
and my right is disregarded by my God"?
28 Do you not know?
Have you not heard?
The LORD is God from of old,
creator of the ends of the earth.
He does not faint or grow weary,
and his knowledge is beyond scrutiny.
29 He gives power to the faint,
abundant strength to the weak.
30 Though young men faint and grow weary,
and youths stagger and fall,
31 They that hope in the LORD will renew their strength,
they will soar on eagles' wings;
They will run and not grow weary,
walk and not grow faint.

CHAPTER 41

See RG 280–95

The Liberator of Israel

1 Keep silence before me, O coastlands;*
let the nations renew their strength.
Let them draw near and speak;
let us come together for judgment.
2 Who has stirred up from the East the champion of justice,
and summoned him to be his attendant?
To him he delivers nations
and subdues kings;
With his sword he reduces them to dust,
with his bow, to driven straw.
3 He pursues them, passing on without loss,
by a path his feet scarcely touch.

40:19 Chains: needed to hold the idol steady when carried in processions; cf. v. 20; Jer 10:4.

40:26 Created: see note on Gn 1:1–2:3. **By name**: for he is their Creator.

40:27–28 The exiles, here called Jacob-Israel (Gn 32:29), must not give way to discouragement: their Lord is the eternal God.

41:1–4 Earlier prophets had spoken of the Assyrians and Babylonians as the Lord's instruments for the punishment of Israel's sins; here the Lord is described as raising up and giving victory to a foreign ruler in order to deliver Israel from the Babylonian exile. The ruler is Cyrus (44:28; 45:1), king of Anshan in Persia, a vassal of the Babylonians. He rebelled against the Babylonian overlords in 556 B.C., and after a series of victories, entered Babylon as victor in 539; the following year he issued a decree which allowed the Jewish captives to return to their homeland (2 Chr 36:22–23; Ezr 1:1–4). For Second Isaiah, the meteoric success of Cyrus was the work of the Lord to accomplish the deliverance promised by earlier prophets.

u: Acts 17:29. *v:* Ps 115:4–7; Jer 10:4. *w:* Is 44:13. *x:* Ps 104:2. *y:* Ps 147:4–5.

4 Who has performed these deeds?
Who has called forth the generations
from the beginning?[z]
I, the LORD, am the first,
and at the last* I am he.
5 The coastlands see, and fear;
the ends of the earth tremble:
they approach, they come on.

6 Each one helps his neighbor,
one says to the other, "Courage!"
7 The woodworker encourages the
goldsmith,
the one who beats with the hammer,
him who strikes on the anvil,
Saying of the soldering, "It is good!"
then fastening it with nails so it will
not totter.
8 But you, Israel, my servant,[a]
Jacob, whom I have chosen,
offspring of Abraham my friend—
9 You whom I have taken from the ends of
the earth
and summoned from its far-off places,
To whom I have said, You are my
servant;
I chose you, I have not rejected you—
10 Do not fear: I am with you;
do not be anxious: I am your God.
I will strengthen you, I will help you,
I will uphold you with my victorious
right hand.

11 Yes, all shall be put to shame and disgrace
who vent their anger against you;
Those shall be as nothing and perish
who offer resistance.
12 You shall seek but not find
those who strive against you;
They shall be as nothing at all
who do battle with you.

13 For I am the LORD, your God,
who grasp your right hand;
It is I who say to you, Do not fear,
I will help you.
14 Do not fear, you worm Jacob,
you maggot Israel;
I will help you—oracle of the LORD;
the Holy One of Israel is your
redeemer.*
15 I will make of you a threshing sledge,
sharp, new, full of teeth,
To thresh the mountains and crush them,
to make the hills like chaff.
16 When you winnow them, the wind shall
carry them off,
the storm shall scatter them.
But you shall rejoice in the LORD;
in the Holy One of Israel you shall
glory.

17 The afflicted and the needy seek water in
vain,
their tongues are parched with thirst.
I, the LORD, will answer them;
I, the God of Israel, will not forsake
them.
18 I will open up rivers on the bare heights,
and fountains in the broad valleys;
I will turn the wilderness into a marshland,
and the dry ground into springs of
water.
19 In the wilderness I will plant the cedar,
acacia, myrtle, and olive;
In the wasteland I will set the cypress,
together with the plane tree and the
pine,
20 That all may see and know,
observe and understand,
That the hand of the LORD has done this,
the Holy One of Israel has created it.

21 Present your case, says the LORD;*
bring forward your arguments, says
the King of Jacob.
22 Let them draw near and foretell to us
what it is that shall happen!

41:4 The first . . . the last: God as the beginning and end encompasses all reality. The same designation is used in 44:6 and 48:12.

41:14 Redeemer: in Hebrew, *go'el*, one who frees others from slavery and avenges their sufferings; cf. Lv 25:48; Dt 19:6, 12. Cf. note on Ru 2:20.

41:21–29 This indictment of Babylonian gods is patterned on a legal trial, in which they are challenged to prove power over events of history and so justify their status as gods (vv. 21–24). Israel's God, on the other hand, has foretold and now brings to pass Israel's deliverance (vv. 25–27). The accused are unable to respond (vv. 28–29). By such polemics (see also 43:12) the prophet declares that all gods other than the Lord are nonexistent; this implicit claim of monotheism later becomes explicit (see 43:10–11; 45:5–7, 14, 18, 21–22; 46:9; and note on 44:6).

z: Is 44:7; 46:10. *a:* Is 44:1–2, 21; 45:4.

What are the things of long ago?
Tell us, that we may reflect on them
and know their outcome;
Or declare to us the things to come,*
23 tell what is to be in the future,
that we may know that you are gods!
Do something, good or evil,
that will put us in awe and in fear.
24 Why, you are nothing
and your work is nought;
to choose you is an abomination!

25 I have stirred up one from the north, and he comes;
from the east I summon him* by name;
He shall trample the rulers down like mud,
like a potter treading clay.
26 Who announced this from the beginning,
that we might know;
beforehand, that we might say, "True"?
Not one of you foretold it, not one spoke;
not one heard you say,
27 "The first news for Zion: here they come,"
or, "I will give Jerusalem a herald of good news."
28 When I look, there is not one,
not one of them to give counsel,
to make an answer when I question them.
29 Ah, all of them are nothing,
their works are nought,
their idols, empty wind!

CHAPTER 42

See RG 280–95

The Servant of the Lord

1 Here is my servant* whom I uphold,
my chosen one with whom I am pleased.
Upon him I have put my spirit;
he shall bring forth justice to the nations.[b]
2 He will not cry out, nor shout,
nor make his voice heard in the street.
3 A bruised reed* he will not break,
and a dimly burning wick he will not quench.
He will faithfully bring forth justice.
4 He will not grow dim or be bruised
until he establishes justice on the earth;
the coastlands* will wait for his teaching.

5 Thus says God, the LORD,
who created the heavens and stretched them out,
who spread out the earth and its produce,
Who gives breath to its people
and spirit to those who walk on it:
6 I, the LORD, have called you for justice,
I have grasped you by the hand;
I formed you, and set you
as a covenant for the people,
a light for the nations,[c]
7 To open the eyes of the blind,
to bring out prisoners from confinement,
and from the dungeon, those who live in darkness.
8 I am the LORD, LORD is my name;
my glory I give to no other,
nor my praise to idols.
9 See, the earlier things have come to pass,
new ones I now declare;
Before they spring forth
I announce them to you.

The Lord's Purpose for Israel

10 Sing to the LORD a new song,
his praise from the ends of the earth:
Let the sea and what fills it resound,
the coastlands, and those who dwell in them.

41:22 Things of long ago . . . things to come: there are no predictions attributed to idols that have since been fulfilled. Second Isaiah makes frequent reference to "things of long ago," sometimes in conjunction with "things to come" or "new things" in connection with the Lord's activity (cf. 42:9; 43:9, 18; 46:9–10; 48:3–8); both the old things (e.g., creation, exodus) and the new things (release from exile) God brings to pass (cf. 51:9–11), which is why he can declare them beforehand.

41:25 I summon him: Cyrus.

42:1–4 Servant: three other passages have been popularly called "servant of the Lord" poems: 49:1–7; 50:4–11; 52:13–53:12. Whether the servant is an individual or a collectivity is not clear (e.g., contrast 49:3 with 49:5). More important is the description of the mission of the servant. In the early Church and throughout Christian tradition, these poems have been applied to Christ; cf. Mt 12:18–21.

42:3 Bruised reed . . . : images to express the gentle manner of the servant's mission.

42:4 Coastlands: for Israel, the world to the west: the islands and coastal nations of the Mediterranean.

b: Is 45:6; 49:6. *c*: Is 45:13.

11 Let the wilderness and its cities cry out,
the villages where Kedar* dwells;
Let the inhabitants of Sela exult,
and shout from the top of the mountains.
12 Let them give glory to the LORD,
and utter his praise in the coastlands.

13 The LORD goes forth like a warrior,
like a man of war he stirs up his fury;
He shouts out his battle cry,
against his enemies he shows his might:[d]
14 For a long time I have kept silent,
I have said nothing, holding myself back;
Now I cry out like a woman in labor,
gasping and panting.
15 * I will lay waste mountains and hills,
all their undergrowth I will dry up;
I will turn the rivers into marshes,
and the marshes I will dry up.[e]
16 I will lead the blind on a way they do not know;
by paths they do not know I will guide them.
I will turn darkness into light before them,
and make crooked ways straight.
These are my promises:
I made them, I will not forsake them.[f]

17 They shall be turned back in utter shame
who trust in idols;
Who say to molten images,
"You are our gods."
18 You deaf ones, listen,*
you blind ones, look and see!
19 Who is blind but my servant,
or deaf like the messenger I send?
Who is blind like the one I restore,
blind like the servant of the LORD?
20 You see many things but do not observe;
ears open, but do not hear.
21 It was the LORD's will for the sake of his justice
to make his teaching great and glorious.

22 This is a people* plundered and despoiled,
all of them trapped in holes,
hidden away in prisons.
They are taken as plunder, with no one to rescue them,
as spoil, with no one to say, "Give back!"
23 Who among you will give ear to this,
listen and pay attention from now on?
24 Who was it that gave Jacob to be despoiled,
Israel to the plunderers?*
Was it not the LORD, against whom we have sinned?
In his ways they refused to walk,
his teaching they would not heed.
25 So he poured out wrath upon them,
his anger, and the fury of battle;
It blazed all around them, yet they did not realize,
it burned them, but they did not take it to heart.

CHAPTER 43

See RG 280–95

Promises of Redemption and Restoration

1 But now, thus says the LORD,
who created you, Jacob, and formed you, Israel:
Do not fear, for I have redeemed you;
I have called you by name: you are mine.
2 When you pass through waters, I will be with you;
through rivers, you shall not be swept away.
When you walk through fire, you shall not be burned,
nor will flames consume you.
3 For I, the LORD, am your God,

42:11 Kedar: cf. note on 21:16. **Sela**: Petra, the capital of Edom.

42:15–16 Active once more, God will remove the obstacles that hinder the exiles' return, and will lead them by new roads to Jerusalem; cf. 40:3–4.

42:18–20 The Lord rebukes his people for their failures, but their role and their mission endure: they remain his servant, his messenger to the nations.

42:22 A people: Israel in exile.

42:24 Plunderers: the Assyrians and Babylonians. **We . . . they**: the switch from first- to third-person speech, though puzzling, does not obscure the fact that "the people" is meant.

d: Ex 14:3. *e*: Ex 9:25; 10:15; 14:21; Ps 105:33–35. *f*: Ex 13:21.

the Holy One of Israel, your savior.
I give Egypt as ransom for you,
Ethiopia and Seba* in exchange for you.
4 Because you are precious in my eyes
and honored, and I love you,
I give people in return for you
and nations in exchange for your life.[g]
5 Fear not, for I am with you;
from the east I will bring back your offspring,
from the west I will gather you.
6 I will say to the north: Give them up!
and to the south: Do not hold them!
Bring back my sons from afar,
and my daughters from the ends of the earth:[h]
7 All who are called by my name
I created for my glory;
I formed them, made them.
8 Lead out the people, blind though they have eyes,
deaf though they have ears.
9 Let all the nations gather together,
let the peoples assemble!
Who among them could have declared this,
or announced to us the earlier things?*
Let them produce witnesses to prove themselves right,
that one may hear and say, "It is true!"
10 You are my witnesses*—oracle of the LORD—
my servant whom I have chosen
To know and believe in me
and understand that I am he.
Before me no god was formed,
and after me there shall be none.
11 I, I am the LORD;
there is no savior but me.
12 It is I who declared, who saved,
who announced, not some strange god among you;
You are my witnesses—oracle of the LORD.
I am God,
13 yes, from eternity I am he;
There is none who can deliver from my hand:
I act and who can cancel it?[i]
14 Thus says the LORD, your redeemer,*
the Holy One of Israel:
For your sake I send to Babylon;
I will bring down all her defenses,
and the Chaldeans shall cry out in lamentation.
15 I am the LORD, your Holy One,
the creator of Israel, your King.
16 Thus says the LORD,
who opens a way in the sea,
a path in the mighty waters,[j]
17 Who leads out chariots and horsemen,
a powerful army,
Till they lie prostrate together, never to rise,
snuffed out, quenched like a wick.[k]
18 Remember not* the events of the past,
the things of long ago consider not;
19 See, I am doing something new!
Now it springs forth, do you not perceive it?
In the wilderness I make a way,

43:3–4 Egypt . . . Ethiopia and Seba: countries which God permitted the Persians to conquer in return for having given Israel its freedom.

43:9 Who among them . . . ?: God, and only God, can foretell the future because it is he who brings it to pass. The argument from prediction is an important theme in Second Isaiah and occurs also in 41:22; 43:10; 44:7–8, 26.

43:10 You are my witnesses: Israel's role as chosen people now takes a new turn as they are given the active role of bearing witness before humankind to the Lord's role in history by proclaiming events beforehand and bringing them to pass; see also 44:8. The false gods, on the other hand, cannot produce such witnesses (v. 9; cf. 44:9). **I am he**: this formula of self-identification, repeated in vv. 13 and 25, is used here to support the assertion that the Lord alone is God; see also 41:4; 46:4; 48:12; 51:12; 52:6. This expression in part may be behind the self-identification formula used by Jesus in John's gospel (cf. Jn 8:58). **Before . . . after**: another example of the same assertion, that the Lord alone is God; see also note on 44:6.

43:14–17 The destruction of Babylon is described in language that recalls the drowning of the Egyptian army in the Red Sea (Ex 14–15).

43:18 Remember not: God's new act of delivering Israel from the Babylonian captivity is presented as so great a marvel as to eclipse even the memory of the exodus from Egypt. This comparison of the return from Babylon to the exodus from Egypt recurs throughout Second Isaiah (cf. 41:17–20; 43:18–21; 48:20–21; 49:8–13; 51:9–11).

g: Dt 4:37; Hos 11:1. *h:* Is 49:22; Ez 16:20. *i:* Is 41:4. *j:* Is 51:10–11; Ex 14:21. *k:* Ex 15:4.

in the wasteland, rivers.
20 Wild beasts honor me,
jackals and ostriches,
For I put water in the wilderness
and rivers in the wasteland
for my chosen people to drink,
21 The people whom I formed for myself,
that they might recount my praise.

22 Yet you did not call upon me, Jacob,*
for you grew weary of me, Israel.
23 You did not bring me sheep for your burnt offerings,
nor honor me with your sacrifices.
I did not exact from you the service of offerings,
nor weary you for frankincense.[l]
24 You did not buy me sweet cane,*
nor did you fill me with the fat of your sacrifices;
Instead, you burdened me with your sins,
wearied me with your crimes.
25 It is I, I, who wipe out,
for my own sake, your offenses;
your sins I remember no more.
26 Would you have me remember, have us come to trial?
Speak up, prove your innocence!
27 Your first father* sinned;
your spokesmen rebelled against me
28 Till I repudiated the holy princes,
put Jacob under the ban,
exposed Israel to scorn.

See RG 280–95

CHAPTER 44

1 Hear then, Jacob, my servant,
Israel, whom I have chosen.
2 Thus says the LORD who made you,
your help, who formed you from the womb:
Do not fear, Jacob, my servant,
Jeshurun,* whom I have chosen.
3 I will pour out water upon the thirsty ground,
streams upon the dry land;
I will pour out my spirit upon your offspring,
my blessing upon your descendants.
4 They shall spring forth amid grass
like poplars beside flowing waters.[m]
5 One shall say, "I am the LORD's,"
another shall be named after Jacob,
And this one shall write on his hand,*
"The LORD's,"
and receive the name Israel.[n]

The True God and False Gods

6 * Thus says the LORD, Israel's king,
its redeemer, the LORD of hosts:
I am the first, I am the last;
there is no God but me.* [o]
7 Who is like me? Let him stand up and declare,
make it evident, and confront me with it.
Who of old announced future events?
Let them foretell to us the things to come.
8 Do not fear or be troubled.
Did I not announce it to you long ago?
I declared it, and you are my witnesses.
Is there any God but me?
There is no other Rock,* I know of none![p]

9 * Those who fashion idols are all nothing;
their precious works are of no avail.
They are their witnesses:*

43:22–28 The reason for the liberation of the Israelites is not their constancy but rather God's faithfulness to his promise (cf. 40:6–8).

43:24 Sweet cane: a fragrant substance used in making incense and the sacred anointing oil; cf. Ex 30:23; Jer 6:20.

43:27 First father: Jacob. **Spokesmen**: leaders, priests, prophets.

44:2 Jeshurun: see note on Dt 32:15; cf. also Dt 33:5, 26.

44:5 Write on his hand: an allusion to the Babylonian custom of tattooing the owner's name on the hand of his slave.

44:6–8 Prediction and fulfillment are here seen as the hallmarks of true divinity. See note on 43:9.

44:6 No god but me: with Second Isaiah, Israel's faith is declared to be explicitly monotheistic. However implicit it may have been, earlier formulas did not exclude the existence of other gods, not even that of the first commandment: "You shall not have other gods besides me" (Ex 20:3). Cf. also note on 41:21–29.

44:8 Rock: place of refuge, a title here used of God; cf., e.g., Dt 32:4, 18; 1 Sm 2:2; Ps 18:3.

44:9–20 A satire on the makers and worshipers of idols.

44:9 Their witnesses: Israel has been called to bear witness to the awesome power of God (cf. 43:10, 12; 44:8), but idol makers cannot testify in support of their creations, for idols cannot act (Dt 4:28; Ps 135:15–18).

l: Jer 6:20. *m*: Is 54:1–3. *n*: Is 43:7; 45:14. *o*: Is 41:4; 43:15; 45:21; 48:3, 12; 51:15; 54:5. *p*: Is 43:10, 12; Dt 32:4.

they see nothing, know nothing,
and so they are put to shame.[q]
10 Who would fashion a god or cast an idol,
that is of no use?
11 Look, all its company will be shamed;
they are artisans, mere human beings!
They all assemble and stand there,
only to cower in shame.
12 The ironsmith fashions a likeness,
he works it over the coals,
Shaping it with hammers,
working it with his strong arm.
With hunger his strength wanes,
without water, he grows faint.[r]
13 The woodworker stretches a line,
and marks out a shape with a stylus.
He shapes it with scraping tools,
with a compass measures it off,
Making it the copy of a man,*
human display, enthroned in a shrine.
14 He goes out to cut down cedars,
takes a holm tree or an oak.
He picks out for himself trees of the forest,
plants a fir, and the rain makes it grow.
15 It is used for fuel:
with some of the wood he warms himself,
makes a fire and bakes bread.
Yet he makes a god and worships it,
turns it into an idol and adores it!
16 Half of it he burns in the fire,
on its embers he roasts meat;
he eats the roast and is full.
He warms himself and says, "Ah!
I am warm! I see the flames!"
17 The rest of it he makes into a god,
an image to worship and adore.
He prays to it and says,
"Help me! You are my god!"
18 They do not know, do not understand;
their eyes are too clouded to see,
their minds, to perceive.
19 He does not think clearly;
he lacks the wit and knowledge to say,
"Half the wood I burned in the fire,
on its embers I baked bread,
I roasted meat and ate.
Shall I turn the rest into an abomination?
Shall I worship a block of wood?"
20 He is chasing ashes!*
A deluded mind has led him astray;
He cannot save himself,
does not say, "This thing in my right hand—is it not a fraud?"

21 Remember these things, Jacob,
Israel, for you are my servant!
I formed you, a servant to me;
Israel, you shall never be forgotten by me:
22 I have brushed away your offenses like a cloud,
your sins like a mist;
return to me, for I have redeemed you.
23 Raise a glad cry, you heavens—the LORD has acted!
Shout, you depths of the earth.
Break forth, mountains, into song,
forest, with all your trees.
For the LORD has redeemed Jacob,
shows his glory through Israel.

Cyrus, Anointed of the Lord, Agent of Israel's Liberation

24 Thus says the LORD, your redeemer,
who formed you from the womb:
I am the LORD, who made all things,
who alone stretched out the heavens,
I spread out the earth by myself.[s]
25 I bring to nought the omens of babblers,
make fools of diviners,
Turn back the wise
and make their knowledge foolish.
26 I confirm the words of my servant,
carry out the plan my messengers announce.
I say to Jerusalem, Be inhabited!
To the cities of Judah, Be rebuilt!
I will raise up their ruins.
27 I say to the deep, Be dry!
I will dry up your rivers.[t]

44:13 Copy of a man: in the biblical view human beings are made in the image of God; here gods are made in the image of human beings.

44:20 Chasing ashes: an exercise in futility.

q: Is 48:5, 7. *r:* Wis 13:11–16. *s:* Is 40:22; Jb 9:8. *t:* Is 42:15; 51:10.

28 I say of Cyrus,* My shepherd!
He carries out my every wish,
Saying of Jerusalem, "Let it be rebuilt,"
and of the temple, "Lay its foundations."[u]

CHAPTER 45

See RG 280–95

1 Thus says the LORD to his anointed,* Cyrus,
whose right hand I grasp,
Subduing nations before him,
stripping kings of their strength,
Opening doors before him,
leaving the gates unbarred:
2 I will go before you
and level the mountains;
Bronze doors* I will shatter,
iron bars I will snap.[v]
3 I will give you treasures of darkness,
riches hidden away,
That you may know I am the LORD,
the God of Israel, who calls you by name.

4 For the sake of Jacob, my servant,
of Israel my chosen one,
I have called you by name,
giving you a title, though you do not know me.[w]
5 I am the LORD, there is no other,
there is no God besides me.
It is I who arm you, though you do not know me,
6 so that all may know, from the rising of the sun
to its setting, that there is none besides me.*
I am the LORD, there is no other.
7 I form the light, and create the darkness,
I make weal and create woe;*
I, the LORD, do all these things.
8 Let justice descend, you heavens, like dew from above,
like gentle rain let the clouds drop it down.
Let the earth open and salvation bud forth;
let righteousness spring up with them!*
I, the LORD, have created this.[x]
9 Woe to anyone who contends with their Maker;[y]
a potsherd among potsherds of the earth!*
Shall the clay say to the potter, "What are you doing?"
or, "What you are making has no handles"?
10 Woe to anyone who asks a father, "What are you begetting?"
or a woman, "What are you giving birth to?"
11 Thus says the LORD,
the Holy One of Israel, his maker:
Do you question me about my children,
tell me how to treat the work of my hands?
12 It was I who made the earth
and created the people upon it;
It was my hands that stretched out the heavens;
I gave the order to all their host.
13 It was I who stirred him* up for justice;
all his ways I make level.
He shall rebuild my city
and let my exiles go free
Without price or payment,
says the LORD of hosts.

44:28 Cyrus: king of Persia (559–529 B.C.); cf. note on 41:1–4.

45:1 Anointed: in Hebrew, *mashiah*, from which the word "Messiah" is derived; from its Greek translation, *Christos*, we have the title "Christ." Applied to kings, "anointed" originally referred only to those of Israel, but it is here given to Cyrus because he is the agent of the Lord.

45:2 Bronze doors: those defending the city gates of Babylon.

45:6 The nations will come to know that Israel's God is the only God; cf. also vv. 20–25.

45:7 Create woe: God created and controls all aspects of creation (light and darkness, order and chaos).

45:8 The Vulgate rendering gave a messianic sense to this verse, using "just one" and "savior" in place of "justice" and "salvation," phraseology taken over in the Advent liturgy, e.g., the "Rorate coeli."

45:9 No one may challenge God's freedom of action, exemplified here by the selection of Cyrus as his anointed.

45:13 Him: Cyrus, called by God for the deliverance and restoration of Israel. **Justice**: the Hebrew word (*sedeq*) has multiple connotations; here it relates to the saving victory that the Lord will give to Cyrus for the deliverance of his people Israel. This word and others from the same root frequently have this connotation in Second Isaiah, occurring as a parallel term with "deliverance," "salvation," etc. Cf. its use in 41:10 (rendered "victorious") and 51:5 (rendered "victory").

u: Jer 3:15; Ez 34:23. *v:* Ps 107:16. *w:* Is 40:26; 44:5. *x:* Ps 72:6; 85:11. *y:* Jer 18:6; Rom 9:20.

14 Thus says the LORD:
The earnings of Egypt, the gain of
Ethiopia,
and the Sabeans,* tall of stature,
Shall come over to you and belong to
you;
they shall follow you, coming in
chains.
Before you they shall bow down,
saying in prayer:
"With you alone is God; and there is
none other,
no other god![z]
15 Truly with you God is hidden,*
the God of Israel, the savior![a]
16 They are put to shame and disgrace, all
of them;
they go in disgrace who carve images.
17 Israel has been saved by the LORD,
saved forever!
You shall never be put to shame or
disgrace
in any future age."

18 For thus says the LORD,
The creator of the heavens,
who is God,
The designer and maker of the earth
who established it,
Not as an empty waste* did he create it,
but designing it to be lived in:
I am the LORD, and there is no other.
19 I have not spoken in secret
from some place in the land of
darkness,
I have not said to the descendants of
Jacob,
"Look for me in an empty waste."
I, the LORD, promise justice,
I declare what is right.

20 Come and assemble, gather together,
you fugitives from among the nations!
They are without knowledge who bear
wooden idols*
and pray to gods that cannot save.
21 Come close and declare;
let them take counsel together:
Who announced this from the beginning,
declared it from of old?
Was it not I, the LORD,
besides whom there is no other God?
There is no just and saving God but me.

22 Turn to me and be safe,
all you ends of the earth,
for I am God; there is no other!
23 By myself I swear,
uttering my just decree,
a word that will not return:
To me every knee shall bend;
by me every tongue shall swear,[b]
24 Saying, "Only in the LORD
are just deeds and power.
Before him in shame shall come
all who vent their anger against him.
25 In the LORD all the descendants of Israel
shall have vindication and glory."

CHAPTER 46

See RG 280–95

The Gods of Babylon

1 Bel bows down, Nebo* stoops,
their idols set upon beasts and cattle;
They must be borne upon shoulders,
a load for weary animals.
2 They stoop and bow down together;
unable to deliver those who bear them,
they too go into captivity.

3 Hear me, O house of Jacob,
all the remnant of the house of Israel,
My burden from the womb,
whom I have carried since birth.[c]
4 Even to your old age I am he,
even when your hair is gray I will
carry you;

45:14 Egypt . . . Ethiopia . . . Sabeans: the Egyptians and their allies who, when conquered by Cyrus, are seen as acknowledging the God of Israel; cf. 43:3.

45:15 God is hidden: i.e., the one known only to Israel, who cannot be represented by wooden or molten images. The concept of the "Deus absconditus," "the hidden God," becomes an important theme in later theology.

45:18 Empty waste: an allusion to Gn 1:2, where the earth is waste and void; the same Hebrew word, *tohu*, is used in both passages. Here it points to devastated Judah and Jerusalem, where God wishes to resettle the returning exiles.

45:20 Who bear wooden idols: in their religious processions. Such gods have feet but cannot walk; cf. Ps 115:7; Bar 6:25.

46:1–4 Bel . . . Nebo: gods of Babylon; their complete helplessness is here contrasted with God's omnipotence; whereas they must be carried about, the Lord carries Israel as a parent does a child.

z: Is 43:3. *a:* Is 55:8; Prv 25:2. *b:* Rom 14:11; Phil 2:10. *c:* Is 44:2.

I have done this, and I will lift you up,
I will carry you to safety.

5 To whom would you liken me as an equal,
compare me, as though we were alike?
6 There are those who pour out gold from a purse
and weigh out silver on the scales;
They hire a goldsmith to make it into a god
before which they bow down in worship.
7 They lift it to their shoulders to carry;
when they set it down, it stays,
and does not move from the place.
They cry out to it, but it cannot answer;
it delivers no one from distress.

8 Remember this and be firm,
take it to heart, you rebels;
9 remember the former things, those long ago:
I am God, there is no other;
I am God, there is none like me.
10 At the beginning I declare the outcome;
from of old, things not yet done.
I say that my plan shall stand,
I accomplish my every desire.
11 I summon from the east a bird of prey,*
from a distant land, one to carry out my plan.
Yes, I have spoken, I will accomplish it;
I have planned it, and I will do it.
12 Listen to me, you fainthearted,
far from the victory of justice:
13 I am bringing on that victory, it is not far off,
my salvation shall not tarry;
I will put salvation within Zion,
give to Israel my glory.

See RG 280–95

CHAPTER 47

*The Fall of Babylon**

1 Come down, sit in the dust,
virgin daughter Babylon;
Sit on the ground, dethroned,
daughter of the Chaldeans.
No longer shall you be called
dainty and delicate.[d]
2 Take the millstone and grind flour,
remove your veil;
Strip off your skirt, bare your legs,
cross through the streams.
3 Your nakedness shall be uncovered,
and your shame be seen;
I will take vengeance,
I will yield to no entreaty,
says 4our redeemer,
Whose name is the LORD of hosts,
the Holy One of Israel.

5 Go into darkness and sit in silence,
daughter of the Chaldeans,
No longer shall you be called
sovereign mistress of kingdoms.
6 Angry at my people,
I profaned my heritage
And gave them into your power;
but you showed them no mercy;
Upon the aged
you laid a very heavy yoke.
7 You said, "I shall remain always,
a sovereign mistress forever!"
You did not take these things to heart,
but disregarded their outcome.[e]
8 Now hear this, voluptuous one,
enthroned securely,
Saying in your heart,
"I, and no one else!*
I shall never be a widow,
bereft of my children"—[f]
9 Both these things shall come to you
suddenly, in a single day:
Complete bereavement and widowhood
shall come upon you
Despite your many sorceries
and the full power of your spells;*
10 Secure in your wickedness,
you said, "No one sees me."
Your wisdom and your knowledge
led you astray,
And you said in your heart,

46:11 From the east a bird of prey: Cyrus; cf. 41:2–4.

47:1–15 A taunt-song, mocking Babylon, once queen of the nations, now a mere slave.

47:8, 10 I, and no one else: Babylon is mockingly presented as making the same claim as the Lord (cf. 45:6, 14, 22; 46:9), a claim that events will soon prove to be false and foolish (v. 11).

47:9–13, 15 Babylon was known for its sorcery and astrology.

d: Dt 28:56. *e:* Is 14:13–14. *f:* Zep 2:15; Rev 18:7.

"I, and no one else!"
11 But upon you shall come an evil
you will not be able to charm away;
Upon you shall fall a disaster
you cannot ward off.
Upon you shall suddenly come
a ruin you cannot imagine.
12 Keep on with your spells
and your many sorceries,
at which you toiled from your youth.
Perhaps you can prevail,
perhaps you can strike terror!
13 You wore yourself out with so many
consultations!
Let the astrologers stand forth to save
you,
The stargazers who forecast at each new
moon
what would happen to you.
14 See, they are like stubble,
fire consumes them;
They cannot deliver themselves
from the spreading flames.
This is no warming ember,
no fire to sit before!
15 Thus do your wizards serve you
with whom you have toiled from your
youth;
They wander their separate ways,
with none to save you.

CHAPTER 48

See RG 280–95

Exhortations to the Exiles

1 Hear this, house of Jacob
called by the name Israel,
sprung from the stock of Judah,
You who swear by the name of the LORD
and invoke the God of Israel
without sincerity, without justice,
2 Though you are named after the holy city
and rely on the God of Israel,
whose name is the LORD of hosts.
3 Things of the past I declared long ago,
they went forth from my mouth, I
announced them;
then suddenly I took action and they
came to be.
4 Because I know that you are stubborn
and that your neck is an iron sinew
and your forehead bronze,
5 I declared them to you of old;
before they took place I informed you,
That you might not say, "My idol did
them,
my statue, my molten image
commanded them."
6 Now that you have heard, look at all this;
must you not admit it?[g]
From now on I announce new things to
you,
hidden events you never knew.
7 Now, not from of old, they are created,
before today you did not hear of them,
so that you cannot claim, "I have
known them."
8 You never heard, you never knew,
they never reached your ears
beforehand.
Yes, I know you are utterly treacherous,
a rebel you were named from the
womb.[h]
9 For the sake of my name I restrain my
anger,
for the sake of my renown I hold it
back from you,
lest I destroy you.
10 See, I refined you, but not like silver;
I tested you in the furnace of
affliction.[i]
11 For my sake, for my own sake, I do this;
why should my name be profaned?
My glory I will not give to another.
12 Listen to me, Jacob,
Israel, whom I called!
I, it is I who am the first,
and am I the last.[j]
13 Yes, my hand laid the foundations of the
earth;
my right hand spread out the
heavens.
When I summon them,
they stand forth at once.[k]
14 All of you assemble and listen:
Who among you declared these
things?

g: Is 42:9. *h:* Is 43:22–24. *i:* Is 1:25; Jer 6:29–30; Zec 13:9; Mal 3:2. *j:* Is 41:4; 44:6; 48:12; Rev 1:8, 17. *k:* Is 40:22, 26; 45:12, 18.

The one the LORD loves* shall do his will
against Babylon and the offspring of
Chaldea.
15 I myself have spoken, I have summoned
him,
I have brought him, and his way
succeeds!
16 Come near to me and hear this!
From the beginning I did not speak in
secret;
At the time it happens, I am there:
"Now the Lord GOD has sent me, and
his spirit."*
17 Thus says the LORD, your redeemer,
the Holy One of Israel:
I am the LORD, your God,
teaching you how to prevail,
leading you on the way you should go.
18 If only you would attend to my
commandments,
your peace would be like a river,
your vindication like the waves of the
sea,
19 Your descendants like the sand,
the offspring of your loins like its
grains,
Their name never cut off
or blotted out from my presence.
20 Go forth from Babylon, flee from
Chaldea!
With shouts of joy declare this,
announce it;
Make it known to the ends of the earth,
Say: "The LORD has redeemed his
servant Jacob.
21 They did not thirst
when he led them through dry lands;
Water from the rock he set flowing for
them;
he cleft the rock, and waters welled
forth."[l]
22 There is no peace* for the wicked,
says the LORD.

B. Expiation of Sin, Spiritual Liberation of Israel

CHAPTER 49

See RG 280–95

*The Servant of the Lord**

1 Hear me, coastlands,
listen, distant peoples.[m]
Before birth the LORD called me,
from my mother's womb he gave me
my name.*
2 He made my mouth like a sharp-edged
sword,
concealed me, shielded by his hand.
He made me a sharpened arrow,
in his quiver he hid me.
3 He said to me, You are my servant,
in you, Israel,* I show my glory.
4 Though I thought I had toiled in vain,
for nothing and for naught spent my
strength,
Yet my right is with the LORD,
my recompense is with my God.[n]
5 For now the LORD has spoken
who formed me as his servant from the
womb,
That Jacob may be brought back to him
and Israel gathered to him;
I am honored in the sight of the LORD,
and my God is now my strength!
6 It is too little, he says, for you to be my
servant,
to raise up the tribes of Jacob,
and restore the survivors of Israel;[o]
I will make you a light to the nations,
that my salvation may reach to the
ends of the earth.*
7 Thus says the LORD,

48:14 The one the LORD loves: the reference is no doubt to Cyrus, who does the Lord's will by overcoming Babylon and releasing Israel from captivity.

48:16 "Now the Lord ... spirit": said by Cyrus; cf. v. 14.

48:22 No peace: while the good news proclaimed by the prophet is directed to the people as a whole, "peace," which can represent the fullness of God's blessings and which would here include deliverance from exile, is not extended to all regardless of disposition.

49:1–7 The second of the four "servant of the Lord" oracles (cf. note on 42:1–4).

49:1 Gave me my name: designated me for a special task or mission (cf. Jer 1:5).

49:3 Israel: the servant is identified with the people of Israel as their ideal representative; however, vv. 5–6 seem to distinguish the servant from Israel.

49:6 The servant's vocation extends beyond the restoration of Israel in order to bring the knowledge of Israel's God to the rest of the earth; cf. Lk 2:32.

l: Ex 17:6; Nm 20:11. *m:* Is 41:9; 43:1; 44:2, 24; 46:3. *n:* Is 40:27. *o:* Is 42:1–6; 44:5; 45:14; Lk 2:32; Acts 13:46–47.

the redeemer, the Holy One of Israel,
To the one despised, abhorred by the nations,
the slave of rulers:
When kings see you, they shall stand up,
and princes shall bow down
Because of the LORD who is faithful,
the Holy One of Israel who has chosen you.[p]

The Liberation and Restoration of Zion

8 Thus says the LORD:
In a time of favor I answer you,*
on the day of salvation I help you;
I form you and set you
as a covenant for the people,
To restore the land
and allot the devastated heritages,[q]
9 To say to the prisoners: Come out!
To those in darkness: Show yourselves!
Along the roadways they shall find pasture,
on every barren height shall their pastures be.[r]
10 They shall not hunger or thirst;
nor shall scorching wind or sun strike them;
For he who pities them leads them
and guides them beside springs of water.[s]
11 I will turn all my mountains into roadway,
and make my highways level.[t]
12 See, these shall come from afar:
some from the north and the west,
others from the land of Syene.*
13 Sing out, heavens, and rejoice, earth,
break forth into song, you mountains,
For the LORD comforts his people
and shows mercy to his afflicted.
14 But Zion said, "The LORD has forsaken me;
my Lord has forgotten me."[u]
15 Can a mother forget her infant,
be without tenderness for the child of her womb?
Even should she forget,
I will never forget you.[v]
16 See, upon the palms of my hands I have engraved you;*
your walls are ever before me.
17 Your children hasten—
your levelers, your destroyers
go forth from you;
18 Look about and see,
they are all gathering and coming to you.
As I live—oracle of the LORD—
you shall don them as jewels,
bedeck yourself like a bride.
19 Though you were waste and desolate,
a land of ruins,
Now you shall be too narrow for your inhabitants,
while those who swallowed you up will be far away.
20 The children of whom you were bereft
shall yet say in your hearing,
"This place is too narrow for me,
make room for me to live in."
21 You shall ask yourself:
"Who has borne me these,
when I was bereft and barren?
Exiled and repudiated,
who has reared them?
I was left all alone;
where then do these come from?"[w]
22 Thus says the Lord GOD:
See, I will lift up my hand to the nations,
and to the peoples raise my signal;
They shall bring your sons in their arms,
your daughters shall be carried on their shoulders.[x]
23 Kings shall be your guardians,
their princesses your nursemaids;
Face to the ground, they shall bow down before you
and lick the dust at your feet.
Then you shall know that I am the LORD,

49:8 You: the individual is not named; perhaps Cyrus or the prophet.

49:12 Syene: now called Aswan, at the first cataract of the Nile in southern Egypt.

49:16 Upon the palms . . . you: for continual remembrance; cf. Ex 13:9, 16; Dt 6:6–9.

p: Is 49:23; 55:5. *q:* 2 Cor 6:2. *r:* Is 42:7, 18–20. *s:* Is 51:14; Rev 7:16. *t:* Is 40:3–4. *u:* Is 40:27. *v:* Is 43:4; 44:21; 46:3–4. *w:* Is 54:1–3. *x:* Is 5:26; 13:2.

none who hope in me shall be
ashamed.
24 Can plunder be taken from a warrior,
or captives rescued from a tyrant?
25 Thus says the LORD:
Yes, captives can be taken from a warrior,
and plunder rescued from a tyrant;
Those who oppose you I will oppose,
and your sons I will save.
26 I will make your oppressors eat their own
flesh,
and they shall be drunk with their own
blood
as though with new wine.
All flesh shall know
that I, the LORD, am your savior,
your redeemer, the Mighty One of
Jacob.[y]

See RG 280–95

CHAPTER 50

Salvation Through the Lord's Servant

1 Thus says the LORD:
Where is the bill of divorce
with which I dismissed your mother?*
Or to which of my creditors
have I sold you?
It was for your sins you were sold,
for your rebellions your mother was
dismissed.[z]

2 Why was no one there when I came?
Why did no one answer when I
called?*
Is my hand too short to ransom?
Have I not the strength to deliver?
See, with my rebuke I dry up the sea,
I turn rivers into wilderness;
Their fish rot for lack of water,
and die of thirst.[a]
3 I clothe the heavens in black,
and make sackcloth their covering.

4 * The Lord GOD has given me
a well-trained tongue,
That I might know how to answer the
weary
a word that will waken them.
Morning after morning
he wakens my ear to hear as disciples
do;
5 The Lord GOD opened my ear;
I did not refuse,
did not turn away.*
6 I gave my back to those who beat me,
my cheeks to those who tore out my
beard;*
My face I did not hide
from insults and spitting.[b]

7 The Lord GOD is my help,
therefore I am not disgraced;
Therefore I have set my face like flint,
knowing that I shall not be put to
shame.[c]
8 He who declares my innocence is near.
Who will oppose me?
Let us appear together.
Who will dispute my right?
Let them confront me.
9 See, the Lord GOD is my help;
who will declare me guilty?
See, they will all wear out like a garment,
consumed by moths.[d]
10 Who among you fears the LORD,*
heeds his servant's voice?
Whoever walk in darkness,
without any light,
Yet trust in the name of the LORD
and rely upon their God![e]
11 All you who kindle flames
and set flares alight,
Walk by the light of your own fire
and by the flares you have burnt!
This is your fate from my hand:

50:1 Responding to the people's complaint of utter abandonment by God, the prophet asserts that their sins were responsible for their banishment. Since there was no bill of divorce, the bond between the Lord and his people still exists and he has the power to deliver them (v. 2).

50:2 Israel's faith in God is weak; the people do not answer God's call, nor believe promises of deliverance.

50:4–11 The third of the four "servant of the Lord" oracles (cf. note on 42:1–4); in vv. 4–9 the servant speaks; in vv. 10–11 God addresses the people directly.

50:5 The servant, like a well-trained disciple, does not refuse the divine vocation.

50:6 He willingly submits to insults and beatings. **Tore out my beard**: a grave and painful insult.

50:10–11 The Lord offers a choice to those who walk in darkness: either trust in the true light (v. 10), or walk in their false light and suffer the consequences.

y: Is 19:2; Ez 38:21; Zec 14:13. *z:* Is 54:6–8; Dt 24:1–4; Mt 19:3; Mk 10:2–4. *a:* Ex 7:18; Ps 105:29. *b:* 2 Sm 10:4–6; Mt 26:67; 27:30. *c:* Ez 3:9. *d:* Is 51:6–8; Ps 102:27. *e:* Is 43:1–2; 44:1–2.

you shall lie down in a place of
torment.

CHAPTER 51

See RG 280–95

Exhortation To Trust in the Lord

1 Listen to me, you who pursue justice,
who seek the LORD;
Look to the rock from which you were hewn,
to the quarry* from which you were taken;[f]
2 Look to Abraham, your father,
and to Sarah, who gave you birth;
Though he was but one when I called him,
I blessed him and made him many.[g]
3 Yes, the LORD shall comfort Zion,
shall comfort all her ruins;
Her wilderness he shall make like Eden,
her wasteland like the garden of the LORD;
Joy and gladness shall be found in her,
thanksgiving and the sound of song.

4 Be attentive to me, my people;*
my nation, give ear to me.
For teaching shall go forth from me,
and my judgment, as light to the peoples.[h]
5 I will make my victory come swiftly;
my salvation shall go forth
and my arm shall judge the nations;
In me the coastlands shall hope,
and my arm they shall await.

6 Raise your eyes to the heavens,
look at the earth below;
Though the heavens vanish like smoke,
the earth wear out like a garment
and its inhabitants die like flies,
My salvation shall remain forever
and my victory shall always be firm.*
7 Hear me, you who know justice,
you people who have my teaching at heart:
Do not fear the reproach of others;
remain firm at their revilings.
8 They shall be like a garment eaten by moths,
like wool consumed by grubs;
But my victory shall remain forever,
my salvation, for all generations.[i]

9 Awake, awake, put on strength,
arm of the LORD!
Awake as in the days of old,
in ages long ago!
Was it not you who crushed Rahab,*
you who pierced the dragon?[j]
10 Was it not you who dried up the sea,
the waters of the great deep,*
You who made the depths of the sea into a way
for the redeemed to pass through?
11 Those whom the LORD has ransomed will return
and enter Zion singing,
crowned with everlasting joy;
They will meet with joy and gladness,
sorrow and mourning will flee.

12 I, it is I who comfort you.
Can you then fear mortals who die,
human beings who are just grass,
13 And forget the LORD, your maker,
who stretched out the heavens
and laid the foundations of earth?
All the day you are in constant dread
of the fury of the oppressor
When he prepares himself to destroy;
but where is the oppressor's fury?

14 The captives shall soon be released;
they shall not die and go down into the pit,
nor shall they want for bread.
15 For I am the LORD, your God,
who stirs up the sea so that its waves roar;
the LORD of hosts by name.[k]
16 I have put my words into your mouth,

51:1 Rock . . . quarry: your glorious ancestry.

51:4–5 The conversion of the nations.

51:6 While the heavens and the earth appear eternal and changeless, they are not so firm and lasting as God's saving will for Israel.

51:9 Rahab: see note on 30:7. **The dragon**: see notes on 27:1; Ps 74:12–17.

51:10 Great deep: a reference to the primeval chaos (cf. Gn 1:2; 7:11; 49:25; Jb 28:14; Ps 36:7; Jon 2:4).

f: Rom 9:30–31. *g:* Ez 33:24; Gn 12:2–4; 22:17. *h:* Is 2:3. *i:* Is 50:9. *j:* Ex 15:16; Jb 9:13; 26:12; Ps 74:13; 89:11. *k:* Jer 31:35.

I covered you, shielded by my hand,
Stretching out the heavens,
laying the foundations of the earth,
saying to Zion: You are my people.

The Cup of the Lord

17 Wake up, wake up!
Arise, Jerusalem,
You who drank at the LORD's hand
the cup of his wrath;
Who drained to the dregs
the bowl of staggering![l]
18 She has no one to guide her
of all the children she bore;
She has no one to take her by the hand,
of all the children she reared!—
19 Your misfortunes are double;
who is there to grieve with you?
Desolation and destruction, famine and sword!
Who is there to comfort you?
20 Your children lie helpless
at every street corner
like antelopes in a net.
They are filled with the wrath of the LORD,
the rebuke of your God.

21 But now, hear this, afflicted one,
drunk, but not with wine,[m]
22 Thus says the LORD, your Master,
your God, who defends his people:
See, I am taking from your hand
the cup of staggering;
The bowl of my wrath
you shall no longer drink.
23 I will put it into the hands of your tormentors,
those who said to you,
"Bow down, that we may walk over you."
So you offered your back like the ground,
like the street for them to walk on.

CHAPTER 52

See RG 280–95

Let Zion Rejoice

1 Awake, awake!
Put on your strength, Zion;
Put on your glorious garments,
Jerusalem, holy city.
Never again shall the uncircumcised
or the unclean enter you.
2 Arise, shake off the dust,
sit enthroned, Jerusalem;
Loose the bonds from your neck,
captive daughter Zion!
3 For thus says the LORD:
For nothing you were sold,
without money you shall be redeemed.

4 For thus says the Lord GOD:
To Egypt long ago my people went down,
to sojourn there;
Assyria, too, oppressed them for nought.
5 But now, what am I to do here?
—oracle of the LORD.
My people have been taken away for nothing;
their rulers mock, oracle of the LORD;
constantly, every day, my name is reviled.
6 Therefore my people shall know my name
on that day, that it is I who speaks:
Here I am!
7 How beautiful upon the mountains*
are the feet of the one bringing good news,
Announcing peace, bearing good news,
announcing salvation, saying to Zion,
"Your God is King!"[n]
8 Listen! Your sentinels raise a cry,
together they shout for joy,
For they see directly, before their eyes,
the LORD's return to Zion.[o]
9 Break out together in song,
O ruins of Jerusalem!
For the LORD has comforted his people,
has redeemed Jerusalem.
10 The LORD has bared his holy arm
in the sight of all the nations;
All the ends of the earth can see
the salvation of our God.

11 Depart, depart, go out from there,
touch nothing unclean!

52:7–10 God leads the people back from Babylon to Zion, from whose ruined walls sentinels greet the returning exiles.

l: Jer 25:15–17; Ez 23:32–34. *m:* Is 29:9. *n:* Is 40:9; Rom 10:15. *o:* Is 62:6.

Out from there!* Purify yourselves,
you who carry the vessels of the LORD.
12 But not in hurried flight will you go out,
nor leave in headlong haste,
For the LORD goes before you,
and your rear guard is the God of Israel.[p]

*Suffering and Triumph of the Servant of the Lord**

13 See, my servant shall prosper,
he shall be raised high and greatly exalted.
14 Even as many were amazed at him—
so marred were his features,
beyond that of mortals
his appearance, beyond that of human beings—[q]
15 So shall he startle many nations,
kings shall stand speechless;
For those who have not been told shall see,
those who have not heard shall ponder it.[r]

CHAPTER 53

See RG 280–95

1 Who would believe what we have heard?*
To whom has the arm of the LORD been revealed?[s]
2 He grew up like a sapling before him,[t]
like a shoot from the parched earth;
He had no majestic bearing to catch our eye,
no beauty to draw us to him.
3 He was spurned and avoided by men,
a man of suffering, knowing pain,
Like one from whom you turn your face,
spurned, and we held him in no esteem.[u]

4 Yet it was our pain that he bore,
our sufferings he endured.
We thought of him as stricken,
struck down by God* and afflicted,[v]
5 But he was pierced for our sins,
crushed for our iniquity.
He bore the punishment that makes us whole,
by his wounds we were healed.[w]
6 We had all gone astray like sheep,
all following our own way;
But the LORD laid upon him*
the guilt of us all.[x]

7 Though harshly treated, he submitted
and did not open his mouth;
Like a lamb led to slaughter
or a sheep silent before shearers,
he did not open his mouth.[y]
8 Seized and condemned, he was taken away.

52:11 From there: from Babylon. **Vessels of the LORD**: taken to Babylon by Nebuchadnezzar, now carried back by the exiles returning in procession to Zion; cf. Ezr 1:7.

52:13–53:12 The last of the "servant of the Lord" oracles (see note on 42:1–4). Taken together, these oracles depict a figure of one called by God for a vocation to Israel and the nations (42:4; 49:5–6); the servant's exaltation both opens and closes the passage (52:13; 53:12). The servant responded in fidelity but has suffered opposition (50:4–6). In this fourth oracle the servant is characterized as "a man of suffering" (53:3) and appears to be unjustly put to death (53:8–9). Those who have witnessed his career somehow recognize that he is innocent, has undergone suffering for their sins (53:4–6), and his death is referred to as a reparation offering (see note on 53:10–11). The servant is described in ways that identify him with Israel (which is frequently referred to as "servant" in the context of Second Isaiah—e.g., 41:8, 9; 44:2, 21; 43:4) and is designated as "Israel" in 49:3; yet Israel outside the "servant of the Lord" oracles is not presented as sinless, but rather in exile because of sin (40:2; 42:21–25) and even as servant as deaf and blind (42:18–19). The servant is thus both identified with Israel and distinguished from it. As with the previous servant poems, this chapter helped the followers of Jesus to interpret his suffering, death, and resurrection; see especially the passion narratives.

53:1–10 What we have heard: this fourth servant oracle is introduced by words of the Lord (52:13–15) but is now continued by speakers who are not identified, perhaps those referred to in 52:15, perhaps Israel (cf. "struck for the sins of his people"—v. 8). The Lord is again the speaker in vv. 11–13.

53:4 Struck down by God: the Bible often sees suffering as a punishment for sin (e.g., Ps 6:2; 32:1–5), yet sin sometimes appears to go unpunished and the innocent often suffer (cf. Ps 73; the Book of Job). In the case of the servant, the onlookers initially judge him guilty because of his suffering but, in some way not explained, they come to understand that his sufferings are for the sins of others. One notes the element of surprise, for such vicarious suffering, in the form described here, is without parallel in the Old Testament.

53:6 The LORD laid upon him: the servant's suffering is no accidental or casual matter, but part of God's plan; see also v. 10. The bystanders' speculation of v. 4 is verified, but not in the sense intended by them.

p: Ex 12:11. *q:* Ps 69:8. *r:* Mi 7:16. *s:* Is 52:10; Jn 12:38; Rom 10:16. *t:* Is 11:1. *u:* Jb 19:18; Ps 31:11–13; Mk 9:11. *v:* Jer 10:19; Mt 8:17. *w:* 1 Cor 15:3; 1 Pt 2:24. *x:* Lv 16:21–22. *y:* Mt 26:63; Acts 8:32.

Who would have thought any more of
his destiny?
For he was cut off from the land of the
living,
struck for the sins of his people.
9 He was given a grave among the wicked,
a burial place with evildoers,
Though he had done no wrong,
nor was deceit found in his mouth.[z]
10 But it was the LORD's will to crush him
with pain.
By making his life as a reparation
offering,*
he shall see his offspring, shall
lengthen his days,
and the LORD's will shall be
accomplished through him.
11 Because of his anguish he shall see the
light;
because of his knowledge he shall be
content;
My servant, the just one, shall justify the
many,
their iniquity he shall bear.
12 Therefore I will give him his portion
among the many,
and he shall divide the spoils with the
mighty,
Because he surrendered himself to death,
was counted among the transgressors,
Bore the sins of many,
and interceded for the transgressors.[a]

See RG 280–95

CHAPTER 54

The New Zion

1 Raise a glad cry, you barren one* who
never bore a child,
break forth in jubilant song, you who
have never been in labor,
For more numerous are the children of
the deserted wife
than the children of her who has a
husband,
says the LORD.[b]
2 Enlarge the space for your tent,
spread out your tent cloths unsparingly;
lengthen your ropes and make firm
your pegs.[c]
3 For you shall spread abroad to the right
and left;
your descendants shall dispossess the
nations
and shall people the deserted cities.*
4 * Do not fear, you shall not be put to
shame;
do not be discouraged, you shall not be
disgraced.
For the shame of your youth you shall
forget,
the reproach of your widowhood no
longer remember.
5 For your husband is your Maker;
the LORD of hosts is his name,
Your redeemer,* the Holy One of Israel,
called God of all the earth.
6 The LORD calls you back,
like a wife forsaken and grieved in
spirit,
A wife married in youth and then cast off,
says your God.[d]
7 For a brief moment I abandoned you,
but with great tenderness I will take
you back.
8 In an outburst of wrath, for a moment
I hid my face from you;
But with enduring love I take pity on you,
says the LORD, your redeemer.

53:10–11 Reparation offering: the Hebrew term *'asham* is used of a particular kind of sacrifice, one that is intended as compensation for that which is due because of guilt. See Lv 5:14–26 and note. **Justify**: the verb means "to be acquitted," "declared innocent," but since the servant bears "their iniquity," an effective rather than simply legal action is suggested.

54:1 Jerusalem, pictured as a wife who had been barren and deserted, now suddenly finds herself with innumerable children (the returning exiles); cf. Gal 4:27 for an application to a new context.

54:3 Those who had taken advantage of the exile to encroach on Jerusalem's territory will be driven out, and the returning exiles will repopulate the cities of Judah.

54:4–8 As with some other Old Testament themes, Second Isaiah uses that of Israel as the Lord's bride in a new manner. Whereas Hosea and Jeremiah had depicted Israel as the Lord's spouse to emphasize both Israel's infidelity and the Lord's continued love (Hos 1–3; Jer 2:2; 3:1–15) and Ezekiel to accuse Israel unsparingly (Ez 16; 23), Second Isaiah speaks only of the love with which the Lord restores the people, speaking tender words with no hint of reproach.

54:5 Redeemer: cf. note on 41:14.

z: 1 Pt 2:22–23; 1 Jn 3:5. *a:* Mk 15:28; Lk 22:37. *b:* Gal 4:27. *c:* Is 49:20. *d:* Mal 2:14–15.

9 This is for me like the days of Noah:
As I swore then that the waters of Noah
should never again flood the earth,
So I have sworn now not to be angry
with you,
or to rebuke you.[e]
10 Though the mountains fall away
and the hills be shaken,
My love shall never fall away from you
nor my covenant of peace* be shaken,
says the LORD, who has mercy on you.[f]

11 O afflicted one,* storm-battered and
unconsoled,
I lay your pavements in carnelians,
your foundations in sapphires;[g]
12 I will make your battlements of rubies,
your gates of jewels,
and all your walls of precious stones.
13 All your children shall be taught by the
LORD;
great shall be the peace of your
children.
14 In justice shall you be established,
far from oppression, you shall not fear,
from destruction, it cannot come near.
15 If there be an attack, it is not my doing;
whoever attacks shall fall before you.

16 See, I have created the smith
who blows on the burning coals
and forges weapons as his work;
It is I also who have created
the destroyer to work havoc.
17 Every weapon fashioned against you
shall fail;
every tongue that brings you to trial
you shall prove false.
This is the lot of the servants of the
LORD,
their vindication from me—oracle of
the LORD.

CHAPTER 55

See RG 280–95

An Invitation to Grace

1 All you who are thirsty,*
come to the water!
You who have no money,
come, buy grain and eat;
Come, buy grain without money,
wine and milk without cost![h]
2 Why spend your money for what is not
bread;
your wages for what does not satisfy?
Only listen to me, and you shall eat well,
you shall delight in rich fare.
3 Pay attention and come to me;
listen, that you may have life.
I will make with you an everlasting
covenant,
the steadfast loyalty promised to
David.[i]
4 As I made him a witness to peoples,
a leader and commander of peoples,
5 So shall you summon a nation you knew
not,
and a nation* that knew you not shall
run to you,
Because of the LORD, your God,
the Holy One of Israel, who has
glorified you.[j]

6 * Seek the LORD while he may be found,
call upon him while he is near.
7 Let the wicked forsake their way,
and sinners their thoughts;
Let them turn to the LORD to find mercy;
to our God, who is generous in
forgiving.
8 For my thoughts are not your thoughts,
nor are your ways my ways—oracle of
the LORD.
9 For as the heavens are higher than the
earth,

54:10 Covenant of peace: this whole section, vv. 9–17, is given to various assurances of God's love for Israel and of safety from various possible threats; the phrase sums up both the positive aspects of *shalom*, which implies a fullness of blessing, and protection from all that might harm. Cf. also 55:3; Nm 25:12; Ez 34:25; 37:26; Mal 2:5.

54:11 Afflicted one: Jerusalem.

55:1–3 The prophet invites all to return, under the figure of a banquet; cf. the covenant banquet in Ex 24:9–11 and wisdom's banquet in Prv 9:1–6. The Lord's covenant with David (2 Sm 7) is now to be extended beyond his dynasty.

55:5 The "nation" is Persia under Cyrus, but the perspective is worldwide.

55:6–9 The invitation to seek the Lord is motivated by the mercy of a God whose "ways" are completely mysterious.

e: Gn 9:15. *f:* Ps 46:3; 76:5. *g:* Rev 21:18–21. *h:* Jn 4:10–15; 6:35; 7:37–39; Rev 21:6; 22:17. *i:* 2 Sm 7:12–16. *j:* Acts 13:34.

so are my ways higher than your ways,
my thoughts higher than your thoughts.

10 * Yet just as from the heavens
the rain and snow come down
And do not return there
till they have watered the earth,
making it fertile and fruitful,
Giving seed to the one who sows
and bread to the one who eats,
11 So shall my word be
that goes forth from my mouth;
It shall not return to me empty,
but shall do what pleases me,
achieving the end for which I sent it.

12 Yes, in joy you shall go forth,
in peace you shall be brought home;
Mountains and hills shall break out in
song before you,
all trees of the field shall clap their
hands.
13 In place of the thornbush, the cypress
shall grow,
instead of nettles,* the myrtle.
This shall be to the LORD's renown,
as an everlasting sign that shall not
fail.

III. Isaiah 56—66

CHAPTER 56

See RG 280–95

*Salvation for the Just**

1 * Thus says the LORD:
Observe what is right, do what is just,
for my salvation is about to come,
my justice, about to be revealed.[k]
2 Happy is the one who does this,
whoever holds fast to it:
Keeping the sabbath without profaning it,
keeping one's hand from doing any
evil.[l]

Obligations and Promises To Share in the Covenant

3 * The foreigner joined to the LORD
should not say,
"The LORD will surely exclude me
from his people";
Nor should the eunuch say,
"See, I am a dry tree."[m]
4 For thus says the LORD:
To the eunuchs who keep my sabbaths,
who choose what pleases me,
and who hold fast to my covenant,[n]
5 I will give them, in my house
and within my walls, a monument and
a name*
Better than sons and daughters;
an eternal name, which shall not be cut
off, will I give them.
6 And foreigners who join themselves to
the LORD,
to minister to him,
To love the name of the LORD,
to become his servants—
All who keep the sabbath without
profaning it
and hold fast to my covenant,

55:10–11 The efficacy of the word of God recalls 40:5, 8.

55:13 Thornbush ... nettles: suggestive of the desert and therefore symbolic of suffering and hardship; **cypress ... myrtle**: suggestive of fertile land and therefore symbolic of joy and strength. **To the LORD's renown**: lit., "to the name of the Lord."

56:1–8 This poem inaugurates the final section of the Book of Isaiah, often referred to as Third or Trito-Isaiah. While Second or Deutero-Isaiah (Is 40–55) gave numerous references to the hopes of the community of Israel during the Babylonian exile (ca. 587–538 B.C.), Third Isaiah witnesses to the struggles and hoped-for blessings of the postexilic community now back in the homeland of Israel. In this opening poem, the references to "keeping the sabbath" (vv. 2, 4, 6), "holding fast to the covenant" (vv. 4, 6) and "God's holy mountain" as a house of prayer (v. 7), all tell of the postexilic community that was establishing itself again in the land according to the pattern of God's word given through the prophet. The poem can be classified as a "prophetic exhortation" in which the prophet gives instruction for those who wish to live according to God's word and covenant. What is important to note are the conditions placed upon the people of God; while Is 40–55 show an unconditional promise of redemption, these final chapters delineate clear expectations for receiving God's salvific promises. Both the expectations and the great promises of God will unfold in the succeeding chapters of Third Isaiah.

56:1 This opening verse echoes themes that are well known throughout the Book of Isaiah: justice and right judgment (1:27; 5:7, 16; 9:6; 16:5; 26:9; 28:17; 32:1, 16; 33:5; 42:1, 4, 6; 45:8, 13, 19), salvation and deliverance (12:3; 26:18; 33:2; 45:8, 21; 46:13; 51:5, 6, 8). These themes will be developed also throughout Third Isaiah.

56:3 Eunuchs had originally been excluded from the community of the Lord; cf. Dt 23:2; Neh 13:1–3; Wis 3:14.

56:5 A monument and a name: literally in Hebrew, "a hand and a name"; a memorial inscription to prevent oblivion for one who had no children; cf. 2 Sm 18:18; Neh 7:5; 13:14.

k: Is 59:9, 14, 19–20. *l:* Is 1:13; 58:13–14; Ex 23:12. *m:* Dt 23:3–5; Neh 13:1–3. *n:* Wis 3:14.

7 * Them I will bring to my holy mountain
and make them joyful in my house of prayer;
Their burnt offerings and their sacrifices
will be acceptable on my altar,
For my house shall be called
a house of prayer for all peoples.[o]
8 * Oracle of the Lord GOD,
who gathers the dispersed of Israel—
Others will I gather to them
besides those already gathered.[p]

*Unworthy Shepherds**

9 All you beasts of the field,*
come to devour,
all you beasts in the forest![q]
10 * All the sentinels of Israel are blind,
they are without knowledge;
They are all mute dogs,
unable to bark;
Dreaming, reclining,
loving their sleep.
11 Yes, the dogs have a ravenous appetite;
they never know satiety,
Shepherds who have no understanding;
all have turned their own way,
each one covetous for gain:
12 "Come, let me bring wine;
let us fill ourselves with strong drink,
And tomorrow will be like today,
or even greater."[r]

CHAPTER 57

See RG 280–95

1 The just have perished,
but no one takes it to heart;
The steadfast are swept away,
while no one understands.
Yet the just are taken away from the presence of evil,
2 * and enter into peace;
They rest upon their couches,
the sincere, who walk in integrity.[s]

*An Idolatrous People**

3 But you, draw near,
you children of a sorceress,
offspring of an adulterer and a prostitute!*
4 Against whom do you make sport,
against whom do you open wide your mouth,
and stick out your tongue?
Are you not rebellious children,
deceitful offspring—
5 You who burn with lust among the oaks,
under every green tree;
You who immolate children in the wadies,
among the clefts of the rocks?*[t]
6 Among the smooth stones* of the wadi is your portion,
they, they are your allotment;

56:7 This verse continues the theme of universalism found in Is 49:6. As Israel was to be "a light to the nations" so that God's "salvation may reach to the ends of the earth," so now does that come to pass as foreigners, faithful to the divine commands, are brought to the Temple by God and joined to the covenant community of Israel.

56:8 For the gathering of the dispersed people of Israel, cf. Jer 23:3; 31:8–9; Ez 11:17. Here the Lord not only gathers the displaced of Israel, but also unites other peoples to them. Cf. Is 60:3–10; 66:18–21.

56:9–57:21 This section is made up of two pronouncements of judgment (56:9–57:2; 57:3–13) and an oracle of salvation (57:14–21), each of which ends with a reversal of imagery and language. While there are harsh indictments against the corrupt leaders of Israel (56:9–12), a promise of peace is offered to those who are just (57:1–2). Then the judgment and its subsequent punishment for idolaters (57:3–13a) change to an announcement of reward for those who place their trust in God (57:13c). And the promises of salvation (57:14–19) then shift to a word of warning to the wicked (57:20–21).

56:9 Beasts of the field: foreign nations, which are invited to come and ravage Israel.

56:10–11 These shepherds of Israel are without "knowledge," a theme developed earlier in the Isaian corpus; cf. 1:3; 6:9–10. Ezekiel 34 has similar condemnatory words against the unfaithful shepherds of Israel.

57:2 Despite their sad fate, the just will ultimately attain peace (most likely in this world); cf. v. 13.

57:3–13 In this courtroom imagery, the idolaters are summoned before the judge (v. 3), their crimes are graphically described (vv. 4–11), their guilt is established, and condemnation is carried out (vv. 12–13b). In contrast to this, v. 13c describes the inheritance of God's land and holy mountain given to those who place their confidence in God instead of in idols.

57:3 Language of sexual infidelity is often used in a figurative way to describe idolatry. Cf. Ez 16:15–22; Hos 2:4–7; Col 3:5.

57:5 Child sacrifice is also attested in 2 Kgs 23:10; Jer 7:31; Ez 16:20; 20:28, 31; 23:37–39.

57:6 Smooth stones: the Hebrew word for this expression has the same consonants as the word for "portion"; instead of making the Lord their portion (cf. Ps 16:5), the people adored

o: 1 Kgs 8:29–30, 41; Mt 21:13. *p:* Ps 147:2. *q:* Jer 12:9–10; Ez 34:5. *r:* Is 22:13; 28:7; Wis 2:7. *s:* Wis 3:1–3. *t:* Dt 12:2; 2 Kgs 17:10; Jer 7:31; 19:5; Ez 20:28, 31.

Indeed, you poured out a drink offering
to them,
and brought up grain offerings.
With these things, should I be
appeased?
7 Upon a towering and lofty mountain
you set up your bed,
and there you went up to offer
sacrifice.[u]
8 Behind the door and the doorpost
you set up your symbol.
Yes, deserting me, you carried up your
bedding;
and spread it wide.
You entered an agreement with them,
you loved their couch, you gazed upon
nakedness.*
9 You approached the king* with oil,
and multiplied your perfumes;
You sent your ambassadors far away,
down even to deepest Sheol.
10 Though worn out with the length of your
journey,
you never said, "It is hopeless";
You found your strength revived,
and so you did not weaken.
11 Whom did you dread and fear,
that you told lies,
And me you did not remember
nor take to heart?
Am I to keep silent and conceal,
while you show no fear of me?
12 I will proclaim your justice*
and your works;
but they shall not help you.
13 * When you cry out,
let your collection of idols save you.
All these the wind shall carry off,
a mere breath shall bear them away;
But whoever takes refuge in me shall
inherit the land,
and possess my holy mountain.

The Way to Peace for God's People

14 And I say:
Build up, build up, prepare the way,
remove every obstacle from my
people's way.* [v]
15 * For thus says the high and lofty One,
the One who dwells forever, whose
name is holy:
I dwell in a high and holy place,
but also with the contrite and lowly of
spirit,
To revive the spirit of the lowly,
to revive the heart of the crushed.
16 For I will not accuse forever,
nor always be angry;
For without me their spirit fails,
the life breath that I have given.[w]
17 Because of their wicked avarice I grew
angry;
I struck them, hiding myself from
them in wrath.
But they turned back, following the way
of their own heart.[x]
18 I saw their ways,
but I will heal them.
I will lead them and restore full comfort
to them

slabs of stone which they took from the streambeds in valleys and set up as idols; cf. Jer 3:9. Therefore, it is implied, they will be swept away as by a sudden torrent of waters carrying them down the rocky-bottomed gorge to destruction and death without burial.

57:8 Nakedness: literally in Hebrew, "hand." In this context, it may euphemistically refer to a phallus.

57:9 The king: in Hebrew, the word for king is *melek*, similar in sound to the Canaanite god Molech, to whom children were offered as a sacrifice in pagan ritual. The expression "your ambassadors" could be a figurative expression for the children whose death served as an offering to this deity.

57:12 Justice: here used sarcastically. The activity described in these verses is far from the justice which God demands of those who are aligned with the covenant (cf. 56:1, 4, 6). In the larger context of Third Isaiah and the whole of the Isaian tradition, justice is a key theological motif. The justice to which God calls Israel will eventually come to its fulfillment in an act of divine intervention (cf. 60:21; 61:3c). Until then, the people of God must strive to live in the ways of justice and right judgment (56:1).

57:13 In v. 6, the smooth stones of the valley are the portion which the unfaithful will receive as their due reward (cf. note on v. 6); while in v. 13c, an inheritance of the land and possession of God's holy mountain will be the portion of the upright.

57:14 The way . . . my people's way: the language and imagery are reminiscent of 40:1–2, but in this context, when the people have already returned, the physical road through the desert is replaced by the spiritual way that leads to redemption.

57:15 The God of Israel is presented in both a transcendent and an immanent manner. God's holiness is the transcendent quality; the immanence is shown in the choice of dwelling among the downtrodden and humble.

u: Jer 2:20; Ez 6:13; Hos 4:13. *v:* Is 40:3–4. *w:* Gn 2:7. *x:* Is 56:11.

and to those who mourn for them,[y]
19 creating words of comfort.*
Peace! Peace to those who are far and near,
says the LORD; and I will heal them.
20 But the wicked are like the tossing sea
which cannot be still,
Its waters cast up mire and mud.[z]
21 There is no peace for the wicked!
says my God.[a]

CHAPTER 58

See RG 280–95

*Reasons for Judgment**

1 Cry out full-throated and unsparingly,
lift up your voice like a trumpet blast;
Proclaim to my people their transgression,
to the house of Jacob their sins.[b]
2 They seek me day after day,
and desire to know my ways,
Like a nation that has done what is just
and not abandoned the judgment of
their God;
They ask of me just judgments,
they desire to draw near to God.
3 "Why do we fast, but you do not see it?
afflict ourselves, but you take no note?"
See, on your fast day you carry out your
own pursuits,
and drive all your laborers.[c]
4 See, you fast only to quarrel and fight
and to strike with a wicked fist!
Do not fast as you do today
to make your voice heard on high!
5 Is this the manner of fasting I would
choose,
a day to afflict oneself?
To bow one's head like a reed,
and lie upon sackcloth and ashes?
Is this what you call a fast,
a day acceptable to the LORD?[d]

*Authentic Fasting That Leads to Blessing**

6 Is this not, rather, the fast that I choose:
releasing those bound unjustly,
untying the thongs of the yoke;
Setting free the oppressed,
breaking off every yoke?[e]
7 Is it not sharing your bread with the hungry,
bringing the afflicted and the homeless
into your house;
Clothing the naked when you see them,
and not turning your back on your own
flesh?[f]
8 Then your light shall break forth like the
dawn,
and your wound shall quickly be healed;
Your vindication shall go before you,
and the glory of the LORD shall be
your rear guard.
9 Then you shall call, and the LORD will
answer,
you shall cry for help, and he will say:
"Here I am!"
If you remove the yoke from among you,
the accusing finger, and malicious
speech;[g]
10 If you lavish your food on the hungry
and satisfy the afflicted;
Then your light shall rise in the darkness,
and your gloom shall become like
midday;
11 Then the LORD will guide you always
and satisfy your thirst in parched places,
will give strength to your bones
And you shall be like a watered garden,
like a flowing spring whose waters
never fail.[h]
12 Your people shall rebuild the ancient ruins;
the foundations from ages past you
shall raise up;
"Repairer of the breach," they shall call
you,
"Restorer of ruined dwellings."[i]

*Authentic Sabbath Observance That Leads to Blessing**

13 If you refrain from trampling the sabbath,
from following your own pursuits on
my holy day;

57:19 Creating words of comfort: lit., "fruit of the lips," perhaps referring to praise and thanksgiving for the divine healing; cf. Hos 14:3.

58:1–5 The prophet is commanded to condemn the formalism of the people, specifically their hypocritical fasting.

58:6–12 Fasting is not genuine without reforming one's way of life. A true social morality will ensure prosperity.

58:13–14 Sabbath observance becomes a cornerstone of postexilic piety; cf. 56:2, 4, 6.

y: Is 61:2. *z:* Jon 2:3–7. *a:* Is 48:22. *b:* Lv 25:9. *c:* 1 Sm 7:6; 1 Kgs 21:12; 1 Mc 3:47; Jl 1:1–2:17. *d:* Zec 7:5. *e:* Is 35:5–6. *f:* Ez 18:7, 16; Mt 25:35. *g:* Am 5:7. *h:* Is 51:3; Ps 24. *i:* Is 61:4.

If you call the sabbath a delight,
the LORD's holy day glorious;
If you glorify it by not following your ways,
seeking your own interests, or pursuing your own affairs—
14 Then you shall delight in the LORD,
and I will make you ride upon the heights of the earth;
I will nourish you with the heritage of Jacob, your father,
for the mouth of the LORD has spoken.[j]

CHAPTER 59

See RG 280–95

Salvation Delayed

1 * No, the hand of the LORD is not too short to save,
nor his ear too dull to hear.[k]
2 Rather, it is your crimes
that separate you from your God,
It is your sins that make him hide his face
so that he does not hear you.
3 For your hands are defiled with blood,
and your fingers with crime;
Your lips speak falsehood,
and your tongue utters deceit.[l]
4 No one brings suit justly,
no one pleads truthfully;
They trust an empty plea and tell lies;
they conceive mischief and bring forth malice.
5 * They hatch adders' eggs,
and weave spiders' webs:
Whoever eats the eggs will die,
if one of them is crushed, it will hatch a viper;[m]
6 Their webs cannot serve as clothing,
nor can they cover themselves with their works.
Their works are evil works,
and deeds of violence are in their hands.
7 Their feet run to evil,
and they hasten to shed innocent blood;
Their thoughts are thoughts of wickedness,
violence and destruction are on their highways.[n]
8 * The way of peace they know not,
and there is no justice on their paths;
Their roads they have made crooked,
no one who walks in them knows peace.

Acknowledgment of Transgressions

9 * That is why judgment is far from us
and justice does not reach us.
We look for light, but there is darkness;
for brightness, and we walk in gloom![o]
10 Like those who are blind we grope along the wall,
like people without eyes we feel our way.
We stumble at midday as if at twilight,
among the vigorous, we are like the dead.
11 Like bears we all growl,
like doves we moan without ceasing.
We cry out for justice, but it is not there;
for salvation, but it is far from us.[p]
12 For our transgressions before you are many,
our sins bear witness against us.
Our transgressions are present to us,
and our crimes we acknowledge:
13 Transgressing, and denying the LORD,
turning back from following our God,
Planning fraud and treachery,
uttering lying words conceived in the heart.
14 Judgment is turned away,
and justice stands far off;
For truth stumbles in the public square,
and uprightness cannot enter.[q]
15 Fidelity is lacking,
and whoever turns from evil is despoiled.

59:1–20 This poem brings together a lament of the postexilic community and a harsh word of judgment from the prophet. After the opening rhetorical question, each of the stanzas begins with a reference to the justice and right judgment which are lacking among the people (vv. 4, 9, 14). Toward the end of the poem, God is depicted as a Divine Warrior (vv. 16–20) who is the only one who can intervene in order to bring redemption. This same Divine Warrior imagery is repeated in a similar fashion in 63:1–6.

59:5–6 The eggs signify evil works, doing positive harm; the webs are devices that serve no useful purpose.

59:9–15 The turning point in the poem comes when the people acknowledge their transgressions and describe the horror of their present state. Light is a metaphor for salvation (cf. 9:1;

j: Hb 3:19. *k:* Is 50:2; Nm 11:23. *l:* Is 1:15. *m:* Jb 20:12–16. *n:* Prv 1:15, 19; 2:8–9, 12–13, 15, 18–19; Rom 3:15. *o:* Am 5:18–19. *p:* Is 38:14. *q:* Jb 28:28.

Divine Intervention

The LORD saw this, and was aggrieved
that there was no justice.
16 He saw that there was no one,
was appalled that there was none to intervene;
Then his own arm brought about the victory,
and his justice sustained him.
17 He put on justice as his breastplate,
victory as a helmet on his head;
He clothed himself with garments of vengeance,
wrapped himself in a mantle of zeal.[r]
18 According to their deeds he repays his enemies
and requites his foes with wrath;
to the coastlands he renders recompense.
19 Those in the west shall fear the name of the LORD,
and those in the east, his glory,
Coming like a pent-up stream
driven on by the breath of the LORD.
20 Then for Zion shall come a redeemer,
to those in Jacob who turn from transgression—oracle of the LORD.[s]
21 * This is my covenant with them,
which I myself have made, says the LORD:
My spirit which is upon you
and my words that I have put in your mouth
Shall not depart from your mouth,
nor from the mouths of your children
Nor the mouths of your children's children
from this time forth and forever, says the LORD.[t]

CHAPTER 60

See RG 280–95

The Dawning of Divine Glory for Zion

1 * Arise! Shine, for your light has come,
the glory of the LORD has dawned upon you.[u]
2 Though darkness covers the earth,
and thick clouds, the peoples,
Upon you the LORD will dawn,
and over you his glory will be seen.
3 Nations shall walk by your light,
kings by the radiance of your dawning.[v]

The Nations Come to Zion

4 Raise your eyes and look about;
they all gather and come to you—
Your sons from afar,
your daughters in the arms of their nurses.[w]
5 Then you shall see and be radiant,
your heart shall throb and overflow.
For the riches of the sea shall be poured out before you,
the wealth of nations shall come to you.
6 Caravans of camels shall cover you,
dromedaries of Midian and Ephah;
All from Sheba shall come
bearing gold and frankincense,
and heralding the praises of the LORD.
7 All the flocks of Kedar shall be gathered for you,
the rams of Nebaioth shall serve your needs;
They will be acceptable offerings on my altar,
and I will glorify my glorious house.
8 Who are these that fly along like a cloud,
like doves to their cotes?
9 The vessels of the coastlands are gathering,
with the ships of Tarshish in the lead,
To bring your children from afar,
their silver and gold with them—
For the name of the LORD, your God,
for the Holy One of Israel who has glorified you.

*Honor and Service for Zion**

10 Foreigners shall rebuild your walls,
their kings shall minister to you;

42:16; 60:1–3, 19–20) and darkness represents sin and disaster.

59:21 This verse makes the transition from chaps. 56–59 to chaps. 60–62. Oracles of judgment yield to oracles about God's redemptive action.

60:1–9 The light the prophet proclaims to Zion symbolizes the blessing to come to her: the glory of the Lord, the return of her children, the wealth of nations who themselves will walk by her light. The passage is famous from its use in the Latin liturgy for the feast of Epiphany.

60:10–18 The glorious promises for the future continue:

r: Wis 5:17–20; Eph 6:14–16; 1 Thes 5:8. *s:* Is 35:4; Rom 11:26–27. *t:* Is 1:27. *u:* Is 40:5; 49:14–26; 51:17–23. *v:* Is 42:6; 45:14; 49:6. *w:* Is 49:18.

Though in my wrath I struck you,
yet in my good will I have shown you mercy.[x]
11 Your gates shall stand open constantly;
day and night they shall not be closed
So that they may bring you the wealth of nations,
with their kings in the vanguard.[y]
12 For the nation or kingdom that will not serve you shall perish;
such nations shall be utterly destroyed![z]
13 The glory of Lebanon shall come to you—
the juniper, the fir, and the cypress all together—
To bring beauty to my sanctuary,
and glory to the place where I stand.[a]
14 The children of your oppressors shall come,
bowing before you;
All those who despised you,
shall bow low at your feet.
They shall call you "City of the LORD,"
"Zion of the Holy One of Israel."
15 No longer forsaken and hated,
with no one passing through,
Now I will make you the pride of the ages,
a joy from generation to generation.
16 You shall suck the milk of nations,
and be nursed at royal breasts;
And you shall know that I, the LORD, am your savior,
your redeemer, the Mighty One of Jacob.
17 Instead of bronze I will bring gold,
instead of iron I will bring silver;
Instead of wood, bronze;
instead of stones, iron.
I will appoint peace your governor,
and justice your ruler.[b]
18 No longer shall violence be heard of in your land,
or plunder and ruin within your borders.
You shall call your walls "Salvation"
and your gates "Praise."

Eternal Light for Zion

19 * No longer shall the sun
be your light by day,
Nor shall the brightness of the moon
give you light by night;
Rather, the LORD will be your light forever,
your God will be your glory.[c]
20 No longer will your sun set,
or your moon wane;
For the LORD will be your light forever,
and the days of your grieving will be over.
21 Your people will all be just;
for all time they will possess the land;
They are the shoot that I planted,
the work of my hands, that I might be glorified.[d]
22 The least one shall become a clan,
the smallest, a mighty nation;
I, the LORD, will swiftly accomplish
these things when the time comes.[e]

CHAPTER 61

See RG 280–95

The Anointed Bearer of Glad Tidings

1 * The spirit of the Lord GOD is upon me,
because the LORD has anointed me;
He has sent me to bring good news to the afflicted,
to bind up the brokenhearted,
To proclaim liberty to the captives,
release to the prisoners,[f]
2 To announce a year of favor from the LORD
and a day of vindication by our God;
To comfort all who mourn;[g]
3 to place on those who mourn in Zion
a diadem instead of ashes,
To give them oil of gladness instead of mourning,

the wealth of the nations (vv. 5, 10), tribute from kings, glorification of the Temple, peace and justice (cf. Ps 85:11).

60:19–20 The theme of light is taken up again, but in an apocalyptic vein: the Lord's radiant presence replaces physical light.

61:1–2 The prophet proclaims that he has been anointed by the Lord to bring good news (cf. 40:9) to the afflicted and to comfort Zion. The background to the "year of favor" is the jubilee year of release from debts (Lv 25:10–11; Is 49:8).

x: Is 54:11–12. *y:* Rev 21:25. *z:* Is 61:2. *a:* Is 35:2; 66:1. *b:* Ps 85:11. *c:* Is 2:5; Rev 21:23; 22:5. *d:* Is 57:13c. *e:* Gn 12:2; 17:6. *f:* Is 40:9; 42:1; 48:16; 52:7; 58:7; Lk 4:18–19. *g:* Mt 5:4.

a glorious mantle instead of a faint
spirit.

Restoration and Blessing

They will be called oaks of justice,
the planting of the LORD to show his
glory.
4 They shall rebuild the ancient ruins,
the former wastes they shall raise up
And restore the desolate cities,
devastations of generation upon
generation.[h]
5 Strangers shall stand ready to pasture
your flocks,
foreigners shall be your farmers and
vinedressers.
6 * You yourselves shall be called "Priests
of the LORD,"
"Ministers of our God" you shall be
called.
You shall eat the wealth of the nations
and in their riches you will boast.[i]
7 Because their shame was twofold*
and disgrace was proclaimed their
portion,
They will possess twofold in their own
land;
everlasting joy shall be theirs.[j]

God's Word of Promise

8 For I, the LORD, love justice,
I hate robbery and wrongdoing;
I will faithfully give them their
recompense,
an everlasting covenant I will make
with them.[k]
9 Their offspring shall be renowned among
the nations,
and their descendants in the midst of
the peoples;
All who see them shall acknowledge
them:
"They are offspring the LORD has
blessed."

Thanksgiving for God's Deliverance

10 * I will rejoice heartily in the LORD,
my being exults in my God;
For he has clothed me with garments of
salvation,
and wrapped me in a robe of justice,
Like a bridegroom adorned with a
diadem,
as a bride adorns herself with her
jewels.[l]
11 As the earth brings forth its shoots,
and a garden makes its seeds spring
up,
So will the Lord GOD make justice spring
up,
and praise before all the nations.

CHAPTER 62

See RG 280–95

A New Name for Zion

1 * For Zion's sake I will not be silent,
for Jerusalem's sake I will not keep
still,
Until her vindication shines forth like the
dawn
and her salvation like a burning torch.[m]
2 Nations shall behold your vindication,
and all kings your glory;
You shall be called by a new name
bestowed by the mouth of the LORD.[n]
3 You shall be a glorious crown in the hand
of the LORD,
a royal diadem in the hand of your
God.
4 No more shall you be called "Forsaken,"
nor your land called "Desolate,"
But you shall be called "My Delight is in
her,"
and your land "Espoused."
For the LORD delights in you,
and your land shall be espoused.[o]
5 For as a young man marries a virgin,
your Builder shall marry you;
And as a bridegroom rejoices in his bride
so shall your God rejoice in you.

61:6 The bestowal of a new name suggests a new identity and mission. The whole people will be priests (cf. Ex 19:6), even ministering to nations who will serve God's people.

61:7 Twofold: Israel was punished double for infidelity (40:2); the blessings of its restoration will also be double.

61:10–11 The new life of the restored Zion is expressed in nuptial (cf. also 62:5) and agricultural (cf. v. 3; 60:21) imagery.

62:1–12 As in chap. 60, the prophet addresses Zion, announcing the reversal of her fortune. Several motifs reappear: light and glory (60:1–3, 19–20), tribute of nations (60:11), and especially the marriage (61:10; cf. also 54:5–8).

h: Is 58:12. *i:* Ex 19:6; 1 Pt 2:9. *j:* Is 40:2. *k:* Is 55:3; 54:9–10; 59:21. *l:* 1 Sm 2:1; Ps 138:1–2. *m:* Is 42:14; 64:22. *n:* Rev 2:17; 3:12. *o:* Is 49:15–16; 54:7–8.

6 Upon your walls, Jerusalem,
I have stationed sentinels;
By day and by night,
they shall never be silent.
You who are to remind the LORD,
take no rest,
7 And give him no rest,
until he re-establishes Jerusalem
And makes it the praise of the earth.

The Blessings of Salvation for God's People

8 * The LORD has sworn by his right hand
and by his mighty arm:
No more will I give your grain
as food to your enemies;
Nor shall foreigners drink the wine,
for which you toiled.[p]
9 But those who harvest shall eat,
and praise the LORD;
Those who gather shall drink
in my holy courts.[q]
10 * Pass through, pass through the gates,
prepare a way for the people;[r]
Build up, build up the highway, clear it
of stones,
raise up a standard over the nations.
11 The LORD has proclaimed
to the ends of the earth:
Say to daughter Zion,
"See, your savior comes!
See, his reward is with him,
his recompense before him."[s]
12 They shall be called "The Holy People,"
"The Redeemed of the LORD."
And you shall be called "Cared For,"
"A City Not Forsaken."[t]

See RG 280–95

CHAPTER 63

*The Divine Warrior**

1 Who is this that comes from Edom,
in crimsoned garments, from Bozrah?
Who is this, glorious in his apparel,
striding in the greatness of his
strength?
"It is I, I who announce vindication,
mighty to save."[u]
2 Why is your apparel red,
and your garments like one who treads
the wine press?[v]
3 "The wine press I have trodden alone,
and from the peoples no one was with
me.
I trod them in my anger,
and trampled them down in my wrath;
Their blood spurted on my garments,
all my apparel I stained.
4 For a day of vindication was in my heart,
my year for redeeming had come.[w]
5 I looked about, but there was no one to
help,
I was appalled that there was no one to
lend support;
So my own arm brought me victory
and my own wrath lent me support.[x]
6 I trampled down the peoples in my anger,
I made them drunk in my wrath,
and I poured out their blood upon the
ground."

Prayer for the Return of God's Favor

7 * The loving deeds of the LORD I will
recall,
the glorious acts of the LORD,
Because of all the LORD has done for us,
the immense goodness to the house of
Israel,
Which he has granted according to his
mercy
and his many loving deeds.[y]
8 He said: "They are indeed my people,
children who are not disloyal."
So he became their savior
9 in their every affliction.
It was not an envoy or a messenger,

62:8–9 Peace and prosperity are indicated by the absence of invaders who would live off the land.

62:10–11 The gates of Babylon are to be opened for the exiles to return, led by the Lord, as in 40:3–5, 10.

63:1–6 Two questions are raised at the approach of a majestic figure coming from Edom. It is the Lord, his garments red with the blood from the judgment battle. Edom (its capital Bozrah) plundered Judah after the fall of Jerusalem; cf. 34:5–17. **Wine press**: here a symbol of a bloody judgment; cf. Lam 1:15; Jl 4:13.

63:7–64:11 This lament of the exilic community recalls God's protection, and especially the memories of the exodus (vv. 7–14), before begging the Lord to come once more to their aid (63:15–64:3), as they confess their sins (64:4–11). The prayer is marked by God's "holy spirit" (63:10–11, 14) and fatherhood (63:8, 9, 16; 64:7).

p: Is 52:10. *q:* Dt 12:17–18; 14:23. *r:* Is 58:14. *s:* Is 40:10. *t:* Is 62:4. *u:* Is 34:6; 49:19. *v:* Rev 19:13. *w:* Is 34:8; 61:2. *x:* Is 59:16. *y:* Is 26:15.

but his presence that saved them.
Because of his love and pity
the LORD redeemed them,
Lifting them up and carrying them
all the days of old.[z]
10 But they rebelled
and grieved his holy spirit;
So he turned to become their enemy,
and warred against them.[a]

11 Then they remembered the days of old, of Moses, his servant:

Where is the one who brought up out of the sea
the shepherd of his flock?
Where is the one who placed in their midst
his holy spirit,[b]
12 Who guided Moses by the hand,
with his glorious arm?
Where is the one who divided the waters before them—
winning for himself an everlasting renown—
13 Who guided them through the depths,
like horses in open country?
14 As cattle going down into the valley,
they did not stumble.
The spirit of the LORD guided them.
Thus you led your people,
to make for yourself a glorious name.
15 Look down from heaven and regard us
from your holy and glorious palace!
Where is your zealous care and your might,
your surge of pity?[c]
Your mercy hold not back!
16 For you are our father.
Were Abraham not to know us,
nor Israel to acknowledge us,
You, LORD, are our father,
our redeemer you are named from of old.
17 Why do you make us wander, LORD,
from your ways,
and harden our hearts so that we do not fear you?*
Return for the sake of your servants,
the tribes of your heritage.
18 Why have the wicked invaded your holy place,
why have our enemies trampled your sanctuary?
19 * Too long have we been like those you do not rule,
on whom your name is not invoked.
Oh, that you would rend the heavens and come down,
with the mountains quaking before you,[d]

CHAPTER 64

See RG 280–95

1 As when brushwood is set ablaze,
or fire makes the water boil!
Then your name would be made known to your enemies
and the nations would tremble before you,
2 While you worked awesome deeds we could not hope for,*
3 such as had not been heard of from of old.
No ear has ever heard, no eye ever seen,
any God but you
working such deeds for those who wait for him.[e]
4 Would that you might meet us doing right,
that we might be mindful of you in our ways!
Indeed, you are angry; we have sinned,
we have acted wickedly.
5 We have all become like something unclean,
all our just deeds are like polluted rags;
We have all withered like leaves,
and our crimes carry us away like the wind.[f]
6 There are none who call upon your name,

63:17 The hardening of the heart (Ex 4:21; 7:3) serves to explain Israel's sins—a motif to induce the Lord to relent.

63:19–64:3 A new theophany, like Sinai of old, is invoked so that Israel's enemies will be humbled by God's intervention.

64:2 The translation here omits some words repeated in the Hebrew from 63:19 ("would that you would come down, with the mountains trembling before you").

z: Dt 4:37–40. *a:* Dt 32:15; Ps 51:12. *b:* Heb 13:20. *c:* Dt 26:15; Bar 2:16. *d:* Ps 144:5; Mk 1:10. *e:* 1 Cor 2:9. *f:* Is 1:30; 34:4.

none who rouse themselves to take
hold of you;
For you have hidden your face from us
and have delivered us up to our crimes.

A Final Plea

7 * Yet, LORD, you are our father;
we are the clay and you our potter:
we are all the work of your hand.
8 Do not be so very angry, LORD,
do not remember our crimes forever;
look upon us, who are all your people!
9 Your holy cities have become a
wilderness;
Zion has become wilderness,
Jerusalem desolation![g]
10 Our holy and glorious house
in which our ancestors praised you
Has been burned with fire;
all that was dear to us is laid waste.
11 Can you hold back, LORD, after all this?
Can you remain silent, and afflict us so
severely?

CHAPTER 65

See RG 280–95

1 * I was ready to respond to those
who did not ask,
to be found by those who did not seek
me.
I said: Here I am! Here I am!
To a nation that did not invoke my
name.[h]
2 I have stretched out my hands all day
to a rebellious people,
Who walk in a way that is not good,
following their own designs;[i]
3 A people who provoke me
continually to my face,
Offering sacrifices in gardens
and burning incense on bricks,
4 Sitting in tombs
and spending the night in caves,
Eating the flesh of pigs,
with broth of unclean meat in their
dishes;
5 Crying out, "Hold back,
do not come near me, lest I render you
holy!"*
These things are smoke in my nostrils,
a fire that burns all the day.
6 See, it stands written before me;
I will not remain quiet until I have
repaid in full
7 Your crimes and the crimes of your
ancestors as well,
says the LORD.
Since they burned incense on the
mountains,
and insulted me on the hills,
I will at once pour out in full measure
their recompense into their laps.

Fate of the Just and Unjust in Israel

8 * Thus says the LORD:
As when the juice is pressed from a
cluster,
and someone says, "Do not destroy it,
for there is still good in it,"
So will I do for the sake of my servants:
I will not destroy them all.
9 From Jacob I will bring forth offspring,
from Judah, those who are to possess
my mountains;
My chosen ones shall possess the land,
my servants shall dwell there.
10 Sharon shall become a pasture for the
flocks,
the Valley of Achor a resting place for
the cattle,
for my people who have sought me.[j]
11 But you who forsake the LORD,
who forget my holy mountain,
Who spread a table for Fortune
and fill cups of mixed wine for Destiny,*

64:7–11 The motifs of father (63:16) and creator (clay and potter, 29:16; 45:9) are adduced to move the Lord to action in view of the damage done to his "holy cities" and "glorious house."

65:1–7 These verses serve as a response to the preceding questions about God's inaction (64:6, 11). It is not God who has been absent, but the people who have walked away from God by idolatrous acts and rituals (vv. 3–4). That is the reason for their punishment (vv. 6–7).

65:5 Render you holy: unclean food is what these people claim has made them sacred! The prophet ridicules them. Sacredness was understood as something communicable (cf. Ex 19:9–15).

65:8 This verse reflects the remnant theology found elsewhere in the Book of Isaiah: 1:8–9; 4:3; 6:11–13; etc.

65:11–12 Destiny: the play on words is found in the Hebrew, in which "destiny" and "destine" are *menî* and *manîthî*.

g: Ps 79:1; Lam 1. *h:* Rom 10:20. *i:* Rom 10:21. *j:* Hos 2:17.

12 You I will destine for the sword;
you shall all bow down for slaughter;
Because I called and you did not answer,
I spoke and you did not listen,
But did what is evil in my sight
and things I do not delight in, you
chose,[k]
13 therefore thus says the Lord GOD:
My servants shall eat,
but you shall go hungry;
My servants shall drink,
but you shall be thirsty;
My servants shall rejoice,
but you shall be put to shame;
14 My servants shall shout
for joy of heart,
But you shall cry out for grief of heart,
and howl for anguish of spirit.
15 You will leave your name for a curse to
my chosen ones
when the Lord GOD slays you,
and calls his servants by another name.
16 Whoever invokes a blessing in the land
shall bless by the God of truth;*
Whoever takes an oath in the land
shall swear by the God of truth;
For the hardships of the past shall be
forgotten
and hidden from my eyes.

A World Renewed

17 * See, I am creating new heavens
and a new earth;
The former things shall not be remembered
nor come to mind.[l]
18 Instead, shout for joy and be glad forever
in what I am creating.
Indeed, I am creating Jerusalem to be a
joy
and its people to be a delight;
19 I will rejoice in Jerusalem
and exult in my people.
No longer shall the sound of weeping be
heard there,
or the sound of crying;
20 No longer shall there be in it
an infant who lives but a few days,
nor anyone who does not live a full
lifetime;
One who dies at a hundred years shall be
considered a youth,
and one who falls short of a hundred
shall be thought accursed.[m]
21 They shall build houses and live in them,
they shall plant vineyards and eat their
fruit;
22 They shall not build and others live there;
they shall not plant and others eat.
As the years of a tree, so the years of my
people;
and my chosen ones shall long enjoy
the work of their hands.
23 They shall not toil in vain,
nor beget children for sudden
destruction;
For they shall be a people blessed by the
LORD
and their descendants with them.
24 Before they call, I will answer;
while they are yet speaking, I will hear.
25 * The wolf and the lamb shall pasture
together,
and the lion shall eat hay like the ox—
but the serpent's food shall be dust.[n]
None shall harm or destroy
on all my holy mountain, says the
LORD.

CHAPTER 66

See RG 280–95

True and False Worship

1 * Thus says the LORD:
The heavens are my throne,
the earth, my footstool.
What house can you build for me?
Where is the place of my rest?[o]
2 My hand made all these things
when all of them came to be—oracle
of the LORD.

65:16 God of truth: lit., "God of Amen," i.e., the one who keeps his word.

65:17–18 The new creation (cf. 66:22) is described with apocalyptic exuberance: long life, material prosperity, and so forth. As the former events in 43:18 are to be forgotten, so also the new creation wipes out memory of the first creation.

65:25 The imagery reflects the ideal era described in 11:6–9; see note there.

66:1–2 The Lord rejects the abuses associated with Temple worship in order to emphasize his concern for the sincere worshiper.

k: Is 66:4; Prv 1:24; Jer 7:13. *l:* Is 66:22; Rev 21:1. *m:* Dt 4:40. *n:* Is 11:6–9. *o:* 2 Sm 7:4–7; 1 Kgs 8:27; Acts 7:49; 17:24.

This is the one whom I approve:
the afflicted one, crushed in spirit,
who trembles at my word.[p]
3 * The one slaughtering an ox, striking a man,
sacrificing a lamb, breaking a dog's neck,
Making an offering of pig's blood,
burning incense, honoring an idol—
These have chosen their own ways,
and taken pleasure in their own abominations.[q]
4 I in turn will choose affliction for them
and bring upon them what they fear.
Because when I called, no one answered,
when I spoke, no one listened.
Because they did what was evil in my sight,
and things I do not delight in they chose,[r]
5 Hear the word of the LORD,
you who tremble at his word!
Your kin who hate you
and cast you out because of my name say,
"May the LORD show his glory,
that we may see your joy";
but they shall be put to shame.
6 A voice roaring from the city,
a voice from the temple;
The voice of the LORD
rendering recompense to his enemies![s]

Blessings of Prosperity and Consolation

7 * Before she is in labor,
she gives birth;[t]
Before her pangs come upon her,
she delivers a male child.
8 Who ever heard of such a thing,
or who ever saw the like?
Can a land be brought forth in one day,
or a nation be born in a single moment?
Yet Zion was scarcely in labor
when she bore her children.
9 Shall I bring a mother to the point of birth,
and yet not let her child be born? says the LORD.
Or shall I who bring to birth
yet close her womb? says your God.
10 * Rejoice with Jerusalem and be glad because of her,
all you who love her;
Rejoice with her in her joy,
all you who mourn over her—[u]
11 So that you may nurse and be satisfied
from her consoling breast;
That you may drink with delight
at her abundant breasts!
12 For thus says the LORD:
I will spread prosperity over her like a river,
like an overflowing torrent,
the wealth of nations.
You shall nurse, carried in her arms,
cradled upon her knees;
13 As a mother comforts her child,
so I will comfort you;
in Jerusalem you shall find your comfort.[v]
14 You will see and your heart shall exult,
and your bodies shall flourish like the grass;
The LORD's power shall be revealed to his servants,
but to his enemies, his wrath.
15 For see, the LORD will come in fire,
his chariots like the stormwind;
To wreak his anger in burning rage
and his rebuke in fiery flames.
16 For with fire the LORD shall enter into judgment,
and, with his sword, against all flesh;
Those slain by the LORD shall be many.[w]

17* Those who sanctify and purify themselves to go into the gardens, following one

66:3–6 The sacrificial abuses listed will only merit punishment. The true worshipers, the downtrodden, are those who "tremble" (vv. 2, 5) at God's word. Although they are ridiculed by those who reject them (v. 5), the latter will be afflicted with divine punishment; their "choice" will be met by the Lord's choice (v. 4).

66:7–9 The renewal of Zion is pictured in terms of a miraculous, instantaneous birth, facilitated by God's intervention.

66:10–16 The poet addresses the children born of Jerusalem, their mother. In v. 13 the metaphor switches to the Lord as mother (cf. 49:15), comforting her charges but destroying the enemies.

66:17 This verse seems to have some connection with 65:2–3.

p: Ps 24:1–2. *q:* Lv 11:7. *r:* Is 65:12; Prv 1:24; Jer 7:13. *s:* Jl 4:16; Am 1:2. *t:* Is 49:18–21; 54:1. *u:* Tb 13:14. *v:* Is 40:1; 49:13. *w:* Lv 11:29.

who stands within, eating pig's flesh, abominable things, and mice, shall all together
come to an end, with their deeds and purposes—oracle of the LORD.
God Gathers the Nations. [18]* I am coming
to gather all nations and tongues; they shall
come and see my glory.[x] [19]I will place a sign
among them; from them I will send survivors to the nations: to Tarshish, Put and
Lud, Mosoch, Tubal and Javan, to the distant
coastlands which have never heard of my
fame, or seen my glory; and they shall proclaim my glory among the nations. [20]They
shall bring all your kin from all the nations
as an offering to the LORD, on horses and in
chariots, in carts, upon mules and dromedaries, to Jerusalem, my holy mountain, says
the LORD, just as the Israelites bring their
grain offering in a clean vessel to the house
of the LORD. [21]Some of these I will take as
priests and Levites, says the LORD.

[22] Just as the new heavens and the new earth
which I am making
Shall endure before me—oracle of the
LORD—
so shall your descendants and your
name endure.[y]
[23] From new moon to new moon,
and from sabbath to sabbath,
All flesh shall come to worship
before me, says the LORD.[z]
[24] * They shall go out and see the corpses[a]
of the people who rebelled against me;
For their worm shall not die,
their fire shall not be extinguished;
and they shall be an abhorrence to all
flesh.

66:18–21 God summons the neighboring nations to Zion and from among them will send some to far distant lands to proclaim the divine glory. **All your kin**: Jews in exile. The "gathering of the people and the nations" is an eschatological motif common in the prophetic tradition; cf. 56:8.

66:24 God's enemies lie dead outside the walls of the New Jerusalem; just as in the past, corpses, filth and refuse lay in the Valley of Hinnom (Gehenna) outside the city; cf. 34:1–4; 2 Kgs 23:10.

x: Is 56:1, 8; 59:20. *y:* Is 65:17; Rev 21:1. *z:* Is 1:13. *a:* Is 1:27–28; Mk 9:45.

See RG 296–309

The Book of Jeremiah

The Book of Jeremiah combines history, biography, and prophecy. It portrays a nation in crisis and introduces the reader to an extraordinary person whom the Lord called to prophesy under the trying circumstances of the final days of the kingdom of Judah. Jeremiah was born, perhaps about 650 B.C., of a priestly family from the village of Anathoth, two and a half miles northeast of Jerusalem. He was called to his task in the thirteenth year of King Josiah (Jer 1:2). Josiah's reform, begun with enthusiasm and hope, ended with his death on the battlefield of Megiddo (609 B.C.) as he attempted to stop the northward march of the Egyptian Pharaoh Neco, who was going to provide assistance to the Assyrians who were in retreat before the Babylonians.

Nineveh, the capital of Assyria, fell in 612 B.C., preparing the way for the new colossus, Babylon, which was soon to put an end to the independence of Judah.

The prophet supported the reform of King Josiah (2 Kgs 22–23), but after the death of Josiah the old idolatry returned. Jeremiah opposed this as well as royal policy toward Babylon. Arrest, imprisonment, and public disgrace were his lot. In the nation's apostasy Jeremiah saw the sealing of its doom. Nebuchadnezzar captured Jerusalem (598 B.C.) and carried King Jehoiachin into exile (Jer 22:24).

During the years 598–587, Jeremiah counseled Zedekiah in the face of bitter opposition. The false prophet Hananiah proclaimed that the yoke of Babylon was broken and a strong pro-Egyptian party in Jerusalem induced Zedekiah to revolt. Nebuchadnezzar took swift vengeance; Jerusalem was destroyed in 587 and its leading citizens sent into exile.

The prophet remained in Jerusalem, but was later forced into Egyptian exile. We do not know the details of his death. The influence of Jeremiah was greater after his death than before. The exiled community read and meditated on the lessons of the prophet; his influence is evident in Ezekiel, some of the psalms, Is 40–66, and Daniel. In the postexilic period, the Book of Jeremiah circulated in various editions.

The book may be divided as follows:

I. Oracles in the Days of Josiah (1:1–6:30)
II. Oracles Primarily from the Days of Jehoiakim (7:1–20:18)
III. Oracles in the Last Years of Jerusalem (21:1–25:38)
IV. The Temple Sermon (26:1–24; cf. 7:1–15)
V. Controversies with the False Prophets (27:1–29:32)
VI. Oracles of the Restoration of Israel and Judah (30:1–35:19)
VII. Jeremiah and the Fall of Jerusalem (36:1–45:5)
VIII. Oracles Against the Nations (46:1–51:64)
IX. Historical Appendix (52:1–34)

I. Oracles in the Days of Josiah

CHAPTER 1

See RG 302

1 The words of Jeremiah, son of Hilkiah, one of the priests from Anathoth,* in
the land of Benjamin. 2 The word of the
LORD came to him in the days of Josiah, son
of Amon, king of Judah, in the thirteenth
year of his reign,[a] 3 and again in the days of
Jehoiakim, son of Josiah, king of Judah, until the end of the eleventh year of Zedekiah,
son of Josiah, king of Judah—down to the
exile of Jerusalem, in the fifth month.[b]

Call of Jeremiah

4 The word of the LORD came to me:
5 Before I formed you in the womb I knew
you,
before you were born I dedicated you,
a prophet to the nations I appointed
you.*[c]
6 "Ah, Lord GOD!" I said,
"I do not know how to speak. I am too
young!"*
7 But the LORD answered me,
Do not say, "I am too young."
To whomever I send you, you shall go;
whatever I command you, you shall
speak.
8 Do not be afraid of them,
for I am with you to deliver you—
oracle of the LORD.

9 Then the LORD extended his hand and
touched my mouth, saying to me,

See, I place my words in your mouth![d]
10 Today I appoint you
over nations and over kingdoms,
To uproot and to tear down,
to destroy and to demolish,
to build and to plant.

11 The word of the LORD came to me: What
do you see, Jeremiah? "I see a branch of the
almond tree,"* I replied. 12 Then the LORD
said to me: You have seen well, for I am
watching over my word to carry it out. 13[e] A
second time the word of the LORD came to
me: What do you see? I replied, "I see a boiling kettle whose mouth is tipped away from
the north."*

14 The LORD said to me, And from the
north evil will pour out over all who dwell in
the land.[f]

15 Look, I am summoning
all the kingdoms of the north—oracle
of the LORD—
Each king shall come and set up his
throne
in the gateways of Jerusalem,
Against all its surrounding walls

1:1 Anathoth: a village about three miles northeast of Jerusalem, to which Solomon had exiled Abiathar the priest (1 Kgs 2:26–27); it is likely that Jeremiah belonged to that priestly family.

1:5 Jeremiah was destined to become a prophet before his birth; cf. Is 49:1, 5; Lk 1:15; Gal 1:15–16. **I knew you**: I loved you and chose you. **I dedicated you**: I set you apart to be a prophet. **The nations**: the neighbors of Judah, along with Assyria, Babylonia, and Egypt.

1:6 I am too young: like Moses (Ex 3:11, 13; 4:10), Jeremiah at first resists God's call. This narrative is perhaps patterned after the story of Moses' call in order to identify Jeremiah as the prophet "like me" in Dt 18:15.

1:11 There is wordplay between the Hebrew noun *shaqed*, "almond tree," and the Hebrew verb *shoqed*, "watcher/watching." Because the almond tree begins to bloom in late winter in Palestine, it is called "the watcher" for the coming of spring. God is also "watcher," observing the fulfillment of the prophetic word.

1:13 Kettle . . . the north: symbol of an invasion from the north; cf. vv. 14–15.

a: Jer 25:3. *b:* Jer 25:1. *c:* Jer 49:1; Gal 1:15–16. *d:* Dt 18:18; Is 6:7. *e:* Ez 11:3, 7; 24:3. *f:* Jer 4:6; 6:1.

and against all the cities of Judah.[g]
16 I will pronounce my sentence against them
for all their wickedness in forsaking me,
In burning incense to other gods,
in bowing down to the works of their hands.[h]
17 But you, prepare yourself;
stand up and tell them
all that I command you.
Do not be terrified on account of them,
or I will terrify you before them;
18 For I am the one who today
makes you a fortified city,
A pillar of iron, a wall of bronze,
against the whole land:
Against Judah's kings and princes,
its priests and the people of the land.[i]
19 They will fight against you, but not prevail over you,
for I am with you to deliver you—
oracle of the LORD.

CHAPTER 2

See RG 302

Infidelity of Israel.* 1 The word of the LORD came to me: 2 Go, cry out this message for Jerusalem to hear!

I remember the devotion* of your youth,
how you loved me as a bride,
Following me in the wilderness,
in a land unsown.[j]
3 Israel was dedicated to the LORD,
the first fruits* of his harvest;
All who ate of it were held guilty,
evil befell them—oracle of the LORD.[k]
4 Listen to the word of the LORD, house of Jacob!
All you clans of the house of Israel,
5 thus says the LORD:
What fault did your ancestors find in me
that they withdrew from me,
Went after emptiness,
and became empty themselves?[l]
6 They did not ask, "Where is the LORD
who brought us up from the land of Egypt,
Who led us through the wilderness,
through a land of wastes and ravines,
A land of drought and darkness,
a land which no one crosses,
where no one dwells?"[m]
7 I brought you into the garden land
to eat its fine fruits,
But you entered and defiled my land,
you turned my heritage into an abomination.[n]
8 The priests did not ask,
"Where is the LORD?"
The experts in the law* did not know me:
the shepherds rebelled against me.
The prophets prophesied by Baal,
and went after useless idols.[o]
9 Therefore I will again accuse you—
oracle of the LORD—
even your children's children I will accuse.[p]
10 Cross to the coast of Cyprus and see,
send to Kedar* and carefully inquire:
Where has anything like this been done?
11 Does any other nation change its gods?—
even though they are not gods at all!
But my people have changed their glory
for useless things.[q]
12 Be horrified at this, heavens;
shudder, be appalled—oracle of the LORD.
13 Two evils my people have done:
they have forsaken me, the source of living waters;
They have dug themselves cisterns,
broken cisterns that cannot hold water.[r]

2:1–3:5 These chapters may contain some of Jeremiah's early preaching. He portrays Israel as the wife of the Lord, faithful only in the beginning, when she walked behind him (2:2–3, 5; 3:1). Consistent with the marriage metaphor, he describes her present unfaithfulness as adultery (2:20; 3:2–3); now she walks behind the Baals.

2:2 Devotion: Heb. *hesed*; Israel's gratitude, fidelity, and love for God.

2:3 First fruits: the first yield of a harvest offered as a sign of dependence on and gratitude toward the Lord of the land, thus divine property. Israel, then, is a gift made to God, set apart for his use; cf. Ex 23:19.

2:8 Experts in the law: the priests. **The shepherds**: the kings and nobles.

2:10 Kedar: a nomadic tribe in north Arabia. Cyprus and Kedar represent west and east.

g: Jer 6:22. *h:* Is 2:8. *i:* Jer 6:27; 15:20; Ez 3:8. *j:* Dt 2:7; 32:9–12; Mi 6:4. *k:* Jer 12:14; Ex 4:22; Dt 7:6; 14:2. *l:* 2 Kgs 17:15; Is 5:4; Mi 6:3. *m:* Ex 20:2–3; Dt 8:14; Is 63:11–14. *n:* Lv 18:24–25; Dt 8:7–10; 32:13–14. *o:* Jer 8:8–9; 23:1, 13. *p:* Ex 20:5. *q:* Jer 16:20; Ps 106:20. *r:* Jer 17:13; Ps 36:9; Is 1:4.

14 Is Israel a slave, a house-born servant?*
Why then has he become plunder?
15 Against him lions roar,
they raise their voices.
They have turned his land into a waste;
his cities are charred ruins, without an inhabitant.[s]
16 Yes, the people of Memphis* and Tahpanhes
shave the crown of your head.
17 Has not forsaking the LORD, your God,
done this to you?[t]
18 And now, why go to Egypt,*
to drink the waters of the Nile?
Why go to Assyria,
to drink the waters of the River?
19 Your own wickedness chastises you,
your own infidelities punish you.
Know then, and see, how evil and bitter
is your forsaking the LORD, your God,
And your showing no fear of me,
oracle of the Lord, the GOD of hosts.[u]
20 Long ago you broke your yoke,[v]
you tore off your bonds.
You said, "I will not serve."
On every high hill, under every green tree,
you sprawled and served as a prostitute.*
21 But I had planted you as a choice vine,
all pedigreed stock;
How could you turn out so obnoxious to me,
a spurious vine?[w]
22 Even if you scour it with lye,
and use much soap,
The stain of your guilt is still before me,
oracle of the Lord GOD.[x]
23 How can you say, "I am not defiled,
I have not pursued the Baals"?
Consider your conduct in the Valley,*
recall what you have done:
A skittish young camel,
running back and forth,
24 a wild donkey bred in the wilderness,
Sniffing the wind in her desire—
who can restrain her lust?
None seeking her need tire themselves;
in her time they will find her.
25 Stop wearing out your feet
and parching your throat!
But you say, "No use! No!
How I love these strangers,
after them I must go."[y]
26 As the thief is shamed when caught,
so shall the house of Israel be shamed:
They, their kings, their princes,
their priests and their prophets;[z]
27 They say to a piece of wood, "You are my father,"
and to a stone, "You gave me birth."
They turn their backs to me, not their faces;
yet in their time of trouble they cry out,
"Rise up and save us!"
28 Where are the gods you made for yourselves?
Let them rise up!
Will they save you in your time of trouble?
For as numerous as your cities
are your gods, O Judah!
And as many as the streets of Jerusalem
are the altars you have set up for Baal.[a]
29 Why are you arguing with me?
You have all rebelled against me—
oracle of the LORD.
30 In vain I struck your children;
correction they did not take.
Your sword devoured your prophets
like a ravening lion.[b]

2:14 House-born servant: one born in the master's house, in contrast to a slave acquired by purchase or as a captive; cf. Lv 22:11.

2:16 Memphis: the capital of Lower Egypt. **Tahpanhes**: a frontier city of Egypt, east of the Delta. **Shave the crown of your head**: an image for Egypt plundering Judah; perhaps a reference to the capture of King Jehoahaz in 609 B.C. (2 Kgs 23:34).

2:18 Egypt and Assyria were the competing foreign powers favored by rival parties within Judah. The desire for such foreign alliances is a further desertion of the Lord, the source of living waters (v. 13), in favor of the above-named powers, symbolized by the waters of the Nile and the Euphrates rivers.

2:20 Served as a prostitute: idolatry (because Israel is the "bride" of God); cf. vv. 2–3.

2:23 The Valley: probably Ben-hinnom, south of Jerusalem, site of the sanctuary of Topheth, where children were sacrificed to Molech; cf. 7:31.

s: Jer 9:11. *t:* Jer 4:18; 30:15. *u:* Prv 5:22; Hos 5:5. *v:* Jer 3:6, 13; Jgs 10:6. *w:* Ex 15:17; Ps 80:9; Is 5:4. *x:* Jb 9:30. *y:* Jer 18:12. *z:* Jer 48:27; Rom 6:21. *a:* Jer 11:13; Dt 32:38; Jgs 10:14. *b:* Jer 5:3; Neh 9:26.

31 You people of this generation,
consider the word of the Lord:
Have I become a wilderness to Israel,
a land of gloom?
Why then do my people say, "We have moved on,
we will not come to you any more"?
32 Does a young woman forget her jewelry,
a bride her sash?
Yet my people have forgotten me
days without number.[c]
33 How well you pick your way
when seeking love!
In your wickedness,
you have gone by ways unclean!
34 On your clothing is
the life-blood of the innocent,
you did not find them committing burglary;
35 Nonetheless you say, "I am innocent;
at least, his anger is turned away from me."
Listen! I will judge you
on that word of yours, "I have not sinned."
36 How frivolous you have become
in changing your course!
By Egypt you will be shamed,
just as you were shamed by Assyria.[d]
37 From there too you will go out,
your hands upon your head;
For the LORD has rejected those in whom you trust,
with them you will have no success.[e]

CHAPTER 3

See RG 302

1 If a man divorces his wife[f]
and she leaves him
and then becomes the wife of another,
Can she return to the first?*
Would not this land be wholly defiled?
But you have played the prostitute with many lovers,
and yet you would return to me!—
oracle of the LORD.
2 Raise your eyes to the heights, and look,
where have men not lain with you?
Along the roadways you waited for them
like an Arabian* in the wilderness.
You defiled the land
by your wicked prostitution.[g]
3 Therefore the showers were withheld,
the spring rain did not fall.
But because you have a prostitute's brow,
you refused to be ashamed.[h]
4 Even now do you not call me, "My father,
you are the bridegroom of my youth?
5 Will he keep his wrath forever,
will he hold his grudge to the end?"
This is what you say; yet you do
all the evil you can.

Judah and Israel. 6 The LORD said to me in
the days of King Josiah: Do you see what rebellious Israel has done? She has gone up
every high mountain, and under every green
tree she has played the prostitute.[i] 7 And I
thought: After she has done all this, she will
return to me. But she did not return. Then,
even though that traitor her sister Judah, saw
8 that, in response to all the adulteries rebel
Israel had committed, I sent her away and
gave her a bill of divorce, nevertheless Judah, the traitor, her sister, was not frightened; she too went off and played the prostitute.[j] 9 With her casual prostitution, she
polluted the land, committing adultery with
stone and wood.[k] 10 In spite of all this, Judah,
the traitor, her sister, did not return to me
wholeheartedly, but insincerely—oracle of
the LORD.

Restoration of Israel. 11 Then the LORD
said to me: Rebel Israel is more just than
traitor Judah.[l] 12 Go, proclaim these words
toward the north, and say:

3:1 Can she return to the first?: i.e., her first husband. Here the Hebrew is emended in light of the Septuagint and Dt 24:1–4, which forbids a man to take back a woman once he has divorced her. The prophet uses this analogy to illustrate the presumption of Judah, the unfaithful wife, who assumes she can easily return to the Lord after worshiping other gods.

3:2 An Arabian: here depicted as a marauder lying in wait for caravans.

c: Jer 13:25; Dt 32:18. *d:* 2 Chr 28:16–21. *e:* 2 Sm 13:19. *f:* Dt 24:1–4. *g:* Ex 16:24–25. *h:* Jer 6:15; 8:12. *i:* Jer 2:20; Dt 12:2. *j:* 2 Kgs 17:6, 18–23; Ez 23:11. *k:* Jer 2:27. *l:* Ez 16:51; 23:11.

Return, rebel Israel—oracle of the LORD—
I will not remain angry with you;
For I am merciful, oracle of the LORD,
I will not keep my anger forever.[m]
13 Only admit your guilt:
how you have rebelled against the
LORD, your God,
How you ran here and there to strangers
under every green tree
and would not listen to my voice—
oracle of the LORD.[n]
14 Return, rebellious children—oracle of
the LORD—*
for I am your master;
I will take you, one from a city, two from
a clan,
and bring you to Zion.[o]
15 I will appoint for you shepherds after my
own heart,
who will shepherd you wisely and
prudently.[p]
16 When you increase in number and are
fruitful in the land—
oracle of the LORD—
They will in those days no longer say,
"The ark of the covenant of the LORD!"
They will no longer think of it, or
remember it,
or miss it, or make another one.

17 At that time they will call Jerusalem "the LORD's throne." All nations will gather together there to honor the name of the LORD at Jerusalem, and they will no longer stubbornly follow their wicked heart.[q] 18 In those days the house of Judah will walk alongside the house of Israel; together they will come from the land of the north to the land which I gave your ancestors as a heritage.[r]

Conditions for Forgiveness

19 I thought:
How I would like to make you my
children!
So I gave you a pleasant land,
the most beautiful heritage among the
nations!
You would call me, "My Father," I thought,
and you would never turn away
from me.[s]
20 But like a woman faithless to her lover,
thus have you been faithless to me,
house of Israel—oracle of the LORD.[t]
21 A cry is heard on the heights!
the plaintive weeping of Israel's
children,
Because they have perverted their way,
they have forgotten the LORD, their
God.
22 Return, rebellious children!
I will heal your rebellions.
"Here we are! We belong to you,
for you are the LORD, our God.[u]
23 Deceptive indeed are the hills,
the mountains, clamorous;
Only in the LORD our God
is Israel's salvation.[v]
24 The shameful thing* has devoured
our ancestors' worth from our youth,
Their sheep and cattle,
their sons and daughters.
25 Let us lie down in our shame,
let our disgrace cover us,
for we have sinned against the LORD,
our God,
We and our ancestors, from our youth to
this day;
we did not listen to the voice of the
LORD, our God."[w]

CHAPTER 4

See RG 302

1 If you return, Israel—oracle of the
LORD—
return to me.
If you put your detestable things out of
my sight,
and do not stray,[x]
2 And swear, "As the LORD lives,"*

3:14–18 A remnant of Israel (v. 14) will reunite with Judah (v. 18). The former Israelite community, represented by the ark of the covenant, will be replaced by a universal alliance, symbolized by Jerusalem, the Lord's throne, to which all nations will be gathered (v. 17).

3:24 The shameful thing: Heb. *bosheth* ("shame"), a term often substituted for the name of Baal, a Canaanite god worshiped at local shrines.

4:2 As the LORD lives: this oath, made sincerely, implies Israel's return and loyal adherence to God. Thus the ancient promises are fulfilled; cf. Gn 12:3; 18:18; 22:18; 26:4; Ps 72:17.

m: Dt 4:29–31. *n:* Jer 2:20, 25; Lv 26:40. *o:* Jer 23:3; Is 10:21–22. *p:* Ez 34:23; Jn 21:15. *q:* Is 2:2. *r:* Jer 30:3; 31:8. *s:* Jer 31:9, 20; Is 63:16. *t:* Jer 5:11. *u:* Hos 3:5. *v:* Jer 14:8. *w:* Jer 16:11–12; 22:21. *x:* Jer 25:5.

in truth, in judgment, and in justice,
Then the nations shall bless themselves
in him
and in him glory.[y]

[3]For to the people of Judah and Jerusalem,
thus says the LORD:
Till your untilled ground,
and do not sow among thorns.[z]
[4] Be circumcised for the LORD,*
remove the foreskins of your hearts,
people of Judah and inhabitants of
Jerusalem;
Or else my anger will break out like fire,
and burn so that no one can quench it,
because of your evil deeds.[a]

The Invasion from the North

[5] Proclaim it in Judah,
in Jerusalem announce it;
Blow the trumpet throughout the land,
call out, "Fill the ranks!"
Say, "Assemble, let us march
to the fortified cities."
[6] Raise the signal—to Zion!
Seek refuge! Don't stand there!
Disaster I bring from the north,
and great destruction.
[7] Up comes the lion from its lair,
the destroyer of nations has set out,
has left its place,
To turn your land into a desolation,
your cities into an uninhabited waste.[b]
[8] So put on sackcloth,
mourn and wail:
"The blazing anger of the LORD
has not turned away from us."[c]
[9] In that day—oracle of the LORD—
The king will lose heart, and the princes;
the priests will be horrified,
and the prophets stunned.
[10] "Ah! Lord GOD," they will say,
"You really did deceive* us
When you said: You shall have peace,
while the sword was at our very
throats."[d]
[11] At that time it will be said
to this people and to Jerusalem,
A scorching wind from the bare heights
comes
through the wilderness toward my
daughter, the people.*
Not to winnow, not to cleanse,
[12] a strong wind from there comes at my
bidding.
Now I too pronounce
sentence upon them.[e]
[13] See! like storm clouds he advances,
like a whirlwind, his chariots;
Swifter than eagles, his horses:
"Woe to us! we are ruined."
[14] Cleanse your heart of evil, Jerusalem,
that you may be saved.
How long will you entertain
wicked schemes?
[15] A voice proclaims it from Dan,
announces wickedness from Mount
Ephraim:
[16] "Make this known to the nations,
announce it against Jerusalem:
Besiegers are coming from the distant
land,
shouting their war cry against the
cities of Judah."[f]
[17] Like watchers in the fields they surround
her,
for she has rebelled against me—
oracle of the LORD.[g]
[18] Your conduct, your deeds, have done this
to you;
how bitter is this evil of yours,
how it reaches to your very heart![h]
[19] My body! my body! how I writhe!*
The walls of my heart!
My heart beats wildly,
I cannot be still;

4:4 The external rite of circumcision accomplishes nothing unless it is accompanied by the removal of blindness and obstinacy of heart. Jeremiah's view is reflected in Rom 2:25, 29; 1 Cor 7:19; Gal 5:6; 6:13, 15.

4:10 You really did deceive: Jeremiah complains that the Lord misled the people by fostering their complacency, leaving them unprepared and unrepentant as judgment approaches.

4:11 My daughter, the people: the covenant people personified as a young woman. Ezekiel 16 presents Israel and Judah as female infants whom the Lord adopts and then abandons and punishes because they desire other lords.

4:19–21 Probably the prophet's own anguish at the coming destruction of Judah.

y: Jer 12:16; Dt 10:20; Is 65:16. *z:* Hos 10:12; Mt 13:7, 22. *a:* Jer 9:24. *b:* Jer 2:15; 5:6. *c:* Jer 6:26; Is 5:25. *d:* Jer 6:14. *e:* Jer 1:16. *f:* Jer 5:15. *g:* Jer 6:3. *h:* Jer 2:17, 19.

For I myself have heard the blast of the
horn,
the battle cry.
20 Ruin upon ruin is reported;
the whole land is laid waste.
In an instant my tents are ravaged;
in a flash, my shelters.[i]
21 How long must I see the signal,
hear the blast of the horn!
22 My people are fools,
they do not know me;
They are senseless children,
without understanding;
They are wise at evil,
but they do not know how to do good.[j]
23 I looked at the earth—it was waste and
void;
at the heavens—their light had gone
out![k]
24 I looked at the mountains—they were
quaking!
All the hills were crumbling!
25 I looked—there was no one;
even the birds of the air had flown
away!
26 I looked—the garden land was a
wilderness,
with all its cities destroyed
before the LORD, before his blazing
anger.[l]
27 For thus says the LORD:
The whole earth shall be waste,
but I will not wholly destroy it.[m]
28 Because of this the earth shall mourn,
the heavens above shall darken;
I have spoken, I will not change my
mind,
I have decided, I will not turn back.[n]
29 At the shout of rider and archer
each city takes to flight;
They shrink into the thickets,
they scale the rocks:
All the cities are abandoned,
no one lives in them.
30 You now who are doomed, what are you
doing
dressing in purple,
bedecking yourself with gold,
Enlarging your eyes with kohl?
You beautify yourself in vain!
Your lovers reject you,
they seek your life.
31 Yes, I hear the cry, like that of a woman
in labor,
like the anguish of a mother bearing
her first child—
The cry of daughter Zion gasping,
as she stretches out her hands:
"Ah, woe is me! I sink exhausted
before my killers!"[o]

CHAPTER 5

See RG 302

Universal Corruption

1 Roam the streets of Jerusalem,
look about and observe,
Search through her squares,
to find even one
Who acts justly
and seeks honesty,
and I will pardon her!
2 They say, "As the LORD lives,"
but in fact they swear falsely.
3 LORD, do your eyes not search for
honesty?
You struck them, but they did not flinch;
you laid them low, but they refused
correction;
They set their faces harder than stone,
and refused to return.[p]
4 I thought: These are only the lowly,
they behave foolishly;
For they do not know the way of the
LORD,
the justice of their God.[q]
5 Let me go to the leaders
and speak with them;
For they must know the way of the LORD,
the justice of their God.
But, one and all, they have broken the
yoke,
torn off the harness.[r]
6 Therefore, lions from the forest slay
them,
wolves of the desert ravage them,
Leopards keep watch round their cities:
all who come out are torn to pieces,

i: Jer 10:20. *j:* Dt 32:5–6, 28. *k:* Is 24:1, 3. *l:* Lv 26:31. *m:* Jer 5:18. *n:* Is 24:4. *o:* Jer 6:24. *p:* Jer 2:30. *q:* Jer 8:7. *r:* Jer 6:13.

For their crimes are many,
their rebellions numerous.
7 Why should I pardon you?
Your children have forsaken me,
they swear by gods that are no gods.
I fed them, but they commit adultery;
to the prostitute's house they throng.
8 They are lustful stallions,
each neighs after the other's wife.[s]
9 Should I not punish them for this?—
oracle of the LORD;
on a nation like this should I not take
vengeance?
10 Climb her terraces, and ravage them,
destroy them completely.
Tear away her tendrils,
they do not belong to the LORD.[t]
11 For they have openly rebelled against me,
both the house of Israel and the house
of Judah—
oracle of the LORD.[u]
12 They denied the LORD,*
saying, "He is nothing,
No evil shall come to us,
neither sword nor famine shall we
see.[v]
13 The prophets are wind,
and the word is not with them.
Let it be done to them!"
14 Therefore, thus says the LORD, the God
of hosts,
because you have said this—
See! I make my words
a fire in your mouth,
And this people the wood
that it shall devour!—
15 Beware! I will bring against you
a nation from far away,
O House of Israel—oracle of the LORD;
A long-lived nation, an ancient nation,
a people whose language you do not
know,
whose speech you cannot understand.[w]
16 Their quivers are like open graves;
all of them are warriors.
17 They will devour your harvest and your
bread,
devour your sons and your daughters,
Devour your sheep and cattle,
devour your vines and fig trees;
With their swords they will beat down
the fortified cities in which you trust.[x]

18 Yet even in those days—oracle of the
LORD—I will not completely destroy you.[y]
19 And when they ask, "Why has the LORD
our God done all these things to us?" say to
them, "As you have abandoned me to serve
foreign gods in your own land, so shall you
serve foreigners in a land not your own."

20 Announce this to the house of Jacob,
proclaim it in Judah:
21 Pay attention to this,
you foolish and senseless people,
Who have eyes and do not see,
who have ears and do not hear.[z]
22 Should you not fear me—oracle of the
LORD—
should you not tremble before me?
I made the sandy shore the sea's limit,
which by eternal decree it may not
overstep.
Toss though it may, it is to no avail;
though its billows roar, they cannot
overstep.[a]
23 But this people's heart is stubborn and
rebellious;
they turn and go away,
24 And do not say in their hearts,
"Let us fear the LORD, our God,
Who gives us rain
early and late,* in its time;
Who watches for us
over the appointed weeks of harvest."[b]
25 Your crimes have prevented these things,
your sins have turned these blessings
away from you.[c]
26 For criminals lurk among my people;
like fowlers they set traps,
but it is human beings they catch.[d]

5:12 They denied the LORD: the people act as though God does not matter and will not interfere.

5:24 Rain early and late: autumn and spring rains respectively. **Appointed weeks of harvest**: the seven weeks between the Passover (Dt 16:9–10) and the feast of Weeks (Pentecost), when it did not ordinarily rain.

s: Jer 13:27. *t:* Jer 2:21. *u:* Jer 3:20. *v:* Jer 14:13; Is 28:15. *w:* Dt 28:49. *x:* Dt 28:31. *y:* Jer 4:27. *z:* Is 6:9. *a:* Jb 38:10–11. *b:* Gn 8:22; Dt 11:14. *c:* Jer 2:17, 19. *d:* Prv 1:11.

27 Their houses are as full of treachery
as a bird-cage is of birds;
Therefore they grow powerful and rich,
28 fat and sleek.
They pass over wicked deeds;
justice they do not defend
By advancing the claim of the orphan
or judging the cause of the poor.[e]
29 Shall I not punish these things?—oracle
of the LORD;
on a nation such as this shall I not take
vengeance?
30 Something shocking and horrible
has happened in the land:
31 The prophets prophesy falsely,
and the priests teach on their own
authority;
Yet my people like it this way;
what will you do when the end comes?[f]

See RG 302

CHAPTER 6

The Enemy at the Gates

1 Seek refuge, Benjaminites,
from the midst of Jerusalem!
Blow the trumpet in Tekoa,
raise a signal over Beth-haccherem;
For disaster threatens from the north,
and mighty destruction.[g]
2 Lovely and delicate
daughter Zion, you are ruined!
3 Against her, shepherds come with their
flocks;*
all around, they pitch their tents
against her;
each one grazes his portion.[h]
4 "Prepare for war against her,
Up! let us rush upon her at midday!"
"Woe to us! the day is waning,
evening shadows lengthen!"
5 "Up! let us rush upon her by night,
destroy her palaces!"[i]
6 For thus says the LORD of hosts:
Hew down her trees,
throw up a siege mound against
Jerusalem.
Woe to the city marked for punishment;
there is nothing but oppression within
her![j]
7 As a well keeps its waters fresh,
so she keeps fresh her wickedness.
Violence and destruction resound in her;
ever before me are wounds and blows.[k]
8 Be warned, Jerusalem,
or I will be estranged from you,
And I will turn you into a wilderness,
a land where no one dwells.
9 Thus says the LORD of hosts:
Glean, glean like a vine
the remnant of Israel;
Pass your hand, like a vintager,
repeatedly over the tendrils.
10 To whom shall I speak?
whom shall I warn, and be heard?
See! their ears are uncircumcised,
they cannot pay attention;
See, the word of the LORD has become
for them
an object of scorn, for which they have
no taste.[l]
11 But the wrath of the LORD brims up
within me,
I am weary of holding it in.
I will pour it out upon the child in the
street,
upon the young men gathered together.
Yes, husband and wife will be taken,
elder with ancient.[m]
12 Their houses will fall to others,
their fields and their wives as well;
For I will stretch forth my hand
against those who dwell in the land—
oracle of the LORD.[n]
13 Small and great alike, all are greedy for
gain;
prophet and priest, all practice fraud.[o]
14 They have treated lightly
the injury to my people:
"Peace, peace!" they say,
though there is no peace.[p]
15 They have acted shamefully, committing
abominations,
yet they are not at all ashamed,

6:3 Shepherds come with their flocks: foreign invaders with their armies.
6:16 Pathways of old: history and the lessons to be learned from it.

e: Jer 12:1; Is 1:23. *f:* Jer 14:14; Mi 2:11. *g:* Jer 1:14–15. *h:* Jer 4:17. *i:* 2 Chr 36:19. *j:* Jer 32:24; Zep 3:1–4. *k:* Is 57:20. *l:* Jer 7:26; 20:8. *m:* Ez 9:6. *n:* Jer 8:10; Dt 28:30–32. *o:* Jer 8:10; 23:11. *p:* Jer 8:11.

they do not know how to blush.
Therefore they will fall among the fallen;
in the time of their punishment they shall stumble,
says the LORD.[q]
16 Thus says the LORD:
Stand by the earliest roads,
ask the pathways of old,*
"Which is the way to good?" and walk it;
thus you will find rest for yourselves.
But they said, "We will not walk it."[r]
17 I raised up watchmen* for them:
"Pay attention to the sound of the trumpet!"
But they said, "We will not pay attention!"
18 Therefore hear, O nations,
and know, O earth,
what I will do with them:
19 See, I bring evil upon this people,
the fruit of their own schemes,
Because they did not pay attention to my words,
because they rejected my law.[s]
20 Of what use to me is incense that comes from Sheba,
or sweet cane from far-off lands?
Your burnt offerings find no favor with me,
your sacrifices do not please me.[t]
21 Therefore, thus says the LORD:
See, I will place before this people
obstacles to trip them up;
Parents and children alike,
neighbors and friends shall perish.[u]
22 Thus says the LORD:
See, a people comes from the land of the north,
a great nation, rising from the very ends of the earth.[v]
23 Bow and javelin they wield;
cruel and pitiless are they.
They sound like the roaring sea
as they ride forth on horses,
Each in his place for battle
against you, daughter Zion.
24 We hear news of them;
our hands hang helpless,
Anguish takes hold of us,
pangs like a woman in childbirth.[w]
25 Do not go out into the field,
do not step into the street,
For the enemy has a sword;
terror on every side!
26 Daughter of my people, dress in sackcloth,
roll in the ashes.
Mourn as for an only child
with bitter wailing:
"How suddenly the destroyer
comes upon us!"[x]
27 * A tester for my people I have appointed you,
to search and test their way.[y]
28 Arch-rebels are they all,
dealers in slander,
bronze and iron, all of them,
destroyers they are.
29 The bellows are scorched,
the lead is consumed by the fire;
In vain has the refiner refined,
the wicked are not drawn off.
30 "Silver rejected" they shall be called,
for the LORD has rejected them.

II. Oracles Primarily from the Days of Jehoiakim

CHAPTER 7

See RG 302

*The Temple Sermon.** 1 The word came
to Jeremiah from the LORD: 2 Stand at the
gate of the house of the LORD and proclaim
this message there: Hear the word of the
LORD, all you of Judah who enter these gates
to worship the LORD! 3 Thus says the LORD
of hosts, the God of Israel: Reform your
ways and your deeds so that I may dwell
with you in this place.[z] 4 Do not put your trust

6:17 Watchmen: the prophets who, like Jeremiah, had upheld God's moral law.

6:27–30 God appoints Jeremiah to be a "tester" of his people. The passage uses the metaphor of the refining of silver: the silver was extracted from lead ore, but the process in ancient times was inexact, so that sometimes all that was left was a scummy mess, to be thrown out.

7:1–15 The Temple of the Lord will not guarantee safety against enemy invasion or any other misfortune.

q: Jer 3:3; 8:12. *r:* Jer 7:23–24; 18:15. *s:* Prv 1:31. *t:* Is 1:11; 43:24. *u:* Is 8:14–15. *v:* Jer 1:15; 5:15. *w:* Jer 4:31. *x:* Jer 25:34; Am 8:10. *y:* Jer 1:18. *z:* Jer 18:11; 26:13.

in these deceptive words: “The temple of the LORD! The temple of the LORD! The temple of the LORD!”[a] [5]Only if you thoroughly reform your ways and your deeds; if each of you deals justly with your neighbor; [6]if you no longer oppress the alien,* the orphan, and the widow; if you no longer shed innocent blood in this place or follow after other gods to your own harm,[b] [7]only then will I let you continue to dwell in this place, in the land I gave your ancestors long ago and forever.[c]

[8]But look at you! You put your trust in deceptive words to your own loss! [9]Do you think you can steal and murder, commit adultery and perjury, sacrifice to Baal, follow other gods that you do not know,[d] [10]and then come and stand in my presence in this house, which bears my name, and say: “We are safe! We can commit all these abominations again!”?[e] [11]Has this house which bears my name become in your eyes a den of thieves? I have seen it for myself!—oracle of the LORD.[f] [12]Go to my place at Shiloh,* where I made my name dwell in the beginning. See what I did to it because of the wickedness of my people Israel.[g] [13]And now, because you have committed all these deeds—oracle of the LORD—because you did not listen, though I spoke to you untiringly, and because you did not answer, though I called you, [14]I will do to this house, which bears my name, in which you trust, and to the place which I gave you and your ancestors, exactly what I did to Shiloh.[h] [15]I will cast you out of my sight, as I cast away all your kindred, all the offspring of Ephraim.[i]

Abuses in Worship. [16]You, now, must not intercede for this people! Do not raise a cry or prayer in their behalf![j] Do not press me, for I will not listen to you! [17]Do you not see what they are doing in the cities of Judah, in the streets of Jerusalem? [18]The children gather wood, their fathers light the fire, and the women knead dough to make cakes for the Queen of Heaven,* while libations are poured out to other gods—all to offend me![k] [19]Are they really offending me—oracle of the LORD—or rather themselves, to their own disgrace?[l] [20]Therefore, thus says the Lord GOD: my anger and my wrath will pour out upon this place, upon human being and beast, upon the trees of the field and the fruits of the earth; it will burn and not be quenched.[m]

[21]Thus says the LORD of hosts, the God of Israel: Heap your burnt offerings upon your sacrifices; eat up the meat! [22]In speaking to your ancestors on the day I brought them out of the land of Egypt, I gave them no command* concerning burnt offering or sacrifice. [23]This rather is what I commanded them: Listen to my voice; then I will be your God and you shall be my people. Walk exactly in the way I command you, so that you may prosper.[n]

[24]But they did not listen to me, nor did they pay attention. They walked in the stubbornness of their evil hearts and turned their backs, not their faces, to me.[o] [25]From the day that your ancestors left the land of Egypt even to this day, I kept on sending all my servants the prophets to you.[p] [26]Yet they have not listened to me nor have they paid attention; they have stiffened their necks and done worse than their ancestors.[q] [27]When you speak all these words to them, they will not listen to you either. When you call to them, they will not answer you. [28]Say to them: This is the nation which does not listen to the voice of the LORD, its God, or take correction. Faithfulness has disappeared; the word itself is banished from their speech.

7:6 The alien: specially protected within Israelite society; cf. Ex 22:20; Nm 9:14; 15:14; Dt 5:14; 28:43.

7:12 Shiloh: an important sanctuary where the ark of the covenant was kept, according to the Books of Joshua, Judges, and 1 Samuel. In response to the corrupt behavior of the priests serving there, God allows the Philistines to destroy Shiloh and take the ark of the covenant. Cf. 1 Sm 1:9; 4:3–4; Ps 78:60, 68–69.

7:18 Queen of Heaven: probably Astarte, goddess of fertility (cf. 1 Sm 31:10; 1 Kgs 11:5), worshiped particularly by women (cf. Jer 44:15–19). Such worship was evidently reinforced during the reign of King Manasseh (2 Kgs 21:3–7) and was revived after Josiah’s death.

7:22 I gave them no command: right conduct rather than formal ritual was God’s will concerning his people (v. 23).

---

a: Mi 3:11. *b:* Ex 22:21–24. *c:* Dt 4:40. *d:* Jer 44:17. *e:* Jer 32:34. *f:* Mt 21:13. *g:* Jos 18:1. *h:* Jer 26:9. *i:* 1 Kgs 9:7; 2 Kgs 17:23. *j:* Jer 11:14; 14:11. *k:* Jer 44:17, 19. *l:* Jb 35:6. *m:* Jer 36:29; 2 Kgs 22:17. *n:* Jer 11:4; Lv 26:3, 12. *o:* Jer 17:23. *p:* 2 Chr 36:15–16; Bar 1:19. *q:* Jer 19:15; 2 Chr 30:8.

29 [r] Cut off your hair* and throw it away!
on the heights raise a lament;
The LORD has indeed rejected and cast off
the generation that draws down his wrath.

30 The people of Judah have done what is
evil in my eyes—oracle of the LORD. They
have set up their detestable things in the
house which bears my name, thereby defiling it.[s] 31 In the Valley of Ben-hinnom* they
go on building the high places of Topheth to
sacrifice their sons and daughters by fire,
something I never commanded or considered. 32 Be assured! Days are coming—oracle
of the LORD—when they will no longer say
"Topheth" or "Valley of Ben-hinnom" but
"Valley of Slaughter." For want of space, Topheth will become burial ground.[t] 33 The
corpses of this people will be food for the
birds of the sky and beasts of the earth, which
no one will drive away.[u] 34 I will silence the
cry of joy, the cry of gladness, the voice of
the bridegroom and the voice of the bride, in
the cities of Judah and in the streets of Jerusalem; for the land will be turned to rubble.[v]

CHAPTER 8

See RG 302

1 At that time—oracle of the LORD—
the bones of the kings and princes of Judah,
the bones of the priests and the prophets, and
the bones of the inhabitants of Jerusalem
will be brought out of their graves[w] 2 and
spread out before the sun, the moon, and the
whole host of heaven,* which they loved and
served, which they followed, consulted, and
worshiped. They will not be gathered up for
burial, but will lie like dung upon the
ground.[x] 3 Death will be preferred to life by
all the survivors of this wicked people who
remain in any of the places to which I banish
them—oracle of the LORD of hosts.

Israel's Conduct Incomprehensible

4 Tell them: Thus says the LORD:
When someone falls, do they not rise again?
if they turn away, do they not turn back?
5 Why then do these people resist
with persistent rebellion?
Why do they cling to deception,
refuse to turn back?[y]
6 I have listened closely:
they speak what is not true;
No one regrets wickedness,
saying, "What have I done?"
Everyone keeps on running their course,
like a horse dashing into battle.[z]
7 Even the stork in the sky
knows its seasons;
Turtledove, swift, and thrush
observe the time of their return,
But my people do not know
the order of the LORD.[a]
8 How can you say, "We are wise,[b]
we have the law of the LORD"?
See, that has been changed into falsehood
by the lying pen of the scribes!*
9 The wise are put to shame,
terrified, and trapped;
Since they have rejected the word of the LORD,
what sort of wisdom do they have?[c]

Shameless in Their Crimes

10 Therefore, I will give their wives to other men,
their fields to new owners.
Small and great alike, all are greedy for gain,
prophet and priest, all practice fraud.[d]
11 They have treated lightly
the injury to the daughter of my people:*

7:29 Hair: the unshorn hair of the nazirite, regarded as sacred because of a vow, temporary or permanent, to abstain from cutting or shaving the hair; nazirites also avoided contact with a corpse and with all products of the vine; cf. Nm 6:4–8. The cutting of this hair was a sign of extreme mourning.

7:31 Valley of Ben-hinnom: this valley was probably south of Jerusalem. **Topheth**: perhaps, "fire pit."

8:2 Host of heaven: the stars, worshiped by other nations and even by the inhabitants of Jerusalem, particularly during the reigns of Manasseh and Amon.

8:8 Lying pen of the scribes: because the teachings and interpretations of the scribes ran counter to the word of the Lord.

8:11 Daughter of my people: see note on 4:11.

r: Jer 9:17–21. *s:* Jer 32:34. *t:* Jer 19:6; 32:35. *u:* Jer 16:4; 34:20. *v:* Jer 16:9. *w:* Bar 2:24. *x:* Dt 4:19. *y:* Jer 5:3; 7:24, 26. *z:* Jb 34:31–32. *a:* Is 1:3. *b:* Mal 2:8; Rom 2:17–23. *c:* 1 Cor 3:20. *d:* Jer 6:13; Dt 28:30.

"Peace, peace!" they say,
though there is no peace.[e]
12 They have acted shamefully; they have done abominable things,
yet they are not at all ashamed,
they do not know how to blush.
Hence they shall be among those who fall;
in their time of punishment they shall stumble,
says the LORD.[f]

Threats of Punishment

13 I will gather them all in—oracle of the LORD:
no grapes on the vine,
No figs on the fig trees,
foliage withered!
Whatever I have given them is gone.
14 Why do we remain here?
Let us assemble and flee to the fortified cities,
where we will meet our doom;
For the LORD our God has doomed us,
he has given us poisoned water to drink,
because we have sinned against the LORD.[g]
15 We wait for peace to no avail;
for a time of healing, but terror comes instead.[h]
16 From Dan is heard
the snorting of horses;
The neighing of stallions
shakes the whole land.
They come to devour the land and everything in it,
the city and its inhabitants.
17 Yes, I will send against you
poisonous snakes.
Against them no charm will work
when they bite you—oracle of the LORD.[i]

The Prophet's Grief over the People's Suffering

18 My joy is gone,
grief is upon me,
my heart is sick.
19 Listen! the cry of the daughter of my people,
far and wide in the land!
"Is the LORD no longer in Zion,
is her King no longer in her midst?"
Why do they provoke me with their idols,
with their foreign nonentities?[j]
20 "The harvest is over, the summer ended,
but we have not yet been saved!"
21 I am broken by the injury of the daughter of my people.
I am in mourning; horror has seized me.[k]
22 Is there no balm in Gilead,*
no healer there?
Why does new flesh not grow
over the wound of the daughter of my people?[l]
23 Oh, that my head were a spring of water,
my eyes a fountain of tears,
That I might weep day and night
over the slain from the daughter of my people!

CHAPTER 9

See RG 302

The Corruption of the People

1 Oh, that I had in the wilderness
a travelers' lodging!
That I might leave my people
and depart from them.
They are all adulterers,
a band of traitors.
2 They ready their tongues like a drawn bow;
with lying, and not with truth,
they are powerful in the land.
They go from evil to evil,
and me they do not know—oracle of the LORD.
3 Be on your guard, everyone against his neighbor;
put no trust in any brother.
Every brother imitates Jacob, the supplanter,*

8:22 Gilead: a region southeast of the Sea of Galilee noted for its healing balm.

9:3 Jacob, the supplanter: in Hebrew, a play on words. In the popular etymology given in Gn 25:26, the name Jacob means "he supplants," for he deprived his brother Esau of his birthright (cf. Gn 25:33).

e: Jer 6:14. *f:* Jer 6:15. *g:* Jer 9:14; 23:15. *h:* Jer 14:19. *i:* Dt 32:24. *j:* Dt 32:21; Mi 4:9. *k:* Jer 14:17. *l:* Jer 46:11.

every neighbor is guilty of slander.
[4] Each one deceives the other,
no one speaks the truth.
They have accustomed their tongues to lying,
they are perverse and cannot repent.[m]
[5] Violence upon violence,
deceit upon deceit:
They refuse to know me—
oracle of the LORD.
[6] Therefore, thus says the LORD of hosts:
I will refine them and test them;
how else should I deal with the daughter of my people?
[7] A murderous arrow is their tongue,
their mouths utter deceit;
They speak peaceably with their neighbors,
but in their hearts they lay an ambush![n]
[8] Should I not punish them for these deeds—oracle of the LORD;
on a nation such as this should I not take vengeance?[o]

Dirge over the Ravaged Land

[9] Over the mountains I shall break out in cries of lamentation,
over the pastures in the wilderness, in a dirge:
They are scorched, and no one crosses them,
no sound of lowing cattle;
Birds of the air as well as beasts,
all have fled and are gone.[p]
[10] I will turn Jerusalem into a heap of ruins,
a haunt of jackals;
The cities of Judah I will make a waste,
where no one dwells.[q]

[11] Who is wise enough to understand this? To whom has the mouth of the LORD spoken? Let him declare it!

Why is the land ravaged,
scorched like a wilderness no one crosses?[r]

[12] The LORD said: Because they have abandoned my law, which I set before them, and did not listen to me or follow it,
[13] but followed instead their stubborn hearts and the Baals, as their ancestors had taught them,[s]
[14] therefore, thus says the LORD of hosts, the God of Israel: See now, I will give this people wormwood to eat and poisoned water to drink.[t]
[15] I will scatter them among nations whom neither they nor their ancestors have known; I will send the sword to pursue them until I have completely destroyed them.[u]

[16] Thus says the LORD of hosts:
Inquire, and call the wailing women to come;
summon the most skilled of them.
[17] Let them come quickly
and raise for us a dirge,
That our eyes may run with tears,
our pupils flow with water.[v]
[18] The sound of the dirge is heard from Zion:
We are ruined and greatly ashamed;
We have left the land,
given up our dwellings!
[19] Hear, you women, the word of the LORD,
let your ears receive the word of his mouth.
Teach your daughters a dirge,
and each other a lament:
[20] Death has come up through our windows,
has entered our citadels,
To cut down children in the street,
young people in the squares.[w]
[21] Corpses shall fall
like dung in the open field,
Like sheaves behind the harvester,
with no one to gather them.

True Glory

[22] Thus says the LORD:
Let not the wise boast of his wisdom,
nor the strong boast of his strength,
nor the rich man boast of his riches;
[23] But rather, let those who boast, boast of this,
that in their prudence they know me,[x]
Know that I, the LORD, act with fidelity,
justice, and integrity on earth.
How I take delight in these—oracle of the LORD.

---

m: Jer 12:6. *n:* Ps 28:3; 62:4. *o:* Jer 5:9, 29. *p:* Jer 4:25; 12:4. *q:* Is 13:22. *r:* Ps 107:43; Hos 14:10. *s:* Jer 7:24; 19:4–5. *t:* Jer 23:15. *u:* Lv 26:33; Dt 28:36, 64. *v:* Jer 14:17. *w:* Jer 14:16. *x:* Prv 21:30.

False Circumcision. 24 See, days are coming—oracle of the LORD—when I will demand an account of all those circumcised in the foreskin:[y] 25 Egypt and Judah, Edom and the Ammonites, Moab, and those who live in the wilderness and shave their temples.* For all the nations are uncircumcised, even the whole house of Israel is uncircumcised at heart.

CHAPTER 10

See RG 302

The Folly of Idolatry. 1 Hear the word the LORD speaks to you, house of Israel.
2 Thus says the LORD:

Do not learn the ways of the nations,
and have no fear of the signs in the heavens,*
even though the nations fear them.[z]
3 For the carvings of the nations are nonentities,
wood cut from the forest,
Fashioned by artisans with the adze,[a]
4 adorned with silver and gold.
With nails and hammers they are fastened,
so they do not fall.[b]
5 Like a scarecrow in a cucumber field are they,
they cannot speak;
They must be carried about,
for they cannot walk.
Do not fear them, they can do no harm,
neither can they do good.[c]
6 No one is like you, LORD,
you are great,
great and mighty is your name.[d]
7 Who would not fear you,
King of the nations,
for it is your due!
Among all the wisest of the nations,
and in all their domains,
there is none like you.[e]
8 One and all they are stupid and senseless,
the instruction from nonentities—only wood!
9 Silver plates brought from Tarshish,
and gold from Ophir,
The work of the artisan
and the handiwork of the smelter,
Clothed with violet and purple—
all of them the work of skilled workers.
10 The LORD is truly God,
he is the living God, the eternal King,
Before whose anger the earth quakes,
whose wrath the nations cannot endure.[f]

11 Thus shall you say of them: The gods that did not make heaven and earth—let these perish from earth and from beneath heaven!* [g]

12 The one who made the earth by his power,
established the world by his wisdom,
and by his skill stretched out the heavens.[h]
13 When he thunders, the waters in the heavens roar,
and he brings up clouds from the end of the earth,
Makes lightning flash in the rain,
and brings forth the wind from his storehouses.
14 Everyone is too stupid to know;
every artisan is put to shame by his idol:
He has molded a fraud,
without breath of life.[i]
15 They are nothing, objects of ridicule;
they will perish in their time of punishment.
16 Jacob's portion is nothing like them:
for he is the maker of everything!
Israel is his very own tribe,
LORD of hosts is his name.[j]

Abandonment of Judah

17 Gather up your bundle from the land,
City living under siege!
18 For thus says the LORD:
Now, at this time
I will sling away the inhabitants of the land;

9:25 Shave their temples: some Arabian tribes practiced this custom. None of the nations who practice circumcision understand the meaning of their action, not even Israel; no one conforms to life under the covenant.

10:2 Signs in the heavens: phenomena in the sky, such as eclipses or comets, used to predict disasters.

10:11 This verse is in Aramaic.

y: Jer 4:4. *z:* Bar 6:6. *a:* Wis 13:11; Is 44:9. *b:* Is 40:19; 41:7. *c:* Ps 115:4–8; Bar 6:15. *d:* Ps 86:8–10. *e:* Jer 5:22; Ps 47:2, 8. *f:* Ps 10:16. *g:* Ps 96:5. *h:* Ps 104:5. *i:* Rom 1:22–23. *j:* Ps 33:12; Jer 31:35.

I will hem them in,
that they may be taken.
19 Woe is me! I am undone,
my wound is beyond healing.
Yet I had thought:
if I make light of my sickness, I can bear it.
20 My tent is ruined,
all its cords are severed.
My children have left me, they are no more:
no one to pitch my tent,
no one to raise its curtains.[k]
21 How stupid are the shepherds!
The LORD they have not sought;
For this reason they have failed,
and all their flocks scattered.[l]
22 Listen! a rumor! here it comes,
a great commotion from the land of the north:
To make the cities of Judah a desolation,
the haunt of jackals.

Prayer of Jeremiah

23 I know, LORD,
that no one chooses their way,
Nor determines their course
nor directs their own step.
24 Correct me, LORD, but with equity,
not in anger, lest you diminish me.
25 Pour out your wrath on the nations that do not know you,
on the tribes that do not call your name;
For they have utterly devoured Jacob,
and laid waste his home.[m]

CHAPTER 11

See RG 302

Plea for Fidelity to the Covenant. 1 The
word that came to Jeremiah from the LORD:
2 Speak to the people of Judah and the inhabitants of Jerusalem, 3 and say to them: Thus
says the LORD, the God of Israel: Cursed be
anyone who does not observe the words of
this covenant,[n] 4 which I commanded your
ancestors the day I brought them up out of
the land of Egypt, that iron furnace, saying:
Listen to my voice and do all that I command
you. Then you shall be my people, and I will
be your God.[o] 5 Thus I will fulfill the oath I
swore to your ancestors, to give them a land
flowing with milk and honey, the one you
have today. "Amen, LORD," I answered.
6 Then the LORD said to me: Proclaim all
these words in the cities of Judah and in the
streets of Jerusalem: Hear the words of this
covenant and obey them. 7 I warned your ancestors unceasingly from the day I brought
them up out of the land of Egypt even to this
day: obey my voice. 8 But they did not listen
or obey. They each walked in the stubbornness of their evil hearts, till I brought upon
them all the threats of this covenant which
they had failed to observe as I commanded
them.[p]
9 A conspiracy has been found, the LORD
said to me, among the people of Judah and
the inhabitants of Jerusalem: 10 They have returned to the crimes of their ancestors who
refused to obey my words. They also have
followed and served other gods; the house of
Israel and the house of Judah have broken the
covenant I made with their ancestors.[q]
11 Therefore, thus says the LORD: See, I am
bringing upon them a disaster they cannot escape. Though they cry out to me, I will not
listen to them.[r] 12 Then the cities of Judah and
the inhabitants of Jerusalem will go and cry
out to the gods to whom they have been offering incense. But these gods will give them
no help whatever in the time of their disaster.[s]

13 For as many as your cities
are your gods, O Judah!
As many as the streets of Jerusalem
are the altars for sacrifice to Baal.[t]

14 Now, you must not intercede for this people; do not raise on their behalf a cry or
prayer! I will not listen when they call to me
in the time of their disaster.[u]

Sacrifices of No Avail

15 What right has my beloved in my house,
while she devises her plots?
Can vows and sacred meat turn away
your disaster from you?
Will you still be jubilant

---

k: Jer 4:20. *l:* Jer 23:1; Ez 34:5–6. *m:* Ps 79:6–7. *n:* Dt 27:26. *o:* Dt 4:20; 1 Kgs 8:51. *p:* 2 Kgs 17:14. *q:* Dt 31:16; Ez 20:21–30. *r:* Jer 14:12; Mi 3:4. *s:* Dt 32:37–38. *t:* Jer 2:28; Hos 10:1. *u:* Jer 7:16; 14:11.

16 when you hear the great tumult?
The LORD has named you
"a spreading olive tree, a pleasure to behold";
Now he sets fire to it,
its branches burn.

17 The LORD of hosts who planted you has decreed disaster for you because of the evil done by the house of Israel and by the house of Judah, who provoked me by sacrificing to Baal.[v]

The Plot Against Jeremiah.
18 I knew it because the LORD informed me: at that time you showed me their doings.
19 Yet I was like a trusting lamb led to slaughter, not knowing that they were hatching plots against me: "Let us destroy the tree in its vigor; let us cut him off from the land of the living, so that his name will no longer be remembered."[w]

20 But, you, LORD of hosts, just Judge,
searcher of mind and heart,
Let me witness the vengeance you take on them,
for to you I have entrusted my cause![x]

21 Therefore, thus says the LORD concerning the men of Anathoth who seek your life and say, "Do not prophesy in the name of the LORD; otherwise you shall die by our hand."[y]
22 Therefore, thus says the LORD of hosts: I am going to punish them. The young men shall die by the sword; their sons and daughters shall die by famine.[z]
23 None shall be spared among them, for I will bring disaster upon the men of Anathoth, the year of their punishment.[a]

See RG 302

CHAPTER 12

1 You would be in the right, O LORD,
if I should dispute with you;
even so, I must lay out the case against you.
Why does the way of the wicked prosper,
why do all the treacherous live in contentment?[b]
2 You planted them; they have taken root,
they flourish and bear fruit as well.
You are upon their lips,
but far from their thoughts.[c]
3 LORD, you know me, you see me,
you have found that my heart is with you.[d]
Pick them out like sheep for the butcher,
set them apart for the day of slaughter.*
4 How long must the land mourn,
the grass of the whole countryside wither?
Because of the wickedness of those who dwell in it
beasts and birds disappear,
for they say, "God does not care about our future."

5 If running against men has wearied you,
how will you race against horses?
And if you are safe only on a level stretch,
what will you do in the jungle of the Jordan?

6 Your kindred and your father's house, even they betray you; they have recruited a force against you. Do not believe them, even when they speak fair words to you.[e]

The Lord's Complaint

7 I have abandoned my house,
cast off my heritage;
The beloved of my soul I have delivered
into the hand of her foes.[f]
8 My heritage has become for me
like a lion in the thicket;
She has raised her voice against me,
therefore she has incurred my hatred.[g]
9 My heritage is a prey for hyenas,
is surrounded by vultures;
Come, gather together, all you wild animals,
come and eat![h]

12:3 Jeremiah calls the Lord to account for allowing the wicked to flourish while he himself is persecuted for his fidelity to the Lord's mission; cf. 20:12. See Jesus' judgment, Mk 9:42. The metaphors indicate that Jeremiah has even greater trials ahead of him.

v: Is 5:2. *w:* Jer 18:18; 20:10; Wis 2:20. *x:* Jer 15:15. *y:* Am 7:13, 16. *z:* Jer 18:21–22. *a:* Jer 23:12. *b:* Jb 21:7; Mal 3:15. *c:* Is 29:13. *d:* Jer 17:18; Jb 23:10. *e:* Jer 9:4. *f:* Ps 78:62; Lam 2:1–2. *g:* Ps 106:40. *h:* 2 Kgs 24:2; Is 56:9.

10 Many shepherds have ravaged my
vineyard,
have trampled down my heritage;
My delightful portion they have turned
into a desert waste.[i]
11 They have made it a mournful waste,
desolate before me,
Desolate, the whole land,
because no one takes it to heart.
12 Upon every height in the wilderness
marauders have appeared.
The LORD has a sword that consumes
the land from end to end:
no peace for any living thing.[j]
13 They have sown wheat and reaped thorns,
they have tired themselves out for no
purpose;
They are shamed by their harvest,
the burning anger of the LORD.

Judah's Neighbors. 14 Thus says the LORD,
against all my evil neighbors* who plunder the
heritage I gave my people Israel as their own:
See, I will uproot them from their land; the
house of Judah I will uproot in their midst.[k]
15 But after uprooting them, I will have
compassion on them again and bring them
back, each to their heritage, each to their
land.[l] 16 And if they truly learn my people's
custom of swearing by my name, "As the
LORD lives," just as they taught my people to
swear by Baal, then they shall be built up in
the midst of my people.[m] 17 But if they do not
obey, I will uproot and destroy that nation
entirely—oracle of the LORD.[n]

See RG 302

CHAPTER 13

*Judah's Corruption.** 1 The LORD said
to me: Go buy yourself a linen loincloth;
wear it on your loins, but do not put it in water. 2 I bought the loincloth, as the LORD commanded, and put it on. 3 A second time the
word of the LORD came to me thus: 4 Take the
loincloth which you bought and are wearing,
and go at once to the Perath; hide it there in
a cleft of the rock. 5 Obedient to the LORD's
command, I went to the Perath and buried
the loincloth. 6 After a long time, the LORD
said to me: Go now to the Perath and fetch
the loincloth which I told you to hide there.
7 So I went to the Perath, looked for the loincloth and took it from the place I had hidden
it. But it was rotted, good for nothing! 8 Then
the word came to me from the LORD: 9 Thus
says the LORD: So also I will allow the pride
of Judah to rot, the great pride of Jerusalem.[o]
10 This wicked people who refuse to obey my
words, who walk in the stubbornness of their
hearts and follow other gods, serving and
worshiping them, will be like this loincloth,
good for nothing.[p] 11 For, as the loincloth
clings to a man's loins, so I made the whole
house of Israel and the whole house of Judah
cling to me—oracle of the LORD—to be my
people, my fame, my praise, my glory. But
they did not listen.[q]

The Broken Wineflask. 12 Now speak to
them this word: Thus says the LORD, the
God of Israel: Every wineflask should be
filled with wine. If they reply, "Do we not
know that every wineflask should be filled
with wine?" 13 say to them: Thus says the
LORD: Beware! I am making all the inhabitants of this land drunk, the kings who sit on
David's throne, the priests and prophets, and
all the inhabitants of Jerusalem.[r] 14 I will
smash them against each other, parents and
children together—oracle of the LORD—
showing no compassion, I will neither spare
nor pity, but I will destroy them.[s]

A Last Warning

15 Listen and give ear, do not be arrogant,
for the LORD speaks.
16 Give glory to the LORD, your God,
before he brings darkness;
Before your feet stumble
on mountains at twilight;

12:14 My evil neighbors: nations surrounding Israel, the land belonging to the Lord; cf. Is 8:8.

13:1–11 In this symbolic action, Jeremiah probably went to the village and spring of Parah, two and a half miles northeast of Anathoth, whose name closely resembled the Hebrew name of the river Euphrates (*Perath*), in order to dramatize the religious corruption of Judah at the hands of the Babylonians.

i: Jer 6:3; Is 63:18. *j:* Is 42:25; 57:21. *k:* 2 Kgs 24:2. *l:* Am 9:14. *m:* Dt 6:13. *n:* Is 60:12. *o:* Prv 16:18. *p:* Jer 2:20; 7:24; 16:11. *q:* Ex 19:5; Dt 26:18–19. *r:* Jer 25:15–18; Is 51:17. *s:* Jer 19:10–11.

Before the light you look for turns to
darkness,
changes into black clouds.[t]
17 If you do not listen to this in your pride,
I will weep many tears in secret;
My eyes will run with tears
for the LORD's flock, led away to exile.[u]

Exile

18 Say to the king and to the queen mother:
come down from your throne;
From your heads
your splendid crowns will fall.[v]
19 The cities of the Negeb are besieged,
with no one to relieve them;
Judah is taken into exile—all of it—
in total exile.

Jerusalem's Disgrace

20 Lift up your eyes and see
those coming in from the north.
Where is the flock entrusted to you,
your splendid sheep?[w]
21 What will you say when rulers are
appointed over you,
those you taught to be allies?
Will not pains seize you
like those of a woman giving birth?[x]
22 If you say to yourself:
"Why have these things happened
to me?"
For your great guilt your skirts are
stripped away
and you are violated.[y]
23 Can Ethiopians change their skin,
leopards their spots?
As easily would you be able to do good,
accustomed to evil as you are.[z]
24 I will scatter them like chaff that flies
on the desert wind.[a]
25 This is your lot, the portion I have
measured out to you—
oracle of the LORD.
Because you have forgotten me,
and trusted in deception,* [b]
26 I now will strip away your skirts,
so that your shame is visible.[c]
27 Your adulteries, your neighings,
your shameless prostitutions:
On the hills, in the fields
I see your detestable crimes.
Woe to you, Jerusalem! How long will
it be
before you are clean?[d]

CHAPTER 14

See RG 302

The Great Drought. 1 The word of the
LORD that came to Jeremiah concerning the
drought:[e]

2 Judah mourns,
her gates are lifeless;
They are bowed to the ground,
and the outcry of Jerusalem goes up.[f]
3 The nobles send their servants for water,
but when they come to the cisterns
They find no water
and return with empty jars.[g]
Confounded, despairing, they cover their
heads
4 because of the ruined soil;
Because there is no rain in the land
the farmers are confounded, they cover
their heads.[h]
5 Even the doe in the field deserts her
young
because there is no grass.
6 The wild donkeys stand on the bare
heights,
gasping for breath like jackals;
Their eyes grow dim;
there is no grass.
7 Even though our crimes bear witness
against us,
act, LORD, for your name's sake—
Even though our rebellions are many,
and we have sinned against you.[i]
8 Hope of Israel, LORD,
our savior in time of need!
Why should you be a stranger in the land,
like a traveler stopping only for a
night?

13:25 Heb. *sheqer*: lit., "deception," often used to designate an idol.

t: Prv 4:18–19; Is 5:30; Am 8:9. *u:* Jer 14:17; Ps 119:136. *v:* Jer 22:26; 2 Kgs 24:12, 15. *w:* Jer 6:22–23. *x:* 2 Kgs 16:7. *y:* Is 47:2–3. *z:* Ps 55:20. *a:* Ps 1:4; 83:14. *b:* Jb 20:29. *c:* Ez 16:32. *d:* Jer 2:20. *e:* Lv 26:19–20. *f:* Is 3:26. *g:* Am 4:8. *h:* Dt 28:23. *i:* Dn 9:4–14.

9 Why are you like someone bewildered,
a champion who cannot save?
You are in our midst, LORD,
your name we bear:
do not forsake us![j]
10 Thus says the LORD about this people:
They so love to wander
that they cannot restrain their feet.
The LORD takes no pleasure in them;
now he remembers their guilt,
and will punish their sins.[k]

11 Then the LORD said to me: Do not intercede for the well-being of this people.[l] 12 If
they fast, I will not listen to their supplication. If they sacrifice burnt offerings or grain
offerings, I will take no pleasure in them.
Rather, I will destroy them with the sword,
famine, and plague.[m]
13 "Ah! Lord GOD," I replied, "it is the
prophets who say to them, 'You shall not see
the sword; famine shall not befall you. Indeed, I will give you lasting peace in this
place.' "[n]
14 These prophets utter lies in my name,
the LORD said to me: I did not send them; I
gave them no command, nor did I speak to
them. They prophesy to you lying visions,
foolish divination, deceptions from their
own imagination.[o] 15 Therefore, thus says the
LORD: Concerning the prophets who prophesy in my name, though I did not send them,
and who say, "Sword and famine shall not
befall this land": by sword and famine shall
these prophets meet their end.[p] 16 The people
to whom they prophesy shall be thrown out
into the streets of Jerusalem because of
famine and the sword. No one shall bury
them, their wives, their sons, or their daughters, for I will pour out upon them their own
wickedness.[q] 17 Speak to them this word:

Let my eyes stream with tears
night and day, without rest,
Over the great destruction which
overwhelms
the virgin daughter of my people,
over her incurable wound.[r]
18 If I walk out into the field,
look! those slain by the sword;
If I enter the city,
look! victims of famine.
Both prophet and priest ply their trade
in a land they do not know.
19 Have you really cast Judah off?
Is Zion loathsome to you?
Why have you struck us a blow
that cannot be healed?
We wait for peace, to no avail;
for a time of healing, but terror comes
instead.[s]
20 We recognize our wickedness, LORD,
the guilt of our ancestors:
we have sinned against you.[t]
21 Do not reject us, for your name's sake,
do not disgrace your glorious throne.
Remember! Do not break your
covenant with us.[u]
22 Among the idols of the nations are there
any that give rain?
Or can the mere heavens send
showers?
Is it not you, LORD,
our God, to whom we look?
You alone do all these things.[v]

CHAPTER 15

See RG 302

1 The LORD said to me: Even if Moses
and Samuel stood before me, my heart
would not turn toward this people. Send
them away from me and let them go.[w] 2 If
they ask you, "Where should we go?" tell
them, Thus says the LORD: Whoever is
marked for death, to death; whoever is
marked for the sword, to the sword; whoever
is marked for famine, to famine; whoever is
marked for captivity, to captivity.[x] 3 Four
kinds of scourge I have decreed against
them—oracle of the LORD—the sword to
kill them; dogs to drag them off; the birds of
the sky and the beasts of the earth to devour
and destroy them.[y] 4 And I will make them an
object of horror to all the kingdoms of the
earth because of what Manasseh, son of
Hezekiah, king of Judah, did in Jerusalem.[z]

j: Is 59:1–2; 63:19. *k:* Jer 2:25. *l:* Jer 11:14; Ex 32:10. *m:* Jer 6:20; Is 1:11, 13. *n:* Jer 4:10; 5:12. *o:* Jer 5:31; 23:16. *p:* Jer 5:12–13. *q:* Jer 7:33; 19:7. *r:* Jer 9:17. *s:* Jer 8:15; 2 Chr 36:16. *t:* Ps 106:6; Dn 9:5, 8. *u:* Jer 14:7; Lv 26:44; Ps 25:11. *v:* Jer 5:24; Zec 10:1. *w:* Ps 99:6; Ez 14:14, 16. *x:* Jer 14:12; Ez 5:12. *y:* Ez 14:21. *z:* Jer 24:9; 2 Kgs 21:11–16; 23:26; 24:3–4.

Scene of Tragedy

5 Who will pity you, Jerusalem,
who will grieve for you?
Who will stop to ask
about your welfare?[a]
6 It is you who have disowned me—oracle
of the LORD—
turned your back upon me;
I stretched out my hand to destroy you,
because I was weary of relenting.[b]
7 I winnowed them with a winnowing fork
at the gates of the land;
I have bereaved, destroyed my people;
they have not turned from their evil
ways.[c]
8 Their widows were more numerous
before me
than the sands of the sea.
I brought against the mother of youths
the destroyer at midday;
Suddenly I struck her
with anguish and terror.
9 The mother of seven faints away,
breathing out her life;
Her sun sets in full day,
she is ashamed, abashed.
Their survivors I will give to the sword
in the presence of their enemies—
oracle of the LORD.[d]

Jeremiah's Complaint

10 Woe to me, my mother, that you gave me
birth!
a man of strife and contention to all
the land!
I neither borrow nor lend,
yet everyone curses me.[e]
11 Tell me, LORD, have I not served you for
their good?
Have I not interceded with you
in time of misfortune and anguish?[f]
12 Can one break iron,
iron from the north, and bronze?
13 * Your wealth and your treasures
I give as plunder, demanding no
payment,
because of all your sins, throughout all
your territory.
14 And I shall enslave you to your enemies
in a land you do not know,
For fire has broken out from my anger,
it is kindled against you.
15 You know, LORD:
Remember me and take care of me,
avenge me on my persecutors.
Because you are slow to anger, do not
banish me;
know that for you I have borne insult.[g]
16 When I found your words, I devoured
them;
your words were my joy, the happiness
of my heart,
Because I bear your name,
LORD, God of hosts.
17 I did not sit celebrating
in the circle of merrymakers;
Under the weight of your hand I sat
alone
because you filled me with rage.[h]
18 Why is my pain continuous,
my wound incurable, refusing to be
healed?
To me you are like a deceptive brook,
waters that cannot be relied on![i]
19 Thus the LORD answered me:
If you come back and I take you back,
in my presence you shall stand;
If you utter what is precious and not what
is worthless,
you shall be my mouth.
Then they will be the ones who turn to
you,
not you who turn to them.
20 And I will make you toward this people
a fortified wall of bronze.
Though they fight against you,
they shall not prevail,
For I am with you,

15:13–14 Though the wording of these verses is close to that in 17:3–4, the present passage is evidently God's word to Jeremiah, whereas 17:3–4 is evidently a word of judgment on Judah. It is noteworthy that the references to "you" in the present passage are singular, until a shift to plural in "against you" in the last line; this "you" is then doubtless a reference to both the prophet and his enemies.

a: Is 51:19. *b:* Am 7:8. *c:* Is 41:16. *d:* 1 Sm 2:5. *e:* Jer 20:14. *f:* Jer 39:11–14. *g:* Jer 11:20; 12:3; Ps 69:8. *h:* Ps 25:4. *i:* Jer 14:19; 30:15.

to save and rescue you—oracle of the
LORD.[j]
21 I will rescue you from the hand of the
wicked,
and ransom you from the power of the
violent.

CHAPTER 16

See RG 302

Jeremiah's Life a Warning. 1This word
came to me from the LORD: 2Do not take a
wife and do not have sons and daughters in
this place, 3for thus says the LORD concerning the sons and daughters born in this place,
the mothers who give them birth, the fathers
who beget them in this land: 4Of deadly disease they shall die. Unlamented and unburied
they will lie like dung on the ground. Sword
and famine will make an end of them, and
their corpses will become food for the birds
of the sky and the beasts of the earth.[k]
5Thus says the LORD: Do not go into a
house of mourning; do not go there to
lament or grieve for them. For I have withdrawn my peace from this people—oracle of
the LORD—my love and my compassion.[l]
6They shall die, the great and the lowly, in
this land, unburied and unlamented.* No one
will gash themselves or shave their heads for
them.[m] 7They will not break bread with the
bereaved to offer consolation for the dead;
they will not give them the cup of consolation to drink over the death of father or
mother.[n]
8Do not enter a house of feasting to sit eating and drinking with them. 9For thus says
the LORD of hosts, the God of Israel: Before
your eyes and in your lifetime, I will silence
in this place the song of joy and the song of
gladness, the song of the bridegroom and the
song of the bride.[o]
10When you proclaim all these words to
this people and they ask you: "Why has the
LORD pronounced all this great disaster
against us? What is our crime? What sin
have we committed against the LORD, our
God?"—[p] 11[q] you shall answer them: It is because your ancestors have forsaken me—oracle of the LORD—and followed other gods
that they served and worshiped; but me they
have forsaken, and my law they did not
keep. 12And you have done worse than your
ancestors. Here you are, every one of you,
walking in the stubbornness of your evil
heart instead of listening to me.[r] 13I will
throw you out of this land into a land that
neither you nor your ancestors have known;
there you can serve other gods day and night
because I will not show you mercy.
Return from Exile. 14Therefore, days are
coming—oracle of the LORD—when it will
no longer be said, "As the LORD lives, who
brought the Israelites out of Egypt";[s] 15but
rather, "As the LORD lives, who brought the
Israelites out of the land of the north and out
of all the countries to which he had banished
them." I will bring them back to the land I
gave their ancestors.[t]
Double Punishment. 16Look!—oracle of
the LORD—I will send many fishermen to
catch them. After that, I will send many
hunters to hunt them out from every mountain and hill and rocky crevice.[u] 17For my
eyes are upon all their ways; they are not
hidden from me, nor does their guilt escape
my sight.[v] 18I will at once repay them double
for their crime and their sin because they
profaned my land with the corpses of their
detestable idols, and filled my heritage with
their abominations.[w]

Conversion of the Nations

19 LORD, my strength, my fortress,
my refuge in the day of distress!
To you nations will come
from the ends of the earth, and say,
"Our ancestors inherited mere frauds,
empty, worthless."[x]
20 Can human beings make for themselves
gods?
But these are not gods at all![y]
21 Therefore, I will indeed give them
knowledge;

16:6–7 These verses refer to popular mourning practices in the land; cf. Dt 14:1–2.

j: Jer 1:18; 6:27. *k:* Jer 7:33; 22:18. *l:* Ez 24:16–17. *m:* Lv 19:28; Dt 14:1. *n:* Ez 24:17. *o:* Jer 7:34; 25:10. *p:* Jer 2:35; 5:19; 13:22. *q:* Jer 22:9; Dt 29:25. *r:* Jer 7:24–26. *s:* Jer 23:7–8. *t:* Jer 24:6. *u:* 2 Kgs 24:2; Lam 4:19. *v:* Jer 32:19; Jb 34:21. *w:* Is 40:2. *x:* Jer 2:11; Is 2:2–3. *y:* Jer 2:11; Gal 4:8.

this time I will make them
acknowledge
My strength and my power:
they shall know that my name is LORD.[z]

See RG 302

CHAPTER 17

The Sin of Judah and Its Punishment

1 The sin of Judah is written
with an iron stylus,
Engraved with a diamond point
upon the tablets of their hearts,[a]

And the horns of their altars, 2 when their
children remember their altars and their
asherahs, beside the green trees, on the high
hills, 3 the peaks in the country.

Your wealth and all your treasures
I give as plunder,
As payment for all your sins
throughout your territory,
4 You will relinquish your hold on your
heritage
which I have given you.
I will enslave you to your enemies
in a land you do not know:
For a fire has broken out from my anger,
burning forever.[b]

True Wisdom

5 Thus says the LORD:
Cursed is the man who trusts in human
beings,
who makes flesh his strength,
whose heart turns away from the
LORD.[c]
6 He is like a barren bush in the wasteland
that enjoys no change of season,
But stands in lava beds in the wilderness,
a land, salty and uninhabited.
7 Blessed are those who trust in the LORD;
the LORD will be their trust.[d]
8 They are like a tree planted beside the
waters
that stretches out its roots to the
stream:
It does not fear heat when it comes,
its leaves stay green;
In the year of drought it shows no
distress,
but still produces fruit.[e]
9 More tortuous than anything is the
human heart,
beyond remedy; who can understand it?
10 I, the LORD, explore the mind
and test the heart,
Giving to all according to their ways,
according to the fruit of their deeds.[f]
11 A partridge that broods but does not
hatch
are those who acquire wealth unjustly:
In midlife it will desert them;
in the end they are only fools.[g]

The Source of Life

12 A throne of glory, exalted from the
beginning,
such is our holy place.[h]
13 O Hope of Israel, LORD!
all who forsake you shall be put to
shame;
The rebels shall be enrolled in the
netherworld;
they have forsaken the LORD, source
of living waters.[i]

Prayer for Vengeance

14 Heal me, LORD, that I may be healed;
save me, that I may be saved,
for you are my praise.
15 See how they say to me,
"Where is the word of the LORD?
Let it come to pass!"[j]
16 Yet I did not press you to send disaster;
the day without remedy I have not
desired.
You know what passed my lips;
it is present before you.
17 Do not become a terror to me,
you are my refuge in the day of
disaster.[k]
18 Let my persecutors be confounded—
not me!
let them be terrified—not me!
Bring upon them the day of disaster,
crush them with double destruction.[l]

z: Am 5:8. *a:* Jb 19:24. *b:* Jer 5:19; Dt 32:22. *c:* Ps 146:2–3. *d:* Ps 1:3. *e:* Is 58:11. *f:* Jer 32:19; 1 Sm 16:7; Eccl 12:14. *g:* Prv 13:11; Lk 12:20. *h:* Jer 14:21. *i:* Jer 2:13. *j:* Is 5:19; 2 Pt 3:4. *k:* Jer 16:19. *l:* Jer 15:15; 18:20–23; Ps 35:5–6.

Observance of the Sabbath. [19]Thus said the LORD to me: Go, stand at the Gate of Benjamin,* where the kings of Judah enter and leave, and at the other gates of Jerusalem.[m] [20]There say to them: Hear the word of the LORD, you kings of Judah, and all Judah, and all you inhabitants of Jerusalem who enter these gates! [21]Thus says the LORD: As you love your lives, take care not to carry burdens on the sabbath, to bring them in through the gates of Jerusalem.[n] [22]Bring no burden from your homes on the sabbath. Do no work whatever, but keep holy the sabbath day, as I commanded your ancestors,[o] [23]though they did not listen or give ear, but stiffened their necks so they could not hear or take correction.[p] [24]If you truly obey me—oracle of the LORD—and carry no burden through the gates of this city on the sabbath, keeping the sabbath day holy and abstaining from all work on it,[q] [25]then, through the gates of this city, kings who sit upon the throne of David will continue to enter, riding in their chariots or upon their horses, along with their princes, and the people of Judah, and the inhabitants of Jerusalem. This city will remain inhabited forever.[r] [26]To it people will come from the cities of Judah and the neighborhood of Jerusalem, from the land of Benjamin and from the Shephelah, from the hill country and the Negeb, to bring burnt offerings and sacrifices, grain offerings, incense, and thank offerings to the house of the LORD.[s] [27]But if you do not obey me and keep holy the sabbath day, if you carry burdens and come through the gates of Jerusalem on the sabbath, I will set fire to its gates—a fire never to be extinguished—and it will consume the palaces of Jerusalem.[t]

See RG 302

CHAPTER 18

The Potter's Vessel.* [1]This word came to Jeremiah from the LORD: [2]Arise and go down to the potter's house; there you will hear my word. [3]I went down to the potter's house and there he was, working at the wheel. [4]Whenever the vessel of clay he was making turned out badly in his hand, he tried again, making another vessel of whatever sort he pleased.[u] [5]Then the word of the LORD came to me: [6]Can I not do to you, house of Israel, as this potter has done?—oracle of the LORD. Indeed, like clay in the hand of the potter, so are you in my hand, house of Israel.[v] [7][w] At one moment I may decree concerning a nation or kingdom that I will uproot and tear down and destroy it; [8]but if that nation against whom I have decreed turns from its evil, then I will have a change of heart regarding the evil which I have decreed.[x] [9]At another moment, I may decree concerning a nation or kingdom that I will build up and plant it; [10]but if that nation does what is evil in my eyes, refusing to obey my voice, then I will have a change of heart regarding the good with which I planned to bless it.[y]

[11]And now, tell this to the people of Judah and the inhabitants of Jerusalem: Thus says the LORD: Look, I am fashioning evil against you and making a plan. Return, all of you, from your evil way; reform your ways and your deeds.[z] [12]But they will say, "No use! We will follow our own devices; each one of us will behave according to the stubbornness of our evil hearts!"[a]

Unnatural Apostasy

13 Therefore thus says the LORD:
Ask among the nations—
who has ever heard the like?
Truly horrible things
virgin Israel has done![b]
14 Does the snow of Lebanon*
desert the rocky heights?
Do the gushing waters dry up
that flow fresh down the mountains?
15 Yet my people have forgotten me:
they offer incense in vain.

17:19 The Gate of Benjamin: this gate, probably part of the Temple area, is otherwise unknown.

18:1–12 The lesson of the potter is that God has the power to destroy or restore, changing his plans accordingly as these nations disobey him or fulfill his will. Cf. Jon 3:10.

18:14 Lebanon: here apparently including Mount Hermon, whose snow-capped peak can be seen from parts of Palestine all year round. The prophet contrasts the certainties of nature with Israel's unnatural desertion of the Lord for idols (v. 15).

m: Jer 7:2. *n:* Neh 13:15–19. *o:* Ex 20:8; 23:12. *p:* Jer 5:3; 7:24. *q:* Is 58:14. *r:* Jer 22:4. *s:* Jer 32:44. *t:* Ez 22:8. *u:* Rom 9:20–21. *v:* Wis 15:7; Is 45:9. *w:* Jer 1:10. *x:* Jer 26:3; Is 55:7; Ez 18:21, 27; Jon 3:10. *y:* Nm 14:22–23. *z:* Jer 7:3; 25:5; 35:15. *a:* Jer 2:25; 7:24. *b:* Jer 2:10–11; 5:30.

They stumble off their paths,
the ways of old,
Traveling on bypaths,
not the beaten track.[c]
16 Their land shall be made a waste,
an object of endless hissing:*
All passersby will be horrified,
shaking their heads.[d]
17 Like the east wind, I will scatter them
before their enemies;
I will show them my back, not my face,
in their day of disaster.[e]

Another Prayer for Vengeance. 18 “Come,”
they said, “let us devise a plot against Jeremiah, for instruction will not perish from the
priests, nor counsel from the wise, nor the
word from the prophets. Come, let us destroy him by his own tongue. Let us pay
careful attention to his every word.”[f]

19 Pay attention to me, O LORD,
and listen to what my adversaries say.
20 Must good be repaid with evil
that they should dig a pit to take my
life?
Remember that I stood before you
to speak on their behalf,
to turn your wrath away from them.[g]
21 So now, give their children* to famine,[h]
deliver them to the power of the sword.
Let their wives be childless and widows;
let their husbands die of pestilence,
their youths be struck down by the
sword in battle.
22 May cries be heard from their homes,
when suddenly you send plunderers
against them.
For they have dug a pit to capture me,
they have hidden snares for my feet;
23 But you, LORD, know
all their planning for my death.
Do not forgive their crime,
and their sin do not blot out from your
sight!
Let them stumble before you,
in the time of your anger act against
them.[i]

CHAPTER 19

See RG 302

Symbol of the Potter's Flask. 1 Thus
said the LORD: Go, buy a potter's earthenware flask. Take along some of the elders of
the people and some of the priests, 2 and go
out toward the Valley of Ben-hinnom, at the
entrance of the Potsherd Gate;* there proclaim the words which I will speak to you:
3 You shall say, Listen to the word of the
LORD, kings of Judah and inhabitants of Jerusalem: Thus says the LORD of hosts, the God
of Israel: I am going to bring such evil upon
this place that the ears of all who hear of it
will ring. 4 All because they have forsaken me
and profaned this place by burning incense to
other gods which neither they nor their ancestors knew; and because the kings of Judah
have filled this place with innocent blood,[j]
5 building high places for Baal to burn their
children in fire as offerings to Baal—something I never considered or said or commanded.[k] 6* Therefore, days are coming—
oracle of the LORD—when this place will no
longer be called Topheth, or the Valley of
Ben-hinnom, but rather, the Valley of
Slaughter.[l] 7 In this place I will foil the plan of
Judah and Jerusalem; I will make them fall
by the sword before their enemies, at the
hand of those who seek their lives. Their
corpses I will give as food to the birds of the
sky and the beasts of the earth.[m] 8 I will make
this city a waste and an object of hissing. Because of all its wounds, every passerby will
be horrified and hiss. 9 I will have them eat
the flesh of their sons and daughters; they
shall eat one another's flesh during the harsh
siege under which their enemies and those
who seek their lives will confine them.[n]
10 And you shall break the flask in the sight
of the men who went with you, 11 and say to

18:16 Hissing: in some ancient Near Eastern cultures hissing was not only a sign of derision but a magical means of keeping demons away; people hissed in order to ward off danger, like whistling in a cemetery.

18:21 Give their children: often an extended family is meant, to be rewarded or punished as a unit.

19:2 Potsherd Gate: perhaps in the south wall of Jerusalem, through which potsherds and other refuse were thrown into the Valley of Ben-hinnom.

19:6 Cf. note on 7:31.

c: Jer 2:13, 32. *d:* Jer 19:8; Lv 26:32; 1 Kgs 9:8. *e:* Prv 1:24–31. *f:* Jer 11:19; Ps 35:15–16. *g:* Ps 35:12. *h:* Ps 109:9–10. *i:* Neh 4:5; Ps 35:4; 37:32–33. *j:* Jer 1:16; 2 Kgs 21:16; 24:4. *k:* Jer 7:31–32; 32:35. *l:* Jer 7:32. *m:* Jer 7:33. *n:* Lv 26:29.

them: Thus says the LORD of hosts: Thus will
I smash this people and this city, as one
smashes a clay pot so that it cannot be repaired. And Topheth shall be its burial place,
for there will be no other place for burial.[o]
12 Thus I will do to this place and to its inhabitants—oracle of the LORD; I will make this
city like Topheth.[p] 13 And the houses of Jerusalem and the houses of the kings of Judah
shall be defiled like the place of Topheth, all
the houses upon whose roofs they burnt incense to the whole host of heaven and poured
out libations to other gods.[q]
14 When Jeremiah returned from Topheth,
where the LORD had sent him to prophesy, he
stood in the court of the house of the LORD
and said to all the people:[r] 15 Thus says the
LORD of hosts, the God of Israel: I will bring
upon this city all the evil I have spoken
against it, because they have become stubborn and have not obeyed my words.[s]

See RG 302

CHAPTER 20

1 Now the priest Pashhur,[t] son of Immer, chief officer in the house of the LORD,*
heard Jeremiah prophesying these things.
2 So he struck the prophet and put him in the
stocks at the upper Gate of Benjamin in the
house of the LORD.[u] 3 The next morning, after Pashhur had released Jeremiah from the
stocks, the prophet said to him:[v] "Instead of
Pashhur, the LORD names you 'Terror on
every side.'* 4 For thus says the LORD: Indeed, I will hand you over to terror, you and
all your friends. Your own eyes shall see
them fall by the sword of their enemies. All
Judah I will hand over to the power of the
king of Babylon,* who shall take them captive to Babylon or strike them down with the
sword. 5 All the wealth of this city, all its resources and its valuables, all the treasures of
the kings of Judah, I will hand over to their
enemies, who will plunder it and carry it
away to Babylon.[w] 6 You, Pashhur, and all
the members of your household shall go into
exile. To Babylon you shall go; there you
shall die and be buried, you and all your
friends, because you have prophesied lies to
them."[x]

Jeremiah's Interior Crisis

7 You seduced me,* LORD, and I let myself
be seduced;
you were too strong for me, and you
prevailed.
All day long I am an object of laughter;
everyone mocks me.
8 Whenever I speak, I must cry out,
violence and outrage I proclaim;
The word of the LORD has brought me
reproach and derision all day long.
9 I say I will not mention him,
I will no longer speak in his name.
But then it is as if fire is burning in my
heart,
imprisoned in my bones;
I grow weary holding back,
I cannot![y]
10 Yes, I hear the whisperings of many:
"Terror on every side!
Denounce! let us denounce him!"
All those who were my friends
are on the watch for any misstep of
mine.
"Perhaps he can be tricked; then we will
prevail,
and take our revenge on him."[z]
11 But the LORD is with me, like a mighty
champion:
my persecutors will stumble, they will
not prevail.
In their failure they will be put to utter
shame,
to lasting, unforgettable confusion.[a]
12 LORD of hosts, you test the just,
you see mind and heart,

20:1 Chief officer in the house of the LORD: head of the Temple police; cf. 29:26. By entering the Temple court (19:14), Jeremiah had put himself under Pashhur's jurisdiction.

20:3 Terror on every side: the name indicates the siege that will beset Jerusalem.

20:4 Babylon: mentioned here for the first time in Jeremiah as the land of exile. The prophecy dates from after 605 B.C., when Nebuchadnezzar defeated Egypt and made the Babylonian (Chaldean) empire dominant in Syria and Palestine.

20:7 You seduced me: Jeremiah accuses the Lord of having deceived him; cf. 15:18.

o: Jer 7:32. *p:* 2 Kgs 23:10. *q:* Jer 32:29. *r:* Jer 26:2. *s:* Jer 7:26; Prv 29:1. *t:* Jer 21:1. *u:* Jer 29:26. *v:* Jer 6:25. *w:* 2 Kgs 20:17; 24:12–16. *x:* Jer 14:13–14; 28:15. *y:* Jer 6:11; Jb 32:18. *z:* Jb 19:19; Ps 31:13; Lk 20:20. *a:* Jer 1:8; 15:20.

Let me see the vengeance you take on
them,
for to you I have entrusted my cause.[b]
13 Sing to the LORD,
praise the LORD,
For he has rescued the life of the poor
from the power of the evildoers![c]

14 Cursed be the day*
on which I was born!
May the day my mother gave me birth
never be blessed![d]
15 Cursed be the one who brought the news
to my father,
"A child, a son, has been born to you!"
filling him with great joy.
16 Let that man be like the cities
which the LORD relentlessly
overthrew;
Let him hear war cries in the morning,
battle alarms at noonday,[e]
17 because he did not kill me in the
womb!
Then my mother would have been my
grave,
her womb confining me forever.[f]
18 Why did I come forth from the womb,
to see sorrow and pain,
to end my days in shame?[g]

III. Oracles in the Last Years of Jerusalem

CHAPTER 21

See RG 302-3

Fate of Zedekiah and Jerusalem. 1 The
word which came to Jeremiah from the
LORD when King Zedekiah* sent Pashhur,
son of Malchiah, and the priest Zephaniah,
son of Maaseiah, to him with this request:
2 Inquire for us of the LORD, because Nebuchadnezzar, king of Babylon, is attacking us.
Perhaps the LORD will act for us in accord
with his wonderful works by making him
withdraw from us. 3 But Jeremiah answered
them: This is what you shall report to Zedekiah: 4 Thus says the LORD, the God of Israel:
I will turn against you the weapons with
which you are fighting the king of Babylon
and the Chaldeans who besiege you outside
the walls. These weapons I will pile up in the
midst of this city,[h] 5 and I myself will fight
against you with outstretched hand and
mighty arm, in anger, wrath, and great rage![i]
6 I will strike down the inhabitants of this
city, human being and beast; they shall die in
a great pestilence.[j] 7 After that—oracle of the
LORD—I will hand over Zedekiah, king of
Judah, and his ministers and the people in
this city who survive pestilence, sword, and
famine, to Nebuchadnezzar, king of Babylon, to their enemies and those who seek
their lives. He shall strike them down with
the edge of the sword, without quarter, without mercy or compassion.[k] 8 And to this people you shall say: Thus says the LORD: See,
I am giving you a choice between the way to
life and the way to death.[l] 9 Whoever remains
in this city shall die by the sword or famine
or pestilence. But whoever leaves and surrenders to the Chaldeans who are besieging
you shall live and escape with his life. 10 I
have set my face against this city, for evil
and not for good—oracle of the LORD. It
shall be given into the power of the king of
Babylon who shall set it on fire.*

*Oracles Regarding the Kings**

11 To the royal house of Judah:
Hear the word of the LORD,
12 house of David!
Thus says the LORD:
Each morning dispense justice,
rescue the oppressed from the hand of
the oppressor,

20:14–18 Deception, sorrow and terror have brought the prophet to the point of despair; nevertheless he maintains confidence in God (vv. 11–13); cf. Jb 3:3–12.

21:1 Zedekiah: brother of Jehoiakim, appointed king by Nebuchadnezzar after he had carried Jehoiachin away to captivity (2 Kgs 24:17). **Pashhur**: different from the one in 20:1–3 but also one of Jeremiah's enemies; cf. 38:1, 4.

21:10 Jeremiah consistently pointed out the uselessness of resistance to Babylon, since the Lord had delivered Judah to Nebuchadnezzar (27:6). Because of this the prophet was denounced and imprisoned as a traitor (37:13–14).

21:11–23:8 This section contains an editor's collection of Jeremiah's oracles against the kings of Judah. They are placed in the chronological order of the kings, and are prefaced by oracles against the kings of Judah in general (21:11–22:9).

b: Jer 11:20. *c:* Ps 35:9–10; 109:30–31. *d:* Jer 15:10; Jb 3:1–10; 10:18. *e:* Gn 19:25; Is 13:19. *f:* Jb 3:10–11; 10:19. *g:* Jb 14:1. *h:* Jer 37:8–10. *i:* Is 63:10; Lam 2:4–5. *j:* Jer 16:4. *k:* Jer 24:8–10; Dt 28:49–50. *l:* Jer 21:9; Dt 30:15, 19.

Or my fury will break out like fire
and burn with no one to quench it
because of your evil deeds.[m]
13 Beware! I am against you, Ruler of the Valley,
Rock of the Plain*—oracle of the LORD.
You say, "Who will attack us,
who can storm our defenses?"
14 I will punish you—oracle of the LORD—
as your deeds deserve!
I will kindle a fire in its forest*
that shall devour all its surroundings.[n]

CHAPTER 22

See RG 302–3

1 Thus says the LORD: Go down to the
palace of the king of Judah and there deliver
this word: 2 You shall say: Listen to the word
of the LORD, king of Judah, who sit on the
throne of David, you, your ministers, and
your people who enter by these gates![o]
3 Thus says the LORD: Do what is right and
just. Rescue the victims from the hand of
their oppressors. Do not wrong or oppress
the resident alien, the orphan, or the widow,
and do not shed innocent blood in this
place.[p] 4 If you carry out these commands,
kings who succeed to the throne of David
will continue to enter the gates of this house,
riding in chariots or mounted on horses, with
their ministers, and their people. 5 But if you
do not obey these commands, I swear by
myself—oracle of the LORD: this house shall
become rubble. 6 For thus says the LORD concerning the house of the king of Judah:

Though you be to me like Gilead,
like the peak of Lebanon,
I swear I shall turn you into a waste,
with cities uninhabited.
7 Against you I will send destroyers,
each with their tools:
They shall cut down your choice cedars,
and cast them into the fire.[q]

8 Many nations will pass by this city and
ask one another: "Why has the LORD done
this to so great a city?"[r] 9 And they will be
told: "Because they have deserted their covenant with the LORD, their God, by worshiping and serving other gods."[s]

Jehoahaz

10 Do not weep for him who is dead,*
nor mourn for him!
Weep rather for him who is going away;
never again to see
the land of his birth.[t]

11 Thus says the LORD concerning Shallum,*
son of Josiah, king of Judah, his father's successor, who left this place: He shall never return, 12 but in the place where they exiled
him, there he shall die; he shall never see this
land again.

Jehoiakim

13 Woe to him who builds his house on wrongdoing,
his roof-chambers on injustice;
Who works his neighbors without pay,*
and gives them no wages.[u]
14 Who says, "I will build myself a spacious house,
with airy rooms,"
Who cuts out windows for it,
panels it with cedar,
and paints it with vermilion.
15 Must you prove your rank among kings*
by competing with them in cedar?

21:13 Ruler of the Valley, Rock of the Plain: Mount Zion, surrounded by valleys, was regarded by the royal house as impregnable. Despite this natural fortification, God derides it as no more than a rock rising from the plain, useless against the attack of his fury.

21:14 Its forest: probably the royal palace, built of cedar wood; cf. 22:14; in 1 Kgs 7:2 the palace is called "the house of the forest of Lebanon."

22:10 Him who is dead: Josiah. His successor, Jehoahaz, was deported by Pharaoh Neco to Egypt, where he died (2 Kgs 23:33–34).

22:11 Shallum: i.e., Jehoahaz; cf. 1 Chr 3:15. This may have been his name at birth, in which case Jehoahaz would have been his throne name.

22:13 Without pay: either by forced labor in public works, or by defrauding the workers. Despite the impoverishment caused in Judah by the payment of foreign tribute, Jehoiakim embarked on a building program in Jerusalem (v. 14); cedar was an expensive building material which had to be imported. Social injustice is the cause of much of the prophetic condemnation of the kings (v. 17).

22:15–16 The rule of Josiah, Jehoiakim's father, shows that authentic kingship is rooted in knowledge of the Lord

m: Jer 4:4; 22:3; Zec 7:9. *n:* 2 Kgs 25:9; 2 Chr 36:19. *o:* Jer 17:20. *p:* Jer 21:12; Ex 22:21–24; Dt 24:17. *q:* Jer 21:14. *r:* Dt 29:24–27. *s:* Jer 19:4; 40:2–3. *t:* 2 Chr 35:23–25. *u:* Lv 19:13; Dt 24:14; Hb 2:9, 12.

Did not your father eat and drink,
And act justly and righteously?
Then he prospered.[v]
16 Because he dispensed justice to the weak and the poor,
he prospered.
Is this not to know me?—
oracle of the LORD.[w]
17 But your eyes and heart are set on nothing
except your own gain,
On shedding innocent blood
and practicing oppression and extortion.[x]

18 Therefore, thus says the LORD concerning Jehoiakim, son of Josiah, king of Judah:

They shall not lament him,
"Alas! my brother"; "Alas! sister."*
They shall not lament him,
"Alas, Lord! alas, Majesty!"[y]
19 The burial of a donkey* he shall be given,
dragged forth and cast out
beyond the gates of Jerusalem.[z]

Jeconiah

20 Climb Lebanon and cry out,*
in Bashan lift up your voice;
Cry out from Abarim,
for all your lovers are crushed.[a]
21 I spoke to you when you were secure,
but you answered, "I will not listen."
This has been your way from your youth,
not to listen to my voice.
22 The wind shall shepherd all your shepherds,
your lovers shall go into exile.
Surely then you shall be ashamed and confounded
because of all your wickedness.
23 You who dwell on Lebanon,
who nest in the cedars,
How you shall groan when pains come upon you,
like the pangs of a woman in childbirth!

24 As I live—oracle of the LORD—even if
you, Coniah,* son of Jehoiakim, king of Judah, were a signet ring[b] on my right hand, I
would snatch you off. 25 I will hand you over
to those who seek your life, to those you
dread: Nebuchadnezzar, king of Babylon,
and the Chaldeans.[c] 26 I will cast you out, you
and the mother who bore you,* into a land
different from the land of your birth; and
there you will die;[d] 27 Neither shall return to
the land for which they yearn.[e]

28 Is this man Coniah a thing despised, to be broken,
a vessel that no one wants?
Why are he and his offspring cast out?
why thrown into a land they do not know?
29 O land, land, land,
hear the word of the LORD—
30 Thus says the LORD:
[f] Write this man down as childless,*
a man who will never prosper in his life!

and creates a society in which the most disadvantaged can expect and receive justice.

22:18 "Alas! my brother"; "Alas! sister": customary cries of mourning.

22:19 The burial of a donkey: no burial at all, except to be cast outside the city as refuse. This prophecy describes the popular feeling toward Jehoiakim rather than the actual circumstances of his burial. According to 2 Kgs 24:5 he was buried with his ancestors in Jerusalem.

22:20–23 The prophet first bids Jerusalem to scale Lebanon, Bashan, and Abarim, i.e., the highest surrounding mountains to the north, northeast, and southeast, and gaze on the ruin of its lovers, i.e., the false leaders of Judah, called its shepherds (v. 22); cf. 2:8. Jerusalem still stands (v. 23), apparently as secure as the heights of Lebanon, but destruction is to follow (cf. v. 6).

22:24 Coniah: a shortened form of Jeconiah, the name Jeremiah gives King Jehoiachin (cf. 24:1). **A signet ring**: the seal used by kings and other powerful figures—a symbol of their power and status—mounted in a ring worn constantly on the hand. The Lord says that even were Jehoiachin such a precious possession, he would reject him. Hg 2:23 uses the same imagery to signal the restoration of Zerubbabel. The words in Jer 22:24–30 date from the short three-month reign of Jehoiachin, before he was deported by Nebuchadnezzar.

22:26 You and the mother who bore you: the queen mother held a special position in the monarchy of Judah, and in the Books of Kings she is invariably mentioned by name along with the king (1 Kgs 15:2; 2 Kgs 18:2). Jehoiachin did indeed die in Babylon.

22:30 Childless: Jehoiachin is considered childless because none of his seven sons became king. His grandson Zerubbabel presided for a time over the Judahite community after the return from exile, but not as king. According to Ezekiel, whose oracles are dated by Jehoiachin's fictitious

v: 2 Sm 5:11; 7:2; 2 Kgs 23:25. *w:* Prv 31:9. *x:* Ez 22:13, 27. *y:* Jer 16:4–7; 1 Kgs 13:30. *z:* Jer 36:30. *a:* Jer 30:14–15; Dt 32:49. *b:* Hg 2:23. *c:* Jer 21:7; 34:20. *d:* 2 Kgs 24:15. *e:* Jer 44:14. *f:* Jer 36:30; 1 Chr 3:16–17; Mt 1:12.

Nor shall any of his descendants prosper,
to sit upon the throne of David,
to rule again over Judah.

See RG 302–3

CHAPTER 23

*A Just Shepherd.** 1[g] Woe to the shepherds who destroy and scatter the flock of
my pasture—oracle of the LORD. 2There-
fore, thus says the LORD, the God of Israel,
against the shepherds who shepherd my people: You have scattered my sheep and driven
them away. You have not cared for them, but
I will take care to punish your evil deeds.[h] 3I
myself will gather the remnant of my flock
from all the lands to which I have banished
them and bring them back to their folds;
there they shall be fruitful and multiply.[i] 4I
will raise up shepherds for them who will
shepherd them so that they need no longer
fear or be terrified; none shall be missing—
oracle of the LORD.[j]

5 See, days are coming—oracle of the
LORD—
when I will raise up a righteous branch
for David;
As king he shall reign and govern wisely,
he shall do what is just and right in the
land.[k]
6 In his days Judah shall be saved,
Israel shall dwell in security.
This is the name to be given him:
"The LORD our justice."[l]

7[m] Therefore, the days are coming—oracle
of the LORD—when they shall no longer say,
"As the LORD lives, who brought the Israelites out of the land of Egypt"; 8but rather, "As
the LORD lives, who brought the descendants
of the house of Israel up from the land of the
north"—and from all the lands to which I
banished them; they shall again live on their
own soil.

*The False Prophets**

9 Concerning the prophets:
My heart is broken within me,
all my bones tremble;
I am like a drunk,
like one overcome by wine,
Because of the LORD,
because of his holy words.
10 The land is filled with adulterers;
because of the curse the land mourns,
the pastures of the wilderness are
withered.[n]
Theirs is an evil course,
theirs is unjust power.
11 Both prophet and priest are godless!
In my very house I find their
wickedness—
oracle of the LORD.[o]
12 Hence their way shall become for them
slippery ground.
Into the darkness they shall be driven,
and fall headlong;
For I will bring disaster upon them,
the year of their punishment—oracle
of the LORD.[p]
13 Among Samaria's prophets
I saw something unseemly:
They prophesied by Baal
and led my people Israel astray.[q]
14 But among Jerusalem's prophets
I saw something more shocking:
Adultery, walking in deception,*
strengthening the power of the
wicked,
so that no one turns from evil;
To me they are all like Sodom,
its inhabitants like Gomorrah.[r]

regnal years, the people expected Jehoiachin to return. Jeremiah's prophecy dispels this hope, despite the words of Hananiah (28:4).

23:1–8 With the false rulers (shepherds) who have governed his people the Lord contrasts himself, the true shepherd, who will in the times of restoration appoint worthy rulers (vv. 1–4). He will provide a new king from David's line who will rule justly, fulfilling royal ideals (vv. 5, 6). "The Lord our justice" is an ironic wordplay on the name of the weak King Zedekiah ("The Lord is justice"). Unlike Zedekiah, the future king will be true to the name he bears. Verses 7–8 may have been added during the exile.

23:9–40 After the collection of oracles against the kings, the editor of the book placed this collection of oracles against the false prophets. With them are associated the priests, for both have betrayed their trust as instructors in the ways of the Lord; cf. 2:8; 4:9; 6:13–14.

23:14 Cf. note on 13:25.

g: Jer 22:22. *h:* Ez 34:4–10; Zec 11:16–17. *i:* Jer 29:14; 32:37. *j:* Jer 3:15; Ez 34:11–12. *k:* Jer 33:14–16; Is 4:2; 9:5–6; 11:1–5. *l:* Dn 9:24. *m:* Jer 16:14–15. *n:* Jer 4:22; 5:7–8; 9:2, 10. *o:* Jer 6:13. *p:* Ps 35:6. *q:* 1 Kgs 18:19. *r:* Jer 29:21–23; Is 1:9–10.

15 Therefore, thus says the LORD of hosts
against the prophets:

Look, I will give them wormwood to eat,
and poisoned water to drink;
For from Jerusalem's prophets
ungodliness has gone forth into the
whole land.[s]
16 Thus says the LORD of hosts:
Do not listen to the words of your
prophets,
who fill you with emptiness;
They speak visions from their own fancy,
not from the mouth of the LORD.[t]
17 They say to those who despise the word
of the LORD,*
"Peace shall be yours";
And to everyone who walks in hardness
of heart,
"No evil shall overtake you."[u]
18 Now, who has stood in the council of the
LORD,
to see him and to hear his word?
Who has heeded his word so as to
announce it?[v]
19 See, the storm of the LORD!
His wrath breaks forth
In a whirling storm
that bursts upon the heads of the
wicked.[w]
20 The anger of the LORD shall not abate
until he has carried out completely
the decisions of his heart.
In days to come
you will understand fully.
21 I did not send these prophets,
yet they ran;
I did not speak to them,
yet they prophesied.[x]
22 Had they stood in my council,
they would have proclaimed my words
to my people,
They would have brought them back
from their evil ways
and from their wicked deeds.
23 Am I a God near at hand only—oracle of
the LORD—[y]
and not a God far off?*
24 Can anyone hide in secret
without my seeing them?—oracle of
the LORD.
Do I not fill
heaven and earth?—oracle of the LORD.

25 I have heard the prophets who prophesy
lies in my name say, "I had a dream! I had a
dream!" 26 How long? Will the hearts of the
prophets who prophesy lies and their own
deceitful fancies ever turn back? 27 By the
dreams they tell each other, they plan to
make my people forget my name, just as
their ancestors forgot my name for Baal.[z]
28 Let the prophets who have dreams tell
their dreams; let those who have my word
speak my word truthfully!

What has straw to do with wheat?*
—oracle of the LORD.[a]
29 Is not my word like fire—oracle of the
LORD—
like a hammer shattering rock?

30 Therefore I am against the prophets—oracle of the LORD—those who steal my words
from each other.[b] 31 Yes, I am against the
prophets—oracle of the LORD—those who
compose their own speeches and call them
oracles. 32 Yes, I am against the prophets who
tell lying dreams—oracle of the LORD—
those who lead my people astray by recounting their reckless lies. It was not I who sent
them or commanded them; they do this people no good at all—oracle of the LORD.[c]
33* And when this people or a prophet or a
priest asks you, "What is the burden of the

23:17–20 Not only are the false prophets personally immoral, but they encourage immorality by prophesying good for evildoers. The true prophet, on the other hand, sees the inevitable consequences of evil behavior.

23:23–24 Near at hand only . . . far off: a divine claim that no one can hide from God and that God is aware of all that happens.

23:28–29 Straw . . . wheat: a contrast between false and true prophecy. True prophecy is also like fire (cf. 5:14; 20:9), producing violent results (v. 29); Jeremiah's own life is a testimony of this.

23:33–40 A wordplay on *massa'*, which means both "oracle" (usually of woe) and "burden." In vv. 34–40 the word *massa'* itself is forbidden to the people under the meaning of a divine oracle.

s: Jer 8:14; 9:14. *t:* Jer 14:14. *u:* Jer 5:12; Ez 13:10; Mi 3:11; Zec 10:2. *v:* Jb 15:8; Is 40:13; 1 Cor 2:16. *w:* Jer 30:23. *x:* Jer 29:9. *y:* Jer 16:17; Ps 139:8. *z:* Jgs 3:7; 8:33. *a:* Nm 12:6. *b:* Dt 18:20. *c:* Jer 28:15–17.

LORD?" you shall answer, "You are the burden, and I cast you off"—oracle of the LORD. 34 If a prophet or a priest or anyone else mentions "the burden of the LORD," I will punish that man and his household. 35 Thus you shall ask, when speaking to one another, "What answer did the LORD give?" or "What did the LORD say?" 36 But "the burden of the LORD" you shall mention no more. For each of you, your own word becomes the burden so that you pervert the words of the living God, the LORD of hosts, our God. 37 Thus shall you ask the prophet, "What answer did the LORD give?" or "What did the LORD say?" 38 But if you ask about "the burden of the LORD," then thus says the LORD: Because you use this phrase, "the burden of the LORD," though I forbade you to use it, 39 therefore I will lift you on high and cast you from my presence, you and the city which I gave to you and your ancestors. 40 And I will bring upon you eternal reproach, eternal shame, never to be forgotten.[d]

CHAPTER 24

See RG 302-3

*The Two Baskets of Figs.** 1 The LORD showed me two baskets of figs placed before the temple of the LORD.[e] This was after Nebuchadnezzar, king of Babylon, had exiled from Jerusalem Jeconiah,* son of Jehoiakim, king of Judah, and the princes of Judah, the artisans and smiths, and brought them to Babylon. 2 One basket contained excellent figs, those that ripen early. But the other basket contained very bad figs, so bad they could not be eaten. 3 Then the LORD said to me: What do you see, Jeremiah?[f] "Figs," I replied; "the good ones are very good, but the bad ones very bad, so bad they cannot be eaten." 4 Thereupon this word of the LORD came to me: 5 Thus says the LORD, the God of Israel: Like these good figs, I will also regard with favor Judah's exiles whom I sent away from this place into the land of the Chaldeans.[g] 6 I will look after them for good and bring them back to this land, to build them up, not tear them down; to plant them, not uproot them.[h] 7 I will give them a heart to know me, that I am the LORD. They shall be my people and I will be their God, for they shall return to me with their whole heart.[i] 8 But like the figs that are bad, so bad they cannot be eaten—yes, thus says the LORD—even so will I treat Zedekiah, king of Judah, and his princes, the remnant of Jerusalem remaining in this land and those who have settled in the land of Egypt.[j] 9 I will make them an object of horror to all the kingdoms of the earth, a reproach and a byword, a taunt and a curse, in all the places to which I will drive them.[k] 10 I will send upon them sword, famine, and pestilence, until they have disappeared from the land which I gave them and their ancestors.[l]

CHAPTER 25

See RG 302-3

Seventy Years of Exile. 1 The word that came to Jeremiah concerning all the people of Judah, in the fourth year of Jehoiakim,* son of Josiah, king of Judah (the first year of Nebuchadnezzar, king of Babylon).[m] 2 This word the prophet Jeremiah spoke to all the people of Judah and all the inhabitants of Jerusalem: 3 Since the thirteenth year of Josiah, son of Amon, king of Judah, to this day—that is, twenty-three years—the word of the LORD has come to me and I spoke to you untiringly, but you would not listen.[n] 4 The LORD kept sending you all his servants the prophets,[o] but you refused to listen or pay attention 5 to this message: Turn back, each of you, from your evil way and from your evil

24:1–10 For Jeremiah, as for Ezekiel, no good could be expected from the people who had been left in Judah under Zedekiah or who had fled into Egypt; a future might be expected only for those who would pass through the purifying experience of the exile to form the new Israel.

24:1 Jeconiah: alternative form of Jehoiachin (cf. note on 22:24).

25:1–14 The fourth year of Jehoiakim: 605 B.C. Officially, the first year of Nebuchadnezzar began the following year; but as early as his victory over Egypt at Carchemish in 605, Nebuchadnezzar wielded dominant power in the Near East. Jeremiah saw in him the fulfillment of his prophecy of the enemy to come from the north (cf. 1:13; 6:22–24). In vv. 11–12 the prophecy of the seventy years' exile occurs for the first time; cf. 29:10. This number signifies that the present generation must die out; cf. forty in the exodus tradition (Nm 14:20–23).

d: Jer 20:11. *e:* Am 8:1–2. *f:* Jer 1:11. *g:* Jer 29:11; Lv 26:44–45. *h:* Jer 12:15; Am 9:15. *i:* Jer 30:22; 31:1; 32:37; Bar 2:31. *j:* Jer 29:18. *k:* Jer 15:4; Dt 28:37. *l:* Jer 14:12. *m:* Jer 36:1. *n:* Jer 1:2. *o:* 2 Chr 36:15.

deeds; then you shall remain in the land which the LORD gave you and your ancestors, from of old and forever. 6 Do not follow other gods to serve and bow down to them; do not provoke me with the works of your hands, or I will bring evil upon you.[p] 7 But you would not listen to me—oracle of the LORD—and so you provoked me with the works of your hands to your own harm.[q] 8 Hence, thus says the LORD of hosts: Since you would not listen to my words, 9 I am about to send for and fetch all the tribes from the north—oracle of the LORD—and I will send for Nebuchadnezzar, king of Babylon, my servant; I will bring them against this land, its inhabitants, and all these neighboring nations. I will doom them, making them an object of horror, of hissing, of everlasting reproach.[r] 10 Among them I will put to an end the song of joy and the song of gladness, the voice of the bridegroom and the voice of the bride, the sound of the millstone and the light of the lamp. 11 This whole land shall be a ruin and a waste. Seventy years these nations shall serve the king of Babylon;[s] 12 but when the seventy years have elapsed, I will punish the king of Babylon and that nation and the land of the Chaldeans for their guilt—oracle of the LORD. Their land I will turn into everlasting waste.[t] 13 Against that land I will fulfill all the words I have spoken against it, all that is written in this book, which Jeremiah prophesied against all the nations. 14 They also shall serve many nations and great kings, and thus I will repay them according to their own deeds and according to the works of their hands.[u]

The Cup of Judgment on the Nations. 15* For thus said the LORD, the God of Israel, to me: Take this cup of the wine of wrath* from my hand and have all the nations to whom I will send you drink it.[v] 16 They shall drink, and retch, and go mad, because of the sword I will send among them.[w] 17 I took the cup from the hand of the LORD and gave it as drink to all the nations to whom the LORD sent me: 18 to Jerusalem, the cities of Judah, its kings and princes, to make them a ruin and a waste, an object of hissing and cursing, as they are today; 19 to Pharaoh, king of Egypt, and his servants, princes, all his people 20 and those of mixed ancestry; all the kings of the land of Uz;* all the kings of the land of the Philistines: Ashkelon, Gaza, Ekron, and the remnant of Ashdod; 21 Edom, Moab, and the Ammonites; 22 all the kings of Tyre, of Sidon, and of the shores beyond the sea;* 23 Dedan and Tema and Buz,* all the desert dwellers who shave their temples; 24 all the kings of Arabia; 25 all the kings of Zimri, of Elam, of the Medes; 26 all the kings of the north, near and far, one after the other; all the kingdoms upon the face of the earth and after them the king of Sheshach* shall drink.

27 Tell them: Thus says the LORD of hosts, the God of Israel: Drink! Get drunk and vomit! Fall, never to rise, before the sword that I will send among you![x] 28 If they refuse to take the cup from your hand and drink, say to them: Thus says the LORD of hosts: You must drink![y] 29 Now that I am inflicting evil on this city, called by my name, how can you possibly escape? You shall not escape! I am calling down the sword upon all the inhabitants of the earth—oracle of the LORD of hosts. 30 As for you, prophesy against them all these words and say to them:

The LORD roars from on high,
  from his holy dwelling he raises his voice;
Mightily he roars over his sheepfold,
  a shout like that of vintagers echoes[z]
  over all the inhabitants of the earth.

25:15–17 Jeremiah is a prophet to the nations (cf. 1:5) as well as to his own people. All the nations mentioned here appear again in the more extensive collection of Jeremiah's oracles against the nations in chaps. 46–51.

25:15 Cup . . . wrath: a metaphor for destruction that occurs often in the Old Testament (cf. Ps 11:6; 75:9; Hb 2:15–16; Ez 23:31–33, etc.).

25:20 Uz: the homeland of legendary Job, in Edomite or Arabian territory.

25:22 The shores beyond the sea: Phoenician commercial colonies located throughout the Mediterranean world.

25:23 Dedan and Tema and Buz: North Arabian tribes.

25:26 Sheshach: a contrived word from the Hebrew letters of Babylon.

p: Jer 7:6–7. *q:* Jer 7:17–19. *r:* Jer 1:15; 43:10. *s:* Lv 26:32–35. *t:* Is 13:20–22. *u:* Jer 27:7; 50:9, 41–42; 51:6, 24. *v:* Rev 14:10. *w:* Jer 51:7. *x:* Ob 16. *y:* Jer 49:12. *z:* Jer 51:14.

31 The uproar spreads
to the end of the earth;
For the LORD has an indictment against
the nations,
he enters into judgment against all
flesh:
The wicked shall be given to the sword—
oracle of the LORD.
32 Thus says the LORD of hosts:
Look! disaster stalks
nation after nation;
A violent storm surges
from the recesses of the earth.

33 On that day, those whom the LORD has
slain will be strewn from one end of the earth
to the other. They will not be mourned, they
will not be gathered, they will not be buried;
they shall lie like dung upon the ground.[a]

34 Howl, you shepherds, and wail!
roll on the ground, leaders of the flock!
The time for your slaughter has come;
like choice rams you shall fall.
35 There is no flight for the shepherds,
no escape for the leaders of the flock.[b]
36 Listen! Wailing from the shepherds,
howling from the leaders of the flock!
For the LORD lays waste their grazing
place;
37 desolate are the peaceful pastures,
from the burning wrath of the LORD.
38 Like a lion he leaves his lair,
and their land is made desolate
By the sweeping sword,
and the burning wrath of the LORD.[c]

IV. The Temple Sermon

CHAPTER 26

See RG 303

Jeremiah Threatened with Death. 1 In
the beginning of the reign* of Jehoiakim, son
of Josiah, king of Judah, this word came
from the LORD: 2 Thus says the LORD: Stand
in the court of the house of the LORD and
speak to the inhabitants of all the cities of Judah who come to worship in the house of the
LORD; whatever I command you, tell them,
and hold nothing back.[d] 3 Perhaps they will
listen and turn, all of them from their evil
way, so that I may repent of the evil I plan to
inflict upon them for their evil deeds.[e] 4 Say
to them: Thus says the LORD: If you do not
obey me, by walking according to the law I
set before you 5 and listening to the words of
my servants the prophets, whom I kept sending you, even though you do not listen to
them,[f] 6 I will treat this house like Shiloh, and
make this city a curse for all the nations of
the earth.[g]

7 Now the priests, the prophets, and all the
people heard Jeremiah speaking these words
in the house of the LORD. 8 When Jeremiah
finished speaking all that the LORD commanded him to speak to all the people, then
the priests, the prophets, and all the people
laid hold of him, crying, "You must die!
9 Why do you prophesy in the name of the
LORD: 'This house shall become like Shiloh,' and 'This city shall be desolate, without
inhabitant'?" And all the people crowded
around Jeremiah in the house of the LORD.
10 When the princes of Judah heard about
these things, they came up from the house of
the king to the house of the LORD and convened at the New Gate of the house of the
LORD. 11 The priests and prophets said to the
princes and to all the people, "Sentence this
man to death! He has prophesied against this
city! You heard it with your own ears."[h]
12 Jeremiah said to the princes and all the
people: "It was the LORD who sent me to
prophesy against this house and city everything you have heard. 13 Now, therefore, reform your ways and your deeds; listen to the
voice of the LORD your God, so that the
LORD will have a change of heart regarding
the evil he has spoken against you.[i] 14 As for
me, I am in your hands; do with me what is
good and right in your eyes. 15 But you
should certainly know that by putting me to
death, you bring innocent blood on yourselves, on this city and its inhabitants. For in
truth it was the LORD who sent me to you, to
speak all these words for you to hear."

26:1 The beginning of the reign: a technical expression for the time between a king's accession to the throne and the beginning of his first official (calendar) year as king. Jehoiakim's first regnal year was 608 B.C.

a: Jer 8:2; 16:4, 6. *b:* Jer 32:4. *c:* Jer 4:7. *d:* Jer 7:2. *e:* Jer 18:3. *f:* Jer 25:4. *g:* Jer 7:12, 14. *h:* Jer 38:4. *i:* Jer 7:3.

16Then the princes and all the people said
to the priests and the prophets, "This man
does not deserve a death sentence; it is in the
name of the LORD, our God, that he speaks to
us." 17At this, some of the elders of the land
arose and said to the whole assembly of the
people, 18"Micah of Moresheth* used to
prophesy in the days of Hezekiah, king of
Judah, and he said to all the people of Judah:
Thus says the LORD of hosts:

Zion shall be plowed as a field,
  Jerusalem, a heap of ruins,
  and the temple mount,
  a forest ridge.[j]

19Did Hezekiah, king of Judah, and all Judah
condemn him to death? Did he not fear the
LORD and entreat the favor of the LORD, so
that the LORD had a change of heart regarding the evil he had spoken against them? We,
however, are about to do great evil against
ourselves."[k]

The Fate of Uriah. 20There was another
man who used to prophesy in the name of
the LORD, Uriah, son of Shemaiah, from Kiriath-jearim; he prophesied against this city
and this land the same message as Jeremiah.
21When King Jehoiakim and all his officers
and princes heard his words, the king sought
to have him killed. But Uriah heard of it and
fled in fear to Egypt. 22Then King Jehoiakim
sent Elnathan, son of Achbor, and others
with him into Egypt, 23and they brought
Uriah out of Egypt and took him to Jehoiakim the king, who struck him down with
the sword and threw his corpse into the common burial ground. 24But the hand of Ahikam, son of Shaphan,* protected Jeremiah,
so they did not hand him over to the people
to be put to death.

V. Controversies with the False Prophets

CHAPTER 27

See RG 303

Serve Babylon or Perish. 1In the beginning of the reign of Zedekiah,* son of Josiah, king of Judah, this word came to Jeremiah from the LORD: 2The LORD said to me:
Make for yourself thongs and yoke bars and
put them on your shoulders. 3Send them to
the kings of Edom, Moab, the Ammonites,
Tyre, and Sidon, through the ambassadors
who have come to Jerusalem to Zedekiah,
king of Judah,* 4and command them to tell
their lords: Thus says the LORD of hosts, the
God of Israel, Thus shall you say to your
lords: 5It was I who made the earth, human
being and beast on the face of the earth, by
my great power, with my outstretched arm;
and I can give them to whomever I think fit.[l]
6Now I have given all these lands into the
hand of Nebuchadnezzar, king of Babylon,
my servant; even the wild animals I have
given him to serve him.[m] 7All nations shall
serve him and his son and his grandson, until the time comes for him and his land; then
many nations and great kings will enslave
him.[n] 8Meanwhile, the nation or the kingdom that will not serve him, Nebuchadnezzar, king of Babylon, or bend its neck under
the yoke of the king of Babylon, I will punish that nation with sword, famine, and
pestilence—oracle of the LORD—until I finish them by his hand.[o]

9You, however, must not listen to your
prophets,* to your diviners and dreamers, to
your soothsayers and sorcerers, who say to
you, "Do not serve the king of Babylon."[p]
10For they prophesy lies to you, so as to

26:18 Micah of Moresheth: the prophet Micah, who appears among the canonical minor prophets (cf. Mi 1:1).

26:24 Ahikam, son of Shaphan: one of Josiah's officials (2 Kgs 22:12) and Jeremiah's friend. He was the father of Gedaliah, who was governor of Judah after Zedekiah's deportation (cf. Jer 39:14; 40:5–7).

27:1–29:32 A special collection of Jeremiah's prophecies dealing with false prophets. Stylistic peculiarities evident in the Hebrew suggest that these three chapters once existed as an independent work.

27:1 Zedekiah: The Hebrew text actually has "Jehoiakim," but the content of the chapter indicates that Zedekiah is intended.

27:3 The time is the fourth year of Zedekiah, 594 B.C., the occasion of a delegation from the neighboring states, doubtless for the purpose of laying plans against Nebuchadnezzar.

27:9 Your prophets: seers and diviners served non-Israelite kings just as the professional prophets served the kings of Judah.

j: Mi 1:1; 3:12. *k:* 2 Chr 32:26. *l:* Jer 32:17. *m:* Jer 25:9; 43:10; Ez 30:21, 25. *n:* Jer 25:11; 2 Chr 36:20. *o:* Jer 25:9; Bar 2:22. *p:* Jer 29:8.

drive you far from your land, making me banish you so that you perish.[q] 11The people that bends the neck to the yoke of the king of Babylon to serve him, I will leave in peace on its own land—oracle of the LORD—to cultivate it and dwell on it.[r]

12To Zedekiah, king of Judah, I spoke the same words: Bend your necks to the yoke of the king of Babylon; serve him and his people, so that you may live.[s] 13Why should you and your people die by sword, famine, and pestilence, in accordance with the word the LORD has spoken to the nation that will not serve the king of Babylon?[t] 14Do not listen to the words of the prophets who say to you, "Do not serve the king of Babylon." They prophesy lies to you![u] 15I did not send them—oracle of the LORD—but they prophesy falsely in my name. As a result I must banish you, and you will perish, you and the prophets who are prophesying to you.[v]

16[w] To the priests and to all the people I said: Thus says the LORD: Do not listen to the words of your prophets who prophesy to you: "The vessels of the house of the LORD will soon be brought back from Babylon," for they prophesy lies to you. 17Do not listen to them! Serve the king of Babylon that you may live. Why should this city become rubble? 18If they were prophets, if the word of the LORD were with them, then they would intercede with the LORD of hosts, that the vessels remaining in the house of the LORD and in the house of the king of Judah and in Jerusalem should not also go to Babylon. 19For thus says the LORD of hosts concerning the pillars, the sea, the stands, and the rest of the vessels remaining in this city, 20which Nebuchadnezzar, king of Babylon, did not take when he exiled Jeconiah, son of Jehoiakim, king of Judah, from Jerusalem to Babylon, along with all the nobles of Judah and Jerusalem— 21thus says the LORD of hosts, the God of Israel, concerning the vessels remaining in the house of the LORD, in the house of the king of Judah, and in Jerusalem:[x] 22To Babylon they shall go, and there they shall remain, until the day I look for them—oracle of the LORD; then I will bring them back and restore them to this place.

CHAPTER 28

See RG 303

The Two Yokes. 1That same year, in the beginning of the reign of Zedekiah, king of Judah, in the fifth month of the fourth year, Hananiah the prophet, son of Azzur, from Gibeon, said to me in the house of the LORD in the sight of the priests and all the people: 2"Thus says the LORD of hosts, the God of Israel: I have broken the yoke of the king of Babylon. 3Within two years I will restore to this place all the vessels of the house of the LORD which Nebuchadnezzar, king of Babylon, took from this place and carried away to Babylon. 4And Jeconiah, son of Jehoiakim, king of Judah, and all the exiles of Judah who went to Babylon, I will bring back to this place—oracle of the LORD—for I will break the yoke of the king of Babylon."

5Jeremiah the prophet answered the prophet Hananiah in the sight of the priests and all the people standing in the house of the LORD, 6and said: Amen! thus may the LORD do! May the LORD fulfill your words that you have prophesied, by bringing back the vessels of the house of the LORD and all the exiles from Babylon to this place! 7But now, listen to the word I am about to speak in your hearing and the hearing of all the people. 8In the past, the prophets who came before you and me prophesied war, disaster, and pestilence against many lands and mighty kingdoms. 9But the prophet who prophesies peace is recognized as the prophet whom the LORD has truly sent only when his word comes to pass.[y]

10Thereupon Hananiah the prophet took the yoke bar from the neck of Jeremiah the prophet and broke it. 11He said in the sight of all the people: "Thus says the LORD: Like this, within two years I will break the yoke of Nebuchadnezzar, king of Babylon, from the neck of all the nations." At that, the prophet Jeremiah went on his way.

12After Hananiah the prophet had broken the yoke bar off the neck of the prophet Jer-

q: Jer 14:13–16. *r:* Bar 2:21. *s:* Jer 38:17. *t:* Jer 24:8–10. *u:* Jer 14:14; 23:21. *v:* Jer 20:6. *w:* Jer 28:3; 2 Chr 36:7, 10, 18. *x:* 2 Kgs 25:13–17; 2 Chr 36:18, 22. *y:* Dt 18:22.

emiah, the word of the LORD came to Jeremiah: 13 Go tell Hananiah this: Thus says the LORD: By breaking a wooden yoke bar, you make an iron yoke! 14 For thus says the LORD of hosts, the God of Israel: A yoke of iron I have placed on the necks of all these nations serving Nebuchadnezzar, king of Babylon, and they shall serve him; even the wild animals I have given him.[z] 15 And Jeremiah the prophet said to Hananiah the prophet: Listen to this, Hananiah! The LORD has not sent you, and you have led this people to rely on deception. 16 For this, says the LORD, I am sending you from the face of the earth; this very year you shall die, because you have preached rebellion against the LORD.[a] 17 Hananiah the prophet died in that year, in the seventh month.

CHAPTER 29

See RG 303

Letter to the Exiles in Babylon. 1 These are the words of the scroll which Jeremiah the prophet sent from Jerusalem to the remaining elders among the exiles, to the priests, the prophets, and all the people whom Nebuchadnezzar exiled from Jerusalem to Babylon. 2 This was after King Jeconiah and the queen mother, the court officials, the princes of Judah and Jerusalem, the artisans and smiths had left Jerusalem.[b] 3 Delivered in Babylon by Elasah,* son of Shaphan, and by Gemariah, son of Hilkiah, whom Zedekiah, king of Judah, sent to the king of Babylon, the letter read:

4 Thus says the LORD of hosts, the God of Israel, to all the exiles whom I exiled from Jerusalem to Babylon: 5 Build houses and live in them; plant gardens and eat their fruits. 6 Take wives and have sons and daughters; find wives for your sons and give your daughters to husbands, so that they may bear sons and daughters. Increase there; do not decrease. 7 Seek the welfare of the city to which I have exiled you; pray for it to the LORD, for upon its welfare your own depends.[c] 8 For thus says the LORD of hosts, the God of Israel: Do not be deceived by the prophets and diviners who are among you; do not listen to those among you who dream dreams,[d] 9 for they prophesy lies to you in my name; I did not send them—oracle of the LORD.[e]

10 For thus says the LORD: Only after seventy years have elapsed for Babylon will I deal with you and fulfill for you my promise to bring you back to this place.[f] 11 For I know well the plans I have in mind for you—oracle of the LORD—plans for your welfare and not for woe, so as to give you a future of hope. 12 When you call me, and come and pray to me, I will listen to you.[g] 13 When you look for me, you will find me. Yes, when you seek me with all your heart, 14 I will let you find me—oracle of the LORD—and I will change your lot; I will gather you together from all the nations and all the places to which I have banished you—oracle of the LORD—and bring you back to the place from which I have exiled you.[h] 15 As for your saying, "The LORD has raised up for us prophets here in Babylon"—

16 Thus says the LORD concerning the king sitting on David's throne and all the people living in this city, your kinsmen who did not go with you into exile; 17 thus says the LORD of hosts: I am sending against them sword, famine, and pestilence. I will make them like rotten figs, so spoiled that they cannot be eaten. 18 I will pursue them with sword, famine, and pestilence, and make them an object of horror to all the kingdoms of the earth, a curse, a desolation, a hissing, and a reproach to all the nations among which I have banished them,[i] 19 because they did not listen to my words—oracle of the LORD—even though I kept sending them my servants the prophets, but they would not listen to them—oracle of the LORD.[j]

20 As for you, listen to the word of the LORD, all you exiles whom I sent away from

29:3 Elasah: probably the brother of Ahikam (cf. 26:24). **Gemariah**: probably the son of the high priest Hilkiah; cf. 2 Kgs 22:4. Zedekiah had dispatched these men to Nebuchadnezzar for some other purpose, possibly the payment of tribute, but Jeremiah took advantage of their mission to send his letter with them.

z: Jer 27:6–7; Dt 28:48. *a:* Dt 13:6. *b:* 2 Kgs 24:15. *c:* 1 Tm 2:1–2. *d:* Jer 27:9, 14. *e:* Jer 5:31. *f:* Jer 25:11; 2 Chr 36:21–22; Ezr 1:1; Dn 9:2; Zec 1:12; 7:5. *g:* Jer 33:3. *h:* Jer 23:3, 8. *i:* Jer 15:4; 24:9; 34:17–18. *j:* Jer 25:4.

Jerusalem to Babylon. 21This is what the LORD of hosts, the God of Israel, says about Ahab, son of Kolaiah, and Zedekiah, son of Maaseiah, who prophesy lies to you in my name: I am handing them over to Nebuchadnezzar, king of Babylon, who will kill them before your eyes.[k] 22And because of them this curse will be used by all the exiles of Judah in Babylon: "May the LORD make you like Zedekiah and Ahab, whom the king of Babylon roasted in fire," 23because they have committed an outrage in Israel, committing adultery with their neighbors' wives, and alleging in my name things I did not command. I know, I am witness—oracle of the LORD.[l]

The False Prophet Shemaiah. 24To Shemaiah, the Nehelamite, say: 25Thus says the LORD of hosts, the God of Israel: Because you sent documents in your own name to all the people in Jerusalem, to Zephaniah, the priest, son of Maaseiah, and to all the priests saying: 26* "It is the LORD who has appointed you priest in place of the priest Jehoiada, to provide officers for the house of the LORD, that you may confine in stocks or pillory any madman who poses as a prophet. 27Why, then, have you not rebuked Jeremiah of Anathoth who poses as a prophet among you? 28For he sent this message to us in Babylon: It will be a long time; build houses to live in; plant gardens and eat their fruit. . . ."

29When the priest Zephaniah read this letter to Jeremiah the prophet, 30the word of the LORD came to Jeremiah: 31Send to all the exiles: Thus says the LORD concerning Shemaiah, the Nehelamite: Because Shemaiah prophesies to you, although I did not send him, and has led you to rely on a lie, 32therefore thus says the LORD, I will punish Shemaiah, the Nehelamite, and his descendants. None of them shall dwell among this people to see the good I will do for this people—oracle of the LORD—because he preached rebellion against the LORD.

VI. Oracles of the Restoration of Israel and Judah

CHAPTER 30

See RG 303

The Restoration.* 1This word came to Jeremiah from the LORD: 2Thus says the LORD, the God of Israel: Write down on a scroll all the words I have spoken to you.[m] 3For indeed, the days are coming—oracle of the LORD—when I will restore the fortunes of my people Israel and Judah—oracle of the LORD. I will bring them back to the land which I gave to their ancestors, and they shall take possession of it.[n]

4These are the words the LORD spoke to Israel and to Judah: 5Thus says the LORD:

We hear a cry of fear:
  terror, not peace.
6 Inquire and see:
  does a male give birth?
Why, then, do I see all these men,
  their hands on their loins
Like women in labor,
  all their faces drained of color?[o]
7 Ah! How mighty is that day—
  there is none like it!
A time of distress for Jacob,
  though he shall be saved from it.[p]

8On that day—oracle of the LORD of hosts—I will break his yoke off your neck and snap your bonds. Strangers shall no longer enslave them;[q] 9instead, they shall serve the LORD, their God, and David, their king,* whom I will raise up for them.[r]

29:26–29 Jeremiah's message to Shemaiah is not completely preserved in the current Hebrew text, hence the incomplete sentence in vv. 25–28.

30:1–31:40 These two chapters contain salvation oracles that originally expressed the double expectation that the Lord would return the exiled survivors of the Northern Kingdom of Israel and reunite Israel and Judah as one kingdom under a just Davidic king. They were probably composed early in Josiah's reign (the reference of v. 9), when he took advantage of Assyria's internal disintegration and asserted control over northern Israel (cf. 2 Kgs 23:15–17). With the destruction of Jerusalem, the oracles were re-worked to include Judah and their fulfillment along with the renewal of the Davidic dynasty became associated with the eschatological "day of the Lord."

30:9 David, their king: a descendant of David ("his leader" in v. 21) who, like his ancestor, would rule a unified kingdom and "walk in the ways of the Lord," as the

k: Jer 14:14. *l:* Jer 23:14. *m:* Jer 36:2; Hb 2:2; Rev 1:11. *n:* Jer 29:14; 31:8, 10, 23; 32:37, 44; Ez 39:25; Am 9:14. *o:* Jer 6:24; 50:43. *p:* Am 5:18; Zep 1:14–15. *q:* Is 14:5–6; Ez 34:27. *r:* Ez 34:23; 37:24; Hos 3:5; Lk 1:69.

[10] But you, my servant Jacob, do not
fear!—oracle of the LORD—
do not be dismayed, Israel!
For I will soon deliver you from places
far away,
your offspring from the land of their
exile;
Jacob shall again find rest,
secure, with none to frighten him,[s]
[11] for I am with you—oracle of the
LORD—to save you.
I will bring to an end all the nations
among whom I have scattered you;
but you I will not bring to an end.
I will chastise you as you deserve,
I will not let you go unpunished.[t]
[12] For thus says the LORD:
Incurable is your wound,
grievous your injury;[u]
[13] There is none to plead your case,
no remedy for your running sore,
no healing for you.
[14] All your lovers have forgotten you,
they do not seek you out.
I struck you as an enemy would strike,
punishing you cruelly.[v]
[15] Why cry out over your wound?
There is no relief for your pain.
Because of your great guilt,
your numerous sins,
I have done this to you.[w]
[16] Yet all who devour you shall be
devoured,
all your enemies shall go into exile.
All who plunder you shall become
plunder,
all who pillage you I will hand over to
be pillaged.[x]
[17] For I will restore your health;
I will heal your injuries—oracle of the
LORD.
"The outcast" they have called you,
"whom no one looks for."[y]
[18] Thus says the LORD:
See! I will restore the fortunes of Jacob's
tents,
on his dwellings I will have compassion;
A city shall be rebuilt upon its own ruins,
a citadel restored where it should be.[z]
[19] From them will come praise,
the sound of people rejoicing.
I will increase them, they will not
decrease,
I will glorify them, they will not be
insignificant.[a]
[20] His children shall be as of old,
his assembly shall stand firm in my
presence,
I will punish all his oppressors.[b]
[21] His leader* shall be one of his own,
and his ruler shall emerge from his
ranks.
He shall approach me when I summon
him;
Why else would he dare
approach me?—oracle of the LORD.
[22] You shall be my people,
and I will be your God.[c]
[23] Look! The storm of the LORD!
His wrath breaks out
In a whirling storm
that bursts upon the heads of the
wicked.[d]
[24] The anger of the LORD will not abate
until he has carried out completely
the decisions of his heart.
In days to come
you will fully understand it.[e]

CHAPTER 31

See RG 303

Good News of the Return

[1] At that time—oracle of the LORD—
I will be the God of all the families of
Israel,

Deuteronomistic historians claimed David did. Other prophets also refer to this idealized ruler as "David"; cf. Ez 34:23–24; 37:24–25; Hos 3:5.

30:21 His leader: cf. v. 9. **Approach me**: i.e., in the sanctuary of the Temple for worship. This new David is given a priestly function to perform on behalf of the assembly. To approach God on one's own brings death; cf. Lv 16:1–2.

31:2–3 Jeremiah describes the exiles of the Northern Kingdom on their way home from the nations where the Assyrians had resettled them (722/721 B.C.). The favor they discover in the wilderness is the appearance of the Lord (v. 3) coming to guide them to Jerusalem. Implicit in these verses is the presentation of the people's return from captivity as a second exodus, a unifying theme in Second Isaiah (chaps. 40–55).

s: Jer 46:27; Is 43:5. *t:* Jer 46:28; Ez 11:16–17; Am 9:8–9. *u:* Jer 10:19; 14:17; 15:18. *v:* Jer 22:22; Lam 1:19. *w:* Jer 15:18. *x:* Jer 2:3. *y:* Jer 33:6. *z:* Jer 33:7, 11; Ezr 6:3–15; Ez 36:10. *a:* Is 35:10; 51:11. *b:* Is 49:26. *c:* Jer 24:7; 31:1, 33; 32:38; Lv 26:12; Ez 11:20; 36:28. *d:* Jer 23:19. *e:* Jer 23:20.

and they shall be my people.[f]
2 * Thus says the LORD:
The people who escaped the sword
find favor in the wilderness.
As Israel comes forward to receive rest,
3 from afar the LORD appears:
With age-old love I have loved you;
so I have kept my mercy toward you.[g]
4 Again I will build you, and you shall stay built,
virgin Israel;
Carrying your festive tambourines,
you shall go forth dancing with merrymakers.
5 You shall again plant vineyards
on the mountains of Samaria;
those who plant them shall enjoy their fruits.[h]
6 Yes, a day will come when the watchmen
call out on Mount Ephraim:
"Come, let us go up to Zion,
to the LORD, our God."[i]

The Road of Return

7 For thus says the LORD:
Shout with joy for Jacob,
exult at the head of the nations;
proclaim your praise and say:
The LORD has saved his people,
the remnant of Israel.[j]
8 Look! I will bring them back
from the land of the north;
I will gather them from the ends of the earth,
the blind and the lame in their midst,
Pregnant women, together with those in labor—
an immense throng—they shall return.[k]
9 With weeping they shall come,
but with compassion I will guide them;
I will lead them to streams of water,
on a level road, without stumbling.
For I am a father to Israel,
Ephraim is my firstborn.[l]
10 Hear the word of the LORD, you nations,
proclaim it on distant coasts, and say:
The One who scattered Israel, now gathers them;
he guards them as a shepherd his flock.
11 The LORD shall ransom Jacob,
he shall redeem him from a hand too strong for him.[m]
12 Shouting, they shall mount the heights of Zion,
they shall come streaming to the LORD's blessings:
The grain, the wine, and the oil,
flocks of sheep and cattle;
They themselves shall be like watered gardens,
never again neglected.[n]
13 Then young women shall make merry and dance,
young men and old as well.
I will turn their mourning into joy,
I will show them compassion and have them rejoice after their sorrows.
14 I will lavish choice portions on the priests,
and my people shall be filled with my blessings—
oracle of the LORD.

End of Rachel's Mourning

15 Thus says the LORD:
In Ramah* is heard the sound of sobbing,
bitter weeping!
Rachel mourns for her children,
she refuses to be consoled
for her children—they are no more![o]
16 Thus says the LORD:
Cease your cries of weeping,
hold back your tears!
There is compensation for your labor—
oracle of the LORD—
they shall return from the enemy's land.

31:15 Ramah: a village about five miles north of Jerusalem, where one tradition locates Rachel's tomb (1 Sm 10:2). The wife of Jacob/Israel, Rachel is the matriarchal ancestor of Ephraim, chief among the northern tribes. She personified Israel as a mother whose grief for her lost children is especially poignant because she had to wait a long time to bear them. Mt 2:18 applies this verse to Herod's slaughter of the innocents.

f: Jer 30:22. *g:* Dt 7:8; 10:15; Is 43:4; 63:9; Hos 11:1, 4. *h:* Dt 28:30; Is 65:21; Am 9:14. *i:* Is 2:3; 27:13; Mi 4:2. *j:* Is 12:6. *k:* Jer 3:18; 23:3, 8; Is 35:5–6. *l:* Ex 4:22. *m:* Is 44:23; 48:20. *n:* Is 58:11. *o:* Mt 2:18.

17 There is hope for your future—oracle of
the LORD—
your children shall return to their own
territory.[p]
18 Indeed, I heard Ephraim rocking in grief:
You chastised me, and I was chastised;
I was like an untamed calf.
Bring me back, let me come back,
for you are the LORD, my God.[q]
19 For after I turned away, I repented;
after I came to myself, I struck my
thigh;*
I was ashamed, even humiliated,
because I bore the disgrace of my
youth.[r]
20 Is Ephraim not my favored son,
the child in whom I delight?
Even though I threaten him,
I must still remember him!
My heart stirs for him,
I must show him compassion!—oracle
of the LORD.[s]

Summons To Return Home

21 Set up road markers,
put up signposts;
Turn your attention to the highway,
the road you walked.
Turn back, virgin Israel,
turn back to these your cities.
22 How long will you continue to hesitate,
rebellious daughter?
The LORD has created a new thing upon
the earth:
woman encompasses man.*

23 Thus says the LORD of hosts, the God of
Israel: When I restore their fortunes in the
land of Judah and in its cities, they shall
again use this greeting: "May the LORD bless
you, Tent of Justice, Holy Mountain!"[t] 24 Judah and all its cities, the farmers and those
who lead the flock shall dwell there together.
25 For I will slake the thirst of the faint; the
appetite of all the weary I will satisfy. 26 At
this I awoke and opened my eyes; my sleep
was satisfying.*

27 See, days are coming—oracle of the
LORD—when I will sow the house of Israel
and the house of Judah with the seed of human beings and the seed of animals. 28 As I
once watched over them to uproot and tear
down, to demolish, to destroy, and to harm,
so I will watch over them to build and to
plant—oracle of the LORD.[u] 29 In those days
they shall no longer say,

"The parents ate unripe grapes,[v]
and the children's teeth are set on
edge,"*

30 but all shall die because of their own iniquity: the teeth of anyone who eats unripe
grapes shall be set on edge.

The New Covenant.* 31 See, days are coming—oracle of the LORD—when I will make
a new covenant with the house of Israel and
the house of Judah.[w] 32 It will not be like the
covenant I made with their ancestors the day
I took them by the hand to lead them out of
the land of Egypt. They broke my covenant,
though I was their master—oracle of the
LORD.[x] 33 But this is the covenant I will make
with the house of Israel after those days—oracle of the LORD. I will place my law within

31:19 Struck my thigh: a gesture signifying grief and dread (cf. Ez 21:17).

31:22 No satisfactory explanation has been given for this text. Jerome, for example, saw the image as a reference to the infant Jesus enclosed in Mary's womb. Since Jeremiah often uses marital imagery in his description of a restored Israel, the phrase may refer to a wedding custom, perhaps women circling the groom in a dance. It may also be a metaphor describing the security of a new Israel, a security so complete that it defies the imagination and must be expressed as hyperbolic role reversal: any danger will be so insignificant that women can protect their men.

31:26 I awoke . . . satisfying: an intrusive comment.

31:29 "The parents . . . on edge": Jeremiah's opponents use this proverb to complain that they are being punished for sins of their ancestors. Jeremiah, however, insists that the Lord knows the depth of their wickedness and holds them accountable for their actions.

31:31–34 The new covenant is an occasional prophetic theme, beginning with Hosea. According to Jeremiah, (a) it lasts forever; (b) its law (*torah*) is written in human hearts; (c) it gives everyone true knowledge of God, making additional instruction (*torah*) unnecessary. The Dead Sea Scroll community claimed they were partners in a "new covenant." The New Testament presents the death and resurrection of Jesus of Nazareth as inaugurating a new covenant open to anyone who professes faith in Jesus the Christ. Cf. Lk 22:20; 1 Cor 11:25; Heb 8:8–12. **Know the LORD**: cf. note on 22:15–16.

p: Jer 29:10–14. *q:* Lv 26:40–42. *r:* Dt 30:1–3. *s:* Hos 11:8. *t:* Jer 30:3; Ps 122:8. *u:* Jer 1:10; 18:7. *v:* Dt 24:16; Ez 18:2. *w:* Jer 32:40; Heb 9:15. *x:* Ex 24:7–8; Dt 5:2.

them, and write it upon their hearts; I will be
their God, and they shall be my people.[y]
34 They will no longer teach their friends and
relatives, "Know the LORD!" Everyone, from
least to greatest, shall know me—oracle of
the LORD—for I will forgive their iniquity
and no longer remember their sin.[z]

Certainty of God's Promise

35 Thus says the LORD,
Who gives the sun to light the day,
moon and stars to light the night;
Who stirs up the sea so that its waves
roar,
whose name is LORD of hosts:[a]
36 If ever this fixed order gives way
before me—oracle of the LORD—
Then would the offspring of Israel cease
as a people before me forever.[b]
37 Thus says the LORD:
If the heavens on high could be
measured,
or the foundations below the earth be
explored,
Then would I reject all the offspring of
Israel
because of all they have done—oracle
of the LORD.

Jerusalem Rebuilt.* 38 See, days are coming—oracle of the LORD—when the city
shall be rebuilt as the LORD's,[c] from the
Tower of Hananel to the Corner Gate. 39 A
measuring line shall be stretched from there
straight to the hill Gareb and then turn to
Goah. 40 The whole valley of corpses and
ashes, all the terraced slopes toward the
Wadi Kidron, as far as the corner of the
Horse Gate at the east, shall be holy to the
LORD. Never again shall the city be uprooted
or demolished.

CHAPTER 32

See RG 303

Pledge of Restoration.* 1 The word
came to Jeremiah from the LORD in the tenth
year of Zedekiah,* king of Judah, the eighteenth year of Nebuchadnezzar. 2 At that time
the army of the king of Babylon was besieging Jerusalem, while Jeremiah the prophet
was confined to the court of the guard, in the
house of the king of Judah.[d] 3 Zedekiah, king
of Judah, had confined him there, saying:
"How dare you prophesy: Thus says the
LORD: I am handing this city over to the king
of Babylon that he may capture it.[e] 4 Zedekiah, king of Judah, shall not escape the
hands of the Chaldeans: he shall indeed be
handed over to the king of Babylon. He shall
speak with him face to face and see him eye
to eye.[f] 5 He shall take Zedekiah to Babylon.
There he shall remain, until I attend to him—
oracle of the LORD. If you fight against the
Chaldeans, you cannot win!"[g]
6* Jeremiah said, This word came to me
from the LORD: 7 Hanamel, son of your uncle
Shallum, will come to you with the offer:[h]
"Purchase my field in Anathoth, since you,
as nearest relative, have the first right of purchase."* 8 And, just as the LORD had said, my
cousin Hanamel came to me in the court of
the guard and said, "Please purchase my
field in Anathoth, in the territory of Benjamin; as nearest relative, you have the first
right of possession—purchase it for your-

31:38–40 The landmarks in these verses outline the borders of Jerusalem during the time of Nehemiah: the Tower of Hananel (Neh 3:1; 12:39) in the northeast and the Corner Gate (2 Kgs 14:13) in the northwest; Goah in the southeast and Gareb Hill in the southwest; the Valley of Ben-hinnom ("the Valley of corpses and ashes"), which met the Wadi Kidron in the southeast, and the Horse Gate in the eastern wall at the southeast corner of the Temple area.

32:1–44 This chapter recounts a prophecy "in action." At the Lord's command, Jeremiah fulfills his family duty to purchase the land of his cousin, carrying out all the legal details, even putting the deed away for safekeeping against the day he will have to produce it to verify his ownership of the land. The Lord defines the meaning of this symbolic action: In the future, Judah will be restored and daily life will return to normal.

32:1 The tenth year of Zedekiah: 588 B.C. **The eighteenth year of Nebuchadnezzar**: dating his reign from his victory at Carchemish; see note on 25:1–14.

32:6–9 Jeremiah's imprisonment by the weak-willed Zedekiah was a technical custody that did not deprive him of all freedom of action.

32:7 The first right of purchase: the obligation of the closest relative to redeem the property of a family member in economic distress so that the ancestral land remains within the family (Lv 25:25–28); see note on Ru 2:20.

y: Jer 32:40; Ez 37:26; Heb 10:16. *z:* Is 54:13. *a:* Gn 1:14–18. *b:* Jer 33:20–21. *c:* Neh 12:38; Zec 14:10–11. *d:* Jer 33:1; 37:20; 38:6; 39:14. *e:* Jer 26:9; 34:2; 37:6–10. *f:* Jer 34:3; 38:18, 23; 39:4–7. *g:* Jer 39:7; 52:11. *h:* Lv 25:24–34; Ru 4:4.

self." Then I knew this was the word of the LORD. 9 So I bought the field in Anathoth from my cousin Hanamel, weighing out for him the silver, seventeen shekels of silver.

10 When I had written and sealed the deed, called witnesses and weighed out the silver on the scales, 11 I accepted the deed of purchase, both the sealed copy, containing title and conditions, and the open copy.* 12 I gave this deed of purchase to Baruch, son of Neriah, son of Mahseiah, in the presence of my cousin Hanamel and the witnesses who had signed the deed of purchase and before all the Judahites sitting around in the court of the guard.[i]

13 In their presence I gave Baruch this charge: 14 Thus says the LORD of hosts, the God of Israel: Take these deeds of purchase, both the sealed and the open deeds, and put them in an earthenware jar,* so they can last a long time. 15 For thus says the LORD of hosts, the God of Israel: They shall again purchase houses and fields and vineyards in this land.

16 After I had given the deed of purchase to Baruch, son of Neriah, I prayed to the LORD: 17 Ah, my Lord GOD! You made the heavens and the earth with your great power and your outstretched arm; nothing is too difficult for you.[j] 18 You continue your kindness through a thousand generations; but you repay the ancestors' guilt upon their children who follow them. Great and mighty God, whose name is LORD of hosts,[k] 19 great in counsel, mighty in deed, whose eyes are fixed on all the ways of mortals, giving to all according to their ways, according to the fruit of their deeds:[l] 20 you performed signs and wonders in the land of Egypt and to this day, in Israel and among all peoples, you have made a name for yourself as on this day.[m] 21 You brought your people Israel out of the land of Egypt with signs and wonders, with a strong hand and an outstretched arm, and great terror. 22 And you gave them this land, as you had sworn to their ancestors to give them, a land flowing with milk and honey.[n] 23 They went in and took possession of it, but they did not listen to your voice. They did not live by your law; they did not do anything you commanded them to do. Then you made all this evil fall upon them.[o] 24 See, the siegeworks have arrived at this city to capture it; the city is handed over to the Chaldeans who are attacking it, with sword, starvation, and disease. What you threatened has happened—you can see it for yourself.[p] 25 Yet you told me, my Lord GOD: Purchase the field with silver and summon witnesses, when the city has already been handed over to the Chaldeans!

26 Then this word of the LORD came to Jeremiah: 27 I am the LORD, the God of all the living! Is anything too difficult for me? 28 Therefore the LORD says: I am handing over this city to the Chaldeans and to Nebuchadnezzar, king of Babylon, and he shall capture it. 29 The Chaldeans who are attacking this city shall go in and set the city on fire, burning it and the houses, on whose roofs incense was burned to Baal and libations were poured out to other gods in order to provoke me.[q] 30 From their youth the Israelites and the Judahites have been doing only what is evil in my eyes; the Israelites have been provoking me with the works of their hands—oracle of the LORD.[r] 31 This city has so stirred my anger and wrath, from the day it was built to this day, that I must put it out of my sight, 32 for all the evil the Israelites and Judahites have done to provoke me—they, their kings, their princes, their priests, and their prophets, the people of Judah and the inhabitants of Jerusalem.[s] 33 They turned their backs to me, not their faces; though I taught them persistently, they would not listen or accept correction.[t] 34 Instead they set up their abominations in the house which bears my name in order to de-

32:11 The sealed copy . . . and the open copy: the legal deed of sale was written on a scroll, which was then rolled up and sealed; a second scroll containing a copy of the legal deed was then rolled around it and left unsealed so the contents of the legal deed would be accessible without destroying the original seal.

32:14 In an earthenware jar: to protect the scroll from drying out and disintegrating. Some of the Dead Sea Scrolls were found in such jars.

i: Jer 36:4. *j:* 2 Kgs 19:15; Jb 42:2. *k:* Ex 20:5–6; 34:6; Dt 5:9. *l:* Jb 34:21; Ps 33:13–15. *m:* Ex 6:6; Dt 4:34; Ps 135:9. *n:* Jer 11:5; Gn 15:18; 17:8; 26:3. *o:* Jer 7:24–26; Dn 9:10–14. *p:* Jer 21:5; 33:4. *q:* Jer 21:10; 37:8–10. *r:* Jer 3:25; 44:8. *s:* Jer 2:26; Is 3:8. *t:* Jer 7:24.

file it.[u] [35]They built high places to Baal in the Valley of Ben-hinnom to sacrifice their sons and daughters to Molech;* I never commanded them to do this, nor did it even enter my mind that they would practice this abomination, so as to bring sin upon Judah.[v]

[36]Now, therefore, thus says the LORD, the God of Israel, concerning this city, which you say is being handed over to the king of Babylon by means of the sword, starvation, and disease: [37]See, I am gathering them from all the lands to which I drove them in my rising fury and great anger; I will bring them back to this place and settle them here in safety.[w] [38]They shall be my people, and I will be their God.[x] [39]I will give them one heart and one way, that they may fear me always, for their own good and the good of their children after them. [40]With them I will make an everlasting covenant, never to cease doing good to them; I will put fear of me in their hearts so that they never turn away from me.[y] [41]I will take delight in doing good to them: I will plant them firmly in this land, with all my heart and soul.[z]

[42]For thus says the LORD: Just as I have brought upon this people all this great evil, so I will bring upon them all the good I have promised them.[a] [43]Fields shall be purchased in this land, about which you say, "It is a wasteland, without human beings or animals, handed over to the Chaldeans."[b] [44]They will purchase fields with silver, write up deeds, seal them, and have them witnessed in the land of Benjamin, in the neighborhood of Jerusalem, in the cities of Judah and of the hill country, in the cities of the Shephelah and the Negeb, when I restore their fortunes—oracle of the LORD.[c]

CHAPTER 33

See RG 303

Restoration of Jerusalem. [1]The word of the LORD came to Jeremiah a second time while he was still confined in the court of the guard: [2]Thus says the LORD who made the earth, giving it shape and stability, LORD is his name: [3]Call to me, and I will answer you; I will tell you great things beyond the reach of your knowledge.[d] [4]Thus says the LORD, the God of Israel, concerning the houses of this city and the houses of the kings of Judah, which are being torn down because of the siegeworks and the sword:[e] [5]men come to battle the Chaldeans, and to fill these houses with the corpses of those whom I have struck down in my raging anger, when I hid my face from this city because of all their wickedness.[f]

[6]Look! I am bringing the city recovery and healing; I will heal them and reveal to them an abundance of lasting peace.[g] [7]I will restore the fortunes of Judah and Israel, and rebuild them as they were in the beginning.[h] [8]I will purify them of all the guilt they incurred by sinning against me; I will forgive all their offenses by which they sinned and rebelled against me.[i] [9]Then this city shall become joy for me, a name of praise and pride, before all the nations of the earth, as they hear of all the good I am doing for them. They shall fear and tremble because of all the prosperity I give it.

[10]Thus says the LORD: In this place, about which you say: "It is a waste without people or animals!" and in the cities of Judah, in the streets of Jerusalem now deserted, without people, without inhabitant, without animal, there shall yet be heard[j] [11]the song of joy, the song of gladness, the song of the bridegroom, the song of the bride, the song of those bringing thank offerings to the house of the LORD: "Give thanks to the LORD of hosts, for the LORD is good; God's love endures forever." For I will restore the fortunes of this land as they were in the beginning, says the LORD.[k]

[12]Thus says the LORD of hosts: In this place, now a waste, without people or animals, and in all its cities there shall again be sheepfolds for the shepherds to rest their

32:35 Molech: a god to whom human sacrifice was offered in the Valley of Ben-hinnom. Here, as in 19:5, he is called "Baal"; see note on Lv 18:21.

u: Jer 7:30; 2 Kgs 21:4–5. *v:* Jer 7:31; 19:5; Ps 106:37–38. *w:* Jer 23:3; 29:14; Is 11:12; Ez 11:17. *x:* Jer 24:7; 31:33. *y:* Jer 31:31–33. *z:* Dt 30:9. *a:* Jer 33:10–14; Zec 8:13. *b:* Jer 33:10. *c:* Jer 17:26; 33:7. *d:* Is 48:6. *e:* Jer 32:24. *f:* Jer 21:4–6. *g:* Is 57:18. *h:* Jer 30:3; 32:44. *i:* Ez 36:25. *j:* Jer 32:43. *k:* 1 Chr 16:34; Ezr 3:11; Ps 136:1.

flocks. 13 In the cities of the hill country, of the Shephelah and the Negeb, in the land of Benjamin and the neighborhood of Jerusalem, and in the cities of Judah, flocks will again pass under the hands of the one who counts them, says the LORD.

14* The days are coming—oracle of the LORD—when I will fulfill the promise I made to the house of Israel and the house of Judah. 15 In those days, at that time, I will make a just shoot spring up for David; he shall do what is right and just in the land.[l] 16 In those days Judah shall be saved and Jerusalem shall dwell safely; this is the name they shall call her: "The LORD our justice." 17 For thus says the LORD: David shall never lack a successor on the throne of the house of Israel,[m] 18 nor shall the priests of Levi ever be lacking before me, to sacrifice burnt offerings, to burn cereal offerings, and to make sacrifices.[n]

19 This word of the LORD also came to Jeremiah: 20 Thus says the LORD: If you can break my covenant with day[o] and my covenant with night so that day and night no longer appear in their proper time, 21 only then can my covenant with my servant David be broken, so that he will not have a descendant to act as king upon his throne, and my covenant with the priests of Levi who minister to me. 22 Just as the host of heaven cannot be numbered and the sands of the sea cannot be counted, so I will multiply the descendants of David my servant and the Levites who minister to me.

23 This word of the LORD came to Jeremiah: 24 Have you not noticed what these people are saying: "The LORD has rejected the two tribes he had chosen"? They hold my people in contempt as if it were no longer a nation in their eyes.[p] 25[q] Thus says the LORD: If I have no covenant with day and night, if I did not establish statutes for heaven and earth, 26 then I will also reject the descendants of Jacob and of David my servant, no longer selecting from his descendants rulers for the offspring of Abraham, Isaac, and Jacob. Yes, I will restore their fortunes and show them mercy.

CHAPTER 34

See RG 303

Fate of Zedekiah. 1 The word which came to Jeremiah from the LORD while Nebuchadnezzar, king of Babylon, and all his army and all the earth's kingdoms under his rule, and all the peoples were attacking Jerusalem and all her cities:[r] 2 Thus says the LORD, the God of Israel: Go to Zedekiah, king of Judah, and tell him: Thus says the LORD: I am handing this city over to the king of Babylon; he will burn it with fire.[s] 3 You yourself shall not escape his hand; rather you will be captured and fall into his hand. You shall see the king of Babylon eye to eye and speak to him face to face. Then you shall go to Babylon.[t]

4 Just hear the word of the LORD, Zedekiah, king of Judah! Then, says the LORD concerning you, you shall not die by the sword. 5 You shall die in peace, and they will burn spices for you as they did for your ancestors, the earlier kings who preceded you, and they shall make lament over you, "Alas, Lord." I myself make this promise—oracle of the LORD.

6 Jeremiah the prophet told all these things to Zedekiah, king of Judah, in Jerusalem, 7 while the army of the king of Babylon was attacking Jerusalem and the remaining cities of Judah, Lachish, and Azekah.* Only these fortified cities were left standing out of all the cities of Judah!

The Pact Broken.* 8 This is the word that came to Jeremiah from the LORD after King

33:14–26 This is the longest continuous passage in the Hebrew text of Jeremiah that is missing from the Greek text of Jeremiah. It is probably the work of a postexilic writer who applied parts of Jeremiah's prophecies to new situations. The hope for an eternal Davidic dynasty (vv. 14–17; cf. 2 Sm 7:11–16) and for a perpetual priesthood and sacrificial system (v. 18) was not realized after the exile. On the canonical authority of the Septuagint, see note on Dn 13:1–14:42.

34:7 Lachish, and Azekah: fortress towns southwest of Jerusalem which Nebuchadnezzar besieged to prevent any help coming to Jerusalem from Egypt. At Lachish, archaeologists found several letters written on ostraca (pottery fragments) dated to 598 or 588 B.C., which mention both Lachish and Azekah.

34:8–22 During the siege of Jerusalem, its citizens made a covenant at Zedekiah's instigation to free Judahites they held in servitude, thus providing additional defenders for the city,

l: Jer 23:5; Ps 72:1–4, 12–14; Is 11:1. *m:* 2 Sm 7:16; 1 Kgs 2:4; Ps 89:4–5, 29, 36–37. *n:* Ez 44:15–16. *o:* Jer 31:36–37; Ps 89:37–38. *p:* Rom 11:1–2. *q:* Jer 31:36–37; 32:44. *r:* Jer 52:4; 2 Kgs 25:1. *s:* Jer 21:10; 32:3, 28. *t:* Jer 32:4; 52:11.

Zedekiah had made a covenant with all the people in Jerusalem to proclaim freedom: 9 Everyone must free their Hebrew slaves, male and female, so that no one should hold another Judahite in servitude.[u] 10 All the princes and the people who entered this covenant agreed to set free their slaves, their male and female servants, so that they should no longer be in servitude. But even though they agreed and freed them, 11 afterward they took back their male and female servants whom they had set free and again forced them into servitude.

12 Then this word of the LORD came to Jeremiah: 13 Thus says the LORD, the God of Israel: I myself made a covenant with your ancestors the day I brought them out of the land of Egypt, out of the house of slavery: 14 Every seventh year each of you must set free all Hebrews who have sold themselves to you; six years they shall serve you, but then you shall let them go free. Your ancestors, however, did not listen to me or obey me. 15 As for you, today you repented and did what is right in my eyes by proclaiming freedom for your neighbor and making a covenant before me in the house which bears my name. 16 But then you again profaned my name by taking back your male and female slaves whom you had just set free for life; you forced them to become your slaves again.[v] 17 Therefore, thus says the LORD: You for your part did not obey me by proclaiming freedom for your families and neighbors. So I now proclaim freedom for you—oracle of the LORD—for the sword, starvation, and disease. I will make you an object of horror to all the kingdoms of the earth. 18* Those who violated my covenant and did not observe the terms of the covenant they made in my presence—I will make them like the calf which they cut in two so they could pass between its parts— 19 the princes of Judah and of Jerusalem, the court officials, the priests, and all the people of the land, who passed between the parts of the calf. 20 These I will hand over to their enemies, to those who seek their lives: their corpses shall become food for the birds of the air and the beasts of the field.[w]

21 Zedekiah, king of Judah, and his princes, I will hand also over to their enemies, to those who seek their lives, to the army of the king of Babylon which is now withdrawing from you.[x] 22 I am giving the command—oracle of the LORD—to bring them back to this city. They shall attack and capture it, and burn it with fire; the cities of Judah I will turn into a waste, where no one dwells.[y]

CHAPTER 35

See RG 303

The Faithful Rechabites. 1 The word that came to Jeremiah from the LORD in the days of Jehoiakim,* son of Josiah, king of Judah: 2 Go to the house* of the Rechabites, speak to them, and bring them to the house of the LORD, to one of the rooms there, and give them wine to drink. 3 So I took Jaazaniah, son of Jeremiah, son of Habazziniah, his brothers and all his sons—the whole house of the Rechabites— 4 and I brought them to the house of the LORD, to the room of the sons of Hanan,* son of Igdaliah, the man of God, next to the room of the princes above the room of Maaseiah, son of Shal-

leaving slave owners with fewer mouths to feed, and making reparation for past violations of the law, which dictated that Hebrew slaves should serve no longer than six years (Dt 15:12–15). But when the siege was temporarily lifted, when the assistance promised by Pharaoh Hophra arrived (cf. Jer 37:5), the inhabitants of Jerusalem broke the covenant and once more pressed their fellow citizens into slavery (v. 11).

34:18–19 Both the Old Testament (Gn 15:10–17) and the eighth century B.C. Sefire inscription indicate that sometimes contracting parties ratified an agreement by walking between dismembered animals, invoking upon themselves the animals' fate if they failed to keep their word. **The covenant**: that mentioned in vv. 10, 15.

35:1 In the days of Jehoiakim: probably in 599 or 598 B.C. (cf. 2 Kgs 24:1–2).

35:2 House: both members of the family of Rechab (cf. v. 3) and the place where they live; cf. note on v. 11. **The Rechabites**: traditionalists who rejected the settled agricultural and urban cultures to which other Israelites had assimilated, maintaining their loyalty to the Lord by perpetuating the semi-nomadic life of their distant ancestors (cf. 2 Kgs 10:15–17). Jeremiah contrasts their adherence to their vows with the Judahites' disregard for divine commands.

35:4 The sons of Hanan: probably disciples of Hanan. **Man of God**: occurring only here in Jeremiah, the title frequently is applied to prophets: e.g., Samuel (1 Sm 9:6–10), Elijah (2 Kgs 1:9–13), Elisha (2 Kgs 4–13). Whatever the function of the sons of Hanan, they encourage Jeremiah by

u: Ex 21:2–4; Lv 25:39, 46; Dt 15:12–15. *v:* Lv 19:12. *w:* Jer 7:33; 16:4; 19:7. *x:* Jer 37:5, 11. *y:* Jer 37:8; 52:7–13; 2 Chr 36:17, 19.

lum, the guard at the entrance. 5I set before the Rechabites bowls full of wine, and cups, and said to them, "Drink some wine."

6"We do not drink wine," they said to me; "Jonadab,* Rechab's son, our father, commanded us, 'Neither you nor your children shall ever drink wine.[z] 7Build no house and sow no seed; do not plant vineyards or own any. You must dwell in tents all your lives, so that you may live long on the land where you live as resident aliens.' 8We have obeyed Jonadab, Rechab's son, our father, in everything that he commanded us: not drinking wine as long as we live—neither we nor our wives nor our sons nor our daughters; 9not building houses to live in; not owning vineyards or fields or crops. 10We live in tents, doing everything our father Jonadab commanded us. 11But when Nebuchadnezzar, king of Babylon, invaded this land, we said, 'Come, let us go into Jerusalem to escape the army of the Chaldeans and the army of the Arameans.'* That is why we are now living in Jerusalem."[a]

12Then the word of the LORD came to Jeremiah: 13Thus says the LORD of hosts, the God of Israel: Go, say to the people of Judah and to the inhabitants of Jerusalem: Will you not take correction and obey my words?—oracle of the LORD.[b] 14The words of Jonadab, Rechab's son, by which he commanded his children not to drink wine, have been upheld: to this day they have not drunk wine; they obeyed their ancestor's command. I, however, have spoken to you time and again. But you did not obey me![c] 15Time and again I sent you all my servants the prophets, saying: Turn away, each of you, from your evil way and reform your actions! Do not follow other gods to serve them that you may remain in the land which I gave you and your ancestors. But you did not pay attention. You did not obey me.[d] 16Yes, the children of Jonadab, Rechab's son, upheld the command which their father laid on them. But this people has not obeyed me! 17Now, therefore, says the LORD God of hosts, the God of Israel: I will soon bring upon Judah and all the inhabitants of Jerusalem every evil with which I threatened them because I spoke but they did not obey, I called but they did not answer.[e]

18But to the house of the Rechabites Jeremiah said: Thus says the LORD of hosts, the God of Israel: Since you have obeyed the command of Jonadab, your father, kept all his commands and done everything he commanded you, 19therefore, thus says the LORD of hosts, the God of Israel: Never shall there fail to be a descendant of Jonadab, Rechab's son, standing in my presence.

VII. Jeremiah and the Fall of Jerusalem

CHAPTER 36

See RG 303

Baruch, the Scribe of Jeremiah. 1In the fourth year of Jehoiakim, son of Josiah, king of Judah, this word came to Jeremiah from the LORD: 2Take a scroll and write on it all the words I have spoken to you about Israel, Judah, and all the nations, from the day I first spoke to you, from the days of Josiah, until today. 3Perhaps, if the house of Judah hears all the evil I have in mind to do to them, so that all of them turn from their evil way, then I can forgive their wickedness and their sin.[f] 4So Jeremiah called Baruch, son of Neriah, and he wrote down on a scroll what Jeremiah said, all the words which the LORD had spoken to him. 5Then Jeremiah commanded Baruch: "I cannot enter the house of the LORD; I am barred* from it. 6So you yourself must go. On a fast day in the hearing of the people in the LORD's house, read

lending him their room. **Maaseiah**: perhaps the father of the priest Zephaniah (29:25; 37:3). **Guard at the entrance**: an important priestly responsibility (cf. 52:24).

35:6 Jonadab: another spelling of Jehonadab, a contemporary of King Jehu; cf. 2 Kgs 10:15–17.

35:11 The army of the Arameans: Nebuchadnezzar enlisted the help of Judah's neighbors in his assault on Jerusalem. **Living in Jerusalem**: the current military threat and the prospect of being killed or captured as plunder drove the Rechabites into the city and away from their tents.

36:5 I am barred: Jeremiah could have been forbidden to enter the Temple for any number of reasons: e.g., his inflammatory preaching (the Temple sermon, 7:1–15; the broken pot); the hostility of Temple guards; the restrictions of arrest.

z: Jgs 4:17, 24; 1 Sm 15:6; 2 Kgs 10:15–17. *a:* 2 Kgs 24:1–2. *b:* Jer 32:33. *c:* Jer 7:13; 25:3; 2 Chr 36:15–16. *d:* Jer 25:4–5, 7. *e:* Jer 11:8–9. *f:* Jer 26:3; Is 55:6–7.

the words of the LORD from the scroll you wrote at my dictation; read them also to all the people of Judah who come up from their cities. [7]Perhaps they will present their supplication before the LORD and will all turn back from their evil way; for great is the anger and wrath with which the LORD has threatened this people."[g]

[8]Baruch, son of Neriah, did everything Jeremiah the prophet commanded; from the scroll he read the LORD's words in the LORD's house. [9]In the ninth month, in the fifth year of Jehoiakim, son of Josiah, king of Judah, all the people of Jerusalem and all those who came from Judah's cities to Jerusalem proclaimed a fast before the LORD. [10]So Baruch read the words of Jeremiah from the scroll in the room of Gemariah,* son of the scribe Shaphan, in the upper court of the LORD's house, at the entrance of the New Temple Gate, in the hearing of all the people.

[11]Now Micaiah, son of Gemariah, son of Shaphan, heard all the words of the LORD read from the scroll. [12]So he went down to the house of the king, into the scribe's chamber,* where the princes were meeting in session: Elishama, the scribe; Delaiah, son of Shemaiah; Elnathan, son of Achbor; Gemariah, son of Shaphan; Zedekiah, son of Hananiah; and the other princes. [13]Micaiah reported to them all that he had heard Baruch read from his scroll in the hearing of the people. [14]The princes immediately sent Jehudi, son of Nethaniah, son of Shelemiah, son of Cushi, to Baruch with the order: "The scroll you read in the hearing of the people—bring it with you and come." Scroll in hand, Baruch, son of Neriah, went to them. [15]"Sit down," they said to him, "and read it in our hearing." Baruch read it in their hearing, [16]and when they had heard all its words, they turned to each other in alarm and said to Baruch, "We have to tell the king all these things." [17]Then they asked Baruch: "Tell us, please, how did you come to write down all these words? Was it at his dictation?" [18]"Yes, he would dictate all these words to me," Baruch answered them, "while I wrote them down with ink in the scroll." [19]The princes said to Baruch, "Go into hiding, you and Jeremiah; do not let anyone know where you are."

[20]They went in to the king, into the courtyard; they had deposited the scroll in the room of Elishama the scribe. When they told the king everything that had happened, [21]the king sent Jehudi to get the scroll. Jehudi brought it from the room of Elishama the scribe, and read it to the king and to all the princes who were attending the king. [22]Now the king was sitting in his winter house, since it was the ninth month, and a fire was burning in the brazier before him. [23]Each time Jehudi finished reading three or four columns, he would cut off the piece with a scribe's knife* and throw it into the fire in the brazier, until the entire scroll was consumed in the fire in the brazier. [24]As they were listening to all these words the king and all his officials did not become alarmed, nor did they tear their garments. [25]And though Elnathan, Delaiah, and Gemariah urged the king not to burn the scroll, he would not listen to them. [26]He commanded Jerahmeel, a royal prince, and Seraiah, son of Azriel, and Shelemiah, son of Abdeel, to arrest Baruch, the scribe, and Jeremiah the prophet. But the LORD had hidden them away.

[27]The word of the LORD came to Jeremiah, after the king burned the scroll and the words Jeremiah had dictated to Baruch: [28]Take another scroll, and write on it all the words in the first scroll, which Jehoiakim, king of Judah, burned. [29]And against Jehoiakim, king of Judah, say this: Thus says the LORD: You are the one who burned that scroll, saying, "Why did you write on it: Babylon's king shall surely come and ravage this land, emptying it of every living thing"? [30]The LORD now says of Jehoiakim, king of Judah:[h] No descendant of his shall sit on David's throne; his corpse shall be thrown out,

36:10 Gemariah: member of a family friendly to Jeremiah with rights to a room in the gateway fortress overlooking the court of the Temple. His father Shaphan had been Josiah's secretary of state (2 Kgs 22:3). From a window in this room Baruch read Jeremiah's scroll to the people.

36:12 The scribe's chamber: the office of the royal secretary.

36:23 A scribe's knife: used to sharpen reed pens.

g: 2 Kgs 22:13. *h:* Jer 22:19.

exposed to heat by day, frost by night.* 31I will punish him and his descendants and his officials for their wickedness; upon them, the inhabitants of Jerusalem, and the people of Judah I will bring all the evil threats to which they did not listen.

32Then Jeremiah took another scroll and gave it to his scribe, Baruch, son of Neriah, who wrote on it at Jeremiah's dictation all the words contained in the scroll which Jehoiakim, king of Judah, had burned in the fire, adding many words like them.

See RG 303

CHAPTER 37

Jeremiah in the Dungeon. 1Zedekiah, son of Josiah, became king, succeeding Coniah, son of Jehoiakim; Nebuchadnezzar, king of Babylon, appointed him king over the land of Judah.[i] 2Neither he, nor his officials, nor the people of the land would listen to the words which the LORD spoke through Jeremiah the prophet. 3Yet King Zedekiah sent Jehucal, son of Shelemiah, and Zephaniah, son of Maaseiah the priest, to Jeremiah the prophet with this request: "Please appeal to the LORD, our God, for us."[j] 4At this time Jeremiah still came and went freely among the people; he had not yet been put into prison.* 5Meanwhile, Pharaoh's army* had set out from Egypt, and when the Chaldeans who were besieging Jerusalem heard this report, they withdrew from the city.[k]

6Then the word of the LORD came to Jeremiah the prophet: 7Thus says the LORD, the God of Israel: Thus you must say to the king of Judah who sent you to consult me: Listen! Pharaoh's army, which has set out to help you, will return to Egypt, its own land.[l] 8The Chaldeans shall return and attack this city; they shall capture it and destroy it by fire.[m]

9Thus says the LORD: Do not deceive yourselves, saying: "The Chaldeans are surely leaving us forever." They are not! 10Even if you could defeat the whole Chaldean army that is now attacking you, and only the wounded remained, each in his tent, these would rise up and destroy the city with fire.[n]

11Now when the Chaldean army withdrew from Jerusalem because of the army of Pharaoh,[o] 12Jeremiah set out from Jerusalem to go to the territory of Benjamin, to receive his share of property among the people. 13But at the Gate of Benjamin, the captain of the guard, by the name of Irijah, son of Shelemiah, son of Hananiah, arrested Jeremiah the prophet, saying, "You are deserting to the Chaldeans!" 14"That is a lie!" Jeremiah answered, "I am not deserting to the Chaldeans." Without listening to him, Irijah kept Jeremiah in custody and brought him to the princes.

15The princes were enraged at Jeremiah and had Jeremiah beaten and imprisoned in the house of Jonathan the scribe, for they were using it as a jail.[p] 16And so Jeremiah went into a room in the dungeon, where he remained many days.

17Then King Zedekiah had him brought to his palace, and he asked him secretly, "Is there any word from the LORD?" "There is!" Jeremiah answered: "You shall be handed over to the king of Babylon."[q] 18Jeremiah then asked King Zedekiah: "How have I wronged you or your officials or this people, that you should put me in prison?[r] 19Where are your own prophets who prophesied for you, saying: 'The King of Babylon will not attack you or this land'? 20Please hear me, my lord king! Grant my petition: do not send me back into the house of Jonathan the scribe, or I shall die there."

21So King Zedekiah ordered that Jeremiah be confined in the court of the guard and given a ration of bread every day from the bakers' street until all the bread in the city was eaten up. Thus Jeremiah remained in the court of the guard.[s]

36:30 Jehoiakim's son Jehoiachin was named king, but reigned only three months; he was better known for his long exile in Babylon. **His corpse shall be thrown out**: just as Jehoiakim had thrown pieces of the scroll into the fire (cf. 22:19).

37:4 Put into prison: as described in 32:1–3. Chronologically, the present episode follows 34:1–7.

37:5 Pharaoh's army: the force sent by Pharaoh Hophra; when they arrived, the Chaldeans temporarily lifted the siege against Jerusalem (cf. 34:21).

i: Jer 52:1; 2 Kgs 24:17; 2 Chr 36:10. *j:* Jer 21:1. *k:* Ez 17:15; 29:6–7. *l:* Ez 17:17. *m:* Jer 34:22. *n:* Jer 21:4. *o:* Zec 14:10. *p:* Jer 38:6–13. *q:* Jer 21:7; 32:3; 34:21. *r:* Jer 26:19. *s:* Jer 32:2; 38:28.

See RG 303

CHAPTER 38

Jeremiah in the Muddy Cistern. [1]Shephatiah, son of Mattan, Gedaliah, son of Pashhur, Jucal, son of Shelemiah, and Pashhur, son of Malchiah, heard the words Jeremiah was speaking to all the people:* [2]Thus says the LORD: Those who remain in this city shall die by means of the sword, starvation, and disease; but those who go out to the Chaldeans shall live. Their lives shall be spared them as spoils of war that they may live.[t] [3]Thus says the LORD: This city shall certainly be handed over to the army of the king of Babylon; he shall capture it.

[4]Then the princes said to the king, "This man ought to be put to death. He is weakening the resolve* of the soldiers left in this city and of all the people, by saying such things to them; he is not seeking the welfare of our people, but their ruin."[u] [5]King Zedekiah answered: "He is in your hands," for the king could do nothing with them. [6]And so they took Jeremiah and threw him into the cistern of Prince Malchiah, in the court of the guard, letting him down by rope. There was no water in the cistern, only mud, and Jeremiah sank down into the mud.[v]

[7]Now Ebed-melech, an Ethiopian, a court official in the king's house, heard that they had put Jeremiah in the cistern. The king happened to be sitting at the Gate of Benjamin, [8]and Ebed-melech went there from the house of the king and said to him, [9]"My lord king, these men have done wrong in all their treatment of Jeremiah the prophet, throwing him into the cistern. He will starve to death on the spot, for there is no more bread in the city."[w] [10]Then the king ordered Ebed-melech the Ethiopian: "Take three men with you, and get Jeremiah the prophet out of the cistern before he dies." [11]Ebed-melech took the men with him, and went first to the linen closet in the house of the king. He took some old, tattered rags and lowered them by rope to Jeremiah in the cistern. [12]Then he said to Jeremiah, "Put these old, tattered rags between your armpits and the ropes." Jeremiah did so, [13]and they pulled him up by rope out of the cistern. But Jeremiah remained in the court of the guard.

[14]King Zedekiah summoned Jeremiah the prophet to meet him at the third entrance of the house of the LORD. "I have a question to ask you," the king said to Jeremiah. "Do not hide anything from me."[x] [15]Jeremiah answered Zedekiah: "If I tell you anything, will you not have me put to death? If I counsel you, you will not listen to me!"[y] [16]But King Zedekiah swore to Jeremiah secretly: "As the LORD lives who gave us our lives, I will not kill you, nor will I hand you over to those men who seek your life."

[17]Jeremiah then said to Zedekiah: "Thus says the LORD God of hosts, the God of Israel: If you will only surrender to the princes of Babylon's king, you shall save your life; this city shall not be destroyed by fire, and you and your household shall live.[z] [18]But if you do not surrender to the princes of Babylon's king, this city shall fall into the hand of the Chaldeans, who shall destroy it by fire, and you shall not escape their hand."[a]

[19]King Zedekiah said to Jeremiah, "I am afraid of the Judahites who have deserted to the Chaldeans; I could be handed over to them, and they will mistreat me."[b] [20]"You will not be handed over to them," Jeremiah answered. "I beg you! Please listen to the voice of the LORD regarding what I tell you so that it may go well with you and your life be spared.[c] [21]But if you refuse to surrender, this is what the LORD has shown: [22]I see all the women who remain in the house of Judah's king being brought out to the princes of Babylon's king, and they are crying:

'They betrayed you, outdid you,
  your good friends!
Now that your feet are sunk in mud,
  they slink away.'[d]

38:1 Jeremiah enjoyed sufficient liberty in the court of the guard (37:21) to speak to the people; cf. 32:6–9. **Gedaliah, son of Pashhur**: the latter is possibly the Pashhur of 20:1. **Pashhur, son of Malchiah**: mentioned in 21:1.

38:4 He is weakening the resolve: lit., "he weakens the hands." One of the Lachish ostraca (cf. note on 34:7) makes the same claim against the princes in Jerusalem.

t: Jer 21:9–10; 39:18; 45:5. *u*: Jer 26:11. *v*: Jer 37:14–15. *w*: Jer 52:6. *x*: Jer 37:16. *y*: Lk 22:67–68. *z*: Jer 27:12–13; 2 Kgs 24:12. *a*: Jer 32:4. *b*: 1 Sm 31:4. *c*: 2 Chr 20:20. *d*: Jb 6:15; 19:13–14, 19.

23 All your wives and children shall be brought out to the Chaldeans, and you shall not escape their hands; you shall be handed over to the king of Babylon, and this city shall be destroyed by fire."[e]

24 Then Zedekiah said to Jeremiah, "Let no one know about this conversation, or you shall die. 25 If the princes should hear I spoke with you and if they should come and ask you, 'Tell us what you said to the king; do not hide it from us, or we will kill you,' or, 'What did the king say to you?' 26 then give them this answer: 'I petitioned the king not to send me back to Jonathan's house lest I die there.' " 27 When all the princes came to Jeremiah and questioned him, he answered them with the very words the king had commanded. They said no more to him, for nothing had been overheard of the conversation. 28 Thus Jeremiah stayed in the court of the guard until the day Jerusalem was taken.[f]

CHAPTER 39

See RG 303

The Capture of Jerusalem. When Jerusalem was taken, 1 in the ninth year of Zedekiah,[g] king of Judah, in the tenth month,* Nebuchadnezzar, king of Babylon, and all his army marched against Jerusalem and placed it under siege. 2 In the eleventh year of Zedekiah, on the ninth day of the fourth month,* the city wall was breached. 3 All the princes of the king of Babylon came and took their seats at the middle gate: Nergal-sharezer of Simmagir, a chief officer; Nebushazban, a high dignitary; and all the rest of the princes of the king of Babylon.* 4 When Zedekiah, king of Judah, and all his warriors saw this, they fled, leaving the city at night by way of the king's garden,* through a gate between the two walls. He went in the direction of the Arabah,[h] 5 but the Chaldean army pursued them; they caught up with Zedekiah in the wilderness near Jericho and took him prisoner. They brought him to Nebuchadnezzar, king of Babylon, in Riblah,* in the land of Hamath, and he pronounced sentence upon him.[i] 6 The king of Babylon executed the sons of Zedekiah at Riblah before his very eyes; the king of Babylon also executed all the nobles of Judah.[j] 7 He then blinded Zedekiah and bound him in chains to bring him to Babylon.[k]

8 The Chaldeans set fire to the king's house and the houses of the people and tore down the walls of Jerusalem.[l] 9 Nebuzaradan, captain of the bodyguard, deported to Babylon the rest of the people left in the city, those who had deserted to him, and the rest of the workers.[m] 10 But Nebuzaradan, captain of the bodyguard, left in the land of Judah some of the poor who had nothing and at the same time gave them vineyards and farms.[n]

Jeremiah Released to Gedaliah's Custody. 11 Concerning Jeremiah, Nebuchadnezzar, king of Babylon, gave these orders through Nebuzaradan, captain of the bodyguard: 12 "Take him and look after him; do not let anything happen to him. Whatever he may ask, you must do for him."[o] 13 Thereupon Nebuzaradan, captain of the bodyguard, and Nebushazban, a high dignitary, and Nergal-sharezer, a chief officer, and all the nobles of the king of Babylon, 14 had Jeremiah taken out of the courtyard of the guard and entrusted to Gedaliah, son of Ahikam, son of Shaphan, to bring him home. And so he remained among the people.[p]

A Word of Comfort for Ebed-melech. 15 While Jeremiah was still imprisoned in the

39:1 In the ninth year . . . in the tenth month: the month Tebet (mid-December to mid-January) of the year 589/588 B.C., according to the Babylonian calendar, whose New Year began in March/April.

39:2 In the eleventh year . . . the ninth day of the fourth month: in July, 587 B.C.

39:3 The Babylonian officers act as a military tribunal or government, headed by Nergal-sharezer, Nebuchadnezzar's son and successor.

39:4 By way of the king's garden: along the southeast side of the city; the royal garden was in the Kidron Valley. **A gate between the two walls**: the southernmost city gate, at the end of the Tyropoeon Valley. **The Arabah**: the southern Jordan Valley. Zedekiah was perhaps trying to escape across the Jordan when he was captured near Jericho.

39:5 Riblah: Nebuchadnezzar's headquarters north of Damascus; Pharaoh Neco had once used the town as a military post (2 Kgs 23:33).

e: Jer 41:10. *f:* Jer 39:14. *g:* Jer 52:4–16; 2 Kgs 25:1–12; Ez 24:1. *h:* Jer 52:7. *i:* Jer 32:4–5; 38:18. *j:* Jer 34:21. *k:* Jer 32:4–5; Ez 12:13. *l:* Jer 21:10; 34:2; 52:13. *m:* 2 Kgs 25:11. *n:* 2 Kgs 25:12, 22. *o:* Jer 40:4. *p:* Jer 26:24; 38:28.

court of the guard, the word of the LORD
came to him: 16 Go, tell this to Ebed-melech
the Ethiopian: Thus says the LORD of hosts,
the God of Israel: See, I am now carrying out
my words against this city, for evil and not
for good; this will happen in your presence
on that day.[q] 17 But on that day I will deliver
you—oracle of the LORD; you shall not be
handed over to the men you dread. 18 I will
make certain that you escape and do not fall
by the sword. Your life will be your spoils of
war because you trusted in me—oracle of
the LORD.[r]

See RG 303

CHAPTER 40

Jeremiah Still in Judah. 1 The word*
which came to Jeremiah from the LORD, after
Nebuzaradan, captain of the bodyguard, had
released him in Ramah, where he found him
a prisoner in chains among the captives of Jerusalem and Judah being exiled to Babylon.[s]
2 The captain of the bodyguard took charge of
Jeremiah and said to him, "The LORD, your
God, decreed ruin for this place. 3 Now he has
made it happen, accomplishing what he decreed; because you sinned against the LORD
and did not listen to his voice, this decree has
been realized against you. 4 Now, I release
you today from the chains upon your hands;
if you want to come with me to Babylon, then
come: I will look out for you. But if you do
not want to come to Babylon, very well. See,
the whole land lies before you; go wherever
you think good and proper.[t] 5 Or go to Gedaliah, son of Ahikam, son of Shaphan, whom
the king of Babylon has set over the cities of
Judah. Stay with him among the people. Or
go wherever you want!" The captain of the
bodyguard gave him food and gifts and let
him go.[u] 6 So Jeremiah went to Gedaliah, son
of Ahikam, in Mizpah,* and dwelt with him
among the people left in the land.[v]

7 When the military leaders still in the field
with their soldiers heard that the king of Babylon had set Gedaliah, son of Ahikam, over
the land and had put him in charge of men,
women, and children, from the poor of the
land who had not been deported to Babylon,
8 they and their soldiers came to Gedaliah in
Mizpah: Ishmael, son of Nethaniah; Johanan, son of Kareah; Seraiah, son of Tanhumeth; the sons of Ephai of Netophah; and
Jezaniah of Beth-maacah. 9 Gedaliah, son of
Ahikam, son of Shaphan, swore an oath to
them and their men: "Do not be afraid to
serve the Chaldeans. Stay in the land and
serve the king of Babylon, so that everything
may go well with you.[w] 10 As for me, I will remain in Mizpah, as your representative before the Chaldeans when they come to us.
You, for your part, harvest the wine, the fruit,
and the oil, store them in jars, and remain in
the cities you occupied." 11 Then all the Judahites in Moab, in Ammon, in Edom, and
those in all other lands heard that the king of
Babylon had left a remnant in Judah and had
set over them Gedaliah, son of Ahikam, son
of Shaphan. 12 They all returned to the land of
Judah from the places to which they had scattered. They went to Gedaliah at Mizpah and
had a rich harvest of wine and fruit.

Assassination of Gedaliah. 13 Now Johanan, son of Kareah, and all the military leaders in the field came to Gedaliah in Mizpah
14 and said to him, "Surely you are aware that
Baalis, the Ammonite king,* has sent Ishmael, son of Nethaniah, to assassinate
you?"[x] But Gedaliah, son of Ahikam, would
not believe them. 15 Then Johanan, son of
Kareah, said secretly to Gedaliah in Mizpah:
"Please let me go and kill Ishmael, son of
Nethaniah; no one will know it. What if he
assassinates you? All the Judahites who
have now rallied behind you would scatter
and the remnant of Judah would perish."
16 Gedaliah, son of Ahikam, answered Johanan, son of Kareah, "You must not do that.
What you are saying about Ishmael is a lie!"

40:1 The word: this "word" does not actually appear until 42:7.

40:6 While Jerusalem had suffered a great deal of damage, the Babylonian leaders' selection of Mizpah as their local headquarters was probably as much a symbolic statement as it was a utilitarian move: Jerusalem and its political and religious worldview had given way to disorder and no longer existed as a symbol of order.

40:14 In an attempt, perhaps, to weaken Babylon's hold on the area and to add Judah to the Ammonite kingdom, Baalis supported Ishmael's claim to the throne of David (cf. 41:1 for Ishmael's genealogy).

q: Jer 21:10; Dn 9:12. *r:* Jer 45:5; Ps 25:3; 37:40. *s:* Jer 39:14. *t:* Jer 39:12. *u:* Jer 39:14; 2 Kgs 25:22. *v:* Jer 39:14. *w:* Jer 27:12–13; 2 Kgs 25:24. *x:* Jer 41:1–3, 10.

CHAPTER 41

See RG 303

1In the seventh month, Ishmael, son of Nethaniah, son of Elishama, of royal descent, one of the king's nobles, came with ten men to Gedaliah, son of Ahikam, at Mizpah.[y] While they were together at table in Mizpah, 2Ishmael, son of Nethaniah, and the ten with him, stood up and struck down Gedaliah, son of Ahikam, son of Shaphan, with swords. They killed him, since the king of Babylon had set him over the land; 3Ishmael also killed all the Judahites of military age who were with Gedaliah and the Chaldean soldiers stationed there.

4The day after the murder of Gedaliah, before anyone learned about it, 5eighty men, in ragged clothes, with beards shaved off and gashes on their bodies, came from Shechem, Shiloh, and Samaria, bringing grain offerings and incense for the house of the LORD. 6Weeping as he went, Ishmael son of Nethaniah, set out from Mizpah to meet them. "Come to Gedaliah, son of Ahikam," he said as he met them. 7Once they were inside the city, Ishmael, son of Nethaniah, and his men slaughtered them and threw them into the cistern. 8Ten of them said to Ishmael: "Do not kill us! We have stores of wheat and barley, oil and honey hidden in the field." So he spared them and did not kill them as he had killed their companions. 9The cistern into which Ishmael threw all the bodies of the men he had killed was the large one King Asa made to defend himself against Baasha, king of Israel; Ishmael, son of Nethaniah, filled this cistern with the slain.[z]

10Ishmael led away the rest of the people left in Mizpah, including the princesses,* whom Nebuzaradan, captain of the bodyguard, had consigned to Gedaliah, son of Ahikam. With these captives, Ishmael, son of Nethaniah, set out to cross over to the Ammonites.

Flight to Egypt. 11But when Johanan, son of Kareah, and the other army leaders with him heard about the crimes Ishmael, son of Nethaniah, had committed, 12they took all their men and set out to attack Ishmael, son of Nethaniah. They overtook him at the great pool in Gibeon.* 13At the sight of Johanan, son of Kareah, and the other army leaders, the people with Ishmael rejoiced; 14all of those whom Ishmael had taken captive from Mizpah went back to Johanan, son of Kareah. 15But Ishmael, son of Nethaniah, escaped from Johanan with eight men and fled to the Ammonites. 16Then Johanan, son of Kareah, and all the military leaders took charge of all the rest of the people whom Ishmael, son of Nethaniah, had taken away from Mizpah after he killed Gedaliah, son of Ahikam—the soldiers, the women with children, and court officials, whom he brought back from Gibeon. 17They set out and stopped at Geruth Chimham near Bethlehem, intending to go into Egypt. 18They were afraid of the Chaldeans, because Ishmael, son of Nethaniah, had slain Gedaliah, son of Ahikam, whom the king of Babylon had set over the land.

CHAPTER 42

See RG 303

1Then all the military leaders, including Johanan, son of Kareah, Azariah, son of Hoshaiah, and all the people, from the least to the greatest, 2approached Jeremiah the prophet and said, "Please grant our petition; pray for us to the LORD, your God, for all this remnant. As you see, only a few of us remain, but once we were many. 3May the LORD, your God, show us the way we should take and what we should do." 4"Very well!" Jeremiah the prophet answered them: "I will pray to the LORD, your God, as you desire; whatever the LORD answers, I will tell you; I will withhold nothing from you."[a] 5And they said to Jeremiah, "May the LORD be a true and faithful witness against us if we do not follow all the instructions the LORD, your God, sends us through you.[b] 6Whether we like it or not, we will obey the command of

41:10 The princesses: the women of Judah's royal house.

41:12 Gibeon: modern El-Jib; northwest of Jerusalem. A huge pit carved into limestone provided water in time of siege, here called the great pool, lit., "many waters"; cf. 2 Sm 2:12–14.

y: Jer 40:14–16; 2 Kgs 25:25. *z:* 1 Kgs 15:16; 2 Chr 16:6. *a:* 1 Sm 3:18. *b:* Jgs 11:10.

the LORD, our God, to whom we are sending you, so that it may go well with us for obeying the command of the LORD, our God."[c]

[7]Ten days passed before the word of the LORD came to Jeremiah. [8]Then he called Johanan, son of Kareah, his army leaders, and all the people, from the least to the greatest, [9]and said to them: Thus says the LORD, the God of Israel, to whom you sent me to offer your petition: [10]If indeed you will remain in this land, I will build you up, and not tear you down; I will plant you, not uproot you; for I repent of the evil I have done you.[d] [11]Do not fear the king of Babylon, as you do now. Do not fear him—oracle of the LORD—for I am with you to save you, to rescue you from his power.[e] [12]I will take pity on you, so that he will have pity on you and let you return to your land.[f] [13]But if you keep saying, "We will not stay in this land," thus disobeying the voice of the LORD, your God, [14]and saying, "No, we will go to the land of Egypt, where we will not see war, nor hear the trumpet alarm, nor hunger for bread. There we will live!"[g] [15]then listen to the word of the LORD, remnant of Judah: Thus says the LORD of hosts, the God of Israel: If you are set on going to Egypt and settling down there once you arrive, [16]the sword you fear shall overtake you in the land of Egypt; the hunger you dread shall pursue you to Egypt and there you shall die.[h] [17]All those determined to go to Egypt to live shall die by the sword, famine, and disease: not one shall survive or escape the evil that I am bringing upon them.[i] [18]For thus says the LORD of hosts, the God of Israel: Just as my furious wrath was poured out upon the inhabitants of Jerusalem, so shall my anger be poured out on you when you reach Egypt. You shall become a malediction and a horror, a curse and a reproach, and you shall never see this place again.[j]

[19]The LORD has spoken to you, remnant of Judah. Do not go to Egypt! Mark well that I am warning you this day. [20]At the cost of your lives you have been deceitful, for you yourselves sent me to the LORD, your God, saying, "Pray for us to the LORD, our God; whatever the LORD, our God, shall say, tell us and we will do it." [21]Today I have told you, but you have not listened to the voice of the LORD your God, in anything that he has sent me to tell you.[k] [22]Have no doubt about this: you shall die by the sword, famine, and disease in the place where you want to go and live.[l]

CHAPTER 43

See RG 303

[1]When Jeremiah finished telling the people all the words the LORD, their God, sent to them, [2]Azariah, son of Hoshaiah, Johanan, son of Kareah, and all the others had the insolence to say to Jeremiah: "You lie; the LORD, our God, did not send you to tell us, 'Do not to go to Egypt to live there.' [3]Baruch, son of Neriah, is inciting you against us, to hand us over to the Chaldeans to be killed or exiled to Babylon."[m]

[4]So Johanan, son of Kareah, and the rest of the leaders and the people did not listen to the voice of the LORD to stay in the land of Judah.[n] [5]Instead, Johanan, son of Kareah, and the military leaders took along all the remnant of Judah who had been dispersed among the nations and then had returned to dwell in the land of Judah: [6]men, women, and children, the princesses and everyone whom Nebuzaradan, captain of the bodyguard, had consigned to Gedaliah, son of Ahikam, son of Shaphan; also Jeremiah, the prophet, and Baruch, son of Neriah.[o] [7]They went to Egypt—they did not listen to the voice of the LORD—and came to Tahpanhes.[p]

Jeremiah in Egypt. [8]The word of the LORD came to Jeremiah in Tahpanhes: [9]Take some large stones in your hand and set them in mortar in the terrace at the entrance to the house of Pharaoh in Tahpanhes, while the Judahites watch. [10]Then say to them: Thus says the LORD of hosts, the God of Israel: I will send for my servant Nebuchadnezzar, king of Babylon. He will place his throne upon these stones which I, Jeremiah, have set up, and stretch his canopy above them.[q]

---

c: Jer 7:23; Dt 5:33; 6:3. *d:* Jer 31:28; 32:41. *e:* Jer 30:10–11. *f:* Ps 106:45–46; Prv 16:7. *g:* Dt 28:68. *h:* Jer 44:13–14, 27. *i:* Jer 29:17–18; 44:14, 28. *j:* Jer 44:12. *k:* Zec 7:11–12. *l:* Jer 44:12; Hos 9:6. *m:* Jer 38:4. *n:* Jer 41:16. *o:* Jer 41:10. *p:* Jer 42:13–14; 44:1. *q:* Jer 27:6; Ez 29:19.

11 He shall come and strike the land of Egypt: with death, those marked for death; with exile, those marked for exile; with the sword, those marked for the sword.[r] 12 He shall set fire to the temples of Egypt's gods, burn the gods and carry them off. He shall pick the land of Egypt clean, as a shepherd picks lice off his cloak, and then depart victorious.[s] 13 He shall smash the obelisks at the Temple of the Sun in the land of Egypt and destroy with fire the temples of the Egyptian gods.

CHAPTER 44

See RG 303

1 The word that came to Jeremiah for all the Judahites who were living in Egypt, those living in Migdol, Tahpanhes, and Memphis, and in Upper Egypt: 2* Thus says the LORD of hosts, the God of Israel: You yourselves have seen all the evil I brought upon Jerusalem and the other cities of Judah. Today they lie in ruins uninhabited,[t] 3 because of the evil they did to provoke me, going after other gods, offering incense and serving other gods they did not know, neither they, nor you, nor your ancestors.[u] 4 Though I repeatedly sent you all my servants the prophets, saying: "You must not commit this abominable deed I hate," 5 they did not listen or incline their ears in order to turn from their evil, no longer offering incense to other gods.[v] 6 Therefore the fury of my anger poured forth and kindled fire in the cities of Judah and the streets of Jerusalem, to turn them into the ruined wasteland they are today.

7 Now thus says the LORD God of hosts, the God of Israel: Why inflict so great an evil upon yourselves, cutting off from Judah man and woman, child and infant, not leaving yourselves even a remnant? 8 Why do you provoke me with the works of your hands, offering sacrifice to other gods here in the land of Egypt where you have come to live? Will you cut yourselves off and become a curse, a reproach among all the nations of the earth?[w] 9 Have you forgotten the evil of your ancestors, the evil of the kings of Judah, the evil of their wives, and your own evil and the evil of your wives—all that they did in the land of Judah and in the streets of Jerusalem?[x] 10 To this day they have not been crushed down, nor have they shown fear. They have not followed my law and my statutes that I set before you and your ancestors.[y]

11 Therefore, thus says the LORD of hosts, the God of Israel: I have set my face against you for evil, to cut off all Judah. 12 I will take away the remnant of Judah who insisted on going to the land of Egypt to live there; in the land of Egypt they shall meet their end. They shall fall by the sword or be consumed by hunger. From the least to the greatest, they shall die by sword or hunger; they shall become a malediction, a horror, a curse, a reproach.[z] 13 Thus I will punish those who live in Egypt, just as I punished Jerusalem, with sword, hunger, and disease, 14 so that none of the remnant of Judah who came to live in the land of Egypt shall escape or survive.[a] No one shall return to the land of Judah. Even though they long to return and live there, they shall not return except as refugees.

15 They answered Jeremiah—all the men who knew that their wives were offering sacrifices to other gods, all the women standing there in the immense crowd, and all the people who lived in Lower and Upper Egypt: 16 "Regarding the word you have spoken to us in the name of the LORD, we are not listening to you.[b] 17 Rather we will go on doing what we proposed; we will offer incense to the Queen of Heaven and pour out libations to her, just as we have done, along with our ancestors, our kings and princes, in the cities of Judah and in the streets of Jerusalem. Then we had plenty to eat, we prospered, and we suffered no misfortune.[c] 18 But ever since we stopped offering sacrifices to the Queen of Heaven and pouring out libations to her, we lack everything and are being destroyed by sword and hunger." 19 And

44:2–30 Chronologically, these are the last of Jeremiah's words to his people. As the narrative ends, Jeremiah meets with rejection. According to tradition, recorded in a much later work, he was murdered in Egypt by fellow Judahites.

r: Jer 46:13; Ez 30:10. *s:* Jer 46:25; Ez 30:13–14. *t:* Jer 34:22; Lv 26:32–33. *u:* Jer 11:17; Dt 32:17. *v:* Jer 7:24, 26; 19:4. *w:* Jer 25:6–7. *x:* 1 Kgs 11:1, 8; Ezr 9:7, 14. *y:* Jer 7:24. *z:* Jer 42:15, 18, 22. *a:* Jer 43:11. *b:* Jer 6:16–17. *c:* Jer 5:3; 7:18.

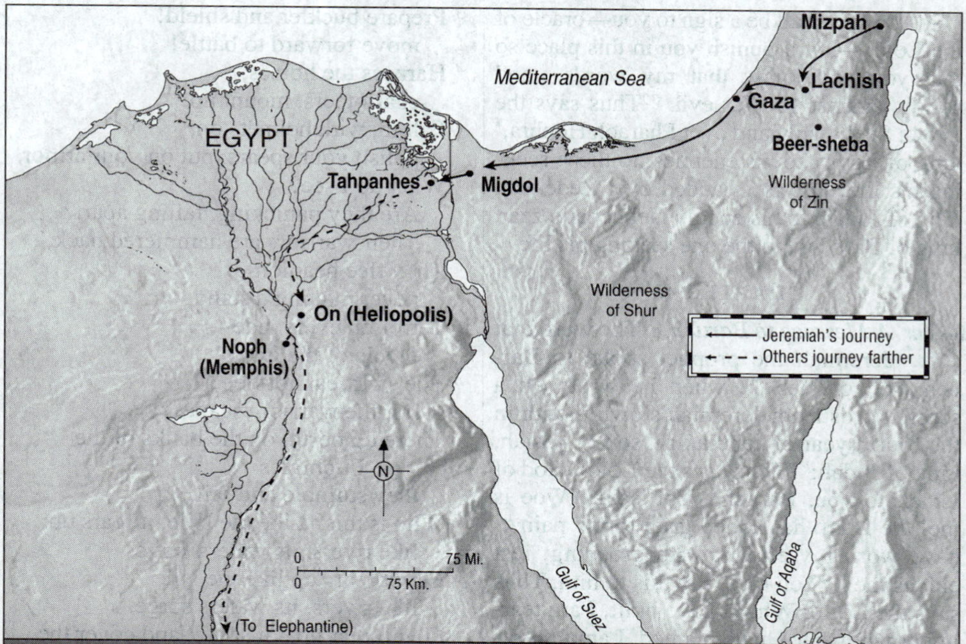

Jeremiah's Journey to Egypt

the women said, "When we offered sacrifices to the Queen of Heaven and poured out
libations to her, did we bake cakes in her image and pour out libations to her without our
husbands' consent?"[d]
[20]To all the people, men and women, who
gave him this answer, Jeremiah said: [21]As
for the sacrifices you offered in the cities of
Judah and in the streets of Jerusalem—you,
your ancestors, your kings and princes, and
the people of the land—did not the LORD remember them? Did it not enter his mind?[e]
[22]The LORD could no longer bear the evil of
your deeds, the abominations you were doing; then your land became a waste, a horror,
a curse, without even one inhabitant, as it is
today.[f] [23]Because you offered sacrifice and
sinned against the LORD, not listening to the
voice of the LORD, not following his law, his
statutes, and his decrees, therefore this evil
has overtaken you, as it is today.[g]
[24]Jeremiah said to all the people and to all
the women: Hear the word of the LORD, all
you Judahites in the land of Egypt: [25]Thus
says the LORD of hosts, the God of Israel:
You and your wives have carried out with
your hands what your mouths have spoken:
"We will go on fulfilling the vows we have
made to offer sacrifice to the Queen of
Heaven and to pour out libations to her."
Very well! keep your vows, fulfill your
vows! [26]And then listen to the word of the
LORD, all you Judahites living in Egypt; I
swear by my own great name, says the
LORD: in the whole land of Egypt, my name
shall no longer be pronounced by the lips of
any Judahite, saying, "As the Lord GOD
lives." [27]I am watching over them for evil,
not for good. All the Judahites in Egypt shall
come to an end by sword or famine until
they are completely destroyed.[h] [28]Those
who escape the sword to return from the
land of Egypt to the land of Judah shall be
few in number. The whole remnant of Judah
who came to Egypt to live shall know whose
word stands, mine or theirs.[i]

d: Jer 7:18. *e:* Jer 11:13. *f:* Jer 15:6. *g:* 2 Kgs 17:15; Dn 9:11–12. *h:* Ezr 7:3–7. *i:* Dt 28:62; Is 10:22.

29 And this shall be a sign to you—oracle of the LORD—I will punish you in this place so that you will know that my words stand solidly against you for evil. 30 Thus says the LORD: See! I will hand over Pharaoh Hophra,* king of Egypt, to his enemies, to those seeking his life, just as I handed over Zedekiah, king of Judah, to his enemy Nebuchadrezzar, king of Babylon, to the one seeking his life.[j]

CHAPTER 45

See RG 303

*A Message to Baruch.** 1 The word that Jeremiah the prophet spoke to Baruch, son of Neriah, when he wrote on a scroll words from Jeremiah's own mouth in the fourth year of Jehoiakim, son of Josiah, king of Judah:[k] 2 Thus says the LORD, God of Israel, to you, Baruch. 3 You said, "Woe is me! the LORD has added grief to my pain.[l] I have worn myself out with groaning; rest eludes me." 4 You must say this to him. Thus says the LORD: What I have built, I am tearing down; what I have planted, I am uprooting: all this land.[m] 5 And you, do you seek great things for yourself? Do not seek them! I am bringing evil on all flesh—oracle of the LORD—but I will grant you your life as spoils of war, wherever you may go.[n]

VIII. Oracles Against the Nations*

CHAPTER 46

See RG 303

1 The word of the LORD that came to Jeremiah the prophet concerning the nations.

Against Egypt. 2 Concerning Egypt. Against the army of Pharaoh Neco, king of Egypt, defeated at Carchemish on the Euphrates* by Nebuchadrezzar, king of Babylon, in the fourth year of Jehoiakim, son of Josiah, king of Judah:

3 Prepare buckler and shield!
move forward to battle!
4 Harness the horses,
charioteers, mount up!
Fall in, with helmets on;
polish your spears, put on your armor.
5 What do I see?
Are they panicking, falling apart?
Their warriors are hammered back,
They flee headlong
never making a stand.
Terror on every side—
oracle of the LORD![o]
6 The swift cannot flee,
nor the warrior escape:
There up north, on the banks of the Euphrates
they stumble and fall.
7 Who is this? Like the Nile, it rears up;
like rivers, its waters surge.
8 Egypt rears up like the Nile,
like rivers, its waters surge.
"I will rear up," it says, "and cover the earth,
destroying the city and its people.[p]
9 Forward, horses!
charge, chariots!
March forth, warriors,
Cush and Put, bearing shields,
Archers of Lud, stretching bows!"
10 Today belongs to the Lord GOD of hosts,
a day of vengeance, vengeance on his foes!
The sword devours and is sated, drunk with their blood:
for the Lord GOD of hosts holds a sacrifice
in the land of the north, on the River Euphrates.[q]
11 Go up to Gilead, procure balm,

44:30 Hophra: killed by his own people. Hophra's successor, Amasis, ruled Egypt when Nebuchadnezzar took control of the country.

45:1–5 At the conclusion of his narrative, Baruch appends a message Jeremiah had given him when he first wrote down Jeremiah's words (cf. 36:4). The future revealed by the prophet overwhelmed Baruch; now he learns his own safety is assured, even though the Lord will destroy Judah.

46:1–51:64 A collection of oracles against foreign nations constitutes the final section of the Hebrew text of Jeremiah; in the Greek text they follow 25:13. The oracles here appear to be arranged in loose chronological order: 46:2 mentions the fourth year of Jehoiakim; the oracles in 50:1–51:64 are evidently from the end of Jeremiah's life.

46:2 Carchemish on the Euphrates: the western terminus of the Mesopotamian trade route, where Nebuchadnezzar defeated Pharaoh Neco in 605 B.C., thus gaining undisputed control of Syria and Palestine.

j: Jer 39:5–7; 46:25–26; Ez 29:3–4; 30:21. *k:* Jer 36:4, 18, 32. *l:* Lam 1:3; 5:5. *m:* Jer 18:7; Is 5:5–6. *n:* Jer 25:26–29. *o:* Jer 6:25; 49:29. *p:* Ez 29:3; 32:2. *q:* Dt 32:42; Is 13:9; Ez 39:17–20.

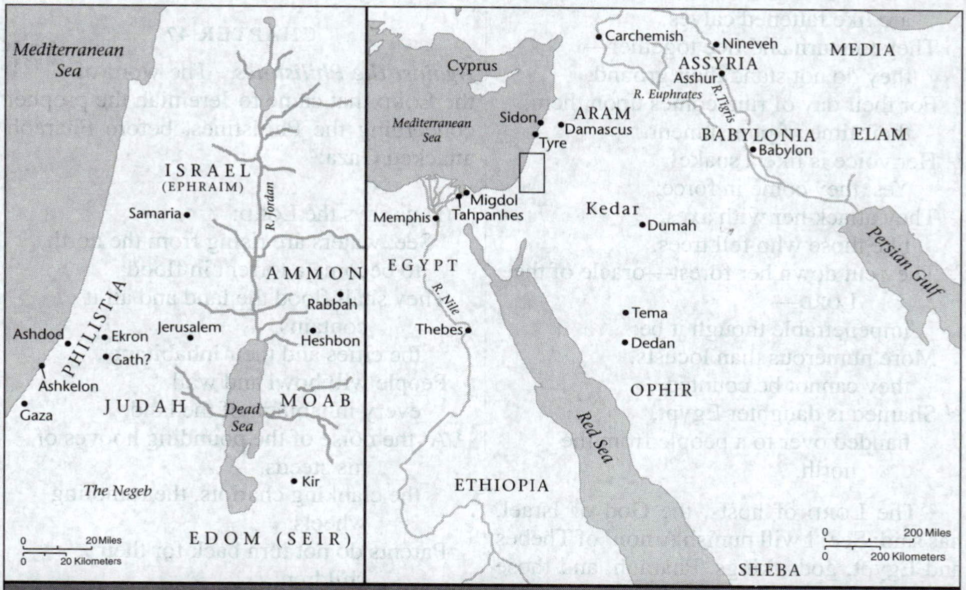

Places Mentioned in the Oracles against the Nations

Virgin daughter Egypt!
No use to multiply remedies;
for you there is no healing.[r]
12 The nations hear your cries,
your screaming fills the earth.
Warrior stumbles against warrior,
both collapse together.[s]

13t The word that the LORD spoke to Jeremiah the prophet when Nebuchadrezzar, king of Babylon, came to attack the land of Egypt:*

14 Proclaim in Egypt, announce in Migdol,
announce in Memphis and Tahpanhes!
Say: Fall in, get ready,
the sword has devoured your neighbors.[u]
15 Why has Apis* fled?
Your champion did not stand,
Because the LORD thrust him down;
16 he stumbled repeatedly then collapsed.
They said to each other,
"Get up! We must return to our own people,
To the land of our birth,
away from the destroying sword."[v]
17 Give Pharaoh, king of Egypt, the name
"Braggart-missed-his-chance."'*
18 As I live, says the King
whose name is LORD of hosts,
Like Tabor above mountains,
like Carmel* above the sea, he comes.
19 Pack your bags for exile,
enthroned daughter Egypt;
Memphis shall become a wasteland,
an empty ruin.
20 Egypt is a beautiful heifer,
a horsefly from the north keeps coming.
21 Even the mercenaries in her ranks

46:13 In 601 B.C. Nebuchadnezzar advanced into Egypt itself, but finally had to withdraw to Syria.

46:15 Apis: the chief god of Memphis; the black bull honored as an incarnation of the god Ptah and, later, of the god Osiris.

46:17 "Braggart-missed-his-chance": the Hebrew phrase may contain a pun on the Pharaoh's name or royal title.

46:18 Tabor . . . Carmel: mountains in Palestine that seem to tower over their surroundings as Nebuchadnezzar towers over the nations in his path as he makes his way toward Egypt.

r: Jer 8:22; 51:8; Ez 30:21–22. *s:* Ez 32:9–12. *t:* Jer 43:10–11; 44:30; Is 19:1. *u:* Jer 44:1. *v:* Lv 26:37.

are like fattened calves;
They too turn and flee together—
they do not stand their ground,
For their day of ruin comes upon them,
their time of punishment.
22 Her voice is like a snake!
Yes, they come in force;
They attack her with axes,
like those who fell trees.
23 They cut down her forest—oracle of the
LORD—
impenetrable though it be;
More numerous than locusts,
they cannot be counted.
24 Shamed is daughter Egypt,
handed over to a people from the
north.

25 The LORD of hosts, the God of Israel,
has said: See! I will punish Amon* of Thebes
and Egypt, gods, kings, Pharaoh, and those
who trust in him.[w] 26 I will hand them over to
those who seek their lives, to Nebuchadrezzar, king of Babylon, and to his officers. But
later, Egypt shall be inhabited again, as in
days of old—oracle of the LORD.[x]

27 But you, my servant Jacob, do not fear;
do not be dismayed, Israel!
Listen! I will deliver you from far-off
lands;
your offspring, from the land of their
exile.
Jacob shall again find rest,
secure, with none to frighten him.[y]
28 You, Jacob my servant, must not fear—
oracle of the LORD—
for I am with you;
I will make an end of all the nations
to which I have driven you,
But of you I will not make an end:
I will chastise you as you deserve,
I cannot let you go unpunished.[z]

CHAPTER 47

See RG 303

Against the Philistines. 1 The word of
the LORD that came to Jeremiah the prophet
concerning the Philistines, before Pharaoh
attacked Gaza:[a]

2 Thus says the LORD:
* See: waters are rising from the north,
to become a torrent in flood;
They shall flood the land and all it
contains,
the cities and their inhabitants.
People will howl and wail,
every inhabitant of the land.
3 At the noise of the pounding hooves of
his steeds,
the clanking chariots, the rumbling
wheels,
Parents do not turn back for their
children;
their hands hang helpless,
4 Because of the day that is coming
to destroy all the Philistines
And cut off from Tyre and Sidon*
the last of their allies.
Yes, the LORD is destroying the
Philistines,
the remnant from the coasts of
Caphtor.[b]
5 Baldness is visited upon Gaza,[c]
Ashkelon is reduced to silence;
Ashdod, remnant of their strength,
how long will you gash yourself?*
6 Ah! Sword of the LORD!
When will you find rest?
Return to your scabbard;
stop, be still!
7 How can it find rest
when the LORD has commanded it?
Against Ashkelon and the seacoast,
there he has appointed it.[d]

46:25 Amon: the sun-god worshiped at Thebes in Upper Egypt.

47:2–7 Nebuchadnezzar's military campaign against Ashkelon in 604 B.C. may provide some historical background for this poem.

47:4 Tyre and Sidon: Phoenician seaports allied commercially with the Philistines and often rebelling against Nebuchadnezzar; cf. 27:1–4. After the capture of Jerusalem, Nebuchadnezzar carried out a partially successful thirteen-year siege of Tyre. **Caphtor**: Crete and other Aegean islands, points of origin for the Philistines and other sea peoples; cf. Am 9:7.

47:5 Baldness . . . gash yourself: close-cropped hair, silence, and ritual slashing of the body express mourning and grief and here represent the mourner's awareness that chaos has overcome order (cf. 41:5).

w: Ez 30:15–16. *x:* Jer 44:30; Ez 30:4; 32:11–12. *y:* Jer 30:10; 43:5. *z:* Jer 30:11. *a:* Ez 25:15–16; Zep 2:4. *b:* Jer 25:22; Ez 25:16–17; Am 1:8; 9:7. *c:* Am 1:7. *d:* Zep 2:5–6.

CHAPTER 48

See RG 303

*Against Moab.** 1 Concerning Moab.
Thus says the LORD of hosts, the God of Israel:

Ah, Nebo! it is ravaged;
Kiriathaim is disgraced, captured;
Disgraced and overthrown is the stronghold:
2 Moab's glory is no more.
In Heshbon they plot evil against her:
"Come! We will put an end to her as a nation."
You, too, Madmen,* shall be silenced;
you the sword stalks!
3 Listen! an outcry from Horonaim,[e]
"Ruin and great destruction!"
4 "Moab is crushed!"
their outcry is heard in Zoar.
5 Up the ascent of Luhith
they go weeping;
At the descent to Horonaim
they hear cries of anguish:
6 "Flee, save your lives!
Be like a wild donkey in the wilderness!"
7 Because you trusted in your works and your treasures,
you also shall be captured.
Chemosh* shall go into exile,
his priests and princes with him.[f]
8 The destroyer comes upon every city,
not a city escapes;
Ruined is the valley,
wasted the plateau—oracle of the LORD.
9 Set up a tombstone for Moab;
it will soon become a complete wasteland,
Its cities turned into ruins
where no one dwells.
10 Cursed are they who do the LORD's work carelessly,
cursed those who keep their sword
from shedding blood.
11 * Moab has been resting from its youth,
suspended above its dregs,
Never poured from flask to flask,
never driven into exile.
Thus it retained its flavor,
its bouquet is not lost.[g]

12 Be assured! The days are coming—oracle of the LORD—when I will send him
wine-makers to decant the wine; they shall
empty its flasks and smash its jars. 13 Chemosh shall disappoint Moab, just as the
house of Israel was disappointed by Bethel,
in which they trusted.[h]

14 How can you say, "We are heroes,
mighty warriors"?
15 The one who ravages Moab and its cities comes up,
the best of its youth go down to slaughter—
oracle of the King, whose name is LORD of hosts.
16 Moab's ruin is near at hand,
its disaster approaches swiftly.
17 Mourn, all you neighbors,
all you who know its name!
Say: How the mighty scepter is broken,
the glorious staff!
18 Come down from glory, sit on the parched ground,
enthroned daughter Dibon;*
Moab's destroyer has fallen upon you,
has shattered your strongholds.[i]
19 Stand along the road, keep watch,
enthroned Aroer;
Ask the fleeing man, the escaping woman:
ask them what has happened.[j]
20 "Moab is put to shame, destroyed."
Wail and cry out,
Proclaim it at the Arnon:
"Moab is destroyed!"[k]

48:1–47 Moab, located east of the Dead Sea, was one of Israel's bitter enemies (cf., e.g., Is 15–16; Am 2:1–3). According to Flavius Josephus, Nebuchadnezzar conquered Moab and Ammon in his twenty-third year (582 B.C.), five years after the destruction of Jerusalem. This chapter is full of local place names in Moab.

48:2 Madmen: a place name, not mentioned elsewhere in the Old Testament.

48:7 Chemosh: chief god of Moab (cf. Nm 21:29).

48:11–12 Moabite wine was known for its high quality. Here the wine is a metaphor for Moab's complacency.

48:18 Dibon, the capital of Moab at that time, is situated on a height. The prophet here offers a personification of the city, pictured as a confident ruler.

e: Is 15:5. *f:* Nm 21:29. *g:* Zep 1:12. *h:* Is 16:12. *i:* Nm 21:30. *j:* Dt 2:36. *k:* Is 16:7.

21 Judgment has come upon the plateau: on
Holon, Jahzah, and Mephaath,[l] 22 on Dibon,
Nebo, and Beth-diblathaim, 23 on Kiria-
thaim, Beth-gamul, and Beth-meon, 24 on
Kerioth and on Bozrah: on all the cities of
the land of Moab, far and near.

25 The horn of Moab is cut off,
its arm is broken—oracle of the LORD.

26 Make him drunk because he set himself
over against the LORD; let Moab swim in his
vomit and become a laughingstock. 27 Has
Israel not been a laughingstock to you? Was
he caught among thieves that you wag your
heads whenever you speak of him?[m]

28 Abandon the cities, take shelter in the crags,
inhabitants of Moab.
Be like the dove that nests
in the walls of a gorge.
29 We have heard of the pride of Moab,[n]
pride beyond bounds:
His loftiness, his pride, his scorn,
his insolent heart.
30 I myself know his arrogance—oracle of the LORD—
liar in word, liar in deed.
31 And so I wail over Moab,
over all Moab I cry,
over the people of Kir-heres I moan.[o]
32 More than for Jazer I weep for you,
vine of Sibmah.
Your tendrils trailed down to the sea,
as far as Jazer they stretched.
Upon your summer harvest and your vintage,
the destroyer has fallen.[p]
33 Joy and gladness are taken away
from the garden land, the land of Moab.
I dry up the wine from the wine vats,
the treader treads no more,
the vintage shout is stilled.

34 The cry of Heshbon and Elealeh is heard
as far as Jahaz; they call from Zoar to Horonaim and to Eglath-shelishiyah; even the
waters of Nimrim turn into a wasteland.[q] 35 I
will leave no one in Moab—oracle of the
LORD—to offer burnt offerings on the high
place or to make sacrifices to their gods.
36 Hence my heart wails like a flute for
Moab; my heart wails like a flute for the
people of Kir-heres: the wealth they accumulated has perished.[r] 37 Every head has
been shaved bald, every beard cut off; every
hand gashed, and all their loins are draped in
sackcloth.[s] 38 On all the rooftops of Moab
and in all its squares there is mourning. I
have shattered Moab like a pot that no one
wants—oracle of the LORD. 39 How terrified
they are, how they wail! How Moab turns its
back in shame! Moab has become a laughingstock and a horror to all its neighbors!

40 For thus says the LORD:
Look there! Like an eagle he swoops,
spreading his wings over Moab.[t]
41 Cities are captured,
strongholds seized:
On that day the hearts of Moab's warriors
become like the heart of a woman in labor.[u]
42 Moab shall be wiped out, a people no more,
because it set itself over against the LORD.[v]
43 Terror, pit, and trap be upon you,
enthroned Moab—oracle of the LORD.[w]
44 Those fleeing the terror
fall into the pit;
Those climbing out of the pit
are caught in the trap;
Ah, yes! I will bring these things upon Moab
in the year of their punishment—
oracle of the LORD.
45 In Heshbon's shadow the fugitives
stop short, exhausted;
For fire blazes up from Heshbon,
and flames up from the house of Sihon:
It consumes the forehead of Moab,
the scalp of the noisemakers.[x]
46 Woe to you, Moab!
You are finished, people of Chemosh!

l: Is 15:4. *m:* Zep 2:8–10. *n:* Is 16:6. *o:* Is 16:7. *p:* Is 16:8–9. *q:* Is 15:4–5. *r:* Is 16:11. *s:* Jer 47:5; Is 15:2–3; Ez 7:18. *t:* Jer 49:22. *u:* Jer 6:24; 30:6. *v:* Zep 2:9–10. *w:* Is 24:17–18. *x:* Nm 21:28–29.

Your sons are taken into exile,
your daughters into captivity.
47 Yet I will restore the fortunes of Moab
in the days to come—oracle of the
LORD.[y]

Thus far the judgment on Moab.

See RG 303

CHAPTER 49

Against the Ammonites. 1 Concerning the Ammonites. Thus says the LORD:

Has Israel no sons?
none to inherit?
Why has Milcom* disinherited Gad,
why are his people living in its cities?
2 Therefore the days are coming—oracle
of the LORD—
when I will sound the battle alarm
against Rabbah of the Ammonites;
It shall become a mound of ruins,
and its villages destroyed by fire.
Israel shall then inherit those who
disinherited it—
oracle of the LORD.[z]
3 Wail, Heshbon, "The ruin is destroyed!"
shriek, villages of Rabbah!
Put on sackcloth and lament!
Run back and forth in the sheepfolds.
For Milcom is going into exile,
taking priest and prince with him.[a]
4 Why boast in your strength,
your ebbing strength, rebellious
daughter?
Why trust in your treasures, saying,
"Who would dare attack me?"
5 See, I am bringing terror upon you—
oracle of the Lord GOD of hosts—
from all around you;
You shall be scattered, each in headlong
flight,
with no one to gather the fugitives.[b]
6 But afterward I will restore the fortunes
of the Ammonites—oracle of the
LORD.

*Against Edom.** 7 Concerning Edom. Thus says the LORD of hosts:

Is there no more wisdom in Teman,*
has counsel perished from the prudent,
is their wisdom gone?
8 Flee, retreat, hide deep for lodging,
inhabitants of Dedan:
For I bring disaster upon Esau*
when I come to punish them.[c]
9 If vintagers came upon you,
they would leave no gleanings;
If thieves by night,
they would destroy as they pleased.[d]
10 So I myself will strip Esau;
I will uncover his lairs so he cannot
hide.
Offspring and family are destroyed,
neighbors, too; he is no more.[e]
11 Leave your orphans behind, I will keep
them alive;
your widows, let them trust in me.[f]

12 For thus says the LORD: Look, even
those not sentenced to drink the cup must
drink it! Shall you then go unpunished? You
shall not! You shall drink every bit of it![g]
13 By myself I have sworn—oracle of the
LORD—Bozrah* shall become an object of
horror, a disgrace, a desolation, and a curse.
Bozrah and all its cities shall become ruins
forever.[h]

14 I have heard a report from the LORD,
a herald has been sent among the
nations:
"Gather together, move against it,
get ready for battle!"
15 I will make you the least among the
nations,
despised by all people![i]
16 The terror you spread,
the pride of your heart, beguiled you.
You denizens of rocks and crevices,
occupying towering peaks:

49:1 Milcom: chief god of the Ammonites (cf. 1 Kgs 11:5). The Ammonites shared a border with Gad, an Israelite tribe in Transjordan (Jos 13:8–10); the Ammonites occupied its territory after the collapse of the Northern Kingdom.

49:7–22 Edom: southeast of the Dead Sea, a traditional enemy who profited from Judah's downfall; cf. Ps 137:7; Lam 4:21–22; Ob 11–12.

49:7 Teman, a district of Edom (cf. Jb 2:11), represents the whole country, which was famous for the wisdom of its sages.

49:8 Esau: Jacob's brother, the traditional ancestor of the Edomites; cf. Gn 36:1.

49:13 Bozrah: capital of Edom.

y: Jer 49:39. *z:* Am 1:14. *a:* Is 15:2–5. *b:* Jer 48:47. *c:* Ez 25:13. *d:* Ob 5. *e:* Mal 1:3. *f:* Dt 10:18; Ps 68:6. *g:* Jer 25:15, 28; Lam 4:21–22. *h:* Is 34:6; Ez 35:3–9; Ob 16. *i:* Ob 2.

16 Though you build your nest high as the
eagle,
from there I will bring you down—
oracle of the LORD.[j]

17 Edom shall become an object of horror.
Passersby recoil in terror, hissing at all its
wounds. 18 As when Sodom, Gomorrah, and
their neighbors were overthrown—oracle of
the LORD—no one shall live in it, nor anyone
settle there.[k]

19 As when a lion comes up from a thicket
of the Jordan
to a permanent pasture,
So in an instant, I will chase them off;
I will establish there whomever I
choose.
For who is like me? Who holds me
accountable?
What shepherd can stand against me?[l]
20 Therefore, listen to the strategy
the LORD devised for Edom;
The plans he has drawn up
against the inhabitants of Teman:
They shall be dragged away, even the
smallest of the flock;
their pasture shall be aghast because of
them.
21 With the din of their collapse the earth
quakes,
to the Red Sea the outcry is heard!
22 Look! like an eagle he soars aloft,
and spreads his wings over Bozrah;
On that day the hearts of Edom's
warriors become
like the heart of a woman in labor.[m]

Against Damascus. 23 Concerning Damascus.

Hamath and Arpad* are shamed,
for they have heard bad news;
Anxious, they surge like the sea
which cannot calm down.[n]
24 Damascus loses heart, turns to flee;
panic has seized it.
Distress and pangs take hold,
like the pain of a woman in labor.
25 How can the glorious city be abandoned,
the town of joy!
26 But now its young men shall fall in its
squares,
all the warriors destroyed on that day—
oracle of the LORD of hosts.
27 I will set fire to the wall of Damascus;
it shall devour the palaces of Ben-
hadad.*

Against Arabia. 28 About Kedar and the
kingdoms of Hazor, which Nebuchadnezzar,
king of Babylon, defeated.

Thus says the LORD:
Rise up, attack Kedar,
destroy the people from the east.[o]
29 Their tents and flocks shall be taken away,
their tent curtains and all their goods;
Their camels they carry off,
they shout over them, "Terror on every
side!"[p]
30 Flee! wander about, hide deep for lodging,
inhabitants of Hazor—oracle of the
LORD;
For Nebuchadnezzar, king of Babylon,
has devised a strategy against
you,
drawn up a plan against you,
31 Get up! set out against a tranquil nation,
living in security—oracle of the LORD—
Without gates or bars,
dwelling alone.
32 Their camels shall become spoils,
their hordes of cattle, plunder;
I will scatter to the winds those who
shave their temples;
from every side I will bring their
ruin—
oracle of the LORD.[q]
33 Hazor shall become a haunt for jackals,
a wasteland forever,
Where no one lives,
no mortal stays.

49:23 Hamath and Arpad: independent Aramean states north of Damascus, the direction from which the invasion is coming. Cf. Is 10:9–10.

49:27 Ben-hadad: a dynastic name for some of the kings who ruled in Damascus; cf. 1 Kgs 15:18, 20.

j: Jer 48:29–30. *k:* Jer 50:40; Dt 29:23. *l:* Jer 12:5; 25:9; 50:44–45. *m:* Jer 4:13. *n:* Is 36:19; 37:13. *o:* Is 21:16. *p:* Jer 4:20. *q:* Jer 9:25.

Against Elam. 34 The word of the LORD that came to Jeremiah the prophet concerning Elam* at the beginning of the reign of Zedekiah, king of Judah:

35 Thus says the LORD of hosts:
Look! I will break the bow of Elam,
the mainstay of their might.
36 I will bring upon Elam the four winds
from the four ends of the heavens:
I will scatter them to all these winds,
until there is no nation
to which the outcasts of Elam have not gone.
37 I will terrify Elam before their foes,
those seeking their life;
I will bring evil upon them,
my burning wrath—oracle of the LORD.
I will send sword after them
until I have finished them off;
38 I will set up my throne in Elam
and destroy from there king and princes—
oracle of the LORD.
39 But at the end of days I will restore
the fortunes of Elam—oracle of the LORD.

CHAPTER 50

See RG 303

The First Oracle Against Babylon.

1 The word the LORD spoke against Babylon,* against the land of the Chaldeans, through Jeremiah the prophet:[r]

2 Proclaim this among the nations,
announce it!
Announce it, do not hide it, but say:
Babylon is captured, Bel* put to shame,
Marduk terrified;
its images are put to shame, its idols shattered.
3 A nation from the north advances
against it,
making the land desolate
So that no one can live there;
human beings and animals have fled.[s]
4 In those days and at that time—oracle of
the LORD—
Israelite and Judahite shall come
together,
Weeping as they come, to seek the LORD,
their God;[t]
5 They shall ask for Zion,
seeking out the way.
"Come, let us join ourselves to the LORD
in an everlasting covenant, never to be forgotten."[u]
6 Lost sheep were my people,
their shepherds misled them,
leading them astray on the mountains;
From mountain to hill they wandered,
forgetting their fold.[v]
7 Whoever happened upon them devoured
them;
their enemies said, "We are not guilty,
Because they sinned against the LORD,
the abode of justice, the hope of their ancestors."[w]
8 Flee from the midst of Babylon,
leave the land of the Chaldeans,
be like rams at the head of the flock.[x]
9 See, I am stirring up against Babylon
a band of great nations from the land
of the north;
They are arrayed against her,
from there she shall be taken.
Their arrows are like the arrows of a
skilled warrior
who never returns empty-handed.[y]
10 Chaldea shall become plunder;
all its plunderers shall be enriched—
oracle of the LORD.
11 Yes, rejoice and exult,
you that plunder my heritage;
Frisk like calves on the grass,
neigh like stallions!
12 Your mother will indeed be put to shame,
she that bore you shall be abashed;
See, the last of the nations,

49:34 Elam: an ancient kingdom east of Babylonia.

50:1–51:58 A collection of miscellaneous oracles against Babylon introducing the story in 51:59–64.

50:2 Bel: originally the title of the god of Nippur in Mesopotamia, later associated with *Merodach* (Marduk), chief god of Babylon (cf. Is 46:1).

r: Jer 51:1; Is 13:1–14; 21:1–10. *s:* Jer 51:48; Is 13:17. *t:* Jer 3:18; Ps 126:6. *u:* Jer 31:31; 32:40. *v:* Is 53:6; 1 Pt 2:25. *w:* Jer 31:23. *x:* Jer 51:6, 45; Is 48:20. *y:* Jer 51:27.

a wilderness, a dry wasteland.[z]
13 Because of the LORD's wrath it shall be uninhabited,
become an utter wasteland;
Everyone who passes by Babylon will be appalled
and hiss at all its wounds.[a]
14 Take your posts encircling Babylon,
you who bend the bow;
Shoot at it, do not spare your arrows,[b]
15 raise the war cry against it on every side.
It surrenders, its bastions fall,
its walls are torn down:*
This is retribution from the LORD! Take retribution on her,
as she has done, do to her;
for she sinned against the LORD.[c]
16 Cut off the sower from Babylon
and those who wield sickles at harvest time!
Before the destroying sword,
all of them turn back to their own people,
all flee to their own land.[d]
17 Israel was a stray sheep
that lions pursued;
The king of Assyria once devoured him;
now Nebuchadnezzar of Babylon
gnaws his bones.[e]
18 Therefore, thus says the LORD of hosts,
the God of Israel:
I will punish the king of Babylon and his land,
as I once punished the king of Assyria;[f]
19 But I will bring Israel back to its pasture,
to feed on Carmel and Bashan,
And on Mount Ephraim and Gilead,
until they have their fill.[g]

20 In those days, at that time—oracle of the LORD:

The guilt of Israel may be sought, but it no longer exists,
the sin of Judah, but it can no longer be found;
for I will forgive the remnant I preserve.[h]
21 Attack the land of Merathaim,
and those who live in Pekod;*
Slaughter and put them under the ban—
oracle of the LORD—
do all I have commanded you.
22 Battle alarm in the land,
great destruction!
23 How the hammer of the whole earth
has been cut off and broken!
What an object of horror
Babylon has become among the nations![i]
24 You ensnared yourself and were caught,
Babylon, before you knew it!
You were discovered and seized,
because you challenged the LORD.[j]
25 The LORD opens his armory,
brings out the weapons of his wrath;
The Lord GOD of hosts has work to do
in the land of the Chaldeans.[k]
26 Come upon them from every side,
open their granaries,
Pile them up in heaps and put them under the ban;
do not leave a remnant.
27 Slay all the oxen,
take them down to slaughter;
Woe to them! their day has come,
the time of their punishment.
28 Listen! the fugitives, the refugees
from the land of Babylon:
They announce in Zion
the retribution of the LORD, our God.[l]
29 Call archers out against Babylon,
all who bend the bow;
Encamp around them;
let no one escape.
Repay them for their deeds;
what they have done, do to them,
For they insulted the LORD,

50:15 Its walls are torn down: the prophet describes the downfall of Babylon in conventional language. Babylon surrendered peacefully to the Persians in 539 B.C.

50:21 Merathaim . . . Pekod: "twice bitter," "punishment," symbolic terms for Babylon that recall the names of regions in the country.

z: Jer 51:43; Is 13:20–22. *a:* Jer 25:12. *b:* Jer 51:11; Is 21:2. *c:* Jer 51:11, 44, 58; Ps 137:8. *d:* Is 13:14. *e:* 2 Kgs 17:24; 18:14. *f:* Is 10:12; 14:24–25. *g:* Jer 23:3; Ez 34:13–14. *h:* Jer 31:34; Is 43:25; Mi 7:19. *i:* Jer 51:20; Is 14:6. *j:* Jer 51:57. *k:* Jer 51:11–12; Is 13:5. *l:* Jer 51:10–11.

the Holy One of Israel.[m]
30 Therefore their young men shall fall in
the squares,
all their warriors shall be stilled on
that day—
oracle of the LORD.[n]
31 I am against you, O Insolence—
oracle of the Lord GOD of hosts;
For your day has come,
the time for me to punish you.
32 Insolence stumbles and falls;
there is no one to raise him up.
I will kindle a fire in his cities
to devour everything around him.
33 Thus says the LORD of hosts:
Oppressed are the people of Israel,
together with the people of Judah;
All their captors hold them fast
and refuse to let them go.
34 Strong is their Redeemer,
whose name is LORD of hosts,
The sure defender of their cause,
who gives rest to their land,
but unrest to those who live in
Babylon.[o]
35 A sword upon the Chaldeans—oracle of
the LORD—
upon the inhabitants of Babylon, her
princes and sages!
36 A sword upon the soothsayers,
and they become fools!
A sword upon the warriors,
and they tremble;
37 A sword upon their motley throng,
and they become women!
A sword upon their treasures,
and they are plundered;[p]
38 A drought upon the waters,
and they dry up!
For it is a land of idols,
soon made frantic by phantoms.[q]
39 Hence, wildcats shall dwell there with
hyenas,
and ostriches occupy it;
Never again shall it be inhabited or
settled,
from age to age.[r]
40 As happened when God overturned
Sodom
and Gomorrah and their neighbors—
oracle of the LORD—
No one shall dwell there,
no mortal shall settle there.[s]
41 See, a people comes from the north,
a great nation, and mighty kings
rising from the ends of the earth.[t]
42 Bow and javelin they wield,
cruel and pitiless are they;
They sound like the roaring sea,
as they ride forth on horses,
Each in place for battle
against you, daughter Babylon.
43 The king of Babylon hears news of them,
and his hands hang helpless;
Anguish takes hold of him,
like the pangs of a woman giving birth.[u]
44 As happens when a lion comes up from a
thicket of the Jordan
to permanent pasture,
So I, in an instant, will chase them off,
and establish there whomever I
choose!
For who is like me? Who can call me to
account?
What shepherd can stand against me?[v]
45 Therefore, hear the strategy of the LORD,
which he has devised against Babylon;
Hear the plans drawn up
against the land of the Chaldeans:
They shall be dragged away, even the
smallest sheep;
their own pasture aghast because of
them.[w]
46 At the cry "Babylon is captured!" the
earth quakes;
the outcry is heard among the nations.[x]

CHAPTER 51

See RG 303

The Second Oracle Against Babylon

1 Thus says the LORD:
See! I rouse against Babylon,
and the inhabitants of Chaldea,
a destroyer wind.*

51:1 The destroyer wind is the fierce dry wind from the east (cf. 4:11).

m: Jer 51:56. *n:* Jer 49:26; 51:4. *o:* Jer 51:36. *p:* Jer 51:30; Na 3:13. *q:* Jer 51:32, 36. *r:* Jer 51:37; Is 13:21–22. *s:* Jer 51:43. *t:* Jer 51:27–28. *u:* Is 13:7. *v:* Jer 49:19. *w:* Jer 51:12, 29. *x:* Jer 51:29.

[2] To Babylon I will send winnowers
to winnow and lay waste the land;
They shall besiege it on every side
on the day of affliction.[y]
[3] How can the archers draw back their bows,
lift their armor?
Do not spare her young men,
put the entire army under the ban.[z]
[4] The slain shall fall in the land of Chaldea,
the wounded, in its streets;[a]
[5] For Israel and Judah are not left widowed
by their God, the LORD of hosts,
Even though the land is full of guilt
against the Holy One of Israel.
[6] Flee from Babylon;
each of you save your own life,
do not perish because of her guilt;
This is a time of retribution from the LORD,
[7] who pays out her due.[b]
Babylon was a golden cup in the hand of the LORD
making the whole earth drunk;
The nations drank its wine,
thus they have gone mad.[c]
[8] Babylon suddenly falls and is broken:
wail over her!
Bring balm for her wounds,
in case she can be healed.[d]
[9] "We have tried to heal Babylon,
but she cannot be healed.
Leave her, each of us must go to our own land."
The judgment against her reaches the heavens,
it touches the clouds.[e]
[10] The LORD has brought forth our vindication;
come, let us tell in Zion
what the LORD, our God, has done.[f]
[11] Sharpen the arrows,
fill the quivers;
The LORD has stirred up the spirit of the kings of the Medes,*
for his resolve is Babylon's destruction.
Yes, it is retribution from the LORD,
retribution for his temple.[g]
[12] Over the walls of Babylon raise a signal,
reinforce the watch;
Post sentries,
arrange ambushes!
For the LORD has both planned and carried out
what he spoke against the inhabitants of Babylon.
[13] You who dwell by mighty waters,
rich in treasure,
Your end has come,
the time at which you shall be cut off![h]
[14] The LORD of hosts has sworn by himself:
I will fill you with people as numerous as locusts,
who shall raise over you a joyous shout!
[15] He made the earth by his power,
established the world by wisdom,
and by his skill stretched out the heavens.[i]
[16] When he thunders, the waters in the heavens roar,
he summons clouds from the ends of the earth,
Makes lightning flash in the rain,
and brings out winds from their storehouses.
[17] Every man is stupid, ignorant;
every artisan is put to shame by his idol:
He molds a fraud,
without life-breath.
[18] They are nothing, a ridiculous work,
that will perish at the time of punishment.
[19] Jacob's portion is nothing like them:
he is the creator of all things.
Israel is his very own tribe;
LORD of hosts is his name.
[20] You are my hammer,
a weapon for war;
With you I shatter nations,
with you I destroy kingdoms.
[21] With you I shatter horse and rider,
with you I shatter chariot and driver.[j]

51:11 Kings of the Medes: the Medes and the Persians lived in the area known today as Iran.

y: Jer 15:7; Is 41:16. *z:* Jer 50:14, 29. *a:* Jer 50:30. *b:* Jer 50:8, 15, 29; Is 48:20. *c:* Rev 14:8; 17:4. *d:* Rev 18:9–18. *e:* Is 13:14; Rev 18:5. *f:* Jer 50:28. *g:* 2 Kgs 17:6; Is 13:17. *h:* Na 2:1. *i:* Jer 10:12. *j:* Dn 7:7, 19, 23.

22 With you I shatter man and woman,
with you I shatter old and young,
with you I shatter the young man and
young woman.[k]
23 With you I shatter shepherd and flock,
with you I shatter farmer and team,
with you I shatter governors and
officers.
24 Thus I will repay Babylon,
all the inhabitants of Chaldea,
For all the evil they committed against
Zion,
before your very eyes—oracle of the
LORD.[l]
25 Beware! I am against you,
destroying mountain—oracle of the
LORD—
destroyer of the entire earth,
I will stretch forth my hand against you,
roll you down over the cliffs,
and make you a burnt mountain:[m]
26 They will not take from you a
cornerstone,
or a foundation stone;
You shall remain ruins forever—
oracle of the LORD.[n]
27 Raise a signal in the land,
sound the trumpet among the nations;
Dedicate nations for war against her,
summon against her the kingdoms:
Ararat, Minni, and Ashkenaz;*
Appoint a recruiting officer against her,
dispatch horses like bristling locusts.[o]
28 Dedicate nations for war against her:
the king of the Medes,
Its governors and all its officers,
every land in its domain.
29 The earth quakes and writhes,
the LORD's plan against Babylon is
carried out,
Turning the land of Babylon
into a wasteland without inhabitants.
30 Babylon's warriors have ceased to fight,
they remain in their strongholds;
Dried up is their strength,
they have become women.
Burned down are their homes,
broken their gates.
31 One runner meets another,
herald meets herald,
Telling the king of Babylon
that his entire city has been taken.[p]
32 The fords have been seized,
marshes set on fire,
warriors panic.

33 For thus says the LORD of hosts, the God
of Israel:

Daughter Babylon is like a threshing
floor
at the time of treading;
Yet a little while,
and the harvest time will come for
her.[q]
34 "He consumed me, defeated me,
Nebuchadnezzar, king of Babylon;
he left me like an empty vessel,
Swallowed me like a sea monster,
filled his belly with my delicacies and
cast me out.
35 Let my torn flesh be visited upon
Babylon,"
says enthroned Zion;
"My blood upon the inhabitants of
Chaldea,"
says Jerusalem.
36 But now, thus says the LORD:
I will certainly defend your cause,
I will certainly avenge you;
I will dry up her sea,
and drain her fountain.
37 Babylon shall become a heap of ruins,
a haunt of jackals;
A place of horror and hissing,
without inhabitants.[r]
38 They roar like lions,
growl like lion cubs.[s]
39 When they are parched, I will set drink
before them
to make them drunk, that they may be
overcome
with everlasting sleep, never to
awaken—
oracle of the LORD.

51:27 Ararat, Minni, and Ashkenaz: regions in eastern Asia Minor under the control of the Medes.

k: Is 13:16, 18. *l:* Jer 25:14; 50:29; Ps 137:8. *m:* Rev 8:7; 18:8–9. *n:* Jer 25:12; Ps 118:22. *o:* Na 3:17. *p:* 2 Chr 30:6; Jb 1:14–18. *q:* Rev 14:15. *r:* Is 25:2. *s:* Na 2:11–12.

40 I will bring them down like lambs to
slaughter,
like rams and goats.
41 How she has been seized, taken captive,
the glory of the whole world!
What a horror Babylon has become
among the nations:[t]
42 against Babylon the sea rises,
she is overwhelmed by roaring waves!
43 Her cities have become wasteland,
a parched and arid land
Where no one lives,
no one passes through.
44 I will punish Bel in Babylon,
and make him vomit up what he
swallowed;
nations shall no longer stream to him.
Even the wall of Babylon falls!
45 Leave her, my people; each of you
save your own life
from the burning wrath of the LORD.

46Do not be discouraged when rumors
spread through the land; this year one rumor
comes, next year another: "Violence in the
land!" or "Ruler against ruler!"[u] 47Realize
that the days are coming when I will punish
the idols of Babylon; the whole land shall be
put to shame, all her slain shall fall in her
midst. 48Then heaven and earth and everything in them shall shout over Babylon with
joy, when the destroyers come against her
from the north—oracle of the LORD.[v] 49Bab-
ylon, too, must fall, you slain of Israel, because by the hand of Babylon the slain of all
the earth have fallen.

50 You who have escaped the sword,
go, do not stand idle;
Remember the LORD from far away,
let Jerusalem come to mind.
51 We are ashamed because we have heard
taunts,
disgrace covers our faces;
strangers have entered sanctuaries in
the LORD's house.[w]

52 Therefore see, the days are coming—
oracle of the LORD—
when I will punish her idols,
and throughout the land the wounded
will groan.
53 Though Babylon scale the heavens,
and make her strong heights
inaccessible,
my destroyers shall reach her—oracle
of the LORD.[x]
54 A sound of crying from Babylon,
great destruction from the land of the
Chaldeans;
55 For the LORD lays Babylon waste,
silences her loud cry,
Waves roaring like mighty waters,
a clamor resounding.
56 For the destroyer comes upon her, upon
Babylon;
warriors are captured, their bows
broken;
The LORD is a God of recompense,
he will surely repay.[y]

57I will make her princes and sages drunk,
with her governors, officers, and warriors,
so that they sleep an everlasting sleep, never
to awaken—oracle of the King, whose name
is LORD of hosts.

58 Thus says the LORD of hosts:
The walls of spacious Babylon shall be
leveled to the ground,
its lofty gates destroyed by fire.
The toil of the peoples is for nothing;
the nations weary themselves for what
the flames consume.[z]

The Prophecy Sent to Babylon. 59The mission Jeremiah the prophet gave to Seraiah,*
son of Neriah, son of Mahseiah, when he
went to Babylon with King Zedekiah, king
of Judah, in the fourth year of his reign; Seraiah was chief quartermaster. 60Jeremiah
wrote down on one scroll the disaster that
would befall Babylon;* all these words were
written against Babylon. 61And Jeremiah

51:59 Seraiah: the brother of Baruch; cf. 32:12. He may have gone to Babylon to explain away the presence of foreign ambassadors in Jerusalem that same year; cf. 27:3.

51:60 Jeremiah prophesied against Babylon, even as he foretold Judah's release from Babylon's power (3:14–18; 32:15; 33:6–9, 12–13); but his scroll against Babylon was thrown in the Euphrates (v. 63). Some of the preceding oracles may have been composed by later writers; see note on 50:1–51:58.

t: Is 13:19. *u:* Mt 24:6–7. *v:* Rev 18:20. *w:* Ps 44:16–17; 78:1–4. *x:* Is 14:13. *y:* Na 1:2. *z:* Hb 2:13.

said to Seraiah: "When you reach Babylon, see that you read all these words aloud,[a] [62]and then say: LORD, you yourself spoke against this place in order to cut it down so that nothing, human being or beast, could live in it, because it is to remain a wasteland forever. [63]When you have finished reading this scroll, tie a stone to it and throw it into the Euphrates,[b] [64]and say: Thus Babylon shall sink. It will never rise, because of the disaster I am bringing upon it." Thus far the words of Jeremiah.

IX. Historical Appendix*

CHAPTER 52

See RG 303

Capture of Jerusalem. [1]Zedekiah was twenty-one years old when he became king; he reigned eleven years in Jerusalem.[c] His mother's name was Hamutal, daughter of Jeremiah from Libnah. [2]He did what was evil in the sight of the LORD, just as Jehoiakim had done. [3]Indeed, the things done in Jerusalem and in Judah so angered the LORD that he cast them out from his presence. Thus Zedekiah rebelled against the king of Babylon. [4][d] In the tenth month of the ninth year of his reign, on the tenth day of the month,* Nebuchadnezzar, king of Babylon, and his entire army advanced against Jerusalem, encamped around it, and built siege walls on every side. [5]The siege of the city continued until the eleventh year of King Zedekiah.

[6]On the ninth day of the fourth month, when famine had gripped the city and the people had no more bread, [7]the city walls were breached. All the soldiers fled and left the city by night through the gate between the two walls which was near the king's garden. With the Chaldeans surrounding the city, they went in the direction of the Arabah. [8]But the Chaldean army pursued the king and overtook Zedekiah in the wilderness near Jericho; his whole army fled from him.

[9]The king, therefore, was arrested and brought to Riblah, in the land of Hamath, to the king of Babylon, who pronounced judgment on him. [10]As Zedekiah looked on, the king of Babylon slaughtered his sons before his eyes! All the nobles of Judah were slaughtered at Riblah. [11]And the eyes of Zedekiah he then blinded, bound him with chains, and the King of Babylon brought him to Babylon and kept him in prison until the day he died.

Destruction of Jerusalem. [12]On the tenth day of the fifth month, this was in the nineteenth year* of Nebuchadnezzar, king of Babylon, Nebuzaradan, captain of the bodyguard, came to Jerusalem as the representative of the king of Babylon. [13]He burned the house of the LORD, the palace of the king, and all the houses of Jerusalem; every large building he destroyed with fire. [14]Then the Chaldean troops with the captain of the guard tore down all the walls that surrounded Jerusalem.

[15]Nebuzaradan, captain of the guard, led into exile the remnant of people left in the city, those who had deserted to the king of Babylon, and the rest of the artisans. [16]But Nebuzaradan, captain of the guard, left behind some of the country's poor as vinedressers and farmers.

[17]The bronze pillars that belonged to the house of the LORD, and the wheeled carts and the bronze sea in the house of the LORD, the Chaldeans broke into pieces; they carried away all the bronze to Babylon. [18]They also took the pots, shovels, snuffers, bowls, pans, and all the bronze vessels used for service; [19]the basins, fire holders, bowls, pots, lampstands, pans, the sacrificial bowls made of gold or silver. Along with these furnishings the captain of the guard carried off [20]the two pillars, the one sea and its base of twelve oxen cast in bronze, and the wheeled carts King Solomon had commissioned for the house of the LORD. The bronze from all these furnishings was impossible to weigh.

52:1–34 One of the editors of the Book of Jeremiah took most of this supplement from 2 Kgs 24:18–25:30 and placed it here to show the fulfillment of Jeremiah's prophecies. The supplement repeats part of the history given in Jeremiah 39–41, but omits the history of Gedaliah in 2 Kgs 25:22–26.

52:4 In the tenth month of the ninth year of his reign, on the tenth day of the month: January 15, 588 B.C. Cf. 39:1.

52:12 On the tenth day of the fifth month . . . nineteenth year: the tenth of Ab—July/August in 587/586 B.C.

a: Jer 50:1–51. *b:* Rev 18:21. *c:* 2 Kgs 24:18–25:21. *d:* Jer 39:1–10.

21 As for the pillars, each of them was
eighteen cubits high and twelve cubits in diameter; each was four fingers thick and hollow inside. 22 A bronze capital five cubits
high crowned the one pillar, and a network
with pomegranates encircled the capital, all
of bronze; and so for the other pillar, with
pomegranates. 23 There were ninety-six
pomegranates on the sides, a hundred pomegranates surrounding the network.
24 The captain of the guard also took Seraiah the high priest, Zephaniah the second
priest, and the three keepers of the entrance.
25 From the city he took one courtier, a commander of soldiers, and seven men in the
personal service of the king still in the city,
the scribe of the army commander who mustered the people of the land, and sixty of the
common people remaining in the city. 26 The
captain of the guard, Nebuzaradan, arrested
them and brought them to the king of Babylon at Riblah, 27 who had them struck down
and executed in Riblah, in the land of Hamath.
Thus Judah was exiled from the land.
28* This is the number of people Nebuchadnezzar led away captive: in his seventh year,
three thousand twenty-three people of Judah; 29 in the eighteenth year of Nebuchadnezzar, eight hundred thirty-two persons
from Jerusalem; 30 in the twenty-third year of
Nebuchadnezzar, Nebuzaradan, captain of
the guard, deported seven hundred forty-five
Judahites: four thousand six hundred persons in all.

Favor Shown to Jehoiachin.* 31[e] In the
thirty-seventh year of the exile of Jehoiachin, king of Judah, on the twenty-fifth
day of the twelfth month, Evil-merodach,
king of Babylon, in the inaugural year of his
reign, raised up Jehoiachin, king of Judah,
and released him from prison. 32 He spoke
kindly to him and gave him a throne higher
than the thrones of the other kings* who
were with him in Babylon. 33 Jehoiachin took
off his prison garb and ate at the king's table
as long as he lived. 34 The allowance given
him by the king of Babylon was a perpetual
allowance, in fixed daily amounts, all the
days of his life until the day of his death.

52:28–30 These verses, missing in the Greek text, do not come from 2 Kgs 25 but from a source using a different chronology. Besides the deportations of 598 and 587 B.C., this passage mentions a final deportation in 582/581, possibly a response to the murder of Gedaliah; cf. Jer 41:2.

52:31–34 In the year 561/560 B.C., Nebuchadnezzar's successor Awel-Marduk (Evil-merodach), who reigned only two years, released Jehoiachin. Babylonian records confirm that Jehoiachin and his family were supported at public expense.

52:32 The other kings: heads of state brought as captives to Babylon.

e: 2 Kgs 25:27–30.

See RG 310–14

The Book of Lamentations

The Book of Lamentations is a collection of five poems that serve as an anguished response to the destruction of Jerusalem in 587 B.C., after a long siege by the invading Babylonian army. (See 2 Kgs 25 for a prose account of the fall of Jerusalem.) Although the poems are traditionally ascribed to the prophet Jeremiah, this is unlikely. The Hebrew text of the book does not mention Jeremiah at all, and it is difficult to square some of the content of the poetry with what one finds in the Book of Jeremiah itself (cf. Lam 1:10; 2:9; 4:17, 20). While there are connections in theme and vocabulary among all five chapters (and especially between chaps. 1 and 2), the poems may have been composed separately and grouped together later. In any case, they are anonymous compositions probably used by survivors of the catastrophe of 587 B.C. in a communal expression of grief and mourning.

Jewish liturgical tradition considers the book one of the "scrolls" (*megillot*); it is read once a year on the ninth of Av (August–September), a fast day commemorating the destruction of both the first Temple in 587 B.C. and the second Temple in A.D. 70. While passages from chap. 3 are often incorporated into Christian services for Holy Thursday or Good Friday, the Church has otherwise tended to neglect the book. It is not hard to see why; a more anguished piece of writing is scarcely imaginable: from its portrayal of

Jerusalem in chaps. 1 and 2 as an abandoned widow exposed to endless dangers, to the broken man of chap. 3, to the bleak description in chap. 4 of the inhabitants of the devastated city, to the final unanswered communal lament of chap. 5, the reader is not so much engaged by the Book of Lamentations as assaulted by it. But with its unsparing focus on destruction, pain, and suffering the book serves an invaluable function as part of Scripture, witnessing to a biblical faith determined to express honestly the harsh realities of a violent world and providing contemporary readers the language to do the same.

As a literary work, the Book of Lamentations combines elements of communal and individual laments (in which the speakers attempt to persuade God to intervene in the face of an acute crisis), funeral dirges (in which a death is mourned), and ancient Near Eastern city-laments (in which the destruction of a city is mourned). The meter is called *Qinah* (lament), that is, each verse normally has three beats followed by two. The poems are acrostics: in chaps. 1–4, the separate stanzas begin with successive letters of the Hebrew alphabet from the first to the last. The last chapter, while not strictly an acrostic, nevertheless partially conforms to the pattern in its use of 22 lines, the number of letters in the Hebrew alphabet. Far from destroying the spontaneous pathos of the songs, this feature conveys the expression of a profound grief that might otherwise seem to be without limit (cf. 2:13).

The book may be divided as follows:

I. The Desolation of Jerusalem (1:1–22).
II. The Lord's Wrath and Zion's Ruin (2:1–22).
III. The Voice of a Suffering Individual (3:1–66).
IV. Miseries of the Besieged City (4:1–22).
V. The Community's Lament to the Lord (5:1–22).

CHAPTER 1

See RG 310–14

*The Desolation of Jerusalem**

1 How solitary sits the city,
once filled with people.
She who was great among the nations
is now like a widow.
Once a princess among the provinces,
now a toiling slave.

2 She weeps incessantly in the night,
her cheeks damp with tears.
She has no one to comfort her
from all her lovers;*
Her friends have all betrayed her,
and become her enemies.[a]

3 Judah has gone into exile,
after oppression and harsh labor;
She dwells among the nations,
yet finds no rest:[b]
All her pursuers overtake her
in the narrow straits.

4 The roads to Zion mourn,
empty of pilgrims to her feasts.
All her gateways are desolate,
her priests groan,
Her young women grieve;
her lot is bitter.[c]

5 Her foes have come out on top,
her enemies are secure;
Because the LORD has afflicted her
for her many rebellions.
Her children have gone away,
captive before the foe.

6 From daughter Zion has gone
all her glory:
Her princes have become like rams
that find no pasture.
They have gone off exhausted
before their pursuers.

7 Jerusalem remembers
in days of wretched homelessness,

1:1–22 In this poem the poet first takes on the persona of an observer describing Jerusalem's abject state after the destruction wrought by the Babylonian army (vv. 1–11a); but the detached tone gives way to a more impassioned appeal when the city itself—personified as the grieving widow and mother Zion—abruptly intrudes upon this description (vv. 9c, 11c–16, 18–22) to demand that God look squarely at her misery.

1:2 Lovers: language of love was typically used to describe the relationship between treaty partners, thus here it connotes Judah's allies (see v. 19).

a: Jer 30:14; Ez 16:37. *b:* Dt 28:65; Jer 45:3. *c:* Is 33:8–9; Jer 14:2.

All the precious things she once had
in days gone by.
But when her people fell into the hands
of the foe,
and she had no help,
Her foes looked on and laughed
at her collapse.

8 Jerusalem has sinned grievously,
therefore she has become a mockery;
Those who honored her now demean
her,
for they saw her nakedness;
She herself groans out loud,
and turns away.[d]

9 Her uncleanness is on her skirt;
she has no thought of her future.
Her downfall is astonishing,
with no one to comfort her.
"Look, O LORD, at my misery;
how the enemy triumphs!"*

10 The foe stretched out his hands
to all her precious things;
She has seen the nations
enter her sanctuary,
Those you forbade to come
into your assembly.[e]

11 All her people groan,
searching for bread;
They give their precious things for food,
to retain the breath of life.
"Look, O LORD, and pay attention
to how I have been demeaned!

12 Come, all who pass by the way,
pay attention and see:
Is there any pain like my pain,
which has been ruthlessly inflicted
upon me,
With which the LORD has tormented me
on the day of his blazing wrath?

13 From on high he hurled fire down
into my very bones;
He spread out a net for my feet,
and turned me back.
He has left me desolate,
in misery all day long.[f]

14 The yoke of my rebellions is bound
together,
fastened by his hand.
His yoke is upon my neck;
he has made my strength fail.
The Lord has delivered me into the grip
of those I cannot resist.

15 All my valiant warriors
my Lord has cast away;
He proclaimed a feast against me
to crush my young men;
My Lord has trodden in the wine press
virgin daughter Judah.

16 For these things I weep—My eyes! My
eyes!
They stream with tears!
How far from me is anyone to comfort,
anyone to restore my life.
My children are desolate;
the enemy has prevailed."[g]

17 Zion stretches out her hands,
with no one to comfort her;
The LORD has ordered against Jacob
his foes all around;
Jerusalem has become in their midst
a thing unclean.

18 "The LORD is in the right;
I had defied his command.
Listen, all you peoples,
and see my pain:
My young women and young men
have gone into captivity.[h]

19 I cried out to my lovers,
but they failed me.[i]
My priests and my elders
perished in the city;
How desperately they searched for food,
to save their lives!

20 Look, O LORD, at the anguish I suffer!
My stomach churns,

1:9 Zion breaks in on the poet's description in v. 9c, albeit briefly, to demand that the Lord face squarely her misery. She takes up the lament in a more sustained fashion in v. 11c.

d: Is 47:2–3; Jer 13:22, 26; Na 3:5. *e:* Dt 23:3–6; Ps 74:4–8; Is 56:6; 66:20–21; Jer 51:51. *f:* Ez 12:13. *g:* Ps 69:21; Eccl 4:1; Jer 13:17; 14:17; Na 3:7. *h:* Dt 28:41. *i:* Jer 30:14.

And my heart recoils within me:
How bitter I am!
Outside the sword bereaves—
indoors, there is death.[j]

21 Hear how I am groaning;
there is no one to comfort me.
All my enemies hear of my misery and rejoice
over what you have done.
Bring on the day you proclaimed,
and let them become like me!

22 Let all their evil come before you
and deal with them
As you have so ruthlessly dealt with me
for all my rebellions.
My groans are many,
my heart is sick."[k]

CHAPTER 2

See RG 310–14

*The Lord's Wrath and Zion's Ruin**

1 How the Lord in his wrath
has abhorred daughter Zion,
Casting down from heaven to earth
the glory of Israel,*
Not remembering his footstool
on the day of his wrath!

2 The Lord has devoured without pity
all of Jacob's dwellings;
In his fury he has razed
daughter Judah's defenses,
Has brought to the ground in dishonor
a kingdom and its princes.

3 In blazing wrath, he cut down entirely
the horn* of Israel;
He withdrew the support of his right hand
when the enemy approached;
He burned against Jacob like a blazing fire
that consumes everything in its path.

4 He bent his bow like an enemy;
the arrow in his right hand
Like a foe, he killed
all those held precious;
On the tent of daughter Zion
he poured out his wrath like fire.

5 The Lord has become the enemy,
he has devoured Israel:
Devoured all its strongholds,
destroyed its defenses,
Multiplied moaning and groaning
throughout daughter Judah.

6 He laid waste his booth like a garden,
destroyed his shrine;*
The LORD has blotted out in Zion
feast day and sabbath,
Has scorned in fierce wrath
king and priest.[l]

7 The Lord has rejected his altar,
spurned his sanctuary;
He has handed over to the enemy
the walls of its strongholds.
They shout in the house of the LORD
as on a feast day.[m]

8 The LORD was bent on destroying
the wall of daughter Zion:
He stretched out the measuring line;*
did not hesitate to devour,
Brought grief on rampart and wall
till both succumbed.[n]

9 Her gates sank into the ground;
he smashed her bars to bits.
Her king and her princes are among the nations;
instruction is wanting,
Even her prophets do not obtain
any vision from the LORD.[o]

2:1–22 This chapter continues to move between the voice of the poet (vv. 1–20) and that of personified Zion (vv. 20–22). The persona of the poet, first portrayed in chap. 1 as a detached observer recounting both the desolation as well as the sins of the city, becomes in this chapter an advocate for Zion in her appeal to the Lord and never once mentions her sins.

2:1 The glory of Israel: the Temple. **His footstool**: the ark of the covenant (1 Chr 28:2; Ps 99:5; 132:7); or again, the Temple (Ez 43:7).

2:3 Horn: a symbol of power and strength; cf. v. 17; 1 Sm 2:1, 10; Ps 89:18, 25; 92:11; 112:9.

2:6 Booth . . . shrine: synonyms for the Temple; cf. Ps 27:5; 74:4, 8. The term for "shrine" in Hebrew (*mo'ed*) figures prominently in the pentateuchal expression "tent of meeting" (*'ohel mo'ed*).

2:8 The measuring line: normally used for building, here employed ironically as an instrument of destruction; cf. Is 34:11; 2 Kgs 21:13.

j: Lam 2:11. *k:* Lam 3:64. *l:* Is 1:13; 5:5. *m:* Ez 24:21. *n:* Jer 52:12–14. *o:* Dt 28:36.

Acrostic Poems in Hebrew

An acrostic poem is one in which the initial letters of each line of poetry follow some sort of pattern. In the Hebrew Bible, all of the acrostic poems are alphabetical acrostics: that is, the first letters of each line (or each group of lines) form the Hebrew alphabet of twenty-two letters.

The following passages in the Bible are acrostics: Psalms 9–10, 25, 34, 37, 111, 112, 119, 145; Proverbs 31:10–31; each chapter in Lamentations except chapter 5, which nevertheless has twenty-two lines; Nahum 1:2–8 (or perhaps 2–10; the acrostic is incomplete). The Hebrew text of Sirach 51:13–30 is also an acrostic. Psalms 34, 37, 112, 119, Proverbs 31, and Sirach 51 are all examples of wisdom literature, and if these texts were used in schools, the acrostic feature may have been an aid to memorization.

Although this kind of pattern in a poem may seem strange to us, we can compare it to the use of rhyme in English poetry. Rhyme is a pattern involving similar sounds at the ends of lines; it is therefore like an acrostic in combining a pattern of sound and meaning. We can admire the artistry involved in such a combination, and perhaps that will give us insight into the enjoyment that acrostic poems may have provided to their original audiences.

In the case of Lamentations, where chapters 1–4 are acrostics, and chapter 5 continues the pattern with its twenty-two lines, there may be a deeper meaning. By expressing grief in a pattern that completes the alphabet, the poet may be expressing two things: the completeness of grief—covering it "from A to Z," as we might say—and also its end. The poetical form helps the poet to channel and contain grief, as mourning rituals can do in other social settings.

10 The elders of daughter Zion
sit silently on the ground;
They cast dust* on their heads
and dress in sackcloth;
The young women of Jerusalem
bow their heads to the ground.[p]

11 My eyes are spent with tears,
my stomach churns;*
My bile is poured out on the ground
at the brokenness of the daughter of my people,
As children and infants collapse
in the streets of the town.[q]

12 They cry out to their mothers,
"Where is bread and wine?"
As they faint away like the wounded
in the streets of the city,
As their life is poured out
in their mothers' arms.

13 To what can I compare you*—to what can I liken you—
O daughter Jerusalem?
What example can I give in order to comfort you,
virgin daughter Zion?
For your breach is vast as the sea;
who could heal you?[r]

14 Your prophets provided you visions
of whitewashed illusion;
They did not lay bare your guilt,
in order to restore your fortunes;

2:10 They cast dust: as a sign of mourning; cf. Jos 7:6; Jb 2:12; Ez 27:30.

2:11 My eyes are spent with tears, my stomach churns: the poet appropriates the emotional language used by Zion in 1:16 and 1:20 to express a progressively stronger commitment to her cause. After describing the systematic dismantling of the city in vv. 5–9, the poet turns to the plight of the inhabitants in vv. 10–12. It is the description of children dying in the streets that finally brings about the poet's emotional breakdown, even as it did for Zion in 1:16.

2:13 To what can I compare you . . . ?: the author calls attention to the poetic task: to find language that speaks adequately of the atrocities and incomparable suffering experienced by Zion, and thus to attempt to offer comfort.

p: Is 3:26. *q*: Lam 1:16, 20; 3:48; Jer 8:18. *r*: Lam 1:12; Jer 8:21.

They saw for you only oracles
of empty deceit.[s]

15 All who pass by on the road,
clap their hands at you;
They hiss and wag their heads
over daughter Jerusalem:
"Is this the city they used to call
perfect in beauty and joy of all the
earth?"[t]

16 They open their mouths against you,
all your enemies;
They hiss and gnash their teeth,
saying, "We have devoured her!
How we have waited for this day—
we have lived to see it!"[u]

17 The LORD has done what he planned.
He has fulfilled the threat
Decreed from days of old,
destroying without pity!
He let the enemy gloat over you
and exalted the horn of your foes.[v]

18 Cry out to the Lord from your heart,
wall of daughter Zion!
Let your tears flow like a torrent
day and night;
Give yourself no rest,
no relief for your eyes.

19 Rise up! Wail in the night,
at the start of every watch;
Pour out your heart like water
before the Lord;
Lift up your hands to him
for the lives of your children,
Who collapse from hunger
at the corner of every street.*

20 "Look, O LORD, and pay attention:
to whom have you been so ruthless?
Must women eat their own offspring,*
the very children they have borne?
Are priest and prophet to be slain
in the sanctuary of the Lord?[w]

21 They lie on the ground in the streets,
young and old alike;
Both my young women and young men
are cut down by the sword;
You killed them on the day of your
wrath,
slaughtered without pity.[x]

22 You summoned as to a feast day
terrors on every side;
On the day of the LORD's wrath,
none survived or escaped.
Those I have borne and nurtured,
my enemy has utterly destroyed."[y]

CHAPTER 3

See RG 310–14

*The Voice of a Suffering Individual**

1 I am one who has known affliction
under the rod of God's anger,[z]
2 One whom he has driven and forced to
walk
in darkness, not in light;
3 Against me alone he turns his hand—
again and again all day long.

4 He has worn away my flesh and my skin,
he has broken my bones;[a]
5 He has besieged me all around
with poverty and hardship;
6 He has left me to dwell in dark places
like those long dead.[b]

2:19 The poet urges Zion to appeal to the Lord once more on behalf of her dying children. The image of Zion's children effectively condenses the metaphorical sense of all residents of the city (young and old alike) into the more poignant picture of actual children at the point of death. It was precisely this image, no doubt well known to survivors of besieged cities, that led to the emotional breakdown of both Zion (1:16) and the poet (2:11). The hope is that the Lord will be similarly affected by such a poignant image and respond with mercy.

2:20 Must women eat their own offspring: extreme famine in a besieged city sometimes led to cannibalism; this becomes a stereotypical way of expressing the nearly unthinkable horrors of war; cf. Lam 4:10; Dt 28:53; 2 Kgs 6:28–29; Bar 2:3; Ez 5:10.

3:1–66 This chapter is focused less on the destruction of Jerusalem than are chaps. 1 and 2 and more on the suffering of an individual. The identity of the individual is never given, and one probably should not search for a specific identification of the speaker. The figure of the representative sufferer makes concrete the pain of the people in a way similar to the personification of Zion as a woman in chaps. 1 and 2. Indeed, in vv. 40–48 the individual voice gives way to a communal voice, returning in vv. 49–66 to the individual sufferer.

s: Is 58:1; Jer 2:8; 23:16; Ez 13:9; 22:28. *t:* Ps 48:3; 50:12; Jer 18:16. *u:* Lam 3:46. *v:* Dt 28:15. *w:* Lam 4:10. *x:* Lam 3:43; 2 Chr 36:17; Jer 6:11. *y:* Jer 42:17. *z:* Jer 20:18. *a:* Jb 30:30; Is 38:13. *b:* Ps 143:3.

7 He has hemmed me in with no escape,
weighed me down with chains;
8 Even when I cry for help,
he stops my prayer;[c]
9 He has hemmed in my ways with fitted
stones,
and made my paths crooked.

10 He has been a bear lying in wait for me,
a lion in hiding![d]
11 He turned me aside and tore me apart,
leaving me ravaged.[e]
12 He bent his bow, and set me up
as a target for his arrow.[f]

13 He pierced my kidneys
with shafts from his quiver.[g]
14 I have become a laughingstock to all my
people,
their taunt all day long;[h]
15 He has sated me with bitterness,
filled me with wormwood.[i]

16 He has made me eat gravel,
trampled me into the dust;
17 My life is deprived of peace,
I have forgotten what happiness is;
18 My enduring hope, I said,
has perished before the LORD.

19 The thought of my wretched
homelessness
is wormwood and poison;
20 Remembering it over and over,
my soul is downcast.
21 But this I will call to mind;*
therefore I will hope:

22 The LORD's acts of mercy are not
exhausted,
his compassion is not spent;[j]
23 They are renewed each morning—
great is your faithfulness!
24 The LORD is my portion, I tell myself,
therefore I will hope in him.[k]

25 The LORD is good to those who trust in
him,
to the one that seeks him;[l]
26 It is good to hope in silence
for the LORD's deliverance.
27 It is good for a person, when young,
to bear the yoke,

28 To sit alone and in silence,
when its weight lies heavy,
29 To put one's mouth in the dust—*
there may yet be hope—
30 To offer one's cheek to be struck,
to be filled with disgrace.[m]

31 For the Lord does not
reject forever;[n]
32 Though he brings grief, he takes pity,
according to the abundance of his
mercy;[o]
33 He does not willingly afflict
or bring grief to human beings.[p]

34 That someone tramples underfoot
all the prisoners in the land,
35 Or denies justice to anyone
in the very sight of the Most High,
36 Or subverts a person's lawsuit—
does the Lord not see?

37 Who speaks so that it comes to pass,
unless the Lord commands it?
38 Is it not at the word of the Most High
that both good and bad take place?[q]
39 What should the living complain
about?
about their sins!

40 * Let us search and examine our ways,
and return to the LORD![r]
41 Let us lift up our hearts as well as our
hands
toward God in heaven!
42 We have rebelled and been obstinate;
you have not forgiven us.

3:21–24 In the midst of a description of suffering, the speaker offers this brief but compelling statement of hope in God's ultimate mercy. It is a hard-won and precarious hope, nearly submerged by the volume and intensity of the surrounding lament, but it is hope nonetheless.

3:29 To put one's mouth in the dust: a sign of humiliation and submission; cf. v. 16; Ps 72:9.

3:40–66 The plural voice in this lament suggests that a communal lament begins here; it then continues in the singular voice in vv. 55–66.

c: Ps 18:41; 22:2; 88:14–15. *d:* Jb 10:16; Hos 13:8. *e:* Lam 1:13. *f:* Lam 2:4; Jb 16:12. *g:* Jb 6:4; Ps 38:3. *h:* Jb 30:9; Ps 69:13. *i:* Jer 9:14; 23:15. *j:* 1 Sm 20:15; Neh 9:31. *k:* Ps 16:5; 73:26. *l:* Ps 130:6; Is 30:18. *m:* Is 50:6; Mt 5:39. *n:* Ps 85:6; 103:9. *o:* 1 Sm 2:6–7; Tb 13:2; Is 54:8. *p:* Ex 34:6–7. *q:* Is 45:7. *r:* Jl 2:12–13.

43 You wrapped yourself in wrath and pursued us,
killing without pity;[s]
44 You wrapped yourself in a cloud,
which no prayer could pierce.
45 You have made us filth and rubbish
among the peoples.[t]

46 They have opened their mouths against us,
all our enemies;
47 Panic and the pit have been our lot,
desolation and destruction;[u]
48 * My eyes stream with tears over the destruction
of the daughter of my people.[v]

49 My eyes will flow without ceasing,
without rest,
50 Until the LORD from heaven
looks down and sees.
51 I am tormented by the sight
of all the daughters of my city.

52 Without cause, my enemies snared me
as though I were a bird;
53 They tried to end my life in the pit,
pelting me with stones.
54 The waters flowed over my head:
and I said, "I am lost!"[w]

55 I have called upon your name, O LORD,[x]
from the bottom of the pit;
56 You heard me call, "Do not let your ear be deaf
to my cry for help."
57 You drew near on the day I called you;
you said, "Do not fear!"

58 You pleaded my case, Lord,
you redeemed my life.
59 You see, LORD, how I am wronged;
do me justice![y]
60 You see all their vindictiveness,
all their plots against me.

61 You hear their reproach, LORD,
all their plots against me,
62 The whispered murmurings of my adversaries,
against me all day long;
63 Look! Whether they sit or stand,
I am the butt of their taunt.

64 Give them what they deserve, LORD,
according to their deeds;
65 Give them hardness of heart;
your curse be upon them;[z]
66 Pursue them in wrath and destroy them
from under the LORD's heaven!

CHAPTER 4

See RG 310–14

*Miseries of the Besieged City**

1 How the gold has lost its luster,
the noble metal changed;
Jewels* lie scattered
at the corner of every street.

2 And Zion's precious children,
worth their weight in gold—
How they are treated like clay jugs,
the work of any potter![a]

3 Even jackals offer their breasts
to nurse their young;
But the daughter of my people is as cruel
as the ostrich* in the wilderness.[b]

4 The tongue of the infant cleaves
to the roof of its mouth in thirst;
Children beg for bread,
but no one gives them a piece.

5 Those who feasted on delicacies
are abandoned in the streets;
Those who reclined on crimson*
now embrace dung heaps.[c]

6 The punishment of the daughter of my people

3:48–51 These verses are more appropriate on the lips of the poet, who speaks of "my city" (v. 51). **Daughters of my city**: here as elsewhere "daughter" may refer to villages dependent on a larger city.

4:1–22 This chapter returns to the focus of chaps. 1 and 2, namely the horrors of a siege. Unlike chaps. 1 and 2, however, the character of personified Zion never interrupts the voice of the poet to protest her abject state. As a result, the emotion of the poem is less intense, while at the same time seeming more grim on account of its lack of petition to the Lord.

4:1–2 Jewels: lit., "holy stones." These precious things designate the children who are abandoned, starving, and killed in the siege of Jerusalem (cf. Zec 9:16). Another explanation is that these are the stones of the destroyed Temple.

4:3 Cruel as the ostrich: see note on Jb 39:14–16. Jerusalem, in her distress, has abandoned her children.

4:5 Crimson: a sign of luxury. Tyrian purple, a red-purple

s: Lam 2:21. *t:* 1 Cor 4:13. *u:* Is 24:17–18; Jer 48:43–44. *v:* Lam 1:16; 2:11; Jer 8:23; 9:17. *w:* Ps 69:2–3; 88:8; Jon 2:4. *x:* Ps 130:1–2. *y:* Ps 35:23–24; 43:1; 119:154. *z:* Jer 11:20; 2 Tm 4:14. *a:* Jer 19:11. *b:* Jb 39:16. *c:* Dt 28:56.

surpassed the penalty of Sodom,
Which was overthrown in an instant
with no hand laid on it.[d]

7 Her princes were brighter than snow,
whiter than milk,
Their bodies more ruddy than coral,
their beauty like the sapphire.

8 Now their appearance is blacker than soot,
they go unrecognized in the streets;
Their skin has shrunk on their bones,
and become dry as wood.[e]

9 Better for those pierced by the sword
than for those pierced by hunger,
Better for those who bleed from wounds
than for those who lack food.

10 The hands of compassionate women
have boiled their own children!
They became their food
when the daughter of my people was shattered.[f]

11 The LORD has exhausted his anger,
poured out his blazing wrath;
He has kindled a fire in Zion
that has consumed her foundations.[g]

12 The kings of the earth did not believe,
nor any of the world's inhabitants,
That foe or enemy could enter
the gates of Jerusalem.

13 Except for the sins of her prophets
and the crimes of her priests,
Who poured out in her midst
the blood of the just.[h]

14 They staggered blindly in the streets,
defiled with blood,
So that people could not touch
even their garments:[i]

15 "Go away! Unclean!" they cried to them,
"Away, away, do not touch!"
If they went away and wandered,
it would be said among the nations,
"They can no longer live here!

16 The presence of the LORD was their portion,
but he no longer looks upon them.
The priests are shown no regard,
the elders, no mercy.

17 Even now our eyes are worn out,
searching in vain for help;
From our watchtower we have watched
for a nation* unable to save.

18 They dogged our every step,
we could not walk in our squares;
Our end drew near, our time was up;
yes, our end had come.

19 Our pursuers were swifter
than eagles in the sky,
In the mountains they were hot on our trail,
they ambushed us in the wilderness.[j]

20 The LORD's anointed—our very lifebreath!—*
was caught in their snares,
He in whose shade we thought
to live among the nations.[k]

21 Rejoice and gloat, daughter Edom,
dwelling in the land of Uz,*
The cup will pass to you as well;
you shall become drunk and strip yourself naked![l]

22 Your punishment is completed, daughter Zion,
the Lord will not prolong your exile;
The Lord will punish your iniquity,
daughter Edom,
will lay bare your sins.[m]

or blue-purple dye produced from shellfish, was very expensive and the only colorfast dye in the ancient Near East. Thus purple or crimson cloth was available only to the wealthy.

4:17 A nation: probably Egypt, which failed to give effective aid against Babylon.

4:20 Our very lifebreath: lit., "the breath of our nostrils," that is, the king. This expression occurs in Egyptian texts of the late second millennium B.C., and may have survived as a royal epithet in the Jerusalem court. After the disaster of 598 B.C. (2 Kgs 24:1–17), Jerusalem could have hoped to live in peace amidst her neighbors; but they (vv. 21–22) as well as Babylon turned against her to ensure her total devastation in 587 B.C.

4:21 Rejoice: the address is sarcastic, since Edom (where Uz may have been located) ravaged the land after the fall of Jerusalem (cf. Ps 137).

d: Gn 19:23–29; 2 Pt 2:6; Jude 7. *e:* Lam 3:4. *f:* Lam 2:20; Dt 28:56–57; 2 Kgs 6:29. *g:* Jer 7:20; Ez 5:13. *h:* Jer 6:13. *i:* Dt 28:29; Is 59:10. *j:* Jer 4:13; Hb 1:8. *k:* Lam 2:9; Ez 19:4, 8. *l:* Lam 1:21; Jer 25:15. *m:* Is 40:2.

See RG 310–14

CHAPTER 5

The Community's Lament to the Lord

[1] Remember, LORD, what has happened to us,
pay attention, and see our disgrace:
[2] Our heritage is turned over to strangers,
our homes, to foreigners.[n]
[3] We have become orphans, without fathers;
our mothers are like widows.
[4] We pay money to drink our own water,
our own wood comes at a price.
[5] With a yoke on our necks, we are driven;
we are worn out, but allowed no rest.
[6] We extended a hand to Egypt and Assyria,
to satisfy our need of bread.*
[7] Our ancestors, who sinned, are no more;
but now we bear their guilt.
[8] Servants* rule over us,
with no one to tear us from their hands.
[9] We risk our lives just to get bread,
exposed to the desert heat;[o]
[10] Our skin heats up like an oven,
from the searing blasts of famine.[p]
[11] Women are raped in Zion,
young women in the cities of Judah;[q]
[12] Princes have been hanged by them,
elders shown no respect.[r]
[13] Young men carry millstones,
boys stagger under loads of wood;
[14] The elders have abandoned the gate,*
the young men their music.
[15] The joy of our hearts has ceased,
dancing has turned into mourning;[s]
[16] The crown has fallen from our head:
woe to us that we sinned!
[17] Because of this our hearts grow sick,
at this our eyes grow dim:
[18] Because of Mount Zion, lying desolate,
and the jackals roaming there!
[19] But you, LORD, are enthroned forever;
your throne stands from age to age.[t]
[20] * Why have you utterly forgotten us,
forsaken us for so long?[u]
[21] Bring us back to you, LORD, that we may return:
renew our days as of old.[v]
[22] For now you have indeed rejected us
and utterly turned your wrath against us.[w]

5:6 Extended a hand: that is, made an alliance. In its state of abjection, Judah was forced to depend on the major powers to the west and the east for subsistence.

5:8 Servants: the Hebrew word for "servant" is also the word used for an official of relatively high status (servant of the ruler; cf. 2 Kgs 25:24, where the term is used to refer to Babylonian rulers over occupied Jerusalem); the author doubtless intends the double meaning here.

5:14 The gate: a place of assembly, where city decisions were made and judgment given by the elders and other community leaders; see note on Ru 4:1.

5:20–22 Unlike most of the laments found in the Book of Psalms, the Book of Lamentations never moves from lament to thanksgiving. It ends with this question still unanswered by God: "Why have you utterly forgotten us?"

n: Ps 79:1. *o:* Lam 1:11. *p:* Lam 4:8. *q:* Zec 14:2. *r:* Lam 4:16. *s:* Jer 16:9; 25:10; Am 8:10. *t:* Ps 9:8; 45:7; 102:13, 27. *u:* Ps 13:2; 42:10; Is 49:14. *v:* Ps 80:19–20. *w:* Jer 14:19.

See RG 315–19

The Book of Baruch

The opening verses ascribe the book to the well-known assistant to Jeremiah (Jer 32:12; 36:4, 32; 45:1). It is a collection of four very different compositions, ending with a work entitled "The Letter of Jeremiah," which circulated separately in major manuscripts of the Greek tradition. The original language may have been Hebrew, but only the Greek and other versions have been preserved. The fictional setting is Babylon, where Baruch reads his scroll to King Jechoniah (Jehoiachin) and the exiles; they react by sending gifts and the scroll to Jerusalem (1:1–14), presumably by the hand of Baruch (1:7). No certain date can be given for the book, but it may have been edited in final form during the last two centuries B.C. The work attempts to explain the trauma of the exile in terms of a Deuteronomic cycle: sin (of Israel), punishment, repentance, and return (cf. Jgs 2; also Dt 28–33).

The prayer of the exiles (2:11–3:8) is a confession of sin and a request for mercy, and has remarkable similarities to Dn 9 and to parts of Jeremiah. The poem on personified Wisdom is concerned with three themes: the importance of Wisdom, the elusive character of Wisdom (cf. Jb 28), and the identification of Wisdom with Torah (cf. Sir 24:23). Baruch's Poem of Consolation resembles parts of Is 40–66, and it offers encouragement to the exiles in view of their eventual return; there are two addresses by personified Zion. The Letter of Jeremiah, unlike the letter in Jer 29, is a polemic against idolatry, a well-known theme (cf. Jer 10:2–11; Ps 115:4–8; 135:15–18; Is 44:9–20; Wis 13:10–15:17). It contains ten warnings that end in a kind of refrain that the idols are not gods and are not to be feared (vv. 14, 22, 28, 39, 44, 51, 56, 64, 68).

The book can be divided thus:

- I. Letter to Jerusalem (1:1–3:8)
  - A. Historical Setting (1:1–9)
  - B. Confession of Guilt (1:10–2:10)
  - C. Prayer for Deliverance (2:11–3:8)
- II. Praise of Wisdom (3:9–4:4)
  - A. Importance of Wisdom (3:9–23)
  - B. Inaccessibility of Wisdom (3:24–36)
  - C. Wisdom Contained in the Law (3:37–4:4)
- III. Baruch's Poem of Consolation (4:5–5:9)
  - A. Baruch Addresses Diaspora (4:5–9a)
  - B. Jerusalem Addresses Neighbors (4:9b–16)
  - C. Jerusalem Addresses Diaspora (4:17–29)
  - D. Baruch Addresses Jerusalem (4:30–5:9)
- IV. Letter of Jeremiah (6:1–72)

I. Letter to Jerusalem

CHAPTER 1

A. Historical Setting

See RG 316–17

*1*Now these are the words of the scroll which Baruch, son of Neriah, son of Mahseiah, son of Zedekiah, son of Hasadiah, son of Hilkiah, wrote in Babylon,[a] *2*in the fifth year, on the seventh day of the month,* at the time the Chaldeans took Jerusalem and destroyed it with fire.[b] *3*[c] Baruch read the words of this scroll in the hearing of Jeconiah, son of Jehoiakim, king of Judah, and all the people who came to the reading:[d] *4*the nobles, kings' sons, elders, and all the people, small and great—all who lived in Babylon by the river Sud.*

*5*They wept, fasted, and prayed before the Lord, *6*and collected such funds as each could afford.[e] *7*These they sent to Jerusalem, to Jehoiakim the priest, son of Hilkiah, son of Shallum, and to the priests and the whole people who were with him in Jerusalem. *8*(At the same time he* received the vessels of the house of the LORD that had been removed from the temple, to restore them to the land of Judah, on the tenth of Sivan. These silver vessels Zedekiah, son of Josiah, king of Judah, had had made *9*[f] after Nebuchadnezzar, king of Babylon, carried off as captives Jeconiah and the princes, the skilled workers, the nobles, and the people of the land from Jerusalem, and brought them to Babylon.)

B. Confession of Guilt

*10*The message was: "We send you funds, with which you are to procure burnt offerings, sin offerings, and frankincense, and to prepare grain offerings; offer these* on the altar of the LORD our God,[g] *11*and pray for the life of Nebuchadnezzar, king of Babylon, and of Belshazzar, his son,* that their lifetimes may be as the days of the heavens above the earth.[h] *12*Pray that the LORD may give us strength, and light to our eyes, that we may live under the protective shadow of

1:2 In the fifth year, on the seventh day of the month: Jerusalem fell on the seventh day of the fifth month in 587 B.C.; cf. 2 Kgs 25:8; Jer 52:12. Either the text read originally "the fifth month," or it refers to the observance of an anniversary of the fall of Jerusalem. The author of this note may have thought of the fifth year (v. 1) of Zedekiah, in view of Jer 28:1; 29:1–3. A "fifth year," again with no month mentioned, is given in Ez 1:2 for the inaugural vision of Ezekiel's prophetic career.

1:4 The river Sud: probably one of the Babylonian canals, not otherwise identified; or possibly a misreading of Ahava; cf. Ezr 8:21, 31.

1:8–9 He: apparently Baruch; less likely Jehoiakim the priest (v. 7). The silver vessels here described are distinct from the vessels referred to in 2 Kgs 25:14 and Ezr 1:7–9.

1:10 Offer these: since 2:26 suggests that the Temple is destroyed, the mention of sacrifices here may be an anachro-

a: Jer 32:12; 36:4; 45:1–5. *b:* 2 Kgs 25:8–10. *c:* 2 Kgs 23:1–2. *d:* 2 Kgs 24:8–17; Jer 22:24–30; 27:20; 51:59–64. *e:* Dt 16:17. *f:* Jer 24:1. *g:* Jer 17:26; 41:5. *h:* Dt 11:21; Ps 89:30; Jer 29:7; Dn 5:1–2; 1 Tm 2:1–2.

Nebuchadnezzar, king of Babylon, and of
Belshazzar, his son, to serve them many
days, and find favor in their sight. 13 Pray for
us to the LORD, our God, for we have sinned
against the LORD, our God. Even to this day
the wrath of the LORD and his anger have not
turned away from us. 14 On the feast day and
during the days of assembly, read aloud in
the house of the LORD this scroll that we
send you:[i]

15* "To the Lord our God belongs justice;
to us, people of Judah and inhabitants of Jerusalem, to be shamefaced, as on this day—[j]
16 to us, our kings, rulers, priests, and prophets, and our ancestors. 17 We have sinned in
the LORD's sight 18 and disobeyed him. We
have not listened to the voice of the LORD,
our God, so as to follow the precepts the
LORD set before us. 19 From the day the LORD
led our ancestors out of the land of Egypt until the present day, we have been disobedient
to the LORD, our God, and neglected to listen
to his voice. 20 Even today evils cling to us,
the curse the LORD pronounced to Moses, his
servant, at the time he led our ancestors out
of the land of Egypt to give us a land flowing
with milk and honey.[k] 21 For we did not listen
to the voice of the LORD, our God, in all the
words of the prophets he sent us, 22 but each
of us has followed the inclinations of our
wicked hearts, served other gods, and done
evil in the sight of the LORD, our God.

CHAPTER 2

See RG 317

1 "So the LORD carried out the warning
he had uttered against us: against our judges,
who governed Israel, against our kings and
princes, and against the people of Israel and
Judah. 2 Nowhere under heaven has anything
been done like what he did in Jerusalem, as
was written in the law of Moses:*[l] 3 that we
would each eat* the flesh of our sons, each
the flesh of our daughters. 4 He has made us
subject to all the kingdoms around us, an object of reproach and horror among all the
peoples around us, where the LORD has scattered us.[m] 5 We are brought low, not raised
high,[n] because we sinned against the LORD,
our God, not listening to his voice.

6 "To the LORD, our God, belongs justice;
to us and to our ancestors, to be shamefaced,
as on this day.[o] 7 All the evils of which the
LORD had warned us have come upon us.
8 We did not entreat the favor of the LORD by
turning, each one, from the designs of our
evil hearts. 9 The LORD kept watch over the
evils, and brought them home to us; for the
LORD is just in all the works he commanded
us to do,[p] 10 but we did not listen to his voice,
or follow the precepts of the LORD which he
had set before us.

C. Prayer for Deliverance

11* "And now, LORD, God of Israel, who led
your people out of the land of Egypt with a
strong hand, with signs and wonders and
great might, and with an upraised arm, so
that you have made for yourself a name to
the present day:[q] 12 we have sinned, we have
committed sacrilege, we have violated all
your statutes, LORD, our God.[r] 13 Withdraw
your anger from us, for we are left few in
number among the nations where you have
scattered us. 14 Hear, LORD, our prayer of
supplication, and deliver us for your own
sake: grant us favor in the sight of those who
brought us into exile, 15 that the whole earth
may know that you are the LORD, our God,

nism. Nevertheless, Jer 41:5 indicates that some people continued to worship at the Temple site after Nebuchadnezzar's destruction of the Temple.

1:11 Nebuchadnezzar ... Belshazzar, his son: Belshazzar was the son of Nabonidus, the last king of Babylon, not of Nebuchadnezzar, the destroyer of Jerusalem. Belshazzar was co-regent for a few years while his father was away in Arabia. Later Jewish tradition seems to have simplified the end of the Babylonian empire (cf. Dn 5:1–2), for three kings came between Nebuchadnezzar and Nabonidus.

1:15–2:10 This confession of sin is similar to Dn 9:7–14, and echoes ideas from Deuteronomy and Jeremiah; cf. also Neh 9.

2:2 Law of Moses: cf. Dt 28:53–57.

2:3 We would each eat: such dreadful events were the result of the prolonged siege of Jerusalem; cf. Lam 2:20.

2:11–35 An earnest appeal for divine mercy, along with confession of sin; cf. Dn 9:15–19.

2:15 Israel: the Israelites claimed descent from the patriarch Jacob, who had received the name Israel in a mysterious encounter with God (Gn 32:29). Thus the Deity was sometimes referred to as "the God of Israel" (Gn 33:20; Ex 5:1).

i: Ex 23:14–17; Lv 23:35–36; Sir 50:6; Hos 9:5. *j:* Bar 2:6; 3:8; Ezr 9:6–15; Neh 9:6–37; Dn 9:4–19. *k:* Lv 26:14–39; Dt 28:15–68. *l:* Dt 28:52–57; 2 Kgs 6:28–29; Jer 19:9; Lam 2:20; 4:10; Ez 5:10; Dn 9:12. *m:* Jer 29:18; Dn 9:16. *n:* Dt 28:13, 43–44. *o:* Bar 1:15; Dn 9:7. *p:* Jer 1:12; 31:28; 44:27; Dn 9:14. *q:* Dt 6:21–22. *r:* Ps 106:6.

and that Israel* and his descendants bear your name.[s] 16 LORD, look down from your holy dwelling and take thought of us; LORD, incline your ear to hear us.[t] 17 Open your eyes and see: it is not the dead in Hades,* whose breath has been taken from within them, who will declare the glory and vindication to the LORD.[u] 18 The person who is deeply grieved, who walks bowed and feeble, with failing eyes and famished soul, will declare your glory and justice, LORD![v]

19 "Not on the just deeds of our ancestors and our kings do we base our plea for mercy in your sight, LORD, our God. 20 You have sent your wrath and anger upon us, as you had warned us through your servants the prophets: 21 Thus says the LORD: Bend your necks and serve the king of Babylon, that you may continue in the land I gave your ancestors;[w] 22* for if you do not listen to the LORD's voice so as to serve the king of Babylon, 23 I will silence from the cities of Judah and from the streets of Jerusalem the cry of joy and the cry of gladness, the voice of the bridegroom and the voice of the bride; and all the land shall be deserted, without inhabitants.[x] 24 But we did not listen to your voice, or serve the king of Babylon, and you carried out the threats you had made through your servants the prophets, that the bones of our kings and the bones of our ancestors would be brought out from their burial places.[y] 25 And indeed, they lie exposed* to the heat of day and the frost of night. They died in great suffering, by famine and sword and plague.[z] 26 And you reduced the house which bears your name* to what it is today, because of the wickedness of the house of Israel and the house of Judah.[a]

God's Promises Recalled. 27 "But with us, Lord, our God, you have dealt in all your clemency and in all your great mercy. 28* Thus you spoke through your servant Moses, the day you ordered him to write down your law in the presence of the Israelites: 29 'If you do not listen to my voice, surely this great and numerous throng will dwindle away among the nations to which I will scatter them.[b] 30 For I know they will not listen to me, because they are a stiff-necked people. But in the land of their exile they shall have a change of heart;[c] 31 they shall know that I, the LORD, am their God. I will give them a heart and ears that listen;[d] 32 and they shall praise me in the land of their exile, and shall remember my name.[e] 33 Then they shall turn back from their stiff-necked stubbornness, and from their evil deeds, because they shall remember the ways of their ancestors, who sinned against the LORD.[f] 34 And I will bring them back to the land I promised on oath to their ancestors, to Abraham, Isaac, and Jacob; and they shall rule it. I will make them increase; they shall not be few. 35 And I will establish for them an eternal covenant: I will be their God, and they shall be my people; and I will never again remove my people Israel from the land I gave them.'[g]

CHAPTER 3

See RG 317

1 "LORD Almighty, God of Israel, the anguished soul, the dismayed spirit cries out to you. 2 Hear, LORD, and have mercy, for you are a merciful God; have mercy on us, who have sinned against you: 3 for you are enthroned forever, while we are perishing forever.[h] 4 LORD Almighty, God of Israel, hear the prayer of the dead of Israel, children who sinned against you; they did not listen to the voice of the LORD, their God, and their evils cling to us.[i] 5 Do not remember the wicked deeds of our ancestors, but remember at this time your power and your name, 6 for you are the LORD our God; and you,

2:17 Hades: this is the Greek translation of Hebrew *sheol*, the nether world.

2:22–24 These words are very similar to Jer 7:34; 27:9, 12.

2:25 They lie exposed: Jeremiah's words threatened Jehoiakim with being left unburied (Jer 22:19; 36:30).

2:26 The house which bears your name: the Temple of Jerusalem; cf. Dt 12:11; Jer 7:11. **What it is today**: during the exile it lay in ruins.

2:28–35 These words do not actually quote anything Moses is recorded as having said, but they present the substance of a passage such as Dt 30:1–10, which envisions exile, repentance, and restoration.

s: Gn 33:20; Sir 36:11; Jer 14:9; 35:17. *t:* Dt 26:15. *u:* Ps 6:6; Is 38:18. *v:* Zep 2:3. *w:* Jer 27:12. *x:* Jer 7:34. *y:* Jer 8:1–2. *z:* Jer 7:34; 14:12; 31:30. *a:* Jer 7:10–15; 11:17. *b:* Lv 26:39. *c:* Dt 30:1–2; 31:27. *d:* Ps 40:7; Jer 24:7; Ez 36:26. *e:* Tb 13:6. *f:* Lv 26:42–45; Dt 30:1–10. *g:* Jer 31:31; Lam 4:22. *h:* Ps 29:10; 102:12–13. *i:* Jer 31:29.

LORD, we will praise! 7This is why you put
into our hearts the fear of you: that we may
call upon your name, and praise you in our
exile, when we have removed from our
hearts all the wickedness of our ancestors
who sinned against you.[j] 8See, today we are
in exile, where you have scattered us, an object of reproach and cursing and punishment
for all the wicked deeds of our ancestors,
who withdrew from the LORD, our God."

II. Praise of Wisdom*

A. Importance of Wisdom

9 Hear, Israel, the commandments of life:
listen, and know prudence![k]
10 How is it, Israel,
that you are in the land of your foes,
grown old in a foreign land,
11 Defiled with the dead,
counted among those destined for Hades?[l]
12 You have forsaken the fountain of wisdom![m]
13 Had you walked in the way of God,
you would have dwelt in enduring peace.[n]
14 Learn where prudence is,
where strength, where understanding;
That you may know also
where are length of days, and life,
where light of the eyes, and peace.[o]
15 Who has found the place of wisdom?[p]
Who has entered into her treasuries?
16 Where are the rulers of the nations,
who lorded it over the wild beasts of the earth,[q]
17 made sport of the birds in the heavens,
Who heaped up the silver,
the gold in which people trust,
whose possessions were unlimited,
18 Who schemed anxiously for money,
their doings beyond discovery?
19 They have vanished, gone down to Hades,
and others have risen up in their stead.
20 Later generations have seen the light of day,
have dwelt on the earth,
But the way to understanding they have not known,
21 they have not perceived her paths or reached her;
their children remain far from the way to her.
22 She has not been heard of in Canaan,*
nor seen in Teman.[r]
23 The descendants of Hagar who seek knowledge on earth,
the merchants of Medan and Tema,[s]
the storytellers and those seeking knowledge—
These have not known the way to wisdom,
nor have they kept her paths in mind.

B. Inaccessibility of Wisdom

24 O Israel, how vast is the dwelling of God,*
how broad the scope of his dominion:
25 Vast and endless,
high and immeasurable!
26 In it were born the giants,*
renowned at the first,
huge in stature, skilled in war.[t]
27 These God did not choose,
nor did he give them the way of understanding;[u]
28 They perished for lack of prudence,
perished through their own folly.[v]
29 Who has gone up to the heavens and taken her,

3:9–4:4 This poem in praise of personified Wisdom utilizes the theme of Jb 28 (where is wisdom to be found?) and it identifies wisdom and law, as in Sir 24:22–23.

3:22–23 Despite the renown for wisdom of the peoples of Canaan and Phoenicia (Ez 28:3–4), of Teman (Jer 49:7), of the descendants of Hagar or the Arabians of Medan and Tema, they did not possess true wisdom, which is found only in the law of God (Bar 4:1).

3:24 The dwelling of God: here, the whole universe; cf. Is 66:1.

3:26 The giants: Gn 6:1–4 reflects a tradition about giants who existed before the flood; this was developed in the noncanonical Book of Enoch.

j: Jer 31:33. *k:* Dt 6:4–5; Prv 4:20–22. *l:* Ps 88:5. *m:* Jer 2:13; Jn 4:10, 14. *n:* Is 48:18. *o:* Prv 3:2; 8:14. *p:* Jb 28:1–28. *q:* Jer 27:6; 1 Cor 1:20. *r:* Jb 2:11; Jer 49:7; Ez 28:4–5; Zec 9:2. *s:* Gn 25:2, 15; Jb 6:19; Jer 25:23. *t:* Gn 6:4; Wis 14:6; Sir 16:7. *u:* 1 Sm 16:7–10. *v:* Sir 10:8.

bringing her down from the clouds?[w]
30 Who has crossed the sea and found her,
bearing her away rather than choice gold?
31 None knows the way to her,
nor has at heart her path.
32 But the one who knows all things knows her;
he has probed her by his knowledge—
The one who established the earth for all time,
and filled it with four-footed animals,
33 Who sends out the lightning, and it goes,
calls it, and trembling it obeys him;
34 Before whom the stars at their posts
shine and rejoice.
35 When he calls them, they answer, "Here we are!"
shining with joy for their Maker.[x]
36 Such is our God;
no other is to be compared to him:

C. Wisdom Contained in the Law

37 * He has uncovered the whole way of understanding,
and has given her to Jacob, his servant,
to Israel, his beloved.[y]
38 Thus she has appeared on earth,
is at home with mortals.[z]

CHAPTER 4

See RG 317–18

1 * She is the book of the precepts of God,
the law that endures forever;
All who cling to her will live,
but those will die who forsake her.[a]
2 Turn, O Jacob, and receive her:
walk by her light toward splendor.[b]
3 Do not give your glory to another,
your privileges to an alien nation.
4 Blessed are we, O Israel;
for what pleases God is known to us![c]

III. Baruch's Poem of Consolation*

A. Baruch Addresses Diaspora

5 Take courage, my people!
Remember, O Israel,
6 You were sold to the nations
not for destruction;
It was because you angered God
that you were handed over to your foes.[d]
7 For you provoked your Maker[e]
with sacrifices to demons and not to God;
8 You forgot the eternal God who nourished you,
and you grieved Jerusalem who nurtured you.
9 She indeed saw coming upon you
the wrath of God; and she said:

B. Jerusalem Addresses Neighbors

"Hear, you neighbors of Zion!
God has brought great mourning upon me,
10 For I have seen the captivity
that the Eternal One has brought
upon my sons and daughters.
11 With joy I nurtured them;
but with mourning and lament I sent them away.
12 Let no one gloat over me,
a widow, bereft of many;
For the sins of my children I am left desolate,
because they turned from the law of God,[f]
13 and did not acknowledge his statutes;
In the ways of God's commandments
they did not walk,
nor did they tread the disciplined paths of his justice.

3:37–38 As in Sir 24:8, Wisdom is given to Israel but also is said to live with all human beings (Prv 8:31).

4:1–4 The poem ends with the identification of Wisdom and Torah, as in Sir 24:22–23; cf. also Dt 4:5–8.

4:5–5:9 The poet addresses the exiles (vv. 5–9a), and then Zion personified is introduced, speaking to the nations and mourning the loss of her children (vv. 9b–16). She then addresses the exiles (vv. 17–29). Finally (4:30–5:9) the poet issues three calls to Jerusalem (4:30, 36; 5:5): she will see her children returning (4:22, 36–37; 5:5).

w: Dt 30:12–13; Sir 24:4; Rom 10:6–7. *x:* Jb 38:7; Ps 147:4; Is 40:26. *y:* Ps 147:19; Sir 24:8–12. *z:* Wis 9:18; Jn 1:14. *a:* Dt 4:6–8; Prv 8:35–36; Sir 24:22. *b:* Prv 4:13, 19. *c:* Dt 4:32–37; 33:29. *d:* Jgs 2:14; Is 50:1; 52:3. *e:* Dt 32:13–18; 1 Cor 10:20. *f:* Lam 1:1, 2, 7.

14 "Let Zion's neighbors come—
Remember the captivity of my sons
and daughters,
brought upon them by the Eternal One.
15 He has brought against them a nation
from afar,
a nation ruthless and of alien speech,
That has neither reverence for old age
nor pity for the child;[g]
16 They have led away this widow's
beloved sons,
have left me solitary, without daughters.

C. Jerusalem Addresses Diaspora

17 What can I do to help you?
18 The one who has brought this evil
upon you
must himself deliver you from your
enemies' hands.[h]
19 Farewell, my children, farewell;
I am left desolate.
20 I have taken off the garment of peace,
have put on sackcloth for my prayer of
supplication;
while I live I will cry out to the Eternal
One.[i]
21 "Take courage, my children; call upon
God;
he will deliver you from oppression,
from enemy hands.[j]
22 I have put my hope for your deliverance
in the Eternal One,
and joy has come to me from the Holy
One
Because of the mercy that will swiftly
reach you
from your eternal Savior.
23 With mourning and lament I sent you
away,
but God will give you back to me
with gladness and joy forever.[k]
24 As Zion's neighbors lately saw you taken
captive,
so shall they soon see God's salvation
come to you,
with great glory and the splendor of
the Eternal One.[l]
25 "My children, bear patiently the wrath[m]
that has come upon you from God;
Your enemies have persecuted you,
but you will soon see their destruction
and trample upon their necks.*
26 My pampered children have trodden
rough roads,
carried off by their enemies like sheep
in a raid.[n]
27 Take courage, my children; call out to God!
The one who brought this upon you
will remember you.[o]
28 As your hearts have been disposed to
stray from God,
so turn now ten times the more to seek
him;
29 For the one who has brought disaster
upon you
will, in saving you, bring you eternal
joy."[p]

D. Baruch Addresses Jerusalem

30 Take courage, Jerusalem!
The one who gave you your name will
console you.[q]
31 Wretched shall be those who harmed
you,
who rejoiced at your downfall;
32 Wretched shall be the cities where your
children were enslaved,
wretched the city that received your
children.[r]
33 As that city rejoiced at your collapse,[s]
and made merry at your downfall,
so shall she grieve over her own
desolation.
34 I will take from her the rejoicing crowds,
and her exultation shall be turned to
mourning:
35 For fire shall come upon her[t]
from the Eternal One, for many a day,
to be inhabited by demons for a long
time.*

4:25 Trample upon their necks: a sign of victory over the enemy (cf. Ps 44:6; Is 14:25). The Israelites considered their enemies to be God's enemies as well.

4:35 Deserts and desolate places were looked upon as the habitation of demons; cf. Tb 8:3; Lk 11:24.

g: Dt 28:49–50; Jer 5:15; 6:22–23. *h:* Jer 32:42. *i:* Jdt 9:1; Est 4:16. *j:* Jer 51:5. *k:* Jer 31:12–13. *l:* Is 60:1–7. *m:* Is 51:23. *n:* Lam 2:22. *o:* Is 40:1. *p:* Is 35:10. *q:* Ps 46:5; Is 60:14. *r:* Jer 51:43. *s:* Is 13:20–22; 47:1–11; Jer 50:13. *t:* Is 34:9–14.

36 Look to the east, Jerusalem;
see the joy that comes to you from God![u]
37 Here come your children whom you sent away,
gathered in from east to west
By the word of the Holy One,
rejoicing in the glory of God.

CHAPTER 5

See RG 318

1 Jerusalem, take off your robe of mourning and misery;
put on forever the splendor of glory from God:[v]
2 Wrapped in the mantle of justice from God,
place on your head the diadem
of the glory of the Eternal One.[w]
3 For God will show your splendor to all under the heavens;
4 you will be named by God forever:
the peace of justice, the glory of God's worship.[x]

5 Rise up, Jerusalem! stand upon the heights;
look to the east and see your children
Gathered from east to west
at the word of the Holy One,
rejoicing that they are remembered by God.
6 Led away on foot by their enemies they left you:
but God will bring them back to you
carried high in glory as on royal thrones.[y]
7 For God has commanded
that every lofty mountain
and the age-old hills be made low,
That the valleys be filled to make level ground,
that Israel may advance securely in the glory of God.[z]
8 The forests and every kind of fragrant tree
have overshadowed Israel at God's command;[a]
9 For God is leading Israel in joy
by the light of his glory,
with the mercy and justice that are his.

IV. Letter of Jeremiah

CHAPTER 6

See RG 318

1 A copy of the letter which Jeremiah
sent to those led captive to Babylon by the
king of the Babylonians, to tell them what
God had commanded him:[b]
For the sins you committed before God,
you are being led captive to Babylon by
Nebuchadnezzar, king of the Babylonians.
2 When you reach Babylon you will be there
many years, a long time—seven generations;* after that I will bring you back from
there in peace. 3 And now in Babylon you
will see gods of silver and gold and wood,
carried shoulder high, to cast fear upon the
nations.[c] 4* Take care that you yourselves do
not become like these foreigners and let not
such fear possess you. 5 When you see the
crowd before them and behind worshiping
them, say in your hearts, "You, Lord, are the
one to be worshiped!"[d] 6 For my angel* is
with you, and he will keep watch on you.[e]
7 Their tongues are smoothed by wood-workers; they are covered with gold and silver—but they are frauds, and cannot speak.[f]
8 People bring gold, as though for a girl fond

6:2 Seven generations: this number may be symbolic. If it is not, it may indicate the date of this composition by an author writing for his contemporaries for whom the conditions of the exile were still realities. He has multiplied the seventy years of Jer 29:10 by three or four.

6:4–72 This whole chapter is a sustained argument against the temptation to worship Babylonian gods. A pattern is repeated throughout the chapter: various reasons are set forth to prove that the idols in the Babylonian temples are not gods (e.g., they are weak, helpless, attended by unworthy ministers); each section is followed by an exhortation not to be deceived, not to worship them. Note the refrain at vv. 14, 22, 28, 39, 44, 51, 56, 64. Israelite religion was aniconic, i.e., it prohibited images; as elsewhere in the Old Testament (e.g., Is 42:17; 44:9–20), the polemic against idols here oversimplifies by identifying the god worshiped with the image that represents it.

6:6 My angel: the prophet assures the people that God's watchful care is with them, just as he was with their ancestors during their journey to the promised land (Ex 23:20).

u: Is 60:4–5. *v:* Is 52:1. *w:* Ex 39:30; Wis 18:24; Is 61:10; 62:3. *x:* Is 1:26; 32:17; Jer 33:16. *y:* Is 49:22. *z:* Is 40:3–4. *a:* Is 41:19. *b:* Jer 29:1. *c:* Is 46:7; Jer 10:1–16. *d:* Dt 6:13; 10:20; Mt 4:10; Lk 4:8. *e:* Ex 23:20. *f:* Ps 135:16.

of dressing up, 9 and prepare crowns for the heads of their gods. Then sometimes the priests filch the gold and silver from their gods and spend it on themselves, 10 or give part of it to harlots* in the brothel. They dress them up in clothes like human beings, these gods of silver and gold and wood. 11 Though they are wrapped in purple clothing, they are not safe from rust and corrosion. 12 Their faces are wiped clean of the cloud of dust which is thick upon them. 13 Each has a scepter, like the human ruler of a district, but none can do away with those that offend against it. 14 Each has in its right hand an ax or dagger, but it cannot save itself from war or pillage. Thus it is known they are not gods; do not fear them.

15 As useless as a broken pot[g] 16 are their gods, set up in their temples, their eyes full of dust from the feet of those who enter. 17 Their courtyards are walled in like those of someone brought to execution for a crime against the king; the priests reinforce their temples with gates and bars and bolts, so they will not be carried off by robbers. 18 They light more lamps for them than for themselves, yet not one of these can they see. 19 They are like any timber in the temple; their hearts, it is said, are eaten away. Though crawling creatures from the ground consume them and their garments, they do not feel it. 20 Their faces become sooty from the smoke in the temple. 21 Bats and swallows alight on their bodies and heads—any bird, and cats as well. 22 Know, therefore, that they are not gods; do not fear them.

23 Gold adorns them, but unless someone wipes away the corrosion, they do not shine; they felt nothing when they were molded. 24 They are bought at whatever price, but there is no spirit in them. 25 Since they have no feet, they are carried shoulder high, displaying to all how worthless they are; even those who worship them are put to shame[h] 26 because, if they fall to the ground, the worshipers must pick them up. They neither move of themselves if one sets them upright, nor come upright if they are tipped over; offerings are set out for them as for the dead.[i] 27* Their priests sell their sacrifices for their own advantage. Likewise their wives cure some of the meat, but they do not share it with the poor and the weak;[j] 28 women ritually unclean or at childbirth handle their sacrifices. From such things, know that they are not gods; do not fear them.

29 How can they be called gods? Women set out the offerings for these gods of silver and gold and wood, 30 and in their temples the priests squat with torn tunic and with shaven hair and beard, and with their heads uncovered.[k] 31 They shout and wail before their gods as others do at a funeral banquet. 32 The priests take some of the clothing from their gods and put it on their wives and children. 33* Whether these gods are treated well or badly by anyone, they cannot repay it. They can neither set up nor remove a king.[l] 34 They cannot give anyone riches or pennies; if one fails to fulfill a vow to them, they will not exact it. 35 They neither save anyone from death, nor deliver the weak from the strong,[m] 36 nor do they restore sight to the blind, or rescue anyone in distress. 37 The widow they do not pity, the orphan they do not help. 38 These gilded and silvered wooden statues are no better than stones from the mountains; their worshipers will be put to shame. 39 How then can it be thought or claimed that they are gods?

40 Even the Chaldeans themselves have no respect for them; for when they see a deaf mute, unable to speak, they bring forward Bel* and expect him to make a sound, as though he could hear. 41 They themselves are unable to reflect and abandon these gods, for they have no sense. 42* And the women, with cords around them, sit by the roads, burning

6:10 Harlots: cult prostitutes, common in some religions of the ancient Near East.

6:27–31 From the viewpoint of Jewish ritual law, the practices named here were grotesque and depraved; cf. Lv 12:2–8; 15:19–23.

6:33–39 All that the Babylonian gods cannot do, the true God does; they have neither power nor inclination to save those in need, unlike the God of Israel, who champions the cause of the weak over the strong, and who defends the widow and the orphan. Cf. 1 Sm 2:7; Ps 68:6; 146:7–9; Is 35:4–5.

6:40 Bel: cf. note on Jer 50:2.

6:42–43 Perhaps a reference to the Babylonian practice of

g: Jer 22:28. *h:* Wis 13:16. *i:* Sir 30:18–19. *j:* Lv 12:4; 15:19–20; Dt 14:28–29. *k:* Lv 10:6; 21:5, 10. *l:* Dn 2:21. *m:* Ps 68:6; 146:7–9.

chaff for incense;[n] 43 and whenever one of
them is taken aside by some passerby who
lies with her, she mocks her neighbor who
has not been thought thus worthy, and has
not had her cord broken. 44 All that is done
for these gods is a fraud; how then can it be
thought or claimed that they are gods?

45 They are produced by woodworkers and
goldsmiths; they are nothing other than what
these artisans wish them to be. 46 Even those
who produce them are not long-lived; 47 how
then can the things they have produced be
gods? They have left frauds and disgrace to
their successors. 48 For when war or disaster
comes upon them, the priests deliberate
among themselves where they can hide with
them. 49 How then can one not understand
that these are not gods, who save themselves
neither from war nor from disaster? 50 Beings
that are wooden, gilded and silvered, they
will later be known for frauds. To all nations
and kings it will be clear that they are not
gods, but human handiwork; and that God's
work is not in them. 51 Is it not obvious that
they are not gods?

52* They set no king over the land, nor do
they give rain. 53 They neither vindicate their
own rights, nor do they rescue anyone
wronged, for they are powerless. 54 They are
like crows in midair. For when fire breaks
out in the temple of these wooden or gilded
or silvered gods, though the priests flee and
are safe, they themselves are burned up in
the fire like timbers. 55 They cannot resist a
king or enemy forces. 56 How then can it be
admitted or thought that they are gods?

They are safe from neither thieves nor bandits, these wooden and silvered and gilded
gods. 57 Anyone who can will strip off the
gold and the silver, and go away with the
clothing that was on them; they cannot help
themselves. 58 How much better to be a king
displaying his valor, or a handy tool in a
house, the joy of its owner, than these false
gods; better the door of a house, protecting
whatever is within, than these false gods; better a wooden post in a palace, than these false
gods![o] 59* The sun and moon and stars are
bright, obedient in the task for which they are
sent. 60 Likewise the lightning, when it
flashes, is a great sight; and the one wind
blows over every land. 61 The clouds, too,
when commanded by God to proceed across
the whole world, fulfill the command; 62 and
fire, sent from on high to burn up the mountains and the forests, carries out its command.
But these false gods are not their equal,
whether in appearance or in power. 63 So it is
unthinkable, and cannot be claimed that they
are gods. They can neither execute judgment,
nor benefit anyone. 64 Know, therefore, that
they are not gods; do not fear them.

65 Kings they can neither curse nor bless.
66 They show the nations no signs in the
heavens, nor do they shine like the sun, nor
give light like the moon. 67 The beasts are
better than they—beasts can help themselves by fleeing to shelter. 68 Thus is it in no
way apparent to us that they are gods; so do
not fear them.

69 For like a scarecrow in a cucumber
patch,[p] providing no protection, are their
wooden, gilded, silvered gods. 70 Just like a
thornbush in a garden on which perches
every kind of bird, or like a corpse hurled
into darkness, are their wooden, gilded, silvered gods. 71 From the rotting of the purple
and the linen upon them, you can know that
they are not gods; they themselves will in
the end be consumed, and be a disgrace in
the land. 72 Better the just who has no idols;
such shall be far from disgrace!

cultic prostitution mentioned by Herodotus, the fifth-century Greek historian. The unbroken cord was a sign that this service had not yet been rendered.

6:52–53 Unlike the God of Israel, the Babylonian gods are unable to set up and depose kings, or to provide life-giving rain.

6:59–62 The elements of nature, obedient to God's orders and accomplishing the divine purpose, are better than the Babylonian gods.

n: Jer 3:2. *o:* Wis 13:10–15; 15:7–17. *p:* Jer 10:5.

See RG 320–35

The Book of Ezekiel

In response to the rebellion of Jehoiakim of Judah in 601 B.C., Nebuchadnezzar, the Babylonian ruler, besieged Jerusalem. When Jehoiakim's successor, Jehoiachin, surrendered in 597, Nebuchadnezzar appointed Zedekiah king and deported to Babylon Jehoiachin and the royal family, along with members of the upper class, including Ezekiel the priest. Five years later, as Zedekiah planned his own revolt against Babylon, Ezekiel became the first prophet to be commissioned outside Judah or Israel (chaps. 1–3). Before Jerusalem is destroyed (587 B.C.), Ezekiel is concerned to convince his audience that they are responsible for the punishment of exile and to justify the Lord's decision to destroy their city and Temple. Later, Ezekiel argues that the Judahites who embrace his preaching are the people whom the Lord has chosen as a new Israel, enlivened by a new heart, imbued with new breath (chaps. 36–37), and restored to a re-created land, Temple, and covenant relationship (chaps. 40–48). Ezekiel is clear on one point: the Lord punishes and restores for one reason—for the sake of his name, in order to demonstrate once and for all that he is Lord.

Ezekiel's symbolic actions or performances foreshadow the inevitable destruction of Jerusalem (4:1–5:4; 12:1–20; 24:15–24). The closely related judgment oracles are directed against increasingly larger groups: the inhabitants of Jerusalem (5:5–17); refugees who have fled into the mountains (6:1–14); Judah's total population, "the four corners of the land" (7:1–27). Particularly chilling is Ez 8–11, the prophet's vision of the violent injustice and idolatrous worship that fills Jerusalem. When Ezekiel protests the Lord's order to slaughter Jerusalem's wicked inhabitants, the Lord refuses to relent; the Lord's glory leaves the Temple, affirming his judgment on Jerusalem (11:22–25), whom Ezekiel portrays as a promiscuous woman, rebel from the beginning, more violent and sinful than Sodom (chap. 16). Appeals for a speedy end to the exile on the basis of a past relationship with the Lord or of Jerusalem's privileged status are futile gestures.

Ezekiel uses stereotypic oracles against the nations (chaps. 25–32) to claim universal sovereignty for Israel's God, to exemplify the consequences of arrogant national pride, and to set the stage for Israel's restoration. In order to demonstrate to all the nations that "I am the Lord," God becomes Israel's just shepherd (34:15) under whose rule a restored people (37:1–14) enjoy prosperity in a restored land. God again acts "for the sake of my name" when the mysterious forces of Gog attack Israel (chaps. 38–39). Their defeat is prelude to Ezekiel's vision of a new Israel whose source of life and prosperity is a well-ordered cult in a new Temple, where the divine glory again dwells (chaps. 40–48).

The Book of Ezekiel has the following divisions:

I. Call of the Prophet (1:1–3:27)
II. Before the Siege of Jerusalem (4:1–24:27)
III. Prophecies Against Foreign Nations (25:1–32:32)
IV. Hope for the Future (33:1–39:29)
V. The New Israel (40:1–48:35)

I. Call of the Prophet

CHAPTER 1

See RG 325–32

The Vision: God on the Cherubim. 1 In
the thirtieth year,* on the fifth day of the
fourth month, while I was among the exiles
by the river Chebar, the heavens opened, and
I saw divine visions.[a]— 2 On the fifth day of
the month—this was the fifth year* of King
Jehoiachin's exile[b]— 3 the word of the LORD
came to the priest Ezekiel, the son of Buzi,

1:1 The thirtieth year, which corresponds to the fifth year of exile (v. 2), has never been satisfactorily explained; possibly it refers to the prophet's age, or the anniversary of the finding of the book of the law in the Temple during Josiah's reform of 622 (2 Kgs 22:1–13). **The river Chebar**: probably a canal near Nippur, southeast of Babylon, one of the sites on which the Jewish exiles were settled.

1:2 The fifth day . . . the fifth year: the end of July, 593 B.C.; cf. v. 1.

a: Ez 10:20; 11:24–25; 43:3; Ps 137:1. *b:* 2 Kgs 24:15.

in the land of the Chaldeans by the river Chebar. There the hand of the LORD came upon him.[c]

4 As I watched, a great stormwind came from the North,* a large cloud with flashing fire, a bright glow all around it, and something like polished metal gleamed at the center of the fire.[d] 5 From within it figures in the likeness of four living creatures* appeared. This is what they looked like:[e] 6 They were in human form, but each had four faces and four wings,[f] 7 and their legs were straight, the soles of their feet like the hooves of a bull, gleaming like polished brass.[g] 8 Human hands were under their wings, and the wings of one touched those of another.[h] 9 Their faces and their wings looked out on all their four sides; they did not turn when they moved, but each went straight ahead.[i]

10* Their faces were like this:[j] each of the four had a human face, and on the right the face of a lion, and on the left, the face of an ox, and each had the face of an eagle. 11 Such were their faces. Their wings were spread out above. On each one, two wings touched one another, and the other two wings covered the body.[k] 12 Each went straight ahead. Wherever the spirit would go, they went; they did not change direction when they moved.[l] 13* And the appearance of the living creatures seemed like burning coals of fire. Something indeed like torches moved back and forth among the living creatures. The fire gleamed intensely, and from it lightning flashed. 14 The creatures darting back and forth flashed like lightning.

15* As I looked at the living creatures, I saw wheels on the ground, one alongside each of the four living creatures.[m] 16 The wheels and their construction sparkled like yellow topaz, and all four of them looked the same: their construction seemed as though one wheel was inside the other. 17 When they moved, they went in any of the four directions without veering as they moved. 18[n] The four of them had rims, high and fearsome—eyes filled the four rims all around. 19 When the living creatures moved, the wheels moved with them; and when the living creatures were raised from the ground, the wheels also were raised. 20 Wherever the spirit would go, they went. And they were raised up together with the living creatures, for the spirit of the living creatures was in the wheels. 21 Wherever the living creatures moved, the wheels moved; when they stood still, the wheels stood still. When they were lifted up from the earth, the wheels were lifted up with them.[o] For the spirit of the living creatures was in the wheels.

22* Above the heads of the living creatures was a likeness of the firmament; it was awesome, stretching upwards like shining crystal over their heads.[p] 23 Beneath the firmament their wings stretched out toward one another; each had two wings covering the body. 24 Then I heard the sound of their wings, like the roaring of mighty waters, like the voice of the Almighty. When they moved, the sound of the tumult was like the din of an army. And when they stood still, they lowered their wings.[q] 25 While they stood with their wings lowered, a voice came from above the firmament over their heads.

26 Above the firmament over their heads was the likeness of a throne that looked like sapphire; and upon this likeness of a throne

1:4 The North: Zaphon, the traditional abode of the gods; see notes on Jb 37:22; Ps 48:3; Is 14:13–15.

1:5 Four living creatures: identified as cherubim in 10:1–2, 20. Known from Assyrian religion as minor guardian deities of palaces and temples, the cherubim were usually portrayed in gigantic sculpture with the bodies of bulls or lions, wings like an eagle and a human head. In the Jerusalem Temple, the Lord was enthroned above in the holy of holies (Is 6:1–2).

1:10 The four faces together represent animate creation: wild animals, domesticated livestock, birds, and human beings. Christian tradition associates them with the four evangelists: the lion with Mark, the ox with Luke, the eagle with John, and the man with Matthew.

1:13–14 The coals and flashing lightning moving among the four creatures and yet coming from them identify this vision as a theophany. See note on 10:2–13.

1:15–21 The repetitions and inconsistencies in the description of the wheels and the direction of their movements evoke the vision's mysterious quality and emphasize the difficulty of describing the divine world in human language.

1:22–23, 26 This symbolic description of God's throne is similar to that in Ex 24:9–10.

c: Ez 3:14, 22; 8:1; 33:22; 37:1; 40:1; 2 Kgs 3:15; Is 8:11. *d:* Ez 8:2; Jb 38:1. *e:* Is 6:2. *f:* Ez 10:14. *g:* Rev 1:15. *h:* Ez 10:8. *i:* Ez 10:22. *j:* Ez 10:14; Rev 4:6–7. *k:* Is 6:2. *l:* Ez 10:16–19. *m:* Ez 10:2. *n:* Ez 10:12; Rev 4:6, 8. *o:* Ez 10:9–12. *p:* Ez 10:1; Gn 1:6. *q:* Ez 3:13; 10:5; 43:2; Rev 1:15.

was seated, up above, a figure that looked
like a human being.* [r] [27]And I saw something like polished metal, like the appearance of fire enclosed on all sides, from what
looked like the waist up; and from what
looked like the waist down, I saw something
like the appearance of fire and brilliant light
surrounding him.[s] [28]Just like the appearance
of the rainbow in the clouds on a rainy day
so was the appearance of brilliance that surrounded him. Such was the appearance of
the likeness of the glory of the LORD. And
when I saw it, I fell on my face and heard a
voice speak.[t]

CHAPTER 2

See RG 325–32

Eating of the Scroll. [1]The voice said
to me: Son of man,* stand up! I wish to speak
to you. [2]As he spoke to me, the spirit* entered into me and set me on my feet, and I
heard the one who was speaking[u] [3]say to me:
Son of man, I am sending you to the Israelites, a nation of rebels who have rebelled
against me; they and their ancestors have
been in revolt against me to this very day.[v]
[4]Their children are bold of face and stubborn
of heart—to them I am sending you. You
shall say to them: Thus says the Lord GOD.[w]
[5]And whether they hear or resist—they are a
rebellious house—they shall know that a
prophet has been among them.[x] [6]But as for
you, son of man, do not fear them or their
words. Do not fear, even though there are
briers or thorns and you sit among scorpions.* Do not be afraid of their words or be
terrified by their looks for they are a rebellious house.[y] [7]You must speak my words to
them, whether they hear or resist, because
they are rebellious.[z] [8]But you, son of man,
hear me when I speak to you and do not rebel
like this rebellious house. Open your mouth
and eat what I am giving you.[a]
[9b] It was then I saw a hand stretched out to
me; in it was a written scroll. [10]He unrolled
it before me; it was covered with writing
front and back. Written on it was: Lamentation, wailing, woe![c]

CHAPTER 3

See RG 325–32

[1]He said to me: Son of man, eat what
you find here: eat this scroll, then go, speak
to the house of Israel. [2]So I opened my
mouth, and he gave me the scroll to eat.
[3d] Son of man, he said to me, feed your
stomach and fill your belly with this scroll I
am giving you. I ate it, and it was as sweet as
honey* in my mouth. [4]Then he said to me,
Son of man, go now to the house of Israel,
and speak my words to them.
[5]Not to a people with obscure speech and
difficult language am I sending you, but to
the house of Israel.[e] [6]Nor to many nations of
obscure speech and difficult language whose
words you cannot understand. For if I were
to send you to these, they would listen to
you.[f] [7]But the house of Israel will refuse to
listen to you, since they refuse to listen to
me. For the whole house of Israel is stubborn
of brow and hard of heart.[g] [8]* Look! I make
your face as hard as theirs, and your brow as
stubborn as theirs.[h] [9]Like diamond, harder
than flint, I make your brow. Do not be
afraid of them, or be terrified by their looks,
for they are a rebellious house.[i]
[10]Then he said to me, Son of man, take
into your heart all my words that I speak to
you; hear them well. [11]Now go to the exiles,
to your own people, and speak to them. Say
to them, whether they hear or refuse to hear:
Thus says the LORD God!

1:26 Looked like a human being: the God who transcends the powers of the human imagination is pictured here in the likeness of an enthroned human king.

2:1 Son of man: in Hebrew, "son/daughter of . . . " is a common idiom expressing affiliation in a group; in this case, "a human being." The title is God's habitual way of addressing the prophet throughout this book, probably used to emphasize the separation of the divine and the human.

2:2 The spirit: lit., wind, breath; a vital power, coming from God, which enables the prophet to hear the divine word; cf. 8:3; 11:1, 24.

2:6 And you sit among scorpions: the prophet must be prepared for bitter opposition.

3:3 As sweet as honey: though the prophet must foretell terrible things, the word of God is sweet to the one who receives it.

3:8 Cf. Jer 1:18. The prophet must face fierce opposition with the determination and resistance shown by his opponents.

r: Rev 1:13. *s:* Ez 8:2. *t:* Rev 4:2–3. *u:* Ez 3:24; Dn 8:18. *v:* Ez 20:8, 13. *w:* Ex 32:9. *x:* Ez 3:11, 27; 33:33. *y:* Dt 31:6. *z:* Ez 3:10–11; Jer 7:27. *a:* Jer 15:16. *b:* Ez 8:3; Rev 10:2. *c:* Zec 5:3; Rev 5:1. *d:* Jer 15:16; Rev 10:9–10. *e:* Is 28:11. *f:* cf. Mt 11:21. *g:* Jer 7:27. *h:* Jer 1:18. *i:* Is 48:4.

12 Then the spirit lifted me up, and I heard behind me a loud rumbling noise as the glory of the LORD* rose from its place:[j] 13 the noise of the wings of the living creatures beating against one another, and the noise of the wheels alongside them, a loud rumbling.[k] 14 And the spirit lifted me up and took me away, and I went off, my spirit angry and bitter, for the hand of the LORD pressed hard on me. 15 Thus I came to the exiles who lived at Tel-abib* by the river Chebar; and there where they dwelt, I stayed among them distraught for seven days. 16[l] At the end of the seven days, the word of the LORD came to me:

The Prophet as Sentinel.* 17 Son of man, I have appointed you a sentinel for the house of Israel.[m] When you hear a word from my mouth, you shall warn them for me.

18 If I say to the wicked, You shall surely die—and you do not warn them or speak out to dissuade the wicked from their evil conduct in order to save their lives—then they shall die for their sin, but I will hold you responsible for their blood. 19 If, however, you warn the wicked and they still do not turn from their wickedness and evil conduct, they shall die for their sin, but you shall save your life.

20 But if the just turn away from their right conduct and do evil when I place a stumbling block before them, then they shall die. Even if you warned them about their sin, they shall still die, and the just deeds that they performed will not be remembered on their behalf. I will, however, hold you responsible for their blood.[n] 21 If, on the other hand, you warn the just to avoid sin, and they do not sin, they will surely live because of the warning, and you in turn shall save your own life.

Ezekiel Mute. 22 The hand of the LORD came upon me there and he said to me: Get up and go out into the plain, where I will speak with you.[o] 23[p] So I got up and went out into the plain. There it was! The glory of the LORD was standing there like the glory I had seen by the river Chebar. Then I fell on my face, 24 but the spirit entered into me, set me on my feet; he spoke to me, and said: Go, shut yourself in your house. 25 As for you, son of man, know that they will put ropes on you and bind you with them, so that you cannot go out among them.[q] 26 And I will make your tongue stick to the roof of your mouth so that you will be mute,* no longer one who rebukes them for being a rebellious house.[r] 27 Only when I speak to you and open your mouth, shall you say to them: Thus says the LORD God: Let those who hear, hear! Let those who resist, resist! They are truly a rebellious house.

II. Before the Siege of Jerusalem

CHAPTER 4

See RG 325–32

Acts Symbolic of Siege and Exile. 1* You, son of man, take a clay tablet; place it in front of you, and draw on it a city, Jerusalem. 2 Lay siege to it: build up siege works, raise a ramp against it, pitch camps and set up battering rams all around it. 3 Then take an iron pan and set it up as an iron wall between you and the city. Set your face toward it and put it under siege. So you must lay siege to it as a sign for the house of Israel.[s] 4 Then lie down on your left side, while I place the guilt of the house of Israel upon you. As many days as you lie like this, you shall bear their guilt. 5 I allot you three hundred and ninety days* during which you must bear the guilt of the house of Israel, the

3:12 The glory of the LORD: the divine presence, manifested here in audible form. Cf. Ex 40:34; Lk 2:9.

3:15 Tel-abib: one of the sites where the exiles were settled, probably near Nippur.

3:17–21 This passage refers to the prophet's role as sentinel, placed here and in chap. 33 as introductions to sections containing judgment oracles and salvation oracles respectively; cf. Hb 2:1.

3:26–27 Mute: here the prophet's inability to speak to the people in exile while Jerusalem was being besieged is seen as a consequence of God's direct intervention (cf. 24:27).

4:1–5:4 The symbolic actions in this section prepare for the series of oracles that follow in 5:5–7:27.

4:5–6 Three hundred and ninety days . . . forty days: a symbol to represent the respective lengths of exile for the Northern Kingdom of Israel and the Southern Kingdom of Judah. Israel had already fallen to Assyria in 722/721 B.C. The numerical value of the Hebrew consonants in the phrase translated "the days of your siege" (v. 8) is three hundred and ninety. Forty years conventionally represents one generation.

j: Ez 8:3; 43:5. *k:* Ez 10:16–17. *l:* Ez 33:7–9; cf. 18:5–18. *m:* Is 52:8; Jer 1:17; Hb 2:1. *n:* Is 8:14. *o:* Ez 1:3; 8:4. *p:* Ez 10:15; 40:3. *q:* Ez 4:8. *r:* Ps 22:15. *s:* Is 8:18.

same number of years they sinned. 6When you have completed this, you shall lie down a second time, on your right side to bear the guilt of the house of Judah forty days; I allot you one day for each year.[t] 7Turning your face toward the siege of Jerusalem, with bared arm* you shall prophesy against it. 8See, I bind you with ropes so that you cannot turn from one side to the other until you have completed the days of your siege.[u]

9* Then take wheat and barley, beans and lentils, millet and spelt; put them into a single pot and make them into bread. Eat it for as many days as you lie upon your side, three hundred and ninety days. 10The food you eat shall be twenty shekels a day by weight; each day you shall eat it. 11And the water you drink shall be the sixth of a hin* by measure; each day you shall drink it. 12And the barley cake you eat you must bake on human excrement in the sight of all. 13The LORD said: Thus the Israelites shall eat their food, unclean, among the nations where I drive them.[v] 14"Oh no, Lord GOD," I protested. "Never have I defiled myself nor have I eaten carrion flesh or flesh torn by wild beasts, nor from my youth till now has any unclean meat entered my mouth."[w] 15Very well, he replied, I will let you use cow manure in place of human dung. You can bake your bread on that. 16Then he said to me: Son of man, I am about to break the staff of bread* in Jerusalem so they shall eat bread which they have weighed out anxiously and drink water which they have measured out fearfully.[x] 17Because they lack bread and water they shall be devastated; each and every one will waste away because of their guilt.[y]

See RG 325–32

CHAPTER 5

1Now you, son of man, take a sharp sword and use it like a barber's razor, to shave your head and your beard. Then take a balance scale for weighing and divide the hair.[z] 2Set a third on fire within the city,* when the days of your siege are completed; place another third around the city and strike it with the sword; the final third scatter to the wind and then unsheathe the sword after it.[a] 3But take a few of the hairs and tie them in the hem of your garment. 4Take some of these and throw them into the fire and burn them in the fire. Because of this, fire will flash out against the whole house of Israel.

5Thus says the Lord GOD: This is Jerusalem! I placed it in the midst of the nations, surrounded by foreign lands. 6But it rebelled against my ordinances more wickedly than the nations, and against my statutes more than the foreign lands around it; they rejected my ordinances and did not walk in my statutes.[b] 7Therefore, thus says the Lord GOD: Because you have caused more uproar than the nations surrounding you, not living by my statutes nor carrying out my judgments, nor even living by the ordinances of the surrounding nations; 8therefore, thus says the Lord GOD: See, I am coming against you!* I will carry out judgments among you while the nations look on.[c] 9Because of all your abominations I will do to you what I have never done before, the like of which I will never do again. 10Therefore, parents will eat their children in your midst, and children will eat their parents.* I will inflict punishments upon you and scatter all who remain to the winds.[d]

11Therefore, as I live, says the Lord GOD, because you have defiled my sanctuary with all your atrocities and all your abominations, I will surely withdraw and not look upon you with pity nor spare you.[e] 12A third of your people shall die of disease or starve to

4:7 Bared arm: a symbol of unrestrained power.

4:9–13 This action represents the scarcity of food during the siege of Jerusalem, and the consequent need to eat whatever is at hand. **Twenty shekels**: about nine ounces. **The sixth of a hin**: about one quart.

4:11 Hin: see note on 45:24.

4:16 Break the staff of bread: reducing the supply of bread that supports life as the walking staff supports a traveler; cf. 5:16; 14:13; Lv 26:26; Ps 105:16; Is 3:1.

5:2 The city: the one drawn on the tablet (4:1).

5:8 I am coming against you: an expression borrowed from the language of warfare in which an enemy attacked another with the sword. "You" in vv. 8–17 is Jerusalem.

5:10 Parents will eat their children . . . parents: the prophet describes the consequences of the prolonged Babylonian siege of Jerusalem in 587/586 B.C. See note on Lam 2:20.

t: Dn 9:24–25; 12:11–12. *u:* Ez 3:25. *v:* Hos 9:4. *w:* Dn 1:8. *x:* Ez 5:16; Lv 26:26. *y:* Lv 26:39. *z:* Is 7:20. *a:* Jer 13:24. *b:* Ez 16:47–51. *c:* Jer 21:5. *d:* Lv 26:29, 33; Dt 28:53; Jer 19:9. *e:* Ez 7:4, 9; 8:18.

death within you; another third shall fall by the sword all around you; a third I will scatter to the winds and pursue them with the sword.[f]

[13]Thus my anger will spend itself; I will vent my wrath against them until I am satisfied. Then they will know that I the LORD spoke in my passion when I spend my wrath upon them.[g] [14]I will make you a desolation and a reproach among the nations around you, in the sight of every passerby.[h] [15]And you will be a reproach and a taunt, a warning and a horror to the nations around you when I execute judgments against you in angry wrath, with furious chastisements. I, the LORD, have spoken! [16]When I loose against you the deadly arrows of starvation that I am sending to destroy you, I will increase starvation and will break your staff of bread.[i] [17]I will send against you starvation and wild beasts who will leave you childless, while disease and bloodshed sweep through you. I will bring the sword against you. I, the LORD, have spoken.[j]

See RG 325–32

CHAPTER 6

Against the Mountains of Israel. [1]The word of the LORD came to me: [2]Son of man, set your face toward the mountains of Israel and prophesy against them:[k] [3]You shall say: Mountains of Israel, hear the word of the Lord GOD. Thus says the Lord GOD to the mountains and hills, to the ravines and valleys:[l] Pay attention! I am bringing a sword against you, and I will destroy your high places.* [4]Your altars shall be laid waste, your incense stands smashed, and I will throw your slain down in front of your idols. [5]Yes, I will lay the corpses of the Israelites in front of their idols, and scatter your bones around your altars.* [m] [6]Wherever you live, cities shall be ruined and high places laid waste, in order that your altars be laid waste and devastated, your idols broken and smashed, your incense altars hacked to pieces, and whatever you have made wiped out.[n] [7]The slain shall fall in your midst, and you shall know that I am the LORD.* [o] [8]But I will spare some of you from the sword to live as refugees among the nations when you are scattered to foreign lands. [9]Then your refugees will remember me among the nations to which they have been exiled, after I have broken their lusting hearts that turned away from me and their eyes that lusted after idols. They will loathe themselves for all the evil they have done, for all their abominations.[p] [10]Then they shall know that I the LORD did not threaten in vain to inflict this evil on them.

[11]Thus says the Lord GOD: Clap your hands, stamp your feet,* and cry "Alas!" for all the evil abominations of the house of Israel! They shall fall by the sword, starvation, and disease.[q] [12]Those far off shall die of disease, those nearby shall fall by the sword, and those who survive and are spared shall perish by starvation; thus will I spend my fury upon them. [13]They shall know that I am the LORD, when their slain lie among their idols, all around their altars, on every high hill and mountaintop, beneath every green tree and leafy oak*—any place they offer sweet-smelling oblations to all their idols.[r] [14]I will stretch out my hand against them; I will make the land a desolate waste, from the wilderness to Riblah,* wherever they live. Thus they shall know that I am the LORD.[s]

6:3 High places: raised platforms usually built on hills outside towns for making sacrifices to the Lord or to Canaanite deities. They became synonymous with places of idolatry after the centralization of worship in the Jerusalem Temple.

6:5 Scatter your bones . . . altars: the bones of the dead defiled a place; cf. 2 Kgs 23:14.

6:7 You shall know that I am the LORD: this formula is repeated after most of Ezekiel's oracles from this point on. Whatever happens to Israel happens at the Lord's command; because the Lord uses the nations to punish or reward Israel for its behavior, Israel will learn that its God has sole rule over the nations and the universe, and will acknowledge that rule in obedience.

6:11 Clap your hands, stamp your feet: these gestures may express grief, even horror, at Israel's infidelities; in 25:6, they are signs of gloating.

6:13 Every green tree and leafy oak: trees often identified with fertility deities and the "tree of life"; sacred groves had a long history in Palestine and throughout the Mediterranean basin as places of worship; cf. Dt 12:2.

6:14 From the wilderness to Riblah: the whole land, from the far south to the far north.

---

f: Ez 6:11–12; Rev 6:8. *g:* Ez 16:42. *h:* Lv 26:32. *i:* Ez 4:16; 14:13; Lv 26:26. *j:* Lv 26:25. *k:* Ez 36:1. *l:* Ez 36:4; Lv 26:30. *m:* Lv 26:30; Jer 8:12. *n:* Lv 26:30. *o:* Ez 11:10–12. *p:* Ez 20:7, 24; Ps 137:1. *q:* Ez 21:14–17. *r:* Ez 20:28; Lv 26:30. *s:* Jer 48:22.

CHAPTER 7

See RG 325–32

The End Has Come. 1 The word of the LORD came to me: 2 Son of man, now say: Thus says the Lord GOD to the land of Israel: An end! The end comes upon the four corners of the land![t] 3 Now the end is upon you; I will unleash my anger against you, judge you according to your ways, and hold against you all your abominations. 4 My eye will not spare you, nor will I have pity; but I will hold your conduct against you, since your abominations remain within you; then shall you know that I am the LORD.[u]

5 Thus says the Lord GOD: Evil upon evil! See it coming! 6 An end is coming, the end is coming; it is ripe for you! See it coming! 7 The crisis has come for you who dwell in the land! The time has come, near is the day: panic, no rejoicing on the mountains.[v] 8 Soon now I will pour out my fury upon you and spend my anger against you; I will judge you according to your ways and hold against you all your abominations.[w] 9 My eye will not spare, nor will I take pity; I will hold your conduct against you since your abominations remain within you, then you shall know that it is I, the LORD, who strikes.[x]

10 The day is here! Look! it is coming! The crisis has come! Lawlessness is blooming, insolence budding; 11 the violent have risen up to wield a scepter of wickedness. But none of them shall remain; none of their crowd, none of their wealth, for none of them are innocent. 12* The time has come, the day dawns. The buyer must not rejoice, nor the seller mourn, for wrath is coming upon all the throng.[y] 13 Assuredly, the seller shall not regain what was sold, as long as they all live; for the vision is for the whole crowd: it shall not be revoked! Yes, because of their guilt, they shall not hold on to life. 14 They will sound the trumpet and get everything ready, but no one will go out to battle, for my wrath weighs upon all the crowd.

15 The sword is outside; disease and hunger are within. Whoever is in the fields will die by the sword; whoever is in the city disease and hunger will devour.[z] 16 If their survivors flee, they will die on the mountains, moaning like doves of the valley on account of their guilt. 17 All their hands will hang limp, and all their knees* turn to water.[a] 18[b] They put on sackcloth, horror clothes them; shame is on all their faces, all their heads are shaved bald.* 19 They fling their silver into the streets, and their gold is considered unclean.[c] Their silver and gold cannot save them on the day of the LORD's wrath. They cannot satisfy their hunger or fill their bellies, for it has been the occasion of their sin. 20* In their beautiful ornaments they took pride; out of them they made their abominable images, their detestable things. For this reason I will make them unclean.[d] 21 I will hand them over as spoils to foreigners, as plunder to the wicked of the earth, so that they may defile them. 22 I will turn my face away from them. My treasure will be defiled; the violent will enter and defile it.[e] 23 They will wreak slaughter, for the land is filled with bloodshed and the city with violence.[f] 24 I will bring in the worst of the nations to take possession of their houses. I will put an end to their proud strength,* and their sanctuaries will be defiled.[g] 25 When anguish comes, they will seek peace, but there is none.[h] 26 Disaster after disaster, rumor upon rumor. They keep seeking a vision from the prophet; instruction from the priest is missing, and counsel from the elders.[i] 27 The king mourns, the prince is terror-stricken, the hands of the common people tremble. I will deal with them according to their ways, and according to their judgments I will judge them. They shall know that I am the LORD.

7:12–13 Normal affairs will cease to have any meaning in view of the disaster that is to come.

7:17 Hands . . . knees: image of profound terror; loss of control of body movement and functions.

7:18 Shaved bald: shaving the head was a sign of mourning.

7:20 Assyrian wall paintings show that statues of deities were often cast in precious metals and then decorated with jewelry. Cf. Is 40:19–20; 41:6–7; 44:9–20.

7:24 Proud strength: misplaced trust in the might and power of their kings and army. Cf. v. 22; 33:28 and related ideas in Is 2:12; 10:12; 13:11; Jer 48:29; Ez 24:21; 30:18.

---

t: Rev 7:1; 20:8. *u:* Ez 5:11; Jer 13:14. *v:* Ez 12:23; 30:3; Am 5:18–19; Zep 1:14. *w:* Ez 20:8, 13, 21. *x:* Ez 22:31; Jer 21:7. *y:* Is 24:2; cf. Mt 24:17–18. *z:* Dt 32:25. *a:* Jer 47:3. *b:* Is 15:2–3; Jer 4:8; 48:3. *c:* Zep 1:7, 18; 2:2. *d:* Jer 10:3–4. *e:* Ps 74:7–8. *f:* Ez 22:9; 24:6. *g:* Lam 2:7. *h:* Jer 6:1. *i:* Jer 18:18; Mi 3:6–7.

See RG 325–32

CHAPTER 8

1 In the sixth year, on the fifth day of the sixth month,* as I was sitting in my house, with the elders of Judah sitting before me, the hand of the Lord GOD fell upon me there.[j] 2 I looked up and there was a figure that looked like a man.* Downward from what looked like his waist, there was fire; from his waist upward, like the brilliance of polished bronze.[k]

Vision of Abominations in the Temple. 3 He stretched out the form of a hand and seized me by the hair of my head. The spirit lifted me up* between earth and heaven and brought me in divine vision to Jerusalem[l] to the entrance of the inner gate facing north where the statue of jealousy that provokes jealousy stood. 4 There I saw the glory of the God of Israel, like the vision I had seen in the plain.[m] 5 He said to me: Son of man, lift your eyes to the north! I looked to the north and there in the entry north of the altar gate was this statue of jealousy.[n] 6 He asked, Son of man, do you see what they are doing? Do you see the great abominations that the house of Israel is practicing here, so that I must depart from my sanctuary? You shall see even greater abominations![o]

7 Then he brought me to the entrance of the courtyard, and there I saw a hole in the wall. 8 Son of man, he ordered, dig through the wall. I dug through the wall—there was a doorway. 9 Go in, he said to me, and see the evil abominations they are doing here. 10 I went in and looked—figures of all kinds of creeping things and loathsome beasts,* all the idols of the house of Israel,[p] pictured around the wall. 11 Before them stood seventy of the elders of the house of Israel. Among them stood Jaazaniah, son of Shaphan, each with censer in hand; a cloud of incense drifted upward.[q] 12 Then he said to me: Do you see, son of man, what the elders of the house of Israel are doing in the dark, each in his idol chamber? They think: "The LORD cannot see us; the LORD has forsaken the land."[r] 13 He said: You will see them practicing even greater abominations.

14 Then he brought me to the entrance of the north gate of the house of the LORD. There women sat and wept for Tammuz.*[s] 15 He said to me: Do you see this, son of man? You will see other abominations, greater than these!

16 Then he brought me into the inner court of the house of the LORD. There at the door of the LORD's temple, between the porch and the altar, were about twenty-five men with their backs to the LORD's temple and their faces toward the east; they were bowing eastward* to the sun.[t] 17 He said: Do you see, son of man? Are the abominable things the house of Judah has done here so slight that they should also fill the land with violence, provoking me again and again? Now they are putting the branch to my nose!* 18 Therefore I in turn will act furiously: my eye will

8:1 In the sixth year, on the fifth day of the sixth month: September, 592 B.C.

8:2 Looked like a man: the divine presence which accompanies Ezekiel in these visions. Cf. 40:3–4.

8:3 The spirit lifted me up: the prophet is transported in vision from Babylon to Jerusalem. Ezekiel may be drawing on his memory of the Temple from before his exile in 598 B.C. **The statue of jealousy**: the statue which provokes the Lord's outrage against the insults of his own people; perhaps the statue of the goddess Asherah set up by Manasseh, king of Judah (cf. 2 Kgs 21:7; 2 Chr 33:7, 15). Although his successor, Josiah, had removed it (2 Kgs 23:6), the statue may have been set up again after his death.

8:10 Creeping things and loathsome beasts: perhaps images of Egyptian deities, often represented in animal form. During the last days of Jerusalem Zedekiah, king of Judah, was allied with Egypt, hoping for protection against the Babylonians.

8:14 Wept for Tammuz: the withering of trees and plants that began in late spring was attributed to the descent of Tammuz, the Mesopotamian god of fertility, to the world of the dead beneath the earth. During the fourth month of the year, female worshipers of Tammuz would wail and mourn the god's disappearance.

8:16 Bowing eastward: sun worship was perhaps introduced as a condition of alliance with other nations. While Josiah removed some elements of this worship (2 Kgs 23:11), Manasseh, for example, built altars to all the "hosts of heaven" in two Temple courtyards (2 Kgs 21:5).

8:17 Putting the branch to my nose: the meaning is uncertain. It may be connected with the social injustice mentioned in v. 17b and in 9:9, e.g., "with their violence they tweak my nose," i.e., "goad my fury." The Masoretic text reads "their noses" as a euphemism for "my nose," thus avoiding the impropriety of these idolaters coming into contact with God even figuratively.

j: Ez 14:1; 33:31. *k:* Ez 1:4, 26–27. *l:* Ez 2:9; 3:12; Dn 14:6. *m:* Ez 3:22. *n:* Ps 78:58. *o:* Ps 78:60. *p:* Ez 23:14. *q:* Nm 11:16. *r:* Is 29:15. *s:* cf. Dn 11:37. *t:* Jb 31:26–28.

not spare, nor will I take pity. Even if they cry out in a loud voice for me to hear, I shall not listen to them.

CHAPTER 9

See RG 325–32

Slaughter of the Idolaters. 1 Then he cried aloud for me to hear: Come, you scourges of the city! 2 And there were six men coming from the direction of the upper gate which faces north, each with a weapon of destruction in his hand. In their midst was a man dressed in linen, with a scribe's case at his waist. They entered and stood beside the bronze altar.[u] 3 Then the glory of the God of Israel moved off the cherub and went up to the threshold of the temple. He called to the man dressed in linen with the scribe's case at his waist,[v] 4[w] and the LORD said to him:* Pass through the city, through the midst of Jerusalem, and mark an X on the foreheads of those who grieve and lament over all the abominations practiced within it. 5 To the others he said in my hearing: Pass through the city after him and strike! Do not let your eyes spare; do not take pity. 6 Old and young, male and female, women and children—wipe them out! But do not touch anyone marked with the X. Begin at my sanctuary. So they began with the elders who were in front of the temple.[x] 7 Defile the temple, he said to them, fill its courts with the slain. Then go out and strike in the city.

8 As they were striking, I was left alone. I fell on my face, crying out, "Alas, Lord GOD! Will you destroy all that is left of Israel when you pour out your fury on Jerusalem?" 9 He answered me: The guilt of the house of Israel and the house of Judah is too great to measure; the land is filled with bloodshed, the city with lawlessness. They think that the LORD has abandoned the land, that he does not see them. 10 My eye, however, will not spare, nor shall I take pity, but I will bring their conduct down upon their heads.

11 Just then the man dressed in linen with the scribe's case at his waist made his report: "I have done as you commanded!"

CHAPTER 10

See RG 325–32

1 Then I looked and there above the firmament over the heads of the cherubim was something like a sapphire, something that looked like a throne.[y] 2* And he said to the man dressed in linen: Go within the wheelwork under the cherubim; fill both your hands with burning coals from the place among the cherubim, then scatter them over the city. As I watched, he entered.[z] 3 Now the cherubim were standing to the south of the temple when the man went in and a cloud filled the inner court. 4 The glory of the LORD had moved off the cherubim to the threshold of the temple; the temple was filled with the cloud, the whole court brilliant with the glory of the LORD. 5 The sound of the wings of the cherubim could be heard as far as the outer court; it was like the voice of God Almighty speaking.[a] 6 He commanded the man dressed in linen: Take fire from within the wheelwork among the cherubim. The man entered and stood by one of the wheels. 7 Thereupon a cherub stretched out a hand from among the cherubim toward the fire in the midst of the cherubim, took some, and put it in the hands of the one dressed in linen. He took it and came out. 8 Something like a human hand was visible under the wings of the cherubim. 9 I also saw four wheels beside the cherubim, one wheel beside each cherub, and the wheels appeared to have the sparkle of yellow topaz. 10 And the appearance of the four all seemed alike, as though one wheel were inside the other. 11 When they moved, they went in any of the four directions without veering as they moved; in whatever direction the first cherub faced, the others followed without veering as they went. 12 Their entire bodies—backs, hands, and wings—and wheels were covered with eyes all around like the four wheels.[b] 13 I heard the wheels

9:4 Ezekiel emphasizes personal accountability; the innocent inhabitants of Jerusalem are spared while the idolatrous are punished. **An X**: lit., the Hebrew letter *taw*.

10:2–13 The burning coals, a sign of the divine presence (cf. 28:14; Ps 18:9), represent the judgment of destruction that God is visiting upon the city; they may also represent the judgment of purification that prepares the land to become the Lord's sanctuary (cf. Is 6:6–7).

u: Ez 10:2; Dn 10:5; 12:6; Rev 8:2; 15:6. *v:* Ez 11:22. *w:* Ex 12:7; Rev 7:2–4; 13:16. *x:* Gn 4:15; Ex 12:7. *y:* Ex 24:10; Rev 4:2. *z:* Rev 8:2. *a:* Jb 40:9. *b:* Ez 1:15–20; Rev 4:6–8.

called "wheelwork." [14]Each living creature had four faces: the first a cherub, the second a human being, the third a lion, the fourth an eagle.[c] [15]* When the cherubim rose up, they were indeed the living creatures I had seen by the river Chebar.[d] [16]When the cherubim moved, the wheels went beside them; when the cherubim lifted up their wings to rise from the earth, even then the wheels did not leave their sides. [17]When they stood still, the wheels stood still; when they rose up, the wheels rose up with them, for the spirit of the living creatures was in them. [18]Then the glory of the LORD left the threshold of the temple and took its place upon the cherubim. [19]The cherubim lifted their wings and rose up from the earth before my eyes as they departed with the wheels beside them. They stopped at the entrance of the eastern gate of the LORD's house, and the glory of the God of Israel was up above them.[e] [20]* These were the living creatures I had seen beneath the God of Israel by the river Chebar. Now I knew they were cherubim.[f] [21]Each of them had four faces and four wings, and something like human hands under their wings. [22]Their faces looked just like the faces I had seen by the river Chebar; and each one went straight ahead.

See RG 325-32

CHAPTER 11

Death for the Remnant in Jerusalem.

[1]The spirit lifted me up and brought me to the east gate of the house of the LORD facing east. There at the entrance of the gate were twenty-five men; among them I saw the public officials Jaazaniah, son of Azzur, and Pelatiah, son of Benaiah. [2]The LORD said to me: Son of man, these are the men who are planning evil and giving wicked counsel in this city. [3]They are saying, "No need to build houses! The city is the pot, and we are the meat."*[g] [4]Therefore prophesy against them, son of man, prophesy! [5]Then the spirit of the LORD fell upon me and told me to say: Thus says the LORD: This is how you talk, house of Israel. I know the things that come into your mind! [6]You have slain many in this city, filled its streets with the slain. [7]Therefore thus says the Lord GOD: The slain whom you piled up in it, that is the meat, the pot is the city. But you I will bring out of it.[h] [8]You fear the sword—that sword I will bring upon you—oracle of the Lord GOD.[i] [9]I will bring you out of the city, hand you over to foreigners, and execute judgments against you. [10]By the sword you shall fall. At the borders of Israel I will judge you so that you will know that I am the LORD. [11]The city shall not be a pot for you, nor shall you be meat within it. At the borders of Israel I will judge you,[j] [12]so you shall know that I am the LORD, whose statutes you did not follow, whose ordinances you did not keep. Instead, you acted according to the ordinances of the nations around you.

[13]While I was prophesying, Pelatiah, the son of Benaiah, dropped dead. I fell down on my face and cried out in a loud voice: "Alas, Lord GOD! You are finishing off what remains of Israel!"*[k]

Restoration for the Exiles. [14]The word of the LORD came to me: [15]* Son of man, the inhabitants of Jerusalem are saying about all your relatives, the other exiles, and all the house of Israel, "They are far away from the

10:15–19 The throne represents God's presence as ruler and protector of the land. In chap. 1, God is revealed as the lord of the world who can appear even in a far-off land; here God is about to abandon the Temple, that is, hand the city over to its enemies. God and the throne return again in 43:1–3.

10:20–22 The repetition of description from the preceding verses is a device intended to suggest the rapid, constantly changing motion of the vision and the difficulty of describing the divine in human language.

11:3 No need to build houses . . . meat: this advice is based on the conviction that invincible Jerusalem will protect its citizens from further danger just as a pot shields the meat inside from the fire. The poorer citizens of Jerusalem and the refugees from nearby villages can now appropriate the property abandoned by the city's wealthier upper class when they were deported (v. 15). The metaphor of the pot and its contents reappears in chap. 24.

11:13 In Ezekiel's vision Pelatiah represents the people left in Jerusalem, "the remnant of Israel." His sudden death in the vision, but not in reality, is a figure for the judgment described in vv. 8–10 and prompts Ezekiel's anguished question about the survival of the people left in the land after the deportations in 597.

11:15–21 Ezekiel insists that those who remained in Judah are doomed; the exiles, under a new covenant, will constitute a new Israel. Cf. chap. 36; Jer 24:7; 29.

c: cf. Gn 3:24. *d:* Ps 137:1. *e:* Ez 43:4. *f:* Ez 1:1. *g:* Ez 24:3; Jer 1:13. *h:* Mi 3:2–3. *i:* Lv 26:25. *j:* 2 Kgs 25:20–21. *k:* Ez 9:8.

LORD. The land is given to us as a possession.”[l] 16 Therefore say: Thus says the Lord GOD: I have indeed sent them far away among the nations, scattered them over the lands, and have been but little sanctuary for them in the lands to which they have gone. 17 Therefore, thus says the Lord GOD, I will gather you from the nations and collect you from the lands through which you were scattered, so I can give you the land of Israel.[m] 18 They will enter it and remove all its atrocities and abominations. 19[n] And I will give them another heart and a new spirit I will put within them. From their bodies I will remove the hearts of stone, and give them hearts of flesh, 20 so that they walk according to my statutes, taking care to keep my ordinances. Thus they will be my people, and I will be their God.[o] 21 But as for those whose hearts are devoted to their atrocities and abominations, I will bring their conduct down upon their heads—oracle of the Lord GOD.

22 Then the cherubim lifted their wings and the wheels alongside them, with the glory of the God of Israel above them.[p] 23* The glory of the LORD rose up from the middle of the city and came to rest on the mountain east of the city.[q] 24 In a vision, the spirit lifted me up and brought me back to the exiles in Chaldea, by the spirit of God. The vision I had seen left me,[r] 25 and I told the exiles everything the LORD had shown me.[s]

See RG 325–32

CHAPTER 12

Acts Symbolic of the Exile. 1 The word of the LORD came to me: 2 Son of man, you live in the midst of a rebellious house; they have eyes to see, but do not see, and ears to hear but do not hear. They are such a rebellious house![t] 3 Now, son of man, during the day while they watch, pack a bag for exile,* and again while they watch, go into exile from your place to another place; perhaps they will see that they are a rebellious house. 4 During the day, while they watch, bring out your bag, an exile’s bag. In the evening, again while they watch, go out as if into exile.[u] 5 While they watch, dig a hole through the wall* and go out through it. 6 While they watch, shoulder your load and go out in darkness. Cover your face so you cannot see the land, for I am making you a sign for the house of Israel![v]

7 I did just as I was commanded. During the day I brought out my bag, an exile’s bag. In the evening while they watched, I dug a hole through the wall with my hands and set out in darkness, shouldering my load.

8 In the morning, the word of the LORD came to me: 9 Son of man, did not the house of Israel, that house of rebels, say, “What are you doing?”[w] 10 Tell them: Thus says the Lord GOD: This load is the prince in Jerusalem and the whole house of Israel within it. 11 Say, I am a sign for you: just as I have done, so it shall be done to them; into exile, as captives they shall go.[x] 12 The prince among them shall shoulder his load in darkness and go out through the hole they dug in the wall to bring him out. His face shall be covered so that he cannot even see the ground.[y] 13[z] I will spread my net over him and he shall be caught in my snare. I will bring him into Babylon, to the land of the Chaldeans, though he shall not see it,* and there he shall die. 14 All his retinue, his aides and all his troops, I will scatter to the winds and pursue them with the sword.[a] 15 Then they shall know that I am the LORD, when I disperse them among the nations and scatter them throughout the lands.[b] 16 But I will let a few of them escape the sword, starvation, and plague, so that they

11:23 The glory of the Lord departs toward the east, to the exiles in Babylon; it will return once the Temple is rebuilt (43:1–3).

12:3–10 An exile’s bag contains bare necessities, probably no more than a bowl, a mat, and a waterskin. The prophet’s action foreshadows the fate of ruler and people (vv. 11–14).

12:5 Through the wall: mud-brick outer wall of a private home. In this symbolic action, Ezekiel represents the enemy forces, and the house wall, the city wall of Jerusalem breached by the Babylonian army.

12:13 Though he shall not see it: according to a Targum, an allusion to Nebuchadnezzar having Zedekiah blinded before deporting him to Babylonia (cf. 2 Kgs 25:7); according to the Septuagint, the king is ashamed of his flight from the city and disguises himself so others will not recognize him.

l: Ez 33:24. *m:* Ez 34:13; 36:28. *n:* Ez 18:31; 36:26; 2 Cor 3:3. *o:* Ex 6:7; Jer 31:33; 32:38. *p:* Ex 24:16. *q:* Zec 14:4. *r:* Ez 37:1. *s:* Ez 3:4, 11. *t:* Is 6:9–10; Jer 5:21; cf. Mt 13:15; Mk 4:12; 8:18. *u:* 2 Kgs 25:4. *v:* Is 8:18. *w:* Ez 20:49; 24:19. *x:* 2 Kgs 25:7; Jer 52:15. *y:* Jer 23:33; 52:7. *z:* Ez 17:20; 19:8; 32:3. *a:* 2 Kgs 25:5; Jer 21:7. *b:* Lv 26:33.

may recount all their abominations among the nations to which they go. Thus they may know that I am the LORD.*

17 The word of the LORD came to me: 18 Son of man, eat your bread trembling and drink your water shaking with fear.[c] 19 And say to the people of the land:* Thus says the Lord GOD about the inhabitants of Jerusalem in the land of Israel: they shall eat their bread in fear and drink their water in horror, because the land will be emptied of what fills it—the lawlessness of all its inhabitants. 20 Inhabited cities shall be in ruins, the land a desolate place. Then you shall know that I am the LORD.

Prophecy Ridiculed. 21 The word of the LORD came to me: 22 Son of man, what is this proverb you have in the land of Israel: "The days drag on, and every vision fails"?*[d] 23 Say to them therefore: Thus says the Lord GOD: I will put an end to that proverb; they shall never use it again in Israel. Say to them instead: "The days are at hand and every vision fulfilled."[e] 24 No longer shall there be any false visions or deceitful divinations within the house of Israel,[f] 25 for whatever word I speak shall happen without delay. In your days, rebellious house, whatever I speak I will bring about—oracle of the Lord GOD.[g]

26 The word of the LORD came to me: 27 Son of man, listen! The house of Israel is saying, "The vision he sees is a long time off; he prophesies for distant times!"[h] 28 Say to them therefore: Thus says the Lord GOD: None of my words shall be delayed any longer. Whatever I say is final; it shall be done—oracle of the Lord GOD.

CHAPTER 13

See RG 325–32

Against the Prophets of Peace. 1 The word of the LORD came to me: 2 Son of man, prophesy against the prophets of Israel, prophesy! Say to those who prophesy their own thoughts: Hear the word of the LORD![i] 3 Thus says the Lord GOD: Woe to those prophets, the fools who follow their own spirit and see nothing.[j] 4 Like foxes among ruins are your prophets, Israel! 5 You did not step into the breach, nor repair the wall around the house of Israel so it would stand firm against attack on the day of the LORD. 6 False visions! Lying divinations! They say, "The oracle of the LORD," even though the LORD did not send them. Then they expect their word to be confirmed![k] 7 Was not the vision you saw false? Did you not report a lying divination when you said, "Oracle of the LORD," even though I never spoke? 8 Therefore thus says the Lord GOD: Because you have spoken falsehood and seen lying visions, therefore, for certain I am coming at you—oracle of the Lord GOD. 9 My hand is against the prophets who see false visions and who make lying divinations. They shall not belong to the community of my people. They shall not be written in the register of the house of Israel, nor shall they enter the land of Israel. Thus you shall know that I am the LORD.[l]

10 Because they led my people astray, saying, "Peace!" when there is no peace, and when a wall is built, they cover it with whitewash,* 11 say then to the whitewashers: I will bring down a flooding rain; hailstones shall fall, and a stormwind shall break forth.[m] 12 When the wall has fallen, will you not be asked: "Where is the whitewash you spread on it?"

13 Therefore thus says the Lord GOD: In my fury I will let loose stormwinds; because of my anger there will be flooding rain, and hailstones will fall with destructive wrath.[n] 14 I will tear down the wall you whitewashed and level it to the ground, laying bare its foundations. When it falls, you shall be crushed beneath it. Thus you shall know that I am the LORD. 15 When I have poured out my

12:16 Both exiles and nations shall know that the exile is divine punishment for Israel's betrayal of the Lord and the covenant, not evidence that the Lord is too weak to fight off the Babylonian deity.

12:19 The people of the land: the exiles in Babylon who, ironically, are now outside the land.

12:22–28 This proverb conveys the skepticism the people of Jerusalem have; cf. Jer 20:7–9.

13:10 The false prophets contributed to popular illusions of security by predictions of peace, like those who whitewash a wall to conceal its defects.

c: Lam 5:9. *d:* Ps 49:4. *e:* Ez 7:7. *f:* Ez 13:23; Jer 14:14; Zec 13:2–4. *g:* Hb 2:3. *h:* cf. Mt 24:48; 2 Pt 3:4. *i:* Jer 23:16, 21–22; 28:15. *j:* Ez 14:9; Nm 16:28; Is 32:6; Jer 23:1, 16, 25–40; Mi 2:11. *k:* cf. Is 30:10. *l:* Ex 32:32. *m:* cf. Ps 18:7–15; 77:17–18. *n:* Rev 11:19; 16:21.

fury on the wall and its whitewashers, it will fall. Then I will say to you: No wall! No whitewashers— [16]the prophets of Israel who prophesy to Jerusalem and see visions of peace for it when there is no peace—oracle of the Lord GOD.[o]

Against Witches. [17]As for you, son of man, now set your face against the daughters of your people who play the prophet from their own thoughts, and prophesy against them.[p] [18]You shall say, Thus says the Lord GOD: Woe to those who sew amulets for the wrists of every arm and make veils* for every head size to snare lives! You ensnare the lives of my people, even as you preserve your own lives! [19]You have profaned me among my people for handfuls of barley and crumbs of bread,* slaying those who should not be slain, and keeping alive those who should not live, lying to my people, who listen to lies. [20]Therefore thus says the Lord GOD: See! I am coming after your amulets by which you ensnare lives like prey. I will tear them from your arms and set free the lives of those you have ensnared like prey.[q] [21]I will tear off your veils and deliver my people from your power, so that they shall never again be ensnared by your hands. Thus you shall know that I am the LORD. [22]Because you discourage the righteous with lies when I did not want them to be distressed, and encourage the wicked so they do not turn from their evil ways and save their lives,[r] [23]therefore you shall no longer see false visions or practice divination again. I will deliver my people from your hand. Thus you shall know that I am the LORD.

CHAPTER 14

See RG 325-32

Idolatry and Unfaithfulness. [1]Some elders of Israel came and sat down before me.[s] [2]Then the word of the LORD came to me: [3]Son of man, these men keep the memory of their idols alive in their hearts, setting the stumbling block of their sin before them. Should I allow myself to be consulted by them? [4]Therefore say to them: Thus says the Lord GOD: If any of the house of Israel who keep the memory of their idols in their hearts, setting the stumbling block of their sin before them, come to a prophet, I the LORD will answer in person because of their many idols, [5]in order to catch the hearts of the house of Israel, estranged from me because of all their idols.

[6]Therefore say to the house of Israel: Thus says the Lord GOD: Return, turn away from your idols; from all your abominations, turn your faces.[t] [7]For if anyone of the house of Israel or any alien residing in Israel who are estranged from me and who keep their idols in their hearts, setting the stumbling block of their sin before them, come to ask a prophet to consult me on their behalf, I the LORD will answer them in person. [8]I will set my face against them and make them a sign and a byword, and cut them off from the midst of my people. Thus you shall know that I am the LORD.

[9][u] As for the prophet, if he speaks a deceiving word, I the LORD am the one who deceives that prophet.* I will stretch out my hand against him and destroy him from the midst of my people Israel. [10]They will be punished for their own sins, the inquirer and the prophet alike, [11]so that the house of Israel may no longer stray from me, no longer defile themselves by all their sins. Then they shall be my people, and I shall be their God—oracle of the Lord GOD.

*Just Cause.** [12]The word of the LORD came to me: [13][v] Son of man, if a land sins

13:18 Sew amulets . . . make veils: used by sorcerers to mark individuals for life or for death. For a small price (v. 19), these women promised protection for the wicked, who, in the Lord's estimation, "should not live" (v. 19), and death for the righteous, "who should not be slain" (v. 19). Both decisions belong to the Lord.

13:19 Handfuls of barley and crumbs of bread: payment for the amulets and scarves.

14:9 The ancient Israelites thought that God could use deception as a means of promoting divine justice; cf. 2 Sm 24:1–3; 1 Kgs 22:19–23.

14:12–23 According to Ezekiel, the people in Jerusalem deserve destruction because they are corrupt. Yet he admits an exception to the principle of individual responsibility when he affirms that some of those deserving death will survive and be reunited with family in exile. The depravity of Jerusalem testifies that the punishment of Jerusalem was just and necessary.

o: Jer 6:14. *p:* Rev 2:20. *q:* Ps 124:7. *r:* Ez 18:21; 33:14–16. *s:* Ez 8:1; 20:1. *t:* Is 2:20; cf. Ez 18:30; 33:11. *u:* cf. 1 Kgs 22:23; 2 Chr 18:22. *v:* Lv 26:26.

against me by breaking faith, and I stretch
out my hand against it, breaking its staff of
bread and setting famine loose upon it, cutting off from it human being and beast
alike— 14 even if these three were in it,
Noah, Daniel, and Job,* they could only
save themselves by their righteousness—
oracle of the Lord GOD.[w] 15 If I summoned
wild beasts to prowl the land, depopulating
it so that it became a wasteland which no
one would cross because of the wild
beasts,[x] 16 and these three were in it, as I
live—oracle of the Lord GOD—I swear
they could save neither sons nor daughters;
they alone would be saved, but the land
would become a wasteland.[y] 17 Or if I bring
the sword upon this land, commanding the
sword to pass through the land cutting off
from it human being and beast alike,[z] 18 and
these three were in it, as I live—oracle of
the Lord GOD—they could save neither
sons nor daughters; they alone would be
saved. 19 Or if I send plague into this land,
pouring out upon it my bloody wrath, cutting off from it human being and beast
alike, 20 even if Noah, Daniel, and Job were
in it, as I live—oracle of the Lord GOD—
they could save neither son nor daughter;
they would save only themselves by their
righteousness.

21 Thus says the Lord GOD: Even though I
send against Jerusalem my four evil punishments—sword, famine, wild beasts, and
plague—to cut off from it human being and
beast alike,[a] 22 there will still be some survivors in it who will bring out sons and
daughters. When they come out to you and
you see their ways and their deeds, you shall
be consoled regarding the evil I brought on
Jerusalem, everything I brought upon it.
23 They shall console you when you see their
ways and their deeds, and you shall know
that not without reason did I do to it everything I did—oracle of the Lord GOD.[b]

CHAPTER 15

See RG 325–32

Parable of the Vine. 1* The word of
the LORD came to me:

2 Son of man,
what makes the wood of the vine
Better than the wood of branches
found on the trees in the forest?[c]
3 Can wood be taken from it
to make something useful?
Can someone make even a peg out of it
on which to hang a vessel?
4 Of course not! If it is fed to the fire for
fuel,
and the fire devours both ends of it,
Leaving the middle charred,
is it useful for anything then?
5 Even when it is whole
it cannot be used for anything;
So when fire has devoured and charred it,
how useful can it be?
6 Therefore, thus says the Lord GOD:
Like vine wood among forest trees,
which I have given as fuel for fire,
So I will give the inhabitants of Jerusalem.
7 I will set my face against them:
Although they have escaped the fire,
the fire will still devour them;
You shall know that I am the LORD,
when I set my face against them.[d]
8 Yes, I will make the land desolate,
because they are so unfaithful—
oracle of the Lord GOD.

CHAPTER 16

See RG 325–32

A Parable of Infidelity. 1 The word of
the LORD came to me: 2 Son of man, make
known to Jerusalem her abominations.[e]
3 You shall say, Thus says the Lord GOD to
Jerusalem: By origin and birth you belong to
the land of the Canaanites; your father was
an Amorite, your mother a Hittite.* [f] 4* As
for your birth, on the day you were born your

14:14 Noah, Daniel, and Job: righteous folk heroes whom Israel shared with other ancient Near Eastern cultures. Daniel was the just judge celebrated in Ugaritic literature, perhaps the model for the hero of Dn 13.

15:1–8 Verses 2–5 point out that the wood of the vinestock may be burned for fuel, fit only for destruction. In vv. 6–8 Ezekiel asserts that Jerusalem has the same destiny.

16:3–4 By origin and birth . . . Hittite: Jerusalem's pre-Israelite origins are the breeding ground for its inability to respond faithfully to the Lord's generosity.

16:4–5 In this chapter, Ezekiel represents Jerusalem and

w: Ez 28:3; Dn 1:6; cf. Gn 6:9; Jb 1:1. *x*: cf. Lv 26:22. *y*: cf. Ez 18:20. *z*: Lv 26:25. *a*: cf. Rev 6:8. *b*: Jer 22:8–9. *c*: cf. Ps 80; Is 5:1–7. *d*: Is 24:18; Am 9:1–4. *e*: cf. Ez 8:17. *f*: cf. Dt 26:5; Gn 23:10; 48:22.

navel cord was not cut; you were not washed with water or anointed; you were not rubbed with salt or wrapped in swaddling clothes.[g] 5No eye looked on you with pity or compassion to do any of these things for you. Rather, on the day you were born you were left out in the field, rejected.

6Then I passed by and saw you struggling in your blood, and I said to you in your blood, "Live!" 7I helped you grow up like a field plant, so that you grew, maturing into a woman with breasts developed and hair grown; but still you were stark naked. 8I passed by you again and saw that you were now old enough for love. So I spread the corner of my cloak* over you to cover your nakedness; I swore an oath to you and entered into covenant with you—oracle of the Lord GOD—and you became mine.[h] 9Then I bathed you with water, washed away your blood, and anointed you with oil.[i] 10I clothed you with an embroidered gown, put leather sandals on your feet; I gave you a fine linen sash and silk robes to wear.[j] 11I adorned you with jewelry, putting bracelets on your arms, a necklace about your neck,[k] 12a ring in your nose, earrings in your ears, and a beautiful crown on your head. 13Thus you were adorned with gold and silver; your garments made of fine linen, silk, and embroidered cloth. Fine flour, honey, and olive oil were your food. You were very, very beautiful, fit for royalty.[l] 14You were renowned among the nations for your beauty, perfected by the splendor I showered on you—oracle of the Lord GOD.

15But you trusted in your own beauty and used your renown to serve as a prostitute. You poured out your prostitution on every passerby—let it be his.[m] 16* You took some of your garments and made for yourself gaudy high places, where you served as a prostitute. It has never happened before, nor will it happen again![n] 17You took the splendid gold and silver ornaments that I had given you and made for yourself male images and served as a prostitute with them. 18You took your embroidered garments to cover them; my oil and my incense you set before them; 19the food I had given you, the fine flour, the oil, and the honey with which I fed you, you set before them as a pleasant odor, says the Lord GOD.[o] 20* [p] The sons and daughters you bore for me you took and offered as sacrifices for them to devour! Was it not enough that you had become a prostitute? 21[q] You slaughtered and immolated my children to them, making them pass through fire. 22In all your abominations and prostitutions you did not remember the days of your youth when you were stark naked, struggling in your blood.[r]

23Then after all your evildoing—woe, woe to you! oracle of the Lord GOD— 24you built yourself a platform and raised up a dais* in every public place.[s] 25[t] At every intersection you built yourself a dais so that you could degrade your beauty by spreading your legs for every passerby, multiplying your prostitutions. 26You served as a prostitute with the Egyptians, your big-membered neighbors, and multiplied your prostitutions to provoke me. 27Therefore I stretched out my hand against you and reduced your allotment, and delivered you over to the whim of

Samaria as unwanted, abandoned sisters whom the Lord rescues and cares for. Here the prophet depicts Jerusalem as a newborn female, abandoned and left to die, an accepted practice in antiquity for females, who were considered financial liabilities by their families. That the infant has no one, not even her mother, to tie off her umbilical cord, wash her clean, and wrap her in swaddling clothes emphasizes Jerusalem's death-like isolation and accentuates the Lord's gracious action in her behalf. The practice of rubbing the skin of newborns with salt is an attested Palestinian custom that survived into the twentieth century.

16:8 I spread the corner of my cloak: one way to acquire a woman for marriage; cf. Ru 3:9. In Dt 23:1 a son's illicit sexual relations with his father's wife is described as "uncovering the edge of the father's garment."

16:16 In the allegory of this chapter the viewpoint often shifts from the figure (prostitution) to the reality (idolatry). A symbol of the woman's depravity supersedes her parents' cruel abandonment when she was an infant. It overrides the loyalty she owes her covenant partner and the care she owes their children.

16:20–21 Also a reference to the practice of child sacrifice introduced under Judah's impious kings; cf. 2 Kgs 16:3; 17:17; Jer 7:31; 19:5; 32:35.

16:24 A platform . . . a dais: associated with rituals borrowed from the Canaanites.

---

g: cf. Lk 2:2. *h:* cf. Ez 16:59; Ru 3:9. *i:* cf. Ru 3:3. *j:* cf. Ps 45:14. *k:* cf. Ez 23:40–42. *l:* Dt 32:13–14; Hos 2:8. *m:* Is 57:7–8. *n:* cf. 2 Kgs 23:7. *o:* Hos 2:13. *p:* Jer 7:31; cf. Lv 18:21; Dt 18:10; 2 Kgs 21:6; 23:10. *q:* cf. 2 Kgs 16:3; 17:17. *r:* Jer 2:2; Hos 2:15; 11:1. *s:* Is 57:7. *t:* Jer 2:20; 3:2; 5:7; Hos 2:4.

your enemies, the Philistines,* who were revolted by your depraved conduct.[u] [28]You also served as a prostitute for the Assyrians, because you were not satisfied. Even after serving as a prostitute for them, you were still not satisfied.[v] [29]You increased your prostitutions again, now going to Chaldea, the land of traders; but despite this, you were still not satisfied.[w]

[30]How wild your lust!—oracle of the Lord GOD—that you did all these works of a shameless prostitute, [31]when you built your platform at every intersection and set up your high place in every public square. But unlike a prostitute, you disdained payment. [32]Adulterous wife, taking strangers in place of her husband! [33]Prostitutes usually receive gifts. But you bestowed gifts on all your lovers, bribing them to come to you for prostitution from every side.[x] [34]Thus in your prostitution you were different from any other woman. No one solicited you for prostitution. Instead, you yourself offered payment; what a reversal!

[35]Therefore, prostitute, hear the word of the LORD! [36]Thus says the Lord GOD: Because you poured out your lust and exposed your nakedness in your prostitution with your lovers and your abominable idols, because you gave the life-blood of your children to them, [37][y] therefore, I will now gather together all your lovers with whom you found pleasure, both those you loved and those you hated; I will gather them against you from all sides and expose you naked for them to see. [38]* I will inflict on you the sentence of adultery and murder; I will bring on you bloody wrath and jealous anger.[z] [39]I will hand you over to them to tear down your platform and demolish your high place, to strip you of your garments and take away your splendid ornaments, leaving you stark naked.[a] [40]They shall lead an assembly against you to stone you and hack you to pieces with their swords.[b] [41][c] They shall set fire to your homes and inflict punishments on you while many women watch. Thus I will put an end to your prostitution, and you shall never again offer payment. [42]When I have spent my fury upon you I will stop being jealous about you, and calm down, no longer angry. [43]Because you did not remember the days of your youth but enraged me with all these things, see, I am bringing down your ways upon your head—oracle of the Lord GOD. Have you not added depravity to your other abominations?

[44]See, everyone who makes proverbs will make this proverb about you, "Like mother, like daughter." [45]Yes, you are truly the daughter of your mother* who rejected her husband and children: you are truly a sister to your sisters who rejected their husbands and children—your mother was a Hittite and your father an Amorite.[d] [46]* Your elder sister was Samaria with her daughters to the north of you; and your younger sister was Sodom and her daughters, south of you.[e] [47]Not only did you walk in their ways and act as abominably as they did, but in a very short time you became more corrupt in all your ways than they were.[f] [48]As I live—oracle of the Lord GOD—I swear that your sister Sodom with her daughters have not done the things you and your daughters have done![g] [49][h] Now look at the guilt of your sister Sodom: she and her daughters were proud, sated with food, complacent in prosperity. They did not give any help to the poor and needy. [50]Instead, they became arrogant and committed

16:27 Philistines: lit., "daughters of the Philistines," a common expression when referring to the various towns that make up a territory.

16:38 As a jealous husband, Yhwh severely punishes Jerusalem for her adultery: i.e., her worship of idols. Adultery was considered a capital crime in ancient Israel; cf. Lv 20:10–14; Nm 5:11–28; Dt 22:22.

16:45 Truly the daughter of your mother: Jerusalem's depraved behavior follows from the bad behavior of its non-Israelite forebears; cf. v. 3.

16:46–47 Jerusalem is so much more corrupt than Samaria, the elder sister in size, and the smaller Sodom that both now appear just and righteous. Ezekiel's reference to Sodom indicates that the city's identification with wickedness and evil was already an established tradition in fifth century B.C. Judah.

u: cf. 2 Chr 28:18. *v:* 2 Kgs 16:7. *w:* cf. Ez 23:14–17. *x:* Hos 8:9–10. *y:* cf. Ez 23:10, 22; Is 47:3; Rev 17:16. *z:* Lv 20:10; Dt 22:22. *a:* cf. 2 Kgs 18:11. *b:* cf. Ez 23:47; Jn 8:5, 7. *c:* 2 Kgs 25:9; cf. Jgs 12:1; 15:6. *d:* cf. Ez 23:2. *e:* Jer 3:8–11; Rev 11:8. *f:* cf. Dt 29:23; 32:32; Is 1:9–10. *g:* cf. Gn 19:25; Mt 10:15; 11:23–24. *h:* cf. Is 1:10; cf. Gn 49:24.

abominations before me; then, as you have
seen, I removed them.[i] 51 Samaria did not
commit half the sins you did. You have done
more abominable things than they did. You
even made your sisters look righteous, with
all the abominations you have done. 52 You,
then, must bear your disgrace, for you have
made a case for your sisters! Because your
sins are more abominable than theirs, they
seem righteous compared to you. Blush for
shame, and bear the disgrace of having made
your sisters appear righteous.

53 I will restore their fortunes, the fortunes
of Sodom and her daughters, the fortunes of
Samaria and her daughters—and your fortunes along with them. 54 Thus you must bear
your disgrace and be ashamed of all you
have done to bring them comfort. 55 Yes,
your sisters, Sodom and her daughters,
Samaria and her daughters, shall return to
the way they were,[j] and you and your daughters shall return to the way you were. 56 Did
you not hold your sister Sodom in bad repute
while you felt proud of yourself, 57 before
your evil was exposed? Now you are like
her, reproached by the Arameans and all
their neighbors, despised on all sides by the
Philistines.[k] 58 The penalty of your depravity
and your abominations—you must bear it
all—oracle of the LORD.

59 For thus says the Lord GOD: I will deal
with you for what you did; you despised an
oath by breaking a covenant.[l] 60 But I will remember the covenant I made with you when
you were young; I will set up an everlasting
covenant* with you.[m] 61 Then you shall remember your ways and be ashamed when you
receive your sisters, those older and younger
than you; I give them to you as daughters, but
not by reason of your covenant. 62 For I will re-
establish my covenant with you, that you may
know that I am the LORD,[n] 63 that you may remember and be ashamed, and never again
open your mouth because of your disgrace,
when I pardon you for all you have done—oracle of the Lord GOD.[o]

CHAPTER 17

See RG 325-32

The Eagles and the Vine. 1 The word
of the LORD came to me: 2 Son of man, propose a riddle, and tell this proverb to the
house of Israel: 3 Thus says the Lord GOD:

The great eagle, with wide wingspan
  and long feathers, with thick plumage,
  many-hued, came to Lebanon.
He plucked the crest of the cedar,[p]
4 broke off its topmost branch,
And brought it to a land of merchants,
  set it in a city of traders.
5 Then he took some native seed
  and planted it in fertile soil;
A shoot beside plentiful waters,
  like a willow he planted it,[q]
6 That it might sprout and become a vine,
  dense and low-lying,
With its branches turned toward him,
  its roots beneath it.
Thus it became a vine, produced branches,
  and put forth shoots.
7 Then another great eagle appeared,
  with wide wingspan, rich in plumage,
And see! This vine bent its roots to him,
  sent out branches for him to water.
From the bed where it was planted,[r]
8 it was transplanted to a fertile field
By abundant waters, to produce
  branches,
  to bear fruit, to become a majestic
  vine.
9 Say: Thus says the Lord GOD: Can it
  thrive?
Will he not tear up its roots
  and strip its fruit?
Then all its green leaves will wither—
  neither strong arm nor mighty nation
  is needed to uproot it.
10 True, it is planted; but will it thrive?
  Will it not wither up
When the east wind strikes it,
  wither in the very bed where it
  sprouted?[s]

16:60 Everlasting covenant: Ezekiel foresees God renewing the covenant of Sinai in a new and spirit-empowered way that will not be fatally broken as in the present exile or force God to abandon Israel again; cf. 11:19–21; 36:25–27; 37:26–28.

i: cf. Gn 18:20–21. *j:* cf. Ez 36:11. *k:* cf. Ez 25:12–14; 35:1–15; 2 Kgs 16:6. *l:* cf. Ez 17:19. *m:* cf. Ez 37:26; Is 55:3; Jer 32:40. *n:* Dt 29:14. *o:* Dn 9:7–8. *p:* Dt 28:49; Jer 49:22; Dn 7:4. *q:* cf. 2 Kgs 24:17. *r:* cf. Ez 31:4–5; Jer 37:5; 44:30. *s:* cf. Ez 19:12.

11* The word of the LORD came to me:

12 Now say to the rebellious house:
Do you not understand this? Tell them!
The king of Babylon came to Jerusalem
and took away its king and officials
and brought them to him in Babylon.[t]
13 After removing the nobles from the land,
he then took one of the royal line
And made a covenant with him,
binding him under oath,[u]
14 To be a humble kingdom,
without high aspirations,
to keep his covenant and so survive.
15 But this one rebelled against him
by sending envoys to Egypt
To obtain horses and a mighty army.
Can he thrive?
Can he escape if he does this?
Can he break a covenant and go free?[v]
16 As I live—oracle of the Lord GOD—
in the house of the king who set him
up to rule,
Whose oath he ignored and whose
covenant he broke,
there in Babylon I swear he shall die![w]
17 Pharaoh shall not help him on the day of
battle,
with a great force and mighty horde,
When ramps are thrown up and siege
works built
for the cutting down of many lives.
18 He ignored his oath, breaking his
covenant;
even though he gave his hand, he did
all these things—
he shall not escape![x]
19 Therefore, thus says the Lord GOD:
As I live, my oath which he spurned,
And my covenant which he broke,
I will bring down on his head.
20 I will spread my net over him,
and he will be caught in my snare.
I will bring him to Babylon
to judge him there
because he broke faith with me.[y]
21 Any among his forces who escape
will fall by the sword,
And whoever might survive
will be scattered to the winds.[z]
Thus you will know that I the LORD have
spoken.
22 Thus says the Lord GOD:
I, too, will pluck from the crest of the
cedar
the highest branch.
From the top a tender shoot
I will break off and transplant*
on a high, lofty mountain.
23 On the mountain height of Israel
I will plant it.
It shall put forth branches and bear fruit,
and become a majestic cedar.
Every small bird will nest under it,
all kinds of winged birds will dwell
in the shade of its branches.[a]
24 Every tree of the field will know
that I am the LORD.
I bring low the high tree,
lift high the lowly tree,
Wither up the green tree,
and make the dry tree bloom.[b]
As I, the LORD, have spoken, so will I do!

CHAPTER 18

See RG 325–32

Personal Responsibility. 1 The word of
the LORD came to me: Son of man, 2 what is
the meaning of this proverb you recite in the
land of Israel:

"Parents eat sour grapes,[c]
but the children's teeth are set on
edge"?*

3 As I live—oracle of the Lord GOD: I swear
that none of you will ever repeat this proverb
in Israel. 4 For all life is mine: the life of the

17:11–21 These verses explain the allegory in vv. 3–10. In 597 B.C., Nebuchadnezzar removed Jehoiachin from the throne and took him into exile; in his place he set Zedekiah, Jehoiachin's uncle, on the throne and received from him the oath of loyalty. But Zedekiah was persuaded to rebel by Pharaoh Hophra of Egypt and thus deserved punishment; cf. 2 Kgs 24:10–25:7.

17:22–23 The Lord will undo the actions of the Babylonian king by rebuilding the Davidic dynasty so the nations realize that only Israel's God can restore a people's destiny.

18:2 Parents ... on edge: a proverb the people quoted to complain that they were being punished for their ancestors' sins; cf. Jer 31:29.

t: 2 Kgs 24:15. *u:* 2 Chr 36:13. *v:* Jer 52:3. *w:* 2 Kgs 24:17; 25:7; Jer 52:11. *x:* cf. 2 Kgs 10:15. *y:* cf. Ez 12:13; 32:3. *z:* Lv 26:33; 2 Kgs 25:5. *a:* Dn 4:12; Hos 14:5–7. *b:* Dn 5:21. *c:* Jer 31:29; cf. Ez 21:19.

parent is like the life of the child, both are mine. Only the one who sins shall die!

[5]If a man is just—if he does what is right, [6]if he does not eat on the mountains,* or raise his eyes to the idols of the house of Israel; if he does not defile a neighbor's wife, or have relations with a woman during her period;[d] [7e] if he oppresses no one, gives back the pledge received for a debt, commits no robbery; gives food to the hungry and clothes the naked; [8]if he does not lend at interest or exact usury; if he refrains from evildoing and makes a fair judgment between two opponents;[f] [9]if he walks by my statutes and is careful to observe my ordinances, that man is just—he shall surely live—oracle of the Lord GOD.[g]

[10]But if he begets a son who is violent and commits murder, or does any of these things,[h] [11]even though the father does none of them—a son who eats on the mountains, defiles the wife of his neighbor, [12]oppresses the poor and needy, commits robbery, does not give back a pledge, raises his eyes to idols, does abominable things, [13]lends at interest and exacts usury—this son certainly shall not live. Because he practiced all these abominations, he shall surely be put to death; his own blood shall be on him.[i]

[14]But, in turn, if he begets a son who sees all the sins his father commits, yet fears and does not imitate him— [15]a son who does not eat on the mountains, or raise his eyes to the idols of the house of Israel, or defile a neighbor's wife; [16]who does not oppress anyone, or exact a pledge, or commit robbery; who gives his food to the hungry and clothes the naked;[j] [17]who refrains from evildoing, accepts no interest or usury, but keeps my ordinances and walks in my statutes—this one shall not die for the sins of his father. He shall surely live! [18]Only the father, since he committed extortion and robbed his brother, and did what was not good among his people—he will die because of his sin! [19]You ask: "Why is not the son charged with the guilt of his father?" Because the son has done what is just and right and has been careful to observe all my statutes—he shall surely live! [20k] Only the one who sins shall die. The son shall not be charged with the guilt of his father, nor shall the father be charged with the guilt of his son. Justice belongs to the just, and wickedness to the wicked.

[21]But if the wicked man turns away from all the sins he has committed, if he keeps all my statutes and does what is just and right, he shall surely live. He shall not die! [22]None of the crimes he has committed shall be remembered against him; he shall live because of the justice he has shown. [23l] Do I find pleasure in the death of the wicked—oracle of the Lord GOD? Do I not rejoice when they turn from their evil way and live?

[24]And if the just turn from justice and do evil, like all the abominations the wicked do, can they do this evil and still live? None of the justice they did shall be remembered, because they acted treacherously and committed these sins; because of this, they shall die.[m] [25n] You say, "The LORD's way is not fair!"* Hear now, house of Israel: Is it my way that is unfair? Are not your ways unfair? [26]When the just turn away from justice to do evil and die, on account of the evil they did they must die. [27]But if the wicked turn from the wickedness they did and do what is right and just, they save their lives; [28]since they turned away from all the sins they committed, they shall live; they shall not die. [29]But the house of Israel says, "The Lord's way is not fair!" Is it my way that is not fair, house of Israel? Is it not your ways that are not fair?

[30o] Therefore I will judge you, house of Israel, all of you according to your ways—oracle of the Lord GOD. Turn, turn back from all your crimes, that they may not be a cause of sin for you ever again. [31]Cast away

18:6 Eat on the mountains: take part in meals after sacrifice at the high places.

18:25 The LORD's way is not fair: this chapter rejects the idea that punishment is transferred from one generation to the next and emphasizes individual responsibility and accountability.

d: Lv 15:19–24; cf. Hos 4:13. *e:* Ex 22:26; Is 58:7; Mt 25:35. *f:* Ex 22:25; Lv 25:35–37; Dt 23:19–20. *g:* Lv 18:5. *h:* cf. Ez 22:6–9. *i:* Ex 22:25; Lv 20:9–11. *j:* cf. Ez 16:49; Is 58:7–10. *k:* Dt 24:16; 2 Kgs 14:6; cf. Mt 16:27; Jn 9:2. *l:* cf. Ez 33:11; 2 Pt 3:9. *m:* cf. 2 Pt 2:20–22. *n:* cf. Ez 33:20. *o:* Jer 35:15; cf. Mt 3:2; Lk 3:3.

from you all the crimes you have committed, and make for yourselves a new heart and a new spirit. Why should you die, house of Israel?[p] 32[q] For I find no pleasure in the death of anyone who dies—oracle of the Lord GOD. Turn back and live!

See RG 325–32

CHAPTER 19

*Allegory of the Lions**

1 As for you, raise a lamentation over the princes of Israel, 2 and say:

What a lioness was your mother,
a lion among lions!
She made her lair among young lions,
to raise her cubs;
3 One cub she raised up,
a young lion he became;
He learned to tear apart prey,
he devoured people.[r]
4 Nations heard about him;
in their pit he was caught;
They took him away with hooks
to the land of Egypt.* [s]
5 When she realized she had waited in vain,
she lost hope.
She took another of her cubs,
and made him a young lion.
6 He prowled among the lions,
became a young lion;
He learned to tear apart prey,
he devoured people.[t]
7 He ravaged their strongholds,
laid waste their cities.
The earth and everything in it were terrified
at the sound of his roar.
8 Nations laid out against him
snares all around;
They spread their net for him,
in their pit he was caught.[u]
9 They put him in fetters and took him away
to the king of Babylon,
So his roar would no longer be heard
on the mountains of Israel.

Allegory of the Vine Branch

10 Your mother was like a leafy vine*
planted by water,
Fruitful and full of branches
because of abundant water.
11 One strong branch grew
into a royal scepter.
So tall it towered among the clouds,
conspicuous in height,
with dense foliage.[v]
12 But she was torn out in fury
and flung to the ground;
The east wind withered her up,
her fruit was plucked away;
Her strongest branch dried up,
fire devoured it.[w]
13 Now she is planted in a wilderness,
in a dry, parched land.[x]
14 Fire flashed from her branch,
and devoured her shoots;
Now she does not have a strong branch,
a royal scepter![y]

This is a lamentation and serves as a lamentation.

CHAPTER 20

See RG 325–32

Israel's History of Infidelity. 1 In the seventh year, on the tenth day of the fifth month,* some of the elders of Israel came to consult the LORD and sat down before me.[z] 2 Then the word of the LORD came to me: 3 Son of man, speak to the elders of Israel and say to them: Thus says the Lord GOD: Have you come to consult me? As I live, I will not allow myself to be consulted by you!—oracle of the Lord GOD.

4 Will you judge them? Will you judge, son of man? Tell them about the abomina-

19:1–9 Some commentators identify Jehoahaz and Zedekiah, sons of the same mother, as the "two young lions"; they were deported to Egypt and Babylon respectively. Cf. 2 Kgs 23:31–34; 24:18–20.

19:4 A common fate for royal prisoners: e.g., Assurbanipal claims he put a ring in the jaw of a captive king and a dog collar around his neck (cf. v. 9). A wall relief shows Esarhaddon holding two royal captives with ropes tied to rings in their lips.

19:10–14 Vine: Judah. **One strong branch**: the Davidic king. This allegory describes the deportation of the Davidic dynasty to Babylon and laments the destruction of the house of David. From Ezekiel's perspective, the arrogance of Judah's kings leads to this tragedy (vv. 12–14).

20:1 The seventh year . . . the fifth month: August 14, 591 B.C.

p: cf. Ez 11:19; 36:26. *q:* cf. Ez 18:23; 33:11. *r:* 2 Kgs 23:31–34. *s:* 2 Chr 36:4. *t:* 2 Kgs 24:9. *u:* 2 Kgs 24:2–15. *v:* Dn 4:11. *w:* Hos 13:15. *x:* cf. Ez 20:35. *y:* cf. Ez 20:47. *z:* cf. Ez 8:1.

tions of their ancestors,[a] [5]and say to them: Thus says the Lord GOD: The day I chose Israel, I swore to the descendants of the house of Jacob; I revealed myself to them in the land of Egypt and swore to them, saying: I am the LORD, your God. [6]That day I swore to bring them out of the land of Egypt to the land I had searched out for them, a land flowing with milk and honey, a jewel among all lands.[b] [7]Then I said to them: Throw away, each of you, the detestable things* that held your eyes; do not defile yourselves with the idols of Egypt: I am the LORD, your God.[c]

[8]But they rebelled and refused to listen to me; none of them threw away the detestable things that held their eyes, nor did they abandon the idols of Egypt. Then I considered pouring out my fury and spending my anger against them there in the land of Egypt.[d] [9]I acted for the sake of my name, that it should not be desecrated in the eyes of the nations among whom they were: in the eyes of the nations I had made myself known to them, to bring them out of the land of Egypt.[e] [10]Therefore I led them out of the land of Egypt and brought them into the wilderness. [11][f] Then I gave them my statutes and made known to them my ordinances, so that everyone who keeps them has life through them. [12][g] I also gave them my sabbaths to be a sign between me and them, to show that it is I, the LORD, who makes them holy.

[13]But the house of Israel rebelled against me in the wilderness. They did not observe my statutes, and they rejected my ordinances that bring life to those who keep them. My sabbaths, too, they desecrated grievously. Then I considered pouring out my fury on them in the wilderness to put an end to them,[h] [14]but I acted for the sake of my name, so it would not be desecrated in the eyes of the nations in whose sight I had brought them out.[i] [15]Nevertheless in the wilderness I swore to them that I would not bring them into the land I had given them—a land flowing with milk and honey, a jewel among all the lands. [16]Their hearts followed after their idols so closely that they did not live by my statutes, but rejected my ordinances and desecrated my sabbaths. [17]But I looked on them with pity, not wanting to destroy them, so I did not put an end to them in the wilderness.

[18]Then I said to their children in the wilderness: Do not follow the statutes of your parents. Do not keep their ordinances. Do not defile yourselves with their idols. [19]I am the LORD, your God: follow my statutes and be careful to observe my ordinances; [20]keep holy my sabbaths as a sign between me and you so that you may know that I am the LORD, your God.[j] [21]But their children rebelled against me: they did not follow my statutes or keep my ordinances that bring life to those who observe them; my sabbaths they desecrated. Then I considered pouring out my fury on them, spending my anger against them in the wilderness; [22]but I stayed my hand, acting for the sake of my name, lest it be desecrated in the eyes of the nations, in whose sight I had brought them out. [23]Nevertheless I swore to them in the wilderness that I would disperse them among the nations and scatter them in other lands, [24]because they did not carry out my ordinances, but rejected my statutes and desecrated my sabbaths, having eyes only for the idols of their ancestors. [25]Therefore I gave them statutes that were not good,* and ordinances through which they could not have life.[k] [26]I let them become defiled by their offerings, by having them

20:7 Detestable things: in the Book of Ezekiel, Israel's continued worship of idols in Egypt and in the wilderness, despite the Lord's powerful deeds on their behalf, is the reason God punishes them so severely; they must learn and acknowledge that he is their only Lord. Cf., e.g., Exodus (5:1–6:9; 14:10–30; 16:1–36) and Numbers (11:1–15; 14:1–12; 20:1–9), where the people's failure to trust Moses and the Lord brings punishment.

20:25–26 I gave them statutes that were not good: because Israel rejected the Lord's life-giving laws, he "gave" laws (e.g., the sacrifice of every firstborn) that would lead only to death and destruction. Dt 12:29–31; Jer 7:31; 19:4–5 may address a popular assumption that the Lord accepted and perhaps required child sacrifice, especially as evidence of great trust during national emergencies (2 Kgs 3:27; Mi 6:7). By combining language from Ex 22:28 with the vocabulary of child sacrifice, Ezekiel suggests that firstborn sons were regularly sacrificed in Israel.

a: cf. Ez 16:2; Mt 23:32. *b:* Ex 3:8; 6:8; Dt 8:7–10. *c:* Ex 20:2–4. *d:* cf. Ez 16:26; Ex 32:7. *e:* cf. Ez 36:22. *f:* Lv 18:5; Dt 4:7–8; Rom 10:5. *g:* Ex 20:8, 10; 31:13; Dt 5:12; Neh 13:17–18. *h:* Jer 11:7–8; 17:21–23. *i:* Is 48:11. *j:* Ex 31:13. *k:* cf. Rom 1:28.

make a fiery offering of every womb's firstborn, in order to ruin them so they might
know that I am the LORD.[l]
27 Therefore speak to the house of Israel,
son of man, and tell them: Thus says the
Lord GOD: In this way also your ancestors
blasphemed me, breaking faith with me.
28 When I brought them to the land I had
sworn to give them, and they saw all its high
hills and leafy trees, there they offered sacrifices, there they made offerings to provoke
me, there they sent up sweet-smelling oblations, there they poured out their libations.[m]
29 So I said to them, "What is this high place*
to which you go?" Thus its name became
"high place" even to this day.[n] 30 Therefore
say to the house of Israel: Thus says the Lord
GOD: Will you defile yourselves in the way
your ancestors did? Will you lust after their
detestable idols? 31 By offering your gifts, by
making your children pass through the fire,
you defile yourselves with all your idols
even to this day. Shall I let myself be consulted by you, house of Israel? As I live—oracle of the Lord GOD—I swear I will not let
myself be consulted by you![o]
32 What has entered your mind shall never
happen: You are thinking, "We shall be like
the nations, like the peoples of foreign lands,
serving wood and stone." 33 As I live—oracle of the Lord GOD—with mighty hand and
outstretched arm, with wrath poured out, I
swear I will be king over you![p] 34 With
mighty hand and outstretched arm, with
wrath poured out, I will bring you out from
the nations and gather you from the countries over which you are scattered;[q] 35* I will
lead you to the wilderness of the peoples and
enter into judgment with you face to face.
36 Just as I entered into judgment with your
ancestors in the wilderness of the land of
Egypt, so will I enter into judgment with
you—oracle of the Lord GOD. 37 Thus I will
make you pass under the staff* and will impose on you the terms of the covenant.[r] 38 I
will sort out from you those who defied me
and rebelled against me; from the land
where they resided as aliens I will bring
them out, but they shall not return to the land
of Israel. Thus you shall know that I am the
LORD.
39 As for you, house of Israel, thus says the
Lord GOD: Go! each of you, and worship
your idols. Listen to me! You shall never
again desecrate my holy name with your offerings and your idols![s] 40 For on my holy
mountain,* on the highest mountain in Israel—oracle of the Lord GOD—there the
whole house of Israel shall worship me;
there in the land I will accept them all, there
I will claim your tributes, the best of your offerings, from all your holy things.[t] 41 As a
sweet-smelling oblation I will accept you,
when I bring you from among the nations
and gather you out of the lands over which
you were scattered; and through you I will
manifest my holiness in the sight of the nations.[u] 42 Thus you shall know that I am the
LORD, when I bring you back to the soil of
Israel, the land I swore to give your ancestors. 43 There you shall remember your ways,
all the deeds by which you defiled yourselves; and you shall loathe yourselves because of all the evil you did.[v] 44 And you shall
know that I am the LORD when I deal with
you thus, for the sake of my name, not according to your evil ways and wanton deeds,
house of Israel—oracle of the Lord GOD.[w]

20:29 High place: a cultic site, originally a hilltop, but often a raised platform in a sacred area. Until Deuteronomy's insistence that official and legitimate worship of the Lord take place only in Jerusalem, these local shrines were popular places for worship (e.g., 1 Sm 9–10) or for consulting the Lord (1 Kgs 3:4–5). In order to unite the Kingdom of Judah politically and religiously, Dt 12:2 demands destruction of the high places. Ezekiel, like other prophets, condemns Israelite worship at these places and identifies this illegitimate worship as one reason for the punishment of exile.

20:35–38 Exile among other lands occasions a new exodus and a new wilderness journey back to Israel. The Lord will eliminate the rebellious, as he did on the first journey, and use the surviving remnant to reveal his power to the nations.

20:37 Pass under the staff: in Lv 27:32–33, a method of counting off animals to select those to be dedicated for the tithe. In Ezekiel, on the other hand, those who survive the selection process are marked for destruction for violating the covenant.

20:40 Holy mountain: the Temple mount and Jerusalem in contrast to "every high hill" in v. 28 (cf. the royal Zion theology in Ps 48:2). Acceptable worship takes place here among a restored people, a theme taken up in chaps. 40–48 (cf. 40:2).

l: Lv 18:21. *m:* Ps 78:57–58. *n:* cf. Ez 16:16. *o:* Ps 106:37–39. *p:* Dt 4:34; 5:1. *q:* Ps 106:47. *r:* Lv 27:3; Jer 33:13. *s:* Ex 20:7. *t:* cf. Ps 2:6; Is 11:9; 56:7. *u:* cf. 2 Cor 2:14. *v:* Lv 26:41. *w:* cf. Ez 36:22.

CHAPTER 21

See RG 325–32

The Sword of the Lord. 1 The word of
the LORD came to me: 2[*] Son of man, turn
your face to the south: preach against the
south, prophesy against the forest land in the
south. 3 Say to the forest in the south: Hear
the word of the LORD! Thus says the Lord
GOD: See! I am kindling a fire in you that
shall devour every green tree as well as
every dry tree. The blazing flame shall not
be quenched so that from south to north
every face shall be scorched by it. 4 All flesh
shall see that I, the LORD, have kindled it; it
shall not be quenched.[x]
5 But I said, "Ah! Lord GOD, they are saying about me, 'Is not this the one who is forever spinning parables?' " 6 Then the word
of the LORD came to me: 7 Son of man, turn
your face toward Jerusalem: preach against
its sanctuary, prophesy against the land of
Israel.[y] 8 Say to the land of Israel: Thus says
the LORD: See! I am coming against you; I
will draw my sword from its scabbard and
cut off from you the righteous and the
wicked.[*] 9 Thus my sword shall come out
from its scabbard against all flesh from
south to north 10 and all flesh shall know that
I, the LORD, have drawn my sword from its
scabbard. It cannot return again.[z]

Act Symbolic of the City's Fall. 11 As for
you, son of man, groan! with shattered loins
and bitter grief, groan in their sight. 12 When
they ask you, "Why are you groaning?" you
shall say: Because of what I heard![*] When it
comes every heart shall melt, every hand fall
helpless; every spirit will grow faint, and
every knee run with water. See, it is coming,
it is here!—oracle of the Lord GOD.

Song of the Sword. 13 The word of the
LORD came to me:[a] 14 Son of man, prophesy!
say: Thus says the LORD:

A sword, a sword has been sharpened,
  a sword, a sword has been burnished:[b]
15 Sharpened to make a slaughter,
  burnished to flash lightning!
Why should I stop now?
  You have rejected the rod and every
    judgment!
16 I have given it over to the burnisher
  that he might hold it in his hand,
A sword sharpened and burnished
  to be put in the hands of an executioner.
17 Cry out and howl, son of man,
  for it is destined for my people,
For all the princes of Israel,
  victims of the sword with my people.
Therefore, slap your thigh,[*]
18   for it is tested, and why not?
Since you rejected my staff,
  should it not happen?—
  oracle of the Lord GOD.
19 As for you, son of man, prophesy,
  and clap your hands!
Let the sword strike twice, a third time.
  It is a sword of slaughter,
A sword for slaughtering,
  whirling around them all,
20 That every heart may tremble;
  for many will be made to stumble.
At all their gates
  I have stationed the sword for slaughter,
Made it flash lightning,
  drawn for slaughter.
21 Slash to the right!
  turn to the left,
  Wherever your edge is directed![c]
22 Then I, too, shall clap my hands,[*]
  and spend my fury.
  I, the LORD, have spoken.

Nebuchadnezzar at the Crossroads. 23 The
word of the LORD came to me: 24 Son of man,
make for yourself two roads over which the
sword of the king of Babylon can come.
Both roads shall start out from the same
land. Then put a signpost at the head of each
road 25 so the sword can come to Rabbah of
the Ammonites or to Judah and its fortress,

21:2–4 In Babylon Ezekiel looks toward Judah, pictured as a forest about to be destroyed by fire.

21:8 Cut off from you the righteous and the wicked: a more complete devastation of Jerusalem than that described in 9:6.

21:12 What I heard: the news of the fall of Jerusalem; cf. 33:21–22.

21:17 Slap your thigh: a gesture signifying grief and dread; cf. Jer 31:19.

21:22 Clap my hands: the Lord declares himself no longer responsible for Judah; cf. 22:13; Nm 24:10; Jb 27:23; Lam 2:15.

x: Lv 26:25. *y:* Lv 26:36. *z:* Is 34:5–6. *a:* Gn 49:10. *b:* cf. 2 Kgs 13:18–19. *c:* Prv 16:33; Zec 10:2.

Jerusalem. 26 For the king of Babylon is standing at the fork of the two roads to read the omens:* he shakes out the arrows, inquires of the teraphim, inspects the liver.[d] 27 Into his right hand has fallen the lot marked "Jerusalem":* to order the slaughter, to raise the battle cry, to set the battering rams against the gates, to throw up a ramp, to build siege works. 28 In the eyes of those bound by oath this seems like a false omen; yet the lot taken in hand exposes the wickedness for which they, still bound by oath, will be taken in hand.

29 Therefore thus says the Lord GOD: Because your guilt has been exposed, your crimes laid bare, your sinfulness revealed in all your deeds—because you have been exposed, you shall be taken in hand.[e] 30 And as for you, depraved and wicked prince of Israel, a day is coming to end your life of crime.[f] 31 Thus says the Lord GOD: Off with the turban and away with the crown! Nothing shall be as it was! Exalt the lowly and bring the exalted low! 32 A ruin, a ruin, a ruin, I shall make it! Nothing will be the same until the one comes to whom I have given it for judgment.[g]

To the Ammonites.* 33 As for you, son of man, prophesy: Thus says the Lord GOD to the Ammonites and their insults:

O sword, sword drawn for slaughter,
burnished to consume, to flash
lightning!
34 Your false visions and lying omens,
Set you over the necks of the slain,
the wicked whose day had come—
an end to their life of crime.
35 Return to your scabbard!
In the place you were created,
In the land of your origin,
I will judge you.
36 I will pour out my anger upon you,
breathing my fiery wrath against you;
I will hand you over to ravagers,
artisans of destruction!
37 You shall be fuel for the fire,
your blood shall flow throughout the
land;
You shall not be remembered,
for I, the LORD, have spoken.

CHAPTER 22

See RG 325–32

Crimes of Jerusalem. 1 The word of the LORD came to me: 2 You,* son of man, will you judge? will you judge the city of bloodshed? Then make known all its abominations, 3 and say: Thus says the Lord GOD: O city that sheds blood within itself so that its time has come, that has made idols for its own defilement: 4 By the blood you shed you have become guilty, and by the idols you made you have become defiled. You have brought on your day, you have come to the end of your years. Therefore I make you an object of scorn for the nations and a laughingstock for all lands.[h] 5 Those near and those far off will mock you: "Defiled of Name! Queen of Tumult!" 6 See! the princes of Israel within you use their power to shed blood.* 7 Within you, father and mother are dishonored; they extort the resident alien in your midst; within you, they oppress orphans and widows.[i] 8 What I consider holy you have rejected, and my sabbaths you have desecrated. 9* In you are those who slander to cause bloodshed; within you are those who feast on the mountains; in your midst are those whose actions are depraved.[j]

21:26 Three forms of divination are mentioned: arrow divination, consisting in the use of differently marked arrows extracted or shaken from a case at random; the consultation of the teraphim or household idols; and liver divination, scrutiny of the configurations of the livers of newly slaughtered animals, a common form of divination in Mesopotamia.

21:27–28 A lot marked "Jerusalem" falls out, which marks the guilt of the city's inhabitants.

21:33–37 In vv. 23–32 Ezekiel imagines Nebuchadnezzar deciding whether to attack Jerusalem or Rabbath-Ammon. As it happened, the Babylonians decided to attack Jerusalem first. Here (vv. 33–37) Ezekiel prophesies to the Ammonites that a nation which serves as an instrument of the Lord's judgment will itself be judged.

22:2–16 This first oracle focuses on Jerusalem as a "city of bloodshed" (cf. Na 3:1). Here transgressions involving blood, the oppression of the poor, and improper cultic practices are seen as interrelated, for blood as the carrier of life is fundamental to both the cultic and social spheres of life.

22:6 To shed blood: a very serious charge in light of the solemn command of God to Noah in Gn 9:6 against human bloodshed.

22:9–11 The charges against Jerusalem echo the commandments of Lv 20:10–18.

d: Is 28:5; Ps 75:8. *e:* Jer 8:11–12; 27:9–10. *f:* cf. Ez 16:3. *g:* Mal 3:19. *h:* Ps 44:13–14. *i:* Ex 22:21–22; 23:9; Dt 5:16. *j:* cf. Ez 18:11.

10 In you are those who uncover the nakedness of their fathers; in you those who coerce women to intercourse during their period.[k] 11 [l] There are those in you who do abominable things with their neighbors' wives, men who defile their daughters-in-law by incest, men who coerce their sisters to intercourse, the daughters of their own fathers. 12 There are those in you who take bribes to shed blood. You exact interest and usury; you extort profit from your neighbor by violence. But me you have forgotten—oracle of the Lord GOD.[m]

13 See, I am clapping my hands because of the profits you extorted and the blood shed in your midst. 14 Will your heart remain firm, will your hands be strong, in the days when I deal with you? I am the LORD; I have spoken, and I will act! 15 I will disperse you among the nations and scatter you over other lands, so that I may purge your filth. 16 In you I will allow myself to be desecrated in the eyes of the nations; thus you shall know that I am the LORD.

17 The word of the LORD came to me: 18* Son of man, the house of Israel has become dross to me. All of them are copper, tin, iron, and lead within a furnace; they have become the dross from silver.[n] 19 Therefore thus says the Lord GOD: Because all of you have become dross, See! I am gathering you within Jerusalem. 20 Just as silver, copper, iron, lead, and tin are gathered within a furnace to be blasted with fire to smelt it, so I will gather you together in my furious wrath, put you in, and smelt you.[o] 21 When I have assembled you, I will blast you with the fire of my anger and smelt you with it. 22 Just as silver is smelted in a furnace, so you shall be smelted in it. Thus you shall know that I, the LORD, have poured out my fury on you.

23 The word of the LORD came to me: 24* Son of man, say to her: You are an unclean land receiving no rain at the time of my fury. 25 A conspiracy of its princes is like a roaring lion tearing prey; they devour people, seizing their wealth and precious things, making many widows within her.[p] 26 Her priests violate my law and desecrate what I consider holy; they do not distinguish between holy and common, nor teach the difference between unclean and clean; they pay no attention to my sabbaths, so that I have been desecrated in their midst.[q] 27 [r] Within her, her officials are like wolves tearing prey, shedding blood and destroying lives to extort profit. 28 [s] And her prophets cover them with whitewash, seeing false visions and performing lying divinations, saying, "Thus says the Lord GOD," although the LORD has not spoken. 29 The people of the land practice extortion and commit robbery; they wrong the poor and the needy, and oppress the resident alien without justice. 30 Thus I have searched among them for someone who would build a wall or stand in the breach before me to keep me from destroying the land; but I found no one. 31 Therefore I have poured out my fury upon them; with my fiery wrath I have consumed them, bringing down their ways upon their heads—oracle of the Lord GOD.

CHAPTER 23

See RG 325–32

The Two Sisters. 1 [t] The word of the LORD came to me: 2 Son of man, there were two women, daughters of the same mother.[u] 3 Even as young girls, they were prostitutes, serving as prostitutes in Egypt. There the Egyptians fondled their breasts and caressed their virgin nipples.[v] 4 Oholah was the name of the elder, and the name of her sister was Oholibah.* They became mine and gave birth to sons and daughters.[w] As for their names: Samaria was Oholah and Jerusalem, Oholibah. 5 [x] Oholah became a prostitute while married to me and lusted after her lovers, the Assyrians: warriors 6 dressed in

22:18–22 The image of smelting metals for purifying the people by the attacks of their enemies is common among the prophets; cf. Is 1:22, 25; Jer 6:27–30.

22:24–31 For a similar oracle, cf. Zep 3:1–8.

23:4 Oholah . . . Oholibah: symbolic names for Samaria, "her own tent," and Jerusalem, "my tent is in her." Cf. Ps 15:1 where "tent" is a synonym for "holy mountain." The names refer to the temple set up in the Northern Kingdom of Samaria (1 Kgs 12:28–29) and the Jerusalem Temple.

k: Lv 18:7–8, 19. *l:* Lv 18:7–20; 20:10–21; Dt 23:1–30; Jer 5:8. *m:* Ez 18:8; Dt 27:25; Am 5:12. *n:* Is 1:21–26; 48:10; Jer 6:27–30. *o:* Hos 8:10; Mal 3:2. *p:* Jer 15:8. *q:* Lv 20:25; Hg 2:11–14. *r:* Mi 3:11; Zep 3:3. *s:* cf. Ez 13:2–10. *t:* cf. Ez 16. *u:* Jer 3:7. *v:* Is 1:21. *w:* Jer 3:6–12. *x:* Hos 5:3; 8:9.

purple, governors and officers, all of them handsome young soldiers, mounted on horses. 7She gave herself as a prostitute to them, to all the Assyrian elite; with all those for whom she lusted, she also defiled herself with their idols. 8She did not abandon the prostitution she had begun with the Egyptians, who had lain with her when she was young, fondling her virgin breasts and pouring out their lust upon her.[y] 9Therefore I handed her over to her lovers, to the Assyrians for whom she lusted. 10[z] They exposed her nakedness; her sons and daughters they took away, and her they killed with the sword. She became a byword for women because of the sentence carried out against her.

11Although her sister Oholibah saw all this, her lust was more depraved than her sister's; she outdid her in prostitution.[a] 12She too lusted after the Assyrians, governors and officers, warriors impeccably clothed, mounted on horses, all of them handsome young soldiers.[b] 13I saw that she had defiled herself—now both had gone down the same path. 14She went further in her prostitution: She saw male figures drawn on the wall, images of Chaldeans drawn with vermilion, 15with sashes tied about their waists, flowing turbans on their heads, all looking like chariot warriors, images of Babylonians, natives of Chaldea. 16As soon as she set eyes on them she lusted for them, and she sent messengers to them in Chaldea.[c] 17The Babylonians came to her, to her love couch; they defiled her with their impurities. But as soon as they had defiled her, she recoiled from them. 18When her prostitution was discovered and her shame revealed, I recoiled from her as I had recoiled from her sister. 19But she increased her prostitution, recalling the days of her youth when she had served as a prostitute in the land of Egypt. 20She lusted for the lechers of Egypt, whose members are like those of donkeys, whose thrusts are like those of stallions.

21You reverted to the depravity of your youth, when Egyptians fondled your breasts, caressing your young nipples. 22Therefore, Oholibah, thus says the Lord GOD: I will now stir up your lovers against you, those from whom you recoiled, and I will bring them against you from every side: 23the men of Babylon and all of Chaldea, Pekod, Shoa and Koa,* along with all the Assyrians, handsome young soldiers, all of them governors and officers, charioteers and warriors, all of them horsemen. 24They shall invade you with armor, chariots and wagons, a horde of peoples; they will array against you on every side bucklers and shields and helmets. I will give them the right of judgment, and they will judge you according to their standards.[d] 25I will direct my jealousy against you, so that they deal with you in fury, cutting off your nose and ears; what is left of you shall fall by the sword. They shall take away your sons and daughters, and what is left of you shall be devoured by fire. 26They shall strip off your clothes and seize your splendid jewelry. 27I will put an end to your depravity and to your prostitution from the land of Egypt; you shall no longer look to them, nor even remember Egypt again.

28For thus says the Lord GOD: I am now handing you over to those whom you hate, to those from whom you recoil. 29They shall treat you with hatred, seizing all that you worked for and leaving you stark naked, so that your indecent nakedness is exposed.[e] Your depravity and prostitution 30brought these things upon you because you served as a prostitute for the nations, defiling yourself with their idols.[f]

31Because you followed your sister's path, I will put her cup into your hand.* [g]

32 Thus says the Lord GOD:[h]

The cup of your sister you shall drink,
deep and wide;
It brings ridicule and mockery,

23:23 Pekod, Shoa and Koa: nations along the Tigris River, part of "greater Babylonia."

23:31 The cup is a metaphor for divine punishment, the lot of all who rebel against the Lord (cf. Ps 75:9; Jer 25:15–16; 51:7; Is 51:21–23; Lam 4:21; Hb 2:15–16).

y: cf. Ez 20:5–8. *z:* cf. Ez 16:37. *a:* Jer 3:8–11. *b:* 2 Kgs 16:7–15; 2 Chr 28:16. *c:* Is 57:8–9. *d:* Jer 30:5–6. *e:* Jer 13:27; Mi 1:11. *f:* Ps 106:37–38. *g:* Ps 75:8; Ob 16; Mt 20:22; Rev 14:10. *h:* Jer 25:15–16.

it holds so much;
33 You will be filled with drunkenness and
grief—
A cup of horror and devastation,
the cup of your sister Samaria;
34 You shall drink it dry,
its very sherds you will gnaw;
And you shall tear out your breasts;
for I have spoken—oracle of the Lord
GOD.

35 Therefore thus says the Lord GOD: You
have forgotten me and cast me behind your
back; now suffer for your depravity and
prostitution.
36* Then the LORD said to me: Son of man,
would you judge Oholah and Oholibah?
Then make known to them their abominations.[i] 37 For they committed adultery, and
blood covers their hands. They committed
adultery with their idols; even the children
they bore for me they burnt as food for them.
38 And they also did this to me: on that day,
they defiled my sanctuary and desecrated
my sabbaths. 39 On the very day they slaughtered their children for their idols, they entered my sanctuary to desecrate it. Thus they
acted within my house![j] 40 Moreover, they
sent for men who had to come from afar;
when a messenger was sent to them, they
came. On their account you bathed, painted
your eyes, and put on jewelry.[k] 41 You sat on
a magnificent couch, set before it a table, on
which to lay my incense and oil. 42 The cries
of a mob! The shouts of men coming in from
the wilderness! They put bracelets on the
women's arms and splendid crowns on their
heads. 43 I said: "That worn-out one still has
adulteries in her! Now they engage her as a
prostitute and she . . . 44 And indeed they did
come in to her as men come in to a prostitute. Thus they came to Oholah and Oholibah, the depraved women. 45 The righteous
shall certainly punish them with sentences
given to adulterers and murderers, for they
committed adultery, and blood is on their
hands.[l]
46 Indeed, thus says the Lord GOD: Raise
up an army against them and hand them over
to terror and plunder. 47 The army will stone
them and hack them to pieces with their
swords. They will kill their sons and daughters and set fire to their houses. 48 Thus I will
put an end to depravity in the land, and all
women will be warned not to imitate your
depravity. 49 They shall inflict on you the
penalty of your depravity, and you shall pay
for your sins of idolatry. Then you shall
know that I am the Lord GOD.[m]

CHAPTER 24

See RG 325–32

Allegory of the Pot.* 1 On the tenth day
of the tenth month, in the ninth year,* the
word of the LORD came to me:[n] 2 Son of man,
write down today's date this very day, for on
this very day the king of Babylon lays siege
to Jerusalem. 3[o] Propose this parable to the
rebellious house and say to them: Thus says
the Lord GOD:

Put the pot on, put it on!
Pour in some water;
4 Add to it pieces of meat,
all choice pieces;
With thigh and shoulder,
with choice cuts fill it.
5 Choose the pick of the flock,
then pile logs beneath it;
Bring it to a boil,
cook all the pieces in it.[p]
6 Therefore thus says the Lord GOD:
Woe to the city full of blood![q]

23:36–49 Unlike vv. 1–35, this short poem juxtaposes the careers of the two sisters and looks to a future punishment. The male lovers of the first poem become the sisters' executioners, and the guests at the love feast a lynch mob. So corrupt and depraved are the two sisters that their executioners win the esteemed title "righteous," for they have acted appropriately as agents of the Lord's judgment.

24:1–14 As the Babylonian siege of Jerusalem begins (588 B.C.), Ezekiel uses allegory to depict Jerusalem and its overconfident inhabitants as a pot of meat set on the fire for boiling (vv. 3–5; cf. 11:3) and left there until only burnt bones remain (v. 10). In vv. 6–8, the innocent blood shed by Jerusalem's inhabitants is the rust that, despite efforts to remove it, coats the interior of the pot filled with meat. Once emptied (v. 8), the rust-encrusted pot is set on hot coals (v. 11), but the rust remains (v. 12). Only the brunt of the Lord's fury can cleanse Jerusalem of its guilt (vv. 13–14).

24:1 The tenth day . . . the ninth year: January 15, 588 B.C. The same wording appears in 2 Kgs 25:1 (Jer 52:4).

i: Is 58:1; Mi 3:8. *j:* 2 Kgs 21:4. *k:* Jer 27:3. *l:* Lv 20:10. *m:* cf. Ez 24:13. *n:* cf. Ez 8:1. *o:* cf. Ez 11:3–12. *p:* Jer 52:24–27. *q:* Na 3:1; Hb 2:12.

A pot containing filth,
whose filth cannot be removed!
Take out its pieces one by one,
for no lot has fallen on their behalf.
7 For her blood is still in her midst;
on a bare rock she left it;
She did not pour it on the ground
to be covered with dirt.*
8 To arouse wrath, to exact vengeance,
I have left her blood on bare rock
not to be covered.
9 Therefore, thus says the Lord GOD:
Woe to the city full of blood!
I will make the pyre great!
10 Pile on the wood, kindle the fire.
Cook the meat, stir the spicy mixture,
char the bones!
11 Then set it empty on the coals,
to heat up until its copper glows,
So its impurities melt,
its filth disappears.
12 * The toil is exhausting,
but the great filth will not come
out—
Filth, even with fire.
13 Even in defiling yourself with
depravity
I would still have cleansed you,
but you would not have your impurity
cleansed.
You will not be cleansed now
until I wreak my fury on you.[r]
14 I, the LORD, have spoken;
it will happen!
I will do it and not hold back!
I will not have pity or relent.
By your conduct and deeds you shall be
judged—
oracle of the Lord GOD.

Ezekiel as a Sign for the Exiles. 15The
word of the LORD came to me: 16Son of man,
with a sudden blow I am taking away from
you the delight of your eyes, but do not
mourn or weep or shed any tears.[s] 17Groan,
moan for the dead, but make no public
lament; bind on your turban, put your sandals on your feet, but do not cover your
beard or eat the bread of mourners.* 18I
spoke to the people in the morning. In the
evening my wife died. The next morning I
did as I had been commanded.[t] 19Then the
people asked me, "Will you not tell us what
all these things you are doing mean for us?"
20I said to them, The word of the LORD came
to me: 21Say to the house of Israel: Thus says
the Lord GOD: I will now desecrate my sanctuary, the pride of your strength, the delight
of your eyes, the concern of your soul. The
sons and daughters you left behind shall fall
by the sword.[u] 22* Then you shall do as I
have done, not covering your beards nor eating the bread of mourning. 23[v] Your turbans
shall remain on your heads, your sandals on
your feet. You shall not mourn or weep, but
you shall waste away because of your sins
and groan to one another. 24Ezekiel shall be
a sign for you: everything he did, you shall
do. When it happens, you shall know that I
am the Lord GOD.

End of Ezekiel's Muteness. 25[w] As for you,
son of man, truly, on the very day I take
away from them their strength, their glorious
joy, the delight of their eyes, the desire of
their soul, the pride of their hearts, their sons
and daughters, 26on that day a survivor will
come to you so that you may hear it with
your own ears.[x] 27On that day, with the survivor, your mouth shall be opened; you shall
speak and be mute* no longer. You shall be a
sign to them, and they shall know that I am
the LORD.

24:7 Blood . . . to be covered with dirt: since blood was sacred to God, it had to be covered with earth (Gn 37:26; Lv 17:13); the blood of innocent victims left uncovered cried out for vengeance; cf. Gn 4:10; Jb 16:18; Is 26:21.

24:12 A cryptic line in Hebrew.

24:17 The bread of mourners: a post-burial meal that mourners shared to comfort one another; cf. 2 Sm 3:35; Jer 16:7. The other gestures mentioned here were also popular mourning customs. Because Ezekiel does not observe any of the mourning customs mentioned, the people are puzzled and ask him to explain.

24:22–24 The fall of the city will be so sudden and final that the exiles will have no time to go into mourning.

24:27 Mute: unable to preach anything but the Lord's judgment against Judah and Jerusalem; cf. 3:27 and note on 33:21–22.

r: Is 22:14; Jer 6:28–30. *s:* Jer 16:5–7. *t:* cf. Ez 12:9. *u:* Lv 26:31. *v:* Is 20:2–3. *w:* cf. Ez 3:22–27. *x:* cf. Ez 33:22.

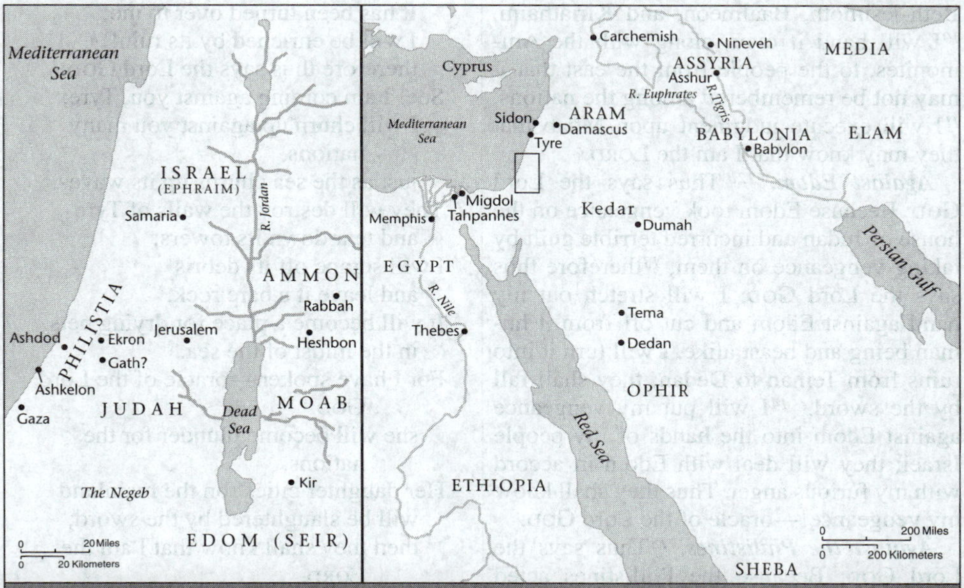

Places Mentioned in the Oracles against the Nations

III. Prophecies Against Foreign Nations*

CHAPTER 25*

See RG 325–32

Against Ammon. [1]The word of the
LORD came to me: [2]Son of man, turn toward
the Ammonites and prophesy against them.[y]
[3]Say to the Ammonites: Hear the word of the
LORD! Thus says the Lord GOD: Because
you jeered at my sanctuary when it was desecrated, at the land of Israel when it was destroyed, and at the house of Judah when they
went into exile, [4]therefore I am giving you to
people from the east* as a possession. They
shall set up their encampments among you
and pitch their tents in your midst; they shall
eat your produce and drink your milk.[z] [5]And
I will turn Rabbah into a pasture for camels
and all of Ammon into a grazing place for
flocks. Then you shall know that I am the
LORD.
[6]For thus says the Lord GOD: Because you
rejoiced over the land of Israel with scorn in
your heart, clapping your hands and stamping your feet, [7]therefore, see, I am stretching
out my hand against you and giving you up
as plunder to the nations. I will cut you off
from the peoples and wipe you out of the
lands. I will destroy you, and you shall know
that I am the LORD.[a]
Against Moab. [8b]Thus says the Lord
GOD: Because Moab said, "See! the house of
Judah is like all the other nations," [9]therefore, I am exposing the whole flank of
Moab* with its cities, the jewels of its land:

25:1–32:32 These chapters form a body of oracles directed against foreign nations. They follow the prophet's condemnation of Judah and oracles announcing its destruction. The unit precedes the announcement of Judah's salvation in chaps. 33–48.

25:1–17 Ezekiel condemns four nations for their reactions to Judah's destruction and exile: Ammon to the east (vv. 2–7); Moab to the southeast (vv. 8–11); Edom to the south (vv. 12–14); Philistia to the west (vv. 15–17). Their hostility was not unprovoked; at one time or another, each one either lost territory to Israel or had been under Israelite control.

25:4 People from the east: nomadic tribes from the desert east of Ammon and Moab (cf. Is 11:14; Jer 49:28), often a threat to outlying towns and villages.

25:9 The whole flank of Moab: the eastern edge of the Moabite plateau, perhaps lightly fortified because the vast desert to the east provided a natural barrier to invasion.

y: Jer 49:1–6; Am 1:13–15; Zep 2:8–11. *z:* Dt 28:33, 51. *a:* Am 1:14–15. *b:* Sir 50:26; Is 15–16; Jer 48; Am 2:1–3.

Beth-jesimoth, Baalmeon, and Kiriathaim.
10 I will hand it over, along with the Ammonites, to the people from the east that it may not be remembered among the nations.
11 I will execute judgment upon Moab that they may know that I am the LORD.[c]

Against Edom.
12[d] Thus says the Lord GOD: Because Edom took vengeance on the house of Judah and incurred terrible guilt by taking vengeance on them,
13 therefore thus says the Lord GOD: I will stretch out my hand against Edom and cut off from it human being and beast alike. I will turn it into ruins from Teman to Dedan; they shall fall by the sword.[e]
14 I will put my vengeance against Edom into the hands of my people Israel; they will deal with Edom in accord with my furious anger. Thus they shall know my vengeance!—oracle of the Lord GOD.[f]

Against the Philistines.
15 Thus says the Lord GOD: Because the Philistines acted vengefully and exacted vengeance with intentional malice, destroying with undying hostility,[g]
16 therefore thus says the Lord GOD: See! I am stretching out my hand against the Philistines, and I will cut off the Cherethites* and wipe out the remnant on the seacoast.
17 Thus I will execute great acts of vengeance on them, punishing them furiously. Then they shall know that I am the LORD, when I wreak my vengeance on them.

See RG 325–32

CHAPTER 26

Against the City of Tyre.
1* On the first day of the eleventh month of the eleventh year, the word of the LORD came to me:

2 * Son of man, because Tyre said of
Jerusalem:
"Aha! The gateway of the peoples is
smashed!
It has been turned over to me;
I will be enriched by its ruin!"[h]
3 therefore thus says the Lord GOD:
See! I am coming against you, Tyre;
I will churn up against you many
nations,
just as the sea churns up its waves.
4 They will destroy the walls of Tyre
and tear down its towers;
I will scrape off its debris
and leave it a bare rock.*
5 It will become a place for drying nets
in the midst of the sea.
For I have spoken—oracle of the Lord
GOD:
she will become plunder for the
nations.
6 Her daughter cities* on the mainland
will be slaughtered by the sword;
then they shall know that I am the
LORD.
7 Indeed thus says the Lord GOD:
I am bringing up against Tyre
from the north, Nebuchadnezzar,
King of Babylon, king of kings,
with horses and chariots, with cavalry,
and a mighty horde of troops.[i]
8 Your daughter cities on the mainland
he shall slay with the sword.
He shall build a siege wall around you,
throw up a ramp against you,
and raise his shields about you.
9 He shall pound your walls with battering-
rams
and break down your towers with his
axes.
10 From the surging of his horses
he will cover you with dust;
from the noise of warhorses,
wheels and chariots.
Your walls will shake

25:16 Cherethites: people from the island of Crete in the Aegean, the Philistines' point of origin. In Zep 2:5, the terms "Philistines," "Cherethites," and "seacoast people" describe the same group of people.

26:1 The Hebrew text does not give a number with the month. This translation assumes a scribal error, the omission of the second occurrence of the number eleven.

26:2 Tyre is pictured rejoicing over Jerusalem's fall to Babylon because now the wealth from caravans and other trade will go to Tyrian merchants.

26:4–5 A bare rock: the Tyre of Ezekiel's time was situated on a rocky island just off the Phoenician coast. During the time of Alexander the Great a causeway was built to connect it to the mainland.

26:6 Daughter cities: tributary towns and villages on the mainland.

c: Am 2:1–3. *d:* 2 Sm 8:13–14; 2 Chr 28:17; Ob 11–14. *e:* cf. Ez 35; Is 34:5–17; 63:1–6; Jer 49:7–11. *f:* cf. Ez 35:11. *g:* Is 14:29–31; Jer 47:1–7; Am 1:6–8; Zep 2:4–7. *h:* Is 23:1–18; Jl 3:4–5; Am 1:9–10; Zec 9:2–4. *i:* Jer 27:6; Na 2:3–4.

when he enters your gates,
even as one enters a city that is breached.
11 With the hooves of his horses
he will trample all your streets;
Your people he will slay by the sword;
your mighty pillars will collapse.[j]
12 They shall plunder your wealth
and pillage your goods;
They will tear down your walls
and demolish your splendid houses.
Your stones, timbers, and debris
they will cast into the sea.
13 I will bring an end to the noise of your songs;
the music of your lyres will be heard no more.
14 I will turn you into bare rock,
you will become a place for drying nets.
You shall never be rebuilt,
for I the LORD have spoken—
oracle of the Lord GOD.
15 Thus says the Lord GOD to Tyre:
At the sound of your downfall,
at the groaning of the wounded,
When victims are slain within you,
will the islands not quake?
16 All the princes of the sea*
will step down from their thrones,
Lay aside their robes,
and strip off their embroidered garments.
Clothed in mourning,
they will sit on the ground
And tremble, horror-struck
and appalled at you.[k]
17 They will raise lament* over you
and say to you:
How you have perished,
gone from the seas,
Renowned City!
Once she was mighty on the sea,
she and her inhabitants,
Those who spread their terror
to all who dwelt nearby.[l]
18 On this, the day of your fall,
the islands quake!
The islands in the sea
are terrified at your passing.
19 Indeed thus says the Lord GOD:
When I make you a ruined city
like cities no longer inhabited,
When I churn up the deep
and its mighty waters cover you,
20 Then I will thrust you down
with those who go down to the pit,*
to those of the bygone age;
I will make you dwell in the netherworld,
in the everlasting ruins,
with those who have gone down to the pit,
So you will never return
or have a place in the land of the living.[m]
21 I will make you a horror,
and you shall be no more;
You shall be sought for,
but never found again—
oracle of the Lord GOD.

CHAPTER 27

See RG 325–32

The Ship Tyre. 1 The word of the LORD came to me: 2 You, son of man, raise a lament over Tyre, 3 and say to Tyre, who sits at the entrance to the sea, trader to peoples on many coastlands, Thus says the Lord GOD:

Tyre, you said, "I am a ship,
perfect in beauty;[n]
4 In the heart of the sea was your territory;
your builders perfected your beauty.[o]
5 With juniper wood from Senir*
they built all your decks;
A cedar from Lebanon they took
to make you a mast.
6 With oaks of Bashan*
they fashioned your oars,

26:16 The princes of the sea: the rulers of the islands and coastal cities leagued commercially with Tyre.

26:17 Lament: the princes sing a funeral dirge at the burial of the personified Tyre; cf. the similar lamentation over Egypt in 32:3–8.

26:20 Those who go down to the pit: the dead, pictured as dwelling in Sheol, a place or cave of darkness. Cf. 32:17–32; Is 14:4–21 for other examples.

27:5 Senir: another name for Mount Hermon; cf. Dt 3:9.

27:6 Bashan: an area in northern Transjordan, noted for its lush growth and great forests (cf. Is 2:13). **Kittim**: here, probably Cyprus.

j: Na 3:11. *k:* cf. Ez 32:10. *l:* cf. Ez 19:1. *m:* cf. Ez 31:14; 32:18, 24, 30. *n:* Is 23:9. *o:* cf. Ez 28:1.

Your bridge, of ivory-inlaid cypress wood
from the coasts of Kittim.
7 Fine embroidered linen from Egypt
became your sail;
Your awnings were made of purple and scarlet
from the coasts of Elishah.* [p]
8 Inhabitants of Sidon* and Arvad
were your oarsmen;
Your own sages, Tyre, were on board,
serving as your sailors.[q]
9 The elders and sages of Gebal
were with you to caulk your seams.
Every ship and sailor on the sea
came to you to carry on trade.[r]
10 Persia and Lud and Put
were warriors in your army;
Shield and helmet they hung on you
to enhance your splendor.
11 The men of Arvad and Helech*
were on your walls all around
And Gamadites on your towers;
they hung their shields around your walls,
they made your beauty perfect.
12 Tarshish traded with you,
so great was your wealth,
Exchanging for your wares
silver, iron, tin, and lead.
13 Javan, Tubal, and Meshech
also traded with you,
Exchanging slaves and bronze vessels
for your merchandise.[s]
14 Horses, steeds, and mules from Beth-togarmah
were exchanged for your wares.
15 Men of Rhodes trafficked with you;
many coastlands were your agents;
Ivory tusks and ebony wood
they brought back as your payment.
16 Edom traded with you for your many wares:
garnets, purple dye, embroidered cloth,
Fine linen, coral, and rubies
they gave you as merchandise.
17 Judah and the land of Israel
trafficked with you:
Minnith wheat, grain,* honey, oil, and balm[t]
they gave you as merchandise.
18 Damascus traded with you for your many wares,
so great was your wealth,
exchanging Helbon wine and Zahar wool.
19 Javan exchanged wrought iron, cassia,
and aromatic cane
from Uzal for your wares.
20 Dedan traded with you for riding gear.[u]
21 Arabia and the sheikhs of Kedar were your agents,
dealing in lambs, rams, and goats.[v]
22 The merchants of Sheba and Raamah
also traded with you,
exchanging for your wares the very best spices,
all kinds of precious stones, and gold.
23 Haran, Canneh, and Eden,
the merchants of Sheba, Asshur, and Chilmad,
24 Traded with you, marketing rich garments,
purple cloth, embroidered fabric,
varicolored carpets, and braided cords.
25 The ships of Tarshish sailed for you with your goods;
You were full and heavily laden
in the heart of the sea.
26 Out into deep waters
your oarsmen brought you;
The east wind shattered you
in the heart of the sea.[w]
27 Your wealth, your goods, your wares,
your sailors, your crew,
The caulkers of your seams,
those who traded for your goods,
All the warriors with you,
the whole crowd with you
Sank into the heart of the sea

27:7 Elishah: perhaps another term for Cyprus.
27:8–9 Sidon . . . Gebal: Phoenician cities in Tyre's orbit of influence; Gebal is classical Byblos.
27:11 Helech: perhaps in Asia Minor; otherwise unknown.
27:17 Grain: most commentators have read "figs," but Hebrew *panag* more properly describes milled grains or prepared meal.

p: Is 19:9–10. *q:* cf. Ez 28:20–23. *r:* Ps 104:26. *s:* cf. Ez 38:2; 39:1. *t:* 1 Kgs 5:9. *u:* Is 21:13. *v:* Is 21:17; Jer 49:28. *w:* Ps 48:7; Jer 18:17.

on the day of your downfall.[x]
28 At the sound of your sailors' shouts
the waves shudder,[y]
29 Down from their ships
come all who ply the oars;
Sailors, all the seafaring crew,
stand on the shore.
30 They raise their voices over you
and shout their bitter cries;
They pour dust on their heads
and cover themselves with ashes.
31 For you they shave their heads bald
and put on sackcloth;
For you they weep bitterly,
in anguished lament.[z]
32 They raise a lament for you;
they wail over you:
"Who was ever destroyed like Tyre
in the midst of the sea?"[a]
33 By exporting your goods by sea
you satisfied many peoples,
With your great wealth and merchandise
you enriched the kings of the earth.[b]
34 Now you are wrecked in the sea,
in the watery depths;
Your wares and all your crew
have fallen down with you.
35 All who dwell on the coastlands
are aghast over you;
Their kings are terrified,
their faces distorted.
36 The traders among the peoples
now hiss at you;
You have become a horror,
you shall be no more.

CHAPTER 28

See RG 325–32

The Prince of Tyre. 1* The word of the LORD came to me: 2 Son of man, say to the prince of Tyre: Thus says the Lord GOD:

Because you are haughty of heart,
you say, "I am a god!
I sit on a god's throne
in the heart of the sea!"
But you are a man, not a god;
yet you pretend
you are a god at heart!
3 Oh yes, you are wiser than Daniel,*
nothing secret is too obscure for you![c]
4 By your wisdom and intelligence
you made yourself rich,
filling your treasuries with gold and
silver.
5 Through your great wisdom in trading
you heaped up riches for yourself—
your heart is haughty because of your
riches.
6 Therefore thus says the Lord GOD:
Because you pretend you are a god at
heart,
7 Therefore, I will bring against you
strangers, the most bloodthirsty of
nations.
They shall draw their swords
against your splendid wisdom,
and violate your radiance.[d]
8 They shall thrust you down into the pit:
you shall die a violent death
in the heart of the sea.
9 Then, face to face with your killers,
will you still say, "I am a god"?
No, you are a man, not a god,
handed over to those who slay you.
10 You shall die the death of the
uncircumcised
handed over to strangers,
for I have spoken—oracle of the Lord
GOD.[e]

11 The word of the LORD came to me: 12 Son of man, raise a lament over the king of Tyre, and say to him: Thus says the Lord GOD:

* You were a seal of perfection,
full of wisdom, perfect in beauty.[f]
13 In Eden, the garden of God, you lived;
precious stones of every kind were
your covering:
Carnelian, topaz, and beryl,

28:1–10 Ezekiel mocks the arrogance of Tyre's leader, who mistakes the city's commercial success for evidence of his divinity. At the hands of a foreign army, commissioned by the only God worthy of the name, this leader dies a humiliating, unceremonious death.

28:3 Wiser than Daniel: see note on 14:14.

28:12–19 Ezekiel describes the leader of Tyre in language that recalls the imagery of Gn 2–3.

x: cf. Ez 28:8. *y:* Jer 49:21. *z:* Is 15:2; Jer 48:37. *a:* Is 23:1–6. *b:* cf. Ez 28:4–5. *c:* cf. Ez 14:14; Dn 1:20; 2:20–23. *d:* cf. Ez 30:11; 31:12; 32:12. *e:* cf. Ez 32:19, 24. *f:* Is 14:12–15.

chrysolite, onyx, and jasper,
sapphire, garnet, and emerald.
Their mounts and settings
were wrought in gold,
fashioned for you the day you were created.[g]
14 With a cherub I placed you;
I put you on the holy mountain of God,*
where you walked among fiery stones.
15 Blameless were you in your ways
from the day you were created,
Until evil was found in you.
16 Your commerce was full of
lawlessness, and you sinned.
Therefore I banished you from the
mountain of God;
the cherub drove you out
from among the fiery stones.[h]
17 Your heart had grown haughty
because of your beauty;
You corrupted your wisdom
because of your splendor.
I cast you to the ground,
I made you a spectacle
in the sight of kings.[i]
18 Because of the enormity of your guilt,
and the perversity of your trade,
you defiled your sanctuary.
I brought fire out of you;
it devoured you;
I made you ashes on the ground
in the eyes of all who see you.[j]
19 All the nations who knew you
are appalled on account of you;
You have become a horror,
never to be again.[k]

Against Sidon. 20The word of the LORD
came to me: 21Son of man, turn your face toward Sidon and prophesy against it. 22Thus
says the Lord GOD:

Watch out! I am against you, Sidon;
I will win glory for myself in your
midst.
They shall know that I am the LORD,
when I deliver judgment upon it
and manifest my holiness in it.
23 I will send disease into it;
blood will fill its streets,
Within it shall fall
those slain by the sword
raised against it on every side.
Then they shall know that I am the LORD.
24 No longer will there be a thorn that tears
or a brier that scratches for the house
of Israel
From the surrounding neighbors
who despise them;
thus they shall know that I am the
LORD.[l]

25Thus says the Lord GOD: When I gather
the house of Israel from the peoples among
whom they are scattered, and I manifest my
holiness through them in the sight of the nations, then they shall live on the land I gave
my servant Jacob.[m] 26They shall dwell on it
securely, building houses and planting vineyards. They shall dwell securely while I execute judgment on all their neighbors who
treated them with contempt; then they shall
know that I, the LORD, am their God.[n]

CHAPTER 29

See RG 325–32

Egypt the Crocodile. 1In the tenth
year, on the twelfth day of the tenth month,*
the word of the LORD came to me: 2Son of
man, turn your face toward Pharaoh, king of
Egypt, and prophesy against him and against
all Egypt.* [o] 3Say to him: Thus says the Lord
GOD:

Pay attention! I am against you,
Pharaoh, king of Egypt,
Great dragon* crouching
in the midst of the Nile,
Who says, "The Nile belongs to me;
I made it myself!"[p]
4 * I will put hooks in your jaws

28:14 The holy mountain of God: the residence of gods in Israelite and non-Israelite myth; cf. Is 14:13. **Fiery stones**: associated with the divine presence; cf. Ez 1:13; Ps 18:13.

29:1 The date is calculated to be January 7, 587 B.C. The siege of Jerusalem had begun a year earlier; cf. 24:1.

29:2 Egypt was allied with Judah against the Babylonians.

29:3 Dragon: Hebrew reads *tannim*, usually translated "jackals," here a byform of *tannin*, the mythical dragon, or sea monster, representing chaos (cf. Is 27:1; 51:9; Jer 51:34; Ps 91:13; Jb 7:12), and the crocodile native to the Nile. **Nile**: the many rivulets of the Nile that branch out into the Delta.

29:4–5 Ezekiel's repetition of detail creates a vivid picture

g: cf. Ez 31:8–9; Gn 2:8, 15. *h:* Gn 3:24. *i:* Is 10:12. *j:* Ob 18. *k:* Lv 26:12. *l:* Nm 33:55. *m:* cf. Ez 20:41. *n:* Lv 25:18–19; Jer 23:6. *o:* Is 19:1–17; Jer 25:19. *p:* cf. Ez 32:2.

and make all the fish of your Nile
Cling to your scales;
I will drag you up from your Nile,
With all the fish of your Nile
clinging to your scales.[q]
5 I will hurl you into the wilderness,
you and all the fish of your Nile.
You will fall into an open field,
you will not be picked up or gathered
together.
To the beasts of the earth
and the birds of the sky
I give you as food.[r]
6 [s] Then all the inhabitants of Egypt
will know that I am the LORD.
Because you were a staff of reeds*
for the house of Israel:
7 When they took hold of you, you would
splinter,
throwing shoulders out of joint.
When they leaned on you, you would
break,
pitching them down headlong.
8 Therefore thus says the Lord GOD:
Look! I am bringing the sword against
you
to cut off from you people and animals.
9 The land of Egypt shall become a
desolate waste;
then they shall know that I am the
LORD.
Because you said, "The Nile belongs
to me;
I made it!"
10 Beware! I am against you
and against your Nile.
I will turn the land of Egypt into ruins,
into a dry, desolate waste,
From Migdol to Syene,*
up to the border of Ethiopia.[t]
11 No foot shall pass through it,
no human being or beast cross it;
it will remain uninhabited for forty
years.
12 I will make the land of Egypt the most
desolate
among desolate lands;
Its cities, the most deserted
among deserted cities for forty years;
I will scatter the Egyptians among the
nations
and disperse them throughout other
lands.[u]
13 But thus says the Lord GOD:
At the end of forty years
I will gather the Egyptians
from among the peoples
where they are scattered;
14 I will restore Egypt's fortunes,
bringing them back to the land of
Pathros,*
the land of their origin.
But there it will be a lowly kingdom,
15 lower than any other kingdom,
no longer able to set itself above the
nations.
I will make them few in number,
so they cannot rule other nations.
16 No longer shall they be security
for the house of Israel,
But a reminder of its iniquity
in turning away to follow them.
Then they shall know that I am the Lord
GOD.[v]

Wages for Nebuchadnezzar. 17 In the
twenty-seventh year on the first day of the
first month,* the word of the LORD came to
me: 18 Son of man, Nebuchadnezzar, the king
of Babylon, has made his army wage a hard

of Egypt's destruction: God hauls the crocodile (Pharaoh) and the fish clinging to it for protection (the Egyptian populace) out of the Nile and lands them in an open field, where their corpses are torn apart by wildlife rather than being properly buried (cf. Dt 28:26; 2 Kgs 9:36–37; Jer 34:20; Ez 39:17–20).

29:6 Staff of reeds: Pharaoh is like a reed that looks sturdy but breaks under pressure. For a similar image, cf. 2 Kgs 18:21 (Is 36:6).

29:10 From Migdol to Syene: from the northeastern to the southern limits of Egypt. Syene is the modern Aswan, at the first cataract of the Nile; Ethiopia (Heb. *kush*) is the territory south of Aswan.

29:14 Pathros: an Egyptian word for upper, i.e., southern, Egypt, above Memphis/Thebes. As silt filled the Delta region and richer land became available there, the population spread north, creating the tradition of a migration from the south (Is 11:11; Jer 44:1, 15).

29:17 In the twenty-seventh year on the first day of the first month: April 26, 571 B.C. This is the latest date attached to any of Ezekiel's prophecies.

q: Is 19:5. *r:* Jer 7:33. *s:* 2 Kgs 18:21; Is 36:6. *t:* cf. Ez 30:4, 6. *u:* Jer 46:19. *v:* Ps 40:5; Is 20:5.

campaign against Tyre;* their heads grew
bald, their shoulders rubbed raw, yet neither
he nor his army received compensation from
Tyre for all the effort they expended against
it.[w] 19Therefore thus says the Lord GOD:[x]
See! I am giving to Nebuchadnezzar, king of
Babylon, the land of Egypt! He will carry off
its wealth, plundering and pillaging whatever he can find to provide pay for his army.
20As payment for his toil I give him the land
of Egypt—oracle of the Lord GOD.

21On that day I will make a horn* sprout
for the house of Israel, and I will let you
again open your mouth in their midst; then
they shall know that I am the LORD.[y]

See RG 325–32

CHAPTER 30

The Day of the Lord Against Egypt.

1The word of the LORD came to me: 2Son of
man, prophesy and say: Thus says the Lord
GOD:

Wail: "Alas the day!"
3 Yes, a day approaches,
a day of the Lord approaches:
A day of dark cloud,
a time appointed for the nations.[z]
4 A sword will come against Egypt,
there will be anguish in Ethiopia,
When the slain fall in Egypt
when its hordes are seized,
its foundations razed.[a]
5 Ethiopia, Put, and Lud,
all the mixed rabble* and Kub,
and the people of allied lands
shall fall by the sword with them.
6 Thus says the LORD:
The pillars of Egypt shall fall,
and its proud strength sink;
From Migdol to Syene,
its people will fall by the sword—
oracle of the Lord GOD.[b]
7 It shall be the most desolate
among desolate lands,
Its cities the most ruined
among ruined cities.
8 They shall know that I am the LORD,
when I set fire to Egypt,
and all its allies are shattered.[c]
9 On that day, messengers from me
will go forth in ships
to terrorize confident Ethiopia.
Anguish will be among them
on Egypt's day—it is certainly
coming!*
10 Thus says the Lord GOD:
I will put an end to Egypt's hordes
by the hand of Nebuchadnezzar, king
of Babylon:
11 He and his army with him,
the most ruthless of nations,
will be brought in to devastate the land.
They will draw their swords against
Egypt
and fill the land with the slain.
12 Then I will dry up the streams of the Nile,
and sell the land into evil hands;
By the hand of foreigners I will devastate
the land and everything in it.
I, the LORD, have spoken.[d]
13 * Thus says the Lord GOD:
I will destroy idols,
and put an end to images in Memphis.
There will never again be a prince
over the land of Egypt.
Instead, I will spread fear
throughout the land of Egypt.[e]
14 I will devastate Pathros,
set fire to Zoan,
and execute judgment against Thebes.[f]
15 I will pour out my wrath on Pelusium,
the fortress of Egypt,

29:18–19 Nebuchadnezzar's thirteen-year siege (587–574 B.C.) ended with Tyre's surrender on the condition that the Babylonian army would not loot and pillage (*pace* 26:3–14). According to Ezekiel, Nebuchadnezzar and his army should collect their wages for serving as God's instrument in Tyre's punishment, by plundering and controlling Egypt.

29:21 A horn: God will give Israel renewed strength. For horn as a symbol of strength, cf. Dt 33:17; Ps 92:11; 132:17. Ezekiel suggests that the Babylonian conquest of Egypt precedes Israel's restoration, an event he expects to witness and acknowledge when God removes his muteness.

30:5 Mixed rabble: mercenaries.

30:9 God spreads panic throughout Ethiopia, ancient Cush, by sending messengers with news of Egypt's fall. Rivers at its borders insulated Ethiopia and made it inaccessible except by boat.

30:13–19 The prophet enumerates a list of major Egyptian cities that shall each bear the judgment proclaimed in the previous oracle, vv. 1–12.

w: Is 26:7–14. *x:* Is 19:4. *y:* Ps 132:17; Lk 1:69. *z:* cf. Ez 7:7; Is 13:6. *a:* Jer 25:19–20. *b:* cf. Ez 29:10. *c:* Jer 49:27. *d:* Is 19:6. *e:* Is 19:13. *f:* Is 19:11, 13; Jer 46:25.

and cut off the troops of Thebes.
16 I will set fire to Egypt;
Pelusium will writhe in anguish,
Thebes will be breached,
and Memphis besieged in daylight.
17 The warriors of On and Pi-beseth
will fall by the sword,
the cities taken captive.
18 In Tahpanhes, the day will turn dark
when I break the scepter of Egypt
there
and put an end to its proud strength.
Dark clouds will cover it,
and its women will go into captivity.[g]
19 I will execute judgment against Egypt
that they may know that I am the LORD.

Pharaoh's Broken Arm. 20 On the seventh
day of the first month in the eleventh year,*
the word of the LORD came to me: 21* Son of
man, I have broken the arm of Pharaoh, king
of Egypt. See! It has not been immobilized
for healing, nor set with a splint to make it
strong enough to grasp a sword.[h] 22 Therefore thus says the Lord GOD: See! I am coming against Pharaoh, king of Egypt. I will
break both his arms, the strong one and the
broken one, making the sword fall from his
hand. 23 I will scatter the Egyptians among
the nations and disperse them throughout
other lands. 24 I will, however, strengthen the
arms of the king of Babylon and put my
sword in his hand so he can bring it against
Egypt for plunder and pillage.[i] 25 When I
strengthen the arms of the king of Babylon,
and the arms of Pharaoh collapse, they shall
know that I am the LORD, because I put my
sword into the hand of the king of Babylon
to wield against the land of Egypt. 26 When I
scatter the Egyptians among the nations and
disperse them throughout other lands, they
shall know that I am the LORD.

CHAPTER 31

See RG 325–32

Allegory of the Cedar. 1 On the first
day of the third month in the eleventh year,*
the word of the LORD came to me: 2 Son of
man, say to Pharaoh, the king of Egypt, and
to his hordes: In your greatness, whom do
you resemble?

3 Assyria! It is Assyria!*
A cedar of Lebanon—
Beautiful branches,
thick shade,
Towering heights,
its crown in the clouds![j]
4 The waters made it grow,
the deep made it tall,
Letting its currents flow
around the place it was planted,
Then sending its channels
to all the other trees of the field.[k]
5 Thereupon it towered in height
above all the trees in the field;
Its branches were numerous
and its boughs long,
Because of the many waters
sent to its shoots.
6 In its branches nested
all the birds of the sky;
Under its boughs all the wild animals
gave birth,
And in its shade* dwelt
all the mighty nations.[l]
7 It was magnificent in size
and in the length of its branches,
For its roots reached down
to the many waters.
8 In the garden of God,
no cedars could rival it,
No juniper could equal its branches,
no plane tree match its boughs.
No tree in the garden of God

30:20 The seventh day of the first month in the eleventh year: April 29, 587 B.C.

30:21–26 This oracle was delivered more than a year into the siege of Jerusalem (24:1). When Pharaoh Hophra came to help Jerusalem, the Babylonians temporarily lifted the siege; cf. Jer 34:21; 37:6–7. In Ezekiel's eyes, Hophra was interfering with the punishment God intended the Babylonians to inflict on Judah. The Babylonians routed the Egyptians, who could not offer Jerusalem any more help; cf. chap. 31.

31:1 The first day of the third month in the eleventh year: June 21, 587 B.C.

31:3 Assyria: this translates *te'ashshur*, which some interpret as "cypress tree." The oracle, however, compares the fate of Pharaoh to the terrible demise of Assyria because of its arrogant pride (cf. Na 1–3). Ezekiel may have drawn on an ancient myth of a cosmic tree of life to emphasize the greatness of Egypt's fall.

31:6 Shade: a metaphor for protection (cf. Lam 4:20).

g: Jer 43:4–7. *h:* Jer 37:10; 44:30; 48:25. *i:* cf. Ez 21:14. *j:* Ps 92:12; Jer 50:18. *k:* Dn 4:10. *l:* Dn 4:12; cf. Mt 13:32.

could match its beauty.[m]
9 I made it beautiful
with abundant foliage,
So that all the trees in Eden
were envious of it.*
10 Therefore, thus says the Lord GOD:
Because it was arrogant about its height,
lifting its crown among the clouds
and exalting itself because of its size,[n]
11 I handed it over to a ruler of nations
to deal with it according to its evil.
I have cast it off,
12 and foreigners have cut it down,
The most ruthless nations,
have hurled it on the mountains.
Its boughs fell into every valley
and its branches lay broken
in every ravine in the land.
All the peoples of the earth
departed from its shade
when it was hurled down.[o]
13 On its fallen trunk
sit all the birds of the sky;
Beside its fallen branches,
are found all the beasts of the field.
14 This has happened so no well-watered
tree
will gain such lofty height,
or lift its crown to the clouds.
Not one of those fed by water
will tower in height over the rest.
For all of them are destined for death,
for the underworld, among mere
mortals,
with those who go down to the pit.
15 Thus says the Lord GOD:
On the day it went down to Sheol,
I made the deep close up
in mourning for it.
I restrained the currents of the deep,
and held back the many waters.
I darkened Lebanon because of it,
and all the trees of the field
languished because of it.
16 At the sound of its fall,
I made nations shudder,
When I cast it down to Sheol
with those who go down to the pit.
In the underworld
all the trees of Eden took comfort:
Lebanon's choicest and best,
all that were fed by the waters.[p]
17 They too will go down to Sheol,
to those slain by the sword,
Its allies* who dwelt
in its shade among the nations.
18 To whom among the trees of Eden
do you compare in glory and greatness?
You will be brought down
with the trees of Eden to the
underworld,
And lie among the uncircumcised,
with those slain by the sword.
Such is Pharaoh and all his hordes—
oracle of the Lord GOD.

CHAPTER 32

See RG 325–32

Lament over Pharaoh. 1 On the first
day of the twelfth month in the twelfth year,*
the word of the LORD came to me: 2 Son of
man, utter a lament over Pharaoh, the king
of Egypt, and say to him:

You liken yourself to a lion among
nations,
but you are like the monster in the sea!
Thrashing about in your streams,
churning the water with your feet,
polluting the streams.[q]
3 Thus says the Lord GOD:
I will cast my net over you
by assembling many armies,
and I will hoist you up in my mesh.
4 I will hurl you onto the land,
cast you into an open field.
I will make all the birds of the sky
roost upon you,
The beasts of the whole earth
gorge themselves on you.
5 I will strew your flesh on the mountains,
and fill the valleys with your corpse.[r]
6 I will drench the land,
pouring out your blood on the
mountain;

31:9 Here Israel's God is responsible for Assyria's splendor, whereas in Is 10:13 Assyria claims to have created its own might.

31:17 Allies: lit., "arm."

32:1 The first day of the twelfth month in the twelfth year: March 3, 585 B.C.

m: Ps 80:10. *n:* Is 2:11. *o:* Dn 4:14. *p:* Is 14:8, 15. *q:* cf. Ez 19:1; 20:3. *r:* Is 34:3.

filling up the ravines with you.
7 When I extinguish you,
I will cover the heavens
and darken all its stars.
The sun I will cover with clouds;
the moon will not give light.[s]
8 All the shining lights in the heavens
I will darken over you;
I will spread darkness over your land—
oracle of the Lord GOD.
9 I will trouble the hearts
of many peoples,
When I bring you captive
among the nations,
to lands you do not know.
10 I will fill many nations with horror;
their kings will shudder at you,
when I brandish my sword in their
faces.
They will tremble violently
fearing for their lives on the day of
your fall.[t]
11 For thus says the Lord GOD:
The sword of the king of Babylon
will come against you.
12 I will cut down your hordes
with the swords of warriors,
all of them, ruthless nations;
They will lay waste the glory of Egypt,
and all its hordes will be destroyed.
13 I will wipe out all the livestock
from the banks of its many waters;
No human foot will disturb them again,
no animal hoof stir them up.
14 Then I will make their waters clear
and their streams flow like oil—
oracle of the Lord GOD.
15 When I make Egypt a wasteland
and the land destitute of everything,
When I strike down all its inhabitants
they shall know that I am the LORD.
16 This is the lamentation
women of all nations will chant;
They will raise it over Egypt;
over all its hordes they will chant it—
oracle of the Lord GOD.

Another Lament over Egypt. 17* On the fifteenth day of that month in the twelfth year, the word of the LORD came to me:

18 Son of man, wail over the hordes of
Egypt—
you and the women of mighty
nations—
Send them down to the underworld,
with those who go down into the pit.
19 Whom do you excel in beauty? Go down!
Be laid to rest with the uncircumcised!
20 Among those slain by the sword they
will fall,
for the sword has been appointed!
Seize Egypt and all its hordes.[u]
21 Out of Sheol the mighty warriors
will speak to him and his allies:
Let them descend and lie down among
the uncircumcised,
those slain by the sword![v]
22 There is Assyria and all its company,
around it are its graves,
all of them slain, fallen by the sword.
23 The graves are set
in the recesses of the pit;
Its company is assembled
around its grave,
All of them slain, fallen by the sword,
those who spread terror in the land of
the living.[w]
24 There is Elam and all its horde
around its grave,
All of them slain, fallen by the sword;
they descended uncircumcised
into the underworld,
Those who spread their terror
in the land of the living.
They bear their disgrace
with those who go down into the pit.
25 Among the slain is set its bed,
with all its horde around its grave;
All of them uncircumcised,
slain by the sword
Because of the terror they spread
in the land of the living.

32:17–32 The description of Pharaoh in Sheol shifts rapidly between the single individual and the collective body, between corpses speaking and corpses lying inert, between singular (his, hers, its) and plural (them, theirs) pronouns to emphasize that all the enemies of Israel come to the same end.

s: Is 3:10. *t:* Rev 18:9–10; 32:12; cf. Ez 31:11–12. *u:* cf. Ez 31:17–18. *v:* Is 14:9. *w:* Is 14:15.

They bear their disgrace
with those who go down into the pit.
Among the slain it is set!
26 There is Meshech and Tubal* and all the hordes
surrounding it with their graves.
All of them uncircumcised,
slain by the sword
Because they spread their terror
in the land of the living.[x]
27 They do not rest with the warriors
who fell in ancient times,
who went down to Sheol fully armed.
Their swords were placed under their heads
and their shields laid over their bones;
For there was terror of these warriors
in the land of the living.
28 But as for you, among the uncircumcised
you will be broken and laid to rest
with those slain by the sword.
29 There is Edom, all its kings and princes,
who, despite their might,
are put with those slain by the sword.
They lie among the uncircumcised,
with those who go down into the pit.[y]
30 There are the generals of the north
and all the Sidonians
Who have gone down with the slain,
because of the terror their might inspired.
They lie uncircumcised
with those slain by the sword,
And bear their shame with those
who have gone down into the pit.[z]
31 When Pharaoh sees them,
he will be consoled on behalf of all his hordes,
slain by the sword—
Pharaoh and all his army—
oracle of the Lord GOD.
32 I spread terror of him
in the land of the living;
Now he is laid among the uncircumcised,
with those slain by the sword—
Pharaoh and all his horde—
oracle of the Lord GOD.

IV. Hope for the Future

CHAPTER 33

See RG 325–32

The Prophet as Sentinel. 1 The word of
the LORD came to me: 2 Son of man, speak to
your people and tell them: When I bring the
sword against a land, if the people of that
land select one of their number as a sentinel*
for them,[a] 3 and the sentinel sees the sword
coming against the land, he should blow the
trumpet to warn the people.[b] 4 If they hear the
trumpet but do not take the warning and a
sword attacks and kills them, their blood
will be on their own heads.[c] 5 They heard the
trumpet blast but ignored the warning; their
blood is on them. If they had heeded the
warning, they could have escaped with their
lives. 6 If, however, the sentinel sees the
sword coming and does not blow the trumpet, so that the sword attacks and takes
someone's life, his life will be taken for his
own sin, but I will hold the sentinel responsible for his blood.

7d You, son of man—I have appointed you
as a sentinel for the house of Israel; when you
hear a word from my mouth, you must warn
them for me. 8 When I say to the wicked,
"You wicked, you must die," and you do not
speak up to warn the wicked about their
ways, they shall die in their sins, but I will
hold you responsible for their blood. 9 If,
however, you warn the wicked to turn from
their ways, but they do not, then they shall
die in their sins, but you shall save your life.

Individual Retribution. 10 As for you, son
of man, speak to the house of Israel: You
people say, "Our crimes and our sins weigh
us down; we are rotting away because of
them. How can we survive?"[e] 11f Answer
them: As I live—oracle of the Lord GOD—I
swear I take no pleasure in the death of the
wicked, but rather that they turn from their

32:26 Meshech and Tubal: see note on 38:2.

33:2 Sentinel: the theme of the sentinel's duty initiates a new commission to announce salvation (chaps. 33–48), just as the same command (3:17–21) opened Ezekiel's ministry to announce judgment (chaps. 3–24).

x: cf. Ez 27:13. *y:* Is 34:5–15. *z:* Jer 25:26. *a:* Lv 26:25. *b:* Hos 5:8; 8:1. *c:* Lv 20:9; Jer 6:17. *d:* Jer 1:17. *e:* Lv 26:16, 39. *f:* Jer 44:7–8; cf. Ez 18:23.

ways and live. Turn, turn from your evil ways! Why should you die, house of Israel? [12]As for you, son of man, say to your people: The justice of the just will not save them on the day they sin; the wickedness of the wicked will not bring about their downfall on the day they turn from their wickedness. No, the just cannot save their lives on the day they sin.[g] [13]Even though I say to the just that they shall surely live, if they, relying on their justice, do wrong, none of their just deeds shall be remembered; because of the wrong they have done, they shall die.[h] [14]And though I say to the wicked that they shall die, if they turn away from sin and do what is just and right— [15]returning pledges, restoring stolen goods, walking by statutes that bring life, doing nothing wrong—they shall surely live; they shall not die.[i] [16]None of the sins they committed shall be remembered against them. If they do what is right and just, they shall surely live.

[17]Your people say, "The way of the LORD is not fair!" But it is their way that is not fair. [18]When the just turn away from justice and do wrong, they shall die for it.[j] [19]When the wicked turn away from wickedness and do what is right and just, because of this they shall live. [20]But still you say, "The way of the LORD is not fair!" I will judge each of you according to your ways, house of Israel.

The Survivor from Jerusalem. [21]On the fifth day of the tenth month,* in the twelfth year of our exile, the survivor came to me from Jerusalem and said, "The city is taken!"[k] [22]The hand of the LORD had come upon me the evening before the survivor arrived and opened my mouth when he reached me in the morning. My mouth was opened, and I was mute no longer.[l]

Those Left in Judah.* [23]The word of the LORD came to me: [24]Son of man, these who live among the ruins in the land of Israel are saying: "Abraham was only one person, yet he was given possession of the land. Since we are many, the land must be given to us as our possession."[m] [25]Therefore say to them: Thus says the Lord GOD: You eat on the mountains, you raise your eyes to your idols, you shed blood—yet you would keep possession of the land?[n] [26]You rely on your swords, you commit abominations, each defiles his neighbor's wife—yet you would keep possession of the land? [27]Say this to them: Thus says the Lord GOD: As I live, those among the ruins shall fall by the sword; those in the open field I have made food for the wild beasts; and those in rocky hideouts and caves shall die by the plague. [28]I will make the land a desolate waste, so that its proud strength will come to an end, and the mountains of Israel shall be so desolate that no one will cross them. [29]Thus they shall know that I am the LORD, when I make the land a desolate waste because of all the abominations they committed.

Popular Misunderstanding. [30]As for you, son of man, your people are talking about you beside the walls and in the doorways of houses. They say to one another, "Let's go hear the latest word that comes from the LORD." [31]My people come to you, gathering as a crowd and sitting in front of you to hear your words, but they will not act on them. Love songs are on their lips, but in their hearts they pursue dishonest gain.[o] [32]For them you are only a singer* of love songs, with a pleasant voice and a clever touch. They listen to your words, but they do not obey them. [33]But when it comes—and it is surely coming!—they shall know that there was a prophet among them.

CHAPTER 34

See RG 325–32

Parable of the Shepherds. [1]The word of the LORD came to me: [2]Son of man,

33:21–22 The fifth day of the tenth month: January 8, 585 B.C. According to Jeremiah (39:2), Jerusalem was taken in July, 587. Some manuscripts read "eleventh" for "twelfth" year (January, 586); even so, there was ample time between the fall of Jerusalem and the arrival of the survivor from that city to journey to Babylon. However, this is the survivor sent to fulfill the promise of Ez 24:25–27, the eyewitness whose arrival would release Ezekiel from his muteness; cf. 3:26–27.

33:23–29 News brought by the survivor furnished the occasion for this prophecy. Like Jeremiah, Ezekiel rejects the idea that those left in Judah have any claim to the land. The new Israel is to be formed from the exiles.

33:32 Singer: perhaps the term indicates an entertainer whom one enjoys and then forgets.

g: cf. Ez 3:20. *h:* Heb 10:38. *i:* Ex 22:1–4, 26. *j:* Jer 18:7–10. *k:* 2 Kgs 25:4, 10; Is 39:1–2. *l:* cf. Ez 3:26–27. *m:* Is 51:2. *n:* Gn 9:4; Jer 7:9–10. *o:* cf. Ez 8:1; Mt 13:22.

prophesy against the shepherds* of Israel.
Prophesy and say to them: To the shepherds,
thus says the Lord GOD: Woe to the shepherds of Israel who have been pasturing
themselves![p] Should not shepherds pasture
the flock? 3You consumed milk, wore wool,
and slaughtered fatlings, but the flock you
did not pasture.[q] 4You did not strengthen the
weak nor heal the sick nor bind up the injured. You did not bring back the stray or
seek the lost but ruled them harshly and bru-
tally.[r] 5So they were scattered for lack of a
shepherd, and became food for all the wild
beasts. They were scattered[s] 6and wandered
over all the mountains and high hills; over
the entire surface of the earth my sheep were
scattered. No one looked after them or
searched for them.

7Therefore, shepherds, hear the word of
the LORD: 8As I live—oracle of the Lord
GOD—because my sheep became plunder,
because my sheep became food for wild
beasts, for lack of a shepherd, because my
shepherds did not look after my sheep, but
pastured themselves and did not pasture my
sheep,[t] 9therefore, shepherds, hear the word
of the LORD: 10Thus says the Lord GOD:
Look! I am coming against these shepherds.
I will take my sheep out of their hand and put
a stop to their shepherding my flock, so that
these shepherds will no longer pasture them.
I will deliver my flock from their mouths so
it will not become their food.[u]

11For thus says the Lord GOD: Look! I myself will search for my sheep and examine
them. 12As a shepherd examines his flock
while he himself is among his scattered
sheep, so will I examine my sheep. I will deliver them from every place where they were
scattered on the day of dark clouds.[v] 13I will
lead them out from among the peoples and
gather them from the lands; I will bring them
back to their own country and pasture them
upon the mountains of Israel, in the ravines
and every inhabited place in the land.[w] 14In
good pastures I will pasture them; on the
mountain heights of Israel will be their grazing land. There they will lie down on good
grazing ground; in rich pastures they will be
pastured on the mountains of Israel.[x] 15I myself will pasture my sheep; I myself will give
them rest—oracle of the Lord GOD. 16The
lost I will search out, the strays I will bring
back, the injured I will bind up, and the sick
I will heal; but the sleek and the strong I will
destroy. I will shepherd them in judgment.

Separation of the Sheep. 17As for you, my
flock, thus says the Lord GOD: I will judge
between one sheep and another, between
rams and goats.[y] 18Was it not enough for you
to graze on the best pasture, that you had to
trample the rest of your pastures with your
hooves? Or to drink the clearest water, that
you had to pollute the rest with your hooves?
19Thus my flock had to graze on what your
hooves had trampled and drink what your
hooves had polluted. 20Therefore thus says
the Lord GOD: Now I will judge between the
fat and the lean. 21Because you push with
flank and shoulder, and butt all the weak
sheep with your horns until you drive them
off, 22I will save my flock so they can no
longer be plundered; I will judge between
one sheep and another. 23[z] I will appoint one
shepherd* over them to pasture them, my
servant David; he shall pasture them and be
their shepherd. 24I, the LORD, will be their
God, and my servant David will be prince in
their midst. I, the LORD, have spoken.[a]

25I will make a covenant of peace with
them and rid the country of wild beasts so
they will dwell securely in the wilderness
and sleep in the forests.[b] 26I will settle them
around my hill and send rain in its season,

34:2 Shepherds: the leaders of the people. A frequent title for kings and deities in the ancient Near East; the ideal ruler took care of his subjects and anticipated their needs. Ezekiel's oracle broadens the reference to include the whole class of Jerusalem's leaders (v. 17). The prophet assures his audience, the exiles in Babylon, that God holds these leaders responsible for what has happened to Jerusalem and will give Israel a new shepherd worthy of the title.

34:23 One shepherd: a future king to rule over a unified, restored Israel, in the image of the idealized David present in the Book of Kings (cf., e.g., 1 Kgs 3:3; 11:38; 2 Kgs 14:3; 22:2). **My servant David**: a common characterization of David; e.g., 1 Kgs 11:34, 36, 38; 2 Kgs 8:19; Ps 36:1; 78:70. See Ez 37:25.

p: Ps 78:70–72; Jn 10:11. *q:* Is 56:11. *r:* Ex 1:13; Zec 11:15–17; Mt 18:12–14. *s:* cf. Mk 6:34. *t:* Jude 12. *u:* Ps 72:14. *v:* Is 40:11; Lk 19:10. *w:* cf. Ez 36:24, 29–30. *x:* Ps 23:2; Is 40:11. *y:* Mt 25:32–33. *z:* Ps 89:4, 20; Jer 23:5–6. *a:* cf. Ez 36:28; Ps 89:49; Jn 10:16. *b:* Is 11:6–9.

the blessing of abundant rain. 27 The trees of the field shall bear their fruits, and the land its crops, and they shall dwell securely on their own soil. They shall know that I am the LORD when I break the bars of their yoke and deliver them from the power of those who enslaved them.[c] 28 They shall no longer be plundered by the nations nor will wild beasts devour them, but they shall dwell securely, with no one to frighten them.[d] 29 I will prepare for them peaceful fields for planting so they are never again swept away by famine in the land or bear taunts from the nations. 30 Thus they shall know that I, the LORD, their God, am with them, and that they are my people, the house of Israel—oracle of the Lord GOD.[e] 31 Yes, you are my flock: you people are the flock of my pasture, and I am your God—oracle of the Lord GOD.[f]

CHAPTER 35

See RG 325–32

*Against Edom.** 1 The word of the LORD came to me: 2 Son of man, set your face against Mount Seir and prophesy against it. 3 Say to it: Thus says the Lord GOD: Watch out! I am against you, Mount Seir. I will stretch out my hand against you and turn you into a desolate waste.[g] 4 Your cities I will turn into ruins, and you shall be a desolation; then you shall know that I am the LORD.[h]

5 Because you nursed a long-standing hatred and handed the Israelites over to the sword at the time of their collapse, at the time of their final punishment,*[i] 6 therefore, as I live—oracle of the Lord GOD—you are guilty of blood, and blood, I swear, shall pursue you. 7 I will make Mount Seir a desolate waste and cut off from it anyone who travels across it and back.[j] 8 I will fill its mountains with the slain; those slain by the sword shall fall on your hills, into your valleys and all your ravines.

9 I will make you a desolation forever,
your cities will not be inhabited,
and you shall know that I am the
LORD.[k]

10 Because you said: The two nations and the two lands* belong to me; let us take possession of them—although the LORD was there— 11 therefore, as I live—oracle of the Lord GOD—I will deal with you according to the anger and envy you dealt out to them in your hatred, and I will make myself known to them when I execute judgment on you,[l] 12 then you shall know that I am the LORD.

I have heard all the insults you spoke against the mountains of Israel, saying: They are desolate; they have been given to us to devour. 13 You boasted against me with your mouths and used insolent words against me. I heard everything! 14 Thus says the Lord GOD: Because you rejoiced that the whole land was desolate, so I will do to you. 15 As you rejoiced over the devastation of the heritage of the house of Israel, the same I will do to you: you will become a ruin, Mount Seir, and the whole of Edom, all of it! Then they shall know that I am the LORD.[m]

CHAPTER 36

See RG 325–32

Regeneration of the Land. 1 As for you, son of man, prophesy to the mountains of Israel and say: Mountains of Israel, hear the word of the LORD! 2 Thus says the Lord GOD: Because the enemy said about you, "Ha! the ancient heights have become our possession," 3 therefore prophesy and say: Thus says the Lord GOD: because you have been ridiculed and hounded on all sides for becoming a possession for the remaining na-

35:1–15 After the fall of Jerusalem, Edom assisted the Babylonians in devastating the land and subduing the population in order to occupy part of Judah's former territory. For this reason these oracles against Edom are found in the context of the city's fall.

35:5 Final punishment: throughout this oracle the prophet echoes the threat against the mountains of Israel found in chaps. 6–7.

35:10 The two nations and the two lands: by presenting Edom's excursion into the southern territory of Judah as its claim to both kingdoms, Ezekiel exaggerates Edom's greed and arrogance. **LORD was there**: Edom's betrayal of Judah becomes an attack on Judah's God, the land's sovereign. In 11:15 and 33:24, Ezekiel condemns Judahites who annex land that does not belong to them. Now the exiles in Babylon learn that even though God had left Jerusalem (chap. 11), he witnesses Edom's insolence and pronounces judgment against it. Cf. 48:35, "The LORD is there!"

c: Lv 26:13; Ps 72:16; Jer 28:10–13. *d:* Jer 30:10. *e:* Ex 6:7. *f:* Ps 28:9. *g:* cf. Ez 25:12–14. *h:* Ob 13. *i:* Ob 11–15. *j:* Jer 46:19. *k:* Is 34:5–6; Ob 10. *l:* Ob 15. *m:* Is 34:11; Ob 12.

tions and have become a byword and a popular jeer,[n] 4therefore, mountains of Israel, hear the word of the Lord GOD: Thus says the Lord GOD to the mountains and hills, to the ravines and valleys, to the desolate ruins and abandoned cities, plundered and mocked by the nations remaining around you:[o] 5therefore thus says the Lord GOD: Truly, with burning jealousy I speak against the remaining nations and against Edom; they all took possession of my land for plunder with wholehearted joy and utter contempt. 6Therefore, prophesy concerning the land of Israel and say to the mountains and hills, to the ravines and valleys: Thus says the Lord GOD: See! in my jealous fury I speak, because you endured the reproach of the nations. 7Therefore, thus says the Lord GOD: I raise my hand and swear: the nations around you shall bear their own reproach.

8But you, mountains of Israel, you will sprout branches and bear fruit for my people Israel, for they are coming soon.[p] 9Look! I am for you! I will turn my face toward you; you will be plowed and planted.[q] 10Upon you I will multiply the whole house of Israel; cities shall be resettled and ruins rebuilt.[r] 11Upon you I will multiply people and animals so they can multiply and be fruitful. I will resettle you as in the past, and make you more prosperous than at your beginning; then you shall know that I am the LORD.[s]

12Upon you I will have them walk, my people Israel. They shall possess you, and you shall be their heritage. Never again shall you rob them of their children.

13Thus says the Lord GOD: Because they say of you, "You devour your own people,* you rob your nation of its children,"[t] 14therefore, you shall never again devour your people or rob your nation of its children—oracle of the Lord GOD. 15I will no longer make you listen to the reproach of nations. You will never again endure insults from the peoples. Never again shall you rob your nation of its children—oracle of the Lord GOD.

Regeneration of the People. 16The word of the LORD came to me: 17Son of man, when the house of Israel lived in its land, they defiled it with their behavior and their deeds. In my sight their behavior was like the impurity of a woman in menstruation.[u] 18So I poured out my fury upon them for the blood they poured out on the ground and for the idols with which they defiled it. 19I scattered them among the nations, and they were dispersed through other lands; according to their behavior and their deeds I carried out judgment against them.[v] 20* But when they came to the nations, where they went, they desecrated my holy name, for people said of them: "These are the people of the LORD, yet they had to leave their land." 21So I relented because of my holy name which the house of Israel desecrated among the nations to which they came. 22Therefore say to the house of Israel: Thus says the Lord GOD: Not for your sake do I act, house of Israel, but for the sake of my holy name, which you desecrated among the nations to which you came.[w] 23But I will show the holiness of my great name, desecrated among the nations, in whose midst you desecrated it. Then the nations shall know that I am the LORD—oracle of the Lord GOD—when through you I show my holiness before their very eyes.[x] 24I will take you away from among the nations, gather you from all the lands, and bring you back to your own soil. 25* [y] I will sprinkle clean water over you to make you clean;

36:13 You devour your own people: i.e., the land destroys its own population; this phrase also occurs in Nm 13:32, where Israelite spies describe Canaan as "a land that devours its inhabitants."

36:20–24 These verses make clear that Israel's restoration is God's initiative, independent of the people's shame and repentance (v. 31). By their wickedness, Israel provoked the exile; its presence among the nations gave the impression that God could not protect his people. God's gracious return of Israel to its land will restore his honor among these same nations.

36:25–26 God's initiative to cleanse Israel (cf. 24:13–14) is the first act in the creation of a new people, no longer disposed to repeating Israel's wicked past (chap. 20). To make this restoration permanent, God replaces Israel's rebellious and obdurate interiority ("heart of stone") with an interiority ("heart of flesh") susceptible to and animated by God's intentions ("my spirit," v. 27).

n: Ob 13. *o:* cf. Ez 6:3. *p:* Lv 26:3–5. *q:* Lv 26:9. *r:* Is 49:8, 17–23. *s:* cf. Gn 1:22, 28. *t:* Nm 13:32. *u:* Ps 106:37–38. *v:* Lv 18:24–28. *w:* cf. Ez 20:44; Dt 9:4–6; Is 37:35. *x:* cf. Ez 20:41; Is 37:23. *y:* Ezr 6:21; Ps 51:2–7.

from all your impurities and from all your idols I will cleanse you. 26[z] I will give you a new heart, and a new spirit I will put within you. I will remove the heart of stone from your flesh and give you a heart of flesh.[a] 27I will put my spirit within you so that you walk in my statutes, observe my ordinances, and keep them.[b] 28You will live in the land I gave to your ancestors; you will be my people, and I will be your God.[c] 29I will deliver you from all your impurities. I will summon the grain and make it plentiful; I will not send famine against you. 30I will increase the fruit on your trees and the crops in your fields so that you no longer endure reproach from the nations because of famine.[d] 31Then you will remember your evil behavior and your deeds that were not good; you will loathe yourselves for your sins and your abominations. 32Not for your sake do I act—oracle of the Lord GOD. Let this be known to you! Be ashamed and humbled because of your behavior, house of Israel.

33Thus says the Lord GOD: When I cleanse you of all your guilt, I will resettle the cities and the ruins will be rebuilt.[e] 34The desolate land will be tilled—once a wasteland in the eyes of every passerby. 35They will say, "This once-desolate land has become like the garden of Eden. The cities once ruined, laid waste and destroyed, are now resettled and fortified."[f] 36Then the surrounding nations that remain shall know that I, the LORD, have rebuilt what was destroyed and replanted what was desolate. I, the LORD, have spoken: I will do it. 37Thus says the Lord GOD: This also I will be persuaded to do for the house of Israel: to multiply them like sheep. 38Like sheep for sacrifice, like the sheep of Jerusalem on its feast days, the ruined cities shall be filled with flocks of people; then they shall know that I am the LORD.[g]

CHAPTER 37

See RG 325–32

Vision of the Dry Bones. * 1The hand of the LORD came upon me, and he led me out in the spirit of the LORD and set me in the center of the broad valley. It was filled with bones. 2He made me walk among them in every direction. So many lay on the surface of the valley! How dry they were! 3He asked me: Son of man, can these bones come back to life? "Lord GOD," I answered, "you alone know that."[h] 4Then he said to me: Prophesy over these bones, and say to them: Dry bones, hear the word of the LORD! 5Thus says the Lord GOD to these bones: Listen! I will make breath enter you so you may come to life. 6I will put sinews on you, make flesh grow over you, cover you with skin, and put breath into you so you may come to life. Then you shall know that I am the LORD. 7I prophesied as I had been commanded. A sound started up, as I was prophesying, rattling like thunder. The bones came together, bone joining to bone. 8As I watched, sinews appeared on them, flesh grew over them, skin covered them on top, but there was no breath in them. 9Then he said to me: Prophesy to the breath, prophesy, son of man! Say to the breath: Thus says the Lord GOD: From the four winds come, O breath, and breathe into these slain that they may come to life.* [i] 10I prophesied as he commanded me, and the breath entered them; they came to life and stood on their feet, a vast army.[j] 11He said to me: Son of man, these bones are the whole house of Israel! They are saying, "Our bones

37:1–14 This account is a figurative description of God's creation of a new Israel. Even though that creation begins with the remains of the old Israel, the exiles under the image of dry bones, depicting a totally hopeless situation, the new Israel is radically different: it is an ideal people, shaped by God's spirit to live the covenant faithfully, something the old Israel, exiles included, were unable to do. While this passage in its present context is not about the doctrine of individual or communal resurrection, many Jewish and Christian commentators suggest that the doctrine is foreshadowed here.

37:9 The Hebrew word *rûah* has multiple related meanings expressed by different English words: wind, spirit, breath. In this translation, *rûah* is rendered "spirit," a powerful force that creates vision and insight (v. 1); "breath," physical energy that quickens and enlivens (vv. 5–6); "wind," invisible physical energy, sometimes destructive, sometimes invigorating (e.g., the rain-bearing winter winds), also a metaphor for restoration and new life (vv. 9–10); "my spirit," a share in God's power so the people observe the law that assures them life in the land (v. 14).

z: Jer 31:33–34. *a:* cf. Rom 8:5–8. *b:* Ps 51:7–11. *c:* Jer 30:22; 31:33. *d:* Lv 26:4–5. *e:* Lv 26:31. *f:* cf. Ez 28:13; 31:9. *g:* 1 Kgs 8:63. *h:* Is 26:19. *i:* Ps 104:30; Is 32:15; Dn 7:2. *j:* cf. Rev 11:11.

are dried up, our hope is lost, and we are cut off." 12 Therefore, prophesy and say to them: Thus says the Lord GOD: Look! I am going to open your graves; I will make you come up out of your graves, my people, and bring you back to the land of Israel.[k] 13 You shall know that I am the LORD, when I open your graves and make you come up out of them, my people! 14 I will put my spirit in you that you may come to life, and I will settle you in your land. Then you shall know that I am the LORD. I have spoken; I will do it—oracle of the LORD.[l]

The Two Sticks. 15* Thus the word of the LORD came to me: 16 As for you, son of man, take one stick and write on it, "Judah and those Israelites associated with it." Then take another stick and write on it: "Joseph, Ephraim's stick, and the whole house of Israel associated with it." 17 Join the two sticks together so they become one stick in your hand. 18 When your people ask you, "Will you not tell us what you mean by all this?" 19 answer them: Thus says the Lord GOD: I will take the stick of Joseph, now in Ephraim's hand, and the tribes of Israel associated with it, and join to it the stick of Judah, making them one stick; they shall become one in my hand.[m] 20 The sticks on which you write, you must hold in your hand in their sight. 21 Say to them: Thus says the Lord GOD: I will soon take the Israelites from among the nations to which they have gone and gather them from all around to bring them back to their land. 22 I will make them one nation in the land, upon the mountains of Israel, and there shall be one king for them all. They shall never again be two nations, never again be divided into two kingdoms.[n]

23 No longer shall they defile themselves with their idols, their abominations, and all their transgressions. I will deliver them from all their apostasy through which they sinned. I will cleanse them so that they will be my people, and I will be their God.[o] 24[p] David my servant shall be king over them; they shall all have one shepherd. They shall walk in my ordinances, observe my statutes, and keep them. 25 They shall live on the land I gave to Jacob my servant, the land where their ancestors lived; they shall live on it always, they, their children, and their children's children, with David my servant as their prince forever. 26[q] I will make a covenant of peace with them; it shall be an everlasting covenant with them. I will multiply them and put my sanctuary among them forever. 27 My dwelling shall be with them; I will be their God, and they will be my people.[r] 28 Then the nations shall know that I, the LORD, make Israel holy, by putting my sanctuary among them forever.

CHAPTER 38

See RG 325-32

First Prophecy Against Gog. 1 The word of the LORD came to me:* 2 Son of man, turn your face against Gog* of the land of Magog, the chief prince of Meshech and Tubal, and prophesy against him.[s] 3 Say: Thus says the Lord GOD: See! I am coming against you, Gog, chief prince of Meshech and Tubal. 4 I will turn you around and put hooks in your jaws to lead you out with all your army, horses and riders, all well armed, a great company, all of them with bucklers and shields, carrying swords: 5[t] Persia, Cush, and Put with them, all with shields and helmets; 6 Gomer and all its troops, Beth-togarmah from the recesses of Zaphon and all its troops—many nations will accompany you. 7 Prepare and get ready, you and the company mobilized for you, but in my service. 8 After many days you will be called to battle; in the last years you will invade a land that has sur-

37:15–22 The symbolic action of joining two sticks into one continues Ezekiel's description of God's future saving action: the unification of Judah and Israel under an ideal ruler.

38:1–39:20 These three oracles against Gog (38:2–13; 14–23; 39:1–20) describe a mythic attack of God against a final enemy of his people sometime in the future. Like the oracles against the nations, their purpose is to strengthen Israel's hope in God, since they end with God's triumph on behalf of the people.

38:2 Gog: the name is symbolic, probably derived from Gyges, king of Lydia. The gloss Magog may be an Akkadian expression, *mat-Gog*, "the land of Gog." Meshech and Tubal, as well as Gomer and Beth-togarmah (v. 6), were countries around the Black Sea, the northernmost countries known to the Israelites. The north was the traditional direction from which invasion was expected; cf. Jer 1:13–15.

k: Is 26:19; Jer 19:14. *l:* cf. Ez 36:27–28; Jer 43:2; Jl 3:1–2. *m:* Zec 10:6. *n:* cf. Ez 17:22; 34:13–14. *o:* cf. Ez 11:18; 36:28; Na 2:2. *p:* Ps 78:70–71; Is 55:4. *q:* Gn 9:16; Nm 25:12; Heb 13:20. *r:* Lv 26:11. *s:* cf. Gn 10:2; Ez 27:13. *t:* Gn 10:2–3, 6.

vived the sword—a people gathered from many nations back to the long-deserted mountains of Israel, brought forth from the nations to dwell securely.[u] [9]You shall come up like a sudden storm, covering the land like a cloud, you and all your troops and the many nations with you.[v]

[10]Thus says the Lord GOD: On that day thoughts shall cross your mind, and you shall devise an evil plan. [11]You will say, "I will invade a land of open villages and attack a peaceful people who live in security—all of them living without city walls, bars, or gates"—[w] [12]in order to plunder and pillage, turning your hand against resettled ruins, against a people gathered from the nations, a people whose concern is cattle and goods, dwelling at the center* of the earth. [13]Sheba and Dedan, the merchants of Tarshish and all its "young lions" shall ask you: "Have you come here to plunder? Have you summoned your army for pillage, to carry off silver and gold, to take away cattle and goods, to seize much plunder?"[x]

Second Prophecy Against Gog. [14]Therefore, prophesy, son of man, and say to Gog: Thus says the Lord GOD: On that day, when my people Israel dwell securely, will you not take action, [15]leaving your base in the recesses of Zaphon,* you and many nations with you, all mounted on horses, a great company, a mighty army?[y] [16]You shall rise up over my people Israel like a cloud covering the land. In those last days, I will let you invade my land so that the nations acknowledge me, when in their sight I show my holiness through you, Gog.

[17]Thus says the Lord GOD: About you I spoke in earlier times through my servants, the prophets of Israel, who prophesied at that time that I would let you invade them. [18]But on that day, the day Gog invades the land of Israel—oracle of the Lord GOD—my fury will flare up in my anger, [19]and in my jealousy, with fiery wrath, I swear on that day there will be a great earthquake in the land of Israel.[z] [20]Before me will tremble the fish of the sea and the birds of the air, the beasts of the field and everything that crawls on the ground, and everyone on the face of the earth. Mountains will be overturned, terraces will collapse, and every wall will fall to the ground.[a] [21]Against him I will summon every terror—oracle of the Lord GOD; every man's sword will be raised against his brother.[b] [22]I will execute judgment on him: disease and bloodshed; flooding rain and hailstones, fire and brimstone, I will rain down on him, on his troops and on the many nations with him.[c] [23]And so I will show my greatness and holiness and make myself known in the sight of many nations. Then they shall know that I am the LORD.[d]

CHAPTER 39

See RG 325-32

Third Prophecy Against Gog. [1]You, son of man, prophesy against Gog, saying: Thus says the Lord GOD: Here I am, Gog, coming at you, chief prince of Meshech and Tubal. [2]I will turn you around, even though I urged you on and brought you up from the recesses of Zaphon and let you attack the mountains of Israel.[e] [3]Then I will strike the bow from your left hand and make the arrows drop from your right. [4]Upon the mountains of Israel you shall fall, you and all your troops and the peoples with you. I will give you as food to birds of prey of every kind and to wild beasts to be eaten. [5]In the open field you shall fall, for I have spoken—oracle of the Lord GOD.[f]

[6]I will send fire against Magog and against those who live securely on the seacoast, and they will know that I am the LORD.[g] [7]I will reveal my holy name among my people Israel, and I will never again allow my holy name to be defiled. Then the nations shall know that I am the LORD, the Holy One of Israel.[h] [8]Yes, it is coming! It shall happen—oracle of the Lord GOD. This is the day I decreed.

[9]Everyone living in the cities of Israel

38:12 Center: lit., "navel." Many ancient peoples spoke of their own homelands as "the navel," that is, the center of the earth.
38:15 Zaphon: cf. note on Jb 37:22.

u: Is 24:22. *v:* Is 25:4; Jer 4:13; Rev 20:8. *w:* Zec 2:4–5. *x:* Gn 10:4, 7. *y:* cf. Ez 39:2. *z:* Is 24:18; Rev 6:12. *a:* Is 42:15. *b:* Is 34:5–6; 66:16. *c:* cf. Rev 9:17; 16:21. *d:* Rev 20:8. *e:* cf. Ez 32:30; 38:6, 15. *f:* cf. Ez 32:4. *g:* Rev 20:9. *h:* Is 12:6.

shall go out and set fire to the weapons, buckler and shield, bows and arrows, clubs and spears; for seven years they shall make fires with them.[i] 10They will not need to bring in wood from the fields or cut down trees in the forests, for they will make fires with the weapons, plundering those who plundered them, pillaging those who pillaged them—oracle of the Lord GOD.

11On that day I will give Gog a place for his tomb in Israel, the Valley of Abarim,* east of the sea. It will block the way of travelers. There Gog shall be buried with all his horde; it shall be called "Valley of Hamon-Gog."[j] 12For seven months the house of Israel shall bury them in order to cleanse the land. 13All the people of the land shall take part in the burials, making a name for themselves on the day I am glorified—oracle of the Lord GOD. 14Men shall be permanently assigned to pass through the land, burying those who lie unburied in order to cleanse the land. For seven months they shall keep searching. 15When these pass through the land and see a human bone, they must set up a marker beside it, until the gravediggers bury it in the Valley of Hamon-Gog. 16Also the name of the city is Hamonah. Thus the land will be cleansed.

17As for you, son of man, thus says the Lord GOD: Say to birds of every kind and to every wild beast: "Assemble! Come from all sides for the sacrifice I am making for you, a great slaughter on the mountains of Israel. You shall eat flesh and drink blood! 18You shall eat the flesh of warriors and drink the blood of the princes of the earth: rams, lambs, and goats, bulls and fatlings from Bashan, all of them.[k] 19From the sacrifice I slaughtered for you, you shall eat fat until you are sated and drink blood until you are drunk. 20At my table you shall be sated with horse and rider, with warrior and soldier of every kind—oracle of the Lord GOD.

Israel's Return. 21Then I will display my glory among the nations, and all the nations will see the judgment I executed, the hand I laid upon them. 22From that day forward the house of Israel shall know that I am the LORD, their God. 23The nations shall know that the house of Israel went into exile because of its sins. Because they betrayed me, I hid my face from them, handing them over to their foes, so they all fell by the sword.[l] 24According to their defilement and their crimes I dealt with them, hiding my face from them.[m]

25Therefore, thus says the Lord GOD: Now I will restore the fortunes of Jacob and take pity on the whole house of Israel; I am zealous for my holy name.[n] 26They will forget their shame and all the infidelities they committed against me when they live securely on their own land with no one to frighten them. 27When I bring them back from the nations and gather them from the lands of their enemies, I will show my holiness through them in the sight of many nations.[o] 28Thus they shall know that I, the LORD, am their God, since I who exiled them among the nations will gather them back to their land, not leaving any of them behind. 29I will no longer hide my face from them once I pour out my spirit upon the house of Israel—oracle of the Lord GOD.[p]

V. The New Israel*

The New Temple

CHAPTER 40

See RG 325–32

The Man with a Measure. 1In the twenty-fifth year of our exile, at the beginning of the year, on the tenth day of the month, fourteen years after the city had been captured, on that very day the hand of the LORD came upon me and brought me back

39:11 The Valley of Abarim: in the Abarim mountains, east of the Jordan. "Abarim" plays on the word *'oberim*, "travelers." **Hamon-Gog**: "the horde of Gog."

40:1–48:35 This lengthy vision of a new Temple and a restored Israel is dated in v. 1 to April 28, 573 B.C. The literary form of the vision is sometimes compared to a mandala, a sacred model through which one can move symbolically to reach the world of the divine. Ezekiel describes the Temple through its boundaries, entrances, and exits in chaps. 40–43; by its sacred and profane use and space in 44–46; and by its central place within the land itself in 47–48. The prophet could not have expected a literal fulfillment of much of what he described. The passage doubtless went through several editorial stages, both from the prophet and from later writers.

i: Ps 46:9; 76:3. *j:* cf. Ez 38:2. *k:* Jer 51:40; Rev 19:17–21. *l:* Ps 30:7; Is 54:8. *m:* 2 Kgs 17:23. *n:* Is 27:13. *o:* cf. Ez 20:41. *p:* cf. Ez 37:9; Is 11:2.

there.[q] 2In a divine vision he brought me to the land of Israel, where he set me down on a very high mountain. In front of me, there was something like a city built on it.[r] 3He brought me there, and there standing in the gateway was a man whose appearance was like bronze! He held in his hand a linen cord and a measuring rod.[s] 4The man said to me, "Son of man, look carefully and listen intently. Pay strict attention to everything I show you, for you have been brought here so that I might show it to you. Then you must tell the house of Israel everything you see." 5There an outer wall completely surrounded the temple. The measuring rod in the man's hand was six cubits long, each cubit being a cubit plus a handbreadth;* he measured the width of the structure, one rod, and its height, one rod.

The East Gate.* 6Going to the gate facing east, he climbed its steps and measured the threshold of the outer gateway as one rod wide.[t] 7Each cell was one rod long and one rod wide, and there were five cubits between the cells; the threshold of the inner gateway adjoining the vestibule of the gate facing the temple was one rod wide. 8He also measured the vestibule of the inner gate, 9eight cubits, and its posts, two cubits each. The vestibule faced the inside. 10On each side of the east gatehouse were three cells, all the same size; their posts were all the same size. 11He measured the width of the gate's entryway, ten cubits, and the length of the gate itself, thirteen cubits. 12The borders in front of the cells on both sides were one cubit, while the cells themselves measured six cubits by six cubits from one opening to the next. 13Next he measured the gatehouse from the back wall of one cell to the back wall of the cell on the opposite side through the openings facing each other, a width of twenty-five cubits. 14All around the courtyard of the gatehouse were posts six cubits high. 15From the front of the gatehouse at its outer entry to the gateway of the porch facing inward, the length was fifty cubits. 16There were recessed windows in the cells on all sides and in the posts on the inner side of the gate. Posts and windows were all around the inside, with palm trees decorating the posts.[u]

The Outer Court. 17Then he brought me to the outer court,* where there were chambers and pavement laid all around the courtyard: thirty chambers facing the pavement.[v] 18The pavement lay alongside the gatehouses, the same length as the gates; this was the lower pavement. 19He measured the length of the pavement from the front of the lower gate to the outside of the inner gate, one hundred cubits. He then moved from the east to the north side.

The North Gate. 20He measured the length and width of the north gate of the outer courtyard. 21Its cells, three on each side, its posts, and its vestibule had the same measurements as those of the first gate, fifty cubits long and twenty-five cubits wide. 22Its windows, its vestibule, and its palm decorations had the same proportions as those of the gate facing east. Seven steps led up to it, and its vestibule faced the inside. 23The inner court had a gate opposite the north gate, just as at the east gate; he measured one hundred cubits from one gate to the other.

The South Gate. 24Then he led me to the south. There, too, facing south, was a gate! He measured its posts and vestibule; they were the same size as the others. 25The gate and its vestibule had windows on both sides, like the other windows, fifty cubits long and twenty-five cubits wide. 26Seven steps led up to it, its vestibule faced inside; and palms decorated each of the posts opposite one another. 27The inner court also had a gate facing south. He measured it from gate to gate, facing south, one hundred cubits.

40:5 A cubit plus a handbreadth: a great cubit. The ordinary cubit consisted of six handbreadths; the great cubit, of seven. In measuring the Temple, a rod six great cubits long was used. The ordinary cubit was about one and a half feet, or, more exactly, 17.5 inches; the large cubit, 20.4 inches.

40:6–16 The gate facing east, leading into the outer court of the Temple, is described more fully than the north and south gates, which, however, have the same dimensions. On the west side of the outer court there is a large building instead of a gate (cf. 41:12).

40:17 The outer court: the court outside the Temple area proper, which had its own inner court (vv. 28–37).

q: 2 Kgs 25:7; Jer 39:1–10; 52:4–11. *r:* Is 2:2; Mi 4:1; Zec 14:10; cf. Rev 21:10. *s:* Zec 2:1–2; Rev 1:15; 11:1; 21:15. *t:* cf. Ez 8:16. *u:* 1 Kgs 6:29, 32, 35. *v:* cf. Ez 41:6; 42:1.

Gates of the Inner Court.* [28]Then he brought me to the inner courtyard by the south gate, where he measured the south gateway; its measurements were the same as the others. [29]Its cells, posts, and vestibule were the same size as the others, fifty cubits long and twenty-five cubits wide. [30]* The vestibules all around were twenty-five cubits long and five cubits wide. [31]Its vestibule faced the outer court; palms decorated its posts, and its stairway had eight steps. [32]Then he brought me to the inner courtyard on the east and measured the gate there; its dimensions were the same as the others. [33]Its cells, posts, and vestibule were the same size as the others. The gate and its vestibule had windows on both sides, fifty cubits long and twenty-five cubits wide. [34]Its vestibule faced the outer court, palms decorated the posts opposite each other, and it had a stairway of eight steps. [35]Then he brought me to the north gate,[w] where he measured the dimensions [36]of its cells, posts, and vestibule; they were the same. The gate and its vestibule had windows on both sides, fifty cubits long and twenty-five cubits wide. [37]Its vestibule faced the outer court; palm trees decorated its posts opposite each other, and it had a stairway of eight steps.

Side Rooms. [38]There was a chamber opening off the vestibule of the gate where burnt offerings were washed.[x] [39]In the vestibule of the gate there were two tables on either side for slaughtering the burnt offerings, purification offerings, and reparation offerings.[y] [40]Two more tables stood along the wall of the vestibule by the entrance of the north gate, and two tables on the other side of the vestibule of the gate. [41]There were thus four tables on one side of the gate and four tables on the other side, eight tables in all, for slaughtering. [42]The four tables for burnt offerings were made of cut stone, one and a half cubits long, one and a half cubits wide, and one cubit high; the instruments used for slaughtering burnt offerings and other sacrifices were kept [43]on shelves the width of one hand, fixed all around the room; but on the tables themselves was the meat for the sacrifices. [44]Outside the inner gatehouse there were two rooms on the inner courtyard, one beside the north gate, facing south, and the other beside the south gate, facing north. [45]He said to me, "This chamber facing south is reserved for the priests who have charge of the temple area, [46]while this chamber facing north is reserved for the priests who have charge of the altar; they are the sons of Zadok,* the only Levites who may come near to minister to the LORD." [47]He measured the courtyard, a square one hundred cubits long and a hundred cubits wide, with the altar standing in front of the temple.[z]

The Temple Building.* [48][a] Then he brought me into the vestibule of the temple and measured the posts, five cubits on each side. The gateway was fourteen cubits wide, its side walls three cubits. [49]The vestibule was twenty cubits long and twelve cubits wide; ten steps led up to it, and there were columns by the posts, one on each side.

CHAPTER 41

See RG 325-32

[1]Then he brought me to the nave and measured the posts; each was six cubits wide.[b] [2]The width of the entrance was ten cubits, and the walls on either side measured five cubits. He measured the nave, forty cubits long and twenty cubits wide.

[3]Then he went inside and measured the posts at the other entrance, two cubits wide. The entrance was six cubits wide, with walls seven cubits long on each side. [4]Next he measured the length and width of the room beyond the nave, twenty cubits long and twenty cubits wide. He said to me, "This is the holy of holies."* [c]

40:28–37 The gates leading into the inner court of the Temple area correspond to the gates leading into the outer court, with the exception that their vestibules are on the outer rather than the inner side.

40:30 The reference to vestibules all around is uncertain, and the verse may have arisen as a partial repetition of v. 29.

40:46 Sons of Zadok: descendants of the priestly line of Zadok; cf. 2 Sm 15:24–29; 1 Kgs 1:32–34; 2:35.

40:48–41:15 The description of Ezekiel's visionary Temple closely follows the description of the Temple of Solomon (1 Kgs 6), along with some crucial differences.

40:49–41:4 Vestibule . . . nave . . . holy of holies: the three divisions of the Temple building in progressing order of sanctity. The last is called "the inner sanctuary" in 1 Kgs 6.

w: cf. Ez 44:4; 47:2. *x:* 2 Chr 4:6. *y:* cf. Ez 46:2. *z:* cf. Ez 41:13–14; 43:14–17. *a:* 1 Kgs 6:2. *b:* 1 Kgs 6:3–5. *c:* 1 Kgs 6:20; cf. Ex 26:33; Heb 9:3–8.

[5]Then he measured the wall of the temple, six cubits wide, and the width of the side chambers stretching all around the temple, four cubits each. [6]* There were thirty side chambers, chamber upon chamber in three stories; terraces on the outside wall of the temple enclosing the side chambers provided support, but there were no supports for the temple wall itself. [7]A broad passageway led up the side chambers, for the house was enclosed all the way up and all the way around. Thus the temple was widened by the ascent that went from the lowest story through the middle one to the highest story.[d] [8]I saw a raised platform all around the temple, the foundation for the side chambers; the width of this terrace was a full rod, six cubits. [9]The width of the outside wall enclosing the side chambers was five cubits. There was an open space between the side chambers of the temple [10]and the other chambers that measured twenty cubits around the temple on all sides. [11]The side chambers had entrances to the open space, one entrance on the north and the other on the south. The width of the wall surrounding the open space was five cubits. [12]The building* opposite the restricted area on the west side was seventy cubits long and ninety cubits wide, with walls five cubits thick all around it. [13]Thus he measured the temple, one hundred cubits long. The restricted area, its building and walls, measured a hundred cubits in length. [14]The temple facade, along with the restricted area to the east, was also one hundred cubits wide. [15]He then measured the building opposite the restricted area which was behind it, together with its terraces on both sides, one hundred cubits.

Interior of the Temple. The inner nave and the outer vestibule [16]were paneled; the windows had recesses and precious wood trim around all three sides except the sill. Paneling covered the walls from the floor up to the windows and even the window sections.[e] [17]Even above the doorway and in the inner part of the temple and outside as well, around all the walls inside and out, [18]were figures of cherubim and palm trees: a palm tree between each pair of cherubim. Each cherub had two faces:[f] [19]the face of a human being looked toward one palm tree and the face of a lion looked toward the other palm tree. Thus the figures covered all the walls around the temple. [20]From the floor to the lintel of the door, cherubim and palm trees decorated the walls. [21]The nave had a square door frame, and inside facing the holy place was something that looked like [22]a wooden altar,* three cubits high, two cubits long, and two cubits wide. It had corners and a wooden base and sides. He said to me, "This is the table that stands before the LORD."[g] [23]The nave had a double door,[h] and the holy place [24]also had a double door; each door had two sections that could move; two sections on one door, and two on the other.[i] [25]Cherubim and palm trees decorated the doors of the nave like the decoration on the walls. Outside a wooden lattice faced the vestibule. [26]There were recessed windows and palm trees on the side walls of the vestibule. The side chambers of the temple also had latticework.

CHAPTER 42

See RG 325–32

Other Structures. [1]Then he led me north to the outer court, bringing me to some chambers on the north side opposite the restricted area and the north building.[j] [2]They were a hundred cubits long on the north side and fifty cubits wide. [3]Built in rows at three different levels, they stood between the twenty cubits of the inner court and the pavement of the outer court. [4]In front of the chambers was a walkway ten cubits wide on the inside of a wall one cubit wide. The doorways faced north. [5]* The upper chambers

41:6 The description of the three stories of rooms surrounding the Temple building can be compared with Solomon's Temple in 1 Kgs 6:6; there a step-like or terraced retaining wall supported the Temple building so no beams or nails from these chambers would enter the Temple wall itself.

41:12 The building: the function of this structure behind the Temple is never specified.

41:22 A wooden altar: the altar of incense, standing in the nave at the entrance to the holy of holies.

42:5–6 The three rows of identical chambers, on different ground levels, necessarily had roofs on correspondingly different levels.

d: 1 Kgs 6:8. *e:* 1 Kgs 6:4, 15. *f:* 1 Kgs 6:18, 29; 7:36. *g:* Ex 25:23; Lv 24:5–9. *h:* 1 Kgs 6:32. *i:* 1 Kgs 6:34. *j:* Ex 27:9.

were shorter because they lost space to the lower and middle tiers of the building. [6]Because they were in three tiers, they did not have foundations like the court, but were set back from the lower and middle levels from the ground up. [7]The outside walls ran parallel to the chambers along the outer court, a length of fifty cubits. [8]The chambers facing the outer court were fifty cubits long; thus the wall along the nave was a hundred cubits. [9]At the base of these chambers, there was an entryway from the east so that one could enter from the outer court [10]where the wall of the court began.

To the south along the side of the restricted area and the building there were also chambers [11]with a walkway in front of them. They looked like the chambers on the north side in length and width, in their exits, their design, and their doorways. [12]At the base of the chambers on the south side there was an entry at the end of a walkway in front of the protective wall by which one could enter from the east. [13]He said to me, "The north and south chambers facing the restricted area are the chambers of the holy place where the priests who approach the LORD shall eat the most holy meals. Here they shall place the most holy offerings: the grain offerings, the purification offerings, and the reparation offerings; for the place is holy.* [k] [14]When the priests have entered, they must not go out again from the holy place into the outer court without leaving the garments in which they ministered because they are holy. They shall put on other garments before approaching the area for the people."[l]

Measuring the Outer Court. [15]When he finished measuring the interior of the temple area, he brought me out by way of the gate facing east and measured all around it. [16]He measured the east side, five hundred cubits by his measuring rod. Then he turned [17]and measured the north side: five hundred cubits by his measuring rod. He turned [18]and measured the south side, five hundred cubits by his measuring rod. [19]He turned and measured the west side, also five hundred cubits by his measuring rod. [20]Thus he measured it on the four sides. It was surrounded by a wall five hundred cubits long and five hundred cubits wide, to separate the sacred from the profane.

Restoration of the Temple

CHAPTER 43

See RG 325–32

The Glory of the Lord Returns. [1]Then he led me to the gate facing east,[m] [2]and there was the glory of the God of Israel coming from the east! His voice was like the roar of many waters, and the earth shone with his glory. [3]The vision I saw was like the vision I had seen when he came to destroy the city and like the vision I had seen by the river Chebar—I fell on my face. [4]The glory of the LORD entered the temple by way of the gate facing east.[n] [5]Then the spirit lifted me up and brought me to the inner court. And there the glory of the LORD filled the temple![o] [6]I heard someone speaking to me from the temple, but the man was standing beside me. [7]The voice said to me: Son of man, do you see the place for my throne, and the place for the soles of my feet? Here I will dwell among the Israelites forever. The house of Israel, neither they nor their kings, will never again defile my holy name, with their prostitutions and the corpses of their kings at their death.[p] [8]When they placed their threshold against my threshold* and their doorpost next to mine, with only a wall between me and them, they defiled my holy name by the abominations they committed, and I devoured them in my wrath.[q] [9]From now on, let them put their prostitution and the corpses of their kings far from me, and I will dwell in their midst forever.[r]

42:13 The function of these chambers is explained again in 46:19–20.

43:8 They placed their threshold against my threshold: in preexilic Jerusalem, the Temple and the palace belonged to the same complex of buildings; kings like Ahaz and Manasseh treated it as their private chapel for the religious practices Ezekiel condemns. In the new Israel the Temple is free, even spatially, from civil jurisdiction; cf. 45:7–8. This is an instance of Ezekiel's broader program to separate the sacred from the secular.

k: Lv 10:12–13, 17. *l:* Ex 29:9; Lv 8:7–9. *m:* 1 Chr 9:18. *n:* cf. Ez 10:19. *o:* cf. Ez 11:24. *p:* 1 Chr 28:2; Ps 132:7; Is 6:1; Jer 3:17. *q:* 1 Kgs 7:1–12. *r:* cf. Ez 37:26–28.

The Law of the Temple. 10 As for you, son of man, describe the temple to the house of Israel so they are ashamed for their sins. Let them measure its layout. 11 If they are ashamed for all they have done, tell them about the layout and design of the temple, its exits and entrances, with all its regulations and instructions; write it down for them to see, that they may carefully observe all its laws and statutes. 12 This is the law for the temple: the entire area on top of the mountain all around will be a most holy place. This is the law for the temple.

The Altar. 13 These were the dimensions of the altar* in cubits, a cubit being one cubit plus a handbreadth. The channel was one cubit deep by one cubit wide, and its rim had a lip one span wide all around it.[s] The height of the altar itself was as follows: 14 from the channel at floor level up to the lower ledge was two cubits, with the ledge one cubit wide; from the lower ledge to the upper ledge, four cubits, with the ledge one cubit wide. 15 The altar hearth was four cubits high, and extending up from the top of the hearth were four horns. 16 The hearth was twelve cubits long and twelve cubits wide, a square with four equal sides. 17 The upper ledge was fourteen cubits long and fourteen cubits wide on all four sides. The rim around it was half a cubit, with a channel one cubit all around. The steps faced east.[t]

18 Then he said to me: Son of man, thus says the Lord GOD: These are the statutes for the altar when it is set up for sacrificing burnt offerings and splashing blood on it.[u] 19 A young bull must be brought as a purification offering to the priests, the Levites descended from Zadok, who come near to serve me—oracle of the Lord GOD.[v] 20 You shall take some of its blood and smear it on the four horns of the altar, and on the four corners of the ledge, and all around its rim. Thus you shall purify and purge it.[w] 21 Then take the bull as purification offering and burn it in the appointed place outside the sanctuary.[x] 22 On the second day present an unblemished male goat as a purification offering, to purify the altar as you did with the bull. 23 When you have completed the purification,[y] you must bring an unblemished young bull and an unblemished ram from the flock 24 and present them before the LORD. The priests shall throw salt on them and sacrifice them as burnt offerings to the LORD. 25 Daily for seven days you shall give a male goat as a purification offering; and a young bull and a ram from the flock, all unblemished,[z] shall be offered 26 for seven days. Thus they shall purge the altar, in order to cleanse and dedicate it. 27 And when these days are over, from the eighth day on, the priests shall sacrifice your burnt offerings and communion offerings on the altar. Then I will be pleased with you—oracle of the Lord GOD.

CHAPTER 44

See RG 325–32

The Closed Gate. 1 Then he brought me back to the outer gate of the sanctuary facing east, but it was closed. 2 The LORD said to me: This gate must remain closed; it must not be opened, and no one should come through it. Because the LORD, the God of Israel, came through it, it must remain closed. 3 Only the prince may sit in it to eat a meal in the presence of the LORD; he must enter through the vestibule of the gate and leave the same way.* [a]

The New Law

Admission to the Temple. 4 Then he brought me by way of the north gate to the facade of the temple. I looked—and the glory of the LORD filled the LORD's house! I fell on my face.[b] 5 The LORD said to me: Son of man, pay close attention, look carefully, and listen intently to everything I tell you about all the statutes and laws of the LORD's house. Pay

43:13–17 The altar: like altars from Assyria and other parts of the ancient Near East, this altar has three parts: a base, a pedestal, and an upper block with a channel cut into the surface on all sides. The rim around the upper block (v. 17) stopped blood and other sacrificial material from falling to the ground.

44:3 Ezekiel imagines a scene like this: The prince stands at the eastern gate of the inner court while his sacrifice is being offered (46:2); he then goes to the vestibule of the outer court to eat the sacrificial meal. The closed outer gate on the eastern side signifies that the Lord has entered the Temple permanently, not to depart again.

s: cf. Ex 20:24. *t:* Ex 20:26. *u:* Ex 29:16; Lv 4:6; 5:9. *v:* Lv 4:3. *w:* Lv 4:7. *x:* Ex 29:14; Lv 4:12; 8:17; cf. Heb 13:11–13. *y:* Ex 29:1. *z:* Ex 29:37; Lv 8:33. *a:* Ex 24:9–11; 2 Chr 26:16–20. *b:* Is 6:4; Rev 15:8.

close attention to the entrance into the temple and all the exits of the sanctuary. 6 Say to that rebellious house, the house of Israel: Thus says the Lord GOD: Enough of all your abominations, house of Israel! 7 You have admitted foreigners, uncircumcised in heart and flesh, into my sanctuary to profane it when you offered me food, the fat and blood.* Thus you have broken my covenant by all your abominations.[c] 8 Instead of caring for the service of my sanctuary, you appointed these foreigners to care for the service of my sanctuary. 9 Thus says the Lord GOD: No foreigners, uncircumcised in heart and flesh, shall ever enter my sanctuary: not even any of the foreigners who live among the Israelites.[d]

Levites. 10 As for the Levites who went far away from me when Israel strayed from me after their idols, they will bear the consequences of their sin. 11 They will serve in my sanctuary only as gatekeepers and temple servants; they will slaughter burnt offerings and sacrifices for the people. They will stand before the people to serve them.[e] 12 Because they used to serve them before their idols, thus becoming a stumbling block to the house of Israel, therefore I have sworn an oath against them, says the Lord GOD, and they will bear the consequences of their sin. 13 They shall no longer come near to serve as my priests, nor shall they touch any of my sacred things or my most sacred offerings, for they must bear their shame, the abominations they committed. 14 Instead I will make them responsible for the service of the temple and all its work, for everything that must be done in it.[f]

Priests. 15 As for the levitical priests, sons of Zadok, who took charge of my sanctuary when the Israelites strayed from me, they may approach me to serve me and stand before me to offer the fat and the blood—oracle of the Lord GOD.[g] 16 They may enter my sanctuary; they may approach my table to serve me and carry out my service.[h] 17 Whenever they enter the gates of the inner court, they shall wear linen garments; they shall not put on anything woolen when they serve at the gates of the inner court or within the temple. 18[i] They shall have linen turbans on their heads and linen undergarments on their loins; they shall not gird themselves with anything that causes sweat. 19[j] And when they go out to the people in the outer court, they shall take off the garments in which they served and leave them in the rooms of the sanctuary, and put on other garments so they do not transmit holiness to the people* by their garments.

20[k] They shall not shave their heads nor let their hair hang loose, but they shall keep their hair carefully trimmed. 21 No priest shall drink wine before he enters the inner court. 22[l] They shall not take as wives either widows or divorced women, but only unmarried women from the line of Israel; however, they may take as wives widows who are widows of priests. 23[m] They shall teach my people to distinguish between sacred and profane and make known to them the difference between clean and unclean. 24[n] In legal cases they shall stand as judges, judging according to my ordinances. They shall observe all my laws and statutes regarding all my appointed feasts, and they shall keep my sabbaths holy.

25[o] They shall not make themselves unclean by going near a dead body; only for their father, mother, son, daughter, brother, or unmarried sister may they make themselves unclean. 26 After he is again clean, he must wait an additional seven days; 27 on the day he enters the inner court to serve in the sanctuary, he shall present a purification offering for himself—oracle of the Lord GOD. 28[p] I will be their heritage: I am their heritage! You shall not give them any property in Israel, for I am

44:7–14 According to Ezekiel, the Levites' priestly role is reduced to the performance of menial tasks as punishment for their misdeeds (cf. vv. 10–14). This demotion was enforced during the restoration of Temple worship under Ezra and Nehemiah; this may explain the small number of Levites willing to return to Jerusalem after the exile.

44:19 Transmit holiness to the people: holiness was considered to have a physical quality that could be communicated from person to person. It is a danger to those who have not prepared themselves to be in God's presence. The priests remove their ceremonial garments out of concern for the people.

c: Lv 26:41. *d:* Jl 4:17; Neh 13:8. *e:* Nm 3:5–37; 1 Chr 26:12–19. *f:* 1 Chr 23:28–32. *g:* 1 Chr 6:50–53. *h:* Lv 3:16–17. *i:* Ex 28:39, 42. *j:* Ex 39:27–29; Lv 6:10–11. *k:* Lv 21:5. *l:* Lv 21:7. *m:* Hg 2:10–13. *n:* Dt 17:8–9. *o:* Lv 21:1–4. *p:* Nm 18:23–24; Dt 18:1–2.

their property! 29[q] They shall eat grain offerings, purification offerings, and reparation offerings; anything under the ban* in Israel belongs to them; 30[r] all the choicest first fruits of
every kind and all the best of your offerings of
every kind shall belong to the priests; the best
of your dough you shall also give to the
priests to bring a blessing upon your house.
31[s] The priests shall not eat anything, whether
bird or animal, that died naturally or was
killed by wild beasts.

CHAPTER 45

See RG 325–32

The Holy Portion. 1 When you apportion the land heritage by heritage, you shall
set apart a holy portion for the LORD, holier
than the rest of the land—twenty-five thousand cubits long and twenty thousand cubits
wide; the entire area shall be holy. 2 Of this
land a square plot, five hundred by five hundred cubits, shall be assigned to the sanctuary, with fifty cubits of free space around it.
3 From this tract also measure off a length of
twenty-five thousand cubits and a width of
ten thousand cubits; on it the sanctuary, the
holy of holies, shall stand. 4 This shall be the
sacred part of the land belonging to the
priests, the ministers of the sanctuary, who
draw near to minister to the LORD; it shall be
a place for their homes and an area set apart
for the sanctuary. 5 There shall also be a strip
twenty-five thousand cubits long and ten
thousand wide for the Levites, the ministers
of the temple, so they have cities to live in.
6 You shall assign a strip five thousand cubits
wide and twenty-five thousand long as the
property of the city parallel to the sacred
tract; this shall belong to the whole house of
Israel. 7 A section shall belong to the prince,
bordering both sides of the sacred tract and
city combined, extending westward on the
west side and eastward on the east side, corresponding in length to one of the tribal portions from the west boundary to the east
boundary 8 of the land. This shall be his
property in Israel so that my princes will no
longer oppress my people, but will leave the
land to the house of Israel according to its
tribes. 9 Thus says the Lord GOD: Enough,
you princes of Israel! Put away violence and
oppression, and do what is just and right!
Stop evicting my people!—oracle of the
Lord GOD.

*Weights and Measures.** 10[t] You shall have
honest scales, an honest ephah, and an honest bath. 11 The ephah and the bath shall be
the same size: the bath equal to one tenth of
a homer, and the ephah equal to one tenth of
a homer; their capacity is based on the homer. 12 The shekel shall be twenty gerahs.
Twenty shekels plus twenty-five shekels
plus fifteen shekels make up a mina* for you.

Offerings. 13 This is the offering you must
make: one sixth of an ephah from each homer of wheat and one sixth of an ephah from
each homer of barley. 14 This is the regulation for oil: for every bath of oil, one tenth of
a bath, computed by the kor,* made up of ten
baths, that is, a homer, for ten baths make a
homer. 15 Also, one sheep from the flock for
every two hundred from the pasture land of
Israel, for the grain offering, the burnt offering, and communion offerings, to make
atonement on their behalf—oracle of the
Lord GOD.[u] 16 All the people of the land shall
be responsible for these offerings to the
prince in Israel. 17 It shall be the duty of the
prince to provide burnt offerings, grain offerings, and libations on feast days, new
moons, and sabbaths, on all the festivals of
the house of Israel. He shall provide the purification offering, grain offering, burnt offering, and communion offerings, to make
atonement on behalf of the house of Israel.[v]

The Passover. 18 Thus says the Lord GOD:
On the first day of the first month you shall
take an unblemished young bull to purify the
sanctuary.[w] 19 The priest shall take some of

44:29 Under the ban: dedicated to the Lord.

45:10–12 Besides the land monopoly fostered by royal greed and collusion with the wealthy (Mi 2:2; Is 3:12–15; 5:8–10), one grave social evil of preexilic Israel was dishonesty in business; cf. Hos 12:8; Am 8:5. **Ephah, bath**: see note on Is 5:10.

45:12 Mina: before the exile, a mina was worth fifty shekels; later, in imitation of Babylonian practice, its value increased to sixty shekels. A shekel weighed slightly less than half an ounce. A shekel's monetary value depended on whether it was gold or silver.

45:14 Kor: a liquid and a dry measure, equal to a homer.

q: Lv 6:16; 27:28. *r:* Nm 15:18–21; 18:12–13. *s:* Lv 11:39. *t:* Lv 19:35–36; Dt 25:13–16; Mi 6:10–12. *u:* Lv 1:4; 6:23. *v:* cf. Ez 46:4–12. *w:* Lv 16:33.

the blood from the purification offering and smear it on the doorposts of the house, on the four corners of the ledge of the altar, and on the doorposts of the gates of the inner courtyard.[x] 20 You shall repeat this on the seventh day of the month for those who have sinned inadvertently or out of ignorance; thus you shall purge the temple.[y] 21 On the fourteenth day of the first month you shall observe the feast of Passover; for seven days unleavened bread must be eaten. 22 On that day the prince shall sacrifice, on his own behalf and on behalf of all the people of the land, a bull as a purification offering. 23 On each of the seven days of the feast he shall sacrifice, as a burnt offering to the LORD, seven bulls and seven rams without blemish, and as a purification offering he shall sacrifice one male goat each day.[z] 24 As a grain offering he shall offer one ephah for each bull and one ephah for each ram and one hin* of oil for each ephah.[a]

The Feast of Booths. 25 In the seventh month, on the fifteenth day of the seventh month, on the feast day and for the next seven days, he shall make the same offerings: the same purification offerings, burnt offerings, grain offerings, and offerings of oil.[b]

CHAPTER 46

See RG 325-32

Sabbaths. 1 Thus says the Lord GOD: The gate of the inner court facing east shall remain closed throughout the six working days, but on the sabbath and on the day of the new moon it shall be open. 2* Then the prince shall enter from outside by way of the vestibule of the gate and remain standing at the doorpost of the gateway while the priests sacrifice his burnt offerings and communion offerings; then he shall bow down in worship at the opening of the gate and leave. But the gate shall not be closed until evening. 3 The people of the land also shall bow down in worship before the LORD at the opening of this gate on the sabbaths and new moons. 4 The burnt offerings which the prince sacrifices to the LORD on the sabbath shall consist of six unblemished lambs and an unblemished ram, 5 together with a grain offering of one ephah for the ram and whatever he pleases for the lambs, and a hin of oil for each ephah. 6[c] On the day of the new moon, he shall provide an unblemished young bull, six lambs, and a ram without blemish, 7 with a grain offering of one ephah for the bull and an ephah for the ram, and for the lambs whatever he can, and for each ephah a hin of oil.[d]

Ritual Laws. 8 When the prince enters, he shall always enter and depart by the vestibule of the gate. 9 When the people of the land come before the LORD to bow down on the festivals, if they enter by the north gate they shall leave by the south gate, and if they enter by the south gate they shall leave by the north gate. They shall not go back by the gate through which they entered; everyone shall leave by the opposite gate. 10 When they come in, the prince shall be with them; he shall also leave with them. 11 On feasts and festivals, the grain offering shall be an ephah for a bull, an ephah for a ram, but for the lambs whatever they please, and a hin of oil with each ephah. 12 When the prince makes a freewill offering to the LORD, whether a burnt offering or communion offering, the gate facing east shall be opened for him, and he shall bring his burnt offering or peace offering as he does on the sabbath. Then he shall leave, and the gate shall be closed after his departure. 13[e] Every day you shall bring as a burnt offering to the LORD an unblemished year-old lamb; you shall offer it every morning, 14 and with it every morning a grain offering of one sixth of an ephah, with a third of a hin of oil to moisten the fine flour. This grain offering for the LORD is a perpetual statute. 15[f] The lamb, the grain offering, and the oil you must bring every morning as a perpetual burnt offering.

45:24 Hin: one sixth of the liquid measure known as a bath.

46:2–12 The prophet describes the inner eastern gateway opening on the inner court of the priests in front of the Temple itself where the altar of sacrifice stands. The people may watch the priests making offerings on sabbaths and feast days only by looking through the open gate; the prince, however, may stand inside the gate, in the vestibule on the edge of the inner court, to observe the offerings. Only priests could stand in the court itself.

x: Lv 16:18–19. *y:* Lv 4:27. *z:* Nm 22:40; 28:16–25. *a:* Nm 28:12–13. *b:* Ex 23:16; 34:22; Lv 23:34–43; Nm 29:12–38. *c:* Lv 22:20. *d:* cf. Nm 28:12. *e:* Ex 29:38; Nm 28:3–8. *f:* Ex 29:42; Nm 28:5–6.

The Prince and the Land. 16 Thus says the Lord GOD: If the prince makes a gift of part of his heritage to any of his sons, it belongs to his sons; that property is their heritage. 17 But if he makes a gift of part of his heritage to one of his servants, it belongs to him until the year of release;* then it reverts to the prince. Only the heritage given to his sons belongs to him.[g] 18 The prince shall not seize any part of the heritage of the people by forcing them off their property. From his own property he shall provide heritage for his sons, so that none of my people will be driven off their property.

The Temple Kitchens. 19 Then he brought me through the entrance at the side of the gateway to the chambers reserved for the priests, which faced north. There I saw a place at the far west end, 20 about which he said to me, "This is the place where the priests cook the reparation offerings and the purification offerings and bake the grain offerings, so they do not have to bring them into the outer court and so transmit holiness to the people."* [h] 21 Then he led me into the outer court and had me cross to the four corners of the court, and there, in each corner, was another court! 22 In all four corners of the courtyard there were courts set off, each forty cubits long by thirty cubits wide, all four of them the same size. 23 A stone wall surrounded them on four sides, and ovens were built along the bottom of the walls all the way around. 24 He said to me, "These are the kitchens where the temple ministers cook the sacrifices of the people."

CHAPTER 47

See RG 325–32

The Wonderful Stream.* 1 Then he brought me back to the entrance of the temple, and there! I saw water flowing out from under the threshold of the temple toward the east, for the front of the temple faced east. The water flowed out toward the right side of the temple to the south of the altar.[i] 2 He brought me by way of the north gate and around the outside to the outer gate facing east; there I saw water trickling from the southern side. 3 When he continued eastward with a measuring cord in his hand, he measured off a thousand cubits and had me wade through the water; it was ankle-deep. 4 He measured off another thousand cubits and once more had me wade through the water; it was up to the knees. He measured another thousand cubits and had me wade through the water; it was up to my waist. 5 Once more he measured off a thousand cubits. Now it was a river I could not wade across. The water had risen so high, I would have to swim—a river that was impassable. 6 Then he asked me, "Do you see this, son of man?" He brought me to the bank of the river and had me sit down. 7 As I was returning, I saw along the bank of the river a great many trees on each side.[j] 8 He said to me, "This water flows out into the eastern district, runs down into the Arabah and empties into the polluted waters of the sea* to freshen them.[k] 9 Wherever it flows, the river teems with every kind of living creature; fish will abound. Where these waters flow they refresh; everything lives where the river goes. 10 Fishermen will stand along its shore from En-gedi to En-eglaim;* it will become a place for drying nets, and it will abound with as many kinds of fish as the Great Sea.[l] 11 Its marshes and swamps shall not be made fresh, but will be left for salt. 12 Along each bank of the river every kind of fruit tree will grow; their leaves will not wither, nor will their fruit fail. Every month they will bear fresh fruit because the waters of the river flow out from the sanctuary. Their fruit is used for food, and their leaves for healing."[m]

46:17 The year of release: the jubilee year; cf. Lv 25:23–55.

46:20 Cf. note on 44:19.

47:1–12 The life and refreshment produced wherever the Temple stream flows evoke the order and abundance of paradise (cf. Gn 1:20–22; 2:10–14; Ps 46:5) and represent the coming transformation Ezekiel envisions for the exiles and their land. Water signifies great blessings and evidence of the Lord's presence (cf. Jl 2:14). This vision of the Temple stream which transforms places of death into places of life is similar in purpose to the oracle of dry bones in 37:1–14: it offers the exiles hope for the future.

47:8 The sea: the Dead Sea, in which nothing can live.

47:10 From En-gedi to En-eglaim: En-gedi is about halfway down the western shore of the Dead Sea; En-eglaim may have been at its northern end.

g: Lv 25:8–17. *h:* Lv 6:20. *i:* cf. Gn 2:10; Ps 46:4; Rev 22:1. *j:* Rev 22:2. *k:* Zec 14:8. *l:* Ps 104:25. *m:* Ps 1:3; Jer 17:8.

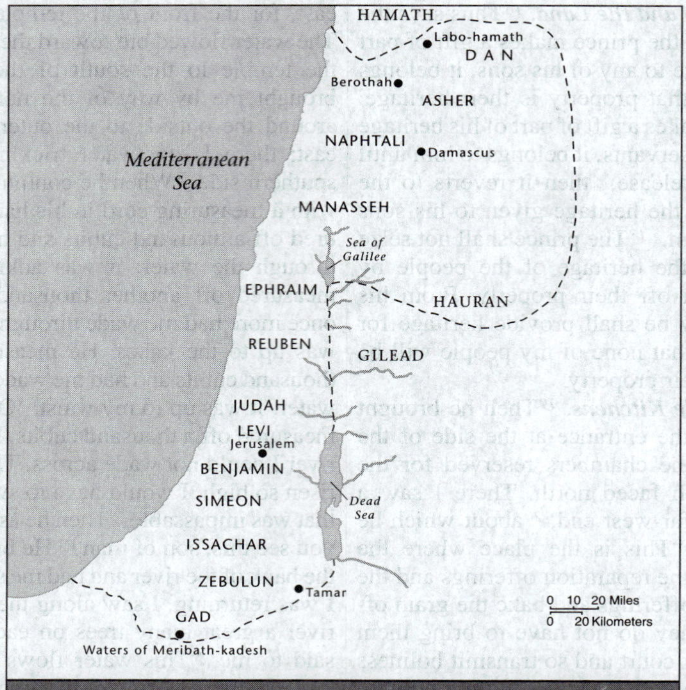

Tribal Territories in the Restored Israel

The New Israel

Boundaries of the Land.* [13]Thus says the Lord GOD: These are the boundaries of the land which you shall apportion among the twelve tribes of Israel, with Joseph having two portions.[n] [14]You shall apportion it equally because I swore to give it to your ancestors as a heritage; this land, then, is your heritage.[o] [15p] These are the borders of the land: on the northern side, from the Great Sea in the direction of Hethlon, Lebo-hamath to Zedad, [16]Berothah, and Sibraim, along the frontiers of Damascus and Hamath, to Hazar-enon, on the border of Hauran.[q] [17]Thus the border extends from the sea to Hazar-enon, north of the border of Damascus, the frontier of Hamath to the north. This is the northern boundary. [18]The eastern border shall be between Damascus and Hauran, while the Jordan will form the border between Gilead and the land of Israel down to the eastern sea as far as Tamar. This is the eastern boundary. [19]The southern border shall go southward from Tamar to the waters of Meribath-kadesh, on to the Wadi of Egypt, and into the Great Sea. This is the southern boundary.[r] [20]The western border shall have the Great Sea as a boundary as far as a point opposite Lebo-hamath. This is the western boundary.

The Northern Portions. [21]You shall divide this land according to the tribes of Israel. [22s] You shall allot it as heritage for yourselves and for the resident aliens in your midst who have fathered children among you. You shall treat them like native Israelites; along with you they shall receive a heritage among the tribes of Israel. [23]In whatever tribe the resi-

47:13–20 These boundaries for a restored Israel correspond to the boundaries of the Davidic kingdom at its fullest extent; they are the "ideal boundaries" of the promised land; cf. Nm 34:3–12.

n: Gn 48:16; Nm 34:2–12. *o:* Gn 12:7; 15:9–21. *p:* Nm 34:1–12. *q:* 2 Sm 8:8. *r:* Nm 34:4; Dt 32:51. *s:* Lv 24:22; Nm 15:29; 26:55–56; Is 56:6–7.

dent alien lives, there you shall assign his heritage—oracle of the Lord GOD.

CHAPTER 48

See RG 325–32

[1]These are the names* of the tribes:

At the northern end, along the side of the way to Hethlon, Lebo-hamath, and Hazar-enon, the border of Damascus, and northward up to the frontier with Hamath, from the eastern border to the western: Dan, one portion. [2]Along the territory of Dan from the eastern border to the western border: Asher, one portion.[t] [3]Along the territory of Asher from the eastern border to the western border: Naphtali, one portion.[u] [4]Along the territory of Naphtali from the eastern border to the western border: Manasseh, one portion.[v] [5]Along the territory of Manasseh from the eastern border to the western border: Ephraim, one portion.[w] [6]Along the territory of Ephraim from the eastern border to the western border: Reuben, one portion.[x] [7]Along the territory of Reuben from the eastern border to the western border: Judah, one portion.[y]

The Sacred Tract. [8]Along the territory of Judah from the eastern border to the western border is the tract you shall set apart, twenty-five thousand cubits wide and as long as one of the portions from the eastern border to the western border. The sanctuary shall stand in the center of the tract. [9]The tract you set apart for the LORD shall be twenty-five thousand cubits long by twenty thousand wide. [10]The sacred tract will be given to the following: the priests shall have twenty-five thousand cubits on the north, ten thousand on the west, ten thousand on the east, and twenty-five thousand on the south. The sanctuary of the LORD shall be in its center. [11]The consecrated priests, the Zadokites, who fulfilled my service and did not stray with the Israelites as the Levites did, [12]shall have their own tract set apart, next to the territory of the Levites, separate from the most holy tract. [13]The Levites shall have territory corresponding to that of the priests, twenty-five thousand cubits long and ten thousand cubits wide. The whole tract shall be twenty-five thousand cubits long and twenty thousand wide. [14]They may not sell or exchange or transfer any of it, the best part of the land, for it is sacred to the LORD. [15]The remaining section, five thousand cubits long and twenty-five thousand cubits wide, is profane land, assigned to the city for dwellings and pasture. The city is at its center. [16]These are the dimensions of the city: the north side, forty-five hundred cubits; the south side, forty-five hundred cubits; the east side, forty-five hundred cubits; and the west side, forty-five hundred cubits.[z] [17]The pasture land for the city extends north two hundred fifty cubits, south two hundred fifty cubits, east two hundred fifty cubits, and west two hundred fifty cubits. [18]The remaining section runs eastward along the sacred tract for ten thousand cubits and westward ten thousand cubits. Its produce shall provide food for the workers of the city. [19]The workers of the city, from all the tribes of Israel, shall cultivate it. [20]The entire sacred tract measures twenty-five thousand by twenty-five thousand cubits; as a square you shall set apart the sacred tract together with the city property.

[21]The remaining land on both sides of the sacred tract and the property of the city shall belong to the prince, extending eastward twenty-five thousand cubits up to the eastern boundary, and westward twenty-five thousand cubits to the western boundary. This portion belongs to the prince and corresponds to the tribal portions. The sacred tract and the sanctuary of the temple shall be in the middle. [22]Except for the Levites' property and the city's property, which are in the middle of the prince's property, the territory between the portion of Judah and the portion of Benjamin shall belong to the prince.

The Southern Portions. [23]These are the remaining tribes:

From the eastern border to the western border: Benjamin, one portion.[a] [24]Along the

48:1–29 This distribution of the land among the tribes does not correspond to the geographical realities of Palestine. It is another idealizing element in Ezekiel's representation of a restored and transformed Israel.

---

t: Jos 19:24–31. *u:* Jos 19:32–39. *v:* Jos 17:1–11. *w:* Jos 16:5–9. *x:* Jos 13:15–21. *y:* Jos 15:1–63. *z:* Rev 21:16. *a:* Jos 18:11–28.

territory of Benjamin from the eastern border to the western border: Simeon, one portion.[b] [25]Along the territory of Simeon from the eastern border to the western border: Issachar, one portion.[c] [26]Along the territory of Issachar from the eastern border to the western border: Zebulun, one portion.[d] [27]Along the territory of Zebulun from the eastern border to the western border: Gad, one portion.[e] [28]Along the territory of Gad shall be the southern border. This boundary shall extend from Tamar to the waters of Meribath-kadesh, and along the Wadi of Egypt to the Great Sea. [29]This is the land you shall apportion as a heritage among the tribes of Israel, and these are their portions—oracle of the Lord GOD.

The Gates of the City. [30]These are the exits from the city: On the north side, measuring forty-five hundred cubits— [31]the gates are named after the tribes of Israel—on the north, three gates: the gate of Reuben, one; the gate of Judah, one; and the gate of Levi, one. [32]On the east side, measuring forty-five hundred cubits, three gates: the gate of Joseph, one; the gate of Benjamin, one; and the gate of Dan, one. [33]On the south side, measuring forty-five hundred cubits, three gates: the gate of Simeon, one; the gate of Issachar, one; and the gate of Zebulun, one. [34]On the west side, measuring forty-five hundred cubits, three gates: the gate of Gad, one; the gate of Asher, one; and the gate of Naphtali, one.[f] [35]The circuit of the city shall be eighteen thousand cubits. From now on the name of the city is "The LORD is there."[g]

b: Jos 19:1–9. *c:* Jos 19:17–23. *d:* Jos 19:10–16. *e:* Jos 13:24–28. *f:* Rev 21:12–13. *g:* Is 2:6; Rev 3:12; 21:3.

See RG 336–43

The Book of Daniel

This book takes its name not from the author, who is actually unknown, but from its hero, who was allegedly among the first Jews deported to Babylon, where he lived at least until 538 B.C. Strictly speaking, the book does not belong to the prophetic writings but rather to a distinctive type of literature known as "apocalyptic," of which it is an early specimen. Apocalyptic writing first appears about 200 B.C. and flourished among Jews and Christians down to the Middle Ages, especially in times of persecution. Apocalyptic literature has its roots in the older teaching of the prophets, who often pointed ahead to the day of the Lord, the consummation of history. For both prophet and apocalyptist there was one Lord of history, who would ultimately vindicate the chosen people. Apocalyptic also has roots in the wisdom tradition. Daniel has the gift of discernment from God. Greek wisdom (represented by the Babylonian "magicians and enchanters") is ridiculed (see especially chaps. 2 and 5), whereas God reveals hidden things to faithful servants.

This work was composed during the bitter persecution carried on by Antiochus IV Epiphanes (167–164 B.C.) and was written to strengthen and comfort the Jewish people in their ordeal. The persecution was occasioned by Antiochus's efforts to unify his kingdom, in face of the rising power of Rome, by continuing the hellenization begun by Alexander the Great; Antiochus tried to force Jews to adopt Greek ways, including religious practices. Severe penalties, including death, were exacted against those who refused (cf., e.g., 1 Mc 1:41–63).

The book contains traditional stories (chaps. 1–6), which tell of the trials and triumphs of the wise Daniel and his three companions. The moral is that people of faith can resist temptation and conquer adversity. The stories bristle with historical problems and have the character of historical novels rather than factual records. What is more important than the question of historicity, and closer to the intention of the author, is the fact that persecuted Jews of the second century B.C. would quickly see the application of these stories to their own plight.

There follows in chaps. 7–12 a series of visions promising deliverance and glory to the Jews in the days to come. The great nations of the ancient world have risen in vain against the Lord; his kingdom shall overthrow existing powers and last forever; in the end the dead will be raised for reward or punishment. Under this apocalyptic imagery some of the best elements of prophetic and sapiential teaching are synthesized: the insistence on right conduct, the divine control over events, the certainty that the kingdom of God will ultimately triumph and humanity attain the goal intended for it at the beginning of creation. The arrival of the kingdom is a central theme of the gospels, where Jesus is identified as the human figure (or "Son of Man") who appears in Daniel's vision in chap. 7. The message in both parts of the first twelve chapters (i.e., chaps. 1–6 and chaps. 7–12) is that history unrolls under the watchful eye of God, who does not abandon those who trust in him and will finally deliver and re-establish them. Moreover, it can be pointed out that chaps. 2 and 7 present the same teaching in different symbolism; 2:31 even describes the king's dream as a "vision."

The added episodes of Susanna, Bel, and the Dragon, found only in the Greek version, are edifying short stories with a didactic purpose (chaps. 13–14). The Greek version also adds a long prayer, numbered in the NAB and the Greek, 3:24–90, between 3:23–24 in the Hebrew text.

These three sections constitute the divisions of the Book of Daniel:

I. Daniel and the Kings of Babylon (1:1–6:29)
II. Daniel's Visions (7:1–12:13)
III. Appendix: Susanna, Bel, and the Dragon (13:1–14:42)

I. Daniel and the Kings of Babylon

CHAPTER 1

See RG 337

The Food Test. [1]In the third year of the reign of Jehoiakim,* king of Judah, King Nebuchadnezzar of Babylon came and laid siege to Jerusalem.[a] [2b]The Lord handed over to him Jehoiakim, king of Judah, and some of the vessels of the temple of God, which he carried off to the land of Shinar* and placed in the temple treasury of his god.

[3]The king told Ashpenaz,* his chief chamberlain, to bring in some of the Israelites, some of the royal line and of the nobility. [4]They should be young men without any defect, handsome, proficient in wisdom, well informed, and insightful, such as could take their place in the king's palace; he was to teach them the language and literature of the Chaldeans. [5]The king allotted them a daily portion of food and wine from the royal table. After three years' training they were to enter the king's service. [6]Among these were Judeans, Daniel, Hananiah, Mishael, and Azariah. [7]* The chief chamberlain changed their names: Daniel to Belteshazzar, Hananiah to Shadrach, Mishael to Meshach, and Azariah to Abednego.

[8]But Daniel was resolved not to defile himself with the king's food or wine; so he begged the chief chamberlain to spare him this defilement.* [9]Though God had given Daniel the favor and sympathy of the chief chamberlain, [10]he said to Daniel, "I am afraid of my lord the king, who allotted your food and drink. If he sees that you look thinner in comparison to the other young men of your age, you will endanger my life with the king." [11]Then Daniel said to the guardian whom the chief chamberlain had put in charge of Daniel, Hananiah, Mishael, and Azariah, [12]"Please test your servants for ten days. Let us be given vegetables to eat and water to drink. [13]Then see how we look in comparison with the other young men who eat from the royal table, and treat your servants according to what you see." [14]He agreed to this request, and tested them for ten days; [15]after ten days they looked healthier and better fed than any

1:1 According to 2 Kgs 24, the siege of Jerusalem took place after the death of Jehoiakim, but 2 Chr 36:5–8 says that Jehoiakim was taken to Babylon.

1:2 Shinar: ancient name for Babylonia, a deliberate archaism in this text; cf. Gn 10:10; 11:2.

1:3 The proper name Ashpenaz is sometimes taken as a title, major-domo.

1:7 Other prominent Jews with Babylonian names include Sheshbazzar and Zerubabbel, who were leaders of the postexilic community.

1:8 This defilement: the bread, meat, and wine of the Gentiles were unclean (Hos 9:3; Tb 1:12; Jdt 10:5; 12:1–2) because they might have been offered to idols; and the meat may not have been drained of blood, as Jewish dietary law requires. This test relates to the attempt of Antiochus to force Jews to eat forbidden foods in contempt of their religion (1 Mc 1:62–63; 2 Mc 6:18; 7:1).

a: 2 Kgs 24:1; 2 Chr 36:6; Jer 25:1. *b:* Dn 5:2; 2 Chr 36:7; Gn 10:10.

of the young men who ate from the royal table. [16]So the steward continued to take away the food and wine they were to receive, and gave them vegetables.

[17]To these four young men God gave knowledge and proficiency in all literature and wisdom, and to Daniel the understanding of all visions and dreams. [18]At the end of the time the king had specified for their preparation, the chief chamberlain brought them before Nebuchadnezzar. [19]When the king had spoken with all of them, none was found equal to Daniel, Hananiah, Mishael, and Azariah; and so they entered the king's service. [20]In any question of wisdom or understanding which the king put to them, he found them ten times better than any of the magicians and enchanters in his kingdom. [21c] Daniel remained there until the first year of King Cyrus.*

See RG 337

CHAPTER 2

Nebuchadnezzar's Dream.* [1]In the second year of his reign, King Nebuchadnezzar had a dream which left his spirit no rest and robbed him of his sleep. [2]So he ordered that the magicians, enchanters, sorcerers, and Chaldeans* be summoned to interpret the dream for him. When they came and presented themselves to the king, [3]he said to them, "I had a dream which will allow my spirit no rest until I know what it means." [4]The Chaldeans answered the king in Aramaic:* "O king, live forever! Tell your servants the dream and we will give its meaning." [5]The king answered the Chaldeans, "This is what I have decided: unless you tell me the dream and its meaning, you shall be cut to pieces and your houses made into a refuse heap. [6]But if you tell me the dream and its meaning, you shall receive from me gifts and presents and great honors. Therefore tell me the dream and its meaning."

[7]Again they answered, "Let the king tell his servants the dream and we will give its meaning." [8]But the king replied: "I know for certain that you are bargaining for time, since you know what I have decided. [9]If you do not tell me the dream, there can be but one decree for you. You have conspired to present a false and deceitful interpretation to me until the crisis is past. Tell me the dream, therefore, that I may be sure that you can also give its correct interpretation."

[10]The Chaldeans answered the king: "There is not a man on earth who can do what you ask, O king; never has any king, however great and mighty, asked such a thing of any magician, enchanter, or Chaldean. [11]What you demand, O king, is too difficult; there is no one who can tell it to the king except the gods, who do not dwell among people of flesh." [12]At this the king became violently angry and ordered all the wise men* of Babylon to be put to death. [13]When the decree was issued that the wise men should be slain, Daniel and his companions were also sought out.

[14]Then Daniel prudently took counsel with Arioch, the chief of the king's guard, who had set out to kill the wise men of Babylon. [15]He asked Arioch, the officer of the king, "What is the reason for this harsh order from the king?" When Arioch told him, [16]Daniel went and asked for time from the king, that he might give him the interpretation.

[17]Daniel went home and informed his companions Hananiah, Mishael, and Azariah, [18]that they might implore the mercy of the God of heaven in regard to this mystery, so that Daniel and his companions might not perish with the rest of the wise men of Babylon. [19]During the night the mystery was re-

1:21 The first year of King Cyrus: the year of this Persian king's conquest of Babylon, 539/538 B.C.

2:1–49 The chronology of v. 1 is in conflict with that of 1:5, 18, and in 2:25 Daniel appears to be introduced to the king for the first time. It seems that the story of this chapter was originally entirely independent of chap. 1 and later retouched slightly to fit its present setting. The Septuagint (Papyrus 967) reads the twelfth year instead of the second.

2:2 Chaldeans: because the Babylonians gave serious study to the stars and planets, "Chaldeans" were identified with astrologers throughout the Hellenistic world.

2:4 Aramaic: a gloss to indicate that at this point the text switches from Hebrew to Aramaic, which continues through the end of chap. 7; at 8:1, the text switches back to Hebrew.

2:12 Wise men: the satire, although directed against the Babylonian diviners in the text, refers to the Hellenistic Greeks, who made special claims to wisdom; the assertion here is that true wisdom comes from God and resides with the Jews. Cf. also chap. 5.

c: Dn 6:29.

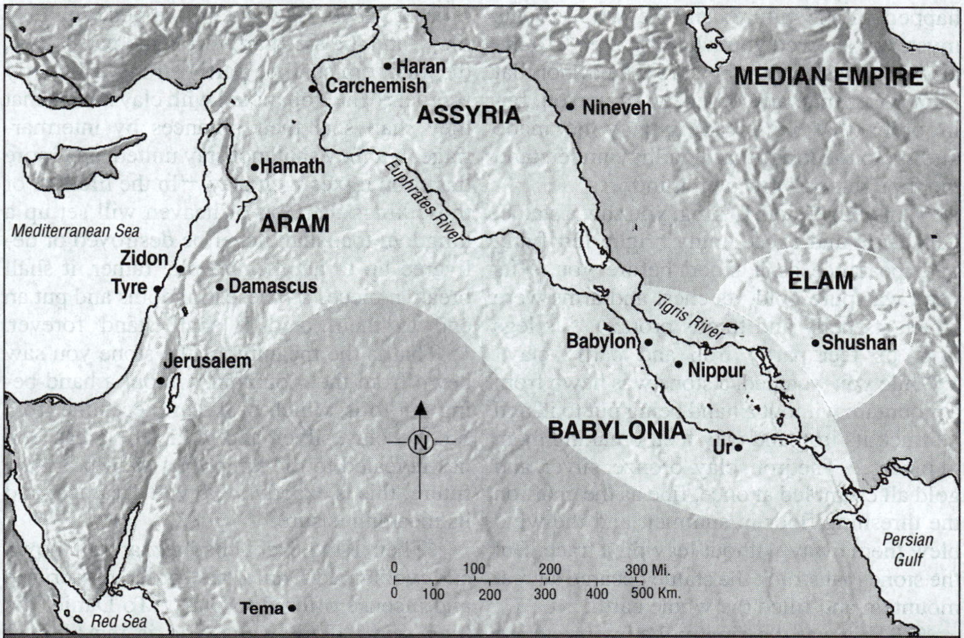

The Neo-Babylonian Empire

vealed to Daniel in a vision, and he blessed the God of heaven:

20 "Blessed be the name of God forever and
ever,
for wisdom and power are his.
21 He causes the changes of the times and
seasons,
establishes kings and deposes them.
He gives wisdom to the wise
and knowledge to those who understand.
22 He reveals deep and hidden things
and knows what is in the darkness,
for the light dwells with him.[d]
23 To you, God of my ancestors,
I give thanks and praise,
because you have given me wisdom
and power.
Now you have shown me what we asked
of you,
you have made known to us the king's
dream."

24 So Daniel went to Arioch, whom the
king had appointed to destroy the wise men
of Babylon, and said to him, "Do not put the
wise men of Babylon to death. Bring me before the king, and I will tell him the interpretation of the dream." Arioch quickly
brought Daniel to the king and said, 25 "I
have found a man among the Judean exiles
who can give the interpretation to the king."
26 The king asked Daniel, whose name was
Belteshazzar, "Can you tell me the dream
that I had and its meaning?" 27 In the king's
presence Daniel made this reply:

"The mystery about which the king has
inquired, the wise men, enchanters, magicians, and diviners could not explain to the
king. 28 But there is a God in heaven who reveals mysteries, and he has shown King
Nebuchadnezzar what is to happen in the
last days; this was your dream, the visions*
you saw as you lay in bed. 29 To you in your
bed there came thoughts about what should

2:28 The visions: lit., "the visions of your head," a phrasing which distinguishes visionary experiences that are personal from those that are observable by others (see 4:2, 7, 10). That Daniel, unlike the Chaldeans, has access to these visions testifies to his God-given wisdom. Actually, this "dream" is more properly an apocalyptic vision; cf. the very

d: Jn 1:9; 8:12; 1 Cor 4:5; 1 Jn 1:6.

happen in the future, and he who reveals mysteries showed you what is to be. 30To me also this mystery has been revealed; not that I am wiser than any other living person, but in order that its meaning may be made known to the king, that you may understand the thoughts of your own mind.

31"In your vision, O king, you saw a statue, very large and exceedingly bright, terrifying in appearance as it stood before you. 32Its head was pure gold, its chest and arms were silver, its belly and thighs bronze, 33its legs iron, its feet partly iron and partly clay.* 34While you watched, a stone was hewn from a mountain without a hand being put to it, and it struck its iron and clay feet, breaking them in pieces. 35The iron, clay, bronze, silver, and gold all crumbled at once, fine as the chaff on the threshing floor in summer, and the wind blew them away without leaving a trace. But the stone that struck the statue became a great mountain and filled the whole earth.

36* "This was the dream; the interpretation we shall also give in the king's presence. 37You, O king, are the king of kings; to you the God of heaven has given dominion and strength, power and glory; 38human beings, wild beasts, and birds of the air, wherever they may dwell, he has handed over to you, making you ruler over them all; you are the head of gold. 39Another kingdom shall take your place, inferior to yours, then a third kingdom, of bronze, which shall rule over the whole earth. 40There shall be a fourth kingdom, strong as iron; it shall break in pieces and subdue all these others, just as iron breaks in pieces and crushes everything else. 41The feet and toes you saw, partly of clay and partly of iron, mean that it shall be a divided kingdom, but yet have some of the hardness of iron. As you saw the iron mixed with clay tile, 42and the toes partly iron and partly clay, the kingdom shall be partly strong and partly fragile. 43The iron mixed with clay means that they shall seal their alliances by intermarriage, but they shall not stay united, any more than iron mixes with clay. 44In the lifetime of those kings the God of heaven will set up a kingdom that shall never be destroyed or delivered up to another people; rather, it shall break in pieces all these kingdoms and put an end to them, and it shall stand forever. 45e That is the meaning of the stone you saw hewn from the mountain without a hand being put to it, which broke in pieces the iron, bronze, clay, silver, and gold. The great God has revealed to the king what shall be in the future; this is exactly what you dreamed, and its meaning is sure."

46Then King Nebuchadnezzar fell down and worshiped Daniel and ordered sacrifice and incense offered to him. 47To Daniel the king said, "Truly your God is the God of gods and Lord of kings and a revealer of mysteries; that is why you were able to reveal this mystery." 48He advanced Daniel to a high post, gave him many generous presents, made him ruler of the whole province of Babylon and chief prefect over all the wise men of Babylon. 49At Daniel's request the king made Shadrach, Meshach, and Abednego administrators of the province of Babylon, while Daniel himself remained at the king's court.

CHAPTER 3

See RG 337

The Fiery Furnace. 1King Nebuchadnezzar had a golden statue made, sixty cubits high and six cubits wide, which he set up in the plain of Dura* in the province of

similar message in Daniel's vision of chap. 7.

2:33 Clay: it has been suggested that the motif of iron mixed with clay implies a hollow metal statue packed with clay to stabilize it. In the interpretation of the dream, however, the mixture is taken as a sign of weakness.

2:36–45 The four successive kingdoms in this apocalyptic perspective are the Babylonian (gold), the Median (silver), the Persian (bronze), and the Hellenistic (iron). The last, after Alexander's death, was divided among his generals (vv. 41–42). Of the kingdoms which emerged from this partitioning, the two that most affected the Jews were the dynasties of the Ptolemies in Egypt and the Seleucids in Syria. They tried in vain, by war and through intermarriage, to restore the unity of Alexander's empire (v. 43). The stone hewn from the mountain is the kingdom of God awaited by the Jews (vv. 44–45). Compare the image of the stone applied to Jesus in Luke 20:17–18.

3:1 Dura: several places in Babylonia bore this name. Probably the present reference is to one located close to Babylon. Giant statues of the type mentioned here were not uncommon in antiquity; a cubit was about a foot and a half. The unrealistic proportions of this statue suggest a comic effect.

e: Mt 21:44; Lk 20:18.

Babylon. 2 He then ordered the satraps,* prefects, and governors, the counselors, treasurers, judges, magistrates and all the officials of the provinces to be summoned to the dedication of the statue which he had set up. 3 The satraps, prefects, and governors, the counselors, treasurers, judges, magistrates and all the officials of the provinces came together for the dedication and stood before the statue which King Nebuchadnezzar had set up. 4 A herald cried out: "Nations and peoples of every language, 5* when you hear the sound of the horn, pipe, zither, dulcimer, harp, double-flute, and all the other musical instruments, you must fall down and worship the golden statue which King Nebuchadnezzar has set up. 6 Whoever does not fall down and worship shall be instantly cast into a white-hot furnace." 7 Therefore, as soon as they heard the sound of the horn, pipe, zither, dulcimer, harp, double-flute, and all the other musical instruments, the nations and peoples of every language all fell down and worshiped the golden statue which King Nebuchadnezzar had set up.

8 At that point, some of the Chaldeans came and accused the Jews 9 to King Nebuchadnezzar: "O king, live forever! 10 O king, you issued a decree that everyone who heard the sound of the horn, pipe, zither, dulcimer, harp, and double-flute, and all the other musical instruments should fall down and worship the golden statue; 11 whoever did not was to be cast into a white-hot furnace. 12 There are certain Jews whom you have made administrators of the province of Babylon: Shadrach, Meshach, and Abednego; these men, O king, have paid no attention to you; they will not serve your god or worship the golden statue which you set up."

13 Nebuchadnezzar flew into a rage and sent for Shadrach, Meshach, and Abednego, who were promptly brought before the king. 14 King Nebuchadnezzar questioned them: "Is it true, Shadrach, Meshach, and Abednego, that you will not serve my god, or worship the golden statue that I set up? 15 Now, if you are ready to fall down and worship the statue I made, whenever you hear the sound of the horn, pipe, zither, dulcimer, harp, double-flute, and all the other musical instruments, then all will be well;* if not, you shall be instantly cast into the white-hot furnace; and who is the God who can deliver you out of my hands?" 16 Shadrach, Meshach, and Abednego answered King Nebuchadnezzar, "There is no need for us to defend ourselves before you in this matter. 17 If our God, whom we serve, can save us* from the white-hot furnace and from your hands, O king, may he save us! 18 But even if he will not, you should know, O king, that we will not serve your god or worship the golden statue which you set up."

19 Nebuchadnezzar's face became livid with utter rage against Shadrach, Meshach, and Abednego. He ordered the furnace to be heated seven times more than usual 20 and had some of the strongest men in his army bind Shadrach, Meshach, and Abednego and cast them into the white-hot furnace. 21 They were bound and cast into the white-hot furnace with their trousers, shirts, hats and other garments, 22 for the king's order was urgent. So huge a fire was kindled in the furnace that the flames devoured the men who threw Shadrach, Meshach, and Abednego into it. 23 But these three fell, bound, into the midst of the white-hot furnace.

Prayer of Azariah.* 24 They walked about in the flames, singing to God and blessing the Lord. 25 Azariah* stood up in the midst of the fire and prayed aloud:

26 "Blessed are you, and praiseworthy,
O Lord, the God of our ancestors,
and glorious forever is your name.
27 For you are just in all you have done;

3:2 Satraps: Persian provincial governors.

3:5 The precise identification of the instruments is disputed. Several of the names are Greek.

3:15 Then all will be well: lacking in Aramaic; this phrase is supplied from the context.

3:17 If our God . . . can save us: the youths do not question the efficacy of the divine power, but whether it will be exercised (v. 18).

3:24–90 These verses are additions to the Aramaic text of Daniel, translated from the Greek form of the book. They were probably first composed in Hebrew or Aramaic, but are no longer extant in the original language. The Roman Catholic Church has always regarded them as part of the canonical Scriptures.

3:25 Azariah: i.e., Abednego; cf. Dn 1:7.

all your deeds are faultless, all your
ways right,
and all your judgments proper.
28 You have executed proper judgments
in all that you have brought upon us
and upon Jerusalem, the holy city of
our ancestors.
By a proper judgment you have done all
this
because of our sins;
29 For we have sinned and transgressed
by departing from you,
and we have done every kind of evil.
30 Your commandments we have not
heeded or observed,
nor have we done as you ordered us
for our good.
31 Therefore all you have brought upon us,
all you have done to us,
you have done by a proper judgment.
32 You have handed us over to our enemies,
lawless and hateful rebels;
to an unjust king, the worst in all the
world.
33 Now we cannot open our mouths;
shame and reproach have come upon us,
your servants, who revere you.
34 For your name's sake, do not deliver us
up forever,
or make void your covenant.
35 Do not take away your mercy from us,
for the sake of Abraham, your beloved,
Isaac your servant, and Israel your
holy one,
36 To whom you promised to multiply their
offspring
like the stars of heaven,
or the sand on the shore of the sea.
37 For we are reduced, O Lord, beyond any
other nation,
brought low everywhere in the world
this day
because of our sins.
38 We have in our day no prince, prophet, or
leader,
no burnt offering, sacrifice, oblation,
or incense,
no place to offer first fruits, to find
favor with you.
39 But with contrite heart and humble spirit
let us be received;
As though it were burnt offerings of rams
and bulls,
or tens of thousands of fat lambs,
40 So let our sacrifice be in your presence
today
and find favor before you;
for those who trust in you cannot be
put to shame.
41 And now we follow you with our whole
heart,
we fear you and we seek your face.
Do not put us to shame,
42 but deal with us in your kindness and
great mercy.
43 Deliver us in accord with your wonders,
and bring glory to your name, O Lord:
44 Let all those be put to shame
who inflict evils on your servants;
Let them be shamed and powerless,
and their strength broken;
45 Let them know that you alone are the
Lord God,
glorious over the whole world."

46 Now the king's servants who had
thrown them in continued to stoke the furnace with naptha, pitch, tow, and brush.
47 The flames rose forty-nine cubits above
the furnace, 48 and spread out, burning the
Chaldeans that it caught around the furnace.
49 But the angel of the Lord went down into
the furnace with Azariah and his companions, drove the fiery flames out of the furnace, 50 and made the inside of the furnace as
though a dew-laden breeze were blowing
through it. The fire in no way touched them
or caused them pain or harm. 51 Then these
three in the furnace with one voice sang, glorifying and blessing God:
52 "Blessed are you, O Lord, the God of our
ancestors,
praiseworthy and exalted above all
forever;
And blessed is your holy and glorious
name,
praiseworthy and exalted above all for
all ages.
53 Blessed are you in the temple of your
holy glory,
praiseworthy and glorious above all
forever.

54 Blessed are you on the throne of your
kingdom,
praiseworthy and exalted above all
forever.
55 Blessed are you who look into the depths
from your throne upon the cherubim,
praiseworthy and exalted above all
forever.
56 Blessed are you in the firmament of
heaven,
praiseworthy and glorious forever.
57 Bless the Lord, all you works of the
Lord,
praise and exalt him above all forever.
58 Angels of the Lord, bless the Lord,
praise and exalt him above all forever.
59 You heavens, bless the Lord,
praise and exalt him above all forever.[f]
60 All you waters above the heavens, bless
the Lord,
praise and exalt him above all forever.
61 All you powers, bless the Lord;
praise and exalt him above all forever.
62 Sun and moon, bless the Lord;
praise and exalt him above all forever.
63 Stars of heaven, bless the Lord;
praise and exalt him above all forever.
64 Every shower and dew, bless the Lord;
praise and exalt him above all forever.
65 All you winds, bless the Lord;
praise and exalt him above all forever.
66 Fire and heat, bless the Lord;
praise and exalt him above all forever.
67 Cold and chill, bless the Lord;
praise and exalt him above all forever.
68 Dew and rain, bless the Lord;
praise and exalt him above all forever.
69 Frost and chill, bless the Lord;
praise and exalt him above all forever.
70 Hoarfrost and snow, bless the Lord;
praise and exalt him above all forever.
71 Nights and days, bless the Lord;
praise and exalt him above all forever.
72 Light and darkness, bless the Lord;
praise and exalt him above all forever.
73 Lightnings and clouds, bless the Lord;
praise and exalt him above all forever.
74 Let the earth bless the Lord,
praise and exalt him above all forever.
75 Mountains and hills, bless the Lord;
praise and exalt him above all forever.
76 Everything growing on earth, bless the
Lord;
praise and exalt him above all forever.
77 You springs, bless the Lord;
praise and exalt him above all forever.
78 Seas and rivers, bless the Lord;
praise and exalt him above all forever.
79 You sea monsters and all water creatures,
bless the Lord;
praise and exalt him above all forever.
80 All you birds of the air, bless the Lord;
praise and exalt him above all forever.
81 All you beasts, wild and tame, bless the
Lord;
praise and exalt him above all forever.
82 All you mortals, bless the Lord;
praise and exalt him above all forever.
83 O Israel, bless the Lord;
praise and exalt him above all forever.
84 Priests of the Lord, bless the Lord;
praise and exalt him above all forever.
85 Servants of the Lord, bless the Lord;
praise and exalt him above all forever.
86 Spirits and souls of the just, bless the
Lord;
praise and exalt him above all forever.
87 Holy and humble of heart, bless the
Lord;
praise and exalt him above all forever.
88 Hananiah, Azariah, Mishael, bless the
Lord;
praise and exalt him above all forever.
For he has delivered us from Sheol,
and saved us from the power of death;
He has freed us from the raging flame
and delivered us from the fire.
89 Give thanks to the Lord, who is good,
whose mercy endures forever.
90 Bless the God of gods, all you who fear
the Lord;
praise and give thanks,
for his mercy endures forever."

Deliverance from the Furnace. 91 Then King
Nebuchadnezzar was startled and rose in
haste, asking his counselors, "Did we not cast
three men bound into the fire?" "Certainly, O

f: Ps 148:4.

king," they answered. [92]"But," he replied, "I
see four men unbound and unhurt, walking in
the fire, and the fourth looks like a son of
God." [93]Then Nebuchadnezzar came to the
opening of the white-hot furnace and called:
"Shadrach, Meshach, and Abednego, servants
of the Most High God, come out." Thereupon
Shadrach, Meshach, and Abednego came out
of the fire. [94]When the satraps, prefects, governors, and counselors of the king came together, they saw that the fire had had no power
over the bodies of these men; not a hair of their
heads had been singed, nor were their garments altered; there was not even a smell of
fire about them. [95]Nebuchadnezzar exclaimed,
"Blessed be the God of Shadrach, Meshach,
and Abednego, who sent his angel to deliver
the servants that trusted in him; they disobeyed
the royal command and yielded their bodies
rather than serve or worship any god except
their own God. [96]Therefore I decree for nations and peoples of every language that whoever blasphemes the God of Shadrach, Meshach, and Abednego shall be cut to pieces and
his house made into a refuse heap. For there is
no other God who can rescue like this." [97]Then
the king promoted Shadrach, Meshach, and
Abednego in the province of Babylon.

[98]* King Nebuchadnezzar to the nations
and peoples of every language, wherever
they dwell on earth: May your peace
abound! [99]It has seemed good to me to publish the signs and wonders which the Most
High God has accomplished in my regard.

[100]How great are his signs, how mighty his wonders;
his kingship is an everlasting kingship,
and his dominion endures through all generations.[g]

CHAPTER 4

See RG 337

Nebuchadnezzar's Madness. [1]I, Nebuchadnezzar, was at home in my palace,
content and prosperous. [2]I had a terrifying
dream as I lay in bed, and the images and my
visions frightened me. [3]So I issued a decree
that all the wise men of Babylon should be
brought before me to give the interpretation
of the dream. [4]When the magicians, enchanters, Chaldeans, and diviners had come
in, I related the dream before them; but none
of them could tell me its meaning. [5]Finally
there came before me Daniel, whose name is
Belteshazzar after the name of my god,* and
in whom is a spirit of the holy gods.[h] I repeated the dream to him: [6]"Belteshazzar,
chief of the magicians, I know that a spirit of
the holy gods is in you and no mystery is too
difficult for you; this is the dream that I saw,
tell me its meaning.

[7]"These were the visions I saw while in
bed: I saw a tree of great height at the center
of the earth. [8]It was large and strong, with its
top touching the heavens, and it could be
seen to the ends of the earth. [9]Its leaves were
beautiful, its fruit abundant, providing food
for all. Under it the wild beasts found shade,
in its branches the birds of the air nested; all
flesh ate of it. [10]In the vision I saw while in
bed, a holy watcher* came down from
heaven [11]and cried aloud in these words:

'Cut down the tree and lop off its branches,
strip off its leaves and scatter its fruit;
Let the beasts flee from beneath it, and the birds from its branches,
[12] but leave its stump in the earth.
Bound with iron and bronze,
let him be fed with the grass of the field
and bathed with the dew of heaven;
let his lot be with the beasts in the grass of the earth.
[13] Let his mind be changed from a human one;
let the mind of a beast be given him,
till seven years pass over him.

3:98–4:34 This section has the form of a letter written by Nebuchadnezzar to his subjects.

4:5 After the name of my god: Belteshazzar, the Babylonian name given to Daniel at the king's orders (1:7), is *Balāṭ-šu-uṣur*, "protect his life." This passage implies a name connected with Bel, a Babylonian god. **A spirit of the holy gods**: or a holy divine spirit; or spirit of a holy God. See also vv. 6, 15; 5:11–12, 14; 6:4.

4:10 A holy watcher: lit., "a watcher and a holy one." Two terms for angels. The term watcher is found in the Bible only in this chapter of Daniel, but it is common in extra-canonical Jewish literature. In 1 Enoch, the fallen angels are called watchers.

g: Dn 4:31; 7:14. *h:* Gn 41:38.

14 By decree of the watchers is this
proclamation,
by order of the holy ones, this
sentence;
That all who live may know
that the Most High is sovereign over
human kingship,
Giving it to whom he wills,
and setting it over the lowliest of
mortals.’[i]

15 “This is the dream that I, King Nebuchadnezzar, had. Now, Belteshazzar, tell me
its meaning. None of the wise men in my
kingdom can tell me the meaning, but you
can, because the spirit of the holy gods is in
you.”
16 Then Daniel, whose name was Belteshazzar, was appalled for a time, dismayed
by his thoughts. “Belteshazzar,” the king
said to him, “do not let the dream or its
meaning dismay you.” “My lord,” Belteshazzar replied, “may this dream be for your
enemies, and its meaning for your foes.
17 The tree that you saw, large and strong, its
top touching the heavens, that could be seen
by the whole earth, 18 its leaves beautiful, its
fruit abundant, providing food for all, under
which the wild beasts lived, and in whose
branches the birds of the air dwelt— 19 you
are that tree, O king, large and strong! Your
majesty has become so great as to touch the
heavens, and your rule reaches to the ends of
the earth. 20 As for the king’s vision of a holy
watcher, who came down from heaven and
proclaimed: ‘Cut down the tree and destroy
it, but leave its stump in the earth. Bound
with iron and bronze, let him be fed with the
grass of the field, and bathed with the dew of
heaven; let his lot be with wild beasts till
seven years pass over him’— 21 here is its
meaning, O king, here is the sentence that
the Most High has passed upon my lord
king: 22[j] You shall be cast out from human
society and dwell with wild beasts; you shall
be given grass to eat like an ox and be bathed
with the dew of heaven; seven years shall
pass over you, until you know that the Most
High is sovereign over human kingship and
gives it to whom he will. 23 The command
that the stump of the tree is to be left means
that your kingdom shall be preserved for
you, once you have learned that heaven is
sovereign. 24 Therefore, O king, may my advice be acceptable to you; atone for your
sins by good deeds,* and for your misdeeds
by kindness to the poor; then your contentment will be long lasting.”
25 All this happened to King Nebuchadnezzar. 26 Twelve months later, as he was
walking on the roof of the royal palace in
Babylon, 27 the king said, “Babylon the
great! Was it not I, with my great strength,
who built it as a royal residence for my
splendor and majesty?” 28 While these words
were still on the king’s lips, a voice spoke
from heaven, “It has been decreed for you,
King Nebuchadnezzar, that your kingship is
taken from you! 29 You shall be cast out from
human society, and shall dwell with wild
beasts; you shall be given grass to eat like an
ox, and seven years shall pass over you, until you learn that the Most High is sovereign
over human kingship and gives it to whom
he will.” 30* At once this was fulfilled. Nebuchadnezzar was cast out from human society, he ate grass like an ox, and his body was
bathed with the dew of heaven, until his hair
grew like the feathers of an eagle, and his
nails like the claws of a bird.
31 When this period was over, I, Nebuchadnezzar, raised my eyes to heaven; my
reason was restored to me, and I blessed the
Most High, I praised and glorified the One
who lives forever,

Whose dominion is an everlasting
dominion,

4:24 Good deeds: the Aramaic word *sidqâ* has the root meaning of “righteousness,” but in a late text such as this could mean “almsgiving.”

4:30–32 There is no historical record that these events happened to Nebuchadnezzar. Scholars have long suspected that the story originally involved Nabonidus, the father of Belshazzar, who was absent from Babylon and lived at Teima in the Arabian desert for a number of years. This suggestion is now strengthened by the Prayer of Nabonidus, found at Qumran, which is closely related to chap. 4. The biblical author’s chief interest was not in the historicity of this popular tale, but in the object lesson it contained for the proud “divine” kings of the Seleucid dynasty.

i: 1 Sm 2:8. *j:* Dn 5:21.

and whose kingdom endures through
all generations.[k]
32 All who live on the earth are counted as
nothing;
he does as he wills with the powers of
heaven
and with those who live on the earth.
There is no one who can stay his hand
or say to him, "What have you done?"

33 At the same time my reason returned to
me, and for the glory of my kingdom, my
majesty and my splendor returned to me. My
counselors and nobles sought me out; I was
restored to my kingdom and became much
greater than before. 34 Now, I, Nebuchadnezzar, praise and exalt and glorify the King of
heaven, all of whose works are right and
ways just; and who is able to humble those
who walk in pride.

CHAPTER 5

See RG 337

The Writing on the Wall. 1 King Belshazzar gave a great banquet for a thousand
of his nobles, with whom he drank. 2 Under
the influence of the wine, he ordered the
gold and silver vessels which Nebuchadnezzar, his father,* had taken from the temple in
Jerusalem, to be brought in so that the king,
his nobles, his consorts, and his concubines
might drink from them. 3 When the gold vessels taken from the temple, the house of God
in Jerusalem, had been brought in, and while
the king, his nobles, his consorts, and his
concubines were drinking 4 wine from them,
they praised their gods of gold and silver,
bronze and iron, wood and stone.

5 Suddenly, opposite the lampstand, the
fingers of a human hand appeared, writing
on the plaster of the wall in the king's palace.
When the king saw the hand that wrote, 6 his
face became pale; his thoughts terrified him,
his hip joints shook, and his knees knocked.
7 The king shouted for the enchanters, Chaldeans, and diviners to be brought in. "Whoever reads this writing and tells me what it
means," he said to the wise men of Babylon,
"shall be clothed in purple, wear a chain of
gold around his neck, and be third in governing the kingdom." 8 But though all the
king's wise men came in, none of them
could either read the writing or tell the king
what it meant. 9 Then King Belshazzar was
greatly terrified; his face became pale, and
his nobles were thrown into confusion.

10 When the queen heard of the discussion
between the king and his nobles, she entered
the banquet hall and said, "O king, live forever! Do not let your thoughts terrify you, or
your face become so pale! 11 There is a man
in your kingdom in whom is a spirit of the
holy gods; during the lifetime of your father
he showed brilliant insight and god-like wisdom. King Nebuchadnezzar, your father,
made him chief of the magicians, enchanters, Chaldeans, and diviners. 12 Because this Daniel, whom the king named
Belteshazzar, has shown an extraordinary
spirit, knowledge, and insight in interpreting
dreams, explaining riddles and solving problems, let him now be summoned to tell you
what this means."

13 Then Daniel was brought into the presence of the king. The king asked him, "Are
you the Daniel, one of the Jewish exiles,
whom my father, the king, brought from Judah? 14 I have heard that the spirit of the gods
is in you, that you have shown brilliant insight and extraordinary wisdom. 15 The wise
men and enchanters were brought in to me to
read this writing and tell me its meaning, but
they could not say what the words meant.
16 But I have heard that you can give interpretations and solve problems; now, if you
are able to read the writing and tell me what
it means, you shall be clothed in purple,
wear a chain of gold around your neck, and
be third in governing the kingdom."

17 Daniel answered the king: "You may
keep your gifts, or give your presents to
someone else; but the writing I will read for
the king, and tell what it means. 18 The Most
High God gave your father Nebuchadnezzar
kingship, greatness, splendor, and majesty.
19 Because he made him so great, the nations
and peoples of every language dreaded and

5:2 Nebuchadnezzar, his father: between Nebuchadnezzar and Belshazzar several kings ruled in Babylon. Belshazzar was the son of Nabonidus, and he acted as regent in Babylon during his father's absence.

k: Dn 3:33; 7:14.

feared him. Whomever he willed, he would kill or let live; whomever he willed, he would exalt or humble. [20]But when his heart became proud and his spirit hardened by insolence, he was put down from his royal throne and deprived of his glory; [21][l] he was cast out from human society and his heart was made like that of a beast; he lived with wild asses, and ate grass like an ox; his body was bathed with the dew of heaven, until he learned that the Most High God is sovereign over human kingship and sets over it whom he will. [22]You, his son, Belshazzar, have not humbled your heart, though you knew all this; [23]you have rebelled against the Lord of heaven. You had the vessels of his temple brought before you, so that you and your nobles, your consorts and your concubines, might drink wine from them; and you praised the gods of silver and gold, bronze and iron, wood and stone, that neither see nor hear nor have intelligence. But the God in whose hand is your very breath and the whole course of your life, you did not glorify. [24]By him was the hand sent, and the writing set down.

[25]"This is the writing that was inscribed: MENE, TEKEL, and PERES.* These words mean: [26]* MENE, God has numbered your kingdom and put an end to it; [27]TEKEL, you have been weighed on the scales and found wanting; [28]PERES, your kingdom has been divided and given to the Medes and Persians."

[29]Then by order of Belshazzar they clothed Daniel in purple, with a chain of gold around his neck, and proclaimed him third in governing the kingdom. [30]That very night Belshazzar, the Chaldean king, was slain:

CHAPTER 6

See RG 337

[1]And Darius the Mede* succeeded to the kingdom at the age of sixty-two.

The Lions' Den. [2]Darius decided to appoint over his entire kingdom one hundred and twenty satraps. [3]These were accountable to three ministers, one of whom was Daniel; the satraps reported to them, so that the king should suffer no loss. [4]Daniel outshone all the ministers and satraps because an extraordinary spirit was in him, and the king considered setting him over the entire kingdom. [5]Then the ministers and satraps tried to find grounds for accusation against Daniel regarding the kingdom. But they could not accuse him of any corruption. Because he was trustworthy, no fault or corruption was to be found in him. [6]Then these men said to themselves, "We shall find no grounds for accusation against this Daniel except in connection with the law of his God." [7]So these ministers and satraps stormed in to the king and said to him, "King Darius, live forever! [8]* [m] All the ministers of the kingdom, the prefects, satraps, counselors, and governors agree that the following prohibition ought to be put in force by royal decree: for thirty days, whoever makes a petition to anyone, divine or human, except to you, O king, shall be thrown into a den of lions. [9]Now, O king, let the prohibition be issued over your signature, immutable and irrevocable* according to the law of the Medes and Persians." [10]So King Darius signed the prohibition into law.

[11]Even after Daniel heard that this law had been signed, he continued his custom of go-

5:25 MENE, TEKEL, and PERES: these seem to be the Aramaic names of weights and monetary values: the mina, the shekel (the sixtieth part of a mina), and the parsu (a half-mina).

5:26–28 Daniel interprets these three terms by a play on the words: *MENE*, connected with the verb meaning to number; *TEKEL*, with the verb meaning to weigh; *PERES*, with the verb meaning to divide. There is also a play on the last term with the word for Persians.

6:1 Darius the Mede: unknown outside of the Book of Daniel. The Median kingdom did not exist at this time because it had already been conquered by Cyrus the Persian. Apparently the author of Daniel is following an apocalyptic view of history, linked to prophecy (cf. Is 13:17–19; Jer 51:11, 28–30), according to which the Medes formed the second of four world kingdoms preceding the messianic times; see note on Dn 2:36–45. The character of Darius the Mede has probably been modeled on that of the Persian king Darius the Great (522–486 B.C.), the second successor of Cyrus. The Persian Darius did appoint satraps over his empire.

6:8–11 The Jews of the second century B.C. could relate the king's attempt to force upon them, under pain of death, the worship of a foreign deity to the decrees of Antiochus IV; cf. 1 Mc 1:41–50.

6:9 Immutable and irrevocable: Est 1:19 and 8:8 also refer to the immutability of Medo-Persian laws. The same idea is found in the historian Diodorus Siculus with reference to the time of Darius III (335–331 B.C.), the last of the Persian kings. Cf. Dn 6:13, 16.

l: Dn 4:22. *m:* Est 1:19.

ing home to kneel in prayer and give thanks to his God in the upper chamber three times a day, with the windows open toward Jerusalem. [12]So these men stormed in and found Daniel praying and pleading before his God. [13]Then they went to remind the king about the prohibition: "Did you not sign a decree, O king, that for thirty days, whoever makes a petition to anyone, divine or human, except to you, O king, shall be cast into a den of lions?" The king answered them, "The decree is absolute, irrevocable under the law of the Medes and Persians." [14]To this they replied, "Daniel, one of the Jewish exiles, has paid no attention to you, O king, or to the prohibition you signed; three times a day he offers his prayer." [15]The king was deeply grieved at this news and he made up his mind to save Daniel; he worked till sunset to rescue him. [16]But these men pressed the king. "Keep in mind, O king," they said, "that under the law of the Medes and Persians every royal prohibition or decree is irrevocable." [17]So the king ordered Daniel to be brought and cast into the lions' den.* To Daniel he said, "Your God, whom you serve so constantly, must save you." [18]To forestall any tampering, the king sealed with his own ring and the rings of the lords the stone that had been brought to block the opening of the den.

[19]Then the king returned to his palace for the night; he refused to eat and he dismissed the entertainers. Since sleep was impossible for him, [20]the king rose very early the next morning and hastened to the lions' den. [21]As he drew near, he cried out to Daniel sorrowfully, "Daniel, servant of the living God, has your God whom you serve so constantly been able to save you from the lions?" [22]Daniel answered the king: "O king, live forever! [23]My God sent his angel and closed the lions' mouths so that they have not hurt me.[n] For I have been found innocent before him; neither have I done you any harm, O king!" [24]This gave the king great joy. At his order Daniel was brought up from the den; he was found to be unharmed because he trusted in his God. [25]The king then ordered the men who had accused Daniel, along with their children and their wives, to be cast into the lions' den. Before they reached the bottom of the den, the lions overpowered them and crushed all their bones.

[26]Then King Darius wrote to the nations and peoples of every language, wherever they dwell on the earth: "May your peace abound! [27]I decree that throughout my royal domain the God of Daniel is to be reverenced and feared:

"For he is the living God, enduring
forever,
whose kingdom shall not be destroyed,
whose dominion shall be without end,
28 A savior and deliverer,
working signs and wonders in heaven
and on earth,
who saved Daniel from the lions'
power."

[29]So Daniel fared well during the reign of Darius and the reign of Cyrus the Persian.[o]

II. Daniel's Visions

CHAPTER 7

See RG 338–42

The Beasts and the Judgment.* [1]In the first year of King Belshazzar of Babylon, as Daniel lay in bed he had a dream, visions in his head. Then he wrote down the dream; the account began: [2]In the vision I saw during the night, suddenly the four winds of heaven stirred up the great sea,* [3]from which emerged four immense beasts,[p] each different from the others. [4]The first was like a lion, but with eagle's wings.* While I watched, the wings were plucked; it was

6:17 The lions' den: a pit too deep to be easily scaled; its opening was blocked with a stone (v. 18).

7:1–27 This vision continues the motif of the four kingdoms from chap. 2; see note on 2:36–45. To the four succeeding world kingdoms, Babylonian, Median, Persian, and Greek, is opposed the heavenly kingdom of God and the kingdom of God's people on earth. The beast imagery of this chapter has been used extensively in the Book of Revelation, where it is applied to the Roman empire, the persecutor of the Church.

7:2 The great sea: the primordial ocean beneath the earth, according to ancient Near Eastern cosmology (Gn 7:11; 49:25). It was thought to contain various monsters (Is 27:1; Jb 7:12), and in particular mythological monsters symbolizing the chaos which God had vanquished in primordial times (Jb 9:13; 26:12; Is 51:9–10; etc.).

7:4 In ancient times the Babylonian empire was commonly

n: 1 Mc 2:60. *o:* Dn 1:21. *p:* Rev 13:1.

raised from the ground to stand on two feet
like a human being, and given a human
mind. 5 The second beast was like a bear;* it
was raised up on one side, and among the
teeth in its mouth were three tusks. It was
given the order, "Arise, devour much flesh."
6 After this I looked and saw another beast,
like a leopard;* on its back were four wings
like those of a bird, and it had four heads. To
this beast dominion was given. 7* After this,
in the visions of the night I saw a fourth
beast, terrifying, horrible, and of extraordinary strength; it had great iron teeth with
which it devoured and crushed, and it trampled with its feet what was left. It differed
from the beasts that preceded it. It had ten
horns. 8 I was considering the ten horns it
had, when suddenly another, a little horn,
sprang out of their midst, and three of the
previous horns were torn away to make
room for it. This horn had eyes like human
eyes, and a mouth that spoke arrogantly.
9* As I watched,

Thrones were set up
  and the Ancient of Days took his
    throne.
His clothing was white as snow,
  the hair on his head like pure wool;
His throne was flames of fire,
  with wheels of burning fire.
10 A river of fire surged forth,
  flowing from where he sat;
Thousands upon thousands were
    ministering to him,
  and myriads upon myriads stood
    before him.[q]

The court was convened, and the books
were opened. 11 I watched, then, from the
first of the arrogant words which the horn
spoke, until the beast was slain and its body
destroyed and thrown into the burning fire.
12 As for the other beasts, their dominion was
taken away, but they were granted a prolon-
gation of life for a time and a season. 13 As
the visions during the night continued, I saw
coming with the clouds of heaven[r]

One like a son of man.*
When he reached the Ancient of Days
  and was presented before him,
14 He received dominion, splendor, and
    kingship;
  all nations, peoples and tongues will
    serve him.
His dominion is an everlasting dominion
  that shall not pass away,
  his kingship, one that shall not be
    destroyed.[s]

15 Because of this, my spirit was anguished and I, Daniel, was terrified by my
visions. 16 I approached one of those present
and asked him the truth of all this; in answer,
he made known to me its meaning: 17 "These
four great beasts stand for four kings which
shall arise on the earth. 18 But the holy ones*
of the Most High shall receive the kingship,
to possess it forever and ever."
19 Then I wished to make certain about the

represented as a winged lion, in the rampant position (raised up on one side). The two wings that were plucked may represent Nebuchadnezzar and Belshazzar. **On two feet like a human being . . . a human mind**: contrasts with what is said in 4:13, 30.

7:5 A bear: represents the Median empire, its three tusks symbolizing its destructive nature; hence, the command: "Arise, devour much flesh."

7:6 A leopard: used to symbolize the swiftness with which Cyrus the Persian established his kingdom. **Four heads**: corresponding to the four Persian kings of 11:2.

7:7–8 Alexander's empire was different from all the others in that it was Western rather than Eastern in inspiration, and far exceeded the others in power. The ten horns represent the kings of the Seleucid dynasty, the only part of the Hellenistic empire that concerned the author. The little horn is Antiochus IV Epiphanes (175–164 B.C.), who usurped the throne and persecuted the Jews.

7:9–10 A vision of the heavenly throne of God (the Ancient of Days), who sits in judgment over the nations. Some of the details of the vision, depicting the divine majesty and omnipotence, are to be found in Ezekiel 1. Others are paralleled in 1 Enoch, a contemporary Jewish apocalypse.

7:13–14 One like a son of man: In contrast to the worldly kingdoms opposed to God, which are represented as grotesque beasts, the coming Kingdom of God is represented by a human figure. Scholars disagree as to whether this figure should be taken as a collective symbol for the people of God (cf. 7:27) or identified as a particular individual, e.g., the archangel Michael (cf. 12:1) or the messiah. The phrase "Son of Man" becomes a title for Jesus in the gospels, especially in passages dealing with the Second Coming (Mk 13 and parallels).

7:18 "Holy ones" in Hebrew and Aramaic literature are nearly always members of the heavenly court or angels (cf. 4:10, 14, 20; 8:13), though here the term is commonly taken to refer to Israel.

q: Rev 5:11. *r:* Mk 13:26; 14:62. *s:* Dn 3:33; 4:31.

fourth beast, so very terrible and different
from the others, devouring and crushing
with its iron teeth and bronze claws, and
trampling with its feet what was left; 20and
about the ten horns on its head, and the other
one that sprang up, before which three horns
fell; and about the horn with the eyes and the
mouth that spoke arrogantly, which appeared greater than its fellows. 21For, as I
watched, that horn made war against the
holy ones and was victorious 22until the Ancient of Days came, and judgment was pronounced in favor of the holy ones of the
Most High, and the time arrived for the holy
ones to possess the kingship. 23He answered
me thus:

"The fourth beast shall be a fourth
kingdom on earth,
different from all the others;
The whole earth it shall devour,
trample down and crush.
24 The ten horns shall be ten kings
rising out of that kingdom;
another shall rise up after them,
Different from those before him,
who shall lay low three kings.
25 He shall speak against the Most High
and wear down the holy ones of the
Most High,
intending to change the feast days and
the law.*
They shall be handed over to him
for a time, two times, and half a time.
26 But when the court is convened,
and his dominion is taken away
to be abolished and completely
destroyed,
27 Then the kingship and dominion and
majesty
of all the kingdoms under the heavens
shall be given to the people of the holy
ones of the Most High,
Whose kingship shall be an everlasting
kingship,
whom all dominions shall serve and
obey."

28This is the end of the report. I, Daniel,
was greatly terrified by my thoughts, and my
face became pale, but I kept the matter to
myself.*

CHAPTER 8

See RG 338–42

*The Ram and the He-goat.** 1After this
first vision, I, Daniel, had another, in the
third year of the reign of King Belshazzar.
2In my vision I saw myself in the fortress of
Susa* in the province of Elam; I was beside
the river Ulai. 3I looked up and saw standing
by the river a ram with two great horns, the
one larger and newer than the other. 4I saw
the ram butting toward the west, north, and
south. No beast could withstand it or be rescued from its power; it did what it pleased
and grew powerful.

5As I was reflecting, a he-goat with a
prominent horn on its forehead suddenly
came from the west across the whole earth
without touching the ground. 6It came to the
two-horned ram I had seen standing by the
river, and rushed toward it with savage
force. 7I saw it reach the ram; enraged, the
he-goat attacked and shattered both its
horns. The ram did not have the strength to
withstand it; the he-goat threw the ram to the
ground and trampled upon it. No one could
rescue the ram from its power.

8The he-goat grew very powerful, but at
the height of its strength the great horn was
shattered, and in its place came up four others, facing the four winds of heaven. 9Out of

7:25 The reference is to the persecution of Antiochus IV and specifically to the disruption of the Temple cult (1 Mc 1:41–64). **A time, two times, and half a time**: an indefinite, evil period of time. Probably here, three and a half years, which becomes the standard period of tribulation in apocalyptic literature (Rev 11:2; 13:5 [in months]; 11:3 [in days]; and cf. 12:14). As seven is the Jewish "perfect" number, half of it signifies great imperfection. Actually, the Temple was desecrated for three years (1 Mc 4:52–54). The duration of the persecution was a little longer, since it was already under way before the Temple was desecrated.

7:28 This verse ends the Aramaic part of the Book of Daniel.

8:1–27 This vision continues images of the preceding one, and develops it in more detail. As explained in vv. 20–22 the two-horned ram represents the combined kingdom of the Medes and Persians, destroyed by Alexander's Hellenistic empire originating in the west. Once again the author is interested only in the Seleucid dynasty, which emerged from the dissolution of Alexander's empire after his death in 323 B.C.

8:2 The fortress of Susa: the royal palace of the Persian kings in the ancient territory of Elam, east of Babylonia. **The river Ulai**: a canal along the northern side of Susa. Some scholars argue that the Hebrew word understood as "river" here should instead be translated "gate."

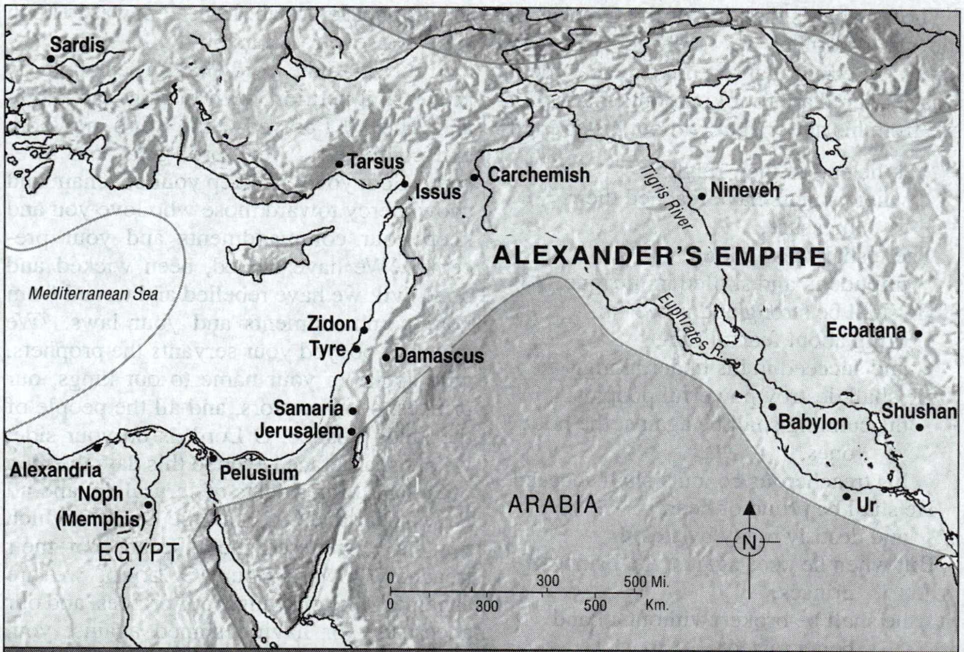

Alexander's Empire

one of them came a little horn* which grew
and grew toward the south, the east, and the
glorious land. 10It grew even to the host of
heaven,* so that it cast down to earth some of
the host and some of the stars and trampled
on them. 11It grew even to the Prince of the
host, from whom the daily sacrifice was removed, and whose sanctuary was cast down.
12The host was given over together with the
daily sacrifice in the course of transgression.
It cast truth to the ground, and was succeeding in its undertaking.
13I heard a holy one speaking, and another
said to whichever one it was that spoke,
"How long shall the events of this vision last
concerning the daily sacrifice, the desolating
sin,* the giving over of the sanctuary and the
host for trampling?" 14He answered him,
"For two thousand three hundred evenings
and mornings; then the sanctuary shall be set
right."
15While I, Daniel, sought the meaning of
the vision I had seen, one who looked like a
man stood before me, 16and on the Ulai I
heard a human voice that cried out, "Gabriel,*
explain the vision to this man." 17When he
came near where I was standing, I fell prostrate in terror. But he said to me, "Understand,
O son of man, that the vision refers to the end
time."* 18As he spoke to me, I fell forward unconscious; he touched me and made me stand
up. 19"I will show you," he said, "what is to
happen in the last days of wrath; for it is for
the appointed time of the end.
20"The two-horned ram you saw represents the kings of the Medes and Persians.*

8:9 A little horn: as in chap. 7, Antiochus IV. **The glorious land**: Israel.

8:10–12 The host of heaven: the angelic host, symbolized by the stars. **The Prince of the host**: the Most High God, whose worship Antiochus suppressed (1 Mc 1:45).

8:13 The desolating sin: the Hebrew contains a wordplay (*shomem*) on the name Baal Shamem ("lord of the heavens," identified by some as the Greek Zeus Olympios). The reference is to some object with which Antiochus profaned the Temple of Jerusalem (2 Mc 6:2), most probably a pagan altar.

8:16 The angel Gabriel is mentioned here for the first time in the Bible. There is wordplay in the preceding verse on *geber*, "manlike figure."

8:17 The end time: the time when God sits in judgment on the wicked (v. 19).

8:20 The Medes and Persians: the Medes had been allies

21 The he-goat is the king of the Greeks, and
the great horn on its forehead is the first
king. 22 The four that rose in its place when it
was shattered are four kingdoms that will issue from his nation, but without his strength.

23 "At the end of their reign,
when sinners have reached their
measure,
There shall arise a king,
impudent, and skilled in intrigue.
24 He shall be strong and powerful,
bring about fearful ruin,
and succeed in his undertaking.
He shall destroy powerful peoples;
25 his cunning shall be against the holy
ones,
his treacherous conduct shall succeed.
He shall be proud of heart
and destroy many by stealth.
But when he rises against the Prince of
princes,
he shall be broken without a hand
being raised.
26 As for the vision of the evenings and the
mornings,
what was spoken is true.
But you, keep this vision secret:
it is for the distant future."

27 I, Daniel, was weak and ill for some
days; then I arose and took care of the king's
affairs. But the vision left me desolate, without understanding.

CHAPTER 9

See RG 338–42

The Seventy Weeks of Years. 1 It was
the first year that Darius,* son of Ahasuerus,
of the race of the Medes, reigned over the
kingdom of the Chaldeans; 2[t] in the first year
of his reign, I, Daniel, perceived in the books
the number of years the LORD had decreed to
the prophet Jeremiah: Jerusalem was to lie in
ruins for seventy years.*

3 I turned to the Lord God, to seek help, in
prayer and petition, with fasting, sackcloth,
and ashes. 4[u] I prayed to the LORD, my God,
and confessed, "Ah, Lord, great and awesome God, you who keep your covenant and
show mercy toward those who love you and
keep your commandments and your precepts! 5 We have sinned, been wicked and
done evil; we have rebelled and turned from
your commandments and your laws. 6 We
have not obeyed your servants the prophets,
who spoke in your name to our kings, our
princes, our ancestors, and all the people of
the land. 7 Justice, O Lord, is on your side;
we are shamefaced even to this day: the men
of Judah, the residents of Jerusalem, and all
Israel, near and far, in all the lands to which
you have scattered them because of their
treachery toward you. 8 O LORD, we are
ashamed, like our kings, our princes, and our
ancestors, for having sinned against you.
9 But to the Lord, our God, belong compassion and forgiveness, though we rebelled
against him 10 and did not hear the voice of
the LORD, our God, by walking in his laws
given through his servants the prophets.
11[v] The curse and the oath written in the law
of Moses, the servant of God, were poured
out over us for our sins, because all Israel
transgressed your law and turned aside, refusing to hear your voice. 12 He fulfilled the
words he spoke against us and against those
who ruled us, by bringing upon us an evil—
no evil so great has happened under heaven
as happened in Jerusalem. 13 As it is written*
in the law of Moses, this evil has come upon
us. We did not appease the LORD, our God,
by turning back from our wickedness and
acting according to your truth, 14 so the LORD

of the Babylonians in destroying the Assyrian empire (late seventh century B.C.), and Cyrus the Persian defeated the Medes en route to conquering the Babylonians. The Book of Daniel, however, treats the Medes and Persians as a dual kingdom; cf. also 5:28; 6:9; and note on 6:1.

9:1 Darius: see note on 6:1.

9:2 Seventy years: Jeremiah was understood to prophesy a Babylonian captivity of seventy years, a round number signifying the complete passing away of the existing generation (Jer 25:11; 29:10). On this view Jeremiah's prophecy was seen to be fulfilled in the capture of Babylon by Cyrus and the subsequent return of the Jews to Palestine. However, the author of Daniel, living during the persecution of Antiochus, extends Jeremiah's number to seventy weeks of years (Dn 9:24), i.e., seven times seventy years, to encompass the period of Seleucid persecution.

9:13 As it is written: the first time that this formula of Scriptural citation is used in the Bible. The reference (v. 11) is to the sanctions of Lv 26:14–16; Dt 28:15–17.

t: Jer 25:11; 29:10. *u:* Ezr 9:6–14; Neh 9:6–37. *v:* Dt 27:15.

kept watch over the evil and brought it upon
us. The LORD, our God, is just in all that he
has done: we did not listen to his voice.
15 “Now, Lord, our God, who led your
people out of the land of Egypt with a strong
hand, and made a name for yourself even to
this day, we have sinned, we are guilty.
16 Lord, in keeping with all your just deeds,
let your anger and your wrath be turned
away from your city Jerusalem, your holy
mountain. On account of our sins and the
crimes of our ancestors, Jerusalem and your
people have become the reproach of all our
neighbors. 17 Now, our God, hear the prayer
and petition of your servant; and for your
own sake, Lord, let your face shine upon
your desolate sanctuary. 18 Give ear, my God,
and listen; open your eyes and look upon our
desolate city upon which your name is invoked. When we present our petition before
you, we rely not on our just deeds, but on
your great mercy. 19 Lord, hear! Lord, pardon! Lord, be attentive and act without delay, for your own sake, my God, because
your name is invoked upon your city and
your people!”
20 I was still praying to the LORD, my God,
confessing my sin and the sin of my people
Israel, presenting my petition concerning the
holy mountain of my God— 21 I was still
praying, when the man, Gabriel, whom I had
seen in vision before, came to me in flight at
the time of the evening offering.* 22 He instructed me in these words: “Daniel, I have
now come to give you understanding.
23 When you began your petition, an answer
was given which I have come to announce,
because you are beloved. Therefore, mark
the answer and understand the vision.

24 “Seventy weeks* are decreed
for your people and for your holy city:
Then transgression will stop and sin will
end,
guilt will be expiated,
Everlasting justice will be introduced,
vision and prophecy ratified,
and a holy of holies will be anointed.
25 Know and understand:
From the utterance of the word
that Jerusalem was to be rebuilt*
Until there is an anointed ruler,
there shall be seven weeks.
In the course of sixty-two weeks
it shall be rebuilt,
With squares and trenches,
in time of affliction.
26 After the sixty-two weeks
an anointed one* shall be cut down
with no one to help him.
And the people of a leader who will
come
shall destroy the city and the
sanctuary.
His end shall come in a flood;
until the end of the war, which is
decreed,
there will be desolation.
27 For one week* he shall make
a firm covenant with the many;
Half the week
he shall abolish sacrifice and offering;
In their place shall be the desolating
abomination

9:21 At the time of the evening offering: between three and four in the afternoon.

9:24 Seventy weeks: i.e., of years. Just as Jeremiah’s seventy years was an approximation (see note on v. 2), the four hundred and ninety years here is not to be taken literally. Similarly, the distribution of the “weeks” in the following verses indicates only relative proportions of the total figure. **A holy of holies**: or “most holy”; could be understood as a place (e.g., the Jerusalem Temple) or a person (cf. 1 Chr 23:13).

9:25 From the utterance . . . to be rebuilt: from the time of Jeremiah’s prophecy. **Anointed ruler**: either Cyrus, who was called the anointed of the Lord to end the exile (Is 45:1), or the high priest Jeshua who presided over the rebuilding of the altar of sacrifice after the exile (Ezr 3:2). **Seven weeks**: forty-nine years, an approximation of the time of the exile. **In the course of sixty-two weeks . . . rebuilt**: a period of four hundred thirty-four years, roughly approximating the interval between the rebuilding of Jerusalem after the exile and the beginning of the Seleucid persecution.

9:26 An anointed one: the high priest Onias III, murdered in 171 B.C., from which the author dates the beginning of the persecution. Onias was in exile when he was killed. **A leader**: Antiochus IV.

9:27 One week: the final phase of the period in view, the time of Antiochus’ persecution. **He**: Antiochus himself. **The many**: the faithless Jews who allied themselves with the Seleucids; cf. 1 Mc 1:11–13. **Half the week**: three and a half years; the Temple was desecrated by Antiochus from 167 to 164 B.C. **The desolating abomination**: see note on 8:13; probably a pagan altar. Jesus refers to this passage in his prediction of the destruction of Jerusalem in Mt 24:15.

until the ruin that is decreed
is poured out upon the desolator."[w]

CHAPTER 10

See RG 338–42

An Angelic Vision.* [1]In the third year of Cyrus, king of Persia, a revelation was given to Daniel, who had been named Belteshazzar. The revelation was certain: a great war;* he understood this from the vision. [2]In those days, I, Daniel, mourned three full weeks. [3]I ate no savory food, took no meat or wine, and did not anoint myself at all until the end of the three weeks.

[4]On the twenty-fourth day of the first month* I was on the bank of the great river, the Tigris. [5]As I looked up, I saw a man* dressed in linen with a belt of fine gold around his waist.[x] [6]His body was like chrysolite, his face shone like lightning, his eyes were like fiery torches, his arms and feet looked like burnished bronze, and the sound of his voice was like the roar of a multitude. [7]I alone, Daniel, saw the vision; but great fear seized those who were with me; they fled and hid themselves, although they did not see the vision. [8]So I was left alone to see this great vision. No strength remained in me; I turned the color of death and was powerless. [9]When I heard the sound of his voice, I fell face forward unconscious.

[10]But then a hand touched me, raising me to my hands and knees. [11]"Daniel, beloved," he said to me, "understand the words which I am speaking to you; stand up, for my mission now is to you." When he said this to me, I stood up trembling. [12]"Do not fear, Daniel," he continued; "from the first day you made up your mind to acquire understanding and humble yourself before God, your prayer was heard. Because of it I started out, [13]but the prince of the kingdom of Persia* stood in my way for twenty-one days, until finally Michael, one of the chief princes, came to help me. I left him there with the prince of the kingdom of Persia, [14]and came to make you understand what shall happen to your people in the last days; for there is yet a vision concerning those days."

[15]While he was speaking thus to me, I fell forward and kept silent. [16]Then something like a hand touched my lips; I opened my mouth and said to the one standing before me, "My lord, I was seized with pangs at the vision and I was powerless. [17]How can my lord's servant speak with you, my lord? For now no strength or even breath is left in me." [18]The one who looked like a man touched me again and strengthened me, saying, [19]"Do not fear, beloved. Peace! Take courage and be strong." When he spoke to me, I grew strong and said, "Speak, my lord, for you have strengthened me." [20]"Do you know," he asked, "why I have come to you? Soon I must fight the prince of Persia again. When I leave, the prince of Greece will come; [21]but I shall tell you what is written in the book of truth.* No one supports me against these except Michael,[y] your prince, [1]and in the first year of Darius the Mede I stood to strengthen him and be his refuge.

CHAPTER 11

See RG 338–42

The Hellenistic Age. [2]"Now I shall tell you the truth.

"Three kings of Persia* are yet to appear; and a fourth shall acquire the greatest riches of all. Strengthened by his riches, he shall stir up all kingdoms, even that of Greece. [3]But a powerful king* shall appear and rule with great might, doing as he wills. [4]No sooner

10:1–12:13 This final vision is concerned with history from the time of Cyrus to the death of Antiochus Epiphanes.

10:1 A great war: or "the service was great," or "a mighty host." The Hebrew is ambiguous.

10:4 The first month: the month Nisan (mid-March to mid-April).

10:5–6 The heavenly person of the vision is probably the angel Gabriel, as in 9:21. **Chrysolite**: or topaz, a yellowish precious stone. Cf. the visions in Ez 1 and 8.

10:13 The prince of the kingdom of Persia: the angelic guardian of Persia. Where older texts speak of the gods of various countries (Dt 32:8), Daniel speaks of "princes." **Michael**: the patron angel of Israel (v. 21).

10:21 The book of truth: a heavenly book in which future events are already recorded; cf. 7:10; 12:1.

11:2 Three kings of Persia: it is unclear which kings are intended because there were more than three Persian kings between Cyrus and the dissolution of the kingdom. The fourth is Xerxes I (486–465 B.C.), the great campaigner against Greece.

11:3 A powerful king: Alexander the Great, who broke Persian dominance by his victory at Issus in 333 B.C.

w: Mt 24:15; 1 Mc 1:54. *x:* Ez 10:2. *y:* Rev 12:7.

shall he appear than his kingdom shall be broken and divided in four directions under
heaven; but not among his descendants or in
keeping with his mighty rule, for his kingdom
shall be torn to pieces and belong to others.
5* "The king of the south shall grow
strong, but one of his princes shall grow
stronger still and govern a domain greater
than his. 6* After some years they shall become allies: the daughter of the king of the
south shall come to the king of the north to
carry out the alliance. But she shall not retain power: and his offspring shall not survive, and she shall be given up, together
with those who brought her, her son, and her
supporter in due time. 7A descendant of her
line shall succeed to his place, and shall
come against the army, enter the stronghold
of the king of the north, attack and conquer
them. 8Even their gods, with their molten
images and their precious vessels of silver
and gold, he shall carry away as spoils of
war into Egypt. For years he shall have nothing to do with the king of the north. 9Then
the latter shall invade the land of the king of
the south, and return to his own country.
10"But his sons shall be aroused and assemble a great armed host, which shall pass
through like a flood and again surge around
the stronghold. 11* The king of the south, enraged, shall go out to fight against the king
of the north, who shall field a great host, but
the host shall be given into his hand. 12When
the host is carried off, in the pride of his
heart he shall bring down tens of thousands,
but he shall not triumph. 13* For the king of
the north shall raise another army, greater
than before; after some years he shall attack
with this large army and great resources. 14In
those times many shall resist the king of the
south, and violent ones among your people
shall rise up in fulfillment of vision, but they
shall stumble. 15* When the king of the north
comes, he shall set up siegeworks and take
the fortified city by storm. The forces of the
south shall not withstand him, and not even
his picked troops shall have the strength to
withstand. 16The invader shall do as he wills,
with no one to withstand him. He shall stop
in the glorious land, and it shall all be in his
power. 17* He shall resolve to come with the
entire strength of his kingdom. He shall
make an alliance with him and give him a
daughter in marriage in order to destroy him,
but this shall not stand. 18* He shall turn to
the coastland and take many prisoners, but a
commander shall put an end to his shameful
conduct, so that he cannot retaliate. 19He
shall turn to the strongholds of his own land,
but shall stumble and fall, to be found no
more. 20* In his stead one shall arise who
will send a collector of tribute through the
glorious kingdom, but he shall soon be destroyed, though not in conflict or in battle.
21* "There shall arise in his place a despi-
cable person, to whom the royal insignia
shall not be given. He shall enter by stealth
and seize the kingdom by fraud. 22Armed
forces shall be completely overwhelmed by
him and crushed, even the prince of the covenant.* 23After making alliances, he shall
treacherously rise to power with only a few
supporters. 24By stealth he shall enter prosperous provinces and do that which his fathers or grandfathers never did; he shall distribute spoil, plunder, and riches among
them and devise plots against their strongholds. 25He shall rouse his strength and
courage to meet the king of the south with a
great army; the king of the south shall go
into battle with a very large and strong army,
but he shall not stand because of the plots

11:5–45 These verses describe the dynastic histories of the Ptolemies in Egypt (the king of the south) and the Seleucids in Syria (the king of the north), the two divisions of the Hellenistic empire that were of interest to the author (v. 6). Verses 10–20 describe the struggle between the two kingdoms for the control of Palestine; the Seleucids were eventually victorious.

11:6 The marriage of Antiochus II Theos and Berenice of Egypt about 250 B.C., which ended in tragedy.

11:11 The battle of Raphia (217 B.C.), in which Egypt defeated Syria.

11:13 Syria defeated Egypt at the battle of Paneas in 200 B.C. Judea then passed under Syrian rule.

11:15 The siege of Sidon after the battle of Paneas.

11:17 Antiochus III, the Great, betrothed his daughter to Ptolemy Epiphanes in 197 B.C.

11:18 The Roman general Scipio defeated Antiochus at Magnesia in 190 B.C.

11:20 Seleucus IV, who sent Heliodorus to Jerusalem (cf. 2 Mc 3).

11:21 Here begins the career of Antiochus IV Epiphanes.

11:22 **The prince of the covenant**: the high priest Onias III, who was murdered.

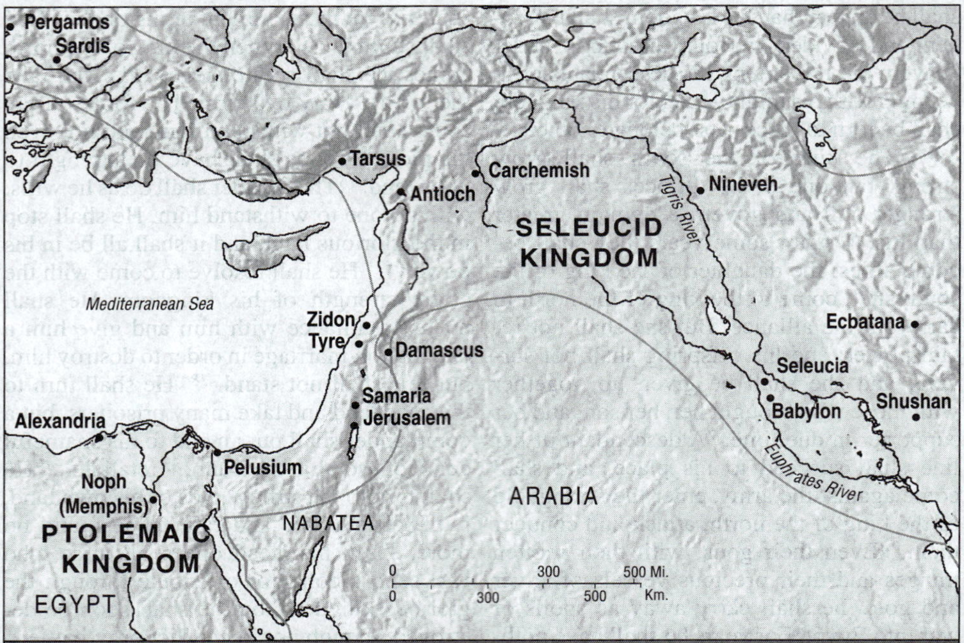

The Ptolemaic and Seleucid Kingdoms

devised against him. 26Even his table companions shall seek to destroy him, his army
shall be overwhelmed, and many shall be
struck down. 27The two kings, resolved on
evil, shall sit at table together and exchange
lies, but they shall have no success, because
the appointed end is not yet.
28"He* shall turn back toward his land
with great riches, his mind set against the
holy covenant; he shall take action and return to his land. 29At the time appointed he
shall come again to the south, but this time it
shall not be as before. 30When ships of the
Kittim* confront him, he shall lose heart and
retreat. Then he shall rage against the holy
covenant and take action; he shall again favor those who forsake the holy covenant.
31Armed forces shall rise at his command
and defile the sanctuary stronghold, abolishing the daily sacrifice and setting up the desolating abomination. 32By his deceit he shall
make some who were disloyal forsake the
covenant; but those who remain loyal to
their God shall take strong action. 33Those
with insight among the people shall instruct
the many; though for a time the sword,
flames, exile, and plunder will cause them to
stumble. 34When they stumble, they will be
helped,* but only a little; many shall join
them, but out of treachery. 35Some of those
with insight shall stumble so that they may
be tested, refined, and purified, until the end
time which is still appointed to come.
36"The king shall do as he wills, exalting
himself and making himself greater than any
god; he shall utter dreadful blasphemies
against the God of gods. He shall prosper
only till the wrath is finished, for what is determined must take place. 37He shall have no
regard for the gods of his ancestors or for the

11:28 He: the king of the north, probably Antiochus IV.

11:30 Kittim: originally this word meant Cypriots or other westerners. It is sometimes used for the Greeks (1 Mc 1:1). Here it refers to the Romans, who forced Antiochus to withdraw from Egypt during his second campaign there.

11:34 Helped: this may be a reference to the Maccabean revolt. The apocalyptic author expects deliverance from God and has little regard for human efforts. In fact, the Maccabees routed the Syrian troops, recaptured Jerusalem, purified and rededicated the Temple, and brought to an end the Syrian persecution.

one in whom women delight;* for no god
shall he have regard, because he shall make
himself greater than all. 38 Instead, he shall
give glory to the god of strongholds;* a god
unknown to his ancestors he shall glorify
with gold, silver, precious stones, and other
treasures. 39 He shall act for those who fortify
strongholds, a people of a foreign god,
whom he has recognized. He shall greatly
honor them; he shall make them rule over
the many and distribute the land as a reward.
40* "At the end time the king of the south
shall engage him in battle but the king of the
north shall overwhelm him with chariots and
horsemen and a great fleet, passing through
the lands like a flood. 41 He shall enter the
glorious land and many shall fall, except
Edom, Moab, and the chief part of Ammon,
which shall escape his power. 42 He shall extend his power over the land, and not even
Egypt shall escape. 43 He shall control the
riches of gold and silver and all the treasures
of Egypt; Libya and Ethiopia shall be in his
entourage. 44 When reports from the east and
the north disturb him, he shall set out with
great fury to destroy many, putting them under the ban. 45 He shall pitch the tents of his
royal pavilion between the sea and the glorious holy mountain, but he shall come to his
end with none to help him.

See RG 338–42

CHAPTER 12

The Resurrection

1 "At that time there shall arise Michael,[z]
the great prince,
guardian of your people;
It shall be a time unsurpassed in distress
since the nation began until that time.
At that time your people shall escape,
everyone who is found written in the
book.*
2 Many of those who sleep*
in the dust of the earth shall awake;
Some to everlasting life,
others to reproach and everlasting
disgrace.[a]
3 But those with insight shall shine brightly
like the splendor of the firmament,
And those who lead the many to justice
shall be like the stars* forever.[b]

4 "As for you, Daniel, keep secret the message and seal the book until the end time;
many shall wander aimlessly and evil shall
increase."
5 I, Daniel, looked and saw two others, one
standing on either bank of the river. 6 One of
them said to the man clothed in linen, who
was upstream, "How long shall it be to the
end of these appalling things?" 7 The man
clothed in linen,[c] who was upstream, lifted
his hands to heaven; and I heard him swear
by him who lives forever that it should be for
a time, two times, and half a time;* and that,
when the power of the destroyer of the holy
people was brought to an end, all these
things should end. 8 I heard, but I did not understand; so I asked, "My lord, what follows
this?" 9 "Go, Daniel," he said, "because the
words are to be kept secret and sealed until
the end time. 10 Many shall be refined, purified, and tested, but the wicked shall prove
wicked; the wicked shall have no understanding, but those with insight shall.
11* From the time that the daily sacrifice is
abolished and the desolating abomination is

11:37 The one in whom women delight: Tammuz. Antiochus favored the cult of Zeus. Daniel takes this to imply the neglect of all other gods, although this does not appear to have been the case.

11:38 The god of strongholds: the god worshiped in the fortress Akra, which Antiochus established in Jerusalem.

11:40–45 In these concluding verses, the events described no longer correspond to the history of the Maccabean period. Daniel imagines the death of Antiochus on the model of Gog in Ez 38–39. Antiochus actually died in Persia.

12:1 Written in the book: cf. 10:21.

12:2 Many of those who sleep: Daniel does not envisage the universal resurrection as later developed. Two groups are distinguished, one that rises to eternal life, the other to reproach and disgrace. Then "those with insight" (11:33–35) are singled out for special honor.

12:3 Like the stars: like the heavenly host, or angels. Cf. Mt 22:30.

12:7 A time, two times, and half a time: see note on 7:25.

12:11 The specific numbers of days given in vv. 11–12 represent attempts to calculate the precise duration of the three and a half years. Most probably, when the first date (1,290 days) passed, the author attempted another calculation. Another, earlier calculation is preserved in 8:14. It is noteworthy, however, that the contradictory numbers were allowed to stand in the text; this is a reminder that it is not possible to calculate a precise date for God's judgment; cf. Mk 13:32.

z: Rev 12:7. *a:* Is 66:24; Mt 25:46; Jn 5:29. *b:* Wis 3:7. *c:* Rev 10:5–6.

set up, there shall be one thousand two hundred and ninety days. [12]Blessed are they who have patience and persevere for the one thousand three hundred and thirty-five days. [13]Go, take your rest, you shall rise for your reward at the end of days."

III. Appendix: Susanna, Bel, and the Dragon*

CHAPTER 13

See RG 342–43

Susanna. [1]In Babylon there lived a man named Joakim, [2]who married a very beautiful and God-fearing woman, Susanna, the daughter of Hilkiah; [3]her parents were righteous and had trained their daughter according to the law of Moses. [4]Joakim was very rich and he had a garden near his house. The Jews had recourse to him often because he was the most respected of them all.

[5]That year, two elders of the people were appointed judges, of whom the Lord said, "Lawlessness has come out of Babylon, that is, from the elders who were to govern the people as judges." [6]These men, to whom all brought their cases, frequented the house of Joakim. [7]When the people left at noon, Susanna used to enter her husband's garden for a walk. [8]When the elders saw her enter every day for her walk, they began to lust for her. [9]They perverted their thinking; they would not allow their eyes to look to heaven, and did not keep in mind just judgments. [10]Though both were enamored of her, they did not tell each other their trouble, [11]for they were ashamed to reveal their lustful desire to have her. [12]Day by day they watched eagerly for her. [13]One day they said to each other, "Let us be off for home, it is time for the noon meal." So they went their separate ways. [14]But both turned back and arrived at the same spot. When they asked each other the reason, they admitted their lust, and then they agreed to look for an occasion when they could find her alone.

[15]One day, while they were waiting for the right moment, she entered as usual, with two maids only, wanting to bathe in the garden, for the weather was warm. [16]Nobody else was there except the two elders, who had hidden themselves and were watching her. [17]"Bring me oil and soap," she said to the maids, "and shut the garden gates while I bathe." [18]They did as she said; they shut the garden gates and left by the side gate to fetch what she had ordered, unaware that the elders were hidden inside.

[19]As soon as the maids had left, the two old men got up and ran to her. [20]"Look," they said, "the garden doors are shut, no one can see us, and we want you. So give in to our desire, and lie with us. [21]If you refuse, we will testify against you that a young man was here with you and that is why you sent your maids away."

[22]"I am completely trapped," Susanna groaned. "If I yield, it will be my death; if I refuse, I cannot escape your power. [23]Yet it is better for me not to do it and to fall into your power than to sin before the Lord." [24]Then Susanna screamed, and the two old men also shouted at her, [25]as one of them ran to open the garden gates. [26]When the people in the house heard the cries from the garden, they rushed in by the side gate to see what had happened to her. [27]At the accusations of the old men, the servants felt very much ashamed, for never had any such thing been said about Susanna.

[28]When the people came to her husband Joakim the next day, the two wicked old men also came, full of lawless intent to put Susanna to death. [29]Before the people they ordered: "Send for Susanna, the daughter of Hilkiah, the wife of Joakim." When she was sent for, [30]she came with her parents, children and all her relatives. [31]Susanna, very delicate and beautiful, [32]was veiled; but those transgressors of the law ordered that she be exposed so as to sate themselves with her beauty. [33]All her companions and the onlookers were weeping.

[34]In the midst of the people the two old

13:1–14:42 The short stories in these two chapters exist now only in Greek and other translations, but probably were first composed in Hebrew or Aramaic. They were never part of the Hebrew-Aramaic Book of Daniel, or of the Hebrew Bible. They are excluded from the Protestant canon of Scripture, but the Catholic Church has always included them among the inspired writings; they existed in the Septuagint, which was used as its Bible by the early church.

men rose up and laid their hands on her head.
[35]As she wept she looked up to heaven, for
she trusted in the Lord wholeheartedly. [36]The
old men said, "As we were walking in the
garden alone, this woman entered with two
servant girls, shut the garden gates and sent
the servant girls away. [37]A young man, who
was hidden there, came and lay with her.
[38]When we, in a corner of the garden, saw
this lawlessness, we ran toward them. [39]We
saw them lying together, but the man we
could not hold, because he was stronger than
we; he opened the gates and ran off. [40]Then
we seized this one and asked who the young
man was, [41]but she refused to tell us. We testify to this." The assembly believed them,
since they were elders and judges of the people, and they condemned her to death.

[42]But Susanna cried aloud: "Eternal God,
you know what is hidden and are aware of
all things before they come to be: [43]you
know that they have testified falsely against
me. Here I am about to die, though I have
done none of the things for which these men
have condemned me."

[44]The Lord heard her prayer. [45]As she was
being led to execution, God stirred up the
holy spirit of a young boy named Daniel,
[46]and he cried aloud: "I am innocent of this
woman's blood." [47]All the people turned and
asked him, "What are you saying?" [48]He
stood in their midst and said, "Are you such
fools, you Israelites, to condemn a daughter
of Israel without investigation and without
clear evidence? [49]Return to court, for they
have testified falsely against her."

[50]Then all the people returned in haste. To
Daniel the elders said, "Come, sit with us
and inform us, since God has given you the
prestige of old age." [51]But he replied, "Separate these two far from one another, and I
will examine them."

[52]After they were separated from each
other, he called one of them and said: "How
you have grown evil with age! Now have
your past sins come to term: [53]passing unjust
sentences, condemning the innocent, and
freeing the guilty,[d] although the Lord says,
'The innocent and the just you shall not put to
death.' [54]Now, then, if you were a witness, tell
me under what tree you saw them together."
[55]"Under a mastic tree,"* he answered. "Your
fine lie has cost you your head," said Daniel;
"for the angel of God has already received the
sentence from God and shall split you in
two." [56]Putting him to one side, he ordered
the other one to be brought. "Offspring of Canaan, not of Judah," Daniel said to him,
"beauty has seduced you, lust has perverted
your heart. [57]This is how you acted with the
daughters of Israel, and in their fear they
yielded to you; but a daughter of Judah did
not tolerate your lawlessness. [58]Now, then,
tell me under what tree you surprised them together." [59]"Under an oak," he said. "Your fine
lie has cost you also your head," said Daniel;
"for the angel of God waits with a sword to
cut you in two so as to destroy you both."

[60]The whole assembly cried aloud, blessing God who saves those who hope in him.
[61]They rose up against the two old men, for
by their own words Daniel had convicted
them of bearing false witness.[e] They condemned them to the fate they had planned
for their neighbor: [62]in accordance with the
law of Moses they put them to death. Thus
was innocent blood spared that day.

[63]Hilkiah and his wife praised God for
their daughter Susanna, with Joakim her
husband and all her relatives, because she
was found innocent of any shameful deed.
[64]And from that day onward Daniel was
greatly esteemed by the people.

CHAPTER 14

See RG 342–43

Bel and the Dragon.* [1]After King
Astyages* was gathered to his ancestors, Cyrus the Persian succeeded to his kingdom.

13:55–59 The contrast between the mastic tree, which is small, and the majestic oak emphasizes the contradiction between the statements of the two elders. In the Greek text there is a play on words between the names of these two trees and the mortal punishment decreed by Daniel for the elders. The mastic tree (*schinon*) sounds like the verb "to split" (*schisai*). The oak tree (*prinon*) suggests a play on *poisai* (to saw).

14:1–22 In chap. 14, readings in the Septuagint differ markedly from those in Theodotion, which is followed here. See individual notes on 1–3a, 10–11, 12–14, 15–17 and 21–22; the translation is that of Collins, *Daniel*, pp. 405ff, with brackets indicating additions to the Septuagint according to Collins.

14:1–3a These verses in the Septuagint Greek text read: "From the prophecy of Habakkuk, son of Joshua, of the tribe

d: Ex 23:7. *e:* Dt 19:18–19.

2 Daniel was a companion of the king and
was held in higher honor than any of the
Friends of the King. 3 The Babylonians had
an idol called Bel,* and every day they provided for it six bushels of fine flour, forty
sheep, and six measures of wine. 4 The king
revered it and went every day to worship it;
but Daniel worshiped only his God. 5 When
the king asked him, "Why do you not worship Bel?" Daniel replied, "Because I do not
revere idols made with hands, but only the
living God who made heaven and earth and
has dominion over all flesh." 6 Then the king
continued, "You do not think Bel is a living
god? Do you not see how much he eats and
drinks every day?" 7 Daniel began to laugh.
"Do not be deceived, O king," he said; "it is
only clay inside and bronze outside; it has
never eaten or drunk anything." 8 Enraged,
the king called his priests and said to them,
"Unless you tell me who it is that consumes
these provisions, you shall die. But if you
can show that Bel consumes them, Daniel
shall die for blaspheming Bel." 9 Daniel said
to the king, "Let it be as you say!"

There were seventy priests of Bel, besides
their wives and children. 10* When the king
went with Daniel into the temple of Bel,
11 the priests of Bel said, "See, we are going
to leave. You, O king, set out the food and
prepare the wine; then shut the door and seal
it with your ring. 12* If you do not find that
Bel has eaten it all when you return in the
morning, we are to die; otherwise Daniel
shall die for his lies against us." 13 They were
not perturbed, because under the table they
had made a secret entrance through which
they always came in to consume the food.
14 After they departed the king set the food
before Bel, while Daniel ordered his servants to bring some ashes, which they scattered through the whole temple; the king
alone was present. Then they went outside,
sealed the closed door with the king's ring,
and departed. 15* The priests entered that
night as usual, with their wives and children,
and they ate and drank everything.

16 Early the next morning, the king came
with Daniel. 17 "Are the seals unbroken,
Daniel?" he asked. And Daniel answered,
"They are unbroken, O king." 18 As soon as
he had opened the door, the king looked at
the table and cried aloud, "You are great, O
Bel; there is no deceit in you." 19* But Daniel laughed and kept the king from entering.
He said, "Look at the floor and consider
whose footprints these are." 20 "I see the
footprints of men, women, and children!"
said the king. 21* In his wrath the king arrested the priests, their wives, and their children. They showed him the secret door by
which they used to enter to consume what
was on the table. 22 The king put them to
death, and handed Bel over to Daniel, who
destroyed it and its temple.

23 There was a great dragon* which the

of Levi. [2] There was a certain man, a priest, whose name was Daniel, son of Abal, a companion of the king of Babylon. [3] There was an idol, Bel, which the Babylonians revered, . . ." This may represent an earlier form of the story, before it was attached to the Book of Daniel. **King Astyages**: the last of the Median kings, defeated by Cyrus in 550 B.C. This story preserves the fiction of a successive Median and Persian rule of Babylon.

14:3 Bel: see note on 4:5.

14:10–11 These verses in the Septuagint Greek text read: "(Now, there were seventy priests of Bel, apart from women and children.) They led the king to the idol shrine. [11] The food was set out in the presence of the king and of Daniel, and mixed wine was brought in and set before Bel. Daniel said, 'You yourself see that these things are laid out, O king. You, therefore, seal the door of temple when it is closed.' [The word pleased the king.]"

14:12–14 Theodotion's vv. 12–13 and 14's "After they departed the king set the food before Bel" are lacking in the Septuagint Greek text, which continues vv. 15–17 from v. 11 as follows: "Then Daniel commanded his attendants to make everyone go out from the temple and sprinkle the whole temple with ashes, unknown to anyone outside. Then he ordered them to apply the seal with the king's ring [and the seals of certain illustrious priests, and so it was done]."

14:15–17 These verses in the Septuagint Greek text read: "[15] On the next day they came to the place. But the priests of Bel had entered through false doors and had eaten all that was set forth for Bel and drunk the wine. Daniel said, 'See whether your seals remain, O priests, and you, O king, see that nothing has happened that seems improper to you.' They found the seal as it had been, and they removed the seal."

14:19 Note that here the king seems unaware of Daniel's ruse.

14:21–22 These verses in the Septuagint Greek text read: "[21] And he went to the house where the priests had come, and he found Bel's food and the wine, and Daniel showed the king the false doors through which the priests entered and consumed what had been set before Bel. [22] The king led them out of the temple of Bel and gave them over to Daniel. He gave Daniel what was expended on him and destroyed Bel."

14:23 Dragon: or "serpent," and see v. 27. Sacred snakes

Babylonians revered. 24 The king said to
Daniel, "You cannot deny that this is a living
god, so worship it." 25 But Daniel answered,
"I worship the Lord, my God, for he is the
living God. 26 Give me permission, O king,
and I will kill this dragon without sword or
club." "I give you permission," the king
said. 27 Then Daniel took some pitch, fat, and
hair; these he boiled together and made into
cakes. He put them into the mouth of the
dragon, and when the dragon ate them, he
burst. "This," he said, "is what you revered."
28 When the Babylonians heard this, they
were angry and turned against the king.
"The king has become a Jew," they said; "he
has destroyed Bel, killed the dragon, and put
the priests to death." 29 They went to the king
and demanded: "Hand Daniel over to us, or
we will kill you and your family." 30 When
he saw himself threatened with violence, the
king was forced to hand Daniel over to them.
31 They threw Daniel into a lions' den,*
where he remained six days. 32 In the den
were seven lions. Two carcasses and two
sheep had been given to them daily, but now
they were given nothing, so that they would
devour Daniel.
33 The prophet Habakkuk was in Judea. He
mixed some bread in a bowl with the stew he
had boiled, and was going to bring it to the
reapers in the field, 34 when an angel of the
Lord told him, "Take the meal you have to
Daniel in the lions' den at Babylon." 35 But
Habakkuk answered, "Sir, I have never seen
Babylon, and I do not know the den!" 36 The
angel of the Lord seized him by the crown of
his head and carried him by the hair;[f] with
the speed of the wind, he set him down in
Babylon above the den. 37 "Daniel, Daniel,"
cried Habakkuk, "take the meal God has
sent you." 38 "You have remembered me, O
God," said Daniel; "you have not forsaken
those who love you." 39 So Daniel ate, but the
angel of God at once brought Habakkuk
back to his own place.
40 On the seventh day the king came to
mourn for Daniel. As he came to the den and
looked in, there was Daniel, sitting there.
41 The king cried aloud, "You are great, O
Lord, the God of Daniel, and there is no
other besides you!" 42 He brought Daniel out,
but those who had tried to destroy him he
threw into the den, and they were devoured
in a moment before his eyes.

are well attested in the ancient world (e.g., in the temple of the god of healing Asclepius at Epidaurus), though evidence for their veneration in Babylon is doubtful.

14:31 A lions' den: this story provides a different account from chap. 6 as to why Daniel was associated with the lions' den.

f: Ez 8:3.

See RG 346–49

The Book of Hosea

Hosea, a prophet from the Northern Kingdom, preached in his homeland, which he addresses as Israel, Jacob or, frequently, Ephraim. Hosea began his mission in a period of prosperity, the last years of Jeroboam II (783–743 B.C.). This was followed by a period of internal instability, with intrigues at the royal court leading to the assassination of several kings. Hosea witnessed the revival of Assyria, the Syro-Ephraimite war, and the numerous treaties the Israelite kings made with Egypt and Assyria to survive. Hosea's long ministry (ca. 750–725) seems to have ended before the capture of Samaria in 722/721.

The only information the text provides us about the life of Hosea concerns his marriage. Even if we cannot reconstruct what happened exactly, the text as it now stands speaks of three moments in the relationship: first love, separation, reunion. This marriage is a symbol of the covenant between the Lord and Israel. Hosea speaks about the first love, the short period of Israel's loyalty in the desert, which was then followed by a long history of unfaithfulness lasting until his day. Hosea accuses Israel of three crimes in particular. Instead of putting their trust in the Lord alone, the people break the covenant: (1) by counting on their own military strength, (2) by making treaties with foreign powers (Assyria and Egypt), and (3) by running after the Baals, the gods of fertility. Israel thus forgets that the Lord is its strength, its covenant partner, and giver of fertility. This unfaithful behavior will lead to Israel's destruction by Assyria, but God's love will have the last word. The back and forth movement from doom to salvation is typical of the Book of Hosea.

Hosea began the Old Testament tradition of describing the relation between the Lord and Israel in terms of marriage (e.g., Jer 3:1; Ez 16:23; Is 50:1). The New Testament uses the marriage imagery to describe the union between Christ and the Church (e.g., Mk 2:19–20; Eph 5:25).

The Hebrew of the Book of Hosea is challenging to translate, possibly because the text is corrupt or because it is written in a nonstandard dialect of Hebrew. As a result, the English translations of the book sometimes offer very different readings of the same passage.

The book, which opens with a superscription (1:1) and ends with a final challenge (14:10), is divided into two major parts:

I. The Prophet's Marriage and Its Symbolism (1:2–3:5)

II. Israel's Guilt, Punishment, and Restoration (4:1–14:9)

CHAPTER 1

See RG 346–47

1* The word of the LORD that came to Hosea son of Beeri, in the days of Uzziah, Jotham,
Ahaz, Hezekiah, kings of Judah, and in the days
of Jeroboam, son of Joash, king of Israel.*

I. The Prophet's Marriage and Its Symbolism

Marriage of Hosea and Gomer. 2When the
LORD began to speak with Hosea, the LORD
said to Hosea: Go, get for yourself a woman
of prostitution* and children of prostitution,
for the land prostitutes itself,[a] turning away
from the LORD.

3So he went and took Gomer, daughter of
Diblaim; and she conceived and bore him a
son. 4Then the LORD said to him: Give him
the name "Jezreel,"* for in a little while I
will punish the house of Jehu for the bloodshed at Jezreel and bring to an end the kingdom of the house of Israel; 5on that day I will
break the bow of Israel in the valley of Jezreel.

6She conceived again and bore a daughter.
The LORD said to him: Give her the name
"Not-Pitied,"* for I will no longer feel pity
for the house of Israel: rather, I will utterly
abhor them. 7* Yet for the house of Judah I
will feel pity; I will save them by the LORD,
their God; but I will not save them by bow or
sword, by warfare, by horses or horsemen.[b]

8After she weaned Not-Pitied, she conceived and bore a son. 9Then the LORD said:
Give him the name "Not-My-People,"* for
you are not my people, and I am not "I am"
for you.

1:1–3 This section begins with Hosea's marriage to Gomer, which symbolizes Israel's relationship to God. Hence the symbolic names of Hosea's children and their later renaming (1:2–9; 2:1–3). The prophet foresees God's punishment for the unfaithful covenant partner, but knows that God's last word is always hope (2:4–25).

1:1 This superscription is from a Judean editor, who lists the kings of Judah in the south first, even though Hosea preached in the Northern Kingdom of Israel.

1:2 A woman of prostitution: this does not necessarily mean that Gomer was a prostitute when Hosea married her; the verse describes the event in its final consequences. Prostitution here may refer to Gomer's participation in the worship of other gods.

1:4 Give him the name "Jezreel": the names of the three children are symbolic, and predict God's punishment in a crescendo. These names are frequently repeated in chaps. 1–2. **Jezreel**: (lit., "God will sow") the strategic valley in northern Israel where Jehu brought the dynasty of Omri to an end through bloodshed (2 Kgs 9–10). Jeroboam II was the next to the last king of the house of Jehu. The prophecy in this verse of the end of the house of Jehu was fulfilled by the murder of Zechariah, son of Jeroboam II (2 Kgs 15:8–10).

1:6 "Not-Pitied": in Hebrew *lo-ruhama*.

1:7 Probably written by a later editor when the prophecies of Hosea circulated in the south, after the dissolution of the Northern Kingdom had occurred. The second part of the verse emphasizes the power of the Lord, who needs no human agents to fulfill the divine will. It may refer to the deliverance of Jerusalem from the siege of Sennacherib in 701 (2 Kgs 19:35–37).

1:9 "Not-My-People": in Hebrew *lo-ammi*. **I am not "I am" for you**: a reference to the divine name revealed to Moses, "I am" (Ex 3:14). This reversal of the relationship marks the end of the covenant (Ex 6:7).

a: Jer 2:20, 23; Ez 23:3. *b:* Zec 4:6.

See RG 346–47

CHAPTER 2

1* The number of the Israelites
will be like the sand of the sea,
which can be neither measured nor counted.[c]
Instead of being told,
"You are Not-My-People,"
They will be called,
"Children of the living God."[d]
2 Then the people of Judah and of Israel
will gather together;
They will appoint for themselves one head
and rise up from the land;
great indeed shall be the day of Jezreel!
3 Say to your brothers, "My People,"
and to your sisters, "Pitied."

*The Lord and Israel His Spouse**

4 Accuse your mother, accuse!
for she is not my wife,
and I am not her husband.*
Let her remove her prostitution from her face.
her adultery from between her breasts,
5 Or I will strip her naked,*
leaving her as on the day of her birth;
I will make her like the wilderness,
make her like an arid land,
and let her die of thirst.
6 I will have no pity on her children,
for they are children of prostitution.
7 Yes, their mother has prostituted herself;
she who conceived them has acted shamefully.
For she said, "I will go after my lovers,*
who give me my bread and my water,
my wool and my flax, my oil and my drink."[e]
8 * Therefore, I will hedge in her way with thorns
and erect a wall against her,
so that she cannot find her paths.
9 If she runs after her lovers, she will not overtake them;
if she seeks them she will not find them.
Then she will say,
"I will go back to my first husband,
for I was better off then than now."[f]
10 She did not know
that it was I who gave her
the grain, the wine, and the oil,
I who lavished upon her silver,
and gold, which they used for Baal,*
11 Therefore I will take back my grain in its time,
and my wine in its season;
I will snatch away my wool and my flax,
which were to cover her nakedness.
12 Now I will lay bare her shame
in full view of her lovers,[g]
and no one can deliver her out of my hand.[h]
13 I will put an end to all her joy,
her festivals, her new moons, her sabbaths—
all her seasonal feasts.
14 I will lay waste her vines and fig trees,
of which she said, "These are the fees
my lovers have given me";
I will turn them into rank growth
and wild animals shall devour them.

2:1–3 These verses abruptly reverse the tone of the judgments of 1:2–9 with words of hope for the covenant people: the name Jezreel is given a positive interpretation in contrast to its negative meaning in 1:4; the child named "Not-Pitied" in 1:6 is renamed "Pitied" in 2:3; the child named "Not-My-People" is renamed "My People." The reversal of these names occurs again in 2:25.

2:4–25 The section contains three oracles of doom (vv. 4–6, 7–9, 10–15), a transition (vv. 16–17), and three oracles of salvation (vv. 18–19, 20–22, 23–25).

2:4 The Lord speaks of Israel, still using the example of Hosea's wife.

2:5 I will strip her naked: it was the husband's responsibility to provide food and clothing for his wife (Ex 21:10) and now, because of her adultery, he takes back his support.

2:7 My lovers: even though Israel had experienced the Lord as the God of the desert, covenant and conquest, the people were inclined to turn to the local fertility deities, the Baals, who were believed to be responsible for agricultural success. They easily forgot that the Lord provides them with everything (v. 10; cf. Dt 7:13), and thus prostituted themselves by worshiping other gods.

2:8 The crop failures sent by the Lord are meant to make Israel see the folly of its ways.

2:10 For Baal: as an offering to Baal or to make statues of Baal.

c: Gn 15:5; 22:17; 32:13. *d:* Rom 9:26–27. *e:* Jer 2:25. *f:* Lk 15:17–18. *g:* Ez 16:37. *h:* Jn 10:29.

15 I will punish her for the days of the Baals,*
for whom she burnt incense,
When she decked herself out with her
rings and her jewelry,
and went after her lovers—
but me she forgot—oracle of the LORD.[i]
16 Therefore,* I will allure her now;
I will lead her into the wilderness[j]
and speak persuasively to her.
17 Then I will give her the vineyards she had,
and the valley of Achor* as a door of
hope.[k]
There she will respond as in the days of
her youth,
as on the day when she came up from
the land of Egypt.

18 On that day—oracle of the LORD—
You shall call me "My husband,"
and you shall never again call me "My
baal."*
19 I will remove from her mouth the names
of the Baals;
they shall no longer be mentioned by
their name.
20 I will make a covenant for them on that
day,[l]
with the wild animals,
With the birds of the air,
and with the things that crawl on the
ground.
Bow and sword and warfare
I will destroy from the land,
and I will give them rest in safety.
21 I will betroth you to me forever:
I will betroth you to me with* justice
and with judgment,
with loyalty and with compassion;
22 I will betroth you to me with fidelity,
and you shall know the LORD.
23 On that day I will respond—oracle of the
LORD—
I will respond to the heavens,
and they will respond to the earth;
24 The earth will respond to the grain, and
wine, and oil,
and these will respond to Jezreel.
25 I will sow her for myself in the land,
and I will have pity on Not-Pitied.
I will say to Not-My-People, "You are
my people,"[m]
and he will say, "My God!"

CHAPTER 3

See RG 346–47

Hosea and His Wife Reunited* 1 Again the LORD said to me:

Go, love a woman
who is loved by her spouse but
commits adultery;
Just as the LORD loves the Israelites,
though they turn to other gods
and love raisin cakes.*

2* So I acquired her for myself for fifteen

2:15 The days of the Baals: feast days of the Baal cult (v. 13), or the whole period of Israel's apostasy.

2:16 Therefore: this word in Hebrew normally introduces an oracle of doom; here, surprisingly, it leads to hope. **Allure**: as though seducing a virgin (Ex 22:15–16). Ordinarily this word connotes deception (Jgs 14:15; 16:5; 1 Kgs 22:20–22).

2:17 Valley of Achor: lit., valley of trouble (Jos 7:26). Here this valley becomes a valley of hope, a new entry into the promised land.

2:18–19 Baal: the word means "lord, master." It was commonly used by women of their husbands, but it is to be shunned as a title for the Lord because of its association with the fertility gods, the Baals. Many Israelites saw little if any difference between the worship of the Lord and the worship of the Baals, thereby dishonoring the true source of the land's fertility.

2:21–22 Betroth . . . with: the betrothal was the legal moment before cohabitation when the dowry was paid to the father of the bride. In this remarriage the Lord gives the bride price to Israel herself "forever." **Justice . . . judgment**: refer to equity and fairness of conduct. The next two terms, "loyalty" (*hesed*), the steadfast love between the covenant partners, and "compassion," maternal love (cf. 1:6; 2:3, 25) are characteristic of Hosea. **You shall know**: not an abstract but a practical knowledge which means acknowledgment of God's will and obedience to his law (4:1; 5:4; 6:3, 6).

3:1–5 Just as the Lord is ready to take Israel back, Hosea takes his wife back. She must undergo a period of purification, just as Israel must experience purification before the restoration of the covenant relationship.

3:1 Raisin cakes: offerings to the fertility goddess Asherah, the female counterpart of Baal, cf. Jer 7:18; 44:19; Dn 14:5–8.

3:2 Just as the Lord offered a new bride price to Israel (2:21–22), so Hosea offers a new bride price to his wife. He returns to her what he has taken away from her (2:5): "fifteen (shekels) of silver"; "a homer of barley," a unit of dry measurement, which according to the etymology means "a mule load"; and "a lethech of barley," which is a half-homer.

i: Jer 2:32. *j:* Jer 2:2–7. *k:* Jos 7:24–26. *l:* Gn 9:8–11; Ez 34:25; Jb 5:23. *m:* Rom 9:25–26; 1 Pt 2:10.

pieces of silver and a homer and a lethech of barley. [3]Then I said to her:

"You will wait for me for many days;
you will not prostitute yourself
Or belong to any man;
I in turn will wait for you."

[4] * For the Israelites will remain many days
without king or prince,
Without sacrifice or sacred pillar,
without ephod or household gods.
[5] Afterward the Israelites will turn back
and seek the LORD, their God,
and David, their king;* [n]
They will come trembling to the LORD
and to his bounty, in the last days.

II. Israel's Guilt, Punishment, and Restoration

CHAPTER 4

See RG 347–49

*Indictment of Israel**

[1] Hear the word of the LORD, Israelites,
for the LORD has a dispute
with the inhabitants of the land:[o]
There is no fidelity, no loyalty,
no knowledge of God in the land.
[2] Swearing, lying, murder,
stealing and adultery break out;*
bloodshed follows bloodshed.[p]
[3] Therefore the land dries up,
and everything that dwells in it
languishes:
The beasts of the field,
the birds of the air,
and even the fish of the sea perish.[q]

Guilt of Priest and of People

[4] But let no one accuse, let no one rebuke;
with you is my dispute, priest!*
[5] You will stumble in the day,
and the prophet will stumble with you
at night;
I will make an end of your mother.*
[6] My people are ruined for lack of
knowledge!
Since you have rejected knowledge,
I will reject you from serving as my
priest;
Since you have forgotten the law of your
God,
I will also forget your children.
[7] The more they multiplied, the more they
sinned against me,
I will change their glory* into shame.[r]
[8] They feed on the sin of my people,
and are greedy for their iniquity.*
[9] Like people, like priest:[s]
I will punish them for their ways,
and repay them for their deeds.
[10] They will eat but not be satisfied,[t]
they will promote prostitution* but not
increase,
Because they have abandoned the LORD,
devoting themselves
[11] to prostitution.

3:4 Israel will lose its political and cultic institutions. **Sacred pillar**: originally perhaps a phallic symbol, representing Baal. These were also used in Israelite worship (cf. notes on Gn 28:18; Ex 34:13). **Ephod**: an instrument used in consulting the deity (1 Sm 23:6–12; 30:7; cf. notes on Ex 28:6, 15–30). **Household gods**: in Hebrew, *teraphim*; images regarded as the tutelary deities of the household (Gn 31:19; Jgs 17:5; 18:14, 17–18).

3:5 David, their king: the king belonging to the line of David who will restore the Israelite nation (Jer 23:5; Ez 34:23, 24). **The last days**: a future time of transformation.

4:1–3 The introduction to the oracles (chaps. 4–11) which begin with "Hear the word of the Lord" (4:1) and end with "oracle of the Lord" (11:11).

4:2 Similar to the decalogue (Ex 20:1–17; cf. Jer 7:9).

4:4–6 Hosea is particularly severe with the priests in the Northern Kingdom who had led the way in the general apostasy from God's law. The prophets here associated with the priests (v. 5) were doubtless cult prophets; cf. Jer 2:8; 4:9–10; 6:13–14; 23:9–40.

4:5 Your mother: the one who gave life to the priest, understood here as an extension of the punishment to his whole family (Am 7:17), or "mother" taken as a metaphor for the community of Israel, of which the priest is a member (Hos 2:4).

4:7 Their glory: possibly connoting "their children." See 9:11: Is 22:24. Or "Glory" may refer to the Lord in contrast to Ba'al. The Hebrew word for shame, *bosheth*, is often substituted for Ba'al in biblical names. See Ishbaal (Heb. *Ishbosheth*, 2 Sm 2:8, 10, 12, 15) and Meribaal (Heb. *Mephibosheth*, 2 Sm 9:6, 10–13).

4:8 The priest receives part of the sacrifice (Lv 6:19; 7:7).

4:10–11 Prostitution: often a synonym for idolatry. The covenant bond was symbolized as the relationship between husband and wife (see chaps. 1–2). Thus, abandoning the Lord for a foreign god was called prostitution or adultery.

n: Jer 30:9; Ez 34:23. *o:* Is 3:10–15; Mi 6:1–5. *p:* Ex 20:13–17. *q:* Is 24:4–7; Zep 1:2–3. *r:* Jer 2:11; Ps 106:20. *s:* Is 24:2. *t:* Mi 6:14.

Aged wine and new wine
take away understanding.[u]
12 My people consult their piece of wood,*
and their wand makes pronouncements
for them,
For the spirit of prostitution has led them
astray;
they prostitute themselves, forsaking
their God.
13 On the mountaintops they offer sacrifice
and on the hills they burn incense,
Beneath oak and poplar and terebinth,
because of their pleasant shade.*
Therefore your daughters prostitute
themselves,
and your daughters-in-law commit
adultery.
14 I will not punish your daughters for their
prostitution,
nor your daughters-in-law for their
adultery,
Because the men themselves consort
with prostitutes,
and with temple women* they offer
sacrifice!
Thus a people without understanding
comes to ruin.
15 Though you prostitute yourself, Israel,
do not let Judah become guilty!
Do not come to Gilgal,*
do not go up to Beth-aven,[v]
do not swear, "As the Lord lives!"[w]
16 For like a stubborn cow,
Israel is stubborn;
Will the LORD now pasture them,
like lambs in a broad meadow?
17 Ephraim* is bound to idols,
let him alone!
18 * When their drinking is over,
they give themselves to prostitution;[x]
they love shame more than their honor.
19 A wind* has bound them up in its wings;[y]
they shall be ashamed because of their
altars.[z]

CHAPTER 5

See RG 347–49

Guilt of the Religious and Political Leaders

1 Hear this, priests,
Pay attention, house of Israel,
Household of the king, give ear![a]
For you are responsible for
judgment.*
But you have been a snare at Mizpah,*
a net spread upon Tabor,
2 a pit dug deep in Shittim.
Now I will discipline them all.
3 I know Ephraim,
and Israel is not hidden from me:
Now, Ephraim, you have practiced
prostitution,
Israel is defiled.
4 Their deeds do not allow them
to return to their God;[b]
For the spirit of prostitution is in them,
and they do not know the LORD.

4:12 Piece of wood: a derogatory term for an idol. **Wand**: a sacred wooden object, perhaps some kind of staff, used for divination.

4:13 The shrines on the "high places" typically had an altar, a grove of trees, and a stone pillar representing a god (Dt 12:2; Jer 2:20).

4:14 Temple women: plural of Heb. *qedesha*; the exact import of the term is disputed. See notes on Gn 38:21 and Dt 23:18–19.

4:15 Gilgal: close to Jericho (Jos 4:19–20; 5:2–9). **Beth-aven**: (lit., "house of iniquity") Hosea's derogatory term for the sanctuary of Bethel (lit., "house of God"), the major shrine of the Northern Kingdom (10:5, 8; cf. Am 5:5). **As the Lord lives**: a legitimate oath formula (1 Sm 26:10, 16), but unacceptable here because Israel is guilty of religious syncretism and the idolatrous worship of other gods.

4:17 Ephraim: the name of one of the sons of Joseph, son of Jacob (Gn 41:52), also used to designate one of the tribes living in the heartland of the Northern Kingdom. Hosea often uses the name Ephraim to refer to the whole Northern Kingdom of Israel. During the latter part of his ministry, after the Assyrians occupied Galilee, Ephraim was all that remained of Israel.

4:18 Cf. v. 11.

4:19 A wind: (Heb. *ruah*), a metaphor for Israel's addiction to the Baal cult, which is nothing but wind, a "spirit (*ruah*) of prostitution" (v. 12).

5:1 For you . . . judgment: possibly "for you are called to judgment."

5:1–2 Mizpah: several places bear this name; the best known is in Benjamin (1 Sm 7:6, 16; 10:17). Perhaps this is a wordplay on *mishpat*, "justice," "judgment." **Tabor**: the mountain that dominates the valley of Jezreel. **Shittim**: in Transjordan, where Israel committed its first act of idolatry with the Baal of Peor (9:10; cf. Nm 25). At these three places the leaders had misled the people by an idolatrous cult or by an abuse of justice.

u: Is 28:7. *v:* Am 4:4. *w:* Am 8:14. *x:* Am 2:8. *y:* Jer 4:11–12. *z:* Is 1:29. *a:* Mi 3:1. *b:* Jer 13:23.

5 The arrogance of Israel bears witness
against him;
Israel and Ephraim stumble because of
their iniquity,
and Judah stumbles with them.
6 With their flocks and herds they will go
to seek the LORD, but will not find him;[c]
he has withdrawn from them.
7 They have betrayed the LORD,
for they have borne illegitimate children;
Now the new moon* will devour them
together with their fields.

*Political Upheavals**

8 Blow the ram's horn in Gibeah,
the trumpet in Ramah!
Sound the alarm in Beth-aven:[d]
"Look behind you, Benjamin!"*
9 Ephraim shall become a wasteland
on the day of punishment:
Among the tribes of Israel
I announce what is sure to be.
10 The princes of Judah have become
like those who move a boundary line;*[e]
Upon them I will pour out
my wrath like water.
11 Ephraim is oppressed, crushed by
judgment,
for he has willingly gone after filth!*
12 I am like a moth for Ephraim,[f]
like rot for the house of Judah.
13 When Ephraim saw his infirmity,
and Judah his sore,
Ephraim went to Assyria,
and sent to the great king.*[g]
But he cannot heal you,
nor take away your sore.
14 For I am like a lion to Ephraim,
like a young lion to the house of Judah;[h]
It is I who tear the prey and depart,
I carry it away and no one can save it.[i]

Insincere Conversion

15 I will go back to my place
until they make reparation
and seek my presence.
In their affliction, they shall look for me.[j]

CHAPTER 6

See RG 347–49

1 "Come, let us return to the
LORD,[k]
For it is he who has torn, but he will
heal us;
he has struck down, but he will bind
our wounds.
2 He will revive us after two days;
on the third day* he will raise us up,[l]
to live in his presence.
3 Let us know, let us strive to know the
LORD;
as certain as the dawn is his coming.
He will come to us like the rain,
like spring rain that waters the earth."[m]
4 What can I do with you, Ephraim?
What can I do with you, Judah?
Your loyalty is like morning mist,
like the dew that disappears early.
5 For this reason I struck them down
through the prophets,
I killed them by the words of my
mouth;*[n]

5:7 New moon: normally a feast day of joy (2:13), but, because of infidelity, it will be a day of destruction.

5:8–14 This passage describes political and military conflict between Judah and Israel. Perhaps some allusion is made to the Syro-Ephraimite war of 735–734 B.C., when a coalition of Arameans and Israelites attempted to dethrone the king of Judah (2 Kgs 16:5; Is 7:1–9). Judah repulsed the attempt with the aid of Assyria, and the latter devastated both Aram and Israel.

5:8 A vision of invasion, from Gibeah and Ramah in northern Judah, into Israel.

5:10 Move a boundary line: invasion by Judah (v. 8) is compared to a case of social injustice (Dt 19:14; 27:17; Prv 23:10–11).

5:11 Filth: Ephraim's reliance on foreign nations and their gods.

5:13 Ephraim went . . . king: in 738 the Israelite king Menahem had to pay tribute to the Assyrian king Tiglath-pileser III, whose vassal he became (2 Kgs 15:19–20). Under the threat of the Syro-Ephraimite invasion King Ahaz of Judah also submitted to Tiglath-pileser (2 Kgs 16:7–9). **Great king**: Heb. *melek-yarev*; may be a proper name: King Yarev, but unknown; or "the defender king": irony about the great king of Assyria (see note on 10:6).

6:2 After two days; on the third day: presumptuous Israel expects that soon God will renew them (cf. Ez 37).

6:5 The word of God proclaimed by the prophets is effective, it accomplished what it promised: punishment.

c: Is 55:6; Jer 29:13; Am 5:4–6; 8:12; Jn 7:34. *d:* Jer 4:5; Jl 2:1. *e:* Dt 19:14; 27:17. *f:* Is 50:9. *g:* 2 Kgs 15:19–20; 16:7–9. *h:* Is 5:29; Am 1:2; 3:12. *i:* Dt 32:39. *j:* Jer 29:13; Ps 78:34. *k:* Lam 3:40. *l:* Lk 24:7, 46; 1 Cor 15:4. *m:* Dt 11:14; Ps 72:6. *n:* Is 11:4; 49:2; Jer 5:14; Heb 4:12–13.

my judgment shines forth like the
light.
6 For it is loyalty that I desire, not
sacrifice,
and knowledge of God rather than
burnt offerings.[o]

Further Crimes of Israel

7 But they, at Adam,* violated the
covenant;
there they betrayed me.

8 Gilead* is a city of evildoers,
tracked with blood.
9 Like brigands lying in wait
is the band of priests.
They murder on the road to Shechem,*
indeed they commit a monstrous
crime.
10 In the house of Israel I have seen a
horrible thing:
there is found Ephraim's prostitution,
Israel is defiled.
11 For you also, Judah,
a harvest* has been appointed!

CHAPTER 7

See RG 347–49

When I would have restored the
fortunes of my people,
1 when I would have healed Israel,
The guilt of Ephraim was revealed,
the wickedness of Samaria:
They practiced falsehood.
Thieves break in,
bandits roam outside.
2 Yet they do not call to mind
that I remember all their wickedness.[p]
Now their crimes surround them,
present to my sight.[q]

*Israel's Domestic Politics**

3 With their wickedness they make the
king rejoice,
the princes too, with their treacherous
deeds.
4 They are all adulterers,*
like a blazing oven,
Which the baker quits stoking,
after the dough's kneading until its
rising.
5 On the day of our king,
they made the princes sick with
poisoned wine;
he extended his hand to the scoffers.
6 For they draw near in ambush
with their hearts like an oven.
All the night their anger sleeps;
in the morning it flares like a blazing
fire.
7 They are all heated like ovens,
and consume their rulers.
All their kings have fallen;
none of them calls upon me.

Israel's Foreign Politics

8 Ephraim is mixed with the nations,*
Ephraim is an unturned cake.
9 Strangers have consumed his strength,
but he does not know it;[r]
Gray hairs are strewn on his head,
but he takes no notice of it.
10 The arrogance of Israel bears witness
against him;
yet they do not return to the LORD,
their God,
nor seek him, despite all this.[s]
11 Ephraim is like a dove,
silly and senseless;
They call upon Egypt,

6:7 At Adam: the violation of the covenant at Adam is mentioned nowhere else in the Bible. The place Adam, the location of which is unknown, may be referred to in Jos 3:16.

6:8 Gilead: city in Transjordan (Gn 31:46–48; 2 Kgs 15:25).

6:9 Shechem: an important ancient religious and political center (Jos 24).

6:11 Harvest: God's judgment, when Judah will reap what it has sown.

7:3–7 This passage perhaps refers to a conspiracy at the royal court. Between the death of Jeroboam II (743 B.C.) and the fall of Samaria (722/721), nearly all the kings were murdered (2 Kgs 15:10, 14, 25, 30).

7:4 Adulterers: the unfaithful nobles who kill the king. Their passion is compared to the fire of the oven. The point of the metaphor is that, like this oven whose fire is always ready to blaze up again, the conspirators are always ready for rebellion.

7:8 Is mixed with the nations: the people reject exclusive allegiance to the Lord, and they now try to find their salvation in alliances with foreign nations. **An unturned cake**: burnt on one side, but not baked at all on the other, and thus worthless.

o: 1 Sm 15:22; Am 5:22–24; Mi 6:6–8; Eccl 4:17; Mt 9:13; 12:7. *p:* Ps 10:11. *q:* Prv 5:21–22. *r:* Jer 5:3; Rev 3:17. *s:* Is 9:12; Am 4:6.

they go to Assyria.
12 When they go I will spread my net
around them,
like birds in the air I will bring them
down.[t]
I will chastise them when I hear of
their assembly.
13 Woe to them, for they have strayed
from me!
Ruin to them, for they have rebelled
against me!
Though I wished to redeem them,
they spoke lies against me.
14 They have not cried to me from their
hearts
when they wailed upon their beds;
For wheat and wine they lacerated
themselves;*
they rebelled against me.
15 Though I trained and strengthened their
arms,
yet they devised evil against me.
16 They have again become useless,
they have been like a treacherous bow.[u]
Their princes shall fall by the sword
because of the insolence of their
tongues;
thus they shall be mocked in the land
of Egypt.

See RG 347–49

CHAPTER 8

Corruption of Cult, Domestic and Foreign Politics

1 Put the trumpet to your lips![v]
One like an eagle* is over the house of
the LORD!
Because they have violated my covenant,
and rebelled against my law,
2 They cry out to me,
"My God! We know you!"
3 But Israel has rejected what is good;
the enemy* shall pursue him.
4 * They made kings, but not by my
authority;
they established princes, but without
my knowledge.
With their silver and gold
they made idols for themselves,
to their own destruction.
5 He has rejected your calf,* Samaria![w]
My wrath is kindled against them;
How long will they be incapable of
innocence
in Israel?
6 An artisan made it,
it is no god at all.[x]
The calf of Samaria
will be dashed to pieces.

7 When they sow the wind,
they will reap the whirlwind;[y]
The stalk of grain that forms no head
can yield no flour;
Even if it could,
strangers would swallow it.
8 Israel is swallowed up;
now they are among the nations,
like a useless vessel.
9 For they went up to Assyria—*
a wild ass off on its own—
Ephraim bargained for lovers.[z]
10 Even though they bargain with the
nations,
I will now gather them* together;
They will soon succumb
under the burden of king and princes.

11 * When Ephraim made many altars to
expiate sin,
they became altars for sinning.

7:14 Lacerated themselves: a ritual to obtain a good harvest from Baal (2:7–10; 1 Kgs 18:28; Jer 16:6; 41:5). This practice was forbidden (Lv 19:28; Dt 14:1).

8:1 Eagle: perhaps an image for Tiglath-pileser III of Assyria, who overran the land of Israel in 733 B.C. (Jer 48:40; 49:22; Ez 17:3).

8:3 Enemy: Assyria.

8:4 Hosea is not against the monarchy, but against the conspiracies at the royal court (see note on 7:3–7). The king should be chosen by God (1 Kgs 19:15–16).

8:5 Calf: a cultic object introduced by Jeroboam I after the separation of the Northern Kingdom from the Southern Kingdom (1 Kgs 12:26–30; cf. Ex 32).

8:9 They went up to Assyria: a reference to the politics of appealing to Assyria (cf. 5:13; 7:11). There is a play on the Hebrew word for "wild ass" (*pere*) and "Ephraim."

8:10 I will now gather them: for judgment and for deportation.

8:11 The altars had become places of self-serving worship (cf. v. 13).

t: Ez 12:13; 32:3. *u:* Ps 78:57. *v:* Jl 2:1. *w:* 1 Kgs 12:28. *x:* Ex 20:4; 34:17; Is 40:19–20; 44:9–20; Jer 10:1–16. *y:* Jb 4:8; Prv 22:8; 2 Cor 9:6; Gal 6:7–8. *z:* Ez 16:32–34.

12 Though I write for him my many
instructions,
they are considered like a stranger's.
13 They love sacrifice,
they sacrifice meat and eat it,
but the LORD is not pleased with them.[a]
Now he will remember their guilt
and punish their sins;[b]
they shall return to Egypt.* [c]
14 Israel has forgotten his maker[d]
and has built palaces.
Judah, too, has fortified many cities,
but I will send fire upon his cities,
to devour their strongholds.[e]

See RG 347–49

CHAPTER 9

From Days of Celebration to Days of Punishment

1 Do not rejoice, Israel,
do not exult like the nations!
For you have prostituted yourself,
abandoning your God,
loving a prostitute's fee
upon every threshing floor.*
2 Threshing floor and wine press will not
nourish them,
the new wine will fail them.

3 They will not dwell in the LORD's land;
Ephraim will return to Egypt,
and in Assyria they will eat unclean
food.
4 They will not pour libations of wine to
the LORD,
and their sacrifices will not please him.
Their bread will be like mourners'
bread,* [f]
that makes unclean all who eat of it;
Their food will be for their own appetites;
it cannot enter the house of the LORD.

5 What will you do on the festival day,
the day of the LORD's feast?*
6 * When they flee from the devastation,
Egypt will gather them, Memphis will
bury them.
Weeds will overgrow their silver treasures,
and thorns, their tents.

7 They have come, the days of punishment!
they have come, the days of
recompense!
Let Israel know it!
"The prophet is a fool,[g]
the man of the spirit is mad!"
Because your iniquity is great,
great, too, is your hostility.
8 * The watchman of Ephraim, the people
of my God, is the prophet;[h]
yet a fowler's snare is on all his ways,
hostility in the house of his God.
9 They have sunk to the depths of
corruption,
as in the days of Gibeah;* [i]
God will remember their iniquity
and punish their sins.

From Former Glory to a History of Corruption

10 Like grapes in the desert,
I found Israel;
Like the first fruits of the fig tree, its first
to ripen,[j]
I looked on your ancestors.
But when they came to Baal-peor* [k]
and consecrated themselves to the
Shameful One,

8:13 Return to Egypt: to punish their violation of the covenant they will experience a reversal of the exodus.

9:1 Threshing floor: an allusion to harvest festivals in honor of Baal, to whom the Israelites had attributed the fertility of the land; cf. 2:7.

9:4 Mourners' bread: bread eaten at funeral rites (Dt 26:14). The presence of a corpse also made all food prepared in that house unclean (Jer 16:5–7).

9:5 The LORD's feast: probably the important autumn feast of Booths, the most important of the Israelite public celebrations (Lv 23:34).

9:6 Instead of gathering for celebration (v. 5), they will be gathered for death. **Memphis**: known for the monumental pyramid tombs. **Silver treasures**: the silver statues of Baal (8:4).

9:8 Prophets, like Hosea himself, are called to be sentinels for Israel, warning Israel of God's coming wrath (see Ez 3:17; 33:7), but often meet rejection.

9:9 The days of Gibeah: the precise allusion is not clear. Perhaps it is a reference to the outrage committed at Gibeah in the days of the judges (Jgs 19–21), or to questions surrounding Saul's kingship at Gibeah (1 Sm 10:26; 14:2; 22:6).

9:10 Baal-peor: where the Israelites consecrated themselves for the first time to Baal (Nm 25; see note on Hos 5:1–2). Baal is here called the Shameful One.

a: Am 5:22. *b:* Jer 14:10. *c:* Dt 28:68. *d:* Dt 32:15, 18; Is 51:13. *e:* Am 1:7, 10, 12, 14; 2:2, 5. *f:* Dt 26:14. *g:* 2 Kgs 9:11; Jn 10:20. *h:* Jer 6:17; Ez 3:17; 33:2, 6, 7. *i:* Jgs 19–21. *j:* Is 28:4; Jer 2:2. *k:* Nm 25.

they became as abhorrent as the thing
they loved.
11 Ephraim is like a bird:
their glory flies away—
no birth, no pregnancy, no conception.[l]
12 Even though they bring up their children,
I will make them childless, until no
one is left.
Indeed, woe to them
when I turn away from them!
13 Ephraim, as I saw, was a tree
planted in a meadow;
But now Ephraim will bring out
his children to the slaughterer!
14 Give them, LORD!
give them what?
Give them a miscarrying womb,
and dry breasts![m]
15 All their misfortune began in Gilgal;*
yes, there I rejected them.
Because of their wicked deeds
I will drive them out of my house.
I will love them no longer;
all their princes are rebels.
16 * Ephraim is stricken,
their root is dried up;[n]
they will bear no fruit.[o]
Were they to bear children,
I would slay the beloved of their womb.
17 My God will disown them
because they have not listened to him;
they will be wanderers among the
nations.[p]

See RG 347–49

CHAPTER 10

Destruction of Idolatrous Cultic Objects

1 [q] Israel is a luxuriant vine
whose fruit matches its growth.
The more abundant his fruit,
the more altars he built;
The more productive his land,
the more sacred pillars* he set up.
2 Their heart is false!
Now they will pay for their guilt:
God will break down their altars
and destroy their sacred pillars.
3 For now they will say,
"We have no king!*
Since we do not fear the LORD,
the king—what could he do for us?"
4 They make promises,
swear false oaths, and make
covenants,
While lawsuits sprout
like poisonous weeds* in the furrows
of a field!
5 The inhabitants of Samaria are afraid
for the calf of Beth-aven;*
Its people mourn for it
and its idolatrous priests wail over it,
—over its glory which has departed
from it.[r]
6 It too will be carried to Assyria,
as an offering to the great king.* [s]
Ephraim will be put to shame,
Israel will be shamed by his schemes.
7 Samaria and her king will disappear,
like a twig upon the waters.
8 The high places of Aven* will be
destroyed,
the sin of Israel;
thorns and thistles will overgrow their
altars.
Then they will cry out to the mountains,
"Cover us!"
and to the hills, "Fall upon us!"[t]

9:15 Gilgal: possibly a reference to Saul's disobedience to Samuel (1 Sm 13:7–14; 15), or to the idolatry practiced in that place (see note on Hos 4:15).

9:16 Wordplay on the Hebrew word for "fruit" (*peri*) and Ephraim (see note on 8:9). The whole passage (vv. 10–17) presents a reversal of Ephraim's name (Gn 41:52). He will have no fruit, a condition which will result in extinction.

10:1 Sacred pillars: see note on 3:4.

10:3 No king: the instability of the monarchy (7:3–7) and its vassalage to foreign kings (7:8–16) render the monarchy ineffective. The kings do the opposite of what they are supposed to do (10:4).

10:4 Lawsuits . . . like poisonous weeds: the administration of justice, which should have been the mainstay of the people, has in corrupt hands become another instrument of oppression; cf. Am 6:12.

10:5 The calf of Beth-aven: see note on 4:15.

10:6 The great king: a title used by the Assyrian kings. See also note on 5:13.

10:8 Aven: wickedness, first of all at Bethel (v. 5), but also at all the high places.

l: Dt 28:18. *m:* Jb 3:11–12; Lk 23:29. *n:* Am 2:9. *o:* Mt 21:19. *p:* Gn 4:12, 14; Dt 28:64–65. *q:* Is 5:1–7. *r:* 1 Sm 4:21–22. *s:* Am 5:27. *t:* Is 2:10, 19; Lk 23:30; Rev 6:16.

War Because of Israel's Wickedness

9 Since the days of Gibeah[u]
you have sinned, Israel.
There they took their stand;
will war not reach them in Gibeah?
Against a perverse people
10 I came and I chastised them;
Peoples will be gathered against them
when I bind them to their two crimes.*
11 Ephraim was a trained heifer,
that loved to thresh;
I myself laid a yoke
upon her beautiful neck;
I will make Ephraim break ground, Judah must plow,
Jacob must harrow for himself:
12 "Sow for yourselves justice,
reap the reward of loyalty;
Break up for yourselves a new field,[v]
for it is time to seek the LORD,
till he comes and rains justice upon you."[w]
13 But you have plowed wickedness,
reaped perversity,
and eaten the fruit of falsehood.
Because you have trusted in your own power,
and in your many warriors,[x]
14 The clamor of war shall break out among your people
and all your fortresses shall be ravaged
As Salman ravaged Beth-arbel* on the day of war,
smashing mothers along with their children.[y]
15 So it will be done to you, Bethel,
because of your utter wickedness:
At dawn* the king of Israel
will utterly disappear.

CHAPTER 11

See RG 347–49

The Disappointment of a Parent

1 * When Israel was a child I loved him,[z]
out of Egypt* I called my son.[a]
2 The more I called them,
the farther they went from me,
Sacrificing to the Baals
and burning incense to idols.
3 Yet it was I who taught Ephraim to walk,
who took them in my arms;[b]
but they did not know that I cared for them.
4 I drew them with human cords,
with bands of love;*
I fostered them like those
who raise an infant to their cheeks;
I bent down to feed them.[c]

5 He shall return to the land of Egypt,[d]
Assyria shall be his king,
because they have refused to repent.
6 The sword shall rage in his cities:
it shall destroy his diviners,
and devour them because of their schemings.
7 My people have their mind set on apostasy;
though they call on God in unison,
he shall not raise them up.

But Love Is Stronger and Restores

8 How could I give you up, Ephraim,
or deliver you up, Israel?
How could I treat you as Admah,
or make you like Zeboiim?* [e]
My heart is overwhelmed,
my pity is stirred.

10:10 Two crimes: the allusion is not clear; a possible reference is the outrage described in Jgs 19.

10:14 As Salman ravaged Beth-arbel: perhaps Salamanu, king of Moab, mentioned in an inscription of Tiglath-pileser III, after an invasion in Gilead (Transjordan), where there was a Beth-arbel, close to present Irbid.

10:15 At dawn: normally the moment of God's victory over Israel's enemies, and thus his salvation (Is 17:14; Ps 46:6). Here it is a reversal of this expectation.

11:1–3 After the image of husband-wife (chaps. 1–3), Hosea uses the image of parent-child (Ex 4:22; Is 1:2; Jer 3:19).

11:1 Out of Egypt: Hosea dates the real beginning of Israel from the time of the exodus. Mt 2:15 applies this text to the return of Jesus from Egypt.

11:4 I drew them . . . with bands of love: perhaps a reversal of the yoke imagery of the previous chapter, i.e., not forcing them like draft animals, but drawing them with kindness and affection.

11:8 Admah . . . Zeboiim: cities in the vicinity of Sodom and Gomorrah (Gn 14:2, 8) and destroyed with them (Gn 19:24–25; Dt 29:22).

u: Jgs 19–21. *v:* Jer 4:3. *w:* Is 45:8; Jl 2:23. *x:* Is 31:1. *y:* Ps 137:9; Am 1:13. *z:* Dt 7:8; 10:15; Jer 2:1–9. *a:* Ex 4:22; Mt 2:15. *b:* Dt 1:31; 8:5. *c:* Dt 8:16. *d:* Dt 17:16. *e:* Dt 29:22.

9 I will not give vent to my blazing anger,
I will not destroy Ephraim again;
For I am God and not a man,[f]
the Holy One present among you;
I will not come in wrath.
10 They shall follow the LORD,
who roars like a lion;[g]
When he roars,
his children shall come frightened
from the west,
11 Out of Egypt they shall come trembling,
like birds,
like doves, from the land of Assyria;
And I will resettle them in their homes,
oracle of the LORD.

See RG 347–49

CHAPTER 12

*Infidelity of Israel**

1 Ephraim has surrounded me with lies,
the house of Israel, with deceit;
Judah still wanders about with gods,
and is faithful to holy ones.*
2 * Ephraim shepherds the wind,
and pursues the east wind all day long.
He multiplies lies and violence:
They make a covenant with Assyria,
and oil is carried to Egypt.

3 The LORD has a dispute with Judah,
and will punish Jacob* for his conduct,
and repay him for his deeds.
4 In the womb he supplanted his brother,[h]
and in his vigor he contended with a
divine being;
5 He contended with an angel and
prevailed,[i]
he wept and entreated him.
At Bethel he met with him,
and there he spoke with him.[j]
6 The LORD is the God of hosts,
the LORD is his name![k]
7 You must return to your God.
Maintain loyalty and justice
and always hope in your God.

8 A merchant who holds a false balance,
he loves to extort!
9 Ephraim has said,
"How rich I have become;
I have made a fortune!"[l]
All his gain will not suffice
for the guilt of his sin.
10 I the LORD have been your God,
since the land of Egypt;[m]
I will again have you live in tents,
as on feast days.
11 I spoke to the prophets,
I granted many visions,[n]
and through the prophets I told parables.
12 In Gilead is falsehood, they have come to
nothing;
in Gilgal they sacrifice bulls,
But their altars are like heaps of stones[o]
in the furrows of the field.

13 Jacob fled to the land of Aram,
and Israel served for a wife;
for a wife he tended sheep.[p]
14 But by a prophet* the LORD brought
Israel out of Egypt,
and by a prophet Israel was tended.[q]
15 Ephraim has aroused bitter anger,
so his Lord shall cast his bloodguilt
upon him
and repay him for his scorn.

CHAPTER 13

See RG 347–49

The Death of Ephraim

1 When Ephraim spoke there was terror;
he was exalted in Israel;*
but he became guilty through Baal and
died.

2 Now they continue to sin,
making for themselves molten images,

12:1–15 This chapter draws a parallel between the history of Israel and events in the life of Jacob-Israel, the ancestor.

12:1 An attack on the idolatry of both kingdoms, Israel and Judah. **Holy ones**: subordinate gods, members of the divine council.

12:2 Hosea frequently condemns the alliances with Assyria and Egypt, the two world powers (7:8–16).

12:3 Jacob: whose name was changed to Israel (Gn 35:10).

12:14 A prophet: Moses.

13:1 Exalted in Israel: Ephraim enjoyed a privileged position in Israel (Gn 48:14–19).

13:2 Kiss calves: apparently a reference to a ritual gesture associated with the worship of Baal represented as a calf (1 Kgs 19:18).

f: Nm 23:19; Is 31:3; Ez 28:2. *g:* Jl 4:16; Am 1:2; Jer 25:30. *h:* Gn 25:26; 27:35–36. *i:* Gn 32:25–30. *j:* Gn 28:12–19; 35:15. *k:* Ex 3:15; Am 4:13. *l:* Rev 3:17. *m:* Ex 20:2. *n:* Ps 74:9. *o:* Gn 31:45–54; Jos 4–5. *p:* Gn 28:5; 29:15–30; 30:31. *q:* Ex 3:7–10; Dt 18:18.

Silver idols according to their skill,[r]
all of them the work of artisans.
"To these, offer sacrifice," they say.
People kiss calves!* [s]
3 Therefore, they will be like a morning cloud
or like the dew that vanishes with the dawn,
Like chaff storm-driven from the threshing floor[t]
or like smoke out of the window.

4 I, the LORD, am your God,
since the land of Egypt;* [u]
Gods apart from me you do not know;
there is no savior but me.[v]
5 I fed you in the wilderness,
in the parched land.
6 When I fed them, they were satisfied;
when satisfied, they became proud,
therefore they forgot me.
7 So, I will be like a lion to them,
like a leopard by the road I will keep watch.
8 [w] I will attack them like a bear robbed of its young,
and tear their hearts from their breasts;
I will devour them on the spot like a lion,
as a wild animal would rip them open.

9 * I destroy you, Israel!
who is there to help you?
10 Where now is your king,
that he may rescue you?
And all your princes,
that they may defend you?
Of whom you said,
"Give me a king and princes"?[x]
11 I give you a king in my anger,
and I take him away in my wrath.*

12 The guilt of Ephraim is wrapped up,
his sin is stored away.
13 * The birth pangs will come for him,[y]
but this is an unwise child,
Who, when it is time, does not present himself
at the mouth of the womb.[z]
14 * Shall I deliver them from the power of Sheol?
shall I redeem them from death?
Where are your plagues, O death!
where is your sting, Sheol![a]
Compassion is hidden from my eyes.

15 Though Ephraim* may flourish among his brothers,
an east wind[b] will come, a wind from the LORD,
rising from the wilderness,
That will dry up his spring,
and leave his fountain dry.
It will loot his treasury
of every precious thing.

CHAPTER 14

See RG 347–49

1 Samaria* has become guilty,
for she has rebelled against her God.
They shall fall by the sword,
their infants shall be dashed to pieces,[c]
their pregnant women shall be ripped open.[d]

Sincere Conversion and New Life

2 Return, Israel, to the LORD, your God;
you have stumbled because of your iniquity.
3 Take with you words,
and return to the LORD;
Say to him, "Forgive all iniquity,

13:4 I, the LORD . . . land of Egypt: according to 1 Kgs 12:28, Jeroboam introduced the calves used in the worship at the sanctuaries in Bethel and Dan with the words: "Here are your gods, O Israel, who brought you up from the land of Egypt."

13:9–10 Only God can save Israel, not the king, whom Israel had requested from the Lord (1 Sm 8:1–9).

13:11 I give you a king . . . in my wrath: the Lord punished the people of the Northern Kingdom by giving them kings who were soon deposed (see notes on 7:3–7 and 8:4).

13:13 Ephraim will die along with its stored-up sin, just as a mother dies along with a child that she cannot deliver.

13:14 God calls upon "death" and "Sheol" to send their auxiliaries, "plagues" and "sting," to punish Israel (Hb 3:5; Ps 91:6). Paul uses this text in a different way to speak about the victory over death (1 Cor 15:54–55).

13:15 Although "Ephraim" is not explicitly mentioned in the text (the Hebrew text has the word "he"), the wordplay with the Hebrew word for "flourish" (*yaphrî'*) suggests the use of "Ephraim" in the translation. **Wind**: possibly Assyria.

14:1 Samaria: the capital of the Northern Kingdom will fall; this is the punishment predicted for Ephraim, the Northern Kingdom.

r: Is 40:19–20; 44:9–20. *s:* 1 Kgs 19:18. *t:* Is 17:13; Zep 2:2; Ps 1:4. *u:* Ex 20:2. *v:* Is 43:11. *w:* 2 Sm 17:8. *x:* 1 Sm 8:5. *y:* Is 26:17–18; Jer 6:24; 22:23. *z:* Is 37:3. *a:* 1 Cor 15:55. *b:* Ez 19:12. *c:* Ps 137:9. *d:* Am 1:13.

and take what is good.
Let us offer the fruit of our lips.[e]
4 * Assyria will not save us,
nor will we mount horses;[f]
We will never again say, 'Our god,'
to the work of our hands;
for in you the orphan finds
compassion."[g]
5 I will heal their apostasy,
I will love them freely;
for my anger is turned away from
them.
6 I will be like the dew for Israel:[h]
he will blossom like the lily;
He will strike root like the Lebanon
cedar,
7 and his shoots will go forth.[i]
His splendor will be like the olive tree
and his fragrance like Lebanon cedar.[j]
8 Again they will live in his shade;
they will raise grain,
They will blossom like the vine,
and his renown will be like the wine of
Lebanon.
9 Ephraim! What more have I to do with
idols?[k]
I have humbled him, but I will take
note of him.
I am like a verdant cypress tree.*
From me fruit will be found for you!

Epilogue

10 * Who is wise enough to understand
these things?[l]
Who is intelligent enough to know
them?
Straight are the paths of the LORD,[m]
the just walk in them,[n]
but sinners stumble in them.

14:4 These good intentions promise a reversal of Israel's sins: no more reliance on "Assyria," i.e., on foreign alliances (see notes on 8:9 and 12:2), on "horses," i.e., on human power (10:13), and on idolatry (8:4–6; 13:2). Israel will trust in the Lord alone.

14:9 Verdant cypress tree: the symbol of lasting life, the opposite of the sacred trees of the Baal cult (4:13). The Lord provides the "fruit" (*peri*) to Israel (2:7, 10), another instance of the wordplay on Ephraim (see notes on 9:16 and 13:15).

14:10 A challenge to the reader in the style of the wisdom literature.

e: Heb 13:15. *f:* Is 31:1. *g:* Lam 5:3. *h:* Is 26:19. *i:* Is 27:6. *j:* Sg 4:11. *k:* 2 Cor 6:16. *l:* Ps 107:43; Jer 9:11; Eccl 8:1. *m:* Dt 32:4. *n:* Dt 8:6; 11:22; Mi 6:8.

See RG 349–51

The Book of Joel

In the two speeches that make up this book, Joel uses an agricultural crisis to measure his audience's knowledge of its God, warn them of a worse disaster if they ignore his preaching, and express his conviction that all faithful Judahites would someday enjoy a secure future. Although the superscription, or title (1:1), does not place Joel's preaching or the book's composition in a specific historical context, internal evidence favors a postexilic date for its composition, probably 450–400 B.C. This evidence includes: Joel's reliance on an established, possibly written, prophetic tradition; the existence of an organized temple liturgy; the dominance of priests and the absence of a king; and vocabulary characteristic of later material like Chronicles and Zechariah.

Inadequate winter rains and a spring locust infestation have devastated Judah's grain fields, vineyards, and orchards. Because the people carry on with business as usual, unaware that this crisis is the work of the Lord in their midst, Joel fears that the Lord may soon deliver a death blow by withholding the rains that normally fall in the late autumn. However, Joel's efforts to avert this crisis are successful. The first speech ends with Joel's assurance that at the end of the next agricultural year the people will enjoy a superabundant harvest.

The second speech begins with a summary description (chap. 3) of the prophet's hope that Judah's God will one day destroy its enemies and make Jerusalem secure once and for all. This divine intervention will create a more inclusive community, cutting across boundaries of gender, class, and age. In Peter's first public speech at Pentecost (Acts 2:16–21), the author uses Jl 3:1–5 to announce the formation of such a community among Christians in Jerusalem and the proximity of the day of the Lord. The rest of Joel's second speech (chap. 4) uses the imagery of drought and locusts from the first speech and introduces the metaphor of a grape harvest and wine making to describe the attack of the Lord's heavenly army on Judah's enemies. In the renewal of Judah's hillsides by the winter rains, the prophet sees the revitalization of the people because the Lord dwells with them.

The Book of Joel may be divided as follows:

I. Announcement of Unprecedented Disaster (1:2–20)
II. The Day of the Lord (2:1–27)
III. The Lord's Final Judgment (3:1–4:21)

See RG 349

CHAPTER 1

1 The word of the LORD which came to Joel, the son of Pethuel.

I. Announcement of Unprecedented Disaster

2 Listen to this, you elders!
Pay attention, all who dwell in the land!
Has anything like this ever happened in your lifetime,
or in the lifetime of your ancestors?
3 Report it to your children.
Have your children report it to their children,
and their children to the next generation.
4 What the cutter left,
the swarming locust has devoured;
What the swarming locust left,
the hopper has devoured;
What the hopper left,
the consuming locust* has devoured.
5 Wake up, you drunkards,* and weep;
wail, all you wine drinkers,
Over the new wine,
taken away from your mouths.
6 For a nation* invaded my land,
powerful and past counting,
With teeth like a lion's,
fangs like those of a lioness.
7 It has stripped bare my vines,
splintered my fig tree,
Shearing off its bark and throwing it away,
until its branches turn white.
8 Wail like a young woman* dressed in sackcloth
for the husband of her youth.
9 Grain offering and libation are cut off
from the house of the LORD;
In mourning are the priests,
the ministers of the LORD.
10 The field is devastated;
the farmland mourns,*
Because the grain is devastated,
the wine has dried up,
the oil has failed.
11 Be appalled, you farmers!
wail, you vinedressers,
Over the wheat and the barley,
because the harvest in the field is ruined.
12 The vine has dried up,
the fig tree has withered;
The pomegranate, even the date palm
and the apple—
every tree in the field has dried up.
Joy itself has dried up
among the people.

Cry Out to the Lord

13 * Gird yourselves and lament, you priests!

1:4 Cutter . . . swarming locust . . . hopper . . . consuming locust: these names may refer to various species of locusts, or to some phases in the insect's life cycle, or to successive waves of locusts ravaging the countryside.

1:5 Drunkards: this metaphor expresses both the urgency behind Joel's preaching and his ironic assessment of his audience. There are no grapes to process into new wine, yet people view their situation as just another agricultural crisis. Joel argues that the problems they now face are lessons the Lord is using to provide the knowledge they lack.

1:6 A nation: the locusts are compared to an invading army, whose numbers are overwhelming. The ravaged landscape resembles the wasteland left behind by marauding troops; the order and peace associated with agricultural productivity (1 Kgs 5:5; Mi 4:4) has been destroyed.

1:8 Like a young woman: this simile personifies Jerusalem as a youthful widow, left unprotected and without resources by her husband's sudden death.

1:10 The farmland mourns: or "the farmland is dried up."

1:13 Judah's situation is so grave and the day of the Lord so imminent that priests must lament day and night if they hope to reverse the divine punishment.

wail, ministers of the altar!
Come, spend the night in sackcloth,
ministers of my God!
For the grain offering and the libation
are withheld from the house of your God.[a]
14 Proclaim a holy fast!
Call an assembly!
Gather the elders,
all who dwell in the land,
To the house of the LORD, your God,
and cry out to the LORD![b]
15 O! The day!*
For near is the day of the LORD,
like destruction from the Almighty it is coming![c]
16 Before our very eyes*
has not food been cut off?
And from the house of our God,
joy and gladness?
17 The seed lies shriveled beneath clods of dirt;*
the storehouses are emptied.
The granaries are broken down,
for the grain is dried up.
18 * How the animals groan!
The herds of cattle are bewildered!
Because they have no pasture,
even the flocks of sheep are starving.
19 To you, LORD, I cry!
for fire has devoured the wilderness pastures,
flame has scorched all the trees in the field.
20 Even the animals in the wild
cry out to you;
For the streams of water have run dry,
and fire has devoured the wilderness pastures.[d]

II. The Day of the Lord

CHAPTER 2

See RG 349–50

The Day Approaches

1 * Blow the horn in Zion,
sound the alarm on my holy mountain!
Let all the inhabitants of the land tremble,
for the day of the LORD is coming![e]
Yes, it approaches,
2 a day of darkness and gloom,
a day of thick clouds!
Like dawn* spreading over the mountains,
a vast and mighty army!
Nothing like it has ever happened in ages past,
nor will the future hold anything like it,
even to the most distant generations.[f]
3 Before it,* fire devours,
behind it flame scorches.
The land before it is like the garden of Eden,
and behind it, a desolate wilderness;
from it nothing escapes.[g]
4 Their appearance is that of horses;
like war horses they run.
5 Like the rumble of chariots
they hurtle across mountaintops;
Like the crackling of fiery flames
devouring stubble;
Like a massive army
in battle formation.[h]

1:15 As in Am 5:18–20, the day of the Lord in Joel's first speech brings punishment, not victory, for Judah. In his second speech, this event means victory for those faithful to the Lord and death for the nations who are the Lord's enemies. **Almighty**: Hebrew *shaddai*. There is wordplay between *shod* ("destruction") and *shaddai*.

1:16 Before our very eyes: Joel's audience should have discerned the significance of the winter drought and the locust invasion they witnessed. **Joy and gladness**: the loss of field crops has reduced Joel's audience to subsistence living, with no means for liturgical or personal celebration, as in v. 12.

1:17 The seed . . . clods of dirt: the meaning of the Hebrew is uncertain. Most commentators use the translation given here, since it fits the prophet's description of an agricultural year plagued by winter drought and a spring locust infestation.

1:18–19 In figurative language, Joel describes how the insufficient winter rain, the locust invasions, and summer's heat on pasture lands and water sources drive domestic and wild animals to cry out for rain.

2:1–11 Joel warns the people about the destruction he sees galloping toward Jerusalem. He combines the imagery of the locust invasion (chap. 1) with language from the holy war tradition in order to describe the Lord leading a heavenly army against the enemy, in this case, Jerusalem.

2:2 Like dawn: from the east comes dark destruction rather than a new day's light.

2:3 Before it: fire precedes and follows the army's advance. Even the ravaged landscape of chap. 1 looks like a lush garden compared to the devastation this army leaves behind.

a: Jer 4:8. *b:* Jl 2:15. *c:* Is 13:6; Ez 30:2–3; Ob 15; Zep 1:7. *d:* Ps 42:2. *e:* Is 13:9; Jer 4:5; 6:1; 51:27; Hos 5:8; Zep 1:16. *f:* Is 13:14; Zep 1:4–15. *g:* Is 13:9; 51:3; Ez 36:35. *h:* Jer 6:23.

[6] Before them peoples tremble,
every face turns pale.[i]
[7] Like warriors they run,
like soldiers they scale walls,
Each advancing in line,
without swerving from the course.
[8] No one crowds the other;
each advances in its own track;
They plunge through the weapons;
they are not checked.
[9] They charge the city,
they run upon the wall,
they climb into the houses;
Through the windows
they enter like thieves.

[10] Before them the earth trembles;
the heavens shake;
Sun and moon are darkened,
and the stars withhold their
brightness.[j]
[11] The LORD raises his voice
at the head of his army;
How immense is his host!
How numerous those who carry out
his command!
How great is the day of the LORD!
Utterly terrifying! Who can survive it?[k]

Return to the Lord

[12] Yet even now—oracle of the LORD—
return to me with your whole heart,
with fasting, weeping, and mourning.
[13] Rend your hearts, not your garments,
and return to the LORD, your God,
For he is gracious and merciful,
slow to anger, abounding in steadfast
love,
and relenting in punishment.[l]
[14] Perhaps he will again relent
and leave behind a blessing,*
Grain offering and libation
for the LORD, your God.[m]
[15] Blow the horn in Zion!
Proclaim a fast,
call an assembly![n]
[16] Gather the people,
sanctify the congregation;
Assemble the elderly;
gather the children,
even infants nursing at the breast;
Let the bridegroom leave his room,
and the bride* her bridal tent.
[17] Between the porch and the altar*
let the priests weep,
let the ministers of the LORD weep and
say:
"Spare your people, LORD!
do not let your heritage become a
disgrace,
a byword among the nations!
Why should they say among the peoples,
'Where is their God?' "[o]

The Lord Relents. [18]Then the LORD grew jealous* for his land and took pity on his people. [19]In response the LORD said to his people:

I am sending you
grain, new wine, and oil,
and you will be satisfied by them;
Never again will I make you
a disgrace among the nations.
[20] The northerner* I will remove far from
you,

2:14 Blessing: the rain that makes possible the grapes and grain (v. 19) that workers will process into Temple offerings.

2:16 Elderly . . . infants . . . bridegroom . . . bride: Jerusalem is in such great danger that even those normally excused from fasting or working are called upon to participate in activities to ward off the imminent catastrophe.

2:17 Between the porch and the altar: the priests stood in the open space between the outdoor altar for burnt offerings and the Temple building.

2:18 Jealous: the Hebrew word describes the passionate empathetic bond the Lord has with Israel. The people's wholehearted participation in Joel's call for fasting and prayer sparks the Lord's longing to protect and love his people Israel. This desire moves him to withhold punishment and to send the blessing of v. 14 instead.

2:20 The northerner: the locusts, pictured as an invading army, which traditionally came from the north (Jer 1:14–15; Ez 26:7; 38:6, 15). Locusts are not usually an annual threat in Palestine, nor are they often associated with the north. However, to demonstrate the extent of the Lord's care for Judah and control over what happens within its borders, Joel assures his audience that the Lord will quickly drive the locusts out of Judah the coming spring, should they reappear. Dead locusts will litter the shores of the "eastern" (the Dead Sea) and the "western" (the Mediterranean) seas.

i: Na 2:11. *j:* Jl 4:15; Is 13:10, 13; Ez 32:7–8; Mt 24:29; Mk 13:24; Lk 21:25–26. *k:* Jer 30:7; Am 5:18; Zep 1:15. *l:* Ex 34:6; Ps 86:5; Jon 4:2. *m:* Jon 3:9. *n:* Jl 1:14. *o:* Ps 42:4, 11; 79:10; 115:2.

driving them out into a dry and
desolate land,
Their vanguard to the eastern sea,
their rearguard to the western sea,
And their stench will rise,
their stink will ascend,
What great deeds the Lord has done!
21 Do not fear, O land!
delight and rejoice,
for the LORD has done great things![p]
22 Do not fear, you animals in the wild,
for the wilderness pastures sprout
green grass.
The trees bear fruit,
the fig tree and the vine produce their
harvest.
23 Children of Zion, delight
and rejoice in the LORD, your God!
For he has faithfully given you the early
rain,*
sending rain down on you,
the early and the late rains as before.[q]
24 The threshing floors will be full of grain,
the vats spilling over with new wine
and oil.
25 I will repay you double
what the swarming locust has eaten,
The hopper, the consuming locust, and
the cutter,
my great army I sent against you.[r]
26 You will eat until you are fully satisfied,
then you will praise the name of the
LORD, your God,
Who acts so wondrously on your behalf!
My people will never again be put to
shame.
27 Then you will know that I am in the
midst of Israel:
I, the LORD, am your God, and there is
no other;
my people will never again be put to
shame.[s]

III. The Lord's Final Judgment

CHAPTER 3

See RG 350

The Day of the Lord[t]

1 * It shall come to pass
I will pour out my spirit upon all flesh.
Your sons and daughters will prophesy,
your old men will dream dreams,
your young men will see visions.
2 Even upon your male and female
servants,
in those days, I will pour out my spirit.
3 I will set signs in the heavens and on the
earth,
blood, fire, and columns of smoke;
4 The sun will darken,
the moon turn blood-red,
Before the day of the LORD arrives,
that great and terrible day.[u]
5 Then everyone who calls upon the name
of the LORD
will escape harm.
For on Mount Zion there will be a
remnant,
as the LORD has said,
And in Jerusalem survivors
whom the LORD will summon.[v]

CHAPTER 4

See RG 350

The Lord's Case Against the Nations

1 For see, in those days and at that time,[w]
when I restore the fortunes
of Judah and Jerusalem,
2 I will gather all the nations
and bring them down to the Valley of
Jehoshaphat.*

2:23 This autumn rain teaches the people to recognize God's compassionate presence in nature and history. There is a play on the double meaning of the Hebrew word *moreh*: "early rain" and "teacher." In the Dead Sea Scrolls, the word is used in the phrase "teacher (= *moreh*) of righteousness."

3:1–5 In many places in the Old Testament, Hebrew *ruah* is God's power, or spirit, bestowed on chosen individuals. The word can also mean "breath" or "wind." In this summary introduction to his second speech, Joel anticipates that the Lord will someday renew faithful Judahites with the divine spirit. In Acts 2:17–21 the author has Peter cite Joel's words to suggest that the newly constituted Christian community, filled with divine life and power, inaugurates the Lord's Day, understood as salvation for all who believe that Jesus of Nazareth is the Christ.

4:2 Valley of Jehoshaphat: one of the symbolic names of the place of punishment for Judah's enemies; the other is "Valley of Decision" (v. 14). The name Jehoshaphat means "the Lord judges." If the popular identification of this place as the Kidron Valley is accurate, Joel may imagine the Lord

p: Ps 126:3. *q*: Hos 10:12. *r*: Jer 5:17. *s*: Is 45:5–6, 18; 46:9. *t*: Is 44:3; Ez 39:28–29; Acts 2:17–21. *u*: Jl 2:10; Mal 3:23. *v*: Ob 17–18; Rom 10:13. *w*: Jer 33:15; 50:4, 20.

There I will enter into judgment with them
on behalf of my people, my heritage,
Israel;
Because they scattered them among the
nations,
they divided up my land.[x]
3 For my people they cast lots,
trading a young boy for the price of a
prostitute,
exchanging a young girl for the wine
they drank.[y]

4* Moreover, what are you doing to me,
Tyre and Sidon, and all the regions of Philistia? Are you paying me back for something?
If you are, I will very quickly turn your
deeds back upon your own head.[z] 5 You took
my silver and my gold and brought my
priceless treasures into your temples! 6 You
sold the people of Judah and Jerusalem to
the Greeks, taking them far from their own
country! 7 Look! I am rousing them from the
place to which you sold them, and I will turn
your deeds back upon your own head. 8 I will
sell your sons and daughters to the Judahites
who will sell them to the Sabeans,* a distant
nation. The LORD has spoken!

The Nations Destroyed

9 Announce this to the nations:
Proclaim a holy war!
Alert the warriors!
Let all the soldiers
report and march![a]
10 * Beat your plowshares into swords,
and your pruning knives into spears;
let the weakling boast, "I am a
warrior!"[b]
11 Hurry and come, all you neighboring
peoples,
assemble there!
Bring down, LORD, your warriors!
12 Let the nations rouse themselves and
come up
to the Valley of Jehoshaphat;
For there I will sit in judgment
upon all the neighboring nations.
13 Wield the sickle,[c]
for the harvest is ripe;
Come and tread,
for the wine press is full;
The vats overflow,
for their crimes are numerous.*
14 Crowds upon crowds
in the Valley of Decision;
For near is the day of the LORD
in the Valley of Decision.[d]
15 Sun and moon are darkened,
and the stars withhold their
brightness,[e]
16 The LORD roars from Zion,
and from Jerusalem raises his
voice,[f]
The heavens and the earth quake,
but the LORD will be a shelter for his
people,
a fortress for the people of Israel.

A Secure Future for Judah

17 Then you will know* that I the LORD am
your God,[g]
dwelling on Zion, my holy mountain;
Jerusalem will be holy,
and strangers will never again travel
through her.

seated above the valley on Mount Zion directing his troops in the destruction of nations in the valley below.

4:4–8 This prose material may be a later addition to the book. It illustrates a common biblical theme (cf. Ps 7:16; 9:16; 35:8; 37:14–15; 57:7), having one's evil deed (selling Judahites into slavery) turned into one's own punishment (being sold into slavery by the Judahites).

4:8 Sabeans: traders from the southwestern tip of the Arabian peninsula, present-day Yemen (cf. 1 Kgs 10:1–2; Ps 72:10; Jer 6:20).

4:10 The Lord directs the troops to forge military weapons out of the agricultural tools necessary for life during peacetime. In Is 2:4 and Mi 4:3, both in contexts presuming the defeat of Israel's enemies, this imagery is reversed.

4:13 Their crimes are numerous: the nations are ripe for punishment. Joel uses the vocabulary of the autumn grape harvest to describe the assault of the Lord's army against these nations. In Is 63:1–6, grape harvest imagery also controls the description of the Lord's return from Edom with blood-spattered clothing after having trod his enemies into the ground as if they were grapes (cf. Jer 25:30).

4:17 Then you will know: this verse further develops the motif of knowledge introduced in 2:27. The Judahites will learn that the Lord is present in their economic prosperity and political autonomy, even though they did not associate God's presence with their crop failure.

x: Is 66:18; Zec 14:2. *y:* Ob 11, 16. *z:* Ob 15. *a:* Jer 6:4. *b:* Is 2:4; Mi 4:3. *c:* Is 63:1–6; Rev 14:15. *d:* Ob 15. *e:* Jl 2:10; 3:4. *f:* Jer 25:30; Am 1:2. *g:* Ob 17; Na 2:1.

18 * On that day
the mountains will drip new wine,
and the hills flow with milk,
All the streams of Judah
will flow with water.
A spring will rise from the house of the
LORD,
watering the Valley of Shittim.[h]
19 Egypt will be a waste,
Edom a desolate wilderness,
Because of violence done to the
Judahites,
because they shed innocent blood in
their land.[i]
20 But Judah will be inhabited forever,
and Jerusalem for all
generations.
21 I will avenge their blood,
and I will not acquit the guilt.
The LORD dwells in Zion.

4:18 Images of agricultural abundance illustrate the harmony and order Joel expects the Lord to establish in Judah; like 2:18–27, this section reverses the deprivation and drought of chap. 1. **A spring . . . house of the LORD**: streams of water flowing from the Temple of an ideal Jerusalem also appear in Ez 47:1. **The Valley of Shittim**: or "the ravine of the acacia trees"; while there is a Shittim east of the Jordan, the reference here is probably to that rocky part of the Kidron Valley southeast of Jerusalem, an arid region where acacia trees flourished.

h: Ez 47:1–12; Am 9:13; Zec 14:8. *i:* Ob 10.

See RG 351–55

The Book of Amos

Amos was a sheepbreeder of Tekoa in Judah, who delivered his oracles in the Northern Kingdom during the prosperous reign of Jeroboam II (786–746 B.C.). He prophesied in Israel at the great cult center of Bethel, from which he was finally expelled by the priest in charge of this royal sanctuary (7:10–17). The poetry of Amos, who denounces the hollow prosperity of the Northern Kingdom, is filled with imagery and language taken from his own pastoral background. The book is an anthology of his oracles and was compiled either by the prophet or by some of his disciples.

The prophecy begins with a sweeping indictment of Damascus, Philistia, Tyre, and Edom; but the forthright herdsman saves his climactic denunciation for Israel, whose injustice and idolatry are sins against the light granted to her. Israel could indeed expect the day of the Lord, but it would be a day of darkness and not light (5:18). When Amos prophesied the overthrow of the sanctuary, the fall of the royal house, and the captivity of the people, it was more than Israelite officialdom could bear. The priest of Bethel drove Amos from the shrine—but not before hearing a terrible sentence pronounced upon himself.

Amos is a prophet of divine judgment, and the sovereignty of the Lord in nature and history dominates his thought. But he was no innovator; his conservatism was in keeping with the whole prophetic tradition calling the people back to the high moral and religious demands of the Lord's revelation.

Amos's message stands as one of the most powerful voices ever to challenge hypocrisy and injustice. He boldly indicts kings, priests, and leaders (6:1; 7:9, 16–17). He stresses the importance and the divine origin of the prophetic word (3:3–8); one must either heed that word in its entirety or suffer its disappearance (8:11–12). Religion without justice is an affront to the God of Israel and, far from appeasing God, can only provoke divine wrath (5:21–27; 8:4–10). The Lord is not some petty national god but the sovereign creator of the cosmos (4:13; 5:8; 9:5–6). Amos alludes to historical forces at work through which God would exercise judgment on Israel (6:14). Several times he mentions deportation as the fate that awaits the people and their corrupt leaders (4:3; 5:5, 27; 7:17), a standard tactic of Assyrian foreign policy during this period. Through the prophetic word and various natural disasters (4:6–12) the Lord has tried to bring Israel to repentance, but to no avail. Israel's rebelliousness has exhausted the divine patience and the destruction of Israel as a nation and as God's people is inevitable (2:4, 13–16; 7:8–9). As it is presented in this book, Amos's message is one of almost unrelieved gloom (but see 5:14–15). A later appendix (9:11–15), however, ends the book on a hopeful note, looking beyond the judgment that had already taken place in fulfillment of Amos's word.

The Book of Amos may be divided as follows:
I. Editorial Introduction (1:1–2)
II. Oracles Against the Nations (1:3–2:16)
III. Threefold Summons to Hear the Word of the Lord (3:1–5:9)
IV. Three Woes (5:7–6:14)
V. Symbolic Visions (7:1–9:10)
VI. Epilogue: Restoration Under a Davidic King (9:11–15)

I. Editorial Introduction

CHAPTER 1

See RG 352

1 The words of Amos, who was one of the sheepbreeders from Tekoa,[a] which he received in a vision concerning Israel in the days of Uzziah, king of Judah, and in the days of Jeroboam, son of Joash, king of Israel, two years before the earthquake.* 2 He said:

The LORD roars from Zion,*
and raises his voice from Jerusalem;
The pastures of the shepherds languish,
and the summit of Carmel withers.[b]

II. Oracles Against the Nations*

Aram

3 Thus says the LORD:

For three crimes of Damascus, and now four—*
I will not take it back—
Because they threshed Gilead
with sledges of iron,
4 I will send fire upon the house of Hazael,
and it will devour the strongholds of Ben-hadad.* [c]
5 I will break the barred gate of Damascus;
From the Valley of Aven* I will cut off the one enthroned,
And the sceptered ruler from Beth-eden;
the people of Aram shall be exiled to Kir,[d] says the LORD.

Philistia

6 Thus says the LORD:

For three crimes of Gaza, and now four—
I will not take it back—
Because they exiled an entire population,
handing them over to Edom,
7 I will send fire upon the wall of Gaza,
and it will devour its strongholds;
8 From Ashdod I will cut off the one enthroned
and the sceptered ruler from Ashkelon;
I will turn my hand against Ekron,
and the last of the Philistines shall perish,
says the Lord GOD.

Tyre

9 Thus says the LORD:

For three crimes of Tyre, and now four—
I will not take it back—
Because they handed over an entire population to Edom,
and did not remember their covenant of brotherhood,*
10 I will send fire upon the wall of Tyre,
and it will devour its strongholds.

1:1 The earthquake: a major earthquake during the reign of Uzziah (ca. 783–742 B.C.), so devastating that it was remembered long afterwards (cf. Zec 14:5). See the description of an earthquake in Amos's final vision (9:1).

1:2 Significantly, the roar comes to the Northern Kingdom from Jerusalem. This verse, perhaps an editorial remark, sets the tone of Amos's message.

1:3–2:16 All the nations mentioned here may have been part of the ideal empire of David-Solomon (cf. 1 Kgs 5:1; 2 Kgs 14:25). Certain standards of conduct were expected not only in their relations with Israel but also with one another.

1:3 For three crimes ... and now four: this formula (N, N+1) is frequent in poetry (e.g., Prv 6:16–19; 30:18–19). The progression "three" followed by "four" here suggests a climax. The fourth crime is one too many and exhausts the Lord's forbearance.

1:4 Hazael ... Ben-hadad: kings of the Arameans whose capital was Damascus (v. 5); they fought against Israel (2 Kgs 13:3) and had long occupied the region of Gilead (v. 3) in Transjordan.

1:5 Valley of Aven: lit., "valley of wickedness," perhaps a distortion of a place name in Aramean territory, identity unknown. **Beth-eden**: an Aramean city-state on the Euphrates, about two hundred miles northeast of Damascus, called *Bit-adini* in Assyro-Babylonian texts. **Kir**: cf. 9:7; probably to be identified with the city of Emar on the Euphrates, a major Aramean center in the Late Bronze Age. One text from this site calls the king of Emar "the king of the people of the land of Kir."

1:9 Did not remember their covenant of brotherhood:

a: Zec 14:5. *b:* Jer 25:30; Jl 4:16. *c:* 2 Kgs 13:3–7; Hos 8:14. *d:* 2 Kgs 16:9.

Edom

[11]Thus says the LORD:

For three crimes of Edom, and now
four—
I will not take it back—
Because he pursued his brother* with the
sword,
suppressing all pity,
Persisting in his anger,
his wrath raging without end,
[12] I will send fire upon Teman,
and it will devour the strongholds of
Bozrah.*

Ammon

[13]Thus says the LORD:

For three crimes of the Ammonites, and
now four—
I will not take it back—
Because they ripped open pregnant
women in Gilead,[e]
in order to extend their territory,
[14] I will kindle a fire upon the wall of
Rabbah,*
and it will devour its strongholds
Amid war cries on the day of battle,
amid stormwind on the day of tempest.
[15] Their king shall go into exile,
he and his princes with him, says the
LORD.

See RG 352

CHAPTER 2

Moab

[1]Thus says the LORD:

For three crimes of Moab, and now
four—
I will not take it back—
Because he burned to ashes*
the bones of Edom's king,
[2] I will send fire upon Moab,
and it will devour the strongholds of
Kerioth;
Moab shall meet death amid uproar,
battle cries and blasts of the ram's
horn.
[3] I will cut off the ruler from its midst,
and all the princes I will slay with him,
says the LORD.

Judah

[4]* Thus says the LORD:

For three crimes of Judah, and now
four—
I will not take it back—
Because they spurned the instruction of
the LORD,[f]
and did not keep his statutes;
Because the lies* which their ancestors
followed
have led them astray,
[5] I will send fire upon Judah,
and it will devour the strongholds of
Jerusalem.

Israel

[6]Thus says the LORD:

For three crimes of Israel,* and now
four—
I will not take it back—
Because they hand over the just for
silver,
and the poor for a pair of sandals;[g]
[7] They trample the heads of the destitute
into the dust of the earth,
and force the lowly out of the way.

standard diplomatic language of this period, meaning "violated the treaty." The violation may not have been against Israel itself but against a fellow "subject" nation of the ideal Davidic-Solomonic empire (cf. 2:1).

1:11 Pursued his brother: "brother" here may denote a fellow vassal or subject of Israel.

1:12 Teman . . . Bozrah: two of the chief cities of Edom; cf. Jer 49:20.

1:14 Rabbah: now called Amman, the modern capital of Jordan.

2:1 He burned to ashes: to the peoples of the Near East, burning the bones of the dead was a particularly heinous crime, as it was believed to cause the spirits of these dead to wander without any hope of interment in their graves, where they could rest in peace.

2:4–8, 12 Unlike the crimes of the nations detailed in this section, which are wrongs against other nations, those of Judah and Israel named here are violations of the Lord's demands.

2:4 The lies: false gods worshiped by the Judahites.

2:6 Israel: Amos's audience would applaud his condemnation of foreign kingdoms in the foregoing seven oracles, especially of Judah. But now he adds an eighth, unexpected oracle—against Israel itself. This is the real "punch line" of this whole section, to which the preceding oracles serve mainly as introduction.

e: 2 Kgs 8:12; 15:16. *f:* Is 5:24. *g:* Am 8:6; Sir 46:19.

Son and father sleep with the same girl,*
profaning my holy name.
8 Upon garments taken in pledge
they recline beside any altar.*[h]
Wine at treasury expense
they drink in their temples.
9 Yet it was I who destroyed the Amorites
before them,
who were as tall as cedars,
and as strong as oak trees.
I destroyed their fruit above
and their roots beneath.[i]
10 It was I who brought you up from the
land of Egypt,
and who led you through the desert for
forty years,
to occupy the land of the Amorites;
11 I who raised up prophets among your
children,
and nazirites* among your young
men.
Is this not so, Israelites?—
oracle of the LORD.
12 But you made the nazirites drink wine,
and commanded the prophets, "Do not
prophesy!"[j]
13 Look, I am groaning beneath you,
as a wagon groans when laden with
sheaves.
14 Flight shall elude the swift,
and the strong shall not retain
strength;[k]
The warrior shall not save his life,
15 nor shall the archer stand his ground;
The swift of foot shall not escape,
nor shall the horseman save his life.
16 And the most stouthearted of warriors
shall flee naked on that day—
oracle of the LORD.

III. Threefold Summons to Hear the Word of the Lord

CHAPTER 3

See RG 353

First Summons

1 Hear this word, Israelites, that the LORD
speaks concerning you,
concerning the whole family I brought
up from the land of Egypt:
2 You alone I have known,*
among all the families of the earth;[l]
Therefore I will punish you
for all your iniquities.

3 * Do two journey together
unless they have agreed?
4 Does a lion roar in the forest
when it has no prey?
Does a young lion cry out from its den
unless it has seized something?
5 Does a bird swoop down on a trap on the
ground
when there is no lure for it?
Does a snare spring up from the ground
without catching anything?
6 Does the ram's horn sound in a city
without the people becoming
frightened?
Does disaster befall a city
unless the LORD has caused it?[m]

7 (Indeed, the Lord GOD does nothing without revealing his plan to his servants the prophets.)

8 The lion has roared,
who would not fear?[n]
The Lord GOD has spoken,
who would not prophesy?

2:7 Son and father sleep with the same girl: the crime condemned here may be the misuse of power by the rich who take unfair advantage of young women from the ranks of the poor and force themselves on them, thus adding oppression to the sin of impurity.

2:8 Upon garments . . . any altar: creditors kept the garments taken as pledges from the poor instead of returning them to their owners before nightfall as the law commanded (Ex 22:25; cf. Dt 24:12). **Wine . . . in their temples**: lavish feasts for the rich, serving the finest wines in great abundance (see 6:4–7) and funded by the treasuries of local temples (e.g., at Dan and Bethel). The Hebrew in this verse is difficult. Another possible translation would be: "And the wine of those who have been fined / they drink in the house of their god."

2:11 Nazirites: see note on Nm 6:2–21. **Oracle of the LORD**: a phrase used extensively in prophetic books to indicate divine speech.

3:2 You alone I have known: precisely because Israel enjoyed a special status among the nations of the world in the eyes of the Lord (but see 9:7) it was called to a high degree of fidelity to God. Because Israel has failed in this expectation, it must experience God's punishment.

3:3–8 The metaphors in these sayings illustrate the principle of cause and effect, and lead up to the conclusion in v. 8.

h: Dt 24:12–13. *i:* Nm 21:21–32; Dt 2:24–37; Jb 18:16; Hos 9:16. *j:* Am 7:13; Nm 6:1–4; Is 30:10; Jer 11:21. *k:* Ps 33:16. *l:* Gn 18:19; Dt 7:6. *m:* Jl 2:1. *n:* Am 1:2.

9 Proclaim this in the strongholds of
Assyria,*
in the strongholds of the land of Egypt:
"Gather on the mount of Samaria,
and see the great disorders within it,
the oppressions within its midst."*
10 They do not know how to do what is
right—
oracle of the LORD—
Storing up in their strongholds
violence and destruction.
11 Therefore thus says the Lord GOD:
An enemy shall surround the land,
tear down your fortresses,
and pillage your strongholds.
12 Thus says the LORD:
As the shepherd rescues from the mouth
of the lion
a pair of sheep's legs or the tip of an
ear,
So shall the Israelites escape,
those who dwell in Samaria,
With the corner of a couch
or a piece of a cot.*

13 Hear and bear witness against the house
of Jacob—
an oracle of the Lord GOD, the God of
hosts:
14 On the day when I punish Israel for its
crimes,
I will also punish the altars of Bethel;
The horns of the altar shall be broken off
and fall to the ground.* [o]
15 I will strike the winter house
and the summer house;
The houses of ivory shall lie in ruin,
and their many rooms shall be no
more—
oracle of the LORD.

CHAPTER 4

See RG 353

Second Summons

1 Hear this word, you cows of Bashan,*
who live on the mount of Samaria:
Who oppress the destitute
and abuse the needy;
Who say to your husbands,
"Bring us a drink!"
2 The Lord GOD has sworn by his holiness:
Truly days are coming upon you
when they shall drag you away with
ropes,
your children with fishhooks;
3 You shall go out through the breached
walls
one in front of the other,
And you shall be exiled to Harmon—*
oracle of the LORD.

4 Come to Bethel* and sin,
to Gilgal and sin all the more!
Each morning bring your sacrifices,
every third day your tithes;
5 Burn leavened bread as a thanksgiving
sacrifice,
proclaim publicly your voluntary
offerings,
For so you love to do, Israelites—
oracle of the Lord GOD.

6 Though I made your teeth
clean of food in all your cities,
and made bread scarce in all your
dwellings,
Yet you did not return to me—
oracle of the LORD.[p]
7 [q] And I withheld the rain from you
when the harvest was still three
months away;

3:9 Assyria: following the Greek version, the Hebrew text has "Ashod." It is supposed that this was a copyist's error: "Assyria" seems intended, in order to parallel "Egypt" in the next line.

3:9 With a keen sense of irony, Amos invites the most powerful oppressors in Israel's memory, past and present—Egypt and Assyria—to see and marvel at the great oppression and injustice being wrought within Samaria by the people of Israel.

3:12 The "escape" is clearly a disaster, not a deliverance.

3:14 On Bethel, see also 4:4; 5:5–6; and 7:13. The prophet is condemning the religiosity and formalism of the worship by Israel's leaders.

4:1 Cows of Bashan: the pampered women of Samaria; Bashan was a region east of the Sea of Galilee, famous for its rich pasture and fattened herds.

4:3 Harmon: or perhaps "Mount Mon"; an unidentified site, probably far to the north of Israel, under the control of Assyria.

4:4 Come to Bethel: Amos's invitation to the people to come and "sin" at two of the major religious centers in Samaria is sarcastic. His point is that sacrifice and worship without justice is an abomination to the God of Israel; cf. 5:21–24.

o: Am 9:1; 1 Kgs 13:1–5. *p*: Wis 12:2, 10. *q*: Jer 14:1–6.

I sent rain upon one city
but not upon another;
One field was watered by rain,
but the one I did not water dried up;
8 Two or three cities staggered to another
to drink water
but were not satisfied;
Yet you did not return to me—
oracle of the LORD.
9 I struck you with blight and mildew;
locusts devoured your gardens and
vineyards,
the caterpillar consumed your fig trees
and olive trees;
Yet you did not return to me—
oracle of the LORD.[r]
10 I sent upon you pestilence like that of
Egypt;[s]
with the sword I killed your young
men and your captured horses,
and to your nostrils I brought the
stench of your camps;
Yet you did not return to me—
oracle of the LORD.
11 I overthrew you
as when God overthrew Sodom and
Gomorrah;
you were like a brand plucked from
the fire,[t]
Yet you did not return to me—
oracle of the LORD.
12 Therefore thus I will do to you,* Israel:
and since I will deal thus with you,
prepare to meet your God, O Israel!
13 The one who forms mountains and
creates winds,
and declares to mortals their thoughts;
Who makes dawn into darkness
and strides upon the heights of the earth,
the LORD, the God of hosts, is his name!

CHAPTER 5

See RG 353–54

*Third Summons**

1 Hear this word which I utter concerning
you,
this dirge, house of Israel:
2 She is fallen, to rise no more,
virgin Israel;
She lies abandoned on her land,
with no one to raise her up.[u]
3 For thus says the Lord GOD
to the house of Israel:
The city that marched out with a
thousand
shall be left with a hundred,
Another that marched out with a hundred
shall be left with ten.
4 For thus says the LORD*
to the house of Israel:
Seek me, that you may live,[v]
5 but do not seek Bethel;
Do not come to Gilgal,
and do not cross over to Beer-sheba;
For Gilgal shall be led into exile
and Bethel shall be no more.
6 * Seek the LORD, that you may live,
lest he flare up against the house of
Joseph* like a fire
that shall consume the house of Israel,
with no one to quench it.

8 The one who made the Pleiades and
Orion,
who turns darkness into dawn,
and darkens day into night;
Who summons the waters of the sea,
and pours them out on the surface of
the earth;[w]
9 Who makes destruction fall suddenly
upon the stronghold

4:12 Therefore thus I will do to you: this climax of vv. 6–12, announcing the sentence the Lord intends to pass on Israel, is open-ended.

5:1–17 These verses form a chiastic section beginning and ending with a lament over Israel (vv. 2, 16–17) and containing a double appeal to "seek" the Lord (vv. 4, 14). This editorial arrangement gives the whole section a negative cast, in effect nullifying the only hopeful verse in Amos (v. 15). Israel is as good as dead.

5:4–5 For thus says the LORD . . . Bethel shall be no more: these two verses continue the sarcasm of 4:4–5, verses in which Amos invites the people to come and "sin" at Bethel and Gilgal. The cult cities of Samaria should have been places where God could be "sought" but, because of the sins of the Northern Kingdom, these cities would cease to exist.

5:6 These verses have been rearranged to achieve the proper sequence according to the best possible manuscript tradition. Cf. the Textual Notes accompanying the translation.

5:6 House of Joseph: the kingdom of Israel or Northern Kingdom, the chief tribes of which were descended from

r: Dt 28:22; Jl 1:4; 2:25; Hg 2:17. *s:* Dt 7:15; 28:27. *t:* Gn 19:24–25; Zec 3:2. *u:* Am 8:13. *v:* Hos 5:6; 10:12. *w:* Am 9:6; Jb 9:9; 38:31.

and brings ruin upon the fortress,
the LORD is his name.

IV. Three Woes

First Woe

7 Woe to those who turn justice into
wormwood
and cast righteousness to the ground,
10 They hate those who reprove at the gate
and abhor those who speak with
integrity;
11 Therefore, because you tax the destitute
and exact from them levies of grain,
Though you have built houses of hewn
stone,
you shall not live in them;
Though you have planted choice
vineyards,
you shall not drink their wine.[x]
12 Yes, I know how many are your crimes,
how grievous your sins:
Oppressing the just, accepting bribes,
turning away the needy at the gate.
13 (Therefore at this time the wise are struck
dumb
for it is an evil time.)
14 Seek good and not evil,
that you may live;
Then truly the LORD, the God of hosts,
will be with you as you claim.
15 Hate evil and love good,
and let justice prevail at the gate;
Then it may be that the LORD, the God of
hosts,
will have pity on the remnant of
Joseph.[y]
16 Therefore, thus says the LORD,
the God of hosts, the Lord:
In every square there shall be
lamentation,
and in every street they shall cry, "Oh,
no!"
They shall summon the farmers to wail
and the professional mourners to
lament.
17 And in every vineyard there shall be
lamentation
when I pass through your midst, says
the LORD.

Second Woe

18 Woe to those who yearn
for the day of the LORD!*
What will the day of the LORD mean for
you?
It will be darkness, not light![z]
19 As if someone fled from a lion
and a bear met him;
Or as if on entering the house
he rested his hand against the wall,
and a snake bit it.
20 Truly, the day of the LORD will be
darkness, not light,
gloom without any brightness!

21 * [a] I hate, I despise your feasts,
I take no pleasure in your solemnities.
22 Even though you bring me your burnt
offerings and grain offerings
I will not accept them;
Your stall-fed communion offerings,
I will not look upon them.
23 Take away from me
your noisy songs;
The melodies of your harps,
I will not listen to them.
24 Rather let justice surge like waters,
and righteousness like an unfailing
stream.

Ephraim and Manasseh, the sons of Joseph; cf. 5:15; 6:6.

5:18 The day of the LORD: first mentioned in Amos, this refers to a specific time in the future, known to the Lord alone, when God's enemies would be decisively defeated. The common assumption among Israelites was that the Lord's foes and Israel's foes were one and the same. But Amos makes it clear that because the people have become God's enemies by refusing to heed the prophetic word, they too would experience the divine wrath on that fateful day. However, during the exile this expression comes to mean a time when God would avenge Israel against its oppressors and bring about its restoration (Jer 50:27; Ez 30:3–5).

5:21–27 The prophet does not condemn cultic activity as such but rather the people's attempt to offer worship with hands unclean from oppression of their fellow Israelites (cf. Ps 15:2–5; 24:3–4). But worship from those who disregard justice and righteousness (v. 24) is never acceptable to the God of Israel. Through the Sinai covenant the love of God and the love of neighbor are inextricably bound together.

x: Am 9:14; Dt 28:30; Zep 1:13. *y:* Jl 2:14; Rom 12:9. *z:* Jer 14:16; Jl 2:1–2, 11; Zep 1:14–18. *a:* Is 1:10–17; Jer 6:20.

25 [b] Did you bring me sacrifices and grain
offerings
for forty years in the desert, O house
of Israel?[c]
26 Yet you will carry away Sukuth,* your
king,
and Kaiwan, your star-image,
your gods that you have made for
yourselves,[d]
27 As I exile you beyond Damascus,
says the LORD,
whose name is the God of hosts.

See RG 354

CHAPTER 6

Third Woe

1 Woe to those who are complacent in
Zion,
secure on the mount of Samaria,
Leaders of the first among nations,
to whom the people of Israel turn.
2 Pass over to Calneh and see,
go from there to Hamath the great,
and down to Gath* of the Philistines.
Are you better than these kingdoms,
or is your territory greater than theirs?
3 You who would put off the day of
disaster,
yet hasten the time of violence!
4 Those who lie on beds of ivory,
and lounge upon their couches;
Eating lambs taken from the flock,
and calves from the stall;
5 Who improvise to the music of the harp,
composing on musical instruments
like David,
6 Who drink wine from bowls,
and anoint themselves with the best
oils,
but are not made ill by the collapse of
Joseph;
7 Therefore, now they shall be the first to
go into exile,
and the carousing of those who
lounged shall cease.

8 The Lord GOD has sworn by his very
self—
an oracle of the LORD, the God of
hosts:
I abhor the pride of Jacob,
I hate his strongholds,
and I will hand over the city with
everything in it;[e]
9 Should there remain ten people
in a single house, these shall die.
10 When a relative or one who prepares the
body picks up the remains
to carry them out of the house,
If he says to someone in the recesses of
the house,
"Is anyone with you?" and the answer
is, "No one,"
Then he shall say, "Silence!"
for no one must mention the name of
the LORD.* [f]
11 Indeed, the LORD has given the command
to shatter the great house to bits,
and reduce the small house to rubble.
12 Can horses run over rock,
or can one plow the sea with oxen?
Yet you have turned justice into gall,
and the fruit of righteousness into
wormwood.[g]
13 You who rejoice in Lodebar,
and say, "Have we not, by our own
strength,
seized Karnaim* for ourselves?"
14 Look, I am raising up against you, house
of Israel—
oracle of the LORD, the God of hosts—

5:26 Sukuth: probably a hebraized form of Assyro-Babylonian *Shukudu* ("the Arrow"), a name of Sirius, the brightest star in the night sky. It was associated with the god Ninurta, who was widely worshiped in Mesopotamia. According to 2 Kgs 17:30 the cult of Sirius was introduced into Samaria by deportees from Babylonia. **Kaiwan:** a hebraized form of an Akkadian name for the planet Saturn, also worshiped as a deity in Mesopotamia.

6:2 Calneh . . . Hamath . . . Gath: city-states overcome by the Assyrians in the eighth century B.C., whose fate should be a lesson to the Israelites. The prophet castigates the leaders for being more intent on pursuing a luxurious lifestyle (vv. 1, 4–6) than reading the signs of the times.

6:10 In this desperate situation there seems to be a profound fear of the Lord, who is the cause of the deaths (cf. 3:6).

6:13 Lodebar . . . Karnaim: two towns recaptured from Judah by Israelite forces during the reign of Jeroboam II (see 2 Kgs 14:25). Some mockery of at least the first of these victories is probably intended by the prophet here, as Lodebar can be translated "nothing."

b: Acts 7:42–43. *c:* Jer 7:21–26. *d:* 2 Kgs 17:30; Jer 2:28. *e:* Is 28:1–4; Jer 51:14. *f:* Zep 1:7. *g:* Am 5:7.

A nation* that shall oppress you
from Lebo-hamath even to the Wadi
Arabah.

V. Symbolic Visions

See RG 351–52, 354

CHAPTER 7

First Vision: The Locust Swarm

1 This is what the Lord GOD showed me: He
was forming a locust swarm when the late
growth began to come up (the late growth
after the king's mowing*). 2 When they had
finished eating the grass in the land, I said:

Forgive, O Lord GOD!
Who will raise up Jacob?
He is so small!

3 The LORD relented concerning this.
"This shall not be," said the Lord GOD.

Second Vision: The Rain of Fire

4 This is what the Lord GOD showed me: He
was summoning a rain of fire. It had devoured the great abyss and was consuming
the fields. 5 Then I said:

Cease, O Lord GOD!
Who will raise up Jacob?
He is so small!

6 The LORD relented concerning this.
"This also shall not be," said the Lord GOD.

Third Vision: The Plummet

7[h] This is what the Lord GOD showed me: He
was standing, plummet in hand, by a wall
built with a plummet.* 8 The Lord GOD asked
me, "What do you see, Amos?" And I answered, "A plummet." Then the LORD said:

See, I am laying the plummet
in the midst of my people Israel;
I will forgive them no longer.
9 The high places of Isaac shall be laid
waste,
and the sanctuaries of Israel made
desolate;
and I will attack the house of
Jeroboam with the sword.

Biographical Interlude: Amos and Amaziah

10 Amaziah, the priest of Bethel, sent word to
Jeroboam, king of Israel: "Amos has conspired against you within the house of Israel;
the country cannot endure all his words.
11 For this is what Amos says:
'Jeroboam shall die by the sword,
and Israel shall surely be exiled from
its land.' "

12 To Amos, Amaziah said: "Off with you,
seer, flee to the land of Judah and there earn
your bread by prophesying! 13 But never
again prophesy in Bethel;[i] for it is the king's
sanctuary and a royal temple." 14 Amos answered Amaziah, "I am not a prophet,* nor
do I belong to a company of prophets. I am
a herdsman and a dresser of sycamores,[j]
15 but the LORD took me from following the
flock, and the LORD said to me, 'Go, prophesy to my people Israel.'[k] 16 Now hear the
word of the LORD:

You say: 'Do not prophesy against Israel,
do not preach against the house of
Isaac.'
17 Therefore thus says the LORD:
Your wife shall become a prostitute in
the city,
and your sons and daughters shall fall
by the sword.
Your land shall be parcelled out by
measuring line,

6:14 A nation: Assyria. **Lebo-hamath . . . Wadi Arabah**: the territorial limits of Solomon's kingdom, north and south respectively, as re-established by Jeroboam II (see 2 Kgs 14:25).

7:1 The king's mowing: the first harvesting of the crops apparently belonged to the king as a kind of tax.

7:7 A plummet: with this vision, the pleas of the prophet (vv. 1–6) disappear, and disaster is announced. One use of the plummet in ancient times was to see how far out of line a wall or building had become, to determine whether it could be repaired or would have to be torn down. Like a structure that had become architecturally unsound, Israel was unsalvageable and would have to be demolished (cf. 2 Kgs 21:13; Is 34:11; Lam 2:8).

7:14 I am not a prophet: Amos reacts strongly to Amaziah's attempt to classify him as a "prophet-for-hire" who "earns [his] bread" by giving oracles in exchange for payment (cf. 1 Sm 9:3–10; Mi 3:5). To disassociate himself from this kind of "professional" prophet, Amos rejects outright the title of *nabi'* ("prophet"). By profession he is a herdsman/sheepbreeder and a dresser of sycamore trees, but God's call has commissioned him to prophesy to Israel.

h: Jer 1:11–14. *i:* Am 2:12. *j:* Am 1:1; 2 Sm 7:8. *k:* Am 3:8.

and you yourself shall die in an
unclean land;
and Israel shall be exiled from its
land."

See RG 354

CHAPTER 8

Fourth Vision: The Summer Fruit

1This is what the Lord GOD showed me: a
basket of end-of-summer fruit.* 2He asked,
"What do you see, Amos?" And I answered,
"A basket of end-of-summer fruit." And the
LORD said to me:

The end has come for my people Israel;
I will forgive them no longer.
3 The temple singers will wail on that
day—
oracle of the Lord GOD.
Many shall be the corpses,
strewn everywhere—Silence![l]
4 Hear this, you who trample upon the
needy
and destroy the poor of the land:
5 "When will the new moon be over," you
ask,
"that we may sell our grain,
And the sabbath,
that we may open the grain-bins?
We will diminish the ephah,*
add to the shekel,
and fix our scales for cheating![m]
6 We will buy the destitute for silver,
and the poor for a pair of sandals;[n]
even the worthless grain we will sell!"
7 The LORD has sworn by the pride of
Jacob:
Never will I forget a thing they have
done!
8 Shall not the land tremble because of
this,
and all who dwell in it mourn?
It will all rise up and toss like the Nile,
and subside like the river of Egypt.[o]
9 On that day—oracle of the Lord GOD—
I will make the sun set at midday
and in broad daylight cover the land
with darkness.
10 I will turn your feasts into mourning
and all your songs into dirges.
I will cover the loins of all with sackcloth
and make every head bald.
I will make it like the time of mourning
for an only child,
and its outcome like a day of bitter
weeping.[p]

11 See, days are coming—oracle of the
Lord GOD—
when I will send a famine upon the
land:
Not a hunger for bread, or a thirst for
water,
but for hearing the word of the LORD.
12 They shall stagger from sea to sea
and wander from north to east
In search of the word of the LORD,
but they shall not find it.[q]

13 On that day, beautiful young women and
young men
shall faint from thirst,
14 Those who swear by Ashima of
Samaria,* [r]
and who say, "By the life of your god,
O Dan,"
"By the life of the Power of Beer-sheba!"
They shall fall, never to rise again.

CHAPTER 9

See RG 354–55

Fifth Vision: The Destruction of the Sanctuary

1I saw the Lord standing beside the altar.
And he said:

Strike the capitals
so that the threshold shakes!

8:1–2 End-of-summer fruit . . . the end has come: the English translation attempts to capture the wordplay of the Hebrew. The Hebrew word for "fruit picked late in the season" is *qayis*, while the word for "end" is *qes*.

8:5 Ephah: see note on Is 5:10.

8:14 Ashima of Samaria: a high-ranking goddess worshiped in Hamath, whose cult was transplanted by the people of that city when they were deported to Samaria by the Assyrians (2 Kgs 17:30). **The Power of Beer-sheba**: possibly an epithet of a deity worshiped in Beer-sheba, either a syncretistic form of the worship of Israel's God or of another god. **Dan . . . Beer-sheba**: the traditional designation for the northern and southern limits of Israel to which the Israelites made pilgrimages.

l: Am 6:10. *m:* Dt 25:13; Hos 12:8. *n:* Am 2:6. *o:* Am 1:1; 9:1, 5. *p:* Tb 2:6; Zec 12:10. *q:* Hos 5:6. *r:* 2 Kgs 17:30.

Break them off on the heads of them
all!
Those who are left I will slay with the
sword.
Not one shall get away,
no survivor shall escape.* [s]
2 Though they dig down to Sheol,
even from there my hand shall take
them;
Though they climb to the heavens,
even from there I shall bring them
down.[t]
3 Though they hide on the summit of
Carmel,
there too I will hunt them down and
take them;
Though they hide from my gaze at the
bottom of the sea,
there I will command the serpent* to
bite them.[u]
4 Though they go into captivity before
their enemies,
there I will command the sword to slay
them.
I will fix my gaze upon them
for evil and not for good.

5 The Lord GOD of hosts,
Who melts the earth with his touch,
so that all who dwell on it mourn,
So that it will all rise up like the Nile,
and subside like the river of Egypt;[v]
6 Who has built his upper chamber in
heaven,
and established his vault over the earth;
Who summons the waters of the sea
and pours them upon the surface of the
earth—
the LORD is his name.[w]

7 Are you not like the Ethiopians to me,
O Israelites?—oracle of the LORD—
Did I not bring the Israelites from the
land of Egypt
as I brought the Philistines from
Caphtor
and the Arameans* from Kir?
8 See, the eyes of the Lord GOD are on this
sinful kingdom,
and I will destroy it from the face of
the earth—
But I will not destroy the house of Jacob
completely—
oracle of the LORD.
9 For see, I have given the command
to sift the house of Israel among all the
nations,
As one sifts with a sieve,
letting no pebble fall to the ground.
10 All sinners among my people shall die by
the sword,
those who say, "Disaster will not reach
or overtake us."[x]

VI. Epilogue: Restoration Under a Davidic King

11 * On that day I will raise up
the fallen hut of David;
I will wall up its breaches,
raise up its ruins,
and rebuild it as in the days of old,[y]

9:1 This vision may describe the destruction of the temple at Bethel and the fulfillment of the oracle in 3:14, linking God's judgment upon Israel with the "punishment" of the altars of Bethel. This dramatic event (perhaps to be identified with the earthquake mentioned in 1:1) symbolizes the end of the Northern Kingdom as the Lord's people, the consequence of their steadfast refusal to heed the prophetic word and return to the God of Israel.

9:3 The serpent: a name for the primeval chaos monster, vanquished by God at the time of creation but not annihilated. He was a personification of the sea, another primary archetype of chaos in the ancient Near East.

9:7 The Ethiopians . . . the Philistines . . . the Arameans: although Israel's relationship to the Lord was special, even unique in some respects (3:2), Israel was not the only people on earth that God cared for. Striking here is the reference to divine intervention in the history of the Philistines and Arameans, not unlike the Lord's saving intervention to bring Israel out of Egypt. **Caphtor**: the island of Crete.

9:11–15 These verses are most likely an editorial supplement to Amos, added to bring the book into harmony with the positive thrust of the prophetic books in general, especially those written after the exile, when the final edition of Amos was probably completed. The editors would have seen the destruction of Samaria in 722/721 B.C. as the fulfillment of Amos's prophecies, but in this epilogue they express the view that destruction was not the Lord's final word for Israel. In Acts 15:15–17, James interprets this passage in a messianic sense. **The fallen hut of David**: the Davidic kingdom, which included what later became the divided Northern and Southern Kingdoms. **All nations claimed in my name**: lit., "all

s: Am 2:13–16. *t:* Ps 139:7–12; Jb 20:6. *u:* Jb 7:12; Is 27:1. *v:* Am 8:8. *w:* Am 5:8. *x:* Jer 5:12; 23:17. *y:* Acts 15:16–17.

12 That they may possess the remnant of Edom,
and all nations claimed in my name—
oracle of the LORD, the one who does this.
13 Yes, days are coming—
oracle of the LORD—
When the one who plows shall overtake the one who reaps
and the vintager, the sower of the seed;
The mountains shall drip with the juice of grapes,
and all the hills shall run with it.[z]
14 I will restore my people Israel,
they shall rebuild and inhabit their ruined cities,
Plant vineyards and drink* the wine,
set out gardens and eat the fruits.[a]
15 I will plant them upon their own ground;
never again shall they be plucked
From the land I have given them—
the LORD, your God, has spoken.

nations over whom my name has been pronounced." This idiom denotes ownership.

9:14 Rebuild . . . inhabit . . . plant . . . drink: in this era of restoration, the Lord nullifies the curse of 5:11, which uses these same four verbs, and turns it into a blessing for Israel.

z: Jl 4:18. *a:* Is 65:21–22.

See RG 356

The Book of Obadiah

This book, the shortest among the twelve minor prophets, is a single twenty-one-verse oracle against Edom. Nothing is known of the author, although his prophecy against Edom, a neighbor and rival of Israel, indicates a date of composition sometime after the Babylonian destruction of Jerusalem in 587 B.C., when the Edomites apparently took advantage of the helpless people of Judah and Jerusalem (v. 11; Ps 137:7). The relations and rivalries between Israel and Edom are reflected in oracles against Edom (Is 34; Ez 35) and in the stories of their ancestors, the brothers Jacob and Esau (Gn 25–33).

The prophecy is a bitter cry for vengeance against Edom for its pride and its crimes. Mount Esau in Edom will be occupied and ravaged by the enemy, while Mount Zion will be restored to its former sanctity and security. The triumphant refrain of Israelite eschatology will be heard once more: "The kingdom is the Lord's!" The opening verses of this prophecy (vv. 1–5) are very similar to part of an oracle against Edom in Jer 49 (vv. 9, 14–16), suggesting that Israel's prophets drew upon traditional language and idioms in the composition of prophetic speech.

The book may be divided as follows:

I. Edom's Fall Decreed (1–7)
II. Edom's Betrayal of Judah (8–14)
III. Edom's Fall and Judah's Restoration (15–21)

Edom's Fall Decreed

1 The vision of Obadiah.
Thus says the Lord GOD concerning Edom:
We have heard a message from the LORD,
and a herald has been sent among the nations:
"Rise up, so we may go to war against it!"[a]
2 Now I make you least among the nations;
you are utterly contemptible.
3 The pride of your heart has deceived you—
you who dwell in mountain crevices,
in your lofty home,*
Who say in your heart,
"Who will bring me down to earth?"
4 Though you soar like the eagle,
and your nest is set among the stars,

3 Edom occupied the mountains southeast of Israel and the Dead Sea.

a: Jer 49:14–16.

From there I will bring you down—
oracle of the LORD.
5 If thieves came to you, robbers by night
—how you have been destroyed!—
would they not steal merely till they
had enough?
If grape pickers came to you,
would they not leave some
gleanings?* [b]
6 * How Esau has been searched out,
his treasures hunted down!
7 To the border they have driven you—
all your allies;
Your partners have deceived you,
they have overpowered you;
Those who eat your bread*
will replace you with foreigners,
who have no understanding.

Edom's Betrayal of Judah

8 On that day—oracle of the LORD—will I
not
make the wise disappear from Edom,
and understanding from Mount Esau?[c]
9 Teman,* your warriors will be terror-
stricken,
so that everyone on Mount Esau will
be cut down.
10 Because of violence to your brother*
Jacob,
disgrace will cover you,
you will be done away with forever![d]
11 On the day you stood by,
the day strangers carried off his
possessions,
And foreigners entered his gates
and cast lots for Jerusalem,
you too were like one of them.* [e]

12 * Do not gloat over the day of your brother,
the day of his disaster;
Do not exult over the people of Judah
on the day of their ruin;
Do not speak haughtily
on the day of distress!
13 Do not enter the gate of my people
on the day of their calamity;
Do not gloat—especially you—over his
misfortune
on the day of his calamity;
Do not lay hands upon his possessions
on the day of his calamity!
14 Do not stand at the crossroads
to cut down his survivors;
Do not hand over his fugitives
on the day of distress!

Edom's Fall and Judah's Restoration

15 Near is the day of the LORD[f]
against all the nations!
As you have done, so will it be done to
you,
your conduct will come back upon
your own head;
16 As you drank* upon my holy mountain,
so will all the nations drink
continually.
Yes, they will drink and swallow,
and will become as though they had
not been.

5 Something of value may escape the thief, and the grape picker always leaves something for the gleaners, but God's devastation of Edom will be complete.

6 With the past tense in vv. 5–7, the prophet presents a future event as if it had already happened.

7 Those who eat your bread: alliances were often established by covenant meals (cf. Gn 31:44–46). When Edom is destroyed, foreigners will replace the Edomites, who were known for wisdom (cf. v. 8; Jer 49:7; Jb 2:11).

9 Teman: a synonym for Edom; perhaps the name of a region or a city, the part representing the whole. **Mount Esau**: whatever its geographic reference, the phrase is an effective representation of Edom's arrogance.

10 Your brother: used with a double meaning referring to the common lineage of Israel and Edom, in which their ancestors were brothers, Jacob and Esau (Gn 25:19–26), and referring also to their political alliance, in which allies were called brothers (cf. Am 1:9, 11).

11 In 587 B.C., Edomites joined the invading Babylonian forces (v. 13) and captured escaping Judahites. The destruction of Jerusalem strengthened and expanded Edom's hold on Judah's southern territory.

12–14 The commands in vv. 12–14 are not to be understood as future prohibitions but as descriptions of crimes Edom in fact already committed on the day of Jerusalem's fall described in v. 11.

16 As you drank: i.e., Judah has suffered the punishment of divine wrath in 587 B.C. The oracle promises a similar fate for the nations, especially Edom (v. 18). The metaphor "drinking the cup of God's wrath" occurs often in the Bible; cf. Jb 21:20; Is 51:17–23; Jer 25:15–16; Rev 14:10.

---

b: Jer 49:9. *c:* Is 29:14; 1 Cor 1:19. *d:* Gn 27:41–45; Ez 25:12–14. *e:* Ps 137:7. *f:* Jl 4:11–12, 14.

17 But on Mount Zion there will be some
who escape;*
the mountain will be holy,
And the house of Jacob will take possession
of those who dispossessed them.[g]
18 The house of Jacob will be a fire,
the house of Joseph a flame,
and the house of Esau stubble.
They will set it ablaze and devour it;
none will survive of the house of Esau,
for the LORD has spoken.

19 They will take possession of the Negeb,*
Mount Esau, the Shephelah, and Philistia,
possess the countryside of Ephraim, the
countryside of Samaria, Benjamin, and Gilead.[h] 20 The exiles of this Israelite army will
possess the Canaanite land as far as
Zarephath,* and the exiles of Jerusalem who
are in Sepharad will possess the cities of the
Negeb. 21 And deliverers* will ascend Mount
Zion to rule Mount Esau, and the kingship
shall be the LORD's.

17–19 The Israelites will be restored and will occupy the lands of those who oppressed them. The survivors of Judah will be rejoined by the returned exiles from northern Israel.

19 Negeb: the area south of Judah and west of Edom. **Gilead**: east of the Jordan River.

20 Zarephath: a town in Phoenicia, north of Tyre; cf. 1 Kgs 17:10. **Sepharad**: perhaps Sardis in western Asia Minor. The later rabbis thought it was Spain.

21 Deliverers: the victorious Israelites who will rule over their enemies, as the ancient judges did; cf. Jgs 3:9, 15, 31; 10:1.

g: Jer 49:2. *h:* Jer 50:19.

See RG 357–58

The Book of Jonah

The story of Jonah has great theological import. It concerns a disobedient prophet who rejected his divine commission, was cast overboard in a storm and swallowed by a great fish, rescued in a marvelous manner, and returned to his starting point. Now he obeys and goes to Nineveh, the capital of Israel's ancient enemy. The Ninevites listen to his message of doom and repent immediately. All, from king to lowliest subject, humble themselves in sackcloth and ashes. Seeing their repentance, God does not carry out the punishment planned for them. At this, Jonah complains, angry because the Lord spares them. This fascinating story caricatures a narrow mentality which would see God's interest extending only to Israel, whereas God is presented as concerned with and merciful to even the inhabitants of Nineveh (4:11), the capital of the Assyrian empire which brought the Northern Kingdom of Israel to an end and devastated Jerusalem in 701. The Lord is free to "repent" and change his mind. Jonah seems to realize this possibility and wants no part in it (4:2; cf. Ex 34:6). But the story also conveys something of the ineluctable character of the prophetic calling.

The book is replete with irony, wherein much of its humor lies. The name "Jonah" means "dove" in Hebrew, but Jonah's character is anything but dove-like. Jonah is commanded to go east to Nineveh but flees toward the westernmost possible point (1:2–3), only to be swallowed by a great fish and dumped back at this starting point (2:1, 11). The sailors pray to their gods, but Jonah is asleep in the hold (1:5–6). The prophet's preaching is a minimum message of destruction, while it is the king of Nineveh who calls for repentance and conversion (3:4–10); the instant conversion of the Ninevites is greeted by Jonah with anger and sulking (4:1). He reproaches the Lord in words that echo Israel's traditional praise of his mercy (4:2; cf. Ex 34:6–7). Jonah is concerned about the loss of the gourd but not about the possible destruction of 120,000 Ninevites (4:10–11).

Unlike other prophetic books, this is not a collection of oracles but the story of a disobedient, narrow-minded prophet who is angry at the outcome of the sole message he delivers (3:4). It is difficult to date but almost certainly is postexilic and may reflect the somewhat narrow, nationalistic reforms of Ezra and Nehemiah. As to genre, it has been classified in various ways, such as parable or satire. The "sign" of Jonah is interpreted in two ways in the New Testament: His experience of three days and nights in the fish is a "type" of the experience of the Son of Man (Mt 12:39–40), and the Ninevites' reaction to the preaching of Jonah is contrasted with the failure of Jesus' generation to obey the preaching of one who is "greater than Jonah" (Mt 12:41–42; Lk 11:29–32).

The Book of Jonah may be divided as follows:
I. Jonah's Disobedience and Flight (1:1–16)
II. Jonah's Prayer (2:1–11)
III. Jonah's Obedience and the Ninevites' Repentance (3:1–10)
IV. Jonah's Anger and God's Reproof (4:1–11)

CHAPTER 1

See RG 357

Jonah's Disobedience and Flight.
1 The word of the LORD came to Jonah,[a] son
of Amittai:* 2 Set out for the great city* of
Nineveh, and preach against it; for their
wickedness has come before me.[b] 3 But Jonah made ready to flee to Tarshish,* away
from the LORD. He went down to Joppa,
found a ship going to Tarshish, paid the fare,
and went down in it to go with them to Tarshish, away from the LORD.
4[c] The LORD, however, hurled a great
wind upon the sea, and the storm was so
great that the ship was about to break up.
5 Then the sailors were afraid and each one
cried to his god. To lighten the ship for themselves, they threw its cargo into the sea.
Meanwhile, Jonah had gone down into the
hold of the ship, and lay there fast asleep.
6 The captain approached him and said,
"What are you doing asleep? Get up, call on
your god! Perhaps this god will be mindful
of us so that we will not perish."
7 Then they said to one another, "Come, let
us cast lots to discover on whose account
this evil has come to us." So they cast lots,
and the lot fell on Jonah.[d] 8 They said to him,
"Tell us why this evil has come to us! What
is your business? Where do you come from?
What is your country, and to what people do
you belong?" 9 "I am a Hebrew," he replied;
"I fear the LORD, the God of heaven, who
made the sea and the dry land."
10 Now the men were seized with great fear
and said to him, "How could you do such a
thing!"—They knew that he was fleeing
from the LORD, because he had told them.
11 They asked, "What shall we do with you,
that the sea may calm down for us?" For the
sea was growing more and more stormy.
12 Jonah responded, "Pick me up and hurl me
into the sea and then the sea will calm down
for you. For I know that this great storm has
come upon you because of me."
13 Still the men rowed hard to return to dry
land, but they could not, for the sea grew
more and more stormy. 14 Then they cried to
the LORD: "Please, O LORD, do not let us
perish for taking this man's life; do not
charge us with shedding innocent blood, for
you, LORD, have accomplished what you desired."* 15 Then they picked up Jonah and
hurled him into the sea, and the sea stopped
raging. 16 Seized with great fear of the LORD,
the men offered sacrifice to the LORD and
made vows.

CHAPTER 2

See RG 357

Jonah's Prayer. 1 But the LORD sent a
great fish to swallow Jonah, and he remained in the belly of the fish three days and
three nights.[e] 2 Jonah prayed to the LORD, his
God, from the belly of the fish:

3 * Out of my distress I called to the LORD,
and he answered me;
From the womb of Sheol* I cried for
help,
and you heard my voice.[f]
4 You cast me into the deep, into the heart
of the sea,
and the flood enveloped me;

1:1 Jonah, son of Amittai: a prophet of this name lived at the time of Jeroboam II (786–746 B.C.).

1:2 Great city: exaggeration is characteristic of this book; the word "great" (Heb. *gadol*) occurs fourteen times.

1:3 Tarshish: identified by many with Tartessus, an ancient Phoenician colony in southwest Spain; precise identification with any particular Phoenician center in the western Mediterranean is uncertain. To the Israelites it stood for the far west.

1:14 Aware that this disaster is a divine punishment on Jonah, the sailors ask that in ridding themselves of him they not be charged with the crime of murder.

2:3–10 These verses, which may have originally been an independent composition, are a typical example of a song of thanksgiving, a common psalm genre (e.g., Ps 116; Is 38:9–20). Such a song is relevant here, since Jonah has not drowned, and the imagery of vv. 4, 6 is appropriate.

2:3 Sheol: Cf. note on Ps 6:6.

a: 2 Kgs 14:25. *b:* Jon 3:3; 4:11. *c:* Mk 4:37–38. *d:* Jos 7:16–18; 1 Sm 14:40–42. *e:* Mt 12:40; 16:4; Lk 11:30; 1 Cor 15:4. *f:* Ps 18:7; 120:1.

All your breakers and your billows
passed over me.[g]
5 Then I said, "I am banished from your
sight!
How will I again look upon your holy
temple?"[h]
6 The waters surged around me up to my
neck;
the deep enveloped me;
seaweed wrapped around my head.[i]
7 I went down to the roots of the
mountains;
to the land whose bars closed behind
me forever,
But you brought my life up from the pit,
O LORD, my God.[j]
8 When I became faint,
I remembered the LORD;
My prayer came to you
in your holy temple.[k]
9 Those who worship worthless idols
abandon their hope for mercy.[l]
10 But I, with thankful voice,
will sacrifice to you;
What I have vowed I will pay:
deliverance is from the LORD.[m]

11 Then the LORD commanded the fish to
vomit Jonah upon dry land.

CHAPTER 3

See RG 357–58

Jonah's Obedience and the Ninevites' Repentance. 1 The word of the LORD came to
Jonah a second time: 2 Set out for the great
city of Nineveh, and announce to it the message that I will tell you. 3 So Jonah set out for
Nineveh, in accord with the word of the
LORD. Now Nineveh was an awesomely great
city; it took three days to walk through it. 4 Jonah began his journey through the city, and
when he had gone only a single day's walk
announcing, "Forty days more and Nineveh
shall be overthrown," 5 the people of Nineveh
believed God; they proclaimed a fast and all
of them, great and small,* put on sackcloth.[n]

6 When the news reached the king of Nineveh, he rose from his throne, laid aside his
robe, covered himself with sackcloth, and sat
in ashes. 7 Then he had this proclaimed
throughout Nineveh:* "By decree of the king
and his nobles, no man or beast, no cattle or
sheep, shall taste anything; they shall not eat,
nor shall they drink water. 8 Man and beast
alike must be covered with sackcloth and call
loudly to God; they all must turn from their
evil way and from the violence of their
hands. 9* Who knows? God may again repent
and turn from his blazing wrath, so that we
will not perish."[o] 10 When God saw by their
actions how they turned from their evil way,
he repented of the evil he had threatened to
do to them; he did not carry it out.

CHAPTER 4

Jonah's Anger and God's Reproof. See RG 358
1 But this greatly displeased Jonah,
and he became angry.* 2 He prayed to the
LORD, "O LORD, is this not what I said while
I was still in my own country? This is why I
fled at first toward Tarshish. I knew that you
are a gracious and merciful God, slow to
anger, abounding in kindness, repenting of
punishment.* [p] 3 So now, LORD, please take
my life from me; for it is better for me to die
than to live."[q] 4 But the LORD asked, "Are
you right to be angry?"*

5 Jonah then left the city for a place to the
east of it, where he built himself a hut and
waited* under it in the shade, to see what
would happen to the city. 6 Then the LORD

3:5 Great and small: the contrast can refer to distinctions of social class (prominent citizens and the poor).

3:7–8 Fasting and wearing sackcloth are signs of human repentance; here they are legislated even for the animals—a humorous touch, perhaps anticipating 4:11.

3:9–10 Scripture frequently presents the Lord as repenting (or, changing his mind) of the evil that he threatens; e.g., Gn 6:6–7; Jer 18:8.

4:1 He became angry: because of his narrow vindictiveness, Jonah did not wish the Lord to forgive the Ninevites.

4:2 Punishment: lit., "evil"; see 1:2, 7, 8; 3:8, 10; 4:1.

4:4 The Lord's question is as unexpected as it is pithy. It is also a mysterious reply to Jonah's wish to die; perhaps it serves to invite Jonah to think over his situation. However, it goes unanswered, and the request and reply will be repeated in vv. 8–9.

4:5 Waited: Jonah still hopes his threat of doom will be fulfilled.

g: Ps 42:8. *h:* Ps 31:23; Is 38:11. *i:* Ps 18:5; 69:2. *j:* Ps 16:10; 30:4. *k:* Ps 5:8; 18:7; 88:3. *l:* Ps 31:7. *m:* Ps 50:14. *n:* Mt 12:41; Lk 11:32. *o:* Jl 2:14. *p:* Ex 34:6–7; Ps 86:5; Jl 2:13. *q:* 1 Kgs 19:4.

God provided a gourd plant.* And when it grew up over Jonah's head, giving shade that relieved him of any discomfort, Jonah was greatly delighted with the plant. 7But the next morning at dawn God provided a worm that attacked the plant, so that it withered. 8And when the sun arose, God provided a scorching east wind; and the sun beat upon Jonah's head till he became faint. Then he wished for death, saying, "It is better for me to die than to live."

9But God said to Jonah, "Do you have a right to be angry over the gourd plant?" Jonah answered, "I have a right to be angry—angry enough to die." 10Then the LORD said, "You are concerned* over the gourd plant which cost you no effort and which you did not grow; it came up in one night and in one night it perished. 11And should I not be concerned over the great city of Nineveh, in which there are more than a hundred and twenty thousand persons who cannot know their right hand from their left, not to mention all the animals?"*

4:6 Gourd plant: the Hebrew word, *qiqayon*, means here a wide-leafed plant of the cucumber or castor-bean variety.

4:10 Concerned: the meaning of the Hebrew verb suggests "pity, care for," and this appears in the Lord's attitude to Nineveh in v. 11. Jonah has shown only a selfish concern over the plant in contrast to the Lord's true "concern" for his creatures.

4:11 A selfish Jonah bemoans his personal loss of a gourd plant for shade without any concern over the threat of loss of life to the Ninevites through the destruction of their city. If a solicitous God provided the plant for a prophet without the latter's effort or merit, how much more is God disposed to show love and mercy toward all people, Jew and Gentile, when they repent of their sins and implore divine pardon. God's care goes beyond human beings to all creation, as in Job 38.

See RG 359–60

The Book of Micah

This book consists of a collection of speeches, proclamations of punishment and of salvation, attributed to the prophet Micah. Following its superscription (1:1), the book has two major sections, each with two parts. The organization of the material is thematic, moving from judgment to salvation in both major sections. In the first section (Mi 1–5), chaps. 1–3 consist almost entirely of prophecies of punishment, and chaps. 4–5 of prophecies of salvation. The second section (chaps. 6–7) also moves from prophecies of punishment (6:1–7:6) to confidence in God's salvation (7:7–20).

Micah was a contemporary of the prophet Isaiah. The book's superscription (1:1) places his prophetic activity during the reigns of three kings of Judah: Jotham, Ahaz, and Hezekiah. It identifies him as a resident of Moresheth, a village in the Judean foothills. The solitary reference to Micah outside the book (Jer 26:17–18) places him in the reign of Hezekiah and reports that he went from his small town to proclaim the word of the Lord in the capital, and asserts that his announcements of judgment against Jerusalem moved the king and the people to repentance. Unlike Isaiah, who was a native of the holy city, Micah was an outsider from the countryside and must have been a controversial figure. He would have been unpopular with the leaders whom he condemned (3:1–4) and the wealthy whom he criticized (2:1–5). He was quick to separate himself from priests and other prophets, whom he considered to be corrupt (3:5–8).

Just how much of the Book of Micah can be traced to the eighth-century prophet is uncertain. Tradition considers all of the words to be the recorded speeches of Micah, and some contemporary commentators agree. On the other hand, some modern scholars have thought of Micah as exclusively a prophet of doom, and therefore attributed as few as three of the seven chapters to him. The style, content, theological viewpoint, and historical perspective of some of the material reflect not the period of the Assyrian threat to Judah in the eighth century but the Babylonian exile in the sixth century B.C. and later. This is particularly evident in chap. 7, but also at other points in the book. The composition of this book, like most other prophetic texts, involved a complex editorial process. This is apparent from the fact that the stirring prophecy of peace and justice in 4:1–5 is virtually identical to Is 2:2–5.

Like Is 1–39, the Book of Micah is focused on Jerusalem, Zion, and the Judean leadership. The

Micah who speaks in this prophetic book knows the tradition that Zion is the Lord's chosen place, but he is critical of the popular view that this election ensures the city's security (2:6–13; 3:9–12). Through the prophetic voice, the Lord announces the impending punishment of God's people by means of military defeat and exile because of their failure to establish justice. After that punishment God will bring the people back to their land and establish perpetual peace. The will of God for human beings is that they do justice, love goodness, and walk humbly with God (6:6–8).

The Book of Micah is divided as follows:

I. Oracles of Punishment (1:2–3:12)
II. Oracles of Salvation (4:1–5:14)
III. Announcement of Judgment (6:1–7:6)
IV. Confidence in God's Future (7:7–20)

CHAPTER 1

See RG 359

1 The word of the LORD which came to Micah of Moresheth in the days of Jotham, Ahaz, and Hezekiah, kings of Judah, which he saw concerning Samaria and Jerusalem.

I. Oracles of Punishment

2 Hear, O peoples, all of you,
give heed, O earth, and all that is in it![a]
Let the Lord GOD be witness against you,
the Lord from his holy temple!*
3 For see, the LORD goes out from his place[b]
and descending, treads upon the heights of the earth.*
4 The mountains melt under him
and the valleys split open,
Like wax before the fire,
like water poured down a slope.
5 All this is for the crime of Jacob,
for the sins of the house of Israel.*
What is the crime of Jacob? Is it not Samaria?
And what is the sin of the house of Judah?
Is it not Jerusalem?
6 So I will make Samaria a ruin in the field,
a place to plant vineyards;
I will throw its stones into the valley,
and lay bare its foundations.*
7 All its carved figures shall be broken to pieces,[c]
all its wages shall be burned in the fire,
and all its idols I will destroy.
As the wages of a prostitute* it gathered them,
and to the wages of a prostitute they shall return.

8 * For this I will lament and wail,
go barefoot and naked;
I will utter lamentation like the jackals,
mourning like the ostriches,[d]
9 For her wound is incurable;
it has come even to Judah.
It has reached to the gate of my people,
even to Jerusalem.
10 * Do not announce it in Gath,
do not weep at all;

1:2 The prophet summons all the peoples to hear the divine accusations against them. What follows in 1:2–3:12 is a series of prophecies of punishment addressed to the capital cities of both the Northern and Southern Kingdoms, Samaria and Jerusalem. The prophecies indict the leaders and main officials, including prophets. Because of the corruption and selfishness of their leaders, Samaria and Jerusalem will fall to their enemies.

1:3 The Lord comes in a theophany which has devastating effects on the natural world (1:4).

1:5 Although the summons (1:2) had been addressed to all people, the Lord speaks against Israel and Judah, identifying their crimes with the respective capital cities of Samaria and Jerusalem. Only Samaria, however, is scheduled for destruction in the announcement of punishment (vv. 6–7).

1:6 The punishment of Samaria will be a military disaster such as the one that actually came at the hands of the Assyrian army in 722/721 B.C.

1:7 The wages of a prostitute: as often in the prophets, prostitution is a metaphor for idolatry (Hos 1–3; 4:14). **They shall return**: i.e., Samaria's idols shall come to nothing just as the wages of a prostitute are counted as nothing.

1:8–16 The prophet laments and wails, singing a funeral song or dirge over the city of Jerusalem. Finally (1:16) he calls upon the people of Jerusalem to join in the mourning.

1:10–15 Not all of the cities and villages in this long list can be located with certainty. However, those which can be identified, including the prophet's hometown, lie southwest of Jerusalem. In the Hebrew, wordplays on the names of these cities abound. The territory involved corresponds to that decimated by the Assyrian king Sennacherib in 701 B.C., during the reign of Hezekiah. **Do not weep at all**: some commentators and translators understand the Hebrew differently. They

a: Dt 32:1; Is 1:2. *b:* Is 26:21; Na 1:5; Hb 3:10. *c:* Hos 9:1. *d:* Jb 30:29.

In Beth-leaphrah
roll in the dust.[e]
11 Pass by,
you who dwell in Shaphir!
The inhabitants of Zaanan
do not come forth from their city.
There is lamentation in Beth-ezel.
It will withdraw its support from you.
12 The inhabitants of Maroth
hope for good,
But evil has come down from the LORD
to the gate of Jerusalem.
13 Harness steeds to the chariots,
inhabitants of Lachish;
You are the beginning of sin
for daughter Zion,
For in you were found
the crimes of Israel.
14 Therefore you must give back the dowry
to Moresheth-gath;
The houses of Achzib* are a dry stream bed
to the kings of Israel.
15 Again I will bring the conqueror to you,
inhabitants of Mareshah;
The glory of Israel shall come
even to Adullam.
16 Make yourself bald, cut off your hair,
for the children whom you cherish;
Make yourself bald as a vulture,
for they are taken from you into exile.*

See RG 359

CHAPTER 2

1* Ah! you plotters of iniquity,
who work out evil on your beds!
In the morning light you carry it out
for it lies within your power.
2 * You covet fields, and seize them;
houses, and take them;
You cheat owners of their houses,
people of their inheritance.
3 Therefore thus says the LORD:
Look, I am planning against this family an evil
from which you cannot free your necks;
Nor shall you walk with head held high,
for it will be an evil time.
4 On that day you shall be mocked,
and there will be bitter lament:
"Our ruin is complete,
our fields are divided among our captors,
The fields of my people are measured out,
and no one can get them back!"*
5 Thus you shall have no one
in the assembly of the LORD
to allot to you a share of land.
6 * "Do not preach," they preach,
"no one should preach of these things!
Shame will not overtake us."
7 How can it be said, house of Jacob,
"Is the LORD short of patience;
are these the Lord's deeds?"
Do not my words promise good
to the one who walks in justice?
8 But you rise up against my people as an enemy:

argue that the translation "in (unknown place name) weep!" fits the context better.

1:14 The houses of Achzib: there is a wordplay here. In the Hebrew, the word translated here as "dry stream bed" is *'achzab*; this word is sometimes translated as "deception" or "disappointment."

1:16 Shaving the head was a sign of mourning; cf. Is 3:24; Am 8:10.

2:1–5 The cry "Ah" (*hoy*) begins a typical prophetic speech that is usually continued, as here (vv. 1–2), by a description of the addressees in terms of their unrighteous activities. This description is an indictment which gives the reasons for punishment announced to a particular group of people (vv. 3–5). The prophet spells out the crimes; the Lord announces the punishment, which corresponds to the crime: those who take the land of others will have their own land taken.

Those who plot iniquity and have the power to do it are wealthy landowners. The evil which they do consists in coveting the fields and houses of others and taking them.

2:2 To covet the "house" and other property of the neighbor was a violation of the Decalogue (Ex 20:17; 34:24; Dt 5:21).

The Lord, as owner of the earth, allotted the land by tribes and families to the people of Israel (Jos 13–19). Losing one's inheritance diminished one's place in the community and threatened the family's economic viability and existence. According to Micah, those who used their power to expand their estates at the expense of weaker Israelites took more than land from them: they were tampering with the divine order.

2:4 Those who take land from the less powerful will in turn have their land taken away by invaders.

2:6–11 This unit is a disputation, an argument in which the prophet is debating with his opponents. The words of the opponents are given to us only as the prophet quotes them. The opponents accuse Micah of being a false prophet, and he re-

e: 2 Sm 1:20.

you have stripped off the garment
from the peaceful,
From those who go their way in
confidence,
as though it were spoils of war.
9 The women of my people you drive out
from their pleasant houses;
From their children you take away
forever the honor I gave them.

10 * "Get up! Leave,
this is no place to rest";
Because of uncleanness that destroys
with terrible destruction.
11 If one possessed of a lying spirit[f]
speaks deceitfully, saying,
"I will preach to you wine and strong
drink,"
that one would be the preacher for this
people.

12 * I will gather you, Jacob, each and every
one,
I will assemble all the remnant of
Israel;
I will group them like a flock in the fold,
like a herd in its pasture;
the noise of the people will resound.

13 The one who makes a breach goes up
before them;
they make a breach and pass through
the gate;
Their king shall go through before them,
the LORD at their head.

CHAPTER 3

See RG 359

1 * And I said:
Hear, you leaders of Jacob,
rulers of the house of Israel!
Is it not your duty to know what is right,
2 you who hate what is good, and love
evil?
You who tear their skin from them,
and their flesh from their bones;[g]
3 Who eat the flesh of my people,
flay their skin from them,
and break their bones;
Who chop them in pieces like flesh in a
kettle,
like meat in a pot.
4 When they cry to the LORD,
he will not answer them;
He will hide his face from them at that
time,
because of the evil they have done.

5 * Thus says the LORD regarding the
prophets:
O you who lead my people astray,
When your teeth have something to bite
you announce peace,
But proclaim war against the one
who fails to put something in your
mouth.[h]
6 Therefore you shall have night, not vision,
darkness, not divination;
The sun shall go down upon the
prophets,
and the day shall be dark for them.[i]
7 Then the seers shall be put to shame,
and the diviners confounded;
They shall all cover their lips,
because there is no answer from God.
8 But as for me, I am filled with power,
with the spirit of the LORD,
with justice and with might;

acts by accusing them of injustice and of preferring prophets and preachers who speak lies (v. 11).

2:10 The meaning of the Hebrew is uncertain.

2:12–13 This announcement of salvation to the "remnant of Israel" stands out dramatically in the context, and is probably a later addition to the words of Micah, coming from the time of the Babylonian exile. The content of the promise and the images are similar to those found in Second Isaiah, the great poet of Israel's salvation and restoration (see Is 40:11; 43:5).

3:1–4 This prophecy of punishment has an introductory call to hear (v. 1a-b) and two major parts, the indictment or reasons for punishment (vv. 1c–3) and the announcement of judgment (v. 4). The prophet accuses the leaders and rulers of Israel of treating the people so badly that their actions are comparable to cannibalism. Those who, above all, should know and maintain justice are the most corrupt of all. In the time of trouble the Lord will withdraw (v. 4); that is, God will abandon the leaders to their fate and refuse to answer their prayers.

3:5–8 This prophecy of punishment concerns and is addressed to false prophets. The prophets in Jerusalem who mislead the people are corrupt because their word can be bought (v. 5). Therefore such prophets, seers, and diviners shall be disgraced, put to shame, left in the dark without vision or answer (vv. 6–7). But Micah is convinced that he is filled with power and the spirit of the Lord, which corresponds to justice and might (v. 8).

---

f: 1 Kgs 22:22–23. *g:* Am 2:7. *h:* Ez 13:10. *i:* Jer 15:9; Am 8:9; Zec 13:3.

To declare to Jacob his crimes
and to Israel his sins.

9 * Hear this, you leaders of the house of Jacob,
you rulers of the house of Israel!
You who abhor justice,
and pervert all that is right;
10 Who build up Zion with bloodshed,
and Jerusalem with wickedness!
11 Its leaders render judgment for a bribe,
the priests teach for pay,
the prophets divine for money,
While they rely on the LORD, saying,
"Is not the LORD in the midst of us?
No evil can come upon us!"[j]
12 Therefore, because of you,
Zion shall be plowed like a field,
and Jerusalem reduced to rubble,
And the mount of the temple
to a forest ridge.[k]

II. Oracles of Salvation

CHAPTER 4

See RG 360

1 * In days to come
the mount of the LORD's house
Shall be established as the highest mountain;
it shall be raised above the hills,
And peoples shall stream to it:[l]
2 Many nations shall come, and say,
"Come, let us climb the LORD's mountain,
to the house of the God of Jacob,
That he may instruct us in his ways,
that we may walk in his paths."
For from Zion shall go forth instruction,
and the word of the LORD from Jerusalem.
3 He shall judge between many peoples
and set terms for strong and distant nations;
They shall beat their swords into plowshares,
and their spears into pruning hooks;
One nation shall not raise the sword against another,
nor shall they train for war again.
4 They shall all sit under their own vines,
under their own fig trees, undisturbed;
for the LORD of hosts has spoken.[m]
5 Though all the peoples walk,
each in the name of its god,
We will walk in the name of the LORD,
our God, forever and ever.

6 * On that day—oracle of the LORD—
I will gather the lame,
And I will assemble the outcasts,
and those whom I have afflicted.
7 I will make of the lame a remnant,
and of the weak a strong nation;
The LORD shall be king over them on Mount Zion,
from now on and forever.[n]

8 And you, O tower of the flock,*
hill of daughter Zion!
To you it shall come:
the former dominion shall be restored,
the reign of daughter Jerusalem.

9 Now why do you cry out so?
Are you without a king?
Or has your adviser perished,
That you are seized with pains

3:9–12 This is the most comprehensive of Micah's prophecies of punishment concerning the leaders in Jerusalem. The indictment (vv. 9–11) includes all political and religious leaders. They combine corruption and greed with a false confidence that the Lord is on their side. But the announcement of judgment (v. 12) is not limited to the punishment of the leaders but includes Mount Zion where the Temple stands and the entire city, thus encompassing the entire population.

4:1–4 This magnificent prophecy of salvation is almost identical to Is 2:2–5, with the exception of its last verse. See also Jl 4:9–10, which transforms the promise into a call to war. It is not known if Micah or an editor of the book picked up the announcement from his contemporary Isaiah or if Isaiah borrowed it from Micah. Perhaps both Isaiah and Micah depended upon another, more ancient tradition. The ground of the prophetic hope voiced here is the justice and grace of the God who has chosen Israel. The basis for peace shall be a just order where all are obedient to the divine will. While the vision is a universal one, including all peoples and nations (vv. 3–4), its center and wellspring is the Temple of the Lord of Israel on Mount Zion in Jerusalem.

4:6–8 An announcement of salvation proclaiming that the Lord will restore the lame and afflicted people of God as a nation on Mount Zion. **Oracle of the LORD**: a phrase used extensively in prophetic books to indicate divine speech.

4:8 Tower of the flock: in Hebrew *migdal-eder*, a place name in Gn 35:21.

j: Ez 22:27; Zep 3:3. *k:* Jer 26:18. *l:* Is 2:2–4. *m:* Hos 14:8; Am 9:14. *n:* Is 6:13; Dn 7:14; Zep 3:19; Lk 1:32.

like a woman in labor?
10 * Writhe, go into labor,
O daughter Zion,
like a woman giving birth;
For now you shall leave the city
and camp in the fields;
To Babylon you shall go,
there you shall be rescued.
There the LORD shall redeem you
from the hand of your enemies.

11 * And now many nations are gathered
against you!
They say, "Let her be profaned,
let our eyes see Zion's downfall!"
12 But they do not know the thoughts of the
LORD,
nor understand his plan:
He has gathered them
like sheaves to the threshing floor.
13 Arise and thresh, O daughter Zion;
your horn I will make iron
And your hoofs I will make bronze,
that you may crush many peoples;
You shall devote their spoils to the LORD,*
their riches to the Lord of the whole
earth.[o]

14 Now grieve, O grieving daughter!*
"They have laid siege against us!"
With the rod they strike on the cheek
the ruler of Israel.

CHAPTER 5

See RG 360

1* But you, Bethlehem-Ephrathah[p]
least among the clans of Judah,
From you shall come forth for me
one who is to be ruler in Israel;
Whose origin is from of old,
from ancient times.
2 Therefore the Lord will give them up,
until the time
when she who is to give birth has
borne,*
Then the rest of his kindred shall return
to the children of Israel.[q]
3 He shall take his place as shepherd
by the strength of the LORD,
by the majestic name of the LORD, his
God;
And they shall dwell securely, for now
his greatness
shall reach to the ends of the earth:
4 he shall be peace.*
If Assyria invades our country
and treads upon our land,
We shall raise against it seven shepherds,
eight of royal standing;
5 They shall tend the land of Assyria with
the sword,
and the land of Nimrod* with the
drawn sword;
They will deliver us from Assyria,
when it invades our land,
when it treads upon our borders.

6 The remnant of Jacob shall be
in the midst of many peoples,
Like dew coming from the LORD,
like showers on the grass,
Which wait for no one,
delay for no human being.
7 And the remnant of Jacob shall be among
the nations,
in the midst of many peoples,
Like a lion among beasts of the forest,
like a young lion among flocks of
sheep;
When it passes through it tramples;

4:10 Frequently the prophets personify the city of Jerusalem as a woman, and here as a woman in labor.

4:11–13 The nations who have ridiculed Zion (v. 11) will be threshed like grain (v. 13).

4:13 Devote their spoils to the LORD: the fulfillment of the ancient ordinance of the holy war in which all plunder taken in the war was "put under the ban," i.e., belonged to the Lord.

4:14 Grieve, O grieving daughter!: the Hebrew actually reflects the ancient Near Eastern mourning practice of afflicting oneself with cuts and gashes, as evidence of grief. A literal rendering would be "gash yourself, O woman who gashes."

5:1–6 Salvation will come through a "messiah," an anointed ruler. The Book of Micah shares with Isaiah the expectation that God will deliver Israel through a king in the line of David. Bethlehem-Ephrathah is the home of the Davidic line.

5:2 These words are sometimes understood as a reference to Isaiah's Emmanuel oracle, given some thirty years earlier (Is 7:14). The Gospel of Matthew reports that the chief priests and scribes cite this passage as the ancient promise of a messiah in the line of David to be born in Bethlehem (Mt 2:5–6).

5:4 Peace: he will not only symbolize but also bring about harmony and wholeness.

5:5 Nimrod: the legendary ancestor of the Mesopotamians; cf. Gn 10:10–12.

o: Is 41:15; Hos 10:11. *p:* Ru 1:2; 1 Sm 17:12; Mt 2:6; Jn 7:42. *q:* Is 7:14; 11:1–2.

it tears and no one can rescue.
8 Your hand shall be lifted above your foes,
and all your enemies shall be cut down.

9 * On that day—oracle of the LORD—
I will destroy the horses from your midst
and ruin your chariots;
10 I will destroy the cities of your land
and tear down all your fortresses.
11 I will destroy the sorcery you practice,
and there shall no longer be
soothsayers among you.
12 I will destroy your carved figures
and the sacred stones* from your
midst;
And you shall no longer worship
the works of your hands.[r]
13 I will tear out the asherahs from your
midst,
and destroy your cities.
14 I will wreak vengeance in anger and
wrath
upon the nations that have not listened.

III. Announcement of Judgment

CHAPTER 6

See RG 360

1 * Hear, then, what the LORD says:
Arise, plead your case before the
mountains,
and let the hills hear your voice![s]
2 Hear, O mountains, the LORD's case,
pay attention, O foundations of the
earth!
For the LORD has a case against his
people;
he enters into trial with Israel.
3 My people, what have I done to you?
how have I wearied you? Answer me![t]
4 I brought you up from the land of Egypt,
from the place of slavery I ransomed
you;
And I sent before you Moses,
Aaron, and Miriam.[u]
5 * My people, remember what Moab's
King Balak planned,
and how Balaam, the son of Beor,
answered him.
Recall the passage from Shittim to
Gilgal,
that you may know the just deeds of
the LORD.[v]
6 * With what shall I come before the
LORD,
and bow before God most high?
Shall I come before him with burnt
offerings,
with calves a year old?[w]
7 Will the LORD be pleased with thousands
of rams,
with myriad streams of oil?
* Shall I give my firstborn for my crime,
the fruit of my body for the sin of my
soul?
8 * You have been told, O mortal, what is
good,
and what the LORD requires of you:
Only to do justice and to love goodness,

5:9–13 The Lord will destroy all those features of the nation's life that have stood between the people and their God. These false supports include horses, chariots, fortifications, and forbidden practices such as sorcery and idolatry.

5:12–13 Sacred stones . . . asherahs: the Hebrew *asherah* is a sacred pole. All forms of idolatry (standing stones and sacred poles were part of forbidden cult practices) were violations of Israel's covenant with the Lord.

6:1–5 The Lord, through the prophet, initiates a legal case against the people. The initial calls (vv. 1–2) signal the beginning of a trial, and the proclamation that the Lord intends to enter into a legal dispute with Israel. One would expect accusations to follow such an introduction, but instead the Lord speaks in self-defense, reciting mighty acts done in behalf of Israel (vv. 3–5).

6:5 The Lord calls for the people to remember the saving events of the past, from the encounters with Balak and Balaam (Nm 22:23) during the wandering in the wilderness to the entrance into the promised land ("from Shittim to Gilgal," Jos 3–5).

6:6–8 These verses continue the previous unit (6:1–5), the dialogue between the Lord and the people in the pattern of a trial. The Lord has initiated proceedings against them, and they ask how to re-establish the broken relationship with God (vv. 6–7), and are given an answer (v. 8). The form of the passage borrows from a priestly liturgical pattern. When worshipers came to the temple, they inquired of the priest concerning the appropriate offering or sacrifice, and the priest answered them (see Ps 15; 24; Is 1:10–17; Am 5:21–24).

6:7 The questions reach their climax with the possibility of child sacrifice, a practice known in antiquity (cf. 2 Kgs 16:3; 21:6).

6:8 To do justice refers to human behavior in relationship to others. *To love goodness* refers to the kind of love and concern which is at the heart of the covenant between the Lord and Israel; it is persistently faithful. **To walk humbly with your God** means to listen carefully to the revealed will of God.

r: Hos 3:4; 10:1–2. *s:* Is 6:2; Ob 1. *t:* Jer 2:5. *u:* Ex 15:20. *v:* Nm 22:23; Jos 3–5. *w:* Hos 6:6; 8:13; Am 5:21.

and to walk humbly with your God.[x]
9 * The LORD cries aloud to the city
(It is prudent to fear your name!):
Hear, O tribe and city assembly,
10 Am I to bear criminal hoarding
and the accursed short ephah?*
11 Shall I acquit crooked scales,
bags of false weights?
12 You whose wealthy are full of violence,
whose inhabitants speak falsehood
with deceitful tongues in their
mouths!
13 I have begun to strike you
with devastation because of your sins.
14 You shall eat, without being satisfied,
food that will leave you empty;
What you acquire, you cannot save;
what you do save, I will deliver up to
the sword.[y]
15 You shall sow, yet not reap,
tread out the olive, yet pour no oil,
crush the grapes, yet drink no wine.[z]
16 You have kept the decrees of Omri,
and all the works of the house of
Ahab,
and you have walked in their counsels;
Therefore I will deliver you up to ruin,
and your citizens to derision;
and you shall bear the reproach of the
nations.

CHAPTER 7

See RG 360

1 Woe is me! I am like the one who
gathers summer fruit,
when the vines have been gleaned;
There is no cluster to eat,
no early fig that I crave.
2 The faithful have vanished from the
earth,
no mortal is just!
They all lie in wait to shed blood,
each one ensnares the other.[a]
3 Their hands succeed at evil;
the prince makes demands,
The judge is bought for a price,
the powerful speak as they please.[b]
4 The best of them is like a brier,
the most honest like a thorn hedge.
The day announced by your sentinels!
Your punishment has come;
now is the time of your confusion.
5 Put no faith in a friend,
do not trust a companion;
With her who lies in your embrace
watch what you say.[c]
6 For the son belittles his father,
the daughter rises up against her
mother,
The daughter-in-law against her
mother-in-law,
and your enemies are members of your
household.[d]

IV. Confidence in God's Future

7 But as for me, I will look to the LORD,
I will wait for God my savior;
my God will hear me![e]
8 * Do not rejoice over me, my enemy!*
though I have fallen, I will arise;
though I sit in darkness, the LORD is
my light.
9 I will endure the wrath of the LORD
because I have sinned against him,
Until he pleads my case,
and establishes my right.
He will bring me forth to the light;
I will see his righteousness.
10 When my enemy sees this,
shame shall cover her:
She who said to me,

6:9–16 The language of the trial resumes as the Lord accuses the people of their sins (vv. 9–12, 16a) and announces their punishment (vv. 13–15, 16b). The city is Jerusalem, and those addressed are its inhabitants. Their wickedness includes cheating in business with false weights and measures, violence, lies, and following the practices of the Israelite kings Omri and Ahab (v. 16a), whose reigns came to symbolize a time of syncretistic worship. The punishment, which has already begun, will include a series of disasters. Finally, the Lord will destroy the city and see that its inhabitants are ridiculed (v. 16b).

6:10 Ephah: see note on Is 5:10.

7:8–20 The book concludes with a collection of confident prayers for deliverance, affirmations of faith, and announcements of salvation. Most of these verses bear the marks of use in worship, and probably arose in the exilic or postexilic periods.

7:8–10 An individual, possibly personified Jerusalem, expresses confidence that the Lord will deliver her from her enemy (cf. Ps 23).

x: Dt 26:16; Zec 7:9; Mt 23:23. *y:* Dt 28:38; Am 5:11; Hg 1:6. *z:* Hos 4:10. *a:* Is 1:21; Hos 4:2. *b:* Is 1:23. *c:* Jer 9:3. *d:* Mt 10:35–36. *e:* Is 8:17.

"Where is the LORD, your God?"
My eyes shall see her downfall;
now she will be trampled* underfoot,
like mud in the streets.
11 * It is the day for building your walls;
on that day your boundaries shall be enlarged.
12 It is the day when those from Assyria to Egypt
shall come to you,
And from Tyre even to the River,
from sea to sea, and from mountain to mountain;[f]
13 And the earth shall be a waste
because of its inhabitants,
as a result of their deeds.

14 * Shepherd your people with your staff,
the flock of your heritage,
That lives apart[g] in a woodland,
in the midst of an orchard.
Let them feed in Bashan and Gilead,
as in the days of old;
15 As in the days when you came from the land of Egypt,
show us wonderful signs.
16 The nations will see and will be put to shame,
in spite of all their strength;
They will put their hands over their mouths;
their ears will become deaf.
17 They will lick the dust like a snake,
like crawling things on the ground;
They will come quaking from their strongholds;
they will tremble in fear of you, the LORD, our God.
18 * Who is a God like you, who removes guilt
and pardons sin for the remnant of his inheritance;
Who does not persist in anger forever,
but instead delights in mercy,[h]
19 And will again have compassion on us,
treading underfoot our iniquities?
You will cast into the depths of the sea all our sins;
20 You will show faithfulness to Jacob,
and loyalty to Abraham,
As you have sworn to our ancestors
from days of old.[i]

7:10 She who said . . . she will be trampled: in the Old Testament, cities are often personified as women. Here, the prophet is speaking of the enemies' cities.

7:11–13 An announcement of salvation to Zion. The walls of Jerusalem will be rebuilt, its inhabitants who are now scattered from Assyria to Egypt shall return, but the other peoples will suffer for their evil deeds.

7:14–17 A prayer that God will care for the people as in ancient days (v. 14) is answered (vv. 15–17) when the Lord promises to do marvelous things. The nations shall be afraid and turn to the Lord.

7:18–20 The final lines of the book contain a hymn of praise for the incomparable God, who pardons sin and delights in mercy. Thus the remnant, those left after the exile, is confident in God's compassion and in the ancient promises sworn to the ancestors.

f: Zec 14:16. *g:* Nm 23:9. *h:* Jer 10:6; Acts 10:43. *i:* Ps 105:6; Is 41:8; 63:16.

See RG 361

The Book of Nahum

Shortly before the fall of Nineveh, the capital of Assyria, in 612 B.C., Nahum uttered his prophecy against the hated city. To understand the prophet's exultant outburst of joy over the impending destruction it is necessary to recall the savage cruelty of Assyria, which had made it the scourge of the ancient Near East for almost three centuries. The royal inscriptions of Assyria afford the best commentary on Nahum's burning denunciation of "the bloody city." In the wake of their conquests, mounds of heads, impaled bodies, enslaved citizens, and avaricious looters testified to the ruthlessness of the Assyrians. Just such a conquest was suffered by Israel, when its capital Samaria fell to the Assyrians in 722/721 B.C., and by Judah, when its capital Jerusalem nearly fell to invading Assyrian armies twenty years later. Little wonder that in 3:19 Judah is shown as joining in the general outburst of joy over the destruction of Nineveh!

But Nahum is not a prophet of unrestrained revenge. He asserts God's moral government of the world. Nineveh's doom is evidence that God stands against oppression and the abuse of power.

As an ancient Near Eastern superpower, Assyria had terrorized its smaller and weaker neighbors, exploiting their economies and subjugating their people for its own ends. Thus Nineveh's demise is viewed as an act of divine justice, and it is greeted by the small, oppressed countries as a time of deliverance, as a moment of renewal, and as a message of peace (2:1; 3:19).

The book is divided as follows:

I. God's Terrifying Appearance (1:2–8)
II. Nineveh's Judgment and Judah's Restoration (1:9–2:1)
III. The Attack on Nineveh (2:2–3:7)
IV. Nineveh's Inescapable Fate (3:8–19)

See RG 361

CHAPTER 1

1 Oracle* concerning Nineveh. The book of the vision of Nahum of Elkosh.

God's Terrifying Appearance

2 * A jealous and avenging God* is the LORD,
an avenger is the LORD, full of wrath;
The LORD takes vengeance on his adversaries,
and rages against his enemies;
3 The LORD is slow to anger, yet great in power;
the LORD will not leave the guilty unpunished.[a]
In stormwind* and tempest he comes,
and clouds are the dust at his feet;
4 He roars at the sea and leaves it dry,
and all the rivers he dries up.
Laid low are Bashan and Carmel,
and the bloom of Lebanon withers;*
5 The mountains quake before him,
and the hills dissolve;
The earth is laid waste before him,
the world and all who dwell in it.
6 * Before his wrath, who can stand firm,
and who can face his blazing anger?[b]
His fury is poured out like fire,
and boulders break apart before him.
7 The LORD is good to those who wait for him,
a refuge on the day of distress,
Taking care of those who look to him for protection,
8 when the flood rages;
He makes an end of his opponents,
and pursues his enemies into darkness.

Nineveh's Judgment and Judah's Restoration

9 What do you plot against the LORD,
the one about to bring total destruction?
No opponent rises a second time!
10 * Like a thorny thicket, they are tangled,
and like drunkards, they are drunk;
like dry stubble, they are utterly consumed.
11 From you has come
one plotting evil against the LORD,
one giving sinister counsel.*
12 Thus says the LORD:
though fully intact and so numerous,
they* shall be mown down and disappear.
Though I have humbled you,
I will humble you no more.
13 Now I will break his yoke off of you,
and tear off your bonds.[c]

1:1 Oracle: (Heb. *Massa'*) a word used frequently to describe a prophetic statement against a foreign nation or occasionally Israel; it is used favorably for Israel in Zec 12:1 and Mal 1:1. **Nahum of Elkosh**: Nahum means "comfort." Elkosh is a clan or village of unknown location, perhaps in southern Judah.

1:2–8 A poem written in the style of the alphabetic psalms (cf. Ps 9; 25; 111; 119) in which each verse unit begins with a successive letter of the Hebrew alphabet. The second half of the alphabet is not represented here.

1:2 A jealous . . . God: see note on Ex 20:5.

1:3–6 In stormwind: the power of God is often pictured by natural forces and cosmic disruption (Ex 19:9–25; Ps 18:8–16; 104:1–9).

1:4 Bashan, Carmel, and Lebanon were famous for their mountainous terrain and lush forests.

1:6–7 When God comes in judgment those who oppose God will be destroyed, and those who trust in God will be saved.

1:10 Thorns (Is 34:13), drunkenness (Lam 4:21; Na 3:11), and burning stubble (Ob 18) are all images of the judgment of God's enemies.

1:11 From you . . . giving sinister counsel: addressed to Nineveh, the capital city of Sennacherib, king of Assyria, who besieged Jerusalem ca. 700 B.C.

1:12–13 They: the enemies of Judah. **You**: Judah. **His yoke**: the dominion of the Assyrian king over Judah.

a: Ex 34:6–7; Jl 2:13. *b:* Is 30:27–28; Zep 1:15. *c:* Is 9:4; 10:27.

14 The LORD has commanded regarding you:*
no descendant will again bear your name;
From the house of your gods I will abolish
the carved and the molten image;
I will make your grave a dung heap.

CHAPTER 2

See RG 361

1 At this moment on the mountains
the footsteps of one bearing good news,
of one announcing peace![d]
Celebrate your feasts, Judah,
fulfill your vows!
For never again will destroyers invade you;*
they are completely cut off.

The Attack on Nineveh

2 One who scatters has come up against you;*
guard the rampart,
Watch the road, brace yourselves,
marshal all your strength!
3 * The LORD will restore the vine of Jacob,
the honor of Israel,
Because ravagers have ravaged them
and ruined their branches.
4 The shields of his warriors are crimsoned,
the soldiers clad in scarlet;
Like fire are the trappings of the chariots
on the day he prepares for war;
the cavalry is agitated!
5 The chariots dash madly through the streets
and wheel in the squares,
Looking like torches,
bolting like lightning.
6 His picked troops are called,
ranks break at their charge;
To the wall they rush,
their screen* is set up.
7 The river gates* are opened,
the palace is washed away.
8 The mistress is led forth captive,
and her maidservants* led away,
Moaning like doves,
beating their breasts.
9 Nineveh is like a pool
whose waters escape;
"Stop! Stop!"
but none turns back.[e]
10 "Plunder the silver, plunder the gold!"
There is no end to the treasure,
to wealth in every precious thing!
11 Emptiness, desolation, waste;
melting hearts and trembling knees,
Churning in every stomach,
every face turning pale![f]
12 Where is the lionesses' den,
the young lions' cave,
Where the lion* went in and out,
and the cub, with no one to disturb them?[g]
13 The lion tore apart enough for his cubs,
and strangled for his lionesses;
He filled his lairs with prey,
and his dens with torn flesh.
14 I now come against you—
oracle of the LORD of hosts—
I will consume your chariots in smoke,
and the sword will devour your young lions;

1:14 You: the king of Assyria.

2:1 For never again will destroyers invade you: prophets are not always absolutely accurate in the things they foresee. Nineveh was destroyed, as Nahum expected, but Judah was later invaded by the Babylonians and (much later) by the Romans. The prophets were convinced that Israel held a key place in God's plan and looked for the people to survive all catastrophes, always blessed by the Lord, though the manner was not always as they expected; the "fallen hut of David" was not rebuilt as Am 9:11 suggests, except in the coming of Jesus, and in a way far different than the prophet expected. Often the prophet speaks in hyperbole, as when Second Isaiah speaks of the restored Jerusalem being built with precious stones (Is 54:12) as a way of indicating a glorious future.

2:2 One who scatters has come up against you: the enemy is about to crush Nineveh, dispersing and deporting its people (v. 8; 3:18).

2:3 This verse does not fit its context well; it may have been the conclusion for the preceding section and have once followed v. 1, or it may be a later scribal addition.

2:6 Their screen: that is, a mantelet, a movable military shelter protecting the besiegers.

2:7 River gates: a network of canals brought water into Nineveh from the Tigris and Khosr Rivers on which the city was located.

2:8 Mistress . . . and her maidservants: either the queen of Nineveh with the ladies of her court, or the city of Nineveh itself, pictured as a noblewoman (3:4).

2:12 The lion: the king of Assyria.

d: Is 52:7; Rom 10:15. *e:* Is 8:7–8. *f:* Jl 2:6. *g:* Ez 19:2–7.

Your preying on the land I will bring to
an end,
the cry of your lionesses will be heard
no more.

CHAPTER 3

See RG 361

1 Ah! The bloody city,
all lies,
Full of plunder,
whose looting never stops![h]
2 The crack of the whip,
the rumbling of wheels;
Horses galloping,
chariots bounding,
3 Cavalry charging,
the flash of the sword,
the gleam of the spear;
A multitude of slain,
a mass of corpses,
Endless bodies
to stumble upon!
4 For the many debaucheries of the
prostitute,
a charming mistress of
witchcraft,
Who enslaved nations with her
prostitution,
and peoples by her witchcraft:[i]
5 * I now come against you—
oracle of the LORD of hosts—
and I will lift your skirt above your
face;
I will show your nakedness to the
nations,
to the kingdoms your shame![j]
6 I will cast filth upon you,
disgrace you and make you a
spectacle;
7 Until everyone who sees you
runs from you saying,
"Nineveh is destroyed;
who can pity her?
Where can I find
any to console you?"

Nineveh's Inescapable Fate

8 Are you better than No-amon* [k]
that was set among the Nile's canals,
Surrounded by waters,
with the river for her rampart
and water for her wall?
9 Ethiopia was her strength,
and Egypt without end;
Put* and the Libyans
were her allies.
10 Yet even she became an exile,
and went into captivity;
Even her little ones were dashed to pieces
at the corner of every street;
For her nobles they cast lots,
and all her great ones were put into
chains.
11 You, too, will drink of this;
you will be overcome;[l]
You, too, will seek
a refuge from the foe.
12 But all your fortresses are fig trees,
bearing early figs;*
When shaken, they fall
into the devourer's mouth.
13 Indeed your troops
are women in your midst;
To your foes are open wide
the gates of your land,
fire has consumed their bars.
14 Draw water for the siege,*
strengthen your fortresses;
Go down into the mud
and tread the clay,
take hold of the brick mold!
15 There the fire will consume you,
the sword will cut you down;
it will consume you like the
grasshoppers.

Multiply like the grasshoppers,
multiply like the locusts![m]
16 You have made your traders* more
numerous

3:5–6 The punishment for adulterous women.

3:8 No-amon: "No" was the Egyptian name of the capital of Upper Egypt, called Thebes by the Greeks; its patron deity was Amon. This great city was destroyed by the Assyrians in 663 B.C.

3:9 Put: a North African people often associated with Egypt and Ethiopia (Jer 46:8–9).

3:12 Early figs: the refugees from Nineveh who escape to presumably secure fortresses.

3:14 An ironic exhortation to prepare the city for a futile defense. **Go down . . . brick mold**: make bricks for the city walls.

3:16 Traders: agents of the economic exploitation that sustained and enriched the Assyrian empire.

h: Is 10:13–14; Hb 2:12. *i:* Mi 1:7; Rev 17:1. *j:* Is 47:3; Jer 13:26. *k:* Jer 46:25. *l:* Jer 25:15–16; Ob 16. *m:* Jer 46:23.

than the stars of the heavens;
like grasshoppers that shed their skins
and fly away.
17 Your sentries are like locusts,
and your scribes like locust
swarms
Gathered on the rubble fences
on a cold day!
Yet when the sun rises, they
vanish,
and no one knows where they have
gone.
18 Your shepherds slumber,
O king of Assyria,
your nobles have gone to rest;
Your people are scattered upon the
mountains,
with none to gather them.
19 There is no healing for your hurt,
your wound is fatal.
All who hear this news of you
clap their hands over you;
For who has not suffered
under your endless malice?

See RG 362–63

The Book of Habakkuk

Habakkuk is the only prophet to devote his entire work to the question of the justice of God's government of the world. In the Bible as a whole, only Job delivers a more pointed challenge to divine rule. Habakkuk's challenge is set up as a dialogue between the prophet and God, in which Habakkuk's opening complaint about injustices in Judean society (1:2–4) is followed in 1:5–11 by God's promise that the perpetrators will be punished by invading Chaldeans, i.e., Babylonians. Habakkuk's second complaint about the violence of the Chaldeans themselves (1:12–2:1) is followed by a second divine response assuring the prophet of the reliability of God's rule and calling for human faithfulness (2:2–4).

This dialogue is followed by a series of observations on the disastrous nature of tyranny (2:5–20), and by a vivid description in chap. 3 of God's appearance to save the people. Chapter 3 may be the prophet's prayer that God fulfill the promises made earlier to Habakkuk, or a hymn praising God's power added to Habakkuk's speeches by editors. In either case, the description of the theophany draws heavily upon ancient traditions in which God establishes order by defeating chaos, symbolized by rebellious waters (see Jb 7:12; Ps 74:13–14; 77:17–21; 89:10–11; Is 51:9).

Two important events frame Habakkuk's prophecy: the great Babylonian (Chaldean) victory over the Egyptians at Carchemish (605 B.C.) and the second Babylonian invasion of Judah (587 B.C.), which ended with the destruction of Jerusalem. The desperate conditions in Judah during these years, arising from internal and external threats, provoked Habakkuk's struggle with difficult and important theological questions about divine justice.

The book may be divided as follows:

I. Habakkuk's First Complaint (1:2–4)
II. God's Response (1:5–11)
III. Habakkuk's Second Complaint (1:12–2:1)
IV. God's Response (2:2–4)
V. Sayings Against Tyrants (2:5–20)
VI. Hymn About God's Reign (3:1–19)

CHAPTER 1

See RG 362–63

1 The oracle which Habakkuk the prophet received in a vision.

Habakkuk's First Complaint

2 How long, O LORD, must I cry for help*
and you do not listen?[a]
Or cry out to you, "Violence!"
and you do not intervene?
3 Why do you let me see iniquity?
why do you simply gaze at evil?

1:2–4 The prophet complains about God's apparent disregard for Judah's internal evils in language that echoes the preaching of prophets like Amos, Isaiah, and Jeremiah.

a: Ps 13:2.

Destruction and violence are before me;[b]
there is strife and discord.
4 This is why the law is numb*
and justice never comes,
For the wicked surround the just;[c]
this is why justice comes forth
perverted.

God's Response

5 * Look over the nations and see!
Be utterly amazed!
For a work is being done in your days
that you would not believe, were it
told.[d]
6 For now I am raising up the Chaldeans,[e]
that bitter and impulsive people,
Who march the breadth of the land
to take dwellings not their own.
7 They are terrifying and dreadful;
their right and their exalted position
are of their own making.
8 Swifter than leopards are their horses,
and faster than desert wolves.
Their horses spring forward;
they come from far away;
they fly like an eagle hastening to
devour.
9 All of them come for violence,
their combined onslaught, a
stormwind
to gather up captives like sand.
10 They scoff at kings,
ridicule princes;
They laugh at any fortress,
heap up an earthen ramp, and
conquer it.
11 Then they sweep through like the wind
and vanish—
they make their own strength their
god!*

Habakkuk's Second Complaint

12 Are you not from of old, O LORD,
my holy God, immortal?[f]
LORD, you have appointed them for
judgment,*
O Rock,* you have set them in place to
punish!
13 Your eyes are too pure to look upon
wickedness,
and the sight of evil you cannot
endure.
Why, then, do you gaze on the faithless
in silence
while the wicked devour those more
just than themselves?
14 You have made mortals like the fish in
the sea,
like creeping things without a leader.
15 He* brings them all up with a hook,
and hauls them away with his net;
He gathers them in his fishing net,
and then rejoices and exults.
16 Therefore he makes sacrifices to his net,*
and burns incense to his fishing net;
For thanks to them his portion is rich,
and his meal lavish.
17 Shall they, then, keep on drawing his
sword
to slaughter nations without mercy?

CHAPTER 2

See RG 362–63

1 I will stand at my guard post,
and station myself upon the rampart;[g]
I will keep watch to see what he will say
to me,

1:4 The law is numb: because the Lord has been silent, the Law, whether in the form of the scroll found in the Temple in the time of Josiah (2 Kgs 22) or in the form of divine instruction given by priests and prophets, has proved ineffective and so appeared to be cold, unreceptive, and powerless. For the Law to be credible, the Lord must see to it that the wicked are punished and the just rewarded.

1:5–7 Habakkuk interprets the Babylonian defeat of Egypt at Carchemish (605 B.C.) as the answer to his complaint: the Lord will send the Chaldean empire against Judah as punishment for their sins.

1:11 The primary aim of military campaigns by ancient Near Eastern rulers was usually the gathering of spoils and the collection of tribute rather than the annexation of territory. However, in the eighth century B.C., the Assyrians began to administer many conquered territories as provinces.

1:12–2:1 Appointed them for judgment: this complaint is directed against the violent Babylonians, the very nation God chose to punish Judah.

1:12 Rock: an ancient title celebrating the Lord's power and fidelity; cf. Dt 32:4; Is 26:4; 30:29; Ps 18:3, 32, 47; 95:1.

1:15 He: the Babylonian king (cf. vv. 6, 13), who easily conquers other nations and treats them as objects for his entertainment and enrichment.

1:16 He makes sacrifices to his net: the leader attributes victory to the military weapons he wields; he and his weapons have won victory, not any god.

b: Ez 45:9. *c:* Is 29:20–21. *d:* Acts 13:41. *e:* Jer 32:28. *f:* Ps 90:2. *g:* Is 21:8.

and what answer he will give to my
complaint.

God's Response

2 Then the LORD answered me and said:
Write down the vision;* [h]
Make it plain upon tablets,
so that the one who reads it may run.
3 For the vision is a witness for the
appointed time,
a testimony to the end; it will not
disappoint.
If it delays, wait for it,
it will surely come, it will not be late.
4 See, the rash have no integrity;
but the just one who is righteous
because of faith shall live.* [i]

Sayings Against Tyrants

5 * Indeed wealth is treacherous;
a proud man does not succeed.
He who opens wide his throat like Sheol,
and is insatiable as death,
Who gathers to himself all the nations,
and collects for himself all the
peoples—
6 Shall not all these take up a taunt against
him,[j]
and make a riddle about him, saying:
Ah! you who store up what is not yours
—how long can it last!—
you who load yourself down with
collateral.
7 Will your debtors* not rise suddenly?
Will they not awake, those who make
you tremble?
You will become their spoil!
8 Because you plundered many nations,
the remaining peoples shall plunder
you;
Because of the shedding of human blood,
and violence done to the land,
to the city and to all who live in it.
9 Ah! you who pursue evil gain for your
household,
setting your nest on high
to escape the reach of misfortune!
10 You have devised shame for your
household,
cutting off many peoples, forfeiting
your own life;
11 For the stone in the wall shall cry out,*
and the beam in the frame shall answer
it!
12 Ah! you who build a city by bloodshed,
and who establish a town with
injustice![k]
13 Is this not from the LORD of hosts:
peoples toil* for what the flames
consume,
and nations grow weary for nothing!
14 But the earth shall be filled
with the knowledge of the LORD's
glory,
just as the water covers the sea.[l]
15 Ah! you who give your neighbors
the cup of your wrath to drink, and
make them drunk,
until their nakedness is seen![m]
16 You are filled with shame instead of
glory;
drink, you too, and stagger!
The cup from the LORD's right hand shall
come around to you,
and utter shame shall cover your glory.

2:2 Write down the vision: the vision is written down for two reasons: so that a herald may carry and proclaim its contents to the people, and so that the reception of the vision and its truth can be verified by its fulfillment (v. 3).

2:4 The just one who is righteous because of faith shall live: the faithful survive the impending doom because they trust in God's justice and wait patiently for God to carry it out. Several New Testament passages cite these words (Rom 1:17; Gal 3:11; cf. Heb 10:38) to confirm the teaching that people receive justification and supernatural life through faith in Christ.

2:5 This verse describes any tyrant who, like the Babylonians, possesses insatiable greed.

2:7 Debtors: the Hebrew term can mean either debtors or creditors, and this double meaning is likely intended: the debtor nations rise up against their creditor nation and become its creditors in the reversal of affairs described here.

2:11–12 The palaces, built at the expense of gross injustice (vv. 6–10), call down vengeance on their builders. This is typical prophetic language for the condemnation of social crimes within Israel and Judah.

2:13 Peoples toil: those oppressed by the Babylonians do not benefit from their work. Verses 13–14 break the pattern of reversal in the oracles that precede and may have been added by an editor.

h: Is 30:8. *i:* Rom 1:17; Gal 3:11; Heb 10:38. *j:* Is 14:4. *k:* Ez 24:6; Mi 3:10; Na 3:1. *l:* Is 11:9. *m:* Jer 51:7; Lam 4:21.

17 For the violence done to Lebanon* shall
cover you,[n]
and the destruction of the animals shall
terrify you;
Because of the shedding of human blood,
and violence done to the land,
to the city and to all who live in it.

18 Of what use is the carved image,*
that its maker should carve it?
Or the molten image, the lying oracle,
that its very maker should trust in it,
and make mute idols?
19 Ah! you who say to wood, "Awake!"
to silent stone, "Arise!"
Can any such thing give oracles?[o]
It is only overlaid with gold and silver,
there is no breath in it at all.
20 But the LORD is in his holy temple;
silence before him, all the earth![p]

See RG 362–63

CHAPTER 3

Hymn About God's Reign

1 Prayer of Habakkuk, the prophet. According to Shigyonot.*

2 O LORD, I have heard your renown,
and am in awe, O LORD, of your work.
In the course of years revive it,*
in the course of years make yourself
known;
in your wrath remember compassion!

3 * God came from Teman,*
the Holy One from Mount Paran.[q]
Selah

His glory covered the heavens,
and his praise filled the earth;
4 his splendor spread like the light.
He raised his horns high,[r]
he rejoiced on the day of his strength.
5 Before him went pestilence,
and plague* followed in his steps.
6 He stood and shook the earth;
he looked and made the nations
tremble.
Ancient mountains were shattered,
the age-old hills bowed low,
age-old orbits* collapsed.

7 The tents of Cushan trembled,
the pavilions of the land of Midian.*
8 Was your anger against the rivers,
O LORD?
your wrath against the rivers,
your rage against the sea,*[s]
That you mounted your steeds,
your victorious chariot?
9 You readied your bow,
you filled your bowstring with arrows.
Selah

You split the earth with rivers;
10 at the sight of you the mountains
writhed.
The clouds poured down water;
the deep roared loudly.

2:17 The violence done to Lebanon: the destruction of the cedar forests of Lebanon, used in lavish building projects by the great conquerors; cf. Is 14:8; 37:24. **The destruction of the animals**: the killing off of the wild animals through excessive hunting by the same conquerors; cf. Bar 3:16.

2:18–20 Idolatrous worship is here shown to be folly by contrasting idols with the majesty of the one true God. Verse 18 may originally have followed v. 19, since the term "Ah!" begins each new saying in this section.

3:1 Shigyonot: a Hebrew technical term no longer understood, but probably a musical notation regarding the following hymn. This term, the references to the leader and stringed instruments at the end of the hymn (v. 19), and the use of the term *selah* in vv. 3, 9, and 13 are found elsewhere in the Bible only in the Psalter, and they indicate that, like the psalms, this poem was once used in worship.

3:2 In the course of years revive it: a plea for God to renew the works of the past.

3:3–15 Cf. the theophanies in Dt 33:2–3; Jgs 5:4–5; Ps 18:8–16; 68:8–9; 77:17–21; 97:1–5; Na 1:3–6, etc. Conventional language is employed to describe the appearance of the Lord, as in Ex 19:16–19.

3:3 Teman: a region in Edom. **Mount Paran**: in the territory of Edom, or the northern part of the Sinai peninsula.

3:5 Pestilence . . . plague: these may be figures who are part of the heavenly armies God leads into battle.

3:6 Age-old orbits: the regular paths through the skies of heavenly bodies are disrupted at the appearance of the divine warrior, as are the ancient mountains on earth. Such cosmic disruption is typical of divine appearances (Ps 18:8; Na 1:5).

3:7 Cushan . . . Midian: the inhabitants of the area southeast of Judah where the divine march originates (Teman, Mount Paran), who are shaken, together with the cosmos, at God's appearance.

3:8 Rivers . . . sea: the forces of chaos personified as *yam* (Sea) and *nahar* (River) try to destroy the order God imposed at creation by sweeping past their boundaries and covering the earth. Their mention here and in v. 15 emphasizes that God is both creator and deliverer, subduing historical enemies and cosmic forces.

n: Is 14:8. *o:* Is 44:18–19. *p:* Ps 11:4. *q:* Dt 33:2. *r:* Ps 18:3. *s:* Ps 74:13; 89:11; Is 51:9; Na 1:4.

The sun* forgot to rise,
11 the moon left its lofty station,[t]
At the light of your flying arrows,
at the gleam of your flashing spear.

12 In wrath you marched on the earth,
in fury you trampled the nations.
13 You came forth to save your people,
to save your anointed one.*
You crushed the back of the wicked,
you laid him bare, bottom to neck.
Selah

14 * You pierced his head with your shafts;
his princes you scattered with your
stormwind,
as food for the poor in unknown
places.
15 You trampled the sea with your horses
amid the churning of the deep waters.

16 I hear, and my body trembles;
at the sound, my lips quiver.
Decay invades my bones,
my legs tremble beneath me.
I await the day of distress
that will come upon the people who
attack us.

17 For though the fig tree does not blossom,
and no fruit appears on the vine,
Though the yield of the olive fails
and the terraces produce no
nourishment,
Though the flocks disappear from the
fold
and there is no herd in the stalls,
18 Yet I will rejoice in the LORD
and exult in my saving God.
19 GOD, my Lord, is my strength;
he makes my feet swift as those of
deer
and enables me to tread upon the
heights.* [u]

For the leader; with stringed instruments.

3:10–11 Sun . . . moon: heavenly figures who, like pestilence and plague (v. 5), serve in God's army, or are startled at God's appearance, as are the ancient constellations (v. 6).

3:13 Your anointed one: the theocratic king, the head of God's people. **The back of the wicked**: this may refer both to God's cosmic enemy, River/Sea, and to the leader of Israel's historical enemy.

3:14 The last two lines of this verse are obscure in Hebrew and difficult to translate.

3:19 The heights: this term can also mean "backs" and may be an image of conquest over the poet's foes.

t: Jos 10:12–13. *u:* Ps 18:32–34.

See RG 363–64

The Book of Zephaniah

Zephaniah's prophecy of judgment on Judah and Jerusalem emphasizes, perhaps more than any other prophecy, the devastation and death that divine judgment will bring. Described as the day of the Lord, the day of judgment is pictured as a time of darkness, of anguish and distress, of destruction and plunder of cities, and of threat to all life, human and animal alike. The major sins motivating this judgment, in Zephaniah's view, are Judah's worship of other deities (1:4–9) and its unjust and abusive leadership (3:1–4).

The title of the prophecy informs us that the ministry of Zephaniah took place during the reign of Josiah (640–609 B.C.), not long before the fall of Jerusalem in 587 B.C. The protest against the worship of false gods and the condemnation of foreign practices (1:8–9) may indicate that Zephaniah spoke during the height of Assyrian influence in the early years of Josiah's reign, before Josiah launched the religious reforms praised by Israel's historians (2 Kgs 22:1–23:30). If so, the prophecy of Zephaniah would be contemporary with the early prophecy of Jeremiah, with which it shares both language and ideas.

Following are the book's four sections:

I. The Day of the Lord: Judgment on Judah (1:2–2:3)
II. Judgment on the Nations (2:4–15)
III. Jerusalem Reproached (3:1–7)
IV. The Nations Punished and Jerusalem Restored (3:8–20)

CHAPTER 1

See RG 363

[1]The word of the LORD which came to Zephaniah, the son of Cushi, the son of Gedaliah, the son of Amariah, the son of Hezekiah,* in the days of Josiah, the son of Amon, king of Judah.

The Day of the Lord: Judgment on Judah

[2] I will completely sweep away all things
from the face of the land—oracle of
the LORD.
[3] I will sweep away human being and
beast alike,
I will sweep away the birds of the sky,
and the fish of the sea.
I will make the wicked stumble;
I will eliminate the people
from the face of the land—oracle of
the LORD.[a]
[4] I will stretch out my hand against
Judah,
and against all the inhabitants of
Jerusalem;
I will eliminate from this place
the last vestige of Baal,
the name of the idolatrous priests.
[5] And those who bow down on the roofs
to the host of heaven,*
And those who bow down to the LORD
but swear by Milcom;[b]
[6] And those who have turned away from
the LORD,
and those who have not sought the
LORD,
who have not inquired of him.

[7] Silence in the presence of the Lord GOD!
for near is the day of the LORD,
Yes, the LORD has prepared a sacrifice,
he has consecrated his guests.* [c]
[8] On the day of the LORD's sacrifice
I will punish the officials and the king's
sons,
and all who dress in foreign apparel.
[9] I will punish, on that day,
all who leap over the threshold,*
Who fill the house of their master
with violence and deceit.
[10] On that day—oracle of the LORD—
A cry will be heard from the Fish Gate,
a wail from the Second Quarter,*
loud crashing from the hills.
[11] Wail, O inhabitants of Maktesh!
for all the merchants are destroyed,
all who weigh out silver, done away
with.
[12] At that time,
I will search Jerusalem with lamps,
I will punish the people
who settle like dregs in wine,*
Who say in their hearts,
"The Lord will not do good,
nor will he do harm."
[13] Their wealth shall be given to plunder
and their houses to devastation;
They will build houses,
but not dwell in them;
They will plant vineyards,
but not drink their wine.[d]
[14] Near is the great day of the LORD,
near and very swiftly coming.
The sound of the day of the LORD!
Piercing—
there a warrior shrieks!
[15] A day of wrath is that day,
a day of distress and anguish,
a day of ruin and desolation,
A day of darkness and gloom,
a day of thick black clouds,[e]
[16] A day of trumpet blasts and battle cries
against fortified cities,
against lofty battlements.[f]

1:1 Hezekiah: it is possible, but not certain, that Zephaniah's ancestor was King Hezekiah who reigned in Judah from 715 to 687 B.C. (2 Kgs 18–20).

1:5 The host of heaven: the sun, moon, planets, and stars, the worship of which became widespread in Judah under Assyrian influence. **Milcom**: the god of the Ammonites; cf. 1 Kgs 11:5, 7, 33; 2 Kgs 23:13.

1:7 He has consecrated his guests: God has consecrated the troops, presumably foreign, who have been invited to share in the spoil on the day of slaughter.

1:9 Leap over the threshold: the reference may be to a religious ritual like that practiced by the priests of the Philistine deity Dagon (1 Sm 5:5).

1:10–11 The Second Quarter . . . Maktesh: sections of Jerusalem (cf. 2 Kgs 22:14).

1:12 Settle like dregs in wine: those who are overconfident because, like the sediment that settles to the bottom of a bottle of wine, they have remained at peace and undisturbed for a long time.

a: Hos 4:3. *b:* Jer 8:2; 2 Kgs 23:13. *c:* Is 34:6; Am 5:18. *d:* Am 5:11. *e:* Is 13:9; Jl 2:1–2. *f:* Am 2:2.

17 I will hem the people in
till they walk like the blind,
because they have sinned against the LORD;
And their blood shall be poured out like dust,
and their bowels like dung.
18 Neither their silver nor their gold
will be able to save them.
On the day of the LORD's wrath,
in the fire of his passion,
all the earth will be consumed.
For he will make an end, yes, a sudden end,
of all who live on the earth.[g]

CHAPTER 2

See RG 363

1* Gather, gather yourselves together,
O nation without shame!
2 Before you are driven away,
like chaff that disappears;
Before there comes upon you
the blazing anger of the LORD;
Before there comes upon you
the day of the LORD's anger.
3 Seek the LORD,
all you humble of the land,
who have observed his law;
Seek justice,
seek humility;
Perhaps you will be sheltered
on the day of the LORD's anger.[h]

Judgment on the Nations

4 For Gaza shall be forsaken,
and Ashkelon shall be a waste,
Ashdod they shall drive out at midday,
and Ekron* shall be uprooted.[i]
5 Ah! You who dwell by the seacoast,
the nation of Cherethites,*
the word of the LORD is against you!
O Canaan, land of the Philistines,
I will leave you to perish without an inhabitant!
6 You shall become fields for shepherds,
and folds for flocks.
7 The seacoast shall belong
to the remnant of the house of Judah;
by the sea they shall pasture.
In the houses of Ashkelon
they shall lie down in the evening.
For the LORD their God will take care of them,
and bring about their restoration.

8 I have heard the taunts uttered by Moab,
and the insults of the Ammonites,*
When they taunted my people
and made boasts against their territory.[j]
9 Therefore, as I live—
oracle of the LORD of hosts—
the God of Israel,
Moab shall become like Sodom,
the Ammonites like Gomorrah:
A field of weeds,
a salt pit,
a waste forever.
The remnant of my people shall plunder them,
the survivors of my nation dispossess them.
10 This will be the recompense for their pride,
because they taunted and boasted against
the people of the LORD of hosts.
11 The LORD shall inspire them with terror
when he makes all the gods of earth waste away;
Then the distant shores of the nations,
each from its own place,
shall bow down to him.

12 You too, O Cushites,*
shall be slain by the sword of the LORD.[k]
13 He will stretch out his hand against the north,

2:1–3 This oracle is a classic description of the day of the Lord as an overwhelming disaster, concluding with a call for repentance and reform. **Nation without shame**: Judah.

2:4 Gaza . . . Ashkelon . . . Ashdod . . . Ekron: cities of the Philistine confederation.

2:5 Cherethites: a synonym for, or subgroup of, the Philistines, which may be associated with Crete, a part of the larger Aegean area from which the Philistines came.

2:8 Moab . . . Ammonites: Judah's neighbors to the East across the Jordan.

2:12 Cushites: the Ethiopians, who had ruled Egypt a generation before Zephaniah's career.

g: Zep 3:8; Jer 4:26–27. *h:* Am 5:14–15. *i:* Jer 47:5; Am 1:6–8. *j:* Jer 48:1; 49:1. *k:* 2 Chr 14:7–14.

to destroy Assyria;
He will make Nineveh a waste,
dry as the desert.[l]
14 In her midst flocks shall lie down,
all the wild life of the hollows;
The screech owl and the desert owl
shall roost in her columns;
The owl shall hoot from the window,
the raven croak from the doorway.[m]
15 Is this the exultant city*
that dwelt secure,
That told itself,
"I and there is no one else"?
How it has become a waste,
a lair for wild animals!
Those who pass by it
hiss, and shake their fists!

See RG 363–64

CHAPTER 3

Jerusalem Reproached

1 Ah! Rebellious and polluted,
the tyrannical city!*
2 It listens to no voice,
accepts no correction;
In the LORD it has not trusted,
nor drawn near to its God.[n]
3 Its officials within it
are roaring lions;
Its judges are desert wolves
that have no bones to gnaw by morning.[o]
4 Its prophets are reckless,
treacherous people;
Its priests profane what is holy,
and do violence to the law.[p]
5 But the LORD in its midst is just,
doing no wrong;
Morning after morning rendering judgment
unfailingly, at dawn;
the wicked, however, know no shame.

6 I have cut down nations,
their battlements are laid waste;
I have made their streets deserted,
with no one passing through;
Their cities are devastated,
with no one dwelling in them.[q]
7 I said, "Surely now you will fear me,
you will accept correction;
They cannot fail to see
all I have brought upon them."
Yet the more eagerly they have done
all their corrupt deeds.

The Nations Punished and Jerusalem Restored

8 Therefore, wait for me—oracle of the LORD—
until the day when I arise as accuser;
For it is my decision to gather nations,
to assemble kingdoms,
In order to pour out upon them my wrath,
all my blazing anger;
For in the fire of my passion
all the earth will be consumed.[r]

9 For then I will make pure
the speech of the peoples,
That they all may call upon the name of the LORD,
to serve him with one accord;
10 From beyond the rivers of Ethiopia
and as far as the recesses of the North,
they shall bring me offerings.

11 On that day
You will not be ashamed
of all your deeds,
when you rebelled against me;
For then I will remove from your midst
the proud braggarts,
And you shall no longer exalt yourself
on my holy mountain.
12 But I will leave as a remnant in your midst
a people humble and lowly,
Who shall take refuge in the name of the LORD—[s]
13 the remnant of Israel.
They shall do no wrong
and speak no lies;
Nor shall there be found in their mouths
a deceitful tongue;

2:15 The exultant city: Nineveh. **Hiss, and shake their fists**: gestures of derision.
3:1 The tyrannical city: Jerusalem.

l: Na 3:7. *m:* Is 34:11. *n:* Jer 2:30; 7:28. *o:* Ez 22:27; Mi 3:11. *p:* Ez 22:26; Hb 1:4. *q:* Jer 2:15. *r:* Zep 1:18; Jl 4:2. *s:* Is 57:13; Ob 17.

They shall pasture and lie down
with none to disturb them.[t]
14 Shout for joy, daughter Zion!
sing joyfully, Israel!
Be glad and exult with all your heart,
daughter Jerusalem![u]
15 The LORD has removed the judgment
against you,
he has turned away your enemies;
The King of Israel, the LORD, is in your
midst,
you have no further misfortune to fear.
16 On that day, it shall be said to
Jerusalem:
Do not fear, Zion,
do not be discouraged!
17 The LORD, your God, is in your midst,
a mighty savior,
Who will rejoice over you with gladness,
and renew you in his love,
Who will sing joyfully because of you,[v]
18 as on festival days.
I will remove disaster from among you,
so that no one may recount your
disgrace.
19 At that time I will deal
with all who oppress you;
I will save the lame,
and assemble the outcasts;
I will give them praise and renown
in every land where they were shamed.[w]
20 At that time I will bring you home,
and at that time I will gather you;
For I will give you renown and praise,
among all the peoples of the earth,
When I bring about your restoration
before your very eyes, says the LORD.[x]

t: Mi 4:4. *u:* Zec 9:9. *v:* Jl 2:27. *w:* Mi 4:6. *x:* Jl 4:1.

See RG 364–65

The Book of Haggai

Haggai's words concern conditions in the Persian province of Judah at the beginning of the postexilic period during the reign of the Persian king Darius I (522–486 B.C.). The community in Judah is struggling with its identity in light of the loss of its statehood through the demise of the monarchy and the destruction of the Temple. Haggai's oracles address both these problems. First, the provincial government, despite its subordination to Persian hegemony, is seen as the legitimate heir to the Davidic monarchy; the governor Zerubbabel, himself a descendant of the Davidic line, and the high priest Joshua together provide political, economic, and religious leadership for the survivors of the Babylonian destruction and the returnees from the Babylonian exile who live together in Judah. Still, the possibility for restoration of Davidic rule is not relinquished but rather is shifted to the eschatological future. Second, the Temple's ruined state is addressed by a rebuilding program. The prophet links the well-being of the community to the work of Temple restoration, and his exhortations to the leaders and the people to begin work on this project are apparently heeded. The brief period of Haggai's ministry (August to December 520 B.C.) marks the resumption of work on the Temple, the symbol of divine presence among the people.

Six date formulas (1:1, 15; 2:1, 10, 18, 20) are an important feature of the Book of Haggai. In their specificity and in their link to the reign of a foreign king (Darius), the dates underscore God's control over history, as do similar chronological references in Zechariah, a prophetic book connected in literary and thematic ways to Haggai.

The prophecies of Haggai can be divided into two major parts:

I. The Restoration of the Temple (1:1–15)
II. Oracles of Encouragement (2:1–23)

CHAPTER 1

See RG 364

Prophetic Call To Work on the Temple.
1 On the first day of the sixth month in the
second year* of Darius the king, the word of

1:1 First day of the sixth month in the second year: August 29, 520 B.C. This is the first of six chronological indicators in Haggai. **Darius**: Darius I, emperor of Persia from 522 to 486 B.C. **Governor**: term used for local rulers of provinces in the Persian imperial structure. **Zerubbabel**: grandson of King Jehoiachin (cf. 2 Kgs 24:8–17).

the LORD came through Haggai the prophet
to the governor of Judah, Zerubbabel,[a] son of
Shealtiel, and to the high priest Joshua, son
of Jehozadak:[b] 2Thus says the LORD of hosts:
This people has said: "Now is not the time to
rebuild the house of the LORD."

3Then the word of the LORD came through
Haggai the prophet: 4Is it time for you to
dwell in your paneled houses while this
house lies in ruins?* [c]

5 Now thus says the LORD of hosts:
Reflect on your experience!*
6 You have sown much, but have brought in little;
you have eaten, but have not been satisfied;[d]
You have drunk, but have not become intoxicated;
you have clothed yourselves, but have not been warmed;
And the hired worker labors for a bag full of holes.

7Thus says the LORD of hosts:

Reflect on your experience!
8 Go up into the hill country;
bring timber, and build the house
that I may be pleased with it,
and that I may be glorified,* says the LORD.
9 You expected much, but it came to little;
and what you brought home, I blew away.
Why is this?—oracle of the LORD* of hosts—
Because my house is the one which lies in ruins,
while each of you runs to your own house.
10 Therefore, the heavens withheld the dew,
and the earth its yield.
11 And I have proclaimed a devastating heat*
upon the land and upon the mountains,
Upon the grain, the new wine, and the olive oil,
upon all that the ground brings forth;
Upon human being and beast alike,
and upon all they produce.

Response of Leaders and People. 12Then
Zerubbabel, son of Shealtiel, and the high
priest Joshua, son of Jehozadak, and all the
remnant of the people* obeyed the LORD
their God, and the words of Haggai the
prophet, since the LORD their God had sent
him; thus the people feared the LORD.
13Then Haggai, the messenger of the LORD,
proclaimed to the people as the message of
the LORD: I am with you!—oracle of the
LORD.
14And so the LORD stirred up the spirit of
the governor of Judah, Zerubbabel, son of
Shealtiel, and the spirit of the high priest
Joshua, son of Jehozadak, and the spirit of
all the remnant of the people,[e] so that they
came to do the work in the house of the
LORD of hosts, their God, 15on the twenty-
fourth day of the sixth month in the second
year* of Darius the king.

1:4 Your paneled houses . . . house lies in ruins: the contrast here is between the unfinished Temple and the completed houses of the Judeans.

1:5 Reflect on your experience: the prophet exhorts the people to consider the futility of their efforts as a result of their neglecting work on the Temple. The following verses call attention to harsh conditions in Judah after the return from exile and the preoccupation of the people with their personal concerns.

1:8 That I may be glorified: for the prophet, the rebuilding of the Temple restores the glory God had lost in the eyes of the nations by the Temple's destruction.

1:9 Oracle of the LORD: a phrase used extensively in prophetic books to indicate divine speech.

1:11 Devastating heat: this pronouncement of natural disaster, which functions as a warning to the people for their failure to rebuild the Temple, concludes the opening oracular section of Haggai.

1:12 The remnant of the people: here the phrase appears to refer to the prophet's audience, but the "remnant" theme, though often in different Hebrew terminology, suggesting especially those whom the Lord will call back from exile and re-establish as his people, is important in the prophets (cf. Is 4:3; 37:31–32; Jl 3:5; Mi 4:7; Ob 17) and in the New Testament (cf. Rom 11:1–10).

1:15 Twenty-fourth day of the sixth month in the second year: September 21, 520 B.C. The resumption of work on the Temple occurred twenty-three days from the beginning of Haggai's prophecy. This date formula repeats in reverse order the formula of v. 1, thereby bringing to conclusion chap. 1; it also initiates the next unit in 2:1.

a: Zec 4:6–10. *b:* Zec 3:1–10. *c:* 2 Sm 7:2. *d:* Lv 26:26; Hos 4:10. *e:* Ezr 1:5; 5:1–2.

CHAPTER 2

See RG 364–65

Assurance of God's Presence. 1On the
twenty-first day of the seventh month,* the
word of the LORD came through Haggai the
prophet: 2Speak to the governor of Judah,
Zerubbabel, son of Shealtiel, and to the high
priest Joshua, son of Jehozadak, and to the
remnant of the people:

3 Who is left among you*
who saw this house in its former glory?
And how do you see it now?
Does it not seem like nothing in your
eyes?[f]
4 Now be strong, Zerubbabel—oracle of
the LORD—
be strong, Joshua, son of Jehozadak,
high priest,
Be strong, all you people of the land—
oracle of the LORD—
and work! For I am with you—oracle
of the LORD of hosts.
5 This is the commitment I made to you
when you came out of Egypt.
My spirit remains in your midst;
do not fear!
6For thus says the LORD of hosts:*
In just a little while,
I will shake the heavens and the earth,[g]
the sea and the dry land.
7 I will shake all the nations,
so that the treasures of all the nations
will come in.
And I will fill this house with glory—
says the LORD of hosts.[h]
8Mine is the silver and mine the gold—oracle of the LORD of hosts.
9 Greater will be the glory of this house[i]
the latter more than the former—says
the LORD of hosts;
And in this place I will give you peace—*
oracle of the LORD of hosts.

Priestly Ruling with Prophetic Interpretation.* 10On the twenty-fourth day of the
ninth month in the second year* of Darius,
the word of the LORD came to Haggai the
prophet: 11Thus says the LORD of hosts: Ask
the priests for a ruling:* 12If someone carries
sanctified meat in the fold of a garment and
the fold touches bread, soup, wine, oil, or
any other food, do they become sanctified?
"No," the priests answered. 13Then Haggai
asked: "If a person defiled from contact with
a corpse touches any of these, do they become defiled?" The priests answered, "They
become defiled."[j] 14Then Haggai replied:

So is this people,* and so is this nation
in my sight—oracle of the LORD—
And so is all the work of their hands;
what they offer there is defiled.

15Now reflect,* from this day forward—

2:1 Twenty-first day of the seventh month: October 17, 520 B.C.

2:3 Who is left among you: i.e., who is old enough to have seen the first Temple prior to its destruction in 587 B.C.? Compare the reaction of priests who were alive then (Ezr 3:12–13).

2:6–9 These verses emphasize that the total fulfillment of God's promises to Israel is on the horizon. Such an eschatological event, which will shake the nations (v. 6; cf. v. 21), finds an echo not only in the political revolts in the Persian empire in 521 but also in the formative events of Israel's history (Ex 19:18; Jgs 5:4; Ps 68:8–9) when God intervened on behalf of the Israelites. The bringing of treasures of all the nations (v. 7) to Jerusalem recalls the visionary passages of Isaiah of the pilgrimage of all nations to Jerusalem (Is 2:2–4; 60:6–9).

2:9 Peace: after God's presence or glory has returned to the Temple, Jerusalem will receive the treasures from the nations, making the Temple more glorious than ever; and from that place God will extend *shalom*, a peace which embraces prosperity, well-being, harmony.

2:10–14 A request for a priestly ruling (Heb. *torah*) is made in the form of a dialogue between Haggai and the priests. Explicit examples where such priestly rulings are quoted are rare in prophetic books. The interchange illustrates an essential role of the priesthood: the interpretation of God's law (cf. Lv 10:9–11).

2:10 Twenty-fourth day of the ninth month in the second year: December 18, 520 B.C.

2:11 Ask the priests for a ruling: i.e., a determination on whether defilement and sanctity can be physically transmitted. The priests are expected to make a legal decision. The answer is that sanctity cannot be transmitted (v. 12) but defilement can (v. 13). Priestly duties are enumerated in Lv 10:10–20.

2:14 So is this people: the prophet's interpretation is that the restored sacrifices were not acceptable because the people's behavior was tainted.

2:15–19 This prophecy is retrospective and should be read with 1:5–11, a description of the conditions of economic deprivation before the rebuilding of the Temple.

f: Ezr 3:10–13. *g*: Heb 12:26. *h*: Is 60:7–11. *i*: 1 Kgs 8:11. *j*: Lv 22:4–7.

before you set stone to stone in the temple of the LORD, 16 what was your experience?

When one went to a heap of grain for
twenty ephahs,
there were only ten;
When one went to a vat to draw fifty
ephahs,*
there were only twenty.[k]

17 I struck you, and all the work of your
hands,
with searing wind, blight, and hail,
yet you did not return to me—oracle
of the LORD.[l]

18 Reflect from this day forward, from the twenty-fourth day of the ninth month.* From the day on which the temple of the LORD was founded, reflect!

19 Is there still seed in the storehouse?
Have the vine, the fig, the
pomegranate,
and the olive tree still not borne fruit?
From this day, I will bless you.*

Future Hope.* 20 The word of the LORD came a second time to Haggai on the twenty-fourth day of the month:* 21 Speak to Zerubbabel, the governor of Judah:

I will shake the heavens and the earth;
22 I will overthrow the thrones of
kingdoms,
and destroy the power of the kingdoms
of the nations.
I will overthrow the chariots and their
riders,
and the riders with their horses
will fall by each other's swords.[m]

23 On that day—oracle of the LORD of hosts—I will take you, my servant, Zerubbabel, son of Shealtiel—oracle of the LORD—and I will make you like a signet ring,* for I have chosen you—oracle of the LORD of hosts.[n]

2:16 Ephahs: see note on Is 5:10.

2:18 Twenty-fourth day of the ninth month: December 18, 520 B.C., the date of the refounding of the Temple (vv. 10, 20), the central date in Haggai.

2:19 I will bless you: from the day of the refounding of the Temple, agricultural plenty and fertility are assured. This link between temple and prosperity is part of the ancient Near Eastern temple ideology that underlies Haggai and Zec 1–8.

2:20–23 This final oracle of hope is uttered on the day of the refounding of the Temple. Unlike the other oracles it is addressed to Zerubbabel alone, who, as a Davidic descendant, will have a servant role in God's future Israelite kingdom to be established when God intervenes to overthrow the nations.

2:20 Twenty-fourth day of the month: December 18, 520 B.C. (as in v. 18).

2:23 Like a signet ring: this promise to Zerubbabel reverses the punishment of his grandfather (Jer 22:23–25). A signet is a ring or other instrument used to mark documents or materials with the equivalent of an official signature. A lower official could thus be authorized to act on behalf of a higher official. Like a signet ring, Zerubbabel represents the Lord.

k: Hos 4:3a. *l:* Am 4:9. *m:* Sir 49:11. *n:* Zec 6:12–13.

See RG 365–68

The Book of Zechariah

The Book of Zechariah, because of its great variation in style, content, and language, is widely believed to be a composite work. Made up of First Zechariah (chaps. 1–8) and Second Zechariah (chaps. 9–14), the book has been attributed to at least two different prophets. The prophecies of First Zechariah can be dated to the late sixth century B.C., contemporary with those of Haggai; the oracles of Second Zechariah are somewhat later.

The most striking feature of First Zechariah is a series of visions in which the prophet describes the centrality of Jerusalem, its Temple, and its leaders, who function both in the politics of the region and of the Persian empire and in God's universal rule. These visions clearly relate to the Temple restoration begun in 520 B.C.

The prophecies of First Zechariah can be divided into three literary units. A brief introductory unit (1:1–6) links the prophecies of chaps. 1–8 with those of Haggai. The visionary unit (1:7–6:15) consists of seven visionary images plus an associated vision dealing with the high priest Joshua. The third unit (7:1–8:23) consists of two parts: (1) an address (7:1–14) to a delegation sent from Bethel in anticipation of the end of the seventy years of exile; (2) a series of oracles

(8:1–23): seven oracles dealing with the restoration of Judah and Zion (vv. 1–17), followed by three oracles of hope concerning Judah and the nations (vv. 18–23).

Coming nearly a century later, the prophecies of Second Zechariah are extraordinarily diverse. A complex assortment of literary genres appears in these six chapters, which consist of two distinct parts (chaps. 9–11 and chaps. 12–14), each introduced by an unusual Hebrew word for "oracle." Despite the diversity of materials, the structural links among the chapters along with verbal and thematic connections point to an overall integrity for Zec 9–14.

Second Zechariah draws heavily on the words and ideas of earlier biblical prophets. The prophet is acutely aware of the devastation that comes from disobedience to God's word, as had been spoken by God's prophetic emissaries. Yet, it was now clear in this century after the rebuilding of the Temple and the repatriation of many of the exiles, that Judah would not soon regain political autonomy and a Davidic king. So the various poems, narratives, oracles, and parables of Second Zechariah maintain the hope of previous prophets by depicting a glorious eschatological restoration. At that time all nations will recognize Jerusalem's centrality and acknowledge God's universal sovereignty.

CHAPTER 1

See RG 365

Call for Obedience. 1 In the second year of Darius,* in the eighth month, the word of the LORD came to the prophet Zechariah, son of Berechiah, son of Iddo: 2 The LORD was very angry with your ancestors.* [a] 3 Say to them: Thus says the LORD of hosts, Return to me—oracle of the LORD* of hosts—and I will return to you, says the LORD of hosts. 4 Do not be like your ancestors to whom the earlier prophets* proclaimed: Thus says the LORD of hosts: Turn from your evil ways and from your wicked deeds.[b] But they did not listen or pay attention to me[c]—oracle of the LORD.— 5 Your ancestors, where are they? And the prophets, can they live forever? 6 But my words and my statutes, with which I charged my servants the prophets, did these not overtake your ancestors?[d] Then they repented* and admitted: "Just as the LORD of hosts intended to treat us according to our ways and deeds, so the LORD has done."

First Vision: Horses Patrolling the Earth.[e] 7 In the second year of Darius, on the twenty-fourth day of Shebat, the eleventh month,* the word of the LORD came to the prophet Zechariah, son of Berechiah, son of Iddo:

8* I looked out in the night,* and there was a man mounted on a red horse standing in the shadows among myrtle trees; and behind him were red, sorrel, and white horses. 9 I asked, "What are these, my lord?"* Then the angel who spoke with me answered, "I will show you what these are." 10 Then the man who was standing among the myrtle trees spoke up and said, "These are the ones whom the LORD has sent to patrol the earth."[f]

1:1 Darius: Darius I, emperor of Persia from 522 to 486 B.C. **The second year . . . eighth month**: October/November 520 B.C., i.e., prior to the latest date in Haggai (Dec. 18, 520 B.C., Hg 2:10). Unlike other prophets, Haggai and Zechariah 1–8 contain specific chronological information, probably because they were sensitive to the imminent end of the expected seventy years of exile. See note on Zec 1:12.

1:2 Your ancestors: refers to the preexilic people of Judah, who were subjected to Babylonian destruction and exile.

1:3 Oracle of the LORD: a phrase used extensively in prophetic books to indicate divine speech.

1:4 Earlier prophets: preexilic prophets of the Lord. There are many allusions to them in Zechariah, indicating their influence on the postexilic community (see 7:7, 12).

1:6 Repented: the Hebrew word *shub* literally means "turn back." This term is often used to speak of repentance as a return to the covenantal relationship between Israel and the Lord.

1:7 The second year . . . eleventh month: February 15, 519 B.C. The largest set of visions (1:7–6:15) is dated to a time just prior to the beginning of the new year in the spring.

1:8–11 Four riders on horses of three different colors are sent by God to patrol the four corners of the earth. Compare the four chariots of the seventh vision, 6:1–8.

1:8 In the night: nighttime, or this night. This setting of darkness is meant only for the first vision.

1:9 My lord: this expression in Hebrew (*'adoni*) is used as a polite form of address. **Angel who spoke with me**: angelic being (not identical to the angel of the Lord who is one of the four horsemen) who serves as an interpreter, bringing a message from God to the prophet, who himself is a messenger of God.

a: Mi 3:7. *b:* Is 55:7. *c:* Lk 20:15. *d:* Zec 7:7–14. *e:* Zec 6:1–7; Rev 5:6; 6:1–9. *f:* Zec 7:5; Jer 25:11–12; 29:10.

11 And they answered the angel of the LORD,*
who was standing among the myrtle trees:
"We have been patrolling the earth, and now
the whole earth rests quietly." 12 Then the angel of the LORD replied, "LORD of hosts, how
long will you be without mercy for Jerusalem and the cities of Judah that have felt
your anger these seventy years?"* [g] 13 To the
angel who spoke with me, the LORD replied
favorably, with comforting words.
Oracular Response. 14 The angel who
spoke with me then said to me, Proclaim:
Thus says the LORD of hosts:

I am jealous for Jerusalem
and for Zion* intensely jealous.[h]
15 I am consumed with anger
toward the complacent nations;*
When I was only a little angry,
they compounded the disaster.[i]
16 Therefore, thus says the LORD:
I return to Jerusalem in mercy;[j]
my house* will be rebuilt there[k]—
oracle of the LORD of hosts—
and a measuring line will be stretched
over Jerusalem.
17 Proclaim further: Thus says the LORD of
hosts:
My cities will again overflow with
prosperity;
the LORD will again comfort Zion,
and will again choose Jerusalem.[l]

CHAPTER 2

See RG 365

*Second Vision: The Four Horns and
the Four Smiths.* 1 I raised my eyes and
looked and there were four horns.* 2 Then I
asked the angel who spoke with me, "What
are those?" He answered, "Those are the
horns that scattered* Judah, Israel, and Jerusalem."[m]
3 Then the LORD showed me four workmen.* 4 And I said, "What are these coming
to do?" And the LORD said, "Those are the
horns that scattered Judah, so that none
could raise their heads any more;[n] and these
have come to terrify them—to cut down the
horns of the nations that raised their horns to
scatter the land of Judah."
*Third Vision: The Man with the Measur-
ing Cord.* 5 I raised my eyes and looked, and
there was a man with a measuring cord* in
his hand.[o] 6 I asked, "Where are you going?"
And he said, "To measure Jerusalem—to see
how great its width is and how great its
length."
7 Then the angel who spoke with me advanced as another angel came out to meet
him 8 and he said to the latter, "Run, speak to
that official:* Jerusalem will be unwalled,
because of the abundance of people and
beasts in its midst.[p] 9 I will be an encircling
wall of fire* for it—oracle of the LORD—and
I will be the glory in its midst."[q]

1:11 Angel of the LORD: chief angelic figure in God's heavenly court, and perhaps the "man" of 1:8.

1:12 These seventy years: allusion to the period of divine anger mentioned in Jer 25:11–12 and 29:10. Here the symbolic number seventy is understood to mark the period without a Temple in Jerusalem. Since these seventy years would have been almost over at this point, this symbolic number would have provided motivation for rebuilding the Temple as a sign of the end of the exile.

1:14 For Jerusalem and for Zion: rather than the usual order, Zion and Jerusalem, elsewhere in the Bible. The reversal highlights the centrality of Jerusalem, which is mentioned in all three of the brief oracles of 1:14–17.

1:15 Complacent nations: probably a reference to the Persian empire, which in its imperial extent included many national groups that maintained separate identities. **Compounded the disaster**: the surrounding nations took advantage of the Lord's anger against Judah to further their own interests.

1:16 My house: the Temple. See note on Hg 1:4. **Measuring line**: a builder's string, not for devastation, as in Is 34:11, but for reconstruction.

2:1 Four horns: symbols of the total political and military might of Judah's imperial adversaries, probably representing Assyria, Babylonia, and Persia. The number four represents universality rather than any specific number of foes.

2:2 Scattered: sent part of the population into exile. This was standard imperial policy initiated in the ancient Near East by the Assyrians for dealing with a conquered state.

2:3 Four workmen: four agents of God's power. The imagery follows that of four horns: the workers cut down, or make ineffectual, the horns, i.e., enemy.

2:5 Measuring cord: a string for measuring, as opposed to a builder's string, 1:16.

2:8 That official: probably the man with the measuring cord of v. 5.

2:9 Encircling wall of fire: divine protection for an unwalled Jerusalem. Urban centers were generally walled, and Jerusalem's walls were eventually rebuilt in the late fifth century B.C. (Neh 2:17–20).

g: Rev 6:10. *h:* Zec 8:2. *i:* Is 47:6. *j:* Is 54:6–10. *k:* Zec 2:5–9. *l:* Zec 2:15; 13:9. *m:* Dt 33:17; Dn 7:8. *n:* Jer 48:25. *o:* Jer 31:38–39; Ez 41:13; Rev 11:1; 21:15. *p:* Is 49:19–20; 54:2–3; Jer 31:27; Ez 38:11. *q:* Rev 21:23; 22:3–5.

Expansion on the Themes of the First Three Visions. 10 Up! Up! Flee from the land of the north*—oracle of the LORD;—For like the four winds of heaven I have dispersed you—oracle of the LORD.[r] 11 Up, Zion! Escape, you who dwell in daughter Babylon! 12 For thus says the LORD of hosts after the LORD's glory had sent me, concerning the nations that have plundered you: Whoever strikes you strikes me directly in the eye.[s] 13 Now I wave my hand over them, and they become plunder for their own servants.[t] Thus you shall know that the LORD of hosts has sent me. 14 Sing and rejoice, daughter Zion! Now, I am coming to dwell in your midst—oracle of the LORD. 15 Many nations will bind themselves to the LORD on that day.[u] They will be my people,* and I will dwell in your midst. Then you shall know that the LORD of hosts has sent me to you. 16 The LORD will inherit Judah[v] as his portion of the holy land,* and the LORD will again choose Jerusalem. 17 Silence, all people, in the presence of the LORD, who stirs forth from his holy dwelling.[w]

CHAPTER 3

See RG 366

Prophetic Vision: Joshua the High Priest. 1 Then he showed me Joshua the high priest standing before the angel of the LORD, while the adversary* stood at his right side to accuse him.[x] 2 And the angel of the LORD said to the adversary, "May the LORD rebuke you, O adversary; may the LORD who has chosen Jerusalem rebuke you![y] Is this not a brand plucked from the fire?"[z]

3* Now Joshua was standing before the angel, clad in filthy garments. 4 Then the angel said to those standing before him, "Remove his filthy garments."[a] And to him he said, "Look, I have taken your guilt from you,[b] and I am clothing you in stately robes." 5 Then he said, "Let them put a clean turban on his head." And they put a clean turban on his head and clothed him with the garments while the angel of the LORD was standing by. 6 Then the angel of the LORD charged Joshua: 7 "Thus says the LORD of hosts: If you walk in my ways and carry out my charge, you will administer my house and watch over my courts;* and I will give you access to those standing here."

Supplementary Oracle. 8 "Hear, O Joshua, high priest! You and your associates who sit before you! For they are signs of things to come!* [c] I will surely bring my servant the Branch. 9 Look at the stone[d] that I have placed before Joshua. On this one stone with seven facets* [e] I will engrave its inscription—oracle of the LORD of hosts—and I will take away the guilt of that land in one day. 10 On that day—oracle of the LORD of hosts—you will invite one another under your vines and fig trees."[f]

2:10 Land of the north: refers to Babylon (v. 11), in a geographic rather than a political sense, as the place from which exiles will return. The designation is "north" because imperial invaders historically entered Palestine from that direction (see Jer 3:18; 23:8).

2:15 Many nations . . . my people: a way of expressing God's relationship to people in covenant language. The covenant between God and Israel (see Jer 31:33; 32:38) is here universalized to include all nations.

2:16 The holy land: the Lord's earthly territory, a designation found only rarely in the Old Testament.

3:1 Adversary: Hebrew *satan*, here, the prosecuting attorney, a figure in the Lord's heavenly courtroom. Cf. Jb 1:6–2:7. Later tradition understands this figure to be Satan.

3:3–4 The filthy garments of Joshua symbolized the guilt of the Israelite people who have become unclean by going into exile. The angel of the Lord purifies the high priest by the removal of his garments.

3:7 If you walk . . . watch over my courts: four components of priestly activity: (1) following God's commandments and teaching them to the people, (2) carrying out cultic functions, (3) participating in the judicial system in certain difficult cases, and (4) administering the laborers and lands in the Temple's domain.

3:8 Signs of things to come: the restoration of the priesthood is a sign of the expected restoration of the Davidic line. **The Branch**: a tree metaphor for the expected future ruler as a descendant of the Davidic dynasty. This imagery also appears in Is 11:1, 10; Jer 23:5; 33:15; and Zec 6:12.

3:9 Stone with seven facets: represents both the precious stones that were part of the high priest's apparel and the building stone (see 4:7, 10) that initiated a major construction project. The seven facets (or "eyes") indicate the totality of its role as an instrument of God's vigilance and action. **Inscription**: can refer both to words engraved on the high priest's apparel (Ex 28:9, 11) and to words chiseled on a cornerstone.

r: Zec 6:5; Is 48:20; Jer 50:8; 51:6. *s:* Dt 32:10; Ps 17:8. *t:* Is 14:2; Zep 3:15. *u:* Is 56:6; 66:18. *v:* Zec 1:17. *w:* Hb 2:20; Zep 1:7; Rev 8:1a. *x:* Jb 1:6–2:7; 1 Chr 21:1. *y:* Jude 9. *z:* Am 4:11. *a:* Lk 15:22; Rev 19:8. *b:* Is 6:7; Jer 31:34; Ez 36:33. *c:* Is 8:18. *d:* Zec 4:7, 10; Is 28:16. *e:* Rev 5:6. *f:* 1 Kgs 5:5; Mi 4:4.

CHAPTER 4

See RG 366

Fourth Vision: The Lampstand and the Two Olive Trees. [1]Then the angel who spoke with me returned and aroused me, like one awakened from sleep. [2]He said to me, "What do you see?" I replied, "I see a lampstand* all of gold,[g] with a bowl on top of it. There are seven lamps on it, with seven spouts on each of the lamps that are on top of it. [3]And beside it are two olive trees,* one on the right of the bowl and one to its left." [4]Then I said to the angel who spoke with me, "What are these things, my lord?" [5]And the angel who spoke with me replied, "Do you not know what these things are?" I said, "No, my lord."

An Oracle. [6]Then he said to me: "This is the word of the LORD to Zerubbabel: Not by might, and not by power, but by my spirit,* [h] says the LORD of hosts. [7]Who are you, O great mountain?* Before Zerubbabel you become a plain. He will bring forth the first stone amid shouts of 'Favor, favor be upon it!' "

[8]Then the word of the LORD came to me: [9]The hands of Zerubbabel have laid the foundations of this house, and his hands will finish it. Thus you shall know that the LORD of hosts has sent me to you. [10]For whoever has scorned such a day of small things will rejoice to see the capstone* in the hand of Zerubbabel.

Resumption of the Vision: Explanation of Lamps and Trees. "These seven are the eyes of the LORD that range over the whole earth."[i] [11]I then asked him, "What are these two olive trees, on the right of the lampstand and on its left?" [12]A second time I asked, "What are the two streams from the olive trees that pour out golden oil through two taps of gold?" [13]He said to me, "Do you not know what these are?" I answered, "No, my lord." [14]Then he said, "These are the two anointed ones* who stand by the Lord of the whole earth."[j]

CHAPTER 5

See RG 366

Fifth Vision: The Flying Scroll. [1]Then I raised my eyes again and saw a flying scroll. [2]He asked me, "What do you see?" I answered, "I see a flying scroll, twenty cubits long and ten cubits wide."* [k] [3]Then he said to me: "This is the curse which is to go forth over the whole land. According to it, every thief and every perjurer* will be expelled. [4]I will send it forth—oracle of the LORD of hosts—so that it will come to the

4:2 Lampstand: receptacle for lamps and one of the furnishings of the main room of the Temple. This visionary object does not correspond to the biblical descriptions of the menorah in either the tabernacle (Ex 25:31–40) or the Solomonic Temple (1 Kgs 7:49) but rather has properties of both. **Seven lamps . . . seven spouts**: seven lamps, each with seven pinched wick holes. Such objects were part of the repertoire of cultic vessels throughout the Old Testament period. Here they symbolize God's eyes, i.e., divine omniscience; see v. 10.

4:3 Olive trees: visionary image that picks up the botanical language describing the Israelite cultic lampstands, with the olive trees specifically connoting fertility, permanence, and righteousness.

4:6 Not by might . . . my spirit: one of the most quoted verses from the Old Testament, particularly in Jewish tradition, which connects it with the theme of Hanukkah, sometimes called the Festival of Lights.

4:7 Great mountain: part of symbolic imagery for the Temple on Mount Zion, as embodiment of the cosmic mountain where heaven and earth connect. **Plain**: leveled ground serving as the foundation area for the construction of the Temple, and symbolizing the foundation of the cosmos. **First stone**: foundation stone of a major public building. Such stones were laid with great ceremony in foundation rituals when monumental buildings were newly built or rebuilt in the biblical world.

4:10 Capstone: topmost stone of a structure, which finishes the construction. This translation is based on the context. Other translations read: "stone of distinction," "plummet," "tin-stone."

4:14 Two anointed ones: two leadership positions in the ideal restored nation. The concept of a state headed by both priestly and political leaders harks back to premonarchic traditions (Aaron and Moses) and finds an echo in the two messianic figures—a Davidic and a levitical messiah—in the Dead Sea Scrolls and in apocryphal literature. See also the two crowns of 6:11–14.

5:2 Twenty cubits long and ten cubits wide: ca. thirty feet by fifteen feet. These dimensions may represent the ratio of height to width in the exposed portion of a scroll being opened for liturgical reading; at the same time it may symbolize the approach to God's presence since the entryway to the Temple has the same measurements (1 Kgs 6:3). The scroll itself may represent God's covenant with the people, insofar as it contains curses against those who break the law.

5:3 Thief . . . perjurer: a pair of miscreants representing all those who disobey God's covenant (see note on v. 2) and who must therefore be punished according to covenant curses.

g: Ex 25:31–40; 1 Kgs 7:49; Rev 11:4. *h:* Hos 1:7. *i:* Zec 1:11; 6:7; Rev 5:6. *j:* Jos 3:11; Mi 4:13; Rev 11:4. *k:* Ez 2:9–10; Rev 10:9–11.

house of the thief, and into the house of the one who swears falsely by my name.[l] It shall lodge within each house, consuming it, timber and stones."

Sixth Vision: The Basket of Wickedness. 5 Then the angel who spoke with me came forward and said to me, "Raise your eyes and look. What is this that comes forth?" 6 I said, "What is it?" And he answered, "This is the basket* that is coming." And he said, "This is their guilt in all the land." 7 Then a leaden cover was lifted, and there was a woman sitting inside the basket.* 8 He said, "This is Wickedness," and he thrust her inside the basket, pushing the leaden weight into the opening.

9 Then I raised my eyes and saw two women coming forth with wind under their wings*—they had wings like the wings of a stork—and they lifted the basket into the air. 10 I said to the angel who spoke with me, "Where are they taking the basket?" 11 He replied, "To build a temple for it in the land of Shinar.* When the temple is constructed, they will set it there on its base."

See RG 366–67

CHAPTER 6

Seventh Vision: Four Chariots.[m] 1 Again I raised my eyes and saw four chariots* coming out from between two mountains; and the mountains were of bronze. 2 The first chariot had red horses, the second chariot black horses, 3 the third chariot white horses, and the fourth chariot dappled horses—all of them strong horses. 4 I asked the angel who spoke with me, "What are these, my lord?" 5 The angel answered me, "These are the four winds of the heavens,* which are coming forth after presenting themselves before the LORD of all the earth.[n] 6 The one with the black horses is going toward the land of the north, and the white horses go toward the west, and the dappled ones go toward the land of the south." 7 These strong horses went out, eager to set about patrolling the earth, for he said, "Go, patrol the earth!" So they patrolled the earth. 8 Then he cried out to me and said, "See, those who go forth to the land of the north provide rest for my spirit in the land of the north."*

The Crowning. 9 Then the word of the LORD came to me: 10 Take from the exiles—Heldai, Tobijah, Jedaiah—and go the same day to the house of Josiah, son of Zephaniah. (These had come from Babylon.) 11 You will take silver and gold, and make crowns;* place one on the head of Joshua, son of Jehozadak, the high priest. 12 And say to him: Thus says the LORD of hosts: There is a man whose name is Branch* [o]—and from his place he will branch out and he will build the temple of the LORD. 13 He will build the temple of the LORD, and taking up the royal insignia, he will sit as ruler upon his throne. The priest will be at his right hand, and between the two of them there will be peaceful understanding.* [p] 14 The other crown will be in the temple of the LORD as a gracious reminder to Heldai, Tobijah, Jedaiah, and the son of Zephaniah. 15 And they who are from

5:6 Basket: literally, ephah, a dry measure; see note on Is 5:10.

5:7 Woman sitting inside the basket: figure representing wickedness or foreign idolatry being transported back to Babylonia (vv. 1–11). Returning exiles were apparently worshiping deities they had learned to accept in Babylonia, and that "wickedness" (v. 8) must be removed.

5:9 Two women . . . wings: composite beings, part human and part animal, similar to the cherubim flanking the holy ark (Ex 25:18–22; 1 Kgs 6:23–28; Ez 10:18–22). Such creatures accompany foreign deities as here, or the biblical God.

5:11 Shinar: land of Babylonia; this name for Babylonia is found also in Gn 1:10; 11:2; 14:1; Is 11:11; and Dn 1:2.

6:1 Four chariots: vehicles with horses of four different colors (vv. 2–3) represent God's presence throughout the world and correspond to the four horses of 1:7–11.

6:5 Four winds of the heavens: four compass directions and therefore the whole world.

6:8 Land of the north: the enemy (cf. 2:10). This emphasis on the land of the north refers to the fact that God will deal with Israel's foes and order will be re-established.

6:11 Crowns: two crowns made of precious metals and representing two high offices (compare the symbolism of the two olive trees in 4:14). One crown is for the high priest Joshua, who, with the governor Zerubbabel, was one of the recognized rulers of the Persian province of Judah. The other crown would have been for a royal ruler, a Davidic descendant. Zerubbabel was a Davidide but could not be king because the Persians would not allow such autonomy. The second crown was thus put in storage in the Temple (v. 14) for the crowning of a future king, or "branch" (see 3:8), from the house of David.

6:12 Branch: future Davidic ruler. See note on 3:8.

6:13 Peaceful understanding: harmonious rule of both the high priest and the king.

l: Ex 20:7, 16. *m:* Rev 6:2–8. *n:* Rev 7:1. *o:* Zec 3:8; Jer 23:5. *p:* Zec 4:14.

afar will come and build the temple of the LORD, and you will know that the LORD of hosts has sent me to you. This will happen if you truly obey the LORD your God.[q]

See RG 366–67

CHAPTER 7

A Question About Fasting. [1]In the fourth year of Darius the king, the word of the LORD came to Zechariah, on the fourth day of the ninth month, Kislev.* [2]Bethel-sarezer sent Regem-melech and his men to implore the favor of the LORD [3]and to ask the priests of the house of the LORD of hosts, and the prophets, "Must I weep and abstain in the fifth month* as I have been doing these many years?" [4]Then the word of the LORD of hosts came to me: [5]Say to all the people of the land and to the priests: When you fasted and lamented in the fifth and in the seventh month* these seventy years, was it really for me that you fasted?[r] [6]When you were eating and drinking, was it not for yourselves that you ate and for yourselves that you drank?

[7]Are these not the words which the LORD proclaimed through the earlier prophets,* when Jerusalem and its surrounding cities were inhabited and secure, when the Negeb and the Shephelah were inhabited? [8]The word of the LORD came to Zechariah: [9]Thus says the LORD of hosts: Judge with true justice, and show kindness and compassion toward each other.[s] [10]Do not oppress the widow or the orphan, the resident alien or the poor;* do not plot evil against one another in your hearts.[t] [11]But they refused to listen; they stubbornly turned their backs and stopped their ears so as not to hear.[u] [12]And they made their hearts as hard as diamond[v] so as not to hear the instruction and the words that the LORD of hosts had sent by his spirit through the earlier prophets. So great anger came from the LORD of hosts: [13]Just as when I called out and they did not listen, so they will call out and I will not listen, says the LORD of hosts. [14]And I will scatter them among all the nations that they do not know.[w] So the land was left desolate behind them with no one moving about, and they made a pleasant land into a wasteland.

See RG 366–67

CHAPTER 8

Seven Oracles: Judah and Zion Restored. [1]Then the word of the LORD of hosts came: [2]Thus says the LORD of hosts:

I am intensely jealous for Zion,[x]
    stirred to jealous wrath for her.

[3]Thus says the LORD:

I have returned to Zion,
    and I will dwell within Jerusalem;
Jerusalem will be called the faithful
    city,* [y]
  and the mountain of the LORD of hosts,
    the holy mountain.

[4]Thus says the LORD of hosts:
Old men and old women will again sit in the streets of Jerusalem, each with staff in hand because of old age.[z] [5]The city will be filled with boys and girls playing in its streets.

[6]Thus says the LORD of hosts:
Even if this should seem impossible in the eyes of the remnant of this people in those days, should it seem impossible in my eyes also?[a]—oracle of the LORD of hosts.

[7]Thus says the LORD of hosts:
I am going to rescue my people from the

7:1 The fourth year of Darius . . . the ninth month, Kislev: December 7, 518 B.C., the last chronological heading in Zechariah.

7:3 Weep . . . fifth month: a mourning ritual commemorating the destruction of Jerusalem and the Temple on the seventh day of the fifth month in the nineteenth year of Nebuchadnezzar's reign (ca. 587/586 B.C.; see 2 Kgs 25:8).

7:5 Seventh month: the time of a fast in memory of the murder of Gedaliah, the governor installed by the Babylonians after they conquered Jerusalem (see 2 Kgs 25:25; Jer 41:1–3). **Seventy years**: see note on 1:12.

7:7, 12 Earlier prophets: see note on 1:4.

7:10 Widow . . . orphan . . . resident alien . . . poor: four categories of socially and economically marginalized persons. Concern for their well-being is commanded in both pentateuchal and prophetic literature.

8:3 Faithful city: a unique biblical epithet for Jerusalem, signaling the importance of the holy city and its leaders for establishing justice in society (see also vv. 8, 16, 19). **Holy mountain**: Jerusalem and its Temple, the sacred center of the holy land (2:16) and of the whole world.

q: Dt 28:1. *r:* Am 5:21. *s:* Is 1:17; 58:6. *t:* Ex 22:20–24; Dt 24:17; Jer 5:28; Mi 2:1. *u:* Ex 32:9; Is 48:4. *v:* Ez 11:19. *w:* Dt 4:27. *x:* Zec 1:14. *y:* Is 1:26. *z:* Dt 4:40. *a:* Jer 32:27.

land of the rising sun, and from the land of the setting sun. [8]I will bring them back to dwell within Jerusalem. They will be my people, and I will be their God,[b] in faithfulness and justice.

[9]Thus says the LORD of hosts:

Let your hands be strong, you who now hear these words which were spoken by the prophets when the foundation of the house of the LORD of hosts was laid* for the building of the temple.[c] [10]For before those days, there were no wages for people, nor hire for animals. Those who came and went were not safe from the enemy, for I set neighbor against neighbor. [11]But now I will not deal with the remnant of this people as in former days—oracle of the LORD of hosts.

[12] For there will be a sowing of peace:
the vine will yield its fruit,
the land will yield its crops,
and the heavens* will yield their dew.

I will give all these things to the remnant of this people to possess. [13]Just as you became a curse among the nations, O house of Judah and house of Israel, so will I save you that you may be a blessing.[d] Do not fear; let your hands be strong.

[14]Thus says the LORD of hosts:

Just as I intended to harm you when your ancestors angered me—says the LORD of hosts—and I did not relent, [15]so again in these days I intend to favor Jerusalem and the house of Judah; do not fear! [16]These then are the things you must do: Speak the truth to one another;[e] judge with honesty and complete justice in your gates.* [f] [17]Let none of you plot evil against another in your heart, nor love a false oath. For all these things I hate—oracle of the LORD.

Three Oracles: Judah and the Nations.

[18]The word of the LORD of hosts came to me:

[19]Thus says the LORD of hosts:

The fast days of the fourth, the fifth, the seventh, and the tenth months* [g] will become occasions of joy and gladness, and happy festivals for the house of Judah.[h] So love faithfulness and peace!

[20]Thus says the LORD of hosts:

There will yet come peoples and inhabitants of many cities;[i] [21]and the inhabitants of one city will approach those of another, and say, "Come! let us go to implore the favor of the LORD and to seek the LORD of hosts. I too am going." [22]Many peoples and strong nations will come to seek the LORD of hosts in Jerusalem and to implore the favor of the LORD.

[23]Thus says the LORD of hosts:

In those days ten people from nations of every language will take hold,[j] yes, will take hold of the cloak of every Judahite and say, "Let us go with you, for we have heard that God is with you."

CHAPTER 9

See RG 367

*Restoration of the Land of Israel**

[1] An oracle:* the word of the LORD is
against the land of Hadrach,
and Damascus is its destination,
For the cities of Aram are the LORD's,

8:9 When the foundation . . . was laid: December 18, 520 B.C., the date of the Temple refoundation ceremony, marking the beginning of the project to restore the Temple (see Hg 2:10, 18, 20).

8:12 Vine . . . land . . . heavens: future prosperity, reversing the hardships of Hg 1:10.

8:16 Gates: important gathering places in ancient Near Eastern cities, where legal proceedings were often carried out.

8:19 Fast days of the fourth, the fifth, the seventh, and the tenth months: all these fast days were probably held in connection with Jerusalem's demise. The fasts of the fourth month (commemorating the departure of Judahite leadership from Jerusalem, 2 Kgs 25:3–7) and of the tenth month (marking the beginning of the siege of Jerusalem, 2 Kgs 25:1) were added to the fasts of the fifth and seventh months mentioned in Zec 7:3 and 5 (see notes).

9:1–8 The opening verses of Second Zechariah delineate the ideal boundaries of a restored Israel. Echoing the ideas of Haggai and First Zechariah (chaps. 1–8), the prophet reiterates the notion that the rebuilt Temple will bring about peace. The areas to be returned to Israel include Syria (Aram), with the cities of Hadrach and Damascus; Phoenicia, with the cities of Tyre and Sidon; and Philistia, with the cities of Ashkelon, Gaza, Ekron, and Ashdod.

9:1 An oracle: this designation also introduces Zec 12:1 and Mal 1:1, suggesting a connection among the three units. The term functions as both a title to the larger literary unit (Zec 9–11) and a part of the message of the opening oracular statement.

b: Zec 13:9; Jer 31:33. *c:* Hg 1:14. *d:* Gn 12:3; Ps 72:17. *e:* Eph 4:25. *f:* Zec 7:9; Dt 21:19; 22:24; Ru 4:1, 11. *g:* Zec 7:1–3; Mt 9:14–15. *h:* Is 35:10; Jer 31:13. *i:* 1 Kgs 8:43. *j:* 1 Sm 15:27; Tb 13:11.

as are all the tribes of Israel.
[2] Hamath also on its border,
Tyre too, and Sidon, no matter how clever they be.
[3] Tyre built itself a stronghold,
and heaped up silver like dust,
and gold like the mud of the streets.
[4] But now the Lord will dispossess it,
and cast its wealth into the sea,
and it will be devoured by fire.
[5] Ashkelon will see it and be afraid;
Gaza too will be in great anguish;
Ekron also, for its hope will wither.
The king will disappear from Gaza,
Ashkelon will not be inhabited,
[6] and the illegitimate will rule in Ashdod.
I will destroy the pride of the Philistines
[7] and take from their mouths their bloody prey,
their disgusting meat from between their teeth.
They will become merely a remnant for our God,[k]
and will be like a clan in Judah;
Ekron will be like the Jebusites.*
[8] I will encamp at my house,
a garrison against invaders;
No oppressor will overrun them again,
for now I have seen their affliction.

*The King's Entry into Jerusalem**

[9] Exult greatly, O daughter Zion!
Shout for joy, O daughter Jerusalem!
Behold: your king* is coming to you,
a just savior is he,
Humble, and riding on a donkey,
on a colt, the foal of a donkey.[l]
[10] He shall banish the chariot from Ephraim,[m]
and the horse from Jerusalem;
The warrior's bow will be banished,
and he will proclaim peace to the nations.[n]
His dominion will be from sea to sea,
and from the River* to the ends of the earth.[o]

Restoration of the People

[11] As for you, by the blood of your covenant,* [p]
I have freed your prisoners from a waterless pit.
[12] Return to a fortress,*
O prisoners of hope;
This very day, I announce
I am restoring double to you.
[13] For I have bent Judah as my bow,
I have set Ephraim as its arrow;
I will arouse your sons, O Zion,
against your sons, O Yavan,*
and I will use you as a warrior's sword.
[14] The LORD will appear over them,
God's arrow will shoot forth as lightning;
The Lord GOD will sound the ram's horn,
and come in a storm from the south.[q]
[15] The LORD of hosts will protect them;
they will devour and conquer with sling stones,
they will drink and become heated as with wine;
they will be full like bowls—like the corners of the altar.[r]

9:7 The Jebusites: the pre-Israelite inhabitants of Jerusalem, conquered by David and incorporated into Israel.

9:9–10 These two verses form the centerpiece of chap. 9. The restoration of a royal figure connects the first part of the chapter (vv. 1–8), which depicts the restored land of Israel, with the second part (vv. 11–17), which concerns the restoration of the people Israel.

9:9 Your king: a just savior, a figure of humble demeanor, but riding on a donkey like royalty in the ancient Near East (Gn 49:11; Jgs 5:10; 10:4). The announcement of the coming of such a king marks a departure from the view of the royal figure as a conquering warrior. This depiction is in keeping with the tone of First Zechariah (3:8; 4:6–10; 6:12) but contrasts with Haggai (2:20–23). New Testament authors apply this prophecy to Jesus' triumphant entry into Jerusalem (Mt 21:4–5; Jn 12:14–15).

9:10 The River: probably the Euphrates; see note on Ps 72:8.

9:11 The blood of your covenant: the covenant between the Lord and Israel sealed with sacrificial blood (Ex 24:8).

9:12 Fortress: the Hebrew word for "fortress" (*bissaron*) plays upon the Hebrew word for Zion (*siyyon*). Those who return to Zion will be protected by the Lord. **O prisoners of hope**: imagery of exile, conveying a sense that the future in Israel will be better.

9:13 Your sons, O Yavan: the reference is to the Greeks and their struggle with the Persians for control of Syria-Palestine and the eastern Mediterranean in the mid-fifth century B.C.

k: Is 4:3. *l*: Is 9:6; 62:11; Jer 23:5; Mt 21:5; Jn 12:15. *m*: Mi 5:9. *n*: Is 2:4; 11:6; Hos 2:20; Eph 2:17. *o*: Ps 72:8. *p*: Ex 24:4–8; Mt 26:28; Heb 13:20. *q*: Dt 33:2; Ps 18:14; Hb 3:4. *r*: Ex 27:3; 38:3; Nm 4:14.

16 And the LORD their God will save them:
the people, like a flock on that day;[s]
For like gemstones of a crown*
they will shine on the land.
17 Then how good and how lovely!
Grain will make the young men
flourish,
and new wine the young women.[t]

See RG 367

CHAPTER 10

The Lord Strengthens Judah and Rescues Ephraim

1 Ask the LORD for rain in the spring
season,[u]
the LORD who brings storm clouds,
and heavy rains,[v]
who gives to everyone grain in the
fields.
2 For the teraphim* have spoken
nonsense,[w]
the diviners have seen false visions;
Deceitful dreams they have told,
empty comfort they have offered.
This is why they wandered like sheep,
wretched, for they have no shepherd.[x]
3 My wrath is kindled against the
shepherds,*
and I will punish the leaders.
For the LORD of hosts attends to the
flock, the house of Judah,
and will make them like a splendid
horse in battle.
4 From them will come the tower,
from them the tent peg,
from them the bow of war,
from them every officer.
5 Together they will be like warriors,
trampling the mud of the streets in
battle.
They will wage war because the LORD is
with them,
and will put the horsemen to shame.
6 I will strengthen the house of Judah,[y]
the house of Joseph* I will save;
I will bring them back, because I have
mercy on them;
they will be as if I had never cast them
off,
for I am the LORD their God, and I will
answer them.[z]
7 Then Ephraim will be like a hero,
and their hearts will be cheered as by
wine.[a]
Their children will see and rejoice—
their hearts will exult in the LORD.
8 I will whistle for them and gather them in;
for I will redeem them
and they will be as numerous as
before.*
9 I sowed them among the nations,
yet in distant lands they will
remember me;
they will bear their children and
return.[b]
10 I will bring them back from the land of
Egypt,
and gather them from Assyria.
To the land of Gilead and to Lebanon I
will bring them,
until no room is found for them.
11 I will cross over to Egypt
and smite the waves of the sea,
and all the depths of the Nile will dry up.
The pride of Assyria will be cast down,
and the scepter of Egypt disappear.
12 I will strengthen them in the LORD,[c]
in whose name they will walk—oracle
of the LORD.

CHAPTER 11

See RG 367–68

The Cry of Trees, Shepherds, and Lions

1 Open your doors, Lebanon,
that fire may devour your cedars!

9:16 Like gemstones of a crown: imagery reminiscent of First Zechariah (3:9; 4:7, 10; 6:11, 14) and evocative of the Temple and the priestly headgear (cf. Ex 29:6 and Lv 8:9).

10:2 Teraphim: household idols or cult objects (see Gn 31:19, 30–35; Jgs 17:5; 1 Sm 19:11–17), or ancestor statuettes (see 2 Kgs 23:24; Hos 3:4).

10:3 Against the shepherds: bad leaders or false prophets.

10:6 The house of Joseph: represents the Northern Kingdom (Israel), as does Ephraim in v. 7 below.

10:8 Gather them in . . . be as numerous as before: God's intention is to bring back the exiles and redeem them as at the time of the exodus. This image, resumed in vv. 10–11, anticipates an expanded population, echoes the ancestral promise (Gn 1:22, 28; 9:1, 7; 35:11), and also suggests an awareness of the acute demographic decline of Jews in Palestine in the Persian period.

s: Ez 34:11. *t:* Jer 31:12–13. *u:* Dt 11:14. *v:* Ps 135:7. *w:* 1 Sm 15:23. *x:* Ez 34:5; Mt 9:36. *y:* Zec 12:5. *z:* Is 41:17. *a:* Ps 104:15. *b:* Dt 30:1–3; Bar 2:30–32. *c:* Zec 12:5.

2 Wail, cypress trees,
for the cedars are fallen,
the mighty are destroyed!
Wail, oaks of Bashan,
for the dense forest is cut down!
3 Listen! the wailing of shepherds,
their glory has been destroyed.
Listen! the roaring of young lions,
the thickets of the Jordan are
destroyed.

*The Shepherd Narrative.** [d] 4 Thus says the
LORD, my God: Shepherd the flock to be
slaughtered.[e] 5 For they who buy them slay
them and are not held accountable; while
those who sell them say, "Blessed be the
LORD, I have become rich!" Even their own
shepherds will not pity them. 6 For I will no
longer pity the inhabitants of the earth—oracle of the LORD.—Yes, I will deliver them
into each other's power, or into the power of
their kings; they will crush the earth, and I
will not deliver it out of their power.
7 So I shepherded the flock to be slaughtered for the merchants of the flock. I took
two staffs: one I called Delight, and the other
Union. Thus I shepherded the flock. 8 In a
single month, I did away with the three shepherds, for I wearied of them, and they disdained me. 9 "I will not shepherd you," I
said. "Whoever is to die shall die; whoever
is to be done away with shall be done away
with; and those who are left shall devour one
another's flesh."
10 Then I took my staff Delight and snapped
it in two, breaking my covenant which I had
made with all peoples. 11 So it was broken on
that day. The merchants of the flock, who
were watching me, understood that this was
the word of the LORD. 12 Then I said to them,
"If it seems good to you, give me my wages;
but if not, withhold them."[f] And they counted
out my wages,[g] thirty pieces of silver. 13 Then
the LORD said to me, Throw it in the treasury—the handsome price at which they valued me. So I took the thirty pieces of silver
and threw them into the treasury in the house
of the LORD. 14 Then I snapped in two my second staff, Union, breaking the kinship between Judah and Israel.
15 The LORD said to me: This time take the
gear of a foolish shepherd.[h] 16 For I am raising up a shepherd in the land who will take
no note of those that disappear, nor seek the
strays, nor heal the injured,[i] nor feed the exhausted; but he will eat the flesh of the fat
ones and tear off their hoofs!

Oracle to the Worthless Shepherd

17 Ah! my worthless shepherd
who forsakes the flock![j]
May the sword fall upon his arm
and upon his right eye;
His arm will surely wither,
and his right eye surely go blind!

CHAPTER 12

See RG 368

*Oracles Concerning the Nations and
Judah.** 1 An oracle:* The word of the LORD
concerning Israel—oracle of the LORD, who
spreads out the heavens, lays the founda-

11:4–17 This narrative has features of an allegory, a parable, and a commissioning narrative. The use of a symbolic action (vv. 7, 10, 14), however, places this text squarely in the tradition of classical prophecy. For example, the staff "Delight" signifies the Mosaic covenant, and the staff "Union" signifies the union of Israel and Judah. Breaking the staffs signifies the breaking of the Mosaic covenant (resulting in the destruction of Jerusalem and the exile) and the historical schism between north and south. In this narrative the prophet is the "shepherd" of God's flock, which is to be slaughtered. The "three shepherds" of v. 8 represent either leaders responsible for the decay in Israelite society or false prophets (cf. vv. 15, 17 and 13:2–6). The service of the good shepherd is contemptuously valued at thirty pieces of silver, the legal indemnity for a gored slave (Ex 21:32). The prophet throws the money into the Temple treasury, showing how poorly God's love is requited (cf. Mt 26:14–16; 27:5). With great rhetorical irony, payment is rejected. The entire wage-payment scenario may be regarded as another symbolic action, embedded within the primary action.

12:1–10 The oracles deal with (1) the status of Judah in relation to other political powers in the world that threaten its existence and (2) the reordering of Judah's internal structures so that its future can be realized. That future is linked to the fortunes of the house of David, which is mentioned five times between 12:7 and 13:1 (12:7, 8, 10, 12; 13:1).

12:1 An oracle: part two of Second Zechariah begins with the same heading as that of part one (9:1; also Mal 1:1), suggesting two distinct blocks of material. The unusual cluster of introductory terms that follow the heading greatly intensifies the claim of prophetic authority, apparently an issue in post-exilic prophecy.

12:2 Cup of reeling: like a cup filled with intoxicating

d: Ez 34:1. *e:* Jer 12:3. *f:* Mt 27:3–10. *g:* 2 Kgs 12:11; 22:4. *h:* Ez 34:1–10. *i:* Is 42:3; Mt 12:20. *j:* Jer 23:1; Jn 10:12–13.

tions of the earth, and fashions the human spirit within:[k] 2See, I will make Jerusalem a cup of reeling* for all peoples round about.[l] Judah will be besieged, even Jerusalem. 3On that day I will make Jerusalem a heavy stone for all peoples. All who attempt to lift it will injure themselves badly, though all the nations of the earth will gather against it. 4On that day—oracle of the LORD—I will strike every horse with fright, and its rider with madness. But over the house of Judah I will keep watch, while I strike blind all the horses of the peoples. 5Then the clans of Judah will say to themselves, "The inhabitants of Jerusalem have their strength in the LORD of hosts, their God."[m] 6On that day I will make the clans of Judah like a brazier of fire in the woodland and like a burning torch among sheaves, and they will devour right and left all the surrounding peoples; but Jerusalem will again inhabit its own place.[n]

7The LORD will save the tents of Judah first, that the glory of the house of David and the glory of the inhabitants of Jerusalem may not be exalted over Judah. 8On that day the LORD will shield the inhabitants of Jerusalem, so that the weakest among them will be like David on that day; and the house of David will be like God, like the angel of the LORD before them.

9On that day I will seek the destruction of all nations that come against Jerusalem.[o] 10I will pour out on the house of David and on the inhabitants of Jerusalem a spirit of mercy and supplication, so that when they look on him whom they have thrust through,* [p] they will mourn for him as one mourns for an only child, and they will grieve for him as one grieves over a firstborn.[q]

Catalogue of Mourners. 11On that day the mourning in Jerusalem will be as great as the mourning for Hadadrimmon in the plain of Megiddo.* 12And the land shall mourn, each family apart: the family of the house of David, and their women; the family of the house of Nathan, and their women; 13the family of the house of Levi, and their women; the family of Shimei, and their women; 14and all the rest of the families, each family apart, and the women apart.

CHAPTER 13

See RG 368

*Oracles Concerning the End of False Prophecy.** 1On that day a fountain will be opened for the house of David* and the inhabitants of Jerusalem, to purify from sin and uncleanness.[r]

2On that day—oracle of the LORD of hosts—I will destroy the names of the idols from the land, so that they will be mentioned no more; I will also remove the prophets and the spirit of uncleanness from the land. 3If any still prophesy, their father and mother who bore them will say, "You will not live, because you have spoken a lie in the name of the LORD." Their father and mother who bore them will thrust them through when they prophesy.[s]

4On that day, all prophets will be ashamed of the visions they prophesy; and they will

drink, Jerusalem will cause the nations to stumble and fall (cf. Is 51:17, 22; Jer 25:15; 49:12; Lam 4:21).

12:10 They look on him . . . thrust through: another possible rendering is "they shall look to me concerning him . . . thrust through." In either case, the victim is an enigmatic figure, perhaps referring to a Davidic descendant, a priestly leader, or even a true prophet. Some historical event, unknown to us from any surviving source, may underlie this reference. The Gospel of John applies this text to the piercing of Christ's side after his death (19:37).

12:11 The mourning for the pierced victim in Jerusalem is compared to the annual ritual mourning in the plain of Megiddo over the death of the Phoenician fertility god, Hadadrimmon. According to others, Hadadrimmon is the name of a place near Megiddo, and the reference would then be to the mourning over the death of King Josiah at the hands of Pharaoh Neco in 609 B.C.; cf. 2 Kgs 23:29–30; 2 Chr 35:22–25.

13:1–6 False prophecy is a major theme of Second Zechariah (chaps. 9–14) and figures in many other passages (10:1–2; 11; 12:10). Problems of idolatry and false prophecy occurred in postexilic Judah as they had in preexilic times. The understanding of the role of the prophet as an intermediary was challenged because (1) there was no king in Jerusalem, and (2) the texts of earlier prophets were beginning to be accorded the authority of prophetic tradition.

13:1 For the house of David: anticipation that a cleansed leadership will enable the re-established monarchy to be rid of the misdeeds of its past.

13:4 Hairy mantle: worn by prophets as a sign of their calling, for example, Elijah (1 Kgs 19:13; 2 Kgs 1:8) and John the Baptist (Mt 3:4).

k: Gn 2:7; Is 42:5. *l:* Is 51:17. *m:* Zec 10:6, 12. *n:* Zec 14:10. *o:* Zec 14:3. *p:* Jn 19:37; Rev 1:7. *q:* Am 8:10. *r:* Ez 36:25; 47:1; Jn 7:38. *s:* Jn 19:34.

not put on the hairy mantle* to mislead,[t] 5 but
each will say, "I am not a prophet. I am a
tiller of the soil, for I have owned land since
my youth."[u] 6 And if anyone asks, "What are
these wounds on your chest?"* each will answer,
"I received these wounds in the house
of my friends."[v]

The Song of the Sword

7 Awake, O sword, against my shepherd,
against the one who is my associate
—oracle of the LORD of hosts.
Strike the shepherd
that the sheep may be scattered;*[w]
I will turn my hand against the little
ones.
8 In all the land—oracle of the LORD—
two thirds of them will be cut off and
perish,
and one third will be left.
9 I will bring the one third through the fire;
I will refine them as one refines silver,[x]
and I will test them as one tests gold.
They will call upon my name, and I will
answer them;[y]
I will say, "They are my people,"[z]
and they will say, "The LORD is my
God."

CHAPTER 14

See RG 368

Devastation and Rescue of Jerusalem.

1* A day is coming for the LORD when the
spoils taken from you will be divided in your
midst. 2 And I will gather all the nations
against Jerusalem for battle: The city will be
taken, houses will be plundered, women
raped; half the city will go into exile, but the
rest of the people will not be removed from
the city. 3 Then the LORD will go forth and
fight against those nations, fighting as on a
day of battle.[a] 4 On that day God's feet will
stand* on the Mount of Olives, which is opposite
Jerusalem to the east. The Mount of
Olives will be split in two from east to west
by a very deep valley,[b] and half of the mountain
will move to the north and half of it to
the south. 5 You will flee by the valley between
the mountains, for the valley between
the mountains will reach to Azal. Thus you
will flee as you fled because of the earthquake*
in the days of Uzziah king of Judah.[c]
Then the LORD, my God, will come, and all
his holy ones with him.[d]

Jerusalem Restored. 6 On that day there
will no longer be cold or frost. 7 There will be
one continuous day—it is known to the
LORD—not day and night, for in the evening
there will be light. 8 On that day, fresh water
will flow from Jerusalem,[e] half to the eastern
sea, and half to the western sea. This will be
so in summer and in winter. 9 The LORD will
be king over the whole earth;[f] on that day the
LORD will be the only one, and the LORD's
name the only one. 10 All the land will turn
into a plain, from Geba to Rimmon, south of
Jerusalem, which will stand exalted in its
place—from the Gate of Benjamin to the
place of the first gate, to the Corner Gate and
from the Tower of Hananel to the king's
wine presses. 11 The city will be inhabited;

13:6 Wounds on your chest: lit., "wounds between your hands." The false prophets, like the prophets of Baal (1 Kgs 18:28), apparently inflicted wounds on themselves. Here it seems that persons accused of false prophecy deny having inflicted wounds on themselves and instead claim that they have received them at the houses of their friends.

13:7 Strike the shepherd . . . may be scattered: in Matthew's Gospel (26:31) Jesus makes use of this text before his arrest in the Garden of Gethsemane and the flight of the disciples.

14:1–21 The marked eschatological thrust of Zec 9–14 culminates in this apocalyptic description, with its astonishing images of the day of the Lord. This last and longest chapter focuses on the restoration of Jerusalem and the return of the people of Zion so that the rest of the world will acknowledge God's sovereignty. Four units constitute this chapter: vv. 1–5 concentrate on the destruction and rescue of Jerusalem and the escape of a remnant; vv. 6–11 describe the transformation of the climate and the topography of Jerusalem; vv. 12–15 depict the defeat of Jerusalem's enemies; and vv. 16–21 outline a vision for the end time, in which even foreign nations will make the pilgrimage to Jerusalem to acknowledge God's universal reign.

14:4 God's feet will stand: a remarkable anthropomorphic image adds emphasis to the traditional Old Testament scene of God appearing on a mountain and causing extreme reactions such as quaking, melting, shattering (see Ex 19:18; Ps 97:5; Hb 3:6). The Mount of Olives is split, which opens a way for those fleeing from the Lord's appearance to escape from Jerusalem.

14:5 Earthquake: Amos 1:1 mentions an earthquake in the time of King Uzziah (cf. Is 6:4).

t: 2 Kgs 1:8; Mt 3:4. *u:* Am 7:14. *v:* 1 Kgs 18:28. *w:* Ez 34:1–8; Mt 26:31. *x:* Is 1:25; 48:10. *y:* Ps 91:15; Is 65:24. *z:* Zec 8:8; Jer 31:31. *a:* Is 31:4. *b:* Mi 1:4. *c:* Am 1:1. *d:* Dt 33:2–3; Mt 16:27; 1 Thes 3:13. *e:* Zec 13:1; Ez 47:1–8; Jl 4:18. *f:* Ps 96:7–10; 97:1; 98:4–6; Rev 11:15.

never again will it be doomed. Jerusalem will dwell securely.[g]

The Fate of Jerusalem's Foes. 12 And this will be the plague with which the LORD will strike all the peoples that have fought against Jerusalem: their flesh will rot while they stand on their feet, and their eyes will rot in their sockets, and their tongues will rot in their mouths.[h] 13 On that day a great panic from the LORD will be upon them.[i] They will seize each other's hands, and their hands will be raised against each other. 14 Even Judah will fight against Jerusalem. The riches of all the surrounding nations will be gathered together—gold, silver, and garments—in great abundance. 15 Like the plague on human beings will be the plague upon the horses, mules, camels, donkeys, and upon all the beasts that are in those camps.

The Future: Jerusalem, Judah, and the Nations. 16 Everyone who is left of all the nations that came against Jerusalem will go up year after year to bow down to the King, the LORD of hosts, and to celebrate the feast of Booths.* [j] 17 Should any of the families of the earth[k] not go up to Jerusalem to bow down to the King, the LORD of hosts, then there will be no rain for them. 18 And if the family of Egypt does not go up or enter, upon them will fall the plague,[l] with which the LORD strikes the nations that do not go up to celebrate the feast of Booths. 19 This will be the punishment of Egypt and the punishment of all the nations that do not go up to celebrate the feast of Booths.

20 On that day, "Holy to the LORD"[m] will be written on the horses' bells.* The pots in the house of the LORD will be as the basins before the altar. 21 Every pot* in Jerusalem and in Judah will be holy to the LORD of hosts. All who come to sacrifice will take them and cook in them. No longer will there be merchants in the house of the LORD of hosts on that day.

14:16 Feast of Booths: fall harvest festival, also known as the "festival of Ingathering" (Ex 23:16; 34:22) or "Booths" (Lv 23:33–36; Dt 16:13–15; 31:9–13). The singling out of this festival indicates its special status in the sacred calendar; it is frequently referred to as "the feast" (1 Kgs 8:1–2; 2 Chr 5:3; Ez 45:25).

14:20 Horses' bells: even these bells, part of the trappings of animals used for war, will become holy in the end time, like the bells of the high priest's garb (cf. Ex 28:34).

14:21 Every pot: vessels used for mundane food preparation will, in the end time, be as holy as Temple vessels.

g: Dt 33:28; Jer 31:40; Rev 22:3. *h:* Is 66:24. *i:* 1 Sm 5:9, 11; 14:18–20; Is 22:5. *j:* Lv 23:33–36; Dt 16:13–15. *k:* Zec 8:20–23; Is 2:1–4; Mi 4:1–3. *l:* Ex 5:3; 9:15. *m:* Lv 23:20; 27:30, 32.

See RG 369–70

The Book of Malachi

This short book may have been written before Nehemiah's first return to Jerusalem in 445 B.C.; it is also possible that it was written while Nehemiah was there, or even later. What seems to be the author's name, *mal'ākî*, is found in 1:1 ("the word of the Lord to Israel through Malachi"), but many believe that this is a pseudonym based on *mal'ākî*, "my messenger," in 3:1 and that the author's real name is unknown. In any case, he shows us attitudes and behaviors characteristic of the Jewish community a few generations after the end of the Babylonian exile, and describes God's response.

God loves Israel (1:2–5), but the people return that love poorly. Taking advantage of the negligent attitude of the priests, they withhold tithes and sacrificial contributions (3:6–11) and cheat God by providing defective goods for sacrifice (1:6–14). People divorce their spouses and marry worshipers of other gods (2:10–16). Sorcerers, adulterers, perjurers, and people who take advantage of workers and the needy abound (3:5). Priests, who could strengthen discipline by their instruction, connive with the people, telling them what they want to hear (2:1–9). Underlying all this is a weary attitude, a cynical notion that nothing is to be gained by doing what God wants and that wrongdoers prosper (2:17; 3:14–15). God condemns the wrongdoing and the underlying attitude, issuing a challenge to immediate reform (3:10–12), but also announcing a general reckoning at a future moment (3:16–21).

The Book of Malachi may be divided as follows:

I. Israel Preferred to Edom (1:2–5)
II. Offense in Sacrifice and Priestly Duty (1:6–2:9)
III. Marriage and Divorce (2:10–16)
IV. Purification and Just Judgment (2:17)
V. The Messenger of the Covenant (3:1–5)
VI. Gifts for God, Blessings for the People (3:6–12)
VII. The Need To Serve God (3:13–21)
VIII. Moses and Elijah (3:22–24)

———

CHAPTER 1

See RG 369

1* An oracle. The word of the LORD to Israel through Malachi.

Israel Preferred to Edom

2 a I love you, says the LORD;
but you say, "How do you love us?"
3 * b Was not Esau Jacob's brother?—
oracle of the LORD.
I loved Jacob, but rejected Esau;
I made his mountains a waste,
his heritage a desert for jackals.
4 c If Edom says, "We have been crushed,
but we will rebuild the ruins,"
Thus says the LORD of hosts:
They indeed may build, but I will tear down,
And they shall be called "territory of wickedness,"
the people with whom the LORD is angry forever.
5 d Your own eyes will see it, and you will say,
"Great is the LORD, even beyond the territory of Israel."

Offense in Sacrifice and Priestly Duty

6 e A son honors his father,
and a servant fears his master;
If, then, I am a father,
where is the honor due to me?
And if I am a master,
where is the fear due to me?
So says the LORD of hosts to you, O priests,
who disdain my name.
But you ask, "How have we disdained your name?"
7 By offering defiled food on my altar!
You ask, "How have we defiled it?"
By saying that the table of the LORD may be disdained!
8 * f When you offer a blind animal for sacrifice,
is there no wrong in that?
When you offer a lame or sick animal,
is there no wrong in that?
Present it to your governor!
Will he be pleased with you—or show you favor?
says the LORD of hosts.
9 So now implore God's favor, that he may have mercy on us!
You are the ones who have done this;
Will he show favor to any of you?
says the LORD of hosts.
10 * Oh, that one of you would just shut the temple gates
to keep you from kindling fire on my altar in vain!
I take no pleasure in you, says the LORD of hosts;

1:1 See note on Zec 9:1.

1:3–5 The thought passes from the person Esau to his descendants, Edom, and from the person Jacob to his descendants, Israel; cf. Gn 25:21–23. In the New Testament, Paul uses this passage as an example of God's freedom of choice in calling the Gentiles to faith (Rom 9:13).

1:8 The sacrificial offering of a lame, sick, or blind animal was forbidden in the law (Lv 22:17–25; Dt 17:1).

1:10–11 The imperfect sacrifices offered by the people of Judah are displeasing to the Lord. **Kindling fire on my altar**: kindle the altar fire for sacrifice. In contrast, the Lord is pleased with the sacrifices offered by other peoples in other places (**the rising of the sun**: the far east; **its setting**: the far west). Since the people of other nations could not be expected to know the Lord's name as did the people of Judah, the rhetorical purpose of this statement is to shame the latter. **Incense offerings**: in the ancient world, the hallmark of an offering made to a god was the smoke it produced on an altar. In the Old Testament, this was true not only of animals (Lv 8:20–21) but also of incense (Ex 30:7), suet (Lv 3:11), and grain offerings (Lv 6:8). In a Christian interpretation of Mal 1:10–11, the "pure offering" of Mal 1:11 is seen as a reference to sacrifice in the Messianic Age. The Council of Trent endorsed this interpretation (DS 1724).

a: Dt 7:8; Ez 16; Hos 11:1; Am 1:11. *b:* Gn 25:23; Rom 9:13. *c:* Is 34:2–15; 63:1–6; Jer 49:7–22; Ob 21. *d:* Is 60. *e:* Prv 1:7; Is 29:13. *f:* Lv 22:17–25; Dt 15:21; 17:1.

and I will not accept any offering from
your hands!
11 [g] From the rising of the sun to its setting,
my name is great among the nations;
Incense offerings are made to my name
everywhere,
and a pure offering;
For my name is great among the nations,
says the LORD of hosts.
12 But you profane it by saying
that the LORD's table is defiled,
and its food may be disdained.
13 You say, "See what a burden this is!"
and you exasperate me, says the LORD
of hosts;
You bring in what is mutilated, or lame,
or sick;
you bring it as an offering!
Will I accept it from your hands?
says the LORD.
14 Cursed is the cheat who has in his flock
an intact male,
and vows it, but sacrifices to the LORD
a defective one instead;
For a great king am I, says the LORD of
hosts,
and my name is feared among the
nations.

CHAPTER 2

See RG 369–70

1 And now, priests, this
commandment is for you:
If you do not listen,
2 [h] And if you do not take to heart
giving honor to my name, says the
LORD of hosts,
I will send a curse upon you
and your blessing I will curse.
In fact, I have already cursed it,
because you do not take it to heart.
3 I will rebuke your offspring;
I will spread dung on your faces,
Dung from your feasts,
and will carry you to it.
4 You should know that I sent you this
commandment
so that my covenant with Levi might
endure,
says the LORD of hosts.
5 [i] My covenant with him was the life and
peace which I gave him,
and the fear he had for me,
standing in awe of my name.
6 [j] Reliable instruction was in his mouth,
no perversity was found upon his lips;
He walked with me in integrity and
uprightness,
and turned many away from evil.
7 [k] For a priest's lips preserve knowledge,
and instruction is to be sought from his
mouth,
because he is the messenger of the
LORD of hosts.
8 But you have turned aside from the way,
and have caused many to stumble by
your instruction;
You have corrupted the covenant of Levi,*
says the LORD of hosts.
9 I, therefore, have made you contemptible
and base before all the people,
For you do not keep my ways,
but show partiality in your instruction.

Marriage and Divorce

10 * [l] Have we not all one father?
Has not one God created us?
Why, then, do we break faith with each
other,
profaning the covenant of our
ancestors?
11 [m] Judah has broken faith; an abominable
thing
has been done in Israel and in
Jerusalem.
Judah has profaned the LORD's holy
place, which he loves,

2:8 The covenant of Levi: not mentioned elsewhere in the Bible. The covenant with Phinehas the grandson of Aaron (Nm 25:11–13) and the Blessing of Levi (Dt 33:8–11) may lie in the background.

2:10–16 Intermarriage of Israelites with foreigners was forbidden according to Dt 7:1–4. After the exile, attempts were made to enforce this law (Ezr 9–10). Foreign marriages are here portrayed as a covenantal violation (v. 10). They were all the more reprehensible when they were accompanied by the divorce of Israelite wives (vv. 14–16), and God finds their sacrifices unacceptable (vv. 13–14). In Mk 10:2–12, Jesus forbids divorce; in Mt 19:3–12, this ideal is maintained with the provision that unlawful marriage may be grounds for divorce (see 1 Cor 7:10–16). **You should be on guard, then,**

g: Ps 113:3; Is 59:19. *h:* Lv 26:14–45; Dt 28:15. *i:* Ez 37:26. *j:* Dt 33:8–11. *k:* Lv 10:10–11; Dt 17:9–10; Hg 2:11–13. *l:* Dt 32:6; Jb 31:15; Mt 23:9; Eph 4:6. *m:* Ezr 9:2; Neh 13:25.

and has married a daughter of a
foreign god.*
12 May the LORD cut off from the man who
does this
both witness and advocate from the
tents of Jacob,
and anyone to bring an offering to the
LORD of hosts!
13 This also you do: the altar of the LORD
you cover
with tears, weeping, and groaning,
Because the Lord no longer takes note of
your offering
or accepts it favorably from your hand.
14 n And you say, "Why?"—
Because the LORD is witness
between you and the wife of your
youth
With whom you have broken faith,
though she is your companion, your
covenanted wife.*
15 o Did he not make them one, with flesh
and spirit?
And what does the One require? Godly
offspring!
You should be on guard, then, for your
life,
and do not break faith with the wife of
your youth.
16 For I hate divorce,
says the LORD, the God of Israel,
And the one who covers his garment
with violence,
says the LORD of hosts.
You should be on guard, then, for your
life,
and you must not break faith.

Purification and Just Judgment

17 You have wearied the LORD with your
words,
yet you say, "How have we wearied
him?"
By saying, "All evildoers
are good in the sight of the LORD,
And he is pleased with them,"
or "Where is the just God?"

CHAPTER 3

See RG 370

The Messenger of the Covenant

1 p Now I am sending my messenger—
he will prepare the way before me;*
And the lord whom you seek will come
suddenly to his temple;
The messenger of the covenant whom
you desire—
see, he is coming! says the LORD of
hosts.
2 But who can endure the day of his
coming?
Who can stand firm when he
appears?
For he will be like a refiner's fire,
like fullers' lye.
3 q He will sit refining and purifying silver,
and he will purify the Levites,
Refining them like gold or silver,
that they may bring offerings to the
LORD in righteousness.
4 Then the offering of Judah and Jerusalem
will please the LORD,
as in ancient days, as in years gone by.
5 I will draw near to you for judgment,
and I will be swift to bear witness
Against sorcerers, adulterers, and
perjurers,
those who deprive a laborer of wages,
Oppress a widow or an orphan,
or turn aside a resident alien,
without fearing me, says the LORD of
hosts.

for your life: a warning of punishment for failure to obey God (cf. Dt 4:9; Jos 23:11; Jer 17:21).

2:11 Daughter of a foreign god: this unusual phrase connotes a woman who does not share the same father/creator (v. 10), since she does not share the same covenant.

2:14 Companion ... covenanted wife: the Hebrew word *haberet* signifies an equal, a partner. This woman, in contrast to the daughter of a foreign god, shares with her husband the same covenant with the Lord.

3:1 My messenger ... before me: Mt 11:10 applies these words to John the Baptist; Mt 11:14 further identifies John as Elijah (see Mal 3:23). Some take God's messenger in v. 1a to be a person distinct from "the lord" and "the messenger of the covenant" in v. 1b; others hold that they are one and the same person. Some consider "the lord" and "the messenger of the covenant" to be divine, while others hold that in the text's literal sense he is a messianic earthly ruler.

n: Gn 31:49–50; Prv 5:18–19. *o:* Gn 2:7, 22–24. *p:* Ex 23:20–22; Is 40:3; Mt 11:10; Mk 1:2; Lk 1:17; 7:27. *q:* Is 1:25; Zec 13:9.

Gifts for God, Blessings for the People

6 For I, the LORD, do not change,*
and you, sons of Jacob, do not cease
to be.
7 [r] Since the days of your ancestors you
have turned aside
from my statutes and have not kept
them.
Return to me, that I may return to you,
says the LORD of hosts.
But you say, "Why should we return?"
8 [s] Can anyone rob God? But you are
robbing me!
And you say, "How have we robbed you?"
Of tithes and contributions!
9 You are indeed accursed,
for you, the whole nation, rob me.
10 [t] Bring the whole tithe
into the storehouse,*
That there may be food in my house.
Put me to the test, says the LORD of
hosts,
And see if I do not open the floodgates of
heaven for you,
and pour down upon you blessing
without measure!
11 I will rebuke the locust for you
so that it will not destroy your crops,
And the vine in the field will not be
barren,
says the LORD of hosts.
12 [u] All the nations will call you blessed,
for you will be a delightful land,
says the LORD of hosts.

The Need To Serve God

13 Your words are too much for me, says the
LORD.
You ask, "What have we spoken
against you?"
14 [v] You have said, "It is useless to serve
God;
what do we gain by observing God's
requirements,
And by going about as mourners*
before the LORD of hosts?
15 But we call the arrogant blessed;
for evildoers not only prosper
but even test God and escape."
16 [w] Then those who fear the LORD spoke
with one another,
and the LORD listened attentively;
A record book* was written before him
of those who fear the LORD and esteem
his name.
17 [x] They shall be mine, says the LORD of
hosts,
my own special possession, on the day
when I take action.
And I will have compassion on them,
as a man has compassion on his son
who serves him.
18 Then you will again distinguish
between the just and the wicked,
Between the person who serves God,
and the one who does not.
19 [y] For the day is coming, blazing like an
oven,
when all the arrogant and all evildoers
will be stubble,
And the day that is coming will set them
on fire,
leaving them neither root nor branch,
says the LORD of hosts.
20 [z] But for you who fear my name, the sun
of justice
will arise with healing in its wings;*
And you will go out leaping like calves
from the stall
21 and tread down the wicked;
They will become dust under the soles of
your feet,
on the day when I take action, says the
LORD of hosts.

3:6–7 Not change: God remains faithful to the covenant even when the human partners break it.

3:10 Storehouse: the temple treasury.

3:14 As mourners: the adverb translated "as mourners" means something like "with a long face."

3:16 Record book: see note on Ex 32:32.

3:20 Wings: a common symbol of the manifestation of a god in the ancient Near East is the winged sun disk found, for example, on premonarchic jar handles. Cf. Nm 6:25; Ps 4:7; 31:17; 34:6; 84:12.

r: Zec 1:3–4; Acts 7:51. *s:* Neh 13:10–14. *t:* Dt 28:2, 12; 2 Chr 31:10–11; Neh 10:38; 13:12; Prv 3:9–10. *u:* Dt 28:10; Is 61:9. *v:* Jb 21:14–15; 22:17; Ps 73:11–12; Is 58:3; Zec 7:2–7. *w:* Rev 20:12. *x:* Ex 19:5; Dt 7:6; Ps 103:13; 135:4. *y:* Is 13:9; 34:8; Jl 3:3; Zep 1:18; 2 Pt 3:7. *z:* Lk 1:78–79.

Moses and Elijah

22 [a] Remember the law of Moses my servant,
whom I charged at Horeb
With statutes and ordinances
for all Israel.
23 [b] Now I am sending to you
Elijah* the prophet,
Before the day of the LORD comes,
the great and terrible day;
24 He will turn the heart of fathers to their sons,
and the heart of sons to their fathers,
Lest I come and strike
the land with utter destruction.

3:23 Elijah: taken up in a whirlwind, according to 2 Kgs 2:11. Here his return seems to be foretold. A Jewish tradition interpreted this literally; the gospels saw Elijah in the person of John the Baptist (Mt 11:13–14; 17:10–13; Mk 9:9–13).

a: Ex 20; Lv 26; Dt 4:1, 5–6. *b:* 2 Kgs 2:10–12; Sir 48:10; Mt 11:13–14; 17:10–13; Mk 9:9–13; Lk 1:17.

THE NEW TESTAMENT

NEW AMERICAN BIBLE

PREFACE TO THE *NEW AMERICAN BIBLE*

First Edition of the New Testament

The New Testament translation has been approached with essentially the same fidelity to the thought and individual style of the biblical writers as was applied in the Old Testament. In some cases, however, the problem of marked literary peculiarities had to be met. What by any Western standard are the limited vocabularies and stylistic infelicities of the evangelists cannot be retained in the exact form in which they appear in the originals without displeasing the modern ear. A compromise is here attempted whereby some measure of the poverty of the evangelists' expression is kept and placed at the service of their message in its richness. Similarly, the syntactical shortcomings of Paul, his frequent lapses into anacoluthon, and the like, are rendered as they occur in his epistles rather than "smoothed out." Only thus, the translators suppose, will contemporary readers have some adequate idea of the kind of writing they have before them. When the prose of the original flows more smoothly, as in Luke, Acts, and Hebrews, it is reflected in the translation.

The Gospel according to John comprises a special case. Absolute fidelity to his technique of reiterated phrasing would result in an assault on the English ear, yet the softening of the vocal effect by substitution of other words and phrases would destroy the effectiveness of his poetry. Again, resort is had to compromise. This is not an easy matter when the very repetitiousness which the author deliberately employed is at the same time regarded by those who read and speak English to be a serious stylistic defect. Only those familiar with the Greek originals can know what a relentless tattoo Johannine poetry can produce. A similar observation could be made regarding other New Testament books as well. Matthew and Mark are given to identical phrasing twice and three times in the same sentence. As for the rhetorical overgrowth and mixed figures of speech in the letters of Peter, James, and Jude, the translator must resist a powerful compulsion to tidy them up if only to render these letters intelligibly.

Without seeking refuge in complaints against the inspired authors, however, the translators of *The New American Bible* here state that what they have attempted is a translation rather than a paraphrase. To be sure, all translation can be called paraphrase by definition. Any striving for complete fidelity will shortly end in infidelity. Nonetheless, it must be pointed out that the temptation to improve overladen sentences by the consolidation or elimination of multiplied adjectives, or the simplification of clumsy hendiadys, has been resisted here. For the most part, rhetorically ineffective words and phrases are retained in this translation in some form, even when it is clear that a Western contemporary writer would never have employed them.

The spelling of proper names in *The New American Bible* follows the customary forms found in most English Bibles since the Authorized Version.

Despite the arbitrary character of the divisions into numbered verses (a scheme which in its present form is only four centuries old), the translators have made a constant effort to keep within an English verse the whole verbal content of the Greek verse. At times the effort has not seemed worth the result since it often does violence to the original author's flow of expression, which preceded it by so many centuries. If this translation had been prepared for purposes of public reading only, the editors would have foregone the effort at an early stage. But since they never departed from the threefold objective of preparing a translation suitable for liturgical use, private reading, and the purposes of students, the last-named consideration prevailed. Those familiar with Greek should be able to discover how the translators of the New Testament have rendered any given original verse of scripture, if their exegetical or theological tasks require them to know this. At the same time, the fact should be set down here that the editors did not commit themselves in the synoptic gospels to rendering repeated words or phrases identically.

This leads to a final consideration: the Greek text used for the New Testament. Here, punctuation and verse division are at least as important as variant readings. In general, Nestle-Aland's *Novum Testamentum Graece* (25th edition, 1963) was followed. Additional help was derived from *The Greek New Testament* (Aland, Black, Metzger, Wikgren), produced for the use of translators by the United Bible Societies in 1966. However, the editors did not confine themselves strictly to these texts; at times, they inclined toward readings otherwise attested. The omission of alternative translations does not mean that the translators think them without merit, but only that in every case they had to make a choice.

Poorly attested readings do not occur in this translation. Doubtful readings of some merit appear within brackets; public readers may include such words or phrases, or omit them entirely without any damage to sense. Parentheses are used, as ordinarily in English, as a punctuation device. Material they enclose is in no sense textually doubtful. It is simply thought to be parenthetical in the intention of the biblical author, even though there is no such punctuation mark in Greek. The difficulty in dealing with quotation marks is well known. Since they do not appear in any form in the original text, wherever they occur here they constitute an editorial decision.

PREFACE TO THE REVISED EDITION

The New Testament of *The New American Bible,* a fresh translation from the Greek text, was first published in complete form in 1970, together with the Old Testament translation that had been completed the previous year. Portions of the New Testament had appeared earlier, in somewhat different form, in the provisional Mass lectionary of 1964 and in the *Lectionary for Mass* of 1970.

Since 1970 many different printings of the New Testament have been issued by a number of publishers, both separately and in complete Bibles, and the text has become widely known both in the United States and in other English-speaking countries. Most American Catholics have been influenced by it because of its widespread use in the liturgy, and it has received a generally favorable reception from many other Christians as well. It has taken its place among the standard contemporary translations of the New Testament, respected for its fidelity to the original and its attempt to render this into current American English.

Although the scriptures themselves are timeless, translations and explanations of them quickly become dated in an era marked by rapid cultural change to a degree never previously experienced. The explosion of biblical studies that has taken place in our century and the changing nature of our language itself require periodic adjustment both in translations and in the accompanying explanatory materials. The experience of actual use of the New Testament of *The New American Bible*, especially in oral proclamation, has provided a basis for further improvement. Accordingly, it was decided in 1978 to proceed with a thorough revision of the New Testament to reflect advances in scholarship and to satisfy needs identified through pastoral experience.

For this purpose a steering committee was formed to plan, organize, and direct the work of revision, to engage collaborators, and to serve as an editorial board to coordinate the work of the various revisers and to determine the final form of the text and the explanatory materials. Guidelines were drawn up and collaborators selected in 1978 and early 1979, and November of 1980 was established as the deadline for manuscripts. From December 1980 through September 1986 the editorial board met a total of fifty times and carefully reviewed and revised all the material in order to ensure accuracy and consistency of approach. The editors also worked together with the bishops' ad hoc committee that was appointed by the National Conference of Catholic Bishops in 1982 to oversee the revision.

The threefold purpose of the translation that was expressed in the preface to the first edition has been maintained in the revision: to provide a version suitable for liturgical proclamation, for private reading, and for purposes of study. Special attention has been given to the first of these purposes, since oral proclamation demands special qualities in a translation, and experience had provided insights and suggestions that could lead to improvement in this area. Efforts have also been made, however, to facilitate devotional reading by providing suitable notes and introductory materials, and to assist the student by achieving greater accuracy and consistency in the translation and supplying more abundant information in the introductions and notes.

The primary aim of the revision is to produce a version as accurate and faithful to the meaning of the Greek original as is possible for a translation. The editors have consequently moved in the direction of a formal-equivalence approach to translation, matching the vocabulary, structure, and even word order of the original as closely as possible in the receptor language. Some other contemporary biblical versions have adopted, in varying degrees, a dynamic-equivalence approach, which attempts to respect the individuality of each language by expressing the meaning of the original in a linguistic structure suited to English, even though this may be very different from the corresponding Greek structure. While this approach often results in fresh and brilliant renderings, it has the disadvantages of more or less radically abandoning traditional biblical and liturgical terminology and phraseology, of expanding the text to include what more properly belongs in notes, commentaries, or preaching, and of tending toward paraphrase. A more formal approach seems better suited to the specific purposes intended for this translation.

At the same time, the editors have wished to produce a version in English that reflects contemporary American usage and is readily understandable to ordinary educated people, but one that will be recognized as dignified speech, on the level of formal rather than colloquial usage. These aims are not in fact contradictory, for there are different levels of language in current use: the language of formal situations is not that of colloquial conversation, though people understand both and may pass from one to the other without adverting to the transition. The liturgy is a formal situation that requires a level of discourse more dignified, formal, and hieratic than the world of business, sport, or informal communication. People readily understand this more formal level even though they may not often use it; our passive vocabulary is much larger than our active vocabulary. Hence this revision, while avoiding archaisms, does not shrink from traditional biblical terms that are easily understood even though not in common use in everyday speech. The level of language consciously aimed at is one appropriate for liturgical proclamation; this may also permit the translation to serve the purposes of devotional reading and serious study.

A particular effort has been made to insure consistency of vocabulary. Always to translate a given Greek word by the same English equivalent would lead to ludicrous results and to infidelity to the meaning of the text. But in passages where a particular Greek term retains the same meaning, it has been rendered in the same way insofar as this has been feasible; this is particularly significant in the case of terms that have a specific theological meaning. The synoptic gospels have been carefully translated so as to reveal both the similarities and the differences of the Greek.

An especially sensitive problem today is the question of discrimination in language. In recent years there has been much discussion about allegations of anti-Jewish expressions in the New Testament and of language that discriminates against various minorities. Above all, however, the question of discrimination against women affects the largest number of people and arouses the greatest degree of interest and concern. At present there is little agreement about these problems or about the best way to deal with them. In all these areas the present translation attempts to display a sensitivity appropriate to the present state of the questions under discussion, which are not yet resolved and in regard to which it is impossible to please everyone, since intelligent and sincere participants in the debate hold mutually contradictory views.

The primary concern in this revision is fidelity to what the text says. When the meaning of the Greek is inclusive of both sexes, the translation seeks to reproduce such inclusivity insofar as this is possible in normal English usage, without resort to inelegant circumlocutions or neologisms that would offend against the dignity of the language. Although the generic sense of *man* is traditional in English, many today reject it; its use has therefore generally been avoided, though it is retained in cases where no fully satisfactory equivalent could be found. English does not possess a gender-inclusive third personal pronoun in the singular, and this translation continues to use the masculine resumptive pronoun after *everyone* or *anyone,* in the traditional way, where this cannot be avoided without infidelity to the meaning.

The translation of the Greek word *adelphos,* particularly in the plural form *adelphoi,* poses an especially delicate problem. While the term literally means *brothers* or other male blood relatives, even in profane Greek the plural can designate two persons, one of either sex, who were born of the same parents. It was adopted by the early Christians to designate, in a figurative sense, the members of the Christian community, who were conscious of a new familial relationship to one another by reason of their adoption as children of God. They are consequently addressed as *adelphoi.* This has traditionally been rendered into English by *brothers* or, more archaically, *brethren.* There has never been any doubt that this designation includes *all* the members of the Christian community, both male and female. Given the absence in English of a corresponding term that explicitly includes both sexes, this translation retains the usage of *brothers,* with the inclusive meaning that has been traditionally attached to it in this biblical context.

Since the New Testament is the product of a particular time and culture, the views expressed in it and the language in which they are expressed reflect a particular cultural conditioning, which sometimes makes them quite different from contemporary ideas and concerns. Discriminatory language should be eliminated insofar as possible whenever it is unfaithful to the meaning of the New Testament, but the text should not be altered in order to adjust it to contemporary concerns. This translation does not introduce any changes, expansions, additions to, or subtractions from the text of scripture. It further retains the traditional biblical ways of speaking about God and about Christ, including the use of masculine nouns and pronouns.

The Greek text followed in this translation is that of the third edition of *The Greek New Testament*, edited by Kurt Aland, Matthew Black, Carlo Martini, Bruce Metzger, and Allen Wikgren, and published by the United Bible Societies in 1975. The same text, with a different critical apparatus and variations in punctuation and typography, was published as the twenty-sixth edition of the Nestle-Aland *Novum Testamentum Graece* in 1979 by the Deutsche Bibelstiftung, Stuttgart. This edition has also been consulted. When variant readings occur, the translation, with few exceptions, follows the reading that was placed in the text of these Greek editions, though the occurrence of the principal variants is pointed out in the notes.

The editors of the Greek text placed square brackets around words or portions of words of which the authenticity is questionable because the evidence of textual witnesses is inconclusive. The same has been done in the translation insofar as it is possible to reproduce this convention in English. It should be possible to read the text either with or without the disputed words, but in English it is not always feasible to provide this alternative, and in some passages the bracketed words must be included to make sense. As in the first edition, parentheses do not indicate textual uncertainty, but are simply a punctuation device to indicate a passage that in the editors' judgment appears parenthetical to the thought of the author.

Citations from the Old Testament are placed within quotation marks; longer citations are set off as block quotations in a separate indented paragraph. The sources of such citations, as well as those of many more or less subtle allusions to the Old Testament, are identified in the biblical cross-reference section at the bottom of each page. Insofar as possible, the translation of such Old Testament citations agrees with that of *The New American Bible* Old Testament whenever the underlying Greek agrees with the Hebrew (or, in some cases, the Aramaic or Greek) text from which the Old Testament translation was made. But citations in the New Testament frequently follow the Septuagint or some other version, or were made from memory; hence, in many cases the translation in the New Testament passage will not agree with what appears in the Old Testament. Some of these cases are explained in the notes.

It is a further aim of the revised edition to supply explanatory materials more abundantly than in the first edition. In most cases the introductions and notes have been entirely rewritten and expanded, and the cross-references checked and revised. It is intended that these materials should reflect the present state of sound biblical scholarship and should be presented in such a form that they can be assimilated by the ordinary intelligent reader without specialized biblical training. While they have been written with the ordinary educated Christian in mind, not all technical vocabulary can be entirely dispensed with in approaching the Bible, any more than in any other field. It is the hope of the editors that these materials, even if they sometimes demand an effort, will help the reader to a fuller and more intelligent understanding of the New Testament and a fruitful appropriation of its meaning for personal spiritual growth.

The New American Bible is a Roman Catholic translation. This revision, however, like the first edition, has been accomplished with the collaboration of scholars from other Christian churches, both among the revisers and on the editorial board, in response to the encouragement of Vatican Council II (*Dei Verbum,* 22). The editorial board expresses gratitude to all who have collaborated in the revision: to all the revisers, consultants, and bishops who contributed to it, to reviewers of the first edition, and to those who voluntarily submitted suggestions. May this translation fulfill its threefold purpose, "so that the word of the Lord may speed forward and be glorified" (2 Thes 3:1).

The Feast of St. Jerome
September 30, 1986

THE GOSPELS

See RG 371–72

The collection of writings that constitutes the New Testament begins with four gospels. Next comes the Acts of the Apostles, followed by twenty-one letters that are attributed to Paul, James, Peter, John, and Jude. Finally, at the end of the early church's scriptures stands the Revelation to John. Virtually all Christians agree that these twenty-seven books constitute the "canon," a term that means "rule" and designates the list of writings that are regarded as authoritative for Christian faith and life.

It is the purpose of this Introduction to describe those features that are common to the four gospels. A similar treatment of the letters of the New Testament is provided in the two Introductions that appear before the Letter to the Romans and before the Letter of James, respectively. The Acts of the Apostles, a work that is both historical and theological, and Revelation, an apocalyptic work, have no counterparts in the New Testament; the special Introductions prefixed to these books treat of the literary characteristics proper to each of them.

While the New Testament contains four writings called "gospels," there is in reality only one gospel running through all of the Christian scriptures, the gospel of and about Jesus Christ. Our English word "gospel" translates the Greek term *euangelion*, meaning "good news." This noun was used in the plural by the Greek translators of the Old Testament to render the Hebrew term for "good news" (2 Sm 4:10; possibly also 2 Sm 18:20, 25). But it is the corresponding verb *euangelizomai*, "to proclaim good news," that was especially significant in preparing for the New Testament idea of "gospel," since this term is used by Deutero-Isaiah of announcing the great victory of God that was to establish his universal kingship and inaugurate the new age (Is 40:9; 52:7; 61:1).

Paul used the word *euangelion* to designate the message that he and the other apostles proclaimed, the "gospel of God" (Rom 1:1; 15:16; 2 Cor 11:7; 1 Thes 2:2, 8, 9). He often referred to it simply as "the gospel" (Rom 1:16; 10:16; 11:28; etc) or, because of its content and origin, as "the gospel of Christ" (Rom 15:19; 1 Cor 9:12; 1 Thes 3:2; etc). Because of its personal meaning for him and his own particular manner of telling the story about Jesus Christ and of explaining the significance of his cross and resurrection, Paul also referred to this message as "my gospel" (Rom 2:16; cf. Gal 1:11; 2:2) or "our gospel" (2 Cor 4:3; 1 Thes 1:5; 2 Thes 2:14).

It was Mark, as far as we know, who first applied the term "gospel" to a book telling the story of Jesus; see Mk 1:1 and the note there. This form of presenting Jesus' life, works, teachings, passion, and resurrection was developed further by the other evangelists; see the Introduction to each gospel. The first three of the canonical gospels, Matthew, Mark, and Luke, are so similar at many points when viewed together, particularly when arranged in parallel columns or lines, that they are called "synoptic" gospels, from the Greek word for such a general view. The fourth gospel, John, often differs significantly from the synoptics in outline and approach. This work never uses the word "gospel" or its corresponding verb; nevertheless, its message concerns the same Jesus, and the reader is urged to believe in him as the Messiah, "that through this belief you may have life in his name" (Jn 20:31).

From the second century onward, the practice arose of designating each of these four books as a "gospel," understood as a title, and of adding a phrase with a name that identified the traditional author, e.g., "The Gospel according to Matthew." The arrangement of the canon that was adopted, with the four gospels grouped together at the beginning followed by Acts, provides a massive focus upon Jesus and allows Acts to serve as a framework for the letters of the New Testament. This order, however, conceals the fact that Luke's two volumes, a gospel and Acts, were intended by their author to go together. It further obscures the point that Paul's letters were written before any of our gospels, though the sayings and deeds of Jesus stand behind all the New Testament writings.

See RG 373–86

The Gospel According to Matthew

The position of the Gospel according to Matthew as the first of the four gospels in the New Testament reflects both the view that it was the first to be written, a view that goes back to the late second century A.D., and the esteem in which it was held by the church; no other was so frequently quoted in the noncanonical literature of earliest Christianity. Although the majority of scholars now reject the opinion about the time of its composition, the high estimation of this work remains. The reason for that becomes clear upon study of the way in which Matthew presents his story of Jesus, the demands of Christian discipleship, and the breaking-in of the new and final age through the ministry but particularly through the death and resurrection of Jesus.

The gospel begins with a narrative prologue (Mt 1:1–2:23), the first part of which is a genealogy of Jesus starting with Abraham, the father of Israel (Mt 1:1–17). Yet at the beginning of that genealogy Jesus is designated as "the son of David, the son of Abraham" (Mt 1:1). The kingly ancestor who lived about a thousand years after Abraham is named first, for this is the genealogy of Jesus Christ, the Messiah, the royal anointed one (Mt 1:16). In the first of the episodes of the infancy narrative that follow the genealogy, the mystery of Jesus' person is declared. He is conceived of a virgin by the power of the Spirit of God (Mt 1:18–25). The first of the gospel's fulfillment citations, whose purpose it is to show that he was the one to whom the prophecies of Israel were pointing, occurs here (Mt 1:23): he shall be named Emmanuel, for in him God is with us.

The announcement of the birth of this newborn king of the Jews greatly troubles not only King Herod but all Jerusalem (Mt 2:1–3), yet the Gentile magi are overjoyed to find him and offer him their homage and their gifts (Mt 2:10–11). Thus his ultimate rejection by the mass of his own people and his acceptance by the Gentile nations is foreshadowed. He must be taken to Egypt to escape the murderous plan of Herod. By his sojourn there and his subsequent return after the king's death he relives the Exodus experience of Israel. The words of the Lord spoken through the prophet Hosea, "Out of Egypt I called my son," are fulfilled in him (Mt 2:15); if Israel was God's son, Jesus is so in a way far surpassing the dignity of that nation, as his marvelous birth and the unfolding of his story show (see Mt 3:17; 4:1–11; 11:27; 14:33; 16:16; 27:54). Back in the land of Israel, he must be taken to Nazareth in Galilee because of the danger to his life in Judea, where Herod's son Archelaus is now ruling (Mt 2:22–23). The sufferings of Jesus in the infancy narrative anticipate those of his passion, and if his life is spared in spite of the dangers, it is because his destiny is finally to give it on the cross as "a ransom for many" (20:28). Thus the word of the angel will be fulfilled, ". . . he will save his people from their sins" (Mt 1:21; cf. Mt 26:28).

In Mt 4:12 Matthew begins his account of the ministry of Jesus, introducing it by the preparatory preaching of John the Baptist (Mt 3:1–12), the baptism of Jesus that culminates in God's proclaiming him his "beloved Son" (Mt 3:13–17), and the temptation in which he proves his true sonship by his victory over the devil's attempt to deflect him from the way of obedience to the Father (Mt 4:1–11). The central message of Jesus' preaching is the coming of the kingdom of heaven and the need for repentance, a complete change of heart and conduct, on the part of those who are to receive this great gift of God (Mt 4:17). Galilee is the setting for most of his ministry; he leaves there for Judea only in Mt 19:1, and his ministry in Jerusalem, the goal of his journey, is limited to a few days (Mt 21:1–25:46).

In this extensive material there are five great discourses of Jesus, each concluding with the formula "When Jesus finished these words" or one closely similar (Mt 7:28; 11:1; 13:53; 19:1; 26:1). These are an important structure of the gospel. In every case the discourse is preceded by a narrative section, each narrative and discourse together constituting a "book" of the gospel. The discourses are, respectively, the "Sermon on the Mount" (Mt 5:3–7:27), the missionary discourse (Mt 10:5–42), the parable discourse (Mt 13:3–52), the "church order" discourse (Mt 18:3–35), and the eschatological discourse (Mt 24:4–25:46). In large measure the material of these discourses came to Matthew from his tradition, but his work in modifying and adding to what he had received is abundantly evident. No other evangelist gives the teaching of Jesus with such elegance and order as he.

In the "Sermon on the Mount" the theme of righteousness is prominent, and even at this early stage of the ministry the note of opposition is struck between Jesus and the Pharisees, who are designated as "the hypocrites" (Mt 6:2, 5, 16). The righteousness of his disciples must surpass that of the scribes and Pharisees; otherwise, in spite of their alleged following of Jesus, they will not enter into the kingdom of heaven (Mt 5:20). Righteousness means doing the will of the heavenly Father (Mt 7:21), and his will is proclaimed in a manner that is startling to all who have identified it with the law of Moses. The antitheses of the Sermon (Mt 5:21–48) both accept (Mt 5:21–30, 43–48) and reject (Mt 5:31–42) elements of that law, and in the former case the understanding of the law's demands is deepened and extended. The antitheses are the best commentary on the meaning of Jesus' claim that he has come not to abolish but to fulfill the law (Mt 5:17). What is meant by fulfillment of the law is not the demand to keep it exactly as it stood before the coming of Jesus, but rather his bringing the law to be a lasting expression of the will of God, and in that fulfillment there is much that will pass away. Should this appear contradictory to his saying that "until heaven and earth pass away" not even the smallest part of the law will pass (Mt 5:18), that time of fulfillment is not the dissolution of the universe but the coming of the new age, which will occur with Jesus' death and resurrection. While righteousness in the new age will continue to mean conduct that is in accordance with the law, it will be conduct in accordance with the law as expounded and interpreted by Jesus (cf. Mt 28:20, ". . . all that I have commanded you").

Though Jesus speaks harshly about the Pharisees in the Sermon, his judgment is not solely a condemnation of them. The Pharisees are portrayed as a negative example for his disciples, and his condemnation of those who claim to belong to him while disobeying his word is no less severe (Mt 7:21–23, 26–27).

In Mt 4:23 a summary statement of Jesus' activity speaks not only of his teaching and proclaiming the gospel but of his "curing every disease and illness among the people"; this is repeated almost verbatim in Mt 9:35. The narrative section that follows the Sermon on the Mount (Mt 8:1–9:38) is composed principally of accounts of those merciful deeds of Jesus, but it is far from being simply a collection of stories about miraculous cures. The nature of the community that Jesus will establish is shown; it will always be under the protection of him whose power can deal with all dangers (Mt 8:23–27), but it is only for those who are prepared to follow him at whatever cost (Mt 8:16–22), not only believing Israelites but Gentiles who have come to faith in him (Mt 8:10–12). The disciples begin to have some insight, however imperfect, into the mystery of Jesus' person. They wonder about him whom "the winds and the sea obey" (Mt 8:27), and they witness his bold declaration of the forgiveness of the paralytic's sins (Mt 9:2). That episode of the narrative moves on two levels. When the crowd sees the cure that testifies to the authority of Jesus, the Son of Man, to forgive sins (Mt 9:6), they glorify God "who had given such authority to human beings" (Mt 9:8). The forgiveness of sins is now not the prerogative of Jesus alone but of "human beings," that is, of the disciples who constitute the community of Jesus, the church. The ecclesial character of this narrative section could hardly be more plainly indicated.

The end of the section prepares for the discourse on the church's mission (Mt 10:5–42). Jesus is moved to pity at the sight of the crowds who are like sheep without a shepherd (Mt 9:36), and he sends out the twelve disciples to make the proclamation with which his own ministry began, "The kingdom of heaven is at hand" (Mt 10:7; cf. Mt 4:17), and to drive out demons and cure the sick as he has done (Mt 10:1). Their mission is limited to Israel (Mt 10:5–6) as Jesus' own was (Mt 15:24), yet in Mt 15:16 that perspective broadens and the discourse begins to speak of the mission that the disciples will have after the resurrection and of the severe persecution that will attend it (Mt 10:18). Again, the discourse moves on two levels: that of the time of Jesus and that of the time of the church.

The narrative section of the third book (Mt 11:2–12:50) deals with the growing opposition to Jesus. Hostility toward him has already been manifested (Mt 8:10; 9:3, 10–13, 34), but here it becomes more intense. The rejection of Jesus comes, as before, from Pharisees, who take "counsel against him to put him to death" (Mt 12:14) and repeat their earlier accusation that he drives out demons because he is in league with demonic power (Mt 12:22–24). But they are not alone in their rejection. Jesus complains of the lack of faith of "this generation" of Israelites (Mt 11:16–19) and reproaches the towns "where most of his mighty deeds had been done" for not heeding his call to repentance (Mt 11:20–24). This dark picture is relieved by Jesus' praise of the Father who has enabled "the childlike" to accept him (Mt 11:25–27), but on the whole the story is one of opposition to his word and blindness to the meaning of his deeds. The whole section ends with his declaring that not even the most intimate blood relationship with him counts for anything; his only true relatives are those who do the will of his heavenly Father (Mt 12:48–50).

The narrative of rejection leads up to the parable discourse (Mt 13:3–52). The reason given for Jesus' speaking to the crowds in parables is that they have hardened themselves against his clear teaching, unlike the disciples to whom knowledge of "the mysteries of the kingdom has been granted" (Mt 13:10–16). In Mt 13:36 he dismisses the crowds and continues the discourse to his disciples alone, who claim, at the end, to have understood all that he has said (Mt 13:51). But, lest the impression be given that the church of Jesus is made up only of true disciples, the explanation of the parable of the weeds among the wheat (Mt 13:37–43), as well as the parable of the net thrown into the sea "which collects fish of every kind" (Mt 13:47–49), shows that it is composed of both the righteous and the wicked, and that separation between the two will be made only at the time of the final judgment.

In the narrative that constitutes the first part of the fourth book of the gospel (Mt 13:54–17:27), Jesus is shown preparing for the establishment of his church with its teaching authority that will supplant the blind guidance of the Pharisees (Mt 15:13–14), whose teaching, curiously said to be that of the Sadducees also, is repudiated by Jesus as the norm for his disciples (Mt 16:6, 11–12). The church of Jesus will be built on Peter (Mt 16:18), who will be given authority to bind and loose on earth, an authority whose exercise will be confirmed in heaven (Mt 16:19). The metaphor of binding and loosing has a variety of meanings, among them that of giving authoritative teaching. This promise is made to Peter directly after he has confessed Jesus to be the Messiah, the Son of the living God (Mt 16:16), a confession that he has made as the result of revelation given to him by the heavenly Father (Mt 16:17); Matthew's ecclesiology is based on his high christology.

Directly after that confession Jesus begins to instruct his disciples about how he must go the way of suffering and death (Mt 16:21). Peter, who has been praised for his confession, protests against this and receives from Jesus the sharpest of rebukes for attempting to deflect Jesus from his God-appointed destiny. The future rock upon whom the church will be built is still a man of "little faith" (see Mt 14:31). Both he and the other disciples must know not only that Jesus will have to suffer and die but that they too will have to follow him on the way of the cross if they are truly to be his disciples (Mt 16:24–25).

The discourse following this narrative (Mt 18:1–35) is often called the "church order" discourse, although that title is perhaps misleading since the emphasis is not on the structure of the church but on the care that the disciples must have for one another in respect to guarding each other's faith in Jesus (Mt 18:6–7), to seeking out those who have wandered from the fold (Mt 18:10–14), and to repeated forgiving of their fellow disciples who have offended them (Mt 18:21–35). But there is also the obligation to correct the sinful fellow Christian and, should one refuse to be corrected, separation from the community is demanded (Mt 18:15–18).

The narrative of the fifth book (Mt 19:1–23:39) begins with the departure of Jesus and his disciples from Galilee for Jerusalem. In the course of their journey Jesus for the third time predicts the passion that awaits him at Jerusalem and also his resurrection (Mt 20:17–19). At his entrance into the city he is hailed as the Son of David by the crowds accompanying him (Mt 21:9). He cleanses the temple (Mt 21:12–17), and in the few days of his Jerusalem ministry he engages in a series of controversies with the Jewish religious leaders (Mt 21:23–27; 22:15–22, 23–33, 34–40, 41–46), meanwhile speaking parables against them (Mt 21:28–32, 33–46), against all those Israelites who have rejected God's invitation to the messianic banquet (Mt 22:1–10), and against all, Jew and Gentile, who have accepted but have shown themselves unworthy of it (Mt 22:11–14). Once again, the perspective of the evangelist includes not only the time of Jesus' ministry but that of the preaching of the gospel after his resurrection. The narrative culminates in Jesus' denunciation of the scribes and Pharisees, reflecting not only his own opposition to them but that of Matthew's church (Mt 23:1–36), and in Jesus' lament over Jerusalem (Mt 23:37–39).

In the discourse of the fifth book (Mt 24:1–25:46), the last of the great structural discourses of the gospel, Jesus predicts the destruction of the temple and his own final coming. The time of the latter is unknown (Mt 24:36, 44), and the disciples are exhorted in various parables to live in readiness for it, a readiness that entails faithful attention to the duties of the interim period (Mt 24:45–25:30). The coming of Jesus will bring with it the great judgment by which the everlasting destiny of all will be determined (Mt 25:31–46).

The story of Jesus' passion and resurrection (Mt 26:1–28:20), the climax of the gospel, throws light on all that has preceded. In Matthew "righteousness" means both the faithful response to the will of God demanded of all to whom that will is announced and also the saving activity of God for his people (see Mt 3:15; 5:6; 6:33). The passion supremely exemplifies both meanings of that central Matthean word. In Jesus' absolute faithfulness to the Father's will that he drink the cup of suffering (Mt 26:39), the incomparable model for Christian obedience is given; in his death "for the forgiveness of sins" (Mt 26:28), the saving power of God is manifested as never before.

Matthew's portrayal of Jesus in his passion combines both the majestic serenity of the obedient Son who goes his destined way in fulfillment of the scriptures (Mt 26:52–54), confident of his ultimate vindication by God, and the depths of fear and abandonment that he feels in face of death (Mt 26:38–39; 27:46). These two aspects are expressed by an Old Testament theme that occurs often in the narrative, i.e., the portrait of the suffering Righteous One who complains to God in his misery, but is certain of eventual deliverance from his terrible ordeal.

The passion-resurrection of God's Son means nothing less than the turn of the ages, a new stage of history, the coming of the Son of Man in his kingdom (Mt 28:18; cf. Mt 16:28). That is the sense of the apocalyptic signs that accompany Jesus' death (Mt 27:51–53) and resurrection (Mt 28:2). Although the old age continues, as it will until the manifestation of Jesus' triumph at his parousia, the final age has now begun. This is known only to those who have seen the Risen One and to those, both Jews and Gentiles, who have believed in their announcement of Jesus' triumph and have themselves become his disciples (cf. Mt 28:19). To them he is constantly, though invisibly, present (Mt 28:20), verifying the name Emmanuel, "God is with us" (cf. Mt 1:23).

The questions of authorship, sources, and the time of composition of this gospel have received many answers, none of which can claim more than a greater or lesser degree of probability. The one now favored by the majority of scholars is the following.

The ancient tradition that the author was the disciple and apostle of Jesus named Matthew (see Mt 10:3) is untenable because the gospel is based, in large part, on the Gospel according to Mark (almost all the verses of that gospel have been utilized in this), and it is hardly likely that a companion of Jesus would have followed so extensively an account that came from one who admittedly never had such an association rather than rely on his own memories. The attribution of the gospel to the disciple Matthew may have been due to his having been responsible for some of the traditions found in it, but that is far from certain.

The unknown author, whom we shall continue to call Matthew for the sake of convenience, drew not only upon the Gospel according to Mark but upon a large body of material (principally, sayings of Jesus) not found in Mark that corresponds, sometimes exactly, to material found also in the Gospel according to Luke. This material, called "Q" (probably from the first letter of the German word Quelle, meaning "source"), represents traditions, written and oral, used by both Matthew and Luke. Mark and Q are sources common to the two other synoptic gospels; hence the name the "Two-Source Theory" given to this explanation of the relation among the synoptics.

In addition to what Matthew drew from Mark and Q, his gospel contains material that is found only there. This is often designated "M," written or oral tradition that was available to the author. Since Mark was written shortly before or shortly after A.D. 70 (see Introduction to Mark), Matthew was composed certainly after that date, which marks the fall of Jerusalem to the Romans at the time of the First Jewish Revolt (A.D. 66–70), and probably at least a decade later since Matthew's use of Mark presupposes a wide diffusion of that gospel. The post-A.D. 70 date is confirmed within the text by Mt 22:7, which refers to the destruction of Jerusalem.

As for the place where the gospel was composed, a plausible suggestion is that it was Antioch, the capital of the Roman province of Syria. That large and important city had a mixed population of Greek-speaking Gentiles and Jews. The tensions between Jewish and Gentile Christians there in the time of Paul (see Gal 2:1–14) in respect to Christian obligation to observe Mosaic law are partially similar to tensions that can be seen between the two groups in Matthew's gospel. The church of Matthew, originally strongly Jewish Christian, had become one in which Gentile Christians were predominant. His gospel answers the question how obedience to the will of God is to be expressed by those who live after the "turn of the ages," the death and resurrection of Jesus.

The principal divisions of the Gospel according to Matthew are the following:

I. The Infancy Narrative (1:1–2:23)
II. The Proclamation of the Kingdom (3:1–7:29)
III. Ministry and Mission in Galilee (8:1–11:1)
IV. Opposition from Israel (11:2–13:53)
V. Jesus, the Kingdom, and the Church (13:54–18:35)
VI. Ministry in Judea and Jerusalem (19:1–25:46)
VII. The Passion and Resurrection (26:1–28:20)

I. The Infancy Narrative

CHAPTER 1

See RG 375–76

The Genealogy of Jesus. [1a]*The book
of the genealogy of Jesus Christ, the son of
David, the son of Abraham.
[2bc]Abraham became the father of Isaac,
Isaac the father of Jacob, Jacob the father of
Judah and his brothers. [3d]Judah became the
father of Perez and Zerah, whose mother
was Tamar. Perez became the father of Hezron,
Hezron the father of Ram, [4e]Ram the father
of Amminadab. Amminadab became
the father of Nahshon, Nahshon the father of
Salmon, [5f]Salmon the father of Boaz, whose
mother was Rahab. Boaz became the father

1:1–2:23 The infancy narrative forms the prologue of the gospel. Consisting of a genealogy and five stories, it presents the coming of Jesus as the climax of Israel's history, and the events of his conception, birth, and early childhood as the fulfillment of Old Testament prophecy. The genealogy is probably traditional material that Matthew edited. In its first two sections (Mt 1:2–11) it was drawn from Ru 4:18–22; 1 Chr 1–3. Except for Jechoniah, Shealtiel, and Zerubbabel, none of the names in the third section (Mt 1:12–16) is found in any Old Testament genealogy. While the genealogy shows the continuity of God's providential plan from Abraham on, discontinuity is also present. The women Tamar (Mt 1:3), Rahab and Ruth (Mt 1:5), and the wife of Uriah, Bathsheba (Mt 1:6), bore their sons through unions that were in varying degrees strange and unexpected. These "irregularities" culminate in the supreme "irregularity" of the Messiah's birth of a virgin mother; the age of fulfillment is inaugurated by a creative act of God. Drawing upon both biblical tradition and Jewish stories, Matthew portrays Jesus as reliving the Exodus experience of Israel and the persecutions of Moses. His rejection by his own people and his passion are foreshadowed by the troubled reaction of "all Jerusalem" to the question of the magi who are seeking the "newborn king of the Jews" (Mt 2:2–3), and by Herod's attempt to have him killed. The magi who do him homage prefigure the Gentiles who will accept the preaching of the gospel. The infancy narrative proclaims who Jesus is, the savior of his people from their sins (Mt 1:21), Emmanuel in whom "God is with us" (Mt 1:23), and the Son of God (Mt 2:15).

1:1 The Son of David, the son of Abraham: two links of the genealogical chain are singled out. Although the later, David is placed first in order to emphasize that Jesus is the royal Messiah. The mention of Abraham may be due not only to his being the father of the nation Israel but to Matthew's interest in the universal scope of Jesus' mission; cf. Gn 22:18 ". . . . in your descendants all the nations of the earth shall find blessing."

a: Gn 5:1 / 1 Chr 17:11 / Gn 22:18. *b:* Lk 3:23–38. *c:* Gn 21:3; 25:26; 29:35; 1 Chr 2:1. *d:* Gn 38:29–30; Ru 4:18; 1 Chr 2:4–9. *e:* Ru 4:19–20; 1 Chr 2:10–11. *f:* Ru 4:21–22; 1 Chr 2:11–12.

of Obed, whose mother was Ruth. Obed became the father of Jesse, [6g]Jesse the father of
David the king.

David became the father of Solomon,
whose mother had been the wife of Uriah.
[7h*]Solomon became the father of Rehoboam, Rehoboam the father of Abijah, Abijah the father of Asaph. [8]Asaph became the
father of Jehoshaphat, Jehoshaphat the father of Joram, Joram the father of Uzziah.
[9]Uzziah became the father of Jotham, Jotham the father of Ahaz, Ahaz the father of
Hezekiah. [10*]Hezekiah became the father of
Manasseh, Manasseh the father of Amos,
Amos the father of Josiah. [11]Josiah became
the father of Jechoniah and his brothers at
the time of the Babylonian exile.

[12i]After the Babylonian exile, Jechoniah
became the father of Shealtiel, Shealtiel the
father of Zerubbabel, [13]Zerubbabel the father
of Abiud. Abiud became the father of Eliakim,
Eliakim the father of Azor, [14]Azor the father
of Zadok. Zadok became the father of Achim,
Achim the father of Eliud, [15]Eliud the father
of Eleazar. Eleazar became the father of Matthan, Matthan the father of Jacob, [16]Jacob the
father of Joseph, the husband of Mary. Of her
was born Jesus who is called the Messiah.

[17*]Thus the total number of generations
from Abraham to David is fourteen generations; from David to the Babylonian exile,
fourteen generations; from the Babylonian
exile to the Messiah, fourteen generations.

The Birth of Jesus. [18*]Now this is how the
birth of Jesus Christ came about. When his
mother Mary was betrothed to Joseph, but before they lived together, she was found with
child through the holy Spirit. [19*]Joseph her
husband, since he was a righteous man, yet
unwilling to expose her to shame, decided to
divorce her quietly. [20j*]Such was his intention
when, behold, the angel of the Lord appeared
to him in a dream and said, "Joseph, son of
David, do not be afraid to take Mary your wife
into your home. For it is through the holy
Spirit that this child has been conceived in her.
[21*]She will bear a son and you are to name
him Jesus, because he will save his people
from their sins." [22]All this took place to fulfill
what the Lord had said through the prophet:

1:7 The successor of Abijah was not Asaph but Asa (see 1 Chr 3:10). Some textual witnesses read the latter name; however, **Asaph** is better attested. Matthew may have deliberately introduced the psalmist Asaph into the genealogy (and in Mt 1:10 the prophet Amos) in order to show that Jesus is the fulfillment not only of the promises made to David (see 2 Sm 7) but of all the Old Testament.

1:10 Amos: some textual witnesses read **Amon**, who was the actual successor of Manasseh (see 1 Chr 3:14).

1:17 Matthew is concerned with fourteen generations, probably because fourteen is the numerical value of the Hebrew letters forming the name of David. In the second section of the genealogy (Mt 1:6b–11), three kings of Judah, Ahaziah, Joash, and Amaziah, have been omitted (see 1 Chr 3:11–12), so that there are fourteen generations in that section. Yet the third (Mt 1:12–16) apparently has only thirteen. Since Matthew here emphasizes that each section has fourteen, it is unlikely that the thirteen of the last was due to his oversight. Some scholars suggest that **Jesus who is called the Messiah** (Mt 1:16b) doubles the final member of the chain: **Jesus**, born within the family of David, opens up the new age as **Messiah**, so that in fact there are fourteen generations in the third section. This is perhaps too subtle, and the hypothesis of a slip not on the part of Matthew but of a later scribe seems likely. On **Messiah**, see note on Lk 2:11.

1:18–25 This first story of the infancy narrative spells out what is summarily indicated in Mt 1:16. The virginal conception of Jesus is the work of the Spirit of God. Joseph's decision to divorce Mary is overcome by the heavenly command that he take her into his home and accept the child as his own. The natural genealogical line is broken but the promises to David are fulfilled; through Joseph's adoption the child belongs to the family of David. Matthew sees the virginal conception as the fulfillment of Is 7:14.

1:18 Betrothed to Joseph: betrothal was the first part of the marriage, constituting a man and woman as husband and wife. Subsequent infidelity was considered adultery. The betrothal was followed some months later by the husband's taking his wife into his home, at which time normal married life began.

1:19 A righteous man: as a devout observer of the Mosaic law, Joseph wished to break his union with someone whom he suspected of gross violation of the law. It is commonly said that the law required him to do so, but the texts usually given in support of that view, e.g., Dt 22:20–21 do not clearly pertain to Joseph's situation. **Unwilling to expose her to shame**: the penalty for proved adultery was death by stoning; cf. Dt 22:21–23.

1:20 The angel of the Lord: in the Old Testament a common designation of God in communication with a human being. **In a dream**: see Mt 2:13, 19, 22. These dreams may be meant to recall the dreams of Joseph, son of Jacob the patriarch (Gn 37:5–11:19). A closer parallel is the dream of Amram, father of Moses, related by Josephus (*Antiquities* 2, 9, 3; (par.) 212, 215–16).

1:21 Jesus: in first-century Judaism the Hebrew name Joshua (Greek *Iēsous*) meaning "Yahweh helps" was interpreted as "Yahweh saves."

g: 2 Sm 12:24; 1 Chr 2:15; 3:5. *h:* 2 Kgs 25:1–21; 1 Chr 3:10–15. *i:* 1 Chr 3:16–19. *j:* 2:13, 19; Lk 1:35.

[23][k]*"Behold, the virgin shall be with child
and bear a son,
and they shall name him Emmanuel,"

which means "God is with us." [24]When Joseph awoke, he did as the angel of the Lord
had commanded him and took his wife into
his home. [25][l]*He had no relations with her
until she bore a son, and he named him Jesus.

CHAPTER 2

See RG 375–76

The Visit of the Magi. [1]*When Jesus
was born in Bethlehem of Judea, in the days
of King Herod, behold, magi from the east
arrived in Jerusalem, [2][m]*saying, "Where is
the newborn king of the Jews? We saw his
star at its rising and have come to do him
homage." [3]When King Herod heard this, he
was greatly troubled, and all Jerusalem with
him. [4]*Assembling all the chief priests and
the scribes of the people, he inquired of them
where the Messiah was to be born. [5][n]They
said to him, "In Bethlehem of Judea, for thus
it has been written through the prophet:

[6] 'And you, Bethlehem, land of Judah,
are by no means least among the rulers
of Judah;
since from you shall come a ruler,
who is to shepherd my people
Israel.' "

[7]Then Herod called the magi secretly and ascertained from them the time of the star's appearance. [8]He sent them to Bethlehem and
said, "Go and search diligently for the child.
When you have found him, bring me word,
that I too may go and do him homage." [9]Af-
ter their audience with the king they set out.
And behold, the star that they had seen at its
rising preceded them, until it came and
stopped over the place where the child was.
[10]They were overjoyed at seeing the star,
[11][o]*and on entering the house they saw the
child with Mary his mother. They prostrated
themselves and did him homage. Then they
opened their treasures and offered him gifts
of gold, frankincense, and myrrh. [12]And
having been warned in a dream not to return
to Herod, they departed for their country by
another way.

The Flight to Egypt. [13]*When they had departed, behold, the angel of the Lord appeared
to Joseph in a dream and said, "Rise, take the
child and his mother, flee to Egypt, and stay
there until I tell you. Herod is going to search
for the child to destroy him." [14]Joseph rose
and took the child and his mother by night
and departed for Egypt. [15][p]*He stayed there
until the death of Herod, that what the Lord
had said through the prophet might be fulfilled, "Out of Egypt I called my son."

1:23 God is with us: God's promise of deliverance to Judah in Isaiah's time is seen by Matthew as fulfilled in the birth of Jesus, in whom God is with his people. The name Emmanuel is alluded to at the end of the gospel where the risen Jesus assures his disciples of his continued presence, ". . . I am with you always, until the end of the age" (Mt 28:20).

1:25 Until she bore a son: the evangelist is concerned to emphasize that Joseph was not responsible for the conception of Jesus. The Greek word translated "until" does not imply normal marital conduct after Jesus' birth, nor does it exclude it.

2:1–12 The future rejection of Jesus by Israel and his acceptance by the Gentiles are retrojected into this scene of the narrative.

2:1 In the days of King Herod: Herod reigned from 37 to 4 B.C. **Magi**: originally a designation of the Persian priestly caste, the word became used of those who were regarded as having more than human knowledge. Matthew's magi are astrologers.

2:2 We saw his star: it was a common ancient belief that a new star appeared at the time of a ruler's birth. Matthew also draws upon the Old Testament story of Balaam, who had prophesied that "A star shall advance from Jacob" (Nm 24:17), though there the star means not an astral phenomenon but the king himself.

2:4 Herod's consultation with the chief priests and scribes has some similarity to a Jewish legend about the child Moses in which the "sacred scribes" warn Pharaoh about the imminent birth of one who will deliver Israel from Egypt and the king makes plans to destroy him.

2:11 Cf. Ps 72:10, 15; Is 60:6. These Old Testament texts led to the interpretation of the magi as kings.

2:13–23 Biblical and nonbiblical traditions about Moses are here applied to the child Jesus, though the dominant Old Testament type is not Moses but Israel (Mt 2:15).

2:13 Flee to Egypt: Egypt was a traditional place of refuge for those fleeing from danger in Palestine (see 1 Kgs 11:40; Jer 26:21), but the main reason why the child is to be taken to Egypt is that he may relive the Exodus experience of Israel.

2:15 The fulfillment citation is taken from Hos 11:1. Israel, God's son, was called out of Egypt at the time of the Exodus; Jesus, the Son of God, will similarly be called out of that land in a new exodus. The father-son relationship between God and the nation is set in a higher key. Here the son is not a group adopted as "son of God," but the child who, as conceived by the holy Spirit, stands in unique relation to God. He is son of David and of Abraham, of Mary and of Joseph, but, above all, of God.

k: Is 7:14 LXX. *l:* Lk 2:7. *m:* Nm 24:17. *n:* Mi 5:1 / 2 Sm 5:2. *o:* Ps 72:10–11, 15; Is 60:6. *p:* Hos 11:1.

The Massacre of the Infants. [16]When Herod realized that he had been deceived by the magi, he became furious. He ordered the massacre of all the boys in Bethlehem and its vicinity two years old and under, in accordance with the time he had ascertained from the magi. [17]Then was fulfilled what had been said through Jeremiah the prophet:

[18] [q*]"A voice was heard in Ramah,
sobbing and loud lamentation;
Rachel weeping for her children,
and she would not be consoled,
since they were no more."

The Return from Egypt. [19]When Herod had died, behold, the angel of the Lord appeared in a dream to Joseph in Egypt [20][r*]and said, "Rise, take the child and his mother and go to the land of Israel, for those who sought the child's life are dead." [21]He rose, took the child and his mother, and went to the land of Israel. [22]*But when he heard that Archelaus was ruling over Judea in place of his father Herod, he was afraid to go back there. And because he had been warned in a dream, he departed for the region of Galilee. [23][s*]He went and dwelt in a town called Nazareth, so that what had been spoken through the prophets might be fulfilled, "He shall be called a Nazorean."

II. The Proclamation of the Kingdom

CHAPTER 3

See RG 376

The Preaching of John the Baptist. [1][t*]In those days John the Baptist appeared, preaching in the desert of Judea [2][u*][and] saying, "Repent, for the kingdom of heaven is at hand!" [3][v*]It was of him that the prophet Isaiah had spoken when he said:

"A voice of one crying out in the desert,
'Prepare the way of the Lord,
make straight his paths.' "

[4][w*]John wore clothing made of camel's hair and had a leather belt around his waist. His

2:18 Jer 31:15 portrays Rachel, wife of the patriarch Jacob, weeping for her children taken into exile at the time of the Assyrian invasion of the northern kingdom (722–21 B.C.). Bethlehem was traditionally identified with Ephrath, the place near which Rachel was buried (see Gn 35:19; 48:7), and the mourning of Rachel is here applied to her lost children of a later age. **Ramah**: about six miles north of Jerusalem. The lamentation of Rachel is so great as to be heard at a far distance.

2:20 For those who sought the child's life are dead: Moses, who had fled from Egypt because the Pharaoh sought to kill him (see Ex 2:15), was told to return there, "for all the men who sought your life are dead" (Ex 4:19).

2:22 With the agreement of the emperor Augustus, Archelaus received half of his father's kingdom, including Judea, after Herod's death. He had the title "ethnarch" (i.e., "ruler of a nation") and reigned from 4 B.C. to A.D. 6.

2:23 Nazareth . . . he shall be called a Nazorean: the tradition of Jesus' residence in Nazareth was firmly established, and Matthew sees it as being in accordance with the foreannounced plan of God. The town of Nazareth is not mentioned in the Old Testament, and no such prophecy can be found there. The vague expression "through the prophets" may be due to Matthew's seeing a connection between Nazareth and certain texts in which there are words with a remote similarity to the name of that town. Some such Old Testament texts are Is 11:1 where the Davidic king of the future is called "a bud" (*nēser*) that shall blossom from the roots of Jesse, and Jgs 13:5, 7 where Samson, the future deliverer of Israel from the Philistines, is called one who shall be consecrated (a *nāzîr*) to God.

3:1 Unlike Luke, Matthew says nothing of the Baptist's origins and does not make him a relative of Jesus. **The desert of Judea**: the barren region west of the Dead Sea extending up the Jordan valley.

3:1–12 Here Matthew takes up the order of Jesus' ministry found in the gospel of Mark, beginning with the preparatory preaching of John the Baptist.

3:2 Repent: the Baptist calls for a change of heart and conduct, a turning of one's life from rebellion to obedience towards God. **The kingdom of heaven is at hand**: "heaven" (lit., "the heavens") is a substitute for the name "God" that was avoided by devout Jews of the time out of reverence. The expression "the kingdom of heaven" occurs only in the gospel of Matthew. It means the effective rule of God over his people. In its fullness it includes not only human obedience to God's word, but the triumph of God over physical evils, supremely over death. In the expectation found in Jewish apocalyptic, the kingdom was to be ushered in by a judgment in which sinners would be condemned and perish, an expectation shared by the Baptist. This was modified in Christian understanding where the kingdom was seen as being established in stages, culminating with the parousia of Jesus.

3:3 See note on Jn 1:23.

3:4 The clothing of John recalls the austere dress of the prophet Elijah (2 Kgs 1:8). The expectation of the return of Elijah from heaven to prepare Israel for the final manifestation of God's kingdom was widespread, and according to Matthew this expectation was fulfilled in the Baptist's ministry (Mt 11:14; 17:11–13).

---

q: Jer 31:15. *r:* Ex 4:19. *s:* 13:54; Mk 1:9; Lk 2:39; 4:34; Jn 19:19. *t:* Mk 1:2–8; Lk 3:2–17. *u:* 4:17; 10:7. *v:* Is 40:3. *w:* 11:7–8; 2 Kgs 1:8; Zec 13:4.

food was locusts and wild honey. [5]At that time Jerusalem, all Judea, and the whole region around the Jordan were going out to him [6*]and were being baptized by him in the Jordan River as they acknowledged their sins.

[7x*]When he saw many of the Pharisees and Sadducees coming to his baptism, he said to them, "You brood of vipers! Who warned you to flee from the coming wrath? [8]Produce good fruit as evidence of your repentance. [9y]And do not presume to say to yourselves, 'We have Abraham as our father.' For I tell you, God can raise up children to Abraham from these stones. [10]Even now the ax lies at the root of the trees. Therefore every tree that does not bear good fruit will be cut down and thrown into the fire. [11z*]I am baptizing you with water, for repentance, but the one who is coming after me is mightier than I. I am not worthy to carry his sandals. He will baptize you with the holy Spirit and fire. [12a*]His winnowing fan is in his hand. He will clear his threshing floor and gather his wheat into his barn, but the chaff he will burn with unquenchable fire."

The Baptism of Jesus. [13b*]Then Jesus came from Galilee to John at the Jordan to be baptized by him. [14*]John tried to prevent him, saying, "I need to be baptized by you, and yet you are coming to me?" [15]Jesus said to him in reply, "Allow it now, for thus it is fitting for us to fulfill all righteousness." Then he allowed him. [16c*]After Jesus was baptized, he came up from the water and behold, the heavens were opened [for him], and he saw the Spirit of God descending like a dove [and] coming upon him. [17d*]And a voice came from the heavens, saying, "This is my beloved Son, with whom I am well pleased."

CHAPTER 4

See RG 376–77

The Temptation of Jesus. [1e*]Then Jesus was led by the Spirit into the desert to

3:6 Ritual washing was practiced by various groups in Palestine between 150 B.C. and A.D. 250. John's baptism may have been related to the purificatory washings of the Essenes at Qumran.

3:7 Pharisees and Sadducees: the former were marked by devotion to the law, written and oral, and the scribes, experts in the law, belonged predominantly to this group. The Sadducees were the priestly aristocratic party, centered in Jerusalem. They accepted as scripture only the first five books of the Old Testament, followed only the letter of the law, rejected the oral legal traditions, and were opposed to teachings not found in the Pentateuch, such as the resurrection of the dead. Matthew links both of these groups together as enemies of Jesus (Mt 16:1, 6, 11, 12; cf. Mk 8:11–13, 15). The threatening words that follow are addressed to them rather than to "the crowds" as in Lk 3:7. **The coming wrath**: the judgment that will bring about the destruction of unrepentant sinners.

3:11 Baptize you with the holy Spirit and fire: the water baptism of John will be followed by an "immersion" of the repentant in the cleansing power of the Spirit of God, and of the unrepentant in the destroying power of God's judgment. However, some see **the holy Spirit** and **fire** as synonymous, and the effect of this "baptism" as either purification or destruction. See note on Lk 3:16.

3:12 The discrimination between the good and the bad is compared to the procedure by which a farmer separates wheat and chaff. The **winnowing fan** was a forklike shovel with which the threshed wheat was thrown into the air. The kernels fell to the ground; the light chaff, blown off by the wind, was gathered and burned up.

3:13–17 The baptism of Jesus is the occasion on which he is equipped for his ministry by the holy Spirit and proclaimed to be the Son of God.

3:14–15 This dialogue, peculiar to Matthew, reveals John's awareness of Jesus' superiority to him as the mightier one who is coming and who will baptize with the holy Spirit (Mt 3:11). His reluctance to admit Jesus among the sinners whom he is baptizing with water is overcome by Jesus' response. **To fulfill all righteousness**: in this gospel to **fulfill** usually refers to fulfillment of prophecy, and **righteousness** to moral conduct in conformity with God's will. Here, however, as in Mt 5:6; 6:33, **righteousness** seems to mean the saving activity of God. **To fulfill all righteousness** is to submit to the plan of God for the salvation of the human race. This involves Jesus' identification with sinners; hence the propriety of his accepting John's baptism.

3:16 The Spirit . . . coming upon him: cf. Is 42:1.

3:17 This is my beloved Son: the Marcan address to Jesus (Mk 1:11) is changed into a proclamation. The Father's voice speaks in terms that reflect Is 42:1; Ps 2:7; Gn 22:2.

4:1–11 Jesus, proclaimed Son of God at his baptism, is subjected to a triple temptation. Obedience to the Father is a characteristic of true sonship, and Jesus is tempted by the devil to rebel against God, overtly in the third case, more subtly in the first two. Each refusal of Jesus is expressed in language taken from the Book of Deuteronomy (Dt 8:3; 6:13, 16). The testings of Jesus resemble those of Israel during the wandering in the desert and later in Canaan, and the victory of Jesus, the true Israel and the true Son, contrasts with the failure of the ancient and disobedient "son," the old Israel. In the temptation account Matthew is almost identical with Luke; both seem to have drawn upon the same source.

x: 12:34; 23:33; Is 59:5. *y:* Jn 8:33, 39; Rom 9:7–8; Gal 4:21–31. *z:* Jn 1:26–27, 33; Acts 1:5. *a:* 13:30; Is 41:16; Jer 15:7. *b:* Mk 1:9–11; Lk 3:21–22; Jn 1:31–34. *c:* Is 42:1. *d:* 12:18; 17:5; Gn 22:2; Ps 2:7; Is 42:1. *e:* Mk 1:12–13; Lk 4:1–13.

be tempted by the devil. [2f*]He fasted for
forty days and forty nights, and afterwards
he was hungry. [3]The tempter approached
and said to him, "If you are the Son of God,
command that these stones become loaves
of bread." [4g*]He said in reply, "It is written:

'One does not live by bread alone,
but by every word that comes forth
from the mouth of God.' "

[5*]Then the devil took him to the holy city,
and made him stand on the parapet of the
temple, [6h]and said to him, "If you are the
Son of God, throw yourself down. For it is
written:

'He will command his angels concerning
you'
and 'with their hands they will support
you,
lest you dash your foot against a stone.' "

[7i]Jesus answered him, "Again it is written,
'You shall not put the Lord, your God, to the
test.' " [8]Then the devil took him up to a very
high mountain, and showed him all the kingdoms of the world in their magnificence,
[9*]and he said to him, "All these I shall give
to you, if you will prostrate yourself and
worship me." [10j]At this, Jesus said to him,
"Get away, Satan! It is written:

'The Lord, your God, shall you worship
and him alone shall you serve.' "

[11]Then the devil left him and, behold, angels
came and ministered to him.

The Beginning of the Galilean Ministry.
[12k*]When he heard that John had been arrested, he withdrew to Galilee. [13l]He left
Nazareth and went to live in Capernaum by
the sea, in the region of Zebulun and Naphtali, [14]that what had been said through Isaiah
the prophet might be fulfilled:

[15 m]"Land of Zebulun and land of Naphtali,
the way to the sea, beyond the Jordan,
Galilee of the Gentiles,
[16 n]the people who sit in darkness
have seen a great light,
on those dwelling in a land
overshadowed by death
light has arisen."

[17o*]From that time on, Jesus began to preach
and say, "Repent, for the kingdom of heaven
is at hand."

The Call of the First Disciples. [18p*]As he
was walking by the Sea of Galilee, he saw
two brothers, Simon who is called Peter, and
his brother Andrew, casting a net into the
sea; they were fishermen. [19]He said to them,
"Come after me, and I will make you fishers
of men." [20*]At once they left their nets and
followed him. [21]He walked along from there
and saw two other brothers, James, the son
of Zebedee, and his brother John. They were
in a boat, with their father Zebedee, mending
their nets. He called them, [22]and immedi-

4:2 Forty days and forty nights: the same time as that during which Moses remained on Sinai (Ex 24:18). The time reference, however, seems primarily intended to recall the forty years during which Israel was tempted in the desert (Dt 8:2).

4:4 Cf. Dt 8:3. Jesus refuses to use his power for his own benefit and accepts whatever God wills.

4:5–7 The devil supports his proposal by an appeal to the scriptures, Ps 91:11a, 12. Unlike Israel (Dt 6:16), Jesus refuses to "test" God by demanding from him an extraordinary show of power.

4:9 The worship of Satan to which Jesus is tempted is probably intended to recall Israel's worship of false gods. His refusal is expressed in the words of Dt 6:13.

4:12–17 Isaiah's prophecy of the light rising upon Zebulun and Naphtali (Is 8:22–9:1) is fulfilled in Jesus' residence at Capernaum. The territory of these two tribes was the first to be devastated (733–32 B.C.) at the time of the Assyrian invasion. In order to accommodate Jesus' move to Capernaum to the prophecy, Matthew speaks of that town as being "in the region of Zebulun and Naphtali" (Mt 4:13), whereas it was only in the territory of the latter, and he understands the sea of the prophecy, the Mediterranean, as the sea of Galilee.

4:17 At the beginning of his preaching Jesus takes up the words of John the Baptist (Mt 3:2) although with a different meaning; in his ministry the kingdom of heaven has already begun to be present (Mt 12:28).

4:18–22 The call of the first disciples promises them a share in Jesus' work and entails abandonment of family and former way of life. Three of the four, Simon, James, and John, are distinguished among the disciples by a closer relation with Jesus (Mt 17:1; 26:37).

4:20 Here and in Mt 4:22, as in Mark (Mk 1:16–20) and unlike the Lucan account (Lk 5:1–11), the disciples' response is motivated only by Jesus' invitation, an element that emphasizes his mysterious power.

f: Ex 24:18; Dt 8:2. *g:* Dt 8:3. *h:* Ps 91:11–12. *i:* Dt 6:16. *j:* 16:23; Dt 6:13. *k:* Mk 1:14–15; Lk 4:14, 31. *l:* Jn 2:12. *m:* Is 8:23 LXX; 9:1. *n:* Lk 1:79. *o:* 3:2. *p:* Mk 1:16–20; Lk 5:1–11.

ately they left their boat and their father and
followed him.

Ministering to a Great Multitude. 23 q *He
went around all of Galilee, teaching in their
synagogues, proclaiming the gospel of the
kingdom, and curing every disease and illness among the people. 24 *His fame spread
to all of Syria, and they brought to him all
who were sick with various diseases and
racked with pain, those who were possessed, lunatics, and paralytics, and he
cured them. 25 r *And great crowds from
Galilee, the Decapolis, Jerusalem, and Judea, and from beyond the Jordan followed
him.

CHAPTER 5

See RG 377–78

The Sermon on the Mount. 1 *When
he saw the crowds, he went up the mountain,
and after he had sat down, his disciples came
to him. 2 He began to teach them, saying:

The Beatitudes

3 s *"Blessed are the poor in spirit,
for theirs is the kingdom of heaven.
4 t *Blessed are they who mourn,
for they will be comforted.
5 u *Blessed are the meek,
for they will inherit the land.
6 *Blessed are they who hunger and thirst
for righteousness,
for they will be satisfied.
7 v Blessed are the merciful,
for they will be shown mercy.
8 w *Blessed are the clean of heart,
for they will see God.
9 Blessed are the peacemakers,
for they will be called children of God.
10 x *Blessed are they who are persecuted
for the sake of righteousness,
for theirs is the kingdom of heaven.

11 y Blessed are you when they insult you and

4:23–25 This summary of Jesus' ministry concludes the narrative part of the first book of Matthew's gospel (Mt 3–4). The activities of his ministry are teaching, proclaiming the gospel, and healing; cf. Mt 9:35.

4:23 Their synagogues: Matthew usually designates the Jewish synagogues as **their synagogue(s)** (Mt 9:35; 10:17; 12:9; 13:54) or, in address to Jews, **your synagogues** (Mt 23:34), an indication that he wrote after the break between church and synagogue.

4:24 Syria: the Roman province to which Palestine belonged.

4:25 The Decapolis: a federation of Greek cities in Palestine, originally ten in number, all but one east of the Jordan.

5:1–7:29 The first of the five discourses that are a central part of the structure of this gospel. It is the discourse section of the first book and contains sayings of Jesus derived from Q and from M. The Lucan parallel is in that gospel's "Sermon on the Plain" (Lk 6:20–49), although some of the sayings in Matthew's "Sermon on the Mount" have their parallels in other parts of Luke. The careful topical arrangement of the sermon is probably not due only to Matthew's editing; he seems to have had a structured discourse of Jesus as one of his sources. The form of that source may have been as follows: four beatitudes (Mt 5:3–4, 6, 11–12), a section on the new righteousness with illustrations (Mt 5:17, 20–24, 27–28, 33–48), a section on good works (Mt 6:1–6, 16–18), and three warnings (Mt 7:1–2, 15–21, 24–27).

5:1–2 Unlike Luke's sermon, this is addressed not only to the disciples but to the crowds (see Mt 7:28).

5:3–12 The form **Blessed are (is)** occurs frequently in the Old Testament in the Wisdom literature and in the psalms. Although modified by Matthew, the first, second, fourth, and ninth beatitudes have Lucan parallels (Mt 5:3 // Lk 6:20; Mt 5:4 // Lk 6:21, 22; Mt 5:6 // Lk 6:21a; Mt 5:11–12 // Lk 5:22–23). The others were added by the evangelist and are probably his own composition. A few manuscripts, Western and Alexandrian, and many versions and patristic quotations give the second and third beatitudes in inverted order.

5:3 The poor in spirit: in the Old Testament, the poor (*anawim*) are those who are without material possessions and whose confidence is in God (see Is 61:1; Zep 2:3; in the NAB the word is translated **lowly** and **humble**, respectively, in those texts). Matthew added **in spirit** in order either to indicate that only the devout poor were meant or to extend the beatitude to all, of whatever social rank, who recognized their complete dependence on God. The same phrase **poor in spirit** is found in the Qumran literature (1QM 14:7).

5:4 Cf. Is 61:2 "(The Lord has sent me) . . . to comfort all who mourn." **They will be comforted**: here the passive is a "theological passive" equivalent to the active "God will comfort them"; so also in Mt 5:6, 7.

5:5 Cf. Ps 37:11, ". . . the meek shall possess the land." In the psalm "the land" means the land of Palestine; here it means the kingdom.

5:6 For righteousness: a Matthean addition. For the meaning of **righteousness** here, see note on Mt 3:14–15.

5:8 Cf. Ps 24:4. Only one "whose heart is clean" can take part in the temple worship. To be with God in the temple is described in Ps 42:2 as "beholding his face," but here the promise to **the clean of heart** is that they will **see God** not in the temple but in the coming kingdom.

5:10 Righteousness here, as usually in Matthew, means conduct in conformity with God's will.

q: 9:35; Mk 1:39; Lk 4:15, 44. *r:* Mk 3:7–8; Lk 6:17–19. *s:* Lk 6:20–23. *t:* Is 61:2–3; Rev 21:4. *u:* Gn 13:15; Ps 37:11. *v:* 18:33; Jas 2:13. *w:* Ps 24:4–5; 73:1. *x:* 1 Pt 2:20; 3:14; 4:14. *y:* 10:22; Acts 5:41.

persecute you and uttter every kind of evil against you [falsely] because of me. [12z*]Rejoice and be glad, for your reward will be great in heaven. Thus they persecuted the prophets who were before you.

The Similes of Salt and Light. [13a*]"You are the salt of the earth. But if salt loses its taste, with what can it be seasoned? It is no longer good for anything but to be thrown out and trampled underfoot. [14b]You are the light of the world. A city set on a mountain cannot be hidden. [15c]Nor do they light a lamp and then put it under a bushel basket; it is set on a lampstand, where it gives light to all in the house. [16d]Just so, your light must shine before others, that they may see your good deeds and glorify your heavenly Father.

Teaching about the Law. [17*]"Do not think that I have come to abolish the law or the prophets. I have come not to abolish but to fulfill. [18e]Amen, I say to you, until heaven and earth pass away, not the smallest letter or the smallest part of a letter will pass from the law, until all things have taken place. [19*]Therefore, whoever breaks one of the least of these commandments and teaches others to do so will be called least in the kingdom of heaven. But whoever obeys and teaches these commandments will be called greatest in the kingdom of heaven. [20]I tell you, unless your righteousness surpasses that of the scribes and Pharisees, you will not enter into the kingdom of heaven.

Teaching about Anger. [21f*]"You have heard that it was said to your ancestors, 'You shall not kill; and whoever kills will be liable to judgment.' [22g*]But I say to you, whoever is angry with his brother will be liable to judgment, and whoever says to his brother, 'Raqa,' will be answerable to the Sanhedrin, and whoever says, 'You fool,' will be liable to

5:12 The prophets who were before you: the disciples of Jesus stand in the line of the persecuted prophets of Israel. Some would see the expression as indicating also that Matthew considered all Christian disciples as prophets.

5:13–16 By their deeds the disciples are to influence the world for good. They can no more escape notice than **a city set on a mountain**. If they fail in good works, they are as useless as flavorless salt or as a lamp whose light is concealed.

5:13 The unusual supposition of salt losing its flavor has led some to suppose that the saying refers to the salt of the Dead Sea that, because chemically impure, could lose its taste.

5:17–20 This statement of Jesus' position concerning the Mosaic law is composed of traditional material from Matthew's sermon documentation (see note on Mt 5:1–7:29), other Q material (cf. Mt 18; Lk 16:17), and the evangelist's own editorial touches. **To fulfill** the law appears at first to mean a literal enforcement of the law in the least detail: **until heaven and earth pass away** nothing of the law **will pass** (Mt 5:18). Yet the "passing away" of heaven and earth is not necessarily the end of the world understood, as in much apocalyptic literature, as the dissolution of the existing universe. The "turning of the ages" comes with the apocalyptic event of Jesus' death and resurrection, and those to whom this gospel is addressed are living in the new and final age, prophesied by Isaiah as the time of "new heavens and a new earth" (Is 65:17; 66:22). Meanwhile, during Jesus' ministry when the kingdom is already breaking in, his mission remains within the framework of the law, though with significant anticipation of the age to come, as the following antitheses (Mt 5:21–48) show.

5:19 Probably **these commandments** means those of the Mosaic law. But this is an interim ethic "until heaven and earth pass away."

5:21–48 Six examples of the conduct demanded of the Christian disciple. Each deals with a commandment of the law, introduced by **You have heard that it was said to your ancestors** or an equivalent formula, followed by Jesus' teaching in respect to that commandment, **But I say to you;** thus their designation as "antitheses." Three of them accept the Mosaic law but extend or deepen it (Mt 5:21–22; 27–28; 43–44); three reject it as a standard of conduct for the disciples (Mt 5:31–32; 33–37; 38–39).

5:21 Cf. Ex 20:13; Dt 5:17. The second part of the verse is not an exact quotation from the Old Testament, but cf. Ex 21:12.

5:22–26 Reconciliation with an offended brother is urged in the admonition of Mt 5:23–24 and the parable of Mt 5:25–26 (Lk 12:58–59). The severity of the judge in the parable is a warning of the fate of unrepentant sinners in the coming judgment by God.

5:22 Anger is the motive behind murder, as the insulting epithets are steps that may lead to it. They, as well as the deed, are all forbidden. **Raqa**: an Aramaic word *rēqāʾ* or *rēqâ* probably meaning "imbecile," "blockhead," a term of abuse. The ascending order of punishment, **judgment** (by a local council?), trial before **the Sanhedrin**, condemnation to **Gehenna**, points to a higher degree of seriousness in each of the offenses. **Sanhedrin**: the highest judicial body of Judaism. **Gehenna**: in Hebrew *gê-hinnōm*, "Valley of Hinnom," or *gê ben-hinnōm*, "Valley of the son of Hinnom," southwest of Jerusalem, the center of an idolatrous cult during the monarchy in which children were offered in sacrifice (see 2 Kgs 23:10; Jer 7:31). In Jos 18:16 (Septuagint, Codex Vaticanus) the Hebrew is transliterated into Greek as *gaienna*, which appears in the New Testament as *geenna*. The concept of punishment of sinners by fire either after death or after the final judgment is found in Jewish apocalyptic literature (e.g., Enoch 90:26) but the name *geenna* is first given to the place of punishment in the New Testament.

z: 2 Chr 36:16; Heb 11:32–38; Jas 5:10. *a:* Mk 9:50; Lk 14:34–35. *b:* Jn 8:12. *c:* Mk 4:21; Lk 8:16; 11:33. *d:* Jn 3:21. *e:* Lk 16:17. *f:* Ex 20:13; Dt 5:17. *g:* Jas 1:19–20.

fiery Gehenna. [23h]Therefore, if you bring your gift to the altar, and there recall that your brother has anything against you, [24]leave your gift there at the altar, go first and be reconciled with your brother, and then come and offer your gift. [25i]Settle with your opponent quickly while on the way to court with him. Otherwise your opponent will hand you over to the judge, and the judge will hand you over to the guard, and you will be thrown into prison. [26]Amen, I say to you, you will not be released until you have paid the last penny.

Teaching about Adultery. [27j*]"You have heard that it was said, 'You shall not commit adultery.' [28]But I say to you, everyone who looks at a woman with lust has already committed adultery with her in his heart. [29k*]If your right eye causes you to sin, tear it out and throw it away. It is better for you to lose one of your members than to have your whole body thrown into Gehenna. [30]And if your right hand causes you to sin, cut it off and throw it away. It is better for you to lose one of your members than to have your whole body go into Gehenna.

Teaching about Divorce. [31l*]"It was also said, 'Whoever divorces his wife must give her a bill of divorce.' [32m]But I say to you, whoever divorces his wife (unless the marriage is unlawful) causes her to commit adultery, and whoever marries a divorced woman commits adultery.

Teaching about Oaths. [33n*]"Again you have heard that it was said to your ancestors, 'Do not take a false oath, but make good to the Lord all that you vow.' [34o*]But I say to you, do not swear at all; not by heaven, for it is God's throne; [35]nor by the earth, for it is his footstool; nor by Jerusalem, for it is the city of the great King. [36]Do not swear by your head, for you cannot make a single hair white or black. [37*]Let your 'Yes' mean 'Yes,' and your 'No' mean 'No.' Anything more is from the evil one.

Teaching about Retaliation. [38p*]"You have heard that it was said, 'An eye for an eye and a tooth for a tooth.' [39q]But I say to you, offer no resistance to one who is evil. When someone strikes you on [your] right cheek, turn the other one to him as well. [40]If anyone wants to go to law with you over your tunic, hand him your cloak as well. [41r*]Should anyone press you into service for one mile, go with him for two miles. [42s]Give to the one who asks of you, and do not turn your back on one who wants to borrow.

5:27 See Ex 20:14; Dt 5:18.

5:29–30 No sacrifice is too great to avoid total destruction in **Gehenna**.

5:31–32 See Dt 24:1–5. The Old Testament commandment that a bill of divorce be given to the woman assumes the legitimacy of divorce itself. It is this that Jesus denies. **(Unless the marriage is unlawful)**: this "exceptive clause," as it is often called, occurs also in Mt 19:9, where the Greek is slightly different. There are other sayings of Jesus about divorce that prohibit it absolutely (see Mk 10:11–12; Lk 16:18; cf. 1 Cor 7:10, 11b), and most scholars agree that they represent the stand of Jesus. Matthew's "exceptive clauses" are understood by some as a modification of the absolute prohibition. It seems, however, that the unlawfulness that Matthew gives as a reason why a marriage must be broken refers to a situation peculiar to his community: the violation of Mosaic law forbidding marriage between persons of certain blood and/or legal relationship (Lv 18:6–18). Marriages of that sort were regarded as incest (*porneia*), but some rabbis allowed Gentile converts to Judaism who had contracted such marriages to remain in them. Matthew's "exceptive clause" is against such permissiveness for Gentile converts to Christianity; cf. the similar prohibition of *porneia* in Acts 15:20, 29. In this interpretation, the clause constitutes no exception to the absolute prohibition of divorce when the marriage is lawful.

5:33 This is not an exact quotation of any Old Testament text, but see Ex 20:7; Dt 5:11; Lv 19:12. The purpose of an oath was to guarantee truthfulness by one's calling on God as witness.

5:34–36 The use of these oath formularies that avoid the divine name is in fact equivalent to swearing by it, for all the things sworn by are related to God.

5:37 Let your 'Yes' mean 'Yes,' and your 'No' mean 'No': literally, "let your speech be 'Yes, yes,' 'No, no.'" Some have understood this as a milder form of oath, permitted by Jesus. In view of Mt 5:34, "Do not swear at all," that is unlikely. **From the evil one**: i.e., from the devil. Oath-taking presupposes a sinful weakness of the human race, namely, the tendency to lie. Jesus demands of his disciples a truthfulness that makes oaths unnecessary.

5:38–42 See Lv 24:20. The Old Testament commandment was meant to moderate vengeance; the punishment should not exceed the injury done. Jesus forbids even this proportionate retaliation. Of the five examples that follow, only the first deals directly with retaliation for evil; the others speak of liberality.

5:41 Roman garrisons in Palestine had the right to requisition the property and services of the native population.

h: Mk 11:25. *i:* 18:34–35; Lk 12:58–59. *j:* Ex 20:14; Dt 5:18. *k:* 18:8–9; Mk 9:43–47. *l:* 19:3–9; Dt 24:1. *m:* Lk 16:18; 1 Cor 7:10–11. *n:* Lv 19:12; Nm 30:3. *o:* Ps 48:3; Sir 23:9; Is 66:1; Jas 5:12. *p:* Ex 21:24; Lv 24:19–20. *q:* Lk 6:29–30. *r:* Lam 3:30. *s:* Dt 15:7–8.

Love of Enemies. [43 tu*]"You have heard that it was said, 'You shall love your neighbor and hate your enemy.' [44]But I say to you, love your enemies, and pray for those who persecute you, [45]that you may be children of your heavenly Father, for he makes his sun rise on the bad and the good, and causes rain to fall on the just and the unjust. [46*]For if you love those who love you, what recompense will you have? Do not the tax collectors do the same? [47*]And if you greet your brothers only, what is unusual about that? Do not the pagans do the same? [48v*]So be perfect, just as your heavenly Father is perfect.

See RG 377–78

CHAPTER 6

Teaching about Almsgiving. [1w*]"[But] take care not to perform righteous deeds in order that people may see them; otherwise, you will have no recompense from your heavenly Father. [2x*]When you give alms, do not blow a trumpet before you, as the hypocrites do in the synagogues and in the streets to win the praise of others. Amen, I say to you, they have received their reward. [3]But when you give alms, do not let your left hand know what your right is doing, [4]so that your almsgiving may be secret. And your Father who sees in secret will repay you.

Teaching about Prayer. [5]"When you pray, do not be like the hypocrites, who love to stand and pray in the synagogues and on street corners so that others may see them. Amen, I say to you, they have received their reward. [6]But when you pray, go to your inner room, close the door, and pray to your Father in secret. And your Father who sees in secret will repay you. [7*]In praying, do not babble like the pagans, who think that they will be heard because of their many words. [8]Do not be like them. Your Father knows what you need before you ask him.

The Lord's Prayer. [9y*]"This is how you are to pray:

Our Father in heaven,
hallowed be your name,

5:43–48 See Lv 19:18. There is no Old Testament commandment demanding hatred of one's enemy, but the "neighbor" of the love commandment was understood as one's fellow countryman. Both in the Old Testament (Ps 139:19–22) and at Qumran (1QS 9:21) hatred of evil persons is assumed to be right. Jesus extends the love commandment to the enemy and the persecutor. His disciples, as children of God, must imitate the example of their Father, who grants his gifts of sun and rain to both the good and the bad.

5:46 Tax collectors: Jews who were engaged in the collection of indirect taxes such as tolls and customs. See note on Mk 2:14.

5:47 Jesus' disciples must not be content with merely usual standards of conduct; see Mt 5:20 where the verb "surpass" (Greek *perisseuō*) is cognate with the **unusual** (*perisson*) of this verse.

5:48 Perfect: in the gospels this word occurs only in Matthew, here and in Mt 19:21. The Lucan parallel (Lk 6:36) demands that the disciples be **merciful**.

6:1–18 The sermon continues with a warning against doing good in order to be seen and gives three examples, almsgiving (Mt 6:2–4), prayer (Mt 6:5–15), and fasting (Mt 6:16–18). In each, the conduct of the hypocrites (Mt 6:2) is contrasted with that demanded of the disciples. The sayings about reward found here and elsewhere (Mt 5:12, 46; 10:41–42) show that this is a genuine element of Christian moral exhortation. Possibly to underline the difference between the Christian idea of reward and that of the hypocrites, the evangelist uses two different Greek verbs to express the rewarding of the disciples and that of the hypocrites; in the latter case it is the verb *apechō*, a commercial term for giving a receipt for what has been paid in full (Mt 6:2, 5, 16).

6:2 The hypocrites: the scribes and Pharisees, see Mt 23:13, 15, 23, 25, 27, 29. The designation reflects an attitude resulting not only from the controversies at the time of Jesus' ministry but from the opposition between Pharisaic Judaism and the church of Matthew. **They have received their reward**: they desire praise and have received what they were looking for.

6:7–15 Matthew inserts into his basic traditional material an expansion of the material on prayer that includes the model prayer, the "Our Father." That prayer is found in Lk 11:2–4 in a different context and in a different form.

6:7 The example of what Christian prayer should be like contrasts it now not with the prayer of the hypocrites but with that of **the pagans**. Their babbling probably means their reciting a long list of divine names, hoping that one of them will force a response from the deity.

6:9–13 Matthew's form of the "Our Father" follows the liturgical tradition of his church. Luke's less developed form also represents the liturgical tradition known to him, but it is probably closer than Matthew's to the original words of Jesus.

6:9 Our Father in heaven: this invocation is found in many rabbinic prayers of the post-New Testament period. **Hallowed be your name**: though the "hallowing" of the divine name could be understood as reverence done to God by human praise and by obedience to his will, this is more probably a petition that God hallow his own name, i.e., that he manifest his glory by an act of power (cf. Ez 36:23), in this case, by the establishment of his kingdom in its fullness.

t: Lk 6:27, 32–36. *u:* Lv 19:18. *v:* Lv 11:44; 19:2; Dt 18:13; Jas 1:4; 1 Pt 1:16; 1 Jn 3:3. *w:* 23:5. *x:* Jn 12:43. *y:* Lk 11:2–4.

10 [z*]your kingdom come,
your will be done,
on earth as in heaven.
11 [a*]Give us today our daily bread;
12 [b*]and forgive us our debts,
as we forgive our debtors;
13 [c*]and do not subject us to the final
test,
but deliver us from the evil one.

14[d*]If you forgive others their transgressions,
your heavenly Father will forgive you. 15[e]But
if you do not forgive others, neither will your
Father forgive your transgressions.

Teaching about Fasting. 16[*]"When you
fast, do not look gloomy like the hypocrites.
They neglect their appearance, so that they
may appear to others to be fasting. Amen, I
say to you, they have received their reward.
17But when you fast, anoint your head and
wash your face, 18so that you may not appear
to others to be fasting, except to your Father
who is hidden. And your Father who sees
what is hidden will repay you.

Treasure in Heaven. 19[f*]"Do not store up
for yourselves treasures on earth, where
moth and decay destroy, and thieves break in
and steal. 20[g]But store up treasures in
heaven, where neither moth nor decay destroy, nor thieves break in and steal. 21For
where your treasure is, there also will your
heart be.

The Light of the Body. 22[h*]"The lamp of
the body is the eye. If your eye is sound,
your whole body will be filled with light;
23but if your eye is bad, your whole body
will be in darkness. And if the light in you is
darkness, how great will the darkness be.

God and Money. 24[i*]"No one can serve
two masters. He will either hate one and love
the other, or be devoted to one and despise the
other. You cannot serve God and mammon.

Dependence on God. 25[j*]"Therefore I tell
you, do not worry about your life, what you
will eat [or drink], or about your body, what
you will wear. Is not life more than food and
the body more than clothing? 26[k]Look at the
birds in the sky; they do not sow or reap,
they gather nothing into barns, yet your
heavenly Father feeds them. Are not you
more important than they? 27[*]Can any of
you by worrying add a single moment to
your life-span? 28Why are you anxious about
clothes? Learn from the way the wild flowers grow. They do not work or spin. 29But I
tell you that not even Solomon in all his

6:10 Your kingdom come: this petition sets the tone of the prayer, and inclines the balance toward divine rather than human action in the petitions that immediately precede and follow it. **Your will be done, on earth as in heaven**: a petition that the divine purpose to establish the kingdom, a purpose present now **in heaven**, be executed **on earth**.

6:11 Give us today our daily bread: the rare Greek word *epiousios*, here **daily**, occurs in the New Testament only here and in Lk 11:3. A single occurrence of the word outside of these texts and of literature dependent on them has been claimed, but the claim is highly doubtful. The word may mean **daily** or "future" (other meanings have also been proposed). The latter would conform better to the eschatological tone of the whole prayer. So understood, the petition would be for a speedy coming of the kingdom (today), which is often portrayed in both the Old Testament and the New under the image of a feast (Is 25:6; Mt 8:11; 22:1–10; Lk 13:29; 14:15–24).

6:12 Forgive us our debts: the word **debts** is used metaphorically of sins, "debts" owed to God (see Lk 11:4). The request is probably for forgiveness at the final judgment.

6:13 Jewish apocalyptic writings speak of a period of severe trial before the end of the age, sometimes called the "messianic woes." This petition asks that the disciples be spared that **final test**.

6:14–15 These verses reflect a set pattern called "Principles of Holy Law." Human action now will be met by a corresponding action of God at the final judgment.

6:16 The only fast prescribed in the Mosaic law was that of the Day of Atonement (Lv 16:31), but the practice of regular fasting was common in later Judaism; cf. *Didache* 9:1.

6:19–34 The remaining material of this chapter is taken almost entirely from Q. It deals principally with worldly possessions, and the controlling thought is summed up in Mt 6:24, the disciple can serve only one master and must choose between God and wealth (**mammon**). See further the note on Lk 16:9.

6:22–23 In this context the parable probably points to the need for the disciple to be enlightened by Jesus' teaching on the transitory nature of earthly riches.

6:24 Mammon: an Aramaic word meaning wealth or property.

6:25–34 Jesus does not deny the reality of human needs (Mt 6:32), but forbids making them the object of anxious care and, in effect, becoming their slave.

6:27 Life-span: the Greek word can also mean "stature." If it is taken in that sense, the word here translated moment (literally, "cubit") must be translated literally as a unit not of time but of spatial measure. The cubit is about eighteen inches.

z: 26:42. *a:* Prv 30:8–9. *b:* 18:21–22; Sir 28:2. *c:* Jn 17:15; 2 Thes 3:3. *d:* 18:35; Sir 28:1–5; Mk 11:25. *e:* Jas 2:13. *f:* Jas 5:2–3. *g:* Lk 12:33–34. *h:* Lk 11:34–36. *i:* Lk 16:13. *j:* Lk 12:22–31. *k:* Ps 145:15–16; 147:9.

splendor was clothed like one of them. [30]*If God so clothes the grass of the field, which grows today and is thrown into the oven tomorrow, will he not much more provide for you, O you of little faith? [31]So do not worry and say, ‘What are we to eat?’ or ‘What are we to drink?’ or ‘What are we to wear?’ [32]All these things the pagans seek. Your heavenly Father knows that you need them all. [33]*But seek first the kingdom [of God] and his righteousness, and all these things will be given you besides. [34]Do not worry about tomorrow; tomorrow will take care of itself. Sufficient for a day is its own evil.

CHAPTER 7

See RG 377–78

Judging Others. [1][l][m]*“Stop judging, that you may not be judged. [2][n]For as you judge, so will you be judged, and the measure with which you measure will be measured out to you. [3]Why do you notice the splinter in your brother’s eye, but do not perceive the wooden beam in your own eye? [4]How can you say to your brother, ‘Let me remove that splinter from your eye,’ while the wooden beam is in your eye? [5]*You hypocrite, remove the wooden beam from your eye first; then you will see clearly to remove the splinter from your brother’s eye.

Pearls before Swine. [6][o]*“Do not give what is holy to dogs, or throw your pearls before swine, lest they trample them underfoot, and turn and tear you to pieces.

The Answer to Prayers. [7][p][q]“Ask and it will be given to you; seek and you will find; knock and the door will be opened to you. [8][r]For everyone who asks, receives; and the one who seeks, finds; and to the one who knocks, the door will be opened. [9]*Which one of you would hand his son a stone when he asks for a loaf of bread, [10]or a snake when he asks for a fish? [11][s]If you then, who are wicked, know how to give good gifts to your children, how much more will your heavenly Father give good things to those who ask him.

The Golden Rule. [12][t]*“Do to others whatever you would have them do to you. This is the law and the prophets.

The Narrow Gate. [13][u]*“Enter through the narrow gate; for the gate is wide and the road broad that leads to destruction, and those who enter through it are many. [14]How narrow the gate and constricted the road that leads to life. And those who find it are few.

False Prophets. [15][v]*“Beware of false prophets, who come to you in sheep’s clothing, but underneath are ravenous wolves. [16][w]By their fruits you will know them. Do

6:30 Of little faith: except for the parallel in Lk 12:28, the word translated **of little faith** is found in the New Testament only in Matthew. It is used by him of those who are disciples of Jesus but whose faith in him is not as deep as it should be (see Mt 8:26; 14:31; 16:8 and the cognate noun in Mt 17:20).

6:33 Righteousness: see note on Mt 3:14–15.

7:1–12 In Mt 7:1 Matthew returns to the basic traditional material of the sermon (Lk 6:37–38, 41–42). The governing thought is the correspondence between conduct toward one’s fellows and God’s conduct toward the one so acting.

7:1 This is not a prohibition against recognizing the faults of others, which would be hardly compatible with Mt 7:5, 6 but against passing judgment in a spirit of arrogance, forgetful of one’s own faults.

7:5 Hypocrite: the designation previously given to the scribes and Pharisees is here given to the Christian disciple who is concerned with the faults of another and ignores his own more serious offenses.

7:6 Dogs and **swine** were Jewish terms of contempt for Gentiles. This saying may originally have derived from a Jewish Christian community opposed to preaching the gospel (**what is holy, pearls**) to Gentiles. In the light of Mt 28:19 that can hardly be Matthew’s meaning. He may have taken the saying as applying to a Christian dealing with an obstinately impenitent fellow Christian (Mt 18:17).

7:9–10 There is a resemblance between a stone and a round loaf of bread and between a serpent and the scaleless fish called *barbut*.

7:12 See Lk 6:31. This saying, known since the eighteenth century as the “Golden Rule,” is found in both positive and negative form in pagan and Jewish sources, both earlier and later than the gospel. **This is the law and the prophets** is an addition probably due to the evangelist.

7:13–28 The final section of the discourse is composed of a series of antitheses, contrasting two kinds of life within the Christian community, that of those who obey the words of Jesus and that of those who do not. Most of the sayings are from Q and are found also in Luke.

7:13–14 The metaphor of the “two ways” was common in pagan philosophy and in the Old Testament. In Christian literature it is found also in the *Didache* (1–6) and the *Epistle of Barnabas* (18–20).

7:15–20 Christian disciples who claimed to speak in the name of God are called **prophets** (Mt 7:15) in Mt 10:41; Mt 23:34. They were presumably an important group within the church of Matthew. As in the case of the Old Testament prophets, there were both true and false ones, and for Matthew the

l: Lk 6:37–38, 41–42. *m:* Rom 2:1–2; 1 Cor 4:5. *n:* Wis 12:22; Mk 4:24. *o:* Prv 23:9. *p:* Mk 11:24; Lk 11:9–13. *q:* 18:19. *r:* Lk 18:1–8; Jn 14:13. *s:* 1 Jn 5:14–15. *t:* Lk 6:31. *u:* Lk 13:24. *v:* 2 Pt 2:1. *w:* 12:33; Lk 6:43–44.

people pick grapes from thornbushes, or figs from thistles? [17]Just so, every good tree bears good fruit, and a rotten tree bears bad fruit. [18]A good tree cannot bear bad fruit, nor can a rotten tree bear good fruit. [19x]Every tree that does not bear good fruit will be cut down and thrown into the fire. [20]So by their fruits you will know them.

The True Disciple. [21y*]"Not everyone who says to me, 'Lord, Lord,' will enter the kingdom of heaven, but only the one who does the will of my Father in heaven. [22za]Many will say to me on that day, 'Lord, Lord, did we not prophesy in your name? Did we not drive out demons in your name? Did we not do mighty deeds in your name?' [23b*]Then I will declare to them solemnly, 'I never knew you. Depart from me, you evildoers.'

The Two Foundations. [24c*]"Everyone who listens to these words of mine and acts on them will be like a wise man who built his house on rock. [25d]The rain fell, the floods came, and the winds blew and buffeted the house. But it did not collapse; it had been set solidly on rock. [26]And everyone who listens to these words of mine but does not act on them will be like a fool who built his house on sand. [27]The rain fell, the floods came, and the winds blew and buffeted the house. And it collapsed and was completely ruined."

[28*]When Jesus finished these words, the crowds were astonished at his teaching, [29e*]for he taught them as one having authority, and not as their scribes.

III. Ministry and Mission in Galilee

CHAPTER 8

See RG 378–79

The Cleansing of a Leper. [1f*]When Jesus came down from the mountain, great crowds followed him. [2*]And then a leper approached, did him homage, and said, "Lord, if you wish, you can make me clean." [3]He stretched out his hand, touched him, and said, "I will do it. Be made clean." His leprosy was cleansed immediately. [4g*]Then Jesus said to him, "See that you tell no one, but go show yourself to the priest, and offer the gift that Moses prescribed; that will be proof for them."

The Healing of a Centurion's Servant. [5h*]When he entered Capernaum, a centurion

difference could be recognized by the quality of their deeds, the **fruits** (Mt 7:16). The mention of **fruits** leads to the comparison with trees, some producing good fruit, others bad.

7:21–23 The attack on the false prophets is continued, but is broadened to include those disciples who perform works of healing and exorcism in the name of Jesus (**Lord**) but live evil lives. Entrance into the kingdom is only for those who do the will of the Father. On the day of judgment (**on that day**) the morally corrupt prophets and miracle workers will be rejected by Jesus.

7:23 I never knew you: cf. Mt 10:33. **Depart from me, you evildoers**: cf. Ps 6:8.

7:24–27 The conclusion of the discourse (cf. Lk 6:47–49). Here the relation is not between saying and doing as in Mt 7:15–23 but between hearing and doing, and the words of Jesus are applied to every Christian (everyone who listens).

7:28–29 When Jesus finished these words: this or a similar formula is used by Matthew to conclude each of the five great discourses of Jesus (cf. Mt 11:1; 13:53; 19:1; 26:1).

7:29 Not as their scribes: scribal instruction was a faithful handing down of the traditions of earlier teachers; Jesus' teaching is based on his own authority. **Their scribes**: for the implications of **their**, see note on Mt 4:23.

8:1–9:38 This narrative section of the second book of the gospel is composed of nine miracle stories, most of which are found in Mark, although Matthew does not follow the Marcan order and abbreviates the stories radically. The stories are arranged in three groups of three, each group followed by a section composed principally of sayings of Jesus about discipleship. Mt 9:35 is an almost verbatim repetition of Mt 4:23. Each speaks of Jesus' teaching, preaching, and healing. The teaching and preaching form the content of Mt 5–7; the healing, that of Mt 8–9. Some scholars speak of a portrayal of Jesus as "Messiah of the Word" in Mt 5–7 and "Messiah of the Deed" in Mt 8–9. That is accurate so far as it goes, but there is also a strong emphasis on discipleship in Mt 8–9; these chapters have not only christological but ecclesiological import.

8:2 A leper: see note on Mk 1:40.

8:4 Cf. Lv 14:2–9. **That will be proof for them**: the Greek can also mean "that will be proof against them." It is not clear whether **them** refers to the priests or the people.

8:5–13 This story comes from Q (see Lk 7:1–10) and is also reflected in Jn 4:46–54. The similarity between the Q story and the Johannine is due to a common oral tradition, not to a common literary source. As in the later story of the daughter of the Canaanite woman (Mt 15:21–28) Jesus here breaks with his usual procedure of ministering only to Israelites and anticipates the mission to the Gentiles.

8:5 A centurion: a military officer commanding a hundred men. He was probably in the service of Herod Antipas, tetrarch of Galilee; see note on Mt 14:1.

x: 3:10. *y:* Is 29:13; Lk 6:46. *z:* Lk 13:26–27. *a:* 25:11–12. *b:* Ps 5:5; 6:9. *c:* Lk 6:47–49. *d:* Prv 10:25. *e:* Mk 1:22; Lk 4:32. *f:* Mk 1:40–44; Lk 5:12–14. *g:* Lv 14:2–32; Lk 17:14. *h:* Lk 7:1–10; Jn 4:46–53.

approached him and appealed to him, [6]saying, “Lord, my servant is lying at home paralyzed, suffering dreadfully.” [7]He said to him, “I will come and cure him.” [8*]The centurion said in reply, “Lord, I am not worthy to have you enter under my roof; only say the word and my servant will be healed. [9]For I too am a person subject to authority, with soldiers subject to me. And I say to one, ‘Go,’ and he goes; and to another, ‘Come here,’ and he comes; and to my slave, ‘Do this,’ and he does it.” [10*]When Jesus heard this, he was amazed and said to those following him, “Amen, I say to you, in no one in Israel have I found such faith. [11i*]I say to you, many will come from the east and the west, and will recline with Abraham, Isaac, and Jacob at the banquet in the kingdom of heaven, [12]but the children of the kingdom will be driven out into the outer darkness, where there will be wailing and grinding of teeth.” [13]And Jesus said to the centurion, “You may go; as you have believed, let it be done for you.” And at that very hour [his] servant was healed.

The Cure of Peter’s Mother-in-Law. [14j*]Jesus entered the house of Peter, and saw his mother-in-law lying in bed with a fever. [15k]He touched her hand, the fever left her, and she rose and waited on him.

Other Healings [16*]When it was evening, they brought him many who were possessed by demons, and he drove out the spirits by a word and cured all the sick, [17l*]to fulfill what had been said by Isaiah the prophet:

> “He took away our infirmities
> and bore our diseases.”

The Would-be Followers of Jesus. [18m*]When Jesus saw a crowd around him, he gave orders to cross to the other side. [19n*]A scribe approached and said to him, “Teacher, I will follow you wherever you go.” [20*]Jesus answered him, “Foxes have dens and birds of the sky have nests, but the Son of Man has nowhere to rest his head.” [21]Another of [his] disciples said to him, “Lord, let me go first and bury my father.” [22*]But Jesus answered him, “Follow me, and let the dead bury their dead.”

The Calming of the Storm at Sea. [23o*]He got into a boat and his disciples followed him. [24*]Suddenly a violent storm came up on

8:8–9 Acquainted by his position with the force of a command, the centurion expresses faith in the power of Jesus’ mere word.

8:10 In no one in Israel: there is good textual attestation (e.g., Codex Sinaiticus) for a reading identical with that of Lk 7:9, “not even in Israel.” But that seems to be due to a harmonization of Matthew with Luke.

8:11–12 Matthew inserts into the story a Q saying (see Lk 13:28–29) about the entrance of Gentiles into the kingdom and the exclusion of those Israelites who, though descended from the patriarchs and members of the chosen nation (**the children of the kingdom**), refused to believe in Jesus. **There will be wailing and grinding of teeth**: the first occurrence of a phrase used frequently in this gospel to describe final condemnation (Mt 13:42, 50; 22:13; 24:51; 25:30). It is found elsewhere in the New Testament only in Lk 13:28.

8:14–15 Cf. Mk 1:29–31. Unlike Mark, Matthew has no implied request by others for the woman’s cure. Jesus acts on his own initiative, and the cured woman rises and waits not on “them” (Mk 1:31) but on **him**.

8:16 By a word: a Matthean addition to Mk 1:34; cf. 8:8.

8:17 This fulfillment citation from Is 53:4 follows the MT, not the LXX. The prophet speaks of the Servant of the Lord who suffers vicariously for the sins (“infirmities”) of others; Matthew takes the **infirmities** as physical afflictions.

8:18–22 This passage between the first and second series of miracles about following Jesus is taken from Q (see Lk 9:57–62). The third of the three sayings found in the source is absent from Matthew.

8:18 The other side: i.e., of the Sea of Galilee.

8:19 Teacher: for Matthew, this designation of Jesus is true, for he has Jesus using it of himself (Mt 10:24, 25; 23:8; 26:18), yet when it is used of him by others they are either his opponents (Mt 9:11; 12:38; 17:24; 22:16, 24, 36) or, as here and in Mt 19:16, well-disposed persons who cannot see more deeply. Thus it reveals an inadequate recognition of who Jesus is.

8:20 Son of Man: see note on Mk 8:31. This is the first occurrence in Matthew of a term that appears in the New Testament only in sayings of Jesus, except for Acts 7:56 and possibly Mt 9:6 (Mk 2:10; Lk 5:24). In Matthew it refers to Jesus in his ministry (seven times, as here), in his passion and resurrection (nine times, e.g., Mt 17:22), and in his glorious coming at the end of the age (thirteen times, e.g., Mt 24:30).

8:22 Let the dead bury their dead: the demand of Jesus overrides what both the Jewish and the Hellenistic world regarded as a filial obligation of the highest importance. See note on Lk 9:60.

8:23 His disciples followed him: the first miracle in the second group (Mt 8:23–9:8) is introduced by a verse that links it with the preceding sayings by the catchword “follow.” In Mark the initiative in entering the boat is taken by the disciples (Mk 4:35–41); here, Jesus enters first and the disciples follow.

8:24 Storm: literally, “earthquake,” a word commonly used in apocalyptic literature for the shaking of the old world

i: 13:42, 50; 22:13; 24:51; 25:30; Lk 13:28–29. *j:* Mk 1:29–34; Lk 4:38–41. *k:* 9:25. *l:* Is 53:4. *m:* Mk 4:35. *n:* Lk 9:57–60. *o:* Mk 4:35–40; Lk 8:22–25.

the sea, so that the boat was being swamped by waves; but he was asleep. [25] [p]*They came and woke him, saying, "Lord, save us! We are perishing!" [26]*He said to them, "Why are you terrified, O you of little faith?" Then he got up, rebuked the winds and the sea, and there was great calm. [27]The men were amazed and said, "What sort of man is this, whom even the winds and the sea obey?"

The Healing of the Gadarene Demoniacs. [28] [q]*When he came to the other side, to the territory of the Gadarenes, two demoniacs who were coming from the tombs met him. They were so savage that no one could travel by that road. [29]*They cried out, "What have you to do with us, Son of God? Have you come here to torment us before the appointed time?" [30]*Some distance away a herd of many swine was feeding. [31] [r]The demons pleaded with him, "If you drive us out, send us into the herd of swine." [32]And he said to them, "Go then!" They came out and entered the swine, and the whole herd rushed down the steep bank into the sea where they drowned. [33]The swineherds ran away, and when they came to the town they reported everything, including what had happened to the demoniacs. [34]Thereupon the whole town came out to meet Jesus, and when they saw him they begged him to leave their district.

CHAPTER 9

See RG 378–79

The Healing of a Paralytic. [1] [s]*He entered a boat, made the crossing, and came into his own town. [2] [t]And there people brought to him a paralytic lying on a stretcher. When Jesus saw their faith, he said to the paralytic, "Courage, child, your sins are forgiven." [3]*At that, some of the scribes said to themselves, "This man is blaspheming." [4]Jesus knew what they were thinking, and said, "Why do you harbor evil thoughts? [5]Which is easier, to say, 'Your sins are forgiven,' or to say, 'Rise and walk'? [6] [u]*But that you may know that the Son of Man has authority on earth to forgive sins"—he then said to the paralytic, "Rise, pick up your stretcher, and go home." [7]He rose and went home. [8]*When the crowds saw this they were struck with awe and glorified God who had given such authority to human beings.

The Call of Matthew. [9] [v]*As Jesus passed

when God brings in his kingdom. All the synoptics use it in depicting the events preceding the parousia of the Son of Man (Mt 24:7; Mk 13:8; Lk 21:11). Matthew has introduced it here and in his account of the death and resurrection of Jesus (Mt 27:51–54; 28:2).

8:25 The reverent plea of the disciples contrasts sharply with their reproach of Jesus in Mk 4:38.

8:26 You of little faith: see note on Mt 6:30. **Great calm**: Jesus' calming the sea may be meant to recall the Old Testament theme of God's control over the chaotic waters (Ps 65:8; 89:10; 93:3–4; 107:29).

8:28 Gadarenes: this is the reading of Codex Vaticanus, supported by other important textual witnesses. The original reading of Codex Sinaiticus was Gazarenes, later changed to Gergesenes, and a few versions have Gerasenes. Each of these readings points to a different territory connected, respectively, with the cities Gadara, Gergesa, and Gerasa (modern Jerash). There is the same confusion of readings in the parallel texts, Mk 5:1 and Lk 8:26; there the best reading seems to be "Gerasenes," whereas "Gadarenes" is probably the original reading in Matthew. The town of Gadara was about five miles southeast of the Sea of Galilee, and Josephus (*Life* 9:42) refers to it as possessing territory that lay on that sea. **Two demoniacs**: Mark (5:1–20) has one.

8:29 What have you to do with us?: see note on Jn 2:4. **Before the appointed time**: the notion that evil spirits were allowed by God to afflict human beings until the time of the final judgment is found in Enoch 16:1 and Jubilees 10:7–10.

8:30 The tending of pigs, animals considered unclean by Mosaic law (Lv 11:6–7), indicates that the population was Gentile.

9:1 His own town: Capernaum; see Mt 4:13.

9:3 Scribes: see note on Mk 2:6. Matthew omits the reason given in the Marcan story for the charge of blasphemy: "Who but God alone can forgive sins?" (Mk 2:7).

9:6 It is not clear whether "But that you may know . . . to forgive sins" is intended to be a continuation of the words of Jesus or a parenthetical comment of the evangelist to those who would hear or read this gospel. In any case, Matthew here follows the Marcan text.

9:8 Who had given such authority to human beings: a significant difference from Mk 2:12 ("They . . . glorified God, saying, 'We have never seen anything like this' "). Matthew's extension to **human beings** of the authority to forgive sins points to the belief that such authority was being claimed by Matthew's church.

9:9–17 In this section the order is the same as that of Mk 2:13–22.

9:9 A man named Matthew: Mark names this tax collector Levi (Mk 2:14). No such name appears in the four lists of the twelve who were the closest companions of Jesus (Mt 10:2–4; Mk 3:16–19; Lk 6:14–16; Acts 1:13 [eleven, because of the defection of Judas Iscariot]), whereas all four list a Matthew, designated in Mt 10:3 as "the tax collector." The

p: Ps 107:28–29. *q:* Mk 5:1–17; Lk 8:26–37. *r:* Lk 4:34, 41. *s:* Mk 2:3–12; Lk 5:18–26. *t:* Lk 7:48. *u:* Jn 5:27. *v:* Mk 2:14–17; Lk 5:27–32.

on from there, he saw a man named Matthew sitting at the customs post. He said to him, "Follow me." And he got up and followed him. [10w*]While he was at table in his house, many tax collectors and sinners came and sat with Jesus and his disciples. [11*]The Pharisees saw this and said to his disciples, "Why does your teacher eat with tax collectors and sinners?" [12*]He heard this and said, "Those who are well do not need a physician, but the sick do. [13x*]Go and learn the meaning of the words, 'I desire mercy, not sacrifice.' I did not come to call the righteous but sinners."

The Question about Fasting. [14y]Then the disciples of John approached him and said, "Why do we and the Pharisees fast [much], but your disciples do not fast?" [15*]Jesus answered them, "Can the wedding guests mourn as long as the bridegroom is with them? The days will come when the bridegroom is taken away from them, and then they will fast. [16*]No one patches an old cloak with a piece of unshrunken cloth, for its fullness pulls away from the cloak and the tear gets worse. [17]People do not put new wine into old wineskins. Otherwise the skins burst, the wine spills out, and the skins are ruined. Rather, they pour new wine into fresh wineskins, and both are preserved."

The Official's Daughter and the Woman with a Hemorrhage. [18z*]While he was saying these things to them, an official came forward, knelt down before him, and said, "My daughter has just died. But come, lay your hand on her, and she will live." [19]Jesus rose and followed him, and so did his disciples. [20*]A woman suffering hemorrhages for twelve years came up behind him and touched the tassel on his cloak. [21a]She said to herself, "If only I can touch his cloak, I shall be cured." [22]Jesus turned around and saw her, and said, "Courage, daughter! Your faith has saved you." And from that hour the woman was cured.

[23]When Jesus arrived at the official's house and saw the flute players and the crowd who were making a commotion, [24*]he said, "Go away! The girl is not dead but sleeping." And they ridiculed him. [25]When the crowd was put out, he came and took her by the hand, and the little girl arose. [26]And news of this spread throughout all that land.

The Healing of Two Blind Men. [27bc*]And

evangelist may have changed the "Levi" of his source to **Matthew** so that this man, whose call is given special notice, like that of the first four disciples (Mt 4:18–22), might be included among the twelve. Another reason for the change may be that the disciple Matthew was the source of traditions peculiar to the church for which the evangelist was writing.

9:10 His house: it is not clear whether **his** refers to Jesus or Matthew. **Tax collectors**: see note on Mt 5:46. Table association with such persons would cause ritual impurity.

9:11 Teacher: see note on Mt 8:19.

9:12 See note on Mk 2:17.

9:13 Go and learn . . . not sacrifice: Matthew adds the prophetic statement of Hos 6:6 to the Marcan account (see also Mt 12:7). If mercy is superior to the temple sacrifices, how much more to the laws of ritual impurity.

9:15 Fasting is a sign of mourning and would be as inappropriate at this time of joy, when Jesus is proclaiming the kingdom, as it would be at a marriage feast. Yet the saying looks forward to the time when Jesus will no longer be with the disciples visibly, the time of Matthew's church. **Then they will fast**: see *Didache* 8:1.

9:16–17 Each of these parables speaks of the unsuitability of attempting to combine the old and the new. Jesus' teaching is not a patching up of Judaism, nor can the gospel be contained within the limits of Mosaic law.

9:18–34 In this third group of miracles, the first (Mt 9:18–26) is clearly dependent on Mark (Mk 5:21–43). Though it tells of two miracles, the cure of the woman had already been included within the story of the raising of the official's daughter, so that the two were probably regarded as a single unit. The other miracles seem to have been derived from Mark and Q respectively, though there Matthew's own editing is much more evident.

9:18 Official: literally, "ruler." Mark calls him "one of the synagogue officials" (Mk 5:22). **My daughter has just died**: Matthew heightens the Marcan "my daughter is at the point of death" (Mk 5:23).

9:20 Tassel: possibly "fringe." The Mosaic law prescribed that tassels be worn on the corners of one's garment as a reminder to keep the commandments (see Nm 15:37–39; Dt 22:12).

9:24 Sleeping: sleep is a biblical metaphor for death (see Ps 87:6 LXX; Dn 12:2; 1 Thes 5:10). Jesus' statement is not a denial of the child's real death, but an assurance that she will be roused from her sleep of death.

9:27–31 This story was probably composed by Matthew out of Mark's story of the healing of a blind man named Bartimaeus (Mk 10:46–52). Mark places the event late in Jesus' ministry, just before his entrance into Jerusalem, and Matthew has followed his Marcan source at that point in his gospel also (see Mt 20:29–34). In each of the Matthean stories the single blind man of Mark becomes two. The reason

w: 11:19; Lk 15:1–2. *x:* 12:7; Hos 6:6. *y:* Mk 2:18–22; Lk 5:33–39. *z:* Mk 5:22–43; Lk 8:41–56. *a:* 14:36; Nm 15:37. *b:* 20:29–34. *c:* 15:22.

as Jesus passed on from there, two blind men followed [him], crying out, "Son of David, have pity on us!" [28]When he entered the house, the blind men approached him and Jesus said to them, "Do you believe that I can do this?" "Yes, Lord," they said to him. [29]Then he touched their eyes and said, "Let it be done for you according to your faith." [30]And their eyes were opened. Jesus warned them sternly, "See that no one knows about this." [31]But they went out and spread word of him through all that land.

The Healing of a Mute Person. [32d*]As they were going out, a demoniac who could not speak was brought to him, [33e]and when the demon was driven out the mute person spoke. The crowds were amazed and said, "Nothing like this has ever been seen in Israel." [34f*]But the Pharisees said, "He drives out demons by the prince of demons."

The Compassion of Jesus. [35g*]Jesus went around to all the towns and villages, teaching in their synagogues, proclaiming the gospel of the kingdom, and curing every disease and illness. [36h*]At the sight of the crowds, his heart was moved with pity for them because they were troubled and abandoned, like sheep without a shepherd. [37i*]Then he said to his disciples, "The harvest is abundant but the laborers are few; [38]so ask the master of the harvest to send out laborers for his harvest."

CHAPTER 10

See RG 379

The Mission of the Twelve. [1j*]Then he summoned his twelve disciples and gave them authority over unclean spirits to drive them out and to cure every disease and every illness. [2*]The names of the twelve apostles are these: first, Simon called Peter, and his brother Andrew; James, the son of Zebedee, and his brother John; [3]Philip and Bartholomew, Thomas and Matthew the tax collector; James, the son of Alphaeus, and Thaddeus; [4]Simon the Cananean, and Judas Iscariot who betrayed him.

The Commissioning of the Twelve. [5k*]Jesus sent out these twelve after instructing them

why Matthew would have given a double version of the Marcan story and placed the earlier one here may be that he wished to add a story of Jesus' curing the blind at this point in order to prepare for Jesus' answer to the emissaries of the Baptist (Mt 11:4–6) in which Jesus, recounting his works, begins with his giving sight to the blind.

9:27 Son of David: this messianic title is connected once with the healing power of Jesus in Mark (Mk 10:47–48) and Luke (Lk 18:38–39) but more frequently in Matthew (see also Mt 12:23; 15:22; 20:30–31).

9:32–34 The source of this story seems to be Q (see Lk 11:14–15). As in the preceding healing of the blind, Matthew has two versions of this healing, the later in Mt 12:22–24 and the earlier here.

9:34 This spiteful accusation foreshadows the growing opposition to Jesus in Mt 11; 12.

9:35 See notes on Mt 4:23–25; Mt 8:1–9:38.

9:36 See Mk 6:34; Nm 27:17; 1 Kgs 22:17.

9:37–38 This Q saying (see Lk 10:2) is only imperfectly related to this context. It presupposes that only God (**the master of the harvest**) can take the initiative in sending out preachers of the gospel, whereas in Matthew's setting it leads into Mt 10 where Jesus does so.

10:1–11:1 After an introductory narrative (Mt 10:1–4), the second of the discourses of the gospel. It deals with the mission now to be undertaken by the disciples (Mt 10:5–15), but the perspective broadens and includes the missionary activity of the church between the time of the resurrection and the parousia.

10:1 His twelve disciples: although, unlike Mark (Mk 3:13–14) and Luke (Lk 6:12–16), Matthew has no story of Jesus' choosing the Twelve, he assumes that the group is known to the reader. The earliest New Testament text to speak of it is 1 Cor 15:5. The number probably is meant to recall the twelve tribes of Israel and implies Jesus' authority to call all Israel into the kingdom. While Luke (Lk 6:13) and probably Mark (Mk 4:10, 34) distinguish between the Twelve and a larger group also termed disciples, Matthew tends to identify the disciples and the Twelve. **Authority . . . every illness**: activities the same as those of Jesus; see Mt 4:23; Mt 9:35; 10:8. The Twelve also share in his proclamation of the kingdom (Mt 10:7). But although he teaches (Mt 4:23; 7:28; 9:35), they do not. Their commission to teach comes only after Jesus' resurrection, after they have been fully instructed by him (Mt 28:20).

10:2–4 Here, for the only time in Matthew, the Twelve are designated **apostles**. The word "apostle" means "one who is sent," and therefore fits the situation here described. In the Pauline letters, the place where the term occurs most frequently in the New Testament, it means primarily one who has seen the risen Lord and has been commissioned to proclaim the resurrection. With slight variants in Luke and Acts, the names of those who belong to this group are the same in the four lists given in the New Testament (see note on Mt 9:9). **Cananean**: this represents an Aramaic word meaning "zealot." The meaning of that designation is unclear (see note on Lk 6:15).

10:5–6 Like Jesus (Mt 15:24), the Twelve are sent only to Israel. This saying may reflect an original Jewish Christian refusal of the mission to the Gentiles, but for Matthew it expresses rather the limitation that Jesus himself observed during his ministry.

d: 12:22–24; Lk 11:14–15. *e:* Mk 2:12; 7:37. *f:* 10:25; Mk 3:22. *g:* 4:23; Lk 8:1. *h:* Nm 27:17; 1 Kgs 22:17; Jer 50:6; Ez 34:5; Mk 6:34. *i:* Lk 10:2; Jn 4:35. *j:* Mk 3:14–19; Lk 6:13–16; Acts 1:13. *k:* Mk 6:7–13; Lk 9:1–6.

thus, "Do not go into pagan territory or enter
a Samaritan town. [6l]Go rather to the lost
sheep of the house of Israel. [7m]As you go,
make this proclamation: 'The kingdom of
heaven is at hand.' [8*]Cure the sick, raise the
dead, cleanse lepers, drive out demons. Without cost you have received; without cost you
are to give. [9n]Do not take gold or silver or
copper for your belts; [10o]no sack for the journey, or a second tunic, or sandals, or walking
stick. The laborer deserves his keep. [11p]What-
ever town or village you enter, look for a worthy person in it, and stay there until you leave.
[12]As you enter a house, wish it peace. [13*]If the
house is worthy, let your peace come upon it;
if not, let your peace return to you. [14q*]Who-
ever will not receive you or listen to your
words—go outside that house or town and
shake the dust from your feet. [15r]Amen, I say
to you, it will be more tolerable for the land of
Sodom and Gomorrah on the day of judgment
than for that town.

Coming Persecutions. [16s]"Behold, I am
sending you like sheep in the midst of
wolves; so be shrewd as serpents and simple
as doves. [17tu*]But beware of people, for they
will hand you over to courts and scourge you
in their synagogues, [18]and you will be led before governors and kings for my sake as a
witness before them and the pagans. [19v]When
they hand you over, do not worry about how
you are to speak or what you are to say. You
will be given at that moment what you are to
say. [20]For it will not be you who speak but the
Spirit of your Father speaking through you.
[21w*]Brother will hand over brother to death,
and the father his child; children will rise up
against parents and have them put to death.
[22*]You will be hated by all because of my
name, but whoever endures to the end will be
saved. [23*]When they persecute you in one
town, flee to another. Amen, I say to you, you
will not finish the towns of Israel before the
Son of Man comes. [24x]No disciple is above
his teacher, no slave above his master. [25*]It is
enough for the disciple that he become like
his teacher, for the slave that he become like
his master. If they have called the master of
the house Beelzebul, how much more those
of his household!

Courage under Persecution. [26yz*]"Therefore do not be afraid of them. Nothing is
concealed that will not be revealed, nor secret that will not be known. [27]What I say to
you in the darkness, speak in the light; what
you hear whispered, proclaim on the housetops. [28a]And do not be afraid of those who
kill the body but cannot kill the soul; rather,
be afraid of the one who can destroy both
soul and body in Gehenna. [29]Are not two
sparrows sold for a small coin? Yet not one
of them falls to the ground without your Father's knowledge. [30]Even all the hairs of
your head are counted. [31]So do not be afraid;

10:8–11 The Twelve have received their own call and mission through God's gift, and the benefits they confer are likewise to be given freely. They are not to take with them money, provisions, or unnecessary clothing; their lodging and food will be provided by those who receive them.

10:13 The greeting of peace is conceived of not merely as a salutation but as an effective word. If it finds no worthy recipient, it will return to the speaker.

10:14 Shake the dust from your feet: this gesture indicates a complete disassociation from such unbelievers.

10:17 The persecutions attendant upon the post-resurrection mission now begin to be spoken of. Here Matthew brings into the discourse sayings found in Mk 13 which deals with events preceding the parousia.

10:21 See Mi 7:6 which is cited in Mt 10:35, 36.

10:22 To the end: the original meaning was probably "until the parousia." But it is not likely that Matthew expected no missionary disciples to suffer death before then, since he envisages the martyrdom of other Christians (Mt 10:21). For him, **the end** is probably that of the individual's life (see Mt 10:28).

10:23 Before the Son of Man comes: since the coming of the Son of Man at the end of the age had not taken place when this gospel was written, much less during the mission of the Twelve during Jesus' ministry, Matthew cannot have meant the coming to refer to the parousia. It is difficult to know what he understood it to be: perhaps the "proleptic parousia" of Mt 28:16–20, or the destruction of the temple in A.D. 70, viewed as a coming of Jesus in judgment on unbelieving Israel.

10:25 Beelzebul: see Mt 9:34 for the charge linking Jesus with "the prince of demons," who is named **Beelzebul** in Mt 12:24. The meaning of the name is uncertain; possibly, "lord of the house."

10:26 The **concealed** and **secret** coming of the kingdom is to be proclaimed by them, and no fear must be allowed to deter them from that proclamation.

l: 15:24. *m:* 3:2; 4:17. *n:* Mk 6:8–9; Lk 9:3; 10:4. *o:* Lk 10:7; 1 Cor 9:14; 1 Tm 5:18. *p:* Mk 6:10–11; Lk 9:4–5; 10:5–12. *q:* Acts 13:51; 18:6. *r:* 11:24; Gn 19:1–29; Jude 7. *s:* Lk 10:3. *t:* Mk 13:9–13; Lk 21:12–19. *u:* Acts 5:40. *v:* Ex 4:11–12; Jer 1:6–10; Lk 12:11–12. *w:* 24:9, 13. *x:* Lk 6:40; Jn 13:16; 15:20. *y:* Lk 12:2–9. *z:* Mk 4:22; Lk 8:17; 1 Tm 5:25. *a:* Jas 4:12.

you are worth more than many sparrows. [32*]Everyone who acknowledges me before others I will acknowledge before my heavenly Father. [33b]But whoever denies me before others, I will deny before my heavenly Father.

Jesus: A Cause of Division. [34c]"Do not think that I have come to bring peace upon the earth. I have come to bring not peace but the sword. [35]For I have come to set

a man 'against his father,
a daughter against her mother,
and a daughter-in-law against her mother-in-law;
36 and one's enemies will be those of his household.'

The Conditions of Discipleship. [37d]"Whoever loves father or mother more than me is not worthy of me, and whoever loves son or daughter more than me is not worthy of me; [38*]and whoever does not take up his cross and follow after me is not worthy of me. [39e*]Whoever finds his life will lose it, and whoever loses his life for my sake will find it.

Rewards. [40f*]"Whoever receives you receives me, and whoever receives me receives the one who sent me. [41*]Whoever receives a prophet because he is a prophet will receive a prophet's reward, and whoever receives a righteous man because he is righteous will receive a righteous man's reward. [42g]And whoever gives only a cup of cold water to one of these little ones to drink because he is a disciple—amen, I say to you, he will surely not lose his reward."

CHAPTER 11

See RG 379–80

[1*]When Jesus finished giving these commands to his twelve disciples, he went away from that place to teach and to preach in their towns.

IV. Opposition from Israel

The Messengers from John the Baptist. [2h*]When John heard in prison of the works of the Messiah, he sent his disciples to him [3*]with this question, "Are you the one who is to come, or should we look for another?" [4]Jesus said to them in reply, "Go and tell John what you hear and see: [5i*]the blind regain their sight, the lame walk, lepers are cleansed, the deaf hear, the dead are raised, and the poor have the good news proclaimed to them. [6]And blessed is the one who takes no offense at me."

Jesus' Testimony to John. [7j*]As they were going off, Jesus began to speak to the crowds

10:32–33 In the Q parallel (Lk 12:8–9), the Son of Man will acknowledge those who have acknowledged Jesus, and those who deny him will be denied (by the Son of Man) before the angels of God at the judgment. Here Jesus and the Son of Man are identified, and the acknowledgment or denial will be before his heavenly Father.

10:38 The first mention of the cross in Matthew, explicitly that of the disciple, but implicitly that of Jesus (and follow after me). Crucifixion was a form of capital punishment used by the Romans for offenders who were not Roman citizens.

10:39 One who denies Jesus in order to save one's earthly life will be condemned to everlasting destruction; loss of earthly life for Jesus' sake will be rewarded by everlasting life in the kingdom.

10:40–42 All who receive the disciples of Jesus receive him, and God who sent him, and will be rewarded accordingly.

10:41 A prophet: one who speaks in the name of God; here, the Christian prophets who proclaim the gospel. **Righteous man**: since righteousness is demanded of all the disciples, it is difficult to take the **righteous man** of this verse and **one of these little ones** (Mt 10:42) as indicating different groups within the followers of Jesus. Probably all three designations are used here of Christian missionaries as such.

11:1 The closing formula of the discourse refers back to the original addressees, the Twelve.

11:2–12:50 The narrative section of the third book deals with the growing opposition to Jesus. It is largely devoted to disputes and attacks relating to faith and discipleship and thus contains much sayings-material, drawn in large part from Q.

11:2 In prison: see Mt 4:12; 14:1–12. **The works of the Messiah**: the deeds of Mt 8–9.

11:3 The question probably expresses a doubt of the Baptist that Jesus is **the one who is to come** (cf. Mal 3:1) because his mission has not been one of fiery judgment as John had expected (Mt 3:2).

11:5–6 Jesus' response is taken from passages of Isaiah (Is 26:19; 29:18–19; 35:5–6; 61:1) that picture the time of salvation as marked by deeds such as those that Jesus is doing. The beatitude is a warning to the Baptist not to disbelieve because his expectations have not been met.

11:7–19 Jesus' rebuke of John is counterbalanced by a reminder of the greatness of the Baptist's function (Mt 11:7–15) that is followed by a complaint about those who have heeded neither John nor Jesus (Mt 11:16–19).

b: Mk 8:38; Lk 9:26; 2 Tm 2:12; Rev 3:5. *c:* Lk 12:51–53. *d:* 16:24–25; Lk 14:26–27. *e:* Mk 8:35; Lk 9:24; Jn 12:25. *f:* Lk 10:16; Jn 12:44; 13:20. *g:* 25:40; Mk 9:41. *h:* Lk 7:18–28. *i:* Is 26:19; 29:18–19; 35:5–6; 61:1. *j:* 3:3, 5.

about John, "What did you go out to the
desert to see? A reed swayed by the wind?
[8]Then what did you go out to see? Someone
dressed in fine clothing? Those who wear
fine clothing are in royal palaces. [9*]Then
why did you go out? To see a prophet? Yes, I
tell you, and more than a prophet. [10k]This is
the one about whom it is written:

'Behold, I am sending my messenger
ahead of you;
he will prepare your way before you.'

[11*]Amen, I say to you, among those born of
women there has been none greater than
John the Baptist; yet the least in the kingdom
of heaven is greater than he. [12l*]From the
days of John the Baptist until now, the kingdom of heaven suffers violence, and the violent are taking it by force. [13*]All the prophets and the law prophesied up to the time of
John. [14m]And if you are willing to accept it,
he is Elijah, the one who is to come. [15]Who-
ever has ears ought to hear.

[16n*]"To what shall I compare this generation? It is like children who sit in marketplaces and call to one another, [17]'We played
the flute for you, but you did not dance, we
sang a dirge but you did not mourn.' [18o]For
John came neither eating nor drinking, and
they said, 'He is possessed by a demon.'
[19p]The Son of Man came eating and drinking and they said, 'Look, he is a glutton and
a drunkard, a friend of tax collectors and sinners.' But wisdom is vindicated by her
works."

Reproaches to Unrepentant Towns.
[20q]Then he began to reproach the towns
where most of his mighty deeds had been
done, since they had not repented. [21r*]"Woe
to you, Chorazin! Woe to you, Bethsaida! For
if the mighty deeds done in your midst had
been done in Tyre and Sidon, they would long
ago have repented in sackcloth and ashes.
[22]But I tell you, it will be more tolerable for
Tyre and Sidon on the day of judgment than
for you. [23s*]And as for you, Capernaum:

'Will you be exalted to heaven?
You will go down to the netherworld.'

For if the mighty deeds done in your midst
had been done in Sodom, it would have remained until this day. [24t]But I tell you, it will
be more tolerable for the land of Sodom on
the day of judgment than for you."

The Praise of the Father. [25u*]At that time
Jesus said in reply, "I give praise to you, Father, Lord of heaven and earth, for although
you have hidden these things from the wise
and the learned you have revealed them to
the childlike. [26]Yes, Father, such has been

11:9–10 In common Jewish belief there had been no prophecy in Israel since the last of the Old Testament prophets, Malachi. The coming of a new prophet was eagerly awaited, and Jesus agrees that John was such. Yet he was **more than a prophet**, for he was the precursor of the one who would bring in the new and final age. The Old Testament quotation is a combination of Mal 3:1; Ex 23:20 with the significant change that the **before me** of Malachi becomes **before you**. The messenger now precedes not God, as in the original, but Jesus.

11:11 John's preeminent greatness lies in his function of announcing the imminence of the kingdom (Mt 3:1). But to be in the kingdom is so great a privilege that the least who has it is greater than the Baptist.

11:12 The meaning of this difficult saying is probably that the opponents of Jesus are trying to prevent people from accepting the kingdom and to snatch it away from those who have received it.

11:13 All the prophets and the law: Matthew inverts the usual order, "law and prophets," and says that both have **prophesied**. This emphasis on the prophetic character of the law points to its fulfillment in the teaching of Jesus and to the transitory nature of some of its commandments (see note on Mt 5:17–20).

11:16–19 See Lk 7:31–35. The meaning of the parable (Mt 11:16–17) and its explanation (Mt 11:18–19b) is much disputed. A plausible view is that the **children** of the parable are two groups, one of which proposes different entertainments to the other that will not agree with either proposal. The first represents John, Jesus, and their disciples; the second those who reject John for his asceticism and Jesus for his table association with those despised by the religiously observant. Mt 11:19c (**her works**) forms an inclusion with Mt 11:2 ("the works of the Messiah"). The original form of the saying is better preserved in Lk 7:35 ". . . wisdom is vindicated by all her children." There John and Jesus are the children of Wisdom; here the works of Jesus the Messiah are those of divine Wisdom, of which he is the embodiment. Some important textual witnesses, however, have essentially the same reading as in Luke.

11:21 Tyre and Sidon were pagan cities denounced for their wickedness in the Old Testament; cf. Jl 3:4–7.

11:23 Capernaum's pride and punishment are described in language taken from the taunt song against the king of Babylon (Is 14:13–15).

11:25–27 This Q saying, identical with Lk 10:21–22 except

k: Ex 23:20; Mal 3:1; Mk 1:2; Lk 1:76. *l:* Lk 16:16. *m:* 17:10–13; Mal 3:23; Lk 1:17. *n:* Lk 7:31–35. *o:* Lk 1:15. *p:* 9:10–11. *q:* Lk 10:12–15. *r:* Jl 4:4–7. *s:* Is 14:13–15. *t:* 10:15. *u:* Lk 10:21–22.

your gracious will. [27v]All things have been handed over to me by my Father. No one knows the Son except the Father, and no one knows the Father except the Son and anyone to whom the Son wishes to reveal him.

The Gentle Mastery of Christ. [28*]"Come to me, all you who labor and are burdened, and I will give you rest. [29w*]Take my yoke upon you and learn from me, for I am meek and humble of heart; and you will find rest for yourselves. [30]For my yoke is easy, and my burden light."

See RG 380

CHAPTER 12

Picking Grain on the Sabbath. [1xy*]At that time Jesus was going through a field of grain on the sabbath. His disciples were hungry and began to pick the heads of grain and eat them. [2]When the Pharisees saw this, they said to him, "See, your disciples are doing what is unlawful to do on the sabbath." [3z*]He said to them, "Have you not read what David did when he and his companions were hungry, [4a]how he went into the house of God and ate the bread of offering, which neither he nor his companions but only the priests could lawfully eat? [5b*]Or have you not read in the law that on the sabbath the priests serving in the temple violate the sabbath and are innocent? [6]I say to you, something greater than the temple is here. [7c*]If you knew what this meant, 'I desire mercy, not sacrifice,' you would not have condemned these innocent men. [8d*]For the Son of Man is Lord of the sabbath."

The Man with a Withered Hand. [9e]Moving on from there, he went into their synagogue. [10*]And behold, there was a man there who had a withered hand. They questioned him, "Is it lawful to cure on the sabbath?" so that they might accuse him. [11*]He said to them, "Which one of you who has a sheep that falls into a pit on the sabbath will not take hold of it and lift it out? [12]How much more valuable a person is than a sheep. So it is lawful to do good on the sabbath." [13]Then he said to the man, "Stretch out your hand." He stretched it out, and it was restored as sound as the other. [14f*]But the Pharisees went out and took counsel against him to put him to death.

for minor variations, introduces a joyous note into this section, so dominated by the theme of unbelief. **While the wise and the learned**, the scribes and Pharisees, have rejected Jesus' preaching and the significance of his mighty deeds, **the childlike** have accepted them. Acceptance depends upon the Father's revelation, but this is granted to those who are open to receive it and refused to the arrogant. Jesus can speak of all mysteries because he is **the Son** and there is perfect reciprocity of knowledge between him and the Father; what has been **handed over** to him is revealed only to those whom he wishes.

11:28–29 These verses are peculiar to Matthew and are similar to Ben Sirach's invitation to learn wisdom and submit to her yoke (Sir 51:23, 26).

11:28 Who labor and are burdened: burdened by the law as expounded by the scribes and Pharisees (Mt 23:4).

11:29 In place of the yoke of the law, complicated by scribal interpretation, Jesus invites the burdened to take the yoke of obedience to his word, under which they **will find rest**; cf. Jer 6:16.

12:1–14 Matthew here returns to the Marcan order that he left in Mt 9:18. The two stories depend on Mk 2:23–28; 3:1–6 respectively, and are the only places in either gospel that deal explicitly with Jesus' attitude toward sabbath observance.

12:1–2 The picking of the heads of grain is here equated with reaping, which was forbidden on the sabbath (Ex 34:21).

12:3–4 See 1 Sm 21:2–7. In the Marcan parallel (Mk 2:25–26) the high priest is called Abiathar, although in 1 Samuel this action is attributed to Ahimelech. The Old Testament story is not about a violation of the sabbath rest; its pertinence to this dispute is that a violation of the law was permissible because of David's men being without food.

12:5–6 This and the following argument (Mt 12:7) are peculiar to Matthew. The temple service seems to be the changing of the showbread on the sabbath (Lv 24:8) and the doubling on the sabbath of the usual daily holocausts (Nm 28:9–10). The argument is that the law itself requires work that breaks the sabbath rest, because of the higher duty of temple service. If temple duties outweigh the sabbath law, how much more does the presence of Jesus, with his proclamation of the kingdom (**something greater than the temple**), justify the conduct of his disciples.

12:7 See note on Mt 9:13.

12:8 The ultimate justification for the disciples' violation of the sabbath rest is that Jesus, the Son of Man, has supreme authority over the law.

12:10 Rabbinic tradition later than the gospels allowed relief to be given to a sufferer on the sabbath if life was in danger. This may also have been the view of Jesus' Pharisaic contemporaries. But the case here is not about one in danger of death.

12:11 Matthew omits the question posed by Jesus in Mk 3:4 and substitutes one about rescuing a sheep on the sabbath, similar to that in Lk 14:5.

12:14 See Mk 3:6. Here the plan to bring about Jesus' death is attributed to the Pharisees only. This is probably due to the situation of Matthew's church, when the sole opponents were the Pharisees.

v: Jn 3:35; 6:46; 7:28; 10:15. *w:* Sir 51:26; Jer 6:16. *x:* Mk 2:23–28; Lk 6:1–5. *y:* Dt 23:26. *z:* 1 Sm 21:2–7. *a:* Lv 24:5–9. *b:* Lv 24:8; Nm 28:9–10. *c:* Hos 6:6. *d:* Jn 5:16–17. *e:* Mk 3:1–6; Lk 6:6–11. *f:* Jn 5:18.

The Chosen Servant. [15*]When Jesus realized this, he withdrew from that place. Many
[people] followed him, and he cured them
all, [16]but he warned them not to make him
known. [17]This was to fulfill what had been
spoken through Isaiah the prophet:

[18] [g]"Behold, my servant whom I have
chosen,
my beloved in whom I delight;
I shall place my spirit upon him,
and he will proclaim justice to the
Gentiles.
[19] *He will not contend or cry out,
nor will anyone hear his voice in the
streets.
[20] A bruised reed he will not break,
a smoldering wick he will not quench,
until he brings justice to victory.
[21] *And in his name the Gentiles will
hope."

Jesus and Beelzebul. [22h*]Then they
brought to him a demoniac who was blind
and mute. He cured the mute person so that
he could speak and see. [23i*]All the crowd
was astounded, and said, "Could this perhaps be the Son of David?" [24j*]But when the
Pharisees heard this, they said, "This man
drives out demons only by the power of
Beelzebul, the prince of demons." [25k*]But he
knew what they were thinking and said to
them, "Every kingdom divided against itself
will be laid waste, and no town or house divided against itself will stand. [26]And if Satan
drives out Satan, he is divided against himself; how, then, will his kingdom stand?
[27*]And if I drive out demons by Beelzebul,
by whom do your own people drive them
out? Therefore they will be your judges.
[28l*]But if it is by the Spirit of God that I drive
out demons, then the kingdom of God has
come upon you. [29*]How can anyone enter a
strong man's house and steal his property,
unless he first ties up the strong man? Then
he can plunder his house. [30m*]Whoever is
not with me is against me, and whoever does
not gather with me scatters. [31n*]Therefore, I
say to you, every sin and blasphemy will be
forgiven people, but blasphemy against the
Spirit will not be forgiven. [32]And whoever
speaks a word against the Son of Man will
be forgiven; but whoever speaks against the
holy Spirit will not be forgiven, either in this
age or in the age to come.

12:15–21 Matthew follows Mk 3:7–12 but summarizes his source in two verses (Mt 12:15, 16) that pick up the withdrawal, the healings, and the command for silence. To this he adds a fulfillment citation from the first Servant Song (Is 42:1–4) that does not correspond exactly to either the Hebrew or the LXX of that passage. It is the longest Old Testament citation in this gospel, emphasizing the meekness of Jesus, the Servant of the Lord, and foretelling the extension of his mission to the Gentiles.

12:15 Jesus' knowledge of the Pharisees' plot and his healing all are peculiar to Matthew.

12:19 The servant's not contending is seen as fulfilled in Jesus' withdrawal from the disputes narrated in Mt 12:1–14.

12:21 Except for a minor detail, Matthew here follows the LXX, although the meaning of the Hebrew ("the coastlands will wait for his teaching") is similar.

12:22–32 For the exorcism, see note on Mt 9:32–34. The long discussion combines Marcan and Q material (Mk 3:22–30; Lk 11:19–20, 23; 12:10). Mk 3:20–21 is omitted, with a consequent lessening of the sharpness of Mt 12:48.

12:23 See note on Mt 9:27.

12:24 See note on Mt 10:25.

12:25–26 Jesus' first response to the Pharisees' charge is that if it were true, Satan would be destroying his own kingdom.

12:27 Besides pointing out the absurdity of the charge, Jesus asks how the work of Jewish exorcists (**your own people**) is to be interpreted. Are they, too, to be charged with collusion with Beelzebul? For an example of Jewish exorcism see Josephus, *Antiquities* 8, 2, 5, 42–49.

12:28 The Q parallel (Lk 11:20) speaks of the "finger" rather than of the "spirit" of God. While the difference is probably due to Matthew's editing, he retains **the kingdom of God** rather than changing it to his usual "kingdom of heaven." **Has come upon you**: see Mt 4:17.

12:29 A short parable illustrates what Jesus is doing. The **strong man** is Satan, whom Jesus has tied up and whose **house** he is plundering. Jewish expectation was that Satan would be chained up in the last days (Rev 20:2); Jesus' exorcisms indicate that those days have begun.

12:30 This saying, already attached to the preceding verses in Q (see Lk 11:23), warns that there can be no neutrality where Jesus is concerned. Its pertinence in a context where Jesus is addressing not the neutral but the bitterly opposed is not clear. The accusation of scattering, however, does fit the situation. Jesus is the shepherd of God's people (Mt 2:6), his mission is to the lost sheep of Israel (Mt 15:24); the Pharisees, who oppose him, are guilty of scattering the sheep.

12:31 **Blasphemy against the Spirit**: the sin of attributing to Satan (Mt 12:24) what is the work of the Spirit of God (Mt 12:28).

g: Is 42:1–4. *h:* 9:32–34; Lk 11:14–15. *i:* 9:27. *j:* 10:25; Mk 3:22. *k:* Mk 3:23–27; Lk 11:17–22. *l:* Lk 11:20. *m:* Lk 11:23. *n:* Mk 3:28–30; Lk 12:10.

A Tree and Its Fruits. 33o*“Either declare the tree good and its fruit is good, or declare the tree rotten and its fruit is rotten, for a tree is known by its fruit. 34p*You brood of vipers, how can you say good things when you are evil? For from the fullness of the heart the mouth speaks. 35A good person brings forth good out of a store of goodness, but an evil person brings forth evil out of a store of evil. 36q*I tell you, on the day of judgment people will render an account for every careless word they speak. 37By your words you will be acquitted, and by your words you will be condemned.”

The Demand for a Sign. 38r*Then some of the scribes and Pharisees said to him, “Teacher, we wish to see a sign from you.” 39*He said to them in reply, “An evil and unfaithful generation seeks a sign, but no sign will be given it except the sign of Jonah the prophet. 40*Just as Jonah was in the belly of the whale three days and three nights, so will the Son of Man be in the heart of the earth three days and three nights. 41*At the judgment, the men of Nineveh will arise with this generation and condemn it, because they repented at the preaching of Jonah; and there is something greater than Jonah here. 42sAt the judgment the queen of the south will arise with this generation and condemn it, because she came from the ends of the earth to hear the wisdom of Solomon; and there is something greater than Solomon here.

The Return of the Unclean Spirit. 43t*“When an unclean spirit goes out of a person it roams through arid regions searching for rest but finds none. 44Then it says, ‘I will return to my home from which I came.’ But upon returning, it finds it empty, swept clean, and put in order. 45Then it goes and brings back with itself seven other spirits more evil than itself, and they move in and dwell there; and the last condition of that person is worse than the first. Thus it will be with this evil generation.”

The True Family of Jesus. 46u*While he was still speaking to the crowds, his mother and his brothers appeared outside, wishing to speak with him. [47*Someone told him, “Your mother and your brothers are standing outside, asking to speak with you.”] 48But he said in reply to the one who told him, “Who is my mother? Who are my brothers?” 49And stretching out his hand toward his disciples, he said, “Here are my mother and my brothers. 50For whoever does the will of my heavenly Father is my brother, and sister, and mother.”

12:33 Declare: literally, “make.” The meaning of this verse is obscure. Possibly it is a challenge to the Pharisees either to declare Jesus and his exorcisms good or both of them bad. A tree is known by its fruit; if the fruit is good, so must the tree be. If the driving out of demons is good, so must its source be.

12:34 The admission of Jesus’ goodness cannot be made by the Pharisees, for they are evil, and the words that proceed from their evil hearts cannot be good.

12:36–37 If on the day of judgment people will be held accountable for even their **careless** words, the vicious accusations of the Pharisees will surely lead to their condemnation.

12:38–42 This section is mainly from Q (see Lk 11:29–32). Mk 8:11–12, which Matthew has followed in Mt 16:1–4, has a similar demand for a sign. The scribes and Pharisees refuse to accept the exorcisms of Jesus as authentication of his claims and demand a sign that will end all possibility of doubt. Jesus’ response is that no such sign will be given. Because his opponents are evil and see him as an agent of Satan, nothing will convince them.

12:38 Teacher: see note on Mt 8:19. In Mt 16:1 the request is for a sign “from heaven” (Mk 8:11).

12:39 Unfaithful: literally, “adulterous.” The covenant between God and Israel was portrayed as a marriage bond, and unfaithfulness to the covenant as adultery; cf. Hos 2:4–14; Jer 3:6–10.

12:40 See Jon 2:1. While in Q the sign was simply Jonah’s preaching to the Ninevites (Lk 11:30, 32), Matthew here adds Jonah’s sojourn **in the belly of the whale** for **three days and three nights**, a prefigurement of Jesus’ sojourn in the abode of the dead and, implicitly, of his resurrection.

12:41–42 The Ninevites who **repented** (see Jon 3:1–10) **and the queen of the south** (i.e., of Sheba; see 1 Kgs 10:1–13) were pagans who responded to lesser opportunities than have been offered to Israel in the ministry of Jesus, **something greater than Jonah** or **Solomon**. At the final judgment they will condemn the faithless **generation** that has rejected him.

12:43–45 Another Q passage; cf. Mt 11:24–26. Jesus’ ministry has broken Satan’s hold over Israel, but the refusal of **this evil generation** to accept him will lead to a worse situation than what preceded his coming.

12:46–50 See Mk 3:31–35. Matthew has omitted Mk 3:20–21 which is taken up in Mk 3:31 (see note on Mt 12:22–32), yet the point of the story is the same in both gospels: natural kinship with Jesus counts for nothing; only one who **does the will** of **his heavenly Father** belongs to his true family.

12:47 This verse is omitted in some important textual witnesses, including Codex Sinaiticus (original reading) and Codex Vaticanus.

---

o: Lk 6:43–45. *p:* 3:7; 23:33; 15:11–12; Lk 3:7. *q:* Jas 3:1–2. *r:* 16:1–4; Jon 2:1; 3:1–10; Mk 8:11–12; Lk 11:29–32. *s:* 1 Kgs 10:1–10. *t:* Lk 11:24–26. *u:* Mk 3:31–35; Lk 8:19–21.

CHAPTER 13

See RG 380

The Parable of the Sower. [1v*]On that day, Jesus went out of the house and sat down by the sea. [2]Such large crowds gathered around him that he got into a boat and sat down, and the whole crowd stood along the shore. [3*]And he spoke to them at length in parables, saying: "A sower went out to sow. [4]And as he sowed, some seed fell on the path, and birds came and ate it up. [5]Some fell on rocky ground, where it had little soil. It sprang up at once because the soil was not deep, [6]and when the sun rose it was scorched, and it withered for lack of roots. [7]Some seed fell among thorns, and the thorns grew up and choked it. [8]But some seed fell on rich soil, and produced fruit, a hundred or sixty or thirtyfold. [9]Whoever has ears ought to hear."

The Purpose of Parables. [10]The disciples approached him and said, "Why do you speak to them in parables?" [11*]He said to them in reply, "Because knowledge of the mysteries of the kingdom of heaven has been granted to you, but to them it has not been granted. [12w*]To anyone who has, more will be given and he will grow rich; from anyone who has not, even what he has will be taken away. [13x*]This is why I speak to them in parables, because 'they look but do not see and hear but do not listen or understand.' [14y]Isaiah's prophecy is fulfilled in them, which says:

'You shall indeed hear but not understand,
you shall indeed look but never see.
[15] Gross is the heart of this people,
they will hardly hear with their ears,
they have closed their eyes,
lest they see with their eyes
and hear with their ears
and understand with their heart and be converted,
and I heal them.'

13:1–53 The discourse in parables is the third great discourse of Jesus in Matthew and constitutes the second part of the third book of the gospel. Matthew follows the Marcan outline (Mk 4:1–35) but has only two of Mark's parables, the five others being from Q and M. In addition to the seven parables, the discourse gives the reason why Jesus uses this type of speech (Mt 13:10–15), declares the blessedness of those who understand his teaching (Mt 13:16–17), explains the parable of the sower (Mt 13:18–23) and of the weeds (Mt 13:36–43), and ends with a concluding statement to the disciples (Mt 13:51–52).

13:3–8 Since in Palestine sowing often preceded ploughing, much of the seed is scattered on ground that is unsuitable. Yet while much is wasted, the seed that falls on good ground bears fruit in extraordinarily large measure. The point of the parable is that, in spite of some failure because of opposition and indifference, the message of Jesus about the coming of the kingdom will have enormous success.

13:3 In parables: the word "parable" (Greek *parabolē*) is used in the LXX to translate the Hebrew *māshāl*, a designation covering a wide variety of literary forms such as axioms, proverbs, similitudes, and allegories. In the New Testament the same breadth of meaning of the word is found, but there it primarily designates stories that are illustrative comparisons between Christian truths and events of everyday life. Sometimes the event has a strange element that is quite different from usual experience (e.g., in Mt 13:33 the enormous amount of dough in the parable of the yeast); this is meant to sharpen the curiosity of the hearer. If each detail of such a story is given a figurative meaning, the story is an allegory. Those who maintain a sharp distinction between parable and allegory insist that a parable has only one point of comparison, and that while parables were characteristic of Jesus' teaching, to see allegorical details in them is to introduce meanings that go beyond their original intention and even falsify it. However, to exclude any allegorical elements from a parable is an excessively rigid mode of interpretation, now abandoned by many scholars.

13:11 Since a parable is figurative speech that demands reflection for understanding, only those who are prepared to explore its meaning can come to know it. To understand is a gift of God, granted to the disciples but not to the crowds. In Semitic fashion, both the disciples' understanding and the crowd's obtuseness are attributed to God. The question of human responsibility for the obtuseness is not dealt with, although it is asserted in Mt 13:13. **The mysteries**: as in Lk 8:10; Mk 4:11 has "the mystery." The word is used in Dn 2:18, 19, 27 and in the Qumran literature (1Qp Heb 7:8; 1QS 3:23; 1QM 3:9) to designate a divine plan or decree affecting the course of history that can be known only when revealed. **Knowledge of the mysteries of the kingdom of heaven** means recognition that the kingdom has become present in the ministry of Jesus.

13:12 In the New Testament use of this axiom of practical "wisdom" (see Mt 25:29; Mk 4:25; Lk 8:18; 19:26), the reference transcends the original level. God gives further understanding to one who accepts the revealed mystery; from the one who does not, he will take it away (note the "theological passive," **more will be given, what he has will be taken away**).

13:13 Because 'they look . . . or understand': Matthew softens his Marcan source, which states that Jesus speaks in parables so that the crowds may not understand (Mk 4:12), and makes such speaking a punishment given **because** they have not accepted his previous clear teaching. However, his citation of Is 6:9–10 in Mt 13:14 supports the harsher Marcan view.

v: Mk 4:1–12; Lk 8:4–10. *w:* 25:29; Mk 4:25; Lk 8:18; 19:26. *x:* Jn 9:39. *y:* Is 6:9–10; Jn 12:40; Acts 28:26–27; Rom 11:8.

The Privilege of Discipleship. [16z*]“But
blessed are your eyes, because they see, and
your ears, because they hear. [17]Amen, I say
to you, many prophets and righteous people
longed to see what you see but did not see it,
and to hear what you hear but did not hear it.

The Explanation of the Parable of the Sower. [18a*]“Hear then the parable of the
sower. [19]The seed sown on the path is the
one who hears the word of the kingdom
without understanding it, and the evil one
comes and steals away what was sown in his
heart. [20]The seed sown on rocky ground is
the one who hears the word and receives it at
once with joy. [21]But he has no root and lasts
only for a time. When some tribulation or
persecution comes because of the word, he
immediately falls away. [22]The seed sown
among thorns is the one who hears the word,
but then worldly anxiety and the lure of
riches choke the word and it bears no fruit.
[23]But the seed sown on rich soil is the one
who hears the word and understands it, who
indeed bears fruit and yields a hundred or
sixty or thirtyfold.”

The Parable of the Weeds among the Wheat. [24*]He proposed another parable to
them. “The kingdom of heaven may be
likened to a man who sowed good seed in his
field. [25*]While everyone was asleep his enemy came and sowed weeds all through the
wheat, and then went off. [26]When the crop
grew and bore fruit, the weeds appeared as
well. [27]The slaves of the householder came
to him and said, ‘Master, did you not sow
good seed in your field? Where have the
weeds come from?’ [28]He answered, ‘An enemy has done this.’ His slaves said to him,
‘Do you want us to go and pull them up?’
[29]He replied, ‘No, if you pull up the weeds
you might uproot the wheat along with
them. [30b*]Let them grow together until harvest; then at harvest time I will say to the
harvesters, “First collect the weeds and tie
them in bundles for burning; but gather the
wheat into my barn.” ’ ”

The Parable of the Mustard Seed. [31c*]He
proposed another parable to them. “The
kingdom of heaven is like a mustard seed
that a person took and sowed in a field. [32d*]It
is the smallest of all the seeds, yet when full-
grown it is the largest of plants. It becomes a
large bush, and the ‘birds of the sky come
and dwell in its branches.’ ”

The Parable of the Yeast. [33e*]He spoke to
them another parable. “The kingdom of

13:16–17 Unlike the unbelieving crowds, the disciples have seen that which the **prophets** and the **righteous** of the Old Testament **longed to see** without having their longing fulfilled.

13:18–23 See Mk 4:14–20; Lk 8:11–15. In this explanation of the parable the emphasis is on the various types of soil on which the seed falls, i.e., on the dispositions with which the preaching of Jesus is received. The second and third types particularly are explained in such a way as to support the view held by many scholars that the explanation derives not from Jesus but from early Christian reflection upon apostasy from the faith that was the consequence of persecution and worldliness respectively. Others, however, hold that the explanation may come basically from Jesus even though it was developed in the light of later Christian experience. The four types of persons envisaged are (1) those who never accept **the word of the kingdom** (Mt 13:19); (2) those who believe for a while but fall away because of **persecution** (Mt 13:20–21); (3) those who believe, but in whom **the word** is choked by **worldly anxiety** and the seduction of **riches** (Mt 13:22); (4) those who respond to **the word** and produce **fruit** abundantly (Mt 13:23).

13:24–30 This parable is peculiar to Matthew. The comparison in Mt 13:24 does not mean that **the kingdom of heaven may be likened** simply to the person in question but to the situation narrated in the whole story. The refusal of the **householder** to allow his **slaves** to separate **the wheat** from **the weeds** while they are still growing is a warning to the disciples not to attempt to anticipate the final judgment of God by a definitive exclusion of sinners from the kingdom. In its present stage it is composed of the good and the bad. The judgment of God alone will eliminate the sinful. Until then there must be patience and the preaching of repentance.

13:25 Weeds: darnel, a poisonous weed that in its first stage of growth resembles wheat.

13:30 Harvest: a common biblical metaphor for the time of God’s judgment; cf. Jer 51:33; Jl 4:13; Hos 6:11.

13:31–33 See Mk 4:30–32; Lk 13:18–21. The parables of the mustard seed and the yeast illustrate the same point: the amazing contrast between the small beginnings of the kingdom and its marvelous expansion.

13:32 See Dn 4:7–9, 17–19 where the birds nesting in the tree represent the people of Nebuchadnezzar’s kingdom. See also Ez 17:23; 31:6.

13:33 Except in this Q parable and in Mt 16:12, **yeast** (or “leaven”) is, in New Testament usage, a symbol of corruption (see Mt 16:6, 11–12; Mk 8:15; Lk 12:1; 1 Cor 5:6–8; Gal 5:9). **Three measures**: an enormous amount, enough to feed a hundred people. The exaggeration of this element of the parable points to the greatness of the kingdom’s effect.

z: Lk 10:23–24; 1 Pt 1:10–12. *a:* Mk 4:13–20; Lk 8:11–15. *b:* 3:12. *c:* Mk 4:30–32; Lk 13:18–19. *d:* Ez 17:23; 31:6; Dn 4:7–9, 17–19. *e:* Lk 13:20–21.

heaven is like yeast that a woman took and mixed with three measures of wheat flour until the whole batch was leavened."

The Use of Parables. [34 f*]All these things Jesus spoke to the crowds in parables. He spoke to them only in parables, [35 g*]to fulfill what had been said through the prophet:

"I will open my mouth in parables,
I will announce what has lain hidden
from the foundation [of the
world]."

The Explanation of the Parable of the Weeds. [36*]Then, dismissing the crowds, he went into the house. His disciples approached him and said, "Explain to us the parable of the weeds in the field." [37*]He said in reply, "He who sows good seed is the Son of Man, [38*]the field is the world, the good seed the children of the kingdom. The weeds are the children of the evil one, [39*]and the enemy who sows them is the devil. The harvest is the end of the age, and the harvesters are angels. [40]Just as weeds are collected and burned [up] with fire, so will it be at the end of the age. [41*]The Son of Man will send his angels, and they will collect out of his kingdom all who cause others to sin and all evildoers. [42 h]They will throw them into the fiery furnace, where there will be wailing and grinding of teeth. [43 i*]Then the righteous will shine like the sun in the kingdom of their Father. Whoever has ears ought to hear.

More Parables. [44 j*]"The kingdom of heaven is like a treasure buried in a field, which a person finds and hides again, and out of joy goes and sells all that he has and buys that field. [45]Again, the kingdom of heaven is like a merchant searching for fine pearls. [46]When he finds a pearl of great price, he goes and sells all that he has and buys it. [47]Again, the kingdom of heaven is like a net thrown into the sea, which collects fish of every kind. [48]When it is full they haul it ashore and sit down to put what is good into buckets. What is bad they throw away. [49]Thus it will be at the end of the age. The angels will go out and separate the wicked from the righteous [50]and throw them into the fiery furnace, where there will be wailing and grinding of teeth.

Treasures New and Old. [51*]"Do you understand all these things?" They answered, "Yes." [52*]And he replied, "Then every scribe

13:34 Only in parables: see Mt 13:10–15.

13:35 The prophet: some textual witnesses read "Isaiah the prophet." The quotation is actually from Ps 78:2; the first line corresponds to the LXX text of the psalm. The psalm's title ascribes it to Asaph, the founder of one of the guilds of temple musicians. He is called "the prophet" (NAB "the seer") in 2 Chr 29:30 but it is doubtful that Matthew averted to that; for him, any Old Testament text that could be seen as fulfilled in Jesus was prophetic.

13:36 Dismissing the crowds: the return of Jesus to the house marks a break with the crowds, who represent unbelieving Israel. From now on his attention is directed more and more to his disciples and to their instruction. The rest of the discourse is addressed to them alone.

13:37–43 In the explanation of the parable of the weeds emphasis lies on the fearful end of the wicked, whereas the parable itself concentrates on patience with them until judgment time.

13:38 The field is the world: this presupposes the resurrection of Jesus and the granting to him of "all power in heaven and on earth" (Mt 28:18).

13:39 The end of the age: this phrase is found only in Matthew (13:40, 49; 24:3; 28:20).

13:41 His kingdom: the **kingdom** of the **Son of Man** is distinguished from that of the Father (Mt 13:43); see 1 Cor 15:24–25. The church is the place where Jesus' kingdom is manifested, but his royal authority embraces the entire world; see note on Mt 13:38.

13:43 See Dn 12:3.

13:44–50 The first two of the last three parables of the discourse have the same point. The **person** who **finds** a buried **treasure** and the **merchant** who finds a **pearl of great price** sell **all** that they have to acquire these finds; similarly, the one who understands the supreme value of the kingdom gives up whatever he must to obtain it. The joy with which this is done is made explicit in the first parable, but it may be presumed in the second also. The concluding parable of the fishnet resembles the explanation of the parable of the weeds with its stress upon the final exclusion of evil persons from the kingdom.

13:44 In the unsettled conditions of Palestine in Jesus' time, it was not unusual to guard valuables by burying them in the ground.

13:51 Matthew typically speaks of the understanding of the disciples.

13:52 Since Matthew tends to identify the disciples and the Twelve (see note on Mt 10:1), this saying about the Christian **scribe** cannot be taken as applicable to all who accept the message of Jesus. While the Twelve are in many ways representative of all who believe in him, they are also distinguished from them in certain respects. The church of Matthew has leaders among whom are a group designated as "scribes" (Mt 23:34). Like the scribes of Israel, they are teachers. It is the Twelve and these their later counterparts to

f: Mk 4:33–34. *g:* Ps 78:2. *h:* 8:12; Rev 21:8. *i:* Dn 12:3. *j:* Prv 2:4; 4:7.

who has been instructed in the kingdom of heaven is like the head of a household who brings from his storeroom both the new and the old." [53]When Jesus finished these parables, he went away from there.

V. Jesus, the Kingdom, and the Church

The Rejection at Nazareth. [54kl*]He came to his native place and taught the people in their synagogue. They were astonished and said, "Where did this man get such wisdom and mighty deeds? [55m]Is he not the carpenter's son? Is not his mother named Mary and his brothers James, Joseph, Simon, and Judas? [56]Are not his sisters all with us? Where did this man get all this?" [57n]And they took offense at him. But Jesus said to them, "A prophet is not without honor except in his native place and in his own house." [58]And he did not work many mighty deeds there because of their lack of faith.

See RG 380–81

CHAPTER 14

Herod's Opinion of Jesus. [1opq*]At that time Herod the tetrarch heard of the reputation of Jesus [2]and said to his servants, "This man is John the Baptist. He has been raised from the dead; that is why mighty powers are at work in him."

The Death of John the Baptist. [3r*]Now Herod had arrested John, bound [him], and put him in prison on account of Herodias, the wife of his brother Philip, [4s]for John had said to him, "It is not lawful for you to have her." [5t]Although he wanted to kill him, he feared the people, for they regarded him as a prophet. [6]But at a birthday celebration for Herod, the daughter of Herodias performed a dance before the guests and delighted Herod [7]so much that he swore to give her whatever she might ask for. [8]Prompted by her mother, she said, "Give me here on a platter the head of John the Baptist." [9]The king was distressed, but because of his oaths and the guests who were present, he ordered that it be given, [10]and he had John beheaded in the prison. [11]His head was brought in on a platter and given to the girl, who took it to her mother. [12]His disciples came and took away the corpse and buried him; and they went and told Jesus.

The Return of the Twelve and the Feeding of the Five Thousand. [13u*]When Jesus heard

whom this verse applies. **The scribe . . . instructed in the kingdom** of heaven knows both the teaching of Jesus (**the new**) and the law and prophets (**the old**) and provides in his own teaching **both the new and the old** as interpreted and fulfilled by **the new**. On the translation **head of a household** (for the same Greek word translated **householder** in Mt 13:27), see note on Mt 24:45–51.

13:54–17:27 This section is the narrative part of the fourth book of the gospel.

13:54 After the Sermon on the Mount the crowds are in admiring astonishment at Jesus' teaching (Mt 7:28); here the astonishment is of those who take **offense at him**. Familiarity with his background and family leads them to regard him as pretentious. Matthew modifies his Marcan source (Mt 6:1–6). Jesus is not the carpenter but **the carpenter's son** (Mt 13:55), "and among his own kin" is omitted (Mt 13:57), **he did not work many mighty deeds** in face of such unbelief (Mt 13:58) rather than the Marcan ". . . he was not able to perform any mighty deed there" (Mt 6:5), and there is no mention of his amazement at his townspeople's lack of faith.

14:1–12 The murder of the Baptist by Herod Antipas prefigures the death of Jesus (see Mt 17:12). The Marcan source (Mk 6:14–29) is much reduced and in some points changed. In Mark Herod reveres John as a holy man and the desire to kill him is attributed to Herodias (Mk 6:19, 20), whereas here that desire is Herod's from the beginning (Mt 14:5).

14:1 Herod the tetrarch: Herod Antipas, son of Herod the Great. When the latter died, his territory was divided among three of his surviving sons, Archelaus who received half of it (Mt 2:23), Herod Antipas who became ruler of Galilee and Perea, and Philip who became ruler of northern Transjordan. Since he received a quarter of his father's domain, Antipas is accurately designated **tetrarch** ("ruler of a fourth [part]"), although in Mt 14:9 Matthew repeats the "king" of his Marcan source (Mk 6:26).

14:3 Herodias was not the wife of Herod's half-brother Philip but of another half-brother, Herod Boethus. The union was prohibited by Lv 18:16; 20:21. According to Josephus (*Antiquities* 18, 5, 2 #116–19), Herod imprisoned and then executed John because he feared that the Baptist's influence over the people might enable him to lead a rebellion.

14:13–21 The feeding of the five thousand is the only miracle of Jesus that is recounted in all four gospels. The principal reason for that may be that it was seen as anticipating the Eucharist and the final banquet in the kingdom (Mt 8:11; 26:29), but it looks not only forward but backward, to the feeding of Israel with manna in the desert at the time of the Exodus (Ex 16), a miracle that in some contemporary Jewish expectation would be repeated in the messianic age (2 Bar 29:8). It may also be meant to recall Elisha's feeding a hundred men with small provisions (2 Kgs 4:42–44).

k: Mk 6:1–6; Lk 4:16–30. *l:* 2:23; Jn 1:46; 7:15. *m:* 12:46; 27:56; Jn 6:42. *n:* Jn 4:44. *o:* Mk 6:14–29. *p:* Lk 9:7–9. *q:* Lk 3:1. *r:* Lk 3:19–20. *s:* Lv 18:16; 20:21. *t:* 21:26. *u:* 15:32–38; Mk 6:32–44; Lk 9:10–17; Jn 6:1–13.

of it, he withdrew in a boat to a deserted place by himself. The crowds heard of this and followed him on foot from their towns. [14]When he disembarked and saw the vast crowd, his heart was moved with pity for them, and he cured their sick. [15]When it was evening, the disciples approached him and said, "This is a deserted place and it is already late; dismiss the crowds so that they can go to the villages and buy food for themselves." [16][Jesus] said to them, "There is no need for them to go away; give them some food yourselves." [17]But they said to him, "Five loaves and two fish are all we have here." [18]Then he said, "Bring them here to me," [19*]and he ordered the crowds to sit down on the grass. Taking the five loaves and the two fish, and looking up to heaven, he said the blessing, broke the loaves, and gave them to the disciples, who in turn gave them to the crowds. [20*]They all ate and were satisfied, and they picked up the fragments left over—twelve wicker baskets full. [21]Those who ate were about five thousand men, not counting women and children.

The Walking on the Water. [22v*]Then he made the disciples get into the boat and precede him to the other side, while he dismissed the crowds. [23w]After doing so, he went up on the mountain by himself to pray. When it was evening he was there alone. [24]Meanwhile the boat, already a few miles offshore, was being tossed about by the waves, for the wind was against it. [25*]During the fourth watch of the night, he came toward them, walking on the sea. [26]When the disciples saw him walking on the sea they were terrified. "It is a ghost," they said, and they cried out in fear. [27*]At once [Jesus] spoke to them, "Take courage, it is I; do not be afraid." [28]Peter said to him in reply, "Lord, if it is you, command me to come to you on the water." [29]He said, "Come." Peter got out of the boat and began to walk on the water toward Jesus. [30x]But when he saw how [strong] the wind was he became frightened; and, beginning to sink, he cried out, "Lord, save me!" [31*]Immediately Jesus stretched out his hand and caught him, and said to him, "O you of little faith, why did you doubt?" [32]After they got into the boat, the wind died down. [33y*]Those who were in the boat did him homage, saying, "Truly, you are the Son of God."

The Healings at Gennesaret. [34z]After making the crossing, they came to land at Gennesaret. [35]When the men of that place recognized him, they sent word to all the surrounding country. People brought to him all those who were sick [36a]and begged him that they might touch only the tassel on his cloak, and as many as touched it were healed.

CHAPTER 15

See RG 380–81

The Tradition of the Elders. [1b*]Then Pharisees and scribes came to Jesus from

14:19 The **taking**, saying the blessing, breaking, and giving to the disciples correspond to the actions of Jesus over the bread at the Last Supper (Mt 26:26). Since they were usual at any Jewish meal, that correspondence does not necessarily indicate a eucharistic reference here. Matthew's silence about Jesus' dividing the fish among the people (Mk 6:41) is perhaps more significant in that regard.

14:20 The fragments left over: as in Elisha's miracle, food was left over after all had been fed. The word **fragments** (Greek *klasmata*) is used, in the singular, of the broken bread of the Eucharist in *Didache* 9:3–4.

14:22–33 The disciples, laboring against the turbulent sea, are saved by Jesus. For his power over the waters, see note on Mt 8:26. Here that power is expressed also by his **walking on the sea** (Mt 14:25; cf. Ps 77:20; Jb 9:8). Matthew has inserted into the Marcan story (Mk 6:45–52) material that belongs to his special traditions on Peter (Mt 14:28–31).

14:25 The fourth watch of the night: between 3 A.M. and 6 A.M. The Romans divided the twelve hours between 6 P.M. and 6 A.M. into four equal parts called "watches."

14:27 It is I: see note on Mk 6:50.

14:31 You of little faith: see note on Mt 6:30. **Why did you doubt?**: the verb is peculiar to Matthew and occurs elsewhere only in Mt 28:17.

14:33 This confession is in striking contrast to the Marcan parallel (Mk 6:51) where the disciples are "completely astounded."

15:1–20 This dispute begins with the question of the Pharisees and scribes why Jesus' disciples are breaking **the tradition of the elders** about washing one's hands before eating (Mt 15:2). Jesus' counterquestion accuses his opponents of breaking **the commandment of God for the sake of** their **tradition** (Mt 15:3) and illustrates this by their interpretation of the commandment of the Decalogue concerning parents (Mt 15:4–6). Denouncing them as hypocrites, he applies to them a derogatory prophecy of Isaiah (Mt 15:7–8). Then with a wider audience (**the crowd**, Mt 15:10) he goes beyond the violation of tradition with which the dispute has started. The parable (Mt 15:11) is an attack on the Mosaic law concerning clean and un-

v: Mk 6:45–52; Jn 6:16–21. *w:* Mk 1:35; Lk 5:16; 6:12. *x:* 8:25–26. *y:* 16:16. *z:* Mk 6:53–56. *a:* 9:20–22. *b:* Mk 7:1–23.

Jerusalem and said, [2c*]"Why do your disciples break the tradition of the elders? They do not wash [their] hands when they eat a meal." [3*]He said to them in reply, "And why do you break the commandment of God for the sake of your tradition? [4d]For God said, 'Honor your father and your mother,' and 'Whoever curses father or mother shall die.' [5*]But you say, 'Whoever says to father or mother, "Any support you might have had from me is dedicated to God," [6]need not honor his father.' You have nullified the word of God for the sake of your tradition. [7]Hypocrites, well did Isaiah prophesy about you when he said:

[8 e*]'This people honors me with their lips,
but their hearts are far from me;
[9 f]in vain do they worship me,
teaching as doctrines human
precepts.' "

[10g]He summoned the crowd and said to them, "Hear and understand. [11]It is not what enters one's mouth that defiles that person; but what comes out of the mouth is what defiles one." [12]Then his disciples approached and said to him, "Do you know that the Pharisees took offense when they heard what you said?" [13*]He said in reply, "Every plant that my heavenly Father has not planted will be uprooted. [14h]Let them alone; they are blind guides [of the blind]. If a blind person leads a blind person, both will fall into a pit." [15*]Then Peter said to him in reply, "Explain [this] parable to us." [16]He said to them, "Are even you still without understanding? [17]Do you not realize that everything that enters the mouth passes into the stomach and is expelled into the latrine? [18i]But the things that come out of the mouth come from the heart, and they defile. [19*]For from the heart come evil thoughts, murder, adultery, unchastity, theft, false witness, blasphemy. [20]These are what defile a person, but to eat with unwashed hands does not defile."

The Canaanite Woman's Faith. [21 j*]Then Jesus went from that place and withdrew to the region of Tyre and Sidon. [22]And behold, a Canaanite woman of that district came and called out, "Have pity on me, Lord, Son of David! My daughter is tormented by a demon." [23]But he did not say a word in answer to her. His disciples came and asked him, "Send her away, for she keeps calling out after us." [24*]He said in reply, "I was sent only to the lost sheep of the house of Israel." [25k]But the woman came and did him homage, saying, "Lord, help me." [26*]He said in reply, "It is not right to take the food of the children and throw it to the dogs." [27]She said, "Please, Lord, for even the dogs eat the scraps that fall from the table of their masters." [28 l*]Then Jesus said to her in reply, "O woman, great is your

clean foods, similar to those antitheses that abrogate the law (Mt 5:31–32, 33–34, 38–39). After a warning to his disciples not to follow the moral guidance of the Pharisees (Mt 15:13–14), he explains the **parable** (Mt 15:15) to them, saying that defilement comes not from what **enters the mouth** (Mt 15:17) but from the evil thoughts and deeds that rise from within, **from the heart** (Mt 15:18–20). The last verse returns to the starting point of the dispute (eating **with unwashed hands**). Because of Matthew's omission of Mk 7:19b, some scholars think that Matthew has weakened the Marcan repudiation of the Mosaic food laws. But that half verse is ambiguous in the Greek, which may be the reason for its omission here.

15:2 The tradition of the elders: see note on Mk 7:5. The purpose of the handwashing was to remove defilement caused by contact with what was ritually unclean.

15:3–4 For the commandment see Ex 20:12 (Dt 5:16); 21:17. The honoring of one's parents had to do with supporting them in their needs.

15:5 See note on Mk 7:11.

15:8 The text of Is 29:13 is quoted approximately according to the Septuagint.

15:13–14 Jesus leads his disciples away from the teaching authority of the Pharisees.

15:15 Matthew specifies **Peter** as the questioner, unlike Mk 7:17. Given his tendency to present the disciples as more understanding than in his Marcan source, it is noteworthy that here he retains the Marcan rebuke, although in a slightly milder form. This may be due to his wish to correct the Jewish Christians within his church who still held to the food laws and thus separated themselves from Gentile Christians who did not observe them.

15:19 The Marcan list of thirteen things that defile (Mk 7:21–22) is here reduced to seven that partially cover the content of the Decalogue.

15:21–28 See note on Mt 8:5–13.

15:24 See note on Mt 10:5–6.

15:26 The children: the people of Israel. **Dogs**: see note on Mt 7:6.

15:28 As in the case of the cure of the centurion's servant (Mt 8:10), Matthew ascribes Jesus' granting the request to the woman's **great faith**, a point not made equally explicit in the Marcan parallel (Mk 7:24–30).

c: Lk 11:38. *d:* Ex 20:12; 21:17; Lv 20:9; Dt 5:16; Prv 20:20. *e:* Is 29:13 LXX. *f:* Col 2:23. *g:* Mk 7:14. *h:* 23:16, 19, 24; Lk 6:39; Jn 9:40. *i:* 12:34. *j:* Mk 7:24–30. *k:* 10:6. *l:* 8:10.

faith! Let it be done for you as you wish." And her daughter was healed from that hour.

The Healing of Many People. [29]Moving on from there Jesus walked by the Sea of Galilee, went up on the mountain, and sat down there. [30m]Great crowds came to him, having with them the lame, the blind, the deformed, the mute, and many others. They placed them at his feet, and he cured them. [31]The crowds were amazed when they saw the mute speaking, the deformed made whole, the lame walking, and the blind able to see, and they glorified the God of Israel.

The Feeding of the Four Thousand. [32n*]Jesus summoned his disciples and said, "My heart is moved with pity for the crowd, for they have been with me now for three days and have nothing to eat. I do not want to send them away hungry, for fear they may collapse on the way." [33]The disciples said to him, "Where could we ever get enough bread in this deserted place to satisfy such a crowd?" [34]Jesus said to them, "How many loaves do you have?" "Seven," they replied, "and a few fish." [35]He ordered the crowd to sit down on the ground. [36*]Then he took the seven loaves and the fish, gave thanks, broke the loaves, and gave them to the disciples, who in turn gave them to the crowds. [37o]They all ate and were satisfied. They picked up the fragments left over—seven baskets full. [38]Those who ate were four thousand men, not counting women and children. [39]And when he had dismissed the crowds, he got into the boat and came to the district of Magadan.

CHAPTER 16

See RG 381–82

The Demand for a Sign. [1p*]The Pharisees and Sadducees came and, to test him, asked him to show them a sign from heaven. [2*]He said to them in reply, "[In the evening you say, 'Tomorrow will be fair, for the sky is red'; [3q]and, in the morning, 'Today will be stormy, for the sky is red and threatening.' You know how to judge the appearance of the sky, but you cannot judge the signs of the times.] [4r*]An evil and unfaithful generation seeks a sign, but no sign will be given it except the sign of Jonah." Then he left them and went away.

The Leaven of the Pharisees and Sadducees. [5s*]In coming to the other side of the sea, the disciples had forgotten to bring bread. [6t*]Jesus said to them, "Look out, and beware of the leaven of the Pharisees and Sadducees." [7*]They concluded among themselves, saying, "It is because we have brought no bread." [8]When Jesus became aware of this he said, "You of little faith, why do you conclude among yourselves that it is because you have no bread? [9u]Do you not yet understand, and do you not remember the five loaves for the five thousand, and how many wicker baskets you took up? [10v]Or the seven loaves for the four thousand, and how many baskets you took up? [11]How do you not comprehend that I was not speaking to you about bread? Beware of the

15:32–39 Most probably this story is a doublet of that of the feeding of the five thousand (Mt 14:13–21). It differs from it notably only in that Jesus takes the initiative, not the disciples (Mt 15:32), and in the numbers: the crowd has been with Jesus **three days** (Mt 15:32), **seven loaves** are multiplied (Mt 15:36), **seven baskets** of fragments remain after the feeding (Mt 15:37), and **four thousand** men are fed (Mt 15:38).

15:36 Gave thanks: see Mt 14:19, "said the blessing." There is no difference in meaning. The thanksgiving was a blessing of God for his benefits.

16:1 A sign from heaven: see note on Mt 12:38–42.

16:2–3 The answer of Jesus in these verses is omitted in many important textual witnesses, and it is very uncertain that it is an original part of this gospel. It resembles Lk 12:54–56 and may have been inserted from there. It rebukes the Pharisees and Sadducees who are able to read indications of coming weather but not the indications of the coming kingdom in the signs that Jesus does offer, his mighty deeds and teaching.

16:4 See notes on Mt 12:39, 40.

16:5–12 Jesus' warning his disciples against **the teaching of the Pharisees and Sadducees** comes immediately before his promise to confer on Peter the authority to bind and to loose on earth (Mt 16:19), an authority that will be confirmed in heaven. Such authority most probably has to do, at least in part, with teaching. The rejection of the teaching authority of the Pharisees (see also Mt 12:12–14) prepares for a new one derived from Jesus.

16:6 Leaven: see note on Mt 13:33. **Sadducees**: Matthew's Marcan source speaks rather of "the leaven of Herod" (Mk 8:15).

16:7–11 The disciples, men **of little faith**, misunderstand Jesus' metaphorical use of **leaven**, forgetting that, as the feeding of the crowds shows, he is not at a loss to provide them with bread.

m: Is 35:5–6. *n:* Mk 8:1–10. *o:* 16:10. *p:* Mk 8:11–21. *q:* Lk 12:54–56. *r:* 12:39; Jon 2:1. *s:* Mk 8:14–21. *t:* Lk 12:1. *u:* 14:17–21; Jn 6:9. *v:* 15:34–38.

leaven of the Pharisees and Sadducees."
12*Then they understood that he was not
telling them to beware of the leaven of
bread, but of the teaching of the Pharisees
and Sadducees.

Peter's Confession about Jesus. 13w*When
Jesus went into the region of Caesarea Philippi he asked his disciples, "Who do people
say that the Son of Man is?" 14x*They
replied, "Some say John the Baptist, others
Elijah, still others Jeremiah or one of the
prophets." 15He said to them, "But who do
you say that I am?" 16y*Simon Peter said in
reply, "You are the Messiah, the Son of the
living God." 17*Jesus said to him in reply,
"Blessed are you, Simon son of Jonah. For
flesh and blood has not revealed this to you,
but my heavenly Father. 18z*And so I say to
you, you are Peter, and upon this rock I will
build my church, and the gates of the netherworld shall not prevail against it. 19a*I will
give you the keys to the kingdom of heaven.

16:12 After his rebuke, the disciples understand that by **leaven** he meant the corrupting influence of the **teaching of the Pharisees and Sadducees**. The evangelist probably understands this **teaching** as common to both groups. Since at the time of Jesus' ministry the two differed widely on points of **teaching**, e.g., the resurrection of the dead, and at the time of the evangelist the Sadducee party was no longer a force in Judaism, the supposed common teaching fits neither period. The disciples' eventual understanding of Jesus' warning contrasts with their continuing obtuseness in the Marcan parallel (Mk 8:14–21).

16:13–20 The Marcan confession of Jesus as Messiah, made by Peter as spokesman for the other disciples (Mk 8:27–29; cf. also Lk 9:18–20), is modified significantly here. The confession is of Jesus both as **Messiah** and as **Son of the living God** (Mt 16:16). Jesus' response, drawn principally from material peculiar to Matthew, attributes the confession to a divine revelation granted to Peter alone (Mt 16:17) and makes him the **rock** on which Jesus **will build** his **church** (Mt 16:18) and the disciple whose authority in the church **on earth** will be confirmed in **heaven**, i.e., by God (Mt 16:19).

16:13 Caesarea Philippi: situated about twenty miles north of the Sea of Galilee in the territory ruled by Philip, a son of Herod the Great, tetrarch from 4 B.C. until his death in A.D. 34 (see note on Mt 14:1). He rebuilt the town of Paneas, naming it **Caesarea** in honor of the emperor, and **Philippi** ("of Philip") to distinguish it from the seaport in Samaria that was also called Caesarea. **Who do people say that the Son of Man is?**: although the question differs from the Marcan parallel (Mk 8:27: "Who . . . that I am?"), the meaning is the same, for Jesus here refers to himself as **the Son of Man** (cf. Mt 16:15).

16:14 John the Baptist: see Mt 14:2. **Elijah**: cf. Mal 3:19; Sir 48:10; and see note on Mt 3:4. **Jeremiah**: an addition of Matthew to the Marcan source.

16:16 The Son of the living God: see Mt 2:15; 3:17. The addition of this exalted title to the Marcan confession eliminates whatever ambiguity was attached to the title Messiah. This, among other things, supports the view proposed by many scholars that Matthew has here combined his source's confession with a post-resurrectional confession of faith in Jesus as **Son of the living God** that belonged to the appearance of the risen Jesus to Peter; cf. 1 Cor 15:5; Lk 24:34.

16:17 Flesh and blood: a Semitic expression for human beings, especially in their weakness. **Has not revealed this . . . but my heavenly Father**: that Peter's faith is spoken of as coming not through human means but through a revelation from God is similar to Paul's description of his recognition of who Jesus was; see Gal 1:15–16, ". . . when he [God] . . . was pleased to reveal his Son to me. . . ."

16:18 You are Peter, and upon this rock I will build my church: the Aramaic word *kēpāʾ* meaning **rock** and transliterated into Greek as *CEphas* is the name by which Peter is called in the Pauline letters (1 Cor 1:12; 3:22; 9:5; 15:4; Gal 1:18; 2:9, 11, 14) except in Gal 2:7–8 ("Peter"). It is translated as *Petros* ("Peter") in Jn 1:42. The presumed original Aramaic of Jesus' statement would have been, in English, "You are the Rock (*Kēpāʾ*) and upon this rock (*kēpāʾ*) I will build my church." The Greek text probably means the same, for the difference in gender between the masculine noun *petros*, the disciple's new name, and the feminine noun *petra* (rock) may be due simply to the unsuitability of using a feminine noun as the proper name of a male. Although the two words were generally used with slightly different nuances, they were also used interchangeably with the same meaning, "rock." **Church**: this word (Greek *ekklēsia*) occurs in the gospels only here and in Mt 18:17 (twice). There are several possibilities for an Aramaic original. Jesus' **church** means the community that he **will** gather and that, like a building, will have Peter as its solid foundation. That function of Peter consists in his being witness to Jesus as **the Messiah, the Son of the living God. The gates of the netherworld shall not prevail against it**: the netherworld (Greek *Hadēs*, the abode of the dead) is conceived of as a walled city whose **gates** will not close in upon the church of Jesus, i.e., it will not be overcome by the power of death.

16:19 The keys to the kingdom of heaven: the image of the keys is probably drawn from Is 22:15–25 where Eliakim, who succeeds Shebnah as master of the palace, is given "the key of the house of David," which he authoritatively "opens" and "shuts" (Mt 22:22). **Whatever you bind . . . loosed in heaven**: there are many instances in rabbinic literature of the binding-loosing imagery. Of the several meanings given there to the metaphor, two are of special importance here: the giving of authoritative teaching, and the lifting or imposing of the ban of excommunication. It is disputed whether the image of **the keys** and that of binding and loosing are different metaphors meaning the same thing. In any case, the promise of **the keys** is given to Peter alone. In Mt 18:18 all the disciples are given the power of binding and loosing, but the context of that verse suggests that there the power of excommunication alone is intended. That the keys are those to the **kingdom of heaven** and that Peter's exercise of authority in the church on earth will be confirmed **in heaven** show an intimate connection between, but not an identification of, the church and the **kingdom of heaven**.

w: Mk 8:27–29; Lk 9:18–20. *x:* 14:2. *y:* Jn 6:69. *z:* Jn 1:42.
a: Is 22:22; Rev 3:7.

Whatever you bind on earth shall be bound
in heaven; and whatever you loose on earth
shall be loosed in heaven." [20b*]Then he
strictly ordered his disciples to tell no one
that he was the Messiah.

The First Prediction of the Passion.
[21cd*]From that time on, Jesus began to show
his disciples that he must go to Jerusalem
and suffer greatly from the elders, the chief
priests, and the scribes, and be killed and on
the third day be raised. [22*]Then Peter took
him aside and began to rebuke him, "God
forbid, Lord! No such thing shall ever happen to you." [23e]He turned and said to Peter,
"Get behind me, Satan! You are an obstacle
to me. You are thinking not as God does, but
as human beings do."

The Conditions of Discipleship. [24f*]Then
Jesus said to his disciples, "Whoever wishes
to come after me must deny himself, take up
his cross, and follow me. [25g*]For whoever
wishes to save his life will lose it, but whoever loses his life for my sake will find it.
[26]What profit would there be for one to gain
the whole world and forfeit his life? Or what
can one give in exchange for his life? [27h*]For
the Son of Man will come with his angels in
his Father's glory, and then he will repay
everyone according to his conduct.
[28*]Amen, I say to you, there are some standing here who will not taste death until they
see the Son of Man coming in his kingdom."

CHAPTER 17

See RG 381-82

The Transfiguration of Jesus. [1i*]After
six days Jesus took Peter, James, and John

16:20 Cf. Mk 8:30. Matthew makes explicit that the prohibition has to do with speaking of Jesus as **the Messiah**; see note on Mk 8:27–30.

16:21–23 This first prediction of the passion follows Mk 8:31–33 in the main and serves as a corrective to an understanding of Jesus' messiahship as solely one of glory and triumph. By his addition of **from that time on** (Mt 16:21) Matthew has emphasized that Jesus' revelation of his coming suffering and death marks a new phase of the gospel. Neither this nor the two later passion predictions (Mt 17:22–23; 20:17–19) can be taken as sayings that, as they stand, go back to Jesus himself. However, it is probable that he foresaw that his mission would entail suffering and perhaps death, but was confident that he would ultimately be vindicated by God (see Mt 26:29).

16:21 He: the Marcan parallel (Mk 8:31) has "the Son of Man." Since Matthew has already designated Jesus by that title (13), its omission here is not significant. The Matthean prediction is equally about the sufferings of the Son of Man. **Must**: this necessity is part of the tradition of all the synoptics; cf. Mk 8:31; Lk 9:21. **The elders, the chief priests, and the scribes**: see note on Mk 8:31. **On the third day**: so also Lk 9:22, against the Marcan "after three days" (Mk 8:31). Matthew's formulation is, in the Greek, almost identical with the pre-Pauline fragment of the kerygma in 1 Cor 15:4 and also with Hos 6:2 which many take to be the Old Testament background to the confession that Jesus was raised on **the third day**. Josephus uses "after three days" and "on the third day" interchangeably (*Antiquities* 7, 11, 6 #280–81; 8, 8, 1–2 #214, 218) and there is probably no difference in meaning between the two phrases.

16:22–23 Peter's refusal to accept Jesus' predicted suffering and death is seen as a satanic attempt to deflect Jesus from his God-appointed course, and the disciple is addressed in terms that recall Jesus' dismissal of the devil in the temptation account (Mt 4:10: "Get away, Satan!"). Peter's satanic purpose is emphasized by Matthew's addition to the Marcan source of the words **You are an obstacle to me.**

16:24–28 A readiness to follow Jesus even to giving up one's life for him is the condition for true discipleship; this will be repaid by him at the final judgment.

16:24 Deny himself: to deny someone is to disown him (see Mt 10:33; 26:34–35) and to deny oneself is to disown oneself as the center of one's existence.

16:25 See notes on Mt 10:38, 39.

16:27 The parousia and final judgment are described in Mt 25:31 in terms almost identical with these.

16:28 Coming in his kingdom: since the **kingdom of the Son of Man** has been described as "the world" and Jesus' sovereignty precedes his final coming in glory (Mt 13:38, 41), the coming in this verse is not the parousia as in the preceding but the manifestation of Jesus' rule after his resurrection; see notes on Mt 13:38, 41.

17:1–8 The account of the transfiguration confirms that Jesus is the **Son** of God (Mt 17:5) and points to fulfillment of the prediction that he will come **in his Father's glory** at the end of the age (Mt 16:27). It has been explained by some as a resurrection appearance retrojected into the time of Jesus' ministry, but that is not probable since the account lacks many of the usual elements of the resurrection-appearance narratives. It draws upon motifs from the Old Testament and noncanonical Jewish apocalyptic literature that express the presence of the heavenly and the divine, e.g., brilliant light, white garments, and the overshadowing cloud.

17:1 These three disciples are also taken apart from the others by Jesus in Gethsemane (Mt 26:37). **A high mountain**: this has been identified with Tabor or Hermon, but probably no specific mountain was intended by the evangelist or by his Marcan source (Mk 9:2). Its meaning is theological rather than geographical, possibly recalling the revelation to Moses on Mount Sinai (Ex 24:12–18) and to Elijah at the same place (1 Kgs 19:8–18; Horeb = Sinai).

b: Mk 8:30; Lk 9:21. *c:* Mk 8:31–9:1; Lk 9:22–27. *d:* 17:22–23; 20:17–19. *e:* 4:10. *f:* Lk 14:27. *g:* Lk 17:33; Jn 12:25. *h:* 25:31–33; Jb 34:11; Ps 62:13; Jer 17:10; 2 Thes 1:7–8. *i:* Mk 9:2–8; Lk 9:28–36.

his brother, and led them up a high mountain
by themselves. [2j*]And he was transfigured
before them; his face shone like the sun and
his clothes became white as light. [3*]And behold, Moses and Elijah appeared to them,
conversing with him. [4*]Then Peter said to
Jesus in reply, "Lord, it is good that we are
here. If you wish, I will make three tents
here, one for you, one for Moses, and one for
Elijah." [5k*]While he was still speaking, behold, a bright cloud cast a shadow over them,
then from the cloud came a voice that said,
"This is my beloved Son, with whom I am
well pleased; listen to him." [6*]When the disciples heard this, they fell prostrate and were
very much afraid. [7]But Jesus came and
touched them, saying, "Rise, and do not be
afraid." [8]And when the disciples raised their
eyes, they saw no one else but Jesus alone.

The Coming of Elijah. [9l*]As they were
coming down from the mountain, Jesus
charged them, "Do not tell the vision to anyone until the Son of Man has been raised
from the dead." [10m*]Then the disciples asked
him, "Why do the scribes say that Elijah
must come first?" [11n*]He said in reply, "Elijah will indeed come and restore all things;
[12o]but I tell you that Elijah has already come,
and they did not recognize him but did to
him whatever they pleased. So also will the
Son of Man suffer at their hands." [13*]Then
the disciples understood that he was speaking to them of John the Baptist.

The Healing of a Boy with a Demon.
[14p*]When they came to the crowd a man approached, knelt down before him, [15*]and
said, "Lord, have pity on my son, for he is a
lunatic and suffers severely; often he falls
into fire, and often into water. [16]I brought
him to your disciples, but they could not
cure him." [17q*]Jesus said in reply, "O faithless and perverse generation, how long will

17:2 His face shone like the sun: this is a Matthean addition; cf. Dn 10:6. **His clothes became white as light**: cf. Dn 7:9 where the clothing of God appears "snow bright." For the white garments of other heavenly beings, see Rev 4:4; 7:9; 19:14.

17:3 See note on Mk 9:5.

17:4 Three tents: the booths in which the Israelites lived during the feast of Tabernacles (cf. Jn 7:2) were meant to recall their ancestors' dwelling in booths during the journey from Egypt to the promised land (Lv 23:39–42). The same Greek word, *skēnē*, here translated **tents**, is used in the LXX for the booths of that feast, and some scholars have suggested that there is an allusion here to that liturgical custom.

17:5 Cloud cast a shadow over them: see note on Mk 9:7. **This is my beloved Son . . . listen to him**: cf. Mt 3:17. The voice repeats the baptismal proclamation about Jesus, with the addition of the command **listen to him**. The latter is a reference to Dt 18:15 in which the Israelites are commanded to **listen to** the prophet like Moses whom God will raise up for them. The command to listen to Jesus is general, but in this context it probably applies particularly to the preceding predictions of his passion and resurrection (Mt 16:21) and of his coming (Mt 16:27, 28).

17:6–7 A Matthean addition; cf. Dn 10:9–10, 18–19.

17:9–13 In response to the disciples' question about the expected return of Elijah, Jesus interprets the mission of the Baptist as the fulfillment of that expectation. But that was not suspected by those who opposed and finally killed him, and Jesus predicts a similar fate for himself.

17:9 The vision: Matthew alone uses this word to describe the transfiguration. **Until the Son of Man has been raised from the dead**: only in the light of Jesus' resurrection can the meaning of his life and mission be truly understood; until then no testimony to **the vision** will lead people to faith.

17:10 See notes on Mt 3:4; 16:14.

17:11–12 The preceding question and this answer may reflect later controversy with Jews who objected to the Christian claims for Jesus that Elijah had not yet come.

17:13 See Mt 11:14.

17:14–20 Matthew has greatly shortened the Marcan story (Mk 9:14–29). Leaving aside several details of the boy's illness, he concentrates on the need for faith, not so much on the part of the boy's father (as does Mark, for Matthew omits Mk 9:22b–24) but on that of his own disciples whose inability to drive out the demon is ascribed to their **little faith** (Mt 17:20).

17:15 A lunatic: this description of the boy is peculiar to Matthew. The word occurs in the New Testament only here and in Mt 4:24 and means one affected or struck by the moon. The symptoms of the boy's illness point to epilepsy, and attacks of this were thought to be caused by phases of the moon.

17:17 Faithless and perverse: so Matthew and Luke (Lk 9:41) against Mark's **faithless** (Mk 9:19). The Greek word here translated **perverse** is the same as that in Dt 32:5 LXX, where Moses speaks to his people. There is a problem in knowing to whom the reproach is addressed. Since the Matthean Jesus normally chides his disciples for their **little faith** (as in Mt 17:20), it would appear that the charge of lack of faith could not be made against them and that the reproach is addressed to unbelievers among the Jews. However in Mt 17:20b (**if you have faith the size of a mustard seed**), which is certainly addressed to the disciples, they appear to have not even the smallest faith; if they had, they would have been able to cure the boy. In the light of Mt 17:20b the reproach of Mt 17:17 could have applied to the disciples. There seems to be an inconsistency between the charge of **little faith** in Mt 17:20a and that of not even a little in Mt 17:20b.

j: 28:3; Dn 7:9; 10:6; Rev 4:4; 7:9; 19:14. *k:* 3:17; Dt 18:15; 2 Pt 1:17. *l:* Mk 9:9–13. *m:* Mal 3:23–24. *n:* Lk 1:17. *o:* 11:14. *p:* Mk 9:14–29; Lk 9:37–43. *q:* Dt 32:5 LXX.

I be with you? How long will I endure you? Bring him here to me." 18*Jesus rebuked him and the demon came out of him, and from that hour the boy was cured. 19Then the disciples approached Jesus in private and said, "Why could we not drive it out?" 20r*He said to them, "Because of your little faith. Amen, I say to you, if you have faith the size of a mustard seed, you will say to this mountain, 'Move from here to there,' and it will move. Nothing will be impossible for you." [21]*

The Second Prediction of the Passion. 22s*As they were gathering in Galilee, Jesus said to them, "The Son of Man is to be handed over to men, 23and they will kill him, and he will be raised on the third day." And they were overwhelmed with grief.

Payment of the Temple Tax. 24t*When they came to Capernaum, the collectors of the temple tax approached Peter and said, "Doesn't your teacher pay the temple tax?" 25*"Yes," he said. When he came into the house, before he had time to speak, Jesus asked him, "What is your opinion, Simon? From whom do the kings of the earth take tolls or census tax? From their subjects or from foreigners?" 26*When he said, "From foreigners," Jesus said to him, "Then the subjects are exempt. 27*But that we may not offend them, go to the sea, drop in a hook, and take the first fish that comes up. Open its mouth and you will find a coin worth twice the temple tax. Give that to them for me and for you."

CHAPTER 18

See RG 381-83

The Greatest in the Kingdom. 1u*At that time the disciples approached Jesus and said, "Who is the greatest in the kingdom of

17:18 The demon came out of him: not until this verse does Matthew indicate that the boy's illness is a case of demoniacal possession.

17:20 The entire verse is an addition of Matthew who (according to the better attested text) omits the reason given for the disciples' inability in Mk 9:29. **Little faith**: see note on Mt 6:30. **Faith the size of a mustard seed . . . and it will move**: a combination of a Q saying (cf. Lk 17:6) with a Marcan saying (cf. Mk 11:23).

17:21 Some manuscripts add, "But this kind does not come out except by prayer and fasting"; this is a variant of the better reading of Mk 9:29.

17:22–23 The second passion prediction (cf. Mt 16:21–23) is the least detailed of the three and may be the earliest. In the Marcan parallel the disciples do not understand (Mk 9:32); here they understand and are **overwhelmed with grief** at the prospect of Jesus' death (Mt 17:23).

17:24–27 Like Mt 14:28–31 and Mt 16:16b–19, this episode comes from Matthew's special material on Peter. Although the question of **the collectors** concerns Jesus' payment of the **temple tax**, it is put to Peter. It is he who receives instruction from Jesus about freedom from the obligation of payment and yet why it should be made. The means of doing so is provided miraculously. The pericope deals with a problem of Matthew's church, whether its members should pay the temple tax, and the answer is given through a word of Jesus conveyed to Peter. Some scholars see here an example of the teaching authority of Peter exercised in the name of Jesus (see Mt 16:19). The specific problem was a Jewish Christian one and may have arisen when the Matthean church was composed largely of that group.

17:24 The temple tax: before the destruction of the Jerusalem temple in A.D. 70 every male Jew above nineteen years of age was obliged to make an annual contribution to its upkeep (cf. Ex 30:11–16; Neh 10:33). After the destruction the Romans imposed upon Jews the obligation of paying that tax for the temple of Jupiter Capitolinus. There is disagreement about which period the story deals with.

17:25 From their subjects or from foreigners?: the Greek word here translated **subjects** literally means "sons."

17:26 Then the subjects are exempt: just as **subjects** are not bound by laws applying to **foreigners**, neither are Jesus and his disciples, who belong to the kingdom of heaven, bound by the duty of paying the temple tax imposed on those who are not of the kingdom. If the Greek is translated "sons," the freedom of Jesus, the Son of God, and of his disciples, children ("sons") of the kingdom (cf. Mt 13:38), is even more clear.

17:27 That we may not offend them: though they are exempt (Mt 17:26), Jesus and his disciples are to avoid giving offense; therefore the tax is to be paid. **A coin worth twice the temple tax**: literally, "a stater," a Greek coin worth two double drachmas. Two double drachmas were equal to the Jewish shekel and the tax was a half-shekel. **For me and for you**: not only Jesus but Peter pays the tax, and this example serves as a standard for the conduct of all the disciples.

18:1–35 This discourse of the fourth book of the gospel is often called the "church order" discourse, but it lacks most of the considerations usually connected with church order, such as various offices in the church and the duties of each, and deals principally with the relations that must obtain among the members of the church. Beginning with the warning that greatness in the **kingdom of heaven** is measured not by rank or power but by childlikeness (Mt 18:1–5), it deals with the care that the disciples must take not to cause the **little ones to sin** or to neglect them if they stray from the community (Mt 18:6–14), the correction of members who sin (Mt 18:15–18), the efficacy of the prayer of the disciples because of the presence of Jesus (Mt 18:19–20), and the forgiveness that must be repeatedly extended to sinful members who repent (Mt 18:21–35).

18:1 The initiative is taken not by Jesus as in the Marcan parallel (Mk 9:33–34) but by the disciples. **Kingdom of heaven**: this may mean **the kingdom** in its fullness, i.e., after the parousia and the final judgment. But what follows about causes of sin, church discipline, and forgiveness, all dealing

r: 21:21; Lk 17:6; 1 Cor 13:2. *s:* 16:21; 20:18–19. *t:* Ex 30:11–16; Neh 10:33. *u:* Mk 9:36–37; Lk 9:46–48.

heaven?" [2]He called a child over, placed it in their midst, [3v*]and said, "Amen, I say to you, unless you turn and become like children, you will not enter the kingdom of heaven. [4w]Whoever humbles himself like this child is the greatest in the kingdom of heaven. [5*]And whoever receives one child such as this in my name receives me.

Temptations to Sin. [6x*]"Whoever causes one of these little ones who believe in me to sin, it would be better for him to have a great millstone hung around his neck and to be drowned in the depths of the sea. [7*]Woe to the world because of things that cause sin! Such things must come, but woe to the one through whom they come! [8y*]If your hand or foot causes you to sin, cut it off and throw it away. It is better for you to enter into life maimed or crippled than with two hands or two feet to be thrown into eternal fire. [9]And if your eye causes you to sin, tear it out and throw it away. It is better for you to enter into life with one eye than with two eyes to be thrown into fiery Gehenna.

The Parable of the Lost Sheep. [10z*]"See that you do not despise one of these little ones, for I say to you that their angels in heaven always look upon the face of my heavenly Father.* [[11]][*a] [12]What is your opinion? If a man has a hundred sheep and one of them goes astray, will he not leave the ninety-nine in the hills and go in search of the stray? [13]And if he finds it, amen, I say to you, he rejoices more over it than over the ninety-nine that did not stray. [14]In just the same way, it is not the will of your heavenly Father that one of these little ones be lost.

A Brother Who Sins. [15b*]"If your brother

with the present age, suggests that the question has to do with rank also in the church, where the kingdom is manifested here and now, although only partially and by anticipation; see notes on Mt 3:2; 4:17.

18:3 Become like children: the child is held up as a model for the disciples not because of any supposed innocence of children but because of their complete dependence on, and trust in, their parents. So must the disciples be, in respect to God.

18:5 Cf. Mt 10:40.

18:6 One of these little ones: the thought passes from the child of Mt 18:2–4 to the disciples, **little ones** because of their becoming **like children**. It is difficult to know whether this is a designation of all who are disciples or of those who are insignificant in contrast to others, e.g., the leaders of the community. Since apart from this chapter the designation **little ones** occurs in Matthew only in Mt 10:42 where it means disciples as such, that is its more likely meaning here. **Who believe in me**: since discipleship is impossible without at least some degree of faith, this further specification seems superfluous. However, it serves to indicate that the warning against causing a **little one** to sin is principally directed against whatever would lead such a one to a weakening or loss of faith. The Greek verb *skandalizein*, here translated **causes . . . to sin**, means literally "causes to stumble"; what the stumbling is depends on the context. It is used of falling away from faith in Mt 13:21. According to the better reading of Mk 9:42, in me is a Matthean addition to the Marcan source. **It would be better . . . depths of the sea**: cf. Mk 9:42.

18:7 This is a Q saying; cf. Lk 17:1. The inevitability of **things that cause sin** (literally, "scandals") does not take away the responsibility of **the one through whom they come.** Mt 18:8–9

18:8 These verses are a doublet of Mt 5:29–30. In that context they have to do with causes of sexual sin. As in the Marcan source from which they have been drawn (Mk 9:42–48), they differ from the first warning about scandal, which deals with causing another person to sin, for they concern what **causes** oneself **to sin** and they do not seem to be related to another's loss of faith, as the first warning is. It is difficult to know how Matthew understood the logical connection between these verses and Mt 18:6–7.

18:10–14 The first and last verses are peculiar to Matthew. The parable itself comes from Q; see Lk 15:3–7. In Luke it serves as justification for Jesus' table-companionship with sinners; here, it is an exhortation for the disciples to seek out fellow disciples who have gone **astray**. Not only must no one cause a fellow disciple to sin, but those who have strayed must be sought out and, if possible, brought back to the community. The joy of the shepherd on finding the sheep, though not absent in Mt 18:13 is more emphasized in Luke. By his addition of Mt 18:10, 14 Matthew has drawn out explicitly the application of the parable to the care of the **little ones**.

18:10 Their angels in heaven . . . my heavenly Father: for the Jewish belief in angels as guardians of nations and individuals, see Dn 10:13, 20–21; Tb 5:4–7; 1QH 5:20–22; as intercessors who present the prayers of human beings to God, see Tb 13:12, 15. The high worth of the **little ones** is indicated by their being represented before God by these heavenly beings.

18:11 Some manuscripts add, "For the Son of Man has come to save what was lost"; cf. Mt 9:13. This is practically identical with Lk 19:10 and is probably a copyist's addition from that source.

18:15–20 Passing from the duty of Christian disciples toward those who have strayed from their number, the discourse now turns to how they are to deal with one who sins and yet remains within the community. First there is to be private correction (Mt 18:15); if this is unsuccessful, further correction before **two or three witnesses** (Mt 18:16); if this fails, the matter is to be brought before the assembled community (the church), and if the sinner refuses to attend to the correction of **the church**, he is to be expelled (Mt 18:17). The church's judgment will be ratified **in heaven**, i.e., by God (Mt

v: 19:14; Mk 10:15; Lk 18:17. *w:* 23:12. *x:* Mk 9:42; Lk 17:1–2. *y:* 5:29–30; Mk 9:43–47. *z:* Ez 34:1–3, 16; Lk 15:3–7. *a:* Lk 19:10. *b:* Lv 19:17; Sir 19:13; Gal 6:1.

sins [against you], go and tell him his fault
between you and him alone. If he listens to
you, you have won over your brother. [16c*]If
he does not listen, take one or two others
along with you, so that 'every fact may be
established on the testimony of two or three
witnesses.' [17d*]If he refuses to listen to them,
tell the church. If he refuses to listen even to
the church, then treat him as you would a
Gentile or a tax collector. [18e*]Amen, I say to
you, whatever you bind on earth shall be
bound in heaven, and whatever you loose on
earth shall be loosed in heaven. [19f*]Again,
[amen,] I say to you, if two of you agree on
earth about anything for which they are to
pray, it shall be granted to them by my heavenly Father. [20g*]For where two or three are
gathered together in my name, there am I in
the midst of them."

The Parable of the Unforgiving Servant.
[21h*]Then Peter approaching asked him,
"Lord, if my brother sins against me, how often must I forgive him? As many as seven
times?" [22*]Jesus answered, "I say to you, not
seven times but seventy-seven times. [23i]That
is why the kingdom of heaven may be
likened to a king who decided to settle accounts with his servants. [24*]When he began
the accounting, a debtor was brought before
him who owed him a huge amount. [25]Since
he had no way of paying it back, his master ordered him to be sold, along with his
wife, his children, and all his property, in
payment of the debt. [26*]At that, the servant
fell down, did him homage, and said, 'Be patient with me, and I will pay you back in full.'
[27]Moved with compassion the master of that
servant let him go and forgave him the loan.

18:18). This three-step process of correction corresponds, though not exactly, to the procedure of the Qumran community; see 1QS 5:25–6:1; 6:24–7:25; CD 9:2–8. The section ends with a saying about the favorable response of God to prayer, even to that of a very small number, for Jesus is in the midst of any gathering of his disciples, however small (Mt 18:19–20). Whether this prayer has anything to do with the preceding judgment is uncertain.

18:15 Your brother: a fellow disciple; see Mt 23:8. The bracketed words, **against you**, are widely attested but they are not in the important codices Sinaiticus and Vaticanus or in some other textual witnesses. Their omission broadens the type of sin in question. **Won over**: literally, "gained."

18:16 Cf. Dt 19:15.

18:17 The church: the second of the only two instances of this word in the gospels; see note on Mt 16:18. Here it refers not to the entire **church** of Jesus, as in Mt 16:18, but to the local congregation. **Treat him . . . a Gentile or a tax collector**: just as the observant Jew avoided the company of Gentiles and tax collectors, so must the congregation of Christian disciples separate itself from the arrogantly sinful member who refuses to repent even when convicted of his sin by the whole **church**. Such a one is to be set outside the fellowship of the community. The harsh language about **Gentile** and **tax collector** probably reflects a stage of the Matthean **church** when it was principally composed of Jewish Christians. That time had long since passed, but the principle of exclusion for such a sinner remained. Paul makes a similar demand for excommunication in 1 Cor 5:1–13.

18:18 Except for the plural of the verbs **bind** and **loose**, this verse is practically identical with Mt 16:19b and many scholars understand it as granting to all the disciples what was previously given to Peter alone. For a different view, based on the different contexts of the two verses, see note on Mt 16:19.

18:19–20 Some take these verses as applying to prayer on the occasion of the church's gathering to deal with the sinner of Mt 18:17. Unless an *a fortiori* argument is supposed, this seems unlikely. God's answer to the prayer of **two or three** envisages a different situation from one that involves the entire congregation. In addition, the object of this prayer is expressed in most general terms as **anything for which they are to pray**.

18:20 For where two or three . . . midst of them: the presence of Jesus guarantees the efficacy of the prayer. This saying is similar to one attributed to a rabbi executed in A.D. 135 at the time of the second Jewish revolt: ". . . When two sit and there are between them the words of the Torah, the divine presence (Shekinah) rests upon them" (*Pirqê 'Abôt* 3:3).

18:21–35 The final section of the discourse deals with the forgiveness that the disciples are to give to their fellow disciples who sin against them. To the question of Peter how often forgiveness is to be granted (Mt 18:21), Jesus answers that it is to be given without limit (Mt 18:22) and illustrates this with the parable of the unmerciful servant (Mt 18:23–34), warning that his **heavenly Father** will give those who do not forgive the same treatment as that given to the unmerciful servant (Mt 18:35). Mt 18:21–22 correspond to Lk 17:4; the parable and the final warning are peculiar to Matthew. That the Parable did not originally belong to this context is suggested by the fact that it really does not deal with repeated forgiveness, which is the point of Peter's question and Jesus' reply.

18:22 Seventy-seven times: the Greek corresponds exactly to the LXX of Gn 4:24. There is probably an allusion, by contrast, to the limitless vengeance of Lamech in the Genesis text. In any case, what is demanded of the disciples is limitless forgiveness.

18:24 A huge amount: literally, "ten thousand talents." The talent was a unit of coinage of high but varying value depending on its metal (gold, silver, copper) and its place of origin. It is mentioned in the New Testament only here and in Mt 25:14–30.

18:26 Pay you back in full: an empty promise, given the size of the debt.

c: Dt 19:15; Jn 8:17; 1 Tm 5:19. *d:* 1 Cor 5:1–13. *e:* 16:19; Jn 20:23. *f:* 7:7–8; Jn 15:7. *g:* 1 Cor 5:4. *h:* 6:12; Lk 17:4. *i:* 25:19.

28*When that servant had left, he found one
of his fellow servants who owed him a much
smaller amount. He seized him and started to
choke him, demanding, 'Pay back what you
owe.' 29Falling to his knees, his fellow servant begged him, 'Be patient with me, and I
will pay you back.' 30But he refused. Instead,
he had him put in prison until he paid back
the debt. 31Now when his fellow servants
saw what had happened, they were deeply
disturbed, and went to their master and reported the whole affair. 32His master summoned him and said to him, 'You wicked servant! I forgave you your entire debt because
you begged me to. 33jShould you not have
had pity on your fellow servant, as I had pity
on you?' 34*Then in anger his master handed
him over to the torturers until he should pay
back the whole debt. 35k*So will my heavenly
Father do to you, unless each of you forgives
his brother from his heart."

VI. Ministry in Judea and Jerusalem

CHAPTER 19

See RG 382–83

Marriage and Divorce. 1*When Jesus
finished these words, he left Galilee and
went to the district of Judea across the Jordan. 2Great crowds followed him, and he
cured them there. 3l*Some Pharisees approached him, and tested him, saying, "Is it
lawful for a man to divorce his wife for any
cause whatever?" 4m*He said in reply, "Have
you not read that from the beginning the
Creator 'made them male and female' 5nand
said, 'For this reason a man shall leave his
father and mother and be joined to his wife,
and the two shall become one flesh'? 6So
they are no longer two, but one flesh. Therefore, what God has joined together, no human being must separate." 7o*They said to

18:28 A much smaller amount: literally, "a hundred denarii." A denarius was the normal daily wage of a laborer. The difference between the two debts is enormous and brings out the absurdity of the conduct of the Christian who has received the great forgiveness of God and yet refuses to forgive the relatively minor offenses done to him.

18:34 Since the debt is so great as to be unpayable, the punishment will be endless.

18:35 The Father's forgiveness, already given, will be withdrawn at the final judgment for those who have not imitated his forgiveness by their own.

19:1–23:39 The narrative section of the fifth book of the gospel. The first part (Mt 19:1–20:34) has for its setting the journey of Jesus from Galilee to Jerusalem; the second (Mt 21:1–23:39) deals with Jesus' ministry in Jerusalem up to the final great discourse of the gospel (Mt 24–25). Matthew follows the Marcan sequence of events, though adding material both special to this gospel and drawn from Q. The second part ends with the denunciation of the scribes and Pharisees (Mt 23:1–36) followed by Jesus' lament over Jerusalem (Mt 23:37–39). This long and important speech raises a problem for the view that Matthew is structured around five other discourses of Jesus (see Introduction) and that this one has no such function in the gospel. However, it is to be noted that this speech lacks the customary concluding formula that follows the five discourses (see note on Mt 7:28), and that those discourses are all addressed either exclusively (Mt 10; 18; 24; 25) or primarily (Mt 5–7; 13) to the disciples, whereas this is addressed primarily to the scribes and Pharisees (Mt 23:13–36). Consequently, it seems plausible to maintain that the evangelist did not intend to give it the structural importance of the five other discourses, and that, in spite of its being composed of sayings-material, it belongs to the narrative section of this book. In that regard, it is similar to the sayings-material of Mt 11:7–30. Some have proposed that Matthew wished to regard it as part of the final discourse of Mt 24–25, but the intervening material (Mt 24:1–4) and the change in matter and style of those chapters do not support that view.

19:1 In giving Jesus' teaching on divorce (Mt 19:3–9), Matthew here follows his Marcan source (Mk 10:2–12) as he does Q in Mt 5:31–32 (cf. Lk 16:18). Mt 19:10–12 are peculiar to Matthew.

19:1 When Jesus finished these words: see note on Mt 7:28–29. **The district of Judea across the Jordan**: an inexact designation of the territory. Judea did not extend **across the Jordan**; the territory east of the river was Perea. The route to Jerusalem by way of Perea avoided passage through Samaria.

19:3 Tested him: the verb is used of attempts of Jesus' opponents to embarrass him by challenging him to do something they think impossible (Mt 16:1; Mk 8:11; Lk 11:16) or by having him say something that they can use against him (Mt 22:18, 35; Mk 10:2; 12:15). **For any cause whatever**: this is peculiar to Matthew and has been interpreted by some as meaning that Jesus was being asked to take sides in the dispute between the schools of Hillel and Shammai on the reasons for divorce, the latter holding a stricter position than the former. It is unlikely, however, that to ask Jesus' opinion about the differing views of two Jewish schools, both highly respected, could be described as "testing" him, for the reason indicated above.

19:4–6 Matthew recasts his Marcan source, omitting Jesus' question about Moses' command (Mk 10:3) and having him recall at once two Genesis texts that show the will and purpose of **the Creator** in making human beings **male and female** (Gn 1:27), namely, that a **man** may **be joined to his wife** in marriage in the intimacy of **one flesh** (Gn 2:24). **What God has** thus **joined** must not be separated by any human being. (The NAB translation of the Hebrew *bāśār* of Gn 2:24 as "body" rather than "flesh" obscures the reference of Matthew to that text.)

19:7 See Dt 24:1–4

j: Sir 28:4. *k:* 6:15; Jas 2:13. *l:* Mk 10:2–12. *m:* Gn 1:27. *n:* Gn 2:24; 1 Cor 6:16; Eph 5:31. *o:* Dt 24:1–4.

him, "Then why did Moses command that the man give the woman a bill of divorce and dismiss [her]?" 8He said to them, "Because of the hardness of your hearts Moses allowed you to divorce your wives, but from the beginning it was not so. 9p*I say to you, whoever divorces his wife (unless the marriage is unlawful) and marries another commits adultery." 10[His] disciples said to him, "If that is the case of a man with his wife, it is better not to marry." 11*He answered, "Not all can accept [this] word, but only those to whom that is granted. 12*Some are incapable of marriage because they were born so; some, because they were made so by others; some, because they have renounced marriage for the sake of the kingdom of heaven. Whoever can accept this ought to accept it."

Blessing of the Children. 13q*Then children were brought to him that he might lay his hands on them and pray. The disciples rebuked them, 14rbut Jesus said, "Let the children come to me, and do not prevent them; for the kingdom of heaven belongs to such as these." 15After he placed his hands on them, he went away.

The Rich Young Man. 16s*Now someone approached him and said, "Teacher, what good must I do to gain eternal life?" 17*He answered him, "Why do you ask me about the good? There is only One who is good. If you wish to enter into life, keep the commandments." 18t*He asked him, "Which ones?" And Jesus replied, " 'You shall not kill; you shall not commit adultery; you shall not steal; you shall not bear false witness; 19honor your father and your mother'; and 'you shall love your neighbor as yourself.' " 20*The young man said to him, "All of these I have observed. What do I still

19:9 Moses' concession to human sinfulness (**the hardness of your hearts**, Mt 19:8) is repudiated by Jesus, and the original will of the Creator is reaffirmed against that concession. **(Unless the marriage is unlawful)**: see note on Mt 5:31–32. There is some evidence suggesting that Jesus' absolute prohibition of divorce was paralleled in the Qumran community (see 11QTemple 57:17–19; CD 4:12b–5:14). Matthew removes Mark's setting of this verse as spoken to the disciples alone "in the house" (Mk 10:10) and also his extension of the divorce prohibition to the case of a woman's divorcing her husband (Mk 10:12), probably because in Palestine, unlike the places where Roman and Greek law prevailed, the woman was not allowed to initiate the divorce.

19:11 [This] word: probably the disciples' **"it is better not to marry"** (Mt 19:10). Jesus agrees but says that celibacy is not for all but only for those **to whom that is granted** by God.

19:12 Incapable of marriage: literally, "eunuchs." Three classes are mentioned, eunuchs from birth, eunuchs by castration, and those who have voluntarily **renounced marriage** (literally, "have made themselves eunuchs") **for the sake of the kingdom**, i.e., to devote themselves entirely to its service. Some scholars take the last class to be those who have been divorced by their spouses and have refused to enter another marriage. But it is more likely that it is rather those who have chosen never to marry, since that suits better the optional nature of the decision: **whoever can . . . ought to accept it**.

19:13–15 This account is understood by some as intended to justify the practice of infant baptism. That interpretation is based principally on the command not to **prevent** the children from coming, since that word sometimes has a baptismal connotation in the New Testament; see Acts 8:36.

19:16–30 Cf. Mk 10:17–31. This story does not set up a "two-tier" morality, that of those who seek (only) **eternal life** (Mt 19:16) and that of those who **wish to be perfect** (Mt 19:21). It speaks rather of the obstacle that riches constitute for the following of Jesus and of the impossibility, humanly speaking, for one who has **many possessions** (Mt 19:22) **to enter the kingdom** (Mt 19:24). Actual renunciation of riches is not demanded of all; Matthew counts the rich Joseph of Arimathea as a disciple of Jesus (Mt 27:57). But only the poor in spirit (Mt 5:3) can **enter the kingdom** and, as here, such poverty may entail the sacrifice of one's **possessions**. The Twelve, who **have given up everything** (Mt 19:27) to follow Jesus, will have as their reward a share in Jesus' (the Son of Man's) **judging the twelve tribes of Israel** (Mt 19:28), and all who have similarly sacrificed family or property for his sake **will inherit eternal life** (Mt 19:29).

19:16 Gain eternal life: this is equivalent to "entering into life" (Mt 19:17) and "being saved" (Mt 19:25); the **life** is that of the new age after the final judgment (see Mt 25:46). It probably is also equivalent here to "entering the kingdom of heaven" (Mt 19:23) or "the kingdom of God" (Mt 19:24), but see notes on Mt 3:2; 4:17; 18:1 for the wider reference of **the kingdom** in Matthew.

19:17 By Matthew's reformulation of the Marcan question and reply (Mk 10:17–18) Jesus' repudiation of the term "good" for himself has been softened. Yet the Marcan assertion that "no one is good but God alone" stands, with only unimportant verbal modification.

19:18–19 The first five commandments cited are from the Decalogue (see Ex 20:12–16; Dt 5:16–20). Matthew omits Mark's "you shall not defraud" (Mk 10:19; see Dt 24:14) and adds Lv 19:18. This combination of commandments of the Decalogue with Lv 19:18 is partially the same as Paul's enumeration of the demands of Christian morality in Rom 13:9.

19:20 Young man: in Matthew alone of the synoptics the questioner is said to be a **young man**; thus the Marcan "from my youth" (Mk 10:20) is omitted.

p: 5:32; Lk 16:18; 1 Cor 7:10–11. *q:* Mk 10:13–16; Lk 18:15–17. *r:* 18:3; Acts 8:36. *s:* Mk 10:17–31; Lk 18:18–30. *t:* Ex 20:12–16; Dt 5:16–20 / Lv 19:18; Rom 13:9.

lack?" [21u*]Jesus said to him, "If you wish to
be perfect, go, sell what you have and give
to [the] poor, and you will have treasure in
heaven. Then come, follow me." [22]When
the young man heard this statement, he
went away sad, for he had many possessions. [23*]Then Jesus said to his disciples,
"Amen, I say to you, it will be hard for one
who is rich to enter the kingdom of heaven.
[24v]Again I say to you, it is easier for a camel
to pass through the eye of a needle than for
one who is rich to enter the kingdom of
God." [25*]When the disciples heard this, they
were greatly astonished and said, "Who
then can be saved?" [26w]Jesus looked at them
and said, "For human beings this is impossible, but for God all things are possible."
[27x]Then Peter said to him in reply, "We have
given up everything and followed you.
What will there be for us?" [28y*]Jesus said to
them, "Amen, I say to you that you who
have followed me, in the new age, when the
Son of Man is seated on his throne of glory,
will yourselves sit on twelve thrones, judging the twelve tribes of Israel. [29]And everyone who has given up houses or brothers or
sisters or father or mother or children or
lands for the sake of my name will receive a
hundred times more, and will inherit eternal
life. [30z*]But many who are first will be last,
and the last will be first.

CHAPTER 20

See RG 382–83

The Workers in the Vineyard. [1*]"The
kingdom of heaven is like a landowner who
went out at dawn to hire laborers for his
vineyard. [2]After agreeing with them for the
usual daily wage, he sent them into his vineyard. [3]Going out about nine o'clock, he saw
others standing idle in the marketplace,
[4*]and he said to them, 'You too go into my
vineyard, and I will give you what is just.'
[5]So they went off. [And] he went out again
around noon, and around three o'clock, and
did likewise. [6]Going out about five o'clock,
he found others standing around, and said to
them, 'Why do you stand here idle all day?'
[7]They answered, 'Because no one has hired
us.' He said to them, 'You too go into my
vineyard.' [8a*]When it was evening the
owner of the vineyard said to his foreman,
'Summon the laborers and give them their
pay, beginning with the last and ending with
the first.' [9]When those who had started about
five o'clock came, each received the usual
daily wage. [10]So when the first came, they
thought that they would receive more, but
each of them also got the usual wage. [11]And

19:21 If you wish to be perfect: **to be perfect** is demanded of all Christians; see Mt 5:48. In the case of this man, it involves selling his possessions and giving to the poor; only so can he **follow** Jesus.

19:23–24 Riches are an obstacle to entering **the kingdom** that cannot be overcome by human power. The comparison with the impossibility of a camel's passing **through the eye of a needle** should not be mitigated by such suppositions as that **the eye of a needle** means a low or narrow gate. **The kingdom of God**: as in Mt 12:28; 21:31, 43 instead of Matthew's usual **kingdom of heaven**.

19:25–26 See note on Mk 10:23–27.

19:28 This saying, directed to the Twelve, is from Q; see Lk 22:29–30. **The new age**: the Greek word here translated "new age" occurs in the New Testament only here and in Ti 3:5. Literally, it means "rebirth" or "regeneration," and is used in Titus of spiritual rebirth through baptism. Here it means the "rebirth" effected by the coming of the kingdom. Since that coming has various stages (see notes on Mt 3:2; 4:17), the **new age** could be taken as referring to the time after the resurrection when the Twelve will govern the true Israel, i.e., the church of Jesus. (For "judge" in the sense of "govern," cf. Jgs 12:8, 9, 11; 15:20; 16:31; Ps 2:10). But since it is connected here with the time when the **Son of Man** will be **seated on his throne of glory**, language that Matthew uses in Mt 25:31 for the time of final judgment, it is more likely that what the Twelve are promised is that they will be joined with Jesus then in judging the people of Israel.

19:30 Different interpretations have been given to this saying, which comes from Mk 10:31. In view of Matthew's associating it with the following parable (Mt 20:1–15) and substantially repeating it (in reverse order) at the end of that parable (Mt 20:16), it may be that his meaning is that all who respond to the call of Jesus, at whatever time (**first** or **last**), will be the same in respect to inheriting the benefits of the kingdom, which is the gift of God.

20:1–16 This parable is peculiar to Matthew. It is difficult to know whether the evangelist composed it or received it as part of his traditional material and, if the latter is the case, what its original reference was. In its present context its close association with Mt 19:30 suggests that its teaching is the equality of all the disciples in the reward of inheriting eternal life.

20:4 What is just: although the wage is not stipulated as in the case of those first hired, it will be fair.

20:8 Beginning with the last . . . the first: this element of the parable has no other purpose than to show how **the first** knew what **the last** were given (Mt 20:12).

u: 5:48; 6:20. *v:* 7:14. *w:* Gn 18:14; Jb 42:2; Lk 1:37. *x:* 4:20, 22. *y:* 25:31; Dn 7:9, 22; Lk 22:30; Rev 3:21; 20:4. *z:* 20:16. *a:* Lv 19:13; Dt 24:15.

on receiving it they grumbled against the landowner, [12]saying, 'These last ones worked only one hour, and you have made them equal to us, who bore the day's burden and the heat.' [13*]He said to one of them in reply, 'My friend, I am not cheating you. Did you not agree with me for the usual daily wage? [14*]Take what is yours and go. What if I wish to give this last one the same as you? [15][Or] am I not free to do as I wish with my own money? Are you envious because I am generous?' [16*]Thus, the last will be first, and the first will be last."

The Third Prediction of the Passion. [17b*]As Jesus was going up to Jerusalem, he took the twelve [disciples] aside by themselves, and said to them on the way, [18]"Behold, we are going up to Jerusalem, and the Son of Man will be handed over to the chief priests and the scribes, and they will condemn him to death, [19]and hand him over to the Gentiles to be mocked and scourged and crucified, and he will be raised on the third day."

The Request of James and John. [20c*]Then the mother of the sons of Zebedee approached him with her sons and did him homage, wishing to ask him for something. [21]He said to her, "What do you wish?" She answered him, "Command that these two sons of mine sit, one at your right and the other at your left, in your kingdom." [22*]Jesus said in reply, "You do not know what you are asking. Can you drink the cup that I am going to drink?" They said to him, "We can." [23]He replied, "My cup you will indeed drink, but to sit at my right and at my left [, this] is not mine to give but is for those for whom it has been prepared by my Father." [24d]When the ten heard this, they became indignant at the two brothers. [25]But Jesus summoned them and said, "You know that the rulers of the Gentiles lord it over them, and the great ones make their authority over them felt. [26]But it shall not be so among you. Rather, whoever wishes to be great among you shall be your servant; [27e]whoever wishes to be first among you shall be your slave. [28f*]Just so, the Son of Man did not come to be served but to serve and to give his life as a ransom for many."

The Healing of Two Blind Men. [29g*]As

20:13 I am not cheating you: literally, "I am not treating you unjustly."

20:14–15 The owner's conduct involves no violation of justice (Mt 20:4, 13), and that all the workers receive the same wage is due only to his generosity to the latest arrivals; the resentment of the first comes from envy.

20:16 See note on Mt 19:30.

20:17–19 Cf. Mk 10:32–34. This is the third and the most detailed of the passion predictions (Mt 16:21–23; 17:22–23). It speaks of Jesus' being **"handed over to the Gentiles"** (Mt 27:2), his being **"mocked"** (Mt 27:27–30), **"scourged"** (Mt 27:26), and **"crucified"** (Mt 27:31, 35). In all but the last of these points Matthew agrees with his Marcan source, but whereas Mark speaks of Jesus' being killed (Mk 10:34), Matthew has the specific **"to be . . . crucified."**

20:20–28 Cf. Mk 10:35–45. The request of the sons of Zebedee, made through their mother, for the highest places of honor in the **kingdom**, and the indignation of **the** other **ten** disciples at this request, show that neither **the two brothers** nor the others have understood that what makes for greatness in the kingdom is not lordly power but humble service. Jesus gives the example, and his ministry of service will reach its highest point when he gives his life for the deliverance of the human race from sin.

20:20–21 The reason for Matthew's making **the mother** the petitioner (cf. Mk 10:35) is not clear. Possibly he intends an allusion to Bathsheba's seeking the kingdom for Solomon; see 1 Kgs 1:11–21. **Your kingdom**: see note on Mt 16:28.

20:22 You do not know what you are asking: the Greek verbs are plural and, with the rest of the verse, indicate that the answer is addressed not to the woman but to her sons. **Drink the cup**: see note on Mk 10:38–40. Matthew omits the Marcan "or be baptized with the baptism with which I am baptized" (Mk 10:38).

20:28 Ransom: this noun, which occurs in the New Testament only here and in the Marcan parallel (Mk 10:45), does not necessarily express the idea of liberation by payment of some price. The cognate verb is used frequently in the LXX of God's liberating Israel from Egypt or from Babylonia after the Exile; see Ex 6:6; 15:13; Ps 77:16 (76 LXX); Is 43:1; 44:22. The liberation brought by Jesus' death will be **for many**; cf. Is 53:12. **Many** does not mean that some are excluded, but is a Semitism designating the collectivity who benefit from the service of the one, and is equivalent to "all." While there are few verbal contacts between this saying and the fourth Servant Song (Is 52:13–53:12), the ideas of that passage are reflected here.

20:29–34 The cure of the blind men is probably symbolic of what will happen to the disciples, now blind to the meaning of Jesus' passion and to the necessity of their sharing his suffering. As the men are given sight, so, after the resurrection, will the disciples come to see that to which they are now blind. Matthew has abbreviated his Marcan source (Mk 10:46–52) and has made Mark's one man two. Such doubling is characteristic of this gospel; see Mt 8:28–34 (Mk 5:1–20) and the note on Mt 9:27–31.

b: 16:21; 17:22–23; Mk 10:32–34; Lk 18:31–33. *c:* Mk 10:35–45. *d:* Lk 22:25–27. *e:* Mk 9:35. *f:* 26:28; Is 53:12; Rom 5:6; 1 Tm 2:6. *g:* Mk 10:46–52; Lk 18:35–43.

they left Jericho, a great crowd followed
him. 30h*Two blind men were sitting by the
roadside, and when they heard that Jesus
was passing by, they cried out, "[Lord,] Son
of David, have pity on us!" 31The crowd
warned them to be silent, but they called out
all the more, "Lord, Son of David, have pity
on us!" 32Jesus stopped and called them and
said, "What do you want me to do for you?"
33They answered him, "Lord, let our eyes be
opened." 34Moved with pity, Jesus touched
their eyes. Immediately they received their
sight, and followed him.

See RG 383–84

CHAPTER 21

The Entry into Jerusalem. 1i*When
they drew near Jerusalem and came to Bethphage on the Mount of Olives, Jesus sent
two disciples, 2*saying to them, "Go into the
village opposite you, and immediately you
will find an ass tethered, and a colt with her.
Untie them and bring them here to me. 3And
if anyone should say anything to you, reply,
'The master has need of them.' Then he will
send them at once." 4*This happened so that
what had been spoken through the prophet
might be fulfilled:

5j*"Say to daughter Zion,
'Behold, your king comes to you,
meek and riding on an ass,
and on a colt, the foal of a beast of
burden.' "

6The disciples went and did as Jesus had ordered them. 7*They brought the ass and the
colt and laid their cloaks over them, and he
sat upon them. 8k*The very large crowd
spread their cloaks on the road, while others
cut branches from the trees and strewed them
on the road. 9l*The crowds preceding him
and those following kept crying out and saying:

"Hosanna to the Son of David;
blessed is he who comes in the name
of the Lord;
hosanna in the highest."

10*And when he entered Jerusalem the
whole city was shaken and asked, "Who is
this?" 11*And the crowds replied, "This is

20:30 [Lord]: some important textual witnesses omit this, but that may be because copyists assimilated this verse to Mt 9:27. **Son of David**: see note on Mt 9:27.

21:1–11 Jesus' coming to Jerusalem is in accordance with the divine will that he must go there (cf. Mt 16:21) to suffer, die, and be raised. He prepares for his entry into the city in such a way as to make it a fulfillment of the prophecy of Zec 9:9 (Mt 21:2) that emphasizes the humility of the **king** who **comes** (Mt 21:5). That prophecy, absent from the Marcan parallel account (Mk 11:1–11) although found also in the Johannine account of the entry (Jn 12:15), is the center of the Matthean story. During the procession from Bethphage to Jerusalem, Jesus is acclaimed as the Davidic messianic king by the crowds who accompany him (Mt 21:9). On his arrival the **whole city was shaken**, and to the inquiry of the amazed populace about Jesus' identity the crowds with him reply that he is **the prophet, from Nazareth in Galilee** (Mt 21:10, 11).

21:1 Bethphage: a village that can no longer be certainly identified. Mark mentions it before Bethany (Mk 11:1), which suggests that it lay to the east of the latter. **The Mount of Olives**: the hill east of Jerusalem that is spoken of in Zec 14:4 as the place where the Lord will come to rescue Jerusalem from the enemy nations.

21:2 An ass tethered, and a colt with her: instead of the one animal of Mk 11:2 Matthew has two, as demanded by his understanding of Zec 9:9.

21:4–5 The prophet: this fulfillment citation is actually composed of two distinct Old Testament texts, Is 62:11 (**Say to daughter Zion**) and Zec 9:9. The **ass** and the **colt** are the same animal in the prophecy, mentioned twice in different ways, the common Hebrew literary device of poetic parallelism. That Matthew takes them as two is one of the reasons why some scholars think that he was a Gentile rather than a Jewish Christian who would presumably not make that mistake (see Introduction).

21:7 Upon them: upon the two animals; an awkward picture resulting from Matthew's misunderstanding of the prophecy.

21:8 Spread . . . on the road: cf. 2 Kgs 9:13. There is a similarity between the cutting and strewing of the branches and the festivities of Tabernacles (Lv 23:39–40); see also 2 Mc 10:5–8 where the celebration of the rededication of the temple is compared to that of Tabernacles.

21:9 Hosanna: the Hebrew means "(O Lord) grant salvation"; see Ps 118:25, but that invocation had become an acclamation of jubilation and welcome. **Blessed is he . . . in the name of the Lord**: see Ps 118:26 and the note on Jn 12:13. **In the highest**: probably only an intensification of the acclamation, although **Hosanna in the highest** could be taken as a prayer, "May God save (him)."

21:10 Was shaken: in the gospels this verb is peculiar to Matthew where it is used also of the earthquake at the time of the crucifixion (Mt 27:51) and of the terror of the guards of Jesus' tomb at the appearance of the angel (Mt 28:4). For Matthew's use of the cognate noun, see note on Mt 8:24.

21:11 The prophet: see Mt 16:14 ("one of the prophets") and 21:46.

---

h: 9:27. *i:* Mk 11:1–11; Lk 19:28–38; Jn 12:12–15. *j:* Is 62:11; Zec 9:9. *k:* 2 Kgs 9:13. *l:* Ps 118:25–26.

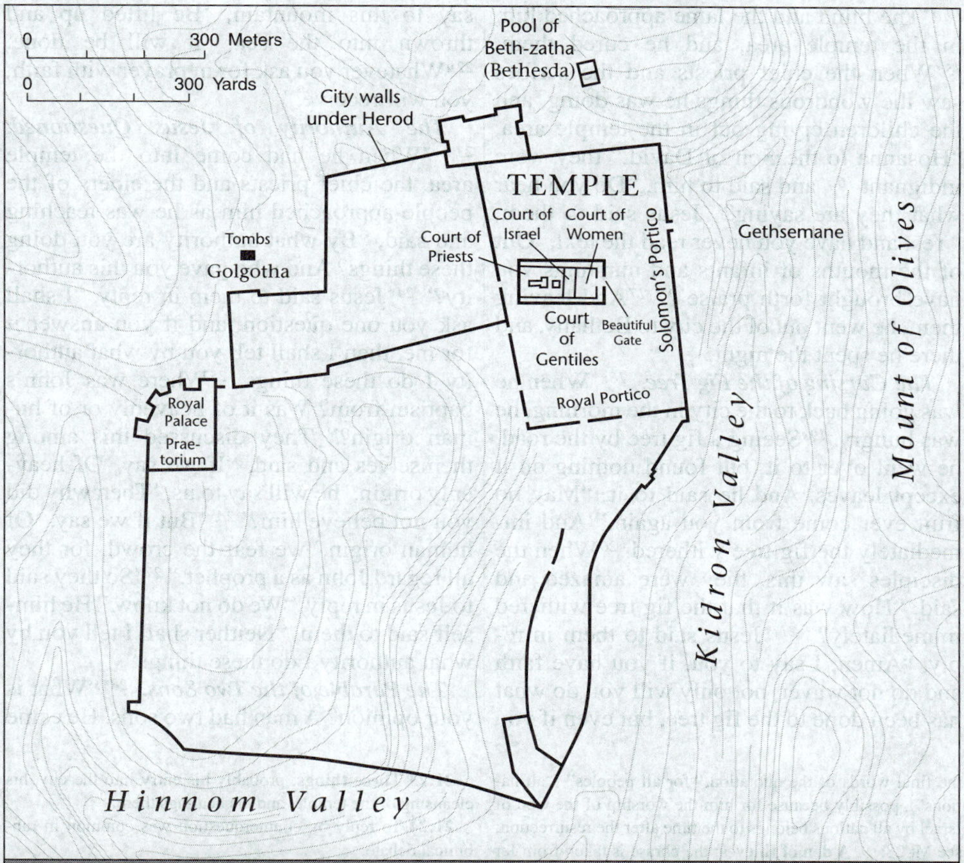

Jerusalem in the Time of Jesus

Jesus the prophet, from Nazareth in Galilee."

The Cleansing of the Temple. *12 mn**Jesus entered the temple area and drove out all those engaged in selling and buying there. He overturned the tables of the money changers and the seats of those who were selling doves. *13 o** And he said to them, "It is written:

'My house shall be a house of prayer,'
but you are making it a den of thieves."

21:12–17 Matthew changes the order of (Mk 11:11, 12, 15) and places the cleansing of the temple on the same day as the entry into Jerusalem, immediately after it. The activities going on in **the temple area** were not secular but connected with the temple worship. Thus Jesus' attack on those so engaged and his charge that they were **making** God's **house of prayer a den of thieves** (Mt 21:12–13) constituted a claim to authority over the religious practices of Israel and were a challenge to the priestly authorities. Mt 21:14–17 are peculiar to Matthew. Jesus' healings and his countenancing the children's cries of praise rouse the indignation of **the chief priests and the scribes** (Mt 21:15). These two groups appear in the infancy narrative (Mt 2:4) and have been mentioned in the first and third passion predictions (Mt 16:21; 20:18). Now, as the passion approaches, they come on the scene again, exhibiting their hostility to Jesus.

21:12 These activities were carried on in the court of the Gentiles, the outermost court of **the temple area**. Animals for sacrifice were sold; the **doves** were for those who could not afford a more expensive offering; see Lv 5:7. **Tables of the money changers**: only the coinage of Tyre could be used for the purchases; other money had to be exchanged for that.

21:13 'My house . . . prayer': cf. Is 56:7. Matthew omits

m: Mk 11:15–19; Lk 19:45–48; Jn 2:14–22. *n:* Lv 5:7. *o:* Is 56:7; Jer 7:11.

[14p*]The blind and the lame approached him in the temple area, and he cured them. [15*]When the chief priests and the scribes saw the wondrous things he was doing, and the children crying out in the temple area, "Hosanna to the Son of David," they were indignant [16q*]and said to him, "Do you hear what they are saying?" Jesus said to them, "Yes; and have you never read the text, 'Out of the mouths of infants and nurslings you have brought forth praise'?" [17]And leaving them, he went out of the city to Bethany, and there he spent the night.

The Cursing of the Fig Tree. [18r*]When he was going back to the city in the morning, he was hungry. [19s]Seeing a fig tree by the road, he went over to it, but found nothing on it except leaves. And he said to it, "May no fruit ever come from you again." And immediately the fig tree withered. [20]When the disciples saw this, they were amazed and said, "How was it that the fig tree withered immediately?" [21t*]Jesus said to them in reply, "Amen, I say to you, if you have faith and do not waver, not only will you do what has been done to the fig tree, but even if you say to this mountain, 'Be lifted up and thrown into the sea,' it will be done. [22u]Whatever you ask for in prayer with faith, you will receive."

The Authority of Jesus Questioned. [23vw*]When he had come into the temple area, the chief priests and the elders of the people approached him as he was teaching and said, "By what authority are you doing these things? And who gave you this authority?" [24*]Jesus said to them in reply, "I shall ask you one question, and if you answer it for me, then I shall tell you by what authority I do these things. [25]Where was John's baptism from? Was it of heavenly or of human origin?" They discussed this among themselves and said, "If we say 'Of heavenly origin,' he will say to us, 'Then why did you not believe him?' [26x*]But if we say, 'Of human origin,' we fear the crowd, for they all regard John as a prophet." [27*]So they said to Jesus in reply, "We do not know." He himself said to them, "Neither shall I tell you by what authority I do these things.

The Parable of the Two Sons. [28*]"What is your opinion? A man had two sons. He came

the final words of the quotation, "for all peoples" ("all nations"), possibly because for him the worship of the God of Israel by all nations belongs to the time after the resurrection; see Mt 28:19. **A den of thieves**: the phrase is taken from Jer 7:11.

21:14 The blind and the lame: according to 2 Sm 5:8 (LXX) **the blind and the lame** were forbidden to enter "the house of the Lord," the temple. These are the last of Jesus' healings in Matthew.

21:15 The wondrous things: the healings.

21:16 'Out of the mouths . . . praise': cf. Ps 8:3 (LXX).

21:18–22 In Mark the effect of Jesus' cursing the fig tree is not immediate; see Mk 11:14, 20. By making it so, Matthew has heightened the miracle. Jesus' act seems arbitrary and ill-tempered, but it is a prophetic action similar to those of Old Testament prophets that vividly symbolize some part of their preaching; see, e.g., Ez 12:1–20. It is a sign of the judgment that is to come upon the Israel that with all its apparent piety lacks the fruit of good deeds (Mt 3:10) and will soon bear the punishment of its fruitlessness (Mt 21:43). Some scholars propose that this story is the development in tradition of a parable of Jesus about the destiny of a fruitless tree, such as Lk 13:6–9. Jesus' answer to the question of the amazed disciples (Mt 21:20) makes the miracle an example of the power of prayer made with unwavering **faith** (Mt 21:21–22).

21:21 See Mt 17:20.

21:23–27 Cf. Mk 11:27–33. This is the first of five controversies between Jesus and the religious authorities of Judaism in Mt 21:23–22:46 Presented in the form of questions and answers.

21:23 These things: probably his entry into the city, his cleansing of the temple, and his healings there.

21:24 To reply by counterquestion was common in rabbinical debate.

21:26 We fear . . . as a prophet: cf. Mt 14:5.

21:27 Since through embarrassment on the one hand and fear on the other the religious authorities claim ignorance of the origin of John's baptism, they show themselves incapable of speaking with authority; hence Jesus refuses to discuss with them the grounds of his authority.

21:28–32 The series of controversies is interrupted by three parables on the judgment of Israel (Mt 21:28–22:14) of which this, peculiar to Matthew, is the first. The second (Mt 21:33–46) comes from Mark (12:1–12), and the third (Mt 22:1–14) from Q; see Lk 14:15–24. This interruption of the controversies is similar to that in Mark, although Mark has only one parable between the first and second controversy. As regards Matthew's first parable, Mt 21:28–30 if taken by themselves could point simply to the difference between saying and doing, a theme of much importance in this gospel (cf. Mt 7:21; 12:50); that may have been the parable's original reference. However, it is given a more specific application by the addition of Mt 21:31–32. The two sons represent, respectively, the religious leaders and the religious outcasts who followed John's call to repentance. By the answer they give to Jesus' question (Mt 21:31) the leaders con-

p: 2 Sm 5:8 LXX. *q:* Ps 8:2 LXX; Wis 10:21. *r:* Mk 11:12–14, 20–24. *s:* Jer 8:13; Lk 13:6–9. *t:* 17:20; Lk 17:6. *u:* 7:7; 1 Jn 3:22. *v:* Mk 11:27–33; Lk 20:1–8. *w:* Jn 2:18. *x:* 14:5.

to the first and said, 'Son, go out and work in
the vineyard today.' [29]He said in reply, 'I
will not,' but afterwards he changed his
mind and went. [30]The man came to the other
son and gave the same order. He said in reply, 'Yes, sir,' but did not go. [31*]Which of the
two did his father's will?" They answered,
"The first." Jesus said to them, "Amen, I say
to you, tax collectors and prostitutes are entering the kingdom of God before you.
[32y*]When John came to you in the way of
righteousness, you did not believe him; but
tax collectors and prostitutes did. Yet even
when you saw that, you did not later change
your minds and believe him.

The Parable of the Tenants. [33za*]"Hear
another parable. There was a landowner who
planted a vineyard, put a hedge around it,
dug a wine press in it, and built a tower.
Then he leased it to tenants and went on a
journey. [34*]When vintage time drew near, he
sent his servants to the tenants to obtain his
produce. [35]But the tenants seized the servants and one they beat, another they killed,
and a third they stoned. [36]Again he sent
other servants, more numerous than the first
ones, but they treated them in the same way.
[37]Finally, he sent his son to them, thinking,
'They will respect my son.' [38*]But when the
tenants saw the son, they said to one another,
'This is the heir. Come, let us kill him and
acquire his inheritance.' [39b*]They seized
him, threw him out of the vineyard, and
killed him. [40]What will the owner of the
vineyard do to those tenants when he
comes?" [41*]They answered him, "He will
put those wretched men to a wretched death
and lease his vineyard to other tenants who
will give him the produce at the proper
times." [42c*]Jesus said to them, "Did you
never read in the scriptures:

'The stone that the builders rejected
has become the cornerstone;
by the Lord has this been done,
and it is wonderful in our eyes'?

[43*]Therefore, I say to you, the kingdom of

demn themselves. There is much confusion in the textual tradition of the parable. Of the three different forms of the text given by important textual witnesses, one has the leaders answer that the son who agreed to go but did not was the one who did the father's will. Although some scholars accept that as the original reading, their arguments in favor of it seem unconvincing. The choice probably lies only between a reading that puts the son who agrees and then disobeys before the son who at first refuses and then obeys, and the reading followed in the present translation. The witnesses to the latter reading are slightly better than those that support the other.

21:31 Entering . . . before you: this probably means "they enter; you do not."

21:32 Cf. Lk 7:29–30. Although the thought is similar to that of the Lucan text, the formulation is so different that it is improbable that the saying comes from Q. **Came to you . . . way of righteousness**: several meanings are possible: that John himself was righteous, that he taught righteousness to others, or that he had an important place in God's plan of salvation. For the last, see note on Mt 3:14–15.

21:33–46 Cf. Mk 12:1–12. In this parable there is a close correspondence between most of the details of the story and the situation that it illustrates, the dealings of God with his people. Because of that heavy allegorizing, some scholars think that it does not in any way go back to Jesus, but represents the theology of the later church. That judgment applies to the Marcan parallel as well, although the allegorizing has gone farther in Matthew. There are others who believe that while many of the allegorical elements are due to church sources, they have been added to a basic parable spoken by Jesus. This view is now supported by the Gospel of Thomas, #65, where a less allegorized and probably more primitive form of the parable is found.

21:33 Planted a vineyard . . . a tower: cf. Is 5:1–2. The vineyard is defined in Is 5:7 as "the house of Israel."

21:34–35 His servants: Matthew has two sendings of **servants** as against Mark's three sendings of a single servant (Mk 11:2–5a) followed by a statement about the sending of "many others" (Mk 11:2, 5b). That these servants stand for the prophets sent by God to Israel is clearly implied but not made explicit here, but see Mt 23:37. **His produce**: cf. Mk 12:2 "some of the produce." The **produce** is the good works demanded by God, and his claim to them is total.

21:38 Acquire his inheritance: if a Jewish proselyte died without heir, the tenants of his land would have final claim on it.

21:39 Threw him out . . . and killed him: the change in the Marcan order where the son is killed and his corpse then thrown out (Mk 12:8) was probably made because of the tradition that Jesus died outside the city of Jerusalem; see Jn 19:17; Heb 13:12.

21:41 They answered: in Mk 12:9 the question is answered by Jesus himself; here the leaders answer and so condemn themselves; cf. Mt 21:31. Matthew adds that the new **tenants** to whom the vineyard will be transferred **will give** the owner **the produce at the proper times.**

21:42 Cf. Ps 118:22–23. The psalm was used in the early church as a prophecy of Jesus' resurrection; see Acts 4:11; 1 Pt 2:7. If, as some think, the original parable ended at Mt 21:39 it was thought necessary to complete it by a reference to Jesus' vindication by God.

21:43 Peculiar to Matthew. **Kingdom of God**: see note on Mt

y: Lk 7:29–30. *z:* Mk 12:1–12; Lk 20:9–19. *a:* Is 5:1–2, 7. *b:* Heb 13:12. *c:* Ps 118:22–23; Is 28:16; Acts 4:11; 1 Pt 2:7.

God will be taken away from you and given
to a people that will produce its fruit. [44 *The
one who falls on this stone will be dashed to
pieces; and it will crush anyone on whom it
falls.]" 45*When the chief priests and the
Pharisees heard his parables, they knew that
he was speaking about them. 46And although
they were attempting to arrest him, they
feared the crowds, for they regarded him as
a prophet.

CHAPTER 22

See RG 383–84

The Parable of the Wedding Feast.
1d*Jesus again in reply spoke to them in parables, saying, 2*"The kingdom of heaven
may be likened to a king who gave a wedding feast for his son. 3*He dispatched his
servants to summon the invited guests to the
feast, but they refused to come. 4A second
time he sent other servants, saying, 'Tell
those invited: "Behold, I have prepared my
banquet, my calves and fattened cattle are
killed, and everything is ready; come to the
feast."' 5Some ignored the invitation and
went away, one to his farm, another to his
business. 6eThe rest laid hold of his servants,
mistreated them, and killed them. 7*The king
was enraged and sent his troops, destroyed
those murderers, and burned their city.
8Then he said to his servants, 'The feast is
ready, but those who were invited were not
worthy to come. 9Go out, therefore, into the
main roads and invite to the feast whomever
you find.' 10*The servants went out into the
streets and gathered all they found, bad and
good alike, and the hall was filled with
guests. 11*But when the king came in to meet
the guests he saw a man there not dressed in
a wedding garment. 12He said to him, 'My
friend, how is it that you came in here without a wedding garment?' But he was reduced
to silence. 13f*Then the king said to his attendants, 'Bind his hands and feet, and cast
him into the darkness outside, where there
will be wailing and grinding of teeth.'
14Many are invited, but few are chosen."

Paying Taxes to the Emperor. 15g*Then the
Pharisees went off and plotted how they
might entrap him in speech. 16*They sent their
disciples to him, with the Herodians, saying,

19:23–24. Its presence here instead of Matthew's usual "kingdom of heaven" may indicate that the saying came from Matthew's own traditional material. **A people that will produce its fruit**: believing Israelites and Gentiles, the church of Jesus.

21:44 The majority of textual witnesses omit this verse. It is probably an early addition to Matthew from Lk 20:18 with which it is practically identical.

21:45 The Pharisees: Matthew inserts into the group of Jewish leaders (Mt 21:23) those who represented the Judaism of his own time.

22:1–14 This parable is from Q; see Lk 14:15–24. It has been given many allegorical traits by Matthew, e.g., the burning of the **city** of the guests who refused the invitation (Mt 22:7), which corresponds to the destruction of Jerusalem by the Romans in A.D. 70. It has similarities with the preceding parable of the tenants: the sending of two groups of **servants** (Mt 22:3, 4), the murder of the **servants** (Mt 22:6) the punishment of the **murderers** (Mt 22:7), and the entrance of a new group into a privileged situation of which the others had proved themselves unworthy (Mt 22:8–10). The parable ends with a section that is peculiar to Matthew (Mt 22:11–14), which some take as a distinct parable. Matthew presents the **kingdom** in its double aspect, already present and something that can be entered here and now (Mt 22:1–10), and something that will be possessed only by those present members who can stand the scrutiny of the final judgment (Mt 22:11–14). The parable is not only a statement of God's judgment on Israel but a warning to Matthew's church.

22:2 Wedding feast: the Old Testament's portrayal of final salvation under the image of a banquet (Is 25:6) is taken up also in Mt 8:11; cf. Lk 13:15.

22:3–4 Servants . . . other servants: probably Christian missionaries in both instances; cf. Mt 23:34.

22:7 See note on Mt 22:1–14.

22:10 Bad and good alike: cf. Mt 13:47.

22:11 A wedding garment: the repentance, change of heart and mind, that is the condition for entrance into the kingdom (Mt 3:2; 4:17) must be continued in a life of good deeds (Mt 7:21–23).

22:13 Wailing and grinding of teeth: the Christian who lacks the wedding garment of good deeds will suffer the same fate as those Jews who have rejected Jesus; see note on Mt 8:11–12.

22:15–22 The series of controversies between Jesus and the representatives of Judaism (see note on Mt 21:23–27) is resumed. As in the first (Mt 21:23–27), here and in the following disputes Matthew follows his Marcan source with few modifications.

22:15 The Pharisees: while Matthew retains the Marcan union of Pharisees and Herodians in this account, he clearly emphasizes the Pharisees' part. They alone are mentioned here, and the Herodians are joined with them only in a prepositional phrase of Mt 22:16. **Entrap him in speech**: the question that they will pose is intended to force Jesus to take either a position contrary to that held by the majority of the people or one that will bring him into conflict with the Roman authorities.

22:16 Herodians: see note on Mk 3:6. They would favor payment of the tax; the Pharisees did not.

d: Lk 14:15–24. *e:* 21:35. *f:* 8:12; 25:30. *g:* Mk 12:13–17; Lk 20:20–26.

"Teacher, we know that you are a truthful man and that you teach the way of God in accordance with the truth. And you are not concerned with anyone's opinion, for you do not regard a person's status. 17*Tell us, then, what is your opinion: Is it lawful to pay the census tax to Caesar or not?" 18Knowing their malice, Jesus said, "Why are you testing me, you hypocrites? 19*Show me the coin that pays the census tax." Then they handed him the Roman coin. 20He said to them, "Whose image is this and whose inscription?" 21h*They replied, "Caesar's." At that he said to them, "Then repay to Caesar what belongs to Caesar and to God what belongs to God." 22When they heard this they were amazed, and leaving him they went away.

The Question about the Resurrection. 23i*On that day Sadducees approached him, saying that there is no resurrection. They put this question to him, 24j*saying, "Teacher, Moses said, 'If a man dies without children, his brother shall marry his wife and raise up descendants for his brother.' 25Now there were seven brothers among us. The first married and died and, having no descendants, left his wife to his brother. 26The same happened with the second and the third, through all seven. 27Finally the woman died. 28Now at the resurrection, of the seven, whose wife will she be? For they all had been married to her." 29*Jesus said to them in reply, "You are misled because you do not know the scriptures or the power of God. 30At the resurrection they neither marry nor are given in marriage but are like the angels in heaven. 31*And concerning the resurrection of the dead, have you not read what was said to you by God, 32k'I am the God of Abraham, the God of Isaac, and the God of Jacob'? He is not the God of the dead but of the living." 33When the crowds heard this, they were astonished at his teaching.

The Greatest Commandment. 34l*When

22:17 Is it lawful: the law to which they refer is the law of God.

22:19 They handed him the Roman coin: their readiness in producing the money implies their use of it and their acceptance of the financial advantages of the Roman administration in Palestine.

22:21 Caesar's: the emperor Tiberius (A.D. 14–37). **Repay to Caesar what belongs to Caesar**: those who willingly use the coin that is Caesar's should **repay** him in kind. The answer avoids taking sides in the question of the lawfulness of the tax. **To God what belongs to God**: Jesus raises the debate to a new level. Those who have hypocritically asked about tax in respect to its relation to the law of **God** should be concerned rather with repaying God with the good deeds that are his due; cf. Mt 21:41, 43.

22:23–33 Here Jesus' opponents are the **Sadducees**, members of the powerful priestly party of his time; see note on Mt 3:7. Denying the resurrection of the dead, a teaching of relatively late origin in Judaism (cf. Dn 12:2), they appeal to a law of the Pentateuch (Dt 25:5–10) and present a case based on it that would make resurrection from the dead ridiculous (Mt 22:24–28). Jesus chides them for knowing neither **the scriptures** nor **the power of God** (Mt 22:29). His argument in respect to God's power contradicts the notion, held even by many proponents as well as by opponents of the teaching, that the life of those raised from the dead would be essentially a continuation of the type of life they had had before death (Mt 22:30). His argument based on the scriptures (Mt 22:31–32) is of a sort that was accepted as valid among Jews of the time.

22:23 Saying that there is no resurrection: in the Marcan parallel (Mk 22:12, 18) the Sadducees are correctly defined as those "who say there is no resurrection"; see also Lk 20:27. Matthew's rewording of Mark can mean that these particular Sadducees deny the resurrection, which would imply that he was not aware that the denial was characteristic of the party. For some scholars this is an indication of his being a Gentile Christian; see note on Mt 21:4–5.

22:24 'If a man dies . . . his brother': this is known as the "law of the levirate," from the Latin *levir*, "brother-in-law." Its purpose was to continue the family line of the deceased brother (Dt 25:6).

22:29 The sexual relationships of this world will be transcended; the risen body will be the work of the creative **power of God**.

22:31–32 Cf. Ex 3:6. In the Pentateuch, which the Sadducees accepted as normative for Jewish belief and practice, God speaks even now (**to you**) of himself as the God of the patriarchs who died centuries ago. He identifies himself in relation to them, and because of their relation to him, the living God, they too are alive. This might appear no argument for the resurrection, but simply for life after death as conceived in Wis 3:1–3. But the general thought of early first-century Judaism was not influenced by that conception; for it human immortality was connected with the existence of the body.

22:34–40 The Marcan parallel (Mk 12:28–34) is an exchange between Jesus and a scribe who is impressed by the way in which Jesus has conducted himself in the previous controversy (Mk 12:28), who compliments him for the answer he gives him (Mk 12:32), and who is said by Jesus to be "not far from the kingdom of God" (Mk 12:34). Matthew has sharpened that scene. The questioner, as the representative of other Pharisees, tests Jesus by his question (Mt 22:34–35), and both his reaction to Jesus' reply and Jesus' commendation of him are lacking.

h: Rom 13:7. *i:* Mk 12:18–27; Lk 20:27–40. *j:* Gn 38:8; Dt 25:5–6. *k:* Ex 3:6. *l:* Mk 12:28–34; Lk 10:25–28.

the Pharisees heard that he had silenced the
Sadducees, they gathered together, [35*]and
one of them [a scholar of the law] tested him
by asking, [36*]"Teacher, which commandment in the law is the greatest?" [37m*]He said
to him, "You shall love the Lord, your God,
with all your heart, with all your soul, and
with all your mind. [38]This is the greatest and
the first commandment. [39n*]The second is
like it: You shall love your neighbor as yourself. [40o*]The whole law and the prophets depend on these two commandments."

The Question about David's Son.
[41p*]While the Pharisees were gathered together, Jesus questioned them, [42*]saying,
"What is your opinion about the Messiah?
Whose son is he?" They replied, "David's."
[43]He said to them, "How, then, does David,
inspired by the Spirit, call him 'lord,' saying:

[44q] 'The Lord said to my lord,
"Sit at my right hand
until I place your enemies under your
feet" '?

[45*]If David calls him 'lord,' how can he be
his son?" [46r]No one was able to answer him
a word, nor from that day on did anyone dare
to ask him any more questions.

CHAPTER 23

See RG 383–84

Denunciation of the Scribes and Pharisees. [1s*]Then Jesus spoke to the
crowds and to his disciples, [2*]saying, "The
scribes and the Pharisees have taken their

22:35 [A scholar of the law]: meaning "scribe." Although this reading is supported by the vast majority of textual witnesses, it is the only time that the Greek word so translated occurs in Matthew. It is relatively frequent in Luke, and there is reason to think that it may have been added here by a copyist since it occurs in the Lucan parallel (Lk 10:25–28). **Tested**: see note on Mt 19:3.

22:36 For the devout Jew all the commandments were to be kept with equal care, but there is evidence of preoccupation in Jewish sources with the question put to Jesus.

22:37–38 Cf. Dt 6:5. Matthew omits the first part of Mark's fuller quotation (Mk 12:29; Dt 6:4–5), probably because he considered its monotheistic emphasis needless for his church. The love of God must engage the total person (**heart, soul, mind**).

22:39 Jesus goes beyond the extent of the question put to him and joins **to the greatest and the first commandment** a **second**, that of **love** of **neighbor**, Lv 19:18; see note on Mt 19:18–19. This combination of the two commandments may already have been made in Judaism.

22:40 The double commandment is the source from which **the whole law and the prophets** are derived.

22:41–46 Having answered the questions of his opponents in the preceding three controversies, Jesus now puts a question to them about the sonship of the Messiah. Their easy response (Mt 22:43a) is countered by his quoting a verse of Ps 110 that raises a problem for their response (43b–45). They are unable to solve it and **from that day on** their questioning of him is ended.

22:41 The Pharisees . . . questioned them: Mark is not specific about who are questioned (Mk 12:35).

22:42–44 David's: this view of the Pharisees was based on such Old Testament texts as Is 11:1–9; Jer 23:5; and Ez 34:23; see also the extrabiblical Psalms of Solomon Ps 17:21. **How, then . . . saying**: Jesus cites Ps 110:1 accepting the Davidic authorship of the psalm, a common view of his time. The psalm was probably composed for the enthronement of a Davidic king of Judah. Matthew assumes that the Pharisees interpret it as referring to the Messiah, although there is no clear evidence that it was so interpreted in the Judaism of Jesus' time. It was widely used in the early church as referring to the exaltation of the risen Jesus. **My lord**: understood as the Messiah.

22:45 Since Matthew presents Jesus both as Messiah (Mt 16:16) and as Son of David (Mt 1:1; see also note on Mt 9:27), the question is not meant to imply Jesus' denial of Davidic sonship. It probably means that although he is the Son of David, he is someone greater, Son of Man and Son of God, and recognized as greater by David who calls him my 'lord.'

23:1–39 The final section of the narrative part of the fifth book of the gospel is a denunciation by Jesus of the scribes and the Pharisees (see note on Mt 3:7). It depends in part on Mark and Q (cf. Mk 12:38–39; Lk 11:37–52; 13:34–35), but in the main it is peculiar to Matthew. (For the reasons against considering this extensive body of sayings-material either as one of the structural discourses of this gospel or as part of the one that follows in Mt 24–25, see note on Mt 19:1–23:39.) While the tradition of a deep opposition between Jesus and the Pharisees is well founded, this speech reflects an opposition that goes beyond that of Jesus' ministry and must be seen as expressing the bitter conflict between Pharisaic Judaism and the church of Matthew at the time when the gospel was composed. The complaint often made that the speech ignores the positive qualities of Pharisaism and of its better representatives is true, but the complaint overlooks the circumstances that gave rise to the invective. Nor is the speech purely anti-Pharisaic. The evangelist discerns in his church many of the same faults that he finds in its opponents and warns his fellow Christians to look to their own conduct and attitudes.

23:2–3 Have taken their seat . . . Moses: it is uncertain whether this is simply a metaphor for Mosaic teaching authority or refers to an actual **chair** on which the teacher sat. It has been proved that there was a seat so designated in synagogues of a later period than that of this gospel. **Do and observe . . . they tell you**: since the Matthean Jesus abrogates Mosaic law (Mt 5:31–42), warns his disciples against the teaching of the Pharisees (Mt 14:1–12), and, in this speech, denounces the Pharisees as blind guides in respect to their teaching on oaths (Mt 23:16–22), this commandment **to ob-**

m: Dt 6:5. *n:* Lv 19:18; Jas 2:8. *o:* Rom 13:8–10; Gal 5:14. *p:* Mk 12:35–37; Lk 20:41–44. *q:* Ps 110:1; Acts 2:35; Heb 1:13. *r:* Lk 20:40. *s:* Mk 12:38–39; Lk 11:37–52; 13:34–35.

seat on the chair of Moses. [3]Therefore, do
and observe all things whatsoever they tell
you, but do not follow their example. For
they preach but they do not practice. [4t*]They
tie up heavy burdens [hard to carry] and lay
them on people's shoulders, but they will not
lift a finger to move them. [5u*]All their works
are performed to be seen. They widen their
phylacteries and lengthen their tassels.
[6v*]They love places of honor at banquets,
seats of honor in synagogues, [7]greetings in
marketplaces, and the salutation 'Rabbi.'
[8*]As for you, do not be called 'Rabbi.' You
have but one teacher, and you are all brothers. [9]Call no one on earth your father; you
have but one Father in heaven. [10]Do not be
called 'Master'; you have but one master,
the Messiah. [11w]The greatest among you
must be your servant. [12x]Whoever exalts
himself will be humbled; but whoever humbles himself will be exalted.
[13y*]"Woe to you, scribes and Pharisees,
you hypocrites. You lock the kingdom of
heaven before human beings. You do not enter yourselves, nor do you allow entrance to
those trying to enter. [[14]]*
[15*]"Woe to you, scribes and Pharisees,
you hypocrites. You traverse sea and land to
make one convert, and when that happens
you make him a child of Gehenna twice as
much as yourselves.
[16z*]"Woe to you, blind guides, who say, 'If

serve all things whatsoever they (the scribes and Pharisees) **tell you** cannot be taken as the evangelist's understanding of the proper standard of conduct for his church. The saying may reflect a period when the Matthean community was largely Jewish Christian and was still seeking to avoid a complete break with the synagogue. Matthew has incorporated this traditional material into the speech in accordance with his view of the course of salvation history, in which he portrays the time of Jesus' ministry as marked by the fidelity to the law, although with significant pointers to the new situation that would exist after his death and resurrection (see note on Mt 5:17–20). The crowds and the disciples (Mt 23:1) are exhorted not to **follow** the **example** of the Jewish leaders, whose deeds do not conform to their teaching (Mt 23:3).

23:4 Tie up heavy burdens: see note on Mt 11:28.

23:5 To the charge of preaching but not practicing (Mt 23:3), Jesus adds that of acting in order to earn praise. The disciples have already been warned against this same fault (see note on Mt 6:1–18). **Phylacteries**: the Mosaic law required that during prayer small boxes containing parchments on which verses of scripture were written be worn on the left forearm and the forehead (see Ex 13:9, 16; Dt 6:8; 11:18). **Tassels**: see note on Mt 9:20. The widening of **phylacteries** and the lengthening of **tassels** were for the purpose of making these evidences of piety more noticeable.

23:6 Cf. Mk 12:38–39. **'Rabbi'**: literally, "my great one," a title of respect for teachers and leaders.

23:8–12 These verses, warning against the use of various titles, are addressed to the disciples alone. While only the title **'Rabbi'** has been said to be used in addressing the scribes and Pharisees (Mt 23:7), the implication is that **Father** and **'Master'** also were. The prohibition of these titles to the disciples suggests that their use was present in Matthew's church. The Matthean Jesus forbids not only the titles but the spirit of superiority and pride that is shown by their acceptance. **Whoever exalts . . . will be exalted**: cf. Lk 14:11.

23:13–36 This series of seven "woes," directed against the **scribes and Pharisees** and addressed to them, is the heart of the speech. The phrase **woe to** occurs often in the prophetic and apocalyptic literature, expressing horror of a sin and punishment for those who commit it. **Hypocrites**: see note on Mt 6:2. The hypocrisy of the **scribes and Pharisees** consists in the difference between their speech and action Mt 23:3 and in demonstrations of piety that have no other purpose than to enhance their reputation as religious persons (Mt 23:5).

23:13 You lock the kingdom of heaven: cf. Mt 16:19 where Jesus tells Peter that he will give him the keys to **the kingdom of heaven**. The purpose of the authority expressed by that metaphor is to give entrance into the kingdom (the kingdom is closed only to those who reject the authority); here the charge is made that the authority of the **scribes and Pharisees** is exercised in such a way as to be an obstacle to entrance. Cf. Lk 11:52 where the accusation against the "scholars of the law" (Matthew's **scribes**) is that they "have taken away the key of knowledge."

23:14 Some manuscripts add a verse here or after Mt 23:12 "Woe to you, scribes and Pharisees, you hypocrites. You devour the houses of widows and, as a pretext, recite lengthy prayers. Because of this, you will receive a very severe condemnation." Cf. Mk 12:40; Lk 20:47. This "woe" is almost identical with Mk 12:40 and seems to be an interpolation derived from that text.

23:15 In the first century A.D. until the First Jewish Revolt against Rome (A.D. 66–70), many Pharisees conducted a vigorous missionary campaign among Gentiles. **Convert**: literally, "proselyte," a Gentile who accepted Judaism fully by submitting to circumcision and all other requirements of Mosaic law. **Child of Gehenna**: worthy of everlasting punishment; for **Gehenna**, see note on Mt 5:22. **Twice as much as yourselves**: possibly this refers simply to the zeal of the **convert**, surpassing that of the one who converted him.

23:16–22 An attack on the casuistry that declared some oaths binding (**one is obligated**) and others not (**it means nothing**) and held the binding oath to be the one made by something of lesser value (**the gold; the gift on the altar**). Such teaching, which inverts the order of values, reveals the teachers to be **blind guides**; cf. Mt 15:14. Since the Matthean Jesus forbids all oaths to his disciples (Mt 5:33–37), this woe does not set up a standard for Christian moral conduct, but ridicules the Pharisees on their own terms.

t: Lk 11:46. *u:* 6:1–6; Ex 13:9, 16; Nm 15:38–39; Dt 6:8; 11:18. *v:* Mk 12:38–39; Lk 11:43; 20:46. *w:* 20:26. *x:* Lk 14:11; 18:14. *y:* Lk 11:52. *z:* 15:14.

one swears by the temple, it means nothing, but if one swears by the gold of the temple, one is obligated.' [17]Blind fools, which is greater, the gold, or the temple that made the gold sacred? [18]And you say, 'If one swears by the altar, it means nothing, but if one swears by the gift on the altar, one is obligated.' [19]You blind ones, which is greater, the gift, or the altar that makes the gift sacred? [20a]One who swears by the altar swears by it and all that is upon it; [21]one who swears by the temple swears by it and by him who dwells in it; [22]one who swears by heaven swears by the throne of God and by him who is seated on it.

[23b*]"Woe to you, scribes and Pharisees, you hypocrites. You pay tithes of mint and dill and cummin, and have neglected the weightier things of the law: judgment and mercy and fidelity. [But] these you should have done, without neglecting the others. [24c*]Blind guides, who strain out the gnat and swallow the camel!

[25d*]"Woe to you, scribes and Pharisees, you hypocrites. You cleanse the outside of cup and dish, but inside they are full of plunder and self-indulgence. [26]Blind Pharisee, cleanse first the inside of the cup, so that the outside also may be clean.

[27*]"Woe to you, scribes and Pharisees, you hypocrites. You are like whitewashed tombs, which appear beautiful on the outside, but inside are full of dead men's bones and every kind of filth. [28e]Even so, on the outside you appear righteous, but inside you are filled with hypocrisy and evildoing.

[29*]"Woe to you, scribes and Pharisees, you hypocrites. You build the tombs of the prophets and adorn the memorials of the righteous, [30f]and you say, 'If we had lived in the days of our ancestors, we would not have joined them in shedding the prophets' blood.' [31g]Thus you bear witness against yourselves that you are the children of those who murdered the prophets; [32]now fill up what your ancestors measured out! [33h]You serpents, you brood of vipers, how can you flee from the judgment of Gehenna? [34i*]Therefore, behold, I send to you prophets

23:23 The Mosaic law ordered tithing of the produce of the land (Lv 27:30; Dt 14:22–23), and the scribal tradition is said here to have extended this law to even the smallest herbs. The practice is criticized not in itself but because it shows the Pharisees' preoccupation with matters of less importance while they neglect **the weightier things of the law**.

23:24 Cf. Lv 11:41–45 that forbids the eating of any "swarming creature." The Pharisees' scrupulosity about minor matters and neglect of greater ones (Mt 23:23) is further brought out by this contrast between straining liquids that might contain a tiny "swarming creature" and yet swallowing **the camel**. The latter was one of the unclean animals forbidden by the law (Lv 11:4), but it is hardly possible that the scribes and Pharisees are being denounced as guilty of so gross a violation of the food laws. To **swallow the camel** is only a hyperbolic way of speaking of their neglect of what is important.

23:25–26 The ritual washing of utensils for dining (cf. Mk 7:4) is turned into a metaphor illustrating a concern for appearances while inner purity is ignored. The **scribes and Pharisees** are compared to cups carefully washed on the outside but filthy within. **Self-indulgence**: the Greek word here translated means lack of self-control, whether in drinking or in sexual conduct.

23:27–28 The sixth **woe**, like the preceding one, deals with concern for externals and neglect of what is **inside**. Since contact with dead bodies, even when one was unaware of it, caused ritual impurity (Nm 19:11–22), tombs were whitewashed so that no one would contract such impurity inadvertently.

23:29–36 The final **woe** is the most serious indictment of all. It portrays the **scribes and Pharisees** as standing in the same line as their **ancestors** who murdered **the prophets** and **the righteous**.

23:29–32 In spite of honoring the slain dead by building their **tombs** and adorning their **memorials**, and claiming that they would not have joined in their ancestors' crimes if they **had lived in** their **days**, the **scribes and Pharisees** are true children of their ancestors and are defiantly ordered by Jesus to **fill up** what those **ancestors measured out**. This order reflects the Jewish notion that there was an allotted measure of suffering that had to be completed before God's final judgment would take place.

23:34–36 There are important differences between the Matthean and the Lucan form of this Q material; cf. Lk 11:49–51. In Luke the one who sends the emissaries is the "wisdom of God." If, as many scholars think, that is the original wording of Q, Matthew, by making Jesus the sender, has presented him as the personified divine wisdom. In Luke, wisdom's emissaries are the Old Testament "prophets" and the Christian "apostles." Matthew's **prophets and wise men and scribes** are probably Christian disciples alone; cf. Mt 10:41 and see note on Mt 13:52. **You will kill**: see Mt 24:9. **Scourge in your synagogues . . . town to town**: see Mt 10:17, 23 and the note on Mt 10:17. **All the righteous blood shed upon the earth**: the slaying of the disciples is in continuity with all the shedding of **righteous blood** beginning with that of **Abel**. The persecution of Jesus' disciples by **this generation** involves the persecutors in the guilt of their murderous ancestors. **The blood of Zechariah**: see note on Lk 11:51. By identifying him as **the son of Barachiah** Matthew understands him to be Zechariah the Old Testament minor prophet; see Zec 1:1.

a: 5:34–35. *b:* Lv 27:30; Dt 14:22; Lk 11:42. *c:* Lv 11:41–45. *d:* Mk 7:4; Lk 11:39. *e:* Lk 16:15; 18:9. *f:* Lk 11:47. *g:* Acts 7:52. *h:* 3:7; 12:34. *i:* 5:12; Gn 4:8; 2 Chr 24:20–22; Zec 1:1; Lk 11:49–51; Rev 18:24.

and wise men and scribes; some of them you will kill and crucify, some of them you will scourge in your synagogues and pursue from town to town, [35]so that there may come upon you all the righteous blood shed upon earth, from the righteous blood of Abel to the blood of Zechariah, the son of Barachiah, whom you murdered between the sanctuary and the altar. [36]Amen, I say to you, all these things will come upon this generation.

The Lament over Jerusalem. [37jk*]"Jerusalem, Jerusalem, you who kill the prophets and stone those sent to you, how many times I yearned to gather your children together, as a hen gathers her young under her wings, but you were unwilling! [38l]Behold, your house will be abandoned, desolate. [39m]I tell you, you will not see me again until you say, 'Blessed is he who comes in the name of the Lord.' "

CHAPTER 24

See RG 383–84

The Destruction of the Temple Foretold. [1n*]Jesus left the temple area and was going away, when his disciples approached him to point out the temple buildings. [2*]He said to them in reply, "You see all these things, do you not? Amen, I say to you, there will not be left here a stone upon another stone that will not be thrown down."

The Beginning of Calamities. [3*]As he was sitting on the Mount of Olives, the disciples approached him privately and said, "Tell us, when will this happen, and what sign will there be of your coming, and of the end of the age?" [4*]Jesus said to them in reply, "See that no one deceives you. [5]For many will come in my name, saying, 'I am the Messiah,' and they will deceive many. [6o*]You will hear of wars and reports of wars;

23:37–39 Cf. Lk 13:34–35. The denunciation of Pharisaic Judaism ends with this lament over **Jerusalem**, which has repeatedly rejected and murdered those whom God has **sent** to her. **How many times**: this may refer to various visits of Jesus to the city, an aspect of his ministry found in John but otherwise not in the synoptics. **As a hen . . . under her wings**: for imagery similar to this, see Ps 17:8; 91:4. **Your house . . . desolate**: probably an allusion to the destruction of the temple in A.D. 70. **You will not see me . . . in the name of the Lord**: Israel will not see Jesus again until he comes in glory for the final judgment. The acclamation has been interpreted in contrasting ways, as an indication that Israel will at last accept Jesus at that time, and as its troubled recognition of him as its dreaded judge who will pronounce its condemnation; in support of the latter view see Mt 24:30.

24:1–25:46 The discourse of the fifth book, the last of the five around which the gospel is structured. It is called the "eschatological" discourse since it deals with the coming of the new age (the *eschaton*) in its fullness, with events that will precede it, and with how the disciples are to conduct themselves while awaiting an event that is as certain as its exact time is unknown to all but the Father (Mt 24:36). The discourse may be divided into two parts, Mt 24:1–44 and Mt 24:45–25:46. In the first, Matthew follows his Marcan source (Mk 13:1–37) closely. The second is drawn from Q and from the evangelist's own traditional material. Both parts show Matthew's editing of his sources by deletions, additions, and modifications. The vigilant waiting that is emphasized in the second part does not mean a cessation of ordinary activity and concentration only on what is to come, but a faithful accomplishment of duties at hand, with awareness that the end, for which the disciples must always be ready, will entail the great judgment by which the everlasting destiny of all will be determined.

24:2 As in Mark, Jesus predicts the destruction of the temple. By omitting the Marcan story of the widow's contribution (Mk 12:41–44) that immediately precedes the prediction in that gospel, Matthew has established a close connection between it and Mt 23:38, ". . . your house will be abandoned desolate."

24:3 The Mount of Olives: see note on Mt 21:1. **The disciples**: cf. Mk 13:3–4 where only Peter, James, John, and Andrew put the question that is answered by the discourse. In both gospels, however, the question is put **privately**: the ensuing discourse is only for those who are **disciples** of Jesus. **When will this happen . . . end of the age?**: Matthew distinguishes carefully between the destruction of the temple (**this**) and the **coming** of Jesus that will bring **the end of the age**. In Mark the two events are more closely connected, a fact that may be explained by Mark's believing that the one would immediately succeed the other. **Coming**: this translates the Greek word *parousia*, which is used in the gospels only here and in Mt 24:27, 37, 39. It designated the official visit of a ruler to a city or the manifestation of a saving deity, and it was used by Christians to refer to the final coming of Jesus in glory, a term first found in the New Testament with that meaning in 1 Thes 2:19. **The end of the age**: see note on Mt 13:39.

24:4–14 This section of the discourse deals with calamities in the world (Mt 24:6–7) and in the church (Mt 24:9–12). The former **must happen** before **the end** comes (Mt 24:6), but they are only the **beginning of the labor pains** (Mt 24:8). (It may be noted that the Greek word translated **the end** in Mt 24:6 and in Mt 24:13–14 is not the same as the phrase "the end of the age" in Mt 24:3 although the meaning is the same.) The latter are sufferings of the church, both from within and without, that will last until **the gospel** is **preached . . . to all nations. Then the end will come** and those who have endured the sufferings with fidelity **will be saved** (Mt 24:13–14).

24:6–7 The disturbances mentioned here are a commonplace of apocalyptic language, as is the assurance that they **must happen** (see Dn 2:28 LXX), for that is the plan of God. **Kingdom against kingdom**: see Is 19:2.

j: Lk 13:34–35; 19:41–44. *k:* 21:35. *l:* Jer 12:7. *m:* Ps 118:26. *n:* Mk 13:1–37; Lk 21:5–36. *o:* Dn 2:28 LXX.

see that you are not alarmed, for these things
must happen, but it will not yet be the end.
[7p]Nation will rise against nation, and kingdom against kingdom; there will be famines
and earthquakes from place to place. [8*]All
these are the beginning of the labor pains.
[9q*]Then they will hand you over to persecution, and they will kill you. You will be hated
by all nations because of my name. [10]And
then many will be led into sin; they will betray and hate one another. [11]Many false
prophets will arise and deceive many; [12]and
because of the increase of evildoing, the
love of many will grow cold. [13r]But the one
who perseveres to the end will be saved.
[14s*]And this gospel of the kingdom will be
preached throughout the world as a witness
to all nations, and then the end will come.

The Great Tribulation. [15t*]"When you see
the desolating abomination spoken of through
Daniel the prophet standing in the holy place
(let the reader understand), [16*]then those in
Judea must flee to the mountains, [17u*]a person
on the housetop must not go down to get
things out of his house, [18]a person in the field
must not return to get his cloak. [19]Woe to
pregnant women and nursing mothers in those
days. [20*]Pray that your flight not be in winter
or on the sabbath, [21v*]for at that time there will
be great tribulation, such as has not been since
the beginning of the world until now, nor ever
will be. [22]And if those days had not been

24:8 The labor pains: the tribulations leading up to the end of the age are compared to the pains of a woman about to give birth. There is much attestation for rabbinic use of the phrase "the woes (or birth pains) of the Messiah" after the New Testament period, but in at least one instance it is attributed to a rabbi who lived in the late first century A.D. In this Jewish usage it meant the distress of the time preceding the coming of the Messiah; here, the **labor pains** precede the coming of the Son of Man in glory.

24:9–12 Matthew has used Mk 13:9–12 in his missionary discourse (Mt 10:17–21) and omits it here. Besides the sufferings, including death, and the hatred of **all nations** that the disciples will have to endure, there will be worse affliction within the church itself. This is described in Mt 24:10–12, which are peculiar to Matthew. **Will be led into sin**: literally, "will be scandalized," probably meaning that they will become apostates; see Mt 13:21 where "fall away" translates the same Greek word as here. **Betray**: in the Greek this is the same word as the **hand over** of Mt 24:9. The handing over to persecution and hatred from outside will have their counterpart within the church. **False prophets**: these are Christians; see note on Mt 7:15–20. **Evildoing**: see Mt 7:23. Because of the apocalyptic nature of much of this discourse, the literal meaning of this description of the church should not be pressed too hard. However, there is reason to think that Matthew's addition of these verses reflects in some measure the condition of his community.

24:14 Except for the last part (**and then the end will come**), this verse substantially repeats Mk 13:10. The Matthean addition raises a problem since what follows in Mt 24:15–23 refers to the horrors of the First Jewish Revolt including the destruction of the temple, and Matthew, writing after that time, knew that the parousia of Jesus was still in the future. A solution may be that the evangelist saw the events of those verses as foreshadowing the cosmic disturbances that he associates with the parousia (Mt 24:29) so that the period in which the former took place could be understood as belonging to **the end**.

24:15–28 Cf. Mk 13:14–23; Lk 17:23–24, 37. A further stage in the tribulations that will precede the coming of the Son of Man, and an answer to the question of Mt 24:3a, "when will this (the destruction of the temple) happen?"

24:15 The desolating abomination: in 167 B.C. the Syrian king Antiochus IV Epiphanes desecrated the temple by setting up in it a statue of Zeus Olympios (see 1 Mc 1:54). That event is referred to in Dn 12:11 LXX as the "desolating abomination" (NAB "horrible abomination") and the same Greek term is used here; cf. also Dn 9:27; 11:31. Although the desecration had taken place before Daniel was written, it is presented there as a future event, and Matthew sees that "prophecy" fulfilled in the desecration of the temple by the Romans. **In the holy place**: the temple; more precise than Mark's **where he should not** (Mk 13:14). **Let the reader understand**: this parenthetical remark, taken from Mk 13:14 invites **the reader** to realize the meaning of Daniel's "prophecy."

24:16 The tradition that the Christians of Jerusalem fled from that city to Pella, a city of Transjordan, at the time of the First Jewish Revolt is found in Eusebius (*Ecclesiastical History*, 3, 5, 3), who attributes the flight to "a certain oracle given by revelation before the war." The tradition is not improbable but the Matthean command, derived from its Marcan source, is vague in respect to the place of flight (**to the mountains**), although some scholars see it as applicable to the flight to Pella.

24:17–19 Haste is essential, and the journey will be particularly difficult for women who are burdened with unborn or infant children.

24:20 On the sabbath: this addition to **in winter** (cf. Mk 13:18) has been understood as an indication that Matthew was addressed to a church still observing the Mosaic law of sabbath rest and the scribal limitations upon the length of journeys that might lawfully be made on that day. That interpretation conflicts with Matthew's view on sabbath observance (cf. Mt 12:1–14). The meaning of the addition may be that those undertaking on the sabbath a journey such as the one here ordered would be offending the sensibilities of law-observant Jews and would incur their hostility.

24:21 For the unparalleled distress of that time, see Dn 12:1.

---

p: Is 19:2. *q:* 10:17. *r:* 10:22. *s:* 28:19; Rom 10:18. *t:* Dn 9:27; 11:31; 12:11; Mk 13:14. *u:* Lk 17:31. *v:* Dn 12:1.

shortened, no one would be saved; but for the sake of the elect they will be shortened. [23w]If anyone says to you then, 'Look, here is the Messiah!' or, 'There he is!' do not believe it. [24]False messiahs and false prophets will arise, and they will perform signs and wonders so great as to deceive, if that were possible, even the elect. [25]Behold, I have told it to you beforehand. [26*]So if they say to you, 'He is in the desert,' do not go out there; if they say, 'He is in the inner rooms,' do not believe it. [27x]For just as lightning comes from the east and is seen as far as the west, so will the coming of the Son of Man be. [28]Wherever the corpse is, there the vultures will gather.

The Coming of the Son of Man. [29y*]"Immediately after the tribulation of those days,

the sun will be darkened,
and the moon will not give its light,
and the stars will fall from the sky,
and the powers of the heavens will be shaken.

[30z*]And then the sign of the Son of Man will appear in heaven, and all the tribes of the earth will mourn, and they will see the Son of Man coming upon the clouds of heaven with power and great glory. [31a*]And he will send out his angels with a trumpet blast, and they will gather his elect from the four winds, from one end of the heavens to the other.

The Lesson of the Fig Tree. [32*]"Learn a lesson from the fig tree. When its branch becomes tender and sprouts leaves, you know that summer is near. [33]In the same way, when you see all these things, know that he is near, at the gates. [34*]Amen, I say to you, this generation will not pass away until all these things have taken place. [35b]Heaven and earth will pass away, but my words will not pass away.

The Unknown Day and Hour. [36c*]"But of that day and hour no one knows, neither the angels of heaven, nor the Son, but the Father alone. [37d*]For as it was in the days of Noah, so it will be at the coming of the Son of Man. [38]In [those] days before the flood, they were eating and drinking, marrying and giving in marriage, up to the day that Noah entered the ark. [39]They did not know until the flood came and carried them all away. So will it be [also] at the coming of the Son of Man. [40e*]Two men will be out in the field; one will

24:26–28 Claims that the Messiah is to be found in some distant or secret place must be ignored. **The coming of the Son of Man** will be as clear as **lightning** is to all and as **the corpse** of an animal is to **vultures**; cf. Lk 17:24, 37. Here there is clear identification of the **Son of Man** and the Messiah; cf. Mt 24:23.

24:29 The answer to the question of Mt 24:3b "What will be the sign of your coming?" **Immediately after . . . those days**: the shortening of time between the preceding **tribulation** and the parousia has been explained as Matthew's use of a supposed device of Old Testament prophecy whereby certainty that a predicted event will occur is expressed by depicting it as imminent. While it is questionable that that is an acceptable understanding of the Old Testament predictions, it may be applicable here, for Matthew knew that the parousia had not come **immediately after** the fall of Jerusalem, and it is unlikely that he is attributing a mistaken calculation of time to Jesus. **The sun . . . be shaken**: cf. Is 13:10, 13.

24:30 The sign of the Son of Man: perhaps this means **the sign** that is the glorious appearance **of the Son of Man**; cf. Mt 12:39–40 where "the sign of Jonah" is Jonah's being in the "belly of the whale." **Tribes of the earth will mourn**: peculiar to Matthew; cf. Zec 12:12–14. **Coming upon the clouds . . . glory**: cf. Dn 7:13 although there the "one like a son of man" comes to God to receive kingship; here **the Son of Man** comes from heaven for judgment.

24:31 Send out his angels: cf. Mt 13:41 where they are sent out to collect the wicked for punishment. **Trumpet blast**: cf. Is 27:13; 1 Thes 4:16.

24:32–35 Cf. Mk 13:28–31.

24:34 The difficulty raised by this verse cannot be satisfactorily removed by the supposition that **this generation** means the Jewish people throughout the course of their history, much less the entire human race. Perhaps for Matthew it means the **generation** to which he and his community belonged.

24:36–44 The statement of Mt 24:34 is now counterbalanced by one that declares that the exact time of the parousia is known only to **the Father** (Mt 24:36), and the disciples are warned to be always ready for it. This section is drawn from Mark and Q (cf. Lk 17:26–27, 34–35; 12:39–40).

24:36 Many textual witnesses omit **nor the Son**, which follows Mk 13:32. Since its omission can be explained by reluctance to attribute this ignorance to **the Son**, the reading that includes it is probably original.

24:37–39 Cf. Lk 17:26–27. **In the days of Noah**: the Old Testament account of the flood lays no emphasis upon what is central for Matthew, i.e., the unexpected coming of the flood upon those who were unprepared for it.

24:40–41 Cf. Lk 17:34–35. **Taken . . . left**: the former probably means **taken** into the kingdom; the latter, **left** for destruction. People in the same situation will be dealt with in opposite ways. In this context, the discrimination between them will be based on their readiness for the coming of the Son of Man.

w: Lk 17:23. *x:* Lk 17:24, 37. *y:* Is 13:10, 13; Ez 32:7; Am 8:9. *z:* Dn 7:13; Zec 12:12–14; Rev 1:7. *a:* Is 27:13; 1 Cor 15:52; 1 Thes 4:16. *b:* Is 40:8. *c:* Acts 1:7. *d:* Gn 6:5–7:23; Lk 17:26–27; 2 Pt 3:6. *e:* Lk 17:34–35.

be taken, and one will be left. [41]Two women
will be grinding at the mill; one will be
taken, and one will be left. [42f*]Therefore,
stay awake! For you do not know on which
day your Lord will come. [43g]Be sure of this:
if the master of the house had known the
hour of night when the thief was coming, he
would have stayed awake and not let his
house be broken into. [44]So too, you also
must be prepared, for at an hour you do not
expect, the Son of Man will come.

The Faithful or the Unfaithful Servant.
[45h*]"Who, then, is the faithful and prudent
servant, whom the master has put in charge
of his household to distribute to them their
food at the proper time? [46]Blessed is that servant whom his master on his arrival finds doing so. [47]Amen, I say to you, he will put him
in charge of all his property. [48*]But if that
wicked servant says to himself, 'My master
is long delayed,' [49]and begins to beat his fellow servants, and eat and drink with drunkards, [50]the servant's master will come on an
unexpected day and at an unknown hour
[51i*]and will punish him severely and assign
him a place with the hypocrites, where there
will be wailing and grinding of teeth.

See RG 383–84

CHAPTER 25

The Parable of the Ten Virgins.
[1*]"Then the kingdom of heaven will be like
ten virgins who took their lamps and went
out to meet the bridegroom. [2*]Five of them
were foolish and five were wise. [3]The foolish ones, when taking their lamps, brought
no oil with them, [4]but the wise brought
flasks of oil with their lamps. [5]Since the
bridegroom was long delayed, they all became drowsy and fell asleep. [6]At midnight,
there was a cry, 'Behold, the bridegroom!
Come out to meet him!' [7]Then all those virgins got up and trimmed their lamps. [8]The
foolish ones said to the wise, 'Give us some
of your oil, for our lamps are going out.'
[9]But the wise ones replied, 'No, for there
may not be enough for us and you. Go instead to the merchants and buy some for
yourselves.' [10]While they went off to buy it,
the bridegroom came and those who were
ready went into the wedding feast with him.
Then the door was locked. [11j*]Afterwards
the other virgins came and said, 'Lord, Lord,
open the door for us!' [12]But he said in reply,
'Amen, I say to you, I do not know you.'
[13k*]Therefore, stay awake, for you know neither the day nor the hour.

The Parable of the Talents. [14l*]"It will be
as when a man who was going on a journey
called in his servants and entrusted his possessions to them. [15*]To one he gave five talents; to another, two; to a third, one—to each
according to his ability. Then he went away.

24:42–44 Cf. Lk 12:39–40. The theme of vigilance and readiness is continued with the bold comparison of the Son of Man to a thief who comes to break into a house.

24:45–51 The second part of the discourse (see note on Mt 24:1–25:46) begins with this parable of **the faithful** or unfaithful **servant**; cf. Lk 12:41–46. It is addressed to the leaders of Matthew's church; **the servant has** been **put in charge** of his master's **household** (Mt 24:45) even though that household is composed of those who are his **fellow servants** (Mt 24:49).

24:45 To distribute . . . proper time: readiness for the master's return means a vigilance that is accompanied by faithful performance of the duty assigned.

24:48 My master . . . delayed: the note of delay is found also in the other parables of this section; cf. Mt 25:5, 19.

24:51 Punish him severely: the Greek verb, found in the New Testament only here and in the Lucan parallel (Lk 12:46), means, literally, "cut in two." **With the hypocrites**: see note on Mt 6:2. Matthew classes the unfaithful Christian leader with the unbelieving leaders of Judaism. **Wailing and grinding of teeth**: see note on Mt 8:11–12.

25:1–13 Peculiar to Matthew.

25:1 Then: at the time of the parousia. **Kingdom . . . will be like**: see note on Mt 13:24–30.

25:2–4 Foolish . . . wise: cf. the contrasted "wise man" and "fool" of Mt 7:24, 26 where the two are distinguished by good deeds and lack of them, and such deeds may be signified by the oil of this parable.

25:11–12 Lord, Lord: cf. Mt 7:21. **I do not know you**: cf. Mt 7:23 where the Greek verb is different but synonymous.

25:13 Stay awake: some scholars see this command as an addition to the original parable of Matthew's traditional material, since in Mt 25:5 all the virgins, wise and foolish, fall asleep. But the wise virgins are adequately equipped for their task, and stay awake may mean no more than to be prepared; cf. Mt 24:42, 44.

25:14–30 Cf. Lk 19:12–27.

25:14 It will be as when . . . journey: literally, "For just as a man who was going on a journey." Although the comparison is not completed, the sense is clear; the kingdom of heaven is like the situation here described. Faithful use of one's gifts will lead to participation in the fullness of the kingdom, lazy inactivity to exclusion from it.

25:15 Talents: see note on Mt 18:24.

f: 25:13; Lk 12:39–40. *g:* 1 Thes 5:2. *h:* Lk 12:41–46. *i:* 13:42; 25:30. *j:* 7:21, 23; Lk 13:25–27. *k:* 24:42; Mk 13:33. *l:* Lk 19:12–27.

Immediately [16]the one who received five talents went and traded with them, and made another five. [17]Likewise, the one who received two made another two. [18*]But the man who received one went off and dug a hole in the ground and buried his master's money. [19]After a long time the master of those servants came back and settled accounts with them. [20*]The one who had received five talents came forward bringing the additional five. He said, 'Master, you gave me five talents. See, I have made five more.' [21m]His master said to him, 'Well done, my good and faithful servant. Since you were faithful in small matters, I will give you great responsibilities. Come, share your master's joy.' [22][Then] the one who had received two talents also came forward and said, 'Master, you gave me two talents. See, I have made two more.' [23]His master said to him, 'Well done, my good and faithful servant. Since you were faithful in small matters, I will give you great responsibilities. Come, share your master's joy.' [24]Then the one who had received the one talent came forward and said, 'Master, I knew you were a demanding person, harvesting where you did not plant and gathering where you did not scatter; [25]so out of fear I went off and buried your talent in the ground. Here it is back.' [26*]His master said to him in reply, 'You wicked, lazy servant! So you knew that I harvest where I did not plant and gather where I did not scatter? [27]Should you not then have put my money in the bank so that I could have got it back with interest on my return? [28]Now then! Take the talent from him and give it to the one with ten. [29n*]For to everyone who has, more will be given and he will grow rich; but from the one who has not, even what he has will be taken away. [30*]And throw this useless servant into the darkness outside, where there will be wailing and grinding of teeth.'

The Judgment of the Nations. [31o*]"When the Son of Man comes in his glory, and all the angels with him, he will sit upon his glorious throne, [32p*]and all the nations will be assembled before him. And he will separate them one from another, as a shepherd separates the sheep from the goats. [33]He will place the sheep on his right and the goats on his left. [34]Then the king will say to those on his right, 'Come, you who are blessed by my Father. Inherit the kingdom prepared for you from the foundation of the world. [35q]For I was hungry and you gave me food, I was thirsty and you gave me drink, a stranger and you welcomed me, [36]naked and you clothed me, ill and you cared for me, in prison and you visited me.' [37*]Then the righteous will answer him and say, 'Lord, when did we see

25:18 Buried his master's money: see note on Mt 13:44.

25:20–23 Although the first two servants have received and doubled large sums, their faithful trading is regarded by the master as fidelity **in small matters** only, compared with **the great responsibilities** now to be given to them. The latter are unspecified. **Share your master's joy**: probably the joy of the banquet of the kingdom; cf. Mt 8:11.

25:26–28 Wicked, lazy servant: this man's inactivity is not negligible but seriously culpable. As punishment, he loses the gift he had received, that is now given to the first servant, whose possessions are already great.

25:29 See note on Mt 13:12 where there is a similar application of this maxim.

25:30 See note on Mt 8:11–12.

25:31–46 The conclusion of the discourse, which is peculiar to Matthew, portrays the final judgment that will accompany the parousia. Although often called a "parable," it is not really such, for the only parabolic elements are the depiction of **the Son of Man** as a **shepherd** and of **the righteous** and the wicked as sheep and goats respectively (Mt 25:32–33). The criterion of judgment will be the deeds of mercy that have been done for the **least** of Jesus' **brothers** (Mt 25:40). A difficult and important question is the identification of these **least brothers**. Are they all people who have suffered hunger, thirst, etc. (Mt 25:35, 36) or a particular group of such sufferers? Scholars are divided in their response and arguments can be made for either side. But leaving aside the problem of what the traditional material that Matthew edited may have meant, it seems that a stronger case can be made for the view that in the evangelist's sense the sufferers are Christians, probably Christian missionaries whose sufferings were brought upon them by their preaching of the gospel. The criterion of judgment for **all the nations** is their treatment of those who have borne to the world the message of Jesus, and this means ultimately their acceptance or rejection of Jesus himself; cf. Mt 10:40, "Whoever receives you, receives me." See note on Mt 16:27.

25:32 All the nations: before the end the gospel will have been preached throughout the world (Mt 24:14); thus the Gentiles will be judged on their response to it. But the phrase **all the nations** includes the Jews also, for at the judgment "the Son of Man . . . will repay everyone according to his conduct" (Mt 16:27).

25:37–40 The righteous will be astonished that in caring for the needs of the sufferers they were ministering to the **Lord** himself. **One of these least brothers of mine**: cf. Mt 10:42.

m: Lk 16:10. *n:* 13:12; Mk 4:25; Lk 8:18; 19:26. *o:* 16:27; Dt 33:2 LXX. *p:* Ez 34:17. *q:* Is 58:7; Ez 18:7.

you hungry and feed you, or thirsty and give you drink? [38]When did we see you a stranger and welcome you, or naked and clothe you? [39]When did we see you ill or in prison, and visit you?' [40r]And the king will say to them in reply, 'Amen, I say to you, whatever you did for one of these least brothers of mine, you did for me.' [41s*]Then he will say to those on his left, 'Depart from me, you accursed, into the eternal fire prepared for the devil and his angels. [42t]For I was hungry and you gave me no food, I was thirsty and you gave me no drink, [43]a stranger and you gave me no welcome, naked and you gave me no clothing, ill and in prison, and you did not care for me.' [44*]Then they will answer and say, 'Lord, when did we see you hungry or thirsty or a stranger or naked or ill or in prison, and not minister to your needs?' [45]He will answer them, 'Amen, I say to you, what you did not do for one of these least ones, you did not do for me.' [46u]And these will go off to eternal punishment, but the righteous to eternal life."

VII. The Passion and Resurrection

CHAPTER 26

See RG 384–86

The Conspiracy against Jesus. [1*]When Jesus finished all these words, he said to his disciples, [2v]"You know that in two days' time it will be Passover, and the Son of Man will be handed over to be crucified." [3*]Then the chief priests and the elders of the people assembled in the palace of the high priest, who was called Caiaphas, [4w]and they consulted together to arrest Jesus by treachery and put him to death. [5*]But they said, "Not during the festival, that there may not be a riot among the people."

The Anointing at Bethany. [6x*]Now when Jesus was in Bethany in the house of Simon the leper, [7]a woman came up to him with an alabaster jar of costly perfumed oil, and poured it on his head while he was reclining at table. [8]When the disciples saw this, they were indignant and said, "Why this waste? [9]It could have been sold for much, and the money given to the poor." [10]Since Jesus knew this, he said to them, "Why do you make trouble for the woman? She has done a good thing for me. [11y]The poor you will always have with you; but you will not always have me. [12*]In pouring this perfumed oil upon my body, she did it to prepare me for burial. [13]Amen, I say to you, wherever this gospel is proclaimed in the whole world, what she has done will be spoken of, in memory of her."

The Betrayal by Judas. [14z*]Then one of the Twelve, who was called Judas Iscariot, went to the chief priests [15a*]and said, "What

25:41 Fire prepared . . . his angels: cf. 1 Enoch 10:13 where it is said of the evil angels and Semyaza, their leader, "In those days they will lead them into the bottom of the fire—and in torment—in the prison (where) they will be locked up forever."

25:44–45 The **accursed** (Mt 25:41) will be likewise astonished that their neglect of the sufferers was neglect of the **Lord** and will receive from him a similar answer.

26:1–28:20 The five books with alternating narrative and discourse (Mt 3:1–25:46) that give this gospel its distinctive structure lead up to the climactic events that are the center of Christian belief and the origin of the Christian church, the passion and resurrection of Jesus. In his passion narrative (Mt 26:26–27) Matthew follows his Marcan source closely but with omissions (e.g., Mk 14:51–52) and additions (e.g., Mt 27:3–10, 19). Some of the additions indicate that he utilized traditions that he had received from elsewhere; others are due to his own theological insight (e.g., Mt 26:28 ". . . for the forgiveness of sins"; Mt 27:52). In his editing Matthew also altered Mark in some minor details. But there is no need to suppose that he knew any passion narrative other than Mark's.

26:1–2 When Jesus finished all these words: see note on Mt 7:28–29. **"You know . . . crucified"**: Matthew turns Mark's statement of the time (Mk 14:1) into Jesus' final prediction of his passion. **Passover**: see note on Mk 14:1.

26:3 Caiaphas was high priest from A.D. 18 to 36.

26:5 Not during the festival: the plan to delay Jesus' arrest and execution until after **the festival** was not carried out, for according to the synoptics he was arrested on the night of Nisan 14 and put to death the following day. No reason is given why the plan was changed.

26:6–13 See notes on Mk 14:3–9 and Jn 12:1–8.

26:12 To prepare me for burial: cf. Mk 14:8. In accordance with the interpretation of this act as Jesus' **burial** anointing, Matthew, more consistent than Mark, changes the purpose of the visit of the women to Jesus' tomb; they do not go to anoint him (Mk 16:1) but "to see the tomb" (Mt 28:1).

26:14 Iscariot: see note on Lk 6:16.

26:15 The motive of avarice is introduced by Judas's question about the price for betrayal, which is absent in the Marcan source (Mk 14:10–11). **Hand him over**: the same Greek

r: 10:40, 42. *s:* 7:23; Lk 13:27. *t:* Jb 22:7; Jas 2:15–16. *u:* Dn 12:2. *v:* Mk 14:1–2; Lk 22:1–2. *w:* Jn 11:47–53. *x:* Mk 14:3–9; Jn 12:1–8. *y:* Dt 15:11. *z:* Mk 14:10–11; Lk 22:3–6. *a:* Zec 11:12.

are you willing to give me if I hand him over to you?" They paid him thirty pieces of silver, 16 and from that time on he looked for an opportunity to hand him over.

Preparations for the Passover. 17 [bc]* On the first day of the Feast of Unleavened Bread, the disciples approached Jesus and said, "Where do you want us to prepare for you to eat the Passover?" 18 *He said, "Go into the city to a certain man and tell him, 'The teacher says, "My appointed time draws near; in your house I shall celebrate the Passover with my disciples." ' " 19 The disciples then did as Jesus had ordered, and prepared the Passover.

The Betrayer. 20 When it was evening, he reclined at table with the Twelve. 21 *And while they were eating, he said, "Amen, I say to you, one of you will betray me." 22 Deeply distressed at this, they began to say to him one after another, "Surely it is not I, Lord?" 23 He said in reply, "He who has dipped his hand into the dish with me is the one who will betray me. 24 [d]* The Son of Man indeed goes, as it is written of him, but woe to that man by whom the Son of Man is betrayed. It would be better for that man if he had never been born." 25 *Then Judas, his betrayer, said in reply, "Surely it is not I, Rabbi?" He answered, "You have said so."

The Lord's Supper. 26 [ef]* While they were eating, Jesus took bread, said the blessing, broke it, and giving it to his disciples said, "Take and eat; this is my body." 27 *Then he took a cup, gave thanks, and gave it to them, saying, "Drink from it, all of you, 28 [g] for this is my blood of the covenant, which will be shed on behalf of many for the forgiveness of sins. 29 *I tell you, from now on I shall not drink this fruit of the vine until the day when I drink it with you new in the kingdom of my Father." 30 *Then, after singing a hymn, they went out to the Mount of Olives.

verb is used to express the saving purpose of God by which Jesus is handed over to death (cf. Mt 17:22; 20:18; 26:2) and the human malice that hands him over. **Thirty pieces of silver**: the price of the betrayal is found only in Matthew. It is derived from Zec 11:12 where it is the wages paid to the rejected shepherd, a cheap price (Zec 11:13). That amount is also the compensation paid to one whose slave has been gored by an ox (Ex 21:32).

26:17 The first day of the Feast of Unleavened Bread: see note on Mk 14:1. Matthew omits Mark's "when they sacrificed the Passover lamb."

26:18 By omitting much of Mk 14:13–15, adding **My appointed time draws near**, and turning the question into a statement, **in your house I shall celebrate the Passover**, Matthew has given this passage a solemnity and majesty greater than that of his source.

26:21 Given Matthew's interest in the fulfillment of the Old Testament, it is curious that he omits the Marcan designation of Jesus' betrayer as "one who is eating with me" (Mk 14:18), since that is probably an allusion to Ps 41:10. However, the shocking fact that the betrayer is one who shares table fellowship with Jesus is emphasized in Mt 26:23.

26:24 It would be better . . . born: the enormity of the deed is such that it would be better not to exist than to do it.

26:25 Peculiar to Matthew. **You have said so**: cf. Mt 26:64; 27:11. This is a half-affirmative. Emphasis is laid on the pronoun and the answer implies that the statement would not have been made if the question had not been asked.

26:26–29 See note on Mk 14:22–24. The Marcan-Matthean is one of the two major New Testament traditions of the words of Jesus when instituting the Eucharist. The other (and earlier) is the Pauline-Lucan (1 Cor 11:23–25; Lk 22:19–20). Each shows the influence of Christian liturgical usage, but the Marcan-Matthean is more developed in that regard than the Pauline-Lucan. The words over the bread and cup succeed each other without the intervening meal mentioned in 1 Cor 11:25; Lk 22:20; and there is parallelism between the consecratory words (**this is my body . . . this is my blood**). Matthew follows Mark closely but with some changes.

26:26 See note on Mt 14:19. **Said the blessing**: a prayer blessing God. **Take and eat**: literally, **Take, eat. Eat** is an addition to Mark's "take it" (literally, "take"; Mk 14:22). **This is my body**: the bread is identified with Jesus himself.

26:27–28 Gave thanks: see note on Mt 15:36. **Gave it to them . . . all of you**: cf. Mk 14:23–24. In the Marcan sequence the disciples drink and then Jesus says the interpretative words. Matthew has changed this into a command to **drink** followed by those words. **My blood**: see Lv 17:11 for the concept that the **blood** is "the seat of life" and that when placed on the altar it "makes atonement." **Which will be shed**: the present participle, "being shed" or "going to be shed," is future in relation to the Last Supper. **On behalf of**: Greek *peri*; see note on Mk 14:24. **Many**: see note on Mt 20:28. **For the forgiveness of sins**: a Matthean addition. The same phrase occurs in Mk 1:4 in connection with John's baptism but Matthew avoids it there (Mt 3:11). He places it here probably because he wishes to emphasize that it is the sacrificial death of Jesus that brings **forgiveness of sins**.

26:29 Although his death will interrupt the table fellowship he has had with the disciples, Jesus confidently predicts his vindication by God and a new table fellowship with them at the banquet of the kingdom.

26:30 See note on Mk 14:26.

b: Mk 14:12–21; Lk 22:7–23. *c:* Ex 12:14–20. *d:* Is 53:8–10. *e:* Mk 14:22–26; Lk 22:14–23; 1 Cor 11:23–25. *f:* 1 Cor 10:16. *g:* Ex 24:8; Is 53:12.

Peter's Denial Foretold. [31hi*]Then Jesus said to them, "This night all of you will have your faith in me shaken, for it is written:

'I will strike the shepherd,
and the sheep of the flock will be
dispersed';

[32]but after I have been raised up, I shall go before you to Galilee." [33]Peter said to him in reply, "Though all may have their faith in you shaken, mine will never be." [34jk*]Jesus said to him, "Amen, I say to you, this very night before the cock crows, you will deny me three times." [35]Peter said to him, "Even though I should have to die with you, I will not deny you." And all the disciples spoke likewise.

The Agony in the Garden. [36lm*]Then Jesus came with them to a place called Gethsemane, and he said to his disciples, "Sit here while I go over there and pray." [37n*]He took along Peter and the two sons of Zebedee, and began to feel sorrow and distress. [38o*]Then he said to them, "My soul is sorrowful even to death. Remain here and keep watch with me." [39p*]He advanced a little and fell prostrate in prayer, saying, "My Father, if it is possible, let this cup pass from me; yet, not as I will, but as you will." [40]When he returned to his disciples he found them asleep. He said to Peter, "So you could not keep watch with me for one hour? [41*]Watch and pray that you may not undergo the test. The spirit is willing, but the flesh is weak." [42q*]Withdrawing a second time, he prayed again, "My Father, if it is not possible that this cup pass without my drinking it, your will be done!" [43]Then he returned once more and found them asleep, for they could not keep their eyes open. [44]He left them and withdrew again and prayed a third time, saying the same thing again. [45r]Then he returned to his disciples and said to them, "Are you still sleeping and taking your rest? Behold, the hour is at hand when the Son of Man is to be handed over to sinners. [46]Get up, let us go. Look, my betrayer is at hand."

The Betrayal and Arrest of Jesus. [47s]While he was still speaking, Judas, one of the Twelve, arrived, accompanied by a large crowd, with swords and clubs, who had come from the chief priests and the eld-

26:31 Will have . . . shaken: literally, "will be scandalized in me"; see note on Mt 24:9–12. **I will strike . . . dispersed**: cf. Zec 13:7.

26:34 Before the cock crows: see note on Mt 14:25. The third watch of the night was called "cockcrow." **Deny me**: see note on Mt 16:24.

26:36–56 Cf. Mk 14:32–52. The account of Jesus in Gethsemane is divided between that of his agony (Mt 26:36–46) and that of his betrayal and arrest (Mt 26:47–56). Jesus' **sorrow and distress** (Mt 26:37) in face of death is unrelieved by the presence of his three disciples who, though urged to **watch with him** (Mt 26:38, 41), fall asleep (Mt 26:40, 43). He prays that **if . . . possible** his death may be avoided (Mt 26:39) but that his Father's will be done (Mt 26:39, 42, 44). Knowing then that his death must take place, he announces to his companions that **the hour** for his being **handed over** has come (Mt 26:45). Judas arrives with an armed band provided by the Sanhedrin and greets Jesus with a kiss, the prearranged sign for his identification (Mt 26:47–49). After his arrest, he rebukes a disciple who has attacked the **high priest's servant** with a **sword** (Mt 26:51–54), and chides those who have come out to seize him with **swords and clubs** as if he were a **robber** (Mt 26:55–56). In both rebukes Jesus declares that the treatment he is how receiving is the fulfillment of the scriptures (Mt 26:55, 56). The subsequent flight of **all the disciples** is itself the fulfillment of his own prediction (cf. 31). In this episode, Matthew follows Mark with a few alterations.

26:36 Gethsemane: the Hebrew name means "oil press" and designates an olive orchard on the western slope of the Mount of Olives; see note on Mt 21:1. The name appears only in Matthew and Mark. The place is called a "garden" in Jn 18:1.

26:37 Peter and the two sons of Zebedee: cf. Mt 17:1.

26:38 Cf. Ps 42:5, 11. In the Septuagint (Ps 41:4, 11) the same Greek word for **sorrowful** is used as here. **To death**: i.e., "enough to die"; cf. Jon 4:9.

26:39 My Father: see note on Mk 14:36. Matthew omits the Aramaic *'abbā'* and adds the qualifier *my*. **This cup**: see note on Mk 10:38–40.

26:41 Undergo the test: see note on Mt 6:13. In that verse "the final test" translates the same Greek word as is here translated **the test**, and these are the only instances of the use of that word in Matthew. It is possible that the passion of Jesus is seen here as an anticipation of the great tribulation that will precede the parousia (see notes on Mt 24:8; 24:21) to which Mt 6:13 refers, and that just as Jesus prays to be delivered from death (Mt 26:39), so he exhorts the disciples to pray that they will not have to **undergo the** great **test** that his passion would be for them. Some scholars, however, understand not undergo (literally, "not enter") **the test** as meaning not that the disciples may be spared **the test** but that they may not yield to the temptation of falling away from Jesus because of his passion even though they will have to endure it.

26:42 Your will be done: cf. Mt 6:10.

h: Mk 14:7–31. *i:* Zec 13:7; Jn 16:32. *j:* Lk 22:33–34; Jn 13:37–38. *k:* 26:69–75. *l:* Mk 14:32–42; Lk 22:39–46. *m:* Jn 18:1. *n:* Heb 5:7. *o:* Ps 42:6, 12; Jon 4:9. *p:* Jn 4:34; 6:38; Phil 2:8. *q:* 6:10; Heb 10:9. *r:* Jn 12:23; 13:1; 17:1. *s:* Mk 14:43–50; Lk 22:47–53; Jn 18:3–11.

ers of the people. [48]His betrayer had arranged a sign with them, saying, "The man I shall kiss is the one; arrest him." [49*]Immediately he went over to Jesus and said, "Hail, Rabbi!" and he kissed him. [50]Jesus answered him, "Friend, do what you have come for." Then stepping forward they laid hands on Jesus and arrested him. [51]And behold, one of those who accompanied Jesus put his hand to his sword, drew it, and struck the high priest's servant, cutting off his ear. [52]Then Jesus said to him, "Put your sword back into its sheath, for all who take the sword will perish by the sword. [53]Do you think that I cannot call upon my Father and he will not provide me at this moment with more than twelve legions of angels? [54]But then how would the scriptures be fulfilled which say that it must come to pass in this way?" [55*]At that hour Jesus said to the crowds, "Have you come out as against a robber, with swords and clubs to seize me? Day after day I sat teaching in the temple area, yet you did not arrest me. [56t]But all this has come to pass that the writings of the prophets may be fulfilled." Then all the disciples left him and fled.

Jesus before the Sanhedrin. [57u*]Those who had arrested Jesus led him away to Caiaphas the high priest, where the scribes and the elders were assembled. [58]Peter was following him at a distance as far as the high priest's courtyard, and going inside he sat down with the servants to see the outcome. [59*]The chief priests and the entire Sanhedrin kept trying to obtain false testimony against Jesus in order to put him to death, [60v*]but they found none, though many false witnesses came forward. Finally two came forward [61]who stated, "This man said, 'I can destroy the temple of God and within three days rebuild it.' " [62]The high priest rose and addressed him, "Have you no answer? What are these men testifying against you?" [63w*]But Jesus was silent. Then the high priest said to him, "I order you to tell us under oath before the living God whether you are the Messiah, the Son of God." [64x*]Jesus said to him in reply, "You have said so. But I tell you:

26:49 Rabbi: see note on Mt 23:6–7. Jesus is so addressed twice in Matthew (Mt 26:25), both times by Judas. For the significance of the closely related address "teacher" in Matthew, see note on Mt 8:19.

26:55 Day after day . . . arrest me: cf. Mk 14:49. This suggests that Jesus had taught for a relatively long period in Jerusalem, whereas Mt 21:1–11 puts his coming to the city for the first time only a few days before.

26:57–68 Following Mk 14:53–65 Matthew presents the nighttime appearance of Jesus before the **Sanhedrin** as a real trial. After **many false witnesses** bring charges against him that do not suffice for the death sentence (Mt 26:60), **two came forward** who charge him with claiming to be able to **destroy the temple . . . and within three days** to **rebuild it** (Mt 26:60–61). Jesus makes no answer even when challenged to do so by **the high priest**, who then orders him to declare **under oath . . . whether** he is the **Messiah, the Son of God** (Mt 26:62–63). Matthew changes Mark's clear affirmative response (Mk 14:62) to the same one as that given to Judas (Mt 26:25), but follows Mark almost verbatim in Jesus' predicting that his judges will see him **(the Son of Man) seated at the right hand of** God **and coming on the clouds of heaven** (Mt 26:64). **The high priest** then charges him with blasphemy (Mt 26:65), a charge with which the other members of **the Sanhedrin** agree by declaring that **he deserves to die** (Mt 26:66). They then attack him (Mt 26:67) and mockingly demand that he **prophesy** (Mt 26:68). This account contains elements that are contrary to the judicial procedures prescribed in the Mishnah, the Jewish code of law that dates in written form from ca. A.D. 200, e.g., trial on a feast day, a night session of the court, pronouncement of a verdict of condemnation at the same session at which testimony was received. Consequently, some scholars regard the account entirely as a creation of the early Christians without historical value. However, it is disputable whether the norms found in the Mishnah were in force at the time of Jesus. More to the point is the question whether the Matthean-Marcan night trial derives from a combination of two separate incidents, a nighttime preliminary investigation (cf. Jn 18:13, 19–24) and a formal trial on the following morning (cf. Lk 22:66–71).

26:57 Caiaphas: see note on Mt 26:3.

26:59 Sanhedrin: see note on Lk 22:66.

26:60–61 Two: cf. Dt 19:15. **I can destroy . . . rebuild it**: there are significant differences from the Marcan parallel (Mk 14:58). Matthew omits "made with hands" and "not made with hands" and changes Mark's "will destroy" and "will build another" to **can destroy** and (can) **rebuild**. The charge is probably based on Jesus' prediction of the temple's destruction; see notes on Mt 23:37–39; 24:2; and Jn 2:19. A similar prediction by Jeremiah was considered as deserving death; cf. Jer 7:1–15; 26:1–8.

26:63 Silent: possibly an allusion to Is 53:7. **I order you . . . living God**: peculiar to Matthew; cf. Mk 14:61.

26:64 You have said so: see note on Mt 26:25. **From now on . . . heaven**: the Son of Man who is to be crucified (cf. Mt 20:19) will be seen in glorious majesty (cf. Ps 110:1) and **coming on the clouds of heaven** (cf. Dn 7:13). **The Power**: see note on Mk 14:61–62.

t: 26:31. *u:* Mk 14:53–65; Lk 22:54–55, 63–71; Jn 18:12–14, 19–24. *v:* Dt 19:15; Jn 2:19; Acts 6:14. *w:* Is 53:7. *x:* Ps 110:1; Dn 7:13.

From now on you will see 'the Son of
Man
seated at the right hand of the Power'
and 'coming on the clouds of
heaven.' "

[65*]Then the high priest tore his robes and said, "He has blasphemed! What further need have we of witnesses? You have now heard the blasphemy; [66]what is your opinion?" They said in reply, "He deserves to die!" [67y*]Then they spat in his face and struck him, while some slapped him, [68]saying, "Prophesy for us, Messiah: who is it that struck you?"

Peter's Denial of Jesus. [69z]Now Peter was sitting outside in the courtyard. One of the maids came over to him and said, "You too were with Jesus the Galilean." [70*]But he denied it in front of everyone, saying, "I do not know what you are talking about!" [71]As he went out to the gate, another girl saw him and said to those who were there, "This man was with Jesus the Nazorean." [72]Again he denied it with an oath, "I do not know the man!" [73*]A little later the bystanders came over and said to Peter, "Surely you too are one of them; even your speech gives you away." [74]At that he began to curse and to swear, "I do not know the man." And immediately a cock crowed. [75a]Then Peter remembered the word that Jesus had spoken: "Before the cock crows you will deny me three times." He went out and began to weep bitterly.

CHAPTER 27

See RG 384–86

Jesus before Pilate. [1b*]When it was morning, all the chief priests and the elders of the people took counsel against Jesus to put him to death. [2]They bound him, led him away, and handed him over to Pilate, the governor.

The Death of Judas. [3cd*]Then Judas, his betrayer, seeing that Jesus had been condemned, deeply regretted what he had done. He returned the thirty pieces of silver to the chief priests and elders, [4]saying, "I have sinned in betraying innocent blood." They said, "What is that to us? Look to it yourself." [5*]Flinging the money into the temple, he departed and went off and hanged himself. [6]The chief priests gathered up the money, but said, "It is not lawful to deposit this in the temple treasury, for it is the price of blood." [7]After consultation, they used it to buy the potter's field as a burial place for foreigners. [8]That is why that field even today is called

26:65 Blasphemed: the punishment for **blasphemy** was death by stoning (see Lv 24:10–16). According to the Mishnah, to be guilty of **blasphemy** one had to pronounce "the Name itself," i.e. Yahweh; cf. **Sanhedrin** 7, 4.5. Those who judge the gospel accounts of Jesus' trial by the later Mishnah standards point out that Jesus uses the surrogate "the Power," and hence no Jewish court would have regarded him as guilty of blasphemy; others hold that the Mishnah's narrow understanding of **blasphemy** was a later development.

26:67–68 The physical abuse, apparently done to Jesus by the members of the Sanhedrin themselves, recalls the sufferings of the Isaian Servant of the Lord; cf. Is 50:6. The mocking challenge to **prophesy** is probably motivated by Jesus' prediction of his future glory (Mt 26:64).

26:70 Denied it in front of everyone: see Mt 10:33. Peter's repentance (Mt 26:75) saves him from the fearful destiny of which Jesus speaks there.

26:73 Your speech . . . away: Matthew explicates Mark's "you too are a Galilean" (Mk 14:70).

27:1–31 Cf. Mk 15:1–20. Matthew's account of the Roman trial before **Pilate** is introduced by a consultation of the Sanhedrin after which Jesus is **handed over to . . . the governor** (Mt 27:1–2). Matthew follows his Marcan source closely but adds some material that is peculiar to him, the death of **Judas** (Mt 27:3–10), possibly the name **Jesus** as the name of **Barabbas** also (Mt 27:16–17), the intervention of Pilate's **wife** (Mt 27:19), Pilate's washing **his hands** in token of his disclaiming responsibility for Jesus' death (Mt 27:24), and the assuming of that responsibility by **the whole people** (Mt 27:25).

27:1 There is scholarly disagreement about the meaning of the Sanhedrin's taking **counsel** (*symboulion elabon*; cf. Mt 12:14; 22:15; 27:7; 28:12); see note on Mk 15:1. Some understand it as a discussion about the strategy for putting their death sentence against **Jesus** into effect since they lacked the right to do so themselves. Others see it as the occasion for their passing that sentence, holding that Matthew, unlike Mark (Mk 14:64), does not consider that it had been passed in the night session (Mt 26:66). Even in the latter interpretation, their handing **him over to Pilate** is best explained on the hypothesis that they did not have competence to put their sentence into effect, as is stated in Jn 18:31.

27:3 The thirty pieces of silver: see Mt 26:15.

27:5–8 For another tradition about the death of Judas, cf. Acts 1:18–19. The two traditions agree only in the purchase of a field with **the money** paid to Judas for his betrayal of Jesus and the name given to **the field, the Field of Blood**. In Acts Judas himself buys the field and its name comes from his own blood shed in his fatal accident on it. **The potter's field**: this designation of the field is based on the fulfillment citation in Mt 27:10.

y: Wis 2:19; Is 50:6. *z:* Mk 14:66–72; Lk 22:56–62; Jn 18:17–18, 25–27. *a:* 26:34. *b:* Mk 15:1; Lk 23:1; Jn 18:28. *c:* Acts 1:18–19. *d:* 26:15.

the Field of Blood. [9]*Then was fulfilled what had been said through Jeremiah the prophet, "And they took the thirty pieces of silver, the value of a man with a price on his head, a price set by some of the Israelites, [10e]and they paid it out for the potter's field just as the Lord had commanded me."

Jesus Questioned by Pilate. [11f]*Now Jesus stood before the governor, and he questioned him, "Are you the king of the Jews?" Jesus said, "You say so." [12g]*And when he was accused by the chief priests and elders, he made no answer. [13]Then Pilate said to him, "Do you not hear how many things they are testifying against you?" [14]But he did not answer him one word, so that the governor was greatly amazed.

The Sentence of Death. [15h]*Now on the occasion of the feast the governor was accustomed to release to the crowd one prisoner whom they wished. [16]*And at that time they had a notorious prisoner called [Jesus] Barabbas. [17]So when they had assembled, Pilate said to them, "Which one do you want me to release to you, [Jesus] Barabbas, or Jesus called Messiah?" [18]*For he knew that it was out of envy that they had handed him over. [19]*While he was still seated on the bench, his wife sent him a message, "Have nothing to do with that righteous man. I suffered much in a dream today because of him." [20i]The chief priests and the elders persuaded the crowds to ask for Barabbas but to destroy Jesus. [21]The governor said to them in reply, "Which of the two do you want me to release to you?" They answered, "Barabbas!" [22]*Pilate said to them, "Then what shall I do with Jesus called Messiah?" They all said, "Let him be crucified!" [23]But he said, "Why? What evil has he done?" They only shouted the louder, "Let him be crucified!" [24j]*When Pilate saw that he was not

27:9–10 Cf. Mt 26:15. Matthew's attributing this text to Jeremiah is puzzling, for there is no such text in that book, and **the thirty pieces of silver** thrown by Judas "into the temple" (Mt 27:5) recall rather Zec 11:12–13. It is usually said that the attribution of the text to Jeremiah is due to Matthew's combining the Zechariah text with texts from Jeremiah that speak of a **potter** (Jer 18:2–3), the buying of a **field** (Jer 32:6–9), or the breaking of a potter's flask at Topheth in the valley of Ben-Hinnom with the prediction that it will become a burial place (Jer 19:1–13).

27:11 King of the Jews: this title is used of Jesus only by pagans. The Matthean instances are, besides this verse, Mt 2:2; 27:29, 37. Matthew equates it with "Messiah"; cf. Mt 2:2, 4 and Mt 27:17, 22 where he has changed "the king of the Jews" of his Marcan source (Mk 15:9, 12) to "(Jesus) called Messiah." The normal political connotation of both titles would be of concern to the Roman **governor**. **You say so**: see note on Mt 26:25. An unqualified affirmative response is not made because Jesus' kingship is not what Pilate would understand it to be.

27:12–14 Cf. Mt 26:62–63. As in the trial before the Sanhedrin, Jesus' silence may be meant to recall Is 53:7. **Greatly amazed**: possibly an allusion to Is 52:14–15.

27:15–26 The choice that Pilate offers **the crowd** between **Barabbas** and **Jesus** is said to be in accordance with a custom of releasing at the Passover feast **one prisoner** chosen by **the crowd** (Mt 27:15). This custom is mentioned also in Mk 15:6 and Jn 18:39 but not in Luke; see note on Lk 23:17. Outside of the gospels there is no direct attestation of it, and scholars are divided in their judgment of the historical reliability of the claim that there was such a practice.

27:16–17 [Jesus] Barabbas: it is possible that the double name is the original reading; **Jesus** was a common Jewish name; see note on Mt 1:21. This reading is found in only a few textual witnesses, although its absence in the majority can be explained as an omission of **Jesus** made for reverential reasons. That name is bracketed because of its uncertain textual attestation. The Aramaic name **Barabbas** means "son of the father"; the irony of the choice offered between him and Jesus, the true son of the Father, would be evident to those addressees of Matthew who knew that.

27:18 Cf. Mk 14:10. This is an example of the tendency, found in varying degree in all the gospels, to present Pilate in a relatively favorable light and emphasize the hostility of the Jewish authorities and eventually of the people.

27:19 Jesus' innocence is declared by a Gentile woman. **In a dream**: in Matthew's infancy narrative, dreams are the means of divine communication; cf. Mt 1:20; 2:12, 13, 19, 22.

27:22 Let him be crucified: incited by the chief priests and elders (Mt 27:20), the crowds demand that Jesus be executed by crucifixion, a peculiarly horrible form of Roman capital punishment. The Marcan parallel, "Crucify him" (Mk 15:3), addressed to Pilate, is changed by Matthew to the passive, probably to emphasize the responsibility of the crowds.

27:24–25 Peculiar to Matthew. **Took water . . . blood**: cf. Dt 21:1–8, the handwashing prescribed in the case of a murder when the killer is unknown. The elders of the city nearest to where the corpse is found must wash their hands, declaring, "Our hands did not shed this blood." **Look to it yourselves**: cf. Mt 27:4. **The whole people**: Matthew sees in those who speak these words **the** entire **people** (Greek *laos*) of Israel. **His blood . . . and upon our children**: cf. Jer 26:15. The responsibility for Jesus' death is accepted by the nation that was God's special possession (Ex 19:5), his own **people** (Hos 2:23), and they thereby lose that high privilege; see Mt 21:43 and the note on that verse. The controversy between Matthew's church and Pharisaic Judaism about which was the true people of God is reflected here. As the Second Vatican Council has pointed out, guilt for Jesus' death is not attributable to all the Jews of his time or to any Jews of later times.

---

e: Zec 11:12–13. *f:* Mk 15:2–5; Lk 23:2–3; Jn 18:29–38. *g:* Is 53:7. *h:* Mk 15:6–15; Lk 23:17–25; Jn 18:39–19:16. *i:* Acts 3:14. *j:* Dt 21:1–8.

succeeding at all, but that a riot was breaking out instead, he took water and washed
his hands in the sight of the crowd, saying, "I
am innocent of this man's blood. Look to it
yourselves." 25 And the whole people said in
reply, "His blood be upon us and upon our
children." 26* Then he released Barabbas to
them, but after he had Jesus scourged, he
handed him over to be crucified.
Mockery by the Soldiers. 27[k]* Then the
soldiers of the governor took Jesus inside
the praetorium and gathered the whole cohort around him. 28* They stripped off his
clothes and threw a scarlet military cloak
about him. 29[l]* Weaving a crown out of
thorns, they placed it on his head, and a
reed in his right hand. And kneeling before
him, they mocked him, saying, "Hail, King
of the Jews!" 30[m]* They spat upon him and
took the reed and kept striking him on the
head. 31 And when they had mocked him,
they stripped him of the cloak, dressed him
in his own clothes, and led him off to crucify him.
The Way of the Cross. 32[n]* As they were
going out, they met a Cyrenian named Simon; this man they pressed into service to
carry his cross.
The Crucifixion. 33[o] And when they came
to a place called Golgotha (which means
Place of the Skull), 34[p]* they gave Jesus wine
to drink mixed with gall. But when he had
tasted it, he refused to drink. 35[q]* After they
had crucified him, they divided his garments
by casting lots; 36 then they sat down and
kept watch over him there. 37* And they
placed over his head the written charge
against him: This is Jesus, the King of the
Jews. 38* Two revolutionaries were crucified
with him, one on his right and the other on
his left. 39[r]* Those passing by reviled him,
shaking their heads 40[s] and saying, "You who
would destroy the temple and rebuild it in
three days, save yourself, if you are the Son
of God, [and] come down from the cross!"
41 Likewise the chief priests with the scribes
and elders mocked him and said, 42* "He
saved others; he cannot save himself. So he
is the king of Israel! Let him come down
from the cross now, and we will believe in
him. 43[t]* He trusted in God; let him deliver
him now if he wants him. For he said, 'I am

27:26 He had Jesus scourged: the usual preliminary to crucifixion.

27:27 The praetorium: the residence of the Roman governor. His usual place of residence was at Caesarea Maritima on the Mediterranean coast, but he went to Jerusalem during the great feasts, when the influx of pilgrims posed the danger of a nationalistic riot. It is disputed whether **the praetorium** in Jerusalem was the old palace of Herod in the west of the city or the fortress of Antonia northwest of the temple area. **The whole cohort**: normally six hundred soldiers.

27:28 Scarlet military cloak: so Matthew as against the royal purple of Mk 15:17 and Jn 19:2.

27:29 Crown out of thorns: probably of long **thorns** that stood upright so that it resembled the "radiant" **crown**, a diadem with spikes worn by Hellenistic kings. The soldiers' purpose was mockery, not torture. **A reed**: peculiar to Matthew; a mock scepter.

27:30 Spat upon him: cf. Mt 26:67 where there also is a possible allusion to Is 50:6.

27:32 See note on Mk 15:21. **Cyrenian named Simon**: Cyrenaica was a Roman province on the north coast of Africa and Cyrene was its capital city. The city had a large population of Greek-speaking Jews. **Simon** may have been living in Palestine or have come there for the Passover as a pilgrim. **Pressed into service**: see note on Mt 5:41.

27:34 Wine . . . mixed with gall: cf. Mk 15:23 where the drink is "wine drugged with myrrh," a narcotic. Matthew's text is probably an inexact allusion to Ps 69:22. That psalm belongs to the class called the individual lament, in which a persecuted just man prays for deliverance in the midst of great suffering and also expresses confidence that his prayer will be heard. That theme of the suffering Just One is frequently applied to the sufferings of Jesus in the passion narratives.

27:35 The clothing of an executed criminal went to his executioner(s), but the description of that procedure in the case of Jesus, found in all the gospels, is plainly inspired by Ps 22:18. However, that psalm verse is quoted only in Jn 19:24.

27:37 The offense of a person condemned to death by crucifixion was written on a tablet that was displayed on his cross. The **charge** against **Jesus** was that he had claimed to be the **King of the Jews** (cf. Mt 27:11), i.e., the Messiah (cf. Mt 27:17, 22).

27:38 Revolutionaries: see note on Jn 18:40 where the same Greek word as that found here is used for Barabbas.

27:39–40 Reviled him . . . heads: cf. Ps 22:8. **You who would destroy . . . three days**; cf. Mt 26:61. **If you are the Son of God**: the same words as those of the devil in the temptation of Jesus; cf. Mt 4:3, 6.

27:42 King of Israel: in their mocking of Jesus the members of the Sanhedrin call themselves and their people not "the Jews" but **Israel**.

27:43 Peculiar to Matthew. **He trusted in God . . . wants him**: cf. Ps 22:9. **He said . . . of God**: probably an allusion to Wis 2:12–20 where the theme of the suffering Just One appears.

k: Mk 15:16–20; Jn 19:2–3. *l:* 27:11. *m:* Is 50:6. *n:* Mk 15:21; Lk 23:26. *o:* Mk 15:22–32; Lk 23:32–38; Jn 19:17–19, 23–24. *p:* Ps 69:21. *q:* Ps 22:19. *r:* Ps 22:8. *s:* 4:3, 6; 26:61. *t:* Ps 22:9; Wis 2:12–20.

the Son of God.' " [44]The revolutionaries
who were crucified with him also kept abusing him in the same way.
The Death of Jesus. [45uv*]From noon onward, darkness came over the whole land
until three in the afternoon. [46w*]And about
three o'clock Jesus cried out in a loud voice,
"*Eli, Eli, lema sabachthani*?" which means,
"My God, my God, why have you forsaken
me?" [47*]Some of the bystanders who heard
it said, "This one is calling for Elijah."
[48x]Immediately one of them ran to get a
sponge; he soaked it in wine, and putting it
on a reed, gave it to him to drink. [49]But the
rest said, "Wait, let us see if Elijah comes to
save him." [50*]But Jesus cried out again in a
loud voice, and gave up his spirit. [51y*]And
behold, the veil of the sanctuary was torn in
two from top to bottom. The earth quaked,
rocks were split, [52z]tombs were opened, and
the bodies of many saints who had fallen
asleep were raised. [53]And coming forth from
their tombs after his resurrection, they entered the holy city and appeared to many.
[54*]The centurion and the men with him who
were keeping watch over Jesus feared
greatly when they saw the earthquake and all
that was happening, and they said, "Truly,
this was the Son of God!" [55*]There were
many women there, looking on from a distance, who had followed Jesus from Galilee,
ministering to him. [56a]Among them were
Mary Magdalene and Mary the mother of
James and Joseph, and the mother of the
sons of Zebedee.
The Burial of Jesus. [57bc*]When it was
evening, there came a rich man from Arimathea named Joseph, who was himself a disciple of Jesus. [58]He went to Pilate and asked
for the body of Jesus; then Pilate ordered it
to be handed over. [59]Taking the body, Joseph
wrapped it [in] clean linen [60]and laid it in his

27:45 Cf. Am 8:9 where on the day of the Lord "the sun will set at midday."

27:46 *Eli, Eli, lema sabachthani?*: Jesus cries out in the words of Ps 22:2, a psalm of lament that is the Old Testament passage most frequently drawn upon in this narrative. In Mark the verse is cited entirely in Aramaic, which Matthew partially retains but changes the invocation of God to the Hebrew *Eli*, possibly because that is more easily related to the statement of the following verse about Jesus' calling for Elijah.

27:47 Elijah: see note on Mt 3:4. This prophet, taken up into heaven (2 Kgs 2:11), was believed to come to the help of those in distress, but the evidences of that belief are all later than the gospels.

27:50 Gave up his spirit: cf. the Marcan parallel (Mk 15:37), "breathed his last." Matthew's alteration expresses both Jesus' control over his destiny and his obedient giving up of his life to God.

27:51–53 Veil of the sanctuary . . . bottom: cf. Mk 15:38; Lk 23:45. Luke puts this event immediately before the death of Jesus. There were two veils in the Mosaic tabernacle on the model of which the temple was constructed, the outer one before the entrance of the Holy Place and the inner one before the Holy of Holies (see Ex 26:31–36). Only the high priest could pass through the latter and that only on the Day of Atonement (see Lv 16:1–18). Probably the torn veil of the gospels is the inner one. The meaning of the scene may be that now, because of Jesus' death, all people have access to the presence of God, or that the temple, its holiest part standing exposed, is now profaned and will soon be destroyed. **The earth quaked . . . appeared to many**: peculiar to Matthew. The earthquake, the splitting of the **rocks**, and especially the resurrection of the dead **saints** indicate the coming of the final age. In the Old Testament the coming of God is frequently portrayed with the imagery of an earthquake (see Ps 68:9; 77:19), and Jesus speaks of the earthquakes that will accompany the "labor pains" that signify the beginning of the dissolution of the old world (Mt 24:7–8). For the expectation of the resurrection of the dead at the coming of the new and final age, see Dn 12:1–3. Matthew knows that the end of the old age has not yet come (Mt 28:20), but the new age has broken in with the death (and resurrection; cf. the earthquake in Mt 28:2) of Jesus; see note on Mt 16:28. **After his resurrection**: this qualification seems to be due to Matthew's wish to assert the primacy of Jesus' **resurrection** even though he has placed the resurrection of the dead **saints** immediately after Jesus' death.

27:54 Cf. Mk 15:39. The Christian confession of faith is made by Gentiles, not only **the centurion**, as in Mark, but the other soldiers **who were keeping watch over Jesus** (cf. Mt 27:36).

27:55–56 Looking on from a distance: cf. Ps 38:12. **Mary Magdalene . . . Joseph**: these two women are mentioned again in Mt 27:61 and Mt 28:1 and are important as witnesses of the reality of the empty tomb. A **James** and **Joseph** are referred to in Mt 13:55 as brothers of Jesus.

27:57–61 Cf. Mk 15:42–47. Matthew drops Mark's designation of **Joseph** of **Arimathea** as "a distinguished member of the council" (the Sanhedrin), and makes him **a rich man** and a **disciple of Jesus**. The former may be an allusion to Is 53:9 (the Hebrew reading of that text is disputed and the one followed in the NAB OT has nothing about the rich, but they are mentioned in the LXX version). That the tomb was the **new tomb of a rich man** and that it was seen by the women are indications of an apologetic intent of Matthew; there could be no question about the identity of Jesus' burial place. **The other Mary**: the mother of James and Joseph (56).

u: Mk 15:33–41; Lk 23:44–49; Jn 19:28–30. *v:* Am 8:9. *w:* Ps 22:2. *x:* Ps 69:21. *y:* Ex 26:31–36; Ps 68:9; 77:19. *z:* Dn 12:1–3. *a:* 13:55. *b:* Mk 15:42–47; Lk 23:50–56; Jn 19:38–42. *c:* Is 53:9.

new tomb that he had hewn in the rock. Then he rolled a huge stone across the entrance to the tomb and departed. [61]But Mary Magdalene and the other Mary remained sitting there, facing the tomb.

The Guard at the Tomb. [62*]The next day, the one following the day of preparation, the chief priests and the Pharisees gathered before Pilate [63d]and said, "Sir, we remember that this impostor while still alive said, 'After three days I will be raised up.' [64*]Give orders, then, that the grave be secured until the third day, lest his disciples come and steal him and say to the people, 'He has been raised from the dead.' This last imposture would be worse than the first." [65*]Pilate said to them, "The guard is yours; go secure it as best you can." [66]So they went and secured the tomb by fixing a seal to the stone and setting the guard.

CHAPTER 28

See RG 386

The Resurrection of Jesus. [1e*]After the sabbath, as the first day of the week was dawning, Mary Magdalene and the other Mary came to see the tomb. [2f*]And behold, there was a great earthquake; for an angel of the Lord descended from heaven, approached, rolled back the stone, and sat upon it. [3g]His appearance was like lightning and his clothing was white as snow. [4]The guards were shaken with fear of him and became like dead men. [5]Then the angel said to the women in reply, "Do not be afraid! I know that you are seeking Jesus the crucified. [6*]He is not here, for he has been raised just

27:62–66 Peculiar to Matthew. The story prepares for Mt 28:11–15 and the Jewish charge that the tomb was empty because the disciples had stolen the body of Jesus (Mt 28:13, 15).

27:62 The next day . . . preparation: the sabbath. According to the synoptic chronology, in that year **the day of preparation** (for the sabbath) was the Passover; cf. Mk 15:42. **The Pharisees**: the principal opponents of Jesus during his ministry and, in Matthew's time, of the Christian church, join with **the chief priests** to guarantee against a possible attempt of Jesus' **disciples** to steal his body.

27:64 This last imposture . . . the first: the claim that Jesus **has been raised from the dead** is clearly the **last imposture; the first** may be either his claim that he would **be raised up** (63) or his claim that he was the one with whose ministry the kingdom of God had come (see Mt 12:28).

27:65 The guard is yours: literally, "have a guard" or "you have a guard." Either the imperative or the indicative could mean that Pilate granted the petitioners some Roman soldiers as guards, which is the sense of the present translation. However, if the verb is taken as an indicative it could also mean that Pilate told them to use their own Jewish guards.

28:1–20 Except for Mt 28:1–8 based on Mk 16:1–8, the material of this final chapter is peculiar to Matthew. Even where he follows Mark, Matthew has altered his source so greatly that a very different impression is given from that of the Marcan account. The two points that are common to the resurrection testimony of all the gospels are that the tomb of Jesus had been found empty and that the risen Jesus had appeared to certain persons, or, in the original form of Mark, that such an appearance was promised as soon to take place (see Mk 16:7). On this central and all-important basis, Matthew has constructed an account that interprets the resurrection as the turning of the ages (Mt 28:2–4), shows the Jewish opposition to Jesus as continuing **to the present** in the claim that the resurrection is a deception perpetrated by the **disciples** who stole his body from the tomb (Mt 28:11–15), and marks a new stage in the mission of **the disciples** once limited to Israel (Mt 10:5–6); now they are to **make disciples of all nations**. In this work they will be strengthened by the presence of the exalted Son of Man, who will be with them **until** the kingdom comes in fullness at **the end of the age** (Mt 28:16–20).

28:1 After the sabbath . . . dawning: since the sabbath ended at sunset, this could mean in the early evening, for **dawning** can refer to the appearance of the evening star; cf. Lk 23:54. However, it is probable that Matthew means the morning dawn of the day after the sabbath, as in the similar though slightly different text of Mark, "when the sun had risen" (Mk 16:2). **Mary Magdalene and the other Mary**: see notes on Mt 27:55–56; 57–61. **To see the tomb**: cf. Mk 16:1–2 where the purpose of the women's visit is to anoint Jesus' body.

28:2–4 Peculiar to Matthew. **A great earthquake**: see note on Mt 27:51–53. **Descended from heaven**: this trait is peculiar to Matthew, although his interpretation of the "young man" of his Marcan source (Mk 16:5) as an **angel** is probably true to Mark's intention; cf. Lk 24:23 where the "two men" of Mt 24:4 are said to be "angels." **Rolled back the stone . . . upon it**: not to allow the risen Jesus to leave the tomb but to make evident that the tomb is empty (see Mt 24:6). Unlike the apocryphal Gospel of Peter (9:35—11:44), the New Testament does not describe the resurrection of Jesus, nor is there anyone who sees it. **His appearance was like lightning . . . snow**: see note on Mt 17:2.

28:6–7 Cf. Mk 16:6–7. **Just as he said**: a Matthean addition referring to Jesus' predictions of his resurrection, e.g., Mt 16:21; 17:23; 20:19. **Tell his disciples**: like the angel of the Lord of the infancy narrative, the angel interprets a fact and gives a commandment about what is to be done; cf. Mt 1:20–21. Matthew omits Mark's "and Peter" (Mk 16:7); considering his interest in Peter, this omission is curious. Perhaps the reason is that the Marcan text may allude to a first appearance of Jesus to Peter alone (cf. 1 Cor 15:5; Lk 24:34) which Matthew has already incorporated into his account of Peter's confession at Caesarea Philippi; see note on Mt 16:16. **He is going . . . Galilee**: like Mk 16:7, a reference to Jesus' prediction at the Last Supper (Mt 26:32; Mk 14:28). Matthew changes Mark's "as he told you" to a declaration of the angel.

d: 12:40; 16:21; 17:23; 20:19. *e:* Mk 16:1–8; Lk 24:1–12; Jn 20:1–10. *f:* 25:51. *g:* 17:2.

as he said. Come and see the place where he
lay. [7h]Then go quickly and tell his disciples,
'He has been raised from the dead, and he is
going before you to Galilee; there you will
see him.' Behold, I have told you." [8*]Then
they went away quickly from the tomb, fearful yet overjoyed, and ran to announce this
to his disciples. [9i*]And behold, Jesus met
them on their way and greeted them. They
approached, embraced his feet, and did him
homage. [10]Then Jesus said to them, "Do not
be afraid. Go tell my brothers to go to Galilee, and there they will see me."

The Report of the Guard. [11*]While they
were going, some of the guard went into the
city and told the chief priests all that had
happened. [12]They assembled with the elders
and took counsel; then they gave a large sum
of money to the soldiers, [13]telling them,
"You are to say, 'His disciples came by night
and stole him while we were asleep.' [14]And
if this gets to the ears of the governor, we
will satisfy [him] and keep you out of trouble." [15]The soldiers took the money and did
as they were instructed. And this story has
circulated among the Jews to the present
[day].

The Commissioning of the Disciples.
[16j*]The eleven disciples went to Galilee, to
the mountain to which Jesus had ordered
them. [17*]When they saw him, they worshiped, but they doubted. [18k*]Then Jesus approached and said to them, "All power in
heaven and on earth has been given to me.
[19l*]Go, therefore, and make disciples of all
nations, baptizing them in the name of the
Father, and of the Son, and of the holy Spirit,
[20m*]teaching them to observe all that I have
commanded you. And behold, I am with you
always, until the end of the age."

28:8 Contrast Mk 16:8 where the women in their fear "said nothing to anyone."

28:9–10 Although these verses are peculiar to Matthew, there are similarities between them and John's account of the appearance of Jesus to Mary Magdalene (Jn 20:17). In both there is a touching of Jesus' body, and a command of Jesus to bear a message to his disciples, designated as his **brothers**. Matthew may have drawn upon a tradition that appears in a different form in John. Jesus' words to the women are mainly a repetition of those of the angel (Mt 28:5a, 7b).

28:11–15 This account indicates that the dispute between Christians and Jews about the empty tomb was not whether the tomb was empty but why.

28:16–20 This climactic scene has been called a "proleptic parousia," for it gives a foretaste of the final glorious coming of the Son of Man (Mt 26:64). Then his triumph will be manifest to all; now it is revealed only to **the disciples**, who are commissioned to announce it to **all nations** and bring them to belief in Jesus and obedience to his commandments.

28:16 The eleven: the number recalls the tragic defection of Judas Iscariot. **To the mountain . . . ordered them**: since the message to the **disciples** was simply that they were to go to Galilee (Mt 28:10), some think that **the mountain** comes from a tradition of the message known to Matthew and alluded to here. For the significance of **the mountain**, see note on Mt 17:1.

28:17 But they doubted: the Greek can also be translated, "but some doubted." The verb occurs elsewhere in the New Testament only in Mt 14:31 where it is associated with Peter's being of "little faith." For the meaning of that designation, see note on Mt 6:30.

28:18 All power . . . me: the Greek word here translated power is the same as that found in the LXX translation of Dn 7:13–14 where one "like a son of man" is given **power** and an everlasting kingdom by God. The risen Jesus here claims universal power, i.e., **in heaven and on earth**.

28:19 Therefore: since universal power belongs to the risen Jesus (Mt 28:18), he gives the eleven a mission that is universal. They are to **make disciples of all nations**. While **all nations** is understood by some scholars as referring only to all Gentiles, it is probable that it included the Jews as well. **Baptizing them**: baptism is the means of entrance into the community of the risen one, the Church. **In the name of the Father . . . holy Spirit**: this is perhaps the clearest expression in the New Testament of trinitarian belief. It may have been the baptismal formula of Matthew's church, but primarily it designates the effect of baptism, the union of the one baptized with the Father, Son, and holy Spirit.

28:20 All that I have commanded you: the moral teaching found in this gospel, preeminently that of the Sermon on the Mount (Mt 5–7). The commandments of Jesus are the standard of Christian conduct, not the Mosaic law as such, even though some of the Mosaic commandments have now been invested with the authority of Jesus. **Behold, I am with you always**: the promise of Jesus' real though invisible presence echoes the name Emmanuel given to him in the infancy narrative; see note on Mt 1:23. **End of the age**: see notes on Mt 13:39 and Mt 24:3.

h: 26:32. *i:* Jn 20:17. *j:* Mk 16:14–16; Lk 24:36–49; Jn 20:19–23. *k:* Dn 7:14 LXX. *l:* Acts 1:8. *m:* 1:23; 13:39; 24:3.

See RG 386–96

The Gospel According to Mark

This shortest of all New Testament gospels is likely the first to have been written, yet it often tells of Jesus' ministry in more detail than either Matthew or Luke (for example, the miracle stories at Mk 5:1–20 or Mk 9:14–29). It recounts what Jesus did in a vivid style, where one incident follows directly upon another. In this almost breathless narrative, Mark stresses Jesus' message about the kingdom of God now breaking into human life as good news (Mk 1:14–15) and Jesus himself as the gospel of God (Mk 1:1; 8:35; 10:29). Jesus is the Son whom God has sent to rescue humanity by serving and by sacrificing his life (Mk 10:45).

The opening verse about good news in Mark (Mk 1:1) serves as a title for the entire book. The action begins with the appearance of John the Baptist, a messenger of God attested by scripture. But John points to a mightier one, Jesus, at whose baptism God speaks from heaven, declaring Jesus his Son. The Spirit descends upon Jesus, who eventually, it is promised, will baptize "with the holy Spirit." This presentation of who Jesus really is (Mk 1:1–13) is rounded out with a brief reference to the temptation of Jesus and how Satan's attack fails. Jesus as Son of God will be victorious, a point to be remembered as one reads of Jesus' death and the enigmatic ending to Mark's Gospel.

The key verses at Mk 1:14–15, which are programmatic, summarize what Jesus proclaims as gospel: fulfillment, the nearness of the kingdom, and therefore the need for repentance and for faith. After the call of the first four disciples, all fishermen (Mk 1:16–20), we see Jesus engaged in teaching (Mk 1:21, 22, 27), preaching (Mk 1:38, 39), and healing (Mk 1:29–31, 34, 40–45), and exorcising demons (1:22–27, 34–39). The content of Jesus' teaching is only rarely stated, and then chiefly in parables (Mk 4) about the kingdom. His cures, especially on the sabbath (Mk 3:1–5); his claim, like God, to forgive sins (Mk 2:3–12); his table fellowship with tax collectors and sinners (Mk 2:14–17); and the statement that his followers need not now fast but should rejoice while Jesus is present (Mk 2:18–22), all stir up opposition that will lead to Jesus' death (Mk 3:6).

In Mark, Jesus is portrayed as immensely popular with the people in Galilee during his ministry (Mk 2:2; 3:7; 4:1). He appoints twelve disciples to help preach and drive out demons, just as he does (Mk 3:13–19). He continues to work many miracles; the blocks Mk 4:35–6:44 and Mk 6:45–7:10 are cycles of stories about healings, miracles at the Sea of Galilee, and marvelous feedings of the crowds. Jesus' teaching in Mk 7 exalts the word of God over "the tradition of the elders" and sees defilement as a matter of the heart, not of unclean foods. Yet opposition mounts. Scribes charge that Jesus is possessed by Beelzebul (Mk 3:22). His relatives think him "out of his mind" (Mk 3:21). Jesus' kinship is with those who do the will of God, in a new eschatological family, not even with mother, brothers, or sisters by blood ties (Mk 3:31–35; cf. Mk 6:1–6). But all too often his own disciples do not understand Jesus (Mk 4:13, 40; 6:52; 8:17–21). The fate of John the Baptist (Mk 6:17–29) hints ominously at Jesus' own passion (Mk 9:13; cf. Mk 8:31).

A breakthrough seemingly comes with Peter's confession that Jesus is the Christ (Messiah; Mk 8:27–30). But Jesus himself emphasizes his passion (Mk 8:31; 9:31; 10:33–34), not glory in the kingdom (Mk 10:35–45). Momentarily he is glimpsed in his true identity when he is transfigured before three of the disciples (Mk 9:2–8), but by and large Jesus is depicted in Mark as moving obediently along the way to his cross in Jerusalem. Occasionally there are miracles (Mk 9:17–27; 10:46–52; 11:12–14, 20–21, the only such account in Jerusalem), sometimes teachings (Mk 10:2–11, 23–31), but the greatest concern is with discipleship (Mk 8:34–9:1; 9:33–50). For the disciples do not grasp the mystery being revealed (Mk 9:32; 10:32, 38). One of them will betray him, Judas (Mk 14:10–11, 43–45); one will deny him, Peter (Mk 14:27, 31, 54, 66–72); all eleven men will desert Jesus (Mk 14:27, 50).

The passion account, with its condemnation of Jesus by the Sanhedrin (Mk 14:53, 55–65; 15:1a) and sentencing by Pilate (Mk 15:1b–15), is prefaced with the entry into Jerusalem (Mk 11:1–11), ministry and controversies there (Mk 11:15–12:44), Jesus' Last Supper with the disciples (Mk 14:1–26), and his arrest at Gethsemane (Mk 14:32–52). A chapter of apocalyptic tone about the destruction of the temple (Mk 13:1–2, 14–23) and the coming of the Son of Man (Mk 13:24–27), a discourse filled with promises (Mk 13:11, 31) and admonitions to be watchful (Mk 13:2, 23, 37), is significant for Mark's Gospel, for it helps one see that God, in Jesus, will be victorious after the cross and at the end of history.

The Gospel of Mark ends in the most ancient manuscripts with an abrupt scene at Jesus' tomb, which the women find empty (Mk 16:1–8). His own prophecy of Mk 14:28 is reiterated, that Jesus goes before the disciples into Galilee; "there you will see him." These words may imply resurrection appearances there, or Jesus' parousia there, or the start of Christian mission, or a return to the roots depicted in Mk 1:9, 14–15 in Galilee. Other hands have attached additional endings after Mk 16:8; see note on Mk 16:9–20.

The framework of Mark's Gospel is partly geographical: Galilee (Mk 1:14–9:49), through the area "across the Jordan" (Mk 10:1) and through Jericho (Mk 10:46–52), to Jerusalem (Mk 11:1–16:8). Only rarely does Jesus go into Gentile territory (Mk 5:1–20; 7:24–37), but those who acknowledge him there and the centurion who confesses Jesus at the cross (Mk 15:39) presage the gospel's expansion into the world beyond Palestine.

Mark's Gospel is even more oriented to christology. Jesus is the Son of God (Mk 1:11; 9:7; 15:39; cf. Mk 1:1; 14:61). He is the Messiah, the anointed king of Davidic descent (Mk 12:35; 15:32), the Greek for which, *Christos*, has, by the time Mark wrote, become in effect a proper name (Mk 1:1; 9:41). Jesus is also seen as Son of Man, a term used in Mark not simply as a substitute for "I" or for humanity in general (cf. Mk 2:10, 27–28; 14:21) or with reference to a mighty figure who is to come (Mk 13:26; 14:62), but also in connection with Jesus' predestined, necessary path of suffering and vindication (Mk 8:31; 10:45).

The unfolding of Mark's story about Jesus is sometimes viewed by interpreters as centered around the term "mystery." The word is employed just once, at Mk 4:11, in the singular, and its content there is the kingdom, the open secret that God's reign is now breaking into human life with its reversal of human values. There is a related sense in which Jesus' real identity remained a secret during his lifetime, according to Mark, although demons and demoniacs knew it (Mk 1:24; 3:11; 5:7); Jesus warned against telling of his mighty deeds and revealing his identity (Mk 1:44; 3:12; 5:43; 7:36; 8:26, 30), an injunction sometimes broken (Mk 1:45; cf. Mk 5:19–20). Further, Jesus teaches by parables, according to Mark, in such a way that those "outside" the kingdom do not understand, but only those to whom the mystery has been granted by God.

Mark thus shares with Paul, as well as with other parts of the New Testament, an emphasis on election (Mk 13:20, 22) and upon the gospel as Christ and his cross (cf. 1 Cor 1:23). Yet in Mark the person of Jesus is also depicted with an unaffected naturalness. He reacts to events with authentic human emotion: pity (Mk 1:44), anger (Mk 3:5), triumph (Mk 4:40), sympathy (Mk 5:36; 6:34), surprise (Mk 6:9), admiration (Mk 7:29; 10:21), sadness (Mk 14:33–34), and indignation (Mk 14:48–49).

Although the book is anonymous, apart from the ancient heading "According to Mark" in manuscripts, it has traditionally been assigned to John Mark, in whose mother's house (at Jerusalem) Christians assembled (Acts 12:12). This Mark was a cousin of Barnabas (Col 4:10) and accompanied Barnabas and Paul on a missionary journey (Acts 12:25; 13:3; 15:36–39). He appears in Pauline letters (2 Tm 4:11; Phlm 24) and with Peter (1 Pt 5:13). Papias (ca. A.D. 135) described Mark as Peter's "interpreter," a view found in other patristic writers. Petrine influence should not, however, be exaggerated. The evangelist has put together various oral and possibly written sources—miracle stories, parables, sayings, stories of controversies, and the passion—so as to speak of the crucified Messiah for Mark's own day.

Traditionally, the gospel is said to have been written shortly before A.D. 70 in Rome, at a time of impending persecution and when destruction loomed over Jerusalem. Its audience seems to have been Gentile, unfamiliar with Jewish customs (hence Mk 7:3–4, 11). The book aimed to equip such Christians to stand faithful in the face of persecution (Mk 13:9–13), while going on with the proclamation of the gospel begun in Galilee (Mk 13:10; 14:9). Modern research often proposes as the author an unknown Hellenistic Jewish Christian, possibly in Syria, and perhaps shortly after the year 70.

The principal divisions of the Gospel according to Mark are the following:

I. The Preparation for the Public Ministry of Jesus (1:1–13)

II. The Mystery of Jesus (1:14–8:26)
III. The Mystery Begins to Be Revealed (8:27–9:32)
IV. The Full Revelation of the Mystery (9:33–16:8)
The Longer Ending (16:9–20)
The Shorter Ending
The Freer Logion (in the note on 16:9–20)

I. The Preparation for the Public Ministry of Jesus

CHAPTER 1

See RG 388–90

[1*]The beginning of the gospel of Jesus Christ [the Son of God].

The Preaching of John the Baptist. [2ab*]As it is written in Isaiah the prophet:

"Behold, I am sending my messenger
ahead of you;
he will prepare your way.
[3 c]A voice of one crying out in the desert:
'Prepare the way of the Lord,
make straight his paths.' "

[4]John [the] Baptist appeared in the desert proclaiming a baptism of repentance for the forgiveness of sins. [5]People of the whole Judean countryside and all the inhabitants of Jerusalem were going out to him and were being baptized by him in the Jordan River as they acknowledged their sins. [6*]John was clothed in camel's hair, with a leather belt around his waist. He fed on locusts and wild honey. [7]And this is what he proclaimed: "One mightier than I is coming after me. I am not worthy to stoop and loosen the thongs of his sandals. [8d*]I have baptized you with water; he will baptize you with the holy Spirit."

The Baptism of Jesus. [9e]It happened in those days that Jesus came from Nazareth of Galilee and was baptized in the Jordan by John. [10*]On coming up out of the water he saw the heavens being torn open and the Spirit, like a dove, descending upon him. [11f]And a voice came from the heavens, "You are my beloved Son; with you I am well pleased."

The Temptation of Jesus. [12g*]At once the Spirit drove him out into the desert, [13]and he remained in the desert for forty days, tempted by Satan. He was among wild beasts, and the angels ministered to him.

1:1–13 The prologue of the Gospel according to Mark begins with the title (Mk 1:1) followed by three events preparatory to Jesus' preaching: (1) the appearance in the Judean wilderness of John, baptizer, preacher of repentance, and precursor of Jesus (Mk 1:2–8); (2) the baptism of Jesus, at which a voice from heaven acknowledges Jesus to be God's Son, and the holy Spirit descends on him (Mk 1:9–11); (3) the temptation of Jesus by Satan (Mk 1:12–13).

1:1 The gospel of Jesus Christ [the Son of God]: the "good news" of salvation in and through Jesus, crucified and risen, acknowledged by the Christian community as Messiah (Mk 8:29; 14:61–62) and Son of God (Mk 1:11; 9:7; 15:39), although some important manuscripts here omit **the Son of God**.

1:2–3 Although Mark attributes the prophecy to Isaiah, the text is a combination of Mal 3:1; Is 40:3; Ex 23:20; cf. Mt 11:10; Lk 7:27. John's ministry is seen as God's prelude to the saving mission of his Son. **The way of the Lord**: this prophecy of Deutero-Isaiah concerning the end of the Babylonian exile is here applied to the coming of Jesus; John the Baptist is to prepare the way for him.

1:6 Clothed in camel's hair . . . waist: the Baptist's garb recalls that of Elijah in 2 Kgs 1:8. Jesus speaks of the Baptist as Elijah who has already come (Mk 9:11–13; Mt 17:10–12; cf. Mal 3:19; Lk 1:17).

1:8–9 Through the life-giving baptism with the holy Spirit (Mk 1:8), Jesus will create a new people of God. But first he identifies himself with the people of Israel in submitting to John's baptism of repentance and in bearing on their behalf the burden of God's decisive judgment (Mk 1:9; cf. Mk 1:4). As in the desert of Sinai, so here in the wilderness of Judea, Israel's sonship with God is to be renewed.

1:10–11 He saw the heavens . . . and the Spirit . . . upon him: indicating divine intervention in fulfillment of promise. Here the descent of the Spirit on Jesus is meant, anointing him for his ministry; cf. Is 11:2; 42:1; 61:1; 63:9. **A voice . . . with you I am well pleased**: God's acknowledgment of Jesus as his unique Son, the object of his love. His approval of Jesus is the assurance that Jesus will fulfill his messianic mission of salvation.

1:12–13 The same Spirit who descended on Jesus in his baptism now drives him into the desert for forty days. The result is radical confrontation and temptation by Satan who attempts to frustrate the work of God. The presence of wild beasts may indicate the horror and danger of the desert regarded as the abode of demons or may reflect the paradise motif of harmony among all creatures; cf. Is 11:6–9. The presence of ministering angels to sustain Jesus recalls the angel who guided the Israelites in the desert in the first Exodus (Ex 14:19; 23:20) and the angel who supplied nourishment to Elijah in the wilderness (1 Kgs 19:5–7). The combined forces

a: Mt 3:1–11; Lk 3:2–16. *b:* Mal 3:1. *c:* Is 40:3; Jn 1:23. *d:* Jn 1:27; Acts 1:5; 11:16. *e:* Mt 3:13–17; Lk 3:21–23; Jn 1:32–33. *f:* Ps 2:7. *g:* Mt 4:1–11; Lk 4:1–13.

II. The Mystery of Jesus

The Beginning of the Galilean Ministry.
14h* After John had been arrested, Jesus came
to Galilee proclaiming the gospel of God:
15i "This is the time of fulfillment. The kingdom of God is at hand. Repent, and believe
in the gospel."

The Call of the First Disciples. 16j* As he
passed by the Sea of Galilee, he saw Simon
and his brother Andrew casting their nets
into the sea; they were fishermen. 17 Jesus
said to them, "Come after me, and I will
make you fishers of men." 18 Then they abandoned their nets and followed him. 19 He
walked along a little farther and saw James,
the son of Zebedee, and his brother John.
They too were in a boat mending their nets.
20 Then he called them. So they left their father Zebedee in the boat along with the hired
men and followed him.

The Cure of a Demoniac. 21k* Then they
came to Capernaum, and on the sabbath he
entered the synagogue and taught. 22l The
people were astonished at his teaching, for he
taught them as one having authority and not
as the scribes. 23* In their synagogue was a
man with an unclean spirit; 24* he cried out,
"What have you to do with us, Jesus of Nazareth? Have you come to destroy us? I know
who you are—the Holy One of God!" 25 Jesus
rebuked him and said, "Quiet! Come out of
him!" 26 The unclean spirit convulsed him
and with a loud cry came out of him. 27 All
were amazed and asked one another, "What
is this? A new teaching with authority. He
commands even the unclean spirits and they
obey him." 28 His fame spread everywhere
throughout the whole region of Galilee.

The Cure of Simon's Mother-in-Law.
29m On leaving the synagogue he entered the
house of Simon and Andrew with James and
John. 30 Simon's mother-in-law lay sick with
a fever. They immediately told him about
her. 31 He approached, grasped her hand, and
helped her up. Then the fever left her and she
waited on them.

Other Healings. 32 When it was evening,
after sunset, they brought to him all who were
ill or possessed by demons. 33 The whole town
was gathered at the door. 34 He cured many
who were sick with various diseases, and he
drove out many demons, not permitting them
to speak because they knew him.

Jesus Leaves Capernaum. 35n Rising very
early before dawn, he left and went off to a
deserted place, where he prayed. 36 Simon and
those who were with him pursued him 37 and
on finding him said, "Everyone is looking for
you." 38 He told them, "Let us go on to the
nearby villages that I may preach there also.
For this purpose have I come." 39 So he went
into their synagogues, preaching and driving
out demons throughout the whole of Galilee.

The Cleansing of a Leper. 40o* A leper
came to him [and kneeling down] begged

of good and evil were present to Jesus in the desert. His sustained obedience brings forth the new Israel of God there where Israel's rebellion had brought death and alienation.

1:14–15 After John had been arrested: in the plan of God, Jesus was not to proclaim the good news of salvation prior to the termination of the Baptist's active mission. **Galilee**: in the Marcan account, scene of the major part of Jesus' public ministry before his arrest and condemnation. **The gospel of God**: not only the good news from God but about God at work in Jesus Christ. **This is the time of fulfillment**: i.e., of God's promises. **The kingdom of God . . . repent**: see note on Mt 3:2.

1:16–20 These verses narrate the call of the first Disciples. See notes on Mt 4:18–22 and Mt 4:20.

1:21–45 The account of a single day's ministry of Jesus on a sabbath in and outside the synagogue of Capernaum (Mk 1:21–31) combines teaching and miracles of exorcism and healing. Mention is not made of the content of the teaching but of the effect of astonishment and alarm on the people. Jesus' teaching with authority, making an absolute claim on the hearer, was in the best tradition of the ancient prophets, not of the scribes. The narrative continues with events that evening (Mk 1:32–34; see notes on Mt 8:14–17) and the next day (Mk 1:35–39). The cleansing in Mk 1:40–45 stands as an isolated story.

1:23 An unclean spirit: so called because of the spirit's resistance to the holiness of God. The spirit knows and fears the power of Jesus to destroy his influence; cf. Mk 1:32, 34; 3:11; 6:13.

1:24–25 The Holy One of God: not a confession but an attempt to ward off Jesus' power, reflecting the notion that use of the precise name of an opposing spirit would guarantee mastery over him. Jesus silenced the cry of the unclean spirit and drove him out of the man.

1:24 What have you to do with us?: see note on Jn 2:4.

1:40 A leper: for the various forms of skin disease, see Lv 13:1–50 and the note on Lv 13:2–4. There are only two instances in the Old Testament in which God is shown to have cured a leper (Nm 12:10–15; 2 Kgs 5:1–14). The law of Mo-

h: Mt 4:12–17; Lk 4:14–15. *i:* Mt 3:2. *j:* Mt 4:18–22; Lk 5:2–11. *k:* Lk 4:31–37. *l:* Mt 7:28–29. *m:* Mt 8:14–16; Lk 4:38–41. *n:* Lk 4:42–44. *o:* Mt 8:2–4; Lk 5:12–14.

him and said, "If you wish, you can make me clean." [41p]Moved with pity, he stretched out his hand, touched him, and said to him, "I do will it. Be made clean." [42q]The leprosy left him immediately, and he was made clean. [43]Then, warning him sternly, he dismissed him at once. [44r]Then he said to him, "See that you tell no one anything, but go, show yourself to the priest and offer for your cleansing what Moses prescribed; that will be proof for them." [45]The man went away and began to publicize the whole matter. He spread the report abroad so that it was impossible for Jesus to enter a town openly. He remained outside in deserted places, and people kept coming to him from everywhere.

CHAPTER 2

See RC 390–91

The Healing of a Paralytic. [1s*]When Jesus returned to Capernaum after some days, it became known that he was at home. [2]Many gathered together so that there was no longer room for them, not even around the door, and he preached the word to them. [3]They came bringing to him a paralytic carried by four men. [4]Unable to get near Jesus because of the crowd, they opened up the roof above him. After they had broken through, they let down the mat on which the paralytic was lying. [5*]When Jesus saw their faith, he said to the paralytic, "Child, your sins are forgiven." [6*]Now some of the scribes were sitting there asking themselves, [7t*]"Why does this man speak that way? He is blaspheming. Who but God alone can forgive sins?" [8]Jesus immediately knew in his mind what they were thinking to themselves, so he said, "Why are you thinking such things in your hearts? [9]Which is easier, to say to the paralytic, 'Your sins are forgiven,' or to say, 'Rise, pick up your mat and walk'? [10*]But that you may know that the Son of Man has authority to forgive sins on earth"— [11]he said to the paralytic, "I say to you, rise, pick up your mat, and go home." [12]He rose, picked up his mat at once, and went away in the sight of everyone. They were all astounded and glorified God, saying, "We have never seen anything like this."

The Call of Levi. [13u*]Once again he went out along the sea. All the crowd came to him and he taught them. [14v*]As he passed by, he saw Levi, son of Alphaeus, sitting at the customs post. He said to him, "Follow me." And he got up and followed him. [15*]While he was at table in his house, many tax collectors and sinners sat with Jesus and his disciples; for there were many who followed him. [16*]Some scribes who were Pharisees saw that he was eating with sinners and tax col-

ses provided for the ritual purification of a leper. In curing the leper, Jesus assumes that the priests will reinstate the cured man into the religious community. See also note on Lk 5:14.

2:1–3:6 This section relates a series of conflicts between Jesus and the scribes and Pharisees in which the growing opposition of the latter leads to their plot to put Jesus to death (Mk 3:6).

2:1 He was at home: to the crowds that gathered in and outside the house Jesus **preached the word**, i.e., the gospel concerning the nearness of the kingdom and the necessity of repentance and faith (Mk 1:14).

2:5 It was the faith of the paralytic and those who carried him that moved Jesus to heal the sick man. Accounts of other miracles of Jesus reveal more and more his emphasis on faith as the requisite for exercising his healing powers (Mk 5:34; 9:23–24; 10:52).

2:6 Scribes: trained in oral interpretation of the written law; in Mark's gospel, adversaries of Jesus, with one exception (Mk 12:28, 34).

2:7 He is blaspheming: an accusation made here and repeated during the trial of Jesus (Mk 14:60–64).

2:10 But that you may know that the Son of Man . . . on earth: although Mk 2:8–9 are addressed to the scribes, the sudden interruption of thought and structure in Mk 2:10 seems not addressed to them nor to the paralytic. Moreover, the early public use of the designation "Son of Man" to unbelieving scribes is most unlikely. The most probable explanation is that Mark's insertion of Mk 2:10 is a commentary addressed to Christians for whom he recalls this miracle and who already accept in faith that Jesus is Messiah and Son of God.

2:13 He taught them: see note on Mk 1:21–45.

2:14 As he passed by: see note on Mk 1:16–20. **Levi, son of Alphaeus**: see note on Mt 9:9. **Customs post**: such tax collectors paid a fixed sum for the right to collect customs duties within their districts. Since whatever they could collect above this amount constituted their profit, the abuse of extortion was widespread among them. Hence, Jewish customs officials were regarded as sinners (Mk 2:16), outcasts of society, and disgraced along with their families. **He got up and followed him**: i.e., became a disciple of Jesus.

2:15 In his house: cf. Mk 2:1; Mt 9:10. Lk 5:29 clearly calls it Levi's house.

2:16–17 This and the following conflict stories reflect a similar pattern: a statement of fact, a question of protest, and a reply by Jesus.

p: 5:30. *q:* Lk 17:14. *r:* Lv 14:2–32. *s:* Mt 9:2–8; Lk 5:18–26. *t:* Is 43:25. *u:* 4:1. *v:* Mt 9:9–13; Lk 5:27–32.

lectors and said to his disciples, "Why does he eat with tax collectors and sinners?" [17*]Jesus heard this and said to them [that], "Those who are well do not need a physician, but the sick do. I did not come to call the righteous but sinners."

The Question about Fasting. [18w*]The disciples of John and of the Pharisees were accustomed to fast. People came to him and objected, "Why do the disciples of John and the disciples of the Pharisees fast, but your disciples do not fast?" [19*]Jesus answered them, "Can the wedding guests fast while the bridegroom is with them? As long as they have the bridegroom with them they cannot fast. [20]But the days will come when the bridegroom is taken away from them, and then they will fast on that day. [21]No one sews a piece of unshrunken cloth on an old cloak. If he does, its fullness pulls away, the new from the old, and the tear gets worse. [22]Likewise, no one pours new wine into old wineskins. Otherwise, the wine will burst the skins, and both the wine and the skins are ruined. Rather, new wine is poured into fresh wineskins."

The Disciples and the Sabbath. [23x*]As he was passing through a field of grain on the sabbath, his disciples began to make a path while picking the heads of grain. [24y]At this the Pharisees said to him, "Look, why are they doing what is unlawful on the sabbath?" [25*]He said to them, "Have you never read what David did when he was in need and he and his companions were hungry? [26z]How he went into the house of God when Abiathar was high priest and ate the bread of offering that only the priests could lawfully eat, and shared it with his companions?" [27a*]Then he said to them, "The sabbath was made for man, not man for the sabbath. [28*]That is why the Son of Man is lord even of the sabbath."

CHAPTER 3

See RG 390–91

A Man with a Withered Hand. [1b*]Again he entered the synagogue. There was a man there who had a withered hand. [2]They watched him closely to see if he would cure him on the sabbath so that they might accuse him. [3]He said to the man with the withered hand, "Come up here before us." [4]Then he said to them, "Is it lawful to do good on the sabbath rather than to do evil, to save life rather than to destroy it?" But they remained silent. [5c]Looking around at them with anger and grieved at their hardness of heart, he said to the man, "Stretch out your hand." He stretched it out and his hand was restored. [6*]The Pharisees went out and im-

2:17 Do not need a physician: this maxim of Jesus with its implied irony was uttered to silence his adversaries who objected that he ate with **tax collectors and sinners** (Mk 2:16). Because the scribes and Pharisees were self-righteous, they were not capable of responding to Jesus' call to repentance and faith in the gospel.

2:18–22 This conflict over the question of fasting has the same pattern as Mk 2:16–17; see notes on Mt 9:15; 9:16–17.

2:19 Can the wedding guests fast?: the bridal metaphor expresses a new relationship of love between God and his people in the person and mission of Jesus to his disciples. It is the inauguration of the new and joyful messianic time of fulfillment and the passing of the old. Any attempt at assimilating the Pharisaic practice of fasting, or of extending the preparatory discipline of John's disciples beyond the arrival of the bridegroom, would be as futile as sewing **a piece of unshrunken cloth on an old cloak** or pouring **new wine into old wineskins** with the resulting destruction of both cloth and wine (Mk 2:21–22). Fasting is rendered superfluous during the earthly ministry of Jesus; cf. Mk 2:20.

2:23–28 This conflict regarding the sabbath follows the same pattern as in Mk 2:18–22.

2:25–26 Have you never read what David did?: Jesus defends the action of his disciples on the basis of 1 Sm 21:2–7 in which an exception is made to the regulation of Lv 24:9 because of the extreme hunger of David and his men. According to 1 Samuel, the priest who gave the bread to David was Ahimelech, father of Abiathar.

2:27 The sabbath was made for man: a reaffirmation of the divine intent of the sabbath to benefit Israel as contrasted with the restrictive Pharisaic tradition added to the law.

2:28 The Son of Man is lord even of the sabbath: Mark's comment on the theological meaning of the incident is to benefit his Christian readers; see note on Mk 2:10.

3:1–5 Here Jesus is again depicted in conflict with his adversaries over the question of sabbath-day observance. His opponents were already ill disposed toward him because they regarded Jesus as a violator of the sabbath. Jesus' question **Is it lawful to do good on the sabbath rather than to do evil?** places the matter in the broader theological context outside the casuistry of the scribes. The answer is obvious. Jesus heals the man with the withered hand in the sight of all and reduces his opponents to silence; cf. Jn 5:17–18.

3:6 In reporting the plot of the Pharisees and Herodians to put Jesus to death after this series of conflicts in Galilee, Mark uses a pattern that recurs in his account of later controversies in Jerusalem (Mk 11:17–18; 12:13–17). The help of the Herodians, supporters of Herod Antipas, tetrarch of Gali-

w: Mt 9:14–17; Lk 5:33–39. *x:* Mt 12:1–8; Lk 6:1–5. *y:* Dt 23:25. *z:* 1 Sm 21:2–7 / Lv 24:5–9. *a:* 2 Mc 5:19. *b:* Mt 12:9–14; Lk 6:6–11. *c:* Lk 14:4.

mediately took counsel with the Herodians against him to put him to death.

The Mercy of Jesus. [7d*]Jesus withdrew toward the sea with his disciples. A large number of people [followed] from Galilee and from Judea. [8]Hearing what he was doing, a large number of people came to him also from Jerusalem, from Idumea, from beyond the Jordan, and from the neighborhood of Tyre and Sidon. [9]He told his disciples to have a boat ready for him because of the crowd, so that they would not crush him. [10e]He had cured many and, as a result, those who had diseases were pressing upon him to touch him. [11f*]And whenever unclean spirits saw him they would fall down before him and shout, "You are the Son of God." [12]He warned them sternly not to make him known.

The Mission of the Twelve. [13g*]He went up the mountain and summoned those whom he wanted and they came to him. [14h*]He appointed twelve [whom he also named apostles] that they might be with him and he might send them forth to preach [15]and to have authority to drive out demons: [16*][he appointed the twelve:] Simon, whom he named Peter; [17i]James, son of Zebedee, and John the brother of James, whom he named Boanerges, that is, sons of thunder; [18]Andrew, Philip, Bartholomew, Matthew, Thomas, James the son of Alphaeus; Thaddeus, Simon the Cananean, [19]and Judas Iscariot who betrayed him.

Blasphemy of the Scribes. [20j*]He came home. Again [the] crowd gathered, making it impossible for them even to eat. [21k]When his relatives heard of this they set out to seize him, for they said, "He is out of his mind." [22l*]The scribes who had come from Jerusalem said, "He is possessed by Beelzebul," and "By the prince of demons he drives out demons."

Jesus and Beelzebul. [23]Summoning them, he began to speak to them in parables, "How can Satan drive out Satan? [24]If a kingdom is divided against itself, that kingdom cannot stand. [25]And if a house is divided against itself, that house will not be able to stand. [26]And if Satan has risen up against himself and is divided, he cannot stand; that is the end of him. [27]But no one can enter a strong man's house to plunder his property unless he first ties up the strong man. Then he can plunder his house. [28m]Amen, I say to you, all sins and all blasphemies that people utter will be forgiven them. [29*]But whoever blasphemes against the holy Spirit will never have forgiveness, but is guilty of an everlasting sin." [30]For they had said, "He has an unclean spirit."

lee and Perea, is needed to take action against Jesus. Both series of conflicts point to their gravity and to the impending passion of Jesus.

3:7–19 This overview of the Galilean ministry manifests the power of Jesus to draw people to himself through his teaching and deeds of power. The crowds of Jews from many regions surround Jesus (Mk 3:7–12). This phenomenon prepares the way for creating a new people of Israel. The choice and mission of the Twelve is the prelude (Mk 3:13–19).

3:11–12 See note on Mk 1:24–25.

3:13 He went up the mountain: here and elsewhere the mountain is associated with solemn moments and acts in the mission and self-revelation of Jesus (Mk 6:46; 9:2–8; 13:3). Jesus acts with authority as he **summoned those whom he wanted and they came to him.**

3:14–15 He appointed twelve [whom he also named apostles] that they might be with him: literally "he made," i.e., instituted them as apostles to extend his messianic mission through them (Mk 6:7–13). See notes on Mt 10:1 and 10:2–4.

3:16 Simon, whom he named Peter: Mark indicates that Simon's name was changed on this occasion. Peter is first in all lists of the apostles (Mt 10:2; Lk 6:14; Acts 1:13; cf. 1 Cor 15:5–8).

3:20–35 Within the narrative of the coming of Jesus' relatives (Mk 3:20–21) is inserted the account of the unbelieving scribes from Jerusalem who attributed Jesus' power over demons to Beelzebul (Mk 3:22–30); see note on Mk 5:21–43. There were those even among the relatives of Jesus who disbelieved and regarded Jesus as **out of his mind** (Mk 3:21). Against this background, Jesus is informed of the arrival of his mother and brothers [and sisters] (Mk 3:32). He responds by showing that not family ties but doing God's will (35) is decisive in the kingdom; cf. note on Mt 12:46–50.

3:20 He came home: cf. Mk 2:1–2 and see note on Mk 2:15.

3:22 By Beelzebul: see note on Mt 10:25. Two accusations are leveled against Jesus: (1) that **he is possessed** by an unclean spirit, and (2) **by the prince of demons he drives out demons.** Jesus answers the second charge by a parable (Mk 3:24–27) and responds to the first charge in Mk 3:28–29.

3:29 Whoever blasphemes against the holy Spirit: this sin is called **an everlasting sin** because it attributes to Satan, who is the power of evil, what is actually the work of the holy Spirit, namely, victory over the demons.

---

d: Mt 4:23–25; 12:15; Lk 6:17–19. *e:* 5:30. *f:* 1:34; Lk 4:41. *g:* Mt 10:1–4; Lk 6:12–16. *h:* 6:7. *i:* Mt 16:18; Jn 1:42. *j:* 2:2. *k:* Jn 10:20. *l:* Mt 12:24–32; Lk 11:15–22; 12:10. *m:* Lk 12:10.

Jesus and His Family. [31n]His mother and his brothers arrived. Standing outside they sent word to him and called him. [32*]A crowd seated around him told him, "Your mother and your brothers [and your sisters] are outside asking for you." [33]But he said to them in reply, "Who are my mother and [my] brothers?" [34]And looking around at those seated in the circle he said, "Here are my mother and my brothers. [35][For] whoever does the will of God is my brother and sister and mother."

CHAPTER 4

See RG 391–92

The Parable of the Sower. [1op*]On another occasion he began to teach by the sea. A very large crowd gathered around him so that he got into a boat on the sea and sat down. And the whole crowd was beside the sea on land. [2]And he taught them at length in parables, and in the course of his instruction he said to them, [3*]"Hear this! A sower went out to sow. [4]And as he sowed, some seed fell on the path, and the birds came and ate it up. [5]Other seed fell on rocky ground where it had little soil. It sprang up at once because the soil was not deep. [6]And when the sun rose, it was scorched and it withered for lack of roots. [7]Some seed fell among thorns, and the thorns grew up and choked it and it produced no grain. [8]And some seed fell on rich soil and produced fruit. It came up and grew and yielded thirty, sixty, and a hundredfold." [9]He added, "Whoever has ears to hear ought to hear."

The Purpose of the Parables. [10]And when he was alone, those present along with the Twelve questioned him about the parables. [11*]He answered them, "The mystery of the kingdom of God has been granted to you. But to those outside everything comes in parables, [12q]so that

'they may look and see but not perceive,
and hear and listen but not understand,
in order that they may not be converted
and be forgiven.' "

[13r*]Jesus said to them, "Do you not understand this parable? Then how will you understand any of the parables? [14]The sower sows the word. [15]These are the ones on the path where the word is sown. As soon as they hear, Satan comes at once and takes away the word sown in them. [16]And these are the ones sown on rocky ground who, when they hear the word, receive it at once with joy. [17]But they have no root; they last only for a time. Then when tribulation or persecution comes because of the word, they quickly fall away. [18]Those sown among thorns are another sort. They are the people who hear the word, [19]but worldly anxiety, the lure of riches, and the craving for other things intrude and choke the word, and it bears no fruit. [20]But those sown on rich soil are the ones who hear the word and accept it and bear fruit thirty and sixty and a hundredfold."

Parable of the Lamp. [21st]He said to them, "Is a lamp brought in to be placed under a bushel basket or under a bed, and not to be placed on a lampstand? [22u]For there is nothing hidden except to be made visible; noth-

3:32 Your brothers: see note on Mk 6:3.

4:1–34 In parables (2): see note on Mt 13:3. The use of parables is typical of Jesus' enigmatic method of teaching the crowds (Mk 4:2–9, 12) as compared with the interpretation of the parables he gives to his disciples (Mk 4:10–25, 33–34) to each group according to its capacity to understand (Mk 4:9–11). The key feature of the parable at hand is the sowing of the seed (3), representing the breakthrough of the kingdom of God into the world. The various types of soil refer to the diversity of response accorded the word of God (Mk 4:4–7). The climax of the parable is the harvest of thirty, sixty, and a hundredfold, indicating the consummation of the kingdom (Mk 4:8). Thus both the present and the future action of God, from the initiation to the fulfillment of the kingdom, is presented through this and other parables (Mk 4:26–29, 30–32).

4:1 By the sea: the shore of the Sea of Galilee or a boat near the shore (Mk 2:13; 3:7–8) is the place where Mark depicts Jesus teaching the crowds. By contrast the mountain is the scene of Jesus at prayer (Mk 6:46) or in the process of forming his disciples (Mk 3:13; 9:2).

4:3–8 See note on Mt 13:3–8.

4:11–12 These verses are to be viewed against their background in Mk 3:6, 22 concerning the unbelief and opposition Jesus encountered in his ministry. It is against this background that the distinction in Jesus' method becomes clear of presenting the kingdom to the disbelieving crowd in one manner and to the disciples in another. To the former it is presented in parables and the truth remains hidden; for the latter the parable is interpreted and the mystery is partially revealed because of their faith; see notes on Mt 13:11 and Mt 13:13.

4:13–20 See note on Mt 13:18–23.

n: Mt 12:46–50; Lk 8:19–21. *o:* Mt 13:1–13; Lk 8:4–10. *p:* 2:13; Lk 5:1. *q:* Is 6:9; Jn 12:40; Acts 28:26; Rom 11:8. *r:* Mt 13:18–23; Lk 8:11–15. *s:* Lk 8:16–18. *t:* Mt 5:15; Lk 11:33. *u:* Mt 10:26; Lk 12:2.

ing is secret except to come to light. [23]Anyone who has ears to hear ought to hear." [24v]He also told them, "Take care what you hear. The measure with which you measure will be measured out to you, and still more will be given to you. [25w]To the one who has, more will be given; from the one who has not, even what he has will be taken away."

Seed Grows of Itself. [26x*]He said, "This is how it is with the kingdom of God; it is as if a man were to scatter seed on the land [27]and would sleep and rise night and day and the seed would sprout and grow, he knows not how. [28]Of its own accord the land yields fruit, first the blade, then the ear, then the full grain in the ear. [29]And when the grain is ripe, he wields the sickle at once, for the harvest has come."

The Mustard Seed. [30y]He said, "To what shall we compare the kingdom of God, or what parable can we use for it? [31]It is like a mustard seed that, when it is sown in the ground, is the smallest of all the seeds on the earth. [32*]But once it is sown, it springs up and becomes the largest of plants and puts forth large branches, so that the birds of the sky can dwell in its shade." [33z]With many such parables he spoke the word to them as they were able to understand it. [34]Without parables he did not speak to them, but to his own disciples he explained everything in private.

The Calming of a Storm at Sea. [35a*]On that day, as evening drew on, he said to them, "Let us cross to the other side." [36]Leaving the crowd, they took him with them in the boat just as he was. And other boats were with him. [37]A violent squall came up and waves were breaking over the boat, so that it was already filling up. [38]Jesus was in the stern, asleep on a cushion. They woke him and said to him, "Teacher, do you not care that we are perishing?" [39*]He woke up, rebuked the wind, and said to the sea, "Quiet! Be still!" The wind ceased and there was great calm. [40]Then he asked them, "Why are you terrified? Do you not yet have faith?" [41b*]They were filled with great awe and said to one another, "Who then is this whom even wind and sea obey?"

CHAPTER 5

See RG 392–93

The Healing of the Gerasene Demoniac. [1c*]They came to the other side of the sea, to the territory of the Gerasenes. [2*]When he got out of the boat, at once a man from the tombs who had an unclean spirit met him. [3]The man had been dwelling among the tombs, and no one could restrain him any longer, even with a chain. [4]In fact, he had frequently been bound with shackles and chains, but the chains had been pulled apart by him and the shackles smashed, and no one was strong enough to subdue him. [5]Night and day among the tombs and on the hillsides he was always crying out and bruising himself with stones. [6]Catching sight of Jesus from a distance, he ran up and prostrated himself before him, [7*]crying out in a loud voice, "What have you to do with me, Jesus, Son of the Most High God? I adjure you by God, do not torment me!" [8](He had been saying to him, "Unclean spirit, come

4:26–29 Only Mark records the parable of the seed's growth. Sower and harvester are the same. The emphasis is on the power of the seed to grow of itself without human intervention (Mk 4:27). Mysteriously it produces **blade** and **ear** and **full grain** (Mk 4:28). Thus the kingdom of God initiated by Jesus in proclaiming the word develops quietly yet powerfully until it is fully established by him at the final judgment (Mk 4:29); cf. Rev 14:15.

4:32 The universality of the kingdom of God is indicated here; cf. Ez 17:23; 31:6; Dn 4:17–19.

4:35–5:43 After the chapter on parables, Mark narrates four miracle stories: Mk 4:35–41; 5:1–20; and two joined together in Mk 5:21–43. See also notes on Mt 8:23–34 and 9:8–26.

4:39 Quiet! Be still!: as in the case of silencing a demon (Mk 1:25), Jesus rebukes the wind and subdues the turbulence of the sea by a mere word; see note on Mt 8:26.

4:41 Jesus is here depicted as exercising power over wind and sea. In the Christian community this event was seen as a sign of Jesus' saving presence amid persecutions that threatened its existence.

5:1 The territory of the Gerasenes: the reference is to pagan territory; cf. Is 65:1. Another reading is "Gadarenes"; see note on Mt 8:28.

5:2–6 The man was an outcast from society, dominated by unclean spirits (Mk 5:8, 13), living among the tombs. The prostration before Jesus (Mk 5:6) indicates Jesus' power over evil spirits.

5:7 What have you to do with me?: cf. Mk 1:24 and see note on Jn 2:4.

---

v: Mt 7:2; Lk 6:38. *w:* Mt 13:12; Lk 19:26. *x:* Jas 5:7. *y:* Mt 13:31–32; Lk 13:18–19. *z:* Mt 13:34. *a:* Mt 8:18, 23–37; Lk 8:22–25. *b:* 1:27. *c:* Mt 8:28–34; Lk 8:26–39.

out of the man!") [9d*]He asked him, "What is your name?" He replied, "Legion is my name. There are many of us." [10]And he pleaded earnestly with him not to drive them away from that territory.

[11*]Now a large herd of swine was feeding there on the hillside. [12]And they pleaded with him, "Send us into the swine. Let us enter them." [13]And he let them, and the unclean spirits came out and entered the swine. The herd of about two thousand rushed down a steep bank into the sea, where they were drowned. [14]The swineherds ran away and reported the incident in the town and throughout the countryside. And people came out to see what had happened. [15]As they approached Jesus, they caught sight of the man who had been possessed by Legion, sitting there clothed and in his right mind. And they were seized with fear. [16]Those who witnessed the incident explained to them what had happened to the possessed man and to the swine. [17]Then they began to beg him to leave their district. [18]As he was getting into the boat, the man who had been possessed pleaded to remain with him. [19*]But he would not permit him but told him instead, "Go home to your family and announce to them all that the Lord in his pity has done for you." [20]Then the man went off and began to proclaim in the Decapolis what Jesus had done for him; and all were amazed.

Jairus's Daughter and the Woman with a Hemorrhage. [21e*]When Jesus had crossed again [in the boat] to the other side, a large crowd gathered around him, and he stayed close to the sea. [22f]One of the synagogue officials, named Jairus, came forward. Seeing him he fell at his feet [23*]and pleaded earnestly with him, saying, "My daughter is at the point of death. Please, come lay your hands on her that she may get well and live." [24]He went off with him, and a large crowd followed him and pressed upon him.

[25]There was a woman afflicted with hemorrhages for twelve years. [26]She had suffered greatly at the hands of many doctors and had spent all that she had. Yet she was not helped but only grew worse. [27]She had heard about Jesus and came up behind him in the crowd and touched his cloak. [28*]She said, "If I but touch his clothes, I shall be cured." [29]Immediately her flow of blood dried up. She felt in her body that she was healed of her affliction. [30]Jesus, aware at once that power had gone out from him, turned around in the crowd and asked, "Who has touched my clothes?" [31]But his disciples said to him, "You see how the crowd is pressing upon you, and yet you ask, 'Who touched me?' " [32]And he looked around to see who had done it. [33]The woman, realizing what had happened to her, approached in fear and trembling. She fell down before Jesus and told him the whole truth. [34g]He said to her, "Daughter, your faith has saved you. Go in peace and be cured of your affliction."

[35*]While he was still speaking, people from the synagogue official's house arrived and said, "Your daughter has died; why trouble the teacher any longer?" [36]Disregarding the message that was reported, Jesus said to the synagogue official, "Do not be afraid; just have faith." [37]He did not allow anyone to accompany him inside except Peter, James, and John, the brother of James.

5:9 Legion is my name: the demons were numerous and the condition of the possessed man was extremely serious; cf. Mt 12:45.

5:11 Herd of swine: see note on Mt 8:30.

5:19 Go home: Jesus did not accept the man's request **to remain with him** as a disciple (Mk 5:18), yet invited him to announce to his own people what the Lord had done for him, i.e., proclaim the gospel message to his pagan family; cf. Mk 1:14, 39; 3:14; 13:10.

5:21–43 The story of the raising to life of Jairus's daughter is divided into two parts: Mk 5:21–24; 5:35–43. Between these two separated parts the account of the cure of the hemorrhage victim (Mk 5:25–34) is interposed. This technique of intercalating or sandwiching one story within another occurs several times in Mk 3:19b–21; Mk 3:22–30 Mk 3:31–35; 6:6b–13; 6:14–29; 6:30; 11:12–14; 11:15–19; 11:20–25; 14:53; 14:54; 14:55–65; 14:66–73.

5:23 Lay your hands on her: this act for the purpose of healing is frequent in Mk 6:5; 7:32–35; 8:23–25; 16:18 and is also found in Mt 9:18; Lk 4:40; 13:13; Acts 9:17; 28:8.

5:28 Both in the case of Jairus and his daughter (Mk 5:23) and in the case of the hemorrhage victim, the inner conviction that physical contact (Mk 5:30) accompanied by faith in Jesus' saving power could effect a cure was rewarded.

5:35 The faith of Jairus was put to a twofold test: (1) that his daughter might be cured and, now that she had died, (2) that she might be restored to life. His faith contrasts with the lack of faith of the crowd.

d: Mt 12:45; Lk 8:2; 11:26. *e:* 2:13. *f:* Mt 9:18–26; Lk 8:41–56. *g:* Lk 7:30.

[38]When they arrived at the house of the synagogue official, he caught sight of a commotion, people weeping and wailing loudly. [39h*]So he went in and said to them, "Why this commotion and weeping? The child is not dead but asleep." [40]And they ridiculed him. Then he put them all out. He took along the child's father and mother and those who were with him and entered the room where the child was. [41*]He took the child by the hand and said to her, "*Talitha koum,*" which means, "Little girl, I say to you, arise!" [42]The girl, a child of twelve, arose immediately and walked around. [At that] they were utterly astounded. [43]He gave strict orders that no one should know this and said that she should be given something to eat.

See RG 392–93

CHAPTER 6

The Rejection at Nazareth. [1i*]He departed from there and came to his native place, accompanied by his disciples. [2*]When the sabbath came he began to teach in the synagogue, and many who heard him were astonished. They said, "Where did this man get all this? What kind of wisdom has been given him? What mighty deeds are wrought by his hands! [3j*]Is he not the carpenter, the son of Mary, and the brother of James and Joses and Judas and Simon? And are not his sisters here with us?" And they took offense at him. [4k*]Jesus said to them, "A prophet is not without honor except in his native place and among his own kin and in his own house." [5*]So he was not able to perform any mighty deed there, apart from curing a few sick people by laying his hands on them. [6]He was amazed at their lack of faith.

The Mission of the Twelve. He went around to the villages in the vicinity teaching. [7l*]He summoned the Twelve and began to send them out two by two and gave them authority over unclean spirits. [8*]He instructed them to take nothing for the journey but a walking stick—no food, no sack, no money in their belts. [9]They were, however, to wear sandals but not a second tunic. [10*]He said to them, "Wherever you enter a house,

5:39 Not dead but asleep: the New Testament often refers to death as sleep (Mt 27:52; Jn 11:11; 1 Cor 15:6; 1 Thes 4:13–15); see note on Mt 9:24.

5:41 Arise: the Greek verb *egeirein* is the verb generally used to express resurrection from death (Mk 6:14, 16; Mt 11:5; Lk 7:14) and Jesus' own resurrection (Mk 16:6; Mt 28:6; Lk 24:6).

6:1 His native place: the Greek word *patris* here refers to Nazareth (cf. Mk 1:9; Lk 4:16, 23–24) though it can also mean native land.

6:2–6 See note on Mt 13:54–58.

6:3 Is he not the carpenter?: no other gospel calls Jesus a carpenter. Some witnesses have "the carpenter's son," as in Mt 13:55. **Son of Mary**: contrary to Jewish custom, which calls a man the son of his father, this expression may reflect Mark's own faith that God is the Father of Jesus (Mk 1:1, 11; 8:38; 13:32; 14:36). **The brother of James . . . Simon**: in Semitic usage, the terms "brother," "sister" are applied not only to children of the same parents, but to nephews, nieces, cousins, half-brothers, and half-sisters; cf. Gn 14:16; 29:15; Lv 10:4. While one cannot suppose that the meaning of a Greek word should be sought in the first place from Semitic usage, the Septuagint often translates the Hebrew *'āh* by the Greek word *adelphos*, "brother," as in the cited passages, a fact that may argue for a similar breadth of meaning in some New Testament passages. For instance, there is no doubt that in v 17, "brother" is used of Philip, who was actually the half-brother of Herod Antipas. On the other hand, Mark may have understood the terms literally; see also 3:31–32; Mt 12:46; 13:55–56; Lk 8:19; Jn 7:3, 5. The question of meaning here would not have arisen but for the faith of the church in Mary's perpetual virginity.

6:4 A prophet is not without honor except . . . in his own house: a saying that finds parallels in other literatures, especially Jewish and Greek, but without reference to a prophet. Comparing himself to previous Hebrew prophets whom the people rejected, Jesus intimates his own eventual rejection by the nation especially in view of the dishonor his own relatives had shown him (Mk 3:21) and now his townspeople as well.

6:5 He was not able to perform any mighty deed there: according to Mark, Jesus' power could not take effect because of a person's lack of faith.

6:7–13 The preparation for the mission of the Twelve is seen in the call (1) of the first disciples to be fishers of men (Mk 1:16–20), (2) then of the Twelve set apart to be with Jesus and to receive authority to preach and expel demons (Mk 3:13–19). Now they are given the specific mission to exercise that authority in word and power as representatives of Jesus during the time of their formation.

6:8–9 In Mark the use of a **walking stick** (Mk 6:8) and **sandals** (Mk 6:9) is permitted, but not in Mt 10:10 nor in Lk 10:4. Mark does not mention any prohibition to visit pagan territory and to enter Samaritan towns. These differences indicate a certain adaptation to conditions in and outside of Palestine and suggest in Mark's account a later activity in the church. For the rest, Jesus required of his apostles a total dependence on God for food and shelter; cf. Mk 6:35–44; 8:1–9.

6:10–11 Remaining in the same house as a guest (Mk 6:10) rather than moving to another offering greater comfort avoided any impression of seeking advantage for oneself and prevented dishonor to one's host. Shaking the dust off one's feet served as testimony against those who rejected the call to repentance.

h: Acts 9:40. *i:* Mt 13:54–58; Lk 4:16–30. *j:* 15:40; Mt 12:46; Jn 6:42. *k:* Jn 4:44. *l:* Mt 10:1, 9–14; Lk 9:15; 10:4–11.

Rulers during New Testament Times

Roman Emperors

27 B.C.–A.D. 14	Augustus
A.D. 14–37	Tiberius
A.D. 37–41	Caligula
A.D. 41–54	Claudius
A.D. 54–68	Nero
A.D. 68–69	Galba; Otho; Vitellius
A.D. 69–79	Vespasian
A.D. 79–81	Titus
A.D. 81–96	Domitian

Herodian Rulers

37–4 B.C.	Herod the Great, king of the Jews
4 B.C.–A.D. 6	Archelaus, ethnarch of Judea
4 B.C.–A.D. 39	Herod Antipas, tetrarch of Galilee and Perea
4 B.C.–A.D. 34	Philip, tetrarch of Iturea, Trachonitis, etc.
A.D. 37–44	Herod Agrippa I, from 37 to 44 king over the former tetrarchy of Philip, and from 41 to 44 over Judea, Galilee, and Perea
A.D. 53–about 100	Herod Agrippa II, king over the former tetrarchy of Philip and Lysanias, and from 56 (or 61) over parts of Galilee and Perea

Procurators of Judea after the Reign of Archelaus to the Reign of Herod Agrippa I

A.D. 6–8	Coponius
A.D. 9–12	M. Ambivius
A.D. 12–15	Annius Rufus
A.D. 15–26	Valerius Gratus
A.D. 26–36	Pontius Pilate
A.D. 37	Marullus
A.D. 37–41	Herennius Capito

Procurators of Palestine from the Reign of Herod Agrippa I to the Jewish Revolt

A.D. 44–about 46	Cuspius Fadus
A.D. about 46–48	Tiberius Alexander
A.D. 48–52	Ventidius Cumanus
A.D. 52–60	M. Antonius Felix
A.D. 60–62	Porcius Festus
A.D. 62–64	Clodius Albinus
A.D. 64–66	Gessius Florus

stay there until you leave from there. [11]Whatever place does not welcome you or listen to you, leave there and shake the dust off your feet in testimony against them." [12]So they went off and preached repentance. [13m*]They drove out many demons, and they anointed with oil many who were sick and cured them.

Herod's Opinion of Jesus. [14no*]King Herod heard about it, for his fame had become widespread, and people were saying, "John the Baptist has been raised from the dead; that is why mighty powers are at work in him." [15p]Others were saying, "He is Elijah"; still others, "He is a prophet like any of the prophets." [16]But when Herod learned of it, he said, "It is John whom I beheaded. He has been raised up."

The Death of John the Baptist. [17q*]Herod was the one who had John arrested and bound in prison on account of Herodias, the wife of his brother Philip, whom he had married. [18r]John had said to Herod, "It is not lawful for you to have your brother's wife." [19*]Herodias harbored a grudge against him and wanted to kill him but was unable to do so. [20]Herod feared John, knowing him to be a righteous and holy man, and kept him in custody. When he heard him speak he was very much perplexed, yet he liked to listen to him. [21]She had an opportunity one day when Herod, on his birthday, gave a banquet for his courtiers, his military officers, and the leading men of Galilee. [22]Herodias's own daughter came in and performed a dance that delighted Herod and his guests. The king said to the girl, "Ask of me whatever you wish and I will grant it to you." [23s]He even swore [many things] to her, "I will grant you whatever you ask of me, even to half of my kingdom." [24]She went out and said to her mother, "What shall I ask for?" She replied, "The head of John the Baptist." [25]The girl hurried back to the king's presence and made her request, "I want you to give me at once on a platter the head of John the Baptist." [26]The king was deeply distressed, but because of his oaths and the guests he did not wish to break his word to her. [27t]So he promptly dispatched an executioner with orders to bring back his head. He went off and beheaded him in the prison. [28]He brought in the head on a platter and gave it to the girl. The girl in turn gave it to her mother. [29]When his disciples heard about it, they came and took his body and laid it in a tomb.

The Return of the Twelve. [30u*]The apostles gathered together with Jesus and reported all they had done and taught. [31v*]He said to them, "Come away by yourselves to a deserted place and rest a while." People were coming and going in great numbers, and they had no opportunity even to eat. [32w]So they went off in the boat by themselves to a deserted place. [33]People saw them leaving and many came to know about it. They hastened there on foot from all the towns and arrived at the place before them.

6:13 Anointed with oil . . . cured them: a common medicinal remedy, but seen here as a vehicle of divine power for healing.

6:14–16 The various opinions about Jesus anticipate the theme of his identity that reaches its climax in Mk 8:27–30.

6:14 King Herod: see note on Mt 14:1.

6:17–29 Similarities are to be noted between Mark's account of the imprisonment and death of John the Baptist in this pericope, and that of the passion of Jesus (Mk 15:1–47). Herod and Pilate, each in turn, acknowledges the holiness of life of one over whom he unjustly exercises the power of condemnation and death (Mk 6:26–27; 15:9–10, 14–15). The hatred of Herodias toward John parallels that of the Jewish leaders toward Jesus. After the deaths of John and of Jesus, well-disposed persons request the bodies of the victims of Herod and of Pilate in turn to give them respectful burial (Mk 6:29; 15:45–46).

6:19 Herodias: see note on Mt 14:3.

6:30 Apostles: here, and in some manuscripts at Mk 3:14, Mark calls apostles (i.e., those sent forth) the Twelve whom Jesus sends as his emissaries, empowering them to preach, to expel demons, and to cure the sick (Mk 6:13). Only after Pentecost is the title used in the technical sense.

6:31–34 The withdrawal of Jesus with his disciples to a desert place to rest attracts a great number of people to follow them. Toward this people of the new exodus Jesus is moved with pity; he satisfies their spiritual hunger by teaching them many things, thus gradually showing himself the faithful shepherd of a new Israel; cf. Nm 27:17; Ez 34:15.

6:35 See note on Mt 14:13–21. Compare this section with Mk 8:1–9. The various accounts of the multiplication of loaves and fishes, two each in Mark and in Matthew and one each in Luke and in John, indicate the wide interest of the early church in their eucharistic gatherings; see, e.g., Mk 6:41; 8:6; 14:22; and recall also the sign of bread in Ex 16; Dt 8:3–16; Ps 78:24–25; 105:40; Wis 16:20–21.

m: Jas 5:14. *n:* Mt 14:1–12. *o:* Lk 9:7–8. *p:* Mt 16:14. *q:* Lk 3:19–20. *r:* Lv 18:16. *s:* Est 5:3. *t:* Lk 9:9. *u:* Lk 9:10. *v:* 3:20; Mt 14:13; Lk 9:10. *w:* Mt 14:13–21; Lk 9:10–17; Jn 6:1–13.

The Feeding of the Five Thousand. [34]When he disembarked and saw the vast crowd, his heart was moved with pity for them, for they were like sheep without a shepherd; and he began to teach them many things. [35*]By now it was already late and his disciples approached him and said, "This is a deserted place and it is already very late. [36]Dismiss them so that they can go to the surrounding farms and villages and buy themselves something to eat." [37]He said to them in reply, "Give them some food yourselves." But they said to him, "Are we to buy two hundred days' wages worth of food and give it to them to eat?" [38]He asked them, "How many loaves do you have? Go and see." And when they had found out they said, "Five loaves and two fish." [39]So he gave orders to have them sit down in groups on the green grass. [40*]The people took their places in rows by hundreds and by fifties. [41*]Then, taking the five loaves and the two fish and looking up to heaven, he said the blessing, broke the loaves, and gave them to [his] disciples to set before the people; he also divided the two fish among them all. [42]They all ate and were satisfied. [43]And they picked up twelve wicker baskets full of fragments and what was left of the fish. [44]Those who ate [of the loaves] were five thousand men.

The Walking on the Water. [45x*]Then he made his disciples get into the boat and precede him to the other side toward Bethsaida, while he dismissed the crowd. [46*]And when he had taken leave of them, he went off to the mountain to pray. [47]When it was evening, the boat was far out on the sea and he was alone on shore. [48*]Then he saw that they were tossed about while rowing, for the wind was against them. About the fourth watch of the night, he came towards them walking on the sea. He meant to pass by them. [49]But when they saw him walking on the sea, they thought it was a ghost and cried out. [50*]They had all seen him and were terrified. But at once he spoke with them, "Take courage, it is I, do not be afraid!" [51]He got into the boat with them and the wind died down. They were [completely] astounded. [52y*]They had not understood the incident of the loaves. On the contrary, their hearts were hardened.

The Healings at Gennesaret. [53z]After making the crossing, they came to land at Gennesaret and tied up there. [54]As they were leaving the boat, people immediately recognized him. [55]They scurried about the surrounding country and began to bring in the sick on mats to wherever they heard he was. [56a]Whatever villages or towns or countryside he entered, they laid the sick in the marketplaces and begged him that they might touch only the tassel on his cloak; and as many as touched it were healed.

CHAPTER 7

See RG 392–93

The Tradition of the Elders. [1b*]Now when the Pharisees with some scribes who

6:40 The people . . . in rows by hundreds and by fifties: reminiscent of the groupings of Israelites encamped in the desert (Ex 18:21–25) and of the wilderness tradition of the prophets depicting the transformation of the wasteland into pastures where the true shepherd feeds his flock (Ez 34:25–26) and makes his people beneficiaries of messianic grace.

6:41 On the language of this verse as eucharistic (cf. Mk 14:22), see notes on Mt 14:19, 20. Jesus observed the Jewish table ritual of blessing God before partaking of food.

6:45–52 See note on Mt 14:22–33.

6:45 To the other side toward Bethsaida: a village at the northeastern shore of the Sea of Galilee.

6:46 He went off to the mountain to pray: see Mk 1:35–38. In Jn 6:15 Jesus withdrew to evade any involvement in the false messianic hopes of the multitude.

6:48 Walking on the sea: see notes on Mt 14:22–33 and on Jn 6:19.

6:50 It is I, do not be afraid!: literally, "I am." This may reflect the divine revelatory formula of Ex 3:14; Is 41:4, 10, 14; 43:1–3, 10, 13. Mark implies the hidden identity of Jesus as Son of God.

6:52 They had not understood . . . the loaves: the revelatory character of this sign and that of the walking on the sea completely escaped the disciples. **Their hearts were hardened**: in Mk 3:5–6 hardness of heart was attributed to those who did not accept Jesus and plotted his death. Here the same disposition prevents the disciples from comprehending Jesus' self-revelation through signs; cf. Mk 8:17.

7:1–23 See note on Mt 15:1–20. Against the Pharisees' narrow, legalistic, and external practices of piety in matters of purification (Mk 7:2–5), external worship (Mk 7:6–7), and observance of commandments, Jesus sets in opposition the true moral intent of the divine law (Mk 7:8–13). But he goes beyond contrasting the law and Pharisaic interpretation of it. The parable of Mk 7:14–15 in effect sets aside the law itself in respect to clean and unclean food. He thereby opens the way for unity between Jew and Gentile in the kingdom of God, intimated by Jesus' departure for pagan territory beyond Galilee. For similar contrast see Mk 2:1–3:6; 3:20–35; 6:1–6.

x: Mt 14:22–32; Jn 6:15–21. *y:* 4:13. *z:* Mt 14:34–36. *a:* 5:27–28; Acts 5:15. *b:* Mt 15:1–20.

had come from Jerusalem gathered around
him, [2]they observed that some of his disciples ate their meals with unclean, that is, unwashed, hands. [3*](For the Pharisees and, in
fact, all Jews, do not eat without carefully
washing their hands, keeping the tradition of
the elders. [4]And on coming from the marketplace they do not eat without purifying
themselves. And there are many other things
that they have traditionally observed, the purification of cups and jugs and kettles [and
beds].) [5*]So the Pharisees and scribes questioned him, "Why do your disciples not follow the tradition of the elders but instead eat
a meal with unclean hands?" [6c]He responded, "Well did Isaiah prophesy about
you hypocrites, as it is written:

'This people honors me with their lips,
but their hearts are far from me;
[7] In vain do they worship me,
teaching as doctrines human precepts.'

[8]You disregard God's commandment but
cling to human tradition." [9]He went on to
say, "How well you have set aside the commandment of God in order to uphold your
tradition! [10d]For Moses said, 'Honor your father and your mother,' and 'Whoever curses
father or mother shall die.' [11*]Yet you say, 'If
a person says to father or mother, "Any support you might have had from me is *qorban*" ' (meaning, dedicated to God), [12]you allow him to do nothing more for his father or
mother. [13]You nullify the word of God in favor of your tradition that you have handed
on. And you do many such things." [14e]He
summoned the crowd again and said to them,
"Hear me, all of you, and understand.
[15]Nothing that enters one from outside can
defile that person; but the things that come
out from within are what defile." [16]*
[17f*]When he got home away from the
crowd his disciples questioned him about the
parable. [18]He said to them, "Are even you
likewise without understanding? Do you not
realize that everything that goes into a person
from outside cannot defile, [19g*]since it enters
not the heart but the stomach and passes out
into the latrine?" (Thus he declared all foods
clean.) [20]"But what comes out of a person,
that is what defiles. [21h]From within people,
from their hearts, come evil thoughts, unchastity, theft, murder, [22]adultery, greed,
malice, deceit, licentiousness, envy, blasphemy, arrogance, folly. [23]All these evils
come from within and they defile."

The Syrophoenician Woman's Faith.
[24i*]From that place he went off to the district
of Tyre. He entered a house and wanted no
one to know about it, but he could not escape
notice. [25]Soon a woman whose daughter had
an unclean spirit heard about him. She came
and fell at his feet. [26j]The woman was a
Greek, a Syrophoenician by birth, and she
begged him to drive the demon out of her
daughter. [27*]He said to her, "Let the children
be fed first. For it is not right to take the food
of the children and throw it to the dogs."

7:3 Carefully washing their hands: refers to ritual purification.

7:5 Tradition of the elders: the body of detailed, unwritten, human laws regarded by the scribes and Pharisees to have the same binding force as that of the Mosaic law; cf. Gal 1:14.

7:11 Qorban: a formula for a gift to God, dedicating the offering to the temple, so that the giver might continue to use it for himself but not give it to others, even needy parents.

7:16 Mk 7:16, "Anyone who has ears to hear ought to hear," is omitted because it is lacking in some of the best Greek manuscripts and was probably transferred here by scribes from Mk 4:9, 23.

7:17 Away from the crowd . . . the parable: in this context of privacy the term **parable** refers to something hidden, about to be revealed to the disciples; cf. Mk 4:10–11, 34. Jesus sets the Mosaic food laws in the context of the kingdom of God where they are abrogated, and he declares moral defilement the only cause of uncleanness.

7:19 (Thus he declared all foods clean): if this bold declaration goes back to Jesus, its force was not realized among Jewish Christians in the early church; cf. Acts 10:1–11:18.

7:24–37 The withdrawal of Jesus to the district of Tyre may have been for a respite (Mk 7:24), but he soon moved onward to Sidon and, by way of the Sea of Galilee, to the Decapolis. These districts provided a Gentile setting for the extension of his ministry of healing because the people there acknowledged his power (Mk 7:29, 37). The actions attributed to Jesus (Mk 7:33–35) were also used by healers of the time.

7:27–28 The figure of a household in which children at table are fed first and then their leftover food is given to the dogs under the table is used effectively to acknowledge the prior claim of the Jews to the ministry of Jesus; however, Jesus accedes to the Gentile woman's plea for the cure of her afflicted daughter because of her faith.

c: Is 29:13. *d:* Ex 21:17; Lv 20:9; Dt 5:16; Eph 6:2. *e:* Mt 15:10–20. *f:* 4:10, 13. *g:* Acts 10:15. *h:* Jer 17:9. *i:* Mt 15:21–28. *j:* Mt 8:29.

[28]She replied and said to him, "Lord, even
the dogs under the table eat the children's
scraps." [29]Then he said to her, "For saying
this, you may go. The demon has gone out of
your daughter." [30]When the woman went
home, she found the child lying in bed and
the demon gone.

The Healing of a Deaf Man. [31][k]Again he
left the district of Tyre and went by way of
Sidon to the Sea of Galilee, into the district
of the Decapolis. [32]And people brought to
him a deaf man who had a speech impediment and begged him to lay his hand on him.
[33]He took him off by himself away from the
crowd. He put his finger into the man's ears
and, spitting, touched his tongue; [34]then he
looked up to heaven and groaned, and said to
him, "*Ephphatha*!" (that is, "Be opened!")
[35]And [immediately] the man's ears were
opened, his speech impediment was removed, and he spoke plainly. [36]*He ordered
them not to tell anyone. But the more he ordered them not to, the more they proclaimed
it. [37][l]They were exceedingly astonished and
they said, "He has done all things well. He
makes the deaf hear and [the] mute speak."

CHAPTER 8

See RG 392–94

The Feeding of the Four Thousand.
[1][m]*In those days when there again was a great
crowd without anything to eat, he summoned
the disciples and said, [2]"My heart is moved
with pity for the crowd, because they have
been with me now for three days and have
nothing to eat. [3]If I send them away hungry to
their homes, they will collapse on the way,
and some of them have come a great distance." [4]His disciples answered him, "Where
can anyone get enough bread to satisfy them
here in this deserted place?" [5]Still he asked
them, "How many loaves do you have?"
"Seven," they replied. [6]*He ordered the crowd
to sit down on the ground. Then, taking the
seven loaves he gave thanks, broke them, and
gave them to his disciples to distribute, and
they distributed them to the crowd. [7]They also
had a few fish. He said the blessing over them
and ordered them distributed also. [8]They ate
and were satisfied. They picked up the fragments left over—seven baskets. [9]There were
about four thousand people.

He dismissed them [10]and got into the boat
with his disciples and came to the region of
Dalmanutha.

The Demand for a Sign. [11][n][o]*The Pharisees came forward and began to argue with
him, seeking from him a sign from heaven to
test him. [12]He sighed from the depth of his
spirit and said, "Why does this generation
seek a sign? Amen, I say to you, no sign will
be given to this generation." [13]Then he left
them, got into the boat again, and went off to
the other shore.

The Leaven of the Pharisees. [14][p]They had
forgotten to bring bread, and they had only
one loaf with them in the boat. [15]*He enjoined them, "Watch out, guard against the
leaven of the Pharisees and the leaven of
Herod." [16]They concluded among themselves that it was because they had no bread.
[17][q]When he became aware of this he said to
them, "Why do you conclude that it is because you have no bread? Do you not yet understand or comprehend? Are your hearts

7:36 The more they proclaimed it: the same verb **proclaim** attributed here to the crowd in relation to the miracles of Jesus is elsewhere used in Mark for the preaching of the gospel on the part of Jesus, of his disciples, and of the Christian community (Mk 1:14; 13:10; 14:9). Implied in the action of the crowd is a recognition of the salvific mission of Jesus; see note on Mt 11:5–6.

8:1–10 The two accounts of the multiplication of loaves and fishes (Mk 8:1–10; 6:31–44) have eucharistic significance. Their similarity of structure and themes but dissimilarity of detail are considered by many to refer to a single event that, however, developed in two distinct traditions, one Jewish Christian and the other Gentile Christian, since Jesus in Mark's presentation (Mk 7:24–37) has extended his saving mission to the Gentiles.

8:6 See note on Mk 6:41.

8:11–12 The objection of the Pharisees that Jesus' miracles are unsatisfactory for proving the arrival of God's kingdom is comparable to the request of the crowd for a sign in Jn 6:30–31. Jesus' response shows that a sign originating in human demand will not be provided; cf. Nm 14:11, 22.

8:15 The leaven of the Pharisees . . . of Herod: the corruptive action of leaven (1 Cor 5:6–8; Gal 5:9) was an apt symbol of the evil dispositions both of the Pharisees (Mk 8:11–13; 7:5–13) and of Herod (Mk 6:14–29) toward Jesus. The disciples of Jesus are warned against sharing such rebellious attitudes toward Jesus; cf. Mk 8:17, 21.

k: Mt 15:29–31. *l:* Mt 15:31. *m:* 6:34–44; Mt 15:32–39. *n:* Mt 12:38–39; 16:1–4. *o:* Lk 11:16. *p:* Mt 16:5–12; Lk 12:1. *q:* 4:13.

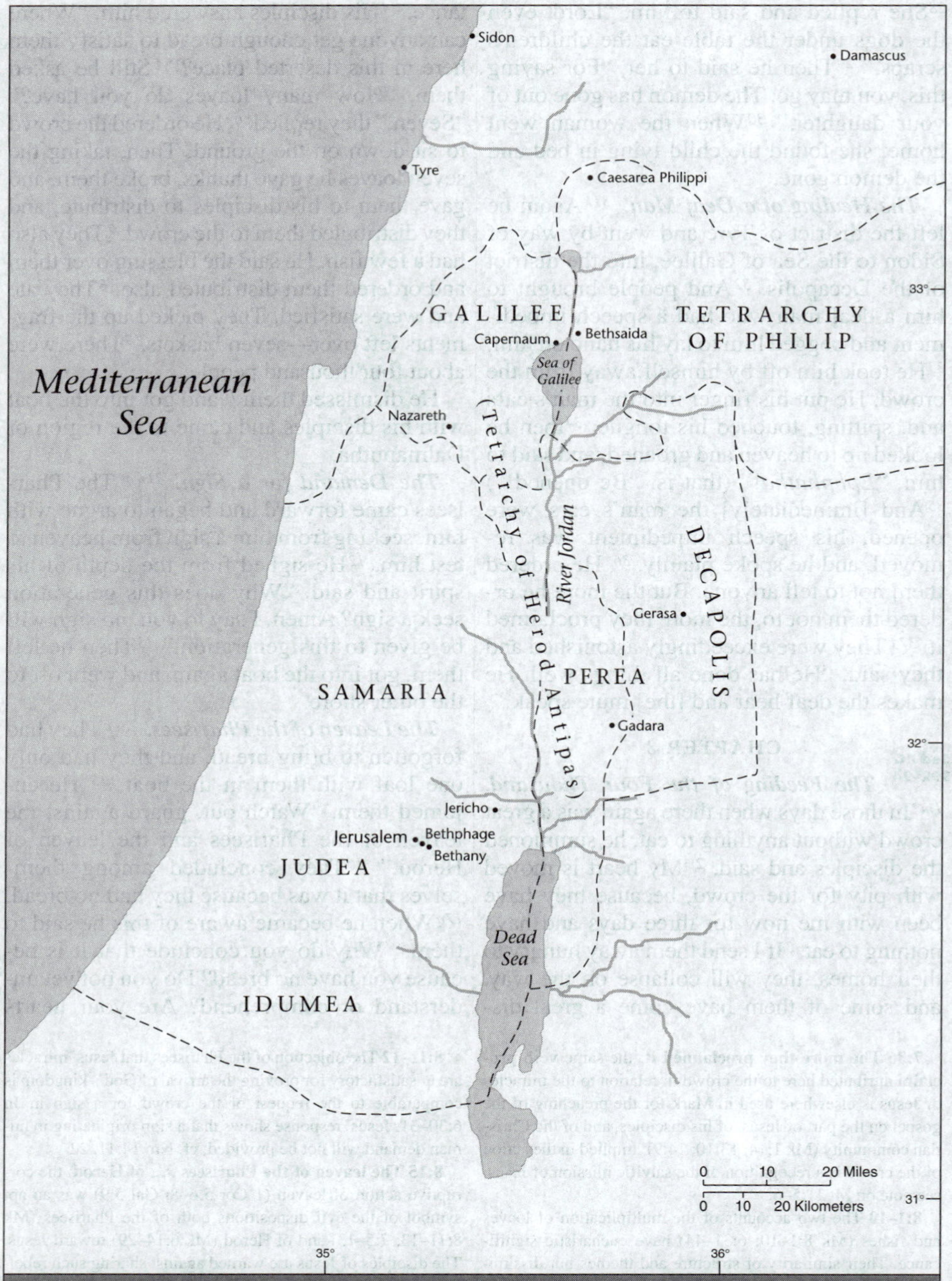

Sites of Jesus' Travels in Galilee and Vicinity

hardened? [18r]Do you have eyes and not see, ears and not hear? And do you not remember, [19]when I broke the five loaves for the five thousand, how many wicker baskets full of fragments you picked up?" They answered him, "Twelve." [20]"When I broke the seven loaves for the four thousand, how many full baskets of fragments did you pick up?" They answered [him], "Seven." [21]He said to them, "Do you still not understand?"

The Blind Man of Bethsaida. [22*]When they arrived at Bethsaida, they brought to him a blind man and begged him to touch him. [23s]He took the blind man by the hand and led him outside the village. Putting spittle on his eyes he laid his hands on him and asked, "Do you see anything?" [24]Looking up he replied, "I see people looking like trees and walking." [25]Then he laid hands on his eyes a second time and he saw clearly; his sight was restored and he could see everything distinctly. [26]Then he sent him home and said, "Do not even go into the village."

III. The Mystery Begins to Be Revealed

Peter's Confession about Jesus. [27t*]Now Jesus and his disciples set out for the villages of Caesarea Philippi. Along the way he asked his disciples, "Who do people say that I am?" [28]They said in reply, "John the Baptist, others Elijah, still others one of the prophets." [29]And he asked them, "But who do you say that I am?" Peter said to him in reply, "You are the Messiah." [30]Then he warned them not to tell anyone about him.

The First Prediction of the Passion. [31u*]He began to teach them that the Son of Man must suffer greatly and be rejected by the elders, the chief priests, and the scribes, and be killed, and rise after three days. [32]He spoke this openly. Then Peter took him aside and began to rebuke him. [33]At this he turned around and, looking at his disciples, rebuked Peter and said, "Get behind me, Satan. You are thinking not as God does, but as human beings do."

The Conditions of Discipleship. [34v*]He summoned the crowd with his disciples and said to them, "Whoever wishes to come after me must deny himself, take up his cross, and follow me. [35w*]For whoever wishes to save his life will lose it, but whoever loses his life for my sake and that of the gospel will save it. [36]What profit is there for one to gain the whole world and forfeit his life? [37]What could one give in exchange for his

8:22–26 Jesus' actions and the gradual cure of the blind man probably have the same purpose as in the case of the deaf man (Mk 7:31–37). Some commentators regard the cure as an intended symbol of the gradual enlightenment of the disciples concerning Jesus' messiahship.

8:27–30 This episode is the turning point in Mark's account of Jesus in his public ministry. Popular opinions concur in regarding him as a prophet. The disciples by contrast believe him to be the Messiah. Jesus acknowledges this identification but prohibits them from making his messianic office known to avoid confusing it with ambiguous contemporary ideas on the nature of that office. See further the notes on Mt 16:13–20.

8:31 Son of Man: an enigmatic title. It is used in Dn 7:13–14 has a symbol of "the saints of the Most High," the faithful Israelites who receive the everlasting kingdom from the Ancient One (God). They are represented by a human figure that contrasts with the various beasts who represent the previous kingdoms of the earth. In the Jewish apocryphal books of 1 Enoch and 4 Ezra the "Son of Man" is not, as in Daniel, a group, but a unique figure of extraordinary spiritual endowments, who will be revealed as the one through whom the everlasting kingdom decreed by God will be established. It is possible though doubtful that this individualization of the Son of Man figure had been made in Jesus' time, and therefore his use of the title in that sense is questionable. Of itself, this expression means simply a human being, or, indefinitely, someone, and there are evidences of this use in pre-Christian times. Its use in the New Testament is probably due to Jesus' speaking of himself in that way, "a human being," and the later church's taking this in the sense of the Jewish apocrypha and applying it to him with that meaning. **Rejected by the elders, the chief priests, and the scribes**: the supreme council called the Sanhedrin was made up of seventy-one members of these three groups and presided over by the high priest. It exercised authority over the Jews in religious matters. See note on Mt 8:20.

8:34–35 This utterance of Jesus challenges all believers to authentic discipleship and total commitment to himself through self-renunciation and acceptance of the cross of suffering, even to the sacrifice of life itself. **Whoever wishes to save his life will lose it . . . will save it**: an expression of the ambivalence of life and its contrasting destiny. Life seen as mere self-centered earthly existence and lived in denial of Christ ends in destruction, but when lived in loyalty to Christ, despite earthly death, it arrives at fullness of life.

8:35 For my sake and that of the gospel: Mark here, as at Mk 10:29 equates Jesus with the gospel.

r: Jer 5:21; Ez 12:2. *s:* 7:33; Jn 9:6. *t:* Mt 16:13–20; Lk 9:18–21. *u:* Mt 16:21–27; Lk 9:22–26. *v:* Mt 10:38–39; 16:24–27; Lk 14:26–27. *w:* Jn 12:25.

life? [38x]Whoever is ashamed of me and of
my words in this faithless and sinful generation, the Son of Man will be ashamed of
when he comes in his Father's glory with the
holy angels."

See RG 393

CHAPTER 9

[1y*]He also said to them, "Amen, I say
to you, there are some standing here who
will not taste death until they see that the
kingdom of God has come in power."

The Transfiguration of Jesus. [2z*]After six
days Jesus took Peter, James, and John and
led them up a high mountain apart by themselves. And he was transfigured before
them, [3]and his clothes became dazzling
white, such as no fuller on earth could
bleach them. [4]Then Elijah appeared to them
along with Moses, and they were conversing
with Jesus. [5*]Then Peter said to Jesus in reply, "Rabbi, it is good that we are here! Let
us make three tents: one for you, one for
Moses, and one for Elijah." [6]He hardly knew
what to say, they were so terrified. [7*]Then a
cloud came, casting a shadow over them;
then from the cloud came a voice, "This is
my beloved Son. Listen to him." [8]Suddenly,
looking around, they no longer saw anyone
but Jesus alone with them.

The Coming of Elijah. [9a*]As they were
coming down from the mountain, he
charged them not to relate what they had
seen to anyone, except when the Son of Man
had risen from the dead. [10]So they kept the
matter to themselves, questioning what rising from the dead meant. [11b]Then they asked
him, "Why do the scribes say that Elijah
must come first?" [12]He told them, "Elijah
will indeed come first and restore all things,
yet how is it written regarding the Son of
Man that he must suffer greatly and be
treated with contempt? [13c]But I tell you that
Elijah has come and they did to him whatever they pleased, as it is written of him."

The Healing of a Boy with a Demon.
[14d*]When they came to the disciples, they saw
a large crowd around them and scribes arguing with them. [15]Immediately on seeing him,
the whole crowd was utterly amazed. They
ran up to him and greeted him. [16]He asked
them, "What are you arguing about with
them?" [17]Someone from the crowd answered
him, "Teacher, I have brought to you my son
possessed by a mute spirit. [18]Wherever it
seizes him, it throws him down; he foams at
the mouth, grinds his teeth, and becomes
rigid. I asked your disciples to drive it out, but
they were unable to do so." [19]He said to them
in reply, "O faithless generation, how long
will I be with you? How long will I endure
you? Bring him to me." [20]They brought the
boy to him. And when he saw him, the spirit
immediately threw the boy into convulsions.
As he fell to the ground, he began to roll

9:1 There are some standing . . . come in power: understood by some to refer to the establishment by God's power of his kingdom on earth in and through the church; more likely, as understood by others, a reference to the imminent parousia.

9:2–8 Mark and Mt 17:1 place the transfiguration of Jesus six days after the first prediction of his passion and death and his instruction to the disciples on the doctrine of the cross; Lk 9:28 has "about eight days." Thus the transfiguration counterbalances the prediction of the passion by affording certain of the disciples insight into the divine glory that Jesus possessed. His glory will overcome his death and that of his disciples; cf. 2 Cor 3:18; 2 Pt 1:16–19. The heavenly voice (Mk 9:7) prepares the disciples to understand that in the divine plan Jesus must die ignominiously before his messianic glory is made manifest; cf. Lk 24:25–27. See further the note on Mt 17:1–8.

9:5 Moses and Elijah represent respectively law and prophecy in the Old Testament and are linked to Mount Sinai; cf. Ex 19:16–20:17; 1 Kgs 19:2, 8–14. They now appear with Jesus as witnesses to the fulfillment of the law and the prophets taking place in the person of Jesus as he appears in glory.

9:7 A cloud came, casting a shadow over them: even the disciples enter into the mystery of his glorification. In the Old Testament the cloud covered the meeting tent, indicating the Lord's presence in the midst of his people (Ex 40:34–35) and came to rest upon the temple in Jerusalem at the time of its dedication (1 Kgs 8:10).

9:9–13 At the transfiguration of Jesus his disciples had seen Elijah. They were perplexed because, according to the rabbinical interpretation of Mal 4:1, Elijah was to come first. Jesus' response shows that Elijah has come, in the person of John the Baptist, to prepare for the day of the Lord. Jesus **must suffer greatly and be treated with contempt** (Mk 9:12) like the Baptist (Mk 9:13); cf. Mk 6:17–29.

9:14–29 The disciples' failure to effect a cure seems to reflect unfavorably on Jesus (Mk 9:14–18, 22). In response Jesus exposes their lack of trust in God (Mk 4:19) and scores their lack of prayer (Mk 4:29), i.e., of conscious reliance on God's power when acting in Jesus' name. For Matthew, see note on Mt 17:14–20. Lk 9:37–43 centers attention on Jesus' sovereign power.

x: Mt 10:33; Lk 12:8. *y:* Mt 16:28; Lk 9:27. *z:* Mt 17:1–13; Lk 9:28–36. *a:* 8:31. *b:* Is 53:3; Mal 3:23. *c:* 1 Kgs 19:2–10. *d:* Mt 17:14–21; Lk 9:37–43.

around and foam at the mouth. [21]Then he questioned his father, "How long has this been happening to him?" He replied, "Since childhood. [22]It has often thrown him into fire and into water to kill him. But if you can do anything, have compassion on us and help us." [23]Jesus said to him, " 'If you can!' Everything is possible to one who has faith." [24]Then the boy's father cried out, "I do believe, help my unbelief!" [25]Jesus, on seeing a crowd rapidly gathering, rebuked the unclean spirit and said to it, "Mute and deaf spirit, I command you: come out of him and never enter him again!" [26]Shouting and throwing the boy into convulsions, it came out. He became like a corpse, which caused many to say, "He is dead!" [27]But Jesus took him by the hand, raised him, and he stood up. [28]When he entered the house, his disciples asked him in private, "Why could we not drive it out?" [29]*He said to them, "This kind can only come out through prayer."

The Second Prediction of the Passion. [30e f]They left from there and began a journey through Galilee, but he did not wish anyone to know about it. [31]He was teaching his disciples and telling them, "The Son of Man is to be handed over to men and they will kill him, and three days after his death he will rise." [32]But they did not understand the saying, and they were afraid to question him.

IV. The Full Revelation of the Mystery

The Greatest in the Kingdom. [33g]*They came to Capernaum and, once inside the house, he began to ask them, "What were you arguing about on the way?" [34]But they remained silent. They had been discussing among themselves on the way who was the greatest. [35h]Then he sat down, called the Twelve, and said to them, "If anyone wishes to be first, he shall be the last of all and the servant of all." [36]Taking a child he placed it in their midst, and putting his arms around it he said to them, [37i]"Whoever receives one child such as this in my name, receives me; and whoever receives me, receives not me but the One who sent me."

Another Exorcist. [38j]*John said to him, "Teacher, we saw someone driving out demons in your name, and we tried to prevent him because he does not follow us." [39]Jesus replied, "Do not prevent him. There is no one who performs a mighty deed in my name who can at the same time speak ill of me. [40k]For whoever is not against us is for us. [41l]Anyone who gives you a cup of water to drink because you belong to Christ, amen, I say to you, will surely not lose his reward.

Temptations to Sin. [42m]"Whoever causes one of these little ones who believe [in me] to sin, it would be better for him if a great millstone were put around his neck and he were thrown into the sea. [43]*If your hand causes you to sin, cut it off. It is better for you to enter into life maimed than with two hands to go into Gehenna, into the unquenchable fire. [*44*]* [45]And if your foot causes you to sin, cut if off. It is better for you to enter into life crippled than with two feet to be thrown into Gehenna. [*46*]* [47]And if your eye causes you to sin, pluck it out. Better for you to enter into the kingdom of God with one eye than with two eyes to be thrown into Gehenna, [48n]where 'their worm does not die, and the fire is not quenched.'

The Simile of Salt. [49]*"Everyone will be

9:29 This kind can only come out through prayer: a variant reading adds "and through fasting."

9:33–37 Mark probably intends this incident and the sayings that follow as commentary on the disciples' lack of understanding (Mk 9:32). Their role in Jesus' work is one of service, especially to the poor and lowly. Children were the symbol Jesus used for the *anawim*, the poor in spirit, the lowly in the Christian community.

9:38–41 Jesus warns against jealousy and intolerance toward others, such as exorcists who do **not follow us**. The saying in Mk 9:40 is a broad principle of the divine tolerance. Even the smallest courtesies shown to those who teach in Jesus' name do not go unrewarded.

9:43, 45, 47 Gehenna: see note on Mt 5:22.

9:44, 46 These verses, lacking in some important early manuscripts, are here omitted as scribal additions. They simply repeat Mk 9:48 itself a modified citation of Is 66:24.

9:49 Everyone will be salted with fire: so the better manuscripts. Some add "every sacrifice will be salted with salt." The purifying and preservative use of salt in food (Lv 2:13) and the refinement effected through fire refer here to compa-

e: 8:31; Mt 17:22–23; Lk 9:43–45. *f:* Jn 7:1. *g:* Mt 18:1–5; Lk 9:46–48. *h:* Mt 20:27. *i:* Mt 10:40; 18:5; Jn 13:20. *j:* Nm 11:28; Lk 9:49–50; 1 Cor 12:3. *k:* Mt 12:30. *l:* Mt 10:42; 1 Cor 3:23. *m:* Mt 5:29–30; 18:6–9; Lk 17:1–2. *n:* Is 66:24.

salted with fire. [50o]Salt is good, but if salt becomes insipid, with what will you restore its flavor? Keep salt in yourselves and you will have peace with one another."

CHAPTER 10

See RG 393–94

Marriage and Divorce. [1]He set out from there and went into the district of Judea [and] across the Jordan. Again crowds gathered around him and, as was his custom, he again taught them. [2p*]The Pharisees approached and asked, "Is it lawful for a husband to divorce his wife?" They were testing him. [3]He said to them in reply, "What did Moses command you?" [4q]They replied, "Moses permitted him to write a bill of divorce and dismiss her." [5]But Jesus told them, "Because of the hardness of your hearts he wrote you this commandment. [6r]But from the beginning of creation, 'God made them male and female. [7s]For this reason a man shall leave his father and mother [and be joined to his wife], [8]and the two shall become one flesh.' So they are no longer two but one flesh. [9]Therefore what God has joined together, no human being must separate." [10]In the house the disciples again questioned him about this. [11t]He said to them, "Whoever divorces his wife and marries another commits adultery against her; [12]and if she divorces her husband and marries another, she commits adultery."

Blessing of the Children. [13uv]And people were bringing children to him that he might touch them, but the disciples rebuked them. [14]When Jesus saw this he became indignant and said to them, "Let the children come to me; do not prevent them, for the kingdom of God belongs to such as these. [15w*]Amen, I say to you, whoever does not accept the kingdom of God like a child will not enter it." [16]Then he embraced them and blessed them, placing his hands on them.

The Rich Man. [17x]As he was setting out on a journey, a man ran up, knelt down before him, and asked him, "Good teacher, what must I do to inherit eternal life?" [18*]Jesus answered him, "Why do you call me good? No one is good but God alone. [19y]You know the commandments: 'You shall not kill; you shall not commit adultery; you shall not steal; you shall not bear false witness; you shall not defraud; honor your father and your mother.' " [20]He replied and said to him, "Teacher, all of these I have observed from my youth." [21]Jesus, looking at him, loved him and said to him, "You are lacking in one thing. Go, sell what you have, and give to [the] poor and you will have treasure in heaven; then come, follow me." [22]At that statement his face fell, and he went away sad, for he had many possessions.

[23z*]Jesus looked around and said to his disciples, "How hard it is for those who have wealth to enter the kingdom of God!" [24]The disciples were amazed at his words. So Jesus again said to them in reply, "Children, how hard it is to enter the kingdom of God! [25]It is easier for a camel to pass through [the] eye of [a] needle than for one who is rich to enter the kingdom of God." [26]They were exceedingly astonished and said among themselves, "Then who can be saved?" [27]Jesus looked at them and said, "For human beings it is im-

rable effects in the spiritual life of the disciples of Jesus.

10:2–9 In the dialogue between Jesus and the Pharisees on the subject of divorce, Jesus declares that the law of Moses permitted divorce (Dt 24:1) only **because of the hardness of your hearts** (Mk 10:4–5). In citing Gn 1:27 and 2:24 Jesus proclaims permanence to be the divine intent from the beginning concerning human marriage (Mk 10:6–8). He reaffirms this with the declaration that **what God has joined together, no human being must separate** (Mk 10:9). See further the notes on Mt 5:31–32; 19:3–9.

10:15 Whoever does not accept the kingdom of God like a child: i.e., in total dependence upon and obedience to the gospel; cf. Mt 18:3–4.

10:18 Why do you call me good?: Jesus repudiates the term "good" for himself and directs it to God, the source of all goodness who alone can grant the gift of eternal life; cf. Mt 19:16–17.

10:23–27 In the Old Testament wealth and material goods are considered a sign of God's favor (Jb 1:10; Ps 128:1–2; Is 3:10). The words of Jesus in Mk 10:23–25 provoke astonishment among the disciples because of their apparent contradiction of the Old Testament concept (Mk 10:24, 26). Since wealth, power, and merit generate false security, Jesus rejects them utterly as a claim to enter the kingdom. Achievement of salvation is beyond human capability and depends solely on the goodness of God who offers it as a gift (Mk 10:27).

o: Lv 2:13; Mt 5:13; Lk 14:34–35; Col 4:6. *p:* Mt 19:3–9. *q:* Dt 24:1–4. *r:* Gn 1:27. *s:* Gn 2:24; 1 Cor 6:16; Eph 5:31. *t:* Mt 5:32; Lk 16:18; 1 Cor 7:10–11. *u:* Mt 19:13–15; Lk 18:15–17. *v:* Lk 9:47. *w:* Mt 18:3. *x:* Mt 19:16–30; Lk 18:18–30. *y:* Ex 20:12–16; Dt 5:16–21. *z:* Prv 11:28.

possible, but not for God. All things are possible for God." [28]Peter began to say to him, "We have given up everything and followed you." [29]Jesus said, "Amen, I say to you, there is no one who has given up house or brothers or sisters or mother or father or children or lands for my sake and for the sake of the gospel [30]who will not receive a hundred times more now in this present age: houses and brothers and sisters and mothers and children and lands, with persecutions, and eternal life in the age to come. [31a]But many that are first will be last, and [the] last will be first."

The Third Prediction of the Passion. [32b]They were on the way, going up to Jerusalem, and Jesus went ahead of them. They were amazed, and those who followed were afraid. Taking the Twelve aside again, he began to tell them what was going to happen to him. [33]"Behold, we are going up to Jerusalem, and the Son of Man will be handed over to the chief priests and the scribes, and they will condemn him to death and hand him over to the Gentiles [34]who will mock him, spit upon him, scourge him, and put him to death, but after three days he will rise."

Ambition of James and John. [35c]Then James and John, the sons of Zebedee, came to him and said to him, "Teacher, we want you to do for us whatever we ask of you." [36]He replied, "What do you wish [me] to do for you?" [37]They answered him, "Grant that in your glory we may sit one at your right and the other at your left." [38d*]Jesus said to them, "You do not know what you are asking. Can you drink the cup that I drink or be baptized with the baptism with which I am baptized?" [39]They said to him, "We can." Jesus said to them, "The cup that I drink, you will drink, and with the baptism with which I am baptized, you will be baptized; [40]but to sit at my right or at my left is not mine to give but is for those for whom it has been prepared." [41]When the ten heard this, they became indignant at James and John. [42e*]Jesus summoned them and said to them, "You know that those who are recognized as rulers over the Gentiles lord it over them, and their great ones make their authority over them felt. [43]But it shall not be so among you. Rather, whoever wishes to be great among you will be your servant; [44]whoever wishes to be first among you will be the slave of all. [45]For the Son of Man did not come to be served but to serve and to give his life as a ransom for many."

The Blind Bartimaeus. [46f*]They came to Jericho. And as he was leaving Jericho with his disciples and a sizable crowd, Bartimaeus, a blind man, the son of Timaeus, sat by the roadside begging. [47]On hearing that it was Jesus of Nazareth, he began to cry out and say, "Jesus, son of David, have pity on me." [48]And many rebuked him, telling him to be silent. But he kept calling out all the more, "Son of David, have pity on me." [49]Jesus stopped and said, "Call him." So they called the blind man, saying to him, "Take courage; get up, he is calling you." [50]He threw aside his cloak, sprang up, and came to Jesus. [51]Jesus said to him in reply, "What do you want me to do for you?" The blind man replied to him, "Master, I want to see." [52]Jesus told him, "Go your way; your faith has saved you." Immediately he received his sight and followed him on the way.

CHAPTER 11

See RG 394

The Entry into Jerusalem. [1g*]When they drew near to Jerusalem, to Bethphage

10:38–40 Can you drink the cup . . . I am baptized?: the metaphor of drinking the cup is used in the Old Testament to refer to acceptance of the destiny assigned by God; see note on Psalm 11:6. In Jesus' case, this involves divine judgment on sin that Jesus the innocent one is to expiate on behalf of the guilty (Mk 14:24; Is 53:5). His baptism is to be his crucifixion and death for the salvation of the human race; cf. Lk 12:50. The request of James and John for a share in the glory (Mk 10:35–37) must of necessity involve a share in Jesus' sufferings, the endurance of tribulation and suffering for the gospel (Mk 10:39). The authority of assigning places of honor in the kingdom is reserved to God (Mk 10:40).

10:42–45 Whatever authority is to be exercised by the disciples must, like that of Jesus, be rendered as service to others (Mk 10:45) rather than for personal aggrandizement (Mk 10:42–44). The service of Jesus is his passion and death for the sins of the human race (Mk 10:45); cf. Mk 14:24; Is 53:11–12; Mt 26:28; Lk 22:19–20.

10:46 See notes on Mt 9:27–31 and 20:29–34.

11:1–11 In Mark's account Jesus takes the initiative in ordering the preparation for his entry into Jerusalem (Mk 11:1–6) even

a: Mt 19:30; Lk 13:30. *b:* 8:31; Mt 20:17–19; Lk 18:31–33. *c:* Mt 20:20–28. *d:* Lk 12:50. *e:* Lk 22:25–27. *f:* Mt 20:29–34; Lk 18:35–43. *g:* Mt 21:1–9; Lk 19:29–38; Jn 12:12–15.

and Bethany at the Mount of Olives, he sent
two of his disciples 2 and said to them, "Go
into the village opposite you, and immediately on entering it, you will find a colt tethered on which no one has ever sat. Untie it
and bring it here. 3 If anyone should say to
you, 'Why are you doing this?' reply, 'The
Master has need of it and will send it back
here at once.' " 4 So they went off and found a
colt tethered at a gate outside on the street,
and they untied it. 5 Some of the bystanders
said to them, "What are you doing, untying
the colt?" 6 They answered them just as Jesus
had told them to, and they permitted them to
do it. 7 So they brought the colt to Jesus and
put their cloaks over it. And he sat on it.
8 Many people spread their cloaks on the road,
and others spread leafy branches that they had
cut from the fields. 9[h] Those preceding him as
well as those following kept crying out:

"Hosanna!
Blessed is he who comes in the name
of the Lord!
10 Blessed is the kingdom of our father
David that is to come!
Hosanna in the highest!"

11[i] He entered Jerusalem and went into the
temple area. He looked around at everything
and, since it was already late, went out to
Bethany with the Twelve.
Jesus Curses a Fig Tree. 12[j]* The next day
as they were leaving Bethany he was hungry. 13 Seeing from a distance a fig tree in
leaf, he went over to see if he could find anything on it. When he reached it he found
nothing but leaves; it was not the time for
figs. 14 And he said to it in reply, "May no
one ever eat of your fruit again!" And his
disciples heard it.

Cleansing of the Temple. 15[k]* They came
to Jerusalem, and on entering the temple
area he began to drive out those selling and
buying there. He overturned the tables of the
money changers and the seats of those who
were selling doves. 16 He did not permit anyone to carry anything through the temple
area. 17[l] Then he taught them saying, "Is it
not written:

'My house shall be called a house of
prayer for all peoples'?
But you have made it a den of
thieves."

18 The chief priests and the scribes came to
hear of it and were seeking a way to put him
to death, yet they feared him because the
whole crowd was astonished at his teaching.
19[m] When evening came, they went out of the
city.
The Withered Fig Tree. 20[n] Early in the
morning, as they were walking along, they
saw the fig tree withered to its roots. 21 Peter
remembered and said to him, "Rabbi, look!
The fig tree that you cursed has withered."
22 Jesus said to them in reply, "Have faith in
God. 23[o] Amen, I say to you, whoever says to
this mountain, 'Be lifted up and thrown into
the sea,' and does not doubt in his heart but
believes that what he says will happen, it
shall be done for him. 24[p] Therefore I tell
you, all that you ask for in prayer, believe
that you will receive it and it shall be yours.
25[q] When you stand to pray, forgive anyone
against whom you have a grievance, so that
your heavenly Father may in turn forgive
you your transgressions. [26]"*

The Authority of Jesus Questioned.
27[r]* They returned once more to Jerusalem.
As he was walking in the temple area, the

as he later orders the preparation of his last Passover supper (Mk 14:12–16). In Mk 10:9–10 the greeting Jesus receives stops short of proclaiming him Messiah. He is greeted rather as the prophet of the coming messianic kingdom. Contrast Mt 21:9.

11:12–14 Jesus' search for fruit on the fig tree recalls the prophets' earlier use of this image to designate Israel; cf. Jer 8:13; 29:14; Jl 1:7; Hos 9:10, 16. Cursing the fig tree is a parable in action representing Jesus' judgment (Mk 11:20) on barren Israel and the fate of Jerusalem for failing to receive his teaching; cf. Is 34:4; Hos 2:12; Lk 13:6–9.

11:15–19 See note on Mt 21:12–17.

11:26 This verse, which reads, "But if you do not forgive, neither will your heavenly Father forgive your transgressions," is omitted in the best manuscripts. It was probably added by copyists under the influence of Mt 6:15.

11:27–33 The mounting hostility toward Jesus came from the chief priests, the scribes, and the elders (Mk 11:27); the Herodians and the Pharisees (Mk 12:13); and the Sadducees

h: 2 Sm 7:16; Ps 118:26. *i:* Mt 21:10, 17. *j:* Mt 21:18–20; Lk 13:6–9. *k:* Mt 21:12–13; Lk 19:45–46; Jn 2:14–16. *l:* Is 56:7; Jer 7:11. *m:* Lk 21:37. *n:* Mt 21:20–22. *o:* Mt 17:20–21; Lk 17:6. *p:* Mt 7:7; Jn 11:22; 14:13. *q:* Mt 6:14; 18:35. *r:* Mt 21:23–27; Lk 20:1–8.

chief priests, the scribes, and the elders approached him [28]and said to him, "By what authority are you doing these things? Or who gave you this authority to do them?" [29]Jesus said to them, "I shall ask you one question. Answer me, and I will tell you by what authority I do these things. [30]Was John's baptism of heavenly or of human origin? Answer me." [31]They discussed this among themselves and said, "If we say, 'Of heavenly origin,' he will say, '[Then] why did you not believe him?' [32]But shall we say, 'Of human origin'?"—they feared the crowd, for they all thought John really was a prophet. [33]So they said to Jesus in reply, "We do not know." Then Jesus said to them, "Neither shall I tell you by what authority I do these things."

See RG 394

CHAPTER 12

Parable of the Tenants. [1 st*]He began to speak to them in parables. "A man planted a vineyard, put a hedge around it, dug a wine press, and built a tower. Then he leased it to tenant farmers and left on a journey. [2]At the proper time he sent a servant to the tenants to obtain from them some of the produce of the vineyard. [3]But they seized him, beat him, and sent him away empty-handed. [4]Again he sent them another servant. And that one they beat over the head and treated shamefully. [5]He sent yet another whom they killed. So, too, many others; some they beat, others they killed. [6]He had one other to send, a beloved son. He sent him to them last of all, thinking, 'They will respect my son.' [7]But those tenants said to one another, 'This is the heir. Come, let us kill him, and the inheritance will be ours.' [8]So they seized him and killed him, and threw him out of the vineyard. [9]What [then] will the owner of the vineyard do? He will come, put the tenants to death, and give the vineyard to others. [10u]Have you not read this scripture passage:

'The stone that the builders rejected
has become the cornerstone;
[11] by the Lord has this been done,
and it is wonderful in our eyes'?"

[12]They were seeking to arrest him, but they feared the crowd, for they realized that he had addressed the parable to them. So they left him and went away.

Paying Taxes to the Emperor. [13vw*]They sent some Pharisees and Herodians to him to ensnare him in his speech. [14]They came and said to him, "Teacher, we know that you are a truthful man and that you are not concerned with anyone's opinion. You do not regard a person's status but teach the way of God in accordance with the truth. Is it lawful to pay the census tax to Caesar or not? Should we pay or should we not pay?" [15]Knowing their hypocrisy he said to them, "Why are you testing me? Bring me a denarius to look at." [16]They brought one to him and he said to them, "Whose image and inscription is this?" They replied to him, "Caesar's." [17x]So Jesus said to them, "Repay to Caesar what belongs to Caesar and to God what belongs to God." They were utterly amazed at him.

The Question about the Resurrection. [18*]Some Sadducees, who say there is no resurrection, came to him and put this question to him, [19y]saying, "Teacher, Moses wrote for us, 'If someone's brother dies, leaving a wife but no child, his brother must take the wife and raise up descendants for his brother.' [20]Now there were seven brothers. The first married a woman and died, leaving no descendants. [21]So the second married her and died, leaving no descendants, and the third likewise. [22]And the seven left no descendants. Last of all the woman also died. [23]At the resurrection

(Mk 12:18). By their rejection of God's messengers, John the Baptist and Jesus, they incurred the divine judgment implied in Mk 11:27–33 and confirmed in the parable of the vineyard tenants (Mk 12:1–12).

12:1–12 The vineyard denotes Israel (Is 5:1–7). The tenant farmers are the religious leaders of Israel. God is the owner of the vineyard. His servants are his messengers, the prophets. The beloved son is Jesus (Mk 1:11; 9:7; Mt 3:17; 17:5; Lk 3:22; 9:35). The punishment of the tenants refers to the religious leaders, and the transfer of the vineyard to others refers to the people of the new Israel.

12:13–34 In the ensuing conflicts (cf. also Mk 2:1–3:6) Jesus vanquishes his adversaries by his responses to their questions and reduces them to silence (Mk 12:34).

12:13–17 See note on Mt 22:15–22.

12:18–27 See note on Mt 22:23–33.

---

s: Mt 21:33–46; Lk 20:9–19. *t:* Is 5:1–7; Jer 2:21. *u:* Ps 118:22–23; Is 28:16. *v:* Mt 22:15–33; Lk 20:20–39. *w:* 3:6. *x:* Rom 13:7. *y:* Dt 25:5.

[when they arise] whose wife will she be?
For all seven had been married to her."
[24]Jesus said to them, "Are you not misled
because you do not know the scriptures or
the power of God? [25]When they rise from
the dead, they neither marry nor are given
in marriage, but they are like the angels in
heaven. [26z]As for the dead being raised,
have you not read in the Book of Moses, in
the passage about the bush, how God told
him, 'I am the God of Abraham, [the] God
of Isaac, and [the] God of Jacob'? [27]He is
not God of the dead but of the living. You
are greatly misled."

The Greatest Commandment. [28a*]One of
the scribes, when he came forward and
heard them disputing and saw how well he
had answered them, asked him, "Which is
the first of all the commandments?" [29]Jesus
replied, "The first is this: 'Hear, O Israel!
The Lord our God is Lord alone! [30b]You
shall love the Lord your God with all your
heart, with all your soul, with all your mind,
and with all your strength.' [31c]The second is
this: 'You shall love your neighbor as yourself.' There is no other commandment
greater than these." [32]The scribe said to him,
"Well said, teacher. You are right in saying,
'He is One and there is no other than he.'
[33d]And 'to love him with all your heart,
with all your understanding, with all your
strength, and to love your neighbor as yourself' is worth more than all burnt offerings
and sacrifices." [34e]And when Jesus saw that
[he] answered with understanding, he said to
him, "You are not far from the kingdom of
God." And no one dared to ask him any more
questions.

The Question about David's Son. [35f*]As
Jesus was teaching in the temple area he
said, "How do the scribes claim that the
Messiah is the son of David? [36g]David himself, inspired by the holy Spirit, said:

'The Lord said to my lord,
"Sit at my right hand
until I place your enemies under your
feet." '

[37]David himself calls him 'lord'; so how is
he his son?" [The] great crowd heard this
with delight.

Denunciation of the Scribes. [38h*]In the
course of his teaching he said, "Beware of
the scribes, who like to go around in long
robes and accept greetings in the marketplaces, [39]seats of honor in synagogues, and
places of honor at banquets. [40]They devour
the houses of widows and, as a pretext, recite lengthy prayers. They will receive a
very severe condemnation."

The Poor Widow's Contribution. [41i*]He
sat down opposite the treasury and observed
how the crowd put money into the treasury.
Many rich people put in large sums. [42]A poor
widow also came and put in two small coins
worth a few cents. [43]Calling his disciples to
himself, he said to them, "Amen, I say to
you, this poor widow put in more than all the
other contributors to the treasury. [44]For they
have all contributed from their surplus
wealth, but she, from her poverty, has contributed all she had, her whole livelihood."

CHAPTER 13

See RG 395

***The Destruction of the Temple Fore-
told.*** [1j*]As he was making his way out of
the temple area one of his disciples said to
him, "Look, teacher, what stones and what
buildings!" [2]Jesus said to him, "Do you see
these great buildings? There will not be one
stone left upon another that will not be
thrown down."

12:28–34 See note on Mt 22:34–40.

12:35–37 Jesus questions the claim of the scribes about the Davidic descent of the Messiah, not to deny it (Mt 1:1; Acts 2:20, 34; Rom 1:3; 2 Tm 2:8) but to imply that he is more than this. His superiority derives from his transcendent origin, to which David himself attested when he spoke of the Messiah with the name "Lord" (Ps 110:1). See also note on Mt 22:41–46.

12:38–40 See notes on Mk 7:1–23 and Mt 23:1–39.

12:41–44 See note on Lk 21:1–4.

13:1–2 The reconstructed temple with its precincts, begun under Herod the Great ca. 20 B.C., was completed only some seven years before it was destroyed by fire in A.D. 70 at the hands of the Romans; cf. Jer 26:18; Mt 24:1–2. For the dating of the reconstruction of the temple, see further the note on Jn 2:20.

z: Ex 3:6. *a:* Mt 22:34–40; Lk 10:25–28. *b:* Dt 6:4–5. *c:* Lv 19:18; Rom 13:9; Gal 5:14; Jas 2:8. *d:* Dt 6:4; Ps 40:7–9. *e:* Mt 22:46; Lk 20:40. *f:* Mt 22:41–45; Lk 20:41–44. *g:* Ps 110:1. *h:* Mt 23:1–7; Lk 11:43; 20:45–47. *i:* Lk 21:1–4. *j:* Mt 24:1–2; Lk 21:5–6.

Parables in the Synoptic Gospels

Parable	Matthew	Mark	Luke
The Weeds among the Wheat	13:24–30		
The Hidden Treasure	13:44		
The Fine Pearl	13:45–46		
The Net	13:47–48		
The Unforgiving Servant	18:23–35		
The Workers in the Vineyard	20:1–16		
The Two Sons	21:28–30		
The Wedding Feast	22:2–14		
The Talents	25:14–30		
The Judgment of the Nations	25:31–46		
Seed Grows of Itself		4:26–29	
Need for Watchfulness		13:32–37	
The Two Debtors			7:41–42
The Good Samaritan			10:30–35
The Persistent Friend			11:5–8
The Rich Fool			12:16–20
The Vigilant and Faithful Servants			12:35–40
The Faithful and Wise Steward			12:42–48
The Barren Fig Tree			13:6–9
The Great Feast			14:15–24
The Tower			14:28–30
The King Marching into Battle			14:31–33
The Lost Coin			15:8–10
The Lost Son			15:11–32
The Dishonest Steward			16:1–8
The Rich Man and Lazarus			16:19–31
Attitude of a Servant			17:7–10
The Persistent Widow			18:2–5
The Pharisee and the Tax Collector			18:9–14
The Ten Gold Coins			19:11–27
The Two Foundations	7:24–29		6:46–49
The Yeast	13:33		13:20–21
The Lost Sheep	18:10–14		15:1–7
The Lamp	5:15	4:21	8:16; 11:33
The New Cloth	9:16	2:21	5:36
The New Wine in Old Wineskins	9:17	2:22	5:37–38
The Sower	13:1–9	4:1–9	8:4–8
The Mustard Seed	13:31–32	4:30–34	13:18–19
The Tenants	21:33–46	12:1–12	20:9–19
The Lesson of the Fig Tree	24:32–35	13:28–31	21:29

The Signs of the End. [3k*]As he was sitting on the Mount of Olives opposite the temple area, Peter, James, John, and Andrew asked him privately, [4]"Tell us, when will this happen, and what sign will there be when all these things are about to come to an end?" [5l]Jesus began to say to them, "See that no one deceives you. [6]Many will come in my name saying, 'I am he,' and they will deceive many. [7]When you hear of wars and reports of wars do not be alarmed; such things must happen, but it will not yet be the end. [8]Nation will rise against nation and kingdom against kingdom. There will be earthquakes from place to place and there will be famines. These are the beginnings of the labor pains.

The Coming Persecution. [9m]"Watch out for yourselves. They will hand you over to the courts. You will be beaten in synagogues. You will be arraigned before governors and kings because of me, as a witness before them. [10*]But the gospel must first be preached to all nations. [11n]When they lead you away and hand you over, do not worry beforehand about what you are to say. But say whatever will be given to you at that hour. For it will not be you who are speaking but the holy Spirit. [12]Brother will hand over brother to death, and the father his child; children will rise up against parents and have them put to death. [13]You will be hated by all because of my name. But the one who perseveres to the end will be saved.

The Great Tribulation. [14op*]"When you see the desolating abomination standing where he should not (let the reader understand), then those in Judea must flee to the mountains, [15q][and] a person on a housetop must not go down or enter to get anything out of his house, [16]and a person in a field must not return to get his cloak. [17]Woe to pregnant women and nursing mothers in those days. [18]Pray that this does not happen in winter. [19r]For those times will have tribulation such as has not been since the beginning of God's creation until now, nor ever will be. [20]If the Lord had not shortened those days, no one would be saved; but for the sake of the elect whom he chose, he did shorten the days. [21]If anyone says to you then, 'Look, here is the Messiah! Look, there he is!' do not believe it. [22]False messiahs and false prophets will arise and will perform signs and wonders in order to mislead, if that were possible, the elect. [23]Be watchful! I have told it all to you beforehand.

The Coming of the Son of Man. [24st]"But in those days after that tribulation

the sun will be darkened,
  and the moon will not give its light,
[25] and the stars will be falling from the sky,
  and the powers in the heavens will be
    shaken.

[26u*]And then they will see 'the Son of Man coming in the clouds' with great power and glory, [27]and then he will send out the angels and gather [his] elect from the four winds, from the end of the earth to the end of the sky.

The Lesson of the Fig Tree. [28v]"Learn a lesson from the fig tree. When its branch becomes tender and sprouts leaves, you know that summer is near. [29]In the same way,

13:3–37 Jesus' prediction of the destruction of the temple (Mk 13:2) provoked questions that the four named disciples put to him in private regarding the time and the sign when all **these things are about to come to an end** (Mk 13:3–4). The response to their questions was Jesus' eschatological discourse prior to his imminent death. It contained instruction and consolation exhorting the disciples and the church to faith and obedience through the trials that would confront them (Mk 13:5–13). The sign is the presence of **the desolating abomination** (Mk 13:14; see Dn 9:27), i.e., of the Roman power profaning the temple. Flight from Jerusalem is urged rather than defense of the city through misguided messianic hope (Mk 13:14–23). Intervention will occur only after destruction (Mk 13:24–27), which will happen before the end of the first Christian generation (Mk 13:28–31). No one but the Father knows the precise time, or that of the parousia (Mk 13:32); hence the necessity of constant vigilance (Mk 13:33–37). Luke sets the parousia at a later date, after "the time of the Gentiles" (Lk 21:24). See also notes on Mt 24:1–25:46.

13:10 The gospel . . . to all nations: the period of the Christian mission.

13:14 The participle **standing** is masculine, in contrast to the neuter at Mt 24:15.

13:26 Son of Man . . . with great power and glory: Jesus cites this text from Dn 7:13 in his response to the high priest, **Are you the Messiah?** (Mk 14:61). In Ex 34:5; Lv 16:2; and Nm 11:25 the clouds indicate the presence of the divinity. Thus in his role of Son of Man, Jesus is a heavenly being who will come in power and glory.

k: Mt 24:3–8; Lk 21:7–11. *l:* Eph 5:6; 2 Thes 2:3. *m:* Mt 24:9–14; Lk 21:12–19. *n:* Mt 10:19–22; Lk 12:11–12. *o:* Mt 24:15–22; Lk 21:20–24. *p:* Dn 9:27; Mt 24:15. *q:* Lk 17:31. *r:* Dn 12:1. *s:* Mt 24:29–31; Lk 21:25–27. *t:* Is 13:10; Ez 32:7; Jl 2:10. *u:* 14:62; Dn 7:13–14. *v:* Mt 24:32–36; Lk 21:29–33.

when you see these things happening, know that he is near, at the gates. [30]Amen, I say to you, this generation will not pass away until all these things have taken place. [31]Heaven and earth will pass away, but my words will not pass away.

Need for Watchfulness. [32]"But of that day or hour, no one knows, neither the angels in heaven, nor the Son, but only the Father. [33w]Be watchful! Be alert! You do not know when the time will come. [34x]It is like a man traveling abroad. He leaves home and places his servants in charge, each with his work, and orders the gatekeeper to be on the watch. [35]Watch, therefore; you do not know when the lord of the house is coming, whether in the evening, or at midnight, or at cockcrow, or in the morning. [36]May he not come suddenly and find you sleeping. [37]What I say to you, I say to all: 'Watch!' "

CHAPTER 14

See RG 395–96

The Conspiracy against Jesus. [1y*]The Passover and the Feast of Unleavened Bread were to take place in two days' time. So the chief priests and the scribes were seeking a way to arrest him by treachery and put him to death. [2]They said, "Not during the festival, for fear that there may be a riot among the people."

The Anointing at Bethany. [3z*]When he was in Bethany reclining at table in the house of Simon the leper, a woman came with an alabaster jar of perfumed oil, costly genuine spikenard. She broke the alabaster jar and poured it on his head. [4]There were some who were indignant. "Why has there been this waste of perfumed oil? [5]It could have been sold for more than three hundred days' wages and the money given to the poor." They were infuriated with her. [6]Jesus said, "Let her alone. Why do you make trouble for her? She has done a good thing for me. [7]The poor you will always have with you, and whenever you wish you can do good to them, but you will not always have me. [8]She has done what she could. She has anticipated anointing my body for burial. [9]Amen, I say to you, wherever the gospel is proclaimed to the whole world, what she has done will be told in memory of her."

The Betrayal by Judas. [10a]Then Judas Iscariot, one of the Twelve, went off to the chief priests to hand him over to them. [11]When they heard him they were pleased and promised to pay him money. Then he looked for an opportunity to hand him over.

Preparations for the Passover. [12b*]On the first day of the Feast of Unleavened Bread, when they sacrificed the Passover lamb, his disciples said to him, "Where do you want us to go and prepare for you to eat the Passover?" [13*]He sent two of his disciples and said to them, "Go into the city and a man will meet you, carrying a jar of water. Follow him. [14]Wherever he enters, say to the master of the house, 'The Teacher says, "Where is my guest room where I may eat

14:1–16:8 In the movement of Mark's gospel the cross is depicted as Jesus' way to glory in accordance with the divine will. Thus the passion narrative is seen as the climax of Jesus' ministry.

14:1 The Passover and the Feast of Unleavened Bread: the connection between the two festivals is reflected in Ex 12:3–20; 34:18; Lv 23:4–8; Nm 9:2–14; 28:16–17; Dt 16:1–8. The Passover commemorated the redemption from slavery and the departure of the Israelites from Egypt by night. It began at sundown after the Passover lamb was sacrificed in the temple in the afternoon of the fourteenth day of the month of Nisan. With the Passover supper on the same evening was associated the eating of unleavened bread. The latter was continued through Nisan 21, a reminder of the affliction of the Israelites and of the haste surrounding their departure. Praise and thanks to God for his goodness in the past were combined at this dual festival with the hope of future salvation. **The chief priests . . . to death**: the intent to put Jesus to death was plotted for a long time but delayed for fear of the crowd (Mk 3:6; 11:18; 12:12).

14:3 At Bethany on the Mount of Olives, a few miles from Jerusalem, in **the house of Simon the leper**, Jesus defends a woman's loving action of anointing his head with perfumed oil in view of his impending death and burial as a criminal, in which case his body would not be anointed. See further the note on Jn 12:7. He assures the woman of the remembrance of her deed in the worldwide preaching of the good news.

14:12 The first day of the Feast of Unleavened Bread . . . the Passover lamb: a less precise designation of the day for sacrificing the Passover lamb as evidenced by some rabbinical literature. For a more exact designation, see note on Mk 14:1. It was actually Nisan 14.

14:13 A man . . . carrying a jar of water: perhaps a prearranged signal, for only women ordinarily carried water in jars. The Greek word used here, however, implies simply a person and not necessarily a male.

w: Mt 24:42; 25:13–15. *x:* Mt 25:14–30; Lk 19:12–27. *y:* Mt 26:2–5; Lk 22:1–2; Jn 11:45–53. *z:* Mt 26:6–13; Jn 12:1–8. *a:* Mt 26:14–16; Lk 22:3–6. *b:* Mt 26:17–19; Lk 22:7–13.

the Passover with my disciples?" ' [15]Then he will show you a large upper room furnished and ready. Make the preparations for us there." [16]The disciples then went off, entered the city, and found it just as he had told them; and they prepared the Passover.

The Betrayer. [17c]When it was evening, he came with the Twelve. [18*]And as they reclined at table and were eating, Jesus said, "Amen, I say to you, one of you will betray me, one who is eating with me." [19]They began to be distressed and to say to him, one by one, "Surely it is not I?" [20]He said to them, "One of the Twelve, the one who dips with me into the dish. [21*]For the Son of Man indeed goes, as it is written of him, but woe to that man by whom the Son of Man is betrayed. It would be better for that man if he had never been born."

The Lord's Supper. [22d*]While they were eating, he took bread, said the blessing, broke it, and gave it to them, and said, "Take it; this is my body." [23]Then he took a cup, gave thanks, and gave it to them, and they all drank from it. [24*]He said to them, "This is my blood of the covenant, which will be shed for many. [25]Amen, I say to you, I shall not drink again the fruit of the vine until the day when I drink it new in the kingdom of God." [26e*]Then, after singing a hymn, they went out to the Mount of Olives.

Peter's Denial Foretold. [27f*]Then Jesus said to them, "All of you will have your faith shaken, for it is written:

'I will strike the shepherd,
  and the sheep will be dispersed.'

[28]But after I have been raised up, I shall go before you to Galilee." [29]Peter said to him, "Even though all should have their faith shaken, mine will not be." [30]Then Jesus said to him, "Amen, I say to you, this very night before the cock crows twice you will deny me three times." [31]But he vehemently replied, "Even though I should have to die with you, I will not deny you." And they all spoke similarly.

The Agony in the Garden. [32gh*]Then they came to a place named Gethsemane, and he said to his disciples, "Sit here while I pray." [33]He took with him Peter, James, and John, and began to be troubled and distressed. [34]Then he said to them, "My soul is sorrowful even to death. Remain here and keep watch." [35]He advanced a little and fell to the ground and prayed that if it were possible the hour might pass by him; [36*]he said, "Abba, Father, all things are possible to you. Take this cup away from me, but not what I will but what you will." [37]When he returned he found them asleep. He said to Peter, "Simon, are you asleep? Could you not keep

14:18 One of you will betray me, one who is eating with me: contrasts the intimacy of table fellowship at the Passover meal with the treachery of the traitor; cf. Ps 41:10.

14:21 The Son of Man indeed goes, as it is written of him: a reference to Ps 41:10 cited by Jesus concerning Judas at the Last Supper; cf. Jn 13:18–19.

14:22–24 The actions and words of Jesus express within the framework of the Passover meal and the transition to a new covenant the sacrifice of himself through the offering of his body and blood in anticipation of his passion and death. His **blood of the covenant** both alludes to the ancient rite of Ex 24:4–8 and indicates the new community that the sacrifice of Jesus will bring into being (Mt 26:26–28; Lk 22:19–20; 1 Cor 11:23–25).

14:24 Which will be shed: see note on Mt 26:27–28. **For many**: the Greek preposition *hyper* is a different one from that at Mt 26:28 but the same as that found at Lk 22:19, 20 and 1 Cor 11:24. The sense of both words is vicarious, and it is difficult in Hellenistic Greek to distinguish between them. For **many** in the sense of "all," see note on Mt 20:28.

14:26 After singing a hymn: Ps 114–118, thanksgiving songs concluding the Passover meal.

14:27–31 Jesus predicted that the Twelve would waver in their faith, even abandon him, despite their protestations to the contrary. Yet he reassured them that after his resurrection he would regather them in Galilee (Mk 16:7; cf. Mt 26:32; 28:7, 10, 16; Jn 21), where he first summoned them to be his followers as he began to preach the good news (Mk 1:14–20).

14:32–34 The disciples who had witnessed the raising to life of the daughter of Jairus (Mk 5:37) and the transfiguration of their Master (Mk 9:2) were now invited to witness his degradation and agony and to watch and pray with him.

14:36 Abba, Father: an Aramaic term, here also translated by Mark, Jesus' special way of addressing God with filial intimacy. The word abba seems not to have been used in earlier or contemporaneous Jewish sources to address God without some qualifier. Cf. Rom 8:15; Gal 4:6 for other occurrences of the Aramaic word in the Greek New Testament. **Not what I will but what you will**: note the complete obedient surrender of the human will of Jesus to the divine will of the Father; cf. Jn 4:34; 8:29; Rom 5:19; Phil 2:8; Heb 5:8.

c: Mt 26:20–24; Lk 22:21–23; Jn 13:21–26. *d:* Mt 26:26–30; Lk 22:19–20; 1 Cor 11:23–25. *e:* Mt 26:30–35; Lk 22:34, 39; Jn 13:36–38. *f:* Zec 13:7; Jn 16:32. *g:* Mt 26:36–46; Lk 22:40–46. *h:* Jn 18:1.

watch for one hour? [38][i]*Watch and pray that you may not undergo the test. The spirit is willing but the flesh is weak." [39]Withdrawing again, he prayed, saying the same thing. [40]Then he returned once more and found them asleep, for they could not keep their eyes open and did not know what to answer him. [41]He returned a third time and said to them, "Are you still sleeping and taking your rest? It is enough. The hour has come. Behold, the Son of Man is to be handed over to sinners. [42]Get up, let us go. See, my betrayer is at hand."

The Betrayal and Arrest of Jesus. [43][j]Then, while he was still speaking, Judas, one of the Twelve, arrived, accompanied by a crowd with swords and clubs who had come from the chief priests, the scribes, and the elders. [44]His betrayer had arranged a signal with them, saying, "The man I shall kiss is the one; arrest him and lead him away securely." [45]He came and immediately went over to him and said, "Rabbi." And he kissed him. [46]At this they laid hands on him and arrested him. [47]One of the bystanders drew his sword, struck the high priest's servant, and cut off his ear. [48]Jesus said to them in reply, "Have you come out as against a robber, with swords and clubs, to seize me? [49]Day after day I was with you teaching in the temple area, yet you did not arrest me; but that the scriptures may be fulfilled." [50]And they all left him and fled. [51]Now a young man followed him wearing nothing but a linen cloth about his body. They seized him, [52]but he left the cloth behind and ran off naked.

Jesus before the Sanhedrin. [53][k]*They led Jesus away to the high priest, and all the chief priests and the elders and the scribes came together. [54]Peter followed him at a distance into the high priest's courtyard and was seated with the guards, warming himself at the fire. [55]The chief priests and the entire Sanhedrin kept trying to obtain testimony against Jesus in order to put him to death, but they found none. [56]Many gave false witness against him, but their testimony did not agree. [57]*Some took the stand and testified falsely against him, alleging, [58][l]"We heard him say, 'I will destroy this temple made with hands and within three days I will build another not made with hands.' " [59]Even so their testimony did not agree. [60]The high priest rose before the assembly and questioned Jesus, saying, "Have you no answer? What are these men testifying against you?" [61]*But he was silent and answered nothing. Again the high priest asked him and said to him, "Are you the Messiah, the son of the Blessed One?" [62][m]Then Jesus answered, "I am;

and 'you will see the Son of Man
seated at the right hand of the Power
and coming with the clouds of
heaven.' "

[63]At that the high priest tore his garments and said, "What further need have we of witnesses? [64]You have heard the blasphemy. What do you think?" They all condemned him as deserving to die. [65][n]Some began to spit on him. They blindfolded him and struck him and said to him, "Prophesy!" And the guards greeted him with blows.

Peter's Denial of Jesus. [66][o]While Peter was below in the courtyard, one of the high priest's maids came along. [67]Seeing Peter warming himself, she looked intently at him

14:38 The spirit is willing but the flesh is weak: the spirit is drawn to what is good yet found in conflict with the flesh, inclined to sin; cf. Ps 51:5, 10. Everyone is faced with this struggle, the full force of which Jesus accepted on our behalf and, through his bitter passion and death, achieved the victory.

14:53 They led Jesus away . . . came together: Mark presents a formal assembly of the whole Sanhedrin (chief priests, elders, and scribes) at night, leading to the condemnation of Jesus (Mk 14:64), in contrast to Lk 22:66, 71 where Jesus is condemned in a daytime meeting of the council; see also Jn 18:13, 19–24.

14:57–58 See notes on Mt 26:60–61 and Jn 2:19.

14:61–62 The Blessed One: a surrogate for the divine name, which Jews did not pronounce. **I am**: indicates Jesus' acknowledgment that he is the Messiah and Son of God; cf. Mk 1:1. Contrast Mt 26:64 and Lk 22:67–70, in which Jesus leaves his interrogators to answer their own question. **You will see the Son of Man . . . with the clouds of heaven**: an allusion to Dn 7:13 and Ps 110:1 portending the enthronement of Jesus as judge in the transcendent glory of God's kingdom. **The Power**: another surrogate for the name of God.

i: Rom 7:5. *j:* Mt 26:47–56; Lk 22:47–53; Jn 18:3–11. *k:* Mt 26:57–68; Lk 22:54–55, 63–65, 67–71; Jn 18:12–13. *l:* 15:29; 2 Cor 5:1. *m:* 13:26; Ps 110:1; Dn 7:13; Mt 24:30. *n:* Lk 22:63–65. *o:* Mt 26:69–75; Lk 22:56–62; Jn 18:16–18, 25–27.

and said, "You too were with the Nazarene, Jesus." [68]*But he denied it saying, "I neither know nor understand what you are talking about." So he went out into the outer court. [Then the cock crowed.] [69]The maid saw him and began again to say to the bystanders, "This man is one of them." [70]Once again he denied it. A little later the bystanders said to Peter once more, "Surely you are one of them; for you too are a Galilean." [71]He began to curse and to swear, "I do not know this man about whom you are talking." [72p]And immediately a cock crowed a second time. Then Peter remembered the word that Jesus had said to him, "Before the cock crows twice you will deny me three times." He broke down and wept.

See RG 395–96

CHAPTER 15

Jesus before Pilate. [1qr]*As soon as morning came, the chief priests with the elders and the scribes, that is, the whole Sanhedrin, held a council. They bound Jesus, led him away, and handed him over to Pilate. [2]*Pilate questioned him, "Are you the king of the Jews?" He said to him in reply, "You say so." [3]The chief priests accused him of many things. [4]Again Pilate questioned him, "Have you no answer? See how many things they accuse you of." [5]Jesus gave him no further answer, so that Pilate was amazed.

The Sentence of Death. [6s]*Now on the occasion of the feast he used to release to them one prisoner whom they requested. [7]*A man called Barabbas was then in prison along with the rebels who had committed murder in a rebellion. [8]The crowd came forward and began to ask him to do for them as he was accustomed. [9]Pilate answered, "Do you want me to release to you the king of the Jews?" [10]For he knew that it was out of envy that the chief priests had handed him over. [11]But the chief priests stirred up the crowd to have him release Barabbas for them instead. [12]Pilate again said to them in reply, "Then what [do you want] me to do with [the man you call] the king of the Jews?" [13]*They shouted again, "Crucify him." [14]Pilate said to them, "Why? What evil has he done?" They only shouted the louder, "Crucify him." [15]*So Pilate, wishing to satisfy the crowd, released Barabbas to them and, after he had Jesus scourged, handed him over to be crucified.

Mockery by the Soldiers. [16t]*The soldiers led him away inside the palace, that is, the praetorium, and assembled the whole cohort. [17]They clothed him in purple and, weaving a crown of thorns, placed it on him. [18]They began to salute him with, "Hail, King of the Jews!" [19]and kept striking his head with a reed and spitting upon him. They knelt before him in homage. [20]And when they had mocked him, they stripped him of the purple cloak, dressed him in his own clothes, and led him out to crucify him.

The Way of the Cross. [21u]*They pressed into service a passer-by, Simon, a Cyrenian, who was coming in from the country, the father of Alexander and Rufus, to carry his cross.

The Crucifixion. [22v]They brought him to the place of Golgotha (which is translated

14:68 [Then the cock crowed]: found in most manuscripts, perhaps in view of Mk 14:30, 72 but omitted in others.

15:1 Held a council: the verb here, *poieō*, can mean either "convene a council" or "take counsel." This reading is preferred to a variant "reached a decision" (cf. Mk 3:6), which Mk 14:64 describes as having happened at the night trial; see note on Mt 27:1–2. **Handed him over to Pilate**: lacking authority to execute their sentence of condemnation (Mk 14:64), the Sanhedrin had recourse to Pilate to have Jesus tried and put to death (Mk 15:15); cf. Jn 18:31.

15:2 The king of the Jews: in the accounts of the evangelists a certain irony surrounds the use of this title as an accusation against Jesus (see note on Mk 15:26). While Pilate uses this term (Mk 15:2, 9, 12), he is aware of the evil motivation of the chief priests who handed Jesus over for trial and condemnation (Mk 15:10; Lk 23:14–16, 20; Mt 27:18, 24; Jn 18:38; 19:4, 6, 12).

15:6–15 See note on Mt 27:15–26.

15:7 Barabbas: see note on Mt 27:16–17.

15:13 Crucify him: see note on Mt 27:22.

15:15 See note on Mt 27:26.

15:16 Praetorium: see note on Mt 27:27.

15:21 They pressed into service . . . Simon, a Cyrenian: a condemned person was constrained to bear his own instrument of torture, at least the crossbeam. The precise naming of Simon and his sons is probably due to their being known among early Christian believers to whom Mark addressed his gospel. See also notes on Mt 27:32; Lk 23:26–32.

p: Jn 13:38. *q:* Mt 27:1–2, 11–14; Lk 23:1–3. *r:* Jn 18:28. *s:* Mt 27:15–26; Lk 23:17–25; Jn 18:39–40. *t:* Mt 27:27–31; Jn 19:2–3. *u:* Mt 27:32; Lk 23:26. *v:* Mt 27:33–51; Lk 23:32–46; Jn 19:17–30.

Place of the Skull). [23]They gave him wine drugged with myrrh, but he did not take it. [24w*]Then they crucified him and divided his garments by casting lots for them to see what each should take. [25*]It was nine o'clock in the morning when they crucified him. [26*]The inscription of the charge against him read, "The King of the Jews." [27x]With him they crucified two revolutionaries, one on his right and one on his left. [[28]]* [29y*]Those passing by reviled him, shaking their heads and saying, "Aha! You who would destroy the temple and rebuild it in three days, [30]save yourself by coming down from the cross." [31]Likewise the chief priests, with the scribes, mocked him among themselves and said, "He saved others; he cannot save himself. [32z]Let the Messiah, the King of Israel, come down now from the cross that we may see and believe." Those who were crucified with him also kept abusing him.

The Death of Jesus. [33]At noon darkness came over the whole land until three in the afternoon. [34a*]And at three o'clock Jesus cried out in a loud voice, "*Eloi, Eloi, lema sabachthani*?" which is translated, "My God, my God, why have you forsaken me?" [35*]Some of the bystanders who heard it said, "Look, he is calling Elijah." [36]One of them ran, soaked a sponge with wine, put it on a reed, and gave it to him to drink, saying, "Wait, let us see if Elijah comes to take him down." [37]Jesus gave a loud cry and breathed his last. [38*]The veil of the sanctuary was torn in two from top to bottom. [39b*]When the centurion who stood facing him saw how he breathed his last he said, "Truly this man was the Son of God!" [40c*]There were also women looking on from a distance. Among them were Mary Magdalene, Mary the mother of the younger James and of Joses, and Salome. [41]These women had followed him when he was in Galilee and ministered to him. There were also many other women who had come up with him to Jerusalem.

The Burial of Jesus. [42d]When it was already evening, since it was the day of preparation, the day before the sabbath, [43*]Joseph of Arimathea, a distinguished member of the council, who was himself awaiting the kingdom of God, came and courageously went to Pilate and asked for the body of Jesus. [44]Pilate was amazed that he was already dead. He summoned the centurion and asked him if Jesus had already died. [45]And when he learned of it from the centurion, he gave the body to Joseph. [46]Having bought a linen cloth, he took him down, wrapped him in the linen cloth and laid him in a tomb that had been hewn out of the rock. Then he rolled a stone against the entrance to the tomb. [47]Mary Magdalene and Mary the mother of Joses watched where he was laid.

CHAPTER 16

See RG 396

The Resurrection of Jesus. [1ef*]When the sabbath was over, Mary Magdalene, Mary, the mother of James, and Salome

15:24 See notes on Mt 27:35 and Jn 19:23–25a.

15:25 It was nine o'clock in the morning: literally, "the third hour," thus between 9 A.M. and 12 noon. Cf. Mk 15:33, 34, 42 for Mark's chronological sequence, which may reflect liturgical or catechetical considerations rather than the precise historical sequence of events; contrast the different chronologies in the other gospels, especially Jn 19:14.

15:26 The inscription . . . the King of the Jews: the political reason for the death penalty falsely charged by the enemies of Jesus. See further the notes on Mt 27:37 and Jn 19:19.

15:28 This verse, "And the scripture was fulfilled that says, 'And he was counted among the wicked,' " is omitted in the earliest and best manuscripts. It contains a citation from Is 53:12 and was probably introduced from Lk 22:37.

15:29 See note on Mt 27:39–40.

15:34 An Aramaic rendering of Ps 22:2. See also note on Mt 27:46.

15:35 Elijah: a verbal link with Eloi (Mk 15:34). See note on Mk 9:9–13; cf. Mal 3:19. See also note on Mt 27:47.

15:38 See note on Mt 27:51–53.

15:39 The closing portion of Mark's gospel returns to the theme of its beginning in the Gentile centurion's climactic declaration of belief that Jesus **was the Son of God**. It indicates the fulfillment of the good news announced in the prologue (Mk 1:1) and may be regarded as the firstfruit of the passion and death of Jesus.

15:40–41 See note on Mt 27:55–56.

15:43 Joseph of Arimathea: see note on Mt 27:57–61.

16:1–8 The purpose of this narrative is to show that the tomb is empty and that Jesus **has been raised** (Mk 16:6) and is **going before you to Galilee** (Mk 16:7) in fulfillment of Mk 14:28. The women find the tomb empty, and an angel stationed there announces to them what has happened. They are told to proclaim the news to Peter and the disciples in order to prepare them for a reunion with him. Mark's composition

w: Ps 22:18. *x:* Lk 23:33. *y:* Jn 2:19. *z:* Lk 23:39. *a:* Ps 22:2. *b:* Mt 27:54–56; Lk 23:47–49. *c:* 6:3; Lk 8:2–3. *d:* Mt 27:57–61; Lk 23:50–56; Jn 19:38–42. *e:* Mt 28:1–8; Lk 24:1–10; Jn 20:1–10. *f:* Mt 28:1; Lk 23:56.

bought spices so that they might go and anoint him. [2]Very early when the sun had risen, on the first day of the week, they came to the tomb. [3]They were saying to one another, "Who will roll back the stone for us from the entrance to the tomb?" [4]When they looked up, they saw that the stone had been rolled back; it was very large. [5g]On entering the tomb they saw a young man sitting on the right side, clothed in a white robe, and they were utterly amazed. [6]He said to them, "Do not be amazed! You seek Jesus of Nazareth, the crucified. He has been raised; he is not here. Behold, the place where they laid him. [7h]But go and tell his disciples and Peter, 'He is going before you to Galilee; there you will see him, as he told you.' " [8]Then they went out and fled from the tomb, seized with trembling and bewilderment. They said nothing to anyone, for they were afraid.

The Longer Ending

The Appearance to Mary Magdalene. [[9i*]When he had risen, early on the first day of the week, he appeared first to Mary Magdalene, out of whom he had driven seven demons. [10j]She went and told his companions who were mourning and weeping. [11]When they heard that he was alive and had been seen by her, they did not believe.

The Appearance to Two Disciples. [12k]After this he appeared in another form to two of them walking along on their way to the country. [13]They returned and told the others; but they did not believe them either.

The Commissioning of the Eleven. [14l][But] later, as the eleven were at table, he appeared to them and rebuked them for their unbelief and hardness of heart because they had not believed those who saw him after he had been raised. [15m]He said to them, "Go into the whole world and proclaim the gospel to every creature. [16]Whoever believes and is baptized will be saved; whoever does not believe will be condemned. [17]These signs will accompany those who believe: in my name they will drive out demons, they will speak new languages. [18n]They will pick up serpents [with their hands], and if they drink any deadly thing, it will not harm them. They will lay hands on the sick, and they will recover."

The Ascension of Jesus. [19o]So then the Lord Jesus, after he spoke to them, was taken up into heaven and took his seat at the right hand of God. [20p]But they went forth and preached everywhere, while the Lord worked with them and confirmed the word through accompanying signs.]

The Shorter Ending

[And they reported all the instructions briefly to Peter's companions. Afterwards Jesus himself, through them, sent forth from east to west the sacred and imperishable proclamation of eternal salvation. Amen.]

of the gospel ends at Mk 16:8 with the women telling no one, because they were afraid. This abrupt termination causes some to believe that the original ending of this gospel may have been lost. See the following note.

16:9–20 This passage, termed the Longer Ending to the Marcan gospel by comparison with a much briefer conclusion found in some less important manuscripts, has traditionally been accepted as a canonical part of the gospel and was defined as such by the Council of Trent. Early citations of it by the Fathers indicate that it was composed by the second century, although vocabulary and style indicate that it was written by someone other than Mark. It is a general resume of the material concerning the appearances of the risen Jesus, reflecting, in particular, traditions found in Lk 24 and Jn 20.

The Freer Logion: Found after v 14 in a fourth-fifth century manuscript preserved in the Freer Gallery of Art, Washington, DC, this ending was known to Jerome in the fourth century. It reads: "And they excused themselves, saying, 'This age of lawlessness and unbelief is under Satan, who does not allow the truth and power of God to prevail over the unclean things dominated by the spirits [or, does not allow the unclean things dominated by the spirits to grasp the truth and power of God]. Therefore reveal your righteousness now.' They spoke to Christ. And Christ responded to them, 'The limit of the years of Satan's power is completed, but other terrible things draw near. And for those who sinned I was handed over to death, that they might return to the truth and no longer sin, in order that they might inherit the spiritual and incorruptible heavenly glory of righteousness. But . . . .' "

16:20 The Shorter Ending: Found after Mk 16:8 before the Longer Ending in four seventh-to-ninth-century Greek manuscripts as well as in one Old Latin version, where it appears alone without the Longer Ending.

g: Jn 20:12. *h:* 14:28. *i:* Mt 28:1–10; Jn 20:11–18. *j:* Lk 24:10–11; Jn 20:18. *k:* Lk 24:13–35. *l:* Lk 24:36–49; 1 Cor 15:5. *m:* 13:10; Mt 28:18–20; Lk 24:47; Jn 20:21. *n:* Mt 10:1; Lk 10:19; Acts 28:3–6. *o:* Lk 24:50–53. *p:* 1 Tm 3:16.

See RG 397–412

The Gospel According to Luke

The Gospel according to Luke is the first part of a two-volume work that continues the biblical history of God's dealings with humanity found in the Old Testament, showing how God's promises to Israel have been fulfilled in Jesus and how the salvation promised to Israel and accomplished by Jesus has been extended to the Gentiles. The stated purpose of the two volumes is to provide Theophilus and others like him with certainty—assurance—about earlier instruction they have received (Lk 1:4). To accomplish his purpose, Luke shows that the preaching and teaching of the representatives of the early church are grounded in the preaching and teaching of Jesus, who during his historical ministry (Acts 1:21–22) prepared his specially chosen followers and commissioned them to be witnesses to his resurrection and to all else that he did (Acts 10:37–42). This continuity between the historical ministry of Jesus and the ministry of the apostles is Luke's way of guaranteeing the fidelity of the Church's teaching to the teaching of Jesus.

Luke's story of Jesus and the church is dominated by a historical perspective. This history is first of all salvation history. God's divine plan for human salvation was accomplished during the period of Jesus, who through the events of his life (Lk 22:22) fulfilled the Old Testament prophecies (Lk 4:21; 18:31; 22:37; 24:26–27, 44), and this salvation is now extended to all humanity in the period of the church (Acts 4:12). This salvation history, moreover, is a part of human history. Luke relates the story of Jesus and the church to events in contemporary Palestinian (Lk 1:5; 3:1–2; Acts 4:6) and Roman (Lk 2:1–2; 3:1; Acts 11:28; 18:2, 12) history for, as Paul says in Acts 26:26, "this was not done in a corner." Finally, Luke relates the story of Jesus and the church to contemporaneous church history. Luke is concerned with presenting Christianity as a legitimate form of worship in the Roman world, a religion that is capable of meeting the spiritual needs of a world empire like that of Rome. To this end, Luke depicts the Roman governor Pilate declaring Jesus innocent of any wrongdoing three times (Luke 23:4, 23:14 and 23:22). . At the same time Luke argues in Acts that Christianity is the logical development and proper fulfillment of Judaism and is therefore deserving of the same toleration and freedom traditionally accorded Judaism by Rome (Acts 13:16–41; 23:6–9; 24:10–21; 26:2–23).

The prominence given to the period of the church in the story has important consequences for Luke's interpretation of the teachings of Jesus. By presenting the time of the church as a distinct phase of salvation history, Luke accordingly shifts the early Christian emphasis away from the expectation of an imminent parousia to the day-to-day concerns of the Christian community in the world. He does this in the gospel by regularly emphasizing the words "each day" (Lk 9:23; cf. Mk 8:34; Lk 11:3; 16:19; 19:47) in the sayings of Jesus. Although Luke still believes the parousia to be a reality that will come unexpectedly (Lk 12:38, 45–46), he is more concerned with presenting the words and deeds of Jesus as guides for the conduct of Christian disciples in the interim period between the ascension and the parousia and with presenting Jesus himself as the model of Christian life and piety.

Throughout the gospel, Luke calls upon the Christian disciple to identify with the master Jesus, who is caring and tender toward the poor and lowly, the outcast, the sinner, and the afflicted, toward all those who recognize their dependence on God (Lk 4:18; 6:20–23; 7:36–50; 14:12–14; 15:1–32; 16:19–31; 18:9–14; 19:1–10; 21:1–4), but who is severe toward the proud and self-righteous, and particularly toward those who place their material wealth before the service of God and his people (Lk 6:24–26; 12:13–21; 16:13–15, 19–31; 18:9–14, 15–25; cf. Lk 1:50–53). No gospel writer is more concerned than Luke with the mercy and compassion of Jesus (Lk 7:41–43; 10:29–37; 13:6–9; 15:11–32). No gospel writer is more concerned with the role of the Spirit in the life of Jesus and the Christian disciple (Lk 1:35, 41; 2:25–27; 4:1, 14, 18; 10:21; 11:13; 24:49), with the importance of prayer (Lk 3:21; 5:16; 6:12; 9:28; 11:1–13; 18:1–8), or with Jesus' concern for women (Lk 7:11–17, 36–50; 8:2–3; 10:38–42). While Jesus calls all humanity

In Acts Luke describes three times when Paul was declared innocent, yet suffered: Acts 23:29; 25:25; and 26:31-32).

to repent (Lk 5:32; 10:13; 11:32; 13:1–5; 15:7–10; 16:30; 17:3–4; 24:47), he is particularly demanding of those who would be his disciples. Of them he demands absolute and total detachment from family and material possessions (Lk 9:57–62; 12:32–34; 14:25–35). To all who respond in faith and repentance to the word Jesus preaches, he brings salvation (Lk 2:30–32; 3:6; 7:50; 8:48, 50; 17:19; 19:9) and peace (Lk 2:14; 7:50; 8:48; 19:38, 42) and life (Lk 10:25–28; 18:26–30).

Early Christian tradition, from the late second century on, identifies the author of this gospel and of the Acts of the Apostles as Luke, a Syrian from Antioch, who is mentioned in the New Testament in Col 4:14, Phlm 24 and 2 Tm 4:11. The prologue of the gospel makes it clear that Luke is not part of the first generation of Christian disciples but is himself dependent upon the traditions he received from those who were eyewitnesses and ministers of the word (Lk 1:2). His two-volume work marks him as someone who was highly literate both in the Old Testament traditions according to the Greek versions and in Hellenistic Greek writings.

Among the likely sources for the composition of this gospel (Lk 1:3) were the Gospel of Mark, a written collection of sayings of Jesus known also to the author of the Gospel of Matthew (Q; see Introduction to Matthew), and other special traditions that were used by Luke alone among the gospel writers. Some hold that Luke used Mark only as a complementary source for rounding out the material he took from other traditions. Because of its dependence on the Gospel of Mark and because details in Luke's Gospel (Lk 13:35a; 19:43–44; 21:20; 23:28–31) imply that the author was acquainted with the destruction of the city of Jerusalem by the Romans in A.D. 70, the Gospel of Luke is dated by most scholars after that date; many propose A.D. 80–90 as the time of composition.

Luke's consistent substitution of Greek names for the Aramaic or Hebrew names occurring in his sources (e.g., Lk 23:33; Mk 15:22; Lk 18:41; Mk 10:51), his omission from the gospel of specifically Jewish Christian concerns found in his sources (e.g., Mk 7:1–23), his interest in Gentile Christians (Lk 2:30–32; 3:6, 38; 4:16–30; 13:28–30; 14:15–24; 17:11–19; 24:47–48), and his incomplete knowledge of Palestinian geography, customs, and practices are among the characteristics of this gospel that suggest that Luke was a non-Palestinian writing to a non-Palestinian audience that was largely made up of Gentile Christians.

The principal divisions of the Gospel according to Luke are the following:

I. The Prologue (1:1–4)
II. The Infancy Narrative (1:5–2:52)
III. The Preparation for the Public Ministry (3:1–4:13)
IV. The Ministry in Galilee (4:14–9:50)
V. The Journey to Jerusalem: Luke's Travel Narrative (9:51–19:27)
VI. The Teaching Ministry in Jerusalem (19:28–21:38)
VII. The Passion Narrative (22:1–23:56)
VIII. The Resurrection Narrative (24:1–53)

I. The Prologue

CHAPTER 1

See RG 401–2

[1a]*Since many have undertaken to
compile a narrative of the events that have
been fulfilled among us, [2b]just as those who
were eyewitnesses from the beginning and
ministers of the word have handed them
down to us, [3]I too have decided, after investigating everything accurately anew, to
write it down in an orderly sequence for
you, most excellent Theophilus, [4]so that
you may realize the certainty of the teachings you have received.

1:1–4 The Gospel according to Luke is the only one of the synoptic gospels to begin with a literary prologue. Making use of a formal, literary construction and vocabulary, the author writes the prologue in imitation of Hellenistic Greek writers and, in so doing, relates his story about Jesus to contemporaneous Greek and Roman literature. Luke is not only interested in the words and deeds of Jesus, but also in the larger context of the birth, ministry, death, and resurrection of Jesus as the fulfillment of the promises of God in the Old Testament. As a second- or third-generation Christian, Luke acknowledges his debt to earlier **eyewitnesses** and **ministers of the word**, but claims that his contribution to this developing tradition is a complete and accurate account, told in an orderly manner, and intended to provide **Theophilus** ("friend of God," literally) and other readers with certainty about earlier teachings they have received.

a: Acts 1:1; 1 Cor 15:3. *b:* 24:48; Jn 15:27; Acts 1:21–22.

II. The Infancy Narrative

Announcement of the Birth of John. [5c*]In
the days of Herod, King of Judea, there was a
priest named Zechariah of the priestly division of Abijah; his wife was from the daughters of Aaron, and her name was Elizabeth.
[6]Both were righteous in the eyes of God, observing all the commandments and ordinances of the Lord blamelessly. [7d*]But they
had no child, because Elizabeth was barren
and both were advanced in years. [8]Once
when he was serving as priest in his division's
turn before God, [9e]according to the practice
of the priestly service, he was chosen by lot to
enter the sanctuary of the Lord to burn incense. [10]Then, when the whole assembly of
the people was praying outside at the hour of
the incense offering, [11]the angel of the Lord
appeared to him, standing at the right of the
altar of incense. [12]Zechariah was troubled by
what he saw, and fear came upon him. [13f*]But
the angel said to him, "Do not be afraid,
Zechariah, because your prayer has been
heard. Your wife Elizabeth will bear you a
son, and you shall name him John. [14]And you
will have joy and gladness, and many will rejoice at his birth, [15g*]for he will be great in the
sight of [the] Lord. He will drink neither wine
nor strong drink. He will be filled with the
holy Spirit even from his mother's womb,
[16]and he will turn many of the children of Israel to the Lord their God. [17h*]He will go before him in the spirit and power of Elijah to
turn the hearts of fathers toward children and
the disobedient to the understanding of the
righteous, to prepare a people fit for the
Lord." [18]Then Zechariah said to the angel,
"How shall I know this? For I am an old man,
and my wife is advanced in years." [19i*]And

1:5–2:52 Like the Gospel according to Matthew, this gospel opens with an infancy narrative, a collection of stories about the birth and childhood of Jesus. The narrative uses early Christian traditions about the birth of Jesus, traditions about the birth and circumcision of John the Baptist, and canticles such as the Magnificat (Lk 1:46–55) and Benedictus (Lk 1:67–79), composed of phrases drawn from the Greek Old Testament. It is largely, however, the composition of Luke who writes in imitation of Old Testament birth stories, combining historical and legendary details, literary ornamentation and interpretation of scripture, to answer in advance the question, "Who is Jesus Christ?" The focus of the narrative, therefore, is primarily christological. In this section Luke announces many of the themes that will become prominent in the rest of the gospel: the centrality of Jerusalem and the temple, the journey motif, the universality of salvation, joy and peace, concern for the lowly, the importance of women, the presentation of Jesus as savior, Spirit-guided revelation and prophecy, and the fulfillment of Old Testament promises. The account presents parallel scenes (diptychs) of angelic announcements of the birth of John the Baptist and of Jesus, and of the birth, circumcision, and presentation of John and Jesus. In this parallelism, the ascendency of Jesus over John is stressed: John is prophet of the Most High (Lk 1:76); Jesus is Son of the Most High (Lk 1:32). John is great in the sight of the Lord (Lk 1:15); Jesus will be Great (a LXX attribute, used absolutely, of God) (Lk 1:32). John will go before the Lord (Lk 1:16–17); Jesus will be Lord (Lk 1:43; 2:11).

1:5 In the days of Herod, King of Judea: Luke relates the story of salvation history to events in contemporary world history. Here and in Lk 3:1–2 he connects his narrative with events in Palestinian history; in Lk 2:1–2 and Lk 3:1 he casts the Jesus story in the light of events of Roman history. Herod the Great, the son of the Idumean Antipater, was declared "King of Judea" by the Roman Senate in 40 B.C., but became the undisputed ruler of Palestine only in 37 B.C. He continued as king until his death in 4 B.C. **Priestly division of Abijah**: a reference to the eighth of the twenty-four divisions of priests who, for a week at a time, twice a year, served in the Jerusalem temple.

1:7 They had no child: though childlessness was looked upon in contemporaneous Judaism as a curse or punishment for sin, it is intended here to present Elizabeth in a situation similar to that of some of the great mothers of important Old Testament figures: Sarah (Gn 15:3; 16:1); Rebekah (Gn 25:21); Rachel (Gn 29:31; 30:1); the mother of Samson and wife of Manoah (Jgs 13:2–3); Hannah (1 Sm 1:2).

1:13 Do not be afraid: a stereotyped Old Testament phrase spoken to reassure the recipient of a heavenly vision (Gn 15:1; Jos 1:9; Dn 10:12, 19 and elsewhere in Lk 1:30; 2:10). **You shall name him John**: the name means "Yahweh has shown favor," an indication of John's role in salvation history.

1:15 He will drink neither wine nor strong drink: like Samson (Jgs 13:4–5) and Samuel (1 Sm 1:11 LXX and 4QSam[a]), John is to be consecrated by Nazirite vow and set apart for the Lord's service.

1:17 He will go before him in the spirit and power of Elijah: John is to be the messenger sent before Yahweh, as described in Mal 3:1–2. He is cast, moreover, in the role of the Old Testament fiery reformer, the prophet Elijah, who according to Mal 4:6 (Mal 3:24) is sent before "the great and terrible day of the Lord comes."

1:19 I am Gabriel: "the angel of the Lord" is identified as Gabriel, the angel who in Dn 9:20–25 announces the seventy weeks of years and the coming of an anointed one, a prince. By alluding to Old Testament themes in Lk 1:17, 19 such as the coming of the day of the Lord and the dawning of the messianic era, Luke is presenting his interpretation of the significance of the births of John and Jesus.

---

c: 1 Chr 24:10. *d:* Gn 18:11; Jgs 13:2–5; 1 Sm 1:5–6. *e:* Ex 30:7. *f:* 1:57, 60, 63; Mt 1:20–21. *g:* 7:33; Nm 6:1–21; Jgs 13:4; 1 Sm 1:11 LXX. *h:* Sir 48:10; Mal 3:1; 3:23–24; Mt 11:14; 17:11–13. *i:* Dn 8:16; 9:21.

the angel said to him in reply, "I am Gabriel,
who stand before God. I was sent to speak to
you and to announce to you this good news.
[20j*]But now you will be speechless and unable to talk until the day these things take
place, because you did not believe my words,
which will be fulfilled at their proper time."
[21]Meanwhile the people were waiting for
Zechariah and were amazed that he stayed
so long in the sanctuary. [22]But when he came
out, he was unable to speak to them, and
they realized that he had seen a vision in the
sanctuary. He was gesturing to them but remained mute. [23]Then, when his days of ministry were completed, he went home. [24]After
this time his wife Elizabeth conceived, and
she went into seclusion for five months, saying, [25k]"So has the Lord done for me at a
time when he has seen fit to take away my
disgrace before others."

Announcement of the Birth of Jesus. [26*]In
the sixth month, the angel Gabriel was sent
from God to a town of Galilee called Nazareth, [27l]to a virgin betrothed to a man named
Joseph, of the house of David, and the virgin's name was Mary. [28m]And coming to her,
he said, "Hail, favored one! The Lord is with
you." [29]But she was greatly troubled at what
was said and pondered what sort of greeting
this might be. [30]Then the angel said to her,
"Do not be afraid, Mary, for you have found
favor with God. [31n]Behold, you will conceive
in your womb and bear a son, and you shall
name him Jesus. [32o*]He will be great and will
be called Son of the Most High, and the Lord
God will give him the throne of David his father, [33p]and he will rule over the house of Jacob forever, and of his kingdom there will be
no end." [34*]But Mary said to the angel, "How
can this be, since I have no relations with a
man?" [35q]And the angel said to her in reply,
"The holy Spirit will come upon you, and the
power of the Most High will overshadow
you. Therefore the child to be born will be
called holy, the Son of God. [36*]And behold,
Elizabeth, your relative, has also conceived a
son in her old age, and this is the sixth month
for her who was called barren; [37r]for nothing
will be impossible for God." [38]Mary said,
"Behold, I am the handmaid of the Lord.
May it be done to me according to your
word." Then the angel departed from her.

Mary Visits Elizabeth. [39]During those days
Mary set out and traveled to the hill country in
haste to a town of Judah, [40]where she entered
the house of Zechariah and greeted Elizabeth.
[41s]When Elizabeth heard Mary's greeting, the
infant leaped in her womb, and Elizabeth,
filled with the holy Spirit, [42t]cried out in a loud
voice and said, "Most blessed are you among
women, and blessed is the fruit of your womb.
[43*]And how does this happen to me, that the
mother of my Lord should come to me? [44]For
at the moment the sound of your greeting
reached my ears, the infant in my womb
leaped for joy. [45u*]Blessed are you who be-

1:20 You will be speechless and unable to talk: Zechariah's becoming mute is the sign given in response to his question in v 18. When Mary asks a similar question in Lk 1:34, unlike Zechariah who was punished for his doubt, she, in spite of her doubt, is praised and reassured (Lk 1:35–37).

1:26–38 The announcement to Mary of the birth of Jesus is parallel to the announcement to Zechariah of the birth of John. In both the angel Gabriel appears to the parent who is troubled by the vision (Lk 1:11–12, 26–29) and then told by the angel not to fear (Lk 1:13, 30). After the announcement is made (Lk 1:14–17, 31–33) the parent objects (Lk 1:18, 34) and a sign is given to confirm the announcement (Lk 1:20, 36). The particular focus of the announcement of the birth of Jesus is on his identity as Son of David (Lk 1:32–33) and Son of God (Lk 1:32, 35).

1:32 Son of the Most High: cf. Lk 1:76 where John is described as "prophet of the Most High." "Most High" is a title for God commonly used by Luke (Lk 1:35, 76; 6:35; 8:28; Acts 7:48; 16:17).

1:34 Mary's questioning response is a denial of sexual relations and is used by Luke to lead to the angel's declaration about the Spirit's role in the conception of this child (Lk 1:35). According to Luke, the virginal conception of Jesus takes place through the holy Spirit, the power of God, and therefore Jesus has a unique relationship to Yahweh: he is Son of God.

1:36–37 The sign given to Mary in confirmation of the angel's announcement to her is the pregnancy of her aged relative Elizabeth. If a woman past the childbearing age could become pregnant, why, the angel implies, should there be doubt about Mary's pregnancy, for **nothing will be impossible for God**.

1:43 Even before his birth, Jesus is identified in Luke as the Lord.

1:45 Blessed are you who believed: Luke portrays Mary as a believer whose faith stands in contrast to the disbelief of Zechariah (Lk 1:20). Mary's role as believer in the infancy narrative should be seen in connection with the explicit mention of

j: 1:45. *k:* Gn 30:23. *l:* 2:5; Mt 1:16, 18. *m:* Jgs 6:12; Ru 2:4; Jdt 13:18. *n:* Gn 16:11; Jgs 13:3; Is 7:14; Mt 1:21–23. *o:* 2 Sm 7:12, 13, 16; Is 9:7. *p:* Dn 2:44; 7:14; Mi 4:7; Mt 28:18. *q:* Mt 1:20. *r:* Gn 18:14; Jer 32:27; Mt 19:26. *s:* 1:15; Gn 25:22 LXX. *t:* 11:27–28; Jgs 5:24; Jdt 13:18; Dt 28:4. *u:* 1:20.

 2 Sam 6

lieved that what was spoken to you by the
Lord would be fulfilled."

The Canticle of Mary. 46[v w*]And Mary
said:

"My soul proclaims the greatness of the
Lord;
47 [x]my spirit rejoices in God my savior.
48 [y]For he has looked upon his handmaid's
lowliness;
behold, from now on will all ages call
me blessed.
49 [z]The Mighty One has done great things
for me,
and holy is his name.
50 [a]His mercy is from age to age
to those who fear him.
51 [b]He has shown might with his arm,
dispersed the arrogant of mind and
heart.
52 [c]He has thrown down the rulers from
their thrones
but lifted up the lowly.
53 [d]The hungry he has filled with good
things;
the rich he has sent away empty.
54 [e]He has helped Israel his servant,
remembering his mercy,
55 [f]according to his promise to our fathers,
to Abraham and to his descendants
forever."

56 Mary remained with her about three
months and then returned to her home.

The Birth of John. 57*When the time arrived for Elizabeth to have her child she gave
birth to a son. 58[g]Her neighbors and relatives
heard that the Lord had shown his great mercy toward her, and they rejoiced with her.
59[h*]When they came on the eighth day to circumcise the child, they were going to call him
Zechariah after his father, 60[i]but his mother
said in reply, "No. He will be called John."
61 But they answered her, "There is no one
among your relatives who has this name."
62 So they made signs, asking his father what
he wished him to be called. 63 He asked for a
tablet and wrote, "John is his name," and all
were amazed. 64[j]Immediately his mouth was
opened, his tongue freed, and he spoke blessing God. 65 Then fear came upon all their
neighbors, and all these matters were discussed throughout the hill country of Judea.
66 All who heard these things took them to
heart, saying, "What, then, will this child be?"
For surely the hand of the Lord was with him.

The Canticle of Zechariah. 67 Then Zechariah his father, filled with the holy Spirit,
prophesied, saying:

68 [k*]"Blessed be the Lord, the God of Israel,
for he has visited and brought
redemption to his people.

her presence among "those who believed" after the resurrection at the beginning of the Acts of the Apostles (Acts 1:14).

1:46–55 Although Mary is praised for being the mother of the Lord and because of her belief, she reacts as the servant in a psalm of praise, the Magnificat. Because there is no specific connection of the canticle to the context of Mary's pregnancy and her visit to Elizabeth, the Magnificat (with the possible exception of v 48) may have been a Jewish Christian hymn that Luke found appropriate at this point in his story. Even if not composed by Luke, it fits in well with themes found elsewhere in Luke: joy and exultation in the Lord; the lowly being singled out for God's favor; the reversal of human fortunes; the fulfillment of Old Testament promises. The loose connection between the hymn and the context is further seen in the fact that a few Old Latin manuscripts identify the speaker of the hymn as Elizabeth, even though the overwhelming textual evidence makes Mary the speaker.

1:57–66 The birth and circumcision of John above all emphasize John's incorporation into the people of Israel by the sign of the covenant (Gn 17:1–12). The narrative of John's circumcision also prepares the way for the subsequent description of the circumcision of Jesus in Lk 2:21. At the beginning of his two-volume work Luke shows those who play crucial roles in the inauguration of Christianity to be wholly a part of the people of Israel. At the end of the Acts of the Apostles (Acts 21:20; 22:3; 23:6–9; 24:14–16; 26:2–8, 22–23) he will argue that Christianity is the direct descendant of Pharisaic Judaism.

1:59 The practice of Palestinian Judaism at this time was to name the child at birth; moreover, though naming a male child after the father is not completely unknown, the usual practice was to name the child after the grandfather (see Lk 1:61). The naming of the child John and Zechariah's recovery from his loss of speech should be understood as fulfilling the angel's announcement to Zechariah in Lk 1:13, 20.

1:68–79 Like the canticle of Mary (Lk 1:46–55) the canticle of Zechariah is only loosely connected with its context. Apart from Lk 1:76–77, the hymn in speaking of **a horn for**

v: 1 Sm 2:1–10. *w:* Ps 35:9; Is 61:10; Heb 3:18. *x:* Ti 3:4; Jude 25. *y:* 11:27; 1 Sm 1:11; 2 Sm 16:12; 2 Kgs 14:26; Ps 113:7. *z:* Dt 10:21; Ps 71:19; 111:9; 126:2–3. *a:* Ps 89:2; 103:13, 17. *b:* Ps 89:10; 118:15; Jer 32:17 (39:17 LXX). *c:* 1 Sm 2:7; 2 Sm 22:28; Jb 5:11; 12:19; Ps 147:6; Sir 10:14; Jas 4:6; 1 Pt 5:5. *d:* 1 Sm 2:5; Ps 107:9. *e:* Ps 98:3; Is 41:8–9. *f:* Gn 13:15; 17:7; 18:18; 22:17–18; Mi 7:20. *g:* 1:14. *h:* 2:21; Gn 17:10, 12; Lv 12:3. *i:* 1:13. *j:* 1:20. *k:* 7:16; Ps 41:13; 72:18; 106:48; 111:9.

69 [l*]He has raised up a horn for our
salvation
within the house of David his servant,
70 even as he promised through the mouth
of his holy prophets from of old:
71 [m]salvation from our enemies and from
the hand of all who hate us,
72 [no]to show mercy to our fathers
and to be mindful of his holy covenant
73 [p]and of the oath he swore to Abraham
our father,
and to grant us that, 74 rescued from the
hand of enemies,
without fear we might worship him 75 [q]in
holiness and righteousness
before him all our days.
76 [r*]And you, child, will be called prophet
of the Most High,
for you will go before the Lord to
prepare his ways,
77 to give his people knowledge of salvation
through the forgiveness of their sins,
78 [st*]because of the tender mercy of our God
by which the daybreak from on high
will visit us
79 to shine on those who sit in darkness and
death's shadow,
to guide our feet into the path of
peace."

80 [u]The child grew and became strong in
spirit, and he was in the desert until the day
of his manifestation to Israel.

CHAPTER 2

See RG 401–3

The Birth of Jesus. 1 [*]In those days a
decree went out from Caesar Augustus that
the whole world should be enrolled. 2 This
was the first enrollment, when Quirinius was
governor of Syria. 3 So all went to be enrolled,
each to his own town. 4 [v]And Joseph too went
up from Galilee from the town of Nazareth to
Judea, to the city of David that is called Bethlehem, because he was of the house and family of David, 5 [w]to be enrolled with Mary, his
betrothed, who was with child. 6 While they

our salvation (Lk 1:69) and **the daybreak from on high** (Lk 1:78) applies more closely to Jesus and his work than to John. Again like Mary's canticle, it is largely composed of phrases taken from the Greek Old Testament and may have been a Jewish Christian hymn of praise that Luke adapted to fit the present context by inserting Lk 1:76–77 to give Zechariah's reply to the question asked in Lk 1:66.

1:69 A horn for our salvation: the horn is a common Old Testament figure for strength (Ps 18:3; 75:5–6; 89:18; 112:9; 148:14). This description is applied to God in Ps 18:2 and is here transferred to Jesus. The connection of the phrase with **the house of David** gives the title messianic overtones and may indicate an allusion to a phrase in Hannah's song of praise (1 Sm 2:10), "the horn of his anointed."

1:76 You will go before the Lord: here **the Lord** is most likely a reference to Jesus (contrast Lk 1:15–17 where Yahweh is meant) and John is presented as the precursor of Jesus.

1:78 The daybreak from on high: three times in the LXX (Jer 23:5; Zec 3:8; 6:12), the Greek word used here for **daybreak** translates the Hebrew word for "scion, branch," an Old Testament messianic title.

2:1–2 Although universal registrations of Roman citizens are attested in 28 B.C., 8 B.C., and A.D. 14 and enrollments in individual provinces of those who are not Roman citizens are also attested, such a universal census of the Roman world under Caesar Augustus is unknown outside the New Testament. Moreover, there are notorious historical problems connected with Luke's dating the census **when Quirinius was governor of Syria**, and the various attempts to resolve the difficulties have proved unsuccessful. P. Sulpicius Quirinius became legate of the province of Syria in A.D. 6–7 when Judea was annexed to the province of Syria. At that time, a provincial census of Judea was taken up. If Quirinius had been legate of Syria previously, it would have to have been before 10 B.C. because the various legates of Syria from 10 B.C. to 4 B.C. (the death of Herod) are known, and such a dating for an earlier census under Quirinius would create additional problems for dating the beginning of Jesus' ministry (Lk 3:1, 23). A previous legateship after 4 B.C. (and before A.D. 6) would not fit with the dating of Jesus' birth in the days of Herod (Lk 1:5; Mt 2:1). Luke may simply be combining Jesus' birth in Bethlehem with his vague recollection of a census under Quirinius (see also Acts 5:37) to underline the significance of this birth for the whole Roman world: through this child born in Bethlehem peace and salvation come to the empire.

2:1 Caesar Augustus: the reign of the Roman emperor Caesar Augustus is usually dated from 27 B.C. to his death in A.D. 14. According to Greek inscriptions, Augustus was regarded in the Roman Empire as "savior" and "god," and he was credited with establishing a time of peace, the *pax Augusta*, throughout the Roman world during his long reign. It is not by chance that Luke relates the birth of Jesus to the time of Caesar Augustus: the real savior (Lk 2:11) and peace-bearer (Lk 2:14; see also Lk 19:38) is the child born in Bethlehem. The great emperor is simply God's agent (like the Persian king Cyrus in Is 44:28–45:1) who provides the occasion for God's purposes to be accomplished. **The whole world**: that is, the whole Roman world: Rome, Italy, and the Roman provinces.

l: Ps 18:3. *m:* Ps 106:10. *n:* Gn 17:7; Lv 26:42; Ps 105:8–9; Mi 7:20. *o:* Ps 106:45–46. *p:* Gn 22:16–17. *q:* Ti 2:12. *r:* Is 40:3; Mal 3:1; Mt 3:3; 11:10. *s:* Is 60:1–2. *t:* Mal 3:20. *u:* 2:40; Mt 3:1. *v:* Mi 5:2; Mt 2:6. *w:* 1:27; Mt 1:18.

were there, the time came for her to have her
child, [7x*]and she gave birth to her firstborn
son. She wrapped him in swaddling clothes
and laid him in a manger, because there was
no room for them in the inn.

[8*]Now there were shepherds in that region
living in the fields and keeping the night
watch over their flock. [9y]The angel of the
Lord appeared to them and the glory of the
Lord shone around them, and they were
struck with great fear. [10]The angel said to
them, "Do not be afraid; for behold, I proclaim to you good news of great joy that will
be for all the people. [11z*]For today in the city
of David a savior has been born for you who
is Messiah and Lord. [12]And this will be a
sign for you: you will find an infant wrapped
in swaddling clothes and lying in a manger."
[13]And suddenly there was a multitude of the
heavenly host with the angel, praising God
and saying:

[14 a*]"Glory to God in the highest
and on earth peace to those on whom
his favor rests."

The Visit of the Shepherds. [15]When the
angels went away from them to heaven, the
shepherds said to one another, "Let us go,
then, to Bethlehem to see this thing that has
taken place, which the Lord has made
known to us." [16]So they went in haste and
found Mary and Joseph, and the infant lying
in the manger. [17]When they saw this, they
made known the message that had been told
them about this child. [18]All who heard it
were amazed by what had been told them by
the shepherds. [19]And Mary kept all these
things, reflecting on them in her heart.
[20]Then the shepherds returned, glorifying
and praising God for all they had heard and
seen, just as it had been told to them.

The Circumcision and Naming of Jesus.
[21b*]When eight days were completed for his
circumcision, he was named Jesus, the name
given him by the angel before he was conceived in the womb.

The Presentation in the Temple. [22c*]When
the days were completed for their purification according to the law of Moses, they
took him up to Jerusalem to present him to

2:7 Firstborn son: the description of Jesus as **firstborn** son does not necessarily mean that Mary had other sons. It is a legal description indicating that Jesus possessed the rights and privileges of the firstborn son (Gn 27; Ex 13:2; Nm 3:12–13; 18:15–16; Dt 21:15–17). See notes on Mt 1:25; Mk 6:3. **Wrapped him in swaddling clothes**: there may be an allusion here to the birth of another descendant of David, his son Solomon, who though a great king was wrapped in swaddling clothes like any other infant (Wis 7:4–6). **Laid him in a manger**: a feeding trough for animals. A possible allusion to Is 1:3 LXX.

2:8–20 The announcement of Jesus' birth to the shepherds is in keeping with Luke's theme that the lowly are singled out as the recipients of God's favors and blessings (see also Lk 1:48, 52).

2:11 The basic message of the infancy narrative is contained in the angel's announcement: this child is **savior, Messiah**, and **Lord**. Luke is the only synoptic gospel writer to use the title **savior** for Jesus (Lk 2:11; Acts 5:31; 13:23; see also Lk 1:69; 19:9; Acts 4:12). As savior, Jesus is looked upon by Luke as the one who rescues humanity from sin and delivers humanity from the condition of alienation from God. The title *christos*, "Christ," is the Greek equivalent of the Hebrew *māšîaḥ*, "Messiah," "anointed one." Among certain groups in first-century Palestinian Judaism, the title was applied to an expected royal leader from the line of David who would restore the kingdom to Israel (see Acts 1:6). The political overtones of the title are played down in Luke and instead the Messiah of the Lord (Lk 2:26) or the Lord's anointed is the one who now brings salvation to all humanity, Jew and Gentile (Lk 2:29–32). Lord is the most frequently used title for Jesus in Luke and Acts. In the New Testament it is also applied to Yahweh, as it is in the Old Testament. When used of Jesus it points to his transcendence and dominion over humanity.

2:14 On earth peace to those on whom his favor rests: the peace that results from the Christ event is for those whom God has favored with his grace. This reading is found in the oldest representatives of the Western and Alexandrian text traditions and is the preferred one; the Byzantine text tradition, on the other hand, reads: "on earth peace, good will toward men." The peace of which Luke's gospel speaks (Lk 2:14; 7:50; 8:48; 10:5–6; 19:38, 42; 24:36) is more than the absence of war of the pax Augusta; it also includes the security and well-being characteristic of peace in the Old Testament.

2:21 Just as John before him had been incorporated into the people of Israel through his circumcision, so too this child (see note on Lk 1:57–66).

2:22–40 The presentation of Jesus in the temple depicts the parents of Jesus as devout Jews, faithful observers of the law of the Lord (Lk 2:23–24, 39), i.e., the law of Moses. In this respect, they are described in a fashion similar to the parents of John (Lk 1:6) and Simeon (Lk 2:25) and Anna (Lk 2:36–37).

2:22 Their purification: syntactically, **their** must refer to Mary and Joseph, even though the Mosaic law never mentions the purification of the husband. Recognizing the problem, some Western scribes have altered the text to read "his purification," understanding the presentation of Jesus in the temple as a form of purification; the Vulgate version has a Latin form that could be either "his" or "her." According to

x: Mt 1:25. *y:* 1:11, 26. *z:* Mt 1:21; 16:16; Jn 4:42; Acts 2:36; 5:31; Phil 2:11. *a:* 19:38. *b:* 1:31; Gn 17:12; Mt 1:21. *c:* Lv 12:2–8.

the Lord, [23][d]just as it is written in the law of
the Lord, "Every male that opens the womb
shall be consecrated to the Lord," [24]and to
offer the sacrifice of "a pair of turtledoves or
two young pigeons," in accordance with the
dictate in the law of the Lord.
[25]*Now there was a man in Jerusalem
whose name was Simeon. This man was
righteous and devout, awaiting the consolation of Israel, and the holy Spirit was upon
him. [26]It had been revealed to him by the
holy Spirit that he should not see death before he had seen the Messiah of the Lord.
[27]He came in the Spirit into the temple; and
when the parents brought in the child Jesus
to perform the custom of the law in regard to
him, [28]he took him into his arms and blessed
God, saying:

[29] "Now, Master, you may let your servant go
in peace, according to your word,
[30] [e]for my eyes have seen your salvation,
[31] which you prepared in sight of all the peoples,
[32] [f]a light for revelation to the Gentiles,
and glory for your people Israel."

[33]The child's father and mother were
amazed at what was said about him; [34][g]and
Simeon blessed them and said to Mary his
mother, "Behold, this child is destined for
the fall and rise of many in Israel, and to be
a sign that will be contradicted [35]*(and you
yourself a sword will pierce) so that the
thoughts of many hearts may be revealed."
[36]There was also a prophetess, Anna, the
daughter of Phanuel, of the tribe of Asher.
She was advanced in years, having lived
seven years with her husband after her marriage, [37]and then as a widow until she was
eighty-four. She never left the temple, but
worshiped night and day with fasting and
prayer. [38][h]And coming forward at that very
time, she gave thanks to God and spoke
about the child to all who were awaiting the
redemption of Jerusalem.

The Return to Nazareth. [39][i]When they
had fulfilled all the prescriptions of the law
of the Lord, they returned to Galilee, to their
own town of Nazareth. [40][j]The child grew
and became strong, filled with wisdom; and
the favor of God was upon him.

The Boy Jesus in the Temple. [41][k]*Each
year his parents went to Jerusalem for the
feast of Passover, [42]and when he was twelve
years old, they went up according to festival
custom. [43]After they had completed its days,
as they were returning, the boy Jesus remained behind in Jerusalem, but his parents
did not know it. [44]Thinking that he was in the
caravan, they journeyed for a day and looked
for him among their relatives and acquaintances, [45]but not finding him, they returned
to Jerusalem to look for him. [46]After three
days they found him in the temple, sitting in
the midst of the teachers, listening to them
and asking them questions, [47]and all who
heard him were astounded at his understand-

the Mosaic law (Lv 12:2–8), the woman who gives birth to a boy is unable for forty days to touch anything sacred or to enter the temple area by reason of her legal impurity. At the end of this period she is required to offer a year-old lamb as a burnt offering and a turtledove or young pigeon as an expiation of sin. The woman who could not afford a lamb offered instead two turtledoves or two young pigeons, as Mary does here. **They took him up to Jerusalem to present him to the Lord**: as the firstborn son (Lk 2:7) Jesus was consecrated to the Lord as the law required (Ex 13:2, 12), but there was no requirement that this be done at the temple. The concept of a presentation at the temple is probably derived from 1 Sm 1:24–28, where Hannah offers the child Samuel for sanctuary services. The law further stipulated (Nm 3:47–48) that the firstborn son should be redeemed by the parents through their payment of five shekels to a member of a priestly family. About this legal requirement Luke is silent.

2:25 Awaiting the consolation of Israel: Simeon here and later Anna who speak about the child to all who were awaiting the redemption of Jerusalem represent the hopes and expectations of faithful and devout Jews who at this time were looking forward to the restoration of God's rule in Israel. The birth of Jesus brings these hopes to fulfillment.

2:35 (And you yourself a sword will pierce): Mary herself will not be untouched by the various reactions to the role of Jesus (34). Her blessedness as mother of the Lord will be challenged by her son who describes true blessedness as "hearing the word of God and observing it" (Lk 11:27–28 and Lk 8:20–21).

2:41–52 This story's concern with an incident from Jesus' youth is unique in the canonical gospel tradition. It presents Jesus in the role of the faithful Jewish boy, raised in the traditions of Israel, and fulfilling all that the law requires. With this episode, the infancy narrative ends just as it began, in the setting of the Jerusalem temple.

d: Ex 13:2, 12. *e:* 3:6; Is 40:5 LXX; 52:10. *f:* Is 42:6; 46:13; 49:6; Acts 13:47; 26:23. *g:* 12:51; Is 8:14; Jn 9:39; Rom 9:33; 1 Cor 1:23; 1 Pt 2:7–8. *h:* Is 52:9. *i:* Mt 2:23. *j:* 1:80; 2:52. *k:* Ex 12:24–27; 23:15; Dt 16:1–8.

ing and his answers. [48]When his parents saw him, they were astonished, and his mother said to him, "Son, why have you done this to us? Your father and I have been looking for you with great anxiety." [49*]And he said to them, "Why were you looking for me? Did you not know that I must be in my Father's house?" [50]But they did not understand what he said to them. [51 l]He went down with them and came to Nazareth, and was obedient to them; and his mother kept all these things in her heart. [52 m]And Jesus advanced [in] wisdom and age and favor before God and man.

III. The Preparation for the Public Ministry

CHAPTER 3

See RG 403–4

The Preaching of John the Baptist. [1 n*]In the fifteenth year of the reign of Tiberius Caesar, when Pontius Pilate was governor of Judea, and Herod was tetrarch of Galilee, and his brother Philip tetrarch of the region of Ituraea and Trachonitis, and Lysanias was tetrarch of Abilene, [2 o*]during the high priesthood of Annas and Caiaphas, the word of God came to John the son of Zechariah in the desert. [3 p*]He went throughout [the] whole region of the Jordan, proclaiming a baptism of repentance for the forgiveness of sins, [4 qr*]as it is written in the book of the words of the prophet Isaiah:

"A voice of one crying out in the desert:
'Prepare the way of the Lord,
make straight his paths.
[5] Every valley shall be filled
and every mountain and hill shall be made low.
The winding roads shall be made straight,
and the rough ways made smooth,
[6 s]and all flesh shall see the salvation of God.' "

2:49 I must be in my Father's house: this phrase can also be translated, "I must be about my Father's work." In either translation, Jesus refers to God as his Father. His divine sonship, and his obedience to his heavenly Father's will, take precedence over his ties to his family.

3:1–20 Although Luke is indebted in this section to his sources, the Gospel of Mark and a collection of sayings of John the Baptist, he has clearly marked this introduction to the ministry of Jesus with his own individual style. Just as the gospel began with a long periodic sentence (Lk 1:1–4), so too this section (Lk 3:1–2). He casts the call of John the Baptist in the form of an Old Testament prophetic call (Lk 3:2) and extends the quotation from Isaiah found in Mk 1:3 (Is 40:3) by the addition of Is 40:4–5 in Lk 3:5–6. In doing so, he presents his theme of the universality of salvation, which he has announced earlier in the words of Simeon (Lk 2:30–32). Moreover, in describing the expectation of the people (Lk 3:15), Luke is characterizing the time of John's preaching in the same way as he had earlier described the situation of other devout Israelites in the infancy narrative (Lk 2:25–26, 37–38). In Lk 3:7–18 Luke presents the preaching of John the Baptist who urges the crowds to reform in view of **the coming wrath** (Lk 3:7, 9: eschatological preaching), and who offers the crowds certain standards for reforming social conduct (Lk 3:10–14: ethical preaching), and who announces to the crowds the coming of **one mightier than** he (Lk 3:15–18: messianic preaching).

3:1 Tiberius Caesar: Tiberius succeeded Augustus as emperor in A.D. 14 and reigned until A.D. 37. The fifteenth year of his reign, depending on the method of calculating his first regnal year, would have fallen between A.D. 27 and 29. **Pontius Pilate**: prefect of Judea from A.D. 26 to 36. The Jewish historian Josephus describes him as a greedy and ruthless prefect who had little regard for the local Jewish population and their religious practices (see Lk 13:1). **Herod**: i.e., Herod Antipas, the son of Herod the Great. He ruled over Galilee and Perea from 4 B.C. to A.D. 39. His official title **tetrarch** means literally, "ruler of a quarter," but came to designate any subordinate prince. **Philip**: also a son of Herod the Great, tetrarch of the territory to the north and east of the Sea of Galilee from 4 B.C. to A.D. 34. Only two small areas of this territory are mentioned by Luke. **Lysanias**: nothing is known about this Lysanias who is said here to have been tetrarch of Abilene, a territory northwest of Damascus.

3:2 During the high priesthood of Annas and Caiaphas: after situating the call of John the Baptist in terms of the civil rulers of the period, Luke now mentions the religious leadership of Palestine (see note on Lk 1:5). Annas had been high priest A.D. 6–15. After being deposed by the Romans in A.D. 15 he was succeeded by various members of his family and eventually by his son-in-law, Caiaphas, who was high priest A.D. 18–36. Luke refers to Annas as high priest at this time (but see Jn 18:13, 19), possibly because of the continuing influence of Annas or because the title continued to be used for the ex-high priest. **The word of God came to John**: Luke is alone among the New Testament writers in associating the preaching of John with a call from God. Luke is thereby identifying John with the prophets whose ministries began with similar calls. In Lk 7:26 John will be described as "more than a prophet"; he is also the precursor of Jesus (Lk 7:27), a transitional figure inaugurating the period of the fulfillment of prophecy and promise.

3:3 See note on Mt 3:2.

3:4 The Essenes from Qumran used the same passage to explain why their community was in the desert studying and observing the law and the prophets (1QS 8:12–15).

l: 2:19. *m:* 1:80; 2:40; 1 Sm 2:26. *n:* Mt 3:1–12; Mk 1:1–8; Jn 1:19–28. *o:* 1:80. *p:* Acts 13:24; 19:4. *q:* Is 40:3–5. *r:* Jn 1:23. *s:* 2:30–31.

[7t]He said to the crowds who came out to be baptized by him, "You brood of vipers! Who warned you to flee from the coming wrath? [8u]Produce good fruits as evidence of your repentance; and do not begin to say to yourselves, 'We have Abraham as our father,' for I tell you, God can raise up children to Abraham from these stones. [9v]Even now the ax lies at the root of the trees. Therefore every tree that does not produce good fruit will be cut down and thrown into the fire."

[10]And the crowds asked him, "What then should we do?" [11]He said to them in reply, "Whoever has two tunics should share with the person who has none. And whoever has food should do likewise." [12w]Even tax collectors came to be baptized and they said to him, "Teacher, what should we do?" [13]He answered them, "Stop collecting more than what is prescribed." [14]Soldiers also asked him, "And what is it that we should do?" He told them, "Do not practice extortion, do not falsely accuse anyone, and be satisfied with your wages."

[15x]Now the people were filled with expectation, and all were asking in their hearts whether John might be the Messiah. [16y*]John answered them all, saying, "I am baptizing you with water, but one mightier than I is coming. I am not worthy to loosen the thongs of his sandals. He will baptize you with the holy Spirit and fire. [17z*]His winnowing fan is in his hand to clear his threshing floor and to gather the wheat into his barn, but the chaff he will burn with unquenchable fire." [18]Exhorting them in many other ways, he preached good news to the people. [19a*]Now Herod the tetrarch, who had been censured by him because of Herodias, his brother's wife, and because of all the evil deeds Herod had committed, [20]added still another to these by [also] putting John in prison.

The Baptism of Jesus. [21b*]After all the people had been baptized and Jesus also had been baptized and was praying, heaven was opened [22c*]and the holy Spirit descended upon him in bodily form like a dove. And a voice came from heaven, "You are my beloved Son; with you I am well pleased."

The Genealogy of Jesus. [23de*]When Jesus began his ministry he was about thirty years of age. He was the son, as was thought, of Joseph, the son of Heli, [24]the son of Matthat, the son of Levi, the son of Melchi, the son of Jannai, the son of Joseph, [25]the son of Mattathias, the son of Amos, the son of Nahum, the son of Esli, the son of Naggai, [26]the son of Maath, the son of Mattathias, the son of Semein, the son of Josech, the son of Joda,

3:16 He will baptize you with the holy Spirit and fire: in contrast to John's baptism with water, Jesus is said to baptize with the holy Spirit and with fire. From the point of view of the early Christian community, the Spirit and fire must have been understood in the light of the fire symbolism of the pouring out of the Spirit at Pentecost (Acts 2:1–4); but as part of John's preaching, the Spirit and fire should be related to their purifying and refining characteristics (Ez 36:25–27; Mal 3:2–3). See note on Mt 3:11.

3:17 Winnowing fan: see note on Mt 3:12.

3:19–20 Luke separates the ministry of John the Baptist from that of Jesus by reporting the imprisonment of John before the baptism of Jesus (Lk 3:21–22). Luke uses this literary device to serve his understanding of the periods of salvation history. With John the Baptist, the time of promise, the period of Israel, comes to an end; with the baptism of Jesus and the descent of the Spirit upon him, the time of fulfillment, the period of Jesus, begins. In his second volume, the Acts of the Apostles, Luke will introduce the third epoch in salvation history, the period of the church.

3:21–22 This episode in Luke focuses on the heavenly message identifying Jesus as Son and, through the allusion to Is 42:1, as Servant of Yahweh. The relationship of Jesus to the Father has already been announced in the infancy narrative (Lk 1:32, 35; 2:49); it occurs here at the beginning of Jesus' Galilean ministry and will reappear in Lk 9:35 before another major section of Luke's gospel, the travel narrative (Lk 9:51–19:27). Elsewhere in Luke's writings (Lk 4:18; Acts 10:38), this incident will be interpreted as a type of anointing of Jesus.

3:21 Was praying: Luke regularly presents Jesus at prayer at important points in his ministry: here at his baptism; at the choice of the Twelve (Lk 6:12); before Peter's confession (Lk 9:18); at the transfiguration (Lk 9:28); when he teaches his disciples to pray (Lk 11:1); at the Last Supper (Lk 22:32); on the Mount of Olives (Lk 22:41); on the cross (Lk 23:46).

3:22 You are my beloved Son; with you I am well pleased: this is the best attested reading in the Greek manuscripts. The Western reading, "You are my Son, this day I have begotten you," is derived from Ps 2:7.

3:23–38 Whereas Mt 1:2 begins the genealogy of Jesus with Abraham to emphasize Jesus' bonds with the people of Israel, Luke's universalism leads him to trace the descent of Jesus beyond Israel to Adam and beyond that to God (Lk 3:38) to stress again Jesus' divine sonship.

t: Mt 12:34. *u:* Jn 8:39. *v:* Mt 7:19; Jn 15:6. *w:* 7:29. *x:* Acts 13:25. *y:* 7:19–20; Jn 1:27; Acts 1:5; 11:16. *z:* Mt 3:12. *a:* Mt 14:3–4; Mk 6:17–18. *b:* Mt 3:13–17; Mk 1:9–11. *c:* 9:35; Ps 2:7; Is 42:1; Mt 12:18; 17:5; Mk 9:7; Jn 1:32; 2 Pt 1:17. *d:* Mt 1:1–17. *e:* 4:22; Jn 6:42.

[27][f]the son of Joanan, the son of Rhesa, the
son of Zerubbabel, the son of Shealtiel, the
son of Neri, [28]the son of Melchi, the son of
Addi, the son of Cosam, the son of Elmadam,
the son of Er, [29]the son of Joshua, the son of
Eliezer, the son of Jorim, the son of Matthat,
the son of Levi, [30]the son of Simeon, the son
of Judah, the son of Joseph, the son of Jonam,
the son of Eliakim, [31][g][h][i*]the son of Melea,
the son of Menna, the son of Mattatha, the
son of Nathan, the son of David, [32]the son of
Jesse, the son of Obed, the son of Boaz, the
son of Sala, the son of Nahshon, [33][j]the son of
Amminadab, the son of Admin, the son of
Arni, the son of Hezron, the son of Perez, the
son of Judah, [34][k][l]the son of Jacob, the son of
Isaac, the son of Abraham, the son of Terah,
the son of Nahor, [35]the son of Serug, the son
of Reu, the son of Peleg, the son of Eber, the
son of Shelah, [36][m]the son of Cainan, the son
of Arphaxad, the son of Shem, the son of
Noah, the son of Lamech, [37]the son of
Methuselah, the son of Enoch, the son of Jared, the son of Mahalaleel, the son of Cainan,
[38]the son of Enos, the son of Seth, the son of
Adam, the son of God.

CHAPTER 4

See RG 403–4

The Temptation of Jesus. [1][n*]Filled
with the holy Spirit, Jesus returned from the
Jordan and was led by the Spirit into the
desert [2][o*]for forty days, to be tempted by the
devil. He ate nothing during those days, and
when they were over he was hungry. [3]The
devil said to him, "If you are the Son of
God, command this stone to become bread."
[4][p]Jesus answered him, "It is written, 'One
does not live by bread alone.' " [5]Then he
took him up and showed him all the kingdoms of the world in a single instant. [6][q]The
devil said to him, "I shall give to you all this
power and their glory; for it has been
handed over to me, and I may give it to
whomever I wish. [7]All this will be yours, if
you worship me." [8][r]Jesus said to him in reply, "It is written:

'You shall worship the Lord, your God,
and him alone shall you serve.' "

[9*]Then he led him to Jerusalem, made him
stand on the parapet of the temple, and said
to him, "If you are the Son of God, throw
yourself down from here, [10][s]for it is written:

'He will command his angels concerning
you,
to guard you,'

[11][t]and:

'With their hands they will support you,
lest you dash your foot against a
stone.' "

[12][u]Jesus said to him in reply, "It also says,
'You shall not put the Lord, your God, to the
test.' " [13][v*]When the devil had finished every
temptation, he departed from him for a time.

IV. The Ministry in Galilee

The Beginning of the Galilean Ministry.
[14][w][x*]Jesus returned to Galilee in the power
of the Spirit, and news of him spread
throughout the whole region. [15]He taught in
their synagogues and was praised by all.

3:31 The son of Nathan, the son of David: in keeping with Jesus' prophetic role in Luke and Acts (e.g., Lk 7:16, 39; 9:8; 13:33; 24:19; Acts 3:22–23; 7:37) Luke traces Jesus' Davidic ancestry through the prophet Nathan (see 2 Sm 7:2) rather than through King Solomon, as Mt 1:6–7.

4:1–13 See note on Mt 4:1–11.

4:1 Filled with the holy Spirit: as a result of the descent of the Spirit upon him at his baptism (Lk 3:21–22), Jesus is now equipped to overcome the devil. Just as the Spirit is prominent at this early stage of Jesus' ministry (Lk 4:1, 14, 18), so too it will be at the beginning of the period of the church in Acts (Acts 1:4; 2:4, 17).

4:2 For forty days: the mention of forty days recalls the forty years of the wilderness wanderings of the Israelites during the Exodus (Dt 8:2).

4:9 To Jerusalem: the Lucan order of the temptations concludes on the parapet of the temple in Jerusalem, the city of destiny in Luke-Acts. It is in Jerusalem that Jesus will ultimately face his destiny (Lk 9:51; 13:33).

4:13 For a time: the devil's opportune time will occur before the passion and death of Jesus (Lk 22:3, 31–32, 53).

4:14 News of him spread: a Lucan theme; see Lk 4:37; 5:15; 7:17.

f: 1 Chr 3:17; Ez 3:2. *g:* 2 Sm 5:14. *h:* 1 Sm 16:1, 18. *i:* Ru 4:17–22; 1 Chr 2:1–15. *j:* Gn 29:35; 38:29. *k:* Gn 21:3; 25:26; 1 Chr 1:34; 28:34. *l:* Gn 11:10–26; 1 Chr 1:24–27. *m:* Gn 4:25–5:32; 1 Chr 1:1–4. *n:* Mt 4:1–11; Mk 1:12–13. *o:* Heb 4:15. *p:* Dt 8:3. *q:* Jer 27:5; Mt 28:18. *r:* Dt 6:13. *s:* Ps 91:11. *t:* Ps 91:12. *u:* Dt 6:16; 1 Cor 10:9. *v:* 22:3; Jn 13:2, 27; Heb 4:15. *w:* Mt 4:12–17; Mk 1:14–15. *x:* 5:15; Mt 3:16.

The Rejection at Nazareth. 16y*He came
to Nazareth, where he had grown up, and
went according to his custom into the synagogue on the sabbath day. He stood up to
read 17and was handed a scroll of the prophet
Isaiah. He unrolled the scroll and found the
passage where it was written:

18 z*"The Spirit of the Lord is upon me,
because he has anointed me
to bring glad tidings to the poor.
He has sent me to proclaim liberty to
captives
and recovery of sight to the blind,
to let the oppressed go free,
19 and to proclaim a year acceptable to the
Lord."

20Rolling up the scroll, he handed it back to
the attendant and sat down, and the eyes of
all in the synagogue looked intently at him.
21*He said to them, "Today this scripture
passage is fulfilled in your hearing." 22aAnd
all spoke highly of him and were amazed at
the gracious words that came from his
mouth. They also asked, "Isn't this the son
of Joseph?" 23*He said to them, "Surely you
will quote me this proverb, 'Physician, cure
yourself,' and say, 'Do here in your native
place the things that we heard were done in
Capernaum.' " 24And he said, "Amen, I say
to you, no prophet is accepted in his own native place. 25b*Indeed, I tell you, there were
many widows in Israel in the days of Elijah
when the sky was closed for three and a half
years and a severe famine spread over the
entire land. 26c*It was to none of these that
Elijah was sent, but only to a widow in
Zarephath in the land of Sidon. 27dAgain,
there were many lepers in Israel during the
time of Elisha the prophet; yet not one of
them was cleansed, but only Naaman the
Syrian." 28When the people in the synagogue heard this, they were all filled with
fury. 29They rose up, drove him out of the
town, and led him to the brow of the hill on
which their town had been built, to hurl him
down headlong. 30But he passed through the
midst of them and went away.

The Cure of a Demoniac. 31e f*Jesus then
went down to Capernaum, a town of Galilee.
He taught them on the sabbath, 32gand they
were astonished at his teaching because he

4:16–30 Luke has transposed to the beginning of Jesus' ministry an incident from his Marcan source, which situated it near the end of the Galilean ministry (Mk 6:1–6a). In doing so, Luke turns the initial admiration (Lk 4:22) and subsequent rejection of Jesus (Lk 4:28–29) into a foreshadowing of the whole future ministry of Jesus.' Moreover, the rejection of Jesus in his own hometown hints at the greater rejection of him by Israel (Acts 13:46).

4:16 According to his custom: Jesus' practice of regularly attending synagogue is carried on by the early Christians' practice of meeting in the temple (Acts 2:46; 3:1; 5:12).

4:18 The Spirit of the Lord is upon me, because he has anointed me: see note on Lk 3:21–22. As this incident develops, Jesus is portrayed as a prophet whose ministry is compared to that of the prophets Elijah and Elisha. Prophetic anointings are known in first-century Palestinian Judaism from the Qumran literature that speaks of prophets as God's anointed ones. **To bring glad tidings to the poor**: more than any other gospel writer Luke is concerned with Jesus' attitude toward the economically and socially poor (see Lk 6:20, 24; 12:16–21; 14:12–14; 16:19–26; 19:8). At times, the poor in Luke's gospel are associated with the downtrodden, the oppressed and afflicted, the forgotten and the neglected (Lk 4:18; 6:20–22; 7:22; 14:12–14), and it is they who accept Jesus' message of salvation.

4:21 Today this scripture passage is fulfilled in your hearing: this sermon inaugurates the time of fulfillment of Old Testament prophecy. Luke presents the ministry of Jesus as fulfilling Old Testament hopes and expectations (Lk 7:22); for Luke, even Jesus' suffering, death, and resurrection are done in fulfillment of the scriptures (Lk 24:25–27, 44–46; Acts 3:18).

4:23 The things that we heard were done in Capernaum: Luke's source for this incident reveals an awareness of an earlier ministry of Jesus in Capernaum that Luke has not yet made use of because of his transposition of this Nazareth episode to the beginning of Jesus' Galilean ministry. It is possible that by use of the future tense you will quote me . . . , Jesus is being portrayed as a prophet.

4:25–26 The references to Elijah and Elisha serve several purposes in this episode: they emphasize Luke's portrait of Jesus as a prophet like Elijah and Elisha; they help to explain why the initial admiration of the people turns to rejection; and they provide the scriptural justification for the future Christian mission to the Gentiles.

4:26 A widow in Zarephath in the land of Sidon: like Naaman the Syrian in Lk 4:27, a non-Israelite becomes the object of the prophet's ministry.

4:31–44 The next several incidents in Jesus' ministry take place in Capernaum and are based on Luke's source, Mk 1:21–39. To the previous portrait of Jesus as prophet (Lk 4:16–30) they now add a presentation of him as teacher (Lk 4:31–32), exorcist (Lk 4:32–37, 41), healer (Lk 4:38–40), and proclaimer of God's kingdom (Lk 4:43).

y: Mt 13:53–58; Mk 6:1–6. *z:* Is 61:1–2; 58:6. *a:* 3:23; Jn 6:42. *b:* 1 Kgs 17:1–7; 18:1; Jas 5:17. *c:* 1 Kgs 17:9. *d:* 2 Kgs 5:1–14. *e:* Mk 1:21–28. *f:* Mt 4:13; Jn 2:12. *g:* Mt 7:28–29.

spoke with authority. [33h]In the synagogue there was a man with the spirit of an unclean demon, and he cried out in a loud voice, [34i*]"Ha! What have you to do with us, Jesus of Nazareth? Have you come to destroy us? I know who you are—the Holy One of God!" [35]Jesus rebuked him and said, "Be quiet! Come out of him!" Then the demon threw the man down in front of them and came out of him without doing him any harm. [36]They were all amazed and said to one another, "What is there about his word? For with authority and power he commands the unclean spirits, and they come out." [37]And news of him spread everywhere in the surrounding region.

The Cure of Simon's Mother-in-Law. [38j*]After he left the synagogue, he entered the house of Simon. Simon's mother-in-law was afflicted with a severe fever, and they interceded with him about her. [39]He stood over her, rebuked the fever, and it left her. She got up immediately and waited on them.

Other Healings. [40k]At sunset, all who had people sick with various diseases brought them to him. He laid his hands on each of them and cured them. [41l*]And demons also came out from many, shouting, "You are the Son of God." But he rebuked them and did not allow them to speak because they knew that he was the Messiah.

Jesus Leaves Capernaum. [42m*]At daybreak, Jesus left and went to a deserted place. The crowds went looking for him, and when they came to him, they tried to prevent him from leaving them. [43n]But he said to them, "To the other towns also I must proclaim the good news of the kingdom of God, because for this purpose I have been sent." [44*]And he was preaching in the synagogues of Judea.

CHAPTER 5

See RG 404–5

The Call of Simon the Fisherman. [1op*]While the crowd was pressing in on Jesus and listening to the word of God, he was standing by the Lake of Gennesaret. [2]He saw two boats there alongside the lake; the fishermen had disembarked and were washing their nets. [3]Getting into one of the boats, the one belonging to Simon, he asked him to put out a short distance from the shore. Then he sat down and taught the crowds from the boat. [4q]After he had finished speaking, he said to Simon, "Put out into deep water and lower your nets for a catch." [5]Simon said in reply, "Master, we have worked hard all night and have caught nothing, but at your command I will lower the nets." [6]When they

4:34 What have you to do with us?: see note on Jn 2:4. **Have you come to destroy us?**: the question reflects the current belief that before the day of the Lord control over humanity would be wrested from the evil spirits, evil destroyed, and God's authority over humanity reestablished. The synoptic gospel tradition presents Jesus carrying out this task.

4:38 The house of Simon: because of Luke's arrangement of material, the reader has not yet been introduced to Simon (cf. Mk 1:16–18, 29–31). Situated as it is before the call of Simon (Lk 5:1–11), it helps the reader to understand Simon's eagerness to do what Jesus says (Lk 5:5) and to follow him (Lk 5:11).

4:41 They knew that he was the Messiah: that is, the Christ (see note on Lk 2:11).

4:42 They tried to prevent him from leaving them: the reaction of these strangers in Capernaum is presented in contrast to the reactions of those in his hometown who rejected him (Lk 4:28–30).

4:44 In the synagogues of Judea: instead of **Judea**, which is the best reading of the manuscript tradition, the Byzantine text tradition and other manuscripts read "Galilee," a reading that harmonizes Luke with Mt 4:23 and Mk 1:39. Up to this point Luke has spoken only of a ministry of Jesus in Galilee. Luke may be using **Judea** to refer to the land of Israel, the territory of the Jews, and not to a specific portion of it.

5:1–11 This incident has been transposed from his source, Mk 1:16–20, which places it immediately after Jesus makes his appearance in Galilee. By this transposition Luke uses this example of Simon's acceptance of Jesus to counter the earlier rejection of him by his hometown people, and since several incidents dealing with Jesus' power and authority have already been narrated, Luke creates a plausible context for the acceptance of Jesus by Simon and his partners. Many commentators have noted the similarity between the wondrous catch of fish reported here (Lk 4:4–9) and the post-resurrectional appearance of Jesus in Jn 21:1–11. There are traces in Luke's story that the post-resurrectional context is the original one: in Lk 4:8 Simon addresses Jesus as **Lord** (a post-resurrectional title for Jesus—see Lk 24:34; Acts 2:36—that has been read back into the historical ministry of Jesus) and recognizes himself as a sinner (an appropriate recognition for one who has denied knowing Jesus—Lk 22:54–62). As used by Luke, the incident looks forward to Peter's leadership in Luke—Acts (Lk 6:14; 9:20; 22:31–32; 24:34; Acts 1:15; 2:14–40; 10:11–18; 15:7–12) and symbolizes the future success of Peter as fisherman (Acts 2:41).

h: 8:28; Mt 8:29; Mk 1:23–24; 5:7. *i:* 4:41; Jn 6:69. *j:* Mt 8:14–15; Mk 1:29–31. *k:* Mt 8:16; Mk 1:32–34. *l:* 4:34; Mt 8:29; Mk 3:11–12. *m:* Mk 1:35–39. *n:* 8:1; Mk 1:14–15. *o:* Mt 4:18–22; Mk 1:16–20. *p:* Mt 13:1–2; Mk 2:13; 3:9–10; 4:1–2. *q:* Jn 21:1–11.

had done this, they caught a great number of
fish and their nets were tearing. [7]They signaled to their partners in the other boat to
come to help them. They came and filled
both boats so that they were in danger of
sinking. [8]When Simon Peter saw this, he fell
at the knees of Jesus and said, "Depart from
me, Lord, for I am a sinful man." [9]For astonishment at the catch of fish they had
made seized him and all those with him,
[10r]and likewise James and John, the sons of
Zebedee, who were partners of Simon. Jesus
said to Simon, "Do not be afraid; from now
on you will be catching men." [11s*]When they
brought their boats to the shore, they left
everything and followed him.

The Cleansing of a Leper. [12t*]Now there
was a man full of leprosy in one of the towns
where he was; and when he saw Jesus, he
fell prostrate, pleaded with him, and said,
"Lord, if you wish, you can make me clean."
[13]Jesus stretched out his hand, touched him,
and said, "I do will it. Be made clean." And
the leprosy left him immediately. [14u*]Then
he ordered him not to tell anyone, but "Go,
show yourself to the priest and offer for your
cleansing what Moses prescribed; that will
be proof for them." [15]The report about him
spread all the more, and great crowds assembled to listen to him and to be cured of
their ailments, [16v]but he would withdraw to
deserted places to pray.

The Healing of a Paralytic. [17w*]One day
as Jesus was teaching, Pharisees and teachers of the law were sitting there who had
come from every village of Galilee and Judea and Jerusalem, and the power of the
Lord was with him for healing. [18]And some
men brought on a stretcher a man who was
paralyzed; they were trying to bring him in
and set [him] in his presence. [19*]But not
finding a way to bring him in because of the
crowd, they went up on the roof and lowered
him on the stretcher through the tiles into the
middle in front of Jesus. [20*]When he saw
their faith, he said, "As for you, your sins are
forgiven." [21x*]Then the scribes and Pharisees began to ask themselves, "Who is this
who speaks blasphemies? Who but God
alone can forgive sins?" [22y]Jesus knew their
thoughts and said to them in reply, "What
are you thinking in your hearts? [23]Which is
easier, to say, 'Your sins are forgiven,' or to
say, 'Rise and walk'? [24z*]But that you may
know that the Son of Man has authority on
earth to forgive sins"—he said to the man
who was paralyzed, "I say to you, rise, pick
up your stretcher, and go home." [25]He stood
up immediately before them, picked up what
he had been lying on, and went home, glorifying God. [26]Then astonishment seized them
all and they glorified God, and, struck with
awe, they said, "We have seen incredible
things today."

The Call of Levi. [27a]After this he went out
and saw a tax collector named Levi sitting at
the customs post. He said to him, "Follow
me." [28*]And leaving everything behind, he

5:11 They left everything: in Mk 1:16–20 and Mt 4:18–22 the fishermen who follow Jesus leave their nets and their father; in Luke, they leave **everything** (see also Lk 5:28; 12:33; 14:33; 18:22), an indication of Luke's theme of complete detachment from material possessions.

5:12 Full of leprosy: see note on Mk 1:40.

5:14 Show yourself to the priest . . . what Moses prescribed: this is a reference to Lv 14:2–9 that gives detailed instructions for the purification of one who had been a victim of leprosy and thereby excluded from contact with others (see Lv 13:45–46, 49; Nm 5:2–3). **That will be proof for them**: see note on Mt 8:4.

5:17–6:11 From his Marcan source, Luke now introduces a series of controversies with Pharisees: controversy over Jesus' power to forgive sins (Lk 5:17–26); controversy over his eating and drinking with tax collectors and sinners (Lk 5:27–32); controversy over not fasting (Lk 5:33–36); and finally two episodes narrating controversies over observance of the sabbath (Lk 5:1–11).

5:17 Pharisees: see note on Mt 3:7.

5:19 Through the tiles: Luke has adapted the story found in Mark to his non-Palestinian audience by changing "opened up the roof" (Mk 2:4 a reference to Palestinian straw and clay roofs) to **through the tiles**, a detail that reflects the Hellenistic Greco-Roman house with tiled roof.

5:20 As for you, your sins are forgiven: literally, "O man, your sins are forgiven you." The connection between the forgiveness of sins and the cure of the paralytic reflects the belief of first-century Palestine (based on the Old Testament: Ex 20:5; Dt 5:9) that sickness and infirmity are the result of sin, one's own or that of one's ancestors (see also Lk 13:2; Jn 5:14; 9:2).

5:21 The scribes: see note on Mk 2:6.

5:24 See notes on Mt 9:6 and Mk 2:10.

5:28 Leaving everything behind: see note on Lk 5:11.

r: Jer 16:16. *s:* Mt 19:27. *t:* Mt 8:2–4; Mk 1:40–45. *u:* 8:56; Lv 14:2–32; Mk 7:36. *v:* Mk 1:35. *w:* Mt 9:1–8; Mk 2:1–12. *x:* 7:49; Is 43:25. *y:* 6:8; 9:47. *z:* Jn 5:8–9, 27. *a:* Mt 9:9–13; Mk 2:13–17.

got up and followed him. [29b]Then Levi gave a great banquet for him in his house, and a large crowd of tax collectors and others were at table with them. [30]The Pharisees and their scribes complained to his disciples, saying, "Why do you eat and drink with tax collectors and sinners?" [31]Jesus said to them in reply, "Those who are healthy do not need a physician, but the sick do. [32]I have not come to call the righteous to repentance but sinners."

The Question about Fasting. [33c]And they said to him, "The disciples of John fast often and offer prayers, and the disciples of the Pharisees do the same; but yours eat and drink." [34*]Jesus answered them, "Can you make the wedding guests fast while the bridegroom is with them? [35]But the days will come, and when the bridegroom is taken away from them, then they will fast in those days." [36*]And he also told them a parable. "No one tears a piece from a new cloak to patch an old one. Otherwise, he will tear the new and the piece from it will not match the old cloak. [37]Likewise, no one pours new wine into old wineskins. Otherwise, the new wine will burst the skins, and it will be spilled, and the skins will be ruined. [38]Rather, new wine must be poured into fresh wineskins. [39*][And] no one who has been drinking old wine desires new, for he says, 'The old is good.' "

CHAPTER 6

See RG 405

Debates about the Sabbath. [1de*]While he was going through a field of grain on a sabbath, his disciples were picking the heads of grain, rubbing them in their hands, and eating them. [2]Some Pharisees said, "Why are you doing what is unlawful on the sabbath?" [3f]Jesus said to them in reply, "Have you not read what David did when he and those [who were] with him were hungry? [4g*][How] he went into the house of God, took the bread of offering, which only the priests could lawfully eat, ate of it, and shared it with his companions." [5]Then he said to them, "The Son of Man is lord of the sabbath."

[6h]On another sabbath he went into the synagogue and taught, and there was a man there whose right hand was withered. [7i]The scribes and the Pharisees watched him closely to see if he would cure on the sabbath so that they might discover a reason to accuse him. [8j]But he realized their intentions and said to the man with the withered hand, "Come up and stand before us." And he rose and stood there. [9]Then Jesus said to them, "I ask you, is it lawful to do good on the sabbath rather than to do evil, to save life rather than to destroy it?" [10]Looking around at them all, he then said to him, "Stretch out your hand." He did so and his hand was restored. [11]But they became enraged and discussed together what they might do to Jesus.

The Mission of the Twelve. [12k*]In those days he departed to the mountain to pray, and he spent the night in prayer to God. [13*]When day came, he called his disciples to himself, and from them he chose Twelve,

5:34–35 See notes on Mt 9:15 and Mk 2:19.

5:34 Wedding guests: literally, "sons of the bridal chamber."

5:36–39 See notes on Mt 9:16–17 and Mk 2:19.

5:39 The old is good: this saying is meant to be ironic and offers an explanation for the rejection by some of the new wine that Jesus offers: satisfaction with old forms will prevent one from sampling the new.

6:1–11 The two episodes recounted here deal with gathering grain and healing, both of which were forbidden on the sabbath. In his defense of his disciples' conduct and his own charitable deed, Jesus argues that satisfying human needs such as hunger and performing works of mercy take precedence even over the sacred sabbath rest. See also notes on Mt 12:1–14 and Mk 2:25–26.

6:4 The bread of offering: see note on Mt 12:5–6.

6:12–16 See notes on Mt 10:1–11:1 and Mk 3:14–15.

6:12 Spent the night in prayer: see note on Lk 3:21.

6:13 He chose Twelve: the identification of this group as the Twelve is a part of early Christian tradition (see 1 Cor 15:5), and in Matthew and Luke, the **Twelve** are associated with the twelve tribes of Israel (Lk 22:29–30; Mt 19:28). After the fall of Judas from his position among the Twelve, the need is felt on the part of the early community to reconstitute this group before the Christian mission begins at Pentecost (Acts 1:15–26). From Luke's perspective, they are an important group who because of their association with Jesus from the time of his baptism to his ascension (Acts 1:21–22) provide the continuity between the historical Jesus and the church of Luke's day and who as the original eyewitnesses guarantee the fidelity of the church's beliefs and practices to the teachings of Jesus (Lk 1:1–4). **Whom he also named apostles**: only Luke among the gospel writers attributes to Jesus the bestowal of the name **apostles** upon the Twelve. See note on Mt 10:2–4. "Apostle" becomes a technical term in

b: 15:1–2. *c:* Mt 9:14–17; Mk 2:18–22. *d:* Mt 12:1–8; Mk 2:23–28. *e:* Dt 23:26. *f:* 1 Sm 21:1–6. *g:* Lv 24:5–9. *h:* Mt 12:9–14; Mk 3:1–6. *i:* 14:1. *j:* 5:22; 9:47. *k:* Mt 10:1–4; Mk 3:13–19.

whom he also named apostles: [14 l*]Simon,
whom he named Peter, and his brother Andrew, James, John, Philip, Bartholomew,
[15*]Matthew, Thomas, James the son of Alphaeus, Simon who was called a Zealot,
[16*]and Judas the son of James, and Judas Iscariot, who became a traitor.

Ministering to a Great Multitude.
[17m*]And he came down with them and stood
on a stretch of level ground. A great crowd of
his disciples and a large number of the people from all Judea and Jerusalem and the
coastal region of Tyre and Sidon [18]came to
hear him and to be healed of their diseases;
and even those who were tormented by unclean spirits were cured. [19]Everyone in the
crowd sought to touch him because power
came forth from him and healed them all.

Sermon on the Plain. [20n*]And raising his
eyes toward his disciples he said:

"Blessed are you who are poor,
for the kingdom of God is yours.
[21 o]Blessed are you who are now hungry,
for you will be satisfied.
Blessed are you who are now weeping,
for you will laugh.
[22 p]Blessed are you when people hate you,
and when they exclude and insult you,
and denounce your name as evil
on account of the Son of Man.

[23q]Rejoice and leap for joy on that day!
Behold, your reward will be great in heaven.
For their ancestors treated the prophets in
the same way.
[24 r]But woe to you who are rich,
for you have received your consolation.
[25 s]But woe to you who are filled now,
for you will be hungry.
Woe to you who laugh now,
for you will grieve and weep.
[26 t]Woe to you when all speak well of you,
for their ancestors treated the false
prophets in this way.

Love of Enemies. [27uv*]"But to you who
hear I say, love your enemies, do good to
those who hate you, [28w]bless those who
curse you, pray for those who mistreat you.

early Christianity for a missionary sent out to preach the word of God. Although Luke seems to want to restrict the title to the Twelve (only in Acts 4:4, 14 are Paul and Barnabas termed apostles), other places in the New Testament show an awareness that the term was more widely applied (1 Cor 15:5–7; Gal 1:19; 1 Cor 1:1; 9:1; Rom 16:7).

6:14 Simon, whom he named Peter: see note on Mk 3:16.

6:15 Simon who was called a Zealot: the Zealots were the instigators of the First Revolt of Palestinian Jews against Rome in A.D. 66–70. Because the existence of the Zealots as a distinct group during the lifetime of Jesus is the subject of debate, the meaning of the identification of Simon as a Zealot is unclear.

6:16 Judas Iscariot: the name **Iscariot** may mean "man from Kerioth."

6:17 The coastal region of Tyre and Sidon: not only Jews from Judea and Jerusalem, but even Gentiles from outside Palestine come to hear Jesus (see Lk 2:31–32; 3:6; 4:24–27).

6:20–49 Luke's "Sermon on the Plain" is the counterpart to Matthew's "Sermon on the Mount" (Mt 5:1–7:27). It is addressed to the disciples of Jesus, and, like the sermon in Matthew, it begins with beatitudes (Lk 6:20–22) and ends with the parable of the two houses (Lk 6:46–49). Almost all the words of Jesus reported by Luke are found in Matthew's version, but because Matthew includes sayings that were related to specifically Jewish Christian problems (e.g., Mt 5:17–20; 6:1–8, 16–18) that Luke did not find appropriate for his predominantly Gentile Christian audience, the "Sermon on the Mount" is considerably longer. Luke's sermon may be outlined as follows: an introduction consisting of blessings and woes (Lk 6:20–26); the love of one's enemies (Lk 6:27–36); the demands of loving one's neighbor (Lk 6:37–42); good deeds as proof of one's goodness (Lk 6:43–45); a parable illustrating the result of listening to and acting on the words of Jesus (Lk 6:46–49). At the core of the sermon is Jesus' teaching on the love of one's enemies (Lk 6:27–36) that has as its source of motivation God's graciousness and compassion for all humanity (Lk 6:35–36) and Jesus' teaching on the love of one's neighbor (Lk 6:37–42) that is characterized by forgiveness and generosity.

6:20–26 The introductory portion of the sermon consists of blessings and woes that address the real economic and social conditions of humanity (the poor—the rich; the hungry—the satisfied; those grieving—those laughing; the outcast—the socially acceptable). By contrast, Matthew emphasizes the religious and spiritual values of disciples in the kingdom inaugurated by Jesus ("poor in spirit," Mt 5:5; "hunger and thirst for righteousness," Mt 5:6). In the sermon, **blessed** extols the fortunate condition of persons who are favored with the blessings of God; the woes, addressed as they are to the disciples of Jesus, threaten God's profound displeasure on those so blinded by their present fortunate situation that they do not recognize and appreciate the real values of God's kingdom. In all the blessings and woes, the present condition of the persons addressed will be reversed in the future.

6:27–36 See notes on Mt 5:43–48 and Mt 5:48.

---

l: Acts 1:13. *m:* Mt 4:23–25; Mk 3:7–10. *n:* Mt 5:1–12. *o:* Ps 126:5–6; Is 61:3; Jer 31:25; Rev 7:16–17. *p:* Jn 15:19; 16:2; 1 Pt 4:14. *q:* 11:47–48; 2 Chr 36:16; Mt 23:30–31. *r:* Jas 5:1. *s:* Is 65:13–14. *t:* Jas 4:4. *u:* Mt 5:38–48. *v:* Prv 25:21; Rom 12:20–21. *w:* Rom 12:14; 1 Pt 3:9.

[29]To the person who strikes you on one cheek, offer the other one as well, and from the person who takes your cloak, do not withhold even your tunic. [30]Give to everyone who asks of you, and from the one who takes what is yours do not demand it back. [31x]Do to others as you would have them do to you. [32]For if you love those who love you, what credit is that to you? Even sinners love those who love them. [33]And if you do good to those who do good to you, what credit is that to you? Even sinners do the same. [34y]If you lend money to those from whom you expect repayment, what credit [is] that to you? Even sinners lend to sinners, and get back the same amount. [35z]But rather, love your enemies and do good to them, and lend expecting nothing back; then your reward will be great and you will be children of the Most High, for he himself is kind to the ungrateful and the wicked. [36]Be merciful, just as [also] your Father is merciful.

Judging Others. [37ab*]"Stop judging and you will not be judged. Stop condemning and you will not be condemned. Forgive and you will be forgiven. [38c]Give and gifts will be given to you; a good measure, packed together, shaken down, and overflowing, will be poured into your lap. For the measure with which you measure will in return be measured out to you." [39d]And he told them a parable, "Can a blind person guide a blind person? Will not both fall into a pit? [40e]No disciple is superior to the teacher; but when fully trained, every disciple will be like his teacher. [41]Why do you notice the splinter in your brother's eye, but do not perceive the wooden beam in your own? [42]How can you say to your brother, 'Brother, let me remove that splinter in your eye,' when you do not even notice the wooden beam in your own eye? You hypocrite! Remove the wooden beam from your eye first; then you will see clearly to remove the splinter in your brother's eye.

A Tree Known by Its Fruit. [43f*]"A good tree does not bear rotten fruit, nor does a rotten tree bear good fruit. [44]For every tree is known by its own fruit. For people do not pick figs from thornbushes, nor do they gather grapes from brambles. [45]A good person out of the store of goodness in his heart produces good, but an evil person out of a store of evil produces evil; for from the fullness of the heart the mouth speaks.

The Two Foundations. [46g]"Why do you call me, 'Lord, Lord,' but not do what I command? [47h*]I will show you what someone is like who comes to me, listens to my words, and acts on them. [48]That one is like a person building a house, who dug deeply and laid the foundation on rock; when the flood came, the river burst against that house but could not shake it because it had been well built. [49]But the one who listens and does not act is like a person who built a house on the ground without a foundation. When the river burst against it, it collapsed at once and was completely destroyed."

CHAPTER 7

See RG 405-6

The Healing of a Centurion's Slave. [1i*]When he had finished all his words to the people, he entered Capernaum. [2*]A centurion there had a slave who was ill and about to die, and he was valuable to him. [3]When he heard about Jesus, he sent elders of the Jews to him, asking him to come and save the life of his slave. [4]They approached Jesus and

6:37–42 See notes on Mt 7:1–12; 7:1; 7:5.

6:43–46 See notes on Mt 7:15–20 and 12:33.

6:47–49 See note on Mt 7:24–27.

7:1–8:3 The episodes in this section present a series of reactions to the Galilean ministry of Jesus and reflect some of Luke's particular interests: the faith of a Gentile (Lk 7:1–10); the prophet Jesus' concern for a widowed mother (Lk 7:11–17); the ministry of Jesus directed to the afflicted and unfortunate of Is 61:1 (Lk 7:18–23); the relation between John and Jesus and their role in God's plan for salvation (Lk 7:24–35); a forgiven sinner's manifestation of love (Lk 7:36–50); the association of women with the ministry of Jesus (Lk 8:1–3).

7:1–10 This story about the faith of the centurion, a Gentile who cherishes the Jewish nation (Lk 7:5), prepares for the story in Acts of the conversion by Peter of the Roman centurion Cornelius who is similarly described as one who is generous to the Jewish nation (Acts 10:2). See also Acts 10:34–35 in the speech of Peter: "God shows no partiality . . . the person who fears him and acts righteously is acceptable to him." See also notes on Mt 8:5–13 and Jn 4:43–54.

7:2 A centurion: see note on Mt 8:5.

---

x: Mt 7:12. *y:* Dt 15:7–8. *z:* Lv 25:35–36. *a:* Mt 7:1–5. *b:* Mt 6:14; Jas 2:13. *c:* Mk 4:24. *d:* Mt 15:14; 23:16–17, 24. *e:* Mt 10:24–25; Jn 13:16; 15:20. *f:* Mt 7:16–20; 12:33, 35. *g:* Mt 7:21; Rom 2:13; Jas 1:22. *h:* Mt 7:24–27. *i:* Mt 8:5–13; Jn 4:43–54.

strongly urged him to come, saying, "He deserves to have you do this for him, [5]for he loves our nation and he built the synagogue for us." [6*]And Jesus went with them, but when he was only a short distance from the house, the centurion sent friends to tell him, "Lord, do not trouble yourself, for I am not worthy to have you enter under my roof. [7]Therefore, I did not consider myself worthy to come to you; but say the word and let my servant be healed. [8]For I too am a person subject to authority, with soldiers subject to me. And I say to one, 'Go,' and he goes; and to another, 'Come here,' and he comes; and to my slave, 'Do this,' and he does it." [9]When Jesus heard this he was amazed at him and, turning, said to the crowd following him, "I tell you, not even in Israel have I found such faith." [10]When the messengers returned to the house, they found the slave in good health.

Raising of the Widow's Son. [11 j*]Soon afterward he journeyed to a city called Nain, and his disciples and a large crowd accompanied him. [12k]As he drew near to the gate of the city, a man who had died was being carried out, the only son of his mother, and she was a widow. A large crowd from the city was with her. [13]When the Lord saw her, he was moved with pity for her and said to her, "Do not weep." [14]He stepped forward and touched the coffin; at this the bearers halted, and he said, "Young man, I tell you, arise!" [15l]The dead man sat up and began to speak, and Jesus gave him to his mother. [16m]Fear seized them all, and they glorified God, exclaiming, "A great prophet has arisen in our midst," and "God has visited his people." [17]This report about him spread through the whole of Judea and in all the surrounding region.

The Messengers from John the Baptist. [18n*]The disciples of John told him about all these things. John summoned two of his disciples [19o]and sent them to the Lord to ask, "Are you the one who is to come, or should we look for another?" [20]When the men came to him, they said, "John the Baptist has sent us to you to ask, 'Are you the one who is to come, or should we look for another?' " [21]At that time he cured many of their diseases, sufferings, and evil spirits; he also granted sight to many who were blind. [22p]And he said to them in reply, "Go and tell John what you have seen and heard: the blind regain their sight, the lame walk, lepers are cleansed, the deaf hear, the dead are raised, the poor have the good news proclaimed to them. [23*]And blessed is the one who takes no offense at me."

Jesus' Testimony to John. [24q*]When the messengers of John had left, Jesus began to speak to the crowds about John. "What did you go out to the desert to see—a reed swayed by the wind? [25]Then what did you go out to see? Someone dressed in fine garments? Those who dress luxuriously and live sumptuously are found in royal palaces. [26r]Then what did you go out to see? A prophet? Yes, I tell you, and more than a prophet. [27s]This is the one about whom scripture says:

7:6 I am not worthy to have you enter under my roof: to enter the house of a Gentile was considered unclean for a Jew; cf. Acts 10:28.

7:11–17 In the previous incident Jesus' power was displayed for a Gentile whose servant was dying; in this episode it is displayed toward a widowed mother whose only son has already died. Jesus' power over death prepares for his reply to John's disciples in Lk 7:22: "the dead are raised." This resuscitation in alluding to the prophet Elijah's resurrection of the only son of a widow of Zarephath (1 Kgs 7:8–24) leads to the reaction of the crowd: "A great prophet has arisen in our midst" (Lk 7:16).

7:18–23 In answer to John's question, **Are you the one who is to come?**—a probable reference to the return of the fiery prophet of reform, Elijah, "before the day of the Lord comes, the great and terrible day" (Mal 3:19)—Jesus responds that his role is rather to bring the blessings spoken of in Is 61:1 to the oppressed and neglected of society (Lk 7:22; cf. Lk 4:18).

7:23 Blessed is the one who takes no offense at me: this beatitude is pronounced on the person who recognizes Jesus' true identity in spite of previous expectations of what "the one who is to come" would be like.

7:24–30 In his testimony to John, Jesus reveals his understanding of the relationship between them: John is the precursor of Jesus (Lk 7:27); John is the messenger spoken of in Mal 3:1 who in Mal 3:19 is identified as Elijah. Taken with the previous episode, it can be seen that Jesus identifies John as precisely the person John envisioned Jesus to be: the Elijah who prepares the way for the coming of the day of the Lord.

j: 4:25–26; 1 Kgs 17:8–24. *k:* 8:42; 1 Kgs 17:17. *l:* 1 Kgs 17:23; 2 Kgs 4:36. *m:* 1:68; 19:44. *n:* Mt 11:2–6. *o:* Mal 3:1; Rev 1:4, 8; 4:8. *p:* 4:18; Is 35:5–6; 61:1. *q:* Mt 11:7–15. *r:* 1:76. *s:* Mal 3:1 / Is 40:3.

'Behold, I am sending my messenger
ahead of you,
he will prepare your way before you.'

[28]I tell you, among those born of women, no one is greater than John; yet the least in the kingdom of God is greater than he." [29t](All the people who listened, including the tax collectors, and who were baptized with the baptism of John, acknowledged the righteousness of God; [30]but the Pharisees and scholars of the law, who were not baptized by him, rejected the plan of God for themselves.)

[31u*]"Then to what shall I compare the people of this generation? What are they like? [32]They are like children who sit in the marketplace and call to one another,

'We played the flute for you, but you did
not dance.
We sang a dirge, but you did not
weep.'

[33]For John the Baptist came neither eating food nor drinking wine, and you said, 'He is possessed by a demon.' [34v]The Son of Man came eating and drinking and you said, 'Look, he is a glutton and a drunkard, a friend of tax collectors and sinners.' [35]But wisdom is vindicated by all her children."

The Pardon of the Sinful Woman. [36w*]A Pharisee invited him to dine with him, and he entered the Pharisee's house and reclined at table. [37xy]Now there was a sinful woman in the city who learned that he was at table in the house of the Pharisee. Bringing an alabaster flask of ointment, [38]she stood behind him at his feet weeping and began to bathe his feet with her tears. Then she wiped them with her hair, kissed them, and anointed them with the ointment. [39]When the Pharisee who had invited him saw this he said to himself, "If this man were a prophet, he would know who and what sort of woman this is who is touching him, that she is a sinner." [40]Jesus said to him in reply, "Simon, I have something to say to you." "Tell me, teacher," he said. [41*]"Two people were in debt to a certain creditor; one owed five hundred days' wages and the other owed fifty. [42]Since they were unable to repay the debt, he forgave it for both. Which of them will love him more?" [43]Simon said in reply, "The one, I suppose, whose larger debt was forgiven." He said to him, "You have judged rightly." [44]Then he turned to the woman and said to Simon, "Do you see this woman? When I entered your house, you did not give me water for my feet, but she has bathed them with her tears and wiped them with her hair. [45]You did not give me a kiss, but she has not ceased kissing my feet since the time I entered. [46]You did not anoint my head with oil, but she anointed my feet with ointment. [47*]So I tell you, her many sins have been forgiven; hence, she has shown great love. But the one to whom little is forgiven, loves little." [48z]He said to her, "Your sins are forgiven." [49a]The others at table said to themselves, "Who is this who even forgives sins?" [50]But he said to the woman, "Your faith has saved you; go in peace."

7:31–35 See note on Mt 11:16–19.

7:36–50 In this story of the pardoning of the sinful woman Luke presents two different reactions to the ministry of Jesus. A Pharisee, suspecting Jesus to be a prophet, invites Jesus to a festive banquet in his house, but the Pharisee's self-righteousness leads to little forgiveness by God and consequently little love shown toward Jesus. The sinful woman, on the other hand, manifests a faith in God (Lk 7:50) that has led her to seek forgiveness for her sins, and because so much was forgiven, she now overwhelms Jesus with her display of love; cf. the similar contrast in attitudes in Lk 18:9–14. The whole episode is a powerful lesson on the relation between forgiveness and love.

7:36 Reclined at table: the normal posture of guests at a banquet. Other oriental banquet customs alluded to in this story include the reception by the host with a kiss (Lk 7:45), washing the feet of the guests (Lk 7:44), and the anointing of the guests' heads (Lk 7:46).

7:41 Days' wages: one denarius is the normal daily wage of a laborer.

7:47 Her many sins have been forgiven; hence, she has shown great love: literally, "her many sins have been forgiven, seeing that she has loved much." That the woman's sins have been forgiven is attested by the great love she shows toward Jesus. Her love is the consequence of her forgiveness. This is also the meaning demanded by the parable in Lk 7:41–43.

t: 3:7, 12; Mt 21:32. *u:* Mt 11:16–19. *v:* 15:2. *w:* 11:37; 14:1. *x:* Mt 26:7; Mk 14:3. *y:* Jn 12:3. *z:* 5:20; Mt 9:20; Mk 2:5. *a:* 5:21.

CHAPTER 8

See RG 405–6

Galilean Women Follow Jesus. [1b*]Afterward he journeyed from one town and village to another, preaching and proclaiming the good news of the kingdom of God. Accompanying him were the Twelve [2c]and some women who had been cured of evil spirits and infirmities, Mary, called Magdalene, from whom seven demons had gone out, [3]Joanna, the wife of Herod's steward Chuza, Susanna, and many others who provided for them out of their resources.

The Parable of the Sower. [4d*]When a large crowd gathered, with people from one town after another journeying to him, he spoke in a parable. [5]"A sower went out to sow his seed. And as he sowed, some seed fell on the path and was trampled, and the birds of the sky ate it up. [6]Some seed fell on rocky ground, and when it grew, it withered for lack of moisture. [7]Some seed fell among thorns, and the thorns grew with it and choked it. [8e]And some seed fell on good soil, and when it grew, it produced fruit a hundredfold." After saying this, he called out, "Whoever has ears to hear ought to hear."

The Purpose of the Parables. [9f]Then his disciples asked him what the meaning of this parable might be. [10g]He answered, "Knowledge of the mysteries of the kingdom of God has been granted to you; but to the rest, they are made known through parables so that 'they may look but not see, and hear but not understand.'

The Parable of the Sower Explained. [11hi*]"This is the meaning of the parable. The seed is the word of God. [12]Those on the path are the ones who have heard, but the devil comes and takes away the word from their hearts that they may not believe and be saved. [13]Those on rocky ground are the ones who, when they hear, receive the word with joy, but they have no root; they believe only for a time and fall away in time of trial. [14]As for the seed that fell among thorns, they are the ones who have heard, but as they go along, they are choked by the anxieties and riches and pleasures of life, and they fail to produce mature fruit. [15]But as for the seed that fell on rich soil, they are the ones who, when they have heard the word, embrace it with a generous and good heart, and bear fruit through perseverance.

The Parable of the Lamp. [16jk*]"No one who lights a lamp conceals it with a vessel or sets it under a bed; rather, he places it on a lampstand so that those who enter may see the light. [17l]For there is nothing hidden that will not become visible, and nothing secret that will not be known and come to light. [18m]Take care, then, how you hear. To anyone who has, more will be given, and from the one who has not, even what he seems to have will be taken away."

Jesus and His Family. [19n*]Then his mother and his brothers came to him but were unable to join him because of the crowd. [20o]He was told, "Your mother and your brothers are standing outside and they

8:1–3 Luke presents Jesus as an itinerant preacher traveling in the company of the Twelve and of the Galilean women who are sustaining them out of their means. These Galilean women will later accompany Jesus on his journey to Jerusalem and become witnesses to his death (Lk 23:49) and resurrection (Lk 24:9–11, where Mary Magdalene and Joanna are specifically mentioned; cf. also Acts 1:14). The association of women with the ministry of Jesus is most unusual in the light of the attitude of first-century Palestinian Judaism toward women. The more common attitude is expressed in Jn 4:27, and early rabbinic documents caution against speaking with women in public.

8:4–21 The focus in this section is on how one should hear the word of God and act on it. It includes the parable of the sower and its explanation (Lk 8:4–15), a collection of sayings on how one should act on the word that is heard (Lk 8:16–18), and the identification of the mother and brothers of Jesus as the ones who hear the word and act on it (Lk 8:19–21). See also notes on Mt 13:1–53 and Mk 4:1–34.

8:4–8 See note on Mt 13:3–8.

8:11–15 On the interpretation of the parable of the sower, see note on Mt 13:18–23.

8:16–18 These sayings continue the theme of responding to the word of God. Those who hear the word must become a light to others (Lk 8:16); even the mysteries of the kingdom that have been made known to the disciples (Lk 8:9–10) must come to light (Lk 8:17); a generous and persevering response to the word of God leads to a still more perfect response to the word.

8:19 His brothers: see note on Mk 6:3.

b: 4:43. *c:* 23:49; 24:10; Mt 27:55–56; Mk 15:40–41; Jn 19:5. *d:* Mt 13:1–9; Mk 4:1–9. *e:* 14:35; Mt 11:15; 13:43; Mk 4:23. *f:* Mt 13:10–13; Mk 4:10–12. *g:* Is 6:9. *h:* Mt 13:18–23; Mk 4:13–20. *i:* 1 Pt 1:23. *j:* Mk 4:21–25. *k:* 11:33; Mt 5:15. *l:* 12:2; Mt 10:26. *m:* 19:26; Mt 13:12; 25:29. *n:* Mt 12:46–50; Mk 3:31–35. *o:* 11:27–28.

wish to see you." 21*He said to them in reply, "My mother and my brothers are those who hear the word of God and act on it."

The Calming of a Storm at Sea. 22p*One day he got into a boat with his disciples and said to them, "Let us cross to the other side of the lake." So they set sail, 23and while they were sailing he fell asleep. A squall blew over the lake, and they were taking in water and were in danger. 24They came and woke him saying, "Master, master, we are perishing!" He awakened, rebuked the wind and the waves, and they subsided and there was a calm. 25Then he asked them, "Where is your faith?" But they were filled with awe and amazed and said to one another, "Who then is this, who commands even the winds and the sea, and they obey him?"

The Healing of the Gerasene Demoniac. 26q*Then they sailed to the territory of the Gerasenes, which is opposite Galilee. 27When he came ashore a man from the town who was possessed by demons met him. For a long time he had not worn clothes; he did not live in a house, but lived among the tombs. 28rWhen he saw Jesus, he cried out and fell down before him; in a loud voice he shouted, "What have you to do with me, Jesus, son of the Most High God? I beg you, do not torment me!" 29For he had ordered the unclean spirit to come out of the man. (It had taken hold of him many times, and he used to be bound with chains and shackles as a restraint, but he would break his bonds and be driven by the demon into deserted places.) 30*Then Jesus asked him, "What is your name?" He replied, "Legion," because many demons had entered him. 31*And they pleaded with him not to order them to depart to the abyss.

32A herd of many swine was feeding there on the hillside, and they pleaded with him to allow them to enter those swine; and he let them. 33The demons came out of the man and entered the swine, and the herd rushed down the steep bank into the lake and was drowned. 34When the swineherds saw what had happened, they ran away and reported the incident in the town and throughout the countryside. 35*People came out to see what had happened and, when they approached Jesus, they discovered the man from whom the demons had come out sitting at his feet. He was clothed and in his right mind, and they were seized with fear. 36Those who witnessed it told them how the possessed man had been saved. 37The entire population of the region of the Gerasenes asked Jesus to leave them because they were seized with great fear. So he got into a boat and returned. 38The man from whom the demons had come out begged to remain with him, but he sent him away, saying, 39"Return home and recount what God has done for you." The man went off and proclaimed throughout the whole town what Jesus had done for him.

Jairus's Daughter and the Woman with a Hemorrhage. 40s*When Jesus returned, the

8:21 The family of Jesus is not constituted by physical relationship with him but by obedience to the word of God. In this, Luke agrees with the Marcan parallel (Mk 3:31–35), although by omitting Mk 3:33 and especially Mk 3:20–21 Luke has softened the Marcan picture of Jesus' natural family. Probably he did this because Mary has already been presented in Lk 1:38 as the obedient handmaid of the Lord who fulfills the requirement for belonging to the eschatological family of Jesus; cf. also Lk 11:27–28.

8:22–56 This section records four miracles of Jesus that manifest his power and authority: (1) the calming of a storm on the lake (Lk 8:22–25); (2) the exorcism of a demoniac (Lk 8:26–39); (3) the cure of a hemorrhaging woman (Lk 8:40–48); (4) the raising of Jairus's daughter to life (49–56). They parallel the same sequence of stories at Mk 4:35–5:43.

8:26 Gerasenes: other manuscripts read Gadarenes or Gergesenes. See also note on Mt 8:28. **Opposite Galilee**: probably Gentile territory (note the presence in the area of pigs—unclean animals to Jews) and an indication that the person who receives salvation (Lk 8:36) is a Gentile.

8:30 What is your name?: the question reflects the popular belief that knowledge of the spirit's name brought control over the spirit. **Legion**: to Jesus' question the demon replies with a Latin word transliterated into Greek. The Roman legion at this period consisted of 5,000 to 6,000 foot soldiers; hence the name implies a very large number of demons.

8:31 Abyss: the place of the dead (Rom 10:7) or the prison of Satan (Rev 20:3) or the subterranean "watery deep" that symbolizes the chaos before the order imposed by creation (Gn 1:2).

8:35 Sitting at his feet: the former demoniac takes the position of a disciple before the master (Lk 10:39; Acts 22:3).

8:40–56 Two interwoven miracle stories, one a healing and the other a resuscitation, present Jesus as master over sickness and death. In the Lucan account, faith in Jesus is responsible for the cure (Lk 8:48) and for the raising to life (Lk 8:50).

p: Mt 8:18, 23–27; Mk 4:35–41. *q:* Mt 8:28–34; Mk 5:1–20. *r:* 4:33–35; Mt 8:29; Mk 1:23–24. *s:* Mt 9:18–26; Mk 5:21–43.

crowd welcomed him, for they were all waiting for him. [41]And a man named Jairus, an official of the synagogue, came forward. He fell at the feet of Jesus and begged him to come to his house, [42*]because he had an only daughter, about twelve years old, and she was dying. As he went, the crowds almost crushed him. [43*]And a woman afflicted with hemorrhages for twelve years, who [had spent her whole livelihood on doctors and] was unable to be cured by anyone, [44]came up behind him and touched the tassel on his cloak. Immediately her bleeding stopped. [45]Jesus then asked, "Who touched me?" While all were denying it, Peter said, "Master, the crowds are pushing and pressing in upon you." [46t]But Jesus said, "Someone has touched me; for I know that power has gone out from me." [47]When the woman realized that she had not escaped notice, she came forward trembling. Falling down before him, she explained in the presence of all the people why she had touched him and how she had been healed immediately. [48u]He said to her, "Daughter, your faith has saved you; go in peace."

[49]While he was still speaking, someone from the synagogue official's house arrived and said, "Your daughter is dead; do not trouble the teacher any longer." [50]On hearing this, Jesus answered him, "Do not be afraid; just have faith and she will be saved." [51]When he arrived at the house he allowed no one to enter with him except Peter and John and James, and the child's father and mother. [52v*]All were weeping and mourning for her, when he said, "Do not weep any longer, for she is not dead, but sleeping." [53]And they ridiculed him, because they knew that she was dead. [54]But he took her by the hand and called to her, "Child, arise!" [55]Her breath returned and she immediately arose. He then directed that she should be given something to eat. [56]Her parents were astounded, and he instructed them to tell no one what had happened.

CHAPTER 9

See RG 405–7

The Mission of the Twelve. [1w*]He summoned the Twelve and gave them power and authority over all demons and to cure diseases, [2]and he sent them to proclaim the kingdom of God and to heal [the sick]. [3*]He said to them, "Take nothing for the journey, neither walking stick, nor sack, nor food, nor money, and let no one take a second tunic. [4x]Whatever house you enter, stay there and leave from there. [5y*]And as for those who do not welcome you, when you leave that town, shake the dust from your feet in testimony against them." [6]Then they set out and went from village to village proclaiming the good news and curing diseases everywhere.

Herod's Opinion of Jesus. [7za*]Herod the tetrarch heard about all that was happening, and he was greatly perplexed because some were saying, "John has been raised from the dead"; [8]others were saying, "Elijah has appeared"; still others, "One of the ancient prophets has arisen." [9b*]But Herod said,

8:42 An only daughter: cf. the son of the widow of Nain whom Luke describes as an "only" son (Lk 7:12; see also Lk 9:38).

8:43 Afflicted with hemorrhages for twelve years: according to the Mosaic law (Lv 15:25–30) this condition would render the woman unclean and unfit for contact with other people.

8:52 Sleeping: her death is a temporary condition; cf. Jn 11:11–14.

9:1–6 Armed with the power and authority that Jesus himself has been displaying in the previous episodes, the Twelve are now sent out to continue the work that Jesus has been performing throughout his Galilean ministry: (1) proclaiming the kingdom (Lk 4:43; 8:1); (2) exorcising demons (Lk 4:33–37, 41; 8:26–39) and (3) healing the sick (Lk 4:38–40; 5:12–16, 17–26; 6:6–10; 7:1–10, 17, 22; Lk 8:40–56).

9:3 Take nothing for the journey: the absolute detachment required of the disciple (Lk 14:33) leads to complete reliance on God (Lk 12:22–31).

9:5 Shake the dust from your feet: see note on Mt 10:14.

9:7–56 This section in which Luke gathers together incidents that focus on the identity of Jesus is introduced by a question that Herod is made to ask in this gospel: "Who then is this about whom I hear such things?"(9) In subsequent episodes, Luke reveals to the reader various answers to Herod's question: Jesus is one in whom God's power is present and who provides for the needs of God's people (10–17); Peter declares Jesus to be "the Messiah of God" (18–21); Jesus says he is the suffering Son of Man (22, 43–45); Jesus is the Master to be followed, even to death (23–27); Jesus is God's son, his Chosen One (28–36).

9:7 Herod the tetrarch: see note on Lk 3:1.

9:9 And he kept trying to see him: this indication of Herod's interest in Jesus prepares for Lk 13:31–33 and for Lk 23:8–12 where Herod's curiosity about Jesus' power to perform miracles remains unsatisfied.

t: 6:19. *u:* 7:50; 17:19; 18:42. *v:* 7:13. *w:* Mt 10:1, 5–15; Mk 6:7–13. *x:* 10:5–7. *y:* 10:10–11; Acts 13:51. *z:* Mt 14:1–12; Mk 6:14–29. *a:* 9:19; Mt 16:14; Mk 8:28. *b:* 23:8.

"John I beheaded. Who then is this about whom I hear such things?" And he kept trying to see him.

The Return of the Twelve and the Feeding of the Five Thousand. [10c]When the apostles returned, they explained to him what they had done. He took them and withdrew in private to a town called Bethsaida. [11]The crowds, meanwhile, learned of this and followed him. He received them and spoke to them about the kingdom of God, and he healed those who needed to be cured. [12]As the day was drawing to a close, the Twelve approached him and said, "Dismiss the crowd so that they can go to the surrounding villages and farms and find lodging and provisions; for we are in a deserted place here." [13d]He said to them, "Give them some food yourselves." They replied, "Five loaves and two fish are all we have, unless we ourselves go and buy food for all these people." [14]Now the men there numbered about five thousand. Then he said to his disciples, "Have them sit down in groups of [about] fifty." [15]They did so and made them all sit down. [16e*]Then taking the five loaves and the two fish, and looking up to heaven, he said the blessing over them, broke them, and gave them to the disciples to set before the crowd. [17]They all ate and were satisfied. And when the leftover fragments were picked up, they filled twelve wicker baskets.

Peter's Confession about Jesus. [18f*]Once when Jesus was praying in solitude, and the disciples were with him, he asked them, "Who do the crowds say that I am?" [19g]They said in reply, "John the Baptist; others, Elijah; still others, 'One of the ancient prophets has arisen.' " [20*]Then he said to them, "But who do you say that I am?" Peter said in reply, "The Messiah of God." [21]He rebuked them and directed them not to tell this to anyone.

The First Prediction of the Passion. [22h]He said, "The Son of Man must suffer greatly and be rejected by the elders, the chief priests, and the scribes, and be killed and on the third day be raised."

The Conditions of Discipleship. [23i j*]Then he said to all, "If anyone wishes to come after me, he must deny himself and take up his cross daily and follow me. [24k]For whoever wishes to save his life will lose it, but whoever loses his life for my sake will save it. [25]What profit is there for one to gain the whole world yet lose or forfeit himself? [26l]Whoever is ashamed of me and of my words, the Son of Man will be ashamed of when he comes in his glory and in the glory of the Father and of the holy angels. [27]Truly I say to you, there are some standing here who will not taste death until they see the kingdom of God."

The Transfiguration of Jesus. [28m*]About eight days after he said this, he took Peter, John, and James and went up the mountain to pray. [29]While he was praying his face changed in appearance and his clothing became dazzling white. [30*]And behold, two men were conversing with him, Moses and

9:16 Then taking . . .: the actions of Jesus recall the institution of the Eucharist in Lk 22:19; see also note on Mt 14:19.

9:18–22 This incident is based on Mk 8:27–33, but Luke has eliminated Peter's refusal to accept Jesus as suffering Son of Man (Mk 8:32) and the rebuke of Peter by Jesus (Mk 8:33). Elsewhere in the gospel, Luke softens the harsh portrait of Peter and the other apostles found in his Marcan source (cf. Lk 22:39–46, which similarly lacks a rebuke of Peter that occurs in the source, Mk 14:37–38).

9:18 When Jesus was praying in solitude: see note on Lk 3:21.

9:20 The Messiah of God: on the meaning of this title in first-century Palestinian Judaism, see notes on Lk 2:11 and on Mt 16:13–20 and Mk 8:27–30.

9:23 Daily: this is a Lucan addition to a saying of Jesus, removing the saying from a context that envisioned the imminent suffering and death of the disciple of Jesus (as does the saying in Mk 8:34–35) to one that focuses on the demands of daily Christian existence.

9:28–36 Situated shortly after the first announcement of the passion, death, and resurrection, this scene of Jesus' transfiguration provides the heavenly confirmation to Jesus' declaration that his suffering will end in glory (Lk 9:32); see also notes on Mt 17:1–8 and Mk 9:2–8.

9:28 Up the mountain to pray: the "mountain" is the regular place of prayer in Luke (see Lk 6:12; 22:39–41).

9:30 Moses and Elijah: the two figures represent the Old Testament law and the prophets. At the end of this episode, the heavenly voice will identify Jesus as the one to be listened to now (Lk 9:35). See also note on Mk 9:5.

c: Mt 14:13–21; Mk 6:30–44; Jn 6:1–14. *d:* 2 Kgs 4:42–44. *e:* 22:19; 24:30–31; Acts 2:42; 20:11; 27:35. *f:* Mt 16:13–20; Mk 8:27–30. *g:* 9:7–8. *h:* 24:7, 26; Mt 16:21; 20:18–19; Mk 8:31; 10:33–34. *i:* Mt 16:24–28; Mk 8:34–9:1. *j:* 14:27; Mt 10:38. *k:* 17:33; Mt 10:39; Jn 12:25. *l:* 12:9; Mt 10:33; 2 Tm 2:12. *m:* Mt 17:1–8; Mk 9:2–8.

Elijah, [31 n*]who appeared in glory and spoke of his exodus that he was going to accomplish in Jerusalem. [32 o*]Peter and his companions had been overcome by sleep, but becoming fully awake, they saw his glory and the two men standing with him. [33*]As they were about to part from him, Peter said to Jesus, "Master, it is good that we are here; let us make three tents, one for you, one for Moses, and one for Elijah." But he did not know what he was saying. [34*]While he was still speaking, a cloud came and cast a shadow over them, and they became frightened when they entered the cloud. [35 p*]Then from the cloud came a voice that said, "This is my chosen Son; listen to him." [36*]After the voice had spoken, Jesus was found alone. They fell silent and did not at that time tell anyone what they had seen.

The Healing of a Boy with a Demon. [37 q*]On the next day, when they came down from the mountain, a large crowd met him. [38]There was a man in the crowd who cried out, "Teacher, I beg you, look at my son; he is my only child. [39]For a spirit seizes him and he suddenly screams and it convulses him until he foams at the mouth; it releases him only with difficulty, wearing him out. [40]I begged your disciples to cast it out but they could not." [41]Jesus said in reply, "O faithless and perverse generation, how long will I be with you and endure you? Bring your son here." [42]As he was coming forward, the demon threw him to the ground in a convulsion; but Jesus rebuked the unclean spirit, healed the boy, and returned him to his father. [43 r]And all were astonished by the majesty of God.

The Second Prediction of the Passion. While they were all amazed at his every deed, he said to his disciples, [44]"Pay attention to what I am telling you. The Son of Man is to be handed over to men." [45]But they did not understand this saying; its meaning was hidden from them so that they should not understand it, and they were afraid to ask him about this saying.

The Greatest in the Kingdom. [46 s t*]An argument arose among the disciples about which of them was the greatest. [47]Jesus realized the intention of their hearts and took a child and placed it by his side [48 u]and said to them, "Whoever receives this child in my name receives me, and whoever receives me receives the one who sent me. For the one who is least among all of you is the one who is the greatest."

Another Exorcist. [49 v]Then John said in reply, "Master, we saw someone casting out demons in your name and we tried to prevent him because he does not follow in our company." [50]Jesus said to him, "Do not prevent him, for whoever is not against you is for you."

V. The Journey to Jerusalem: Luke's Travel Narrative

Departure for Jerusalem; Samaritan Inhospitality. [51 w*]When the days for his being taken

9:31 His exodus that he was going to accomplish in Jerusalem: Luke identifies the subject of the conversation as the **exodus** of Jesus, a reference to the death, resurrection, and ascension of Jesus that will take place in Jerusalem, the city of destiny (see Lk 9:51). The mention of exodus, however, also calls to mind the Israelite Exodus from Egypt to the promised land.

9:32 They saw his glory: the **glory** that is proper to God is here attributed to Jesus (see Lk 24:26).

9:33 Let us make three tents: in a possible allusion to the feast of Tabernacles, Peter may be likening his joy on the occasion of the transfiguration to the joyful celebration of this harvest festival.

9:34 Over them: it is not clear whether **them** refers to Jesus, Moses, and Elijah, or to the disciples. For the cloud casting its shadow, see note on Mk 9:7.

9:35 Like the heavenly voice that identified Jesus at his baptism prior to his undertaking the Galilean ministry (Lk 3:22), so too here before the journey to the city of destiny is begun (Lk 9:51) the heavenly voice again identifies Jesus as Son. Listen to him: the two representatives of Israel of old depart (Lk 9:33) and Jesus is left alone (Lk 9:36) as the teacher whose words must be heeded (see also Acts 3:22).

9:36 At that time: i.e., before the resurrection.

9:37–43a See note on Mk 9:14–29.

9:46–50 These two incidents focus on attitudes that are opposed to Christian discipleship: rivalry and intolerance of outsiders.

9:51–18:14 The Galilean ministry of Jesus finishes with the previous episode and a new section of Luke's gospel be-

n: 9:22; 13:33. *o:* Jn 1:14; 2 Pt 1:16. *p:* 3:22; Dt 18:15; Ps 2:7; Is 42:1; Mt 3:17; 12:18; Mk 1:11; 2 Pt 1:17–18. *q:* Mt 17:14–18; Mk 9:14–27. *r:* 18:32–34; Mt 17:22–23; Mk 9:30–32. *s:* Mt 18:1–5; Mk 9:33–37. *t:* 22:24. *u:* 10:16; Mt 10:40; Jn 13:20. *v:* Mk 9:38–40. *w:* 9:53; 13:22, 33; 17:11; 18:31; 19:28; 24:51; Acts 1:2, 9–11, 22.

up were fulfilled, he resolutely determined to journey to Jerusalem, [52x*]and he sent messengers ahead of him. On the way they entered a Samaritan village to prepare for his reception there, [53]but they would not welcome him because the destination of his journey was Jerusalem. [54y]When the disciples James and John saw this they asked, "Lord, do you want us to call down fire from heaven to consume them?" [55]Jesus turned and rebuked them, [56]and they journeyed to another village.

The Would-be Followers of Jesus. [57z*]As they were proceeding on their journey someone said to him, "I will follow you wherever you go." [58]Jesus answered him, "Foxes have dens and birds of the sky have nests, but the Son of Man has nowhere to rest his head." [59]And to another he said, "Follow me." But he replied, "[Lord,] let me go first and bury my father." [60*]But he answered him, "Let the dead bury their dead. But you, go and proclaim the kingdom of God." [61a]And another said, "I will follow you, Lord, but first let me say farewell to my family at home." [62][To him] Jesus said, "No one who sets a hand to the plow and looks to what was left behind is fit for the kingdom of God."

CHAPTER 10

See RG 406-7

The Mission of the Seventy-two. [1b*]After this the Lord appointed seventy [-two] others whom he sent ahead of him in pairs to every town and place he intended to visit. [2c]He said to them, "The harvest is abundant but the laborers are few; so ask the master of the harvest to send out laborers for his harvest. [3d]Go on your way; behold, I am sending you like lambs among wolves. [4ef*]Carry no money bag, no sack, no sandals; and greet no one along the way. [5*]Into whatever house you enter, first say, 'Peace to this household.' [6*]If a peaceful person lives

gins, the journey to Jerusalem. This journey is based on Mk 10:1–52 but Luke uses his Marcan source only in Lk 18:15–19:27. Before that point he has inserted into his gospel a distinctive collection of sayings of Jesus and stories about him that he has drawn from Q, a collection of sayings of Jesus used also by Matthew, and from his own special traditions. All of the material collected in this section is loosely organized within the framework of a journey of Jesus to Jerusalem, the city of destiny, where his exodus (suffering, death, resurrection, ascension) is to take place (Lk 9:31), where salvation is accomplished, and from where the proclamation of God's saving word is to go forth (Lk 24:47; Acts 1:8). Much of the material in the Lucan travel narrative is teaching for the disciples. During the course of this journey Jesus is preparing his chosen Galilean witnesses for the role they will play after his exodus (Lk 9:31): they are to be his witnesses to the people (Acts 10:39; 13:31) and thereby provide certainty to the readers of Luke's gospel that the teachings they have received are rooted in the teachings of Jesus (Lk 1:1–4).

9:51–55 Just as the Galilean ministry began with a rejection of Jesus in his hometown, so too the travel narrative begins with the rejection of him by Samaritans. In this episode Jesus disassociates himself from the attitude expressed by his disciples that those who reject him are to be punished severely. The story alludes to 2 Kgs 1:10, 12 where the prophet Elijah takes the course of action Jesus rejects, and Jesus thereby rejects the identification of himself with Elijah.

9:51 Days for his being taken up: like the reference to his exodus in Lk 9:31 this is probably a reference to all the events (suffering, death, resurrection, ascension) of his last days in Jerusalem. **He resolutely determined**: literally, "he set his face."

9:52 Samaritan: Samaria was the territory between Judea and Galilee west of the Jordan river. For ethnic and religious reasons, the Samaritans and the Jews were bitterly opposed to one another (see Jn 4:9).

9:57–62 In these sayings Jesus speaks of the severity and the unconditional nature of Christian discipleship. Even family ties and filial obligations, such as burying one's parents, cannot distract one no matter how briefly from proclaiming the kingdom of God. The first two sayings are paralleled in Mt 8:19–22; see also notes there.

9:60 Let the dead bury their dead: i.e., let the spiritually dead (those who do not follow) bury their physically dead. See also note on Mt 8:22.

10:1–12 Only the Gospel of Luke contains two episodes in which Jesus sends out his followers on a mission: the first (Lk 10:1–6) is based on the mission in Mk 6:6b–13 and recounts the sending out of the Twelve; here in Lk 10:1–12 a similar report based on Q becomes the sending out of seventy-two in this gospel. The episode continues the theme of Jesus preparing witnesses to himself and his ministry. These witnesses include not only the Twelve but also the seventy-two who may represent the Christian mission in Luke's own day. Note that the instructions given to the Twelve and to the seventy-two are similar and that what is said to the seventy-two in Lk 10:4 is directed to the Twelve in Lk 22:35.

10:1 Seventy[-two]: important representatives of the Alexandrian and Caesarean text types read "seventy," while other important Alexandrian texts and Western readings have "seventy-two."

10:4 Carry no money bag . . . greet no one along the way: because of the urgency of the mission and the single-mindedness required of missionaries, attachment to material possessions should be avoided and even customary greetings should not distract from the fulfillment of the task.

10:5 First say, 'Peace to this household': see notes on Lk 2:14 and Mt 10:13.

10:6 A peaceful person: literally, "a son of peace."

x: Mal 3:1. *y:* 2 Kgs 1:10, 12. *z:* Mt 8:19–22. *a:* 1 Kgs 19:20. *b:* Mk 6:7. *c:* Mt 9:37–38; Jn 4:35. *d:* Mt 10:16. *e:* Mt 10:7–14. *f:* 9:3; 2 Kgs 4:29.

there, your peace will rest on him; but if not,
it will return to you. [7g]Stay in the same
house and eat and drink what is offered to
you, for the laborer deserves his payment.
Do not move about from one house to another. [8h]Whatever town you enter and they
welcome you, eat what is set before you,
[9i]cure the sick in it and say to them, 'The
kingdom of God is at hand for you.'
[10j]Whatever town you enter and they do not
receive you, go out into the streets and say,
[11k]'The dust of your town that clings to our
feet, even that we shake off against you.' Yet
know this: the kingdom of God is at hand.
[12l]I tell you, it will be more tolerable for
Sodom on that day than for that town.

Reproaches to Unrepentant Towns.
[13mn*]"Woe to you, Chorazin! Woe to you,
Bethsaida! For if the mighty deeds done in
your midst had been done in Tyre and Sidon,
they would long ago have repented, sitting
in sackcloth and ashes. [14]But it will be more
tolerable for Tyre and Sidon at the judgment
than for you. [15o*]And as for you, Capernaum, 'Will you be exalted to heaven? You
will go down to the netherworld.' " [16p]Who-
ever listens to you listens to me. Whoever
rejects you rejects me. And whoever rejects
me rejects the one who sent me."

Return of the Seventy-two. [17]The seventy
[-two] returned rejoicing, and said, "Lord,
even the demons are subject to us because of
your name." [18q*]Jesus said, "I have observed
Satan fall like lightning from the sky. [19r]Be-
hold, I have given you the power 'to tread
upon serpents' and scorpions and upon the
full force of the enemy and nothing will harm
you. [20s]Nevertheless, do not rejoice because
the spirits are subject to you, but rejoice because your names are written in heaven."

Praise of the Father. [21tu*]At that very moment he rejoiced [in] the holy Spirit and
said, "I give you praise, Father, Lord of
heaven and earth, for although you have hidden these things from the wise and the
learned you have revealed them to the childlike. Yes, Father, such has been your gracious will. [22v]All things have been handed
over to me by my Father. No one knows who
the Son is except the Father, and who the Father is except the Son and anyone to whom
the Son wishes to reveal him."

The Privileges of Discipleship. [23w]Turning
to the disciples in private he said, "Blessed
are the eyes that see what you see. [24]For I say
to you, many prophets and kings desired to
see what you see, but did not see it, and to
hear what you hear, but did not hear it."

The Greatest Commandment. [25xy*]There
was a scholar of the law who stood up to test
him and said, "Teacher, what must I do to inherit eternal life?" [26]Jesus said to him,
"What is written in the law? How do you
read it?" [27z]He said in reply, "You shall love
the Lord, your God, with all your heart, with
all your being, with all your strength, and
with all your mind, and your neighbor as
yourself." [28a]He replied to him, "You have

10:13–16 The call to repentance that is a part of the proclamation of the kingdom brings with it a severe judgment for those who hear it and reject it.

10:15 The netherworld: the underworld, the place of the dead (Acts 2:27, 31) here contrasted with heaven; see also note on Mt 11:23.

10:18 I have observed Satan fall like lightning: the effect of the mission of the seventy-two is characterized by the Lucan Jesus as a symbolic fall of Satan. As the kingdom of God is gradually being established, evil in all its forms is being defeated; the dominion of Satan over humanity is at an end.

10:21 Revealed them to the childlike: a restatement of the theme announced in Lk 8:10: the mysteries of the kingdom are revealed to the disciples. See also note on Mt 11:25–27.

10:25–37 In response to a question from a Jewish legal expert about inheriting eternal life, Jesus illustrates the superiority of love over legalism through the story of the good Samaritan. The law of love proclaimed in the "Sermon on the Plain" (Lk 6:27–36) is exemplified by one whom the legal expert would have considered ritually impure (see Jn 4:9). Moreover, the identity of the "neighbor" requested by the legal expert (Lk 10:29) turns out to be a Samaritan, the enemy of the Jew (see note on Lk 9:52).

10:25 Scholar of the law: an expert in the Mosaic law, and probably a member of the group elsewhere identified as the scribes (Lk 5:21).

g: 9:4; Mt 10:10; 1 Cor 9:6–14; 1 Tm 5:18. *h:* 1 Cor 10:27. *i:* Mt 3:2; 4:17; Mk 1:15. *j:* 9:5. *k:* Acts 13:51; 18:6. *l:* Mt 10:15; 11:24. *m:* Mt 11:20–24. *n:* Is 23; Ez 26–28; Jl 3:4–8; Am 1:1–10; Zec 9:2–4. *o:* Is 14:13–15. *p:* Mt 10:40; Jn 5:23; 13:20; 15:23. *q:* Is 14:12; Jn 12:31; Rev 12:7–12. *r:* Ps 91:13; Mk 16:18. *s:* Ex 32:32; Dn 12:1; Mt 7:22; Phil 4:3; Heb 12:23; Rev 3:5; 21:27. *t:* Mt 11:25–27. *u:* 1 Cor 1:26–28. *v:* Jn 3:35; 10:15. *w:* Mt 13:16–17. *x:* Mt 22:34–40; Mk 12:28–34. *y:* 18:18; Mt 19:16; Mk 10:17. *z:* Lv 19:18; Dt 6:5; 10:12; Jos 22:5; Mt 19:19; 22:37–39; Rom 13:9; Gal 5:14; Jas 2:8. *a:* Lv 18:5; Prv 19:16; Rom 10:5; Gal 3:12.

answered correctly; do this and you will
live."
The Parable of the Good Samaritan. 29But
because he wished to justify himself, he said
to Jesus, "And who is my neighbor?" 30Jesus
replied, "A man fell victim to robbers as he
went down from Jerusalem to Jericho. They
stripped and beat him and went off leaving
him half-dead. 31*A priest happened to be going down that road, but when he saw him, he
passed by on the opposite side. 32Likewise a
Levite came to the place, and when he saw
him, he passed by on the opposite side. 33But
a Samaritan traveler who came upon him was
moved with compassion at the sight. 34He
approached the victim, poured oil and wine
over his wounds and bandaged them. Then
he lifted him up on his own animal, took him
to an inn and cared for him. 35The next day
he took out two silver coins and gave them to
the innkeeper with the instruction, 'Take care
of him. If you spend more than what I have
given you, I shall repay you on my way
back.' 36Which of these three, in your opinion, was neighbor to the robbers' victim?"
37He answered, "The one who treated him
with mercy." Jesus said to him, "Go and do
likewise."
Martha and Mary. 38b*As they continued
their journey he entered a village where a
woman whose name was Martha welcomed
him. 39*She had a sister named Mary [who]
sat beside the Lord at his feet listening to
him speak. 40Martha, burdened with much
serving, came to him and said, "Lord, do you
not care that my sister has left me by myself
to do the serving? Tell her to help me." 41The
Lord said to her in reply, "Martha, Martha,
you are anxious and worried about many
things. 42*There is need of only one thing.
Mary has chosen the better part and it will
not be taken from her."

CHAPTER 11

See RG 406-8

The Lord's Prayer. 1c*He was praying
in a certain place, and when he had finished,
one of his disciples said to him, "Lord, teach
us to pray just as John taught his disciples."
2*He said to them, "When you pray, say:

Father, hallowed be your name,
your kingdom come.
3 *Give us each day our daily bread
4 and forgive us our sins
for we ourselves forgive everyone in
debt to us,
and do not subject us to the final test."

Further Teachings on Prayer. 5dAnd he
said to them, "Suppose one of you has a
friend to whom he goes at midnight and says,
'Friend, lend me three loaves of bread, 6for a
friend of mine has arrived at my house from a
journey and I have nothing to offer him,' 7and
he says in reply from within, 'Do not bother
me; the door has already been locked and my
children and I are already in bed. I cannot get
up to give you anything.' 8I tell you, if he does
not get up to give him the loaves because of
their friendship, he will get up to give him
whatever he needs because of his persistence.

10:31–32 Priest . . . Levite: those religious representatives of Judaism who would have been expected to be models of "neighbor" to the victim pass him by.

10:38–42 The story of Martha and Mary further illustrates the importance of hearing the words of the teacher and the concern with women in Luke.

10:39 Sat beside the Lord at his feet: it is remarkable for first-century Palestinian Judaism that a woman would assume the posture of a disciple at the master's feet (see also Lk 8:35; Acts 22:3), and it reveals a characteristic attitude of Jesus toward women in this gospel (see Lk 8:2–3).

10:42 There is need of only one thing: some ancient versions read, "there is need of few things"; another important, although probably inferior, reading found in some manuscripts is, "there is need of few things, or of one."

11:1–13 Luke presents three episodes concerned with prayer. The first (Lk 11:1–4) recounts Jesus teaching his disciples the Christian communal prayer, the "Our Father"; the second (Lk 11:5–8), the importance of persistence in prayer; the third (Lk 11:9–13), the effectiveness of prayer.

11:1–4 The Matthean form of the "Our Father" occurs in the "Sermon on the Mount" (Mt 6:9–15); the shorter Lucan version is presented while Jesus is at prayer (see note on Lk 3:21) and his disciples ask him to teach them to pray just as John taught his disciples to pray. In answer to their question, Jesus presents them with an example of a Christian communal prayer that stresses the fatherhood of God and acknowledges him as the one to whom the Christian disciple owes daily sustenance (Lk 11:3), forgiveness (Lk 11:4), and deliverance from the final trial (Lk 11:4). See also notes on Mt 6:9–13.

11:2 Your kingdom come: in place of this petition, some early church Fathers record: "May your holy Spirit come upon us and cleanse us," a petition that may reflect the use of the "Our Father" in a baptismal liturgy.

11:3–4 Daily bread: see note on Mt 6:11. **The final test**: see note on Mt 6:13.

b: Jn 11:1; 12:2–3. *c:* Mt 6:9–15. *d:* 18:1–5.

The Answer to Prayer. [9][e][f]"And I tell you, ask and you will receive; seek and you will find; knock and the door will be opened to you. [10]For everyone who asks, receives; and the one who seeks, finds; and to the one who knocks, the door will be opened. [11]What father among you would hand his son a snake when he asks for a fish? [12]Or hand him a scorpion when he asks for an egg? [13][*]If you then, who are wicked, know how to give good gifts to your children, how much more will the Father in heaven give the holy Spirit to those who ask him?"

Jesus and Beelzebul. [14][g]He was driving out a demon [that was] mute, and when the demon had gone out, the mute person spoke and the crowds were amazed. [15][h]Some of them said, "By the power of Beelzebul, the prince of demons, he drives out demons." [16][i]Others, to test him, asked him for a sign from heaven. [17]But he knew their thoughts and said to them, "Every kingdom divided against itself will be laid waste and house will fall against house. [18]And if Satan is divided against himself, how will his kingdom stand? For you say that it is by Beelzebul that I drive out demons. [19][*]If I, then, drive out demons by Beelzebul, by whom do your own people drive them out? Therefore they will be your judges. [20][j]But if it is by the finger of God that [I] drive out demons, then the kingdom of God has come upon you. [21]When a strong man fully armed guards his palace, his possessions are safe. [22][*]But when one stronger than he attacks and overcomes him, he takes away the armor on which he relied and distributes the spoils. [23][k]Whoever is not with me is against me, and whoever does not gather with me scatters.

The Return of the Unclean Spirit. [24][l]"When an unclean spirit goes out of someone, it roams through arid regions searching for rest but, finding none, it says, 'I shall return to my home from which I came.' [25]But upon returning, it finds it swept clean and put in order. [26][m]Then it goes and brings back seven other spirits more wicked than itself who move in and dwell there, and the last condition of that person is worse than the first."

True Blessedness. [27][n][*]While he was speaking, a woman from the crowd called out and said to him, "Blessed is the womb that carried you and the breasts at which you nursed." [28]He replied, "Rather, blessed are those who hear the word of God and observe it."

The Demand for a Sign. [29][o][p][*]While still more people gathered in the crowd, he said to them, "This generation is an evil generation; it seeks a sign, but no sign will be given it, except the sign of Jonah. [30]Just as Jonah became a sign to the Ninevites, so will the Son of Man be to this generation. [31][q]At the judgment the queen of the south will rise with the men of this generation and she will condemn them, because she came from the ends of the earth to hear the wisdom of Solomon, and there is something greater than Solomon here. [32][r]At the judgment the men of Nineveh will arise with this generation and condemn it, because at the preaching of Jonah they repented, and there is something greater than Jonah here.

The Simile of Light. [33][s]"No one who lights a lamp hides it away or places it [under a bushel basket], but on a lampstand so that those who enter might see the light. [34][t]The lamp of the body is your eye. When your eye is sound, then your whole body is filled with

11:13 The holy Spirit: this is a Lucan editorial alteration of a traditional saying of Jesus (see Mt 7:11). Luke presents the gift of the holy Spirit as the response of the Father to the prayer of the Christian disciple.

11:19 Your own people: the Greek reads "your sons." Other Jewish exorcists (see Acts 19:13–20), who recognize that the power of God is active in the exorcism, would themselves convict the accusers of Jesus. See also note on Mt 12:27.

11:22 One stronger: i.e., Jesus. Cf. Lk 3:16 where John the Baptist identifies Jesus as "more powerful than I."

11:27–28 The beatitude in Lk 11:28 should not be interpreted as a rebuke of the mother of Jesus; see note on Lk 8:21. Rather, it emphasizes (like Lk 2:35) that attentiveness to God's word is more important than biological relationship to Jesus.

11:29–32 The "sign of Jonah" in Luke is the preaching of the need for repentance by a prophet who comes from afar. Cf. Mt 12:38–42 (and see notes there) where the "sign of Jonah" is interpreted by Jesus as his death and resurrection.

e: Mt 7:7–11. *f:* Mt 21:22; Mk 11:24; Jn 14:13; 15:7; 1 Jn 5:14–15. *g:* Mt 12:22–30; Mk 3:20–27. *h:* Mt 9:34. *i:* Mt 12:38; 16:1; Mk 8:11; 1 Cor 1:22. *j:* Ex 8:19. *k:* 9:50; Mk 9:40. *l:* Mt 12:43–45. *m:* Jn 5:14. *n:* 1:28, 42, 48. *o:* Mt 12:38–42; Mk 8:12. *p:* Mt 16:1, 4; Jn 6:30; 1 Cor 1:22. *q:* 1 Kgs 10:1–10; 2 Chr 9:1–12. *r:* Jon 3:8, 10. *s:* 8:16; Mt 5:15; Mk 4:21. *t:* Mt 6:22–23.

light, but when it is bad, then your body is in darkness. [35]Take care, then, that the light in you not become darkness. [36]If your whole body is full of light, and no part of it is in darkness, then it will be as full of light as a lamp illuminating you with its brightness."

Denunciation of the Pharisees and Scholars of the Law. [37uv*]After he had spoken, a Pharisee invited him to dine at his home. He entered and reclined at table to eat. [38w]The Pharisee was amazed to see that he did not observe the prescribed washing before the meal. [39x]The Lord said to him, "Oh you Pharisees! Although you cleanse the outside of the cup and the dish, inside you are filled with plunder and evil. [40]You fools! Did not the maker of the outside also make the inside? [41]But as to what is within, give alms, and behold, everything will be clean for you. [42y]Woe to you Pharisees! You pay tithes of mint and of rue and of every garden herb, but you pay no attention to judgment and to love for God. These you should have done, without overlooking the others. [43z]Woe to you Pharisees! You love the seat of honor in synagogues and greetings in marketplaces. [44a*]Woe to you! You are like unseen graves over which people unknowingly walk."

[45b*]Then one of the scholars of the law said to him in reply, "Teacher, by saying this you are insulting us too." [46]And he said, "Woe also to you scholars of the law! You impose on people burdens hard to carry, but you yourselves do not lift one finger to touch them. [47c]Woe to you! You build the memorials of the prophets whom your ancestors killed. [48]Consequently, you bear witness and give consent to the deeds of your ancestors, for they killed them and you do the building. [49d*]Therefore, the wisdom of God said, 'I will send to them prophets and apostles; some of them they will kill and persecute' [50]in order that this generation might be charged with the blood of all the prophets shed since the foundation of the world, [51e*]from the blood of Abel to the blood of Zechariah who died between the altar and the temple building. Yes, I tell you, this generation will be charged with their blood! [52f]Woe to you, scholars of the law! You have taken away the key of knowledge. You yourselves did not enter and you stopped those trying to enter." [53g]When he left, the scribes and Pharisees began to act with hostility toward him and to interrogate him about many things, [54h]for they were plotting to catch him at something he might say.

CHAPTER 12

See RG 406-8

The Leaven of the Pharisees. [1i*]Meanwhile, so many people were crowding together that they were trampling one another underfoot. He began to speak, first to his disciples, "Beware of the leaven—that is, the hypocrisy—of the Pharisees.

Courage under Persecution. [2jk*]"There is nothing concealed that will not be revealed, nor secret that will not be known. [3]Therefore whatever you have said in the darkness will be heard in the light, and what you have whispered behind closed doors will be proclaimed on the housetops. [4]I tell you, my friends, do

11:37–54 This denunciation of the Pharisees (Lk 11:39–44) and the scholars of the law (Lk 11:45–52) is set by Luke in the context of Jesus' dining at the home of a Pharisee. Controversies with or reprimands of Pharisees are regularly set by Luke within the context of Jesus' eating with Pharisees (see Lk 5:29–39; 7:36–50; 14:1–24). A different compilation of similar sayings is found in Mt 23 (see also notes there).

11:44 Unseen graves: contact with the dead or with human bones or graves (see Nm 19:16) brought ritual impurity. Jesus presents the Pharisees as those who insidiously lead others astray through their seeming attention to the law.

11:45 Scholars of the law: see note on Lk 10:25.

11:49 I will send to them prophets and apostles: Jesus connects the mission of the church (apostles) with the mission of the Old Testament prophets who often suffered the rebuke of their contemporaries.

11:51 From the blood of Abel to the blood of Zechariah: the murder of Abel is the first murder recounted in the Old Testament (Gn 4:8). The Zechariah mentioned here may be the Zechariah whose murder is recounted in 2 Chr 24:20–22, the last murder presented in the Hebrew canon of the Old Testament.

12:1 See notes on Mk 8:15 and Mt 16:5–12.

12:2–9 Luke presents a collection of sayings of Jesus exhorting his followers to acknowledge him and his mission fearlessly and assuring them of God's protection even in times of persecution. They are paralleled in Mt 10:26–33.

u: 20:45–47; Mt 23:1–36; Mk 12:38–40. *v:* 7:36; 14:1. *w:* Mt 15:2; Mk 7:2–5. *x:* Mt 23:25–26. *y:* Lv 27:30; Mt 23:23. *z:* 20:46; Mt 23:6; Mk 12:38–39. *a:* Mt 23:27. *b:* Mt 23:4. *c:* Mt 23:29–32. *d:* Mt 23:34–36. *e:* Gn 4:8; 2 Chr 24:20–22. *f:* Mt 23:13. *g:* 6:11; Mt 22:15–22. *h:* 20:20. *i:* Mt 16:6; Mk 8:15. *j:* Mt 10:26–33. *k:* 8:17; Mk 4:22.

not be afraid of those who kill the body but after that can do no more. [5*]I shall show you whom to fear. Be afraid of the one who after killing has the power to cast into Gehenna; yes, I tell you, be afraid of that one. [6*]Are not five sparrows sold for two small coins? Yet not one of them has escaped the notice of God. [7l]Even the hairs of your head have all been counted. Do not be afraid. You are worth more than many sparrows. [8]I tell you, everyone who acknowledges me before others the Son of Man will acknowledge before the angels of God. [9m]But whoever denies me before others will be denied before the angels of God.

Sayings about the holy Spirit. [10n*]"Everyone who speaks a word against the Son of Man will be forgiven, but the one who blasphemes against the holy Spirit will not be forgiven. [11o]When they take you before synagogues and before rulers and authorities, do not worry about how or what your defense will be or about what you are to say. [12]For the holy Spirit will teach you at that moment what you should say."

Saying against Greed. [13*]Someone in the crowd said to him, "Teacher, tell my brother to share the inheritance with me." [14p]He replied to him, "Friend, who appointed me as your judge and arbitrator?" [15q]Then he said to the crowd, "Take care to guard against all greed, for though one may be rich, one's life does not consist of possessions."

Parable of the Rich Fool. [16]Then he told them a parable. "There was a rich man whose land produced a bountiful harvest. [17]He asked himself, 'What shall I do, for I do not have space to store my harvest?' [18]And he said, 'This is what I shall do: I shall tear down my barns and build larger ones. There I shall store all my grain and other goods [19rs]and I shall say to myself, "Now as for you, you have so many good things stored up for many years, rest, eat, drink, be merry!" ' [20]But God said to him, 'You fool, this night your life will be demanded of you; and the things you have prepared, to whom will they belong?' [21*]Thus will it be for the one who stores up treasure for himself but is not rich in what matters to God."

Dependence on God. [22t]He said to [his] disciples, "Therefore I tell you, do not worry about your life and what you will eat, or about your body and what you will wear. [23]For life is more than food and the body more than clothing. [24u]Notice the ravens: they do not sow or reap; they have neither storehouse nor barn, yet God feeds them. How much more important are you than birds! [25]Can any of you by worrying add a moment to your life-span? [26]If even the smallest things are beyond your control, why are you anxious about the rest? [27v]Notice how the flowers grow. They do not toil or spin. But I tell you, not even Solomon in all his splendor was dressed like one of them. [28]If God so clothes the grass in the field that grows today and is thrown into the oven tomorrow, will he not much more provide for you, O you of little faith? [29]As for you, do not seek what you are to eat and what you are to drink, and do not worry anymore. [30]All the nations of the world seek for these things, and your Father knows that you need them. [31]Instead, seek his kingdom, and these other things will be given you besides. [32w]Do not be afraid any longer, little flock, for your Father is pleased to give you the kingdom. [33x]Sell your belongings and give

12:5 Gehenna: see note on Mt 5:22.

12:6 Two small coins: the Roman copper coin, the assarion (Latin *as*), was worth about one-sixteenth of a denarius (see note on Lk 7:41).

12:10–12 The sayings about the holy Spirit are set in the context of fearlessness in the face of persecution (Lk 12:2–9; cf. Mt 12:31–32). The holy Spirit will be presented in Luke's second volume, the Acts of the Apostles, as the power responsible for the guidance of the Christian mission and the source of courage in the face of persecution.

12:13–34 Luke has joined together sayings contrasting those whose focus and trust in life is on material possessions, symbolized here by the rich fool of the parable (Lk 12:16–21), with those who recognize their complete dependence on God (Lk 12:21), those whose radical detachment from material possessions symbolizes their heavenly treasure (Lk 12:33–34).

12:21 Rich in what matters to God: literally, "rich for God."

l: 12:24; 21:18; Acts 27:34. *m:* 9:26; Mk 8:38; 2 Tm 2:12. *n:* Mt 12:31–32; Mk 3:28–29. *o:* 21:12–15; Mt 10:17–20; Mk 13:11. *p:* Ex 2:14; Acts 7:27. *q:* 1 Tm 6:9–10. *r:* Mt 6:19–21; 1 Tm 6:17. *s:* Sir 11:19. *t:* Mt 6:25–34. *u:* 12:7. *v:* 1 Kgs 10:4–7; 2 Chr 9:3–6. *w:* 22:29; Rev 1:6. *x:* 18:22; Mt 6:20–21; Mk 10:21.

alms. Provide money bags for yourselves that do not wear out, an inexhaustible treasure in heaven that no thief can reach nor moth destroy. [34]For where your treasure is, there also will your heart be.

Vigilant and Faithful Servants. [35y*]"Gird your loins and light your lamps [36z]and be like servants who await their master's return from a wedding, ready to open immediately when he comes and knocks. [37]Blessed are those servants whom the master finds vigilant on his arrival. Amen, I say to you, he will gird himself, have them recline at table, and proceed to wait on them. [38]And should he come in the second or third watch and find them prepared in this way, blessed are those servants. [39a]Be sure of this: if the master of the house had known the hour when the thief was coming, he would not have let his house be broken into. [40]You also must be prepared, for at an hour you do not expect, the Son of Man will come."

[41]Then Peter said, "Lord, is this parable meant for us or for everyone?" [42]And the Lord replied, "Who, then, is the faithful and prudent steward whom the master will put in charge of his servants to distribute [the] food allowance at the proper time? [43]Blessed is that servant whom his master on arrival finds doing so. [44]Truly, I say to you, he will put him in charge of all his property. [45*]But if that servant says to himself, 'My master is delayed in coming,' and begins to beat the menservants and the maidservants, to eat and drink and get drunk, [46]then that servant's master will come on an unexpected day and at an unknown hour and will punish him severely and assign him a place with the unfaithful. [47b]That servant who knew his master's will but did not make preparations nor act in accord with his will shall be beaten severely; [48]and the servant who was ignorant of his master's will but acted in a way deserving of a severe beating shall be beaten only lightly. Much will be required of the person entrusted with much, and still more will be demanded of the person entrusted with more.

Jesus: A Cause of Division. [49*]"I have come to set the earth on fire, and how I wish it were already blazing! [50c*]There is a baptism with which I must be baptized, and how great is my anguish until it is accomplished! [51de]Do you think that I have come to establish peace on the earth? No, I tell you, but rather division. [52]From now on a household of five will be divided, three against two and two against three; [53f]a father will be divided against his son and a son against his father, a mother against her daughter and a daughter against her mother, a mother-in-law against her daughter-in-law and a daughter-in-law against her mother-in-law."

Signs of the Times. [54g]He also said to the crowds, "When you see [a] cloud rising in the west you say immediately that it is going to rain—and so it does; [55]and when you notice that the wind is blowing from the south you say that it is going to be hot—and so it is. [56]You hypocrites! You know how to interpret the appearance of the earth and the sky; why do you not know how to interpret the present time?

Settlement with an Opponent. [57h]"Why do you not judge for yourselves what is right? [58]If you are to go with your opponent before a magistrate, make an effort to settle the matter on the way; otherwise your opponent will turn you over to the judge, and the judge hand you over to the constable, and the constable throw you into prison. [59*]I say to you, you will not be released until you have paid the last penny."

12:35–48 This collection of sayings relates to Luke's understanding of the end time and the return of Jesus. Luke emphasizes for his readers the importance of being faithful to the instructions of Jesus in the period before the parousia.

12:45 My master is delayed in coming: this statement indicates that early Christian expectations for the imminent return of Jesus had undergone some modification. Luke cautions his readers against counting on such a delay and acting irresponsibly. Cf. the similar warning in Mt 24:48.

12:49–53 Jesus' proclamation of the kingdom is a refining and purifying fire. His message that meets with acceptance or rejection will be a source of conflict and dissension even within families.

12:50 Baptism: i.e., his death.

12:59 The last penny: Greek, **lepton**, a very small amount. Mt 5:26 has for "the last penny" the Greek word *kodrantēs* (Latin *quadrans*, "farthing").

y: Mt 24:45–51. *z:* Mt 25:1–13; Mk 13:35–37. *a:* Mt 24:43–44; 1 Thes 5:2. *b:* Jas 4:17. *c:* Mk 10:38–39. *d:* Mt 10:34–35. *e:* 2:14. *f:* Mi 7:6. *g:* Mt 16:2–3. *h:* Mt 5:25–26.

CHAPTER 13

See RG 407-8

A Call to Repentance. [1*] At that time some people who were present there told him about the Galileans whose blood Pilate had mingled with the blood of their sacrifices. [2i] He said to them in reply, "Do you think that because these Galileans suffered in this way they were greater sinners than all other Galileans? [3j] By no means! But I tell you, if you do not repent, you will all perish as they did! [4*] Or those eighteen people who were killed when the tower at Siloam fell on them—do you think they were more guilty than everyone else who lived in Jerusalem? [5] By no means! But I tell you, if you do not repent, you will all perish as they did!"

The Parable of the Barren Fig Tree. [6k*] And he told them this parable: "There once was a person who had a fig tree planted in his orchard, and when he came in search of fruit on it but found none, [7] he said to the gardener, 'For three years now I have come in search of fruit on this fig tree but have found none. [So] cut it down. Why should it exhaust the soil?' [8] He said to him in reply, 'Sir, leave it for this year also, and I shall cultivate the ground around it and fertilize it; [9] it may bear fruit in the future. If not you can cut it down.' "

Cure of a Crippled Woman on the Sabbath. [10*] He was teaching in a synagogue on the sabbath. [11] And a woman was there who for eighteen years had been crippled by a spirit; she was bent over, completely incapable of standing erect. [12] When Jesus saw her, he called to her and said, "Woman, you are set free of your infirmity." [13] He laid his hands on her, and she at once stood up straight and glorified God. [14l] But the leader of the synagogue, indignant that Jesus had cured on the sabbath, said to the crowd in reply, "There are six days when work should be done. Come on those days to be cured, not on the sabbath day." [15m*] The Lord said to him in reply, "Hypocrites! Does not each one of you on the sabbath untie his ox or his ass from the manger and lead it out for watering? [16n*] This daughter of Abraham, whom Satan has bound for eighteen years now, ought she not to have been set free on the sabbath day from this bondage?" [17] When he said this, all his adversaries were humiliated; and the whole crowd rejoiced at all the splendid deeds done by him.

The Parable of the Mustard Seed. [18o*] Then he said, "What is the kingdom of God like? To what can I compare it? [19p] It is like a mustard seed that a person took and

13:1–5 The death of the Galileans at the hands of Pilate (Lk 13:1) and the accidental death of those on whom the tower fell (Lk 13:4) are presented by the Lucan Jesus as timely reminders of the need for all to repent, for the victims of these tragedies should not be considered outstanding sinners who were singled out for punishment.

13:1 The slaughter of the Galileans by Pilate is unknown outside Luke; but from what is known about Pilate from the Jewish historian Josephus, such a slaughter would be in keeping with the character of Pilate. Josephus reports that Pilate had disrupted a religious gathering of the Samaritans on Mount Gerizim with a slaughter of the participants (*Antiquities* 18, 4, 1 #86–87), and that on another occasion Pilate had killed many Jews who had opposed him when he appropriated money from the temple treasury to build an aqueduct in Jerusalem (*Jewish War* 2, 9, 4 #175–77; *Antiquities* 18, 3, 2 #60–62).

13:4 Like the incident mentioned in Lk 13:1 nothing of this accident in Jerusalem is known outside Luke and the New Testament.

13:6–9 Following on the call to repentance in Lk 13:1–5, the parable of the barren fig tree presents a story about the continuing patience of God with those who have not yet given evidence of their repentance (see Lk 3:8). The parable may also be alluding to the delay of the end time, when punishment will be meted out, and the importance of preparing for the end of the age because the delay will not be permanent (Lk 13:8–9).

13:10–17 The cure of the crippled woman on the sabbath and the controversy that results furnishes a parallel to an incident that will be reported by Luke in 14:1–6, the cure of the man with dropsy on the sabbath. A characteristic of Luke's style is the juxtaposition of an incident that reveals Jesus' concern for a man with an incident that reveals his concern for a woman; cf., e.g., Lk 7:11–17 and Lk 8:49–56.

13:15–16 If the law as interpreted by Jewish tradition allowed for the untying of bound animals on the sabbath, how much more should this woman who has been bound by Satan's power be freed on the sabbath from her affliction.

13:16 **Whom Satan has bound**: affliction and infirmity are taken as evidence of Satan's hold on humanity. The healing ministry of Jesus reveals the gradual wresting from Satan of control over humanity and the establishment of God's kingdom.

13:18–21 Two parables are used to illustrate the future proportions of the kingdom of God that will result from its deceptively small beginning in the preaching and healing ministry of Jesus. They are paralleled in Mt 13:31–33 and Mk 4:30–32.

i: Jn 9:2. *j:* Jn 8:24. *k:* Jer 8:13; Heb 3:17; Mt 21:19; Mk 11:13. *l:* 6:7; 14:3; Ex 20:8–11; Dt 5:12–15; Mt 12:10; Mk 3:2–4; Jn 5:16; 7:23; 9:14, 16. *m:* 14:5; Dt 22:4; Mt 12:11. *n:* 19:9. *o:* Mt 13:31–32; Mk 4:30–32. *p:* Ez 17:23–24; 31:6.

planted in the garden. When it was fully grown, it became a large bush and 'the birds of the sky dwelt in its branches.' "

The Parable of the Yeast. [20q]Again he said, "To what shall I compare the kingdom of God? [21]It is like yeast that a woman took and mixed [in] with three measures of wheat flour until the whole batch of dough was leavened."

The Narrow Door; Salvation and Rejection. [22*]He passed through towns and villages, teaching as he went and making his way to Jerusalem. [23]Someone asked him, "Lord, will only a few people be saved?" He answered them, [24rs]"Strive to enter through the narrow gate, for many, I tell you, will attempt to enter but will not be strong enough. [25t]After the master of the house has arisen and locked the door, then will you stand outside knocking and saying, 'Lord, open the door for us.' He will say to you in reply, 'I do not know where you are from.' [26]And you will say, 'We ate and drank in your company and you taught in our streets.' [27u]Then he will say to you, 'I do not know where [you] are from. Depart from me, all you evildoers!' [28v]And there will be wailing and grinding of teeth when you see Abraham, Isaac, and Jacob and all the prophets in the kingdom of God and you yourselves cast out. [29w]And people will come from the east and the west and from the north and the south and will recline at table in the kingdom of God. [30x]For behold, some are last who will be first, and some are first who will be last."

Herod's Desire to Kill Jesus. [31]At that time some Pharisees came to him and said, "Go away, leave this area because Herod wants to kill you." [32*]He replied, "Go and tell that fox, 'Behold, I cast out demons and I perform healings today and tomorrow, and on the third day I accomplish my purpose. [33y*]Yet I must continue on my way today, tomorrow, and the following day, for it is impossible that a prophet should die outside of Jerusalem.'

The Lament over Jerusalem. [34z]"Jerusalem, Jerusalem, you who kill the prophets and stone those sent to you, how many times I yearned to gather your children together as a hen gathers her brood under her wings, but you were unwilling! [35a]Behold, your house will be abandoned. [But] I tell you, you will not see me until [the time comes when] you say, 'Blessed is he who comes in the name of the Lord.' "

CHAPTER 14

See RG 406-8

Healing of the Man with Dropsy on the Sabbath. [1bc*]On a sabbath he went to dine at the home of one of the leading Pharisees, and the people there were observing him carefully. [2*]In front of him there was a man suffering from dropsy. [3d]Jesus spoke to the scholars of the law and Pharisees in reply, asking, "Is it lawful to cure on the sabbath or not?" [4]But they kept silent; so he took the man and, after he had healed him, dismissed him. [5e*]Then he said to them, "Who among you, if your son or ox falls into a cistern, would not immediately pull him out on the sabbath day?" [6f]But they were unable to answer his question.

13:22–30 These sayings of Jesus follow in Luke upon the parables of the kingdom (Lk 13:18–21) and stress that great effort is required for entrance into the kingdom (Lk 13:24) and that there is an urgency to accept the present opportunity to enter because the narrow door will not remain open indefinitely (Lk 13:25). Lying behind the sayings is the rejection of Jesus and his message by his Jewish contemporaries (Lk 13:26) whose places at table in the kingdom will be taken by Gentiles from the four corners of the world (Lk 13:29). Those called last (the Gentiles) will precede those to whom the invitation to enter was first extended (the Jews). See also Lk 14:15–24.

13:32 Nothing, not even Herod's desire to kill Jesus, stands in the way of Jesus' role in fulfilling God's will and in establishing the kingdom through his exorcisms and healings.

13:33 It is impossible that a prophet should die outside of Jerusalem: Jerusalem is the city of destiny and the goal of the journey of the prophet Jesus. Only when he reaches the holy city will his work be accomplished.

14:1–6 See note on Lk 13:10–17.

14:2 Dropsy: an abnormal swelling of the body because of the retention and accumulation of fluid.

14:5 Your son or ox: this is the reading of many of the oldest and most important New Testament manuscripts. Because of the strange collocation of **son** and **ox**, some copyists have altered it to "your ass or ox," on the model of the saying in Lk 13:15.

q: Mt 13:33. *r:* Mt 7:13–14, 21–23. *s:* Mk 10:25. *t:* Mt 25:10–12. *u:* Ps 6:9; Mt 7:23; 25:41. *v:* Mt 8:11–12. *w:* Ps 107:2–3. *x:* Mt 19:20; 20:16; Mk 10:31. *y:* 2:38; Jn 6:30; 8:20. *z:* 19:41–44; Mt 23:37–39. *a:* 19:38; 1 Kgs 9:7–8; Ps 118:26; Jer 7:4–7, 13–15; 12:7; 22:5. *b:* 6:6–11; 13:10–17. *c:* 11:37. *d:* 6:9; Mk 3:4. *e:* 13:15; Dt 22:4; Mt 12:11. *f:* Mt 22:46.

Conduct of Invited Guests and Hosts.
[7g]*He told a parable to those who had been
invited, noticing how they were choosing
the places of honor at the table. [8h]"When
you are invited by someone to a wedding
banquet, do not recline at table in the place
of honor. A more distinguished guest than
you may have been invited by him, [9]and the
host who invited both of you may approach
you and say, 'Give your place to this man,"
and then you would proceed with embarrassment to take the lowest place. [10]Rather,
when you are invited, go and take the lowest
place so that when the host comes to you he
may say, 'My friend, move up to a higher
position.' Then you will enjoy the esteem of
your companions at the table. [11i]For everyone who exalts himself will be humbled, but
the one who humbles himself will be exalted." [12j]Then he said to the host who invited him, "When you hold a lunch or a dinner, do not invite your friends or your
brothers or your relatives or your wealthy
neighbors, in case they may invite you back
and you have repayment. [13]Rather, when
you hold a banquet, invite the poor, the crippled, the lame, the blind; [14k]blessed indeed
will you be because of their inability to repay you. For you will be repaid at the resurrection of the righteous."

The Parable of the Great Feast. [15]*One of
his fellow guests on hearing this said to him,
"Blessed is the one who will dine in the kingdom of God." [16l]He replied to him, "A man
gave a great dinner to which he invited many.
[17]When the time for the dinner came, he dispatched his servant to say to those invited,
'Come, everything is now ready.' [18]But one
by one, they all began to excuse themselves.
The first said to him, 'I have purchased a
field and must go to examine it; I ask you,
consider me excused.' [19]And another said, 'I
have purchased five yoke of oxen and am on
my way to evaluate them; I ask you, consider
me excused.' [20]And another said, 'I have just
married a woman, and therefore I cannot
come.' [21]The servant went and reported this
to his master. Then the master of the house in
a rage commanded his servant, 'Go out
quickly into the streets and alleys of the town
and bring in here the poor and the crippled,
the blind and the lame.' [22]The servant reported, 'Sir, your orders have been carried
out and still there is room.' [23]The master then
ordered the servant, 'Go out to the highways
and hedgerows and make people come in
that my home may be filled. [24]For, I tell you,
none of those men who were invited will
taste my dinner.' "

Sayings on Discipleship. [25]*Great crowds
were traveling with him, and he turned and
addressed them, [26mn]*"If anyone comes to
me without hating his father and mother,
wife and children, brothers and sisters, and
even his own life, he cannot be my disciple.
[27o]Whoever does not carry his own cross
and come after me cannot be my disciple.
[28]Which of you wishing to construct a tower
does not first sit down and calculate the cost
to see if there is enough for its completion?
[29]Otherwise, after laying the foundation and
finding himself unable to finish the work the
onlookers should laugh at him [30]and say,
'This one began to build but did not have the
resources to finish.' [31]Or what king marching into battle would not first sit down and
decide whether with ten thousand troops he
can successfully oppose another king ad-

14:7–14 The banquet scene found only in Luke provides the opportunity for these teachings of Jesus on humility and presents a setting to display Luke's interest in Jesus' attitude toward the rich and the poor (see notes on Lk 4:18; 6:20–26; 12:13–34).

14:15–24 The parable of the great dinner is a further illustration of the rejection by Israel, God's chosen people, of Jesus' invitation to share in the banquet in the kingdom and the extension of the invitation to other Jews whose identification as the poor, crippled, blind, and lame (Lk 14:21) classifies them among those who recognize their need for salvation, and to Gentiles (Lk 14:23). A similar parable is found in Mt 22:1–10.

14:25–33 This collection of sayings, most of which are peculiar to Luke, focuses on the total dedication necessary for the disciple of Jesus. No attachment to family (Lk 14:26) or possessions (Lk 14:33) can stand in the way of the total commitment demanded of the disciple. Also, acceptance of the call to be a disciple demands readiness to accept persecution and suffering (Lk 14:27) and a realistic assessment of the hardships and costs (Lk 14:28–32).

14:26 Hating his father . . .: cf. the similar saying in Mt 10:37. The disciple's family must take second place to the absolute dedication involved in following Jesus (see also Lk 9:59–62).

g: 11:43; Mt 23:6; Mk 12:38–39. *h:* Prv 25:6–7. *i:* 18:14. *j:* 6:32–35. *k:* Jn 5:29. *l:* Mt 22:2–10. *m:* Mt 10:37–38. *n:* 9:57–62; 18:29; Jn 12:25. *o:* 9:23; Mt 16:24; Mk 8:34.

vancing upon him with twenty thousand troops? [32]But if not, while he is still far away, he will send a delegation to ask for peace terms. [33p]In the same way, everyone of you who does not renounce all his possessions cannot be my disciple.

The Simile of Salt. [34q*]"Salt is good, but if salt itself loses its taste, with what can its flavor be restored? [35r]It is fit neither for the soil nor for the manure pile; it is thrown out. Whoever has ears to hear ought to hear."

See RG 406-8

CHAPTER 15

The Parable of the Lost Sheep. [1s*]The tax collectors and sinners were all drawing near to listen to him, [2t]but the Pharisees and scribes began to complain, saying, "This man welcomes sinners and eats with them." [3]So to them he addressed this parable. [4uvw]"What man among you having a hundred sheep and losing one of them would not leave the ninety-nine in the desert and go after the lost one until he finds it? [5]And when he does find it, he sets it on his shoulders with great joy [6]and, upon his arrival home, he calls together his friends and neighbors and says to them, 'Rejoice with me because I have found my lost sheep.' [7x]I tell you, in just the same way there will be more joy in heaven over one sinner who repents than over ninety-nine righteous people who have no need of repentance.

The Parable of the Lost Coin. [8*]"Or what woman having ten coins and losing one would not light a lamp and sweep the house, searching carefully until she finds it? [9]And when she does find it, she calls together her friends and neighbors and says to them, 'Rejoice with me because I have found the coin that I lost.' [10]In just the same way, I tell you, there will be rejoicing among the angels of God over one sinner who repents."

The Parable of the Lost Son. [11]Then he said, "A man had two sons, [12]and the younger son said to his father, 'Father, give me the share of your estate that should come to me.' So the father divided the property between them. [13y]After a few days, the younger son collected all his belongings and set off to a distant country where he squandered his inheritance on a life of dissipation. [14]When he had freely spent everything, a severe famine struck that country, and he found himself in dire need. [15]So he hired himself out to one of the local citizens who sent him to his farm to tend the swine. [16]And he longed to eat his fill of the pods on which the swine fed, but nobody gave him any. [17]Coming to his senses he thought, 'How many of my father's hired workers have more than enough food to eat, but here am I, dying from hunger. [18]I shall get up and go to my father and I shall say to him, "Father, I have sinned against heaven and against you. [19]I no longer deserve to be called your son; treat me as you would treat one of your hired workers." ' [20]So he got up and went back to his father. While he was still a long way off, his father caught sight of him, and was filled with compassion. He ran to his son, embraced him and kissed him. [21]His son said to him, 'Father, I have sinned against heaven and against you; I no longer deserve to be called your son.' [22]But his father ordered his servants, 'Quickly bring the finest robe and put it on him; put a ring on his finger and sandals on his feet. [23]Take the fattened calf and slaughter it. Then let us celebrate with a feast, [24]because this son of mine was dead, and has come to life again; he was lost, and has been found.' Then the celebration began. [25]Now the older son had been out in the field and, on his way back, as he neared the house, he heard the sound of music and dancing. [26]He called one of the servants and asked what this might mean. [27]The servant said to him, 'Your brother has returned and

14:34–35 The simile of salt follows the sayings of Jesus that demanded of the disciple total dedication and detachment from family and possessions and illustrates the condition of one who does not display this total commitment. The half-hearted disciple is like salt that cannot serve its intended purpose. See the simile of salt in Mt 5:13 and the note there.

15:1–32 To the parable of the lost sheep (Lk 15:1–7) that Luke shares with Matthew (Mt 18:12–14), Luke adds two parables (the lost coin, Lk 15:8–10; the prodigal son, Lk 15:11–32) from his own special tradition to illustrate Jesus' particular concern for the lost and God's love for the repentant sinner.

15:8 Ten coins: literally, "ten drachmas." A drachma was a Greek silver coin.

---

p: 5:11. *q:* Mt 5:13; Mk 9:50. *r:* 8:8; Mt 11:15; 13:9; Mk 4:9, 23. *s:* Mt 9:10–13. *t:* 5:30; 19:7. *u:* Mt 18:12–14. *v:* 19:10. *w:* Ez 34:11–12, 16. *x:* Ez 18:23. *y:* Prv 29:3.

your father has slaughtered the fattened calf because he has him back safe and sound.' [28]He became angry, and when he refused to enter the house, his father came out and pleaded with him. [29]He said to his father in reply, 'Look, all these years I served you and not once did I disobey your orders; yet you never gave me even a young goat to feast on with my friends. [30]But when your son returns who swallowed up your property with prostitutes, for him you slaughter the fattened calf.' [31]He said to him, 'My son, you are here with me always; everything I have is yours. [32]But now we must celebrate and rejoice, because your brother was dead and has come to life again; he was lost and has been found.' "

See RG 406–8

CHAPTER 16

The Parable of the Dishonest Steward. [1*]Then he also said to his disciples, "A rich man had a steward who was reported to him for squandering his property. [2]He summoned him and said, 'What is this I hear about you? Prepare a full account of your stewardship, because you can no longer be my steward.' [3]The steward said to himself, 'What shall I do, now that my master is taking the position of steward away from me? I am not strong enough to dig and I am ashamed to beg. [4]I know what I shall do so that, when I am removed from the stewardship, they may welcome me into their homes.' [5]He called in his master's debtors one by one. To the first he said, 'How much do you owe my master?' [6*]He replied, 'One hundred measures of olive oil.' He said to him, 'Here is your promissory note. Sit down and quickly write one for fifty.' [7*]Then to another he said, 'And you, how much do you owe?' He replied, 'One hundred kors of wheat.' He said to him, 'Here is your promissory note; write one for eighty.' [8z*]And the master commended that dishonest steward for acting prudently.

Application of the Parable. "For the children of this world are more prudent in dealing with their own generation than are the children of light. [9a*]I tell you, make friends for yourselves with dishonest wealth, so that when it fails, you will be welcomed into eternal dwellings. [10b*]The person who is trustworthy in very small matters is also trustworthy in great ones; and the person who is dishonest in very small matters is also dishonest in great ones. [11]If, therefore, you are not trustworthy with dishonest wealth, who will trust you with true wealth? [12]If you are not trustworthy with what belongs to another, who will give you what is yours? [13c*]No servant can serve two masters. He will either hate one and love the other, or be devoted to one and despise the other. You cannot serve God and mammon."

16:1–8a The parable of the dishonest steward has to be understood in the light of the Palestinian custom of agents acting on behalf of their masters and the usurious practices common to such agents. The dishonesty of the steward consisted in the squandering of his master's property (Lk 16:1) and not in any subsequent graft. The master commends the dishonest steward who has forgone his own usurious commission on the business transaction by having the debtors write new notes that reflected only the real amount owed the master (i.e., minus the steward's profit). The dishonest steward acts in this way in order to ingratiate himself with the debtors because he knows he is being dismissed from his position (Lk 16:3). The parable, then, teaches the prudent use of one's material goods in light of an imminent crisis.

16:6 One hundred measures: literally, "one hundred baths." A bath is a Hebrew unit of liquid measurement equivalent to eight or nine gallons.

16:7 One hundred kors: a **kor** is a Hebrew unit of dry measure for grain or wheat equivalent to ten or twelve bushels.

16:8b–13 Several originally independent sayings of Jesus are gathered here by Luke to form the concluding application of the parable of the dishonest steward.

16:8b–9 The first conclusion recommends the prudent use of one's wealth (in the light of the coming of the end of the age) after the manner of the children of this world, represented in the parable by the dishonest steward.

16:9 Dishonest wealth: literally, "mammon of iniquity." Mammon is the Greek transliteration of a Hebrew or Aramaic word that is usually explained as meaning "that in which one trusts." The characterization of this wealth as **dishonest** expresses a tendency of wealth to lead one to dishonesty. **Eternal dwellings**: or, "eternal tents," i.e., heaven.

16:10–12 The second conclusion recommends constant fidelity to those in positions of responsibility.

16:13 The third conclusion is a general statement about the incompatibility of serving God and being a slave to riches. To be dependent upon wealth is opposed to the teachings of Jesus who counseled complete dependence on the Father as one of the characteristics of the Christian disciple (Lk 12:22–39). **God and mammon**: see note on Lk 16:9. Mammon is used here as if it were itself a god.

---

z: Eph 5:8; 1 Thes 5:5. *a:* 12:33. *b:* 19:17; Mt 25:20–23. *c:* Mt 6:24.

A Saying against the Pharisees. [14*]The Pharisees, who loved money, heard all these things and sneered at him. [15d]And he said to them, "You justify yourselves in the sight of others, but God knows your hearts; for what is of human esteem is an abomination in the sight of God.

Sayings about the Law. [16e*]"The law and the prophets lasted until John; but from then on the kingdom of God is proclaimed, and everyone who enters does so with violence. [17f]It is easier for heaven and earth to pass away than for the smallest part of a letter of the law to become invalid.

Sayings about Divorce. [18g]"Everyone who divorces his wife and marries another commits adultery, and the one who marries a woman divorced from her husband commits adultery.

The Parable of the Rich Man and Lazarus. [19*]"There was a rich man who dressed in purple garments and fine linen and dined sumptuously each day. [20]And lying at his door was a poor man named Lazarus, covered with sores, [21h]who would gladly have eaten his fill of the scraps that fell from the rich man's table. Dogs even used to come and lick his sores. [22]When the poor man died, he was carried away by angels to the bosom of Abraham. The rich man also died and was buried, [23*]and from the netherworld, where he was in torment, he raised his eyes and saw Abraham far off and Lazarus at his side. [24]And he cried out, 'Father Abraham, have pity on me. Send Lazarus to dip the tip of his finger in water and cool my tongue, for I am suffering torment in these flames.' [25i]Abraham replied, 'My child, remember that you received what was good during your lifetime while Lazarus likewise received what was bad; but now he is comforted here, whereas you are tormented. [26]Moreover, between us and you a great chasm is established to prevent anyone from crossing who might wish to go from our side to yours or from your side to ours.' [27]He said, 'Then I beg you, father, send him to my father's house, [28]for I have five brothers, so that he may warn them, lest they too come to this place of torment.' [29]But Abraham replied, 'They have Moses and the prophets. Let them listen to them.' [30*]He said, 'Oh no, father Abraham, but if someone from the dead goes to them, they will repent.' [31j]Then Abraham said, 'If they will not listen to Moses and the prophets, neither will they be persuaded if someone should rise from the dead.' "

CHAPTER 17

See RG 406-8

Temptations to Sin. [1k]He said to his disciples, "Things that cause sin will inevitably occur, but woe to the person through whom they occur. [2]It would be better for him if a millstone were put around his neck and he be thrown into the sea than for him to cause one of these little ones to sin. [3l*]Be on your guard! If your brother sins, rebuke him; and if he repents, forgive him. [4m]And if he wrongs you seven times in one day and returns to you seven times saying, 'I am sorry,' you should forgive him."

Saying of Faith. [5]And the apostles said to

16:14–18 The two parables about the use of riches in chap. 16 are separated by several isolated sayings of Jesus on the hypocrisy of the Pharisees (Lk 16:14–15), on the law (Lk 16:16–17), and on divorce (Lk 16:18).

16:14–15 The Pharisees are here presented as examples of those who are slaves to wealth (see Lk 16:13) and, consequently, they are unable to serve God.

16:16 John the Baptist is presented in Luke's gospel as a transitional figure between the period of Israel, the time of promise, and the period of Jesus, the time of fulfillment. With John, the fulfillment of the Old Testament promises has begun.

16:19–31 The parable of the rich man and Lazarus again illustrates Luke's concern with Jesus' attitude toward the rich and the poor. The reversal of the fates of the rich man and Lazarus (Lk 16:22–23) illustrates the teachings of Jesus in Luke's "Sermon on the Plain" (Lk 6:20–21, 24–25).

16:19 The oldest Greek manuscript of Luke dating from ca. A.D. 175–225 records the name of the rich man as an abbreviated form of "Nineveh," but there is very little textual support in other manuscripts for this reading. "Dives" of popular tradition is the Latin Vulgate's translation for "rich man" (Lk 16:19–31).

16:23 The netherworld: see note on Lk 10:15.

16:30–31 A foreshadowing in Luke's gospel of the rejection of the call to repentance even after Jesus' resurrection.

17:3 Be on your guard: the translation takes Lk 17:3a as the conclusion to the saying on scandal in Lk 17:1–2. It is not impossible that it should be taken as the beginning of the saying on forgiveness in Lk 17:3b–4.

d: 18:9–14. *e:* Mt 11:12–13. *f:* Mt 5:18. *g:* Mt 5:32; 19:9; Mk 10:11–12; 1 Cor 7:10–11. *h:* Mt 15:27; Mk 7:28. *i:* 6:24–25. *j:* Jn 5:46–47; 11:44–48. *k:* Mt 18:6–7. *l:* Mt 18:15. *m:* Mt 6:14; 18:21–22, 35; Mk 11:25.

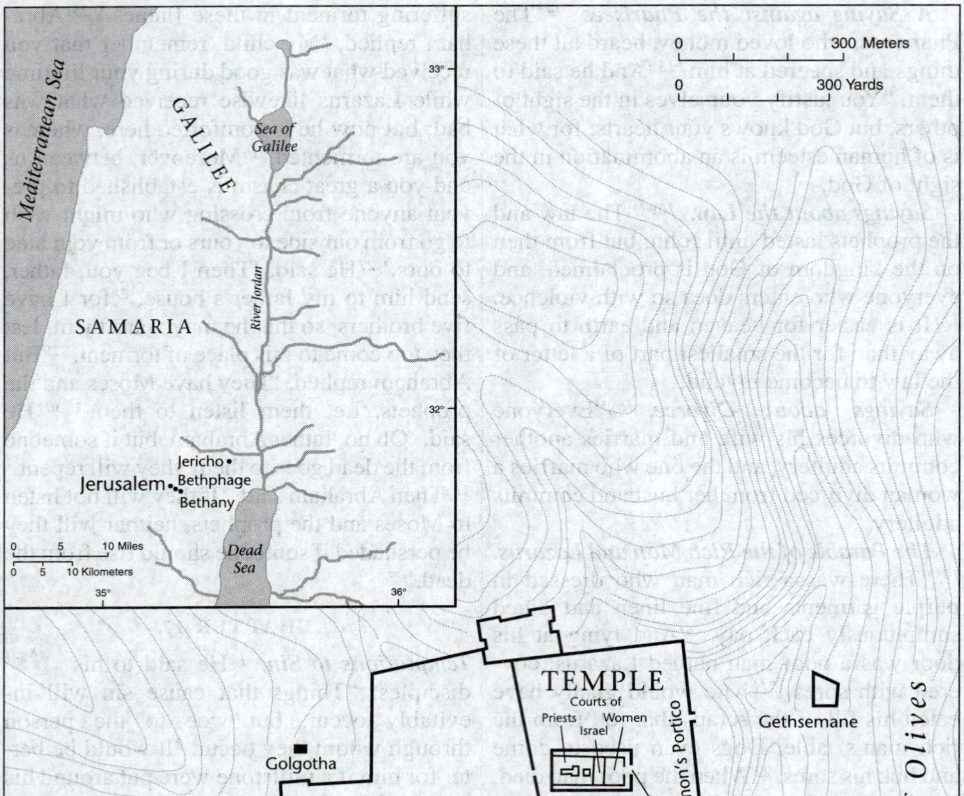

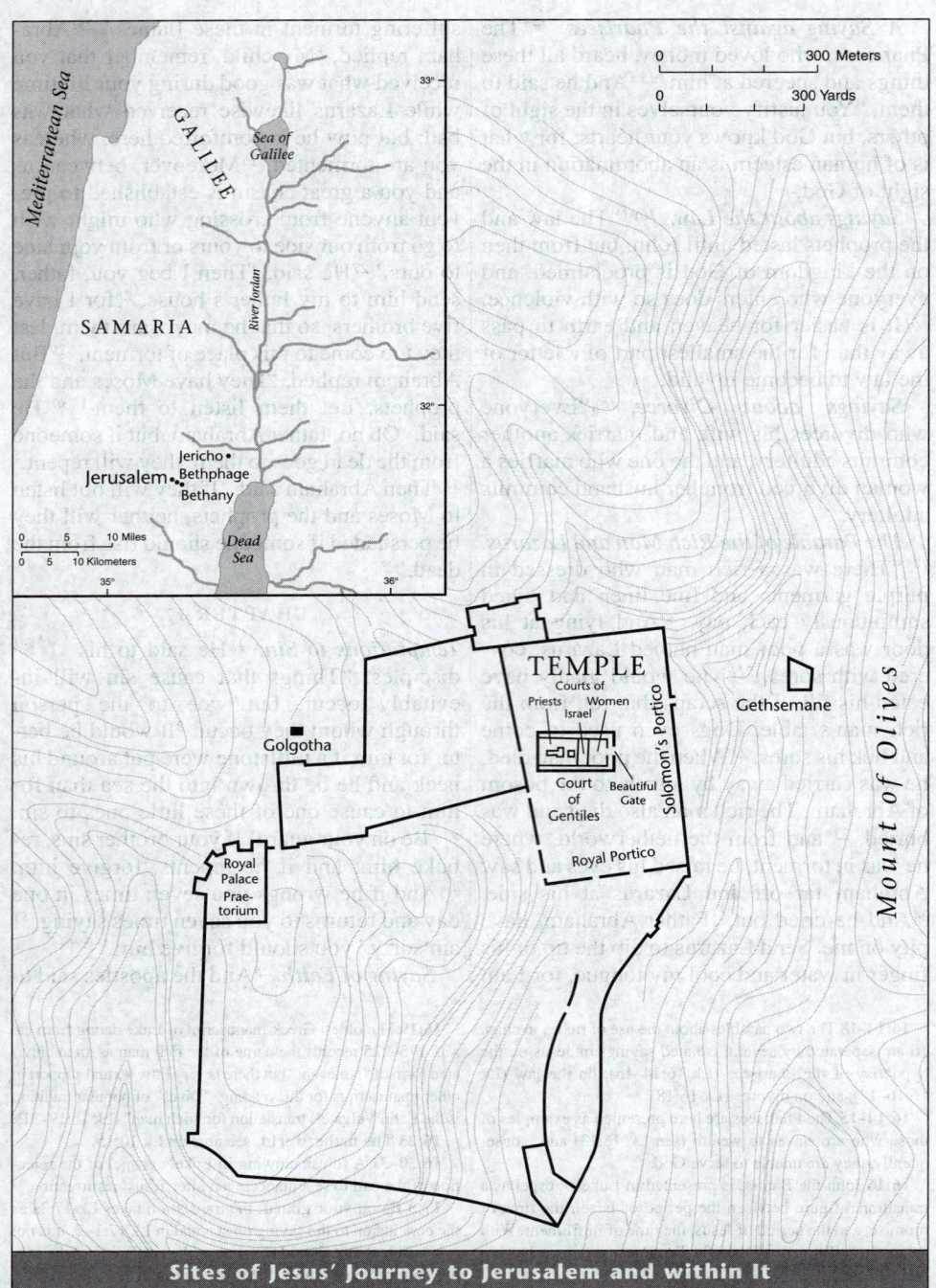

Sites of Jesus' Journey to Jerusalem and within It

the Lord, "Increase our faith." [6n]The Lord replied, "If you have faith the size of a mustard seed, you would say to [this] mulberry tree, 'Be uprooted and planted in the sea,' and it would obey you.

Attitude of a Servant. [7*]"Who among you would say to your servant who has just come in from plowing or tending sheep in the field, 'Come here immediately and take your place at table'? [8]Would he not rather say to him, 'Prepare something for me to eat. Put on your apron and wait on me while I eat and drink. You may eat and drink when I am finished'? [9]Is he grateful to that servant because he did what was commanded? [10]So should it be with you. When you have done all you have been commanded, say, 'We are unprofitable servants; we have done what we were obliged to do.' "

The Cleansing of Ten Lepers. [11o*]As he continued his journey to Jerusalem, he traveled through Samaria and Galilee. [12]As he was entering a village, ten lepers met [him]. They stood at a distance from him [13p]and raised their voice, saying, "Jesus, Master! Have pity on us!" [14q*]And when he saw them, he said, "Go show yourselves to the priests." As they were going they were cleansed. [15]And one of them, realizing he had been healed, returned, glorifying God in a loud voice; [16]and he fell at the feet of Jesus and thanked him. He was a Samaritan. [17]Jesus said in reply, "Ten were cleansed, were they not? Where are the other nine? [18]Has none but this foreigner returned to give thanks to God?" [19r]Then he said to him, "Stand up and go; your faith has saved you."

The Coming of the Kingdom of God. [20s*]Asked by the Pharisees when the kingdom of God would come, he said in reply, "The coming of the kingdom of God cannot be observed, [21t*]and no one will announce, 'Look, here it is,' or, 'There it is.' For behold, the kingdom of God is among you."

The Day of the Son of Man. [22]Then he said to his disciples, "The days will come when you will long to see one of the days of the Son of Man, but you will not see it. [23u]There will be those who will say to you, 'Look, there he is,' [or] 'Look, here he is.' Do not go off, do not run in pursuit. [24v]For just as lightning flashes and lights up the sky from one side to the other, so will the Son of Man be [in his day]. [25w]But first he must suffer greatly and be rejected by this generation. [26x]As it was in the days of Noah, so it will be in the days of the Son of Man; [27]they were eating and drinking, marrying and giving in marriage up to the day that Noah entered the ark, and the flood came and destroyed them all. [28y]Similarly, as it was in the days of Lot: they were eating, drinking, buying, selling, planting, building; [29]on the day when Lot left Sodom, fire and brimstone rained from the sky to destroy them all. [30]So it will be on the day the Son of Man is revealed. [31za]On that day, a person who is on the housetop and whose belongings are in the house must not go down to get them, and likewise a person in the field must not return to what was left

17:7–10 These sayings of Jesus, peculiar to Luke, which continue his response to the apostles' request to increase their faith (Lk 17:5–6), remind them that Christian disciples can make no claim on God's graciousness; in fulfilling the exacting demands of discipleship, they are only doing their duty.

17:11–19 This incident recounting the thankfulness of the cleansed Samaritan leper is narrated only in Luke's gospel and provides an instance of Jesus holding up a non-Jew (Lk 17:18) as an example to his Jewish contemporaries (cf. Lk 10:33 where a similar purpose is achieved in the story of the good Samaritan). Moreover, it is the faith in Jesus manifested by the foreigner that has brought him salvation (Lk 17:19; cf. the similar relationship between faith and salvation in Lk 7:50; 8:48, 50).

17:11 Through Samaria and Galilee: or, "between Samaria and Galilee."

17:14 See note on Lk 5:14.

17:20–37 To the question of the Pharisees about the time of the coming of God's kingdom, Jesus replies that the kingdom is **among you** (Lk 17:20–21). The emphasis has thus been shifted from an imminent observable coming of the kingdom to something that is already present in Jesus' preaching and healing ministry. Luke has also appended further traditional sayings of Jesus about the unpredictable suddenness of the day of the Son of Man, and assures his readers that in spite of the delay of that day (Lk 12:45), it will bring judgment unexpectedly on those who do not continue to be vigilant.

17:21 Among you: the Greek preposition translated as **among** can also be translated as "within." In the light of other statements in Luke's gospel about the presence of the kingdom (see Lk 10:9, 11; 11:20) "among" is to be preferred.

n: Mt 17:20; 21:21; Mk 11:23. *o:* 9:51–53; 13:22, 33; 18:31; 19:28; Jn 4:4. *p:* 18:38; Mt 9:27; 15:22. *q:* 5:14; Lv 14:2–32; Mt 8:4; Mk 1:44. *r:* 7:50; 18:42. *s:* Jn 3:3. *t:* 17:23; Mt 24:23; Mk 13:21. *u:* 17:21; Mt 24:23, 26; Mk 13:21. *v:* Mt 24:27. *w:* 9:22; 18:32–33; Mt 16:21; 17:22–23; 20:18–19; Mk 8:31; 9:31; 10:33–34. *x:* Gn 6–8; Mt 24:37–39. *y:* Gn 18:20–21; 19:1–29. *z:* Gn 19:17, 26. *a:* Mt 24:17–18; Mk 13:15–16.

behind. [32]Remember the wife of Lot. [33b]Whoever seeks to preserve his life will lose it, but whoever loses it will save it. [34]I tell you, on that night there will be two people in one bed; one will be taken, the other left. [35c]And there will be two women grinding meal together; one will be taken, the other left." [[36]]* [37d]They said to him in reply, "Where, Lord?" He said to them, "Where the body is, there also the vultures will gather."

CHAPTER 18

See RG 406-8

The Parable of the Persistent Widow. [1e*]Then he told them a parable about the necessity for them to pray always without becoming weary. He said, [2]"There was a judge in a certain town who neither feared God nor respected any human being. [3]And a widow in that town used to come to him and say, 'Render a just decision for me against my adversary.' [4]For a long time the judge was unwilling, but eventually he thought, 'While it is true that I neither fear God nor respect any human being, [5f*]because this widow keeps bothering me I shall deliver a just decision for her lest she finally come and strike me.'" [6]The Lord said, "Pay attention to what the dishonest judge says. [7]Will not God then secure the rights of his chosen ones who call out to him day and night? Will he be slow to answer them? [8]I tell you, he will see to it that justice is done for them speedily. But when the Son of Man comes, will he find faith on earth?"

The Parable of the Pharisee and the Tax Collector. [9g]He then addressed this parable to those who were convinced of their own righteousness and despised everyone else. [10]"Two people went up to the temple area to pray; one was a Pharisee and the other was a tax collector. [11]The Pharisee took up his position and spoke this prayer to himself, 'O God, I thank you that I am not like the rest of humanity—greedy, dishonest, adulterous—or even like this tax collector. [12h]I fast twice a week, and I pay tithes on my whole income.' [13i]But the tax collector stood off at a distance and would not even raise his eyes to heaven but beat his breast and prayed, 'O God, be merciful to me a sinner.' [14j]I tell you, the latter went home justified, not the former; for everyone who exalts himself will be humbled, and the one who humbles himself will be exalted."

Saying on Children and the Kingdom. [15k*]People were bringing even infants to him that he might touch them, and when the disciples saw this, they rebuked them. [16]Jesus, however, called the children to himself and said, "Let the children come to me and do not prevent them; for the kingdom of God belongs to such as these. [17l]Amen, I say to you, whoever does not accept the kingdom of God like a child will not enter it."

The Rich Official. [18mn]An official asked him this question, "Good teacher, what must I do to inherit eternal life?" [19]Jesus answered him, "Why do you call me good? No one is good but God alone. [20o]You know the com-

17:36 The inclusion of Lk 17:36 "There will be two men in the field; one will be taken, the other left behind," in some Western manuscripts appears to be a scribal assimilation to Mt 24:40.

18:1–14 The particularly Lucan material in the travel narrative concludes with two parables on prayer. The first (Lk 18:1–8) teaches the disciples the need of persistent prayer so that they not fall victims to apostasy (Lk 18:8). The second (Lk 18:9–14) condemns the self-righteous, critical attitude of the Pharisee and teaches that the fundamental attitude of the Christian disciple must be the recognition of sinfulness and complete dependence on God's graciousness. The second parable recalls the story of the pardoning of the sinful woman (Lk 7:36–50) where a similar contrast is presented between the critical attitude of the Pharisee Simon and the love shown by the pardoned sinner.

18:5 Strike me: the Greek verb translated as strike means "to strike under the eye" and suggests the extreme situation to which the persistence of the widow might lead. It may, however, be used here in the much weaker sense of "to wear one out."

18:15–19:27 Luke here includes much of the material about the journey to Jerusalem found in his Marcan source (Lk 10:1–52) and adds to it the story of Zacchaeus (Lk 19:1–10) from his own particular tradition and the parable of the gold coins (minas) (Lk 19:11–27) from Q, the source common to Luke and Matthew.

18:15–17 The sayings on children furnish a contrast to the attitude of the Pharisee in the preceding episode (Lk 18:9–14) and that of the wealthy official in the following one (Lk 18:18–23) who think that they can lay claim to God's favor by their own merit. The attitude of the disciple should be marked by the receptivity and trustful dependence characteristic of the child.

b: 9:24; Mt 10:39; 16:25; Mk 8:35; Jn 12:25. *c:* Mt 24:40–41. *d:* Jb 39:30; Mt 24:28. *e:* Rom 12:12; Col 4:2; 1 Thes 5:17. *f:* 11:8. *g:* 16:5; Mt 23:25–28. *h:* Mt 23:23. *i:* Ps 51:3. *j:* 14:11; Mt 23:12. *k:* Mt 19:13–15; Mk 10:13–16. *l:* Mt 18:3. *m:* Mt 19:16–30; Mk 10:17–31. *n:* 10:25. *o:* Ex 20:12–16; Dt 5:16–20.

mandments, 'You shall not commit adultery; you shall not kill; you shall not steal; you shall not bear false witness; honor your father and your mother.' " [21]And he replied, "All of these I have observed from my youth." [22 p*]When Jesus heard this he said to him, "There is still one thing left for you: sell all that you have and distribute it to the poor, and you will have a treasure in heaven. Then come, follow me." [23]But when he heard this he became quite sad, for he was very rich.

On Riches and Renunciation. [24]Jesus looked at him [now sad] and said, "How hard it is for those who have wealth to enter the kingdom of God! [25]For it is easier for a camel to pass through the eye of a needle than for a rich person to enter the kingdom of God." [26]Those who heard this said, "Then who can be saved?" [27 q]And he said, "What is impossible for human beings is possible for God." [28]Then Peter said, "We have given up our possessions and followed you." [29 r]He said to them, "Amen, I say to you, there is no one who has given up house or wife or brothers or parents or children for the sake of the kingdom of God [30]who will not receive [back] an overabundant return in this present age and eternal life in the age to come."

The Third Prediction of the Passion. [31 s*]Then he took the Twelve aside and said to them, "Behold, we are going up to Jerusalem and everything written by the prophets about the Son of Man will be fulfilled. [32 t]He will be handed over to the Gentiles and he will be mocked and insulted and spat upon; [33]and after they have scourged him they will kill him, but on the third day he will rise." [34 u]But they understood nothing of this; the word remained hidden from them and they failed to comprehend what he said.

The Healing of the Blind Beggar. [35 v]Now as he approached Jericho a blind man was sitting by the roadside begging, [36]and hearing a crowd going by, he inquired what was happening. [37]They told him, "Jesus of Nazareth is passing by." [38 w*]He shouted, "Jesus, Son of David, have pity on me!" [39]The people walking in front rebuked him, telling him to be silent, but he kept calling out all the more, "Son of David, have pity on me!" [40]Then Jesus stopped and ordered that he be brought to him; and when he came near, Jesus asked him, [41 x]"What do you want me to do for you?" He replied, "Lord, please let me see." [42 y]Jesus told him, "Have sight; your faith has saved you." [43]He immediately received his sight and followed him, giving glory to God. When they saw this, all the people gave praise to God.

CHAPTER 19

See RG 408

Zacchaeus the Tax Collector. [1*]He came to Jericho and intended to pass through the town. [2]Now a man there named Zacchaeus, who was a chief tax collector and also a wealthy man, [3]was seeking to see who Jesus was; but he could not see him because of the crowd, for he was short in stature. [4]So he ran ahead and climbed a sycamore tree in order to see Jesus, who was about to pass that way.

18:22 Detachment from material possessions results in the total dependence on God demanded of one who would inherit eternal life. **Sell all that you have**: the original saying (cf. Mk 10:21) has characteristically been made more demanding by Luke's addition of "all."

18:31–33 The details included in this third announcement of Jesus' suffering and death suggest that the literary formulation of the announcement has been directed by the knowledge of the historical passion and death of Jesus.

18:31 Everything written by the prophets . . . will be fulfilled: this is a Lucan addition to the words of Jesus found in the Marcan source (Mk 10:32–34). Luke understands the events of Jesus' last days in Jerusalem to be the fulfillment of Old Testament prophecy, but, as is usually the case in Luke-Acts, the author does not specify which Old Testament prophets he has in mind; cf. Lk 24:25, 27, 44; Acts 3:8; 13:27; 26:22–23.

18:38 Son of David: the blind beggar identifies Jesus with a title that is related to Jesus' role as Messiah (see note on Lk 2:11). Through this Son of David, salvation comes to the blind man. Note the connection between salvation and house of David mentioned earlier in Zechariah's canticle (Lk 1:69). See also note on Mt 9:27.

19:1–10 The story of the tax collector Zacchaeus is unique to this gospel. While a rich man (Lk 19:2), Zacchaeus provides a contrast to the rich man of Lk 18:18–23 who cannot detach himself from his material possessions to become a follower of Jesus. Zacchaeus, according to Luke, exemplifies the proper attitude toward wealth: he promises to give half of his possessions to the poor (Lk 19:8) and consequently is the recipient of salvation (Lk 19:9–10).

p: 12:33; Sir 29:11; Mt 6:20. *q:* Mk 14:36. *r:* 14:26. *s:* 24:25–27, 44; Mt 20:17–19; Mk 10:32–34; Acts 3:18. *t:* 9:22, 44. *u:* Mk 9:32. *v:* Mt 20:29–34; Mk 10:46–52. *w:* 17:13; Mt 9:27; 15:22. *x:* Mk 10:36. *y:* 7:50; 17:19.

[5]When he reached the place, Jesus looked up
and said to him, "Zacchaeus, come down
quickly, for today I must stay at your house."
[6]And he came down quickly and received him
with joy. [7z]When they all saw this, they began
to grumble, saying, "He has gone to stay at the
house of a sinner." [8a]But Zacchaeus stood
there and said to the Lord, "Behold, half of my
possessions, Lord, I shall give to the poor, and
if I have extorted anything from anyone I shall
repay it four times over." [9b*]And Jesus said to
him, "Today salvation has come to this house
because this man too is a descendant of Abraham. [10c*]For the Son of Man has come to seek
and to save what was lost."

The Parable of the Ten Gold Coins.
[11d*]While they were listening to him speak,
he proceeded to tell a parable because he
was near Jerusalem and they thought that the
kingdom of God would appear there immediately. [12e]So he said, "A nobleman went off
to a distant country to obtain the kingship for
himself and then to return. [13*]He called ten
of his servants and gave them ten gold coins
and told them, 'Engage in trade with these
until I return.' [14]His fellow citizens, however, despised him and sent a delegation after him to announce, 'We do not want this
man to be our king.' [15]But when he returned
after obtaining the kingship, he had the servants called, to whom he had given the
money, to learn what they had gained by
trading. [16]The first came forward and said,
'Sir, your gold coin has earned ten additional
ones.' [17f]He replied, 'Well done, good servant! You have been faithful in this very
small matter; take charge of ten cities.'
[18]Then the second came and reported, 'Your
gold coin, sir, has earned five more.' [19]And
to this servant too he said, 'You, take charge
of five cities.' [20]Then the other servant came
and said, 'Sir, here is your gold coin; I kept
it stored away in a handkerchief, [21]for I was
afraid of you, because you are a demanding
person; you take up what you did not lay
down and you harvest what you did not
plant.' [22]He said to him, 'With your own
words I shall condemn you, you wicked servant. You knew I was a demanding person,
taking up what I did not lay down and harvesting what I did not plant; [23]why did you
not put my money in a bank? Then on my return I would have collected it with interest.'
[24]And to those standing by he said, 'Take the
gold coin from him and give it to the servant
who has ten.' [25]But they said to him, 'Sir, he
has ten gold coins.' [26g]'I tell you, to everyone who has, more will be given, but from
the one who has not, even what he has will
be taken away. [27]Now as for those enemies
of mine who did not want me as their king,
bring them here and slay them before me.'"

VI. The Teaching Ministry in Jerusalem

The Entry into Jerusalem. [28h*]After he had
said this, he proceeded on his journey up to

19:9 A descendant of Abraham: literally, "a son of Abraham." The tax collector Zacchaeus, whose repentance is attested by his determination to amend his former ways, shows himself to be a true descendant of Abraham, the true heir to the promises of God in the Old Testament. Underlying Luke's depiction of Zacchaeus as a descendant of Abraham, the father of the Jews (Lk 1:73; 16:22–31), is his recognition of the central place occupied by Israel in the plan of salvation.

19:10 This verse sums up for Luke his depiction of the role of Jesus as savior in this gospel.

19:11–27 In this parable Luke has combined two originally distinct parables: (1) a parable about the conduct of faithful and productive servants (Lk 19:13, 15b–26) and (2) a parable about a rejected king (Lk 19:12, 14–15a, 27). The story about the conduct of servants occurs in another form in Mt 25:14–20. The story about the rejected king may have originated with a contemporary historical event. After the death of Herod the Great, his son Archelaus traveled to Rome to receive the title of king. A delegation of Jews appeared in Rome before Caesar Augustus to oppose the request of Archelaus. Although not given the title of king, Archelaus was made ruler over Judea and Samaria. As the story is used by Luke, however, it furnishes a correction to the expectation of the imminent end of the age and of the establishment of the kingdom in Jerusalem (Lk 19:11). Jesus is not on his way to Jerusalem to receive the kingly power; for that, he must go away and only after returning from the distant country (a reference to the parousia) will reward and judgment take place.

19:13 Ten gold coins: literally, "ten minas." A mina was a monetary unit that in ancient Greece was the equivalent of one hundred drachmas.

19:28–21:38 With the royal entry of Jesus into Jerusalem, a new section of Luke's gospel begins, the ministry of Jesus in Jerusalem before his death and resurrection. Luke suggests that this was a lengthy ministry in Jerusalem (Lk 19:47; 20:1;

z: 5:30; 15:2. *a:* Ex 21:37; Nm 5:6–7; 2 Sm 12:6. *b:* 13:16; Mt 21:31. *c:* 15:4–10; Ez 34:16. *d:* Mt 25:14–30. *e:* Mk 13:34. *f:* 16:10. *g:* 8:18; Mt 13:12; Mk 4:25. *h:* Mt 21:1–11; Mk 11:1–11; Jn 12:12–19.

Jerusalem. [29i]As he drew near to Bethphage
and Bethany at the place called the Mount of
Olives, he sent two of his disciples. [30j]He
said, "Go into the village opposite you, and as
you enter it you will find a colt tethered on
which no one has ever sat. Untie it and bring
it here. [31]And if anyone should ask you, 'Why
are you untying it?' you will answer, 'The
Master has need of it.' " [32k]So those who had
been sent went off and found everything just
as he had told them. [33]And as they were untying the colt, its owners said to them, "Why are
you untying this colt?" [34]They answered,
"The Master has need of it." [35l]So they
brought it to Jesus, threw their cloaks over the
colt, and helped Jesus to mount. [36]As he rode
along, the people were spreading their cloaks
on the road; [37]and now as he was approaching
the slope of the Mount of Olives, the whole
multitude of his disciples began to praise God
aloud with joy for all the mighty deeds they
had seen. [38m*]They proclaimed:

"Blessed is the king who comes
in the name of the Lord.
Peace in heaven
and glory in the highest."

[39*]Some of the Pharisees in the crowd said to
him, "Teacher, rebuke your disciples." [40]He
said in reply, "I tell you, if they keep silent,
the stones will cry out!"

The Lament for Jerusalem. [41no*]As he
drew near, he saw the city and wept over it,
[42p]saying, "If this day you only knew what
makes for peace—but now it is hidden from
your eyes. [43q*]For the days are coming upon
you when your enemies will raise a palisade
against you; they will encircle you and hem
you in on all sides. [44r]They will smash you
to the ground and your children within you,
and they will not leave one stone upon another within you because you did not recognize the time of your visitation."

The Cleansing of the Temple. [45st*]Then
Jesus entered the temple area and proceeded
to drive out those who were selling things,
[46u]saying to them, "It is written, 'My house
shall be a house of prayer, but you have
made it a den of thieves.' " [47vw]And every
day he was teaching in the temple area. The
chief priests, the scribes, and the leaders of
the people, meanwhile, were seeking to put
him to death, [48]but they could find no way to
accomplish their purpose because all the
people were hanging on his words.

CHAPTER 20

See RG 408-9

The Authority of Jesus Questioned.
[1x*]One day as he was teaching the people in
the temple area and proclaiming the good
news, the chief priests and scribes, together
with the elders, approached him [2y]and said

21:37–38; 22:53) and it is characterized by Jesus' daily teaching in the temple (Lk 21:37–38). For the story of the entry of Jesus into Jerusalem, see also Mt 21:1–11; Mk 11:1–10; Jn 12:12–19 and the notes there.

19:38 Blessed is the king who comes in the name of the Lord: only in Luke is Jesus explicitly given the title **king** when he enters Jerusalem in triumph. Luke has inserted this title into the words of Ps 118:26 that heralded the arrival of the pilgrims coming to the holy city and to the temple. Jesus is thereby acclaimed as **king** (see Lk 1:32) and as the one who comes (see Mal 3:1; Lk 7:19). **Peace in heaven . . .**: the acclamation of the disciples of Jesus in Luke echoes the announcement of the angels at the birth of Jesus (Lk 2:14). The peace Jesus brings is associated with the salvation to be accomplished here in Jerusalem.

19:39 Rebuke your disciples: this command, found only in Luke, was given so that the Roman authorities would not interpret the acclamation of Jesus as king as an uprising against them; cf. Lk 23:2–3.

19:41–44 The lament for Jerusalem is found only in Luke. By not accepting Jesus (the one who mediates peace), Jerusalem will not find peace but will become the victim of devastation.

19:43–44 Luke may be describing the actual disaster that befell Jerusalem in A.D. 70 when it was destroyed by the Romans during the First Revolt.

19:45–46 Immediately upon entering the holy city, Jesus in a display of his authority enters the temple (see Mal 3:1–3) and lays claim to it after cleansing it that it might become a proper place for his teaching ministry in Jerusalem (Lk 19:47; 20:1; 21:37; 22:53). See Mt 21:12–17; Mk 11:15–19; Jn 2:13–17 and the notes there.

20:1–47 The Jerusalem religious leaders or their representatives, in an attempt to incriminate Jesus with the Romans and to discredit him with the people, pose a number of questions to him (about his authority, 2; about payment of taxes, Lk 20:22; about the resurrection, Lk 20:28–33).

---

i: Zec 14:4. *j:* Nm 19:2; Dt 21:3; 1 Sm 6:7; Zec 9:9. *k:* 22:13. *l:* 2 Kgs 9:13. *m:* 2:14; Ps 118:26. *n:* 13:34–35. *o:* 2 Kgs 8:11–12; Jer 14:17; 15:5. *p:* 8:10; Is 6:9–10; Mt 13:14; Mk 4:12; Acts 28:26–27; Rom 11:8, 10. *q:* Is 29:3. *r:* 1:68; 21:6; Ps 137:9; Mt 24:2; Mk 13:2. *s:* Mt 21:12–13; Mk 11:15–17; Jn 2:13–17. *t:* 3:1 / Hos 9:15. *u:* Is 56:7; Jer 7:11. *v:* 20:19; 22:2; Mt 21:46; Mk 11:18; 12:12; 14:1–2; Jn 5:18; 7:30. *w:* 21:37; 22:53; Jn 18:20. *x:* Mt 21:23–27; Mk 11:27–33. *y:* Acts 4:7.

to him, "Tell us, by what authority are you doing these things? Or who is the one who gave you this authority?" 3He said to them in reply, "I shall ask you a question. Tell me, 4[z]was John's baptism of heavenly or of human origin?" 5[a]They discussed this among themselves, and said, "If we say, 'Of heavenly origin,' he will say, 'Why did you not believe him?' 6But if we say, 'Of human origin,' then all the people will stone us, for they are convinced that John was a prophet." 7So they answered that they did not know from where it came. 8Then Jesus said to them, "Neither shall I tell you by what authority I do these things."

The Parable of the Tenant Farmers. 9[bc]*Then he proceeded to tell the people this parable. "[A] man planted a vineyard, leased it to tenant farmers, and then went on a journey for a long time. 10[d]At harvest time he sent a servant to the tenant farmers to receive some of the produce of the vineyard. But they beat the servant and sent him away empty-handed. 11So he proceeded to send another servant, but him also they beat and insulted and sent away empty-handed. 12Then he proceeded to send a third, but this one too they wounded and threw out. 13[e]The owner of the vineyard said, 'What shall I do? I shall send my beloved son; maybe they will respect him.' 14But when the tenant farmers saw him they said to one another, 'This is the heir. Let us kill him that the inheritance may become ours.' 15*So they threw him out of the vineyard and killed him. What will the owner of the vineyard do to them? 16He will come and put those tenant farmers to death and turn over the vineyard to others." When the people heard this, they exclaimed, "Let it not be so!" 17[f]But he looked at them and asked, "What then does this scripture passage mean:

'The stone which the builders rejected
has become the cornerstone'?

18Everyone who falls on that stone will be dashed to pieces; and it will crush anyone on whom it falls." 19[g]The scribes and chief priests sought to lay their hands on him at that very hour, but they feared the people, for they knew that he had addressed this parable to them.

Paying Taxes to the Emperor. 20[hi]*They watched him closely and sent agents pretending to be righteous who were to trap him in speech, in order to hand him over to the authority and power of the governor. 21[j]They posed this question to him, "Teacher, we know that what you say and teach is correct, and you show no partiality, but teach the way of God in accordance with the truth. 22*Is it lawful for us to pay tribute to Caesar or not?" 23Recognizing their craftiness he said to them, 24*"Show me a denarius; whose image and name does it bear?" They replied, "Caesar's." 25[k]So he said to them, "Then repay to Caesar what belongs to Caesar and to God what belongs to God." 26They were unable to trap him by something he might say before the people, and so amazed were they at his reply that they fell silent.

The Question about the Resurrection. 27[lm]*Some Sadducees, those who deny that there is a resurrection, came forward and put

20:9–19 This parable about an absentee landlord and a tenant farmers' revolt reflects the social and economic conditions of rural Palestine in the first century. The synoptic gospel writers use the parable to describe how the rejection of the landlord's son becomes the occasion for the vineyard to be taken away from those to whom it was entrusted (the religious leadership of Judaism that rejects the teaching and preaching of Jesus; Lk 20:19).

20:15 They threw him out of the vineyard and killed him: cf. Mk 12:8. Luke has altered his Marcan source and reports that the murder of the son takes place outside the vineyard to reflect the tradition of Jesus' death outside the walls of the city of Jerusalem (see Heb 13:12).

20:20 The governor: i.e., Pontius Pilate, the Roman administrator responsible for the collection of taxes and maintenance of order in Palestine.

20:22 Through their question the agents of the Jerusalem religious leadership hope to force Jesus to take sides on one of the sensitive political issues of first-century Palestine. The issue of nonpayment of taxes to Rome becomes one of the focal points of the First Jewish Revolt (A.D. 66–70) that resulted in the Roman destruction of Jerusalem and the temple. See also note on Mt 22:15–22.

20:24 Denarius: a Roman silver coin (see note on Lk 7:41).

20:27 Sadducees: see note on Mt 3:7.

z: 3:3, 16. *a:* Mt 21:32. *b:* Mt 21:33–46; Mk 12:1–12. *c:* Is 5:1–7. *d:* 2 Chr 36:15–16. *e:* 3:22. *f:* Ps 118:22; Is 28:16. *g:* 19:47–48; 22:2; Mt 21:46; Mk 11:18; 12:12; 14:1–2; Jn 5:18; 7:30. *h:* Mt 22:15–22; Mk 12:13–17. *i:* 11:54. *j:* Jn 3:2. *k:* Rom 13:6–7. *l:* Mt 22:23–33; Mk 12:18–27. *m:* Acts 23:8.

this question to him, 28n*saying, "Teacher,
Moses wrote for us, 'If someone's brother
dies leaving a wife but no child, his brother
must take the wife and raise up descendants
for his brother.' 29Now there were seven
brothers; the first married a woman but died
childless. 30Then the second 31and the third
married her, and likewise all the seven died
childless. 32Finally the woman also died.
33Now at the resurrection whose wife will
that woman be? For all seven had been married to her." 34Jesus said to them, "The children of this age marry and remarry; 35but
those who are deemed worthy to attain to the
coming age and to the resurrection of the
dead neither marry nor are given in marriage. 36*They can no longer die, for they are
like angels; and they are the children of God
because they are the ones who will rise.
37oThat the dead will rise even Moses made
known in the passage about the bush, when
he called 'Lord' the God of Abraham, the
God of Isaac, and the God of Jacob; 38pand
he is not God of the dead, but of the living,
for to him all are alive." 39Some of the
scribes said in reply, "Teacher, you have answered well." 40qAnd they no longer dared
to ask him anything.

The Question about David's Son. 41r*Then
he said to them, "How do they claim that the
Messiah is the Son of David? 42sFor David
himself in the Book of Psalms says:

'The Lord said to my lord,
"Sit at my right hand
43 till I make your enemies your
footstool." '

44Now if David calls him 'lord,' how can he
be his son?"

Denunciation of the Scribes. 45tThen,
within the hearing of all the people, he said
to [his] disciples, 46u"Be on guard against
the scribes, who like to go around in long
robes and love greetings in marketplaces,
seats of honor in synagogues, and places of
honor at banquets. 47They devour the houses
of widows and, as a pretext, recite lengthy
prayers. They will receive a very severe condemnation."

CHAPTER 21

See RG 408–9

The Poor Widow's Contribution.
1v*When he looked up he saw some wealthy
people putting their offerings into the treasury 2and he noticed a poor widow putting in
two small coins. 3He said, "I tell you truly,
this poor widow put in more than all the rest;
4for those others have all made offerings
from their surplus wealth, but she, from her
poverty, has offered her whole livelihood."

The Destruction of the Temple Foretold.
5w*While some people were speaking about
how the temple was adorned with costly
stones and votive offerings, he said, 6x"All

20:28–33 The Sadducees' question, based on the law of levirate marriage recorded in Dt 25:5–10, ridicules the idea of the resurrection. Jesus rejects their naive understanding of the resurrection (Lk 20:35–36) and then argues on behalf of the resurrection of the dead on the basis of the written law (Lk 20:37–38) that the Sadducees accept. See also notes on Mt 22:23–33.

20:36 Because they are the ones who will rise: literally, "being sons of the resurrection."

20:41–44 After successfully answering the three questions of his opponents, Jesus now asks them a question. Their inability to respond implies that they have forfeited their position and authority as the religious leaders of the people because they do not understand the scriptures. This series of controversies between the religious leadership of Jerusalem and Jesus reveals Jesus as the authoritative teacher whose words are to be listened to (see Lk 9:35). See also notes on Mt 22:41–46.

21:1–4 The widow is another example of the poor ones in this gospel whose detachment from material possessions and dependence on God leads to their blessedness (Lk 6:20). Her simple offering provides a striking contrast to the pride and pretentiousness of the scribes denounced in the preceding section (Lk 20:45–47). The story is taken from Mk 12:41–44.

21:5–36 Jesus' eschatological discourse in Luke is inspired by Mk 13 but Luke has made some significant alterations to the words of Jesus found there. Luke maintains, though in a modified form, the belief in the early expectation of the end of the age (see Lk 21:27, 28, 31, 32, 36), but, by focusing attention throughout the gospel on the importance of the day-to-day following of Jesus and by reinterpreting the meaning of some of the signs of the end from Mk 13 he has come to terms with what seemed to the early Christian community to be a delay of the parousia. Mark, for example, described the desecration of the Jerusalem temple by the Romans (Mk 13:14) as the apocalyptic symbol (see Dn 9:27; 12:11) accompanying the end of the age and the coming of the Son of Man. Luke (Lk 21:20–24), however, removes the apocalyptic setting and separates the historical destruction of Jerusalem from the signs of the coming of the Son of Man by a period that he refers to as "the times of the Gentiles" (Lk 21:24). See also notes on Mt 24:1–36 and Mk 13:1–37.

n: Gn 38:8; Dt 25:5. *o:* Ex 3:2, 6, 15–16. *p:* Rom 14:8–9. *q:* Mt 22:46; Mk 12:34. *r:* Mt 22:41–45; Mk 12:35–37. *s:* Ps 110:1. *t:* 11:37–54; Mt 23:1–36; Mk 12:38–40. *u:* 14:7–11. *v:* Mk 12:41–44. *w:* Mt 24:1–2; Mk 13:1–2. *x:* 19:44.

that you see here—the days will come when there will not be left a stone upon another stone that will not be thrown down."

The Signs of the End. [7y]Then they asked him, "Teacher, when will this happen? And what sign will there be when all these things are about to happen?" [8z*]He answered, "See that you not be deceived, for many will come in my name, saying, 'I am he,' and 'The time has come.' Do not follow them! [9]When you hear of wars and insurrections, do not be terrified; for such things must happen first, but it will not immediately be the end." [10a]Then he said to them, "Nation will rise against nation, and kingdom against kingdom. [11]There will be powerful earthquakes, famines, and plagues from place to place; and awesome sights and mighty signs will come from the sky.

The Coming Persecution. [12bc*]"Before all this happens, however, they will seize and persecute you, they will hand you over to the synagogues and to prisons, and they will have you led before kings and governors because of my name. [13]It will lead to your giving testimony. [14]Remember, you are not to prepare your defense beforehand, [15d*]for I myself shall give you a wisdom in speaking that all your adversaries will be powerless to resist or refute. [16ef]You will even be handed over by parents, brothers, relatives, and friends, and they will put some of you to death. [17]You will be hated by all because of my name, [18g]but not a hair on your head will be destroyed. [19h]By your perseverance you will secure your lives.

The Great Tribulation. [20ij*]"When you see Jerusalem surrounded by armies, know that its desolation is at hand. [21k]Then those in Judea must flee to the mountains. Let those within the city escape from it, and let those in the countryside not enter the city, [22]for these days are the time of punishment when all the scriptures are fulfilled. [23l]Woe to pregnant women and nursing mothers in those days, for a terrible calamity will come upon the earth and a wrathful judgment upon this people. [24m*]They will fall by the edge of the sword and be taken as captives to all the Gentiles; and Jerusalem will be trampled underfoot by the Gentiles until the times of the Gentiles are fulfilled.

The Coming of the Son of Man. [25no]"There will be signs in the sun, the moon, and the stars, and on earth nations will be in dismay, perplexed by the roaring of the sea and the waves. [26p*]People will die of fright in anticipation of what is coming upon the world, for the powers of the heavens will be shaken. [27q]And then they will see the Son of Man coming in a cloud with power and great glory. [28r]But when these signs begin to happen, stand erect and raise your heads because your redemption is at hand."

The Lesson of the Fig Tree. [29s]He taught them a lesson. "Consider the fig tree and all the other trees. [30]When their buds burst open, you see for yourselves and know that summer is now near; [31]in the same way, when you see these things happening, know that the kingdom of God is near. [32t]Amen, I say to you, this generation will not pass away until all these things have taken place. [33u]Heaven and earth will pass away, but my words will not pass away.

21:8 The time has come: in Luke, the proclamation of the imminent end of the age has itself become a false teaching.

21:12 Before all this happens . . .: to Luke and his community, some of the signs of the end just described (Lk 21:10–11) still lie in the future. Now in dealing with the persecution of the disciples (Lk 21:12–19) and the destruction of Jerusalem (Lk 21:20–24) Luke is pointing to eschatological signs that have already been fulfilled.

21:15 A wisdom in speaking: literally, "a mouth and wisdom."

21:20–24 The actual destruction of Jerusalem by Rome in A.D. 70 upon which Luke and his community look back provides the assurance that, just as Jesus' prediction of Jerusalem's destruction was fulfilled, so too will be his announcement of their final redemption (Lk 21:27–28).

21:24 The times of the Gentiles: a period of indeterminate length separating the destruction of Jerusalem from the cosmic signs accompanying the coming of the Son of Man.

21:26 The powers of the heavens: the heavenly bodies mentioned in Lk 21:25 and thought of as cosmic armies.

y: Mt 24:3–14; Mk 13:3–13. *z:* 17:23; Mk 13:5, 6, 21; 1 Jn 2:18. *a:* 2 Chr 15:6; Is 19:2. *b:* 12:11–12; Mt 10:17–20; Mk 13:9–11. *c:* Jn 16:2; Acts 25:24. *d:* Acts 6:10. *e:* Mt 10:21–22. *f:* 12:52–53. *g:* 12:7; 1 Sm 14:45; Mt 10:30; Acts 27:34. *h:* 8:15. *i:* Mt 24:15–21; Mk 13:14–19. *j:* 19:41–44. *k:* 17:31. *l:* 1 Cor 7:26. *m:* Tb 14:5; Ps 79:1; Is 63:18; Jer 21:7; Rom 11:25; Rev 11:2. *n:* Mt 24:29–31; Mk 13:24–27. *o:* Wis 5:22; Is 13:10; Ez 32:7; Jl 2:10; 3:3–4; 4:15; Rev 6:12–14. *p:* Hg 2:6, 21. *q:* Dn 7:13–14; Mt 26:64; Rev 1:7. *r:* 2:38. *s:* Mt 24:32–35; Mk 13:28–31. *t:* 9:27; Mt 16:28. *u:* 16:17.

Exhortation to be Vigilant. [34v]"Beware that your hearts do not become drowsy from carousing and drunkenness and the anxieties of daily life, and that day catch you by surprise [35]like a trap. For that day will assault everyone who lives on the face of the earth. [36w]Be vigilant at all times and pray that you have the strength to escape the tribulations that are imminent and to stand before the Son of Man."

Ministry in Jerusalem. [37x]During the day, Jesus was teaching in the temple area, but at night he would leave and stay at the place called the Mount of Olives. [38]And all the people would get up early each morning to listen to him in the temple area.

VII. The Passion Narrative

CHAPTER 22

See RG 409–10

The Conspiracy against Jesus. [1y*]Now the feast of Unleavened Bread, called the Passover, was drawing near, [2z]and the chief priests and the scribes were seeking a way to put him to death, for they were afraid of the people. [3ab*]Then Satan entered into Judas, the one surnamed Iscariot, who was counted among the Twelve, [4]and he went to the chief priests and temple guards to discuss a plan for handing him over to them. [5]They were pleased and agreed to pay him money. [6]He accepted their offer and sought a favorable opportunity to hand him over to them in the absence of a crowd.

Preparations for the Passover. [7cd]When the day of the feast of Unleavened Bread arrived, the day for sacrificing the Passover lamb, [8]he sent out Peter and John, instructing them, "Go and make preparations for us to eat the Passover." [9]They asked him, "Where do you want us to make the preparations?" [10*]And he answered them, "When you go into the city, a man will meet you carrying a jar of water. Follow him into the house that he enters [11]and say to the master of the house, 'The teacher says to you, "Where is the guest room where I may eat the Passover with my disciples?"' [12]He will show you a large upper room that is furnished. Make the preparations there." [13e]Then they went off and found everything exactly as he had told them, and there they prepared the Passover.

The Last Supper. [14f]When the hour came, he took his place at table with the apostles. [15*]He said to them, "I have eagerly desired to eat this Passover with you before I suffer, [16g]for, I tell you, I shall not eat it [again] until there is fulfillment in the kingdom of God." [17*]Then he took a cup, gave thanks, and said, "Take this and share it among yourselves; [18]for I tell you [that] from this time on I shall not drink of the fruit of the vine until the kingdom of God comes."

22:1–23:56a The passion narrative. Luke is still dependent upon Mark for the composition of the passion narrative but has incorporated much of his own special tradition into the narrative. Among the distinctive sections in Luke are: (1) the tradition of the institution of the Eucharist (Lk 22:15–20); (2) Jesus' farewell discourse (Lk 22:21–38); (3) the mistreatment and interrogation of Jesus (Lk 22:63–71); (4) Jesus before Herod and his second appearance before Pilate (Lk 23:6–16); (5) words addressed to the women followers on the way to the crucifixion (Lk 23:27–32); (6) words to the penitent thief (Lk 23:39–41); (7) the death of Jesus (Lk 23:46, 47b–49). Luke stresses the innocence of Jesus (Lk 23:4, 14–15, 22) who is the victim of the powers of evil (Lk 22:3, 31, 53) and who goes to his death in fulfillment of his Father's will (Lk 22:42, 46). Throughout the narrative Luke emphasizes the mercy, compassion, and healing power of Jesus (Lk 22:51; 23:43) who does not go to death lonely and deserted, but is accompanied by others who follow him on the way of the cross (Lk 23:26–31, 49).

22:1 Feast of Unleavened Bread, called the Passover: see note on Mk 14:1.

22:3 Satan entered into Judas: see note on Lk 4:13.

22:10 A man will meet you carrying a jar of water: see note on Mk 14:13.

22:15 This Passover: Luke clearly identifies this last supper of Jesus with the apostles as a Passover meal that commemorated the deliverance of the Israelites from slavery in Egypt. Jesus reinterprets the significance of the Passover by setting it in the context of the kingdom of God (Lk 22:16). The "deliverance" associated with the Passover finds its new meaning in the blood that will be shed (Lk 22:20).

22:17 Because of a textual problem in Lk 22:19–20 some commentators interpret this cup as the eucharistic cup.

v: 12:45–46; Mt 24:48–50; 1 Thes 5:3, 6–7. *w:* Mk 13:33. *x:* 19:47; 22:39. *y:* Mt 26:1–5; Mk 14:1–2; Jn 11:47–53. *z:* 19:47–48; 20:19; Mt 21:46; Mk 12:12; Jn 5:18; 7:30. *a:* Mt 26:14–16; Mk 14:10–11; Jn 13:2, 27. *b:* Acts 1:17. *c:* Mt 26:17–19; Mk 14:12–16. *d:* Ex 12:6, 14–20. *e:* 19:32. *f:* Mt 26:20, 26–30; Mk 14:17, 22–26; 1 Cor 11:23–25. *g:* 13:29.

[19h*]Then he took the bread, said the blessing, broke it, and gave it to them, saying, "This is my body, which will be given for you; do this in memory of me." [20i]And likewise the cup after they had eaten, saying, "This cup is the new covenant in my blood, which will be shed for you.

The Betrayal Foretold. [21j]"And yet behold, the hand of the one who is to betray me is with me on the table; [22]for the Son of Man indeed goes as it has been determined; but woe to that man by whom he is betrayed." [23]And they began to debate among themselves who among them would do such a deed.

The Role of the Disciples. [24k*]Then an argument broke out among them about which of them should be regarded as the greatest. [25l*]He said to them, "The kings of the Gentiles lord it over them and those in authority over them are addressed as 'Benefactors'; [26m]but among you it shall not be so. Rather, let the greatest among you be as the youngest, and the leader as the servant. [27]For who is greater: the one seated at table or the one who serves? Is it not the one seated at table? I am among you as the one who serves. [28]It is you who have stood by me in my trials; [29n]and I confer a kingdom on you, just as my Father has conferred one on me, [30o]that you may eat and drink at my table in my kingdom; and you will sit on thrones judging the twelve tribes of Israel.

Peter's Denial Foretold. [31pq*]"Simon, Simon, behold Satan has demanded to sift all of you like wheat, [32]but I have prayed that your own faith may not fail; and once you have turned back, you must strengthen your brothers." [33r]He said to him, "Lord, I am prepared to go to prison and to die with you." [34s]But he replied, "I tell you, Peter, before the cock crows this day, you will deny three times that you know me."

Instructions for the Time of Crisis. [35t]He said to them, "When I sent you forth without a money bag or a sack or sandals, were you in need of anything?" "No, nothing," they replied. [36u*]He said to them, "But now one who has a money bag should take it, and likewise a sack, and one who does not have a sword should sell his cloak and buy one. [37v]For I tell you that this scripture must be fulfilled in me, namely, 'He was counted among the wicked'; and indeed what is written about me is coming to fulfillment." [38*]Then they said, "Lord, look, there are two swords here." But he replied, "It is enough!"

The Agony in the Garden. [39w]Then going out he went, as was his custom, to the Mount of Olives, and the disciples followed him. [40x]When he arrived at the place he said to them, "Pray that you may not undergo the test." [41y]After withdrawing about a stone's throw from them and kneeling, he prayed, [42z]saying, "Father, if you are willing, take this cup away from me; still, not my will but yours be done." [[43*]And to strengthen him

22:19c–20 Which will be given . . . do this in memory of me: these words are omitted in some important Western text manuscripts and a few Syriac manuscripts. Other ancient text types, including the oldest papyrus manuscript of Luke dating from the late second or early third century, contain the longer reading presented here. The Lucan account of the words of institution of the Eucharist bears a close resemblance to the words of institution in the Pauline tradition (see 1 Cor 11:23–26). See also notes on Mt 26:26–29; 26:27–28; and Mk 14:22–24.

22:24–38 The Gospel of Luke presents a brief farewell discourse of Jesus; compare the lengthy farewell discourses and prayer in Jn 13–17.

22:25 'Benefactors': this word occurs as a title of rulers in the Hellenistic world.

22:31–32 Jesus' prayer for Simon's faith and the commission to strengthen his brothers anticipates the post-resurrectional prominence of Peter in the first half of Acts, where he appears as the spokesman for the Christian community and the one who begins the mission to the Gentiles (Acts 10–11).

22:31 All of you: literally, "you." The translation reflects the meaning of the Greek text that uses a second person plural pronoun here.

22:36 In contrast to the ministry of the Twelve and of the seventy-two during the period of Jesus (Lk 9:3; 10:4), in the future period of the church the missionaries must be prepared for the opposition they will face in a world hostile to their preaching.

22:38 It is enough!: the farewell discourse ends abruptly with these words of Jesus spoken to the disciples when they take literally what was intended as figurative language about being prepared to face the world's hostility.

22:43–44 These verses, though very ancient, were probably not part of the original text of Luke. They are absent from

h: 24:30; Acts 27:35. *i:* Ex 24:8; Jer 31:31; 32:40; Zec 9:11. *j:* Ps 41:10; Mt 26:21–25; Mk 14:18–21; Jn 13:21–30. *k:* 9:46; Mt 18:1; Mk 9:34. *l:* Mt 20:25–27; Mk 10:42–44; Jn 13:3–16. *m:* Mt 23:11; Mk 9:35. *n:* 12:32. *o:* Mt 19:28. *p:* Mt 26:33–35; Mk 14:29–31; Jn 13:37–38. *q:* Jb 1:6–12; Am 9:9. *r:* 22:54. *s:* 22:54–62. *t:* 9:3; 10:4; Mt 10:9–10; Mk 6:7–9. *u:* 22:49. *v:* Is 53:12. *w:* Mt 26:30, 36–46; Mk 14:26, 32–42; Jn 18:1–2. *x:* 22:46. *y:* Heb 5:7–8. *z:* Mt 6:10.

an angel from heaven appeared to him. [44]He
was in such agony and he prayed so fervently that his sweat became like drops of
blood falling on the ground.] [45]When he rose
from prayer and returned to his disciples, he
found them sleeping from grief. [46a]He said
to them, "Why are you sleeping? Get up and
pray that you may not undergo the test."

The Betrayal and Arrest of Jesus.
[47b]While he was still speaking, a crowd approached and in front was one of the Twelve,
a man named Judas. He went up to Jesus to
kiss him. [48]Jesus said to him, "Judas, are you
betraying the Son of Man with a kiss?"
[49c]His disciples realized what was about to
happen, and they asked, "Lord, shall we
strike with a sword?" [50d]And one of them
struck the high priest's servant and cut off
his right ear. [51*]But Jesus said in reply,
"Stop, no more of this!" Then he touched the
servant's ear and healed him. [52e]And Jesus
said to the chief priests and temple guards
and elders who had come for him, "Have
you come out as against a robber, with
swords and clubs? [53f]Day after day I was
with you in the temple area, and you did not
seize me; but this is your hour, the time for
the power of darkness."

Peter's Denial of Jesus. [54gh]After arresting him they led him away and took him into
the house of the high priest; Peter was following at a distance. [55]They lit a fire in the
middle of the courtyard and sat around it, and
Peter sat down with them. [56]When a maid
saw him seated in the light, she looked intently at him and said, "This man too was
with him." [57]But he denied it saying,
"Woman, I do not know him." [58]A short
while later someone else saw him and said,
"You too are one of them"; but Peter answered, "My friend, I am not." [59]About an
hour later, still another insisted, "Assuredly,
this man too was with him, for he also is a
Galilean." [60]But Peter said, "My friend, I do
not know what you are talking about." Just as
he was saying this, the cock crowed, [61i*]and
the Lord turned and looked at Peter; and Peter remembered the word of the Lord, how he
had said to him, "Before the cock crows today, you will deny me three times." [62]He
went out and began to weep bitterly. [63j]The
men who held Jesus in custody were ridiculing and beating him. [64]They blindfolded him
and questioned him, saying, "Prophesy! Who
is it that struck you?" [65]And they reviled him
in saying many other things against him.

Jesus before the Sanhedrin. [66kl*]When
day came the council of elders of the people
met, both chief priests and scribes, and they
brought him before their Sanhedrin. [67m]They
said, "If you are the Messiah, tell us," but he
replied to them, "If I tell you, you will not
believe, [68]and if I question, you will not respond. [69n]But from this time on the Son of
Man will be seated at the right hand of the
power of God." [70]They all asked, "Are you
then the Son of God?" He replied to them,
"You say that I am." [71]Then they said, "What
further need have we for testimony? We
have heard it from his own mouth."

CHAPTER 23

See RG 410–11

Jesus before Pilate. [1o*]Then the
whole assembly of them arose and brought

the oldest papyrus manuscripts of Luke and from manuscripts of wide geographical distribution.

22:51 And healed him: only Luke recounts this healing of the injured servant.

22:61 Only Luke recounts that **the Lord turned and looked at Peter**. This look of Jesus leads to Peter's weeping bitterly over his denial (Lk 22:62).

22:66–71 Luke recounts one daytime trial of Jesus (Lk 22:66–71) and hints at some type of preliminary nighttime investigation (Lk 22:54–65). Mark (and Matthew who follows Mark) has transferred incidents of this day into the nighttime interrogation with the result that there appear to be two Sanhedrin trials of Jesus in Mark (and Matthew); see note on Mk 14:53.

22:66 Sanhedrin: the word is a Hebraized form of a Greek word meaning a "council," and refers to the elders, chief priests, and scribes who met under the high priest's leadership to decide religious and legal questions that did not pertain to Rome's interests. Jewish sources are not clear on the competence of the Sanhedrin to sentence and to execute during this period.

23:1–5, 13–25 Twice Jesus is brought before Pilate in Luke's account, and each time Pilate explicitly declares Jesus innocent of any wrongdoing (Lk 23:4, 14, 22). This stress on the innocence of Jesus before the Roman authorities is also characteris-

a: 22:40. *b:* Mt 26:47–56; Mk 14:43–50; Jn 18:3–4. *c:* 22:36. *d:* Jn 18:26. *e:* 22:37. *f:* 19:47; 21:37; Jn 7:30; 8:20; Col 1:13. *g:* Mt 26:57–58, 69–75; Mk 14:53–54, 66–72; Jn 18:12–18, 25–27. *h:* 22:33. *i:* 22:34. *j:* Mt 26:67–68; Mk 14:65. *k:* Mt 26:59–66; Mk 14:55–64. *l:* Mt 27:1; Mk 15:1. *m:* Jn 3:12; 8:45; 10:24. *n:* Ps 110:1; Dn 7:13–14; Acts 7:56. *o:* Mt 27:1–2, 11–14; Mk 15:1–5; Jn 18:28–38.

him before Pilate. [2][p]They brought charges against him, saying, "We found this man misleading our people; he opposes the payment of taxes to Caesar and maintains that he is the Messiah, a king." [3][q]Pilate asked him, "Are you the king of the Jews?" He said to him in reply, "You say so." [4][r]Pilate then addressed the chief priests and the crowds, "I find this man not guilty." [5]But they were adamant and said, "He is inciting the people with his teaching throughout all Judea, from Galilee where he began even to here."

Jesus before Herod. [6][*]On hearing this Pilate asked if the man was a Galilean; [7][s]and upon learning that he was under Herod's jurisdiction, he sent him to Herod who was in Jerusalem at that time. [8][t]Herod was very glad to see Jesus; he had been wanting to see him for a long time, for he had heard about him and had been hoping to see him perform some sign. [9][u]He questioned him at length, but he gave him no answer. [10][v]The chief priests and scribes, meanwhile, stood by accusing him harshly. [11][w][Even] Herod and his soldiers treated him contemptuously and mocked him, and after clothing him in resplendent garb, he sent him back to Pilate. [12]Herod and Pilate became friends that very day, even though they had been enemies formerly. [13]Pilate then summoned the chief priests, the rulers, and the people [14][x]and said to them, "You brought this man to me and accused him of inciting the people to revolt. I have conducted my investigation in your presence and have not found this man guilty of the charges you have brought against him, [15]nor did Herod, for he sent him back to us. So no capital crime has been committed by him. [16][y]Therefore I shall have him flogged and then release him." [[17]][*]

The Sentence of Death. [18][z]But all together they shouted out, "Away with this man! Release Barabbas to us." [19](Now Barabbas had been imprisoned for a rebellion that had taken place in the city and for murder.) [20]Again Pilate addressed them, still wishing to release Jesus, [21]but they continued their shouting, "Crucify him! Crucify him!" [22]Pilate addressed them a third time, "What evil has this man done? I found him guilty of no capital crime. Therefore I shall have him flogged and then release him." [23]With loud shouts, however, they persisted in calling for his crucifixion, and their voices prevailed. [24]The verdict of Pilate was that their demand should be granted. [25]So he released the man who had been imprisoned for rebellion and murder, for whom they asked, and he handed Jesus over to them to deal with as they wished.

The Way of the Cross. [26][a][*]As they led him away they took hold of a certain Simon, a Cyrenian, who was coming in from the country; and after laying the cross on him, they made him carry it behind Jesus. [27]A large crowd of people followed Jesus, including many women who mourned and lamented him. [28][b]Jesus turned to them and said, "Daughters of Jerusalem, do not weep for me; weep instead for yourselves and for your children, [29]for indeed, the days are coming when people will say, 'Blessed are the barren, the wombs that never bore and the breasts that never nursed.' [30][c]At that time people will say to the mountains, 'Fall upon us!' and to the hills, 'Cover us!' [31]for if these things are done when the wood is green what

tic of John's gospel (Jn 18:38; 19:4, 6). Luke presents the Jerusalem Jewish leaders as the ones who force the hand of the Roman authorities (Lk 23:1–2, 5, 10, 13, 18, 21, 23–25).

23:6–12 The appearance of Jesus before Herod is found only in this gospel. Herod has been an important figure in Luke (Lk 9:7–9; 13:31–33) and has been presented as someone who has been curious about Jesus for a long time. His curiosity goes unrewarded. It is faith in Jesus, not curiosity, that is rewarded (Lk 7:50; 8:48, 50; 17:19).

23:17 This verse, "He was obliged to release one prisoner for them at the festival," is not part of the original text of Luke. It is an explanatory gloss from Mk 15:6 (also Mt 27:15) and is not found in many early and important Greek manuscripts. On its historical background, see notes on Mt 27:15–26.

23:26–32 An important Lucan theme throughout the gospel has been the need for the Christian disciple to follow in the footsteps of Jesus. Here this theme comes to the fore with the story of Simon of Cyrene who takes up the cross and follows Jesus (see Lk 9:23; 14:27) and with the large crowd who likewise follow Jesus on the way of the cross. See also note on Mk 15:21.

p: 20:22–25; Acts 17:7; 24:5. *q:* 22:70; 1 Tm 6:13. *r:* 23:14, 22, 41; Mt 27:24; Jn 19:4, 6; Acts 13:28. *s:* 3:1; 9:7. *t:* 9:9; Acts 4:27–28. *u:* Mk 15:5. *v:* Mt 27:12; Mk 15:3. *w:* Mt 27:28–30; Mk 15:17–19; Jn 19:2–3. *x:* 23:4, 22, 41. *y:* 23:22; Jn 19:12–14. *z:* Mt 27:20–26; Mk 15:6–7, 11–15; Jn 18:38b–40; 19:14–16; Acts 3:13–14. *a:* Mt 27:32, 38; Mk 15:21, 27; Jn 19:17. *b:* 19:41–44; 21:23–24. *c:* Hos 10:8; Rev 6:16.

will happen when it is dry?" [32]Now two others, both criminals, were led away with him to be executed.

The Crucifixion. [33de]When they came to the place called the Skull, they crucified him and the criminals there, one on his right, the other on his left. [34f*][Then Jesus said, "Father, forgive them, they know not what they do."] They divided his garments by casting lots. [35gh]The people stood by and watched; the rulers, meanwhile, sneered at him and said, "He saved others, let him save himself if he is the chosen one, the Messiah of God." [36i]Even the soldiers jeered at him. As they approached to offer him wine [37]they called out, "If you are King of the Jews, save yourself." [38]Above him there was an inscription that read, "This is the King of the Jews."

[39*]Now one of the criminals hanging there reviled Jesus, saying, "Are you not the Messiah? Save yourself and us." [40]The other, however, rebuking him, said in reply, "Have you no fear of God, for you are subject to the same condemnation? [41j]And indeed, we have been condemned justly, for the sentence we received corresponds to our crimes, but this man has done nothing criminal." [42k]Then he said, "Jesus, remember me when you come into your kingdom." [43l]He replied to him, "Amen, I say to you, today you will be with me in Paradise."

The Death of Jesus. [44mn*]It was now about noon and darkness came over the whole land until three in the afternoon [45o]because of an eclipse of the sun. Then the veil of the temple was torn down the middle. [46p]Jesus cried out in a loud voice, "Father, into your hands I commend my spirit"; and when he had said this he breathed his last. [47*]The centurion who witnessed what had happened glorified God and said, "This man was innocent beyond doubt." [48q]When all the people who had gathered for this spectacle saw what had happened, they returned home beating their breasts; [49r]but all his acquaintances stood at a distance, including the women who had followed him from Galilee and saw these events.

The Burial of Jesus. [50s]Now there was a virtuous and righteous man named Joseph who, though he was a member of the council, [51t]had not consented to their plan of action. He came from the Jewish town of Arimathea and was awaiting the kingdom of God. [52]He went to Pilate and asked for the body of Jesus. [53u]After he had taken the body down, he wrapped it in a linen cloth and laid him in a rock-hewn tomb in which no one had yet been buried. [54]It was the day of preparation, and the sabbath was about to begin. [55v]The women who had come from Galilee with him followed behind, and when they had seen the tomb and the way in which his body was laid in it, [56w]they returned and prepared spices and perfumed oils. Then they rested on the sabbath according to the commandment.

VIII. The Resurrection Narrative

CHAPTER 24

See RG 411–12

The Resurrection of Jesus. [1x*]But at daybreak on the first day of the week they

23:34 [Then Jesus said, "Father, forgive them, they know not what they do."]: this portion of Lk 23:34 does not occur in the oldest papyrus manuscript of Luke and in other early Greek manuscripts and ancient versions of wide geographical distribution.

23:39–43 This episode is recounted only in this gospel. The penitent sinner receives salvation through the crucified Jesus. Jesus' words to the penitent thief reveal Luke's understanding that the destiny of the Christian is "to be with Jesus."

23:44 Noon . . . three in the afternoon: literally, the sixth and ninth hours. See note on Mk 15:25.

23:47 This man was innocent: or, "This man was righteous."

24:1–53 The resurrection narrative in Luke consists of five sections: (1) the women at the empty tomb (Lk 23:56b–24:12); (2) the appearance to the two disciples on the way to Emmaus (Lk 24:13–35); (3) the appearance to the disciples in Jerusalem (Lk 24:36–43); (4) Jesus' final instructions (Lk 24:44–49); (5) the ascension (Lk 24:50–53). In Luke, all the resurrection appearances take place in and around Jerusalem; moreover, they are all recounted as having taken place on Easter Sunday. A consistent theme throughout

d: Mt 27:33–44; Mk 15:22–32; Jn 19:17–24. *e:* 22:37; Is 53:12. *f:* Nm 15:27–31; Ps 22:19; Mt 5:44; Acts 7:60. *g:* Ps 22:8–9. *h:* 4:23. *i:* Ps 69:22; Mt 27:48; Mk 15:36. *j:* 23:4, 14, 22. *k:* 9:27; 23:2, 3, 38. *l:* 2 Cor 12:3; Rev 2:7. *m:* Mt 27:45–56; Mk 15:33–41; Jn 19:25–30. *n:* Am 8:9. *o:* Ex 26:31–33; 36:35. *p:* Ps 31:6; Acts 7:59. *q:* 18:13; Zec 12:10. *r:* 8:1–3; 23:55–56; 24:10; Ps 38:12. *s:* Mt 27:57–61; Mk 15:42–47; Jn 19:38–42; Acts 13:29. *t:* 2:25, 38. *u:* 19:30; Acts 13:29. *v:* 8:2; 23:49; 24:10. *w:* Ex 12:16; 20:10; Dt 5:14. *x:* Mt 28:1–8; Mk 16:1–8; Jn 20:1–17.

took the spices they had prepared and went to the tomb. [2]They found the stone rolled away from the tomb; [3]but when they entered, they did not find the body of the Lord Jesus. [4y]While they were puzzling over this, behold, two men in dazzling garments appeared to them. [5z]They were terrified and bowed their faces to the ground. They said to them, "Why do you seek the living one among the dead? [6*]He is not here, but he has been raised. Remember what he said to you while he was still in Galilee, [7a]that the Son of Man must be handed over to sinners and be crucified, and rise on the third day." [8b]And they remembered his words. [9c*]Then they returned from the tomb and announced all these things to the eleven and to all the others. [10d]The women were Mary Magdalene, Joanna, and Mary the mother of James; the others who accompanied them also told this to the apostles, [11]but their story seemed like nonsense and they did not believe them. [12e*]But Peter got up and ran to the tomb, bent down, and saw the burial cloths alone; then he went home amazed at what had happened.

The Appearance on the Road to Emmaus. [13f*]Now that very day two of them were going to a village seven miles from Jerusalem called Emmaus, [14]and they were conversing about all the things that had occurred. [15]And it happened that while they were conversing and debating, Jesus himself drew near and walked with them, [16g*]but their eyes were prevented from recognizing him. [17]He asked them, "What are you discussing as you walk along?" They stopped, looking downcast. [18]One of them, named Cleopas, said to him in reply, "Are you the only visitor to Jerusalem who does not know of the things that have taken place there in these days?" [19h]And he replied to them, "What sort of things?" They said to him, "The things that happened to Jesus the Nazarene, who was a prophet mighty in deed and word before God and all the people, [20]how our chief priests and rulers both handed him over to a sentence of death and crucified him. [21i]But we were hoping that he would be the one to redeem Israel; and besides all this, it is now the third day since this took place. [22j]Some women from our group, however, have astounded us: they were at the tomb early in the morning [23]and did not find his body; they came back and reported that they had indeed seen a vision of angels who announced that he was alive. [24k]Then some of those with us went to the tomb and found things just as the women had described, but him they did not see." [25l]And he said to them, "Oh, how foolish you are! How slow of heart to believe all that the prophets spoke! [26*]Was it not neces-

the narrative is that the suffering, death, and resurrection of Jesus were accomplished in fulfillment of Old Testament promises and of Jewish hopes (Lk 24:19a, 21, 26–27, 44, 46). In his second volume, Acts, Luke will argue that Christianity is the fulfillment of the hopes of Pharisaic Judaism and its logical development (see Acts 24:10–21).

24:6 He is not here, but he has been raised: this part of the verse is omitted in important representatives of the Western text tradition, but its presence in other text types and the slight difference in wording from Mt 28:6 and Mk 16:6 argue for its retention.

24:9 The women in this gospel do not flee from the tomb and tell no one, as in Mk 16:8 but return and tell the disciples about their experience. The initial reaction to the testimony of the women is disbelief (Lk 24:11).

24:12 This verse is missing from the Western textual tradition but is found in the best and oldest manuscripts of other text types.

24:13–35 This episode focuses on the interpretation of scripture by the risen Jesus and the recognition of him in the breaking of the bread. The references to the quotations of scripture and explanation of it (Lk 24:25–27), the kerygmatic proclamation (Lk 24:34), and the liturgical gesture (Lk 24:30) suggest that the episode is primarily catechetical and liturgical rather than apologetic.

24:13 Seven miles: literally, "sixty stades." A stade was 607 feet. Some manuscripts read "160 stades" or more than eighteen miles. The exact location of Emmaus is disputed.

24:16 A consistent feature of the resurrection stories is that the risen Jesus was different and initially unrecognizable (Lk 24:37; Mk 16:12; Jn 20:14; 21:4).

24:26 That the Messiah should suffer . . .: Luke is the only New Testament writer to speak explicitly of a suffering Messiah (Lk 24:26, 46; Acts 3:18; 17:3; 26:23). The idea of a suffering Messiah is not found in the Old Testament or in other Jewish literature prior to the New Testament period, although the idea is hinted at in Mk 8:31–33. See notes on Mt 26:63 and 26:67–68.

y: 2 Mc 3:26; Acts 1:10. *z:* Acts 2:9. *a:* 9:22, 44; 17:25; 18:32–33; Mt 16:21; 17:22–23; Mk 9:31; Acts 17:3. *b:* Jn 2:22. *c:* Mk 16:10–11; Jn 20:18. *d:* 8:2–3; Mk 16:9. *e:* Jn 20:3–7. *f:* Mk 16:12–13. *g:* Jn 20:14; 21:4. *h:* Mt 2:23; 21:11; Acts 2:22. *i:* 1:54, 68; 2:38. *j:* 24:1–11; Mt 28:1–8; Mk 16:1–8. *k:* Jn 20:3–10. *l:* 9:22; 18:31; 24:44; Acts 3:24; 17:3.

sary that the Messiah should suffer these
things and enter into his glory?" [27m]Then beginning with Moses and all the prophets, he
interpreted to them what referred to him in
all the scriptures. [28]As they approached the
village to which they were going, he gave
the impression that he was going on farther.
[29]But they urged him, "Stay with us, for it is
nearly evening and the day is almost over."
So he went in to stay with them. [30]And it
happened that, while he was with them at
table, he took bread, said the blessing, broke
it, and gave it to them. [31]With that their eyes
were opened and they recognized him, but
he vanished from their sight. [32]Then they
said to each other, "Were not our hearts
burning [within us] while he spoke to us on
the way and opened the scriptures to us?"
[33]So they set out at once and returned to
Jerusalem where they found gathered together the eleven and those with them
[34n]who were saying, "The Lord has truly
been raised and has appeared to Simon!"
[35]Then the two recounted what had taken
place on the way and how he was made
known to them in the breaking of the bread.

The Appearance to the Disciples in Jerusalem. [36o p*]While they were still speaking about this, he stood in their midst and
said to them, "Peace be with you." [37q]But
they were startled and terrified and thought
that they were seeing a ghost. [38]Then he said
to them, "Why are you troubled? And why do
questions arise in your hearts? [39*]Look at my
hands and my feet, that it is I myself. Touch
me and see, because a ghost does not have
flesh and bones as you can see I have."
[40r]And as he said this, he showed them his
hands and his feet. [41]While they were still in-
credulous for joy and were amazed, he asked
them, "Have you anything here to eat?"
[42s]They gave him a piece of baked fish; [43]he
took it and ate it in front of them.

[44t]He said to them, "These are my words
that I spoke to you while I was still with you,
that everything written about me in the law
of Moses and in the prophets and psalms
must be fulfilled." [45u]Then he opened their
minds to understand the scriptures. [46v*]And
he said to them, "Thus it is written that the
Messiah would suffer and rise from the dead
on the third day [47w]and that repentance, for
the forgiveness of sins, would be preached in
his name to all the nations, beginning from
Jerusalem. [48x]You are witnesses of these
things. [49y*]And [behold] I am sending the
promise of my Father upon you; but stay in
the city until you are clothed with power
from on high."

The Ascension. [50z*]Then he led them
[out] as far as Bethany, raised his hands, and
blessed them. [51]As he blessed them he parted
from them and was taken up to heaven.
[52a]They did him homage and then returned to
Jerusalem with great joy, [53*]and they were
continually in the temple praising God.

24:36–43, 44–49 The Gospel of Luke, like each of the other gospels (Mt 28:16–20; Mk 16:14–15; Jn 20:19–23), focuses on an important appearance of Jesus to the Twelve in which they are commissioned for their future ministry. As in Lk 24:6, 12, so in Lk 24:36, 40 there are omissions in the Western text.

24:39–42 The apologetic purpose of this story is evident in the concern with the physical details and the report that Jesus ate food.

24:46 See note on Lk 24:26.

24:49 The promise of my Father: i.e., the gift of the holy Spirit.

24:50–53 Luke brings his story about the time of Jesus to a close with the report of the ascension. He will also begin the story of the time of the church with a recounting of the ascension. In the gospel, Luke recounts the ascension of Jesus on Easter Sunday night, thereby closely associating it with the resurrection. In Acts 1:3, 9–11; 13:31 he historicizes the ascension by speaking of a forty-day period between the resurrection and the ascension. The Western text omits some phrases in Lk 24:51, 52 perhaps to avoid any chronological conflict with Acts 1 about the time of the ascension.

24:53 The Gospel of Luke ends as it began (Lk 1:9), in the Jerusalem temple.

---

m: 24:44; Dt 18:15; Ps 22:1–18; Is 53; 1 Pt 1:10–11. *n:* 1 Cor 15:4–5. *o:* Mk 16:14–19; Jn 20:19–20. *p:* 1 Cor 15:5. *q:* Mt 14:26. *r:* Jn 21:5, 9–10, 13. *s:* Acts 10:41. *t:* 18:31; 24:27; Mt 16:21; Jn 5:39, 46. *u:* Jn 20:9. *v:* 9:22; Is 53; Hos 6:2. *w:* Mt 3:2; 28:19–20; Mk 16:15–16; Acts 10:41. *x:* Acts 1:8. *y:* Jn 14:26; Acts 1:4; 2:3–4. *z:* Mk 16:19; Acts 1:9–11. *a:* Acts 1:12.

See RG 412–23

The Gospel According to John

The Gospel according to John is quite different in character from the three synoptic gospels. It is highly literary and symbolic. It does not follow the same order or reproduce the same stories as the synoptic gospels. To a much greater degree, it is the product of a developed theological reflection and grows out of a different circle and tradition. It was probably written in the 90s of the first century.

The Gospel of John begins with a magnificent prologue, which states many of the major themes and motifs of the gospel, much as an overture does for a musical work. The prologue proclaims Jesus as the preexistent and incarnate Word of God who has revealed the Father to us. The rest of the first chapter forms the introduction to the gospel proper and consists of the Baptist's testimony about Jesus (there is no baptism of Jesus in this gospel—John simply points him out as the Lamb of God), followed by stories of the call of the first disciples, in which various titles predicated of Jesus in the early church are presented.

The gospel narrative contains a series of "signs"—the gospel's word for the wondrous deeds of Jesus. The author is primarily interested in the significance of these deeds, and so interprets them for the reader by various reflections, narratives, and discourses. The first sign is the transformation of water into wine at Cana (Jn 2:1–11); this represents the replacement of the Jewish ceremonial washings and symbolizes the entire creative and transforming work of Jesus. The second sign, the cure of the royal official's son (Jn 4:46–54) simply by the word of Jesus at a distance, signifies the power of Jesus' life-giving word. The same theme is further developed by other signs, probably for a total of seven. The third sign, the cure of the paralytic at the pool with five porticoes in chap. 5, continues the theme of water offering newness of life. In the preceding chapter, to the woman at the well in Samaria Jesus had offered living water springing up to eternal life, a symbol of the revelation that Jesus brings; here Jesus' life-giving word replaces the water of the pool that failed to bring life. Jn 6 contains two signs, the multiplication of loaves and the walking on the waters of the Sea of Galilee. These signs are connected much as the manna and the crossing of the Red Sea are in the Passover narrative and symbolize a new exodus. The multiplication of the loaves is interpreted for the reader by the discourse that follows, where the bread of life is used first as a figure for the revelation of God in Jesus and then for the Eucharist. After a series of dialogues reflecting Jesus' debates with the Jewish authorities at the Feast of Tabernacles in Jn 7; 8, the sixth sign is presented in Jn 9, the sign of the young man born blind. This is a narrative illustration of the theme of conflict in the preceding two chapters; it proclaims the triumph of light over darkness, as Jesus is presented as the Light of the world. This is interpreted by a narrative of controversy between the Pharisees and the young man who had been given his sight by Jesus, ending with a discussion of spiritual blindness and spelling out the symbolic meaning of the cure. And finally, the seventh sign, the raising of Lazarus in chap. 11, is the climax of signs. Lazarus is presented as a token of the real life that Jesus, the Resurrection and the Life, who will now ironically be put to death because of his gift of life to Lazarus, will give to all who believe in him once he has been raised from the dead.

After the account of the seven signs, the "hour" of Jesus arrives, and the author passes from sign to reality, as he moves into the discourses in the upper room that interpret the meaning of the passion, death, and resurrection narratives that follow. The whole gospel of John is a progressive revelation of the glory of God's only Son, who comes to reveal the Father and then returns in glory to the Father. The author's purpose is clearly expressed in what must have been the original ending of the gospel at the end of Jn 20: "Now Jesus did many other signs in the presence of [his] disciples that are not written in this book. But these are written that you may [come to] believe that Jesus is the Messiah, the Son of God, and that through this belief you may have life in his name."

Critical analysis makes it difficult to accept the idea that the gospel as it now stands was written by one person. Jn 21 seems to have been added after the gospel was completed; it exhibits a Greek style somewhat different from that of the rest of the work. The prologue (Jn 1:1–18) apparently contains an independent hymn, subsequently adapted to serve as a preface to the gospel. Within the gospel itself there are also some inconsistencies, e.g., there are two endings of Jesus' discourse in the upper room (Jn 14:31; 18:1). To solve these problems, scholars have proposed various rearrangements that would produce a smoother order. However, most have come to the conclusion that the inconsistencies were probably produced by subsequent editing in which homogeneous materials were added to a shorter original.

Other difficulties for any theory of eyewitness authorship of the gospel in its present form are presented by its highly developed theology and by certain elements of its literary style. For instance, some of the wondrous deeds of Jesus have been worked into highly effective dramatic scenes (Jn 9); there has been a careful attempt to have these followed by discourses that explain them (Jn 5; 6); and the sayings of Jesus have been oven into long discourses of a quasi-poetic form resembling the speeches of personified Wisdom in the Old Testament.

The polemic between synagogue and church produced bitter and harsh invective, especially regarding the hostility toward Jesus of the authorities—Pharisees and Sadducees—who are combined and referred to frequently as "the Jews" (see note on Jn 1:19). These opponents are even described in Jn 8:44 as springing from their father the devil, whose conduct they imitate in opposing God by rejecting Jesus, whom God has sent. On the other hand, the author of this gospel seems to take pains to show that women are not inferior to men in the Christian community: the woman at the well in Samaria (Jn 4) is presented as a prototype of a missionary (Jn 4:4–42), and the first witness of the resurrection is a woman (Jn 20:11–18).

The final editing of the gospel and arrangement in its present form probably dates from between A.D. 90 and 100. Traditionally, Ephesus has been favored as the place of composition, though many support a location in Syria, perhaps the city of Antioch, while some have suggested other places, including Alexandria.

The principal divisions of the Gospel according to John are the following:

I. Prologue (1:1–18)
II. The Book of Signs (1:19–12:50)
III. The Book of Glory (13:1–20:31)
IV. Epilogue: The Resurrection Appearance in Galilee (21:1–25)

I. Prologue

CHAPTER 1

See RG 415–16

1 a*In the beginning was the Word,
and the Word was with God,
and the Word was God.
2 He was in the beginning with God.
3 b*All things came to be through him,
and without him nothing came to be.
What came to be 4 c through him was life,
and this life was the light of the human race;
5 d*the light shines in the darkness,
and the darkness has not overcome it.

1:1–18 The prologue states the main themes of the gospel: life, light, truth, the world, testimony, and the preexistence of Jesus Christ, the incarnate *Logos*, who reveals God the Father. In origin, it was probably an early Christian hymn. Its closest parallel is in other christological hymns, Col 1:15–20 and Phil 2:6–11. Its core (Jn 1:1–5, 10–11, 14) is poetic in structure, with short phrases linked by "staircase parallelism," in which the last word of one phrase becomes the first word of the next. Prose inserts (at least Jn 1:6–8, 15) deal with John the Baptist.

1:1 In the beginning: also the first words of the Old Testament (Gn 1:1). **Was**: this verb is used three times with different meanings in this verse: existence, relationship, and predication. **The Word** (Greek *logos*): this term combines God's dynamic, creative word (Genesis), personified preexistent Wisdom as the instrument of God's creative activity (Proverbs), and the ultimate intelligibility of reality (Hellenistic philosophy). **With God**: the Greek preposition here connotes communication with another. **Was God**: lack of a definite article with "God" in Greek signifies predication rather than identification.

1:3 What came to be: while the oldest manuscripts have no punctuation here, the corrector of Bodmer Papyrus P^{75}, some manuscripts, and the Ante-Nicene Fathers take this phrase with what follows, as staircase parallelism. Connection with Jn 1:3 reflects fourth-century anti-Arianism.

1:5 The ethical dualism of light and darkness is paralleled in intertestamental literature and in the Dead Sea Scrolls. **Overcome**: "comprehend" is another possible translation, but cf. Jn 12:35; Wis 7:29–30.

a: 10:30; Gn 1:1–5; Jb 28:12–27; Prv 8:22–25; Wis 9:1–2; 1 Jn 1:1–2; Col 1:1, 15; Rev 3:14; 19:13. *b:* Ps 33:9; Wis 9:1; Sir 42:15; 1 Cor 8:6; Col 1:16; Heb 1:2; Rev 3:14. *c:* 5:26; 8:12; 1 Jn 1:2. *d:* 3:19; 8:12; 9:5; 12:35, 46; Wis 7:29–30; 1 Thes 5:4; 1 Jn 2:8.

6e* A man named John was sent from God.
7f* He came for testimony, to testify to the
light, so that all might believe through him.
8g He was not the light, but came to testify to
the light. 9h The true light, which enlightens
everyone, was coming into the world.

10 He was in the world,
and the world came to be through him,
but the world did not know him.
11 * He came to what was his own,
but his own people did not accept him.

12i But to those who did accept him he gave
power to become children of God, to those
who believe in his name, 13j* who were born
not by natural generation nor by human
choice nor by a man's decision but of God.

14 k* And the Word became flesh
and made his dwelling among us,
and we saw his glory,
the glory as of the Father's only Son,
full of grace and truth.

15l* John testified to him and cried out, saying, "This was he of whom I said, 'The one
who is coming after me ranks ahead of me
because he existed before me.' " 16* From his
fullness we have all received, grace in place
of grace, 17m because while the law was
given through Moses, grace and truth came
through Jesus Christ. 18n* No one has ever
seen God. The only Son, God, who is at the
Father's side, has revealed him.

II. The Book of Signs

John the Baptist's Testimony to Himself.

19* And this is the testimony of John. When
the Jews from Jerusalem sent priests and
Levites [to him] to ask him, "Who are

1:6 John was **sent** just as Jesus was "sent" (Jn 4:34) in divine mission. Other references to John the Baptist in this gospel emphasize the differences between them and John's subordinate role.

1:7 Testimony: the testimony theme of John is introduced, which portrays Jesus as if on trial throughout his ministry. All testify to Jesus: John the Baptist, the Samaritan woman, scripture, his works, the crowds, the Spirit, and his disciples.

1:11 What was his own . . . his own people: first a neuter, literally, "his own property/possession" (probably = Israel), then a masculine, "his own people" (the Israelites).

1:13 Believers in Jesus become children of God not through any of the three natural causes mentioned but through God who is the immediate cause of the new spiritual life. **Were born**: the Greek verb can mean "begotten" (by a male) or "born" (from a female or of parents). The variant "he who was begotten," asserting Jesus' virginal conception, is weakly attested in Old Latin and Syriac versions.

1:14 Flesh: the whole person, used probably against docetic tendencies (cf. 1 Jn 4:2; 2 Jn 7). **Made his dwelling**: literally, "pitched his tent/tabernacle." Cf. the tabernacle or tent of meeting that was the place of God's presence among his people (Ex 25:8–9). The incarnate Word is the new mode of God's presence among his people. The Greek verb has the same consonants as the Aramaic word for God's presence (Shekinah). **Glory**: God's visible manifestation of majesty in power, which once filled the tabernacle (Ex 40:34) and the temple (1 Kgs 8:10–11, 27), is now centered in Jesus. **Only Son**: Greek, *monogenēs*, but see note on Jn 1:18. **Grace and truth**: these words may represent two Old Testament terms describing Yahweh in covenant relationship with Israel (cf. Ex 34:6), thus God's "love" and "fidelity." The Word shares Yahweh's covenant qualities.

1:15 This verse, interrupting Jn 1:14, 16 seems drawn from Jn 1:30.

1:16 Grace in place of grace: replacement of the Old Covenant with the New (cf. Jn 1:17). Other possible translations are "grace upon grace" (accumulation) and "grace for grace" (correspondence).

1:18 The only Son, God: while the vast majority of later textual witnesses have another reading, "the Son, the only one" or "the only Son," the translation above follows the best and earliest manuscripts, *monogenēs theos*, but takes the first term to mean not just "Only One" but to include a filial relationship with the Father, as at Lk 9:38 ("only child") or Heb 11:17 ("only son") and as translated at Jn 1:14. The Logos is thus "only Son" and God but not Father/God.

1:19–51 The testimony of John the Baptist about the Messiah and Jesus' self-revelation to the first disciples. This section constitutes the introduction to the gospel proper and is connected with the prose inserts in the prologue. It develops the major theme of testimony in four scenes: John's negative testimony about himself; his positive testimony about Jesus; the revelation of Jesus to Andrew and Peter; the revelation of Jesus to Philip and Nathanael.

1:19 The Jews: throughout most of the gospel, the "Jews" does not refer to the Jewish people as such but to the hostile authorities, both Pharisees and Sadducees, particularly in Jerusalem, who refuse to believe in Jesus. The usage reflects the atmosphere, at the end of the first century, of polemics between church and synagogue, or possibly it refers to Jews as representative of a hostile world (Jn 1:10–11).

e: Mt 3:1; Mk 1:4; Lk 3:2–3. *f:* 1:19–34; 5:33. *g:* 5:35. *h:* 3:19; 8:12; 9:39; 12:46. *i:* 3:11–12; 5:43–44; 12:46–50; Gal 3:26; 4:6–7; Eph 1:5; 1 Jn 3:2. *j:* 3:5–6. *k:* Ex 16:10; 24:17; 25:8–9; 33:22; 34:6; Sir 24:4, 8; Is 60:1; Ez 43:7; Jl 4:17; Heb 2:14; 1 Jn 1:2; 4:2; 2 Jn 7. *l:* 1:30; 3:27–30. *m:* 7:19; Ex 31:18; 34:28. *n:* 5:37; 6:46; Ex 33:20; Jgs 13:21–22; 1 Tm 6:16; 1 Jn 4:12.

you?” 20o*he admitted and did not deny it,
but admitted, “I am not the Messiah.”
21p*So they asked him, “What are you
then? Are you Elijah?” And he said, “I am
not.” “Are you the Prophet?” He answered,
“No.” 22So they said to him, “Who are you,
so we can give an answer to those who sent
us? What do you have to say for yourself?”
23q*He said:

“I am ‘the voice of one crying out in the
desert,
“Make straight the way of the Lord,” ’

as Isaiah the prophet said.” 24*Some Pharisees were also sent. 25rThey asked him,
“Why then do you baptize if you are not the
Messiah or Elijah or the Prophet?” 26s*John
answered them, “I baptize with water; but
there is one among you whom you do not
recognize, 27the one who is coming after me,
whose sandal strap I am not worthy to untie.” 28*This happened in Bethany across the
Jordan, where John was baptizing.

John the Baptist’s Testimony to Jesus.
29t*The next day he saw Jesus coming toward him and said, “Behold, the Lamb of
God, who takes away the sin of the world.
30u*He is the one of whom I said, ‘A man is
coming after me who ranks ahead of me because he existed before me.’ 31*I did not
know him, but the reason why I came baptizing with water was that he might be made
known to Israel.” 32v*John testified further,
saying, “I saw the Spirit come down like a
dove from the sky and remain upon him. 33wI
did not know him, but the one who sent me
to baptize with water told me, ‘On
whomever you see the Spirit come down and
remain, he is the one who will baptize with
the holy Spirit.’ 34x*Now I have seen and testified that he is the Son of God.”

The First Disciples. 35yThe next day John
was there again with two of his disciples,
36*and as he watched Jesus walk by, he said,
“Behold, the Lamb of God.” 37*The two disciples heard what he said and followed
Jesus. 38Jesus turned and saw them following him and said to them, “What are you
looking for?” They said to him, “Rabbi”
(which translated means Teacher), “where

1:20 Messiah: the anointed agent of Yahweh, usually considered to be of Davidic descent. See further the note on Jn 1:41.

1:21 Elijah: the Baptist did not claim to be Elijah returned to earth (cf. Mal 3:19; Mt 11:14). **The Prophet**: probably the prophet like Moses (Dt 18:15; cf. Acts 3:22).

1:23 This is a repunctuation and reinterpretation (as in the synoptic gospels and Septuagint) of the Hebrew text of Is 40:3 which reads, “A voice cries out: In the desert prepare the way of the Lord.”

1:24 Some Pharisees: other translations, such as “Now they had been sent from the Pharisees,” misunderstand the grammatical construction. This is a different group from that in Jn 1:19; the priests and Levites would have been Sadducees, not Pharisees.

1:26 I baptize with water: the synoptics add “but he will baptize you with the holy Spirit” (Mk 1:8) or “. . . holy Spirit and fire” (Mt 3:11; Lk 3:16). John’s emphasis is on purification and preparation for a better baptism.

1:28 Bethany across the Jordan: site unknown. Another reading is “Bethabara.”

1:29 The Lamb of God: the background for this title may be the victorious apocalyptic lamb who would destroy evil in the world (Rev 5–7; 17:14); the paschal lamb, whose blood saved Israel (Ex 12); and/or the suffering servant led like a lamb to the slaughter as a sin-offering (Is 53:7, 10).

1:30 He existed before me: possibly as Elijah (to come, Jn 1:27); for the evangelist and his audience, Jesus’ preexistence would be implied (see note on Jn 1:1).

1:31 I did not know him: this gospel shows no knowledge of the tradition (Lk 1) about the kinship of Jesus and John the Baptist. **The reason why I came baptizing with water**: in this gospel, John’s baptism is not connected with forgiveness of sins; its purpose is revelatory, that Jesus may be made known to Israel.

1:32 Like a dove: a symbol of the new creation (Gn 8:8) or the community of Israel (Hos 11:11). **Remain**: the first use of a favorite verb in John, emphasizing the permanency of the relationship between Father and Son (as here) and between the Son and the Christian. Jesus is the permanent bearer of the Spirit.

1:34 The Son of God: this reading is supported by good Greek manuscripts, including the Chester Beatty and Bodmer Papyri and the Vatican Codex, but is suspect because it harmonizes this passage with the synoptic version: “This is my beloved Son” (Mt 3:17; Mk 1:11; Lk 3:22). The poorly attested alternate reading, “God’s chosen One,” is probably a reference to the Servant of Yahweh (Is 42:1).

1:36 John the Baptist’s testimony makes his disciples’ following of Jesus plausible.

1:37 The two disciples: Andrew (Jn 1:40) and, traditionally, John, son of Zebedee (see note on Jn 13:23).

o: 3:28; Lk 3:15; Acts 13:25. *p:* Dt 18:15, 18; 2 Kgs 2:11; Sir 48:10; Mal 3:1, 23; Mt 11:14; 17:11–13; Mk 9:13; Acts 3:22. *q:* Is 40:3; Mt 3:3; Mk 1:2; Lk 3:4. *r:* Ez 36:25; Zec 13:1; Mt 16:14. *s:* Mt 3:11; Mk 1:7–8; Lk 3:16; Acts 13:25. *t:* 1:36; Ex 12; Is 53:7; Rev 5–7; 17:14. *u:* 1:15; Mt 3:11; Mk 1:7; Lk 3:16. *v:* Sg 5:2; Is 11:2; Hos 11:11; Mt 3:16; Mk 1:10; Lk 3:21–22. *w:* Is 42:1; Mt 3:11; Mk 1:8; Lk 3:16. *x:* Is 42:1; Mt 3:17; Mk 1:11; Lk 9:35. *y:* Mt 4:18–22; Mk 1:16–20; Lk 5:1–11.

are you staying?" [39*]He said to them, "Come, and you will see." So they went and saw where he was staying, and they stayed with him that day. It was about four in the afternoon. [40]Andrew, the brother of Simon Peter, was one of the two who heard John and followed Jesus. [41z*]He first found his own brother Simon and told him, "We have found the Messiah" (which is translated Anointed). [42a*]Then he brought him to Jesus. Jesus looked at him and said, "You are Simon the son of John; you will be called Cephas" (which is translated Peter).

[43*]The next day he decided to go to Galilee, and he found Philip. And Jesus said to him, "Follow me." [44]Now Philip was from Bethsaida, the town of Andrew and Peter. [45b]Philip found Nathanael and told him, "We have found the one about whom Moses wrote in the law, and also the prophets, Jesus son of Joseph, from Nazareth." [46]But Nathanael said to him, "Can anything good come from Nazareth?" Philip said to him, "Come and see." [47*]Jesus saw Nathanael coming toward him and said of him, "Here is a true Israelite. There is no duplicity in him." [48c*]Nathanael said to him, "How do you know me?" Jesus answered and said to him, "Before Philip called you, I saw you under the fig tree." [49d*]Nathanael answered him, "Rabbi, you are the Son of God; you are the King of Israel." [50*]Jesus answered and said to him, "Do you believe because I told you that I saw you under the fig tree? You will see greater things than this." [51e*]And he said to him, "Amen, amen, I say to you, you will see the sky opened and the angels of God ascending and descending on the Son of Man."

CHAPTER 2

See RG 416–17

The Wedding at Cana. [1f*]On the third day there was a wedding in Cana in Galilee, and the mother of Jesus was there. [2]Jesus and his disciples were also invited to the wedding. [3]When the wine ran short, the mother of Jesus said to him, "They have no wine." [4g*][And] Jesus said to her, "Woman, how does your concern affect me? My hour

1:39 Four in the afternoon: literally, the tenth hour, from sunrise, in the Roman calculation of time. Some suggest that the next day, beginning at sunset, was the sabbath; they would have stayed with Jesus to avoid travel on it.

1:41 Messiah: the Hebrew word *māšîaḥ*, "anointed one" (see note on Lk 2:11), appears in Greek as the transliterated *messias* only here and in Jn 4:25. Elsewhere the Greek translation *christos* is used.

1:42 Simon, the son of John: in Mt 16:17, Simon is called **Bariona**, "son of Jonah," a different tradition for the name of Simon's father. **Cephas**: in Aramaic = the Rock; cf. Mt 16:18. Neither the Greek equivalent **Petros** nor, with one isolated exception, **Cephas** is attested as a personal name before Christian times.

1:43 He: grammatically, could be Peter, but logically is probably Jesus.

1:47 A true Israelite. There is no duplicity in him: Jacob was the first to bear the name "Israel" (Gn 32:29), but Jacob was a man of duplicity (Gn 27:35–36).

1:48 Under the fig tree: a symbol of messianic peace (cf. Mi 4:4; Zec 3:10).

1:49 Son of God: this title is used in the Old Testament, among other ways, as a title of adoption for the Davidic king (2 Sm 7:14; Ps 2:7; 89:27), and thus here, with **King of Israel**, in a messianic sense. For the evangelist, Son of God also points to Jesus' divinity (cf. Jn 20:28).

1:50 Possibly a statement: "You [singular] believe because I saw you under the fig tree."

1:51 The double "Amen" is characteristic of John. **You** is plural in Greek. The allusion is to Jacob's ladder (Gn 28:12).

2:1–6:71 Signs revealing Jesus as the Messiah to all Israel. "Sign" (*sēmeion*) is John's symbolic term for Jesus' wondrous deeds (see Introduction). The Old Testament background lies in the Exodus story (cf. Dt 11:3; 29:2). John is interested primarily in what the *sēmeia* signify: God's intervention in human history in a new way through Jesus.

2:1–11 The first sign. This story of replacement of Jewish ceremonial washings (Jn 2:6) presents the initial revelation about Jesus at the outset of his ministry. He manifests his glory; the disciples believe. There is no synoptic parallel.

2:1 Cana: unknown from the Old Testament. **The mother of Jesus**: she is never named in John.

2:4 This verse may seek to show that Jesus did not work miracles to help his family and friends, as in the apocryphal gospels. **Woman**: a normal, polite form of address, but unattested in reference to one's mother. Cf. also Jn 19:26. **How does your concern affect me?**: literally, "What is this to me and to you?"—a Hebrew expression of either hostility (Jgs 11:12; 2 Chr 35:21; 1 Kgs 17:18) or denial of common interest (Hos 14:9; 2 Kgs 3:13). Cf. Mk 1:24; 5:7 used by demons to Jesus. **My hour has not yet come**: the translation as a question ("Has not my hour now come?"), while preferable grammatically and supported by Greek Fathers, seems unlikely from a comparison with Jn 7:6, 30. The "hour" is that of Jesus' passion, death, resurrection, and ascension (Jn 13:1).

z: 4:25. *a:* Mt 16:18; Mk 3:16. *b:* 21:2. *c:* Mi 4:4; Zec 3:10. *d:* 12:13; Ex 4:22; Dt 14:1; 2 Sm 7:14; Jb 1:6; 2:1; 38:7; Ps 2:7; 29:1; 89:27; Wis 2:18; Sir 4:10; Dn 3:92; Hos 11:1; Mt 14:33; 16:16; Mk 13:32. *e:* Gn 28:10–17; Dn 7:13. *f:* 4:46; Jgs 14:12; Tb 11:8. *g:* 7:30; 8:20; 12:23; 13:1; Jgs 11:12; 1 Kgs 17:18; 2 Kgs 3:13; 2 Chr 35:21; Hos 14:9; Mk 1:24; 5:7; 7:30; 8:20; 12:23; 13:1.

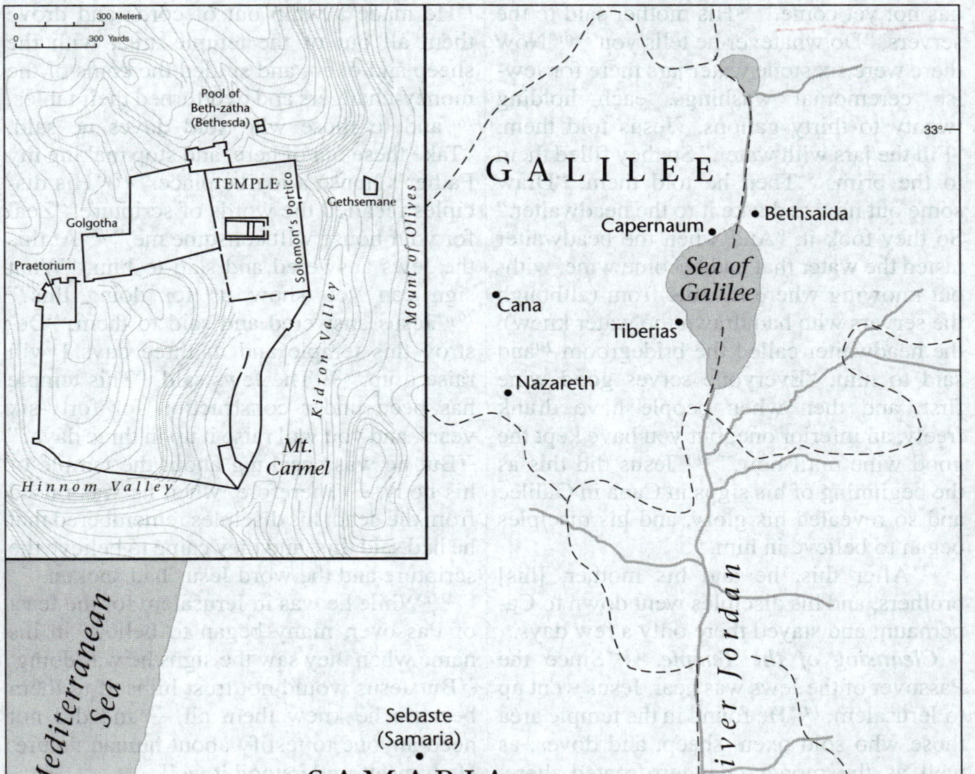

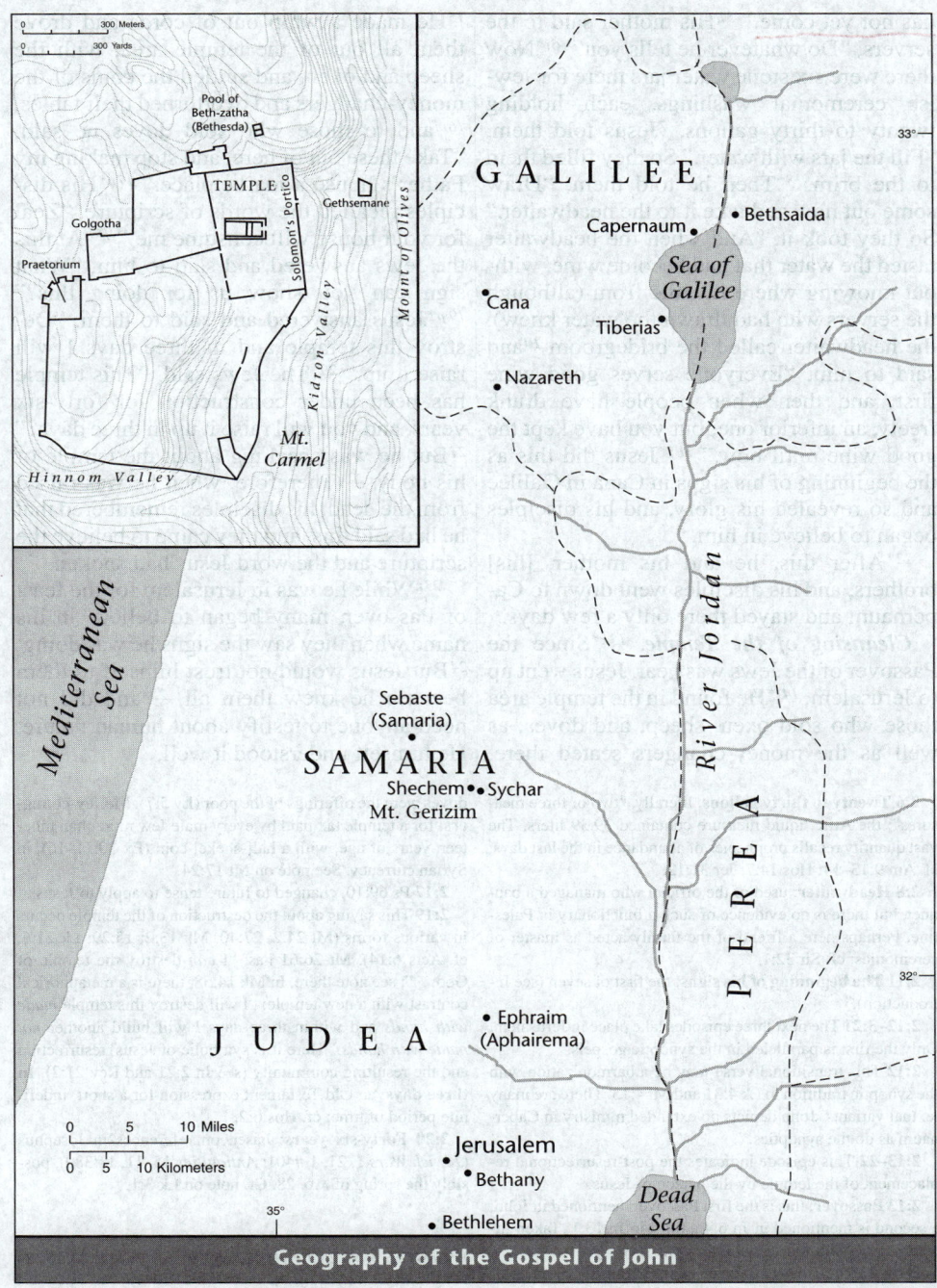

Geography of the Gospel of John

has not yet come." [5h]His mother said to the servers, "Do whatever he tells you." [6i*]Now there were six stone water jars there for Jewish ceremonial washings, each holding twenty to thirty gallons. [7]Jesus told them, "Fill the jars with water." So they filled them to the brim. [8*]Then he told them, "Draw some out now and take it to the headwaiter." So they took it. [9]And when the headwaiter tasted the water that had become wine, without knowing where it came from (although the servers who had drawn the water knew), the headwaiter called the bridegroom [10]and said to him, "Everyone serves good wine first, and then when people have drunk freely, an inferior one; but you have kept the good wine until now." [11j*]Jesus did this as the beginning of his signs in Cana in Galilee and so revealed his glory, and his disciples began to believe in him.

[12*]After this, he and his mother, [his] brothers, and his disciples went down to Capernaum and stayed there only a few days.

Cleansing of the Temple. [13k*]Since the Passover of the Jews was near, Jesus went up to Jerusalem. [14l*]He found in the temple area those who sold oxen, sheep, and doves, as well as the money-changers seated there. [15]He made a whip out of cords and drove them all out of the temple area, with the sheep and oxen, and spilled the coins of the money-changers and overturned their tables, [16m]and to those who sold doves he said, "Take these out of here, and stop making my Father's house a marketplace." [17n*]His disciples recalled the words of scripture, "Zeal for your house will consume me." [18o]At this the Jews answered and said to him, "What sign can you show us for doing this?" [19p*]Jesus answered and said to them, "Destroy this temple and in three days I will raise it up." [20*]The Jews said, "This temple has been under construction for forty-six years, and you will raise it up in three days?" [21]But he was speaking about the temple of his body. [22q]Therefore, when he was raised from the dead, his disciples remembered that he had said this, and they came to believe the scripture and the word Jesus had spoken.

[23r]While he was in Jerusalem for the feast of Passover, many began to believe in his name when they saw the signs he was doing. [24]But Jesus would not trust himself to them because he knew them all, [25s]and did not need anyone to testify about human nature. He himself understood it well.

2:6 Twenty to thirty gallons: literally, "two or three measures"; the Attic liquid measure contained 39.39 liters. The vast quantity recalls prophecies of abundance in the last days; cf. Am 9:13–14; Hos 14:7; Jer 31:12.

2:8 Headwaiter: used of the official who managed a banquet, but there is no evidence of such a functionary in Palestine. Perhaps here a friend of the family acted as master of ceremonies; cf. Sir 32:1.

2:11 The beginning of his signs: the first of seven (see Introduction).

2:12–3:21 The next three episodes take place in Jerusalem. Only the first is paralleled in the synoptic gospels.

2:12 This transitional verse may be a harmonization with the synoptic tradition in Lk 4:31 and Mt 4:13. There are many textual variants. John depicts no extended ministry in Capernaum as do the synoptics.

2:13–22 This episode indicates the post-resurrectional replacement of the temple by the person of Jesus.

2:13 Passover: this is the first Passover mentioned in John; a second is mentioned in Jn 6:4 a third in Jn 13:1. Taken literally, they point to a ministry of at least two years.

2:14–22 The other gospels place the cleansing of the temple in the last days of Jesus' life (Matthew, on the day Jesus entered Jerusalem; Mark, on the next day). The order of events in the gospel narratives is often determined by theological motives rather than by chronological data.

2:14 Oxen, sheep, and doves: intended for sacrifice. The doves were the offerings of the poor (Lv 5:7). **Money-changers**: for a temple tax paid by every male Jew more than nineteen years of age, with a half-shekel coin (Ex 30:11–16), in Syrian currency. See note on Mt 17:24.

2:17 Ps 69:10, changed to future tense to apply to Jesus.

2:19 This saying about the destruction of the temple occurs in various forms (Mt 24:2; 27:40; Mk 13:2; 15:29; Lk 21:6; cf. Acts 6:14). Mt 26:61 has: "I *can* destroy the temple of God. . ."; see note there. In Mk 14:58, there is a metaphorical contrast with a new temple: "I will destroy this temple *made with hands* and within three days I will build another *not made with hands*." Here it is symbolic of Jesus' resurrection and the resulting community (see Jn 2:21 and Rev 21:2). **In three days**: an Old Testament expression for a short, indefinite period of time; cf. Hos 6:2.

2:20 Forty-six years: based on references in Josephus (*Jewish Wars* 1, 21, 1 #401; *Antiquities* 15, 11, 1 #380), possibly the spring of A.D. 28. Cf. note on Lk 3:1.

h: Gn 41:55. *i:* 3:25; Lv 11:33; Am 9:13–14; Mt 15:2; 23:25–26; Mk 7:2–4; Lk 11:38. *j:* 4:54. *k:* Mt 21:12–13; Mk 11:15–17; Lk 19:45–46. *l:* Ex 30:11–16; Lv 5:7. *m:* Zec 14:21. *n:* Ps 69:9. *o:* 6:30. *p:* Mt 24:2; 26:61; 27:40; Mk 13:2; 14:58; 15:29; Lk 21:6; Acts 6:14. *q:* 5:39; 12:16; 14:26; 20:9; Mt 12:6; Lk 24:6–8; Rev 21:22. *r:* 4:45. *s:* 1 Kgs 8:39; Ps 33:15; 94:11; Sir 42:18; Jer 17:10; 20:12.

anothen

CHAPTER 3

See RG 417–18

Nicodemus. [1t*]Now there was a Pharisee named Nicodemus, a ruler of the Jews. [2u]He came to Jesus at night and said to him, "Rabbi, we know that you are a teacher who has come from God, for no one can do these signs that you are doing unless God is with him." [3*]Jesus answered and said to him, "Amen, amen, I say to you, no one can see the kingdom of God without being born from above." [4v]Nicodemus said to him, "How can a person once grown old be born again? Surely he cannot reenter his mother's womb and be born again, can he?" [5w]Jesus answered, "Amen, amen, I say to you, no one can enter the kingdom of God without being born of water and Spirit. [6x]What is born of flesh is flesh and what is born of spirit is spirit. [7]Do not be amazed that I told you, 'You must be born from above.' [8y*]The wind blows where it wills, and you can hear the sound it makes, but you do not know where it comes from or where it goes; so it is with everyone who is born of the Spirit." [9]Nicodemus answered and said to him, "How can this happen?" [10]Jesus answered and said to him, "You are the teacher of Israel and you do not understand this? [11z]Amen, amen, I say to you, we speak of what we know and we testify to what we have seen, but you people do not accept our testimony. [12a]If I tell you about earthly things and you do not believe, how will you believe if I tell you about heavenly things? [13b]No one has gone up to heaven except the one who has come down from heaven, the Son of Man. [14c*]And just as Moses lifted up the serpent in the desert, so must the Son of Man be lifted up, [15*]so that everyone who believes in him may have eternal life."

[16d*]For God so loved the world that he gave his only Son, so that everyone who believes in him might not perish but might have eternal life. [17e*]For God did not send his Son into the world to condemn the world, but that the world might be saved through him. [18f]Whoever believes in him will not be condemned, but whoever does not believe has already been condemned, because he has not believed in the name of the only Son of God. [19g*]And this is the verdict, that the light came into the world, but people preferred darkness to light, because their works were evil. [20h]For everyone who does wicked things hates the light and does not come toward the light, so that his works might not be exposed. [21i]But whoever lives the truth comes to the light, so that his works may be clearly seen as done in God.

Final Witness of the Baptist. [22j*]After this, Jesus and his disciples went into the region of

3:1–21 Jesus instructs Nicodemus on the necessity of a new birth from above. This scene in Jerusalem at Passover exemplifies the faith engendered by signs (Jn 2:23). It continues the self-manifestation of Jesus in Jerusalem begun in Jn 2. This is the first of the Johannine discourses, shifting from dialogue to monologue (Jn 3:11–15) to reflection of the evangelist (Jn 3:16–21). The shift from singular through Jn 3:10 to plural in Jn 3:11 may reflect the early church's controversy with the Jews.

3:1 A ruler of the Jews: most likely a member of the Jewish council, the Sanhedrin; see note on Mk 8:31.

3:3 Born: see note on Jn 1:13. **From above**: the Greek adverb *anōthen* means both "from above" and "again." Jesus means "from above" (see Jn 3:31) but Nicodemus misunderstands it as "again." This misunderstanding serves as a springboard for further instruction.

3:8 Wind: the Greek word *pneuma* (as well as the Hebrew *rûah*) means both "wind" and "spirit." In the play on the double meaning, "wind" is primary.

3:14 Lifted up: in Nm 21:9 Moses simply "mounted" a serpent upon a pole. John here substitutes a verb implying glorification. Jesus, exalted to glory at his cross and resurrection, represents healing for all.

3:15 Eternal life: used here for the first time in John, this term stresses quality of life rather than duration.

3:16 Gave: as a gift in the incarnation, and also "over to death" in the crucifixion; cf. Rom 8:32.

3:17–19 Condemn: the Greek root means both judgment and condemnation. Jesus' purpose is to save, but his coming provokes judgment; some condemn themselves by turning from the light.

3:19 Judgment is not only future but is partially realized here and now.

3:22–26 Jesus' ministry in Judea is only loosely connected with Jn 2:13–3:21; cf. Jn 1:19–36. Perhaps John the Baptist's further testimony was transposed here to give meaning to "water" in Jn 3:5. Jesus is depicted as baptizing (Jn 3:22); contrast Jn 4:2.

t: 7:50–51; 19:39. *u:* 9:4, 16, 33; 10:21; 11:10; 13:30; Mt 22:16; Mk 12:14; Lk 20:21. *v:* 1:13. *w:* 1:32; 7:39; 19:30, 34–35; Is 32:15; 44:3; Ez 36:25–27; Jl 3:1–2. *x:* 6:63; 1 Cor 15:44–50. *y:* Eccl 11:4–5; Acts 2:2–4. *z:* 3:32, 34; 8:14; Mt 11:27. *a:* 6:62–65; Wis 9:16–17; 1 Cor 15:40; 2 Cor 5:1; Phil 2:10; 3:19–20. *b:* 1:18; 6:62; Dn 7:13; Rom 10:6; Eph 4:9. *c:* 8:28; 12:32, 34; Nm 21:4–9; Wis 16:5–7. *d:* 1 Jn 4:9. *e:* 5:22, 30; 8:15–18; 12:47. *f:* 5:24; Mk 16:16. *g:* 1:5, 9–11; 8:12; 9:5. *h:* Jb 24:13–17. *i:* Gn 47:29 LXX; Jos 2:14 LXX; 2 Sm 2:6 LXX; 15:20 LXX; Tb 4:6 LXX; 13:6; Is 26:10 LXX; Mt 5:14–16. *j:* 4:1–2.

Judea, where he spent some time with them baptizing. [23*]John was also baptizing in Aenon near Salim, because there was an abundance of water there, and people came to be baptized, [24k*]for John had not yet been imprisoned. [25*]Now a dispute arose between the disciples of John and a Jew about ceremonial washings. [26l]So they came to John and said to him, "Rabbi, the one who was with you across the Jordan, to whom you testified, here he is baptizing and everyone is coming to him." [27m]John answered and said, "No one can receive anything except what has been given him from heaven. [28n]You yourselves can testify that I said [that] I am not the Messiah, but that I was sent before him. [29o*]The one who has the bride is the bridegroom; the best man, who stands and listens to him, rejoices greatly at the bridegroom's voice. So this joy of mine has been made complete. [30p]He must increase; I must decrease."

The One from Heaven. [31q*]The one who comes from above is above all. The one who is of the earth is earthly and speaks of earthly things. But the one who comes from heaven [is above all]. [32r]He testifies to what he has seen and heard, but no one accepts his testimony. [33s]Whoever does accept his testimony certifies that God is trustworthy. [34*]For the one whom God sent speaks the words of God. He does not ration his gift of the Spirit. [35t]The Father loves the Son and has given everything over to him. [36u]Whoever believes in the Son has eternal life, but whoever disobeys the Son will not see life, but the wrath of God remains upon him.

CHAPTER 4

See RG 417–18

[1*]Now when Jesus learned that the Pharisees had heard that Jesus was making and baptizing more disciples than John [2*](although Jesus himself was not baptizing, just his disciples), [3]he left Judea and returned to Galilee.

The Samaritan Woman. [4*]He had to pass through Samaria. [5v*]So he came to a town of Samaria called Sychar, near the plot of land that Jacob had given to his son Joseph. [6]Jacob's well was there. Jesus, tired from his journey, sat down there at the well. It was about noon.

[7]A woman of Samaria came to draw water. Jesus said to her, "Give me a drink." [8]His disciples had gone into the town to buy food. [9w*]The Samaritan woman said to him, "How can you, a Jew, ask me, a Samaritan woman, for a drink?" (For Jews use nothing in common with Samaritans.) [10x*]Jesus answered and said to her, "If you knew the gift of God and who is saying to you, 'Give me a drink,' you would have asked him and he would have given you living water." [11*][The

3:23 Aenon near Salim: site uncertain, either in the upper Jordan valley or in Samaria.

3:24 A remark probably intended to avoid objections based on a chronology like that of the synoptics (Mt 4:12; Mk 1:14).

3:25 A Jew: some think Jesus is meant. Many manuscripts read "Jews."

3:29 The best man: literally, "the friend of the groom," the *shoshben* of Jewish tradition, who arranged the wedding. Competition between him and the groom would be unthinkable.

3:31–36 It is uncertain whether these are words by the Baptist, Jesus, or the evangelist. They are reflections on the two preceding scenes.

3:34 His gift: of God or to Jesus, perhaps both. This verse echoes Jn 5:8.

4:1–42 Jesus in Samaria. The self-revelation of Jesus continues with his second discourse, on his mission to "half-Jews." It continues the theme of replacement, here with regard to cult (Jn 4:21). Water (Jn 4:7–15) serves as a symbol (as at Cana and in the Nicodemus episode).

4:2 An editorial refinement of Jn 3:22, perhaps directed against followers of John the Baptist who claimed that Jesus imitated him.

4:4 He had to: a theological necessity; geographically, Jews often bypassed Samaria by taking a route across the Jordan.

4:5 Sychar: Jerome identifies this with Shechem, a reading found in Syriac manuscripts.

4:9 Samaritan women were regarded by Jews as ritually impure, and therefore Jews were forbidden to drink from any vessel they had handled.

4:10 Living water: the water of life, i.e., the revelation that Jesus brings; the woman thinks of "flowing water," so much more desirable than stagnant cistern water. On John's device of such misunderstanding, cf. note on Jn 3:3.

4:11 Sir: the Greek *kyrios* means "master" or "lord," as a respectful mode of address for a human being or a deity; cf. Jn 4:19. It is also the word used in the Septuagint for the Hebrew *'adônai*, substituted for the tetragrammaton YHWH.

k: Mt 4:12; 14:3; Mk 1:14; 6:17; Lk 3:20. *l:* 1:26, 32–34, 36. *m:* 19:11; 1 Cor 4:7; 2 Cor 3:5; Heb 5:4. *n:* 1:20–23; Lk 3:15. *o:* 15:11; 17:13; Mt 9:15. *p:* 2 Sm 3:1. *q:* 8:23. *r:* 3:11. *s:* 8:26; 12:44–50; 1 Jn 5:10. *t:* 13:3; Mt 11:27; 28:18; Lk 10:22. *u:* 3:16; 1 Jn 5:13. *v:* Gn 33:18–19; 48:22; Jos 24:32. *w:* Sir 50:25–26; Mt 10:5. *x:* Sir 24:20–21; Is 55:1; Jer 2:13.

woman] said to him, "Sir, you do not even have a bucket and the well is deep; where then can you get this living water? [12y]Are you greater than our father Jacob, who gave us this well and drank from it himself with his children and his flocks?" [13]Jesus answered and said to her, "Everyone who drinks this water will be thirsty again; [14z]but whoever drinks the water I shall give will never thirst; the water I shall give will become in him a spring of water welling up to eternal life." [15]The woman said to him, "Sir, give me this water, so that I may not be thirsty or have to keep coming here to draw water."

[16]Jesus said to her, "Go call your husband and come back." [17]The woman answered and said to him, "I do not have a husband." Jesus answered her, "You are right in saying, 'I do not have a husband.' [18a]For you have had five husbands, and the one you have now is not your husband. What you have said is true." [19b]The woman said to him, "Sir, I can see that you are a prophet. [20c*]Our ancestors worshiped on this mountain; but you people say that the place to worship is in Jerusalem." [21]Jesus said to her, "Believe me, woman, the hour is coming when you will worship the Father neither on this mountain nor in Jerusalem. [22d]You people worship what you do not understand; we worship what we understand, because salvation is from the Jews. [23*]But the hour is coming, and is now here, when true worshipers will worship the Father in Spirit and truth; and indeed the Father seeks such people to worship him. [24e]God is Spirit, and those who worship him must worship in Spirit and truth." [25f*]The woman said to him, "I know that the Messiah is coming, the one called the Anointed; when he comes, he will tell us everything." [26g*]Jesus said to her, "I am he, the one who is speaking with you."

[27*]At that moment his disciples returned, and were amazed that he was talking with a woman, but still no one said, "What are you looking for?" or "Why are you talking with her?" [28]The woman left her water jar and went into the town and said to the people, [29]"Come see a man who told me everything I have done. Could he possibly be the Messiah?" [30]They went out of the town and came to him. [31]Meanwhile, the disciples urged him, "Rabbi, eat." [32]But he said to them, "I have food to eat of which you do not know." [33]So the disciples said to one another, "Could someone have brought him something to eat?" [34h]Jesus said to them, "My food is to do the will of the one who sent me and to finish his work. [35i*]Do you not say, 'In four months the harvest will be here'? I tell you, look up and see the fields ripe for the harvest. [36j*]The reaper is already receiving his payment and gathering crops for eternal life, so that the sower and reaper can rejoice together. [37k]For here the saying is verified that 'One sows and another reaps.' [38]I sent you to reap what you have not worked for; others have done the work, and you are sharing the fruits of their work."

[39*]Many of the Samaritans of that town began to believe in him because of the word of the woman who testified, "He told me everything I have done." [40]When the Samaritans came to him, they invited him to stay with them; and he stayed there two days. [41]Many more began to believe in him be-

4:20 This mountain: Gerizim, on which a temple was erected in the fourth century B.C. by Samaritans to rival Mount Zion in Jerusalem; cf. Dt 27:4 (Mount Ebal = the Jews' term for Gerizim).

4:23 In Spirit and truth: not a reference to an interior worship within one's own spirit. The Spirit is the spirit given by God that reveals truth and enables one to worship God appropriately (Jn 14:16–17). Cf. "born of water and Spirit" (Jn 3:5).

4:25 The expectations of the Samaritans are expressed here in Jewish terminology. They did not expect a messianic king of the house of David but a prophet like Moses (Dt 18:15).

4:26 I am he: it could also be translated "I am," an Old Testament self-designation of Yahweh (Is 43:3, etc.); cf. Jn 6:20; 8:24, 28, 58; 13:19; 18:5–6, 8. See note on Mk 6:50.

4:27 Talking with a woman: a religious and social restriction that Jesus is pictured treating as unimportant.

4:35 'In four months . . . ': probably a proverb; cf. Mt 9:37–38.

4:36 Already: this word may go with the preceding verse rather than with Jn 4:36.

4:39 The woman is presented as a missionary, described in virtually the same words as the disciples are in Jesus' prayer (Jn 17:20).

y: 8:53; Mt 12:41. *z:* 6:35, 58; 7:37–39; Is 44:3; 49:10; Jl 4:18; Rev 7:16; 21:6. *a:* 2 Kgs 17:24–34. *b:* 9:17; Hos 1:3. *c:* Dt 11:29; 27:4; Jos 8:33; Ps 122:1–5. *d:* 2 Kgs 17:27; Ps 76:2–3. *e:* 2 Cor 3:17. *f:* 1:41. *g:* 9:37. *h:* 5:30, 36; 6:38; 9:4; 17:4. *i:* Mt 9:37–38; Lk 10:2; Rev 14:15. *j:* Ps 126:5–6; Am 9:13–14. *k:* Dt 20:6; 28:30; Jb 31:8; Mi 6:15.

cause of his word, [42l]and they said to the woman, "We no longer believe because of your word; for we have heard for ourselves, and we know that this is truly the savior of the world."

Return to Galilee. [43*]After the two days, he left there for Galilee. [44m*]For Jesus himself testified that a prophet has no honor in his native place. [45]When he came into Galilee, the Galileans welcomed him, since they had seen all he had done in Jerusalem at the feast; for they themselves had gone to the feast.

Second Sign at Cana. [46n*]Then he returned to Cana in Galilee, where he had made the water wine. Now there was a royal official whose son was ill in Capernaum. [47]When he heard that Jesus had arrived in Galilee from Judea, he went to him and asked him to come down and heal his son, who was near death. [48o]Jesus said to him, "Unless you people see signs and wonders, you will not believe." [49]The royal official said to him, "Sir, come down before my child dies." [50p]Jesus said to him, "You may go; your son will live." The man believed what Jesus said to him and left. [51]While he was on his way back, his slaves met him and told him that his boy would live. [52]He asked them when he began to recover. They told him, "The fever left him yesterday, about one in the afternoon." [53]The father realized that just at that time Jesus had said to him, "Your son will live," and he and his whole household came to believe. [54q][Now] this was the second sign Jesus did when he came to Galilee from Judea.

CHAPTER 5

See RG 418

Cure on a Sabbath. [1r*]After this, there was a feast of the Jews, and Jesus went up to Jerusalem. [2s*]Now there is in Jerusalem at the Sheep [Gate] a pool called in Hebrew Bethesda, with five porticoes. [3*]In these lay a large number of ill, blind, lame, and crippled. [4]* [5]One man was there who had been ill for thirty-eight years. [6]When Jesus saw him lying there and knew that he had been ill for a long time, he said to him, "Do you want to be well?" [7]The sick man answered him, "Sir, I have no one to put me into the pool when the water is stirred up; while I am on my way, someone else gets down there before me." [8t]Jesus said to him, "Rise, take up your mat, and walk." [9u]Immediately the man became well, took up his mat, and walked.

Now that day was a sabbath. [10v]So the Jews said to the man who was cured, "It is the sabbath, and it is not lawful for you to carry your mat." [11]He answered them, "The man who made me well told me, 'Take up

4:43–54 Jesus' arrival in Cana in Galilee; the second sign. This section introduces another theme, that of the life-giving word of Jesus. It is explicitly linked to the first sign (Jn 2:11). The royal official believes (Jn 4:50). The natural life given his son is a sign of eternal life.

4:44 Probably a reminiscence of a tradition as in Mk 6:4. Cf. Gospel of Thomas 4:31: "No prophet is acceptable in his village, no physician heals those who know him."

4:46–54 The story of the cure of the royal official's son may be a third version of the cure of the centurion's son (Mt 8:5–13) or servant (Lk 7:1–10). Cf. also Mt 15:21–28; Mk 7:24–30.

5:1–47 The self-revelation of Jesus continues in Jerusalem at a feast. The third sign (cf. Jn 2:11; 4:54) is performed, the cure of a paralytic by Jesus' life-giving word. The water of the pool fails to bring life; Jesus' word does.

5:1 The reference in Jn 5:45–46 to Moses suggests that the feast was Pentecost. The connection of that feast with the giving of the law to Moses on Sinai, attested in later Judaism, may already have been made in the first century. The feast could also be Passover (cf. Jn 6:4). John stresses that the day was a sabbath (Jn 5:9).

5:2 There is no noun with **Sheep**. "Gate" is supplied on the grounds that there must have been a gate in the NE wall of the temple area where animals for sacrifice were brought in; cf. Neh 3:1, 32; 12:39. **Hebrew**: more precisely, Aramaic. **Bethesda**: preferred to variants "Be(th)zatha" and "Bethsaida"; *bêt-'eśdatayin* is given as the name of a double pool northeast of the temple area in the Qumran Copper Roll. **Five porticoes**: a pool excavated in Jerusalem actually has five porticoes.

5:3 The Caesarean and Western recensions, followed by the Vulgate, add "waiting for the movement of the water." Apparently an intermittent spring in the pool bubbled up occasionally (see Jn 5:7). This turbulence was believed to cure.

5:4 Toward the end of the second century in the West and among the fourth-century Greek Fathers, an additional verse was known: "For [from time to time] an angel of the Lord used to come down into the pool; and the water was stirred up, so the first one to get in [after the stirring of the water] was healed of whatever disease afflicted him." The angel was a popular explanation of the turbulence and the healing powers attributed to it. This verse is missing from all early Greek

l: 1 Jn 4:14. *m:* Mt 13:57; Mk 6:4; Lk 4:24. *n:* 2:1–11; Mt 8:5–13; 15:21–28; Mk 7:24–30; Lk 7:1–10. *o:* 2:18, 23; Wis 8:8; Mt 12:38; 1 Cor 1:22. *p:* 1 Kgs 17:23. *q:* 2:11. *r:* 6:4. *s:* Neh 3:1, 32; 12:39. *t:* Mt 9:6; Mk 2:11; Lk 5:24; Acts 3:6. *u:* Mk 2:12; Lk 5:25; 9:14. *v:* Ex 20:8; Jer 17:21–27; Mk 3:2; Lk 13:10 / 14:1.

your mat and walk.' " [12]They asked him,
"Who is the man who told you, 'Take it up
and walk'?" [13w]The man who was healed
did not know who it was, for Jesus had
slipped away, since there was a crowd
there. [14x*]After this Jesus found him in the
temple area and said to him, "Look, you are
well; do not sin any more, so that nothing
worse may happen to you." [15]The man went
and told the Jews that Jesus was the one
who had made him well. [16y]Therefore, the
Jews began to persecute Jesus because he
did this on a sabbath. [17z*]But Jesus answered them, "My Father is at work until
now, so I am at work." [18a]For this reason
the Jews tried all the more to kill him, because he not only broke the sabbath but he
also called God his own father, making
himself equal to God.

The Work of the Son. [19b*]Jesus answered
and said to them, "Amen, amen, I say to
you, a son cannot do anything on his own,
but only what he sees his father doing; for
what he does, his son will do also. [20c]For the
Father loves his Son and shows him everything that he himself does, and he will show
him greater works than these, so that you
may be amazed. [21d*]For just as the Father
raises the dead and gives life, so also does
the Son give life to whomever he wishes.
[22e*]Nor does the Father judge anyone, but
he has given all judgment to his Son, [23]so
that all may honor the Son just as they honor
the Father. Whoever does not honor the Son
does not honor the Father who sent him.
[24f]Amen, amen, I say to you, whoever hears
my word and believes in the one who sent
me has eternal life and will not come to condemnation, but has passed from death to
life. [25g]Amen, amen, I say to you, the hour
is coming and is now here when the dead
will hear the voice of the Son of God, and
those who hear will live. [26h]For just as the
Father has life in himself, so also he gave to
his Son the possession of life in himself.
[27i]And he gave him power to exercise judgment, because he is the Son of Man. [28j*]Do
not be amazed at this, because the hour is
coming in which all who are in the tombs
will hear his voice [29k]and will come out,
those who have done good deeds to the resurrection of life, but those who have done
wicked deeds to the resurrection of condemnation.

[30l]"I cannot do anything on my own; I
judge as I hear, and my judgment is just, because I do not seek my own will but the will
of the one who sent me.

Witnesses to Jesus. [31m]"If I testify on my
own behalf, my testimony cannot be verified. [32*]But there is another who testifies on
my behalf, and I know that the testimony he
gives on my behalf is true. [33n]You sent
emissaries to John, and he testified to the
truth. [34o]I do not accept testimony from a
human being, but I say this so that you may

manuscripts and the earliest versions, including the original Vulgate. Its vocabulary is markedly non-Johannine.

5:14 While the cure of the paralytic in Mk 2:1–12 is associated with the forgiveness of sins, Jesus never drew a one-to-one connection between sin and suffering (cf. Jn 9:3; Lk 12:1–5), as did Ez 18:20.

5:17 Sabbath observance (10) was based on God's resting on the seventh day (cf. Gn 2:2–3; Ex 20:11). Philo and some rabbis insisted that God's providence remains active on the sabbath, keeping all things in existence, giving life in birth and taking it away in death. Other rabbis taught that God rested from creating, but not from judging (=ruling, governing). Jesus here claims the same authority to work as the Father, and, in the discourse that follows, the same divine prerogatives: power over life and death (Jn 5:21, 24–26) and judgment (Jn 5:22, 27).

5:19 This proverb or parable is taken from apprenticeship in a trade: the activity of a son is modeled on that of his father. Jesus' dependence on the Father is justification for doing what the Father does.

5:21 Gives life: in the Old Testament, a divine prerogative (Dt 32:39; 1 Sm 2:6; 2 Kgs 5:7; Tb 13:2; Is 26:19; Dn 12:2).

5:22 Judgment: another divine prerogative, often expressed as acquittal or condemnation (Dt 32:36; Ps 43:1).

5:28–29 While Jn 5:19–27 present realized eschatology, Jn 5:28–29 are future eschatology; cf. Dn 12:2.

5:32 Another: likely the Father, who in four different ways gives testimony to Jesus, as indicated in the verse groupings Jn 5:33–34, 36, 37–38, 39–40.

w: Mt 8:18; 13:36; Mk 4:36; 7:17. *x:* 8:11; 9:2; Ez 18:20. *y:* 7:23; Mt 12:8. *z:* Ex 20:11. *a:* 7:1, 25; 8:37, 40; 10:33, 36; 14:28; Gn 3:5–6; Wis 2:16; Mt 26:4; 2 Thes 2:4. *b:* 3:34; 8:26; 12:49; 9:4; 10:30. *c:* 3:35. *d:* 11:25; Dt 32:39; 1 Sm 2:6; 2 Kgs 5:7; Tb 13:2; Wis 16:13; Is 26:19; Dn 7:10, 13; 12:2; Rom 4:17; 2 Cor 1:9. *e:* Acts 10:42; 17:31. *f:* 3:18; 8:51; 1 Jn 3:14. *g:* 5:28; 8:51; 11:25–26; Eph 2:1; 5:14; Rev 3:1. *h:* 1:4; 1 Jn 5:11. *i:* 5:22; Dn 7:13, 22; Mt 25:31; Lk 21:36. *j:* 11:43. *k:* Dn 12:2; Mt 16:27; 25:46; Acts 24:15; 2 Cor 5:10. *l:* 6:38. *m:* 8:13–14, 18. *n:* 1:19–27; Mt 11:10–11. *o:* 1 Jn 5:9.

be saved. [35p*]He was a burning and shining lamp, and for a while you were content to rejoice in his light. [36q]But I have testimony greater than John's. The works that the Father gave me to accomplish, these works that I perform testify on my behalf that the Father has sent me. [37r]Moreover, the Father who sent me has testified on my behalf. But you have never heard his voice nor seen his form, [38s]and you do not have his word remaining in you, because you do not believe in the one whom he has sent. [39t*]You search the scriptures, because you think you have eternal life through them; even they testify on my behalf. [40]But you do not want to come to me to have life.

Unbelief of Jesus' Hearers. [41*]"I do not accept human praise; [42u]moreover, I know that you do not have the love of God in you. [43v]I came in the name of my Father, but you do not accept me; yet if another comes in his own name, you will accept him. [44w]How can you believe, when you accept praise from one another and do not seek the praise that comes from the only God? [45x]Do not think that I will accuse you before the Father: the one who will accuse you is Moses, in whom you have placed your hope. [46y]For if you had believed Moses, you would have believed me, because he wrote about me. [47]But if you do not believe his writings, how will you believe my words?"

CHAPTER 6

See RG 418–19

Multiplication of the Loaves. [1z*]After this, Jesus went across the Sea of Galilee [of Tiberias]. [2]A large crowd followed him, because they saw the signs he was performing on the sick. [3]Jesus went up on the mountain, and there he sat down with his disciples. [4a]The Jewish feast of Passover was near. [5b*]When Jesus raised his eyes and saw that a large crowd was coming to him, he said to Philip, "Where can we buy enough food for them to eat?" [6*]He said this to test him, because he himself knew what he was going to do. [7c*]Philip answered him, "Two hundred days' wages worth of food would not be enough for each of them to have a little [bit]." [8]One of his disciples, Andrew, the brother of Simon Peter, said to him, [9d*]"There is a boy here who has five barley loaves and two fish; but what good are these for so many?" [10e*]Jesus said, "Have the people recline." Now there was a great deal of grass in that place. So the men reclined, about five thousand in number. [11f]Then Jesus took the loaves, gave thanks, and distributed them to those who were reclining, and also as much of the fish as they wanted. [12]When they had had their fill, he said to his disciples, "Gather the fragments left over, so that nothing will be wasted." [13*]So they collected them, and filled twelve wicker baskets with fragments from the five barley

5:35 Lamp: cf. Ps 132:17—"I will place a lamp for my anointed (= David)," and possibly the description of Elijah in Sir 48:1. But only **for a while**, indicating the temporary and subordinate nature of John's mission.

5:39 You search: this may be an imperative: "Search the scriptures, because you think that you have eternal life through them."

5:41 Praise: the same Greek word means "praise" or "honor" (from others) and "glory" (from God). There is a play on this in Jn 5:44.

6:1–15 This story of the multiplication of the loaves is the fourth sign (cf. note on Jn 5:1–47). It is the only miracle story found in all four gospels (occurring twice in Mark and Matthew). See notes on Mt 14:13–21; 15:32–39. John differs on the roles of Philip and Andrew, the proximity of Passover (Jn 6:4), and the allusion to Elisha (see Jn 6:9). The story here symbolizes the food that is really available through Jesus. It connotes a new exodus and has eucharistic overtones.

6:1 [Of Tiberias]: the awkward apposition represents a later name of the Sea of Galilee. It was probably originally a marginal gloss.

6:5 Jesus takes the initiative (in the synoptics, the disciples do), possibly pictured as (cf. Jn 6:14) the new Moses (cf. Nm 11:13).

6:6 Probably the evangelist's comment; in this gospel Jesus is never portrayed as ignorant of anything.

6:7 Days' wages: literally, "denarii"; a Roman denarius is a day's wage in Mt 20:2.

6:9 Barley loaves: the food of the poor. There seems an allusion to the story of Elisha multiplying the barley bread in 2 Kgs 4:42–44.

6:10 Grass: implies springtime, and therefore Passover. **Five thousand**: so Mk 6:39, 44 and parallels.

6:13 Baskets: the word describes the typically Palestinian wicker basket, as in Mk 6:43 and parallels.

p: 1:8; Ps 132:17; Sir 48:1. *q:* 10:25. *r:* 8:18; Dt 4:12, 15; 1 Jn 5:9. *s:* 1 Jn 2:14. *t:* 12:16; 19:28; 20:9; Lk 24:27, 44; 1 Pt 1:10. *u:* 1 Jn 2:15. *v:* Mt 24:5, 24. *w:* 12:43. *x:* Dt 31:26. *y:* 5:39; Dt 18:15; Lk 16:31; 24:44. *z:* Mt 14:13–21; Mk 6:32–44; Lk 9:10–17. *a:* 2:13; 11:55. *b:* Nm 11:13. *c:* Mt 20:2. *d:* 2 Kgs 4:42–44. *e:* Mt 14:21; Mk 6:44. *f:* 21:13.

loaves that had been more than they could
eat. [14g*]When the people saw the sign he had
done, they said, "This is truly the Prophet,
the one who is to come into the world."
[15h]Since Jesus knew that they were going to
come and carry him off to make him king, he
withdrew again to the mountain alone.

Walking on the Water. [16i*]When it was
evening, his disciples went down to the sea,
[17]embarked in a boat, and went across the
sea to Capernaum. It had already grown
dark, and Jesus had not yet come to them.
[18]The sea was stirred up because a strong
wind was blowing. [19j*]When they had
rowed about three or four miles, they saw
Jesus walking on the sea and coming near
the boat, and they began to be afraid. [20*]But
he said to them, "It is I. Do not be afraid."
[21]They wanted to take him into the boat, but
the boat immediately arrived at the shore to
which they were heading.

The Bread of Life Discourse. [22*]The next
day, the crowd that remained across the sea
saw that there had been only one boat there,
and that Jesus had not gone along with his
disciples in the boat, but only his disciples
had left. [23*]Other boats came from Tiberias
near the place where they had eaten the
bread when the Lord gave thanks. [24]When
the crowd saw that neither Jesus nor his disciples were there, they themselves got into
boats and came to Capernaum looking for
Jesus. [25]And when they found him across the
sea they said to him, "Rabbi, when did you
get here?" [26]Jesus answered them and said,
"Amen, amen, I say to you, you are looking
for me not because you saw signs but because you ate the loaves and were filled.
[27k*]Do not work for food that perishes but
for the food that endures for eternal life,
which the Son of Man will give you. For on
him the Father, God, has set his seal." [28]So
they said to him, "What can we do to accomplish the works of God?" [29]Jesus answered and said to them, "This is the work of
God, that you believe in the one he sent."
[30l]So they said to him, "What sign can you
do, that we may see and believe in you?
What can you do? [31m*]Our ancestors ate
manna in the desert, as it is written:

'He gave them bread from heaven to eat.' "

[32n]So Jesus said to them, "Amen, amen, I say
to you, it was not Moses who gave the bread
from heaven; my Father gives you the true
bread from heaven. [33]For the bread of God is
that which comes down from heaven and
gives life to the world."

[34o]So they said to him, "Sir, give us this
bread always." [35p*]Jesus said to them, "I am
the bread of life; whoever comes to me will
never hunger, and whoever believes in me
will never thirst. [36q]But I told you that although you have seen [me], you do not believe. [37]Everything that the Father gives me
will come to me, and I will not reject anyone
who comes to me, [38r]because I came down
from heaven not to do my own will but the
will of the one who sent me. [39s]And this is the
will of the one who sent me, that I should not

6:14 The Prophet: probably the prophet like Moses (see note on Jn 1:21). **The one who is to come into the world**: probably Elijah; cf. Mal 3:1; 4:5.

6:16–21 The fifth sign is a nature miracle, portraying Jesus sharing Yahweh's power. Cf. the parallel stories following the multiplication of the loaves in Mk 6:45–52 and Mt 14:22–33.

6:19 Walking on the sea: although the Greek (cf. Jn 6:16) could mean "on the seashore" or "by the sea" (cf. Jn 21:1), the parallels, especially Mt 14:25, make clear that Jesus walked upon the water. John may allude to Jb 9:8: God "treads upon the crests of the sea."

6:20 It is I: literally, "I am." See also notes on Jn 4:26 and Mk 6:50.

6:22–71 Discourse on the bread of life; replacement of the manna. Jn 6:22–34 serve as an introduction, Jn 6:35–59 constitute the discourse proper, Jn 6:60–71 portray the reaction of the disciples and Peter's confession.

6:23 Possibly a later interpolation, to explain how the crowd got to Capernaum.

6:27 The food that endures for eternal life: cf. Jn 4:14, on water "springing up to eternal life."

6:31 Bread from heaven: cf. Ex 16:4, 15, 32–34 and the notes there; Ps 78:24. The manna, thought to have been hidden by Jeremiah (2 Mc 2:5–8), was expected to reappear miraculously at Passover, in the last days.

6:35–59 Up to Jn 6:50 "bread of life" is a figure for God's revelation in Jesus; in Jn 6:51–58, the eucharistic theme comes to the fore. There may thus be a break between Jn 6:50–51.

---

g: Dt 18:15, 18; Mal 3:1, 23; Acts 3:22. *h:* 18:36. *i:* Mt 14:22–27; Mk 6:45–52. *j:* Jb 9:8; Ps 29:3–4; 77:20; Is 43:16. *k:* 6:50, 51, 54, 58. *l:* Mt 16:1–4; Lk 11:29–30. *m:* Ex 16:4–5; Nm 11:7–9; Ps 78:24. *n:* Mt 6:11. *o:* 4:15. *p:* Is 55:1–3; Am 8:11–13. *q:* 20:29. *r:* 4:34; Mt 26:39; Heb 10:9. *s:* 10:28–29; 17:12; 18:9.

lose anything of what he gave me, but that I should raise it [on] the last day. [40t]For this is the will of my Father, that everyone who sees the Son and believes in him may have eternal life, and I shall raise him [on] the last day."

[41]The Jews murmured about him because he said, "I am the bread that came down from heaven," [42u]and they said, "Is this not Jesus, the son of Joseph? Do we not know his father and mother? Then how can he say, 'I have come down from heaven'?" [43v*]Jesus answered and said to them, "Stop murmuring among yourselves. [44]No one can come to me unless the Father who sent me draw him, and I will raise him on the last day. [45w]It is written in the prophets:

'They shall all be taught by God.'

Everyone who listens to my Father and learns from him comes to me. [46x]Not that anyone has seen the Father except the one who is from God; he has seen the Father. [47]Amen, amen, I say to you, whoever believes has eternal life. [48]I am the bread of life. [49y]Your ancestors ate the manna in the desert, but they died; [50]this is the bread that comes down from heaven so that one may eat it and not die. [51z]I am the living bread that came down from heaven; whoever eats this bread will live forever; and the bread that I will give is my flesh for the life of the world."

[52]The Jews quarreled among themselves, saying, "How can this man give us [his] flesh to eat?" [53]Jesus said to them, "Amen, amen, I say to you, unless you eat the flesh of the Son of Man and drink his blood, you do not have life within you. [54*]Whoever eats my flesh and drinks my blood has eternal life, and I will raise him on the last day. [55]For my flesh is true food, and my blood is true drink. [56]Whoever eats my flesh and drinks my blood remains in me and I in him. [57a]Just as the living Father sent me and I have life because of the Father, so also the one who feeds on me will have life because of me. [58]This is the bread that came down from heaven. Unlike your ancestors who ate and still died, whoever eats this bread will live forever." [59]These things he said while teaching in the synagogue in Capernaum.

The Words of Eternal Life. [60*]Then many of his disciples who were listening said, "This saying is hard; who can accept it?" [61]Since Jesus knew that his disciples were murmuring about this, he said to them, "Does this shock you? [62*]What if you were to see the Son of Man ascending to where he was before? [63*]It is the spirit that gives life, while the flesh is of no avail. The words I have spoken to you are spirit and life. [64b]But there are some of you who do not believe." Jesus knew from the beginning the ones who would not believe and the one who would betray him. [65]And he said, "For this reason I have told you that no one can come to me unless it is granted him by my Father."

[66]As a result of this, many [of] his disciples returned to their former way of life and no longer accompanied him. [67]Jesus then said to the Twelve, "Do you also want to leave?" [68]Simon Peter answered him, "Master, to whom shall we go? You have the words of eternal life. [69c]We have come to believe and are convinced that you are the Holy One of God." [70]Jesus answered them, "Did I not choose you twelve? Yet is not one of you a devil?" [71d]He was referring to Judas, son of Simon the Iscariot; it was he who would betray him, one of the Twelve.

6:43 Murmuring: the word may reflect the Greek of Ex 16:2, 7–8.

6:54–58 Eats: the verb used in these verses is not the classical Greek verb used of human eating, but that of animal eating: "munch," "gnaw." This may be part of John's emphasis on the reality of the flesh and blood of Jesus (cf. Jn 6:55), but the same verb eventually became the ordinary verb in Greek meaning "eat."

6:60–71 These verses refer more to themes of Jn 6:35–50 than to those of Jn 6:51–58 and seem to be addressed to members of the Johannine community who found it difficult to accept the high christology reflected in the bread of life discourse.

6:62 This unfinished conditional sentence is obscure. Probably there is a reference to Jn 6:49–51. Jesus claims to be **the bread that comes down from heaven** (Jn 6:50); this claim provokes incredulity (Jn 6:60); and so Jesus is pictured as asking what his disciples will say when he goes up to heaven.

6:63 Spirit . . . flesh: probably not a reference to the eucharistic body of Jesus but to the supernatural and the natural, as in Jn 3:6. **Spirit and life**: all Jesus said about the bread of life is the revelation of the Spirit.

---

t: 1 Jn 2:25. *u:* Mt 13:54–57; Mk 6:1–4; Lk 4:22. *v:* Ex 16:2, 7, 8; Lk 4:22. *w:* Is 54:13; Jer 31:33–34. *x:* 1:18; 7:29; Ex 33:20. *y:* 1 Cor 10:3, 5. *z:* Mt 26:26–27; Lk 22:19. *a:* 5:26. *b:* 13:11. *c:* 11:27; Mt 16:16; Mk 1:24; Lk 4:34. *d:* 12:4; 13:2, 27.

CHAPTER 7*

See RG 419

The Feast of Tabernacles. [1e]After this, Jesus moved about within Galilee; but he did not wish to travel in Judea, because the Jews were trying to kill him. [2f]But the Jewish feast of Tabernacles was near. [3*]So his brothers said to him, "Leave here and go to Judea, so that your disciples also may see the works you are doing. [4g]No one works in secret if he wants to be known publicly. If you do these things, manifest yourself to the world." [5]For his brothers did not believe in him. [6*]So Jesus said to them, "My time is not yet here, but the time is always right for you. [7h]The world cannot hate you, but it hates me, because I testify to it that its works are evil. [8*]You go up to the feast. I am not going up to this feast, because my time has not yet been fulfilled." [9]After he had said this, he stayed on in Galilee.

[10]But when his brothers had gone up to the feast, he himself also went up, not openly but [as it were] in secret. [11]The Jews were looking for him at the feast and saying, "Where is he?" [12]And there was considerable murmuring about him in the crowds. Some said, "He is a good man," [while] others said, "No; on the contrary, he misleads the crowd." [13i]Still, no one spoke openly about him because they were afraid of the Jews.

The First Dialogue. [14*]When the feast was already half over, Jesus went up into the temple area and began to teach. [15j*]The Jews were amazed and said, "How does he know scripture without having studied?" [16]Jesus answered them and said, "My teaching is not my own but is from the one who sent me. [17k*]Whoever chooses to do his will shall know whether my teaching is from God or whether I speak on my own. [18]Whoever speaks on his own seeks his own glory, but whoever seeks the glory of the one who sent him is truthful, and there is no wrong in him. [19l]Did not Moses give you the law? Yet none of you keeps the law. Why are you trying to kill me?" [20m*]The crowd answered, "You are possessed! Who is trying to kill you?" [21n*]Jesus answered and said to them, "I performed one work and all of you are amazed [22o]because of it. Moses gave you circumcision—not that it came from Moses but rather from the patriarchs—and you circumcise a man on the sabbath. [23p]If a man can receive circumcision on a sabbath so that the law of Moses may not be broken, are you angry with me because I made a whole person well on a sabbath? [24q]Stop judging by appearances, but judge justly."

[25]So some of the inhabitants of Jerusalem said, "Is he not the one they are trying to

7:1–8 These chapters contain events about the feast of Tabernacles (Sukkoth, Ingathering: Ex 23:16; Tents, Booths: Dt 16:13–16), with its symbols of booths (originally built to shelter harvesters), rain (water from Siloam poured on the temple altar), and lights (illumination of the four torches in the Court of the Women). They continue the theme of the replacement of feasts (Passover, Jn 2:13; 6:4; Hanukkah, Jn 10:22; Pentecost, Jn 5:1), here accomplished by Jesus as the Living Water. These chapters comprise seven miscellaneous controversies and dialogues. There is a literary inclusion with Jesus in hiding in Jn 7:4, 10; 8:59. There are frequent references to attempts on his life: Jn 7:1, 13, 19, 25, 30, 32, 44; 8:37, 40, 59.

7:3 Brothers: these relatives (cf. Jn 2:12 and see note on Mk 6:3) are never portrayed as disciples until after the resurrection (Acts 1:14). Mt 13:55 and Mk 6:3 give the names of four of them. Jesus has already performed works/signs in Judea; cf. Jn 2:23; 3:2; 4:45; 5:8.

7:6 Time: the Greek word means "opportune time," here a synonym for Jesus' "hour" (see note on Jn 2:4), his death and resurrection. In the wordplay, any time is suitable for Jesus' brothers, because they are not dependent on God's will.

7:8 I am not going up: an early attested reading "not yet" seems a correction, since Jesus in the story does go up to the feast. "Go up," in a play on words, refers not only to going up to Jerusalem but also to exaltation at the cross, resurrection, and ascension; cf. Jn 3:14; 6:62; 20:17.

7:14–31 Jesus teaches in the temple; debate with the Jews.

7:15 Without having studied: literally, "How does he know letters without having learned?" Children were taught to read and write by means of the scriptures. But here more than Jesus' literacy is being discussed; the people are wondering how he can teach like a rabbi. Rabbis were trained by other rabbis and traditionally quoted their teachers.

7:17 To do his will: presumably a reference back to the "work" of Jn 6:29: belief in the one whom God has sent.

7:20 You are possessed: literally, "You have a demon." The insane were thought to be possessed by a demoniacal spirit.

7:21 One work: the cure of the paralytic (Jn 5:1–9) because of the reference to the sabbath (Jn 7:22; 5:9–10).

---

e: 5:18; 8:37, 40. *f:* Ex 23:16; Lv 23:34; Nm 29:12; Dt 16:13–16; Zec 14:16–19. *g:* 14:22. *h:* 15:18. *i:* 9:22; 19:38; 20:19. *j:* Lk 2:47. *k:* 6:29. *l:* Acts 7:53. *m:* 8:48–49; 10:20. *n:* 5:1–9. *o:* Gn 17:10; Lv 12:3. *p:* 5:2–9, 16; Mt 12:11–12; Lk 14:5. *q:* 8:15; Lv 19:15; Is 11:3–4.

kill? [26*]And look, he is speaking openly and
they say nothing to him. Could the authorities have realized that he is the Messiah?
[27r]But we know where he is from. When the
Messiah comes, no one will know where he
is from." [28s]So Jesus cried out in the temple
area as he was teaching and said, "You know
me and also know where I am from. Yet I did
not come on my own, but the one who sent
me, whom you do not know, is true. [29t]I
know him, because I am from him, and he
sent me." [30u]So they tried to arrest him, but
no one laid a hand upon him, because his
hour had not yet come. [31v]But many of the
crowd began to believe in him, and said,
"When the Messiah comes, will he perform
more signs than this man has done?"

Officers Sent to Arrest Jesus. [32*]The
Pharisees heard the crowd murmuring about
him to this effect, and the chief priests and
the Pharisees sent guards to arrest him.
[33w]So Jesus said, "I will be with you only a
little while longer, and then I will go to the
one who sent me. [34x]You will look for me but
not find [me], and where I am you cannot
come." [35*]So the Jews said to one another,
"Where is he going that we will not find
him? Surely he is not going to the dispersion
among the Greeks to teach the Greeks, is he?
[36]What is the meaning of his saying, 'You
will look for me and not find [me], and
where I am you cannot come'?"

Rivers of Living Water. [37y*]On the last
and greatest day of the feast, Jesus stood up
and exclaimed, "Let anyone who thirsts
come to me and drink. [38z*]Whoever believes
in me, as scripture says:

'Rivers of living water will flow from
within him.' "

[39a*]He said this in reference to the Spirit that
those who came to believe in him were to receive. There was, of course, no Spirit yet,
because Jesus had not yet been glorified.

***Discussion about the Origins of the Mes-
siah.*** [40b*]Some in the crowd who heard
these words said, "This is truly the Prophet."
[41]Others said, "This is the Messiah." But
others said, "The Messiah will not come
from Galilee, will he? [42c]Does not scripture
say that the Messiah will be of David's family and come from Bethlehem, the village
where David lived?" [43]So a division occurred in the crowd because of him. [44]Some
of them even wanted to arrest him, but no
one laid hands on him.

[45]So the guards went to the chief priests
and Pharisees, who asked them, "Why did
you not bring him?" [46]The guards answered,
"Never before has anyone spoken like this
one." [47]So the Pharisees answered them,
"Have you also been deceived? [48d]Have any
of the authorities or the Pharisees believed in
him? [49]But this crowd, which does not know
the law, is accursed." [50e]Nicodemus, one of
their members who had come to him earlier,
said to them, [51f]"Does our law condemn a
person before it first hears him and finds out

7:26 The authorities: the members of the Sanhedrin (same term as Jn 3:1).

7:32–36 Jesus announces his approaching departure (cf. also Jn 8:21; 12:36; 13:33) and complete control over his destiny.

7:35 Dispersion: or "diaspora": Jews living outside Palestine. **Greeks**: probably refers to the Gentiles in the Mediterranean area; cf. Jn 12:20.

7:37, 39 Promise of living water through the Spirit.

7:38 Living water: not an exact quotation from any Old Testament passage; in the gospel context the gift of the Spirit is meant; cf. Jn 3:5. **From within him**: either Jesus or the believer; if Jesus, it continues the Jesus-Moses motif (water from the rock, Ex 17:6; Nm 20:11) as well as Jesus as the new temple (cf. Ez 47:1). Grammatically, it goes better with the believer.

7:39 No Spirit yet: Codex Vaticanus and early Latin, Syriac, and Coptic versions add "given." In this gospel, the sending of the Spirit cannot take place until Jesus' glorification through his death, resurrection, and ascension; cf. Jn 20:22.

7:40–53 Discussion of the Davidic lineage of the Messiah.

7:53–8:11 The story of the woman caught in adultery is a later insertion here, missing from all early Greek manuscripts. A Western text-type insertion, attested mainly in Old Latin translations, it is found in different places in different manuscripts: here, or after Jn 7:36 or at the end of this gospel, or after Lk 21:38, or at the end of that gospel. There are many non-Johannine features in the language, and there are also many doubtful readings within the passage. The style and motifs are similar to those of Luke, and it fits better with the general situation at the end of Lk 21: but it was probably inserted here because of the allusion to Jer 17:13 (cf. note on Jn 8:6) and the statement, "I do not judge anyone," in Jn 8:15. The Catholic Church accepts this passage as canonical scripture.

---

r: Heb 7:3. *s:* 8:19. *t:* 6:46; 8:55. *u:* 7:44; 8:20; Lk 4:29–30. *v:* 2:11; 10:42; 11:45. *w:* 13:33; 16:16. *x:* 8:21; 12:36; 13:33, 36; 16:5; Dt 4:29; Prv 1:28; Is 55:6; Hos 5:6. *y:* Rev 21:6. *z:* 4:10, 14; 19:34; Is 12:3; Ez 47:1. *a:* 16:7. *b:* Dt 18:15, 18. *c:* 2 Sm 7:12–14; Ps 89:3–4; 132:11; Mi 5:1; Mt 2:5–6. *d:* 12:42. *e:* 3:1; 19:39. *f:* Dt 1:16–17.

what he is doing?" [52]They answered and said to him, "You are not from Galilee also, are you? Look and see that no prophet arises from Galilee."

CHAPTER 8

See RG 419–20

A Woman Caught in Adultery. [[53*]Then each went to his own house, [1g*]while Jesus went to the Mount of Olives. [2]But early in the morning he arrived again in the temple area, and all the people started coming to him, and he sat down and taught them. [3]Then the scribes and the Pharisees brought a woman who had been caught in adultery and made her stand in the middle. [4]They said to him, "Teacher, this woman was caught in the very act of committing adultery. [5h*]Now in the law, Moses commanded us to stone such women. So what do you say?" [6*]They said this to test him, so that they could have some charge to bring against him. Jesus bent down and began to write on the ground with his finger. [7i*]But when they continued asking him, he straightened up and said to them, "Let the one among you who is without sin be the first to throw a stone at her." [8]Again he bent down and wrote on the ground. [9]And in response, they went away one by one, beginning with the elders. So he was left alone with the woman before him. [10j]Then Jesus straightened up and said to her, "Woman, where are they? Has no one condemned you?" [11k]She replied, "No one, sir." Then Jesus said, "Neither do I condemn you. Go, [and] from now on do not sin any more."]

The Light of the World. [12l*]Jesus spoke to them again, saying, "I am the light of the world. Whoever follows me will not walk in darkness, but will have the light of life." [13]So the Pharisees said to him, "You testify on your own behalf, so your testimony cannot be verified." [14m*]Jesus answered and said to them, "Even if I do testify on my own behalf, my testimony can be verified, because I know where I came from and where I am going. But you do not know where I come from or where I am going. [15n*]You judge by appearances, but I do not judge anyone. [16o]And even if I should judge, my judgment is valid, because I am not alone, but it is I and the Father who sent me. [17p*]Even in your law it is written that the testimony of two men can be verified. [18q]I testify on my behalf and so does the Father who sent me." [19r]So they said to him, "Where is your father?" Jesus answered, "You know neither me nor my Father. If you knew me, you would know my Father also." [20s]He spoke these words while teaching in the treasury in the temple area. But no one arrested him, because his hour had not yet come.

Jesus, the Father's Ambassador. [21t*]He said to them again, "I am going away and you will look for me, but you will die in your sin. Where I am going you cannot come." [22*]So the Jews said, "He is not going to kill himself, is he, because he said, 'Where I am going you cannot come'?" [23u]He said to them, "You belong to what is below, I belong to what is above. You belong to this world,

8:1 Mount of Olives: not mentioned elsewhere in the gospel tradition outside of passion week.

8:5 Lv 20:10 and Dt 22:22 mention only death, but Dt 22:23–24 prescribes stoning for a betrothed virgin.

8:6 Cf. Jer 17:13 (RSV): "Those who turn away from thee shall be written in the earth, for they have forsaken the LORD, the fountain of living water"; cf. Jn 7:38.

8:7 The first stones were to be thrown by the witnesses (Dt 17:7).

8:12–20 Jesus the light of the world. Jesus replaces the four torches of the illumination of the temple as the light of joy.

8:14 My testimony can be verified: this seems to contradict Jn 5:31 but the emphasis here is on Jesus' origin from the Father and his divine destiny. **Where I am going**: indicates Jesus' passion and glorification.

8:15 By appearances: literally, "according to the flesh." **I do not judge anyone**: superficial contradiction of Jn 5:22, 27, 30; here the emphasis is that the judgment is not by material standards.

8:17 Your law: a reflection of later controversy between church and synagogue.

8:21–30 He whose ambassador I am is with me. Jesus' origin is from God; he can reveal God.

8:21 You will die in your sin: i.e., of disbelief; cf. Jn 8:24. **Where I am going you cannot come**: except through faith in Jesus' passion-resurrection.

8:22 The Jews suspect that he is referring to his death. Johannine irony is apparent here; Jesus' death will not be self-inflicted but destined by God.

---

g: Lk 21:37–38. *h:* Lv 20:10; Dt 22:22–29. *i:* Dt 17:7. *j:* Ez 33:11. *k:* 5:14. *l:* 1:4–5, 9; 12:46; Ex 13:22; Is 42:6; Zec 14:8. *m:* 5:31. *n:* 12:47; 1 Sm 16:7. *o:* 5:30. *p:* Dt 17:6; 19:15; Nm 35:30. *q:* 5:23, 37. *r:* 7:28; 14:7; 15:21. *s:* 7:30. *t:* 7:34; 13:33. *u:* 3:31; 17:14; 18:36.

but I do not belong to this world. 24v*That is why I told you that you will die in your sins. For if you do not believe that I AM, you will die in your sins." 25w*So they said to him, "Who are you?" Jesus said to them, "What I told you from the beginning. 26xI have much to say about you in condemnation. But the one who sent me is true, and what I heard from him I tell the world." 27They did not realize that he was speaking to them of the Father. 28ySo Jesus said [to them], "When you lift up the Son of Man, then you will realize that I AM, and that I do nothing on my own, but I say only what the Father taught me. 29The one who sent me is with me. He has not left me alone, because I always do what is pleasing to him." 30Because he spoke this way, many came to believe in him.

Jesus and Abraham. 31*Jesus then said to those Jews who believed in him, "If you remain in my word, you will truly be my disciples, 32zand you will know the truth, and the truth will set you free." 33a*They answered him, "We are descendants of Abraham and have never been enslaved to anyone. How can you say, 'You will become free'?" 34bJesus answered them, "Amen, amen, I say to you, everyone who commits sin is a slave of sin. 35c*A slave does not remain in a household forever, but a son always remains. 36So if a son frees you, then you will truly be free. 37I know that you are descendants of Abraham. But you are trying to kill me, because my word has no room among you. 38*I tell you what I have seen in the Father's presence; then do what you have heard from the Father."

39d*They answered and said to him, "Our father is Abraham." Jesus said to them, "If you were Abraham's children, you would be doing the works of Abraham. 40But now you are trying to kill me, a man who has told you the truth that I heard from God; Abraham did not do this. 41eYou are doing the works of your father!" [So] they said to him, "We are not illegitimate. We have one Father, God." 42fJesus said to them, "If God were your Father, you would love me, for I came from God and am here; I did not come on my own, but he sent me. 43Why do you not understand what I am saying? Because you cannot bear to hear my word. 44gYou belong to your father the devil and you willingly carry out your father's desires. He was a murderer from the beginning and does not stand in truth, because there is no truth in him. When he tells a lie, he speaks in character, because he is a liar and the father of lies. 45But because I speak the truth, you do not believe me. 46hCan any of you charge me with sin? If I am telling the truth, why do you not believe me? 47iWhoever belongs to God hears the words of God; for this reason you do not listen, because you do not belong to God."

48*The Jews answered and said to him, "Are we not right in saying that you are a Samaritan and are possessed?" 49Jesus answered, "I am not possessed; I honor my Father, but you dishonor me. 50jI do not seek my own glory; there is one who seeks it and

8:24, 28 I AM: an expression that late Jewish tradition understood as Yahweh's own self-designation (Is 43:10); see note on Jn 4:26. Jesus is here placed on a par with Yahweh.

8:25 What I told you from the beginning: this verse seems textually corrupt, with several other possible translations: "(I am) what I say to you"; "Why do I speak to you at all?" The earliest attested reading (Bodmer Papyrus P^{66}) has (in a second hand), "I told you at the beginning what I am also telling you (now)." The answer here (cf. Prv 8:22) seems to hinge on a misunderstanding of Jn 8:24 "*that* I AM" as "*what* I am."

8:31–59 Jesus' origin ("before Abraham") and destiny are developed; the truth will free them from sin (Jn 8:34) and death (Jn 8:51).

8:31 Those Jews who believed in him: a rough editorial suture, since in Jn 8:37 they are described as trying to kill Jesus.

8:33 Have never been enslaved to anyone: since, historically, the Jews were enslaved almost continuously, this verse is probably Johannine irony, about slavery to sin.

8:35 A slave . . . a son: an allusion to Ishmael and Isaac (Gn 16; 21), or to the release of a slave after six years (Ex 21:2; Dt 15:12).

8:38 The Father: i.e., God. It is also possible, however, to understand the second part of the verse as a sarcastic reference to descent of the Jews from the devil (Jn 8:44), "You do what you have heard from [your] father."

8:39 The works of Abraham: Abraham believed; cf. Rom 4:11–17; Jas 2:21–23.

8:48 Samaritan: therefore interested in magical powers; cf. Acts 7:14–24.

v: Ex 3:14; Dt 32:39; Is 43:10. *w:* 10:24. *x:* 12:44–50. *y:* 3:14; 12:32, 34. *z:* Is 42:7; Gal 4:31. *a:* Mt 3:9. *b:* Rom 6:16–17. *c:* Gn 21:10; Gal 4:30; Heb 3:5–6. *d:* Gn 26:5; Rom 4:11–17; Jas 2:21–23. *e:* Mal 2:10. *f:* 1 Jn 5:1. *g:* Gn 3:4; Wis 1:13; 2:24; Acts 13:10; 1 Jn 3:8–15. *h:* Heb 4:15; 1 Pt 2:22; 1 Jn 3:5. *i:* 10:26; 1 Jn 4:6. *j:* 7:18.

he is the one who judges. [51k]Amen, amen, I say to you, whoever keeps my word will never see death.” [52][So] the Jews said to him, “Now we are sure that you are possessed. Abraham died, as did the prophets, yet you say, ‘Whoever keeps my word will never taste death.’ [53l*]Are you greater than our father Abraham, who died? Or the prophets, who died? Who do you make yourself out to be?” [54]Jesus answered, “If I glorify myself, my glory is worth nothing; but it is my Father who glorifies me, of whom you say, ‘He is our God.’ [55m]You do not know him, but I know him. And if I should say that I do not know him, I would be like you a liar. But I do know him and I keep his word. [56n*]Abraham your father rejoiced to see my day; he saw it and was glad. [57*]So the Jews said to him, “You are not yet fifty years old and you have seen Abraham?” [58o*]Jesus said to them, “Amen, amen, I say to you, before Abraham came to be, I AM.” [59p]So they picked up stones to throw at him; but Jesus hid and went out of the temple area.

CHAPTER 9

See RG 420

The Man Born Blind. [1q*]As he passed by he saw a man blind from birth. [2r*]His disciples asked him, “Rabbi, who sinned, this man or his parents, that he was born blind?” [3s]Jesus answered, “Neither he nor his parents sinned; it is so that the works of God might be made visible through him. [4t]We have to do the works of the one who sent me while it is day. Night is coming when no one can work. [5u]While I am in the world, I am the light of the world.” [6v]When he had said this, he spat on the ground and made clay with the saliva, and smeared the clay on his eyes, [7w*]and said to him, “Go wash in the Pool of Siloam” (which means Sent). So he went and washed, and came back able to see.

[8]His neighbors and those who had seen him earlier as a beggar said, “Isn’t this the one who used to sit and beg?” [9]Some said, “It is,” but others said, “No, he just looks like him.” He said, “I am.” [10]So they said to him, “[So] how were your eyes opened?” [11]He replied, “The man called Jesus made clay and anointed my eyes and told me, ‘Go to Siloam and wash.’ So I went there and washed and was able to see.” [12]And they said to him, “Where is he?” He said, “I don’t know.”

[13]They brought the one who was once blind to the Pharisees. [14x*]Now Jesus had made clay and opened his eyes on a sabbath. [15]So then the Pharisees also asked him how he was able to see. He said to them, “He put clay on my eyes, and I washed, and now I can see.” [16y]So some of the Pharisees said, “This man is not from God, because he does not keep the sabbath.” [But] others said, “How can a sinful man do such signs?” And there was a division among them. [17z]So they said to the blind man again, “What do you have to say about him, since he opened your eyes?” He said, “He is a prophet.”

[18]Now the Jews did not believe that he had been blind and gained his sight until they summoned the parents of the one who had gained his sight. [19]They asked them, “Is this your son, who you say was born blind? How does he

8:53 Are you greater than our father Abraham?: cf. Jn 4:12.

8:56 He saw it: this seems a reference to the birth of Isaac (Gn 17:7; 21:6), the beginning of the fulfillment of promises about Abraham’s seed.

8:57 The evidence of the third-century Bodmer Papyrus P^{75} and the first hand of Codex Sinaiticus indicates that the text originally read: “How can Abraham have seen you?”

8:58 Came to be, I AM: the Greek word used for “came to be” is the one used of all creation in the prologue, while the word used for “am” is the one reserved for the Logos.

9:1–10:21 Sabbath healing of the man born blind. This fifth sign is introduced to illustrate the saying, “I am the light of the world” (Jn 8:12; 9:5). The narrative of conflict about Jesus contrasts Jesus (light) with the Jews (blindness, Jn 9:39–41). The theme of water is reintroduced in the reference to the pool of Siloam. Ironically, Jesus is being judged by the Jews, yet the Jews are judged by the Light of the world; cf. Jn 3:19–21.

9:2 See note on Jn 5:14, and Ex 20:5, that parents’ sins were visited upon their children. Jesus denies such a cause and emphasizes the purpose: the infirmity was providential.

9:7 Go wash: perhaps a test of faith; cf. 2 Kgs 5:10–14. The water tunnel Siloam (= Sent) is used as a symbol of Jesus, sent by his Father.

9:14 In using spittle, kneading clay, and healing, Jesus had broken the sabbath rules laid down by Jewish tradition.

k: 5:24–29; 6:40, 47; 11:25–26. *l:* 4:12. *m:* 7:28–29. *n:* Gn 17:17; Mt 13:17; Lk 17:22. *o:* 1:30; 17:5. *p:* 10:31, 39; 11:8; Lk 4:29–30. *q:* Is 42:7. *r:* Ex 20:5; Ez 18:20; Lk 13:2. *s:* 5:14; 11:4. *t:* 11:9–10; 12:35–36. *u:* 8:12. *v:* 5:11; Mk 7:33; 8:23. *w:* 2 Kgs 5:10–14. *x:* 5:9. *y:* 3:2; Mt 12:10–11; Lk 13:10–11; 14:1–4. *z:* 4:19.

now see?" [20]His parents answered and said, "We know that this is our son and that he was born blind. [21]We do not know how he sees now, nor do we know who opened his eyes. Ask him, he is of age; he can speak for himself." [22a*]His parents said this because they were afraid of the Jews, for the Jews had already agreed that if anyone acknowledged him as the Messiah, he would be expelled from the synagogue. [23b]For this reason his parents said, "He is of age; question him."

[24c*]So a second time they called the man who had been blind and said to him, "Give God the praise! We know that this man is a sinner." [25]He replied, "If he is a sinner, I do not know. One thing I do know is that I was blind and now I see." [26]So they said to him, "What did he do to you? How did he open your eyes?" [27]He answered them, "I told you already and you did not listen. Why do you want to hear it again? Do you want to become his disciples, too?" [28]They ridiculed him and said, "You are that man's disciple; we are disciples of Moses! [29d]We know that God spoke to Moses, but we do not know where this one is from." [30]The man answered and said to them, "This is what is so amazing, that you do not know where he is from, yet he opened my eyes. [31e]We know that God does not listen to sinners, but if one is devout and does his will, he listens to him. [32*]It is unheard of that anyone ever opened the eyes of a person born blind. [33f]If this man were not from God, he would not be able to do anything." [34]They answered and said to him, "You were born totally in sin, and are you trying to teach us?" Then they threw him out.

[35]When Jesus heard that they had thrown him out, he found him and said, "Do you believe in the Son of Man?" [36]He answered and said, "Who is he, sir, that I may believe in him?" [37g]Jesus said to him, "You have seen him and the one speaking with you is he." [38]He said, "I do believe, Lord," and he worshiped him. [39h*]Then Jesus said, "I came into this world for judgment, so that those who do not see might see, and those who do see might become blind."

[40i]Some of the Pharisees who were with him heard this and said to him, "Surely we are not also blind, are we?" [41j]Jesus said to them, "If you were blind, you would have no sin; but now you are saying, 'We see,' so your sin remains.

CHAPTER 10

See RG 420

The Good Shepherd. [1k*]"Amen, amen, I say to you, whoever does not enter a sheepfold through the gate but climbs over elsewhere is a thief and a robber. [2]But whoever enters through the gate is the shepherd of the sheep. [3]The gatekeeper opens it for him, and the sheep hear his voice, as he calls his own sheep by name and leads them out. [4l*]When he has driven out all his own, he walks ahead of them, and the sheep follow him, because they recognize his voice. [5]But they will not follow a stranger; they will run away from him, because they do not recognize the voice of strangers." [6*]Although Jesus used this figure of speech, they did not realize what he was trying to tell them.

9:22 This comment of the evangelist (in terms used again in Jn 12:42; Jn 16:2) envisages a situation after Jesus' ministry. Rejection/excommunication from the synagogue of Jews who confessed Jesus as Messiah seems to have begun ca. A.D. 85, when the curse against the *mînîm* or heretics was introduced into the "Eighteen Benedictions."

9:24 Give God the praise!: an Old Testament formula of adjuration to tell the truth; cf. Jos 7:19; 1 Sm 6:5 LXX. Cf. Jn 5:41.

9:32 A person born blind: the only Old Testament cure from blindness is found in Tobit (cf. Tb 7:7; 11:7–13; 14:1–2), but Tobit was not born blind.

9:39–41 These verses spell out the symbolic meaning of the cure; the Pharisees are not the innocent blind, willing to accept the testimony of others.

10:1–21 The good shepherd discourse continues the theme of attack on the Pharisees that ends Jn 9. The figure is allegorical: the hired hands are the Pharisees who excommunicated the cured blind man. It serves as a commentary on Jn 9. For the shepherd motif, used of Yahweh in the Old Testament, cf. Ex 34; Gn 48:15; 49:24; Mi 7:14; Ps 23:1–4; 80:1.

10:1 Sheepfold: a low stone wall open to the sky.

10:4 Recognize his voice: the Pharisees do not recognize Jesus, but the people of God, symbolized by the blind man, do.

10:6 Figure of speech: John uses a different word for illustrative speech than the "parable" of the synoptics, but the idea is similar.

---

a: 7:13; 12:42; 16:2; 19:38. *b:* 12:42. *c:* Jos 7:19; 1 Sm 6:5 LXX. *d:* Ex 33:11. *e:* 10:21; Ps 34:16; 66:18; Prv 15:29; Is 1:15. *f:* 3:2. *g:* 4:26; Dn 7:13. *h:* Mt 13:33–35. *i:* Mt 15:14; 23:26; Rom 2:19. *j:* 15:22. *k:* Gn 48:15; 49:24; Ps 23:1–4; 80:2; Jer 23:1–4; Ez 34:1–31; Mi 7:14. *l:* Mi 2:12–13.

[7*]So Jesus said again, "Amen, amen, I say to you, I am the gate for the sheep. [8*]All who came [before me] are thieves and robbers, but the sheep did not listen to them. [9]I am the gate. Whoever enters through me will be saved, and will come in and go out and find pasture. [10]A thief comes only to steal and slaughter and destroy; I came so that they might have life and have it more abundantly. [11m]I am the good shepherd. A good shepherd lays down his life for the sheep. [12n]A hired man, who is not a shepherd and whose sheep are not his own, sees a wolf coming and leaves the sheep and runs away, and the wolf catches and scatters them. [13]This is because he works for pay and has no concern for the sheep. [14]I am the good shepherd, and I know mine and mine know me, [15o]just as the Father knows me and I know the Father; and I will lay down my life for the sheep. [16p*]I have other sheep that do not belong to this fold. These also I must lead, and they will hear my voice, and there will be one flock, one shepherd. [17q]This is why the Father loves me, because I lay down my life in order to take it up again. [18r*]No one takes it from me, but I lay it down on my own. I have power to lay it down, and power to take it up again. This command I have received from my Father."

[19s]Again there was a division among the Jews because of these words. [20t]Many of them said, "He is possessed and out of his mind; why listen to him?" [21u]Others said, "These are not the words of one possessed; surely a demon cannot open the eyes of the blind, can he?"

Feast of the Dedication. [22v*]The feast of the Dedication was then taking place in Jerusalem. It was winter. [23*]And Jesus walked about in the temple area on the Portico of Solomon. [24w*]So the Jews gathered around him and said to him, "How long are you going to keep us in suspense? If you are the Messiah, tell us plainly." [25x*]Jesus answered them, "I told you and you do not believe. The works I do in my Father's name testify to me. [26y]But you do not believe, because you are not among my sheep. [27]My sheep hear my voice; I know them, and they follow me. [28z]I give them eternal life, and they shall never perish. No one can take them out of my hand. [29a*]My Father, who has given them to me, is greater than all, and no one can take them out of the Father's hand. [30b*]The Father and I are one."

[31c]The Jews again picked up rocks to stone him. [32]Jesus answered them, "I have shown you many good works from my Father. For which of these are you trying to stone me?" [33d]The Jews answered him, "We are not stoning you for a good work but for blasphemy. You, a man, are making yourself God." [34e*]Jesus answered them, "Is it not written in

10:7–10 In Jn 10:7–8, the figure is of a gate for the shepherd to come to the sheep; in Jn 10:9–10, the figure is of a gate for the sheep to **come in and go out**.

10:8 [Before me]: these words are omitted in many good early manuscripts and versions.

10:16 Other sheep: the Gentiles, possibly a reference to "God's dispersed children" of Jn 11:52 destined to be gathered into one, or "apostolic Christians" at odds with the community of the beloved disciple.

10:18 Power to take it up again: contrast the role of the Father as the efficient cause of the resurrection in Acts 2:24; 4:10; etc.; Rom 1:4; 4:24. Yet even here is added: **This command I have received from my Father**.

10:22 Feast of the Dedication: an eight-day festival of lights (Hebrew, Hanukkah) held in December, three months after the feast of Tabernacles (Jn 7:2), to celebrate the Maccabees' rededication of the altar and reconsecration of the temple in 164 B.C., after their desecration by Antiochus IV Epiphanes (Dn 8:13; 9:27; cf. 1 Mc 4:36–59; 2 Mc 1:18–2:19; 10:1–8).

10:23 Portico of Solomon: on the east side of the temple area, offering protection against the cold winds from the desert.

10:24 Keep us in suspense: literally, "How long will you take away our life?" Cf. Jn 11:48–50. **If you are the Messiah, tell us plainly**: cf. Lk 22:67. This is the climax of Jesus' encounters with the Jewish authorities. There has never yet been an open confession before them.

10:25 I told you: probably at Jn 8:25 which was an evasive answer.

10:29 The textual evidence for the first clause is very divided; it may also be translated: "As for the Father, what he has given me is greater than all," or "My Father is greater than all, in what he has given me."

10:30 This is justification for Jn 10:29; it asserts unity of power and reveals that the words and deeds of Jesus are the words and deeds of God.

10:34 This is a reference to the judges of Israel who, since they exercised the divine prerogative to judge (Dt 1:17), were

m: Ps 23:1–4; Is 40:11; 49:9–10; Heb 13:20; Rev 7:17. *n:* Zec 11:17. *o:* 15:13; 1 Jn 3:16. *p:* 11:52; Is 56:8; Jer 23:3; Ez 34:23; 37:24; Mi 2:12. *q:* Heb 10:10. *r:* 19:11. *s:* 7:43; 9:16. *t:* 7:20; 8:48. *u:* 3:2. *v:* 1 Mc 4:54, 59. *w:* Lk 22:67. *x:* 8:25 / 5:36; 10:38. *y:* 8:45, 47. *z:* Dt 32:39. *a:* Wis 3:1; Is 43:13. *b:* 1:1; 12:45; 14:9; 17:21. *c:* 8:59. *d:* 5:18; 19:7; Lv 24:16. *e:* Ps 82:6.

your law, 'I said, "You are gods" '? [35]If it calls them gods to whom the word of God came, and scripture cannot be set aside, [36f*]can you say that the one whom the Father has consecrated and sent into the world blasphemes because I said, 'I am the Son of God'? [37]If I do not perform my Father's works, do not believe me; [38g]but if I perform them, even if you do not believe me, believe the works, so that you may realize [and understand] that the Father is in me and I am in the Father." [39][Then] they tried again to arrest him; but he escaped from their power.

[40h]He went back across the Jordan to the place where John first baptized, and there he remained. [41*]Many came to him and said, "John performed no sign, but everything John said about this man was true." [42i]And many there began to believe in him.

See RG 420

CHAPTER 11

The Raising of Lazarus. [1j*]Now a man was ill, Lazarus from Bethany, the village of Mary and her sister Martha. [2]Mary was the one who had anointed the Lord with perfumed oil and dried his feet with her hair; it was her brother Lazarus who was ill. [3]So the sisters sent word to him, saying, "Master, the one you love is ill." [4k*]When Jesus heard this he said, "This illness is not to end in death, but is for the glory of God, that the Son of God may be glorified through it." [5]Now Jesus loved Martha and her sister and Lazarus. [6]So when he heard that he was ill, he remained for two days in the place where he was. [7]Then after this he said to his disciples, "Let us go back to Judea." [8l]The disciples said to him, "Rabbi, the Jews were just trying to stone you, and you want to go back there?" [9mn]Jesus answered, "Are there not twelve hours in a day? If one walks during the day, he does not stumble, because he sees the light of this world. [10*]But if one walks at night, he stumbles, because the light is not in him." [11]He said this, and then told them, "Our friend Lazarus is asleep, but I am going to awaken him." [12]So the disciples said to him, "Master, if he is asleep, he will be saved." [13o]But Jesus was talking about his death, while they thought that he meant ordinary sleep. [14]So then Jesus said to them clearly, "Lazarus has died. [15]And I am glad for you that I was not there, that you may believe. Let us go to him." [16p*]So Thomas, called Didymus, said to his fellow disciples, "Let us also go to die with him."

[17]When Jesus arrived, he found that Lazarus had already been in the tomb for four days. [18*]Now Bethany was near Jerusalem, only about two miles away. [19q]And many of the Jews had come to Martha and Mary to comfort them about their brother. [20]When Martha heard that Jesus was coming, she went to meet him; but Mary sat at home. [21r]Martha said to Jesus, "Lord, if you had been here, my brother would not have died. [22][But] even now I know that whatever you ask of God, God will give you." [23]Jesus said

called "gods"; cf. Ex 21:6, besides Ps 82:6 from which the quotation comes.

10:36 Consecrated: this may be a reference to the rededicated altar at the Hanukkah feast; see note on Jn 10:22.

10:41 Performed no sign: this is to stress the inferior role of John the Baptist. The Transjordan topography recalls the great witness of John the Baptist to Jesus, as opposed to the hostility of the authorities in Jerusalem.

11:1–44 The raising of Lazarus, the longest continuous narrative in John outside of the passion account, is the climax of the signs. It leads directly to the decision of the Sanhedrin to kill Jesus. The theme of life predominates. Lazarus is a token of the real life that Jesus dead and raised will give to all who believe in him. Johannine irony is found in the fact that Jesus' gift of life leads to his own death. The story is not found in the synoptics, but cf. Mk 5:21 and parallels; Lk 7:11–17. There are also parallels between this story and Luke's parable of the rich man and poor Lazarus (Lk 16:19–31). In both a man named Lazarus dies; in Luke, there is a request that he return to convince his contemporaries of the need for faith and repentance, while in John, Lazarus does return and some believe but others do not.

11:4 Not to end in death: this is misunderstood by the disciples as referring to physical death, but it is meant as spiritual death.

11:10 The light is not in him: the ancients apparently did not grasp clearly the entry of light **through** the eye; they seem to have thought of it as being **in** the eye; cf. Lk 11:34; Mt 6:23.

11:16 Called Didymus: **Didymus** is the Greek word for twin. Thomas is derived from the Aramaic word for twin; in an ancient Syriac version and in the Gospel of Thomas (80:11–12) his given name, Judas, is supplied.

11:18 About two miles: literally, "about fifteen stades"; a stade was 607 feet.

f: 5:18. *g:* 14:10–11, 20. *h:* 1:28. *i:* 2:23; 7:31; 8:30. *j:* 12:1–8; Lk 10:38–42; 16:19–31. *k:* 9:3, 24. *l:* 8:59; 10:31. *m:* 12:35; 1 Jn 2:10. *n:* 8:12; 9:4. *o:* Mt 9:24. *p:* 14:5, 22. *q:* 12:9, 17–18. *r:* 11:32.

to her, "Your brother will rise." 24[s] Martha
said to him, "I know he will rise, in the resurrection on the last day." 25[t] Jesus told her,
"I am the resurrection and the life; whoever
believes in me, even if he dies, will live,
26 and everyone who lives and believes in me
will never die. Do you believe this?" 27[u]* She
said to him, "Yes, Lord. I have come to believe that you are the Messiah, the Son of
God, the one who is coming into the world."
28 When she had said this, she went and
called her sister Mary secretly, saying, "The
teacher is here and is asking for you." 29 As
soon as she heard this, she rose quickly and
went to him. 30 For Jesus had not yet come
into the village, but was still where Martha
had met him. 31 So when the Jews who were
with her in the house comforting her saw
Mary get up quickly and go out, they followed her, presuming that she was going to
the tomb to weep there. 32 When Mary came
to where Jesus was and saw him, she fell at
his feet and said to him, "Lord, if you had
been here, my brother would not have died."
33* When Jesus saw her weeping and the
Jews who had come with her weeping, he
became perturbed and deeply troubled,
34 and said, "Where have you laid him?"
They said to him, "Sir, come and see."
35[v] And Jesus wept. 36 So the Jews said, "See
how he loved him." 37 But some of them said,
"Could not the one who opened the eyes of
the blind man have done something so that
this man would not have died?"
38 So Jesus, perturbed again, came to the
tomb. It was a cave, and a stone lay across it.
39 Jesus said, "Take away the stone." Martha,
the dead man's sister, said to him, "Lord, by
now there will be a stench; he has been dead
for four days." 40 Jesus said to her, "Did I not
tell you that if you believe you will see the
glory of God?" 41* So they took away the
stone. And Jesus raised his eyes and said,
"Father, I thank you for hearing me. 42[w] I
know that you always hear me; but because
of the crowd here I have said this, that they
may believe that you sent me." 43* And when
he had said this, he cried out in a loud voice,
"Lazarus, come out!" 44 The dead man came
out, tied hand and foot with burial bands,
and his face was wrapped in a cloth. So Jesus
said to them, "Untie him and let him go."

Session of the Sanhedrin. 45[x] Now many
of the Jews who had come to Mary and seen
what he had done began to believe in him.
46 But some of them went to the Pharisees and
told them what Jesus had done. 47[y] So the
chief priests and the Pharisees convened the
Sanhedrin and said, "What are we going to
do? This man is performing many signs. 48* If
we leave him alone, all will believe in him,
and the Romans will come and take away
both our land and our nation." 49[z]* But one of
them, Caiaphas, who was high priest that
year, said to them, "You know nothing, 50 nor
do you consider that it is better for you that
one man should die instead of the people, so
that the whole nation may not perish." 51 He
did not say this on his own, but since he was
high priest for that year, he prophesied that
Jesus was going to die for the nation, 52* and
not only for the nation, but also to gather into
one the dispersed children of God. 53[a] So
from that day on they planned to kill him.
54* So Jesus no longer walked about in public among the Jews, but he left for the region
near the desert, to a town called Ephraim, and
there he remained with his disciples.

11:27 The titles here are a summary of titles given to Jesus earlier in the gospel.

11:33 Became perturbed: a startling phrase in Greek, literally, "He snorted in spirit," perhaps in anger at the presence of evil (death).

11:41 Father: in Aramaic, "*abba*". See note on Mk 14:36.

11:43 Cried out in a loud voice: a dramatization of Jn 5:28; "the hour is coming when all who are in the tombs will hear his voice."

11:48 The Romans will come: Johannine irony; this is precisely what happened after Jesus' death.

11:49 That year: emphasizes the conjunction of the office and the year. Actually, Caiaphas was high priest A.D. 18–36. The Jews attributed a gift of prophecy, sometimes unconscious, to the high priest.

11:52 Dispersed children of God: perhaps the "other sheep" of Jn 10:16.

11:54 Ephraim is usually located about twelve miles northeast of Jerusalem, where the mountains descend into the Jordan valley.

s: 5:29; 6:39–40, 44, 54; 12:48; Is 2:2; Mi 4:1; Acts 23:8; 24:15. *t:* 5:24; 8:51; 14:6; Dn 12:2. *u:* 1:9; 6:69. *v:* Lk 19:41. *w:* 12:30. *x:* Lk 16:31. *y:* 12:19; Mt 26:3–5; Lk 22:2; Acts 4:16. *z:* 18:13–14. *a:* 5:18; 7:1; Mt 12:14.

The Last Passover. [55b*]Now the Passover of the Jews was near, and many went up from the country to Jerusalem before Passover to purify themselves. [56]They looked for Jesus and said to one another as they were in the temple area, "What do you think? That he will not come to the feast?" [57]For the chief priests and the Pharisees had given orders that if anyone knew where he was, he should inform them, so that they might arrest him.

See RG 420

CHAPTER 12

The Anointing at Bethany. [1cd*]Six days before Passover Jesus came to Bethany, where Lazarus was, whom Jesus had raised from the dead. [2e]They gave a dinner for him there, and Martha served, while Lazarus was one of those reclining at table with him. [3f*]Mary took a liter of costly perfumed oil made from genuine aromatic nard and anointed the feet of Jesus and dried them with her hair; the house was filled with the fragrance of the oil. [4]Then Judas the Iscariot, one [of] his disciples, and the one who would betray him, said, [5*]"Why was this oil not sold for three hundred days' wages and given to the poor?" [6g]He said this not because he cared about the poor but because he was a thief and held the money bag and used to steal the contributions. [7*]So Jesus said, "Leave her alone. Let her keep this for the day of my burial. [8h]You always have the poor with you, but you do not always have me."

[9i][The] large crowd of the Jews found out that he was there and came, not only because of Jesus, but also to see Lazarus, whom he had raised from the dead. [10]And the chief priests plotted to kill Lazarus too, [11j]because many of the Jews were turning away and believing in Jesus because of him.

The Entry into Jerusalem. [12k*]On the next day, when the great crowd that had come to the feast heard that Jesus was coming to Jerusalem, [13l*]they took palm branches and went out to meet him, and cried out:

"Hosanna!
Blessed is he who comes in the name of
the Lord,
[even] the king of Israel."

[14]Jesus found an ass and sat upon it, as is written:

[15 m*]"Fear no more, O daughter Zion;
see, your king comes, seated upon an
ass's colt."

[16n*]His disciples did not understand this at first, but when Jesus had been glorified they remembered that these things were written about him and that they had done this for him. [17*]So the crowd that was with him when he called Lazarus from the tomb and raised him from death continued to testify. [18]This

11:55 Purify: prescriptions for purity were based on Ex 19:10–11, 15; Nm 9:6–14; 2 Chr 30:1–3, 15–18.

12:1–8 This is probably the same scene of anointing found in Mk 14:3–9 (see note there) and Mt 26:6–13. The anointing by a penitent woman in Lk 7:36–38 is different. Details from these various episodes have become interchanged.

12:3 The feet of Jesus: so Mk 14:3; but in Mt 26:6, Mary anoints Jesus' head as a sign of regal, messianic anointing.

12:5 Days' wages: literally, "denarii." A denarius is a day's wage in Mt 20:2; see note on Jn 6:7.

12:7 Jesus' response reflects the rabbinical discussion of what was the greatest act of mercy, almsgiving or burying the dead. Those who favored proper burial of the dead thought it an essential condition for sharing in the resurrection.

12:12–19 In John, the entry into Jerusalem follows the anointing whereas in the synoptics it precedes. In John, the crowd, not the disciples, are responsible for the triumphal procession.

12:13 Palm branches: used to welcome great conquerors; cf. 1 Mc 13:51; 2 Mc 10:7. They may be related to the *lûlāb*, the twig bundles used at the feast of Tabernacles. **Hosanna**: see Ps 118:25–26. The Hebrew word means: "(O Lord), grant salvation." **He who comes in the name of the Lord**: referred in Ps 118:26 to a pilgrim entering the temple gates, but here a title for Jesus (see notes on Mt 11:3 and Jn 6:14; 11:27). **The king of Israel**: perhaps from Zep 3:14–15 in connection with the next quotation from Zec 9:9.

12:15 Daughter Zion: Jerusalem. **Ass's colt**: symbol of peace, as opposed to the war horse.

12:16 They had done this: the antecedent of **they** is ambiguous.

12:17–18 There seem to be two different crowds in these verses. There are some good witnesses to the text that have another reading for Jn 12:17: "Then the crowd that was with him began to testify that he had called Lazarus out of the tomb and raised him from the dead."

---

b: 2:13; 5:1; 6:4; 18:28; Ex 19:10–11, 15; Nm 9:6–14; 19:12; Dt 16:6; 2 Chr 30:1–3, 15–18. *c:* Mt 26:6–13; Mk 14:3–9. *d:* 11:1. *e:* Lk 10:38–42. *f:* 11:2. *g:* 13:29. *h:* Dt 15:11. *i:* 11:19. *j:* 11:45. *k:* Mt 21:1–16; Mk 11:1–10; Lk 19:28–40. *l:* 1:49; Lv 23:40; 1 Mc 13:51; 2 Mc 10:7; Rev 7:9. *m:* Is 40:9; Zec 9:9. *n:* 2:22.

was [also] why the crowd went to meet him,
because they heard that he had done this sign.
[19o*]So the Pharisees said to one another,
"You see that you are gaining nothing. Look,
the whole world has gone after him."

The Coming of Jesus' Hour. [20p*]Now
there were some Greeks among those who
had come up to worship at the feast.
[21q*]They came to Philip, who was from
Bethsaida in Galilee, and asked him, "Sir,
we would like to see Jesus." [22r]Philip went
and told Andrew; then Andrew and Philip
went and told Jesus. [23s*]Jesus answered
them, "The hour has come for the Son of
Man to be glorified. [24t*]Amen, amen, I say
to you, unless a grain of wheat falls to the
ground and dies, it remains just a grain of
wheat; but if it dies, it produces much fruit.
[25u*]Whoever loves his life loses it, and whoever hates his life in this world will preserve
it for eternal life. [26v]Whoever serves me
must follow me, and where I am, there also
will my servant be. The Father will honor
whoever serves me.

[27w*]"I am troubled now. Yet what should I
say? 'Father, save me from this hour'? But it
was for this purpose that I came to this hour.
[28x]Father, glorify your name." Then a voice
came from heaven, "I have glorified it and
will glorify it again." [29y]The crowd there
heard it and said it was thunder; but others
said, "An angel has spoken to him." [30z]Jesus
answered and said, "This voice did not come
for my sake but for yours. [31a*]Now is the
time of judgment on this world; now the
ruler of this world will be driven out. [32b]And
when I am lifted up from the earth, I will
draw everyone to myself." [33]He said this indicating the kind of death he would die.
[34c*]So the crowd answered him, "We have
heard from the law that the Messiah remains
forever. Then how can you say that the Son
of Man must be lifted up? Who is this Son of
Man?" [35d]Jesus said to them, "The light will
be among you only a little while. Walk while
you have the light, so that darkness may not
overcome you. Whoever walks in the dark
does not know where he is going. [36e]While
you have the light, believe in the light, so
that you may become children of the light."

Unbelief and Belief among the Jews. After he had said this, Jesus left and hid from
them. [37f*]Although he had performed so
many signs in their presence they did not believe in him, [38g*]in order that the word which
Isaiah the prophet spoke might be fulfilled:

"Lord, who has believed our preaching,
to whom has the might of the Lord
been revealed?"

12:19 The whole world: the sense is that everyone is following Jesus, but John has an ironic play on **world**; he alludes to the universality of salvation (Jn 3:17; 4:42).

12:20–36 This announcement of glorification by death is an illustration of "the whole world" (19) going after him.

12:20 Greeks: not used here in a nationalistic sense. These are probably Gentile proselytes to Judaism; cf. Jn 7:35.

12:21–22 Philip . . . Andrew: the approach is made through disciples who have distinctly Greek names, suggesting that access to Jesus was mediated to the Greek world through his disciples. Philip and Andrew were from Bethsaida (Jn 1:44); Galileans were mostly bilingual. **See**: here seems to mean "have an interview with."

12:23 Jesus' response suggests that only after the crucifixion could the gospel encompass both Jew and Gentile.

12:24 This verse implies that through his death Jesus will be accessible to all. **It remains just a grain of wheat**: this saying is found in the synoptic triple and double traditions (Mk 8:35; Mt 16:25; Lk 9:24; Mt 10:39; Lk 17:33). John adds the phrases (Jn 12:25) **in this world** and **for eternal life**.

12:25 His life: the Greek word *psychē* refers to a person's natural life. It does not mean "soul," for Hebrew anthropology did not postulate body/soul dualism in the way that is familiar to us.

12:27 I am troubled: perhaps an allusion to the Gethsemane agony scene of the synoptics.

12:31 Ruler of this world: Satan.

12:34 There is no passage in the Old Testament that states precisely that the **Messiah remains forever**. Perhaps the closest is Ps 89:37.

12:37–50 These verses, on unbelief of the Jews, provide an epilogue to the Book of Signs.

12:38–41 John gives a historical explanation of the disbelief of the Jewish people, not a psychological one. The Old Testament had to be fulfilled; the disbelief that met Isaiah's message was a foreshadowing of the disbelief that Jesus encountered. In Jn 12:42 and also in Jn 3:20 we see that there is no negation of freedom.

---

o: 11:47–48. *p:* Acts 10:2. *q:* 1:44. *r:* 1:40. *s:* 2:4. *t:* Is 53:10–12; 1 Cor 15:36. *u:* Mt 10:39; 16:25; Mk 8:35; Lk 9:24; 17:33. *v:* 14:3; 17:24; Mt 16:24; Mk 8:34; Lk 9:23. *w:* 6:38; 18:11; Mt 26:38–39; Mk 14:34–36; Lk 22:42; Heb 5:7–8. *x:* 2:11; 17:5; Dn 4:31, 34. *y:* Ex 9:28; 2 Sm 22:14; Jb 37:4; Ps 29:3; Lk 22:43; Acts 23:9. *z:* 11:42. *a:* 16:11; Lk 10:18; Rev 12:9. *b:* 3:14; 8:28; Is 52:13. *c:* Ps 89:5; 110:4; Is 9:7; Dn 7:13–14; Rev 20:1–6. *d:* 9:4; 11:10; Jb 5:14. *e:* Eph 5:8. *f:* Dt 29:2–4; Mk 4:11–12; Rom 9–11. *g:* Is 53:1; Rom 10:16.

[39]For this reason they could not believe,
because again Isaiah said:

[40 h]"He blinded their eyes
and hardened their heart,
so that they might not see with their eyes
and understand with their heart and be
converted,
and I would heal them."

[41 i*]Isaiah said this because he saw his glory
and spoke about him. [42 j]Nevertheless,
many, even among the authorities, believed
in him, but because of the Pharisees they
did not acknowledge it openly in order not
to be expelled from the synagogue. [43 k]For
they preferred human praise to the glory of
God.

Recapitulation. [44 l]Jesus cried out and
said, "Whoever believes in me believes not
only in me but also in the one who sent me,
[45 m]and whoever sees me sees the one who
sent me. [46 n]I came into the world as light, so
that everyone who believes in me might not
remain in darkness. [47 o]And if anyone hears
my words and does not observe them, I do
not condemn him, for I did not come to condemn the world but to save the world.
[48 p]Whoever rejects me and does not accept
my words has something to judge him: the
word that I spoke, it will condemn him on
the last day, [49 q]because I did not speak on
my own, but the Father who sent me commanded me what to say and speak. [50]And I
know that his commandment is eternal life.
So what I say, I say as the Father told me."

III. The Book Of Glory*

CHAPTER 13

See RG 420–21

The Washing of the Disciples' Feet.
[1 r*]Before the feast of Passover, Jesus knew
that his hour had come to pass from this
world to the Father. He loved his own in the
world and he loved them to the end. [2 s*]The
devil had already induced Judas, son of Simon the Iscariot, to hand him over. So, during supper, [3 t]fully aware that the Father had
put everything into his power and that he
had come from God and was returning to
God, [4]he rose from supper and took off his
outer garments. He took a towel and tied it
around his waist. [5 u*]Then he poured water
into a basin and began to wash the disciples'
feet and dry them with the towel around his
waist. [6]He came to Simon Peter, who said to
him, "Master, are you going to wash my
feet?" [7]Jesus answered and said to him,
"What I am doing, you do not understand
now, but you will understand later." [8 v]Peter
said to him, "You will never wash my feet."
Jesus answered him, "Unless I wash you,
you will have no inheritance with me." [9]Si-
mon Peter said to him, "Master, then not
only my feet, but my hands and head as
well." [10 w*]Jesus said to him, "Whoever has
bathed has no need except to have his feet
washed, for he is clean all over; so you are
clean, but not all." [11 x]For he knew who
would betray him; for this reason, he said,
"Not all of you are clean."

12:41 His glory: Isaiah saw the glory of Yahweh enthroned in the heavenly temple, but in John the antecedent of his is Jesus.

13:1–19:42 The Book of Glory. There is a major break here; the word "sign" is used again only in Jn 20:30. In this phase of Jesus' return to the Father, the discourses (Jn 13–17) precede the traditional narrative of the passion (Jn 18–20) to interpret them for the Christian reader. This is the only extended example of esoteric teaching of disciples in John.

13:1–20 Washing of the disciples' feet. This episode occurs in John at the place of the narration of the institution of the Eucharist in the synoptics. It may be a dramatization of Lk 22:27—"I am your servant." It is presented as a "model" ("pattern") of the crucifixion. It symbolizes cleansing from sin by sacrificial death.

13:1 Before the feast of Passover: this would be Thursday evening, before the day of preparation; in the synoptics, the Last Supper is a Passover meal taking place, in John's chronology, on Friday evening. **To the end**: or, "completely."

13:2 Induced: literally, "The devil put into the heart that Judas should hand him over."

13:5 The act of washing another's feet was one that could not be required of the lowliest Jewish slave. It is an allusion to the humiliating death of the crucifixion.

13:10 Bathed: many have suggested that this passage is a symbolic reference to baptism. The Greek root involved is used in baptismal contexts in 1 Cor 6:11; Eph 5:26; Ti 3:5; Heb 10:22.

h: Is 6:9–10; Mt 13:13–15; Mk 4:12. *i:* 5:39; Is 6:1, 4. *j:* 9:22. *k:* 5:44. *l:* 13:20; 14:1. *m:* 14:7–9. *n:* 1:9; 8:12. *o:* 3:17. *p:* Lk 10:16; Heb 4:12. *q:* 14:10, 31; Dt 18:18–19. *r:* 2:4; 7:30; 8:20; Mt 26:17, 45; Mk 14:12, 41; Lk 22:7. *s:* 6:71; 17:12; Mt 26:20–21; Mk 14:17–18; Lk 22:3. *t:* 3:35. *u:* 1 Sm 25:41. *v:* 2 Sm 20:1. *w:* 15:3. *x:* 6:70.

[12]So when he had washed their feet [and] put his garments back on and reclined at table again, he said to them, "Do you realize what I have done for you? [13y]You call me 'teacher' and 'master,' and rightly so, for indeed I am. [14]If I, therefore, the master and teacher, have washed your feet, you ought to wash one another's feet. [15z]I have given you a model to follow, so that as I have done for you, you should also do. [16a*]Amen, amen, I say to you, no slave is greater than his master nor any messenger greater than the one who sent him. [17]If you understand this, blessed are you if you do it. [18b]I am not speaking of all of you. I know those whom I have chosen. But so that the scripture might be fulfilled, 'The one who ate my food has raised his heel against me.' [19]From now on I am telling you before it happens, so that when it happens you may believe that I AM. [20c]Amen, amen, I say to you, whoever receives the one I send receives me, and whoever receives me receives the one who sent me."

Announcement of Judas's Betrayal. [21d]When he had said this, Jesus was deeply troubled and testified, "Amen, amen, I say to you, one of you will betray me." [22]The disciples looked at one another, at a loss as to whom he meant. [23e*]One of his disciples, the one whom Jesus loved, was reclining at Jesus' side. [24]So Simon Peter nodded to him to find out whom he meant. [25f]He leaned back against Jesus' chest and said to him, "Master, who is it?" [26*]Jesus answered, "It is the one to whom I hand the morsel after I have dipped it." So he dipped the morsel and [took it and] handed it to Judas, son of Simon the Iscariot. [27g]After he took the morsel, Satan entered him. So Jesus said to him, "What you are going to do, do quickly." [28][Now] none of those reclining at table realized why he said this to him. [29h]Some thought that since Judas kept the money bag, Jesus had told him, "Buy what we need for the feast," or to give something to the poor. [30]So he took the morsel and left at once. And it was night.

The New Commandment. [31*]When he had left, Jesus said, "Now is the Son of Man glorified, and God is glorified in him. [32i][If God is glorified in him,] God will also glorify him in himself, and he will glorify him at once. [33j]My children, I will be with you only a little while longer. You will look for me, and as I told the Jews, 'Where I go you cannot come,' so now I say it to you. [34k*]I give you a new commandment: love one another. As I have loved you, so you also should love one another. [35]This is how all will know that you are my disciples, if you have love for one another."

Peter's Denial Predicted. [36l]Simon Peter said to him, "Master, where are you going?" Jesus answered [him], "Where I am going, you cannot follow me now, though you will follow later." [37]Peter said to him, "Master, why can't I follow you now? I will lay down my life for you." [38m]Jesus answered, "Will you lay down your life for me? Amen, amen, I say to you, the cock will not crow before you deny me three times."

13:16 Messenger: the Greek has *apostolos*, the only occurrence of the term in John. It is not used in the technical sense here.

13:23 The one whom Jesus loved: also mentioned in Jn 19:26; 20:2; 21:7. A disciple, called "another disciple" or "the other disciple," is mentioned in Jn 18:15 and Jn 20:2; in the latter reference he is identified with the disciple whom Jesus loved. There is also an unnamed disciple in Jn 1:35–40; see note on Jn 1:37.

13:26 Morsel: probably the bitter herb dipped in salt water.

13:31–17:26 Two farewell discourses and a prayer. These seem to be Johannine compositions, including sayings of Jesus at the Last Supper and on other occasions, modeled on similar farewell discourses in Greek literature and the Old Testament (of Moses, Joshua, David).

13:31–38 Introduction: departure and return. Terms of coming and going predominate. These verses form an introduction to the last discourse of Jesus, which extends through Jn 14–17. In it John has collected Jesus' words to his own (Jn 13:1). There are indications that several speeches have been fused together, e.g., in Jn 14:31 and Jn 17:1.

13:34 I give you a new commandment: this puts Jesus on a par with Yahweh. The commandment itself is not new; cf. Lv 19:18 and the note there.

y: Mt 23:8, 10. *z:* Lk 22:27; 1 Pt 2:21. *a:* 15:20; Mt 10:24; Lk 6:40. *b:* Ps 41:10. *c:* Mt 10:40; Mk 9:37; Lk 9:48. *d:* Mt 26:21–25; Mk 14:18–21; Lk 22:21–23. *e:* 19:26; 20:2; 21:7, 20; Mt 10:37. *f:* 21:20. *g:* 13:2; Lk 22:3. *h:* 12:5–6. *i:* 17:1–5. *j:* 7:33; 8:21. *k:* 15:12–13, 17; Lv 19:18; 1 Thes 4:9; 1 Jn 2:7–10; 3:23; 2 Jn 5. *l:* Mk 14:27; Lk 22:23. *m:* 18:27; Mt 26:33–35; Mk 14:29–31; Lk 22:33–34.

CHAPTER 14

See RG 420–21

Last Supper Discourses. [1*]"Do not let your hearts be troubled. You have faith in God; have faith also in me. [2]In my Father's house there are many dwelling places. If there were not, would I have told you that I am going to prepare a place for you? [3n*]And if I go and prepare a place for you, I will come back again and take you to myself, so that where I am you also may be. [4*]Where [I] am going you know the way." [5]Thomas said to him, "Master, we do not know where you are going; how can we know the way?" [6o*]Jesus said to him, "I am the way and the truth and the life. No one comes to the Father except through me. [7p*]If you know me, then you will also know my Father. From now on you do know him and have seen him." [8q*]Philip said to him, "Master, show us the Father, and that will be enough for us." [9r]Jesus said to him, "Have I been with you for so long a time and you still do not know me, Philip? Whoever has seen me has seen the Father. How can you say, 'Show us the Father'? [10s]Do you not believe that I am in the Father and the Father is in me? The words that I speak to you I do not speak on my own. The Father who dwells in me is doing his works. [11t]Believe me that I am in the Father and the Father is in me, or else, believe because of the works themselves. [12u]Amen, amen, I say to you, whoever believes in me will do the works that I do, and will do greater ones than these, because I am going to the Father. [13v]And whatever you ask in my name, I will do, so that the Father may be glorified in the Son. [14]If you ask anything of me in my name, I will do it.

The Advocate. [15w]"If you love me, you will keep my commandments. [16x*]And I will ask the Father, and he will give you another Advocate to be with you always, [17y*]the Spirit of truth, which the world cannot accept, because it neither sees nor knows it. But you know it, because it remains with you, and will be in you. [18*]I will not leave you orphans; I will come to you. [19z]In a little while the world will no longer see me, but you will see me, because I live and you will live. [20a]On that day you will realize that I am in my Father and you are in me and I in you. [21b]Whoever has my commandments and observes them is the one who loves me. And whoever loves me will be loved by my Father, and I will love him and reveal myself to him." [22c*]Judas, not the Iscariot, said to him, "Master, [then] what happened that you will reveal yourself to us and not to the world?" [23d]Jesus answered and said to him, "Whoever loves me will keep my

14:1–31 Jesus' departure and return. This section is a dialogue marked off by a literary inclusion in Jn 14:1, 27: "Do not let your hearts be troubled."

14:1 You have faith: could also be imperative: "Have faith."

14:3 Come back again: a rare Johannine reference to the parousia; cf. 1 Jn 2:28.

14:4 The way: here, of Jesus himself; also a designation of Christianity in Acts 9:2; 19:9, 23; 22:4; 24:14, 22.

14:6 The truth: in John, the divinely revealed reality of the Father manifested in the person and works of Jesus. The possession of truth confers knowledge and liberation from sin (Jn 8:32).

14:7 An alternative reading, "If you knew me, then you would have known my Father also," would be a rebuke, as in Jn 8:19.

14:8 Show us the Father: Philip is pictured asking for a theophany like Ex 24:9–10; 33:18.

14:16 Another Advocate: Jesus is the first advocate (*paraclete*); see 1 Jn 2:1, where Jesus is an advocate in the sense of intercessor in heaven. The Greek term derives from legal terminology for an advocate or defense attorney, and can mean spokesman, mediator, intercessor, comforter, consoler, although no one of these terms encompasses the meaning in John. The Paraclete in John is a teacher, a witness to Jesus, and a prosecutor of the world, who represents the continued presence on earth of the Jesus who has returned to the Father.

14:17 The Spirit of truth: this term is also used at Qumran, where it is a moral force put into a person by God, as opposed to the spirit of perversity. It is more personal in John; it will teach the realities of the new order (Jn 14:26), and testify to the truth (Jn 14:6). While it has been customary to use masculine personal pronouns in English for the Advocate, the Greek word for "spirit" is neuter, and the Greek text and manuscript variants fluctuate between masculine and neuter pronouns.

14:18 I will come to you: indwelling, not parousia.

14:22 Judas, not the Iscariot: probably not the brother of Jesus in Mk 6:3 // Mt 13:55 or the apostle named Jude in Lk 6:16 but Thomas (see note on Jn 11:16), although other readings have "Judas the Cananean."

n: 12:26; 17:24; 1 Jn 2:28. *o:* 8:31–47. *p:* 8:19; 12:45. *q:* Ex 24:9–10; 33:18. *r:* 1:18; 10:30; 12:45; 2 Cor 4:4; Col 1:15; Heb 1:3. *s:* 1:1; 10:37–38; 12:49. *t:* 10:38. *u:* 1:50; 5:20. *v:* 15:7, 16; 16:23–24; Mt 7:7–11. *w:* 15:10; Dt 6:4–9; Ps 119; Wis 6:18; 1 Jn 5:3; 2 Jn 6. *x:* 15:26; Lk 24:49; 1 Jn 2:1. *y:* 16:13; Mt 28:20; 2 Jn 1–2. *z:* 16:16. *a:* 10:38; 17:21; Is 2:17; 4:2–3. *b:* 16:27; 1 Jn 2:5; 3:24. *c:* 7:4; Acts 10:40–41. *d:* Rev 3:20.

word, and my Father will love him, and we will come to him and make our dwelling with him. [24]Whoever does not love me does not keep my words; yet the word you hear is not mine but that of the Father who sent me.

[25]"I have told you this while I am with you. [26e]The Advocate, the holy Spirit that the Father will send in my name—he will teach you everything and remind you of all that [I] told you. [27f*]Peace I leave with you; my peace I give to you. Not as the world gives do I give it to you. Do not let your hearts be troubled or afraid. [28g*]You heard me tell you, 'I am going away and I will come back to you.' If you loved me, you would rejoice that I am going to the Father; for the Father is greater than I. [29h]And now I have told you this before it happens, so that when it happens you may believe. [30*]I will no longer speak much with you, for the ruler of the world is coming. He has no power over me, [31i]but the world must know that I love the Father and that I do just as the Father has commanded me. Get up, let us go.

CHAPTER 15

See RG 420–21

The Vine and the Branches. [1j*]"I am the true vine, and my Father is the vine grower. [2*]He takes away every branch in me that does not bear fruit, and every one that does he prunes so that it bears more fruit. [3k]You are already pruned because of the word that I spoke to you. [4]Remain in me, as I remain in you. Just as a branch cannot bear fruit on its own unless it remains on the vine, so neither can you unless you remain in me. [5]I am the vine, you are the branches. Whoever remains in me and I in him will bear much fruit, because without me you can do nothing. [6l*]Anyone who does not remain in me will be thrown out like a branch and wither; people will gather them and throw them into a fire and they will be burned. [7m]If you remain in me and my words remain in you, ask for whatever you want and it will be done for you. [8n]By this is my Father glorified, that you bear much fruit and become my disciples. [9o]As the Father loves me, so I also love you. Remain in my love. [10p]If you keep my commandments, you will remain in my love, just as I have kept my Father's commandments and remain in his love.

[11q]"I have told you this so that my joy may be in you and your joy may be complete. [12r]This is my commandment: love one another as I love you. [13s*]No one has greater love than this, to lay down one's life for one's friends. [14]You are my friends if you do what I command you. [15t*]I no longer call you slaves, because a slave does not know what his master is doing. I have called you friends, because I have told you everything I have heard from my Father. [16u]It was not you who chose me, but I who chose you and appointed you to go and bear fruit that will remain, so that whatever you ask the Father in my name he may give you. [17v]This I command you: love one another.

14:27 Peace: the traditional Hebrew salutation *šālôm*; but Jesus' "Shalom" is a gift of salvation, connoting the bounty of messianic blessing.

14:28 The Father is greater than I: because he **sent**, **gave**, etc., and Jesus is "a man who has told you the truth that I heard from God" (Jn 8:40).

14:30 The ruler of the world: Satan; cf. Jn 12:31; 16:11.

15:1–16:4 Discourse on the union of Jesus with his disciples. His words become a monologue and go beyond the immediate crisis of the departure of Jesus.

15:1–17 Like Jn 10:1–5, this passage resembles a parable. Israel is spoken of as a vineyard at Is 5:1–7; Mt 21:33–46 and as a vine at Ps 80:9–17; Jer 2:21; Ez 15:2; 17:5–10; 19:10; Hos 10:1. The identification of the vine as the Son of Man in Ps 80:15 and Wisdom's description of herself as a vine in Sir 24:17 are further background for portrayal of Jesus by this figure. There may be secondary eucharistic symbolism here; cf. Mk 14:25 "the fruit of the vine."

15:2 Takes away . . . prunes: in Greek there is a play on two related verbs.

15:6 Branches were cut off and dried on the wall of the vineyard for later use as fuel.

15:13 For one's friends: or: "those whom one loves." In Jn 15:9–13a, the words for love are related to the Greek *agapaō*. In Jn 15:13b–15, the words for love are related to the Greek *phileō*. For John, the two roots seem synonymous and mean "to love"; cf. also Jn 21:15–17. The word *philos* is used here.

15:15 Slaves . . . friends: in the Old Testament, Moses (Dt 34:5), Joshua (Jos 24:29), and David (Ps 89:21) were called "servants" or "slaves of Yahweh"; only Abraham (Is 41:8; 2 Chr 20:7; cf. Jas 2:23) was called a "friend of God."

e: 15:26; 16:7, 13–14; Ps 51:13; Is 63:10. *f:* 16:33; Eph 2:14–18. *g:* 8:40. *h:* 13:19; 16:4. *i:* 6:38. *j:* Ps 80:9–17; Is 5:1–7; Jer 2:21; Ez 15:2; 17:5–10; 19:10. *k:* 13:10. *l:* Ez 15:6–7; 19:10–14. *m:* 14:13; Mt 7:7; Mk 11:24; 1 Jn 5:14. *n:* Mt 5:16. *o:* 17:23. *p:* 8:29; 14:15. *q:* 16:22; 17:13. *r:* 13:34. *s:* Rom 5:6–8; 1 Jn 3:16. *t:* Dt 34:5; Jos 24:29; 2 Chr 20:7; Ps 89:21; Is 41:8; Rom 8:15; Gal 4:7; Jas 2:23. *u:* 14:13; Dt 7:6. *v:* 13:34; 1 Jn 3:23; 4:21.

The World's Hatred. [18w*]"If the world hates you, realize that it hated me first. [19x]If you belonged to the world, the world would love its own; but because you do not belong to the world, and I have chosen you out of the world, the world hates you. [20y*]Remember the word I spoke to you, 'No slave is greater than his master.' If they persecuted me, they will also persecute you. If they kept my word, they will also keep yours. [21z*]And they will do all these things to you on account of my name, because they do not know the one who sent me. [22a*]If I had not come and spoken to them, they would have no sin; but as it is they have no excuse for their sin. [23b]Whoever hates me also hates my Father. [24c]If I had not done works among them that no one else ever did, they would not have sin; but as it is, they have seen and hated both me and my Father. [25d*]But in order that the word written in their law might be fulfilled, 'They hated me without cause.'

[26e*]"When the Advocate comes whom I will send you from the Father, the Spirit of truth that proceeds from the Father, he will testify to me. [27f]And you also testify, because you have been with me from the beginning.

CHAPTER 16

See RG 420-21

[1]"I have told you this so that you may not fall away. [2g*]They will expel you from the synagogues; in fact, the hour is coming when everyone who kills you will think he is offering worship to God. [3h]They will do this because they have not known either the Father or me. [4i*]I have told you this so that when their hour comes you may remember that I told you.

Jesus' Departure; Coming of the Advocate. "I did not tell you this from the beginning, because I was with you. [5j*]But now I am going to the one who sent me, and not one of you asks me, 'Where are you going?' [6]But because I told you this, grief has filled your hearts. [7k]But I tell you the truth, it is better for you that I go. For if I do not go, the Advocate will not come to you. But if I go, I will send him to you. [8*]And when he comes he will convict the world in regard to sin and righteousness and condemnation: [9l]sin, because they do not believe in me; [10]righteousness, because I am going to the Father and you will no longer see me; [11m]condemnation, because the ruler of this world has been condemned.

[12]"I have much more to tell you, but you cannot bear it now. [13n*]But when he comes, the Spirit of truth, he will guide you to all truth. He will not speak on his own, but he will speak what he hears, and will declare to you the things that are coming. [14]He will glorify me, because he will take from what is

15:18–16:4 The hostile reaction of the world. There are synoptic parallels, predicting persecution, especially at Mt 10:17–25; 24:9–10.

15:20 The word I spoke to you: a reference to Jn 13:16.

15:21 On account of my name: the idea of persecution for Jesus' name is frequent in the New Testament (Mt 10:22; 24:9; Acts 9:14). For John, association with Jesus' name implies union with Jesus.

15:22, 24 Jesus' words (**spoken**) and deeds (**works**) are the great motives of credibility. **They have seen and hated**: probably means that they have seen his works and still have hated; but the Greek can be read: "have seen both me and my Father and still have hated both me and my Father." **Works . . . that no one else ever did**: so Yahweh in Dt 4:32–33.

15:25 In their law: law is here used as a larger concept than the Pentateuch, for the reference is to Ps 35:19 or Ps 69:5. See notes on Jn 10:34; 12:34. **Their** law reflects the argument of the church with the synagogue.

15:26 Whom I will send: in Jn 14:16, 26 the Paraclete is to be sent by the Father, at the request of Jesus. Here the Spirit comes from both Jesus and the Father in mission; there is no reference here to the eternal procession of the Spirit.

16:2 Hour: of persecution, not Jesus' "hour" (see note on Jn 2:4).

16:4b–33 A duplicate of Jn 14:1–31 on departure and return.

16:5 Not one of you asks me: the difficulty of reconciling this with Simon Peter's question in Jn 13:36 and Thomas' words in Jn 14:5 strengthens the supposition that the last discourse has been made up of several collections of Johannine material.

16:8–11 These verses illustrate the forensic character of the Paraclete's role: in the forum of the disciples' conscience he prosecutes the world. He leads believers to see (a) that the basic sin was and is refusal to believe in Jesus; (b) that, although Jesus was found guilty and apparently died in disgrace, in reality righteousness has triumphed, for Jesus has returned to his Father; (c) finally, that it is the ruler of this world, Satan, who has been condemned through Jesus' death (Jn 12:32).

16:13 Declare to you the things that are coming: not a reference to new predictions about the future, but interpretation of what has already occurred or been said.

---

w: 7:7; 14:17; Mt 10:22; 24:9; Mk 13:13; Lk 6:22; 1 Jn 3:13. *x:* 17:14–16; 1 Jn 4:5. *y:* 13:16; Mt 10:24. *z:* 8:19; 16:3. *a:* 8:21, 24; 9:41. *b:* 5:23; Lk 10:16; 1 Jn 2:23. *c:* 3:2; 9:32; Dt 4:32–33. *d:* Ps 35:19; 69:4. *e:* 14:16, 26; Mt 10:19–20. *f:* Lk 1:2; Acts 1:8. *g:* 9:22; 12:42; Mt 10:17; Lk 21:12; Acts 26:11. *h:* 15:21. *i:* 13:19; 14:29. *j:* 7:33; 13:36; 14:5. *k:* 7:39; 14:16–17, 26; 15:26. *l:* 8:21–24; 15:22. *m:* 12:31. *n:* 14:17, 26; 15:26; Ps 25:5; 143:10; 1 Jn 2:27; Rev 7:17.

mine and declare it to you. [15]Everything that the Father has is mine; for this reason I told you that he will take from what is mine and declare it to you.

[16o]"A little while and you will no longer see me, and again a little while later and you will see me." [17]So some of his disciples said to one another, "What does this mean that he is saying to us, 'A little while and you will not see me, and again a little while and you will see me,' and 'Because I am going to the Father'?" [18]So they said, "What is this 'little while' [of which he speaks]? We do not know what he means." [19]Jesus knew that they wanted to ask him, so he said to them, "Are you discussing with one another what I said, 'A little while and you will not see me, and again a little while and you will see me'? [20p]Amen, amen, I say to you, you will weep and mourn, while the world rejoices; you will grieve, but your grief will become joy. [21q]When a woman is in labor, she is in anguish because her hour has arrived; but when she has given birth to a child, she no longer remembers the pain because of her joy that a child has been born into the world. [22r]So you also are now in anguish. But I will see you again, and your hearts will rejoice, and no one will take your joy away from you. [23s]On that day you will not question me about anything. Amen, amen, I say to you, whatever you ask the Father in my name he will give you. [24]Until now you have not asked anything in my name; ask and you will receive, so that your joy may be complete.

[25t*]"I have told you this in figures of speech. The hour is coming when I will no longer speak to you in figures but I will tell you clearly about the Father. [26u]On that day you will ask in my name, and I do not tell you that I will ask the Father for you. [27]For the Father himself loves you, because you have loved me and have come to believe that I came from God. [28v]I came from the Father and have come into the world. Now I am leaving the world and going back to the Father." [29]His disciples said, "Now you are talking plainly, and not in any figure of speech. [30*]Now we realize that you know everything and that you do not need to have anyone question you. Because of this we believe that you came from God." [31]Jesus answered them, "Do you believe now? [32w*]Behold, the hour is coming and has arrived when each of you will be scattered to his own home and you will leave me alone. But I am not alone, because the Father is with me. [33x]I have told you this so that you might have peace in me. In the world you will have trouble, but take courage, I have conquered the world."

CHAPTER 17

See RG 420–21

The Prayer of Jesus. [1y*]When Jesus had said this, he raised his eyes to heaven and said, "Father, the hour has come. Give glory to your son, so that your son may glorify you, [2z*]just as you gave him authority over all people, so that he may give eternal life to all you gave him. [3a*]Now this is eternal life, that they should know you, the only true God,

16:25 See note on Jn 10:6. Here, possibly a reference to Jn 15:1–16 or Jn 16:21.

16:30 The reference is seemingly to the fact that Jesus could anticipate their question in Jn 16:19. The disciples naively think they have the full understanding that is the climax of "the hour" of Jesus' death, resurrection, and ascension (Jn 16:25), but the only part of the hour that is at hand for them is their share in the passion (Jn 16:32).

16:32 You will be scattered: cf. Mk 14:27 and Mt 26:31, where both cite Zec 13:7 about the sheep being dispersed.

17:1–26 Climax of the last discourse(s). Since the sixteenth century, this chapter has been called the "high priestly prayer" of Jesus. He speaks as intercessor, with words addressed directly to the Father and not to the disciples, who supposedly only overhear. Yet the prayer is one of petition, for immediate (Jn 17:6–19) and future (Jn 17:20–21) disciples. Many phrases reminiscent of the Lord's Prayer occur. Although still in the world (Jn 17:13), Jesus looks on his earthly ministry as a thing of the past (Jn 17:4, 12). Whereas Jesus has up to this time stated that the disciples could follow him (Jn 13:33, 36), now he wishes them to be with him in union with the Father (Jn 17:12–14).

17:1 The action of looking up to heaven and the address Father are typical of Jesus at prayer; cf. Jn 11:41 and Lk 11:2.

17:2 Another possible interpretation is to treat the first line of the verse as parenthetical and the second as an appositive to the clause that ends v 1: **so that your son may glorify you (just as . . . all people), so that he may give eternal life. . . .**

17:3 This verse was clearly added in the editing of the gospel as a reflection on the preceding verse; Jesus nowhere else refers to himself as Jesus Christ.

o: 7:33; 14:19. *p:* Ps 126:6. *q:* Is 26:17–18; Jer 31:13; Mi 4:9. *r:* 14:19; 15:11; 20:20. *s:* 14:13. *t:* Mt 13:34–35. *u:* 14:13. *v:* 1:1. *w:* 8:29; Zec 13:7; Mt 26:31; Mk 14:27. *x:* 14:27. *y:* 13:31. *z:* 3:35; Mt 28:18. *a:* 1:17; Wis 14:7; 15:3; 1 Jn 5:20.

and the one whom you sent, Jesus Christ. [4]I glorified you on earth by accomplishing the work that you gave me to do. [5b]Now glorify me, Father, with you, with the glory that I had with you before the world began.

[6*]"I revealed your name to those whom you gave me out of the world. They belonged to you, and you gave them to me, and they have kept your word. [7]Now they know that everything you gave me is from you, [8]because the words you gave to me I have given to them, and they accepted them and truly understood that I came from you, and they have believed that you sent me. [9c]I pray for them. I do not pray for the world but for the ones you have given me, because they are yours, [10d]and everything of mine is yours and everything of yours is mine, and I have been glorified in them. [11]And now I will no longer be in the world, but they are in the world, while I am coming to you. Holy Father, keep them in your name that you have given me, so that they may be one just as we are. [12e]When I was with them I protected them in your name that you gave me, and I guarded them, and none of them was lost except the son of destruction, in order that the scripture might be fulfilled. [13f]But now I am coming to you. I speak this in the world so that they may share my joy completely. [14g]I gave them your word, and the world hated them, because they do not belong to the world any more than I belong to the world. [15h*]I do not ask that you take them out of the world but that you keep them from the evil one. [16]They do not belong to the world any more than I belong to the world. [17i]Consecrate them in the truth. Your word is truth. [18j]As you sent me into the world, so I sent them into the world. [19]And I consecrate myself for them, so that they also may be consecrated in truth.

[20]"I pray not only for them, but also for those who will believe in me through their word, [21k]so that they may all be one, as you, Father, are in me and I in you, that they also may be in us, that the world may believe that you sent me. [22]And I have given them the glory you gave me, so that they may be one, as we are one, [23]I in them and you in me, that they may be brought to perfection as one, that the world may know that you sent me, and that you loved them even as you loved me. [24l*]Father, they are your gift to me. I wish that where I am they also may be with me, that they may see my glory that you gave me, because you loved me before the foundation of the world. [25m]Righteous Father, the world also does not know you, but I know you, and they know that you sent me. [26*]I made known to them your name and I will make it known, that the love with which you loved me may be in them and I in them."

CHAPTER 18

See RG 421–22

Jesus Arrested. [1n*]When he had said this, Jesus went out with his disciples across the Kidron valley to where there was a garden, into which he and his disciples entered. [2]Judas his betrayer also knew the place, because Jesus had often met there with his disciples. [3o*]So Judas got a band of soldiers and guards from the chief priests and the Pharisees and went there with lanterns, torches, and weapons. [4]Jesus, knowing everything that was going to happen to him, went out and said to them, "Whom are you looking for?"

17:6 I revealed your name: perhaps the name **I AM**; cf. Jn 8:24, 28, 58; 13:19.

17:15 Note the resemblance to the petition of the Lord's Prayer, "deliver us from the evil one." Both probably refer to the devil rather than to abstract evil.

17:24 Where I am: Jesus prays for the believers ultimately to join him in heaven. Then they will not see his glory as in a mirror but clearly (2 Cor 3:18; 1 Jn 3:2).

17:26 I will make it known: through the Advocate.

18:1–14 John does not mention the agony in the garden and the kiss of Judas, nor does he identify the place as Gethsemane or the Mount of Olives.

18:1 Jesus went out: see Jn 14:31 where it seems he is leaving the supper room. **Kidron valley**: literally, "the winter-flowing Kidron"; this wadi has water only during the winter rains.

18:3 Band of soldiers: seems to refer to Roman troops, either the full cohort of 600 men (1/10 of a legion), or more likely the maniple of 200 under their tribune (Jn 18:12). In this case, John is hinting at Roman collusion in the action against Jesus before he was brought to Pilate. The lanterns and torches may be symbolic of the hour of darkness.

b: 1:1, 2; 12:28; Phil 2:6, 9–11. *c:* 17:20. *d:* 16:15; 2 Thes 1:10, 12. *e:* 13:18; 18:9; Ps 41:10; Mt 26:24; Acts 1:16. *f:* 15:11. *g:* 15:19. *h:* Mt 6:13; 2 Thes 3:3; 1 Jn 5:18. *i:* 1 Pt 1:22 *j:* 20:21–22. *k:* 10:30; 14:10–11, 20. *l:* 14:3; 1 Thes 4:17. *m:* 1:10. *n:* 2 Sm 15:23; Mt 26:30, 36; Mk 14:26, 32; Lk 22:39. *o:* Mt 26:47–51; Mk 14:43–44; Lk 22:47.

[5*]They answered him, "Jesus the Nazorean." He said to them, "I AM." Judas his betrayer was also with them. [6]When he said to them, "I AM," they turned away and fell to the ground. [7]So he again asked them, "Whom are you looking for?" They said, "Jesus the Nazorean." [8]Jesus answered, "I told you that I AM. So if you are looking for me, let these men go." [9p*]This was to fulfill what he had said, "I have not lost any of those you gave me." [10*]Then Simon Peter, who had a sword, drew it, struck the high priest's slave, and cut off his right ear. The slave's name was Malchus. [11q*]Jesus said to Peter, "Put your sword into its scabbard. Shall I not drink the cup that the Father gave me?"

[12r]So the band of soldiers, the tribune, and the Jewish guards seized Jesus, bound him, [13s*]and brought him to Annas first. He was the father-in-law of Caiaphas, who was high priest that year. [14t]It was Caiaphas who had counseled the Jews that it was better that one man should die rather than the people.

Peter's First Denial. [15u*]Simon Peter and another disciple followed Jesus. Now the other disciple was known to the high priest, and he entered the courtyard of the high priest with Jesus. [16]But Peter stood at the gate outside. So the other disciple, the acquaintance of the high priest, went out and spoke to the gatekeeper and brought Peter in. [17]Then the maid who was the gatekeeper said to Peter, "You are not one of this man's disciples, are you?" He said, "I am not." [18]Now the slaves and the guards were standing around a charcoal fire that they had made, because it was cold, and were warming themselves. Peter was also standing there keeping warm.

The Inquiry before Annas. [19v]The high priest questioned Jesus about his disciples and about his doctrine. [20w*]Jesus answered him, "I have spoken publicly to the world. I have always taught in a synagogue or in the temple area where all the Jews gather, and in secret I have said nothing. [21]Why ask me? Ask those who heard me what I said to them. They know what I said." [22x]When he had said this, one of the temple guards standing there struck Jesus and said, "Is this the way you answer the high priest?" [23]Jesus answered him, "If I have spoken wrongly, testify to the wrong; but if I have spoken rightly, why do you strike me?" [24y*]Then Annas sent him bound to Caiaphas the high priest.

Peter Denies Jesus Again. [25z]Now Simon Peter was standing there keeping warm. And they said to him, "You are not one of his disciples, are you?" He denied it and said, "I am not." [26]One of the slaves of the high priest, a relative of the one whose ear Peter had cut off, said, "Didn't I see you in the garden with him?" [27*]Again Peter denied it. And immediately the cock crowed.

The Trial before Pilate. [28a*]Then they brought Jesus from Caiaphas to the praetorium. It was morning. And they themselves did not enter the praetorium, in order not to

18:5 Nazorean: the form found in Mt 26:71 (see note on Mt 2:23) is here used, not **Nazarene** of Mark. **I AM**: or "I am he," but probably intended by the evangelist as an expression of divinity (cf. their appropriate response in Jn 18:6); see note on Jn 8:24. John sets the confusion of the arresting party against the background of Jesus' divine majesty.

18:9 The citation may refer to Jn 6:39; 10:28; or Jn 17:12.

18:10 Only John gives the names of the two antagonists; both John and Luke mention the right ear.

18:11 The theme of the cup is found in the synoptic account of the agony (Mk 14:36 and parallels).

18:13 Annas: only John mentions an inquiry before Annas; cf. Jn 18:16, 19–24; see note on Lk 3:2. It is unlikely that this nighttime interrogation before Annas is the same as the trial before Caiaphas placed by Matthew and Mark at night and by Luke in the morning.

18:15–16 Another disciple . . . the other disciple: see note on Jn 13:23.

18:20 I have always taught . . . in the temple area: cf. Mk 14:49 for a similar statement.

18:24 Caiaphas: see Mt 26:3, 57; Lk 3:2; and the notes there. John may leave room here for the trial before Caiaphas described in the synoptic gospels.

18:27 Cockcrow was the third Roman division of the night, lasting from midnight to 3 A.M.

18:28 Praetorium: see note on Mt 27:27. **Morning**: literally, "the early hour," or fourth Roman division of the night, 3 to 6 A.M. **The Passover**: the synoptic gospels give the impression that the Thursday night supper was the Passover meal (Mk 14:12); for John that meal is still to be eaten Friday night.

---

p: 6:39; 10:28; 17:12. *q:* Mt 20:22; 26:39; Mk 10:38; Lk 22:42. *r:* Mt 26:57–58; Mk 14:53–54; Lk 22:54–55. *s:* Lk 3:2. *t:* 11:49–50. *u:* Mt 26:58, 69–70; Mk 14:54, 66–68; Lk 22:54–57. *v:* Mt 26:59–66; Mk 14:55–64; Lk 22:66–71. *w:* 6:59; 7:14, 26; Is 48:16; Mt 26:55; Mk 4:23; Lk 19:47; 22:53. *x:* Acts 23:2. *y:* Mt 26:57. *z:* Mt 26:71–75; Mk 14:69–72; Lk 22:58–62. *a:* Mt 27:1–2, 11–25; Mk 15:1–5; Lk 23:1–5.

be defiled so that they could eat the Passover. [29]So Pilate came out to them and said, "What charge do you bring [against] this man?" [30]They answered and said to him, "If he were not a criminal, we would not have handed him over to you." [31*]At this, Pilate said to them, "Take him yourselves, and judge him according to your law." The Jews answered him, "We do not have the right to execute anyone," [32b*]in order that the word of Jesus might be fulfilled that he said indicating the kind of death he would die. [33]So Pilate went back into the praetorium and summoned Jesus and said to him, "Are you the King of the Jews?" [34]Jesus answered, "Do you say this on your own or have others told you about me?" [35c]Pilate answered, "I am not a Jew, am I? Your own nation and the chief priests handed you over to me. What have you done?" [36d]Jesus answered, "My kingdom does not belong to this world. If my kingdom did belong to this world, my attendants [would] be fighting to keep me from being handed over to the Jews. But as it is, my kingdom is not here." [37e*]So Pilate said to him, "Then you are a king?" Jesus answered, "You say I am a king. For this I was born and for this I came into the world, to testify to the truth. Everyone who belongs to the truth listens to my voice." [38f]Pilate said to him, "What is truth?"

When he had said this, he again went out to the Jews and said to them, "I find no guilt in him. [39*]But you have a custom that I release one prisoner to you at Passover. Do you want me to release to you the King of the Jews?" [40*]They cried out again, "Not this one but Barabbas!" Now Barabbas was a revolutionary.

CHAPTER 19

See RG 421–22

[1g*]Then Pilate took Jesus and had him scourged. [2]And the soldiers wove a crown out of thorns and placed it on his head, and clothed him in a purple cloak, [3]and they came to him and said, "Hail, King of the Jews!" And they struck him repeatedly. [4h]Once more Pilate went out and said to them, "Look, I am bringing him out to you, so that you may know that I find no guilt in him." [5i]So Jesus came out, wearing the crown of thorns and the purple cloak. And he said to them, "Behold, the man!" [6j]When the chief priests and the guards saw him they cried out, "Crucify him, crucify him!" Pilate said to them, "Take him yourselves and crucify him. I find no guilt in him." [7k*]The Jews answered, "We have a law, and according to that law he ought to die, because he made himself the Son of God." [8]Now when Pilate heard this statement, he became even more afraid, [9l]and went back into the praetorium and said to Jesus, "Where are you from?" Jesus did not answer him. [10]So Pilate said to him, "Do you not speak to me? Do you not know that I have power to release you and I have power to crucify you?" [11m]Jesus answered [him], "You would have no power over me if it had not been given to you from above. For this reason the one who handed me over to you has the greater sin." [12n*]Consequently, Pilate tried to release him; but the

18:31 We do not have the right to execute anyone: only John gives this reason for their bringing Jesus to Pilate. Jewish sources are not clear on the competence of the Sanhedrin at this period to sentence and to execute for political crimes.

18:32 The Jewish punishment for blasphemy was stoning (Lv 24:16). In coming to the Romans to ensure that Jesus would be crucified, the Jewish authorities fulfilled his prophecy that he would be **exalted** (Jn 3:14; 12:32–33). There is some historical evidence, however, for Jews crucifying Jews.

18:37 You say I am a king: see Mt 26:64 for a similar response to the high priest. It is at best a reluctant affirmative.

18:39 See note on Mt 27:15.

18:40 Barabbas: see note on Mt 27:16–17. **Revolutionary**: a guerrilla warrior fighting for nationalistic aims, though the term can also denote a robber. See note on Mt 27:38.

19:1 Luke places the mockery of Jesus at the midpoint in the trial when Jesus was sent to Herod. Mark and Matthew place the scourging and mockery at the end of the trial after the sentence of death. Scourging was an integral part of the crucifixion penalty.

19:7 Made himself the Son of God: this question was not raised in John's account of the Jewish interrogations of Jesus as it was in the synoptic account. Nevertheless, see Jn 5:18; 8:53; 10:36.

19:12 Friend of Caesar: a Roman honorific title bestowed upon high-ranking officials for merit.

b: 3:14; 8:28; 12:32–33. *c:* 1:11. *d:* 1:10; 8:23. *e:* 8:47; 1 Tm 6:13. *f:* Mt 27:15–26; Mk 15:6–15; Lk 23:18–25; Acts 3:14. *g:* Mt 27:27–31; Mk 15:16–20; Lk 23:13–25. *h:* 18:38. *i:* Is 52:14. *j:* 18:31; 19:15. *k:* 10:33–36; Lv 24:16. *l:* 7:28. *m:* 3:27; 10:18; Rom 13:1. *n:* Acts 17:7.

Jews cried out, "If you release him, you are not a Friend of Caesar. Everyone who makes himself a king opposes Caesar."

13*When Pilate heard these words he brought Jesus out and seated him on the judge's bench in the place called Stone Pavement, in Hebrew, Gabbatha. 14*It was preparation day for Passover, and it was about noon. And he said to the Jews, "Behold, your king!" 15They cried out, "Take him away, take him away! Crucify him!" Pilate said to them, "Shall I crucify your king?" The chief priests answered, "We have no king but Caesar." 16*Then he handed him over to them to be crucified.

The Crucifixion of Jesus. So they took Jesus, 17o*and carrying the cross himself he went out to what is called the Place of the Skull, in Hebrew, Golgotha. 18There they crucified him, and with him two others, one on either side, with Jesus in the middle. 19*Pilate also had an inscription written and put on the cross. It read, "Jesus the Nazorean, the King of the Jews." 20Now many of the Jews read this inscription, because the place where Jesus was crucified was near the city; and it was written in Hebrew, Latin, and Greek. 21pSo the chief priests of the Jews said to Pilate, "Do not write 'The King of the Jews,' but that he said, 'I am the King of the Jews.' " 22Pilate answered, "What I have written, I have written."

23qr*When the soldiers had crucified Jesus, they took his clothes and divided them into four shares, a share for each soldier. They also took his tunic, but the tunic was seamless, woven in one piece from the top down. 24So they said to one another, "Let's not tear it, but cast lots for it to see whose it will be," in order that the passage of scripture might be fulfilled [that says]:

"They divided my garments among them,
and for my vesture they cast lots."

This is what the soldiers did. 25s*Standing by the cross of Jesus were his mother and his mother's sister, Mary the wife of Clopas, and Mary of Magdala. 26t*When Jesus saw his mother and the disciple there whom he loved, he said to his mother, "Woman,

19:13 Seated him: others translate "(Pilate) sat down." In John's thought, Jesus is the real judge of the world, and John may here be portraying him seated on the judgment bench. **Stone pavement**: in Greek *lithostrotos*; under the fortress Antonia, one of the conjectured locations of the praetorium, a massive stone pavement has been excavated. **Gabbatha** (Aramaic rather than Hebrew) probably means "ridge, elevation."

19:14 Noon: Mk 15:25 has Jesus crucified "at the third hour," which means either 9 A.M. or the period from 9 to 12. Noon, the time when, according to John, Jesus was sentenced to death, was the hour at which the priests began to slaughter Passover lambs in the temple; see Jn 1:29.

19:16 He handed him over to them to be crucified: in context this would seem to mean "handed him over to the chief priests." Lk 23:25 has a similar ambiguity. There is a polemic tendency in the gospels to place the guilt of the crucifixion on the Jewish authorities and to exonerate the Romans from blame. But John later mentions the Roman soldiers (Jn 19:23), and it was to these soldiers that Pilate handed Jesus over.

19:17 Carrying the cross himself: a different picture from that of the synoptics, especially Lk 23:26 where Simon of Cyrene is made to carry the cross, walking behind Jesus. In John's theology, Jesus remained in complete control and master of his destiny (cf. Jn 10:18). **Place of the Skull**: the Latin word for skull is *Calvaria*; hence "Calvary." **Golgotha** is actually an Aramaic rather than a Hebrew word.

19:19 The inscription differs with slightly different words in each of the four gospels. John's form is fullest and gives the equivalent of the Latin *INRI = Iesus Nazarenus Rex Iudaeorum*. Only John mentions its polyglot character (Jn 19:20) and Pilate's role in keeping the title unchanged (Jn 19:21–22).

19:23–25a While all four gospels describe the soldiers casting lots to divide Jesus' garments (see note on Mt 27:35), only John quotes the underlying passage from Ps 22:19, and only John sees each line of the poetic parallelism literally carried out in two separate actions (Jn 19:23–24).

19:25 It is not clear whether four women are meant, or three (i.e., **Mary the wife of Cl[e]opas** [cf. Lk 24:18] is in apposition with **his mother's sister**) or two (his mother and his mother's sister, i.e., Mary of Cl[e]opas and Mary of Magdala). Only John mentions the mother of Jesus here. The synoptics have a group of women looking on from a distance at the cross (Mk 15:40).

19:26–27 This scene has been interpreted literally, of Jesus' concern for his mother; and symbolically, e.g., in the light of the Cana story in Jn 2 (the presence of the mother of Jesus, the address **woman**, and the mention of the **hour**) and of the upper room in Jn 13 (the presence of the beloved disciple; the **hour**). Now that the hour has come (Jn 19:28), Mary (a symbol of the church?) is given a role as the mother of Christians (personified by the beloved disciple); or, as a representative of those seeking salvation, she is supported by the disciple who interprets Jesus' revelation; or Jewish and Gentile Christianity (or Israel and the Christian community) are reconciled.

o: Mt 27:32–37; Mk 15:21–26; Lk 23:26–35. *p:* 18:33; Lk 19:14. *q:* Mt 27:38–44; Mk 15:27–32; Lk 23:36–43. *r:* Ps 22:19; Mt 27:35; Mk 15:24; Lk 23:34. *s:* Mt 27:55; Mk 15:40–41; Lk 8:2; 23:49. *t:* 13:23.

behold, your son." [27]Then he said to the disciple, "Behold, your mother." And from that hour the disciple took her into his home.

[28uv*]After this, aware that everything was now finished, in order that the scripture might be fulfilled, Jesus said, "I thirst." [29*]There was a vessel filled with common wine. So they put a sponge soaked in wine on a sprig of hyssop and put it up to his mouth. [30w*]When Jesus had taken the wine, he said, "It is finished." And bowing his head, he handed over the spirit.

The Blood and Water. [31x]Now since it was preparation day, in order that the bodies might not remain on the cross on the sabbath, for the sabbath day of that week was a solemn one, the Jews asked Pilate that their legs be broken and they be taken down. [32]So the soldiers came and broke the legs of the first and then of the other one who was crucified with Jesus. [33]But when they came to Jesus and saw that he was already dead, they did not break his legs, [34y*]but one soldier thrust his lance into his side, and immediately blood and water flowed out. [35z*]An eyewitness has testified, and his testimony is true; he knows that he is speaking the truth, so that you also may [come to] believe. [36a]For this happened so that the scripture passage might be fulfilled:

"Not a bone of it will be broken."

[37b]And again another passage says:

"They will look upon him whom they
have pierced."

The Burial of Jesus. [38c*]After this, Joseph of Arimathea, secretly a disciple of Jesus for fear of the Jews, asked Pilate if he could remove the body of Jesus. And Pilate permitted it. So he came and took his body. [39d]Nicodemus, the one who had first come to him at night, also came bringing a mixture of myrrh and aloes weighing about one hundred pounds. [40]They took the body of Jesus and bound it with burial cloths along with the spices, according to the Jewish burial custom. [41]Now in the place where he had been crucified there was a garden, and in the garden a new tomb, in which no one had yet been buried. [42]So they laid Jesus there because of the Jewish preparation day; for the tomb was close by.

CHAPTER 20

See RG 421–22

The Empty Tomb. [1ef*]On the first day of the week, Mary of Magdala came to the tomb early in the morning, while it was still dark, and saw the stone removed from the tomb. [2*]So she ran and went to Simon Peter and to the other disciple whom Jesus loved, and told them, "They have taken the Lord

19:28 The scripture . . . fulfilled: either in the scene of Jn 19:25–27, or in the **I thirst** of Jn 19:28. If the latter, Ps 22:16; 69:22 deserve consideration.

19:29 Wine: John does not mention the drugged wine, a narcotic that Jesus refused as the crucifixion began (Mk 15:23), but only this final gesture of kindness at the end (Mk 15:36). **Hyssop**, a small plant, is scarcely suitable for carrying a sponge (Mark mentions a reed) and may be a symbolic reference to the hyssop used to daub the blood of the paschal lamb on the doorpost of the Hebrews (Ex 12:22).

19:30 Handed over the spirit: there is a double nuance of dying (giving up the last breath or spirit) and that of passing on the holy Spirit; see Jn 7:39 which connects the giving of the Spirit with Jesus' glorious return to the Father, and Jn 20:22 where the author portrays the conferral of the Spirit.

19:34–35 John probably emphasizes these verses to show the reality of Jesus' death, against the docetist heretics. In the blood and water there may also be a symbolic reference to the Eucharist and baptism.

19:35 He knows: it is not certain from the Greek that this **he** is the **eyewitness** of the first part of the sentence. **May [come to] believe**: see note on Jn 20:31.

19:38–42 In the first three gospels there is no anointing on Friday. In Matthew and Luke the women come to the tomb on Sunday morning precisely to anoint Jesus.

20:1–31 The risen Jesus reveals his glory and confers the Spirit. This story fulfills the basic need for testimony to the resurrection. What we have here is not a record but a series of single stories.

20:1–10 The story of the empty tomb is found in both the Matthean and the Lucan traditions; John's version seems to be a fusion of the two.

20:1 Still dark: according to Mark the sun had risen, Matthew describes it as "dawning," and Luke refers to early dawn. Mary sees the stone removed, not the empty tomb.

20:2 Mary runs away, not directed by an angel/young man as in the synoptic accounts. The plural "we" in the second part of her statement might reflect a tradition of more women going to the tomb.

u: Mt 27:45–56; Mk 15:33–41; Lk 23:44–49. *v:* Ps 22:16; 69:22. *w:* 4:34; 10:18; 17:4; Lk 23:46. *x:* Ex 12:16; Dt 21:23. *y:* Nm 20:11; 1 Jn 5:6. *z:* 7:37–39; 21:24. *a:* Ex 12:46; Nm 9:12; Ps 34:21. *b:* Nm 21:9; Zec 12:10; Rev 1:7. *c:* Mt 27:57–60; Mk 15:42–46; Lk 23:46–49. *d:* 3:1–2; 7:50; Ps 45:9. *e:* Mt 28:1–10; Mk 16:1–11; Lk 24:1–12. *f:* 19:25.

from the tomb, and we don't know where they put him." [3*]So Peter and the other disciple went out and came to the tomb. [4]They both ran, but the other disciple ran faster than Peter and arrived at the tomb first; [5]he bent down and saw the burial cloths there, but did not go in. [6g*]When Simon Peter arrived after him, he went into the tomb and saw the burial cloths there, [7h]and the cloth that had covered his head, not with the burial cloths but rolled up in a separate place. [8]Then the other disciple also went in, the one who had arrived at the tomb first, and he saw and believed. [9i*]For they did not yet understand the scripture that he had to rise from the dead. [10]Then the disciples returned home.

The Appearance to Mary of Magdala. [11j*]But Mary stayed outside the tomb weeping. And as she wept, she bent over into the tomb [12]and saw two angels in white sitting there, one at the head and one at the feet where the body of Jesus had been. [13]And they said to her, "Woman, why are you weeping?" She said to them, "They have taken my Lord, and I don't know where they laid him." [14k]When she had said this, she turned around and saw Jesus there, but did not know it was Jesus. [15l]Jesus said to her, "Woman, why are you weeping? Whom are you looking for?" She thought it was the gardener and said to him, "Sir, if you carried him away, tell me where you laid him, and I will take him." [16*]Jesus said to her, "Mary!" She turned and said to him in Hebrew, "Rabbouni," which means Teacher. [17m*]Jesus said to her, "Stop holding on to me, for I have not yet ascended to the Father. But go to my brothers and tell them, 'I am going to my Father and your Father, to my God and your God.' " [18]Mary of Magdala went and announced to the disciples, "I have seen the Lord," and what he told her.

Appearance to the Disciples. [19n*]On the evening of that first day of the week, when the doors were locked, where the disciples were, for fear of the Jews, Jesus came and stood in their midst and said to them, "Peace be with you." [20o*]When he had said this, he showed them his hands and his side. The disciples rejoiced when they saw the Lord. [21p*][Jesus] said to them again, "Peace be

20:3–10 The basic narrative is told of Peter alone in Lk 24:12, a verse missing in important manuscripts and which may be borrowed from tradition similar to John. Cf. also Lk 24:24.

20:6–8 Some special feature about the state of the burial cloths caused the beloved disciple to believe. Perhaps the details emphasized that the grave had not been robbed.

20:9 Probably a general reference to the scriptures is intended, as in Lk 24:26 and 1 Cor 15:4. Some individual Old Testament passages suggested are Ps 16:10; Hos 6:2; Jon 2:1, 2, 10.

20:11–18 This appearance to Mary is found only in John, but cf. Mt 28:8–10 and Mk 16:9–11.

20:16 Rabbouni: Hebrew or Aramaic for "my master."

20:17 Stop holding on to me: see Mt 28:9, where the women take hold of his feet. **I have not yet ascended**: for John and many of the New Testament writers, the ascension in the theological sense of going to the Father to be glorified took place with the resurrection as one action. This scene in John dramatizes such an understanding, for by Easter night Jesus is glorified and can give the Spirit. Therefore his ascension takes place immediately after he has talked to Mary. In such a view, the ascension after forty days described in Acts 1:1–11 would be simply a termination of earthly appearances or, perhaps better, an introduction to the conferral of the Spirit upon the early church, modeled on Elisha's being able to have a (double) share in the spirit of Elijah if he saw him being taken up (same verb as ascending) into heaven (2 Kgs 2:9–12). **To my Father and your Father, to my God and your God**: this echoes Ru 1:16: "Your people shall be my people, and your God my God." The Father of Jesus will now become the Father of the disciples because, once ascended, Jesus can give them the Spirit that comes from the Father and they can be reborn as God's children (Jn 3:5). That is why he calls them **my brothers**.

20:19–29 The appearances to the disciples, without or with Thomas (cf. Jn 11:16; 14:5), have rough parallels in the other gospels only for Jn 20:19–23; cf. Lk 24:36–39; Mk 16:14–18.

20:19 The disciples: by implication from Jn 20:24 this means ten of the Twelve, presumably in Jerusalem. **Peace be with you**: although this could be an ordinary greeting, John intends here to echo Jn 14:27. The theme of rejoicing in Jn 20:20 echoes Jn 16:22.

20:20 Hands and . . . side: Lk 24:39–40 mentions "hands and feet," based on Ps 22:17.

20:21 By means of this sending, the Eleven were made apostles, that is, "those sent" (cf. Jn 17:18), though John does not use the noun in reference to them (see note on Jn 13:16). A solemn mission or "sending" is also the subject of the post-resurrection appearances to the Eleven in Mt 28:19; Lk 24:47; Mk 16:15.

g: Lk 24:12. *h:* 11:44; 19:40. *i:* Acts 2:26–27; 1 Cor 15:4. *j:* Mk 16:9–11. *k:* 21:4; Mk 16:12; Lk 24:16; 1 Cor 15:43–44. *l:* Mt 28:9–10. *m:* Acts 1:9. *n:* Mt 28:16–20; Mk 16:14–18; Lk 24:36–44. *o:* 14:27. *p:* 17:18; Mt 28:19; Mk 16:15; Lk 24:47–48.

with you. As the Father has sent me, so I send you." [22q*]And when he had said this, he breathed on them and said to them, "Receive the holy Spirit. [23r*]Whose sins you forgive are forgiven them, and whose sins you retain are retained."

Thomas. [24]Thomas, called Didymus, one of the Twelve, was not with them when Jesus came. [25s]So the other disciples said to him, "We have seen the Lord." But he said to them, "Unless I see the mark of the nails in his hands and put my finger into the nailmarks and put my hand into his side, I will not believe." [26t]Now a week later his disciples were again inside and Thomas was with them. Jesus came, although the doors were locked, and stood in their midst and said, "Peace be with you." [27]Then he said to Thomas, "Put your finger here and see my hands, and bring your hand and put it into my side, and do not be unbelieving, but believe." [28u*]Thomas answered and said to him, "My Lord and my God!" [29v*]Jesus said to him, "Have you come to believe because you have seen me? Blessed are those who have not seen and have believed."

Conclusion. [30w*]Now Jesus did many other signs in the presence of [his] disciples that are not written in this book. [31x]But these are written that you may [come to] believe that Jesus is the Messiah, the Son of God, and that through this belief you may have life in his name.

IV. Epilogue: The Resurrection Appearance in Galilee

CHAPTER 21

See RG 422

The Appearance to the Seven Disciples. [1y*]After this, Jesus revealed himself again to his disciples at the Sea of Tiberias. He revealed himself in this way. [2*]Together were Simon Peter, Thomas called Didymus, Nathanael from Cana in Galilee, Zebedee's sons, and two others of his disciples. [3z*]Simon Peter said to them, "I am going fishing." They said to him, "We also will come with you." So they went out and got into the boat, but that night they caught nothing. [4a]When it was already dawn, Jesus was standing on the shore; but the disciples did not realize that it was Jesus. [5b]Jesus said to them, "Children, have you caught anything to eat?" They answered him, "No." [6]So he said to them, "Cast the net over the right side of the boat and you will find something." So they cast it, and were not able to pull it in because of the number of fish. [7]So the disciple whom Jesus loved said to Peter, "It is the Lord." When Simon Peter heard that it was the Lord, he tucked in his garment, for he was lightly clad, and jumped into the sea. [8]The other disciples came in the boat, for they were not far from shore, only about a hundred yards, dragging

20:22 This action recalls Gn 2:7, where God breathed on the first man and gave him life; just as Adam's life came from God, so now the disciples' new spiritual life comes from Jesus. Cf. also the revivification of the dry bones in Ez 37. This is the author's version of Pentecost. Cf. also the note on Jn 19:30.

20:23 The Council of Trent defined that this power to forgive sins is exercised in the sacrament of penance. See Mt 16:19; Mt 18:18.

20:28 My Lord and my God: this forms a literary inclusion with the first verse of the gospel: "and the Word was God."

20:29 This verse is a beatitude on future generations; faith, not sight, matters.

20:30–31 These verses are clearly a conclusion to the gospel and express its purpose. While many manuscripts read **come to believe**, possibly implying a missionary purpose for John's gospel, a small number of quite early ones read "continue to believe," suggesting that the audience consists of Christians whose faith is to be deepened by the book; cf. Jn 19:35.

21:1–23 There are many non-Johannine peculiarities in this chapter, some suggesting Lucan Greek style; yet this passage is closer to John than Jn 7:53–8:11. There are many Johannine features as well. Its closest parallels in the synoptic gospels are found in Lk 5:1–11 and Mt 14:28–31. Perhaps the tradition was ultimately derived from John but preserved by some disciple other than the writer of the rest of the gospel. The appearances narrated seem to be independent of those in Jn 20. Even if a later addition, the chapter was added before publication of the gospel, for it appears in all manuscripts.

21:2 Zebedee's sons: the only reference to James and John in this gospel (but see note on Jn 1:37). Perhaps the phrase was originally a gloss to identify, among the five, the **two others of his disciples**. The anonymity of the latter phrase is more Johannine (Jn 1:35). The total of seven may suggest the community of the disciples in its fullness.

21:3–6 This may be a variant of Luke's account of the catch of fish; see note on Lk 5:1–11.

q: Gn 2:7; Ez 37:9; 1 Cor 15:45. *r:* Mt 16:19; 18:18. *s:* 1 Jn 1:1. *t:* 21:14. *u:* 1:1. *v:* 4:48; Lk 1:45; 1 Pt 1:8. *w:* 21:25. *x:* 3:14, 15; 1 Jn 5:13. *y:* Mt 26:32; 28:7. *z:* Mt 4:18; Lk 5:4–10. *a:* 20:14; Mt 28:17; Lk 24:16. *b:* Lk 24:41.

the net with the fish. 9c*When they climbed out on shore, they saw a charcoal fire with fish on it and bread. 10Jesus said to them, "Bring some of the fish you just caught." 11d*So Simon Peter went over and dragged the net ashore full of one hundred fifty-three large fish. Even though there were so many, the net was not torn. 12*Jesus said to them, "Come, have breakfast." And none of the disciples dared to ask him, "Who are you?" because they realized it was the Lord. 13eJesus came over and took the bread and gave it to them, and in like manner the fish. 14f*This was now the third time Jesus was revealed to his disciples after being raised from the dead.

Jesus and Peter. 15*When they had finished breakfast, Jesus said to Simon Peter, "Simon, son of John, do you love me more than these?" He said to him, "Yes, Lord, you know that I love you." He said to him, "Feed my lambs." 16He then said to him a second time, "Simon, son of John, do you love me?" He said to him, "Yes, Lord, you know that I love you." He said to him, "Tend my sheep." 17gHe said to him the third time, "Simon, son of John, do you love me?" Peter was distressed that he had said to him a third time, "Do you love me?" and he said to him, "Lord, you know everything; you know that I love you." [Jesus] said to him, "Feed my sheep. 18h*Amen, amen, I say to you, when you were younger, you used to dress yourself and go where you wanted; but when you grow old, you will stretch out your hands, and someone else will dress you and lead you where you do not want to go." 19iHe said this signifying by what kind of death he would glorify God. And when he had said this, he said to him, "Follow me."

The Beloved Disciple. 20jPeter turned and saw the disciple following whom Jesus loved, the one who had also reclined upon his chest during the supper and had said, "Master, who is the one who will betray you?" 21When Peter saw him, he said to Jesus, "Lord, what about him?" 22k*Jesus said to him, "What if I want him to remain until I come? What concern is it of yours? You follow me." 23*So the word spread among the brothers that that disciple would not die. But Jesus had not told him that he would not die, just "What if I want him to remain until I come? [What concern is it of yours?]"

Conclusion. 24l*It is this disciple who testifies to these things and has written them, and we know that his testimony is true. 25mThere are also many other things that Jesus did, but if these were to be described individually, I do not think the whole world would contain the books that would be written.

21:9, 12–13 It is strange that Jesus already has fish since none have yet been brought ashore. This meal may have had eucharistic significance for early Christians since Jn 21:13 recalls Jn 6:11 which uses the vocabulary of Jesus' action at the Last Supper; but see also note on Mt 14:19.

21:11 The exact number 153 is probably meant to have a symbolic meaning in relation to the apostles' universal mission; Jerome claims that Greek zoologists catalogued 153 species of fish. Or 153 is the sum of the numbers from 1 to 17. Others invoke Ez 47:10.

21:12 None . . . dared to ask him: is Jesus' appearance strange to them? Cf. Lk 24:16; Mk 16:12; Jn 20:14. The disciples do, however, recognize Jesus **before** the breaking of the bread (opposed to Lk 24:35).

21:14 This verse connects Jn 20 and 21; cf. Jn 20:19, 26.

21:15–23 This section constitutes Peter's rehabilitation and emphasizes his role in the church.

21:15–17 In these three verses there is a remarkable variety of synonyms: two different Greek verbs for **love** (see note on Jn 15:13); two verbs for **feed/tend**; two nouns for **sheep**; two verbs for **know**. But apparently there is no difference of meaning. The threefold confession of Peter is meant to counteract his earlier threefold denial (Jn 18:17, 25, 27). The First Vatican Council cited these verses in defining that Jesus after his resurrection gave Peter the jurisdiction of supreme shepherd and ruler over the whole flock.

21:15 More than these: probably "more than these disciples do" rather than "more than you love them" or "more than you love these things [fishing, etc.]."

21:18 Originally probably a proverb about old age, now used as a figurative reference to the crucifixion of Peter.

21:22 Until I come: a reference to the parousia.

21:23 This whole scene takes on more significance if the disciple is already dead. The death of the apostolic generation caused problems in the church because of a belief that Jesus was to have returned first. Loss of faith sometimes resulted; cf. 2 Pt 3:4.

21:24 Who . . . has written them: this does not necessarily mean he wrote them with his own hand. The same expression is used in Jn 19:22 of Pilate, who certainly would not have written the inscription himself. **We know**: i.e., the Christian community; cf. Jn 1:14, 16.

c: Lk 24:41–43. *d:* 2 Chr 2:16. *e:* Lk 24:42. *f:* 20:19, 26. *g:* 13:37–38; 18:15–18, 25–27; Mt 26:69–75; Mk 14:66–72; Lk 22:55–62. *h:* Acts 21:11, 14; 2 Pt 1:14. *i:* 13:36. *j:* 13:25. *k:* Mt 16:28. *l:* 19:35. *m:* 20:30.

See RG 423–38

The Acts of the Apostles

The Acts of the Apostles, the second volume of Luke's two-volume work, continues Luke's presentation of biblical history, describing how the salvation promised to Israel in the Old Testament and accomplished by Jesus has now under the guidance of the holy Spirit been extended to the Gentiles. This was accomplished through the divinely chosen representatives (Acts 10:41) whom Jesus prepared during his historical ministry (Acts 1:21–22) and commissioned after his resurrection as witnesses to all that he taught (Acts 1:8; 10:37–43; Lk 24:48). Luke's preoccupation with the Christian community as the Spirit-guided bearer of the word of salvation rules out of his book detailed histories of the activity of most of the preachers. Only the main lines of the roles of Peter and Paul serve Luke's interest.

Peter was the leading member of the Twelve (Acts 1:13, 15), a miracle worker like Jesus in the gospel (Acts 3:1–10; 5:1–11, 15; 9:32–35, 36–42), the object of divine care (Acts 5:17–21; 12:6–11), and the spokesman for the Christian community (Acts 2:14–36; 3:12–26; 4:8–12; 5:29–32; 10:34–43; 15:7–11), who, according to Luke, was largely responsible for the growth of the community in the early days (Acts 2:4; 4:4). Paul eventually joined the community at Antioch (Acts 11:25–26), which subsequently commissioned him and Barnabas to undertake the spread of the gospel to Asia Minor. This missionary venture generally failed to win the Jews of the diaspora to the gospel but enjoyed success among the Gentiles (Acts 13:14–14:27).

Paul's refusal to impose the Mosaic law upon his Gentile converts provoked very strong objection among the Jewish Christians of Jerusalem (Acts 15:1), but both Peter and James supported his position (Acts 15:6–21). Paul's second and third missionary journeys (Acts 16:36–21:16) resulted in the same pattern of failure among the Jews generally but of some success among the Gentiles. Paul, like Peter, is presented as a miracle worker (Acts 14:8–18; 19:12; 20:7–12; 28:7–10) and the object of divine care (Acts 16:25–31).

In Acts, Luke has provided a broad survey of the church's development from the resurrection of Jesus to Paul's first Roman imprisonment, the point at which the book ends. In telling this story, Luke describes the emergence of Christianity from its origins in Judaism to its position as a religion of worldwide status and appeal. Originally a Jewish Christian community in Jerusalem, the church was placed in circumstances impelling it to include within its membership people of other cultures: the Samaritans (Acts 8:4–25), at first an occasional Gentile (Acts 8:26–30; 10:1–48), and finally the Gentiles on principle (Acts 11:20–21). Fear on the part of the Jewish people that Christianity, particularly as preached to the Gentiles, threatened their own cultural heritage caused them to be suspicious of Paul's gospel (Acts 13:42–45; 15:1–5; 28:17–24). The inability of Christian missionaries to allay this apprehension inevitably created a situation in which the gospel was preached more and more to the Gentiles. Toward the end of Paul's career, the Christian communities, with the exception of those in Palestine itself (Acts 9:31), were mainly of Gentile membership. In tracing the emergence of Christianity from Judaism, Luke is insistent upon the prominence of Israel in the divine plan of salvation (see note on Acts 1:26; see also Acts 2:5–6; 3:13–15; 10:36; 13:16–41; 24:14–15) and that the extension of salvation to the Gentiles has been a part of the divine plan from the beginning (see Acts 15:13–18; 26:22–23).

In the development of the church from a Jewish Christian origin in Jerusalem, with its roots in Jewish religious tradition, to a series of Christian communities among the Gentiles of the Roman empire, Luke perceives the action of God in history laying open the heart of all humanity to the divine message of salvation. His approach to the history of the church is motivated by his theological interests. His history of the apostolic church is the story of a Spirit-guided community and a Spirit-guided spread of the Word of God (Acts 1:8). The travels of Peter and Paul are in reality the travels of the Word of God as it spreads from Jerusalem, the city of destiny for Jesus, to Rome, the capital of the civilized world of Luke's day. Nonetheless, the historical data he utilizes are of value for the understanding of the church's early life and development and as general background to the Pauline epistles. In the interpretation of Acts, care must be exercised to determine Luke's theological aims and interests and to evaluate his historical data without either exaggerating their literal accuracy or underestimating their factual worth.

Finally, an apologetic concern is evident throughout Acts. By stressing the continuity between Judaism and Christianity (Acts 13:16–41; 23:6–9; 24:10–21; 26:2–23), Luke argues that Christianity is deserving of the same toleration accorded Judaism by Rome. Part of Paul's defense before Roman authorities is to show that Christianity is not a disturber of the peace of the Roman Empire (Acts 24:5, 12–13; 25:7–8). Moreover, when he stands before Roman authorities, he is declared innocent of any crime against the empire (Acts 18:13–15; 23:29; 25:25–27; 26:31–32). Luke tells his story with the hope that Christianity will be treated as fairly.

Concerning the date of Acts, see the Introduction to the Gospel according to Luke.

The principal divisions of the Acts of the Apostles are the following:

- I. The Preparation for the Christian Mission (1:1–2:13)
- II. The Mission in Jerusalem (2:14–8:3)
- III. The Mission in Judea and Samaria (8:4–9:43)
- IV. The Inauguration of the Gentile Mission (10:1–15:35)
- V. The Mission of Paul to the Ends of the Earth (15:36–28:31)

I. The Preparation For The Christian Mission

CHAPTER 1

See RG 426

The Promise of the Spirit. [1a*]In the
first book, Theophilus, I dealt with all that
Jesus did and taught [2b]until the day he was
taken up, after giving instructions through
the holy Spirit to the apostles whom he had
chosen. [3c*]He presented himself alive to
them by many proofs after he had suffered,
appearing to them during forty days and
speaking about the kingdom of God.
[4d*]While meeting with them, he enjoined
them not to depart from Jerusalem, but to
wait for "the promise of the Father about
which you have heard me speak; [5e]for John
baptized with water, but in a few days you
will be baptized with the holy Spirit."

The Ascension of Jesus. [6*]When they had
gathered together they asked him, "Lord, are
you at this time going to restore the kingdom
to Israel?" [7f*]He answered them, "It is not for
you to know the times or seasons that the Father has established by his own authority.
[8g*]But you will receive power when the holy
Spirit comes upon you, and you will be my
witnesses in Jerusalem, throughout Judea
and Samaria, and to the ends of the earth."

1:1–26 This introductory material (Acts 1:1–2) connects Acts with the Gospel of Luke, shows that the apostles were instructed by the risen Jesus (Acts 1:3–5), points out that the parousia or second coming in glory of Jesus will occur as certainly as his ascension occurred (Acts 1:6–11), and lists the members of the Twelve, stressing their role as a body of divinely mandated witnesses to his life, teaching, and resurrection (Acts 1:12–26).

1:3 Appearing to them during forty days: Luke considered especially sacred the interval in which the appearances and instructions of the risen Jesus occurred and expressed it therefore in terms of the sacred number forty (cf. Dt 8:2). In his gospel, however, Luke connects the ascension of Jesus with the resurrection by describing the ascension on Easter Sunday evening (Lk 24:50–53). What should probably be understood as one event (resurrection, glorification, ascension, sending of the Spirit—the paschal mystery) has been historicized by Luke when he writes of a visible ascension of Jesus after forty days and the descent of the Spirit at Pentecost. For Luke, the ascension marks the end of the appearances of Jesus except for the extraordinary appearance to Paul. With regard to Luke's understanding of salvation history, the ascension also marks the end of the time of Jesus (Lk 24:50–53) and signals the beginning of the time of the church.

1:4 The promise of the Father: the holy Spirit, as is clear from the next verse. This gift of the Spirit was first promised in Jesus' final instructions to his chosen witnesses in Luke's gospel (Lk 24:49) and formed part of the continuing instructions of the risen Jesus on the kingdom of God, of which Luke speaks in Acts 1:3.

1:6 The question of the disciples implies that in believing Jesus to be the Christ (see note on Lk 2:11) they had expected him to be a political leader who would restore self-rule to Israel during his historical ministry. When this had not taken place, they ask if it is to take place at this time, the period of the church.

1:7 This verse echoes the tradition that the precise time of the parousia is not revealed to human beings; cf. Mk 13:32; 1 Thes 5:1–3.

1:8 Just as Jerusalem was the city of destiny in the Gospel of Luke (the place where salvation was accomplished), so here at the beginning of Acts, Jerusalem occupies a central position. It is the starting point for the mission of the Christian disciples to "the ends of the earth," the place where the apostles were situated and the doctrinal focal point in the early days of the community (Acts 15:2, 6). **The ends of the earth**: for Luke, this means Rome.

a: Lk 1:1–4. *b:* Mt 28:19–20; Lk 24:44–49; Jn 20:22; 1 Tm 3:16. *c:* 10:41; 13:31. *d:* Jn 14:16, 17, 26. *e:* 11:16; Mt 3:11; Mk 1:8; Lk 3:16; Jn 1:26; Eph 1:13. *f:* Mt 24:36; 1 Thes 5:1–2. *g:* 2:1–13; 10:39; Is 43:10; Mt 28:19; Lk 24:47–48.

[9h]When he had said this, as they were looking on, he was lifted up, and a cloud took him from their sight. [10i]While they were looking intently at the sky as he was going, suddenly two men dressed in white garments stood beside them. [11j]They said, "Men of Galilee, why are you standing there looking at the sky? This Jesus who has been taken up from you into heaven will return in the same way as you have seen him going into heaven." [12k]Then they returned to Jerusalem from the mount called Olivet, which is near Jerusalem, a sabbath day's journey away.

The First Community in Jerusalem. [13]When they entered the city they went to the upper room where they were staying, Peter and John and James and Andrew, Philip and Thomas, Bartholomew and Matthew, James son of Alphaeus, Simon the Zealot, and Judas son of James. [14l]All these devoted themselves with one accord to prayer, together with some women, and Mary the mother of Jesus, and his brothers.

The Choice of Judas's Successor. [15]During those days Peter stood up in the midst of the brothers (there was a group of about one hundred and twenty persons in the one place). He said, [16m]"My brothers, the scripture had to be fulfilled which the holy Spirit spoke beforehand through the mouth of David, concerning Judas, who was the guide for those who arrested Jesus. [17]He was numbered among us and was allotted a share in this ministry. [18n*]He bought a parcel of land with the wages of his iniquity, and falling headlong, he burst open in the middle, and all his insides spilled out. [19]This became known to everyone who lived in Jerusalem, so that the parcel of land was called in their language 'Akeldama,' that is, Field of Blood. [20o]For it is written in the Book of Psalms:

'Let his encampment become desolate,
and may no one dwell in it.'

And:

'May another take his office.'

[21]Therefore, it is necessary that one of the men who accompanied us the whole time the Lord Jesus came and went among us, [22p]beginning from the baptism of John until the day on which he was taken up from us, become with us a witness to his resurrection." [23]So they proposed two, Joseph called Barsabbas, who was also known as Justus, and Matthias. [24]Then they prayed, "You, Lord, who know the hearts of all, show which one of these two you have chosen [25]to take the place in this apostolic ministry from which Judas turned away to go to his own place." [26q*]Then they gave lots to them, and the lot fell upon Matthias, and he was counted with the eleven apostles.

CHAPTER 2

See RG 426–27

The Coming of the Spirit. [1r*]When the time for Pentecost was fulfilled, they were all in one place together. [2s*]And suddenly there came from the sky a noise like a strong driving wind, and it filled the entire house in which they were. [3t*]Then there appeared to them tongues as of fire, which parted and

1:18 Luke records a popular tradition about the death of Judas that differs from the one in Mt 27:5, according to which Judas hanged himself. Here, although the text is not certain, Judas is depicted as purchasing a piece of property with the betrayal money and being killed on it in a fall.

1:26 The need to replace Judas was probably dictated by the symbolism of the number twelve, recalling the twelve tribes of Israel. This symbolism also indicates that for Luke (see Lk 22:30) the Christian church is a reconstituted Israel.

2:1–41 Luke's pentecostal narrative consists of an introduction (Acts 2:1–13), a speech ascribed to Peter declaring the resurrection of Jesus and its messianic significance (Acts 2:14–36), and a favorable response from the audience (Acts 2:37–41). It is likely that the narrative telescopes events that took place over a period of time and on a less dramatic scale. The Twelve were not originally in a position to proclaim publicly the messianic office of Jesus without incurring immediate reprisal from those religious authorities in Jerusalem who had brought about Jesus' death precisely to stem the rising tide in his favor.

2:2 There came from the sky a noise like a strong driving wind: wind and spirit are associated in Jn 3:8. The sound of a great rush of wind would herald a new action of God in the history of salvation.

2:3 Tongues as of fire: see Ex 19:18 where fire symbolizes the presence of God to initiate the covenant on Sinai. Here the holy Spirit acts upon the apostles, preparing them to proclaim the new covenant with its unique gift of the Spirit (Acts 2:38).

h: 2 Kgs 2:11; Mk 16:19; Lk 24:51. *i:* Jn 20:17. *j:* Lk 24:51; Eph 4:8–10; 1 Pt 3:22; Rev 1:7. *k:* Lk 6:14–16. *l:* Lk 23:49. *m:* Ps 41:10; Lk 22:47. *n:* Mt 27:3–10. *o:* Ps 69:26; 109:8; Jn 17:12. *p:* 1:8–9; 10:39. *q:* Prv 16:33. *r:* Lv 23:15–21; Dt 16:9–11. *s:* Jn 3:8. *t:* Lk 3:16.

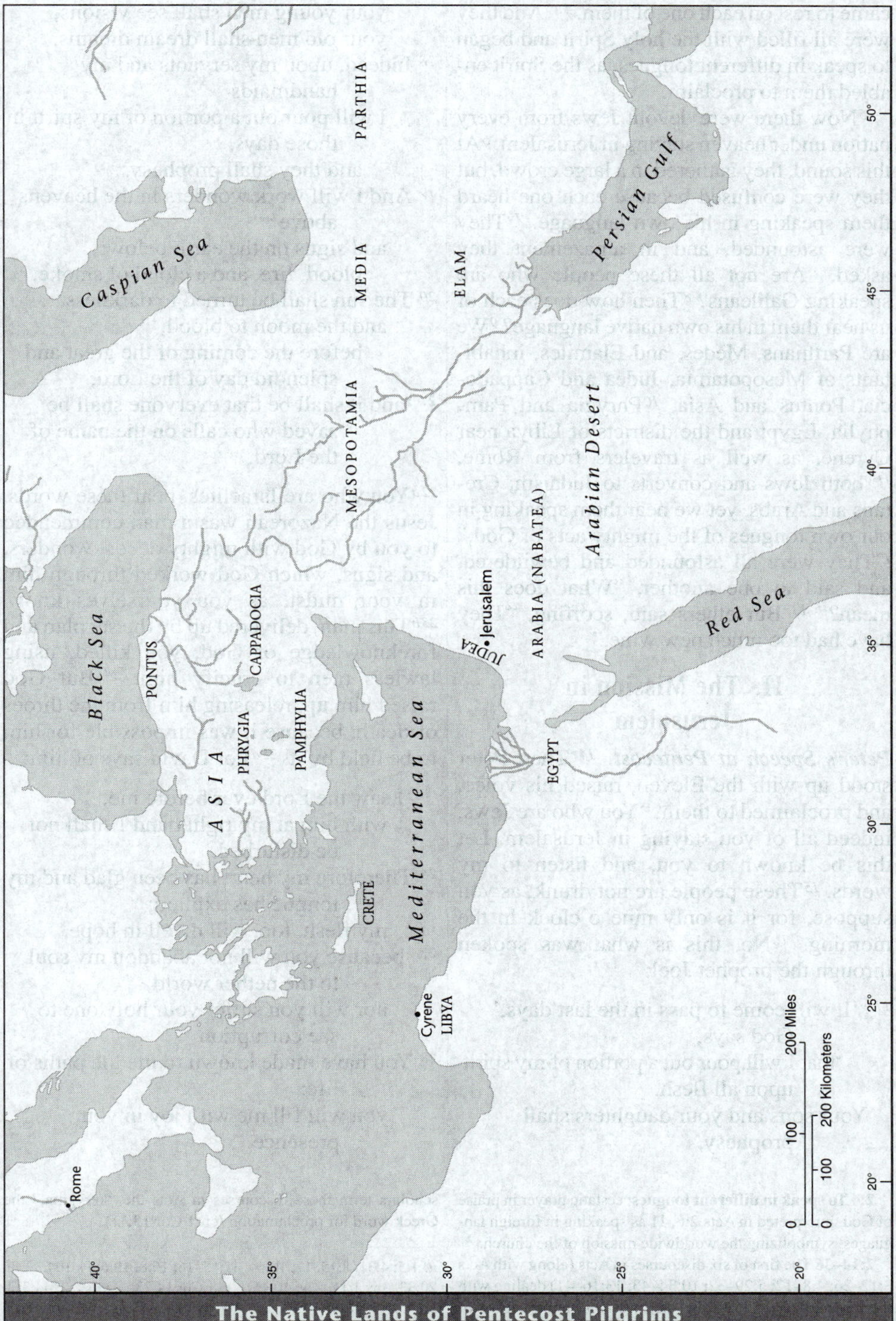

The Native Lands of Pentecost Pilgrims

came to rest on each one of them. [4u*]And they
were all filled with the holy Spirit and began
to speak in different tongues, as the Spirit enabled them to proclaim.

[5]Now there were devout Jews from every
nation under heaven staying in Jerusalem. [6]At
this sound, they gathered in a large crowd, but
they were confused because each one heard
them speaking in his own language. [7v]They
were astounded, and in amazement they
asked, "Are not all these people who are
speaking Galileans? [8]Then how does each of
us hear them in his own native language? [9]We
are Parthians, Medes, and Elamites, inhabitants of Mesopotamia, Judea and Cappadocia, Pontus and Asia, [10]Phrygia and Pamphylia, Egypt and the districts of Libya near
Cyrene, as well as travelers from Rome,
[11w]both Jews and converts to Judaism, Cretans and Arabs, yet we hear them speaking in
our own tongues of the mighty acts of God."
[12]They were all astounded and bewildered,
and said to one another, "What does this
mean?" [13x]But others said, scoffing, "They
have had too much new wine."

II. The Mission in Jerusalem

Peter's Speech at Pentecost. [14*]Then Peter
stood up with the Eleven, raised his voice,
and proclaimed to them, "You who are Jews,
indeed all of you staying in Jerusalem. Let
this be known to you, and listen to my
words. [15]These people are not drunk, as you
suppose, for it is only nine o'clock in the
morning. [16]No, this is what was spoken
through the prophet Joel:

[17 y]'It will come to pass in the last days,'
God says,
'that I will pour out a portion of my spirit
upon all flesh.
Your sons and your daughters shall
prophesy,
your young men shall see visions,
your old men shall dream dreams.
[18] Indeed, upon my servants and my
handmaids
I will pour out a portion of my spirit in
those days,
and they shall prophesy.
[19] And I will work wonders in the heavens
above
and signs on the earth below:
blood, fire, and a cloud of smoke.
[20] The sun shall be turned to darkness,
and the moon to blood,
before the coming of the great and
splendid day of the Lord,
[21 z]and it shall be that everyone shall be
saved who calls on the name of
the Lord.'

[22a]You who are Israelites, hear these words.
Jesus the Nazorean was a man commended
to you by God with mighty deeds, wonders,
and signs, which God worked through him
in your midst, as you yourselves know.
[23b]This man, delivered up by the set plan and
foreknowledge of God, you killed, using
lawless men to crucify him. [24c]But God
raised him up, releasing him from the throes
of death, because it was impossible for him
to be held by it. [25d]For David says of him:

'I saw the Lord ever before me,
with him at my right hand I shall not
be disturbed.
[26] Therefore my heart has been glad and my
tongue has exulted;
my flesh, too, will dwell in hope,
[27 e]because you will not abandon my soul
to the nether world,
nor will you suffer your holy one to
see corruption.
[28] You have made known to me the paths of
life;
you will fill me with joy in your
presence.'

2:4 To speak in different tongues: ecstatic prayer in praise of God, interpreted in Acts 2:6, 11 as speaking in foreign languages, symbolizing the worldwide mission of the church.

2:14–36 The first of six discourses in Acts (along with Acts 3:12–26; 4:8–12; 5:29–32; 10:34–43; 13:16–41) dealing with the resurrection of Jesus and its messianic import. Five of these are attributed to Peter, the final one to Paul. Modern scholars term these discourses in Acts the "kerygma," the Greek word for proclamation (cf. 1 Cor 15:11).

u: 1:5; 4:31; 8:15, 17; 10:44; 11:15–16; 15:8; 19:6; Ps 104:30; Jn 20:33. *v:* 1:11. *w:* 10:46. *x:* 1 Cor 14:23. *y:* Is 2:2; 44:3; Jl 3:1–5. *z:* Rom 10:13. *a:* 10:38; Lk 24:19. *b:* 1 Thes 2:15. *c:* 13:34. *d:* Ps 16:8–11. *e:* 13:35.

[29]My brothers, one can confidently say to you about the patriarch David that he died and was buried, and his tomb is in our midst to this day. [30f]But since he was a prophet and knew that God had sworn an oath to him that he would set one of his descendants upon his throne, [31g]he foresaw and spoke of the resurrection of the Messiah, that neither was he abandoned to the netherworld nor did his flesh see corruption. [32]God raised this Jesus; of this we are all witnesses. [33h*]Exalted at the right hand of God, he received the promise of the holy Spirit from the Father and poured it forth, as you [both] see and hear. [34i]For David did not go up into heaven, but he himself said:

'The Lord said to my Lord,
"Sit at my right hand
35 until I make your enemies your
footstool." '

[36j]Therefore let the whole house of Israel know for certain that God has made him both Lord and Messiah, this Jesus whom you crucified."

[37k]Now when they heard this, they were cut to the heart, and they asked Peter and the other apostles, "What are we to do, my brothers?" [38l*]Peter [said] to them, "Repent and be baptized, every one of you, in the name of Jesus Christ for the forgiveness of your sins; and you will receive the gift of the holy Spirit. [39m]For the promise is made to you and to your children and to all those far off, whomever the Lord our God will call." [40n]He testified with many other arguments, and was exhorting them, "Save yourselves from this corrupt generation." [41o]Those who accepted his message were baptized, and about three thousand persons were added that day.

Communal Life. [42pq*]They devoted themselves to the teaching of the apostles and to the communal life, to the breaking of the bread and to the prayers. [43r]Awe came upon everyone, and many wonders and signs were done through the apostles. [44s]All who believed were together and had all things in common; [45]they would sell their property and possessions and divide them among all according to each one's need. [46]Every day they devoted themselves to meeting together in the temple area and to breaking bread in their homes. They ate their meals with exultation and sincerity of heart, [47]praising God and enjoying favor with all the people. And every day the Lord added to their number those who were being saved.

CHAPTER 3

See RG 427

Cure of a Crippled Beggar. [1*]Now Peter and John were going up to the temple

2:33 At the right hand of God: or "by the right hand of God."

2:38 Repent and be baptized: repentance is a positive concept, a change of mind and heart toward God reflected in the actual goodness of one's life. It is in accord with the apostolic teaching derived from Jesus (Acts 2:42) and ultimately recorded in the four gospels. Luke presents baptism in Acts as the expected response to the apostolic preaching about Jesus and associates it with the conferring of the Spirit (Acts 1:5; 10:44–48; 11:16).

2:42–47 The first of three summary passages (along with Acts 4:32–37; 5:12–16) that outline, somewhat idyllically, the chief characteristics of the Jerusalem community: adherence to the teachings of the Twelve and the centering of its religious life in the eucharistic liturgy (Acts 2:42); a system of distribution of goods that led wealthier Christians to sell their possessions when the needs of the community's poor required it (Acts 2:44 and the note on Acts 4:32–37); and continued attendance at the temple, since in this initial stage there was little or no thought of any dividing line between Christianity and Judaism (Acts 2:46).

3:1–4:31 This section presents a series of related events: the dramatic cure of a lame beggar (Acts 3:1–10) produces a large audience for the kerygmatic discourse of Peter (Acts 3:11–26). The Sadducees, taking exception to the doctrine of resurrection, have Peter, John, and apparently the beggar as well, arrested (Acts 4:1–4) and brought to trial before the Sanhedrin. The issue concerns the authority by which Peter and John publicly teach religious doctrine in the temple (Acts 4:5–7). Peter replies with a brief summary of the kerygma, implying that his authority is prophetic (Acts 4:8–12). The court warns the apostles to abandon their practice of invoking prophetic authority in the name of Jesus (Acts 4:13–18). When Peter and John reply that the prophetic role cannot be abandoned to satisfy human objections, the court nevertheless releases them, afraid to do otherwise since the beggar, lame from birth and over forty years old, is a well-known figure in Jerusalem and the facts of his cure are common property (Acts 4:19–22). The narrative concludes with a prayer of the Christian community imploring divine aid against threats of persecution (Acts 4:23–31).

3:1 For the three o'clock hour of prayer: literally, "at the ninth hour of prayer." With the day beginning at 6 A.M., the ninth hour would be 3 P.M.

f: 2 Sm 7:12; Ps 132:11. *g:* 13:35; Ps 16:10. *h:* 1:4–5. *i:* Ps 110:1. *j:* 9:22; Rom 10:9; Phil 2:11. *k:* Lk 3:10. *l:* 3:19; 16:31; Lk 3:3. *m:* Is 57:19; Jl 3:5; Eph 2:17. *n:* Dt 32:5; Ps 78:8; Lk 9:41; Phil 2:15. *o:* 2:47; 4:4; 5:14; 6:7; 11:21, 24; 21:20. *p:* 4:32–35. *q:* 1:14; 6:4. *r:* 5:12–16. *s:* 4:32, 34–35.

area for the three o'clock hour of prayer. [2t]And a man crippled from birth was carried and placed at the gate of the temple called "the Beautiful Gate" every day to beg for alms from the people who entered the temple. [3]When he saw Peter and John about to go into the temple, he asked for alms. [4]But Peter looked intently at him, as did John, and said, "Look at us." [5]He paid attention to them, expecting to receive something from them. [6u*]Peter said, "I have neither silver nor gold, but what I do have I give you: in the name of Jesus Christ the Nazorean, [rise and] walk." [7]Then Peter took him by the right hand and raised him up, and immediately his feet and ankles grew strong. [8v]He leaped up, stood, and walked around, and went into the temple with them, walking and jumping and praising God. [9]When all the people saw him walking and praising God, [10]they recognized him as the one who used to sit begging at the Beautiful Gate of the temple, and they were filled with amazement and astonishment at what had happened to him.

Peter's Speech. [11w]As he clung to Peter and John, all the people hurried in amazement toward them in the portico called "Solomon's Portico." [12x]When Peter saw this, he addressed the people, "You Israelites, why are you amazed at this, and why do you look so intently at us as if we had made him walk by our own power or piety? [13y*]The God of Abraham, [the God] of Isaac, and [the God] of Jacob, the God of our ancestors, has glorified his servant Jesus whom you handed over and denied in Pilate's presence, when he had decided to release him. [14z*]You denied the Holy and Righteous One and asked that a murderer be released to you. [15a*]The author of life you put to death, but God raised him from the dead; of this we are witnesses. [16]And by faith in his name, this man, whom you see and know, his name has made strong, and the faith that comes through it has given him this perfect health, in the presence of all of you. [17b*]Now I know, brothers, that you acted out of ignorance, just as your leaders did; [18c*]but God has thus brought to fulfillment what he had announced beforehand through the mouth of all the prophets, that his Messiah would suffer. [19d]Repent, therefore, and be converted, that your sins may be wiped away, [20*]and that the Lord may grant you times of refreshment and send you the Messiah already appointed for you, Jesus, [21*]whom heaven must receive until the times of universal

3:6–10 The miracle has a dramatic cast; it symbolizes the saving power of Christ and leads the beggar to enter the temple, where he hears Peter's proclamation of salvation through Jesus.

3:13 Has glorified: through the resurrection and ascension of Jesus, God reversed the judgment against him on the occasion of his trial. **Servant**: the Greek word can also be rendered as "son" or even "child" here and also in Acts 3:26; 4:25 (applied to David); Acts 4:27; and Acts 4:30. Scholars are of the opinion, however, that the original concept reflected in the words identified Jesus with the suffering Servant of the Lord of Is 52:13–53:12.

3:14 The Holy and Righteous One: so designating Jesus emphasizes his special relationship to the Father (see Lk 1:35; 4:34) and emphasizes his sinlessness and religious dignity that are placed in sharp contrast with the guilt of those who rejected him in favor of Barabbas.

3:15 The author of life: other possible translations of the Greek title are "leader of life" or "pioneer of life." The title clearly points to Jesus as the source and originator of salvation.

3:17 Ignorance: a Lucan motif, explaining away the actions not only of the people but also of their leaders in crucifying Jesus. On this basis the presbyters in Acts could continue to appeal to the Jews in Jerusalem to believe in Jesus, even while affirming their involvement in his death because they were unaware of his messianic dignity. See also Acts 13:27 and Lk 23:34.

3:18 Through the mouth of all the prophets: Christian prophetic insight into the Old Testament saw the crucifixion and death of Jesus as the main import of messianic prophecy. The Jews themselves did not anticipate a suffering Messiah; they usually understood the Servant Song in Is 52:13–53:12 to signify their own suffering as a people. In his typical fashion (cf. Lk 18:31; 24:25, 27, 44), Luke does not specify the particular Old Testament prophecies that were fulfilled by Jesus. See also note on Lk 24:26.

3:20 The Lord . . . and send you the Messiah already appointed for you, Jesus: an allusion to the parousia or second coming of Christ, judged to be imminent in the apostolic age. This reference to its nearness is the only explicit one in Acts. Some scholars believe that this verse preserves a very early christology, in which the title "Messiah" (Greek "Christ") is applied to him as of his parousia, his second coming (contrast Acts 2:36). This view of a future messiahship of Jesus is not found elsewhere in the New Testament.

3:21 The times of universal restoration: like "the times of refreshment" (Acts 3:20), an apocalyptic designation of the messianic age, fitting in with the christology of Acts 3:20 that associates the messiahship of Jesus with his future coming.

t: 14:8–10. *u:* 4:10. *v:* Is 35:6; Lk 7:22. *w:* 5:12; Jn 10:23. *x:* 14:15. *y:* Ex 3:6, 15; Is 52:13; Lk 23:14–25. *z:* Mt 27:20–21; Mk 15:11; Lk 23:18; Jn 18:40. *a:* 4:10; 5:31 / 1:8; 2:32. *b:* 13:27; Lk 23:34; 1 Cor 2:8; 1 Tm 1:13. *c:* Lk 18:31. *d:* 2:38.

restoration of which God spoke through the
mouth of his holy prophets from of old.
22[e]*For Moses said:

'A prophet like me will the Lord, your
God, raise up for you
from among your own kinsmen;
to him you shall listen in all that he may
say to you.
23 [f]Everyone who does not listen to that
prophet
will be cut off from the people.'

24Moreover, all the prophets who spoke,
from Samuel and those afterwards, also announced these days. 25[g]You are the children
of the prophets and of the covenant that God
made with your ancestors when he said to
Abraham, 'In your offspring all the families
of the earth shall be blessed.' 26[h]For you
first, God raised up his servant and sent him
to bless you by turning each of you from
your evil ways."

CHAPTER 4

See RG 427–28

1*While they were still speaking to the
people, the priests, the captain of the temple
guard, and the Sadducees confronted them,
2[i]disturbed that they were teaching the people
and proclaiming in Jesus the resurrection of
the dead. 3They laid hands on them and put
them in custody until the next day, since it
was already evening. 4But many of those who
heard the word came to believe and [the]
number of men grew to [about] five thousand.

Before the Sanhedrin. 5On the next day,
their leaders, elders, and scribes were assembled in Jerusalem, 6with Annas the high
priest, Caiaphas, John, Alexander, and all
who were of the high-priestly class. 7They
brought them into their presence and questioned them, "By what power or by what
name have you done this?" 8[j]Then Peter,
filled with the holy Spirit, answered them,
"Leaders of the people and elders: 9If we are
being examined today about a good deed
done to a cripple, namely, by what means he
was saved, 10then all of you and all the people of Israel should know that it was in the
name of Jesus Christ the Nazorean whom
you crucified, whom God raised from the
dead; in his name this man stands before you
healed. 11[k]*He is 'the stone rejected by you,
the builders, which has become the cornerstone.' 12 [l]*There is no salvation through
anyone else, nor is there any other name under heaven given to the human race by
which we are to be saved."

13Observing the boldness of Peter and
John and perceiving them to be uneducated,
ordinary men, they were amazed, and they
recognized them as the companions of Jesus.
14Then when they saw the man who had
been cured standing there with them, they
could say nothing in reply. 15So they ordered
them to leave the Sanhedrin, and conferred
with one another, saying, 16"What are we to
do with these men? Everyone living in
Jerusalem knows that a remarkable sign was
done through them, and we cannot deny it.
17[m]But so that it may not be spread any further among the people, let us give them a
stern warning never again to speak to anyone in this name."

18So they called them back and ordered
them not to speak or teach at all in the name
of Jesus. 19[n]Peter and John, however, said to
them in reply, "Whether it is right in the
sight of God for us to obey you rather than

3:22 A loose citation of Dt 18:15, which teaches that the Israelites are to learn the will of Yahweh from no one but their prophets. At the time of Jesus, some Jews expected a unique prophet to come in fulfillment of this text. Early Christianity applied this tradition and text to Jesus and used them especially in defense of the divergence of Christian teaching from traditional Judaism.

4:1 The priests, the captain of the temple guard, and the Sadducees: the priests performed the temple liturgy; the temple guard was composed of Levites, whose captain ranked next after the high priest. The Sadducees, a party within Judaism at this time, rejected those doctrines, including bodily resurrection, which they believed alien to the ancient Mosaic religion. The Sadducees were drawn from priestly families and from the lay aristocracy.

4:11 Early Christianity applied this citation from Ps 118:22 to Jesus; cf. Mk 12:10; 1 Pt 2:7.

4:12 In the Roman world of Luke's day, salvation was often attributed to the emperor who was hailed as "savior" and "god." Luke, in the words of Peter, denies that deliverance comes through anyone other than Jesus.

e: 7:37; Dt 18:15, 18. *f:* Lv 23:29; Dt 18:19. *g:* Gn 12:3; 18:18; 22:18; Sir 44:19–21; Gal 3:8–9. *h:* 13:46; Rom 1:16. *i:* 23:6–8; 24:21. *j:* Mt 10:20. *k:* Ps 118:22; Is 28:16; Mt 21:42; Mk 12:10; Lk 20:17; Rom 9:33; 1 Pt 2:7. *l:* Mt 1:21; 1 Cor 3:11. *m:* 5:28. *n:* 5:29–32.

God, you be the judges. [20]It is impossible for us not to speak about what we have seen and heard." [21]After threatening them further, they released them, finding no way to punish them, on account of the people who were all praising God for what had happened. [22]For the man on whom this sign of healing had been done was over forty years old.

Prayer of the Community. [23]After their release they went back to their own people and reported what the chief priests and elders had told them. [24]And when they heard it, they raised their voices to God with one accord and said, "Sovereign Lord, maker of heaven and earth and the sea and all that is in them, [25][o]you said by the holy Spirit through the mouth of our father David, your servant:

'Why did the Gentiles rage
    and the peoples entertain folly?
[26] The kings of the earth took their stand
    and the princes gathered together
        against the Lord and against his
            anointed.'

[27][p]*Indeed they gathered in this city against your holy servant Jesus whom you anointed, Herod and Pontius Pilate, together with the Gentiles and the peoples of Israel, [28]to do what your hand and [your] will had long ago planned to take place. [29]And now, Lord, take note of their threats, and enable your servants to speak your word with all boldness, [30]as you stretch forth [your] hand to heal, and signs and wonders are done through the name of your holy servant Jesus." [31][q]*As they prayed, the place where they were gathered shook, and they were all filled with the holy Spirit and continued to speak the word of God with boldness.

Life in the Christian Community. [32]*The community of believers was of one heart and mind, and no one claimed that any of his possessions was his own, but they had everything in common. [33]With great power the apostles bore witness to the resurrection of the Lord Jesus, and great favor was accorded them all. [34][r]There was no needy person among them, for those who owned property or houses would sell them, bring the proceeds of the sale, [35]and put them at the feet of the apostles, and they were distributed to each according to need.

[36][s]Thus Joseph, also named by the apostles Barnabas (which is translated "son of encouragement"), a Levite, a Cypriot by birth, [37]sold a piece of property that he owned, then brought the money and put it at the feet of the apostles.

CHAPTER 5

See RG 427–28

Ananias and Sapphira. [1]*A man named Ananias, however, with his wife Sapphira, sold a piece of property. [2]He retained for himself, with his wife's knowledge, some of the purchase price, took the remainder, and put it at the feet of the apostles. [3][t]But Peter said, "Ananias, why has Satan filled your heart so that you lied to the holy Spirit and retained part of the price of the land? [4]While it remained unsold, did it not remain yours? And when it was sold, was it not still under your control? Why did you contrive this deed? You have lied not to human beings, but to God." [5]When Ananias heard these words, he fell down and breathed his last,

4:27 Herod: Herod Antipas, ruler of Galilee and Perea from 4 B.C. to A.D. 39, who executed John the Baptist and before whom Jesus was arraigned; cf. Lk 23:6–12.

4:31 The place . . . shook: the earthquake is used as a sign of the divine presence in Ex 19:18; Is 6:4. Here the shaking of the building symbolizes God's favorable response to the prayer. Luke may have had as an additional reason for using the symbol in this sense the fact that it was familiar in the Hellenistic world. Ovid and Virgil also employ it.

4:32–37 This is the second summary characterizing the Jerusalem community (see note on Acts 2:42–47). It emphasizes the system of the distribution of goods and introduces Barnabas, who appears later in Acts as the friend and companion of Paul, and who, as noted here (Acts 4:37), endeared himself to the community by a donation of money through the sale of property. This sharing of material possessions continues a practice that Luke describes during the historical ministry of Jesus (Lk 8:3) and is in accord with the sayings of Jesus in Luke's gospel (Lk 12:33; 16:9, 11, 13).

5:1–11 The sin of Ananias and Sapphira did not consist in the withholding of part of the money but in their deception of the community. Their deaths are ascribed to a lie to the holy Spirit (Acts 5:3, 9), i.e., they accepted the honor accorded them by the community for their generosity, but in reality they were not deserving of it.

o: Ps 2:1–2. *p:* Lk 23:12–13. *q:* 2:4. *r:* 2:44–45. *s:* 9:27; 11:22, 30; 12:25; 13:15; 1 Cor 9:6; Gal 2:1, 9, 13; Col 4:10. *t:* Lk 22:3; Jn 13:2.

and great fear came upon all who heard of it. [6]The young men came and wrapped him up, then carried him out and buried him.

[7]After an interval of about three hours, his wife came in, unaware of what had happened. [8]Peter said to her, "Tell me, did you sell the land for this amount?" She answered, "Yes, for that amount." [9]Then Peter said to her, "Why did you agree to test the Spirit of the Lord? Listen, the footsteps of those who have buried your husband are at the door, and they will carry you out." [10]At once, she fell down at his feet and breathed her last. When the young men entered they found her dead, so they carried her out and buried her beside her husband. [11u]And great fear came upon the whole church and upon all who heard of these things.

Signs and Wonders of the Apostles. [12v*]Many signs and wonders were done among the people at the hands of the apostles. They were all together in Solomon's portico. [13]None of the others dared to join them, but the people esteemed them. [14]Yet more than ever, believers in the Lord, great numbers of men and women, were added to them. [15w]Thus they even carried the sick out into the streets and laid them on cots and mats so that when Peter came by, at least his shadow might fall on one or another of them. [16]A large number of people from the towns in the vicinity of Jerusalem also gathered, bringing the sick and those disturbed by unclean spirits, and they were all cured.

Trial before the Sanhedrin. [17x*]Then the high priest rose up and all his companions, that is, the party of the Sadducees, and, filled with jealousy, [18]laid hands upon the apostles and put them in the public jail. [19y]But during the night, the angel of the Lord opened the doors of the prison, led them out, and said, [20]"Go and take your place in the temple area, and tell the people everything about this life." [21]When they heard this, they went to the temple early in the morning and taught. When the high priest and his companions arrived, they convened the Sanhedrin, the full senate of the Israelites, and sent to the jail to have them brought in. [22]But the court officers who went did not find them in the prison, so they came back and reported, [23]"We found the jail securely locked and the guards stationed outside the doors, but when we opened them, we found no one inside." [24]When they heard this report, the captain of the temple guard and the chief priests were at a loss about them, as to what this would come to. [25]Then someone came in and reported to them, "The men whom you put in prison are in the temple area and are teaching the people." [26z]Then the captain and the court officers went and brought them in, but without force, because they were afraid of being stoned by the people.

[27]When they had brought them in and made them stand before the Sanhedrin, the high priest questioned them, [28a]"We gave you strict orders [did we not?] to stop teaching in that name. Yet you have filled Jerusalem with your teaching and want to bring this man's blood upon us." [29b]But Peter and the apostles said in reply, "We must obey God rather than men. [30c*]The God of our ancestors raised Jesus, though you had him killed by hanging him on a tree. [31d*]God exalted him at his right hand as leader and savior to grant Israel repentance and for-

5:12–16 This, the third summary portraying the Jerusalem community, underscores the Twelve as its bulwark, especially because of their charismatic power to heal the sick; cf. Acts 2:42–47; 4:32–37.

5:17–42 A second action against the community is taken by the Sanhedrin in the arrest and trial of the Twelve; cf. Acts 4:1–3. The motive is the jealousy of the religious authorities over the popularity of the apostles (Acts 5:17) who are now charged with the defiance of the Sanhedrin's previous order to them to abandon their prophetic role (Acts 5:28; cf. Acts 4:18). In this crisis the apostles are favored by a miraculous release from prison (Acts 5:18–24). (For similar incidents involving Peter and Paul, see Acts 12:6–11; 16:25–29.) The real significance of such an event, however, would be manifest only to people of faith, not to unbelievers; since the Sanhedrin already judged the Twelve to be inauthentic prophets, it could disregard reports of their miracles. When the Twelve immediately resumed public teaching, the Sanhedrin determined to invoke upon them the penalty of death (Acts 5:33) prescribed in Dt 13:6–10. Gamaliel's advice against this course finally prevailed, but it did not save the Twelve from the punishment of scourging (Acts 5:40) in a last endeavor to shake their conviction of their prophetic mission.

5:30 Hanging him on a tree: that is, crucifying him (cf. also Gal 3:13).

5:31 At his right hand: see note on Acts 2:33.

u: 2:43; 5:5; 19:17. *v:* 2:43; 6:8; 14:3; 15:12. *w:* 19:11–12; Mk 6:56. *x:* 4:1–3, 6. *y:* 12:7–10; 16:25–26. *z:* Lk 20:19. *a:* Mt 27:25. *b:* 4:19. *c:* 2:23–24. *d:* 2:38.

giveness of sins. [32e]We are witnesses of these things, as is the holy Spirit that God has given to those who obey him."

[33]When they heard this, they became infuriated and wanted to put them to death. [34f*]But a Pharisee in the Sanhedrin named Gamaliel, a teacher of the law, respected by all the people, stood up, ordered the men to be put outside for a short time, [35]and said to them, "Fellow Israelites, be careful what you are about to do to these men. [36*]Some time ago, Theudas appeared, claiming to be someone important, and about four hundred men joined him, but he was killed, and all those who were loyal to him were disbanded and came to nothing. [37]After him came Judas the Galilean at the time of the census. He also drew people after him, but he too perished and all who were loyal to him were scattered. [38]So now I tell you, have nothing to do with these men, and let them go. For if this endeavor or this activity is of human origin, it will destroy itself. [39]But if it comes from God, you will not be able to destroy them; you may even find yourselves fighting against God." They were persuaded by him. [40g]After recalling the apostles, they had them flogged, ordered them to stop speaking in the name of Jesus, and dismissed them. [41h]So they left the presence of the Sanhedrin, rejoicing that they had been found worthy to suffer dishonor for the sake of the name. [42i]And all day long, both at the temple and in their homes, they did not stop teaching and proclaiming the Messiah, Jesus.

CHAPTER 6

See RG 428

The Need for Assistants. [1j*]At that time, as the number of disciples continued to grow, the Hellenists complained against the Hebrews because their widows were being neglected in the daily distribution. [2*]So the Twelve called together the community of the disciples and said, "It is not right for us to neglect the word of God to serve at table. [3]Brothers, select from among you seven reputable men, filled with the Spirit and wisdom, whom we shall appoint to this task, [4]whereas we shall devote ourselves to prayer and to the ministry of the word." [5]The proposal was acceptable to the whole community, so they chose Stephen, a man filled with faith and the holy Spirit, also Philip, Prochorus, Nicanor, Timon, Parmenas, and Nicholas of Antioch, a convert to Judaism. [6k*]They presented these men to the apostles who prayed and laid hands on them. [7l]The word of God continued to spread, and the number of the disciples in Jerusalem increased greatly; even a large group of priests were becoming obedient to the faith.

Accusation against Stephen. [8*]Now Ste-

5:34 Gamaliel: in Acts 22:3, Paul identifies himself as a disciple of this Rabbi Gamaliel I who flourished in Jerusalem between A.D. 25 and 50.

5:36–37 Gamaliel offers examples of unsuccessful contemporary movements to argue that if God is not the origin of this movement preached by the apostles it will perish by itself. The movement initiated by Theudas actually occurred when C. Cuspius Fadus was governor, A.D. 44–46. Luke's placing of Judas the Galilean after Theudas and at the time of the census (see note on Lk 2:1–2) is an indication of the vagueness of his knowledge of these events.

6:1–7 The Hellenists . . . the Hebrews: the Hellenists were not necessarily Jews from the diaspora, but were more probably Palestinian Jews who spoke only Greek. The Hebrews were Palestinian Jews who spoke Hebrew or Aramaic and who may also have spoken Greek. Both groups belong to the Jerusalem Jewish Christian community. The conflict between them leads to a restructuring of the community that will better serve the community's needs. The real purpose of the whole episode, however, is to introduce Stephen as a prominent figure in the community whose long speech and martyrdom will be recounted in Acts 7.

6:2–4 The essential function of the Twelve is the "service of the word," including development of the kerygma by formulation of the teachings of Jesus.

6:2 To serve at table: some commentators think that it is not the serving of food that is described here but rather the keeping of the accounts that recorded the distribution of food to the needy members of the community. In any case, after Stephen and the others are chosen, they are never presented carrying out the task for which they were appointed (Acts 6:2–3). Rather, two of their number, Stephen and Philip, are presented as preachers of the Christian message. They, the Hellenist counterpart of the Twelve, are active in the ministry of the word.

6:6 They . . . laid hands on them: the customary Jewish way of designating persons for a task and invoking upon them the divine blessing and power to perform it.

6:8–8:1 The summary (Acts 6:7) on the progress of the Jerusalem community, illustrated by the conversion of the priests, is followed by a lengthy narrative regarding Stephen. Stephen's defense is not a response to the charges made

e: Lk 24:48; Jn 15:26. *f:* 22:3. *g:* Mt 10:17; Acts 4:17–18. *h:* Mt 5:10–11; 1 Pt 4:13. *i:* 2:46; 5:20–21, 25; 8:35; 17:3; 18:5, 28; 19:4–5. *j:* 2:45; 4:34–35. *k:* 1:24; 13:3; 14:23. *l:* 9:31; 12:24; 16:5; 19:20; 28:30–31.

phen, filled with grace and power, was working great wonders and signs among the people. [9]Certain members of the so-called Synagogue of Freedmen, Cyrenians, and Alexandrians, and people from Cilicia and Asia, came forward and debated with Stephen, [10m]but they could not withstand the wisdom and the spirit with which he spoke. [11n]Then they instigated some men to say, "We have heard him speaking blasphemous words against Moses and God." [12]They stirred up the people, the elders, and the scribes, accosted him, seized him, and brought him before the Sanhedrin. [13*]They presented false witnesses who testified, "This man never stops saying things against [this] holy place and the law. [14o]For we have heard him claim that this Jesus the Nazorean will destroy this place and change the customs that Moses handed down to us." [15]All those who sat in the Sanhedrin looked intently at him and saw that his face was like the face of an angel.

See RG 428–29

CHAPTER 7

Stephen's Discourses. [1]Then the high priest asked, "Is this so?" [2p*]And he replied, "My brothers and fathers, listen. The God of glory appeared to our father Abraham while he was in Mesopotamia, before he had settled in Haran, [3q]and said to him, 'Go forth from your land and [from] your kinsfolk to the land that I will show you.' [4r]So he went forth from the land of the Chaldeans and settled in Haran. And from there, after his father died, he made him migrate to this land where you now dwell. [5s]Yet he gave him no inheritance in it, not even a foot's length, but he did promise to give it to him and his descendants as a possession, even though he was childless. [6t]And God spoke thus, 'His descendants shall be aliens in a land not their own, where they shall be enslaved and oppressed for four hundred years; [7u]but I will bring judgment on the nation they serve,' God said, 'and after that they will come out and worship me in this place.' [8v]Then he gave him the covenant of circumcision, and so he became the father of Isaac, and circumcised him on the eighth day, as Isaac did Jacob, and Jacob the twelve patriarchs.

[9w]"And the patriarchs, jealous of Joseph, sold him into slavery in Egypt; but God was with him [10x]and rescued him from all his afflictions. He granted him favor and wisdom before Pharaoh, the king of Egypt, who put him in charge of Egypt and [of] his entire household. [11y]Then a famine and great affliction struck all Egypt and Canaan, and our ancestors could find no food; [12z]but when Jacob heard that there was grain in Egypt, he sent our ancestors there a first time. [13a]The second time, Joseph made himself known to his brothers, and Joseph's family became known to Pharaoh. [14b]Then Joseph sent for his father Jacob, inviting him and his whole clan, seventy-five persons; [15c]and Jacob

against him but takes the form of a discourse that reviews the fortunes of God's word to Israel and leads to a prophetic declaration: a plea for the hearing of that word as announced by Christ and now possessed by the Christian community. The charges that Stephen depreciated the importance of the temple and the Mosaic law and elevated Jesus to a stature above Moses (Acts 6:13–14) were in fact true. Before the Sanhedrin, no defense against them was possible. With Stephen, who thus perceived the fuller implications of the teachings of Jesus, the differences between Judaism and Christianity began to appear. Luke's account of Stephen's martyrdom and its aftermath shows how the major impetus behind the Christian movement passed from Jerusalem, where the temple and law prevailed, to Antioch in Syria, where these influences were less pressing.

6:13 False witnesses: here, and in his account of Stephen's execution (Acts 7:54–60), Luke parallels the martyrdom of Stephen with the death of Jesus.

7:2–53 Stephen's speech represents Luke's description of Christianity's break from its Jewish matrix. Two motifs become prominent in the speech: (Acts 7:1) Israel's reaction to God's chosen leaders in the past reveals that the people have consistently rejected them; and (Acts 7:2) Israel has misunderstood God's choice of the Jerusalem temple as the place where he is to be worshiped.

7:2 God . . . appeared to our father Abraham . . . in Mesopotamia: the first of a number of minor discrepancies between the data of the Old Testament and the data of Stephen's discourse. According to Gn 12:1, God first spoke to Abraham in Haran. The main discrepancies are these: in Acts 7:16 it is said that Jacob was buried in Shechem, whereas Gn 50:13 says he was buried at Hebron; in the same verse it is said that the tomb was purchased by Abraham, but in Gn 33:19 and Jos 24:32 the purchase is attributed to Jacob himself.

m: Lk 21:15. *n:* Mt 26:59–61; Mk 14:55–58; Acts 21:21. *o:* Mt 26:59–61; 27:40; Jn 2:19. *p:* Gn 11:31; 12:1; Ps 29:3. *q:* Gn 12:1. *r:* Gn 12:5; 15:7. *s:* Gn 12:7; 13:15; 15:2; 16:1; Dt 2:5. *t:* Gn 15:13–14. *u:* Ex 3:12. *v:* Gn 17:10–14; 21:2–4. *w:* Gn 37:11, 28; 39:2, 3, 21, 23. *x:* Gn 41:37–43; Ps 105:21; Wis 10:13–14. *y:* Gn 41:54–57; 42:5. *z:* Gn 42:1–2. *a:* Gn 45:3–4, 16. *b:* Gn 45:9–11, 18–19; 46:27; Ex 1:5 LXX; Dt 10:22. *c:* Gn 46:5–6; 49:33.

went down to Egypt. And he and our ancestors died 16d and were brought back to Shechem and placed in the tomb that Abraham had purchased for a sum of money from the sons of Hamor at Shechem.

17e "When the time drew near for the fulfillment of the promise that God pledged to Abraham, the people had increased and become very numerous in Egypt, 18f until another king who knew nothing of Joseph came to power [in Egypt]. 19 He dealt shrewdly with our people and oppressed [our] ancestors by forcing them to expose their infants, that they might not survive. 20g At this time Moses was born, and he was extremely beautiful. For three months he was nursed in his father's house; 21h but when he was exposed, Pharaoh's daughter adopted him and brought him up as her own son. 22 Moses was educated [in] all the wisdom of the Egyptians and was powerful in his words and deeds.

23i "When he was forty years old, he decided to visit his kinsfolk, the Israelites. 24 When he saw one of them treated unjustly, he defended and avenged the oppressed man by striking down the Egyptian. 25 He assumed [his] kinsfolk would understand that God was offering them deliverance through him, but they did not understand. 26j The next day he appeared to them as they were fighting and tried to reconcile them peacefully, saying, 'Men, you are brothers. Why are you harming one another?' 27 Then the one who was harming his neighbor pushed him aside, saying, 'Who appointed you ruler and judge over us? 28 Are you thinking of killing me as you killed the Egyptian yesterday?' 29k Moses fled when he heard this and settled as an alien in the land of Midian, where he became the father of two sons.

30l "Forty years later, an angel appeared to him in the desert near Mount Sinai in the flame of a burning bush. 31 When Moses saw it, he was amazed at the sight, and as he drew near to look at it, the voice of the Lord came, 32 'I am the God of your fathers, the God of Abraham, of Isaac, and of Jacob.' Then Moses, trembling, did not dare to look at it. 33 But the Lord said to him, 'Remove the sandals from your feet, for the place where you stand is holy ground. 34 I have witnessed the affliction of my people in Egypt and have heard their groaning, and I have come down to rescue them. Come now, I will send you to Egypt.' 35m This Moses, whom they had rejected with the words, 'Who appointed you ruler and judge?' God sent as [both] ruler and deliverer, through the angel who appeared to him in the bush. 36n This man led them out, performing wonders and signs in the land of Egypt, at the Red Sea, and in the desert for forty years. 37o It was this Moses who said to the Israelites, 'God will raise up for you, from among your own kinsfolk, a prophet like me.' 38p It was he who, in the assembly in the desert, was with the angel who spoke to him on Mount Sinai and with our ancestors, and he received living utterances to hand on to us.

39q "Our ancestors were unwilling to obey him; instead, they pushed him aside and in their hearts turned back to Egypt, 40r saying to Aaron, 'Make us gods who will be our leaders. As for that Moses who led us out of the land of Egypt, we do not know what has happened to him.' 41s So they made a calf in those days, offered sacrifice to the idol, and reveled in the works of their hands. 42tu Then God turned and handed them over to worship the host of heaven, as it is written in the book of the prophets:

'Did you bring me sacrifices and
offerings
for forty years in the desert, O house
of Israel?
43 No, you took up the tent of Moloch
and the star of [your] god Rephan,
the images that you made to
worship.
So I shall take you into exile beyond
Babylon.'

44v Our ancestors had the tent of testimony in the desert just as the One who spoke to Moses directed him to make it according to the

d: Gn 23:3–20; 33:19; 49:29–30; 50:13; Jos 24:32. *e:* Ex 1:7. *f:* Ex 1:8. *g:* Ex 2:2; Heb 11:23. *h:* Ex 2:3–10. *i:* Ex 2:11–12. *j:* Ex 2:13–14. *k:* Ex 2:15, 21–22; 18:3–4. *l:* Ex 3:2–3. *m:* Ex 2:14. *n:* Ex 7:3, 10; 14:21; Nm 14:33. *o:* Dt 18:15; Acts 3:22. *p:* Ex 19:3; 20:1–17; Dt 5:4–22; 6:4–25. *q:* Nm 14:3. *r:* Ex 32:1, 23. *s:* Ex 32:4–6. *t:* Am 5:25–27. *u:* Jer 7:18; 8:2; 19:13. *v:* Ex 25:9, 40.

pattern he had seen. [45w]Our ancestors who
inherited it brought it with Joshua when they
dispossessed the nations that God drove out
from before our ancestors, up to the time of
David, [46x]who found favor in the sight of
God and asked that he might find a dwelling
place for the house of Jacob. [47y]But Solomon
built a house for him. [48z]Yet the Most High
does not dwell in houses made by human
hands. As the prophet says:

[49] [a]'The heavens are my throne,
the earth is my footstool.
What kind of house can you build for me?
says the Lord,
or what is to be my resting place?
[50] Did not my hand make all these things?'

Conclusion. [51]"You stiff-necked people,
uncircumcised in heart and ears, you always
oppose the holy Spirit; you are just like your
ancestors. [52b]Which of the prophets did your
ancestors not persecute? They put to death
those who foretold the coming of the righteous one, whose betrayers and murderers
you have now become. [53c]You received the
law as transmitted by angels, but you did not
observe it."

Stephen's Martyrdom. [54]When they heard
this, they were infuriated, and they ground
their teeth at him. [55d]*But he, filled with the
holy Spirit, looked up intently to heaven and
saw the glory of God and Jesus standing at the
right hand of God, [56]and he said, "Behold, I
see the heavens opened and the Son of Man
standing at the right hand of God." [57]*But
they cried out in a loud voice, covered their
ears, and rushed upon him together. [58e]They
threw him out of the city, and began to stone
him. The witnesses laid down their cloaks at
the feet of a young man named Saul. [59f]*As
they were stoning Stephen, he called out,
"Lord Jesus, receive my spirit." [60g]Then he
fell to his knees and cried out in a loud voice,
"Lord, do not hold this sin against them"; and
when he said this, he fell asleep.

CHAPTER 8

See RG 428–30

[1h]*Now Saul was consenting to his
execution.

Persecution of the Church. On that day,
there broke out a severe persecution of the
church in Jerusalem, and all were scattered
throughout the countryside of Judea and
Samaria, except the apostles. [2]Devout men
buried Stephen and made a loud lament over
him. [3i]*Saul, meanwhile, was trying to destroy the church; entering house after house
and dragging out men and women, he
handed them over for imprisonment.

III. The Mission in Judea and Samaria

Philip in Samaria. [4j]Now those who had
been scattered went about preaching the
word. [5k]Thus Philip went down to [the] city

7:55 He . . . saw . . . Jesus standing at the right hand of God: Stephen affirms to the Sanhedrin that the prophecy Jesus made before them has been fulfilled (Mk 14:62).

7:57 Covered their ears: Stephen's declaration, like that of Jesus, is a scandal to the court, which regards it as blasphemy.

7:59 Compare Lk 23:34, 46.

8:1–40 Some idea of the severity of the persecution that now breaks out against the Jerusalem community can be gathered from Acts 22:4 and Acts 26:9–11. Luke, however, concentrates on the fortunes of the word of God among people, indicating how the dispersal of the Jewish community resulted in the conversion of the Samaritans (Acts 8:4–17, 25). His narrative is further expanded to include the account of Philip's acceptance of an Ethiopian (Acts 8:26–39).

8:1 All were scattered . . . except the apostles: this observation leads some modern scholars to conclude that the persecution was limited to the Hellenist Christians and that the Hebrew Christians were not molested, perhaps because their attitude toward the law and temple was still more in line with that of their fellow Jews (see the charge leveled against the Hellenist Stephen in Acts 6:13–14). Whatever the facts, it appears that the Twelve took no public stand regarding Stephen's position, choosing, instead, to await the development of events.

8:3 Saul . . . was trying to destroy the church: like Stephen, Saul was able to perceive that the Christian movement contained the seeds of doctrinal divergence from Judaism. A pupil of Gamaliel, according to Acts 22:3, and totally dedicated to the law as the way of salvation (Gal 1:13–14), Saul accepted the task of crushing the Christian movement, at least insofar as it detracted from the importance of the temple and the law. His vehement opposition to Christianity reveals how difficult it was for a Jew of his time to accept a messianism that differed so greatly from the general expectation.

w: Jos 3:14–17; 18:1; 2 Sm 7:5–7. *x:* 2 Sm 7:1–2; 1 Kgs 8:17; Ps 132:1–5. *y:* 1 Kgs 6:1; 1 Chr 17:12. *z:* 17:24. *a:* Is 66:1–2. *b:* 2 Chr 36:16; Mt 23:31, 34. *c:* Gal 3:19; Heb 2:2. *d:* Mt 26:64; Mk 14:62; Lk 22:69; Acts 2:34. *e:* 22:20. *f:* Ps 31:6; Lk 23:46. *g:* Mt 27:46, 50; Mk 15:34; Lk 23:46. *h:* 22:20. *i:* 9:1, 13; 22:4; 26:9–11; 1 Cor 5:9; Gal 1:13. *j:* 11:19. *k:* 6:5; 21:8–9.

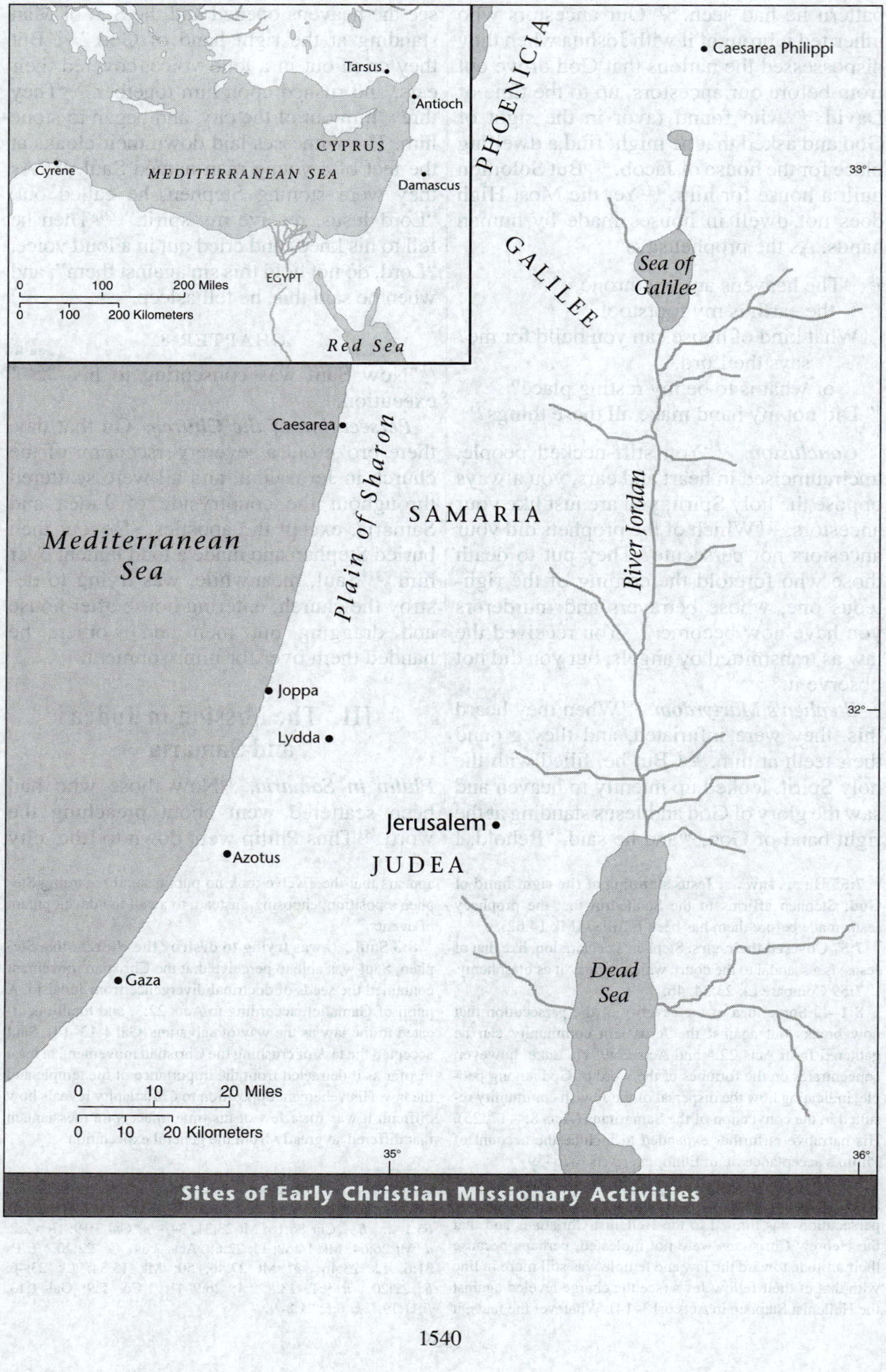

Sites of Early Christian Missionary Activities

of Samaria and proclaimed the Messiah to them. [6]With one accord, the crowds paid attention to what was said by Philip when they heard it and saw the signs he was doing. [7l]For unclean spirits, crying out in a loud voice, came out of many possessed people, and many paralyzed and crippled people were cured. [8]There was great joy in that city.

Simon the Magician. [9*]A man named Simon used to practice magic in the city and astounded the people of Samaria, claiming to be someone great. [10]All of them, from the least to the greatest, paid attention to him, saying, "This man is the 'Power of God' that is called 'Great.' " [11]They paid attention to him because he had astounded them by his magic for a long time, [12m]but once they began to believe Philip as he preached the good news about the kingdom of God and the name of Jesus Christ, men and women alike were baptized. [13]Even Simon himself believed and, after being baptized, became devoted to Philip; and when he saw the signs and mighty deeds that were occurring, he was astounded.

[14]Now when the apostles in Jerusalem heard that Samaria had accepted the word of God, they sent them Peter and John, [15]who went down and prayed for them, that they might receive the holy Spirit, [16*]for it had not yet fallen upon any of them; they had only been baptized in the name of the Lord Jesus. [17n]Then they laid hands on them and they received the holy Spirit.

[18*]When Simon saw that the Spirit was conferred by the laying on of the apostles' hands, he offered them money [19]and said, "Give me this power too, so that anyone upon whom I lay my hands may receive the holy Spirit." [20]But Peter said to him, "May your money perish with you, because you thought that you could buy the gift of God with money. [21]You have no share or lot in this matter, for your heart is not upright before God. [22]Repent of this wickedness of yours and pray to the Lord that, if possible, your intention may be forgiven. [23]For I see that you are filled with bitter gall and are in the bonds of iniquity." [24]Simon said in reply, "Pray for me to the Lord, that nothing of what you have said may come upon me." [25]So when they had testified and proclaimed the word of the Lord, they returned to Jerusalem and preached the good news to many Samaritan villages.

Philip and the Ethiopian. [26*]Then the angel of the Lord spoke to Philip, "Get up and head south on the road that goes down from Jerusalem to Gaza, the desert route." [27o*]So he got up and set out. Now there was an Ethiopian eunuch, a court official of the Candace, that is, the queen of the Ethiopians, in charge of her entire treasury, who had come to Jerusalem to worship, [28]and was returning home. Seated in his chariot, he was reading the prophet Isaiah. [29]The Spirit said to Philip, "Go and join up with that chariot." [30*]Philip ran up and heard him reading Isaiah the prophet and said, "Do you understand what you are reading?" [31p]He replied, "How can I, unless someone instructs me?" So he invited

8:9–13, 18–24 Sorcerers were well known in the ancient world. Probably the incident involving Simon and his altercation with Peter is introduced to show that the miraculous charisms possessed by members of the Christian community (Acts 8:6–7) were not to be confused with the magic of sorcerers.

8:16 Here and in Acts 10:44–48 and Acts 19:1–6, Luke distinguishes between baptism in the name of the Lord Jesus and the reception of the Spirit. In each case, the Spirit is conferred through members of the Twelve (Peter and John) or their representative (Paul). This may be Luke's way of describing the role of the church in the bestowal of the Spirit. Elsewhere in Acts, baptism and the Spirit are more closely related (Acts 1:5; 11:16).

8:18–20 Simon attempts to buy the gift of God (Acts 8:20) with money. Peter's cursing of Simon's attempt so to use his money expresses a typically Lucan attitude toward material wealth (cf. Lk 6:24; 12:16–21; 16:13).

8:26–40 In the account of the conversion of the Ethiopian eunuch, Luke adduces additional evidence to show that the spread of Christianity outside the confines of Judaism itself was in accord with the plan of God. He does not make clear whether the Ethiopian was originally a convert to Judaism or, as is more probable, a "God-fearer" (Acts 10:1), i.e., one who accepted Jewish monotheism and ethic and attended the synagogue but did not consider himself bound by other regulations such as circumcision and observance of the dietary laws. The story of his conversion to Christianity is given a strong supernatural cast by the introduction of an angel (Acts 8:26), instruction from the holy Spirit (Acts 8:29), and the strange removal of Philip from the scene (8:39).

8:27 The Candace: Candace is not a proper name here but the title of a Nubian queen.

8:30–34 Philip is brought alongside the carriage at the very moment when the Ethiopian is pondering the meaning of Is 53:7–8, a passage that Christianity, from its earliest origins, has applied to Jesus; cf. note on Acts 3:13.

l: Mk 16:17. *m:* 1:3; 19:8; 28:23, 31. *n:* 2:4; 4:31; 10:44–47; 15:8–9; 19:2, 6. *o:* Is 56:3–5. *p:* Jn 16:13.

Philip to get in and sit with him. [32q]This was
the scripture passage he was reading:

"Like a sheep he was led to the slaughter,
and as a lamb before its shearer is
silent,
so he opened not his mouth.
[33] In [his] humiliation justice was denied
him.
Who will tell of his posterity?
For his life is taken from the earth."

[34]Then the eunuch said to Philip in reply, "I
beg you, about whom is the prophet saying
this? About himself, or about someone
else?" [35]Then Philip opened his mouth and,
beginning with this scripture passage, he
proclaimed Jesus to him. [36r]As they traveled
along the road they came to some water, and
the eunuch said, "Look, there is water. What
is to prevent my being baptized?" [[37]]*
[38]Then he ordered the chariot to stop, and
Philip and the eunuch both went down into
the water, and he baptized him. [39s]When
they came out of the water, the Spirit of the
Lord snatched Philip away, and the eunuch
saw him no more, but continued on his way
rejoicing. [40t]Philip came to Azotus, and went
about proclaiming the good news to all the
towns until he reached Caesarea.

CHAPTER 9

See RG 430–31

Saul's Conversion. [1uv*]Now Saul,
still breathing murderous threats against the
disciples of the Lord, went to the high priest
[2*]and asked him for letters to the synagogues in Damascus, that, if he should find
any men or women who belonged to the
Way, he might bring them back to Jerusalem
in chains. [3w]On his journey, as he was nearing Damascus, a light from the sky suddenly
flashed around him. [4x]He fell to the ground
and heard a voice saying to him, "Saul, Saul,
why are you persecuting me?" [5y]He said,
"Who are you, sir?" The reply came, "I am
Jesus, whom you are persecuting. [6z]Now get
up and go into the city and you will be told
what you must do." [7a]The men who were
traveling with him stood speechless, for they
heard the voice but could see no one. [8b*]Saul
got up from the ground, but when he opened
his eyes he could see nothing; so they led
him by the hand and brought him to Damascus. [9]For three days he was unable to see,
and he neither ate nor drank.

Saul's Baptism. [10c]There was a disciple in
Damascus named Ananias, and the Lord said
to him in a vision, "Ananias." He answered,
"Here I am, Lord." [11d]The Lord said to him,
"Get up and go to the street called Straight
and ask at the house of Judas for a man from
Tarsus named Saul. He is there praying,
[12]and [in a vision] he has seen a man named
Ananias come in and lay [his] hands on him,
that he may regain his sight." [13e*]But Ananias replied, "Lord, I have heard from many
sources about this man, what evil things he
has done to your holy ones in Jerusalem.
[14f]And here he has authority from the chief
priests to imprison all who call upon your
name." [15g]But the Lord said to him, "Go, for

8:37 The oldest and best manuscripts of Acts omit this verse, which is a Western text reading: "And Philip said, 'If you believe with all your heart, you may.' And he said in reply, 'I believe that Jesus Christ is the Son of God.' "

9:1–19 This is the first of three accounts of Paul's conversion (with Acts 22:3–16 and Acts 26:2–18) with some differences of detail owing to Luke's use of different sources. Paul's experience was not visionary but was precipitated by the appearance of Jesus, as he insists in 1 Cor 15:8. The words of Jesus, "Saul, Saul, why are you persecuting me?" related by Luke with no variation in all three accounts, exerted a profound and lasting influence on the thought of Paul. Under the influence of this experience he gradually developed his understanding of justification by faith (see the letters to the Galatians and Romans) and of the identification of the Christian community with Jesus Christ (see 1 Cor 12:27). That Luke would narrate this conversion three times is testimony to the importance he attaches to it. This first account occurs when the word is first spread to the Gentiles. At this point, the conversion of the hero of the Gentile mission is recounted. The emphasis in the account is on Paul as a divinely chosen instrument (Acts 9:15).

9:2 The Way: a name used by the early Christian community for itself (Acts 18:26; 19:9, 23; 22:4; 24:14, 22). The Essene community at Qumran used the same designation to describe its mode of life.

9:8 He could see nothing: a temporary blindness (Acts 9:18) symbolizing the religious blindness of Saul as persecutor (cf. Acts 26:18).

9:13 Your holy ones: literally, "your saints."

q: Is 53:7–8 LXX. *r:* 10:47. *s:* 1 Kgs 18:12. *t:* 21:8. *u:* 8:3; 9:13; 22:4; 1 Cor 15:9; Gal 1:13–14. *v:* 9:14; 26:10. *w:* 1 Cor 9:1; 15:8; Gal 1:16. *x:* 22:6; 26:14. *y:* 22:8; 26:15; Mt 25:40. *z:* 22:10; 26:16. *a:* 22:9; 26:13–14. *b:* 22:11. *c:* 22:12–16. *d:* 21:39. *e:* 8:3; 9:1. *f:* 9:1–2; 26:10; 1 Cor 1:2; 2 Tm 2:22. *g:* 22:15; 26:1; 27:24.

this man is a chosen instrument of mine to carry my name before Gentiles, kings, and Israelites, [16]and I will show him what he will have to suffer for my name." [17]So Ananias went and entered the house; laying his hands on him, he said, "Saul, my brother, the Lord has sent me, Jesus who appeared to you on the way by which you came, that you may regain your sight and be filled with the holy Spirit." [18]Immediately things like scales fell from his eyes and he regained his sight. He got up and was baptized, [19*]and when he had eaten, he recovered his strength.

Saul Preaches in Damascus. He stayed some days with the disciples in Damascus, [20*]and he began at once to proclaim Jesus in the synagogues, that he is the Son of God. [21]All who heard him were astounded and said, "Is not this the man who in Jerusalem ravaged those who call upon this name, and came here expressly to take them back in chains to the chief priests?" [22]But Saul grew all the stronger and confounded [the] Jews who lived in Damascus, proving that this is the Messiah.

Saul Visits Jerusalem. [23]After a long time had passed, the Jews conspired to kill him, [24h]but their plot became known to Saul. Now they were keeping watch on the gates day and night so as to kill him, [25]but his disciples took him one night and let him down through an opening in the wall, lowering him in a basket.

[26i*]When he arrived in Jerusalem he tried to join the disciples, but they were all afraid of him, not believing that he was a disciple. [27]Then Barnabas took charge of him and brought him to the apostles, and he reported to them how on the way he had seen the Lord and that he had spoken to him, and how in Damascus he had spoken out boldly in the name of Jesus. [28]He moved about freely with them in Jerusalem, and spoke out boldly in the name of the Lord. [29*]He also spoke and debated with the Hellenists, but they tried to kill him. [30j]And when the brothers learned of this, they took him down to Caesarea and sent him on his way to Tarsus.

The Church at Peace. [31*]The church throughout all Judea, Galilee, and Samaria was at peace. It was being built up and walked in the fear of the Lord, and with the consolation of the holy Spirit it grew in numbers.

Peter Heals Aeneas at Lydda. [32]As Peter was passing through every region, he went down to the holy ones living in Lydda. [33]There he found a man named Aeneas, who had been confined to bed for eight years, for he was paralyzed. [34]Peter said to him, "Aeneas, Jesus Christ heals you. Get up and make your bed." He got up at once. [35]And all the inhabitants of Lydda and Sharon saw him, and they turned to the Lord.

Peter Restores Tabitha to Life. [36*]Now in Joppa there was a disciple named Tabitha (which translated means Dorcas). She was completely occupied with good deeds and almsgiving. [37]Now during those days she fell sick and died, so after washing her, they laid [her] out in a room upstairs. [38]Since Lydda was near Joppa, the disciples, hearing that Peter was there, sent two men to him with the request, "Please come to us without delay." [39]So Peter got up and went with them. When he arrived, they took him to the room upstairs where all the widows came to him weeping and showing him the tunics and cloaks that Dorcas had made while she

9:19–30 This is a brief resume of Paul's initial experience as an apostolic preacher. At first he found himself in the position of being regarded as an apostate by the Jews and suspect by the Christian community of Jerusalem. His acceptance by the latter was finally brought about through his friendship with Barnabas (Acts 9:27).

9:20 Son of God: the title "Son of God" occurs in Acts only here, but cf. the citation of Ps 2:7 in Paul's speech at Antioch in Pisidia (Acts 13:33).

9:26 This visit of Paul to Jerusalem is mentioned by Paul in Gal 1:18.

9:29 Hellenists: see note on Acts 6:1–7.

9:31–43 In the context of the period of peace enjoyed by the community through the cessation of Paul's activities against it, Luke introduces two traditions concerning the miraculous power exercised by Peter as he was making a tour of places where the Christian message had already been preached. The towns of Lydda, Sharon, and Joppa were populated by both Jews and Gentiles and their Christian communities may well have been mixed.

9:36 Tabitha (**Dorcas**), respectively the Aramaic and Greek words for "gazelle," exemplifies the right attitude toward material possessions expressed by Jesus in the Lucan Gospel (Lk 6:30; 11:41; 12:33; 18:22; 19:8).

h: 2 Cor 11:32–33. *i:* Gal 1:18. *j:* 11:25.

was with them. [40k]Peter sent them all out and knelt down and prayed. Then he turned to her body and said, "Tabitha, rise up." She opened her eyes, saw Peter, and sat up. [41]He gave her his hand and raised her up, and when he had called the holy ones and the widows, he presented her alive. [42]This became known all over Joppa, and many came to believe in the Lord. [43 l *]And he stayed a long time in Joppa with Simon, a tanner.

IV. The Inauguration of the Gentile Mission

CHAPTER 10

See RG 431

The Vision of Cornelius. [1m*]Now in Caesarea there was a man named Cornelius, a centurion of the Cohort called the Italica, [2*]devout and God-fearing along with his whole household, who used to give alms generously to the Jewish people and pray to God constantly. [3*]One afternoon about three o'clock, he saw plainly in a vision an angel of God come in to him and say to him, "Cornelius." [4]He looked intently at him and, seized with fear, said, "What is it, sir?" He said to him, "Your prayers and almsgiving have ascended as a memorial offering before God. [5]Now send some men to Joppa and summon one Simon who is called Peter. [6n]He is staying with another Simon, a tanner, who has a house by the sea." [7*]When the angel who spoke to him had left, he called two of his servants and a devout soldier from his staff, [8]explained everything to them, and sent them to Joppa.

The Vision of Peter. [9*]The next day, while they were on their way and nearing the city, Peter went up to the roof terrace to pray at about noontime. [10]He was hungry and wished to eat, and while they were making preparations he fell into a trance. [11o]He saw heaven opened and something resembling a large sheet coming down, lowered to the ground by its four corners. [12]In it were all the earth's four-legged animals and reptiles and the birds of the sky. [13]A voice said to him, "Get up, Peter. Slaughter and eat." [14p]But Peter said, "Certainly not, sir. For never have I eaten anything profane and unclean." [15q]The voice spoke to him again, a second time, "What God has made clean, you are not to call profane." [16]This happened three times, and then the object was taken up into the sky.

[17*]While Peter was in doubt about the meaning of the vision he had seen, the men sent by Cornelius asked for Simon's house and arrived at the entrance. [18]They called out inquiring whether Simon, who is called Peter, was staying there. [19r]As Peter was pondering the vision, the Spirit said [to him], "There are three men here looking for you. [20]So get up, go downstairs, and accompany them without hesitation, because I have sent them." [21]Then Peter went down to the men

9:43 The fact that Peter lodged with a tanner would have been significant to both the Gentile and Jewish Christians, for Judaism considered the tanning occupation unclean.

10:1–48 The narrative centers on the conversion of Cornelius, a Gentile and a "God-fearer" (see note on Acts 8:26–40). Luke considers the event of great importance, as is evident from his long treatment of it. The incident is again related in Acts 11:1–18 where Peter is forced to justify his actions before the Jerusalem community and alluded to in Acts 15:7–11 where at the Jerusalem "Council" Peter supports Paul's missionary activity among the Gentiles. The narrative divides itself into a series of distinct episodes, concluding with Peter's presentation of the Christian kerygma (Acts 10:4–43) and a pentecostal experience undergone by Cornelius' household preceding their reception of baptism (Acts 10:44–48).

10:1 The Cohort called the Italica: this battalion was an auxiliary unit of archers formed originally in Italy but transferred to Syria shortly before A.D. 69.

10:2 Used to give alms generously: like Tabitha (Acts 9:36), Cornelius exemplifies the proper attitude toward wealth (see note on Acts 9:36).

10:3 About three o'clock: literally, "about the ninth hour." See note on Acts 3:1.

10:7 A devout soldier: by using this adjective, Luke probably intends to classify him as a "God-fearer" (see note on Acts 8:26–40).

10:9–16 The vision is intended to prepare Peter to share the food of Cornelius' household without qualms of conscience (Acts 10:48). The necessity of such instructions to Peter reveals that at first not even the apostles fully grasped the implications of Jesus' teaching on the law. In Acts, the initial insight belongs to Stephen.

10:9 At about noontime: literally, "about the sixth hour."

10:17–23 The arrival of the Gentile emissaries with their account of the angelic apparition illuminates Peter's vision: he is to be prepared to admit Gentiles, who were considered unclean like the animals of his vision, into the Christian community.

k: Mk 5:40–41. *l:* 10:6. *m:* 10:30–33. *n:* 9:43. *o:* 11:5–12. *p:* Lv 11:1–47; Ez 4:14. *q:* Mk 7:15–19; Gal 2:12. *r:* 13:2.

and said, "I am the one you are looking for.
What is the reason for your being here?"
22s They answered, "Cornelius, a centurion,
an upright and God-fearing man, respected
by the whole Jewish nation, was directed by
a holy angel to summon you to his house and
to hear what you have to say." 23 So he invited them in and showed them hospitality.
The next day he got up and went with
them, and some of the brothers from Joppa
went with him. 24* On the following day he
entered Caesarea. Cornelius was expecting
them and had called together his relatives
and close friends. 25t When Peter entered,
Cornelius met him and, falling at his feet,
paid him homage. 26 Peter, however, raised
him up, saying, "Get up. I myself am also a
human being." 27 While he conversed with
him, he went in and found many people
gathered together 28u* and said to them, "You
know that it is unlawful for a Jewish man to
associate with, or visit, a Gentile, but God
has shown me that I should not call any person profane or unclean. 29 And that is why I
came without objection when sent for. May
I ask, then, why you summoned me?"
30* Cornelius replied, "Four days ago at this
hour, three o'clock in the afternoon, I was at
prayer in my house when suddenly a man in
dazzling robes stood before me and said,
31 'Cornelius, your prayer has been heard and
your almsgiving remembered before God.
32 Send therefore to Joppa and summon Simon, who is called Peter. He is a guest in the
house of Simon, a tanner, by the sea.' 33 So I
sent for you immediately, and you were kind
enough to come. Now therefore we are all
here in the presence of God to listen to all that
you have been commanded by the Lord."

Peter's Speech. 34v* Then Peter proceeded
to speak and said, "In truth, I see that God
shows no partiality. 35 Rather, in every nation
whoever fears him and acts uprightly is acceptable to him. 36w* You know the word
[that] he sent to the Israelites as he proclaimed peace through Jesus Christ, who is
Lord of all, 37x what has happened all over
Judea, beginning in Galilee after the baptism
that John preached, 38y* how God anointed
Jesus of Nazareth with the holy Spirit and
power. He went about doing good and healing all those oppressed by the devil, for God
was with him. 39* We are witnesses of all that
he did both in the country of the Jews and [in]
Jerusalem. They put him to death by hanging
him on a tree. 40 This man God raised [on] the
third day and granted that he be visible,
41z not to all the people, but to us, the witnesses chosen by God in advance, who ate
and drank with him after he rose from the

10:24–27 So impressed is Cornelius with the apparition that he invites close personal friends to join him in his meeting with Peter. But his understanding of the person he is about to meet is not devoid of superstition, suggested by his falling down before him. For a similar experience of Paul and Barnabas, see Acts 14:11–18.

10:28 Peter now fully understands the meaning of his vision; see note on Acts 10:17–23.

10:30 Four days ago: literally, "from the fourth day up to this hour."

10:34–43 Peter's speech to the household of Cornelius typifies early Christian preaching to Gentiles.

10:34–35 The revelation of God's choice of Israel to be the people of God did not mean he withheld the divine favor from other people.

10:36–43 These words are more directed to Luke's Christian readers than to the household of Cornelius, as indicated by the opening words, "You know." They trace the continuity between the preaching and teaching of Jesus of Nazareth and the proclamation of Jesus by the early community. The emphasis on this divinely ordained continuity (Acts 10:41) is meant to assure Luke's readers of the fidelity of Christian tradition to the words and deeds of Jesus.

10:36 To the Israelites: Luke, in the words of Peter, speaks of the prominent position occupied by Israel in the history of salvation.

10:38 Jesus of Nazareth: God's revelation of his plan for the destiny of humanity through Israel culminated in Jesus of Nazareth. Consequently, the ministry of Jesus is an integral part of God's revelation. This viewpoint explains why the early Christian communities were interested in conserving the historical substance of the ministry of Jesus, a tradition leading to the production of the four gospels.

10:39 We are witnesses: the apostolic testimony was not restricted to the resurrection of Jesus but also included his historical ministry. This witness, however, was theological in character; the Twelve, divinely mandated as prophets, were empowered to interpret his sayings and deeds in the light of his redemptive death and resurrection. The meaning of these words and deeds was to be made clear to the developing Christian community as the bearer of the word of salvation (cf. Acts 1:21–26). **Hanging him on a tree**: see note on 5:30.

s: Lk 7:4–5. *t:* 14:13–15; Rev 19:10. *u:* Gal 2:11–16. *v:* Dt 10:17; 2 Chr 19:7; Jb 34:19; Wis 6:7; Rom 2:11; Gal 2:6; Eph 6:9; 1 Pt 1:17. *w:* Is 52:7; Na 2:1. *x:* Mt 4:12; Mk 1:14; Lk 4:14. *y:* Is 61:1; Lk 4:18. *z:* Lk 24:41–43.

dead. 42a*He commissioned us to preach to
the people and testify that he is the one appointed by God as judge of the living and the
dead. 43To him all the prophets bear witness,
that everyone who believes in him will receive forgiveness of sins through his name."
The Baptism of Cornelius. 44b*While Peter
was still speaking these things, the holy Spirit
fell upon all who were listening to the word.
45The circumcised believers who had accompanied Peter were astounded that the gift of
the holy Spirit should have been poured out
on the Gentiles also, 46for they could hear
them speaking in tongues and glorifying God.
Then Peter responded, 47c"Can anyone withhold the water for baptizing these people,
who have received the holy Spirit even as we
have?" 48He ordered them to be baptized in
the name of Jesus Christ. 49Then they invited
him to stay for a few days.

See RG 430-31

CHAPTER 11

The Baptism of the Gentiles Ex-
plained. 1*Now the apostles and the brothers
who were in Judea heard that the Gentiles too
had accepted the word of God. 2So when Peter went up to Jerusalem the circumcised believers confronted him, 3*saying, "You entered the house of uncircumcised people and
ate with them." 4Peter began and explained it
to them step by step, saying, 5d"I was at
prayer in the city of Joppa when in a trance I
had a vision, something resembling a large
sheet coming down, lowered from the sky by
its four corners, and it came to me. 6Looking
intently into it, I observed and saw the four-
legged animals of the earth, the wild beasts,
the reptiles, and the birds of the sky. 7I also
heard a voice say to me, 'Get up, Peter.
Slaughter and eat.' 8But I said, 'Certainly
not, sir, because nothing profane or unclean
has ever entered my mouth.' 9But a second
time a voice from heaven answered, 'What
God has made clean, you are not to call profane.' 10This happened three times, and then
everything was drawn up again into the sky.
11Just then three men appeared at the house
where we were, who had been sent to me
from Caesarea. 12*The Spirit told me to accompany them without discriminating.
These six brothers also went with me, and we
entered the man's house. 13eHe related to us
how he had seen [the] angel standing in his
house, saying, 'Send someone to Joppa and
summon Simon, who is called Peter, 14who
will speak words to you by which you and all
your household will be saved.' 15fAs I began
to speak, the holy Spirit fell upon them as it
had upon us at the beginning, 16gand I remembered the word of the Lord, how he had
said, 'John baptized with water but you will
be baptized with the holy Spirit.' 17hIf then
God gave them the same gift he gave to us
when we came to believe in the Lord Jesus
Christ, who was I to be able to hinder God?"
18When they heard this, they stopped object-
ing and glorified God, saying, "God has then
granted life-giving repentance to the Gentiles
too."

The Church at Antioch. 19i*Now those
who had been scattered by the persecution
that arose because of Stephen went as far as
Phoenicia, Cyprus, and Antioch, preaching
the word to no one but Jews. 20There were

10:42 As judge of the living and the dead: the apostolic preaching to the Jews appealed to their messianic hope, while the preaching to Gentiles stressed the coming divine judgment; cf. 1 Thes 1:10.

10:44 Just as the Jewish Christians received the gift of the Spirit, so too do the Gentiles.

11:1–18 The Jewish Christians of Jerusalem were scandalized to learn of Peter's sojourn in the house of the Gentile Cornelius. Nonetheless, they had to accept the divine directions given to both Peter and Cornelius. They concluded that the setting aside of the legal barriers between Jew and Gentile was an exceptional ordinance of God to indicate that the apostolic kerygma was also to be directed to the Gentiles. Only in Acts 15 at the "Council" in Jerusalem does the evangelization of the Gentiles become the official position of the church leadership in Jerusalem.

11:3 You entered . . .: alternatively, this could be punctuated as a question.

11:12 These six brothers: companions from the Christian community of Joppa (see Acts 10:23).

11:19–26 The Jewish Christian antipathy to the mixed community was reflected by the early missionaries generally. The few among them who entertained a different view succeeded in introducing Gentiles into the community at Antioch (in Syria). When the disconcerted Jerusalem community sent Barnabas to investigate, he was so favorably impressed by what he observed that he persuaded his friend Saul to participate in the Antioch mission.

a: 1:8; 3:15; 17:31; Lk 24:48; Rom 14:9; 2 Tm 4:1. *b:* 11:15; 15:8. *c:* 8:36. *d:* 10:11–20. *e:* 10:3–5, 22, 30–32. *f:* 10:44. *g:* 1:5; 19:4; Lk 3:16. *h:* 15:8–9. *i:* 8:1–4.

some Cypriots and Cyrenians among them, however, who came to Antioch and began to speak to the Greeks as well, proclaiming the Lord Jesus. [21]The hand of the Lord was with them and a great number who believed turned to the Lord. [22]The news about them reached the ears of the church in Jerusalem, and they sent Barnabas [to go] to Antioch. [23]When he arrived and saw the grace of God, he rejoiced and encouraged them all to remain faithful to the Lord in firmness of heart, [24]for he was a good man, filled with the holy Spirit and faith. And a large number of people was added to the Lord. [25]Then he went to Tarsus to look for Saul, [26*]and when he had found him he brought him to Antioch. For a whole year they met with the church and taught a large number of people, and it was in Antioch that the disciples were first called Christians.

The Prediction of Agabus. [27*]At that time some prophets came down from Jerusalem to Antioch, [28j]and one of them named Agabus stood up and predicted by the Spirit that there would be a severe famine all over the world, and it happened under Claudius. [29k]So the disciples determined that, according to ability, each should send relief to the brothers who lived in Judea. [30*]This they did, sending it to the presbyters in care of Barnabas and Saul.

CHAPTER 12

See RG 431

Herod's Persecution of the Christians. [1*]About that time King Herod laid hands upon some members of the church to harm them. [2*]He had James, the brother of John, killed by the sword, [3*]and when he saw that this was pleasing to the Jews he proceeded to arrest Peter also. (It was [the] feast of Unleavened Bread.) [4]He had him taken into custody and put in prison under the guard of four squads of four soldiers each. He intended to bring him before the people after Passover. [5l]Peter thus was being kept in prison, but prayer by the church was fervently being made to God on his behalf.

[6]On the very night before Herod was to bring him to trial, Peter, secured by double chains, was sleeping between two soldiers, while outside the door guards kept watch on the prison. [7]Suddenly the angel of the Lord stood by him and a light shone in the cell. He tapped Peter on the side and awakened him, saying, "Get up quickly." The chains fell from his wrists. [8]The angel said to him, "Put on your belt and your sandals." He did so. Then he said to him, "Put on your cloak and follow me." [9]So he followed him out, not realizing that what was happening through the angel was real; he thought he was seeing a vision. [10]They passed the first guard, then the second, and came to the iron gate leading out to the city, which opened for them by itself. They emerged and made their way down an alley, and suddenly the angel left him. [11]Then Peter recovered his senses and said, "Now I know for certain that [the] Lord sent his angel and rescued me from the hand of Herod and from all that the Jewish people had been expecting." [12m]When he realized this, he went to the house of Mary, the mother of John who is called Mark, where there were many people gathered in prayer. [13]When he knocked on the gateway door, a maid named Rhoda came to answer it. [14]She was so overjoyed when she recognized Peter's voice that, in-

11:26 Christians: "Christians" is first applied to the members of the community at Antioch because the Gentile members of the community enable it to stand out clearly from Judaism.

11:27–30 It is not clear whether the prophets from Jerusalem came to Antioch to request help in view of the coming famine or whether they received this insight during their visit there. The former supposition seems more likely. Suetonius and Tacitus speak of famines during the reign of Claudius (A.D. 41–54), while the Jewish historian Josephus mentions a famine in Judea in A.D. 46–48. Luke is interested, rather, in showing the charity of the Antiochene community toward the Jewish Christians of Jerusalem despite their differences on mixed communities.

11:30 Presbyters: this is the same Greek word that elsewhere is translated "elders," primarily in reference to the Jewish community.

12:1–19 Herod Agrippa ruled Judea A.D. 41–44. While Luke does not assign a motive for his execution of James and his intended execution of Peter, the broad background lies in Herod's support of Pharisaic Judaism. The Jewish Christians had lost the popularity they had had in Jerusalem (Acts 2:47), perhaps because of suspicions against them traceable to the teaching of Stephen.

12:2 James, the brother of John: this James, the son of Zebedee, was beheaded by Herod Agrippa ca. A.D. 44.

12:3, 4 Feast of Unleavened Bread . . . Passover: see note on Lk 22:1.

j: 21:10. *k:* 12:25. *l:* Jas 5:16. *m:* 12:25; 15:37.

stead of opening the gate, she ran in and announced that Peter was standing at the gate.
[15]They told her, "You are out of your mind,"
but she insisted that it was so. But they kept
saying, "It is his angel." [16]But Peter continued to knock, and when they opened it, they
saw him and were astounded. [17*]He motioned to them with his hand to be quiet and
explained [to them] how the Lord had led
him out of the prison, and said, "Report this
to James and the brothers." Then he left and
went to another place. [18n]At daybreak there
was no small commotion among the soldiers over what had become of Peter.
[19]Herod, after instituting a search but not
finding him, ordered the guards tried and
executed. Then he left Judea to spend some
time in Caesarea.

Herod's Death. [20*]He had long been
very angry with the people of Tyre and Sidon, who now came to him in a body. After
winning over Blastus, the king's chamberlain, they sued for peace because their
country was supplied with food from the
king's territory. [21]On an appointed day,
Herod, attired in royal robes, [and] seated
on the rostrum, addressed them publicly.
[22]The assembled crowd cried out, "This is
the voice of a god, not of a man." [23]At once
the angel of the Lord struck him down because he did not ascribe the honor to God,
and he was eaten by worms and breathed
his last. [24o]But the word of God continued
to spread and grow.

Mission of Barnabas and Saul. [25p*]After
Barnabas and Saul completed their relief
mission, they returned to Jerusalem, taking
with them John, who is called Mark.

CHAPTER 13

See RG 431

[1*]Now there were in the church at
Antioch prophets and teachers: Barnabas,
Symeon who was called Niger, Lucius of Cyrene, Manaen who was a close friend of Herod
the tetrarch, and Saul. [2]While they were worshiping the Lord and fasting, the holy Spirit
said, "Set apart for me Barnabas and Saul for
the work to which I have called them." [3]Then,
completing their fasting and prayer, they laid
hands on them and sent them off.

First Mission Begins in Cyprus. [4*]So
they, sent forth by the holy Spirit, went down
to Seleucia and from there sailed to Cyprus.
[5*]When they arrived in Salamis, they proclaimed the word of God in the Jewish synagogues. They had John also as their assistant. [6*]When they had traveled through the
whole island as far as Paphos, they met a
magician named Bar-Jesus who was a Jewish false prophet. [7]He was with the proconsul Sergius Paulus, a man of intelligence,
who had summoned Barnabas and Saul and
wanted to hear the word of God. [8]But Elymas the magician (for that is what his name

12:17 To James: this James is not the son of Zebedee mentioned in Acts 12:2, but is James, the "brother of the Lord" (Gal 1:19), who in Acts 15; 21 is presented as leader of the Jerusalem Christian community. **He left and went to another place**: the conjecture that Peter left for Rome at this time has nothing to recommend it. His chief responsibility was still the leadership of the Jewish Christian community in Palestine (see Gal 2:7). The concept of the great missionary effort of the church was yet to come (see Acts 13:1–3).

12:20–23 Josephus gives a similar account of Herod's death that occurred in A.D. 44. Early Christian tradition considered the manner of it to be a divine punishment upon his evil life. See 2 Kgs 19:35 for the figure of the angel of the Lord in such a context.

12:25 They returned to Jerusalem: many manuscripts read "from Jerusalem," since Acts 11:30 implies that Paul and Barnabas are already in Jerusalem. This present verse could refer to a return visit or subsequent relief mission.

13:1–3 The impulse for the first missionary effort in Asia Minor is ascribed to the prophets of the Antiochene community, under the inspiration of the holy Spirit. Just as the Jerusalem community had earlier been the center of missionary activity, so too Antioch becomes the center from which the missionaries Barnabas and Saul are sent out.

13:4–14:27 The key event in Luke's account of the first missionary journey is the experience of Paul and Barnabas at Pisidian Antioch (Acts 13:14–52). The Christian kerygma proclaimed by Paul in the synagogue was favorably received. Some Jews and "God-fearers" (see note on Acts 8:26–40) became interested and invited the missionaries to speak again on the following sabbath (Acts 13:42). By that time, however, the appearance of a large number of Gentiles from the city had so disconcerted the Jews that they became hostile toward the apostles (Acts 13:44–50). This hostility of theirs appears in all three accounts of Paul's missionary journeys in Acts, the Jews of Iconium (Acts 14:1–2) and Beroea (Acts 17:11) being notable exceptions.

13:5 John: that is, John Mark (see Acts 12:12, 25).

13:6 A magician named Bar-Jesus who was a Jewish false prophet: that is, he posed as a prophet. Again Luke takes the opportunity to dissociate Christianity from the magical acts of the time (Acts 13:7–11); see also Acts 8:18–24.

n: 5:22–24. *o:* 6:7. *p:* 11:29–30.

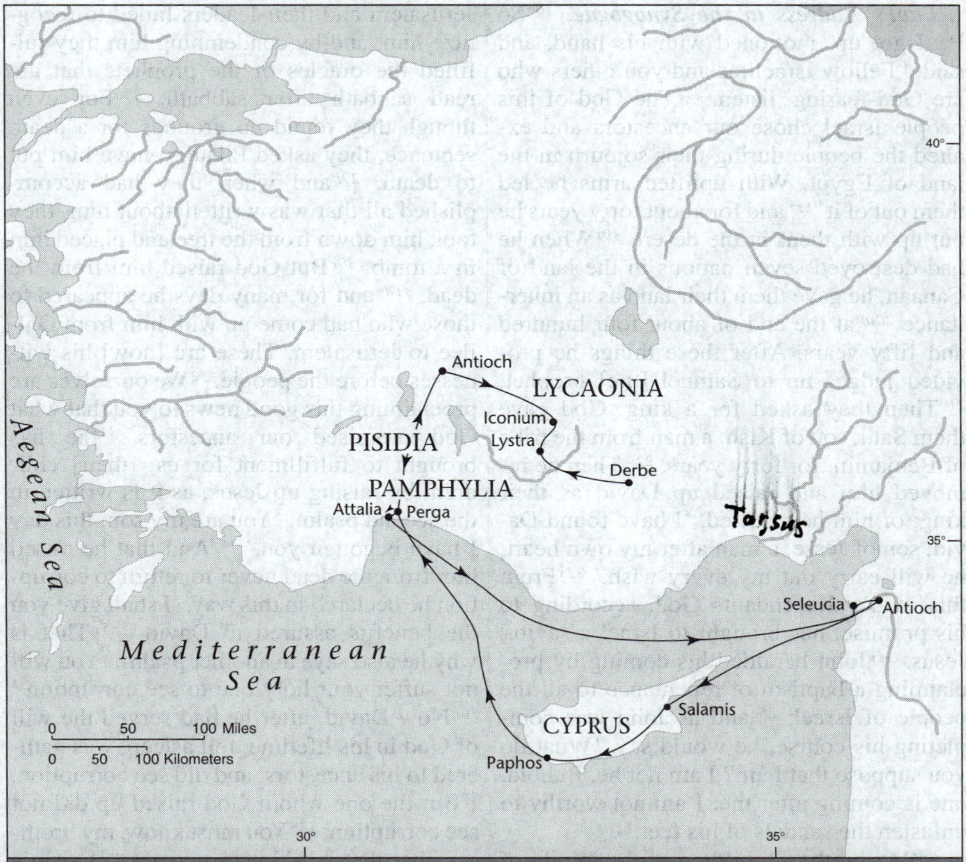

First Missionary Journey of Paul

means) opposed them in an attempt to turn the proconsul away from the faith. [9*]But Saul, also known as Paul, filled with the holy Spirit, looked intently at him [10]and said, "You son of the devil, you enemy of all that is right, full of every sort of deceit and fraud. Will you not stop twisting the straight paths of [the] Lord? [11]Even now the hand of the Lord is upon you. You will be blind, and unable to see the sun for a time." Immediately a dark mist fell upon him, and he went about seeking people to lead him by the hand. [12]When the proconsul saw what had happened, he came to believe, for he was astonished by the teaching about the Lord.

Paul's Arrival at Antioch in Pisidia. [13q]From Paphos, Paul and his companions set sail and arrived at Perga in Pamphylia. But John left them and returned to Jerusalem. [14]They continued on from Perga and reached Antioch in Pisidia. On the sabbath they entered [into] the synagogue and took their seats. [15]After the reading of the law and the prophets, the synagogue officials sent word to them, "My brothers, if one of you has a word of exhortation for the people, please speak."

13:9 Saul, also known as Paul: there is no reason to believe that his name was changed from Saul to Paul upon his conversion. The use of a double name, one Semitic (Saul), the other Greco-Roman (Paul), is well attested (cf. Acts 1:23, Joseph Justus; Acts 12:12, 25, John Mark).

q: 15:38.

Paul's Address in the Synagogue. [16*]So Paul got up, motioned with his hand, and said, "Fellow Israelites and you others who are God-fearing, listen. [17r]The God of this people Israel chose our ancestors and exalted the people during their sojourn in the land of Egypt. With uplifted arms he led them out of it [18s*]and for about forty years he put up with them in the desert. [19t]When he had destroyed seven nations in the land of Canaan, he gave them their land as an inheritance [20u*]at the end of about four hundred and fifty years. After these things he provided judges up to Samuel [the] prophet. [21v]Then they asked for a king. God gave them Saul, son of Kish, a man from the tribe of Benjamin, for forty years. [22w]Then he removed him and raised up David as their king; of him he testified, 'I have found David, son of Jesse, a man after my own heart; he will carry out my every wish.' [23x]From this man's descendants God, according to his promise, has brought to Israel a savior, Jesus. [24y]John heralded his coming by proclaiming a baptism of repentance to all the people of Israel; [25z]and as John was completing his course, he would say, 'What do you suppose that I am? I am not he. Behold, one is coming after me; I am not worthy to unfasten the sandals of his feet.'

[26]"My brothers, children of the family of Abraham, and those others among you who are God-fearing, to us this word of salvation has been sent. [27]The inhabitants of Jerusalem and their leaders failed to recognize him, and by condemning him they fulfilled the oracles of the prophets that are read sabbath after sabbath. [28a]For even though they found no grounds for a death sentence, they asked Pilate to have him put to death, [29b]and when they had accomplished all that was written about him, they took him down from the tree and placed him in a tomb. [30c]But God raised him from the dead, [31d*]and for many days he appeared to those who had come up with him from Galilee to Jerusalem. These are [now] his witnesses before the people. [32]We ourselves are proclaiming this good news to you that what God promised our ancestors [33e]he has brought to fulfillment for us, [their] children, by raising up Jesus, as it is written in the second psalm, 'You are my son; this day I have begotten you.' [34f]And that he raised him from the dead never to return to corruption he declared in this way, 'I shall give you the benefits assured to David.' [35g]That is why he also says in another psalm, 'You will not suffer your holy one to see corruption.' [36h]Now David, after he had served the will of God in his lifetime, fell asleep, was gathered to his ancestors, and did see corruption. [37]But the one whom God raised up did not see corruption. [38*]You must know, my brothers, that through him forgiveness of sins is being proclaimed to you, [and] in regard to everything from which you could not be justified under the law of Moses, [39i]in him

13:16–41 This is the first of several speeches of Paul to Jews proclaiming that the Christian church is the logical development of Pharisaic Judaism (see also Acts 24:10–21; 26:2–23).

13:16 Who are God-fearing: see note on Acts 8:26–40.

13:18 Put up with: some manuscripts read "sustained."

13:20 At the end of about four hundred and fifty years: the manuscript tradition makes it uncertain whether the mention of four hundred and fifty years refers to the sojourn in Egypt before the Exodus, the wilderness period and the time of the conquest (see Ex 12:40–41), as the translation here suggests, or to the time between the conquest and the time of Samuel, the period of the judges, if the text is read, "After these things, for about four hundred and fifty years, he provided judges."

13:31 The theme of the Galilean witnesses is a major one in the Gospel of Luke and in Acts and is used to signify the continuity between the teachings of Jesus and the teachings of the church and to guarantee the fidelity of the church's teachings to the words of Jesus.

13:38–39 Justified: the verb is the same as that used in Paul's letters to speak of the experience of justification and, as in Paul, is here connected with the term "to have faith" ("every believer"). But this seems the only passage about Paul in Acts where justification is mentioned. In Lucan fashion it is paralleled with "forgiveness of sins" (a theme at Acts 2:38; 3:19; 5:31; 10:43) based on Jesus' resurrection (Acts 13:37) rather than his cross, and is put negatively (Acts 13:38). Therefore, some would translate, "in regard to everything from which you could not be acquitted . . . every believer is acquitted."

r: Ex 6:1, 6; 12:51. *s:* Ex 16:1, 35; Nm 14:34. *t:* Dt 7:1; Jos 14:1–2. *u:* Jgs 2:16; 1 Sm 3:20. *v:* 1 Sm 8:5, 19; 9:16; 10:1, 20–21, 24; 11:15. *w:* 1 Sm 13:14; 16:12–13; Ps 89:20–21. *x:* Is 11:1. *y:* Mt 3:1–2; Mk 1:4–5; Lk 3:2–3. *z:* Mt 3:11; Mk 1:7; Lk 3:16; Jn 1:20, 27. *a:* Mt 27:20, 22–23; Mk 15:13–14; Lk 23:4, 14–15, 21–23; Jn 19:4–6, 15. *b:* Mt 27:59–60; Mk 15:46; Lk 23:53; Jn 19:38, 41–42. *c:* 2:24, 32; 3:15; 4:10; 17:31. *d:* 1:3, 8; 10:39, 41; Mt 28:8–10, 16–20; Mk 16:9, 12–20; Lk 24:13–53; Jn 20:11–29; 21:1–23. *e:* Ps 2:7. *f:* Is 55:3. *g:* Ps 16:10. *h:* 2:29; 1 Kgs 2:10. *i:* Rom 3:20.

every believer is justified. [40]Be careful, then, that what was said in the prophets not come about:

[41] [j]'Look on, you scoffers,
be amazed and disappear.
For I am doing a work in your days,
a work that you will never believe
even if someone tells you.' "

[42]As they were leaving, they invited them to speak on these subjects the following sabbath. [43]After the congregation had dispersed, many Jews and worshipers who were converts to Judaism followed Paul and Barnabas, who spoke to them and urged them to remain faithful to the grace of God.

Address to the Gentiles. [44]On the following sabbath almost the whole city gathered to hear the word of the Lord. [45]When the Jews saw the crowds, they were filled with jealousy and with violent abuse contradicted what Paul said. [46][k]*Both Paul and Barnabas spoke out boldly and said, "It was necessary that the word of God be spoken to you first, but since you reject it and condemn yourselves as unworthy of eternal life, we now turn to the Gentiles. [47][l]For so the Lord has commanded us, 'I have made you a light to the Gentiles, that you may be an instrument of salvation to the ends of the earth.' "

[48]The Gentiles were delighted when they heard this and glorified the word of the Lord. All who were destined for eternal life came to believe, [49]and the word of the Lord continued to spread through the whole region. [50]The Jews, however, incited the women of prominence who were worshipers and the leading men of the city, stirred up a persecution against Paul and Barnabas, and expelled them from their territory. [51][m]*So they shook the dust from their feet in protest against them and went to Iconium. [52]The disciples were filled with joy and the holy Spirit.

CHAPTER 14

See RG 432

Paul and Barnabas at Iconium. [1]In Iconium they entered the Jewish synagogue together and spoke in such a way that a great number of both Jews and Greeks came to believe, [2]although the disbelieving Jews stirred up and poisoned the minds of the Gentiles against the brothers. [3][n]So they stayed for a considerable period, speaking out boldly for the Lord, who confirmed the word about his grace by granting signs and wonders to occur through their hands. [4]The people of the city were divided: some were with the Jews; others, with the apostles. [5][o]When there was an attempt by both the Gentiles and the Jews, together with their leaders, to attack and stone them, [6]they realized it and fled to the Lycaonian cities of Lystra and Derbe and to the surrounding countryside, [7]where they continued to proclaim the good news.

Paul and Barnabas at Lystra. [8]*At Lystra there was a crippled man, lame from birth, who had never walked. [9]He listened to Paul speaking, who looked intently at him, saw that he had the faith to be healed, [10]and called out in a loud voice, "Stand up straight on your feet." He jumped up and began to walk about. [11][p]When the crowds saw what Paul had done, they cried out in Lycaonian, "The gods have come down to us in human form." [12]*They called Barnabas "Zeus" and Paul "Hermes," because he was the chief speaker. [13]And the priest of Zeus, whose temple was at the entrance to the city, brought oxen and garlands to the gates, for he together with the people intended to offer sacrifice.

[14]*The apostles Barnabas and Paul tore their garments when they heard this and

13:46 The refusal to believe frustrates God's plan for his chosen people; however, no adverse judgment is made here concerning their ultimate destiny. Again, Luke, in the words of Paul, speaks of the priority of Israel in the plan for salvation (see Acts 10:36).

13:51 See note on Lk 9:5.

14:8–18 In an effort to convince his hearers that the divine power works through his word, Paul cures the cripple. However, the pagan tradition of the occasional appearance of gods among human beings leads the people astray in interpreting the miracle. The incident reveals the cultural difficulties with which the church had to cope. Note the similarity of the miracle worked here by Paul to the one performed by Peter in Acts 3:2–10.

14:12 Zeus . . . Hermes: in Greek religion, Zeus was the chief of the Olympian gods, the "father of gods and men"; Hermes was a son of Zeus and was usually identified as the herald and messenger of the gods.

14:14 Tore their garments: a gesture of protest.

---

j: Heb 1:5. *k:* 3:26; Rom 1:16. *l:* Is 49:6. *m:* Mt 10:14; Mk 6:11; Lk 9:5; 10:11. *n:* Mk 16:17–20. *o:* 2 Tm 3:11. *p:* 28:6.

rushed out into the crowd, shouting, [15q*]"Men, why are you doing this? We are of the same nature as you, human beings. We proclaim to you good news that you should turn from these idols to the living God, 'who made heaven and earth and sea and all that is in them.' [16r]In past generations he allowed all Gentiles to go their own ways; [17s]yet, in bestowing his goodness, he did not leave himself without witness, for he gave you rains from heaven and fruitful seasons, and filled you with nourishment and gladness for your hearts." [18]Even with these words, they scarcely restrained the crowds from offering sacrifice to them.

[19t]However, some Jews from Antioch and Iconium arrived and won over the crowds. They stoned Paul and dragged him out of the city, supposing that he was dead. [20]But when the disciples gathered around him, he got up and entered the city. On the following day he left with Barnabas for Derbe.

End of the First Mission. [21]After they had proclaimed the good news to that city and made a considerable number of disciples, they returned to Lystra and to Iconium and to Antioch. [22u]They strengthened the spirits of the disciples and exhorted them to persevere in the faith, saying, "It is necessary for us to undergo many hardships to enter the kingdom of God." [23*]They appointed presbyters for them in each church and, with prayer and fasting, commended them to the Lord in whom they had put their faith. [24]Then they traveled through Pisidia and reached Pamphylia. [25]After proclaiming the word at Perga they went down to Attalia. [26v]From there they sailed to Antioch, where they had been commended to the grace of God for the work they had now accomplished. [27]And when they arrived, they called the church together and reported what God had done with them and how he had opened the door of faith to the Gentiles. [28]Then they spent no little time with the disciples.

CHAPTER 15

See RG 432

Council of Jerusalem. [1wx*]Some who had come down from Judea were instructing the brothers, "Unless you are circumcised according to the Mosaic practice, you cannot be saved." [2]Because there arose no little dissension and debate by Paul and Barnabas with them, it was decided that Paul, Barnabas, and some of the others should go up to Jerusalem to the apostles and presbyters about this question. [3]They were sent on their journey by the church, and passed through Phoenicia and Samaria telling of the conversion of the Gentiles, and brought great joy to all the brothers. [4]When they arrived in Jerusalem, they were welcomed by the church, as well as by the apostles and the presbyters, and they reported what God had done with them. [5]But some from the party of the Pharisees who had become believers stood up and said, "It is necessary to circumcise them and direct them to observe the Mosaic law."

[6*]The apostles and the presbyters met together to see about this matter. [7y*]After

14:15–17 This is the first speech of Paul to Gentiles recorded by Luke in Acts (cf. Acts 17:22–31). Rather than showing how Christianity is the logical outgrowth of Judaism, as he does in speeches before Jews, Luke says that God excuses past Gentile ignorance and then presents a natural theology arguing for the recognition of God's existence and presence through his activity in natural phenomena.

14:23 They appointed presbyters: the communities are given their own religious leaders by the traveling missionaries. The structure in these churches is patterned on the model of the Jerusalem community (Acts 11:30; 15:2, 5, 22; 21:18).

15:1–35 The Jerusalem "Council" marks the official rejection of the rigid view that Gentile converts were obliged to observe the Mosaic law completely. From here to the end of Acts, Paul and the Gentile mission become the focus of Luke's writing.

15:1–5 When some of the converted Pharisees of Jerusalem discover the results of the first missionary journey of Paul, they urge that the Gentiles be taught to follow the Mosaic law. Recognizing the authority of the Jerusalem church, Paul and Barnabas go there to settle the question of whether Gentiles can embrace a form of Christianity that does not include this obligation.

15:6–12 The gathering is possibly the same as that recalled by Paul in Gal 2:1–10. Note that in Acts 15:2 it is only the apostles and presbyters, a small group, with whom Paul and Barnabas are to meet. Here Luke gives the meeting a public character because he wishes to emphasize its doctrinal significance (see Acts 15:22).

15:7–11 Paul's refusal to impose the Mosaic law on the Gentile Christians is supported by Peter on the ground that within his own experience God bestowed the holy Spirit upon

q: 3:12; 10:26; Ex 20:11; Ps 146:6. *r:* 17:30. *s:* Wis 13:1. *t:* 2 Cor 11:25; 2 Tm 3:11. *u:* 1 Thes 3:3. *v:* 13:1–3. *w:* Gal 2:1–9. *x:* Lv 12:3; Gal 5:2. *y:* 10:27–43.

much debate had taken place, Peter got up and said to them, “My brothers, you are well aware that from early days God made his choice among you that through my mouth the Gentiles would hear the word of the gospel and believe. [8z]And God, who knows the heart, bore witness by granting them the holy Spirit just as he did us. [9a]He made no distinction between us and them, for by faith he purified their hearts. [10b]Why, then, are you now putting God to the test by placing on the shoulders of the disciples a yoke that neither our ancestors nor we have been able to bear? [11c*]On the contrary, we believe that we are saved through the grace of the Lord Jesus, in the same way as they.” [12]The whole assembly fell silent, and they listened while Paul and Barnabas described the signs and wonders God had worked among the Gentiles through them.

James on Dietary Law. [13*]After they had fallen silent, James responded, “My brothers, listen to me. [14*]Symeon has described how God first concerned himself with acquiring from among the Gentiles a people for his name. [15]The words of the prophets agree with this, as is written:

16 [d]‘After this I shall return
and rebuild the fallen hut of David;
from its ruins I shall rebuild it
and raise it up again,
17 so that the rest of humanity may seek out the Lord,
even all the Gentiles on whom my name is invoked.
Thus says the Lord who accomplishes these things,
18 known from of old.’

[19e]It is my judgment, therefore, that we ought to stop troubling the Gentiles who turn to God, [20f]but tell them by letter to avoid pollution from idols, unlawful marriage, the meat of strangled animals, and blood. [21]For Moses, for generations now, has had those who proclaim him in every town, as he has been read in the synagogues every sabbath.”

Letter of the Apostles. [22]Then the apostles and presbyters, in agreement with the whole church, decided to choose representatives and to send them to Antioch with Paul and Barnabas. The ones chosen were Judas, who was called Barsabbas, and Silas, leaders among the brothers. [23]This is the letter delivered by them: “The apostles and the presbyters, your brothers, to the brothers in Antioch, Syria, and Cilicia of Gentile origin: greetings. [24]Since we have heard that some of our number [who went out] without any mandate from us have upset you with their teachings and disturbed your peace of mind, [25]we have with one accord decided to choose representatives and to send them to you along with our beloved Barnabas and Paul, [26]who have dedicated their lives to the name of our Lord Jesus Christ. [27]So we are sending Judas and Silas who will also convey this same message by word of mouth: [28g]‘It is the decision of the holy Spirit and of us not to place on you any burden beyond these necessities, [29h]namely, to abstain from meat sacrificed to idols, from blood, from

Cornelius and his household without preconditions concerning the adoption of the Mosaic law (see Acts 10:44–47).

15:11 In support of Paul, Peter formulates the fundamental meaning of the gospel: that all are invited to be saved through faith in the power of Christ.

15:13–35 Some scholars think that this apostolic decree suggested by James, the immediate leader of the Jerusalem community, derives from another historical occasion than the meeting in question. This seems to be the case if the meeting is the same as the one related in Gal 2:1–10. According to that account, nothing was imposed upon Gentile Christians in respect to Mosaic law; whereas the decree instructs Gentile Christians of mixed communities to abstain from meats sacrificed to idols and from blood-meats, and to avoid marriage within forbidden degrees of consanguinity and affinity (Lv 18), all of which practices were especially abhorrent to Jews. Luke seems to have telescoped two originally independent incidents here: the first a Jerusalem “Council” that dealt with the question of circumcision, and the second a Jerusalem decree dealing mainly with Gentile observance of dietary laws (see Acts 21:25 where Paul seems to be learning of the decree for the first time).

15:14 Symeon: elsewhere in Acts he is called either Peter or Simon. The presence of the name Symeon here suggests that, in the source Luke is using for this part of the Jerusalem “Council” incident, the name may have originally referred to someone other than Peter (see Acts 13:1 where the Antiochene Symeon Niger is mentioned). As the text now stands, however, it is undoubtedly a reference to Simon Peter (Acts 15:7).

z: 10:44–48. *a:* 10:34–35. *b:* Mt 23:4; Gal 5:1. *c:* Gal 2:16; 3:11; Eph 2:5–8. *d:* Am 9:11–12. *e:* 15:28–29; 21:25. *f:* Gn 9:4; Lv 3:17; 17:10–14. *g:* 15:19–20. *h:* Gn 9:4; Lv 3:17; 17:10–14.

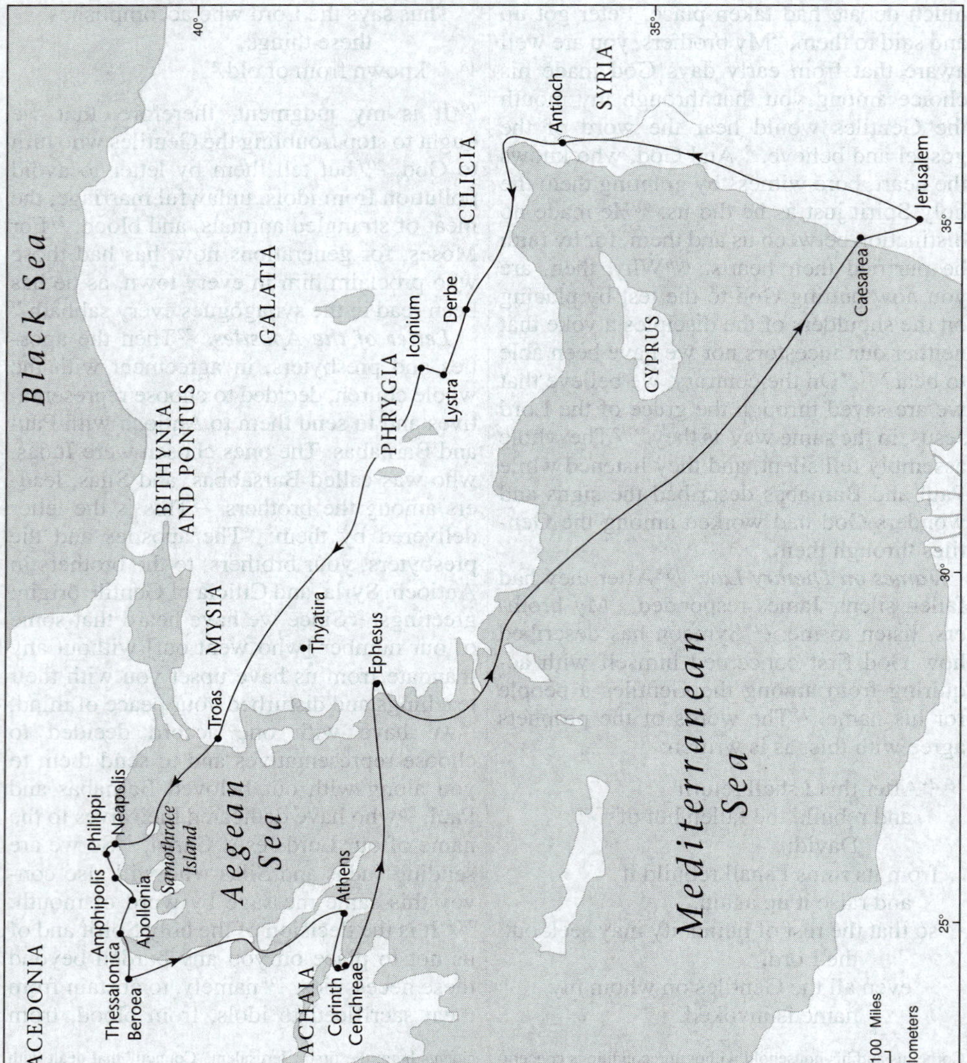

Second Missionary Journey of Paul

meats of strangled animals, and from unlawful marriage. If you keep free of these, you will be doing what is right. Farewell.' "

Delegates at Antioch. [30]And so they were sent on their journey. Upon their arrival in Antioch they called the assembly together and delivered the letter. [31]When the people read it, they were delighted with the exhortation. [32]Judas and Silas, who were themselves prophets, exhorted and strengthened the brothers with many words. [33]After they had spent some time there, they were sent off with greetings of peace from the brothers to those who had commissioned them. [[34]]* [35]But Paul and Barnabas remained in Antioch, teaching and proclaiming with many others the word of the Lord.

V. The Mission of Paul to the Ends of the Earth

Paul and Barnabas Separate. [36]* After some time, Paul said to Barnabas, "Come, let us make a return visit to see how the brothers are getting on in all the cities where we proclaimed the word of the Lord." [37]Barnabas wanted to take with them also John, who was called Mark, [38][i]but Paul insisted that they should not take with them someone who had deserted them at Pamphylia and who had not continued with them in their work. [39]So sharp was their disagreement that they separated. Barnabas took Mark and sailed to Cyprus. [40]But Paul chose Silas and departed after being commended by the brothers to the grace of the Lord. [41]He traveled through Syria and Cilicia bringing strength to the churches.

CHAPTER 16

See RG 432-33

Paul in Lycaonia: Timothy. [1][j]He reached [also] Derbe and Lystra where there was a disciple named Timothy, the son of a Jewish woman who was a believer, but his father was a Greek. [2][k]The brothers in Lystra and Iconium spoke highly of him, [3]*and Paul wanted him to come along with him. On account of the Jews of that region, Paul had him circumcised, for they all knew that his father was a Greek. [4]As they traveled from city to city, they handed on to the people for observance the decisions reached by the apostles and presbyters in Jerusalem. [5]Day after day the churches grew stronger in faith and increased in number.

Through Asia Minor. [6]They traveled through the Phrygian and Galatian territory because they had been prevented by the holy Spirit from preaching the message in the province of Asia. [7]*When they came to Mysia, they tried to go on into Bithynia, but the Spirit of Jesus did not allow them, [8]so they crossed through Mysia and came down to Troas. [9]During [the] night Paul had a vision. A Macedonian stood before him and implored him with these words, "Come over to Macedonia and help us." [10]*When he had seen the vision, we sought passage to Macedonia at once, concluding that God had called us to proclaim the good news to them.

15:34 Some manuscripts add, in various wordings, "But Silas decided to remain there."

15:36–18:22 This continuous narrative recounts Paul's second missionary journey. On the internal evidence of the Lucan account, it lasted about three years. Paul first visited the communities he had established on his first journey (Acts 16:1–5), then pushed on into Macedonia, where he established communities at Philippi, Thessalonica, and Beroea (Acts 16:7–17:5). To escape the hostility of the Jews of Thessalonica, he left for Greece and while resident in Athens attempted, without success, to establish an effective Christian community there. From Athens he proceeded to Corinth and, after a stay of a year and a half, returned to Antioch by way of Ephesus and Jerusalem (Acts 17:16–18:22). Luke does not concern himself with the structure or statistics of the communities but aims to show the general progress of the gospel in the Gentile world as well as its continued failure to take root in the Jewish community.

16:3 Paul had him circumcised: he did this in order that Timothy might be able to associate with the Jews and so perform a ministry among them. Paul did not object to the Jewish Christians' adherence to the law. But he insisted that the law could not be imposed on the Gentiles. Paul himself lived in accordance with the law, or as exempt from the law, according to particular circumstances (see 1 Cor 9:19–23).

16:7 The Spirit of Jesus: this is an unusual formulation in Luke's writings. The parallelism with Acts 16:6 indicates its meaning, the holy Spirit.

16:10–17 This is the first of the so-called "we-sections" in Acts, where Luke writes as one of Paul's companions. The other passages are Acts 20:5–15; 21:1–18; 27:1–28:16. Scholars debate whether Luke may not have used the first person plural simply as a literary device to lend color to the narrative. The realism of the narrative, however, lends weight to the argument that the "we" includes Luke or another companion of Paul whose data Luke used as a source.

i: 13:13. *j:* 1 Tm 1:2; 2 Tm 1:5. *k:* Phil 2:20.

Into Europe. 11*We set sail from Troas, making a straight run for Samothrace, and on the next day to Neapolis, 12and from there to Philippi, a leading city in that district of Macedonia and a Roman colony. We spent some time in that city. 13On the sabbath we went outside the city gate along the river where we thought there would be a place of prayer. We sat and spoke with the women who had gathered there. 14*One of them, a woman named Lydia, a dealer in purple cloth, from the city of Thyatira, a worshiper of God, listened, and the Lord opened her heart to pay attention to what Paul was saying. 15After she and her household had been baptized, she offered us an invitation, "If you consider me a believer in the Lord, come and stay at my home," and she prevailed on us.

Imprisonment at Philippi. 16*As we were going to the place of prayer, we met a slave girl with an oracular spirit, who used to bring a large profit to her owners through her fortune-telling. 17She began to follow Paul and us, shouting, "These people are slaves of the Most High God, who proclaim to you a way of salvation." 18She did this for many days. Paul became annoyed, turned, and said to the spirit, "I command you in the name of Jesus Christ to come out of her." Then it came out at that moment.

19When her owners saw that their hope of profit was gone, they seized Paul and Silas and dragged them to the public square before the local authorities. 20*They brought them before the magistrates and said, "These people are Jews and are disturbing our city 21and are advocating customs that are not lawful for us Romans to adopt or practice." 22lThe crowd joined in the attack on them, and the magistrates had them stripped and ordered them to be beaten with rods. 23After inflicting many blows on them, they threw them into prison and instructed the jailer to guard them securely. 24When he received these instructions, he put them in the innermost cell and secured their feet to a stake.

Deliverance from Prison. 25About midnight, while Paul and Silas were praying and singing hymns to God as the prisoners listened, 26there was suddenly such a severe earthquake that the foundations of the jail shook; all the doors flew open, and the chains of all were pulled loose. 27When the jailer woke up and saw the prison doors wide open, he drew [his] sword and was about to kill himself, thinking that the prisoners had escaped. 28But Paul shouted out in a loud voice, "Do no harm to yourself; we are all here." 29He asked for a light and rushed in and, trembling with fear, he fell down before Paul and Silas. 30Then he brought them out and said, "Sirs, what must I do to be saved?" 31And they said, "Believe in the Lord Jesus and you and your household will be saved." 32So they spoke the word of the Lord to him and to everyone in his house. 33He took them in at that hour of the night and bathed their wounds; then he and all his family were baptized at once. 34He brought them up into his house and provided a meal and with his household rejoiced at having come to faith in God.

35*But when it was day, the magistrates sent the lictors with the order, "Release those men." 36The jailer reported the[se] words to Paul, "The magistrates have sent orders that you be released. Now, then, come out and go in peace." 37m*But Paul said to them, "They have beaten us publicly, even though we are Roman citizens and have not been tried, and have thrown us into prison. And now, are they going to release us se-

16:11–40 The church at Philippi became a flourishing community to which Paul addressed one of his letters (see Introduction to the Letter to the Philippians).

16:14 A worshiper of God: a "God-fearer." See note on Acts 8:26–40.

16:16 With an oracular spirit: literally, "with a Python spirit." The Python was the serpent or dragon that guarded the Delphic oracle. It later came to designate a "spirit that pronounced oracles" and also a ventriloquist who, it was thought, had such a spirit in the belly.

16:20 Magistrates: in Greek, *stratēgoi*, the popular designation of the *duoviri*, the highest officials of the Roman colony of Philippi.

16:35 The lictors: the equivalent of police officers, among whose duties were the apprehension and punishment of criminals.

16:37 Paul's Roman citizenship granted him special privileges in regard to criminal process. Roman law forbade under severe penalty the beating of Roman citizens (see also Acts 22:25).

l: 2 Cor 11:25; Phil 1:30; 1 Thes 2:2. *m:* 22:25.

cretly? By no means. Let them come themselves and lead us out." [38n]The lictors reported these words to the magistrates, and they became alarmed when they heard that they were Roman citizens. [39]So they came and placated them, and led them out and asked that they leave the city. [40]When they had come out of the prison, they went to Lydia's house where they saw and encouraged the brothers, and then they left.

CHAPTER 17

See RG 433–34

Paul in Thessalonica. [1o]When they took the road through Amphipolis and Apollonia, they reached Thessalonica, where there was a synagogue of the Jews. [2]Following his usual custom, Paul joined them, and for three sabbaths he entered into discussions with them from the scriptures, [3p]expounding and demonstrating that the Messiah had to suffer and rise from the dead, and that "This is the Messiah, Jesus, whom I proclaim to you." [4]Some of them were convinced and joined Paul and Silas; so, too, a great number of Greeks who were worshipers, and not a few of the prominent women. [5q]But the Jews became jealous and recruited some worthless men loitering in the public square, formed a mob, and set the city in turmoil. They marched on the house of Jason, intending to bring them before the people's assembly. [6*]When they could not find them, they dragged Jason and some of the brothers before the city magistrates, shouting, "These people who have been creating a disturbance all over the world have now come here, [7r*]and Jason has welcomed them. They all act in opposition to the decrees of Caesar and claim instead that there is another king, Jesus." [8]They stirred up the crowd and the city magistrates who, upon hearing these charges, [9]took a surety payment from Jason and the others before releasing them.

Paul in Beroea. [10]The brothers immediately sent Paul and Silas to Beroea during the night. Upon arrival they went to the synagogue of the Jews. [11s]These Jews were more fair-minded than those in Thessalonica, for they received the word with all willingness and examined the scriptures daily to determine whether these things were so. [12]Many of them became believers, as did not a few of the influential Greek women and men. [13]But when the Jews of Thessalonica learned that the word of God had now been proclaimed by Paul in Beroea also, they came there too to cause a commotion and stir up the crowds. [14t]So the brothers at once sent Paul on his way to the seacoast, while Silas and Timothy remained behind. [15]After Paul's escorts had taken him to Athens, they came away with instructions for Silas and Timothy to join him as soon as possible.

Paul in Athens. [16*]While Paul was waiting for them in Athens, he grew exasperated at the sight of the city full of idols. [17]So he debated in the synagogue with the Jews and with the worshipers, and daily in the public square with whoever happened to be there. [18*]Even some of the Epicurean and Stoic philosophers engaged him in discussion. Some asked, "What is this scavenger trying

17:6–7 The accusations against Paul and his companions echo the charges brought against Jesus in Lk 23:2.

17:7 There is another king, Jesus: a distortion into a political sense of the apostolic proclamation of Jesus and the kingdom of God (see Acts 8:12).

17:16–21 Paul's presence in Athens sets the stage for the great discourse before a Gentile audience in Acts 17:22–31. Although Athens was a politically insignificant city at this period, it still lived on the glories of its past and represented the center of Greek culture. The setting describes the conflict between Christian preaching and Hellenistic philosophy.

17:18 Epicurean and Stoic philosophers: for the followers of Epicurus (342–271 B.C.), the goal of life was happiness attained through sober reasoning and the searching out of motives for all choice and avoidance. The Stoics were followers of Zeno, a younger contemporary of Alexander the Great. Zeno and his followers believed in a type of pantheism that held that the spark of divinity was present in all reality and that, in order to be free, each person must live "according to nature." **This scavenger**: literally, "seed-picker," as of a bird that picks up grain. The word is later used of scrap collectors and of people who take other people's ideas and propagate them as if they were their own. **Promoter of foreign deities**: according to Xenophon, Socrates was accused of promoting new deities. The accusation against Paul echoes the charge against Socrates. **'Jesus' and 'Resurrection'**: the Athenians are presented as misunderstanding Paul from the outset; they think he is preaching about Jesus and a goddess named **Anastasis**, i.e., Resurrection.

n: 22:29. *o:* 1 Thes 2:1–2. *p:* 3:18; Lk 24:25–26, 46. *q:* Rom 16:21. *r:* Lk 23:2; Jn 19:12–15. *s:* Jn 5:39. *t:* 1 Thes 3:1–2.

to say?" Others said, "He sounds like a promoter of foreign deities," because he was preaching about 'Jesus' and 'Resurrection.' [19u*]They took him and led him to the Areopagus and said, "May we learn what this new teaching is that you speak of? [20]For you bring some strange notions to our ears; we should like to know what these things mean." [21]Now all the Athenians as well as the foreigners residing there used their time for nothing else but telling or hearing something new.

Paul's Speech at the Areopagus. [22*]Then Paul stood up at the Areopagus and said:

"You Athenians, I see that in every respect you are very religious. [23*]For as I walked around looking carefully at your shrines, I even discovered an altar inscribed, 'To an Unknown God.' What therefore you unknowingly worship, I proclaim to you. [24v]The God who made the world and all that is in it, the Lord of heaven and earth, does not dwell in sanctuaries made by human hands, [25]nor is he served by human hands because he needs anything. Rather it is he who gives to everyone life and breath and everything. [26*]He made from one the whole human race to dwell on the entire surface of the earth, and he fixed the ordered seasons and the boundaries of their regions, [27w]so that people might seek God, even perhaps grope for him and find him, though indeed he is not far from any one of us. [28*]For 'In him we live and move and have our being,' as even some of your poets have said, 'For we too are his offspring.' [29x]Since therefore we are the offspring of God, we ought not to think that the divinity is like an image fashioned from gold, silver, or stone by human art and imagination. [30]God has overlooked the times of ignorance, but now he demands that all people everywhere repent [31y]because he has established a day on which he will 'judge the world with justice' through a man he has appointed, and he has provided confirmation for all by raising him from the dead."

[32]When they heard about resurrection of the dead, some began to scoff, but others said, "We should like to hear you on this some other time." [33]And so Paul left them. [34]But some did join him, and became believers. Among them were Dionysius, a member of the Court of the Areopagus, a woman named Damaris, and others with them.

CHAPTER 18

See RG 434

Paul in Corinth. [1]After this he left Athens and went to Corinth. [2z*]There he met a Jew named Aquila, a native of Pontus, who had recently come from Italy with his wife Priscilla because Claudius had ordered all the Jews to leave Rome. He went to visit them [3]and, because he practiced the same trade, stayed with them and worked, for they were tentmakers by trade. [4]Every sabbath, he

17:19 To the Areopagus: the "Areopagus" refers either to the Hill of Ares west of the Acropolis or to the Council of Athens, which at one time met on the hill but which at this time assembled in the Royal Colonnade (**Stoa Basileios**).

17:22–31 In Paul's appearance at the Areopagus he preaches his climactic speech to Gentiles in the cultural center of the ancient world. The speech is more theological than christological. Paul's discourse appeals to the Greek world's belief in divinity as responsible for the origin and existence of the universe. It contests the common belief in a multiplicity of gods supposedly exerting their powers through their images. It acknowledges that the attempt to find God is a constant human endeavor. It declares, further, that God is the judge of the human race, that the time of the judgment has been determined, and that it will be executed through a man whom God raised from the dead. The speech reflects sympathy with pagan religiosity, handles the subject of idol worship gently, and appeals for a new examination of divinity, not from the standpoint of creation but from the standpoint of judgment.

17:23 'To an Unknown God': ancient authors such as Pausanias, Philostratus, and Tertullian speak of Athenian altars with no specific dedication as altars of "unknown gods" or "nameless altars."

17:26 From one: many manuscripts read "from one blood." **Fixed . . . seasons**: or "fixed limits to the epochs."

17:28 'In him we live and move and have our being': some scholars understand this saying to be based on an earlier saying of Epimenides of Knossos (6th century B.C.). **'For we too are his offspring'**: here Paul is quoting Aratus of Soli, a third-century B.C. poet from Cilicia.

18:2 Aquila . . . Priscilla: both may already have been Christians at the time of their arrival in Corinth (see Acts 18:26). According to 1 Cor 16:19, their home became a meeting place for Christians. **Claudius**: the Emperor Claudius expelled the Jews from Rome ca. A.D. 49. The Roman historian Suetonius gives as reason for the expulsion disturbances among the Jews "at the instigation of Chrestos," probably meaning disputes about the messiahship of Jesus.

u: 1 Cor 1:22. *v:* 7:48–50; Gn 1:1; 1 Kgs 8:27; Is 42:5. *w:* Jer 23:23; Wis 13:6; Rom 1:19. *x:* 19:26; Is 40:18–20; 44:10–17; Rom 1:22–23. *y:* 10:42. *z:* Rom 16:3.

entered into discussions in the synagogue, attempting to convince both Jews and Greeks. [5]When Silas and Timothy came down from Macedonia, Paul began to occupy himself totally with preaching the word, testifying to the Jews that the Messiah was Jesus. [6a*]When they opposed him and reviled him, he shook out his garments and said to them, "Your blood be on your heads! I am clear of responsibility. From now on I will go to the Gentiles." [7b*]So he left there and went to a house belonging to a man named Titus Justus, a worshiper of God; his house was next to a synagogue. [8c*]Crispus, the synagogue official, came to believe in the Lord along with his entire household, and many of the Corinthians who heard believed and were baptized. [9d]One night in a vision the Lord said to Paul, "Do not be afraid. Go on speaking, and do not be silent, [10]for I am with you. No one will attack and harm you, for I have many people in this city." [11]He settled there for a year and a half and taught the word of God among them.

Accusations before Gallio. [12*]But when Gallio was proconsul of Achaia, the Jews rose up together against Paul and brought him to the tribunal, [13*]saying, "This man is inducing people to worship God contrary to the law." [14]When Paul was about to reply, Gallio spoke to the Jews, "If it were a matter of some crime or malicious fraud, I should with reason hear the complaint of you Jews; [15]but since it is a question of arguments over doctrine and titles and your own law, see to it yourselves. I do not wish to be a judge of such matters." [16]And he drove them away from the tribunal. [17]They all seized Sosthenes, the synagogue official, and beat him in full view of the tribunal. But none of this was of concern to Gallio.

Return to Syrian Antioch. [18e*]Paul remained for quite some time, and after saying farewell to the brothers he sailed for Syria, together with Priscilla and Aquila. At Cenchreae he had his hair cut because he had taken a vow. [19]When they reached Ephesus, he left them there, while he entered the synagogue and held discussions with the Jews. [20]Although they asked him to stay for a longer time, he did not consent, [21]but as he said farewell he promised, "I shall come back to you again, God willing." Then he set sail from Ephesus. [22*]Upon landing at Caesarea, he went up and greeted the church and then went down to Antioch. [23*]After staying there some time, he left and traveled in orderly sequence through the Galatian country and Phrygia, bringing strength to all the disciples.

Apollos. [24f*]A Jew named Apollos, a native of Alexandria, an eloquent speaker, arrived in Ephesus. He was an authority on the scriptures. [25]He had been instructed in the Way of the Lord and, with ardent spirit, spoke and taught accurately about Jesus, although he knew only the baptism of John. [26*]He began to speak boldly in the synagogue; but when Priscilla and Aquila heard him, they took him aside and explained to him the Way [of God] more accurately. [27]And when he wanted to cross to Achaia, the brothers encouraged him and wrote to the disciples there to welcome him. After his arrival he gave great assistance

18:6 Shook out his garments: a gesture indicating Paul's repudiation of his mission to the Jews there; cf. Acts 28:17–31.

18:7 A worshiper of God: see note on Acts 8:26–40.

18:8 Crispus: in 1 Cor 1:14 Paul mentions that Crispus was one of the few he himself baptized at Corinth.

18:12 When Gallio was proconsul of Achaia: Gallio's proconsulship in Achaia is dated to A.D. 51–52 from an inscription discovered at Delphi. This has become an important date in establishing a chronology of the life and missionary work of Paul.

18:13 Contrary to the law: Gallio (Acts 18:15) understands this to be a problem of Jewish, not Roman, law.

18:18 He had his hair cut because he had taken a vow: a reference to a Nazirite vow (see Nm 6:1–21, especially, 6:18) taken by Paul (see also Acts 21:23–27).

18:22 He went up and greeted the church: "going up" suggests a visit to the church in Jerusalem.

18:23–21:16 Luke's account of Paul's third missionary journey devotes itself mainly to his work at Ephesus (Acts 19:1–20:1). There is a certain restiveness on Paul's part and a growing conviction that the Spirit bids him return to Jerusalem and prepare to go to Rome (Acts 19:21).

18:24, 25 Apollos appears as a preacher who knows the teaching of Jesus in the context of John's baptism of repentance. Aquila and Priscilla instruct him more fully. He is referred to in 1 Cor 1:12; 3:5–6, 22.

18:26 The Way [of God]: for the Way, see note on Acts 9:2. Other manuscripts here read "the Way of the Lord," "the word of the Lord," or simply "the Way."

---

a: 13:51; Mt 10:14; 27:24–25; Mk 6:11; Lk 9:5; 10:10–11. *b:* 13:46–47; 28:28. *c:* 1 Cor 1:14. *d:* Jer 1:8. *e:* 21:24; Nm 6:18. *f:* 1 Cor 1:12.

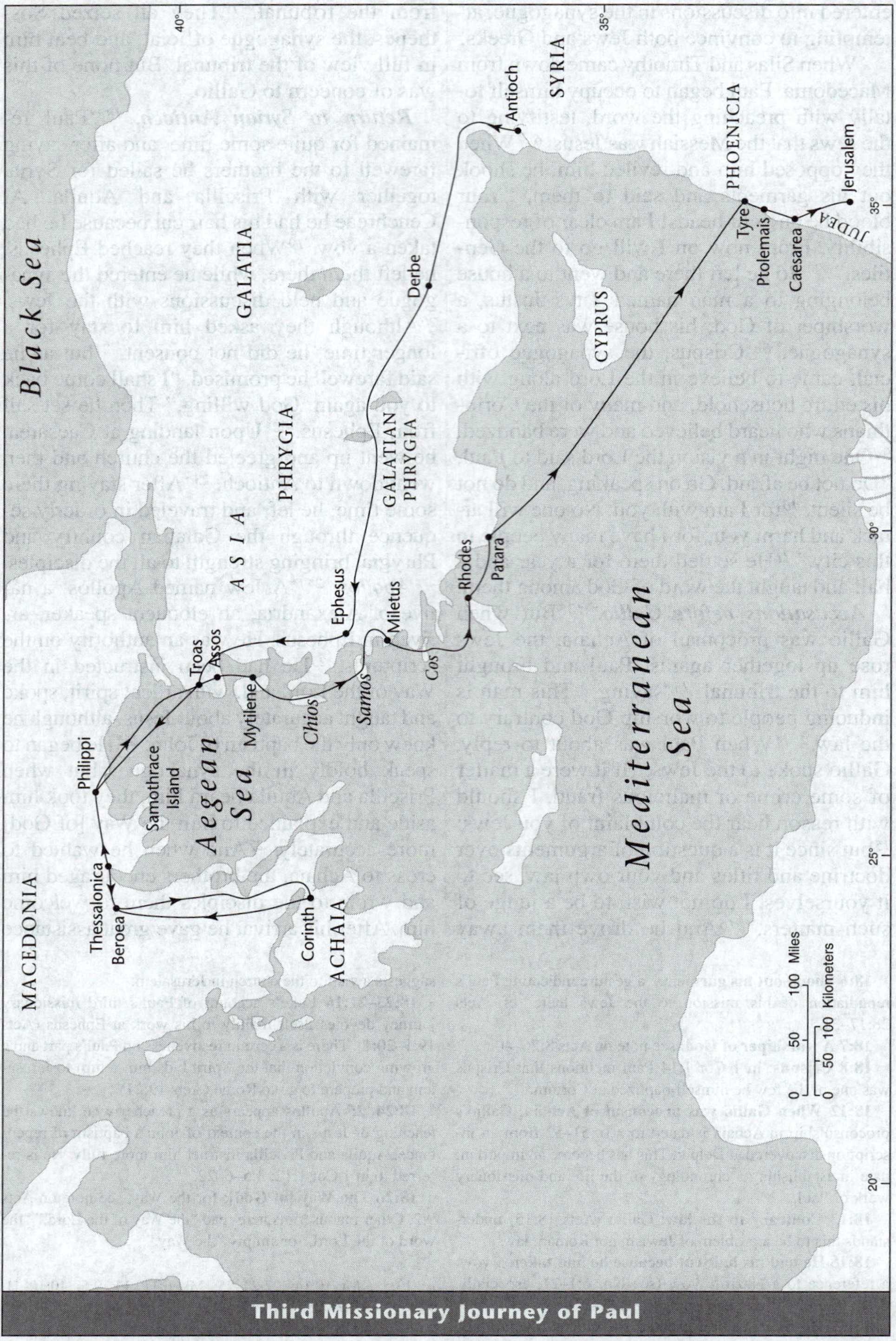

Third Missionary Journey of Paul

to those who had come to believe through grace. [28]He vigorously refuted the Jews in public, establishing from the scriptures that the Messiah is Jesus.

CHAPTER 19

See RG 434–35

Paul in Ephesus. [1*]While Apollos was in Corinth, Paul traveled through the interior of the country and came [down] to Ephesus where he found some disciples. [2]He said to them, "Did you receive the holy Spirit when you became believers?" They answered him, "We have never even heard that there is a holy Spirit." [3]He said, "How were you baptized?" They replied, "With the baptism of John." [4g]Paul then said, "John baptized with a baptism of repentance, telling the people to believe in the one who was to come after him, that is, in Jesus." [5]When they heard this, they were baptized in the name of the Lord Jesus. [6h]And when Paul laid [his] hands on them, the holy Spirit came upon them, and they spoke in tongues and prophesied. [7]Altogether there were about twelve men.

[8]He entered the synagogue, and for three months debated boldly with persuasive arguments about the kingdom of God. [9]But when some in their obstinacy and disbelief disparaged the Way before the assembly, he withdrew and took his disciples with him and began to hold daily discussions in the lecture hall of Tyrannus. [10]This continued for two years with the result that all the inhabitants of the province of Asia heard the word of the Lord, Jews and Greeks alike. [11]So extraordinary were the mighty deeds God accomplished at the hands of Paul [12i]that when face cloths or aprons that touched his skin were applied to the sick, their diseases left them and the evil spirits came out of them.

The Jewish Exorcists. [13]Then some itinerant Jewish exorcists tried to invoke the name of the Lord Jesus over those with evil spirits, saying, "I adjure you by the Jesus whom Paul preaches." [14]When the seven sons of Sceva, a Jewish high priest, tried to do this, [15]the evil spirit said to them in reply, "Jesus I recognize, Paul I know, but who are you?" [16]The person with the evil spirit then sprang at them and subdued them all. He so overpowered them that they fled naked and wounded from that house. [17]When this became known to all the Jews and Greeks who lived in Ephesus, fear fell upon them all, and the name of the Lord Jesus was held in great esteem. [18]Many of those who had become believers came forward and openly acknowledged their former practices. [19]Moreover, a large number of those who had practiced magic collected their books and burned them in public. They calculated their value and found it to be fifty thousand silver pieces. [20]Thus did the word of the Lord continue to spread with influence and power.

Paul's Plans. [21j]When this was concluded, Paul made up his mind to travel through Macedonia and Achaia, and then to go on to Jerusalem, saying, "After I have been there, I must visit Rome also." [22]Then he sent to Macedonia two of his assistants, Timothy and Erastus, while he himself stayed for a while in the province of Asia.

The Riot of the Silversmiths. [23]About that time a serious disturbance broke out concerning the Way. [24*]There was a silversmith named Demetrius who made miniature silver shrines of Artemis and provided no little work for the craftsmen. [25]He called a meeting of these and other workers in related crafts and said, "Men, you know well that our prosperity derives from this work. [26k]As you can now see and hear, not only in Ephesus but throughout most of the province of Asia this Paul has persuaded and misled a great number of people by saying that gods made by hands are not gods at all. [27]The dan-

19:1–6 Upon his arrival in Ephesus, Paul discovers other people at the same religious stage as Apollos, though they seem to have considered themselves followers of Christ, not of the Baptist. On the relation between baptism and the reception of the Spirit, see note on Acts 8:16.

19:24 Miniature silver shrines of Artemis: the temple of Artemis at Ephesus was one of the seven wonders of the ancient world. Artemis, originally the Olympian virgin hunter, moon goddess, and goddess of wild nature, was worshiped at Ephesus as an Asian mother goddess and goddess of fertility. She was one of the most widely worshiped female deities in the Hellenistic world (see Acts 18:27).

g: 1:5; 11:16; 13:24–25; Mt 3:11; Mk 1:8; Lk 3:16. *h:* 8:15–17; 10:44, 46. *i:* 5:15–16; Lk 8:44–47. *j:* 23:11; Rom 1:13; 15:22–32. *k:* 17:29.

ger grows, not only that our business will be discredited, but also that the temple of the great goddess Artemis will be of no account, and that she whom the whole province of Asia and all the world worship will be stripped of her magnificence."

[28]When they heard this, they were filled with fury and began to shout, "Great is Artemis of the Ephesians!" [29l]The city was filled with confusion, and the people rushed with one accord into the theater, seizing Gaius and Aristarchus, the Macedonians, Paul's traveling companions. [30]Paul wanted to go before the crowd, but the disciples would not let him, [31*]and even some of the Asiarchs who were friends of his sent word to him advising him not to venture into the theater. [32]Meanwhile, some were shouting one thing, others something else; the assembly was in chaos, and most of the people had no idea why they had come together. [33]Some of the crowd prompted Alexander, as the Jews pushed him forward, and Alexander signaled with his hand that he wished to explain something to the gathering. [34]But when they recognized that he was a Jew, they all shouted in unison, for about two hours, "Great is Artemis of the Ephesians!" [35*]Finally the town clerk restrained the crowd and said, "You Ephesians, what person is there who does not know that the city of the Ephesians is the guardian of the temple of the great Artemis and of her image that fell from the sky? [36]Since these things are undeniable, you must calm yourselves and not do anything rash. [37]The men you brought here are not temple robbers, nor have they insulted our goddess. [38]If Demetrius and his fellow craftsmen have a complaint against anyone, courts are in session, and there are proconsuls. Let them bring charges against one another. [39]If you have anything further to investigate, let the matter be settled in the lawful assembly, [40*]for, as it is, we are in danger of being charged with rioting because of today's conduct. There is no cause for it. We shall [not] be able to give a reason for this demonstration." With these words he dismissed the assembly.

CHAPTER 20

See RG 434–35

Journey to Macedonia and Greece. [1m]When the disturbance was over, Paul had the disciples summoned and, after encouraging them, he bade them farewell and set out on his journey to Macedonia. [2]As he traveled throughout those regions, he provided many words of encouragement for them. Then he arrived in Greece, [3]where he stayed for three months. But when a plot was made against him by the Jews as he was about to set sail for Syria, he decided to return by way of Macedonia.

Return to Troas. [4n]Sopater, the son of Pyrrhus, from Beroea, accompanied him, as did Aristarchus and Secundus from Thessalonica, Gaius from Derbe, Timothy, and Tychicus and Trophimus from Asia [5o*]who went on ahead and waited for us at Troas. [6*]We sailed from Philippi after the feast of Unleavened Bread, and rejoined them five days later in Troas, where we spent a week.

Eutychus Restored to Life. [7*]On the first day of the week when we gathered to break bread, Paul spoke to them because he was going to leave on the next day, and he kept on speaking until midnight. [8]There were many lamps in the upstairs room where we

19:31 Asiarchs: the precise status and role of the Asiarchs is disputed. They appear to have been people of wealth and influence who promoted the Roman imperial cult and who may also have been political representatives in a league of cities in the Roman province of Asia.

19:35 Guardian of the temple: this title was accorded by Rome to cities that provided a temple for the imperial cult. Inscriptional evidence indicates that Ephesus was acknowledged as the temple keeper of Artemis and of the imperial cult. **That fell from the sky**: many scholars think that this refers to a meteorite that was worshiped as an image of the goddess.

19:40 Some manuscripts omit the negative in **[not] be able**, making the meaning, "There is no cause for which we shall be able to give a reason for this demonstration."

20:5 The second "we-section" of Acts begins here. See note on Acts 16:10–17.

20:6 Feast of Unleavened Bread: see note on Lk 22:1.

20:7 The first day of the week: the day after the sabbath and the first day of the Jewish week, apparently chosen originally by the Jerusalem community for the celebration of the liturgy of the Eucharist in order to relate it to the resurrection of Christ.

l: Col 4:10. *m:* 1 Cor 16:1. *n:* Rom 16:21. *o:* 21:29; 2 Tm 4:20.

were gathered, [9]and a young man named Eutychus who was sitting on the window sill was sinking into a deep sleep as Paul talked on and on. Once overcome by sleep, he fell down from the third story and when he was picked up, he was dead. [10 p]*Paul went down, threw himself upon him, and said as he embraced him, "Don't be alarmed; there is life in him." [11]Then he returned upstairs, broke the bread, and ate; after a long conversation that lasted until daybreak, he departed. [12]And they took the boy away alive and were immeasurably comforted.

Journey to Miletus. [13]We went ahead to the ship and set sail for Assos where we were to take Paul on board, as he had arranged, since he was going overland. [14]When he met us in Assos, we took him aboard and went on to Mitylene. [15]We sailed away from there on the next day and reached a point off Chios, and a day later we reached Samos, and on the following day we arrived at Miletus. [16]*Paul had decided to sail past Ephesus in order not to lose time in the province of Asia, for he was hurrying to be in Jerusalem, if at all possible, for the day of Pentecost.

Paul's Farewell Speech at Miletus. [17]From Miletus he had the presbyters of the church at Ephesus summoned. [18]When they came to him, he addressed them, "You know how I lived among you the whole time from the day I first came to the province of Asia. [19]I served the Lord with all humility and with the tears and trials that came to me because of the plots of the Jews, [20]and I did not at all shrink from telling you what was for your benefit, or from teaching you in public or in your homes. [21]I earnestly bore witness for both Jews and Greeks to repentance before God and to faith in our Lord Jesus. [22]But now, compelled by the Spirit, I am going to Jerusalem. What will happen to me there I do not know, [23 q]except that in one city after another the holy Spirit has been warning me that imprisonment and hardships await me. [24 r]Yet I consider life of no importance to me, if only I may finish my course and the ministry that I received from the Lord Jesus, to bear witness to the gospel of God's grace.

[25]"But now I know that none of you to whom I preached the kingdom during my travels will ever see my face again. [26]And so I solemnly declare to you this day that I am not responsible for the blood of any of you, [27]for I did not shrink from proclaiming to you the entire plan of God. [28 s]*Keep watch over yourselves and over the whole flock of which the holy Spirit has appointed you overseers, in which you tend the church of God that he acquired with his own blood. [29 t]I know that after my departure savage wolves will come among you, and they will not spare the flock. [30 u]And from your own group, men will come forward perverting the truth to draw the disciples away after them. [31 v]So be vigilant and remember that for three years, night and day, I unceasingly admonished each of you with tears. [32]And now I commend you to God and to that gracious word of his that can build you up and give you the inheritance among all who are consecrated. [33]I have never wanted anyone's silver or gold or clothing. [34 w]You know well that these very hands have served my needs and my companions. [35 x]In every way I have shown you that by hard work of that sort we must help the weak, and keep in mind the words of the Lord Jesus who himself said, 'It is more blessed to give than to receive.' "

20:10 The action of Paul in throwing himself upon the dead boy recalls that of Elijah in 1 Kgs 17:21 where the son of the widow of Zarephath is revived and that of Elisha in 2 Kgs 4:34 where the Shunamite woman's son is restored to life.

20:16–35 Apparently aware of difficulties at Ephesus and neighboring areas, Paul calls the presbyters together at Miletus, about thirty miles from Ephesus. He reminds them of his dedication to the gospel (Acts 20:18–21), speaks of what he is about to suffer for the gospel (Acts 20:22–27), and admonishes them to guard the community against false prophets, sure to arise upon his departure (Acts 20:28–31). He concludes by citing a saying of Jesus (Acts 20:35) not recorded in the gospel tradition. Luke presents this farewell to the Ephesian presbyters as Paul's last will and testament.

20:28 Overseers: see note on Phil 1:1. **The church of God**: because the clause "that he acquired with his own blood" following "the church of God" suggests that "his own blood" refers to God's blood, some early copyists changed "the church of God" to "the church of the Lord." Some prefer the translation "acquired with the blood of his own," i.e., Christ.

p: 1 Kgs 17:17–24; 2 Kgs 4:30–37; Mt 9:24; Mk 5:39; Lk 8:52. *q:* 9:16. *r:* 2 Tm 4:7. *s:* Jn 21:15–17; 1 Pt 5:2. *t:* Jn 10:12. *u:* Mt 7:15; 2 Pt 2:1–3; 1 Jn 2:18–19. *v:* 1 Thes 2:11. *w:* 1 Cor 4:12; 1 Thes 2:9; 2 Thes 3:8. *x:* Sir 4:31.

[36]When he had finished speaking he knelt down and prayed with them all. [37]They were all weeping loudly as they threw their arms around Paul and kissed him, [38]for they were deeply distressed that he had said that they would never see his face again. Then they escorted him to the ship.

CHAPTER 21

See RG 435–36

Arrival at Tyre. [1*]When we had taken leave of them we set sail, made a straight run for Cos, and on the next day for Rhodes, and from there to Patara. [2]Finding a ship crossing to Phoenicia, we went on board and put out to sea. [3]We caught sight of Cyprus but passed by it on our left and sailed on toward Syria and put in at Tyre where the ship was to unload cargo. [4]There we sought out the disciples and stayed for a week. They kept telling Paul through the Spirit not to embark for Jerusalem. [5]At the end of our stay we left and resumed our journey. All of them, women and children included, escorted us out of the city, and after kneeling on the beach to pray, [6]we bade farewell to one another. Then we boarded the ship, and they returned home.

Arrival at Ptolemais and Caesarea. [7]We continued the voyage and came from Tyre to Ptolemais, where we greeted the brothers and stayed a day with them. [8y*]On the next day we resumed the trip and came to Caesarea, where we went to the house of Philip the evangelist, who was one of the Seven, and stayed with him. [9]He had four virgin daughters gifted with prophecy. [10*]We had been there several days when a prophet named Agabus came down from Judea. [11z*]He came up to us, took Paul's belt, bound his own feet and hands with it, and said, "Thus says the holy Spirit: This is the way the Jews will bind the owner of this belt in Jerusalem, and they will hand him over to the Gentiles." [12]When we heard this, we and the local residents begged him not to go up to Jerusalem. [13a]Then Paul replied, "What are you doing, weeping and breaking my heart? I am prepared not only to be bound but even to die in Jerusalem for the name of the Lord Jesus." [14b*]Since he would not be dissuaded we let the matter rest, saying, "The Lord's will be done."

Paul and James in Jerusalem. [15]After these days we made preparations for our journey, then went up to Jerusalem. [16]Some of the disciples from Caesarea came along to lead us to the house of Mnason, a Cypriot, a disciple of long standing, with whom we were to stay. [17*]When we reached Jerusalem the brothers welcomed us warmly. [18]The next day, Paul accompanied us on a visit to James, and all the presbyters were present. [19]He greeted them, then proceeded to tell them in detail what God had accomplished among the Gentiles through his ministry. [20]They praised God when they heard it but said to him, "Brother, you see how many thousands of believers there are from among the Jews, and they are all zealous observers of the law. [21]They have been informed that you are teaching all the Jews who live among the Gentiles to abandon Moses and that you are telling them not to circumcise their children or to observe their customary practices. [22]What is to be done? They will surely hear that you have arrived. [23c*]So do what we tell you. We have four men who have taken a vow. [24*]Take these men and purify yourself

21:1–18 The third "we-section" of Acts (see note on Acts 16:10–17).

21:8 One of the Seven: see note on Acts 6:2–4.

21:10 Agabus: mentioned in Acts 11:28 as the prophet who predicted the famine that occurred when Claudius was emperor.

21:11 The symbolic act of Agabus recalls those of Old Testament prophets. Compare Is 20:2; Ez 4:1; Jer 13:1.

21:14 The Christian disciples' attitude reflects that of Jesus (see Lk 22:42).

21:17–26 The leaders of the Jewish Christians of Jerusalem inform Paul that the Jews there believe he has encouraged the Jews of the diaspora to abandon the Mosaic law. According to Acts, Paul had no objection to the retention of the law by the Jewish Christians of Jerusalem and left the Jews of the diaspora who accepted Christianity free to follow the same practice.

21:23–26 The leaders of the community suggest that Paul, on behalf of four members of the Jerusalem community, make the customary payment for the sacrifices offered at the termination of the Nazirite vow (see Nm 6:1–24) in order to impress favorably the Jewish Christians in Jerusalem with his high regard for the Mosaic law. Since Paul himself had once made this vow (Acts 18:18), his respect for the law would be on public record.

21:24 Pay their expenses: according to Nm 6:14–15 the Nazirite had to present a yearling lamb for a holocaust, a yearling ewe lamb for a sin offering, and a ram for a peace offering, along with food and drink offerings, upon completion of the period of the vow.

y: 6:5; 8:5–6. *z:* 11:28; 20:23. *a:* 19:15–16. *b:* Mt 6:10; 26:39; Mk 14:36; Lk 22:42. *c:* 18:18; Nm 6:1–21.

with them, and pay their expenses that they
may have their heads shaved. In this way
everyone will know that there is nothing to
the reports they have been given about you
but that you yourself live in observance of
the law. [25d*]As for the Gentiles who have
come to believe, we sent them our decision
that they abstain from meat sacrificed to
idols, from blood, from the meat of strangled
animals, and from unlawful marriage." [26e]So
Paul took the men, and on the next day after
purifying himself together with them entered
the temple to give notice of the day when the
purification would be completed and the offering made for each of them.
Paul's Arrest. [27]When the seven days were
nearly completed, the Jews from the province
of Asia noticed him in the temple, stirred up
the whole crowd, and laid hands on him,
[28f*]shouting, "Fellow Israelites, help us. This
is the man who is teaching everyone everywhere against the people and the law and this
place, and what is more, he has even brought
Greeks into the temple and defiled this sacred
place." [29]For they had previously seen Trophimus the Ephesian in the city with him and
supposed that Paul had brought him into the
temple. [30]The whole city was in turmoil with
people rushing together. They seized Paul and
dragged him out of the temple, and immediately the gates were closed. [31*]While they
were trying to kill him, a report reached the
cohort commander that all Jerusalem was rioting. [32]He immediately took soldiers and
centurions and charged down on them. When
they saw the commander and the soldiers they
stopped beating Paul. [33]The cohort commander came forward, arrested him, and ordered him to be secured with two chains; he
tried to find out who he might be and what he
had done. [34]Some in the mob shouted one
thing, others something else; so, since he was
unable to ascertain the truth because of the
uproar, he ordered Paul to be brought into the
compound. [35]When he reached the steps, he
was carried by the soldiers because of the violence of the mob, [36g*]for a crowd of people
followed and shouted, "Away with him!"
[37]Just as Paul was about to be taken into the
compound, he said to the cohort commander,
"May I say something to you?" He replied,
"Do you speak Greek? [38h*]So then you are
not the Egyptian who started a revolt some
time ago and led the four thousand assassins
into the desert?" [39]Paul answered, "I am a
Jew, of Tarsus in Cilicia, a citizen of no mean
city; I request you to permit me to speak to the
people." [40*]When he had given his permission, Paul stood on the steps and motioned
with his hand to the people; and when all was
quiet he addressed them in Hebrew.

CHAPTER 22

See RG 436

*Paul's Defense before the Jerusalem
Jews.* [1*]"My brothers and fathers, listen to
what I am about to say to you in my defense." [2]When they heard him addressing
them in Hebrew they became all the more
quiet. And he continued, [3i]"I am a Jew, born
in Tarsus in Cilicia, but brought up in this

21:25 Paul is informed about the apostolic decree, seemingly for the first time (see note on Acts 15:13–35). The allusion to the decree was probably introduced here by Luke to remind his readers that the Gentile Christians themselves were asked to respect certain Jewish practices deriving from the law.

21:28 The charges against Paul by the diaspora Jews are identical to the charges brought against Stephen by diaspora Jews in Acts 6:13. **Brought Greeks into the temple**: non-Jews were forbidden, under penalty of death, to go beyond the Court of the Gentiles. Inscriptions in Greek and Latin on a stone balustrade marked off the prohibited area.

21:31 Cohort commander: literally, "the leader of a thousand in a cohort." At this period the Roman cohort commander usually led six hundred soldiers, a tenth of a legion; but the number in a cohort varied.

21:36 Away with him: at the trial of Jesus before Pilate in Lk 23:18, the people similarly shout, "Away with this man."

21:38 The Egyptian: according to the Jewish historian Josephus, an Egyptian gathered a large crowd on the Mount of Olives to witness the destruction of the walls of Jerusalem that would fall at the Egyptian "prophet's" word. The commotion was put down by the Roman authorities and the Egyptian escaped, but only after thousands had been killed. **Four thousand assassins**: literally, *sicarii*. According to Josephus, these were political nationalists who removed their opponents by assassination with a short dagger, called in Latin a *sica*.

21:40 In Hebrew: meaning, perhaps, in Aramaic, which at this time was the Semitic tongue in common use.

22:1–21 Paul's first defense speech is presented to the Jerusalem crowds. Luke here presents Paul as a devout Jew (Acts 22:3) and zealous persecutor of the Christian community (Acts 22:4–5), and then recounts the conversion of Paul for the second time in Acts (see note on Acts 9:1–19).

d: 15:19–20, 28–29. *e:* 1 Cor 9:20. *f:* Rom 15:31. *g:* 22:22; Lk 23:18; Jn 19:15. *h:* 5:36–37. *i:* 5:34; 26:4–5; 2 Cor 11:22; Gal 1:13–14; Phil 3:5–6.

city. At the feet of Gamaliel I was educated strictly in our ancestral law and was zealous for God, just as all of you are today. [4][j]I persecuted this Way to death, binding both men and women and delivering them to prison. [5]Even the high priest and the whole council of elders can testify on my behalf. For from them I even received letters to the brothers and set out for Damascus to bring back to Jerusalem in chains for punishment those there as well.

[6][k]"On that journey as I drew near to Damascus, about noon a great light from the sky suddenly shone around me. [7][l]I fell to the ground and heard a voice saying to me, 'Saul, Saul, why are you persecuting me?' [8][m]I replied, 'Who are you, sir?' And he said to me, 'I am Jesus the Nazorean whom you are persecuting.' [9][n]My companions saw the light but did not hear the voice of the one who spoke to me. [10][o]I asked, 'What shall I do, sir?' The Lord answered me, 'Get up and go into Damascus, and there you will be told about everything appointed for you to do.' [11][p]Since I could see nothing because of the brightness of that light, I was led by hand by my companions and entered Damascus.

[12][q]"A certain Ananias, a devout observer of the law, and highly spoken of by all the Jews who lived there, [13]came to me and stood there and said, 'Saul, my brother, regain your sight.' And at that very moment I regained my sight and saw him. [14]Then he said, 'The God of our ancestors designated you to know his will, to see the Righteous One, and to hear the sound of his voice; [15]*for you will be his witness before all to what you have seen and heard. [16]Now, why delay? Get up and have yourself baptized and your sins washed away, calling upon his name.'

[17]"After I had returned to Jerusalem and while I was praying in the temple, I fell into a trance [18]and saw the Lord saying to me, 'Hurry, leave Jerusalem at once, because they will not accept your testimony about me.' [19][r]But I replied, 'Lord, they themselves know that from synagogue to synagogue I used to imprison and beat those who believed in you. [20][s]And when the blood of your witness Stephen was being shed, I myself stood by giving my approval and keeping guard over the cloaks of his murderers.' [21][t]*Then he said to me, 'Go, I shall send you far away to the Gentiles.'"

Paul Imprisoned. [22][u]*They listened to him until he said this, but then they raised their voices and shouted, "Take such a one as this away from the earth. It is not right that he should live." [23]And as they were yelling and throwing off their cloaks and flinging dust into the air, [24]the cohort commander ordered him to be brought into the compound and gave instruction that he be interrogated under the lash to determine the reason why they were making such an outcry against him. [25][v]*But when they had stretched him out for the whips, Paul said to the centurion on duty, "Is it lawful for you to scourge a man who is a Roman citizen and has not been tried?" [26]When the centurion heard this, he went to the cohort commander and reported it, saying, "What are you going to do? This man is a Roman citizen." [27]Then the commander came and said to him, "Tell me, are you a Roman citizen?" "Yes," he answered. [28]The commander replied, "I acquired this citizenship for a large sum of money." Paul said, "But I was born one." [29]At once those who were going to interrogate him backed away from him, and the commander became alarmed when he realized that he was a Roman citizen and that he had had him bound.

22:15 His witness: like the Galilean followers during the historical ministry of Jesus, Paul too, through his experience of the risen Christ, is to be a witness to the resurrection (compare Acts 1:8; 10:39–41; Lk 24:48).

22:21 Paul endeavors to explain that his position on the law has not been identical with that of his audience because it has been his prophetic mission to preach to the Gentiles to whom the law was not addressed and who had no faith in it as a way of salvation.

22:22 Paul's suggestion that his prophetic mission to the Gentiles did not involve his imposing the law on them provokes the same opposition as occurred in Pisidian Antioch (Acts 13:45).

22:25 Is it lawful for you to scourge a man who is a Roman citizen and has not been tried?: see note on Acts 16:37.

j: 8:3; 9:1–2; 22:19; 26:9–11; Phil 3:6. *k:* 9:3; 26:13; 1 Cor 15:8. *l:* 9:4; 26:14. *m:* 9:5; 26:15; Mt 25:40. *n:* 9:7; 26:13–14. *o:* 9:6; 26:16. *p:* 9:8. *q:* 9:10–19. *r:* 8:3; 9:1–2; 22:4–5; 26:9–11. *s:* 7:58; 8:1. *t:* 9:15; Gal 2:7–9. *u:* 21:36; Lk 23:18; Jn 19:15. *v:* 16:37.

Paul before the Sanhedrin. [30]The next day, wishing to determine the truth about why he was being accused by the Jews, he freed him and ordered the chief priests and the whole Sanhedrin to convene. Then he brought Paul down and made him stand before them.

See RG 436

CHAPTER 23

[1w]Paul looked intently at the Sanhedrin and said, "My brothers, I have conducted myself with a perfectly clear conscience before God to this day." [2*]The high priest Ananias ordered his attendants to strike his mouth. [3x*]Then Paul said to him, "God will strike you, you whitewashed wall. Do you indeed sit in judgment upon me according to the law and yet in violation of the law order me to be struck?" [4]The attendants said, "Would you revile God's high priest?" [5y*]Paul answered, "Brothers, I did not realize he was the high priest. For it is written, 'You shall not curse a ruler of your people.' "

[6z]Paul was aware that some were Sadducees and some Pharisees, so he called out before the Sanhedrin, "My brothers, I am a Pharisee, the son of Pharisees; [I] am on trial for hope in the resurrection of the dead." [7]When he said this, a dispute broke out between the Pharisees and Sadducees, and the group became divided. [8a]For the Sadducees say that there is no resurrection or angels or spirits, while the Pharisees acknowledge all three. [9]A great uproar occurred, and some scribes belonging to the Pharisee party stood up and sharply argued, "We find nothing wrong with this man. Suppose a spirit or an angel has spoken to him?" [10]The dispute was so serious that the commander, afraid that Paul would be torn to pieces by them, ordered his troops to go down and rescue him from their midst and take him into the compound. [11b*]The following night the Lord stood by him and said, "Take courage. For just as you have borne witness to my cause in Jerusalem, so you must also bear witness in Rome."

Transfer to Caesarea. [12]When day came, the Jews made a plot and bound themselves by oath not to eat or drink until they had killed Paul. [13]There were more than forty who formed this conspiracy. [14]They went to the chief priests and elders and said, "We have bound ourselves by a solemn oath to taste nothing until we have killed Paul. [15]You, together with the Sanhedrin, must now make an official request to the commander to have him bring him down to you, as though you meant to investigate his case more thoroughly. We on our part are prepared to kill him before he arrives." [16]The son of Paul's sister, however, heard about the ambush; so he went and entered the compound and reported it to Paul. [17*]Paul then called one of the centurions and requested, "Take this young man to the commander; he has something to report to him." [18]So he took him and brought him to the commander and explained, "The prisoner Paul called me and asked that I bring this young man to you; he has something to say to you." [19]The commander took him by the hand, drew him aside, and asked him privately, "What is it you have to report to me?" [20]He replied, "The Jews have conspired to ask you to bring Paul down to the Sanhedrin tomorrow, as though they meant to inquire about him more thoroughly, [21]but do not believe them. More than forty of them are lying in wait for him; they have bound themselves by oath not to eat or drink until they have killed him. They are now ready and only wait for your consent." [22]As the commander dismissed the young man he directed him, "Tell no one that you gave me this information."

23:2 The high priest Ananias: Ananias, son of Nedebaeus, was high priest from A.D. 47 to 59.

23:3 God will strike you: Josephus reports that Ananias was later assassinated in A.D. 66 at the beginning of the First Revolt.

23:5 Luke portrays Paul as a model of one who is obedient to the Mosaic law. Paul, because of his reverence for the law (Ex 22:27), withdraws his accusation of hypocrisy, "whitewashed wall" (cf. Mt 23:27), when he is told Ananias is the high priest.

23:11 The occurrence of the vision of Christ consoling Paul and assuring him that he will be his witness in Rome prepares the reader for the final section of Acts: the journey of Paul and the word he preaches to Rome under the protection of the Romans.

23:17 Centurions: a centurion was a military officer in charge of one hundred soldiers.

w: 24:16. *x:* Ez 13:10–15; Mt 23:27. *y:* Ex 22:27. *z:* 24:15, 21; 26:5; Phil 3:5. *a:* Mt 22:23; Lk 20:27. *b:* 19:21.

[23]*Then he summoned two of the centurions and said, "Get two hundred soldiers ready to go to Caesarea by nine o'clock tonight, along with seventy horsemen and two hundred auxiliaries. [24]Provide mounts for Paul to ride and give him safe conduct to Felix the governor." [25]Then he wrote a letter with this content: [26]*"Claudius Lysias to his excellency the governor Felix, greetings. [27c]This man, seized by the Jews and about to be murdered by them, I rescued after intervening with my troops when I learned that he was a Roman citizen. [28]I wanted to learn the reason for their accusations against him so I brought him down to their Sanhedrin. [29d]I discovered that he was accused in matters of controversial questions of their law and not of any charge deserving death or imprisonment. [30]Since it was brought to my attention that there will be a plot against the man, I am sending him to you at once, and have also notified his accusers to state [their case] against him before you."

[31]So the soldiers, according to their orders, took Paul and escorted him by night to Antipatris. [32]The next day they returned to the compound, leaving the horsemen to complete the journey with him. [33]When they arrived in Caesarea they delivered the letter to the governor and presented Paul to him. [34]When he had read it and asked to what province he belonged, and learned that he was from Cilicia, [35]he said, "I shall hear your case when your accusers arrive." Then he ordered that he be held in custody in Herod's praetorium.

CHAPTER 24

See RG 436

Trial before Felix. [1]Five days later the high priest Ananias came down with some elders and an advocate, a certain Tertullus, and they presented formal charges against Paul to the governor. [2]When he was called, Tertullus began to accuse him, saying, "Since we have attained much peace through you, and reforms have been accomplished in this nation through your provident care, [3]we acknowledge this in every way and everywhere, most excellent Felix, with all gratitude. [4]But in order not to detain you further, I ask you to give us a brief hearing with your customary graciousness. [5e]*We found this man to be a pest; he creates dissension among Jews all over the world and is a ringleader of the sect of the Nazoreans. [6f]He even tried to desecrate our temple, but we arrested him. [7]* [8]If you examine him you will be able to learn from him for yourself about everything of which we are accusing him." [9]The Jews also joined in the attack and asserted that these things were so.

[10]*Then the governor motioned to him to speak and Paul replied, "I know that you have been a judge over this nation for many years and so I am pleased to make my defense before you. [11]As you can verify, not more than twelve days have passed since I went up to Jerusalem to worship. [12]Neither in the temple, nor in the synagogues, nor anywhere in the city did they find me arguing with anyone or instigating a riot among the people. [13]Nor can they prove to you the accusations they are now making against me. [14g]But this I do admit to you, that according to the Way, which they call a sect, I worship the God of our ancestors and I believe everything that is in accordance with the law and written in the prophets. [15h]I have

23:23 By nine o'clock tonight: literally, "by the third hour of the night." The night hours began at 6 P.M. **Two hundred auxiliaries**: the meaning of the Greek is not certain. It seems to refer to spearmen from the local police force and not from the cohort of soldiers, which would have numbered only 500–1000 men.

23:26–30 The letter emphasizes the fact that Paul is a Roman citizen and asserts the lack of evidence that he is guilty of a crime against the empire. The tone of the letter implies that the commander became initially involved in Paul's case because of his Roman citizenship, but this is not an exact description of what really happened (see Acts 21:31–33; 22:25–29).

23:26 M. Antonius Felix was procurator of Judea from A.D. 52 to 60. His procuratorship was marked by cruelty toward and oppression of his Jewish subjects.

24:5 Nazoreans: that is, followers of Jesus of Nazareth.

24:7 The Western text has added here a verse (really 6b–8a) that is not found in the best Greek manuscripts. It reads, "and would have judged him according to our own law, but the cohort commander Lysias came and violently took him out of our hands and ordered his accusers to come before you."

24:10–21 Whereas the advocate Tertullus referred to Paul's activities on his missionary journeys, the apostle narrowed the charges down to the riot connected with the incident in the temple (see Acts 21:27–30; 24:17–20). In his defense, Paul stresses the continuity between Christianity and Judaism.

c: 21:30–34; 22:27. *d:* 18:14–15; 25:18–19. *e:* 24:14; Lk 23:2. *f:* 21:28. *g:* 24:5. *h:* Dn 12:2; Jn 5:28–29.

the same hope in God as they themselves have that there will be a resurrection of the righteous and the unrighteous. [16i]Because of this, I always strive to keep my conscience clear before God and man. [17j]After many years, I came to bring alms for my nation and offerings. [18k]While I was so engaged, they found me, after my purification, in the temple without a crowd or disturbance. [19]But some Jews from the province of Asia, who should be here before you to make whatever accusation they might have against me— [20]or let these men themselves state what crime they discovered when I stood before the Sanhedrin, [21l]unless it was my one outcry as I stood among them, that 'I am on trial before you today for the resurrection of the dead.' "

[22]Then Felix, who was accurately informed about the Way, postponed the trial, saying, "When Lysias the commander comes down, I shall decide your case." [23]He gave orders to the centurion that he should be kept in custody but have some liberty, and that he should not prevent any of his friends from caring for his needs.

Captivity in Caesarea. [24*]Several days later Felix came with his wife Drusilla, who was Jewish. He had Paul summoned and listened to him speak about faith in Christ Jesus. [25]But as he spoke about righteousness and self-restraint and the coming judgment, Felix became frightened and said, "You may go for now; when I find an opportunity I shall summon you again." [26]At the same time he hoped that a bribe would be offered him by Paul, and so he sent for him very often and conversed with him.

[27*]Two years passed and Felix was succeeded by Porcius Festus. Wishing to ingratiate himself with the Jews, Felix left Paul in prison.

CHAPTER 25

See RG 436

Appeal to Caesar. [1]Three days after his arrival in the province, Festus went up from Caesarea to Jerusalem [2*]where the chief priests and Jewish leaders presented him their formal charges against Paul. They asked him [3]as a favor to have him sent to Jerusalem, for they were plotting to kill him along the way. [4]Festus replied that Paul was being held in custody in Caesarea and that he himself would be returning there shortly. [5]He said, "Let your authorities come down with me, and if this man has done something improper, let them accuse him."

[6]After spending no more than eight or ten days with them, he went down to Caesarea, and on the following day took his seat on the tribunal and ordered that Paul be brought in. [7]When he appeared, the Jews who had come down from Jerusalem surrounded him and brought many serious charges against him, which they were unable to prove. [8]In defending himself Paul said, "I have committed no crime either against the Jewish law or against the temple or against Caesar." [9*]Then Festus, wishing to ingratiate himself with the Jews, said to Paul in reply, "Are you willing to go up to Jerusalem and there stand trial before me on these charges?" [10]Paul answered, "I am standing before the tribunal of Caesar; this is where I should be tried. I have committed no crime against the Jews, as you very well know. [11]If I have committed a crime or done anything deserving death, I do not seek to escape the death penalty; but if there is no substance to the charges they are bringing against me, then no one has the right to hand me over to them. I appeal to Caesar." [12]Then Festus, after conferring with his council, replied, "You have appealed to Caesar. To Caesar you will go."

24:24, 25 The way of Christian discipleship greatly disquiets Felix, who has entered into an adulterous marriage with Drusilla, daughter of Herod Agrippa I. This marriage provides the background for the topics Paul speaks about and about which Felix does not want to hear.

24:27 Very little is known of Porcius Festus who was a procurator of Judea from A.D. 60 to 62.

25:2 Even after two years the animosity toward Paul in Jerusalem had not subsided (see Acts 24:27).

25:9–12 Paul refuses to acknowledge that the Sanhedrin in Jerusalem has any jurisdiction over him now (Acts 25:11). Paul uses his right as a Roman citizen to appeal his case to the jurisdiction of the Emperor (Nero, ca. A.D. 60) (Acts 25:12). This move broke the deadlock between Roman protective custody of Paul and the plan of his enemies to kill him (25:3).

i: 23:1. *j:* Rom 15:25–26; Gal 2:10. *k:* 21:26–30. *l:* 23:6; 24:15.

Paul before King Agrippa. [13*]When a few days had passed, King Agrippa and Bernice arrived in Caesarea on a visit to Festus. [14m]Since they spent several days there, Festus referred Paul's case to the king, saying, "There is a man here left in custody by Felix. [15]When I was in Jerusalem the chief priests and the elders of the Jews brought charges against him and demanded his condemnation. [16]I answered them that it was not Roman practice to hand over an accused person before he has faced his accusers and had the opportunity to defend himself against their charge. [17]So when [they] came together here, I made no delay; the next day I took my seat on the tribunal and ordered the man to be brought in. [18n]His accusers stood around him, but did not charge him with any of the crimes I suspected. [19]Instead they had some issues with him about their own religion and about a certain Jesus who had died but who Paul claimed was alive. [20]Since I was at a loss how to investigate this controversy, I asked if he were willing to go to Jerusalem and there stand trial on these charges. [21]And when Paul appealed that he be held in custody for the Emperor's decision, I ordered him held until I could send him to Caesar." [22]Agrippa said to Festus, "I too should like to hear this man." He replied, "Tomorrow you will hear him."

[23]The next day Agrippa and Bernice came with great ceremony and entered the audience hall in the company of cohort commanders and the prominent men of the city and, by command of Festus, Paul was brought in. [24]And Festus said, "King Agrippa and all you here present with us, look at this man about whom the whole Jewish populace petitioned me here and in Jerusalem, clamoring that he should live no longer. [25]I found, however, that he had done nothing deserving death, and so when he appealed to the Emperor, I decided to send him. [26]But I have nothing definite to write about him to our sovereign; therefore I have brought him before all of you, and particularly before you, King Agrippa, so that I may have something to write as a result of this investigation. [27]For it seems senseless to me to send up a prisoner without indicating the charges against him."

CHAPTER 26

See RG 436

King Agrippa Hears Paul. [1]Then Agrippa said to Paul, "You may now speak on your own behalf." So Paul stretched out his hand and began his defense. [2*]"I count myself fortunate, King Agrippa, that I am to defend myself before you today against all the charges made against me by the Jews, [3]especially since you are an expert in all the Jewish customs and controversies. And therefore I beg you to listen patiently. [4*]My manner of living from my youth, a life spent from the beginning among my people and in Jerusalem, all [the] Jews know. [5o]They have known about me from the start, if they are willing to testify, that I have lived my life as a Pharisee, the strictest party of our religion. [6p]But now I am standing trial because of my hope in the promise made by God to our ancestors. [7]Our twelve tribes hope to attain to that promise as they fervently worship God day and night; and on account of this hope I am accused by Jews, O king. [8]Why is it thought unbelievable among you that God raises the dead? [9q]I myself once thought that I had to do many things against the name of Jesus the Nazorean, [10r]and I did so in Jerusalem. I imprisoned many of the holy ones with the authorization I received from the chief priests, and when they were to be put to death I cast my vote against them. [11]Many times, in synagogue after synagogue, I punished them in an attempt to force them to blaspheme; I was so enraged against them that I pursued them even to foreign cities.

[12]"On one such occasion I was traveling to Damascus with the authorization and com-

25:13 King Agrippa and Bernice: brother and sister, children of Herod Agrippa I whose activities against the Jerusalem community are mentioned in Acts 12:1–19. Agrippa II was a petty ruler over small areas in northern Palestine and some villages in Perea. His influence on the Jewish population of Palestine was insignificant.

26:2–23 Paul's final defense speech in Acts is now made before a king (see Acts 9:15). In the speech Paul presents himself as a zealous Pharisee and Christianity as the logical development of Pharisaic Judaism. The story of his conversion is recounted for the third time in Acts in this speech (see note on Acts 9:1–19).

26:4 Among my people: that is, among the Jews.

m: 24:27. *n:* 18:14–15; 23:29. *o:* Phil 3:5–6; Gal 1:13–14; 2 Cor 11:22. *p:* 23:6; 24:15, 21; 28:20. *q:* 8:3; 9:1–2; 22:19; Phil 3:6. *r:* 9:14.

mission of the chief priests. [13st]At midday,
along the way, O king, I saw a light from the
sky, brighter than the sun, shining around me
and my traveling companions. [14u*]We all fell
to the ground and I heard a voice saying to
me in Hebrew, 'Saul, Saul, why are you persecuting me? It is hard for you to kick against
the goad.' [15v]And I said, 'Who are you, sir?'
And the Lord replied, 'I am Jesus whom you
are persecuting. [16w*]Get up now, and stand
on your feet. I have appeared to you for this
purpose, to appoint you as a servant and witness of what you have seen [of me] and what
you will be shown. [17x]I shall deliver you
from this people and from the Gentiles to
whom I send you, [18y*]to open their eyes that
they may turn from darkness to light and
from the power of Satan to God, so that they
may obtain forgiveness of sins and an inheritance among those who have been consecrated by faith in me.'

[19]"And so, King Agrippa, I was not disobedient to the heavenly vision. [20]On the
contrary, first to those in Damascus and in
Jerusalem and throughout the whole country
of Judea, and then to the Gentiles, I preached
the need to repent and turn to God, and to do
works giving evidence of repentance.
[21z]That is why the Jews seized me [when I
was] in the temple and tried to kill me.
[22a*]But I have enjoyed God's help to this
very day, and so I stand here testifying to
small and great alike, saying nothing different from what the prophets and Moses foretold, [23b*]that the Messiah must suffer and
that, as the first to rise from the dead, he
would proclaim light both to our people and
to the Gentiles."

Reactions to Paul's Speech. [24]While Paul
was so speaking in his defense, Festus said
in a loud voice, "You are mad, Paul; much
learning is driving you mad." [25]But Paul
replied, "I am not mad, most excellent Festus; I am speaking words of truth and reason.
[26*]The king knows about these matters and
to him I speak boldly, for I cannot believe
that [any] of this has escaped his notice; this
was not done in a corner. [27*]King Agrippa,
do you believe the prophets? I know you believe." [28]Then Agrippa said to Paul, "You
will soon persuade me to play the Christian." [29]Paul replied, "I would pray to God
that sooner or later not only you but all who
listen to me today might become as I am except for these chains."

[30]Then the king rose, and with him the
governor and Bernice and the others who sat
with them. [31*]And after they had withdrawn
they said to one another, "This man is doing
nothing [at all] that deserves death or imprisonment." [32c]And Agrippa said to Festus,
"This man could have been set free if he had
not appealed to Caesar."

CHAPTER 27

See RG 436–37

Departure for Rome. [1*]When it was
decided that we should sail to Italy, they
handed Paul and some other prisoners over

26:14 In Hebrew: see note on Acts 21:40. **It is hard for you to kick against the goad**: this proverb is commonly found in Greek literature and in this context signifies the senselessness and ineffectiveness of any opposition to the divine influence in his life.

26:16 The words of Jesus directed to Paul here reflect the dialogues between Christ and Ananias (Acts 9:15) and between Ananias and Paul (Acts 22:14–15) in the two previous accounts of Paul's conversion.

26:18 To open their eyes: though no mention is made of Paul's blindness in this account (cf. Acts 9:8–9, 12, 18; 22:11–13), the task he is commissioned to perform is the removal of other people's spiritual blindness.

26:22 Saying nothing different from what the prophets and Moses foretold: see note on Lk 18:31.

26:23 That the Messiah must suffer: see note on Lk 24:26.

26:26 Not done in a corner: for Luke, this Greek proverb expresses his belief that he is presenting a story about Jesus and the church that is already well known. As such, the entire history of Christianity is public knowledge and incontestable. Luke presents his story in this way to provide "certainty" to his readers about the instructions they have received (Lk 1:4).

26:27, 28 If the Christian missionaries proclaim nothing different from what the Old Testament prophets had proclaimed (Acts 26:22–23), then the logical outcome for the believing Jew, according to Luke, is to become a Christian.

26:31–32 In recording the episode of Paul's appearance before Agrippa, Luke wishes to show that, when Paul's case was judged impartially, no grounds for legal action against him were found (see Acts 23:29; 25:25).

27:1–28:16 Here Luke has written a stirring account of adventure on the high seas, incidental to his main purpose of showing how well Paul got along with his captors and how

s: 9:7. *t:* 9:3; 22:6. *u:* 9:4; 22:7. *v:* 9:5; 22:8; Mt 25:40. *w:* 9:6; 22:10; Ez 2:1. *x:* Jer 1:7. *y:* Is 42:7, 16; 61:1 LXX; Col 1:13. *z:* 21:31. *a:* 3:18; Lk 24:26–27, 44–47. *b:* Is 42:6; 49:6; Lk 2:32; 1 Cor 15:20–23. *c:* 25:11–12.

to a centurion named Julius of the Cohort Augusta. [2d]We went on board a ship from Adramyttium bound for ports in the province of Asia and set sail. Aristarchus, a Macedonian from Thessalonica, was with us. [3]On the following day we put in at Sidon where Julius was kind enough to allow Paul to visit his friends who took care of him. [4]From there we put out to sea and sailed around the sheltered side of Cyprus because of the headwinds, [5]and crossing the open sea off the coast of Cilicia and Pamphylia we came to Myra in Lycia.

Storm and Shipwreck. [6]There the centurion found an Alexandrian ship that was sailing to Italy and put us on board. [7]For many days we made little headway, arriving at Cnidus only with difficulty, and because the wind would not permit us to continue our course we sailed for the sheltered side of Crete off Salmone. [8]We sailed past it with difficulty and reached a place called Fair Havens, near which was the city of Lasea.

[9e*]Much time had now passed and sailing had become hazardous because the time of the fast had already gone by, so Paul warned them, [10]"Men, I can see that this voyage will result in severe damage and heavy loss not only to the cargo and the ship, but also to our lives." [11]The centurion, however, paid more attention to the pilot and to the owner of the ship than to what Paul said. [12]Since the harbor was unfavorably situated for spending the winter, the majority planned to put out to sea from there in the hope of reaching Phoenix, a port in Crete facing west-northwest, there to spend the winter.

[13]A south wind blew gently, and thinking they had attained their objective, they weighed anchor and sailed along close to the coast of Crete. [14]Before long an offshore wind of hurricane force called a "Northeaster" struck. [15]Since the ship was caught up in it and could not head into the wind we gave way and let ourselves be driven. [16]We passed along the sheltered side of an island named Cauda and managed only with difficulty to get the dinghy under control. [17]They hoisted it aboard, then used cables to undergird the ship. Because of their fear that they would run aground on the shoal of Syrtis, they lowered the drift anchor and were carried along in this way. [18]We were being pounded by the storm so violently that the next day they jettisoned some cargo, [19]and on the third day with their own hands they threw even the ship's tackle overboard. [20]Neither the sun nor the stars were visible for many days, and no small storm raged. Finally, all hope of our surviving was taken away.

[21]When many would no longer eat, Paul stood among them and said, "Men, you should have taken my advice and not have set sail from Crete and you would have avoided this disastrous loss. [22]I urge you now to keep up your courage; not one of you will be lost, only the ship. [23]For last night an angel of the God to whom [I] belong and whom I serve stood by me [24f]and said, 'Do not be afraid, Paul. You are destined to stand before Caesar; and behold, for your sake, God has granted safety to all who are sailing with you.' [25]Therefore, keep up your courage, men; I trust in God that it will turn out as I have been told. [26]We are destined to run aground on some island."

[27]On the fourteenth night, as we were still being driven about on the Adriatic Sea, toward midnight the sailors began to suspect that they were nearing land. [28]They took soundings and found twenty fathoms; a little farther on, they again took soundings and found fifteen fathoms. [29]Fearing that we would run aground on a rocky coast, they dropped four anchors from the stern and prayed for day to come. [30]The sailors then tried to abandon ship; they lowered the dinghy to the sea on the pretext of going to lay out anchors from the bow. [31]But

his prophetic influence saved the lives of all on board. The recital also establishes the existence of Christian communities in Puteoli and Rome. This account of the voyage and shipwreck also constitutes the final "we-section" in Acts (see note on Acts 16:10–17).

27:1 Cohort Augusta: the presence of a Cohort Augusta in Syria during the first century A.D. is attested in inscriptions. Whatever the historical background to this information given by Luke may be, the name Augusta serves to increase the prominence and prestige of the prisoner Paul whose custodians bear so important a Roman name.

27:9 The time of the fast: the fast kept on the occasion of the Day of Atonement (Lv 16:29–31), which occurred in late September or early October.

d: 19:29; 20:4. *e:* Lv 16:29–31. *f:* 23:11.

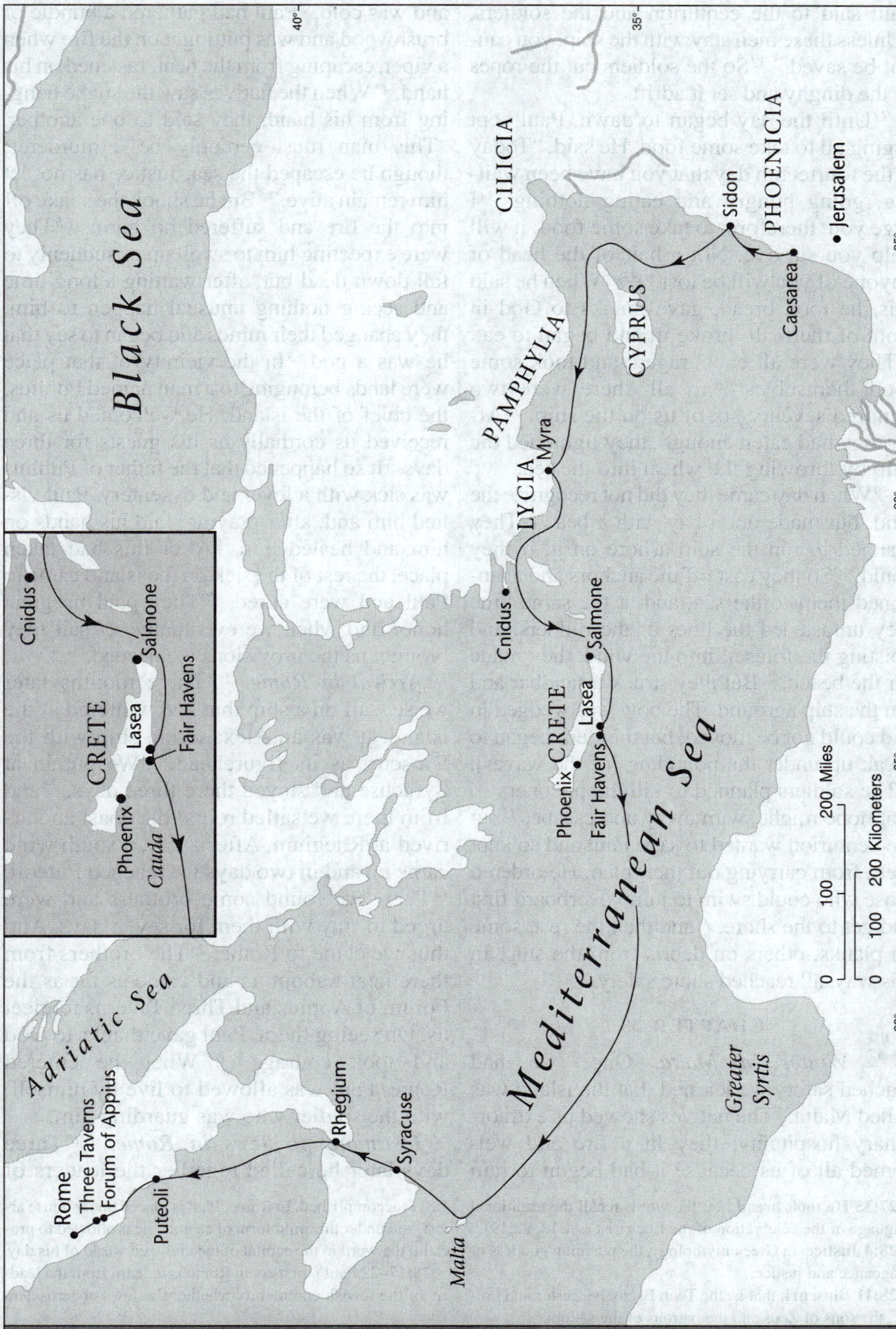

Paul's Journey to Rome

Paul said to the centurion and the soldiers, "Unless these men stay with the ship, you cannot be saved." [32]So the soldiers cut the ropes of the dinghy and set it adrift.

[33]Until the day began to dawn, Paul kept urging all to take some food. He said, "Today is the fourteenth day that you have been waiting, going hungry and eating nothing. [34]I urge you, therefore, to take some food; it will help you survive. Not a hair of the head of anyone of you will be lost." [35g*]When he said this, he took bread, gave thanks to God in front of them all, broke it, and began to eat. [36]They were all encouraged, and took some food themselves. [37]In all, there were two hundred seventy-six of us on the ship. [38]After they had eaten enough, they lightened the ship by throwing the wheat into the sea.

[39]When day came they did not recognize the land, but made out a bay with a beach. They planned to run the ship ashore on it, if they could. [40]So they cast off the anchors and abandoned them to the sea, and at the same time they unfastened the lines of the rudders, and hoisting the foresail into the wind, they made for the beach. [41]But they struck a sandbar and ran the ship aground. The bow was wedged in and could not be moved, but the stern began to break up under the pounding [of the waves]. [42]The soldiers planned to kill the prisoners so that none might swim away and escape, [43]but the centurion wanted to save Paul and so kept them from carrying out their plan. He ordered those who could swim to jump overboard first and get to the shore, [44]and then the rest, some on planks, others on debris from the ship. In this way, all reached shore safely.

CHAPTER 28

See RG 436–37

Winter in Malta. [1]Once we had reached safety we learned that the island was called Malta. [2]The natives showed us extraordinary hospitality; they lit a fire and welcomed all of us because it had begun to rain and was cold. [3]Paul had gathered a bundle of brushwood and was putting it on the fire when a viper, escaping from the heat, fastened on his hand. [4*]When the natives saw the snake hanging from his hand, they said to one another, "This man must certainly be a murderer; though he escaped the sea, Justice has not let him remain alive." [5]But he shook the snake off into the fire and suffered no harm. [6h]They were expecting him to swell up or suddenly to fall down dead but, after waiting a long time and seeing nothing unusual happen to him, they changed their minds and began to say that he was a god. [7]In the vicinity of that place were lands belonging to a man named Publius, the chief of the island. He welcomed us and received us cordially as his guests for three days. [8]It so happened that the father of Publius was sick with a fever and dysentery. Paul visited him and, after praying, laid his hands on him and healed him. [9]After this had taken place, the rest of the sick on the island came to Paul and were cured. [10]They paid us great honor and when we eventually set sail they brought us the provisions we needed.

Arrival in Rome. [11*]Three months later we set sail on a ship that had wintered at the island. It was an Alexandrian ship with the Dioscuri as its figurehead. [12]We put in at Syracuse and stayed there three days, [13]and from there we sailed round the coast and arrived at Rhegium. After a day, a south wind came up and in two days we reached Puteoli. [14]There we found some brothers and were urged to stay with them for seven days. And thus we came to Rome. [15]The brothers from there heard about us and came as far as the Forum of Appius and Three Taverns to meet us. On seeing them, Paul gave thanks to God and took courage. [16*]When he entered Rome, Paul was allowed to live by himself, with the soldier who was guarding him.

Testimony to Jews in Rome. [17i*]Three days later he called together the leaders of

27:35 He took bread . . .: the words recall the traditional language of the celebration of the Eucharist (see Lk 22:19).

28:4 Justice: in Greek mythology, the pursuing goddess of vengeance and justice.

28:11 Dioscuri: that is, the Twin Brothers, Castor and Pollux, the sons of Zeus and the patrons of the sailors.

28:16 With Paul's arrival in Rome, the programmatic spread of the word of the Lord to "the ends of the earth" (Acts 1:8) is accomplished. In Rome, Paul is placed under house arrest, and under this mild form of custody he is allowed to proclaim the word in the capital of the civilized world of his day.

28:17–22 Paul's first act in Rome is to learn from the leaders of the Jewish community whether the Jews of Jerusalem

g: Mt 15:36; Mk 6:41; 8:6; Lk 22:19; 1 Cor 11:23–24. *h:* 14:11. *i:* 24:12–13; 25:8.

the Jews. When they had gathered he said to
them, "My brothers, although I had done
nothing against our people or our ancestral
customs, I was handed over to the Romans
as a prisoner from Jerusalem. [18j]After trying my case the Romans wanted to release
me, because they found nothing against me
deserving the death penalty. [19k]But when
the Jews objected, I was obliged to appeal to
Caesar, even though I had no accusation to
make against my own nation. [20l*]This is the
reason, then, I have requested to see you
and to speak with you, for it is on account of
the hope of Israel that I wear these chains."
[21]They answered him, "We have received
no letters from Judea about you, nor has any
of the brothers arrived with a damaging report or rumor about you. [22m]But we should
like to hear you present your views, for we
know that this sect is denounced everywhere."
[23]So they arranged a day with him and
came to his lodgings in great numbers. From
early morning until evening, he expounded
his position to them, bearing witness to the
kingdom of God and trying to convince
them about Jesus from the law of Moses and
the prophets. [24]Some were convinced by
what he had said, while others did not believe. [25*]Without reaching any agreement
among themselves they began to leave; then
Paul made one final statement. "Well did the
holy Spirit speak to your ancestors through
the prophet Isaiah, saying:

[26 n]'Go to this people and say:
You shall indeed hear but not understand.
You shall indeed look but never see.
[27] Gross is the heart of this people;
they will not hear with their ears;
they have closed their eyes,
so they may not see with their eyes
and hear with their ears
and understand with their heart and be converted,
and I heal them.'

[28o]Let it be known to you that this salvation
of God has been sent to the Gentiles; they
will listen." [29]*
[30*]He remained for two full years in his
lodgings. He received all who came to him,
[31]and with complete assurance and without
hindrance he proclaimed the kingdom of
God and taught about the Lord Jesus Christ.

plan to pursue their case against him before the Roman jurisdiction. He is informed that no such plan is afoot, but that the Jews of Rome have heard the Christian teaching denounced. Paul's offer to explain it to them is readily accepted.

28:20 The hope of Israel: in the words of Paul (Acts 23:6), Luke has identified this hope as hope in the resurrection of the dead.

28:25–28 Paul's final words in Acts reflect a major concern of Luke's writings: how the salvation promised in the Old Testament, accomplished by Jesus, and offered first to Israel (Acts 13:26), has now been offered to and accepted by the Gentiles. Quoting Is 6:9–10, Paul presents the scriptural support for his indictment of his fellow Jews who refuse to accept the message he proclaims. Their rejection leads to its proclamation among the Gentiles.

28:29 The Western text has added here a verse that is not found in the best Greek manuscripts: "And when he had said this, the Jews left, seriously arguing among themselves."

28:30–31 Although the ending of Acts may seem to be abrupt, Luke has now completed his story with the establishment of Paul and the proclamation of Christianity in Rome. Paul's confident and unhindered proclamation of the gospel in Rome forms the climax to the story whose outline was provided in Acts 1:8—"You will be my witnesses in Jerusalem . . . and to the ends of the earth."

j: 23:29; 25:25; 26:31–32. *k:* 25:11. *l:* 23:6; 24:15, 21; 26:6–8. *m:* 24:5, 14. *n:* Is 6:9–10; Mt 13:14–15; Mk 4:12; Lk 8:10; Jn 12:40; Rom 11:8. *o:* 13:46; 18:6; Ps 67:2; Is 40:5 LXX; Lk 3:6.

See RG 439–41

NEW TESTAMENT LETTERS

In the New Testament canon, between the Acts of the Apostles and Revelation, there are twenty-one documents that take the form of letters or epistles. Most of these are actual letters, but some are more like treatises in the guise of letters. In a few cases even some of the more obvious elements of the letter form are absent; see the Introductions to Hebrews and to 1 John.

The virtually standard form found in these documents, though with some variation, is dependent upon the conventions of letter writing common in the ancient world, but these were modified to suit the purposes of Christian writers. The New Testament letters usually begin with a greeting including an identification of the sender or senders and of the recipients. Next comes a prayer, usually in the form of a thanksgiving. The body of the letter provides an exposition of Christian teaching, usually provoked by concrete circumstances, and generally also draws conclusions regarding ethical behavior. There often follows a discussion of practical matters, such as the writer's travel plans, and the letter concludes with further advice and a formula of farewell.

Fourteen of the twenty-one letters have been traditionally attributed to Paul. One of these, the Letter to the Hebrews, does not itself claim to be the work of Paul; when it was accepted into the canon after much discussion, it was attached at the very end of the Pauline corpus. The other thirteen identify Paul as their author, but most scholars believe that some of them were actually written by his disciples; see the Introductions to Ephesians, Colossians, 2 Thessalonians, and 1 Timothy.

Four of the letters in the Pauline corpus (Ephesians, Philippians, Colossians, and Philemon) are called the "Captivity Epistles" because in each of them the author speaks of being in prison at the time of writing. Three others (1–2 Timothy and Titus) are known as the "Pastoral Epistles" because, addressed to individuals rather than communities, they give advice to disciples about caring for the flock. The letters of the Pauline corpus are arranged in roughly descending order of length from Romans to Philemon, with Hebrews added at the end.

The other seven letters of the New Testament that follow the Pauline corpus are collectively referred to as the "Catholic Epistles." This term, which means "universal," refers to the fact that most of them are directed not to a single Christian community, as are most of the Pauline letters, but to a wider audience; see the Introduction to the catholic letters. Three of them (1–2–3 John) are closely related to the fourth gospel and thus belong to the Johannine corpus. The catholic letters, like those of the Pauline corpus, are also arranged in roughly descending order of length, but the three Johannine letters are kept together and Jude is placed at the end.

The genuine letters of Paul are earlier in date than any of our written gospels. The dates of the other New Testament letters are more difficult to determine, but for the most part they belong to the second and third Christian generations rather than to the first.

See RG 441–50

The Letter to the Romans

Of all the letters of Paul, that to the Christians at Rome has long held pride of place. It is the longest and most systematic unfolding of the apostle's thought, expounding the gospel of God's righteousness that saves all who believe (Rom 1:16–17); it reflects a universal outlook, with special implications for Israel's relation to the church (Rom 9–11). Yet, like all Paul's letters, Romans too arose out of a specific situation, when the apostle wrote from Greece, likely Corinth, between A.D. 56 and 58 (cf. Acts 20:2–3).

Paul at that time was about to leave for Jerusalem with a collection of funds for the impoverished Jewish Christian believers there, taken up from his predominantly Gentile congregations (Rom 15:25–27). He planned then to travel on to Rome and to enlist support there for a mission to Spain (Rom 15:24, 28). Such a journey had long been on his mind (Rom 1:9–13; 15:23). Now, with much missionary preaching successfully accomplished in the East (Rom 15:19), he sought new opportunities in the West (Rom 15:20–21), in order to complete the divine plan of evangelization in the Roman world. Yet he recognized that the visit to Jerusalem would be hazardous (Rom 15:30–32), and we know from Acts that Paul was arrested there and came to Rome only in chains, as a prisoner (Acts 21–28, especially Acts 21:30–33 and Acts 28:14, 30–31).

The existence of a Christian community in Rome antedates Paul's letter there. When it arose, likely within the sizable Jewish population at Rome, and how, we do not know. The Roman historian Suetonius mentions an edict of the Emperor Claudius about A.D. 49 ordering the expulsion of Jews from Rome in connection with a certain "Chrestus," probably involving a dispute in the Jewish community over Jesus as the Messiah ("Christus"). According to Acts 18:2, Aquila and Priscilla (or Prisca, as in Rom 16:3) were among those driven out; from them, in Corinth, Paul may have learned about conditions in the church at Rome.

Opinions vary as to whether Jewish or Gentile Christians predominated in the house churches (cf. Rom 16:5) in the capital city of the empire at the time Paul wrote. Perhaps already by then Gentile Christians were in the majority. Paul speaks in Romans of both Jews and Gentiles (Rom 3:9, 29; see note on Rom 1:14). The letter also refers to those "weak in faith" (Rom 14:1) and those "who are strong" (Rom 15:1); this terminology may reflect not so much differences between believers of Jewish and of Gentile background, respectively, as an ascetic tendency in some converts (Rom 14:2) combined with Jewish laws about clean and unclean foods (Rom 14:14, 20). The issues were similar to problems that Paul had faced in Corinth (1 Cor 8). If Rom 16 is part of the letter to Rome (see note on Rom 16:1–23), then Paul had considerable information about conditions in Rome through all these people there whom he knew, and our letter does not just reflect a generalized picture of an earlier situation in Corinth.

In any case, Paul writes to introduce himself and his message to the Christians at Rome, seeking to enlist their support for the proposed mission to Spain. He therefore employs formulations likely familiar to the Christians at Rome; see note on the confessional material at Rom 1:3–4 and compare Rom 3:25–26; 4:25. He cites the Old Testament frequently (Rom 1:17; 3:10–18; 4; 9:7, 12–13, 15, 17, 25–29, 33; 10:5–13, 15–21; 15:9–12). The gospel Paul presents is meant to be a familiar one to those in Rome, even though they heard it first from other preachers.

As the outline below shows, this gospel of Paul (see Rom 16:25) finds its center in salvation and justification through faith in Christ (Rom 1:16–17). While God's wrath is revealed against all sin and wickedness of Gentile and Jew alike (Rom 1:18–3:20), God's power to save by divine righteous or justifying action in Christ is also revealed (Rom 1:16–17; 3:21–5:21). The consequences and implications for those who believe are set forth (Rom 6:1–8:39), as are results for those in Israel (Rom 9–11) who, to Paul's great sorrow (Rom 9:1–5), disbelieve. The apostle's hope is that, just as rejection of the gospel by some in Israel has led to a ministry of salvation for non-Jews, so one day, in God's mercy, "all Israel" will be saved (Rom 11:11–15, 25–29, 30–32). The fuller ethical response of believers is also drawn out, both with reference to life in

Christ's body (Rom 12) and with regard to the world (Rom 13:1–7), on the basis of the eschatological situation (Rom 13:11–14) and conditions in the community (Rom 14:1–15:13).

Others have viewed Romans more in the light of Paul's earlier, quite polemical Letter to the Galatians and so see the theme as the relationship between Judaism and Christianity, a topic judged to be much in the minds of the Roman Christians. Each of these religious faiths claimed to be the way of salvation based upon a covenant between God and a people chosen and made the beneficiary of divine gifts. But Christianity regarded itself as the prophetic development and fulfillment of the faith of the Old Testament, declaring that the preparatory Mosaic covenant must now give way to the new and more perfect covenant in Jesus Christ. Paul himself had been the implacable advocate of freedom of Gentiles from the laws of the Mosaic covenant and, especially in Galatia, had refused to allow attempts to impose them on Gentile converts to the gospel. He had witnessed the personal hostilities that developed between the adherents of the two faiths and had written his strongly worded Letter to the Galatians against those Jewish Christians who were seeking to persuade Gentile Christians to adopt the religious practices of Judaism. For him, the purity of the religious understanding of Jesus as the source of salvation would be seriously impaired if Gentile Christians were obligated to amalgamate the two religious faiths.

Still others find the theme of Israel and the church as expressed in Rom 9–11 to be the heart of Romans. Then the implication of Paul's exposition of justification by faith rather than by means of law is that the divine plan of salvation works itself out on a broad theological plane to include the whole of humanity, despite the differences in the content of the given religious system to which a human culture is heir. Romans presents a plan of salvation stretching from Adam through Abraham and Moses to Christ (Rom 4; 5) and on to the future revelation at Christ's parousia (Rom 8:18–25). Its outlook is universal.

Paul's Letter to the Romans is a powerful exposition of the doctrine of the supremacy of Christ and of faith in Christ as the source of salvation. It is an implicit plea to the Christians at Rome, and to all Christians, to hold fast to that faith. They are to resist any pressure put on them to accept a doctrine of salvation through works of the law (see note on Rom 10:4). At the same time they are not to exaggerate Christian freedom as an abdication of responsibility for others (Rom 12:1–2) or as a repudiation of God's law and will (see notes on Rom 3:9–26; 3:31; 7:7–12, 13–25).

The principal divisions of the Letter to the Romans are the following:

I. Address (1:1–15)
II. Humanity Lost without the Gospel (1:16–3:20)
III. Justification through Faith in Christ (3:21–5:21)
IV. Justification and the Christian Life (6:1–8:39)
V. Jews and Gentiles in God's Plan (9:1–11:36)
VI. The Duties of Christians (12:1–15:13)
VII. Conclusion (15:14–16:27)

I. Address

CHAPTER 1

See RG 442-45

Greeting. 1[a]*Paul, a slave of Christ Jesus, called to be an apostle and set apart for the gospel of God, 2[b]which he promised previously through his prophets in the holy

1:1–7 In Paul's letters the greeting or *praescriptio* follows a standard form, though with variations. It is based upon the common Greco-Roman epistolary practice, but with the addition of Semitic and specifically Christian elements. The three basic components are: name of sender; name of addressee; greeting. In identifying himself, Paul often adds phrases to describe his apostolic mission; this element is more developed in Romans than in any other letter. Elsewhere he associates coworkers with himself in the greeting: Sosthenes (1 Corinthians), Timothy (2 Corinthians; Philippians; Philemon) Silvanus (1 Thessalonians—2 Thessalonians). The standard secular greeting was the infinitive *chairein*, "greetings." Paul uses instead the similar-sounding *charis*, "grace," together with the Semitic greeting *šālôm* (Greek *eirēnē*), "peace." These gifts, foreshadowed in God's dealings with Israel (see Nm 6:24–26), have been poured out abundantly in Christ, and Paul wishes them to his readers. In Romans the Pauline *praescriptio* is expanded and expressed in a formal tone; it emphasizes Paul's office as apostle to the Gentiles. Rom 1:3–4 stress the gospel or *kerygma*, Rom 1:2 the fulfillment of God's promise, and Rom 1:1, 5 Paul's office. On his call, see Gal 1:15–16; 1 Cor 9:1; 15:8–10; Acts 9:1–22; 22:3–16; 26:4–18.

1:1 Slave of Christ Jesus: Paul applies the term slave to himself in order to express his undivided allegiance to the Lord of the church, the Master of all, including slaves and

a: Gal 1:10; Phil 1:1; Jas 1:1 / Acts 9:15; 13:2; 1 Cor 1:1; Gal 1:15; Ti 1:1. *b:* 16:25–26; Ti 1:2.

scriptures, [3c*]the gospel about his Son, descended from David according to the flesh, [4d]but established as Son of God in power according to the spirit of holiness through resurrection from the dead, Jesus Christ our Lord. [5e*]Through him we have received the grace of apostleship, to bring about the obedience of faith, for the sake of his name, among all the Gentiles, [6f]among whom are you also, who are called to belong to Jesus Christ; [7g*]to all the beloved of God in Rome, called to be holy. Grace to you and peace from God our Father and the Lord Jesus Christ.

Thanksgiving. [8h*]First, I give thanks to my God through Jesus Christ for all of you, because your faith is heralded throughout the world. [9i]God is my witness, whom I serve with my spirit in proclaiming the gospel of his Son, that I remember you constantly, [10j*]always asking in my prayers that somehow by God's will I may at last find my way clear to come to you. [11k]For I long to see you, that I may share with you some spiritual gift so that you may be strengthened, [12]that is, that you and I may be mutually encouraged by one another's faith, yours and mine. [13l*]I do not want you to be unaware, brothers, that I often planned to come to you, though I was prevented until now, that I might harvest some fruit among you, too, as among the rest of the Gentiles. [14*]To Greeks and non-Greeks alike, to the wise and the ignorant, I am under obligation; [15m]that is why I am eager to preach the gospel also to you in Rome.

II. Humanity Lost without the Gospel

God's Power for Salvation. [16n*]For I am not ashamed of the gospel. It is the power of God for the salvation of everyone who be-

masters. "No one can serve (i.e., be a slave to) two masters," said Jesus (Mt 6:24). It is this aspect of the slave-master relationship rather than its degrading implications that Paul emphasizes when he discusses Christian commitment.

1:3–4 Paul here cites an early confession that proclaims Jesus' sonship as messianic descendant of David (cf. Mt 22:42; 2 Tm 2:8; Rev 22:16) and as Son of God by the resurrection. As "life-giving spirit" (1 Cor 15:45), Jesus Christ is able to communicate the Spirit to those who believe in him.

1:5 Paul recalls his apostolic office, implying that the Romans know something of his history. **The obedience of faith**: as Paul will show at length in chaps. 6–8 and 12–15, faith in God's justifying action in Jesus Christ relates one to God's gift of the new life that is made possible through the death and resurrection of Jesus Christ and the activity of the holy Spirit (see especially Rom 8:1–11).

1:7 Called to be holy: Paul often refers to Christians as "the holy ones" or "the saints." The Israelite community was called a "holy assembly" because they had been separated for the worship and service of the Lord (see Lv 11:44; 23:1–44). The Christian community regarded its members as sanctified by baptism (Rom 6:22; 15:16; 1 Cor 6:11; Eph 5:26–27). Christians are called to holiness (1 Cor 1:2; 1 Thes 4:7), that is, they are called to make their lives conform to the gift they have already received.

1:8 In Greco-Roman letters, the greeting was customarily followed by a prayer. The Pauline letters usually include this element (except Galatians and 1 Timothy, 2 Timothy) expressed in Christian thanksgiving formulas and usually stating the principal theme of the letter. In 2 Corinthians the thanksgiving becomes a blessing, and in Ephesians it is preceded by a lengthy blessing. Sometimes the thanksgiving is blended into the body of the letter, especially in 1 Thessalonians. In Romans it is stated briefly.

1:10–12 Paul lays the groundwork for his more detailed statement in Rom 15:22–24 about his projected visit to Rome.

1:13 Brothers is idiomatic for all Paul's "kin in Christ," all those who believe in the gospel; it includes women as well as men (cf. Rom 4:3).

1:14 Greeks and non-Greeks: literally, "Greeks and barbarians." As a result of Alexander's conquests, Greek became the standard international language of the Mediterranean world. **Greeks** in Paul's statement therefore means people who know Greek or who have been influenced by Greek culture. **Non-Greeks** were people whose cultures remained substantially unaffected by Greek influences. Greeks called such people "barbarians" (cf. Acts 28:2), meaning people whose speech was foreign. Roman citizens would scarcely classify themselves as such, and Nero, who was reigning when Paul wrote this letter, prided himself on his admiration for Greek culture. **Under obligation**: Paul will expand on the theme of obligation in Rom 13:8; 15:1, 27.

1:16–17 The principal theme of the letter is salvation through faith. **I am not ashamed of the gospel**: Paul is not ashamed to proclaim the gospel, despite the criticism that Jews and Gentiles leveled against the proclamation of the crucified savior; cf. 1 Cor 1:23–24. Paul affirms, however, that it is precisely through the crucifixion and resurrection of Jesus that God's saving will and power become manifest. **Jew first** (cf. Rom 2:9–10) means that Jews especially, in view of the example of Abraham (Rom 4), ought to be the leaders in the response of faith.

---

c: 9:5; 2 Sm 7:12; Mt 1:1; Mk 12:35; Jn 7:42; Acts 13:22–23; 2 Tm 2:8; Rev 22:16. *d:* 10:9; Acts 13:33; Phil 3:10. *e:* 15:15; Gal 2:7, 9 / 15:18; Acts 9:15; 26:16–18; Gal 1:16; 2:7, 9. *f:* 1 Cor 1:9. *g:* Nm 6:25–26; 1 Cor 1:2–3; 2 Cor 1:1–2. *h:* 16:19; 1 Thes 1:8. *i:* 2 Cor 1:23; Eph 1:16; Phil 1:8; 1 Thes 1:2; 2:5, 10; 2 Tm 1:3. *j:* 15:23, 32; Acts 18:21; 1 Cor 4:19; 1 Thes 2:17. *k:* 1 Thes 2:17; 3:10. *l:* 15:22; Jn 15:16; Acts 19:21. *m:* Acts 28:30–31. *n:* Ps 119:46; 1 Cor 1:18, 24 / 2:9; Acts 3:26; 13:46.

lieves: for Jew first, and then Greek. [17o*]For in it is revealed the righteousness of God from faith to faith; as it is written, "The one who is righteous by faith will live."

Punishment of Idolators. [18p*]The wrath of God is indeed being revealed from heaven against every impiety and wickedness of those who suppress the truth by their wickedness. [19q]For what can be known about God is evident to them, because God made it evident to them. [20r]Ever since the creation of the world, his invisible attributes of eternal power and divinity have been able to be understood and perceived in what he has made. As a result, they have no excuse; [21s]for although they knew God they did not accord him glory as God or give him thanks. Instead, they became vain in their reasoning, and their senseless minds were darkened. [22t]While claiming to be wise, they became fools [23u]and exchanged the glory of the immortal God for the likeness of an image of mortal man or of birds or of four-legged animals or of snakes.

[24v*]Therefore, God handed them over to impurity through the lusts of their hearts for the mutual degradation of their bodies. [25w]They exchanged the truth of God for a lie and revered and worshiped the creature rather than the creator, who is blessed forever. Amen. [26]Therefore, God handed them over to degrading passions. Their females exchanged natural relations for unnatural, [27x]and the males likewise gave up natural relations with females and burned with lust for one another. Males did shameful things with males and thus received in their own persons the due penalty for their perversity. [28]And since they did not see fit to acknowledge God, God handed them over to their undiscerning mind to do what is improper. [29y]They are filled with every form of wickedness, evil, greed, and malice; full of envy, murder, rivalry, treachery, and spite. They are gossips [30]and scandalmongers and they hate God. They are insolent, haughty, boastful, ingenious in their wickedness, and rebellious toward their parents. [31]They are senseless, faithless, heartless, ruthless. [32z]Although they know the just decree of God that all who practice such things deserve death, they not only do them but give approval to those who practice them.

1:17 In it is revealed the righteousness of God from faith to faith: the gospel centers in Jesus Christ, in whom God's saving presence and righteousness in history have been made known. Faith is affirmation of the basic purpose and meaning of the Old Testament as proclamation of divine promise (Rom 1:2; 4:13) and exposure of the inability of humanity to effect its salvation even through covenant law. Faith is the gift of the holy Spirit and denotes acceptance of salvation as God's righteousness, that is, God's gift of a renewed relationship in forgiveness and power for a new life. Faith is response to God's total claim on people and their destiny. **The one who is righteous by faith will live**: see note on Heb 2:4.

1:18–3:20 Paul aims to show that all humanity is in a desperate plight and requires God's special intervention if it is to be saved.

1:18–32 In this passage Paul uses themes and rhetoric common in Jewish-Hellenistic mission proclamation (cf. Wis 13:1–14:31) to indict especially the non-Jewish world. The close association of idolatry and immorality is basic, but the generalization needs in all fairness to be balanced against the fact that non-Jewish Christian society on many levels displayed moral attitudes and performance whose quality would challenge much of contemporary Christian culture. Romans themselves expressed abhorrence over devotion accorded to animals in Egypt. Paul's main point is that the wrath of God does not await the end of the world but goes into action at each present moment in humanity's history when misdirected piety serves as a facade for self-interest.

1:18 The wrath of God: God's reaction to human sinfulness, an Old Testament phrase that expresses the irreconcilable opposition between God and evil (see Is 9:11, 16, 18, 20; 10:4; 30:27). It is not contrary to God's universal love for his creatures, but condemns Israel's turning aside from the covenant obligations. Hosea depicts Yahweh as suffering intensely at the thought of having to punish Israel (Hos 11:8–9). God's wrath was to be poured forth especially on the "Day of Yahweh" and thus took on an eschatological connotation (see Zep 1:15).

1:24 In order to expose the depth of humanity's rebellion against the Creator, **God handed them over to impurity through the lusts of their hearts**. Instead of curbing people's evil interests, God abandoned them to self-indulgence, thereby removing the facade of apparent conformity to the divine will. Subsequently Paul will show that the Mosaic law produces the same effect; cf. Rom 5:20; 7:13–24. The divine judgment expressed here is related to the theme of hardness of heart described in Rom 9:17–18.

---

o: 3:21–22; Heb 2:4; Gal 3:11; Heb 10:38. *p:* 2:5, 8–9; Is 66:15; Eph 5:6; Col 3:6. *q:* Wis 13–19; Acts 14:15–17; 17:23–29. *r:* Jb 12:7–9; Ps 8:4; 19:2; Sir 17:7–9; Is 40:26; Acts 14:17; 17:25–28. *s:* Eph 4:17–18. *t:* Wis 13:1–9; Is 5:21; Jer 10:14; Acts 17:29–30; 1 Cor 1:19–21. *u:* Dt 4:15–19; Ps 106:20; Wis 11:15; 12:24; 13:10–19; Jer 2:11. *v:* Wis 12:25; 14:22–31; Acts 7:41–42; Eph 4:19. *w:* 9:5; Jer 13:25–27. *x:* Lv 18:22; 20:13; Wis 14:26; 1 Cor 6:9; 1 Tm 1:10. *y:* 13:13; Mt 15:19; Mk 7:21–22; Gal 5:19–21; 2 Tm 3:2–4. *z:* Acts 8:1; 2 Thes 2:12.

CHAPTER 2

See RG 444–45

God's Just Judgment. [1a*]Therefore, you are without excuse, every one of you who passes judgment. For by the standard by which you judge another you condemn yourself, since you, the judge, do the very same things. [2]We know that the judgment of God on those who do such things is true. [3b]Do you suppose, then, you who judge those who engage in such things and yet do them yourself, that you will escape the judgment of God? [4c]Or do you hold his priceless kindness, forbearance, and patience in low esteem, unaware that the kindness of God would lead you to repentance? [5d]By your stubbornness and impenitent heart, you are storing up wrath for yourself for the day of wrath and revelation of the just judgment of God, [6e*]who will repay everyone according to his works: [7]eternal life to those who seek glory, honor, and immortality through perseverance in good works, [8f]but wrath and fury to those who selfishly disobey the truth and obey wickedness. [9]Yes, affliction and distress will come upon every human being who does evil, Jew first and then Greek. [10g]But there will be glory, honor, and peace for everyone who does good, Jew first and then Greek. [11h*]There is no partiality with God.

Judgment by the Interior Law. [12i*]All who sin outside the law will also perish without reference to it, and all who sin under the law will be judged in accordance with it. [13j]For it is not those who hear the law who are just in the sight of God; rather, those who observe the law will be justified. [14k]For when the Gentiles who do not have the law by nature observe the prescriptions of the law, they are a law for themselves even though they do not have the law. [15*]They show that the demands of the law are written in their hearts, while their conscience also bears witness and their conflicting thoughts accuse or even defend them [16l]on the day when, according to my gospel, God will judge people's hidden works through Christ Jesus.

Judgment by the Mosaic Law. [17m*]Now if you call yourself a Jew and rely on the law and boast of God [18n]and know his will and are able to discern what is important since you are instructed from the law, [19o]and if you are confident that you are a guide for the blind and a light for those in darkness, [20p]that you are a trainer of the foolish and teacher of the simple, because in the law you have the formulation of knowledge and truth— [21q]then you who teach another, are you failing to teach yourself? You who preach against stealing, do you steal? [22]You who forbid adultery, do you commit adultery? You who detest idols, do you rob temples? [23]You who boast of the law, do you dis-

2:1–3:20 After his general indictment of the Gentile, Paul shows that in spite of special revelation Jews enjoy no advantage in moral status before God (Rom 3:1–8). With the entire human race now declared guilty before God (Rom 3:9–20), Paul will then be able to display the solution for the total problem: salvation through God's redemptive work that is revealed in Christ Jesus for all who believe (Rom 3:21–31).

2:1–11 As a first step in his demonstration that Jews enjoy no real moral supremacy over Gentiles, Paul explains that the final judgment will be a review of performance, not of privilege. From this perspective Gentiles stand on an equal footing with Jews, and Jews cannot condemn the sins of Gentiles without condemning themselves.

2:6 Will repay everyone according to his works: Paul reproduces the Septuagint text of Ps 62:12 and Prv 24:12.

2:11 No partiality with God: this sentence is not at variance with the statements in Rom 2:9–10. Since Jews are the first to go under indictment, it is only fair that they be given first consideration in the distribution of blessings. Basic, of course, is the understanding that God accepts no bribes (Dt 10:17).

2:12–16 Jews cannot reasonably demand from Gentiles the standard of conduct inculcated in the Old Testament since God did not address its revelation to them. Rather, God made it possible for Gentiles to know instinctively the difference between right and wrong. But, as Paul explained in Rom 1:18–32, humanity misread the evidence of God's existence, power, and divinity, and "while claiming to be wise, they became fools" (Rom 1:22).

2:15 Paul expands on the thought of Jer 31:33; Wis 17:11.

2:17–29 Mere possession of laws is no evidence of virtue. By eliminating circumcision as an elitist moral sign, Paul clears away the last obstacle to his presentation of justification through faith without claims based on the receipt of circumcision and its attendant legal obligations.

---

a: Mt 7:1–2. *b:* Wis 16:15–16. *c:* 3:25–26; 9:22; Wis 11:23; 15:1; 2 Pt 3:9, 15. *d:* Ex 33:3; Acts 7:51; Rev 6:17; 11:18. *e:* Ps 62:12; Prv 24:12; Sir 16:14; Mt 16:27; Jn 5:29; 2 Cor 5:10. *f:* 2 Thes 1:8. *g:* 1:16; 3:9. *h:* Dt 10:17; 2 Chr 19:7; Sir 35:12–13; Acts 10:34; Gal 2:6; Eph 6:9; Col 3:25; 1 Pt 1:17. *i:* 3:19. *j:* Mt 7:21; Lk 6:46–49; 8:21; Jas 1:22–25; 1 Jn 3:7. *k:* Acts 10:35. *l:* Acts 10:42; 17:31. *m:* Is 48:1–2; Mi 3:11; Phil 3:4–6. *n:* Phil 1:10. *o:* Mt 15:14; Lk 6:39. *p:* 2 Tm 3:15. *q:* Ps 50:16–21; Mt 23:3–4.

honor God by breaking the law? [24r*]For, as it
is written, "Because of you the name of God
is reviled among the Gentiles."
[25st]Circumcision, to be sure, has value if
you observe the law; but if you break the
law, your circumcision has become uncircumcision. [26u]Again, if an uncircumcised
man keeps the precepts of the law, will he
not be considered circumcised? [27]Indeed,
those who are physically uncircumcised but
carry out the law will pass judgment on you,
with your written law and circumcision, who
break the law. [28v]One is not a Jew outwardly.
True circumcision is not outward, in the
flesh. [29w]Rather, one is a Jew inwardly, and
circumcision is of the heart, in the spirit, not
the letter; his praise is not from human beings but from God.

CHAPTER 3

See RG 444–45

Answers to Objections. [1*]What advantage is there then in being a Jew? Or
what is the value of circumcision? [2x]Much,
in every respect. [For] in the first place, they
were entrusted with the utterances of God.
[3y]What if some were unfaithful? Will their
infidelity nullify the fidelity of God? [4z*]Of
course not! God must be true, though every
human being is a liar, as it is written:

"That you may be justified in your
words,
and conquer when you are judged."

[5a]But if our wickedness provides proof of
God's righteousness, what can we say? Is
God unjust, humanly speaking, to inflict his
wrath? [6]Of course not! For how else is God
to judge the world? [7]But if God's truth redounds to his glory through my falsehood,
why am I still being condemned as a sinner?
[8b]And why not say—as we are accused and
as some claim we say—that we should do
evil that good may come of it? Their penalty
is what they deserve.

Universal Bondage to Sin. [9c*]Well, then,
are we better off? Not entirely, for we have
already brought the charge against Jews and
Greeks alike that they are all under the domination of sin, [10d]as it is written:

"There is no one just, not one,
11 there is no one who understands,
there is no one who seeks God.
12 All have gone astray; all alike are
worthless;
there is not one who does good,
[there is not] even one.
13 [e]Their throats are open graves;
they deceive with their tongues;
the venom of asps is on their lips;
14 [f]their mouths are full of bitter cursing.
15 [g]Their feet are quick to shed blood;
16 ruin and misery are in their ways,
17 and the way of peace they know not.
18 [h]There is no fear of God before their
eyes."

[19i*]Now we know that what the law says is
addressed to those under the law, so that
every mouth may be silenced and the whole
world stand accountable to God, [20j*]since no

2:24 According to Is 52:5 the suffering of Israel prompts her enemies to revile God. Paul uses the passage in support of his point that the present immorality of Israelites is the cause of such defamation.

3:1–4 In keeping with the popular style of diatribe, Paul responds to the objection that his teaching on the sinfulness of all humanity detracts from the religious prerogatives of Israel. He stresses that Jews have remained the vehicle of God's revelation despite their sins, though this depends on the fidelity of God.

3:4 Though every human being is a liar: these words reproduce the Greek text of Ps 116:11. The rest of the verse is from Ps 51:6.

3:9–20 Well, then, are we better off?: this phrase can also be translated "Are we at a disadvantage?" but the latter version does not substantially change the overall meaning of the passage. Having explained that Israel's privileged status is guaranteed by God's fidelity, Paul now demonstrates the infidelity of the Jews by a catena of citations from scripture, possibly derived from an existing collection of *testimonia*. These texts show that all human beings share the common burden of sin. They are linked together by mention of organs of the body: throat, tongue, lips, mouth, feet, eyes.

3:19 The law: Paul here uses the term in its broadest sense to mean all of the scriptures; none of the preceding texts is from the Torah or Pentateuch.

3:20 No human being will be justified in his sight: these words are freely cited from Ps 143:2. In place of the psalmist's "no living person," Paul substitutes "no human being" (literally "no flesh," a Hebraism), and he adds "by observing the law."

r: Is 52:5; Ez 36:20; 2 Pt 2:2. *s:* Jer 4:4; 9:24–25. *t:* 1 Cor 7:19; Gal 5:3. *u:* Gal 5:6. *v:* Jn 7:24; 8:15, 39. *w:* Dt 30:6; Jer 4:4; 9:25; Col 2:11 / 1 Cor 4:5; 2 Cor 10:18. *x:* 9:4; Dt 4:7–8; Ps 103:7; 147:19–20. *y:* 9:6; 11:1, 29; Ps 89:30–37; 2 Tm 2:13. *z:* Ps 116:11 / Ps 51:6. *a:* 9:14; Jb 34:12–17. *b:* 6:1. *c:* 1:18–2:25; 3:23; Sir 8:5. *d:* Ps 14:1–3; 53:2–4; Eccl 7:20. *e:* Ps 5:10; 140:4. *f:* Ps 10:7. *g:* Prv 1:16; Is 59:7–8. *h:* Ps 36:2. *i:* 7:7. *j:* Ps 143:2; Gal 2:16 / 7:7.

human being will be justified in his sight by
observing the law; for through the law
comes consciousness of sin.

III. Justification through Faith in Christ

Justification apart from the Law. [21k*]But
now the righteousness of God has been manifested apart from the law, though testified to
by the law and the prophets, [22l]the righteousness of God through faith in Jesus
Christ for all who believe. For there is no
distinction; [23m]all have sinned and are deprived of the glory of God. [24n]They are justified freely by his grace through the
redemption in Christ Jesus, [25o*]whom God
set forth as an expiation, through faith, by
his blood, to prove his righteousness because of the forgiveness of sins previously
committed, [26]through the forbearance of
God—to prove his righteousness in the present time, that he might be righteous and justify the one who has faith in Jesus.
[27p*]What occasion is there then for boasting? It is ruled out. On what principle, that of
works? No, rather on the principle of faith.
[28q]For we consider that a person is justified
by faith apart from works of the law. [29r]Does
God belong to Jews alone? Does he not belong to Gentiles, too? Yes, also to Gentiles,
[30s]for God is one and will justify the circumcised on the basis of faith and the uncircumcised through faith. [31t*]Are we then annulling the law by this faith? Of course not!
On the contrary, we are supporting the law.

CHAPTER 4

See RG 445

Abraham Justified by Faith. [1u*]What
then can we say that Abraham found, our ancestor according to the flesh? [2*]Indeed, if
Abraham was justified on the basis of his
works, he has reason to boast; but this was
not so in the sight of God. [3v*]For what does

3:21–31 These verses provide a clear statement of Paul's "gospel," i.e., the principle of justification by faith in Christ. God has found a means of rescuing humanity from its desperate plight: Paul's general term for this divine initiative is the righteousness of God (Rom 3:21). Divine mercy declares the guilty innocent and makes them so. God does this not as a result of the law but apart from it (Rom 3:21), and not because of any merit in human beings but through forgiveness of their sins (Rom 3:24), in virtue of the redemption wrought in Christ Jesus for all who believe (Rom 3:22, 24–25). God has manifested his righteousness in the coming of Jesus Christ, whose saving activity inaugurates a new era in human history.

3:21 But now: Paul adopts a common phrase used by Greek authors to describe movement from disaster to prosperity. The expressions indicate that Rom 3:21–26 are the consolatory answer to Rom 3:9–20.

3:25 Expiation: this rendering is preferable to "propitiation," which suggests hostility on the part of God toward sinners. As Paul will be at pains to point out (Rom 5:8–10), it is humanity that is hostile to God.

3:27–31 People cannot boast of their own holiness, since it is God's free gift (Rom 3:27), both to the Jew who practices circumcision out of faith and to the Gentile who accepts faith without the Old Testament religious culture symbolized by circumcision (Rom 3:29–30).

3:27 Principle of faith: literally, "law of faith." Paul is fond of wordplay involving the term "law"; cf. Rom 7:21, 23; 8:2. Since "law" in Greek may also connote "custom" or "principle," his readers and hearers would have sensed no contradiction in the use of the term after the negative statement concerning law in Rom 3:20.

3:31 We are supporting the law: giving priority to God's intentions. God is the ultimate source of law, and the essence of law is fairness. On the basis of the Mosaic covenant, God's justice is in question if those who sinned against the law are permitted to go free (see Rom 3:23–26). In order to rescue all humanity rather than condemn it, God thinks of an alternative: the law or "principle" of faith (Rom 3:27). What can be more fair than to admit everyone into the divine presence on the basis of forgiveness grasped by faith? Indeed, this principle of faith antedates the Mosaic law, as Paul will demonstrate in Rom 4, and does not therefore mark a change in divine policy.

4:1–25 This is an expanded treatment of the significance of Abraham's faith, which Paul discusses in Gal 3:6–18; see notes there.

4:2–5 Rom 4:2 corresponds to Rom 4:4, and Rom 4:3–5. The Greek term here rendered **credited** means "made an entry." The context determines whether it is credit or debit. Rom 4:8 speaks of "recording sin" as a debit. Paul's repeated use of accountants' terminology in this and other passages can be traced both to the Old Testament texts he quotes and to his business activity as a tentmaker. The commercial term in Gn 15:6, "credited it to him," reminds Paul in Rom 4:7–8 of Ps 32:2, in which the same term is used and applied to forgiveness of sins. Thus Paul is able to argue that Abraham's faith involved receipt of forgiveness of sins and that all believers benefit as he did through faith.

4:3 Jas 2:24 appears to conflict with Paul's statement. However, James combats the error of extremists who used the doctrine of justification through faith as a screen for moral self- determination. Paul discusses the subject of holiness in greater detail than does James and beginning with Rom 6

k: Is 51:6–8; Acts 10:43. *l:* 1:17; Gal 2:16; Phil 3:9. *m:* 3:9; 5:12. *n:* Eph 2:8; Ti 3:7 / 5:1–2; Eph 1:7. *o:* Lv 16:12–15; Acts 17:31; 1 Jn 4:10. *p:* 8:2; 1 Cor 1:29–31. *q:* 5:1; Gal 2:16. *r:* 10:12. *s:* Dt 6:4; Gal 3:20; Jas 2:19 / 4:11–12. *t:* 8:4; Mt 5:17. *u:* Gal 3:6–9. *v:* Gn 15:6; Gal 3:6; Jas 2:14, 20–24.

the scripture say? "Abraham believed God,
and it was credited to him as righteousness."
[4w]A worker's wage is credited not as a gift,
but as something due. [5]But when one does
not work, yet believes in the one who justifies the ungodly, his faith is credited as righteousness. [6]So also David declares the
blessedness of the person to whom God
credits righteousness apart from works:

[7 x]"Blessed are they whose iniquities are
forgiven
and whose sins are covered.
[8] Blessed is the man whose sin the Lord
does not record."

[9y*]Does this blessedness apply only to the
circumcised, or to the uncircumcised as
well? Now we assert that "faith was credited
to Abraham as righteousness." [10]Under what
circumstances was it credited? Was he circumcised or not? He was not circumcised,
but uncircumcised. [11z]And he received the
sign of circumcision as a seal on the righteousness received through faith while he
was uncircumcised. Thus he was to be the
father of all the uncircumcised who believe,
so that to them [also] righteousness might be
credited, [12]as well as the father of the circumcised who not only are circumcised but
also follow the path of faith that our father
Abraham walked while still uncircumcised.

Inheritance through Faith. [13a]It was not
through the law that the promise was made to
Abraham and his descendants that he would
inherit the world, but through the righteousness that comes from faith. [14b]For if those
who adhere to the law are the heirs, faith is
null and the promise is void. [15c*]For the law
produces wrath; but where there is no law,
neither is there violation. [16d]For this reason,
it depends on faith, so that it may be a gift,
and the promise may be guaranteed to all his
descendants, not to those who only adhere to
the law but to those who follow the faith of
Abraham, who is the father of all of us, [17e]as
it is written, "I have made you father of many
nations." He is our father in the sight of God,
in whom he believed, who gives life to the
dead and calls into being what does not exist.
[18f]He believed, hoping against hope, that he
would become "the father of many nations,"
according to what was said, "Thus shall your
descendants be." [19g]He did not weaken in
faith when he considered his own body as
[already] dead (for he was almost a hundred
years old) and the dead womb of Sarah.
[20*]He did not doubt God's promise in unbelief; rather, he was empowered by faith and
gave glory to God [21h]and was fully convinced that what he had promised he was
also able to do. [22i]That is why "it was credited to him as righteousness." [23]But it was
not for him alone that it was written that "it
was credited to him"; [24j]it was also for us, to
whom it will be credited, who believe in the
one who raised Jesus our Lord from the dead,
[25k]who was handed over for our transgressions and was raised for our justification.

shows how justification through faith introduces one to the gift of a new life in Christ through the power of the holy Spirit.

4:9 Blessedness: evidence of divine favor.

4:15 Law has the negative function of bringing the deep-seated rebellion against God to the surface in specific sins; see note on Rom 1:18–32.

4:20 He did not doubt God's promise in unbelief: any doubts Abraham might have had were resolved in commitment to God's promise. Heb 11:8–12 emphasizes the faith of Abraham and Sarah.

5:1–11 Popular piety frequently construed reverses and troubles as punishment for sin; cf. Jn 9:2. Paul therefore assures believers that God's justifying action in Jesus Christ is a declaration of peace. The crucifixion of Jesus Christ displays God's initiative in certifying humanity for unimpeded access into the divine presence. Reconciliation is God's gift of pardon to the entire human race. Through faith one benefits personally from this pardon or, in Paul's term, is justified. The ultimate aim of God is to liberate believers from the pre-Christian self as described in Rom 1–3. Since this liberation will first find completion in the believer's resurrection, salvation is described as future in Rom 5:10. Because this fullness of salvation belongs to the future it is called the Christian hope. Paul's Greek term for hope does not, however, suggest a note of uncertainty, to the effect: "I wonder whether God really means it." Rather, God's promise in the gospel fills believers with expectation and anticipation for the climactic gift of unalloyed commitment in the holy Spirit to the performance of the will of God. The persecutions that attend Christian commitment are to teach believers patience and to strengthen this hope, which will not disappoint them because the holy Spirit dwells in their hearts and imbues them with God's love (Rom 5:5).

w: 11:6. *x:* Ps 32:1–2. *y:* 4:3. *z:* Gn 17:10–11; Gal 3:6–8. *a:* Gn 12:7; 18:18; 22:17–18; Sir 44:21; Gal 3:16–18, 29. *b:* Gal 3:18. *c:* 3:20; 5:13; 7:8; Gal 3:19. *d:* Sir 44:19; Gal 3:7–9. *e:* Gn 17:5; Heb 11:19 / Is 48:13. *f:* Gn 15:5. *g:* Gn 17:17; Heb 11:11. *h:* Gn 18:14; Lk 1:37. *i:* Gn 15:6. *j:* 10:9; 1 Pt 1:21. *k:* Is 53:4–5, 12; 1 Cor 15:17; 1 Pt 1:3 / 8:11.

See RG 445–46

CHAPTER 5

Faith, Hope, and Love. [1l*]Therefore,
since we have been justified by faith, we
have peace with God through our Lord Jesus
Christ, [2m]through whom we have gained access [by faith] to this grace in which we
stand, and we boast in hope of the glory of
God. [3]Not only that, but we even boast of
our afflictions, knowing that affliction produces endurance, [4n]and endurance, proven
character, and proven character, hope, [5o]and
hope does not disappoint, because the love
of God has been poured out into our hearts
through the holy Spirit that has been given to
us. [6]For Christ, while we were still helpless,
yet died at the appointed time for the ungodly. [7*]Indeed, only with difficulty does
one die for a just person, though perhaps for
a good person one might even find courage
to die. [8p]But God proves his love for us in
that while we were still sinners Christ died
for us. [9q]How much more then, since we are
now justified by his blood, will we be saved
through him from the wrath. [10r]Indeed, if,
while we were enemies, we were reconciled
to God through the death of his Son, how
much more, once reconciled, will we be
saved by his life. [11]Not only that, but we also
boast of God through our Lord Jesus Christ,
through whom we have now received reconciliation.

Humanity's Sin through Adam. [12s*]There-
fore, just as through one person sin entered
the world, and through sin, death, and thus
death came to all, inasmuch as all sinned—
[13t]for up to the time of the law, sin was in the
world, though sin is not accounted when
there is no law. [14u]But death reigned from
Adam to Moses, even over those who did
not sin after the pattern of the trespass of
Adam, who is the type of the one who was to
come.

Grace and Life through Christ. [15]But the
gift is not like the transgression. For if by
that one person's transgression the many
died, how much more did the grace of God
and the gracious gift of the one person
Jesus Christ overflow for the many. [16]And
the gift is not like the result of the one person's sinning. For after one sin there was
the judgment that brought condemnation;
but the gift, after many transgressions,
brought acquittal. [17]For if, by the transgression of one person, death came to reign
through that one, how much more will
those who receive the abundance of grace
and of the gift of justification come to reign
in life through the one person Jesus Christ.
[18v]In conclusion, just as through one transgression condemnation came upon all, so
through one righteous act acquittal and life
came to all. [19w]For just as through the disobedience of one person the many were
made sinners, so through the obedience of
one the many will be made righteous.
[20x*]The law entered in so that transgression
might increase but, where sin increased,
grace overflowed all the more, [21y]so that,
as sin reigned in death, grace also might
reign through justification for eternal life
through Jesus Christ our Lord.

5:1 We have peace: a number of manuscripts, versions, and church Fathers read "Let us have peace"; cf. Rom 14:19.

5:7 In the world of Paul's time the **good person** is especially one who is magnanimous to others.

5:12–21 Paul reflects on the sin of Adam (Gn 3:1–13) in the light of the redemptive mystery of Christ. Sin, as used in the singular by Paul, refers to the dreadful power that has gripped humanity, which is now in revolt against the Creator and engaged in the exaltation of its own desires and interests. But no one has a right to say, "Adam made me do it," for all are culpable (Rom 5:12): Gentiles under the demands of the law written in their hearts (Rom 2:14–15), and Jews under the Mosaic covenant. Through the Old Testament law, the sinfulness of humanity that was operative from the beginning (Rom 5:13) found further stimulation, with the result that sins were generated in even greater abundance. According to Rom 5:15–21, God's act in Christ is in total contrast to the disastrous effects of the virus of sin that invaded humanity through Adam's crime.

5:12 Inasmuch as all sinned: others translate "because all sinned," and understand v 13 as a parenthetical remark. Unlike Wis 2:24, Paul does not ascribe the entry of death to the devil.

5:20 The law entered in: sin had made its entrance (12); now the law comes in alongside sin. See notes on Rom 1:18–32; 5:12–21. **Where sin increased, grace overflowed all the more**: Paul declares that grace outmatches the productivity of sin.

l: 3:24–28; Gal 2:16. *m:* Eph 2:18; 3:12. *n:* 2 Cor 12:9–10; Jas 1:2–4; 1 Pt 1:5–7; 4:12–14. *o:* 8:14–16; Ps 22:5–6; 25:20. *p:* Jn 3:16; 1 Jn 4:10, 19. *q:* 1:18; 1 Thes 1:10. *r:* 8:7–8; 2 Cor 5:18; Col 1:21–22. *s:* Gn 2:17; 3:1–19; Wis 2:24 / 3:19, 23. *t:* 4:15. *u:* 1 Cor 15:21. *v:* 1 Cor 15:21–22. *w:* Is 53:11; Phil 2:8–9. *x:* 4:15; 7:7–8; Gal 3:19. *y:* 6:23.

IV. Justification and the Christian Life

CHAPTER 6

See RG 446

Freedom from Sin; Life in God. [1z*]What then shall we say? Shall we persist in sin that grace may abound? Of course not! [2a]How can we who died to sin yet live in it? [3b]Or are you unaware that we who were baptized into Christ Jesus were baptized into his death? [4c]We were indeed buried with him through baptism into death, so that, just as Christ was raised from the dead by the glory of the Father, we too might live in newness of life.

[5d]For if we have grown into union with him through a death like his, we shall also be united with him in the resurrection. [6e]We know that our old self was crucified with him, so that our sinful body might be done away with, that we might no longer be in slavery to sin. [7]For a dead person has been absolved from sin. [8f]If, then, we have died with Christ, we believe that we shall also live with him. [9g]We know that Christ, raised from the dead, dies no more; death no longer has power over him. [10h]As to his death, he died to sin once and for all; as to his life, he lives for God. [11i]Consequently, you too must think of yourselves as [being] dead to sin and living for God in Christ Jesus.

[12j*]Therefore, sin must not reign over your mortal bodies so that you obey their desires. [13k]And do not present the parts of your bodies to sin as weapons for wickedness, but present yourselves to God as raised from the dead to life and the parts of your bodies to God as weapons for righteousness. [14l]For sin is not to have any power over you, since you are not under the law but under grace.

[15m]What then? Shall we sin because we are not under the law but under grace? Of course not! [16no]Do you not know that if you present yourselves to someone as obedient slaves, you are slaves of the one you obey, either of sin, which leads to death, or of obedience, which leads to righteousness? [17*]But thanks be to God that, although you were once slaves of sin, you have become obedient from the heart to the pattern of teaching to which you were entrusted. [18]Freed from sin, you have become slaves of righteousness. [19]I am speaking in human terms because of the weakness of your nature. For just as you presented the parts of your bodies as slaves to impurity and to lawlessness for lawlessness, so now present them as slaves to righteousness for sanctification. [20p*]For when you were slaves of sin, you were free from righteousness. [21q]But what profit did you get then from the things of which you are now ashamed? For the end of those things is death. [22r*]But now that you have been freed from sin and have become slaves of God, the benefit that you have leads to sanctification,

6:1–11 To defend the gospel against the charge that it promotes moral laxity (cf. Rom 3:5–8), Paul expresses himself in the typical style of spirited diatribe. God's display of generosity or grace is not evoked by sin but, as stated in Rom 5:8 is the expression of God's love, and this love pledges eternal life to all believers (Rom 5:21). Paul views the present conduct of the believers from the perspective of God's completed salvation when the body is resurrected and directed totally by the holy Spirit. Through baptism believers share the death of Christ and thereby escape from the grip of sin. Through the resurrection of Christ the power to live anew becomes reality for them, but the fullness of participation in Christ's resurrection still lies in the future. But life that is lived in dedication to God now is part and parcel of that future. Hence anyone who sincerely claims to be interested in that future will scarcely be able to say, "Let us sin so that grace may prosper" (cf. Rom 6:1).

6:12–19 Christians have been released from the grip of sin, but sin endeavors to reclaim its victims. The antidote is constant remembrance that divine grace has claimed them and identifies them as people who are alive only for God's interests.

6:17 In contrast to humanity, which was handed over to self-indulgence (Rom 1:24–32), believers are **entrusted** ("handed over") to God's **pattern of teaching**, that is, the new life God aims to develop in Christians through the productivity of the holy Spirit. Throughout this passage Paul uses the slave-master model in order to emphasize the fact that one cannot give allegiance to both God and sin.

6:20 You were free from righteousness: expressed ironically, for such freedom is really tyranny. The commercial metaphors in Rom 6:21–23 add up only one way: sin is a bad bargain.

6:22 Sanctification: or holiness.

z: 3:5–8. *a:* 1 Pt 4:1. *b:* Gal 3:27. *c:* Col 2:12; 1 Pt 3:21–22. *d:* Phil 3:10–11; 2 Tm 2:11. *e:* Gal 5:24; 6:14; Eph 4:22–23. *f:* 1 Thes 4:17. *g:* Acts 13:34; 1 Cor 15:26; 2 Tm 1:10; Rev 1:18. *h:* Heb 9:26–28; 1 Pt 3:18. *i:* 2 Cor 5:15; 1 Pt 2:24. *j:* Gn 4:7. *k:* 12:1; Eph 2:5 / 5:14; Col 3:5. *l:* Gal 5:18; 1 Jn 3:6. *m:* 5:17, 21. *n:* Jn 8:32–36. *o:* Jn 8:31–34; 2 Pt 2:19. *p:* Jn 8:34. *q:* 8:6, 13; Prv 12:28; Ez 16:61, 63. *r:* 1 Pt 1:9.

and its end is eternal life. [23s]For the wages of sin is death, but the gift of God is eternal life in Christ Jesus our Lord.

CHAPTER 7

See RG 446

Freedom from the Law. [1*]Are you unaware, brothers (for I am speaking to people who know the law), that the law has jurisdiction over one as long as one lives? [2t]Thus a married woman is bound by law to her living husband; but if her husband dies, she is released from the law in respect to her husband. [3]Consequently, while her husband is alive she will be called an adulteress if she consorts with another man. But if her husband dies she is free from that law, and she is not an adulteress if she consorts with another man.

[4]In the same way, my brothers, you also were put to death to the law through the body of Christ, so that you might belong to another, to the one who was raised from the dead in order that we might bear fruit for God. [5u]For when we were in the flesh, our sinful passions, awakened by the law, worked in our members to bear fruit for death. [6v]But now we are released from the law, dead to what held us captive, so that we may serve in the newness of the spirit and not under the obsolete letter.

Acquaintance with Sin through the Law. [7w*]What then can we say? That the law is sin? Of course not! Yet I did not know sin except through the law, and I did not know what it is to covet except that the law said, "You shall not covet." [8x]But sin, finding an opportunity in the commandment, produced in me every kind of covetousness. Apart from the law sin is dead. [9]I once lived outside the law, but when the commandment came, sin became alive; [10y]then I died, and the commandment that was for life turned out to be death for me. [11z]For sin, seizing an opportunity in the commandment, deceived me and through it put me to death. [12a]So then the law is holy, and the commandment is holy and righteous and good.

Sin and Death. [13b*]Did the good, then, become death for me? Of course not! Sin, in order that it might be shown to be sin, worked death in me through the good, so that sin might become sinful beyond measure through the commandment. [14c]We know that the law is spiritual; but I am carnal, sold into slavery to sin. [15]What I do, I do not understand. For I do not do what I want, but I do what I hate. [16]Now if I do what I do not want, I concur that the law is good. [17]So now it is no longer I who do it, but sin that dwells in me. [18d]For I know that good does not dwell in me, that is, in my flesh. The willing is ready at hand, but doing the good is not. [19]For I do not do the good I want, but I do the evil I do not want. [20]Now if [I] do what I do not want, it is no longer I who do it, but sin that dwells in me. [21]So, then, I discover the principle that when I want to do right, evil is at hand. [22]For I take delight in the law of God, in my inner self, [23e*]but I see in my members another principle at war with the law of my mind, taking me captive to the

7:1–6 Paul reflects on the fact that Christians have a different understanding of the law because of their faith in Christ. Law binds the living, not the dead, as exemplified in marriage, which binds in life but is dissolved through death. Similarly, Christians who through baptism have died with Christ to sin (cf. Rom 6:2–4) are freed from the law that occasioned transgressions, which in turn were productive of death. Now that Christians are joined to Christ, the power of Christ's resurrection makes it possible for them to bear the fruit of newness of life for God.

7:7–25 In this passage Paul uses the first person singular in the style of diatribe for the sake of argument. He aims to depict the disastrous consequences when a Christian reintroduces the law as a means to attain the objective of holiness pronounced in Rom 6:22.

7:7–12 The apostle defends himself against the charge of identifying the law with sin. Sin does not exist in law but in human beings, whose sinful inclinations are not overcome by the proclamation of law.

7:13–25 Far from improving the sinner, law encourages sin to expose itself in transgressions or violations of specific commandments (see Rom 1:24; 5:20). Thus persons who do not experience the justifying grace of God, and Christians who revert to dependence on law as the criterion for their relationship with God, will recognize a rift between their reasoned desire for the goodness of the law and their actual performance that is contrary to the law. Unable to free themselves from the slavery of sin and the power of death, they can only be rescued from defeat in the conflict by the power of God's grace working through Jesus Christ.

7:23 As in Rom 3:27 Paul plays on the term **law**, which in Greek can connote custom, system, or **principle**.

s: Gn 2:17; Gal 6:7–9; Jas 1:15. *t:* 1 Cor 7:39. *u:* 6:21; 8:6, 13. *v:* 8:2; 2 Cor 3:6. *w:* 3:20; Ex 20:17; Dt 5:21. *x:* 5:13, 20; 1 Cor 15:56 / 4:15. *y:* Lv 18:5. *z:* Gn 3:13; Heb 3:13. *a:* 1 Tm 1:8. *b:* 4:15; 5:20. *c:* 8:7–8; Ps 51:7. *d:* Gn 6:5; 8:21; Phil 2:13. *e:* Gal 5:17; 1 Pt 2:11.

law of sin that dwells in my members. [24]Miserable one that I am! Who will deliver me from this mortal body? [25f]Thanks be to God through Jesus Christ our Lord. Therefore, I myself, with my mind, serve the law of God but, with my flesh, the law of sin.

CHAPTER 8

See RG 446–47

The Flesh and the Spirit. [1*]Hence, now there is no condemnation for those who are in Christ Jesus. [2g]For the law of the spirit of life in Christ Jesus has freed you from the law of sin and death. [3h]For what the law, weakened by the flesh, was powerless to do, this God has done: by sending his own Son in the likeness of sinful flesh and for the sake of sin, he condemned sin in the flesh, [4i]so that the righteous decree of the law might be fulfilled in us, who live not according to the flesh but according to the spirit. [5]For those who live according to the flesh are concerned with the things of the flesh, but those who live according to the spirit with the things of the spirit. [6j]The concern of the flesh is death, but the concern of the spirit is life and peace. [7k]For the concern of the flesh is hostility toward God; it does not submit to the law of God, nor can it; [8l]and those who are in the flesh cannot please God. [9m]But you are not in the flesh; on the contrary, you are in the spirit, if only the Spirit of God dwells in you. Whoever does not have the Spirit of Christ does not belong to him. [10n]But if Christ is in you, although the body is dead because of sin, the spirit is alive because of righteousness. [11]If the Spirit of the one who raised Jesus from the dead dwells in you, the one who raised Christ from the dead will give life to your mortal bodies also, through his Spirit that dwells in you. [12]Consequently, brothers, we are not debtors to the flesh, to live according to the flesh. [13o]For if you live according to the flesh, you will die, but if by the spirit you put to death the deeds of the body, you will live.

Children of God through Adoption. [14p*]For those who are led by the Spirit of God are children of God. [15q*]For you did not receive a spirit of slavery to fall back into fear, but you received a spirit of adoption, through which we cry, "*Abba,* Father!" [16r]The Spirit itself bears witness with our spirit that we are children of God, [17s]and if children, then heirs, heirs of God and joint heirs with Christ, if only we suffer with him so that we may also be glorified with him.

Destiny of Glory. [18t*]I consider that the sufferings of this present time are as nothing compared with the glory to be revealed for us. [19]For creation awaits with eager expectation the revelation of the children of God; [20u]for creation was made subject to futility, not of its own accord but because of the one who subjected it, in hope [21v]that creation it-

8:1–13 After his warning in Rom 7 against the wrong route to fulfillment of the objective of holiness expressed in Rom 6:22, Paul points his addressees to the correct way. Through the redemptive work of Christ, Christians have been liberated from the terrible forces of sin and death. Holiness was impossible so long as the **flesh** (or our "old self"), that is, self-interested hostility toward God (Rom 8:7), frustrated the divine objectives expressed in the law. What is worse, sin used the law to break forth into all manner of lawlessness (Rom 8:8). All this is now changed. At the cross God broke the power of sin and pronounced sentence on it (Rom 8:3). Christians still retain the flesh, but it is alien to their new being, which is life in the spirit, namely the new self, governed by the holy Spirit. Under the direction of the holy Spirit Christians are able to fulfill the divine will that formerly found expression in the law (Rom 8:4). The same Spirit who enlivens Christians for holiness will also resurrect their bodies at the last day (Rom 8:11). Christian life is therefore the experience of a constant challenge to put to death the evil deeds of the body through life of the spirit (Rom 8:13).

8:14–17 Christians, by reason of the Spirit's presence within them, enjoy not only new life but also a new relationship to God, that of adopted children and heirs through Christ, whose sufferings and glory they share.

8:15 Abba: see note on Mk 14:36.

8:18–27 The glory that believers are destined to share with Christ far exceeds the sufferings of the present life. Paul considers the destiny of the created world to be linked with the future that belongs to the believers. As it shares in the penalty of corruption brought about by sin, so also will it share in the benefits of redemption and future glory that comprise the ultimate liberation of God's people (Rom 8:19–22). After patient endurance in steadfast expectation, the full harvest of the Spirit's presence will be realized. On earth believers enjoy the firstfruits, i.e., the Spirit, as a guarantee of the total liberation of their bodies from the influence of the rebellious old self (Rom 8:23).

f: 1 Cor 15:57. *g:* 7:23–24; 2 Cor 3:17. *h:* Acts 13:38; 15:10 / Jn 3:16–17; 2 Cor 5:21; Gal 3:13; 4:4; Phil 2:7; Col 1:22; Heb 2:17; 4:15; 1 Jn 4:9. *i:* Gal 5:16–25. *j:* 6:21; 7:5; 8:13; Gal 6:8. *k:* 5:10; Jas 4:4. *l:* 1 Jn 2:16. *m:* 1 Cor 3:16. *n:* Gal 2:20; 1 Pt 4:6. *o:* Gal 5:24; 6:8; Eph 4:22–24. *p:* Gal 5:18. *q:* Mk 14:36; Gal 4:5–6; 2 Tm 1:7. *r:* Jn 1:12; Gal 3:26–29. *s:* Gal 4:7; 1 Pt 4:13; 5:1. *t:* 2 Cor 4:17. *u:* Gn 3:17–19. *v:* 2 Pt 3:12–13; Rev 21:1.

self would be set free from slavery to corruption and share in the glorious freedom of
the children of God. [22w]We know that all creation is groaning in labor pains even until
now; [23x]and not only that, but we ourselves,
who have the firstfruits of the Spirit, we also
groan within ourselves as we wait for adoption, the redemption of our bodies. [24y]For in
hope we were saved. Now hope that sees for
itself is not hope. For who hopes for what
one sees? [25]But if we hope for what we do
not see, we wait with endurance.
[26]In the same way, the Spirit too comes to
the aid of our weakness; for we do not know
how to pray as we ought, but the Spirit itself
intercedes with inexpressible groanings.
[27z]And the one who searches hearts knows
what is the intention of the Spirit, because it
intercedes for the holy ones according to
God's will.

God's Indomitable Love in Christ. [28a*]We
know that all things work for good for those
who love God, who are called according to
his purpose. [29b*]For those he foreknew he
also predestined to be conformed to the image of his Son, so that he might be the firstborn among many brothers. [30c]And those he
predestined he also called; and those he
called he also justified; and those he justified
he also glorified.
[31d*]What then shall we say to this? If God
is for us, who can be against us? [32e]He who
did not spare his own Son but handed him
over for us all, how will he not also give us
everything else along with him? [33f]Who
will bring a charge against God's chosen
ones? It is God who acquits us. [34g]Who will
condemn? It is Christ [Jesus] who died,
rather, was raised, who also is at the right
hand of God, who indeed intercedes for us.
[35]What will separate us from the love of
Christ? Will anguish, or distress, or persecution, or famine, or nakedness, or peril, or the
sword? [36h]As it is written:

"For your sake we are being slain all the
day;
we are looked upon as sheep to be
slaughtered."

[37i]No, in all these things we conquer overwhelmingly through him who loved us.
[38j*]For I am convinced that neither death,
nor life, nor angels, nor principalities, nor
present things, nor future things, nor powers,
[39*]nor height, nor depth, nor any other creature will be able to separate us from the love
of God in Christ Jesus our Lord.

V. Jews And Gentiles in God's Plan

CHAPTER 9

See RG 447–48

Paul's Love for Israel. [1k*]I speak the
truth in Christ, I do not lie; my conscience
joins with the holy Spirit in bearing me wit-

8:28–30 These verses outline the Christian vocation as it was designed by God: **to be conformed to the image of his Son**, who is to **be the firstborn among many brothers** (Rom 8:29). God's redemptive action on behalf of the believers has been in process before the beginning of the world. Those whom God chooses are **those he foreknew** (Rom 8:29) or elected. Those who are **called** (Rom 8:30) are **predestined** or predetermined. These expressions do not mean that God is arbitrary. Rather, Paul uses them to emphasize the thought and care that God has taken for the Christian's salvation.

8:28 We know that all things work for good for those who love God: a few ancient authorities have God as the subject of the verb, and some translators render: "We know that God makes everything work for good for those who love God . . . ."

8:29 Image: while man and woman were originally created in God's image (Gn 1:26–27), it is through baptism into Christ, the image of God (2 Cor 4:4; Col 1:15), that we are renewed according to the image of the Creator (Col 3:10).

8:31–39 The all-conquering power of God's love has overcome every obstacle to Christians' salvation and every threat to separate them from God. That power manifested itself fully when God's own Son was delivered up to death for their salvation. Through him Christians can overcome all their afflictions and trials.

8:38 Present things and **future things** may refer to astrological data. Paul appears to be saying that the gospel liberates believers from dependence on astrologers.

8:39 Height, depth may refer to positions in the zodiac, positions of heavenly bodies relative to the horizon. In astrological documents the term for "height" means "exaltation" or the position of greatest influence exerted by a planet. Since hostile spirits were associated with the planets and stars, Paul includes **powers** (Rom 8:38) in his list of malevolent forces.

9:1–11:36 Israel's unbelief and its rejection of Jesus as sav-

w: 2 Cor 5:2–5. *x:* 2 Cor 1:22; Gal 5:5. *y:* 2 Cor 5:7; Heb 11:1. *z:* Ps 139:1; 1 Cor 4:5. *a:* Eph 1:4–14; 3:11. *b:* Eph 1:5; 1 Pt 1:2. *c:* Is 45:25; 2 Thes 2:13–14. *d:* Ps 118:6; Heb 13:6. *e:* Jn 3:16. *f:* Is 50:8. *g:* Ps 110:1; Heb 7:25; 1 Jn 2:1. *h:* Ps 44:23; 1 Cor 4:9; 15:30; 2 Cor 4:11; 2 Tm 3:12. *i:* 1 Jn 5:4. *j:* 1 Cor 3:22; Eph 1:21; 1 Pt 3:22. *k:* 2 Cor 11:31; 1 Tm 2:7.

ness [2]that I have great sorrow and constant
anguish in my heart. [3l]For I could wish that I
myself were accursed and separated from
Christ for the sake of my brothers, my kin according to the flesh. [4m]They are Israelites;
theirs the adoption, the glory, the covenants,
the giving of the law, the worship, and the
promises; [5n*]theirs the patriarchs, and from
them, according to the flesh, is the Messiah.
God who is over all be blessed forever. Amen.

God's Free Choice. [6o]But it is not that the
word of God has failed. For not all who are
of Israel are Israel, [7p]nor are they all children of Abraham because they are his descendants; but "It is through Isaac that descendants shall bear your name." [8q]This
means that it is not the children of the flesh
who are the children of God, but the children
of the promise are counted as descendants.
[9r]For this is the wording of the promise,
"About this time I shall return and Sarah will
have a son." [10s*]And not only that, but also
when Rebecca had conceived children by
one husband, our father Isaac— [11]before
they had yet been born or had done anything,
good or bad, in order that God's elective
plan might continue, [12t]not by works but by
his call—she was told, "The older shall
serve the younger." [13u*]As it is written:

"I loved Jacob
but hated Esau."

[14v*]What then are we to say? Is there injustice on the part of God? Of course not!
[15w]For he says to Moses:

"I will show mercy to whom I will,
I will take pity on whom I will."

[16x]So it depends not upon a person's will or
exertion, but upon God, who shows mercy.
[17y]For the scripture says to Pharaoh, "This is
why I have raised you up, to show my power
through you that my name may be proclaimed throughout the earth." [18z*]Conse-
quently, he has mercy upon whom he wills,
and he hardens whom he wills.

[19a*]You will say to me then, "Why [then]
does he still find fault? For who can oppose
his will?" [20b]But who indeed are you, a human being, to talk back to God? Will what

ior astonished and puzzled Christians. It constituted a serious problem for them in view of God's specific preparation of Israel for the advent of the Messiah. Paul addresses himself here to the essential question of how the divine plan could be frustrated by Israel's unbelief. At the same time, he discourages both complacency and anxiety on the part of Gentiles. To those who might boast of their superior advantage over Jews, he warns that their enjoyment of the blessings assigned to Israel can be terminated. To those who might anxiously ask, "How can we be sure that Israel's fate will not be ours?" he replies that only unbelief can deprive one of salvation.

9:1–5 The apostle speaks in strong terms of the depth of his grief over the unbelief of his own people. He would willingly undergo a curse himself for the sake of their coming to the knowledge of Christ (Rom 9:3; cf. Lv 27:28–29). His love for them derives from God's continuing choice of them and from the spiritual benefits that God bestows on them and through them on all of humanity (Rom 9:4–5).

9:5 Some editors punctuate this verse differently and prefer the translation, "Of whom is Christ according to the flesh, who is God over all." However, Paul's point is that God **who is over all** aimed to use Israel, which had been entrusted with every privilege, in outreach to the entire world through the Messiah.

9:10 Children by one husband, our father Isaac: Abraham had two children, Ishmael and Isaac, by two wives, Hagar and Sarah, respectively. In that instance Isaac, although born later than Ishmael, became the bearer of the messianic promise. In the case of twins born to Rebecca, God's elective procedure is seen even more dramatically, and again the younger, contrary to Semitic custom, is given the preference.

9:13 The literal rendering, **"Jacob I loved, but Esau I hated,"** suggests an attitude of divine hostility that is not implied in Paul's statement. In Semitic usage "hate" means to love less; cf. Lk 14:26 with Mt 10:37. Israel's unbelief reflects the mystery of the divine election that is always operative within it. Mere natural descent from Abraham does not ensure the full possession of the divine gifts; it is God's sovereign prerogative to bestow this fullness upon, or to withhold it from, whomsoever he wishes; cf. Mt 3:9; Jn 8:39. The choice of Jacob over Esau is a case in point.

9:14–18 The principle of divine election does not invite Christians to theoretical inquiry concerning the nonelected, nor does this principle mean that God is unfair in his dealings with humanity. The instruction concerning divine election is a part of the gospel and reveals that the gift of faith is the enactment of God's mercy (Rom 9:16). God raised up Moses to display that mercy, and Pharaoh to display divine severity in punishing those who obstinately oppose their Creator.

9:18 The basic biblical principle is: those who will not see or hear *shall* not see or hear. On the other hand, the same God who thus makes stubborn or hardens the heart can reconstruct it through the work of the holy Spirit.

9:19–29 The apostle responds to the objection that if God rules over faith through the principle of divine election, God

---

l: Ex 32:32. *m:* 3:2; Ex 4:22; Dt 7:6; 14:1–2. *n:* Mt 1:1–16; Lk 3:23–38 / 1:25; Ps 41:14. *o:* Nm 23:19 / Mt 3:9. *p:* Gn 21:12; Gal 3:29. *q:* Gal 4:23, 28. *r:* Gn 18:10, 14. *s:* Gn 25:21. *t:* 11:5–6 / Gn 25:23–24. *u:* Mal 1:3. *v:* Dt 32:4. *w:* Ex 33:19. *x:* Eph 2:8; Ti 3:5. *y:* Ex 9:16. *z:* 11:30–32; Ex 4:21; 7:3. *a:* 3:7; Wis 12:12. *b:* Wis 15:7; Is 29:16; 45:9; Jer 18:6.

is made say to its maker, "Why have you created me so?" [21]Or does not the potter have a right over the clay, to make out of the same lump one vessel for a noble purpose and another for an ignoble one? [22c]What if God, wishing to show his wrath and make known his power, has endured with much patience the vessels of wrath made for destruction? [23]This was to make known the riches of his glory to the vessels of mercy, which he has prepared previously for glory, [24]namely, us whom he has called, not only from the Jews but also from the Gentiles.

Witness of the Prophets. [25d*]As indeed he says in Hosea:

"Those who were not my people I will
call 'my people,'
and her who was not beloved I will
call 'beloved.'
[26e]And in the very place where it was said
to them, 'You are not my people,'
there they shall be called children of
the living God."

[27f]And Isaiah cries out concerning Israel, "Though the number of the Israelites were like the sand of the sea, only a remnant will be saved; [28]for decisively and quickly will the Lord execute sentence upon the earth." [29g]And as Isaiah predicted:

"Unless the Lord of hosts had left us
descendants,
we would have become like Sodom
and have been made like Gomorrah."

Righteousness Based on Faith. [30h*]What then shall we say? That Gentiles, who did not pursue righteousness, have achieved it, that is, righteousness that comes from faith; [31i]but that Israel, who pursued the law of righteousness, did not attain to that law? [32j*]Why not? Because they did it not by faith, but as if it could be done by works. They stumbled over the stone that causes stumbling, [33k]as it is written:

"Behold, I am laying a stone in Zion
that will make people stumble
and a rock that will make them fall,
and whoever believes in him shall not be
put to shame."

CHAPTER 10

See RG 447–48

[1l*]Brothers, my heart's desire and prayer to God on their behalf is for salvation. [2m]I testify with regard to them that they have zeal for God, but it is not discerning. [3n]For, in their unawareness of the righteousness that comes from God and their attempt to establish their own [righteousness], they did not submit to the righteousness of God. [4o*]For Christ is the end of the law for the justification of everyone who has faith.

cannot then accuse unbelievers of sin (Rom 9:19). For Paul, this objection is in the last analysis a manifestation of human insolence, and his "answer" is less an explanation of God's ways than the rejection of an argument that places humanity on a level with God. At the same time, Paul shows that God is far less arbitrary than appearances suggest, for God endures **with much patience** (Rom 9:22) a person like the Pharaoh of the Exodus.

9:25 Beloved: in Semitic discourse means "preferred" or "favorite" (cf. Rom 9:13). See Hos 2:1.

9:30–33 In the conversion of the Gentiles and, by contrast, of relatively few Jews, the Old Testament prophecies are seen to be fulfilled; cf. Rom 9:25–29. Israel feared that the doctrine of justification through faith would jeopardize the validity of the Mosaic law, and so they never reached their goal of righteousness that they had sought to attain through meticulous observance of the law (Rom 9:31). Since Gentiles, including especially Greeks and Romans, had a great regard for righteousness, Paul's statement concerning Gentiles in Rom 9:30 is to be understood from a Jewish perspective: quite evidently they had not been interested in "God's" righteousness, for it had not been revealed to them; but now in response to the proclamation of the gospel they respond in faith.

9:32 Paul discusses Israel as a whole from the perspective of contemporary Jewish rejection of Jesus as Messiah. The Old Testament and much of Jewish noncanonical literature in fact reflect a fervent faith in divine mercy.

10:1–13 Despite Israel's lack of faith in God's act in Christ, Paul does not abandon hope for her salvation (Rom 10:1). However, Israel must recognize that the Messiah's arrival in the person of Jesus Christ means the termination of the Mosaic law as the criterion for understanding oneself in a valid relationship to God. Faith in God's saving action in Jesus Christ takes precedence over any such legal claim (Rom 10:6).

10:4 The Mosaic legislation has been superseded by God's action in Jesus Christ. Others understand end here in the sense that Christ is the goal of the law, i.e., the true meaning of the Mosaic law, which cannot be correctly understood apart from him. Still others believe that both meanings are intended.

c: 2:4; Wis 12:20–21; Jer 50:25. *d:* Hos 2:25. *e:* Hos 2:1. *f:* Is 10:22–23; Hos 2:1 / 11:5 / Is 28:22. *g:* Is 1:9; Mt 10:15. *h:* 10:4, 20. *i:* 10:3. *j:* Is 8:14. *k:* Is 28:16; 1 Pt 2:6–8. *l:* 9:1, 3. *m:* Acts 22:3. *n:* 9:31–32; Phil 3:9. *o:* Acts 13:38–39; 2 Cor 3:14; Heb 8:13.

[5p*]Moses writes about the righteousness that comes from [the] law, "The one who does these things will live by them." [6q]But the righteousness that comes from faith says, "Do not say in your heart, 'Who will go up into heaven?' (that is, to bring Christ down) [7r*]or 'Who will go down into the abyss?' (that is, to bring Christ up from the dead)." [8s]But what does it say?

"The word is near you,
in your mouth and in your heart"

(that is, the word of faith that we preach), [9t*]for, if you confess with your mouth that Jesus is Lord and believe in your heart that God raised him from the dead, you will be saved. [10]For one believes with the heart and so is justified, and one confesses with the mouth and so is saved. [11u]For the scripture says, "No one who believes in him will be put to shame." [12v]For there is no distinction between Jew and Greek; the same Lord is Lord of all, enriching all who call upon him. [13w]For "everyone who calls on the name of the Lord will be saved."

[14x*]But how can they call on him in whom they have not believed? And how can they believe in him of whom they have not heard? And how can they hear without someone to preach? [15y*]And how can people preach unless they are sent? As it is written, "How beautiful are the feet of those who bring [the] good news!" [16z]But not everyone has heeded the good news; for Isaiah says, "Lord, who has believed what was heard from us?" [17a]Thus faith comes from what is heard, and what is heard comes through the word of Christ. [18b]But I ask, did they not hear? Certainly they did; for

"Their voice has gone forth to all the earth,
and their words to the ends of the world."

[19c]But I ask, did not Israel understand? First Moses says:

"I will make you jealous of those who are not a nation;
with a senseless nation I will make you angry."

[20d]Then Isaiah speaks boldly and says:

"I was found [by] those who were not seeking me;
I revealed myself to those who were not asking for me."

[21]But regarding Israel he says, "All day long I stretched out my hands to a disobedient and contentious people."

CHAPTER 11

See RG 447–48

The Remnant of Israel. [1ef*]I ask, then, has God rejected his people? Of course not! For I too am an Israelite, a descendant of Abraham, of the tribe of Benjamin. [2]God has not rejected his people whom he foreknew. Do you not know what the scripture says about Elijah, how he pleads with God against Israel? [3g]"Lord, they have

10:5–6 The subject of the verb **says** (Rom 10:6) is **righteousness** personified. Both of the statements in Rom 10:5, 6 derive from Moses, but Paul wishes to contrast the language of law and the language of faith.

10:7 Here Paul blends Dt 30:13 and Ps 107:26.

10:9–11 To confess Jesus as Lord was frequently quite hazardous in the first century (cf. Mt 10:18; 1 Thes 2:2; 1 Pt 2:18–21; 3:14). For a Jew it could mean disruption of normal familial and other social relationships, including great economic sacrifice. In the face of penalties imposed by the secular world, Christians are assured that **no one who believes in** Jesus **will be put to shame** (Rom 10:11).

10:14–21 The gospel has been sufficiently proclaimed to Israel, and Israel has adequately understood God's plan for the messianic age, which would see the gospel brought to the uttermost parts of the earth. As often in the past, Israel has not accepted the prophetic message; cf. Acts 7:51–53.

10:15 How beautiful are the feet of those who bring [the] good news: in Semitic fashion, the parts of the body that bring the messenger with welcome news are praised; cf. Lk 11:27.

11:1–10 Although Israel has been unfaithful to the prophetic message of the gospel (Rom 10:14–21), God remains faithful to Israel. Proof of the divine fidelity lies in the existence of Jewish Christians like Paul himself. The unbelieving Jews, says Paul, have been blinded by the Christian teaching concerning the Messiah.

p: Lv 18:5; Gal 3:12. *q:* Dt 9:4; 30:12. *r:* Dt 30:13; 1 Pt 3:19. *s:* Dt 30:14. *t:* 1 Cor 12:3. *u:* 9:33; Is 28:16. *v:* 1:16; 3:22, 29; Acts 10:34; 15:9, 11; Gal 3:28; Eph 2:14. *w:* Jl 3:5; Acts 2:21. *x:* Acts 8:31. *y:* Is 52:7; Na 2:1; Eph 6:15. *z:* Is 53:1; Jn 12:38. *a:* Jn 17:20. *b:* Ps 19:5; Mt 24:14. *c:* 11:11, 14; Dt 32:21. *d:* 9:30; Is 65:1–2. *e:* 1 Sm 12:22; Ps 94:14. *f:* 2 Cor 11:22; Phil 3:5. *g:* 1 Kgs 19:10, 14.

killed your prophets, they have torn down
your altars, and I alone am left, and they are
seeking my life.” [4h]But what is God’s response to him? “I have left for myself seven
thousand men who have not knelt to Baal.”
[5i]So also at the present time there is a remnant, chosen by grace. [6j]But if by grace, it is
no longer because of works; otherwise grace
would no longer be grace. [7k]What then?
What Israel was seeking it did not attain, but
the elect attained it; the rest were hardened,
[8l]as it is written:

“God gave them a spirit of deep sleep,
eyes that should not see
and ears that should not hear,
down to this very day.”

[9m]And David says:

“Let their table become a snare and a trap,
a stumbling block and a retribution for them;
[10] let their eyes grow dim so that they may not see,
and keep their backs bent forever.”

The Gentiles’ Salvation. [11n*]Hence I ask,
did they stumble so as to fall? Of course not!
But through their transgression salvation has
come to the Gentiles, so as to make them
jealous. [12]Now if their transgression is enrichment for the world, and if their diminished number is enrichment for the Gentiles,
how much more their full number.

[13o]Now I am speaking to you Gentiles.
Inasmuch then as I am the apostle to the
Gentiles, I glory in my ministry [14]in order to
make my race jealous and thus save some of
them. [15]For if their rejection is the reconciliation of the world, what will their acceptance be but life from the dead? [16p*]If the
firstfruits are holy, so is the whole batch of
dough; and if the root is holy, so are the
branches.

[17q]But if some of the branches were broken off, and you, a wild olive shoot, were
grafted in their place and have come to share
in the rich root of the olive tree, [18r]do not
boast against the branches. If you do boast,
consider that you do not support the root; the
root supports you. [19]Indeed you will say,
“Branches were broken off so that I might be
grafted in.” [20s]That is so. They were broken
off because of unbelief, but you are there because of faith. So do not become haughty,
but stand in awe. [21t]For if God did not spare
the natural branches, [perhaps] he will not
spare you either. [22u]See, then, the kindness
and severity of God: severity toward those
who fell, but God’s kindness to you, provided you remain in his kindness; otherwise
you too will be cut off. [23v]And they also, if
they do not remain in unbelief, will be
grafted in, for God is able to graft them in
again. [24]For if you were cut from what is by
nature a wild olive tree, and grafted, contrary to nature, into a cultivated one, how
much more will they who belong to it by nature be grafted back into their own olive tree.

God’s Irrevocable Call. [25w*]I do not want
you to be unaware of this mystery, brothers,
so that you will not become wise [in] your
own estimation: a hardening has come upon
Israel in part, until the full number of the
Gentiles comes in, [26xy]and thus all Israel will
be saved, as it is written:

11:11–15 The unbelief of the Jews has paved the way for the preaching of the gospel to the Gentiles and for their easier acceptance of it outside the context of Jewish culture. Through his mission to the Gentiles Paul also hopes to fill his fellow Jews with jealousy. Hence he hastens to fill the entire Mediterranean world with the gospel. Once all the Gentile nations have heard the gospel, Israel as a whole is expected to embrace it. This will be tantamount to resurrection of the dead, that is, the reappearance of Jesus Christ with all the believers at the end of time.

11:16–24 Israel remains holy in the eyes of God and stands as a witness to the faith described in the Old Testament because of **the firstfruits** (or the first piece baked) (Rom 11:16), that is, the converted remnant, and **the root** that **is holy**, that is, the patriarchs (Rom 11:16). The Jews’ failure to believe in Christ is a warning to Gentile Christians to be on guard against any semblance of anti-Jewish arrogance, that is, failure to recognize their total dependence on divine grace.

11:25–29 In God’s design, Israel’s unbelief is being used to grant the light of faith to the Gentiles. Meanwhile, Israel remains dear to God (cf. Rom 9:13), still the object of special providence, the mystery of which will one day be revealed.

h: 1 Kgs 19:18. *i:* 9:27. *j:* 4:4; Gal 3:18. *k:* 9:31. *l:* Dt 29:3; Is 29:10; Mt 13:13–15; Acts 28:26–27. *m:* Ps 69:23–24; 35:8. *n:* Acts 13:46; 18:6; 28:28 / 10:19; Dt 32:21. *o:* 1:5. *p:* Nm 15:17–21; Ez 44:30; Neh 10:36–38. *q:* Eph 2:11–19. *r:* 1 Cor 1:31. *s:* 12:16. *t:* 1 Cor 10:12. *u:* Jn 15:2, 4; Heb 3:14. *v:* 2 Cor 3:16. *w:* Prv 3:7 / 12:16; Mk 13:10; Lk 21:24; Jn 10:16. *x:* Ps 14:7; Is 59:20–21. *y:* Mt 23:39.

"The deliverer will come out of Zion,
he will turn away godlessness from
Jacob;
[27 z]and this is my covenant with them
when I take away their sins."

[28a]In respect to the gospel, they are enemies
on your account; but in respect to election,
they are beloved because of the patriarchs.
[29b]For the gifts and the call of God are irrevocable.

Triumph of God's Mercy. [30*]Just as you
once disobeyed God but have now received
mercy because of their disobedience, [31]so
they have now disobeyed in order that, by
virtue of the mercy shown to you, they too
may [now] receive mercy. [32c]For God delivered all to disobedience, that he might have
mercy upon all.

[33d*]Oh, the depth of the riches and wisdom and knowledge of God! How inscrutable are his judgments and how unsearchable his ways!

[34 e*]"For who has known the mind of the
Lord
or who has been his counselor?"
[35 f*]"Or who has given him anything
that he may be repaid?"

[36g]For from him and through him and for
him are all things. To him be glory forever.
Amen.

VI. The Duties of Christians

CHAPTER 12

See RG 448

Sacrifice of Body and Mind. [1h*]I urge
you therefore, brothers, by the mercies of
God, to offer your bodies as a living sacrifice, holy and pleasing to God, your spiritual
worship. [2i]Do not conform yourselves to this
age but be transformed by the renewal of
your mind, that you may discern what is the
will of God, what is good and pleasing and
perfect.

Many Parts in One Body. [3j]For by the
grace given to me I tell everyone among
you not to think of himself more highly
than one ought to think, but to think
soberly, each according to the measure of
faith that God has apportioned. [4k]For as in
one body we have many parts, and all the
parts do not have the same function, [5*]so
we, though many, are one body in Christ
and individually parts of one another.
[6l*]Since we have gifts that differ according
to the grace given to us, let us exercise

11:30–32 Israel, together with the Gentiles who have been handed over to all manner of vices (Rom 1), **has been delivered . . . to disobedience**. The conclusion of Rom 11:32 repeats the thought of Rom 5:20, "Where sin increased, grace overflowed all the more."

11:33–36 This final reflection celebrates the wisdom of God's plan of salvation. As Paul has indicated throughout these chapters, both Jew and Gentile, despite the religious recalcitrance of each, have received the gift of faith. The methods used by God in making this outreach to the world stagger human comprehension but are at the same time a dazzling invitation to abiding faith.

11:34 The citation is from the Greek text of Is 40:13. Paul does not explicitly mention Isaiah in this verse, nor Job in 11:35.

11:35 Paul quotes from an old Greek version of Jb 41:3a, which differs from the Hebrew text (Jb 41:11a).

12:1–13:14 Since Christ marks the termination of the Mosaic law as the primary source of guidance for God's people (Rom 10:4), the apostle explains how Christians can function, in the light of the gift of justification through faith, in their relation to one another and the state.

12:1–8 The Mosaic code included elaborate directions on sacrifices and other cultic observances. The gospel, however, invites believers to present their **bodies as a living sacrifice** (Rom 12:1). Instead of being limited by specific legal maxims, Christians are liberated for the exercise of good judgment as they are confronted with the many and varied decisions required in the course of daily life. To assist them, God distributes a variety of gifts to the fellowship of believers, including those of prophecy, teaching, and exhortation (Rom 12:6–8). Prophets assist the community to understand the will of God as it applies to the present situation (Rom 12:6). Teachers help people to understand themselves and their responsibilities in relation to others (Rom 12:7). One who **exhorts** offers encouragement to the community to exercise their faith in the performance of all that is pleasing to God (Rom 12:8). Indeed, this very section, beginning with Rom 12:1, is a specimen of Paul's own style of exhortation.

12:5 One body in Christ: on the church as the body of Christ, see 1 Cor 12:12–27.

12:6 Everyone has some gift that can be used for the benefit of the community. When the instruction on justification through faith is correctly grasped, the possessor of a gift will understand that it is not an instrument of self-aggrandizement. Possession of a gift is not an index to quality of faith. Rather, the gift is a challenge to faithful use.

z: Is 27:9; Jer 31:33–34. *a:* 15:8; 1 Thes 2:15–16. *b:* 9:6; Nm 23:19; Is 54:10. *c:* Gal 3:22; 1 Tm 2:4. *d:* Jb 11:7–8; Ps 139:6, 17–18; Wis 17:1; Is 55:8–9. *e:* Jb 15:8; Wis 9:13; Is 40:13; Jer 23:18; 1 Cor 2:11–16. *f:* Jb 41:3; Is 40:14. *g:* 1 Cor 8:6; Col 1:16–17. *h:* 2 Cor 1:3 / 6:13; 1 Pt 2:5. *i:* Eph 4:17, 22–23; 1 Pt 1:14 / Eph 5:10, 17; Phil 1:10. *j:* 15:15 / Phil 2:3 / 1 Cor 12:11; Eph 4:7. *k:* 1 Cor 12:12, 27; Eph 4:25. *l:* 1 Cor 12:4–11, 28–31; Eph 4:7–12; 1 Pt 4:10–11 / 2 Cor 9:7.

them: if prophecy, in proportion to the faith; [7]if ministry, in ministering; if one is a teacher, in teaching; [8*]if one exhorts, in exhortation; if one contributes, in generosity; if one is over others, with diligence; if one does acts of mercy, with cheerfulness.

Mutual Love. [9m]Let love be sincere; hate what is evil, hold on to what is good; [10n]love one another with mutual affection; anticipate one another in showing honor. [11o]Do not grow slack in zeal, be fervent in spirit, serve the Lord. [12p]Rejoice in hope, endure in affliction, persevere in prayer. [13q]Contribute to the needs of the holy ones, exercise hospitality. [14rs*]Bless those who persecute [you], bless and do not curse them. [15t]Rejoice with those who rejoice, weep with those who weep. [16u]Have the same regard for one another; do not be haughty but associate with the lowly; do not be wise in your own estimation. [17v]Do not repay anyone evil for evil; be concerned for what is noble in the sight of all. [18w]If possible, on your part, live at peace with all. [19x]Beloved, do not look for revenge but leave room for the wrath; for it is written, "Vengeance is mine, I will repay, says the Lord." [20y]Rather, "if your enemy is hungry, feed him; if he is thirsty, give him something to drink; for by so doing you will heap burning coals upon his head." [21]Do not be conquered by evil but conquer evil with good.

CHAPTER 13

See RG 448

Obedience to Authority. [1z*]Let every person be subordinate to the higher authorities, for there is no authority except from God, and those that exist have been established by God. [2]Therefore, whoever resists authority opposes what God has appointed, and those who oppose it will bring judgment upon themselves. [3a]For rulers are not a cause of fear to good conduct, but to evil. Do you wish to have no fear of authority? Then do what is good and you will receive approval from it, [4b]for it is a servant of God for your good. But if you do evil, be afraid, for it does not bear the sword without purpose; it is the servant of God to inflict wrath on the evildoer. [5c]Therefore, it is necessary to be subject not only because of the wrath but also because of conscience. [6]This is why you also pay taxes, for the authorities are ministers of God, devoting themselves to this very thing. [7d]Pay to all their dues, taxes to whom taxes are due, toll to whom toll is due, respect to whom respect is due, honor to whom honor is due.

Love Fulfills the Law. [8e*]Owe nothing to anyone, except to love one another; for the

12:8 Over others: usually taken to mean "rule over" but possibly "serve as a patron." Wealthier members in Greco-Roman communities were frequently asked to assist in public service projects. In view of the references to contributing **in generosity** and to **acts of mercy**, Paul may have in mind people like Phoebe (Rom 16:1–2), who is called a **benefactor** (or "patron") because of the services she rendered to many Christians, including Paul.

12:14–21 Since God has justified the believers, it is not necessary for them to take justice into their own hands by taking vengeance. God will ultimately deal justly with all, including those who inflict injury on the believers. This question of personal rights as a matter of justice prepares the way for more detailed consideration of the state as adjudicator.

13:1–7 Paul must come to grips with the problem raised by a message that declares people free from the law. How are they to relate to Roman authority? The problem was exacerbated by the fact that imperial protocol was interwoven with devotion to various deities. Paul builds on the traditional instruction exhibited in Wis 6:1–3, according to which kings and magistrates rule by consent of God. From this perspective, then, believers who render obedience to the governing authorities are obeying the one who is highest in command. At the same time, it is recognized that Caesar has the responsibility to make just ordinances and to commend uprightness; cf. Wis 6:4–21. That Caesar is not entitled to obedience when such obedience would nullify God's prior claim to the believers' moral decision becomes clear in the light of the following verses.

13:8–10 When love directs the Christian's moral decisions, the interest of law in basic concerns, such as familial relationships, sanctity of life, and security of property, is safeguarded (Rom 13:9). Indeed, says Paul, the same applies to any **other commandment** (Rom 13:9), whether one in the Mosaic code or one drawn up by local magistrates under imperial authority. Love anticipates the purpose of public legislation, namely, to secure the best interests of the citizenry. Since Caesar's obligation is to punish the wrongdoer (Rom 13:4), the Christian who acts in love is free from all legitimate indictment.

m: 2 Cor 6:6; 1 Tm 1:5; 1 Pt 1:22 / Am 5:15. *n:* Jn 13:34; 1 Thes 4:9; 1 Pt 2:17; 2 Pt 1:7 / Phil 2:3. *o:* Acts 18:25. *p:* 5:2–3; Col 4:2; 1 Thes 5:17. *q:* Heb 13:2; 1 Pt 4:9. *r:* Mt 5:38–48; 1 Cor 4:12; 1 Pt 3:9. *s:* Lk 6:27–28. *t:* Ps 35:13; Sir 7:34; 1 Cor 12:26. *u:* 15:5; Phil 2:2–3 / 11:20; Prv 3:7; Is 5:21. *v:* Prv 3:4; 1 Thes 5:15; 1 Pt 3:9. *w:* Heb 12:14. *x:* Lv 19:18; Dt 32:35, 41; Mt 5:39; 1 Cor 6:6–7; Heb 10:30. *y:* Prv 25:21–22; Mt 5:44. *z:* Prv 8:15–16; Wis 6:3; Jn 19:11; 1 Pt 2:13–17; Ti 3:1. *a:* 1 Pt 2:13–14; 3:13. *b:* 12:19. *c:* 1 Pt 2:19. *d:* Mt 22:21; Mk 12:17; Lk 20:25. *e:* Jn 13:34; Gal 5:14.

one who loves another has fulfilled the law. [9f]The commandments, “You shall not commit adultery; you shall not kill; you shall not steal; you shall not covet,” and whatever other commandment there may be, are summed up in this saying, [namely] “You shall love your neighbor as yourself.” [10g]Love does no evil to the neighbor; hence, love is the fulfillment of the law.

Awareness of the End of Time. [11h*]And do this because you know the time; it is the hour now for you to awake from sleep. For our salvation is nearer now than when we first believed; [12i]the night is advanced, the day is at hand. Let us then throw off the works of darkness [and] put on the armor of light; [13j*]let us conduct ourselves properly as in the day, not in orgies and drunkenness, not in promiscuity and licentiousness, not in rivalry and jealousy. [14k]But put on the Lord Jesus Christ, and make no provision for the desires of the flesh.

See RG 448

CHAPTER 14

To Live and Die for Christ. [1lm*]Welcome anyone who is weak in faith, but not for disputes over opinions. [2n]One person believes that one may eat anything, while the weak person eats only vegetables. [3o]The one who eats must not despise the one who abstains, and the one who abstains must not pass judgment on the one who eats; for God has welcomed him. [4p]Who are you to pass judgment on someone else’s servant? Before his own master he stands or falls. And he will be upheld, for the Lord is able to make him stand. [5q*][For] one person considers one day more important than another, while another person considers all days alike. Let everyone be fully persuaded in his own mind. [6]Whoever observes the day, observes it for the Lord. Also whoever eats, eats for the Lord, since he gives thanks to God; while whoever abstains, abstains for the Lord and gives thanks to God. [7]None of us lives for oneself, and no one dies for oneself. [8r*]For if we live, we live for the Lord, and if we die, we die for the Lord; so then, whether we live or die, we are the Lord’s. [9s]For this is why Christ died and came to life, that he might be Lord of both the dead and the living. [10t]Why then do you judge your brother? Or you, why do you look down on your brother? For we shall all stand before the judgment seat of God; [11u]for it is written:

“As I live, says the Lord, every knee
shall bend before me,
and every tongue shall give praise to
God.”

[12v]So [then] each of us shall give an account of himself [to God].

Consideration for the Weak Conscience. [13w]Then let us no longer judge one another, but rather resolve never to put a stumbling block or hindrance in the way of a brother. [14x]I know and am convinced in the Lord

13:11–14 These verses provide the motivation for the love that is encouraged in Rom 13:8–10.

13:13 Let us conduct ourselves properly as in the day: the behavior described in Rom 1:29–30 is now to be reversed. Secular moralists were fond of making references to people who could not wait for nightfall to do their carousing. Paul says that Christians claim to be people of the new day that will dawn with the return of Christ. Instead of planning for nighttime behavior they should be concentrating on conduct that is consonant with avowed interest in the Lord’s return.

14:1–15:6 Since Christ spells termination of the law, which included observance of specific days and festivals as well as dietary instruction, the jettisoning of long-practiced customs was traumatic for many Christians brought up under the Mosaic code. Although Paul acknowledges that in principle no food is a source of moral contamination (Rom 14:14), he recommends that the consciences of Christians who are scrupulous in this regard be respected by other Christians (Rom 14:21). On the other hand, those who have scruples are not to sit in judgment on those who know that the gospel has liberated them from such ordinances (Rom 14:10). See 1 Cor 8; 10.

14:5 Since the problem to be overcome was humanity’s perverted mind or judgment (Rom 1:28), Paul indicates that the mind of the Christian is now able to function with appropriate discrimination (cf. Rom 12:2).

14:8 The Lord: Jesus, our Master. The same Greek word, *kyrios*, was applied to both rulers and holders of slaves. Throughout the Letter to the Romans Paul emphasizes God’s total claim on the believer; see note on Rom 1:1.

f: Ex 20:13–17 / Lv 19:18; Dt 5:17–21; Mt 5:43–44; 19:18–19; 22:39; Mk 12:31; Lk 10:27; Gal 5:14; Jas 2:8. *g:* Mt 22:40; 1 Cor 13:4–7. *h:* Eph 5:8–16; 1 Thes 5:5–7. *i:* Jn 8:12; 1 Thes 5:4–8; 1 Jn 2:8 / 2 Cor 6:7; 10:4; Eph 5:11; 6:13–17. *j:* Lk 21:34; Eph 5:18. *k:* Gal 3:27; 5:16; Eph 4:24; 6:11. *l:* 1 Cor 8:1–13. *m:* 15:1, 7; 1 Cor 9:22. *n:* Gn 1:29; 9:3; 1 Cor 8:1–13; 10:14–33. *o:* Col 2:16. *p:* 2:1; Mt 7:11; Jas 4:11–12. *q:* Gal 4:10. *r:* Lk 20:38; 2 Cor 5:15; Gal 2:20; 1 Thes 5:10. *s:* Acts 10:42. *t:* Acts 17:31; 2 Cor 5:10. *u:* Is 49:18 / Is 45:23; Phil 2:10–11. *v:* Gal 6:5. *w:* 1 Cor 8:9, 13. *x:* Mk 7:5, 20; Acts 10:15; 1 Cor 10:25–27; 1 Tm 4:4.

Jesus that nothing is unclean in itself; still, it is unclean for someone who thinks it unclean. [15y]If your brother is being hurt by what you eat, your conduct is no longer in accord with love. Do not because of your food destroy him for whom Christ died. [16z]So do not let your good be reviled. [17a]For the kingdom of God is not a matter of food and drink, but of righteousness, peace, and joy in the holy Spirit; [18]whoever serves Christ in this way is pleasing to God and approved by others. [19b*]Let us then pursue what leads to peace and to building up one another. [20c]For the sake of food, do not destroy the work of God. Everything is indeed clean, but it is wrong for anyone to become a stumbling block by eating; [21]it is good not to eat meat or drink wine or do anything that causes your brother to stumble. [22]Keep the faith [that] you have to yourself in the presence of God; blessed is the one who does not condemn himself for what he approves. [23d*]But whoever has doubts is condemned if he eats, because this is not from faith; for whatever is not from faith is sin.

CHAPTER 15

See RG 448–49

Patience and Self-Denial. [1e]We who are strong ought to put up with the failings of the weak and not to please ourselves; [2f]let each of us please our neighbor for the good, for building up. [3g*]For Christ did not please himself; but, as it is written, "The insults of those who insult you fall upon me." [4h]For whatever was written previously was written for our instruction, that by endurance and by the encouragement of the scriptures we might have hope. [5i*]May the God of endurance and encouragement grant you to think in harmony with one another, in keeping with Christ Jesus, [6]that with one accord you may with one voice glorify the God and Father of our Lord Jesus Christ.

God's Fidelity and Mercy. [7j*]Welcome one another, then, as Christ welcomed you, for the glory of God. [8k]For I say that Christ became a minister of the circumcised to show God's truthfulness, to confirm the promises to the patriarchs, [9l]but so that the Gentiles might glorify God for his mercy. As it is written:

"Therefore, I will praise you among the Gentiles
and sing praises to your name."

[10m*]And again it says:

"Rejoice, O Gentiles, with his people."

[11n]And again:

"Praise the Lord, all you Gentiles,
and let all the peoples praise him."

[12o]And again Isaiah says:

"The root of Jesse shall come,
raised up to rule the Gentiles;
in him shall the Gentiles hope."

[13p]May the God of hope fill you with all joy and peace in believing, so that you may abound in hope by the power of the holy Spirit.

VII. Conclusion

Apostle to the Gentiles. [14*]I myself am convinced about you, my brothers, that you your-

14:19 some manuscripts, versions, and church Fathers read, "We then pursue . . ."; cf. Rom 5:1.

14:23 Whatever is not from faith is sin: Paul does not mean that all the actions of unbelievers are sinful. He addresses himself to the question of intracommunity living. **Sin** in the singular is the dreadful power described in Rom 5:12–14.

15:3 Liberation from the law of Moses does not make the scriptures of the old covenant irrelevant. Much consolation and motivation for Christian living can be derived from the Old Testament, as in the citation from Ps 69:10. Because this psalm is quoted several times in the New Testament, it has been called indirectly messianic.

15:5 Think in harmony: a Greco-Roman ideal. Not rigid uniformity of thought and expression but thoughtful consideration of other people's views finds expression here.

15:7–13 True oneness of mind is found in pondering the ultimate mission of the church: to bring it about that God's name be glorified throughout the world and that Jesus Christ be universally recognized as God's gift to all humanity. Paul here prepares his addressees for the climactic appeal he is about to make.

15:10 Paul's citation of Dt 32:43 follows the Greek version.

15:14–33 Paul sees himself as apostle and benefactor in

y: 1 Cor 8:11–13. *z:* 2:24; Ti 2:5. *a:* 1 Cor 8:8. *b:* 12:18 / 15:2. *c:* 1 Cor 8:11–13; 10:28–29; Ti 1:15. *d:* Ti 1:15; Jas 4:17. *e:* 14:1–2. *f:* 14:1, 19; 1 Cor 9:19; 10:24, 33. *g:* Ps 69:10. *h:* 4:23–24; 1 Mc 12:9; 1 Cor 10:11; 2 Tm 3:16. *i:* 12:16; Phil 2:2; 4:2. *j:* 14:1. *k:* Mt 15:24 / Mi 7:20; Acts 3:25. *l:* 11:30 / 2 Sm 22:50; Ps 18:50. *m:* Dt 32:43. *n:* Ps 117:1. *o:* Is 11:10; Rev 5:5; 22:16. *p:* 5:1–2.

selves are full of goodness, filled with all knowledge, and able to admonish one another. 15[q]But I have written to you rather boldly in some respects to remind you, because of the grace given me by God 16[r]to be a minister of Christ Jesus to the Gentiles in performing the priestly service of the gospel of God, so that the offering up of the Gentiles may be acceptable, sanctified by the holy Spirit. 17In Christ Jesus, then, I have reason to boast in what pertains to God. 18[s]For I will not dare to speak of anything except what Christ has accomplished through me to lead the Gentiles to obedience by word and deed, 19*by the power of signs and wonders, by the power of the Spirit [of God], so that from Jerusalem all the way around to Illyricum I have finished preaching the gospel of Christ. 20[t]*Thus I aspire to proclaim the gospel not where Christ has already been named, so that I do not build on another's foundation, 21[u]*but as it is written:

> "Those who have never been told of him
> shall see,
> and those who have never heard of
> him shall understand."

Paul's Plans; Need for Prayers. 22That is why I have so often been prevented from coming to you. 23[v]But now, since I no longer have any opportunity in these regions and since I have desired to come to you for many years, 24[w]I hope to see you in passing as I go to Spain and to be sent on my way there by you, after I have enjoyed being with you for a time. 25[x]*Now, however, I am going to Jerusalem to minister to the holy ones. 26[y]*For Macedonia and Achaia have decided to make some contribution for the poor among the holy ones in Jerusalem; 27[z]they decided to do it, and in fact they are indebted to them, for if the Gentiles have come to share in their spiritual blessings, they ought also to serve them in material blessings. 28So when I have completed this and safely handed over this contribution to them, I shall set out by way of you to Spain; 29and I know that in coming to you I shall come in the fullness of Christ's blessing.

30[a]I urge you, [brothers,] by our Lord Jesus Christ and by the love of the Spirit, to join me in the struggle by your prayers to God on my behalf, 31that I may be delivered from the disobedient in Judea, and that my ministry for Jerusalem may be acceptable to the holy ones, 32so that I may come to you with joy by the will of God and be refreshed together with you. 33[b]The God of peace be with all of you. Amen.

CHAPTER 16

See RG 449

Phoebe Commended. 1[c]*I commend to you Phoebe our sister, who is [also] a minister of the church at Cenchreae, 2that you may receive her in the Lord in a manner wor-

the priestly service of the gospel and so sketches plans for a mission in Spain, supported by those in Rome.

15:14 Full of goodness: the opposite of what humanity was filled with according to Rom 1:29–30.

15:19 Illyricum: Roman province northwest of Greece on the eastern shore of the Adriatic.

15:20 I aspire: Paul uses terminology customarily applied to philanthropists. Unlike some philanthropists of his time, Paul does not engage in cheap competition for public acclaim. This explanation of his missionary policy is to assure the Christians in Rome that he is also not planning to remain in that city and build on other people's foundations (cf. 2 Cor 10:12–18). However, he does solicit their help in sending him on his way to Spain, which was considered the limit of the western world. Thus Paul's addressees realize that evangelization may be understood in the broader sense of mission or, as in Rom 1:15, of instruction within the Christian community that derives from the gospel.

15:21 The citation from Is 52:15 concerns the Servant of the Lord. According to Isaiah, the Servant is first of all Israel, which was to bring the knowledge of Yahweh to the nations. In Rom 9–11 Paul showed how Israel failed in this mission. Therefore, he himself undertakes almost singlehandedly Israel's responsibility as the Servant and moves as quickly as possible with the gospel through the Roman empire.

15:25–27 Paul may have viewed the contribution he was gathering from Gentile Christians for the poor in Jerusalem (cf. 2 Cor 8–9) as a fulfillment of the vision of Is 60:5–6. In confidence that the messianic fulfillment was taking place, Paul stresses in Rom 14–16 the importance of harmonious relationships between Jews and Gentiles.

15:26 Achaia: the Roman province of southern Greece.

16:1–23 Some authorities regard these verses as a later addition to the letter, but in general the evidence favors the view that they were included in the original. Paul endeavors through the long list of greetings (Rom 16:3–16, 21–23) to establish strong personal contact with congregations that he has not personally encountered before. The combination of Jewish and Gentile names dramatically attests the unity in the

q: 1:5; 12:3. *r:* 11:13; Phil 2:17. *s:* Acts 15:12; 2 Cor 12:12. *t:* 2 Cor 10:13–18. *u:* Is 52:15. *v:* 1:10–13; Acts 19:21–22. *w:* 1 Cor 16:6. *x:* Acts 19:21; 20:22. *y:* 1 Cor 16:1; 2 Cor 8:1–4; 9:2, 12. *z:* 9:4 / 1 Cor 9:11. *a:* 2 Cor 1:11; Phil 1:27; Col 4:3; 2 Thes 3:1. *b:* 16:20; 2 Cor 13:11; Phil 4:9; 1 Thes 5:23; 2 Thes 3:16; Heb 13:20. *c:* Acts 18:18.

thy of the holy ones, and help her in whatever
she may need from you, for she has been a
benefactor to many and to me as well.

Paul's Greetings. [3d*]Greet Prisca and Aquila, my co-workers in Christ Jesus, [4]who
risked their necks for my life, to whom not
only I am grateful but also all the churches of
the Gentiles; [5e*]greet also the church at their
house. Greet my beloved Epaenetus, who was
the firstfruits in Asia for Christ. [6]Greet Mary,
who has worked hard for you. [7*]Greet Andronicus and Junia, my relatives and my fellow prisoners; they are prominent among the
apostles and they were in Christ before me.
[8]Greet Ampliatus, my beloved in the Lord.
[9]Greet Urbanus, our co-worker in Christ, and
my beloved Stachys. [10]Greet Apelles, who is
approved in Christ. Greet those who belong to
the family of Aristobulus. [11]Greet my relative
Herodion. Greet those in the Lord who belong
to the family of Narcissus. [12]Greet those
workers in the Lord, Tryphaena and Tryphosa.
Greet the beloved Persis, who has worked
hard in the Lord. [13f*]Greet Rufus, chosen in
the Lord, and his mother and mine. [14]Greet
Asyncritus, Phlegon, Hermes, Patrobas, Her-
mas, and the brothers who are with them.
[15]Greet Philologus, Julia, Nereus and his sister, and Olympas, and all the holy ones who
are with them. [16g]Greet one another with a
holy kiss. All the churches of Christ greet you.

Against Factions. [17h*]I urge you, brothers,
to watch out for those who create dissensions
and obstacles, in opposition to the teaching
that you learned; avoid them. [18i]For such
people do not serve our Lord Christ but their
own appetites, and by fair and flattering
speech they deceive the hearts of the innocent. [19j]For while your obedience is known
to all, so that I rejoice over you, I want you to
be wise as to what is good, and simple as to
what is evil; [20k*]then the God of peace will
quickly crush Satan under your feet. The
grace of our Lord Jesus be with you.

Greetings from Corinth. [21l]Timothy, my
co-worker, greets you; so do Lucius and Jason and Sosipater, my relatives. [22]I, Tertius,
the writer of this letter, greet you in the
Lord. [23m*]Gaius, who is host to me and to
the whole church, greets you. Erastus, the
city treasurer, and our brother Quartus greet
you. [24]*

Doxology. [[25 n*]Now to him who can
strengthen you, according to my gospel and
the proclamation of Jesus Christ, according
to the revelation of the mystery kept secret
for long ages [26o]but now manifested through
the prophetic writings and, according to the
command of the eternal God, made known
to all nations to bring about the obedience of
faith, [27p]to the only wise God, through Jesus
Christ be glory forever and ever. Amen.]

gospel that transcends previous barriers of nationality, religious ceremony, or racial status.

16:1 Minister: in Greek, *diakonos*; see note on Phil 1:1.

16:3 Prisca and Aquila: presumably the couple mentioned at Acts 18:2; 1 Cor 16:19; 2 Tm 4:19.

16:5 The church at their house: i.e., that meets there. Such local assemblies (cf. 1 Cor 16:19; Col 4:15; Phlm 2) might consist of only one or two dozen Christians each. It is understandable, therefore, that such smaller groups might experience difficulty in relating to one another on certain issues. **Firstfruits**: cf. Rom 8:23; 11:16; 1 Cor 16:15.

16:7 The name Junia is a woman's name. One ancient Greek manuscript and a number of ancient versions read the name "Julia." Most editors have interpreted it as a man's name, Junias.

16:13 This Rufus cannot be identified to any degree of certainty with the Rufus of Mk 15:21.

16:17–18 Paul displays genuine concern for the congregations in Rome by warning them against self-seeking teachers. It would be a great loss, he intimates, if their obedience, which is known to all (cf. Rom 1:8), would be diluted.

16:20 This verse contains the only mention of Satan in Romans.

16:23 This Erastus is not necessarily to be identified with the Erastus of Acts 19:22 or of 2 Tm 4:20.

16:24 Some manuscripts add, similarly to Rom 16:20, "The grace of our Lord Jesus Christ be with you all. Amen."

16:25–27 This doxology is assigned variously to the end of Rom 14; 15; 16 in the manuscript tradition. Some manuscripts omit it entirely. Whether written by Paul or not, it forms an admirable conclusion to the letter at this point.

16:25 Paul's gospel reveals **the mystery kept secret for long ages**: justification and salvation through faith, with all the implications for Jews and Gentiles that Paul has developed in the letter.

d: Acts 18:2, 18–26; 1 Cor 16:19; 2 Tm 4:19. *e:* 1 Cor 16:19; Col 4:15; Phlm 2 / 1 Cor 16:15. *f:* Mk 15:21. *g:* 1 Cor 16:20; 2 Cor 13:12; 1 Thes 5:26; 1 Pt 5:14. *h:* Mt 7:15; Ti 3:10. *i:* Phil 3:18–19; Col 2:4; 2 Pt 2:3. *j:* 1:8; Mt 10:16; 1 Cor 14:20. *k:* 15:33; Gn 3:15; Lk 10:19 / 1 Cor 16:23; 1 Thes 5:28; 2 Thes 3:18. *l:* Acts 16:1–2; 19:22; 20:4; 1 Cor 4:17; 16:10; Phil 2:19–22; Heb 13:23. *m:* Acts 19:29; 1 Cor 1:14 / 2 Tm 4:20. *n:* 1 Cor 2:7; Eph 1:9; 3:3–9; Col 1:26. *o:* 2 Tm 1:10 / 1:5; Eph 3:4–5, 9; 1 Pt 1:20. *p:* 11:36; Gal 1:5; Eph 3:20–21; Phil 4:20; 1 Tm 1:17; 2 Tm 4:18; Heb 13:21; 1 Pt 4:11; 2 Pt 3:18; Jude 25; Rev 1:6.

See RG 450–58

The First Letter to the Corinthians

Paul's first letter to the church of Corinth provides us with a fuller insight into the life of an early Christian community of the first generation than any other book of the New Testament. Through it we can glimpse both the strengths and the weaknesses of this small group in a great city of the ancient world, men and women who had accepted the good news of Christ and were now trying to realize in their lives the implications of their baptism. Paul, who had founded the community and continued to look after it as a father, responds both to questions addressed to him and to situations of which he had been informed. In doing so, he reveals much about himself, his teaching, and the way in which he conducted his work of apostleship. Some things are puzzling because we have the correspondence only in one direction. For the person studying this letter, it seems to raise as many questions as it answers, but without it our knowledge of church life in the middle of the first century would be much poorer.

Paul established a Christian community in Corinth about the year 51, on his second missionary journey. The city, a commercial crossroads, was a melting pot full of devotees of various pagan cults and marked by a measure of moral depravity not unusual in a great seaport. The Acts of the Apostles suggests that moderate success attended Paul's efforts among the Jews in Corinth at first, but that they soon turned against him (Acts 18:1–8). More fruitful was his year and a half spent among the Gentiles (Acts 18:11), which won to the faith many of the city's poor and underprivileged (1 Cor 1:26). After his departure the eloquent Apollos, an Alexandrian Jewish Christian, rendered great service to the community, expounding "from the scriptures that the Messiah is Jesus" (Acts 18:24–28).

While Paul was in Ephesus on his third journey (1 Cor 16:8; Acts 19:1–20), he received disquieting news about Corinth. The community there was displaying open factionalism, as certain members were identifying themselves exclusively with individual Christian leaders and interpreting Christian teaching as a superior wisdom for the initiated few (1 Cor 1:10–4:21). The community lacked the decisiveness to take appropriate action against one of its members who was living publicly in an incestuous union (1 Cor 5:1–13). Other members engaged in legal conflicts in pagan courts of law (1 Cor 6:1–11); still others may have participated in religious prostitution (1 Cor 6:12–20) or temple sacrifices (1 Cor 10:14–22).

The community's ills were reflected in its liturgy. In the celebration of the Eucharist certain members discriminated against others, drank too freely at the agape, or fellowship meal, and denied Christian social courtesies to the poor among the membership (1 Cor 11:17–22). Charisms such as ecstatic prayer, attributed freely to the impulse of the holy Spirit, were more highly prized than works of charity (1 Cor 13:1–2, 8), and were used at times in a disorderly way (1 Cor 14:1–40). Women appeared at the assembly without the customary head-covering (1 Cor 11:3–16), and perhaps were quarreling over their right to address the assembly (1 Cor 14:34–35).

Still other problems with which Paul had to deal concerned matters of conscience discussed among the faithful members of the community: the eating of meat that had been sacrificed to idols (1 Cor 8:1–13), the use of sex in marriage (1 Cor 7:1–7), and the attitude to be taken by the unmarried toward marriage in view of the possible proximity of Christ's second coming (1 Cor 7:25–40). There was also a doctrinal matter that called for Paul's attention, for some members of the community, despite their belief in the resurrection of Christ, were denying the possibility of general bodily resurrection.

To treat this wide spectrum of questions, Paul wrote this letter from Ephesus about the year 56. The majority of the Corinthian Christians may well have been quite faithful. Paul writes on their behalf to guard against the threats posed to the community by the views and conduct of various minorities. He writes with confidence in the authority of his apostolic mission, and he presumes that the Corinthians, despite their deficiencies, will recognize and accept it. On the other hand, he does not hesitate to exercise his authority as his judgment dictates in each situation, even going so far as to promise a direct confrontation with recalcitrants, should the abuses he scores remain uncorrected (1 Cor 4:18–21).

The letter illustrates well the mind and character of Paul. Although he is impelled to insist on his office as founder of the community, he recognizes that he is only one servant of God among many and generously acknowledges the labors of Apollos (1 Cor 3:5–8). He provides us in this letter with many valuable examples of his method of theological reflection and exposition. He always treats the questions at issue on the level of the purity of Christian teaching and conduct. Certain passages of the letter are of the greatest importance for the understanding of early Christian teaching on the Eucharist (1 Cor 10:14–22; 11:17–34) and on the resurrection of the body (1 Cor 15:1–58).

Paul's authorship of 1 Corinthians, apart from a few verses that some regard as later interpolations, has never been seriously questioned. Some scholars have proposed, however, that the letter as we have it contains portions of more than one original Pauline letter. We know that Paul wrote at least two other letters to Corinth (see 1 Cor 5:9; 2 Cor 2:3–4) in addition to the two that we now have; this theory holds that the additional letters are actually contained within the two canonical ones. Most commentators, however, find 1 Corinthians quite understandable as a single coherent work.

The principal divisions of the First Letter to the Corinthians are the following:

- I. Address (1:1–9)
- II. Disorders in the Corinthian Community (1:10–6:20)
  - A. Divisions in the Church (1:10–4:21)
  - B. Moral Disorders (5:1–6:20)
- III. Answers to the Corinthians' Questions (7:1–11:1)
  - A. Marriage and Virginity (7:1–40)
  - B. Offerings to Idols (8:1–11:1)
- IV. Problems in Liturgical Assemblies (11:2–14:40)
  - A. Women's Headdresses (11:3–16)
  - B. The Lord's Supper (11:17–34)
  - C. Spiritual Gifts (12:1–14:40)
- V. The Resurrection (15:1–58)
  - A. The Resurrection of Christ (15:1–11)
  - B. The Resurrection of the Dead (15:12–34)
  - C. The Manner of the Resurrection (15:35–58)
- VI. Conclusion (16:1–24)

I. Address

CHAPTER 1

See RG 452-53

Greeting. [1a*]Paul, called to be an
apostle of Christ Jesus by the will of God,
and Sosthenes our brother, [2b]to the church
of God that is in Corinth, to you who have
been sanctified in Christ Jesus, called to be
holy, with all those everywhere who call
upon the name of our Lord Jesus Christ,
their Lord and ours. [3]Grace to you and
peace from God our Father and the Lord
Jesus Christ.

Thanksgiving. [4]I give thanks to my God
always on your account for the grace of God
bestowed on you in Christ Jesus, [5]that in him
you were enriched in every way, with all discourse and all knowledge, [6*]as the testimony
to Christ was confirmed among you, [7c]so
that you are not lacking in any spiritual gift
as you wait for the revelation of our Lord
Jesus Christ. [8d]He will keep you firm to the
end, irreproachable on the day of our Lord
Jesus [Christ]. [9e]God is faithful, and by him
you were called to fellowship with his Son,
Jesus Christ our Lord.

II. Disorders in the Corinthian Community

A. Divisions in the Church

Groups and Slogans. [10f*]I urge you, brothers, in the name of our Lord Jesus Christ,

1:1–9 Paul follows the conventional form for the opening of a Hellenistic letter (cf. Rom 1:1–7), but expands the opening with details carefully chosen to remind the readers of their situation and to suggest some of the issues the letter will discuss.

1:1 Called . . . by the will of God: Paul's mission and the church's existence are grounded in God's initiative. God's call, grace, and fidelity are central ideas in this introduction, emphasized by repetition and wordplays in the Greek.

1:6 The testimony: this defines the purpose of Paul's mission (see also 1 Cor 15:15 and the note on 1 Cor 2:1). The forms of his testimony include oral preaching and instruction, his letters, and the life he leads as an apostle.

1:10–4:21 The first problem Paul addresses is that of divisions within the community. Although we are unable to

a: Rom 1:1. *b:* Acts 18:1–11. *c:* Ti 2:13. *d:* Phil 1:6. *e:* 1 Jn 1:3. *f:* Phil 2:2.

that all of you agree in what you say, and
that there be no divisions among you, but
that you be united in the same mind and in
the same purpose. [11]For it has been reported
to me about you, my brothers, by Chloe's
people, that there are rivalries among you.
[12g*]I mean that each of you is saying, "I belong to Paul," or "I belong to Apollos," or
"I belong to Cephas," or "I belong to
Christ." [13*]Is Christ divided? Was Paul crucified for you? Or were you baptized in the
name of Paul? [14h]I give thanks [to God] that
I baptized none of you except Crispus and
Gaius, [15]so that no one can say you were
baptized in my name. [16i](I baptized the
household of Stephanas also; beyond that I
do not know whether I baptized anyone
else.) [17j*]For Christ did not send me to baptize but to preach the gospel, and not with
the wisdom of human eloquence, so that the
cross of Christ might not be emptied of its
meaning.

Paradox of the Cross. [18k]The message of
the cross is foolishness to those who are perishing, but to us who are being saved it is the
power of God. [19l]For it is written:

"I will destroy the wisdom of the wise,
and the learning of the learned I will
set aside."

[20m]Where is the wise one? Where is the
scribe? Where is the debater of this age? Has
not God made the wisdom of the world foolish? [21*]For since in the wisdom of God the
world did not come to know God through
wisdom, it was the will of God through the
foolishness of the proclamation to save
those who have faith. [22n]For Jews demand
signs and Greeks look for wisdom, [23o]but we
proclaim Christ crucified, a stumbling block
to Jews and foolishness to Gentiles, [24]but to
those who are called, Jews and Greeks alike,
Christ the power of God and the wisdom of
God. [25]For the foolishness of God is wiser
than human wisdom, and the weakness of
God is stronger than human strength.

The Corinthians and Paul. [26*]Consider
your own calling, brothers. Not many of you
were wise by human standards, not many
were powerful, not many were of noble birth.
[27p]Rather, God chose the foolish of the world
to shame the wise, and God chose the weak

reconstruct the situation in Corinth completely, Paul clearly traces the divisions back to a false self-image on the part of the Corinthians, coupled with a false understanding of the apostles who preached to them (cf. 1 Cor 4:6, 9; 9:1–5) and of the Christian message itself. In these chapters he attempts to deal with those underlying factors and to bring the Corinthians back to a more correct perspective.

1:12 I belong to: the activities of Paul and Apollos in Corinth are described in Acts 18. **Cephas** (i.e., "the Rock," a name by which Paul designates Peter also in 1 Cor 3:22; 9:5; 15:5 and in Gal 1:18; 2:9, 11, 14) may well have passed through Corinth; he could have baptized some members of the community either there or elsewhere. The reference to **Christ** may be intended ironically here.

1:13–17 The reference to baptism and the contrast with preaching the gospel in v 17a suggest that some Corinthians were paying special allegiance to the individuals who initiated them into the community.

1:17b–18 The basic theme of 1 Cor 1–4 is announced. Adherence to individual leaders has something to do with differences in rhetorical ability and also with certain presuppositions regarding wisdom, eloquence, and effectiveness (power), which Paul judges to be in conflict with the gospel and the cross.

1:17b Not with the wisdom of human eloquence: both of the nouns employed here involve several levels of meaning, on which Paul deliberately plays as his thought unfolds. **Wisdom** (*sophia*) may be philosophical and speculative, but in biblical usage the term primarily denotes practical knowledge such as is demonstrated in the choice and effective application of means to achieve an end. The same term can designate the arts of building (cf. 1 Cor 3:10) or of persuasive speaking (cf. 1 Cor 2:4) or effectiveness in achieving salvation. **Eloquence** (*logos*): this translation emphasizes one possible meaning of the term *logos* (cf. the references to rhetorical style and persuasiveness in 1 Cor 2:1, 4). But the term itself may denote an internal reasoning process, plan, or intention, as well as an external word, speech, or message. So by his expression *ouk en sophia logou* in the context of gospel preaching, Paul may intend to exclude both human ways of reasoning or thinking about things and human rhetorical technique. **Human**: this adjective does not stand in the Greek text but is supplied from the context. Paul will begin immediately to distinguish between *sophia* and *logos* from their divine counterparts and play them off against each other.

1:21–25 True wisdom and power are to be found paradoxically where one would least expect them, in the place of their apparent negation. To human eyes the crucified Christ symbolizes impotence and absurdity.

1:26–2:5 The pattern of God's wisdom and power is exemplified in their own experience, if they interpret it rightly (1 Cor 1:26–31), and can also be read in their experience of Paul as he first appeared among them preaching the gospel (1 Cor 2:1–5).

---

g: 3:4, 22; 16:12; Acts 18:24–28. *h:* Acts 18:8 / Rom 16:23. *i:* 16:15–17. *j:* 2:1, 4. *k:* 2:14 / Rom 1:16. *l:* Is 29:14. *m:* Is 19:12. *n:* Mt 12:38; 16:1 / Acts 17:18–21. *o:* 2:2; Gal 3:1 / Gal 5:11. *p:* Jas 2:5.

of the world to shame the strong, [28]and God chose the lowly and despised of the world, those who count for nothing, to reduce to nothing those who are something, [29q*]so that no human being might boast before God. [30r]It is due to him that you are in Christ Jesus, who became for us wisdom from God, as well as righteousness, sanctification, and redemption, [31s]so that, as it is written, "Whoever boasts, should boast in the Lord."

CHAPTER 2

See RG 452–53

[1t*]When I came to you, brothers, proclaiming the mystery of God, I did not come with sublimity of words or of wisdom. [2u]For I resolved to know nothing while I was with you except Jesus Christ, and him crucified. [3*]I came to you in weakness and fear and much trembling, [4v*]and my message and my proclamation were not with persuasive [words of] wisdom, but with a demonstration of spirit and power, [5w]so that your faith might rest not on human wisdom but on the power of God.

The True Wisdom. [6*]Yet we do speak a wisdom to those who are mature, but not a wisdom of this age, nor of the rulers of this age who are passing away. [7*]Rather, we speak God's wisdom, mysterious, hidden, which God predetermined before the ages for our glory, [8*]and which none of the rulers of this age knew; for, if they had known it, they would not have crucified the Lord of glory. [9x]But as it is written:

"What eye has not seen, and ear has not heard,
and what has not entered the human heart,
what God has prepared for those who love him,"

[10y]this God has revealed to us through the Spirit.

For the Spirit scrutinizes everything, even the depths of God. [11]Among human beings, who knows what pertains to a person except the spirit of the person that is within? Similarly, no one knows what pertains to God except the Spirit of God. [12]We have not received the spirit of the world but the Spirit that is from God, so that we may understand the things freely given us by God. [13*]And we speak about them not with words taught by

1:29–31 "Boasting (about oneself)" is a Pauline expression for the radical sin, the claim to autonomy on the part of a creature, the illusion that we live and are saved by our own resources. "Boasting in the Lord" (1 Cor 1:31), on the other hand, is the acknowledgment that we live only from God and for God.

2:1 The mystery of God: God's secret, known only to himself, is his plan for the salvation of his people; it is clear from 1 Cor 1:18–25; 2:2, 8–10 that this secret involves Jesus and the cross. In place of **mystery**, other good manuscripts read "testimony" (cf. 1 Cor 1:6).

2:3 The **weakness** of the crucified Jesus is reflected in Paul's own bearing (cf. 2 Cor 10–13). **Fear and much trembling**: reverential fear based on a sense of God's transcendence permeates Paul's existence and preaching. Compare his advice to the Philippians to work out their salvation with "fear and trembling" (Phil 2:12), because God is at work in them just as his exalting power was paradoxically at work in the emptying, humiliation, and obedience of Jesus to death on the cross (Phil 2:6–11).

2:4 Among many manuscript readings here the best is either "not with the persuasion of wisdom" or "not with persuasive words of wisdom," which differ only by a nuance. Whichever reading is accepted, the inefficacy of human wisdom for salvation is contrasted with the power of the cross.

2:6–3:4 Paul now asserts paradoxically what he has previously been denying. To the Greeks who "are looking for wisdom" (1 Cor 1:22), he does indeed bring a wisdom, but of a higher order and an entirely different quality, the only wisdom really worthy of the name. The Corinthians would be able to grasp Paul's preaching as wisdom and enter into a wisdom-conversation with him if they were more open to the Spirit and receptive to the new insight and language that the Spirit teaches.

2:7–10a God's wisdom: his plan for our salvation. This was his own eternal secret that no one else could fathom, but in this new age of salvation he has graciously revealed it to us. For the pattern of God's secret, hidden to others and now revealed to the Church, cf. also Rom 11:25–36; 16:25–27; Eph 1:3–10; 3:3–11; Col 1:25–28.

2:8 The rulers of this age: this suggests not only the political leaders of the Jews and Romans under whom Jesus was crucified (cf. Acts 4:25–28) but also the cosmic powers behind them (cf. Eph 1:20–23; 3:10). **They would not have crucified the Lord of glory**: they became the unwitting executors of God's plan, which will paradoxically bring about their own conquest and submission (1 Cor 15:24–28).

2:13 In spiritual terms: the Spirit teaches spiritual people a new mode of perception (1 Cor 2:12) and an appropriate language by which they can share their self-understanding, their knowledge about what God has done in them. The final phrase in 1 Cor 2:13 can also be translated "describing spiritual realities to spiritual people," in which case it prepares for 1 Cor 2:14–16.

q: Eph 2:9. *r:* Rom 4:17 / 6:11; Rom 3:24–26; 2 Cor 5:21 / Eph 1:7; Col 1:14; 1 Thes 5:23. *s:* Jer 9:23; 2 Cor 10:17. *t:* 1:17. *u:* 1:23; Gal 6:14. *v:* 4:20; Rom 15:19; 1 Thes 1:5. *w:* 2 Cor 4:7. *x:* Is 64:3. *y:* Mt 11:25; 13:11; 16:17.

human wisdom, but with words taught by the Spirit, describing spiritual realities in spiritual terms.

[14]*Now the natural person does not accept what pertains to the Spirit of God, for to him it is foolishness, and he cannot understand it, because it is judged spiritually. [15]*The spiritual person, however, can judge everything but is not subject to judgment by anyone.

[16z]For "who has known the mind of the Lord, so as to counsel him?" But we have the mind of Christ.

CHAPTER 3

See RG 452–53

[1]*Brothers, I could not talk to you as spiritual people, but as fleshly people, as infants in Christ. [2a]I fed you milk, not solid food, because you were unable to take it. Indeed, you are still not able, even now, [3b]*for you are still of the flesh. While there is jealousy and rivalry among you, are you not of the flesh and behaving in an ordinary human way? [4c]Whenever someone says, "I belong to Paul," and another, "I belong to Apollos," are you not merely human?

The Role of God's Ministers. [5]*What is Apollos, after all, and what is Paul? Ministers through whom you became believers, just as the Lord assigned each one. [6d]I planted, Apollos watered, but God caused the growth. [7]Therefore, neither the one who plants nor the one who waters is anything, but only God, who causes the growth. [8]The one who plants and the one who waters are equal, and each will receive wages in proportion to his labor. [9e]For we are God's co-workers; you are God's field, God's building.

[10]*According to the grace of God given to me, like a wise master builder I laid a foundation, and another is building upon it. But each one must be careful how he builds upon it, [11]for no one can lay a foundation other than the one that is there, namely, Jesus Christ. [12]If anyone builds on this foundation with gold, silver, precious stones, wood, hay, or straw, [13f]*the work of each will come to light, for the Day will disclose it. It will be revealed with fire, and the fire [itself] will test the quality of each one's work. [14]If the work stands that someone built upon the foundation, that person will receive a wage. [15]*But if someone's work is burned up, that

2:14 The natural person: see note on 1 Cor 3:1.

2:15 The spiritual person . . . is not subject to judgment: since spiritual persons have been given knowledge of what pertains to God (1 Cor 2:11–12), they share in God's own capacity to judge. One to whom the mind of the Lord (and of Christ) is revealed (1 Cor 2:16) can be said to share in some sense in God's exemption from counseling and criticism.

3:1–4 The Corinthians desire a sort of wisdom dialogue or colloquy with Paul; they are looking for solid, adult food, and he appears to disappoint their expectations. Paul counters: if such a dialogue has not yet taken place, the reason is that they are still at an immature stage of development (cf. 1 Cor 2:6).

3:1 Spiritual people . . . fleshly people: Paul employs two clusters of concepts and terms to distinguish what later theology will call the "natural" and the "supernatural." (1) The natural person (1 Cor 2:14) is one whose existence, perceptions, and behavior are determined by purely natural principles, the *psychē* (1 Cor 2:14) and the *sarx* (flesh, a biblical term that connotes creatureliness, 1 Cor 3:1, 3). Such persons are only infants (1 Cor 3:1); they remain on a purely human level (*anthrōpoi*, 1 Cor 3:4). (2) On the other hand, they are called to be animated by a higher principle, the **pneuma**, God's spirit. They are to become spiritual (*pneumatikoi*, 1 Cor 3:1) and mature (1 Cor 2:6) in their perceptions and behavior (cf. Gal 5:16–26). The culmination of existence in the Spirit is described in 1 Cor 15:44–49.

3:3–4 Jealousy, rivalry, and divisions in the community are symptoms of their arrested development; they reveal the immaturity both of their self-understanding (1 Cor 3:4) and of the judgments about their apostles (1 Cor 3:21).

3:5–4:5 The Corinthians tend to evaluate their leaders by the criteria of human wisdom and to exaggerate their importance. Paul views the role of the apostles in the light of his theology of spiritual gifts (cf. 1 Cor 12–14, where the charism of the apostle heads the lists). The essential aspects of all spiritual gifts (1 Cor 12:4–6 presents them as gifts of grace, as services, and as modes of activity) are exemplified by the apostolate, which is a gift of grace (1 Cor 3:10) through which God works (1 Cor 3:9) and a form of service (1 Cor 3:5) for the common good (elsewhere expressed by the verb "build up," suggested here by the image of the building, 1 Cor 3:9). The apostles serve the church, but their accountability is to God and to Christ (1 Cor 4:1–5).

3:5 Ministers: for other expressions of Paul's understanding of himself as minister or steward to the church, cf. 1 Cor 4:1; 9:17, 19–27; 2 Cor 3:6–9; 4:1; 5:18; 6:3–4; and 2 Cor 11:23 (the climax of Paul's defense).

3:10–11 There are diverse functions in the service of the community, but each individual's task is serious, and each will stand accountable for the quality of his contribution.

3:13 The Day: the great day of Yahweh, the day of judgment, which can be a time of either gloom or joy. Fire both destroys and purifies.

3:15 Will be saved: although Paul can envision very harsh divine punishment (cf. 1 Cor 3:17), he appears optimistic about the success of divine corrective means both here and elsewhere (cf. 1 Cor 5:5; 11:32 [discipline]). The text of 1 Cor 3:15 has sometimes been used to support the notion of purgatory, though it does not envisage this.

z: Wis 9:13; Is 40:13; Rom 11:34. *a:* Heb 5:12–14. *b:* Jas 3:13–16. *c:* 1:12. *d:* Acts 18:1–11, 24–28. *e:* Eph 2:20–22; 1 Pt 2:5. *f:* Mt 3:11–12; 2 Thes 1:7–10.

one will suffer loss; the person will be saved,
but only as through fire. [16g]Do you not know
that you are the temple of God, and that the
Spirit of God dwells in you? [17*]If anyone destroys God's temple, God will destroy that
person; for the temple of God, which you
are, is holy.

[18h]Let no one deceive himself. If anyone
among you considers himself wise in this
age, let him become a fool so as to become
wise. [19i]For the wisdom of this world is foolishness in the eyes of God, for it is written:

"He catches the wise in their own ruses,"

[20j]and again:

"The Lord knows the thoughts of the
wise, that they are vain."

[21k*]So let no one boast about human beings,
for everything belongs to you, [22]Paul or Apollos or Cephas, or the world or life or death, or
the present or the future: all belong to you,
[23]and you to Christ, and Christ to God.

CHAPTER 4

See RG 452–53

[1l]Thus should one regard us: as servants of Christ and stewards of the mysteries
of God. [2]Now it is of course required of
stewards that they be found trustworthy. [3]It
does not concern me in the least that I be
judged by you or any human tribunal; I do
not even pass judgment on myself; [4m]I am
not conscious of anything against me, but I
do not thereby stand acquitted; the one who
judges me is the Lord. [5]Therefore, do not
make any judgment before the appointed
time, until the Lord comes, for he will bring
to light what is hidden in darkness and will
manifest the motives of our hearts, and then
everyone will receive praise from God.

Paul's Life as Pattern. [6*]I have applied
these things to myself and Apollos for your
benefit, brothers, so that you may learn from
us not to go beyond what is written, so that
none of you will be inflated with pride in favor of one person over against another. [7]Who
confers distinction upon you? What do you
possess that you have not received? But if
you have received it, why are you boasting as
if you did not receive it? [8*]You are already
satisfied; you have already grown rich; you
have become kings without us! Indeed, I
wish that you had become kings, so that we
also might become kings with you.

[9n*]For as I see it, God has exhibited us
apostles as the last of all, like people sen-

3:17 Holy: i.e., "belonging to God." The cultic sanctity of the community is a fundamental theological reality to which Paul frequently alludes (cf. 1 Cor 1:2, 30; 6:11; 7:14).

3:21–23 These verses pick up the line of thought of 1 Cor 1:10–13. If the Corinthians were genuinely wise (1 Cor 3:18–20), their perceptions would be reversed, and they would see everything in the world and all those with whom they exist in the church in their true relations with one another. Paul assigns all the persons involved in the theological universe a position on a scale: God, Christ, church members, church leaders. Read from top to bottom, the scale expresses ownership; read from bottom to top, the obligation to serve. This picture should be complemented by similar statements such as those in 1 Cor 8:6 and 1 Cor 15:20–28.

4:6–21 This is an emotionally charged peroration to the discussion about divisions. It contains several exhortations and statements of Paul's purpose in writing (cf. 1 Cor 4:6, 14–17, 21) that counterbalance the initial exhortation at 1 Cor 1:10.

4:6 That you may learn from us not to go beyond what is written: the words "to go" are not in the Greek, but have here been added as the minimum necessary to elicit sense from this difficult passage. It probably means that the Corinthians should avoid the false wisdom of vain speculation, contenting themselves with Paul's proclamation of the cross, which is the fulfillment of God's promises in the Old Testament (what is written). **Inflated with pride**: literally, "puffed up," i.e., arrogant, filled with a sense of self-importance. The term is particularly Pauline, found in the New Testament only in 1 Cor 4:6, 18–19; 5:2; 8:1; 13:4; Col 2:18 (cf. the related noun at 2 Cor 12:20). It sometimes occurs in conjunction with the theme of "boasting," as in 1 Cor 4:6–7 here.

4:8 Satisfied . . . rich . . . kings: these three statements could also be punctuated as questions continuing the series begun in v 7. In any case these expressions reflect a tendency at Corinth toward an overrealized eschatology, a form of self-deception that draws Paul's irony. The underlying attitude has implications for the Corinthians' thinking about other issues, notably morality and the resurrection, that Paul will address later in the letter.

4:9–13 A rhetorically effective catalogue of the circumstances of apostolic existence, in the course of which Paul ironically contrasts his own sufferings with the Corinthians' illusion that they have passed beyond the folly of the passion and have already reached the condition of glory. His language echoes that of the beatitudes and woes, which assert a future reversal of present conditions. Their present sufferings ("to this very hour," 11) place the apostles in the class of those to whom the beatitudes promise future relief (Mt 5:3–11; Lk 6:20–23); whereas the Corinthians' image of themselves as "already" filled, rich,

g: 6:19; 2 Cor 6:16; Eph 2:20–22. *h:* 8:2; Is 5:21; Gal 6:3. *i:* 1:20 / Jb 5:13. *j:* Ps 94:11. *k:* 4:6 / Rom 8:32. *l:* Ti 1:7; 1 Pt 4:10. *m:* 2 Cor 1:12; Rom 2:16; 2 Cor 5:10. *n:* 15:31; Rom 8:36; 2 Cor 4:8–12; 11:23 / Heb 10:33.

tenced to death, since we have become a spectacle to the world, to angels and human beings alike. [10o]We are fools on Christ's account, but you are wise in Christ; we are weak, but you are strong; you are held in honor, but we in disrepute. [11p]To this very hour we go hungry and thirsty, we are poorly clad and roughly treated, we wander about homeless [12q]and we toil, working with our own hands. When ridiculed, we bless; when persecuted, we endure; [13]when slandered, we respond gently. We have become like the world's rubbish, the scum of all, to this very moment.

[14*]I am writing you this not to shame you, but to admonish you as my beloved children. [15r]Even if you should have countless guides to Christ, yet you do not have many fathers, for I became your father in Christ Jesus through the gospel. [16s]Therefore, I urge you, be imitators of me. [17t]For this reason I am sending you Timothy, who is my beloved and faithful son in the Lord; he will remind you of my ways in Christ [Jesus], just as I teach them everywhere in every church.

[18*]Some have become inflated with pride, as if I were not coming to you. [19]But I will come to you soon, if the Lord is willing, and I shall ascertain not the talk of these inflated people but their power. [20u]For the kingdom of God is not a matter of talk but of power. [21v]Which do you prefer? Shall I come to you with a rod, or with love and a gentle spirit?

B. Moral Disorders

CHAPTER 5

See RG 453

A Case of Incest. [1w*]It is widely reported that there is immorality among you, and immorality of a kind not found even among pagans—a man living with his father's wife. [2*]And you are inflated with pride. Should you not rather have been sorrowful? The one who did this deed should be expelled from your midst. [3x]I, for my part, although absent in body but present in spirit, have already, as if present, pronounced judgment on the one who has committed this deed, [4]in the name of [our] Lord Jesus: when you have gathered together and I am with you in spirit with the power of the Lord Jesus, [5y*]you are to deliver this man to Satan for the destruction of his flesh, so that his spirit may be saved on the day of the Lord.

[6z*]Your boasting is not appropriate. Do you not know that a little yeast leavens all

ruling (1 Cor 4:8), as wise, strong, and honored (1 Cor 4:10) places them paradoxically in the position of those whom the woes threaten with future undoing (Lk 6:24–26). They have lost sight of the fact that the reversal is predicted for the future.

4:14–17 My beloved children: the close of the argument is dominated by the tender metaphor of the father who not only gives his children life but also educates them. Once he has begotten them through his preaching, Paul continues to present the gospel to them existentially, by his life as well as by his word, and they are to learn, as children do, by imitating their parents (1 Cor 4:16). The reference to the **rod** in 1 Cor 4:21 belongs to the same image-complex. So does the image of the **ways** in 1 Cor 4:17: the ways that Paul teaches everywhere, "his ways in Christ Jesus," mean a behavior pattern quite different from the human ways along which the Corinthians are walking (1 Cor 3:3).

4:18–21 1 Cor 4:20 picks up the contrast between a certain kind of talk (*logos*) and true power (*dynamis*) from 1 Cor 1:17–18 and 1 Cor 2:4–5. The kingdom, which many of them imagine to be fully present in their lives (1 Cor 4:8), will be rather unexpectedly disclosed in the strength of Paul's encounter with them, if they make a powerful intervention on his part necessary. Compare the similar ending to an argument in 2 Cor 13:1–4, 10.

5:1–6:20 Paul now takes up a number of other matters that require regulation. These have come to his attention by hearsay (1 Cor 5:1), probably in reports brought by "Chloe's people" (1 Cor 1:11).

5:1–13 Paul first deals with the incestuous union of a man with his stepmother (1 Cor 5:1–8) and then attempts to clarify general admonitions he has given about associating with fellow Christians guilty of immorality (1 Cor 5:9–13). Each of these three brief paragraphs expresses the same idea: the need of separation between the holy and the unholy.

5:2 Inflated with pride: this remark and the reference to **boasting** in 1 Cor 5:6 suggest that they are proud of themselves despite the infection in their midst, tolerating and possibly even approving the situation. The attitude expressed in 1 Cor 6:2, 13 may be influencing their thinking in this case.

5:5 Deliver this man to Satan: once the sinner is expelled from the church, the sphere of Jesus' lordship and victory over sin, he will be in the region outside over which Satan is still master. **For the destruction of his flesh**: the purpose of the penalty is medicinal: through affliction, sin's grip over him may be destroyed and the path to repentance and reunion laid open. With Paul's instructions for an excommunication ceremony here, contrast his recommendations for the reconciliation of a sinner in 2 Cor 2:5–11.

5:6 A little yeast: yeast, which induces fermentation, is a

o: 1:18; 3:18; 2 Cor 11:19 / 2:3; 2 Cor 13:9. *p:* Rom 8:35; 2 Cor 11:23–27. *q:* Acts 9:6–14; 18:3; 20:34; 1 Thes 2:9 / 1 Pt 3:9. *r:* Gal 4:19; Phlm 10. *s:* 11:1; Phil 3:17; 4:9; 1 Thes 1:6; 2 Thes 3:7, 9. *t:* 16:10; Acts 19:22. *u:* 2:4; 1 Thes 1:5. *v:* 2 Cor 1:23; 10:2. *w:* Lv 18:7–8; 20:11; Dt 27:20. *x:* Col 2:5. *y:* 1 Tm 1:20. *z:* Gal 5:9.

the dough? [7a*]Clear out the old yeast, so that
you may become a fresh batch of dough,
inasmuch as you are unleavened. For our
paschal lamb, Christ, has been sacrificed.
[8b]Therefore, let us celebrate the feast, not
with the old yeast, the yeast of malice and
wickedness, but with the unleavened bread
of sincerity and truth.

[9*]I wrote you in my letter not to associate
with immoral people, [10c]not at all referring
to the immoral of this world or the greedy
and robbers or idolaters; for you would then
have to leave the world. [11d]But I now write
to you not to associate with anyone named a
brother, if he is immoral, greedy, an idolater,
a slanderer, a drunkard, or a robber, not even
to eat with such a person. [12]For why should
I be judging outsiders? Is it not your business to judge those within? [13e]God will
judge those outside. "Purge the evil person
from your midst."

See RG 453

CHAPTER 6

Lawsuits before Unbelievers. [1*]How
can any one of you with a case against another dare to bring it to the unjust for judgment instead of to the holy ones? [2f*]Do you
not know that the holy ones will judge the
world? If the world is to be judged by you, are
you unqualified for the lowest law courts?
[3]Do you not know that we will judge angels?
Then why not everyday matters? [4]If, therefore, you have courts for everyday matters, do
you seat as judges people of no standing in
the church? [5]I say this to shame you. Can it be
that there is not one among you wise enough
to be able to settle a case between brothers?
[6]But rather brother goes to court against
brother, and that before unbelievers?

[7g]Now indeed [then] it is, in any case, a failure on your part that you have lawsuits against
one another. Why not rather put up with injustice? Why not rather let yourselves be
cheated? [8]Instead, you inflict injustice and
cheat, and this to brothers. [9h*]Do you not
know that the unjust will not inherit the kingdom of God? Do not be deceived; neither for-
nicators nor idolaters nor adulterers nor boy
prostitutes nor sodomites [10]nor thieves nor the
greedy nor drunkards nor slanderers nor robbers will inherit the kingdom of God. [11i]That
is what some of you used to be; but now you
have had yourselves washed, you were sanctified, you were justified in the name of the
Lord Jesus Christ and in the Spirit of our God.

Sexual Immorality. [12j*]"Everything is

natural symbol for a source of corruption that becomes all-pervasive. The expression is proverbial.

5:7–8 In the Jewish calendar, Passover was followed immediately by the festival of Unleavened Bread. In preparation for this feast all traces of old bread were removed from the house, and during the festival only unleavened bread was eaten. The sequence of these two feasts provides Paul with an image of Christian existence: Christ's death (the true Passover celebration) is followed by the life of the Christian community, marked by newness, purity, and integrity (a perpetual feast of unleavened bread). Paul may have been writing around Passover time (cf. 1 Cor 16:5); this is a little Easter homily, the earliest in Christian literature.

5:9–13 Paul here corrects a misunderstanding of his earlier directives against associating with immoral fellow Christians. He concedes the impossibility of avoiding contact with sinners in society at large but urges the Corinthians to maintain the inner purity of their own community.

6:1–11 Christians at Corinth are suing one another before pagan judges in Roman courts. A barrage of rhetorical questions (1 Cor 6:1–9) betrays Paul's indignation over this practice, which he sees as an infringement upon the holiness of the Christian community. 6:2–3: The principle to which Paul appeals is an eschatological prerogative promised to Christians: they are to share with Christ the judgment of the world (cf. Dn 7:22, 27). Hence they ought to be able to settle minor disputes within the community.

6:9–10 A catalogue of typical vices that exclude from the kingdom of God and that should be excluded from God's church. Such lists (cf. 1 Cor 5:10) reflect the common moral sensibility of the New Testament period.

6:9 The Greek word translated as **boy prostitutes** may refer to catamites, i.e., boys or young men who were kept for purposes of prostitution, a practice not uncommon in the Greco-Roman world. In Greek mythology this was the function of Ganymede, the "cupbearer of the gods," whose Latin name was Catamitus. The term translated **sodomites** refers to adult males who indulged in homosexual practices with such boys. See similar condemnations of such practices in Rom 1:26–27; 1 Tm 1:10.

6:12–20 Paul now turns to the opinion of some Corinthians that sexuality is a morally indifferent area (1 Cor 6:12–13). This leads him to explain the mutual relation between the Lord Jesus and our bodies (1 Cor 6:13b) in a densely packed paragraph that contains elements of a profound theology of sexuality (1 Cor 6:15–20).

6:12–13 Everything is lawful for me: the Corinthians may have derived this slogan from Paul's preaching about Christian freedom, but they mean something different by it:

a: Ex 12:1–13; Dt 16:1–2; 1 Pt 1:19. *b:* Ex 12:15–20; 13:7; Dt 16:3. *c:* 10:27; Jn 17:15. *d:* Mt 18:17; 2 Thes 3:6, 14; 2 Jn 10. *e:* Dt 13:6; 17:7; 22:24. *f:* Wis 3:8; Mt 19:28; Rev 20:4. *g:* Mt 5:38–42; Rom 12:17–21; 1 Thes 5:15. *h:* 15:50; Gal 5:19–21; Eph 5:5. *i:* Ti 3:3–7. *j:* 10:23.

lawful for me," but not everything is beneficial. "Everything is lawful for me," but I will
not let myself be dominated by anything.
[13]"Food for the stomach and the stomach for
food," but God will do away with both the
one and the other. The body, however, is not
for immorality, but for the Lord, and the
Lord is for the body; [14k]God raised the Lord
and will also raise us by his power.

[15l*]Do you not know that your bodies are
members of Christ? Shall I then take Christ's
members and make them the members of a
prostitute? Of course not! [16m][Or] do you not
know that anyone who joins himself to a prostitute becomes one body with her? For "the
two," it says, "will become one flesh." [17n]But
whoever is joined to the Lord becomes one
spirit with him. [18*]Avoid immorality. Every
other sin a person commits is outside the body,
but the immoral person sins against his own
body. [19o*]Do you not know that your body is a
temple of the holy Spirit within you, whom
you have from God, and that you are not your
own? [20p]For you have been purchased at a
price. Therefore glorify God in your body.

III. Answers to the Corinthians' Questions

A. Marriage and Virginity

CHAPTER 7

See RG 453-54

Advice to the Married. [1*]Now in regard to the matters about which you wrote:
"It is a good thing for a man not to touch a
woman," [2]but because of cases of immorality every man should have his own wife, and
every woman her own husband. [3]The husband should fulfill his duty toward his wife,
and likewise the wife toward her husband.
[4]A wife does not have authority over her own
body, but rather her husband, and similarly a
husband does not have authority over his
own body, but rather his wife. [5]Do not deprive each other, except perhaps by mutual
consent for a time, to be free for prayer, but
then return to one another, so that Satan may
not tempt you through your lack of self-control. [6*]This I say by way of concession, however, not as a command. [7q*]Indeed, I wish
everyone to be as I am, but each has a partic-

they consider sexual satisfaction a matter as indifferent as food, and they attribute no lasting significance to bodily functions (1 Cor 6:13a). Paul begins to deal with the slogan by two qualifications, which suggest principles for judging sexual activity. **Not everything is beneficial**: cf. 1 Cor 10:23, and the whole argument of 1 Cor 8–10 on the finality of freedom and moral activity. **Not let myself be dominated**: certain apparently free actions may involve in fact a secret servitude in conflict with the lordship of Jesus.

6:15b–16 A prostitute: the reference may be specifically to religious prostitution, an accepted part of pagan culture at Corinth and elsewhere; but the prostitute also serves as a symbol for any sexual relationship that conflicts with Christ's claim over us individually. **The two . . . will become one flesh**: the text of Gn 2:24 is applied positively to human marriage in Matthew and Mark, and in Eph 5:29–32: love of husband and wife reflect the love of Christ for his church. The application of the text to union with a prostitute is jarring, for such a union is a parody, an antitype of marriage, which does conflict with Christ's claim over us. This explains the horror expressed in 15b.

6:18 Against his own body: expresses the intimacy and depth of sexual disorder, which violates the very orientation of our bodies.

6:19–20 Paul's vision becomes trinitarian. **A temple**: sacred by reason of God's gift, his indwelling Spirit. **Not your own**: but "for the Lord," who acquires ownership by the act of redemption. **Glorify God in your body**: the argument concludes with a positive imperative to supplement the negative "avoid immorality" of 1 Cor 6:18. Far from being a terrain that is morally indifferent, the area of sexuality is one in which our relationship with God (and his Christ and his Spirit) is very intimately expressed: he is either highly glorified or deeply offended.

7:1–40 Paul now begins to answer questions addressed to him by the Corinthians (1 Cor 7:1–11:1). The first of these concerns marriage. This chapter contains advice both to the married (1–16) and to the unmarried (1 Cor 7:25–38) or widowed (1 Cor 7:39–40); these two parts are separated by 1 Cor 7:17–24, which enunciate a principle applicable to both.

7:1–16 It seems that some Christians in Corinth were advocating asceticism in sexual matters. The pattern **it is a good thing . . . , but** occurs twice (1 Cor 7:1–2, 8–9; cf. 1 Cor 7:26), suggesting that in this matter as in others the Corinthians have seized upon a genuine value but are exaggerating or distorting it in some way. Once again Paul calls them to a more correct perspective and a better sense of their own limitations. The phrase it is a **good thing** (1 Cor 7:1) may have been the slogan of the ascetic party at Corinth.

7:1–7 References to Paul's own behavior (1 Cor 7:7–8) suggest that his celibate way of life and his preaching to the unmarried (cf. 1 Cor 7:25–35) have given some the impression that asceticism within marriage, i.e., suspension of normal sexual relations, would be a laudable ideal. Paul points to their experience of widespread immorality to caution them against overestimating their own strength (1 Cor 7:2); as individuals they may not have the particular gift that makes such asceticism feasible (1 Cor 7:7) and hence are to abide by the principle to be explained in 1 Cor 7:17–24.

7:6 By way of concession: this refers most likely to the

k: Rom 8:11; 2 Cor 4:14. *l:* 12:27; Rom 6:12–13; 12:5; Eph 5:30. *m:* Gn 2:24; Mt 19:5; Mk 10:8; Eph 5:31. *n:* Rom 8:9–10; 2 Cor 3:17. *o:* 3:16–17; Rom 5:5. *p:* 3:23; 7:23; Acts 20:28 / Rom 12:1; Phil 1:20. *q:* Mt 19:11–12.

ular gift from God, one of one kind and one of another.

[8r*]Now to the unmarried and to widows I say: It is a good thing for them to remain as they are, as I do, [9]but if they cannot exercise self-control they should marry, for it is better to marry than to be on fire. [10s*]To the married, however, I give this instruction (not I, but the Lord): A wife should not separate from her husband [11]—and if she does separate she must either remain single or become reconciled to her husband—and a husband should not divorce his wife.

[12*]To the rest I say (not the Lord): If any brother has a wife who is an unbeliever, and she is willing to go on living with him, he should not divorce her; [13]and if any woman has a husband who is an unbeliever, and he is willing to go on living with her, she should not divorce her husband. [14t]For the unbelieving husband is made holy through his wife, and the unbelieving wife is made holy through the brother. Otherwise your children would be unclean, whereas in fact they are holy.

[15*]If the unbeliever separates, however, let him separate. The brother or sister is not bound in such cases; God has called you to peace. [16]For how do you know, wife, whether you will save your husband; or how do you know, husband, whether you will save your wife?

The Life That the Lord Has Assigned. [17*]Only, everyone should live as the Lord has assigned, just as God called each one. I give this order in all the churches. [18u]Was someone called after he had been circumcised? He should not try to undo his circumcision. Was an uncircumcised person called? He should not be circumcised. [19v]Circumcision means nothing, and uncircumcision means nothing; what matters is keeping God's commandments. [20]Everyone should remain in the state in which he was called.

[21]Were you a slave when you were called? Do not be concerned but, even if you can gain your freedom, make the most of it. [22w]For the slave called in the Lord is a freed person in the Lord, just as the free person who has been called is a slave of Christ. [23x]You have been purchased at a price. Do not become slaves to human beings. [24]Brothers, everyone should continue before God in the state in which he was called.

Advice to Virgins and Widows. [25*]Now in regard to virgins I have no commandment from the Lord, but I give my opinion as one who by the Lord's mercy is trustworthy. [26y]So this is what I think best because of the present distress: that it is a good thing for a person to remain as he is. [27]Are you bound to a wife? Do not seek a separation. Are you free of a wife? Then do not look for a wife. [28]If you marry, however, you do not sin, nor does an unmarried woman sin if she marries; but such people will experience affliction in their earthly life, and I would like to spare you that.

[29z*]I tell you, brothers, the time is running out. From now on, let those having wives act

concession mentioned in 1 Cor 7:5a: temporary interruption of relations for a legitimate purpose.

7:7 A particular gift from God: use of the term **charisma** suggests that marriage and celibacy may be viewed in the light of Paul's theology of spiritual gifts (1 Cor 7:12–14).

7:8 Paul was obviously unmarried when he wrote this verse. Some interpreters believe that he had previously been married and widowed; there is no clear evidence either for or against this view, which was expressed already at the end of the second century by Clement of Alexandria.

7:10–11 (Not I, but the Lord): Paul reminds the married of Jesus' principle of nonseparation (Mk 10:9). This is one of his rare specific references to the teaching of Jesus.

7:12–14 To the rest: marriages in which only one partner is a baptized Christian. Jesus' prohibition against divorce is not addressed to them, but Paul extends the principle of nonseparation to such unions, provided they are marked by peacefulness and shared sanctification.

7:15–16 If the unbeliever separates: the basis of the "Pauline privilege" in Catholic marriage legislation.

7:17–24 On the ground that distinct human conditions are less significant than the whole new existence opened up by God's call, Paul urges them to be less concerned with changing their states of life than with answering God's call where it finds them. The principle applies both to the married state (1 Cor 7:1–16) and to the unmarried (1 Cor 7:25–38).

7:25–28 Paul is careful to explain that the principle of 1 Cor 7:17 does not bind under sin but that present earthly conditions make it advantageous for the unmarried to remain as they are (1 Cor 7:28). These remarks must be complemented by the statement about "particular gifts" from 1 Cor 7:7.

7:29–31 The world . . . is passing away: Paul advises Christians to go about the ordinary activities of life in a manner different from those who are totally immersed in them and unaware of their transitoriness.

r: 1 Tm 5:11–16 / 9:5. *s:* Mt 5:32; 19:9. *t:* Rom 11:16. *u:* 1 Mc 1:15 / Acts 15:1–2. *v:* Rom 2:25, 29; Gal 5:6; 6:15. *w:* Eph 6:5–9; Col 3:11; Phlm 16. *x:* 6:20. *y:* 8. *z:* Rom 13:11.

as not having them, [30]those weeping as not weeping, those rejoicing as not rejoicing, those buying as not owning, [31]those using the world as not using it fully. For the world in its present form is passing away.

[32]I should like you to be free of anxieties. An unmarried man is anxious about the things of the Lord, how he may please the Lord. [33a]But a married man is anxious about the things of the world, how he may please his wife, [34b]and he is divided. An unmarried woman or a virgin is anxious about the things of the Lord, so that she may be holy in both body and spirit. A married woman, on the other hand, is anxious about the things of the world, how she may please her husband. [35c]I am telling you this for your own benefit, not to impose a restraint upon you, but for the sake of propriety and adherence to the Lord without distraction.

[36*]If anyone thinks he is behaving improperly toward his virgin, and if a critical moment has come and so it has to be, let him do as he wishes. He is committing no sin; let them get married. [37]The one who stands firm in his resolve, however, who is not under compulsion but has power over his own will, and has made up his mind to keep his virgin, will be doing well. [38]So then, the one who marries his virgin does well; the one who does not marry her will do better.

[39d*]A wife is bound to her husband as long as he lives. But if her husband dies, she is free to be married to whomever she wishes, provided that it be in the Lord. [40e]She is more blessed, though, in my opinion, if she remains as she is, and I think that I too have the Spirit of God.

B. Offerings to Idols

CHAPTER 8

See RG 454–55

Knowledge Insufficient. [1f*]Now in regard to meat sacrificed to idols: we realize that "all of us have knowledge"; knowledge inflates with pride, but love builds up. [2]If anyone supposes he knows something, he does not yet know as he ought to know. [3g]But if one loves God, one is known by him.

[4h]So about the eating of meat sacrificed to idols: we know that "there is no idol in the world," and that "there is no God but one." [5]Indeed, even though there are so-called gods in heaven and on earth (there are, to be sure, many "gods" and many "lords"), [6i*]yet for us there is

7:36–38 The passage is difficult to interpret, because it is unclear whether Paul is thinking of a father and his unmarried daughter (or slave), or of a couple engaged in a betrothal or spiritual marriage. The general principles already enunciated apply: there is no question of sin, even if they should marry, but staying as they are is "better" (for the reasons mentioned in 1 Cor 7:28–35). Once again the **charisma** of 1 Cor 7:7 which applies also to the unmarried (1 Cor 7:8–9), is to be presupposed.

7:36 A critical moment has come: either because the woman will soon be beyond marriageable age, or because their passions are becoming uncontrollable (cf. 1 Cor 7:9).

7:39–40 Application of the principles to the case of widows. If they do choose to remarry, they ought to prefer Christian husbands.

8:1–11:1 The Corinthians' second question concerns meat that has been sacrificed to idols; in this area they were exhibiting a disordered sense of liberation that Paul here tries to rectify. These chapters contain a sustained and unified argument that illustrates Paul's method of theological reflection on a moral dilemma. Although the problem with which he is dealing is dated, the guidelines for moral decisions that he offers are of lasting validity. Essentially Paul urges them to take a communitarian rather than an individualistic view of their Christian freedom. Many decisions that they consider pertinent only to their private relationship with God have, in fact, social consequences. Nor can moral decisions be determined by merely theoretical considerations; they must be based on concrete circumstances, specifically on the value and needs of other individuals and on mutual responsibility within the community. Paul here introduces the theme of "building up" (*oikodomē*), i.e., of contributing by individual action to the welfare and growth of the community. This theme will be further developed in 1 Cor 14; see note on 1 Cor 14:3b–5. Several years later Paul would again deal with the problem of meat sacrificed to idols in Rom 14:1–15:6.

8:1a Meat sacrificed to idols: much of the food consumed in the city could have passed through pagan religious ceremonies before finding its way into markets and homes. **"All of us have knowledge"**: a slogan, similar to 1 Cor 6:12, which reveals the self-image of the Corinthians. 1 Cor 8:4 will specify the content of this knowledge.

8:6 This verse rephrases the monotheistic confession of v 4 in such a way as to contrast it with polytheism (1 Cor 8:5) and to express our relationship with the one God in concrete, i.e., in personal and Christian terms. **And for whom we exist**: since the Greek contains no verb here and the action intended must be inferred from the preposition *eis*, another translation is equally possible: "toward whom we return." **Through whom all things**: the earliest reference in the New Testament to Jesus' role in creation.

a: Lk 14:20. *b:* 1 Tm 5:5. *c:* Lk 10:39–42. *d:* Rom 7:2. *e:* 25. *f:* Rom 15:14 / 13:1–13; Rom 14:15, 19. *g:* Rom 8:29; Gal 4:9; *h:* 10:19; Dt 6:4. *i:* Mal 2:10 / Rom 11:36; Eph 4:5–6 / 1:2–3 / Jn 1:3; Col 1:16.

one God, the Father,
from whom all things are and for
whom we exist,
and one Lord, Jesus Christ,
through whom all things are and
through whom we exist.

Practical Rules. [7j]But not all have this
knowledge. There are some who have
been so used to idolatry up until now that,
when they eat meat sacrificed to idols,
their conscience, which is weak, is defiled.
[8k*]Now food will not bring us closer to
God. We are no worse off if we do not eat,
nor are we better off if we do. [9l]But make
sure that this liberty of yours in no way becomes a stumbling block to the weak. [10]If
someone sees you, with your knowledge, reclining at table in the temple of an idol, may
not his conscience too, weak as it is, be "built
up" to eat the meat sacrificed to idols?
[11m]Thus through your knowledge, the weak
person is brought to destruction, the brother
for whom Christ died. [12]When you sin in this
way against your brothers and wound their
consciences, weak as they are, you are sinning against Christ. [13n*]Therefore if food
causes my brother to sin, I will never eat
meat again, so that I may not cause my
brother to sin.

CHAPTER 9

See RG 455

Paul's Rights as an Apostle. [1o*]Am I
not free? Am I not an apostle? Have I not
seen Jesus our Lord? Are you not my work in
the Lord? [2]Although I may not be an apostle
for others, certainly I am for you, for you are
the seal of my apostleship in the Lord.
[3*]My defense against those who would
pass judgment on me is this. [4*]Do we not
have the right to eat and drink? [5]Do we not
have the right to take along a Christian
wife, as do the rest of the apostles, and the
brothers of the Lord, and Cephas? [6p]Or is it
only myself and Barnabas who do not have
the right not to work? [7q]Who ever serves as
a soldier at his own expense? Who plants a
vineyard without eating its produce? Or
who shepherds a flock without using some
of the milk from the flock? [8]Am I saying
this on human authority, or does not the law
also speak of these things? [9r]It is written in
the law of Moses, "You shall not muzzle an
ox while it is treading out the grain." Is God
concerned about oxen, [10s]or is he not really
speaking for our sake? It was written for
our sake, because the plowman should
plow in hope, and the thresher in hope of
receiving a share. [11t]If we have sown spiritual seed for you, is it a great thing that we
reap a material harvest from you? [12u*]If

8:8–9 Although the food in itself is morally neutral, extrinsic circumstances may make the eating of it harmful. **A stumbling block**: the image is that of tripping or causing someone to fall (cf. 1 Cor 8:13; 9:12; 10:12, 32; 2 Cor 6:3; Rom 14:13, 20–1). This is a basic moral imperative for Paul, a counterpart to the positive imperative to "build one another up"; compare the expression "giving offense" as opposed to "pleasing" in 1 Cor 10:32–33.

8:13 His own course is clear: he will avoid any action that might harm another Christian. This statement prepares for the paradigmatic development in 1 Cor 9.

9:1–27 This chapter is an emotionally charged expansion of Paul's appeal to his own example in 1 Cor 8:13; its purpose is to reinforce the exhortation of 1 Cor 8:9. The two opening questions introduce the themes of Paul's freedom and his apostleship (1 Cor 9:1), themes that the chapter will develop in reverse order, 1 Cor 9:1–18 treating the question of his apostleship and the rights that flow from it, and 1 Cor 9:19–27 exploring dialectically the nature of Paul's freedom. The language is highly rhetorical, abounding in questions, wordplays, paradoxes, images, and appeals to authority and experience. The argument is unified by repetitions; its articulations are highlighted by inclusions and transitional verses.

9:3 My defense against those who would pass judgment on me: the reference to a defense (*apologia*) is surprising, and suggests that Paul is incorporating some material here that he has previously used in another context. The defense will touch on two points: the fact of Paul's rights as an apostle (1 Cor 9:4–12a and 1 Cor 9:13–14) and his nonuse of those rights (1 Cor 9:12b and 1 Cor 9:15–18).

9:4–12a Apparently some believe that Paul is not equal to the other apostles and therefore does not enjoy equal privileges. His defense on this point (here and in 1 Cor 9:13–14) reinforces the assertion of his apostolic character in 1 Cor 9:2. It consists of a series of analogies from natural equity (7) and religious custom (1 Cor 9:13) designed to establish his equal right to support from the churches (1 Cor 9:4–6, 11–12a); these analogies are confirmed by the authority of the law (1 Cor 9:8–10) and of Jesus himself (1 Cor 9:14).

9:12 It appears, too, that suspicion or misunderstanding has been created by Paul's practice of not living from his

j: 10:28; Rom 14:23 / Rom 14:1; 15:1. *k:* Rom 14:17. *l:* Rom 14:13, 20–21. *m:* Rom 14:15, 20. *n:* Mt 18:6; Rom 14:20–21. *o:* 1 Cor 9:19 / 2 Cor 12:12 / 15:8–9 / Acts 9:17; 26:16. *p:* Acts 4:36–37; 13:1–2; Gal 2:1, 9, 13; Col 4:10. *q:* 2 Tm 2:3–4. *r:* Dt 25:4; 1 Tm 5:18. *s:* 2 Tm 2:6. *t:* Rom 15:27. *u:* 2 Cor 11:7–12; 12:13–18; 2 Thes 3:6–12.

others share this rightful claim on you, do not we still more?

Reason for Not Using His Rights. Yet we have not used this right. On the contrary, we endure everything so as not to place an obstacle to the gospel of Christ. [13v*]Do you not know that those who perform the temple services eat [what] belongs to the temple, and those who minister at the altar share in the sacrificial offerings? [14w]In the same way, the Lord ordered that those who preach the gospel should live by the gospel.

[15x*]I have not used any of these rights, however, nor do I write this that it be done so in my case. I would rather die. Certainly no one is going to nullify my boast. [16y]If I preach the gospel, this is no reason for me to boast, for an obligation has been imposed on me, and woe to me if I do not preach it! [17z]If I do so willingly, I have a recompense, but if unwillingly, then I have been entrusted with a stewardship. [18a]What then is my recompense? That, when I preach, I offer the gospel free of charge so as not to make full use of my right in the gospel.

All Things to All. [19b*]Although I am free in regard to all, I have made myself a slave to all so as to win over as many as possible. [20]To the Jews I became like a Jew to win over Jews; to those under the law I became like one under the law—though I myself am not under the law—to win over those under the law. [21]To those outside the law I became like one outside the law—though I am not outside God's law but within the law of Christ—to win over those outside the law. [22c]To the weak I became weak, to win over the weak. I have become all things to all, to save at least some. [23]All this I do for the sake of the gospel, so that I too may have a share in it.

[24d*]Do you not know that the runners in the stadium all run in the race, but only one wins the prize? Run so as to win. [25e]Every athlete exercises discipline in every way. They do it to win a perishable crown, but we an imperishable one. [26]Thus I do not run aimlessly; I do not fight as if I were shadowboxing. [27*]No, I drive my body and train it, for fear that, after having preached to others, I myself should be disqualified.

CHAPTER 10

See RG 454–55

Warning against Overconfidence. [1f*]I do not want you to be unaware, brothers, that our ancestors were all under the cloud and all passed through the sea, [2g]and all of them were baptized into Moses in the cloud and in the sea. [3]All ate the same spiritual food,

preaching. The first reason he asserts in defense of this practice is an entirely apostolic one; it anticipates the developments to follow in 1 Cor 9:19–22. He will give a second reason in 1 Cor 9:15–18.

9:13–14 The position of these verses produces an interlocking of the two points of Paul's defense. These arguments by analogy (1 Cor 9:13) and from authority (1 Cor 9:14) belong with those of 1 Cor 9:7–10 and ground the first point. But Paul defers them until he has had a chance to mention "the gospel of Christ" (1 Cor 9:12b), after which it is more appropriate to mention Jesus' injunction to his preachers and to argue by analogy from the sacred temple service to his own liturgical service, the preaching of the gospel (cf. Rom 1:9; 15:16).

9:15–18 Paul now assigns a more personal motive to his nonuse of his right to support. His preaching is not a service spontaneously undertaken on his part but a stewardship imposed by a sort of divine compulsion. Yet to merit any reward he must bring some spontaneous quality to his service, and this he does by freely renouncing his right to support. The material here is quite similar to that contained in Paul's "defense" at 2 Cor 11:5–12; 12:11–18.

9:19–23 In a rhetorically balanced series of statements Paul expands and generalizes the picture of his behavior and explores the paradox of apostolic freedom. It is not essentially freedom from restraint but freedom for service—a possibility of constructive activity.

9:24–27 A series of miniparables from sports, appealing to readers familiar with Greek gymnasia and the nearby Isthmian games.

9:27 For fear that . . . I myself should be disqualified: a final paradoxical turn to the argument: what appears at first a free, spontaneous renunciation of rights (1 Cor 9:12–18) seems subsequently to be required for fulfillment of Paul's stewardship (to preach effectively he must reach his hearers wherever they are, 1 Cor 9:19–22), and finally is seen to be necessary for his own salvation (1 Cor 9:23–27). Mention of the possibility of disqualification provides a transition to 1 Cor 10.

10:1–5 Paul embarks unexpectedly upon a panoramic survey of the events of the Exodus period. The privileges of Israel in the wilderness are described in terms that apply strictly only to the realities of the new covenant ("baptism," "spiritual food and drink"); interpreted in this way they point forward to the Christian experience (1 Cor 10:1–4). But those privileges did not guarantee God's permanent pleasure (1 Cor 10:5).

v: Nm 18:8, 31; Dt 18:1–5. *w:* Mt 10:10; Lk 10:7–8. *x:* 2 Cor 11:9–10. *y:* Acts 26:14–18. *z:* 4:1; Gal 2:7. *a:* 2 Cor 11:7–12. *b:* Mt 20:26–27. *c:* 10:33; Rom 15:1; 2 Cor 11:29. *d:* Heb 12:1. *e:* 2 Tm 2:5 / 2 Tm 4:7–8; Jas 1:12; 1 Pt 5:4. *f:* Ex 13:21–22; 14:19–20 / Ex 14:21–22, 26–30. *g:* Rom 6:3; Gal 3:27 / Ex 16:4–35.

They despised the S-N food.

S-N

[4h*]and all drank the same spiritual drink, for they drank from a spiritual rock that followed them, and the rock was the Christ. [5i]Yet God was not pleased with most of them, for they were struck down in the desert.

[6j*]These things happened as examples for us, so that we might not desire evil things, as they did. [7k]And do not become idolaters, as some of them did, as it is written, "The people sat down to eat and drink, and rose up to revel." [8l]Let us not indulge in immorality as some of them did, and twenty-three thousand fell within a single day. [9m*]Let us not test Christ as some of them did, and suffered death by serpents. [10n]Do not grumble as some of them did, and suffered death by the destroyer. [11*]These things happened to them as an example, and they have been written down as a warning to us, upon whom the end of the ages has come. [12*]Therefore whoever thinks he is standing secure should take care not to fall. [13o]No trial has come to you but what is human. God is faithful and will not let you be tried beyond your strength; but with the trial he will also provide a way out, so that you may be able to bear it.

Warning against Idolatry. [14p*]Therefore, my beloved, avoid idolatry. [15]I am speaking as to sensible people; judge for yourselves what I am saying. [16q]The cup of blessing that we bless, is it not a participation in the blood of Christ? The bread that we break, is it not a participation in the body of Christ? [17r]Because the loaf of bread is one, we, though many, are one body, for we all partake of the one loaf.

[18s]Look at Israel according to the flesh; are not those who eat the sacrifices participants in the altar? [19]So what am I saying? That meat sacrificed to idols is anything? Or that an idol is anything? [20t*]No, I mean that what they sacrifice, [they sacrifice] to demons, not to God, and I do not want you to become participants with demons. [21u]You cannot drink the cup of the Lord and also the cup of demons. You cannot partake of the table of the Lord and of the table of demons. [22v]Or are we provoking the Lord to jealous anger? Are we stronger than he?

Seek the Good of Others. [23w*]"Everything is lawful," but not everything is beneficial. "Everything is lawful," but not everything builds up. [24x]No one should seek his own advantage, but that of his neighbor. [25*]Eat any-

10:4 A spiritual rock that followed them: the Torah speaks only about a rock from which water issued, but rabbinic legend amplified this into a spring that followed the Israelites throughout their migration. Paul uses this legend as a literary type: he makes the rock itself accompany the Israelites, and he gives it a spiritual sense. **The rock was the Christ**: in the Old Testament, Yahweh is the Rock of his people (cf. Dt 32, Moses' song to Yahweh the Rock). Paul now applies this image to the Christ, the source of the living water, the true Rock that accompanied Israel, guiding their experiences in the desert.

10:6–13 This section explicitates the typological value of these Old Testament events: the desert experiences of the Israelites are examples, meant as warnings, to deter us from similar sins (idolatry, immorality, etc.) and from a similar fate.

10:9 Christ: to avoid Paul's concept of Christ present in the wilderness events, some manuscripts read "the Lord."

10:11 Upon whom the end of the ages has come: it is our period in time toward which past ages have been moving and in which they arrive at their goal.

10:12–13 Take care not to fall: the point of the whole comparison with Israel is to caution against overconfidence, a sense of complete security (1 Cor 10:12). This warning is immediately balanced by a reassurance, based, however, on God (1 Cor 10:13).

10:14–22 The warning against idolatry from 1 Cor 10:7 is now repeated (1 Cor 10:14) and explained in terms of the effect of sacrifices: all sacrifices, Christian (1 Cor 10:16–17), Jewish (1 Cor 10:18), or pagan (1 Cor 10:20), establish communion. But communion with Christ is exclusive, incompatible with any other such communion (1 Cor 10:21). Compare the line of reasoning at 1 Cor 6:15.

10:20 To demons: although Jews denied divinity to pagan gods, they often believed that there was some nondivine reality behind the idols, such as the dead, or angels, or demons. The explanation Paul offers in 1 Cor 10:20 is drawn from Dt 32:17: the power behind the idols, with which the pagans commune, consists of demonic powers hostile to God.

10:23–11:1 By way of peroration Paul returns to the opening situation (1 Cor 8) and draws conclusions based on the intervening considerations (1 Cor 9–10).

10:23–24 He repeats in the context of this new problem the slogans of liberty from 1 Cor 6:12, with similar qualifications. Liberty is not merely an individual perfection, nor an end in itself, but is to be used for the common good. The language of 1 Cor 10:24 recalls the descriptions of Jesus' self-emptying in Phil 2.

10:25–30 A summary of specific situations in which the eating of meat sacrificed to idols could present problems of conscience. Three cases are considered. In the first (the marketplace, 1 Cor 10:25–26) and the second (at table, 1 Cor 10:27), there is no need to be concerned with whether food has passed through a pagan

h: Ex 17:1–7; Nm 20:7–11; Dt 8:15. *i:* Nm 14:28–38; Jude 5. *j:* Nm 11:4, 34. *k:* Ex 32:6. *l:* Nm 25:1–9. *m:* Nm 21:5–9. *n:* Nm 14:2–37; 16:1–35. *o:* Mt 6:13; Jas 1:13–14 / 1:9. *p:* 1 Jn 5:21. *q:* Mt 26:26–29; Acts 2:42. *r:* Rom 12:5; Eph 4:4. *s:* Lv 7:6. *t:* Dt 32:17. *u:* 2 Cor 6:14–18. *v:* Dt 32:21 / Eccl 6:10. *w:* 6:12. *x:* Rom 15:2; Phil 2:4, 21.

thing sold in the market, without raising questions on grounds of conscience, [26y]for "the earth and its fullness are the Lord's." [27]If an unbeliever invites you and you want to go, eat whatever is placed before you, without raising questions on grounds of conscience. [28]But if someone says to you, "This was offered in sacrifice," do not eat it on account of the one who called attention to it and on account of conscience; [29]I mean not your own conscience, but the other's. For why should my freedom be determined by someone else's conscience? [30z]If I partake thankfully, why am I reviled for that over which I give thanks?

[31]So whether you eat or drink, or whatever you do, do everything for the glory of God. [32*]Avoid giving offense, whether to Jews or Greeks or the church of God, [33a]just as I try to please everyone in every way, not seeking my own benefit but that of the many, that they may be saved.

CHAPTER 11

See RG 454–56

[1b]Be imitators of me, as I am of Christ.

IV. Problems In Liturgical Assemblies

[2c*]I praise you because you remember me in everything and hold fast to the traditions, just as I handed them on to you.

A. Women's Headdresses

Man and Woman. [3d*]But I want you to know that Christ is the head of every man, and a husband the head of his wife, and God the head of Christ. [4*]Any man who prays or prophesies with his head covered brings shame upon his head. [5]But any woman who prays or prophesies with her head unveiled brings shame upon her head, for it is one and the same thing as if she had had her head shaved. [6]For if a woman does not have her head veiled, she may as well have her hair cut off. But if it is shameful for a woman to have her hair cut off or her head shaved, then she should wear a veil.

[7e*]A man, on the other hand, should not cover his head, because he is the image and glory of God, but woman is the glory of

sacrifice or not, for the principle of 1 Cor 8:4–6 still stands, and the whole creation belongs to the one God. But in the third case (1 Cor 10:28), the situation changes if someone present explicitly raises the question of the sacrificial origin of the food; eating in such circumstances may be subject to various interpretations, some of which could be harmful to individuals. Paul is at pains to insist that the enlightened Christian conscience need not change its judgment about the neutrality, even the goodness, of the food in itself (1 Cor 10:29–30); yet the total situation is altered to the extent that others are potentially endangered, and this calls for a different response, for the sake of others.

10:32–11:1 In summary, the general rule of mutually responsible use of their Christian freedom is enjoined first negatively (1 Cor 10:32), then positively, as exemplified in Paul (1 Cor 10:33), and finally grounded in Christ, the pattern for Paul's behavior and theirs (1 Cor 11:1; cf. Rom 15:1–3).

11:2–14:40 This section of the letter is devoted to regulation of conduct at the liturgy. The problems Paul handles have to do with the dress of women in the assembly (1 Cor 11:3–16), improprieties in the celebration of community meals (1 Cor 11:17–34), and the use of charisms or spiritual gifts (1 Cor 12:1–14:40). The statement in 1 Cor 11:2 introduces all of these discussions, but applies more appropriately to the second (cf. the mention of praise in 1 Cor 11:17 and of tradition in 1 Cor 11:23).

11:3–16 Women have been participating in worship at Corinth without the head-covering normal in Greek society of the period. Paul's stated goal is to bring them back into conformity with contemporary practice and propriety. In his desire to convince, he reaches for arguments from a variety of sources, though he has space to develop them only sketchily and is perhaps aware that they differ greatly in persuasiveness.

11:3 A husband the head of his wife: the specific problem suggests to Paul the model of the head as a device for clarifying relations within a hierarchical structure. The model is similar to that developed later in greater detail and nuance in Eph 5:21–33. It is a hybrid model, for it grafts onto a strictly theological scale of existence (cf. 1 Cor 3:21–23) the hierarchy of sociosexual relations prevalent in the ancient world: men, dominant, reflect the active function of Christ in relation to his church; women, submissive, reflect the passive role of the church with respect to its savior. This gives us the functional scale: God, Christ, man, woman.

11:4–6 From man's direct relation to Christ, Paul infers that his head should not be covered. But woman, related not directly to Christ on the scale but to her husband, requires a covering as a sign of that relationship. **Shameful . . . to have her hair cut off**: certain less honored classes in society, such as lesbians and prostitutes, are thought to have worn their hair close-cropped.

11:7–9 The hierarchy of v 3 is now expressed in other metaphors: the image (*eikōn*) and the reflected glory (*doxa*). Paul is alluding basically to the text of Gn 1:27, in which mankind as a whole, the male-female couple, is created in God's image and given the command to multiply and together dominate the lower creation. But Gn 1:24 is interpreted here in the light of the second creation narrative in Gn 2, in which each of the sexes is created separately (first the man and then the woman from man and for him, to be his helpmate, Gn

y: Ps 24:1; 50:12. *z:* Rom 14:6; 1 Tm 4:3–4. *a:* 9:22; Rom 15:2. *b:* 4:16; Phil 3:17. *c:* 15:3; 2 Thes 2:15. *d:* Eph 5:23. *e:* Gn 1:26–27; 5:1.

man. [8][f]For man did not come from woman, but woman from man; [9][g]nor was man created for woman, but woman for man; [10][*]for this reason a woman should have a sign of authority on her head, because of the angels. [11][h][*]Woman is not independent of man or man of woman in the Lord. [12][i]For just as woman came from man, so man is born of woman; but all things are from God.

[13][*]Judge for yourselves: is it proper for a woman to pray to God with her head unveiled? [14]Does not nature itself teach you that if a man wears his hair long it is a disgrace to him, [15]whereas if a woman has long hair it is her glory, because long hair has been given [her] for a covering? [16]But if anyone is inclined to be argumentative, we do not have such a custom, nor do the churches of God.

B. The Lord's Supper

An Abuse at Corinth. [17][*]In giving this instruction, I do not praise the fact that your meetings are doing more harm than good. [18][j]First of all, I hear that when you meet as a church there are divisions among you, and to a degree I believe it; [19][*]there have to be factions among you in order that [also] those who are approved among you may become known. [20]When you meet in one place, then, it is not to eat the Lord's supper, [21]for in eating, each one goes ahead with his own supper, and one goes hungry while another gets drunk. [22][k]Do you not have houses in which you can eat and drink? Or do you show contempt for the church of God and make those who have nothing feel ashamed? What can I say to you? Shall I praise you? In this matter I do not praise you.

Tradition of the Institution. [23][l][*]For I received from the Lord what I also handed on to you, that the Lord Jesus, on the night he was handed over, took bread, [24]and, after he had given thanks, broke it and said, "This is my body that is for you. Do this in remembrance of me." [25][m]In the same way also the cup, after supper, saying, "This cup is the new covenant in my blood. Do this, as often as you drink it, in remembrance of me." [26]For as often as you eat this bread and drink the cup, you proclaim the death of the Lord until he comes.

[27][*]Therefore whoever eats the bread or drinks the cup of the Lord unworthily will have to answer for the body and blood of the

2:20–23), and under the influence of the story of the fall, as a result of which the husband rules over the woman (Gn 3:16). This interpretation splits the single image of God into two, at different degrees of closeness.

11:10 A sign of authority: "authority" (*exousia*) may possibly be due to mistranslation of an Aramaic word for "veil"; in any case, the connection with 1 Cor 11:9 indicates that the covering is a sign of woman's subordination. **Because of the angels**: a surprising additional reason, which the context does not clarify. Presumably the reference is to cosmic powers who might inflict harm on women or whose function is to watch over women or the cult.

11:11–12 These parenthetical remarks relativize the argument from Gn 2–3. **In the Lord**: in the Christian economy the relation between the sexes is characterized by a mutual dependence, which is not further specified. And even in the natural order conditions have changed: the mode of origin described in Gn 2 has been reversed (1 Cor 11:12a). But the ultimately significant fact is the origin that all things have in common (1 Cor 11:12b).

11:13–16 The argument for conformity to common church practice is summed up and pressed home. 1 Cor 11:14–15 contain a final appeal to the sense of propriety that contemporary Greek society would consider "natural" (cf. 1 Cor 11:5–6).

11:17–34 Paul turns to another abuse connected with the liturgy, and a more serious one, for it involves neglect of basic Christian tradition concerning the meaning of the Lord's Supper. Paul recalls that tradition for them and reminds them of its implications.

11:19 That . . . those who are approved among you may become known: Paul situates their divisions within the context of the eschatological separation of the authentic from the inauthentic and the final revelation of the difference. The notion of authenticity-testing recurs in the injunction to self-examination in view of present and future judgment (1 Cor 11:28–32).

11:23–25 This is the earliest written account of the institution of the Lord's Supper in the New Testament. The narrative emphasizes Jesus' action of self-giving (expressed in the words over the bread and the cup) and his double command to repeat his own action.

11:27 It follows that the only proper way to celebrate the Eucharist is one that corresponds to Jesus' intention, which fits with the meaning of his command to reproduce his action in the proper spirit. If the Corinthians eat and drink unworthily, i.e., without having grasped and internalized the meaning of his death for them, **they will have to answer for the body and blood**, i.e., will be guilty of a sin against the Lord himself (cf. 1 Cor 8:12).

f: Gn 2:21–23. *g:* Gn 2:18. *h:* Gal 3:27–28. *i:* 8:6; Rom 11:36. *j:* 1:10–12; Gal 5:20. *k:* Jas 2:1–7. *l:* 2; 15:3 / 10:16–17; Mt 26:26–29; Mk 14:22–25; Lk 22:14–20. *m:* Ex 24:8; 2 Cor 3:6; Heb 8:6–13.

Lord. [28*]A person should examine himself, and so eat the bread and drink the cup. [29*]For anyone who eats and drinks without discerning the body, eats and drinks judgment on himself. [30]That is why many among you are ill and infirm, and a considerable number are dying. [31]If we discerned ourselves, we would not be under judgment; [32n]but since we are judged by [the] Lord, we are being disciplined so that we may not be condemned along with the world.

[33]Therefore, my brothers, when you come together to eat, wait for one another. [34]If anyone is hungry, he should eat at home, so that your meetings may not result in judgment. The other matters I shall set in order when I come.

C. Spiritual Gifts

CHAPTER 12

See RG 456–57

Unity and Variety. [1*]Now in regard to spiritual gifts, brothers, I do not want you to be unaware. [2o*]You know how, when you were pagans, you were constantly attracted and led away to mute idols. [3p]Therefore, I tell you that nobody speaking by the spirit of God says, "Jesus be accursed." And no one can say, "Jesus is Lord," except by the holy Spirit.

[4q*]There are different kinds of spiritual gifts but the same Spirit; [5]there are different forms of service but the same Lord; [6]there are different workings but the same God who produces all of them in everyone. [7]To each individual the manifestation of the Spirit is given for some benefit. [8r]To one is given through the Spirit the expression of wisdom; to another the expression of knowledge according to the same Spirit; [9]to another faith by the same Spirit; to another gifts of healing by the one Spirit; [10s]to another mighty deeds; to another prophecy; to another discernment of spirits; to another varieties of tongues; to another interpretation of tongues. [11t]But one and the same Spirit produces all of these, distributing them individually to each person as he wishes.

One Body, Many Parts. [12u*]As a body is one though it has many parts, and all the parts of the body, though many, are one body, so also Christ. [13v]For in one Spirit we were all baptized into one body, whether Jews or Greeks, slaves or free persons, and we were all given to drink of one Spirit.

[14]Now the body is not a single part, but many. [15]If a foot should say, "Because I am not a hand I do not belong to the body," it does not for this reason belong any less to

11:28 Examine himself: the Greek word is similar to that for "approved" in 1 Cor 11:19, which means "having been tested and found true." The self-testing required for proper eating involves **discerning the body** (1 Cor 11:29), which, from the context, must mean understanding the sense of Jesus' death (1 Cor 11:26), perceiving the imperative to unity that follows from the fact that Jesus gives himself to all and requires us to repeat his sacrifice in the same spirit (1 Cor 11:18–25).

11:29–32 Judgment: there is a series of wordplays in these verses that would be awkward to translate literally into English; it includes all the references to judgment (*krima*, 1 Cor 11:29, 34; *krinō*, 1 Cor 11:31, 32) discernment (*diakrinō*, 1 Cor 11:29, 31), and condemnation (*katakrinō*, 1 Cor 11:32). The judgment is concretely described as the illness, infirmity, and death that have visited the community. These are signs that the power of Jesus' death is not yet completely recognized and experienced. Yet even the judgment incurred is an expression of God's concern; it is a medicinal measure meant to rescue us from condemnation with God's enemies.

12:1–14:40 Ecstatic and charismatic activity were common in early Christian experience, as they were in other ancient religions. But the Corinthians seem to have developed a disproportionate esteem for certain phenomena, especially tongues, to the detriment of order in the liturgy. Paul's response to this development provides us with the fullest exposition we have of his theology of the charisms.

12:2–3 There is an experience of the Spirit and an understanding of ecstatic phenomena that are specifically Christian and that differ, despite apparent similarities, from those of the pagans. It is necessary to discern which spirit is leading one; ecstatic phenomena must be judged by their effect (1 Cor 12:2). 1 Cor 12:3 illustrates this by an example: power to confess Jesus as Lord can come only from the Spirit, and it is inconceivable that the Spirit would move anyone to curse the Lord.

12:4–6 There are some features common to all charisms, despite their diversity: all are **gifts** (*charismata*), grace from outside ourselves; all are forms of **service** (*diakoniai*), an expression of their purpose and effect; and all are workings (*energēmata*), in which God is at work. Paul associates each of these aspects with what later theology will call one of the persons of the Trinity, an early example of "appropriation."

12:12–26 The image of **a body** is introduced to explain Christ's relationship with believers (1 Cor 12:12). 1 Cor 12:13 applies this model to the church: by baptism all, despite diversity of ethnic or social origins, are integrated into one organism. 1 Cor 12:14–26 then develop the need for diversity of function among the parts of a body without threat to its unity.

n: Dt 8:5; Heb 12:5–11. *o:* Eph 2:11–18. *p:* Rom 10:9; 1 Jn 4:2–3. *q:* Rom 12:6; Eph 4:7, 11. *r:* 2:6–13. *s:* 14:5, 26, 39; Acts 2:4. *t:* 7:7; Eph 4:7. *u:* 10:17; Rom 12:4–5; Eph 2:16; Col 3:15. *v:* Gal 3:28; Eph 2:13–18; Col 3:11 / Jn 7:37–39.

the body. [16]Or if an ear should say, "Because
I am not an eye I do not belong to the body,"
it does not for this reason belong any less to
the body. [17]If the whole body were an eye,
where would the hearing be? If the whole
body were hearing, where would the sense
of smell be? [18]But as it is, God placed the
parts, each one of them, in the body as he intended. [19]If they were all one part, where
would the body be? [20]But as it is, there are
many parts, yet one body. [21]The eye cannot
say to the hand, "I do not need you," nor
again the head to the feet, "I do not need
you." [22]Indeed, the parts of the body that
seem to be weaker are all the more necessary, [23]and those parts of the body that we
consider less honorable we surround with
greater honor, and our less presentable parts
are treated with greater propriety, [24]whereas
our more presentable parts do not need this.
But God has so constructed the body as to
give greater honor to a part that is without it,
[25]so that there may be no division in the
body, but that the parts may have the same
concern for one another. [26]If [one] part suffers, all the parts suffer with it; if one part is
honored, all the parts share its joy.

Application to Christ. [27w*]Now you are
Christ's body, and individually parts of it.
[28x*]Some people God has designated in the
church to be, first, apostles; second, prophets; third, teachers; then, mighty deeds; then
gifts of healing, assistance, administration,
and varieties of tongues. [29]Are all apostles?
Are all prophets? Are all teachers? Do all
work mighty deeds? [30]Do all have gifts of
healing? Do all speak in tongues? Do all interpret? [31]Strive eagerly for the greatest spiritual gifts.

The Way of Love. But I shall show you a
still more excellent way.

CHAPTER 13

See RG 456–57

[1y*]If I speak in human and angelic
tongues, but do not have love, I am a resounding gong or a clashing cymbal. [2z]And
if I have the gift of prophecy and comprehend all mysteries and all knowledge; if I
have all faith so as to move mountains, but
do not have love, I am nothing. [3a]If I give
away everything I own, and if I hand my
body over so that I may boast but do not
have love, I gain nothing.

[4b*]Love is patient, love is kind. It is not
jealous, [love] is not pompous, it is not inflated, [5c]it is not rude, it does not seek its
own interests, it is not quick-tempered, it
does not brood over injury, [6]it does not rejoice over wrongdoing but rejoices with the
truth. [7d]It bears all things, believes all things,
hopes all things, endures all things.

[8*]Love never fails. If there are prophecies,
they will be brought to nothing; if tongues,
they will cease; if knowledge, it will be
brought to nothing. [9]For we know partially
and we prophesy partially, [10]but when the

12:27–30 Paul now applies the image again to the church as a whole and its members (1 Cor 12:27). The lists in 1 Cor 12:28–30 spell out the parallelism by specifying the diversity of functions found in the church (cf. Rom 12:6–8; Eph 4:11).

12:28 First, apostles: apostleship was not mentioned in 1 Cor 12:8–10, nor is it at issue in these chapters, but Paul gives it pride of place in his listing. It is not just one gift among others but a prior and fuller gift that includes the others. They are all demonstrated in Paul's apostolate, but he may have developed his theology of charisms by reflecting first of all on his own grace of apostleship (cf. 1 Cor 3:5–4:14; 9:1–27; 2 Cor 2:14–6:13; 10:1–13:30, esp. 1 Cor 11:23 and 12:12).

13:1–13 This chapter involves a shift of perspective and a new point. All or part of the material may once have been an independent piece in the style of Hellenistic eulogies of virtues, but it is now integrated, by editing, into the context of 1 Cor 12–14 (cf. the reference to tongues and prophecy) and into the letter as a whole (cf. the references to knowledge and to behavior). The function of 1 Cor 13 within the discussion of spiritual gifts is to relativize all the charisms by contrasting them with the more basic, pervasive, and enduring value that gives them their purpose and their effectiveness. The rhetoric of this chapter is striking.

13:1–3 An inventory of gifts, arranged in careful gradation: neither tongues (on the lowest rung), nor prophecy, knowledge, or faith, nor even self-sacrifice has value unless informed by love.

13:4–7 This paragraph is developed by personification and enumeration, defining love by what it does or does not do. The Greek contains fifteen verbs; it is natural to translate many of them by adjectives in English.

13:8–13 The final paragraph announces its topic, **Love never fails** (1 Cor 13:8), then develops the permanence of love in contrast to the charisms (1 Cor 13:9–12), and finally asserts love's superiority even over the other "theological virtues" (1 Cor 13:13).

w: Rom 12:5–8; Eph 1:23; 4:12; 5:30; Col 1:18, 24. *x:* Eph 2:20; 3:5; 4:11. *y:* 8:1; 16:14; Rom 12:9–10; 13:8–10. *z:* 4:1; 14:2 / 1:5; 8:1–3; 12:8 / Mt 17:20; 21:21; Col 2:3. *a:* Mt 6:2. *b:* Eph 4:2 / 4:6, 18; 5:2; 8:1. *c:* 10:24, 33; Phil 2:4, 21; 1 Thes 5:15. *d:* Prv 10:12; 1 Pt 4:8.

perfect comes, the partial will pass away. [11]When I was a child, I used to talk as a child, think as a child, reason as a child; when I became a man, I put aside childish things. [12e]At present we see indistinctly, as in a mirror, but then face to face. At present I know partially; then I shall know fully, as I am fully known. [13f*]So faith, hope, love remain, these three; but the greatest of these is love.

CHAPTER 14

See RG 456–57

Prophecy Greater than Tongues. [1g*]Pursue love, but strive eagerly for the spiritual gifts, above all that you may prophesy. [2*]For one who speaks in a tongue does not speak to human beings but to God, for no one listens; he utters mysteries in spirit. [3h*]On the other hand, one who prophesies does speak to human beings, for their building up, encouragement, and solace. [4]Whoever speaks in a tongue builds himself up, but whoever prophesies builds up the church. [5]Now I should like all of you to speak in tongues, but even more to prophesy. One who prophesies is greater than one who speaks in tongues, unless he interprets, so that the church may be built up.

[6*]Now, brothers, if I should come to you speaking in tongues, what good will I do you if I do not speak to you by way of revelation, or knowledge, or prophecy, or instruction? [7]Likewise, if inanimate things that produce sound, such as flute or harp, do not give out the tones distinctly, how will what is being played on flute or harp be recognized? [8]And if the bugle gives an indistinct sound, who will get ready for battle? [9]Similarly, if you, because of speaking in tongues, do not utter intelligible speech, how will anyone know what is being said? For you will be talking to the air. [10]It happens that there are many different languages in the world, and none is meaningless; [11]but if I do not know the meaning of a language, I shall be a foreigner to one who speaks it, and one who speaks it a foreigner to me. [12]So with yourselves: since you strive eagerly for spirits, seek to have an abundance of them for building up the church.

Need for Interpretation. [13*]Therefore, one who speaks in a tongue should pray to be able to interpret. [14*][For] if I pray in a tongue, my spirit is at prayer but my mind is unproductive. [15i]So what is to be done? I will pray with the spirit, but I will also pray with the mind. I will sing praise with the

13:13 In speaking of love, Paul is led by spontaneous association to mention faith and hope as well. They are already a well-known triad (cf. 1 Thes 1:3), three interrelated (cf. 1 Cor 13:7) features of Christian life, more fundamental than any particular charism. **The greatest . . . is love**: love is operative even within the other members of the triad (7), so that it has a certain primacy among them. Or, if the perspective is temporal, love will remain (cf. "never fails," 1 Cor 13:8) even when faith has yielded to sight and hope to possession.

14:1–5 1 Cor 14:1b returns to the thought of 1 Cor 12:31a and reveals Paul's primary concern. The series of contrasts in 1 Cor 14:2–5 discloses the problem at Corinth: a disproportionate interest in tongues, with a corresponding failure to appreciate the worth of prophecy. Paul attempts to clarify the relative values of those gifts by indicating the kind of communication achieved in each and the kind of effect each produces.

14:2–3a They involve two kinds of communication: tongues, private speech toward God in inarticulate terms that need interpretation to be intelligible to others (see 1 Cor 14:27–28); prophecy, communication with others in the community.

14:3b–5 They produce two kinds of effect. One who speaks in tongues **builds himself up**; it is a matter of individual experience and personal perfection, which inevitably recalls Paul's previous remarks about being inflated, seeking one's own good, pleasing oneself. But a prophet **builds up the church**: the theme of "building up" or "edifying" others, the main theme of the letter, comes to clearest expression in this chapter (1 Cor 14:3, 4, 5, 12, 17). It has been anticipated at 1 Cor 8:1 and 1 Cor 10:23, and by the related concept of "the beneficial" in 1 Cor 6:12; 10:23; 12:7; etc.

14:6–12 Sound, in order to be useful, must be intelligible. This principle is illustrated by a series of analogies from music (1 Cor 14:7–8) and from ordinary human speech (1 Cor 14:10–11); it is applied to the case at hand in 1 Cor 14:9, 12.

14:13–19 The charism of interpretation lifts tongues to the level of intelligibility, enabling them to produce the same effect as prophecy (cf. 1 Cor 14:5, 26–28).

14:14–15 My spirit: Paul emphasizes the exclusively ecstatic, nonrational quality of tongues. The tongues at Pentecost are also described as an ecstatic experience (Acts 2:4, 12–13), though Luke superimposes further interpretations of his own. **My mind**: the ecstatic element, dominant in earliest Old Testament prophecy as depicted in 1 Sm 10:5–13; 19:20–24, seems entirely absent from Paul's notion of prophecy and completely relegated to tongues. He emphasizes the role of reason when he specifies instruction as a function of prophecy (1 Cor 14:6, 19, 31). But he does not exclude intuition and emotion; cf. references to encouragement and consolation (1 Cor 14:3, 31) and the scene describing the ideal exercise of prophecy (1 Cor 14:24–25).

e: 2 Cor 5:7; Heb 11:1 / 2 Tm 2:19; 1 Jn 3:2. *f:* Col 1:4; 1 Thes 1:3; 5:8. *g:* 5, 12, 39. *h:* 4–5, 12, 17, 26; 3:9; 8:1, 10; 10:23. *i:* Eph 5:19; Col 3:16.

spirit, but I will also sing praise with the mind. [16]Otherwise, if you pronounce a blessing [with] the spirit, how shall one who holds the place of the uninstructed say the "Amen" to your thanksgiving, since he does not know what you are saying? [17]For you may be giving thanks very well, but the other is not built up. [18]I give thanks to God that I speak in tongues more than any of you, [19]but in the church I would rather speak five words with my mind, so as to instruct others also, than ten thousand words in a tongue.

Functions of These Gifts. [20][j*]Brothers, stop being childish in your thinking. In respect to evil be like infants, but in your thinking be mature. [21][k]It is written in the law:

"By people speaking strange tongues
 and by the lips of foreigners
I will speak to this people,
 and even so they will not listen to me,

says the Lord." [22]Thus, tongues are a sign not for those who believe but for unbelievers, whereas prophecy is not for unbelievers but for those who believe.

[23][l*]So if the whole church meets in one place and everyone speaks in tongues, and then uninstructed people or unbelievers should come in, will they not say that you are out of your minds? [24]But if everyone is prophesying, and an unbeliever or uninstructed person should come in, he will be convinced by everyone and judged by everyone, [25][m]and the secrets of his heart will be disclosed, and so he will fall down and worship God, declaring, "God is really in your midst."

Rules of Order. [26][n*]So what is to be done, brothers? When you assemble, one has a psalm, another an instruction, a revelation, a tongue, or an interpretation. Everything should be done for building up. [27]If anyone speaks in a tongue, let it be two or at most three, and each in turn, and one should interpret. [28]But if there is no interpreter, the person should keep silent in the church and speak to himself and to God.

[29]Two or three prophets should speak, and the others discern. [30]But if a revelation is given to another person sitting there, the first one should be silent. [31]For you can all prophesy one by one, so that all may learn and all be encouraged. [32]Indeed, the spirits of prophets are under the prophets' control, [33*]since he is not the God of disorder but of peace.

As in all the churches of the holy ones, [34][o]women should keep silent in the churches, for they are not allowed to speak, but should be subordinate, as even the law says. [35]But if they want to learn anything,

14:20–22 The Corinthians pride themselves on tongues as a sign of God's favor, a means of direct communication with him (2:28). To challenge them to a more mature appraisal, Paul draws from scripture a less flattering explanation of what speaking in tongues may signify. Isaiah threatened the people that if they failed to listen to their prophets, the Lord would speak to them (in punishment) through the lips of Assyrian conquerors (Is 28:11–12). Paul compresses Isaiah's text and makes God address his people directly. Equating tongues with foreign languages (cf. 1 Cor 14:10–11), Paul concludes from Isaiah that **tongues are a sign not for those who believe**, i.e., not a mark of God's pleasure for those who listen to him but a mark of his displeasure with those in the community who are faithless, who have not heeded the message that he has sent through the prophets.

14:23–25 Paul projects the possible missionary effect of two hypothetical liturgical experiences, one consisting wholly of tongues, the other entirely of prophecy. **Uninstructed** (*idiōtai*): the term may simply mean people who do not speak or understand tongues, as in 1 Cor 14:16, where it seems to designate Christians. But coupled with the term "unbelievers" it may be another way of designating those who have not been initiated into the community of faith; some believe it denotes a special class of non-Christians who are close to the community, such as catechumens. **Unbelievers** (*apistoi*): he has shifted from the inner-community perspective of 1 Cor 14:22; the term here designates non-Christians (cf. 1 Cor 6:6; 7:15; 10:27).

14:26–33a Paul concludes with specific directives regarding exercise of the gifts in their assemblies. Verse 26 enunciates the basic criterion in the use of any gift: it must contribute to "building up."

14:33b–36 Verse 33b may belong with what precedes, so that the new paragraph would begin only with 1 Cor 14:34. 1 Cor 14:34–35 change the subject. These two verses have the theme of submission in common with 1 Cor 14:11 despite differences in vocabulary, and a concern with what is or is not becoming; but it is difficult to harmonize the injunction to silence here with 1 Cor 11 which appears to take it for granted that women do pray and prophesy aloud in the assembly (cf. 1 Cor 11:5, 13). Hence the verses are often considered an interpolation, reflecting the discipline of later churches; such an interpolation would have to have antedated our manuscripts, all of which contain them, though some transpose them to the very end of the chapter.

j: Mt 10:16; Rom 16:19; Eph 4:14. *k:* Is 28:11–12; Dt 28:49. *l:* Acts 2:6, 13. *m:* 4:5 / Is 45:14; Zec 8:23. *n:* Eph 4:12. *o:* 1 Tm 2:11–15; 1 Pt 3:1.

they should ask their husbands at home. For it is improper for a woman to speak in the church. [36]Did the word of God go forth from you? Or has it come to you alone?

[37]If anyone thinks that he is a prophet or a spiritual person, he should recognize that what I am writing to you is a commandment of the Lord. [38]If anyone does not acknowledge this, he is not acknowledged. [39]So, [my] brothers, strive eagerly to prophesy, and do not forbid speaking in tongues, [40]but everything must be done properly and in order.

V. The Resurrection

A. The Resurrection of Christ

CHAPTER 15

See RG 457

The Gospel Teaching. [1*]Now I am reminding you, brothers, of the gospel I preached to you, which you indeed received and in which you also stand. [2]Through it you are also being saved, if you hold fast to the word I preached to you, unless you believed in vain. [3p*]For I handed on to you as of first importance what I also received: that Christ died for our sins in accordance with the scriptures; [4q]that he was buried; that he was raised on the third day in accordance with the scriptures; [5r]that he appeared to Cephas, then to the Twelve. [6]After that, he appeared to more than five hundred brothers at once, most of whom are still living, though some have fallen asleep. [7]After that he appeared to James, then to all the apostles. [8s]Last of all, as to one born abnormally, he appeared to me. [9t*]For I am the least of the apostles, not fit to be called an apostle, because I persecuted the church of God. [10]But by the grace of God I am what I am, and his grace to me has not been ineffective. Indeed, I have toiled harder than all of them; not I, however, but the grace of God [that is] with me. [11]Therefore, whether it be I or they, so we preach and so you believed.

B. The Resurrection of the Dead

Results of Denial. [12*]But if Christ is preached as raised from the dead, how can some among you say there is no resurrection of the dead? [13u]If there is no resurrection of the dead, then neither has Christ been raised. [14]And if Christ has not been raised, then empty [too] is our preaching; empty, too, your faith. [15v]Then we are also false witnesses to God, because we testified against God that he raised Christ, whom he did not raise if in fact the dead are not raised. [16]For if the dead are not raised, nei-

15:1–58 Some consider this chapter an earlier Pauline composition inserted into the present letter. The problem that Paul treats is clear to a degree: some of the Corinthians are denying the resurrection of the dead (1 Cor 15:12), apparently because of their inability to imagine how any kind of bodily existence could be possible after death (1 Cor 15:35). It is plausibly supposed that their attitude stems from Greek anthropology, which looks with contempt upon matter and would be content with the survival of the soul, and perhaps also from an overrealized eschatology of gnostic coloration, such as that reflected in 2 Tm 2:18, which considers the resurrection a purely spiritual experience already achieved in baptism and in the forgiveness of sins. Paul, on the other hand, will affirm both the essential corporeity of the resurrection and its futurity. His response moves through three steps: a recall of the basic kerygma about Jesus' resurrection (1 Cor 15:1–11), an assertion of the logical inconsistencies involved in denial of the resurrection (1 Cor 15:12–34), and an attempt to perceive theologically what the properties of the resurrected body must be (1 Cor 15:35–58).

15:1–11 Paul recalls the tradition (1 Cor 15:3–7), which he can presuppose as common ground and which provides a starting point for his argument. This is the fundamental content of all Christian preaching and belief (1 Cor 15:1–2, 11).

15:3–7 The language by which Paul expresses the essence of the "gospel" (1 Cor 15:1) is not his own but is drawn from older credal formulas. This credo highlights Jesus' death for our sins (confirmed by his burial) and Jesus' resurrection (confirmed by his appearances) and presents both of them as fulfillment of prophecy. **In accordance with the scriptures**: conformity of Jesus' passion with the scriptures is asserted in Mt 16:1; Lk 24:25–27, 32, 44–46. Application of some Old Testament texts (Ps 2:7; 16:8–11) to his resurrection is illustrated by Acts 2:27–31; 13:29–39; and Is 52:13–53:12 and Hos 6:2 may also have been envisaged.

15:9–11 A persecutor may have appeared disqualified (*ouk . . . hikanos*) from apostleship, but in fact God's grace has qualified him. Cf. the remarks in 2 Corinthians about his qualifications (2 Cor 2:16; 3:5) and his greater labors (2 Cor 11:23). These verses are parenthetical, but a nerve has been touched (the references to his abnormal birth and his activity as a persecutor may echo taunts from Paul's opponents), and he is instinctively moved to self-defense.

15:12–19 Denial of the resurrection (1 Cor 15:12) involves logical inconsistencies. The basic one, stated twice (1 Cor 15:13, 16), is that if there is no such thing as (bodily) resurrection, then it has not taken place even in Christ's case.

p: 11:23 / 1 Pt 2:24; 3:18 / Is 53:4–12. *q:* Acts 2:23–24 / Ps 16:8–11; Hos 6:1–2; Jon 2:1. *r:* Mk 16:14; Mt 28:16–17; Lk 24:36; Jn 20:19. *s:* 9:1; Acts 9:3–6; Gal 1:16. *t:* Acts 8:3; 9:1–2; Gal 1:23; Eph 3:8; 1 Tm 1:15. *u:* 1 Thes 4:14. *v:* Acts 5:32.

ther has Christ been raised, [17*]and if Christ has not been raised, your faith is vain; you are still in your sins. [18]Then those who have fallen asleep in Christ have perished. [19]If for this life only we have hoped in Christ, we are the most pitiable people of all.

Christ the Firstfruits. [20w*]But now Christ has been raised from the dead, the firstfruits of those who have fallen asleep. [21*]For since death came through a human being, the resurrection of the dead came also through a human being. [22x]For just as in Adam all die, so too in Christ shall all be brought to life, [23y]but each one in proper order: Christ the firstfruits; then, at his coming, those who belong to Christ; [24z*]then comes the end, when he hands over the kingdom to his God and Father, when he has destroyed every sovereignty and every authority and power. [25a]For he must reign until he has put all his enemies under his feet. [26b*]The last enemy to be destroyed is death, [27c*]for "he subjected everything under his feet." But when it says that everything has been subjected, it is clear that it excludes the one who subjected everything to him. [28d]When everything is subjected to him, then the Son himself will [also] be subjected to the one who subjected everything to him, so that God may be all in all.

Practical Arguments. [29*]Otherwise, what will people accomplish by having themselves baptized for the dead? If the dead are not raised at all, then why are they having themselves baptized for them?

[30e*]Moreover, why are we endangering ourselves all the time? [31f]Every day I face death; I swear it by the pride in you [brothers] that I have in Christ Jesus our Lord. [32g]If at Ephesus I fought with beasts, so to speak, what benefit was it to me? If the dead are not raised:

"Let us eat and drink,
for tomorrow we die."

[33]Do not be led astray:

"Bad company corrupts good morals."

15:17–18 The consequences for the Corinthians are grave: both forgiveness of sins and salvation are an illusion, despite their strong convictions about both. Unless Christ is risen, their faith does not save.

15:20–28 After a triumphant assertion of the reality of Christ's resurrection (1 Cor 15:20a), Paul explains its positive implications and consequences. As a soteriological event of both human (1 Cor 15:20–23) and cosmic (1 Cor 15:24–28) dimensions, Jesus' resurrection logically and necessarily involves ours as well.

15:20 The firstfruits: the portion of the harvest offered in thanksgiving to God implies the consecration of the entire harvest to come. Christ's resurrection is not an end in itself; its finality lies in the whole harvest, ourselves.

15:21–22 Our human existence, both natural and supernatural, is corporate, involves solidarity. **In Adam . . . in Christ**: the Hebrew word *'ādām* in Genesis is both a common noun for mankind and a proper noun for the first man. Paul here presents Adam as at least a literary type of Christ; the parallelism and contrast between them will be developed further in 1 Cor 15:45–49 and in Rom 5:12–21.

15:24–28 Paul's perspective expands to cosmic dimensions, as he describes the climax of history, **the end**. His viewpoint is still christological, as in 1 Cor 15:20–23. 1 Cor 15:24, 28 describe Christ's final relations to his enemies and his Father in language that is both royal and military; 1 Cor 15:25–28 insert a proof from scripture (Ps 110:1; 8:6) into this description. But the viewpoint is also theological, for God is the ultimate agent and end, and likewise soteriological, for we are the beneficiaries of all the action.

15:26 The last enemy . . . is death: a parenthesis that specifies the final fulfillment of the two Old Testament texts just referred to, Ps 110:1 and Ps 8:7. Death is not just one cosmic power among many, but the ultimate effect of sin in the universe (cf. 1 Cor 15:56; Rom 5:12). Christ defeats death where it prevails, in our bodies. The destruction of the last enemy is concretely the "coming to life" (1 Cor 15:22) of "those who belong to Christ" (1 Cor 15:23).

15:27b–28 The one who subjected everything to him: the Father is the ultimate agent in the drama, and the final end of the process, to whom the Son and everything else is ordered (24, 28). **That God may be all in all**: his reign is a dynamic exercise of creative power, an outpouring of life and energy through the universe, with no further resistance. This is the supremely positive meaning of "subjection": that God may fully be God.

15:29–34 Paul concludes his treatment of logical inconsistencies with a listing of miscellaneous Christian practices that would be meaningless if the resurrection were not a fact.

15:29 Baptized for the dead: this practice is not further explained here, nor is it necessarily mentioned with approval, but Paul cites it as something in their experience that attests in one more way to belief in the resurrection.

15:30–34 A life of sacrifice, such as Paul describes in 1 Cor 4:9–13 and 2 Corinthians, would be pointless without the prospect of resurrection; a life of pleasure, such as that expressed in the Epicurean slogan of 1 Cor 15:32, would be far more consistent. **I fought with beasts**: since Paul does not elsewhere mention a combat with beasts at Ephesus, he may be speaking figuratively about struggles with adversaries.

w: Rom 8:11; Col 1:18; 1 Thes 4:14. *x:* Gn 3:17–19; Rom 5:12–19. *y:* 1 Thes 4:15–17. *z:* Eph 1:22. *a:* Ps 110:1. *b:* Rom 6:9; 2 Tm 1:10; Rev 20:14; 21:4. *c:* Ps 8:7; Eph 1:22; Phil 3:21. *d:* Eph 4:6; Col 3:11. *e:* 2 Cor 4:8–12; 11:23–27. *f:* Ps 44:23; Rom 8:36. *g:* 4:9; 2 Cor 4:10–11 / Wis 2:5–7; Is 22:13.

[34h]Become sober as you ought and stop sinning. For some have no knowledge of God; I say this to your shame.

C. The Manner of the Resurrection

[35*]But someone may say, "How are the dead raised? With what kind of body will they come back?"

The Resurrection Body. [36i*]You fool! What you sow is not brought to life unless it dies. [37]And what you sow is not the body that is to be but a bare kernel of wheat, perhaps, or of some other kind; [38j]but God gives it a body as he chooses, and to each of the seeds its own body. [39*]Not all flesh is the same, but there is one kind for human beings, another kind of flesh for animals, another kind of flesh for birds, and another for fish. [40]There are both heavenly bodies and earthly bodies, but the brightness of the heavenly is one kind and that of the earthly another. [41]The brightness of the sun is one kind, the brightness of the moon another, and the brightness of the stars another. For star differs from star in brightness.

[42*]So also is the resurrection of the dead. It is sown corruptible; it is raised incorruptible. [43k]It is sown dishonorable; it is raised glorious. It is sown weak; it is raised powerful. [44]It is sown a natural body; it is raised a spiritual body. If there is a natural body, there is also a spiritual one.

[45l*]So, too, it is written, "The first man, Adam, became a living being," the last Adam a life-giving spirit. [46]But the spiritual was not first; rather the natural and then the spiritual. [47]The first man was from the earth, earthly; the second man, from heaven. [48]As was the earthly one, so also are the earthly, and as is the heavenly one, so also are the heavenly. [49m*]Just as we have borne the image of the earthly one, we shall also bear the image of the heavenly one.

The Resurrection Event. [50n*]This I declare, brothers: flesh and blood cannot inherit the kingdom of God, nor does corruption inherit incorruption. [51o*]Behold, I tell you a mystery. We shall not all fall asleep,

15:35–58 Paul imagines two objections that the Corinthians could raise: one concerning the manner of the resurrection (*how*?), the other pertaining to the qualities of the risen body (*what kind*?). These questions probably lie behind their denial of the resurrection (1 Cor 15:12), and seem to reflect the presumption that no kind of body other than the one we now possess would be possible. Paul deals with these objections in inverse order, in 1 Cor 15:36–49 and 1 Cor 15:50–58. His argument is fundamentally theological and its appeal is to the understanding.

15:35–49 Paul approaches the question of the nature of the risen body (*what kind of body*?) by means of two analogies: the seed (1 Cor 15:36–44) and the first man, Adam (1 Cor 15:45–49).

15:36–38 The analogy of the seed: there is a change of attributes from seed to plant; the old life-form must be lost for the new to emerge. By speaking about the seed as a **body** that dies and comes to life, Paul keeps the point of the analogy before the reader's mind.

15:39–41 The expression "its own body" (1 Cor 15:38) leads to a development on the marvelous diversity evident in bodily life.

15:42–44 The principles of qualitative difference before and after death (1 Cor 15:36–38) and of diversity on different levels of creation (1 Cor 15:39–41) are now applied to the human body. **Before**: a body animated by a lower, natural life-principle (*psychē*) and endowed with the properties of natural existence (corruptibility, lack of glory, weakness). **After**: a body animated by a higher life-principle (*pneuma*; cf. 1 Cor 15:45) and endowed with other qualities (incorruptibility, glory, power, spirituality), which are properties of God himself.

15:45 The analogy of **the first man, Adam**, is introduced by a citation from Gn 2:7. Paul alters the text slightly, adding the adjective **first**, and translating the Hebrew *'ādām* twice, so as to give it its value both as a common noun (**man**) and as a proper name (**Adam**). 1 Cor 15:45b then specifies similarities and differences between the two Adams. **The last Adam**, Christ (cf. 1 Cor 15:21–22) has become **a . . . spirit** (*pneuma*), a life-principle transcendent with respect to the natural soul (*psychē*) of the first Adam (on the terminology here, cf. note on 1 Cor 3:1). Further, he is not just alive, but life-giving, a source of life for others.

15:49 We shall also bear the image: although it has less manuscript support, this reading better fits the context's emphasis on futurity and the transforming action of God; on future transformation as conformity to the image of the Son, cf. Rom 8:29; Phil 3:21. The majority reading, "let us bear the image," suggests that the image of the heavenly man is already present and exhorts us to conform to it.

15:50–57 These verses, an answer to the first question of 1 Cor 15:35, explain theologically how the change of properties from one image to another will take place: God has the power to transform, and he will exercise it.

15:50–53 Flesh and blood . . . corruption: living persons and the corpses of the dead, respectively. In both cases, the gulf between creatures and God is too wide to be bridged unless God himself transforms us.

15:51–52 A mystery: the last moment in God's plan is disclosed; cf. notes on 1 Cor 2:1, 7–10a. The final trumpet and the awakening of the dead are stock details of the apocalyptic scenario. **We shall not all fall asleep**: Paul expected that some of

h: Mt 22:29; Mk 12:24. *i:* Jn 12:24. *j:* Gn 1:11. *k:* Phil 3:20–21; Col 3:4. *l:* Gn 2:7 / Jn 5:21–29; 2 Cor 3:6, 17. *m:* Gn 5:3 / Rom 8:29; Phil 3:21. *n:* Jn 3:3–6. *o:* 1 Thes 4:14–17.

but we will all be changed, [52p]in an instant, in the blink of an eye, at the last trumpet. For the trumpet will sound, the dead will be raised incorruptible, and we shall be changed. [53q]For that which is corruptible must clothe itself with incorruptibility, and that which is mortal must clothe itself with immortality. [54r*]And when this which is corruptible clothes itself with incorruptibility and this which is mortal clothes itself with immortality, then the word that is written shall come about:

"Death is swallowed up in victory.
[55 s]Where, O death, is your victory?
Where, O death, is your sting?"

[56t*]The sting of death is sin, and the power of sin is the law. [57u]But thanks be to God who gives us the victory through our Lord Jesus Christ.

[58]Therefore, my beloved brothers, be firm, steadfast, always fully devoted to the work of the Lord, knowing that in the Lord your labor is not in vain.

VI. Conclusion

CHAPTER 16

See RG 457–58

The Collection. [1v*]Now in regard to the collection for the holy ones, you also should do as I ordered the churches of Galatia. [2]On the first day of the week each of you should set aside and save whatever he can afford, so that collections will not be going on when I come. [3]And when I arrive, I shall send those whom you have approved with letters of recommendation to take your gracious gift to Jerusalem. [4*]If it seems fitting that I should go also, they will go with me.

Paul's Travel Plans. [5w*]I shall come to you after I pass through Macedonia (for I am going to pass through Macedonia), [6]and perhaps I shall stay or even spend the winter with you, so that you may send me on my way wherever I may go. [7x]For I do not wish to see you now just in passing, but I hope to spend some time with you, if the Lord permits. [8y*]I shall stay in Ephesus until Pentecost, [9z]because a door has opened for me wide and productive for work, but there are many opponents.

[10a]If Timothy comes, see that he is without fear in your company, for he is doing the work of the Lord just as I am. [11]Therefore, no one should disdain him. Rather, send him on his way in peace that he may come to me, for I am expecting him with the brothers. [12b]Now in regard to our brother Apollos, I urged him strongly to go to you with the brothers, but it was not at all his will that he go now. He will go when he has an opportunity.

Exhortation and Greetings. [13]Be on your guard, stand firm in the faith, be courageous, be strong. [14]Your every act should be done with love.

[15c]I urge you, brothers—you know that the household of Stephanas is the firstfruits of Achaia and that they have devoted them-

his contemporaries might still be alive at Christ's return; after the death of Paul and his whole generation, copyists altered this statement in various ways. **We will all be changed**: the statement extends to all Christians, for Paul is not directly speaking about anyone else. Whether they have died before the end or happen still to be alive, all must be transformed.

15:54–55 Death is swallowed up in victory: scripture itself predicts death's overthrow. **O death**: in his prophetic vision Paul may be making Hosea's words his own, or imagining this cry of triumph on the lips of the risen church.

15:56 The sting of death is sin: an explanation of Hosea's metaphor. Death, scorpion-like, is equipped with a sting, sin, by which it injects its poison. Christ defeats sin, the cause of death (Gn 3:19; Rom 5:12).

16:1–4 This paragraph contains our earliest evidence for a project that became a major undertaking of Paul's ministry. The collection for the church at Jerusalem was a symbol in his mind for the unity of Jewish and Gentile Christianity. Cf. Gal 2:10; Rom 15:25–29; 2 Cor 8–9 and the notes to this last passage.

16:1 In regard to the collection: it has already begun in Galatia and Macedonia (cf. 2 Cor 8), and presumably he has already instructed the Corinthians about its purpose.

16:4 That I should go also: presumably Paul delivered the collection on his final visit to Jerusalem; cf. Rom 15:25–32; Acts 24:14.

16:5–12 The travel plans outlined here may not have materialized precisely as Paul intended; cf. 2 Cor 1:8–2:13; 7:4–16.

16:8 In Ephesus until Pentecost: this tells us the place from which he wrote the letter and suggests he may have composed it about Easter time (cf. 1 Cor 5:7–8).

p: Jl 2:1; Zec 9:14; Mt 24:31; Rev 11:15–18. *q:* 2 Cor 5:2–4. *r:* Is 25:8; 2 Cor 5:4; 2 Tm 1:10; Heb 2:14–15. *s:* Hos 13:14. *t:* Rom 4:15; 7:7, 13. *u:* Jn 16:33; 1 Jn 5:4. *v:* Acts 24:17; Rom 15:25–32; 2 Cor 8–9; Gal 2:10. *w:* Acts 19:21; Rom 15:26; 2 Cor 1:15–16. *x:* Acts 18:21. *y:* 15:32; Acts 18:19; 19:1–10. *z:* Acts 14:27; 2 Cor 2:12. *a:* 4:17; Acts 16:1; 19:22; Phil 2:19–23. *b:* 1:12; 3:4–6, 22; Acts 18:24–28. *c:* 1:16.

selves to the service of the holy ones— [16]be subordinate to such people and to everyone who works and toils with them. [17]I rejoice in the arrival of Stephanas, Fortunatus, and Achaicus, because they made up for your absence, [18d]for they refreshed my spirit as well as yours. So give recognition to such people.

[19e*]The churches of Asia send you greetings. Aquila and Prisca together with the church at their house send you many greetings in the Lord. [20f]All the brothers greet you. Greet one another with a holy kiss.

[21g]I, Paul, write you this greeting in my own hand. [22h*]If anyone does not love the Lord, let him be accursed. *Marana tha.* [23i]The grace of the Lord Jesus be with you. [24]My love to all of you in Christ Jesus.

16:19–24 These paragraphs conform to the normal epistolary conclusion, but their language is overlaid with liturgical coloration as well. The **greetings** of the Asian churches are probably to be read, along with the letter, in the liturgy at Corinth, and the union of the church is to be expressed by a holy kiss (1 Cor 16:19–20). Paul adds to this his own greeting (1 Cor 16:21) and blessings (1 Cor 16:23–24).

16:22 Accursed: literally, "anathema." This expression (cf. 1 Cor 12:3) is a formula for exclusion from the community; it may imply here a call to self-examination before celebration of the Eucharist, in preparation for the Lord's coming and judgment (cf. 1 Cor 11:17–34). *Marana tha*: an Aramaic expression, probably used in the early Christian liturgy. As understood here ("O Lord, come!"), it is a prayer for the early return of Christ. If the Aramaic words are divided differently (*Maran atha*, "Our Lord has come"), it becomes a credal declaration. The former interpretation is supported by what appears to be a Greek equivalent of this acclamation in Rev 22:20 "Amen. Come, Lord Jesus!"

d: 1 Thes 5:12–13. *e:* Acts 18:2, 18, 26; Rom 16:3–5. *f:* Rom 16:16; 2 Cor 13:12; 1 Thes 5:26; 1 Pt 5:14. *g:* Gal 6:11; Col 4:18; 2 Thes 3:17. *h:* 12:3; Rom 9:3; Gal 1:8–9; Rev 22:20. *i:* Rom 16:20.

See RG 458–64

The Second Letter to the Corinthians

The Second Letter to the Corinthians is the most personal of all of Paul's extant writings, and it reveals much about his character. In it he deals with one or more crises that have arisen in the Corinthian church. The confrontation with these problems caused him to reflect deeply on his relationship with the community and to speak about it frankly. One moment he is venting his feelings of frustration and uncertainty, the next he is pouring out his relief and affection. The importance of the issues at stake between them calls forth from him an enormous effort of personal persuasion, as well as doctrinal considerations that are of great value for us. Paul's ability to produce profound theological foundations for what may at first sight appear to be rather commonplace circumstances is perhaps nowhere better exemplified than in Second Corinthians. The emotional tone of the letter, its lack of order, and our ignorance of some of its background do not make it easy to follow, but it amply repays the effort required of the reader.

Second Corinthians is rich and varied in content. The interpretation of Exodus in chapter 3, for instance, offers a striking example of early apologetic use of the Old Testament. Paul's discussion of the collection in chaps. 8–9 contains a theology of sharing of possessions, of community of goods among Christian churches, which is both balanced and sensitive. Furthermore, the closing chapters provide an illustration of early Christian invective and polemic, because the conflict with intruders forces Paul to assert his authority. But in those same chapters Paul articulates the vision and sense of values that animate his own apostolate, revealing his faith that Jesus' passion and resurrection are the pattern for all Christian life and expressing a spirituality of ministry unsurpassed in the New Testament.

The letter is remarkable for its rhetoric. Paul falls naturally into the style and argumentation of contemporary philosophic preachers, employing with ease the stock devices of the "diatribe." By a barrage of questions, by challenges both serious and ironic, by paradox heaped upon paradox, even by insults hurled at his opponents, he strives to awaken in his hearers a true sense of values and an appropriate response. All his argument centers on the destiny of Jesus, in which a paradoxical reversal of values is revealed. But Paul appeals to his own personal experience as well. In passages of great rhetorical power (2 Cor 4:7–15; 6:3–10; 11:21–29; 12:5–10; 13:3–4) he enumerates the circumstances of his ministry and the tribulations he has had to endure for Jesus and the gospel, in the hope of illustrating the pattern of Jesus' existence in his own and of drawing the Corinthians into a reappraisal of the values they cherish. Similar passages in the same style in his other letters (cf. especially Rom 8:31–39; 1 Cor 1:26–31; 4:6–21; 9:1–27; 13:1–13; Phil 4:10–19) confirm Paul's familiarity with contemporary rhetoric and demonstrate how effectively it served to express his vision of Christian life and ministry.

Second Corinthians was occasioned by events and problems that developed after Paul's first letter reached Corinth. We have no information about these circumstances except what is contained in the letter itself, which of course supposes that they are known to the readers. Consequently the reconstruction of the letter's background is an uncertain enterprise about which there is not complete agreement.

The letter deals principally with these three topics: (1) a crisis between Paul and the Corinthians, occasioned at least partially by changes in his travel plans (2 Cor 1:12–2:13), and the successful resolution of that crisis (2 Cor 7:5–16); (2) further directives and encouragement in regard to the collection for the church in Jerusalem (2 Cor 8:1–9:15); (3) the definition and defense of Paul's ministry as an apostle. Paul's reflections on this matter are occasioned by visitors from other churches who passed through Corinth, missionaries who differed from Paul in a variety of ways, both in theory and in practice. Those differences led to comparisons. Either the visitors themselves or some of the local church members appear to have sown confusion among the Corinthians with regard to Paul's authority or his style, or both. Paul deals at length with aspects of this situation in 2 Cor 2:14–7:4 and again in 2 Cor 10:1–13:10, though the manner of treatment and the thrust of the argument differ in each of these sections.

Scholars have noticed a lack of continuity in this document. For example, the long section of 2 Cor 2:14–7:4 seems abruptly spliced into the narrative of a crisis and its resolution. Identical or similar topics, moreover, seem to be treated several times during the letter (compare 2 Cor 2:14–7:4 with 2 Cor 10:1–13:10, and 2 Cor 8:1–24 with 2 Cor 9:1–15). Many judge, therefore, that this letter as it stands incorporates several briefer letters sent to Corinth over a certain span of time. If this is so, then Paul himself or, more likely, some other editor clearly took care to gather those letters together and impose some literary unity upon the collection, thus producing the document that has come down to us as the Second Letter to the Corinthians. Others continue to regard it as a single letter, attributing its inconsistencies to changes of perspective in Paul that may have been occasioned by the arrival of fresh news from Corinth during its composition. The letter, or at least some sections of it, appears to have been composed in Macedonia (2 Cor 2:12–13; 7:5–6; 8:1–4; 9:2–4). It is generally dated about the autumn of A.D. 57; if it is a compilation, of course, the various parts may have been separated by intervals of at least some months.

The principal divisions of the Second Letter to the Corinthians are the following:

- I. Address (1:1–11)
- II. The Crisis between Paul and the Corinthians (1:12–7:16)
  - A. Past Relationships (1:12–2:13)
  - B. Paul's Ministry (2:14–7:4)
  - C. Resolution of the Crisis (7:5–16)
- III. The Collection for Jerusalem (8:1–9:15)
- IV. Paul's Defense of His Ministry (10:1–13:10)
- V. Conclusion (13:11–13)

I. Address

CHAPTER 1

See RG 459–60

Greeting. 1 [a]*Paul, an apostle of
Christ Jesus by the will of God, and Timothy
our brother, to the church of God that is in
Corinth, with all the holy ones throughout
Achaia: 2 grace to you and peace from God
our Father and the Lord Jesus Christ.

1:1–11 The opening follows the usual Pauline form, except that the thanksgiving takes the form of a doxology or glorification of God (2 Cor 1:3). This introduces a meditation on the experience of suffering and encouragement shared by Paul and the Corinthians (2 Cor 1:4–7), drawn, at least in part, from Paul's reflections on a recent affliction (2 Cor 1:8–10). The section ends with a modified and delayed allusion to thanksgiving (2 Cor 1:11).

a: Eph 1:1; Col 1:1 / 1:19; Acts 16; Rom 1:7; 1 Cor 1:2.

Thanksgiving. [3b*]Blessed be the God and Father of our Lord Jesus Christ, the Father of compassion and God of all encouragement, [4c]who encourages us in our every affliction, so that we may be able to encourage those who are in any affliction with the encouragement with which we ourselves are encouraged by God. [5*]For as Christ's sufferings overflow to us, so through Christ does our encouragement also overflow. [6]If we are afflicted, it is for your encouragement and salvation; if we are encouraged, it is for your encouragement, which enables you to endure the same sufferings that we suffer. [7*]Our hope for you is firm, for we know that as you share in the sufferings, you also share in the encouragement.

[8d*]We do not want you to be unaware, brothers, of the affliction that came to us in the province of Asia; we were utterly weighed down beyond our strength, so that we despaired even of life. [9e*]Indeed, we had accepted within ourselves the sentence of death, that we might trust not in ourselves but in God who raises the dead. [10f]He rescued us from such great danger of death, and he will continue to rescue us; in him we have put our hope [that] he will also rescue us again, [11g]as you help us with prayer, so that thanks may be given by many on our behalf for the gift granted us through the prayers of many.

II. The Crisis Between Paul and the Corinthians

A. Past Relationships

Paul's Sincerity and Constancy. [12*]For our boast is this, the testimony of our conscience that we have conducted ourselves in the world, and especially toward you, with the simplicity and sincerity of God, [and] not by human wisdom but by the grace of God. [13]For we write you nothing but what you can read and understand, and I hope that you will understand completely, [14h]as you have come to understand us partially, that we are your boast as you also are ours, on the day of [our] Lord Jesus.

[15*]With this confidence I formerly intended to come to you so that you might receive a double favor, [16i]namely, to go by way of you to Macedonia, and then to come to you again on my return from Macedonia, and have you send me on my way to Judea. [17j*]So when I intended this, did I act lightly?

1:3 God of all encouragement: Paul expands a standard Jewish blessing so as to state the theme of the paragraph. The theme of "encouragement" or "consolation" (*paraklēsis*) occurs ten times in this opening, against a background formed by multiple references to "affliction" and "suffering."

1:5 Through Christ: the Father of compassion is the Father of our Lord Jesus (2 Cor 1:3); Paul's sufferings and encouragement (or "consolation") are experienced in union with Christ. Cf. Lk 2:25: the "consolation of Israel" is Jesus himself.

1:7 You also share in the encouragement: the eschatological reversal of affliction and encouragement that Christians expect (cf. Mt 5:4; Lk 6:24) permits some present experience of reversal in the Corinthians' case, as in Paul's.

1:8 Asia: a Roman province in western Asia Minor, the capital of which was Ephesus.

1:9–10 The sentence of death: it is unclear whether Paul is alluding to a physical illness or to an external threat to life. The result of the situation was to produce an attitude of faith in God alone. **God who raises the dead**: rescue is the constant pattern of God's activity; his final act of encouragement is the resurrection.

1:12–2:13 The autobiographical remarks about the crisis in Asia Minor lead into consideration of a crisis that has arisen between Paul and the Corinthians. Paul will return to this question, after a long digression, in 2 Cor 7:5–16. Both of these sections deal with travel plans Paul had made, changes in the plans, alternative measures adopted, a breach that opened between him and the community, and finally a reconciliation between them.

1:12–14 Since Paul's own conduct will be under discussion here, he prefaces the section with a statement about his habitual behavior and attitude toward the community. He protests his openness, single-mindedness, and conformity to God's grace; he hopes that his relationship with them will be marked by mutual understanding and pride, which will constantly increase until it reaches its climax at the judgment. Two references to boasting frame this paragraph (2 Cor 1:12, 14), the first appearances of a theme that will be important in the letter, especially in 2 Cor 10–13; the term is used in a positive sense here (cf. note on 1 Cor 1:29–31).

1:15 I formerly intended to come: this plan reads like a revision of the one mentioned in 1 Cor 16:5. Not until 2 Cor 1:23–2:1 will Paul tell us something his original readers already knew, that he has canceled one or the other of these projected visits.

1:17 Did I act lightly?: the subsequent change of plans casts suspicion on the original intention, creating the impression that Paul is vacillating and inconsistent or that **human considera-**

b: 1 Cor 15:24; Eph 1:3; 1 Pt 1:3 / Rom 15:5. *c:* 7:6–7, 13; 1 Thes 3:6–8; 2 Thes 2:16. *d:* Acts 20:18–19; 1 Cor 15:32. *e:* 4:7–11; Rom 4:17. *f:* 2 Tm 4:18. *g:* 4:15; 9:12. *h:* Phil 2:16; 1 Thes 2:19–20. *i:* 1 Cor 16:5–9; Acts 19:21. *j:* Mt 5:37; Jas 5:12.

Or do I make my plans according to human
considerations, so that with me it is "yes,
yes" and "no, no"? [18*]As God is faithful, our
word to you is not "yes" and "no." [19k]For the
Son of God, Jesus Christ, who was proclaimed to you by us, Silvanus and Timothy
and me, was not "yes" and "no," but "yes"
has been in him. [20l]For however many are
the promises of God, their Yes is in him;
therefore, the Amen from us also goes
through him to God for glory. [21m*]But the
one who gives us security with you in Christ
and who anointed us is God; [22n]he has also
put his seal upon us and given the Spirit in
our hearts as a first installment.

Paul's Change of Plan. [23o*]But I call
upon God as witness, on my life, that it is to
spare you that I have not yet gone to Corinth.
[24]Not that we lord it over your faith; rather,
we work together for your joy, for you stand
firm in the faith.

CHAPTER 2

See RG 460–61

[1]For I decided not to come to you
again in painful circumstances. [2]For if I inflict pain upon you, then who is there to
cheer me except the one pained by me?
[3*]And I wrote as I did so that when I came I
might not be pained by those in whom I
should have rejoiced, confident about all of
you that my joy is that of all of you. [4]For out
of much affliction and anguish of heart I
wrote to you with many tears, not that you
might be pained but that you might know the
abundant love I have for you.

The Offender. [5*]If anyone has caused
pain, he has caused it not to me, but in some
measure (not to exaggerate) to all of you.
[6]This punishment by the majority is enough
for such a person, [7p]so that on the contrary
you should forgive and encourage him instead, or else the person may be overwhelmed by excessive pain. [8]Therefore, I
urge you to reaffirm your love for him. [9q]For
this is why I wrote, to know your proven
character, whether you were obedient in
everything. [10]Whomever you forgive anything, so do I. For indeed what I have forgiven, if I have forgiven anything, has been
for you in the presence of Christ, [11r]so that

tions keep dictating shifts in his goals and projects (cf. the counterclaim of 2 Cor 1:12). **"Yes, yes" and "no, no"**: stating something and denying it in the same or the next breath; being of two minds at once, or from one moment to the next.

1:18–22 As God is faithful: unable to deny the change in plans, Paul nonetheless asserts the firmness of the original plan and claims a profound constancy in his life and work. He grounds his defense in God himself, who is firm and reliable; this quality can also be predicated in various ways of those who are associated with him. Christ, Paul, and the Corinthians all participate in analogous ways in the constancy of God. A number of the terms here, which appear related only conceptually in Greek or English, would be variations of the same root, *'mn*, in a Semitic language, and thus naturally associated in a Semitic mind, such as Paul's. These include the words **yes** (2 Cor 1:17–20), **faithful** (2 Cor 1:18), **Amen** (2 Cor 1:20), **gives us security** (2 Cor 1:21), **faith, stand firm** (2 Cor 1:24).

1:21–22 The commercial terms **gives us security, seal, first installment** are here used analogously to refer to the process of initiation into the Christian life, perhaps specifically to baptism. The passage is clearly trinitarian. The Spirit is the **first installment** or "down payment" of the full messianic benefits that God guarantees to Christians. Cf. Eph 1:13–14.

1:23–24 I have not yet gone to Corinth: some suppose that Paul received word of some affair in Corinth, which he decided to regulate by letter even before the first of his projected visits (cf. 2 Cor 1:16). Others conjecture that he did pay the first visit, was offended there (cf. 2 Cor 2:5), returned to Ephesus, and sent a letter (2 Cor 2:3–9) in place of the second visit. The expressions **to spare you** (2 Cor 1:23) and **work together for your joy** (2 Cor 1:24) introduce the major themes of the next two paragraphs, which are remarkable for insistent repetition of key words and ideas. These form two clusters of terms in the English translation: (1) cheer, rejoice, encourage, joy; (2) pain, affliction, anguish. These clusters reappear when Paul resumes treatment of this subject in 2 Cor 7:5–16.

2:3–4 I wrote as I did: we learn for the first time about the sending of a letter in place of the proposed visit. Paul mentions the letter in passing, but emphasizes his motivation in sending it: to avoid being saddened by them (cf. 1 Cor 2:1), and to help them realize the depth of his love. Another motive will be added in 2 Cor 7:12—to bring to light their own concern for him. **With many tears**: it has been suggested that we may have all or part of this "tearful letter" somewhere in the Corinthian correspondence, either in 1 Cor 5 (the case of the incestuous man), or in 1 Corinthians as a whole, or in 2 Cor 2:10–13. None of these hypotheses is entirely convincing. See note on 2 Cor 13:1.

2:5–11 The nature of the **pain** (2 Cor 2:5) is unclear, though some believe an individual at Corinth rejected Paul's authority, thereby scandalizing many in the community. In any case, action has been taken, and Paul judges the measures adequate to right the situation (2 Cor 2:6). The follow-up directives he now gives are entirely positive: forgive, encourage, love. **Overwhelmed** (2 Cor 2:7): a vivid metaphor (literally "swallowed") that Paul employs positively at 2 Cor 5:4 and in 1 Cor 15:54 (2 Cor 2:7). It is often used to describe satanic activity (cf. 1 Pt 5:8); note the reference to Satan here in 2 Cor 2:11.

k: Acts 16:1–3; 1 Thes 1:1; 2 Thes 1:1. *l:* 1 Cor 14:16; Rev 3:14. *m:* 1 Jn 2:20, 27. *n:* Eph 1:13–14; 4:30 / 5:5; Rom 5:5; 8:16, 23. *o:* 13:2. *p:* Col 3:13. *q:* 7:15. *r:* Eph 4:27.

we might not be taken advantage of by Satan, for we are not unaware of his purposes.
Paul's Anxiety. 12s*When I went to Troas
for the gospel of Christ, although a door was
opened for me in the Lord, 13t*I had no relief
in my spirit because I did not find my
brother Titus. So I took leave of them and
went on to Macedonia.

B. Paul's Ministry

Ministers of a New Covenant. 14*But thanks
be to God, who always leads us in triumph in
Christ and manifests through us the odor of
the knowledge of him in every place. 15uFor
we are the aroma of Christ for God among
those who are being saved and among those
who are perishing, 16*to the latter an odor of
death that leads to death, to the former an
odor of life that leads to life. Who is qualified for this? 17vFor we are not like the many
who trade on the word of God; but as out of
sincerity, indeed as from God and in the
presence of God, we speak in Christ.

CHAPTER 3

See RG 460–61

1w*Are we beginning to commend
ourselves again? Or do we need, as some do,
letters of recommendation to you or from
you? 2*You are our letter, written on our
hearts, known and read by all, 3x*shown to

2:12–13 I had no relief: Paul does not explain the reason for his anxiety until he resumes the thread of his narrative at 2 Cor 7:5: he was waiting to hear how the Corinthians would respond to his letter. Since 2 Cor 7:5–16 describes their response in entirely positive terms, we never learn in detail why he found it necessary to defend and justify his change of plans, as in 2 Cor 1:15–24. Was this portion of the letter written before the arrival of Titus with his good news (2 Cor 7:6–7)?

2:13 Macedonia: a Roman province in northern Greece.

2:14–7:4 This section constitutes a digression within the narrative of the crisis and its resolution (2 Cor 1:12–2:13 and 2 Cor 7:5–16). The main component (2 Cor 2:14–6:10) treats the nature of Paul's ministry and his qualifications for it; this material bears some similarity to the defense of his ministry in chaps. 10–13, but it may well come from a period close to the crisis. This is followed by a supplementary block of material quite different in character and tone (2 Cor 6:14–7:1). These materials may have been brought together into their present position during final editing of the letter; appeals to the Corinthians link them to one another (2 Cor 6:11–13) and lead back to the interrupted narrative (2 Cor 7:2–4).

2:14–6:10 The question of Paul's adequacy (2 Cor 2:16; cf. 2 Cor 3:5) and his credentials (2 Cor 3:1–2) has been raised. Paul responds by an extended treatment of the nature of his ministry. It is a ministry of glory (2 Cor 3:7–4:6), of life (2 Cor 4:7–5:10), of reconciliation (2 Cor 5:11–6:10).

2:14–16a The initial statement plunges us abruptly into another train of thought. Paul describes his personal existence and his function as a preacher in two powerful images (2 Cor 2:14) that constitute a prelude to the development to follow.

2:14a Leads us in triumph in Christ: this metaphor of a festive parade in honor of a conquering military hero can suggest either a positive sharing in Christ's triumph or an experience of defeat, being led in captivity and submission (cf. 2 Cor 4:8–11; 1 Cor 4:9). Paul is probably aware of the ambiguity, as he is in the case of the next metaphor.

2:14b–16a The odor of the knowledge of him: incense was commonly used in triumphal processions. The metaphor suggests the gradual diffusion of the knowledge of God through the apostolic preaching. **The aroma of Christ**: the image shifts from the fragrance Paul diffuses to the aroma that he is. Paul is probably thinking of the "sweet odor" of the sacrifices in the Old Testament (e.g., Gn 8:21; Ex 29:18) and perhaps of the metaphor of wisdom as a sweet odor (Sir 24:15). **Death . . . life**: the aroma of Christ that comes to them through Paul is perceived differently by various classes of people. To some his preaching and his life (cf. 1 Cor 1:17–2:6) are perceived as death, and the effect is death for them; others perceive him, despite appearances, as **life**, and the effect is life for them. This fragrance thus produces a separation and a judgment (cf. the function of the "light" in John's gospel).

2:16b–17 Qualified: Paul may be echoing either the self-satisfied claims of other preachers or their charges about Paul's deficiencies. No one is really qualified, but the apostle contrasts himself with those who dilute or falsify the preaching for personal advantage and insists on his totally good conscience: his ministry is from God, and he has exercised it with fidelity and integrity (cf. 2 Cor 3:5–6).

3:1 Paul seems to allude to certain preachers who pride themselves on their written credentials. Presumably they reproach him for not possessing similar credentials and compel him to spell out his own qualifications (2 Cor 4:2; 5:12; 6:4). The Corinthians themselves should have performed this function for Paul (2 Cor 5:12; cf. 2 Cor 12:11). Since he is forced to find something that can recommend him, he points to them: their very existence constitutes his **letter** of recommendation (2 Cor 3:1–2). Others who engage in self-commendation will also be mentioned in 2 Cor 10:12–18.

3:2–3 Mention of "letters of recommendation" generates a series of metaphors in which Paul plays on the word "letter": (1) the community is Paul's letter of recommendation (2 Cor 3:2a); (2) they are a letter engraved on his affections for all to see and read (2 Cor 3:2b); (3) they are a letter from Christ that Paul merely delivers (2 Cor 3:3a); (4) they are a letter written by the Spirit on the tablets of human hearts (2 Cor 3:3b). One image dissolves into another.

3:3 This verse contrasts Paul's letter with those **written . . . in ink** (like the credentials of other preachers) and those **written . . . on tablets of stone** (like the law of Moses). These contrasts suggest that the other preachers may have claimed special relationship with Moses. If they were Judaizers zealous for the Mosaic law, that would explain the detailed contrast between the old and the new covenants (2 Cor 3:6; 4:7–6:10). If they were charismatics who claimed Moses as their model, that

s: Acts 16:8. *t:* 7:6; 1 Tm 1:3. *u:* 4:3; 1 Cor 1:18. *v:* 4:2; 1 Cor 5:8. *w:* Acts 18:27; Rom 16:1; 1 Cor 16:3. *x:* Ex 24:12; 31:18; 32:15–19 / Jer 31:33; Ez 11:19; 36:26–27.

be a letter of Christ administered by us, written not in ink but by the Spirit of the living
God, not on tablets of stone but on tablets
that are hearts of flesh.
4*Such confidence we have through
Christ toward God. 5yNot that of ourselves
we are qualified to take credit for anything
as coming from us; rather, our qualification
comes from God, 6z*who has indeed qualified us as ministers of a new covenant, not of
letter but of spirit; for the letter brings death,
but the Spirit gives life.

Contrast with the Old Covenant. 7a*Now
if the ministry of death, carved in letters on
stone, was so glorious that the Israelites
could not look intently at the face of Moses
because of its glory that was going to fade,
8*how much more will the ministry of the
Spirit be glorious? 9For if the ministry of
condemnation was glorious, the ministry of
righteousness will abound much more in
glory. 10Indeed, what was endowed with
glory has come to have no glory in this respect because of the glory that surpasses it.
11For if what was going to fade was glorious,
how much more will what endures be glorious.
12*Therefore, since we have such hope, we
act very boldly 13*and not like Moses, who
put a veil over his face so that the Israelites
could not look intently at the cessation of
what was fading. 14*Rather, their thoughts
were rendered dull, for to this present day the
same veil remains unlifted when they read the
old covenant, because through Christ it is
taken away. 15bTo this day, in fact, whenever
Moses is read, a veil lies over their hearts,
16cbut whenever a person turns to the Lord the
veil is removed. 17*Now the Lord is the Spirit,
and where the Spirit of the Lord is, there is

would explain the extended treatment of Moses himself and his glory (2 Cor 3:7–4:6). **Hearts of flesh**: cf. Ezekiel's contrast between the heart of flesh that the Spirit gives and the heart of stone that it replaces (Ez 36:26); the context is covenant renewal and purification that makes observance of the law possible.

3:4–6 These verses resume 2 Cor 2:1–3:3. Paul's confidence (2 Cor 3:4) is grounded in his sense of God-given mission (2 Cor 2:17), the specifics of which are described in 2 Cor 3:1–3. 2 Cor 3:5–6 return to the question of his qualifications (2 Cor 2:16), attributing them entirely to God. 2 Cor 3:6 further spells out the situation described in v 3b and "names" it: Paul is living within **a new covenant**, characterized by the Spirit, which **gives life**. The usage of a **new covenant** is derived from Jer 31:31–33 a passage that also speaks of writing on the heart; cf. 2 Cor 3:2.

3:6 This verse serves as a topic sentence for 2 Cor 3:7–6:10. For the contrast between **letter** and **spirit**, cf. Rom 2:29; 7:5–6.

3:7–4:6 Paul now develops the contrast enunciated in 2 Cor 3:6b in terms of the relative glory of the two covenants, insisting on the greater glory of the new. His polemic seems directed against individuals who appeal to the glorious Moses and fail to perceive any comparable glory either in Paul's life as an apostle or in the gospel he preaches. He asserts in response that Christians have a glory of their own that far surpasses that of Moses.

3:7 The ministry of death: from his very first words, Paul describes the Mosaic covenant and ministry from the viewpoint of their limitations. They lead to **death** rather than life (2 Cor 3:6–7; cf. 2 Cor 4:7–5:10), to **condemnation** rather than reconciliation (2 Cor 3:9; cf. 2 Cor 5:11–6:10). **Was so glorious**: the basic text to which Paul alludes is Ex 34:29–35 to which his opponents have undoubtedly laid claim. **Going to fade**: Paul concedes the glory of Moses' covenant and ministry, but grants them only temporary significance.

3:8–11 How much more: the argument "from the less to the greater" is repeated three times (2 Cor 3:8, 9, 11). 2 Cor 3:10 expresses another point of view: the difference in glory is so great that only the new covenant and ministry can properly be called "glorious" at all.

3:12 Such hope: the glory is not yet an object of experience, but that does not lessen Paul's confidence. **Boldly**: the term *parrēsia* expresses outspoken declaration of Christian conviction (cf. 2 Cor 4:1–2). Paul has nothing to hide and no reason for timidity.

3:13–14a Not like Moses: in Exodus Moses veiled his face to protect the Israelites from God's reflected glory. Without impugning Moses' sincerity, Paul attributes another effect to the veil. Since it lies between God's glory and the Israelites, it explains how they could fail to notice the glory disappearing. **Their thoughts were rendered dull**: the problem lay with their understanding. This will be expressed in 2 Cor 3:14b–16 by a shift in the place of the veil: it is no longer over Moses' face but over their perception.

3:14b–16 The parallelism in these verses makes it necessary to interpret corresponding parts in relation to one another. **To this present day**: this signals the shift of Paul's attention to his contemporaries; his argument is typological, as in 1 Cor 10. The Israelites of Moses' time typify the Jews of Paul's time, and perhaps also Christians of Jewish origin or mentality who may not recognize the temporary character of Moses' glory. **When they read the old covenant**: the lasting dullness prevents proper appraisal of Moses' person and covenant. When his writings are read in the synagogue, a veil still impedes their understanding. **Through Christ**: i.e., in the new covenant. **Whenever a person turns to the Lord**: Moses in Exodus appeared before God without the veil and gazed on his face unprotected. Paul applies that passage to converts to Christianity: when they turn to the Lord fully and authentically, the impediment to their understanding is removed.

3:17 The Lord is the Spirit: the "Lord" to whom the Christian turns (2 Cor 3:16) is the Spirit of whom Paul has been speak-

y: Jn 3:27. *z:* Eph 3:7 / Jer 31:31–34. *a:* Ex 34:29–35. *b:* Rom 11:7–10. *c:* Ex 34:34.

freedom. [18d*]All of us, gazing with unveiled face on the glory of the Lord, are being transformed into the same image from glory to glory, as from the Lord who is the Spirit.

See RG 461–62

CHAPTER 4

Integrity in the Ministry. [1*]Therefore, since we have this ministry through the mercy shown us, we are not discouraged. [2e]Rather, we have renounced shameful, hidden things; not acting deceitfully or falsifying the word of God, but by the open declaration of the truth we commend ourselves to everyone's conscience in the sight of God. [3f*]And even though our gospel is veiled, it is veiled for those who are perishing, [4g]in whose case the god of this age has blinded the minds of the unbelievers, so that they may not see the light of the gospel of the glory of Christ, who is the image of God. [5*]For we do not preach ourselves but Jesus Christ as Lord, and ourselves as your slaves for the sake of Jesus. [6h*]For God who said, "Let light shine out of darkness," has shone in our hearts to bring to light the knowledge of the glory of God on the face of [Jesus] Christ.

The Paradox of the Ministry. [7*]But we hold this treasure in earthen vessels, that the surpassing power may be of God and not from us. [8i*]We are afflicted in every way, but not constrained; perplexed, but not driven to despair; [9]persecuted, but not abandoned; struck down, but not destroyed; [10j*]always carrying about in the body the dying of Jesus, so that the life of Jesus may also be manifested in our body. [11k]For we who live are constantly being given up to death for the sake of Jesus, so that the life of Jesus may be manifested in our mortal flesh.

[12*]So death is at work in us, but life in

ing, the life-giving Spirit of the living God (2 Cor 3:6, 8), the inaugurator of the new covenant and ministry, who is also the Spirit of Christ. **The Spirit of the Lord**: the Lord here is the living God (2 Cor 3:3), but there may also be an allusion to Christ as Lord (2 Cor 3:14, 16). **Freedom**: i.e., from the ministry of death (2 Cor 3:7) and the covenant that condemned (2 Cor 3:9).

3:18 Another application of the veil image. **All of us . . . with unveiled face**: Christians (Israelites from whom the veil has been removed) are like Moses, standing in God's presence, beholding and reflecting his glory. **Gazing**: the verb may also be translated "contemplating as in a mirror"; 2 Cor 4:6 would suggest that the mirror is Christ himself. **Are being transformed**: elsewhere Paul speaks of transformation, conformity to Jesus, God's image, as a reality of the end time, and even 2 Cor 3:12 speaks of the glory as an object of hope. But the life-giving Spirit, the distinctive gift of the new covenant, is already present in the community (cf. 2 Cor 1:22, the "first installment"), and the process of transformation has already begun. **Into the same image**: into the image of God, which is Christ (2 Cor 4:4).

4:1–2 A ministry of this sort generates confidence and forthrightness; cf. 2 Cor 1:12–14; 2:17.

4:3–4 Though our gospel is veiled: the final application of the image. Paul has been reproached either for obscurity in his preaching or for his manner of presenting the gospel. But he confidently asserts that there is no veil over his gospel. If some fail to perceive its light, that is because of unbelief. The veil lies over their eyes (2 Cor 3:14), a blindness induced by Satan, and a sign that they are headed for destruction (cf. 2 Cor 2:15).

4:5 We do not preach ourselves: the light seen in his gospel is the glory of Christ (2 Cor 4:4). Far from preaching himself, the preacher should be a transparent medium through whom Jesus is perceived (cf. 2 Cor 4:10–11). **Your slaves**: Paul draws attention away from individuals as such and toward their role in relation to God, Christ, and the community; cf. 1 Cor 3:5; 2 Cor 4:1.

4:6 Autobiographical allusion to the episode at Damascus clarifies the origin and nature of Paul's service; cf. Acts 9:1–19; 22:3–16; 26:2–18. **"Let light shine out of darkness"**: Paul seems to be thinking of Gn 1:3 and presenting his apostolic ministry as a new creation. There may also be an allusion to Is 9:1 suggesting his prophetic calling as servant of the Lord and light to the nations; cf. Is 42:6, 16; 49:6; 60:1–2, and the use of light imagery in Acts 26:13–23. **To bring to light the knowledge**: Paul's role in the process of revelation, expressed at the beginning under the image of the odor and aroma (2 Cor 2:14–15), is restated now, at the end of this first moment of the development, in the imagery of light and glory (2 Cor 4:3–6).

4:7–5:10 Paul now confronts the difficulty that his present existence does not appear glorious at all; it is marked instead by suffering and death. He deals with this by developing the topic already announced in 2 Cor 3:3, 6, asserting his faith in the presence and ultimate triumph of life, in his own and every Christian existence, despite the experience of death.

4:7 This treasure: the glory that he preaches and into which they are being transformed. **In earthen vessels**: the instruments God uses are human and fragile; some imagine small terracotta lamps in which light is carried.

4:8–9 A catalogue of his apostolic trials and afflictions. Yet in these the negative never completely prevails; there is always some experience of rescue, of salvation.

4:10–11 Both the negative and the positive sides of the experience are grounded christologically. The logic is similar to that of 2 Cor 1:3–11. His sufferings are connected with Christ's, and his deliverance is a sign that he is to share in Jesus' resurrection.

4:12–15 His experience does not terminate in himself, but in others (12, 15; cf. 2 Cor 1:4–5). Ultimately, everything is ordered even beyond the community, toward God (2 Cor 4:15; cf. 2 Cor 1:11).

d: Rom 8:29–30; 12:2; Gal 4:19; Phil 3:10, 20–21 / 4:4–6; 1 Cor 15:49; Col 1:15; 3:9–11; 1 Jn 3:2. *e:* 2:17; 1 Thes 2:4–7. *f:* 2:15–16; 2 Thes 2:10. *g:* Jn 12:31–36 / 1 Tm 1:11. *h:* Gn 1:3; Is 9:1; Acts 26:13–23; Gal 1:15–16 / Jn 8:12; Heb 1:3. *i:* 6:4–10; 1 Cor 4:9–13. *j:* Col 1:24. *k:* Rom 8:36; 1 Cor 15:31.

you. [13l]*Since, then, we have the same spirit of faith, according to what is written, "I believed, therefore I spoke," we too believe and therefore speak, [14m]knowing that the one who raised the Lord Jesus will raise us also with Jesus and place us with you in his presence. [15n]Everything indeed is for you, so that the grace bestowed in abundance on more and more people may cause the thanksgiving to overflow for the glory of God.

[16o]*Therefore, we are not discouraged; rather, although our outer self is wasting away, our inner self is being renewed day by day. [17p]For this momentary light affliction is producing for us an eternal weight of glory beyond all comparison, [18q]as we look not to what is seen but to what is unseen; for what is seen is transitory, but what is unseen is eternal.

CHAPTER 5

See RG 462

Our Future Destiny. [1r]*For we know that if our earthly dwelling, a tent, should be destroyed, we have a building from God, a dwelling not made with hands, eternal in heaven. [2s]*For in this tent we groan, longing to be further clothed with our heavenly habitation [3]*if indeed, when we have taken it off, we shall not be found naked. [4t]*For while we are in this tent we groan and are weighed down, because we do not wish to be unclothed but to be further clothed, so that what is mortal may be swallowed up by life. [5u]*Now the one who has prepared us for this very thing is God, who has given us the Spirit as a first installment.

[6]*So we are always courageous, although we know that while we are at home in the body we are away from the Lord, [7]for we

4:13–14 Like the Psalmist, Paul clearly proclaims his faith, affirming life within himself despite death (2 Cor 4:10–11) and the life-giving effect of his experience upon the church (2 Cor 4:12, 14–15). **And place us with you in his presence**: Paul imagines God presenting him and them to Jesus at the parousia and the judgment; cf. 2 Cor 11:2; Rom 14:10.

4:16–18 In a series of contrasts Paul explains the extent of his faith in life. Life is not only already present and revealing itself (2 Cor 4:8–11, 16) but will outlast his experience of affliction and dying: it is eternal (2 Cor 4:17–18).

4:16 Not discouraged: i.e., despite the experience of death. Paul is still speaking of himself personally, but he assumes his faith and attitude will be shared by all Christians. **Our outer self**: the individual subject of ordinary perception and observation, in contrast to the interior and hidden self, which undergoes renewal. **Is being renewed day by day**: this suggests a process that has already begun; cf. 2 Cor 3:18. The renewal already taking place even in Paul's dying is a share in the life of Jesus, but this is recognized only by faith (2 Cor 4:13, 18; 2 Cor 5:7).

5:1 Our earthly dwelling: the same contrast is restated in the imagery of a dwelling. The language recalls Jesus' saying about the destruction of the temple and the construction of another building **not made with hands** (Mk 14:58), a prediction later applied to Jesus' own body (Jn 2:20).

5:2–5 2 Cor 5:2–3 and 4 are largely parallel in structure. **We groan, longing**: see note on 2 Cor 5:5. **Clothed with our heavenly habitation**: Paul mixes his metaphors, adding the image of the garment to that of the building. **Further clothed**: the verb means strictly "to put one garment on over another." Paul may desire to put the resurrection body on over his mortal body, without dying; 2 Cor 5:2, 4 permit this meaning but do not impose it. Or perhaps he imagines the resurrection body as a garment put on over the Christ-garment first received in baptism (Gal 3:27) and preserved by moral behavior (Rom 13:12–14; Col 3:12; cf. Mt 22:11–13). Some support for this interpretation may be found in the context; cf. the references to baptism (2 Cor 5:5), to judgment according to works (2 Cor 5:10), and to present renewal (2 Cor 4:16), an idea elsewhere combined with the image of "putting on" a new nature (Eph 4:22–24; Col 3:1–5, 9–10).

5:3 When we have taken it off: the majority of witnesses read "when we have put it on," i.e., when we have been clothed (in the resurrection body), then we shall not be without a body (naked). This seems mere tautology, though some understand it to mean: whether we are "found" (by God at the judgment) clothed or naked depends upon whether we have preserved or lost our original investiture in Christ (cf. the previous note). In this case to "put it on" does not refer to the resurrection body, but to keeping intact the Christ-garment of baptism. The translation follows the western reading (Codex Bezae, Tertullian), the sense of which is clear: to "take it off" is to shed our mortal body in death, after which we shall be clothed in the resurrection body and hence not "naked" (cf. 1 Cor 15:51–53).

5:4 We do not wish to be unclothed: a clear allusion to physical death (2 Cor 4:16; 5:1). Unlike the Greeks, who found dissolution of the body desirable (cf. Socrates), Paul has a Jewish horror of it. He seems to be thinking of the "intermediate period," an interval between death and resurrection. **Swallowed up by life**: cf. 1 Cor 15:54.

5:5 God has created us for resurrected bodily life and already prepares us for it by the gift of the Spirit in baptism. **The Spirit as a first installment**: the striking parallel to 2 Cor 5:1–5 in Rom 8:17–30 describes Christians who have received the "firstfruits" (cf. "first installment" here) of the Spirit as "groaning" (cf. 2 Cor 5:2, 4 here) for the resurrection, the complete redemption of their bodies. In place of clothing and building, Rom 8 uses other images for the resurrection: adoption and conformity to the image of the Son.

5:6–9 Tension between present and future is expressed by

l: Ps 116:10. *m:* Rom 4:24–25; 8:11; 1 Cor 6:14; 1 Thes 4:14. *n:* 1:11. *o:* 4:1, 1. *p:* Mt 5:11–12; Rom 8:18. *q:* Rom 8:24–25; Heb 11:1. *r:* Is 38:12 / Col 3:1–4 / Mk 14:58; Col 2:11; Heb 9:11, 24. *s:* Rom 8:23 / 1 Cor 15:51–54. *t:* Is 25:8; 1 Cor 15:54. *u:* 1:22.

walk by faith, not by sight. [8v]Yet we are courageous, and we would rather leave the body and go home to the Lord. [9]Therefore, we aspire to please him, whether we are at home or away. [10w*]For we must all appear before the judgment seat of Christ, so that each one may receive recompense, according to what he did in the body, whether good or evil.

The Ministry of Reconciliation. [11x*]Therefore, since we know the fear of the Lord, we try to persuade others; but we are clearly apparent to God, and I hope we are also apparent to your consciousness. [12y]We are not commending ourselves to you again but giving you an opportunity to boast of us, so that you may have something to say to those who boast of external appearance rather than of the heart. [13*]For if we are out of our minds, it is for God; if we are rational, it is for you. [14z*]For the love of Christ impels us, once we have come to the conviction that one died for all; therefore, all have died. [15a]He indeed died for all, so that those who live might no longer live for themselves but for him who for their sake died and was raised.

[16*]Consequently, from now on we regard no one according to the flesh; even if we once knew Christ according to the flesh, yet now we know him so no longer. [17b]So whoever is in Christ is a new creation: the old things have passed away; behold, new things have come. [18*]And all this is from God, who has reconciled us to himself through Christ and given us the ministry of reconciliation, [19c]namely, God was reconciling the world to himself in Christ, not counting their trespasses against them and entrusting to us the message of reconciliation. [20d]So we are ambassadors for Christ, as if God were appealing through us. We implore you on behalf of Christ, be reconciled to God. [21e*]For our sake he made him to be sin who did not know sin, so that we might become the righteousness of God in him.

CHAPTER 6

See RG 462

The Experience of the Ministry. [1f*]Working together, then, we appeal to you not to receive the grace of God in vain. [2g*]For he says:

another spatial image, the metaphor of the country and its citizens. At present we are like citizens in exile or far away from home. The Lord is the distant homeland, believed in but unseen (2 Cor 5:7).

5:10 We must all appear: the verb is ambiguous: we are scheduled to "appear" for judgment, at which we will be "revealed" as we are (cf. 2 Cor 11; 2:14; 4:10–11).

5:11–15 This paragraph is transitional. Paul sums up much that has gone before. Still playing on the term "appearance," he reasserts his transparency before God and the Corinthians, in contrast to the self-commendation, boasting, and preoccupation with externals that characterize some others (cf. 2 Cor 1:12–14; 2:14; 3:1; 3:7–4:6). 2 Cor 5:14 recalls 2 Cor 3:7–4:6, and sums up 2 Cor 4:7–5:10.

5:13 Out of our minds: this verse confirms that a concern for ecstasy and charismatic experience may lie behind the discussion about "glory" in 2 Cor 3:7–4:6. Paul also enjoys such experiences but, unlike others, does not make a public display of them or consider them ends in themselves. **Rational**: the Greek virtue *sōphrosynē*, to which Paul alludes, implies reasonableness, moderation, good judgment, self-control.

5:14–15 These verses echo 2 Cor 4:14 and resume the treatment of "life despite death" from 2 Cor 4:7–5:10.

5:16–17 Consequently: the death of Christ described in 2 Cor 5:14–15 produces a whole new order (2 Cor 5:17) and a new mode of perception (2 Cor 5:16). **According to the flesh**: the natural mode of perception, characterized as "fleshly," is replaced by a mode of perception proper to the Spirit. Elsewhere Paul contrasts what Christ looks like according to the old criteria (weakness, powerlessness, folly, death) and according to the new (wisdom, power, life); cf. 2 Cor 5:15, 21; 1 Cor 1:17–3:3. Similarly, he describes the paradoxical nature of Christian existence, e.g., in 2 Cor 4:10–11, 14. **A new creation**: rabbis used this expression to describe the effect of the entrance of a proselyte or convert into Judaism or of the remission of sins on the Day of Atonement. The new order created **in Christ** is the new covenant (2 Cor 3:6).

5:18–21 Paul attempts to explain the meaning of God's action by a variety of different categories; his attention keeps moving rapidly back and forth from God's act to his own ministry as well. **Who has reconciled us to himself**: i.e., he has brought all into oneness. **Not counting their trespasses**: the reconciliation is described as an act of justification (cf. "righteousness," 2 Cor 5:21); this contrasts with the covenant that condemned (2 Cor 3:8). **The ministry of reconciliation**: Paul's role in the wider picture is described: entrusted with the message of reconciliation (2 Cor 5:19), he is Christ's ambassador, through whom God appeals (2 Cor 5:20a). In v 20b Paul acts in the capacity just described.

5:21 This is a statement of God's purpose, expressed paradoxically in terms of sharing and exchange of attributes. As Christ became our righteousness (1 Cor 1:30), we become God's righteousness (cf. 2 Cor 5:14–15).

6:1–10 This paragraph is a single long sentence in the Greek, interrupted by the parenthesis of 2 Cor 5:2. The one main verb is "we appeal." In this paragraph Paul both exercises his min-

v: Phil 1:21–23. *w:* Mt 16:27; 25:31–46; Rom 2:16; 14:10–11. *x:* 1:12–14. *y:* 3:1 / 1:14; Phil 1:26. *z:* Rom 6:1–6. *a:* Rom 4:25; 6:4–11; 14:9; Col 3:3–4. *b:* Gal 6:15; Eph 2:15 / Is 43:18–21; Rev 21:5. *c:* Rom 5:10–11; Col 1:20. *d:* Eph 6:20; Phlm 9. *e:* Is 53:6–9; Gal 3:13 / Rom 3:24–26; 1 Cor 1:30; 1 Pt 2:24; 1 Jn 3:5–8. *f:* 1 Cor 3:9; 1 Thes 3:2. *g:* Is 49:8.

"In an acceptable time I heard you,
and on the day of salvation I helped
you."

Behold, now is a very acceptable time; behold, now is the day of salvation. [3h*]We
cause no one to stumble in anything, in order
that no fault may be found with our ministry;
[4i*]on the contrary, in everything we commend ourselves as ministers of God, through
much endurance, in afflictions, hardships,
constraints, [5j]beatings, imprisonments, riots, labors, vigils, fasts; [6k*]by purity, knowledge, patience, kindness, in a holy spirit, in
unfeigned love, [7l]in truthful speech, in the
power of God; with weapons of righteousness at the right and at the left; [8*]through
glory and dishonor, insult and praise. We are
treated as deceivers and yet are truthful; [9m]as
unrecognized and yet acknowledged; as dying and behold we live; as chastised and yet
not put to death; [10n]as sorrowful yet always
rejoicing; as poor yet enriching many; as
having nothing and yet possessing all things.

[11*]We have spoken frankly to you, Corinthians; our heart is open wide. [12o]You are not
constrained by us; you are constrained by
your own affections. [13p]As recompense in
kind (I speak as to my children), be open
yourselves.

Call to Holiness. [14*]Do not be yoked with
those who are different, with unbelievers.
For what partnership do righteousness and
lawlessness have? Or what fellowship does
light have with darkness? [15]What accord has
Christ with Beliar? Or what has a believer in
common with an unbeliever? [16q*]What
agreement has the temple of God with idols?
For we are the temple of the living God; as
God said:

istry of reconciliation (cf. 2 Cor 5:20) and describes how his ministry is exercised: the "message of reconciliation" (2 Cor 5:19) is lived existentially in his apostolic experience.

6:1 Not to receive . . . in vain: i.e., conform to the gift of justification and new creation. The context indicates how this can be done concretely: become God's righteousness (2 Cor 5:21), not live for oneself (2 Cor 5:15) be reconciled with Paul (2 Cor 6:11–13; 7:2–3).

6:2 In an acceptable time: Paul cites the Septuagint text of Is 49:8; the Hebrew reads "in a time of favor"; it is parallel to "on the day of salvation." **Now**: God is bestowing favor and salvation at this very moment, as Paul is addressing his letter to them.

6:3 Cause no one to stumble: the language echoes that of 1 Cor 8–10 as does the expression "no longer live for themselves" in 2 Cor 5:15. **That no fault may be found**: i.e., at the eschatological judgment (cf. 1 Cor 4:2–5).

6:4a This is the central assertion, the topic statement for the catalogue that follows. **We commend ourselves**: Paul's self-commendation is ironical (with an eye on the charges mentioned in 2 Cor 3:1–3) and paradoxical (pointing mostly to experiences that would not normally be considered points of pride but are perceived as such by faith). Cf. also the self-commendation in 2 Cor 11:23–29. **As ministers of God**: the same Greek word, *diakonos*, means "minister" and "servant"; cf. 2 Cor 11:23, the central assertion in a similar context, and 1 Cor 3:5.

6:4b–5 Through much endurance: this phrase functions as a subtitle; it is followed by an enumeration of nine specific types of trials endured.

6:6–7a A list of virtuous qualities in two groups of four, the second fuller than the first.

6:8b–10 A series of seven rhetorically effective antitheses, contrasting negative external impressions with positive inner reality. Paul perceives his existence as a reflection of Jesus' own and affirms an inner reversal that escapes outward observation. The final two members illustrate two distinct kinds of paradox or apparent contradiction that are characteristic of apostolic experience.

6:11–13 Paul's tone becomes quieter, but his appeal for acceptance and affection is emotionally charged. References to the heart and their mutual relations bring the development begun in 2 Cor 2:14–3:3 to an effective conclusion.

6:14–7:1 Language and thought shift noticeably here. Suddenly we are in a different atmosphere, dealing with a quite different problem. Both the vocabulary and the thought, with their contrast between good and evil, are more characteristic of Qumran documents or the Book of Revelation than they are of Paul. Hence, critics suspect that this section was inserted by another hand.

6:14–16a The opening injunction to separate from unbelievers is reinforced by five rhetorical questions to make the point that Christianity is not compatible with paganism. Their opposition is emphasized also by the accumulation of five distinct designations for each group. These verses are a powerful statement of God's holiness and the exclusiveness of his claims.

6:16c–18 This is a chain of scriptural citations carefully woven together. God's covenant relation to his people and his presence among them (2 Cor 6:16) is seen as conditioned on cultic separation from the profane and cultically impure (2 Cor 6:17); that relation is translated into the personal language of the parent-child relationship, an extension to the community of the language of 2 Sm 7:14 (2 Cor 6:18). Some remarkable parallels to this chain are found in the final chapters of Revelation. God's presence among his people (Rev 21:22) is expressed there, too, by applying 2 Sm 7:14 to the community (Rev 21:7). There is a call to separation (Rev 18:4) and exclusion of the unclean from the community and its liturgy (Rev 21:27). The title "Lord Almighty" (*Pantokratōr*) occurs in the New Testament only here in 2 Cor 6:18 and nine times in Revelation.

h: 1 Cor 9:12; 10:32 / 8:20–21. *i:* 4:8–11; 11:23–27; 1 Cor 4:9–13. *j:* Acts 16:23. *k:* Gal 5:22–23. *l:* 10:4; Rom 13:12; Eph 6:11–17. *m:* 4:10–11; Rom 8:36. *n:* Rom 8:32; 1 Cor 3:21. *o:* 7:3. *p:* Gal 4:19. *q:* 1 Cor 10:20–21 / 1 Cor 3:16–17; 6:19 / Ex 25:8; 29:45; Lv 26:12; Jer 31:1; 32:38; Ez 37:27.

"I will live with them and move among
them,
and I will be their God
and they shall be my people.
17 [r]Therefore, come forth from them
and be separate," says the Lord,
"and touch nothing unclean;
then I will receive you
18 [s]and I will be a father to you,
and you shall be sons and daughters to
me,
says the Lord Almighty."

CHAPTER 7

See RG 462

1 Since we have these promises, beloved, let us cleanse ourselves from every defilement of flesh and spirit, making holiness perfect in the fear of God.

2 *Make room for us; we have not wronged anyone, or ruined anyone, or taken advantage of anyone. 3 [t]I do not say this in condemnation, for I have already said that you are in our hearts, that we may die together and live together. 4 I have great confidence in you, I have great pride in you; I am filled with encouragement, I am overflowing with joy all the more because of all our affliction.

C. Resolution of the Crisis

Paul's Joy in Macedonia. 5 [u]*For even when we came into Macedonia, our flesh had no rest, but we were afflicted in every way—external conflicts, internal fears. 6 [v]But God, who encourages the downcast, encouraged us by the arrival of Titus, 7 and not only by his arrival but also by the encouragement with which he was encouraged in regard to you, as he told us of your yearning, your lament, your zeal for me, so that I rejoiced even more. 8 [w]*For even if I saddened you by my letter, I do not regret it; and if I did regret it ([for] I see that that letter saddened you, if only for a while), 9 I rejoice now, not because you were saddened, but because you were saddened into repentance; for you were saddened in a godly way, so that you did not suffer loss in anything because of us. 10 For godly sorrow produces a salutary repentance without regret, but worldly sorrow produces death. 11 For behold what earnestness this godly sorrow has produced for you, as well as readiness for a defense, and indignation, and fear, and yearning, and zeal, and punishment. In every way you have shown yourselves to be innocent in the matter. 12 [x]So then even though I wrote to you, it was not on account of the one who did the wrong, or on account of the one who suffered the wrong, but in order that your concern for us might be made plain to you in the sight of God. 13 *For this reason we are encouraged.

And besides our encouragement, we rejoice even more because of the joy of Titus, since his spirit has been refreshed by all of you. 14 For if I have boasted to him about you, I was not put to shame. No, just as everything we said to you was true, so our boasting before Titus proved to be the truth. 15 [y]And his heart goes out to you all the more,

7:2–4 These verses continue the thought of 2 Cor 6:11–13, before the interruption of 2 Cor 6:14–7:1. 2 Cor 7:4 serves as a transition to the next section: the four themes it introduces (confidence; pride or "boasting"; encouragement; joy in affliction) are developed in 2 Cor 7:5–16. All have appeared previously in the letter.

7:5–16 This section functions as a peroration or formal summing up of the whole first part of the letter, 2 Cor 1–7. It deals with the restoration of right relations between Paul and the Corinthians, and it is marked by fullness and intensity of emotion.

7:5–7 Paul picks up the thread of the narrative interrupted at 2 Cor 2:13 (2 Cor 7:5) and describes the resolution of the tense situation there depicted (2 Cor 7:6–7). Finally Titus arrives and his coming puts an end to Paul's restlessness (2 Cor 2:13; 2 Cor 7:5), casts out his fears, and reverses his mood. The theme of encouragement and affliction is reintroduced (cf. 2 Cor 1:3–11); here, too, encouragement is traced back to God and is described as contagious (2 Cor 7:6). The language of joy and sorrow also reappears in 2 Cor 7:7 (cf. 2 Cor 1:23–2:1 and the note on 2 Cor 1:23–24).

7:5 Macedonia: see note on 2 Cor 2:13.

7:8–12 Paul looks back on the episode from the viewpoint of its ending. The goal of their common activity, promotion of their joy (2 Cor 1:24), has been achieved, despite and because of the sorrow they felt. That sorrow was God-given. Its salutary effects are enumerated fully and impressively in 2 Cor 7:10–11; not the least important of these is that it has revealed to them the attachment they have to Paul.

7:13–16 Paul summarizes the effect of the experience on Titus: encouragement, joy, love, relief. Finally, he describes its effects on himself: encouragement, joy, confidence, pride or "boasting" (i.e., the satisfaction resulting from a boast that proves well-founded; cf. 2 Cor 7:4; 1:12, 14).

r: Is 52:11; Ez 20:34, 41; Rev 18:4; 21:27. *s:* 2 Sm 7:14; Ps 2:7; Is 43:6; Jer 31:9; Rev 21:7 / Rev 4:8; 11:17; 15:3; 21:22. *t:* 6:11–13. *u:* 2:13. *v:* 7:13–14; 1 Thes 3:6–8. *w:* 2:2–4; Heb 12:11. *x:* 2:3, 9; 7:8. *y:* 2:9.

as he remembers the obedience of all of you,
when you received him with fear and trembling. [16]I rejoice, because I have confidence
in you in every respect.

III. The Collection for Jerusalem

CHAPTER 8

See RG 462–63

Generosity in Giving. [1z*]We want you
to know, brothers, of the grace of God that
has been given to the churches of Macedonia, [2*]for in a severe test of affliction, the
abundance of their joy and their profound
poverty overflowed in a wealth of generosity on their part. [3*]For according to their
means, I can testify, and beyond their means,
spontaneously, [4a]they begged us insistently
for the favor of taking part in the service to
the holy ones, [5*]and this, not as we expected,
but they gave themselves first to the Lord
and to us through the will of God, [6b*]so that
we urged Titus that, as he had already begun,
he should also complete for you this gracious act also. [7c*]Now as you excel in every
respect, in faith, discourse, knowledge, all
earnestness, and in the love we have for you,
may you excel in this gracious act also.
[8]I say this not by way of command, but to
test the genuineness of your love by your
concern for others. [9d*]For you know the gracious act of our Lord Jesus Christ, that for
your sake he became poor although he was

8:1–9:15 Paul turns to a new topic, the collection for the church in Jerusalem. There is an early precedent for this project in the agreement mentioned in Gal 2:6–10. According to Acts, the church at Antioch had sent Saul and Barnabas to Jerusalem with relief (Acts 11:27–30). Subsequently Paul organized a project of relief for Jerusalem among his own churches. Our earliest evidence for it comes in 1 Cor 16:1–4—after it had already begun (see notes there); by the time Paul wrote Rom 15:25–28 the collection was completed and ready for delivery. 2 Cor 8–9 contain what appear to be two letters on the subject. In them Paul gives us his fullest exposition of the meaning he sees in the enterprise, presenting it as an act of Christian charity and as an expression of the unity of the church, both present and eschatological. These chapters are especially rich in the recurrence of key words, on which Paul plays; it is usually impossible to do justice to these wordplays in the translation.

8:1–24 This is a letter of recommendation for Titus and two unnamed companions, written from Macedonia probably at least a year later than 1 Cor 16. The recommendation proper is prefaced by remarks about the ideals of sharing and equality within the Christian community (2 Cor 8:1–15). Phil 4:10–20 shows that Paul has reflected on his personal experience of need and relief in his relations with the community at Philippi; he now develops his reflections on the larger scale of relations between his Gentile churches and the mother church in Jerusalem.

8:1–5 The example of the Macedonians, a model of what ought to be happening at Corinth, provides Paul with the occasion for expounding his theology of "giving."

8:1 The grace of God: the fundamental theme is expressed by the Greek noun *charis*, which will be variously translated throughout these chapters as "grace" (2 Cor 8:1; 9:8, 14), "favor" (2 Cor 8:4), "gracious act" (2 Cor 8:6, 7, 9) or "gracious work" (2 Cor 8:19), to be compared to "gracious gift" (1 Cor 16:3). The related term, *eucharistia*, "thanksgiving," also occurs at 2 Cor 9:11, 12. The wordplay is not superficial; various mutations of the same root signal inner connection between aspects of a single reality, and Paul consciously exploits the similarities in vocabulary to highlight that connection.

8:2 Three more terms are now introduced. **Test** (*dokimē*): the same root is translated as "to test" (2 Cor 8:8) and "evidence" (2 Cor 9:13); it means to be tried and found genuine. **Abundance**: variations on the same root lie behind "overflow" (2 Cor 8:2; 9:12), "excel" (2 Cor 8:7), "surplus" (2 Cor 8:14), "superfluous" (2 Cor 9:1) "make abundant" and "have an abundance" (2 Cor 9:8). These expressions of fullness contrast with references to need (2 Cor 8:14; 9:12). **Generosity**: the word *haplotēs* has nuances of both simplicity and sincerity; here and in 2 Cor 9:11, 13 it designates the singleness of purpose that manifests itself in generous giving.

8:3–4 Paul emphasizes the spontaneity of the Macedonians and the nature of their action. **They begged us insistently**: the same root is translated as "urge," "appeal," "encourage" (2 Cor 8:6, 17; 9:5). **Taking part**: the same word is translated "contribution" in 2 Cor 9:13 and a related term as "partner" in 2 Cor 8:23. **Service** (*diakonia*): this word occurs also in 2 Cor 9:1, 13 as "service"; in 2 Cor 9:12 it is translated "administration," and in 2 Cor 8:19, 20 the corresponding verb is rendered "administer."

8:5 They gave themselves . . . to the Lord and to us: on its deepest level their attitude is one of self-giving.

8:6 Titus: 1 Cor 16 seemed to leave the organization up to the Corinthians, but apparently Paul has sent Titus to initiate the collection as well; 2 Cor 8:16–17 will describe Titus' attitude as one of shared concern and cooperation.

8:7 The charitable service Paul is promoting is seen briefly and in passing within the perspective of Paul's theology of the charisms. **Earnestness** (*spoudē*): this or related terms occur also in 2 Cor 8:22 ("earnest") and 2 Cor 8:8, 16, 17 ("concern").

8:9 The dialectic of Jesus' experience, expressed earlier in terms of life and death (2 Cor 5:15), sin and righteousness (2 Cor 5:21), is now rephrased in terms of poverty and wealth. Many scholars think this is a reference to Jesus' preexistence with God (his "wealth") and to his incarnation and death (his "poverty"), and they point to the similarity between this verse and Phil 2:6–8. Others interpret the wealth and poverty as succeeding phases of Jesus' earthly existence, e.g., his sense of intimacy with God and then the desolation and the feeling of abandonment by God in his death (cf. Mk 15:34).

z: 11:9; Rom 15:26. *a:* Acts 24:17; Rom 15:31. *b:* 2:13; 7:6–7, 13–14; 8:16, 23; 12:18. *c:* 1 Cor 1:5. *d:* 6:10; Phil 2:6–8.

rich, so that by his poverty you might become rich. [10e]And I am giving counsel in this matter, for it is appropriate for you who began not only to act but to act willingly last year: [11*]complete it now, so that your eager willingness may be matched by your completion of it out of what you have. [12*]For if the eagerness is there, it is acceptable according to what one has, not according to what one does not have; [13]not that others should have relief while you are burdened, but that as a matter of equality [14]your surplus at the present time should supply their needs, so that their surplus may also supply your needs, that there may be equality. [15f]As it is written:

> "Whoever had much did not have more,
> and whoever had little did not have less."

Titus and His Collaborators. [16*]But thanks be to God who put the same concern for you into the heart of Titus, [17]for he not only welcomed our appeal but, since he is very concerned, he has gone to you of his own accord. [18g*]With him we have sent the brother who is praised in all the churches for his preaching of the gospel. [19h]And not only that, but he has also been appointed our traveling companion by the churches in this gracious work administered by us for the glory of the Lord [himself] and for the expression of our eagerness. [20*]This we desire to avoid, that anyone blame us about this lavish gift administered by us, [21i]for we are concerned for what is honorable not only in the sight of the Lord but also in the sight of others. [22]And with them we have sent our brother whom we often tested in many ways and found earnest, but who is now much more earnest because of his great confidence in you. [23]As for Titus, he is my partner and coworker for you; as for our brothers, they are apostles of the churches, the glory of Christ. [24*]So give proof before the churches of your love and of our boasting about you to them.

CHAPTER 9

See RG 462–63

God's Indescribable Gift. [1*]Now about the service to the holy ones, it is superfluous for me to write to you, [2j*]for I know your eagerness, about which I boast of you to the Macedonians, that Achaia has been ready since last year; and your zeal has stirred up most of them. [3*]Nonetheless, I sent the brothers so that our boast about you might not prove empty in this case, so that you might be ready, as I said, [4]for fear that if any Macedonians come with me and find you not ready we might be put to shame (to say nothing of you) in this conviction. [5]So I thought it necessary to encourage the brothers to go on ahead to you and arrange in advance for your promised gift, so that in this

8:11 Eager: the word *prothymia* also occurs in 2 Cor 8:12, 19; 9:2.

8:12–15 Paul introduces the principle of **equality** into the discussion. The goal is not impoverishment but sharing of resources; balance is achieved at least over the course of time. In 2 Cor 8:15 Paul grounds his argument unexpectedly in the experience of Israel gathering manna in the desert: equality was achieved, independently of personal exertion, by God, who gave with an even hand according to need. Paul touches briefly here on the theme of "living from God."

8:16–24 In recommending Titus and his companions, Paul stresses their personal and apostolic qualities, their good dispositions toward the Corinthians, and their authority as messengers of the churches and representatives of Christ.

8:18 The brother: we do not know the identity of this coworker of Paul, nor of the third companion mentioned below in 2 Cor 8:22.

8:20–22 That anyone blame us: 2 Cor 12:16–18 suggests that misunderstandings may indeed have arisen concerning Paul's management of the collection through the messengers mentioned here, but those same verses seem to imply that the Corinthians by and large would recognize the honesty of Paul's conduct in this area as in others (cf. 2 Cor 6:3).

8:24 As Paul began by holding up the Macedonians as examples to be imitated, he closes by exhorting the Corinthians to show their love (by accepting the envoys and by cooperating as the Macedonians do), thus justifying the pride Paul demonstrates because of them before other churches.

9:1–15 Quite possibly this was originally an independent letter, though it deals with the same subject and continues many of the same themes. In that case, it may have been written a few weeks later than 2 Cor 8, while the delegation there mentioned was still on its way.

9:2 Achaia: see note on Rom 15:26.

9:3 I sent the brothers: the Greek aorist tense here could be epistolary, referring to the present; in that case Paul would be sending them now, and 2 Cor 9:9 would merely conclude the letter of recommendation begun in 2 Cor 9:8. But the aorist may also refer to a sending that is past as Paul writes; then 2 Cor 9:9, with its apparently fresh beginning, is a follow-up message entrusted to another carrier.

e: 9:2; 1 Cor 16:1–4. *f:* Ex 16:18. *g:* 12:18. *h:* 1 Cor 16:3–4. *i:* Rom 12:17. *j:* 8:10; Rom 15:26.

way it might be ready as a bountiful gift and
not as an exaction.
[6k]Consider this: whoever sows sparingly
will also reap sparingly, and whoever sows
bountifully will also reap bountifully. [7l]Each
must do as already determined, without sadness or compulsion, for God loves a cheerful
giver. [8*]Moreover, God is able to make
every grace abundant for you, so that in all
things, always having all you need, you may
have an abundance for every good work.
[9m]As it is written:

"He scatters abroad, he gives to the poor;
his righteousness endures forever."

[10n]The one who supplies seed to the sower
and bread for food will supply and multiply
your seed and increase the harvest of your
righteousness.
[11*]You are being enriched in every way for
all generosity, which through us produces
thanksgiving to God, [12]for the administration
of this public service is not only supplying
the needs of the holy ones but is also overflowing in many acts of thanksgiving to God.
[13o]Through the evidence of this service, you
are glorifying God for your obedient confession of the gospel of Christ and the generosity of your contribution to them and to all
others, [14]while in prayer on your behalf they
long for you, because of the surpassing grace
of God upon you. [15p]Thanks be to God for
his indescribable gift!

IV. Paul's Defense of His Ministry

CHAPTER 10

See RG 463–64

Accusation of Weakness. [1*]Now I
myself, Paul, urge you through the gentleness
and clemency of Christ, I who am humble
when face to face with you, but brave toward
you when absent, [2q*]I beg you that, when
present, I may not have to be brave with that
confidence with which I intend to act boldly

9:8–10 The behavior to which he exhorts them is grounded in God's own pattern of behavior. God is capable of overwhelming generosity, as scripture itself attests (2 Cor 9:9), so that they need not fear being short. He will provide in abundance, both supplying their natural needs and increasing their righteousness. Paul challenges them to godlike generosity and reminds them of the fundamental motive for encouragement: God himself cannot be outdone.

9:11–15 Paul's vision broadens to take in all the interested parties in one dynamic picture. His language becomes liturgically colored and conveys a sense of fullness. With a final play on the words *charis* and *eucharistia* (see note on 2 Cor 8:1), he describes a circle that closes on itself: the movement of grace overflowing from God to them and handed on from them through Paul to others is completed by the prayer of praise and thanksgiving raised on their behalf to God.

10:1–13:10 These final chapters have their own unity of structure and theme and could well have formed the body of a separate letter. They constitute an **apologia** on Paul's part, i.e., a legal defense of his behavior and his ministry; the writing is emotionally charged and highly rhetorical. In the central section (2 Cor 11:16–12:10), the **apologia** takes the form of a boast. This section is prepared for by a prologue (2 Cor 11:1–15) and followed by an epilogue (2 Cor 12:11–18), which are similar in content and structure. These sections, in turn, are framed by an introduction (2 Cor 10:1–18) and a conclusion (2 Cor 12:19–13:10), both of which assert Paul's apostolic authority and confidence and define the purpose of the letter. The structure that results from this disposition of the material is chiastic, i.e., the first element corresponds to the last, the second to the second last, etc., following the pattern a b c b', a'.

10:1–18 Paul asserts his apostolic authority and expresses the confidence this generates in him. He writes in response to certain opinions that have arisen in the community and certain charges raised against him and in preparation for a forthcoming visit in which he intends to set things in order. This section gives us an initial glimpse of the situation in Corinth that Paul must address; much of its thematic material will be taken up again in the finale (2 Cor 12:19–13:10).

10:1–2 A strong opening plunges us straight into the conflict. Contrasts dominate here: presence versus absence, gentleness-clemency-humility versus boldness-confidence-bravery. **Through the gentleness and clemency of Christ**: the figure of the gentle Christ, presented in a significant position before any specifics of the situation are suggested, forms a striking contrast to the picture of the bold and militant Paul (2 Cor 10:2–6); this tension is finally resolved in 2 Cor 13:3–4. **Absent . . . present**: this same contrast, with a restatement of the purpose of the letter, recurs in 2 Cor 13:10, which forms an inclusion with 2 Cor 10:1–2.

10:2b–4a Flesh: the Greek word *sarx* can express both the physical life of the body without any pejorative overtones (as in "we are in the flesh," 3) and our natural life insofar as it is marked by limitation and weakness (as in the other expressions) in contrast to the higher life and power conferred by the Spirit; cf. note on 1 Cor 3:1. The wordplay is intended to express the paradoxical situation of a life already taken over by the Spirit but not yet seen as such except by faith. Lack of empirical evidence of the Spirit permits misunderstanding and misjudgment, but Paul resolutely denies that his behavior and effectiveness are as limited as some suppose.

k: Prv 11:24–25. *l:* Prv 22:8 LXX. *m:* Ps 112:9. *n:* Is 55:10. *o:* 8:4; Rom 15:31. *p:* Rom 5:15–16. *q:* 13:2, 10; 1 Cor 4:21.

against some who consider us as acting according to the flesh. [3*]For, although we are in the flesh, we do not battle according to the flesh, [4r]for the weapons of our battle are not of flesh but are enormously powerful, capable of destroying fortresses. We destroy arguments [5]and every pretension raising itself against the knowledge of God, and take every thought captive in obedience to Christ, [6s]and we are ready to punish every disobedience, once your obedience is complete.

[7t*]Look at what confronts you. Whoever is confident of belonging to Christ should consider that as he belongs to Christ, so do we. [8u]And even if I should boast a little too much of our authority, which the Lord gave for building you up and not for tearing you down, I shall not be put to shame. [9*]May I not seem as one frightening you through letters. [10v]For someone will say, "His letters are severe and forceful, but his bodily presence is weak, and his speech contemptible." [11w]Such a person must understand that what we are in word through letters when absent, that we also are in action when present.

[12x*]Not that we dare to class or compare ourselves with some of those who recommend themselves. But when they measure themselves by one another and compare themselves with one another, they are without understanding. [13*]But we will not boast beyond measure but will keep to the limits God has apportioned us, namely, to reach even to you. [14]For we are not overreaching ourselves, as though we did not reach you; we indeed first came to you with the gospel of Christ. [15]We are not boasting beyond measure, in other people's labors; yet our hope is that, as your faith increases, our influence among you may be greatly enlarged, within our proper limits, [16y]so that we may preach the gospel even beyond you, not boasting of work already done in another's sphere. [17z*]"Whoever boasts, should boast in the Lord." [18a*]For it is not the one who recommends himself who is approved, but the one whom the Lord recommends.

CHAPTER 11

See RG 463–64

Preaching without Charge. [1b*]If only you would put up with a little foolishness

10:3b–6 Paul is involved in combat. The strong military language and imagery are both an assertion of his confidence in the divine power at his disposal and a declaration of war against those who underestimate his resources. The threat is echoed in 2 Cor 13:2–3.

10:7–8 Belonging to Christ . . . so do we: these phrases already announce the pattern of Paul's boast in 2 Cor 11:21b–29, especially 2 Cor 11:22–23. **For building you up and not for tearing you down**: Paul draws on the language by which Jeremiah described the purpose of the prophetic power the Lord gave to him (Jer 1:9–10; 12:16–17; 24:6). Though Paul's power may have destructive effects on others (2 Cor 10:2–6), its intended effect on the community is entirely constructive (cf. 2 Cor 13:10). **I shall not be put to shame**: his assertions will not be refuted; they will be revealed as true at the judgment.

10:9–10 Paul cites the complaints of some who find him lacking in personal forcefulness and holds out the threat of a personal **parousia** (both "return" and "presence") that will be forceful, indeed will be a demonstration of Christ's own power (cf. 2 Cor 13:2–4).

10:12–18 Paul now qualifies his claim to boldness, indicating its limits. He distinguishes his own behavior from that of others, revealing those "others" as they appear to him: as self-recommending, immoderately boastful, encroaching on territory not assigned to them, and claiming credit not due to them.

10:13 Will keep to the limits: the notion of proper limits is expressed here by two terms with overlapping meanings, *metron* and *kanōn*, which are played off against several expressions denoting overreaching or expansion beyond a legitimate sphere.

10:17 Boast in the Lord: there is a legitimate boasting, in contrast to the immoderate boasting to which 2 Cor 10:13, 15 allude. God's work through Paul in the community is the object of his boast (2 Cor 10:13–16; 2 Cor 1:12–14) and constitutes his recommendation (2 Cor 3:1–3). Cf. notes on 2 Cor 1:12–14 and 1 Cor 1:29–31.

10:18 Approved: to be approved is to come successfully through the process of testing for authenticity (cf. 2 Cor 13:3–7 and the note on 2 Cor 8:2). **Whom the Lord recommends**: self-commendation is a premature and unwarranted anticipation of the final judgment, which the Lord alone will pass (cf. 1 Cor 4:3–5). Paul alludes to this judgment throughout 2 Cor 10–13, frequently in final or transitional positions; cf. 2 Cor 11:15; 12:19a; 13:3–7.

11:1–15 Although these verses continue to reveal information about Paul's opponents and the differences he perceives between them and himself, 2 Cor 11:1 signals a turn in Paul's thought. This section constitutes a prologue to the boasting that he will undertake in 2 Cor 11:16–12:10, and it bears remarkable similarities to the section that follows the central boast, 2 Cor 12:11–18.

11:1 Put up with a little foolishness from me: this verse indicates more clearly than the general statement of intent in 2 Cor 10:13 the nature of the project Paul is about to undertake. He alludes ironically to the Corinthians' toleration for others. **Foolishness**: Paul qualifies his project as folly from beginning to end; see note on 2 Cor 11:16–12:10.

r: 6:7; 13:2–3; 1 Cor 1:25; Eph 6:10–14. *s:* 2:9. *t:* 1 Cor 1:12. *u:* 13:10. *v:* 1 Cor 2:3. *w:* 13:1–2. *x:* 3:1–2; 4:2; 5:12; 6:4; 10:18; 12:11. *y:* Rom 15:20–21. *z:* Jer 9:22–23; 1 Cor 1:31. *a:* 13:3–9. *b:* 11:21; 12:11.

from me! Please put up with me. [2c*]For I am
jealous of you with the jealousy of God,
since I betrothed you to one husband to present you as a chaste virgin to Christ. [3d*]But I
am afraid that, as the serpent deceived Eve
by his cunning, your thoughts may be corrupted from a sincere [and pure] commitment to Christ. [4e*]For if someone comes and
preaches another Jesus than the one we
preached, or if you receive a different spirit
from the one you received or a different
gospel from the one you accepted, you put up
with it well enough. [5f*]For I think that I am
not in any way inferior to these "superapostles." [6g*]Even if I am untrained in speaking, I am not so in knowledge; in every way
we have made this plain to you in all things.

[7h*]Did I make a mistake when I humbled
myself so that you might be exalted, because
I preached the gospel of God to you without
charge? [8]I plundered other churches by accepting from them in order to minister to
you. [9i]And when I was with you and in need,
I did not burden anyone, for the brothers
who came from Macedonia supplied my
needs. So I refrained and will refrain from
burdening you in any way. [10j]By the truth of
Christ in me, this boast of mine shall not be
silenced in the regions of Achaia. [11k*]And
why? Because I do not love you? God
knows I do!

[12]And what I do I will continue to do, in
order to end this pretext of those who seek a
pretext for being regarded as we are in the
mission of which they boast. [13*]For such
people are false apostles, deceitful workers,
who masquerade as apostles of Christ.
[14]And no wonder, for even Satan masquerades as an angel of light. [15]So it is not
strange that his ministers also masquerade as
ministers of righteousness. Their end will
correspond to their deeds.

11:2 Paul gives us a sudden glimpse of the theological values that are at stake. **The jealousy of God**: the perspective is that of the covenant, described in imagery of love and marriage, as in the prophets; cf. 1 Cor 10:22. **I betrothed you**: Paul, like a father (cf. 2 Cor 12:14), betroths the community to Christ as his bride (cf. Eph 5:21–33) and will present her to him at his second coming. Cf. Mt 25:1–13 and the nuptial imagery in Rev 21.

11:3 As the serpent deceived Eve: before Christ can return for the community Paul fears a repetition of the primal drama of seduction. Corruption of minds is satanic activity (see 2 Cor 2:11; 4:4). Satanic imagery recurs in 2 Cor 11:13–15, 20; 12:7b, 16–17; see notes on these passages.

11:4 Preaches another Jesus: the danger is specified, and Paul's opponents are identified with the cunning serpent. The battle for minds has to do with the understanding of Jesus, the Spirit, the gospel; the Corinthians have flirted with another understanding than the one that Paul handed on to them as traditional and normative.

11:5 These "superapostles": this term, employed again in 2 Cor 12:11b, designates the opponents of whom Paul has spoken in 2 Cor 10 and again in 2 Cor 11:4. They appear to be intruders at Corinth. Their preaching is marked at least by a different emphasis and style, and they do not hesitate to accept support from the community. Perhaps these itinerants appeal to the authority of church leaders in Jerusalem and even carry letters of recommendation from them. But it is not those distant leaders whom Paul is attacking here. The intruders are "superapostles" not in the sense of the "pillars" at Jerusalem (Gal 2), but in their own estimation. They consider themselves superior to Paul as apostles and ministers of Christ, and they are obviously enjoying some success among the Corinthians. Paul rejects their claim to be apostles in any superlative sense (*hyperlian*), judging them bluntly as "false apostles," ministers of Satan masquerading as apostles of Christ (2 Cor 11:13–15). On the contrary, he himself will claim to be a superminister of Christ (*hyper egō*, 2 Cor 11:23).

11:6 Apparently found deficient in both rhetorical ability (cf. 2 Cor 10:10) and knowledge (cf. 2 Cor 10:5), Paul concedes the former charge but not the latter. **In every way**: in all their contacts with him revelation has been taking place. Paul, through whom God reveals the knowledge of himself (2 Cor 2:14), and in whom the death and life of Jesus are revealed (2 Cor 4:10–11; cf. 2 Cor 6:4), also demonstrates his own role as the bearer of true knowledge. Cf. 1 Cor 1:18–2:16.

11:7–10 Abruptly Paul passes to another reason for complaints: his practice of preaching without remuneration (cf. 1 Cor 9:3–18). He deftly defends his practice by situating it from the start within the pattern of Christ's own self-humiliation (cf. 2 Cor 10:1) and reduces objections to absurdity by rhetorical questions (cf. 2 Cor 12:13).

11:11–12 Paul rejects lack of affection as his motive (possibly imputed to him by his opponents) and states his real motive, a desire to emphasize the disparity between himself and the others (cf. 2 Cor 11:19–21). The topic of his gratuitous service will be taken up once more in 2 Cor 12:13–18. 1 Cor 9:15–18 gives a different but complementary explanation of his motivation.

11:13–15 Paul picks up again the imagery of 2 Cor 11:3 and applies it to the opponents: they are false apostles of Christ, really serving another master. **Deceitful . . . masquerade**: deception and simulation, like cunning (2 Cor 11:3), are marks of the satanic. **Angel of light**: recalls the contrast between light and darkness, Christ and Beliar at 2 Cor 6:14–15. **Ministers of righteousness**: recalls the earlier contrast between the ministry of condemnation and that of righteousness (2 Cor 3:9). **Their end**: the section closes with another allusion to the judgment, when all participants in the final conflict will be revealed or unmasked and dealt with as they deserve.

c: Hos 2:21–22; Eph 5:26–27. *d:* Gn 3:1–6. *e:* Gal 1:6–9. *f:* 12:11. *g:* 1 Cor 1:5, 17; 2:1–5. *h:* 12:13–18; Acts 18:3; 1 Cor 9:6–18. *i:* Phil 4:15, 18. *j:* 1 Cor 9:15. *k:* 12:15.

Paul's Boast: His Labors. 16*I repeat, no one should consider me foolish; but if you do, accept me as a fool, so that I too may boast a little. 17What I am saying I am not saying according to the Lord but as in foolishness, in this boastful state. 18Since many boast according to the flesh, I too will boast. 19For you gladly put up with fools, since you are wise yourselves. 20*For you put up with it if someone enslaves you, or devours you, or gets the better of you, or puts on airs, or slaps you in the face. 21*To my shame I say that we were too weak!

But what anyone dares to boast of (I am speaking in foolishness) I also dare. 22l*Are they Hebrews? So am I. Are they Israelites? So am I. Are they descendants of Abraham? So am I. 23m*Are they ministers of Christ? (I am talking like an insane person.) I am still more, with far greater labors, far more imprisonments, far worse beatings, and numerous brushes with death. 24nFive times at the hands of the Jews I received forty lashes minus one. 25oThree times I was beaten with rods, once I was stoned, three times I was shipwrecked, I passed a night and a day on the deep; 26on frequent journeys, in dangers from rivers, dangers from robbers, dangers from my own race, dangers from Gentiles, dangers in the city, dangers in the wilderness, dangers at sea, dangers among false brothers; 27pin toil and hardship, through many sleepless nights, through hunger and thirst, through frequent fastings, through cold and exposure. 28And apart from these things, there is the daily pressure upon me of my anxiety for all the churches. 29qWho is weak, and I am not weak? Who is led to sin, and I am not indignant?

Paul's Boast: His Weakness. 30*If I must boast, I will boast of the things that show my weakness. 31*The God and Father of the Lord Jesus knows, he who is blessed forever, that I do not lie. 32At Damascus, the governor under King Aretas guarded the city of Damascus, in order to seize me, 33rbut I was lowered in a basket through a window in the wall and escaped his hands.

CHAPTER 12

See RG 463–64

1*I must boast; not that it is profitable, but I will go on to visions and revelations of

11:16–12:10 Paul now accepts the challenge of his opponents and indulges in boasting similar to theirs, but with differences that he has already signaled in 2 Cor 10:12–18 and that become clearer as he proceeds. He defines the nature of his project and unmistakably labels it as folly at the beginning and the end (2 Cor 11:16–23; 12:11). Yet his boast does not spring from ignorance (2 Cor 11:21; 12:6) nor is it concerned merely with human distinctions (2 Cor 11:18). Paul boasts "in moderation" (2 Cor 10:13, 15) and "in the Lord" (2 Cor 10:17).

11:16–29 The first part of Paul's boast focuses on labors and afflictions, in which authentic service of Christ consists.

11:16–21 These verses recapitulate remarks already made about the foolishness of boasting and the excessive toleration of the Corinthians. They form a prelude to the boast proper.

11:20 Paul describes the activities of the "others" in terms that fill out the picture drawn in vv 3–4, 13–15. Much of the vocabulary suggests fleshly or even satanic activity. **Enslaves**: cf. Gal 2:4. **Devours**: cf. 1 Pt 5:8. **Gets the better**: the verb *lambanō* means "to take," but is used in a variety of senses; here it may imply financial advantage, as in the English colloquialism "to take someone." It is similarly used at 2 Cor 12:16 and is there connected with cunning and deceit. **Puts on airs**: the same verb is rendered "raise oneself" (2 Cor 10:5) and "be too elated" (2 Cor 12:7).

11:21 Paul ironically concedes the charge of personal weakness from 2 Cor 10:1–18 but will refute the other charge there mentioned, that of lack of boldness, accepting the challenge to demonstrate it by his boast.

11:22 The opponents apparently pride themselves on their "Jewishness." Paul, too, can claim to be a Jew by race, religion, and promise. **Descendants of Abraham**: elsewhere Paul distinguishes authentic from inauthentic heirs of Abraham and the promise (Rom 4:13–18; 9:7–13; 11:1; Gal 3:9, 27–29; cf. Jn 8:33–47). Here he grants his opponents this title in order to concentrate on the principal claim that follows.

11:23b–29 Service of the humiliated and crucified Christ is demonstrated by trials endured for him. This rhetorically impressive catalogue enumerates many of the labors and perils Paul encountered on his missionary journeys.

11:23a Ministers of Christ . . . I am still more: the central point of the boast (cf. note on 2 Cor 11:5). **Like an insane person**: the climax of his folly.

11:30–12:10 The second part of Paul's boast, marked by a change of style and a shift in focus. After recalling the project in which he is engaged, he states a new topic: his weaknesses as matter for boasting. Everything in this section, even the discussion of privileges and distinctions, will be integrated into this perspective.

11:31–32 The episode at Damascus is symbolic. It aptly illustrates Paul's weakness but ends in deliverance (cf. 2 Cor 4:7–11).

12:1–4 In the body or out of the body: he seemed no longer confined to bodily conditions, but he does not claim to understand the mechanics of the experience. Caught up: i.e., in ecstasy. **The third heaven . . . Paradise**: ancient cosmolo-

l: Acts 22:3 / Rom 11:1; Phil 3:5–6. *m:* 6:5; Acts 16:22–24; 1 Cor 15:31–32. *n:* Dt 25:2–3. *o:* Acts 14:19; 27:43–44. *p:* 1 Cor 4:11. *q:* 1 Cor 9:22. *r:* Acts 9:23–25.

the Lord. [2]I know someone in Christ who,
fourteen years ago (whether in the body or
out of the body I do not know, God knows),
was caught up to the third heaven. [3]And I
know that this person (whether in the body
or out of the body I do not know, God
knows) [4s]was caught up into Paradise and
heard ineffable things, which no one may utter. [5*]About this person I will boast, but
about myself I will not boast, except about
my weaknesses. [6]Although if I should wish
to boast, I would not be foolish, for I would
be telling the truth. But I refrain, so that no
one may think more of me than what he sees
in me or hears from me [7t*]because of the
abundance of the revelations. Therefore, that
I might not become too elated, a thorn in the
flesh was given to me, an angel of Satan, to
beat me, to keep me from being too elated.
[8u*]Three times I begged the Lord about this,
that it might leave me, [9v*]but he said to me,
"My grace is sufficient for you, for power is
made perfect in weakness." I will rather
boast most gladly of my weaknesses, in order that the power of Christ may dwell with
me. [10w*]Therefore, I am content with weaknesses, insults, hardships, persecutions, and
constraints, for the sake of Christ; for when
I am weak, then I am strong.

Selfless Concern for the Church. [11x*]I
have been foolish. You compelled me, for I
ought to have been commended by you. For
I am in no way inferior to these "superapostles," even though I am nothing. [12y*]The

gies depicted a multitiered universe. Jewish intertestamental literature contains much speculation about the number of heavens. Seven is the number usually mentioned, but the Testament of Levi (2:7–10; 3:1–4) speaks of three; God himself dwelt in the third of these. Without giving us any clear picture of the cosmos, Paul indicates a mental journey to a nonearthly space, set apart by God, in which secrets were revealed to him. **Ineffable things**: i.e., privileged knowledge, which it was not possible or permitted to divulge.

12:5–7 This person: the indirect way of referring to himself has the effect of emphasizing the distance between that experience and his everyday life, just as the indirect **someone in Christ** (2 Cor 12:2) and all the passive verbs emphasize his passivity and receptivity in the experience. The revelations were not a personal achievement, nor were they meant to draw attention to any quality of his own.

12:7 That I might not become too elated: God assures that there is a negative component to his experience, so that he cannot lose proper perspective; cf. 2 Cor 1:9; 4:7–11. **A thorn in the flesh**: variously interpreted as a sickness or physical disability, a temptation, or a handicap connected with his apostolic activity. But since Hebrew "thorn in the flesh," like English "thorn in my side," refers to persons (cf. Nm 33:55; Ez 28:24), Paul may be referring to some especially persistent and obnoxious opponent. The language of 2 Cor 12:7–8 permits this interpretation. If this is correct, the frequent appearance of singular pronouns in depicting the opposition may not be merely a stylistic variation; the singular may be provoked and accompanied by the image of one individual in whom criticism of Paul's preaching, way of life, and apostolic consciousness is concentrated, and who embodies all the qualities Paul attributes to the group. **An angel of Satan**: a personal messenger from Satan; cf. the satanic language already applied to the opponents in 2 Cor 11:3, 13–15, 20.

12:8 Three times: his prayer was insistent, like that of Jesus in Gethsemane, a sign of how intolerable he felt the thorn to be.

12:9 But he said to me: Paul's petition is denied; release and healing are withheld for a higher purpose. The Greek perfect tense indicates that Jesus' earlier response still holds at the time of writing. **My grace is sufficient for you**: this is not a statement about the sufficiency of grace in general. Jesus speaks directly to Paul's situation. **Is made perfect**: i.e., is given most fully and manifests itself fully.

12:9b–10a Paul draws the conclusion from the autobiographical anecdote and integrates it into the subject of this part of the boast. **Weaknesses**: the apostolic hardships he must endure, including active personal hostility, as specified in a final catalogue (2 Cor 12:10a). **That the power of Christ may dwell with me**: Paul pinpoints the ground for the paradoxical strategy he has adopted in his self-defense.

12:10 When I am weak, then I am strong: Paul recognizes a twofold pattern in the resolution of the weakness-power (and death-life) dialectic, each of which looks to Jesus as the model and is experienced in him. The first is personal, involving a reversal in oneself (Jesus, 2 Cor 13:4a; Paul, 2 Cor 1:9–10; 4:10–11; 6:9). The second is apostolic, involving an effect on others (Jesus, 2 Cor 5:14–15; Paul, 2 Cor 1:6; 4:12; 13:9). The specific kind of "effectiveness in ministry" that Paul promises to demonstrate on his arrival (2 Cor 13:4b; cf. 2 Cor 10:1–11) involves elements of both; this, too, will be modeled on Jesus' experience and a participation in that experience (2 Cor 9; 13:3b).

12:11–18 This brief section forms an epilogue or concluding observation to Paul's boast, corresponding to the prologue in 2 Cor 11:1–15. A four-step sequence of ideas is common to these two sections: Paul qualifies his boast as folly (2 Cor 11:1; 12:11a), asserts his noninferiority to the "superapostles" (2 Cor 11:5; 12:11b), exemplifies this by allusion to charismatic endowments (2 Cor 11:6; 12:12), and finally denies that he has been a financial burden to the community (2 Cor 11:7–12; 12:13–18).

12:12 Despite weakness and affliction (suggested by the mention **of endurance**), his ministry has been accompanied by demonstrations of power (cf. 1 Cor 2:3–4). **Signs of an apostle**: visible proof of belonging to Christ and of mediating Christ's power, which the opponents require as touchstones of apostleship (2 Cor 12:11; cf. 2 Cor 13:3).

s: Lk 23:43; Rev 2:7. *t:* Nm 33:55; Jos 23:13; Ez 28:24. *u:* Mt 26:39–44. *v:* 4:7. *w:* 6:4–5; Rom 5:3 / Phil 4:13. *x:* 11:5. *y:* Rom 15:19; 1 Thes 1:5.

signs of an apostle were performed among
you with all endurance, signs and wonders,
and mighty deeds. [13z*]In what way were you
less privileged than the rest of the churches,
except that on my part I did not burden you?
Forgive me this wrong!
[14]Now I am ready to come to you this third
time. And I will not be a burden, for I want
not what is yours, but you. Children ought
not to save for their parents, but parents for
their children. [15]I will most gladly spend and
be utterly spent for your sakes. If I love you
more, am I to be loved less? [16a]But granted
that I myself did not burden you, yet I was
crafty and got the better of you by deceit.
[17]Did I take advantage of you through any of
those I sent to you? [18b]I urged Titus to go and
sent the brother with him. Did Titus take advantage of you? Did we not walk in the same
spirit? And in the same steps?
Final Warnings and Appeals. [19*]Have you
been thinking all along that we are defending
ourselves before you? In the sight of God we
are speaking in Christ, and all for building
you up, beloved. [20c*]For I fear that when I
come I may find you not such as I wish, and
that you may find me not as you wish; that
there may be rivalry, jealousy, fury, selfishness, slander, gossip, conceit, and disorder.
[21*]I fear that when I come again my God may
humiliate me before you, and I may have to
mourn over many of those who sinned earlier
and have not repented of the impurity, immorality, and licentiousness they practiced.

CHAPTER 13

See RG 463–64

[1d*]This third time I am coming to you.
"On the testimony of two or three witnesses
a fact shall be established." [2*]I warned those
who sinned earlier and all the others, and I
warn them now while absent, as I did when
present on my second visit, that if I come
again I will not be lenient, [3*]since you are
looking for proof of Christ speaking in me.
He is not weak toward you but powerful in
you. [4]For indeed he was crucified out of

12:13–18 Paul insists on his intention to continue refusing support from the community (cf. 2 Cor 11:8–12). In defending his practice and his motivation, he once more protests his love (cf. 2 Cor 11:11) and rejects the suggestion of secret self-enrichment. He has recourse here again to language applied to his opponents earlier: "cunning" (2 Cor 11:3), "deceit" (2 Cor 11:13), "got the better of you" (see note on 2 Cor 11:20), "take advantage" (2 Cor 2:11).

12:19–13:10 This concludes the development begun in 2 Cor 10. In the chiastic arrangement of the material (see note on 2 Cor 10:1–13:10), this final part corresponds to the opening; there are important similarities of content between the two sections as well.

12:19 This verse looks back at the previous chapters and calls them by their proper name, a defense, an apologia (cf. 1 Cor 9:3). Yet Paul insists on an important distinction: he has indeed been speaking for their benefit, but the ultimate judgment to which he submits is God's (cf. 1 Cor 4:3–5). This verse also leads into the final section, announcing two of its themes: judgment and building up.

12:20 I fear that . . .: earlier Paul expressed fear that the Corinthians were being victimized, exploited, seduced from right thinking by his opponents (2 Cor 11:3–4, 19–21). Here he alludes unexpectedly to moral disorders among the Corinthians themselves. The catalogue suggests the effects of factions that have grown up around rival apostles.

12:21 Again: one can also translate, "I fear that when I come my God may again humiliate me." Paul's allusion to the humiliation and mourning that may await him recall the mood he described in 2 Cor 2:1–4, but there is no reference here to any individual such as there is in 2 Cor 2:5–11. The crisis of 2 Cor 2 has happily been resolved by integration of the offender and repentance (2 Cor 7:4–16), whereas 2 Cor 12:21 is preoccupied with still unrepentant sinners. The sexual sins recall 1 Cor 5–7.

13:1 This third time I am coming: designation of the forthcoming visit as the "third" (cf. 2 Cor 12:14) may indicate that, in addition to his founding sojourn in Corinth, Paul had already made the first of two visits mentioned as planned in 2 Cor 1:15, and the next visit will be the long-postponed second of these. If so, the materials in 2 Cor 1:12–2:13 plus 2 Cor 7:4–16 and 2 Cor 10–13 may date from the same period of time, presumably of some duration, between Paul's second and third visit, though it is not clear that they are addressing the same crisis. The chronology is too unsure and the relations between sections of 2 Corinthians too unclear to yield any certainty. The hypothesis that 2 Cor 10–13 are themselves the "tearful letter" mentioned at 2 Cor 2:3–4 creates more problems than it solves.

13:2 I warned those who sinned earlier: mention of unrepentant sinners (2 Cor 12:21 and here) and of an oral admonition given them on an earlier visit complicates the picture at the very end of Paul's development. It provides, in fact, a second explanation for the show of power that has been threatened from the beginning (2 Cor 10:1–6), but a different reason for it, quite unsuspected until now. It is not clear whether Paul is merely alluding to a dimension of the situation that he has not previously had occasion to mention, or whether some other community crisis, not directly connected with that behind 2 Cor 10–13, has influenced the final editing. **I will not be lenient**: contrast Paul's hesitation and reluctance to inflict pain in 2 Cor 1:23 and 2 Cor 2:1–4. The next visit will bring the showdown.

13:3–4 Paul now gives another motive for severity when he comes, the charge of weakness leveled against him as an apostle. The motive echoes more closely the opening section

z: 11:9–12. *a:* 11:3, 13. *b:* 2:13; 8:16, 23. *c:* 1 Cor 1:11; 3:3. *d:* Dt 19:15; Mt 18:16; Jn 8:17; Heb 10:28.

weakness, but he lives by the power of God. So also we are weak in him, but toward you we shall live with him by the power of God.

5*Examine yourselves to see whether you are living in faith. Test yourselves. Do you not realize that Jesus Christ is in you?—unless, of course, you fail the test. 6I hope you will discover that we have not failed. 7But we pray to God that you may not do evil, not that we may appear to have passed the test but that you may do what is right, even though we may seem to have failed. 8For we cannot do anything against the truth, but only for the truth. 9For we rejoice when we are weak but you are strong. What we pray for is your improvement.

10e*I am writing this while I am away, so that when I come I may not have to be severe in virtue of the authority that the Lord has given me to build up and not to tear down.

V. Conclusion

11*Finally, brothers, rejoice. Mend your ways, encourage one another, agree with one another, live in peace, and the God of love and peace will be with you. 12fGreet one another with a holy kiss. All the holy ones greet you.

13gThe grace of the Lord Jesus Christ and the love of God and the fellowship of the holy Spirit be with all of you.

(2 Cor 10:1–18) and the intervening development (especially 2 Cor 11:30–12:10). **Proof of Christ speaking in me**: the threat of 2 Cor 10:1–2 is reworded to recall Paul's conformity with the pattern of Christ, his insertion into the interplay of death and life, weakness and power (cf. note on 2 Cor 12:10b).

13:5–9 Paul turns the challenge mentioned in 2 Cor 13:3 on them: they are to put themselves to the test to demonstrate whether Christ is in them. These verses involve a complicated series of plays on the theme of *dokimē* (testing, proof, passing and failing a test). Behind this stands the familiar distinction between present human judgment and final divine judgment. This is the final appearance of the theme (cf. 2 Cor 10:18; 11:15; 12:19).

13:10 Authority . . . to build up and not to tear down: Paul restates the purpose of his letter in language that echoes 2 Cor 10:2, 8, emphasizing the positive purpose of his authority in their regard. This verse forms an inclusion with the topic sentence of the section (2 Cor 12:19), as well as with the opening of this entire portion of the letter (2 Cor 10:1–2).

13:11–13 These verses may have originally concluded 2 Cor 10–13, but they have nothing specifically to do with the material of that section. It is also possible to consider them a conclusion to the whole of 2 Corinthians in its present edited form. The exhortations are general, including a final appeal for peace in the community. The letter ends calmly, after its many storms, with the prospect of ecclesial unity and divine blessing. The final verse is one of the clearest trinitarian passages in the New Testament.

e: 10:8. *f:* Rom 16:16; 1 Cor 16:20 / Phil 4:22; 1 Thes 5:26; 1 Pt 5:14. *g:* Rom 16:20; 1 Cor 16:23.

See RG 464–71

The Letter to the Galatians

The Galatians to whom the letter is addressed were Paul's converts, most likely among the descendants of Celts who had invaded western and central Asia Minor in the third century B.C. and had settled in the territory around Ancyra (modern Ankara, Turkey). Paul had passed through this area on his second missionary journey (Acts 16:6) and again on his third (Acts 18:23). It is less likely that the recipients of this letter were Paul's churches in the southern regions of Pisidia, Lycaonia, and Pamphylia where he had preached earlier in the Hellenized cities of Perge, Iconium, Pisidian Antioch, Lystra, and Derbe (Acts 13:13–14:27); this area was part of the Roman province of Galatia, and some scholars think that South Galatia was the destination of this letter.

If it is addressed to the Galatians in the north, the letter was probably written around A.D. 54 or 55, most likely from Ephesus after Paul's arrival there for a stay of several years on his third missionary journey (Acts 19; 20:31). On the South Galatian theory, the date would be earlier, perhaps A.D. 48–50. Involved is the question of how one relates the events of Gal 2:1–10 to the "Council of Jerusalem" described in Acts 15 (see notes on each passage).

In any case, the new Christians whom Paul is addressing were converts from paganism (Gal 4:8–9) who were now being enticed by other missionaries to add the observances of the Jewish law, including the rite of circumcision, to the cross of Christ as a means of salvation. For, since Paul's visit, some other interpretation of Christianity had been brought to these neophytes, probably by converts from Judaism (the name "Judaizers" is sometimes applied to them); it has specifically been suggested that they were Jewish Christians who had come from the austere Essene sect.

These interlopers insisted on the necessity of following certain precepts of the Mosaic law along with faith in Christ. They were undermining Paul's authority also, asserting that he had not been trained by Jesus himself, that his gospel did not agree with that of the original and true apostles in Jerusalem, that he had kept from his converts in Galatia the necessity of accepting circumcision and other key obligations of the Jewish law, in order more easily to win them to Christ, and that his gospel was thus not the full and authentic one held by "those of repute" in Jerusalem (Gal 2:2). Some scholars also see in Galatians 5; 6 another set of opponents against whom Paul writes, people who in their emphasis on the Spirit set aside all norms for conduct and became libertines in practice.

When Paul learned of the situation, he wrote this defense of his apostolic authority and of the correct understanding of the faith. He set forth the unique importance of Christ and his redemptive sacrifice on the cross, the freedom that Christians enjoy from the old burdens of the law, the total sufficiency of Christ and of faith in Christ as the way to God and to eternal life, and the beauty of the new life of the Spirit. Galatians is thus a summary of basic Pauline theology. Its themes were more fully and less polemically developed in the Letter to the Romans.

Autobiographically, the letter gives us Paul's own accounts of how he came to faith (Gal 1:15–24), the agreement in "the truth of the gospel" (Gal 2:5, 14) that he shared with the Jewish Christian leaders in Jerusalem, James, Cephas, and John (Gal 2:1–10), and the rebuke he had to deliver to Cephas in Antioch for inconsistency, contrary to the gospel, on the issue of table fellowship in the racially mixed church of Jewish and Gentile Christians in Antioch (Gal 2:11–14; cf. Gal 2:15–21). At the conclusion of the letter (Gal 6:11–18), Paul wrote in his own hand (cf. 2 Thes 3:17–18) a vivid summary of the message to the Galatians.

In his vigorous emphasis on the absolute preeminence of Christ and his cross as God's way to salvation and holiness, Paul stresses Christian freedom and the ineffectiveness of the Mosaic law for gaining divine favor and blessings (Gal 3:19–29). The pious Jew saw in the law a way established by God to win divine approval by a life of meticulous observance of ritual, social, and moral regulations. But Paul's profound insight into the higher designs of God in Christ led him to understand and welcome the priority of promise and faith (shown in the experience of Abraham, Gal 3:6–18) and the supernatural gifts of the Spirit (Gal 3:2–5; 5:16–6:10). His enthusiasm for this new vision of the life of grace in Christ and of the uniquely salvific role of Christ's redemptive death on the cross shines through this whole letter.

The principal divisions of the Letter to the Galatians are the following:

I. Address (1:1–5)
II. Loyalty to the Gospel (1:6–10)
III. Paul's Defense of His Gospel and His Authority (1:11–2:21)
IV. Faith and Liberty (3:1–4:31)
V. Exhortation to Christian Living (5:1–6:10)
VI. Conclusion (6:11–18)

I. Address

CHAPTER 1

See RG 466–67

Greeting. 1ab*Paul, an apostle not
from human beings nor through a human being but through Jesus Christ and God the Father who raised him from the dead, 2*and all
the brothers who are with me, to the churches
of Galatia: 3grace to you and peace from God
our Father and the Lord Jesus Christ, 4c*who

1:1–5 See note on Rom 1:1–7, concerning the greeting.

1:1 Apostle: because of attacks on his authority in Galatia, Paul defends his apostleship. He is not an apostle commissioned by a congregation (Phil 2:25; 2 Cor 8:23) or even by prophets (1 Tm 1:18; 4:14) but **through Jesus Christ and God the Father**.

1:2 All the brothers: fellow believers in Christ, male and female; cf. Gal 3:27–28. Paul usually mentions the co-sender(s) at the start of a letter, but the use of all is unique, adding weight to the letter. **Galatia**: central Turkey more likely than the Roman province of Galatia; see Introduction.

1:4 The greeting in v 3 is expanded by a christological for-

a: Rom 1:1–7; 1 Cor 1:1–3. *b:* 1:11–12. *c:* 2:20; Eph 5:2; 1 Tm 2:6 / 1 Jn 5:19 / Rom 12:2; Eph 5:16; Heb 10:10.

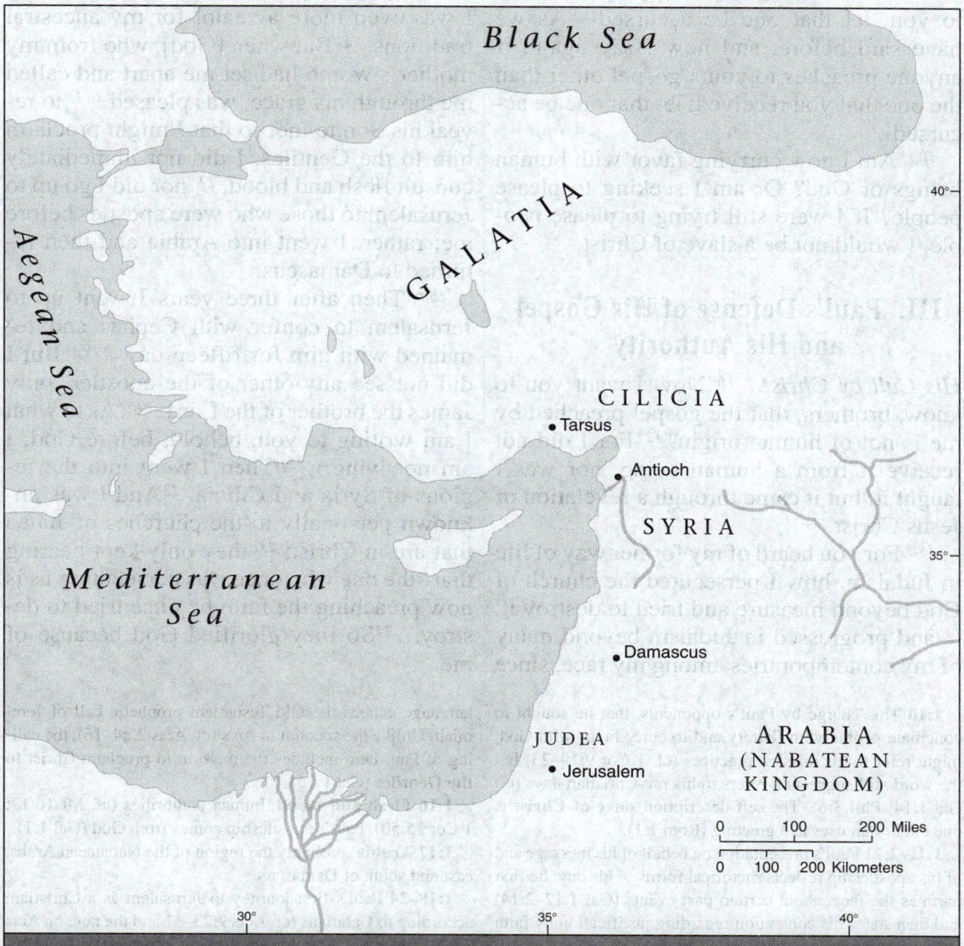

Paul's Journeys to Asia Minor

gave himself for our sins that he might rescue us from the present evil age in accord with the will of our God and Father, [5d]to whom be glory forever and ever. Amen.

II. Loyalty To The Gospel

[6e*]I am amazed that you are so quickly forsaking the one who called you by [the] grace [of Christ] for a different gospel [7](not that there is another). But there are some who are disturbing you and wish to pervert the gospel of Christ. [8f*]But even if we or an angel from heaven should preach [to you] a gospel other than the one that we preached

mula that stresses deliverance through the Lord Jesus from a world dominated by Satan; cf. 2 Cor 4:4; Eph 2:2; 6:12.

1:6–10 In place of the usual thanksgiving (see note on Rom 1:8), Paul, with little to be thankful for in the Galatian situation, expresses amazement at the way his converts are deserting the gospel of Christ for a perverted message. He reasserts the one gospel he has preached (Gal 1:7–9) and begins to defend himself (Gal 1:10).

1:6 The one who called you: God or Christ, though in actuality Paul was the divine instrument to call the Galatians.

1:8 Accursed: in Greek, **anathema**; cf. Rom 9:3; 1 Cor 12:3; 16:22.

d: Rom 16:27; 2 Tm 4:18. *e:* 5:8, 10; Acts 15:1, 24; 2 Cor 11:4. *f:* 1 Cor 16:22 / 5:3, 21; 2 Cor 13:2.

to you, let that one be accursed! [9]As we have said before, and now I say again, if anyone preaches to you a gospel other than the one that you received, let that one be accursed!

[10g*]Am I now currying favor with human beings or God? Or am I seeking to please people? If I were still trying to please people, I would not be a slave of Christ.

III. Paul's Defense of His Gospel and His Authority

His Call by Christ. [11h*]Now I want you to know, brothers, that the gospel preached by me is not of human origin. [12*]For I did not receive it from a human being, nor was I taught it, but it came through a revelation of Jesus Christ.

[13i*]For you heard of my former way of life in Judaism, how I persecuted the church of God beyond measure and tried to destroy it, [14j]and progressed in Judaism beyond many of my contemporaries among my race, since I was even more a zealot for my ancestral traditions. [15k]But when [God], who from my mother's womb had set me apart and called me through his grace, was pleased [16l*]to reveal his Son to me, so that I might proclaim him to the Gentiles, I did not immediately consult flesh and blood, [17*]nor did I go up to Jerusalem to those who were apostles before me; rather, I went into Arabia and then returned to Damascus.

[18m*]Then after three years I went up to Jerusalem to confer with Cephas and remained with him for fifteen days. [19n*]But I did not see any other of the apostles, only James the brother of the Lord. [20o](As to what I am writing to you, behold, before God, I am not lying.) [21p]Then I went into the regions of Syria and Cilicia. [22]And I was unknown personally to the churches of Judea that are in Christ; [23q]they only kept hearing that "the one who once was persecuting us is now preaching the faith he once tried to destroy." [24]So they glorified God because of me.

1:10 This charge by Paul's opponents, that he sought to conciliate people with flattery and to curry favor with God, might refer to his mission practices (cf. 1 Cor 9:19–23) but the word **still** suggests it refers to his pre-Christian days (cf. Gal 1:14; Phil 3:6). The self-description **slave of Christ** is one Paul often uses in a greeting (Rom 1:1).

1:11–2:21 Paul's presentation on behalf of his message and of his apostleship reflects rhetorical forms of his day: he first narrates the facts about certain past events (Gal 1:12–2:14) and then states his contention regarding justification by faith as the gospel message (Gal 2:15–21). Further arguments follow from both experience and scripture in Galatians 3; 4 before he draws out the ethical consequences (Gal 5:1–6:10). The specific facts that he takes up here to show that his gospel is not a human invention (Gal 1:11) but **came through a revelation of Jesus Christ** (Gal 1:12) deal with his own calling as a Christian missionary (Gal 1:13–17), his initial relations with the apostles in Jerusalem (Gal 1:18–24), a later journey to Jerusalem (Gal 2:1–10), and an incident in Antioch involving Cephas and persons from James (Gal 2:11–14). The content of Paul's revealed gospel is then set forth in the heart of the letter (Gal 2:15–21).

1:12 Although Paul received his gospel **through a revelation** from Christ, this did not exclude his use of early Christian confessional formulations. See note on Gal 1:4.

1:13–17 Along with Phil 3:4–11, which also moves from autobiography to its climax in a discussion on justification by faith (cf. Gal 2:15–21), this passage is Paul's chief account of the change from his **former way of life** (Gal 1:13) to service as a Christian missionary (Gal 1:16); cf. Acts 9:1–22; 22:4–16; 26:9–18. Paul himself does not use the term "conversion" but stresses revelation (Gal 1:12, 16). In Gal 1:15 his language echoes the Old Testament prophetic call of Jeremiah. Unlike the account in Acts (cf. Acts 22:4–16), the calling of Paul here includes the mission to proclaim Christ **to the Gentiles** (Gal 1:16).

1:16 Flesh and blood: human authorities (cf. Mt 16:17; 1 Cor 15:50). Paul's apostleship comes from God (Gal 1:1).

1:17 Arabia: probably the region of the Nabataean Arabs, east and south of Damascus.

1:18–24 Paul's first journey to Jerusalem as a Christian, according to Galatians (cf. Acts 9:23–31 and the note on Acts 12:25). He is quite explicit about contacts there, testifying under oath (Gal 1:20). On returning to Syria (perhaps specifically Damascus, cf. Gal 1:17) **and Cilicia** (including his home town Tarsus, cf. Acts 9:30; 22:3), Paul most likely engaged in missionary work. He underscores the fact that Christians in Judea knew of him only by reputation.

1:18 After three years: two years and more, since Paul's call. To **confer with** Cephas may mean simply "pay a visit" or more specifically "get information from" him about Jesus, over a two-week period. **Cephas**: Aramaic name of Simon (Peter); cf. Mt 16:16–18 and the notes there.

1:19 James the brother of the Lord: not one of the Twelve, but a brother of Jesus (see note on Mk 6:3). He played an important role in the Jerusalem church (see note on Gal 2:9), the leadership of which he took over from Peter (Acts 12:17). Paul may have regarded James as an apostle.

g: 2 Cor 5:11 / 1 Thes 2:4. *h:* 1 Cor 15:1 / 1:1; Eph 3:3. *i:* Acts 8:1–3; 9:1–2; 1 Cor 15:9. *j:* Acts 26:4–5. *k:* Is 49:1; Jer 1:4. *l:* 1:11–12; Rom 1:5; 1 Cor 15:10; Acts 9:3–9 / 2:2, 7 / Mt 16:17. *m:* Acts 9:26–30 / Jn 1:42. *n:* 2:9; Mt 13:55; Acts 12:17. *o:* Rom 9:1; 2 Cor 11:31. *p:* Acts 9:30. *q:* 1:13.

CHAPTER 2

See RG 467–68

The Council of Jerusalem. [1r*]Then
after fourteen years I again went up to
Jerusalem with Barnabas, taking Titus along
also. [2s*]I went up in accord with a revelation, and I presented to them the gospel that
I preach to the Gentiles—but privately to
those of repute—so that I might not be running, or have run, in vain. [3t*]Moreover, not
even Titus, who was with me, although he
was a Greek, was compelled to be circumcised, [4u*]but because of the false brothers secretly brought in, who slipped in to spy on
our freedom that we have in Christ Jesus,
that they might enslave us— [5v*]to them we
did not submit even for a moment, so that
the truth of the gospel might remain intact
for you. [6w]But from those who were reputed
to be important (what they once were makes
no difference to me; God shows no partiality)—those of repute made me add nothing.
[7x*]On the contrary, when they saw that I had
been entrusted with the gospel to the uncircumcised, just as Peter to the circumcised,
[8]for the one who worked in Peter for an
apostolate to the circumcised worked also in
me for the Gentiles, [9y*]and when they recognized the grace bestowed upon me, James
and Cephas and John, who were reputed to
be pillars, gave me and Barnabas their right
hands in partnership, that we should go to
the Gentiles and they to the circumcised.
[10z*]Only, we were to be mindful of the poor,
which is the very thing I was eager to do.

Peter's Inconsistency at Antioch. [11a*]And
when Cephas came to Antioch, I opposed him
to his face because he clearly was wrong.

2:1–10 Paul's second journey to Jerusalem, according to Galatians, involved a private meeting with **those of repute** (Gal 2:2). At issue was a Gentile, Titus, and the question of circumcision, which **false brothers** (Gal 2:4) evidently demanded for him. Paul insists that the gospel he preaches (Gal 2:2; cf. Gal 1:9, 11) remained intact with no addition by those of repute (Gal 2:6); that **Titus** was not **compelled** to accept circumcision (Gal 2:3); and that he and the reputed **pillars** in Jerusalem agreed on how each would advance the missionary task (Gal 1:7–10). Usually, Gal 1:1–10 is equated with the "Council of Jerusalem," as it is called, described in Acts 15. See notes on Acts 15:6–12, 13–35, the latter concerning the "decree" that Paul does not mention.

2:1 After fourteen years: thirteen or more years, probably reckoned from the return to Syria and Cilicia (Gal 1:21), though possibly from Paul's calling as a Christian (Gal 1:15). **Barnabas**: cf. Gal 2:9, 13; 1 Cor 9:6. A Jewish Christian missionary, with whom Paul worked (Acts 4:36–37; 11:22, 25, 30; 12:25; 13:1–3; 15:2). **Titus**: a missionary companion of Paul (2 Cor 2:13; 7:6, 13–15; 8:6, 16, 23; 12:18), non-Jewish (Gal 2:3), never mentioned in Acts.

2:2 A revelation: cf. Gal 1:1, 12. Paul emphasizes it was God's will, not Jerusalem authority, that led to the journey. Acts 15:2 states that the church in Antioch appointed Paul and Barnabas for the task. **Those of repute**: leaders of the Jerusalem church; the term, while positive, may be slightly ironic (cf. Gal 1:6, 9). **Run, in vain**: while Paul presents a positive picture in what follows, his missionary work in Galatia would have been to no purpose if his opponents were correct that circumcision is needed for complete faith in Christ.

2:3 Not even a Gentile Christian like Titus was compelled to receive the rite of circumcision. The Greek text could be interpreted that he voluntarily accepted circumcision, but this is unlikely in the overall argument.

2:4 False brothers: Jewish Christians who took the position that Gentile Christians must first become Jews through circumcision and observance of the Mosaic law in order to become Christians; cf. Acts 15:1.

2:5 The truth of the gospel: the true gospel, in contrast to the false one of the opponents (Gal 1:6–9); the gospel of grace, used as a norm (Gal 2:14).

2:7–9 Some think that actual "minutes" of the meeting are here quoted. Paul's apostleship to the Gentiles (Gal 1:16) is recognized alongside that of Peter to the Jews. Moreover, the right to proclaim the gospel without requiring circumcision and the Jewish law is sealed by a handshake. That Paul and colleagues **should go to the Gentiles** did not exclude his preaching to the Jews as well (Rom 1:13–16) or Cephas to Gentile areas.

2:9 James and Cephas and John: see notes on Gal 1:18, 19; on Peter and John as leaders in the Jerusalem church, cf. Acts 3:1 and Acts 8:14. The order here, with James first, may reflect his prominence in Jerusalem after Peter (Cephas) departed (Acts 12:17).

2:10 The poor: Jerusalem Christians or a group within the church there (cf. Rom 15:26). The collection for them was extremely important in Paul's thought and labor (cf. Rom 15:25–28; 1 Cor 16:1–4; 2 Cor 8–9).

2:11–14 The decision reached in Jerusalem (Gal 2:3–7) recognized the freedom of Gentile Christians from the Jewish law. But the problem of table fellowship between Jewish Christians, who possibly still kept kosher food regulations, and Gentile believers was not yet settled. When Cephas first came to the racially mixed community of Jewish and Gentile Christians in Antioch (Gal 2:12), he ate with non-Jews. Pressure from persons arriving later from Jerusalem caused him and Barnabas to draw back. Paul therefore publicly rebuked Peter's inconsistency toward the gospel (Gal 2:14). Some think that what Paul said on that occasion extends through Gal 2:16, 21.

2:11 Clearly was wrong: literally, "stood condemned," by himself and also by Paul. His action in breaking table fellow-

r: Acts 15:2. *s:* 1:11–12, 16 / 1:16 / Phil 2:16. *t:* 2 Cor 2:13; 7:6–7; 8:16–17; 12:18; Ti 1:4 / 2:14; 6:12. *u:* 5:1; Acts 15:1, 24. *v:* 2:14; 4:16. *w:* Dt 10:17; Rom 2:11. *x:* 1:15–16; Acts 9:15; 15:12; 22:21; Rom 1:5. *y:* Rom 15:15 / 1:18–19; Jn 1:42; Acts 12:17 / 2:1. *z:* Acts 11:29–30; Rom 15:25–28; 1 Cor 16:1–4; 2 Cor 8:9. *a:* 1:18 / Acts 11:19–30; 15:1–2.

[12b*]For, until some people came from James, he used to eat with the Gentiles; but when they came, he began to draw back and separated himself, because he was afraid of the circumcised. [13c*]And the rest of the Jews [also] acted hypocritically along with him, with the result that even Barnabas was carried away by their hypocrisy. [14d*]But when I saw that they were not on the right road in line with the truth of the gospel, I said to Cephas in front of all, "If you, though a Jew, are living like a Gentile and not like a Jew, how can you compel the Gentiles to live like Jews?"

Faith and Works. [15*]We, who are Jews by nature and not sinners from among the Gentiles, [16e*][yet] who know that a person is not justified by works of the law but through faith in Jesus Christ, even we have believed in Christ Jesus that we may be justified by faith in Christ and not by works of the law, because by works of the law no one will be justified. [17*]But if, in seeking to be justified in Christ, we ourselves are found to be sinners, is Christ then a minister of sin? Of course not! [18*]But if I am building up again those things that I tore down, then I show myself to be a transgressor. [19f*]For through the law I died to the law, that I might live for God. I have been crucified with Christ; [20g]yet I live, no longer I, but Christ lives in me; insofar as I now live in the flesh, I live by faith in the Son of God who has loved me and given himself up for me. [21h]I do not nullify the grace of God; for if justification comes through the law, then Christ died for nothing.

IV. Faith and Liberty

CHAPTER 3

See RG 468–70

Justification by Faith. [1i*]O stupid Galatians! Who has bewitched you, before whose eyes Jesus Christ was publicly portrayed as crucified? [2j*]I want to learn only this from you: did you receive the Spirit from works of the law, or from faith in what you heard? [3k*]Are you so stupid? After beginning with the Spirit, are you now ending with the flesh? [4*]Did you experience so many things

ship was especially grievous if the eating involved the meal at the Lord's supper (cf. 1 Cor 11:17–25).

2:12 Some people came from James: strict Jewish Christians (cf. Acts 15:1, 5; 21:20–21), either sent by James (Gal 1:19; 2:9) or claiming to be from the leader of the Jerusalem church. **The circumcised**: presumably Jewish Christians, not Jews.

2:13 The Jews: Jewish Christians, like Barnabas. **Hypocrisy**: literally, "pretense," "play-acting"; moral insincerity.

2:14 Compel the Gentiles to live like Jews: that is, conform to Jewish practices, such as circumcision (Gal 2:3–5) or regulations about food (Gal 2:12).

2:15–21 Following on the series of incidents cited above, Paul's argument, whether spoken to Cephas at Antioch or only now articulated, is pertinent to the Galatian situation, where believers were having themselves circumcised (Gal 6:12–13) and obeying other aspects of Jewish law (Gal 4:9–10; 5:1–4). He insists that salvation is by faith in Christ, not by works of the law. His teaching on the gospel concerns justification by faith (Gal 2:16) in relation to sin (Gal 2:17), law (Gal 2:19), life in Christ (Gal 2:19–20), and grace (Gal 2:21).

2:16 No one will be justified: Ps 143:2 is reflected.

2:17 A minister of sin: literally, "a servant of sin" (cf. Rom 15:8), an agent of sin, one who promotes it. This is possibly a claim by opponents that justification on the basis of faith in Christ makes Christ an abettor of sin when Christians **are found to be sinners**. Paul denies the conclusion (cf. Rom 6:1–4).

2:18 To return to observance of the law as the means to salvation would entangle one not only in inevitable transgressions of it but also in the admission that it was wrong to have abandoned the law in the first place.

2:19 Through the law I died to the law: this is variously explained: the law revealed sin (Rom 7:7–9) and led to death and then to belief in Christ; or, the law itself brought the insight that law cannot justify (Gal 2:16; Ps 143:2); or, the "law of Christ" (Gal 6:2) led to abandoning the Mosaic law; or, the law put Christ to death (cf. Gal 3:13) and so provided a way to our salvation, through baptism into Christ, through which we die (**crucified with Christ**; see Rom 6:6). Cf. also Gal 3:19–25 on the role of the law in reference to salvation.

3:1–14 Paul's contention that justification comes not through the law or the works of the law but by faith in Christ and in his death (Gal 2:16, 21) is supported by appeals to Christian experience (Gal 3:1–5) and to scripture (Gal 3:6–14). The gift of God's Spirit to the Galatians came from the gospel received in faith, not from doing what the law enjoins. The story of Abraham shows that faith in God brings **righteousness** (Gal 3:6; Gn 15:6). The promise to Abraham (Gal 3:8; Gn 12:3) extends to the Gentiles (Gal 3:14)

3:1 Stupid: not just senseless, for they were in danger of deserting their salvation.

3:2 Faith in what you heard: Paul's message received with faith. The Greek can also mean "the proclamation of the faith" or "a hearing that comes from faith."

3:3 On the contrast of **Spirit** and **flesh**, cf. Rom 8:1–11. Having received the Spirit, they need not be circumcised now.

3:4 Experience so many things: probably the **mighty deeds** of Gal 1:5 but possibly the experience of sufferings.

---

b: Acts 10:15, 28; 11:3. *c:* 2:1, 9. *d:* 2:5 / 1:18; 2:9 / 2:3. *e:* 3:2, 11; Ps 143:1–2; Rom 3:20, 28; 4:5; 11:6; Eph 2:8–9; Phil 3:9. *f:* 6:14; Rom 6:6, 8, 10; 7:6. *g:* 1:4; Rom 8:10–11; Col 3:3–4. *h:* 5:2. *i:* 5:7; 1 Cor 1:23. *j:* 2:16 / 3:14; Rom 10:17. *k:* 5:16–18.

in vain?—if indeed it was in vain. [5l]Does, then, the one who supplies the Spirit to you and works mighty deeds among you do so from works of the law or from faith in what you heard? [6m*]Thus Abraham "believed God, and it was credited to him as righteousness."

[7n*]Realize then that it is those who have faith who are children of Abraham. [8o]Scripture, which saw in advance that God would justify the Gentiles by faith, foretold the good news to Abraham, saying, "Through you shall all the nations be blessed." [9p]Consequently, those who have faith are blessed along with Abraham who had faith. [10q*]For all who depend on works of the law are under a curse; for it is written, "Cursed be everyone who does not persevere in doing all the things written in the book of the law." [11r]And that no one is justified before God by the law is clear, for "the one who is righteous by faith will live." [12s]But the law does not depend on faith; rather, "the one who does these things will live by them." [13t]Christ ransomed us from the curse of the law by becoming a curse for us, for it is written, "Cursed be everyone who hangs on a tree," [14u]that the blessing of Abraham might be extended to the Gentiles through Christ Jesus, so that we might receive the promise of the Spirit through faith.

The Law Did Not Nullify the Promise. [15v*]Brothers, in human terms I say that no one can annul or amend even a human will once ratified. [16w*]Now the promises were made to Abraham and to his descendant. It does not say, "And to descendants," as referring to many, but as referring to one, "And to your descendant," who is Christ. [17x*]This is what I mean: the law, which came four hundred and thirty years afterward, does not annul a covenant previously ratified by God, so as to cancel the promise. [18y*]For if the inheritance comes from the law, it is no longer from a promise; but God bestowed it on Abraham through a promise.

[19z*]Why, then, the law? It was added for

3:6 Abraham . . . righteousness: see Gn 15:6; Rom 4:3. The Galatians like Abraham heard with faith and experienced justification. This first argument forms the basis for the further scriptural evidence that follows.

3:7–9 Faith is what matters, for **Abraham** and the **children of Abraham**, in contrast to the claims of the opponents that circumcision and observance of the law are needed to bring the promised blessing of Gn 12:3; cf. Gn 18:18; Sir 44:21; Acts 3:25.

3:10–14 Those **who depend** not on promise and faith but **on works of the law are under a curse** because they do **not persevere in doing all the things written in the book of the law** (Gal 3:10; Dt 27:26) in order to gain life (Gal 3:12; Lv 18:5; cf. Rom 10:5). But scripture teaches that **no one is justified before God by the law** (Gal 3:11; Heb 2:4, adapted from the Greek version of Habakkuk; cf. Rom 1:17; Heb 10:38). Salvation, then, depends on faith in Christ who died on the cross (Gal 3:13), taking upon himself a curse found in Dt 21:23 (about executed criminals hanged in public view), to free us from **the curse of the law** (Gal 3:13). That the Gentile Galatians have received the promised Spirit (Gal 3:14) by faith and in no other way returns the argument to the experience cited in Gal 3:1–5.

3:15–18 A third argument to support Paul's position that salvation is not through the law but by promise (Gal 3:1–14) comes from legal practice and scriptural history. A legal agreement or **human will**, duly **ratified**, is unalterable (Gal 3:15). God's **covenant** with **Abraham** and its repeated promises (Gn 12:2–3, 7; 13:15; 17:7–8; 22:16–18; 24:7) is not superseded by **the law**, which came much later, in the time of Moses. **The inheritance** (of the Spirit and the blessings) is by promise, not by law (Gal 3:18). Paul's argument hinges on the fact that the same Greek word, *diathēkē*, can be rendered as **will** or testament (Gal 3:15) and as **covenant** (Gal 3:17).

3:16 Descendant: literally, "and to his seed." The Hebrew, as in Gn 12:7; 15:18; 22:17–18, is a collective singular, traditionally rendered as a plural, **descendants**, but taken by Paul in its literal number to refer to **Christ** as descendant of Abraham.

3:17 Four hundred and thirty years afterward: follows Ex 12:40 in the Greek (Septuagint) version, in contrast to Gn 15:13 and Acts 7:6, for chronology.

3:18 This refutes the opponents' contention that the promises of God are fulfilled only as a reward for human observance of the law.

3:19–22 A digression: if the Mosaic law, then, does not save or **bring life**, why was it given? Elsewhere, Paul says the law served to show what sin is (Rom 3:20; 7:7–8). Here the further implication is that the law in effect served to produce transgressions. Moreover, it was received at second hand **by angels**, through a **mediator**, not directly from God (Gal 3:19). The law does not, however, oppose God's purposes, for it carries out its function (Gal 3:22), so that **righteousness** comes by **faith** and **promise**, not by human works of the law.

3:19 The descendant: Christ (Gal 3:16). **By angels**: Dt 33:2–4 stressed their presence as enhancing the importance of the law; Paul uses their role to diminish its significance (cf. Acts 7:38, 53). **A mediator**: Moses. But in a covenant of

l: 2:16. *m:* Gn 15:6; Rom 4:3; Jas 2:23. *n:* 3:29; Rom 4:11–12 / Sir 44:19–21. *o:* Gn 12:3; 18:17–19; Acts 3:25. *p:* Rom 4:16. *q:* Dt 27:26; Jas 2:10. *r:* 2:16; Heb 2:4; Rom 1:17. *s:* Lv 18:5; Rom 10:5. *t:* Dt 21:23; Rom 8:3; 2 Cor 5:21. *u:* 3:2–3, 5; Is 44:3; Jl 3:1–2; Acts 2:33. *v:* Rom 3:5 / Heb 9:16–17. *w:* Gn 12:7; 13:15; 17:8; 22:17; 24:7; Mt 1:1. *x:* Ex 12:40. *y:* Rom 4:16; 11:6. *z:* Rom 4:15; 5:20; 7:7, 13 / Acts 7:38, 53.

transgressions, until the descendant came to
whom the promise had been made; it was
promulgated by angels at the hand of a mediator. [20a]Now there is no mediator when
only one party is involved, and God is one.
[21b]Is the law then opposed to the promises
[of God]? Of course not! For if a law had
been given that could bring life, then righteousness would in reality come from the
law. [22c]But scripture confined all things under the power of sin, that through faith in
Jesus Christ the promise might be given to
those who believe.
What Faith Has Brought Us. [23d*]Before
faith came, we were held in custody under
law, confined for the faith that was to be revealed. [24e*]Consequently, the law was our
disciplinarian for Christ, that we might be
justified by faith. [25f]But now that faith has
come, we are no longer under a disciplinarian. [26g*]For through faith you are all children of God in Christ Jesus. [27h*]For all of
you who were baptized into Christ have
clothed yourselves with Christ. [28i]There is
neither Jew nor Greek, there is neither slave
nor free person, there is not male and female; for you are all one in Christ Jesus.
[29j]And if you belong to Christ, then you are
Abraham's descendant, heirs according to
the promise.

CHAPTER 4

See RG 469–70

God's Free Children in Christ. [1*]I
mean that as long as the heir is not of age, he
is no different from a slave, although he is
the owner of everything, [2]but he is under the
supervision of guardians and administrators
until the date set by his father. [3k*]In the same
way we also, when we were not of age, were
enslaved to the elemental powers of the
world. [4l]But when the fullness of time had
come, God sent his Son, born of a woman,
born under the law, [5m]to ransom those under
the law, so that we might receive adoption.
[6n*]As proof that you are children, God sent
the spirit of his Son into our hearts, crying
out, "Abba, Father!" [7o]So you are no longer
a slave but a child, and if a child then also an
heir, through God.
Do Not Throw This Freedom Away. [8p*]At
a time when you did not know God, you became slaves to things that by nature are not

promise, where all depends on the one God, no mediator is needed (Gal 3:20).

3:23–29 Paul adds a further argument in support of righteousness or justification by faith and through God's promise rather than by works of the law (Gal 2:16; 3:22): as **children of God, baptized into Christ**, the Galatians are all **Abraham's descendant** and **heirs** of **the promise** to Abraham (Gal 3:8, 14, 16–18, 29). The teaching in Gal 3:23–25, that since **faith** (Christianity) **has come, we are no longer under** the law, could be taken with the previous paragraph on the role of the Mosaic law, but it also fits here as a contrast between the situation **before faith** (Gal 3:23) and the results after faith has come (Gal 3:25–29).

3:24–25 Disciplinarian: the Greek *paidagōgos* referred to a slave who escorted a child to school but did not teach or tutor; hence, a guardian or monitor. Applying this to the law fits the role of the law described in Gal 3:19–25.

3:26 Children of God: literally "sons," in contrast to the young child under the disciplinarian in Gal 3:24–25. The term includes males and females (Gal 3:28).

3:27–28 Likely a formula used at baptism that expresses racial, social-economic, and sexual equality in Christ (cf. Col 3:11).

3:27 Clothed yourselves with Christ: literally, "have put on Christ"; cf. Rom 13:14; Eph 4:24; Col 3:10. Baptismal imagery, traceable to the Old Testament (Jb 29:14; Is 59:17) but also found in pagan mystery cults.

4:1–7 What Paul has argued in Gal 3:26–29 is now elaborated in terms of the Christian as **the heir** (Gal 4:1, 7; cf. Gal 3:18, 29) freed from control by others. Again, as in Gal 3:2–5, the proof that Christians are children of God is the gift of the Spirit of Christ relating them intimately to God.

4:1, 3 Not of age: an infant or minor.

4:3 The elemental powers of the world: while the term can refer to the "elements" like earth, air, fire, and water or to elementary forms of religion, the sense here is more likely that of celestial beings that were thought in pagan circles to control the world; cf. Gal 4:8; Col 2:8, 20.

4:6 Children: see note on Gal 3:26; here in contrast to the infant or young person **not of age** (Gal 3:1, 3). **Abba**: cf. Mk 14:36 and the note; Rom 8:15.

4:8–11 On the basis of the arguments advanced from Gal 3:1 through Gal 4:7, Paul now launches his appeal to the Galatians with the question, **how can you turn back** to the slavery of the law (Gal 4:9)? The question is posed with reference to bondage to the **elemental powers** (see note on Gal 4:3) because the Galatians had originally been converted to Christianity from paganism, not Judaism (Gal 4:8). The use of the direct question is like Gal 3:3–5.

4:8 Things that by nature are not gods: or "gods that by nature do not exist."

a: Dt 6:4. *b:* Rom 7:7, 10; 8:2–4. *c:* Rom 3:9–20, 23; 11:32. *d:* 4:3–5; 5:18. *e:* 2:16. *f:* Rom 10:4. *g:* 4:5–7; Jn 1:12; Rom 8:14–17. *h:* Rom 6:3; 13:14; Eph 4:24. *i:* Rom 10:12; 1 Cor 12:13; Col 3:11. *j:* 3:7, 14, 16, 18; Rom 4:16–17; 9:7 / 4:1, 7; Rom 4:13–14; 8:17; Heb 6:12; Jas 2:5. *k:* 3:23 / 4:9; Col 2:20. *l:* Mk 1:15. *m:* 3:13, 26. *n:* 3:26; Rom 8:15. *o:* 3:29; Rom 8:16–17. *p:* 1 Cor 12:2.

gods; [9q]but now that you have come to know God, or rather to be known by God, how can you turn back again to the weak and destitute elemental powers? Do you want to be slaves to them all over again? [10r*]You are observing days, months, seasons, and years. [11*]I am afraid on your account that perhaps I have labored for you in vain.

Appeal to Former Loyalty. [12s*]I implore you, brothers, be as I am, because I have also become as you are. You did me no wrong; [13*]you know that it was because of a physical illness that I originally preached the gospel to you, [14]and you did not show disdain or contempt because of the trial caused you by my physical condition, but rather you received me as an angel of God, as Christ Jesus. [15*]Where now is that blessedness of yours? Indeed, I can testify to you that, if it had been possible, you would have torn out your eyes and given them to me. [16]So now have I become your enemy by telling you the truth? [17t*]They show interest in you, but not in a good way; they want to isolate you, so that you may show interest in them. [18]Now it is good to be shown interest for good reason at all times, and not only when I am with you. [19u]My children, for whom I am again in labor until Christ be formed in you! [20]I would like to be with you now and to change my tone, for I am perplexed because of you.

An Allegory on Christian Freedom. [21*]Tell me, you who want to be under the law, do you not listen to the law? [22v]For it is written that Abraham had two sons, one by the slave woman and the other by the freeborn woman. [23w]The son of the slave woman was born naturally, the son of the freeborn through a promise. [24x]Now this is an allegory. These women represent two covenants. One was from Mount Sinai, bearing children for slavery; this is Hagar. [25*]Hagar represents Sinai, a mountain in Arabia; it corresponds to the present Jerusalem, for she is in slavery along with her children. [26y]But the Jerusalem above is freeborn, and she is our mother. [27z*]For it is written:

"Rejoice, you barren one who bore no
children;
break forth and shout, you who were
not in labor;
for more numerous are the children of the
deserted one
than of her who has a husband."

4:10 This is likely a reference to ritual observances from the Old Testament, promoted by opponents: sabbaths or Yom Kippur, new moon, Passover or Pentecost, sabbatical years.

4:11 Cf. Gal 2:2. If the Galatians become **slaves . . . all over again** to the law (Gal 4:9), Paul will have worked in vain among them.

4:12–20 A strongly personal section. Paul appeals to past ties between the Galatians and himself. He speaks sharply of the opponents (Gal 4:17–18) and pastorally to the Galatians (Gal 4:19–20).

4:12 Because I have also become as you are: a terse phrase in Greek, meaning "Be as I, Paul, am," i.e., living by faith, independent of the law, for, in spite of my background in Judaism (Gal 1:13), I have become as you Galatians are now, a brother in Christ.

4:13 Physical illness: because its nature is not described, some assume an eye disease (Gal 4:15); others, epilepsy; some relate it to 2 Cor 12:7–9. **Originally**: this may also be translated "formerly" or "on the first (of two) visit(s)"; cf. Acts 16:6; 18:23.

4:15 That blessedness of yours: possibly a reference to the Galatians' initial happy reception of Paul (Gal 4:14) and of his gospel (Gal 1:6; 3:1–4) and their felicitation at such blessedness, but the phrase could also refer ironically to earlier praise by Paul of the Galatians, no longer possible when they turn from the gospel to the claims of the opponents (Gal 4:17–18; 1:7). If the word is a more literal reference to a beatitude, Gal 3:26–28 may be in view.

4:17 Isolate you: that is, from the blessings of the gospel and/or from Paul.

4:21–31 Paul supports his appeal for the gospel (Gal 4:9; 1:6–9; 2:16; 3:2) by a further argument from scripture (cf. Gal 3:6–18). It involves the relationship of **Abraham** (Gal 3:6–16) to his wife, Sarah, the **freeborn woman**, and to Hagar, **the slave woman**, and the contrast between the sons born to each, **Isaac**, child of promise, and Ishmael, son of Hagar (Gn 16; 21). Only through Isaac is the promise of God preserved. This **allegory** (Gal 4:24), with its equation of the Sinai covenant and Mosaic law with slavery and of the promise of God with freedom, Paul uses only in light of previous arguments. His quotation of Gn 21:10 at Gal 4:30 suggests on a scriptural basis that the Galatians should expel those who are troubling them (Gal 1:7).

4:25 Hagar represents Sinai . . .: some manuscripts have what seems a geographical note, "For Sinai is a mountain in Arabia."

4:27 Is 54:1 in the Septuagint translation is applied to Sarah as the **barren one** (in Gn 15) who ultimately becomes the mother not only of Isaac but now of numerous children, i.e., of all those who believe, the **children of the promise** (Gal 4:28).

---

q: 4:3; Col 2:20. *r:* Col 2:16–20. *s:* 1 Cor 11:1. *t:* 1:7; 6:12; Acts 20:30. *u:* 1 Cor 4:14–15; 2 Cor 6:13; 1 Thes 2:7–8. *v:* Gn 16:15; 21:2–3. *w:* Gn 17:16; Rom 4:19–20; 9:7–9. *x:* 3:17 / Ex 19:20 / Gn 16:1. *y:* Heb 12:22; Rev 21:2. *z:* Is 54:1.

[28a]Now you, brothers, like Isaac, are children of the promise. [29]But just as then the child of the flesh persecuted the child of the spirit, it is the same now. [30b]But what does the scripture say?

"Drive out the slave woman and her son!
For the son of the slave woman shall
not share the inheritance with the son"

of the freeborn. [31c]Therefore, brothers, we are children not of the slave woman but of the freeborn woman.

V. Exhortation to Christian Living

CHAPTER 5

See RG 470

The Importance of Faith. [1d*]For freedom Christ set us free; so stand firm and do not submit again to the yoke of slavery.

[2e]It is I, Paul, who am telling you that if you have yourselves circumcised, Christ will be of no benefit to you. [3f*]Once again I declare to every man who has himself circumcised that he is bound to observe the entire law. [4]You are separated from Christ, you who are trying to be justified by law; you have fallen from grace. [5g]For through the Spirit, by faith, we await the hope of righteousness. [6h*]For in Christ Jesus, neither circumcision nor uncircumcision counts for anything, but only faith working through love.

Be Not Misled. [7*]You were running well; who hindered you from following [the] truth? [8i*]That enticement does not come from the one who called you. [9j]A little yeast leavens the whole batch of dough. [10k]I am confident of you in the Lord that you will not take a different view, and that the one who is troubling you will bear the condemnation, whoever he may be. [11l*]As for me, brothers, if I am still preaching circumcision, why am I still being persecuted? In that case, the stumbling block of the cross has been abolished. [12*]Would that those who are upsetting you might also castrate themselves!

Freedom for Service. [13m*]For you were called for freedom, brothers. But do not use this freedom as an opportunity for the flesh; rather, serve one another through love. [14n*]For the whole law is fulfilled in one statement, namely, "You shall love your neighbor as yourself." [15]But if you go on biting and devouring one another, beware that you are not consumed by one another.

[16o*]I say, then: live by the Spirit and you will certainly not gratify the desire of the

5:1–6 Paul begins the exhortations, continuing through Gal 6:10, with an appeal to the Galatians to side with freedom instead of slavery (Gal 5:1). He reiterates his message of justification or righteousness by faith instead of law and circumcision (Gal 5:2–5); cf. Gal 2:16; 3:3. Faith, not circumcision, is what counts (Gal 5:6).

5:1 Freedom: Paul stresses as the conclusion from the allegory in Gal 4:21–31 this result of Christ's work for us. It is a principle previously mentioned (Gal 2:4), the responsible use of which Gal 5:13 will emphasize.

5:3 Cf. Gal 3:10–12. Just as those who seek to live by the law must carry out all its contents, so those who have faith and live by promise must stand firm in their freedom (Gal 5:1, 13).

5:6 Cf. Rom 2:25–26; 1 Cor 7:19; Gal 6:15. The Greek for **faith working through love** or "faith expressing itself through love" can also be rendered as "faith energized by (God's) love."

5:7–12 Paul addresses the Galatians directly: with questions (Gal 5:7, 11), a proverb (Gal 5:9), a statement (Gal 5:8), and biting sarcasm (Gal 5:12), seeking to persuade the Galatians to break with those trying to add law and circumcision to Christ as a basis for salvation.

5:7 Running well: as in an athletic contest; cf. Gal 2:2; 1 Cor 9:24–26; Phil 2:16; 3:14.

5:8 The one who called you: see note on Gal 1:6.

5:11 Preaching circumcision: this could refer to Paul's pre-Christian period (possibly as a missionary for Judaism); more probably it arose as a charge from opponents, based perhaps on the story in Acts 16:1–3 that Paul had circumcised Timothy "on account of the Jews." Unlike the Gentile Titus in Gal 2:3 Timothy was the son of a Jewish mother. **The stumbling block of the cross**: cf. 1 Cor 1:23.

5:12 A sarcastic half-wish that their knife would go beyond mere circumcision; cf. Phil 3:2 and the note there.

5:13–26 In light of another reminder of the freedom of the gospel (Gal 5:13; cf. Gal 5:1), Paul elaborates on what believers are called to do and be: they fulfill the law by love of neighbor (Gal 5:14–15), walking in the Spirit (Gal 5:16–26), as is illustrated by concrete **fruit of the Spirit** in their lives.

5:13 Serve . . . through love: cf. Gal 5:6.

5:14 Lv 19:18, emphasized by Jesus (Mt 22:39; Lk 10:27); cf. Rom 13:8–10.

5:16–25 Spirit . . . flesh: cf. Gal 3:3 and the note on Rom 8:1–13.

a: Rom 9:8. *b:* Gn 21:10. *c:* 3:29; Jn 8:35. *d:* 2:4; 4:5, 9; Jn 8:32, 36. *e:* 2:21; Acts 15:1–29. *f:* 3:10; Rom 2:25; Jas 2:10. *g:* Rom 8:23, 25. *h:* 3:28; 6:15; 1 Cor 7:19. *i:* 1:6. *j:* 1 Cor 5:6. *k:* 1:7. *l:* 6:12, 14; 1 Cor 1:23. *m:* 5:1 / Rom 6:18; 1 Cor 8:9; 1 Pt 2:16. *n:* Lv 19:18; Mt 22:39; Rom 13:8–10. *o:* 5:24–25; Rom 8:5.

flesh. [17p]For the flesh has desires against the Spirit, and the Spirit against the flesh; these are opposed to each other, so that you may not do what you want. [18q]But if you are guided by the Spirit, you are not under the law. [19r*]Now the works of the flesh are obvious: immorality, impurity, licentiousness, [20s]idolatry, sorcery, hatreds, rivalry, jealousy, outbursts of fury, acts of selfishness, dissensions, factions, [21*]occasions of envy, drinking bouts, orgies, and the like. I warn you, as I warned you before, that those who do such things will not inherit the kingdom of God. [22t]In contrast, the fruit of the Spirit is love, joy, peace, patience, kindness, generosity, faithfulness, [23u]gentleness, self-control. Against such there is no law. [24v]Now those who belong to Christ [Jesus] have crucified their flesh with its passions and desires. [25w]If we live in the Spirit, let us also follow the Spirit. [26x]Let us not be conceited, provoking one another, envious of one another.

CHAPTER 6

See RG 470–71

Life in the Community of Christ. [1y*]Brothers, even if a person is caught in some transgression, you who are spiritual should correct that one in a gentle spirit, looking to yourself, so that you also may not be tempted. [2z*]Bear one another's burdens, and so you will fulfill the law of Christ. [3a]For if anyone thinks he is something when he is nothing, he is deluding himself. [4*]Each one must examine his own work, and then he will have reason to boast with regard to himself alone, and not with regard to someone else; [5b]for each will bear his own load.

[6c*]One who is being instructed in the word should share all good things with his instructor. [7]Make no mistake: God is not mocked, for a person will reap only what he sows, [8d]because the one who sows for his flesh will reap corruption from the flesh, but the one who sows for the spirit will reap eternal life from the spirit. [9e]Let us not grow tired of doing good, for in due time we shall reap our harvest, if we do not give up. [10f*]So then, while we have the opportunity, let us do good to all, but especially to those who belong to the family of the faith.

VI. Conclusion

Final Appeal. [11g*]See with what large letters I am writing to you in my own hand! [12h*]It is those who want to make a good appearance in the flesh who are trying to compel you to

5:19–23 Such lists of vices and virtues (cf. Rom 1:29–31; 1 Cor 6:9–10) were common in the ancient world. Paul contrasts **works of the flesh** (Gal 5:19) with **fruit** (not "works") **of the Spirit** (Gal 5:22). Not law, but the Spirit, leads to such traits.

5:21 Occasions of envy: after the Greek word *phthonoi*, "envies," some manuscripts add a similar sounding one, *phonoi*, "murders."

6:1–10 The ethical exhortations begun at Gal 5:1 continue with a variety of admonitions to the community (**brothers**: see note on Gal 1:2). Nearly every sentence contains a separate item of practical advice; the faith and freedom of the gospel underlie each maxim. Tensions and temptation within communal life have previously been addressed in Gal 5:15, 26 and Gal 6:1 continues with a case in which a **person is caught in some transgression** such as those in Gal 5:19–21; cf. Gal 2:17.

6:2 The law of Christ: cf. Rom 8:2; 1 Cor 9:21; Gal 5:14. The principle of love for others is meant. **To bear one another's burdens** is to "serve one another through love" (Gal 5:13).

6:4–5 Self-examination is the cure for self-deception. Compare what you are with what you were before, and give the glory to God; cf. Rom 6:19–22. **Load**: used elsewhere of a soldier's pack. Correcting one's own conduct avoids burdening others with it.

6:6 Implies oral instruction in the faith by catechists; these are to be remunerated for their service; cf. Rom 15:27.

6:10 The family of the faith: the Christian household or church. Doing good has a universal object (**to all**), but the local community makes specific the reality of those to be served.

6:11–18 A postscript in Paul's own hand, as was his practice (see 1 Cor 16:21; 2 Thes 3:17). Paul summarizes his appeal against his opponents (Gal 6:12–13), then returns to his message of glorying in the cross, not in circumcision, as the means of salvation (Gal 6:14–15; cf. Gal 5:11). A benediction follows at Gal 6:16. In the polemical spirit that the attack on his apostleship called forth (Gal 1:11–2:21), Paul reasserts his missionary credentials (Gal 6:17) before giving a final benediction (Gal 6:18).

6:11 Large letters: in contrast to the finer hand of the scribe who wrote the letter up to this point. The larger Greek letters make Paul's message even more emphatic. Some find a hint of poor eyesight on Paul's part. See note on Gal 4:13.

6:12–15 The Jewish Christian opponents wished **not** to **be persecuted**, possibly by Jews. But since Judaism seems to have had a privileged status as a religion in the Roman empire, circumcised Christians might, if taken as Jews, thereby

p: Rom 7:15, 23; 8:6. *q:* Rom 6:14; 8:14. *r:* Rom 1:29–31; 1 Cor 6:9–10; Col 3:5–6, 8. *s:* Rev 22:15. *t:* Eph 5:9 / 1 Cor 13:4–7; 2 Cor 6:6; 1 Tm 4:12; 2 Pt 1:6. *u:* 1 Tm 1:9. *v:* 2:19; Rom 6:6; 8:13. *w:* 5:16. *x:* Phil 2:3. *y:* Mt 18:15; Jas 5:19 / 1 Cor 10:12–13. *z:* Col 3:13 / 1 Cor 9:21. *a:* 1 Cor 3:18; 8:2; 2 Cor 12:11. *b:* Rom 14:12. *c:* 1 Cor 9:14. *d:* Prv 11:18; Rom 8:6, 13. *e:* 2 Thes 3:13; Heb 12:1–3. *f:* 1 Thes 5:15. *g:* 1 Cor 16:21. *h:* 5:2, 11.

have yourselves circumcised, only that they may not be persecuted for the cross of Christ. [13]*Not even those having themselves circumcised observe the law themselves; they only want you to be circumcised so that they may boast of your flesh. [14i]*But may I never boast except in the cross of our Lord Jesus Christ, through which the world has been crucified to me, and I to the world. [15j]*For neither does circumcision mean anything, nor does uncircumcision, but only a new creation. [16k]*Peace and mercy be to all who follow this rule and to the Israel of God.

[17l]*From now on, let no one make troubles for me; for I bear the marks of Jesus on my body.

[18m]The grace of our Lord Jesus Christ be with your spirit, brothers. Amen.

avoid persecution from the Romans. In any case, Paul instead stresses conformity with **the cross of our Lord Jesus Christ**; cf. Gal 2:19–21; 5:11.

6:13 Those having themselves circumcised: other manuscripts read, "those who have had themselves circumcised."

6:14 Through which: or "through whom."

6:15 New creation: or "new creature"; cf. 2 Cor 5:17.

6:16 This rule: the principle in Gal 6:14, 15. **The Israel of God**: while the church may be meant (the phrase can be translated "to all who follow this rule, even the Israel of God"; cf. Gal 6:10; 1 Cor 10:18), the reference may also be to God's ancient people, Israel; cf. Ps 125:5; 128:6.

6:17 The marks of Jesus: slaves were often branded by marks (stigmata) burned into their flesh to show to whom they belonged; so also were devotees of pagan gods. Paul implies that instead of outdated circumcision, his body bears the scars of his apostolic labors (2 Cor 11:22–31), such as floggings (Acts 16:22; 2 Cor 11:25) and stonings (Acts 14:19), that mark him as belonging to the Christ who suffered (cf. Rom 6:3; 2 Cor 4:10; Col 1:24) and will protect his own.

i: 2:20; 1 Cor 2:2. *j:* 5:6; 1 Cor 7:19 / 2 Cor 5:17. *k:* Ps 125:5; 128:6. *l:* 2 Cor 4:10. *m:* Phil 4:23; 2 Tm 4:22; Phlm 25.

See RG 471–75

The Letter to the Ephesians

Ephesians is the great Pauline letter about the church. It deals, however, not so much with a congregation in the city of Ephesus in Asia Minor as with the worldwide church, the head of which is Christ (Eph 4:15), the purpose of which is to be the instrument for making God's plan of salvation known throughout the universe (Eph 3:9–10). Yet this ecclesiology is anchored in God's saving love, shown in Jesus Christ (Eph 2:4–10), and the whole of redemption is rooted in the plan and accomplishment of the triune God (Eph 1:3–14). The language is often that of doxology (Eph 1:3–14) and prayer (cf. Eph 1:15–23; 3:14–19), indeed of liturgy and hymns (Eph 3:20–21; 5:14).

The majestic chapters of Ephesians emphasize the unity in the church of Christ that has come about for both Jews and Gentiles within God's household (Eph 1:15–2:22, especially Eph 2:11–22) and indeed the "seven unities" of church, Spirit, hope; one Lord, faith, and baptism; and the one God (Eph 4:4–6). Yet the concern is not with the church for its own sake but rather as the means for mission in the world (Eph 3:1–4:24). The gifts Christ gives its members are to lead to growth and renewal (Eph 4:7–24). Ethical admonition is not lacking either; all aspects of human life and relationships are illumined by the light of Christ (Eph 4:25–6:20).

The letter is seemingly addressed by Paul to Christians in Ephesus (Eph 1:1), a place where the apostle labored for well over two years (Acts 19:10). Yet there is a curiously impersonal tone to the writing for a community with which Paul was so intimately acquainted (cf. Eph 3:2 and Eph 4:21). There are no personal greetings (cf. Eph 6:23). More significantly, important early manuscripts omit the words "in Ephesus" (see note on Eph 1:1). Many therefore regard the letter as an encyclical or "circular letter" sent to a number of churches in Asia Minor, the addressees to be designated in each place by its bearer, Tychicus (Eph 6:21–22). Others think that Ephesians is the letter referred to in Col 4:16 as "to the Laodiceans."

Paul, who is designated as the sole author at Eph 1:1, is described in almost unparalleled terms with regard to the significant role he has in God's plan for bringing the Gentiles to faith in Christ (Eph 3:1–12). Yet at the time of writing he is clearly in prison (Eph 3:1; 4:1; 6:20), suffering afflictions (Eph 3:13). Traditionally this "Captivity Epistle" has, along with Colossians, Philippians, and Philemon, been dated to an imprisonment in Rome, likely in A.D. 61–63. Others appeal to an earlier imprisonment, perhaps in Caesarea (Acts 23:27–27:2). Since the early nineteenth century, however, much of critical scholarship has considered the letter's style and use of words (especially when compared with Colossians), its concept of the church, and other points of doctrine put forward by the writer as grounds for serious doubt about authorship by Paul. The letter may then be the work of a secretary writing at the apostle's direction or of a later disciple who sought to develop Paul's ideas for a new situation around A.D. 80–100.

The principal divisions of the Letter to the Ephesians are the following:

I. Address (1:1–14)
II. Unity of the Church in Christ (1:15–2:22)
III. World Mission of the Church (3:1–4:24)
IV. Daily Conduct, an Expression of Unity (4:25–6:20)
V. Conclusion (6:21–24).

I. Address

CHAPTER 1

See RG 472–73

Greeting. [1a*]Paul, an apostle of
Christ Jesus by the will of God, to the holy
ones who are [in Ephesus] faithful in Christ
Jesus: [2b]grace to you and peace from God
our Father and the Lord Jesus Christ.

The Father's Plan of Salvation. [3c*]Blessed
be the God and Father of our Lord Jesus
Christ, who has blessed us in Christ with
every spiritual blessing in the heavens, [4d]as
he chose us in him, before the foundation of
the world, to be holy and without blemish
before him. In love [5e]he destined us for
adoption to himself through Jesus Christ, in
accord with the favor of his will, [6f]for the
praise of the glory of his grace that he
granted us in the beloved.

Fulfillment through Christ. [7g]In him we
have redemption by his blood, the forgiveness of transgressions, in accord with the
riches of his grace [8h]that he lavished upon
us. In all wisdom and insight, [9i*]he has made
known to us the mystery of his will in accord
with his favor that he set forth in him [10j]as a
plan for the fullness of times, to sum up all
things in Christ, in heaven and on earth.

Inheritance through the Spirit. [11k]In him
we were also chosen, destined in accord
with the purpose of the One who accomplishes all things according to the intention
of his will, [12*]so that we might exist for the

1:1–2 For the epistolary form used at the beginning of letters, see note on Rom 1:1–7. Twenty-two of the thirty Greek words in Eph 1:1–2 also occur in Col 1:1–2.

1:1 [In Ephesus]: the phrase is lacking in important early witnesses such as P^{46} (3rd cent.), and Sinaiticus and Vaticanus (4th cent.), appearing in the latter two as a fifth-century addition. Basil and Origen mention its absence from manuscripts. See Introduction. Without the phrase, the Greek can be rendered, as in Col 1:2, "to the holy ones and faithful brothers in Christ."

1:3–14 While a Pauline letter usually continues after the greeting with a prayer of thanksgiving, as in Eph 1:15–23 below, Ephesians first inserts a blessing of God for the blessings Christians have experienced, as in 2 Cor 1:3–4 and 1 Pt 1:3–12. The blessing here, akin to a Jewish *berakah*, is rich in images almost certainly drawn from hymns and liturgy. Many ideas here are also found in Col 1:3–23. Certain phrases are frequently repeated, such as **in Christ** (Eph 1:3, 10, 12) or **in him** (Eph 1:4, 7, 9, 11, 13) or **in the beloved** (Eph 1:6) and **(for) the praise of (his) glory** (Eph 1:6, 12, 14). Some terms like **chose** (Eph 1:4) and **destined** (Eph 1:5) reflect Old Testament theology (Dt 7:7; 9:4–6; 23:5) or Pauline themes (**redemption**, Eph 1:7, 14; **grace**, Eph 1:6, 7) or specific emphases in Colossians (**forgiveness**, Col 1:14). A triadic structure is discernible in Eph 1:3–14: **God** the **Father** (Eph 1:3–6, 8, 11), **Christ** (Eph 1:3, 5, 7–10, 12), and the **Spirit** (Eph 1:13–14). The spiritual blessings Christians have received through Christ (Eph 1:3) are gratefully enumerated: the call to holiness (Eph 1:4; cf. Col 1:22); the gift of divine **adoption** establishing a unique spiritual relationship with God the Father through Christ (Eph 1:5; cf. Gal 4:5); liberation from sin through Christ's sacrificial death (Eph 1:7); revelation of God's plan of salvation in Christ (Eph 1:9; cf. Eph 3:3–4; Rom 16:25); the gift of election and faith in Christ bestowed upon Jewish Christians (see note on Eph 1:12, **we who first hoped in Christ**); and finally, the same gift granted to Gentiles (Eph 1:13, **you also**). In the Christ-centered faith and existence of the Christian communities the apostle sees the predetermined **plan** of God to bring all creation under the final rule of Christ (Eph 1:4–5, 9–10) being **made known** (Eph 1:9) and carried through, to God's glory (Eph 1:6, 12, 14).

1:3 In the heavens: literally, "in the heavenlies" or "in the heavenly places," a term in Ephesians for the divine realm.

1:9 Mystery: as in Rom 16:25; Col 1:26, 27 and elsewhere, a secret of God now revealed in the **plan** to save and **sum up all things in Christ** (Eph 1:10); cf. Eph 3:3–6.

1:12 We who first hoped: probably Jewish Christians (contrast Eph 1:13, **you**, the Gentiles); possibly the people of Israel, "we who already enjoyed the hope of Christ," or perhaps present hope in contrast to future redemption (cf. Eph 1:14).

a: Rom 1:7; 1 Cor 1:1–2; Col 1:1. *b:* Col 1:2. *c:* 2:6; 2 Cor 1:3. *d:* 5:27; Jn 15:16; 17:24; Rom 8:29; 2 Thes 2:13. *e:* Jn 1:12; 1 Jn 3:1. *f:* Mt 3:17; Col 1:13. *g:* 2:7–13; Rom 3:24; Col 1:14, 20. *h:* Col 1:9. *i:* 3:3, 9; Rom 16:25. *j:* Gal 4:4; Col 1:16, 20. *k:* Is 46:10; Rom 8:28; Col 1:12; Rev 4:11.

praise of his glory, we who first hoped in
Christ. [13l]*In him you also, who have heard
the word of truth, the gospel of your salvation, and have believed in him, were sealed
with the promised holy Spirit, [14m]*which is
the first installment of our inheritance toward redemption as God's possession, to the
praise of his glory.

II. Unity of the Church in Christ

The Church as Christ's Body. [15n]*Therefore,
I, too, hearing of your faith in the Lord Jesus
and of your love for all the holy ones, [16o]do
not cease giving thanks for you, remembering you in my prayers, [17p]that the God of our
Lord Jesus Christ, the Father of glory, may
give you a spirit of wisdom and revelation
resulting in knowledge of him. [18q]May the
eyes of [your] hearts be enlightened, that
you may know what is the hope that belongs
to his call, what are the riches of glory in his
inheritance among the holy ones, [19r]and
what is the surpassing greatness of his power
for us who believe, in accord with the exercise of his great might, [20s]which he worked
in Christ, raising him from the dead and
seating him at his right hand in the heavens,
[21t]far above every principality, authority,
power, and dominion, and every name that is
named not only in this age but also in the one
to come. [22u]And he put all things beneath his
feet and gave him as head over all things to
the church, [23v]*which is his body, the fullness of the one who fills all things in every
way.

CHAPTER 2

See RG 472–73

Generosity of God's Plan. [1w]*You
were dead in your transgressions and sins
[2x]*in which you once lived following the

1:13 Sealed: by God, in baptism; cf. Eph 4:30; 2 Cor 1:22.

1:14 First installment: down payment by God on full salvation, as at 2 Cor 1:22.

1:15–23 See note on Rom 1:8 for the thanksgiving form in a letter. Much of the content parallels thoughts in Col 1:3–20. The prayer moves from God and Christ (Eph 1:17, 20–21) to the Ephesians (Eph 1:17–19) and the church (Eph 1:22–23). Paul asks that the blessing imparted by God the Father (Eph 1:3) to the Ephesians will be strengthened in them through the message of the gospel (Eph 1:13, 17–19). Those blessings are seen in the context of God's **might** in establishing the sovereignty of Christ over all other creatures (Eph 1:19–21) and in appointing him **head** of the church (Eph 1:22–23). For the allusion to angelic spirits in Eph 1:21, see Rom 8:38 and Col 1:16. Here, as in 1 Cor 15:24–25 and Col 2:15, every such **principality** and **power** is made subject to Christ.

1:15 Your faith . . . your love: some manuscripts omit the latter phrase, but cf. Col 1:4.

1:23 His body: the church (Eph 1:22); cf. note on Col 1:18. Only in Ephesians and Colossians is Christ the **head** of the **body**, in contrast to the view in 1 Cor 12 and Rom 12:4–8 where Christ is equated with the entire body or community. **Fullness**: see note on Col 1:19. Some take **the one who fills** as God, others as Christ (cf. Eph 4:10). If in Christ "dwells the fullness of the deity bodily" (Col 2:9), then, as God "fills" Christ, Christ in turn fills the church and the believer (Eph 3:19; 5:18). But the difficult phrases here may also allow the church to be viewed as the "complement" of Christ who is "being filled" as God's plan for the universe is carried out through the church (cf. Eph 3:9–10).

2:1–22 The gospel of **salvation** (Eph 1:13) that God **worked in Christ** (Eph 1:20) is reiterated in terms of what God's **great love** (Eph 2:4), expressed in Christ, means for us. The passage sometimes addresses **you**, Gentiles (Eph 2:1–2, 8, 11–13, 19, 22), but other times speaks of **all of us** who believe (Eph 2:3–7, 10, 14, 18). In urging people to **remember** their grim past when they were **dead** in sins (Eph 2:1–3, 11–12) and what they are **now in Christ** (Eph 2:4–10, 13), the author sees both Jew and Gentile reconciled with God, now **one new person**, a new humanity, **one body**, **the household of God**, **a temple** and **dwelling place** of God's Spirit (Eph 2:15–16, 19–22). The presentation falls into two parts, the second stressing more the meaning for the church.

2:1–10 The recipients of Paul's letter have experienced, in their redemption from **transgressions and sins**, the effect of Christ's supremacy over the power of the devil (Eph 2:1–2; cf. Eph 6:11–12), who rules not from the netherworld but from the air between God in heaven and human beings on earth. Both Jew and Gentile have experienced, through Christ, God's free gift of salvation that already marks them for a future heavenly destiny (Eph 2:3–7). The language **dead**, **raised us up**, and **seated us . . . in the heavens** closely parallels Jesus' own passion and Easter experience. The terms in Eph 2:8–9 describe salvation in the way Paul elsewhere speaks of justification: **by grace**, **through faith**, **the gift of God**, **not from works**; cf. Gal 2:16–21; Rom 3:24–28. Christians are a newly created people in Christ, fashioned by God for a life of goodness (Eph 2:10).

2:1–7 These verses comprise one long sentence in Greek, the main verb coming in Eph 2:5, God **brought us to life**, the object you/us **dead in . . . transgressions** being repeated in Eph 2:1, 5; cf. Col 2:13.

2:2 Age of this world: or "aeon," a term found in gnostic thought, possibly synonymous with the **rulers of this world**, but also reflecting the Jewish idea of "two ages," this present evil age and "the age to come"; cf. 1 Cor 3:19; 5:10; 7:31; Gal 1:4; Ti 2:12. **The disobedient**: literally, "the sons of disobedience," a Semitism as at Is 30:9.

l: 4:30; Acts 2:33; Col 1:5–6. *m:* 2 Cor 1:22; 5:5. *n:* Col 1:3–4; Phlm 4–5. *o:* Col 1:3, 9. *p:* 3:14, 16; Col 1:9–10; 1 Jn 5:20. *q:* 4:4; Col 1:12, 27. *r:* 2 Cor 13:4; Col 1:11; 2:12. *s:* Ps 110:1; Heb 1:3. *t:* Phil 2:9; Col 1:16; 1 Pt 3:22. *u:* 4:15; Ps 8:7; Mt 28:18; Col 1:18. *v:* 4:10, 12; Rom 12:5; 1 Cor 12:27; Col 1:19. *w:* Col 1:21; 2:13. *x:* 6:12; Jn 12:31; Col 1:13.

age of this world, following the ruler of the
power of the air, the spirit that is now at
work in the disobedient. [3y]All of us once
lived among them in the desires of our
flesh, following the wishes of the flesh and
the impulses, and we were by nature children of wrath, like the rest. [4]But God, who
is rich in mercy, because of the great love
he had for us, [5z*]even when we were dead
in our transgressions, brought us to life
with Christ (by grace you have been saved),
[6a]raised us up with him, and seated us with
him in the heavens in Christ Jesus, [7b]that in
the ages to come he might show the immeasurable riches of his grace in his kindness to us in Christ Jesus. [8c]For by grace
you have been saved through faith, and this
is not from you; it is the gift of God; [9d]it is
not from works, so no one may boast.
[10e]For we are his handiwork, created in
Christ Jesus for the good works that God
has prepared in advance, that we should
live in them.

One in Christ. [11*]Therefore, remember
that at one time you, Gentiles in the flesh,
called the uncircumcision by those called
the circumcision, which is done in the flesh
by human hands, [12f*]were at that time without Christ, alienated from the community of
Israel and strangers to the covenants of
promise, without hope and without God in
the world. [13g]But now in Christ Jesus you
who once were far off have become near by
the blood of Christ.
[14h*]For he is our peace, he who made both
one and broke down the dividing wall of enmity, through his flesh, [15i*]abolishing the
law with its commandments and legal
claims, that he might create in himself one
new person in place of the two, thus establishing peace, [16j]and might reconcile both
with God, in one body, through the cross,
putting that enmity to death by it. [17k]He
came and preached peace to you who were
far off and peace to those who were near,
[18l]for through him we both have access in
one Spirit to the Father.
[19m]So then you are no longer strangers
and sojourners, but you are fellow citizens
with the holy ones and members of the
household of God, [20n*]built upon the foundation of the apostles and prophets, with
Christ Jesus himself as the capstone.
[21o]Through him the whole structure is held
together and grows into a temple sacred in
the Lord; [22p]in him you also are being built
together into a dwelling place of God in the
Spirit.

III. World Mission of the Church

CHAPTER 3

See RG 473

Commission to Preach God's Plan.
[1q*]Because of this, I, Paul, a prisoner of

2:5 Our relation through baptism **with Christ**, the risen Lord, is depicted in terms of realized eschatology, as already exaltation, though Eph 2:7 brings in the future aspect too.

2:11–22 The Gentiles lacked Israel's messianic expectation, lacked the various **covenants** God made with **Israel**, lacked **hope** of salvation and knowledge of the true **God** (Eph 2:11–12); but through Christ all these religious barriers between Jew and Gentile have been transcended (Eph 2:13–14) by the abolition of the Mosaic covenant-law (Eph 2:15) for the sake of uniting Jew and Gentile into a single religious community (Eph 2:15–16), imbued with the same holy **Spirit** and worshiping the same **Father** (Eph 2:18). The Gentiles are now included in God's **household** (Eph 2:19) as it arises upon the **foundation** of **apostles** assisted by those endowed with the prophetic gift (Eph 3:5), the preachers of Christ (Eph 2:20; cf. 1 Cor 12:28). With Christ as the **capstone** (Eph 2:20; cf. Is 28:16; Mt 21:42), they are being built into the holy **temple** of God's people where the divine presence dwells (Eph 2:21–22).

2:12 The community of Israel: or "commonwealth"; cf. Eph 4:18. **The covenants**: cf. Rom 9:4: with Abraham, with Moses, with David.

2:14–16 The elaborate imagery here combines pictures of Christ as **our peace** (Is 9:5), his crucifixion, the ending of the Mosaic law (cf. Col 2:14), reconciliation (2 Cor 5:18–21), and the destruction of **the dividing wall** such as kept people from God in the temple or a barrier in the heavens.

2:15 One new person: a corporate body, the Christian community, made up of Jews and Gentiles, replacing ancient divisions; cf. Rom 1:16.

2:20 Capstone: the Greek can also mean cornerstone or keystone.

3:1–13 Paul reflects on his mission to the Gentiles. He alludes to his call and appointment to the apostolic office (Eph 3:2–3) and how his **insight** through revelation, as well as that of the other apostles and charismatic prophets in the church (Eph 3:4–5), has

y: Col 3:6–7. *z:* Rom 5:8; 6:13; Col 2:13. *a:* Rom 8:10–11; Phil 3:20; Col 2:12. *b:* 1:7. *c:* Rom 3:24; Gal 2:16. *d:* 1 Cor 1:29. *e:* 4:24; Ti 2:14. *f:* Rom 9:4; Col 1:21, 27. *g:* 2:17; Is 57:19; Col 1:20. *h:* Gal 3:28. *i:* 2 Cor 5:17; Col 2:14. *j:* Col 1:20, 22. *k:* Is 57:19; Zec 9:10. *l:* 3:12. *m:* Heb 12:22–23. *n:* Is 28:16; Rev 21:14. *o:* 1 Cor 3:16; Col 2:19. *p:* 1 Pt 2:5. *q:* Phil 1:7, 13; Col 1:24–29; 4:18; Phlm 9; 2 Tm 2:9.

Christ [Jesus] for you Gentiles— [2r*]if, as I
suppose, you have heard of the stewardship
of God's grace that was given to me for your
benefit, [3s*][namely, that] the mystery was
made known to me by revelation, as I have
written briefly earlier. [4]When you read this
you can understand my insight into the mystery of Christ, [5t]which was not made known
to human beings in other generations as it
has now been revealed to his holy apostles
and prophets by the Spirit, [6u]that the Gentiles are coheirs, members of the same body,
and copartners in the promise in Christ Jesus
through the gospel.

[7v]Of this I became a minister by the gift of
God's grace that was granted me in accord
with the exercise of his power. [8w]To me, the
very least of all the holy ones, this grace was
given, to preach to the Gentiles the inscrutable riches of Christ, [9x*]and to bring to
light [for all] what is the plan of the mystery
hidden from ages past in God who created all
things, [10y*]so that the manifold wisdom of
God might now be made known through the
church to the principalities and authorities in
the heavens. [11]This was according to the eternal purpose that he accomplished in Christ
Jesus our Lord, [12z]in whom we have boldness
of speech and confidence of access through
faith in him. [13a]So I ask you not to lose heart
over my afflictions for you; this is your glory.

Prayer for the Readers. [14*]For this reason
I kneel before the Father, [15]from whom
every family in heaven and on earth is
named, [16b]that he may grant you in accord
with the riches of his glory to be strengthened with power through his Spirit in the inner self, [17c]and that Christ may dwell in your
hearts through faith; that you, rooted and
grounded in love, [18d]may have strength to
comprehend with all the holy ones what is
the breadth and length and height and depth,
[19e]and to know the love of Christ that surpasses knowledge, so that you may be filled
with all the fullness of God.

[20f]Now to him who is able to accomplish
far more than all we ask or imagine, by the
power at work within us, [21]to him be glory in
the church and in Christ Jesus to all generations, forever and ever. Amen.

CHAPTER 4

See RG 473–74

Unity in the Body. [1g*]I, then, a prisoner for the Lord, urge you to live in a manner worthy of the call you have received,
[2h]with all humility and gentleness, with pa-

deepened understanding of God's plan of salvation in Christ. Paul is the special herald (Eph 3:7) of a new **promise** to the **Gentiles** (Eph 3:6): that the divine plan includes them in the spiritual benefits promised to Israel. Not only is this unique apostolic role his; Paul also has been given the task of explaining to all the divine **plan** of salvation (Eph 3:8–9), once **hidden**. Through **the church**, God's plan to save through Christ is becoming manifest to angelic beings (Eph 3:10; cf. Eph 1:21), in accord with God's **purpose** (Eph 3:11). The fulfillment of the plan in Christ gives the whole church more **confidence** through **faith** in God (Eph 3:12). The readers of this letter are also thereby encouraged to greater confidence despite Paul's imprisonment (Eph 3:13).

3:1 A prisoner of Christ: see Introduction. Paul abruptly departs from his train of thought at the end of Eph 3:1 leaving an incomplete sentence.

3:2 Stewardship: the Greek is the same term employed at Eph 1:10 for the **plan** that God administers (Col 1:25) and in which Paul plays a key role.

3:3–4 The mystery: God's resolve to deliver Gentiles along with Israel through Christ; cf. notes on Eph 1:10; 3:9.

3:9 [For all]: while some think this phrase was added so as to yield the sense "to enlighten all about the plan . . . ," it is more likely that some manuscripts and Fathers omitted it accidentally or to avoid the idea that **all** conflicted with Paul's assignment to preach to **the Gentiles** (Eph 3:8) specifically.

3:10 Principalities and authorities: see note on Eph 1:15–23 regarding Eph 3:21.

3:14–21 The apostle prays that those he is addressing may, like the rest of the church, deepen their understanding of God's plan of salvation in Christ. It is a plan that affects the whole universe (Eph 3:15) with **the breadth and length and height and depth** of God's love in Christ (Eph 3:18) or possibly the universe in all its dimensions. The apostle prays that they may perceive the redemptive love of Christ for them and be completely immersed in the fullness of God (Eph 3:19). The prayer concludes with a doxology to God (Eph 3:20–21).

3:14–15 Every family: in the Greek there is wordplay on the word for **the Father** (*patria, patēr*). The phrase could also mean "God's whole family" (cf. Eph 2:21).

4:1–16 A general plea for unity in the church. Christians have been fashioned through the **Spirit** into a single harmonious religious community (one **body**, Eph 4:4, 12; cf. Eph 4:16), belonging to a single **Lord** (in contrast to the many gods of the pagan world), and by one way of salvation through **faith**, brought out especially by the significance of **baptism** (Eph 4:1–6; cf. Rom 6:1–11). But Christian unity is

r: Col 1:25. *s:* 1:9–10; Col 1:26. *t:* Col 1:26. *u:* 2:13, 18–19. *v:* Rom 15:15; Col 1:25, 29. *w:* 1 Cor 15:8–10; Gal 1:16; 2:7–9. *x:* Rom 16:25; Col 1:26–27. *y:* 1 Pt 1:12. *z:* Rom 5:1–2; Heb 4:16. *a:* Col 1:22, 24; 2 Tm 2:10. *b:* 6:10; Rom 7:22; 2 Cor 4:16; Col 1:11. *c:* Jn 14:23; Col 1:23; 2:7. *d:* Col 2:2. *e:* Col 2:3, 9. *f:* Rom 16:25–27; Col 1:29. *g:* 3:1; Col 1:10. *h:* Col 3:12–13.

tience, bearing with one another through
love, 3[i]striving to preserve the unity of the
spirit through the bond of peace: 4[j*]one
body and one Spirit, as you were also called
to the one hope of your call; 5[k]one Lord, one
faith, one baptism; 6[l]one God and Father of
all, who is over all and through all and in all.

Diversity of Gifts. 7[m]But grace was given
to each of us according to the measure of
Christ's gift. 8[n*]Therefore, it says:

"He ascended on high and took prisoners
captive;
he gave gifts to men."

9What does "he ascended" mean except that
he also descended into the lower [regions] of
the earth? 10The one who descended is also
the one who ascended far above all the heavens, that he might fill all things.

11[o*]And he gave some as apostles, others
as prophets, others as evangelists, others as
pastors and teachers, 12[*]to equip the holy
ones for the work of ministry, for building
up the body of Christ, 13[p*]until we all attain
to the unity of faith and knowledge of the
Son of God, to mature manhood, to the extent of the full stature of Christ, 14[q]so that we
may no longer be infants, tossed by waves
and swept along by every wind of teaching
arising from human trickery, from their cunning in the interests of deceitful scheming.
15[r*]Rather, living the truth in love, we should
grow in every way into him who is the head,
Christ, 16[s]from whom the whole body,
joined and held together by every supporting
ligament, with the proper functioning of
each part, brings about the body's growth
and builds itself up in love.

Renewal in Christ. 17[t*]So I declare and
testify in the Lord that you must no longer
live as the Gentiles do, in the futility of their
minds; 18[u]darkened in understanding, alienated from the life of God because of their ignorance, because of their hardness of heart,
19[v]they have become callous and have
handed themselves over to licentiousness for
the practice of every kind of impurity to excess. 20That is not how you learned Christ,
21assuming that you have heard of him and
were taught in him, as truth is in Jesus,
22[w]that you should put away the old self of
your former way of life, corrupted through
deceitful desires, 23[x]and be renewed in the
spirit of your minds, 24[y*]and put on the new
self, created in God's way in righteousness
and holiness of truth.

more than adherence to a common belief. It is manifested in the exalted Christ's gifts to individuals to serve so as to make the community more Christlike (Eph 4:11–16). This teaching on Christ as the source of the gifts is introduced in Eph 4:8 by a citation of Ps 68:18, which depicts Yahweh triumphantly leading Israel to salvation in Jerusalem. It is here understood of Christ, ascending **above all the heavens**, the **head** of the church; through his redemptive death, resurrection, and ascension he has become the source of the church's spiritual gifts. The "descent" of Christ (Eph 4:9–10) refers more probably to the incarnation (cf. Phil 2:6–8) than to Christ's presence after his death in the world of the dead (cf. 1 Pt 3:19).

4:4–6 The "seven unities" (church, **Spirit**, **hope**; **Lord**, **faith** in Christ [Eph 1:13], **baptism**; **one God**) reflect the triune structure of later creeds in reverse.

4:8–10 While the emphasis is on an ascension and gift-giving by Christ, there is also a reference in taking **prisoners captive** to the aeons and powers mentioned at Eph 1:21; 2:2; 3:10; 6:12.

4:11 Concerning this list of ministers, cf. 1 Cor 12:28 and Rom 12:6–8. **Evangelists**: missionary preachers (cf. Acts 21:8; 2 Tm 4:5), not those who wrote gospels. **Pastors and teachers**: a single group in the Greek, shepherding congregations.

4:12 The ministerial leaders in Eph 4:11 are to equip the whole people of God for their **work of ministry**.

4:13 Mature manhood: literally, "a perfect man" (cf. Col 1:28), possibly the "one new person" of Eph 2:15, though there *anthrōpos* suggests humanity, while here *anēr* is the term for male. This personage becomes visible in the church's growing to its fullness in the unity of those who believe in Christ.

4:15–16 The head, Christ: cf. Col 1:18 and contrast 1 Cor 12:12–27 and Rom 12:4–5 where Christ is identified with the whole body, including the head. The imagery may derive from ancient views in medicine, the **head** coordinating and caring for the body, each **ligament** (perhaps the ministers of Eph 4:11) supporting the whole. But as at Eph 2:19–22, where the temple is depicted as a growing organism, there may also be the idea here of growing toward the capstone, Christ.

4:17–24 Paul begins to indicate how the new life in Christ contrasts with the Gentiles' old way of existence. Literally, **the old self** (Eph 4:22) and **the new self** (Eph 4:24) are "the old man" and "the new man" (*anthrōpos*, person), as at Eph 2:15; cf. note on Eph 4:13.

4:24 Put on: in baptism. See note on Gal 3:27.

---

i: Col 3:14–15. *j:* Rom 12:5; 1 Cor 10:17; 12:12–13. *k:* 1 Cor 8:6. *l:* 1 Cor 12:6. *m:* Rom 12:3, 6; 1 Cor 12:28. *n:* Ps 68:19; Col 2:15. *o:* 1 Cor 12:28. *p:* Col 1:28. *q:* 1 Cor 14:20; Col 2:4, 8; Heb 13:9; Jas 1:6. *r:* 1 Cor 11:3; Col 1:18; 2:19. *s:* Col 2:19. *t:* Rom 1:21. *u:* Col 1:21; 1 Pt 1:14. *v:* Col 3:5. *w:* Rom 8:13; Gal 6:8; Col 3:9. *x:* Rom 12:2. *y:* Gn 1:26–27; Col 3:10.

IV. Daily Conduct, an Expression of Unity

Rules for the New Life. [25z*]Therefore, putting away falsehood, speak the truth, each one to his neighbor, for we are members one of another. [26a*]Be angry but do not sin; do not let the sun set on your anger, [27b]and do not leave room for the devil. [28c*]The thief must no longer steal, but rather labor, doing honest work with his [own] hands, so that he may have something to share with one in need. [29d]No foul language should come out of your mouths, but only such as is good for needed edification, that it may impart grace to those who hear. [30*]And do not grieve the holy Spirit of God, with which you were sealed for the day of redemption. [31e]All bitterness, fury, anger, shouting, and reviling must be removed from you, along with all malice. [32f][And] be kind to one another, compassionate, forgiving one another as God has forgiven you in Christ.

CHAPTER 5

See RG 473–74

[1g*]So be imitators of God, as beloved children, [2h]and live in love, as Christ loved us and handed himself over for us as a sacrificial offering to God for a fragrant aroma. [3i]Immorality or any impurity or greed must not even be mentioned among you, as is fitting among holy ones, [4j]no obscenity or silly or suggestive talk, which is out of place, but instead, thanksgiving. [5k]Be sure of this, that no immoral or impure or greedy person, that is, an idolater, has any inheritance in the kingdom of Christ and of God.

Duty to Live in the Light. [6l*]Let no one deceive you with empty arguments, for because of these things the wrath of God is coming upon the disobedient. [7]So do not be associated with them. [8m]For you were once darkness, but now you are light in the Lord. Live as children of light, [9n]for light produces every kind of goodness and righteousness and truth. [10o]Try to learn what is pleasing to the Lord. [11p]Take no part in the fruitless works of darkness; rather expose them, [12]for it is shameful even to mention the things done by them in secret; [13q]but everything exposed by the light becomes visible, [14r*]for everything that becomes visible is light. Therefore, it says:

> "Awake, O sleeper,
>   and arise from the dead,
> and Christ will give you light."

[15s*]Watch carefully then how you live, not as foolish persons but as wise, [16]making the most of the opportunity, because the days are evil. [17]Therefore, do not continue in ignorance, but try to understand what is the will of the Lord. [18t]And do not get drunk on wine, in which lies debauchery, but be filled with the Spirit, [19u]addressing one another [in] psalms and hymns and spiritual songs, singing and playing to the Lord in your hearts, [20v]giving thanks always and for everything in the name of our Lord Jesus Christ to God the Father.

Wives and Husbands. [21w*]Be subordinate

4:25–6:20 For similar exhortations to a morally good life in response to God's gift of faith, see notes on Rom 12:1–13:14 and Gal 5:13–26.

4:26 If angry, seek reconciliation that day, not giving the devil (Eph 6:11) opportunity to lead into sin.

4:28 Honest work: literally, "the good." **His [own] hands**: some manuscripts have the full phrase as in 1 Cor 4:12.

4:30 See note on Eph 1:13.

5:1 Imitators of God: in forgiving (Eph 4:32) and in loving (as exhibited in how **Christ loved us**).

5:6 See note on Eph 2:2.

5:14 An early Christian hymn, possibly from a baptismal liturgy. For the content compare Eph 2:5–6; 3:9 and Is 60:1.

5:15–16, 19–20 The wording is similar to Col 4:5 and Eph 3:16–17.

5:21–6:9 Cf. notes on Col 3:18–4:1 and 1 Pt 2:18–3:7 for a similar listing of household duties where the inferior is admonished first (**wives**, Eph 5:22; **children**, Eph 6:1; **slaves**, Eph 6:5), then the superior (**husbands**, Eph 5:25; **fathers**, Eph 6:4; **masters**, Eph 6:9). Paul varies this pattern by an emphasis on mutuality (see Eph 5:20); use of Old Testament material about **father and mother** in Eph 6:2; the judgment to come for slave-owners (**you have a Master in heaven**, Eph 6:9); and above all the initial principle of subordination **to one another** under **Christ**, thus effectively undermining exclusive claims to domination by one party. Into the section on **wives** and **husbands** an elaborate teach-

z: Zec 8:16. *a:* Ps 4:5 LXX; Mt 5:22. *b:* 2 Cor 2:11. *c:* 1 Thes 4:11. *d:* 5:4; Col 3:16; 4:6. *e:* Col 3:8. *f:* Mt 6:14; Col 3:12–13. *g:* Mt 5:45, 48. *h:* Ex 29:18; Ps 40:7; Gal 2:20; 1 Jn 3:16. *i:* Gal 5:19; Col 3:5. *j:* 4:29; Col 3:8. *k:* 1 Cor 6:9–10; Gal 5:21; Col 3:5. *l:* Rom 1:18; Col 2:4, 8. *m:* 2:11–13; Jn 12:36; Col 1:12–13. *n:* Gal 5:22. *o:* Rom 12:2. *p:* Rom 13:12. *q:* Jn 3:20–21. *r:* Is 26:19; 60:1. *s:* Col 4:5. *t:* Prv 23:31 LXX; Lk 21:34. *u:* Ps 33:2–3; Col 3:16. *v:* Col 3:17. *w:* 1 Pt 5:5.

to one another out of reverence for Christ. [22x]Wives should be subordinate to their husbands as to the Lord. [23y]For the husband is head of his wife just as Christ is head of the church, he himself the savior of the body. [24]As the church is subordinate to Christ, so wives should be subordinate to their husbands in everything. [25z]Husbands, love your wives, even as Christ loved the church and handed himself over for her [26a]to sanctify her, cleansing her by the bath of water with the word, [27b]that he might present to himself the church in splendor, without spot or wrinkle or any such thing, that she might be holy and without blemish. [28]So [also] husbands should love their wives as their own bodies. He who loves his wife loves himself. [29]For no one hates his own flesh but rather nourishes and cherishes it, even as Christ does the church, [30c]because we are members of his body.

[31 d]"For this reason a man shall leave [his]
father and [his] mother
and be joined to his wife,
and the two shall become one flesh."

[32e]This is a great mystery, but I speak in reference to Christ and the church. [33]In any case, each one of you should love his wife as himself, and the wife should respect her husband.

See RG 473–74

CHAPTER 6

Children and Parents. [1f]Children, obey your parents [in the Lord], for this is right. [2g]"Honor your father and mother." This is the first commandment with a promise, [3]"that it may go well with you and that you may have a long life on earth." [4h]Fathers, do not provoke your children to anger, but bring them up with the training and instruction of the Lord.

Slaves and Masters. [5i]Slaves, be obedient to your human masters with fear and trembling, in sincerity of heart, as to Christ, [6j]not only when being watched, as currying favor, but as slaves of Christ, doing the will of God from the heart, [7]willingly serving the Lord and not human beings, [8]knowing that each will be requited from the Lord for whatever good he does, whether he is slave or free. [9k]Masters, act in the same way toward them, and stop bullying, knowing that both they and you have a Master in heaven and that with him there is no partiality.

Battle against Evil. [10*]Finally, draw your strength from the Lord and from his mighty power. [11l]Put on the armor of God so that you may be able to stand firm against the tactics of the devil. [12m]For our struggle is not with flesh and blood but with the principalities, with the powers, with the world rulers of this present darkness, with the evil spirits in the heavens. [13n]Therefore, put on the armor of God, that you may be able to resist on the evil day and, having done everything, to hold your ground. [14o]So stand fast with your loins girded in truth, clothed with righteousness as a breastplate, [15p]and your feet shod in readiness for the gospel of peace. [16q]In all circumstances, hold faith as a shield, to quench all [the] flaming arrows of the evil one. [17r]And take the helmet of salvation and the sword of the Spirit, which is the word of God.

Constant Prayer. [18s]With all prayer and supplication, pray at every opportunity in

ing on **Christ** and **the church** has been woven (Eph 5:22–33).

5:21–33 The apostle exhorts married Christians to a strong mutual love. Holding with Gn 2:24 that marriage is a divine institution (Eph 5:31), Paul sees Christian marriage as taking on a new meaning symbolic of the intimate relationship of love between Christ and the church. The wife should serve her husband in the same spirit as that of the church's service to Christ (Eph 5:22, 24), and the husband should care for his wife with the devotion of Christ to the church (Eph 5:25–30). Paul gives to the Genesis passage its highest meaning in the light of the union of Christ and the church, of which Christlike loyalty and devotion in Christian marriage are a clear reflection (Eph 5:31–33).

6:10–20 A general exhortation to courage and prayer. Drawing upon the imagery and ideas of Is 11:5; 59:16–17; and Wis 5:17–23, Paul describes the Christian in terms of the dress and equipment of Roman soldiers. He observes, however, that the Christian's readiness for combat is not directed against human beings but against the spiritual powers of evil (Eph 6:10–17; cf. Eph 1:21; 2:2; 3:10). Unique importance is placed upon prayer (Eph 6:18–20).

x: Col 3:18–4:1; 1 Pt 3:1–7. *y:* 1 Cor 11:3; Col 1:18. *z:* Col 3:19; 1 Tm 2:6. *a:* Rom 6:4; Ti 3:5–7. *b:* 2 Cor 11:2; Col 1:22. *c:* Rom 12:5; 1 Cor 6:15. *d:* Gn 2:24; Mt 19:5; Mk 10:7–8. *e:* Rev 19:7. *f:* Prv 6:20; Sir 3:1–6; Col 3:20. *g:* Ex 20:12; Dt 5:16. *h:* Col 3:21–22. *i:* Col 3:22–25; 1 Tm 6:1–2; Ti 2:9–10. *j:* 1 Pt 2:18. *k:* Col 4:1. *l:* Rom 13:12; 2 Cor 6:7; 10:4; Jas 4:7. *m:* 1:21; 2:2; Col 1:13. *n:* Rom 13:12. *o:* Wis 5:17–20; Is 11:5; Lk 12:35; 1 Thes 5:8. *p:* Is 52:7. *q:* 1 Pt 5:9. *r:* Is 59:17; 1 Thes 5:8. *s:* Mt 26:41; Col 4:2–3.

the Spirit. To that end, be watchful with all
perseverance and supplication for all the
holy ones [19t]and also for me, that speech
may be given me to open my mouth, to make
known with boldness the mystery of the
gospel [20u]for which I am an ambassador in
chains, so that I may have the courage to
speak as I must.

V. Conclusion

A Final Message. [21v*]So that you also may
have news of me and of what I am doing,
Tychicus, my beloved brother and trustworthy minister in the Lord, will tell you
everything. [22w]I am sending him to you for
this very purpose, so that you may know
about us and that he may encourage your
hearts.

[23]Peace be to the brothers, and love with
faith, from God the Father and the Lord
Jesus Christ. [24x]Grace be with all who love
our Lord Jesus Christ in immortality.

6:21–24 Tychicus: the bearer of the letter; see note on Col 4:7. Eph 6:21–22 parallel Col 4:7–8, often word for word. If Ephesians is addressed to several Christian communities (see Introduction), it is understandable that no greetings to individual members of these communities should have been included in it.

t: Acts 4:29; Col 4:3; 2 Thes 3:1. *u:* 2 Cor 5:20; Col 4:4. *v:* Acts 20:4; Col 4:7; 2 Tm 4:12. *w:* Col 4:8. *x:* 1 Pt 1:8.

See RG 475–78

The Letter to the Philippians

Philippi, in northeastern Greece, was a city of some importance in the Roman province of Macedonia. Lying on the great road from the Adriatic coast to Byzantium, the Via Egnatia, and in the midst of rich agricultural plains near the gold deposits of Mt. Pangaeus, it was in Paul's day a Roman town (Acts 16:21), with a Greek-Macedonian population and a small group of Jews (see Acts 16:13). Originally founded in the sixth century B.C. as Krenides by the Thracians, the town was taken over after 360 B.C. by Philip II of Macedon, the father of Alexander the Great, and was renamed for himself, "Philip's City." The area became Roman in the second century B.C. On the plains near Philippi in October 42 B.C., Antony and Octavian decisively defeated the forces of Brutus and Cassius, the slayers of Julius Caesar. Octavian (Augustus) later made Philippi a Roman colony and settled many veterans of the Roman armies there.

Paul, according to Acts (Acts 16:9–40), established at Philippi the first Christian community in Europe. He came to Philippi, via its harbor town of Neapolis (modern Kavalla), on his second missionary journey, probably in A.D. 49 or 50, accompanied by Silas and Timothy (Acts 15:40; 16:3; cf. Phil 1:1) and Luke, if he is to be included in the "we" references of Acts 16:10–17. The Acts account tells of the conversion of a business woman, Lydia; the exorcism of a slave girl; and, after an earthquake, while Paul and Silas were imprisoned in Philippi, the faith and baptism of a jailer and his family. None of these persons, however, is directly mentioned in Philippians (cf. the notes on Phil 4:2 and Phil 4:3). Acts 16 concludes its account by describing how Paul (and Silas), asked by the magistrates to leave Philippi, went on to Thessalonica (Acts 17:1–10), where several times his loyal Philippians continued to support him with financial aid (Phil 4:16). Later, Paul may have passed through Philippi on his way from Ephesus to Greece (Acts 20:1–2), and he definitely stopped there on his fateful trip to Jerusalem (Acts 20:6).

Paul's letter to the Christians at Philippi was written while he was in a prison somewhere (Phil 1:7, 13, 14, 17), indeed in danger of death (Phil 1:20–23). Although under guard for preaching Christ, Paul rejoices at the continuing progress of the gospel (Phil 1:12–26) and expresses gratitude for the Philippians' renewed concern and help in an expression of thanks most clearly found at Phil 4:10–20. Much of the letter is devoted to instruction about unity and humility within the Christian community at Philippi (Phil 1:27–2:18) and exhortations to growth, joy, and peace in their life together (Phil 4:1–9). The letter seems to be drawing to a close at the end of what we number as Phil 2, as Paul reports the plans of his helper Timothy and of Epaphroditus (whom the Philippians had sent to aid Paul) to come to Philippi (Phil 2:19–3:1), and even Paul's own expectation that he will go free and come to Philippi (Phil 1:25–26; 2:24). Yet quite abruptly at Phil 3:2, Paul erupts into warnings against false teachers who threaten to impose on the Philippians the burdens of the Mosaic law, including circumcision. The section that follows, Phil 3:2–21, is a vigorous attack on these Judaizers (cf. Gal 2:11–3:29) or Jewish Christian teachers (cf. 2 Cor 11:12–23), giving us insights into Paul's own life story (Phil 3:4–6) and into the doctrine of justification, the Christian life, and ultimate hope (Phil 3:7–21).

The location of Paul's imprisonment when he wrote to the Philippians, and thus the date of the letter, are uncertain. The traditional view has been that it stems from Paul's confinement in Rome, between A.D. 59 and 63 (cf. Acts 28:14–31). One modern view suggests the period when he was imprisoned at Caesarea, on the coast of Palestine, A.D. 57 or 58 (Acts 23:23–26:32); another suggests Corinth (cf. 2 Cor 11:9). Much recent scholarship favors Ephesus, around A.D. 55, a situation referred to in 2 Cor 1:8 concerning "the affliction that came to us" in Asia Minor (cf. also 1 Cor 15:32). The reference at Phil 1:13 to the "praetorium" (cf. also Phil 4:22) can be understood to mean the imperial guard or government house at Ephesus (or Caesarea), or the praetorian camp in Rome. Involved in a decision are the several journeys back and forth between Philippi and wherever Paul is imprisoned, mentioned in the letter (Phil 2:25–28; 4:14); this factor causes many to prefer Ephesus because of its proximity to Philippi. The Ephesian hypothesis dates the composition of Philippians to the mid-50s when most of Paul's major letters were written.

There is also a likelihood, according to some scholars, that the letter as we have it is a composite from parts of three letters by Paul to the Philippians. Seemingly Phil 4:10–20 is a brief note of appreciation for help sent through Epaphroditus. The long section from Phil 1:3 to Phil 3:1 is then another letter, with news of Paul's imprisonment and reports on Timothy and Epaphroditus (who has fallen ill while with Paul), along with exhortations to the Philippians about Christian conduct; and Phil 3:2–21 a third communication warning about threats to Philippian Christianity. The other verses in Phil 4 and Phil 1:1–2, are variously assigned by critics to these three underlying letters, which an editor presumably put together to produce a picture of Paul writing earnestly from prison (Phil 1–2), facing opponents of the faith (Phil 3), and with serene joy advising and thanking his Philippians (Phil 4). If all four chapters were originally a unity, then one must assume that a break occurred between the writing of Phil 3:1 and Phil 3:2, possibly involving the receipt of bad news from Philippi, and that Paul had some reasons for delaying his words of thanks for the aid brought by Epaphroditus till the end of his letter.

This beautiful letter is rich in insights into Paul's theology and his apostolic love and concern for the gospel and his converts. In Philippians, Paul reveals his human sensitivity and tenderness, his enthusiasm for Christ as the key to life and death (Phil 1:21), and his deep feeling for those in Christ who dwell in Philippi. With them he shares his hopes and convictions, his anxieties and fears, revealing the total confidence in Christ that constitutes faith (Phil 3:8–10). The letter incorporates a hymn about the salvation that God has brought about through Christ (Phil 2:6–11), applied by Paul to the relations of Christians with one another (Phil 2:1–5). Philippians has been termed "the letter of joy" (Phil 4:4, 10). It is the rejoicing of faith, based on true understanding of Christ's unique role in the salvation of all who profess his lordship (Phil 2:11; 3:8–12, 14, 20–21).

The principal divisions of the Letter to the Philippians are the following:

I. Address (1:1–11)
II. Progress of the Gospel (1:12–26)
III. Instructions for the Community (1:27–2:18)
IV. Travel Plans of Paul and His Assistants (2:19–3:1)
V. Polemic: Righteousness and the Goal in Christ (3:2–21)
VI. Instructions for the Community (4:1–9)
VII. Gratitude for the Philippians' Generosity (4:10–20)
VIII. Farewell (4:21–23)

I. Address

CHAPTER 1

See RG 476

Greeting. [1a*]Paul and Timothy,
slaves of Christ Jesus, to all the holy ones in
Christ Jesus who are in Philippi, with the
overseers and ministers: [2b*]grace to you and
peace from God our Father and the Lord
Jesus Christ.

Thanksgiving. [3c*]I give thanks to my
God at every remembrance of you, [4]pray-
ing always with joy in my every prayer for
all of you, [5]because of your partnership for
the gospel from the first day until now. [6d*]I
am confident of this, that the one who began a good work in you will continue to
complete it until the day of Christ Jesus. [7]It
is right that I should think this way about all
of you, because I hold you in my heart, you
who are all partners with me in grace, both
in my imprisonment and in the defense and
confirmation of the gospel. [8e]For God is my
witness, how I long for all of you with the
affection of Christ Jesus. [9f]And this is my
prayer: that your love may increase ever
more and more in knowledge and every
kind of perception, [10g]to discern what is of
value, so that you may be pure and blameless for the day of Christ, [11h]filled with the
fruit of righteousness that comes through
Jesus Christ for the glory and praise of
God.

II. Progress of the Gospel

[12i*]I want you to know, brothers, that my situation has turned out rather to advance the
gospel, [13j*]so that my imprisonment has become well known in Christ throughout the
whole praetorium and to all the rest, [14*]and
so that the majority of the brothers, having
taken encouragement in the Lord from my

1:1–2 See note on Rom 1:1–7, concerning the greeting.

1:1 Slaves: Paul usually refers to himself at the start of a letter as an apostle. Here he substitutes a term suggesting the unconditional obligation of himself and Timothy to the service of Christ, probably because, in view of the good relationship with the Philippians, he wishes to stress his status as a co-servant rather than emphasize his apostolic authority. Reference to Timothy is a courtesy: Paul alone writes the letter, as the singular verb throughout shows (Phil 1:3–26), and the reference (Phil 2:19–24) to Timothy in the third person. **Overseers**: the Greek term *episkopos* literally means "one who oversees" or "one who supervises," but since the second century it has come to designate the "bishop," the official who heads a local church. In New Testament times this office had not yet developed into the form that it later assumed, though it seems to be well on the way to such development in the Pastorals; see 1 Tm 3:2 and Ti 1:7, where it is translated bishop. At Philippi, however (and at Ephesus, according to Acts 20:28), there was more than one *episkopos*, and the precise function of these officials is uncertain. In order to distinguish this office from the later stages into which it developed, the term is here translated as **overseers**. **Ministers**: the Greek term *diakonoi* is used frequently in the New Testament to designate "servants," "attendants," or "ministers." Paul refers to himself and to other apostles as "ministers of God" (2 Cor 6:4) or "ministers of Christ" (2 Cor 11:23). In the Pastorals (1 Tm 3:8, 12) the *diakonos* has become an established official in the local church; hence the term is there translated as **deacon**. The *diakonoi* at Philippi seem to represent an earlier stage of development of the office; we are uncertain about their precise functions. Hence the term is here translated as **ministers**. See Rom 16:1, where Phoebe is described as a *diakonos* (minister) of the church of Cenchreae.

1:2 The gifts come **from** Christ the Lord, not simply through him from the Father; compare the christology in Phil 2:6–11.

1:3–11 As in Rom 1:8–15 and all the Pauline letters except Galatians, a thanksgiving follows, including a direct prayer for the Philippians (Phil 1:9–11); see note on Rom 1:8. On their **partnership for the gospel** (Phil 1:5), cf. Phil 1:29–30; 4:10–20. Their devotion to the faith and to Paul made them his pride and joy (Phil 4:1). The characteristics thus manifested are evidence of the community's continuing preparation for the Lord's parousia (Phil 1:6, 10). Paul's especially warm relationship with the Philippians is suggested here (Phil 1:7–8) as elsewhere in the letter. The eschatology serves to underscore a concern for ethical growth (Eph 1:9–11), which appears throughout the letter.

1:6 The day of Christ Jesus: the parousia or triumphant return of Christ, when those loyal to him will be with him and share in his eternal glory; cf. Phil 1:10; 2:16; 3:20–21; 1 Thes 4:17; 5:10; 2 Thes 1:10; 1 Cor 1:8.

1:12–26 The body of the letter begins with an account of Paul's present **situation**, i.e., his **imprisonment** (Phil 1:12–13; see Introduction), and then goes on with advice for the Philippians (Phil 1:27–2:18). The **advance of the gospel** (Phil 1:12) and the **progress** of the Philippians **in the faith** (Phil 1:25) frame what is said.

1:13 Praetorium: either the praetorian guard in the city where Paul was imprisoned or the governor's official residence in a Roman province (cf. Mk 15:16; Acts 23:35). See Introduction on possible sites.

1:14–18 Although Paul is imprisoned, Christians there nonetheless go on preaching Christ. But they do so with varied motives, **some** with personal hostility toward Paul, others out of personal ambition.

a: Rom 1:1; 2 Cor 1:1; 1 Thes 1:1; Phlm 1 / 1 Tm 3:1–13. *b:* Rom 1:7; Gal 1:3; Phlm 3. *c:* Rom 1:8; 1 Cor 1:4; 1 Thes 1:2. *d:* 2:13 / 1:10; 2:16; 1 Cor 1:8. *e:* Rom 1:9; 2 Cor 1:23; 1 Thes 2:5. *f:* Eph 3:14–19; Col 1:9–10; Phlm 6. *g:* Rom 2:18; 12:2 / 1:6. *h:* Jn 15:8. *i:* Eph 3:1; 6:20; 2 Tm 2:9; Phlm 9. *j:* 4:22.

imprisonment, dare more than ever to proclaim the word fearlessly.
[15]Of course, some preach Christ from envy and rivalry, others from good will. [16]The latter act out of love, aware that I am here for the defense of the gospel; [17]the former proclaim Christ out of selfish ambition, not from pure motives, thinking that they will cause me trouble in my imprisonment. [18k*]What difference does it make, as long as in every way, whether in pretense or in truth, Christ is being proclaimed? And in that I rejoice.

Indeed I shall continue to rejoice, [19l*]for I know that this will result in deliverance for me through your prayers and support from the Spirit of Jesus Christ. [20m]My eager expectation and hope is that I shall not be put to shame in any way, but that with all boldness, now as always, Christ will be magnified in my body, whether by life or by death.
[21n]For to me life is Christ, and death is gain.
[22o]If I go on living in the flesh, that means fruitful labor for me. And I do not know which I shall choose. [23p]I am caught between the two. I long to depart this life and be with Christ, [for] that is far better. [24]Yet that I remain [in] the flesh is more necessary for your benefit. [25]And this I know with confidence, that I shall remain and continue in the service of all of you for your progress and joy in the faith, [26]so that your boasting in Christ Jesus may abound on account of me when I come to you again.

III. Instructions for the Communtiy

Steadfastness in Faith. [27q*]Only, conduct yourselves in a way worthy of the gospel of Christ, so that, whether I come and see you or am absent, I may hear news of you, that you are standing firm in one spirit, with one mind struggling together for the faith of the gospel, [28]not intimidated in any way by your opponents. This is proof to them of destruction, but of your salvation. And this is God's doing. [29r]For to you has been granted, for the sake of Christ, not only to believe in him but also to suffer for him. [30s*]Yours is the same struggle as you saw in me and now hear about me.

CHAPTER 2

See RG 476–77

Plea for Unity and Humility. [1*]If there is any encouragement in Christ, any solace in love, any participation in the Spirit, any compassion and mercy, [2t]complete my joy by being of the same mind, with the same love, united in heart, thinking one thing. [3u]Do nothing out of selfishness or out of vainglory; rather, humbly regard others as more important than yourselves, [4v]each looking out not for his own interests, but [also] everyone for those of others.

[5*]Have among yourselves the same attitude that is also yours in Christ Jesus,

1:18 Rejoice: a major theme in the letter; see Introduction.

1:19–25 Paul earnestly debates his prospects of martyrdom or continued missionary labor. While he may **long to depart this life** and thus **be with Christ** (Phil 1:23), his overall and final expectation is that he will be delivered from this imprisonment and **continue in the service** of the Philippians and of others (Phil 1:19, 25; Phil 2:24). In either case, Christ is central (Phil 1:20–21); if to live means Christ for Paul, death means to be united with Christ in a deeper sense.

1:19 Result in deliverance for me: an echo of Jb 13:16, hoping that God will turn suffering to ultimate good and deliverance from evil.

1:27–30 Ethical admonition begins at this early point in the letter, emphasizing steadfastness and congregational unity in the face of possible suffering. The **opponents** (Phil 1:28) are those in Philippi, probably pagans, who oppose the gospel cause. **This is proof . . .** (Phil 1:28) may refer to the whole outlook and conduct of the Philippians, turning out for their salvation but to the judgment of the opponents (cf. 2 Cor 2:15–16), or possibly the sentence refers to the opinion of the opponents, who hold that the obstinacy of the Christians points to the destruction of such people as defy Roman authority (though in reality, Paul holds, such faithfulness leads to salvation).

1:30 A reference to Paul's earlier imprisonment in Philippi (Acts 16:19–24; 1 Thes 2:2) and to his present confinement.

2:1–11 The admonition to likemindedness and unity (Phil 2:2–5) is based on the believers' threefold experience with Christ, God's love, and the Spirit. The appeal to humility (Phil 2:3) and to obedience (Phil 2:12) is rooted in christology, specifically in a statement about Christ Jesus (Phil 2:6–11) and his humbling of self and obedience to the point of death (Phil 2:8).

2:5 Have . . . the same attitude that is also yours in Christ Jesus: or, "that also Christ Jesus had." While it is often held that Christ here functions as a model for moral imitation, it is

k: 4:10. *l:* Jb 13:16 / 2 Cor 1:11. *m:* 1 Cor 6:20; 1 Pt 4:16. *n:* Gal 2:20. *o:* Rom 1:13. *p:* 2 Cor 5:8. *q:* Eph 4:1; Col 1:10; 1 Thes 2:12 / 4:3. *r:* Mt 5:10; 10:38; Mk 8:34; Acts 5:41. *s:* 1:13; Acts 16:22–24. *t:* Rom 15:5; 1 Cor 1:10. *u:* Rom 12:3, 10; Gal 5:26. *v:* 1 Cor 10:24, 33; 13:5.

6 [w]*Who, though he was in the form of God,
did not regard equality with God
something to be grasped.
7 [x]*Rather, he emptied himself,
taking the form of a slave,
coming in human likeness;
and found human in appearance,
8 [y]*he humbled himself,
becoming obedient to death,
even death on a cross.
9 [z]*Because of this, God greatly exalted him
and bestowed on him the name
that is above every name,
10 [a]*that at the name of Jesus
every knee should bend,
of those in heaven and on earth and
under the earth,
11 [b]*and every tongue confess that
Jesus Christ is Lord,
to the glory of God the Father.

Obedience and Service in the World. 12 [c]*So
then, my beloved, obedient as you have always been, not only when I am present but
all the more now when I am absent, work out
your salvation with fear and trembling.
13 [d]For God is the one who, for his good purpose, works in you both to desire and to
work. 14 [e]Do everything without grumbling
or questioning, 15 [f]*that you may be blameless and innocent, children of God without
blemish in the midst of a crooked and perverse generation, among whom you shine
like lights in the world, 16 [g]as you hold on to
the word of life, so that my boast for the day
of Christ may be that I did not run in vain or
labor in vain. 17 [h]*But, even if I am poured out
as a libation upon the sacrificial service of
your faith, I rejoice and share my joy with all
of you. 18 [i]In the same way you also should
rejoice and share your joy with me.

IV. Travel Plans of Paul and His Assistants

Timothy and Paul. 19 [j]*I hope, in the Lord
Jesus, to send Timothy to you soon, so that I
too may be heartened by hearing news of

not the historical Jesus but the entire Christ event that Phil 2:6–11 depict. Therefore, the appeal is to have in relations among yourselves that same relationship you have in Jesus Christ, i.e., serving one another as you serve Christ (Phil 2:4).

2:6–11 Perhaps an early Christian hymn quoted here by Paul. The short rhythmic lines fall into two parts, Phil 2:6–8 where the subject of every verb is Christ, and Phil 2:9–11 where the subject is God. The general pattern is thus of Christ's humiliation and then exaltation. More precise analyses propose a division into six three-line stanzas (Phil 2:6; 7abc, 7d–8, 9, 10, 11) or into three stanzas (Phil 2:6–7ab, 7cd–8, 9–11). Phrases such as **even death on a cross** (Phil 2:8c) are considered by some to be additions (by Paul) to the hymn, as are Phil 2:10c, 11c.

2:6 Either a reference to Christ's preexistence and those aspects of divinity that he was willing to give up in order to serve in human form, or to what the man Jesus refused to grasp at to attain divinity. Many see an allusion to the Genesis story: unlike Adam, Jesus, **though . . . in the form of God** (Gn 1:26–27), did not reach out for **equality with God**, in contrast with the first Adam in Gn 3:5–6.

2:7 Taking the form of a slave, coming in human likeness: or ". . . taking the form of a slave. Coming in human likeness, and found human in appearance." While it is common to take Phil 2:6, 7 as dealing with Christ's preexistence and Phil 2:8 with his incarnate life, so that lines Phil 2:7b, 7c are parallel, it is also possible to interpret so as to exclude any reference to preexistence (see note on Phil 2:6) and to take Phil 2:6–8 as presenting two parallel stanzas about Jesus' human state (Phil 2:6–7b; 7cd–8); in the latter alternative, **coming in human likeness** begins the second stanza and parallels 6a to some extent.

2:8 There may be reflected here language about the servant of the Lord, Is 52:13–53:12 especially Is 53:12.

2:9 The name: "Lord" (Phil 2:11), revealing the true nature of the one who is named.

2:10–11 Every knee should bend . . . every tongue confess: into this language of Is 45:23 there has been inserted a reference to the three levels in the universe, according to ancient thought, **heaven**, **earth**, **under the earth**.

2:11 Jesus Christ is Lord: a common early Christian acclamation; cf. 1 Cor 12:3; Rom 10:9. But doxology to God the Father is not overlooked here (Phil 2:11c) in the final version of the hymn.

2:12–18 Paul goes on to draw out further ethical implications for daily life (Phil 2:14–18) from the salvation God works in Christ.

2:12 Fear and trembling: a common Old Testament expression indicating awe and seriousness in the service of God (cf. Ex 15:16; Jdt 2:28; Ps 2:11; Is 19:16).

2:15–16 Generation . . . as you hold on to . . .: or ". . . generation. Among them shine like lights in the world because you hold the word of life. . . ."

2:17 Libation: in ancient religious ritual, the pouring out on the ground of a liquid offering as a sacrifice. Paul means that he may be facing death.

2:19–3:1 The plans of Paul and his assistants for future

w: Jn 1:1–2; 17:5; Col 2:9; Heb 1:3. *x:* Is 53:3, 11; Jn 1:14; Rom 8:3; 2 Cor 8:9; Gal 4:4; Heb 2:14, 17. *y:* Mt 26:39; Jn 10:17; Heb 5:8; 12:2. *z:* Acts 2:33; Mt 23:12; Eph 1:20–21; Heb 1:3–4. *a:* Is 45:23; Jn 5:23; Rom 14:11; Rev 5:13. *b:* Acts 2:36; Rom 10:9; 1 Cor 12:3. *c:* Ps 2:11; 1 Cor 2:3; 2 Cor 7:15. *d:* 1:6; 1 Cor 12:6; 15:10; 2 Cor 3:5. *e:* 1 Cor 10:10; 1 Pt 4:9. *f:* 1 Thes 3:13 / Dt 32:5; Mt 10:16; Acts 2:40 / Dn 12:3; Mt 5:14, 16; Eph 5:8. *g:* 1 Thes 2:19 / Is 49:4; 65:23; Gal 2:2. *h:* Rom 15:16; 2 Tm 4:6. *i:* 3:1; 4:4. *j:* Acts 16:1–3; 17:14–15; 1 Cor 4:17; 16:10.

you. [20]For I have no one comparable to him for genuine interest in whatever concerns you. [21k]For they all seek their own interests, not those of Jesus Christ. [22]But you know his worth, how as a child with a father he served along with me in the cause of the gospel. [23]He it is, then, whom I hope to send as soon as I see how things go with me, [24*]but I am confident in the Lord that I myself will also come soon.

Epaphroditus. [25 l*]With regard to Epaphroditus, my brother and co-worker and fellow soldier, your messenger and minister in my need, I consider it necessary to send him to you. [26]For he has been longing for all of you and was distressed because you heard that he was ill. [27]He was indeed ill, close to death; but God had mercy on him, not just on him but also on me, so that I might not have sorrow upon sorrow. [28]I send him therefore with the greater eagerness, so that, on seeing him, you may rejoice again, and I may have less anxiety. [29m]Welcome him then in the Lord with all joy and hold such people in esteem, [30]because for the sake of the work of Christ he came close to death, risking his life to make up for those services to me that you could not perform.

CHAPTER 3

See RG 477

Concluding Admonitions. [1n*]Finally, my brothers, rejoice in the Lord. Writing the same things to you is no burden for me but is a safeguard for you.

V. Polemic: Righteousness and the Goal in Christ

Against Legalistic Teachers. [2o*]Beware of the dogs! Beware of the evil-workers! Beware of the mutilation! [3p*]For we are the circumcision, we who worship through the Spirit of God, who boast in Christ Jesus and do not put our confidence in flesh, [4q]although I myself have grounds for confidence even in the flesh.

Paul's Autobiography. If anyone else thinks he can be confident in flesh, all the more can I. [5r*]Circumcised on the eighth day, of the race of Israel, of the tribe of Benjamin, a Hebrew of Hebrew parentage, in observance of the law a Pharisee, [6s]in zeal I

travel are regularly a part of a Pauline letter near its conclusion; cf. Rom 15:22–29; 1 Cor 16:5–12.

2:19 Timothy: already known to the Philippians (Acts 16:1–15; cf. 1 Cor 4:17; 16:10).

2:24 I myself will also come soon: cf. Phil 1:19–25 for the significance of this statement.

2:25 Epaphroditus: sent by the Philippians as their **messenger** (literally, "apostle") to aid Paul in his imprisonment, he had fallen seriously ill; Paul commends him as he sends him back to Philippi.

3:1 Finally . . . rejoice: the adverb often signals the close of a letter; cf. Phil 4:8; 2 Cor 13:11. While the verb could also be translated "good-bye" or "farewell," although it is never so used in Greek epistolography, the theme of joy has been frequent in the letter (Phil 1:18; 2:2, 18); note also Phil 4:4 and the addition of "always" there as evidence for the meaning "rejoice." To write **the same things** may refer to what Paul has previously taught in Philippi or to what he has just written or to what follows.

3:2–21 An abrupt change in content and tone, either because Paul at this point responds to disturbing news he has just heard about a threat to the faith of the Philippians in the form of false teachers, or because part of another Pauline letter was inserted here; see Introduction. The chapter describes these teachers in strong terms as **dogs**. The persons meant are evidently different from the rival preachers of Phil 1:14–18 and the opponents of Phil 1:28. Since Phil 3:2–4 emphasize Jewish terms like **circumcision** (Phil 3:2–3, 5), some relate them to the "Judaizers" of the Letter to the Galatians. Other phrases make them appear more like the false teachers of 2 Cor 11:12–15, the **evil-workers**. The latter part of the chapter depicts the **many** who are **enemies** of Christ's cross in terms that may sound more Gentile or even "gnostic" than Jewish (Phil 3:18–19). Accordingly, some see two groups of false teachers in Phil 3, others one group characterized by a claim of having attained "perfect maturity" (Phil 3:12–15).

3:2–11 Paul sets forth the Christian claim, especially using personal, autobiographical terms that are appropriate to the situation. He presents his own experience in coming to know Christ Jesus in terms of **righteousness** or justification (cf. Rom 1:16–17; 3:21–5:11; Gal 2:5–11), contrasting the **righteousness from God** through faith and that of one's own **based on the law** as two exclusive ways of pleasing God.

3:2 Beware of the mutilation: literally, "incision," an ironic wordplay on "circumcision"; cf. Gal 5:12. There may be an association with the self-inflicted mutilations of the prophets of Baal (1 Kgs 18:28) and of devotees of Cybele who slashed themselves in religious frenzy.

3:3 We are the circumcision: the true people of God, seed and offspring of Abraham (Gal 3:7, 29; 6:15). **Spirit of God**: some manuscripts read "worship God by the Spirit."

3:5 Circumcised on the eighth day: as the law required (Gn 17:12; Lv 12:3).

k: 1 Cor 13:5; 2 Tm 4:10. *l:* 4:10–11, 15–16, 18. *m:* 1 Cor 16:18. *n:* 2:18; 4:4. *o:* Ps 22:17, 21; Rev 22:15 / 2 Cor 11:13 / Gal 5:6, 12. *p:* Rom 2:28–29; Col 2:11. *q:* 2 Cor 11:18, 21–23. *r:* Lk 1:59; 2:21 / Acts 22:3; 23:6; 26:5. *s:* Acts 8:3; 22:4; 26:9–11.

persecuted the church, in righteousness based on the law I was blameless.

Righteousness from God. [7t*][But] whatever gains I had, these I have come to consider a loss because of Christ. [8]More than that, I even consider everything as a loss because of the supreme good of knowing Christ Jesus my Lord. For his sake I have accepted the loss of all things and I consider them so much rubbish, that I may gain Christ [9u]and be found in him, not having any righteousness of my own based on the law but that which comes through faith in Christ, the righteousness from God, depending on faith [10v]to know him and the power of his resurrection and [the] sharing of his sufferings by being conformed to his death, [11w]if somehow I may attain the resurrection from the dead.

Forward in Christ. [12x*]It is not that I have already taken hold of it or have already attained perfect maturity, but I continue my pursuit in hope that I may possess it, since I have indeed been taken possession of by Christ [Jesus]. [13]Brothers, I for my part do not consider myself to have taken possession. Just one thing: forgetting what lies behind but straining forward to what lies ahead, [14y]I continue my pursuit toward the goal, the prize of God's upward calling, in Christ Jesus. [15]Let us, then, who are "perfectly mature" adopt this attitude. And if you have a different attitude, this too God will reveal to you. [16*]Only, with regard to what we have attained, continue on the same course.

Wrong Conduct and Our Goal. [17z*]Join with others in being imitators of me, brothers, and observe those who thus conduct themselves according to the model you have in us. [18a]For many, as I have often told you and now tell you even in tears, conduct themselves as enemies of the cross of Christ. [19b]Their end is destruction. Their God is their stomach; their glory is in their "shame." Their minds are occupied with earthly things. [20c*]But our citizenship is in heaven, and from it we also await a savior, the Lord Jesus Christ. [21d]He will change our lowly body to conform with his glorified body by the power that enables him also to bring all things into subjection to himself.

VI. Instructions for the Community

CHAPTER 4

See RG 477–78

Live in Concord. [1e*]Therefore, my brothers, whom I love and long for, my joy and crown, in this way stand firm in the Lord, beloved.

[2*]I urge Euodia and I urge Syntyche to come to a mutual understanding in the Lord. [3f*]Yes, and I ask you also, my true yoke-

3:7 Loss: his knowledge of Christ led Paul to reassess the ways of truly pleasing and serving God. His reevaluation indicates the profound and lasting effect of his experience of the meaning of Christ on the way to Damascus some twenty years before (Gal 1:15–16; Acts 9:1–22).

3:12–16 To be **taken possession of by Christ** does not mean that one has already arrived at perfect spiritual maturity. Paul and the Philippians instead press on, trusting in God.

3:12 Attained perfect maturity: possibly an echo of the concept in the mystery religions of being an initiate, admitted to divine secrets.

3:16 Some manuscripts add, probably to explain Paul's cryptic phrase, "thinking alike."

3:17–21 Paul and those who live a life centered in Christ, envisaging both his suffering and resurrection, provide a model that is the opposite of opponents who reject Christ's cross (cf. 1 Cor 1:23).

3:17 Being imitators of me: not arrogance, but humble simplicity, since all his converts know that Paul is wholly dedicated to imitating Christ (1 Cor 11:1; cf. also Phil 4:9; 1 Thes 1:6; 2 Thes 3:7, 9; 1 Cor 4:6).

3:20 Citizenship: Christians constitute a colony of heaven, as Philippi was a *colonia* of Rome (Acts 16:12). The hope Paul expresses involves the final coming of Christ, not a status already attained, such as the opponents claim.

4:1–9 This series of ethical admonitions rests especially on the view of Christ and his coming (cf. Phil 4:5) in Phil 3:20–21. Paul's instructions touch on unity within the congregation, joy, prayer, and the Christian outlook on life.

4:2 Euodia . . . Syntyche: two otherwise unknown women in the Philippian congregation; on the advice to them, cf. Phil 2:2–4.

4:3 Yokemate: or "comrade," although the Greek *syzygos* could also be a proper name. **Clement**: otherwise unknown, although later writers sought to identify him with Clement, bishop of Rome (Eusebius, *Ecclesiastical History* 3.15.1).

t: Mt 13:44, 46; Lk 14:33. *u:* Rom 3:21–22. *v:* Rom 6:3–5; 8:17; Gal 6:17. *w:* Jn 11:23–26; Acts 4:2; Rev 20:5–6. *x:* 1 Tm 6:12, 19. *y:* 1 Cor 9:24–25; 2 Tm 4:7. *z:* 1 Cor 4:16; 11:1; 1 Thes 1:7; 1 Pt 5:3. *a:* 1 Cor 1:17, 23; Gal 6:12. *b:* Rom 8:5–6; 16:18. *c:* Eph 2:6, 19; Col 3:1–3; Heb 12:22. *d:* Rom 8:23, 29; 1 Cor 15:42–57; 2 Cor 3:18; 5:1–5 / 1 Cor 15:27–28. *e:* 1 Thes 2:19–20. *f:* Ex 32:32–33; Ps 69:29; Dn 12:1; Lk 10:20; Rev 3:5; 13:8; 17:8; 20:12, 15; 21:27.

mate, to help them, for they have struggled at my side in promoting the gospel, along with Clement and my other co-workers, whose names are in the book of life.

Joy and Peace. [4g*]Rejoice in the Lord always. I shall say it again: rejoice! [5h*]Your kindness should be known to all. The Lord is near. [6i]Have no anxiety at all, but in everything, by prayer and petition, with thanksgiving, make your requests known to God. [7j]Then the peace of God that surpasses all understanding will guard your hearts and minds in Christ Jesus.

[8k*]Finally, brothers, whatever is true, whatever is honorable, whatever is just, whatever is pure, whatever is lovely, whatever is gracious, if there is any excellence and if there is anything worthy of praise, think about these things. [9l*]Keep on doing what you have learned and received and heard and seen in me. Then the God of peace will be with you.

VII. Gratitude for the Philippians' Generosity

[10m*]I rejoice greatly in the Lord that now at last you revived your concern for me. You were, of course, concerned about me but lacked an opportunity. [11n]Not that I say this because of need, for I have learned, in whatever situation I find myself, to be self-sufficient. [12]I know indeed how to live in humble circumstances; I know also how to live with abundance. In every circumstance and in all things I have learned the secret of being well fed and of going hungry, of living in abundance and of being in need. [13o]I have the strength for everything through him who empowers me. [14]Still, it was kind of you to share in my distress.

[15*]You Philippians indeed know that at the beginning of the gospel, when I left Macedonia, not a single church shared with me in an account of giving and receiving, except you alone. [16]For even when I was at Thessalonica you sent me something for my needs, not only once but more than once. [17]It is not that I am eager for the gift; rather, I am eager for the profit that accrues to your account. [18p*]I have received full payment and I abound. I am very well supplied because of what I received from you through Epaphroditus, "a fragrant aroma," an acceptable sacrifice, pleasing to God. [19q]My God will fully supply whatever you need, in accord with his glorious riches in Christ Jesus. [20r]To our God and Father, glory forever and ever. Amen.

VIII. Farewell

[21*]Give my greetings to every holy one in Christ Jesus. The brothers who are with me send you their greetings; [22s*]all the holy ones send you their greetings, especially those of Caesar's household. [23]The grace of the Lord Jesus Christ be with your spirit.

4:4 Rejoice: see note on Phil 3:1.

4:5 Kindness: considerateness, forbearance, fairness. **The Lord is near**: most likely a reference to Christ's parousia (Phil 1:6, 10; 3:20–21; 1 Cor 16:22), although some sense an echo of Ps 119:151 and the perpetual presence of the Lord.

4:8 The language employs terms from Roman Stoic thought.

4:9 Cf. note on Phil 3:17.

4:10–20 Paul, more directly than anywhere else in the letter (cf. Phil 1:3–5), here thanks the Philippians for their gift of money sent through Epaphroditus (Phil 2:25). Paul's own policy was **to be self-sufficient** as a missionary, supporting himself by his own labor (1 Thes 2:5–9; 1 Cor 9:15–18; cf. Acts 18:2–3). In spite of this reliance on self and on God to provide (Phil 4:11–13) Paul accepted gifts from the Philippians **not only once but more than once** (Phil 4:16) when he was in Thessalonica (Acts 17:1–9), as he does now, in prison (**my distress**, Phil 4:14). While commercial terms appear in the passage, like **an account of giving and receiving** (Phil 4:15) and **received full payment** (Phil 4:18), Paul is most concerned about the spiritual growth of the Philippians (10, 17, 19); he emphasizes that God will care for their needs, through Christ.

4:15 The beginning of the gospel: it was at Philippi that Paul first preached Christ in Europe, going on from there to Thessalonica and Beroea (Acts 16:9–17:14).

4:18 Aroma . . . sacrifice: Old Testament cultic language (cf. Gn 8:21; Ex 29:18, 25, 41; Lv 1:9, 13; Ez 20:41) applied to the Philippians' gift; cf. Eph 5:2; 2 Cor 2:14–16.

4:21–23 On the usual greetings at the conclusion of a letter, see note on 1 Cor 16:19–24. Inclusion of greetings from **all the holy ones** in the place from which Paul writes would involve even the Christians of Phil 1:14–18 who had their differences with Paul.

4:22 Those of Caesar's household: minor officials or even slaves and freedmen, found in Ephesus or Rome, among other places.

g: 2:18; 3:1. *h:* Ti 3:2 / Ps 145:18; Heb 10:37; Jas 5:8–9. *i:* Mt 6:25–34; 1 Pt 5:7 / Col 4:2. *j:* Jn 14:27; Col 3:15. *k:* Rom 12:17. *l:* 1 Thes 4:1 / Rom 15:33; 16:20; 1 Cor 14:33; 1 Thes 5:23. *m:* 1:18; 2:25; 1 Cor 9:11; 2 Cor 11:9. *n:* 1 Cor 4:11; 2 Cor 6:10; 11:27 / 2 Cor 12:9–10. *o:* Col 1:29; 2 Tm 4:17. *p:* Gn 8:21; Ex 29:18; Eph 5:2; Heb 13:16. *q:* 1 Thes 3:11, 13. *r:* Rom 16:27; Eph 5:20. *s:* 1:13.

See RG 478–80

The Letter to the Colossians

This letter is addressed to a congregation at Colossae in the Lycus Valley in Asia Minor, east of Ephesus. At the time of writing, Paul had not visited there, the letter says (Col 1:4; 2:1). The community had apparently been established by Epaphras of Colossae (Col 1:7; 4:12; Phlm 23). Problems, however, had arisen, brought on by teachers who emphasized Christ's relation to the universe (cosmos). Their teachings stressed angels (Col 2:18; "principalities and powers," Col 2:15), which were connected with astral powers and cultic practices (see note on Col 2:16) and rules about food and drink and ascetical disciplines (Col 2:16, 18). These teachings, Paul insists, detract from the person and work of Christ for salvation as set forth magnificently in a hymnic passage at Col 1:15–20 and reiterated throughout the letter. Such teachings are but "shadows"; Christ is "reality" (Col 2:17).

For help in dealing with these problems that the new teachers posed at Colossae, Epaphras sought out Paul, who was then imprisoned (Col 4:10, 18) at a place that the letter does not mention. Paul, without entering into debate over the existence of angelic spirits or their function, simply affirms that Christ possesses the sum total of redemptive power (Col 1:19) and that the spiritual renewal of the human person occurs through contact in baptism with the person of Christ, who died and rose again (Col 2:9–14). It is unnecessary for the Christian to be concerned about placating spirits (Col 2:15) or avoiding imagined defilement through ascetical practices in regard to food and drink (Col 2:20–23). True Christian asceticism consists in the conquering of personal sins (Col 3:5–10) and the practice of love of neighbor in accordance with the standard set by Christ (Col 3:12–16).

Paul commends the community as a whole (Col 1:3–8); this seems to indicate that, though the Colossians have been under pressure to adopt the false doctrines, they have not yet succumbed. The apostle expresses his prayerful concern for them (Col 1:9–14). His preaching has cost him persecution, suffering, and imprisonment, but he regards these as reflective of the sufferings of Christ, a required discipline for the sake of the gospel (see note on 1:24; cf. 1:29; 2:1). His instructions to the Christian family and to slaves and masters require a new spirit of reflection and action. Love, obedience, and service are to be rendered "in the Lord" (Col 3:18–4:1).

Colossians follows the outline of a typical Pauline letter. It is distinguished by the poetic lines in Col 1:15–20 concerning who Christ is and what Christ means in creation and redemption. This hymn may be compared with similar passages in Phil 2:6–11; 1 Tm 3:16; and Jn 1:1–18. It was apparently familiar liturgical material to the author, the audience, and the false teachers. In Col 1:21–2:7, however, Paul interprets the relation between the body of Christ, which he insists is the church (Col 1:18), and the world or cosmos to be one not simply of Christ's preexistence and rule but one of missionary advance into the world by the spreading of the word (Col 1:25, 28). In this labor of the missionary body of Christ, Paul as a minister plays a prime part in bringing Christ and the gospel as hope to the Gentiles (Col 1:23, 25, 27). To "every creature under heaven" the word is to be proclaimed, so that everyone receives Christ, is established in faith, and walks in Christ (Col 1:28; 2:6, 7).

Paul wrote the Letter to the Colossians while in prison, but his several imprisonments leave the specific place and date of composition uncertain. On this point the same problem exists as with Ephesians and Philippians (see the Introductions to these letters). Traditionally the house arrest at Rome, in which Paul enjoyed a certain restricted freedom in preaching (see Acts 28:16–28), or a second Roman imprisonment has been claimed as the setting. Others suggest a still earlier imprisonment at Caesarea (see Acts 23:12–27:1) or in Ephesus (see Acts 19). Still others regard the letter as the work of some pupil or follower of Paul, writing in his name. In any case, the contents are often closely paralleled by thoughts in Ephesians.

The principal divisions of the Letter to the Colossians are the following:

I. Address (1:1–14)
II. The Preeminence of Christ (1:15–2:3)
III. Warnings against False Teachers (2:4–23)
IV. The Ideal Christian Life in the World (3:1–4:6)
V. Conclusion (4:7–18)

I. Address

CHAPTER 1

See RG 479

Greeting. [1a*]Paul, an apostle of
Christ Jesus by the will of God, and Timothy
our brother, [2]to the holy ones and faithful
brothers in Christ in Colossae: grace to you
and peace from God our Father.

Thanksgiving. [3b*]We always give thanks
to God, the Father of our Lord Jesus Christ,
when we pray for you, [4]for we have heard of
your faith in Christ Jesus and the love that
you have for all the holy ones [5c]because of
the hope reserved for you in heaven. Of this
you have already heard through the word of
truth, the gospel, [6]that has come to you. Just
as in the whole world it is bearing fruit and
growing, so also among you, from the day
you heard it and came to know the grace of
God in truth, [7d*]as you learned it from Epaphras our beloved fellow slave, who is a
trustworthy minister of Christ on your behalf [8]and who also told us of your love in the
Spirit.

Prayer for Continued Progress. [9e*]There-
fore, from the day we heard this, we do not
cease praying for you and asking that you
may be filled with the knowledge of his will
through all spiritual wisdom and understanding [10]to live in a manner worthy of the
Lord, so as to be fully pleasing, in every
good work bearing fruit and growing in the
knowledge of God, [11]strengthened with
every power, in accord with his glorious
might, for all endurance and patience, with
joy [12f*]giving thanks to the Father, who has
made you fit to share in the inheritance of
the holy ones in light. [13]He delivered us
from the power of darkness and transferred
us to the kingdom of his beloved Son, [14g]in
whom we have redemption, the forgiveness
of sins.

II. The Preeminence of Christ—His Person and Work

[15 h*]He is the image of the invisible God,
the firstborn of all creation.
[16 i*]For in him were created all things in
heaven and on earth,
the visible and the invisible,

1:1–2 For the epistolary form used by Paul at the beginning of his letters, see note on Rom 1:1–7. On **holy ones** or "God's people," see note on Rom 1:7. Awareness of their calling helps this group to be **faithful brothers** and sisters **in Christ**, i.e., dedicated to the tasks implied in their calling.

1:3–8 On thanksgiving at the start of a letter, see note on Rom 1:8. The apostle, recalling his own prayers for them and the good report about them he has received (Col 1:3–4), congratulates the Colossians upon their acceptance of Christ and their faithful efforts to live the gospel (Col 3:6–8). To encourage them he mentions the success of the gospel elsewhere (Col 1:6) and assures them that his knowledge of their community is accurate, since he has been in personal contact with Epaphras (Col 1:7–8), who likely had evangelized Colossae and other cities in the Lycus Valley of Asia Minor (cf. Col 4:12, 13; Phlm 23). On **faith, love,** and **hope** (Col 1:4, 5, 8), see note on 1 Cor 13:13; cf. 1 Thes 1:3; 5:8.

1:7 Epaphras: now with Paul but a Colossian, founder of the church there.

1:9–14 Moved by Epaphras' account, the apostle has prayed and continues to pray fervently for the Colossians that, in their response to the gospel, they **may be filled with the knowledge of** God's **will** (Col 1:9; cf. Col 3:10). Paul expects a mutual interaction between their life according to the gospel and this knowledge (Col 1:10), yielding results (**fruit**, Col 1:10; cf. Col 1:6) **in every good work**: growth, strength, **endurance**, **patience**, **with joy** (Col 1:11), and the further giving of thanks (Col 1:12).

1:12–14 A summary about **redemption** by **the Father** precedes the statement in Col 1:15–20 about the **beloved Son** who is God's love in person (Col 1:13). Christians share the **inheritance . . . in light** with **the holy ones**, here probably the angels (Col 1:12). The imagery reflects the Exodus (**delivered . . . transferred**) and Jesus' theme of the **kingdom. Redemption** is explained as **forgiveness of sins** (cf. Acts 2:38; Rom 3:24–25; Eph 1:7).

1:15–20 As the poetic arrangement indicates, these lines are probably an early Christian hymn, known to the Colossians and taken up into the letter from liturgical use (cf. Phil 2:6–11; 1 Tm 3:16). They present Christ as the mediator of creation (Col 1:15–18a) and of redemption (Col 1:18b–20). There is a parallelism between **firstborn of all creation** (Col 1:15) and firstborn from the dead (Col 1:18). While many of the phrases were at home in Greek philosophical use and even in gnosticism, the basic ideas also reflect Old Testament themes about Wisdom found in Prv 8:22–31; Wis 7:22–8:1; and Sir 1:4. See also notes on what is possibly a hymn in Jn 1:1–18.

1:15 Image: cf. Gn 1:27. Whereas the man and the woman were originally created in the image and likeness of God (see also Gn 1:26), Christ as image (2 Cor 4:4) of the **invisible God** (Jn 1:18) now shares this new nature in baptism with those redeemed (cf. Col 3:10–11).

1:16–17 Christ (though not mentioned by name) is preeminent and supreme as God's agent in the creation of **all things** (cf. Jn 1:3), as prior to **all things** (Col 1:17; cf. Heb 1:3).

a: Eph 1:1. *b:* Eph 1:15–16; Phlm 4–5. *c:* Eph 1:13, 18; 1 Pt 1:4. *d:* Phlm 23. *e:* Eph 1:15–17; 5:17; Phil 1:9. *f:* 3:17; Jn 8:12; Acts 26:18; 1 Tm 6:16; 1 Pt 2:9. *g:* Eph 1:7. *h:* Ps 89:28; Jn 1:3, 18; 2 Cor 4:4. *i:* 1 Cor 8:6; Eph 1:10, 21.

whether thrones or dominions or
principalities or powers;
all things were created through him
and for him.
17 He is before all things,
and in him all things hold together.
18 [j]*He is the head of the body, the
church.
He is the beginning, the firstborn from
the dead,
that in all things he himself might be
preeminent.
19 *For in him all the fullness was pleased
to dwell,
20 [k]*and through him to reconcile all
things for him,
making peace by the blood of his cross
[through him], whether those on earth
or those in heaven.

21 [l]*And you who once were alienated and
hostile in mind because of evil deeds 22 he
has now reconciled in his fleshly body
through his death, to present you holy, without blemish, and irreproachable before him,
23 provided that you persevere in the faith,
firmly grounded, stable, and not shifting
from the hope of the gospel that you heard,
which has been preached to every creature
under heaven, of which I, Paul, am a minister.

Christ in Us. 24 *Now I rejoice in my sufferings for your sake, and in my flesh I am
filling up what is lacking in the afflictions of
Christ on behalf of his body, which is the
church, 25 of which I am a minister in accordance with God's stewardship given to me to
bring to completion for you the word of
God, 26 [m]the mystery hidden from ages and
from generations past. But now it has been
manifested to his holy ones, 27 [n]to whom God
chose to make known the riches of the glory
of this mystery among the Gentiles; it is
Christ in you, the hope for glory. 28 [o]It is he
whom we proclaim, admonishing everyone
and teaching everyone with all wisdom, that
we may present everyone perfect in Christ.
29 [p]For this I labor and struggle, in accord
with the exercise of his power working
within me.

1:18 Church: such a reference seemingly belongs under "redemption" in the following lines, not under the "creation" section of the hymn. Stoic thought sometimes referred to the world as "the body of Zeus." Pauline usage is to speak of the church as the body of Christ (1 Cor 12:12–27; Rom 12:4–5). Some think that the author of Colossians has inserted the reference to the church here so as to define "head of the body" in Paul's customary way. See Col 1:24. **Preeminent**: when Christ was raised by God as **firstborn from the dead** (cf. Acts 26:23; Rev 1:5), he was placed over the community, the church, that he had brought into being, but he is also indicated as crown of the whole new creation, over **all things**. His further role is to **reconcile all things** (Col 1:20) for God or possibly "to himself."

1:19 Fullness: in gnostic usage this term referred to a spiritual world of beings above, between God and the world; many later interpreters take it to refer to **the fullness of the deity** (Col 2:9); the reference could also be to the fullness of grace (cf. Jn 1:16).

1:20 The blood of his cross: the most specific reference in the hymn to redemption through Christ's death, a central theme in Paul; cf. Col 2:14–15; 1 Cor 1:17, 18, 23. **[Through him]**: the phrase, lacking in some manuscripts, seems superfluous but parallels the reference to reconciliation through Christ earlier in the verse.

1:21–23 Paul, in applying this hymn to the Colossians, reminds them that they have experienced the reconciling effect of Christ's death. He sees the effects of the cross in the redemption of human beings, not of cosmic powers such as those referred to in Col 1:16, 20 (**all things**). Paul also urges adherence to Christ in faith and begins to point to his own role as minister (Col 1:23), sufferer (Col 1:24), and proclaimer (Col 1:27–28) of this gospel.

1:24–2:3 As the community at Colossae was not personally known to Paul (see Introduction), he here invests his teaching with greater authority by presenting a brief sketch of his apostolic ministry and sufferings as they reflect those of Christ on behalf of the church (24). The preaching of God's word (Col 1:25) carries out the divine plan (**the mystery**, Col 1:26) to make Christ known to the Gentiles (Col 1:27). It teaches the God-given wisdom about Christ (Col 1:28), whose power works mightily in the apostle (Col 1:29). Even in those communities that do not know him personally (Col 2:1), he can increase the perception of God in Christ, unite the faithful more firmly in love, and so bring encouragement to them (Col 2:2). He hopes that his apostolic authority will make the Colossians perceive more readily the defects in the teaching of others who have sought to delude them, the next concern in the letter.

1:24 What is lacking: although variously interpreted, this phrase does not imply that Christ's atoning death on the cross was defective. It may refer to the apocalyptic concept of a quota of "messianic woes" to be endured before the end comes; cf. Mk 13:8, 19–20, 24 and the note on Mt 23:29–32. Others suggest that Paul's mystical unity with Christ allowed him to call his own **sufferings the afflictions of Christ**.

j: 1 Cor 11:3; 12:12, 27; 15:20; Eph 1:22–23; Rev 1:5. *k:* 2 Cor 5:18–19; Eph 1:10. *l:* Eph 2:14–16. *m:* Rom 16:25–26; 1 Cor 2:7; Eph 3:3, 9. *n:* 3:4; Rom 8:10. *o:* Eph 4:13. *p:* 2:1; 4:12; Phil 4:13.

CHAPTER 2

See RG 479–80

1*For I want you to know how great a
struggle I am having for you and for those in
Laodicea and all who have not seen me face
to face, 2qthat their hearts may be encouraged as they are brought together in love, to
have all the richness of fully assured understanding, for the knowledge of the mystery
of God, Christ, 3rin whom are hidden all the
treasures of wisdom and knowledge.

III. Warnings against False Teachers

A General Admonition. 4s*I say this so that
no one may deceive you by specious arguments. 5tFor even if I am absent in the flesh,
yet I am with you in spirit, rejoicing as I observe your good order and the firmness of
your faith in Christ. 6So, as you received
Christ Jesus the Lord, walk in him, 7urooted
in him and built upon him and established in
the faith as you were taught, abounding in
thanksgiving. 8v*See to it that no one captivate you with an empty, seductive philosophy according to human tradition, according
to the elemental powers of the world and not
according to Christ.

Sovereign Role of Christ. 9w*For in him
dwells the whole fullness of the deity bodily,
10and you share in this fullness in him, who
is the head of every principality and power.
11x*In him you were also circumcised with a
circumcision not administered by hand, by
stripping off the carnal body, with the circumcision of Christ. 12yYou were buried
with him in baptism, in which you were also
raised with him through faith in the power of
God, who raised him from the dead. 13zAnd
even when you were dead [in] transgressions and the uncircumcision of your flesh,
he brought you to life along with him, having forgiven us all our transgressions;
14a*obliterating the bond against us, with its
legal claims, which was opposed to us, he
also removed it from our midst, nailing it to
the cross; 15b*despoiling the principalities
and the powers, he made a public spectacle
of them, leading them away in triumph by it.

Practices Contrary to Faith. 16c*Let no
one, then, pass judgment on you in matters
of food and drink or with regard to a festival
or new moon or sabbath. 17dThese are shad-

2:1 Laodicea: chief city in Phrygia, northwest of Colossae; cf. Col 4:13, 16; Rev 3:14–22.

2:4–23 In face of the threat posed by false teachers (Col 2:4), the Colossians are admonished to adhere to the gospel as it was first preached to them (Col 2:6), steeping themselves in it with grateful hearts (Col 2:7). They must reject religious teachings originating in any source except the gospel (Col 2:8) because in Christ alone will they have access to God, **the deity** (Col 2:9). So fully has Christ enlightened them that they need no other source of religious knowledge or virtue (Col 2:10). They do not require **circumcision** (Col 2:11), for **in baptism** their whole being has been affected by Christ (Col 2:12) through forgiveness of sin and resurrection to a new life (Col 2:13; cf. Col 3:1 and Rom 6:1–11). On the cross Christ canceled the record of the debt that stood against us with all its claims (Col 2:14), i.e., he eliminated the law (cf. Eph 2:15) that human beings could not observe—and that could not save them. He forgave sins against the law (Col 2:14) and exposed as false and misleading (Col 2:15) all other powers (cf. Col 1:16) that purport to offer salvation. Therefore, the Colossians are not to accept judgments from such teachers on **food and drink** or to keep certain religious festivals or engage in certain cultic practices (Col 2:16), for the Colossians would thereby risk severing themselves from Christ (Col 2:19). If, when they accepted the gospel, they believed in Christ as their savior, they must be convinced that their salvation cannot be achieved by appeasing ruling spirits through dietary practices or through a wisdom gained simply by means of harsh asceticism (Col 2:20–23).

2:8 Elemental powers of the world: see note on Gal 4:3.

2:9 Fullness of the deity: the divine nature, not just attributes; see note on Col 1:19.

2:11 A description of baptism (Col 2:12) in symbolic terms of the Old Testament rite for entry into the community. The false teachers may have demanded physical circumcision of the Colossians.

2:14 The elaborate metaphor here about how God canceled the legal claims against us through Christ's cross depicts not Christ being nailed to the cross by men but **the bond . . . with its legal claims** being nailed to the cross by God.

2:15 The picture derives from the **public spectacle** and **triumph** of a Roman emperor's victory parade, where captives marched in subjection. **The principalities and the powers** are here conquered, not reconciled (cf. Col 1:16, 20). An alternate rendering for **by it** (the cross) is "by him" (Christ).

2:16 Festival or new moon or sabbath: yearly, monthly, and weekly observances determined by religious powers associated with a calendar set by the heavenly bodies, sun, moon, and stars (cf. Col 2:8).

q: 1:26–27; Eph 3:18–19. *r:* Prv 2:4–5; Is 45:3; Rom 11:33; 1 Cor 1:30. *s:* Eph 4:14. *t:* 1 Cor 5:3; Phil 1:27. *u:* Eph 2:20–22; 3:17. *v:* Gal 4:3; Eph 5:6. *w:* 1:19; Eph 3:19. *x:* 1:22; Jer 4:4; Rom 2:25–29; Phil 3:3. *y:* Rom 6:3–4. *z:* Eph 2:1, 5. *a:* Eph 2:14–15. *b:* 1:16, 20; 2 Cor 2:14; Eph 1:21. *c:* Rom 14:3–4; 1 Tm 4:3. *d:* Heb 8:5; 10:1.

ows of things to come; the reality belongs to
Christ. [18e*]Let no one disqualify you, de-
lighting in self-abasement and worship of
angels, taking his stand on visions, inflated
without reason by his fleshly mind, [19f]and
not holding closely to the head, from whom
the whole body, supported and held together
by its ligaments and bonds, achieves the
growth that comes from God.

[20]If you died with Christ to the elemental
powers of the world, why do you submit to
regulations as if you were still living in the
world? [21]"Do not handle! Do not taste! Do
not touch!" [22g]These are all things destined
to perish with use; they accord with human
precepts and teachings. [23]While they have a
semblance of wisdom in rigor of devotion
and self-abasement [and] severity to the
body, they are of no value against gratification of the flesh.

IV. The Ideal Christian Life in the World

CHAPTER 3

See RG 480

Mystical Death and Resurrection.
[1h*]If then you were raised with Christ, seek
what is above, where Christ is seated at the
right hand of God. [2]Think of what is above,
not of what is on earth. [3i]For you have died,
and your life is hidden with Christ in God.
[4]When Christ your life appears, then you too
will appear with him in glory.

Renunciation of Vice. [5j*]Put to death,
then, the parts of you that are earthly: immorality, impurity, passion, evil desire, and
the greed that is idolatry. [6k*]Because of these
the wrath of God is coming [upon the dis-
obedient]. [7]By these you too once conducted
yourselves, when you lived in that way.
[8l*]But now you must put them all away:
anger, fury, malice, slander, and obscene language out of your mouths. [9m]Stop lying to
one another, since you have taken off the old
self with its practices [10n*]and have put on the
new self, which is being renewed, for knowledge, in the image of its creator. [11o*]Here
there is not Greek and Jew, circumcision and
uncircumcision, barbarian, Scythian, slave,
free; but Christ is all and in all.

[12p]Put on then, as God's chosen ones, holy
and beloved, heartfelt compassion, kindness,
humility, gentleness, and patience, [13q]bear-
ing with one another and forgiving one another, if one has a grievance against another;
as the Lord has forgiven you, so must you
also do. [14r]And over all these put on love,
that is, the bond of perfection. [15s]And let the
peace of Christ control your hearts, the peace
into which you were also called in one body.
And be thankful. [16t]Let the word of Christ
dwell in you richly, as in all wisdom you
teach and admonish one another, singing
psalms, hymns, and spiritual songs with gratitude in your hearts to God. [17u]And whatever
you do, in word or in deed, do everything in
the name of the Lord Jesus, giving thanks to
God the Father through him.

The Christian Family. [18v*]Wives, be sub-

2:18 Ascetic practices encouraged by the false teachers included subjection of self humbly to their rules, worship of angels, and cultivation of visions, though exact details are unclear.

3:1–4 By retaining the message of the gospel that the risen, living Christ is the source of their salvation, the Colossians will be free from false religious evaluations of the things of the world (Col 3:1–2). They have died to these; but one day **when Christ . . . appears**, they will live with Christ in the presence of God (Col 3:3–4).

3:5–17 In lieu of false asceticism and superstitious festivals, the apostle reminds the Colossians of the moral life that is to characterize their response to God through Christ. He urges their participation in the liturgical hymns and prayers that center upon God's plan of salvation in Christ (Col 3:16).

3:5, 8 The two lists of five vices each are similar to enumerations at Rom 1:29–31 and Gal 5:19–21.

3:6 The wrath of God: see note on Rom 1:18. Many manuscripts add, as at Eph 5:6, "upon the disobedient."

3:8–10 Put . . . away; have taken off; have put on: the terms may reflect baptismal practice, taking off garments and putting on new ones after being united with Christ, here translated into ethical terms.

3:10 Image: see note on Col 1:15.

3:11 Scythian: a barbarous people from north of the Black Sea.

3:18–4:6 After general recommendations that connect family life and the social condition of slavery with the service of Christ (Col 3:18–4:1), Paul requests prayers for himself, especially in view of his imprisonment (Col 3:2–3), and rec-

e: 2:23; Mt 24:4. *f:* Eph 2:21–22; 4:16. *g:* Is 29:13. *h:* 2:12; Ps 110:1; Phil 3:20; Eph 2:6. *i:* Rom 6:2–5. *j:* Mt 15:19; Rom 1:29–30; Gal 5:19–21; Eph 5:3, 5. *k:* Rom 1:18. *l:* Eph 4:22, 25, 31. *m:* Rom 6:4, 6; Eph 4:22–25; Heb 12:1; 1 Pt 2:1; 4:2. *n:* Gn 1:26–27. *o:* 1 Cor 12:13; Gal 3:27–28. *p:* Eph 4:1–2, 32; 1 Thes 5:15. *q:* Mt 6:14; 18:21–35; Eph 4:32. *r:* Rom 13:8–10. *s:* Rom 12:5; 1 Cor 12:12; Eph 2:16; 4:3–4; Phil 4:7. *t:* Eph 5:19–20. *u:* 1 Cor 10:31. *v:* Eph 5:22; Ti 2:5; 1 Pt 3:1.

ordinate to your husbands, as is proper in the Lord. [19]Husbands, love your wives, and avoid any bitterness toward them. [20w]Children, obey your parents in everything, for this is pleasing to the Lord. [21x]Fathers, do not provoke your children, so they may not become discouraged.

Slaves and Masters. [22y*]Slaves, obey your human masters in everything, not only when being watched, as currying favor, but in simplicity of heart, fearing the Lord. [23]Whatever you do, do from the heart, as for the Lord and not for others, [24]knowing that you will receive from the Lord the due payment of the inheritance; be slaves of the Lord Christ. [25z]For the wrongdoer will receive recompense for the wrong he committed, and there is no partiality.

CHAPTER 4

See RG 480

[1]Masters, treat your slaves justly and fairly, realizing that you too have a Master in heaven.

Prayer and Apostolic Spirit. [2a]Persevere in prayer, being watchful in it with thanksgiving; [3b]at the same time, pray for us, too, that God may open a door to us for the word, to speak of the mystery of Christ, for which I am in prison, [4]that I may make it clear, as I must speak. [5c]Conduct yourselves wisely toward outsiders, making the most of the opportunity. [6]Let your speech always be gracious, seasoned with salt, so that you know how you should respond to each one.

V. Conclusion

Tychicus and Onesimus. [7d*]Tychicus, my beloved brother, trustworthy minister, and fellow slave in the Lord, will tell you all the news of me. [8]I am sending him to you for this very purpose, so that you may know about us and that he may encourage your hearts, [9e]together with Onesimus, a trustworthy and beloved brother, who is one of you. They will tell you about everything here.

From Paul's Co-Workers. [10f*]Aristarchus, my fellow prisoner, sends you greetings, as does Mark the cousin of Barnabas (concerning whom you have received instructions; if he comes to you, receive him), [11*]and Jesus, who is called Justus, who are of the circumcision; these alone are my co-workers for the kingdom of God, and they have been a comfort to me. [12g*]Epaphras sends you greetings; he is one of you, a slave of Christ [Jesus], always striving for you in his prayers so that you may be perfect and fully assured in all the will of God. [13*]For I can testify that he works very hard for you and for those in Laodicea and those in Hierapolis. [14h*]Luke the beloved physician sends greetings, as does Demas.

A Message for the Laodiceans. [15*]Give greetings to the brothers in Laodicea and to Nympha and to the church in her house. [16*]And when this letter is read before you, have it read also in the church of the Laodiceans, and you yourselves read the one from

ommends friendly relations and meaningful discussions of Christian teaching with outsiders, i.e., non-Christians (Col 3:5–6). See note on Eph 5:21–6:9.

3:22–25 Slaves: within this table of duties in family and societal relations, involving wives and husbands, children and parents (Col 3:18–21), such as also appears in Eph 5:22–6:9, slaves here receive special attention because of the case of Onesimus the slave returning to his master (Col 4:9; Phlm 10–12).

4:7–18 Paul concludes with greetings and information concerning various Christians known to the Colossians.

4:7 Tychicus: Acts 20:4 mentions his role in the collection for Jerusalem; Eph 6:21 repeats what is said here; see also 2 Tm 4:12; Ti 3:12.

4:10 Aristarchus: a Thessalonian who was with Paul at Ephesus and Caesarea and on the voyage to Rome (Acts 19:29; 20:4; 27:2). **Mark**: also referred to at Phlm 24 and 2 Tm 4:11 and, as "John Mark," in Acts (Acts 12:12, 25; 13:13; 15:37–40). See also 1 Pt 5:13 and the note there. Traditionally the author of the second gospel.

4:11 Jesus: a then common Jewish name, the Greek form of Joshua.

4:12 Epaphras: see notes on Col 1:3–8 and Col 1:7.

4:13 Laodicea: see note on Col 2:1. **Hierapolis**: a city northeast of Laodicea and northwest of Colossae.

4:14 Luke: only here described as a medical doctor; cf. Phlm 24 and 2 Tm 4:11. Traditionally the author of the third gospel. **Demas**: cf. Phlm 24; he later deserted Paul (2 Tm 4:10).

4:15 Nympha and . . . her house: some manuscripts read a masculine for the house-church leader, "Nymphas and . . . his house."

4:16 The one from Laodicea: either a letter by Paul that

w: Eph 6:1. *x:* Eph 6:4. *y:* Eph 6:5; 1 Tm 6:1; Ti 2:9–10; 1 Pt 2:18. *z:* Rom 2:11. *a:* Lk 18:1; Rom 12:12; Eph 6:18–20; 1 Thes 5:17. *b:* Rom 15:30; 1 Cor 16:9; Eph 6:19; 2 Thes 3:1. *c:* Eph 5:15–16. *d:* Acts 20:4; Eph 6:21–22; Phil 1:12. *e:* Phlm 10–11. *f:* Acts 19:29; 20:4; 27:2 / Acts 12:12, 25; 13:13; 15:37, 40; 2 Tm 4:11; Phlm 24; 1 Pt 5:13. *g:* 1:7; Rom 15:30. *h:* Phlm 24; 2 Tm 4:10–11.

Laodicea. 17i*And tell Archippus, "See that you fulfill the ministry that you received in the Lord."

18j*The greeting is in my own hand, Paul's. Remember my chains. Grace be with you.

has been lost or the Letter to the Ephesians (cf. note on Eph 1:1 **in Ephesus**).

4:17 Fulfill the ministry: usually taken to mean that **Archippus**, the son of Philemon and Apphia (Phlm 1–2), is "pastor" at Colossae. An alternate interpretation is that Archippus, not Philemon, is the owner of the slave Onesimus and that Paul is asking Archippus to complete the service he has received in the Lord by sending Onesimus back to minister to Paul in his captivity (cf. Phlm 20).

4:18 My own hand: a postscript in Paul's own hand was his custom; cf. Gal 6:11–18 and 2 Thes 3:17–18.

i: Phlm 2. *j:* 1 Cor 16:21; Gal 6:11; Eph 3:1; 2 Thes 3:17.

See RG 481–84

The First Letter to the Thessalonians

When Paul parted from Barnabas (Acts 15:36–41) at the beginning of what is called his second missionary journey, he chose Silvanus (Silas) as his traveling companion. Soon afterwards he took Timothy along with him (Acts 16:1–3). Paul was now clearly at the head of his own missionary band. About A.D. 50, he arrived in Greece for the first time. In making converts in Philippi and, soon afterwards, in Thessalonica, he was beset by persecution from Jews and Gentiles alike. Moving on to Beroea, he was again harassed by enemies from Thessalonica and hurriedly left for Athens (Acts 16:11–17:15). Silvanus and Timothy remained behind for a while. Paul soon sent Timothy back to Thessalonica to strengthen that community in its trials (1 Thes 3:1–5). Timothy and Silvanus finally returned to Paul when he reached Corinth (Acts 18:1–18), probably in the early summer of A.D. 51. Timothy's return with a report on conditions at Thessalonica served as the occasion for Paul's first letter (1 Thes 3:6–8).

The letter begins with a brief address (1 Thes 1:1) and concludes with a greeting (1 Thes 5:26–28). The body of the letter consists of two major parts. The first (1 Thes 1:2–3:13) is a set of three sections of thanksgiving connected by two *apologiae* (defenses) dealing, respectively, with the missionaries' previous conduct and their current concerns. Paul's thankful optimism regarding the Thessalonians' spiritual welfare is tempered by his insistence on their recognition of the selfless love shown by the missionaries. In an age of itinerant peddlers of new religions, Paul found it necessary to emphasize not only the content of his gospel but also his manner of presenting it, for both attested to God's grace as freely bestowed and powerfully effected.

The second part of the letter (1 Thes 4:1–5:25) is specifically hortatory or parenetic. The superabundant love for which Paul has just prayed (1 Thes 3:12–13) is to be shown practically by living out the norms of conduct that he has communicated to them. Specific "imperatives" of Christian life, principles for acting morally, stem from the "indicative" of one's relationship to God through Christ by the sending of the holy Spirit. Thus, moral conduct is the practical, personal expression of one's Christian faith, love, and hope.

The principal divisions of the First Letter to the Thessalonians are the following:

I. Address (1:1–10)
II. Previous Relations with the Thessalonians (2:1–3:13)
III. Specific Exhortations (4:1–5:25)
IV. Final Greeting (5:26–28)

I. Address

CHAPTER 1

See RG 482

Greeting. 1a*Paul, Silvanus, and Timothy to the church of the Thessalonians in God the Father and the Lord Jesus Christ: grace to you and peace.

Thanksgiving for Their Faith. 2bWe give thanks to God always for all of you, remembering you in our prayers, unceasingly 3*calling to mind your work of faith and labor of

1:1 On the address, see note on Rom 1:1–7.

1:3 Faith . . . love . . . hope: this, along with 1 Thes 5:8, is the earliest mention in Christian literature of the three "theological virtues" (see 1 Cor 13:13). The order here stresses eschatological hope, in line with the letter's emphasis on the Lord's second, triumphal coming, or parousia (1 Thes 1:10; 2:12, 19; 3:13;

a: Acts 15:40; 16:1–3, 19; 17:14–15; 2 Thes 1:1–2. *b:* 2 Thes 1:3.

love and endurance in hope of our Lord Jesus Christ, before our God and Father, [4c]knowing, brothers loved by God, how you were chosen. [5d]For our gospel did not come to you in word alone, but also in power and in the holy Spirit and [with] much conviction. You know what sort of people we were [among] you for your sake. [6*]And you became imitators of us and of the Lord, receiving the word in great affliction, with joy from the holy Spirit, [7e]so that you became a model for all the believers in Macedonia and in Achaia. [8f]For from you the word of the Lord has sounded forth not only in Macedonia and [in] Achaia, but in every place your faith in God has gone forth, so that we have no need to say anything. [9g]For they themselves openly declare about us what sort of reception we had among you, and how you turned to God from idols to serve the living and true God [10h]and to await his Son from heaven, whom he raised from [the] dead, Jesus, who delivers us from the coming wrath.

II. Previous Relations with the Thessalonians

CHAPTER 2

See RG 482–83

Paul's Ministry Among Them. [1]For you yourselves know, brothers, that our reception among you was not without effect. [2i]Rather, after we had suffered and been insolently treated, as you know, in Philippi, we drew courage through our God to speak to you the gospel of God with much struggle. [3]Our exhortation was not from delusion or impure motives, nor did it work through deception. [4j*]But as we were judged worthy by God to be entrusted with the gospel, that is how we speak, not as trying to please human beings, but rather God, who judges our hearts. [5]Nor, indeed, did we ever appear with flattering speech, as you know, or with a pretext for greed—God is witness— [6k]nor did we seek praise from human beings, either from you or from others, [7*]although we were able to impose our weight as apostles of Christ. Rather, we were gentle among you, as a nursing mother cares for her children. [8]With such affection for you, we were determined to share with you not only the gospel of God, but our very selves as well, so dearly beloved had you become to us. [9l]You recall, brothers, our toil and drudgery. Working night and day in order not to burden any of you, we proclaimed to you the gospel of God. [10]You are witnesses, and so is God, how devoutly and justly and blamelessly we behaved toward you believers. [11m]As you know, we treated each one of you as a father treats his children, [12n]exhorting and encouraging you and insisting that you conduct yourselves as worthy of the God who calls you into his kingdom and glory.

Further Thanksgiving. [13]And for this reason we too give thanks to God unceasingly, that, in receiving the word of God from hearing us, you received not a human word but, as it truly is, the word of God, which is now at work in you who believe. [14*]For you, brothers, have become imitators of the churches of God that are in Judea in Christ Jesus. For you suffer the same things from your compatriots as they did from the Jews, [15o*]who killed both the Lord Jesus and the

4:13–5:11; 5:23).

1:6 Imitators: the Pauline theme of "imitation" (see 1 Thes 2:14; 1 Cor 4:16; 11:1; 2 Thes 3:9) is rooted in Paul's view of solidarity in Christ through sharing in Jesus' cross and in the Spirit of the risen Lord.

2:4 Judged worthy: Paul regards "worthiness" not as grounded in one's own talent or moral self-righteousness but in God's discernment of genuinely selfless attitudes and actions (see 2 Cor 10:17–18).

2:7 Gentle: many excellent manuscripts read "infants" (*nēpioi*), but "gentle" (*ēpioi*) better suits the context here.

2:14 Luke's picture of the persecutions at Philippi (by Gentiles) and in Thessalonica and Beroea (by Jews) seems to be considerably schematized (Acts 16:11–40; 17:1–15). Paul pictures the Thessalonian community as composed of converts from paganism (1 Thes 1:9) and speaks here of persecution by their (pagan) compatriots rather than by Jews.

2:15–16 Paul is speaking of historical opposition on the part of Palestinian Jews in particular and does so only some twenty years after Jesus' crucifixion. Even so, he quickly proceeds to depict the persecutors typologically, in apocalyptic terms. His remarks give no grounds for anti-Semitism to those willing to understand him, especially in view of

c: 2 Thes 2:13. *d:* Acts 13:52; 17:1–9. *e:* 2 Thes 1:4; 1 Cor 4:16; 11:1 / 2:14; Phil 3:17. *f:* Rom 1:8. *g:* Acts 14:15; Gal 4:8 / 4:5. *h:* Rom 2:1–16; 5:9; 13:4 / 5:9. *i:* Acts 16:19–17:10. *j:* Gal 1:10. *k:* Jn 5:41, 44; 1 Cor 10:31; 2 Cor 4:17. *l:* Acts 20:34; 1 Cor 4:12; 9:3–18; 2 Thes 3:7–9. *m:* Acts 20:31. *n:* 1 Pt 5:10 / 4:7; 2 Thes 2:14. *o:* Acts 2:23; 7:52.

prophets and persecuted us; they do not
please God, and are opposed to everyone,
[16p]trying to prevent us from speaking to the
Gentiles that they may be saved, thus constantly filling up the measure of their sins.
But the wrath of God has finally begun to
come upon them.

Paul's Recent Travel Plans. [17q]Brothers,
when we were bereft of you for a short time,
in person, not in heart, we were all the more
eager in our great desire to see you in person.
[18r]We decided to go to you—I, Paul, not
only once but more than once—yet Satan
thwarted us. [19s]For what is our hope or joy or
crown to boast of in the presence of our Lord
Jesus at his coming if not you yourselves?
[20]For you are our glory and joy.

CHAPTER 3

See RG 482–83

[1t]That is why, when we could bear it
no longer, we decided to remain alone in
Athens [2u]and sent Timothy, our brother and
co-worker for God in the gospel of Christ, to
strengthen and encourage you in your faith,
[3*]so that no one be disturbed in these afflictions. For you yourselves know that we are
destined for this. [4v]For even when we were
among you, we used to warn you in advance
that we would undergo affliction, just as has
happened, as you know. [5]For this reason,
when I too could bear it no longer, I sent to
learn about your faith, for fear that somehow
the tempter had put you to the test and our
toil might come to nothing.
[6]But just now Timothy has returned to us
from you, bringing us the good news of your
faith and love, and that you always think
kindly of us and long to see us as we long to
see you. [7]Because of this, we have been reassured about you, brothers, in our every distress and affliction, through your faith. [8]For
we now live, if you stand firm in the Lord.

Concluding Thanksgiving and Prayer.
[9*]What thanksgiving, then, can we render to
God for you, for all the joy we feel on your
account before our God? [10]Night and day we
pray beyond measure to see you in person
and to remedy the deficiencies of your faith.
[11]Now may God himself, our Father, and our
Lord Jesus direct our way to you, [12w]and
may the Lord make you increase and abound
in love for one another and for all, just as we
have for you, [13x]so as to strengthen your
hearts, to be blameless in holiness before our
God and Father at the coming of our Lord
Jesus with all his holy ones. [Amen.]

III. Specific Exhortations

CHAPTER 4

See RG 483–84

General Exhortations. [1]Finally, brothers, we earnestly ask and exhort you in the
Lord Jesus that, as you received from us how
you should conduct yourselves to please
God—and as you are conducting yourselves—
you do so even more. [2*]For you know what instructions we gave you through the Lord Jesus.

Holiness in Sexual Conduct. [3*]This is the

Paul's pride in his own ethnic and religious background (Rom 9:1–5; 10:1; 11:1–3; Phil 3:4–6). Sinful conduct (1 Thes 2:16) is itself an anticipation of the ultimate wrath or judgment of God (Rom 1:18–2:5), whether or not it is perceived as such.

3:3 We are destined: the Greek phraseology and the context suggest Paul's concern to alert his readers to difficulties he knew they would necessarily face and to enable them to see their present experience in the light of what he warned them would happen in the future. This line of thought is followed in 2 Thes 2:1–15.

3:9–10 The tension between Paul's optimism concerning the Thessalonians' faith and his worries about their perseverance remains unresolved. Perhaps this is accounted for not only by the continuing harassment but also by the shortness of his own stay in Thessalonica (even if that were over twice as long as the conventional three weeks that Luke assigns to it, Acts 17:2).

4:2 Instructions: these include specific guidelines on the basis of the Lord's authority, not necessarily sayings Jesus actually uttered. More profoundly, as 1 Thes 4:8 implies, the instructions are practical principles that Paul worked out in accordance with his understanding of the role of the Spirit.

4:3–8 Many think that this passage deals with a variety of moral regulations (fornication, adultery, sharp business practices). It can be more specifically interpreted as bringing general norms to bear on a specific problem, namely, marriage within degrees of consanguinity (as between uncle and niece) forbidden in Jewish law but allowed according to a Greek heiress law, which would insure retention of an inheritance within the family and perhaps thereby occasion divorce. In that case, "immorality" (1 Thes 4:3) should be rendered as "unlawful marriage" and "this matter" (1 Thes 4:6) as "a lawsuit." The phrase in 1 Thes 4:4, "acquire a wife for himself," has often been interpreted to mean "control one's body."

p: Gn 15:16; 2 Mc 6:14 / Rom 1:18; 2:5–6. *q:* 3:10; Rom 1:10–11. *r:* Rom 15:22. *s:* 2 Cor 1:14; Phil 2:16; 4:1. *t:* Acts 17:14. *u:* Acts 16:1–2; 1 Cor 3:5–9. *v:* Acts 14:22; 2 Thes 2:5–7; 2 Tm 3:12. *w:* 4:9–10; 2 Thes 1:3. *x:* 5:23; 1 Cor 1:8.

will of God, your holiness: that you refrain from immorality, [4]that each of you know how to acquire a wife for himself in holiness and honor, [5y]not in lustful passion as do the Gentiles who do not know God; [6]not to take advantage of or exploit a brother in this matter, for the Lord is an avenger in all these things, as we told you before and solemnly affirmed. [7]For God did not call us to impurity but to holiness. [8z]Therefore, whoever disregards this, disregards not a human being but God, who [also] gives his holy Spirit to you.

Mutual Charity. [9a]On the subject of mutual charity you have no need for anyone to write you, for you yourselves have been taught by God to love one another. [10b]Indeed, you do this for all the brothers throughout Macedonia. Nevertheless we urge you, brothers, to progress even more, [11]and to aspire to live a tranquil life, to mind your own affairs, and to work with your [own] hands, as we instructed you, [12]that you may conduct yourselves properly toward outsiders and not depend on anyone.

Hope for the Christian Dead. [13]We do not want you to be unaware, brothers, about those who have fallen asleep, so that you may not grieve like the rest, who have no hope. [14c]For if we believe that Jesus died and rose, so too will God, through Jesus, bring with him those who have fallen asleep. [15d*]Indeed, we tell you this, on the word of the Lord, that we who are alive, who are left until the coming of the Lord, will surely not precede those who have fallen asleep. [16e]For the Lord himself, with a word of command, with the voice of an archangel and with the trumpet of God, will come down from heaven, and the dead in Christ will rise first. [17*]Then we who are alive, who are left, will be caught up together with them in the clouds to meet the Lord in the air. Thus we shall always be with the Lord. [18]Therefore, console one another with these words.

CHAPTER 5

See RG 483–84

Vigilance. [1f]Concerning times and seasons, brothers, you have no need for anything to be written to you. [2g]For you yourselves know very well that the day of the Lord will come like a thief at night. [3]When people are saying, "Peace and security," then sudden disaster comes upon them, like labor pains upon a pregnant woman, and they will not escape.

[4h]But you, brothers, are not in darkness, for that day to overtake you like a thief. [5*]For all of you are children of the light and children of the day. We are not of the night or of darkness. [6i]Therefore, let us not sleep as the rest do, but let us stay alert and sober. [7]Those who sleep go to sleep at night, and those who are drunk get drunk at night. [8j]But since we are of the day, let us be sober, putting on the breastplate of faith and love and the helmet that is hope for salvation. [9]For God did not destine us for wrath, but to gain salvation through our Lord Jesus Christ, [10*]who died for us, so that whether we are awake or asleep we may live together with him. [11k]Therefore, encourage one another and build one another up, as indeed you do.

Church Order. [12]We ask you, brothers, to respect those who are laboring among you and who are over you in the Lord and who

4:15 Coming of the Lord: Paul here assumes that the second coming, or parousia, will occur within his own lifetime but insists that the time or season is unknown (1 Thes 5:1–2). Nevertheless, the most important aspect of the parousia for him was the fulfillment of union with Christ. His pastoral exhortation focuses first on hope for the departed faithful, then (1 Thes 5:1–3) on the need of preparedness for those who have to achieve their goal.

4:17 Will be caught up together: literally, snatched up, carried off; cf. 2 Cor 12:2; Rev 12:5. From the Latin verb here used, *rapiemur*, has come the idea of "the rapture," when believers will be transported away from the woes of the world; this construction combines this verse with Mt 24:40–41 (see note there) // Lk 17:34–35 and passages from Revelation in a scheme of millennial dispensationalism.

5:5 Children of the light: that is, belonging to the daylight of God's personal revelation and expected to achieve it (an analogous development of imagery that appears in Jn 12:36).

5:10 Characteristically, Paul plays on words suggesting ultimate and anticipated death and life. Union with the crucified and risen Lord at his parousia is anticipated in some measure in contrasted states of our temporal life. The essential element he urges is our indestructible personal union in Christ's own life (see Rom 5:1–10).

y: Ps 79:6; Jer 10:25; 2 Thes 1:8; 1 Pt 3:7. *z:* Lk 10:16. *a:* Jn 6:45; 13:34; 1 Jn 2:20–21, 27; 4:7. *b:* 2 Thes 3:6–12. *c:* 1 Cor 15:3–4, 12, 20. *d:* 1 Cor 15:51; Rev 14:13; 20:4–6. *e:* Mt 24:31; 1 Cor 15:23, 52. *f:* Mt 24:36–45. *g:* 2 Pt 3:10. *h:* Eph 5:8–9. *i:* Mt 24:42; Rom 13:12–13; 1 Pt 5:8. *j:* Is 59:17; Rom 13:11–14; Eph 6:11, 14–17. *k:* Rom 15:2; 1 Cor 8:1; 14:12, 26; Eph 4:29.

admonish you, [13]and to show esteem for them with special love on account of their work. Be at peace among yourselves.

[14]We urge you, brothers, admonish the idle, cheer the fainthearted, support the weak, be patient with all. [15l]See that no one returns evil for evil; rather, always seek what is good [both] for each other and for all. [16]Rejoice always. [17]Pray without ceasing. [18m]In all circumstances give thanks, for this is the will of God for you in Christ Jesus. [19*]Do not quench the Spirit. [20]Do not despise prophetic utterances. [21]Test everything; retain what is good. [22]Refrain from every kind of evil.

Concluding Prayer. [23n*]May the God of peace himself make you perfectly holy and may you entirely, spirit, soul, and body, be preserved blameless for the coming of our Lord Jesus Christ. [24]The one who calls you is faithful, and he will also accomplish it. [25]Brothers, pray for us [too].

IV. Final Greeting

[26*]Greet all the brothers with a holy kiss. [27]I adjure you by the Lord that this letter be read to all the brothers. [28]The grace of our Lord Jesus Christ be with you.

5:19–21 Paul's buoyant encouragement of charismatic freedom sometimes occasioned excesses that he or others had to remedy (see 1 Cor 14; 2 Thes 2:1–15; 2 Pt 3:1–16).

5:23 Another possible translation is, "May the God of peace himself make you perfectly holy and sanctify your spirit fully, and may both soul and body be preserved blameless for the coming of our Lord Jesus Christ." In either case, Paul is not offering an anthropological or philosophical analysis of human nature. Rather, he looks to the wholeness of what may be called the supernatural and natural aspects of a person's service of God.

5:26 Kiss: the holy embrace (see Rom 16:16; 1 Cor 16:20; 2 Cor 13:12; 1 Pt 5:14) was a greeting of respect and affection, perhaps given during a liturgy at which Paul's letter would have been read.

l: Prv 20:22; Mt 5:38–42; Rom 12:17. *m:* Eph 5:20. *n:* 2 Thes 3:16.

See RG 484-86

The Second Letter to the Thessalonians

This letter is addressed to the same church as the letter that precedes it in the canon and contains many expressions parallel to those in the First Letter to the Thessalonians, indeed verbatim with them. Yet other aspects of the contents of the Second Letter to the Thessalonians suggest a more impersonal tone and changed circumstances in the situation at Thessalonica.

The letter begins with an address (2 Thes 1:1–2) that expands only slightly on that of 1 Thes 1:1. It ends with a greeting insisting on its Pauline authority in the face of false claims made in Paul's name (see note on 2 Thes 2:2). The body of the letter falls into three short parts, of which the second is notoriously difficult (2 Thes 2).

The opening thanksgiving and prayer (2 Thes 1:3–12) speak of the Thessalonians' increasing faith and love in the face of outside persecution. God's eventual judgment against persecutors and his salvation for the faithful are already evidenced by the very fact of persecution. The second part (2 Thes 2:1–17), the heart of the letter, deals with a problem threatening the faith of the community. A message involving a prophetic oracle and apparently a forged letter, possibly presented at a liturgical gathering (cf. 2 Thes 2:2 and 1 Cor 14:26–33), to the effect that the day of the Lord and all that it means have already come, has upset the life of the Thessalonian church.

The writer counters their preoccupation with the date of the parousia (or coming again of the Lord Jesus from heaven, 2 Thes 2:1) by recalling Paul's teaching concerning what must happen first and by going on to describe what will happen at the Lord's coming (2 Thes 2:8); he indicates the twofold process by which the "activity of Satan" and God's actions (2 Thes 2:9–11) are working out, namely, a growing division between believers and those who succumb to false prophecy and "the lie." He concludes by insisting on Pauline traditions and by praying for divine strength (2 Thes 2:13–17). The closing part of the letter (2 Thes 3:1–16) deals in particular with the apostle's directives and model style of life and with correction of disorderly elements within the community.

Traditional opinion holds that this letter was written shortly after 1 Thessalonians. Occasionally it has been argued that 2 Thessalonians was written first or that the two letters are addressed to different segments within the church at Thessalonica (2 Thessalonians being directed to the Jewish Christians there) or even that 2 Thessalonians was originally written to some other nearby place where Paul carried out mission work, such as Philippi or Beroea. Increasingly in recent times, however, the opinion has been advanced that 2 Thessalonians is a pseudepigraph, that is, a letter written authoritatively in Paul's name, to maintain apostolic traditions in a later period, perhaps during the last two decades of the first century.

In any case, the presumed audience of Second Thessalonians and certain features of its style and content require that it be read and studied in a Pauline context, particularly that provided by 1 Thessalonians. At the same time, and especially if the letter is regarded as not by Paul himself, its apocalyptic presentation of preconditions for the parousia (2 Thes 2:1–12) may profit from and require recourse to a wider biblical basis for interpretation, namely Old Testament books such as Daniel and Isaiah and especially, in the New Testament, the synoptic apocalyptic discourse (Mk 13; Mt 24–25; Lk 21:5–36) and the Book of Revelation.

The principal divisions of the Second Letter to the Thessalonians are the following:

I. Address (1:1–12)
II. Warning against Deception Concerning the Parousia (2:1–17)
III. Concluding Exhortations (3:1–16)
IV. Final Greetings (3:17–18)

I. Address

CHAPTER 1

See RG 485

Greeting. [1a*]Paul, Silvanus, and Timothy to the church of the Thessalonians in God our Father and the Lord Jesus Christ: [2]grace to you and peace from God [our] Father and the Lord Jesus Christ.

Thanksgiving. [3b*]We ought to thank God always for you, brothers, as is fitting, because your faith flourishes ever more, and the love of every one of you for one another grows ever greater. [4]Accordingly, we ourselves boast of you in the churches of God regarding your endurance and faith in all your persecutions and the afflictions you endure.

[5c]This is evidence of the just judgment of God, so that you may be considered worthy of the kingdom of God for which you are suffering. [6]For it is surely just on God's part to repay with afflictions those who are afflicting you, [7]and to grant rest along with us to you who are undergoing afflictions, at the revelation of the Lord Jesus from heaven with his mighty angels, [8d]in blazing fire, inflicting punishment on those who do not acknowledge God and on those who do not obey the gospel of our Lord Jesus. [9e]These will pay the penalty of eternal ruin, separated from the presence of the Lord and from the glory of his power, [10f*]when he comes to be glorified among his holy ones and to be marveled at on that day among all who have believed, for our testimony to you was believed.

Prayer. [11g]To this end, we always pray for you, that our God may make you worthy of his calling and powerfully bring to fulfillment every good purpose and every effort of faith, [12h*]that the name of our Lord Jesus may be glorified in you, and you in him, in accord with the grace of our God and Lord Jesus Christ.

1:1–2 On the address, see note on Rom 1:1–7 and cf. 1 Thes 1:1.

1:3–12 On the thanksgiving, see note on Rom 1:8 and cf. 1 Thes 1:2–10. Paul's gratitude to God for the faith and love of the Thessalonians (2 Thes 1:3) and his Christian pride in their faithful endurance (2 Thes 1:4–5) contrast with the condemnation announced for those who afflict them, a judgment to be carried out at the parousia (2 Thes 1:6–10), which is described in vivid language drawn from Old Testament apocalyptic. A prayer for the fulfillment of God's purpose in the Thessalonians (2 Thes 1:11–12) completes the section, as is customary in a Pauline letter (cf. 1 Thes 1:2–3).

1:10 Among his holy ones: in the Old Testament, this term can refer to an angelic throng (cf. also Jude 14), but here, in parallel with **among all who have believed**, it can refer to the triumphant people of God.

1:12 The grace of our God and Lord Jesus Christ: the Greek can also be translated, "the grace of our God and of the Lord Jesus Christ."

a: 1 Thes 1:1. *b:* 1 Cor 1:4; 1 Thes 1:2; 3:12. *c:* Phil 1:28; 1 Thes 2:12. *d:* Ps 79:5–6; Is 66:15; Jer 10:25. *e:* Is 2:10, 19, 21. *f:* Ps 89:8; Dn 7:18–22, 27; 1 Thes 3:13. *g:* 1 Thes 1:2–3. *h:* Is 66:5.

II. Warning against Deception Concerning the Parousia

CHAPTER 2

See RG 485–86

Christ and the Lawless One. [1i*]We
ask you, brothers, with regard to the coming
of our Lord Jesus Christ and our assembling
with him, [2j*]not to be shaken out of your
minds suddenly, or to be alarmed either by a
"spirit," or by an oral statement, or by a letter allegedly from us to the effect that the
day of the Lord is at hand. [3*]Let no one deceive you in any way. For unless the apostasy comes first and the lawless one is revealed, the one doomed to perdition, [4k*]who
opposes and exalts himself above every so-
called god and object of worship, so as to
seat himself in the temple of God, claiming
that he is a god— [5]do you not recall that
while I was still with you I told you these
things? [6*]And now you know what is restraining, that he may be revealed in his
time. [7l*]For the mystery of lawlessness is

2:1–17 The Thessalonians have been **shaken** by a message purporting to come from Paul himself that **the day of the Lord** is already present. He warns against this deception in eschatology by citing a scenario of events that must first occur (2 Thes 2:3–12) before the end will come. The overall point Paul makes is the need to reject such lies as Satan sends; he also reaffirms the Thessalonians in their calling (2 Thes 2:13–14). They are to uphold what Paul himself has taught (2 Thes 2:15). There is a concluding prayer for their strengthening (2 Thes 2:16–17). As in 2 Thes 1:8–10, the Old Testament provides a good deal of coloring; cf. especially Is 14:13–14; 66:15, 18–21; Ez 28:2–9; Dn 11:36–37. The contents of 2 Thes 2:3b–8 may come from a previously existing apocalypse. The details have been variously interpreted. An alternative to the possibilities noted below understands that an oracular utterance, supposedly coming from a prophetic spirit (2 Thes 2:2–3a), has so disrupted the community's thinking that its effects may be compared to those of the mania connected with the worship of the Greek god Dionysus. On this view, the writer seems to allude in 2 Thes 2:6–8 to Dionysiac "seizure," although, of course, ironically, somewhat as Paul alludes to witchcraft ("an evil eye") in Gal 3:1 in speaking of the threat to faith posed by those disturbing the Galatians (Gal 1:6–7; 5:10b). On this view of 2 Thes 2:2, the Greek participles *katechon* (rendered above as **what is restraining**) and *katechōn* (**the one who restrains**) are to be translated "the seizing power" in 2 Thes 2:6 and "the seizer" in 2 Thes 2:7. They then allude to a pseudocharismatic force or spirit of Dionysiac character that has suddenly taken hold of the Thessalonian community (see 2 Thes 2:2). The addressees **know** (2 Thes 2:6) this force or spirit because of the problem it is causing. This pseudocharismatic force or spirit is a kind of anticipation and advance proof of the ultimate, climactic figure (**the lawless one** or the rebel, 2 Thes 2:3), of which the community has been warned (see note on 1 Thes 3:3). It is, however, only the beginning of the end that the latter's manifestation entails; the end is not yet. For in the course of the **mystery of lawlessness** (2 Thes 2:7), false prophetism, after it ceases in the Thessalonian community, will be manifested in the world at large (2 Thes 2:8–12), where it will also be eliminated in turn by the Lord Jesus.

2:2 "Spirit": a Spirit-inspired utterance or ecstatic revelation. **An oral statement**: literally, a "word" or pronouncement, not necessarily of ecstatic origin. **A letter allegedly sent by us**: possibly a forged letter, so that Paul calls attention in 2 Thes 3:17 to his practice of concluding a genuine letter with a summary note or greeting in his own hand, as at Gal 6:11–18 and elsewhere.

2:3b–5 This incomplete sentence (anacoluthon, 2 Thes 2:4) recalls what the Thessalonians had already been taught, an apocalyptic scenario depicting, in terms borrowed especially from Dn 11:36–37 and related verses, human self-assertiveness against God in **the temple of God** itself. **The lawless one** represents the climax of such activity in this account.

2:4 Seat himself in the temple of God: a reflection of the language in Dn 7:23–25; 8:9–12; 9:27; 11:36–37; 12:11 about the attempt of Antiochus IV Epiphanes to set up a statue of Zeus in the Jerusalem temple and possibly of the Roman emperor Caligula to do a similar thing (Mk 13:14). Here the imagery suggests an attempt to install someone in the place of God, **claiming that he is a god** (cf. Ez 28:2). Usually, it is the Jerusalem temple that is assumed to be meant; on the alternative view sketched above (see note on 2 Thes 2:1–17), **the temple** refers to the Christian community.

2:6–7 What is restraining . . . the one who restrains: neuter and masculine, respectively, of a force and person holding back the lawless one. The Thessalonians know what is meant (2 Thes 2:6), but the terms, seemingly found only in this passage and in writings dependent on it, have been variously interpreted. Traditionally, 2 Thes 2:6 has been applied to the Roman empire and 2 Thes 2:7 to the Roman emperor (in Paul's day, Nero) as bulwarks holding back chaos (cf. Rom 13:1–7). A second interpretation suggests that cosmic or angelic powers are binding Satan (2 Thes 2:9) and so restraining him; some relate this to an anti-Christ figure (1 Jn 2:18) or to Michael the archangel (Rev 12:7–9; 20:1–3). A more recent view suggests that it is the preaching of the Christian gospel that restrains the end, for in God's plan the end cannot come until the gospel is preached to all nations (Mk 13:10); in that case, Paul as missionary preacher par excellence is "the one who restrains," whose removal (death) will bring the end (2 Thes 2:7). On the alternative view (see note on 2 Thes 2:1–17), the phrases should be referred to that which and to him who seizes (a prophet) in ecstasy so as to have him speak pseudo-oracles.

2:7–12 The lawless one and **the one who restrains** are involved in an activity or process, **the mystery of lawlessness**, behind which **Satan** stands (2 Thes 2:9). The action of the **Lord [Jesus]** in overcoming the lawless one is described in Old Testament language (**with the breath of his mouth**; cf.

i: 1 Thes 4:13–17. *j:* Mt 24:6; 1 Cor 14:26, 32–33; 1 Thes 5:1–2. *k:* Dn 11:36–37; Ez 28:2. *l:* Mt 13:36–43; Acts 20:29; Gal 5:10; 2 Pt 2:1; Rev 22:11.

already at work. But the one who restrains is to do so only for the present, until he is removed from the scene. [8m]And then the lawless one will be revealed, whom the Lord [Jesus] will kill with the breath of his mouth and render powerless by the manifestation of his coming, [9n]the one whose coming springs from the power of Satan in every mighty deed and in signs and wonders that lie, [10]and in every wicked deceit for those who are perishing because they have not accepted the love of truth so that they may be saved. [11]Therefore, God is sending them a deceiving power so that they may believe the lie, [12]that all who have not believed the truth but have approved wrongdoing may be condemned.

[13o*]But we ought to give thanks to God for you always, brothers loved by the Lord, because God chose you as the firstfruits for salvation through sanctification by the Spirit and belief in truth. [14p]To this end he has [also] called you through our gospel to possess the glory of our Lord Jesus Christ. [15*]Therefore, brothers, stand firm and hold fast to the traditions that you were taught, either by an oral statement or by a letter of ours.

[16]May our Lord Jesus Christ himself and God our Father, who has loved us and given us everlasting encouragement and good hope through his grace, [17]encourage your hearts and strengthen them in every good deed and word.

III. Concluding Exhortations

CHAPTER 3

See RG 486

Request for Prayers. [1q*]Finally, brothers, pray for us, so that the word of the Lord may speed forward and be glorified, as it did among you, [2]and that we may be delivered from perverse and wicked people, for not all have faith. [3r]But the Lord is faithful; he will strengthen you and guard you from the evil one. [4s]We are confident of you in the Lord that what we instruct you, you [both] are doing and will continue to do. [5]May the Lord direct your hearts to the love of God and to the endurance of Christ.

Neglect of Work. [6*]We instruct you, brothers, in the name of [our] Lord Jesus Christ, to shun any brother who conducts himself in a disorderly way and not according to the tradition they received from us. [7]For you know how one must imitate us. For we did not act in a disorderly way among you, [8t]nor did we eat food received free from anyone. On the contrary, in toil and drudgery, night and day we worked, so as not to burden any of you. [9u]Not that we do not have the right. Rather, we wanted to present ourselves as a model for you, so that you might imitate us. [10v]In fact, when we were with you, we instructed you that if anyone was unwilling to work, neither should that one eat. [11w]We hear that some are conducting themselves among you in a

Is 11:4; Jb 4:9; Rev 19:15). His **coming** is literally the Lord's "parousia." The biblical concept of the "holy war," eschatologically conceived, may underlie the imagery.

2:13 As the firstfruits: there is also strong manuscript evidence for the reading, "God chose you from the beginning," thus providing a focus on God's activity from beginning to end; **firstfruits** is a Pauline term, however; cf. Rom 8:23; 11:16; 16:5 among other references.

2:15 Reference to **an oral statement** and a **letter** (2 Thes 2:2) and the content here, including a formula of conclusion (cf. 1 Cor 16:13; Gal 5:1), suggest that 2 Thes 2:1–15 or even 2 Thes 2:1–17 are to be taken as a literary unit, notwithstanding the incidental thanksgiving formula in 2 Thes 2:13.

3:1–18 The final chapter urges the Thessalonians to pray for Paul and his colleagues (2 Thes 3:1–2) and reiterates confidence in the Thessalonians (2 Thes 3:3–5), while admonishing them about a specific problem in their community that has grown out of the intense eschatological speculation, namely, not to work but to become instead disorderly busybodies (2 Thes 3:6–15). A benediction (2 Thes 3:16) and postscript in Paul's own hand round out the letter. On 2 Thes 3:17–18, cf. note on 2 Thes 2:2.

3:6 Some members of the community, probably because they regarded the parousia as imminent or the new age of the Lord to be already here (2 Thes 2:2), had apparently ceased to work for a living. The disciplinary problem they posed could be rooted in distorted thinking about Paul's own teaching (cf. 1 Thes 2:16; 3:3–4; 5:4–5) or, more likely, in a forged letter (2 Thes 2:2) and the type of teaching dealt with in 2 Thes 2:1–15. The apostle's own moral teaching, reflected in his selfless labors for others, was rooted in a deep doctrinal concern for the gospel message (cf. 1 Thes 2:3–10).

m: Is 11:4; Rev 19:15. *n:* Mt 24:24; Rev 13:13. *o:* 1 Thes 2:13; 5:9. *p:* Rom 5:1–10; 8:29–30; 1 Thes 4:7; 5:9. *q:* Eph 6:19; Col 4:3. *r:* 1 Thes 5:24 / 1 Cor 16:13 / Mt 6:13. *s:* 2 Cor 7:16; 1 Thes 4:1–2. *t:* 1 Thes 2:9. *u:* Mt 10:10; Phil 3:17. *v:* 1 Thes 4:11. *w:* 1 Thes 5:14.

disorderly way, by not keeping busy but
minding the business of others. [12]Such
people we instruct and urge in the Lord
Jesus Christ to work quietly and to eat their
own food. [13]But you, brothers, do not be
remiss in doing good. [14]If anyone does not
obey our word as expressed in this letter,
take note of this person not to associate
with him, that he may be put to shame.
[15x]Do not regard him as an enemy but admonish him as a brother. [16y]May the Lord
of peace himself give you peace at all
times and in every way. The Lord be with
all of you.

IV. Final Greetings

[17z]This greeting is in my own hand, Paul's.
This is the sign in every letter; this is how I
write. [18]The grace of our Lord Jesus Christ
be with all of you.

x: 2 Cor 2:7; Gal 6:1. *y:* Jn 14:27; Rom 15:33. *z:* 1 Cor 16:21; Gal 6:11.

See RG 487–89

The First Letter to Timothy

The three letters, First and Second Timothy and Titus, form a distinct group within the Pauline corpus. In the collection of letters by the Apostle to the Gentiles, they differ from the others in form and contents. All three suggest they were written late in Paul's career. The opponents are not "Judaizers" as in Galatians but false teachers stressing "knowledge" (*gnōsis*; see note on 1 Tm 6:20–21). Attention is given especially to correct doctrine and church organization. Jesus' second coming recedes into the background compared to references in Paul's earlier letters (though not Colossians and Ephesians). The three letters are addressed not to congregations but to those who shepherd congregations (Latin, *pastores*). These letters were first named "Pastoral Epistles" in the eighteenth century because they all are concerned with the work of a pastor in caring for the community or communities under his charge.

The first of the Pastorals, 1 Timothy, is presented as having been written from Macedonia. Timothy, whom Paul converted, was of mixed Jewish and Gentile parentage (Acts 16:1–3). He was the apostle's companion on both the second and the third missionary journeys (Acts 16:3; 19:22) and was often sent by him on special missions (Acts 19:22; 1 Cor 4:17; 1 Thes 3:2). In 1 Timothy (1 Tm 1:3), he is described as the administrator of the entire Ephesian community.

The letter instructs Timothy on his duty to restrain false and useless teaching (1 Tm 1:3–11; 4:1–5; 6:3–16) and proposes principles pertaining to his relationship with the older members of the community (1 Tm 5:1–2) and with the presbyters (5:17–22). It gives rules for aid to widows (1 Tm 5:3–8) and their selection for charitable ministrations (1 Tm 5:9–16) and also deals with liturgical celebrations (1 Tm 2:1–15), selections for the offices of bishop and deacon (1 Tm 3:1–13), relation of slaves with their masters (1 Tm 6:1–2), and obligations of the wealthier members of the community (1 Tm 6:17–19). This letter also reminds Timothy of the prophetic character of his office (1 Tm 1:12–20) and encourages him in his exercise of it (1 Tm 4:6–16). The central passage of the letter (1 Tm 3:14–16) expresses the principal motive that should guide the conduct of Timothy—preservation of the purity of the church's doctrine against false teaching. On this same note the letter concludes (1 Tm 6:20–21).

From the late second century to the nineteenth, Pauline authorship of the three Pastoral Epistles went unchallenged. Since then, the attribution of these letters to Paul has been questioned. Most scholars are convinced that Paul could not have been responsible for the vocabulary and style, the concept of church organization, or the theological expressions found in these letters. A second group believes, on the basis of statistical evidence, that the vocabulary and style are Pauline, even if at first sight the contrary seems to be the case. They state that the concept of church organization in the letters is not as advanced as the questioners of Pauline authorship hold since the notion of hierarchical order in a religious community existed in Israel before the time of Christ, as evidenced in the Dead Sea Scrolls. Finally, this group sees affinities between the theological thought of the Pastorals and that of the unquestionably genuine letters of Paul. Other scholars, while conceding a degree of validity to the positions mentioned above, suggest that the apostle made use of a secretary who was responsible for the composition of the letters. A fourth group of scholars believes that these letters are the work of a compiler, that they are based on traditions about Paul in his later years, and that they include, in varying amounts, actual fragments of genuine Pauline correspondence.

If Paul is considered the more immediate author, the Pastorals are to be dated between the end of his first Roman imprisonment (Acts 28:16) and his execution under Nero (A.D. 63–67); if they are regarded as only more remotely Pauline, their date may be as late as the early second century. In spite of these problems of authorship and dating, the Pastorals are illustrative of early Christian life and remain an important element of canonical scripture.

The principal divisions of the First Letter to Timothy are the following:

I. Address (1:1–2)
II. Sound Teaching (1:3–20)
III. Problems of Discipline (2:1–4:16)
IV. Duties toward Others (5:1–6:2a)
V. False Teaching and True Wealth (6:2b–19)
VI. Final Recommendation and Warning (6:20–21)

I. Address

CHAPTER 1

See RG 487-88

Greeting. [1a*]Paul, an apostle of Christ
Jesus by command of God our savior and of
Christ Jesus our hope, [2b]to Timothy, my true
child in faith: grace, mercy, and peace from
God the Father and Christ Jesus our Lord.

II. Sound Teaching

Warning against False Doctrine. [3c*]I repeat
the request I made of you when I was on my
way to Macedonia, that you stay in Ephesus
to instruct certain people not to teach false
doctrines [4d*]or to concern themselves with
myths and endless genealogies, which promote speculations rather than the plan of
God that is to be received by faith. [5e]The aim
of this instruction is love from a pure heart,
a good conscience, and a sincere faith.
[6f]Some people have deviated from these and
turned to meaningless talk, [7]wanting to be
teachers of the law, but without understanding either what they are saying or what they
assert with such assurance.

[8g*]We know that the law is good, provided that one uses it as law, [9]with the understanding that law is meant not for a righteous person but for the lawless and unruly,
the godless and sinful, the unholy and profane, those who kill their fathers or mothers,
murderers, [10h*]the unchaste, sodomites, kidnappers, liars, perjurers, and whatever else is
opposed to sound teaching, [11i]according to
the glorious gospel of the blessed God, with
which I have been entrusted.

Gratitude for God's Mercy. [12j*]I am grateful to him who has strengthened me, Christ
Jesus our Lord, because he considered me
trustworthy in appointing me to the ministry.

1:1–2 For the Pauline use of the conventional epistolary form, see note on Rom 1:1–7.

1:3–7 Here Timothy's initial task **in Ephesus** (cf. Acts 20:17–35) is outlined: to suppress the idle religious speculations, probably about Old Testament figures (1 Tm 1:3–4, but see note on 1 Tm 6:20–21), which do not contribute to the development of love within the community (1 Tm 1:5) but rather encourage similar useless conjectures (1 Tm 1:6–7).

1:4 The **plan of God that is to be received by faith**: the Greek may also possibly mean "God's trustworthy plan" or "the training in faith that God requires."

1:8–11 Those responsible for the speculations that are to be suppressed by Timothy do not present the Old Testament from the Christian viewpoint. The Christian values the Old Testament not as a system of law but as the first stage in God's revelation of his saving plan, which is brought to fulfillment in the good news of salvation through faith in Jesus Christ.

1:10 Sodomites: see 1 Cor 6:9 and the note there.

1:12–17 Present gratitude for the Christian apostleship leads Paul to recall an earlier time when he had been a fierce persecutor of the Christian communities (cf. Acts 26:9–11) until his conversion by intervention of divine mercy through the appearance of Jesus. This and his subsequent apostolic experience testify to the saving purpose of Jesus' incarnation. The fact of his former ignorance of the truth has not kept the apostle from regarding himself as having been the worst of sinners (1 Tm 1:15). Yet he was chosen to be an apostle, that God might manifest his firm will to save sinful humanity through Jesus Christ (1 Tm 1:16). The recounting of so great a mystery leads to a spontaneous outpouring of adoration (1 Tm 1:17).

a: 2:3; Lk 1:47; Ti 1:3; 2:10 / Col 1:27. *b:* 2 Tm 1:2; Ti 1:4. *c:* Acts 20:1. *d:* 4:7; Ti 1:14; 3:9; 2 Pt 1:16. *e:* Rom 13:10. *f:* 6:4, 20; Ti 1:10. *g:* Rom 7:12, 16. *h:* 4:6; 6:3; 2 Tm 4:3; Ti 1:9; 2:1. *i:* Ti 1:3. *j:* Phil 4:13 / Acts 9:15; Gal 1:15–16.

[13k]I was once a blasphemer and a persecutor
and an arrogant man, but I have been mercifully treated because I acted out of ignorance
in my unbelief. [14l]Indeed, the grace of our
Lord has been abundant, along with the faith
and love that are in Christ Jesus. [15m*]This
saying is trustworthy and deserves full acceptance: Christ Jesus came into the world
to save sinners. Of these I am the foremost.
[16]But for that reason I was mercifully
treated, so that in me, as the foremost, Christ
Jesus might display all his patience as an example for those who would come to believe
in him for everlasting life. [17n*]To the king of
ages, incorruptible, invisible, the only God,
honor and glory forever and ever. Amen.
Responsibility of Timothy. [18o*]I entrust
this charge to you, Timothy, my child, in accordance with the prophetic words once spoken about you. Through them may you fight
a good fight [19p]by having faith and a good
conscience. Some, by rejecting conscience,
have made a shipwreck of their faith,
[20q*]among them Hymenaeus and Alexander,
whom I have handed over to Satan to be
taught not to blaspheme.

III. Problems of Discipline

CHAPTER 2

Prayer and Conduct. [1r*]First of all,
then, I ask that supplications, prayers,
See RG 488
petitions, and thanksgivings be offered for
everyone, [2]for kings and for all in authority,
that we may lead a quiet and tranquil life in
all devotion and dignity. [3s]This is good and
pleasing to God our savior, [4t]who wills
everyone to be saved and to come to knowledge of the truth.

[5 u]For there is one God.
There is also one mediator between God
and the human race,
Christ Jesus, himself human,
[6 v*]who gave himself as ransom for all.

This was the testimony at the proper time.
[7w]For this I was appointed preacher and
apostle (I am speaking the truth, I am not lying), teacher of the Gentiles in faith and
truth.
[8*]It is my wish, then, that in every place
the men should pray, lifting up holy hands,

1:15 This saying is trustworthy: this phrase regularly introduces in the Pastorals a basic truth of early Christian faith; cf. 1 Tm 3:1; 4:9; 2 Tm 2:11; Ti 3:8.

1:17 King of ages: through Semitic influence, the Greek expression could mean "everlasting king"; it could also mean "king of the universe."

1:18–20 Timothy is to be mindful of his calling, which is here compared to the way Barnabas and Saul were designated by Christ as prophets for missionary service; cf. Acts 13:1–3. Such is probably the sense of the allusion to the prophetic words (1 Tm 1:18). His task is not to yield, whether in doctrine or in conduct, to erroneous opinions, taking warning from what has already happened at Ephesus in the case of Hymenaeus and Alexander (1 Tm 1:19–20).

1:18 The prophetic words once spoken about you: the Greek may also be translated, "the prophecies that led (me) to you." It probably refers to testimonies given by charismatic figures in the Christian communities. **Fight a good fight**: this translation preserves the play on words in Greek. The Greek terms imply a lengthy engagement in battle and might well be translated "wage a good campaign."

1:20 Hymenaeus: mentioned in 2 Tm 2:17 as saying that the resurrection has already taken place (in baptism). **Alexander**: probably the Alexander mentioned in 2 Tm 4:14 as the coppersmith who "did me a great deal of harm." **Whom I have handed over to Satan**: the same terms are used in the condemnation of the incestuous man in 1 Cor 5:5.

2:1–7 This marked insistence that the liturgical prayer of the community concern itself with the needs of all, whether Christian or not, and especially of those in authority, may imply that a disposition existed at Ephesus to refuse prayer for pagans. In actuality, such prayer aids the community to achieve peaceful relationships with non-Christians (1 Tm 2:2) and contributes to salvation, since it derives its value from the presence within the community of Christ, who is the one and only savior of all (1 Tm 2:3–6). The vital apostolic mission to the Gentiles (1 Tm 2:7) reflects Christ's purpose of universal salvation. 1 Tm 2:5 contains what may well have been a very primitive creed. Some interpreters have called it a Christian version of the Jewish *shema*: "Hear, O Israel, the LORD is our God, the LORD alone . . ." (Dt 6:4–5). The assertion in 1 Tm 2:7, "I am speaking the truth, I am not lying," reminds one of similar affirmations in Rom 9:1; 2 Cor 11:31; and Gal 1:20.

2:6 The testimony: to make sense of this overly concise phrase, many manuscripts supply "to which" (or "to whom"); two others add "was given." The translation has supplied "this was."

2:8–15 The prayer of the community should be unmarred by internal dissension (1 Tm 2:8); cf. Mt 5:21–26; 6:14; Mk 11:25. At the liturgical assembly the dress of women should be appro-

k: Acts 8:3; 9:1–2; 1 Cor 15:9; Gal 1:13. *l:* Rom 5:20; 2 Tm 1:13. *m:* Lk 15:2; 19:10. *n:* Rom 16:27. *o:* 4:14 / 6:12; 2 Tm 4:7; Jude 3. *p:* 3:9. *q:* 2 Tm 2:17; 4:14 / 1 Cor 5:5. *r:* Eph 6:18; Phil 4:6. *s:* 1:1; 4:10. *t:* 2 Tm 3:7; 2 Pt 3:9. *u:* 1 Cor 8:6; Heb 8:6; 9:15; 12:24 / Rom 5:15. *v:* Mk 10:45; Gal 1:4; 2:20; Eph 5:25; Ti 2:14. *w:* Acts 9:15; 1 Cor 9:1; Gal 2:7–8.

without anger or argument. [9x]Similarly, [too,] women should adorn themselves with proper conduct, with modesty and self-control, not with braided hairstyles and gold ornaments, or pearls, or expensive clothes, [10y]but rather, as befits women who profess reverence for God, with good deeds. [11z]A woman must receive instruction silently and under complete control. [12*]I do not permit a woman to teach or to have authority over a man. She must be quiet. [13a]For Adam was formed first, then Eve. [14b]Further, Adam was not deceived, but the woman was deceived and transgressed. [15c]But she will be saved through motherhood, provided women persevere in faith and love and holiness, with self-control.

See RG 488

CHAPTER 3

Qualifications of Various Ministers. [1d*]This saying is trustworthy: whoever aspires to the office of bishop desires a noble task. [2]Therefore, a bishop must be irreproachable, married only once, temperate, self-controlled, decent, hospitable, able to teach, [3e]not a drunkard, not aggressive, but gentle, not contentious, not a lover of money. [4]He must manage his own household well, keeping his children under control with perfect dignity; [5]for if a man does not know how to manage his own household, how can he take care of the church of God? [6*]He should not be a recent convert, so that he may not become conceited and thus incur the devil's punishment. [7f]He must also have a good reputation among outsiders, so that he may not fall into disgrace, the devil's trap.

[8*]Similarly, deacons must be dignified, not deceitful, not addicted to drink, not greedy for sordid gain, [9]holding fast to the mystery of the faith with a clear conscience. [10]Moreover, they should be tested first; then, if there is nothing against them, let them serve as deacons. [11g*]Women, similarly, should be dignified, not slanderers, but temperate and faithful in everything. [12]Deacons may be married only once and must manage their children and their households well. [13]Thus those who serve well as deacons gain good standing and much confidence in their faith in Christ Jesus.

The Mystery of Our Religion. [14*]I am writing you about these matters, although I hope to visit you soon. [15h]But if I should be delayed, you should know how to behave in the house-

priate to the occasion (2 Tm 2:9); their chief adornment is to be reputation for good works (2 Tm 2:10). Women are not to take part in the charismatic activity of the assembly (1 Tm 2:11–12; cf. 1 Cor 14:34) or exercise authority; their conduct there should reflect the role of man's helpmate (2 Tm 2:13; cf. Gn 2:18) and not the later relationship of Eve to Adam (2 Tm 2:14; cf. Gn 3:6–7). As long as women perform their role as wives and mothers in faith and love, their salvation is assured (2 Tm 2:15).

2:12 A man: this could also mean "her husband."

3:1–7 The passage begins by commending those who aspire to the office of bishop (*episkopos*; see note on Phil 1:1) within the community, but this first sentence (1 Tm 3:1) may also imply a warning about the great responsibilities involved. The writer proceeds to list the qualifications required: personal stability and graciousness; talent for teaching (1 Tm 3:2); moderation in habits and temperament (1 Tm 3:3); managerial ability (1 Tm 3:4); and experience in Christian living (1 Tm 3:5–6). Moreover, the candidate's previous life should provide no grounds for the charge that he did not previously practice what he now preaches. No list of qualifications for presbyters appears in 1 Timothy. The presbyter-bishops here and in Titus (see note on Ti 1:5–9) lack certain functions reserved here for Paul and Timothy.

3:1 This saying is trustworthy: the saying introduced is so unlike others after this phrase that some later Western manuscripts read, "This saying is popular." It is understood by some interpreters as concluding the preceding section (1 Tm 2:8–15). **Bishop**: literally, "overseer"; see note on Phil 1:1.

3:6 The devil's punishment: this phrase could mean the punishment once incurred by the devil (objective genitive) or a punishment brought about by the devil (subjective genitive).

3:8–13 Deacons, besides possessing the virtue of moderation (1 Tm 3:8), are to be outstanding for their faith (1 Tm 3:9) and well respected within the community (1 Tm 3:10). Women in the same role, although some interpreters take them to mean wives of deacons, must be dignified, temperate, dedicated, and not given to malicious talebearing (1 Tm 3:11). Deacons must have shown stability in marriage and have a good record with their families (1 Tm 3:12), for such experience prepares them well for the exercise of their ministry on behalf of the community (1 Tm 3:13). See further the note on Phil 1:1.

3:11 Women: this seems to refer to women deacons but may possibly mean wives of deacons. The former is preferred because the word is used absolutely; if deacons' wives were meant, a possessive "their" would be expected. Moreover, they are also introduced by the word "similarly," as in 1 Tm 3:8; this parallel suggests that they too exercised ecclesiastical functions.

3:14–16 In case there is some delay in the visit to Timothy at Ephesus planned for the near future, the present letter is being sent on ahead to arm and enlighten him in his task of preserving sound Christian conduct in the Ephesian church. The care he must exercise over this community is required by the

x: 1 Pt 3:3–5. *y:* 5:10; 1 Pt 3:1. *z:* 1 Cor 14:34–35. *a:* Gn 1:27; 2:7, 22; 1 Cor 11:8–9. *b:* Gn 3:6, 13; 2 Cor 11:3. *c:* 5:14. *d:* Ti 1:6–9. *e:* Heb 13:5. *f:* 2 Cor 8:21; 2 Tm 2:26. *g:* Ti 2:3. *h:* Eph 2:19–22.

hold of God, which is the church of the living God, the pillar and foundation of truth. [16i*]Undeniably great is the mystery of devotion,

Who was manifested in the flesh,
vindicated in the spirit,
seen by angels,
proclaimed to the Gentiles,
believed in throughout the world,
taken up in glory.

CHAPTER 4

See RG 488

False Asceticism. [1j*]Now the Spirit explicitly says that in the last times some will turn away from the faith by paying attention to deceitful spirits and demonic instructions [2]through the hypocrisy of liars with branded consciences. [3k]They forbid marriage and require abstinence from foods that God created to be received with thanksgiving by those who believe and know the truth. [4l]For everything created by God is good, and nothing is to be rejected when received with thanksgiving, [5*]for it is made holy by the invocation of God in prayer.

Counsel to Timothy. [6*]If you will give these instructions to the brothers, you will be a good minister of Christ Jesus, nourished on the words of the faith and of the sound teaching you have followed. [7m]Avoid profane and silly myths. Train yourself for devotion, [8n]for, while physical training is of limited value, devotion is valuable in every respect, since it holds a promise of life both for the present and for the future. [9o]This saying is trustworthy and deserves full acceptance. [10p*]For this we toil and struggle, because we have set our hope on the living God, who is the savior of all, especially of those who believe.

[11*]Command and teach these things. [12q*]Let no one have contempt for your youth, but set an example for those who believe, in speech, conduct, love, faith, and purity. [13*]Until I arrive, attend to the reading, exhortation, and teaching. [14r*]Do not neglect the gift you have, which was conferred on you through the prophetic word with the imposition of hands of the presbyterate. [15]Be diligent in these matters, be absorbed in them, so that your progress may be evident

profound nature of Christianity. It centers in Christ, appearing in human flesh, vindicated by the holy Spirit; the mystery of his person was revealed to the angels, announced to the Gentiles, and accepted by them in faith. He himself was taken up (through his resurrection and ascension) to the divine glory (1 Tm 3:16). This passage apparently includes part of a liturgical hymn used among the Christian communities in and around Ephesus. It consists of three couplets in typical Hebrew balance: flesh-spirit (contrast), seen-proclaimed (complementary), world-glory (contrast).

3:16 Who: the reference is to Christ, who is himself "the mystery of our devotion." Some predominantly Western manuscripts read "which," harmonizing the gender of the pronoun with that of the Greek word for mystery; many later (eighth/ninth century on), predominantly Byzantine manuscripts read "God," possibly for theological reasons.

4:1–5 Doctrinal deviations from the true Christian message within the church have been prophesied, though the origin of the prophecy is not specified (1 Tm 4:1–2); cf. Acts 20:29–30. The letter warns against a false asceticism that prohibits marriage and regards certain foods as forbidden, though they are part of God's good creation (1 Tm 4:3).

4:5 The invocation of God in prayer: literally, "the word of God and petition." The use of "word of God" without an article in Greek suggests that it refers to the name of God being invoked in blessing rather than to the "word of God" proclaimed to the community.

4:6–10 Timothy is urged to be faithful, both in his teaching and in his own life, as he looks only to God for salvation.

4:10 Struggle: other manuscripts and patristic witnesses read "suffer reproach."

4:11–16 Timothy is urged to preach and teach with confidence, relying on the gifts and the mission that God has bestowed on him.

4:12 Youth: some commentators find this reference a sign of pseudepigraphy. Timothy had joined Paul as a missionary already in A.D. 49, some fifteen years before the earliest supposed date of composition.

4:13 Reading: the Greek word refers to private or public reading. Here, it probably designates the public reading of scripture in the Christian assembly.

4:14 Prophetic word: this may mean the utterance of a Christian prophet designating the candidate or a prayer of blessing accompanying the rite. **Imposition of hands**: this gesture was used in the Old Testament to signify the transmission of authority from Moses to Joshua (Nm 27:18–23; Dt 34:9). The early Christian community used it as a symbol of installation into an office: the Seven (Acts 6:6) and Paul and Barnabas (Acts 13:3). **Of the presbyterate**: this would mean that each member of the college of presbyters imposed hands and appears to contradict 2 Tm 1:6, in which Paul says that he imposed hands on Timothy. This latter text, however, does not exclude participation by others in the rite. Some prefer to translate "for the presbyterate," and thus understand it to designate the office into which Timothy was installed rather than the agents who installed him.

i: Jn 1:14; Rom 1:3–4. *j:* 2 Tm 3:1; 4:3; 2 Pt 3:3; Jude 18. *k:* Gn 9:3; Rom 14:6; 1 Cor 10:30–31. *l:* Gn 1:31; Acts 10:15. *m:* 1:4; 2 Tm 2:16; Ti 1:14. *n:* 6:6. *o:* 1:15; 2 Tm 2:11; Ti 3:8. *p:* 2:4; Ti 2:11. *q:* 1 Cor 16:11; Ti 2:15 / Phil 3:17. *r:* 5:22; Acts 6:6; 8:17; 2 Tm 1:6.

to everyone. [16]Attend to yourself and to your teaching; persevere in both tasks, for by doing so you will save both yourself and those who listen to you.

IV. Duties toward Others

CHAPTER 5

See RG 488–89

[1s*]Do not rebuke an older man, but appeal to him as a father. Treat younger men as brothers, [2]older women as mothers, and younger women as sisters with complete purity.

Rules for Widows. [3]Honor widows who are truly widows. [4]But if a widow has children or grandchildren, let these first learn to perform their religious duty to their own family and to make recompense to their parents, for this is pleasing to God. [5t]The real widow, who is all alone, has set her hope on God and continues in supplications and prayers night and day. [6]But the one who is self-indulgent is dead while she lives. [7]Command this, so that they may be irreproachable. [8]And whoever does not provide for relatives and especially family members has denied the faith and is worse than an unbeliever.

[9]Let a widow be enrolled if she is not less than sixty years old, married only once, [10u]with a reputation for good works, namely, that she has raised children, practiced hospitality, washed the feet of the holy ones, helped those in distress, involved herself in every good work. [11]But exclude younger widows, for when their sensuality estranges them from Christ, they want to marry [12]and will incur condemnation for breaking their first pledge. [13v]And furthermore, they learn to be idlers, going about from house to house, and not only idlers but gossips and busybodies as well, talking about things that ought not to be mentioned. [14w]So I would like younger widows to marry, have children, and manage a home, so as to give the adversary no pretext for maligning us. [15]For some have already turned away to follow Satan. [16*]If any woman believer has widowed relatives, she must assist them; the church is not to be burdened, so that it will be able to help those who are truly widows.

Rules for Presbyters. [17x*]Presbyters who preside well deserve double honor, especially those who toil in preaching and teaching. [18y]For the scripture says, "You shall not muzzle an ox when it is threshing," and, "A worker deserves his pay." [19z]Do not accept an accusation against a presbyter unless it is supported by two or three witnesses. [20a]Reprimand publicly those who do sin, so that the rest also will be afraid. [21]I charge you before God and Christ Jesus and the elect angels to keep these rules without prejudice, doing nothing out of favoritism. [22b]Do not lay hands too readily on anyone, and do not share in another's sins.

5:1–16 After a few words of general advice based on common sense (1 Tm 5:1–2), the letter takes up, in its several aspects, the subject of widows. The first responsibility for their care belongs to the family circle, not to the Christian community as such (1 Tm 5:3–4, 16). The widow left without the aid of relatives may benefit the community by her prayer, and the community should consider her material sustenance its responsibility (1 Tm 5:5–8). Widows who wish to work directly for the Christian community should not be accepted unless they are well beyond the probability of marriage, i.e., sixty years of age, married only once, and with a reputation for good works (1 Tm 5:9–10). Younger widows are apt to be troublesome and should be encouraged to remarry (1 Tm 5:11–15).

5:16 Woman believer: some early Latin manuscripts and Fathers have a masculine here, while most later manuscripts and patristic quotations conflate the two readings, perhaps to avoid unfair restriction to women.

5:17–25 The function of presbyters is not exactly the same as that of the *episkopos*, "bishop" (1 Tm 3:1); in fact, the relation of the two at the time of this letter is obscure (but cf. note on Ti 1:5–9). The Pastorals seem to reflect a transitional stage that developed in many regions of the church into the monarchical episcopate of the second and third centuries. The presbyters possess the responsibility of preaching and teaching, for which functions they are supported by the community (1 Tm 5:17–18). The realization that their position subjects them to adverse criticism is implied in the direction to Timothy (1 Tm 5:19–20) to make sure of the truth of any accusation against them before public reproof is given. He must be as objective as possible in weighing charges against presbyters (1 Tm 5:21), learning from his experience to take care in selecting them (1 Tm 5:22). Some scholars take 1 Tm 5:22 as a reference not to ordination of presbyters but to reconciliation of public sinners. The letter now sounds an informal note of personal concern in its advice to Timothy not to be so ascetic that he even avoids wine (1 Tm 5:23). Judgment concerning the fitness of candidates to serve as presbyters is easy with persons of open conduct, more difficult and prolonged with those of greater reserve (1 Tm 5:24–25).

s: Lv 19:32; Ti 2:2. *t:* Jer 49:11; Lk 2:37; 18:7. *u:* Jn 13:14; Heb 13:2. *v:* 2 Thes 3:11. *w:* 1 Cor 7:9. *x:* 1 Cor 16:18; Phil 2:29. *y:* Dt 25:4; 1 Cor 9:8 / Mt 10:10; Lk 10:7. *z:* Dt 17:6; 19:15; Mt 18:16; 2 Cor 13:1. *a:* Gal 2:14; Eph 5:11; 2 Tm 4:2; Ti 1:9, 13. *b:* 4:14; 2 Tm 1:6.

Keep yourself pure. [23]Stop drinking only water, but have a little wine for the sake of your stomach and your frequent illnesses.

[24]Some people's sins are public, preceding them to judgment; but other people are followed by their sins. [25]Similarly, good works are also public; and even those that are not cannot remain hidden.

See RG 489

CHAPTER 6

Rules for Slaves. [1c*]Those who are under the yoke of slavery must regard their masters as worthy of full respect, so that the name of God and our teaching may not suffer abuse. [2d*]Those whose masters are believers must not take advantage of them because they are brothers but must give better service because those who will profit from their work are believers and are beloved.

V. False Teaching and True Wealth

Teach and urge these things. [3e]Whoever teaches something different and does not agree with the sound words of our Lord Jesus Christ and the religious teaching [4]is conceited, understanding nothing, and has a morbid disposition for arguments and verbal disputes. From these come envy, rivalry, insults, evil suspicions, [5f]and mutual friction among people with corrupted minds, who are deprived of the truth, supposing religion to be a means of gain. [6g*]Indeed, religion with contentment is a great gain. [7h]For we brought nothing into the world, just as we shall not be able to take anything out of it. [8i]If we have food and clothing, we shall be content with that. [9j]Those who want to be rich are falling into temptation and into a trap and into many foolish and harmful desires, which plunge them into ruin and destruction. [10]For the love of money is the root of all evils, and some people in their desire for it have strayed from the faith and have pierced themselves with many pains.

Exhortations to Timothy. [11k*]But you, man of God, avoid all this. Instead, pursue righteousness, devotion, faith, love, patience, and gentleness. [12l]Compete well for the faith. Lay hold of eternal life, to which you were called when you made the noble confession in the presence of many witnesses. [13m]I charge [you] before God, who gives life to all things, and before Christ Jesus, who gave testimony under Pontius Pilate for the noble confession, [14]to keep the commandment without stain or reproach until the appearance of our Lord Jesus Christ [15n]that the blessed and only ruler will make manifest at the proper time, the King of kings and Lord of lords, [16o]who alone has immortality, who dwells in unapproachable light, and whom no human being has seen or can see. To him be honor and eternal power. Amen.

Right Use of Wealth. [17p*]Tell the rich in the present age not to be proud and not to rely on so uncertain a thing as wealth but rather on God, who richly provides us with all things for our enjoyment. [18]Tell them to do good, to be rich in good works, to be generous, ready to share, [19q]thus accumulating as treasure a good foundation for the future, so as to win the life that is true life.

6:1–2 Compare the tables for household duties, such as that of Col 3:18–4:1. Domestic relationships derive new meaning from the Christian faith.

6:1 Our teaching: this refers to the teaching of the Christian community.

6:2b–10 Timothy is exhorted to maintain steadfastly the position outlined in this letter, not allowing himself to be pressured into any other course. He must realize that false teachers can be discerned by their pride, envy, quarrelsomeness, and greed for material gain. 1 Tm 6:6 is rather obscure and is interpreted, and therefore translated, variously. The suggestion seems to be that the important gain that religion brings is spiritual, but that there is material gain, too, up to the point of what is needed for physical sustenance (cf. 1 Tm 6:17–19).

6:6 Contentment: the word *autarkeia* is a technical Greek philosophical term for the virtue of independence from material goods (Aristotle, Cynics, Stoics).

6:11–16 Timothy's position demands total dedication to God and faultless witness to Christ (1 Tm 6:11–14) operating from an awareness, through faith, of the coming revelation in Jesus of the invisible God (1 Tm 6:15–16).

6:11 Man of God: a title applied to Moses and the prophets (Dt 33:1; 1 Sm 2:27; 1 Kgs 12:22; 13:1; etc.).

6:17–19 Timothy is directed to instruct the rich, advising them to make good use of their wealth by aiding the poor.

c: Eph 6:5; Ti 2:9–10. *d:* Phlm 16. *e:* Gal 1:6–9; 2 Tm 1:13; Ti 1:1. *f:* 2 Tm 3:8; 4:4; Ti 1:14. *g:* 4:8; Phil 4:11–12; Heb 13:5. *h:* Jb 1:21; Eccl 5:14. *i:* Prv 30:8. *j:* Prv 23:4; 28:22. *k:* 2 Tm 2:22. *l:* 1 Cor 9:26; 2 Tm 4:7. *m:* Jn 18:36–37; 19:11. *n:* 2 Mc 13:4; Rev 17:14. *o:* Ex 33:20; Ps 104:2. *p:* Ps 62:11; Lk 12:20. *q:* Mt 6:20.

VI. Final Recommendation and Warning

20r*O Timothy, guard what has been entrusted to you. Avoid profane babbling and the absurdities of so-called knowledge.
21sBy professing it, some people have deviated from the faith.

Grace be with all of you.

6:20–21 A final solemn warning against the heretical teachers, with what seems to be a specific reference to gnosticism, the great rival and enemy of the church for two centuries and more (the Greek word for "knowledge" is *gnōsis*). If gnosticism is being referred to here, it is probable that the warnings against "speculations" and "myths and genealogies" (cf. especially 1 Tm 1:4; Ti 3:9) involve allusions to that same kind of heresy. Characteristic of the various gnostic systems of speculation was an elaborate mythology of innumerable superhuman intermediaries, on a descending scale ("genealogies"), between God and the world. Thus would be explained the emphasis upon Christ's being the one mediator (as in 1 Tm 2:5). Although fully developed gnosticism belonged to the second and later centuries, there are signs that incipient forms of it belonged to Paul's own period.

r: 2 Tm 1:14 / 4:7. *s:* 1:6; 2 Tm 2:18.

See RG 489–91

The Second Letter to Timothy

The authorship and date of this letter, as one of the Pastoral Epistles, are discussed in the Introduction to the First Letter to Timothy.

The tone here is more personal than in First Timothy, for this letter addresses Timothy in vivid terms (2 Tm 1:6–14; 2:1–13) and depicts Paul's courage and hope in the face of discouragements late in the course of his apostolic ministry (2 Tm 1:15–18; 3:10–17; 4:9–18). Indeed, the letter takes on the character of a final exhortation and testament from Paul to the younger Timothy (2 Tm 4:1–8). Paul is portrayed as a prisoner (2 Tm 1:8, 16; 2:9) in Rome (2 Tm 1:17), and there is a hint that Timothy may be in Ephesus (2 Tm 2:17). The letter reveals that, with rare exceptions, Christians have not rallied to Paul's support (2 Tm 1:15–18) and takes a pessimistic view of the outcome of his case (2 Tm 4:6). It describes Paul as fully aware of what impends, looking to God, not to human beings, for his deliverance (2 Tm 4:3–8, 18). It recalls his mission days with Timothy (2 Tm 1:3–5; cf. Acts 16:1–4). It points to his preaching of the gospel as the reason for his imprisonment and offers Timothy, as a motive for steadfastness, his own example of firmness in faith despite adverse circumstances (2 Tm 1:6–14). The letter suggests that Timothy should prepare others to replace himself as Paul has prepared Timothy to replace him (2 Tm 2:1–2). Paul urges him not to desist out of fear from preserving and spreading the Christian message (2 Tm 2:3–7). It presents the resurrection of Jesus and his messianic role as the heart of the gospel for which Paul has been ready to lay down his life (2 Tm 2:8–9) and thus not only to express his own conviction fully but to support the conviction of others (2 Tm 2:10–13).

This letter, like the preceding one, urges Timothy to protect the community from the inevitable impact of false teaching (2 Tm 2:14–3:9), without fear of the personal attacks that may result (2 Tm 3:10–13). It recommends that he rely on the power of the scriptures, on proclamation of the word, and on sound doctrine (2 Tm 3:14–4:2), without being troubled by those who do not accept him (2 Tm 4:3–5). The letter poignantly observes in passing that Paul has need of his reading materials and his cloak (2 Tm 4:13) and, what will be best of all, a visit from Timothy.

On the theory of authorship by Paul himself, Second Timothy appears to be the last of the three Pastoral Epistles. The many scholars who argue that the Pastorals are products of the Pauline school often incline toward Second Timothy as the earliest of the three and the one most likely to have actual fragments of material from Paul himself.

The principal divisions of the Second Letter to Timothy are the following:

I. Address (1:1–5)
II. Exhortations to Timothy (1:6–2:13)
III. Instructions Concerning False Teaching (2:14–4:8)
IV. Personal Requests and Final Greetings (4:9–22)

I. Address

CHAPTER 1

See RG 490

Greeting. [1a*]Paul, an apostle of Christ Jesus by the will of God for the promise of life in Christ Jesus, [2]to Timothy, my dear child: grace, mercy, and peace from God the Father and Christ Jesus our Lord.

Thanksgiving. [3b*]I am grateful to God, whom I worship with a clear conscience as my ancestors did, as I remember you constantly in my prayers, night and day. [4*]I yearn to see you again, recalling your tears, so that I may be filled with joy, [5c]as I recall your sincere faith that first lived in your grandmother Lois and in your mother Eunice and that I am confident lives also in you.

II. Exhortations to Timothy

The Gifts Timothy Has Received. [6d*]For this reason, I remind you to stir into flame the gift of God that you have through the imposition of my hands. [7e]For God did not give us a spirit of cowardice but rather of power and love and self-control. [8f*]So do not be ashamed of your testimony to our Lord, nor of me, a prisoner for his sake; but bear your share of hardship for the gospel with the strength that comes from God.

[9g*]He saved us and called us to a holy life, not according to our works but according to his own design and the grace bestowed on us in Christ Jesus before time began, [10h]but now made manifest through the appearance of our savior Christ Jesus, who destroyed death and brought life and immortality to light through the gospel, [11i*]for which I was appointed preacher and apostle and teacher. [12j*]On this account I am suffering these things; but I am not ashamed, for I know him in whom I have believed and am confident that he is able to guard what has been entrusted to me until that day. [13k]Take as your norm the sound words that you heard from me, in the faith and love that are in Christ Jesus. [14l]Guard this rich trust with the help of the holy Spirit that dwells within us.

Paul's Suffering. [15m*]You know that everyone in Asia deserted me, including Phygelus and Hermogenes. [16n*]May the Lord grant mercy to the family of Onesiphorus because he often gave me new heart and was not ashamed of my chains. [17]But when he came to Rome, he promptly searched for me and found me. [18o*]May the

1:1–2 For the formula of address and greeting, see note on Rom 1:1–7.

1:1 The promise of life in Christ Jesus: that God grants through union with Christ in faith and love; cf. Col 3:4; 1 Tm 4:8.

1:3 As my ancestors did: this emphasizes the continuity of Judaism and Christianity; for a similar view, see Rom 9:3–5; Phil 3:4–6.

1:4–5 Purportedly written from prison in Rome (2 Tm 1:8, 17; 4:6–8) shortly before the writer's death, the letter recalls the earlier sorrowful parting from Timothy, commending him for his faith and expressing the longing to see him again.

1:6 The gift of God: the grace resulting from the conferral of an ecclesiastical office. **The imposition of my hands**: see note on 1 Tm 4:14.

1:8 Do not be ashamed of your testimony to our Lord: i.e., of preaching and suffering for the sake of the gospel.

1:9–10 Redemption from sin and the call to holiness of life are not won by personal deeds but are freely and graciously bestowed according to God's eternal plan; cf. Eph 1:4.

1:11 Teacher: the overwhelming majority of manuscripts and Fathers read "teacher of the nations," undoubtedly a harmonization with 1 Tm 2:7.

1:12 He is able to guard . . . until that day: the intervening words can also be translated "what I have entrusted to him" (i.e., the fruit of his ministry) as well as "what has been entrusted to me" (i.e., the faith). The same difficult term occurs in 2 Tm 1:14, where it is modified by the adjective "rich" and used without a possessive.

1:15 Keen disappointment is expressed, here and later (2 Tm 4:16), that the Christians of the province of Asia, especially Phygelus and Hermogenes, should have abandoned the writer and done nothing to defend his case in court.

1:16–18 The family of Onesiphorus because he . . . of my chains: Onesiphorus seems to have died before this letter was written. His family is mentioned twice (here and in 2 Tm 4:19), though it was Onesiphorus himself who was helpful to Paul in prison and rendered much service to the community of Ephesus. Because the apostle complains of abandonment by all in Asia during his second imprisonment and trial, the assistance of Onesiphorus seems to have been given to Paul during his first Roman imprisonment (A.D. 61–63).

1:18 Lord . . . Lord: the first "Lord" here seems to refer to Christ, the second "Lord" to the Father.

a: 1 Tm 4:8. *b:* 1 Tm 3:9 / Phil 3:5. *c:* 1 Tm 1:5 / Acts 16:1. *d:* 1 Tm 4:14; 5:22 / Acts 6:6; 8:17. *e:* Rom 5:5; 8:15; 1 Cor 2:4. *f:* 2:3, 15; Rom 1:16. *g:* Eph 2:8–9; Ti 3:5 / Eph 1:4; Ti 1:2. *h:* Rom 16:26; 1 Pt 1:20 / 1 Tm 6:14 / Phil 3:20; Ti 1:4; 2:13; 2 Pt 1:11 / 1 Cor 15:54–55; Heb 2:14 / 1 Cor 15:53–54. *i:* 1 Tm 2:7. *j:* 1 Pt 4:16 / 1 Tm 1:10–11. *k:* 1 Tm 1:14. *l:* 1 Tm 6:20 / Rom 8:11. *m:* 4:16. *n:* 4:19. *o:* Jude 21.

Lord grant him to find mercy from the Lord on that day. And you know very well the services he rendered in Ephesus.

CHAPTER 2

See RG 490

Timothy's Conduct. [1]*So you, my child, be strong in the grace that is in Christ Jesus. [2]And what you heard from me through many witnesses entrust to faithful people who will have the ability to teach others as well. [3p]Bear your share of hardship along with me like a good soldier of Christ Jesus. [4q]To satisfy the one who recruited him, a soldier does not become entangled in the business affairs of life. [5r]Similarly, an athlete cannot receive the winner's crown except by competing according to the rules. [6s]The hardworking farmer ought to have the first share of the crop. [7t]Reflect on what I am saying, for the Lord will give you understanding in everything.

[8u]*Remember Jesus Christ, raised from the dead, a descendant of David: such is my gospel, [9v]for which I am suffering, even to the point of chains, like a criminal. But the word of God is not chained. [10w]Therefore, I bear with everything for the sake of those who are chosen, so that they too may obtain the salvation that is in Christ Jesus, together with eternal glory. [11x]This saying is trustworthy:

If we have died with him
we shall also live with him;
[12y]if we persevere
we shall also reign with him.
But if we deny him
he will deny us.
[13z]If we are unfaithful
he remains faithful,
for he cannot deny himself.

III. Instructions Concerning False Teaching

Warning against Useless Disputes. [14a]*Remind people of these things and charge them before God to stop disputing about words. This serves no useful purpose since it harms those who listen. [15b]Be eager to present yourself as acceptable to God, a workman who causes no disgrace, imparting the word of truth without deviation. [16c]Avoid profane, idle talk, for such people will become more and more godless, [17d]and their teaching will spread like gangrene. Among them are Hymenaeus and Philetus, [18e]who have deviated from the truth by saying that [the] resurrection has already taken place and are upsetting the faith of some. [19f]Nevertheless, God's solid foundation stands, bearing this inscription, "The Lord knows those who are his"; and, "Let everyone who calls upon the name of the Lord avoid evil."

[20]In a large household there are vessels not only of gold and silver but also of wood

2:1–7 This passage manifests a characteristic deep concern for safeguarding the faith and faithfully transmitting it through trustworthy people (2 Tm 2:1–2; cf. 2 Tm 1:14; 1 Tm 6:20; Ti 1:9). Comparisons to the soldier's detachment, the athlete's sportsmanship, and the farmer's arduous work as the price of recompense (2 Tm 2:4–6) emphasize the need of singleness of purpose in preaching the word, even at the cost of hardship, for the sake of Christ (2 Tm 2:3).

2:8–13 The section begins with a sloganlike summary of Paul's gospel about Christ (2 Tm 2:8) and concludes with what may be part of an early Christian hymn (2 Tm 2:11b–12a; most exegetes include the rest of 2 Tm 2:12 and all of 2 Tm 2:13 as part of the quotation). The poetic lines suggest that through baptism Christians die spiritually with Christ and hope to live with him and reign with him forever, but the Christian life includes endurance, witness, and even suffering, as the final judgment will show and as Paul's own case makes clear; while he is imprisoned for preaching the gospel (2 Tm 2:9), his sufferings are helpful to the elect for obtaining the salvation and glory available in Christ (2 Tm 2:10), who will be true to those who are faithful and will disown those who deny him (2 Tm 2:12–13).

2:14–19 For those who dispute about mere words (cf. 2 Tm 2:23–24) and indulge in irreligious talk to the detriment of their listeners (2 Tm 2:16–19), see notes on 1 Tm 1:3–7; 6:20–21. Hymenaeus and Philetus (2 Tm 2:17), while accepting the Christian's mystical death and resurrection in Christ through baptism, claimed that baptized Christians are already risen with Christ in this life and thus that there is no future bodily resurrection or eternal glory to come. The first quotation in 2 Tm 2:19 is from Nm 16:5; the other quotation is from some unidentified Jewish or Christian writing.

2:14 Before God: many ancient manuscripts read "before the Lord."

---

p: 1:8; 4:5; Phlm 2. *q:* 1 Cor 9:6. *r:* 1 Cor 9:25. *s:* 1 Cor 9:7–10. *t:* Prv 2:6. *u:* Rom 1:3; 1 Cor 15:4, 20 / Rom 2:16; Gal 1:11; 2:2. *v:* Phil 1:12–14. *w:* Col 1:24; 1 Tm 1:15. *x:* Rom 6:8. *y:* Mt 10:22, 33; Lk 12:9. *z:* Nm 23:19; Rom 3:3–4; 1 Cor 10:13; Ti 1:2. *a:* 1 Tm 6:4. *b:* 1:8; 2 Cor 6:7; Eph 1:13; Col 1:5. *c:* 1 Tm 4:7. *d:* 1 Tm 1:20. *e:* 2 Thes 2:2. *f:* Is 28:16; 1 Cor 3:10–15 / Nm 16:5; Jn 10:14.

and clay, some for lofty and others for humble use. [21g]If anyone cleanses himself of these things, he will be a vessel for lofty use, dedicated, beneficial to the master of the house, ready for every good work. [22h*]So turn from youthful desires and pursue righteousness, faith, love, and peace, along with those who call on the Lord with purity of heart. [23i]Avoid foolish and ignorant debates, for you know that they breed quarrels. [24j]A slave of the Lord should not quarrel, but should be gentle with everyone, able to teach, tolerant, [25k]correcting opponents with kindness. It may be that God will grant them repentance that leads to knowledge of the truth, [26l*]and that they may return to their senses out of the devil's snare, where they are entrapped by him, for his will.

CHAPTER 3

See RG 490

The Dangers of the Last Days. [1m*]But understand this: there will be terrifying times in the last days. [2n]People will be self-centered and lovers of money, proud, haughty, abusive, disobedient to their parents, ungrateful, irreligious, [3]callous, implacable, slanderous, licentious, brutal, hating what is good, [4]traitors, reckless, conceited, lovers of pleasure rather than lovers of God, [5o]as they make a pretense of religion but deny its power. Reject them. [6p]For some of these slip into homes and make captives of women weighed down by sins, led by various desires, [7q]always trying to learn but never able to reach a knowledge of the truth. [8r]Just as Jannes and Jambres opposed Moses, so they also oppose the truth—people of depraved mind, unqualified in the faith. [9]But they will not make further progress, for their foolishness will be plain to all, as it was with those two.

Paul's Example and Teaching. [10*]You have followed my teaching, way of life, purpose, faith, patience, love, endurance, [11s]persecutions, and sufferings, such as happened to me in Antioch, Iconium, and Lystra, persecutions that I endured. Yet from all these things the Lord delivered me. [12t]In fact, all who want to live religiously in Christ Jesus will be persecuted. [13]But wicked people and charlatans will go from bad to worse, deceivers and deceived. [14u]But you, remain faithful to what you have learned and believed, because you know from whom you learned it, [15v]and that from infancy you have known [the] sacred scriptures, which are capable of giving you wisdom for salvation through faith in Christ Jesus. [16w*]All scripture is inspired by God and is useful for teaching, for refutation, for correction, and for training in righteousness, [17x]so that one who belongs to God may be competent, equipped for every good work.

CHAPTER 4

See RG 490–91

Solemn Charge. [1y*]I charge you in the presence of God and of Christ Jesus, who will

2:22 Those who call on the Lord: those who believe in Christ and worship him as Lord, i.e., Christians (Acts 9:14–16, 20–21; Rom 10:12–13; cf. 2 Tm 2:19, literally, "Everyone who names the name of the Lord").

2:26 Some interpreters would render this passage, "Thus they may come to their senses and, forced to do his (i.e., God's) will, may escape the devil's trap." This interpretation of the Greek is possible, but the one accepted in the text seems more likely.

3:1–9 The moral depravity and false teaching that will be rampant in the last days are already at work (2 Tm 3:1–5). The frivolous and superficial, too, devoid of the true spirit of religion, will be easy victims of those who pervert them by falsifying the truth (2 Tm 3:6–8), just as Jannes and Jambres, Pharaoh's magicians of Egypt (Ex 7:11–12, 22), discredited the truth in Moses' time. Exodus does not name the magicians, but the two names are widely found in much later Jewish, Christian, and even pagan writings. Their origins are legendary.

3:10–17 Paul's example for Timothy includes persecution, a frequent emphasis in the Pastorals. Timothy is to be steadfast to what he has been taught and to scripture. The scriptures are the source of wisdom, i.e., of belief in and loving fulfillment of God's word revealed in Christ, through whom salvation is given.

3:16–17 Useful for teaching . . . every good work: because as God's word the scriptures share his divine authority. It is exercised through those who are ministers of the word.

3:16 All scripture is inspired by God: this could possibly also be translated, "All scripture inspired by God is useful for. . . ." In this classic reference to inspiration, God is its principal author, with the writer as the human collaborator. Thus the scriptures are the word of God in human language. See also 2 Pt 1:20–21.

4:1–5 The gravity of the obligation incumbent on Timothy

g: 3:17. *h:* Gal 5:22; 1 Tm 6:11 / Rom 10:13; 1 Cor 1:2. *i:* 1 Tm 1:4; 4:7; 6:4; Ti 3:9. *j:* 1 Tm 3:2–3. *k:* 3:7; 1 Tm 2:4. *l:* 1 Tm 3:7. *m:* 1 Tm 4:1; 2 Pt 3:3; Jude 18. *n:* Rom 1:29–31. *o:* Rom 2:20–22; Ti 1:16. *p:* Ti 1:11. *q:* 2:25. *r:* Ex 7:11, 22; 1 Tm 6:5. *s:* Acts 13:50; 14:5, 19 / Ps 34:20. *t:* Jn 15:20; Acts 14:22. *u:* 2:2. *v:* Jn 5:39. *w:* Rom 15:4; 2 Pt 1:19–21. *x:* 2:21. *y:* 1 Tm 5:21; 6:14 / Acts 10:42; Rom 14:9–10; 1 Pt 4:5.

judge the living and the dead, and by his appearing and his kingly power: [2z]proclaim the word; be persistent whether it is convenient or inconvenient; convince, reprimand, encourage through all patience and teaching. [3a*]For the time will come when people will not tolerate sound doctrine but, following their own desires and insatiable curiosity, will accumulate teachers [4b]and will stop listening to the truth and will be diverted to myths. [5]But you, be self-possessed in all circumstances; put up with hardship; perform the work of an evangelist; fulfill your ministry.

Reward for Fidelity. [6c*]For I am already being poured out like a libation, and the time of my departure is at hand. [7d*]I have competed well; I have finished the race; I have kept the faith. [8e*]From now on the crown of righteousness awaits me, which the Lord, the just judge, will award to me on that day, and not only to me, but to all who have longed for his appearance.

IV. Personal Requests and Final Greetings

Paul's Loneliness. [9*]Try to join me soon, [10f*]for Demas, enamored of the present world, deserted me and went to Thessalonica, Crescens to Galatia, and Titus to Dalmatia. [11g]Luke is the only one with me. Get Mark and bring him with you, for he is helpful to me in the ministry. [12h]I have sent Tychicus to Ephesus. [13i]When you come, bring the cloak I left with Carpus in Troas, the papyrus rolls, and especially the parchments.

[14j*]Alexander the coppersmith did me a great deal of harm; the Lord will repay him according to his deeds. [15]You too be on guard against him, for he has strongly resisted our preaching.

[16k]At my first defense no one appeared on my behalf, but everyone deserted me. May it not be held against them! [17l]But the Lord stood by me and gave me strength, so that through me the proclamation might be completed and all the Gentiles might hear it. And I was rescued from the lion's mouth. [18m]The Lord will rescue me from every evil threat and will bring me safe to his heavenly kingdom. To him be glory forever and ever. Amen.

Final Greeting. [19n*]Greet Prisca and Aq-

to preach the word can be gauged from the solemn adjuration: in the presence of God, and of Christ coming as universal judge, and by his appearance and his kingly power (2 Tm 4:1). Patience, courage, constancy, and endurance are required despite the opposition, hostility, indifference, and defection of many to whom the truth has been preached (2 Tm 4:2–5).

4:3 Insatiable curiosity: literally, "with itching ears."

4:6 The apostle recognizes his death through martyrdom to be imminent. He regards it as an act of worship in which his blood will be poured out in sacrifice; cf. Ex 29:38–40; Phil 2:17.

4:7 At the close of his life Paul could testify to the accomplishment of what Christ himself foretold concerning him at the time of his conversion, "I will show him what he will have to suffer for my name" (Acts 9:16).

4:8 When the world is judged at the parousia, all who have eagerly looked for the Lord's appearing and have sought to live according to his teachings will be rewarded. The crown is a reference to the laurel wreath placed on the heads of victorious athletes and conquerors in war; cf. 2 Tm 2:5; 1 Cor 9:25.

4:9–13 Demas either abandoned the work of the ministry for worldly affairs or, perhaps, gave up the faith itself (2 Tm 4:10). Luke (2 Tm 4:11) may have accompanied Paul on parts of his second and third missionary journeys (Acts 16:10–12; 20:5–7). Notice the presence of the first personal pronoun "we" in these Acts passages, suggesting to some that Luke (or at least some traveling companion of Paul's) was the author of Acts. Mark, once rejected by Paul (Acts 13:13; 15:39), is now to render him a great service (2 Tm 4:11); cf. Col 4:10; Phlm 24. For Tychicus, see Eph 6:21; cf. also Acts 20:4; Col 4:7.

4:10 Galatia: some manuscripts read "Gaul" or "Gallia."

4:14–18 Alexander: an opponent of Paul's preaching (2 Tm 4:14–15), perhaps the one who is mentioned in 1 Tm 1:20. Despite Paul's abandonment by his friends in the province of Asia (cf. 2 Tm 1:15–16), the divine assistance brought this first trial to a successful issue, even to the point of making the gospel message known to those who participated in or witnessed the trial (2 Tm 4:16–17).

4:19 Prisca and Aquila: they assisted Paul in his ministry in Corinth (Acts 18:2–3) and Ephesus (Acts 18:19, 26; 1 Cor 16:19). They risked death to save his life, and all the Gentile communities are indebted to them (Rom 16:3–5).

z: Acts 20:20, 31; 1 Tm 5:20. *a:* 1 Tm 4:1. *b:* 1 Tm 1:4; 4:7; Ti 1:14. *c:* Phil 2:17. *d:* 1 Tm 1:18; 6:12; Jude 3 / Acts 20:24; 1 Cor 9:24; Heb 12:1. *e:* 2:5; Wis 5:16; 1 Cor 9:25; Phil 3:14; Jas 1:12; 1 Pt 5:4; Rev 2:10. *f:* Col 4:14; Phlm 24 / 2 Cor 2:13; 7:6–7; 8:23; Gal 2:3; Ti 1:4. *g:* Col 4:14; Phlm 24 / Col 4:10; Phlm 24. *h:* Acts 20:4; Eph 6:21; Col 4:7. *i:* Acts 16:8; 20:6. *j:* 1 Tm 1:20 / 2 Sm 3:39; Ps 28:4; 62:12; Prv 24:12; Rom 2:6. *k:* 1:15. *l:* Acts 23:11; 27:23; Phil 4:13 / 1 Mc 2:60; Ps 22:22; Dn 6:23. *m:* 2 Cor 1:10 / Rom 16:27. *n:* Acts 18:2; Rom 16:3; 1 Cor 16:19 / 1:16.

uila and the family of Onesiphorus.
20 o *Erastus remained in Corinth, while I left Trophimus sick at Miletus.
21 *Try to get here before winter. Eubulus, Pudens, Linus, Claudia, and all the brothers send greetings.
22 p The Lord be with your spirit. Grace be with all of you.

4:20 Erastus: he was the treasurer of the city of Corinth (Rom 16:24); cf. also Acts 19:22. **Trophimus**: from the province of Asia, he accompanied Paul from Greece to Troas (Acts 20:4–5).

4:21 Linus: Western tradition sometimes identified this Linus with the supposed successor of Peter as bishop of Rome, and Claudia as the mother of Linus (*Apostolic Constitutions*, fourth century).

o: Acts 19:22; Rom 16:24 / Acts 20:4; 21:29. *p:* Gal 6:18; Phil 4:23; Col 4:18; 1 Tm 6:21; Ti 3:15.

See RG 491–93

The Letter to Titus

The third of the Pastoral Epistles in the New Testament is addressed to a different co-worker of Paul than are First and Second Timothy. The situation is different, too, for Titus is addressed as the person in charge of developing the church on the large Mediterranean island of Crete (Ti 1:5), a place Paul had never, according to the New Testament, visited. The tone is closer to that of First Timothy as three topics of church life and structure are discussed: presbyter-bishops (see note on Ti 1:5–9), groups with which one must work in the church (Ti 2:1–10), and admonitions for conduct based on the grace and love of God that appeared in Jesus Christ (Ti 2:11–3:10). The warmer personal tone of Second Timothy is replaced by emphasis on church office and on living in the society of the day, in which deceivers and heretics abound (Ti 1:10–16; 3:9–10).

The Pauline assistant who is addressed, Titus, was a Gentile Christian, but we are nowhere informed of his place of birth or residence. He went from Antioch with Paul and Barnabas to Jerusalem (Gal 2:1; cf. Acts 15:2). According to 2 Corinthians (2 Cor 2:13; 7:6, 13–14), he was with Paul on his third missionary journey; his name, however, does not appear in Acts. Besides being the bearer of Paul's severe letter to the Corinthians (2 Cor 7:6–8), he had the responsibility of taking up the collection in Corinth for the Christian community of Jerusalem (2 Cor 8:6, 16–19, 23). In the present letter (Ti 1:5), he is mentioned as the administrator of the Christian community in Crete, charged with the task of organizing it through the appointment of presbyters and bishops (Ti 1:5–9; here the two terms refer to the same personages).

The letter instructs Titus about the character of the assistants he is to choose in view of the pastoral difficulties peculiar to Crete (Ti 1:5–16). It suggests the special individual and social virtues that the various age groups and classes in the Christian community should be encouraged to acquire (Ti 2:1–10). The motivation for transformation of their lives comes from christology, especially the redemptive sacrifice of Christ and his future coming, as applied through baptism and justification (Ti 2:11–14; 3:4–8). The community is to serve as a leaven for Christianizing the social world about it (Ti 3:1–3). Good works are to be the evidence of their faith in God (Ti 3:8); those who engage in religious controversy are, after suitable warning, to be ignored (Ti 3:9–11).

The authorship and date of the Letter to Titus are discussed in the Introduction to 1 Timothy. Those who assume authorship by Paul himself usually place Titus after 1 Timothy and before 2 Timothy. Others see it as closely related to 1 Timothy, in a growing emphasis on church structure and opposition to heresy, later than the letters of Paul himself and 2 Timothy. It has also been suggested that, if the three Pastorals once circulated as a literary unit, Titus was meant to be read ahead of 1 and 2 Timothy.

The principal divisions of the Letter to Titus are the following:

I. Address (1:1–4)
II. Pastoral Charge (1:5–16)
III. Teaching the Christian Life (2:1–3:15)

I. Address

CHAPTER 1

See RG 491–92

Greeting. [1a*]Paul, a slave of God and apostle of Jesus Christ for the sake of the faith of God's chosen ones and the recognition of religious truth, [2b]in the hope of eternal life that God, who does not lie, promised before time began, [3c]who indeed at the proper time revealed his word in the proclamation with which I was entrusted by the command of God our savior, [4d]to Titus, my true child in our common faith: grace and peace from God the Father and Christ Jesus our savior.

II. Pastoral Charge

Titus in Crete. [5*]For this reason I left you in Crete so that you might set right what remains to be done and appoint presbyters in every town, as I directed you, [6e]on condition that a man be blameless, married only once, with believing children who are not accused of licentiousness or rebellious. [7]For a bishop as God's steward must be blameless, not arrogant, not irritable, not a drunkard, not aggressive, not greedy for sordid gain, [8]but hospitable, a lover of goodness, temperate, just, holy, and self-controlled, [9f]holding fast to the true message as taught so that he will be able both to exhort with sound doctrine and to refute opponents. [10*]For there are also many rebels, idle talkers and deceivers, especially the Jewish Christians. [11]It is imperative to silence them, as they are upsetting whole families by teaching for sordid gain what they should not. [12*]One of them, a prophet of their own, once said, "Cretans have always been liars, vicious beasts, and lazy gluttons." [13g]That testimony is true. Therefore, admonish them sharply, so that they may be sound in the faith, [14h]instead of paying attention to Jewish myths and regulations of people who have repudiated the truth. [15i]To the clean all things are clean, but to those who are defiled and unbelieving nothing is clean; in fact, both their minds and their consciences are tainted. [16]They claim to know God, but by their deeds they deny him. They are vile and disobedient and unqualified for any good deed.

III. Teaching the Christian Life

CHAPTER 2

See RG 492

Christian Behavior. [1j*]As for yourself, you must say what is consistent with sound doctrine, namely, [2]that older men should be temperate, dignified, self-controlled, sound in faith, love, and endurance. [3]Similarly, older women should be reverent in their behavior, not slanderers, not addicted to drink, teaching what is good, [4]so that they may train younger women to love their husbands and children, [5k]to be self-controlled, chaste, good homemakers, under the control of their husbands, so that the word of God may not be discredited.

1:1–4 On the epistolary form, see note on Rom 1:1–7. The apostolate is the divinely appointed mission to lead others to the true faith and through it to eternal salvation (1–3).

1:5–9 This instruction on the selection and appointment of presbyters, substantially identical with that in 1 Tm 3:1–7 on a bishop (see note there), was aimed at strengthening the authority of Titus by apostolic mandate; cf. Ti 2:15. In Ti 1:5, 7 and Acts 20:17, 28, the terms *episkopos* and *presbyteros* ("bishop" and "presbyter") refer to the same persons. Deacons are not mentioned in Titus. See also note on Phil 1:1.

1:10–16 This adverse criticism of the defects within the community is directed especially against certain Jewish Christians, who busy themselves with useless speculations over persons mentioned in the Old Testament, insist on the observance of Jewish ritual purity regulations, and thus upset whole families by teaching things they have no right to teach; cf. Ti 3:9; 1 Tm 1:3–10.

1:10 Jewish Christians: literally, "those of the circumcision."

1:12 Cretans . . . gluttons: quoted from Epimenides, a Cretan poet of the sixth century B.C.

2:1–10 One of Titus' main tasks in Crete is to become acquainted with the character of the Cretans and thereby learn to cope with its deficiencies (see Ti 1:12). The counsel is not only for Titus himself but for various classes of people with whom he must deal: older men and women (Ti 2:2–4), younger women and men (Ti 2:4–7), and slaves (Ti 2:9–10); cf. Eph 6:1–9; Col 3:18–4:1.

a: 1 Tm 2:4; 4:3; 2 Tm 2:25; 3:7; Heb 10:26. *b:* 3:7; 2 Tm 1:1; 1 Jn 2:25. *c:* 2:10; 3:4; Ps 24:5; 1 Tm 1:1; 2:3; 4:10; Jude 25. *d:* 2:13; 3:6; Phil 3:20; 2 Tm 1:10; 2 Pt 1:1, 11; 2:20; 3:2, 18. *e:* 1 Tm 3:2–7; 2 Tm 2:24–26. *f:* 1:13; 2:1–2, 8; 1 Tm 1:10; 6:3; 2 Tm 1:13; 4:3. *g:* 1:9. *h:* 3:9; 1 Tm 1:4; 4:7; 2 Tm 4:4; 2 Pt 1:16. *i:* Mk 7:18–23; Acts 10:15; Rom 14:14–23. *j:* 1:9, 13; 2:8; 1 Tm 1:10; 6:3; 2 Tm 1:13; 4:3. *k:* 1 Cor 11:3; 14:34; Eph 5:22–24; Col 3:18; 1 Tm 2:11–15; 1 Pt 3:1–6.

[6]Urge the younger men, similarly, to control themselves, [7]showing yourself as a
model of good deeds in every respect, with
integrity in your teaching, dignity, [8]and
sound speech that cannot be criticized, so
that the opponent will be put to shame without anything bad to say about us.

[9][l]Slaves are to be under the control of
their masters in all respects, giving them satisfaction, not talking back to them [10][m]or
stealing from them, but exhibiting complete
good faith, so as to adorn the doctrine of God
our savior in every way.

Transformation of Life. [11][n*]For the grace
of God has appeared, saving all [12]and training us to reject godless ways and worldly desires and to live temperately, justly, and devoutly in this age, [13][o*]as we await the
blessed hope, the appearance of the glory of
the great God and of our savior Jesus Christ,
[14][p]who gave himself for us to deliver us
from all lawlessness and to cleanse for himself a people as his own, eager to do what is
good.

[15][q]Say these things. Exhort and correct
with all authority. Let no one look down on
you.

CHAPTER 3

See RG 492–93

[1][r*]Remind them to be under the control of magistrates and authorities, to be obedient, to be open to every good enterprise.
[2]They are to slander no one, to be peaceable,
considerate, exercising all graciousness toward everyone. [3][s]For we ourselves were
once foolish, disobedient, deluded, slaves to
various desires and pleasures, living in malice and envy, hateful ourselves and hating
one another.

[4] [t]But when the kindness and generous love
of God our savior appeared,
[5] [u]not because of any righteous deeds we had done
but because of his mercy,
he saved us through the bath of rebirth
and renewal by the holy Spirit,
[6] [v]whom he richly poured out on us
through Jesus Christ our savior,
[7] [w]so that we might be justified by his grace
and become heirs in hope of eternal life.

[8][x*]This saying is trustworthy.

Advice to Titus. I want you to insist on
these points, that those who have believed in
God be careful to devote themselves to good
works; these are excellent and beneficial to
others. [9][y*]Avoid foolish arguments, genealogies, rivalries, and quarrels about the law,
for they are useless and futile. [10][z]After a first
and second warning, break off contact with
a heretic, [11]realizing that such a person is
perverted and sinful and stands self-con-
demned.

Directives, Greetings, and Blessing.
[12][a*]When I send Artemas to you, or Tychicus,

2:11–15 Underlying the admonitions for moral improvement in Ti 2:1–10 as the moving force is the constant appeal to God's revelation of salvation in Christ, with its demand for transformation of life.

2:13 The blessed hope, the appearance: literally, "the blessed hope and appearance," but the use of a single article in Greek strongly suggests an epexegetical, i.e., explanatory sense. **Of the great God and of our savior Jesus Christ**: another possible translation is "of our great God and savior Jesus Christ."

3:1–8 The list of Christian duties continues from Ti 2:9–10, undergirded again as in Ti 2:11–13 by appeal to what God in Christ has done (Ti 2:4–7; cf. Ti 2:11–14). The spiritual renewal of the Cretans, signified in God's merciful gift of baptism (Ti 3:4–7), should be reflected in their improved attitude toward civil authority and in their Christian relationship with all (Ti 3:1–3).

3:1 Magistrates and authorities: some interpreters understand these terms as referring to the principalities and powers of the heavenly hierarchy. **To be open to every good enterprise**: this implies being good citizens. It could also be translated "ready to do every sort of good work" (as Christians); cf. Ti 3:14.

3:8–11 In matters of good conduct and religious doctrine, Titus is to stand firm.

3:9 See note on 1 Tm 6:20–21.

3:12–15 Artemas or **Tychicus** (2 Tm 4:12) is to replace

l: 1 Cor 7:21–22; Eph 6:5–8; Col 3:22–25; 1 Tm 6:1–2; 1 Pt 2:18. *m:* 1:3; 3:4; Ps 24:5; 1 Tm 1:1; 2:3; 4:10; Jude 25. *n:* 1 Tm 2:4; 4:10. *o:* 1 Cor 1:7; Phil 3:20; 1 Thes 1:10 / 2 Tm 1:10 / 1:4; 3:6; 2 Pt 1:1, 11; 2:20; 3:2, 18. *p:* Gal 1:4; 2:20; Eph 5:2, 25; 1 Tm 2:6; 1 Pt 1:18–19 / Ps 130:8. *q:* 1 Tm 4:12. *r:* Rom 13:1–7; 1 Tm 2:1–2; 1 Pt 2:13–14. *s:* 1 Cor 6:9–11; Eph 2:1–3; 5:8; Col 3:5–7; 1 Pt 4:3. *t:* 1:3; 2:10; Ps 24:5; 1 Tm 1:1; 2:3; 4:10; Jude 25. *u:* Dt 9:5; Eph 2:4–5, 8–9; 2 Tm 1:9. *v:* 1:4; 2:13; Phil 3:20; 2 Tm 1:10; 2 Pt 1:1, 11; 2:20; 3:2, 18. *w:* 1:2; 2 Tm 1:1; 1 Jn 2:25. *x:* 1 Tm 1:15; 3:1; 4:9; 2 Tm 2:11. *y:* 1 Tm 1:4; 4:7; 2 Tm 2:23. *z:* Mt 18:15–18; Rom 16:17; 1 Cor 5:11; 2 Thes 3:6, 14–15. *a:* Acts 20:4; Eph 6:21; Col 4:7; 2 Tm 4:12.

try to join me at Nicopolis, where I have decided to spend the winter. [13b]Send Zenas the lawyer and Apollos on their journey soon, and see to it that they have everything they need. [14c]But let our people, too, learn to devote themselves to good works to supply urgent needs, so that they may not be unproductive. [15d]All who are with me send you greetings. Greet those who love us in the faith.

Grace be with all of you.

Titus, who will join Paul in his winter sojourn at Nicopolis in Epirus, on the western coast of Greece.

b: Acts 18:24–26; 1 Cor 1:12; 3:4–6, 22; 4:6; 16:12. *c:* 2:14; 3:8; Heb 10:24; 1 Pt 3:13. *d:* Heb 13:25.

See RG 493–95

The Letter to Philemon

This short letter addressed to three specific individuals was written by Paul during an imprisonment, perhaps in Rome between A.D. 61 and 63 (see the Introduction to Colossians for other possible sites). It concerns Onesimus, a slave from Colossae (Col 4:9), who had run away from his master, perhaps guilty of theft in the process (Phlm 18). Onesimus was converted to Christ by Paul (Phlm 10). Paul sends him back to his master (Phlm 12) with this letter asking that he be welcomed willingly by his old master (Phlm 8–10, 14, 17) not just as a slave but as a brother in Christ (Phlm 16). Paul uses very strong arguments (especially Phlm 19) in his touching appeal on behalf of Onesimus. It is unlikely that Paul is subtly hinting that he would like to retain Onesimus as his own slave, lent to Paul by his master. Rather, he suggests he would like to have Onesimus work with him for the gospel (Phlm 13, 20–21). There is, however, little evidence connecting this Onesimus with a bishop of Ephesus of the same name mentioned by Ignatius of Antioch (ca. A.D. 110).

Paul's letter deals with an accepted institution of antiquity, human slavery. But Paul breathes into this letter the spirit of Christ and of equality within the Christian community. He does not attack slavery directly, for this is something the Christian communities of the first century were in no position to do, and the expectation that Christ would soon come again militated against social reforms. Yet Paul, by presenting Onesimus as "brother, beloved . . . to me, but even more so to you" (Phlm 16), voiced an idea revolutionary in that day and destined to break down worldly barriers of division "in the Lord."

See RG 494

Address and Greeting. [1a*]Paul, a prisoner for Christ Jesus, and Timothy our brother, to Philemon, our beloved and our co-worker, [2b*]to Apphia our sister, to Archippus our fellow soldier, and to the church at your house. [3c*]Grace to you and peace from God our Father and the Lord Jesus Christ.

Thanksgiving. [4d*]I give thanks to my God always, remembering you in my prayers, [5*]as I hear of the love and the faith you have in the Lord Jesus and for all the holy ones, [6e*]so that your partnership in the faith may become effective in recognizing every good there is in us that leads to Christ.

Plea for Onesimus. [7f*]For I have experi-

1 Prisoner: as often elsewhere (cf. Romans, 1 Corinthians, Galatians especially), the second word in Greek enunciates the theme and sets the tone of the letter. Here it is the prisoner appealing rather than the apostle commanding.

2 Apphia our sister: sister is here used (like brother) to indicate a fellow Christian. **The church at your house: your** here is singular. It more likely refers to Philemon than to the last one named, Archippus; Philemon is then the owner of the slave Onesimus (Phlm 10). An alternate view is that the actual master of the slave is Archippus and that the one to whom the letter is addressed, Philemon, is the most prominent Christian there; see note on Col 4:17.

3 Grace . . . and peace: for this greeting, which may be a combination of Greek and Aramaic epistolary formulae, see note on Rom 1:1–7.

4 In my prayers: literally, "at the time of my prayers."

5 Holy ones: a common term for members of the Christian community (so also Phlm 7).

6 In us: some good ancient manuscripts have *in you* (plural). **That leads to Christ: leads to** translates the Greek preposition *eis*, indicating direction or purpose.

7 Encouragement: the Greek word *paraklēsis* is cognate with the verb translated "urge" in Phlm 9, 10, and serves as an introduction to Paul's plea. **Hearts**: literally, "bowels," expressing in Semitic fashion the seat of the emotions, one's "inmost self." The same Greek word is used in Phlm 12 and

a: 9; Eph 3:1; 4:1; Phil 1:7, 13. *b:* Col 4:17. *c:* Rom 1:7; Gal 1:3; Phil 1:2. *d:* Rom 1:8–9; Eph 1:15–16. *e:* Phil 1:9; Col 1:9. *f:* 2 Cor 7:4.

enced much joy and encouragement from your love, because the hearts of the holy ones have been refreshed by you, brother. [8*]Therefore, although I have the full right in Christ to order you to do what is proper, [9g*]I rather urge you out of love, being as I am, Paul, an old man, and now also a prisoner for Christ Jesus. [10h]I urge you on behalf of my child Onesimus, whose father I have become in my imprisonment, [11*]who was once useless to you but is now useful to [both] you and me. [12]I am sending him, that is, my own heart, back to you. [13i*]I should have liked to retain him for myself, so that he might serve me on your behalf in my imprisonment for the gospel, [14j]but I did not want to do anything without your consent, so that the good you do might not be forced but voluntary. [15*]Perhaps this is why he was away from you for a while, that you might have him back forever, [16k*]no longer as a slave but more than a slave, a brother, beloved especially to me, but even more so to you, as a man and in the Lord. [17]So if you regard me as a partner, welcome him as you would me. [18*]And if he has done you any injustice or owes you anything, charge it to me. [19l]I, Paul, write this in my own hand: I will pay. May I not tell you that you owe me your very self. [20]Yes, brother, may I profit from you in the Lord. Refresh my heart in Christ.

[21]With trust in your compliance I write to you, knowing that you will do even more than I say. [22m]At the same time prepare a guest room for me, for I hope to be granted to you through your prayers.

Final Greetings. [23n*]Epaphras, my fellow prisoner in Christ Jesus, greets you, [24o]as well as Mark, Aristarchus, Demas, and Luke, my co-workers. [25]The grace of the Lord Jesus Christ be with your spirit.

again in Phlm 20, where it forms a literary inclusion marking off the body of the letter.

8 Full right: often translated "boldness," the Greek word *parrēsia* connotes the full franchise of speech, as the right of a citizen to speak before the body politic, claimed by the Athenians as their privilege (Euripides).

9 Old man: some editors conjecture that Paul here used a similar Greek word meaning "ambassador" (cf. Eph 6:20). This conjecture heightens the contrast with "prisoner" but is totally without manuscript support.

11 Useless . . . useful: here Paul plays on the name Onesimus, which means "useful" or "beneficial." The verb translated "profit" in Phlm 20 is cognate.

13 Serve: the Greek *diakoneō* could connote a ministry.

15 Was away from: literally, "was separated from," but the same verb means simply "left" in Acts 18:1. It is a euphemism for his running away.

16 As a man: literally, "in the flesh." With this and the following phrase, Paul describes the natural and spiritual orders.

18–19 Charge it to me . . . I will pay: technical legal and commercial terms in account keeping and acknowledgment of indebtedness.

23–24 Epaphras: a Colossian who founded the church there (Col 1:7) and perhaps also in Laodicea and Hierapolis (Col 2:1; 4:12–13). **Aristarchus**: a native of Thessalonica and fellow worker of Paul (Acts 19:29; 20:4; 27:2). For Mark, Demas, and Luke, see 2 Tm 4:9–13 and the note there.

g: 1; Eph 3:1; 4:1; Phil 1:7, 13. *h*: 1 Cor 4:14–15; Gal 4:19; Col 4:9. *i*: Phil 2:30. *j*: 2 Cor 9:7; 1 Pt 5:2. *k*: 1 Tm 6:2. *l*: Gal 6:11; 2 Thes 3:17. *m*: Heb 13:19. *n*: Col 1:7; 4:12–13. *o*: Acts 12:12, 15; 13:13; 15:37–39; 19:29; 20:4; 27:2; Col 4:10, 14; 2 Tm 4:10–13.

See RG 496-501

The Letter to the Hebrews

As early as the second century, this treatise, which is of great rhetorical power and force in its admonition to faithful pilgrimage under Christ's leadership, bore the title "To the Hebrews." It was assumed to be directed to Jewish Christians. Usually Hebrews was attached in Greek manuscripts to the collection of letters by Paul. Although no author is mentioned (for there is no address), a reference to Timothy (Heb 13:23) suggested connections to the circle of Paul and his assistants. Yet the exact audience, the author, and even whether Hebrews is a letter have long been disputed. Apollos

The author saw the addressees in danger of apostasy from their Christian faith. This danger was due not to any persecution from outsiders but to a weariness with the demands of Christian life and a growing indifference to their calling (Heb 2:1; 4:14; 6:1–12; 10:23–32). The author's main theme, the priesthood and sacrifice of Jesus (Heb 3–10), is not developed for its own sake but as a means of restoring their lost fervor and strengthening them in their faith. Another important theme of the letter is that of the pilgrimage of the people of God to the heavenly Jerusalem (11:10; 12:1–3, 18–29; 13:14). This theme is intimately connected with that of Jesus' ministry in the heavenly sanctuary (Heb 9:11–10:22).

The author calls this work a "message of encouragement" (Heb 13:22), a designation that is given to a synagogue sermon in Acts 13:15. Hebrews is probably therefore a written homily, to which the author gave an epistolary ending (Heb 13:22–25).

The author begins with a reminder of the preexistence, incarnation, and exaltation of Jesus (Heb 1:3) that proclaimed him the climax of God's word to humanity (Heb 1:1–3). He dwells upon the dignity of the person of Christ, superior to the angels (Heb 1:4–2:2). Christ is God's final word of salvation communicated (in association with accredited witnesses to his teaching: cf. Heb 2:3–4) not merely by word but through his suffering in the humanity common to him and to all others (Heb 2:5–16). This enactment of salvation went beyond the pattern known to Moses, faithful prophet of God's word though he was, for Jesus as high priest expiated sin and was faithful to God with the faithfulness of God's own Son (Heb 2:17–3:6).

Just as the infidelity of the people thwarted Moses' efforts to save them, so the infidelity of any Christian may thwart God's plan in Christ (3:6–4:13). Christians are to reflect that it is their humanity that Jesus took upon himself, with all its defects save sinfulness, and that he bore the burden of it until death out of obedience to God. God declared this work of his Son to be the cause of salvation for all (Heb 4:14–5:10). Although Christians recognize this fundamental teaching, they may grow weary of it and of its implications, and therefore require other reflections to stimulate their faith (5:11–6:20).

Therefore, the author presents to the readers for their reflection the everlasting priesthood of Christ (Heb 7:1–28), a priesthood that fulfills the promise of the Old Testament (Heb 8:1–13). It also provides the meaning God ultimately intended in the sacrifices of the Old Testament (Heb 9:1–28): these pointed to the unique sacrifice of Christ, which alone obtains forgiveness of sins (Heb 10:1–18). The trial of faith experienced by the readers should resolve itself through their consideration of Christ's ministry in the heavenly sanctuary and his perpetual intercession there on their behalf (Heb 7:25; 8:1–13). They should also be strengthened by the assurance of his foreordained parousia, and by the fruits of faith that they have already enjoyed (Heb 10:19–39).

It is in the nature of faith to recognize the reality of what is not yet seen and is the object of hope, and the saints of the Old Testament give striking example of that faith (Heb 11:1–40). The perseverance to which the author exhorts the readers is shown forth in the early life of Jesus. Despite the afflictions of his ministry and the supreme trial of his suffering and death, he remained confident of the triumph that God would bring him (Heb 12:1–3). The difficulties of human life have meaning when they are accepted as God's discipline (Heb 12:4–13), and if Christians persevere in fidelity to the word in which they have believed, they are assured of possessing forever the unshakable kingdom of God (Heb 12:14–29).

The letter concludes with specific moral commandments (Heb 13:1–17), in the course of which the author recalls again his central theme of the sacrifice of Jesus and the courage needed to associate oneself with it in faith (Heb 13:9–16).

As early as the end of the second century, the church of Alexandria in Egypt accepted Hebrews as a letter of Paul, and that became the view commonly held in the East. Pauline authorship was contested in the West into the fourth century, but then accepted. In the sixteenth century, doubts about that position were again raised, and the modern consensus is that the letter was not written by Paul. There is, however, no widespread agreement on any of the other suggested authors, e.g., Barnabas, Apollos, or Prisc(ill)a and Aquila. The document itself has no statement about its author.

Among the reasons why Pauline authorship has been abandoned are the great difference of vocabulary and style between Hebrews and Paul's letters, the alternation of doctrinal teaching with moral exhortation, the different manner of citing the Old Testament, and the resemblance between the thought of Hebrews and that of Alexandrian Judaism. The Greek of the letter is in many ways the best in the New Testament.

Since the letter of Clement of Rome to the Corinthians, written about A.D. 96, most probably cites Hebrews, the upper limit for the date of composition is reasonably certain. While the letter's references in the present tense to the Old Testament sacrificial worship do not necessarily show that temple worship was still going on, many older commentators and a growing number of recent ones favor the view that it was and that the author wrote before the destruction of the temple of Jerusalem in A.D. 70. In that case, the argument of the letter is more easily explained as directed toward Jewish Christians rather than those of Gentile origin, and the persecutions they have suffered in the past (cf. Heb 10:32–34) may have been connected with the disturbances that preceded the expulsion of the Jews from Rome in A.D. 49 under the emperor Claudius. These were probably caused by disputes between Jews who accepted Jesus as the Messiah and those who did not.

The principal divisions of the Letter to the Hebrews are the following:

I. Introduction (1:1–4)
II. The Son Higher than the Angels (1:5–2:18)
III. Jesus, Faithful and Compassionate High Priest (3:1–5:10)
IV. Jesus' Eternal Priesthood and Eternal Sacrifice (5:11–10:39)
V. Examples, Discipline, Disobedience (11:1–12:29)
VI. Final Exhortation, Blessing, Greetings (13:1–25)

I. Introduction

CHAPTER 1

See RG 497–98

1 *In times past, God spoke in partial
and various ways to our ancestors through the
prophets; 2 [a]in these last days, he spoke to us
through a son, whom he made heir of all things
and through whom he created the universe,

3 [b]who is the refulgence of his glory,
the very imprint of his being,
and who sustains all things by his mighty word.
When he had accomplished purification from sins,
he took his seat at the right hand of the Majesty on high,
4 [c]as far superior to the angels
as the name he has inherited is more excellent than theirs.

II. The Son Higher than the Angels

Messianic Enthronement. 5 [d]*For to
which of the angels did God ever say:

"You are my son; this day I have begotten you"?

Or again:

"I will be a father to him, and he shall be a son to me"?

1:1–4 The letter opens with an introduction consisting of a reflection on the climax of God's revelation to the human race in his Son. The divine communication was initiated and maintained during Old Testament times in fragmentary and varied ways through **the prophets** (Heb 1:1), including Abraham, Moses, and all through whom God spoke. But now **in these last days** (Heb 1:2) the final age, God's revelation of his saving purpose is achieved **through a son**, i.e., one who is Son, whose role is redeemer and mediator of creation. He was made **heir of all things** through his death and exaltation to glory, yet he existed before he appeared as man; through him God **created the universe**. Heb 1:3–4, which may be based upon a liturgical hymn, assimilate the Son to the personified Wisdom of the Old Testament as **refulgence of** God's **glory** and **imprint of his being** (Heb 1:3; cf. Wis 7:26). These same terms are used of the Logos in Philo. The author now turns from the cosmological role of the preexistent Son to the redemptive work of Jesus: he brought about purification from sins and has been exalted to the right hand of God (see Ps 110:1). The once-humiliated and crucified Jesus has been declared God's Son, and this name shows his superiority to the angels. The reason for the author's insistence on that superiority is, among other things, that in some Jewish traditions angels were mediators of the old covenant (see Acts 7:53; Gal 3:19). Finally, Jesus' superiority to the angels emphasizes the superiority of the new covenant to the old because of the heavenly priesthood of Jesus.

1:5–14 Jesus' superiority to the angels is now demonstrated by a series of seven Old Testament texts. Some scholars see in the stages of Jesus' exaltation an order corresponding to that of enthronement ceremonies in the ancient Near East, especially in Egypt, namely, elevation to divine status (Heb 1:5–6); presentation to the angels and proclamation of everlasting lordship (Heb 1:7–12); enthronement and conferral of royal power (Heb 1:13). The citations from the Psalms in Heb 1:5, 13 were traditionally used of Jesus' messianic sonship (cf. Acts 13:33) through his resurrection and exaltation (cf. Acts 2:33–35); those in Heb 1:8, 10–12 are concerned with his divine kingship and his creative

a: Is 2:2; Jer 23:20; Ez 38:16; Dn 10:14 / Jn 3:17; Rom 8:3; Gal 4:4 / Prv 8:30; Wis 7:22; Jn 1:3; 1 Cor 8:6; Col 1:16. *b:* Wis 7:26; 2 Cor 4:4; Col 1:15 / 8:1; 10:12; 12:2; Mk 16:19; Acts 2:33; 7:55–56; Rom 8:34; Eph 1:20; Col 3:1; 1 Pt 3:22. *c:* Eph 1:21; Phil 2:9–11. *d:* Ps 2:7 / 2 Sm 7:14.

6[e]*And again, when he leads the first-born into the world, he says:

"Let all the angels of God worship him."

7[f]Of the angels he says:

"He makes his angels winds
and his ministers a fiery flame";

8[g]*but of the Son:

"Your throne, O God, stands forever and ever;
and a righteous scepter is the scepter of your kingdom.
9 You loved justice and hated wickedness;
therefore God, your God, anointed you
with the oil of gladness above your companions";

10[h]and:

"At the beginning, O Lord, you established the earth,
and the heavens are the works of your hands.
11 They will perish, but you remain;
and they will all grow old like a garment.
12 You will roll them up like a cloak,
and like a garment they will be changed.
But you are the same, and your years will have no end."

13[i]But to which of the angels has he ever said:

"Sit at my right hand
until I make your enemies your footstool"?

14[j]Are they not all ministering spirits sent to serve, for the sake of those who are to inherit salvation?

CHAPTER 2

See RG 497–98

Exhortation to Faithfulness. 1*Therefore, we must attend all the more to what we have heard, so that we may not be carried away. 2[k]For if the word announced through angels proved firm, and every transgression and disobedience received its just recompense, 3[l]how shall we escape if we ignore so great a salvation? Announced originally through the Lord, it was confirmed for us by those who had heard. 4[m]God added his testimony by signs, wonders, various acts of power, and distribution of the gifts of the holy Spirit according to his will.

Exaltation through Abasement. 5*For it was not to angels that he subjected the world to come, of which we are speaking. 6[n]Instead, someone has testified somewhere:

"What is man that you are mindful of him,

function. The central quotation in Heb 1:7 serves to contrast the angels with the Son. The author quotes it according to the Septuagint translation, which is quite different in meaning from that of the Hebrew ("You make the winds your messengers, and flaming fire your ministers"). The angels are only **sent to serve . . . those who are to inherit salvation** (Heb 1:14).

1:6 And again, when he leads: the Greek could also be translated "And when he again leads" in reference to the parousia.

1:8–12 O God: the application of the name "God" to the Son derives from the preexistence mentioned in Heb 1:2–3; the psalmist had already used it of the Hebrew king in the court style of the original. See note on Ps 45:6. It is also important for the author's christology that in Heb 1:10–12 an Old Testament passage addressed to God is redirected to Jesus.

2:1–4 The author now makes a transition into exhortation, using an a fortiori argument (as at Heb 7:21–22; 9:13–14; 10:28–29; 12:25). The **word announced through angels** (Heb 2:2), the Mosaic law, is contrasted with the more powerful word that Christians have received (Heb 2:3–4). Christ's supremacy strengthens Christians against being **carried away** from their faith.

2:5–18 The humanity and the suffering of Jesus do not constitute a valid reason for relinquishing the Christian faith. Ps 8:5–6 is also applied to Jesus in 1 Cor 15:27; Eph 1:22; and probably 1 Pt 3:22. This christological interpretation, therefore, probably reflects a common early Christian tradition, which may have originated in the expression **the son of man** (Heb 2:6). The psalm contrasts God's greatness with man's relative insignificance but also stresses the superiority of man to the rest of creation, of which he is lord. Hebrews applies this christologically: Jesus lived a truly human existence, **lower than the angels**, in the days of his earthly life, particularly in his suffering and death; now, **crowned with glory and honor**, he is raised above all creation. The author considers all things as already **subject to him** because of his exaltation (Heb 2:8–9), though **we do not see** this yet. The reference to Jesus as **leader** (Heb 2:10) sounds the first note of an important leitmotif in Hebrews: the journey of the people of God to the sabbath rest (Heb 4:9), the heavenly sanctuary, following Jesus, their "forerunner" (Heb 6:20). It was fitting that God should make him **perfect through suffering**, consecrated by obedient suffering. Because he is perfected as high priest, Jesus is then able to consecrate his people (Heb 2:11); access to God is

e: Dt 32:43 LXX; Ps 97:7. *f:* Ps 104:4 LXX. *g:* Ps 45:7–8. *h:* Ps 102:26–28. *i:* Ps 110:1. *j:* Ps 91:11; Dn 7:10. *k:* Acts 7:38, 53; Gal 3:19. *l:* 10:29; 12:25. *m:* Mk 16:20; Acts 14:3; 19:11. *n:* Ps 8:5–7.

or the son of man that you care for
him?
[7] You made him for a little while lower
than the angels;
you crowned him with glory and honor,
[8] [o]subjecting all things under his feet."

In "subjecting" all things [to him], he left
nothing not "subject to him." Yet at present
we do not see "all things subject to him,"
[9p]but we do see Jesus "crowned with glory
and honor" because he suffered death, he
who "for a little while" was made "lower
than the angels," that by the grace of God he
might taste death for everyone.
[10q]For it was fitting that he, for whom and
through whom all things exist, in bringing
many children to glory, should make the
leader to their salvation perfect through suffering. [11]He who consecrates and those who
are being consecrated all have one origin.
Therefore, he is not ashamed to call them
"brothers," [12r]saying:

"I will proclaim your name to my
brothers,
in the midst of the assembly I will
praise you";

[13s]and again:

"I will put my trust in him";

and again:

"Behold, I and the children God has
given me."

[14t]Now since the children share in blood and
flesh, he likewise shared in them, that
through death he might destroy the one who
has the power of death, that is, the devil,
[15]and free those who through fear of death
had been subject to slavery all their life.
[16]Surely he did not help angels but rather the
descendants of Abraham; [17u]therefore, he
had to become like his brothers in every
way, that he might be a merciful and faithful
high priest before God to expiate the sins of
the people. [18]Because he himself was tested
through what he suffered, he is able to help
those who are being tested.

III. Jesus, Faithful and Compassionate High Priest

CHAPTER 3

See RG 498–99

Jesus, Superior to Moses. [1*]There-
fore, holy "brothers," sharing in a heavenly
calling, reflect on Jesus, the apostle and high
priest of our confession, [2v]who was faithful
to the one who appointed him, just as Moses
was "faithful in [all] his house." [3w]But he is
worthy of more "glory" than Moses, as the

made possible by each of these two consecrations. If Jesus is able to help human beings, it is because he has become one of us; we are his "brothers." The author then cites three Old Testament texts as proofs of this unity between ourselves and the Son. Ps 22:22 is interpreted so as to make Jesus the singer of this lament, which ends with joyful praise of the Lord in the assembly of "brothers." The other two texts are from Is 8:17, 18. The first of these seems intended to display in Jesus an example of the trust in God that his followers should emulate. The second curiously calls these followers "children"; probably this is to be understood to mean children of Adam, but the point is our solidarity with Jesus. By sharing human nature, including the ban of death, Jesus broke the power of the devil over death (Heb 2:4); the author shares the view of Hellenistic Judaism that death was not intended by God and that it had been introduced into the world by the devil. The **fear of death** (Heb 2:15) is a religious fear based on the false conception that death marks the end of a person's relations with God (cf. Ps 115:17–18; Is 38:18). Jesus deliberately allied himself with the **descendants of Abraham** (Heb 2:16) in order to be a **merciful and faithful high priest**. This is the first appearance of the central theme of Hebrews, Jesus the great high priest expiating the **sins of the people** (Heb 2:17), as one who experienced the same tests as they (Heb 2:18).

3:1–6 The author now takes up the two qualities of Jesus mentioned in Heb 2:17, but in inverse order: faithfulness (Heb 3:1–4:13) and mercy (Heb 4:14–5:10). Christians are called holy "brothers" because of their common relation to him (Heb 2:11), **the apostle**, a designation for Jesus used only here in the New Testament (cf. Jn 13:16; 17:3), meaning one sent as God's final word to us (Heb 1:2). He is compared with Moses probably because he is seen as mediator of the new covenant (Heb 9:15) just as Moses was of the old (Heb 9:19–22, including his sacrifice). But when the author of Hebrews speaks of Jesus' sacrifice, he does not consider Moses as the Old Testament antitype, but rather the high priest on the Day of Atonement (Heb 9:6–15). Moses' faithfulness **"in [all] his house"** refers back to Nm 12:7, on which this section is a midrashic commentary. In Heb 3:3–6, the author does not indicate that he thinks of either Moses or Christ as the founder of the household. **His house** (Heb 3:2, 5, 6) means God's house, not that of Moses or Christ; in the case of Christ, compare Heb 3:6 with Heb 10:21. The **house** of Heb 3:6

o: Mt 28:18; 1 Cor 15:25–28; Eph 1:20–23; Phil 3:21; 1 Pt 3:22. *p:* Phil 2:6–11. *q:* 12:2; Is 53:4 / Rom 11:36; 1 Cor 8:6. *r:* Ps 22:23. *s:* Is 8:17, 18. *t:* Is 25:8; Hos 13:14; Jn 12:31; Rom 6:9; 1 Cor 15:54–55; 2 Tm 1:10; Rev 12:10. *u:* 4:15; 5:1–3. *v:* Nm 12:7. *w:* 2 Cor 3:7–8.

founder of a house has more "honor" than
the house itself. [4]Every house is founded by
someone, but the founder of all is God. [5]Mo-
ses was "faithful in all his house" as a "servant" to testify to what would be spoken,
[6x]*but Christ was faithful as a son placed
over his house. We are his house, if [only]
we hold fast to our confidence and pride in
our hope.
Israel's Infidelity a Warning. [7y]*Therefore, as the holy Spirit says:

"Oh, that today you would hear his
voice,
8 'Harden not your hearts as at the
rebellion
in the day of testing in the desert,
9 [z]where your ancestors tested and tried
me
and saw my works [10]for forty
years.
Because of this I was provoked with
that generation
and I said, "They have always been
of erring heart,
and they do not know my ways."
11 As I swore in my wrath,
"They shall not enter into my
rest." ' "

[12]Take care, brothers, that none of you may
have an evil and unfaithful heart, so as to
forsake the living God. [13]Encourage yourselves daily while it is still "today," so that
none of you may grow hardened by the deceit of sin. [14a]We have become partners of
Christ if only we hold the beginning of the
reality firm until the end, [15b]for it is said:

"Oh, that today you would hear his
voice:
'Harden not your hearts as at the
rebellion.' "

[16c]Who were those who rebelled when they
heard? Was it not all those who came out of
Egypt under Moses? [17d]With whom was he
"provoked for forty years"? Was it not those
who had sinned, whose corpses fell in the
desert? [18e]And to whom did he "swear that
they should not enter into his rest," if not to
those who were disobedient? [19]And we see
that they could not enter for lack of faith.

CHAPTER 4

See RG 498–99

The Sabbath Rest. [1]Therefore, let us
be on our guard while the promise of entering into his rest remains, that none of you
seem to have failed. [2]For in fact we have received the good news just as they did. But
the word that they heard did not profit them,
for they were not united in faith with those
who listened. [3f]For we who believed enter
into [that] rest, just as he has said:

"As I swore in my wrath,
'They shall not enter into my rest,' "

is the Christian community; the author suggests its continuity with Israel by speaking not of two houses but of only one. Heb 3:6 brings out the reason why Jesus is superior to Moses: the latter was the faithful **servant** laboring **in** the house founded by God, but Jesus is God's **son**, placed **over** the house.

3:6 The majority of manuscripts add "firm to the end," but these words are not found in the three earliest and best witnesses and are probably an interpolation derived from Heb 3:14.

3:7–4:13 The author appeals for steadfastness of faith in Jesus, basing his warning on the experience of Israel during the Exodus. In the Old Testament the Exodus had been invoked as a symbol of the return of Israel from the Babylonian exile (Is 42:9; 43:16–21; 51:9–11). In the New Testament the redemption was similarly understood as a new exodus, both in the experience of Jesus himself (Lk 9:31) and in that of his followers (1 Cor 10:1–4). The author cites Ps 95:7–11, a salutary example of hardness of heart, as a warning against the danger of growing weary and giving up the journey. To call God **living** (Heb 3:12) means that he reveals himself in his works (cf. Jos 3:10; Jer 10:11). The **rest** (Heb 3:11) into which Israel was to enter was only a foreshadowing of that rest to which Christians are called. They are to remember the example of Israel's revolt in the desert that cost a whole generation the loss of the promised land (Heb 3:15–19; cf. Nm 14:20–29). In Heb 4:1–11, the symbol of **rest** is seen in deeper dimension: because the promise to the ancient Hebrews foreshadowed that given to Christians, it is **good news**; and because the promised land was the place of rest that God provided for his people, it was a share in his own rest, which he enjoyed after he had finished his creative work (Heb 3:3–4; cf. Gn 2:2). The author attempts to read this meaning of God's rest into Ps 95:7–11 (Heb 3:6–9). The Greek form of the name of Joshua, who led Israel into the promised land, is Jesus (Heb 3:8). The author plays upon the name but stresses the superiority of Jesus, who leads his followers into heavenly rest. Heb 3:12, 13 are meant as a continuation of the warning, for the word of God brings judgment as well as salvation. Some would capitalize **the word of God** and see it as a personal title of Jesus, comparable to that of Jn 1:1–18.

x: 10:21; Eph 2:19; 1 Tm 3:15; 1 Pt 4:17. *y:* Ps 95:7–11. *z:* Ex 17:7; Nm 20:2–5. *a:* Rom 8:17. *b:* Ps 95:7–8. *c:* Nm 14:1–38; Dt 1:19–40. *d:* Nm 14:29. *e:* Nm 14:22–23; Dt 1:35. *f:* 3:11; Ps 95:11.

and yet his works were accomplished at the foundation of the world. [4g]For he has spoken somewhere about the seventh day in this manner, "And God rested on the seventh day from all his works"; [5h]and again, in the previously mentioned place, "They shall not enter into my rest." [6]Therefore, since it remains that some will enter into it, and those who formerly received the good news did not enter because of disobedience, [7i]he once more set a day, "today," when long afterwards he spoke through David, as already quoted:

"Oh, that today you would hear his voice:
'Harden not your hearts.' "

[8j]Now if Joshua had given them rest, he would not have spoken afterwards of another day. [9]Therefore, a sabbath rest still remains for the people of God. [10]And whoever enters into God's rest, rests from his own works as God did from his. [11]Therefore, let us strive to enter into that rest, so that no one may fall after the same example of disobedience.

[12k]Indeed, the word of God is living and effective, sharper than any two-edged sword, penetrating even between soul and spirit, joints and marrow, and able to discern reflections and thoughts of the heart. [13l]No creature is concealed from him, but everything is naked and exposed to the eyes of him to whom we must render an account.

Jesus, Compassionate High Priest. [14m*]Therefore, since we have a great high priest who has passed through the heavens, Jesus, the Son of God, let us hold fast to our confession. [15n]For we do not have a high priest who is unable to sympathize with our weaknesses, but one who has similarly been tested in every way, yet without sin. [16o]So let us confidently approach the throne of grace to receive mercy and to find grace for timely help.

CHAPTER 5

See RG 498–99

[1*]Every high priest is taken from among men and made their representative before God, to offer gifts and sacrifices for sins. [2*]He is able to deal patiently with the ignorant and erring, for he himself is beset by weakness [3p]and so, for this reason, must make sin offerings for himself as well as for the people. [4q]No one takes this honor upon himself but only when called by God, just as Aaron was. [5r]In the same way, it was not Christ who glorified himself in becoming high priest, but rather the one who said to him:

"You are my son;
this day I have begotten you";

[6s*]just as he says in another place:

"You are a priest forever
according to the order of Melchizedek."

4:14–16 These verses, which return to the theme first sounded in Heb 2:16–3:1, serve as an introduction to the section that follows. The author here alone calls Jesus **a great high priest** (Heb 4:14), a designation used by Philo for the Logos; perhaps he does so in order to emphasize Jesus' superiority over the Jewish high priest. He has **been tested in every way, yet without sin** (Heb 4:15); this indicates an acquaintance with the tradition of Jesus' temptations, not only at the beginning (as in Mk 1:13) but throughout his public life (cf. Lk 22:28). Although the reign of the exalted Jesus is a theme that occurs elsewhere in Hebrews, and Jesus' throne is mentioned in Heb 1:8, **the throne of grace** (Heb 4:16) refers to the throne of God. The similarity of Heb 4:16 to Heb 10:19–22 indicates that the author is thinking of our confident access to God, made possible by the priestly work of Jesus.

5:1–10 The true humanity of Jesus (see note on Heb 2:5–18) makes him a more rather than a less effective high priest to the Christian community. In Old Testament tradition, the high priest was identified with the people, guilty of personal sin just as they were (Heb 5:1–3). Even so, the office was of divine appointment (Heb 5:4), as was also the case with the sinless Christ (Heb 5:5). For Heb 5:6, see note on Ps 110:4. Although Jesus was Son of God, he was destined as a human being to learn obedience by accepting the suffering he had to endure (Heb 5:8). Because of his perfection through this experience of human suffering, he is the cause of salvation for all (Heb 5:9), a **high priest according to the order of Melchizedek** (Heb 5:10; cf. Heb 5:6 and Heb 7:3).

5:1 To offer gifts and sacrifices for sins: the author is thinking principally of the Day of Atonement rite, as is clear from Heb 9:7. This ritual was celebrated to atone for "all the sins of the Israelites" (Lv 16:34).

5:2 Deal patiently: the Greek word *metriopathein* occurs only here in the Bible; this term was used by the Stoics to designate the golden mean between excess and defect of passion. Here it means rather the ability to sympathize.

5:6–8 The author of Hebrews is the only New Testament writer to cite Ps 110:4, here and in Heb 7:17, 21, to show that Jesus has been called by God to his role as priest. Heb 5:7–8 deal with his ability to sympathize with sinners, because of his own experience of the trials and weakness of human nature, especially fear of death. In his present exalted state,

g: Gn 2:2. *h:* Ps 95:11. *i:* 3:7–8, 15; Ps 95:7–8. *j:* Dt 31:7; Jos 22:4. *k:* Wis 18:15–16; Is 49:2; Eph 6:17; Rev 1:16; 2:12. *l:* Jb 34:21–22; Ps 90:8; 139:2–4. *m:* 9:11, 24. *n:* 2:17–18; 5:2. *o:* 8:1; 10:19, 22, 35; 12:2; Eph 3:12. *p:* Lv 9:7; 16:15–17, 30, 34. *q:* Ex 28:1. *r:* Ps 2:7. *s:* Ps 110:4.

[7t*]In the days when he was in the flesh, he offered prayers and supplications with loud cries and tears to the one who was able to save him from death, and he was heard because of his reverence. [8u*]Son though he was, he learned obedience from what he suffered; [9v]and when he was made perfect, he became the source of eternal salvation for all who obey him, [10w]declared by God high priest according to the order of Melchizedek.

IV. Jesus' Eternal Priesthood and Eternal Sacrifice

Exhortation to Spiritual Renewal. [11*]About this we have much to say, and it is difficult to explain, for you have become sluggish in hearing. [12x]Although you should be teachers by this time, you need to have someone teach you again the basic elements of the utterances of God. You need milk, [and] not solid food. [13]Everyone who lives on milk lacks experience of the word of righteousness, for he is a child. [14]But solid food is for the mature, for those whose faculties are trained by practice to discern good and evil.

CHAPTER 6

See RG 499

[1y]Therefore, let us leave behind the basic teaching about Christ and advance to maturity, without laying the foundation all over again: repentance from dead works and faith in God, [2z*]instruction about baptisms and laying on of hands, resurrection of the dead and eternal judgment. [3]And we shall do this, if only God permits. [4a*]For it is impossible in the case of those who have once been enlightened and tasted the heavenly gift and shared in the holy Spirit [5*]and tasted the good word of God and the powers of the age to come, [6b*]and then have fallen away, to bring them to repentance again, since they are recrucifying the Son of God for themselves and holding him up to contempt. [7c]Ground that has absorbed the rain falling upon it repeatedly and brings forth crops useful to those for whom it is cultivated receives a blessing from God. [8d]But if it produces thorns and thistles, it is rejected; it will soon be cursed and finally burned.

---

weakness is foreign to him, but he understands what we suffer because of his previous earthly experience.

5:7 He offered prayers . . . to the one who was able to save him from death: at Gethsemane (cf. Mk 14:35), though some see a broader reference (see note on Jn 12:27).

5:8 Son though he was: two different though not incompatible views of Jesus' sonship coexist in Hebrews, one associating it with his exaltation, the other with his preexistence. The former view is the older one (cf. Rom 1:4).

5:11–6:20 The central section of Hebrews (5:11–10:39) opens with a reprimand and an appeal. Those to whom the author directs his teaching about Jesus' priesthood, which is **difficult to explain**, have become **sluggish in hearing** and forgetful of even **the basic elements** (Heb 5:12). But rather than treating of basic teachings, the author apparently believes that the challenge of more advanced ones may shake them out of their inertia (**therefore**, Heb 6:1). The six examples of **basic teaching** in Heb 6:1–3 are probably derived from a traditional catechetical list. No effort is made to address apostates, for their very hostility to the Christian message cuts them off completely from Christ (Heb 6:4–8). This harsh statement seems to rule out repentance after apostasy, but perhaps the author deliberately uses hyperbole in order to stress the seriousness of abandoning Christ. With Heb 6:9 a milder tone is introduced, and the criticism of the community (Heb 6:1–3, 9) is now balanced by an expression of confidence that its members are living truly Christian lives, and that God will justly reward their efforts (Heb 6:10). The author is concerned especially about their persevering (Heb 6:11–12), citing in this regard the achievement of Abraham, who relied on God's promise and on God's oath (Heb 6:13–18; cf. Gn 22:16), and proposes to them as a firm anchor of Christian hope the high priesthood of Christ, who is now living with God (Heb 6:19–20).

6:2 Instruction about baptisms: not simply about Christian baptism but about the difference between it and similar Jewish rites, such as proselyte baptism, John's baptism, and the washings of the Qumran sectaries. **Laying on of hands**: in Acts 8:17; 19:6 this rite effects the infusion of the holy Spirit; in Acts 6:6; 13:3; 1 Tm 4:14; 5:22; 2 Tm 1:6 it is a means of conferring some ministry or mission in the early Christian community.

6:4 Enlightened and tasted the heavenly gift: this may refer to baptism and the Eucharist, respectively, but more probably means the neophytes' enlightenment by faith and their experience of salvation.

6:5 Tasted the good word of God and the powers of the age to come: the proclamation of the **word of God** was accompanied by signs of the Spirit's power (1 Thes 1:5; 1 Cor 2:4).

6:6 They are recrucifying the Son of God for themselves: a colorful description of the malice of apostasy, which is portrayed as again crucifying and deriding the Son of God.

t: Mt 26:38–44; Mk 14:34–40; Lk 22:41–46; Jn 12:27. *u:* Rom 5:19; Phil 2:8. *v:* 7:24–25, 28. *w:* 6:20; Ps 110:4. *x:* 1 Cor 3:1–3. *y:* 9:14. *z:* 9:10; Mk 7:4 / Acts 6:6; 8:17; 13:3; 19:6; 1 Tm 4:14; 5:22; 2 Tm 1:6. *a:* 10:26, 32; Ps 34:6; 2 Cor 4:6. *b:* 2 Pt 2:21. *c:* Gn 1:11–12; Dt 11:11. *d:* Gn 3:17–18; Mt 7:16; 13:7; Mk 4:7; Lk 8:7.

[9]But we are sure in your regard, beloved,
of better things related to salvation, even
though we speak in this way. [10]For God is
not unjust so as to overlook your work and
the love you have demonstrated for his name
by having served and continuing to serve the
holy ones. [11e]We earnestly desire each of
you to demonstrate the same eagerness for
the fulfillment of hope until the end, [12f*]so
that you may not become sluggish, but imitators of those who, through faith and patience, are inheriting the promises.

God's Promise Immutable. [13g*]When God
made the promise to Abraham, since he had
no one greater by whom to swear, "he swore
by himself," [14h]and said, "I will indeed bless
you and multiply" you. [15i*]And so, after patient waiting, he obtained the promise. [16]Hu-
man beings swear by someone greater than
themselves; for them an oath serves as a
guarantee and puts an end to all argument.
[17j]So when God wanted to give the heirs of
his promise an even clearer demonstration of
the immutability of his purpose, he intervened with an oath, [18k*]so that by two immutable things, in which it was impossible
for God to lie, we who have taken refuge
might be strongly encouraged to hold fast to
the hope that lies before us. [19l*]This we have
as an anchor of the soul, sure and firm, which
reaches into the interior behind the veil,
[20m]where Jesus has entered on our behalf as
forerunner, becoming high priest forever according to the order of Melchizedek.

CHAPTER 7

See RG 498–99

Melchizedek, a Type of Christ. [1n*]This
"Melchizedek, king of Salem and priest of
God Most High," "met Abraham as he returned from his defeat of the kings" and
"blessed him." [2*]And Abraham apportioned
to him "a tenth of everything." His name
first means righteous king, and he was also
"king of Salem," that is, king of peace.
[3o*]Without father, mother, or ancestry, without beginning of days or end of life, thus
made to resemble the Son of God, he remains a priest forever.

[4p*]See how great he is to whom the patriarch "Abraham [indeed] gave a tenth" of his
spoils. [5q]The descendants of Levi who receive the office of priesthood have a com-

6:12 Imitators of those . . . inheriting the promises: the author urges the addressees to imitate the faith of the holy people of the Old Testament, who now possess the promised goods of which they lived in hope. This theme will be treated fully in Heb 6:11.

6:13 He swore by himself: God's promise to Abraham, which he confirmed by an oath ("I swear by myself," Gn 22:16) was the basis for the hope of all Abraham's descendants.

6:15 He obtained the promise: this probably refers not to Abraham's temporary possession of the land but to the eschatological blessings that Abraham and the other patriarchs have now come to possess.

6:18 Two immutable things: the promise and the oath, both made by God.

6:19 Anchor . . . into the interior behind the veil: a mixed metaphor. The Holy of Holies, beyond the veil that separates it from the Holy Place (Ex 26:31–33), is seen as the earthly counterpart of the heavenly abode of God. This theme will be developed in Heb 9.

7:1–3 Recalling the meeting between Melchizedek and Abraham described in Gn 14:17–20, the author enhances the significance of this priest by providing the popular etymological meaning of his name and that of the city over which he ruled (Heb 7:2). Since Genesis gives no information on the parentage or the death of Melchizedek, he is seen here as a type of Christ, representing a priesthood that is unique and eternal (Heb 7:3).

7:1 The author here assumes that Melchizedek was a priest of the God of Israel (cf. Gn 14:22 and the note there).

7:2 In Gn 14, the Hebrew text does not state explicitly who gave tithes to whom. The author of Hebrews supplies Abraham as the subject, according to a contemporary interpretation of the passage. This supports the argument of the midrash and makes it possible to see in Melchizedek a type of Jesus. The messianic blessings of righteousness and peace are foreshadowed in the names "Melchizedek" and "Salem."

7:3 Without father, mother, or ancestry, without beginning of days or end of life: this is perhaps a quotation from a hymn about Melchizedek. The rabbis maintained that anything not mentioned in the Torah does not exist. Consequently, since the Old Testament nowhere mentions Melchizedek's ancestry, birth, or death, the conclusion can be drawn that he **remains . . . forever**.

7:4–10 The tithe that Abraham gave to Melchizedek (Heb 7:4), a practice later followed by the levitical priesthood (Heb 7:5), was a gift (Heb 7:6) acknowledging a certain superiority in Melchizedek, the foreign priest (Heb 7:7). This is further indicated by the fact that the institution of the levitical priesthood was sustained by hereditary succession in the tribe of Levi, whereas the absence of any mention of Melchizedek's death in Genesis implies that his personal priesthood is permanent (Heb 7:8). The levitical priesthood itself, through Abraham, its ancestor, paid tithes to Melchizedek, thus acknowledging the superiority of his priesthood over its own (Heb 7:9–10).

e: 3:14. *f:* 5:11; Gal 3:14; Eph 1:13–14. *g:* Gn 22:16. *h:* Gn 22:17. *i:* 12; Rom 4:20. *j:* 12. *k:* Nm 23:19; 1 Sm 15:29; Jn 8:17; 2 Tm 2:13. *l:* 10:20; Ex 26:31–33; Lv 16:2. *m:* 5:10; Ps 110:4. *n:* Gn 14:17–20. *o:* 4:14; 6:6; 10:29. *p:* Gn 14:20. *q:* Nm 18:21 / Gn 35:11.

mandment according to the law to exact
tithes from the people, that is, from their
brothers, although they also have come from
the loins of Abraham. [6]But he who was not
of their ancestry received tithes from Abraham and blessed him who had received the
promises. [7*]Unquestionably, a lesser person
is blessed by a greater. [8]In the one case, mortal men receive tithes; in the other, a man of
whom it is testified that he lives on. [9*]One
might even say that Levi himself, who receives tithes, was tithed through Abraham,
[10]for he was still in his father's loins when
Melchizedek met him.

[11r*]If, then, perfection came through the
levitical priesthood, on the basis of which
the people received the law, what need
would there still have been for another priest
to arise according to the order of Melchizedek, and not reckoned according to the order of Aaron? [12]When there is a change of
priesthood, there is necessarily a change of
law as well. [13*]Now he of whom these things
are said belonged to a different tribe, of
which no member ever officiated at the altar.
[14s*]It is clear that our Lord arose from Judah,
and in regard to that tribe Moses said nothing about priests. [15*]It is even more obvious
if another priest is raised up after the likeness of Melchizedek, [16*]who has become so,
not by a law expressed in a commandment
concerning physical descent but by the
power of a life that cannot be destroyed.
[17t]For it is testified:

> "You are a priest forever
> according to the order of
> Melchizedek."

[18u]On the one hand, a former commandment
is annulled because of its weakness and uselessness, [19*]for the law brought nothing to
perfection; on the other hand, a better hope
is introduced, through which we draw near
to God. [20*]And to the degree that this happened not without the taking of an oath—for
others became priests without an oath, [21v]but
he with an oath, through the one who said to
him:

> "The Lord has sworn, and he will not
> repent:
> 'You are a priest forever' "—

7:7 A lesser person is blessed by a greater: though this sounds like a principle, there are some examples in the Old Testament that do not support it (cf. 2 Sm 14:22; Jb 31:20). The author may intend it as a statement of a liturgical rule.

7:9 Levi: for the author this name designates not only the son of Jacob mentioned in Genesis but the priestly tribe that was thought to be descended from him.

7:11–14 The levitical priesthood was not typified by the priesthood of Melchizedek, for Ps 110:4 speaks of a priesthood of a new order, the order of Melchizedek, to arise in messianic times (Heb 7:11). Since the levitical priesthood served the Mosaic law, a new priesthood (Heb 7:12) would not come into being without a change in the law itself. Thus Jesus was not associated with the Old Testament priesthood, for he was a descendant of the tribe of Judah, which had never exercised the priesthood (Heb 7:13–14).

7:13 He of whom these things are said: Jesus, the priest "according to the order of Melchizedek." According to the author's interpretation, Ps 110 spoke prophetically of Jesus.

7:14 Judah: the author accepts the early Christian tradition that Jesus was descended from the family of David (cf. Mt 1:1–2, 16, 20; Lk 1:27; 2:4; Rom 1:3). The Qumran community expected two Messiahs, one descended from Aaron and one from David; Hebrews shows no awareness of this view or at least does not accept it. Our author's view is not attested in contemporaneous Judaism.

7:15–19 Jesus does not exercise a priesthood through family lineage but through his immortal existence (15–16), fulfilling Ps 110:4 (Heb 7:17; cf. Heb 7:3). Thus he abolishes forever both the levitical priesthood and the law it serves, because neither could effectively sanctify people (Heb 7:18) by leading them into direct communication with God (Heb 7:19).

7:16 A life that cannot be destroyed: the life to which Jesus has attained by virtue of his resurrection; it is his exaltation rather than his divine nature that makes him priest. The Old Testament speaks of the Aaronic priesthood as eternal (see Ex 40:15); our author does not explicitly consider this possible objection to his argument but implicitly refutes it in Heb 7:23–24.

7:19 A better hope: this hope depends upon the sacrifice of the Son of God; through it we "approach the throne of grace" (Heb 4:16); cf. Heb 6:19, 20.

7:20–25 As was the case with the promise to Abraham (Heb 6:13), though not with the levitical priesthood, the eternal priesthood of the order of Melchizedek was confirmed by God's oath (Heb 7:20–21); cf. Ps 110:4. Thus Jesus becomes the guarantee of a permanent covenant (Heb 7:22) that does not require a succession of priests as did the levitical priesthood (Heb 7:23) because his high priesthood is eternal and unchangeable (Heb 7:24). Consequently, Jesus is able to save all who draw near to God through him since he is their everliving intercessor (Heb 7:25).

7:20 An oath: God's oath in Ps 110:4.

r: 5:6; Ps 110:4. *s:* Gn 49:10; Is 11:1; Mt 1:1–2, 16, 20; 2:6; Lk 1:27; 2:4; Rom 1:3; Rev 5:5. *t:* 5:6; Ps 110:4. *u:* 10:1. *v:* Ps 110:4.

[22w*]to that same degree has Jesus [also] become the guarantee of an [even] better covenant. [23]Those priests were many because
they were prevented by death from remaining in office, [24x]but he, because he remains
forever, has a priesthood that does not pass
away. [25y*]Therefore, he is always able to
save those who approach God through him,
since he lives forever to make intercession
for them.

[26z*]It was fitting that we should have such
a high priest: holy, innocent, undefiled, separated from sinners, higher than the heavens.
[27a*]He has no need, as did the high priests, to
offer sacrifice day after day, first for his own
sins and then for those of the people; he did
that once for all when he offered himself.
[28b]For the law appoints men subject to weakness to be high priests, but the word of the
oath, which was taken after the law, appoints
a son, who has been made perfect forever.

CHAPTER 8

See RG 499

Heavenly Priesthood of Jesus. [1c*]The
main point of what has been said is this: we
have such a high priest, who has taken his
seat at the right hand of the throne of the
Majesty in heaven, [2d*]a minister of the
sanctuary and of the true tabernacle that the
Lord, not man, set up. [3e]Now every high
priest is appointed to offer gifts and sacrifices; thus the necessity for this one also to
have something to offer. [4f]If then he were
on earth, he would not be a priest, since
there are those who offer gifts according to
the law. [5g]They worship in a copy and
shadow of the heavenly sanctuary, as Moses
was warned when he was about to erect the
tabernacle. For he says, "See that you make
everything according to the pattern shown
you on the mountain." [6h]Now he has obtained so much more excellent a ministry as
he is mediator of a better covenant, enacted
on better promises.

Old and New Covenants. [7*]For if that
first covenant had been faultless, no place
would have been sought for a second one.
[8i*]But he finds fault with them and says:

7:22 An [even] better covenant: better than the Mosaic covenant because it will be eternal, like the priesthood of Jesus upon which it is based. Heb 7:12 argued that a change of priesthood involves a change of law; since "law" and "covenant" are used correlatively, a new covenant is likewise instituted.

7:25 To make intercession: the intercession of the exalted Jesus, not the sequel to his completed sacrifice but its eternal presence in heaven; cf. Rom 8:34.

7:26 This verse with its list of attributes is reminiscent of Heb 7:3 and is perhaps a hymnic counterpart to it, contrasting the exalted Jesus with Melchizedek.

7:26–28 Jesus is precisely the high priest whom the human race requires, holy and sinless, installed far above humanity (Heb 7:26); one having no need to offer sacrifice daily for sins but making a single offering of himself (Heb 7:27) once for all. The law could only appoint high priests with human limitations, but the fulfillment of God's oath regarding the priesthood of Melchizedek (Ps 110:4) makes the Son of God the perfect priest forever (Heb 7:28).

7:27 Such daily sacrifice is nowhere mentioned in the Mosaic law; only on the Day of Atonement is it prescribed that the high priest must **offer sacrifice . . . for his own sins and then for those of the people** (Lv 16:11–19). **Once for all**: this translates the Greek words *ephapax/hapax* that occur eleven times in Hebrews.

8:1–6 The Christian community has in Jesus the kind of high priest described in Heb 7:26–28. In virtue of his ascension Jesus has taken his place at God's right hand in accordance with Ps 110:1 (Heb 8:1), where he presides over the heavenly sanctuary established by God himself (Heb 8:2). Like every high priest, he has his offering to make (Heb 8:3; cf. Heb 9:12, 14), but it differs from that of the levitical priesthood in which he had no share (Heb 8:4) and which was in any case but a shadowy reflection of the true offering in the heavenly sanctuary (Heb 8:5). But Jesus' ministry in the heavenly sanctuary is that of mediator of a superior covenant that accomplishes what it signifies (Heb 8:6).

8:2 The sanctuary: the Greek term could also mean "holy things" but bears the meaning "sanctuary" elsewhere in Hebrews (Heb 9:8, 12, 24, 25; 10:19; 13:11). **The true tabernacle**: the heavenly tabernacle **that the Lord . . . set up** is contrasted with the earthly tabernacle that Moses set up in the desert. **True** means "real" in contradistinction to a mere "copy and shadow" (Heb 8:5); compare the Johannine usage (e.g., Jn 1:9; 6:32; 15:1). The idea that the earthly sanctuary is a reflection of a heavenly model may be based upon Ex 25:9, but probably also derives from the Platonic concept of a real world of which our observable world is merely a shadow.

8:7–13 Since the first covenant was deficient in accomplishing what it signified, it had to be replaced (Heb 8:7), as Jeremiah (Jer 31:31–34) had prophesied (Heb 8:8–12). Even in the time of Jeremiah, the first covenant was antiquated (Heb 8:13). In Heb 7:22–24, the superiority of the new covenant was seen in the permanence of its priesthood; here the superiority is based on better promises, made explicit in the citation of Jer 31:31–34 (LXX: 38), namely, in the immediacy of the people's knowledge of God (Heb 8:11) and in the forgiveness of sin (Heb 8:12).

w: 8:6–10; 9:15–20; 10:29; 12:24; 13:20. *x:* 5:6; 13:8. *y:* Rom 8:34; 1 Jn 2:1; Rev 1:18. *z:* 4:14, 15. *a:* 5:3; 9:12, 25–28; 10:11–14; Ex 29:38–39; Lv 16:6, 11, 15–17; Nm 28:3–4; Is 53:10; Rom 6:10. *b:* 5:1, 2, 9. *c:* 1:3; 4:14; 7:26–28. *d:* 9:11; Ex 33:7; Nm 24:6 LXX. *e:* 5:1. *f:* 7:13. *g:* 9:23; Ex 25:40; Acts 7:44; Col 2:17. *h:* 7:22; 9:15. *i:* Jer 31:31–34.

"Behold, the days are coming, says the
Lord,
when I will conclude a new covenant
with the house of Israel and the
house of Judah.
9 It will not be like the covenant I made
with their fathers
the day I took them by the hand to lead
them forth from the land of
Egypt;
for they did not stand by my covenant
and I ignored them, says the Lord.
10 [j]But this is the covenant I will establish
with the house of Israel
after those days, says the Lord:
I will put my laws in their minds
and I will write them upon their hearts.
I will be their God,
and they shall be my people.
11 And they shall not teach, each one his
fellow citizen
and kinsman, saying, 'Know the
Lord,'
for all shall know me,
from least to greatest.
12 For I will forgive their evildoing
and remember their sins no more."

13 [k*]When he speaks of a "new" covenant, he
declares the first one obsolete. And what has
become obsolete and has grown old is close
to disappearing.

CHAPTER 9

See RG 500

The Worship of the First Covenant.

1 [*]Now [even] the first covenant had regulations for worship and an earthly sanctuary.
2 [l*]For a tabernacle was constructed, the
outer one, in which were the lampstand, the
table, and the bread of offering; this is called
the Holy Place. 3 [m*]Behind the second veil
was the tabernacle called the Holy of Holies,
4 [n*]in which were the gold altar of incense
and the ark of the covenant entirely covered
with gold. In it were the gold jar containing
the manna, the staff of Aaron that had
sprouted, and the tablets of the covenant.
5 [o*]Above it were the cherubim of glory
overshadowing the place of expiation. Now
is not the time to speak of these in detail.
6 [p*]With these arrangements for worship,
the priests, in performing their service, go
into the outer tabernacle repeatedly, 7 [q*]but
the high priest alone goes into the inner one
once a year, not without blood that he offers

8:8–12 In citing Jeremiah the author follows the Septuagint; some apparent departures from it may be the result of a different Septuagintal text rather than changes deliberately introduced.

8:13 Close to disappearing: from the prophet's perspective, not that of the author of Hebrews.

9:1–10 The regulations for worship under the old covenant permitted all the priests to enter the Holy Place (Heb 2:6), but only the high priest to enter the Holy of Holies and then only once a year (Heb 9:3–5, 7). The description of the sanctuary and its furnishings is taken essentially from Ex 25–26. This exclusion of the people from the Holy of Holies signified that they were not allowed to stand in God's presence (Heb 9:8) because their offerings and sacrifices, which were merely symbols of their need of spiritual renewal (Heb 9:10), could not obtain forgiveness of sins (Heb 9:9).

9:2 The outer one: the author speaks of the **outer tabernacle** (Heb 9:6) and **the inner one** (Heb 9:7) rather than of one Mosaic tabernacle divided into two parts or sections.

9:3 The second veil: what is meant is the veil that divided the Holy Place from the Holy of Holies. It is here called **the second**, because there was another veil at the entrance to the Holy Place, or "outer tabernacle" (Ex 26:36).

9:4 The gold altar of incense: Ex 30:6 locates this altar in the Holy Place, i.e., the first tabernacle, rather than in the Holy of Holies. Neither is there any Old Testament support for the assertion that the jar of manna and the staff of Aaron were in the ark of the covenant. For the tablets of the covenant, see Ex 25:16.

9:5 The place of expiation: the gold "mercy seat" (Greek *hilastērion*, as in Rom 3:25), where the blood of the sacrificial animals was sprinkled on the Day of Atonement (Lv 16:14–15). This rite achieved "expiation" or atonement for the sins of the preceding year.

9:6 In performing their service: the priestly services that had to be performed regularly in the Holy Place or **outer tabernacle** included burning incense on the incense altar twice each day (Ex 30:7), replacing the loaves on the table of the bread of offering once each week (Lv 24:8), and constantly caring for the lamps on the lampstand (Ex 27:21).

9:7 Not without blood: blood was essential to Old Testament sacrifice because it was believed that life was located in the blood. Hence blood was especially sacred, and its outpouring functioned as a meaningful symbol of cleansing from sin and reconciliation with God. Unlike Hebrews, the Old Testament never says that the blood is "offered." The author is perhaps retrojecting into his description of Mosaic ritual a concept that belongs to the New Testament antitype, as Paul does when he speaks of the Israelites' passage through the sea as a "baptism" (1 Cor 10:2).

j: 10:16–17. *k:* Rom 10:4. *l:* Ex 25:23–30. *m:* Ex 26:31–34. *n:* Ex 16:32–34; 25:10, 16, 21; 30:1–10; Lv 16:12–13; Nm 17:2–7, 16–26. *o:* Ex 25:16–22; 26:34; Lv 16:14–15. *p:* Ex 27:21; 30:7; Lv 24:8. *q:* Ex 30:10; Lv 16:1–14.

for himself and for the sins of the people. [8]In this way the holy Spirit shows that the way into the sanctuary had not yet been revealed while the outer tabernacle still had its place. [9*]This is a symbol of the present time, in which gifts and sacrifices are offered that cannot perfect the worshiper in conscience [10r]but only in matters of food and drink and various ritual washings: regulations concerning the flesh, imposed until the time of the new order.

Sacrifice of Jesus. [11s*]But when Christ came as high priest of the good things that have come to be, passing through the greater and more perfect tabernacle not made by hands, that is, not belonging to this creation, [12t]he entered once for all into the sanctuary, not with the blood of goats and calves but with his own blood, thus obtaining eternal redemption. [13u*]For if the blood of goats and bulls and the sprinkling of a heifer's ashes can sanctify those who are defiled so that their flesh is cleansed, [14v*]how much more will the blood of Christ, who through the eternal spirit offered himself unblemished to God, cleanse our consciences from dead works to worship the living God.

[15w*]For this reason he is mediator of a new covenant: since a death has taken place for deliverance from transgressions under the first covenant, those who are called may receive the promised eternal inheritance. [16*]Now where there is a will, the death of the testator must be established. [17]For a will takes effect only at death; it has no force while the testator is alive. [18]Thus not even the first covenant was inaugurated without blood. [19x*]When every commandment had been proclaimed by Moses to all the people according to the law, he took the blood of calves [and goats], together with water and crimson wool and hyssop, and sprinkled both the book itself and all the people, [20y]saying, "This is 'the blood of the covenant which God has enjoined upon you.' " [21z*]In the same way, he sprinkled also the taberna-

9:9 The present time: this expression is equivalent to the "present age," used in contradistinction to the "age to come."

9:11–14 Christ, the high priest of the spiritual blessings foreshadowed in the Old Testament sanctuary, has actually entered the true sanctuary of heaven that is not of human making (Heb 9:11). His place there is permanent, and his offering is his own blood that won eternal redemption (Heb 9:12). If the sacrifice of animals could bestow legal purification (Heb 9:13), how much more effective is the blood of the sinless, divine Christ who spontaneously offered himself to purge the human race of sin and render it fit for the service of God (Heb 9:14).

9:11 The good things that have come to be: the majority of later manuscripts here read "the good things to come"; cf. Heb 10:1.

9:13 A heifer's ashes: ashes from a red heifer that had been burned were mixed with water and used for the cleansing of those who had become ritually defiled by touching a corpse; see Nm 19:9, 14–21.

9:14 Through the eternal spirit: this expression does not refer either to the holy Spirit or to the divine nature of Jesus but to the life of the risen Christ, "a life that cannot be destroyed" (Heb 7:16).

9:15–22 Jesus' role as **mediator of the new covenant** is based upon his sacrificial **death** (cf. Heb 8:6). His death has effected **deliverance from transgressions**, i.e., deliverance from sins committed under the old covenant, which the Mosaic sacrifices were incapable of effacing. Until this happened, the **eternal inheritance** promised by God could not be obtained (Heb 9:15). This effect of his work follows the human pattern by which a last will and testament becomes effective only with the death of the testator (Heb 9:16–17). The Mosaic covenant was also associated with death, for Moses made use of blood to seal the pact between God and the people (Heb 9:18–21). In Old Testament tradition, guilt could normally not be remitted without the use of blood (Heb 9:22; cf. Lv 17:11).

9:16–17 A will . . . death of the testator: the same Greek word *diathēkē*, meaning "covenant" in Heb 9:15, 18, is used here with the meaning **will**. The new covenant, unlike the old, is at the same time a will that requires the **death of the testator**. Jesus as eternal Son is the one who established the new covenant together with his Father, author of both covenants; at the same time he is the testator whose death puts his **will** into effect.

9:19–20 A number of details here are different from the description of this covenant rite in Ex 24:5–8. Exodus mentions only calves ("young bulls," NAB), not goats (but this addition in Hebrews is of doubtful authenticity), says nothing of the use of **water and crimson wool and hyssop** (these features probably came from a different rite; cf. Lv 14:3–7; Nm 19:6–18), and describes Moses as splashing blood on the altar, whereas Hebrews says he sprinkled it on the book (but both book and altar are meant to symbolize the agreement of God). The words of Moses are also slightly different from those in Exodus and are closer to the words of Jesus at the Last Supper in Mk 14:24; Mt 26:28.

9:21 According to Exodus, the tabernacle did not yet exist at the time of the covenant rite. Moreover, nothing is said of sprinkling it with blood at its subsequent dedication (Ex 40:9–11).

---

r: 13:9; Lv 11; 14:8; Nm 19:11–21; Col 2:16. *s:* 4:14; 10:1, 20. *t:* 7:27; Mt 26:28. *u:* 10:4; Lv 16:6–16; Nm 19:9, 14–21. *v:* 10:10; Rom 5:9; 1 Tm 3:9; Ti 2:14; 1 Pt 1:18–19; 1 Jn 1:7; Rev 1:5. *w:* 1 Tm 2:5. *x:* 12–13. *y:* Ex 24:3–8; Mt 26:28; Mk 14:24. *z:* Ex 40:9; Lv 8:15, 19.

cle and all the vessels of worship with blood.
[22a*]According to the law almost everything
is purified by blood, and without the shedding of blood there is no forgiveness.
[23b*]Therefore, it was necessary for the
copies of the heavenly things to be purified
by these rites, but the heavenly things themselves by better sacrifices than these. [24c]For
Christ did not enter into a sanctuary made by
hands, a copy of the true one, but heaven itself, that he might now appear before God
on our behalf. [25]Not that he might offer himself repeatedly, as the high priest enters each
year into the sanctuary with blood that is not
his own; [26d*]if that were so, he would have
had to suffer repeatedly from the foundation
of the world. But now once for all he has appeared at the end of the ages to take away sin
by his sacrifice. [27e]Just as it is appointed that
human beings die once, and after this the
judgment, [28f*]so also Christ, offered once to
take away the sins of many, will appear a
second time, not to take away sin but to
bring salvation to those who eagerly await
him.

CHAPTER 10

See RG 500

One Sacrifice instead of Many.
[1g*]Since the law has only a shadow of the
good things to come, and not the very image of them, it can never make perfect
those who come to worship by the same
sacrifices that they offer continually each
year. [2]Otherwise, would not the sacrifices
have ceased to be offered, since the worshipers, once cleansed, would no longer
have had any consciousness of sins? [3h]But
in those sacrifices there is only a yearly remembrance of sins, [4i]for it is impossible
that the blood of bulls and goats take away
sins. [5j*]For this reason, when he came into
the world, he said:

"Sacrifice and offering you did not
desire,
but a body you prepared for me;

9:22 Without the shedding of blood there is no forgiveness: in fact, ancient Israel did envisage other means of obtaining forgiveness; the Old Testament mentions contrition of heart (Ps 51:17), fasting (Jl 2:12), and almsgiving (Sir 3:29). The author is limiting his horizon to the sacrificial cult, which did always involve the shedding of blood for its expiatory and unitive value.

9:23–28 Since the blood of animals became a cleansing symbol among Old Testament prefigurements, it was necessary that the realities foreshadowed be brought into being by a shedding of blood that was infinitely more effective by reason of its worth (Heb 9:23). Christ did not simply prefigure the heavenly realities (Heb 9:24) by performing an annual sacrifice with a blood not his own (Heb 9:25); he offered the single sacrifice of himself as the final annulment of sin (Heb 9:26). Just as death is the unrepeatable act that ends a person's life, so Christ's offering of himself for all is the unrepeatable sacrifice that has once for all achieved redemption (Heb 9:27–28).

9:26 At the end of the ages: the use of expressions such as this shows that the author of Hebrews, despite his interest in the Platonic concept of an eternal world above superior to temporal reality here below, nevertheless still clings to the Jewish Christian eschatology with its sequence of "the present age" and "the age to come."

9:28 To take away the sins of many: the reference is to Is 53:12. Since the Greek verb *anapherō* can mean both "to take away" and "to bear," the author no doubt intended to play upon both senses: Jesus took away sin by bearing it himself. See the similar wordplay in Jn 1:29. **Many** is used in the Semitic meaning of "all" in the inclusive sense, as in Mk 14:24. **To those who eagerly await him**: Jesus will appear **a second time** at the parousia, as the high priest reappeared on the Day of Atonement, emerging from the Holy of Holies, which he had entered to **take away sin**. This dramatic scene is described in Sir 50:5–11.

10:1–10 Christian faith now realizes that the Old Testament sacrifices did not effect the spiritual benefits to come but only prefigured them (Heb 10:1). For if the sacrifices had actually effected the forgiveness of sin, there would have been no reason for their constant repetition (Heb 10:2). They were rather a continual reminder of the people's sins (Heb 10:3). It is not reasonable to suppose that human sins could be removed by the blood of animal sacrifices (Heb 10:4). Christ, therefore, is here shown to understand his mission in terms of Ps 40:5–7, cited according to the Septuagint (Heb 10:5–7). Jesus acknowledged that the Old Testament sacrifices did not remit the sins of the people and so, perceiving the will of God, offered his own body for this purpose (Heb 10:8–10).

10:1 A shadow of the good things to come: the term **shadow** was used in Heb 8:5 to signify the earthly counterpart of the Platonic heavenly reality. But here it means a prefiguration of what is to come in Christ, as it is used in the Pauline literature; cf. Col 2:17.

10:5–7 A passage from Ps 40:7–9 is placed in the mouth of the Son at his incarnation. As usual, the author follows the Septuagint text. There is a notable difference in Heb 10:5 (Ps 40:6), where the Masoretic text reads "ears you have dug for me" ("ears open to obedience you gave me," NAB), but most Septuagint manuscripts have "a body you prepared for me," a reading obviously more suited to the interpretation of Hebrews.

a: Lv 17:11. *b:* Jb 15:15. *c:* 7:25; Rom 8:34; 1 Jn 2:1–2. *d:* 7:27; Jn 1:29; Gal 4:4. *e:* Gn 3:19. *f:* 10:10; Is 53:12. *g:* 8:5; Col 2:17. *h:* Lv 16:21; Nm 5:15 LXX. *i:* Is 1:11; Mi 6:6–8. *j:* Ps 40:7–9.

6 holocausts and sin offerings you took no
delight in.
7 Then I said, 'As is written of me in the
scroll,
Behold, I come to do your will,
O God.' "

8k*First he says, "Sacrifices and offerings,
holocausts and sin offerings, you neither desired nor delighted in." These are offered according to the law. 9lThen he says, "Behold, I
come to do your will." He takes away the first
to establish the second. 10mBy this "will," we
have been consecrated through the offering of
the body of Jesus Christ once for all.
11n*Every priest stands daily at his ministry, offering frequently those same sacrifices
that can never take away sins. 12oBut this one
offered one sacrifice for sins, and took his
seat forever at the right hand of God; 13*now
he waits until his enemies are made his footstool. 14pFor by one offering he has made
perfect forever those who are being consecrated. 15*The holy Spirit also testifies to us,
for after saying:

16q"This is the covenant I will establish
with them after those days, says
the Lord:
'I will put my laws in their hearts,
and I will write them upon their
minds,' "

17r*he also says:

"Their sins and their evildoing
I will remember no more."

18Where there is forgiveness of these, there
is no longer offering for sin.

Recalling the Past. 19s*Therefore, brothers, since through the blood of Jesus we
have confidence of entrance into the sanctuary 20t*by the new and living way he
opened for us through the veil, that is, his

10:8 Sacrifices and offerings, holocausts and sin offerings: these four terms taken from the preceding passage of Ps 40 (with the first two changed to plural forms) are probably intended as equivalents to the four principal types of Old Testament sacrifices: peace offerings (Lv 3, here called **sacrifices**); cereal offerings (Lv 2, here called **offerings**); **holocausts** (Lv 1); and **sin offerings** (Lv 4–5). This last category includes the guilt offerings of Lv 5:14–19.

10:11–18 Whereas the levitical priesthood offered daily sacrifices that were ineffectual in remitting sin (Heb 10:11), Jesus offered a single sacrifice that won him a permanent place at God's right hand. There he has only to await the final outcome of his work (Heb 10:12–13; cf. Ps 110:1). Thus he has brought into being in his own person the new covenant prophesied by Jeremiah (Jer 31:33–34) that has rendered meaningless all other offerings for sin (Heb 10:14–18).

10:13 Until his enemies are made his footstool: Ps 110:1 is again used; the reference here is to the period of time between the enthronement of Jesus and his second coming. The identity of the **enemies** is not specified; cf. 1 Cor 15:25–27.

10:15–17 The testimony of the scriptures is now invoked to support what has just preceded. The passage cited is a portion of the new covenant prophecy of Jer 31:31–34, which the author previously used in Heb 8:8–12.

10:17 He also says: these words are not in the Greek text, which has only *kai*, "also," but the expression **"after saying"** in Heb 10:15 seems to require such a phrase to divide the Jeremiah text into two sayings. Others understand "the Lord says" of Heb 10:16 (here rendered **says the Lord**) as outside the quotation and consider Heb 10:16b as part of the second saying. Two ancient versions and a number of minuscules introduce the words "then he said" or a similar expression at the beginning of Heb 10:17.

10:19–39 Practical consequences from these reflections on the priesthood and the sacrifice of Christ should make it clear that Christians may now have direct and confident access to God through the person of Jesus (Heb 10:19–20), who rules God's house as high priest (Heb 10:21). They should approach God with sincerity and faith, in the knowledge that through baptism their sins have been remitted (Heb 10:22), reminding themselves of the hope they expressed in Christ at that event (Heb 10:23). They are to encourage one another to Christian love and activity (Heb 10:24), not refusing, no matter what the reason, to participate in the community's assembly, especially in view of the parousia (Heb 10:25; cf. 1 Thes 4:13–18). If refusal to participate in the assembly indicates rejection of Christ, no sacrifice exists to obtain forgiveness for so great a sin (Heb 10:26); only the dreadful judgment of God remains (Heb 10:27). For if violation of the Mosaic law could be punished by death, how much worse will be the punishment of those who have turned their backs on Christ by despising his sacrifice and disregarding the gifts of the holy Spirit (Heb 10:28–29). Judgment belongs to the Lord, and he enacts it by his living presence (Heb 10:30–31). There was a time when the spirit of their community caused them to welcome and share their sufferings (Heb 10:32–34). To revitalize that spirit is to share in the courage of the Old Testament prophets (cf. Is 26:20; Heb 2:3–4), the kind of courage that must distinguish the faith of the Christian (Heb 10:35–39).

10:20 Through the veil, that is, his flesh: the term **flesh** is used pejoratively. As the temple veil kept people from entering the Holy of Holies (it was rent at Christ's death, Mk 15:38), so the flesh of Jesus constituted an obstacle to approaching God.

10:21 The house of God: this refers back to Heb 3:6, "we are his house."

k: 5–6; Ps 40:7. *l:* 7; Ps 40:8; Mt 26:39; Mk 14:36; Lk 22:42; Jn 6:38. *m:* 9:12, 14. *n:* 7:27; Dt 10:8; 18:7. *o:* Ps 110:1. *p:* 9:28. *q:* 8:10; Jer 31:33. *r:* 8:12; Jer 31:34. *s:* 3:6; 4:16; 6:19–20; Eph 1:7; 3:12. *t:* Jn 14:6 / 6:19–20; 9:8, 11–12; Mt 27:51; Mk 15:38; Lk 23:45.

flesh, [21u*]and since we have "a great priest
over the house of God," [22v*]let us approach
with a sincere heart and in absolute trust,
with our hearts sprinkled clean from an evil
conscience and our bodies washed in pure
water. [23w]Let us hold unwaveringly to our
confession that gives us hope, for he who
made the promise is trustworthy. [24]We must
consider how to rouse one another to love
and good works. [25x*]We should not stay
away from our assembly, as is the custom
of some, but encourage one another, and
this all the more as you see the day drawing
near.

[26y*]If we sin deliberately after receiving
knowledge of the truth, there no longer remains sacrifice for sins [27z]but a fearful
prospect of judgment and a flaming fire
that is going to consume the adversaries.
[28a*]Anyone who rejects the law of Moses is
put to death without pity on the testimony
of two or three witnesses. [29b]Do you not
think that a much worse punishment is due
the one who has contempt for the Son of
God, considers unclean the covenant-blood
by which he was consecrated, and insults
the spirit of grace? [30c]We know the one who
said:

"Vengeance is mine; I will repay,"

and again:

"The Lord will judge his people."

[31d]It is a fearful thing to fall into the hands of
the living God.

[32e*]Remember the days past when, after
you had been enlightened, you endured a
great contest of suffering. [33f]At times you
were publicly exposed to abuse and affliction; at other times you associated yourselves with those so treated. [34g]You even
joined in the sufferings of those in prison
and joyfully accepted the confiscation of
your property, knowing that you had a better
and lasting possession. [35h]Therefore, do not
throw away your confidence; it will have
great recompense. [36i]You need endurance to
do the will of God and receive what he has
promised.

[37 j*]"For, after just a brief moment,
he who is to come shall come;
he shall not delay.
[38 k]But my just one shall live by faith,
and if he draws back I take no pleasure
in him."

[39]We are not among those who draw back
and perish, but among those who have faith
and will possess life.

V. Examples, Discipline, Disobedience

CHAPTER 11

See RG 500

Faith of the Ancients. [1l*]Faith is the
realization of what is hoped for and evidence

10:22 With our hearts sprinkled clean from an evil conscience: as in Heb 9:13 (see note there), the sprinkling motif refers to the Mosaic rite of cleansing from ritual impurity. This could produce only an external purification, whereas sprinkling with the blood of Christ (Heb 9:14) cleanses the **conscience. Washed in pure water**: baptism is elsewhere referred to as a washing; cf. 1 Cor 6:11; Eph 5:26.

10:25 Our assembly: the liturgical **assembly** of the Christian community, probably for the celebration of the Eucharist. **The day**: this designation for the parousia also occurs in the Pauline letters, e.g., Rom 2:16; 1 Cor 3:13; 1 Thes 5:2.

10:26 If we sin deliberately: verse 29 indicates that the author is here thinking of apostasy; cf. Heb 3:12; 6:4–8.

10:28 Rejects the law of Moses: evidently not any sin against the law, but idolatry. Dt 17:2–7 prescribed capital punishment for idolaters who were convicted on the testimony of two or three witnesses.

10:32 After you had been enlightened: "enlightenment" is an ancient metaphor for baptism (cf. Eph 5:14; Jn 9:11), but see Heb 6:4 and the note there.

10:37–38 In support of his argument, the author uses Heb 2:3–4 in a wording almost identical with the text of the Codex Alexandrinus of the Septuagint but with the first and second lines of Heb 10:4 inverted. He introduces it with a few words from Is 26:20: **after just a brief moment**. Note the Pauline usage of Heb 2:4 in Rom 1:17; Gal 3:11.

11:1–40 This chapter draws upon the people and events of the Old Testament to paint an inspiring portrait of religious faith, firm and unyielding in the face of any obstacles that confront it. These pages rank among the most eloquent and lofty to be found in the Bible. They expand the theme announced in Heb 6:12, to which the author now returns (Heb 10:39). The material of this chapter is developed chronologically. Heb 11:3–7 draw upon the first nine chapters of Genesis (Gn 1–9);

u: 3:6. *v:* 9:13–14; Ez 36:25; 1 Cor 6:11; Ti 3:5; 1 Pt 3:21. *w:* 3:1, 6; 4:14; 1 Cor 10:13. *x:* Rom 13:12; 1 Cor 3:13. *y:* 3:12; 6:4–8. *z:* 31; 9:27; Is 26:11 LXX; Zep 1:18. *a:* Dt 17:6. *b:* 6:6. *c:* Dt 32:35, 36; Rom 12:19. *d:* 27; Mt 10:28; Lk 12:4–5. *e:* 6:4. *f:* 1 Cor 4:9. *g:* 13:3; Mt 6:19–20; Lk 12:33–34. *h:* 4:16. *i:* Lk 21:19. *j:* Is 26:20; Heb 2:3. *k:* Heb 2:4; Rom 1:17; Gal 3:11. *l:* 1:3; 3:14; Rom 8:24; 2 Cor 4:18.

of things not seen. [2]Because of it the ancients were well attested. [3m*]By faith we understand that the universe was ordered by the word of God, so that what is visible came into being through the invisible. [4n*]By faith Abel offered to God a sacrifice greater than Cain's. Through this he was attested to be righteous, God bearing witness to his gifts, and through this, though dead, he still speaks. [5o]By faith Enoch was taken up so that he should not see death, and "he was found no more because God had taken him." Before he was taken up, he was attested to have pleased God. [6p*]But without faith it is impossible to please him, for anyone who approaches God must believe that he exists and that he rewards those who seek him. [7q]By faith Noah, warned about what was not yet seen, with reverence built an ark for the salvation of his household. Through this he condemned the world and inherited the righteousness that comes through faith.

[8r]By faith Abraham obeyed when he was called to go out to a place that he was to receive as an inheritance; he went out, not knowing where he was to go. [9s]By faith he sojourned in the promised land as in a foreign country, dwelling in tents with Isaac and Jacob, heirs of the same promise; [10t]for he was looking forward to the city with foundations, whose architect and maker is God. [11u]By faith he received power to generate, even though he was past the normal age—and Sarah herself was sterile—for he thought that the one who had made the promise was trustworthy. [12v]So it was that there came forth from one man, himself as good as dead, descendants as numerous as the stars in the sky and as countless as the sands on the seashore.

[13w]All these died in faith. They did not receive what had been promised but saw it and greeted it from afar and acknowledged themselves to be strangers and aliens on earth, [14]for those who speak thus show that they are seeking a homeland. [15]If they had been thinking of the land from which they had come, they would have had opportunity to return. [16x]But now they desire a better homeland, a heavenly one. Therefore, God is not ashamed to be called their God, for he has prepared a city for them.

[17y]By faith Abraham, when put to the test, offered up Isaac, and he who had received the promises was ready to offer his only son, [18z]of whom it was said, "Through Isaac descendants shall bear your name." [19a*]He reasoned that God was able to raise even from

Heb 11:8–22, upon the period of the patriarchs; Heb 11:23–31, upon the time of Moses; Heb 11:32–38, upon the history of the judges, the prophets, and the Maccabean martyrs. The author gives the most extensive description of faith provided in the New Testament, though his interest does not lie in a technical, theological definition. In view of the needs of his audience he describes what authentic faith does, not what it is in itself. Through faith God guarantees the blessings to be hoped for from him, providing evidence in the gift of faith that what he promises will eventually come to pass (Heb 11:1). Because they accepted in faith God's guarantee of the future, the biblical personages discussed in Heb 11:3–38 were themselves commended by God (Heb 11:2). Christians have even greater reason to remain firm in faith since they, unlike the Old Testament men and women of faith, have perceived the beginning of God's fulfillment of his messianic promises (Heb 11:39–40).

11:1 Faith is the realization . . . evidence: the author is not attempting a precise definition. There is dispute about the meaning of the Greek words *hypostasis* and *elenchos*, here translated **realization** and **evidence**, respectively. *Hypostasis* usually means "substance," "being" (as translated in Heb 1:3), or "reality" (as translated in Heb 3:14); here it connotes something more subjective, and so **realization** has been chosen rather than "assurance" (RSV). *Elenchos*, usually "proof," is used here in an objective sense and so translated **evidence** rather than the transferred sense of "(inner) conviction" (RSV).

11:3 By faith . . . God: this verse does not speak of the faith of the Old Testament men and women but is in the first person plural. Hence it seems out of place in the sequence of thought.

11:4 The "Praise of the Ancestors" in Sir 44:1–50:21 gives a similar list of heroes. The Cain and Abel narrative in Gn 4:1–16 does not mention Abel's faith. It says, however, that God "looked with favor on Abel and his offering" (Gn 4:4); in view of v 6 the author probably understood God's favor to have been activated by Abel's faith. **Though dead, he still speaks**: possibly because his blood "cries out to me from the soil" (Gn 4:10), but more probably a way of saying that the repeated story of Abel provides ongoing witness to faith.

11:6 One must believe not only that God *exists* but that he is concerned about human conduct; the Old Testament defines folly as the denial of this truth; cf. Ps 52:2.

11:19 As a symbol: Isaac's "return from death" is seen as

m: Gn 1:3; Ps 33:6; Wis 9:1; Jn 1:3. *n:* 12:24; Gn 4:4, 10. *o:* Gn 5:24; Sir 44:16. *p:* Wis 4:10. *q:* Gn 6:8–22; Sir 44:17–18; Mt 24:37–39; Lk 17:26–27; 1 Pt 3:20; 2 Pt 2:5. *r:* Gn 12:1–4; 15:7–21; Sir 44:19–22; Acts 7:2–8; Rom 4:16–22. *s:* Gn 12:8; 13:12; 23:4; 26:3; 35:27. *t:* 12:22; 13:14; Rev 21:10–22. *u:* Gn 17:19; 21:2; Rom 4:19–21 / 1 Cor 10:13. *v:* Gn 15:5; 22:17; 32:13; Ex 32:13; Dt 10:22; Dn 3:36. *w:* Gn 23:4; Ps 39:13. *x:* 13:14; Ex 3:6. *y:* Gn 22:1–10; Sir 44:20; 1 Mc 2:52; Jas 2:21. *z:* Gn 21:12 LXX; Rom 9:7. *a:* Rom 4:16–22.

the dead, and he received Isaac back as a symbol. [20b*]By faith regarding things still to come Isaac blessed Jacob and Esau. [21c]By faith Jacob, when dying, blessed each of the sons of Joseph and "bowed in worship, leaning on the top of his staff." [22d]By faith Joseph, near the end of his life, spoke of the Exodus of the Israelites and gave instructions about his bones.

[23e]By faith Moses was hidden by his parents for three months after his birth, because they saw that he was a beautiful child, and they were not afraid of the king's edict. [24f*]By faith Moses, when he had grown up, refused to be known as the son of Pharaoh's daughter; [25]he chose to be ill-treated along with the people of God rather than enjoy the fleeting pleasure of sin. [26]He considered the reproach of the Anointed greater wealth than the treasures of Egypt, for he was looking to the recompense. [27g]By faith he left Egypt, not fearing the king's fury, for he persevered as if seeing the one who is invisible. [28h]By faith he kept the Passover and sprinkled the blood, that the Destroyer of the firstborn might not touch them. [29i]By faith they crossed the Red Sea as if it were dry land, but when the Egyptians attempted it they were drowned. [30j]By faith the walls of Jericho fell after being encircled for seven days. [31k]By faith Rahab the harlot did not perish with the disobedient, for she had received the spies in peace.

[32l]What more shall I say? I have not time to tell of Gideon, Barak, Samson, Jephthah, of David and Samuel and the prophets, [33m]who by faith conquered kingdoms, did what was righteous, obtained the promises; they closed the mouths of lions, [34n]put out raging fires, escaped the devouring sword; out of weakness they were made powerful, became strong in battle, and turned back foreign invaders. [35o]Women received back their dead through resurrection. Some were tortured and would not accept deliverance, in order to obtain a better resurrection. [36p]Others endured mockery, scourging, even chains and imprisonment. [37q]They were stoned, sawed in two, put to death at sword's point; they went about in skins of sheep or goats, needy, afflicted, tormented. [38r]The world was not worthy of them. They wandered about in deserts and on mountains, in caves and in crevices in the earth.

[39]Yet all these, though approved because of their faith, did not receive what had been promised. [40*]God had foreseen something better for us, so that without us they should not be made perfect.

CHAPTER 12

See RG 500–501

God our Father. [1*]Therefore, since we are surrounded by so great a cloud of witnesses, let us rid ourselves of every burden and sin that clings to us and persevere in running the race that lies before us [2s]while keeping our eyes fixed on Jesus, the leader and perfecter of faith. For the sake of the joy

a **symbol** of Christ's resurrection. Others understand the words *en parabolē* to mean "in figure," i.e., the word **dead** is used figuratively of Isaac, since he did not really die. But in the one other place that *parabolē* occurs in Hebrews, it means symbol (Heb 9:9).

11:20–22 Each of these three patriarchs, Isaac, Jacob, and Joseph, had faith in the future fulfillment of God's promise and renewed this faith when near death.

11:24–27 The reason given for Moses' departure from Egypt differs from the account in Ex 2:11–15. The author also gives a christological interpretation of his decision to share the trials of his people.

11:40 So that without us they should not be made perfect: the heroes of the Old Testament obtained their recompense only after the saving work of Christ had been accomplished. Thus they already enjoy what Christians who are still struggling do not yet possess in its fullness.

12:1–13 Christian life is to be inspired not only by the Old Testament men and women of faith (Heb 12:1) but above all by Jesus. As the architect of Christian faith, he had himself to endure the cross before receiving the glory of his triumph (Heb 12:2). Reflection on his sufferings should give his followers courage to continue the struggle, if necessary even to the shedding of blood (Heb 12:3–4). Christians should regard their own sufferings as the affectionate correction of the Lord, who loves them as a father loves his children.

12:1 That clings to us: the meaning is uncertain, since the Greek word *euperistatos*, translated **cling**, occurs only here. The papyrus P^{46} and one minuscule read *euperispastos*, "easily distracting," which also makes good sense.

b: Gn 27:27–40. *c:* Gn 27:38–40; 47:31 LXX; 48:15–16. *d:* Gn 50:24–25. *e:* Ex 2:2; Acts 7:20. *f:* Ex 2:10–15; Acts 7:23–29. *g:* Ex 2:15; Acts 7:29. *h:* Ex 12:21–23; Wis 18:25; 1 Cor 10:10. *i:* Ex 14:22–28. *j:* Jos 6:12–21. *k:* Jos 2:1–21; 6:22–25; Jas 2:25. *l:* Jgs 4:6–22; 6:11–8:32; 11:1–12:7. *m:* Dn 6:23. *n:* Dn 3:22–25, 49–50. *o:* 1 Kgs 17:17–24; 2 Kgs 4:18–37; 2 Mc 6:18–7:42. *p:* 2 Chr 36:16; Jer 20:2; 37:15. *q:* 2 Chr 24:21. *r:* 1 Mc 2:28–30. *s:* 2:10; Ps 110:1; Phil 2:6–8.

that lay before him he endured the cross, despising its shame, and has taken his seat at
the right of the throne of God. [3]Consider
how he endured such opposition from sinners, in order that you may not grow weary
and lose heart. [4]In your struggle against sin
you have not yet resisted to the point of
shedding blood. [5][t]You have also forgotten
the exhortation addressed to you as sons:

"My son, do not disdain the discipline of
the Lord
or lose heart when reproved by him;
[6] for whom the Lord loves, he disciplines;
he scourges every son he
acknowledges."

[7][u]Endure your trials as "discipline"; God
treats you as sons. For what "son" is there
whom his father does not discipline? [8]If you
are without discipline, in which all have
shared, you are not sons but bastards. [9][v]Be-
sides this, we have had our earthly fathers to
discipline us, and we respected them.
Should we not [then] submit all the more to
the Father of spirits and live? [10]They disciplined us for a short time as seemed right to
them, but he does so for our benefit, in order
that we may share his holiness. [11][w]At the
time, all discipline seems a cause not for joy
but for pain, yet later it brings the peaceful
fruit of righteousness to those who are
trained by it.

[12][x]So strengthen your drooping hands and
your weak knees. [13][y]Make straight paths for
your feet, that what is lame may not be dislocated but healed.

Penalties of Disobedience. [14][z]Strive for
peace with everyone, and for that holiness
without which no one will see the Lord.
[15][a]*See to it that no one be deprived of the
grace of God, that no bitter root spring up and
cause trouble, through which many may become defiled, [16][b]that no one be an immoral or
profane person like Esau, who sold his
birthright for a single meal. [17][c]For you know
that later, when he wanted to inherit his father's blessing, he was rejected because he
found no opportunity to change his mind,
even though he sought the blessing with tears.

[18][d]*You have not approached that which
could be touched and a blazing fire and
gloomy darkness and storm [19][e]and a trumpet
blast and a voice speaking words such that
those who heard begged that no message be
further addressed to them, [20][f]for they could
not bear to hear the command: "If even an
animal touches the mountain, it shall be
stoned." [21][g]Indeed, so fearful was the spectacle that Moses said, "I am terrified and
trembling." [22][h]No, you have approached
Mount Zion and the city of the living God,
the heavenly Jerusalem, and countless angels in festal gathering, [23][i]*and the assembly
of the firstborn enrolled in heaven, and God
the judge of all, and the spirits of the just
made perfect, [24][j]*and Jesus, the mediator of

12:15–17 Esau serves as an example in two ways: his **profane** attitude illustrates the danger of apostasy, and his inability to secure a blessing afterward illustrates the impossibility of repenting after falling away (see Heb 6:4–6).

12:18–29 As a final appeal for adherence to Christian teaching, the two covenants, of Moses and of Christ, are compared. The Mosaic covenant, the author argues, is shown to have originated in fear of God and threats of divine punishment (Heb 12:18–21). The covenant in Christ gives us direct access to God (Heb 12:22), makes us members of the Christian community, God's children, a sanctified people (Heb 12:23), who have Jesus as mediator to speak for us (Heb 12:24). Not to heed the voice of the risen Christ is a graver sin than the rejection of the word of Moses (Heb 12:25–26). Though Christians fall away, God's kingdom in Christ will remain and his justice will punish those guilty of deserting it (Heb 12:28–29).

12:18 This remarkably beautiful passage contrasts two great assemblies of people: that of the Israelites gathered at Mount Sinai for the sealing of the old covenant and the promulgation of the Mosaic law, and that of the followers of Jesus gathered at **Mount Zion, the heavenly Jerusalem**, the assembly of the **new covenant**. This latter scene, marked by the presence of **countless angels** and of **Jesus** with his redeeming **blood**, is reminiscent of the celestial liturgies of the Book of Revelation.

12:23 The assembly of the firstborn enrolled in heaven: this expression may refer to the angels of Heb 12:22, or to the heroes of the Old Testament (see Heb 11), or to the entire assembly of the new covenant.

12:24 Speaks more eloquently: the blood of Abel, the first human blood to be shed, is contrasted with that of Jesus. Abel's blood cried out from the earth for vengeance, but the blood of Jesus has opened the way for everyone, providing cleansing and access to God (Heb 10:19).

t: Prv 3:11–12 / Dt 8:5; 1 Cor 11:32. *u:* Prv 13:24; Sir 30:1. *v:* Nm 16:22; 27:16 LXX. *w:* 2 Cor 4:17; Phil 1:11; Jas 3:18. *x:* Is 35:3; Sir 25:23; Jb 4:3–4. *y:* Prv 4:26 LXX. *z:* Rom 12:18; 14:19. *a:* Dt 29:18 (17 LXX). *b:* Gn 25:33. *c:* Gn 27:34–38. *d:* Ex 19:12–14; Dt 4:11; 5:22–23. *e:* Ex 19:16, 19; 20:18–19. *f:* Ex 19:12–13. *g:* Dt 9:19. *h:* Gal 4:26; Rev 21:2. *i:* Lk 10:20; Rev 5:11. *j:* 7:22; 8:6; 9:15 / 11:4; Gn 4:10.

a new covenant, and the sprinkled blood that speaks more eloquently than that of Abel.

[25k]See that you do not reject the one who speaks. For if they did not escape when they refused the one who warned them on earth, how much more in our case if we turn away from the one who warns from heaven. [26l]His voice shook the earth at that time, but now he has promised, "I will once more shake not only earth but heaven." [27m]That phrase, "once more," points to [the] removal of shaken, created things, so that what is unshaken may remain. [28n]Therefore, we who are receiving the unshakable kingdom should have gratitude, with which we should offer worship pleasing to God in reverence and awe. [29o]For our God is a consuming fire.

VI. Final Exhortation, Blessing, Greetings

CHAPTER 13

See RG 501

[1*]Let mutual love continue. [2p]Do not neglect hospitality, for through it some have unknowingly entertained angels. [3q]Be mindful of prisoners as if sharing their imprisonment, and of the ill-treated as of yourselves, for you also are in the body. [4r]Let marriage be honored among all and the marriage bed be kept undefiled, for God will judge the immoral and adulterers. [5s]Let your life be free from love of money but be content with what you have, for he has said, "I will never forsake you or abandon you." [6t]Thus we may say with confidence:

"The Lord is my helper,
[and] I will not be afraid.
What can anyone do to me?"

[7]Remember your leaders who spoke the word of God to you. Consider the outcome of their way of life and imitate their faith. [8u]Jesus Christ is the same yesterday, today, and forever.

[9v*]Do not be carried away by all kinds of strange teaching. It is good to have our hearts strengthened by grace and not by foods, which do not benefit those who live by them. [10*]We have an altar from which those who serve the tabernacle have no right to eat. [11w]The bodies of the animals whose blood the high priest brings into the sanctuary as a sin offering are burned outside the camp. [12x]Therefore, Jesus also suffered outside the gate, to consecrate the people by his own blood. [13]Let us then go to him outside the camp, bearing the reproach that he bore. [14y]For here we have no lasting city, but we seek the one that is to come. [15z]Through him [then] let us continually offer God a sacrifice of praise, that is, the fruit of lips that confess his name. [16a]Do not neglect to do good and to share what you have; God is pleased by sacrifices of that kind.

[17*]Obey your leaders and defer to them, for they keep watch over you and will have to give an account, that they may fulfill their task with joy and not with sorrow, for that would be of no advantage to you.

[18]Pray for us, for we are confident that we have a clear conscience, wishing to act rightly in every respect. [19]I especially ask for

13:1–16 After recommendations on social and moral matters (Heb 13:1–6), the letter turns to doctrinal issues. The fact that the original leaders are dead should not cause the recipients of this letter to lose their faith (Heb 13:7), for Christ still lives and he remains always the same (Heb 13:8). They must not rely for their personal sanctification on regulations concerning foods (Heb 13:9), nor should they entertain the notion that Judaism and Christianity can be intermingled (Heb 13:10; cf. notes on Gal 2:11–14; 2:15–21). As Jesus died separated from his own people, so must the Christian community remain apart from the religious doctrines of Judaism (Heb 13:11–14). Christ must be the heart and center of the community (Heb 13:15–16).

13:9 Strange teaching: this doctrine about **foods** probably refers to the Jewish food laws; in view of Heb 13:10, however, the author may be thinking of the Mosaic sacrificial banquets.

13:10 We have an altar: this does not refer to the Eucharist, which is never clearly mentioned in Hebrews, but to the sacrifice of Christ.

13:17–25 Recommending obedience to the leaders of the community, the author asks for prayers (Heb 13:17–19). The letter concludes with a blessing (Heb 13:20–21), a final request for the acceptance of its message (Heb 13:22), information regarding Timothy (Heb 13:23), and general greetings (Heb 13:24–25).

---

k: Ex 20:19. *l:* Ex 19:18; Jgs 5:4–5; Ps 68:9; Hg 2:6. *m:* Is 66:22; Mt 24:35; Mk 13:31; Lk 21:33. *n:* Dn 7:14, 18 / Rom 1:9. *o:* Dt 4:24; Is 33:14. *p:* Gn 18:3; 19:2–3; Jgs 6:11–22; Tb 5:4. *q:* Mt 25:36. *r:* 1 Cor 5:13; Eph 5:5. *s:* Dt 31:6, 8; Jos 1:5. *t:* Ps 27:1–3; 118:6. *u:* 1:12; 7:24; Rev 1:17. *v:* Rom 14:17; 1 Cor 8:8; Eph 4:14; Col 2:16. *w:* Ex 29:14; Lv 16:27. *x:* Mt 21:39; Mk 12:8; Lk 20:15; Jn 19:17. *y:* 11:10, 14. *z:* Hos 14:3. *a:* Phil 4:18.

your prayers that I may be restored to you very soon.

[20b*]May the God of peace, who brought up from the dead the great shepherd of the sheep by the blood of the eternal covenant, Jesus our Lord, [21]furnish you with all that is good, that you may do his will. May he carry out in you what is pleasing to him through Jesus Christ, to whom be glory forever [and ever]. Amen.

[22]Brothers, I ask you to bear with this message of encouragement, for I have written to you rather briefly. [23c]I must let you know that our brother Timothy has been set free. If he comes soon, I shall see you together with him. [24]Greetings to all your leaders and to all the holy ones. Those from Italy send you greetings. [25d]Grace be with all of you.

13:20–21 These verses constitute one of the most beautiful blessings in the New Testament. The resurrection of Jesus is presupposed throughout Hebrews, since it is included in the author's frequently expressed idea of his exaltation, but this is the only place where it is explicitly mentioned.

b: Is 63:11; Zec 9:11; Jn 10:11; Acts 2:24; Rom 15:33. *c:* Acts 16:1. *d:* Ti 3:15.

THE CATHOLIC LETTERS

See RG 501–20

In addition to the thirteen letters attributed to Paul and the Letter to the Hebrews, the New Testament contains seven other letters. Three of these are attributed to John, two to Peter, and one each to James and Jude, all personages of the apostolic age. The term "catholic letter" first appears, with reference only to 1 John, in the writings of Apollonius of Ephesus, a second-century apologist, known only from a citation in Eusebius's *Ecclesiastical History*. Eusebius himself (A.D. 260–340) used the term to refer to all seven letters.

The reason for the term "catholic," which means "universal," was the perception that these letters, unlike those of Paul, which were directed to a particular local church, were apparently addressed more generally to the universal church. This designation is not entirely accurate, however. On the one hand, Hebrews has no specifically identified addressees, and originally this was probably true of Ephesians as well. On the other hand, 3 John is addressed to a named individual, 2 John to a specific, though unnamed, community, and 1 Peter to a number of churches that are specified as being located in Asia Minor.

While all seven of these writings begin with an epistolary formula, several of them do not appear to be real letters in the modern sense of the term. In the ancient world it was not unusual to cast an exhortation in the form of a letter for literary effect, a phenomenon comparable to the "open letter" that is sometimes used today.

With the exception of 1 Peter and 1 John, the ancient church showed reluctance to include the catholic letters in the New Testament canon. The reason for this was widespread doubt whether they had actually been written by the apostolic figures to whom they are attributed. The early Christians saw the New Testament as the depository of apostolic faith; therefore, they wished to include only the testimony of apostles. Today we distinguish more clearly between the authorship of a work and its canonicity: even though written by other, later witnesses than those whose names they bear, these writings nevertheless testify to the apostolic faith and constitute canonical scripture. By the late fourth or early fifth centuries, most objections had been overcome in both the Greek and Latin churches (though not in the Syriac), and all seven of the catholic letters have since been acknowledged as canonical.

The Letter of James

See RG 501–6

The person to whom this letter is ascribed can scarcely be one of the two members of the Twelve who bore the name James (see Mt 10:2–3; Mk 3:17–18; Lk 6:14–15), for he is not identified as an apostle but only as "slave of God and of the Lord Jesus Christ" (Jas 1:1). This designation most probably refers to the third New Testament personage named James, a relative of Jesus who is usually called "brother of the Lord" (see Mt 13:55; Mk 6:3). He was the leader of the Jewish Christian community in Jerusalem whom Paul acknowledged as one of the "pillars" (Gal 2:9). In Acts he appears as the authorized spokesman for the Jewish Christian position in the early Church

(Acts 12:17; 15:13–21). According to the Jewish historian Josephus (*Antiquities* 20, 9, 1 §§201–203), he was stoned to death by the Jews under the high priest Ananus II in A.D. 62.

The letter is addressed to "the twelve tribes in the dispersion." In Old Testament terminology the term "twelve tribes" designates the people of Israel; the "dispersion" or "diaspora" refers to the non-Palestinian Jews who had settled throughout the Greco-Roman world (see Jn 7:35). Since in Christian thought the church is the new Israel, the address probably designates the Jewish Christian churches located in Palestine, Syria, and elsewhere. Or perhaps the letter is meant more generally for all Christian communities, and the "dispersion" has the symbolic meaning of exile from our true home, as it has in the address of 1 Peter (1 Pt 1:1). The letter is so markedly Jewish in character that some scholars have regarded it as a Jewish document subsequently "baptized" by a few Christian insertions, but such an origin is scarcely tenable in view of the numerous contacts discernible between the Letter of James and other New Testament literature.

From the viewpoint of its literary form, James is a letter only in the most conventional sense; it has none of the characteristic features of a real letter except the address. It belongs rather to the genre of parenesis or exhortation and is concerned almost exclusively with ethical conduct. It therefore falls within the tradition of Jewish wisdom literature, such as can be found in the Old Testament (Proverbs, Sirach) and in the extracanonical Jewish literature (Testaments of the Twelve Patriarchs, the Books of Enoch, the Manual of Discipline found at Qumran). More specifically, it consists of sequences of didactic proverbs, comparable to Tb 4:5–19, to many passages in Sirach, and to sequences of sayings in the synoptic gospels. Numerous passages in James treat of subjects that also appear in the synoptic sayings of Jesus, especially in Matthew's Sermon on the Mount, but the correspondences are too general to establish any literary dependence. James represents a type of early Christianity that emphasized sound teaching and responsible moral behavior. Ethical norms are derived not primarily from christology, as in Paul, but from a concept of salvation that involves conversion, baptism, forgiveness of sin, and expectation of judgment (Jas 1:17; 4:12).

Paradoxically, this very Jewish work is written in an excellent Greek style, which ranks among the best in the New Testament and appears to be the work of a trained Hellenistic writer. Those who continue to regard James of Jerusalem as its author are therefore obliged to suppose that a secretary must have put the letter into its present literary form. This assumption is not implausible in the light of ancient practice. Some regard the letter as one of the earliest writings in the New Testament and feel that its content accurately reflects what we would expect of the leader of Jewish Christianity. Moreover, they argue that the type of Jewish Christianity reflected in the letter cannot be situated historically after the fall of Jerusalem in A.D. 70.

Others, however, believe it more likely that James is a pseudonymous work of a later period. In addition to its Greek style, they observe further that (a) the prestige that the writer is assumed to enjoy points to the later legendary reputation of James; (b) the discussion of the importance of good works seems to presuppose a debate subsequent to that in Paul's own day; (c) the author does not rely upon prescriptions of the Mosaic law, as we would expect from the historical James; (d) the letter contains no allusions to James's own history and to his relationship with Jesus or to the early Christian community of Jerusalem. For these reasons, many recent interpreters assign James to the period A.D. 90–100.

The principal divisions of the Letter of James are the following:

I. Address (1:1)
II. The Value of Trials and Temptation (1:2–18)
III. Exhortations and Warnings (1:19–5:12)
IV. The Power of Prayer (5:13–20)

I. Address

CHAPTER 1

See RG 502

[1a*]James, a slave of God and of the
Lord Jesus Christ, to the twelve tribes in the
dispersion, greetings.

II. The Value of Trials and Temptation

Perseverance in Trial. [2b*]Consider it all joy,
my brothers, when you encounter various
trials, [3*]for you know that the testing of your
faith produces perseverance. [4]And let perseverance be perfect, so that you may be perfect and complete, lacking in nothing. [5c*]But
if any of you lacks wisdom, he should ask
God who gives to all generously and ungrudgingly, and he will be given it. [6d]But he
should ask in faith, not doubting, for the one
who doubts is like a wave of the sea that is
driven and tossed about by the wind. [7]For
that person must not suppose that he will receive anything from the Lord, [8]since he is a
man of two minds, unstable in all his ways.
[9e*]The brother in lowly circumstances
should take pride in his high standing,
[10f]and the rich one in his lowliness, for he
will pass away "like the flower of the field."
[11]For the sun comes up with its scorching
heat and dries up the grass, its flower
droops, and the beauty of its appearance
vanishes. So will the rich person fade away
in the midst of his pursuits.

Temptation. [12g*]Blessed is the man who
perseveres in temptation, for when he has
been proved he will receive the crown of life
that he promised to those who love him.
[13h*]No one experiencing temptation should
say, "I am being tempted by God"; for God
is not subject to temptation to evil, and he
himself tempts no one. [14]Rather, each person
is tempted when he is lured and enticed by
his own desire. [15]Then desire conceives and
brings forth sin, and when sin reaches maturity it gives birth to death.

[16*]Do not be deceived, my beloved brothers: [17*]all good giving and every perfect gift
is from above, coming down from the Father
of lights, with whom there is no alteration or
shadow caused by change. [18i*]He willed to
give us birth by the word of truth that we
may be a kind of firstfruits of his creatures.

1:1 James, a slave of God and of the Lord Jesus Christ: a declaration of the writer's authority for instructing the Christian communities; cf. Rom 1:1. Regarding the identity of the author, see Introduction. **Dispersion**: see Introduction.

1:2 Consider it all joy . . . various trials: a frequent teaching of the New Testament derived from the words and sufferings of Jesus (Mt 5:10–12; Jn 10:11; Acts 5:41).

1:3–8 The sequence of testing, perseverance, and being perfect and complete indicates the manner of attaining spiritual maturity and full preparedness for the coming of Christ (Jas 5:7–12; cf. 1 Pt 1:6–7; Rom 5:3–5). These steps require wisdom (Jas 1:5).

1:5 Wisdom: a gift that God readily grants to all who ask in faith and that sustains the Christian in times of trial. It is a kind of knowledge or understanding not accessible to the unbeliever or those who doubt, which gives the recipient an understanding of the real importance of events. In this way a Christian can deal with adversity with great calm and hope (cf. 1 Cor 2:6–12).

1:9–11 Throughout his letter (see Jas 2:5; 4:10, 13–16; 5:1–6), the author reaffirms the teaching of Jesus that worldly prosperity is not necessarily a sign of God's favor but can even be a hindrance to proper humility before God (cf. Lk 6:20–25; 12:16–21; 16:19–31).

1:12 Temptation: the Greek word used here is the same one used for "trials" in Jas 1:2. **The crown of life**: in ancient Palestine, crowns or wreaths of flowers were worn at festive occasions as signs of joy and honor. In the Hellenistic world, wreaths were given as a reward to great statesmen, soldiers, athletes. **Life**: here means eternal life. **He promised**: some manuscripts read "God" or "the Lord," while the best witnesses do not specify the subject of "promised."

1:13–15 It is contrary to what we know of God for God to be the author of human temptation (Jas 1:13). In the commission of a sinful act, one is first beguiled by passion (Jas 1:14), then consent is given, which in turn causes the sinful act. When sin permeates the entire person, it incurs the ultimate penalty of death (Jas 1:15).

1:16–18 The author here stresses that God is the source of all good and of good alone, and the evil of temptation does not come from him.

1:17 All good giving and every perfect gift may be a proverb written in hexameter. **Father of lights**: God is here called the Father of the heavenly luminaries, i.e., the stars, sun, and moon that he created (Gn 1:14–18). Unlike orbs moving from nadir to zenith, he never changes or diminishes in brightness.

1:18 Acceptance of the gospel message, **the word of truth**, constitutes new birth (Jn 3:5–6) and makes the recipient the **firstfruits** (i.e., the cultic offering of the earliest grains, symbolizing the beginning of an abundant harvest) of a new creation; cf. 1 Cor 15:20; Rom 8:23.

---

a: Jn 7:35; 1 Pt 1:1. *b:* Rom 5:3–5; 1 Pt 1:6; 4:13–16. *c:* Prv 2:2–6; Wis 9:4, 9–12. *d:* Mt 7:7; Mk 11:24. *e:* 2:5. *f:* Is 40:6–7. *g:* 1 Cor 9:25; 2 Tm 4:8; 1 Pt 5:4; Rev 2:10. *h:* Sir 15:11–20; 1 Cor 10:13. *i:* Jn 1:12–13; 1 Pt 1:23.

III. Exhortations and Warnings

Doers of the Word. [19j*]Know this, my dear
brothers: everyone should be quick to hear,
slow to speak, slow to wrath, [20k]for the wrath
of a man does not accomplish the righteousness of God. [21l]Therefore, put away all filth
and evil excess and humbly welcome the
word that has been planted in you and is able
to save your souls.
[22m]Be doers of the word and not hearers
only, deluding yourselves. [23]For if anyone is
a hearer of the word and not a doer, he is like
a man who looks at his own face in a mirror.
[24]He sees himself, then goes off and
promptly forgets what he looked like.
[25n*]But the one who peers into the perfect
law of freedom and perseveres, and is not a
hearer who forgets but a doer who acts, such
a one shall be blessed in what he does.
[26o*]If anyone thinks he is religious and does
not bridle his tongue but deceives his heart, his
religion is vain. [27p*]Religion that is pure and
undefiled before God and the Father is this: to
care for orphans and widows in their affliction
and to keep oneself unstained by the world.

CHAPTER 2

See RG 502–3

Sin of Partiality. [1*]My brothers,
show no partiality as you adhere to the faith
in our glorious Lord Jesus Christ. [2]For if a
man with gold rings on his fingers and in
fine clothes comes into your assembly, and a
poor person in shabby clothes also comes in,
[3]and you pay attention to the one wearing
the fine clothes and say, "Sit here, please,"
while you say to the poor one, "Stand there,"
or "Sit at my feet," [4*]have you not made distinctions among yourselves and become
judges with evil designs?
[5q*]Listen, my beloved brothers. Did not
God choose those who are poor in the world
to be rich in faith and heirs of the kingdom
that he promised to those who love him? [6]But
you dishonored the poor person. Are not the
rich oppressing you? And do they themselves
not haul you off to court? [7r]Is it not they who
blaspheme the noble name that was invoked
over you? [8s*]However, if you fulfill the royal
law according to the scripture, "You shall
love your neighbor as yourself," you are doing well. [9t]But if you show partiality, you
commit sin, and are convicted by the law as
transgressors. [10u]For whoever keeps the
whole law, but falls short in one particular,
has become guilty in respect to all of it. [11v]For
he who said, "You shall not commit adultery,"
also said, "You shall not kill." Even if you do
not commit adultery but kill, you have become a transgressor of the law. [12w*]So speak
and so act as people who will be judged by the

1:19–25 To **be quick to hear** the gospel is to accept it readily and to act in conformity with it, removing from one's soul whatever is opposed to it, so that it may take root and effect salvation (Jas 1:19–21). To listen to the gospel message but not practice it is failure to improve oneself (Jas 1:22–24). Only conformity of life to the perfect law of true freedom brings happiness (Jas 1:25).

1:25 Peers into the perfect law: the image of a person doing this is paralleled to that of hearing God's word. The **perfect law** applies the Old Testament description of the Mosaic law to the gospel of Jesus Christ that brings freedom.

1:26–27 A practical application of Jas 1:22 is now made.

1:26 For control of the tongue, see note on Jas 3:1–12.

1:27 In the Old Testament, orphans and widows are classical examples of the defenseless and oppressed.

2:1–13 In the Christian community there must be no discrimination or favoritism based on status or wealth (Jas 2:2–4; cf. Mt 5:3; 11:5; 23:6; 1 Cor 1:27–29). Divine favor rather consists in God's election and promises (Jas 2:5). The rich who oppress the poor blaspheme the name of Christ (Jas 2:6–7). By violating one law of love of neighbor, they offend against the whole law (Jas 2:8–11). On the other hand, conscious awareness of the final judgment helps the faithful to fulfill the whole law (Jas 2:12).

2:4 When Christians show favoritism to the rich they are guilty of the worst kind of prejudice and discrimination. The author says that such Christians set themselves up as judges who judge not by divine law but by the basest, self-serving motives.

2:5 The poor, "God's poor" of the Old Testament, were seen by Jesus as particularly open to God for belief in and reliance on him alone (Lk 6:20). God's law cannot tolerate their oppression in any way (Jas 2:9).

2:8 Royal: literally, "kingly"; because the Mosaic law came from God, the universal king. There may be an allusion to Jesus' uses of this commandment in his preaching of the kingdom of God (Mt 22:39; Mk 12:31; Lk 10:27).

2:12–13 The law upon which the last judgment will be based is the law of freedom. As Jesus taught, mercy (which participates in God's own loving mercy) includes forgiveness of those who wrong us (see Mt 6:12, 14–15).

j: Prv 14:17; Sir 5:11. *k:* Eph 4:26. *l:* Col 3:8. *m:* Mt 7:26; Rom 2:13. *n:* 2:12; Ps 19:8; Rom 8:2. *o:* 3:2; Ps 34:14. *p:* Ex 22:21. *q:* 1 Cor 1:26–28; Rev 2:9. *r:* 1 Pt 4:4. *s:* Lv 19:18; Mt 22:39; Rom 13:9. *t:* Dt 1:17. *u:* Gal 3:10. *v:* Ex 20:13–14; Dt 5:17–18. *w:* 1:25; Rom 8:2.

law of freedom. [13x]For the judgment is merciless to one who has not shown mercy; mercy triumphs over judgment.

Faith and Works. [14y*]What good is it, my brothers, if someone says he has faith but does not have works? Can that faith save him? [15]If a brother or sister has nothing to wear and has no food for the day, [16z]and one of you says to them, "Go in peace, keep warm, and eat well," but you do not give them the necessities of the body, what good is it? [17]So also faith of itself, if it does not have works, is dead.

[18]Indeed someone may say, "You have faith and I have works." Demonstrate your faith to me without works, and I will demonstrate my faith to you from my works. [19]You believe that God is one. You do well. Even the demons believe that and tremble. [20]Do you want proof, you ignoramus, that faith without works is useless? [21a]Was not Abraham our father justified by works when he offered his son Isaac upon the altar? [22]You see that faith was active along with his works, and faith was completed by the works. [23b]Thus the scripture was fulfilled that says, "Abraham believed God, and it was credited to him as righteousness," and he was called "the friend of God." [24]See how a person is justified by works and not by faith alone. [25c]And in the same way, was not Rahab the harlot also justified by works when she welcomed the messengers and sent them out by a different route? [26]For just as a body without a spirit is dead, so also faith without works is dead.

CHAPTER 3

See RG 503–4

Power of the Tongue. [1*]Not many of you should become teachers, my brothers, for you realize that we will be judged more strictly, [2d]for we all fall short in many respects. If anyone does not fall short in speech, he is a perfect man, able to bridle his whole body also. [3]If we put bits into the mouths of horses to make them obey us, we also guide their whole bodies. [4]It is the same with ships: even though they are so large and driven by fierce winds, they are steered by a very small rudder wherever the pilot's inclination wishes. [5]In the same way the tongue is a small member and yet has great pretensions.

Consider how small a fire can set a huge forest ablaze. [6]The tongue is also a fire. It exists among our members as a world of malice, defiling the whole body and setting the entire course of our lives on fire, itself set on fire by Gehenna. [7]For every kind of beast and bird, of reptile and sea creature, can be tamed and has been tamed by the human species, [8e]but no human being can tame the tongue. It is a restless evil, full of deadly poison. [9]With it we bless the Lord and Father, and with it we curse human beings who are made in the likeness of God. [10]From the same mouth come blessing and cursing. This need not be so, my brothers. [11]Does a spring gush forth from the same opening both pure and brackish water? [12f]Can a fig tree, my brothers, produce olives, or a grapevine figs? Neither can salt water yield fresh.

True Wisdom. [13g*]Who among you is wise and understanding? Let him show his works by a good life in the humility that comes from wisdom. [14]But if you have bitter jealousy and selfish ambition in your hearts, do not boast and be false to the truth. [15]Wisdom of this kind does not come down from above but is earthly, unspiritual, demonic.

2:14–26 The theme of these verses is the relationship of faith and works (deeds). It has been argued that the teaching here contradicts that of Paul (see especially Rom 4:5–6). The problem can only be understood if the different viewpoints of the two authors are seen. Paul argues against those who claim to participate in God's salvation because of their good deeds as well as because they have committed themselves to trust in God through Jesus Christ (Paul's concept of faith). Paul certainly understands, however, the implications of true faith for a life of love and generosity (see Gal 5:6, 13–15). The author of James is well aware that proper conduct can only come about with an authentic commitment to God in faith (Jas 2:18, 26). Many think he was seeking to correct a misunderstanding of Paul's view.

3:1–12 The use and abuse of the important role of teaching in the church (Jas 3:1) are here related to the good and bad use of the tongue (Jas 3:9–12), the instrument through which teaching was chiefly conveyed (see Sir 5:11–6:1; 28:12–26).

3:13–18 This discussion of true wisdom is related to the previous reflection on the role of the teacher as one who is in control of his speech. The qualities of the wise man endowed from above are detailed (Jas 3:17–18; cf. Gal 5:22–23), in contrast to the qualities of earthbound wisdom (Jas 3:14–16; cf. 2 Cor 12:20).

x: Mt 5:7; 6:14–15; 18:32–33. *y:* Mt 25:31–46; Gal 5:6. *z:* 1 Jn 3:17. *a:* Gn 22:9–12; Heb 11:17. *b:* Gn 15:6; Rom 4:3; Gal 3:6 / 2 Chr 20:7; Is 41:8. *c:* Jos 2:1–21. *d:* 1:26; Prv 13:3; Sir 28:12–26. *e:* Ps 140:4. *f:* Mt 7:16–17. *g:* Eph 4:1–2.

[16]For where jealousy and selfish ambition
exist, there is disorder and every foul practice. [17h]But the wisdom from above is first of
all pure, then peaceable, gentle, compliant,
full of mercy and good fruits, without inconstancy or insincerity. [18i]And the fruit of righteousness is sown in peace for those who
cultivate peace.

CHAPTER 4

See RG 504–5

Causes of Division. [1j*]Where do the
wars and where do the conflicts among you
come from? Is it not from your passions
that make war within your members? [2]You
covet but do not possess. You kill and envy
but you cannot obtain; you fight and wage
war. You do not possess because you do
not ask. [3]You ask but do not receive, because you ask wrongly, to spend it on your
passions. [4k*]Adulterers! Do you not know
that to be a lover of the world means enmity with God? Therefore, whoever wants
to be a lover of the world makes himself an
enemy of God. [5*]Or do you suppose that
the scripture speaks without meaning when
it says, "The spirit that he has made to
dwell in us tends toward jealousy"? [6l*]But
he bestows a greater grace; therefore, it
says:

"God resists the proud,
but gives grace to the humble."

[7m]So submit yourselves to God. Resist the
devil, and he will flee from you. [8n]Draw near
to God, and he will draw near to you.
Cleanse your hands, you sinners, and purify
your hearts, you of two minds. [9]Begin to
lament, to mourn, to weep. Let your laughter
be turned into mourning and your joy into
dejection. [10o]Humble yourselves before the
Lord and he will exalt you.

[11*]Do not speak evil of one another, brothers. Whoever speaks evil of a brother or
judges his brother speaks evil of the law and
judges the law. If you judge the law, you are
not a doer of the law but a judge. [12p]There is
one lawgiver and judge who is able to save
or to destroy. Who then are you to judge
your neighbor?

Warning against Presumption. [13*]Come
now, you who say, "Today or tomorrow we
shall go into such and such a town, spend a
year there doing business, and make a
profit"— [14q*]you have no idea what your life
will be like tomorrow. You are a puff of
smoke that appears briefly and then disappears. [15*]Instead you should say, "If the Lord
wills it, we shall live to do this or that." [16]But

4:1–12 The concern here is with the origin of conflicts in the Christian community. These are occasioned by love **of the world**, which **means enmity with God** (4). Further, the conflicts are bound up with failure to pray properly (cf. Mt 7:7–11; Jn 14:13; 15:7; 16:23), that is, not asking God at all or using God's kindness only for one's pleasure (Jas 4:2–3). In contrast, the proper dispositions are submission to God, repentance, humility, and resistance to evil (Jas 4:7–10).

4:1–3 Passions: the Greek word here (literally, "pleasures") does not indicate that pleasure is evil. Rather, as the text points out (Jas 4:2–3), it is the manner in which one deals with needs and desires that determines good or bad. The motivation for any action can be wrong, especially if one does not pray properly but seeks only selfish enjoyment (Jas 4:3).

4:4 Adulterers: a common biblical image for the covenant between God and his people is the marriage bond. In this image, breaking the covenant with God is likened to the unfaithfulness of adultery.

4:5 The meaning of this saying is difficult because the author of James cites, probably from memory, a passage that is not in any extant manuscript of the Bible. Other translations of the text with a completely different meaning are possible: "The Spirit that he (God) made to dwell in us yearns (for us) jealously," or, "He (God) yearns jealously for the spirit that he has made to dwell in us." If this last translation is correct, the author perhaps had in mind an apocryphal religious text that echoes the idea that God is zealous for his creatures; cf. Ex 20:5; Dt 4:24; Zec 8:2.

4:6 The point of this whole argument is that God wants the happiness of all, but that selfishness and pride can make that impossible. We must work with him in humility (Jas 4:10).

4:11 Slander of a fellow Christian does not break just one commandment but makes mockery of the authority of law in general and therefore of God.

4:13–17 The uncertainty of life (Jas 4:14), its complete dependence on God, and the necessity of submitting to God's will (Jas 4:15) all help one know and do what is right (Jas 4:17). To disregard this is to live in pride and arrogance (Jas 4:16); failure to do what is right is a sin (Jas 4:17).

4:14 Some important Greek manuscripts here have, "You who have no idea what tomorrow will bring. Why, what is your life?"

4:15 If the Lord wills it: often in piety referred to as the "*conditio Jacobaea*," the condition James says we should employ to qualify all our plans.

h: 1:17; Wis 7:22–23. *i:* Mt 5:9. *j:* Rom 7:23; 1 Pt 2:11. *k:* Mt 6:24; Lk 16:13; Rom 8:7; 1 Jn 2:15–16. *l:* Jb 22:29; Prv 3:34; Mt 23:12; 1 Pt 5:5. *m:* 1 Pt 5:8–9. *n:* Zec 1:3; Mal 3:7. *o:* Jb 5:11; Mt 23:12; Lk 14:11; 18:14; 1 Pt 5:6. *p:* Mt 7:1; Rom 2:1; 14:4. *q:* Prv 27:1 / Ps 39:6–7.

now you are boasting in your arrogance. All
such boasting is evil. 17r*So for one who
knows the right thing to do and does not do
it, it is a sin.

CHAPTER 5

See RG 505–6

Warning to the Rich. 1s*Come now,
you rich, weep and wail over your impending miseries. 2tYour wealth has rotted away,
your clothes have become moth-eaten,
3uyour gold and silver have corroded, and
that corrosion will be a testimony against
you; it will devour your flesh like a fire. You
have stored up treasure for the last days.
4vBehold, the wages you withheld from the
workers who harvested your fields are crying aloud, and the cries of the harvesters
have reached the ears of the Lord of hosts.
5wYou have lived on earth in luxury and
pleasure; you have fattened your hearts for
the day of slaughter. 6x*You have condemned; you have murdered the righteous
one; he offers you no resistance.

Patience and Oaths. 7*Be patient, therefore, brothers, until the coming of the Lord.
See how the farmer waits for the precious
fruit of the earth, being patient with it until it
receives the early and the late rains. 8yYou
too must be patient. Make your hearts firm,
because the coming of the Lord is at hand.
9Do not complain, brothers, about one another, that you may not be judged. Behold,
the Judge is standing before the gates.
10Take as an example of hardship and patience, brothers, the prophets who spoke in
the name of the Lord. 11zIndeed we call
blessed those who have persevered. You
have heard of the perseverance of Job, and
you have seen the purpose of the Lord, because "the Lord is compassionate and merciful."

12a*But above all, my brothers, do not
swear, either by heaven or by earth or with
any other oath, but let your "Yes" mean
"Yes" and your "No" mean "No," that you
may not incur condemnation.

IV. The Power of Prayer

Anointing of the Sick. 13Is anyone among
you suffering? He should pray. Is anyone in
good spirits? He should sing praise. 14b*Is
anyone among you sick? He should summon
the presbyters of the church, and they should
pray over him and anoint [him] with oil in
the name of the Lord, 15*and the prayer of
faith will save the sick person, and the Lord
will raise him up. If he has committed any
sins, he will be forgiven.

Confession and Intercession. 16Therefore,
confess your sins to one another and pray for
one another, that you may be healed. The fervent prayer of a righteous person is very

4:17 It is a sin: those who live arrogantly, forgetting the contingency of life and our dependence on God (Jas 4:13–16), are guilty of sin.

5:1–6 Continuing with the theme of the transitory character of life on earth, the author points out the impending ruin of the godless. He denounces the unjust rich, whose victims cry to heaven for judgment on their exploiters (Jas 5:4–6). The decay and corrosion of the costly garments and metals, which symbolize wealth, prove them worthless and portend the destruction of their possessors (Jas 5:2–3).

5:6 The author does not have in mind any specific crime in his readers' communities but rather echoes the Old Testament theme of the harsh oppression of the righteous poor (see Prv 1:11; Wis 2:10, 12, 20).

5:7–11 Those oppressed by the unjust rich are reminded of the need for patience, both in bearing the sufferings of human life (Jas 5:9) and in their expectation of the coming of the Lord. It is then that they will receive their reward (Jas 5:7–8, 10–11; cf. Heb 10:25; 1 Jn 2:18).

5:7 The early and the late rains: an expression related to the agricultural season in ancient Palestine (see Dt 11:14; Jer 5:24; Jl 2:23).

5:12 This is the threat of condemnation for the abuse of swearing oaths (cf. Mt 5:33–37). **By heaven or by earth**: these words were substitutes for the original form of an oath, to circumvent its binding force and to avoid pronouncing the holy name of God (see Ex 22:10).

5:14 In case of sickness a Christian should ask for the presbyters of the church, i.e., those who have authority in the church (cf. Acts 15:2, 22–23; 1 Tm 5:17; Ti 1:5). They are to pray over the person and anoint with oil; oil was used for medicinal purposes in the ancient world (see Is 1:6; Lk 10:34). In Mk 6:13, the Twelve anoint the sick with oil on their missionary journey. **In the name of the Lord**: by the power of Jesus Christ.

5:15 The results of the prayer and anointing are physical health and forgiveness of sins. The Roman Catholic Church (Council of Trent, Session 14) declared that this anointing of the sick is a sacrament "instituted by Christ and promulgated by blessed James the apostle."

r: Lk 12:47. s: Lk 6:24. t: Mt 6:19. u: Ps 21:10; Prv 11:4; Jdt 16:17. v: Lv 19:13; Dt 24:14–15; Mal 3:5. w: Jer 12:3; Lk 16:19–25. x: Wis 2:10–20. y: Lk 21:19; Heb 10:36 / Heb 10:25; 1 Pt 4:7. z: Ex 34:6; Ps 103:8. a: Mt 5:34–37. b: Mk 6:13.

powerful. [17c]Elijah was a human being like
us; yet he prayed earnestly that it might not
rain, and for three years and six months it did
not rain upon the land. [18d]Then he prayed
again, and the sky gave rain and the earth
produced its fruit.

Conversion of Sinners. [19e]My brothers, if
anyone among you should stray from the truth
and someone bring him back, [20f*]he should
know that whoever brings back a sinner from
the error of his way will save his soul from
death and will cover a multitude of sins.

5:20 When a Christian is instrumental in the conversion of a sinner, the result is forgiveness of sins and a reinstatement of the sinner to the life of grace.

c: 1 Kgs 17:1; Lk 4:25. *d:* 1 Kgs 18:45. *e:* Mt 18:15; Gal 6:1. *f:* Prv 10:12; 1 Pt 4:8.

See RG 506–10

The First Letter of Peter

This letter begins with an address by Peter to Christian communities located in five provinces of Asia Minor (1 Pt 1:1), including areas evangelized by Paul (Acts 16:6–7; 18:23). Christians there are encouraged to remain faithful to their standards of belief and conduct in spite of threats of persecution. Numerous allusions in the letter suggest that the churches addressed were largely of Gentile composition (1 Pt 1:14, 18; 2:9–10; 4:3–4), though considerable use is made of the Old Testament (1 Pt 1:24; 2:6–7, 9–10, 22; 3:10–12).

The contents following the address both inspire and admonish these "chosen sojourners" (1 Pt 1:1) who, in seeking to live as God's people, feel an alienation from their previous religious roots and the society around them. Appeal is made to Christ's resurrection and the future hope it provides (1 Pt 1:3–5) and to the experience of baptism as new birth (1 Pt 1:3, 23–25; 3:21). The suffering and death of Christ serve as both source of salvation and example (1 Pt 1:19; 2:21–25; 3:18). What Christians are in Christ, as a people who have received mercy and are to proclaim and live according to God's call (1 Pt 2:9–10), is repeatedly spelled out for all sorts of situations in society (1 Pt 2:11–17), work (even as slaves, 1 Pt 2:18–20), the home (1 Pt 3:1–7), and general conduct (1 Pt 3:8–12; 4:1–11). But over all hangs the possibility of suffering as a Christian (1 Pt 3:13–17). In 1 Pt 4:12–19 persecution is described as already occurring, so that some have supposed the letter was addressed both to places where such a "trial by fire" was already present and to places where it might break out.

The letter constantly mingles moral exhortation (*paraklēsis*) with its catechetical summaries of mercies in Christ. Encouragement to fidelity in spite of suffering is based upon a vision of the meaning of Christian existence. The emphasis on baptism and allusions to various features of the baptismal liturgy suggest that the author has incorporated into his exposition numerous homiletic, credal, hymnic, and sacramental elements of the baptismal rite that had become traditional at an early date.

From Irenaeus in the late second century until modern times, Christian tradition regarded Peter the apostle as author of this document. Since he was martyred at Rome during the persecution of Nero between A.D. 64 and 67, it was supposed that the letter was written from Rome shortly before his death. This is supported by its reference to "Babylon" (1 Pt 5:13), a code name for Rome in the early church.

Some modern scholars, however, on the basis of a number of features that they consider incompatible with Petrine authenticity, regard the letter as the work of a later Christian writer. Such features include the cultivated Greek in which it is written, difficult to attribute to a Galilean fisherman, together with its use of the Greek Septuagint translation when citing the Old Testament; the similarity in both thought and expression to the Pauline literature; and the allusions to widespread persecution of Christians, which did not occur until at least the reign of Domitian (A.D. 81–96). In this view the letter would date from the end of the first century or even the beginning of the second, when there is evidence for persecution of Christians in Asia Minor (the letter of Pliny the Younger to Trajan, A.D. 111–12).

Other scholars believe, however, that these objections can be met by appeal to use of a secretary, Silvanus, mentioned in 1 Pt 5:12. Such secretaries often gave literary expression to the author's thoughts in their own style and language. The persecutions may refer to local harassment rather than to systematic repression by the state. Hence there is nothing in the document incompatible with Petrine authorship in the 60s.

Still other scholars take a middle position. The many literary contacts with the Pauline literature, James, and 1 John suggest a common fund of traditional formulations rather than direct dependence upon Paul. Such liturgical and catechetical traditions must have been very ancient and in some cases of Palestinian origin.

Yet it is unlikely that Peter addressed a letter to the Gentile churches of Asia Minor while Paul was still alive. This suggests a period after the death of the two apostles, perhaps A.D. 70–90. The author would be a disciple of Peter in Rome, representing a Petrine group that served as a bridge between the Palestinian origins of Christianity and its flowering in the Gentile world. The problem addressed would not be official persecution but the difficulty of living the Christian life in a hostile, secular environment that espoused different values and subjected the Christian minority to ridicule and oppression.

The principal divisions of the First Letter of Peter are the following:

I. Address (1:1–2)
II. The Gift and Call of God in Baptism (1:3–2:10)
III. The Christian in a Hostile World (2:11–4:11)
IV. Advice to the Persecuted (4:12–5:11)
V. Conclusion (5:12–14)

I. Address

CHAPTER 1

See RG 507-8

Greeting. [1a]*Peter, an apostle of
Jesus Christ, to the chosen sojourners of the
dispersion in Pontus, Galatia, Cappadocia,
Asia, and Bithynia, [2b]in the foreknowledge
of God the Father, through sanctification by
the Spirit, for obedience and sprinkling with
the blood of Jesus Christ: may grace and
peace be yours in abundance.

II. The Gift and Call of God in Baptism

Blessing. [3c]*Blessed be the God and Father
of our Lord Jesus Christ, who in his great
mercy gave us a new birth to a living hope
through the resurrection of Jesus Christ from
the dead, [4d]to an inheritance that is imperishable, undefiled, and unfading, kept in
heaven for you [5]who by the power of God
are safeguarded through faith, to a salvation
that is ready to be revealed in the final time.
[6e]*In this you rejoice, although now for a little while you may have to suffer through
various trials, [7f]so that the genuineness of
your faith, more precious than gold that is
perishable even though tested by fire, may
prove to be for praise, glory, and honor at the
revelation of Jesus Christ. [8g]Although you
have not seen him you love him; even
though you do not see him now yet believe
in him, you rejoice with an indescribable
and glorious joy, [9]as you attain the goal of
[your] faith, the salvation of your souls.
[10]*Concerning this salvation, prophets

1:1–2 The introductory formula names **Peter** as the writer (but see Introduction). In his comments to the presbyters (1 Pt 5:1), the author calls himself a "fellow presbyter." He addresses himself to the Gentile converts of Asia Minor. Their privileged status as a **chosen** and sanctified people makes them worthy of God's **grace** and **peace**. In contrast is their actual existence as aliens and **sojourners**, scattered among pagans, far from their true country.

1:1 Dispersion: literally, diaspora; see Jas 1:1 and Introduction to that letter. **Pontus . . . Bithynia**: five provinces in Asia Minor, listed in clockwise order from the north, perhaps in the sequence in which a messenger might deliver the letter.

1:3–5 A prayer of praise and thanksgiving to God who bestows the gift of new life and hope in baptism (**new birth**, 1 Pt 1:3) **through the resurrection of Jesus Christ from the dead.** The new birth is a sign of an **imperishable inheritance** (1 Pt 1:4), of **salvation** that is still in the future (**to be revealed in the final time**, 1 Pt 1:5).

1:6–9 As the glory of Christ's resurrection was preceded by his sufferings and death, the new life of faith that it bestows is to be subjected to many **trials** (1 Pt 1:6) while achieving its goal: the glory of the fullness of **salvation** (1 Pt 1:9) at the coming of Christ (1 Pt 1:7).

1:10–12 The **Spirit of Christ** (1 Pt 1:11) is here shown to have been present in the prophets, moving them to search, investigate, and prophesy about the **grace** of **salvation** that was to come (1 Pt 1:10), and in the apostles impelling them to preach the fulfillment of salvation in the message of Christ's sufferings and glory (1 Pt 1:12).

a: Jas 1:1. *b:* Rom 8:29. *c:* Ti 3:5. *d:* Mt 6:19–20. *e:* Jas 1:2–3. *f:* 1 Cor 3:13. *g:* 2 Cor 5:6–7.

who prophesied about the grace that was to be yours searched and investigated it, [11h]investigating the time and circumstances that the Spirit of Christ within them indicated when it testified in advance to the sufferings destined for Christ and the glories to follow them. [12]It was revealed to them that they were serving not themselves but you with regard to the things that have now been announced to you by those who preached the good news to you [through] the holy Spirit sent from heaven, things into which angels longed to look.

Obedience. [13*]Therefore, gird up the loins of your mind, live soberly, and set your hopes completely on the grace to be brought to you at the revelation of Jesus Christ. [14*]Like obedient children, do not act in compliance with the desires of your former ignorance [15i]but, as he who called you is holy, be holy yourselves in every aspect of your conduct, [16j]for it is written, "Be holy because I [am] holy."

Reverence. [17k]Now if you invoke as Father him who judges impartially according to each one's works, conduct yourselves with reverence during the time of your sojourning, [18l]realizing that you were ransomed from your futile conduct, handed on by your ancestors, not with perishable things like silver or gold [19m*]but with the precious blood of Christ as of a spotless unblemished lamb. [20]He was known before the foundation of the world but revealed in the final time for you, [21]who through him believe in God who raised him from the dead and gave him glory, so that your faith and hope are in God.

Mutual Love. [22n*]Since you have purified yourselves by obedience to the truth for sincere mutual love, love one another intensely from a [pure] heart. [23o*]You have been born anew, not from perishable but from imperishable seed, through the living and abiding word of God, [24p]for:

"All flesh is like grass,
and all its glory like the flower of the field;
the grass withers,
and the flower wilts;
[25] but the word of the Lord remains forever."

This is the word that has been proclaimed to you.

CHAPTER 2

See RG 508-9

God's House and People. [1q*]Rid yourselves of all malice and all deceit, insincerity, envy, and all slander; [2]like newborn infants, long for pure spiritual milk so that through it you may grow into salvation, [3r*]for you have tasted that the Lord is good. [4s*]Come to him, a living stone, rejected by human beings but chosen and precious in the sight of God, [5t*]and, like living stones, let yourselves be built into a spiritual house to be a holy priesthood to offer spiritual sacri-

1:13–25 These verses are concerned with the call of God's people to holiness and to mutual love by reason of their redemption through the blood of Christ (1 Pt 1:18–21).

1:13 Gird up the loins of your mind: a figure reminiscent of the rite of Passover when the Israelites were in flight from their oppressors (Ex 12:11), and also suggesting the vigilance of the Christian people in expectation of the parousia of Christ (Lk 12:35).

1:14–16 The **ignorance** here referred to (1 Pt 1:14) was their former lack of knowledge of God, leading inevitably to godless conduct. Holiness (1 Pt 1:15–16), on the contrary, is the result of their call to the knowledge and love of God.

1:19 Christians have received the redemption prophesied by Isaiah (Is 52:3), through the blood (Jewish symbol of life) of the spotless lamb (Is 53:7, 10; Jn 1:29; Rom 3:24–25; cf. 1 Cor 6:20).

1:22–25 The new birth of Christians (1 Pt 1:23) derives from Christ, the **imperishable seed** or sowing that produces a new and lasting existence in those who accept the gospel (1 Pt 1:24–25), with the consequent duty of loving **one another** (1 Pt 1:22).

1:23 The living and abiding word of God: or, "the word of the living and abiding God."

2:1–3 Growth toward salvation is seen here as two steps: first, stripping away all that is contrary to the new life in Christ; second, the nourishment (**pure spiritual milk**) that the newly baptized have received.

2:3 Tasted that the Lord is good: cf. Ps 34:8.

2:4–8 Christ is the cornerstone (cf. Is 28:16) that is the foundation of the spiritual edifice of the Christian community (1 Pt 2:5). To unbelievers, Christ is an obstacle and a stumbling block on which they are destined to fall (1 Pt 2:8); cf. Rom 11:11.

2:5 Let yourselves be built: the form of the Greek word could also be indicative passive, "you are being built" (cf. 2 Pt 2:9).

h: Is 52:13–53:12; Dn 9:24. *i:* Mt 5:48; 1 Jn 3:3. *j:* Lv 11:44; 19:2. *k:* 2:11. *l:* Is 52:3; 1 Cor 6:20. *m:* Ex 12:5; Jn 1:29; Heb 9:14. *n:* Rom 12:10. *o:* 1 Jn 3:9. *p:* Is 40:6–8. *q:* Jas 1:21. *r:* Ps 34:9. *s:* Ps 118:22; Mt 21:42; Acts 4:11. *t:* Eph 2:21–22.

fices acceptable to God through Jesus Christ. [6u]For it says in scripture:

"Behold, I am laying a stone in Zion,
a cornerstone, chosen and precious,
and whoever believes in it shall not be
put to shame."

[7v]Therefore, its value is for you who have faith, but for those without faith:

"The stone which the builders rejected
has become the cornerstone,"

[8w]and

"A stone that will make people
stumble,
and a rock that will make them fall."

They stumble by disobeying the word, as is their destiny.

[9x*]But you are "a chosen race, a royal priesthood, a holy nation, a people of his own, so that you may announce the praises" of him who called you out of darkness into his wonderful light.

[10 y]Once you were "no people"
but now you are God's people;
you "had not received mercy"
but now you have received mercy.

III. The Christian in a Hostile World

Christian Examples. [11z*]Beloved, I urge you as aliens and sojourners to keep away from worldly desires that wage war against the soul. [12]Maintain good conduct among the Gentiles, so that if they speak of you as evildoers, they may observe your good works and glorify God on the day of visitation.

Christian Citizens. [13a*]Be subject to every human institution for the Lord's sake, whether it be to the king as supreme [14]or to governors as sent by him for the punishment of evildoers and the approval of those who do good. [15]For it is the will of God that by doing good you may silence the ignorance of foolish people. [16b]Be free, yet without using freedom as a pretext for evil, but as slaves of God. [17c]Give honor to all, love the community, fear God, honor the king.

Christian Slaves. [18d*]Slaves, be subject to your masters with all reverence, not only to those who are good and equitable but also to those who are perverse. [19]For whenever anyone bears the pain of unjust suffering because of consciousness of God, that is a grace. [20]But

2:9–10 The prerogatives of ancient Israel mentioned here are now more fully and fittingly applied to the Christian people: "a chosen race" (cf. Is 43:20–21) indicates their divine election (Eph 1:4–6); "a royal priesthood" (cf. Ex 19:6) to serve and worship God in Christ, thus continuing the priestly functions of his life, passion, and resurrection; "a holy nation" (Ex 19:6) reserved for God, a people he claims for his own (cf. Mal 3:17) in virtue of their baptism into his death and resurrection. This transcends all natural and national divisions and unites the people into one community to glorify the one who led them from the darkness of paganism to the light of faith in Christ. From being "no people" deprived of all mercy, they have become the very people of God, the chosen recipients of his mercy (cf. Hos 1:9; 2:23).

2:11–3:12 After explaining the doctrinal basis for the Christian community, the author makes practical applications in terms of the virtues that should prevail in all the social relationships of the members of the community: good example to Gentile neighbors (1 Pt 2:11–12); respect for human authority (1 Pt 2:13–17); obedience, patience, and endurance of hardship in domestic relations (1 Pt 2:18–25); Christian behavior of husbands and wives (1 Pt 3:1–7); mutual charity (1 Pt 3:8–12).

2:11 Aliens and sojourners: no longer signifying absence from one's native land (Gn 23:4), this image denotes rather their estrangement from the world during their earthly pilgrimage (see also 1 Pt 1:1, 17).

2:13–17 True Christian freedom is the result of being servants of God (16; see note on 1 Pt 2:18–23). It includes reverence for God, esteem for every individual, and committed love for fellow Christians (1 Pt 2:17). Although persecution may threaten, subjection to human government as urged (1 Pt 2:13, 17) and concern for the impact of Christians' conduct on those who are not Christians (1 Pt 2:12, 15).

2:18–21 Most of the labor in the commercial cities of first-century Asia Minor was performed by a working class of slaves. The sense of freedom contained in the gospel undoubtedly caused great tension among Christian slaves: witness the special advice given concerning them here and in 1 Cor 7:21–24; Eph 6:5–8; Col 3:22–25; Philemon. The point made here does not have so much to do with the institution of slavery, which the author does not challenge, but with the nonviolent reaction (1 Pt 2:20) of slaves to unjust treatment. Their patient suffering is compared to that of Jesus (1 Pt 2:21), which won righteousness for all humanity.

u: Is 28:16. *v:* Ps 118:22; Mt 21:42; Lk 20:17; Acts 4:11. *w:* Is 8:14; Rom 9:33. *x:* Ex 19:6; Is 61:6; Rev 1:6; 20:6. *y:* Hos 1:9; 2:25 / Hos 1:6. *z:* Gal 5:24. *a:* Rom 13:1–7. *b:* Gal 5:13. *c:* Prv 24:21; Mt 22:21. *d:* Eph 6:5.

what credit is there if you are patient when
beaten for doing wrong? But if you are patient
when you suffer for doing what is good, this
is a grace before God. [21e*]For to this you have
been called, because Christ also suffered for
you, leaving you an example that you should
follow in his footsteps.

[22 f*]"He committed no sin,
and no deceit was found in his mouth."

[23g]When he was insulted, he returned no insult; when he suffered, he did not threaten;
instead, he handed himself over to the one
who judges justly. [24h]He himself bore our
sins in his body upon the cross, so that, free
from sin, we might live for righteousness.
By his wounds you have been healed. [25i*]For
you had gone astray like sheep, but you have
now returned to the shepherd and guardian
of your souls.

See RG 508–9

CHAPTER 3

Christian Spouses. [1*]Likewise, you
wives should be subordinate to your husbands so that, even if some disobey the
word, they may be won over without a word
by their wives' conduct [2j]when they observe
your reverent and chaste behavior. [3k]Your
adornment should not be an external one:
braiding the hair, wearing gold jewelry, or
dressing in fine clothes, [4]but rather the hidden character of the heart, expressed in the
imperishable beauty of a gentle and calm
disposition, which is precious in the sight of
God. [5]For this is also how the holy women
who hoped in God once used to adorn themselves and were subordinate to their husbands; [6]thus Sarah obeyed Abraham, calling
him "lord." You are her children when you
do what is good and fear no intimidation.

[7l*]Likewise, you husbands should live
with your wives in understanding, showing
honor to the weaker female sex, since we are
joint heirs of the gift of life, so that your
prayers may not be hindered.

Christian Conduct. [8*]Finally, all of you,
be of one mind, sympathetic, loving toward
one another, compassionate, humble. [9m]Do
not return evil for evil, or insult for insult;
but, on the contrary, a blessing, because to
this you were called, that you might inherit a
blessing. [10n]For:

"Whoever would love life
and see good days
must keep the tongue from evil
and the lips from speaking deceit,
[11] must turn from evil and do good,
seek peace and follow after it.
[12] For the eyes of the Lord are on the
righteous
and his ears turned to their prayer,
but the face of the Lord is against
evildoers."

Christian Suffering. [13*]Now who is going to harm you if you are enthusiastic for

2:21 Suffered: some ancient manuscripts and versions read "died" (cf. 1 Pt 3:18).

2:22–25 After the quotation of Is 53:9b, the passage describes Jesus' passion with phrases concerning the Suffering Servant from Is 53:4–12, perhaps as employed in an early Christian confession of faith; cf. 1 Pt 1:18–21 and 1 Pt 3:18–22.

2:25 The shepherd and guardian of your souls: the familiar shepherd and flock figures express the care, vigilance, and love of God for his people in the Old Testament (Ps 23; Is 40:11; Jer 23:4–5; Ez 34:11–16) and of Jesus for all humanity in the New Testament (Mt 18:10–14; Lk 15:4–7; Jn 10:1–16; Heb 13:20).

3:1–6 The typical marital virtues of women of the ancient world, obedience, reverence, and chastity (1 Pt 3:1–2), are outlined here by the author, who gives them an entirely new motivation: Christian wives are to be virtuous so that they may be instrumental in the conversion of their husbands. In imitation of **holy women** in the past (1 Pt 3:5) they are to cultivate the interior life (1 Pt 3:4) instead of excessive concern with their appearance (1 Pt 3:3).

3:7 Husbands who do not respect their wives will have as little success in prayer as those who, according to Paul, have no love: their prayers will be "a resounding gong or a clashing cymbal" (1 Cor 13:1). Consideration for others is shown as a prerequisite for effective prayer also in Mt 5:23–24; 1 Cor 11:20–22; Jas 4:3. After all, whatever the social position of women in the world and in the family, they are equal recipients of the gift of God's salvation. Paul is very clear on this point, too (see 1 Cor 11:11–12; Gal 3:28).

3:8–12 For the proper ordering of Christian life in its various aspects as described in 1 Pt 2:11–3:9, there is promised the blessing expressed in Ps 34:13–17. In the Old Testament this refers to longevity and prosperity; here, it also refers to eternal life.

3:13–22 This exposition, centering on 1 Pt 3:17, runs as follows: by his suffering and death Christ the righteous one saved the unrighteous (1 Pt 3:18); by his resurrection he received new life in the spirit, which he communicates to be-

e: Mt 16:24. *f:* Is 53:9. *g:* Mt 5:39. *h:* Is 53:4, 12 / Is 53:5. *i:* Is 53:6. *j:* 1 Cor 7:12–16; Eph 5:22–24; Col 3:18; 1 Tm 2:9–15. *k:* 1 Tm 2:9–10. *l:* Eph 5:25–33; Col 3:19. *m:* Mt 5:44; Lk 6:28; Rom 12:14. *n:* Ps 34:13–17.

what is good? [14]But even if you should suffer because of righteousness, blessed are you. Do not be afraid or terrified with fear of them, [15o]but sanctify Christ as Lord in your hearts. Always be ready to give an explanation to anyone who asks you for a reason for your hope, [16]but do it with gentleness and reverence, keeping your conscience clear, so that, when you are maligned, those who defame your good conduct in Christ may themselves be put to shame. [17]For it is better to suffer for doing good, if that be the will of God, than for doing evil.

[18p*]For Christ also suffered for sins once, the righteous for the sake of the unrighteous, that he might lead you to God. Put to death in the flesh, he was brought to life in the spirit. [19*]In it he also went to preach to the spirits in prison, [20q]who had once been disobedient while God patiently waited in the days of Noah during the building of the ark, in which a few persons, eight in all, were saved through water. [21r*]This prefigured baptism, which saves you now. It is not a removal of dirt from the body but an appeal to God for a clear conscience, through the resurrection of Jesus Christ, [22s]who has gone into heaven and is at the right hand of God, with angels, authorities, and powers subject to him.

CHAPTER 4

See RG 509–10

Christian Restraint. [1*]Therefore, since Christ suffered in the flesh, arm yourselves also with the same attitude (for whoever suffers in the flesh has broken with sin), [2]so as not to spend what remains of one's life in the flesh on human desires, but on the will of God. [3t]For the time that has passed is sufficient for doing what the Gentiles like to do: living in debauchery, evil desires, drunkenness, orgies, carousing, and wanton idolatry. [4]They are surprised that you do not plunge into the same swamp of profligacy, and they vilify you; [5u]but they will give an account to him who stands ready to judge the living and the dead. [6*]For this is why the gospel was preached even to the dead that, though condemned in the flesh in human estimation, they might live in the spirit in the estimation of God.

Christian Charity. [7*]The end of all things is at hand. Therefore, be serious and sober for prayers. [8v*]Above all, let your love for one another be intense, because love covers a multitude of sins. [9w]Be hospitable to one another without complaining. [10x]As each one has received a gift, use it to serve one another as good stewards of God's varied grace. [11y*]Whoever preaches, let it be with the words of God; whoever serves, let it be

lievers through the baptismal bath that cleanses their consciences from sin. As Noah's family was saved **through water**, so Christians are saved through the waters of baptism (1 Pt 3:19–22). Hence they need not share the fear of sinners; they should rather rejoice in suffering because of their hope in Christ. Thus their innocence disappoints their accusers (1 Pt 3:13–16; cf. Mt 10:28; Rom 8:35–39).

3:18 Suffered: very many ancient manuscripts and versions read "died." **Put to death in the flesh**: affirms that Jesus truly died as a human being. **Brought to life in the spirit**: that is, in the new and transformed existence freed from the limitations and weaknesses of natural human life (cf. 1 Cor 15:45).

3:19 The spirits in prison: it is not clear just who these spirits are. They may be the spirits of the sinners who died in the flood, or angelic powers, hostile to God, who have been overcome by Christ (cf. 1 Pt 3:22; Gn 6:4; Enoch 6–36, especially 21:6; 2 Enoch 7:1–5).

3:21 Appeal to God: this could also be translated "pledge," that is, a promise on the part of Christians to live with a good conscience before God, or a pledge from God of forgiveness and therefore a good conscience for us.

4:1–6 Willingness to suffer with Christ equips the Christian with the power to conquer sin (1). Christ is here portrayed as the judge to whom those guilty of pagan vices must render an account (1 Pt 4:5; cf. Jn 5:22–27; Acts 10:42; 2 Tm 4:1).

4:6 The dead: these may be the sinners of the flood generation who are possibly referred to in 1 Pt 3:19. But many scholars think that there is no connection between these two verses, and that **the dead** here are Christians who have died since hearing the preaching of the gospel.

4:7–11 The inner life of the eschatological community is outlined as **the end** (the parousia of Christ) and the judgment draws near in terms of seriousness, sobriety, prayer, and love expressed through hospitality and the use of one's gifts for the glory of God and of Christ.

4:8 Love covers a multitude of sins: a maxim based on Prv 10:12; see also Ps 32:1; Jas 5:20.

4:11 Some scholars feel that this doxology concludes the part of the homily addressed specifically to the newly baptized, begun in 1 Pt 1:3; others that it concludes a baptismal liturgy. Such doxologies do occur within a New Testament letter, e.g., Rom 9:5. Some propose that 1 Pt 4:11 was an al-

o: Is 8:12. *p:* 1 Cor 15:45. *q:* Gn 7:7, 17; 2 Pt 2:5. *r:* Eph 5:26; Heb 10:22. *s:* Eph 1:20–21. *t:* Eph 2:2–3; 4:17–19; Col 3:7; Ti 3:3. *u:* Acts 10:42; 2 Tm 4:1. *v:* Prv 10:12; Jas 5:20. *w:* Heb 13:2. *x:* Rom 12:6–8; 1 Cor 12:4–11. *y:* 1 Cor 10:31.

with the strength that God supplies, so that
in all things God may be glorified through
Jesus Christ, to whom belong glory and dominion forever and ever. Amen.

IV. Advice to the Persecuted

Trial of Persecution. [12z*]Beloved, do not be
surprised that a trial by fire is occurring
among you, as if something strange were
happening to you. [13a]But rejoice to the extent that you share in the sufferings of
Christ, so that when his glory is revealed you
may also rejoice exultantly. [14b]If you are insulted for the name of Christ, blessed are
you, for the Spirit of glory and of God rests
upon you. [15]But let no one among you be
made to suffer as a murderer, a thief, an evildoer, or as an intriguer. [16]But whoever is
made to suffer as a Christian should not be
ashamed but glorify God because of the
name. [17c]For it is time for the judgment to
begin with the household of God; if it begins
with us, how will it end for those who fail to
obey the gospel of God?

[18 d]"And if the righteous one is barely
saved,
where will the godless and the sinner
appear?"

[19]As a result, those who suffer in accord with
God's will hand their souls over to a faithful
creator as they do good.

CHAPTER 5

See RG 509-10

Advice to Presbyters. [1*]So I exhort
the presbyters among you, as a fellow presbyter and witness to the sufferings of Christ
and one who has a share in the glory to be revealed. [2e]Tend the flock of God in your
midst, [overseeing] not by constraint but
willingly, as God would have it, not for
shameful profit but eagerly. [3]Do not lord it
over those assigned to you, but be examples
to the flock. [4f*]And when the chief Shepherd is revealed, you will receive the unfading crown of glory.

Advice to the Community. [5g*]Likewise,
you younger members, be subject to the
presbyters. And all of you, clothe yourselves
with humility in your dealings with one another, for:

"God opposes the proud
but bestows favor on the humble."

[6h]So humble yourselves under the mighty
hand of God, that he may exalt you in due
time. [7i]Cast all your worries upon him because he cares for you.

[8j]Be sober and vigilant. Your opponent
the devil is prowling around like a roaring
lion looking for [someone] to devour. [9]Re-
sist him, steadfast in faith, knowing that
your fellow believers throughout the world
undergo the same sufferings. [10k]The God of
all grace who called you to his eternal glory
through Christ [Jesus] will himself restore,
confirm, strengthen, and establish you after
you have suffered a little. [11]To him be dominion forever. Amen.

ternate ending, with 1 Pt 4:12–5:14 being read in places where persecution was more pressing. But such doxologies usually do not occur at the end of letters (the only examples are 2 Pt 3:18, Jude 25, and Rom 16:27, the last probably a liturgical insertion).

4:12–19 The suffering to which the author has already frequently referred is presented in more severe terms. This has led some scholars to see these verses as referring to an actual persecution. Others see the heightening of the language as only a rhetorical device used at the end of the letter to emphasize the suffering motif.

5:1–4 In imitation of Christ, the chief shepherd, those entrusted with a pastoral office are to tend the flock by their care and example.

5:1 Presbyters: the officially appointed leaders and teachers of the Christian community (cf. 1 Tm 5:17–18; Ti 1:5–8; Jas 5:14).

5:4 See note on 1 Pt 2:25.

5:5–11 The community is to be subject to the presbyters and to show humility toward one another and trust in God's love and care (1 Pt 5:5–7). With sobriety, alertness, and steadfast faith they must resist the evil one; their sufferings are shared with Christians everywhere (1 Pt 5:8–9). They will be strengthened and called to eternal glory (1 Pt 5:10–11).

5:5 Younger members: this may be a designation for office-holders of lesser rank.

---

z: 1:6–7; 3:14, 17. *a:* Rom 5:3–5; 8:17; 2 Tm 2:12. *b:* Acts 5:41 / Is 11:2. *c:* Lk 23:31; 2 Thes 1:8. *d:* Prv 11:31 LXX. *e:* Acts 20:28; Ti 1:7. *f:* Wis 5:15–16; 1 Cor 9:25; 2 Tm 4:8; Jas 1:12. *g:* Prv 3:34. *h:* Jb 22:29; Jas 4:10. *i:* Ps 55:23; Mt 6:25–33; Lk 12:22–31; Phil 4:6. *j:* 1 Thes 5:6. *k:* Rom 8:18; 2 Cor 4:17.

V. Conclusion

12 *I write you this briefly through Silvanus, whom I consider a faithful brother, exhorting you and testifying that this is the true grace of God. Remain firm in it. 13 *The chosen one at Babylon sends you greeting, as does Mark, my son. 14 [l]Greet one another with a loving kiss. Peace to all of you who are in Christ.

5:12 Silvanus: the companion of Paul (see 2 Cor 1:19; 1 Thes 1:1; 2 Thes 1:1). Jews and Jewish Christians, like Paul, often had a Hebrew name (Saoul, Silas) and a Greek or Latin name (Paul, Silvanus). On Silvanus's possible role as amanuensis, see Introduction.

5:13 The chosen one: feminine, referring to the Christian community (*ekklēsia*) at **Babylon**, the code name for Rome in Rev 14:8; 17:5; 18:2. **Mark, my son**: traditionally a prominent disciple of Peter and co-worker at the church in Rome, perhaps the John Mark referred to in Acts 12:12, 25; 13:5, 13; and in Acts 15:37–39, a companion of Barnabas. Perhaps this is the same Mark mentioned as Barnabas's cousin in Col 4:10, a co-worker with Paul in Phlm 24 (see also 2 Tm 4:11).

l: Rom 16:16; 1 Cor 16:20; 2 Cor 13:12.

See RG 510-13

The Second Letter of Peter

This letter can be appreciated both for its positive teachings and for its earnest warnings. It seeks to strengthen readers in faith (2 Pt 1:1), hope for the future (2 Pt 3:1–10), knowledge (2 Pt 1:2, 6, 8), love (2 Pt 1:7), and other virtues (2 Pt 1:5–6). This aim is carried out especially by warning against false teachers, the condemnation of whom occupies the long central section of the letter (2 Pt 2:1–22). A particular crisis is the claim by "scoffers" that there will be no second coming of Jesus, a doctrine that the author vigorously affirms (2 Pt 3:1–10). The concept of God's "promises" is particularly precious in the theology of 2 Peter (2 Pt 1:4; 3:4, 9, 13). Closing comments at 2 Pt 3:17–18 well sum up the twin concerns: that you not "be led into" error and "fall" but instead "grow in grace" and "knowledge" of Jesus Christ.

Second Peter is clearly structured in its presentation of these points. It reminds its readers of the divine authenticity of Christ's teaching (2 Pt 1:3–4), continues with reflections on Christian conduct (2 Pt 1:5–15), then returns to the exalted dignity of Jesus by incorporating into the text the apostolic witness to his transfiguration (2 Pt 1:16–18). It takes up the question of the interpretation of scripture by pointing out that it is possible to misunderstand the sacred writings (2 Pt 1:19–21) and that divine punishment will overtake false teachers (2 Pt 2:1–22). It proclaims that the parousia is the teaching of the Lord and of the apostles and is therefore an eventual certainty (2 Pt 3:1–13). At the same time, it warns that the meaning of Paul's writings on this question should not be distorted (2 Pt 3:14–18).

In both content and style this letter is very different from 1 Peter, which immediately precedes it in the canon. The opening verse attributes it to "Symeon Peter, a slave and apostle of Jesus Christ." Moreover, the author in 2 Pt 3:1 calls his work a "second letter," referring probably to 1 Peter as his first, and in 2 Pt 1:18 counts himself among those present at the transfiguration of Jesus.

Nevertheless, acceptance of 2 Peter into the New Testament canon met with great resistance in the early church. The oldest certain reference to it comes from Origen in the early third century. While he himself accepted both Petrine letters as canonical, he testifies that others rejected 2 Peter. As late as the fifth century some local churches still excluded it from the canon, but eventually it was universally adopted. The principal reason for the long delay was the persistent doubt that the letter stemmed from the apostle Peter.

Among modern scholars there is wide agreement that 2 Peter is a pseudonymous work, i.e., one written by a later author who attributed it to Peter according to a literary convention popular at the time. It gives the impression of being more remote in time from the apostolic period than 1 Peter; indeed, many think it is the latest work in the New Testament and assign it to the first or even the second quarter of the second century.

The principal reasons for this view are the following. The author refers to the apostles and "our ancestors" as belonging to a previous generation, now dead (2 Pt 3:2–4). A collection of Paul's letters exists and appears to be well known, but disputes have arisen about the interpretation of them (2 Pt 3:14–16). The passage about false teachers

(2 Pt 2:1–18) contains a number of literary contacts with Jude 4–16, and it is generally agreed that 2 Peter depends upon Jude, not vice versa. Finally, the principal problem exercising the author is the false teaching of "scoffers" who have concluded from the delay of the parousia that the Lord is not going to return. This could scarcely have been an issue during the lifetime of Simon Peter.

The Christians to whom the letter is addressed are not identified, though it may be the intent of 2 Pt 3:1 to identify them with the churches of Asia Minor to which 1 Peter was sent. Except for the epistolary greeting in 2 Pt 1:1–2, 2 Peter does not have the features of a genuine letter at all, but is rather a general exhortation cast in the form of a letter. The author must have been a Jewish Christian of the dispersion for, while his Jewish heritage is evident in various features of his thought and style, he writes in the rather stilted literary Greek of the Hellenistic period. He appeals to tradition against the twin threat of doctrinal error and moral laxity, which appear to reflect an early stage of what later developed into full-blown gnosticism. Thus he forms a link between the apostolic period and the church of subsequent ages.

The principal divisions of the Second Letter of Peter are the following:

I. Address (1:1–2)
II. Exhortation to Christian Virtue (1:3–21)
III. Condemnation of the False Teachers (2:1–22)
IV. The Delay of the Second Coming (3:1–16)
V. Final Exhortation and Doxology (3:17–18)

I. Address

CHAPTER 1

See RG 000-00

Greeting. [1]*Symeon Peter, a slave and apostle of Jesus Christ, to those who have received a faith of equal value to ours through the righteousness of our God and savior Jesus Christ: [2]*may grace and peace be yours in abundance through knowledge of God and of Jesus our Lord.

II. Exhortation to Christian Virtue

The Power of God's Promise. [3][a]*His divine power has bestowed on us everything that makes for life and devotion, through the knowledge of him who called us by his own glory and power. [4][b]Through these, he has bestowed on us the precious and very great promises, so that through them you may come to share in the divine nature, after escaping from the corruption that is in the world because of evil desire. [5][c]*For this very reason, make every effort to supplement your faith with virtue, virtue with knowledge, [6]knowledge with self-control, self-control with endurance, endurance with devotion, [7]devotion with mutual affection, mutual affection with love. [8]If these are yours and increase in abundance, they will keep you from being idle or unfruitful in the knowledge of our Lord Jesus Christ. [9][d]Anyone who lacks them is blind and shortsighted, forgetful of the cleansing of his past sins. [10]*Therefore, brothers, be all the

1:1 Symeon Peter: on the authorship of 2 Peter, see Introduction; on the spelling here of the Hebrew name *Sim'ôn*, cf. Acts 15:14. The greeting is especially similar to those in 1 Peter and Jude. The words translated **our God and savior Jesus Christ** could also be rendered "our God and the savior Jesus Christ"; cf. 2 Pt 1:11; 2:20; 3:2, 18.

1:2 Knowledge: a key term in the letter (2 Pt 1:3, 8; 2:20; 3:18), perhaps used as a Christian emphasis against gnostic claims.

1:3–4 Christian life in its fullness is a gift of divine power effecting a knowledge of Christ and the bestowal of divine promises (2 Pt 3:4, 9). **To share in the divine nature**, escaping from a corrupt world, is a thought found elsewhere in the Bible but expressed only here in such Hellenistic terms, since it is said to be accomplished through knowledge (2 Pt 1:3); cf. 2 Pt 1:2; 2:20; but see also Jn 15:4; 17:22–23; Rom 8:14–17; Heb 3:14; 1 Jn 1:3; 3:2.

1:3 By his own glory and power: the most ancient papyrus and the best codex read "through glory and power."

1:5–9 Note the climactic gradation of qualities (2 Pt 1:5–7), beginning with faith and leading to the fullness of Christian life, which is love; cf. Rom 5:3–4; Gal 5:6, 22 for a similar series of "virtues," though the program and sense here are different than in Paul. The fruit of these is knowledge of Christ (2 Pt 1:8) referred to in 2 Pt 1:3; their absence is spiritual blindness (2 Pt 1:9).

1:10–11 Perseverance in the Christian vocation is the best preventative against losing it and the safest provision for attaining its goal, the kingdom. **Kingdom of . . . Christ**, instead of "God," is unusual; cf. Col 1:13 and Mt 13:41, as well as the **righteousness of . . . Christ** (2 Pt 1:1).

a: 2 Cor 4:6; 1 Pt 2:9. *b:* 2 Cor 7:1; 1 Jn 2:15. *c:* Gal 5:22–23. *d:* 1 Jn 2:9, 11.

more eager to make your call and election
firm, for, in doing so, you will never stumble.
[11]For, in this way, entry into the eternal kingdom of our Lord and savior Jesus Christ will
be richly provided for you.

Apostolic Witness. [12*]Therefore, I will always remind you of these things, even
though you already know them and are established in the truth you have. [13*]I think it
right, as long as I am in this "tent," to stir
you up by a reminder, [14e]since I know that I
will soon have to put it aside, as indeed our
Lord Jesus Christ has shown me. [15]I shall
also make every effort to enable you always
to remember these things after my departure.
[16f*]We did not follow cleverly devised
myths when we made known to you the
power and coming of our Lord Jesus Christ,
but we had been eyewitnesses of his majesty.
[17g*]For he received honor and glory from
God the Father when that unique declaration
came to him from the majestic glory, "This is
my Son, my beloved, with whom I am well
pleased." [18*]We ourselves heard this voice
come from heaven while we were with him
on the holy mountain. [19h]Moreover, we possess the prophetic message that is altogether
reliable. You will do well to be attentive to it,
as to a lamp shining in a dark place, until day
dawns and the morning star rises in your
hearts. [20*]Know this first of all, that there is
no prophecy of scripture that is a matter of
personal interpretation, [21]for no prophecy
ever came through human will; but rather human beings moved by the holy Spirit spoke
under the influence of God.

III. Condemnation of the False Teachers

CHAPTER 2

See RG 511–12

False Teachers. [1i*]There were also
false prophets among the people, just as there
will be false teachers among you, who will introduce destructive heresies and even deny the
Master who ransomed them, bringing swift
destruction on themselves. [2j]Many will follow their licentious ways, and because of
them the way of truth will be reviled. [3k]In their
greed they will exploit you with fabrications,
but from of old their condemnation has not
been idle and their destruction does not sleep.

Lessons from the Past. [4l*]For if God did

1:12–19 The purpose in writing is to call to mind the apostle's witness to the truth, even as he faces the end of his life (2 Pt 1:12–15), his eyewitness testimony to Christ (1 Pt 1:16–18), and the true prophetic message (2 Pt 1:19) through the Spirit in scripture (2 Pt 1:20–21), in contrast to what false teachers are setting forth (2 Pt 2).

1:13 Tent: a biblical image for transitory human life (Is 38:12), here combined with a verb that suggests not folding or packing up a tent but its being discarded in death (cf. 2 Cor 5:1–4).

1:16 Coming: in Greek *parousia*, used at 2 Pt 3:4, 12 of the second coming of Christ. The word was used in the extrabiblical writings for the visitation of someone in authority; in Greek cult and Hellenistic Judaism it was used for the manifestation of the divine presence. That the apostles **made known** has been interpreted to refer to Jesus' transfiguration (2 Pt 1:17) or to his entire first coming or to his future coming in power (2 Pt 3).

1:17 The author assures the readers of the reliability of the apostolic message (including Jesus' power, glory, and coming; cf. note on 2 Pt 1:16) by appeal to the transfiguration of Jesus in glory (cf. Mt 17:1–8 and parallels) and by appeal to the prophetic message (2 Pt 1:19; perhaps Nm 24:17). Here, as elsewhere, the New Testament insists on continued reminders as necessary to preserve the historical facts about Jesus and the truths of the faith; cf. 2 Pt 3:1–2; 1 Cor 11:2; 15:1–3. **My Son, my beloved**: or, "my beloved Son."

1:18 We: at Jesus' transfiguration, referring to Peter, James, and John (Mt 17:1).

1:20–21 Often cited, along with 2 Tm 3:16, on the "inspiration" of scripture or against private interpretation, these verses in context are directed against the false teachers of 2 Pt 2 and clever tales (2 Pt 1:16). The prophetic word in scripture comes admittedly through **human beings** (2 Pt 1:21), but **moved by the holy Spirit**, not from their own interpretation, and is a matter of what the author and Spirit intended, not the **personal interpretation** of false teachers. Instead of **under the influence of God**, some manuscripts read "holy ones of God."

2:1–3 The pattern of **false prophets** among the Old Testament people of God will recur through **false teachers** in the church. Such destructive opinions of heretical sects bring loss of faith in Christ, contempt for the way of salvation (cf. 2 Pt 2:21), and immorality.

2:4–6 The false teachers will be punished just as surely and as severely as were the fallen **angels** (2 Pt 2:4; cf. Jude 6; Gn 6:1–4), the sinners of Noah's day (2 Pt 2:5; Gn 7:21–23), and the inhabitants of the cities of the Plain (2 Pt 2:6; Jude 7; Gn 19:25). Whereas there are three examples in Jude 5–7 (Exodus and wilderness; rebellious angels; Sodom and Gomorrah), 2 Peter omitted the first of these, has inserted a new illustration about Noah (2 Pt 2:5) between Jude's second and third examples, and listed the resulting three examples in their Old Testament order (Gn 6; 7; 19).

e: Is 38:12; Jn 21:18–19. *f:* Lk 9:28–36; Jn 1:14. *g:* Ps 2:7; Mt 17:4–6. *h:* Lk 1:78–79; Rev 2:28. *i:* Mt 24:11, 24; 1 Tm 4:1; Jude 4. *j:* Is 52:5. *k:* Rom 16:18. *l:* Jude 6.

not spare the angels when they sinned, but
condemned them to the chains of Tartarus and
handed them over to be kept for judgment;
[5m*]and if he did not spare the ancient world,
even though he preserved Noah, a herald of
righteousness, together with seven others,
when he brought a flood upon the godless
world; [6n]and if he condemned the cities of
Sodom and Gommorah [to destruction], reducing them to ashes, making them an example for the godless [people] of what is coming; [7]and if he rescued Lot, a righteous man
oppressed by the licentious conduct of unprincipled people [8](for day after day that righteous man living among them was tormented
in his righteous soul at the lawless deeds that
he saw and heard), [9o]then the Lord knows
how to rescue the devout from trial and to
keep the unrighteous under punishment for
the day of judgment, [10p*]and especially those
who follow the flesh with its depraved desire
and show contempt for lordship.

False Teachers Denounced. Bold and arrogant, they are not afraid to revile glorious
beings, [11q*]whereas angels, despite their superior strength and power, do not bring a reviling judgment against them from the Lord.
[12r]But these people, like irrational animals
born by nature for capture and destruction,
revile things that they do not understand,
and in their destruction they will also be destroyed, [13s*]suffering wrong as payment for
wrongdoing. Thinking daytime revelry a delight, they are stains and defilements as they
revel in their deceits while carousing with
you. [14]Their eyes are full of adultery and insatiable for sin. They seduce unstable people, and their hearts are trained in greed. Accursed children! [15t*]Abandoning the straight
road, they have gone astray, following the
road of Balaam, the son of Bosor, who loved
payment for wrongdoing, [16u]but he received
a rebuke for his own crime: a mute beast
spoke with a human voice and restrained the
prophet's madness.

[17v]These people are waterless springs
and mists driven by a gale; for them the
gloom of darkness has been reserved.
[18w*]For, talking empty bombast, they seduce with licentious desires of the flesh
those who have barely escaped from people
who live in error. [19x]They promise them
freedom, though they themselves are slaves
of corruption, for a person is a slave of
whatever overcomes him. [20y]For if they,
having escaped the defilements of the
world through the knowledge of [our] Lord
and savior Jesus Christ, again become entangled and overcome by them, their last
condition is worse than their first. [21z*]For it
would have been better for them not to have
known the way of righteousness than after
knowing it to turn back from the holy commandment handed down to them. [22a*]What

2:4 Chains of Tartarus: cf. Jude 6; other manuscripts in 2 Peter read "pits of Tartarus." **Tartarus**: a term borrowed from Greek mythology to indicate the infernal regions.

2:5–10a Although God did not spare the sinful, he kept and saved the righteous, such as **Noah** (2 Pt 2:5) and **Lot** (2 Pt 2:7), and **he knows how to rescue the devout** (2 Pt 2:9), who are contrasted with the false teachers of the author's day. On Noah, cf. Gn 5:32–9:29, especially 7:1. On Lot, cf. Gn 13 and 19.

2:10b–22 Some take 2 Pt 2:10b, 11 with the preceding paragraph. Others begin the new paragraph with 2 Pt 2:10a, supplying from 2 Pt 2:9 **The Lord knows how . . . to keep . . . under punishment**, with reference to God and probably specifically Christ (2 Pt 2:1). The conduct of the false teachers is described and condemned in language similar to that of Jude 8–16. This arrogance knows no bounds; animal-like, they are due to be caught and destroyed. They seduce even those who have knowledge of Christ (2 Pt 2:20).

2:10b Glorious beings: literally, "glories"; cf. Jude 8. While some think that illustrious personages are meant or even political officials behind whom (fallen) angels stand, it is more likely that the reference is to glorious angelic beings (cf. Jude 9).

2:11 From the Lord: some manuscripts read "before the Lord"; cf. Jude 9.

2:13 Suffering wrong: some manuscripts read "receiving a reward." **In their deceits**: some manuscripts read "in their love feasts" (Jude 12).

2:15 Balaam, the son of Bosor: in Nm 22:5, Balaam is said to be the son of Beor, and it is this name that turns up in a few ancient Greek manuscripts by way of "correction" of the text. Balaam is not portrayed in such a bad light in Nm 22. His evil reputation and his **madness** (2 Pt 2:16), and possibly his surname Bosor, may have come from a Jewish tradition about him in the first/second century, of which we no longer have any knowledge.

2:18 Barely escaped: some manuscripts read "really escaped."

2:21 Commandment handed down: cf. 2 Pt 3:2 and Jude 3.

2:22 The second proverb is of unknown origin, while the first appears in Prv 26:11.

m: Gn 8:15–19; Heb 11:7. *n:* Gn 19:24–25; Jude 7. *o:* 1 Cor 10:13; Rev 3:10. *p:* Jude 8. *q:* Jude 9. *r:* Ps 49:13–15; Jude 10. *s:* Jude 12. *t:* Nm 31:16; Jude 11. *u:* Nm 22:28–33. *v:* Jude 12–13. *w:* Jude 16. *x:* Jn 8:34; Rom 6:16–17. *y:* Mt 12:45. *z:* Ez 3:20. *a:* Prv 26:11.

is expressed in the true proverb has happened to them, “The dog returns to its own
vomit,” and “A bathed sow returns to wal-
lowing in the mire.”

IV. The Delay of the Second Coming

CHAPTER 3

See RG 512

Denial of the Parousia. [1*]This is
now, beloved, the second letter I am writing
to you; through them by way of reminder I
am trying to stir up your sincere disposition,
[2b]to recall the words previously spoken by
the holy prophets and the commandment of
the Lord and savior through your apostles.
[3c*]Know this first of all, that in the last days
scoffers will come [to] scoff, living according to their own desires [4d*]and saying,
“Where is the promise of his coming? From
the time when our ancestors fell asleep,
everything has remained as it was from the
beginning of creation.” [5e*]They deliberately
ignore the fact that the heavens existed of
old and earth was formed out of water and
through water by the word of God;
[6f*]through these the world that then existed
was destroyed, deluged with water. [7g]The
present heavens and earth have been reserved by the same word for fire, kept for the
day of judgment and of destruction of the
godless.
[8h*]But do not ignore this one fact,
beloved, that with the Lord one day is like a
thousand years and a thousand years like one
day. [9i]The Lord does not delay his promise,
as some regard “delay,” but he is patient
with you, not wishing that any should perish
but that all should come to repentance.
[10j*]But the day of the Lord will come like a
thief, and then the heavens will pass away
with a mighty roar and the elements will be
dissolved by fire, and the earth and everything done on it will be found out.

Exhortation to Preparedness. [11k*]Since
everything is to be dissolved in this way,
what sort of persons ought [you] to be,
conducting yourselves in holiness and devotion, [12l*]waiting for and hastening the
coming of the day of God, because of
which the heavens will be dissolved in

3:1–4 The false teachers not only flout Christian morality (cf. Jude 8–19); they also deny the second coming of Christ and the judgment (2 Pt 3:4; cf. 2 Pt 3:7). They seek to justify their licentiousness by arguing that the promised return of Christ has not been realized and the world is the same, no better than it was before (2 Pt 3:3–4). The author wishes to strengthen the faithful against such errors by reminding them in this **second letter** of the instruction in 1 Peter and of the teaching of the **prophets** and of Christ, conveyed through the **apostles** (2 Pt 3:1–2; cf. Jude 17); cf. 1 Pt 1:10–12, 16–21, especially 16–21; Eph 2:20.

3:3 Scoffers: cf. Jude 18, where, however, only the passions of the scoffers are mentioned, not a denial on their part of Jesus' parousia.

3:4–7 The false teachers tried to justify their immorality by pointing out that the promised **coming** (*parousia*) of the Lord has not yet occurred, even though early Christians expected it in their day. They thus insinuate that God is not guiding the world's history anymore, since nothing has changed and the first generation of Christians, **our ancestors** (2 Pt 3:4), has all died by this time. The author replies that, just as God destroyed the earth by water in the flood (2 Pt 3:5–6, cf. 2 Pt 2:5), so he will destroy it along with the false teachers on judgment day (7). **The word of God**, which called the world into being (Gn 1; Ps 33:6) and **destroyed** it by the waters of a flood, will destroy it again by fire on **the day of judgment** (2 Pt 3:5–7).

3:5 Formed out of water and through water: Gn 1:2, 6–8 is reflected as well as Greek views that water was the basic element from which all is derived.

3:6 Destroyed, deluged with water: cf. 2 Pt 2:5; Gn 7:11–8:2.

3:8–10 The scoffers' objection (2 Pt 3:4) is refuted also by showing that **delay** of the Lord's second coming is not a failure to fulfill his word but rather a sign of his patience: God is giving time for repentance before the final judgment (cf. Wis 11:23–26; Ez 18:23; 33:11).

3:8 Cf. Ps 90:4.

3:10 Like a thief: Mt 24:43; 1 Thes 5:2; Rev 3:3. **Will be found out**: cf. 1 Cor 3:13–15. Some few versions read, as the sense may demand, “will not be found out”; many manuscripts read “will be burned up”; there are further variants in other manuscripts, versions, and Fathers. Total destruction is assumed (2 Pt 3:11).

3:11–16 The second coming of Christ and the judgment of the world are the doctrinal bases for the moral exhortation to readiness through vigilance and a virtuous life; cf. Mt 24:42, 50–51; Lk 12:40; 1 Thes 5:1–11; Jude 20–21.

3:12 Flames . . . fire: although this is the only New Testament passage about a final conflagration, the idea was common in apocalyptic and Greco-Roman thought. **Hastening**: eschatology is here used to motivate ethics (2 Pt 3:11), as elsewhere in the New Testament. Jewish sources and Acts 3:19–20 assume that proper ethical conduct can help bring the promised day of the Lord; cf. 2 Pt 3:9. Some render the phrase, however, “desiring it earnestly.”

---

b: Jude 17. *c:* 1 Tm 4:1; 2 Tm 3:1; Jude 18. *d:* Is 5:19. *e:* Gn 1:2, 6, 8; Ps 24:2. *f:* Gn 7:21. *g:* Is 51:6; Mt 3:12. *h:* Ps 90:4. *i:* Ez 18:23; 1 Tm 2:4. *j:* Is 66:15–16; Mt 24:29. *k:* Acts 3:19–21. *l:* Is 34:4; Heb 10:27.

flames and the elements melted by fire. [13m*]But according to his promise we await new heavens and a new earth in which righteousness dwells.

[14]Therefore, beloved, since you await these things, be eager to be found without spot or blemish before him, at peace. [15n]And consider the patience of our Lord as salvation, as our beloved brother Paul, according to the wisdom given to him, also wrote to you, [16*]speaking of these things as he does in all his letters. In them there are some things hard to understand that the ignorant and unstable distort to their own destruction, just as they do the other scriptures.

V. Final Exhortation and Doxology

[17o*]Therefore, beloved, since you are forewarned, be on your guard not to be led into the error of the unprincipled and to fall from your own stability. [18p]But grow in grace and in the knowledge of our Lord and savior Jesus Christ. To him be glory now and to the day of eternity. [Amen.]

3:13 New heavens and a new earth: cf. Is 65:17; 66:22. The divine promises will be fulfilled after the day of judgment will have passed. The universe will be transformed by the reign of God's **righteousness** or justice; cf. Is 65:17–18; Acts 3:21; Rom 8:18–25; Rev 21:1.

3:16 These things: the teachings of this letter find parallels in Paul, e.g., God's will to save (Rom 2:4; 9:22–23; 1 Cor 1:7–8), the coming of Christ (1 Thes 4:16–17; 1 Cor 15:23–52), and preparedness for the judgment (Col 1:22–23; Eph 1:4–14; 4:30; 5:5–14). **Other scriptures**: used to guide the faith and life of the Christian community. The letters of Paul are thus here placed on the same level as books of the Old Testament. Possibly other New Testament writings could also be included.

3:17–18 To avoid the dangers **of error** and loss of **stability** Christians are **forewarned** to be **on guard** and to **grow in grace and knowledge** (2 Pt 1:2) of Christ. The doxology (2 Pt 3:18) recalls 1 Pt 4:11. Some manuscripts add **Amen**.

m: Is 65:17; 66:22; Rom 8:21; Rev 21:1, 27. *n:* Rom 8:19; Jude 24. *o:* Mk 13:5; Heb 2:1. *p:* Rom 16:27.

See RG 513–16

The First Letter of John

Early Christian tradition identified this work as a letter of John the apostle. Because of its resemblance to the fourth gospel in style, vocabulary, and ideas, it is generally agreed that both works are the product of the same school of Johannine Christianity. The terminology and the presence or absence of certain theological ideas in 1 John suggest that it was written after the gospel; it may have been composed as a short treatise on ideas that were developed more fully in the fourth gospel. To others, the evidence suggests that 1 John was written after the fourth gospel as part of a debate on the proper interpretation of that gospel. Whatever its relation to the gospel, 1 John may be dated toward the end of the first century. Unlike 2 and 3 John, it lacks in form the salutation and epistolary conclusion of a letter. These features, its prologue, and its emphasis on doctrinal teaching make it more akin to a theological treatise than to most other New Testament letters.

The purpose of the letter is to combat certain false ideas, especially about Jesus, and to deepen the spiritual and social awareness of the Christian community (1 Jn 3:17). Some former members (1 Jn 2:19) of the community refused to acknowledge Jesus as the Christ (1 Jn 2:22) and denied that he was a true man (1 Jn 4:2). The specific heresy described in this letter cannot be identified exactly, but it is a form of docetism or gnosticism; the former doctrine denied the humanity of Christ to insure that his divinity was untainted, and the latter viewed the appearance of Christ as a mere stepping-stone to higher knowledge of God. These theological errors are rejected by an appeal to the reality and continuity of the apostolic witness to Jesus. The author affirms that authentic Christian love, ethics, and faith take place only within the historical revelation and sacrifice of Jesus Christ. The fullness of Christian life as fellowship with the Father must be based on true belief and result in charitable living; knowledge of God and love for one another are inseparable, and error in one area inevitably affects the other. Although the author recognizes that Christian doctrine presents intangible mysteries of faith about Christ, he insists that the concrete Christian life brings to light the deeper realities of the gospel.

The structure and language of the letter are straightforward yet repetitious. The author sets forth the striking contrasts between light and darkness, Christians and the world, and truth and error to illustrate the threats and responsibilities of Christian life. The result is not one of theological argument but one of intense religious conviction expressed in simple truths. The letter is of particular value for its declaration of the humanity and divinity of Christ as an apostolic teaching and for its development of the intrinsic connection between Christian moral conduct and Christian doctrine.

The principal divisions of the First Letter of John are the following:

I. Prologue (1:1–4)
II. God as Light (1:5–3:10)
III. Love for One Another (3:11–5:12)
IV. Epilogue (5:13–21)

I. Prologue

CHAPTER 1

See RG 514

The Word of Life

1 [a]*What was from the beginning,
what we have heard,
what we have seen with our eyes,
what we looked upon
and touched with our hands
concerns the Word of life—
2 [b]for the life was made visible;
we have seen it and testify to it
and proclaim to you the eternal life
that was with the Father and was made
visible to us—
3 [c]what we have seen and heard
we proclaim now to you,
so that you too may have fellowship with
us;
for our fellowship is with the Father
and with his Son, Jesus Christ.
4 [d]We are writing this so that our joy may
be complete.

II. God as Light

God is Light. 5*Now this is the message that
we have heard from him and proclaim to
you: God is light, and in him there is no
darkness at all. 6[e]If we say, "We have fellowship with him," while we continue to
walk in darkness, we lie and do not act in
truth. 7[f]But if we walk in the light as he is in
the light, then we have fellowship with one
another, and the blood of his Son Jesus
cleanses us from all sin. 8[g]*If we say, "We
are without sin," we deceive ourselves, and
the truth is not in us. 9[h]If we acknowledge
our sins, he is faithful and just and will forgive our sins and cleanse us from every
wrongdoing. 10[i]If we say, "We have not
sinned," we make him a liar, and his word is
not in us.

CHAPTER 2

See RG 514–15

Christ and His Commandments.
1 [j]*My children, I am writing this to you so
that you may not commit sin. But if anyone
does sin, we have an Advocate with the Father, Jesus Christ the righteous one. 2[k]He is
expiation for our sins, and not for our sins
only but for those of the whole world.

1:1–4 There is a striking parallel to the prologue of the gospel of John (Jn 1:1–18), but the emphasis here is not on the preexistent Word but rather on the apostles' witness to the incarnation of life by their experience of the historical Jesus. He is **the Word of life** (1 Jn 1:1; cf. Jn 1:4), **the eternal life that was with the Father and was made visible** (1 Jn 1:2; cf. Jn 1:14), and was **heard, seen, looked upon**, and **touched** by the apostles. The purpose of their teaching is to share that **life**, called **fellowship . . . with the Father and with his Son, Jesus Christ**, with those who receive their witness (1 Jn 1:3; Jn 1:14, 16).

1:5–7 Light is to be understood here as truth and goodness; **darkness** here is error and depravity (cf. Jn 3:19–21; 17:17; Eph 5:8). To **walk** in light or darkness is to live according to truth or error, not merely intellectual but moral as well. Fellowship with God and with one another consists in a life according to the truth as found in God and in Christ.

1:8–10 Denial of the condition of sin is self-deception and even contradictory of divine revelation; there is also the continual possibility of sin's recurrence. Forgiveness and deliverance from sin through Christ are assured through acknowledgment of them and repentance.

2:1 Children: like the term "beloved," this is an expression of pastoral love (cf. Jn 13:33; 21:5; 1 Cor 4:14). **Advocate**: for the use of the term, see Jn 14:16. Forgiveness of sin is assured through Christ's intercession and expiation or "offering"; the death of Christ effected the removal of sin.

---

a: 2:13; Jn 1:1, 14; 20:20, 25, 27. *b:* Jn 15:27; 17:5. *c:* Jn 17:21; Acts 4:20. *d:* Jn 15:11; 2 Jn 12. *e:* Jn 12:35. *f:* Mt 26:28; Rom 3:24–25; Heb 9:14; 1 Pt 1:19; Rev 1:5. *g:* 2 Chr 6:36; Prv 20:9. *h:* Prv 28:13; Jas 5:16. *i:* 5:10. *j:* Jn 14:16; Heb 7:25. *k:* 4:10.

[3l*]The way we may be sure that we know him is to keep his commandments. [4m]Whoever says, "I know him," but does not keep his commandments is a liar, and the truth is not in him. [5n]But whoever keeps his word, the love of God is truly perfected in him. This is the way we may know that we are in union with him: [6]whoever claims to abide in him ought to live [just] as he lived.

The New Commandment. [7o*]Beloved, I am writing no new commandment to you but an old commandment that you had from the beginning. The old commandment is the word that you have heard. [8p*]And yet I do write a new commandment to you, which holds true in him and among you, for the darkness is passing away, and the true light is already shining. [9q]Whoever says he is in the light, yet hates his brother, is still in the darkness. [10r]Whoever loves his brother remains in the light, and there is nothing in him to cause a fall. [11]Whoever hates his brother is in darkness; he walks in darkness and does not know where he is going because the darkness has blinded his eyes.

Members of the Community. [12s*]I am writing to you, children, because your sins have been forgiven for his name's sake.

[13t]I am writing to you, fathers, because you know him who is from the beginning.

I am writing to you, young men, because you have conquered the evil one.

[14]I write to you, children, because you know the Father.

I write to you, fathers, because you know him who is from the beginning.

I write to you, young men, because you are strong and the word of God remains in you, and you have conquered the evil one.

[15u*]Do not love the world or the things of the world. If anyone loves the world, the love of the Father is not in him. [16*]For all that is in the world, sensual lust, enticement for the eyes, and a pretentious life, is not from the Father but is from the world. [17v]Yet the world and its enticement are passing away. But whoever does the will of God remains forever.

Antichrists. [18w*]Children, it is the last hour; and just as you heard that the antichrist was coming, so now many antichrists have appeared. Thus we know this is the last hour. [19*]They went out from us, but they were not really of our number; if they had been, they would have remained with us. Their desertion shows that none of them was of our number. [20x*]But you have the anointing that comes

2:3–6 The way we may be sure: to those who claim, "I have known Christ and therefore I know him," our author insists on not mere intellectual knowledge but obedience to God's commandments in a life conformed to the example of Christ; this confirms our knowledge of him and is **the love of God . . . perfected**. Disparity between moral life and the commandments proves improper belief.

2:7–11 The author expresses the continuity and freshness of mutual charity in Christian experience. Through Christ the commandment of love has become the **light** defeating the **darkness** of evil in a new age. All hatred as darkness is incompatible with the light and Christian life. Note also the characteristic Johannine polemic in which a positive assertion is emphasized by the negative statement of its opposite.

2:8 Which holds true in him and among you: literally, "a thing that holds true in him and in you."

2:12–17 The Christian community that has experienced the grace of God through forgiveness of sin and knowledge of Christ is armed against the evil one.

2:12 For his name's sake: because of Christ our sins are forgiven.

2:15 The world: all that is hostile toward God and alienated from him. Love of the **world** and love of God are thus mutually exclusive; cf. Jas 4:4.

2:16 Sensual lust: literally, "the lust of the flesh," inordinate desire for physical gratification. **Enticement for the eyes**: literally, "the lust of the eyes," avarice or covetousness; the eyes are regarded as the windows of the soul. **Pretentious life**: literally, "pride of life," arrogance or ostentation in one's earthly style of life that reflects a willful independence from God and others.

2:18 It is the last hour: literally, "a last hour," the period between the death and resurrection of Christ and his second coming. **The antichrist**: opponent or adversary of Christ; the term appears only in 1 John–2 John, but "pseudochrists" (translated "false messiahs") in Mt 24:24 and Mk 13:22, and Paul's "lawless one" in 2 Thes 2:3, are similar figures. **Many antichrists**: Matthew, Mark, and Revelation seem to indicate a collectivity of persons, here related to the false teachers.

2:19 Not really of our number: the apostate teachers only proved their lack of faith by leaving the community.

2:20 The anointing that comes from the holy one: this anointing is in the Old Testament sense of receiving the Spirit of God. The **holy one** probably refers to Christ. True knowledge is the gift of the Spirit (cf. Is 11:2), and the function of the Spirit is to lead Christians to the truth (Jn 14:17, 26; 16:13).

l: Jn 14:15; 15:10. *m:* 4:20. *n:* Jn 14:23. *o:* 3:11; Dt 6:5; Mt 22:37–40. *p:* Jn 13:34 / Jn 1:5; Rom 13:12. *q:* Jn 8:12. *r:* Eccl 2:14; Jn 11:10. *s:* 1 Cor 6:11. *t:* 1:1; Jn 1:1. *u:* Rom 8:7–8; Jas 4:4; 2 Pt 1:4. *v:* Is 40:8; Mt 7:21; 1 Cor 7:31; 1 Pt 4:2. *w:* 1 Tm 4:1. *x:* Jn 14:26.

from the holy one, and you all have knowledge. [21y]I write to you not because you do not know the truth but because you do, and because every lie is alien to the truth. [22z*]Who is the liar? Whoever denies that Jesus is the Christ. Whoever denies the Father and the Son, this is the antichrist. [23a]No one who denies the Son has the Father, but whoever confesses the Son has the Father as well.

Life from God's Anointing. [24b*]Let what you heard from the beginning remain in you. If what you heard from the beginning remains in you, then you will remain in the Son and in the Father. [25c]And this is the promise that he made us: eternal life. [26]I write you these things about those who would deceive you. [27]As for you, the anointing that you received from him remains in you, so that you do not need anyone to teach you. But his anointing teaches you about everything and is true and not false; just as it taught you, remain in him.

Children of God. [28*]And now, children, remain in him, so that when he appears we may have confidence and not be put to shame by him at his coming. [29]If you consider that he is righteous, you also know that everyone who acts in righteousness is begotten by him.

See RG 514–15

CHAPTER 3

[1d*]See what love the Father has bestowed on us that we may be called the children of God. Yet so we are. The reason the world does not know us is that it did not know him. [2e*]Beloved, we are God's children now; what we shall be has not yet been revealed. We do know that when it is revealed we shall be like him, for we shall see him as he is. [3f]Everyone who has this hope based on him makes himself pure, as he is pure.

Avoiding Sin. [4*]Everyone who commits sin commits lawlessness, for sin is lawlessness. [5g]You know that he was revealed to take away sins, and in him there is no sin. [6]No one who remains in him sins; no one who sins has seen him or known him. [7]Children, let no one deceive you. The person who acts in righteousness is righteous, just as he is righteous. [8h]Whoever sins belongs to the devil, because the devil has sinned from the beginning. Indeed, the Son of God was revealed to destroy the works of the devil. [9*]No one who is begotten by God commits sin, because God's seed remains in him; he cannot sin because he is begotten by God. [10]In this way, the children of God and the children of the devil are made plain; no one who fails to act in righteousness belongs to God, nor anyone who does not love his brother.

III. Love for One Another

[11i*]For this is the message you have heard from the beginning: we should love one another, [12j]unlike Cain who belonged to the evil one and slaughtered his brother. Why

2:22–23 Certain gnostics denied that the earthly Jesus was the Christ; to deny knowledge of the Son is to deny the Father, since only through the Son has God been fully revealed (Jn 1:18; 14:8–9).

2:24 Continuity with the apostolic witness as proclaimed in the prologue is the safeguard of right belief.

2:28–29 Our confidence at his judgment is based on the daily assurance of salvation. Our actions reflect our true relation to him.

3:1–3 The greatest sign of God's love is the gift of his Son (Jn 3:16) that has made Christians true children of God. This relationship is a present reality and also part of the life to come; true knowledge of God will ultimately be gained, and Christians prepare themselves now by virtuous lives in imitation of the Son.

3:2 When it is revealed: or "when he is revealed" (the subject of the verb could be Christ).

3:4 Lawlessness: a reference to the activity of the antichrist, so it is expressed as hostility toward God and a rejection of Christ. The author goes on to contrast the states of sin and righteousness. Christians do not escape sin but realize that when they sin they cease to have fellowship with God. Virtue and sin distinguish the children of God from the children of the devil.

3:9 A habitual sinner is a child of the devil, while a child of God, who by definition is in fellowship with God, cannot sin. **Seed**: Christ or the Spirit who shares the nature of God with the Christian.

3:11–18 Love, even to the point of self-sacrifice, is the point of the commandment. The story of Cain and Abel (1 Jn 3:12–15; Gn 4:1–16) presents the rivalry of two brothers, in a contrast of evil and righteousness, where envy led to murder. For Christians, proof of deliverance is love toward others, after the example of Christ. This includes concrete acts of charity, out of our material abundance.

y: 3:19; 2 Pt 1:12. *z:* 2 Thes 2:4. *a:* Jn 14:7–9. *b:* Jn 14:23. *c:* Jn 5:24; 10:28; 17:2. *d:* Jn 1:12; Eph 1:5 / Jn 15:21; 17:25. *e:* Phil 3:21. *f:* 2:6. *g:* Is 53:9; Jn 1:29; 8:46; 1 Pt 2:22. *h:* Jn 8:44; 12:31–32. *i:* 2:7; Jn 13:34; 15:12, 17. *j:* Gn 4:8; Jude 11.

did he slaughter him? Because his own works were evil, and those of his brother righteous. [13k]Do not be amazed, [then,] brothers, if the world hates you. [14l]We know that we have passed from death to life because we love our brothers. Whoever does not love remains in death. [15m]Everyone who hates his brother is a murderer, and you know that no murderer has eternal life remaining in him. [16n]The way we came to know love was that he laid down his life for us; so we ought to lay down our lives for our brothers. [17o]If someone who has worldly means sees a brother in need and refuses him compassion, how can the love of God remain in him? [18p]Children, let us love not in word or speech but in deed and truth.

Confidence before God. [19*][Now] this is how we shall know that we belong to the truth and reassure our hearts before him [20]in whatever our hearts condemn, for God is greater than our hearts and knows everything. [21]Beloved, if [our] hearts do not condemn us, we have confidence in God [22q]and receive from him whatever we ask, because we keep his commandments and do what pleases him. [23r]And his commandment is this: we should believe in the name of his Son, Jesus Christ, and love one another just as he commanded us. [24s]Those who keep his commandments remain in him, and he in them, and the way we know that he remains in us is from the Spirit that he gave us.

CHAPTER 4

See RG 515–16

Testing the Spirits. [1t*]Beloved, do not trust every spirit but test the spirits to see whether they belong to God, because many false prophets have gone out into the world. [2u]This is how you can know the Spirit of God: every spirit that acknowledges Jesus Christ come in the flesh belongs to God, [3v*]and every spirit that does not acknowledge Jesus does not belong to God. This is the spirit of the antichrist that, as you heard, is to come, but in fact is already in the world. [4]You belong to God, children, and you have conquered them, for the one who is in you is greater than the one who is in the world. [5w]They belong to the world; accordingly, their teaching belongs to the world, and the world listens to them. [6x]We belong to God, and anyone who knows God listens to us, while anyone who does not belong to God refuses to hear us. This is how we know the spirit of truth and the spirit of deceit.

God's Love and Christian Life. [7*]Beloved, let us love one another, because love is of God; everyone who loves is begotten by God and knows God. [8]Whoever is without love does not know God, for God is love. [9y]In this way the love of God was revealed to us: God sent his only Son into the world so that we might have life through him. [10z]In this is love: not that we have loved God, but that he loved us and sent his Son as expiation for our sins. [11]Beloved, if God so loved us, we also must love one another. [12a]No one has ever

3:19–24 Living a life of faith in Jesus and of Christian love assures us of abiding in God no matter what our feelings may at times tell us. Our obedience gives us confidence in prayer and trust in God's judgment. This obedience includes our belief in Christ and love for one another.

3:19b–20 This difficult passage may also be translated "we shall be at peace before him in whatever our hearts condemn, for . . ." or "and before God we shall convince our hearts, if our hearts condemn us, that God is greater than our hearts."

4:1–6 Deception is possible in spiritual phenomena and may be tested by its relation to Christian doctrine (cf. 1 Cor 12:3): those who fail to acknowledge Jesus Christ in the flesh are false prophets and belong to the antichrist. Even though these false prophets are well received in the world, the Christian who belongs to God has a greater power in the truth.

4:3 Does not acknowledge Jesus: some ancient manuscripts add "Christ" and/or "to have come in the flesh" (cf. 1 Jn 4:2), and others read "every spirit that annuls (or severs) Jesus."

4:7–12 Love as we share in it testifies to the nature of God and to his presence in our lives. One who loves shows that one is a child of God and knows God, for God's very being is love; one without love is without God. The revelation of the nature of God's love is found in the free gift of his Son to us, so that we may share life with God and be delivered from our sins. The love we have for one another must be of the same sort: authentic, merciful; this unique Christian love is our proof that we know God and can "see" the invisible God.

k: Mt 24:9; Jn 15:18; 17:14. *l:* Lv 19:17; Jn 5:24. *m:* Jn 8:44. *n:* Mt 20:28; Jn 10:11; 15:13. *o:* Dt 15:7, 11; Jas 2:15–16. *p:* Jas 1:22. *q:* 5:15; Mt 7:7–11; 21:22; Jn 14:13–14. *r:* Jn 13:34; 15:17. *s:* 4:13; Jn 14:21–23. *t:* 2:18; Mt 24:24. *u:* 1 Cor 12:3; 1 Thes 5:21. *v:* 3:22. *w:* Jn 15:19. *x:* Jn 8:47; 10:16. *y:* Jn 3:16. *z:* Rom 5:8. *a:* Jn 1:18; 1 Tm 6:16.

seen God. Yet, if we love one another, God remains in us, and his love is brought to perfection in us.

[13*]This is how we know that we remain in him and he in us, that he has given us of his Spirit. [14]Moreover, we have seen and testify that the Father sent his Son as savior of the world. [15]Whoever acknowledges that Jesus is the Son of God, God remains in him and he in God. [16]We have come to know and to believe in the love God has for us.

God is love, and whoever remains in love remains in God and God in him. [17b]In this is love brought to perfection among us, that we have confidence on the day of judgment because as he is, so are we in this world. [18]There is no fear in love, but perfect love drives out fear because fear has to do with punishment, and so one who fears is not yet perfect in love. [19]We love because he first loved us. [20c*]If anyone says, "I love God," but hates his brother, he is a liar; for whoever does not love a brother whom he has seen cannot love God whom he has not seen. [21d]This is the commandment we have from him: whoever loves God must also love his brother.

CHAPTER 5

See RG 515-16

Faith is Victory over the World. [1e*]Everyone who believes that Jesus is the Christ is begotten by God, and everyone who loves the father loves [also] the one begotten by him. [2]In this way we know that we love the children of God when we love God and obey his commandments. [3f]For the love of God is this, that we keep his commandments. And his commandments are not burdensome, [4g]for whoever is begotten by God conquers the world. And the victory that conquers the world is our faith. [5h]Who [indeed] is the victor over the world but the one who believes that Jesus is the Son of God?

[6i*]This is the one who came through water and blood, Jesus Christ, not by water alone, but by water and blood. The Spirit is the one that testifies, and the Spirit is truth. [7]So there are three that testify, [8j]the Spirit, the water, and the blood, and the three are of one accord. [9k]If we accept human testimony, the testimony of God is surely greater. Now the testimony of God is this, that he has testified on behalf of his Son. [10l]Whoever believes in the Son of God has this testimony within himself. Whoever does not believe God has made him a liar by not believing the testimony God has given about his Son. [11m]And this is the testimony: God gave us eternal life, and this life is in his Son. [12]Whoever possesses the Son has life; whoever does not possess the Son of God does not have life.

IV. Epilogue

Prayer for Sinners. [13n*]I write these things to you so that you may know that you have

4:13–21 The testimony of the Spirit and that of faith join the testimony of love to confirm our knowledge of God. Our love is grounded in the confession of Jesus as the Son of God and the example of God's love for us. Christian life is founded on the knowledge of God as love and on his continuing presence that relieves us from fear of judgment (1 Jn 4:16–18). What Christ is gives us confidence, even as we live and love in this world. Yet Christian love is not abstract but lived in the concrete manner of love for one another.

4:20 Cannot love God: some ancient manuscripts read "how can he love . . . ?"

5:1–5 Children of God are identified not only by their love for others (1 Jn 4:7–9) and for God (1 Jn 5:1–2) but by their belief in the divine sonship of Jesus Christ. Faith, the acceptance of Jesus in his true character and the obedience in love to God's commands (1 Jn 5:3), is the source of the Christian's power in the world and conquers the world of evil (1 Jn 5:4–5), even as Christ overcame the world (Jn 16:33).

5:6–12 Water and blood (1 Jn 5:6) refers to Christ's baptism (Mt 3:16–17) and to the shedding of his blood on the cross (Jn 19:34). **The Spirit** was present at the baptism (Mt 3:16; Mk 1:10; Lk 3:22; Jn 1:32, 34). **The testimony** to Christ as the Son of God is confirmed by divine witness (1 Jn 5:7–9), greater by far than the two legally required human witnesses (Dt 17:6). To deny this is to deny God's truth; cf. Jn 8:17–18. The gist of the divine witness or **testimony** is that **eternal life** (1 Jn 5:11–12) is given in Christ and nowhere else. To **possess the Son** is not acceptance of a doctrine but of a person who lives now and provides life.

5:13–21 As children of God we have confidence in prayer because of our intimate relationship with him (1 Jn 5:14–15). In love, we pray (1 Jn 5:16–17) for those who are in **sin**, but not in **deadly sin** (literally, "sin unto death"), probably referring to apostasy or activities brought on under the antichrist; cf. Mk 3:29; Heb 6:4–6; 10:26–31. Even in the latter case, however, prayer, while not enjoined, is not forbidden. The letter concludes with a summary of the themes of the letter (1 Jn 5:18–20). There is a sharp antithesis between the children of God and those belonging to the world and to the evil one. The

b: 2:28. *c:* 2:4. *d:* Jn 13:34; 14:15, 21; 15:17. *e:* Jn 8:42; 1 Pt 1:23. *f:* Jn 14:15. *g:* Jn 16:33. *h:* 1 Cor 15:57. *i:* Jn 15:26; 19:34. *j:* Jn 5:32, 36; 15:26. *k:* Jn 5:32, 37. *l:* Jn 3:33. *m:* 1:2; Jn 1:4; 5:21, 26; 17:3. *n:* Jn 1:12; 20:31.

eternal life, you who believe in the name of
the Son of God. [14][o]And we have this confidence in him, that if we ask anything according to his will, he hears us. [15]And if we
know that he hears us in regard to whatever
we ask, we know that what we have asked
him for is ours. [16][p]If anyone sees his brother
sinning, if the sin is not deadly, he should
pray to God and he will give him life. This is
only for those whose sin is not deadly. There
is such a thing as deadly sin, about which I
do not say that you should pray. [17]All
wrongdoing is sin, but there is sin that is not
deadly.

[18]We know that no one begotten by God
sins; but the one begotten by God he protects,
and the evil one cannot touch him. [19]We know
that we belong to God, and the whole world is
under the power of the evil one. [20][q]We also
know that the Son of God has come and has
given us discernment to know the one who is
true. And we are in the one who is true, in his
Son Jesus Christ. He is the true God and eternal
life. [21]Children, be on your guard against idols.

Son reveals the God of truth; Christians dwell in the true God, **in his Son**, and have eternal life. The final verse (1 Jn 5:21) voices a perennial warning about **idols**, any type of rival to God.

o: 3:21–22; Mt 7:7; Jn 14:13–14. *p:* Mt 12:31. *q:* Jer 24:7; Jn 17:3; Eph 1:17.

See RG 516–17

The Second Letter of John

Written in response to similar problems, the Second and Third Letters of John are of the same length, perhaps determined by the practical consideration of the writing space on one piece of papyrus. In each letter the writer calls himself "the Presbyter," and their common authorship is further evidenced by internal similarities in style and wording, especially in the introductions and conclusions. The literary considerations that link 2 John and 3 John also link them with the First Letter and the Gospel of John. The concern with "truth," christology, mutual love, the new commandment, antichrist, and the integrity of witness to the earthly Jesus mark these works as products of the Johannine school. The identity of the Presbyter is problematic. The use of the title implies more than age, and refers to his position of leadership in the early church. The absence of a proper name indicates that he was well known and acknowledged in authority by the communities to which he writes. Although traditionally attributed to John the apostle, these letters were probably written by a disciple or scribe of an apostle. The traditional place and date of composition, Ephesus at the end of the first century, are plausible for both letters.

The Second Letter is addressed to "the chosen Lady" and "to her children." This literary image of a particular Christian community reflects the specific destination and purpose of the letter. Unlike 1 John, this brief letter is not a theological treatise but a reply to problems within the church. The Johannine themes of love and truth are used to support practical advice on Christian living. The Presbyter encourages community members to show their Christianity by adhering to the great commandment of mutual love and to the historical truth about Jesus. The false teaching present among them is a spiritualizing christology that may tempt some members to discount teachings about the incarnation and death of Jesus the Christ; cf. 1 Jn 4:2. For their protection the Presbyter forbids hospitality toward unknown or "progressive" Christians to prevent their infiltration of the community. The Second Letter preserves the Johannine concerns of doctrinal purity and active love in the form of pastoral advice to a threatened community.

See RG 516–17

[1][a]*The Presbyter to the chosen Lady
and to her children whom I love in

1 The chosen Lady: literally, "elected"; this could also be translated "Kyria (a woman's name) chosen (by God)" or "the lady Electa" or "Electa Kyria." The adjective "chosen" is applied to all Christians at the beginning of other New Testament letters (1 Pt 1:1; Ti 1:1). The description is of a specific community with "children" who are its members. **The truth**: the affirmation of Jesus in the flesh and in contrast to false teaching (1 Jn 1:7).

a: Jn 8:32; 3 Jn 1.

truth—and not only I but also all who know the truth— [2]because of the truth that dwells in us and will be with us forever. [3*]Grace, mercy, and peace will be with us from God the Father and from Jesus Christ the Father's Son in truth and love.

[4b*]I rejoiced greatly to find some of your children walking in the truth just as we were commanded by the Father. [5c]But now, Lady, I ask you, not as though I were writing a new commandment but the one we have had from the beginning: let us love one another. [6d*]For this is love, that we walk according to his commandments; this is the commandment, as you heard from the beginning, in which you should walk.

[7e*]Many deceivers have gone out into the world, those who do not acknowledge Jesus Christ as coming in the flesh; such is the deceitful one and the antichrist. [8*]Look to yourselves that you do not lose what we worked for but may receive a full recompense. [9f*]Anyone who is so "progressive" as not to remain in the teaching of the Christ does not have God; whoever remains in the teaching has the Father and the Son. [10g*]If anyone comes to you and does not bring this doctrine, do not receive him in your house or even greet him; [11]for whoever greets him shares in his evil works.

[12h*]Although I have much to write to you, I do not intend to use paper and ink. Instead, I hope to visit you and to speak face to face so that our joy may be complete. [13*]The children of your chosen sister send you greetings.

3 Grace, mercy, and peace: like 1 Timothy; 2 Timothy this letter adds mercy to the terms used frequently in a salutation to describe Christian blessing; it appears only here in the Johannine writings. The author also puts the blessing in relation to **truth** and **love**, the watchwords of the Johannine teaching. **The Father's Son**: the title that affirms the close relationship of Christ to God; similar variations of this title occur elsewhere (Jn 1:14; 3:35), but the precise wording is not found elsewhere in the New Testament.

4 Some of your children: this refers to those whom the Presbyter has recently encountered, but it may also indicate the presence of false doctrine in the community: the Presbyter encourages those who have remained faithful. **Walking in the truth**: an expression used in the Johannine writings to describe a way of living in which the Christian faith is visibly expressed; cf. 1 Jn 1:6–7; 2:6, 11; 3 Jn 3.

6 His commandments: cf. 1 Jn 3:23; 2:7–8; 4:21; obedience to the commandment of faith and love includes all others.

7 The antichrist: see 1 Jn 2:18–19, 22; 4:3.

8 You (plural): it is not certain whether this means the Christians addressed or includes the Presbyter, since some of the ancient Greek manuscripts and Greek Fathers have "we."

9 Anyone who is so "progressive": literally, "Anyone who goes ahead." Some gnostic groups held the doctrine of the Christ come in the flesh to be a first step in belief, which the more advanced and spiritual believer surpassed and abandoned in his knowledge of the spiritual Christ. The author affirms that fellowship with God may be gained only by holding to the complete doctrine of Jesus Christ (1 Jn 2:22–23; 4:2; 5:5–6).

10–11 At this time false teachers were considered so dangerous and divisive as to be shunned completely. From this description they seem to be wandering preachers. We see here a natural suspicion of early Christians concerning such itinerants and can envisage the problems faced by missionaries such as those mentioned in 3 Jn 10.

12 Our joy: a number of other Greek manuscripts read "your joy."

13 Chosen sister: the community of which the Presbyter is now a part greets you (singular), the community of the Lady addressed.

b: 3 Jn 3. *c:* Jn 13:34; 15:12; 1 Jn 4:7. *d:* Jn 13:34; 14:15; 1 Jn 5:3. *e:* 1 Jn 2:22; 4:2. *f:* Jn 8:31; 1 Jn 2:23; 4:15. *g:* Rom 16:17; 2 Thes 3:6. *h:* Jn 15:11; 1 Jn 1:4; 3 Jn 13.

See RG 517–18

The Third Letter of John

The Third Letter of John preserves a brief glimpse into the problems of missionary activity and local autonomy in the early church. In contrast to the other two letters of John, this work was addressed to a specific individual, Gaius. This letter is less theological in content and purpose. The author's goal was to secure hospitality and material support for his missionaries, and the Presbyter is writing to another member of the church who has welcomed missionaries in the past. The Presbyter commends Gaius for his hospitality and encourages his future help. He indicates he may come to challenge the policy of Diotrephes that is based on evil gossip.

The problems of the Presbyter in this short letter provide us with valuable evidence of the flexible and personal nature of authority in the early church. The Presbyter writes to Gaius, whom perhaps he had converted or instructed, on the basis of their personal links. The brothers have also confirmed him as a loyal Christian in action and belief. Gaius accepted the missionaries from the Presbyter and presumably will accept Demetrius on the Presbyter's recommendation. In contrast, Diotrephes refuses to receive either letters or friends of the Presbyter. Although he is portrayed as ambitious and hostile, he perhaps exemplifies the cautious and sectarian nature of early Christianity; for its own protection the local community mistrusted missionaries as false teachers. Most interestingly, Diotrephes seems comfortable in ignoring the requests of the Presbyter. The Presbyter seems to acknowledge that only a personal confrontation with Diotrephes will remedy the situation (3 Jn 10). The division, however, may also rest on doctrinal disagreement in which Gaius and the other "friends" accept the teaching of the Presbyter, and Diotrephes does not; the missionaries are not received for suspicion of theological error. Diotrephes has thus been viewed by some as an overly ambitious local upstart trying to thwart the advance of orthodox Christianity, by others as an orthodox church official suspicious of the teachings of the Presbyter and those in the Johannine school who think as he does, or by still others as a local leader anxious to keep the debates in the Johannine community out of his own congregation.

This brief letter and the situation that it mirrors show us how little we know about some details of early development in the church: schools of opinion existed around which questions of faith and life were discussed, and personal ties as well as doctrine and authority played a role in what happened amid divisions and unity.

See RG 517–18

[1a*]The Presbyter to the beloved Gaius
whom I love in truth.

[2]Beloved, I hope you are prospering in
every respect and are in good health, just as
your soul is prospering. [3b*]I rejoiced
greatly when some of the brothers came
and testified to how truly you walk in the
truth. [4c]Nothing gives me greater joy than
to hear that my children are walking in the
truth.

[5d*]Beloved, you are faithful in all you do
for the brothers, especially for strangers;
[6e*]they have testified to your love before the
church. Please help them in a way worthy of
God to continue their journey. [7*]For they
have set out for the sake of the Name and
are accepting nothing from the pagans.
[8]Therefore, we ought to support such persons,
so that we may be co-workers in the
truth.

[9*]I wrote to the church, but Diotrephes,
who loves to dominate, does not acknowledge
us. [10*]Therefore, if I come, I will draw
attention to what he is doing, spreading evil
nonsense about us. And not content with
that, he will not receive the brothers, hindering
those who wish to do so and expelling
them from the church.

[11f*]Beloved, do not imitate evil but imitate
good. Whoever does what is good is of
God; whoever does what is evil has never
seen God. [12g*]Demetrius receives a good report
from all, even from the truth itself. We
give our testimonial as well, and you know
our testimony is true.

1 Beloved Gaius: a frequent form of address for fellow Christians in New Testament epistolary literature.

3 The brothers: in this letter, the term may refer to Christians who have been missionaries and received hospitality from Gaius (3 Jn 5–6). **Walk in the truth**: the common Johannine term to describe Christian living; this description presents Gaius as following the teachings of the Presbyter in contrast to Diotrephes.

5 You are faithful in all you do: Gaius's aid to the missionaries is a manifestation of his true Christian faith.

6 Help them . . . to continue their journey: the Presbyter asks Gaius not only to continue to welcome the missionaries to his community but also to equip them for further travels.

7 The Name: of Jesus Christ (cf. Acts 5:41; 1 Jn 2:12; 3:23; 5:13). **Accepting nothing**: not expecting support from the pagans to whom they preach the gospel, so that they will not be considered as beggars; they required support from other Christians; cf. Paul's complaints to the Corinthians (1 Cor 9:3–12).

9 Who loves to dominate: the Presbyter does not deny Diotrephes' place as leader but indicates that his ambition may have caused him to disregard his letter and his influence.

10 If I come: the Presbyter may visit the community to challenge the actions of Diotrephes toward himself and the missionaries. **Will not receive the brothers**: Diotrephes may have been critical of the teachings of the Presbyter and sought to maintain doctrinal purity; cf. 1 Jn 2:19 and 2 Jn 10–11.

11 Do not imitate evil: Gaius should not be influenced by the behavior of Diotrephes.

12 Demetrius: because of the fear of false teachers,

a: 2 Jn 1. *b:* 5; Gal 6:10; 2 Jn 4. *c:* 1 Thes 2:11–12; 1 Tm 1:2; 2 Tm 1:2; 1 Jn 2:1; 2 Jn 4. *d:* Rom 12:13; Gal 6:10; Heb 13:2. *e:* Acts 15:3; Col 1:10; 1 Thes 2:12. *f:* 1 Jn 2:29; 3:6, 10. *g:* Jn 19:35; 21:24; 1 Tm 3:7.

[13][h]I have much to write to you, but I do
not wish to write with pen and ink. [14]Instead,
I hope to see you soon, when we can talk
face to face. [15][i]*Peace be with you. The
friends greet you; greet the friends there
each by name.

Demetrius, perhaps the bearer of the letter, is provided with a recommendation from the Presbyter; cf. 2 Cor 3:1; Rom 16:1. **Even from the truth itself**: this refers probably to the manner of Demetrius's life that testifies to his true belief; cf. Gaius above (3 Jn 3).

15 Friends: although a Johannine term for Christians (Jn 15:15), the word here may refer to those in the community loyal to the Presbyter and to Gaius.

h: 2 Jn 12. *i:* Jn 20:19, 21, 26; Eph 6:23; 1 Pt 5:14.

See RG 519–20

The Letter of Jude

This letter is by its address attributed to "Jude, a slave of Jesus Christ and brother of James" (Jude 1). Since he is not identified as an apostle, this designation can hardly be meant to refer to the Jude or Judas who is listed as one of the Twelve (Lk 6:16; Acts 1:13; cf. Jn 14:22). The person intended is almost certainly the other Jude, named in the gospels among the relatives of Jesus (Mt 13:55; Mk 6:3), and the James who is listed there as his brother is the one to whom the Letter of James is attributed (see the Introduction to James). Nothing else is known of this Jude, and the apparent need to identify him by reference to his better-known brother indicates that he was a rather obscure personage in the early church.

The letter is addressed in the most general terms to "those who are called, beloved in God the Father and kept safe for Jesus Christ" (Jude 1), hence apparently to all Christians. But since its purpose is to warn the addressees against false teachers, the author must have had in mind one or more specific Christian communities located in the unidentified region where the errors in question constituted a danger. While the letter contains some Semitic features, there is nothing to identify the addressees specifically as Jewish Christians; indeed, the errors envisaged seem to reflect an early form of gnosticism, opposed to law, that points rather to the cultural context of the Gentile world. Like James and 2 Peter, the Letter of Jude manifests none of the typical features of the letter form except the address.

There is so much similarity between Jude and 2 Peter, especially Jude 4–16 and 2 Pt 2:1–18, that there must be a literary relationship between them. Since there is no evidence for the view that both authors borrowed from the same source, it is usually supposed that one of them borrowed from the other. Most scholars believe that Jude is the earlier of the two, principally because he quotes two apocryphal Jewish works, the Assumption of Moses (Jude 9) and the Book of Enoch (Jude 14–15) as part of his structured argument, whereas 2 Peter omits both references. Since there was controversy in the early church about the propriety of citing noncanonical literature that included legendary material, it is more probable that a later writer would omit such references than that he would add them.

Many interpreters today consider Jude a pseudonymous work dating from the end of the first century or even later. In support of this view they adduce the following arguments: (a) the apostles are referred to as belonging to an age that has receded into the past (Jude 17–18); (b) faith is understood as a body of doctrine handed down by a process of tradition (Jude 3); (c) the author's competent Greek style shows that he must have had a Hellenistic cultural formation; (d) the gnostic character of the errors envisaged fits better into the early second century than into a period several decades earlier. While impressive, these arguments are not entirely compelling and do not completely rule out the possibility of composition around the year A.D. 80, when the historical Jude may still have been alive.

This little letter is an urgent note by an author who intended to write more fully about salvation to an unknown group of readers, but who was forced by dangers from false teachers worming their way into the community (Jude 3–4) to dash off a warning against them (Jude 5–16) and to deliver some pressing Christian admonitions (Jude 17–23). The letter is justly famous for its majestic closing doxology (24–25).

See RG 519-20

Address and Greeting. [1a*]Jude, a slave of Jesus Christ and brother of James, to those who are called, beloved in God the Father and kept safe for Jesus Christ: [2b]may mercy, peace, and love be yours in abundance.

Occasion for Writing. [3c*]Beloved, although I was making every effort to write to you about our common salvation, I now feel a need to write to encourage you to contend for the faith that was once for all handed down to the holy ones. [4d]For there have been some intruders, who long ago were designated for this condemnation, godless persons, who pervert the grace of our God into licentiousness and who deny our only Master and Lord, Jesus Christ.

The False Teachers. [5e*]I wish to remind you, although you know all things, that [the] Lord who once saved a people from the land of Egypt later destroyed those who did not believe. [6f*]The angels too, who did not keep to their own domain but deserted their proper dwelling, he has kept in eternal chains, in gloom, for the judgment of the great day. [7g*]Likewise, Sodom, Gomorrah, and the surrounding towns, which, in the same manner as they, indulged in sexual promiscuity and practiced unnatural vice, serve as an example by undergoing a punishment of eternal fire.

[8*]Similarly, these dreamers nevertheless also defile the flesh, scorn lordship, and revile glorious beings. [9h*]Yet the archangel Michael, when he argued with the devil in a dispute over the body of Moses, did not venture to pronounce a reviling judgment upon him but said, "May the Lord rebuke you!" [10i]But these people revile what they do not understand and are destroyed by what they know by nature like irrational animals. [11j*]Woe to them! They followed the way of Cain, abandoned themselves to Balaam's error for the sake of gain, and perished in the rebellion of Korah. [12k*]These are blemishes on your love feasts, as they carouse fearlessly and look after themselves. They are

1 Jude . . . brother of James: for the identity of the author of this letter, see Introduction. **To those who are called**: the vocation to the Christian faith is God's free gift to those whom he loves and whom he safely protects in Christ until the Lord's second coming.

3–4 Our common salvation: the teachings of the Christian faith derived from the apostolic preaching and to be kept by the Christian community.

5 For this first example of divine punishment on those who had been saved but did not then keep faith, see Nm 14:28–29 and the note there. Some manuscripts have the word "once" (*hapax* as at Jude 3) after "you know"; some commentators have suggested that it means "knowing one thing" or "you know all things once for all." Instead of "[the] Lord" manuscripts vary, having "Jesus," "God," or no subject stated.

6 This second example draws on Gn 6:1–4 as elaborated in the apocryphal Book of Enoch (cf. Jude 14): heavenly beings came to earth and had sexual intercourse with women. God punished them by casting them out of heaven into darkness and bondage.

7 Practiced unnatural vice: literally, "went after alien flesh." This example derives from Gn 19:1–25, especially 4–11, when the townsmen of Sodom violated both hospitality and morality by demanding that Lot's two visitors (really messengers of Yahweh) be handed over to them so that they could abuse them sexually. **Unnatural vice**: this refers to the desire for intimacies by human beings with angels (the reverse of the example in Jude 6). Sodom (whence "sodomy") and Gomorrah became proverbial as object lessons for God's punishment on sin (Is 1:9; Jer 50:40; Am 4:11; Mt 10:15; 2 Pt 2:6).

8 Dreamers: the writer returns to the false teachers of Jude 4, applying charges from the three examples in Jude 5, 6, 7. This may apply to claims they make for revelations they have received by night (to the author, hallucinations). **Defile the flesh**: this may mean bodily pollutions from the erotic dreams of sexual license (Jude 7). **Lordship . . . glorious beings**: these may reflect the Lord (Jude 5; Jesus, Jude 4) whom they spurn and the angels (Jude 6; cf. note on 2 Pt 2:10, here, as there, literally, "glories").

9 The archangel Michael . . . judgment: a reference to an incident in the apocryphal Assumption of Moses. Dt 34:6 had said of Moses, literally in Greek, "they buried him" or "he (God?) buried him" (taken to mean "he was buried"). The later account tells how Michael, who was sent to bury him, was challenged by the devil's interest in the body. Our author draws out the point that if an archangel refrained from reviling even the devil, how wrong it is for mere human beings to revile glorious beings (angels).

11 Cain . . . Balaam . . . Korah: examples of rebellious men and of the punishment their conduct incurred; cf. Gn 4:8–16; Nm 16:1–35; 31:16. See note on 2 Pt 2:15.

12 Blemishes on your love feasts: or "hidden rocks" or "submerged reefs" (cf. Jude 13). The opponents engaged in scandalous conduct in connection with community gatherings called **love feasts** (agape meals), which were associated with eucharistic celebrations at certain stages of early Christian practice; cf. 1 Cor 11:18–34 and the note on 2 Pt 2:13.

a: Mt 13:55; Mk 6:3; Acts 12:17; Rom 1:7. *b:* Gal 6:16; 1 Tm 1:2; 2 Pt 1:2. *c:* 17, 20; 1 Tm 6:12. *d:* Gal 2:4; 2 Tm 3:6; 2 Pt 2:1. *e:* Nm 14:35; 1 Cor 10:5; Heb 3:16, 17. *f:* 2 Pt 2:4, 9. *g:* Dt 29:22–24; Mt 25:41; 2 Thes 1:8–9; 2 Pt 2:6; 3:7. *h:* Dn 10:21; 12:1. *i:* 2 Pt 2:12. *j:* Gn 4:8–16; 1 Jn 3:12 / Nm 31:15–16; 2 Pt 2:15; Rev 2:14 / Nm 16:19–35. *k:* 2 Pt 2:13, 17.

waterless clouds blown about by winds, fruitless trees in late autumn, twice dead and uprooted. [13]They are like wild waves of the sea, foaming up their shameless deeds, wandering stars for whom the gloom of darkness has been reserved forever.

[14l*]Enoch, of the seventh generation from Adam, prophesied also about them when he said, "Behold, the Lord has come with his countless holy ones [15]to execute judgment on all and to convict everyone for all the godless deeds that they committed and for all the harsh words godless sinners have uttered against him." [16m]These people are complainers, disgruntled ones who live by their desires; their mouths utter bombast as they fawn over people to gain advantage.

Exhortations. [17n]But you, beloved, remember the words spoken beforehand by the apostles of our Lord Jesus Christ, [18o*]for they told you, "In [the] last time there will be scoffers who will live according to their own godless desires." [19p]These are the ones who cause divisions; they live on the natural plane, devoid of the Spirit. [20q]But you, beloved, build yourselves up in your most holy faith; pray in the holy Spirit. [21r]Keep yourselves in the love of God and wait for the mercy of our Lord Jesus Christ that leads to eternal life. [22*]On those who waver, have mercy; [23*]save others by snatching them out of the fire; on others have mercy with fear, abhorring even the outer garment stained by the flesh.

Doxology. [24s*]To the one who is able to keep you from stumbling and to present you unblemished and exultant, in the presence of his glory, [25t]to the only God, our savior, through Jesus Christ our Lord be glory, majesty, power, and authority from ages past, now, and for ages to come. Amen.

14–15 Cited from the apocryphal Book of Enoch 1:9.

18 This is the substance of much early Christian preaching rather than a direct quotation of any of the various New Testament passages on this theme (see Mk 13:22; Acts 20:30; 1 Tm 4:1–3; 2 Pt 3:3).

22 Have mercy: some manuscripts read "convince," "confute," or "reprove." Others have "even though you waver" or "doubt" instead of **who waver**.

23 With fear: some manuscripts connect the phrase "with fear" with the imperative "save" or with the participle "snatching." Other manuscripts omit the phrase "on others have mercy," so that only two groups are envisioned. Rescue of those led astray and caution in the endeavor are both enjoined. **Outer garment stained by the flesh**: the imagery may come from Zec 3:3–5, just as that of **snatching . . . out of the fire** comes from Zec 3:2; the very garments of the godless are to be abhorred because of their contagion.

24–25 With this liturgical statement about the power of God to keep the faithful from stumbling, and praise to him through Jesus Christ, the letter reaches its conclusion by returning to the themes with which it began (Jude 1–2).

l: Mt 16:27; Heb 12:22–23. *m:* 18; 1 Cor 10:10; 2 Pt 2:10, 18. *n:* Heb 2:3; 2 Pt 3:2. *o:* 1 Tm 4:1; 2 Tm 3:1–5; 2 Pt 3:3. *p:* 1 Cor 2:14; Jas 3:15. *q:* 2; Eph 6:18; Col 2:7. *r:* Ti 2:13. *s:* 2 Cor 4:14; 1 Pt 4:13. *t:* Rom 11:36; 1 Tm 1:17.

See RG 520–25

The Revelation to John

The Apocalypse, or Revelation to John, the last book of the Bible, is one of the most difficult to understand because it abounds in unfamiliar and extravagant symbolism, which at best appears unusual to the modern reader. Symbolic language, however, is one of the chief characteristics of apocalyptic literature, of which this book is an outstanding example. Such literature enjoyed wide popularity in both Jewish and Christian circles from ca. 200 B.C. to A.D. 200.

This book contains an account of visions in symbolic and allegorical language borrowed extensively from the Old Testament, especially Ezekiel, Zechariah, and Daniel. Whether or not these visions were real experiences of the author or simply literary conventions employed by him is an open question.

This much, however, is certain: symbolic descriptions are not to be taken as literal descriptions, nor is the symbolism meant to be pictured realistically. One would find it difficult and repulsive to visualize a lamb with seven horns and seven eyes; yet Jesus Christ is described in precisely such words (Rev 5:6). The author used these images to suggest Christ's universal (seven) power (horns) and knowledge (eyes). A significant feature of apocalyptic writing is the use of symbolic colors, metals, garments (Rev 1:13–16; 3:18; 4:4; 6:1–8; 17:4; 19:8), and numbers (*four* signifies the world, *six* imperfection, *seven* totality or perfection, *twelve* Israel's tribes or the apostles, *one thousand* immensity). Finally the vindictive language in the book (Rev 6:9–10; 18:1–19:4) is also to be understood symbolically and not literally. The cries for vengeance on the lips of Christian martyrs that sound so harsh are in fact literary devices the author employed to evoke in the reader and hearer a feeling of horror for apostasy and rebellion that will be severely punished by God.

The lurid descriptions of the punishment of Jezebel (Rev 2:22) and of the destruction of the great harlot, Babylon (Rev 16:9–19:2), are likewise literary devices. The metaphor of Babylon as harlot would be wrongly construed if interpreted literally. On the other hand, the stylized figure of the woman clothed with the sun (Rev 12:1–6), depicting the New Israel, may seem to be a negative stereotype. It is necessary to look beyond the literal meaning to see that these images mean to convey a sense of God's wrath at sin in the former case and trust in God's providential care over the church in the latter.

The Book of Revelation cannot be adequately understood except against the historical background that occasioned its writing. Like Daniel and other apocalypses, it was composed as resistance literature to meet a crisis. The book itself suggests that the crisis was ruthless persecution of the early church by the Roman authorities; the harlot Babylon symbolizes pagan Rome, the city on seven hills (17:9). The book is, then, an exhortation and admonition to Christians of the first century to stand firm in the faith and to avoid compromise with paganism, despite the threat of adversity and martyrdom; they are to await patiently the fulfillment of God's mighty promises. The triumph of God in the world of men and women remains a mystery, to be accepted in faith and longed for in hope. It is a triumph that unfolded in the history of Jesus of Nazareth and continues to unfold in the history of the individual Christian who follows the way of the cross, even, if necessary, to a martyr's death.

Though the perspective is eschatological—ultimate salvation and victory are said to take place at the end of the present age when Christ will come in glory at the parousia—the book presents the decisive struggle of Christ and his followers against Satan and his cohorts as already over. Christ's overwhelming defeat of the kingdom of Satan ushered in the everlasting reign of God (Rev 11:15; 12:10). Even the forces of evil unwittingly carry out the divine plan (Rev 17:17), for God is the sovereign Lord of history.

The Book of Revelation had its origin in a time of crisis, but it remains valid and meaningful for Christians of all time. In the face of apparently insuperable evil, either from within or from without, all Christians are called to trust in Jesus' promise, "Behold, I am with you always, until the end of the age" (Mt 28:20). Those who remain steadfast in their faith and confidence in the risen Lord need have no fear. Suffering, persecution, even death by martyrdom, though remaining impenetrable mysteries of evil, do not comprise an absurd dead end. No matter what adversity or sacrifice Christians may endure, they will in the end triumph over Satan and his forces because of their fidelity to Christ the victor. This is the enduring message of the book; it is a message of hope and consolation and challenge for all who dare to believe.

The author of the book calls himself John (Rev 1:1, 4, 9; 22:8), who because of his Christian faith has been exiled to the rocky island of Patmos, a Roman penal colony. Although he never claims to be John the apostle, whose name is attached to the fourth gospel, he was so identified by several of the early church Fathers, including Justin, Irenaeus, Clement of Alexandria, Tertullian, Cyprian, and Hippolytus. This identification, however, was denied by other Fathers, including Denis of Alexandria, Eusebius of Caesarea, Cyril of Jerusalem, Gregory Nazianzen, and John Chrysostom. Indeed, vocabulary, grammar, and style make it doubtful that the book could have been put into its present form by the same person(s) responsible for the fourth gospel. Nevertheless, there are definite linguistic and theological affinities between the two books. The tone of the letters to the seven churches (Rev 1:4–3:22) is indicative of the great authority the author enjoyed over the Christian communities in Asia. It is possible, therefore, that he was a disciple of John the apostle, who is traditionally associated with that part of the world. The date of the book in its present form is probably near the end of the reign of Domitian (A.D. 81–96), a fierce persecutor of the Christians.

The principal divisions of the Book of Revelation are the following:

I. Prologue (1:1–3)

II. Letters to the Churches of Asia (1:4–3:22)
III. God and the Lamb in Heaven (4:1–5:14)
IV. The Seven Seals, Trumpets, and Plagues, with Interludes (6:1–16:21)
V. The Punishment of Babylon and the Destruction of Pagan Nations (17:1–20:15)
VI. The New Creation (21:1–22:5)
VII. Epilogue (22:6–21)

I. Prologue

CHAPTER 1

See RG 521–22

1a*The revelation of Jesus Christ,
which God gave to him, to show his servants
what must happen soon. He made it known
by sending his angel to his servant John,
2who gives witness to the word of God and
to the testimony of Jesus Christ by reporting
what he saw. 3b*Blessed is the one who reads
aloud and blessed are those who listen to this
prophetic message and heed what is written
in it, for the appointed time is near.

II. Letters to the Churches of Asia

Greeting. 4c*John, to the seven churches in
Asia: grace to you and peace from him who
is and who was and who is to come, and
from the seven spirits before his throne,
5d*and from Jesus Christ, the faithful witness,
the firstborn of the dead and ruler of
the kings of the earth. To him who loves us
and has freed us from our sins by his blood,
6ewho has made us into a kingdom, priests
for his God and Father, to him be glory and
power forever [and ever]. Amen.

7 fBehold, he is coming amid the clouds,
and every eye will see him,
even those who pierced him.
All the peoples of the earth will lament him.
Yes. Amen.

8g*"I am the Alpha and the Omega," says the
Lord God, "the one who is and who was and
who is to come, the almighty."

The First Vision. 9*I, John, your brother,
who share with you the distress, the kingdom,
and the endurance we have in Jesus,
found myself on the island called Patmos
because I proclaimed God's word and gave
testimony to Jesus. 10*I was caught up in
spirit on the Lord's day and heard behind me
a voice as loud as a trumpet, 11*which said,
"Write on a scroll what you see and send it
to the seven churches: to Ephesus, Smyrna,
Pergamum, Thyatira, Sardis, Philadelphia,

1:1–3 This prologue describes the source, contents, and audience of the book and forms an inclusion with the epilogue (Rev 22:6–21), with its similar themes and expressions.

1:3 Blessed is the one: this is the first of seven beatitudes in this book; the others are in Rev 14:13; 16:15; 19:9; 20:6; 22:7, 14. **This prophetic message**: literally, "the words of the prophecy"; so Rev 22:7, 10, 18, 19 by inclusion. **The appointed time**: when Jesus will return in glory; cf. Rev 1:7; 3:11; 22:7, 10, 12, 20.

1:4–8 Although Revelation begins and ends (Rev 22:21) with Christian epistolary formulae, there is nothing between Rev 4; 22 resembling a letter. The author here employs the standard word order for greetings in Greek letter writing: "N. to N., greetings . . ."; see note on Rom 1:1.

1:4 Seven churches in Asia: Asia refers to the Roman province of that name in western Asia Minor (modern Turkey); these representative churches are mentioned by name in Rev 1:11, and each is the recipient of a message (Rev 2:1–3:22). **Seven** is the biblical number suggesting fullness and completeness; thus the seer is writing for the whole church.

1:5 Freed us: the majority of Greek manuscripts and several early versions read "washed us"; but "freed us" is supported by the best manuscripts and fits well with Old Testament imagery, e.g., Is 40:2.

1:8 The Alpha and the Omega: the first and last letters of the Greek alphabet. In Rev 22:13 the same words occur together with the expressions "the First and the Last, the Beginning and the End"; cf. Rev 1:17; 2:8; 21:6; Is 41:4; 44:6.

1:9–20 In this first vision, the seer is commanded to write what he sees to the seven churches (Rev 1:9–11). He sees Christ in glory, whom he depicts in stock apocalyptic imagery (Rev 1:12–16), and hears him describe himself in terms meant to encourage Christians by emphasizing his victory over death (Rev 1:17–20).

1:9 Island called Patmos: one of the Sporades islands in the Aegean Sea, some fifty miles south of Ephesus, used by the Romans as a penal colony. **Because I proclaimed God's word**: literally, "on account of God's word."

1:10 The Lord's day: Sunday. **As loud as a trumpet**: the imagery is derived from the theophany at Sinai (Ex 19:16, 19; cf. Heb 12:19 and the trumpet in other eschatological settings in Is 27:13; Jl 2:1; Mt 24:31; 1 Cor 15:52; 1 Thes 4:16).

1:11 Scroll: a papyrus roll.

a: 22:6–8, 20; Dn 2:28 / 19:10. *b:* 22:7 / Lk 11:28. *c:* 8; 4:8; 11:17; 16:5; Ex 3:14. *d:* 3:14; 1 Cor 15:20; Col 1:18 / Heb 9:14; 1 Pt 1:19; 1 Jn 1:7. *e:* Ex 19:6; 1 Pt 2:9. *f:* Dn 7:13 / Zec 12:10; Mt 24:30; Jn 19:37. *g:* 17; 21:6; 22:13; Is 41:4; 44:6; 48:12.

and Laodicea." [12*]Then I turned to see whose voice it was that spoke to me, and when I turned, I saw seven gold lampstands [13h*]and in the midst of the lampstands one like a son of man, wearing an ankle-length robe, with a gold sash around his chest. [14*]The hair of his head was as white as white wool or as snow, and his eyes were like a fiery flame. [15*]His feet were like polished brass refined in a furnace, and his voice was like the sound of rushing water. [16i*]In his right hand he held seven stars. A sharp two-edged sword came out of his mouth, and his face shone like the sun at its brightest.

[17j*]When I caught sight of him, I fell down at his feet as though dead. He touched me with his right hand and said, "Do not be afraid. I am the first and the last, [18*]the one who lives. Once I was dead, but now I am alive forever and ever. I hold the keys to death and the netherworld. [19*]Write down, therefore, what you have seen, and what is happening, and what will happen afterwards. [20*]This is the secret meaning of the seven stars you saw in my right hand, and of the seven gold lampstands: the seven stars are the angels of the seven churches, and the seven lampstands are the seven churches.

CHAPTER 2

See RG 522

To Ephesus. [1*]"To the angel of the church in Ephesus, write this:

" 'The one who holds the seven stars in his right hand and walks in the midst of the seven gold lampstands says this: [2*]"I know your works, your labor, and your endurance, and that you cannot tolerate the wicked; you have tested those who call themselves apostles but are not, and discovered that they are impostors. [3]Moreover, you have endurance and have suffered for my name, and you have not grown weary. [4]Yet I hold this against you: you have lost the love you had at first. [5]Realize how far you have fallen. Repent, and do the works you did at first. Otherwise, I will come to you and remove

1:12–16 A symbolic description of Christ in glory. The metaphorical language is not to be understood literally; cf. Introduction.

1:13 Son of man: see note on Mk 8:31. **Ankle-length robe**: Christ is priest; cf. Ex 28:4; 29:5; Wis 18:24; Zec 3:4. **Gold sash**: Christ is king; cf. Ex 28:4; 1 Mc 10:89; 11:58; Dn 10:5.

1:14 Hair . . . as white as white wool or as snow: Christ is eternal, clothed with the dignity that belonged to the "Ancient of Days"; cf. Rev 1:18; Dn 7:9. **His eyes were like a fiery flame**: Christ is portrayed as all-knowing; cf. Rev 2:23; Ps 7:10; Jer 17:10; and similar expressions in Rev 2:18; 19:12; cf. Dn 10:6.

1:15 His feet . . . furnace: Christ is depicted as unchangeable; cf. Ez 1:27; Dn 10:6. The Greek word translated "refined" is unconnected grammatically with any other word in the sentence. **His voice . . . water**: Christ speaks with divine authority; cf. Ez 1:24.

1:16 Seven stars: in the pagan world, Mithras and the Caesars were represented with seven stars in their right hand, symbolizing their universal dominion. **A sharp two-edged sword**: this refers to the word of God (cf. Eph 6:17; Heb 4:12) that will destroy unrepentant sinners; cf. Rev 2:16; 19:15; Wis 18:15; Is 11:4; 49:2. **His face . . . brightest**: this symbolizes the divine majesty of Christ; cf. Rev 10:1; 21:23; Jgs 5:31; Is 60:19; Mt 17:2.

1:17 It was an Old Testament belief that for sinful human beings to see God was to die; cf. Ex 19:21; 33:20; Jgs 6:22–23; Is 6:5.

1:18 Netherworld: Greek Hades, Hebrew Sheol, the abode of the dead; cf. Rev 20:13–14; Nm 16:33.

1:19 What you have seen, and what is happening, and what will happen afterwards: the three parts of the Book of Revelation, the vision (Rev 1:10–20), the situation in the seven churches (Rev 2–3), and the events of Rev 6–22.

1:20 Secret meaning: literally, "mystery." **Angels**: these are the presiding spirits of the seven churches. Angels were thought to be in charge of the physical world (cf. Rev 7:1; 14:18; 16:5) and of nations (Dn 10:13; 12:1), communities (the seven churches), and individuals (Mt 18:10; Acts 12:15). Some have seen in the "angel" of each of the seven churches its pastor or a personification of the spirit of the congregation.

2:1–3:22 Each of the seven letters follows the same pattern: address; description of the exalted Christ; blame and/or praise for the church addressed; threat and/or admonition; final exhortation and promise to all Christians.

2:1–7 The letter to Ephesus praises the members of the church there for their works and virtues, including discerning false teachers (Rev 2:2–3), but admonishes them to repent and return to their former devotion (Rev 2:4–5). It concludes with a reference to the Nicolaitans (see note on Rev 2:6) and a promise that the victor will have access to eternal life (Rev 2:7).

2:1 Ephesus: this great ancient city had a population of ca. 250,000; it was the capital of the Roman province of Asia and the commercial, cultural, and religious center of Asia. The other six churches were located in the same province, situated roughly in a circle; they were selected for geographical reasons rather than for the size of their Christian communities. **Walks in the midst of the seven gold lampstands**: this signifies that Christ is always present in the church; see note on Rev 1:4.

2:2 Who call themselves . . . impostors: this refers to unauthorized and perverse missionaries; cf. Acts 20:29–30.

h: Dn 7:13; 10:5. *i:* Heb 4:12. *j:* Dn 8:18 / 1:8.

your lampstand from its place, unless you repent. [6*]But you have this in your favor: you hate the works of the Nicolaitans, which I also hate.

[7k*]" ' "Whoever has ears ought to hear what the Spirit says to the churches. To the victor I will give the right to eat from the tree of life that is in the garden of God." '

To Smyrna. [8*]"To the angel of the church in Smyrna, write this:

" 'The first and the last, who once died but came to life, says this: [9l*]"I know your tribulation and poverty, but you are rich. I know the slander of those who claim to be Jews and are not, but rather are members of the assembly of Satan. [10]Do not be afraid of anything that you are going to suffer. Indeed, the devil will throw some of you into prison, that you may be tested, and you will face an ordeal for ten days. Remain faithful until death, and I will give you the crown of life.

[11m*]" ' "Whoever has ears ought to hear what the Spirit says to the churches. The victor shall not be harmed by the second death." '

To Pergamum. [12*]"To the angel of the church in Pergamum, write this:

" 'The one with the sharp two-edged sword says this: [13*]"I know that you live where Satan's throne is, and yet you hold fast to my name and have not denied your faith in me, not even in the days of Antipas, my faithful witness, who was martyred among you, where Satan lives. [14n*]Yet I have a few things against you. You have some people there who hold to the teaching of Balaam, who instructed Balak to put a stumbling block before the Israelites: to eat food sacrificed to idols and to play the harlot. [15]Likewise, you also have some people who hold to the teaching of [the] Nicolaitans. [16]Therefore, repent. Otherwise, I will come to you quickly and wage war against them with the sword of my mouth.

[17o*]" ' "Whoever has ears ought to hear what the Spirit says to the churches. To the victor I shall give some of the hidden manna; I shall also give a white amulet upon which is inscribed a new name, which no one knows except the one who receives it." '

2:6 Nicolaitans: these are perhaps the impostors of Rev 2:2; see note on Rev 2:14–15. There is little evidence for connecting this group with Nicolaus, the proselyte from Antioch, mentioned in Acts 6:5.

2:7 Victor: referring to any Christian individual who holds fast to the faith and does God's will in the face of persecution. **The tree of life that is in the garden of God**: this is a reference to the tree in the primeval paradise (Gn 2:9); cf. Rev 22:2, 14, 19. The decree excluding humanity from the tree of life has been revoked by Christ.

2:8–11 The letter to Smyrna encourages the Christians in this important commercial center by telling them that although they are impoverished, they are nevertheless rich, and calls those Jews who are slandering them members of the assembly of Satan (Rev 2:9). There is no admonition; rather, the Christians are told that they will suffer much, even death, but the time of tribulation will be short compared to their eternal reward (Rev 2:10), and they will thus escape final damnation (Rev 2:11).

2:8 Smyrna: modern Izmir, ca. thirty miles north of Ephesus, and the chief city of Lydia, with a temple to the goddess Roma. It was renowned for its loyalty to Rome, and it also had a large Jewish community very hostile toward Christians.

2:9–10 The church in Smyrna was materially poor but spiritually rich. Accusations made by Jewish brethren there occasioned the persecution of Christians; cf. Acts 14:2, 19; 17:5, 13.

2:11 The second death: this refers to the eternal death, when sinners will receive their final punishment; cf. Rev 20:6, 14–15; 21:8.

2:12–17 The letter to Pergamum praises the members of the church for persevering in their faith in Christ even in the midst of a pagan setting and in face of persecution and martyrdom (Rev 2:13). But it admonishes them about members who advocate an unprincipled morality (Rev 2:14; cf. 2 Pt 2:15; Jude 11) and others who follow the teaching of the Nicolaitans (Rev 2:15; see note there). It urges them to repent (Rev 2:16) and promises them the hidden manna and Christ's amulet (Rev 2:17).

2:12 Pergamum: modern Bergama, ca. forty-five miles northeast of Smyrna, a center for various kinds of pagan worship. It also had an outstanding library (the word **parchment** is derived from its name).

2:13 Satan's throne: the reference is to emperor worship and other pagan practices that flourished in Pergamum, perhaps specifically to the white marble altar erected and dedicated to Zeus by Eumenes II (197–160 B.C.).

2:14–15 Like Balaam, the biblical prototype of the religious compromiser (cf. Nm 25:1–3; 31:16; 2 Pt 2:15; Jude 11), the Nicolaitans in Pergamum and Ephesus (Rev 2:6) accommodated their Christian faith to paganism. They abused the principle of liberty enunciated by Paul (1 Cor 9:19–23).

2:17 The hidden manna: this is the food of life; cf. Ps 78:24–25. **White amulet**: literally, "white stone," on which was written a magical name, whose power could be tapped by one who knew the secret name. It is used here as a symbol of victory and joy; cf. Rev 3:4–5. **New name**: this is a reference to the Christian's rebirth in Christ; cf. Rev 3:12; 19:12; Is 62:2; 65:15.

k: 11, 17, 29; 3:6, 13, 22; 13:9; Mt 11:15. *l:* Jas 2:5. *m:* 20:6, 14; 21:8. *n:* Nm 22–24; 25:1–3; 31:16; 2 Pt 2:15; Jude 11. *o:* Is 62:2; 65:15.

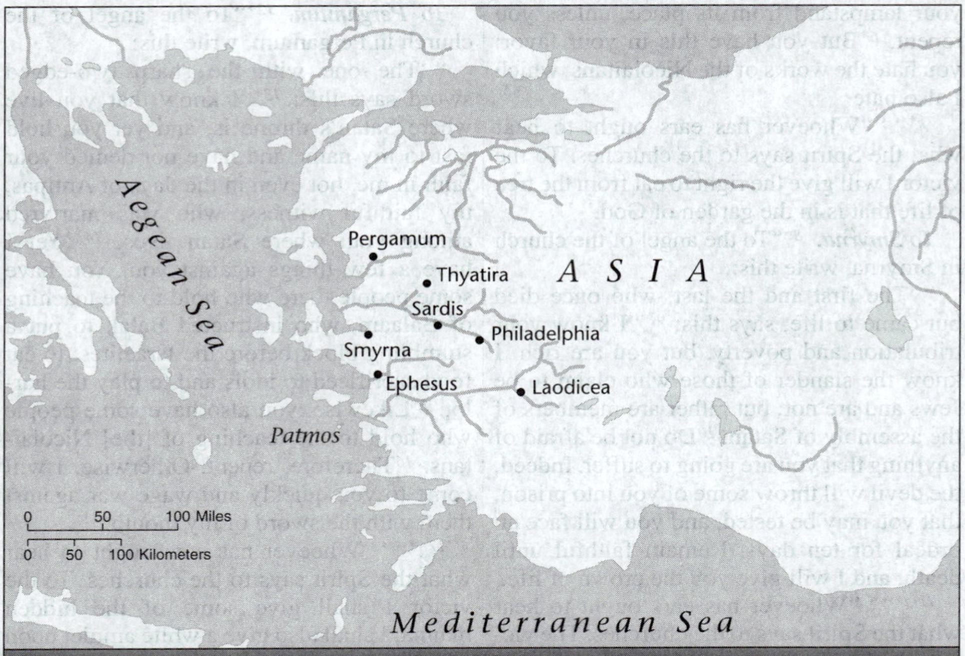

The Seven Churches

To Thyatira. [18]*"To the angel of the church in Thyatira, write this:

" 'The Son of God, whose eyes are like a fiery flame and whose feet are like polished brass, says this: [19]"I know your works, your love, faith, service, and endurance, and that your last works are greater than the first. [20]*Yet I hold this against you, that you tolerate the woman Jezebel, who calls herself a prophetess, who teaches and misleads my servants to play the harlot and to eat food sacrificed to idols. [21]I have given her time to repent, but she refuses to repent of her harlotry. [22]So I will cast her on a sickbed and plunge those who commit adultery with her into intense suffering unless they repent of her works. [23][p]*I will also put her children to death. Thus shall all the churches come to know that I am the searcher of hearts and minds and that I will give each of you what your works deserve. [24]*But I say to the rest of you in Thyatira, who do not uphold this teaching and know nothing of the so-called deep secrets of Satan: on you I will place no further burden, [25]except that you must hold fast to what you have until I come.

[26][q]*" ' "To the victor, who keeps to my
ways until the end,

2:18–29 The letter to Thyatira praises the progress in virtue of this small Christian community (Rev 2:19) but admonishes them for tolerating a false prophet who leads them astray (Rev 2:20). Her fate is sealed, but there is hope of repentance for her followers (Rev 2:21–22). Otherwise, they too shall die (Rev 2:23). They are warned against Satanic power or knowledge (Rev 2:24–25). Those who remain faithful will share in the messianic reign, having authority over nations (Rev 2:26–27), and will in fact possess Christ himself (Rev 2:8).

2:18 Thyatira: modern Akhisar, ca. forty miles southeast of Pergamum, a frontier town famous for its workers' guilds (cf. Acts 16:14), membership in which may have involved festal meals in pagan temples.

2:20 The scheming and treacherous Jezebel of old (cf. 1 Kgs 19:1–2; 21:1–14; 2 Kgs 9:22, 30–34) introduced pagan customs into the religion of Israel; this new Jezebel was doing the same to Christianity.

2:23 Children: spiritual descendants.

2:24 The so-called deep secrets of Satan: literally, "the deep things of Satan," a scathing reference to the perverse teaching of the Nicolaitans (Rev 2:15).

2:26–28 The Christian who perseveres in faith will share in

p: 1 Sm 16:7; Jer 11:20; 17:10. *q:* 12:5; Ps 2:8–9.

I will give authority over the nations.
27 He will rule them with an iron rod.
Like clay vessels will they be
smashed,
28 just as I received authority from my Father.
And to him I will give the morning star.
29" ' "Whoever has ears ought to hear
what the Spirit says to the churches." '

CHAPTER 3

See RG 522

To Sardis. 1*"To the angel of the
church in Sardis, write this:
" 'The one who has the seven spirits of
God and the seven stars says this: "I know
your works, that you have the reputation of
being alive, but you are dead. 2 Be watchful
and strengthen what is left, which is going to
die, for I have not found your works complete
in the sight of my God. 3[r]Remember then
how you accepted and heard; keep it, and repent. If you are not watchful, I will come like
a thief, and you will never know at what hour
I will come upon you. 4[s]However, you have a
few people in Sardis who have not soiled their
garments; they will walk with me dressed in
white, because they are worthy.
5[t]*" ' "The victor will thus be dressed in
white, and I will never erase his name from the
book of life but will acknowledge his name in
the presence of my Father and of his angels.
6" ' "Whoever has ears ought to hear what
the Spirit says to the churches." '

To Philadelphia. 7[u]*"To the angel of the
church in Philadelphia, write this:

" 'The holy one, the true,
who holds the key of David,
who opens and no one shall close,
who closes and no one shall open,

says this:
8*" ' "I know your works (behold, I have
left an open door before you, which no one
can close). You have limited strength, and
yet you have kept my word and have not denied my name. 9[v]Behold, I will make those
of the assembly of Satan who claim to be
Jews and are not, but are lying, behold I will
make them come and fall prostrate at your
feet, and they will realize that I love you.
10*Because you have kept my message of
endurance, I will keep you safe in the time of
trial that is going to come to the whole world
to test the inhabitants of the earth. 11[w]I am
coming quickly. Hold fast to what you have,
so that no one may take your crown.
12[x]*" ' "The victor I will make into a pillar
in the temple of my God, and he will never

Christ's messianic authority (cf. Ps 2:8–9) and resurrection victory over death, symbolized by the morning star; cf. Rev 22:16.

2:26 Who keeps to my ways: literally, "who keeps my works."

3:1–6 The letter to Sardis does not praise the community but admonishes its members to watchfulness, mutual support, and repentance (Rev 3:2–3). The few who have remained pure and faithful will share Christ's victory and will be inscribed in the book of life (Rev 3:4–5).

3:1 Sardis: this city, located ca. thirty miles southeast of Thyatira, was once the capital of Lydia, known for its wealth at the time of Croesus (6th century B.C.). Its citadel, reputed to be unassailable, was captured by surprise, first by Cyrus and later by Antiochus. The church is therefore warned to be on guard.

3:5 In white: white is a sign of victory and joy as well as resurrection; see note on Rev 2:17. **The book of life**: the roll in which the names of the redeemed are kept; cf. Rev 13:8; 17:8; 20:12, 15; 21:27; Phil 4:3; Dn 12:1. They will be acknowledged by Christ in heaven; cf. Mt 10:32.

3:7–13 The letter to Philadelphia praises the Christians there for remaining faithful even with their limited strength (Rev 3:8). Members of the assembly of Satan are again singled out (Rev 3:9; see Rev 2:9). There is no admonition; rather, the letter promises that they will be kept safe at the great trial (Rev 3:10–11) and that the victors will become pillars of the heavenly temple, upon which three names will be inscribed: God, Jerusalem, and Christ (Rev 3:12).

3:7 Philadelphia: modern Alasehir, ca. thirty miles southeast of Sardis, founded by Attalus II Philadelphus of Pergamum to be an "open door" (Rev 3:8) for Greek culture; it was destroyed by an earthquake in A.D. 17. Rebuilt by money from the Emperor Tiberius, the city was renamed Neo-Caesarea; this may explain the allusions to "name" in Rev 3:12. **Key of David**: to the heavenly city of David (cf. Is 22:22), "the new Jerusalem" (Rev 3:12), over which Christ has supreme authority.

3:8 An open door: opportunities for sharing and proclaiming the faith; cf. Acts 14:27; 1 Cor 16:9; 2 Cor 2:12.

3:10 My message of endurance: this does not refer to a saying of Jesus about patience but to the example of Christ's patient endurance. **The inhabitants of the earth**: literally, "those who live on the earth." This expression, which also occurs in Rev 6:10; 8:13; 11:10; 13:8, 12, 14; 17:2, 8, always refers to the pagan world.

3:12 Pillar: this may be an allusion to the rebuilding of the city; see note on v 7. **New Jerusalem**: it is described in Rev 21:10–22:5.

r: Mt 24:42–44; Mk 13:33; 1 Thes 5:2; 2 Pt 3:10. *s:* 7:13–14. *t:* Ps 69:29; Dn 12:1 / Mt 10:32. *u:* Is 22:22; Mt 16:19. *v:* 2:9 / Is 45:14; 60:14. *w:* 2:25; 22:7, 20. *x:* 21:2–3; Ez 48:35 / 19:13.

leave it again. On him I will inscribe the name of my God and the name of the city of my God, the new Jerusalem, which comes down out of heaven from my God, as well as my new name.

[13]" ' "Whoever has ears ought to hear what the Spirit says to the churches." '

To Laodicea. [14y*]"To the angel of the church in Laodicea, write this:

" 'The Amen, the faithful and true witness, the source of God's creation, says this: [15*]"I know your works; I know that you are neither cold nor hot. I wish you were either cold or hot. [16*]So, because you are lukewarm, neither hot nor cold, I will spit you out of my mouth. [17z*]For you say, 'I am rich and affluent and have no need of anything,' and yet do not realize that you are wretched, pitiable, poor, blind, and naked. [18*]I advise you to buy from me gold refined by fire so that you may be rich, and white garments to put on so that your shameful nakedness may not be exposed, and buy ointment to smear on your eyes so that you may see. [19a]Those whom I love, I reprove and chastise. Be earnest, therefore, and repent.

[20*]" ' "Behold, I stand at the door and knock. If anyone hears my voice and opens the door, [then] I will enter his house and dine with him, and he with me. [21b]I will give the victor the right to sit with me on my throne, as I myself first won the victory and sit with my Father on his throne.

[22]" ' "Whoever has ears ought to hear what the Spirit says to the churches." ' "

III. God and the Lamb in Heaven

CHAPTER 4

See RG 522–23

Vision of Heavenly Worship. [1*]After this I had a vision of an open door to heaven, and I heard the trumpetlike voice that had spoken to me before, saying, "Come up here and I will show you what must happen afterwards." [2c*]At once I was caught up in spirit. A throne was there in heaven, and on the throne sat [3]one whose appearance sparkled like jasper and carnelian. Around the throne was a halo as brilliant as an emerald. [4d*]Surrounding the throne I saw twenty-four other thrones on which twenty-four elders sat, dressed in white garments and with gold crowns on their heads. [5*]From the throne came flashes of lightning,

3:14–22 The letter to Laodicea reprimands the community for being lukewarm (Rev 3:15–16), but no particular faults are singled out. Their material prosperity is contrasted with their spiritual poverty, the violet tunics that were the source of their wealth with the white robe of baptism, and their famous eye ointment with true spiritual perception (Rev 3:17–18). But Christ's chastisement is inspired by love and a desire to be allowed to share the messianic banquet with his followers in the heavenly kingdom (Rev 3:9–21).

3:14 Laodicea: ca. forty miles southeast of Philadelphia and ca. eighty miles east of Ephesus, a wealthy industrial and commercial center, with a renowned medical school. It exported fine woolen garments and was famous for its eye salves. It was so wealthy that it was proudly rebuilt without outside aid after the devastating earthquake of A.D. 60/61. **The Amen**: this is a divine title (cf. Hebrew text of Is 65:16) applied to Christ; cf. 2 Cor 1:20. **Source of God's creation**: literally, "the beginning of God's creation," a concept found also in Jn 1:3; Col 1:16–17; Heb 1:2; cf. Prv 8:22–31; Wis 9:1–2.

3:15–16 Halfhearted commitment to the faith is nauseating to Christ; cf. Rom 12:11.

3:16 Spit: literally, "vomit." The image is that of a beverage that should be either hot or cold. Perhaps there is an allusion to the hot springs of Hierapolis across the Lycus river from Laodicea, which would have been lukewarm by the time they reached Laodicea.

3:17 Economic prosperity occasioned spiritual bankruptcy.

3:18 Gold . . . fire: God's grace. **White garments**: symbol of an upright life; the city was noted for its violet/purple cloth. **Ointment . . . eyes**: to remove spiritual blindness; one of the city's exports was eye ointment (see note on Rev 3:14).

3:20 Christ invites all to the messianic banquet in heaven; cf. Is 25:6; Lk 14:15; 22:30.

4:1–11 The seer now describes a vision of the heavenly court in worship of God enthroned. He reverently avoids naming or describing God but pictures twenty-four elders in priestly and regal attire (Rev 4:4) and God's throne and its surroundings made of precious gems and other symbols that traditionally express the majesty of God (Rev 4:5–6). Universal creation is represented by the four living creatures (Rev 4:6–7). Along with the twenty-four elders, they praise God unceasingly in humble adoration (Rev 4:8–11).

4:1 The ancients viewed heaven as a solid vault, entered by way of actual doors.

4:2–8 Much of the imagery here is taken from Ez 1:10.

4:4 Twenty-four elders: these represent the twelve tribes of Israel and the twelve apostles; cf. Rev 21:12–14.

4:5 Flashes of lightning, rumblings, and peals of thunder: as in other descriptions of God's appearance or activity; cf. Rev 8:5; 11:19; 16:18; Ex 19:16; Ez 1:4, 13. **The seven spirits of God**: the seven "angels of the presence" as in Rev 8:2 and Tb 12:15.

y: 1:5. *z*: Prv 13:7; Lk 12:21. *a*: Prv 3:11–12; 1 Cor 11:32; Heb 12:5–11. *b*: Lk 22:28–30; Mt 19:28. *c*: Is 6:1 / Ez 1:26–28. *d*: Is 24:23.

rumblings, and peals of thunder. Seven flaming torches burned in front of the throne,
which are the seven spirits of God. [6e*]In front
of the throne was something that resembled a
sea of glass like crystal.

In the center and around the throne, there
were four living creatures covered with eyes
in front and in back. [7*]The first creature resembled a lion, the second was like a calf,
the third had a face like that of a human being, and the fourth looked like an eagle in
flight. [8f*]The four living creatures, each of
them with six wings, were covered with eyes
inside and out. Day and night they do not
stop exclaiming:

"Holy, holy, holy is the Lord God
almighty,
who was, and who is, and who is to
come."

[9]Whenever the living creatures give glory
and honor and thanks to the one who sits on
the throne, who lives forever and ever, [10]the
twenty-four elders fall down before the one
who sits on the throne and worship him, who
lives forever and ever. They throw down
their crowns before the throne, exclaiming:

[11 g]"Worthy are you, Lord our God,
to receive glory and honor and power,
for you created all things;
because of your will they came to be
and were created."

CHAPTER 5

See RG 522–23

The Scroll and the Lamb. [1h*]I saw a
scroll in the right hand of the one who sat on
the throne. It had writing on both sides and
was sealed with seven seals. [2]Then I saw a
mighty angel who proclaimed in a loud
voice, "Who is worthy to open the scroll and
break its seals?" [3]But no one in heaven or on
earth or under the earth was able to open the
scroll or to examine it. [4]I shed many tears
because no one was found worthy to open
the scroll or to examine it. [5i*]One of the elders said to me, "Do not weep. The lion of
the tribe of Judah, the root of David, has triumphed, enabling him to open the scroll
with its seven seals."

[6j*]Then I saw standing in the midst of the
throne and the four living creatures and the
elders a Lamb that seemed to have been
slain. He had seven horns and seven eyes;
these are the [seven] spirits of God sent out
into the whole world. [7]He came and received
the scroll from the right hand of the one who
sat on the throne. [8]When he took it, the four
living creatures and the twenty-four elders
fell down before the Lamb. Each of the elders held a harp and gold bowls filled with incense, which are the prayers of the holy
ones. [9]They sang a new hymn:

"Worthy are you to receive the scroll
and to break open its seals,

4:6 A sea of glass like crystal: an image adapted from Ez 1:22–26. **Four living creatures**: these are symbols taken from Ez 1:5–21; they are identified as cherubim in Ez 10:20. **Covered with eyes**: these suggest God's knowledge and concern.

4:7 Lion . . . calf . . . human being . . . eagle: these symbolize, respectively, what is noblest, strongest, wisest, and swiftest in creation. **Calf**: traditionally translated "ox," the Greek word refers to a heifer or young bull. Since the second century, these four creatures have been used as symbols of the evangelists Mark, Luke, Matthew, and John, respectively.

4:8 Six wings: like the seraphim of Is 6:2.

5:1–14 The seer now describes a papyrus roll in God's right hand (Rev 5:1) with seven seals indicating the importance of the message. A mighty angel asks who is worthy to open the scroll, i.e., who can accomplish God's salvific plan (Rev 5:2). There is despair at first when no one in creation can do it (Rev 5:3–4). But the seer is comforted by an elder who tells him that Christ, called the lion of the tribe of Judah, has won the right to open it (Rev 5:5). Christ then appears as a Lamb, coming to receive the scroll from God (Rev 5:6–7), for which he is acclaimed as at a coronation (Rev 5:8–10). This is followed by a doxology of the angels (Rev 5:11–12) and then finally by the heavenly church united with all of creation (Rev 5:13–14).

5:1 A scroll: a papyrus roll possibly containing a list of afflictions for sinners (cf. Ez 2:9–10) or God's plan for the world. **Sealed with seven seals**: it is totally hidden from all but God. Only the Lamb (Rev 5:7–9) has the right to carry out the divine plan.

5:5 The lion of the tribe of Judah, the root of David: these are the messianic titles applied to Christ to symbolize his victory; cf. Rev 22:16; Gn 49:9; Is 11:1, 10; Mt 1:1.

5:6 Christ is the Paschal Lamb without blemish, whose blood saved the new Israel from sin and death; cf. Ex 12; Is 53:7; Jn 1:29, 36; Acts 8:32; 1 Pt 1:18–19. This is the main title for Christ in Revelation, used twenty-eight times. **Seven horns and seven eyes**: Christ has the fullness (see note on Rev 1:4) of power (horns) and knowledge (eyes); cf. Zec 4:7. **[Seven] spirits**: as in Rev 1:4; 3:1; 4:5.

e: Ex 24:10. *f:* Is 6:2–3 / 1:4, 8; 11:17; 16:5. *g:* Rom 4:17; 16:27. *h:* Is 29:11. *i:* Is 11:1, 10; Rom 15:12. *j:* Jn 1:29.

for you were slain and with your blood
you purchased for God
those from every tribe and tongue,
people and nation.
10 [k]You made them a kingdom and priests
for our God,
and they will reign on earth."

11 [l]*I looked again and heard the voices of
many angels who surrounded the throne and
the living creatures and the elders. They
were countless in number, 12 and they cried
out in a loud voice:

"Worthy is the Lamb that was slain
to receive power and riches, wisdom
and strength,
honor and glory and blessing."

13 Then I heard every creature in heaven and
on earth and under the earth and in the sea,
everything in the universe, cry out:

"To the one who sits on the throne and to
the Lamb
be blessing and honor, glory and
might,
forever and ever."

14 The four living creatures answered,
"Amen," and the elders fell down and worshiped.

IV. The Seven Seals, Trumpets, and Plagues, with Interludes

CHAPTER 6

See RG 523

The First Six Seals. 1 *Then I watched
while the Lamb broke open the first of the
seven seals, and I heard one of the four living creatures cry out in a voice like thunder,
"Come forward." 2 [m]*I looked, and there was
a white horse, and its rider had a bow. He
was given a crown, and he rode forth victorious to further his victories.

3 When he broke open the second seal, I
heard the second living creature cry out,
"Come forward." 4 [n]*Another horse came
out, a red one. Its rider was given power to
take peace away from the earth, so that people would slaughter one another. And he was
given a huge sword.

5 *When he broke open the third seal, I
heard the third living creature cry out,
"Come forward." I looked, and there was a
black horse, and its rider held a scale in his
hand. 6 [o]*I heard what seemed to be a voice
in the midst of the four living creatures. It
said, "A ration of wheat costs a day's pay,
and three rations of barley cost a day's pay.
But do not damage the olive oil or the wine."

7 When he broke open the fourth seal, I

5:11 Countless: literally, "100,000,000 plus 1,000,000," used by the author to express infinity.

6:1–16:21 A series of seven disasters now begins as each seal is broken (Rev 6:1–8:1), followed by a similar series as seven trumpets sound (Rev 8:2–11:19) and as seven angels pour bowls on the earth causing plagues (Rev 15:1–16:21). These gloomy sequences are interrupted by longer or shorter scenes suggesting the triumph of God and his witnesses (e.g., Rev 7; 10; 11; 12; 13; 14).

6:1–17 This chapter provides a symbolic description of the contents of the sealed scroll. The breaking of the first four seals reveals four riders. The first rider (of a white horse) is a conquering power (Rev 6:1–2), the second (red horse) a symbol of bloody war (Rev 6:3–4), the third (black horse) a symbol of famine (Rev 6:5–6), the fourth (pale green horse) a symbol of Death himself, accompanied by Hades (the netherworld) as his page (Rev 6:7–8). Rev 6:8b summarizes the role of all four riders. The breaking of the fifth seal reveals Christian martyrs in an attitude of sacrifice as blood poured out at the foot of an altar begging God for vindication, which will come only when their quota is filled; but they are given a white robe symbolic of victory (Rev 6:9–11). The breaking of the sixth seal reveals typical apocalyptic signs in the sky and the sheer terror of all people at the imminent divine judgment (Rev 6:12–17).

6:1–8 The imagery is adapted from Zec 1:8–10; 6:1–8.

6:2 White horse . . . bow: this may perhaps allude specifically to the Parthians on the eastern border of the Roman empire. Expert in the use of the bow, they constantly harassed the Romans and won a major victory in A.D. 62; see note on Rev 9:13–21. But the Old Testament imagery typifies the history of oppression of God's people at all times.

6:4 Huge sword: this is a symbol of war and violence; cf. Ez 21:14–17.

6:5 Black horse: this is a symbol of famine, the usual accompaniment of war in antiquity; cf. Lv 26:26; Ez 4:12–13. The scale is a symbol of shortage of food with a corresponding rise in price.

6:6 A day's pay: literally, "a denarius," a Roman silver coin that constitutes a day's wage in Mt 20:2. Because of the famine, food was rationed and sold at an exorbitant price. A liter of flour was considered a day's ration in the Greek historians Herodotus and Diogenes Laertius. **Barley**: food of the poor (Jn 6:9, 13; cf. 2 Kgs 7:1, 16, 18); it was also used to feed animals; cf. 1 Kgs 5:8. **Do not damage**: the olive and the vine are to be used more sparingly in time of famine.

k: 1:6; Ex 19:6; Is 61:6. *l:* Dn 7:10; Jude 14–15. *m:* Zec 1:8–10; 6:1–3. *n:* Ez 21:14–16. *o:* Lv 26:26; Ez 4:16–17.

heard the voice of the fourth living creature
cry out, "Come forward." 8p*I looked, and
there was a pale green horse. Its rider was
named Death, and Hades accompanied him.
They were given authority over a quarter of
the earth, to kill with sword, famine, and
plague, and by means of the beasts of the
earth.
9*When he broke open the fifth seal, I saw
underneath the altar the souls of those who
had been slaughtered because of the witness
they bore to the word of God. 10*They cried
out in a loud voice, "How long will it be, holy
and true master, before you sit in judgment
and avenge our blood on the inhabitants of
the earth?" 11Each of them was given a white
robe, and they were told to be patient a little
while longer until the number was filled of
their fellow servants and brothers who were
going to be killed as they had been.
12q*Then I watched while he broke open
the sixth seal, and there was a great earthquake; the sun turned as black as dark sackcloth and the whole moon became like blood.
13*The stars in the sky fell to the earth like unripe figs shaken loose from the tree in a strong
wind. 14r*Then the sky was divided like a torn
scroll curling up, and every mountain and island was moved from its place. 15*The kings
of the earth, the nobles, the military officers,
the rich, the powerful, and every slave and
free person hid themselves in caves and
among mountain crags. 16sThey cried out to
the mountains and the rocks, "Fall on us and
hide us from the face of the one who sits on
the throne and from the wrath of the Lamb,
17*because the great day of their wrath has
come and who can withstand it?"

CHAPTER 7

See RG 523

The 144,000 Sealed. 1t*After this I
saw four angels standing at the four corners
of the earth, holding back the four winds of
the earth so that no wind could blow on land
or sea or against any tree. 2*Then I saw another angel come up from the East, holding
the seal of the living God. He cried out in a
loud voice to the four angels who were given
power to damage the land and the sea, 3u"Do
not damage the land or the sea or the trees
until we put the seal on the foreheads of the
servants of our God." 4v*I heard the number
of those who had been marked with the seal,
one hundred and forty-four thousand
marked from every tribe of the Israelites:
5*twelve thousand were marked from the

6:8 Pale green: symbol of death and decay; cf. Ez 14:21.

6:9 The altar: this altar corresponds to the altar of holocausts in the temple in Jerusalem; see also Rev 11:1. **Because of the witness . . . word of God**: literally, "because of the word of God and the witness they had borne."

6:10 Holy and true master: Old Testament usage as well as the context indicates that this is addressed to God rather than to Christ.

6:12–14 Symbolic rather than literal description of the cosmic upheavals attending the day of the Lord when the martyrs' prayer for vindication (Rev 6:10) would be answered; cf. Am 8:8–9; Is 34:4; 50:3; Jl 2:10; 3:3–4; Mt 24:4–36; Mk 13:5–37; Lk 21:8–36.

6:12 Dark sackcloth: for mourning, sackcloth was made from the skin of a black goat.

6:13 Unripe figs: literally, "summer (or winter) fruit."

6:14 Was divided: literally, "was split," like a broken papyrus roll torn in two, each half then curling up to form a roll on either side.

6:15 Nobles: literally, "courtiers," "grandees." **Military officers**: literally, "commanders of 1,000 men," used in Josephus and other Greek authors as the equivalent of the Roman *tribunus militum*. The listing of various ranks of society represents the universality of terror at the impending doom.

6:17 Their: this reading is attested in the best manuscripts, but the vast majority read "his" in reference to the wrath of the Lamb in the preceding verse.

7:1–17 An interlude of two visions precedes the breaking of the seventh seal, just as two more will separate the sixth and seventh trumpets (Rev 10). In the first vision (Rev 7:1–8), the elect receive the seal of the living God as protection against the coming cataclysm; cf. Rev 14:1; Ez 9:4–6; 2 Cor 1:22; Eph 1:13; 4:30. The second vision (Rev 7:9–17) portrays the faithful Christians before God's throne to encourage those on earth to persevere to the end, even to death.

7:1 The four corners of the earth: the earth is seen as a table or rectangular surface.

7:2 East: literally, "rising of the sun." The east was considered the source of light and the place of paradise (Gn 2:8). **Seal**: whatever was marked by the impression of one's signet ring belonged to that person and was under his protection.

7:4–9 One hundred and forty-four thousand: the square of twelve (the number of Israel's tribes) multiplied by a thousand, symbolic of the new Israel (cf. Rev 14:1–5; Gal 6:16; Jas 1:1) that embraces people **from every nation, race, people, and tongue** (Rev 7:9).

7:5–8 Judah is placed first because of Christ; cf. "the Lion of the tribe of Judah" (Rev 5:5). Dan is omitted because of a later tradition that the antichrist would arise from it.

p: Ez 14:21. *q:* Jl 3:4; Mt 24:29. *r:* Is 34:4 / 16:20. *s:* Is 2:19; Hos 10:8; Lk 23:30. *t:* Jer 49:36; Zec 6:5. *u:* Ex 12:7–14; Ez 9:4; 2 Cor 1:22; Eph 1:13; 4:30. *v:* 14:1.

tribe of Judah, twelve thousand from the
tribe of Reuben, twelve thousand from the
tribe of Gad, [6]twelve thousand from the tribe
of Asher, twelve thousand from the tribe of
Naphtali, twelve thousand from the tribe of
Manasseh, [7]twelve thousand from the tribe
of Simeon, twelve thousand from the tribe of
Levi, twelve thousand from the tribe of Issachar, [8]twelve thousand from the tribe of
Zebulun, twelve thousand from the tribe of
Joseph, and twelve thousand were marked
from the tribe of Benjamin.

Triumph of the Elect. [9*]After this I had a
vision of a great multitude, which no one
could count, from every nation, race, people,
and tongue. They stood before the throne
and before the Lamb, wearing white robes
and holding palm branches in their hands.
[10*]They cried out in a loud voice:

"Salvation comes from our God, who is
seated on the throne,
and from the Lamb."

[11]All the angels stood around the throne and
around the elders and the four living creatures. They prostrated themselves before the
throne, worshiped God, [12]and exclaimed:

"Amen. Blessing and glory, wisdom and
thanksgiving,
honor, power, and might
be to our God forever and ever.
Amen."

[13]Then one of the elders spoke up and said to
me, "Who are these wearing white robes,
and where did they come from?" [14w*]I said
to him, "My lord, you are the one who
knows." He said to me, "These are the ones
who have survived the time of great distress;
they have washed their robes and made them
white in the blood of the Lamb.

[15]"For this reason they stand before God's
throne
and worship him day and night in his
temple.
The one who sits on the throne will
shelter them.
[16 x]They will not hunger or thirst anymore,
nor will the sun or any heat strike them.
[17 y*]For the Lamb who is in the center of
the throne will shepherd them
and lead them to springs of life-giving
water,
and God will wipe away every tear
from their eyes."

CHAPTER 8

See RG 523

The Seven Trumpets. [1z*]When he
broke open the seventh seal, there was silence in heaven for about half an hour.
[2a]And I saw that the seven angels who stood
before God were given seven trumpets.

The Gold Censer. [3b*]Another angel came
and stood at the altar, holding a gold censer.
He was given a great quantity of incense to offer, along with the prayers of all the holy ones,
on the gold altar that was before the throne.
[4]The smoke of the incense along with the
prayers of the holy ones went up before God
from the hand of the angel. [5c]Then the angel
took the censer, filled it with burning coals
from the altar, and hurled it down to the earth.
There were peals of thunder, rumblings,
flashes of lightning, and an earthquake.

The First Four Trumpets. [6d]The seven an-

7:9 White robes . . . palm branches: symbols of joy and victory; see note on Rev 3:5.

7:10 Salvation comes from: literally, "(let) salvation (be ascribed) to." A similar hymn of praise is found at the fall of the dragon (Rev 12:10) and of Babylon (Rev 19:1).

7:14 Time of great distress: fierce persecution by the Romans; cf. Introduction.

7:17 Life-giving water: literally, "the water of life," God's grace, which flows from Christ; cf. Rev 21:6; 22:1, 17; Jn 4:10, 14.

8:1–13 The breaking of the seventh seal produces at first silence and then seven symbolic disasters, each announced by a trumpet blast, of which the first four form a unit as did the first four seals. A minor liturgy (Rev 8:3–5) is enclosed by a vision of seven angels (Rev 8:2, 6). Then follow the first four trumpet blasts, each heralding catastrophes modeled on the plagues of Egypt affecting the traditional prophetic third (cf. Ez 5:12) of the earth, sea, fresh water, and stars (Rev 8:7–12). Finally, there is a vision of an eagle warning of the last three trumpet blasts (Rev 8:13).

8:1 Silence in heaven: as in Zep 1:7, a prelude to the eschatological woes that are to follow; cf. Introduction.

8:3 Altar: there seems to be only one altar in the heavenly temple, corresponding to the altar of holocausts in Rev 6:9, and here to the altar of incense in Jerusalem; cf. also Rev 9:13; 11:1; 14:18; 16:7.

w: Mt 24:21. *x:* Is 49:10. *y:* 21:4; Is 25:8. *z:* Heb 2:20; Zep 1:7; Zec 2:17. *a:* 4:5; Tb 12:15. *b:* Ps 141:2; Tb 12:12. *c:* Ez 10:2; Ps 11:6 / 4:5; 11:19; 16:18. *d:* 16:1–21.

gels who were holding the seven trumpets prepared to blow them.

[7*]When the first one blew his trumpet, there came hail and fire mixed with blood, which was hurled down to the earth. A third of the land was burned up, along with a third of the trees and all green grass.

[8e*]When the second angel blew his trumpet, something like a large burning mountain was hurled into the sea. A third of the sea turned to blood, [9*]a third of the creatures living in the sea died, and a third of the ships were wrecked.

[10f]When the third angel blew his trumpet, a large star burning like a torch fell from the sky. It fell on a third of the rivers and on the springs of water. [11g*]The star was called "Wormwood," and a third of all the water turned to wormwood. Many people died from this water, because it was made bitter.

[12h]When the fourth angel blew his trumpet, a third of the sun, a third of the moon, and a third of the stars were struck, so that a third of them became dark. The day lost its light for a third of the time, as did the night.

[13*]Then I looked again and heard an eagle flying high overhead cry out in a loud voice, "Woe! Woe! Woe to the inhabitants of the earth from the rest of the trumpet blasts that the three angels are about to blow!"

See RG 523

CHAPTER 9

The Fifth Trumpet. [1i*]Then the fifth angel blew his trumpet, and I saw a star that had fallen from the sky to the earth. It was given the key for the passage to the abyss. [2j]It opened the passage to the abyss, and smoke came up out of the passage like smoke from a huge furnace. The sun and the air were darkened by the smoke from the passage. [3k*]Locusts came out of the smoke onto the land, and they were given the same power as scorpions of the earth. [4]They were told not to harm the grass of the earth or any plant or any tree, but only those people who did not have the seal of God on their foreheads. [5*]They were not allowed to kill them but only to torment them for five months; the torment they inflicted was like that of a scorpion when it stings a person. [6l]During that time these people will seek death but will not find it, and they will long to die but death will escape them.

[7m*]The appearance of the locusts was like that of horses ready for battle. On their heads they wore what looked like crowns of gold; their faces were like human faces, [8n]and they had hair like women's hair. Their teeth were like lions' teeth, [9]and they had chests like iron breastplates. The sound of their wings was like the sound of many horse-drawn chariots racing into battle. [10]They had tails like scorpions, with stingers; with their tails they had power to harm people for five months. [11*]They had as their king the angel of the abyss, whose name in Hebrew is Abaddon and in Greek Apollyon.

[12]The first woe has passed, but there are two more to come.

8:7 This woe resembles the seventh plague of Egypt (Ex 9:23–24); cf. Jl 3:3.

8:8–11 The background of these two woes is the first plague of Egypt (Ex 7:20–21).

8:9 Creatures living in the sea: literally, "creatures in the sea that had souls."

8:11 Wormwood: an extremely bitter and malignant plant symbolizing the punishment God inflicts on the ungodly; cf. Jer 9:12–14; 23:15.

8:13 Woe! Woe! Woe: each of the three woes pronounced by the angel represents a separate disaster; cf. Rev 9:12; 11:14. The final woe, released by the seventh trumpet blast, includes the plagues of Rev 16.

9:1–12 The fifth trumpet heralds a woe containing elements from the eighth and ninth plagues of Egypt (Ex 10:12–15, 21–23) but specifically reminiscent of the invasion of locusts in Jl 1:4–2:10.

9:1 A star: late Judaism represented fallen powers as stars (Is 14:12–15; Lk 10:18; Jude 13), but a comparison with Rev 1:20 and Rev 20:1 suggests that here it means an angel. **The passage to the abyss**: referring to Sheol, the netherworld, where Satan and the fallen angels are kept for a thousand years, to be cast afterwards into the pool of fire; cf. Rev 20:7–10. The abyss was conceived of as a vast subterranean cavern full of fire. Its only link with the earth was a kind of passage or mine shaft, which was kept locked.

9:3 Scorpions: their poisonous sting was proverbial; Ez 2:6; Lk 11:12.

9:5 For five months: more or less corresponding to the life-span of locusts.

9:7–10 Eight characteristics are listed to show the eschatological and diabolical nature of these locusts.

9:11 Abaddon: Hebrew (more precisely, Aramaic) for destruction or ruin. **Apollyon**: Greek for the "Destroyer."

e: Ex 7:20. *f:* Is 14:12. *g:* Jer 9:14. *h:* Ex 10:21–23. *i:* 20:1. *j:* Gn 19:28. *k:* Ex 10:12–15; Wis 16:9. *l:* Jb 3:21. *m:* Jl 2:4. *n:* Jl 1:6.

The Sixth Trumpet. [13o*]Then the sixth angel blew his trumpet, and I heard a voice coming from the [four] horns of the gold altar before God, [14*]telling the sixth angel who held the trumpet, "Release the four angels who are bound at the banks of the great river Euphrates." [15]So the four angels were released, who were prepared for this hour, day, month, and year to kill a third of the human race. [16]The number of cavalry troops was two hundred million; I heard their number. [17p*]Now in my vision this is how I saw the horses and their riders. They wore red, blue, and yellow breastplates, and the horses' heads were like heads of lions, and out of their mouths came fire, smoke, and sulfur. [18]By these three plagues of fire, smoke, and sulfur that came out of their mouths a third of the human race was killed. [19]For the power of the horses is in their mouths and in their tails; for their tails are like snakes, with heads that inflict harm.

[20q*]The rest of the human race, who were not killed by these plagues, did not repent of the works of their hands, to give up the worship of demons and idols made from gold, silver, bronze, stone, and wood, which cannot see or hear or walk. [21]Nor did they repent of their murders, their magic potions, their unchastity, or their robberies.

See RG 523

CHAPTER 10

The Angel with the Small Scroll.

[1*]Then I saw another mighty angel come down from heaven wrapped in a cloud, with a halo around his head; his face was like the sun and his feet were like pillars of fire. [2*]In his hand he held a small scroll that had been opened. He placed his right foot on the sea and his left foot on the land, [3r]and then he cried out in a loud voice as a lion roars. When he cried out, the seven thunders raised their voices, too. [4]When the seven thunders had spoken, I was about to write it down; but I heard a voice from heaven say, "Seal up what the seven thunders have spoken, but do not write it down." [5]Then the angel I saw standing on the sea and on the land raised his right hand to heaven [6s*]and swore by the one who lives forever and ever, who created heaven and earth and sea and all that is in them, "There shall be no more delay. [7t*]At the time when you hear the seventh angel blow his trumpet, the mysterious plan of God shall be fulfilled, as he promised to his servants the prophets."

[8]Then the voice that I had heard from heaven spoke to me again and said, "Go, take the scroll that lies open in the hand of the angel who is standing on the sea and on the land." [9*]So I went up to the angel and told him to give me the small scroll. He said to me, "Take and swallow it. It will turn your stomach sour, but in your mouth it will taste as sweet as honey." [10u]I took the small scroll

9:13–21 The sixth trumpet heralds a woe representing another diabolical attack symbolized by an invasion by the Parthians living east of the Euphrates; see note on Rev 6:2. At the appointed time (Rev 9:15), the frightful horses act as God's agents of judgment. The imaginative details are not to be taken literally; see Introduction and the note on Rev 6:12–14.

9:13 [Four]: many Greek manuscripts and versions omit the word. The horns were situated at the four corners of the altar (Ex 27:2; 30:2–3); see note on Rev 8:3.

9:14–15 The four angels: they are symbolic of the destructive activity that will be extended throughout the universe.

9:17 Blue: literally, "hyacinth-colored." **Yellow**: literally, "sulfurous."

9:20 The works of their hands: i.e., the gods their hands had made.

10:1–11:14 An interlude in two scenes (Rev 10:1–11 and Rev 11:1–14) precedes the sounding of the seventh trumpet; cf. Rev 7:1–17. The first vision describes an angel astride sea and land like a colossus, with a small scroll open, the contents of which indicate that the end is imminent (Rev 10). The second vision is of the measuring of the temple and of two witnesses, whose martyrdom means that the kingdom of God is about to be inaugurated.

10:2 He placed . . . on the land: this symbolizes the universality of the angel's message, as does the figure of the small scroll open to be read.

10:3 The seven thunders: God's voice announcing judgment and doom; cf. Ps 29:3–9, where thunder, as the voice of Yahweh, is praised seven times.

10:6 Heaven and earth and sea: the three parts of the universe. **No more delay**: cf. Dn 12:7; Heb 2:3.

10:7 The mysterious plan of God: literally, "the mystery of God," the end of the present age when the forces of evil will be put down (Rev 17:1–19:4, 11–21; 20:7–10; cf. 2 Thes 2:6–12; Rom 16:25–26), and the establishment of the reign of God when all creation will be made new (Rev 21:1–22:5).

10:9–10 The small scroll was sweet because it predicted the final victory of God's people; it was sour because it also announced their sufferings. Cf. Ez 3:1–3.

o: Ex 30:1–3. *p:* Jb 41:10–13. *q:* Ps 135:15–17; Is 17:8; Dn 5:4. *r:* Ps 29:3–9; Jer 25:30; Am 3:8. *s:* Dt 32:40; Dn 12:7 / Ez 12:28. *t:* Am 3:7. *u:* Ez 3:1–3.

from the angel's hand and swallowed it. In
my mouth it was like sweet honey, but when
I had eaten it, my stomach turned sour.
[11*]Then someone said to me, "You must
prophesy again about many peoples, nations, tongues, and kings."

CHAPTER 11

See RG 523

The Two Witnesses. [1v*]Then I was
given a measuring rod like a staff and I was
told, "Come and measure the temple of God
and the altar, and count those who are worshiping in it. [2*]But exclude the outer court of
the temple; do not measure it, for it has been
handed over to the Gentiles, who will trample the holy city for forty-two months. [3*]I
will commission my two witnesses to prophesy for those twelve hundred and sixty days,
wearing sackcloth." [4w*]These are the two olive trees and the two lampstands that stand
before the Lord of the earth. [5*]If anyone
wants to harm them, fire comes out of their
mouths and devours their enemies. In this
way, anyone wanting to harm them is sure to
be slain. [6x]They have the power to close up
the sky so that no rain can fall during the time
of their prophesying. They also have power
to turn water into blood and to afflict the
earth with any plague as often as they wish.
[7y*]When they have finished their testimony, the beast that comes up from the
abyss will wage war against them and conquer them and kill them. [8*]Their corpses will
lie in the main street of the great city, which
has the symbolic names "Sodom" and
"Egypt," where indeed their Lord was crucified. [9*]Those from every people, tribe,
tongue, and nation will gaze on their corpses
for three and a half days, and they will not
allow their corpses to be buried. [10]The inhabitants of the earth will gloat over them
and be glad and exchange gifts because
these two prophets tormented the inhabitants
of the earth. [11z]But after the three and a half
days, a breath of life from God entered them.
When they stood on their feet, great fear fell
on those who saw them. [12a]Then they heard
a loud voice from heaven say to them,
"Come up here." So they went up to heaven
in a cloud as their enemies looked on. [13*]At
that moment there was a great earthquake,
and a tenth of the city fell in ruins. Seven
thousand people were killed during the
earthquake; the rest were terrified and gave
glory to the God of heaven.

[14]The second woe has passed, but the
third is coming soon.

The Seventh Trumpet. [15*]Then the sev-

10:11 This further prophecy is contained in chaps. 12–22.

11:1 The temple and altar symbolize the new Israel; see note on Rev 7:4–9. The worshipers represent Christians. The measuring of the temple (cf. Ez 40:3–42:20; 47:1–12; Zec 2:5–6) suggests that God will preserve the faithful remnant (cf. Is 4:2–3) who remain true to Christ (Rev 14:1–5).

11:2 The outer court: the Court of the Gentiles. **Trample . . . forty-two months**: the duration of the vicious persecution of the Jews by Antiochus IV Epiphanes (Dn 7:25; 12:7); this persecution of three and a half years (half of seven, counted as 1260 days in Rev 11:3; 12:6) became the prototype of periods of trial for God's people; cf. Lk 4:25; Jas 5:17. The reference here is to the persecution by the Romans; cf. Introduction.

11:3 The two witnesses, wearing sackcloth symbolizing lamentation and repentance, cannot readily be identified. Do they represent Moses and Elijah, or the Law and the Prophets, or Peter and Paul? Most probably they refer to the universal church, especially the Christian martyrs, fulfilling the office of witness (two because of Dt 19:15; cf. Mk 6:7; Jn 8:17).

11:4 The two olive trees and the two lampstands: the martyrs who stand in the presence of the Lord; the imagery is taken from Zec 4:8–14, where the olive trees refer to Zerubbabel and Joshua.

11:5–6 These details are derived from stories of Moses, who turned **water into blood** (Ex 7:17–20), and of Elijah, who called down fire from heaven (1 Kgs 18:36–40; 2 Kgs 1:10) and closed up the sky for three years (1 Kgs 17:1; cf. 18:1).

11:7 The beast . . . from the abyss: the Roman emperor Nero, who symbolizes the forces of evil, or the antichrist (Rev 13:1, 8; 17:8); cf. Dn 7:2–8, 11–12, 19–22 and Introduction.

11:8 The great city: this expression is used constantly in Revelation for Babylon, i.e., Rome; cf. Rev 14:8; 16:19; 17:18; 18:2, 10, 21. **"Sodom" and "Egypt"**: symbols of immorality (cf. Is 1:10) and oppression of God's people (cf. Ex 1:11–14). **Where indeed their Lord was crucified**: not the geographical but the symbolic Jerusalem that rejects God and his witnesses, i.e., Rome, called Babylon in Rev 16–18; see note on Rev 17:9 and Introduction.

11:9–12 Over the martyrdom (Rev 11:7) of the two witnesses, now called prophets, the ungodly rejoice **for three and a half days**, a symbolic period of time; see note on Rev 11:2. Afterwards they go in triumph to heaven, as did Elijah (2 Kgs 2:11).

11:13 Seven thousand people: a symbolic sum to represent all social classes (seven) and large numbers (thousands); cf. Introduction.

11:15–19 The seventh trumpet proclaims the coming of God's reign after the victory over diabolical powers; see note on Rev 10:7.

v: Ez 40:3–5 / Zec 2:5–9. *w:* Zec 4:3, 14. *x:* Ex 7:17. *y:* Dn 7:21. *z:* Ez 37:5, 10. *a:* 2 Kgs 2:11.

enth angel blew his trumpet. There were loud voices in heaven, saying, "The kingdom of the world now belongs to our Lord and to his Anointed, and he will reign forever and ever." 16The twenty-four elders who sat on their thrones before God prostrated themselves and worshiped God 17and said:

"We give thanks to you, Lord God
    almighty,
  who are and who were.
For you have assumed your great power
  and have established your reign.
18 bThe nations raged,
  but your wrath has come,
  and the time for the dead to be judged,
and to recompense your servants, the
    prophets,
  and the holy ones and those who fear
    your name,
  the small and the great alike,
and to destroy those who destroy the
    earth."

19Then God's temple in heaven was opened, and the ark of his covenant could be seen in the temple. There were flashes of lightning, rumblings, and peals of thunder, an earthquake, and a violent hailstorm.

CHAPTER 12

See RG 523

The Woman and the Dragon. 1c*A great sign appeared in the sky, a woman clothed with the sun, with the moon under her feet, and on her head a crown of twelve stars. 2*She was with child and wailed aloud in pain as she labored to give birth. 3d*Then another sign appeared in the sky; it was a huge red dragon, with seven heads and ten horns, and on its heads were seven diadems. 4eIts tail swept away a third of the stars in the sky and hurled them down to the earth. Then the dragon stood before the woman about to give birth, to devour her child when she gave birth. 5f*She gave birth to a son, a male child, destined to rule all the nations with an iron rod. Her child was caught up to God and his throne. 6*The woman herself fled into the desert where she had a place prepared by God, that there she might be taken care of for twelve hundred and sixty days.

7*Then war broke out in heaven; Michael and his angels battled against the dragon. The dragon and its angels fought back, 8but they did not prevail and there was no longer any place for them in heaven. 9g*The huge dragon, the ancient serpent, who is called the Devil and Satan, who deceived the whole

12:1–14:20 This central section of Revelation portrays the power of evil, represented by a dragon, in opposition to God and his people. First, the dragon pursues the woman about to give birth, but her son is saved and "caught up to God and his throne" (Rev 12:5). Then Michael and his angels cast the dragon and his angels out of heaven (Rev 12:7–9). After this, the dragon tries to attack the boy indirectly by attacking members of his church (Rev 12:13–17). A beast, symbolizing the Roman empire, then becomes the dragon's agent, mortally wounded but restored to life and worshiped by all the world (Rev 13:1–10). A second beast arises from the land, symbolizing the antichrist, which leads people astray by its prodigies to idolize the first beast (Rev 13:11–18). This is followed by a vision of the Lamb and his faithful ones, and the proclamation of imminent judgment upon the world in terms of the wine of God's wrath (Rev 14:1–20).

12:1 The woman adorned with the sun, the moon, and the stars (images taken from Gn 37:9–10) symbolizes God's people in the Old and the New Testament. The Israel of old gave birth to the Messiah (Rev 12:5) and then became the new Israel, the church, which suffers persecution by the dragon (Rev 12:6, 13–17); cf. Is 50:1; 66:7; Jer 50:12. This corresponds to a widespread myth throughout the ancient world that a goddess pregnant with a savior was pursued by a horrible monster; by miraculous intervention, she bore a son who then killed the monster.

12:2 Because of Eve's sin, the woman gives birth in distress and pain (Gn 3:16; cf. Is 66:7–14).

12:3 Huge red dragon: the Devil or Satan (cf. Rev 12:9; 20:2), symbol of the forces of evil, a mythical monster known also as Leviathan (Ps 74:13–14) or Rahab (Jb 26:12–13; Ps 89:11). **Seven diadems**: these are symbolic of the fullness of the dragon's sovereignty over the kingdoms of this world; cf. Christ with many diadems (Rev 19:12).

12:5 Rule . . . iron rod: fulfilled in Rev 19:15; cf. Ps 2:9. **Was caught up to God**: reference to Christ's ascension.

12:6 God protects the persecuted church in the desert, the traditional Old Testament place of refuge for the afflicted, according to the typology of the Exodus; see note on Rev 11:2.

12:7–12 Michael, mentioned only here in Revelation, wins a victory over the dragon. A hymn of praise follows.

12:7 Michael: the archangel, guardian and champion of Israel; cf. Dn 10:13, 21; 12:1; Jude 9. In Hebrew, the name Michael means "Who can compare with God?"; cf. Rev 13:4.

12:9 The ancient serpent: who seduced Eve (Gn 3:1–6), mother of the human race; cf. Rev 20:2; Eph 6:11–12. **Was thrown down**: allusion to the expulsion of Satan from heaven; cf. Lk 10:18.

b: Ps 2:1, 5 / Am 3:7. *c:* Gn 37:9. *d:* Dn 7:7. *e:* Dn 8:10. *f:* Is 66:7 / Ps 2:9. *g:* Gn 3:1–4; Lk 10:18.

world, was thrown down to earth, and its angels were thrown down with it.
10*Then I heard a loud voice in heaven say:

"Now have salvation and power come,
and the kingdom of our God
and the authority of his Anointed.
For the accuser of our brothers is cast out,
who accuses them before our God day
and night.
11 They conquered him by the blood of the
Lamb
and by the word of their testimony;
love for life did not deter them from
death.
12 Therefore, rejoice, you heavens,
and you who dwell in them.
But woe to you, earth and sea,
for the Devil has come down to you in
great fury,
for he knows he has but a short time."

13h When the dragon saw that it had been
thrown down to the earth, it pursued the
woman who had given birth to the male
child. 14i*But the woman was given the two
wings of the great eagle, so that she could fly
to her place in the desert, where, far from the
serpent, she was taken care of for a year, two
years, and a half-year. 15*The serpent, however, spewed a torrent of water out of his
mouth after the woman to sweep her away
with the current. 16But the earth helped the
woman and opened its mouth and swallowed the flood that the dragon spewed out
of its mouth. 17j*Then the dragon became
angry with the woman and went off to wage
war against the rest of her offspring, those
who keep God's commandments and bear
witness to Jesus. 18*It took its position on the
sand of the sea.

CHAPTER 13

See RG 523

The First Beast. 1k*Then I saw a beast
come out of the sea with ten horns and seven
heads; on its horns were ten diadems, and on
its heads blasphemous name[s]. 2l*The beast
I saw was like a leopard, but it had feet like a
bear's, and its mouth was like the mouth of a
lion. To it the dragon gave its own power and
throne, along with great authority. 3*I saw
that one of its heads seemed to have been
mortally wounded, but this mortal wound
was healed. Fascinated, the whole world followed after the beast. 4*They worshiped the
dragon because it gave its authority to the
beast; they also worshiped the beast and said,
"Who can compare with the beast or who can
fight against it?"
5m*The beast was given a mouth uttering
proud boasts and blasphemies, and it was
given authority to act for forty-two months.
6It opened its mouth to utter blasphemies
against God, blaspheming his name and his
dwelling and those who dwell in heaven. 7nIt
was also allowed to wage war against the
holy ones and conquer them, and it was
granted authority over every tribe, people,
tongue, and nation. 8oAll the inhabitants of

12:10 The accuser: the meaning of the Hebrew word "Satan," found in Rev 12:9; Jb 1–2; Zec 3:1; 1 Chr 21:1; he continues to accuse Christ's disciples.

12:14 Great eagle: symbol of the power and swiftness of divine help; cf. Ex 19:4; Dt 32:11; Is 40:31.

12:15 The serpent is depicted as the sea monster; cf. Rev 13:1; Is 27:1; Ez 32:2; Ps 74:13–14.

12:17 Although the church is protected by God's special providence (Rev 12:16), the individual Christian is to expect persecution and suffering.

12:17 It took its position: many later manuscripts and versions read "I took my position," thus connecting the sentence to the following paragraph.

13:1–10 This wild beast, combining features of the four beasts in Dn 7:2–28, symbolizes the Roman empire; the seven heads represent the emperors; see notes on Rev 17:10 and Rev 17:12–14. The blasphemous names are the divine titles assumed by the emperors.

13:2 Satan (Rev 12:9), the prince of this world (Jn 12:31), commissioned the beast to persecute the church (Rev 13:5–7).

13:3 This may be a reference to the popular legend that Nero would come back to life and rule again after his death (which occurred in A.D. 68 from a self-inflicted stab wound in the throat); cf. Rev 13:14; Rev 17:8. Domitian (A.D. 81–96) embodied all the cruelty and impiety of Nero. Cf. Introduction.

13:4 Worshiped the beast: allusion to emperor worship, which Domitian insisted upon and ruthlessly enforced. **Who can compare with the beast**: perhaps a deliberate parody of the name Michael; see note on Rev 12:7.

13:5–6 Domitian, like Antiochus IV Epiphanes (Dn 7:8, 11, 25), demanded that he be called by divine titles such as "our lord and god" and "Jupiter." See note on Rev 11:2.

13:5 Forty-two months: this is the same duration as the profanation of the holy city (Rev 11:2), the prophetic mission of the two witnesses (Rev 11:3), and the retreat of the woman into the desert (Rev 12:6, 14).

---

h: Gn 3:15. *i*: Ex 19:4; Dn 7:25; 12:7. *j*: Gn 3:15. *k*: 2 Thes 2:3–12. *l*: Dn 7:3–6. *m*: Dn 7:8, 11, 25; 8:14; 9:27; 11:36; 12:7. *n*: Dn 7:21. *o*: 3:5; 17:8; 20:12.

the earth will worship it, all whose names were not written from the foundation of the world in the book of life, which belongs to the Lamb who was slain.

[9 p]Whoever has ears ought to hear these
words.
[10 q]Anyone destined for captivity goes into
captivity.
Anyone destined to be slain by the sword
shall be slain by the sword.

Such is the faithful endurance of the holy ones.

The Second Beast. [11*]Then I saw another beast come up out of the earth; it had two horns like a lamb's but spoke like a dragon. [12]It wielded all the authority of the first beast in its sight and made the earth and its inhabitants worship the first beast, whose mortal wound had been healed. [13r]It performed great signs, even making fire come down from heaven to earth in the sight of everyone. [14]It deceived the inhabitants of the earth with the signs it was allowed to perform in the sight of the first beast, telling them to make an image for the beast who had been wounded by the sword and revived. [15s]It was then permitted to breathe life into the beast's image, so that the beast's image could speak and [could] have anyone who did not worship it put to death. [16t]It forced all the people, small and great, rich and poor, free and slave, to be given a stamped image on their right hands or their foreheads, [17]so that no one could buy or sell except one who had the stamped image of the beast's name or the number that stood for its name.

[18u*]Wisdom is needed here; one who understands can calculate the number of the beast, for it is a number that stands for a person. His number is six hundred and sixty-six.

CHAPTER 14

See RG 523

The Lamb's Companions. [1v*]Then I looked and there was the Lamb standing on Mount Zion, and with him a hundred and forty-four thousand who had his name and his Father's name written on their foreheads. [2]I heard a sound from heaven like the sound of rushing water or a loud peal of thunder. The sound I heard was like that of harpists playing their harps. [3w]They were singing [what seemed to be] a new hymn before the throne, before the four living creatures and the elders. No one could learn this hymn except the hundred and forty-four thousand who had been ransomed from the earth. [4x*]These are they who were not defiled with women; they are virgins and these are the ones who follow the Lamb wherever he goes. They have been ransomed as the firstfruits of the human race for God and the Lamb. [5y*]On their lips no deceit has been found; they are unblemished.

The Three Angels. [6*]Then I saw another

13:11–18 The second beast is described in terms of the false prophets (cf. Rev 16:13; 19:20; 20:10) who accompany the false messiahs (the first beast); cf. Mt 24:24; Mk 13:22; 2 Thes 2:9; cf. also Dt 13:2–4. Christians had either to worship the emperor and his image or to suffer martyrdom.

13:18 Each of the letters of the alphabet in Hebrew as well as in Greek has a numerical value. Many possible combinations of letters will add up to 666, and many candidates have been nominated for this infamous number. The most likely is the emperor Caesar Nero (see note on Rev 13:3), the Greek form of whose name in Hebrew letters gives the required sum. (The Latin form of this name equals 616, which is the reading of a few manuscripts.) Nero personifies the emperors who viciously persecuted the church. It has also been observed that "6" represents imperfection, falling short of the perfect number "7," and is represented here in a triple or superlative form.

14:1–5 Now follows a tender and consoling vision of the Lamb and his companions.

14:1 Mount Zion: in Jerusalem, the traditional place where the true remnant, the Israel of faith, is to be gathered in the messianic reign; cf. 2 Kgs 19:30–31; Jl 3:5; Ob 17; Mi 4:6–8; Zep 3:12–20. **A hundred and forty-four thousand**: see note on Rev 7:4–9. **His Father's name . . . foreheads**: in contrast to the pagans who were marked with the name or number of the beast (Rev 13:16–17).

14:4 Virgins: metaphorically, because they never indulged in any idolatrous practices, which are considered in the Old Testament to be adultery and fornication (Rev 2:14–15, 20–22; 17:1–6; cf. Ez 16:1–58; 23:1–49). The parallel passages (Rev 7:3; 22:4) indicate that the 144,000 whose foreheads are sealed represent all Christian people.

14:5 No deceit: because they did not deny Christ or do homage to the beast. Lying is characteristic of the opponents of Christ (Jn 8:44), but the Suffering Servant spoke no falsehood (Is 53:9; 1 Pt 2:22). **Unblemished**: a cultic term taken from the vocabulary of sacrificial ritual.

14:6–13 Three angels proclaim imminent judgment on the pagan world, calling all peoples to worship God the creator.

p: Mt 13:9. *q:* Jer 15:2. *r:* Dt 13:2–4; Mt 24:24; 2 Thes 2:9–10. *s:* Dn 3:5–7, 15. *t:* 14:9; 16:2; 19:20; 20:4. *u:* 17:9. *v:* Jl 3:5; Ob 17; Acts 2:21. *w:* Ps 33:3; 96:1; 98:1; Is 42:10. *x:* Jer 2:2; Jas 1:18. *y:* Zep 3:13.

angel flying high overhead, with everlasting good news to announce to those who dwell on earth, to every nation, tribe, tongue, and people. [7z]He said in a loud voice, "Fear God and give him glory, for his time has come to sit in judgment. Worship him who made heaven and earth and sea and springs of water."

[8a*]A second angel followed, saying:

"Fallen, fallen is Babylon the great,
that made all the nations drink
the wine of her licentious passion."

[9]A third angel followed them and said in a loud voice, "Anyone who worships the beast or its image, or accepts its mark on forehead or hand, [10*]will also drink the wine of God's fury, poured full strength into the cup of his wrath, and will be tormented in burning sulfur before the holy angels and before the Lamb. [11b]The smoke of the fire that torments them will rise forever and ever, and there will be no relief day or night for those who worship the beast or its image or accept the mark of its name." [12c*]Here is what sustains the holy ones who keep God's commandments and their faith in Jesus.

[13d*]I heard a voice from heaven say, "Write this: Blessed are the dead who die in the Lord from now on." "Yes," said the Spirit, "let them find rest from their labors, for their works accompany them."

The Harvest of the Earth. [14e*]Then I looked and there was a white cloud, and sitting on the cloud one who looked like a son of man, with a gold crown on his head and a sharp sickle in his hand. [15f]Another angel came out of the temple, crying out in a loud voice to the one sitting on the cloud, "Use your sickle and reap the harvest, for the time to reap has come, because the earth's harvest is fully ripe." [16]So the one who was sitting on the cloud swung his sickle over the earth, and the earth was harvested.

[17]Then another angel came out of the temple in heaven who also had a sharp sickle. [18*]Then another angel [came] from the altar, [who] was in charge of the fire, and cried out in a loud voice to the one who had the sharp sickle, "Use your sharp sickle and cut the clusters from the earth's vines, for its grapes are ripe." [19g]So the angel swung his sickle over the earth and cut the earth's vintage. He threw it into the great wine press of God's fury. [20*]The wine press was trodden outside the city and blood poured out of the wine press to the height of a horse's bridle for two hundred miles.

CHAPTER 15

See RG 523

The Seven Last Plagues. [1*]Then I saw in heaven another sign, great and awe-inspiring: seven angels with the seven last plagues, for through them God's fury is accomplished.

[2h*]Then I saw something like a sea of glass mingled with fire. On the sea of glass

Babylon (Rome) will fall, and its supporters will be tormented forever.

14:6 Everlasting good news: that God's eternal reign is about to begin; see note on Rev 10:7.

14:8 This verse anticipates the lengthy dirge over Babylon (Rome) in Rev 18:1–19:4. The oracle of Is 21:9 to Babylon is applied here.

14:10–11 The wine of God's fury: image taken from Is 51:17; Jer 25:15–16; 49:12; 51:7; Ez 23:31–34. Eternal punishment in the fiery pool of burning sulfur (or "fire and brimstone"; cf. Gn 19:24) is also reserved for the Devil, the beast, and the false prophet (Rev 19:20; 20:10; 21:8).

14:12 In addition to **faith in Jesus**, the seer insists upon the necessity and value of works, as in Rev 2:23; 20:12–13; 22:12; cf. Mt 16:27; Rom 2:6.

14:13 See note on Rev 1:3. According to Jewish thought, people's actions followed them as witnesses before the court of God.

14:14–20 The reaping of the harvest symbolizes the gathering of the elect in the final judgment, while the reaping and treading of the grapes symbolizes the doom of the ungodly (cf. Jl 4:12–13; Is 63:1–6) that will come in Rev 19:11–21.

14:18 Altar: there was only one altar in the heavenly temple; see notes above on Rev 6:9; 8:3; 11:1.

14:20 Two hundred miles: literally sixteen hundred stades. The *stadion*, a Greek unit of measurement, was about 607 feet in length, approximately the length of a furlong.

15:1–16:21 The seven bowls, the third and last group of seven after the seven seals and the seven trumpets, foreshadow the final cataclysm. Again, the series is introduced by a heavenly prelude, in which the victors over the beast sing the canticle of Moses (Rev 15:2–4).

15:1–4 A vision of the victorious martyrs precedes the vision of woe in Rev 15:5–16:21; cf. Rev 7:9–12.

15:2 Mingled with fire: fire symbolizes the sanctity involved in facing God, reflected in the trials that have prepared the victorious Christians or in God's wrath.

z: 2:10; Mt 10:28. *a:* 18:2–3; Is 21:9; Jer 51:8 / Is 51:17; Jer 25:15–17. *b:* 19:3. *c:* 12:17. *d:* Mt 11:28–29; 2 Thes 1:7; Heb 4:10. *e:* 1:7; Dn 7:13. *f:* Jl 4:13; Mt 13:36–43. *g:* 19:15; Is 63:1–6. *h:* 7:9, 14; 13:15–18.

were standing those who had won the victory over the beast and its image and the
number that signified its name. They were
holding God's harps, [3i*]and they sang the
song of Moses, the servant of God, and the
song of the Lamb:

"Great and wonderful are your works,
Lord God almighty.
Just and true are your ways,
O king of the nations.
[4 j]Who will not fear you, Lord,
or glorify your name?
For you alone are holy.
All the nations will come
and worship before you,
for your righteous acts have been
revealed."

[5*]After this I had another vision. The temple
that is the heavenly tent of testimony
opened, [6k]and the seven angels with the
seven plagues came out of the temple. They
were dressed in clean white linen, with a
gold sash around their chests. [7]One of the
four living creatures gave the seven angels
seven gold bowls filled with the fury of God,
who lives forever and ever. [8 l]Then the temple became so filled with the smoke from
God's glory and might that no one could enter it until the seven plagues of the seven angels had been accomplished.

CHAPTER 16

See RG 523

The Seven Bowls. [1*]I heard a loud
voice speaking from the temple to the seven
angels, "Go and pour out the seven bowls of
God's fury upon the earth."

[2*]The first angel went and poured out his
bowl on the earth. Festering and ugly sores
broke out on those who had the mark of the
beast or worshiped its image.

[3*]The second angel poured out his bowl on
the sea. The sea turned to blood like that from
a corpse; every creature living in the sea died.

[4m]The third angel poured out his bowl on
the rivers and springs of water. These also
turned to blood. [5n]Then I heard the angel in
charge of the waters say:

"You are just, O Holy One,
who are and who were,
in passing this sentence.
[6 o]For they have shed the blood of the holy
ones and the prophets,
and you [have] given them blood to
drink;
it is what they deserve."

[7p]Then I heard the altar cry out,

"Yes, Lord God almighty,
your judgments are true and just."

[8]The fourth angel poured out his bowl on the
sun. It was given the power to burn people
with fire. [9q]People were burned by the
scorching heat and blasphemed the name of
God who had power over these plagues, but
they did not repent or give him glory.

[10r*]The fifth angel poured out his bowl on
the throne of the beast. Its kingdom was
plunged into darkness, and people bit their
tongues in pain [11s]and blasphemed the God
of heaven because of their pains and sores.
But they did not repent of their works.

[12*]The sixth angel emptied his bowl on
the great river Euphrates. Its water was dried
up to prepare the way for the kings of the
East. [13t*]I saw three unclean spirits like frogs
come from the mouth of the dragon, from

15:3 The song of Moses: the song that Moses and the Israelites sang after their escape from the oppression of Egypt (Ex 15:1–18). The martyrs have escaped from the oppression of the Devil. **Nations**: many other Greek manuscripts and versions read "ages."

15:5–8 Seven angels receive the bowls of God's wrath.

15:5 Tent of testimony: the name of the meeting tent in the Greek text of Ex 40. Cf. 2 Mc 2:4–7.

16:1–21 These seven bowls, like the seven seals (Rev 6:1–17; 8:1) and the seven trumpets (Rev 8:2–9:21; 11:15–19), bring on a succession of disasters modeled in part on the plagues of Egypt (Ex 7–12). See note on Rev 6:12–14.

16:2 Like the sixth Egyptian plague (Ex 9:8–11).

16:3–4 Like the first Egyptian plague (Ex 7:20–21). The same woe followed the blowing of the second trumpet (Rev 8:8–9).

16:10 The throne of the beast: symbol of the forces of evil. **Darkness**: like the ninth Egyptian plague (Ex 10:21–23); cf. Rev 9:2.

16:12 The kings of the East: Parthians; see notes on Rev 6:2 and Rev 17:12–13. **East**: literally, "rising of the sun," as in Rev 7:2.

16:13 Frogs: possibly an allusion to the second Egyptian

i: Ps 92:6; 98:1 / Dt 32:4; Ps 145:17. *j:* Ps 86:9–10; Jer 10:7. *k:* 19:8. *l:* 1 Kgs 8:10; Is 6:4. *m:* Ex 7:14–24. *n:* 1:4. *o:* Ez 35:6; Mt 23:34–35. *p:* Dn 3:27; Tb 3:2. *q:* Am 4:6. *r:* Ex 10:21–23. *s:* Ex 9:8–11 / Jer 5:3. *t:* Ex 8:2–3.

the mouth of the beast, and from the mouth of the false prophet. [14u]These were demonic spirits who performed signs. They went out to the kings of the whole world to assemble them for the battle on the great day of God the almighty. [15v*](“Behold, I am coming like a thief.” Blessed is the one who watches and keeps his clothes ready, so that he may not go naked and people see him exposed.) [16*]They then assembled the kings in the place that is named Armageddon in Hebrew.

[17w]The seventh angel poured out his bowl into the air. A loud voice came out of the temple from the throne, saying, “It is done.” [18x]Then there were lightning flashes, rumblings, and peals of thunder, and a great earthquake. It was such a violent earthquake that there has never been one like it since the human race began on earth. [19*]The great city was split into three parts, and the gentile cities fell. But God remembered great Babylon, giving it the cup filled with the wine of his fury and wrath. [20*]Every island fled, and mountains disappeared. [21y]Large hailstones like huge weights came down from the sky on people, and they blasphemed God for the plague of hail because this plague was so severe.

V. The Punishment of Babylon and the Destruction of Pagan Nations

CHAPTER 17

See RG 523–24

Babylon the Great. [1z*]Then one of the seven angels who were holding the seven bowls came and said to me, “Come here. I will show you the judgment on the great harlot who lives near the many waters. [2a*]The kings of the earth have had intercourse with her, and the inhabitants of the earth became drunk on the wine of her harlotry.” [3b*]Then he carried me away in spirit to a deserted place where I saw a woman seated on a scarlet beast that was covered with blasphemous names, with seven heads and ten horns. [4c*]The woman was wearing purple and scarlet and adorned with gold, precious stones, and pearls. She held in her hand a gold cup that was filled with the abominable and sordid deeds of her harlotry. [5]On her forehead was written a name, which is a mystery, “Babylon the great, the mother of harlots and of the abominations of the earth.” [6*]I saw that the woman was drunk on the blood of the holy ones and on the blood of the witnesses to Jesus.

Meaning of the Beast and Harlot When I saw her I was greatly amazed. [7]The angel said to me, “Why are you amazed? I will explain to you the mystery of the woman and of the beast that carries her, the beast with the seven heads and the ten horns. [8d*]The beast that you saw existed once but now exists no longer. It will come up from the abyss and is headed for destruction. The inhabitants of the earth whose names have not been written in the book of life from the foundation of the world shall be amazed when they see the beast, because it existed once but exists no longer, and yet it will

plague (Ex 7:25–8:11). **The false prophet**: identified with the two-horned second beast (Rev 13:11–18 and the note there).

16:15 Like a thief: as in Rev 3:3 (cf. Mt 24:42–44; 1 Thes 5:2). **Blessed**: see note on Rev 1:3.

16:16 Armageddon: in Hebrew, this means “Mountain of Megiddo.” Since Megiddo was the scene of many decisive battles in antiquity (Jgs 5:19–20; 2 Kgs 9:27; 2 Chr 35:20–24), the town became the symbol of the final disastrous rout of the forces of evil.

16:19 The great city: Rome and the empire.

16:20–21 See note on Rev 6:12–14. **Hailstones**: as in the seventh Egyptian plague (Ex 9:23–24); cf. Rev 8:7. **Like huge weights**: literally, “weighing a talent,” about one hundred pounds.

17:1–19:10 The punishment of Babylon is now described as a past event and, metaphorically, under the image of the great harlot who leads people astray into idolatry.

17:1–6 Babylon, the symbolic name (Rev 17:5) of Rome, is graphically described as “the great harlot.”

17:2 Intercourse . . . harlotry: see note on Rev 14:4. The pagan kings subject to Rome adopted the cult of the emperor.

17:3 Scarlet beast: see note on Rev 13:1–10. **Blasphemous names**: divine titles assumed by the Roman emperors; see note on Rev 13:5–6.

17:6 Reference to the great wealth and idolatrous cults of Rome.

17:6b–18 An interpretation of the vision is here given.

17:8 Allusion to the belief that the dead Nero would return to power (Rev 17:11); see note on Rev 13:3.

u: 1 Cor 1:8. *v:* Mt 24:42–44 / 3:17. *w:* Is 66:6. *x:* Mk 13:19. *y:* Ex 9:22–26. *z:* Jer 50:38; 51:13. *a:* Jer 51:7. *b:* 13:1. *c:* 18:16. *d:* 13:3–4 / 3:5; 13:8; 20:12.

come again. [9e*]Here is a clue for one who
has wisdom. The seven heads represent
seven hills upon which the woman sits.
They also represent seven kings: [10*]five
have already fallen, one still lives, and the
last has not yet come, and when he comes
he must remain only a short while. [11*]The
beast that existed once but exists no longer
is an eighth king, but really belongs to the
seven and is headed for destruction.
[12f*]The ten horns that you saw represent
ten kings who have not yet been crowned;
they will receive royal authority along with
the beast for one hour. [13]They are of one
mind and will give their power and authority to the beast. [14g]They will fight with the
Lamb, but the Lamb will conquer them, for
he is Lord of lords and king of kings, and
those with him are called, chosen, and
faithful."

[15]Then he said to me, "The waters that
you saw where the harlot lives represent
large numbers of peoples, nations, and
tongues. [16h*]The ten horns that you saw and
the beast will hate the harlot; they will leave
her desolate and naked; they will eat her
flesh and consume her with fire. [17]For God
has put it into their minds to carry out his
purpose and to make them come to an agreement to give their kingdom to the beast until
the words of God are accomplished. [18]The
woman whom you saw represents the great
city that has sovereignty over the kings of
the earth."

CHAPTER 18

See RG 524

The Fall of Babylon. [1i*]After this I
saw another angel coming down from
heaven, having great authority, and the earth
became illumined by his splendor. [2j*]He
cried out in a mighty voice:

"Fallen, fallen is Babylon the great.
She has become a haunt for demons.
She is a cage for every unclean spirit,
a cage for every unclean bird,
[a cage for every unclean] and
disgusting [beast].
[3 k*]For all the nations have drunk
the wine of her licentious passion.
The kings of the earth had intercourse
with her,
and the merchants of the earth grew
rich from her drive for luxury."

[4l*]Then I heard another voice from heaven
say:

"Depart from her, my people,
so as not to take part in her sins
and receive a share in her plagues,
[5 m]for her sins are piled up to the sky,
and God remembers her crimes.
[6 n]Pay her back as she has paid others.
Pay her back double for her deeds.
Into her cup pour double what she
poured.
[7 o]To the measure of her boasting and
wantonness

17:9 Here is a clue: literally, "Here a mind that has wisdom." **Seven hills**: of Rome.

17:10 There is little agreement as to the identity of the Roman emperors alluded to here. The number seven (Rev 17:9) suggests that all the emperors are meant; see note on Rev 1:4.

17:11 The beast: Nero; see note on Rev 17:8.

17:12–13 Ten kings who have not yet been crowned: perhaps Parthian satraps who are to accompany the revived Nero (the beast) in his march on Rome to regain power; see note on Rev 13:3. In Rev 19:11–21, the Lamb and his companions will conquer them.

17:16–18 The ten horns: the ten pagan kings (Rev 17:12) who unwittingly fulfill God's will against harlot Rome, the great city; cf. Ez 16:37.

18:1–19:4 A stirring dirge over the fall of Babylon-Rome. The perspective is prophetic, as if the fall of Rome had already taken place. The imagery here, as elsewhere in this book, is not to be taken literally. The vindictiveness of some of the language, borrowed from the scathing Old Testament prophecies against Babylon, Tyre, and Nineveh (Is 23; 24; 27; Jer 50–51; Ez 26–27), is meant to portray symbolically the inexorable demands of God's holiness and justice; cf. Introduction. The section concludes with a joyous canticle on the future glory of heaven.

18:2 Many Greek manuscripts and versions omit **a cage for every unclean . . . beast.**

18:3–24 Rome is condemned for her immorality, symbol of idolatry (see note on Rev 14:4), and for persecuting the church; cf. Rev 19:2.

18:4 Depart from her: not evacuation of the city but separation from sinners, as always in apocalyptic literature.

e: 13:18. *f:* Dn 7:24. *g:* 19:11–21; 2 Mc 13:4; 1 Tm 6:15 / Rom 1:6; 1 Pt 2:9; Jude 1. *h:* Ez 16:37–41; 23:25–29. *i:* Ez 43:2. *j:* 14:8; Is 21:9; Jer 50:2–3; 51:8. *k:* 17:2; Jer 51:7. *l:* Is 48:20; Jer 50:8. *m:* Jer 51:9. *n:* Jer 50:15 / Jer 16:18. *o:* Is 47:8–9.

repay her in torment and grief;
for she said to herself,
'I sit enthroned as queen;
I am no widow,
and I will never know grief.'
8 Therefore, her plagues will come in one day,
pestilence, grief, and famine;
she will be consumed by fire.
For mighty is the Lord God who judges her."

9The kings of the earth who had intercourse
with her in their wantonness will weep and
mourn over her when they see the smoke of
her pyre. 10They will keep their distance for
fear of the torment inflicted on her, and they
will say:

"Alas, alas, great city,
Babylon, mighty city.
In one hour your judgment has come."

11*The merchants of the earth will weep and
mourn for her, because there will be no more
markets for their cargo: 12their cargo of gold,
silver, precious stones, and pearls; fine
linen, purple silk, and scarlet cloth; fragrant
wood of every kind, all articles of ivory and
all articles of the most expensive wood,
bronze, iron, and marble; 13*cinnamon,
spice, incense, myrrh, and frankincense;
wine, olive oil, fine flour, and wheat; cattle
and sheep, horses and chariots, and slaves,
that is, human beings.

14 [p]"The fruit you craved
has left you.
All your luxury and splendor are gone,
never again will one find them."

15The merchants who deal in these goods,
who grew rich from her, will keep their distance for fear of the torment inflicted on her.
Weeping and mourning, 16[q]they cry out:

"Alas, alas, great city,
wearing fine linen, purple and scarlet,
adorned [in] gold, precious stones, and pearls.
17 In one hour this great wealth has been ruined."

Every captain of a ship, every traveler at sea,
sailors, and seafaring merchants stood at a
distance 18and cried out when they saw the
smoke of her pyre, "What city could compare with the great city?" 19[r]They threw dust
on their heads and cried out, weeping and
mourning:

"Alas, alas, great city,
in which all who had ships at sea
grew rich from her wealth.
In one hour she has been ruined.
20 [s]Rejoice over her, heaven,
you holy ones, apostles, and prophets.
For God has judged your case against her."

21[t]A mighty angel picked up a stone like a
huge millstone and threw it into the sea and
said:

"With such force will Babylon the great city be thrown down,
and will never be found again.
22 [u]No melodies of harpists and musicians,
flutists and trumpeters,
will ever be heard in you again.
No craftsmen in any trade
will ever be found in you again.
No sound of the millstone
will ever be heard in you again.
23 [v]No light from a lamp
will ever be seen in you again.
No voices of bride and groom
will ever be heard in you again.
Because your merchants were the great ones of the world,
all nations were led astray by your magic potion.
24 [w]In her was found the blood of prophets and holy ones
and all who have been slain on the earth."

18:11 Ironically, the merchants weep not so much for Babylon-Rome, but for their lost markets; cf. Ez 27:36.
18:13 Spice: an unidentified spice plant called in Greek *amōmon*.

p: Hos 10:5 / Am 6:7. *q:* 17:4. *r:* Ez 27:27–32. *s:* 19:1–2; Dt 32:43. *t:* Jer 51:63–64; Ez 26:21. *u:* Is 24:8; Ez 26:13. *v:* Jer 7:34; 16:9; 25:10. *w:* 16:6.

CHAPTER 19

See RG 524

[1*]After this I heard what sounded like
the loud voice of a great multitude in
heaven, saying:

"Alleluia!
Salvation, glory, and might belong to our
God,
2 [x]for true and just are his judgments.
He has condemned the great harlot
who corrupted the earth with her
harlotry.
He has avenged on her the blood of his
servants."

[3y]They said a second time:

"Alleluia! Smoke will rise from her
forever and ever."

[4]The twenty-four elders and the four living
creatures fell down and worshiped God who
sat on the throne, saying, "Amen. Alleluia."
The Victory Song. [5z*]A voice coming
from the throne said:

"Praise our God, all you his servants,
[and] you who revere him, small and
great."

[6]Then I heard something like the sound of a
great multitude or the sound of rushing water or mighty peals of thunder, as they said:

"Alleluia!
The Lord has established his reign,
[our] God, the almighty.
7 [a*]Let us rejoice and be glad
and give him glory.
For the wedding day of the Lamb has
come,
his bride has made herself ready.
8 [b*]She was allowed to wear
a bright, clean linen garment."

(The linen represents the righteous deeds of
the holy ones.)
[9c*]Then the angel said to me, "Write this:
Blessed are those who have been called to
the wedding feast of the Lamb." And he said
to me, "These words are true; they come
from God." [10d*]I fell at his feet to worship
him. But he said to me, "Don't! I am a fellow servant of yours and of your brothers
who bear witness to Jesus. Worship God.
Witness to Jesus is the spirit of prophecy."

The King of Kings. [11e*]Then I saw the
heavens opened, and there was a white
horse; its rider was [called] "Faithful and
True." He judges and wages war in righteousness. [12f*]His eyes were [like] a fiery
flame, and on his head were many diadems.
He had a name inscribed that no one knows
except himself. [13g*]He wore a cloak that had
been dipped in blood, and his name was
called the Word of God. [14h]The armies of
heaven followed him, mounted on white
horses and wearing clean white linen.
[15i*]Out of his mouth came a sharp sword to
strike the nations. He will rule them with an
iron rod, and he himself will tread out in the
wine press the wine of the fury and wrath of

19:1, 3, 4, 6 Alleluia: found only here in the New Testament, this frequent exclamation of praise in the Hebrew psalms was important in Jewish liturgy.

19:5–10 A victory song follows, sung by the entire church, celebrating the marriage of the Lamb, the union of the Messiah with the community of the elect.

19:7 The wedding day of the Lamb: symbol of God's reign about to begin (Rev 21:1–22:5); see note on Rev 10:7. **His bride**: the church; cf. 2 Cor 11:2; Eph 5:22–27. Marriage is one of the biblical metaphors used to describe the covenant relationship between God and his people; cf. Hos 2:16–22; Is 54:5–6; 62:5; Ez 16:6–14. Hence, idolatry and apostasy are viewed as adultery and harlotry (Hos 2:4–13; Ez 16:15–63); see note on Rev 14:4.

19:8 See note on Rev 14:12.

19:9 Blessed: see note on Rev 1:3.

19:10 The spirit of prophecy: as the prophets were inspired to proclaim God's word, so the Christian is called to give witness to the Word of God (Rev 19:13) made flesh; cf. Rev 1:2; 6:9; 12:17.

19:11–16 Symbolic description of the exalted Christ (cf. Rev 1:13–16) who together with the armies of heaven overcomes the beast and its followers; cf. Rev 17:14.

19:12 A name: in Semitic thought, the name conveyed the reality of the person; cf. Mt 11:27; Lk 10:22.

19:13 Had been dipped in: other Greek manuscripts and versions read "had been sprinkled with"; cf. Rev 19:15. **The Word of God**: Christ is the revelation of the Father; cf. Jn 1:1, 14; 1 Jn 2:14.

19:15 The treading of the wine press is a prophetic symbol used to describe the destruction of God's enemies; cf. Is 63:1–6; Jl 4:13.

x: Dn 3:27 / Jer 51:48–49. *y:* 14:11; Is 34:10. *z:* 11:18; Ps 115:13. *a:* Mt 22:9; Eph 5:27. *b:* 15:6; Is 61:10; Mt 22:11–12. *c:* Mt 8:11; Lk 14:15. *d:* 22:8–9. *e:* Is 11:4. *f:* 1:14–16; 2:18 / Lk 10:22. *g:* Is 63:1 / Jn 1:1. *h:* 15:6; 19:8. *i:* 14:20; Is 63:3.

God the almighty. [16j]He has a name written on his cloak and on his thigh, "King of kings and Lord of lords."

[17*]Then I saw an angel standing on the sun. He cried out [in] a loud voice to all the birds flying high overhead, "Come here. Gather for God's great feast, [18k]to eat the flesh of kings, the flesh of military officers, and the flesh of warriors, the flesh of horses and of their riders, and the flesh of all, free and slave, small and great." [19]Then I saw the beast and the kings of the earth and their armies gathered to fight against the one riding the horse and against his army. [20l*]The beast was caught and with it the false prophet who had performed in its sight the signs by which he led astray those who had accepted the mark of the beast and those who had worshiped its image. The two were thrown alive into the fiery pool burning with sulfur. [21]The rest were killed by the sword that came out of the mouth of the one riding the horse, and all the birds gorged themselves on their flesh.

See RG 524

CHAPTER 20

The Thousand-year Reign. [1m*]Then I saw an angel come down from heaven, holding in his hand the key to the abyss and a heavy chain. [2n*]He seized the dragon, the ancient serpent, which is the Devil or Satan, and tied it up for a thousand years [3]and threw it into the abyss, which he locked over it and sealed, so that it could no longer lead the nations astray until the thousand years are completed. After this, it is to be released for a short time.

[4o*]Then I saw thrones; those who sat on them were entrusted with judgment. I also saw the souls of those who had been beheaded for their witness to Jesus and for the word of God, and who had not worshiped the beast or its image nor had accepted its mark on their foreheads or hands. They came to life and they reigned with Christ for a thousand years. [5]The rest of the dead did not come to life until the thousand years were over. This is the first resurrection. [6*]Blessed and holy is the one who shares in the first resurrection. The second death has no power over these; they will be priests of God and of Christ, and they will reign with him for [the] thousand years.

[7*]When the thousand years are completed, Satan will be released from his prison. [8p*]He will go out to deceive the nations at the four corners of the earth, Gog and Magog, to gather them for battle; their number is like the sand of the sea. [9q*]They invaded the breadth of the earth and surrounded the camp of the holy ones and the beloved city. But fire came down from heaven and consumed them. [10]The Devil who had led them astray was thrown into the pool of fire and sulfur, where the beast and the false prophet were. There they will be tormented day and night forever and ever.

The Large White Throne. [11r*]Next I saw a large white throne and the one who was sitting on it. The earth and the sky fled from his

19:17–21 The certainty of Christ's victory is proclaimed by an angel, followed by a reference to the mustering of enemy forces and a fearsome description of their annihilation. The gruesome imagery is borrowed from Ez 39:4, 17–20.

19:20 Beast . . . false prophet: see notes on Rev 13. **The fiery pool . . . sulfur**: symbol of God's punishment (Rev 14:10; 20:10, 14–15), different from the abyss; see note on Rev 9:1.

20:1–6 Like the other numerical values in this book, the thousand years are not to be taken literally; they symbolize the long period of time between the chaining up of Satan (a symbol for Christ's resurrection-victory over death and the forces of evil) and the end of the world. During this time God's people share in the glorious reign of God that is present to them by virtue of their baptismal victory over death and sin; cf. Rom 6:1–8; Jn 5:24–25; 16:33; 1 Jn 3:14; Eph 2:1.

20:1 Abyss: see note on Rev 9:1.

20:2 Dragon . . . serpent . . . Satan: see notes on Rev 12:3, 9, 10, 15.

20:4 Beast . . . mark: see Rev 13 and its notes.

20:6 Blessed: see note on Rev 1:3. **Second death**: see note on Rev 2:11. **Priests**: as in Rev 1:6; 5:10; cf. 1 Pt 2:9.

20:7–10 A description of the symbolic battle to take place when Satan is released at the end of time, when the thousand years are over; see note on Rev 20:1–6.

20:8 Gog and Magog: symbols of all pagan nations; the names are taken from Ez 38:1–39:20.

20:9 The breadth of the earth: Palestine. **The beloved city**: Jerusalem; see note on Rev 14:1.

20:11–15 A description of the final judgment. After the intermediate reign of Christ, all the dead are raised and judged, thus inaugurating the new age.

---

j: 17:14; 2 Mc 13:4. *k*: Ez 39:17–20. *l*: 14:10. *m*: 9:1. *n*: Gn 3:1. *o*: Mt 19:28. *p*: Ez 38:2, 9, 16. *q*: Ez 38:22. *r*: 2 Pt 3:7, 10, 12.

presence and there was no place for them.
12s*I saw the dead, the great and the lowly,
standing before the throne, and scrolls were
opened. Then another scroll was opened, the
book of life. The dead were judged according to their deeds, by what was written in the
scrolls. 13*The sea gave up its dead; then
Death and Hades gave up their dead. All the
dead were judged according to their deeds.
14t*Then Death and Hades were thrown into
the pool of fire. (This pool of fire is the second death.) 15Anyone whose name was not
found written in the book of life was thrown
into the pool of fire.

VI. The New Creation

CHAPTER 21

See RG 524

The New Heaven and the New Earth.
1u*Then I saw a new heaven and a new earth.
The former heaven and the former earth had
passed away, and the sea was no more. 2v*I
also saw the holy city, a new Jerusalem,
coming down out of heaven from God, prepared as a bride adorned for her husband.
3w*I heard a loud voice from the throne saying, "Behold, God's dwelling is with the human race. He will dwell with them and they
will be his people and God himself will always be with them [as their God]. 4xHe will
wipe every tear from their eyes, and there
shall be no more death or mourning, wailing
or pain, [for] the old order has passed away."
5y*The one who sat on the throne said,
"Behold, I make all things new." Then he
said, "Write these words down, for they are
trustworthy and true." 6z*He said to me,
"They are accomplished. I [am] the Alpha
and the Omega, the beginning and the end.
To the thirsty I will give a gift from the
spring of life-giving water. 7a*The victor
will inherit these gifts, and I shall be his
God, and he will be my son. 8b*But as for
cowards, the unfaithful, the depraved, murderers, the unchaste, sorcerers, idol-worshipers, and deceivers of every sort, their lot
is in the burning pool of fire and sulfur,
which is the second death."

The New Jerusalem. 9*One of the seven
angels who held the seven bowls filled with
the seven last plagues came and said to me,
"Come here. I will show you the bride, the
wife of the Lamb." 10cHe took me in spirit to
a great, high mountain and showed me the
holy city Jerusalem coming down out of
heaven from God. 11dIt gleamed with the
splendor of God. Its radiance was like that of
a precious stone, like jasper, clear as crystal.
12It had a massive, high wall, with twelve
gates where twelve angels were stationed
and on which names were inscribed, [the
names] of the twelve tribes of the Israelites.
13eThere were three gates facing east, three
north, three south, and three west. 14f*The
wall of the city had twelve courses of stones
as its foundation, on which were inscribed
the twelve names of the twelve apostles of
the Lamb.

20:12 The book of life: see note on Rev 3:5. **Judged . . . scrolls**: see note on Rev 14:12.

20:13 Hades: the netherworld; see note on Rev 1:18.

20:14 Second death: see note on Rev 2:11.

21:1–22:5 A description of God's eternal kingdom in heaven under the symbols of a new heaven and a new earth; cf. Is 65:17–25; 66:22; Mt 19:28.

21:1 Sea . . . no more: because as home of the dragon it was doomed to disappear; cf. Jb 7:12.

21:2 New Jerusalem . . . bride: symbol of the church (Gal 4:26); see note on Rev 19:7.

21:3–4 Language taken from Ez 37:27; Is 25:8; 35:10; cf. Rev 7:17.

21:3 People: other ancient manuscripts read a plural, "peoples."

21:5 The one . . . on the throne: God himself; cf. Rev 4:1–11.

21:6 They are accomplished: God's reign has already begun; see note on Rev 20:1–6. **Alpha . . . Omega**: see note on Rev 1:8. **Life-giving water**: see note on Rev 7:17.

21:7 The victor: over the forces of evil; see the conclusions of the seven letters (Rev 2:7, 11, 17, 26; 3:5, 12, 21). **He will be my son**: the victorious Christian enjoys divine affiliation by adoption (Gal 4:4–7; Rom 8:14–17); see note on Rev 2:26–28.

21:8 Cowards: their conviction is so weak that they deny Christ in time of trial and become traitors. **Second death**: see note on Rev 2:11.

21:9–22:5 Symbolic descriptions of the new Jerusalem, the church. Most of the images are borrowed from Ez 40–48.

21:9 The bride, the wife of the Lamb: the church (Rev 21:2), the new Jerusalem (Rev 21:10); cf. 2 Cor 11:2.

21:14 Courses of stones . . . apostles: literally, "twelve foundations"; cf. Eph 2:19–20.

s: Rom 2:6. *t:* 1 Cor 15:26, 54–55. *u:* Is 65:17; 66:22; Rom 8:19–23; 2 Pt 3:13. *v:* 19:7–9. *w:* Ez 37:27. *x:* 7:17; Is 25:8; 35:10. *y:* Is 43:19; 2 Cor 5:17. *z:* 22:17; Ps 36:8–9; Is 55:1. *a:* 2 Sm 7:14. *b:* 22:15; Rom 1:29–32. *c:* Ez 40:2. *d:* Heb 11:10. *e:* Ez 48:31–35. *f:* Eph 2:20.

15*The one who spoke to me held a gold measuring rod to measure the city, its gates, and its wall. 16*The city was square, its length the same as [also] its width. He measured the city with the rod and found it fifteen hundred miles in length and width and height. 17*He also measured its wall: one hundred and forty-four cubits according to the standard unit of measurement the angel used. 18*The wall was constructed of jasper, while the city was pure gold, clear as glass. 19gThe foundations of the city wall were decorated with every precious stone; the first course of stones was jasper, the second sapphire, the third chalcedony, the fourth emerald, 20the fifth sardonyx, the sixth carnelian, the seventh chrysolite, the eighth beryl, the ninth topaz, the tenth chrysoprase, the eleventh hyacinth, and the twelfth amethyst. 21lThe twelve gates were twelve pearls, each of the gates made from a single pearl; and the street of the city was of pure gold, transparent as glass.

22h*I saw no temple in the city, for its temple is the Lord God almighty and the Lamb. 23i*The city had no need of sun or moon to shine on it, for the glory of God gave it light, and its lamp was the Lamb. 24j*The nations will walk by its light, and to it the kings of the earth will bring their treasure. 25During the day its gates will never be shut, and there will be no night there. 26The treasure and wealth of the nations will be brought there, 27kbut nothing unclean will enter it, nor any[one] who does abominable things or tells lies. Only those will enter whose names are written in the Lamb's book of life.

CHAPTER 22

See RG 524

1l*Then the angel showed me the river of life-giving water, sparkling like crystal, flowing from the throne of God and of the Lamb 2*down the middle of its street. On either side of the river grew the tree of life that produces fruit twelve times a year, once each month; the leaves of the trees serve as medicine for the nations. 3Nothing accursed will be found there anymore. The throne of God and of the Lamb will be in it, and his servants will worship him. 4*They will look upon his face, and his name will be on their foreheads. 5mNight will be no more, nor will they need light from lamp or sun, for the Lord God shall give them light, and they shall reign forever and ever.

VII. Epilogue

6n*And he said to me, "These words are trustworthy and true, and the Lord, the God of prophetic spirits, sent his angel to show his servants what must happen soon." 7o*"Behold, I am coming soon." Blessed is the one who keeps the prophetic message of this book.

8It is I, John, who heard and saw these things, and when I heard and saw them I fell down to worship at the feet of the angel who showed them to me. 9pBut he said to me,

21:15–17 The city is shaped like a gigantic cube, a symbol of perfection (cf. 1 Kgs 6:19–20). The measurements of the city and its wall are multiples of the symbolic number twelve; see note on Rev 7:4–9.

21:16 Fifteen hundred miles: literally, twelve thousand stades, about 12,000 furlongs (see note on Rev 14:20); the number is symbolic: twelve (the apostles as leaders of the new Israel) multiplied by 1,000 (the immensity of Christians); cf. Introduction. **In length and width and height**: literally, "its length and width and height are the same."

21:17 One hundred and forty-four cubits: the cubit was about eighteen inches in length. **Standard unit of measurement the angel used**: literally, "by a human measure, i.e., an angel's."

21:18–21 The gold and precious gems symbolize the beauty and excellence of the church; cf. Ex 28:15–21; Tb 13:16–17; Is 54:11–12.

21:22 Christ is present throughout the church; hence, no temple is needed as an earthly dwelling for God; cf. Mt 18:20; 28:20; Jn 4:21.

21:23 Lamp . . . Lamb: cf. Jn 8:12.

21:24–27 All men and women of good will are welcome in the church; cf. Is 60:1, 3, 5, 11. **The . . . book of life**: see note on Rev 3:5.

22:1, 17 Life-giving water: see note on Rev 7:17.

22:2 The tree of life: cf. Rev 22:14; see note on Rev 2:7. **Fruit . . . medicine**: cf. Ez 47:12.

22:4 Look upon his face: cf. Mt 5:8; 1 Cor 13:12; 1 Jn 3:2.

22:6–21 The book ends with an epilogue consisting of a series of warnings and exhortations and forming an inclusion with the prologue by resuming its themes and expressions; see note on Rev 1:1–3.

22:7, 12, 20 I am coming soon: Christ is the speaker; see note on Rev 1:3.

22:7, 14 Blessed: see note on Rev 1:3.

---

g: Is 54:11–12. *h:* Jn 2:19–20. *i:* Is 60:1–2, 19–20. *j:* Is 60:11. *k:* Is 35:8; 52:1; Zec 13:2 / 3:5; 20:12. *l:* Ez 47:1–12. *m:* Is 60:20. *n:* 1:1. *o:* 12, 20 / 1:3. *p:* 19:10.

"Don't! I am a fellow servant of yours and of your brothers the prophets and of those who keep the message of this book. Worship God."

[10]*Then he said to me, "Do not seal up the prophetic words of this book, for the appointed time is near. [11]Let the wicked still act wickedly, and the filthy still be filthy. The righteous must still do right, and the holy still be holy."

[12q]"Behold, I am coming soon. I bring with me the recompense I will give to each according to his deeds. [13r]*I am the Alpha and the Omega, the first and the last, the beginning and the end."

[14s]*Blessed are they who wash their robes so as to have the right to the tree of life and enter the city through its gates. [15t]Outside are the dogs, the sorcerers, the unchaste, the murderers, the idol-worshipers, and all who love and practice deceit.

[16u]*"I, Jesus, sent my angel to give you this testimony for the churches. I am the root and offspring of David, the bright morning star."

[17v]*The Spirit and the bride say, "Come." Let the hearer say, "Come." Let the one who thirsts come forward, and the one who wants it receive the gift of life-giving water.

[18]I warn everyone who hears the prophetic words in this book: if anyone adds to them, God will add to him the plagues described in this book, [19w]and if anyone takes away from the words in this prophetic book, God will take away his share in the tree of life and in the holy city described in this book.

[20x]*The one who gives this testimony says, "Yes, I am coming soon." Amen! Come, Lord Jesus!

[21]The grace of the Lord Jesus be with all.

22:10 The appointed time: see note on Rev 1:3.

22:13 Christ applies to himself words used by God in Rev 1:8.

22:14 The city: heavenly Jerusalem; see note on Rev 21:2.

22:16 The root . . . of David: see note on Rev 5:5. **Morning star**: see note on Rev 2:26–28.

22:17 Bride: the church; see note on Rev 21:2.

22:20 Come, Lord Jesus: a liturgical refrain, similar to the Aramaic expression *Marana tha*—"Our Lord, come!"—in 1 Cor 16:22; cf. note there. It was a prayer for the coming of Christ in glory at the parousia; see note on Rev 1:3.

q: 7, 20 / Ps 62:12; 2 Tm 4:14. *r*: 1:8; 21:6; Is 41:4; 44:6. *s*: 7:14–15; 22:2. *t*: 21:8; Rom 1:29–32. *u*: 1:1, 11–12; 22:6 / 2:28. *v*: 21:6; Is 55:1. *w*: Dt 4:2. *x*: 7, 12 / Acts 3:20–21; 1 Cor 15:23; 16:22.

GLOSSARY
MEASURES AND WEIGHTS
LECTIONARY

GLOSSARY

A

Abba (Aram. "father"), the word Jesus (Mk 14:36 and many other places) and, following him, the early church (Rom 8:15) used to address God.

Abaddon (Heb. "place of destruction"), the realm of the dead (Jb 26:6; Prv 15:11; Ps 88:10–12; Rev 9:11).

accession the act of taking one's place as a ruler.

acrostic a literary device in which the first letter of each line of poetry occurs according to a predetermined pattern. In the poetry of the Hebrew Bible all acrostics are alphabetical: the individual lines of a poem (or occasionally small groups of lines) begin with the twenty-two letters of the Hebrew alphabet in order. (This would be equivalent to the first line of an English poem beginning with A, the second with B, etc.) The acrostic form, besides giving the esthetic pleasure of a pattern, may have been intended to make memorization easier. It may also have been intended as a way of expressing completeness: in Lamentations, for instance, the acrostic format of the individual chapters might have been used to express both the completeness of the outpouring of grief and its finality. The following poems in the Bible are acrostics: Psalms 9–10; 25; 34; 37; 111; 112; 119; 145; Proverbs 31:10–31; Lamentations 1; 2; 3; 4 (ch 5 is not an acrostic, but preserves part of the form by having 22 lines, the number of letters in the Hebrew alphabet); Nahum 1:2–8 (or 9) (incomplete). In the Hebrew text of Sirach, 51:13–30 is acrostic.

Adonai (Heb. "my Lord") a divine title and the word generally substituted for the tetragrammaton, **YHWH,** when the Bible is read aloud.

allegorical a method of reading a text as an allegory; explaining or interpreting elements in a narrative as if they stood for something else. Paul uses an allegorical method in Galatians 4:22–26. "Allegorical interpretation," such as that used by **Philo Judaeus** to draw out the meaning of the Bible, is an effort to make an allegory out of a writing that was not originally intended to be one, but that is, in the view of the interpreter, presenting a hidden meaning that the allegorical interpretation will reveal.

allegory an extended comparison which directly describes one reality while indirectly describing something entirely different. An allegory as a narrative uses action, setting, and characters to point symbolically to something else. Biblical allegories include the "Song of the Vineyard" in Isaiah 5, in which the story of the vineyard is also the story of Judah, and the parable of the sower in Matthew 13:1–8 and 18–23. Allegory is infrequent in present-day literature, but allegorical treatments or uses of art still occur: The statue of Justice in courthouses uses allegorical elements: a beautiful woman (justice attracts us), blindfolded (justice is indifferent to external appearance), holding balancing scales (justice weighs the merits of a case in a publicly observable way) and a sword (justice can punish), all of which express our ideals of justice.

alleluia a Greek and Latin form of a Hebrew verb, meaning "Praise the Lord." See **hallelujah.**

Amorites according to the Bible, one of the native nations of Canaan. Amorites are attested in other ancient Near Eastern documents from the third millennium and onwards as residents of Syria who migrated to Mesopotamia and other areas. They spoke a language related to Hebrew.

anachronism an element in a story that is out of place because it did not exist at the time of the story. Anachronisms can be valuable clues to when a particular narrative was written.

anawim the Hebrew word for "the poor," "the afflicted," "the meek or humble." Often used in Psalms for the group to which the Psalmist belongs.

anoint touch or rub with oil. Both things and people can be anointed. Anointing was a sign that the person or thing was dedicated to God: kings (1 Kgs 1:39) and priests (Lv 8:30) were anointed, as were the bodies of those who had died (Lk 23:56).

anthropomorphic (Gr. "human form") language that presents God in human or human-like terms. "Your right hand, O LORD, magnificent in power, your right hand, O LORD, has shattered the enemy" (Ex 15:6).

antithesis the contrast of ideas through closely contrasted words: "A mild answer calms wrath, but a harsh word stirs up anger" (Prv 15:1).

antithetic parallelism two parallel lines related to one another by opposition (e.g., Prv 10:4, "The slack hand impoverishes, but the hand of the diligent enriches").

aphorism a short, memorable saying. Many of the Proverbs are aphorisms, as are many of Jesus' statements.

apocalypse (Gr. *apokalypsis,* "removal of the veil, revelation") a narrative literary genre in which an angel or other heavenly being communicates to a human being the divine plan for history and the arrangement of the supernatural order. Many apocalypses are a series of visions of heaven and earth that are then explained. Apocalypses are a feature of late biblical religion.

apocalyptic having the character of an apocalypse; assuming the existence of a supernatural realm closely related to the natural; maintaining the imminence of a final judgment.

Apocrypha (Gr. "hidden things") a group of about 20 mostly Jewish works, many of which were included in the **Septuagint,** but which were not accepted into the Jewish canon of the Bible. All of these works are extra-canonical for Protestants; some are canonical for Roman Catholics; a few more are canonical for Orthodox Christians. See **deuterocanonical.**

apodictic law law stated absolutely, as in the Decalogue's "you shall not," rather than casuistically, "if a person . . . " See **casuistic law.**

apologia (Gr. "explanation") a defense of one's actions or beliefs, usually in a formal speech or written document.

apostasy abandoning a set of beliefs, or the position of having abandoned them.

apostle (Gr. "one who is sent"), a delegate or representative. In the New Testament, an apostle was one who had known Jesus and could witness to the resurrection (Acts 1:21–22) or a preacher of the gospel who had been called by God (1 Cor 12:28; Rom 16:7).

apostrophe an address to an absent person or personified object. There is an apostrophe to Assyria in Isaiah 10:5.

Aramaic a Semitic language used widely in Mesopotamia and the Land of Israel during the Persian period, though it developed earlier. In the mid-first millennium, it eventually replaced Akkadian as the lingua franca of the ancient near eastern world. It became the ordinary language of Jews and is the language of much rabbinic commentary. The Aramaic translation of the Bible is the Targum.

Arameans a Semitic people living in the area of Syria from the second millennium onwards. Some biblical texts suggest particular kinship between Israel and the Arameans (see esp. Dt 26:5). Damascus was their main city.

Ark (for the Torah) a box or cabinet, typically of wood, in which the Torah scrolls are stored at the front of the synagogue. It is often finely decorated, reflecting the centrality of the Torah scrolls to Judaism.

Ark of the Covenant the chest (Heb. *'aron*) in the Tabernacle or Temple that contained the Pact (Heb. *'edut*) (Ex 40:20), or the tablets (Dt 10:2), or that served as the throne of the LORD (1 Sm 4:4).

Armageddon the traditional site of the final battle between good and evil (Rev 16:16), possibly derived from Megiddo, a battle site in Israel's history (Jgs 5:19; 2 Kgs 9:27).

Asherah (pl. Asherim) Canaanite goddess, wife or consort of El; her sacred symbol, a pole or tree, was the object of prophetic condemnation.

Assyria a Mesopotamian world power, in addition to Egypt and Babylonia. Its capital cities included Asshur and Nineveh. The Assyrian empire conquered the northern kingdom of Israel in 722 and exiled its people. The Assyrians were well-known for their massive building projects, and for their cruelty in war.

'atbash a form of cipher in which a word is transformed into a code by letter substitution, in which the last letter of the alphabet is substituted for the first, the next-to-last for the second, and so on: *alef* becomes *tav, bet* becomes *shin, gimel* becomes *resh,* and so on. (In English, A would become Z, B would become Y, etc.) Using this method, Jeremiah transforms Babylon into Sheshach (Jer 25:26; 51:41): "b–b–l" or *bet-bet-lamed* becomes "sh-sh-k" or *shin-shin-kaf.*

atonement the expiation for sin, or reparation for an injury committed against another. The Hebrew *kapparah* (with possible root meaning "to cover") refers to ritual cleansing of the Temple precincts.

B

baal (Heb. "master," "lord," "husband") the chief god of the Canaanite religion; the storm god.

Babylonia a Mesopotamian world power. It often competed against Assyria, which it conquered in 612 B.C. Its major city was Babylon, Akkadian for "gate of the gods." Its main god became Marduk, and its religion and literature were extremely influential, even on its arch-rival Assyria. Babylonia destroyed the First Temple in 586, and was conquered by Cyrus the Great in 539.

Babylonian Exile the forced relocation of some of the population of Judah, perhaps the ruling portion of it, after the conquest by Babylonia in 595–586 B.C. The exile ended with the permitted return to the land under Cyrus (beginning ca. 538 B.C.).

Babylonian Talmud see **Talmud.**

ban (Heb. *herem*) the devotion of war booty (including people) in its entirety to the deity (see esp. Dt 20:17), or the forfeiture of goods (e.g., idols) from which no benefit is permissible. See ***herem.***

baptism ritual purification by immersion in water, a practice in use throughout the ancient Mediterranean world. New Testament baptism, based on the reported practice of John the Baptist (Mk 1:4) may have been derived from Jewish purification ritual (Lv 15:18), but Paul's connection of baptism with the death and resurrection of Christ (Rom 6:1–14) changed its meaning from purification to initiation into a new community and new identity.

basilica a church built according to an ancient Roman plan, with a rectangular nave and a semicircular apse at one end; also, a Catholic church with certain ceremonial or liturgical privileges.

B.C.E. before the Common Era, an alternative to B.C.

Bedouin an Arab nomad; in general, a member of a nomadic desert tribe.

Beelzebul (also Baalzebul, Baalzebub, Beelzebub) the ruler of the demons (Mt 12:24–27). It is based on the Hebrew *Baalzebul,* "lord of heaven," a title of the Phoenician god at Ekron (2 Kgs 1:2–18), transformed (probably as a derogatory name) into Baalzebub, "lord of the flies."

behemoth a mythical beast, sometimes identified with the hippopotamus (Jb 40:15–24) who represents violent forces in the world.

berit (Heb. "treaty") a term that may be used of a treaty between two individuals, groups, or nations, or between God and Israel. See **covenant.**

bicolon: unit of Hebrew poetry composed of two *cola,* or lines (sometimes called a *distich*).

Book of the Covenant see **Covenant Collection**.

Booths, Feast of the final harvest festival of grapes and olives, falling usually within our month of October. It was called "Booths" because the harvesters lived in the fields in makeshift tents or booths. Also called Tabernacles, Sukkoth.

C

Canaan a designation for the area roughly equivalent to the land of Israel in pre-biblical Mesopotamian and Egyptian documents. In the Bible, it most often refers to the pre-Israelite land of Israel.

canon (Gr. "measuring rod") the rule by which something is determined to belong or not to a category. Christian tradition uses the word for the official list of the individual books that make up the Scriptures. The canon of the Catholic church is more extensive than that of the Protestant churches, but less extensive than that of the Orthodox churches.

canonical criticism the interpretation of a biblical text based upon its final form, rather than interpretation built up from viewing it as an assemblage of smaller, pre-existing units.

casemate two parallel walls, joined by short cross-walls. The small rooms, like closets, that result were sometimes used for storage and sometimes filled with rubble or earth to strengthen them.

casuistic law (also called "case law") the form of law dealing with the treatment of specific cases. It is frequently in the form of "if/when . . . then" formulae. Most ancient near eastern law collections are formulated this way.

C.E. common era; equivalent to the christological term A.D.

ceramic typology dating different levels of an archeological site by classifying the pieces of pottery found in them according to the approximate eras in which they were made.

chaos complete lack of order. In ancient Near Eastern mythology, chaos was sometimes personified as divine beings who had to be conquered by other gods to establish an orderly, habitable universe.

charisma a gift of spiritual grace, particularly a gift of one of the manifestations of the Holy Spirit in the New Testament church.

charismatic (Gr. "gifted, graced") characterized by the ability to influence or lead others; personally magnetic; talented.

cherubim mythical, composite creatures with body parts from various animals; they often had wings and human heads. They were commonly guardians of temples and palaces in the ancient near east.

chiasm, chiasmus (from Gr. "chi," the letter that resembles an "X") inverting the second pair of terms in a parallel structure, so that the corresponding terms, if laid out in a square, would form an X. The resultant pattern is ABBA, ABCBA, ABCCBA, etc. "The king takes delight (A) in honest lips (B), and the man who speaks what is right (B) he loves (A)" (Prv 16:13). Chiasmus can also describe the structure of an entire passage, and it can involve several terms or parts of a passage, each of which has an analog that occurs in the reverse order of the original list of terms or sequence of parts.

Christ (Gr. "anointed"), the translation of the Hebrew *mashshiach,* "messiah." In the New Testament and in general usage, Christ always refers to Jesus of Nazareth, though in contrast to New Testament usage (where it is always a title, "the anointed one"), in general use today "Christ" is simply an alternative name for Jesus.

Christian Hebraists Christian scholars, inspired by the examples of Origen and Jerome, who taught the importance of returning to the Hebrew text of the Christian Old Testament, and who therefore studied Hebrew with rabbinic scholars and influenced Christian Bible translation and commentary to rely on the Hebrew and not on the Latin Vulgate text. The beginnings of Christian Hebraism are generally traced to Andrew of St. Victor (d. 1175), a monk at the Abbey of St. Victor in Paris, where Hugh of St. Victor (d. 1141) had established a school specializing in biblical exposition. There was a significant renaissance of Christian Hebraism during the Renaissance.

Christology the theological doctrines covering the nature of Christ.

chronicle an account of events in the order in which they occurred.

Chronicler the name for the unknown author of the books of Chronicles; sometimes also applied to the author of Ezra and Nehemiah.

church fathers see **patristic writers.**

circumcision the removal of the foreskin of the penis. In the Bible it is a sign of entry into the covenant community, whether the circumcision is meant literally (Jos 5:5–7) or metaphorically ("uncircumcised hearts," Lv 26:41). In the writings of Paul, "the circumcised" and "the uncircumcised" (Gal 2:7) refer to Jews and Gentiles, respectively.

citadel a stronghold or fortress, whether standing alone or serving as the inner fortification of a city.

clan a social unit of those considered to be descended from one common ancestor; several clans constitute a tribe.

climax (Gr. "ladder"), a series of clauses in which each succeeding clause repeats the important term from the previous clause, each clause in turn making a more important point: ". . . affliction produces endurance, and endurance, proven character, and proven character, hope . . ." (Rom 5:3–4).

codex a manuscript of separate leaves of writing, bound into a unit along one edge. Modern books are a development of the codex.

colon (pl. *cola*) a single line of poetry (also known as a *stich*).

colophon (Gr. "summit," by extension "finishing touch") a notice, usually printed at the end of a book, giving information about authorship: Sirach 50:27.

Community Rule (or "Rule of the Community") a scroll from the Dead Sea community, 1QS, that sets out the communal arrangements under which the community functioned, or at least those that they held up as an ideal: holding property in common; eating, blessing, and advising one another in unity; preparing for the eschaton; and training new members of the community in their responsibilities.

concordance a word index to a given text, listing each occurrence of a given word along with a context line so that scholars may better see how a particular word is used.

concubine a woman who is the sexual partner of a man, and is legally recognized as such, but who does not have the full status of a wife.

cosmology any account (mythical or otherwise) of the origin of the world.

cosmos (Gr. "order, regularity") the created world of order, stability, relative permanence; the opposite of chaos.

Council of Trent the twenty-ninth ecumenical council of the Catholic Church (1545–1563), held after the Protestant Reformation had begun. Among other decisions, it defined the books that are included in the Catholic canon of Scripture.

covenant (Heb. ***berit***) a treaty between God and Israel. Some covenants have specific conditions or treaty stipulations, while others are covenants of grant. The biblical notion of covenant between God and Israel, especially as it appears in Deuteronomy, may reflect a theologized reworking of treaties between Assyrian kings and their vassals.

Covenant Code another term for **Covenant Collection.**

Covenant Collection Exodus 20:19–23:33, which details the terms of the covenant between God and Israel.

cult rituals and religious practices at a place of worship. The cult of the Jerusalem Temple means the religious practices carried out there, with no judgment about their value.

cult prostitute one available for sexual intercourse with worshipers at the temple of a god. The biblical accusation (Dt 23:17–18; 1 Kgs 14:24) that non-Israelite religions have cult prostitutes may be a polemical exaggeration.

Cyrus king of Persia (559–530 B.C.). He defeated Media in 550 and conquered most of the ancient Near East, including Babylonia, allowing the Jewish exiles in Babylonia to return to the land beginning about 538.

D

D the Deuteronomic source, which covers almost the entire book of Deuteronomy (except for sections of the last few chapters).

Davidic dynasty the direct descendants of King David, who reigned in Jerusalem from the tenth century through the sixth. An attempt to reinstitute this dynasty after the return from exile was not successful.

Day of Atonement (Heb. **Yom Kippur**) commemorated on the tenth day of the seventh month in the fall. It was a day of fasting and abstinence, as well as performance of certain key Temple rituals (see Lv. 16).

Day of the LORD the time mentioned in many prophetic books where God appears as a warrior, sometimes fighting against Israel, sometimes against Israel's enemies. The earliest text to mention this Day is Amos 5:18.

Dead Sea Scrolls a group of manuscripts found in 1947 in caves near the Dead Sea, at wadi Qumran. The scrolls were probably the library of an Essene settlement that flourished at the site from the second century B.C. until it was destroyed by the Romans in A.D. 68. The library included Hebrew manuscripts of biblical books older than those previously known, and other scrolls regulating the life of the community that shed light on the variety of Jewish belief and practice in the time of Jesus.

decalogue (Gr. "ten words") the traditional name for the list of commandments in Exodus 20:1–17 and Deuteronomy 5:6–21.

defilement a state of ritual impurity caused by contact with a corpse or other impure object. Priestly literature in the Torah is especially concerned with defilement and removing defilement.

demon (Gr. *daimon,* "spirit") a spiritual or nonphysical being, generally hostile to human beings, but in most Old Testament passages still under God's control (see Jb 1 and 2). A common Hebrew name was *satan,* meaning "adversary." By the time of the New Testament demons were generally regarded as hostile to God as well, and therefore evil, or the cause of bad influences—disease, mental distress—on human beings.

demonic marked by spiritual evil, like a demon.

deuterocanon, deuterocanonical (Gr. "second canon") those books or portions of books not included in the Hebrew canon but accepted as canonical by some Christian churches (Roman Catholic and Orthodox) because they were included in the Septuagint.

Deutero-Isaiah the general term for the portion of Isaiah beginning with chapter 40. Most scholars consider Deutero-Isaiah to consist of chapters 40–55 (or 40–54). These chapters are primarily concerned with the promise of return from exile and the events leading up to the decree of Cyrus (538 B.C.) permitting the exiles to return to Judah and rebuild their city and Temple. See **Trito-Isaiah.**

deuteronomistic pertaining to the editor(s) of the history comprised in the books of Joshua, Judges, Samuel, and Kings, as prefaced by the book of Deuteronomy. The term is also applied to the style of these books, reflecting concern for such matters as obedience to the laws given in Deuteronomy, centralized worship in Jerusalem, and support for the Davidic dynasty.

Deuteronomistic History the account in the books Deuteronomy, Joshua, Judges, Samuel, and Kings, that portrays the history of Israel as a partial failure to keep the covenant faithfully, and the consequences of that failure in the subsequent history of the people. These books show significant theological and linguistic similarities, suggesting that they have a common editor or editors.

deuteronomistic having the qualities or the theology of the **Deuteronomistic History.**

diaspora (Gr. "dispersal") the scattering of Jews outside the land of Israel.

diatribe an argument against a position, or one critical of a person or group. Diatribe often includes an imagined dialogue between opposing viewpoints, as in the book of Job.

Didache (Gr. "teaching") an early Christian writing, dating from around A.D. 150 but including earlier materials. It consists of moral exhortation, a manual of church order, and guidance for community life. It is valuable for providing insight into the concerns of early Christian communities. It contains material similar to that in the Pastoral Letters (1 and 2 Tm and Ti).

discernment the ability to distinguish between what is valuable and what is not, especially in the spiritual or moral realms.

disciple a follower, an adherent of a particular teaching.

divination the effort to learn about the future or the current situation, particularly such an effort undertaken by occult means, such as consulting mediums.

divine warrior God in the role of leader of the heavenly armies, usually seen as fighting for Israel.

doctrine (Lat. *doctrina,* "teaching") the beliefs or tenets held by a particular group; Christian doctrines are rooted in the person of Christ.

documentary hypothesis a theory about the formation of the first five books of the Bible, Genesis through Deuteronomy. The hypothesis holds that there are four traditions underlying these books, naming them after a chief characteristic of each: "J" or the "Yahwist" ("J" from the German spelling "Jahveh") uses the divine name "YHWH" (the LORD) consistently and contains much of the oldest material; "E" or the "Elohist" uses the divine name "Elohim" (God) fairly consistently and contains traditions from the northern kingdom of Israel; "P" or the "Priestly" writer is concerned largely with legal codes and matters of religious practice; and "D" or the "Deuteronomist" represents the traditions gathered mostly in Deuteronomy and continued through the deuteronomistic history in Joshua, Judges, Samuel, and Kings. There have been many modifications in the documentary hypothesis, and most scholars now agree that these "documents" are much more like streams of tradition, at least partly oral, than they are like fully-conceived, written texts that could be combined in a cut-and-paste process.

doxology (Gr. "word of glory") a prayer of praise to God, or one glorifying God.

dualism the religious view that reality consists of two basic elements, often seen as "good" and "evil." Some dualistic thought is primarily ethical, arguing that human actions ultimately fall into one category or the other; other dualistic philosophies see good and evil as the basic constituents of the nature of the universe.

dynasty a ruling family; when a leader dies, the next leader is always chosen from among the family members.

E

E one of the four sources or traditions in the Torah, which characteristically refers to God as *elohim.* More recently, as scholars have examined the texts more closely, they speak of a JE tradition, since E as a separate source is difficult to isolate entirely. It may represent the traditions and practices of the inhabitants of the northern areas of Israel.

early Christian writings besides the books contained in the New Testament, many other writings from the first century or so of the Christian church are known to have survived, or are quoted or referred to by later writers. These writings include letters, gospels, narrative books like the Acts of the Apostles, apocalypses, and collections of teachings. In some cases these works provide direct evidence of teachings that were later rejected by the main body of Christians. In other cases they contain similar material, or parallel arguments, to those in parts of the New Testament, such as the instructions to local churches in the Pastoral Letters. In still other cases, they provide further examples of kinds of literature found in the New Testament.

ecclesiology the theological study of the church; the doctrines that concern the nature of the Christian community.

ecumenism (from the Greek *oikoumene,* "the whole inhabited world") any attempts to deal with the relations between different Christian groups, or to think about ways in which divisions among them might be overcome. Since the Second Vatican Council (1963–65), ecumenical activity has become a major goal of the Catholic Church.

ecumenical (from **ecumenism**) aimed at fostering ecumenism, or characterized by aims supporting ecumenism; having the character of ecumenism.

edom/Edomites the territory and people to the south of Judah, first attested in late second millennium texts. Edom is identified in Genesis 36 with Esau, Jacob's brother. The enmity between these brothers and that between Judah and Edom mirror each other.

eisegesis (Gr. "lead into"; opposed to **exegesis,** "lead out of") the practice of reading into the text what one desires to find there, rather than reading out of the text to determine what it actually says.

El a Canaanite deity popular in the second millennium. In the texts from Ugarit, he is a significant deity, but is often depicted as old and is largely supplanted by Baal.

Elohim the Hebrew word usually translated "God," though its plural form is sometimes translated "gods" (e.g., Gn 6:2, "sons of elohim," NAB note: "sons of the gods"). It is originally a common noun (a god), though it is often used as a proper noun for The God of Israel, even though it is a plural form.

Elohist the putative author of the E source (see **E**).

ephod two different objects are called an ephod: (1) the linen apron worn by priests in the Temple; (2) a device used to divine the will of God. The second kind of ephod was carried in priestly garments, which may explain why the same word was used for both (1 Sm 2:18). "Ephod" in Judges 8:27 seems to be an idol rather than a priestly garment.

Ephraim the most important tribe of the **Northern Kingdom.**

Epicureans a Greek philosophical school, founded by Epicurus, who taught that human beings naturally seek pleasure, and that the best way to achieve this pursuit was in moderation, since moderation permits the longest possible life of pleasure-seeking.

epigraph an inscription, usually carved or etched in stone.

Epiphanes a title, "[God] made manifest," adopted by Antiochus IV, the ruler of the part of the Greek empire that included Israel during the second century B.C. He was the king who forced pagan worship to occur in the Jerusalem Temple, thus provoking the revolt of the Maccabees.

epiphany (Gr. "manifestation, appearance") usually the appearance of a god or divine being in a form that can be seen by human beings.

epistle a letter, sometimes intended for public reading and therefore written according to a particular literary form.

epithet a word or phrase that characterizes a person or thing, and that can often be used by itself to refer to the person. The name "Maccabeus," or "Hammer," is an epithet of Judas, the son of Mattathias and leader of the Jewish revolt against Antiochus IV in 167 B.C.

eschatological, eschatology (Gr. *eschata,* "last things") a concern with the end time, or the end of the world as we know it, whether that involves a new historical era radically discontinuous from this one, or an entirely new cosmos after the destruction of the current one.

Essenes a communal society in Judaism around the first century B.C. to the first century A.D. that kept the law with utmost rigor and lived apart in communities that were similar in some respects to later monastic groups. It is generally agreed that the Dead Sea Scrolls of Qumran were collected and preserved by an Essene community.

etiology (Gr. *aition,* "cause") an explanation for a word, an event, or a natural phenomenon. An etiological story is one that posits a particular cause (not necessarily the right cause) for some event. For example, the story at the end of Genesis 32 explains why Israelites do not eat the thigh muscle.

Eucharist a ritual or service of thanksgiving, centering on the sharing of bread and wine, based on the final meal Jesus shared with his followers before his trial and crucifixion; also called Communion, the Lord's Supper, and the Mass.

euphemism the substitution of an inoffensive word for one that is too explicit or impolite. The word "feet" in Isaiah 6:2; 7:20 (NAB: "between the legs") and possibly Ruth 3:4, 7, 8, 14 is a euphemism for "genitals."

evangelist (from Greek *euangelion,* "good news") the author of a gospel.

exegesis (Gr. "lead out of") the explanation or interpretation of the meaning of a written text.

exhortation urging a particular course of action or behavior by argument or advice.

Exile the forced removal of a people from its land, and the community in which they lived in the foreign land. The Israelites of the northern kingdom were exiled by the Assyrians in the late eighth century, and the Judeans were exiled by the Babylonians in the early sixth century. Specifically, "the Exile" is the period from 586 to approximately 539 B.C. During this time the ruling classes of Judah were forced to leave Judah and live in Babylonia. See **Babylonian Exile.**

F

fable an illustrative story in which animals or plants have speaking parts. Judges 9:8–15 is a fable about the dangers of kingship in which plants speak.

Fertile Crescent the agriculturally fertile areas of Egypt, Israel, and Mesopotamia, forming a rough arc from the Nile through the coastal regions of Israel to the Tigris-Euphrates basin.

Festival of Weeks see **Shavuot.**

festival scrolls the five short books that are read on five holy days in the Jewish calendar: Song of Songs on Passover, Ruth on Pentecost (Weeks or Shavuoth), Lamentations on 9 Ab (the date of the Temple's destruction), Ecclesiastes on Booths (Sukkoth), and Esther on Purim.

First Temple the Temple in Jerusalem from Solomon's time (tenth century) until the destruction of Jerusalem by the Babylonians in 586 B.C. The First Temple period extends from the tenth to sixth centuries B.C.

form criticism the interpretation of a text—a parable, a psalm, a proverb—with particular attention to the structure of the text and to the original setting of that form out of which it arose. Form criticism attempts to recover the original context, audience, or situation of a particular kind of literature, before the unit was made a part of a larger narrative such as a gospel or a historical book with its own context, audience, and situation.

Former Prophets the name in the Hebrew Bible for the first part of the longer section called "the Prophets." The Former Prophets are Joshua, Judges, Samuel, and Kings.

fundamentalist in its narrow meaning, a conservative Protestant who holds to the five fundamentals: the sole authority of Scripture; the Virgin Birth of Jesus Christ; the doctrine of the substitutionary atonement of the death of Christ; the physical, bodily resurrection of Christ; and the literal Second Coming of Christ to judge the world. In a wider sense, a fundamentalist is any rigidly conservative adherent to a belief system who regards all those outside the belief system as without hope of salvation and who treats the sacred text of the tradition as an infallible guide to belief and action.

G

Galilee the northernmost geographical area of Israel.

Gehenna the place of punishment after death (e.g., see Mt 5:22). The name means "valley of Hinnom," a place south of Jerusalem that had been thought to be the area where children were burnt as sacrificial offerings: Josiah (2 Kgs 23:10) destroyed the site, but its associations with burning and evil remained and developed into the image of burning punishment that is found in the New Testament.

genealogy a list or history of the ancestors of an individual or group.

genre a form of literature with particular characteristics. The detective story is a genre. Once a genre is established, the audience for it knows what to expect and can respond more easily to any given work. Biblical genres include oracles, laments, proverbs, hymns, parables, letters, gospels, and apocalypses.

gentile a non-Jew.

Gilgamesh the Babylonian and Assyrian epic, whose hero, Gilgamesh, travels the world in search of immortality. Among the characters he encounters is Utnapishtim, whose tale of the flood has parallels with the biblical account of Noah (Gn chs 6–9). This epic explores the tension between nature and culture and addresses the mortality of human beings.

glean to gather or collect, usually by hand, grain that is left behind by reapers. People too poor to own their own fields were permitted to glean in the fields of those better off (Lv 19:9–10; Dt 24:19–24).

gnosticism (from Gk. *gnosis,* "knowledge") a philosophy that regards spirit and matter as opposites. According to gnostic teaching, human beings are spirits trapped or imprisoned in matter; the material world is an illusion or the work of an inferior, even demonic, divine being; and the purpose of life is to learn how to free oneself from material things (including the body) and attain eternal life in the spiritual realm. This is accomplished by learning specialized or secret knowledge about the nature of reality; it is from this emphasis on knowledge that gnosticism gets its name. Gnostic teachings were often in the form of secret doctrines or mysteries, and many mystery religions were gnostic. Gnosticism, though influential during the first few centuries of the Christian church's existence, was ultimately rejected by what became the main body of Christians, and most of the gnostic writings were lost or suppressed. Because gnosticism itself did not continue as an established form of Christianity, it did not develop an "orthodox" or systematic body of thought, and most of what is attributed to it as a philosophy has had to be assembled from disparate sources that do not always agree with each other in every particular.

God, names for see **Adonai, Elohim, YHWH.**

Greek Bible a general term for the variety of ancient translations of the Bible into Greek in antiquity, including the Septuagint and the translations of Aquila, Symmachus, and Theodotion.

H

Hades the abode of the dead in Greek religion, used in the New Testament as the general name for the place where souls go after death (e.g., see Mt 11:23; Acts 2:27).

haggadah (poss. from Heb. *huggad,* "things said" or "what is told") the nonlegal portions of the Talmud and Midrash (see ***halakhah***). Haggadah is concerned with explicating the meaning of Scripture in the moral sense, and with elaborating on the stories in the Bible. As such, it is more akin to preaching than to legal analysis, and many haggadic collections are homiletical in character. The legal sections, called *halakhah,* are concerned with understanding the obligations placed on the believer by the biblical text; *haggadah*, by contrast, contains ethical teaching as well as illustrative narrative, prayers, legends, and folklore.

Haggadah of Pesah ("telling of Passover") the liturgical recitation, used at the Passover **seder;** also the book that contains the recitation and instructions of the seder.

halakhah (Heb. "way," from *halakh* "go"; pl. *halakhot*) the legal portions of the Talmud, or any legal ruling according to Jewish law.

Hallel (Heb. "praise") Psalms 113–118, which are recited on major Jewish festivals.

hallelujah a Hebrew acclamation, "Praise Yah!" It is frequent in the Psalms.

Hammurabi Babylonian monarch (ruled 1792–1750 B.C.), responsible for the formulation of a legal collection (the Code [or Laws] of Hammurabi) that is one of the earliest collections of case law on various subjects.

Hasidic, Hasidim (Heb. *Hasid,* "pious one") (1) a Jewish group in the Maccabean period, concerned with re-establishing Jewish practices in ritual and purity laws. The Hasidim supported the Maccabees for a time; they may have been the precursors of the Sadducees. (2) a renewal movement that began in the mid-eighteenth century in eastern Europe under the influence of the Baal Shem Tov ("master of the good Name"), R. Yisrael ben Eliezer (ca. 1700–1760).

Hasmonean the dynasty descended from the Maccabee brothers. It ruled Israel from 135 to 36 B.C.; the last Hasmonean was overthrown by Herod the Great.

Hasmonean Revolt the uprising led by the family of Mattathias Heshmon against the Seleucid ruler Antiochus IV Epiphanes beginning in 166 B.C., particularly by Mattathias' son Judah (or Judas) Maccabeus ("the hammer"), which succeeded in liberating Jerusalem and the surrounding territory from Seleucid rule in 164. When the Temple, which had been desecrated by Antiochus, was retaken by the Jews, it was rededicated, an event commemorated in the festival of Hanukkah ("dedication").

Hebrew Bible a term used to refer to what Christians call the (Protestant) Old Testament. Though the two terms refer to basically the same body of writings, the order of books in the Hebrew Bible (i.e., the Jewish Bible) differs from that found in the Old Testament.

Hellenism a general term for the spread of Greek culture, politics, and language around the Mediterranean in the period after the conquests of Alexander the Great (d. 323 B.C.).

Hellenistic Greek-speaking or influenced by Greek culture after the time of Alexander.

Hellenize bring under the influence of Greek language and culture.

herem (Heb. "ban") the total dedication of conquest to God; later, the exile or suspension of someone from the community ("excommunication").

heresy (Gr. *hairesis,* "choice") an opinion or belief contrary to the accepted doctrine of the Catholic Church; an unorthodox position.

hermeneutics (Gr. "interpretation") the theory and practice of interpretation.

Herodian followers and members of the court of Herod the Great and his sons (36 B.C. to A.D. 40).

Hexateuch (Gr. "six scrolls") a grouping of the first six books in the Bible—Genesis through Joshua—to complete the narrative with the conquest of the Land that is in Joshua. See **Pentateuch, Tetrateuch.**

high places shrines, usually on a hill or a raised platform, where worship, especially sacrifices, took place. Because they were outside of Jerusalem and sometimes, though not always, used for other gods, they were regularly condemned in the Deuteronomistic History, though in earlier writings, and even in the narratives in Kings, there are clear indications that sacrifice and worship took place in numerous locations throughout Israel.

higher criticism the effort to distinguish among the sources of biblical documents, and to trace them back to their origins, so far as that is possible; distinguished from textual criticism ("lower criticism"), which is concerned with establishing the most accurate text in its final form. See **documentary hypothesis.**

historical-critical method interpreting a text by trying to understand its original setting and audience, and what it would have meant when it was originally written or spoken. This method uses the tools of historical research to understand the conditions of the past, and critical tools to understand the traditions and developments that lie behind the surface of the text. It is also an umbrella term that includes such methods as form criticism and redaction criticism.

holocaust a sacrifice entirely consumed by fire, a whole burnt offering.

holy war battles conducted under divine guidance in which the LORD fought for Israel in the role of divine warrior (Jgs 6).

homiletical having the character or function of a sermon.

hortatory characteristic of writing or speech that aims at changing the behavior of the hearers or inspiring them to a particular course of action.

hosanna a Hebrew word, meaning "Save!" that was used as a cry of acclamation (Ps 118:26; Mt 21:9).

household code a list of rules or prescribed behaviors for the members of an extended family and their servants living under one roof. There are household codes in some of the New Testament letters, for instance Ephesians 5:22–6:9.

Hyksos the mostly Semitic rulers of Egypt during the period 1665–1560 B.C. (approximately).

hyperbole exaggeration for effect. "Will the LORD be pleased with thousands of rams, with myriad streams of oil?" (Mi 6:7).

hypostasis (Gr. "that which stands under," i.e., the real nature or essence of anything; pl. *hypostases*) a Greek philosophical term, meaning both "essential being" or what defines a thing as a member of a class of things and "individual being" or what a thing is in itself. It was used by, among others, the neo-Platonist mystics. It refers to the three constitutive orders of reality, the One, Mind, and Soul, each of which is an hypostasis.

hyssop a shrub related to mint. It was used as a medicine and, because of its leafy branches, for ritual sprinkling of water or blood (Ex 12:22).

I

idolatry the worship of anything other than what the worshiper defines as the true God.

Idumea the Greek form of the name Edom; province in the Land during Persian, Hellenistic, and Roman times, located south of Judah (Yehud), between the Dead Sea and the Mediterranean.

Ignatius, Letters of early Christian writings of instruction. The author, Ignatius, bishop of Antioch, wrote them (seven are known to have survived) on his way to martyrdom in Rome. They are largely concerned with overcoming divisions in local churches, combating false teaching, and conducting one's life properly. They therefore are very similar to some of the canonical New Testament letters, particularly 1 and 2 Timothy and Titus. The letters of Ignatius are addressed to the Ephesians, the Magnesians, the Trallians, the Romans, the Philadelphians, and the Smyrnians, as well as one to Polycarp, bishop of Smyrna.

impurity a ritual state which forbade the impure individual to partake in Temple rituals. See **defilement**.

incarnation (Lat., "enfleshment") the belief that a divine being has become human in some form.

incubation the practice of sleeping in a particular place, or in contact with particular things (animal skins, the ground) to induce dreams that might provide divine guidance.

inerrancy the doctrine that the biblical materials are without error. In its most expansive form, as held for instance by Protestant fundamentalists, inerrancy includes the assertion that in the original manuscripts of the biblical books, there are no errors of fact, whether theological, historical, or scientific. A more restrained version of the doctrine would claim that the Bible is an inerrant guide in matters of faith but that it may contain historical errors or assertions that cannot be reconciled with present-day science. Vatican II expressed it this way: "Therefore, since everything asserted by the inspired authors or sacred writers must be held to be asserted by the Holy Spirit, it follows that the books of Scriptures must be acknowledged as teaching firmly, faithfully, and without error that truth which God wanted put into the sacred writings for the sake of our salvation" (Document on Revelation, *Dei Verbum,* n. 11). The final phrase, "for the sake of our salvation"—that is, not for the sake of giving us historical or scientific information—establishes the limits of inerrancy.

inspiration the belief that the words uttered by a human being are really the words of a divine being. In the ancient world, prophets and oracles were thought to be inspired. In Christian tradition, the notion of inspiration was eventually applied to the whole Bible. Inspiration in a more expanded sense speaks of an inspired tradition, in which numerous authors, anonymous contributors, editors, and others all worked together more or less consciously to create the biblical materials; in this view, God used all these people and their human traditions to express the Bible's teachings. The Second Vatican Council affirms the inspiration of Scripture, but warns that God speaks "through men in human fashion" so that careful attention must be given "to what the sacred writers really intended" (*Dogmatic Constitution on Divine Revelation,* III.12).

interpolation an insertion of material into a previously existent text. In the absence of textual evidence, e.g. differing forms of a manuscript for a given text, interpolation must be inferred and is often the subject of scholarly disagreement.

interpretation There are a number of different methods of interpreting the Bible, each meant to answer different questions. In general, the purpose of interpretation is to help make the meaning of the text clear, but this sometimes means not only understanding the sentences and paragraphs that we read today, but also understanding the possible ways by which they came to be written, trying to determine the original context of the story or saying, and looking at the different stages through which a biblical text does on its way to its final form. So interpreters are interested in examining the meanings of words used in the Bible, the historical religious, or social background of a particular story or saying, the process by which a story was written down, how groups of stories were combined into a longer narrative, how different biblical writers treated the same materials, what the original audience would have gotten out of a story, how a saying was adapted to address the concerns of later readers, and many similar paths of investigation. Terms used by biblical interpreters include: canonical criticism, documentary hypothesis, form criticism, redaction criticism, source criticism, synoptic problem, tradition criticism, textual criticism.

interregnum an interruption or gap between the end of one reign or dynasty and the beginning of the next.

intertextuality the interrelationship between

one part of a text (or collection of texts) and other parts. Intertextuality can take the form of recurrent images (the vineyard in Is 5:1–10 and 27:2–4), quotation and/or inner biblical interpretation (Jer 25:11–12 is partly quoted in Dn 9:2 before it is reinterpreted; 1 Cor 3:20 quotes Ps 94:11), or allusion (Is 54:8 alludes to the promise made to Noah in Gn 9:11).

irony, ironic a characteristic of literature in which the reader or listener knows more than the characters about the situation in the story. A character in an ironic situation is missing a vital piece of information that is known to the audience. By extension, an ironic aspect of a story, situation, or fact is one that from the outside looks very different than it does from the inside. Irony thus becomes a rhetorical technique in which the author's plain or literal meaning (what the words mean in the dictionary sense) is different from, even in conflict with, the author's intended meaning (what the words mean in their context, with particular emphasis, etc.). Saying "My! Don't you look lovely!" to someone dressed in old work clothes who has just finished a strenuous and messy task is an example of irony in this sense.

Isis the Egyptian mother-goddess, wife of Osiris, the god of vegetation and hence of regeneration.

Israel the name for both the kingdom of twelve tribal groups, of which David and Solomon were kings, and for the northern section of this kingdom, which split off after the death of Solomon and began a separate political existence under Jeroboam (1 Kgs 12). See **Northern Kingdom, Southern Kingdom.**

J

J the posited document or narrative tradition that is one of the constituent parts of the Torah (Pentateuch), according to a scholarly hypothesis codified by J. Wellhausen and subsequently developed by numerous biblical researchers. J is usually understood to be the earliest source, and is Judean; it frequently depicts God, for whom it uses the tetragrammaton (YHWH, misvocalized Jehovah, thus J), in very anthropomorphic terms.

Jerome (ca. 340–420) Christian theologian and translator. Beginning in 382, he produced a Latin version of the Bible, the Old Testament of which was based not on a previous Latin version nor on the Greek text (Septuagint) but on the Hebrew. To do this, Jerome studied Hebrew with rabbis of the time, an unusual step for a Christian. His version, which became known as the **Vulgate** ("common") because it was the translation into commonly used Latin in the Western world, was completed in 405.

Jerusalem Talmud also called the Palestinian Talmud or the Talmud of the Land of Israel—none of these titles is fully accurate. This Talmud, mostly reflecting traditions of the Galilean rabbis of the third and fourth centuries A.D., is a commentary on several tractates of the Mishnah. It was ultimately seen as less authoritative than the longer, more comprehensive, and more carefully edited **Babylonian Talmud**. See **Talmud.**

Joseph and Aseneth an ancient Greek novel about Joseph's life in Egypt, his marriage to the haughty daughter of an Egyptian priest, and her conversion to faith in Joseph's God, and their triumph over a plot to kill them.

Josephus a Hellenistic Jewish historian who lived from about A.D. 37 to about A.D. 100. Four of his writings have survived: *The Jewish War,* an account of the rebellion against Rome in A.D. 66–70, with background information starting at about 200 B.C.; *The Antiquities of the Jews,* a complete history from the creation up to the point where *The Jewish War* begins; *Against Apion,* a defense of Judaism; and an autobiography, the *Life*. Josephus provides invaluable historical information about Judaism and its background from 200 B.C. to A.D. 100; his account of the rebellion, in which he was involved, is in part that of an eyewitness. He also provides first-hand information about the Essenes and the Pharisees, because at one time or another he was associated with both groups, as well as giving information about the Sadducees. Josephus is important to scholars in trying to understand the religious context in which Jesus lived and from which early Christianity and rabbinic Judaism developed.

Jubilee (Heb. *yovel,* perhaps "ram" from the sounding of the ram's horn to mark the beginning of the observance) the year of release for slaves and return of ancestral lands to their original owners (or descendants of the owners), to occur every 50 years (after seven sabbaths of years) (Lv ch 25). It is a cornerstone of Priestly ideology, but it is uncertain if it was ever practiced.

Judah the major tribal group of the southern kingdom. According to the biblical text, after the death of Solomon, the kingdom was divided into two, with Judah in the south and Israel in the north. The capital of Judah was Jerusalem.

Judea the Roman name for the area of Judah.

K

kabbalah "what is received," that is, matter handed to one. In the twelfth century and later, however, *kabbalah* came to mean esoteric or in some sense mystical teaching. *Kabbalah* taught that God was inaccessible by direct experience and could only be apprehended through emanations of the Godhead; Torah in kabbalistic teaching had a hidden meaning, and meditation on texts was a method of ascent to a mystical vision.

kaddish (Aram. "holiness, sanctification") prayer in praise of God that is recited at the conclusion of a principal section of the synagogue service; a special type of kaddish is also recited in memory of the deceased.

Kiddush short for *kiddush ha-yom,* "sanctification of the day," both the ceremony and the prayer that proclaims the holiness of the Sabbath (or festival), recited over wine before the Sabbath (or festival) meal.

kohen (Heb. "priest") a member of the hereditary group within the Levites, traditionally supposed to be descended from Aaron or Zadok, who alone were allowed to serve as Temple priests.

kosher (Heb. "fit" or "proper") a general term used in post-biblical texts for dietary laws; usually applied to food, but also to other ritual objects and practices. Most dietary laws apply to meat: It may not be consumed with blood in it, certain kinds of internal fat are not to be eaten, it may not be consumed along with dairy products, and some meats (e.g., pork), sea creatures (e.g., shellfish), and "creeping things" (e.g., snails) are not permitted.

L

lament a poem of grief or mourning. See **qinah meter.**

Latter Prophets the canonical division of Nevi'im that includes the books of Isaiah, Jeremiah, Ezekiel, and the Twelve.

law the usual English translation of Hebrew *torah,* which more generally means "teaching, instruction." *Torah* is also the name for the first five books of the Hebrew Bible, Genesis through Deuteronomy.

lectionary a list of readings of Scripture passages for Sabbaths and holy days (in Judaism) or Sundays and holy days (in Christianity). Christian lectionaries also sometimes include readings for weekdays. Lectionaries are partly designed to read certain portions of the Bible—for instance, the Torah, in Jewish lectionaries, or the first three Gospels, in Christian lectionaries—completely through, in order, over a lectionary cycle of a year or several years. In addition, in Christian lectionaries important seasons (e.g., Christmas or Easter) have their own specific readings outside the continuous readings. In the synagogue, the Torah reading is followed by what is called a Haftarah reading (*haphtarah* is Hebrew for "conclusion, completion") from one of the prophets; in addition, the five **festival scrolls** are read on five holy days. In many Christian churches, the Gospel reading is preceded by a reading from the Hebrew Scriptures, a psalm, and a reading from elsewhere in the New Testament, usually a letter. The Gospel of John is read during Easter season.

legate an official representative.

legend, legendary a popular story, sometimes exaggerated or romanticized, about a holy or righteous person or a special place. The characters in legends can themselves be legendary, like Paul Bunyan, or they can be real historical personages about whom stories are told, like George Washington and the cherry tree. Characters that are legendary are those who are famous enough to have legends told about their exploits. Many of the stories told about Elijah and especially Elisha have legendary elements.

leviathan the monster of the sea in Canaanite mythology, who is defeated by Baal. It is sometimes identified with the crocodile (Jb 41:1) and represents the forces of watery chaos that must be overcome at creation (Ps 74:1–17) and that will be finally defeated at the end of time (Is 27:1). In the book of Revelation, the dragon, the enemy of God, is identified with the sea (17:1, 3), and in the new creation there is no more sea (21:1).

levirate marriage (from Lat. *levir,* "husband's brother") the provision that if a man died without an heir to carry on his name, his brother would marry the widow and the first son she bore would be regarded as the dead brother's heir. This practice is dealt with in Deuteronomy 25:5–10, but it is unclear whether it was actually carried out to any extent; by rabbinic times *halitzah,* the ceremony that released the levir from this obligation, was preferred.

Levite (from Heb. "descendant of Levi") originally the tribe or group from which priests were chosen; later, after the establishment of the Zadokites as priests (1 Kgs 1), a subordinate Temple servant who assisted the priests in their duties (see Ex 32:28; Nm 3:18; Ez 4:10–14).

lex talionis (Lat. "law [of retribution] in kind") punishment fitting the crime. See **talion.**

liminal (Lat. *limina,* "threshhold") the term for rites or practices that governed life passages, such as entry into puberty or marriage.

literal meaning the "plain sense" of a text, as opposed to an allegorical, homiletical, or spiritual interpretation.

literary criticism the older name for **source criticism.**

liturgy the form or rite for communal, public worship.

LXX the roman numeral 70, the standard abbreviation for the **Septuagint.**

M

Ma'at Egyptian goddess of reason and order; her name literally means "truth."

malediction curse; opposite of benediction, "blessing."

martyr (Gr. "witness") a person who demonstrates loyalty by remaining faithful even when being threatened with death or being killed.

Martyrdom of Isaiah a Greco-Roman, Jewish work that is the origin of the legend that Isaiah died by being sawn in two. It is alluded to in Hebrews 11:37.

Masoretic text the text of the Hebrew Bible, established by Jewish scholars (called Masoretes). (*Masorah* means "tradition.") The text consists of the Hebrew consonants, vowel signs, accent markings, and other notes. Texts derived from this effort date from circa A.D. 900 to 1000. The Masoretic text is the only complete form of the Hebrew Bible that has come down to us, though individual manuscripts of books are among the Dead Sea Scrolls.

matrilineal tracing descent through female ancestors. See **patrilineal.**

matzah unleavened bread, associated with Passover, but also used with certain sacrifices.

Mesopotamia (Gr. "between the rivers") the area between the Tigris and Euphrates rivers.

messiah the Hebrew word for "anointed." A king could be referred to as "the LORD's anointed" (1 Sm 24:6); even a foreign king could be so called (Is 45:1). Later the term came to be used of the expected savior of the Jewish people and was taken over by Christians to refer to Jesus, whom they believed to be the messiah (Gr. *christos,* "anointed").

Messiah (Heb. *mashshiach,* "anointed [one]") a title for the king or other servant or agent of God (priest, prophet, or even non-Israelite Cyrus in Is 45:1).

metaphor a direct comparison between two things: "The LORD is my shepherd" (Ps 23:1). See **simile.**

metonymy a figure of speech in which a word is used in place of another word to which it is closely related. "The coastlands have seen and are afraid" (Is 41:5) means "the inhabitants of the coastlands," that is, foreigners.

mezuzah (Heb. "doorpost") a parchment on which are written the paragraphs of the Shema (Dt 6:4–9; 11:13–21), and on the back of which *sh-d-y* ("Shaddai," "Almighty") is written so as to be visible through a small opening in the case. *Sh-d-y* is interpreted as an acronym for *shomer delatot Yisrael,* "guardian of the doors of Israel."

midrash, midrashic (Heb. *derash* "inquire") interpretation to draw out meanings from a text that are other than, or go beyond, the "plain sense."

Minor Prophets (so-called because compared to the Major Prophets, Isaiah, Jeremiah, and Ezekiel, they are much shorter) the books from

Hosea through Malachi; in the Hebrew Bible they are treated as one collection, "The Book of the Twelve."

mitzvah (Heb. "commandment") a religious obligation; by extension, any good deed.

Moab/Moabites the territory and inhabitants south and east of the Dead Sea.

Molech the title—"king"—of the Ammonite god. The worshipers of this god were accused of child sacrifice.

motif an image or character type that recurs throughout a literary work. The Servant motif occurs in Isaiah at 42:1–4; 49:1–6; 50:4–11; 52:13–53:12.

mystery in the New Testament, a divine truth that is kept hidden or secret by God until the right moment for it to be revealed (see Rom 16:25–26). A "mystery" in this sense is a revelation about God's plan (Eph 1:9–10). The later, theological meaning of "mystery," a religious teaching that is based on a revelation from God or other divine messenger, rather than on conclusions from reasoning, and that therefore can never be fully understood by reason alone, is not present in the New Testament.

mystery religion any one of various religious groups in the Greek and Roman empires that practiced secret rites of initiation. These rites often involved rituals enacting the myth of creation of other underlying teaching about the meaning of the universe according to the particular group. Mystery religions taught that the real meaning of life could not be learned without divine guidance and that such guidance was available in their secret teachings and practices. These secret rites were themselves known as "mysteries" and had the sense of a revelation from the divine realm that is similar to some of the New Testament uses of "mystery."

myth a story that expresses a spiritual truth or basic conviction of a culture through narrative. In particular myths give explanations of origins, often through the struggles of divine beings or superhuman creatures. Because the Bible firmly maintains the teaching that there is only one God, in biblical myths the presence of multiple deities has faded out, but the titanic struggle between good and evil is still maintained, as in the story of Paradise in Genesis 2–3, or the Tower of Babel story in Genesis 11:1–9. Such stories, for example, express the impossibility of human efforts to attain the level of God. Myths are not meant to be taken literally.

N

narrative a connected, orderly account of an incident, or a longer account including many incidents. Narratives can be historical, fictional, legendary, mythical, or a combination of types.

Negev the high plateau south of the central hill country of Israel.

Neoplatonism a development of **Platonism.** It originated with Plotinus (ca. 204–270) and saw the universe as a series of emanations flowing out from the One, the unknowable source of all. The emanations, Mind, the realm of knowledge, and Soul, the realm of thought and activity, are called hypostases. All of existence is a balance between emanation, or movement outward, and contemplation or return, movement back toward the One. The individual's task is to return to the One by contemplation, involving a progressive detachment from the world of matter and sense and ultimately from all categories of thought until the One can be grasped in an indescribable void of thought. There may be early neoplatonic influences in the Wisdom of Solomon 7:25.

Nevi'im the Prophets, the second division of the Hebrew Scriptures.

new moon the beginning of any month in the Jewish calendar.

Northern Kingdom the political assembly of tribal groups that split off from the kingdom of Israel after Solomon's death (1 Kgs 12). This newly-formed kingdom was itself called Israel, and in some of the prophets (e.g., Hos 8:11), Ephraim, after its largest tribe.

novel a fictional work in prose. Ancient novels were often **romances**.

O

obelisk a four-sided stone shaft, usually tapered and topped with a pyramid, characteristic of ancient Egypt.

Old Latin the Latin translation of the Bible based on the Greek text, the Septuagint. The Old Latin version was replaced by Jerome's Latin translation, the **Vulgate.**

oracle a statement uttered by a prophet or other sacred person, purporting to be the words of a deity.

oracular having the qualities of an oracle or sacred speech.

Oral Torah a synonym for the **Mishnah** and **Talmud.** According to traditional rabbinic belief, the Oral Law was given to Moses on Mount Sinai along with the written law, the Torah. The Oral Law was, however, as its name suggests, originally transmitted orally alongside the Torah, as the authoritative interpretation of the Torah. As a result of historical exigencies, it was committed to writing by the rabbis, in stages, in the first millennium A.D.

ordination a formal ceremony and process by which certain members of the community are set apart for religious service, for instance as priests (Lv 8:1–46).

oxymoron (Gr. "swift-slow") combining two terms that appear contradictory. "For the foolishness of God is wiser than human wisdom, and the weakness of God is stronger than human strength" (1 Cor 1:25).

P

P the Priestly document in the Torah, comprised of both narratives and laws. It is concerned, among other things, with laws and regulations, ritual practices, the proper conduct of the Temple worship, holiness and purity, and genealogies. P may also have had a hand in the shaping or redaction of the Torah.

paleography the study of ancient writing, used to date manuscripts.

Palestine a name derived from the Roman designation *Provincia Syria Palaestina,* "Syro-Palestinian Province," which replaced *Provincia Judaea* after the revolt of A.D. 135; *Palaestina* was the Roman spelling of "Philistine," and the designation was probably intended as a derogation of Jewish claims to the territory.

Palestinian Talmud the **Jerusalem Talmud** or Talmud Yerushalmi; see **Talmud.**

parable a statement or story that uses figurative or imaginative language to evoke a reality that lies beyond the literal level of the story or statement. A parable makes its point by analogy, or the comparison of a known fact, situation, or experience with one that is less familiar. The analogy is usually not made explicit; for instance, in the parable of the Prodigal Son (Lk 15:11–32) the father is meant to represent, by analogy, the merciful action of God's forgiveness, but this is not stated. Sometimes an interpretation is added, however, as with the parable of the Sower (Mk 4:1–8, interpreted in vv. 14–20).

paraenesis moral exhortation.

parallelism a characteristic feature of biblical Hebrew poetry in which the second line of a unit in some way echoes the meaning or grammatical structure of the first line. This can take the form of a repetition of the meaning, or of a statement of opposites, or of a further statement that serves to extend or modify the first line in some way. Psalms and Proverbs are largely composed in parallelistic form and demonstrate the great degree of variation that the form permits.

parousia (Gr. "coming") the second coming of Christ; the expected return of the messiah at the end of the age or the end of the world.

Paschal pertaining to the Passover (ultimately from the Gr. *pascha,* derived from Heb. *pesah*).

Passover (Heb. *pesach,* prob. "protection"; others "pass over") the name of the festival commemorating the Exodus from Egypt. The first day involves the sacrifice of the lamb, which took place on the eve of the Exodus (14 Nisan); the rest of the festival, the "festival of unleavened bread," was probably originally a festival marking the beginning of the spring barley harvest.

Passover *Haggadah, Haggadah* of Pesah the "telling" of the Passover story in the context of the household liturgy of Pesah, which accompanies the ritual meal, the **seder.**

patriarchs the founding fathers of Israel: Abraham, Isaac, and Jacob.

patrilineal tracing one's descent through male ancestors. See **matrilineal.**

patristic writers the theologians of the early Christian centuries, from the time of the close of the New Testament period (sometime after A.D. 100) to about the fifth century. Clement, Irenaeus, Origen, and Jerome are patristic figures of importance to biblical studies.

penitential psalms Psalms 6; 32; 38; 51; 102; 130; and 143, used in Christian services of repentance from the earliest times, and by the Middle Ages in regular use during Lent.

Pentapolis the five cities of the **Philistines:** Ashdod, Ashkelon, Ekron, Gath, Gaza.

Pentateuch (Gr. "five scrolls") the first five books of the Bible—Genesis through Deuteronomy—regarded as a unit after its final editing during or after the Exile. The traditional term in Judaism for this collection of books is **Torah,** "teaching." Although these five books are traditionally grouped together, they contain markedly different kinds of writing—prehistory, narrative, law, ritual instruction, and so on—and scholars have investigated the materials of which they are composed. Deuteronomy is largely a separate work that was probably attached to the first four books at a later stage, leading some scholars to speak of a **Tetrateuch** consisting of Genesis through Numbers; and it is also the case that the actual narrative climax of the story, the conquest of the Land, is given in the book of Joshua, leading other scholars to speak of a **Hexateuch** consisting of Genesis through Joshua.

Pentecost (Gr. "fiftieth [day]") the Greek name for the Jewish festival of Weeks (Shavuoth), which occurs 50 days after Passover. On the Pentecost after Jesus' crucifixion, according to Acts chapter 2, the Holy Spirit descended on his followers and inspired them to speak in different languages.

Persian era the period of domination of the Persian empire over the Near East, beginning at around 550 B.C. when Cyrus the Great, King of Persia, defeated the Medes, and lasting until about 330 B.C., when Alexander the Great of Macedon conquered the lands surrounding the Mediterranean and brought them under Greek rule. It was during the Persian era that the Israelites were allowed to return to their land from exile (537 B.C.) and rebuild the Temple (515 B.C. or thereafter).

Persian period the era from approximately 539–333 B.C., from the time of Cyrus the Great until the Greek conquest under Alexander.

personification representing an idea, a value, or other abstract thought as a person. Wisdom is personified as a woman in Proverbs 8.

Pesach the Hebrew word usually translated "Passover."

Pharisees a movement among Jews in the first century A.D., according to Josephus and the writings in the New Testament. The Pharisees were concerned to extend Jewish practice into all areas of life, and followed the tradition of interpretation (**Oral Law**) associated with the schools of Hillel and Shammai. They were thus proponents of a Jewish identity separate from the larger non-Jewish culture that surrounded Judea, but were also opponents of the more conservative Sadducees, who did not accept their traditions of oral law. See **Sadducees.**

Philistines a group from the "Sea Peoples," who invaded and settled on the coastal region of Canaan. They had been repulsed from an invasion of Egypt (ca. 1190 B.C.). The five major Philistine cities (the **Pentapolis**) were Ashkelon, Ashdod, Ekron, Gath, and Gaza.

Philo Judaeus Hellenistic Jewish philosopher (ca. 20 B.C.–A.D. 50) of Alexandria, Egypt. Philo worked out a system that tried to interpret biblical concepts and beliefs in terms of the philosophy of Plato and his followers. In this system, God cannot be known directly, but only through intermediate beings; the soul, the higher element in the human person, is always attempting to return to God, its origin, although if this task is not far enough along at the time of the individual's death, the soul may have to transmigrate into another body and try again. In Philo's view, the best insights of Greek philosophy were compatible with the religion of the Hebrew Scriptures and could be found in the Bible by means of allegorical interpretation, which he used in his own interpretive works. He influenced Jewish writers like the author of the Wisdom of Solomon and Christian theologians such as Clement, Origen, and Ambrose.

Phoenicians the people who lived in the area north of Israel, in part of what is present-day

Lebanon. Their chief cities were Tyre and Sidon. The Phoenicians were known throughout the eastern Mediterranean region as merchants, and for producing a reddish-purple dye, from which they apparently got their name (*phoinix* is the Greek word for the color of the dye).

phylacteries (Gr. *phulakterion,* "amulet," from *phulax,* "guard") see **tefillin.**

Platonism a particular philosophy derived from the teaching of Plato, saying that there is a profound difference, even an opposition, between the realm of matter and the realm of spirit, and that the world of sense experience is essentially an illusion, deriving what reality it has from a correspondence with a true, ultimately real world of Forms. The influence of Platonism on religious thought can be seen in the Wisdom of Solomon; it is also apparent in the thought of **Philo Judaeus** and Christian thinkers like Clement, Origen, and Augustine.

pogrom an officially encouraged, organized massacre of a minority group.

polemic, polemical (Gr. *polemos,* "war") an argument or debate in the form of an attack on one's opponent or on the opposing position. Polemical speech is characterized by verbal attacks, exaggerated language, and sometimes violent imagery.

Polycarp, Letter of an early Christian letter of instruction. it was written by Polycarp, bishop of Smyrna, and addressed to the church of Philippi. It gives advice about dealing with problems in the congregation, exhorts readers to behave in a moral fashion, and combats false teachings. It is therefore similar to many canonical New Testament writings, some of which (like the Gospels and Paul's letters) Polycarp seems to know.

potsherd a broken piece of pottery. Examination of such pieces allows archeologists to date the different levels of a site according to the type of pottery represented at a given level.

primogeniture the social arrangement by which the eldest son inherits a father's title or the bulk of the father's property.

proem a short introduction or preface to a literary text.

prophet (Gr. *prophetes,* "speak out" or "speak forth") the LXX translation of *nabi'* ("one who is called"), the standard Hebrew term for prophet. Synonyms include "seer," "man of God," and "visionary." Besides the authors of the prophetic books, Moses, Samuel, and others are called prophets. Prophets do not so much predict the future, as the current use would imply, as they speak about the situation of their own time and what it will result in if nothing changes.

Prophets, The the second division of the Hebrew Scriptures.

proverb (Heb. *mashal,* "comparison") a short statement of traditional wisdom, supported by long experience and expressed in memorable form. In Hebrew proverbs, generally the second line repeats or develops, sometimes by contrast, the thought of the first line. This feature is called parallelism and is common in Hebrew poetry. Proverbs are quoted in many books of the Bible, but the major collection is in the book of Proverbs. There are also proverbs in the Wisdom of Solomon and, in a longer "essay" form, in Sirach (Ecclesiasticus).

psalm (from Gr. *psalmos*) a song accompanied by musical instruments. In the Bible these songs cover a wide variety of styles and greatly differing content; psalms appear in many places (e.g., 1 Sm 2:1–10; Jon 2:1–9), but the principal collection of them is found in the book of Psalms. The Hebrew name for this book is *Tehillim,* meaning "praises," even though the majority of the psalms are not hymns of praise but spread over many other categories such as laments, prayers of thanksgiving and confidence, wisdom, and psalms of royalty.

pseudonymous written or published under a false name (e.g., Testaments of the Twelve Patriarchs). Most pseudonymous writing is attributed to someone much better known than the actual writer, to give the text the benefit of the presumed authority of the famous person.

Ptolemies the rulers of Egypt and its surrounding areas after the breakup of the Greek empire of Alexander the Great, following his death.

Purim the festival that commemorates the delivery of the Jews in Persia from destruction, as recounted in the book of Esther. It is celebrated on 14 or 15 Adar.

Q

Q see **synoptic problem.**

qinah meter a metrical pattern consisting of a line with three stresses followed by a line with two stresses; it is primarily used in psalms of lament or complaint, and in the book of Lamentations, though it can also express joy (Ps 65).

Qumran Community the settlement near Wadi Qumran at the Dead Sea, most likely composed of Essenes. The Qumran group was a sectarian Jewish community that kept its own practices in opposition to the established community in Jerusalem and Judea; the library of this group was discovered in 1948 and is known as the Dead Sea Scrolls.

R

rabbi (Aram. "teacher") a Jewish religious leader who studied Torah and its associated commentaries, particularly the Talmud, and offered his own teaching based on that study.

reader-response criticism analyzing a text by looking at the relationship between the text and its reader, including the clues within the text that guide the reader in drawing meaning from it.

redaction criticism the study of how already existing textual units—narratives of incidents, laws, proverbs, or other isolatable pieces that can be disentangled by **source criticism**—were combined into larger texts by the activities of editors called "redactors." Redaction criticism concentrates on the perspective of the editor, trying to deduce what editorial intentions can be understood from the way smaller units are arranged, expanded, and combined.

redactor an editor who works with already existing units to combine them into larger wholes.

resident alien a foreigner with legal rights living in Israel or an Israelite residing in the territory of another tribe.

revelation (Lat. "remove the veil," translating Gr. *apokalypsis*) belief or insight granted to a human being by a deity or heavenly being.

rhetoric (Gr. *rhetor,* "speaker, orator") the art or study of persuasive speech or writing.

Roman Period the period from 63 B.C. onwards, marking the beginning of Roman rule of Judea.

romance a popular storytelling technique in the ancient Mediterranean world that recounted the situation of young lovers and how they overcome obstacles to their marriage. Tobit is the purest romance in biblical literature. In early Christianity the form was modified to tell the stories of early converts and martyrs and the obstacles to their faith.

Rosh ha-Shanah (Heb. "head [i.e., beginning] of the year") the fall New Year in the Jewish calendar, 1 Tishri. (Rosh Ha-Shanah is now observed for two days.) The beginning of the religious calendar is 1 Nisan.

S

sackcloth rough cloth, often made from animal hair. A garment made of sackcloth is uncomfortable and is worn to indicate penitence or grief.

sacrifice (Lat. "make holy") the practice of giving something of value to God to show one's devotion or commitment. In Israelite religion, sacrifice, usually of an animal or bird (though grain and wine were also offered), was carried out by the ritual destruction of part or all of it by fire on an altar; by chasing it off into the wilderness; by letting it fly away; or by pouring it out on the ground or against the side of the altar. By giving to God something of value, the offerer symbolized the bonding of self with God or the reunion with God after a sinful or unclean person received forgiveness and purification. Christianity took over this idea of sacrifice and applied it to the death of Jesus Christ, teaching that Christ's sacrifice was an atonement for human sin. In modern-day Christianity, sacrifice usually entails doing without things of value (money, material possessions, or time) by giving them away, to the church to promote its work of worship and service, to any organization engaged in the service of others, or directly to those in need.

Sadducees a movement among Jews in the first century A.D., according to Josephus and the New Testament. They held to a strict application of Torah and to maintaining Temple worship according to its mandate; to continue the Temple practices without interference, the Sadducees were apparently willing to collaborate with the occupying Roman power to some extent, including accepting Roman interference in the choice of high priest. They were opposed to the Pharisees in not accepting the traditions of oral law as a guide to Torah practices, and they were also opposed to the political activists who wished to rebel against Roman rule, fearing that any rebellion would bring an end to the limited autonomy under which they could maintain Temple worship. See **Pharisees.**

Samaritan Pentateuch a text of the Torah in Hebrew used by the **Samaritans.** This text disagrees with the Masoretic text at many points. Some of these disagreements reflect Samaritan beliefs (e.g., in the religious importance of Mt. Gerizim), but others are supported by the **Dead Sea Scrolls** and reflect an alternate textual tradition.

Samaritans the descendants of the population of Samaria (northern kingdom) after the invasion of that kingdom and the deportation of the inhabitants in 722 B.C. The Samaritans regard themselves as descended from the Jewish remnant after the deportation, but the returning exiles from the southern kingdom (after the Babylonian Exile) did not regard them as Jews, seeing them rather as descendants of foreigners who had been settled there after the Jewish population had been removed. Therefore, beginning with Ezra and Nehemiah, the leadership forbade intermarriage between Samaritans and Jews. The Samaritans maintained worship (with a Temple on Mt. Gerizim) and the Torah (but not the rest of the Bible), although their calendar is not the same as the Jewish calendar.

Sanhedrin (ultimately from Gr. *synedria* from *syn-* and *hedra,* "with seat," i.e., "council") the religious court, whose membership was drawn from the Jewish ruling classes, that held ruling authority over the territory of Palestine under the Roman empire. The Sanhedrin was responsible for census-taking and taxation, as well as for acting as a court that would decide cases on its own and also, after preliminary determination, send cases on to the Roman governors.

scribe in general, one who could write, especially official documents, and take down dictation for letters, legal proceedings, etc. In the New Testament, a scribe was a lawyer, one who was expert in the requirements and meaning of Jewish law.

scroll a long strip of parchment (treated leather) or papyrus (reeds split, moistened, and pressed together), on which a text was written in columns. The scroll was read by unrolling one side while rolling up the other, to expose successive columns of text.

Second Isaiah see **Deutero-Isaiah.**

Second Temple the Temple constructed ca. 515 B.C. by the returning exiles, and continued and expanded over the course of time, until its destruction by the Romans in A.D. 70.

sect a religious grouping that emphasizes strict adherence to particular teachings and excludes those who do not conform.

seder (Heb. "order") the ritual meal and recitation of Passover eve. Also, the major divisions of the Mishnah (pl. *sedarim*).

Seleucid Empire the political entity that ruled over Syria and (at times) Judea after the death of Alexander the Great. The Seleucid ruler Antiochus IV "Epiphanes" desecrated the Temple in 167 B.C., leading to the Maccabean revolt and the rededication of the Temple in 164 B.C., an event commemorated in the festival of Hanukkah.

Seleucids (after Seleucus, the general who was the first of this ruling group) the rulers of Syria and its surrounding areas after the breakup of the Greek empire of Alexander the Great, following his death.

Septuagint the ancient Greek translation of the Hebrew Scriptures. The Septuagint was translated over a lengthy period beginning probably in the third century B.C. Traditionally there were 72 translators, a number that is rounded off to 70 and, in roman numerals, used as the abbreviation for this translation (LXX). The Septuagint was prepared for the use of Jews who lived outside the land of Israel and whose main language was Greek. It is important for several reasons: it translated a version of the Hebrew text that is older than the currently available Hebrew (Masoretic) text (see **Masoretic text**); it contains additional works, the Apocryphal/Deuterocanonical Books, most of which were originally written in Greek; and it was the Bible of early Christians and therefore represents what they thought of as Scripture.

Shabbat (Heb. "cessation") the Sabbath day.

Shavuot the festival of "Weeks," (also "Pentecost," Gr. for "fiftieth" [day]) the spring harvest, occurring, according to Priestly texts, 50 days (seven full weeks) after Passover.

Shekhinah a post-biblical term for the "dwelling" or "presence" of God with Israel; by extension, the divine manifestation in the community's life, or the sense of divine immanence within the world.

Shema the first word, used as a title, of the exhortation (Dt 6:4), "Hear, O Israel! The LORD is our God, the LORD alone!" (or, "the LORD our God, the LORD is one"); also the name of perhaps the most important and best-known prayer in Judaism, comprised of Deuteronomy 6:4–9; 11:13–21 and Numbers 15:37–41.

Sheol the underworld or abode of the dead. In the Hebrew Bible (Old Testament), all deceased descended to Sheol; there is no concept of a separate heaven and hell.

shofar the ram's horn for ceremonial use. In ancient Israel it was sounded to announce the anointing of a king or as a summons to war or to sound an alarm; today, in the synagogue, it is sounded on the High Holy Days.

simile a comparison, using "like" or "as" rather than, as in metaphor, linking two things directly. "[He] made my feet swift as a deer's" (Ps 18:34).

source criticism the effort to discover the sources or documents behind a text and to explore how the sources were combined into larger units. See **documentary hypothesis.**

Southern Kingdom the remaining part of the undivided kingdom of Israel, after the northern tribes withdrew from Israel at Solomon's death (1 Kgs 12). It is also called Judah.

Stoics Greek philosophers in the Hellenistic and Roman periods, who taught that emotions should be strictly controlled by reason.

Sukkot (Heb. "booths") the autumn harvest festival ("festival of ingathering"), during which it is customary, following Leviticus 23:42–43, to dwell in temporary booths. See **Tabernacles, feast of.**

suzerain the lord or ruler to whom loyalty is due in a covenant relationship. (Although the term is actually Old French for "sovereign," and originally applied to the feudal relationship of lord to peasant or subsidiary, it has been adapted for the ancient Near Eastern covenant system.)

synagogue (Gr. "coming together with") an assembly; a congregation. For Jews who were too distant from the Temple to worship at it, and for all Jews after the final destruction of the Temple by the Romans in A.D. 70, the synagogue became the only form of worship. Services consisted of prayer, song, and study of the sacred text.

syncretism the incorporation into one religion of practices and teachings derived from another, or the effort to combine two different religious traditions into a third, composite religion.

synonymous parallelism an imprecise term used for the type of **parallelism** where the second line or *colon* of a *bicolon* echoes the meaning of the first in different terms, for example, Isaiah 1:3, "An ox knows its owner, and an ass its master's manger: But Israel does not know, my people has not understood."

Synoptic Gospels Matthew, Mark, and Luke. "Synoptic" means "view together" and is applied to these writings because they, unlike John, can be readily compared.

synoptic problem the observation that in many passages Matthew and Luke repeat with only minor changes what Mark says, yet in other passages they do not follow Mark, or include stories or sayings that Mark does not have, yet match each other very closely. (They also each include material that none of the others have, but that is not a characteristic that needs to be explained.) Many commentators, from the earliest years of Christianity, have tried to understand the relationship among the Synoptic Gospels. According to the most widely held theory, Matthew and Luke relied on Mark and on another document (now lost) that contained mostly sayings of Jesus; this second document is referred to as "Q" from the German word "Quelle," meaning "source." In addition, Matthew and Luke each had their own sources.

T

tabernacle the portable sanctuary used by the Israelites during their wanderings in the wilderness. Exodus chapters 25–30 contain instructions for building it; the construction is narrated in Exodus chapters 35–40. It was eventually replaced by the Temple.

Tabernacles, Feast of the final harvest festival of grapes and olives, falling within our month of October. It was also called the "Feast of Booths" because the harvesters lived in the field in makeshift tents or booths. See **Sukkot.**

tablet a slab, typically of clay, with a smoothed surface that can be inscribed with a text.

talion (Lat. *talio,* "in kind" from *talis,* "like," "such like") a punishment that is of the same kind as the crime: exacting an equivalent penalty, such as an equal economic loss for theft, or death for murder, or "an eye for an eye." Talion is well-attested in Mesopotamian law, and in some biblical legal collections.

Talmud (Heb. "teaching") the title of the two great collections of rabbinic teaching, the Jerusalem Talmud or Talmud Yerushalmi and the Babylonian Talmud or Talmud Bavli. The Talmuds were compiled beginning after A.D. 200, as an extensive commentary on the Mishnah; they consist of comments on, and extensions of, the Mishnah sections to work out the application of Jewish teaching to everyday life, but they also include much other material, and information and teaching on a wide range of topics. The form of the Talmuds is that passages of the Mishnah are commented on by rabbinic teachings (called *gemara*). The Mishnah is not treated in its entirety. At the beginning of the Talmud's formation, the two centers of rabbinic study (the land of Israel and Babylonia) were in contact with each other and the commentary therefore reflected a common effort; later, especially with the completion of the Talmud in Israel (ca. A.D. 400), the Babylonian effort continued to refine and extend the applications, and it was the Talmud developed in Babylonia (completion after A.D. 500) that was distributed worldwide, under the auspices of the academies that continued to work in Babylon until the beginning of the second millennium A.D.

tefillin small black leather boxes containing biblical passages from Exodus 13:1–10; 13:11–16 and Deuteronomy 6:4–9; 11:13–21. Two are worn during weekday morning prayer: one on the head (above the space between the eyes, just below the hairline) and one on the (left) arm (see e.g., Dt 6:8). Also called "phylacteries."

tel a mound formed by repeated construction, occupation, and destruction of buildings on a particular site.

Temple the central place of worship for Israelite religion in Jerusalem, referring either to the first Temple built by Solomon or the Second Temple of Zerubbabel that was enlarged and rebuilt by Herod the Great.

testament (Lat. *testamentum,* "will, covenant"; translating Gr. *diatheke,* "covenant") an agreement, especially between God and human beings; also, the collections of books detailing various covenants between God and human beings: the "Old Testament" or "first covenant," that between God and Noah, Abraham, Moses, and the Israelites in general; and the "New Testament" or "new covenant" established by Jesus Christ.

Tetrateuch the first four books of the Bible, Genesis through Numbers, regarded as an edited collection to which Deuteronomy was then attached. See **Pentateuch.**

Text any fixed, written form of words; particularly, any writing that is subject to historical investigation, interpretation, exegesis, or homiletics.

textual criticism the effort to establish, by scholarly assessment of manuscript copies and other sources, an accurate version of a text according to what the original author had written.

theodicy the theological effort to justify the goodness of God in the face of suffering.

theophany (Gr. "appearance of god") the temporary appearance or manifestation of a divine being in a form that can be apprehended by the human senses.

Third Isaiah see **Trito-Isaiah.**

Thomas, Gospel of an early collection of sayings attributed to Jesus. It contains no miracle stories and no account of Jesus' deeds, his birth, his death, or the resurrection. Some of the sayings resemble those in the canonical Gospels, but others reflect a philosophy that regards spirit and matter as radically different and opposed to each other; in this view, life on earth is one of spirits trapped in matter, and the purpose of life is to free oneself from matter and attain eternal life in the spiritual realm. This philosophy, called **gnosticism,** was rejected by the main body of early Christians, and this may explain why the Gospel of Thomas was never accepted as canonical.

thresh to beat gathered stalks of grain to separate the grain from the stems and husks. See **winnow**. A threshing floor, a flat area used for threshing grain, was often built on a hilltop to catch the breeze necessary for winnowing. This hilltop location made a threshing floor an ideal location for holding sacrifices (1 Chr 21:18–27).

threshing floor a location where the usable portion of grain is separated from its outer covering. Grain is threshed by being beaten to crack the husks and separate the grain from the stems. It is then winnowed by being tossed in a flat basket in a breeze, allowing the husks (chaff), which are lighter, to blow away. A good location for this process is a flat area on a hilltop; this was also an ideal spot for offering sacrifice (see 1 Chr 21:18–27).

toledoth (Heb. "generations") lists of descendants; also, histories of ancestors and their descendants.

Torah (Heb. "teaching, instruction") the first division of the Hebrew Scriptures, consisting of Genesis through Deuteronomy. The word (and hence the title) is sometimes translated "law," but this translation can be misleading since the full collection of books contains much more than law codes and regulations.

tradition (Lat. *traditio*, "what is handed on") the means by which beliefs, customs, stories, laws, religious practices, and other cultural phenomena are handed down from one generation to the next. The Bible is in part a record of traditions, first among the Hebrew people and then among the Christians. The Bible itself was first represented in tradition: in traditional stories and beliefs, in religious practices, and so on; only later was it written down and handed on in that form. The study of tradition—of how things are handed on, and how they change or stay the same during the process—is of great importance for understanding the Bible and the beliefs that are based on it.

tradition criticism the interpretation of the history of a tradition, including stages such as oral transmission, the alteration of a tradition to address a changed situation, and the examination of particular kinds of traditions, such as the explanation of place names, the development of religious practices, or the growth or disuse of social practices.

Transjordan the area to the east of the Jordan River.

transmission history an account, usually inferred, of how a text came down to the present from its originator. Steps in transmission history can include oral transmission, redaction, manuscript copying, and scribal emendation.

Trito-Isaiah the scholarly term for chs 56–66 (or 55–66) of Isaiah. These chapters are primarily concerned with the life of the returned exiles in the province of Yehud (the Persian name for Judah) after 538 B.C. Some scholars doubt the separate existence of Trito-Isaiah; others maintain that it is not the product of one author, but a collection of diverse oracles by different members of a "school of Isaiah" collected during the Persian period.

Twelve, Book of the the Hebrew Bible's designation for the **Minor Prophets.**

typology (Gr. *typos,* the raised design on a seal for imprinting in wax, then by extension a pattern or model) understanding persons or events, especially in the New Testament, by referring them to Old Testament "types," such as the Exodus (1 Cor 10:1–6); Solomon (Lk 11:31); or narratives like that of Jonah (Lk 11:29–30).

U

uncircumcised, the Gentiles (Rom 4:9; Gal 2:7).

unleavened bread (Heb. *matzah, matzot*) bread made without yeast; also the festival that follows **Passover.**

V

vassal the underlord in a covenant relationship, who is granted power and control over people in a particular area in return for loyalty to the suzerain.

Vatican II the Council of Catholic bishops under the leadership of Popes John XXIII and Paul VI, held 1962–1965 in the Vatican. It undertook numerous reforms, including establishing vernacular liturgies and issuing decrees on ecumenism, relations with Judaism and other religions, and the Church and the modern world. The Council also promoted the study and reading of the Scriptures and encouraged new Catholic translations and commentaries to help the understanding of nonexperts.

Vulgate (Lat., "common") the Latin translation of the Bible begun by St. Jerome in the fourth century A.D., completed 405. Jerome translated his version directly from the Hebrew (unlike that of the previous Latin version [the "Old Latin" or "Vetus Latina"], which was translated from the Septuagint) and Greek texts and also separated the Old Testament text that was not part of the Hebrew Bible, but included in the Septuagint, into a separate section of "deuterocanonical" books. In the Middle Ages the Vulgate became the standard translation of the Bible for Western Christians. With the Protestant Reformation, its authority was questioned, but was reaffirmed by the Roman Catholic Church at the Council of Trent (1546).

W

wadi (Arabic) a stream bed or valley that is dry for part of the year; an arroyo or gulch.

Weeks, Feast of Shavuoth or Pentecost.

winnow to separate grain from its husks (called chaff) after it has been threshed. The threshed grain is placed in a wide, flat basket and tossed repeatedly into the air, allowing a breeze to blow away the lighter chaff while the grain drops back down into the basket.

wisdom literature Job, Proverbs, and Ecclesiastes in the Hebrew Bible; Sirach and Wisdom in the Septuagint; and some Psalms, for example, 37. Wisdom literature is concerned with insight, instruction, meditation of the meaning of life, and moral exhortation. It does not generally concern itself with key events in Israel's history, such as the Exodus; central teachings, such as the covenant; or focal institutions, such as the Davidic monarchy, prophecy, or the Temple.

Writings the third division of the Hebrew Scriptures.

X

xenophobia fear of, or contempt for, foreigners; racial exclusiveness.

Y

Yehud designation of the province of Judea during Persian times.

YHWH the name of God, which conventionally remains unpronounced and is represented in the text by the Hebrew letters *yod-he-vav-he* and the vowels for the title *Adonai,* "my Lord." In standard English translations, YHWH is represented by the word LORD written in capital and small capital letters. The original vocalization and meaning of this name is unknown, though it is connected to the verb *h-y-h,* "be" or "become," most likely in a causitive sense, "he who causes to be."

Yom Kippur (Heb. "day of atonement") the solemn fast observed each year on 10 Tishri, according to the command recorded in Leviticus 23:26–32. The observance involves abstention of various kinds and focuses on personal and communal repentance (teshuvah). The prayer services begin with the evening service and continue through the next day, with a morning service, an additional service, an afternoon service, and a concluding service.

Z

Zealot a member of the Jewish revolutionary movement during the Roman occupation of Palestine; an advocate of armed resistance in Roman rule.

ziggurat a temple-tower in ancient Mesopotamia. Ziggurats are presumed to represent a mount, on the top of which the earthly and divine realms merged.

Zion the name of the fortified hill within Jerusalem and thus, by extension, an alternative name for Jerusalem itself.

MEASURES AND WEIGHTS

The modern equivalents for biblical measures and weights are presented in the following tables.

Hebrew Measures of Capacity: Liquid Measures

HEBREW	NAB	EQUIVALENCE	U.S. MEASURES	METRIC UNITS
kor	kor	10 baths	60.738 gallons	230 liters
bat	bath	6 hins	6.073 gallons	23 liters
hin	hin	3 kabs	1.012 gallons	3.829 liters
qab	kab	4 logs	1.4349 quarts	1.276 liters
log	log		.674 pint	.32 liter

Hebrew Measures of Capacity: Dry Measures

HEBREW	NAB	EQUIVALENCE	U.S. MEASURES	METRIC UNITS
homer	homer	2 lethechs	6.524 bushels	229.7 liters
kor	measure, cor	2 lethechs	6.524 bushels	229.7 liters
letek	lethech, measure	5 ephahs	3.262 bushels	114.8 liters
ʾepah	ephah, measure	3 seahs	20.878 quarts	22.9 liters
tseʾah	measure	3.33 omers	6.959 quarts	7.7 liters
ʿomer	omer	1.8 kabs	2.087 quarts	2.3 liters
ʿissaron	tenth part (of ephah)			
qab	kab		1.159 quarts	1.3 liters

Measures of Capacity in the New Testament

GREEK	NAB	EQUIVALENCE	U.S. MEASURES	METRIC UNITS
batos	measure	(Hebrew) *bat*	6.073 gallons	23 liters
koros	kor	(Hebrew) *kor*	60.738 gallons or 6.524 bushels	230 liters
saton	measure	(Hebrew) *tseʾah*	6.959 dry quarts	7.71 liters
metretes	measure		10.3 gallons	39 liters
choinix	ration		.98 dry quart	1.079 liters
modios	bushel	(Latin) modius	7.68 dry quarts	8.458 liters

Hebrew Measures of Length

HEBREW	NAB	EQUIVALENCE	U.S. MEASURES	METRIC UNITS
ʾammaḥ	cubit	2 spans	17.49 inches	.443 meter
zeret	span	3 handbreadths	8.745 inches	.221 meter
topaḥ, tepaḥ	handbreadth	4 fingers	2.915 inches	.074 meter
ʾetsbaʿ	finger		.728 inch	.019 meter

The cubit described in Ezekiel 40:5; 43:13 is equal to seven (not six) handbreadths, namely 20.405 inches.

Measures of Length in the New Testament

GREEK	NAB	U.S. MEASURES	METRIC UNITS
pechus	cubit	about 1.5 feet	.456 meter
orguia	fathom	about 72.44 inches	1.839 meters
stadion	stade	about 606 feet	184.7 meters
milion	mile	about 4,854 feet	1.482 kilometers

Hebrew Weights

HEBREW	NAB	EQUIVALENCE	U.S. UNITS	METRIC UNITS
kikkar	talent	60 minas	75.558 pounds	34.3 kilograms
maneh	mina	50 shekels	20.148 ounces	571.2 grams
sheqel	shekel	2 bekas	176.29 grains	11.42 grams
beqaʿ	bekah, half a shekel	10 gerahs	88.14 grains	5.71 grams
gerah	gerah		8.81 grains	.57 gram

The practice of weighing unmarked ingots of metal used in commercial transactions prior to the invention of money explains that the names of the units of weight were used later as indications of value, and as names for monetary standards. There is, however, no direct relation between the shekel-weight and the weight of a shekel piece.

Weights in the New Testament

GREEK	NAB	EQUIVALENCE	U.S. UNITS	METRIC UNITS
talenton	talent	(Hebrew) talent	75.558 pounds	34.3 kilograms
mna	gold coin	(Hebrew) mina	20.148 ounces	571.2 grams
litra	pound	(Latin) libra	.719 pound	326.4 grams

LECTIONARY

THE NEW 3-YEAR CYCLE OF READINGS FOR SUNDAY MASS

See pp. 1814–1815 for Readings of Feasts that displace the Sunday Readings.
Guide: 1 refers to Reading I; 2 refers to Reading II; 3 refers to Gospel reading.

YEAR A
2011 2014 2017 2020 2023 2026 2029

Advent Season

1st Sunday of Advent
1 Is 2:1–5
2 Rom 13:11–14
3 Mt 24:37–44

2nd Sunday of Advent
1 Is 11:1–10
2 Rom 15:4–9
3 Mt 3:1–12

3rd Sunday of Advent
1 Is 35:1–6a, 10
2 Jas 5:7–10
3 Mt 11:2–11

4th Sunday of Advent
1 Is 7:10–14
2 Rom 1:1–7
3 Mt 1:18–24

Christmas Season

Christmas Vigil
1 Is 62:1–5
2 Acts 13:16–17, 22–25
3 Mt 1:1–25

Christmas (At Midnight)
1 Is 9:1–6
2 Ti 2:11–14
3 Lk 2:1–14

Christmas (At Dawn)
1 Is 62:11–12
2 Ti 3:4–7
3 Lk 2:15–20

Christmas (During the Day)
1 Is 52:7–10
2 Heb 1:1–6
3 Jn 1:1–18

Sunday After Christmas (Holy Family)
1 Sir 3:3–7, 14–17a
2 Col 3:12–21
3 Mt 2:13–15, 19–23

January 1 (Solemnity of Mary, Mother of God)
1 Nm 6:22–27
2 Gal 4:4–7
3 Lk 2:16–21

2nd Sunday After Christmas
1 Sir 24:1–4, 12–16
2 Eph 1:3–6, 15–18
3 Jn 1:1–18

Epiphany
1 Is 60:1–6
2 Eph 3:2–3a, 5–6
3 Mt 2:1–12

Sunday After Epiphany (Baptism of the Lord)
1 Is 42:1–4, 6–7
2 Acts 10:34–38
3 Mt 3:13–17

Lenten Season

Ash Wednesday
1 Jl 2:12–18
2 2 Cor 5:20–6:2
3 Mt 6:1–6, 16–18

1st Sunday of Lent
1 Gn 2:7–9; 3:1–7
2 Rom 5:12–19
3 Mt 4:1–11

2nd Sunday of Lent
1 Gn 12:1–4a
2 2 Tm 1:8b–10
3 Mt 17:1–9

3rd Sunday of Lent
1 Ex 17:3–7
2 Rom 5:1–2, 5–8
3 Jn 4:5–42

4th Sunday of Lent
1 1 Sm 16:1b, 6–7, 10–13a
2 Eph 5:8–14
3 Jn 9:1–41

5th Sunday of Lent
1 Ez 37:12–14
2 Rom 8:8–11
3 Jn 11:1–45

Passion Sunday (Palm Sunday)
Procession: Mt 21:1–11
1 Is 50:4–7
2 Phil 2:6–11
3 Mt 26:14–27:66

Easter Triduum and Easter Season

Mass of Lord's Supper
1 Ex 12:1–8, 11–14
2 1 Cor 11:23–26
3 Jn 13:1–15

Good Friday
1 Is 52:13–53:12
2 Heb 4:14–16; 5:7–9
3 Jn 18:1–19:42

Easter Vigil
1 Gn 1:1–2:2
Gn 22:1–18
Ex 14:15–15:1

Is 54:5–14
Is 55:1–11
Bar 3:9–15, 32–4:4
Ez 36:16–17a, 18–28
2 Rom 6:3–11
3 Mt 28:1–10

Easter Sunday
1 Acts 10:34a, 37–43
2 Col 3:1–4
or 1 Cor 5:6b–8
3 Jn 20:1–9
or Mt 28:1–10
Evening: 3 Lk 24:13–35

2nd Sunday of Easter
1 Acts 2:42–47
2 1 Pt 1:3–9
3 Jn 20:19–31

3rd Sunday of Easter
1 Acts 2:14, 22–33
2 1 Pt 1:17–21
3 Lk 24:13–35

4th Sunday of Easter
1 Acts 2:14a, 36–41
2 1 Pt 2:20b–25
3 Jn 10:1–10

5th Sunday of Easter
1 Acts 6:1–7
2 1 Pt 2:4–9
3 Jn 14:1–12

6th Sunday of Easter
1 Acts 8:5–8, 14–17
2 1 Pt 3:15–18
3 Jn 14:15–21

Ascension of Our Lord
1 Acts 1:1–11
2 Eph 1:17–23
3 Mt 28:16–20

7th Sunday of Easter
1 Acts 1:12–14
2 1 Pt 4:13–16
3 Jn 17:1–11a

Pentecost Vigil
1 Gn 11:1–9
or Ex 19:3–8a, 16–20b
or Ez 37:1–14
or Jl 3:1–5
2 Rom 8:22–27
3 Jn 7:37–39

Mass of the Day
1 Acts 2:1–11
2 1 Cor 12:3b–7, 12–13
3 Jn 20:19–23

Solemnities of the Lord During Ordinary Time

Trinity Sunday (Sunday after Pentecost)
1 Ex 34:4b–6, 8–9
2 2 Cor 13:11–13
3 Jn 3:16–18

Corpus Christi
1 Dt 8:2–3, 14b–16a
2 1 Cor 10:16–17
3 Jn 6:51–58

Sacred Heart of Jesus
1 Dt 7:6–11
2 1 Jn 4:7–16
3 Mt 11:25–30

Ordinary Time

1st Sunday
(See Baptism of the Lord, above)

2nd Sunday
1 Is 49:3, 5–6
2 1 Cor 1:1–3
3 Jn 1:29–34

3rd Sunday
1 Is 8:23b–9:3
2 1 Cor 1:10–13, 17
3 Mt 4:12–23

4th Sunday
1 Zep 2:3; 3:12–13
2 1 Cor 1:26–31
3 Mt 5:1–12a

5th Sunday
1 Is 58:7–10
2 1 Cor 2:1–5
3 Mt 5:13–16

6th Sunday
1 Sir 15:16–21
2 1 Cor 2:6–10
3 Mt 5:17–37

7th Sunday
1 Lv 19:1–2, 17–18
2 1 Cor 3:16–23
3 Mt 5:38–48

8th Sunday
1 Is 49:14–15
2 1 Cor 4:1–5
3 Mt 6:24–34

9th Sunday
1 Dt 11:18, 26–28, 32
2 Rom 3:21–25a, 28
3 Mt 7:21–27

10th Sunday
1 Hos 6:3–6
2 Rom 4:18–25
3 Mt 9:9–13

11th Sunday
1 Ex 19:2–6a
2 Rom 5:6–11
3 Mt 9:36–10:8

12th Sunday
1 Jer 20:10–13
2 Rom 5:12–15
3 Mt 10:26–33

13th Sunday
1 2 Kgs 4:8–11, 14–16a
2 Rom 6:3–4, 8–11
3 Mt 10:37–42

14th Sunday
1 Zec 9:9–10
2 Rom 8:9, 11–13
3 Mt 11:25–30

15th Sunday
1 Is 55:10–11
2 Rom 8:18–23
3 Mt 13:1–23

16th Sunday
1 Wis 12:13, 16–19
2 Rom 8:26–27
3 Mt 13:24–43

17th Sunday
1 1 Kgs 3:5, 7–12
2 Rom 8:28–30
3 Mt 13:44–52

18th Sunday
1 Is 55:1–3
2 Rom 8:35, 37–39
3 Mt 14:13–21

19th Sunday
1 1 Kgs 19:9a, 11–13a
2 Rom 9:1–5
3 Mt 14:22–33

20th Sunday
1 Is 56:1, 6–7
2 Rom 11:13–15, 29–32
3 Mt 15:21–28

21st Sunday
1 Is 22:19–23
2 Rom 11:33–36
3 Mt 16:13–20

22nd Sunday
1 Jer 20:7–9
2 Rom 12:1–2
3 Mt 16:21–27

23rd Sunday
1 Ez 33:7–9
2 Rom 13:8–10
3 Mt 18:15–20

24th Sunday
1 Sir 27:30–28:7
2 Rom 14:7–9
3 Mt 18:21–35

25th Sunday
1 Is 55:6–9
2 Phil 1:20c–24, 27a
3 Mt 20:1–16a

26th Sunday
1 Ez 18:25–28
2 Phil 2:1–11
3 Mt 21:28–32

27th Sunday
1 Is 5:1–7
2 Phil 4:6–9
3 Mt 21:33–43

28th Sunday
1 Is 25:6–10a
2 Phil 4:12–14, 19–20
3 Mt 22:1–14

29th Sunday
1 Is 45:1, 4–6
2 1 Thes 1:1–5b
3 Mt 22:15–21

30th Sunday
1 Ex 22:20–26
2 1 Thes 1:5c–10
3 Mt 22:34–40

31st Sunday
1 Mal 1:14b–2:2b, 8–10
2 1 Thes 2:7b–9, 13
3 Mt 23:1–12

32nd Sunday
1 Wis 6:12–16
2 1 Thes 4:13–18
3 Mt 25:1–13

33rd Sunday
1 Prv 31:10–13, 19–20, 30–31
2 1 Thes 5:1–6
3 Mt 25:14–30

34th Sunday (Christ the King)
1 Ez 34:11–12, 15–17
2 1 Cor 15:20–26, 28
3 Mt 25:31–46

YEAR B
2012 2015 2018 2021 2024 2027 2030

Advent Season

1st Sunday of Advent
1 Is 63:16b–17, 19b; 64:2b–7
2 1 Cor 1:3–9
3 Mk 13:33–37

2nd Sunday of Advent
1 Is 40:1–5, 9–11
2 2 Pt 3:8–14
3 Mk 1:1–8

3rd Sunday of Advent
1 Is 61:1–2a, 10–11
2 1 Thes 5:16–24
3 Jn 1:6–8, 19–28

4th Sunday of Advent
1 2 Sm 7:1–5, 8b–12, 14a, 16
2 Rom 16:25–27
3 Lk 1:26–38

Christmas Season

Christmas Vigil
1 Is 62:1–5
2 Acts 13:16–17, 22–25
3 Mt 1:1–25

Christmas (At Midnight)
1 Is 9:1–6
2 Ti 2:11–14
3 Lk 2:1–14

Christmas (At Dawn)
1 Is 62:11–12
2 Ti 3:4–7
3 Lk 2:15–20

Christmas (During the Day)
1 Is 52:7–10
2 Heb 1:1–6
3 Jn 1:1–18

Sunday After Christmas (Holy Family)
1 Gn 15:1–6; 21:1–3
2 Heb 11:8, 11–12, 17–19
3 Lk 2:22–40 or 22, 39–40

January 1 (Solemnity of Mary, Mother of God)
1 Nm 6:22–27
2 Gal 4:4–7
3 Lk 2:16–21

2nd Sunday After Christmas
1 Sir 24:1–2, 8–12
2 Eph 1:3–6, 15–18
3 Jn 1:1–18

Epiphany
1 Is 60:1–6
2 Eph 3:2–3a, 5–6
3 Mt 2:1–12

Sunday After Epiphany (Baptism of the Lord)
1 Is 55:1–11
2 1 Jn 5:1–9
3 Mk 1:7–11

Lenten Season

Ash Wednesday
1 Jl 2:12–18
2 2 Cor 5:20–6:2
3 Mt 6:1–6, 16–18

1st Sunday of Lent
1 Gn 9:8–15
2 1 Pt 3:18–22
3 Mk 1:12–15

2nd Sunday of Lent
1 Gn 22:1–2, 9a, 10–13, 15–18
2 Rom 8:31b–34
3 Mk 9:2–10

3rd Sunday of Lent
1 Ex 20:1–17
2 1 Cor 1:22–25
3 Jn 2:13–25

4th Sunday of Lent
1 2 Chr 36:14–16, 19–23
2 Eph 2:4–10
3 Jn 3:14–21

5th Sunday of Lent
1 Jer 31:31–34
2 Heb 5:7–9
3 Jn 12:20–33

Passion Sunday (Palm Sunday)
Procession: Mk 11:1–10 or Jn 12:12–16
1 Is 50:4–7
2 Phil 2:6–11
3 Mk 14:1–15,47

Easter Triduum and Easter Season

Mass of Lord's Supper
1 Ex 12:1–8, 11–14
2 1 Cor 11:23–26
3 Jn 13:1–15

Good Friday
1 Is 52:13–53:12
2 Heb 4:14–16; 5:7–9
3 Jn 18:1–19:42

Easter Vigil
1 Gn 1:1–2:2
Gn 22:1–18
Ex 14:15–15:1
Is 54:5–14
Is 55:1–11
Bar 3:9–15, 32–4:4
Ez 36:16–28
2 Rom 6:3–11
3 Mk 16:1–7

Easter Sunday
1 Acts 10:34a, 37–43
2 Col 3:1–4 or 1 Cor 5:6b–8
3 Jn 20:1–9 or Mk 16:1–8
Evening: 3 Lk 24:13–35

2nd Sunday of Easter
1 Acts 4:32–35
2 1 Jn 5:1–6
3 Jn 20:19–31

3rd Sunday of Easter
1 Acts 3:13–15, 17–19
2 1 Jn 2:1–5a
3 Lk 24:35–48

4th Sunday of Easter
1 Acts 4:8–12
2 1 Jn 3:1–2
3 Jn 10:11–18

5th Sunday of Easter
1 Acts 9:26–31
2 1 Jn 3:18–24
3 Jn 15:1–8

6th Sunday of Easter
1 Acts 10:25–26, 34–35, 44–48
2 1 Jn 4:7–10
3 Jn 15:9–17

Ascension of Our Lord
1 Acts 1:1–11
2 Eph 1:17–23 or 4:1–13
3 Mk 16:15–20

7th Sunday of Easter
1 Acts 1:15–17, 20a, 20c–26
2 1 Jn 4:11–16
3 Jn 17:11b–19

Pentecost Vigil
1 Gn 11:1–9 or Ex 19:3–8a, 16–20b or Ez 37:1–14 or Jl 3:1–5
2 Rom 8:22–27
3 Jn 7:37–39

Mass of the Day
1 Acts 2:1–11
2 1 Cor 12:3b–7, 12–13
3 Jn 20:19–23
Pentecost-Optional
2 Gal 5:16–25

3 Jn 15:26–27; 16:12–15

Solemnities of the Lord During Ordinary Time

Trinity Sunday (Sunday after Pentecost)
1 Dt 4:32–34, 39–40
2 Rom 8:14–17
3 Mt 28:16–20

Corpus Christi
1 Ex 24:3–8
2 Heb 9:11–15
3 Mk 14:12–16, 22–26

Sacred Heart of Jesus
1 Hos 11:1, 3–4, 8c–9
2 Eph 3:8–12, 14–19
3 Jn 19:31–37

Ordinary Time

1st Sunday
(See Baptism of the Lord, above)

2nd Sunday
1 1 Sm 3:3b–10, 19
2 1 Cor 6:13c–15a, 17–20
3 Jn 1:35–42

3rd Sunday
1 Jon 3:1–5, 10
2 1 Cor 7:29–31
3 Mk 1:14–20

4th Sunday
1 Dt 18:15–20
2 1 Cor 7:32–35
3 Mk 1:21–28

5th Sunday
1 Jb 7:1–4, 6–7
2 1 Cor 9:16–19, 22–23
3 Mk 1:29–39

6th Sunday
1 Lv 13:1–2, 45–46
2 1 Cor 10:31–11:1
3 Mk 1:40–45

7th Sunday
1 Is 43:18–19, 21–22, 24b–25
2 2 Cor 1:18–22
3 Mk 2:1–12

8th Sunday
1 Hos 2:16b, 17b, 21–22
2 2 Cor 3:1b–6
3 Mk 2:18–22

9th Sunday
1 Dt 5:12–15
2 2 Cor 4:6–11
3 Mk 2:23–3:6

10th Sunday
1 Gn 3:9–15
2 2 Cor 4:13–5:1
3 Mk 3:20–35

11th Sunday
1 Ez 17:22–24
2 2 Cor 5:6–10
3 Mk 4:26–34

12th Sunday
1 Jb 38:1, 8–11
2 2 Cor 5:14–17
3 Mk 4:35–41

13th Sunday
1 Wis 1:13–15; 2:23–24
2 2 Cor 8:7, 9, 13–15
3 Mk 5:21–43

14th Sunday
1 Ez 2:2–5
2 2 Cor 12:7–10
3 Mk 6:1–6

15th Sunday
1 Am 7:12–15
2 Eph 1:3–14
3 Mk 6:7–13

16th Sunday
1 Jer 23:1–6
2 Eph 2:13–18
3 Mk 6:30–34

17th Sunday
1 2 Kgs 4:42–44
2 Eph 4:1–6
3 Jn 6:1–15

18th Sunday
1 Ex 16:2–4, 12–15
2 Eph 4:17, 20–24
3 Jn 6:24–35

19th Sunday
1 1 Kgs 19:4–8
2 Eph 4:30–5:2
3 Jn 6:41–51

20th Sunday
1 Prv 9:1–6
2 Eph 5:15–20
3 Jn 6:51–58

21st Sunday
1 Jos 24:1–2a, 15–17, 18b
2 Eph 5:21–32
3 Jn 6:60–69

22nd Sunday
1 Dt 4:1–2, 6–8
2 Jas 1:17–18, 21b–22, 27
3 Mk 7:1–8, 14–15, 21–23

23rd Sunday
1 Is 35:4–7a
2 Jas 2:1–5
3 Mk 7:31–37

24th Sunday
1 Is 50:5–9a
2 Jas 2:14–18
3 Mk 8:27–35

25th Sunday
1 Wis 2:12, 17–20
2 Jas 3:16–4:3
3 Mk 9:30–37

26th Sunday
1 Nm 11:25–29
2 Jas 5:1–6
3 Mk 9:38–43, 45, 47–48

27th Sunday
1 Gn 2:18–24
2 Heb 2:9–11
3 Mk 10:2–16

28th Sunday
1 Wis 7:7–11
2 Heb 4:12–13
3 Mk 10:17–30

29th Sunday
1 Is 53:10–11
2 Heb 4:14–16
3 Mk 10:35–45

30th Sunday
1 Jer 31:7–9
2 Heb 5:1–6
3 Mk 10:46–52

31st Sunday
1 Dt 6:2–6
2 Heb 7:23–28
3 Mk 12:28b–34

32nd Sunday
1 1 Kgs 17:10–16
2 Heb 9:24–28
3 Mk 12:38–44

33rd Sunday
1 Dn 12:1–3
2 Heb 10:11–14, 18
3 Mk 13:24–32

34th Sunday (Christ the King)
1 Dn 7:13–14
2 Rev 1:5–8
3 Jn 18:33b–37

YEAR C
2013 2016 2019 2022 2025 2028 2031

Advent Season

1st Sunday of Advent
1 Jer 33:14–16
2 1 Thes 3:12–4:2
3 Lk 21:25–28, 34–36

2nd Sunday of Advent
1 Bar 5:1–9
2 Phil 1:4–6, 8–11
3 Lk 3:1–6

3rd Sunday of Advent
1 Zep 3:14–18a
2 Phil 4:4–7
3 Lk 3:10–18

4th Sunday of Advent
1 Mi 5:1–4a
2 Heb 10:5–10
3 Lk 1:39–45

Christmas Season

Christmas Vigil
1 Is 62:1–6
2 Acts 13:16–17, 22–25
3 Mt 1:1–25

Christmas (At Midnight)
1 Is 9:1–6
2 Ti 2:11–14
3 Lk 2:1–14

Christmas (At Dawn)
1 Is 62:11–12

2 Ti 3:4–7
3 Lk 2:15–20

Christmas (During the Day)
1 Is 57:7–10
2 Heb 1:1–6
3 Jn 1:1–18

Sunday After Christmas (Holy Family)
1 1 Sm 1:20–22, 24–28
2 1 Jn 3:1–2, 21–24
3 Lk 2:41–52

January 1 (Solemnity of Mary, Mother of God)
1 Nm 6:22–27
2 Gal 4:4–7
3 Lk 2:16–21

2nd Sunday After Christmas
1 Sir 24:1–2, 8–12
2 Eph 1:3–6, 15–18
3 Jn 1:1–18

Epiphany
1 Is 60:1–6
2 Eph 3:2–3a, 5–6
3 Mt 2:1–12

Sunday After Epiphany (Baptism of the Lord)
1 Is 40:1–5, 9–11
2 Ti 2:11–14; 3:4–7
3 Lk 3:15–16, 21–22

Lenten Season

Ash Wednesday
1 Jl 2:12–18
2 2 Cor 5:20–6:2
3 Mt 6:1–6, 16–18

1st Sunday of Lent
1 Dt 26:4–10
2 Rom 10:8–13
3 Lk 4:1–13

2nd Sunday of Lent
1 Gn 15:5–12, 17–18
2 Phil 3:17–4:1
3 Lk 9:28b–36

3rd Sunday of Lent
1 Ex 3:1–8a, 13–15
2 1 Cor 10:1–6, 10–12
3 Lk 13:1–9

4th Sunday of Lent
1 Jos 5:9a, 10–12
2 2 Cor 5:17–21
3 Lk 15:1–3, 11–32

5th Sunday of Lent
1 Is 43:16–21
2 Phil 3:8–14
3 Jn 8:1–11

Passion Sunday (Palm Sunday)
Procession: Lk 19:28–40
1 Is 50:4–7
2 Phil 2:6–11
3 Lk 22:14–23:56

Easter Triduum and Easter Season

Mass of Lord's Supper
1 Ex 12:1–8, 11–14
2 1 Cor 11:23–26
3 Jn 13:1–15

Good Friday
1 Is 52:13–53:12
2 Heb 4:14–16; 5:7–9
3 Jn 18:1–19:42

Easter Vigil
1 Gn 1:1–2:2
Gn 22:1–18
Ex 14:15–15:1
Is 54:5–14
Is 55:1–11
Bar 3:9–15, 32–4:4
Ez 36:16–28
2 Rom 6:3–11
3 Lk 24:1–12

Easter Sunday
1 Acts 10:34a, 37–43
2 Col 3:1–4 or 1 Cor 5:6b–8
3 Jn 20:1–9 or Lk 24:1–12
Evening: 3 Lk 24:13–35

2nd Sunday of Easter
1 Acts 5:12–16
2 Rev 1:9–11a, 12–13, 17–19
3 Jn 20:19–31

3rd Sunday of Easter
1 Acts 5:27b–32, 40b–41
2 Rev 5:11–14
3 Jn 21:1–19 or 1–14

4th Sunday of Easter
1 Acts 13:14, 43–52
2 Rev 7:9, 14b–17
3 Jn 10:27–30

5th Sunday of Easter
1 Acts 14:21b–27
2 Rev 21:1–5a
3 Jn 13:31–33a, 34–35

6th Sunday of Easter
1 Acts 15:1–2, 22–29
2 Rev 21:10–14, 22–23
3 Jn 14:23–29

Ascension of the Lord
1 Acts 1:1–11
2 Eph 1:17–23 or Heb 9:24–28; 10:19–23
3 Lk 24:46–53

7th Sunday of Easter
1 Acts 7:55–60
2 Rev 22:12–14, 16–17, 20
3 Jn 17:20–26

Pentecost Vigil
1 Gn 11:1–9 or Ex 19:3–8a, 16–20b or Ez 37:1–14 or Jl 3:1–5
2 Rom 8:22–27
3 Jn 7:37–39

Mass of the Day
1 Acts 2:1–11
2 1 Cor 12:3b–7, 12–13 or Rom 8:8–27
3 Jn 20:19–23 or Jn 14:15–16, 23b–26

Solemnities of the Lord During Ordinary Time

Trinity Sunday (Sunday After Pentecost)
1 Prv 8:22–31
2 Rom 5:1–5
3 Jn 16:12–15

Corpus Christi
1 Gn 14:18–20
2 1 Cor 11:23–26
3 Lk 9:11b–17

Sacred Heart of Jesus
1 Ez 34:11–16
2 Rom 5:5b–11
3 Lk 15:3–7

Ordinary Time

1st Sunday
(See Baptism of the Lord, above)

2nd Sunday
1 Is 62:1–5
2 1 Cor 12:4–11
3 Jn 2:1–12

3rd Sunday
1 Neh 8:2–4a, 5–6, 8–10
2 1 Cor 12:12–30
3 Lk 1:1–4; 4:14–21

4th Sunday
1 Jer 1:4–5, 17–19
2 1 Cor 12:31–13:13
3 Lk 4:21–30

5th Sunday
1 Is 6:1–2a, 3–8
2 1 Cor 15:1–11
3 Lk 5:1–11

6th Sunday
1 Jer 17:5–8
2 1 Cor 15:12, 16–20
3 Lk 6:17, 20–26

7th Sunday
1 1 Sm 26:2, 7–9, 12–13, 22–23
2 1 Cor 15:45–49
3 Lk 6:27–38

8th Sunday
1 Sir 27:5–8
2 1 Cor 15:54–58
3 Lk 6:39–45

9th Sunday
1 1 Kgs 8:41–43
2 Gal 1:1–2, 6–10
3 Lk 7:1–10

10th Sunday
1 1 Kgs 17:17–24
2 Gal 1:11–19
3 Lk 7:11–17

11th Sunday
1 2 Sm 12:7–10, 13
2 Gal 2:16, 19–21
3 Lk 7:36–8:3

12th Sunday
1 Zec 12:10–11
2 Gal 3:26–29
3 Lk 9:18–24

13th Sunday
1 1 Kgs 19:16b, 19–21
2 Gal 5:1, 13–18
3 Lk 9:51–62

14th Sunday
1 Is 66:10–14c
2 Gal 6:14–18
3 Lk 10:1–12, 17–20

15th Sunday
1 Dt 30:10–14
2 Col 1:15–20
3 Lk 10:25–37

16th Sunday
1 Gn 18:1–10a
2 Col 1:24–28
3 Lk 10:38–42

17th Sunday
1 Gn 18:20–32
2 Col 2:12–14
3 Lk 11:1–13

18th Sunday
1 Eccl 1:2; 2:21–23
2 Col 3:1–5, 9–11
3 Lk 12:13–31

19th Sunday
1 Wis 18:6–9
2 Heb 11:1–2, 8–19
3 Lk 12:32–48

20th Sunday
1 Jer 38:4–6, 8–10
2 Heb 12:1–4
3 Lk 12:49–53

21st Sunday
1 Is 66:18–21
2 Heb 12:5–7, 11–13
3 Lk 13:22–30

22nd Sunday
1 Sir 3:19–21, 30–31
2 Heb 12:18–19, 22–24a
3 Lk 14:1, 7–14

23rd Sunday
1 Wis 9:13–19
2 Phlm 9b–10, 12–17
3 Lk 14:25–33

24th Sunday
1 Ex 32:7–11, 13–14
2 1 Tm 1:12–17
3 Lk 15:1–32

25th Sunday
1 Am 8:4–7
2 1 Tm 2:1–8
3 Lk 16:1–13

26th Sunday
1 Am 6:1a, 4–7
2 1 Tm 6:11–16
3 Lk 16:19–31

27th Sunday
1 Hb 1:2–3; 2:2–4
2 2 Tm 1:6–8, 13–14
3 Lk 17:5–10

28th Sunday
1 2 Kgs 5:14–17
2 2 Tm 2:8–13
3 Lk 17:11–19

29th Sunday
1 Ex 17:8–13
2 2 Tm 3:14–4:2
3 Lk 18:1–8

30th Sunday
1 Sir 35:15b–17, 20–22a
2 2 Tm 4:6–8, 16–18
3 Lk 18:9–14

31st Sunday
1 Wis 11:23–12:2
2 2 Thes 1:11–2:2
3 Lk 19:1–10

32nd Sunday
1 2 Mc 7:1–2, 9–14
2 2 Thes 2:16–3:5
3 Lk 20:27–38

33rd Sunday
1 Mal 3:19–20a
2 2 Thes 3:7–12
3 Lk 21:5–19

34th Sunday (Christ the King)
1 2 Sm 5:1–3
2 Col 1:12–20
3 Lk 23:35–43

READINGS FOR THE MAJOR FEASTS OF THE YEAR

Feb. 2: Presentation of the Lord
1 Mal 3:1–4
2 Heb 2:14–18
3 Lk 2:22–40

Mar. 19: Joseph, Husband of Mary
1 2 Sm 7:4–5a, 12–14a, 16
2 Rom 4:13, 16–18, 22
3 Mt 1:16, 18–21, 24a
or Lk 2:41–51a

Mar. 25: Annunciation
1 Is 7:10–14
2 Heb 10:4–10
3 Lk 1:26–28

June 24: John the Baptist Vigil
1 Jer 1:4–10
2 1 Pt 1:8–12
3 Lk 1:5–17

Mass of the Day
1 Is 49:1–6
2 Acts 13:22–26
3 Lk 1:57–66, 80

June 29: Peter and Paul Vigil
1 Acts 3:1–10
2 Gal 1:11–20
3 Jn 21:15–19

Mass of the Day
1 Acts 12:1–11
2 2 Tm 4:6–8, 17–18
3 Mt 16:13–19

Aug. 6: Transfiguration
1 Dn 7:9–10, 13–14
2 2 Pt 1:16–19
3 (A) Mt 7:1–9
(B) Mk 9:2–10
(C) Lk 9:28b–36

Aug. 15: Assumption Vigil
1 1 Chr 15:3–4, 15; 16:1–2
2 1 Cor 15:54–57
3 Lk 11:27–28

Mass of the Day
1 Rev 11:19a; 12:1–6a, 10ab
2 1 Cor 15:20–26
3 Lk 1:39–56

Sept. 14: Triumph of the Cross
1 Nm 21:4–9
2 Phil 2:6–11
3 Jn 3:13–17

Nov. 1: All Saints
1 Rev 7:2–4, 9–14
2 1 Jn 3:1–3
3 Mt 5:1–12a

Nov. 2: All Souls First Mass
1 Jb 19:1, 23–27
2 1 Cor 15:51–57
3 Jn 6:37–40

Second Mass
1 Wis 3:1–9
2 Phil 3:20–21
3 Jn 11:17–27

Third Mass
1 2 Mc 12:43–46
2 Rev 14:13
3 Jn 14:1–6
(Other Readings may be chosen)

Nov. 9: Dedication of St. John Lateran
1 2 Chr 5:6–10, 13–6:2
2 1 Cor 3:9–13, 16–17
3 Lk 19:1–10
(Other Readings may be chosen)

Dec. 8: Immaculate Conception
1 Gn 3:9–15, 20
2 Eph 1:3–6, 11–12
3 Lk 1:26–38

WEEKDAY READINGS

Advent Season

First Week of Advent
Monday: Is 2:1–5 (Year A Is 4:2–6); Mt 8:5–11
Tuesday: Is 11:1–10; Lk 10:21–24
Wednesday: Is 25:6–10a; Mt 15:29–37
Thursday: Is 26:1–6; Mt 7:21, 24–27
Friday: Is 29:17–24; Mt 9:27–31
Saturday: Is 30:19–21, 23–26; Mt 9:35–10:1, 6–8

Second Week of Advent
Monday: Is 35:1–10; Lk 5:17–26
Tuesday: Is 40:1–11; Mt 18:12–14
Wednesday: Is 40:25–31; Mt 11:28–30
Thursday: Is 41:13–20; Mt 11:11–15
Friday: Is 48:17–19; Mt 11:16–19
Saturday: Sir 48:1–4, 9–11; Mt 17:10–13

Third Week of Advent
Monday: Num 24:2–7, 15–17a; Mt 21:23–27
Tuesday: Zep 3:1–2, 9–13; Mt 21:28–32
Wednesday: Is 45:6b–8, 18, 21b–25; Lk 7:18b–23
Thursday: Is 54:1–10; Lk 7:24–30
Friday: Is 56:1–3a, 6–8; Jn 5:33–36
Dec. 17: Gn 49:2, 8–10; Mt 1:1–17
Dec. 18: Jer 23:5–8; Mt 1:18–24
Dec. 19: Jgs 13:2–7, 24–25a; Lk 1:5–25
Dec. 20: Is 7:10–14; Lk 1:26–38
Dec. 21: Sg 2:8–14 or Zep 3:14–18a; Lk 1:39–45
Dec. 22: 1 Sm 1:24–28; Lk 1:46–56
Dec. 23: Mal 3:1–4, 23–24; Lk 1:57–66
Dec. 24: 2 Sm 7:1–5, 8b–11, 16; Lk 1:67–79

Christmas Season

Octave of Christmas
Second day (St. Stephen): Acts 6:8–10; 7:54–59; Mt 10:17–22
Third day (St. John): 1 Jn 1:1–4; Jn 20:2–8
Fourth day (Holy Innocents): 1 Jn 1:5–2:2; Mt 2:13–18
Fifth day: 1 Jn 2:3–11; Lk 2:22–35
Sixth day: 1 Jn 2:12–17; Lk 2:36–40
Seventh day: 1 Jn 2:18–21; Jn 1:1–18
January 2: 1 Jn 2:22–28; Jn 1:19–28
January 3: 1 Jn 2:29–3:6; Jn 1:29–34
January 4: 1 Jn 3:7–10; Jn 1:35–42
January 5: 1 Jn 3:11–21; Jn 1:43–51
January 6 (if Epiphany not celebrated): 1 Jn 5:5–13; Mk 1:6b–11
Readings may vary slightly depending on when Epiphany is celebrated

Week After Epiphany
Monday after Epiphany: 1 Jn 3:22–4:6; Mt 4:12–17, 23–25
Tuesday after Epiphany: 1 Jn 4:7–10; Mk 6:34–44
Wednesday after Epiphany: 1 Jn 4:11–18; Mk 6:45–52
Thursday after Epiphany: 1 Jn 4:19–5:4; Lk 4:14–22a
Friday after Epiphany: 1 Jn 5:5–13; Lk 5:12–16
Saturday after Epiphany: 1 Jn 5:14–21; Jn 3:22–30

Lenten Season
Ash Wednesday: Jl 2:12–18; 2 Cor 5:20–6:2; Mt 6:1–6, 16–18
Thursday after Ash Wednesday: Dt 30:15–20; Lk 9:22–25
Friday after Ash Wednesday: Is 58:1–9a; Mt 9:14–15
Saturday after Ash Wednesday: Is 58:9b–14; Lk 5:27–32

First Week of Lent
Monday: Lv 19:1–2, 11–18; Mt 25:31–46
Tuesday: Is 55:10–11; Mt 6:7–15
Wednesday: Jon 3:1–10; Lk 11:29–32
Thursday: Est C:12, 14–16, 23–25; Mt 7:7–12
Friday: Ez 18:21–28; Mt 5:20–26
Saturday: Dt 26:16–19; Mt 5:43–48

Second Week of Lent
Monday: Dn 9:4b–10; Lk 6:36–38
Tuesday: Is 1:10, 16–20; Mt 23:1–12
Wednesday: Jer 18:18–20; Mt 20:17–28
Thursday: Jer 17:5–10; Lk 16:19–31
Friday: Gn 37:3–4, 12–13a, 17b–28; Mt 21:33–43, 45–46
Saturday: Mi 7:14–15, 18–20; Lk 15:1–3, 11–32

Third Week of Lent
Monday: 2 Kgs 5:1–15a; Lk 4:24–30
Tuesday: Dn 3:25, 34–43; Mt 18:21–35

Wednesday: Dt 4:1, 5–9; Mt 5:17–19
Thursday: Jer 7:23–28; Lk 11:14–23
Friday: Hos 14:2–10; Mk 12:28b–34
Saturday: Hos 6:1–6; Lk 18:19–24

Fourth Week of Lent
Monday: Is 65:17–21; Jn 4:43–54
Tuesday: Ez 47:1–9, 12; Jn 5:1–3a, 5–16
Wednesday: Is 49:8–15; Jn 5:17–30
Thursday: Ex 32:7–14; Jn 5:31–47
Friday: Wis 2:1a, 12–22; Jn 7:1–2, 10, 25–30
Saturday: Jer 11:18–20; Jn 7:40–53

Fifth Week of Lent
Monday: Dn 13:1–9, 15–17, 19–30, 33–62; Jn 8:1–11 (Year C: Jn 8:12–20)
Tuesday: Nm 21:4–9; Jn 8:21–30
Wednesday: Dn 3:14–20, 91–92, 95; Jn 8:31–42
Thursday: Gn 17:3–9; Jn 8:51–59
Friday: Jer 20:10–13; Jn 10:31–42
Saturday: Ez 37:21–28; Jn 11:45–56

Holy Week
Monday: Is 42:1–7; Jn 12:1–11
Tuesday: Is 49:1–6; Jn 13:21–33, 36–38
Wednesday: Is 50:4–9a; Mt 26:14–25
Thursday Chrism Mass: Is 61:1–3a, 6a, 8b–9; Rev 1:5–8; Lk 4:16–21

Easter Season

Octave of Easter
Monday: Acts 2:14, 22–32; Mt 28:8–15
Tuesday: Acts 2:36–41; Jn 20:11–18
Wednesday: Acts 3:1–10; Lk 24:13–35
Thursday: Acts 3:11–26; Lk 24:35–48
Friday: Acts 4:1–12; Jn 21:1–14
Saturday: Acts 4:13–21; Mk 16:9–15

Second Week of Easter
Monday: Acts 4:23–31; Jn 3:1–8
Tuesday: Acts 4:32–37; Jn 3:7–15
Wednesday: Acts 5:17–26; Jn 3:16–21
Thursday: Acts 5:27–33; Jn 3:31–36
Friday: Acts 5:34–42; Jn 6:1–15
Saturday: Acts 6:1–7; Jn 6:16–21

Third Week of Easter
Monday: Acts 6:8–15; Jn 6:22–29
Tuesday: Acts 7:51–8:1a; Jn 6:30–35
Wednesday: Acts 8:1–8; Jn 6:35–40
Thursday: Acts 8:26–40; Jn 6:44–51
Friday: Acts 9:1–20; Jn 6:52–59
Saturday: Acts 9:31–42; Jn 6:60–69

Fourth Week of Easter
Monday: Acts 11:1–18; Jn 10:1–10 (Year A: Jn 10:11–18)
Tuesday: Acts 11:19–26; Jn 10:22–30
Wednesday: Acts 12:24–13:5a; Jn 12:44–50
Thursday: Acts 13:13–25; Jn 13:16–20
Friday: Acts 13:26–33; Jn 14:1–6
Saturday: Acts 13:44–52; Jn 14:7–14

Fifth Week of Easter
Monday: Acts 14:5–18; Jn 14:21–26
Tuesday: Acts 14:19–28; Jn 14:27–31a
Wednesday: Acts 15:1–6; Jn 15:1–8
Thursday: Acts 15:7–21; Jn 15:9–11
Friday: Acts 15:22–31; Jn 15:12–17
Saturday: Acts 16:1–10; Jn 15:18–21

Sixth Week of Easter
Monday: Acts 16:11–15; Jn 15:26–16:4a
Tuesday: Acts 16:22–34; Jn 16:5–11
Wednesday: Acts 17:15, 22–18:1; Jn 16:12–15
Thursday: Acts 18:1–8; Jn 16:16–20
Friday: Acts 18:9–18; Jn 16:20–23a
Saturday: Acts 18:23–28; Jn 16:23b–28

Seventh Week of Easter
Monday: Acts 19:1–8; Jn 16:29–33
Tuesday: Acts 20:17–27; Jn 17:1–11a
Wednesday: Acts 20:28–38; Jn 17:11b–19
Thursday: Acts 22:30; 23:6–11; Jn 17:20–26
Friday: Acts 25:13–21; Jn 21:15–19
Saturday: Acts 28:16–20, 30–31; Jn 21:20–25

Season of the Year
(I is the reading for Year 1; II is the reading for Year II; the Gospel is the same each year)

Week One
Monday: I – Heb 1:1–6; II – 1 Sm 1:1–8; Mk 1:14–20
Tuesday: I – Heb 2:5–12; II – 1 Sm 1:9–20; Mk 1:21–28
Wednesday: I – Heb 2:14–18; II – 1 Sm 3:1–10, 19–20; Mk 1:29–39
Thursday: I – Heb 3:7–14; II – 1 Sm 4:1–11; Mk 1:40–45
Friday: I – Heb 4:1–5, 11; II – 1 Sm 8:4–7, 10–22a; Mk 2:1–12
Saturday: I – Heb 4:12–16; II – 1 Sm 9:1–14, 17–19; 10:1a; Mk 2:13–17

Week Two
Monday: I – Heb 5:1–10; II – 1 Sm 15:16–23; Mk 2:18–22
Tuesday: I – Heb 6:10–20; II – 1 Sm 16:1–13; Mk 2:23–28
Wednesday: I – Heb 7:1–3, 15–17; II – 1 Sm 17:32–33, 37, 40–51; Mk 3:1–6
Thursday: I – Heb 7:25–8:6; II – 1 Sm 18:6–9; 19:1–7; Mk 3:7–12
Friday: I – Heb 8:6–13; II – 1 Sm 24:3–21; Mk 3:13–19

Saturday: I – Heb 9:2–3, 11–14; II – 2 Sm 1:1–4, 11–12, 19, 23–27; Mk 3:20–21

Week Three

Monday: I – Heb 9:15, 24–28; II – 2 Sm 5:1–7, 10; Mk 3:22–30

Tuesday: I – Heb 10:1–10; II – 2 Sm 6:12b–15, 17–19; Mk 3:31–35

Wednesday: I – Heb 10:11–18; II – 2 Sm 7:4–17; Mk 4:1–20

Thursday: I – Heb 10:19–25; II – 2 Sm 7:18–19, 24–29; Mk 4:21–25

Friday: I – Heb 10:32–39; II – 2 Sm 11:1–4a, 5–10a, 13–17; Mk 4:26–34

Saturday: I – Heb 11:1–2, 8–9; II – 2 Sm 12:1–7a, 10–17; Mk 4:35–41

Week Four

Monday: I – Heb 11:32–40; II – 2 Sm 15:13–14, 30; 16:5–13a; Mk 5:1–20

Tuesday: I – Heb 12:1–4; II – 2 Sm 18:9–10, 14b, 24–25a, 30–19:3; Mk 5:21–43

Wednesday: I – Heb 12:4–7, 11–15; II – 2 Sm 24:2, 9–17; Mk 6:1–6

Thursday: I – Heb 12:18–19, 21–24; II – 1 Kgs 2:1–4, 10–12; Mk 6:7–13

Friday: I – Heb 13:1–8; II – Sir 47:2–11; Mk 6:14–29

Saturday: 1 – Heb 13:15–17, 20–21; II – 1 Kgs 3:4–13; Mk 6:30–34

Week Five

Monday: I – Gn 1:1–19; II – 1 Kgs 8:1–7, 9–13; Mk 6:53–56

Tuesday: I – Gn 1:20–2:4a; II – 1 Kgs 8:22–23, 27–30; Mk 7:1–13

Wednesday: I – Gn 2:4b–9, 15–17; II – 1 Kgs 10:1–10; Mk 7:14–23

Thursday: I – Gn 2:18–25; II – 1 Kgs 11:4–13; Mk 7:24–30

Friday: I – Gn 3:1–8; II – 1 Kgs 11:29–32; 12:19; Mk 7:31–37

Saturday: I – Gn 3:9–24; II – 1 Kgs 12:26–32; 13:33–34; Mk 8:1–10

Week Six

Monday: I – Gn 4:1–15, 25; II – Jas 1:1–11; Mk 8:11–13

Tuesday: I – Gn 6:5–8; 7:1–5, 10; II – Jas 1:12–18; Mk 8:14–21

Wednesday: I – Gn 8:6–13, 20–22; II – Jas 1:19–27; Mk 8:22–26

Thursday: I – Gn 9:1–13; II – Jas 2:1–9; Mk 8:27–33

Friday: I – Gn 11:1–9; II – Jas 2:14–24, 26; Mk 8:34–9:1

Saturday: I – Heb 11:1–7; II – Jas 3:1–10; Mk 9:2–13

Week Seven

Monday: I – Sir 1:1–10; II – Jas 3:13–18; Mk 9:14–29

Tuesday: I – Sir 2:1–11; II – Jas 4:1–10; Mk 9:30–37

Wednesday: I – Sir 4:11–19; II – Jas 4:13–17; Mk 9:38–40

Thursday: I – Sir 5:1–8; II – Jas 5:1–6; Mk 9:41–50

Friday: I – Sir 6:5–17; II – Jas 5:9–12; Mk 10:1–12

Saturday: I – Sir 17:1–15; II – Jas 5:13–20; Mk 10:13–16

Week Eight

Monday: I – Sir 17:19–27; II – 1 Pt 1:3–9; Mk 10:17–27

Tuesday: I – Sir 35:1–12; II – 1 Pt 1:10–16; Mk 10:28–31

Wednesday: I – Sir 36:1, 5–6, 10–17; II – 1 Pt 1:18–25; Mk 10:32–45

Thursday: I – Sir 42:15–25; II – 1 Pt 2:2–5, 9–12; Mk 10:46–52

Friday: I – Sir 44:1, 9–13; II – 1 Pt 4:7–13; Mk 11:11–26

Saturday: I – Sir 51:12b–20; II – Jude 17:20b–25; Mk 11:27–33

Week Nine

Monday: I – Tb 1:1a–2; 2:1–9; II – 2 Pt 1:2–7; Mk 12:1–12

Tuesday: I – Tb 2:9–14; II – 2 Pt 3:12–15a, 17–18; Mk 12:13–17

Wednesday: I – Tb 3:1–11, 16; II – 2 Tm 1:1–3, 6–12; Mk 12:18–27

Thursday: I – Tb 6:10–11; 7:1, 9–17; 8:4–7; II – 2 Tm 2:8–15; Mk 12:28b–34

Friday: I – Tb 11:5–17; II – 2 Tm 3:10–17; Mk 12:35–37

Saturday: I – Tb 12:1, 5–15, 20; II – 2 Tm 4:1–8; Mk 12:38–44

Week Ten

Monday: I – 2 Cor 1:1–7; II – 1 Kgs 17:1–6; Mt 5:1–12

Tuesday: I – 2 Cor 1:18–22; II – 1 Kgs 17:7–16; Mt 5:13–16

Wednesday: I – 2 Cor 3:4–11; II – 1 Kgs 18:20–39; Mt 5:17–19

Thursday: I – 2 Cor 3:15–4:1, 3–6; II – 1 Kgs 18:41–46; Mt 5:20–26

Friday: I – 2 Cor 4:7–15; II – 1 Kgs 19:9a, 11–16; Mt 5:27–32

Saturday: I – 2 Cor 5:14–21; II – 1 Kgs 19:19–21; Mt 5:33–37

Week Eleven

Monday: I – 2 Cor 6:1–10; II – 1 Kgs 21:1–16; Mt 5:38–42

Tuesday: I – 2 Cor 8:1–9; II – 1 Kgs 21:17–29; Mt 5:43–48

Wednesday: I – 2 Cor 9:6–11; II – 1 Kgs 2:1, 6–14; Mt 6:1–6, 16–18

Thursday: I – 2 Cor 11:1–11; II – Sir 48:1–15; Mt 6:7–15

Friday: I – 2 Cor 11:18, 21b–30; II – 2 Kgs 11:1–4, 9–18, 20; Mt 6:19–23

Saturday: I – 2 Cor 12:1–10; II – 2 Chr 24:17–25; Mt 6:24–34

Week Twelve

Monday: I – Gn 12:1–9; II – 2 Kgs 17:5–8, 13–15a, 18; Mt 7:1–5

Tuesday: I – Gn 13:2, 5–8; II – 2 Kgs 19:9b–11, 14–21, 31–35a, 36; Mt 7:6, 12–14

Wednesday: I – Gn 15:1–12, 17–18; II – 2 Kgs 22:8–13; 23:1–3; Mt 7:15–20

Thursday: I – Gn 16:1–12, 15–16; II – 2 Kgs 24:8–17; Mt 7:21–29

Friday: I – Gn 17:1, 9–10, 15–22; II – 2 Kgs 25:1–12; Mt 8:1–4
Saturday: I – Gn 18:1–15; II – Lam 2:2, 10–14, 18–19; Mt 8:5–17

Week Thirteen
Monday: I – Gn 18:16–33; II – Am 2:6–10, 13–16; Mt 8:18–22
Tuesday: I – Gn 19:15–29; II – Am 3:1–8; 4:11–12; Mt 8:23–27
Wednesday: I – Gn 21:5, 8–20; II – Am 5:14–15, 21–24; Mt 8:28–34
Thursday: I – Gn 22:1–19; II – Am 7:10–17; Mt 9:1–8
Friday: I – Gn 23:1–4, 19; 24:1–8, 62–67; II – Am 8:4–6, 9–12; Mt 9:9–13
Saturday: I – Gn 27:1–5, 15–29; II – Am 9:11–15; Mt 9:14–17

Week Fourteen
Monday: I – Gn 28:10–22a; II – Hos 2:16, 17b–18, 21–22; Mt 9:18–26
Tuesday: I – Gn 32:22–33; II – Hos 8:4–7, 11–13; Mt 9:32–38
Wednesday: I – Gn 41:51–57; 42:5–7a, 17–24a; II – Hos 10:1–3, 7–8, 12; Mt 10:1–7
Thursday: I – Gn 44:18–21, 23b–29; 45:1–5; II – Hos 11:1, 3–4, 8c–9; Mt 10:7–15
Friday: I – Gn 46:1–7, 28–30; II – Hos 14:2–10; Mt 10:16–23
Saturday: I – Gn 49:29–33; 50:15–24; II – Is 6:1–8; Mt 10:24–33

Week Fifteen
Monday: I – Ex 1:8–14, 22; II – Is 1:10–17; Mt 10:34–11:1
Tuesday: I – Ex 2:1–15a; II – Is 7:1–9; Mt 11:20–24
Wednesday: I – Ex 3:1–6, 9–12; II – Is 10:5–7, 13–16; Mt 11:25–27
Thursday: I – Ex 3:13–20; II – Is 26:7–9, 12, 16–19; Mt 11:28–30
Friday: I – Ex 11:10–12, 14; II – Is 38:1–6, 21–22, 7–8; Mt 12:1–8
Saturday: I – Ex 12:37–42; II – Mi 2:1–5; Mt 12:14–21

Week Sixteen
Monday: I – Ex 14:5–18; II – Mi 6:1–4, 6–8; Mt 12:38–42
Tuesday: I – Ex 14:21–15:1; II – Mi 7:14–15, 18–20; Mt 12:46–50
Wednesday: I – Ex 16:1–5, 9–15; II – Jer 1:1, 4–10; Mt 13:1–9
Thursday: I – Ex 19:1–2, 9–11, 16–20b; II – Jer 2:1–3, 7–8, 12–13; Mt 13:10–17
Friday: I – Ex 20:1–17; II – Jer 3:14–17; Mt 13:18–23
Saturday: I – Ex 24:3–8; II – Jer 7:1–11; Mt 13:24–30

Week Seventeen
Monday: I – Ex 32:15–24, 30–34; II – Jer 13:1–11; Mt 13:31–35
Tuesday: I – Ex 33:7–11; 34:5b–9, 28; II – Jer 14:17–22; Mt 13:36–43
Wednesday: I – Ex 34:29–34; II – Jer 15:10, 16–21; Mt 13:44–46
Thursday: I – Ex 40:16–21, 34–38; II – Jer 18:1–6; Mt 13:47–53
Friday: I – Lv 23:1, 4–11, 15–16, 27, 34b–37; II – Jer 26:1–9; Mt 13:54–58
Saturday: I – Lv 25:1, 8–17; II – Jer 26:11–16, 24; Mt 14:1–12

Week Eighteen
Monday: I – Nm 11:4b–15; II – Jer 28:1–17; Mt 14:13–21 or Mt 14:22–36
Tuesday: I – Nm 12:1–13; II – Jer 30:1–2, 12–15, 18–22; Mt 14:22–36 or Mt 15:1–2, 10–14
Wednesday: I – Nm 13:1–2a, 25–14:1, 26–29, 34–35; II – Jer 31:1–7; Mt 15:21–28
Thursday: I – Nm 20:1–13; II – Jer 31:31–34; Mt 16:13–23
Friday: I – Dt 4:32–40; II – Na 2:1, 3; 3:1–3, 6–7; Mt 16:24–28
Saturday: I – Dt 6:4–13; II – Hb 1:12–2:4; Mt 17:14–20

Week Nineteen
Monday: I – Dt 10:12–22; II – Ez 1:2–5, 24–28c; Mt 17:22–27
Tuesday: I – Dt 31:1–8; II – Ez 2:8–3:4; Mt 18:1–5, 10, 12–14
Wednesday: I – Dt 34:1–12; II – Ez 9:1–7; 10:18–22; Mt 18:15–20
Thursday: I – Jos 3:7–10a, 11, 13–17; II – Ez 12:1–12; Mt 18:21–19:1
Friday: I – Jos 24:1–13; II – Ez 16:1–15, 60, 63; Mt 19:3–12
Saturday: I – Jos 24:14–29; II – Ez 18:1–10, 13b, 30–32; Mt 19:13–15

Week Twenty
Monday: I – Jgs 2:11–19; II – Ez 24:15–24; Mt 19:16–22
Tuesday: I – Jgs 6:11–24a; II – Ez 28:1–10; Mt 19:23–30
Wednesday: I – Jgs 9:6–15; II – Ez 34:1–11; Mt 20:1–16a
Thursday: I – Jgs 11:29–39a; II – Ez 36:23–28; Mt 22:1–14
Friday: I – Ru 1:1, 3–6, 14b–16, 22; II – Ez 37:1–14; Mt 22:34–40
Saturday: I – Ru 2:1–3, 8–11; 4:13–17; II – Ez 43:1–7a; Mt 23:1–12

Week Twenty-one
Monday: I – 1 Thes 1:2b–5, 8b–10; II – 2 Thes 1:1–5, 11b–12; Mt 23:13–22
Tuesday: I – 1 Thes 2:1–8; II – 2 Thes 2:1–3a, 13–17; Mt 23:23–26
Wednesday: I – 1 Thes 2:9–13; II – 2 Thes 3:6–10, 16–18; Mt 23:27–32
Thursday: I – 1 Thes 3:7–13; II – 1 Cor 1:1–9; Mt 24:42–51
Friday: I – 1 Thes 4:1–8; II – 1 Cor 1:17–25; Mt 25:1–13
Saturday: I – 1 Thes 4:9–12; II – 1 Cor 1:26–31; Mt 25:14–30

Week Twenty-two
Monday: I – 1 Thes 4:13–18; II – 1 Cor 2:1–5; Lk 4:16–30
Tuesday: I – 1 Thes 5:1–6, 9–11; II – 1 Cor 2:10b–16; Lk 4:31–37
Wednesday: I – Col 1:1–8; II – 1 Cor 3:1–9; Lk 4:38–44
Thursday: I – Col 1:9–14; II – 1 Cor 3:18–23; Lk 5:1–11
Friday: I – Col 1:15–20; II – 1 Cor 4:1–5; Lk 5:33–39
Saturday: I – Col 1:21–23; II – 1 Cor 4:9–15; Lk 6:1–5

Week Twenty-three
Monday: I – Col 1:24–2:3; II – 1 Cor 5:1–8; Lk 6:6–11
Tuesday: I – Col 2:6–15; II – 1 Cor 6:1–11; Lk 6:12–19
Wednesday: I – Col 3:1–11; II – 1 Cor 7:25–31; Lk 6:20–26
Thursday: I – Col 3:12–17; II – 1 Cor 8:1b–7, 11–13; Lk 6:27–38
Friday: I – 1 Tm 1:1–2, 12–14; II – 1 Cor 9:16–19, 22b–27; Lk 6:39–42
Saturday: I – 1 Tm 1:15–17; II – 1 Cor 10:14–22a; Lk 6:43–49

Week Twenty-four
Monday: I – 1 Tm 2:1–8; II – 1 Cor 11:17–26, 33; Lk 7:1–10
Tuesday: I – 1 Tm 3:1–13; II – 1 Cor 12:12–14, 27–31a; Lk 7:11–17
Wednesday: I – 1 Tm 3:14–16; II – 1 Cor 12:31–13:13; Lk 7:31–35
Thursday: I – 1 Tm 4:12–16; II – 1 Cor 15:1–11; Lk 7:36–50
Friday: I – 1 Tm 6:2c–12; II – 1 Cor 15:12–20; Lk 8:1–3
Saturday: I – 1 Tm 6:13–16; II – 1 Cor 15:36–37, 42–49; Lk 8:4–15

Week Twenty-five
Monday: I – Ezr 1:1–6; II – Prv 3:27–34; Lk 8:16–18
Tuesday: I – Ezr 6:7–8, 12b, 14–20; II – Prv 21:1–6, 10–13; Lk 8:19–21
Wednesday: I – Ezr 9:5–9; II – Prv 30:5–9; Lk 9:1–6
Thursday: I – Hg 1:1–8; II – Eccl 1:2–11; Lk 9:7–9
Friday: I – Hg 1:15b–2:9; II – Eccl 3:1–11; Lk 9:18–22
Saturday: I – Zec 2:5–9a, 14–15a; II – Eccl 11:9–12:8; Lk 9:43b–45

Week Twenty-six
Monday: I – Zec 8:1–8; II – Jb 1:6–22; Lk 9:46–50
Tuesday: I – Zec 8:20–23; II – Jb 3:1–3, 11–17, 20–23; Lk 9:51–56
Wednesday: I – Neh 2:1–8; II – Jb 9:1–12, 14–16; Lk 9:57–62
Thursday: I – Neh 8:1–4a, 5–6, 7b–12; II – Jb 19:12–27; Lk 10:1–12
Friday: I – Bar 1:15–22; II – Jb 38:1, 12–21; 40:3–5; Lk 10:13–16
Saturday: I – Bar 4:5–12, 27–29; II – Jb 42:1–3, 5–6, 12–17; Lk 10:17–24

Week Twenty-seven
Monday: I – Jon 1:1–2:1, 11; II – Gal 1:6–12; Lk 10:25–37
Tuesday: I – Jon 3:1–10; II – Gal 1:13–24; Lk 10:38–42
Wednesday: I – Jon 4:1–11; II – Gal 2:1–2, 7–14; Lk 11:1–4
Thursday: I – Mal 3:13–20a; II – Gal 3:1–5; Lk 11:5–13
Friday: I – Jl 1:13–15; 2:1–2; II – Gal 3:7–14; Lk 11:15–26
Saturday: I – Jl 4:12–21; II – Gal 3:22–29; Lk 11:27–28

Week Twenty-eight
Monday: I – Rom 1:1–7; II – Gal 4:22–24, 26–27; Lk 11:29–32
Tuesday: I – Rom 1:16–25; II – Gal 5:1–6; Lk 11:37–41
Wednesday: I – Rom 2:1–11; II – Gal 5:18–25; Lk 11:42–46
Thursday: I – Rom 3:21–29; II – Eph 1:3–10; Lk 11:47–54
Friday: I – Rom 4:1–8; II – Eph 1:11–14; Lk 12:1–7
Saturday: I – Rom 4:13, 16–18; II – Eph 1:15–23; Lk 12:8–12

Week Twenty-nine
Monday: I – Rom 4:20–25; II – Eph 2:1–10; Lk 12:13–21
Tuesday: I – Rom 5:12, 15b, 17–19, 20b–21; II – Eph 2:12–22; Lk 12:35, 38
Wednesday: I – Rom 6:12–18; II – Eph 3:2–12; Lk 12:39–48
Thursday: I – Rom 6:19–23; II – Eph 3:14–21; Lk 12:49–53
Friday: I – Rom 7:18–25a; II – Eph 4:1–6; Lk 12:54–59
Saturday: I – Rom 8:1–11; II – Eph 4:7–16; Lk 13:1–9

Week Thirty
Monday: I – Rom 8:12–17; II – Eph 4:32–5:8; Lk 13:10–17
Tuesday: I – Rom 8:18–25; II – Eph 5:21–33; Lk 13:18–21
Wednesday: I – Rom 8:26–30; II – Eph 6:1–9; Lk 13:22–30
Thursday: I – Rom 3:31b–39; II – Eph 6:10–20; Lk 13:31–35
Friday: I – Rom 9:1–5; II – Phil 1:1–11; Lk 14:1–6
Saturday: I – Rom 11:1–2a, 11–12, 25–29; II – Phil 1:18b–26; Lk 14:1, 7–11

Week Thirty-one
Monday: I – Rom 11:29–36; II – Phil 2:1–4; Lk 14:12–14
Tuesday: I – Rom 12:5–16a; II – Phil 2:5–11; Lk 14:15–24
Wednesday: I – Rom 13:8–10; II – Phil 2:12–18; Lk 14:25–33
Thursday: I – Rom 14:7–12; II – Phil 3:3–8a; Lk 15:1–10
Friday: I – Rom 15:14–21; II – Phil 3:17–4:1; Lk 16:1–8
Saturday: I – Rom 16:3–9, 16, 22–27; II – Phil 4:10–19; Lk 16:9–15

Week Thirty-two
Monday: I – Wis 1:1–7; II – Ti 1:1–9; Lk 17:1–6
Tuesday: I – Wis 2:23–3:9; II – Ti 2:1–8, 11–14; Lk 17:7–10
Wednesday: I – Wis 6:1–11; II – Ti 3:1–7; Lk 17:11–19

Thursday: I – Wis 7:22–8:1; II – Phlm 7–20; Lk 17:20–25
Friday: I – Wis 13:1–9; II – 2 Jn 4–9; Lk 17:26–37
Saturday: I – Wis 18:14–16; 19:6–9; II – 3 Jn 5–8; Lk 18:1–8

Week Thirty-three
Monday: I – 1 Mc 1:10–15, 41–43, 54, 57, 62, 64; II – Rev 1:1–4; 2:1–5a; Lk 18:35–43
Tuesday: I – 2 Mc 6:18–31; II – Rev 3:1–6, 14–22; Lk 19:1–10
Wednesday: I – 2 Mc 7:1, 20–31; II – Rev 4:1–11; Lk 19:11–28
Thursday: I – 1 Mc 2:15–29; II – Rev 5:1–10; Lk 19:41–44
Friday: I – 1 Mc 4:36–37, 52–59; II – Rev 10:8–11; Lk 19:45–48
Saturday: I – 1 Mc 6:1–13; II – Rev 11:4–12; Lk 20:27–40

Week Thirty-four
Monday: I – Dn 1:1–6, 8–20; II – Rev 14:1–3, 4b–5; Lk 21:1–4
Tuesday: I – Dn 2:31–45; II – Rev 14:14–19; Lk 21:5–11
Wednesday: I – Dn 5:1–6, 13–14, 16–17, 23–28; II – Rev 15:1–4; Lk 21:12–19
Thursday: I – Dn 6:11–28; II – Rev 18:1–2, 21–23; 19:1–3, 9a; Lk 21:20–28
Friday: I – Dn 7:2–14; II – Rev 20:1–4; 20:11–21:2; Lk 21:29–33
Saturday: I – Dn 7:15–27; II – Rev 22:1–7; Lk 21:34–36

INDEX TO READING GUIDE

INDEX TO READING GUIDE

Aaron, 119, 126, 129
Abdon, 161–62
Abigail, 177
Abimelech, 160–61
Abraham
  biblical history and, 34–36
  in Genesis, 107, 110–12
  in Pauline Epistles, 445, 469, 470
Absalom, 181–82, 185
Acts of the Apostles, 423–38
  guide to reading specific passages, 425–37
  biblical history of, 30, 52
  as entertainment, 425
  main themes and theology of, 437–38
  missions
    to Gentiles, 430–32
    in Jerusalem, 426–29
    in Judah and Samaria, 429–31
    preparation for, 426–27
    to rest of empire, 432–37
  organization and structure, 425–26
  Paul (*See* Paul)
  persecution in
    arrest and imprisonment of Paul in Jerusalem, 436
    martyrdom of James and imprisonment of Peter, 431
    trial and death of Stephen, 428–29
    trial of apostles John and Peter, 427
  Peter (*See* Peter)
  as salvation history, 424–25
actualization, 22
Adam, Jesus as second, 445–46
Adapa, 104–5
Adonijah, 184–85
aggiornamento, 19
agriculture vs. pastoralism in ancient Israel, 42, 43, 106
Ahab, 190–91
Ahasuerus, king of Persia, 223
Ahaz, 195–96
Ahmose, Pharaoh, 37
Akenaten, Pharaoh, 38, 118
Albert the Great, 61
Albright, William F., 31, 35, 41
Alcuin, 58
Alexander the Great, 11, 227, 272
Alexandria (Egypt)
  biblical interpretation, Alexandrian school of, 17, 56–57
  Jewish community, origins of Wisdom in, 272
  scriptural tradition based in, 272
allegory. *See also* symbolism
  Bible, allegorical approach to, 17–18, 54–58, 60, 62
  of the shepherds, in Zechariah, 367–68
  Song of Songs, allegorical interpretation of, 268–69, 271
  Alt, Albrecht, 40
alternative versions of biblical text. *See* transmission history
Amalekites, 175
Amarna Letters, 41
Amasa, 182
Ambrose of Milan, 57, 59
Amenhotep III, Pharaoh, 38, 118
Amnon, 181
Amos, 351–55
  guide to reading specific passages, 352–55
  blunt style of, 351–52
  covenant and, 353
  dating of, 344
  the Day of the Lord in, 349, 354
  foreign nations, oracles against, 352
  main themes and theology of, 344, 345
  modern relevance of, 355
  radical monotheism and concern with idol worship, 353–54
Amos the prophet, career of, 351
anagogical approach to Bible, 18, 62
analytic philosophical approach to reading Bible, 8
Andrew of St. Victor, 60, 61
angels and demons. *See also* Satan
  in Daniel, 338, 339, 341
  in Ezekiel, 326
  Gabriel, 341

angels and demons (*cont.*)
  Jesus as higher than angels, in Hebrews, 497–98
  in Luke, 401, 403, 411
  Michael, 341
  Raphael, 216, 217
  in Tobit, 216, 217
Anselm, 59
anthropological and ethnological study of biblical texts, 21, 94
Antiochene school of biblical interpretation, 17, 56–57, 60
Antiochus IV Epiphanes, 52, 226–29, 232–33, 272, 336, 339
ʾApiru or Habiru, 38
Apocalypse. *See* Revelation
apocalypticism. *See* eschatology
apocrypha
  Catholic, 5, 204, 226, 315, 318, 362, 519
  Protestant (*See* deuterocanonical texts)
Apollinaris of Laodicea, 57
Apollos, 424, 434, 452, 463
apologetic literature, 1 Peter as, 506–7
apostles. *See* Acts of the Apostles, discipleship, and specific apostles, e.g. Peter
Arad Letters, 44
Aram and Arameans, 188, 189, 192–96
archaeology
  biblical interpretation and, 21
  history and significance of, 31–33
  of Israelite settlement in Canaan, 42–43
  of New Testament/Roman period, 53
  of Pentateuch, 94
  of Persian period, 51
  of tenth century (monarchy period), 46–47
Aristotle, 57, 60, 63
ark and tent of covenant. *See also* covenant between God and Israel
  as battle palladium in 1Samuel, 171–72
  in Exodus, 123
  moved to Jerusalem by David in the books of Samuel, 179
arrogance denounced in James, 505
Artaxerxes I, king of Persia, 51
Ashtaroth, 157–58
Asmodeus, 217
Assurbanipal, 296
Assyria
  annals of kings of, 44
  conquest of kingdom of Israel by, 196
  invasion of kingdom of Judah by, 196
  prophets' emergence and, 281, 296, 320–21
  sudden collapse of, 196
  vassal treaties, 124
Athaliah, 179, 193–94
atonement. *See* sin and atonement
Atonement, Day of, 131
Atrahasis, 105
Augustine of Hippo, 17, 57–58, 59, 60
authority of Bible, 27–28

B

Baal, 105, 157–58, 190, 194, 347–48
Babel, tower of, 107
Babylonian creation myths borrowed in Genesis, 104–6
Babylonian documentary evidence of Israelite monarchy, 44
Babylonian exile and return
  Baruch and, 315–16, 319
  biblical history of, 11, 46, 50, 51
  Daniel and, 336
  Davidic dynasty ended by, 180
  Ezekiel and, 320–21
  Isaiah's relationship to, 280
  Israel, fall of kingdom of, 196
  Jeremiah's relationship to, 296–99
  Jerusalem
    rebuilding and repopulation of, 212, 214
    siege and destruction of, 46, 47, 50, 180, 197
  Joshua's foreshadowing of, 150, 155
  Judah, fall of kingdom of, 197–98, 204
  Lamentations connection to, 310
  restoration of Judah in Ezra and Nehemiah, 207–9
  Temple
    destruction of, 187, 197, 310–11
    rebuilding of, 207–9, 364–65
Babylon's fall in Revelation, 523–24
Balaam, 140–41, 375
baptism. *See also* John the Baptist
  the Bible in the Lectionary and, 76, 78, 81–82, 84
  in Colossians, 479
  in 1 Corinthians, 451, 452, 453, 454, 458
  dialogue between Jesus and Nicodemus, in John, 417
  disciples' mission to preach, in Luke, 411
  ecumenical movement and, 206
  in Ephesians, 474
  in Galatians, 466, 467, 470
  as gift of Spirit vs. John the Baptist's baptism with water, in Luke, 403, 429, 434
  Jesus' baptism
    in John, 416
    in Luke, 403, 405
    Mark opening with, 371, 388
    in Matthew, 376
  Jewish baptismal sects, continuation of, 435
  in 1 Peter, 506, 509
  in Philemon, 494
  in Romans, 446
Barak, 159
Barnabas, 431–32, 487
Bartimaeus, 393–94
Baruch, 315–19
Basil, 56
Bathsheba, 181, 185
Bede, 58
Bel and the dragon, 343
Benedict XV, Pope, 18
Benedictines, 58, 63

Benedictus, 402
Bible. *See also* Epistles; Gospels; Judaism and Jewish Bible; New Testament; Old Testament
  authority of, 27–28
  canon (*See* canon)
  chapters and verses, division of text into, 6, 61
  different ways of approaching, 8
  earliest manuscripts of, 6
  historical background to (*See* biblical history)
  historical value and accuracy of, 5–6
  importance and significance of, 3
  languages used in, 3
  nature of, 25–27
  prayer and study as context for, 7–9
  and tradition, 24–25
  as tradition, 23–24
  unity and diversity of, 3, 5
biblical criticism. *See also* form criticism; literary criticism; source criticism; individual books of Bible
  canonical criticism, 22, 94
  early examples of, 65–66
  historical criticism, 20–21, 65
  historical-critical method, 20, 21, 65
  of Pentateuch, 90–94
  reader-response criticism of Pentateuch, 94
  redaction criticism, 21, 94
  rhetorical criticism, 21, 94
  Second Vatican Council's acceptance of, 19
  semiotic analysis, 21
  Sixtus of Siena foreshadowing, 64
  structural analysis, 21, 94
  textual criticism, 6, 20
  types of, 6, 20–21
biblical history, 4, 10–12. *See also* under individual books of Bible
  archaeology and, 31–33 (*See also* archaeology)
  Babylonian exile and return, 11
  Bronze Age, 33–38, 42
  ethnicity of early Israelites, problem of, 32
  exodus story, 10–11, 36–38, 117–18
  Hasmoneans and Herodians, 12, 52–53
  Hellenic period, 11–12, 52, 227
  Iron I Age, 38–43
  Iron II Age, 43–50
  judges, period of, 11, 38–43
  Luke's use of, 397
  monarchy period of Israelite history, 11, 43–50
  patriarchal period, 10, 34–36
  of Pentateuch, 94–96, 97
  Persian period, 50–52, 208, 223, 316
  Peter Comestor's Historia scholastica, 60–61
  Roman conquest, 12, 52–53
  settlement of Israel, 10–11, 38–43
  value and accuracy of, 5–6, 30–31
biblical research institutions and journals, 22–23, 65, 67
bishops in the early church, 56, 476, 488–89, 492
Boaz, 164, 166, 167–69
Body of Christ, Church described as, 472–73
Bonaventure, 61
Book of Consolation in Jeremiah, 305
Bossuet, Jacques-Benigne, 65
Bright, John, 41
Bronze Age in biblical history, 33–38, 42
Brown, Raymond E., 65, 67

C

Cain and Abel, 106
Cajetan, Cardinal (Thomas de Vio), 64
Calvin, Jean, 64
Cana, miracle at, 416–17
Canaan and Canaanites
  biblical history and, 39–43
  Joshua and, 151–52, 154–55
  Ruth reflecting life in, 166
  Samuel and, 171–72
  Song of Songs, cultic interpretation of, 269–70
  at time of Pentateuch, 97
  Wisdom, personification of, 260–61
  wisdom tradition, 236
cannibalism, 312
canon. *See also* apocrypha
  Baruch, 315, 319
  books accepted by Catholics and Orthodox but not Jews or Protestants (*See* deuterocanonical texts)
  Daniel, 336
  Esther, 222
  formation of, 4–5, 26, 54, 55, 272, 277–79
  of Jewish Bible, 4, 5, 276–77
  Maccabees, 230
  of Orthodox Churches, 4, 5, 226, 315
  of Protestant Churches, 5, 26, 272, 336
  Wisdom and Sirach, 272, 276–77, 279
canonical criticism, 22, 94
Canticles in Luke, 402, 412
Cappadocian Fathers, 56
captivity letters of Paul, 475
Cassiodorus, 57
Catena Aurea (Thomas Aquinas), 62
Catholic Epistles, 510. *See also* 1 Peter; 2 Peter; James; 1 John; 2 John; 3 John; Jude
Catholic life and the Bible, 16–29
  Biblical period to Enlightenment, 17–18
  nineteenth and early twentieth centuries, 18
  twentieth century, pre- and post-Vatican II practice compared, 16–17
  Second Vatican Council, pronouncements of, 18–19
  in modern era, 9, 19–20
  abiding principles of, 18
  Amos, modern relevance of, 355
  authority of Bible, 27–28
  Baruch in, 319
  creation story, Church use of, 107–8
  Ecclesiastes, modern use of, 266–67
  education, 28
  Esther, Christian reading of, 225
  Haggai, modern relevance of, 365
  Hosea, modern relevance of, 348–49

Catholic life and the Bible (*cont.*)
interpretive history and methods (*See* interpretation of the Bible)
Jonah, modern relevance of, 358
Judith as model for image of women in Church, 221
Lamentations in, 314
liturgy (*See* Lectionary; liturgy)
1 and 2 Maccabees and, 230, 233–34
nature of Bible, 25–27
Petrine foundation in Matthew, 382
piety, 28
priesthood, Catholic, and 1 Chronicles, 202–3
Proverbs, modern use of, 261
Psalms, modern use of, 251–54
research institutions and journals, 22–23, 65, 67
theology, 17, 28
tradition
Bible and, 24–25
Bible as, 23–24
Wisdom and Sirach, modern use of, 279
chapters and verses
division of biblical text into, 6, 61
Esther, arrangement of, 222
Kings, arrangement of, 186
chariot in Ezekiel, and chariot mysticism, 334
chiasm, 182, 219, 329
child-minder analogy in Galatians, 469–70
Chloe, 452
Christology
in Colossians, 479, 480
in 1 Corinthians, 457
of Hebrews, 496–501
in Luke, 402
in Mark, 387
in Matthew, 378–79
in Philippians, 476
Chronicler's History, 199. *See also* 1 Chronicles; 2 Chronicles; Ezra; Nehemiah
1 Chronicles, 199–203
guide to reading specific passages, 200–201
biblical history of, 11, 46
Catholic concept of priesthood and, 202–3
division of Chronicles into two books, 199
organization and structure of, 199
placement in relationship to other books of Bible, 199–200
sources used in, 46
theology of, 199, 201–2
2 Chronicles, 203–7
guide to reading specific passages, 203–4
biblical history of, 11, 46
division of Chronicles into two books, 199
placement in relationship to other books of Bible, 199–200
Samaritans and problem of religious diversity, 205–7
sources used in, 46
theological purpose of, 204–5
Church. *See* Catholic life and the Bible; early church
Church councils. *See* councils of the Church
Church Fathers (patristics), 17, 18, 59, 62
Church year reflected in Lectionary, 78–79
circular letters
Ephesians sometimes regarded as, 472
Galatians as, 464
cities and towns
Jericho, battle of, 151, 152
Jerusalem (*See* Jerusalem)
Levites, towns set aside for, 154
refuge, cities of, 153
Clarius, Isidorus, 64
clean and unclean. *See* purity laws
Clement of Alexandria, 17, 279
clergy. *See* ministry
Collings, Adela Yarbro, 67
Collins, J., 65
Colossians, 471, 478–80
combat myth
in Ezekiel, 325, 331
in First Isaiah, 284–85
commentaries on the Bible, 62
Communion. *See* Eucharist
communion of saints, 500
community, Christian, stress on
in Acts, 425, 427, 437
in 1 Corinthians, 451, 452–53
in Ephesians, 472–74
in Galatians, 470–71
in James, 502–3
in Johannine epistles, 513–18
in John, 421
in Mark, 395
in Matthew, 382–83
Paul's deep attachment to companions, 486–87, 489
in 1 Peter, 508, 509–10
in Philippians, 475, 476–77
in Romans, 449
in 1 Timothy, 488–89
concordances, 61
confessions of faith
in 2 Chronicles, 204
in Deuteronomy, 146
in Ezra and Nehemiah, 212, 214
laments or confessions in Jeremiah, 304–5, 307
confidence and thanksgiving, psalms of, 245, 246–48, 252
conscience in 1 Corinthians, 454–55
Constantinople, ecumenical council of (381 A.D.), 57
1 Corinthians, 450–58
guide to reading specific passages, 451, 452–58
community divisions and squabbles in, 451, 452–53
dating of, 450
dress and decorum in, 456
liturgical issues in, 455–57
organization and structure, 451–52
Paul's answers to questions asked by Corinthians, 453–55
resurrection of the dead in, 457

2 Corinthians, 450, 458–64
guide to reading specific passages in, 459–64
crisis in relationship between Paul and Corinthians, 460–64
Jerusalem Church, collections for, 462–63
organization and structure, 459, 460
Cornelius, conversion of, 431
councils of the Church
Constantinople, ecumenical council of (381 A.D.), 57
Florence, 230
Trent (*See* Trent, Council of)
Vatican II (*See* Second Vatican Council)
Counter-Reformation, 18, 63–64
covenant between God and Israel. *See also* ark and tent of covenant; land of Israel, promise of
in Amos, 353
in 2 Corinthians, 461
with David in Samuel, 180
in Deuteronomy, 143–44, 146, 147
in Exodus, 122–24
in Galatians, 469–70
in Hebrews, 497, 499
in Hosea, 346
in Jeremiah, 306–7
in Leviticus, 129, 130
Nehemiah, agreement to observe Torah in, 214
in 1 Peter, 507
in Psalms, 252, 253–54
creation
in Ezekiel, 105, 325
in Genesis, 104, 105, 107–8
Psalms, praised in, 250
Revelation, new creation revealed in, 524
Crossan, John Dominic, 67
crucifixion, death, and resurrection of Jesus
in Hebrews, 499, 500, 501
in John, 421–22, 423
in Luke, 410–12
in Mark, 388–89, 394–96
in Matthew, 384–86
theology of cross
in 1 Corinthians, 457
in Philippians, 476
cultic or liturgical interpretation of Song of Songs, 268, 269–70
cultural sensitivities in Biblical translations, 7
Cyprian of Carthage, 57
Cyrus Cylinder, 51
Cyrus the Persian, 51, 280, 290, 315

D

D. *See* Deuteronomic History
Damascus, Pope, 57
Daniel, 336–43
guide to reading specific passages, 336–43
"additions" to, 336, 342–43
affirmation of gentile environment in, 336–37, 338
angels and demons in, 338, 339, 341
Aramaic used in, 3
Baruch's relationship to, 315, 316
biblical history of, 11–12, 52
canonicity of, 336
dating of, 336
eschatological genre in, 338–40
on importance of fidelity to Jewish faith, 337–38
organization and structure of, 336
prophecy in, 339–40, 341
symbolism as used in, 338–41
Darius the Mede, 51, 336, 337
dating, 4, 23–24. *See also* individual books of the Bible
of exodus from Egypt, 118
of minor prophets, 344
of patriarchal period, 35
of Pentateuch, 96
Song of Deborah as possibly oldest text in Bible, 159
of Synoptic Gospels, 371–72
David
administration of, 180, 182
ark moved to Jerusalem by, 179
Bathsheba and, 181, 185
biblical history of, 11, 45, 46
in 1 Chronicles, 200–201
death of, 182–85
dynasty of, 179–80
family of, 178–82
as fugitive, 176–77
Goliath and, 175–76
Jonathan and, 174–78, 181, 182
kingship of, 178–82, 200–201
Moabites, connection to, 165
in Samuel, 175–83
Saul and, 175–77
Solomon's accession to kingship and, 184–85
Temple, desire to build, 179, 186, 201
Davidic kingship, promised return of. *See* Messianism in Old Testament
Day of Atonement, 131
the Day of the Lord, 349–50, 354, 363, 370
deacons in the early church, 291, 428, 449, 461, 476, 488–89
Dead Sea Scrolls (Qumran community)
Davidic Messiah-figure in, 160
early biblical manuscripts provided by, 6
Essenes, identified with, 53
interpretation of the Bible, influence on, 21
Isaiah's influence on, 294
Jeremiah, transmission history of, 308
key to scriptures for, 17
1 Maccabees not part of, 230
religious diversity indicated by, 53
Sirach scroll found among, 279
written materials, evidence drawn from, 31
death
of David, 182–85
farewell/deathbed speeches in Bible, 143, 154, 182–83, 185, 228, 491
of Jesus (*See* crucifixion, death, and resurrection of Jesus)

death (*cont.*)
resurrection from (*See* resurrection of the dead)
of Stephen protomartyr, 428–29
Deborah, 159
Dei verbum (1965), 18–19, 24–28, 67, 84. *See also* Second Vatican Council
Delilah, 162–63
Demetrius, 518
demons. *See* angels and demons; Satan
desert of Sinai, Israelites wandering in
in Genesis, 121–22
in Numbers, 135–36
desert, temptation of Jesus in, 376, 388, 389, 404
deterministic view of history, 339
deuterocanonical texts, 5, 86. *See also* 1 and 2 Maccabees; Baruch; Judith; Sirach; Tobit; Wisdom
Deutero-Isaiah. *See under* Isaiah
Deuteronomistic History (D), 39. *See also* Joshua; Judges; Kings; 1 and 2 Samuel
Chronicles illustrating sources not used by, 46
God as principal character of, 170
Jeremiah influenced by, 301, 304
kingdoms of Judah and Israel, use of chronicles of, 45–46
not a history in modern sense, 184
Pentateuch and, 91, 93
relationship of Deuteronomy to, 148
Deuteronomy, 141–48
Baruch alluding to, 316
biblical history of, 10–11
dating and historical development of, 142, 144–45
Ezekiel and, 333
Lamentations' relationship to, 313
main themes and theology of, 145–47
mixed law and narrative genre, 86
organization and structure of, 142–44
relationship to other books of Bible, 144–45, 145, 147, 148
theology of, 142
unique style of, 144
Deutero-Pauline letters, 439, 471. *See also* Colossians; Ephesians; 2 Thessalonians; 1 Timothy; 2 Timothy; Titus
Deutero-Zechariah, 365
Diaspora Judaism
Esther reflecting, 223–25
2 Maccabees letters to Jews in Egypt, 231
Septuagint created for, 221, 272
special difficulties faced by, 225
Tobit reflecting, 216, 218
Wisdom possibly originating in Alexandrine Jewish community, 272
diatribe, 441–42, 503
Didache, 4
Dio Cassius, 52
Diodore of Tarsus, 56
Diodorus Siculus, 50, 52
Diotrephes, 518
discipleship. *See also* Acts of the Apostles
in John, 416
in Luke, 404–5, 407–8, 411, 412
in Mark, 387–88, 390, 392, 393–94, 395–96
Mary as first disciple, 400–401
in Matthew, 378–79, 380, 381, 385
distribution of lands among Israelites, in Joshua, 152–53
divine election. *See* covenant between God and Israel
Divino Afflante Spiritus (1943), 18, 19, 66
divorce, Malachi on, 369–70
documentary evidence, 31. *See also* Dead Sea Scrolls
Amarna Letters, 41
earliest surviving biblical manuscripts, 6
Harris Papyrus I, 38
interpretation of Bible via, 21
Mari and Nuzi texts, 35
for monarchy period of Israelite history, 43–44
for Persian period, 51
Ugaritic texts, 21
Dominicans, 61, 63
Donahue, J., 65
Donatism, 57
doublets and repetition, 333–34
dramatic interpretation of Song of Songs, 270, 271
dress and decorum in 1 Corinthians, 456
dualism
in Hebrews, 497
in 1 John, 513
in John (Gospel of), 414
in 1 Thessalonians, 481
in Wisdom, 274

E

E. *See* Elohist source
early church
canon, formation of, 4–5
interpretation and study of Bible in, 17, 54–58
Jewish heritage in Matthew, 373–74
ministry in (*See* ministry)
Old Testament as Bible of, 17
persecution of (*See* persecution of early church)
tradition as process in, 23–24
Ecclesiastes, 262–67
main themes and theology of, 263–66
modern use of, 266–67
organization and structure of, 263
Solomon's association with, 262–63
Ecclesiasticus (Sirach), 276–79, 315
École Biblique, 22–23, 65
ecumenical movement
Ezra's and Nehemiah's exclusivism and modern call to inclusion, 209–11, 214–15
Lectionary and, 83
place of Bible in, 16–17
Second Vatican Council and, 206–7
universalism of Zechariah, 368
Edom and Edomites, 113, 157, 188, 193, 195, 196, 356

education
  Catholic use of Bible in, 28
  Lectionary used in, 83–84
  Matthew, catechetical or teaching function of, 373
  medieval monasticism and, 58
  Proverbs, teacher-student aspect of, 255, 256–57
  Titus, pastoral teaching addressed in, 492
effects, history of, 22
Egypt. *See also* exodus from Egypt, and individual pharaohs
  Diaspora Jews of, 231, 272
  documentary evidence of Israelite monarchy, 44
  exodus story and, 10–11, 36–38, 117–18
  involvement in separate kingdoms of Judah and Israel, 188, 189, 197
  Ptolemaic dynasty, 11, 53, 227, 272
  at time of Pentateuch, 97
  wisdom tradition, 236
  withdrawal from Palestine in early Iron I Age, 38–39
Ehud, 158–59
election, divine. *See* covenant between God and Israel
Elephantine Papyri, 51
Eli, judgment against house of, 170–71, 172
Elijah
  Amos and, 352
  in 1 Chronicles, 200
  Deuteronomy and, 145, 146
  in James, 501, 505
  Jonah and, 358
  in Kings, 190–92
  in Luke, 404, 405, 406, 411
  in Mark, 389
  in Matthew, 376
Elisha, 145, 146, 191–94, 404, 405
Elohist source (E), 91, 92–93
  in Genesis, 109
  in Numbers, 137, 141
Elon, 161–62
emptiness as motif of Ruth, 167
Enlightenment, 18, 65
Enuma Elish, 104, 105
Epaphras, 478, 479
Epaphroditus, 477
Ephesians, 471–75
Epicureans, 512
Epistles. *See also* Pauline Epistles, and individual letters
  biblical history of, 52
  Catholic Epistles, 510 (*See also* 1 Peter; 2 Peter; James; 1 John; 2 John; 3 John; Jude)
  circulars (*See* circular letters)
  Deutero-Pauline letters, 439, 471 (*See also* Colossians; Ephesians; 2 Thessalonians; 1 Timothy; 2 Timothy; Titus)
  literary style of, 440
  Pastoral Letters (1 and 2 Timothy; Titus), 486–93
  Pauline (*See* Pauline Epistles)
  Revelation's use of epistolary mode, 522
Erasmus, Desiderius, 18, 63–64
Esau, 113
eschatology
  in Daniel, 338, 339–40
  the Day of the Lord, 349–50, 354, 363, 370
  history as viewed by, 339, 341–42
  in Luke, 409
  in Mark, 395
  in Matthew, 376, 384, 385
  of 2 Peter, 510, 512–13
  Revelation as, 521 (*See also* Revelation)
  in 1 and 2 Thessalonians, 481, 483–86
  of Wisdom, 273
  in Zechariah, 368
Essenes, 12, 53, 205–6, 230, 27–29
Esther, 222–26
Etana, 104
ethics, Christian
  in Colossians, 480
  in 1 Corinthians, 453–55, 456
  in Ephesians, 473–74
  Galatians, exhortations for Christian living in, 470–71
  James as moral exhortation, 501, 503–6
  Jude on God's grace and, 520
  1 Peter on relationship of Christians to world, 508–9
  slavery in Philemon, 493–95
  in 1 Thessalonians, 483–84
  in 2 Thessalonians, 486
ethnic exclusivism in Ezra and Nehemiah and modern call to inclusivism, 209–11, 214–15
ethnicity of early Israelites, problem of, 32
Eucharist. *See also* Last Supper
  in Acts, 437
  the Bible in Catholic life and, 28
  the Bible in the Lectionary and, 76, 78
  in 1 Corinthians, 307, 451, 452, 456, 458
  ecumenical movement and, 206
  Exodus passages associated with, in early church, 120
  in John, 418–19
  in Jude, 520
  in Luke, 307
  in Mark, 393
  role of sacrifice in Leviticus and, 125
Eusebius of Caesarea, 56
Eustathius of Antioch, 56
evil, problem of (theodicy), in Job, 239–40
exclusivism in Ezra and Nehemiah and modern call to inclusivism, 209–11, 214–15
exegesis. *See* interpretation of the Bible
exile, Israelite. *See* Babylonian exile and return; Diaspora Judaism
Exodus, 115–24
  guide to reading specific passages, 117–23
  Amos' perspective on, 353
  biblical history of, 10–11, 36–38, 117–18
  Deuteronomy's update of covenant law of, 147
  Ezekiel drawing on tradition of, 324

Exodus (*cont.*)
  Jeremiah drawing on tradition of, 300–301
  mixed law and narrative genre, 86
  organization and structure of, 115–17
  Second Isaiah, "new exodus" announced in, 289–90
exodus from Egypt (as event)
  biblical history and, 10–11, 36–38
  dating of, 118
  Egyptian setting of, 10–11, 36–38, 117–18
  narrative of, 120–22
  Wisdom on special providence of God during, 275
experience and tradition, relationship in Job between, 241–42
Ezekiel, 320–35
  guide to reading specific passages, 326–32
  biblical history, 320–21
  biography of prophet in, 322–23
  creation narrative in, 105
  dating of, 321–22
  in Jewish and Christian tradition, 334
  literary structure of, 325–28
  theology of, 332–33
  traditions used in, 105, 324–25
  transmission history of, 334–35
Ezra, 207–11
  guide to reading specific passages, 208–10
  Aramaic used in, 3, 208
  biblical history of, 11, 50, 51–52
  division of Ezra and Nehemiah into two books, 199, 207, 211
  exclusivism in, 209–11
  mixed marriages in, 209
  relationship to Nehemiah, 211
  restoration of Judah on return from exile, 207–9
  theology of, 210

F

faith, Christian concept of
  Abraham as model of faith in Romans, 445
  in Galatians, 468–70
  in Hebrews, 498–99, 500
  in James, 502, 503
  in John, 414, 415, 418–19
  justification in Romans, 443–44, 445
  in Luke, 408
  in Matthew, 381
  1 Peter on gift and call of God, 507
false gods. *See* idols, Israelite worship of
false teachings, warnings against
  in Colossians, 480
  in 2 Peter, 511–12
  in 1 Timothy, 487–88
  in 2 Timothy, 490
  in Titus, 492
farewell/deathbed speeches in Bible, 143, 154, 182–83, 185, 228, 491
Fathers of the Church (patristics), 17, 18, 59, 62
Felix, Roman Procurator, 52, 436
fertility ritual, interpretation of Song of Songs as, 269–70
Festus, Roman Procurator, 52, 436
First Isaiah. *See under* Isaiah
First Zechariah, 365
Fitzmeyer, J., 65
Flavius Josephus, 50, 52, 60, 224
flood story in Genesis, 106–7
Florence, Council of, 230
foreign nations, oracles concerning, 305
  minor prophets generally, 344
  Amos, 35
  Ezekiel, 330
  Jeremiah, 30
  Joel, 350–51
  Jonah, 357–58
  Obadiah, 356
  Zechariah, 368
  Zephaniah, 363
forgiveness. *See* sin and atonement
form criticism, 21
  of Genesis, 102
  of Pentateuch, 91–92, 93–94
former prophets. *See* Joshua; Judges; Kings; Samuel
Francis of Assisi, 61
Franciscans, 61, 63

G

Gabriel (archangel), 341
Gaius, 517–18
Galatians, 464–71
  guide to reading specific passages, 466–71
  defense of Pauline ministry and authority in, 467–68
  exhortations for Christian living in, 470–71
  Gentile and Jewish Christianity in, 465–68
  James, voice resembling, 502
  law, requirement to observe, 467–70
  organization and structure of, 466
  theology of, 468–70
Gallia of Achaia, proconsul, 52
Gallus, Thomas, 61
gender issues. *See also* women
  feminist biblical interpretation, 21
  inclusive language, 7, 72–74
  Lectionary and, 84
  rise in number of women biblical scholars, 67
genealogies
  in 1 Chronicles, 200
  in Genesis, 101–2, 106, 107, 108
  in Luke, 403–4
  in Matthew, 375
  in Ruth, 169
Genesis, 100–115
  guide to reading specific passages, 104–15
  biblical criticism of, 102–4
  biblical history of, 34–35, 109–10
  creation narrative in, 104, 105, 107–8
  Elohist source, 109

genealogical or *Toledoth* name lists, division of text by, 101–2, 106, 107, 108
medieval interest in, 59
as narrative genre, 86
Near Eastern mythic traditions reflected in, 102, 104–5, 106
organization and structure, 100–102,
patriarchal ancestor narratives of, 108–15
Priestly source, 102, 103–4
theology of, 102–4
Yahwist source, 102, 103
Gentile and Jewish Christianity
in Acts, 428, 430–32, 437
in Colossians, 480
in Galatians, 465–66, 467–68
in Luke, 398–99, 412
in Mark, 392, 396
in Matthew, 380
1 Peter, audience of, 506, 507
in Romans, 444–45, 448, 449
Gezer Calendar, 44
Gideon, 159–60
Gihon, spring of, 44, 185
Gilbert the Universal, 59
Gilgamesh, 105, 106
glossa, 59, 61, 62
gnosis or knowledge
in Corinthians, 454–55, 463, 464
in 1 Timothy, 487–88
God
appearances to Jacob, 113–14
conditional nature of promises to Israel, 147
consistency in dealings with Israel, 147
fear of, in Proverbs, 258–59
jealousy of, 329, 330, 361, 504
Jesus as
in Hebrews, 497–98
in John, 414–15, 422–23
as mystery in Job, 242
names for, 7, 91, 119
1 Peter on gift and call of, 507
presence in Esther, 224
presence in Ruth, 167
as principal character of 1 and 2 Samuel, 170
in Psalms, 249–50
Revelation's vision of God and the Lamb in heaven, 522–23
theophany
in Exodus, 119
in Habakkuk, 362
in Luke, 406
in Micah, 359
Goliath, 175–76
Gomer, 346
Good Samaritan, 399, 400, 407
the good shepherd. *See* sheep and shepherds
Gospels. *See also* John (Gospel of); Luke; Mark; Matthew
biblical history of, 52
Pauline Epistles, "Gospel" message of, 440
1 Peter on Gospel life to which Christians are called, 507–8
relative dating and order of, 371–72
source criticism of, 372
Synoptic Gospels, 371–72, 413
grace
Jude on, 520
1 Peter on gift and call of God, 507
Grant, R. M., 55
gratitude, confidence, and thanksgiving, psalms of, 245, 246–48, 252
Greek additions to Esther, 222–23
Greek culture
biblical history and, 11–12, 52, 227
interpretive tradition, 54
Maccabees' response to Hellenization, 227, 232–33, 272
Sirach as response to Hellenization, 276
theology, Hellenization of, 276
Wisdom influenced by, 272, 276
wisdom literature and, 272
Greek edition of Bible. *See* Septuagint
Gregory of Nyssa, 56
Gregory the Great, Pope, 58, 59
Gunkel, Hermann, 92

H

Habakkuk, 344, 362–43
Habiru or *ʿApiru,* 38
Haggai, 344, 345, 364–65
Haimo, 58
Haman the Agagite, 223
Hanukkah, 229
Harnack, Adolf von, 56
Harrington, D., 65
Harris Papyrus I, 38
Hasidim, 205, 230
Hasmoneans, 12, 52, 227, 230. *See also* entries in Maccabees
Hazael, 193
Hebrew Bible. *See* Judaism and Jewish Bible; Old Testament
Hebrews, 496–501
argumentative structure of, 496
audience of, 497
Christology of, 496–501
high priest, Jesus as, 498–99, 501
liturgy influenced by, 496
prologue, 497
as sermon, 496, 501
symbolism of, 497
Hellenic period and Hellenization. *See* Greek culture
Henri de Lubac, 63
hermeneutics, 22, 62, 63
Herodian dynasty
in Acts, 431, 436
biblical history and, 12, 52–53
Hasmoneans succeeded by, 12, 230

Herodian dynasty (*cont.*)
in John, 413
in Luke, 398, 403, 406, 410
in Mark, 391, 392, 394
in Matthew, 375, 381, 383
political and religious diversity, 206
Herodotus, 30, 50
Hezekiah, 33, 44, 46, 49, 50, 196, 204
high priest
Jesus as, in Hebrews, 498–99, 501
in Zechariah, 36
Hilary of Poitiers, 59
historical criticism, 20–21, 65
historical-critical method, 20, 21, 65
history
Acts of the Apostles as salvation history, 424–25
ancient concepts of, 95
of archaeology, 31–32
of Bible study and interpretation, 17–18, 21–22, 54–64
of biblical period (*See* biblical history)
Chronicler's History, 199 (*See also* 1 Chronicles; 2 Chronicles; Ezra; Nehemiah)
deterministic view of, 339
Deuteronomistic (*See* Deuteronomistic History)
of effects, 22
eschatological view o, 339, 341–42
historical approach to reading and study of Bible, 8
Joachim of Fiore's theology of, 61
Luke as, 397
Mark's account of God's triumph in, 395
minor prophets' understanding of, 345
Pentateuch as, 89–90
of transmission of text (*See* transmission history)
value and accuracy of Bible for, 5–6, 30–31
Hittite vassal treaties, 124
Holiness Code, 131–33
Holofernes, 218–22
Holy Spirit
Church as guided by, in Acts, 437
gifts of, in 1 Corinthians, 456–57
life according to, in 1 Thessalonians, 484
Pentecost, 426–27
Romans on, 447
holy war, in Numbers, 138–39
Homer, 54
Horemhab, Pharaoh, 118
Hosea, 346–49
Baal and idol cults, concern with, 346–48
dating of, 344, 346
Lamentations' relationship to, 313
main themes and theology of, 344, 345
marriage metaphor in, 346–47
modern relevance of, 348–49
"household code" of New Testament Epistles, 480, 488
Hugh of St. Cher, 61, 62
Hugh of St. Victor, 60–61
Humanism, Renaissance, 18
humanist stress on individual behavior in wisdom literature, 235–36, 258–60
humor
Bel and the dragon, 343
in Jonah, 357
Hyksos, 36, 37, 118
hymns, psalms regarded as, 244–45, 253

I

Ibzam, 161–62
idols, Israelite worship of
Amos' concern with, 353–54
golden calf incident in desert of Sinai, 123, 138, 142
Hosea's concern with, 346–48
in Judges, 157–58, 162–63
in Kings, 184, 190, 194
Malachi's marriage metaphors and, 369–70
Solomon's marriage to non-Israelite women and, 188
immigrant peoples, 225. *See also* Diaspora Judaism
immoral behavior/sexual conduct
in 1 Corinthians, 453
in 1 Thessalonians, 483
inclusion of Gentiles in Christian mission. *See* Gentiles and Christianity
inclusive language, 7, 72–74
inclusivism, modern call to, and exclusivism in Ezra and Nehemiah, 209–11, 214–15
inculturation, 22
individual behavior in wisdom literature, humanist stress on, 235–36, 258–60
inerrancy of Bible, 26
inspiration of Bible, 26
inspirational approach to reading Bible, 8
interpretation of the Bible, 54–67
in early Church (100–500), 17, 54–58
in Middle Ages (500–1500), 18, 57, 58–63
in early modern period (1500–1650), 63–64
emergence of modern Catholic biblical criticism (1650–1943), 64–66
coming of age of modern Catholic biblical criticism (1943–2000), 66–67
allegorical approach, 17–18, 54–58, 60, 62
anagogical approach, 18, 62
Catholic research institutions and journals, 22–23, 65, 67
Catholic Study Bible, use of, 13–15
different approaches to, 8
in First Isaiah, 287
historiography of, 17–18, 21–22, 54–64
Lectionary used for biblical study, 83–84
literal approach, 17–18, 56–58, 62
methods of, 20–22
moral or tropological approach, 18, 62
Pentateuch, 90–94
Philemon, interpretive problems posed by, 493
prayer, reading, and study, 7–9
Revelation, 520–21

Song of Songs, 268–71
translations as, 68, 69, 74
The Interpretation of the Bible in the Church (Pontifical Biblical Commission), 9, 19–20, 69–70
Irenaeus of Lyons, 55–56, 58, 64
Iron I Age, 38–43
Iron II Age, 43–50
Isaac, 111–12
Isaiah, 280–95
dating of, 280, 288
First Isaiah, 281–87
biblical history of, 281–82
interpretation of scripture in, 287
literary structure of, 282–84
Messianism in, 285–87
theology of, 284
traditions used in, 284–85
influence on later biblical books, 294–95
Judah, association with kingdom of, 301
Lamentations' relationship to, 312
organization and structure of, 280–81, 288, 292
Philip's instruction about, in Acts, 429
Second Isaiah (Deutero-Isaiah), 287–91
Baruch alluding to, 316
continuities and discontinuities with First Isaiah, 288–90
and Davidic kingship, 290
"new exodus" announced in, 289–90
organization and structure of, 288
the servant of the Lord in, 290–91
theology of, 284, 293, 294
Third Isaiah (Trito-Isaiah), 291–92, 293
traditions used in, 284–85, 292
unity of entire book, 292–94
word pairs in, 293–94
Israel, kingdom of
biblical history, 45–48
Jeremiah's association with, 301
in Kings
separation of Judah from, 188–89
Nadab to Omri, 189–90
house of Omri and Ahab, 190–94
Jehu to Jeroboam II, 194–95
final collapse of, 196
bias against Israel in, 184
Song of Songs, possible origins of, 267

J

J. *See* Yahwist source
Jacob, 112–14
Jael, 159
Jahwist source. *See* Yahwist source
Jair, 161
James, 501–6
arrogance denounced in, 505
discrimination and law of love in, 502–3
faith in, 502, 503
friendship with God or world in, 504–5
literary style and structure of, 501
as moral exhortation, 501, 503–6
on patience, 505
power of the tongue in, 503–4, 505
on prayer, 505
theology of, 502, 504
those of two minds addressed in, 502
two measures of, 502
Jason of Cyrene, 52
jealousy of God, 329, 330, 361, 504
Jehoshaphat, 191, 204
Jehu, 194
Jephthah, 161
Jeremiah, 296–309
guide to reading specific passages, 301–3
Aramaic used in, 3
"authentic words" of, 303–4
biblical history, 296–97
biography of prophet, 299–300
Book of Consolation, 305
dating of, 297–99
"Deuteronomic" sections of, 301, 304
influence on other biblical books, 309
Isaiah's influence on, 294
laments or confessions, 304–5, 307
main themes and theology of, 305–8
oracles concerning foreign nations, 305
organization and structure of, 303–5
traditions used by, 300–301
transmission history of, 308–9
Jeremiah the prophet
Baruch as secretary of, 315
biography of, 299–300
Lamentations, authorship of, 312
Letter of Jeremiah, 309, 315, 318, 319
Jericho, battle of, 151, 152
Jeroboam I, 188, 189
Jeroboam II, 195
Jerome, 7, 17, 57, 59, 60, 62, 199
Jerusalem. *See also* Temple
archaeology of, 42, 47, 53
ark moved to, 179
Babylonian siege and destruction of, 46, 47, 50, 180, 197
biblical history of, 11
capture by David, 176, 178–79
Deuteronomic History's emphasis on, 93
Isaiah of (*See* First Isaiah, *under* Isaiah)
Jesus and (*See* Jesus)
under kingdom of Judah, 48–50
new creation revealed in Revelation, 524
Paul's arrest and imprisonment in, 436
in Persian period, 52
pilgrimage psalms associated with, 246, 248, 249
political centralization in, 170
rebuilding and repopulation after return from exile, 212, 214
restriction of Temple to, 93, 96, 123, 146, 147
Roman sack of, 53
Zephaniah on, 363–64

Jerusalem Church
  establishment of, 426–29
  Gentile mission confirmed by, 432, 467–68
  Paul's collections for, 449, 462–63, 467
Jesus
  authority of
    in Luke, 408–9
    in Matthew, 384–85
  baptism of (*See* baptism)
  birth and origins of
    in Luke, 401–3
    in Matthew, 374–76
  crucifixion, death, and resurrection (*See* crucifixion, death, and resurrection of Jesus)
  family of, 391
  Galilean ministry of
    in Luke, 404–8
    in Mark, 388
    in Matthew, 377–81
  as God
    in Hebrews, 497–98
    in John, 414–15, 422–23
  as healer
    in John, 418, 419
    in Luke, 404, 405–6
    in Mark, 390, 394
    in Matthew, 378–79
  Jeremiah, identified with, 309
  in Jerusalem
    in John, 417
    in Luke, 408–11
    in Mark, 388–89, 393–94
    in Matthew, 383–84
  Jerusalem, journey to
    in Luke, 406–8
    in Mark, 388, 393–94
    in Matthew, 381–83
  Jewish heritage in Matthew, 373–74, 375
  on law, in Matthew, 383–84
  as Messiah (*See* Messiah, Jesus as)
  miracles of (*See* miracles of Jesus)
  mission of (*See* mission of Jesus/Church)
  opponents of (*See also* Pharisees)
    in John, 419
    in Luke, 404–5, 406, 409–10
    in Mark, 390–91, 394, 395
    in Matthew, 379–80, 381, 384
  Pauline Epistles rarely speaking directly of, 440
  Philippians on example of, 476–77
  preparation for ministry
    in Luke, 403–4
    in Mark, 388, 389
    in Matthew, 376
  as prophet, 385
  as second Adam, 445–46
  as Son of Man (*See* Son of Man)
  Synoptic Gospels' portrayal of, 372
  in Temple
    in John, 417
    in Luke, 408–9
    in Mark, 394–95
    in Matthew, 384
  theology of (*See* Christology)
  Transfiguration theophany in Luke, 406
Jewish Christians. *See* Gentile and Jewish Christianity
Jews and Jewish Bible generally. *See* Judaism and Jewish Bible
Jezebel, 190, 191
Joab, 181–82, 184, 185
Joachim of Fiore, 61
Joash, 194
Job, 236–43
  guide to reading, 242–43
  literary style of, 237–38
  main themes and theology of, 238–43
  organization and structure of, 238
Joel, 344, 345, 349–51
Johannine Christianity, 513–18, 522
John, Gospel of, 412–23
  guide to reading specific passages, 413–14, 415–22
  Book of Glory, 420–22
  Book of Signs, 416–20
  double ending of, 412–13
  epilogue, 422
  main themes and theology of, 414–15, 422–23
  organization and structure of, 415
  Passion narrative, 421–22, 423
  prologue on divine word, 415–16
  Synoptic Gospels, relationship to, 413
  transmission history, 412–13
  use of symbols, irony, and misunderstanding in, 413–14, 416
1 John, 513–16
2 John, 513, 516–17
3 John, 513, 517–18
John the Baptist
  in Acts, 429
  Elijah, identified with, 200, 389
  Jeremiah, identified with, 309
  in John, 414, 416, 417–18
  in Lectionary, 82
  in Luke, 398, 401–3, 405, 406, 408, 429
  in Mark, 387, 388, 389, 390, 392
  in Matthew, 374, 376, 379, 381
  as Messiah, 370
  new Exodus of Hosea and, 347
  as prophet, 368
John Cassian, 58
John Chrysostom, 17, 56
John XXIII, Pope, 19, 66
John Paul II, Pope, 19, 69, 107
Jonah, 210, 344, 357–59
Jonah the prophet, in 2 Kings, 45, 195
Jonathan and David, 174–78, 181, 182
Jonathan Maccabee, 229
Joseph son of Jacob, 36, 114–15, 115, 224
Josephus, 50, 52, 60, 224

Joshua, 149–56
guide to reading specific passages, 150–54
biblical history of, 10–11, 39–41
organization and structure of, 149
problem of violence and conquest in, 154–56
theology of, 150–51, 154–56
Joshua, in Zechariah, 366
Josiah
"Book of the Law" of, 144–45, 197, 296, 321
reign of, 197, 204, 296, 297–98, 321
Judah, kingdom of
Babylonian exile, 197–98, 204
biblical history, 45–46, 48–50
in 2 Chronicles, 203–4
Isaiah's association with, 301
in Kings
separation from Israel, 188–89
Jehoshaphat and Ahaziah, 191–92
Jehoram, 193
Athaliah and Joash, 195
Amaziah to Ahaz, 195–96
final years of, 196–98
bias in favor of Judah, 184
restoration on return from exile in Ezra and Nehemiah, 207–9
Judaism and Jewish Bible. *See also* individual books
in Acts, 437
baptismal sects, Jewish, continuation into third century, 435
canonical books, 4, 5, 276–77
Christians of Jewish origin or allegiance (*See* Gentile and Jewish Christianity)
of Diaspora (*See* Diaspora Judaism)
Esther, Judaism of, 222
Ezekiel's importance to, 334
God, names for, 7
Hebrews on, 496, 497
interpretive tradition, 54–55, 60
John (Gospel of) and, 413–14, 416
Judith, Judaism of, 220–21
Lectionary's need to be responsive to, 84
Leviticus' importance to, 125
Luke and, –99
Matthew and, 373–74, 375, 384
nationalism of (*See* nationalism, Jewish)
in 1 Peter, 507
placement of Chronicles, 200
placement of prophets, 280
placement of Ruth, 165–66
prayer and study as basis for reading Bible, 8
Rashi and other Jewish commentors' influence on Christian interpreters, 60, 62
Romans on, 447–48
Rome, Jewish revolts against, 12, 52, 53
Tobit, Judaism of, 216–17
Judaizers. *See* Gentile and Jewish Christianity
Judas
betrayal of Jesus by, 385, 386, 395, 409–10, 420
replacement of, 410, 426
wages, significance of, 367
Judas Maccabee, 229, 233–34
Jude, 510, 519–20
Judges, 156–64
guide to reading specific passages, 157–64
biblical history of, 11, 39–40
chaotic nature of early Israelite settlement reflected in, 163–64
organization and structure of, 156–57, 158
theology of, 157–58, 164
judges, historical period of, 11, 38–43, 157–58
judgment. *See* eschatology; sin and atonement
Judith, 218–22
guide to reading specific passages, 218–19
dating of, 221
Esther and, 222
heroine, character and nature of, 219–20
ironic character of, 210
Judaism of, 220–21
literary form of, 218
organization and structure of, 219
theology of, 221
women, as model for, 219–20, 221
justification in Romans, 443–44, 445
Justin Martyr, 55, 79

K

Kenyon, Kathleen, 31, 35
King James Bible, 63, 71
1 and 2 Kings, 183–98
guide to reading specific passages, 184–98
authorship and dating of, 184
biblical history of, 11, 45–46
Deuteronomy and 2 Kings, 144–45
division into two books, 184
sources for, 45–46, 184
theology of, 184, 194–95, 198
kings, period of. *See* monarchy period
knowledge or gnosis
in Corinthians, 454–55, 463, 464
in 1 Timothy, 487–88
Kuntillet ʿAjrud Inscriptions, 44

L

Lachish Letters, 44
Lagrange, M.-J., 65
Lamb of God
Jesus as, 76, 416, 522–24
Revelation's vision of, 522–23
Lamentabili (1907), 66
Lamentations, 310–14
laments
in Jeremiah, 304–5, 307
Job as type of, 238
psalms regarded as, 244, 246, 252
types of, 311
land distribution in Joshua, 152–53

land of Israel, promise of. *See also* covenant between God and Israel; settlement of Israel
  conditional nature of, 147, 154
  in Joshua, 152
land redemption in Ruth, 168
Langton, Stephen, 61
language, living and changing nature of, 68
languages used in Bible, 3, 208, 222–23
Last Supper. *See also* Eucharist
  in John, 420–21
  in Luke, 409–10
  in Mark, 395
latter prophets. *See* minor or latter prophets
law. *See also* Torah
  in Deuteronomy, 146–47
  in Galatians, 467–70
  Gentile Christians' requirement to observe, 467–68
  Jesus on, in Matthew, 383–84
  justification in Romans and, 443–44, 445
  Leviticus as law genre, 86
  Pentateuch, mixed law and narrative genres of, 87–88
  purity (*See* purity laws)
  will and testament compared, 469
lawsuits
  in 1 Corinthians, 453
  Job as type of, 238
Lazarus, raising of, 81, 413, 420
Lazarus the poor man at the gate, 407
leadership, Christian. *See* ministry
Leclercq, Jean, 58, 59
lectio divina, 22, 58
lectio electa, lectio continua, and *lectio semicontinua,* 79
Lectionary, 28, 76–84
  Church year reflected in, 78–79
  ecumenical import of, 83
  organization of
    Advent-Christmas season, 82
    Lent-Easter season, 81–82
    Ordinary Time, 80–81, 82–83
    Sundays, 79–82
    weekdays, 82–83
  prayer and study, as basis for, 83–84
  principles governing, 76–79
  reasons for having, 77–78
  responsorial psalms, 83
  revision of, 77, 84
Leo XIII, Pope, 18, 61, 65, 66
Letter of Jeremiah, 309, 315, 318, 319
letters. *See* Epistles
levirate marriage in Ruth, 168
Levites
  in Judges, 163
  Numbers' concern with, 138
  as sole legitimate priests, 180 (*See also* priesthood, Israelite)
  Temple personnel in 1 Chronicles, 202
  towns set aside for, 154
Leviticus, 125–33
  guide to reading specific passages, 127–33
  Christian vs. Jewish perceptions of, 125
  as law genre, 86
  literary unity and diversity of, 126–27
  organization and structure of, 126, 127
liberation theology, 21
literal approach to Bible, 17–18, 56–58, 62
literal interpretation of Song of Songs, 270–71
literary criticism, 20, 66
  apologetic literature, 1 Peter as, 506–7
  Epistles, style of, 440
  Ezekiel, literary structure of, 325–26
  First Isaiah, literary structure of, 282–84
  James, style and structure of, 501
  Job, literary style of, 237–38
  Judith, literary form of, 218
  of Lamentations, 311–12
  Leviticus, literary unity and diversity of, 126–27
  Numbers, literary unity of, 137
  Pentateuch, as literary work, 90
  Tobit, literary form of, 215–16
literary evidence. *See* documentary evidence
liturgical or cultic interpretation of Song of Songs, 269–70
liturgy
  Bible, liturgical use of, 28, 76–84, 252 (*See also* Lectionary)
  centrality of worship in Luke, 412
  in 1 Corinthians, 455–57
  Hebrews' influence on, 496
  ritual, Zechariah's appreciation of, 366–67
  in 1 Thessalonians intended as part of, 484
Loisy, Alfred, 66
Lombard, Peter, 59, 62
Louis XIV, king of France, 65
love, Christian law of
  in James, 502–4
  in John, 421, 423
  in Matthew, 377
  in 1 Thessalonians, 484
Luke, 397–412
  guide to reading specific passages, 399, 401–12
  Canticles, 402
  eschatology in, 409
  Galilean ministry in, 404–6
  as history or narrative, 397
  infancy narrative, 401–3
  Jerusalem
    journey to, 406–8
    ministry in, 408–10
  main themes and theology of, 399–400, 412
  Mark compared, 398
  organization and structure of, 398, 401
  preparation for ministry in, 403–4
  prologue, 401
  regarded as new Deuteronomy, 148
  sources of, 397, 398
  tragedy of Israel in, 398–99

Luther, Martin, 18, 62, 63–64, 319
LXX. *See* Septuagint

M

1 Maccabees, 226–31
  guide to reading specific passages, 227–30
  biblical history of, 11–12, 52
  in Catholic tradition, 230
  Hanukkah and, 228
  Hasmoneans, legitimacy of, 227, 230
  as history, 226–27
  militancy of, 228
  relationship to 2 Maccabees, 231
  theology of, 226–27
2 Maccabees, 11–12, 52, 231–34
3 and 4 Maccabees, 226
Maccabees literature generally, 226
  Catholic tradition and, 230, 233–34
  Hellenization, Jewish response to, 227, 232–33, 272
Magnificat, 402, 405
major prophets. *See* Ezekiel; Isaiah; Jeremiah
Malachi, 344, 345, 369–70
Malta, Paul's shipwreck on, 437
Manasseh, 46, 145, 196, 204, 296
manuscript evidence. *See* documentary evidence
Marcion of Pontus, 55, 56
Marduk, 104
Mari texts, 35
Mark, 387–97
  guide to reading specific passages, 388–96
  crucifixion, death, and resurrection, 388–89, 394–96
  as earliest Gospel, 371–72, 386
  eschatology in, 395
  Galilean ministry, 388, 389–93
  Jerusalem, journey to, 388, 393–94
  Luke compared, 398
  main themes and theology of, 387–88
  as narrative, 387
  organization and structure of, 388
  preparation for ministry, 388, 389
marriage
  in 1 Corinthians, 453–54
  Hosea, marriage metaphor in, 346–47
  "household code" of New Testament Epistles, 480, 488
  kidnapping of women for wives in Judges, 163–64
  levirate marriage in Ruth, 168
  Malachi on, 369–70
  to non-Israelites (*See* mixed marriages)
  Song of Songs interpreted as wedding drama, 268, 270–71
martyrdom. *See* persecution of early church
Marxist history and Peasant Revolt model of Israelite settlement, 41–42
Mary and Martha, 400
Mary, mother of God
  as first disciple, 400–401
  Luke's infancy narrative and, 401–3
  Mariology, 63
Masada, 53
material possessions
  community sharing in Acts, 427–28
  James' denunciation of arrogance of, 505
  in Luke, 407
  Solomon, wealth of, 186, 188
Mattathias, 227–28
Matthew, 373–86
  guide to reading specific passages, 374–86
  catechetical or teaching function of, 373
  Deuteronomy cited in, 148
  as earliest Gospel, 371–72
  eschatology in, 376, 384, 385
  Galilean ministry of Jesus in, 377–81
  Jerusalem
    Jesus in, 383–84
    Jesus' journey to, 381–83
  Jewish heritage of Jesus and early church in, 373–74, 375
  Jonah in belly of whale in, 358
  Judaism critiqued in, 374
  medieval interest in, 59
  as narrative, 373
  organization and structure of, 374
  origins of Jesus in, 374–76
  preparation for ministry of Jesus in, 376
Medieval period, interpretation of the Bible in, 18, 57, 58–63
Megilloth or Scrolls, 165, 263, 267. *See also* Ecclesiastes; Esther; Lamentations; Ruth; Song of Songs
Meier, J., 65
Melchizedek, 91, 496, 497, 499
mercy, forgiveness, and tolerance as positive values, 358
Meribaal, 181, 182
merkabah (chariot) mysticism, 334
Merneptah, Pharaoh, 38, 118
Mesha of Moab, Stela of, 44, 192
Mesopotamia
  city laments of, 311–12
  at time of Pentateuch, 97
  wisdom tradition, 236
Messiah, Jesus as
  in John, 414, 418–20, 422–23
  in Luke, 406, 408
  in Mark, 396
  in Matthew, 375–76, 384
Messiah, John the Baptist as, 370
Messianism in Old Testament. *See also* eschatology
  Davidic dynasty and, 180
  the Day of the Lord, 349–50, 354, 363, 370
  in First Isaiah, 285–87
  Jeremiah, use of Davidic kingship tradition in, 300, 301
  in Second Isaiah, 290–91
  the servant of the Lord in Second Isaiah, 290–91
  in Zechariah, 467
metaphor in Hosea, 346, 348

Micah, 344, 359–61
Micah in Judges, 162
Michael (archangel), 228, 339–42, 367, 519
Michal, 176, 179
Middle Ages, interpretation of the Bible in, 18, 57, 58–63
Midrash
  Judith regarded as, 218
  Nicholas of Lyra's familiarity with, 62
  Romans using form of, 447
  as source for Chronicles, 46
  use of Hebrew in, 208
  in wisdom literature, 273, 275
migrant peoples, 225. *See also* Diaspora Judaism
Military Invasion model of Israelite settlement history, 41
ministry
  bishops, 56, 476, 488–89, 492
  deacons, 291, 428, 449, 461, 476, 488–89
  Johannine Christianity, split in, 513–18
  leadership in Matthew, 382
  of Paul (*See* Paul)
  in 1 Peter, 510
  in 1 and 2 Timothy, 486–91
  in Titus, 492–93
minor or latter prophets, 280, 344–45. *See also* Amos; Hosea; Zechariah
  the Day of the Lord in, 349–50, 354, 363, 370
  Habakkuk, 344, 362–63
  Haggai, 344, 345, 364–65
  Joel, 344, 345, 349–51
  Jonah, 210, 344, 357–59
  Malachi, 344, 345, 369–70
  Micah, 344, 359–61
  Nahum, 344, 361
  Obadiah, 344, 356
  Zephaniah, 344, 345, 363–64
miracles of Jesus
  in John, 416–20
  in Luke, 404, 405–6
  in Mark, 390, 392–94
  in Matthew, 377, 378–79, 380
mission of Jesus/Church
  in Acts (*See* Acts of the Apostles)
  in John, 418
  in Luke, 406, 412
  Mark on, 389–95, 396
  Matthew on, 379
  Paul, missions of (*See* Paul)
  Peter, missions of
    to Gentiles, 423, 431–32, 466, 467–68
    to Jerusalem, 427–29
Mitchell, Margaret, 67
mixed marriages
  in Ezra and Nehemiah, 209, 214
  Malachi on, 369–70
  in Ruth, 166
  of Solomon, 188
Moab and Moabites
  in Kings, 192
  as national state, 157
  in Ruth, 165, 166, 169
Moabite Stela, 44, 192
Modernism, 18
monarchy period. *See also* David; Israel, kingdom of; Judah, kingdom of; Solomon
  biblical history of, 11, 43–50
  consequences of monarchy in Samuel, 183
  emergence in Samuel, 172–73
  royal psalms, 245, 249
  Saul, 173–78, 200
  United Monarchy, 45–47
  Zechariah's understanding of, 366
monastic culture and scriptural interpretation, 58, 61, 63
moral or tropological approach to Bible, 18, 62
Mordecai, 223
Moses. *See also* exodus from Egypt
  as author of Pentateuch, 65, 95–96
  confrontation with Pharaoh, 119–20
  Deuteronomy framed as farewell speech of, 143
  God's choice of, 118–19, 120
  Jeremiah drawing on tradition of, 300
  Jesus compared, 498–99
murmuring tradition, in Numbers, 139
mythic traditions used in Bible. *See* Near Eastern mythic traditions used in Bible

N

Naaman, 192
NAB. See New American Bible
Naboth's vineyard, 191
Nahum, 344, 361
names for God, 7, 91, 119
Naomi, 164–69
narrative
  Luke as, 398
  Mark as, 387
  Matthew as, 373
  in Pentateuch, 87–88
narrative analysis, 21
Nathan the prophet, 170, 181
nationalism, Jewish
  in Esther, 225
  ethnic exclusivism in Ezra and Nehemiah, 209–11, 214–15
  1 Maccabees, militancy of, 228
  in Psalms, 248–49, 250, 253–54
natural world celebrated in Psalms, 250
Nazirites, 135, 162–63, 170
Near Eastern mythic traditions used in Bible, 30–31
  in Ezekiel, 325
  in First Isaiah, 284–85
  in Genesis, 102, 104–5, 106
  in Job, 237
  in Psalms, 284–85
  in Second Isaiah, 289

Nebuchadnezzar, 197, 297, 321, 337
Nehemiah, 211–15
  guide to reading specific passages, 211–12, 215
  biblical history of, 11, 50, 51–52
  division of Ezra and Nehemiah into two books, 199, 207, 211
  exclusivism in, 214–15
  main themes and theology of, 212–15
  relationship to Ezra, 211
  restoration of Judah on return from exile, 207–8
  Torah and, 212–14
Nero, emperor, 387, 424
New American Bible (NAB)
  on Daniel, 342
  Deuteronomy in, 141–42, 147
  on Ecclesiastes, 262
  on Hosea, 346
  inclusive language used in, 7, 72
  on John, 413
  on Jude, 519
  on Luke, 397
  order of Psalms in, 243
  Pentateuch, 86, 91
  placement of Ruth in, 165
  on Synoptic Gospels, 371
  as translation, 7, 71, 74–75
  versification of Esther in, 222
  versification of Kings in, 186
New Testament. *See also* Gospels, Epistles, and individual books
  biblical history of, 11–12, 52–53
  Christian concept of, 55
  Davidic descent of Jesus in, 180
  Deuteronomy and, 148
  Ezekiel, allusions to, 334
  inclusivism of, 215
  Isaiah's influence on, 291, 295
  Jeremiah's influence on, 309
  Pentateuch cited in, 90–91
  Psalms and, 251
  the servant of the Lord in Second Isaiah, influence of, 291
  Sirach as influence on, 279
  source materials, 23–24
  tradition and creativity in, 23–24
  wisdom literature, influence of, 275
Nicholas of Damascus, 52
Nicholas of Lyra, 62, 63
Nicodemus, Jesus' dialogue with, 417
Noah and flood story in Genesis, 106–7
Nomadic Infiltration model of Israelite settlement history, 40
North African traditions of biblical exegesis and translation, 57
Northern Kingdom. *See* Israel, kingdom of
Nostra Aetate (1965), 225
Noth, Martin, 40
novel
  Acts of the Apostles resembling popular novels of first and second centuries A.D., 425
  Esther as, 223
  first six chapters of Daniel as, 336
  Judith as, 218
  Tobit as, 215, 217
Numbers, 133–41
  guide to reading specific passages, 134–47
  biblical history of, 10–11
  connections with other books of Pentateuch, 133–34
  literary unity of, 137
  main themes and theology of, 137–41
  mixed law and narrative genre, 86
  organization and structure of, 134, 135
  origins of name, 133
  Priestly, Elohist, and Yahwist sources in, 137, 141
Nunc Dimittis, 402
Nuzi texts, 35

O

Obadiah, 344, 356
offerings. *See* sacrifice and offerings
Old Testament. *See also* Judaism and Jewish Bible, and individual books
  as Bible of Jesus and early church, 17
  Christian concept of, 55
  parts of, 86
  source materials, 23
  tradition and creativity in, 23
Olivi, Peter, 61
one sanctuary principle
  civil war in Joshua and, 154
  Deuteronomy's stress on, 147
  Jerusalem, restriction of Temple to, 93, 96, 123, 146, 147
  Northern Kingdom's cultic centers, 189, 195
Onesimus, 480, 493–95
onomasticon, 237
oracles. *See* prophets and prophecy
oral transmission of Biblical text, 6, 334
Origen, 17, 56–57, 58, 59, 270
Orthodox Churches, canonical books of, 4, 5, 226, 315
Osiek, Carolyn, 67
Othniel, 158

P

P. *See* Priestly source
parables
  in Luke, 406–8, 412
  in Mark, 39
  in Matthew, 380, 383
parallelism
  in Exodus, 120
  in Job, 238
  in Judith, 219
  in Luke, 401, 402
  in Proverbs, 255, 256

parallelism (*cont.*)
translation of, 75
in Wisdom, 273
parenesis, 501
Pascendi dominici gregis (1908), 66
Paschasius Radbertus, 58
Passion narratives. *See* crucifixion, death, and resurrection of Jesus
Pastoral Letters (1 and 2 Timothy and Titus), 486–93
pastoralism vs. agriculture in ancient Israel, 42, 43, 106. *See also* sheep and shepherds
patience, James on, 505
patriarchal period
ancestor narratives of Genesis, 108–15
in biblical history, 10, 34–36
patristics, 17, 18, 59, 62
Paul
apostolic identification of, 440
arrests, imprisonments, and martyrdom of
in Ephesus, 475, 477
impending martyrdom, Paul's words regarding, 490–91
in Jerusalem, 436
in Rome, 436, 475, 476, 490–91
companions of, 486–87, 489
conversion of, 43
examples in letters drawn from own life as trait of, 455, 477, 479
Jerusalem Church, collections for, 449, 462–63, 467
life of, 439
Malta, shipwreck on, 437
ministry of
in Colossians, 479
in 2 Corinthians, 460–62, 463–64
in Galatians, 467–68
in 1 Thessalonians, 482–83
missions of, 486
first missionary journey, 431–32
journey to Rome, 436–37
second missionary journey, 432–34
third missionary journey, 434–36
travels outlined in Philippians, 477
Rome
arrest and imprisonment in, 436, 475, 476
journey to, 436–37
sources of information about, 439
Spain, intended mission to, 449
Paul VI, Pope, 66, 107, 225
Pauline Epistles, 439–40. *See also* 1 Corinthians; 2 Corinthians; Galatians; Romans
captivity letters, 475
circulation in Christian community, 440–41
Deutero-Pauline letters, 439, 471 (*See also* Colossians; Ephesians; 2 Thessalonians; 1 Timothy; 2 Timothy; Titus)
as earliest New Testament documents, 23, 27
"Gospel" message of, 440
medieval interest in, 59
Philemon, 493–95
Philippians, 475–78
1 Thessalonians, 481, 482–84
traditional nature of, 23
Peasant Revolt model of Israelite settlement history, 41–42
Pekah, 195
Pentateuch, 85–99. *See also* Deuteronomy; Exodus; Genesis; Leviticus; Numbers
defined, 85
historical background of, 94–96, 97
as historical document, 89–90
interpretation and biblical criticism of, 90–94
as literary work, 90
Moses as author of, 65, 95–96
NAB text of, 86
New Testament citation of, 90–91
organization and structure of, 88–89
diagrammed, 87–89
historical records contributing to, 94–95
mixed law and narrative genres, 87–88
"plot," 88
reasons behind, 85
symmetry and unity of five books, 88–89
Reformation and post-Reformation scholarship on, 91
sources for, 91, 94–95
theology of, 89, 96–98
as Torah, 23, 85, 86 (*See also* Torah)
transmission history of, 94
Pentecost, 426–27
Perkins, Pheme, 67
persecution of early church
in Acts (*See* Acts of the Apostles)
by Nero, 387
Paul's arrests and imprisonments (*see* Paul)
in 1 Peter, 505, 508–9
in Revelation, 523–24
Persian period, 50–52, 208, 223–25, 316
Peter
authorship of 1 and 2 Peter, 505, 510
calling in Luke, 404
Gentiles accepted as Christians by, 431, 466, 467–68
importance as leader in Matthew, 382
missions
to Gentiles, 430–31, 466, 467–68
to Jerusalem, 427
trials and imprisonments, 427, 431
1 Peter, 505–10
as apologetic, 506–7
audience for, 505
authorship of, 505
on community, 508, 509–10
gift and call of God in, 507
on Gospel life to which Christians are called, 507–8
on relationship of Christians to world, 508–9
2 Peter, 510–13, 519
Peter Comestor or Manducator, 60–61

Peter Lombard, 59, 62
Petrie, W. M. Flinders, 31
Pharisees
in Acts, 428, 436
angels, belief in, 217
Hasmonean dynasty, groups evolving in opposition to, 12
in John, 413, 420
in Luke, 400, 404–5, 406, 409, 453
in Mark, 388, 391, 392, 394, 453
in Matthew, 373, 374, 378–80, 382–84, 453
Paul as, 439, 465
resurrection of the dead, acceptance of concept of, 278
Sirach and, 277
spiritual ancestors of, 230
Philemon, 493–95
Philippians, 475–78
Philistines
emergence of, 38
in Judges, 162–63
in Samuel, 171–72, 174–78
Philo of Alexandria, 52, 54
philosophical approach to reading Bible, 8
Phoebe, 449
piety
Catholic use of Bible in, 28
Job, disinterested piety as theme of, 240–41
of psalms, 246–49
pilgrimage and processional psalms, 246, 249, 252–54
Pius V, Pope, 77
Pius X, Pope, 18, 65, 66
Pius XII, Pope, 18, 19, 66–67
Plato and Platonism, 54, 67, 497
Pliny the Elder, 52
poetry
in Baruch, 318
in Hosea, 346, 347
in Job, 237–38
of Lamentations, 312
of minor prophets, 344
of Psalms, 251
of Revelation, 522, 523
Song of Songs as collection of, 267
political issues in Biblical translations, 7
Polybius, 52
Pontius Pilate
in Acts, 436
in John, 413, 421–22, 423
in Luke, 398, 409, 410
in Mark, 395
in Matthew, 384, 385
poor, sick, and disabled, Christian concern for. *See also* Jesus: as healer
Jerusalem Church, collections for, 449, 462–63, 467
in Luke, 400
Paul on Christian priority of, 467
Peter on Christian priority of, 427
Populorum Progressio (1967), 107
praise and thanksgiving, psalms of, 243, 245, 247–53
prayer
in Baruch, 317
Bible as basis for, 7–9
James on, 505
Lamentations as, 311, 313–14
lectio divina and, 22
Lectionary as used for, 83–84
in Luke, 408, 412
2 Maccabees, prayers for living and dead in, 233–34
Psalms used as, 252
presbyters, 435, 488, 492
priesthood, Catholic, and 1 Chronicles, 202–3
priesthood, Israelite
David's sons, 180
Ezekiel drawing on tradition of, 324–32
Jesus as high priest, in Hebrews, 498–99, 501
Levites as sole legitimate priests, 180 (*See also* Levites)
Leviticus, establishment of priesthood of Aaron in, 129
Malachi's criticism of, 369
Numbers' concern with, 138
Temple personnel in 1 Chronicles, 202
Zechariah on, 36
priesthood of early church. *See* ministry
Priestly source (P), 91, 93
in Genesis, 102, 103–4
Leviticus identified with, 126
in Numbers, 137, 141
problem of evil or theodicy, in Job, 239–40
processional and pilgrimage psalms, 246, 249, 252–54
promised land. *See* land of Israel, promise of
prophets and prophecy. *See also* individual prophets, e.g. Deborah, Samuel
Assyrian dominance and emergence of, 281
in Daniel, 339–40, 341
decline of, in Zechariah, 368
against foreign nations (*See* foreign nations, oracles concerning)
foreign nations, oracles concerning, 305
former prophets (*See* 1 and 2 Kings; 1 and 2 Samuel; Joshua; Judges)
Jesus as prophet, 385
John the Baptist as prophet, 368
major prophets (*See* Ezekiel; Isaiah; Jeremiah)
minor or latter prophets (*See* minor or latter prophets)
placement of books of, 280
psalms, prophetic, 246, 249
Revelation as prophecy, 521
true vs. false prophets in Jeremiah, 307–8
zeal or lack of zeal, 358
Protestant Churches
canonical books of, 5, 26, 272, 336
concept of lectionary and, 77, 83

Protestant Churches (*cont.*)
history of Bible study, 18
methodological indistinguishability of modern Catholic exegesis from, 67
Reformation, 18, 24, 25, 63–64, 91, 272
"Scripture alone" principle, 24, 25
Proverbs, 254–62
humanist stress on individual behavior in, 258–60
main themes and theology of, 258–60
modern use of, 261
nature of *mashal* or proverbs of, 255–56
organization and structure of, 254–55
Sirach compared, 278
Solomon as traditional author of, 254–55
teacher-student aspect of, 255, 256-57
"the way of wisdom" in, 256, 257–58
Providentissimus Deus (1893), 18, 19, 65, 66
Psalms, 243–54
medieval interest in, 59
modern use of, 251–54
Near Eastern mythic traditions used in, 284–85
organization and structure of, 243
piety of, 246–49
responsorial psalms in Lectionary, 83
theology of, 249–51
types of, 244–46
Psalter, 243. *See also* Psalms
Ptolemaic dynasty, 11, 53, 227, 272
Purim, 223–24
purity laws
in Daniel, 337
in Ezekiel, 325
in Leviticus, 129–31
in Nehemiah, 214
in Numbers, 136
Pythagoras and Pythagoreans, 54

Q

Q (posited *Quelle* manuscript), 23, 372, 397, 398
Qoheleth, 262–63. *See also* Ecclesiastes
Qumran community. *See* Dead Sea Scrolls

R

Rabanus Maurus, 58
Ralph, 59
Ramesses II, Pharaoh, 36, 38, 118
Ramesses III, Pharaoh, 37, 118
Raphael (archangel), 216–18
Rashi (Rabbi Solomon bar Isaac of Troyes), 60, 62
reader-response criticism of Pentateuch, 94
Rebekah, 111–12
redaction criticism, 21, 94
redemption of land in Ruth, 168
Redemptor Hominis (1979), 107
Reformation, 18, 24, 25, 63–64, 91, 272. *See also* Protestant Churches
refuge, Israelite cities of, 153
Rehoboam, 188–89, 204
Reisner, George, 31
religious diversity in Israel, 205–7
religious sensitivities in Biblical translations, 7
Remigius of Auxerre, 58
Renaissance, 18
repentance. *See* sin and atonement
repetition and doublets, 333–34
resurrection of the dead
in 1 Corinthians, 457
Jesus' espousal of, in Luke, 408–9
Jesus' resurrection (*See* crucifixion, death, and resurrection of Jesus)
in John, 414, 420
judgment and restoration of Israel in Jeremiah, 308
in 2 Maccabees, 233–34
Sadducee vs. Pharisee position on, 278
Sirach's rejection of, 278
in 1 Thessalonians, 483–84
retribution, theory of, in Wisdom Books, 236, 238–39, 259, 263, 264, 266, 277–78
return from exile. *See* Babylonian exile and return
Revelation, 520–25
Babylon (Roman empire), fall of, 523–24
cosmic conflicts envisioned in, 523
epistolary mode, use of, 522
as eschatology, 521
God and the Lamb in heaven, 522–23
interpretation of, 520–21
Johannine affinities of, 522
new creation revealed in, 524
organization and structure of, 521–22
as prophecy, 521
revelation, Catholic concept of, 25–26
Revue biblique, 22–23, 65, 66
rhetorical criticism, 21, 94
Richard of St. Victor, 60
riches. *See* material possessions
ritual purity. *See* purity laws
ritual, Zechariah's appreciation of, 366–67
Roman Christians, 441
in Acts, 424
Mark probably written for, 387
Pauline Epistle to (*See* Romans)
Paul's arrest and imprisonment in Rome, 436
Paul's mission to, 436–37
Roman empire
biblical history and, 12, 52–53
census story in Luke's infancy narrative, 403
fall of Babylon in Revelation associated with, 523–24
Greco-Roman interpretive tradition, 54
Jewish revolts against, 12, 52, 53
Luke's attention to, 397, 408
Romans, 441–50
guide to reading specific passages, 442–49
Abraham as model of faith in, 445
on community, 448
as diatribe, 441–42

on Gentile and Jewish Christians, 444–45, 448, 449
Jesus as second Adam in, 445–46
on Judaism and Jewish Bible, 447–48
justification in, 443–44, 445
organization and structure of, 442
spirit and flesh in, 446–47
theological anthropology of, 446
royal psalms, 245, 248
Royal Testament, 262
Ruth, 164–69
guide to reading specific passages, 166–69
dating of, 165
emptiness as motif of, 167
organization and structure of, 165
placement in relationship to other books of Bible, 165–66
theology of, 166, 167, 169

S

sacrifice and offerings
Jesus as, in Hebrews, 500, 501
in Leviticus, 128–29, 133
one sanctuary only, biblical stress on (*See* one sanctuary principle)
Sadducees
in Acts, 436
angels, rejection of concept of, 217
denial of divine providence by, 512
in John, 413
in Luke, 409
in Mark, 394
in Matthew, 383
resurrection of the dead, rejection of concept of, 278
Sirach and, 277, 279
willingness to compromise with foreign occupiers, 230
Sadoleto, Jacopo, 64
saints
communion of, 500
intercession of, 234
salvation. *See also* eschatology; Messiah, Jesus as; Messianism in Old Testament; sin and atonement
Acts of the Apostles as salvation history, 424–25, 437
in John, 414, 416, 423
justification in Romans, 443–44, 445
universality of, 399–400, 412, 437, 444–45, 481 (*See also* ecumenical movement; entries at inclusive; Gentiles and Christianity)
Samaria Ostraca, 44
Samaritans, 196, 205–6, 399, 406, 417, 418, 419, 429, 434
Samson, 162
1 and 2 Samuel, 169–83
guide to reading specific passages, 170–83
authorship and dating, 169–70
biblical history of, 11, 44–45
division into two books, 169
organization and structure of, 170, 182
theology of, 170, 180, 182
Samuel the prophet
as author of 1 Samuel, 169–70
birth of, 170
Eli and, 170–71
Israelite monarchy and, 172–73
Saul and, 173–74
Sarah and Abraham, 110–11, 470
Sarah and Tobit, 215–18
Satan
in Job, 236–43
in John, 419, 420
in Jude, 519
in Luke, 404, 407, 410
in Mark, 388, 389
in Matthew, 376, 381, 382
in Pauline Epistles, 460, 464
in Revelation, 523
temptation of Jesus in the desert, 376, 388, 389, 404
as viewed in New Testament times, 217
in Zechariah, 366
Saul, 173–78, 200
scapegoat ritual, 366–67
Schleiermacher, Friedrich, 65
scholarly research institutions and journals, 22–23, 65, 67
Schüssler-Fiorenza, Elizabeth, 67
scribes and Pharisees. *See* Jesus: opponents of; Pharisees
Scrolls or *Megilloth,* 165, 263, 267. *See also* Ecclesiastes; Esther; Lamentations; Ruth; Song of Songs
Second Isaiah. *See under* Isaiah
Second Vatican Council
Dei verbum (1965), 18–19, 24–28, 67, 84
ecumenism encouraged by, 206–7
on interpretation of scripture, 66–67
Lectionary revision ordered by, 77, 84
on nature of Bible, 25–26
renewed Catholic emphasis on Bible via, 8, 16, 18–19, 76
on tradition, 24–25
Second Zechariah, 365
Seleucids, 11–12, 52, 226–29, 231–32, 272
semiotic analysis, 21
Senior, D., 65
Sennacherib, king of Assyria, 196
Sentences (Peter Lombard), 59, 62
Septuagint (LXX), 68
canonicity affected by, 5, 55
creation for Diaspora Jews, 221, 272
interpretation of Bible and, 54
name of book of Numbers taken from, 133
placement of Chronicles in, 199
Sermon on the Mount, in Matthew, 377–78

Sermon on the Plain, in Luke, 405
the servant of the Lord in Second Isaiah, 290–91
Seti I, Pharaoh, 118
settlement of Israel
biblical history of, 10–11, 38–43
in Joshua, 149–54
in Numbers, 136–37, 139–40, 140
sexual conduct/immoral behavior
in 1 Corinthians, 453
in 1 Thessalonians, 483
Shalmaneser III, Assyrian king, 44
Shamgar, 159
Sheba, Queen of, 188
sheep and shepherds
agriculture vs. pastoralism in ancient Israel, 42, 43, 106
cultural issues and biblical translation, 70, 73
David as shepherd, 176, 179
in Ezekiel, 330, 331, 333, 334
in Jeremiah, 301
in John, 81, 413, 420, 422
Joseph son of Jacob as shepherd, 115
Lamb of God
Jesus as, 76, 416, 522–24
Revelation's vision of, 522–23
in Luke's infancy narrative, 403
in Mark, 331
in Matthew, 379
in 1 Peter, 510
Song of Songs, shepherd in, 267, 270
Zechariah, allegory of the shepherds in, 367–68
shepherds. *See* sheep and shepherds
Sheshbazzar, 51
Sheshonq I, Pharaoh, 44
Shishak, Pharaoh, 189, 204
Shunem, woman of, 193
sick. *See* Jesus: as healer; poor, sick, and disabled, Christian concern for
Siloam Tunnel inscription, 44
Simeon, 402
Simon Maccabee, 229
Simon Magus, 429–30
Simon, Richard, 64–65, 91
sin and atonement
Day of Atonement, 131
doom and restoration in Ezekiel, 326, 329–32
Hosea, marriage metaphor in, 346–47
in Jeremiah, 307, 308
justification in Romans, 443–44, 445
in Luke, 406–7
in Mark, 390
in Matthew, 376
mercy, forgiveness, and tolerance as positive values, 358
in minor prophets, 344–45
retribution, theory of, 236, 238–39, 277–78
Sinai desert, Israelites wandering in
in Genesis, 121–22
in Numbers, 135–36
Sirach (Ecclesiasticus), 276–79, 315
Sisera, 159
Sixtus of Siena, 64
Skeptics, 512
slavery
Israelite enslavement in Egypt, 96, 116, 120–22, 155–56
1 Peter on, 508
Philemon on, 493–95
Temple slaves, 202
Smalley, Beryl, 59, 60
sociological study of biblical texts, 19, 21, 94
Solomon
accession to kingship, 184–85
administration of, 186
biblical history of, 11, 34, 45, 46
in 1 Chronicles, 201
in 2 Chronicles, 203
David's family, place in, 178–79, 180–82
death of, 188
in Kings, 184–88
reign of, 185–88
in Samuel, 178–82
Song of Songs associated with, 267
Temple, building of, 186–87, 201, 203
wealth of, 186, 188
wisdom literature attributed to, 255, 262–63, 267, 272, 274
wisdom of, 186, 188
Son of Man
in Daniel, 340
in Ezekiel, 333
Jesus as
in Acts, 429
in John, 416, 417
in Luke, 405, 407, 409, 410, 411
in Mark, 387, 394, 395
in Matthew, 360, 384, 385
in Revelation, 429, 522
translation issues, 73, 74
Song of Songs, 267–71
dating and geographic associations of, 267
interpretations of, 268–71
medieval interest in, 59
organization and structure of, 267
Solomon, association with, 267
speakers of, 268
theological value of, 271
as wisdom literature, 271
women as portrayed in, 270–71
Sosthenes, 457
source criticism, 21
of Genesis, 102–4
of Pentateuch, 92–94
of Synoptic Gospels, 372, 397, 398
Southern Kingdom. *See* Judah, kingdom of
Spain, Paul's intended mission to, 449
speech, power of, in James, 503–4, 505
Spinoza, Baruch, 18

Spirit. *See* Holy Spirit
Spiritus Paracletus (1920), 18
Stephen protomartyr
  Gentles, mission to, 466
  trial and death of, 428–29
Stoics, 54
Strabo, 52
structural analysis, 21, 94
study of Bible. *See* interpretation of the Bible
Suetonius, 52
suffering as positive value. *See also* crucifixion, death, and resurrection of Jesus; persecution of early church
  in Acts, 437
  in 2 Corinthians, 464
  in Hebrews, 500, 501
  in James, 505
  in Job, 236–37, 241
  in Lamentations, 313–14
  in Luke, 406, 407
  in 2 Maccabees, 233
  in 1 Peter, 508–9
  in Philippians, 475, 476–77
  in Psalms, 246–47
  in 2 Timothy, 490–91
  in Tobit, 215–18
the suffering servant in Second Isaiah, 290–91
Summa Theologica (Thomas Aquinas), 61–62
Susanna and the elders, 342–43
symbolism. *See also* allegory
  in Daniel, 338–39, 340–41
  in Hebrews, 497
  in Hosea, 346, 348
  in 2 John, 516
  in John (Gospel of), 413
  metaphor in Hosea, 346, 348
Synoptic Gospels, 371–72, 413. *See also* Luke; Mark; Matthew

T

Tabitha and Talitha, healings of, 430–31
Tacitus, 52
Talmud
  Ezra, 208, 210
  glossed Bibles compared, 59
  Jeremiah, 309
  Leviticus, 125
  1 Maccabees, 229
  Nehemiah, 213
  Nicholas of Lyra's familiarity with, 62
  Sirach, 279
Tamar, 181
Tanakh. *See* Judaism and Jewish Bible
Temple
  Babylonian destruction of, 187, 197, 310–11
  building of, 179, 186–87, 201, 203
  in Ezekiel, 326, 329, 332
  Herodian structure, 53
  importance to Judaism of, 179, 201–2
  Jesus in (*See* Jesus)
  one sanctuary, biblical stress on (*See* one sanctuary principle)
  personnel of, 202
  processional and pilgrimage psalms, 246, 249, 252–54
  rebuilding on return from Babylonian exile, 207–9, 364–65
  Romans, final destruction by, 12, 53
  slaves, 202
temptation of Jesus in the desert, 376, 388, 389, 4 04
Tertullian, 57, 58
text evidence. *See* documentary evidence
text, versions of. *See* transmission history
textual criticism, 6, 20
Textus Receptus, 63
thanksgiving
  psalms of, 245, 246–49, 251, 253
  1 Thessalonians, as theme of, 483
theodicy or problem of evil, in Job, 239–40
Theodore of Mopsuestia, 17, 56
theology. *See also under* individual books of Bible
  as approach to reading Bible, 8
  Catholic, attention to Bible paid by, 17, 28
  of covenant between God and Israel, 123–24
  Hellenization of, 276
  of history (Joachim of Fiore), 61
  identity with scriptural interpretation in early church, 58
  of Jesus (*See* Christology)
  of minor prophets, 344–45
  of Pentateuch, 89, 97–98
  relationship to scriptural interpretation in modern church, 67
  speech, implications of, 504
theophany. *See under* God
Therapeutae, 54
1 Thessalonians, 481, 482–84
2 Thessalonians, 481, 484–86
Third Isaiah, 291–92, 293
Third Zechariah, 365
Thomas Aquinas, 18, 60, 61–62, 64
Thomas Gallus, 61
Thutmose I, Pharaoh, 118
Thutmose II, Pharaoh, 118
Thutmose III, Pharaoh, 37, 118
Tiglath-pileser III, Assyrian king, 44
1 Timothy, 486–89
2 Timothy, 486–87, 489–91
Timothy, companion of Paul, 477, 487
Titus, 486–87, 491–93
Titus, companion of Paul, 487
Titus, emperor, 53
Tobit, 215–18
Tola, 161
Toledoth or genealogical name lists, division of Genesis by, 101–2, 106, 107, 108
tongue, power of, in James, 503–4, 505

Torah. *See also* law
Baruch and, 317–18
Genesis and, 104
James on, 503, 505
Joshua and, 150, 151, 152, 154, 155, 156
Judges and, 156
Kings and, 184–86, 189, 191, 196, 199
lectio continua, 79
Leviticus and, 125
Nehemiah and, 212–14
Numbers and, 133
Paul on justification and, 443, 444
Pentateuch as, 23, 85, 86 (*See also* Pentateuch)
1 Peter's use of, 508
Philo of Alexandria on, 54
Psalms' organization possibly patterned after, 246
Ruth and, 166, 169
Samuel and, 185, 186, 194
torah (priestly or authoritative teaching)
in Baruch, 316
in Ezekiel, 325, 326, 329
towns. *See* cities and towns
tradition
Bible and, 24–25
Bible as, 23–24
in Ezekiel, 324–25
in Isaiah, 284–85, 292
Near Eastern (*See* Near Eastern mythic traditions used in Bible)
2 Peter on authority of shared tradition, 511
relationship between experience and tradition in Job, 241–42
Sirach's valorization of, 277–78
Transfiguration, 406
translations of the Bible, 68–75. *See also* Septuagint; Vulgate
ancient translations, 6, 57, 221, 227
cultural influences on, 69–70
early modern editions, 18, 63–64
fidelity to original text, 68–69, 70–72
formal vs. dynamic equivalence, 69, 70–72
inclusive language, 7, 72–74
interpretive nature of, 68, 69, 74
Jerome's Vulgate, 57, 63, 64, 199
languages used in original texts, 3, 208, 222–23
living and changing nature of language and, 68
multiple translations, purpose of and comparison of, 70–72
NAB, 7, 71, 74–75 *(See also New American Bible)*
oral and written transmission of text, 6
principles associated with, 68–70
status and authority of, 64, 65, 66
table of modern English translations, 71
transmission history, 6
of Ezekiel, 334–35
of Jeremiah, 308–9
John, Gospel of, 412–13
of Pentateuch, 94
Trent, Council of
canon formed under, 4, 26, 230, 319
on interpretation of scripture, 64
Missal set in use by, 77
Trinity, 61
Trito-Isaiah, 291–92, 293
Trito-Zechariah, 365
tropological or moral approach to Bible, 18, 62
Tutankhamun, Pharaoh, 118
twelve minor prophets. *See* minor or latter prophets
twelve tribes of Israel
migration of Dan and decimation of Benjamin in Judges, 163–64
role in Numbers, 139–40, 140
"two-source hypothesis," 372
Tyconius, 57
Tyndale, William, 63
typological (allegorical) approach to Bible, 17–18, 54–58, 60, 62

U

Ugaritic texts, 21
unclean and clean. *See* purity laws
United Monarchy, 45–47. *See also* David; Saul; Solomon
unity of Church. *See also* community, Christian stress on
Ephesians on, 472–73
Philippians on, 475, 476–77
universalism. *See* ecumenical movement; entries at inclusive; Gentiles and Christianity; salvation
Urban IV, Pope, 62
Uriah the Hittite, 181, 189

V

vanity as theme of Ecclesiastes, 263, 265
Vashti, Queen of Persia, 223
Vatican II. *See* Second Vatican Council
The Venerable Bede, 58
verses. *See* chapters and verses
versions of biblical text. *See* transmission history
Victorine canons, interpretive school of, 59–60
Vio, Thomas de (Cardinal Cajetan), 64
virginity
in 1 Corinthians, 453–54
of Mary, significance of, 402–3
Vulgate (Latin editions of Bible)
alternative readings established in Correctium Bibliae, 61
Clarius's, 64
Erasmus's, 18, 63
Jerome's, 57, 63, 64, 199
status and authority for purposes of dogma, 64, 65, 66

W

Walafrid of Strabo, 58, 59
"the way of wisdom" in Proverbs, 256, 257–58
wealth. *See* material possessions
Wellhausen, Julius, 65, 91

wisdom literature, 235–36. *See also* Ecclesiastes; Job; Proverbs
in Baruch, 317–18
Hellenization and, 272
humanist stress on individual behavior in, 235–36, 258–60
New Testament influence of, 275
personification of Wisdom in, 260–61, 274–75
psalms regarded as, 245–46, 249, 253
retribution, theory of, 236, 238–39, 277–78
Sirach (Ecclesiasticus), 276–79, 315
Solomon's association with, 255, 262–63, 267, 272, 274
Song of Songs as form of, 271
Wisdom (of Solomon), 272–76
wisdom, Paul on, 464
women. *See also* gender issues, marriage, and specific women in the Bible, e.g. Deborah
childless widows in Ruth, 166
in 1 Corinthians, 456
in Ezekiel, 330
"household code" of New Testament Epistles, 480, 488
Judith
composite nature of heroine in, 219–20
as model for image of women in Church, 221
in Luke, 399–402, 405–6, 410–11
1 Peter on, 509
Sirach on, 278
Song of Songs' portrayal of, 270–71
in 1 Timothy, 488
in Titus, 492
Wisdom, personification of, 260–61
in Zechariah, 366
world, relationship of Christians to
James, friendship with God or world in, 504–5
Luke on what is due to Caesar and God, 408
1 Peter on, 508–9
worship. *See* Lectionary; liturgy
Wright, G. Ernest, 31, 41
written evidence. *See* documentary evidence

Y

Yadin, Yigael, 31
Yahwist source (J), 91, 92
in Genesis, 102, 103
in Leviticus, 129
in Numbers, 137, 141

Z

Zechariah, 365–68
guide to reading specific passages, 367–68
dating of, 344
eschatology in, 368
main themes and theology of, 344, 345
multiple authorship of, 365–66
portrayal of community leaders in, 366
ritual, appreciation of, 366–67
Zechariah father of John the Baptist in Luke, 401–2
Zedekiah, 197, 204, 297, 298–99, 321
Zenon papyri, 52
Zephaniah, 344, 345, 363–64
Zerubabbel, 51, 366
Zionism. *See* nationalism, Jewish

COLLABORATORS
on the Old Testament of the *New American Bible* 1970

BISHOPS' COMMITTEE OF THE CONFRATERNITY OF CHRISTIAN DOCTRINE

Most Rev. Charles P. Greco, D.D., *Chairman* Most Rev. Joseph T. McGucken, S.T.D. Most Rev. Vincent S. Waters, D.D.
Most Rev. Romeo Blanchette, D.D. Most Rev. Christopher J. Weldon, D.D.

EDITORS IN CHIEF

Rev. Louis F. Hartman, C.SS.R., S.S.L., LING. OR. L., *Chairman* Rev. Msgr. Patrick W. Skehan, S.T.D., LL.D., *Vice-Chairman*
Rev. Stephen J. Hartdegen, O.F.M., S.S.L., *Secretary*

ASSOCIATE EDITORS AND TRANSLATORS

Rev. Edward P. Arbez, S.S., S.T.D. Rev. Msgr. Edward J. Byrne, PH.D., S.T.D. Rev. Edward A. Cerny, S.S., S.T.D.
Rev. James E. Coleran, S.J., S.T.L., S.S.L. Rev. John J. Collins, S.J., M.A., S.S.L.
Sr. M. Emmanuel Collins, O.S.F., PH.D. Prof. Frank M. Cross Jr., PH.D. Rev. Patrick Cummins, O.S.B., S.T.D.
Rev. Antonine A. DeGuglielmo, O.F.M., S.T.D., S.S.L., S.S.LECT. GEN. Rev. Alexander A. Di Lella, O.F.M., S.T.L., S.S.L., PH.D.
Most Rev. John J. Dougherty, S.T.L., S.S.D. William A. Dowd, S.J., S.T.D., S.S.L. Prof. David Noel Freedman, PH.D.
Rev. Michael J. Fruenthaner, S.J., S.T.D., S.S.D. Rev. Msgr. Maurice A. Hofer, S.S.L Rev. Justin Krellner, O.S.B., S.T.D.
Rev. Joseph L. Lilly, C.M., S.T.D., S.S.L. Rev. Roderick F. MacKenzie, S.J., M.A., S.S.D.
Rev. Edward A. Mangan, C.SS.R., S.S.L. Rev. Daniel W. Martin, C.M., S.T.L., S.S.L. Rev. William H. McClellan, S.J.
Rev. James McGlinchey, C.M., S.T.D. Rev. Frederick Moriarty, S.J., S.S.L., S.T.D. Rev. Richard T. Murphy, O.P., S.T.D., S.S.D.
Rev. Roland E. Murphy, O. CARM., M.A., S.T.D., S.S.L. Rev. Msgr. William R. Newton, M.S., S.S.D.
Rev. Everhard Olinger, O.S.B. Rev. Charles H. Pickar, O.S.A., S.T.L., S.S.L.
Rev. Christopher Rehwinkel, O.F.M., S.T.D., S.S. LECT. GEN. Rev. Msgr. John R. Rowan, S.T.D., S.S.L.,
Prof. J.A. Sanders, PH.D. Rev. Edward F. Siegman, C.PP.S., S.T.D., S.S.L. Rev. Msgr. Matthew P. Stapleton, S.T.D., S.S.L.
Rev. Msgr. John E. Steinmueller, S.T.D., S.S.L. Rev. John Ujlaki, O.S.B., LITT.D.
Rev. Bruce Vawter, C.M., S.T.L., S.S.D. Rev. John B. Weisengoff, S.T.D., S.S.L.

COLLABORATORS
on the Revised Psalms of the *New American Bible* 1991

BISHOPS' AD HOC COMMITTEE

Most Rev. Enrique San Pedro, S.J. Most Rev. Richard Sklba, D.D. Most Rev. Donald W. Trautman, S.T.D., S.S.L.
Most Rev. Emil A. Wcela Most Rev. John F. Whealon, S.S.L., *Chairman*

BOARD OF EDITORS

Rev. Richard Clifford, S.J. Br. Aloysius Fitzgerald, F.S.C. Rev. Joseph Jensen, O.S.B. Rev. Roland Murphy, O.CARM.
Sr. Irene Nowell, O.S.B. Dr. Judith Sanderson

REVISERS

Prof. Gary Anderson Rev. Michael L. Barré, S.S. Rev. Christopher T. Begg Dr. Joseph Blenkinsopp
Rev. Anthony R. Ceresko, O.S.F.S. Rev. Richard J. Clifford, S.J. Rev. Aelred Cody, O.S.B. Prof. Michael D. Coogan
Rev. Alexander A. Di Lella, O.F.M. Dr. Robert A. Di Vito Br. Aloysius Fitzgerald, F.S.C. Rev. Michael D. Guinan, O.F.M.
Rev. William L. Holladay Rev. William Irwin, C.S.B. Rev. Joseph Jensen, O.S.B. Rev. John S. Kselman
Rev. Leo Laberge, O.M.I. Dr. Conrad E. L'Heureux Dr. Paul G. Mosca Rev. Dr. Roland E. Murphy, O.CARM.
Dr. Michael Patrick O'Connor Rev. Brian J. Peckham, S.J. Prof. Jimmy J. Roberts Sr. Eileen M. Schuller, O.S.U.
Dr. Byron E. Shafer Prof. Mark S. Smith Prof. Matitiahu Tesvat Dr. Eugene C. Ulrich
Prof. James C. VanderKam Rev. Jerome T. Walsh

ENGLISH CONSULTANTS

Dr. Catherine Dunn
Br. Daniel Burke, F.S.C.

BUSINESS MANAGER

Charles A. Buggé

COLLABORATORS
on the Revised New Testament of the *New American Bible* 1986

BISHOPS' AD HOC COMMITTEE

Most Rev. Theodore E. McCarrick, D.D. Most Rev. Richard J. Sklba, D.D. Most Rev. J. Francis Stafford, D.D.
Most Rev. John F. Whealon, D.D., *Chairman*

BOARD OF EDITORS

Rev. Msgr. Myles M. Bourke Rev. Francis T. Gignac, S.J., *Chairman*
Rev. Stephen J. Hartdegen, O.F.M., *Secretary* Rev. John H. Reumann

REVISERS

Rev. Msgr. Myles M. Bourke Rev. Frederick W. Danker Rev. Alexander A. Di Lella, O.F.M. Rev. Charles H. Giblin, S.J.
Rev. Francis T. Gignac, S.J. Rev. Stephen J. Hartdegen, O.F.M. Dr. Maurya P. Horgan Rev. John R. Keating, S.J.
Rev. John Knox Dr. Paul J. Kobelski Dr. J. Rebecca Lyman Br. Elliott C. Maloney, O.S.B. Dr. Janet A. Timbie

CONSULTANTS

Rev. Joseph Jensen, O.S.B. Rev. Aidan Kavanagh, O.S.B. Dr. Marianne Sawicki

BUSINESS MANAGER

Charles A. Buggé

WORD PROCESSOR

Suzanna Jordan

COLLABORATORS
on the Old Testament of the *New American Bible* 2010

BISHOPS' COMMITTEE ON DOCTRINE
SUBCOMMITTEE ON THE TRANSLATION OF SCRIPTURE TEXT

Most Rev. Arthur J. Serratelli, *Chairman* Justin Cardinal Rigali Most Rev. Blase J. Cupich
Most Rev. Richard J. Sklba Most Rev. Anthony B. Taylor

BOARD OF EDITORS

Dr. Deirdre A. Dempsey Dr. Robert A. Di Vito Rev. Francis T. Gignac, S.J. Rev. Joseph Jensen, O.S.B., *Chairman*
Rev. Dale Lauderville, O.S.B. Rev. Roland E. Murphy, O.CARM. + Dr. Kathleen S. Nash
Sr. Irene Nowell, O.S.B. Rev. James P. M. Walsh, S.J.

REVISERS

Dr. Gary A. Anderson Reverend Michael L. Barré, S.S. Reverend Christopher T. Begg Dr. Joseph Blenkinsopp
Reverend Lawrence Boadt, C.S.P. + Professor Edward F. Campbell Professor Anthony Ceresko, OSFS +
Reverend Richard J. Clifford, S.J. Reverend Aelred Cody, O.S.B. Dr. John J. Collins Professor Michael D. Coogan
Reverend T.J. Jeremy Corley Dr. Toni Craven Dr. James L. Crenshaw Reverend Alexander A. Di Lella, O.F.M.
Dr. Robert A. Di Vito Brother Aloysius Fitzgerald, F.S.C. + Reverend Joseph A. Fitzmyer, S.J. Dr. Carole R. Fontaine
Reverend Daniel J. Harrington, S.J. Dr. Richard S. Hess Dr. Theodore Hiebert Dr. William L. Holladay Dr. Tod Linafelt
Dr. P. Kyle McCarter, Jr. Dr. Carol Meyers Dr. Eric Meyers Dr. Patrick D. Miller, Jr.
Reverend Craig E. Morrison, O. CARM. Dr. Paul G. Mosca Dr. Kathleen S. Nash Professor Robert A. Oden, Jr.
Reverend Gregory J. Polan, O.S.B. Dr. James J.M. Roberts Dr. William M. Soll Dr. Gene M. Tucker
Dr. Eugene C. Ulrich Reverend Walter A. Vogels, W.F. Reverend Jerome T. Walsh
Reverend Addison G. Wright, S.S. Dr. David P. Wright

BUSINESS MANAGERS

Charles Buggé Mary Elizabeth Sperry

WORD PROCESSORS

Ellen Coughlin Nancy Hartnagel

COLLABORATORS
on the Book of Psalms of the *New American Bible* 2010

BISHOPS' COMMITTEE ON DOCTRINE

SUBCOMMITTEE ON THE TRANSLATION OF SCRIPTURE TEXT

Most Rev. Arthur J. Serratelli, *Chairman* Justin Cardinal Rigali Most Rev. Blase J. Cupich
Most Rev. Richard J. Sklba Most Rev. Anthony B. Taylor

BOARD OF EDITORS

Rev. Joseph Mindling, OFM CAP. Rev. J. Edward Owens, O.SS.T.

REVISERS

Rev. Michael L. Barré, S.S. Dr. Corrine L. Carvalho Dr. Robert A. Di Vito Dr. Robert D. Miller II, SFO
Rev. Joseph Mindling, OFM CAP. Rev. J. Edward Owens, O.SS.T. Dr. Eugene C. Ulrich

BUSINESS MANAGER

Mary Elizabeth Sperry

A CONCORDANCE TO THE *NEW AMERICAN BIBLE*

SPECIAL SYMBOLS

*	*GOD, *LORD and *LORD'S index the proper name of God *(Yahweh)* typeset in small capital letters (GOD, LORD, LORD's) in the NAB.
→	An arrow following an entry heading points to related words for additional study
=	An equals sign marks an alternate proper name for additional study (e.g., ISRAEL = JACOB)

John R. Kohlenberger III

TABLE OF ABBREVIATIONS

Acts	Acts
Am	Amos
Bar.	Baruch
1 Chr.	1 Chronicles
2 Chr.	2 Chronicles
1 Cor	1 Corinthians
2 Cor	2 Corinthians
Col.	Colossians
Dn	Daniel
Dt	Deuteronomy
Eccl	Ecclesiastes
Eph	Ephesians
Est.	Esther
Ex	Exodus
Ez	Ezekiel
Ezr.	Ezra
Gal	Galatians
Gn	Genesis
Hb.	Habakkuk
Hg	Haggai
Heb	Hebrews
Hos	Hosea
Is	Isaiah
Jas	James
Jgs	Judges
Jdt	Judith
Jb.	Job
Jl.	Joel
Jer.	Jeremiah
Jn.	John
1 Jn.	1 John
2 Jn.	2 John
3 Jn.	3 John
Jon	Jonah
Jos	Joshua
Jude	Jude
1 Kgs	1 Kings
2 Kgs	2 Kings
Lam.	Lamentations
Lk	Luke
Lv.	Leviticus
Mal	Malachi
1 Mc.	1 Maccabees
2 Mc.	2 Maccabees
Mi	Micah
Mk	Mark
Mt	Matthew
Na	Nahum
Neh.	Nehemiah
Nm	Numbers
Ob	Obadiah
Phil	Philippians
Phlm	Philemon
1 Pt	1 Peter
2 Pt	2 Peter
Prv	Proverbs
Ps.	Psalms
Rev	Revelation
Rom	Romans
Ru	Ruth
1 Sm.	1 Samuel
2 Sm.	2 Samuel
Sir	Sirach
Sg	Song of Songs
Tb	Tobit
1 Thes	1 Thessalonians
2 Thes	2 Thessalonians
Ti	Titus
1 Tm.	1 Timothy
2 Tm.	2 Timothy
Wis	Wisdom
Zec	Zechariah
Zep.	Zephaniah

OTHER

S	Shorter Ending of Mark
Pr:	Sirach Prologue

A

AARON

Genealogy (Ex 6:16-20; Jos 21:4, 10; 1 Ch 6:3-15). Priesthood of (Ex 28:1; Nm 17; Heb 5:1-4; 7), vestments of (Ex 28; 39), consecration of (Ex 29), ordination of (Lv 8).

Spokesman for Moses (Ex 4:14-16, 27–31; 7:1-2). Supported Moses' hands in battle (Ex 17:8-13). Built golden calf (Ex 32; Dt 9:20). Spoke against Moses (Nm 12). Priesthood opposed (Nm 16); staff budded (Nm 17). Forbidden to enter the promised land (Nm 20:1-12). Death of (Nm 20:22-29; 33:38-39). Praise of (Sir 45:6-22).

ABANDON → ABANDONED

Dt	4:31	God, he will not **a** or destroy you,
2 Ch	15:2	but if you **a** him, he will **a** you.
Acts	2:27	because you will not **a** my soul

ABANDONED → ABANDON

Jgs	2:13	Because they had **a** the LORD
2 Ch	12:5	You have **a** me, and so I have **a** you
Sir	49:4	They **a** the Law of the Most High,
Is	54:7	For a brief moment I **a** you,

ABBA

Mk	14:36	he said, "**A**, Father, all things are
Rom	8:15	through which we cry, "**A**, Father!"
Gal	4:6	our hearts, crying out, "**A**, Father!"

ABEDNEGO → =AZARIAH

Deported to Babylon with Daniel (Dn 1:1-6). Name changed from Azariah (Dn 1:7). Refused defilement by food (Dn 1:8-20). Refused idol worship (Dn 3:1-12); saved from furnace (Dn 3:13-30).

ABEL

Second son of Adam (Gn 4:2). Offered acceptable sacrifice (Gn 4:4; Heb 11:4; 12:24). Murdered by Cain (Gn 4:8; Mt 23:35; Lk 11:51; 1 Jn 3:12).

ABIATHAR

High priest in days of Saul and David (1 Sm 22; 2 Sm 15; 1 Kgs 1–2; Mk 2:26). Escaped Saul's slaughter of priests (1 Sm 22:18-23). Supported David in Absalom's revolt (2 Sm 15:24-29). Supported Adonijah (1 Kgs 1:7-42); deposed by Solomon (1 Kgs 2:22-35; cf. 1 Sm 2:31-35).

ABIDE

Ps	15:1	LORD, who may **a** in your tent?
	91:1	who **a** in the shade of the Almighty,
Wis	3:9	the faithful shall **a** with him in love:

ABIGAIL

1. Sister of David (1 Ch 2:16-17).

2. Wife of Nabal (1 Sm 25:30); pled for his life with David (1 Sm 25:14-35). Became David's wife after Nabal's death (1 Sm 25:36-42).

ABIHU

Son of Aaron (Ex 6:23; 24:1, 9); killed for offering illicit fire (Lv 10; Nm 3:2-4; 1 Ch 24:1-2).

ABIJAH

1. Second son of Samuel (1 Ch 6:28); a corrupt judge (1 Sm 8:1-5).

2. An Aaronic priest (1 Ch 24:10; Lk 1:5).

3. Son of Jeroboam I; died as prophesied by Ahijah (1 Kgs 14:1-18).

4. Son of Rehoboam, also called Abijam; king of Judah who fought Jeroboam I attempting to reunite Israel (1 Kgs 14:31–15:8; 2 Ch 12:16–14:1).

ABILITY → ABLE

Mt	25:15	to each according to his **a**.

ABIMELECH

1. King of Gerar who took Abraham's wife Sarah, believing her to be his sister (Gn 20). Covenanted with Abraham (Gn 21:22-33).

2. King of Gerar who took Isaac's wife Rebekah, believing her to be his sister (Gn 26:1-11). Covenanted with Isaac (Gn 26:12-31).

3. Son of Gideon (Jgs 8:31). Attempted to become king (Jgs 9).

ABIRAM

Sided with Dathan in rebellion against Moses and Aaron (Nm 16; 26:9; Dt 11:6; Sir 45:18).

ABISHAI

Son of Zeruiah, David's sister (1 Sm 26:6; 1 Ch 2:16). One of David's chief warriors (1 Ch 11:15-21): against Edom (1 Ch 18:12-13), Ammon (2 Sm 10), Absalom (2 Sm 18), Sheba (2 Sm 20). Wanted to kill Saul (1 Sm 26), killed Abner (2 Sm 2:18-27; 3:22-39).

ABLE → ABILITY

Ex	18:25	He picked out **a** men from all Israel
Jdt	11:18	of them will be **a** to withstand you.
Rom	14:4	for the Lord is **a** to make him stand.
2 Cor	9:8	God is **a** to make every grace
Eph	6:11	you may be **a** to stand firm against
2 Tm	1:12	that he is **a** to guard what has been
Heb	2:18	he is **a** to help those who are being
	5:2	He is **a** to deal patiently
	7:25	he is always **a** to save those who
Rev	5:3	or under the earth was **a** to open

ABNER

Cousin of Saul and commander of his army (1 Sm 14:50; 17:55-57; 26). Made Ish-Bosheth king after Saul (2 Sm 2:8-10), but later defected to David (2 Sm 3:6-21). Killed Asahel (2 Sm 2:18-32), for which he was killed by Joab and Abishai (2 Sm 3:22-39).

ABOLISH → ABOLISHING

Mt	5:17	think that I have come to **a** the law
	5:17	I have come not to **a** but to fulfill.

ABOLISHING → ABOLISH

Dn	11:31	**a** the daily sacrifice and setting

ABOMINABLE → ABOMINATION

2 Ch	28:3	accordance with the **a** practices
Ez	7:20	of them they made their **a** images,

ABOMINATION → ABOMINABLE, ABOMINATIONS

1 Mc	6:7	they had pulled down the **a**
Prv	6:16	hates, yes, seven are an **a** to him;
Dn	9:27	be the desolating **a** until the ruin

ABOMINATIONS → ABOMINATION

Ez	44:7	broken my covenant by all your **a**.
Rev	17:5	of harlots and of the **a** of the earth."

ABOUND

Rom	6:1	we persist in sin that grace may **a**?

ABOVE

Dt	4:39	the LORD is God in the heavens **a**
Jn	3:7	you, 'You must be born from **a**.'
Phil	2:9	him the name that is **a** every name,
Col	3:2	Think of what is **a**, not of what is

ABRAHAM

Abram, son of Terah (Gn 11:26-27), husband of Sarah (Gn 11:29).

Covenant relation with the LORD (Gn 12:1-3; 13:14-17; 15; 17; 22:15-18; Ex 2:24; Neh 9:8; Ps 105; Mi 7:20; Lk 1:68-75; Rom 4; Heb 6:13-15).

Called from Ur, via Haran, to Canaan (Gn 12:1; Acts 7:2-4; Heb 11:8-10). Moved to Egypt, nearly lost Sarah to Pharoah (Gn

12:10-20). Divided the land with Lot; settled in Hebron (Gn 13). Saved Lot from four kings (Gn 14:1-16); blessed by Melchizedek (Gn 14:17-20; Heb 7:1-20). Declared righteous by faith (Gn 15:6; Rom 4:3; Gal 3:6-9; 1 Mc 2:52). Fathered Ishmael by Hagar (Gn 16).

Name changed from Abram (Gn 17:5; Neh 9:7). Circumcised (Gn 17; Rom 4:9-12). Entertained three visitors (Gn 18); promised a son by Sarah (Gn 18:9-15; 17:16). Questioned destruction of Sodom and Gomorrah (Gn 18:16-33). Moved to Gerar; nearly lost Sarah to Abimelech (Gn 20). Fathered Isaac by Sarah (Gn 21:1-7; Acts 7:8; Heb 11:11-12); sent away Hagar and Ishmael (Gn 21:8-21; Gal 4:22-30). Covenant with Abimelech (Gn 21:22-32). Tested by offering Isaac (Gn 22; Heb 11:17-19; Jas 2:21-24). Sarah died; bought field of Ephron for burial (Gn 23). Secured wife for Isaac (Gn 24). Fathered children by Keturah (Gn 25:1-6; 1 Ch 1:32-33). Death (Gn 25:7-11).

Called servant of God (Gn 26:24), friend of God (2 Ch 20:7; Is 41:8; Jas 2:23), prophet (Gn 20:7), father of Israel (Ex 3:15; Is 51:2; Mt 3:9; Jn 8:39-58). Praised (Sir 44:19–45:1).

ABSALOM

Son of David by Maacah (2 Sm 3:3; 1 Ch 3:2). Killed Amnon for rape of his sister Tamar; banished by David (2 Sm 13). Returned to Jerusalem; received by David (2 Sm 14). Rebelled against David (2 Sm 15–17). Killed (2 Sm 18).

ABSENT

1 Cor 5: 3 although **a** in body but present
Col 2: 5 For even if I am **a** in the flesh, yet I

ABUNDANCE → ABUNDANTLY

2 Cor 9: 8 you may have an **a** for every good

ABUNDANTLY → ABUNDANCE

Jn 10: 10 might have life and have it more **a**.

ABYSS

Lk 8: 31 not to order them to depart to the **a**.
Rom 10: 7 or 'Who will go down into the **a**?'

ACCEPT → ACCEPTED

Mt 19: 11 "Not all can **a** [this] word, but only
Jn 1: 11 but his own people did not **a** him.

ACCEPTED → ACCEPT

Lk 4: 24 no prophet is **a** in his own native

ACCESS

Rom 5: 2 through whom we have gained **a**
Eph 2: 18 through him we both have **a** in one

ACCORDING

Sir 16: 12 judges people, each **a** to their deeds.
Mt 9: 29 it be done for you **a** to your faith."
Rom 8: 4 who live not **a** to the flesh but **a**
Heb 2: 4 gifts of the holy Spirit **a** to his will.
1 Jn 5: 14 that if we ask anything **a** to his will,
Rev 20: 12 The dead were judged **a** to their

ACCOUNT

Mt 12: 36 of judgment people will render an **a**
Heb 4: 13 him to whom we must render an **a**.

ACCURSED → CURSE

Rom 9: 3 I could wish that I myself were **a**
Rev 22: 3 Nothing **a** will be found there

ACCUSE → ACCUSER

Zec 3: 1 stood at his right side to **a** him.
Mt 12: 10 so that they might **a** him.

ACCUSER → ACCUSE

Rev 12: 10 For the **a** of our brothers is cast out,

ACHAN

Sinned at Jericho; stoned (Jos 7; 22:20; 1 Ch 2:7).

ACHISH

King of Gath before whom David feigned insanity (1 Sm 21:10-15). Later "ally" of David (2 Sm 27–29).

ACKNOWLEDGE

Mt 10: 32 others I will **a** before my heavenly
Rom 1: 28 since they did not see fit to **a** God,

ACT → ACTED, ACTIVE, ACTS

Ps 37: 5 trust in him and he will **a**

ACTED → ACT

Ez 20: 9 I **a** for the sake of my name, that it
Acts 3: 17 that you **a** out of ignorance, just as
1 Tm 1: 13 been mercifully treated because I **a**

ACTIVE → ACT

Jas 2: 22 faith was **a** along with his works,

ACTS → ACT

Ex 6: 6 arm and with mighty **a** of judgment.
Ps 71: 15 day after day your **a** of deliverance,
Mt 7: 24 **a** on them will be like a wise man
Jas 1: 25 who forgets but a doer who **a**,

ADAM

First man (Tb 8:6; Gn 1:26–2:25; Rom 5:14; 1 Tm 2:13). Sin of (Gn 3; Hos 6:7 [note]; Rom 5:12-21). Children of (Gn 4:1–5:5). Death of (Gn 5:5; Rom 5:12-21; 1 Cor 15:22).

ADD

Dt 4: 2 you shall not **a** to what I command
Prv 30: 6 **A** nothing to his words, lest he
Lk 12: 25 of you by worrying **a** a moment

ADMONISH

Col 3: 16 you teach and **a** one another,

ADONIJAH

1. Son of David by Haggith (2 Sm 3:4; 1 Ch 3:2). Attempted to be king after David; killed at Solomon's order (1 Kgs 1–2).

2. Levite; teacher of the Law (2 Ch 17:8).

ADOPTION

Rom 8: 15 fear, but you received a spirit of **a**,
8: 23 within ourselves as we wait for **a**,
Gal 4: 5 the law, so that we might receive **a**.

ADORNED → ADORNMENT

Lk 21: 5 how the temple was **a** with costly
Rev 17: 4 purple and scarlet and **a** with gold,
21: 2 God, prepared as a bride **a** for her

ADORNMENT → ADORNED

Prv 3: 22 to your soul, and an **a** for your neck.

ADULTERERS → ADULTERY

Jer 23: 10 The land is filled with **a**;
1 Cor 6: 9 nor idolaters nor **a** nor boy

ADULTERESS → ADULTERY

Lv 20: 10 and the **a** shall be put to death.

ADULTERY → ADULTERERS, ADULTERESS

Ex 20: 14 You shall not commit **a**.
Jer 3: 9 committing **a** with stone and wood.
Mt 5: 28 lust has already committed **a**
Lk 16: 18 and marries another commits **a**,
Jn 8: 3 a woman who had been caught in **a**

ADVANTAGE

Rom 3: 1 What **a** is there then in being a Jew?
1 Cor 10: 24 No one should seek his own **a**,

ADVERSARIES → ADVERSARY

2 Sm 22: 49 you have exalted me above my **a**,

ADVERSARY

Zec 3: 2 angel of the LORD said to the **a**,

1 Tm 5:14 so as to give the a no pretext

ADVICE
2 Ch 10:13 Ignoring the a the elders had given
Tb 4:18 do not think lightly of any useful a.
Prv 8:14 Mine are counsel and a;
Sir 37:11 Seek no a from a woman about her

ADVOCATE
Jn 14:26 The A, the holy Spirit
15:26 the A comes whom I will send you
1 Jn 2:1 sin, we have an A with the Father,

AFFLICTED → AFFLICTION
2 Cor 4:8 We are a in every way, but not

AFFLICTION → AFFLICTED
Dt 16:3 the bread of a, so that you may
Ps 25:18 Look upon my a and suffering;
2 Cor 4:17 this momentary light a is producing

AFRAID → FEAR
Gn 3:10 but I was a, because I was naked,
Ex 3:6 face, for he was a to look at God.
Dt 20:3 Do not be weakhearted or a,
Mt 10:31 So do not be a; you are worth more
28:10 Jesus said to them, "Do not be a.
Lk 12:32 Do not be a any longer, little flock,
Heb 13:6 is my helper, [and] I will not be a.

AGABUS
A Christian prophet (Acts 11:28; 21:10).

AGAG
King of Amalekites; not killed by Saul (1 Sm 15).

AGAIN
Jb 14:14 to die, and live a, all the days of my
Jn 14:3 I will come back a and take you
Heb 6:6 to bring them to repentance a,

AGE → AGES
Gn 21:2 bore Abraham a son in his old a,
Mt 28:20 you always, until the end of the a."
Gal 1:4 us from the present evil a in accord

AGES → AGE
1 Cor 2:7 God predetermined before the a
Col 1:26 the mystery hidden from a
1 Tm 1:17 To the king of a, incorruptible,

AGREE
Mt 18:19 you, if two of you a on earth
Mk 14:56 him, but their testimony did not a.

AGRIPPA
Descendant of Herod; king before whom Paul argued his case in Caesarea (Acts 25:13–26:32).

AHAB
1. Son of Omri; king of Israel (1 Kgs 16:28–22:40), husband of Jezebel (1 Kgs 16:31). Promoted Baal worship (1 Kgs 16:31-33); opposed by Elijah (1 Kgs 17:1; 18; 21), a prophet (1 Kgs 20:35-43), Micaiah (1 Kgs 22:1-28). Defeated Ben-Hadad (1 Kgs 20). Killed for failing to kill Ben-Hadad and for murder of Naboth (1 Kgs 20:35–21:40).
2. A false prophet (Jer 29:21-22).

AHASUERUS → =ARTAXERXES
King of Persia (Ezr 4:6), husband of Esther (called Artaxerxes in Est 11:1; 12:2; 13:1; 16:1). Deposed Vashti; replaced her with Esther (Est 1–2). Sealed Haman's edict to annihilate the Jews (Est 3). Received Esther without having called her (Est 5:1-8). Honored Mordecai (Est 6). Hanged Haman (Est 7). Issued edict allowing Jews to defend themselves (Est 8). Promoted Mordecai (Est 8:1-2, 15; 9:4; 10).

AHAZ
Son of Jotham; king of Judah, (2 Kgs 16; 2 Ch 28; Mt 1:9). Idolatry of (2 Kgs 16:3-4, 10-18; 2 Ch 28:1-4, 22-25). Defeated by Aram and Israel (2 Kgs 16:5-6; 2 Ch 28:5-15). Sought help from Assyria rather than the LORD (2 Kgs 16:7-9; 2 Ch 28:16-21; Is 7).

AHAZIAH → =JEHOAHAZ
1. Son of Ahab; king of Israel (1 Kgs 22:51-2 Kgs 1:18; 2 Ch 20:35-37). Made an unsuccessful alliance with Jehoshaphat (2 Ch 20:35-37). Died for seeking Baal rather than the LORD (2 Kgs 1).
2. Son of Jehoram; king of Judah (2 Kgs 8:25-29; 9:14-29), also called Jehoahaz (2 Ch 21:17–22:9; 25:23). Killed by Jehu while visiting Joram (2 Kgs 9:14-29; 2 Ch 22:1-9).

AHEAD
Mt 11:10 I am sending my messenger a
Phil 3:13 but straining forward to what lies a,

AHIJAH
1. Priest during Saul's reign (1 Sm 14:3,18).
2. Prophet of Shiloh (1 Kgs 11:29-39; 14:1-18).

AHIKAM
Father of Gedaliah (2 Kgs 25:22), protector of Jeremiah (Jer 26:24).

AHIMAAZ
1. Father-in-law of Saul (1 Sm 14:50).
2. Son of Zadok, the high priest, loyal to David (2 Sm 15:27,36; 17:17-20; 18:19-33).

AHIMELECH
1. Priest who helped David in his flight from Saul (1 Sm 21–22).
2. One of David's warriors (1 Sm 26:6).

AHITHOPHEL
One of David's counselors who sided with Absalom (2 Sm 15:12, 31-37; 1 Ch 27:33-34); committed suicide when his advice was ignored (2 Sm 16:15–17:23).

AI
Jos 7:4 but they fled before the army at A,

AIR
Eph 2:2 the ruler of the power of the a,
1 Thes 4:17 the clouds to meet the Lord in the a.
Rev 16:17 poured out his bowl into the a.

ALARMED
Mk 13:7 and reports of wars do not be a;
2 Thes 2:2 or to be a either by a "spirit,"

ALEXANDER
1 Mc 1:1 After A the Macedonian,

ALIEN → ALIENS
Lv 19:34 you shall love the a as yourself;
Dt 24:17 You shall not deprive the resident a

ALIENS → ALIEN
Gn 15:13 your descendants will reside as a
1 Pt 2:11 I urge you as a and sojourners

ALIVE → LIVE
Gn 6:19 to keep them a along with you.
Acts 1:3 He presented himself a to them
1 Thes 4:17 Then we who are a, who are left,
Rev 1:18 but now I am a forever and ever.
19:20 The two were thrown a

ALL
Gn 6:13 that the end of a mortals has come,
Dt 8:3 by a that comes forth from the mouth
Sir 7:29 With a your soul fear God
Jer 29:13 you seek me with a your heart,
Lk 10:27 God, with a your heart, with a your

Rom 3:23 **a** have sinned and are deprived
6:10 death, he died to sin once and for **a**;
1 Cor 15:51 We shall not **a** fall asleep, but we will **a** be changed,
2 Cor 5:15 He indeed died for **a**, so that those
Eph 1:23 the one who fills **a** things in every
Col 3:11 but Christ is **a** and in **a**.
2 Tm 3:16 **A** scripture is inspired by God and is
2 Pt 3:9 that **a** should come to repentance.
Rev 21:5 "Behold, I make **a** things new."

ALMIGHTY → MIGHT
Gn 17:1 to Abram and said: I am God the **A**.
Ex 6:3 As God the **A** I appeared
Ps 91:1 who abide in the shade of the **A**,
Bar 3:1 "LORD **A**, God of Israel,
Rev 1:8 was and who is to come, the **a**."
21:22 for its temple is the Lord God **a**

ALMS → ALMSGIVING
Tb 12:8 It is better to give **a** than to store
Mt 6:2 When you give **a**, do not blow

ALMSGIVING → ALMS
Sir 7:10 Do not be impatient in prayer or neglect **a**.

ALONE
Gn 2:18 It is not good for the man to be **a**.
Dt 6:4 LORD is our God, the LORD **a**!
Is 2:11 and the LORD **a** will be exalted,
Mk 2:7 Who but God **a** can forgive sins?"
10:18 No one is good but God **a**.
Jas 2:24 by works and not by faith **a**.

ALPHA
Rev 1:8 "I am the **A** and the Omega,"
22:13 I am the **A** and the Omega, the first

ALTAR → ALTARS
Gn 22:9 put him on top of the wood on the **a**.
Ex 27:1 You shall make an **a** of acacia
30:1 burning incense you shall make an **a**
Ezr 3:2 began building the **a** of the God
Jdt 4:12 The **a**, too, they draped in sackcloth;
1 Mc 1:54 upon the **a** of burnt offerings,
4:47 built a new **a** like the former one.
Mt 5:24 leave your gift there at the **a**,
Heb 13:10 We have an **a** from which those
Jas 2:21 he offered his son Isaac upon the **a**?
Rev 6:9 I saw underneath the **a** the souls

ALTARS → ALTAR
Ex 34:13 Tear down their **a**;
Nm 3:31 the **a**, the utensils of the sanctuary
1 Mc 2:45 about and tore down the pagan **a**;

ALWAYS
Mt 28:20 I am with you **a**, until the end
Lk 18:1 to pray **a** without becoming weary.
Phil 4:4 Rejoice in the Lord **a**. I shall say it

AMALEK
Ex 17:8 Then **A** came and waged war
1 Sm 15:3 attack **A**, and put under the ban

AMASA
Nephew of David (1 Ch 2:17). Commander of Absalom's forces (2 Sm 17:24-27). Returned to David (2 Sm 19:13). Killed by Joab (2 Sm 20:4-13).

AMAZED
Mt 8:27 The men were **a** and said,
Mk 6:6 He was **a** at their lack of faith.

AMAZIAH
1. Son of Joash; king of Judah (2 Kgs 14; 2 Ch 25). Defeated Edom (2 Kgs 14:7; 2 Ch 25:5-13); defeated by Israel for worshiping Edom's gods (2 Kgs 14:8-14; 2 Ch 25:14-24).
2. Idolatrous priest; opposed Amos (Am 7:10-17).

AMBASSADOR → AMBASSADORS
Eph 6:20 for which I am an **a** in chains,

AMBASSADORS → AMBASSADOR
2 Cor 5:20 So we are **a** for Christ, as if God

AMBITION
Jas 3:14 and selfish **a** in your hearts, do not

AMEN
Dt 27:15 all the people shall answer, "**A**!"
2 Cor 1:20 the **A** from us also goes through him
Rev 3:14 " 'The **A**, the faithful and true

AMMONITES
Gn 19:38 He is the ancestor of the **A** of today.
Jer 49:6 I will restore the fortunes of the **A**—

AMNON
Firstborn of David (2 Sm 3:2; 1 Ch 3:1). Killed by Absalom for raping his sister Tamar (2 Sm 13).

AMON
1. Son of Manasseh; king of Judah (2 Kgs 21:18-26; 1 Ch 3:14; 2 Ch 33:21-25).
2. Ruler of Samaria (1 Kgs 22:26; 2 Ch 18:25).

AMORITES
Gn 15:16 of the **A** is not yet complete.
Nm 21:31 So Israel settled in the land of the **A**.

AMOS
Prophet from Tekoa (Am 1:1; 7:10-17; Tb 2:6).

ANANIAS
1. Early disciple; died for lying to God (Acts 5:1-11).
2. Disciple who baptized Saul (Acts 9:10-19).
3. High priest at Paul's arrest (Acts 22:30–24:1).

ANCESTORS
Acts 5:30 The God of our **a** raised Jesus,
Heb 1:1 ways to our **a** through the prophets;

ANCHOR
Heb 6:19 This we have as an **a** of the soul,

ANCIENT
Ps 24:7 be lifted, you **a** portals, that the king
Dn 7:9 and the **A** of Days took his throne.
Rev 20:2 He seized the dragon, the **a** serpent,

ANDREW
Apostle; brother of Simon Peter (Mt 4:18; 10:2; Mk 1:16-18, 29; 3:18; 13:3; Lk 6:14; Jn 1:35-44; 6:8-9; 12:22; Acts 1:13).

ANGEL → ANGELS, ARCHANGEL
Ex 3:2 There the **a** of the LORD appeared
23:20 I am sending an **a** before you,
Nm 22:22 and the **a** of the LORD took
1 Ch 21:15 sent an **a** to Jerusalem to destroy it;
Tb 5:4 found the **a** Raphael standing before
5:4 not know that this was an **a** of God).
1 Mc 7:41 your **a** went out and killed
Ps 34:8 The **a** of the LORD encamps
Is 37:36 the **a** of the LORD went forth
Dn 3:49 the **a** of the Lord went down
3:95 who sent his **a** to deliver
13:59 "for the **a** of God waits
14:34 when an **a** of the Lord told him,
Mt 1:20 the **a** of the Lord appeared to him
Lk 1:26 the **a** Gabriel was sent from God
Acts 5:19 the **a** of the Lord opened the doors
2 Cor 11:14 even Satan masquerades as an **a**
Gal 1:8 an **a** from heaven should preach

ANGELS → ANGEL
Gn 19: 1 The two **a** reached Sodom
Tb 11: 14 name, and blessed be all his holy **a**.
Ps 103: 20 all you his **a**, mighty in strength,
Mk 12: 25 but they are like the **a** in heaven.
Lk 4: 10 will command his **a** concerning you,
Jn 1: 51 opened and the **a** of God ascending
Acts 23: 8 say that there is no resurrection or **a**
Rom 8: 38 nor life, nor **a**, nor principalities,
1 Cor 6: 3 you not know that we will judge **a**?
Col 2: 18 in self-abasement and worship of **a**,
Heb 2: 7 for a little while lower than the **a**;
1 Pt 1: 12 things into which **a** longed to look.
2 Pt 2: 4 if God did not spare the **a** when they
Rev 1: 20 the seven stars are the **a** of the seven
7: 1 this I saw four **a** standing at the four
21: 12 gates where twelve **a** were stationed

ANGER → ANGRY
Ex 34: 6 slow to **a** and abounding in love
1 Kgs 16: 13 the God of Israel, to **a** by their idols.
Ps 30: 6 For his **a** lasts but a moment;
Prv 12: 16 Fools immediately show their **a**,
Is 48: 9 sake of my name I restrain my **a**,
Jl 2: 13 slow to **a**, abounding in steadfast
Jon 4: 2 slow to **a**, abounding in kindness,
Mk 3: 5 Looking around at them with **a**
Eph 4: 26 do not let the sun set on your **a**,

ANGRY → ANGER
Jer 3: 12 I will not remain **a** with you;
Mt 5: 22 whoever is **a** with his brother will

ANGUISH
Zep 1: 15 a day of distress and **a**, a day of ruin

ANIMAL → ANIMALS
Gn 1: 25 God made every kind of wild **a**, every kind of tame **a**,
Ps 50: 10 For every **a** of the forest is mine,

ANIMALS → ANIMAL
Gn 2: 19 out of the ground all the wild **a**
3: 14 this, cursed are you among all the **a**,
9: 2 come upon all the **a** of the earth

ANNA
1. Prophetess; spoke of the child Jesus (Lk 2:36-38).
2. Wife of Tobit (Tb 1:20; 2:1, 11).

ANNAS
High priest A.D. 6–15 (Lk 3:2; Jn 18:13, 24; Acts 4:6).

ANOINT → ANOINTED, ANOINTING
Ex 30: 30 and his sons you shall also **a**
1 Sm 15: 1 to **a** you king over his people Israel.
Ps 23: 5 You **a** my head with oil;

ANOINTED → ANOINT
1 Sm 2: 10 king, and exalt the horn of his **a**!"
26: 9 can lay a hand on the LORD's **a**
1 Ch 16: 22 "Do not touch my **a**, to my
Ps 2: 2 the LORD and against his **a** one:
Is 61: 1 me, because the LORD has **a** me;
Dn 9: 24 and a holy of holies will be **a**.
9: 26 sixty-two weeks an **a** one shall be
Zec 4: 14 are the two **a** ones who stand
Lk 4: 18 because he has **a** me to bring glad
Jn 1: 41 Messiah" (which is translated **A**).
12: 3 nard and **a** the feet of Jesus

ANOINTING → ANOINT
Ex 30: 25 and blend them into sacred **a** oil,
1 Jn 2: 27 the **a** that you received from him
2: 27 his **a** teaches you about everything

ANOTHER
Prv 27: 2 Let **a** praise you, not your own
Is 48: 11 My glory I will not give to **a**.
Jn 14: 16 he will give you **a** Advocate to be
Gal 1: 7 (not that there is **a**). But there are

ANSWER → ANSWERED
1 Kgs 18: 37 **A** me, LORD! **A** me, that this
Jb 30: 20 I cry to you, but you do not **a** me;
Prv 15: 1 A mild **a** turns back wrath,
Is 65: 24 Before they call, I will **a**;
Lk 23: 9 him at length, but he gave him no **a**.

ANSWERED → ANSWER
1 Ch 21: 26 who **a** him by sending down fire
Ps 118: 21 I thank you for you **a** me;

ANT
Prv 6: 6 Go to the **a**, O sluggard, study her

ANTICHRIST
1 Jn 2: 18 as you heard that the **a** was coming,
2: 22 the Father and the Son, this is the **a**.
4: 3 This is the spirit of the **a** that, as you
2 Jn 1: 7 such is the deceitful one and the **a**.

ANTIOCH
Acts 11: 26 it was in **A** that the disciples were
13: 1 were in the church at **A** prophets
Gal 2: 11 And when Cephas came to **A**,

ANTIOCHUS
Antiochus IV Epiphanes, king of the Syrian Greeks B.C. 175-164 (1 Mc 1:10-19). Plundered the temple in Jerusalem (1 Mc 1:20-28). Attempted to force the Hellenization of the Jewish people (1 Mc 1:41-53), including defiling the altar and holy place (1 Mc 1:54-64). His policies sparked the Maccabean revolt.

ANXIETIES
1 Cor 7: 32 I should like you to be free of **a**.

ANYTHING
Gn 18: 14 Is **a** too marvelous for the LORD
Jer 32: 27 Is **a** too difficult for me?
Mt 18: 19 of you agree on earth about **a**
Jn 16: 23 you will not question me about **a**.

APART
Rom 3: 21 God has been manifested **a**

APOLLOS
Christian from Alexandria, learned in the Scriptures; instructed by Aquila and Priscilla (Acts 18:24-28). At Corinth (Acts 19:1; 1 Cor 1:12; 3; Ti 3:13).

APOSTASY
1 Mc 2: 15 of enforcing the **a** came to the city

APOSTLE → APOSTLES
Rom 11: 13 then as I am the **a** to the Gentiles,
1 Cor 9: 1 Am I not an **a**? Have I not seen
2 Cor 12: 12 of an **a** were performed among you
Heb 3: 1 Jesus, the **a** and high priest of our

APOSTLES → APOSTLE
See also Andrew, Bartholomew, Barnabas, James, John, Judas, Matthew, Matthias, Nathanael, Paul, Peter, Philip, Simon, Thaddaeus, Thomas.
Mt 10: 2 names of the twelve **a** are these:
Lk 6: 13 Twelve, whom he also named **a**:
Acts 2: 43 and signs were done through the **a**.
1 Cor 12: 28 in the church to be, first, **a**;
Eph 2: 20 built upon the foundation of the **a**
4: 11 And he gave some as **a**, others as
Rev 21: 14 names of the twelve **a** of the Lamb.

APPEAL
Acts 25:11 me over to them. I **a** to Caesar."
1 Pt 3:21 an **a** to God for a clear conscience,

APPEAR → APPEARANCE, APPEARANCES, APPEARED, APPEARING
Mt 24:30 of the Son of Man will **a** in heaven,
2 Cor 5:10 we must all **a** before the judgment
Heb 9:28 sins of many, will **a** a second time,

APPEARANCE → APPEAR
1 Sm 16:7 Do not judge from his **a** or from his
16:7 not see as a mortal, who sees the **a**.
2 Cor 5:12 who boast of external **a** rather than

APPEARANCES → APPEAR
Jn 7:24 Stop judging by **a**, but judge

APPEARED → APPEAR
1 Cor 15:5 that he **a** to Cephas,
Heb 9:26 now once for all he has **a** at the end

APPEARING → APPEAR
Acts 1:3 **a** to them during forty days

APPETITES
Rom 16:18 our Lord Christ but their own **a**,

APPLE
Dt 32:10 guarded them as the **a** of his eye.

APPOINT → APPOINTED
1 Sm 8:5 your example, **a** a king over us,
Is 60:17 I will **a** peace your governor,

APPOINTED → APPOINT
Hb 1:12 LORD, you have **a** them for judgment,
Mk 3:16 [he **a** the twelve:] Simon, whom he
Acts 3:20 send you the Messiah already **a**
Heb 9:27 Just as it is **a** that human beings die

APPROACH
Heb 4:16 So let us confidently **a** the throne

AQUILA
Husband of Priscilla; co-worker with Paul, instructor of Apollos (Acts 18; Rom 16:3; 1 Cor 16:19; 2 Tm 4:19).

ARABIANS
1 Mc 5:39 they have also hired **A** to help them,

ARAM → ARAMAIC, ARAMEAN
Jgs 10:6 the gods of **A**, the gods of Sidon,
2 Ch 16:7 you relied on the king of **A** and did
16:7 king of **A** has escaped your power.

ARAMAIC → ARAM
2 Kgs 18:26 "Please speak to your servants in **A**;
Ezr 4:7 The document was written in **A**
Dn 2:4 Chaldeans answered the king in **A**:

ARAMEAN → ARAM
Dt 26:5 was a refugee **A** who went down

ARARAT
Gn 8:4 came to rest on the mountains of **A**.

ARAUNAH
2 Sm 24:16 the threshing floor of **A** the Jebusite.

ARCHANGEL → ANGEL
Jude 1:9 Yet the **a** Michael, when he argued

ARCHITECT
Heb 11:10 whose **a** and maker is God.

AREOPAGUS
Acts 17:22 Paul stood up at the **A** and said:

ARGUMENT → ARGUMENTS
Lk 9:46 An **a** arose among the disciples
1 Tm 2:8 up holy hands, without anger or **a**.

ARGUMENTS → ARGUMENT
2 Cor 10:4 We destroy **a**
Col 2:4 one may deceive you by specious **a**.

ARIMATHEA
Jn 19:38 Joseph of **A**, secretly a disciple

ARISE → ARISES, RISE
Sg 2:10 lover speaks and says to me, "**A**,
Mt 24:11 Many false prophets will **a**

ARISES → ARISE, RISE
1 Mc 14:41 until a trustworthy prophet **a**.

ARK
Gn 6:14 Make yourself an **a** of gopherwood,
Ex 25:10 You shall make an **a** of acacia
1 Sm 4:11 The **a** of God was captured,
1 Kgs 8:9 There was nothing in the **a**
2 Mc 2:4 and the **a** should accompany him,
1 Pt 3:20 Noah during the building of the **a**,
Rev 11:19 the **a** of his covenant could be seen

ARM → ARMIES, ARMOR, ARMS, ARMY
Ex 6:6 redeem you by my outstretched **a**
Dt 7:19 and outstretched **a**
2 Ch 32:8 He has only an **a** of flesh, but we
Jb 40:9 Have you an **a** like that of God,
Is 53:1 whom has the **a** of the LORD been

ARMIES → ARM
1 Sm 17:36 because he has insulted the **a**
Lk 21:20 you see Jerusalem surrounded by **a**,
Rev 19:14 The **a** of heaven followed him,

ARMOR → ARM
Wis 5:17 He shall take his zeal for **a** and arm
Rom 13:12 darkness [and] put on the **a** of light;
Eph 6:11 Put on the **a** of God so that you may

ARMS → ARM
Prv 31:17 she exerts her **a** with vigor.
Hos 11:3 to walk, who took them in my **a**;

ARMY → ARM
Ex 15:4 and **a** he hurled into the sea;
Ps 27:3 Though an **a** encamp against me,
33:16 A king is not saved by a great **a**,
Rev 19:19 riding the horse and against his **a**.

AROMA
2 Cor 2:15 For we are the **a** of Christ for God

ARRESTED
Mt 14:3 Now Herod had **a** John,
26:50 they laid hands on Jesus and **a** him.

ARROGANCE → ARROGANT
1 Mc 1:24 much blood and spoke with great **a**.
Prv 8:13 Pride, **a**, the evil way,

ARROGANT → ARROGANCE
Ps 73:3 of the **a** when I saw the prosperity
Dn 7:11 the first of the **a** words

ARROW → ARROWS
Ps 64:8 God shoots an **a** at them;
Is 49:2 He made me a sharpened **a**, in his

ARROWS → ARROW
1 Sm 20:20 month I will shoot **a** to the side

Eph 6: 16 to quench all [the] flaming **a**

ARTAXERXES → =AHASUERUS

1. King of Persia; allowed rebuilding of temple under Ezra (Ezr 4; 7), and of walls of Jerusalem under his cupbearer Nehemiah (Neh 2; 5:14; 13:6).

2. See Ahasuerus.

ARTEMIS

Acts 19: 27 of the great goddess **A** will be of no

ASA

King of Judah (1 Kgs 15:8-24; 1 Ch 3:10; 2 Ch 14–16). Godly reformer (2 Ch 15); in later years defeated Israel with help of Aram, not the LORD (1 Kgs 15:16-22; 2 Ch 16).

ASAHEL

Nephew of David, one of his warriors (2 Sm 23:24; 1 Ch 2:16; 11:26; 27:7). Killed by Abner (2 Sm 2); avenged by Joab (2 Sm 3:22-39).

ASAPH

1. Recorder to Hezekiah (2 Kgs 18:18, 37; Is 36:3, 22).

2. Levitical musician (1 Ch 6:39; 15:17-19; 16:4-7, 37), seer (2 Ch 29:30). Sons of (1 Ch 25; 2 Ch 5:12; 20:14; 29:13; 35:15; Ezr 2:41; 3:10; Neh 7:44; 11:17; 12:27-47). Psalms of (2 Ch 29:30; Ps 50; 73–83).

ASCEND → ASCENDING, ASCENTS

Ps 139: 8 If I **a** to the heavens, you are there;

ASCENDING → ASCEND

Jn 1: 51 the angels of God **a** and descending

ASCENTS → ASCEND

Songs of ascents (Ps 120-134).

ASHAMED → SHAME

Is 29: 22 No longer shall Jacob be **a**,
Mk 8: 38 Whoever is **a** of me and of my
8: 38 the Son of Man will be **a**
Rom 1: 16 For I am not **a** of the gospel.
Heb 2: 11 he is not **a** to call them "brothers,"
11: 16 God is not **a** to be called their God,

ASHER

Son of Jacob by Zilpah (Gn 30:13; 35:26; 46:17; Ex 1:4; 1 Ch 2:2). Tribe of blessed (Gn 49:20; Dt 33:24-25), numbered (Nm 1:40-41; 26:44-47), allotted land (Jos 10:24-31; Ez 48:2), failed to fully possess (Jgs 1:31-32), failed to support Deborah (Jgs 5:17), supported Gideon (Jgs 6:35; 7:23) and David (1 Ch 12:36), 12,000 from (Rev 7:6).

ASHERAH → ASHERAHS, ASTARTE

Dt 16: 21 You shall not plant an **a** of any kind
1 Kgs 18: 19 four hundred prophets of **A** who eat
2 Ch 15: 16 had made an obscene object for **A**;

ASHERAHS → ASHERAH

Jgs 3: 7 and served the Baals and the **A**,
2 Kgs 17: 10 They set up pillars and **a** for themselves

ASHES

Gn 18: 27 Lord, though I am only dust and **a**!
Jdt 4: 11 and sprinkled **a** on their heads,
Est 4: 1 put on sackcloth and **a**, and went
Jb 42: 6 have said, and repent in dust and **a**.
Jon 3: 6 himself with sackcloth, and sat in **a**.
Mt 11: 21 have repented in sackcloth and **a**.

ASIA

Acts 16: 6 the message in the province of **A**.
Rev 1: 4 John, to the seven churches in **A**:

ASIDE → SIDE

Ex 32: 8 They have quickly turned **a**
Dt 28: 14 not turning **a**, either to the right

ASK

Ps 2: 8 **A** it of me, and I will give you
Mt 6: 8 what you need before you **a** him.
7: 7 "**A** and it will be given to you;
Jn 16: 24 **a** and you will receive, so that your
Jas 4: 3 You **a** but do not receive,
4: 3 because you **a** wrongly, to spend it
1 Jn 5: 14 if we **a** anything according to his

ASLEEP → SLEEP

Jon 1: 5 hold of the ship, and lay there fast **a**.
Mt 8: 24 swamped by waves; but he was **a**.

ASSEMBLE → ASSEMBLY

Zep 3: 8 to **a** kingdoms, In order to pour
Rev 16: 14 of the whole world to **a** them

ASSEMBLY → ASSEMBLE

Neh 8: 2 priest brought the law before the **a**,
Ps 149: 1 his praise in the **a** of the faithful.
Heb 12: 23 and the **a** of the firstborn enrolled

ASSIGNED

1 Cor 3: 5 just as the Lord **a** each one.
7: 17 should live as the Lord has **a**, just as

ASSYRIA

2 Kgs 18: 11 The king of **A** then deported the Israelites to **A**
Jer 50: 18 as I once punished the king of **A**;

ASTARTE → ASHERAH

1 Kgs 11: 5 Solomon followed **A**, the goddess

ASTONISHED

Lk 2: 48 they were **a**, and his mother said

ASTRAY → STRAY

Dt 30: 17 but are led **a** and bow down to other
Is 53: 6 We had all gone **a** like sheep,
Mt 18: 12 sheep and one of them goes **a**,
1 Pt 2: 25 For you had gone **a** like sheep,

ASYLUM

Nm 35: 11 cities to serve as cities of **a**,

ATE → EAT

Gn 3: 6 she took some of its fruit and **a** it;
3: 6 who was with her, and he **a** it.
Ex 16: 35 The Israelites **a** the manna for forty
Ps 78: 25 Man **a** the bread of the angels;
Ez 3: 3 I **a** it, and it was as sweet as honey
Mt 14: 20 They all **a** and were satisfied,
15: 37 They all **a** and were satisfied.

ATHALIAH

Granddaughter of Omri; wife of Jehoram and mother of Ahaziah; encouraged their evil ways (2 Kgs 8:18, 27; 2 Ch 22:2). At death of Ahaziah she made herself queen, killing all his sons but Joash (2 Kgs 11:1-3; 2 Ch 22:10-12); killed six years later when Joash revealed (2 Kgs 11:4-16; 2 Ch 23:1-15).

ATHLETE

2 Tm 2: 5 an **a** cannot receive the winner's

ATONE → ATONEMENT, ATONING

Sir 3: 3 Those who honor their father **a** for sins;

ATONEMENT → ATONES

Ex 29: 36 as a purification offering, to make **a**.
32: 30 be able to make **a** for your sin."
Lv 23: 28 because it is the Day of **A**, when **a** is

ATONING → ATONE

Ex 30: 10 with the blood of the **a** purification offering.

ATTAIN → ATTAINED

Phil 3: 11 if somehow I may **a** the resurrection

ATTAINED → ATTAIN
Phil 3:16 with regard to what we have **a**,

AUTHOR
Acts 3:15 The **a** of life you put to death,

AUTHORITIES → AUTHORITY
Rom 13: 1 be subordinate to the higher **a**,

AUTHORITY → AUTHORITIES
Mk 1:27 A new teaching with **a**.
Lk 5:24 the Son of Man has **a** on earth
Rom 13: 1 for there is no **a** except from God,
1 Cor 11:10 a woman should have a sign of **a**
1 Tm 2:12 to teach or to have **a** over a man.
Rev 12:10 our God and the **a** of his Anointed.

AVENGE → VENGEANCE
Dt 32:43 he will **a** the blood of his servants,
1 Mc 2:67 observe the law, and **a** your people.
Rev 6:10 **a** our blood on the inhabitants

AVENGER → VENGEANCE
Nm 35:12 of asylum from the **a** of blood,
Ps 8: 3 your foes, to silence enemy and **a**.
1 Thes 4: 6 the Lord is an **a** in all these things,

AVENGING → VENGEANCE
Na 1: 2 A jealous and **a** God is the LORD,

AVOID → AVOIDED
2 Tm 2:16 **A** profane, idle talk, for such people
Ti 3: 9 **A** foolish arguments, genealogies,

AVOIDED → AVOID
Prv 16: 6 by the fear of the LORD evil is **a**.

AWAKE
Ps 44:24 **A**! Why do you sleep, O Lord?
57: 9 **A**, my soul; **a**, lyre and harp!
Is 51: 9 **A**, **a**, put on strength,
Dn 12: 2 sleep in the dust of the earth shall **a**;
Eph 5:14 "**A**, O sleeper, and arise

AWE → AWESOME
Is 29:23 Jacob, be in **a** of the God of Israel.
Mt 9: 8 saw this they were struck with **a**
Acts 2:43 **A** came upon everyone, and many
Rom 11:20 not become haughty, but stand in **a**.

AWESOME → AWE
Dt 10:17 mighty and **a**, who has no favorites,
Neh 1: 5 great and **a** God, you preserve your
Ps 65: 6 You answer us with **a** deeds
68:36 **A** is God in his holy place, the God
Dn 9: 4 great and **a** God, you who keep your

AX
Mt 3:10 Even now the **a** lies at the root

AZARIAH → =ABEDNEGO, =UZZIAH
1. King of Judah; see Uzziah (2 Kgs 15:1-7).
2. Prophet (2 Ch 15:1-8).
3. Opponent of Jeremiah (Jer 43:2).
4. Jewish exile; see Abednego (Dn 1:6-19).

AZAZEL
Lv 16: 8 is for the LORD and which for **A**.

B

BAAL → BAALS
Nm 25: 3 attached itself to the **B** of Peor,
Jgs 2:13 and served **B** and the Astartes,
1 Kgs 18:25 Elijah then said to the prophets of **B**,
19:18 every knee that has not bent to **B**,
Jer 2: 8 The prophets prophesied by **B**,
Rom 11: 4 men who have not knelt to **B**."

BAALS → BAAL
Jgs 3: 7 and served the **B** and the Asherahs,
1 Sm 7: 4 So the Israelites removed their **B**

BAASHA
King of Israel (1 Kgs 15:16–16:7; 2 Ch 16:1-6).

BABEL → BABYLON
Gn 11: 9 That is why it was called **B**,

BABES
Ps 8: 3 with the mouths of **b** and infants.

BABYLON → BABEL
2 Kgs 24:15 He deported Jehoiachin to **B**,
Ps 137: 1 the rivers of **B** there we sat weeping
Is 14: 4 taunt-song against the king of **B**:
21: 9 out and says, 'Fallen, fallen is **B**!
Jer 25:11 nations shall serve the king of **B**;
Dn 14:36 he set him down in **B** above the den.
1 Pt 5:13 chosen one at **B** sends you greeting,
Rev 14: 8 "Fallen, fallen is **B** the great,

BACK
Gn 19:26 But Lot's wife looked **b**, and she

BAD
Prv 20:14 "**B**, **b**!" says the buyer, then goes
Mt 7:17 fruit, and a rotten tree bears **b** fruit.
1 Cor 15:33 "**B** company corrupts good

BALAAM
Prophet who attempted to curse Israel (Nm 22–24; Dt 23:4-5; 2 Pt 2:15; Jude 11; Rev 2:14). Killed in Israel's vengeance on Midianites (Nm 31:8; Jos 13:22).

BALAK
Moabite king who hired Balaam to curse Israel (Nm 22–24; Jos 24:9; Mi 6:5).

BALANCE
Is 40:12 in scales and the hills in a **b**?

BALM
Jer 8:22 Is there no **b** in Gilead, no healer

BAPTISM → BAPTIZE
Mk 1: 4 in the desert proclaiming a **b**
10:38 be baptized with the **b** with which I
Lk 20: 4 was John's **b** of heavenly
Acts 18:25 although he knew only the **b**
19: 3 They replied, "With the **b** of John."
Rom 6: 4 with him through **b** into death,
Eph 4: 5 one Lord, one faith, one **b**;
Col 2:12 You were buried with him in **b**,
1 Pt 3:21 This prefigured **b**, which saves you

BAPTISMS → BAPTIZE
Heb 6: 2 instruction about **b** and laying

BAPTIST → BAPTIZE
Mt 3: 1 In those days John the **B** appeared,
11:11 been none greater than John the **B**;
14: 8 on a platter the head of John the **B**."
16:14 "Some say John the **B**,

BAPTIZE → BAPTISM, BAPTISMS, BAPTIST, BAPTIZED, BAPTIZING
Mt 3:11 He will **b** you with the holy Spirit
Lk 3:16 He will **b** you with the holy Spirit
1 Cor 1:17 For Christ did not send me to **b**

BAPTIZED → BAPTIZE
Mt 3:13 to John at the Jordan to be **b** by him.
Acts 1: 5 for John **b** with water, but in a few
2:38 "Repent and be **b**, every one
Rom 6: 3 we who were **b** into Christ Jesus
6: 3 Christ Jesus were **b** into his death?

1 Cor 10: 2 all of them were **b** into Moses
12: 13 in one Spirit we were all **b** into one

BAPTIZING → BAPTIZE
Mt 28: 19 **b** them in the name of the Father,
Jn 4: 1 and **b** more disciples than John

BARABBAS
Prisoner released by Pilate instead of Jesus (Mt 27:16-26; Mk 15:7-15; Lk 23:18-19; Jn 18:40).

BARAK
Judge who fought with Deborah against Canaanites (Jgs 4–5; 1 Sm 12:11; Heb 11:32).

BARBARIAN
Col 3: 11 circumcision and uncircumcision, **b**,

BARBS
Nm 33: 55 remain will become **b** in your eyes

BARE → BARED
Ps 18: 16 the world's foundations lay **b**,

BARED → BARE
Is 52: 10 The LORD has **b** his holy arm

BARN → BARNS
Lk 12: 24 they have neither storehouse nor **b**,

BARNABAS → =JOSEPH
Disciple, originally Joseph (Acts 4:36), prophet (Acts 13:1), apostle (Acts 14:14). Brought Paul to apostles (Acts 9:27), Antioch (Acts 11:22-29; Gal 2:1-13), on the first missionary journey (Acts 13–14). Together at Jerusalem Council, they separated over John Mark (Acts 15). Later co-workers (1 Cor 9:6; Col 4:10).

BARNS → BARN
Dt 28: 8 upon you, on your **b** and on all your
Ps 144: 13 May our **b** be full with every kind
Lk 12: 18 I shall tear down my **b** and build

BARREN
Gn 11: 30 Sarai was **b**; she had no child.
Ex 23: 26 no woman in your land will be **b**
1 Sm 2: 5 The **b** wife bears seven sons,
Is 54: 1 you **b** one who never bore a child,
Lk 1: 7 because Elizabeth was **b** and both

BARTHOLOMEW → =NATHANAEL?
Apostle (Mt 10:3; Mk 3:18; Lk 6:14; Acts 1:13). Possibly also called Nathanael (Jn 1:45-49; 21:2).

BARUCH
Jeremiah's secretary (Jer 32:12-16; 36; 43:1-6; 45:1-2). Deuterocanonical book ascribed to (Bar 1:1, 3, 8).

BARZILLAI
1. Gileadite who aided David during Absalom's revolt (2 Sm 17:27; 19:31-39).
2. Son-in-law of 1. (Ezr 2:61; Neh 7:63).

BASHAN
Nm 21: 33 king of **B**, advanced against them
Ps 22: 13 fierce bulls of **B** encircle me.
Mi 7: 14 Let them feed in **B** and Gilead,

BASIN
Jn 13: 5 he poured water into a **b** and began

BASKET
Ex 2: 3 she took a papyrus **b**, daubed it
Mt 5: 15 and then put it under a bushel **b**;
Acts 9: 25 in the wall, lowering him in a **b**.

BATHING
2 Sm 11: 2 From the roof he saw a woman **b**;

BATHSHEBA
Wife of Uriah; committed adultery with and married David (2 Sm 11; Ps 51), mother of Solomon (2 Sm 12:24; 1 Kgs 1–2; 1 Ch 3:5).

BATTLE
1 Sm 17: 47 For the **b** belongs to the LORD,
2 Ch 20: 15 for the **b** is not yours but God's.
Eccl 9: 11 the swift, nor the **b** by the valiant,
Rev 16: 14 them for the **b** on the great day
20: 8 and Magog, to gather them for **b**;

BEAR → BEARS, BIRTH, BIRTHRIGHT, BORE, BORN, CHILDBEARING, FIRSTBORN
Gn 4: 13 "My punishment is too great to **b**.
17: 19 your wife Sarah is to **b** you a son,
Is 7: 14 pregnant and about to **b** a son,
Mt 1: 23 shall be with child and **b** a son,
7: 18 A good tree cannot **b** bad fruit,
7: 18 nor can a rotten tree **b** good fruit.
Jn 15: 2 branch in me that does not **b** fruit,
Gal 6: 2 **B** one another's burdens, and so you

BEARS → BEAR
1 Cor 13: 7 It **b** all things, believes all things,

BEAST → BEASTS
Rev 11: 7 the **b** that comes up from the abyss
13: 18 can calculate the number of the **b**,
16: 2 on those who had the mark of the **b**
19: 20 The **b** was caught and with it
19: 20 who had accepted the mark of the **b**

BEASTS → BEAST
Dn 7: 3 which emerged four immense **b**,
Mk 1: 13 He was among wild **b**,

BEAT → BEATEN, BEATING
Is 2: 4 They shall **b** their swords

BEATEN → BEAT
2 Cor 11: 25 Three times I was **b** with rods,
1 Pt 2: 20 if you are patient when **b** for doing

BEATING → BEAT
Lk 22: 63 custody were ridiculing and **b** him.

BEAUTIFUL → BEAUTY
Gn 12: 11 "I know that you are a **b** woman.
Tb 6: 12 girl is wise, courageous, and very **b**;
Jb 42: 15 women were as **b** as the daughters
Is 52: 7 How **b** upon the mountains are
Dn 13: 2 who married a very **b**
Acts 3: 2 temple called "the **B** Gate" every
Rom 10: 15 "How **b** are the feet of those who

BEAUTY → BEAUTIFUL
2 Sm 14: 25 praised for his **b** than Absalom,
Jdt 16: 9 his eyes, her **b** captivated his mind,
1 Mc 2: 12 laid waste, our **b**, our glory.
Ps 27: 4 To gaze on the LORD's **b**, to visit
Prv 6: 25 Do not lust in your heart after her **b**,
31: 30 Charm is deceptive and **b** fleeting;
Wis 13: 3 in their **b** they thought them gods,
13: 3 original source of **b** fashioned them.
Sir 9: 8 do not gaze upon **b** that is not yours;
Dn 13: 56 said to him, "**b** has seduced you,
1 Pt 3: 4 in the imperishable **b** of a gentle

BED
Gn 47: 31 Israel bowed at the head of the **b**.
Ps 36: 5 On his **b** he hatches plots; he sets
Heb 13: 4 the marriage **b** be kept undefiled,

BEE → BEES
Sir 11: 3 The **b** is least among winged

Is 7:18 and for the **b** in the land of Assyria.

BEER-SHEBA
Gn 21:31 This is why the place is called **B**;
1 Sm 3:20 Israel from Dan to **B** came to know

BEES → BEE
Jgs 14: 8 there was a swarm of **b** in the lion's

BEFORE
Ex 33: 2 Jebusites, I will send an angel **b** you
Is 43:10 **B** me no god was formed,
65:24 **B** they call, I will answer;
Mal 3: 1 he will prepare the way **b** me;
Mt 6: 8 what you need **b** you ask him.
Lk 22:61 to him, "**B** the cock crows today,
Heb 12: 2 that lay **b** him he endured the cross,

BEGGAR
Jn 9: 8 had seen him earlier as a **b** said,

BEGINNING
Gn 1: 1 In the **b**, when God created
Ps 111:10 of the LORD is the **b** of wisdom;
Prv 1: 7 the LORD is the **b** of knowledge;
Eccl 7: 8 is the end of a thing than its **b**;
Is 40:21 Was it not told you from the **b**?
Mt 24: 8 All these are the **b** of the labor
Jn 1: 1 In the **b** was the Word,
1 Jn 1: 1 What was from the **b**, what we have
2 Jn 1: 6 as you heard from the **b**,
Rev 21: 6 and the Omega, the **b** and the end.

BEGOT → BEGOTTEN
Dt 32: 6 Is he not your father who **b** you,

BEGOTTEN → BEGOT
Acts 13:33 are my son; this day I have **b** you.'
Heb 1: 5 are my son; this day I have **b** you"?

BEHEADED → HEAD
Lk 9: 9 But Herod said, "John I **b**.
Rev 20: 4 of those who had been **b** for their

BEHEMOTH
Jb 40:15 Look at **B**, whom I made along

BEHIND
Is 38:17 **B** your back you cast all my sins.
Mt 16:23 turned and said to Peter, "Get **b** me,
Phil 3:13 forgetting what lies **b** but straining

BEING
Gn 2: 7 life, and the man became a living **b**.
Dt 6: 5 with your whole **b**, and with your whole
1 Cor 15:45 became a living **b**," the last Adam
Heb 1: 3 the very imprint of his **b**, and who

BEL
Babylonian deity (Is 46:1; Jer 50:2; 51:44; Bar 6:40; Dn 14:3-28).

BELIEF → BELIEVE
2 Thes 2:13 by the Spirit and **b** in truth.

BELIEVE → BELIEF, BELIEVED, BELIEVER, BELIEVES
Ex 4: 5 is so they will **b** that the LORD,
Prv 14:15 The naive **b** everything, but the
Jer 12: 6 Do not **b** them, even when they
Mt 18: 6 one of these little ones who **b** in me
24:23 or, 'There he is!' do not **b** it.
Mk 1:15 Repent, and **b** in the gospel."
9:24 out, "I do **b**, help my unbelief!"
Lk 24:25 of heart to **b** all that the prophets
Jn 1: 7 so that all might **b** through him.
3:18 but whoever does not **b** has already
6:29 God, that you **b** in the one he sent."
10:38 them, even if you do not **b** me,
17:20 those who will **b** in me through their
20:29 to **b** because you have seen me?
Acts 16:31 "**B** in the Lord Jesus and you
28:24 he had said, while others did not **b**.
Rom 3:22 faith in Jesus Christ for all who **b**.
10: 9 **b** in your heart that God raised him
1 Thes 4:14 For if we **b** that Jesus died and rose,
Heb 11: 6 anyone who approaches God must **b**
Jas 2:19 You **b** that God is one. You do well.
2:19 Even the demons **b**
1 Pt 1: 8 you do not see him now yet **b**
Jude 1: 5 later destroyed those who did not **b**.

BELIEVED → BELIEVE
Ex 14:31 They **b** in the LORD and in Moses
Jdt 14:10 of Israel had done, **b** firmly in God.
Jn 12:38 "Lord, who has **b** our preaching,
20: 8 at the tomb first, and he saw and **b**.
Acts 2:44 All who **b** were together and had all
Rom 4: 3 "Abraham **b** God, and it was
10:16 who has **b** what was heard
2 Cor 4:13 is written, "I **b**, therefore I spoke,"
Gal 3: 6 Thus Abraham "**b** God, and it was
1 Tm 3:16 Gentiles, **b** in throughout the world,
Heb 4: 3 For we who **b** enter into [that] rest,
Jas 2:23 that says, "Abraham **b** God, and it

BELIEVER → BELIEVE
2 Cor 6:15 Or what has a **b** in common

BELIEVES → BELIEVE
Jn 3:15 everyone who **b** in him may have
11:26 lives and **b** in me will never die.
Rom 9:33 whoever **b** in him shall not be put
10:10 For one **b** with the heart and so is
1 Cor 13: 7 It bears all things, **b** all things,

BELLY
Gn 3:14 On your **b** you shall crawl, and dust
Lv 11:42 Whether it crawls on its **b**,
Mt 12:40 was in the **b** of the whale three days

BELONG → BELONGS
Jn 10:16 sheep that do not **b** to this fold.
15:19 because you do not **b** to the world,
1 Cor 12:15 "Because I am not a hand I do not **b**

BELONGS → BELONG
Ps 22:29 For kingship **b** to the LORD,
62:12 I have heard: Strength **b** to God;

BELOVED → LOVE
Mt 3:17 "This is my **b** Son, with whom I am
12:18 chosen, my **b** in whom I delight;
17: 5 "This is my **b** Son, with whom I am
Col 3:12 holy and **b**, heartfelt compassion,
Rev 20: 9 of the holy ones and the **b** city.

BELSHAZZAR
King of Babylon (Dn 5; Bar 1:11-12).

BELT
1 Sm 18: 4 dress, even his sword, bow, and **b**.
Is 11: 5 and faithfulness a **b** upon his hips.
Mk 1: 6 with a leather **b** around his waist.

BELTESHAZZAR → See DANIEL

BEN-HADAD
1. King of Syria in time of Asa (1 Kgs 15:18-20; 2 Ch 16:2-4).
2. King of Syria in time of Ahab (1 Kgs 20; 2 Kgs 6:24; 8:7-15).
3. King of Syria in time of Jehoahaz (2 Kgs 13:3, 24-25; Jer 49:27; Am 1:4).

BENAIAH
A commander of David's army (2 Sm 8:18; 20:23; 23:20-30); loyal to Solomon (1 Kgs 1:8–2:46; 4:4).

BEND → BENT
Phil 2: 10 name of Jesus every knee should **b**,

BENEFICIAL → BENEFIT
1 Cor 6: 12 for me," but not everything is **b**.
10: 23 is lawful," but not everything is **b**.

BENEFIT
Gal 5: 2 Christ will be of no **b** to you.

BENJAMIN → BENJAMINITE
Twelfth son of Jacob by Rachel (Gn 35:16-24; 46:19-21; 1 Ch 2:2). Jacob refused to send him to Egypt, but relented (Gn 42–45). Tribe of blessed (Gn 49:27; Dt 33:12), numbered (Nm 1:37; 26:41), allotted land (Jos 18:11-28; Ez 48:23), failed to fully possess (Jgs 1:21), nearly obliterated (Jgs 20–21), sided with Ish-Bosheth (2 Sm 2), but turned to David (1 Ch 12:2, 29). 12,000 from (Rev 7:8).

BENJAMINITE → BENJAMIN
Jgs 3: 15 of Gera, a **B** who was left-handed.
1 Sm 9: 21 "Am I not a **B**, from the smallest

BENT → BEND
Jn 8: 6 Jesus **b** down and began to write
20: 5 he **b** down and saw the burial cloths

BEREAVES
Lam 1: 20 Outside the sword **b**—

BESIDES
Wis 12: 13 is there any god **b** you who have
Is 45: 21 **b** whom there is no other God?
Dn 14: 41 and there is no other **b** you!"

BEST → GOOD
Dt 33: 21 He saw that the **b** should be his,

BETHANY
Mt 26: 6 when Jesus was in **B** in the house
Jn 11: 1 Lazarus from **B**, the village of Mary

BETHEL
Gn 12: 8 on to the hill country east of **B**,
28: 19 He named that place **B**,
1 Sm 7: 16 passing through **B**,

BETHLEHEM
Ru 4: 11 Bestow a name in **B**!
1 Sm 17: 12 an Ephrathite named Jesse from **B**
Mt 2: 1 When Jesus was born in **B** of Judea,
Lk 2: 15 to **B** to see this thing that has taken

BETRAY
Jn 13: 11 For he knew who would **b** him;

BETTER → GOOD
1 Sm 15: 22 Obedience is **b** than sacrifice,
Tb 12: 8 It is **b** to give alms than to store
Ps 63: 4 For your love is **b** than life;
Prv 15: 16 **B** a little with fear of the LORD
27: 5 **B** is an open rebuke than a love
Eccl 2: 24 There is nothing **b** for mortals than
9: 4 "A live dog is **b** off than a dead
Sir 40: 26 exult, but **b** than either, fear of God.
Dn 1: 20 he found them ten times **b** than any
Mt 5: 29 It is **b** for you to lose one of your
Mk 14: 21 It would be **b** for that man if he had
Jn 11: 50 do you consider that it is **b** for you
Phil 1: 23 be with Christ, [for] that is far **b**.
Heb 7: 22 guarantee of an [even] **b** covenant.
9: 23 by **b** sacrifices than these.
1 Pt 3: 17 For it is **b** to suffer for doing good,

BETWEEN
Gn 3: 15 I will put enmity **b** you
3: 15 and **b** your offspring and hers;
9: 13 serve as a sign of the covenant **b** me
16: 5 May the LORD decide **b** you
Is 2: 4 He shall judge **b** the nations, and set
Ez 34: 17 I will judge **b** one sheep and another, **b** rams and goats.
Rom 10: 12 For there is no distinction **b** Jew
1 Tm 2: 5 one mediator **b** God and the human

BEWARE
Eccl 12: 12 As to more than these, my son, **b**.
Phil 3: 2 **B** of the dogs! **B** of the evil workers!
3: 2 **B** of the mutilation!

BEYOND
Ps 147: 5 in power, with wisdom **b** measure.
2 Cor 4: 17 weight of glory **b** all comparison,

BEZALEL
Judahite craftsman in charge of building the tabernacle (Ex 31:1-11; 35:30–39:31).

BILDAD
One of Job's friends (Jb 2:11; 8; 18; 25; 42:9).

BILHAH
Servant of Rachel, mother of Jacob's sons Dan and Naphtali (Gn 30:1-7; 35:25; 46:23-25).

BIND → BINDS
Dt 6: 8 **B** them on your arm as a sign
Mt 16: 19 Whatever you **b** on earth shall be

BINDS → BIND
Jb 5: 18 For he wounds, but he **b** up;

BIRD → BIRDS
Gn 7: 3 of every **b** of the air, seven pairs,
Lv 20: 25 detestable through any beast or **b**

BIRDS → BIRD
Gn 1: 21 teems, and all kinds of winged **b**.
1: 22 and let the **b** multiply on the earth.
Jer 7: 33 will be food for the **b** of the sky
Mt 6: 26 Look at the **b** in the sky; they do not
Rev 19: 21 all the **b** gorged themselves on their

BIRTH → BEAR
Dt 32: 18 you forgot the God who gave you **b**.
Eccl 3: 2 A time to give **b**, and a time to die;
Jas 1: 18 He willed to give us **b** by the word
1 Pt 1: 3 his great mercy gave us a new **b**

BIRTHRIGHT → BEAR, RIGHT
Heb 12: 16 who sold his **b** for a single meal.

BISHOP
1 Tm 3: 1 the office of **b** desires a noble task.
Ti 1: 7 For a **b** as God's steward must be

BIT → BITE, BITS
Ps 32: 9 with **b** and bridle their temper is

BITE → BIT
Sir 21: 2 a serpent that will **b** you if you go

BITS → BIT
Jas 3: 3 If we put **b** into the mouths

BITTER → BITTERNESS
Ex 1: 14 making life **b** for them with hard
12: 8 with unleavened bread and **b** herbs.
15: 23 drink its water, because it was too **b**.
Ru 1: 13 daughters, my lot is too **b** for you,
Rev 8: 11 this water, because it was made **b**.

BITTERNESS → BITTER
Prv 14:10 The heart knows its own **b**, and its
Eph 4:31 All **b**, fury, anger, shouting,

BLACK
Zec 6:2 horses, the second chariot **b** horses,
Mt 5:36 make a single hair white or **b**.
Rev 6:5 and there was a **b** horse, and its

BLAMELESS
Gn 17:1 Walk in my presence and be **b**.
1 Mc 4:42 He chose **b** priests,
Jb 1:1 In the land of Uz there was a **b**
Ps 37:18 LORD knows the days of the **b**;
Phil 2:15 that you may be **b** and innocent,
1 Thes 5:23 be preserved **b** for the coming
Ti 1:7 bishop as God's steward must be **b**,

BLASPHEME → BLASPHEMED, BLASPHEMER, BLASPHEMERS, BLASPHEMES, BLASPHEMIES, BLASPHEMOUS
Acts 26:11 in an attempt to force them to **b**;
1 Tm 1:20 over to Satan to be taught not to **b**.

BLASPHEMED → BLASPHEME
Ez 20:27 this way also your ancestors **b** me,
Mt 26:65 tore his robes and said, "He has **b**!

BLASPHEMER → BLASPHEME
1 Tm 1:13 I was once a **b** and a persecutor

BLASPHEMERS → BLASPHEME
Sir 3:16 who neglect their father are like **b**;

BLASPHEMES → BLASPHEME
Lv 24:15 who **b** God shall bear the penalty;
Lk 12:10 but the one who **b** against the holy

BLASPHEMIES → BLASPHEME
Mk 3:28 and all **b** that people utter will be
Rev 13:6 its mouth to utter **b** against God,

BLASPHEMOUS → BLASPHEME
Acts 6:11 heard him speaking **b** words against
Rev 13:1 and on its heads **b** name[s].

BLAZING
Heb 12:18 which could be touched and a **b** fire

BLEMISH
Ex 12:5 be a year-old male and without **b**.
Eph 5:27 she might be holy and without **b**.

BLESS → BLESSED, BLESSING, BLESSINGS
Gn 12:2 you a great nation, and I will **b** you;
17:16 I will **b** her, and I will give you
22:17 I will **b** you and make your
26:3 and I will be with you and **b** you;
Ex 20:24 I will come to you and **b** you.
Nm 6:24 The LORD **b** you and keep you!
23:20 I was summoned to **b**; I will **b**;
Dt 7:13 He will love and **b** and multiply
7:13 he will **b** the fruit of your womb
30:16 God, will **b** you in the land you are
1 Ch 29:20 "Now **b** the LORD your God!"
Tb 4:19 At all times **b** the Lord, your God,
12:6 "**B** God and give him thanks before all
Ps 5:13 For you, LORD, **b** the just one;
29:11 may the LORD **b** his people
34:2 I will **b** the LORD at all times;
103:1 **B** the LORD, my soul;
109:28 Though they curse, may you **b**;
Hg 2:19 From this day, I will **b** you.
Lk 6:28 **b** those who curse you,
Rom 12:14 **B** those who persecute [you],
1 Cor 4:12 When ridiculed, we **b**;
Jas 3:9 With it we **b** the Lord and Father,

BLESSED → BLESS
Gn 1:22 and God **b** them, saying:
2:3 God **b** the seventh day and made it
14:19 He **b** Abram with these words:
Nm 24:9 **B** are those who bless you,
Tb 3:11 "**B** are you, merciful God!
3:11 "**B** be your holy and honorable name
Jdt 13:17 saying with one accord, "**B** are you,
Jb 1:21 **b** be the name of the LORD!"
42:12 Thus the LORD **b** the later days
Ps 1:1 **B** is the man who does not walk
33:12 **B** is the nation whose God is
84:13 **b** the man who trusts in you!
118:26 **B** is he who comes in the name
Jer 17:7 **B** are those who trust
Dn 3:26 "**B** are you, and praiseworthy,
Mt 5:3 "**B** are the poor in spirit, for theirs
16:17 said to him in reply, "**B** are you,
Mk 10:16 Then he embraced them and **b** them,
Lk 1:42 "Most **b** are you among women,
1:42 and **b** is the fruit of your womb.
6:20 "**B** are you who are poor,
Jn 12:13 **B** is he who comes in the name
20:29 **B** are those who have not seen
Acts 20:35 said, 'It is more **b** to give than
Gal 3:8 you shall all the nations be **b**."
Eph 1:3 **B** be the God and Father of our Lord
1:3 who has **b** us in Christ with every
1 Pt 3:14 because of righteousness, **b** are you.
Rev 1:3 **B** is the one who reads aloud and **b**
22:7 **B** is the one who keeps

BLESSING → BLESS
Gn 12:2 name great, so that you will be a **b**.
22:18 the nations of the earth will find **b**,
27:36 and now he has taken away my **b**."
27:36 "Have you not saved a **b** for me?"
Dt 11:26 I set before you this day a **b**
Neh 13:2 our God turned the curse into a **b**."
Tb 8:15 are you, God, with every pure **b**!
Ez 34:26 in its season, the **b** of abundant rain.
Mal 3:10 down upon you **b** without measure!
Mk 14:22 he took bread, said the **b**, broke it,
1 Cor 10:16 The cup of **b** that we bless, is it not
Gal 3:14 that the **b** of Abraham might be
Eph 1:3 every spiritual **b** in the heavens,
Rev 5:12 strength, honor and glory and **b**."
7:12 "Amen. **B** and glory,

BLESSINGS → BLESS
Dt 28:2 All these **b** will come upon you
Jos 8:34 of the law, the **b** and the curses,
Ps 21:7 make him the pattern of **b** forever,
Prv 10:6 **B** are for the head of the just;
Rom 15:27 come to share in their spiritual **b**,
15:27 also to serve them in material **b**.

BLIND → BLINDED, BLINDNESS
Ex 4:11 another mute or deaf, seeing or **b**?
Dt 27:18 be anyone who misleads the **b**
Ps 146:8 the LORD gives sight to the **b**.
Is 35:5 Then the eyes of the **b** shall see,
42:19 Who is **b** but my servant, or deaf
Mt 11:5 the **b** regain their sight, the lame
Lk 6:39 "Can a **b** person guide a **b** person?
Jn 9:25 One thing I do know is that I was **b**
Rom 2:19 that you are a guide for the **b**
2 Pt 1:9 Anyone who lacks them is **b**

BLINDED → BLIND
Jn 12:40 "He **b** their eyes and hardened their

2 Cor 4: 4 of this age has **b** the minds

BLINDNESS → BLIND
Dt 28: 28 you with madness, **b** and panic,

BLOCK
Sir 31: 7 It is a stumbling **b** for fools;
Is 44: 19 Shall I worship a **b** of wood?"
Rom 11: 9 a stumbling **b** and a retribution
1 Cor 1: 23 crucified, a stumbling **b** to Jews

BLOOD → BLOODSHED
Gn 4: 10 Your brother's **b** cries out to me
9: 6 Anyone who sheds the **b** of a human being shall that one's **b** be shed;
Ex 7: 17 Nile and it will be changed into **b**.
12: 13 for you the **b** will mark the houses
12: 13 Seeing the **b**, I will pass over you;
24: 8 he took the **b** and splashed it
24: 8 "This is the **b** of the covenant
Lv 1: 5 shall offer its **b** by splashing it on all
3: 17 You shall not eat any fat or any **b**.
17: 11 since the life of the flesh is in the **b**,
17: 11 because it is the **b** as life that makes
Nm 35: 33 can have no expiation for the **b** shed
35: 33 on it except through the **b** of the one
Ps 72: 14 for precious is their **b** in his sight.
Is 1: 11 In the **b** of calves, lambs, and goats
Mt 27: 8 even today is called the Field of **B**.
Mk 14: 24 "This is my **b** of the covenant,
Lk 22: 44 sweat became like drops of **b** falling
Jn 6: 53 of the Son of Man and drink his **b**,
19: 34 immediately **b** and water flowed
Acts 2: 20 and the moon to **b**,
Rom 5: 9 since we are now justified by his **b**,
1 Cor 11: 25 cup is the new covenant in my **b**.
Eph 1: 7 him we have redemption by his **b**,
6: 12 our struggle is not with flesh and **b**
Heb 9: 12 not with the **b** of goats and calves
9: 12 goats and calves but with his own **b**,
9: 22 almost everything is purified by **b**,
9: 22 of **b** there is no forgiveness.
1 Jn 5: 6 one who came through water and **b**,
5: 6 by water alone, but by water and **b**.
Rev 1: 5 has freed us from our sins by his **b**,
5: 9 with your **b** you purchased for God
6: 12 and the whole moon became like **b**.
12: 11 conquered him by the **b** of the Lamb

BLOODSHED → BLOOD, SHED
Is 5: 7 He waited for judgment, but see, **b**!

BLOSSOMS
Ex 25: 33 shaped like almond **b**, each with its

BLOT
Ps 51: 3 your abundant compassion **b** out my

BLOW
Jl 2: 1 **B** the horn in Zion, sound the alarm
Rev 8: 6 seven trumpets prepared to **b** them.

BOAST → BOASTING
Prv 27: 1 Do not **b** about tomorrow, for you
Rom 2: 23 You who **b** of the law, do you
1 Cor 1: 31 boasts, should **b** in the Lord."
2 Cor 11: 30 If I must **b**, I will **b** of the things
Gal 6: 14 may I never **b** except in the cross
Eph 2: 9 is not from works, so no one may **b**.

BOASTING → BOAST
1 Cor 5: 6 Your **b** is not appropriate.

BOAZ
Bethlehemite who showed favor to Ruth (Ru 2), married her (Ru 4). Ancestor of David (Ru 4:18-22; 1 Ch 2:12-15), Jesus (Mt 1:5-16; Lk 3:23-32).

BODIES → BODY
Rom 12: 1 to offer your **b** as a living sacrifice,
1 Cor 6: 15 not know that your **b** are members
Heb 10: 22 and our **b** washed in pure water.

BODILY → BODY
Lk 3: 22 upon him in **b** form like a dove.
Col 2: 9 the whole fullness of the deity **b**,

BODY → BODIES, BODILY
Mi 6: 7 the fruit of my **b** for the sin of my
Mt 6: 22 "The lamp of the **b** is the eye.
Mk 14: 22 and said, "Take it; this is my **b**."
Lk 12: 4 not be afraid of those who kill the **b**
Jn 2: 21 speaking about the temple of his **b**.
Rom 7: 24 will deliver me from this mortal **b**?
1 Cor 6: 13 the Lord, and the Lord is for the **b**;
10: 17 are one **b**, for we all partake
15: 44 It is sown a natural **b**; it is raised a spiritual **b**.
2 Cor 5: 8 we would rather leave the **b** and go
Eph 4: 4 one **b** and one Spirit, as you were
Col 2: 19 from whom the whole **b**,

BOLDNESS
Eph 3: 12 in whom we have **b** of speech

BONE → BONES
Gn 2: 23 is **b** of my bones and flesh of my
Ez 37: 7 bones came together, **b** joining to **b**.

BONES → BONE
Ex 12: 46 You shall not break any of its **b**.
Ps 34: 21 He watches over all his **b**;

BOOK → BOOKS
Jos 1: 8 Do not let this **b** of the law depart
Ps 69: 29 they be blotted from the **b** of life;
Rev 21: 27 are written in the Lamb's **b** of life.

BOOKS → BOOK
Eccl 12: 12 making of many **b** there is no end,
Dn 7: 10 convened, and the **b** were opened.
Jn 21: 25 whole world would contain the **b**

BOOTHS
Lv 23: 34 month is the LORD's feast of **B**,
Ezr 3: 4 kept the feast of **B** in the manner
Zec 14: 16 and to celebrate the feast of **B**.

BORE → BEAR
Ps 22: 11 since my mother **b** me you are my God.
Mt 8: 17 our infirmities and **b** our diseases."
1 Pt 2: 24 He himself **b** our sins in his body

BORN → BEAR
Is 66: 8 or a nation be **b** in a single moment?
Lk 2: 11 of David a savior has been **b** for you
Jn 3: 7 you, 'You must be **b** from above.'
1 Cor 15: 8 as to one **b** abnormally, he appeared
1 Pt 1: 23 You have been **b** anew,

BORROW → BORROWER, BORROWS
Dt 28: 12 to many nations but **b** from none.
Mt 5: 42 your back on one who wants to **b**.

BORROWER → BORROW
Prv 22: 7 and the **b** is the slave of the lender.

BORROWS → BORROW
Ps 37: 21 The wicked one **b** but does not

BOW → BOWED
Gn 9: 13 I set my **b** in the clouds to serve as
Ex 20: 5 you shall not **b** down before them
Ps 95: 6 Enter, let us **b** down in worship;

BOWED → BOW
Ps 146: 8 raises up those who are **b** down;

BOWLS
Rev 16: 1 pour out the seven **b** of God's fury

BOY → BOYS
Lk 2: 43 the **b** Jesus remained behind

BOYS → BOY
Ex 1: 18 done this, allowing the **b** to live?"

BRANCH → BRANCHES
Is 4: 2 The **b** of the LORD will be beauty
Jn 15: 2 He takes away every **b** in me

BRANCHES → BRANCH
Jn 15: 5 I am the vine, you are the **b**.
Rom 11: 21 if God did not spare the natural **b**,

BREAD
Gn 3: 19 sweat of your brow you shall eat **b**,
Ex 12: 8 eating it roasted with unleavened **b**
Dt 8: 3 it is not by **b** alone that people live,
Ps 136: 25 gives **b** to all flesh, for his mercy
Eccl 11: 1 Send forth your **b** upon the face
Wis 16: 20 and furnished them **b** from heaven,
Sir 15: 3 will feed him with the **b** of learning,
Mt 6: 11 Give us today our daily **b**;
Lk 4: 4 'One does not live by **b** alone.' "
Jn 6: 35 said to them, "I am the **b** of life;
Acts 2: 42 to the breaking of the **b**
1 Cor 10: 17 Because the loaf of **b** is one, we,
11: 26 For as often as you eat this **b**

BREAK → BROKEN, BROKENHEARTED
Mt 6: 19 destroy, and thieves **b** in and steal.
Jn 19: 33 dead, they did not **b** his legs,

BREASTPIECE → BREASTPLATE
Ex 28: 15 The **b** of decision you shall

BREASTPLATE → BREASTPIECE
Wis 5: 18 Shall put on righteousness for a **b**,
Is 59: 17 He put on justice as his **b**, victory as
Eph 6: 14 clothed with righteousness as a **b**,

BREATH
Gn 2: 7 blew into his nostrils the **b** of life,
6: 17 sky in which there is the **b** of life;
Eccl 12: 7 the life **b** returns to God who gave
2 Thes 2: 8 will kill with the **b** of his mouth

BRIBE
Dt 16: 19 you shall not take a **b**, for a **b** blinds

BRIDE → BRIDEGROOM
Is 62: 5 in his **b** so shall your God rejoice
Rev 19: 7 come, his **b** has made herself ready.
21: 9 I will show you the **b**, the wife

BRIDEGROOM → BRIDE
Mt 9: 15 wedding guests mourn as long as the **b** is
Jn 3: 29 The one who has the bride is the **b**;

BRIDLE
Ps 32: 9 bit and **b** their temper is curbed,
Jas 3: 2 man, able to **b** his whole body also.

BRIGHT → BRIGHTNESS
Mt 17: 5 a **b** cloud cast a shadow over them,
Rev 22: 16 of David, the **b** morning star."

BRIGHTNESS → BRIGHT
Am 5: 20 not light, gloom without any **b**!

BRING → BRINGS, BROUGHT
Gn 6: 19 all living creatures you shall **b** two
Eccl 12: 14 because God will **b** to judgment
Jer 24: 6 good and **b** them back to this land,
Mt 10: 34 I have come to **b** peace
10: 34 I have come to **b** not peace
Rom 10: 15 of those who **b** [the] good news!"

BRINGS → BRING
Jas 5: 20 know that whoever **b** back a sinner

BROKE → BREAK
Ex 32: 19 **b** them on the base of the mountain.
Jer 31: 32 They **b** my covenant, though I was
Mt 14: 19 he said the blessing, **b** the loaves,
1 Cor 11: 24 he had given thanks, **b** it and said,

BROKEN → BREAK
Rom 11: 20 They were **b** off because

BROKENHEARTED → BREAK, HEART
Ps 147: 3 Healing the **b**, and binding up their
Is 61: 1 to bind up the **b**, To proclaim liberty

BRONZE
Nm 21: 9 Moses made a **b** serpent
Dt 28: 23 over your heads will be like **b**
Dn 10: 6 and feet looked like burnished **b**,

BROOD
Mt 3: 7 he said to them, "You **b** of vipers!
Lk 13: 34 a hen gathers her **b** under her wings,

BROTHER → BROTHER'S, BROTHER-IN-LAW, BROTHERS
Gn 4: 8 Cain attacked his **b** Abel and killed
Mt 5: 24 first and be reconciled with your **b**,
10: 21 **B** will hand over **b** to death,

BROTHER'S → BROTHER
Dt 25: 7 does not want to marry his **b** wife,
25: 7 to perpetuate his **b** name in Israel
Mk 6: 18 for you to have your **b** wife."

BROTHER-IN-LAW → BROTHER
Gn 38: 8 in fulfillment of your duty as **b**,

BROTHERS → BROTHER
Gn 9: 25 of slaves shall he be to his **b**."
37: 11 So his **b** were furious at him but his
Mk 3: 33 "Who are my mother and [my] **b**?"
Lk 22: 32 back, you must strengthen your **b**."
Heb 2: 11 he is not ashamed to call them "**b**,"

BROUGHT → BRING
Gn 15: 7 I am the LORD who **b** you
Jgs 2: 1 I **b** you up from Egypt and led you
2 Ch 36: 18 princes, all these he **b** to Babylon.
Ezr 6: 5 and **b** to Babylon be sent back;
1 Tm 6: 7 For we **b** nothing into the world,

BUILD → BUILDERS, BUILDING, BUILDS, BUILT, REBUILD
Gn 11: 4 let us **b** ourselves a city and a tower
Dt 6: 10 fine, large cities that you did not **b**,
Ps 127: 1 Unless the LORD **b** the house, they labor in vain who **b**.
Is 57: 14 **B** up, **b** up, prepare the way,
Mt 16: 18 upon this rock I will **b** my church,

BUILDERS → BUILD
Ps 118: 22 The stone the **b** rejected has become
Mk 12: 10 that the **b** rejected has become
1 Pt 2: 7 which the **b** rejected has become

BUILDING → BUILD
1 Cor 3: 9 you are God's field, God's **b**.
2 Cor 5: 1 destroyed, we have a **b** from God,
Eph 4: 12 for **b** up the body of Christ,

BUILDS → BUILD
Prv 14: 1 Wisdom **b** her house, but Folly tears

1 Cor 3:10 each one must be careful how he **b**
8:1 inflates with pride, but love **b** up.
10:23 is lawful," but not everything **b** up.

BUILT → BUILD
Tb 13:16 of Jerusalem will be **b** with sapphire
13:16 of Jerusalem will be **b** with gold,
1 Mc 4:47 **b** a new altar like the former one.
Prv 9:1 Wisdom has **b** her house, she has set
Eph 2:20 **b** upon the foundation

BULLS
1 Ch 29:21 a thousand **b**, a thousand rams,
Ps 22:13 Many **b** surround me; fierce **b**
Heb 10:4 it is impossible that the blood of **b**

BURDEN → BURDENS, BURDENSOME
Mt 11:30 my yoke is easy, and my **b** light."

BURDENS → BURDEN
Lk 11:46 You impose on people **b** hard
Gal 6:2 Bear one another's **b**, and so you

BURDENSOME → BURDEN
1 Jn 5:3 And his commandments are not **b**,

BURIED → BURY
Rom 6:4 We were indeed **b** with him through
1 Cor 15:4 that he was **b**; that he was raised

BURN → BURNED, BURNING, BURNT
Ex 3:3 sight. Why does the bush not **b** up?"
21:25 **b** for **b**, wound for wound,
Lk 3:17 his barn, but the chaff he will **b**

BURNED → BURN
Jn 15:6 them into a fire and they will be **b**.
1 Cor 3:15 But if someone's work is **b** up,

BURNING → BURN
Ps 79:5 your jealous anger keep **b** like fire?
Lk 24:32 not our hearts **b** [within us] while he

BURNT → BURN
Ex 40:6 Put the altar for **b** offerings in front
Lv 1:3 If a person's offering is a **b** offering
1 Sm 15:22 "Does the LORD delight in **b** offerings
1 Mc 1:45 to prohibit **b** offerings, sacrifices,
4:56 and joyfully offered **b** offerings and
Ps 51:18 a **b** offering you would not accept.
Hos 6:6 knowledge of God rather than **b** offerings.
Mi 6:6 Shall I come before him with **b** offerings,
Mk 12:33 is worth more than all **b** offerings

BURY → BURIED
Lk 9:60 him, "Let the dead **b** their dead.

BUSH
Ex 3:2 to him as fire flaming out of a **b**.
3:2 looked, although the **b** was on fire,

BUY → BUYS
Rev 3:18 I advise you to **b** from me gold
3:18 **b** ointment to smear on your eyes

BUYS → BUY
Mt 13:44 sells all that he has and **b** that field.

BYWORD → WORD
Jb 17:6 I am made a **b** of the people;
Ps 44:15 You make us a **b** among the nations;

C

CAESAREA
Mt 16:13 of **C** Philippi he asked his disciples,
Acts 10:1 Now in **C** there was a man named
25:4 Paul was being held in custody in **C**

CAIAPHAS
High priest at trial of Jesus (Mt 26:3, 57; Lk 3:2; Jn 11:49; 18:13-28); at trial of disciples (Acts 4:6).

CAIN
Firstborn of Adam (Gn 4:1), murdered brother Abel (Gn 4:1-25; Heb 11:4; 1 Jn 3:12; Jude 11).

CALAMITIES
1 Sm 10:19 saves you from all your evils and **c**,

CALEB
Judahite who spied out Canaan (Nm 13:6); allowed to enter land (Nm 13:30–14:38; Dt 1:36; Sir 46:7-9; 1 Mc 2:56). Given Hebron (Jos 14:6–15:19).

CALF → CALVES
Ex 32:4 it with a tool, made a molten **c**.
Lk 15:23 Take the fattened **c** and slaughter it.

CALL → CALLED, CALLING
Dt 4:26 I **c** heaven and earth this day
1 Sm 3:5 "I did not **c** you," Eli answered.
1 Kgs 18:24 You shall **c** upon the name of your
18:24 and I will **c** upon the name
Ps 61:3 From the ends of the earth I **c**;
Prv 8:1 Does not Wisdom **c**,
Is 65:24 Before they **c**, I will answer;
Mt 9:13 I did not come to **c** the righteous
Lk 6:46 "Why do you **c** me, 'Lord, Lord,'
Jn 15:15 I no longer **c** you slaves,
Rom 10:12 of all, enriching all who **c** upon him.
11:29 and the **c** of God are irrevocable.

CALLED → CALL
2 Sm 22:7 In my distress I **c** out: LORD!
Is 43:1 I have **c** you by name:
Mt 23:8 As for you, do not be **c** 'Rabbi.'
1 Cor 7:15 God has **c** you to peace.
1 Jn 3:1 we may be **c** the children of God.

CALLING → CALL
Phil 3:14 the prize of God's upward **c**,

CALVES → CALF
1 Kgs 12:28 took counsel, made two **c** of gold,

CAMEL
Mt 23:24 out the gnat and swallow the **c**!
Mk 10:25 for a **c** to pass through [the] eye

CANA
Jn 2:1 third day there was a wedding in **C**

CANAAN → CANAANITE, CANAANITES
Gn 9:25 "Cursed be **C**! The lowest of slaves
Nm 13:2 men to reconnoiter the land of **C**,
1 Ch 16:18 "To you will I give the land of **C**,

CANAANITE → CANAAN
Gn 28:1 "You shall not marry a **C** woman!
Mt 15:22 a **C** woman of that district came

CANAANITES → CANAAN
Ex 33:2 Driving out the **C**, Amorites,
Jgs 3:5 the Israelites settled among the **C**,

CAPERNAUM
Mt 4:13 and went to live in **C** by the sea,
Jn 6:59 teaching in the synagogue in **C**.

CAPTIVE → CAPTIVITY
2 Kgs 24:16 of Babylon brought **c** to Babylon.
Rom 7:23 taking me **c** to the law of sin
Eph 4:8 on high and took prisoners **c**;

CAPTIVITY → CAPTIVE
Dt 28:41 with you, for they will go into **c**.

Ezr 8:35 those who had returned from the **c**,

CARE → CARELESS, CARES
Ps 8: 5 a son of man that you **c** for him?
Heb 2: 6 the son of man that you **c** for him?
Jas 1:27 to **c** for orphans and widows in their

CARELESS → CARE
Mt 12:36 for every **c** word they speak.

CARES → CARE
1 Pt 5: 7 upon him because he **c** for you.

CARMEL
1 Kgs 18:20 the prophets gather on Mount **C**.

CARPENTER'S
Mt 13:55 Is he not the **c** son? Is not his

CARRY
Lk 14:27 Whoever does not **c** his own cross

CASE
Is 41:21 Present your **c**, says the LORD;

CAST
Est 9:24 to destroy them and had **c** the *pur*,
Ps 22:19 for my clothing they **c** lots.
55:23 **C** your care upon the LORD,
Prv 16:33 Into the bag the lot is **c**,
Jn 19:24 and for my vesture they **c** lots."
1 Pt 5: 7 **C** all your worries upon him

CAUGHT
2 Cor 12: 2 was **c** up to the third heaven.
1 Thes 4:17 will be **c** up together with them

CAUSE
Ps 9: 5 For you upheld my right and my **c**,
Jn 15:25 fulfilled, 'They hated me without **c**.'

CAVE
Gn 23: 9 he will sell me the **c** of Machpelah
1 Sm 22: 1 and escaped to the **c** of Adullam.

CEASE
Gn 8:22 and day and night shall not **c**.
Jer 31:36 of Israel **c** as a people before me
1 Cor 13: 8 if tongues, they will **c**;

CEDAR
2 Sm 7: 2 "Here I am living in a house of **c**,
Ps 92:13 tree, shall grow like a **c** of Lebanon.

CELEBRATE
1 Cor 5: 8 Therefore let us **c** the feast,

CENSER → CENSERS
Ez 8:11 of Shaphan, each with **c** in hand;
Rev 8: 3 stood at the altar, holding a gold **c**.

CENSERS → CENSER
Lv 10: 1 Nadab and Abihu took their **c** and,

CENSUS
Nm 1: 2 Take a **c** of the whole community

CENTURION
Mt 8: 5 a **c** approached him and appealed
Lk 23:47 The **c** who witnessed what had
Acts 10: 1 a **c** of the Cohort called the Italica,

CEPHAS → =PETER
Name given to the apostle Peter (Jn 1:42; 1 Cor 1:12; 3:22; 9:5; 15:5; Gal 1:18; 2:9, 11, 14).

CHAFF
Ps 1: 4 They are like **c** driven by the wind.
Lk 3:17 his barn, but the **c** he will burn

CHAINED → CHAINS
2 Tm 2: 9 But the word of God is not **c**.

CHAINS → CHAINED
Eph 6:20 for which I am an ambassador in **c**,
Heb 11:36 even **c** and imprisonment.
2 Pt 2: 4 them to the **c** of Tartarus

CHALDEANS
Gn 15: 7 of the **C** to give you this land as
Dn 1: 4 the language and literature of the **C**.

CHANGE → CHANGED, CHANGERS
1 Kgs 8:47 they have a **c** of heart in the land
Jas 1:17 no alteration or shadow caused by **c**.

CHANGED → CHANGE
1 Cor 15:51 all fall asleep, but we will all be **c**,
Heb 1:12 and like a garment they will be **c**.

CHANGERS → CHANGE
Mk 11:15 overturned the tables of the money **c**
Jn 2:15 spilled the coins of the money-**c**

CHARACTER
Rom 5: 4 endurance, proven **c**, and proven **c**,

CHARGE
Mk 15:26 of the **c** against him read,
Rom 8:33 will bring a **c** against God's chosen
1 Cor 9:18 I offer the gospel free of **c** so as not

CHARIOT → CHARIOTS
2 Kgs 2:11 a fiery **c** and fiery horses came
Ps 104: 3 You make the clouds your **c**;

CHARIOTS → CHARIOT
Ex 14:28 it covered the **c** and the horsemen.
Zec 6: 1 and saw four **c** coming

CHARM
Prv 31:30 **C** is deceptive and beauty fleeting;

CHEEK
Mt 5:39 strikes you on (your) right **c**,

CHEERFUL
2 Cor 9: 7 compulsion, for God loves a **c** giver.

CHEMOSH
1 Kgs 11: 7 then built a high place to **C**,
Jer 48: 7 **C** shall go into exile, his priests

CHERUB → CHERUBIM
Ps 18:11 Mounted on a **c** he flew,
Ez 28:14 With a **c** I placed you; I put you

CHERUBIM → CHERUB
Gn 3:24 man, stationing the **c** and the fiery
Ex 25:18 Make two **c** of beaten gold
2 Ch 3:11 of the **c** spanned twenty cubits:
Ps 80: 2 Seated upon the **c**, shine forth
Heb 9: 5 Above it were the **c** of glory

CHIEF
Mk 15: 3 The **c** priests accused him of many
1 Pt 5: 4 when the **c** Shepherd is revealed,

CHILD → CHILDBEARING, CHILDISH, CHILDREN
Gn 17:17 "Can a **c** be born to a man who is
Sir 4:10 Then God will call you his **c**,
Is 11: 6 with a little **c** to guide them.
49:15 tenderness for the **c** of her womb?
Hos 11: 1 When Israel was a **c** I loved him,
Mt 1:18 with **c** through the holy Spirit.
Mk 10:15 of God like a **c** will not enter it."
1 Cor 13:11 When I was a **c**, I used to talk as a **c**, think as a **c**, reason as a **c**;

Gal 4: 7 So you are no longer a slave but a **c**, and if a **c** then also an heir,
Rev 12: 4 to devour her **c** when she gave birth.

CHILDBEARING → CHILD, BEAR
Gn 3: 16 I will intensify your toil in **c**;

CHILDISH → CHILD
1 Cor 13: 11 I became a man, I put aside **c** things.

CHILDREN → CHILD
Ex 12: 26 When your **c** ask you, 'What does
Dt 6: 7 Keep repeating them to your **c**.
11: 19 Teach them to your **c**,
Mt 3: 9 you, God can raise up **c** to Abraham
Lk 18: 16 "Let the **c** come to me and do not
Jn 1: 12 he gave power to become **c** of God,
Rom 8: 14 by the Spirit of God are **c** of God.
Eph 6: 4 do not provoke your **c** to anger,
1 Jn 3: 10 the **c** of God and the **c** of the devil

CHOOSE → CHOOSES, CHOSE, CHOSEN
Dt 30: 19 **C** life, then, that you and your

CHOOSES → CHOOSE
Dt 12: 14 place which the LORD **c** in one

CHOSE → CHOOSE
Dt 4: 37 ancestors he **c** their descendants
Neh 9: 7 are the LORD God who **c** Abram,
Mk 13: 20 for the sake of the elect whom he **c**,
1 Cor 1: 27 God **c** the foolish of the world
1: 27 and God **c** the weak of the world

CHOSEN → CHOOSE
Is 42: 1 my **c** one with whom I am pleased.
Mt 22: 14 Many are invited, but few are **c**."
Rom 11: 5 time there is a remnant, **c** by grace.
1 Pt 2: 6 a cornerstone, **c** and precious,
2: 9 But you are "a **c** race, a royal

CHRIST → CHRISTIAN, CHRISTIANS, MESSIAH
Rom 5: 6 For **C**, while we were still helpless,
8: 35 will separate us from the love of **C**?
10: 4 For **C** is the end of the law
1 Cor 1: 23 but we proclaim **C** crucified,
3: 11 one that is there, namely, Jesus **C**.
11: 1 Be imitators of me, as I am of **C**.
15: 3 that **C** died for our sins
Gal 5: 1 For freedom **C** set us free;
Eph 4: 15 way into him who is the head, **C**,
Phil 1: 21 For to me life is **C**, and death is
2: 11 tongue confess that Jesus **C** is Lord,
Col 1: 27 it is **C** in you, the hope for glory.
Rev 20: 4 they reigned with **C** for a thousand

CHRISTIAN → CHRIST
Acts 26: 28 soon persuade me to play the **C**."
1 Pt 4: 16 suffer as a **C** should not be ashamed

CHRISTIANS → CHRIST
Acts 11: 26 that the disciples were first called **C**.

CHURCH
Mt 16: 18 and upon this rock I will build my **c**,
Acts 8: 1 persecution of the **c** in Jerusalem,
1 Cor 12: 28 God has designated in the **c** to be,
14: 4 whoever prophesies builds up the **c**.
Col 1: 18 He is the head of the body, the **c**.

CIRCUMCISE → CIRCUMCISED, CIRCUMCISION
Gn 17: 11 **C** the flesh of your foreskin.
Dt 10: 16 **C** therefore the foreskins of your
Lk 1: 59 on the eighth day to **c** the child,
Jn 7: 22 and you **c** a man on the sabbath.

CIRCUMCISED → CIRCUMCISE
Gn 17: 10 every male among you shall be **c**.
1 Mc 1: 60 women who had their children **c**,
Acts 15: 1 "Unless you are **c** according
Gal 6: 13 they only want you to be **c** so
Col 2: 11 were also **c** with a circumcision not

CIRCUMCISION → CIRCUMCISE
Rom 2: 29 and **c** is of the heart, in the spirit,
Gal 5: 6 neither **c** nor uncircumcision counts

CISTERN
Prv 5: 15 Drink water from your own **c**,
Jer 38: 6 him into the **c** of Prince Malchiah,

CITIES → CITY
Gn 19: 25 He overthrew those **c** and the whole
Jos 20: 2 for yourselves the **c** of refuge
Rev 16: 19 three parts, and the gentile **c** fell.

CITIZENSHIP
Phil 3: 20 But our **c** is in heaven, and from it

CITY → CITIES
1 Ch 11: 7 therefore was called the **C** of David.
Ps 127: 1 Unless the LORD guard the **c**,
Prv 31: 31 her deeds praise her at the **c** gates.
Lam 1: 1 How solitary sits the **c**, once filled
Dn 9: 24 for your people and for your holy **c**:
Mt 5: 14 A **c** set on a mountain cannot be
Heb 12: 22 Zion and the **c** of the living God,
Rev 21: 2 I also saw the holy **c**, a new

CLAP
Ps 47: 2 All you peoples, **c** your hands;
Is 55: 12 trees of the field shall **c** their hands.

CLAY
Is 45: 9 Shall the **c** say to the potter,
Jer 18: 6 like **c** in the hand of the potter,
Rom 9: 21 the potter have a right over the **c**,
2 Tm 2: 20 and silver but also of wood and **c**,

CLEAN → CLEANSE, CLEANSING
Gn 7: 2 Of every **c** animal, take with you
Lv 10: 10 and between what is **c** and what is
Mk 7: 19 (Thus he declared all foods **c**.)
Jn 13: 10 for he is **c** all over; so you are **c**, but not all."
Acts 10: 15 "What God has made **c**, you are not
Heb 10: 22 our hearts sprinkled **c** from an evil

CLEANSE → CLEAN
Ps 51: 4 and from my sin **c** me.
Sir 38: 10 **c** your heart of every sin.
1 Jn 1: 9 and **c** us from every wrongdoing.

CLEANSING → CLEAN
Eph 5: 26 **c** her by the bath of water
2 Pt 1: 9 forgetful of the **c** of his past sins.

CLEAR
Ps 19: 9 The command of the LORD is **c**,
1 Tm 3: 9 of the faith with a **c** conscience.
Rev 21: 18 the city was pure gold, **c** as glass.

CLINGS
Gn 2: 24 father and mother and **c** to his wife,
Heb 12: 1 of every burden and sin that **c** to us

CLOAK
Ex 22: 26 it is the **c** for his body.
Heb 1: 12 You will roll them up like a **c**,

CLOTHE → CLOTHED, CLOTHING
1 Pt 5: 5 **c** yourselves with humility in your

CLOTHED → CLOTHE
2 Cor 5: 2 to be further **c** with our heavenly

Gal 3:27 into Christ have **c** yourselves
Rev 12: 1 in the sky, a woman **c** with the sun,

CLOTHING → CLOTHE
Ps 22:19 for my **c** they cast lots.

CLOUD → CLOUDS
Ex 13:21 of a column of **c** to show them
1 Kgs 8:10 the **c** filled the house of the LORD
18:44 "There is a **c** as small as a man's
Ez 10: 4 the temple was filled with the **c**,
Mk 9: 7 Then a **c** came, casting a shadow
9: 7 then from the **c** came a voice,
Lk 21:27 of Man coming in a **c** with power
Heb 12: 1 by so great a **c** of witnesses, let us
Rev 14:14 I looked and there was a white **c**,
14:14 on the **c** one who looked like a son

CLOUDS → CLOUD
Gn 9:13 my bow in the **c** to serve as a sign
Dn 7:13 with the **c** of heaven One like a son
Mt 24:30 Man coming upon the **c** of heaven
1 Thes 4:17 them in the **c** to meet the Lord
Rev 1: 7 he is coming amid the **c**, and every

CLUSTER
Nm 13:23 a branch with a single **c** of grapes

COALS
Ps 11: 6 rains upon the wicked fiery **c**
Prv 25:22 For live **c** you will heap on their
Rom 12:20 by so doing you will heap burning **c**

COIN
Mt 17:27 you will find a **c** worth twice
22:19 Show me the **c** that pays the census
Lk 15: 9 me because I have found the **c** that I

COLD
Zec 14: 6 that day there will no longer be **c**
Mt 24:12 the love of many will grow **c**.
Rev 3:16 neither hot nor **c**, I will spit you

COLLECTOR → COLLECTORS
Mt 10: 3 Thomas and Matthew the tax **c**;
Lk 18:10 a Pharisee and the other was a tax **c**.
19: 2 who was a chief tax **c**

COLLECTORS → COLLECTOR
Mt 5:46 Do not the tax **c** do the same?
11:19 a friend of tax **c** and sinners.'

COLT
Zec 9: 9 donkey, on a **c**, the foal of a donkey.
Jn 12:15 comes, seated upon an ass's **c**."

COME → COMES, COMING
Ps 144: 5 incline your heavens and **c** down;
Is 59:20 Then for Zion shall **c** a redeemer,
Zec 14: 5 will **c**, and all his holy ones
Mt 6:10 your kingdom **c**, your will be done,
Lk 7:20 ask, 'Are you the one who is to **c**,
Jn 6:37 the Father gives me will **c** to me,
Rev 1: 4 is and who was and who is to **c**,
22:20 Amen! **C**, Lord Jesus!

COMES → COME
Ps 118:26 Blessed is he who **c** in the name
Lk 19:38 "Blessed is the king who **c**
Jn 14: 6 No one **c** to the Father except

COMFORT → COMFORTED, COMFORTERS, COMFORTS
Is 40: 1 **C**, give **c** to my people, says your

COMFORTED → COMFORT
Mt 5: 4 they who mourn, for they will be **c**.

COMFORTERS → COMFORT
Jb 16: 2 Troublesome **c**, all of you!
Ps 69:21 was none, for **c**, but found none.

COMFORTS → COMFORT
Is 66:13 As a mother **c** her child, so I will

COMING → COME
Mal 3: 2 who can endure the day of his **c**?
2 Pt 3: 4 "Where is the promise of his **c**?
Rev 22:20 says, "Yes, I am **c** soon." Amen!

COMMAND → COMMANDED, COMMANDMENT, COMMANDMENTS
Dt 1:26 you defied the **c** of the LORD,

COMMANDED → COMMAND
Gn 7: 5 complied, just as the LORD had **c**.
Ex 40:32 altar, as the LORD had **c** Moses.
Jos 1:16 "We will do all you have **c** us,
Mt 28:20 to observe all that I have **c** you.
Jn 14:31 that I do just as the Father has **c** me.

COMMANDMENT → COMMAND
Dt 6: 1 This then is the **c**, the statutes and
Mt 22:38 This is the greatest and the first **c**.
Rom 7:12 and the **c** is holy and righteous
1 Jn 3:23 And his **c** is this: we should believe

COMMANDMENTS → COMMAND
Ex 20: 6 those who love me and keep my **c**.
Eccl 12:13 Fear God and keep his **c**, for this
Mt 19:17 wish to enter into life, keep the **c**."
22:40 prophets depend on these two **c**."
Jn 14:15 you love me, you will keep my **c**.
1 Cor 7:19 what matters is keeping God's **c**.
1 Jn 5: 3 of God is this, that we keep his **c**. And his **c** are not burdensome,
Rev 14:12 the holy ones who keep God's **c**

COMMIT → COMMITS
Dt 5:18 You shall not **c** adultery.
2 Kgs 17:21 causing them to **c** a great sin.
Mt 5:27 was said, 'You shall not **c** adultery.

COMMITS → COMMIT
Jn 8:34 everyone who **c** sin is a slave of sin.

COMMON
Acts 2:44 together and had all things in **c**;

COMPANY
1 Cor 15:33 "Bad **c** corrupts good morals."

COMPARE
Prv 8:11 and no treasures can **c** with her.]
Lk 7:31 to what shall I **c** the people of this

COMPASSION → COMPASSIONATE
Ps 103:13 As a father has **c** on his children,
103:13 so the LORD has **c** on those who
Col 3:12 and beloved, heartfelt **c**, kindness,

COMPASSIONATE → COMPASSION
Sir 2:11 For the Lord is **c** and merciful;
Jas 5:11 Lord, because "the Lord is **c**

COMPETING
2 Tm 2: 5 crown except by **c** according

COMPLAINING → COMPLAINT
1 Pt 4: 9 hospitable to one another without **c**.

COMPLAINT → COMPLAINING
Jb 10: 1 I will give myself up to **c**;
Ps 142: 3 Before him I pour out my **c**,
Hb 2: 1 what answer he will give to my **c**.

COMPLETED
Gn 2: 2 On the seventh day God **c** the work

CONCEITED
Gal 5: 26 Let us not be **c**, provoking one
1 Tm 6: 4 is **c**, understanding nothing, and has
3: 6 so that he may not become **c**

CONCEIVE
Lk 1: 31 you will **c** in your womb and bear

CONDEMN → CONDEMNATION, CONDEMNED
Lk 11: 31 this generation and she will **c** them,
Jn 3: 17 Son into the world to **c** the world,
Rom 8: 34 Who will **c**? It is Christ [Jesus] who
1 Jn 3: 21 if [our] hearts do not **c** us, we have

CONDEMNATION → CONDEMN
Mk 12: 40 They will receive a very severe **c**."
Rom 5: 18 as through one transgression **c** came
Jas 5: 12 "No," that you may not incur **c**.

CONDEMNED → CONDEMN
Mt 12: 37 and by your words you will be **c**."
Jn 3: 18 believes in him will not be **c**,
3: 18 does not believe has already been **c**,
16: 11 the ruler of this world has been **c**.
1 Cor 11: 32 that we may not be **c** along

CONDUCT
Tb 4: 14 and discipline yourself in all your **c**.
Sir 37: 17 The root of all **c** is the heart;
Rom 13: 3 are not a cause of fear to good **c**,
1 Pt 1: 15 in every aspect of your **c**,

CONFESS → CONFESSES, CONFESSION
Lv 5: 5 person shall **c** the wrong committed,
16: 21 he shall **c** over it all the iniquities
Phil 2: 11 every tongue **c** that Jesus Christ is

CONFESSES → CONFESS
Rom 10: 10 and one **c** with the mouth and so is
1 Jn 2: 23 whoever **c** the Son has the Father as

CONFESSION → CONFESS
1 Tm 6: 12 when you made the noble **c**
Heb 4: 14 Son of God, let us hold fast to our **c**.

CONFIDENCE
Phil 3: 3 Jesus and do not put our **c** in flesh,
Heb 10: 19 of Jesus we have **c** of entrance

CONFIRM
2 Sm 7: 25 **c** the promise that you have spoken
Rom 15: 8 to **c** the promises to the patriarchs,

CONFORMED
Rom 8: 29 predestined to be **c** to the image

CONFUSE
Gn 11: 7 go down and there **c** their language,

CONQUER → CONQUERED, CONQUERS
Rev 17: 14 but the Lamb will **c** them, for he is

CONQUERED → CONQUER
Jn 16: 33 take courage, I have **c** the world."
Heb 11: 33 who by faith **c** kingdoms, did what
1 Jn 2: 13 because you have **c** the evil one.

CONQUERS → CONQUER
1 Jn 5: 4 is begotten by God **c** the world.
5: 4 victory that **c** the world is our faith.

CONSCIENCE
Rom 2: 15 while their **c** also bears witness
1 Cor 8: 7 to idols, their **c**, which is weak,
1 Tm 1: 5 heart, a good **c**, and a sincere faith.
1 Pt 3: 21 but an appeal to God for a clear **c**,

CONSECRATE → CONSECRATED
Ex 13: 2 **C** to me every firstborn;

CONSECRATED → CONSECRATE
2 Ch 7: 16 **c** this house that my name may be

CONSIDER → CONSIDERED
Jas 1: 2 **C** it all joy, my brothers, when you

CONSIDERED → CONSIDER
Prv 17: 28 fools, keeping silent, are **c** wise;

CONSOLATION
Lk 2: 25 and devout, awaiting the **c** of Israel,

CONSULT → CONSULTED
Is 40: 14 Whom did he **c** to gain knowledge?

CONSULTED → CONSULT
Ez 20: 3 not allow myself to be **c** by you!—

CONSUME → CONSUMED, CONSUMING
Nm 16: 21 that I may **c** them at once.
Jn 2: 17 "Zeal for your house will **c** me."

CONSUMED → CONSUME
Ex 3: 2 bush was on fire, it was not being **c**.
Ps 90: 7 Truly we are **c** by your anger,
Zep 3: 8 of my passion all the earth will be **c**.
Gal 5: 15 that you are not **c** by one another.

CONSUMING → CONSUME
Heb 12: 29 For our God is a **c** fire.

CONTAIN
Jn 21: 25 the whole world would **c** the books

CONTEMPT
Mk 9: 12 suffer greatly and be treated with **c**?
Heb 6: 6 themselves and holding him up to **c**.

CONTEND
Jude 1: 3 to encourage you to **c** for the faith

CONTENT → CONTENTMENT
Sir 29: 23 or much, be **c** with what you have:
2 Cor 12: 10 Therefore, I am **c** with weaknesses,
Heb 13: 5 money but be **c** with what you have,

CONTENTMENT → CONTENT
1 Tm 6: 6 religion with **c** is a great gain.

CONTRIBUTE
Rom 12: 13 **C** to the needs of the holy ones,

CONTRITE
Ps 51: 19 My sacrifice, O God, is a **c** spirit;

CONVERT
Mt 23: 15 traverse sea and land to make one **c**,
1 Tm 3: 6 He should not be a recent **c**,

CONVICT
Jude 1: 15 and to **c** everyone for all the godless

CONVINCE → CONVINCED
Acts 28: 23 trying to **c** them about Jesus
2 Tm 4: 2 **c**, reprimand, encourage through all

CONVINCED → CONVINCE
Rom 8: 38 For I am **c** that neither death,

COPY
Dt 17: 18 he shall write a **c** of this law
Heb 9: 24 made by hands, a **c** of the true one,

CORDS
2 Sm 22: 6 The **c** of Sheol tightened;
Hos 11: 4 I drew them with human **c**,

CORNELIUS
First Gentile Christian (Acts 10).

CORNERSTONE → STONE
Ps 118: 22 builders rejected has become the **c**.
Is 28: 16 A precious **c** as a sure foundation;
Lk 20: 17 builders rejected has become the **c**'?
1 Pt 2: 6 in Zion, a **c**, chosen and precious,

CORRECTING → CORRECTION
2 Tm 2: 25 **c** opponents with kindness.

CORRECTION → CORRECTING
Jer 5: 3 laid them low, but they refused **c**;
2 Tm 3: 16 refutation, for **c**, and for training

CORRUPT → CORRUPTION
Gn 6: 11 the earth was **c** in the view of God
Acts 2: 40 yourselves from this **c** generation."

CORRUPTION → CORRUPT
Acts 2: 31 netherworld nor did his flesh see **c**.
2 Pt 1: 4 escaping from the **c** that is

COST
1 Ch 21: 24 burnt offerings that **c** me nothing."
Lk 14: 28 and calculate the **c** to see if there is

COUNCIL
Jer 23: 18 has stood in the **c** of the LORD,

COUNSEL → COUNSELOR, COUNSELORS
Is 28: 29 wonderful is his **c** and great his

COUNSELOR → COUNSEL
Rom 11: 34 of the Lord or who has been his **c**?"

COUNSELORS → COUNSEL
Prv 11: 14 security lies in many **c**.
24: 6 and victory depends on many **c**.

COUNT → COUNTED
Ps 90: 12 Teach us to **c** our days aright,

COUNTED → COUNT
Gn 13: 16 your descendants too might be **c**.
Mt 10: 30 all the hairs of your head are **c**.

COURAGE → COURAGEOUS
Jn 16: 33 but take **c**, I have conquered

COURAGEOUS → COURAGE
1 Mc 2: 64 be **c** and strong in keeping the law,
1 Cor 16: 13 firm in the faith, be **c**, be strong.

COURT → COURTS
Ex 27: 9 also make a **c** for the tabernacle.
Dn 7: 10 The **c** was convened, and the books
Mt 5: 25 while on the way to **c** with him.
1 Cor 6: 6 brother goes to **c** against brother,

COURTS → COURT
Ps 84: 11 in your **c** than a thousand elsewhere.
96: 8 Bring gifts and enter his **c**;

COVENANT → COVENANTS
Gn 6: 18 I will establish my **c** with you.
9: 9 I am now establishing my **c**
15: 18 that day the LORD made a **c**
Ex 2: 24 was mindful of his **c** with Abraham,
19: 5 obey me completely and keep my **c**,
24: 7 Taking the book of the **c**, he read it
Lv 26: 42 I will remember my **c** with Jacob,
26: 42 and also my **c** with Abraham I will
Jgs 2: 1 I will never break my **c** with you,
1 Kgs 8: 23 you keep **c** and love toward your
Ezr 10: 3 enter into a **c** before our God
Jdt 9: 13 planned dire things against your **c**,
1 Mc 1: 15 and abandoned the holy **c**;
Ps 105: 8 He remembers forever his **c**,
Sir 28: 7 remember the **c** of the Most High,
Is 61: 8 an everlasting **c** I will make
Jer 31: 31 I will make a new **c** with the house
Ez 16: 60 I will remember the **c** I made
16: 60 set up an everlasting **c** with you.
Mal 3: 1 of the **c** whom you desire—
Lk 22: 20 "This cup is the new **c** in my blood,
1 Cor 11: 25 "This cup is the new **c** in my blood.
2 Cor 3: 6 qualified us as ministers of a new **c**,
Heb 7: 22 the guarantee of an [even] better **c**.
12: 24 the mediator of a new **c**,
Rev 11: 19 the ark of his **c** could be seen

COVENANTS → COVENANT
Rom 9: 4 glory, the **c**, the giving of the law,
Gal 4: 24 These women represent two **c**.

COVER → COVERED
Ex 33: 22 will **c** you with my hand until I have
Jas 5: 20 death and will **c** a multitude of sins.

COVERED → COVER
Ez 10: 12 wheels were **c** with eyes all around

COVET
Ex 20: 17 You shall not **c** your neighbor's
Rom 7: 7 I did not know what it is to **c** except
7: 7 the law said, "You shall not **c**."
Jas 4: 2 You **c** but do not possess.

CRAFTY
2 Cor 12: 16 yet I was **c** and got the better of you

CRAWLING
Gn 1: 24 tame animals, **c** things, and every kind

CREATE → CREATED, CREATING, CREATION, CREATOR
Ps 51: 12 A clean heart **c** for me, God;
Eph 2: 15 that he might **c** in himself one new

CREATED → CREATE
Gn 1: 1 when God **c** the heavens
1: 27 God **c** mankind in his image;
1: 27 in the image of God he **c** them;
1: 27 male and female he **c** them.
Sir 1: 4 all other things wisdom was **c**;
Mal 2: 10 Has not one God **c** us?
1 Cor 11: 9 nor was man **c** for woman,
Eph 2: 10 **c** in Christ Jesus for the good works
Col 1: 16 in him were **c** all things in heaven
1: 16 all things were **c** through him
1 Tm 4: 4 For everything **c** by God is good,
Rev 4: 11 and power, for you **c** all things;
4: 11 will they came to be and were **c**."

CREATING → CREATE
Is 65: 17 I am **c** new heavens and a new earth;

CREATION → CREATE
Gn 2: 3 from all the work he had done in **c**.
Mk 10: 6 But from the beginning of **c**,
Rom 8: 19 For **c** awaits with eager expectation
2 Cor 5: 17 So whoever is in Christ is a new **c**:
Gal 6: 15 uncircumcision, but only a new **c**.
Col 1: 15 invisible God, the firstborn of all **c**.
2 Pt 3: 4 as it was from the beginning of **c**."

CREATOR → CREATE
Eccl 12: 1 Remember your **C** in the days
Rom 1: 25 the creature rather than the **c**, who is
Col 3: 10 for knowledge, in the image of its **c**.
1 Pt 4: 19 over to a faithful **c** as they do good.

CREATURE → CREATURES
Rom 1:25 and worshiped the **c** rather than

CREATURES → CREATURE
Ps 104:24 the earth is full of your **c**.
Ez 1:5 likeness of four living **c** appeared.
Rev 4:6 there were four living **c** covered
19:4 and the four living **c** fell down

CREDIT
Lk 6:33 good to you, what **c** is that to you?
1 Pt 2:20 But what **c** is there if you are patient

CRIED → CRY
Ex 2:23 under their bondage and **c** out,
Nm 20:16 When we **c** to the LORD, he heard
Jgs 3:9 But when the Israelites **c**
Ps 22:6 To you they **c** out and they escaped;
Mt 27:46 about three o'clock Jesus **c**

CRIMINAL → CRIMINALS
Jn 18:30 "If he were not a **c**, we would not
2 Tm 2:9 even to the point of chains, like a **c**.

CRIMINALS → CRIMINAL
Lk 23:32 both **c**, were led away with him

CROOKED
Dt 32:5 basely, a twisted and **c** generation!
Eccl 1:15 What is **c** cannot be made straight,
Phil 2:15 without blemish in the midst of a **c**

CROSS → CROSSROADS
Dt 31:3 your God, who will **c** before you;
31:3 (It is Joshua who will **c** before you,
Mk 15:30 by coming down from the **c**."
Lk 14:27 Whoever does not carry his own **c**
1 Cor 1:18 The message of the **c** is foolishness
Gal 6:14 in the **c** of our Lord Jesus Christ,
Phil 2:8 obedient to death, even death on a **c**.
Col 1:20 by the blood of his **c** [through him],
Heb 12:2 lay before him he endured the **c**,

CROSSROADS → CROSS, ROAD
Prv 8:2 road, at the **c** she takes her stand;

CROWD → CROWDS
Mk 8:2 heart is moved with pity for the **c**,
14:43 accompanied by a **c** with swords

CROWDS → CROWD
Mt 7:28 words, the **c** were astonished at his

CROWN → CROWNED, CROWNS
Prv 4:9 a glorious **c** will she bestow
Jn 19:2 the soldiers wove a **c** out of thorns
Phil 4:1 my joy and **c**, in this way stand firm
2 Tm 4:8 on the **c** of righteousness awaits me,
1 Pt 5:4 you will receive the unfading **c**
Rev 6:2 He was given a **c**, and he rode forth
14:14 man, with a gold **c** on his head

CROWNED → CROWN
Ps 8:6 a god, **c** him with glory and honor.
Heb 2:9 but we do see Jesus "**c** with glory

CROWNS → CROWN
Rev 4:10 They throw down their **c** before

CRUCIFIED → CRUCIFY
Mt 27:22 They all said, "Let him be **c**!"
Lk 24:7 be handed over to sinners and be **c**,
Acts 4:10 Christ the Nazorean whom you **c**,
Rom 6:6 that our old self was **c** with him,
1 Cor 1:23 but we proclaim Christ **c**,
Gal 2:19 I have been **c** with Christ;

CRUCIFY → CRUCIFIED
Lk 23:21 continued their shouting, "**C** him!
Jn 19:15 him away, take him away! **C** him!"
19:15 said to them, "Shall I **c** your king?"

CRUSH → CRUSHED
Jb 6:9 that God would decide to **c** me,
Is 53:10 it was the LORD's will to **c** him
Rom 16:20 of peace will quickly **c** Satan under

CRUSHED → CRUSH
Ps 34:19 saves those whose spirit is **c**.

CRY → CRIED, CRYING
Ex 2:23 their bondage their **c** for help went
Ps 5:3 Attend to the sound of my **c**,
Hb 1:2 must I **c** for help and you do not
1:2 Or **c** out to you, "Violence!"
Mk 15:37 Jesus gave a loud **c** and breathed his

CRYING → CRY
Mk 1:3 A voice of one **c** out in the desert:

CRYSTAL
Ez 1:22 upwards like shining **c** over their
Rev 22:1 sparkling like **c**,

CUP
Ps 23:5 my head with oil; my **c** overflows.
Jer 25:15 Take this **c** of the wine of wrath
Mt 10:42 And whoever gives only a **c** of cold
26:39 is possible, let this **c** pass from me;
Mk 10:38 Can you drink the **c** that I drink
Lk 22:17 Then he took a **c**, gave thanks,
1 Cor 11:25 In the same way also the **c**,
11:25 "This **c** is the new covenant in my
Rev 14:10 full strength into the **c** of his wrath,

CURED
Mt 8:16 spirits by a word and **c** all the sick,
Acts 5:16 unclean spirits, and they were all **c**.

CURSE → ACCURSED, CURSED, CURSES
Gn 12:3 bless you and **c** those who **c** you.
Lv 24:16 death for uttering the LORD's name in a **c**.
Nm 22:12 with them and do not **c** this people,
Dt 21:23 anyone who is hanged is a **c** of God.
23:5 Pethor in Aram Naharaim, to **c** you.
Jb 2:9 **C** God and die!"
Ps 109:28 Though they **c**, may you bless;
Sir 4:5 do not give them reason to **c** you.
Mk 14:71 He began to **c** and to swear, "I do
Lk 6:28 bless those who **c** you,
Rom 12:14 [you], bless and do not **c** them.
Gal 3:13 ransomed us from the **c** of the law by becoming a **c** for us,

CURSED → CURSE
Gn 3:17 it, **C** is the ground because of you!
9:25 he said: "**C** be Caanan!
27:29 **C** be those who curse you,
Nm 23:8 on the one whom God has not **c**?
Jb 3:1 Job opened his mouth and **c** his day.
Mk 11:21 fig tree that you **c** has withered."
Gal 3:10 "**C** be everyone who does not
Heb 6:8 it will soon be **c** and finally burned.

CURSES → CURSE
2 Ch 34:24 all the **c** written in the book that was

CUSTOM → CUSTOMS
Jn 18:39 But you have a **c** that I release one

CUSTOMS → CUSTOM
1 Mc 1:42 and abandon their particular **c**.
Acts 16:21 are advocating **c** that are not lawful

CUT
Ps 37: 9 Those who do evil will be **c** off,
Is 53: 8 For he was **c** off from the land
Mt 3: 10 not bear good fruit will be **c** down
Mk 9: 43 your hand causes you to sin, **c** it off.
Rom 11: 22 otherwise you too will be **c** off.

CYMBAL → CYMBALS
1 Cor 13: 1 a resounding gong or a clashing **c**.

CYMBALS → CYMBAL
2 Sm 6: 5 harps, tambourines, sistrums, and **c**.
Neh 12: 27 hymns and the music of **c**, harps,
Ps 150: 5 Give praise with crashing **c**,

CYRUS
Persian king who allowed exiles to return (2 Ch 36:22-Ezr 1:8), to rebuild temple (Ezr 5:13–6:14), as appointed by the LORD (Is 44:28–45:13).

D

DAGON
Jgs 16: 23 offer a great sacrifice to their god **D**
1 Sm 5: 2 and brought it into the temple of **D**,

DAILY → DAY
Mt 6: 11 Give us today our **d** bread;
Lk 9: 23 take up his cross **d** and follow me.

DAMASCUS
Acts 9: 3 as he was nearing **D**, a light

DAN
1. Son of Jacob by Bilhah (Gn 30:4-6; 35:25; 46:23). Tribe of blessed (Gn 49:16-17; Dt 33:22), numbered (Nm 1:39; 26:43), allotted land (Jos 19:40-48; Ez 48:1), failed to fully possess (Jgs 1:34-35), failed to support Deborah (Jgs 5:17), possessed Dan (Jgs 18).
2. Northernmost city in Israel (Gn 14:14; Jgs 18; 20:1).

DANCE
Ps 150: 4 Give praise with tambourines and **d**,
Eccl 3: 4 a time to mourn, and a time to **d**.
Lk 7: 32 the flute for you, but you did not **d**.

DANIEL → =BELTESHAZZAR
1. Hebrew exile to Babylon, name changed to Belteshazzar (Dn 1:6-7). Refused to eat unclean food (Dn 1:8-21). Interpreted Nebuchadnezzar's dreams (Dn 2; 4), writing on the wall (Dn 5). Thrown into lion's den (Dn 6; 14:31-42). Visions of (Dn 7–12). Saves Susanna (Dn 13). Destroys Bel and its priests (Dn 14).
2. Son of David (1 Ch 3:1).

DARE
Mt 22: 46 did anyone **d** to ask him any more

DARIUS
1. King of Persia (Ezr 4:5), allowed rebuilding of temple (Ezr 5–6).
2. Mede who conquered Babylon (Dn 5:31).

DARK → DARKNESS
Ps 139: 12 Darkness is not **d** for you, and night
2 Pt 1: 19 it, as to a lamp shining in a **d** place,

DARKNESS → DARK
Gn 1: 2 with **d** over the abyss and a mighty
Ex 10: 22 there was dense **d** throughout
Dt 5: 23 the voice from the midst of the **d**,
Zep 1: 15 desolation, A day of **d** and gloom,
Mt 4: 16 who sit in **d** have seen a great light,
6: 23 bad, your whole body will be in **d**. And if the light in you is **d**, how great will the **d** be.
Jn 1: 5 the light shines in the **d**, and the **d**
Eph 5: 8 For you were once **d**, but now you
Col 1: 13 He delivered us from the power of **d**
1 Jn 1: 5 light, and in him there is no **d** at all.

DATHAN
Involved in Korah's rebellion against Moses and Aaron (Nm 16:1-27; 26:9; Dt 11:6; Ps 106:17; Sir 45:18).

DAUGHTER → DAUGHTERS
Ex 2: 5 Pharaoh's **d** came down to bathe
Jdt 10: 12 "I am a **d** of the Hebrews, and I am
Est 2: 7 Mordecai adopted her as his own **d**.
Ps 9: 15 salvation in the gates of **d** Zion.
Lam 2: 1 in his wrath has abhorred **d** Zion,
Mi 7: 6 the **d** rises up against her mother,
Zec 9: 9 Exult greatly, O **d** Zion!
9: 9 Shout for joy, O **d** Jerusalem!
Mt 14: 6 the **d** of Herodias performed a dance
Lk 12: 53 a mother against her **d** and a **d**

DAUGHTERS → DAUGHTER
Gn 6: 4 with the **d** of human beings,
19: 36 Thus the two **d** of Lot became
Nm 27: 1 The **d** of Zelophehad,
Dt 12: 31 their sons and **d** to their gods.
Jb 42: 15 women were as beautiful as the **d**
Acts 2: 17 sons and your **d** shall prophesy,
2 Cor 6: 18 and you shall be sons and **d** to me,

DAVID
Son of Jesse (Ru 4:17-22; 1 Ch 2:13-15), ancestor of Jesus (Mt 1:1-17; Lk 3:31). Wives and children (1 Sm 18; 25:39-44; 2 Sm 3:2-5; 5:13-16; 11:27; 1 Ch 3:1-9).
Anointed king by Samuel (1 Sm 16:1-13). Musician to Saul (1 Sm 16:14-23; 18:10). Killed Goliath (1 Sm 17). Relation with Jonathan (1 Sm 18:1-4; 19-20; 23:16-18; 2 Sm 1). Disfavor of Saul (1 Sm 18:6–23:29). Spared Saul's life (1 Sm 24; 26). Among Philistines (1 Sm 21:10-14; 27-30). Lament for Saul and Jonathan (2 Sm 1).
Anointed king of Judah (2 Sm 2:1-11). Conflict with house of Saul (2 Sm 2–4). Anointed king of Israel (2 Sm 5:1-4; 1 Ch 11:1-3). Conquered Jerusalem (2 Sm 5:6-10; 1 Ch 11;4-9). Brought ark to Jerusalem (2 Sm 6; 1 Ch 13; 15–16). The LORD promised eternal dynasty (2 Sm 7; 1 Ch 17; Ps 132). Showed kindness to Mephibosheth (2 Sm 9). Adultery with Bathsheba, murder of Uriah (2 Sm 11–12). Son Amnon raped daughter Tamar; killed by Absalom (2 Sm 13). Absalom's revolt (2 Sm 14–17); death (2 Sm 18). Sheba's revolt (2 Sm 20). Victories: Philistines (2 Sm 5:17-25; 21:15-22; 1 Ch 14:8-17; 20:4-8), Ammonites (2 Sm 10; 1 Ch 19), various (2 Sm 8; 1 Ch 18). Mighty men (2 Sm 23:8-39; 1 Ch 11–12). Punished for numbering army (2 Sm 24; 1 Ch 21). Appointed Solomon king (1 Kgs 1:28–2:9). Prepared for building of temple (1 Ch 22–29). Last words (2 Sm 23:1-7). Death (1 Kgs 2:10-12; 1 Ch 29:28).
Psalmist (Mt 22:43-45), musician (Am 6:5), prophet (2 Sm 23:2-7; Acts 1:16; 2:30).
Psalms of: 2 (Acts 4:25), 3–32, 34–41, 51–65, 68–70, 86, 95 (Heb 4:7), 101, 103, 108-110, 122, 124, 131, 133, 138-145.

DAWN → DAWNS
Is 14: 12 O Morning Star, son of the **d**!
Hos 6: 3 as certain as the **d** is his coming.

DAWNS → DAWN
Ps 97: 11 Light **d** for the just, and gladness
2 Pt 1: 19 until day **d** and the morning star

DAY → DAILY, DAYS
Gn 1: 5 God called the light "**d**,"
1: 5 and morning followed—the first **d**.
8: 22 and **d** and night shall not cease.
Ex 13: 21 Thus they could travel both **d**
20: 8 Remember the sabbath **d**—
Jos 1: 8 Recite it by **d** and by night, that you
Ps 1: 2 on his law he meditates **d** and night.
118: 24 This is the **d** the LORD has made;
Is 66: 8 a land be brought forth in one **d**,

Jl 1:15 O! The **d**! For near is the **d**
Zec 14:1 A **d** is coming for the LORD
Mal 3:2 But who can endure the **d** of his
Mt 25:13 you know neither the **d** nor the hour.
Lk 11:3 Give us each **d** our daily bread
24:46 and rise from the dead on the third **d**
Jn 6:40 I shall raise him [on] the last **d**."
Rom 14:5 considers one **d** more important
2 Cor 6:2 on the **d** of salvation I helped you."
6:2 behold, now is the **d** of salvation.
1 Thes 5:2 the **d** of the Lord will come like
2 Pt 3:8 the Lord one **d** is like a thousand
3:8 and a thousand years like one **d**.
3:10 the **d** of the Lord will come like
1 Jn 4:17 the **d** of judgment because as he is,
Rev 1:10 caught up in spirit on the Lord's **d**
16:14 on the great **d** of God the almighty.

DAYS → DAY
Gn 1:14 the seasons, the **d** and the years,
7:4 seven **d** from now I will bring rain
7:4 rain down on the earth for forty **d**
Ex 24:18 He was on the mountain for forty **d**
1 Kgs 19:8 he walked forty **d** and forty nights
1 Mc 4:56 For eight **d** they celebrated
Mk 1:13 remained in the desert for forty **d**,
Eph 5:16 opportunity, because the **d** are evil.
2 Tm 3:1 will be terrifying times in the last **d**.
Heb 1:2 in these last **d**, he spoke to us

DEACONS
1 Tm 3:8 Similarly, **d** must be dignified,

DEAD → DEATH, DIE, DIED, DYING
Dt 18:11 spirits, or seeks oracles from the **d**.
Ps 115:17 The **d** do not praise the LORD,
Eccl 9:4 live dog is better off than a **d** lion."
Mt 8:22 me, and let the **d** bury their **d**."
Mk 12:27 He is not God of the **d**
Lk 24:5 seek the living one among the **d**?
Rom 6:11 of yourselves as [being] **d** to sin
Eph 2:1 You were **d** in your transgressions
Col 1:18 the firstborn from the **d**, that in all
1 Pt 4:5 ready to judge the living and the **d**.
Rev 1:5 the firstborn of the **d** and ruler
20:12 I saw the **d**, the great and the lowly,
20:12 The **d** were judged according

DEAF
Ex 4:11 Who makes another mute or **d**,
Is 29:18 that day the **d** shall hear the words
Lk 7:22 lepers are cleansed, the **d** hear,

DEATH → DEAD
Dt 30:19 I have set before you life and **d**,
Ru 1:17 if even **d** separates me from you!"
Ps 22:16 you lay me in the dust of **d**.
Prv 18:21 **D** and life are in the power
Sg 8:6 For Love is strong as **D**, longing is
Sir 15:17 Before everyone are life and **d**,
Hos 13:14 shall I redeem them from **d**?
13:14 Where are your plagues, O **d**!
Mt 16:28 who will not taste **d** until they see
Jn 5:24 but has passed from **d** to life.
Rom 6:23 For the wages of sin is **d**,
1 Cor 15:55 Where, O **d**, is your victory?
15:55 Where, O **d**, is your sting?"
2 Cor 2:16 to the latter an odor of **d** that leads to **d**,
Heb 2:14 through **d** he might destroy the one who has the power of **d**,
1 Jn 3:14 that we have passed from **d** to life
3:14 does not love remains in **d**.
Rev 1:18 I hold the keys to **d**
20:14 Then **D** and Hades were thrown
20:14 (This pool of fire is the second **d**.
21:4 and there shall be no more **d**

DEBAUCHERY
Eph 5:18 in which lies **d**, but be filled

DEBORAH
Prophetess; led victory over Canaanites (Jgs 4–5).

DEBTS
Dt 15:1 you shall have a remission of **d**,
Mt 6:12 and forgive us our **d**, as we forgive

DECEIT → DECEITFUL, DECEIVE, DECEIVED, DECEIVERS
Dt 32:4 without **d**, just and upright is he!
1 Pt 2:22 and no **d** was found in his mouth."

DECEITFUL → DECEIT
Ps 35:20 in the land they fashion **d** speech.
Zep 3:13 be found in their mouths a **d** tongue;
1 Tm 4:1 faith by paying attention to **d** spirits

DECEIVE → DECEIT
Eph 5:6 Let no one **d** you with empty
1 Jn 1:8 are without sin," we **d** ourselves,
Rev 20:8 to **d** the nations at the four corners

DECEIVED → DECEIT
1 Tm 2:14 Adam was not **d**, but the woman was **d** and transgressed.

DECEIVERS → DECEIT
Ti 1:10 idle talkers and **d**,
2 Jn 1:7 Many **d** have gone

DECISION
Prv 16:33 from the LORD comes every **d**.

DECLARED
Mk 7:19 (Thus he **d** all foods clean.)

DECREASE
Jn 3:30 He must increase; I must **d**."

DECREE → DECREED
Ps 2:7 I will proclaim the **d** of the LORD,
Lk 2:1 In those days a **d** went

DECREED → DECREE
Dn 9:24 "Seventy weeks are **d** for your

DEDICATED → DEDICATION
1 Kgs 8:63 all the Israelites **d** the house

DEDICATION → DEDICATED
2 Ch 7:9 they had celebrated the **d** of the altar
Ezr 6:16 celebrated the **d** of this house
1 Mc 4:56 eight days they celebrated the **d**

DEED → DEEDS
Jer 32:10 I had written and sealed the **d**,
Col 3:17 in word or in **d**, do everything

DEEDS → DEED
Dt 3:24 or on earth can perform **d**
Ps 9:2 I will declare all your wondrous **d**.
Jer 50:29 Repay them for their **d**;
Rev 19:8 linen represents the righteous **d**

DEFEND
Ps 72:4 he may **d** the oppressed among
Prv 31:9 justly, **d** the needy and the poor!

DEFILE → DEFILED
Nm 35:34 Do not **d** the land in which you live
Mk 7:15 one from outside can **d** that person;
7:15 come out from within are what **d**."

DEFILED → DEFILE
1 Mc 1:37 they **d** the sanctuary.
Ps 79:1 they have **d** your holy temple;

DEFRAUD
Mk 10:19 you shall not **d**; honor your father

DEITY
Col 2:9 the whole fullness of the **d** bodily,

DELAY
Ps 70:6 LORD, do not **d**!
Heb 10:37 to come shall come; he shall not **d**.

DELIGHT → DELIGHTS
1 Sm 15:22 "Does the LORD **d** in burnt
Ps 40:9 I **d** to do your will, my God;
Prv 8:30 I was his **d** day by day,
Zec 11:7 took two staffs: one I called **D**,
Rom 7:22 For I take **d** in the law of God,

DELIGHTS → DELIGHT
Ps 5:5 You are not a god who **d** in evil;

DELILAH
Philistine who betrayed Samson (Jgs 16:4-22).

DELIVER → DELIVERANCE, DELIVERER
Mt 27:43 let him **d** him now if he wants him.

DELIVERANCE → DELIVER
Est 4:14 and **d** will come to the Jews
Phil 1:19 this will result in **d** for me through

DELIVERER → DELIVER
Rom 11:26 "The **d** will come out of Zion,

DEMON → DEMONIACS, DEMONIC, DEMONS
Tb 3:8 the wicked **d** Asmodeus kept killing
6:8 a woman who is afflicted by a **d**
Mt 11:18 they said, 'He is possessed by a **d**.'
17:18 him and the **d** came out of him,
Jn 10:21 surely a **d** cannot open the eyes

DEMONIACS → DEMON
Mt 8:28 two **d** who were coming

DEMONIC → DEMON
Rev 16:14 These were **d** spirits who performed

DEMONS → DEMON
Dt 32:17 They sacrificed to **d**, to "no-gods,"
Bar 4:7 your Maker with sacrifices to **d**
Lk 11:18 it is by Beelzebul that I drive out **d**.
1 Cor 10:20 [they sacrifice] to **d**, not to God,
10:20 you to become participants with **d**.
Jas 2:19 Even the **d** believe that and tremble.
Rev 9:20 to give up the worship of **d**

DEN
Jer 7:11 become in your eyes a **d** of thieves?
Mk 11:17 you have made it a **d** of thieves."

DENARIUS
Mk 12:15 Bring me a **d** to look at."

DENIED → DENY
Mt 26:70 But he **d** it in front of everyone,
1 Tm 5:8 family members has **d** the faith
Rev 3:8 my word and have not **d** my name.

DENIES → DENY
Lk 12:9 whoever **d** me before others will be
1 Jn 2:22 Whoever **d** that Jesus is the Christ.
2:22 Whoever **d** the Father and the Son,

DENY → DENIED, DENIES
Mt 16:24 to come after me must **d** himself,
2 Tm 2:12 But if we **d** him he will **d** us.
2 Pt 2:1 even **d** the Master who ransomed

DEPART
Gn 49:10 The scepter shall never **d**
Phil 1:23 I long to **d** this life and be

DEPRAVED
2 Pt 2:10 follow the flesh with its **d** desire

DEPRIVE
1 Cor 7:5 Do not **d** each other, except perhaps

DEPTH → DEPTHS
Rom 11:33 the **d** of the riches and wisdom
Eph 3:18 breadth and length and height and **d**,

DEPTHS → DEPTH
Ps 130:1 Out of the **d** I call to you, LORD;
1 Cor 2:10 everything, even the **d** of God.

DESCENDANTS
Gn 15:18 To your **d** I give this land,
Dt 4:37 your ancestors he chose their **d**
Is 44:3 offspring, my blessing upon your **d**.
Rom 9:7 of Abraham because they are his **d**;

DESCENDED → DESCENDING
Eph 4:9 also **d** into the lower [regions]

DESCENDING → DESCENDED
Mk 1:10 the Spirit, like a dove, **d** upon him.
Jn 1:51 and **d** on the Son of Man."

DESERT
Ps 106:14 In the **d** they gave in to their

DESERTED
Mk 8:4 satisfy them here in this **d** place?"

DESERVE
Rev 2:23 give each of you what your works **d**.

DESIRE → DESIRED, DESIRES
Is 46:10 shall stand, I accomplish my every **d**.
Hos 6:6 For it is loyalty that I **d**,
Mt 9:13 meaning of the words, 'I **d** mercy,
Jas 1:14 is lured and enticed by his own **d**.

DESIRED → DESIRE
Lk 22:15 them, "I have eagerly **d** to eat this

DESIRES → DESIRE
Sir 18:30 guide, but keep your **d** in check.
2 Tm 4:3 following their own **d** and insatiable

DESOLATE → DESOLATING
Ex 23:29 lest the land become **d** and the wild
1 Mc 1:39 Her sanctuary became **d** as
Mt 23:38 your house will be abandoned, **d**.

DESOLATING → DESOLATE
Mk 13:14 you see the **d** abomination standing

DESPAIR → DESPAIRED
2 Cor 4:8 perplexed, but not driven to **d**;

DESPAIRED → DESPAIR
2 Cor 1:8 strength, so that we **d** even of life.

DESPISE → DESPISED
Prv 1:7 fools **d** wisdom and discipline.
Lk 16:13 be devoted to one and **d** the other.

DESPISED → DESPISE
1 Cor 1:28 chose the lowly and **d** of the world,

DESTINED
Eph 1:5 he **d** us for adoption to himself
1 Pt 1:11 to the sufferings **d** for Christ

DESTROY → DESTROYED, DESTROYER, DESTRUCTION
Gn 6: 13 So I am going to **d** them
Est 3: 6 he sought to **d** all the Jews,
Mt 10: 28 of the one who can **d** both soul
Jn 10: 10 only to steal and slaughter and **d**;
Jas 4: 12 judge who is able to save or to **d**.
1 Jn 3: 8 God was revealed to **d** the works

DESTROYED → DESTROY
1 Cor 15: 26 The last enemy to be **d** is death,
2 Cor 5: 1 should be **d**, we have a building

DESTROYER → DESTROY
Ex 12: 23 not let the **d** come into your houses
1 Cor 10: 10 did, and suffered death by the **d**.

DESTRUCTION → DESTROY
Mt 7: 13 and the road broad that leads to **d**,
Rom 9: 22 the vessels of wrath made for **d**?
2 Pt 3: 16 and unstable distort to their own **d**,

DEVIL
Mt 4: 1 the desert to be tempted by the **d**.
Lk 8: 12 but the **d** comes and takes away
Jn 8: 44 You belong to your father the **d**
Eph 4: 27 and do not leave room for the **d**.
6: 11 firm against the tactics of the **d**.
Heb 2: 14 the power of death, that is, the **d**,
Jas 4: 7 Resist the **d**, and he will flee
1 Pt 5: 8 Your opponent the **d** is prowling
1 Jn 3: 8 Whoever sins belongs to the **d**, because the **d** has sinned
3: 8 to destroy the works of the **d**.
Jude 1: 9 with the **d** in a dispute over the body
Rev 12: 9 who is called the **D** and Satan,
20: 2 serpent, which is the **D** or Satan,

DEVOTED → DEVOTION
Ps 116: 15 eyes of the LORD is the death of his **d**.
Mt 6: 24 or be **d** to one and despise the other.

DEVOTION → DEVOTED
Wis 10: 12 that he might know that **d** to God is
1 Tm 4: 7 Train yourself for **d**,
2 Pt 1: 3 everything that makes for life and **d**,

DEVOUR → DEVOURING
1 Pt 5: 8 lion looking for [someone] to **d**.
Rev 12: 4 to **d** her child when she gave birth.

DEVOURING → DEVOUR
Gal 5: 15 you go on biting and **d** one another,

DEW
Jgs 6: 37 and if **d** is on the fleece alone,

DICTATE
Jer 36: 18 he would **d** all these words to me,"

DIE → DEAD
Gn 2: 17 when you eat from it you shall **d**.
3: 4 "You certainly will not **d**!
Ex 11: 5 firstborn in the land of Egypt will **d**,
Ru 1: 17 Where you **d** I will **d**, and there be
Jb 2: 9 Curse God and **d**!"
Prv 10: 21 many, but fools **d** for want of sense.
Eccl 3: 2 A time to give birth, and a time to **d**;
Is 22: 13 and drink, for tomorrow we **d**!"
Jer 31: 30 but all shall **d** because of their own
Mt 26: 35 "Even though I should have to **d**
Jn 11: 26 and believes in me will never **d**.
Rom 14: 8 and if we **d**, we **d** for the Lord;
14: 8 whether we live or **d**, we are
1 Cor 15: 32 eat and drink, for tomorrow we **d**."
Heb 9: 27 that human beings **d** once,

DIED → DEAD
Rom 5: 6 yet **d** at the appointed time
1 Cor 15: 3 that Christ **d** for our sins
Gal 2: 19 For through the law I **d** to the law,

DIFFERENT
2 Cor 11: 4 if you receive a **d** spirit from the one
11: 4 or a **d** gospel from the one you
Gal 1: 6 [the] grace [of Christ] for a **d** gospel

DILIGENCE
Rom 12: 8 if one is over others, with **d**;

DINAH
Only daughter of Jacob, by Leah (Gn 30:21; 46:15). Raped by Shechem; avenged by Simeon and Levi (Gn 34).

DIRECT → DIRECTS
2 Thes 3: 5 May the Lord **d** your hearts

DIRECTS → DIRECT
Prv 16: 9 the way, but the LORD **d** the steps.

DISAPPOINT
Rom 5: 5 and hope does not **d**,

DISCERNMENT
1 Cor 12: 10 to another **d** of spirits;

DISCIPLE → DISCIPLES
Mt 10: 24 No **d** is above his teacher, no slave
Lk 14: 26 his own life, he cannot be my **d**.

DISCIPLES → DISCIPLE
Is 8: 16 seal the instruction with my **d**.
Mt 26: 56 Then all the **d** left him and fled.
28: 19 and make **d** of all nations,
Lk 6: 13 day came, he called his **d** to himself,
Jn 8: 31 in my word, you will truly be my **d**,
Acts 11: 26 the **d** were first called Christians.

DISCIPLINE → DISCIPLINED
Prv 5: 23 They will die from lack of **d**,
Heb 12: 5 do not disdain the **d** of the Lord

DISCIPLINED → DISCIPLINE
1 Cor 11: 32 we are being **d** so that we may not

DISEASE → DISEASES
Mt 4: 23 curing every **d** and illness among
9: 35 and curing every **d** and illness.

DISEASES → DISEASE
Ex 15: 26 any of the **d** with which I afflicted
Mt 8: 17 our infirmities and bore our **d**."

DISGRACE
1 Mc 4: 58 the people now that the **d** brought
Prv 11: 2 When pride comes, **d** comes;

DISHONEST
Lk 16: 10 the person who is **d** in very small matters is also **d** in great ones.

DISHONOR
Jn 8: 49 I honor my Father, but you **d** me.
Acts 5: 41 worthy to suffer **d** for the sake

DISMAYED
Jos 1: 9 Do not fear nor be **d**,

DISOBEDIENT → DISOBEY
Rom 10: 21 long I stretched out my hands to a **d**
Ti 3: 3 we ourselves were once foolish, **d**,

DISOBEY → DISOBEYING, DISOBEDIENT
Lv 26: 27 you **d** and continue hostile to me,

DISOBEYING → DISOBEDIENT
1 Pt 2: 8 They stumble by **d** the word, as is

DISPERSION
Jn 7:35 not going to the **d** among the Greeks

DISQUALIFIED → DISQUALIFY
1 Cor 9:27 to others, I myself should be **d**.

DISQUALIFY → DISQUALIFIED
Col 2:18 Let no one **d** you,

DISSENSIONS
Gal 5:20 fury, acts of selfishness, **d**, factions,

DISTINCTION → DISTINCTIONS
Rom 3:22 all who believe. For there is no **d**;

DISTINCTIONS → DISTINCTION
Jas 2: 4 you not made **d** among yourselves

DISTRESS
Dt 4:30 In your **d**, when all these things
Jgs 2:15 and they were in great **d**.
2 Sm 22: 7 In my **d** I called out: LORD!
Ps 81: 8 In **d** you called and I rescued you;
Jer 30: 7 A time of **d** for Jacob, though he
Rom 8:35 Will anguish, or **d**, or persecution,

DISTRIBUTED
Acts 4:35 they were **d** to each according

DIVIDE → DIVIDED
Ps 22:19 they **d** my garments among them;

DIVIDED → DIVIDE
Lk 11:18 And if Satan is **d** against himself,

DIVINATION → DIVINE
1 Sm 15:23 For a sin of **d** is rebellion,
2 Kgs 17:17 They practiced augury and **d**.

DIVINE → DIVINATION
2 Pt 1: 4 may come to share in the **d** nature,

DIVORCE → DIVORCED
Dt 24: 1 he writes out a bill of **d** and hands it
Is 50: 1 Where is the bill of **d** with which I
Jer 3: 8 her away and gave her a bill of **d**,
Mal 2:16 For I hate **d**, says the LORD,
Mt 5:31 his wife must give her a bill of **d**.'
19: 3 a man to **d** his wife for any cause
1 Cor 7:11 and a husband should not **d** his wife.

DIVORCED → DIVORCE
Lv 21: 7 nor a woman who has been **d** by her
Mt 5:32 marries a **d** woman commits

DOCTRINE → DOCTRINES
2 Tm 4: 3 people will not tolerate sound **d** but,
Ti 1: 9 be able both to exhort with sound **d**

DOCTRINES → DOCTRINE
Mk 7: 7 me, teaching as **d** human precepts.'
1 Tm 1: 3 certain people not to teach false **d**

DOEG
Edomite; Saul's chief shepherd; murdered 85 priests at Nob (1 Sm 21:7; 22:6-23; Ps 52).

DOERS → DOES, DONE
Jas 1:22 Be **d** of the word and not hearers

DOES → DOERS
Ps 135: 6 Whatever the LORD desires he **d**
Eccl 3:14 whatever God **d** will endure forever;
Mk 3:35 [For] whoever **d** the will of God is

DOG → DOGS
Jgs 7: 5 the water as a **d** does with its tongue
2 Pt 2:22 "The **d** returns to its own vomit,"

DOGS → DOG
Prv 26:11 As **d** return to their vomit, so fools
Mt 7: 6 "Do not give what is holy to **d**,
15:26 the children and throw it to the **d**."
Phil 3: 2 Beware of the **d**! Beware of the evil
Rev 22:15 Outside are the **d**, the sorcerers,

DOMINION
Gn 1:26 Let them have **d** over the fish
Ps 110: 2 from Zion. Have **d** over your enemies!
Dn 7:14 His **d** is an everlasting **d** that shall

DONE → DOERS
Mt 6:10 come, your will be **d**, on earth as
26:42 my drinking it, your will be **d**!"
Rev 16:17 from the throne, saying, "It is **d**."

DOOM → DOOMED
Dt 32:35 and their **d** is rushing upon them!

DOOMED → DOOM
Ps 102:21 prisoners, to release those **d** to die."

DOOR → DOORPOSTS
Mt 7: 7 and the **d** will be opened to you.
Rev 3:20 I stand at the **d** and knock.
3:20 hears my voice and opens the **d**,

DOORPOSTS → DOOR
Ex 12: 7 apply it to the two **d** and the lintel

DORCAS
Disciple; raised from the dead (Acts 9:36-43).

DOUBLE
Dt 21:17 giving him a **d** share of whatever he
1 Sm 1: 5 but he would give a **d** portion
2 Kgs 2: 9 "May I receive a **d** portion of your
Rev 18: 6 Pay her back **d** for her deeds.
18: 6 her cup pour **d** what she poured.

DOUBT → DOUBTED, DOUBTING
Mt 14:31 you of little faith, why did you **d**?"

DOUBTED → DOUBT
Mt 28:17 him, they worshiped, but they **d**.

DOUBTING → DOUBT
Jas 1: 6 not **d**, for the one who doubts is like

DOUGH
Ex 12:39 The **d** they had brought out of Egypt
Gal 5: 9 yeast leavens the whole batch of **d**.

DOVE
Gn 8: 8 Then he released a **d**, to see
Mk 1:10 like a **d**, descending upon him.

DRAGON
Is 27: 1 he will slay the **d** in the sea.
Dn 14:23 There was a great **d**
Rev 12: 3 it was a huge red **d**, with seven
20: 2 He seized the **d**, the ancient serpent,

DRANK → DRINK
Mk 14:23 it to them, and they all **d** from it.
1 Cor 10: 4 and all **d** the same spiritual drink,
10: 4 for they **d** from a spiritual rock

DRAW
Jn 12:32 earth, I will **d** everyone to myself."
Jas 4: 8 **D** near to God, and he will **d** near

DREAM → DREAMER, DREAMS
1 Kgs 3: 5 appeared to Solomon in a **d** at night.
Dn 7: 1 as Daniel lay in bed he had a **d**,
7: 1 Then he wrote down the **d**;
Mt 1:20 of the Lord appeared to him in a **d**

Acts 2: 17 your old men shall **d** dreams.

DREAMER → DREAM
Gn 37: 19 to one another: "Here comes that **d**!

DREAMS → DREAM
Nm 12: 6 to them, in **d** I speak to them;
1 Sm 28: 6 neither in **d** nor by Urim nor
Sir 34: 7 For **d** have led many astray,

DRIED → DRY
Jos 5: 1 that the LORD had **d** up the waters
Is 51: 10 Was it not you who **d** up the sea,

DRINK → DRANK, DRUNK, DRUNKARD, DRUNKARDS, DRUNKENNESS
Ex 32: 6 Then they sat down to eat and **d**,
Eccl 9: 7 and **d** your wine with a merry heart,
Is 22: 13 "Eat and **d**, for tomorrow we die!"
Mt 20: 22 Can you **d** the cup that I am going to **d**?"
Jn 18: 11 Shall I not **d** the cup that the Father
Rom 14: 17 of God is not a matter of food and **d**,
1 Cor 12: 13 we were all given to **d** of one Spirit.
Rev 14: 10 will also **d** the wine of God's fury,

DRIVE → DROVE
Ex 23: 30 little I will **d** them out before you,
Mk 11: 15 the temple area he began to **d**

DROSS
Ps 119: 119 Like **d** you regard all the wicked
Is 1: 25 and refine your **d** in the furnace,
Ez 22: 18 house of Israel has become **d** to me.

DROVE → DRIVE
Jos 24: 18 our approach the LORD **d** out all
Mk 1: 12 At once the Spirit **d** him

DRUNK → DRINK
Gn 9: 21 became **d**, and lay naked inside his
1 Sm 1: 13 Eli, thinking she was **d**,
Jn 2: 10 and then when people have **d** freely,
Acts 2: 15 These people are not **d**, as you
Eph 5: 18 And do not get **d** on wine,

DRUNKARD → DRINK
Mt 11: 19 he is a glutton and a **d**, a friend
1 Cor 5: 11 a slanderer, a **d**, or a robber,
1 Tm 3: 3 not a **d**, not aggressive, but gentle,

DRUNKARDS → DRINK
Prv 23: 21 For **d** and gluttons come to poverty,

DRUNKENNESS → DRINK
Tb 4: 15 let **d** accompany you on your way.

DRY → DRIED
Gn 1: 9 basin, so that the **d** land may appear.
Ex 14: 16 may pass through the sea on **d** land.
Jos 3: 17 of the LORD stood on **d** ground
3: 17 while all Israel crossed on **d** ground,
Jgs 6: 37 while all the ground is **d**, I shall
Ez 37: 4 **D** bones, hear the word

DUE
1 Ch 16: 29 to the LORD the glory **d** his name!
Mal 1: 6 father, where is the honor **d** to me?
1: 6 a master, where is the fear **d** to me?
Rom 13: 7 taxes to whom taxes are **d**, toll to whom toll is **d**,

DULL
Is 6: 10 **d** their ears and close their eyes;
59: 1 to save, nor his ear too **d** to hear.

DUST
Gn 13: 16 make your descendants like the **d**
1 Sm 2: 8 He raises the needy from the **d**;
Ps 103: 14 formed, remembers that we are **d**.
Eccl 3: 20 both were made from the **d**, and to the **d** they both return.
Na 1: 3 and clouds are the **d** at his feet;
Mt 10: 14 and shake the **d** from your feet.

DWELL → DWELLING, DWELLS
Ex 25: 8 for me, that I may **d** in their midst.
Ps 23: 6 I will **d** in the house of the LORD
Eph 3: 17 Christ may **d** in your hearts through
Col 1: 19 all the fullness was pleased to **d**,
Rev 21: 3 He will **d** with them and they will

DWELLING → DWELL
Dt 12: 11 chooses as the **d** place for his name
1 Kgs 8: 27 "Is God indeed to **d** on earth?
Jn 14: 2 house there are many **d** places.
Eph 2: 22 being built together into a **d** place

DWELLS → DWELL
Jn 14: 10 The Father who **d** in me is doing his
Rom 7: 17 I who do it, but sin that **d** in me.
1 Cor 3: 16 and that the Spirit of God **d** in you?
Col 2: 9 in him **d** the whole fullness

DYING → DEAD
2 Cor 6: 9 as **d** and behold we live;

E

EAGLE → EAGLES'
Ez 1: 10 an ox, and each had the face of an **e**.
17: 3 The great **e**, with wide wingspan
Rev 4: 7 the fourth looked like an **e** in flight.

EAGLES' → EAGLE
Is 40: 31 strength, they will soar on **e** wings;

EAR → EARS
Lk 22: 51 Then he touched the servant's **e**
1 Cor 2: 9 and **e** has not heard, and what has

EARLY
Dt 11: 14 land, the **e** rain and the late rain,
Lk 24: 22 were at the tomb **e** in the morning
Jas 5: 7 patient with it until it receives the **e**

EARS → EAR
Is 35: 5 see, and the **e** of the deaf be opened;
Mt 11: 15 Whoever has **e** ought to hear.
Rev 2: 7 " ' "Whoever has **e** ought to hear

EARTH → EARTHLY, EARTHQUAKE, EARTHQUAKES
Gn 1: 1 God created the heavens and the **e**—
6: 11 the **e** was corrupt in the view of God
Ex 19: 5 all peoples, though all the **e** is mine.
Ps 37: 11 But the poor will inherit the **e**,
47: 3 feared, the great king over all the **e**,
Sir 40: 11 All that is of **e** returns to **e**, and what
Is 6: 3 All the **e** is filled with his glory!"
65: 17 creating new heavens and a new **e**;
Jer 23: 24 Do I not fill heaven and **e**?—
Mt 24: 35 Heaven and **e** will pass away,
Lk 5: 24 of Man has authority on **e** to forgive
2 Pt 3: 13 and a new **e** in which righteousness
Rev 21: 1 I saw a new heaven and a new **e**.
21: 1 and the former **e** had passed away,

EARTHLY → EARTH
Jn 3: 12 If I tell you about **e** things and you
2 Cor 5: 1 For we know that if our **e** dwelling,

EARTHQUAKE → EARTH
1 Kgs 19: 11 after the wind, an **e**—but the LORD was not in the **e**;
Mt 28: 2 And behold, there was a great **e**;
Acts 16: 26 there was suddenly such a severe **e**

Rev 6: 12 sixth seal, and there was a great **e**;

EARTHQUAKES → EARTH
Mt 24: 7 famines and **e** from place to place.

EASIER → EASY
Mt 9: 5 Which is **e**, to say, 'Your sins are
Lk 16: 17 It is **e** for heaven and earth to pass
18: 25 For it is **e** for a camel to pass

EAST
Gn 2: 8 in the **e**, and placed there the man
Ps 103: 12 As far as the **e** is from the west,
Mt 2: 1 behold, magi from the **e** arrived

EASY → EASIER
Mt 11: 30 For my yoke is **e**, and my burden

EAT → ATE, EATING, EATS
Gn 2: 16 You are free to **e** from any
Ex 12: 11 This is how you are to **e** it:
12: 11 in hand, you will **e** it in a hurry.
Lv 11: 4 you shall not **e** any of the following
Eccl 2: 24 nothing better for mortals than to **e**
Mt 26: 26 it to his disciples said, "Take and **e**;
Acts 10: 13 "Get up, Peter. Slaughter and **e**."
1 Cor 10: 31 So whether you **e** or drink,

EATING → EAT
Lk 7: 34 The Son of Man came **e**
1 Cor 8: 4 So about the **e** of meat sacrificed

EATS → EAT
Jn 6: 51 whoever **e** this bread will live
1 Cor 11: 27 Therefore whoever **e** the bread

EDEN
Gn 2: 8 LORD God planted a garden in **E**,
Is 51: 3 wilderness he shall make like **E**,
Ez 28: 13 In **E**, the garden of God, you lived;

EDOM → =ESAU
Gn 25: 30 That is why he was called **E**.
Nm 20: 18 But **E** answered him, "You shall
Ob 1: 1 says the Lord GOD concerning **E**:
Mal 1: 4 If **E** says, "We have been crushed,

EFFORT
2 Pt 1: 5 make every **e** to supplement your

EGYPT
Gn 12: 10 so Abram went down to **E**
37: 28 the Ishmaelites, who took him to **E**.
47: 27 Thus Israel settled in the land of **E**,
Ex 1: 8 of Joseph, rose to power in **E**.
12: 40 had stayed in **E** was four hundred
Jos 15: 47 as far as the Wadi of **E** and the coast
Neh 9: 18 God who brought you up from **E**,'
Ps 78: 51 He struck all the firstborn of **E**,
Hos 11: 1 loved him, out of **E** I called my son.
Mt 2: 15 "Out of **E** I called my son."
Rev 11: 8 names "Sodom" and "**E**,"

EHUD
Judge of Israel (Jgs 3:12-30).

ELAH
1. Son of Baasha; king of Israel (1 Kgs 16:6-14).
2. Valley in which David fought Goliath (1 Sm 17:2, 19; 21:9).

ELDERS
Ex 24: 1 and seventy of the **e** of Israel.
Jgs 2: 7 of those **e** who outlived Joshua
Is 3: 14 into judgment with the people's **e**
Mt 27: 12 accused by the chief priests and **e**,
Mk 7: 3 hands, keeping the tradition of the **e**.
Rev 4: 4 thrones on which twenty-four **e** sat,

ELEAZAR
1. Third son of Aaron (Ex 6:23-25). Succeeded Aaron as high priest (Nm 20:26; Dt 10:6). Allotted land to tribes (Jos 14:1). Death (Jos 24:33).
2. Brother of Judas Maccabeus (1 Mc 2:5; 6:43-46).

ELECT → ELECTION
Mt 24: 22 sake of the **e** they will be shortened.
Mk 13: 22 mislead, if that were possible, the **e**.

ELECTION → ELECT
Rom 11: 28 but in respect to **e**, they are beloved
2 Pt 1: 10 eager to make your call and **e** firm,

ELEMENTS
Heb 5: 12 someone teach you again the basic **e**
2 Pt 3: 10 and the **e** will be dissolved by fire,

ELEVEN
Mt 28: 16 The **e** disciples went to Galilee,
Acts 1: 26 he was counted with the **e** apostles.

ELI
1. High priest in youth of Samuel (1 Sm 1–4). Blessed Hannah (1 Sm 1:12-18); raised Samuel (1 Sm 2:11-26). Prophesied against because of wicked sons (1 Sm 2:27-36). Death of Eli and sons (1 Sm 4:11-22).
2. "Eli, Eli, lema sabachthani?" (Mt 27:46).

ELIAKIM → =JEHOIAKIM
1. Original name of Jehoiakim (2 Kgs 23:34; 2 Ch 36:4).
2. Hezekiah's palace administrator (2 Kgs 18:17-37; 19:2; Is 36:1-22; 37:2).

ELIEZER
1. Servant of Abraham (Gn 15:2).
2. Son of Moses (Ex 18:4; 1 Ch 23:15-17).

ELIHU
A friend of Job (Jb 32–37).

ELIJAH
Prophet; predicted famine in Israel (1 Kgs 17:1; Jas 5:17). Fed by ravens (1 Kgs 17:2-6). Raised Sidonian widow's son (1 Kgs 17:7-24). Defeated prophets of Baal at Carmel (1 Kgs 18:16-46). Ran from Jezebel (1 Kgs 19:1-9). Prophesied death of Azariah (2 Kgs 1). Succeeded by Elisha (1 Kgs 19:19-21; 2 Kgs 2:1-18). Taken to heaven in whirlwind (2 Kgs 2:11-12; Sir 48:1-12; 1 Mc 2:58).
Return prophesied (Mal 4:5-6); equated with John the Baptist (Mt 17:9-13; Mk 9:9-13; Lk 1:17). Appeared with Moses in transfiguration of Jesus (Mt 17:1-8; Mk 9:1-8).

ELIMELECH
Ru 1: 3 **E**, the husband of Naomi, died,

ELIPHAZ
A friend of Job (Jb 4–5; 15; 22; 42:7, 9).

ELISHA
Prophet; successor of Elijah (1 Kgs 19:16-21; Sir 48:12-14); inherited his mantle (2 Kgs 2:1-18). Purified bad water (2 Kgs 2:19-22). Cursed young men (2 Kgs 2:23-25). Aided Israel's defeat of Moab (2 Kgs 3). Provided widow with oil (2 Kgs 4:1-7). Raised Shunammite woman's son (2 Kgs 4:8-37). Purified food (2 Kgs 4:38-41). Fed 100 men (2 Kgs 4:42-44). Healed Naaman's leprosy (2 Kgs 5). Made axhead float (2 Kgs 6:1-7). Captured Arameans (2 Kgs 6:8-23). Political adviser to Israel (2 Kgs 6:24–8:6; 9:1-3; 13:14-19), Aram (2 Kgs 8:7-15). Death (2 Kgs 13:20).

ELIZABETH
Mother of John the Baptist (Lk 1:5-58).

ELKANAH
Husband of Hannah, father of Samuel (1 Sm 1–2).

EMMANUEL
Is 7: 14 about to bear a son, shall name him **E**.
8: 8 will fill the width of your land, **E**!
Mt 1: 23 and they shall name him **E**,"

EMMAUS
Lk 24: 13 miles from Jerusalem called **E**,

EMPTIED → EMPTY
1 Cor 1: 17 cross of Christ might not be **e** of its
Phil 2: 7 Rather, he **e** himself,

EMPTY → EMPTIED, EMPTY-HANDED
Ru 3: 17 not go back to your mother-in-law **e**.' "
Eph 5: 6 one deceive you with **e** arguments,

EMPTY-HANDED → EMPTY, HAND
Ex 23: 15 No one shall appear before me **e**.

ENCOURAGEMENT
Acts 4: 36 (which is translated "son of **e**"),
Rom 15: 5 and **e** grant you to think in harmony
Phil 2: 1 If there is any **e** in Christ,

END → ENDS
Gn 6: 13 that the **e** of all mortals has come,
Prv 14: 12 right, but the **e** of it leads to death!
Eccl 12: 12 making of many books there is no **e**,
Mt 24: 13 perseveres to the **e** will be saved.
28: 20 you always, until the **e** of the age."
Jn 13: 1 world and he loved them to the **e**.
Rom 10: 4 For Christ is the **e** of the law
Rev 22: 13 the last, the beginning and the **e**."

ENDOR
1 Sm 28: 7 is a woman in **E** who is a medium."

ENDS → END
Ps 2: 8 your possession, the **e** of the earth.
Is 40: 28 of old, creator of the **e** of the earth.
Rom 10: 18 their words to the **e** of the world."

ENDURANCE → ENDURE
Rom 5: 3 knowing that affliction produces **e**,
Heb 10: 36 You need **e** to do the will of God
2 Pt 1: 6 self-control with **e**, **e** with devotion,
Rev 1: 9 and the **e** we have in Jesus,

ENDURE → ENDURANCE, ENDURED, ENDURES
Mal 3: 2 who can **e** the day of his coming?

ENDURED → ENDURE
Heb 12: 2 that lay before him he **e** the cross,

ENDURES → ENDURE
1 Ch 16: 41 LORD, "whose love **e** forever,"
Sir 40: 17 cut off, and righteousness **e** forever.
Bar 4: 1 of God, the law that **e** forever;
Mt 10: 22 whoever **e** to the end will be saved.
Jn 6: 27 for the food that **e** for eternal life,
1 Cor 13: 7 things, hopes all things, **e** all things.

ENEMIES → ENEMY
Ex 23: 22 I will be an enemy to your **e**
Jdt 8: 35 you to take vengeance upon our **e**!"
Est 9: 5 The Jews struck down all their **e**
1 Mc 4: 36 "Now that our **e** have been crushed,
Ps 110: 1 I make your **e** your footstool."
Mt 5: 44 love your **e**, and pray for those who
Lk 20: 43 I make your **e** your footstool." '
Rom 5: 10 if, while we were **e**, we were

ENEMY → ENEMIES, ENMITY
Mt 13: 39 the **e** who sows them is the devil.
1 Cor 15: 26 The last **e** to be destroyed is death,
Jas 4: 4 of the world makes himself an **e**

ENJOY → ENJOYMENT
Eccl 9: 9 **E** life with the wife you love,

ENJOYMENT → ENJOY
1 Tm 6: 17 provides us with all things for our **e**.

ENLIGHTENED → LIGHT
Eph 1: 18 May the eyes of [your] hearts be **e**,
Heb 6: 4 case of those who have once been **e**

ENLIGHTENS → LIGHT
Jn 1: 9 which **e** everyone, was coming

ENMITY → ENEMY
Gn 3: 15 I will put **e** between you
Jas 4: 4 of the world means **e** with God?

ENOCH
Walked with God and taken by him (Gn 5:18-24; Heb 11:5; Sir 44:16). Prophet (Jude 14).

ENSLAVE → SLAVE
Gal 2: 4 Christ Jesus, that they might **e** us—

ENTER
Ex 40: 35 Moses could not **e** the tent
Nm 20: 24 he shall not **e** the land I have given
Ps 95: 11 "They shall never **e** my rest."
Mt 5: 20 you will not **e** into the kingdom
7: 13 "**E** through the narrow gate;
7: 13 those who **e** through it are many.
Mk 10: 15 of God like a child will not **e** it."
Jn 3: 5 no one can **e** the kingdom of God
Heb 3: 11 wrath, "They shall not **e** into my
Rev 21: 27 but nothing unclean will **e** it,
21: 27 Only those will **e** whose names are

ENTHRONED → THRONE
1 Ch 13: 6 by the name "LORD **e**

ENTRUSTED → TRUST
Lk 12: 48 required of the person **e** with much,
12: 48 of the person **e** with more.
2 Tm 1: 12 to guard what has been **e** to me until

ENVY
Mk 7: 22 deceit, licentiousness, **e**, blasphemy,
Rom 1: 29 full of **e**, murder, rivalry, treachery,

EPHOD
Ex 28: 6 The **e** they shall make of gold
Jgs 8: 27 Gideon made an **e** out of the gold

EPHRAIM
1. Second son of Joseph (Gn 41:52; 46:20). Blessed as firstborn by Jacob (Gn 48). Tribe of numbered (Nm 1:33; 26:37), blessed (Dt 33:17), allotted land (Jos 16:4-9; Ez 48:5), failed to fully possess (Jos 16:10; Jgs 1:29).
2. Term for the Northern Kingdom (Is 7:17; Hos 5).

EQUAL → EQUALITY
Is 40: 25 To whom can you liken me as an **e**?
46: 5 whom would you liken me as an **e**,
Jn 5: 18 father, making himself **e** to God.

EQUALITY → EQUAL
Phil 2: 6 of God, did not regard **e** with God

EQUIPPED
2 Tm 3: 17 competent, **e** for every good work.

ESAU → =EDOM
Firstborn of Isaac, twin of Jacob (Gn 25:21-26). Also called Edom (Gn 25:30). Sold Jacob his birthright (Gn 25:29-34); lost blessing (Gn 27). Married Hittites (Gn 26:34), Ishmaelites (Gn 28:6-9). Reconciled to Jacob (Gn 33). Genealogy (Gn 36). The LORD chose Jacob over Esau (Mal 1:2-3), but gave Esau land (Dt 2:2-12). Descendants eventually obliterated (Ob 1-21; Jer 49:7-22).

ESCAPE
Ps 68:21 **e** from death is the LORD God's.
Rom 2:3 that you will **e** the judgment
1 Thes 5:3 woman, and they will not **e**.
Heb 12:25 they did not **e** when they refused

ESTABLISH → ESTABLISHED
Gn 6:18 I will **e** my covenant with you.
Dt 28:9 The LORD will **e** you as a holy
Ps 89:5 and **e** your throne through all ages."
Rom 10:3 to **e** their own [righteousness],

ESTABLISHED → ESTABLISH
Ps 89:3 For I said, "My mercy is **e** forever;
Jer 10:12 power, **e** the world by his wisdom,
2 Pt 1:12 and are **e** in the truth you have.

ESTHER
Jewess, originally named Hadassah, who lived in Persia; cousin of Mordecai (Est 2:7). Chosen queen of Xerxes (Est 2:8-18). Persuaded by Mordecai to foil Haman's plan to exterminate the Jews (Est 3–4). Revealed Haman's plans to Xerxes, resulting in Haman's death (Est 7), the Jews' preservation (Est 8–9), Mordecai's exaltation (Est 8:15; 9:4; 10). Decreed celebration of Purim (Est 9:18-32).

ETERNAL → ETERNITY
Mt 25:46 these will go off to **e** punishment,
25:46 but the righteous to **e** life."
Mk 10:17 what must I do to inherit **e** life?"
Jn 3:16 not perish but might have **e** life.
4:14 of water welling up to **e** life."
10:28 I give them **e** life, and they shall
Rom 5:21 **e** life through Jesus Christ our Lord.
2 Cor 4:17 us an **e** weight of glory beyond all
Heb 5:9 he became the source of **e** salvation
1 Jn 5:13 you may know that you have **e** life,

ETERNITY → ETERNAL
Sir 42:21 he is from all **e** one and the same,
2 Pt 3:18 be glory now and to the day of **e**.

EUNUCH → EUNUCHS
Acts 8:27 Now there was an Ethiopian **e**,

EUNUCHS → EUNUCH
Is 56:4 To the **e** who keep my sabbaths,

EUPHRATES
Gn 2:14 The fourth river is the **E**.
15:18 of Egypt to the Great River, the **E**,
Rev 16:12 his bowl on the great river **E**.

EUTYCHUS
Acts 20:9 and a young man named **E** who was

EVANGELIST → EVANGELISTS
Acts 21:8 we went to the house of Philip the **e**,
2 Tm 4:5 perform the work of an **e**;

EVANGELISTS → EVANGELIST
Eph 4:11 others as **e**, others as pastors

EVE
Gn 3:20 man gave his wife the name "**E**,"
4:1 had intercourse with his wife **E**,
Tb 8:6 you made his wife **E** to be his helper
2 Cor 11:3 as the serpent deceived **E** by his
1 Tm 2:13 For Adam was formed first, then **E**.

EVENING
Gn 1:5 **E** came, and morning followed—
Eccl 11:6 at **e** do not let your hand be idle:
Zec 14:7 night, for in the **e** there will be light.

EVERLASTING → LAST
Gn 9:16 remember the **e** covenant between

EVERY → EVERYTHING
Gn 7:23 The LORD wiped out **e** being
Ex 11:5 **E** firstborn in the land of Egypt will
Eccl 12:14 God will bring to judgment **e** work,
Is 45:23 To me **e** knee shall bend; by me **e**
Mt 12:25 "**E** kingdom divided against itself
Rom 14:11 Lord, **e** knee shall bend before me,
14:11 **e** tongue shall give praise to God."
Phil 2:10 name of Jesus **e** knee should bend,
2 Tm 3:17 equipped for **e** good work.
1 Jn 4:1 do not trust **e** spirit but test
Rev 21:4 He will wipe **e** tear from their eyes,

EVERYTHING → EVERY
Gn 1:31 God looked at **e** he had made,
Ex 19:8 together, "**E** the LORD has said,
Eccl 3:1 There is an appointed time for **e**,
1 Cor 10:31 you do, do **e** for the glory of God.
1 Tm 4:4 For **e** created by God is good,
2 Pt 1:3 has bestowed on us **e** that makes

EVIL → EVILDOERS, EVILS
Gn 6:5 was always nothing but **e**,
Ex 32:22 know how the people are prone to **e**.
Tb 12:7 good, and **e** will not overtake you.
Prv 8:13 fear of the LORD is hatred of **e**;]
8:13 Pride, arrogance, the **e** way,
Sir 7:1 Do no **e**, and **e** will not overtake
Is 5:20 Those who call **e** good, and good **e**,
Ez 7:5 says the Lord GOD: **E** upon **e**!
Dn 9:13 law of Moses, this **e** has come upon us.
Mt 6:13 test, but deliver us from the **e** one.
12:35 an **e** person brings forth **e** out of a store of **e**.
Jn 17:15 that you keep them from the **e** one.
Rom 12:17 Do not repay anyone **e** for **e**;
Eph 5:16 opportunity, because the days are **e**.
1 Pt 2:16 using freedom as a pretext for **e**,
1 Jn 5:18 and the **e** one cannot touch him.
2 Jn 1:11 greets him shares in his **e** works.
3 Jn 1:11 do not imitate **e** but imitate good.
1:11 does what is **e** has never seen God.

EVILDOERS → EVIL
Ps 34:17 The LORD's face is against **e**
Lk 13:27 Depart from me, all you **e**!'
1 Pt 2:12 so that if they speak of you as **e**,

EVILS → EVIL
1 Tm 6:10 love of money is the root of all **e**,

EXALT → EXALTED, EXALTS
Prv 4:8 Extol her, and she will **e** you;
Jas 4:10 before the Lord and he will **e** you.

EXALTED → EXALT
Ps 97:9 all the earth, **e** far above all gods.
Is 2:11 and the LORD alone will be **e**,
Phil 2:9 God greatly **e** him and bestowed

EXALTS → EXALT
Prv 14:34 Justice **e** a nation, but sin is
Sir 7:11 there is One who **e** and humbles.
Lk 14:11 For everyone who **e** himself will be

EXAMINE
1 Cor 11:28 A person should **e** himself, and so
2 Cor 13:5 **E** yourselves to see whether you are

EXAMPLES
1 Cor 10:6 These things happened as **e** for us,
1 Pt 5:3 to you, but be **e** to the flock.

EXCELLENCE → EXCELLENT
Phil 4:8 if there is any **e** and if there is

EXCELLENT → EXCELLENCE
1 Cor 12: 31 I shall show you a still more **e** way.
Heb 1: 4 has inherited is more **e** than theirs.

EXCEPT
2 Sm 22: 32 Truly, who is God **e** the LORD?
Mt 11: 27 No one knows the Son **e** the Father,
11: 27 no one knows the Father **e** the Son
Lk 11: 29 will be given it, **e** the sign of Jonah.
Jn 14: 6 comes to the Father **e** through me.

EXCHANGED
Ps 106: 20 They **e** their glory for the image
Rom 1: 23 **e** the glory of the immortal God

EXCUSE
Jn 15: 22 as it is they have no **e** for their sin.
Rom 1: 20 As a result, they have no **e**;

EXHORT
Ti 2: 15 **E** and correct with all authority.

EXILE
2 Kgs 25: 11 guard, led into **e** the last of the army
Ezr 6: 21 who had returned from the **e** and all

EXIST → EXISTED, EXISTS
1 Cor 8: 6 all things are and for whom we **e**,
Heb 2: 10 and through whom all things **e**,

EXISTED → EXIST
2 Pt 3: 5 the fact that the heavens **e** of old

EXISTS → EXIST
Heb 11: 6 God must believe that he **e**

EXPECTING
Lk 6: 35 to them, and lend **e** nothing back;

EXPLAIN → EXPLAINED
2 Ch 9: 2 that Solomon could not **e** it to her.

EXPLAINED → EXPLAIN
Mk 4: 34 his own disciples he **e** everything

EXPLAINING → EXPLAIN
Dn 5: 12 **e** riddles and solving problems,

EXPLOIT
Lv 19: 13 You shall not **e** your neighbor.

EXPOSE → EXPOSED
Mt 1: 19 yet unwilling to **e** her to shame,
Eph 5: 11 works of darkness; rather **e** them,

EXPOSED → EXPOSE
Jn 3: 20 so that his works might not be **e**.
Eph 5: 13 everything **e** by the light becomes
Heb 10: 33 times you were publicly **e** to abuse

EYE → EYES, EYEWITNESSES
Ex 21: 24 **e** for **e**, tooth for tooth,
Ps 17: 8 Keep me as the apple of your **e**;
Mt 5: 29 If your right **e** causes you to sin,
5: 38 said, 'An **e** for an **e** and a tooth
7: 3 the splinter in your brother's **e**,
7: 3 the wooden beam in your own **e**?
Mk 10: 25 to pass through [the] **e** of [a] needle
1 Cor 15: 52 in the blink of an **e**, at the last
Rev 1: 7 and every **e** will see him, even those

EYES → EYE
Gn 3: 7 the **e** of both of them were opened,
2 Ch 16: 9 The **e** of the LORD roam over
Ps 121: 1 I raise my **e** toward the mountains.
Prv 3: 7 Do not be wise in your own **e**,
22: 12 The **e** of the LORD watch over
Ez 1: 18 **e** filled the four rims all around.
Dn 10: 6 his **e** were like fiery torches,
Zec 4: 10 "These seven are the **e**
Mt 9: 30 And their **e** were opened.
13: 15 they have closed their **e**, lest
Lk 24: 31 With that their **e** were opened
Eph 1: 18 May the **e** of [your] hearts be
1 Pt 3: 12 For the **e** of the Lord are
1 Jn 2: 16 lust, enticement for the **e**,
Rev 1: 14 and his **e** were like a fiery flame.
4: 6 four living creatures covered with **e**
21: 4 He will wipe every tear from their **e**,

EYEWITNESSES → EYE, WITNESS
Lk 1: 2 just as those who were **e**
2 Pt 1: 16 but we had been **e** of his majesty.

EZEKIEL
Priest called to be prophet to the exiles (Ez 1–3; Sir 49:8). Symbolically acted out destruction of Jerusalem (Ez 4–5; 12; 24).

EZRA
Priest and teacher of the Law who led a return of exiles to Israel to reestablish temple and worship (Ezr 7–8). Corrected intermarriage of priests (Ezr 9–10). Read Law at celebration of Feast of Tabernacles (Neh 8). Participated in dedication of Jerusalem's walls (Neh 12).

F

FACE → FACES
Ex 3: 6 Moses hid his **f**, for he was afraid
34: 30 radiant the skin of his **f** had become,
Nm 6: 25 The LORD let his **f** shine
12: 8 **f** to **f** I speak to him, plainly and not
Ps 4: 7 show us the light of your **f**!"
51: 13 Do not drive me from before your **f**,
Is 54: 8 for a moment I hid my **f** from you;
Ez 39: 29 I will no longer hide my **f**
Lk 9: 29 While he was praying his **f** changed
2 Cor 3: 7 intently at the **f** of Moses because
Rev 1: 16 and his **f** shone like the sun at its

FACES → FACE
Ez 1: 6 but each had four **f** and four wings,
Rev 9: 7 their **f** were like human **f**,

FACTIONS
1 Cor 11: 19 there have to be **f** among you
Gal 5: 20 acts of selfishness, dissensions, **f**,

FAIL → FAILED
Dt 31: 6 he will never **f** you or forsake you.
Ez 47: 12 will not wither, nor will their fruit **f**.

FAILED → FAIL
Rom 9: 6 it is not that the word of God has **f**.

FAINT
Ps 142: 4 When my spirit is **f** within me,
Is 40: 31 grow weary, walk and not grow **f**.

FAITH → FAITHFUL, FAITHFULNESS, FAITHLESS
Ps 146: 6 that is in them, Who keeps **f** forever,
Is 7: 9 Unless your **f** is firm, you shall not
Hb 2: 4 is righteous because of **f** shall live.
Mt 17: 20 to them, "Because of your little **f**.
17: 20 if you have **f** the size of a mustard
Mk 2: 5 When Jesus saw their **f**, he said
Lk 7: 50 the woman, "Your **f** has saved you;
18: 8 comes, will he find **f** on earth?"
Acts 3: 16 And by **f** in his name, this man,
Rom 1: 17 the righteousness of God from **f** to **f**;
1: 17 one who is righteous by **f** will live."
3: 28 a person is justified by **f** apart
1 Cor 13: 13 So **f**, hope, love remain, these three;
Gal 3: 11 one who is righteous by **f** will live."

5: 6 but only **f** working through love.
Eph 4: 5 one Lord, one **f**, one baptism;
Phil 3: 9 which comes through **f** in Christ,
1 Tm 6: 11 righteousness, devotion, **f**, love,
2 Tm 4: 7 finished the race; I have kept the **f**.
Heb 11: 1 **F** is the realization of what is hoped
12: 2 Jesus, the leader and perfecter of **f**.
Jas 2: 17 So also **f** of itself, if it does not have
2: 24 by works and not by **f** alone.
2 Pt 1: 1 those who have received a **f** of equal
1 Jn 5: 4 that conquers the world is our **f**.
Jude 1: 3 contend for the **f** that was once
Rev 2: 13 and have not denied your **f** in me,

FAITHFUL → FAITH
Dt 32: 4 A **f** God, without deceit,
Ps 4: 4 works wonders for his **f** one;
Wis 3: 9 the **f** shall abide with him in love:
Mi 7: 2 The **f** have vanished from the earth,
Zec 8: 3 Jerusalem will be called the **f** city,
Mt 24: 45 then, is the **f** and prudent servant,
1 Cor 10: 13 God is **f** and will not let you be tried
1 Thes 5: 24 The one who calls you is **f**, and he
1 Pt 4: 19 over to a **f** creator as they do good.
1 Jn 1: 9 he is **f** and just and will forgive our
Rev 1: 5 and from Jesus Christ, the **f** witness,
19: 11 its rider was [called] "**F** and True."

FAITHFULNESS → FAITH
Ps 26: 3 I walk guided by your **f**.
Is 11: 5 his waist, and **f** a belt upon his hips.
Lam 3: 23 great is your **f**!
Gal 5: 22 patience, kindness, generosity, **f**,

FAITHLESS → FAITH
Mt 17: 17 reply, "O **f** and perverse generation,

FALL → FALLEN, FALLING
Ps 91: 7 Though a thousand **f** at your side,
Prv 16: 18 and a haughty spirit before a **f**.
Sir 28: 23 who forsake the Lord will **f** victim
Lk 10: 18 have observed Satan **f** like lightning
Rom 9: 33 and a rock that will make them **f**,
1 Cor 10: 12 secure should take care not to **f**.
Heb 10: 31 It is a fearful thing to **f**

FALLEN → FALL
2 Sm 1: 19 How can the warriors have **f**!
Is 14: 12 How you have **f** from the heavens,
21: 9 He calls out and says, '**F**, **f** is
Rev 9: 1 I saw a star that had **f** from the sky
18: 2 "**F**, **f** is Babylon the great.

FALLING → FALL
Lk 22: 44 like drops of blood **f** on the ground.]

FALSE
Mt 7: 15 "Beware of **f** prophets, who come
Mk 13: 22 **F** messiahs and **f** prophets will arise
2 Pt 2: 1 also **f** prophets among the people,
2: 1 there will be **f** teachers among you,
Rev 16: 13 and from the mouth of the **f** prophet.
20: 10 the beast and the **f** prophet were.

FAMILIES → FAMILY
Acts 3: 25 your offspring all the **f** of the earth
Ti 1: 11 as they are upsetting whole **f**

FAMILY → FAMILIES
Gal 6: 10 who belong to the **f** of the faith.
Eph 3: 15 from whom every **f** in heaven

FAMINE
Gn 12: 10 since the **f** in the land was severe.
41: 27 they are seven years of **f**.
Ru 1: 1 the judges there was a **f** in the land;
Ps 37: 19 in days of **f** they will be satisfied.
Am 8: 11 when I will send a **f** upon the land:
Jer 14: 12 will destroy them with the sword, **f**,
Acts 11: 28 would be a severe **f** all over
Rom 8: 35 or persecution, or **f**, or nakedness,

FAR
Is 57: 19 Peace to those who are **f** and near,
Jer 23: 23 and not a God **f** off?
Mk 7: 6 lips, but their hearts are **f** from me;
12: 34 "You are not **f** from the kingdom

FAST → FASTED, FASTING
Is 58: 5 Is this what you call a **f**, a day
Mt 6: 16 "When you **f**, do not look gloomy
Lk 18: 12 I **f** twice a week, and I pay tithes

FASTED → FAST
Mt 4: 2 He **f** for forty days and forty nights,

FASTING → FAST
Mt 6: 16 they may appear to others to be **f**.

FATE
Ps 81: 16 him, but their **f** is fixed forever.

FATHER → FATHER'S
Gn 2: 24 That is why a man leaves his **f**
Ex 20: 12 Honor your **f** and your mother,
21: 15 Whoever strikes **f** or mother shall be
2 Sm 7: 14 I will be a **f** to him, and he shall be
Ps 89: 27 cry to me, 'You are my **f**, my God,
Prv 28: 24 Whoever defrauds **f** or mother
Wis 2: 16 and boasts that God is his **F**.
Sir 3: 3 Those who honor their **f** atone
Is 8: 4 learns to say, "My **f**, my mother,"
Jer 3: 19 would call me, "My **F**," I thought,
Mal 1: 6 A son honors his **f**, and a servant
1: 6 I am a **f**, where is the honor due
Mt 6: 9 Our **F** in heaven, hallowed be your
28: 19 baptizing them in the name of the **F**,
Lk 18: 20 honor your **f** and your mother.' "
Jn 5: 18 but he also called God his own **f**,
8: 44 You belong to your **f** the devil
8: 44 because he is a liar and the **f** of lies.
14: 6 comes to the **F** except through me.
Rom 8: 15 through which we cry, "Abba, **F**!"
Gal 4: 6 our hearts, crying out, "Abba, **F**!"
Eph 6: 2 "Honor your **f** and mother."
Heb 1: 5 "I will be a **f** to him, and he shall be
12: 9 all the more to the **F** of spirits
Jas 1: 17 coming down from the **F** of lights,
Rev 3: 5 his name in the presence of my **F**

FATHER'S → FATHER
Lk 2: 49 that I must be in my **F** house?"
Jn 1: 14 the glory as of the **F** only Son,
2: 16 here, and stop making my **F** house
10: 29 can take them out of the **F** hand.
14: 2 In my **F** house there are many

FAULT
Sir 11: 7 Before investigating, do not find **f**;
Rom 9: 19 "Why (then) does he still find **f**?

FAVOR → FAVORED
Gn 6: 8 But Noah found **f** with the LORD.
Ex 33: 12 You have found **f** with me.
Ps 30: 6 lasts but a moment; his **f** a lifetime.
Is 49: 8 In a time of **f** I answer you,

FAVORED → FAVOR
Lk 1: 28 coming to her, he said, "Hail, **f** one!

FEAR → AFRAID, FEARED, FEARS
Dt 6: 13 The LORD, your God, shall you **f**;
Ps 19: 10 The **f** of the LORD is pure,
23: 4 the shadow of death, I will **f** no evil,
27: 1 and my salvation; whom should I **f**?
Prv 1: 7 **F** of the LORD is the beginning
Eccl 12: 13 all is heard: **F** God and keep his
Sir 1: 11 The **f** of the Lord is glory and
Phil 2: 12 work out your salvation with **f**
1 Pt 3: 14 be afraid or terrified with **f** of them,
1 Jn 4: 18 There is no **f** in love, but perfect love drives out **f**
Rev 14: 7 voice, "**F** God and give him glory,

FEARED → FEAR
Ex 14: 31 Egypt, the people **f** the LORD.
Jb 1: 1 Job, who **f** God and avoided evil.
Hg 1: 12 thus the people **f** the LORD.

FEARS → FEAR
Jdt 16: 16 one who **f** the Lord is forever great.
Ps 34: 5 me, delivered me from all my **f**.
Prv 31: 30 the woman who **f** the LORD is
Sir 15: 1 Whoever **f** the LORD will do this;

FED → FEED
Dt 8: 16 **f** you in the wilderness with manna,
Ps 80: 6 You have **f** them the bread of tears,

FEED → FED, FEEDS
Jn 21: 15 He said to him, "**F** my lambs."
Rom 12: 20 "if your enemy is hungry, **f** him;

FEEDS → FED
Is 40: 11 Like a shepherd he **f** his flock;

FEET → FOOT
Ps 8: 7 of your hands, put all things at his **f**:
119: 105 Your word is a lamp for my **f**, a light
Dn 2: 33 its **f** partly iron and partly clay.
Mt 22: 44 your enemies under your **f**" '?
Lk 24: 39 Look at my hands and my **f**, that it
Jn 12: 3 nard and anointed the **f** of Jesus
13: 5 began to wash the disciples' **f**
Rom 16: 20 quickly crush Satan under your **f**.
1 Cor 15: 25 has put all his enemies under his **f**.
Rev 1: 15 His **f** were like polished brass

FELLOWSHIP
2 Cor 6: 14 Or what **f** does light have
1 Jn 1: 3 so that you too may have **f** with us;
1: 3 for our **f** is with the Father

FEMALE
Gn 1: 27 male and **f** he created them.
Mk 10: 6 'God made them male and **f**.
Gal 3: 28 free person, there is not male and **f**;

FESTIVALS
Lv 23: 2 declare holy days. These are my **f**:

FEVER
Dt 28: 22 will strike you with consumption, **f**,
Mk 1: 30 mother-in-law lay sick with a **f**.

FEW
Ps 105: 12 When they were **f** in number,
Mt 22: 14 Many are invited, but **f** are chosen."
Lk 13: 23 will only a **f** people be saved?"

FIDELITY
Tb 3: 2 All your ways are mercy and **f**;
Ps 25: 5 Guide me by your **f** and teach me,

FIELD → FIELDS
Prv 31: 16 She picks out a **f** and acquires it;
Mt 13: 44 is like a treasure buried in a **f**,
13: 44 sells all that he has and buys that **f**.
24: 40 Two men will be out in the **f**;
1 Cor 3: 9 you are God's **f**, God's building.

FIELDS → FIELD
Lk 2: 8 in that region living in the **f**
Jn 4: 35 up and see the **f** ripe for the harvest.

FIG → FIGS
Gn 3: 7 so they sewed **f** leaves together
Hb 3: 17 though the **f** tree does not blossom,
Mt 24: 32 "Learn a lesson from the **f** tree.
Lk 13: 6 a person who had a **f** tree planted

FIGHT → FOUGHT
Ex 14: 14 The LORD will **f** for you;
1 Tm 1: 18 Through them may you **f** a good **f**

FIGS → FIG
Jer 24: 1 of **f** placed before the temple
Lk 6: 44 For people do not pick **f**

FILL → FILLED, FULL, FULLNESS
Gn 1: 28 **f** the earth and subdue it.
9: 1 fertile and multiply and **f** the earth.
Ps 72: 19 may he **f** all the earth with his glory.
Jer 23: 24 Do I not **f** heaven and earth?—
Eph 4: 10 heavens, that he might **f** all things.

FILLED → FILL
Ex 1: 7 that the land was **f** with them.
40: 34 of the LORD **f** the tabernacle.
1 Kgs 8: 11 of the LORD had **f** the house
Ez 43: 5 glory of the LORD **f** the temple!
Lk 1: 15 He will be **f** with the holy Spirit
Acts 2: 4 they were all **f** with the holy Spirit
Eph 5: 18 debauchery, but be **f** with the Spirit,

FILTHY
Zec 3: 3 before the angel, clad in **f** garments.
Rev 22: 11 still act wickedly, and the **f** still be **f**.

FIND → FINDS, FOUND
Dt 4: 29 you shall indeed **f** him if you search
Prv 18: 22 To **f** a wife is to **f** happiness,
Jer 29: 13 you look for me, you will **f** me.
Mt 11: 29 and you will **f** rest for your selves.
16: 25 loses his life for my sake will **f** it.
Lk 11: 9 seek and you will **f**;

FINDS → FIND
Prv 8: 35 For whoever **f** me **f** life, and wins

FINGER
Dt 9: 10 by God's own **f**, with a copy of all
Mt 23: 4 they will not lift a **f** to move them.
Lk 11: 20 if it is by the **f** of God that [I] drive

FINISHED
Ex 40: 33 Thus Moses **f** all the work.
Jn 19: 30 taken the wine, he said, "It is **f**."

FIRE
Ex 3: 2 appeared to him as **f** flaming
3: 2 although the bush was on **f**, it was
13: 21 of a column of **f** to give them light.
Lv 9: 24 **F** came forth from the LORD's
Nm 11: 1 the LORD's **f** burned among them
Dt 4: 24 is a consuming **f**, a jealous God.
1 Kgs 19: 12 after the earthquake, **f**—but the LORD was not in the **f**;
19: 12 after the **f**, a light silent sound.
2 Ch 7: 1 **f** came down from heaven
Is 66: 24 die, their **f** shall not be extinguished;
Dn 3: 92 walking in the **f**, and the fourth
Mal 3: 2 For he will be like a refiner's **f**,
Mt 3: 11 you with the holy Spirit and **f**.

Mk 9:43 Gehenna, into the unquenchable **f**.
Acts 2:3 appeared to them tongues as of **f**,
1 Cor 3:13 It will be revealed with **f**, and the **f**
Heb 12:29 For our God is a consuming **f**.
Jas 3:6 The tongue is also a **f**.
3:6 itself set on **f** by Gehenna.
2 Pt 3:10 the elements will be dissolved by **f**,
Rev 20:14 were thrown into the pool of **f**.
20:14 (This pool of **f** is the second death.

FIRM
Is 7:9 Unless your faith is **f**, you shall not be **f**!
2 Cor 1:24 your joy, for you stand **f** in the faith.

FIRST → FIRSTBORN
Gn 1:5 and morning followed—the **f** day.
Is 41:4 am the **f**, and at the last I am he.
Mt 6:33 But seek **f** the kingdom (of God)
Mk 10:31 But many that are **f** will be last,
10:31 last, and [the] last will be **f**."
16:2 had risen, on the **f** day of the week,
Acts 11:26 disciples were **f** called Christians.
Rom 1:16 for Jew **f**, and then Greek.
1 Cor 15:45 it is written, "The **f** man, Adam,
1 Thes 4:16 and the dead in Christ will rise **f**.
1 Jn 4:19 We love because he **f** loved us.
Rev 1:17 not be afraid. I am the **f** and the last,
20:5 This is the **f** resurrection.

FIRSTBORN → BEAR, FIRST
Gn 25:34 Esau treated his right as **f** with disdain.
Ex 4:22 says the LORD: Israel is my son, my **f**.
12:29 at midnight the LORD struck down every **f**
13:2 Consecrate to me every **f**;
Ps 78:51 He struck all the **f** of Egypt,
Zec 12:10 for him as one grieves over a **f**.
Lk 2:7 and she gave birth to her **f** son.
Col 1:15 invisible God, the **f** of all creation.
Rev 1:5 the **f** of the dead and ruler of

FISH
Gn 1:26 Let them have dominion over the **f**
Jon 2:1 But the LORD sent a great **f**
2:1 in the belly of the **f** three days
Mt 7:10 or a snake when he asks for a **f**?
Jn 6:9 has five barley loaves and two **f**;

FIVE
1 Sm 17:40 David selected **f** smooth stones
Mt 14:19 Taking the **f** loaves and the two fish,
1 Cor 14:19 church I would rather speak **f** words

FLAME → FLAMES
Is 10:17 a **f**, That burns and consumes its
Rev 19:12 His eyes were [like] a fiery **f**,

FLAMES → FLAME
Dn 3:49 drove the fiery **f** out of the furnace,

FLED → FLEE
Ex 2:15 But Moses **f** from Pharaoh and went
Mk 14:50 And they all left him and **f**.
Rev 12:6 The woman herself **f** into the desert
20:11 and the sky **f** from his presence

FLEE → FLED
Ps 11:1 me, "**F** like a bird to the mountains!
139:7 From your presence, where can I **f**?
Is 30:17 if five threaten, you shall **f**.
Jas 4:7 the devil, and he will **f** from you.

FLESH
Gn 2:23 is bone of my bones and **f** of my **f**;
Jb 19:26 off, and from my **f** I will see God:
Mt 16:17 For **f** and blood has not revealed this
26:41 spirit is willing, but the **f** is weak."
Jn 1:14 the Word became **f** and made his
3:6 What is born of **f** is **f** and what is
Rom 8:4 who live not according to the **f**
8:13 For if you live according to the **f**,
2 Cor 12:7 a thorn in the **f** was given to me,
Gal 5:19 Now the works of the **f** are obvious:
Eph 6:12 For our struggle is not with **f**
1 Pt 1:24 "All **f** is like grass, and all its glory
1 Jn 4:2 Jesus Christ come in the **f** belongs

FLOCK
Is 40:11 Like a shepherd he feeds his **f**;
Mt 26:31 the sheep of the **f** will be dispersed';
Lk 12:32 little **f**, for your Father is pleased
Jn 10:16 voice, and there will be one **f**,
1 Pt 5:3 to you, but be examples to the **f**.

FLOGGED
Acts 5:40 they had them **f**, ordered them

FLOOD
Gn 7:7 ark because of the waters of the **f**.
9:15 waters will never again become a **f**
Ps 29:10 LORD sits enthroned above the **f**!
2 Pt 2:5 he brought a **f** upon the godless

FLOW → FLOWING
Zec 14:8 fresh water will **f** from Jerusalem,
Jn 7:38 of living water will **f** from within

FLOWER
Is 40:7 The grass withers, the **f** wilts,
1 Pt 1:24 all its glory like the **f** of the field;
1:24 the grass withers, and the **f** wilts;

FLOWING → FLOW
Ex 3:8 land, a land **f** with milk and honey,
Jos 5:6 us, a land **f** with milk and honey.
Ez 47:1 I saw water **f** out from under
Rev 22:1 **f** from the throne of God

FOE
Ex 23:22 to your enemies and a **f** to your foes.
Ps 60:13 Give us aid against the **f**;

FOLLOW → FOLLOWED
Ex 16:4 see whether they **f** my instructions
1 Kgs 18:21 If the LORD is God, **f** him; if Baal, **f** him."
Lk 9:23 and take up his cross daily and **f** me.
Jn 10:27 I know them, and they **f** me.
Rev 14:4 the ones who **f** the Lamb wherever

FOLLOWED → FOLLOW
Jgs 2:12 They **f** other gods, the gods
Mk 1:18 they abandoned their nets and **f** him.
Rev 13:3 the whole world **f** after the beast.

FOLLY → FOOL
Prv 13:16 prudently but the foolish parade **f**.
26:4 answer fools according to their **f**,
Eccl 2:13 as much profit over **f** as light has
Mk 7:22 envy, blasphemy, arrogance, **f**.

FOOD → FOODS
Gn 1:30 I give all the green plants for **f**.
1 Mc 1:63 to die rather than to be defiled with **f**
Mt 6:25 Is not life more than **f** and the body
Jn 6:55 For my flesh is true **f**, and my blood
1 Cor 8:8 Now **f** will not bring us closer

FOODS → FOOD
Mk 7:19 (Thus he declared all **f** clean.)
1 Tm 4:3 require abstinence from **f** that God

FOOL → FOLLY, FOOLISH, FOOLISHNESS, FOOLS
Ps 14:1 The **f** says in his heart, "There is no

Prv 15: 5 The f spurns a father's instruction,
20: 3 strife, while every f starts a quarrel.
Mt 5: 22 says, 'You f,' will be liable to fiery

FOOLISH → FOOL
Prv 17: 25 A f son is vexation to his father,
Jer 5: 21 to this, you f and senseless people,
Mt 25: 2 Five of them were f and five were
1 Cor 1: 20 made the wisdom of the world f?
Ti 3: 3 For we ourselves were once f,

FOOLISHNESS → FOOL
1 Cor 1: 18 of the cross is f to those who are
3: 19 wisdom of this world is f in the eyes

FOOLS → FOOL
Prv 1: 7 f despise wisdom and discipline.
10: 21 many, but f die for want of sense.
Rom 1: 22 claiming to be wise, they became f
1 Cor 4: 10 We are f on Christ's account,

FOOT → FEET, FOOTSTOOL
Ps 91: 12 lest you strike your f against a stone.
Mt 18: 8 If your hand or f causes you to sin,
Lk 4: 11 you dash your f against a stone.' "

FOOTSTOOL → FOOT
Ps 110: 1 while I make your enemies your f."
Is 66: 1 are my throne, the earth, my f.
Heb 10: 13 until his enemies are made his f.

FOREHEAD → FOREHEADS
Ex 13: 9 your hand and a reminder on your f,
1 Sm 17: 49 and struck the Philistine on the f.

FOREHEADS → FOREHEAD
Ez 9: 4 an X on the f of those who grieve
Rev 7: 3 put the seal on the f of the servants
13: 16 image on their right hands or their f,
20: 4 nor had accepted its mark on their f

FOREIGN → FOREIGNER, FOREIGNERS
Ps 81: 10 There shall be no f god among you;
Prv 2: 16 a f woman with her smooth words,

FOREIGNER → FOREIGN
Ex 12: 43 No f may eat of it.
1 Cor 14: 11 I shall be a f to one who speaks it, and one who speaks it a f to me.

FOREIGNERS → FOREIGN
1 Cor 14: 21 by the lips of f I will speak to this

FOREKNEW → KNOW
Rom 8: 29 For those he f he also predestined
11: 2 not rejected his people whom he f.

FORERUNNER → RUN
Heb 6: 20 Jesus has entered on our behalf as f,

FORESKIN
Gn 17: 14 flesh of his f has not been cut away,

FOREVER
Gn 3: 22 tree of life, and eats of it and lives f?
6: 3 shall not remain in human beings f,
Ex 3: 15 This is my name f; this is my title
2 Sm 7: 13 I will establish his royal throne f.
1 Ch 16: 15 He remembers f his covenant
Ps 19: 10 of the LORD is pure, enduring f.
110: 4 "You are a priest f in the manner
117: 2 the faithfulness of the LORD is f.
Eccl 3: 14 whatever God does will endure f;
Wis 5: 15 But the righteous live f,
Is 40: 8 but the word of our God stands f."
51: 6 My salvation shall remain f and my
Jn 6: 51 whoever eats this bread will live f;
Heb 5: 6 "You are a priest f according
13: 8 is the same yesterday, today, and f.
1 Pt 1: 25 the word of the Lord remains f."
Rev 1: 18 dead, but now I am alive f and ever.
11: 15 and he will reign f and ever."
22: 5 and they shall reign f and ever.

FORFEIT
Mk 8: 36 gain the whole world and f his life?

FORGAVE → FORGIVE
Ps 85: 3 You f the guilt of your people,

FORGET → FORGOT, FORGOTTEN
Dt 6: 12 be careful not to f the LORD,
Ps 137: 5 If I f you, Jerusalem, may my right hand f.
Prv 4: 5 Do not f or turn aside
Is 49: 15 Can a mother f her infant,
49: 15 Even should she f, I will never f

FORGIVE → FORGAVE, FORGIVEN, FORGIVENESS, FORGIVING
Ex 32: 32 Now if you would only f their sin!
Sir 5: 6 my many sins he will f."
Mt 6: 12 and f us our debts, as we f our
Lk 5: 24 has authority on earth to f sins"—
1 Jn 1: 9 just and will f our sins and cleanse

FORGIVEN → FORGIVE
Lv 4: 20 on their behalf, that they may be f.
Ps 32: 1 fault is removed, whose sin is f.
Mt 12: 31 sin and blasphemy will be f people,
12: 31 against the Spirit will not be f.
Mk 2: 9 'Your sins are f,' or to say, 'Rise,
Rom 4: 7 are they whose iniquities are f
Eph 4: 32 one another as God has f you

FORGIVENESS → FORGIVE
Mk 1: 4 of repentance for the f of sins.
3: 29 the holy Spirit will never have f,
Col 1: 14 we have redemption, the f of sins.
Heb 9: 22 the shedding of blood there is no f.

FORGIVING → FORGIVE
Ex 34: 7 and f wickedness, rebellion, and sin;
Ps 86: 5 you are good and f, most merciful
Eph 4: 32 f one another as God has forgiven

FORGOT → FORGET
Dt 32: 18 you f the God who gave you birth.
Jer 23: 27 just as their ancestors f my name

FORGOTTEN → FORGET
Ps 77: 10 Has God f how to show mercy,
Is 49: 14 my Lord has f me."
Heb 12: 5 f the exhortation addressed to you as

FORM → FORMED, FORMLESS
Gn 1: 2 and the earth was without f or shape,
Lk 3: 22 upon him in bodily f like a dove.

FORMED → FORM
Gn 2: 7 the LORD God f the man
Ps 139: 13 You f my inmost being; you knit me
Gal 4: 19 in labor until Christ be f in you!

FORMLESS → FORM
Wis 11: 17 the universe from f matter, to send

FORSAKE → FORSAKEN
Dt 31: 6 he will never fail you or f you.
Jos 1: 5 I will not leave you nor f you.
Jer 17: 13 all who f you shall be put to shame;
Heb 13: 5 said, "I will never f you or abandon

FORSAKEN → FORSAKE
Mt 27: 46 my God, why have you f me?"

FORTRESS
2 Sm 22: 2 my rock, my **f**, my deliverer,
Ps 71: 3 for you are my rock and **f**.

FORTY
Gn 7: 4 rain down on the earth for **f** days and **f** nights,
Nm 14: 34 reconnoitering the land—**f** days—
14: 34 one year for each day: **f** years.
1 Kgs 19: 8 he walked **f** days and **f** nights
Jon 3: 4 "**F** days more and Nineveh shall be
Mt 4: 2 He fasted for **f** days and **f** nights,
Heb 3: 17 was he "provoked for **f** years"?

FOUGHT → FIGHT
Jos 10: 42 the God of Israel, **f** for Israel.
Rev 12: 7 The dragon and its angels **f** back,

FOUND → FIND
Is 55: 6 Seek the LORD while he may be **f**,
65: 1 be **f** by those who did not seek me.
Lk 15: 24 he was lost, and has been **f**.'
Rom 10: 20 "I was **f** [by] those who were not
Rev 20: 15 whose name was not **f** written

FOUNDATION → FOUNDATIONS
Ezr 3: 6 though the **f** of the LORD's temple
Is 28: 16 A precious cornerstone as a sure **f**;
1 Cor 3: 11 no one can lay a **f** other than the one
Eph 2: 20 built upon the **f** of the apostles
2 Tm 2: 19 God's solid **f** stands, bearing this

FOUNDATIONS → FOUNDATION
1 Kgs 6: 37 The **f** of the LORD's house were
Heb 11: 10 looking forward to the city with **f**,

FOUNTAIN
Ps 36: 10 For with you is the **f** of life,
Prv 16: 22 Good sense is a **f** of life to those
Zec 13: 1 that day a **f** will be opened

FOUR
Ez 1: 5 of **f** living creatures appeared.
10: 14 Each living creature had **f** faces:
Rev 4: 6 there were **f** living creatures covered

FOXES
Lk 9: 58 "**F** have dens and birds of the sky

FRAGRANT
Ex 25: 6 anointing oil and for the **f** incense;
Eph 5: 2 offering to God for a **f** aroma.

FRANKINCENSE → INCENSE
Is 60: 6 shall come bearing gold and **f**,
Mt 2: 11 and offered him gifts of gold, **f**,

FREE → FREED, FREEDOM
Ps 146: 7 The LORD sets prisoners **f**;
Sir 15: 14 them subject to their own **f** choice.
Jn 8: 32 truth, and the truth will set you **f**."
Gal 3: 28 there is neither slave nor **f** person,
Eph 6: 8 he does, whether he is slave or **f**.

FREED → FREE
Rev 1: 5 has **f** us from our sins by his blood,

FREEDOM → FREE
2 Cor 3: 17 the Spirit of the Lord is, there is **f**.
Gal 5: 1 For **f** Christ set us free;
1 Pt 2: 16 yet without using **f** as a pretext

FRIEND → FRIENDS
Prv 17: 17 A **f** is a **f** at all times, and a brother
Sir 7: 18 Do not barter a **f** for money,
Mt 11: 19 a **f** of tax collectors and sinners.'
Jas 2: 23 and he was called "the **f** of God."

FRIENDS → FRIEND
Jb 2: 11 three of Job's **f** heard of all
Prv 18: 24 but there are true **f** more loyal
Jn 15: 13 to lay down one's life for one's **f**.
15: 15 I have called you **f**, because I have

FRUIT → FRUITFUL, FRUITS
Gn 3: 6 So she took some of its **f** and ate it;
Dt 28: 4 Blessed be the **f** of your womb,
Ps 1: 3 of water, that yields its **f** in season;
Prv 8: 19 My **f** is better than gold, even pure
Ez 47: 12 river every kind of **f** tree will grow;
47: 12 will not wither, nor will their **f** fail.
Mt 3: 8 Produce good **f** as evidence of your
Lk 1: 42 and blessed is the **f** of your womb.
6: 44 every tree is known by its own **f**.
Jn 15: 2 branch in me that does not bear **f**,
15: 2 he prunes so that it bears more **f**.
Gal 5: 22 contrast, the **f** of the Spirit is love,
Col 1: 10 in every good work bearing **f**
Heb 13: 15 the **f** of lips that confess his name.
Rev 22: 2 that produces **f** twelve times a year,

FRUITFUL → FRUIT
Ex 1: 7 the Israelites were **f** and prolific.

FRUITS → FRUIT
Prv 3: 9 with first **f** of all your produce;
Mt 7: 16 By their **f** you will know them.

FULFILL → FULFILLED
Eccl 5: 4 a vow than make it and not **f** it.
Mt 5: 17 I have come not to abolish but to **f**.
Gal 6: 2 and so you will **f** the law of Christ.
Jas 2: 8 if you **f** the royal law according

FULFILLED → FULFILL
Lk 24: 44 the prophets and psalms must be **f**."
Rom 8: 4 decree of the law might be **f** in us,

FULL → FILL
Jn 1: 14 only Son, **f** of grace and truth.

FULLNESS → FILL
Jn 1: 16 From his **f** we have all received,
1 Cor 10: 26 "the earth and its **f** are the Lord's."
Gal 4: 4 But when the **f** of time had come,
Eph 1: 10 as a plan for the **f** of times, to sum
3: 19 may be filled with all the **f** of God.
Col 1: 19 him all the **f** was pleased to dwell,
2: 9 him dwells the whole **f** of the deity

FURNACE
Is 48: 10 I tested you in the **f** of affliction.
Dn 3: 6 be instantly cast into a white-hot **f**."
3: 49 went down into the **f** with Azariah
3: 49 drove the fiery flames out of the **f**,
Mt 13: 42 will throw them into the fiery **f**,

FURY
Rom 2: 8 **f** to those who selfishly disobey
Rev 16: 19 the cup filled with the wine of his **f**

FUTURE
Prv 24: 20 For the evil have no **f**, the lamp
Jer 31: 17 There is hope for your **f**—
1 Cor 3: 22 life or death, or the present or the **f**:
1 Tm 6: 19 treasure a good foundation for the **f**,

G

GABRIEL
Angel who interpreted Daniel's visions (Dn 8:16-26; 9:20-27); announced births of John (Lk 1:11-20), Jesus (Lk 1:26-38).

GAD
1. Son of Jacob by Zilpah (Gn 30:9-11; 35:26; 1 Ch 2:2). Tribe

of blessed (Gn 49:19; Dt 33:20-21), numbered (Nm 1:25; 26:18), allotted land east of the Jordan (Nm 32; 34:14; Jos 18:7; 22), west (Ez 48:27-28), 12,000 from (Rev 7:5).

2. Prophet; seer of David (1 Sm 22:5; 2 Sm 24:11-19; 1 Ch 29:29).

GAIN
Lk 9:25 one to **g** the whole world yet lose
Phil 1:21 to me life is Christ, and death is **g**.
3:8 so much rubbish, that I may **g** Christ
1 Tm 6:5 religion to be a means of **g**.

GALILEAN → GALILEE
Mt 26:69 "You too were with Jesus the **G**."

GALILEANS → GALILEE
Acts 2:7 these people who are speaking **G**?

GALILEE → GALILEAN, GALILEANS
Mt 4:15 the Jordan, **G** of the Gentiles,
Jn 7:41 Messiah will not come from **G**,

GAMALIEL
Pharisee (Acts 5:34-39), teacher of Paul (Acts 22:5).

GARDEN
Gn 2:8 The LORD God planted a **g**
Ez 28:13 In Eden, the **g** of God, you lived;
Jn 19:41 he had been crucified there was a **g**, and in the **g** a new tomb,

GARMENT → GARMENTS
Ps 102:27 they all wear out like a **g**;

GARMENTS → GARMENT
Gn 3:21 for the man and his wife **g** of skin,

GATE → GATES
Mt 7:13 "Enter through the narrow **g**;
7:13 for the **g** is wide and the road broad
Jn 10:7 say to you, I am the **g** for the sheep.
Heb 13:12 Jesus also suffered outside the **g**,

GATES → GATE
Gn 24:60 of the **g** of their enemies!"
Dt 6:9 of your houses and on your **g**.
Ps 100:4 Enter his **g** with thanksgiving,
Mt 16:18 the **g** of the netherworld shall not
Rev 21:21 The twelve **g** were twelve pearls,
21:21 each of the **g** made from a single

GATH
1 Sm 17:4 champion named Goliath of **G** came
2 Sm 1:20 Do not report it in **G**, as good news

GATHER → GATHERED
Ex 16:4 to go out and **g** their daily portion;
Ru 2:7 'I would like to **g** the gleanings
Is 11:12 nations and **g** the outcasts of Israel;
Mt 12:30 and whoever does not **g** with me
Lk 13:34 to **g** your children together as a hen

GATHERED → GATHER
Mt 18:20 or three are **g** together in my name,

GAVE → GIVE
Ex 31:18 he **g** him the two tablets
Neh 9:15 heaven you **g** them in their hunger,
Eccl 12:7 life breath returns to God who **g** it.
Mt 25:35 I was hungry and you **g** me food,
25:35 I was thirsty and you **g** me drink,
Jn 1:12 who did accept him he **g** power
3:16 the world that he **g** his only Son,
Eph 4:11 And he **g** some as apostles, others as
1 Tm 2:6 who **g** himself as ransom for all.

GEDALIAH
Governor of Judah (2 Kgs 25:22-26; Jer 39–41).

GEHAZI
Servant of Elisha (2 Kgs 4:12–5:27; 8:4-5).

GENEALOGY
Mt 1:1 The book of the **g** of Jesus Christ,

GENERATION → GENERATIONS
Ex 20:6 the thousandth **g** of those who love
34:7 children to the third and fourth **g**!
Mt 12:39 evil and unfaithful **g** seeks a sign,
Lk 21:32 this **g** will not pass away until all

GENERATIONS → GENERATION
Is 51:8 forever, my salvation, for all **g**.

GENEROSITY
Rom 12:8 if one contributes, in **g**; if one is
Gal 5:22 patience, kindness, **g**, faithfulness,

GENTILE → GENTILES
1 Mc 1:14 according to the **G** custom.
Mt 18:17 treat him as you would a **G** or a tax
Gal 2:14 are living like a **G** and not like

GENTILES → GENTILE
1 Mc 1:11 a covenant with the **G** all around us;
Lk 21:24 be taken as captives to all the **G**;
21:24 underfoot by the **G** until the times
Acts 15:19 to stop troubling the **G** who turn
Rom 3:29 Does he not belong to **G**, too?
Gal 3:8 God would justify the **G** by faith,
Eph 4:17 you must no longer live as the **G** do,

GENTLE → GENTLENESS
1 Pt 3:4 in the imperishable beauty of a **g**

GENTLENESS → GENTLE
Gal 5:23 **g**, self-control. Against such there is
1 Tm 6:11 faith, love, patience, and **g**.

GETHSEMANE
Mk 14:32 Then they came to a place named **G**,

GHOST
Mt 14:26 "It is a **g**," they said, and they cried
Lk 24:39 because a **g** does not have flesh

GIANT
Sir 47:4 As a youth he struck down the **g**

GIBEON
Jos 10:12 Sun, stand still at **G**, Moon,
1 Kgs 3:5 In **G** the LORD appeared

GIDEON
Judge, also called Jerubbaal; freed Israel from Midianites (Jgs 6–8; Heb 11:32). The fleece (Jgs 8:36-40).

GIFT → GIFTS
Nm 18:7 I give you your priesthood as a **g**.
Mt 5:23 if you bring your **g** to the altar,
Jn 4:10 "If you knew the **g** of God and who
Acts 2:38 you will receive the **g** of the holy
Rom 6:23 the **g** of God is eternal life in Christ
1 Cor 7:7 each has a particular **g** from God,
Jas 1:17 and every perfect **g** is from above,
Rev 21:6 the thirsty I will give a **g**

GIFTS → GIFT
Mt 2:11 treasures and offered him **g** of gold,
Lk 11:13 how to give good **g** to your children,
Rom 11:29 For the **g** and the call of God are
1 Cor 12:1 Now in regard to spiritual **g**,
14:1 but strive eagerly for the spiritual **g**,
Eph 4:8 he gave **g** to men."

GILGAL
Jos 5:9 Therefore the place is called **G**

1 Sm 7:16 **G** and Mizpah and judging Israel

GIRL
Ex 1:16 but if it is a **g**, she may live."
Mk 5:41 means, "Little **g**, I say to you,

GIVE → GAVE, GIVEN, GIVER, GIVES
Gn 9:3 I **g** them all to you as I did the green
12:7 your descendants I will **g** this land.
1 Kgs 3:5 Whatever you ask I shall **g** you.
Tb 12:9 Those who **g** alms will enjoy a full
Prv 25:21 are hungry, **g** them food to eat,
25:21 if thirsty, **g** something to drink;
30:15 has two daughters: "**G**," and "**G**."
Ez 36:26 I will **g** you a new heart, and a new
36:26 and **g** you a heart of flesh.
Mt 6:11 **G** us today our daily bread;
7:6 "Do not **g** what is holy to dogs,
Mk 10:45 to **g** his life as a ransom for many."
Jn 10:28 I **g** them eternal life, and they shall
Acts 20:35 said, 'It is more blessed to **g** than

GIVEN → GIVE
Mt 7:7 "Ask and it will be **g** to you;
Mk 4:25 To the one who has, more will be **g**;
Lk 22:19 is my body, which will be **g** for you;
Rom 5:5 the holy Spirit that has been **g** to us.

GIVER → GIVE
2 Cor 9:7 for God loves a cheerful **g**.

GIVES → GIVE
2 Cor 3:6 brings death, but the Spirit **g** life.
Jas 4:6 proud, but **g** grace to the humble."

GLAD → GLADNESS
Ps 16:9 Therefore my heart is **g**, my soul
90:15 Make us **g** as many days as you
Mt 5:12 Rejoice and be **g**, for your reward
Acts 2:26 Therefore my heart has been **g**

GLADNESS → GLAD
Ps 51:14 Restore to me the **g** of your salvation;
100:2 serve the LORD with **g**;
Is 16:10 orchards are taken away joy and **g**,
Zep 3:17 Who will rejoice over you with **g**,
Heb 1:9 you with the oil of **g** above your

GLASS
Rev 4:6 resembled a sea of **g** like crystal.
21:18 the city was pure gold, clear as **g**.

GLEAN
Ru 2:2 **g** grain in the field of anyone who

GLOOM
Is 9:1 in a land of **g** a light has shone.
Jl 2:2 a day of darkness and **g**, a day

GLORIFIED → GLORY
Jn 13:31 "Now is the Son of Man **g**, and God is **g** in him.
17:4 I **g** you on earth by accomplishing
Acts 3:13 has **g** his servant Jesus whom you
Rom 8:30 and those he justified he also **g**.

GLORIFY → GLORY
Ps 86:12 all my heart, **g** your name forever,
Jn 17:1 son, so that your son may **g** you,
1 Cor 6:20 Therefore, **g** God in your body.
Rev 15:4 not fear you, Lord, or **g** your name?

GLORIOUS → GLORY
Jdt 16:13 great are you and **g**,
Dn 3:26 and **g** forever is your name.
Jas 2:1 the faith in our **g** Lord Jesus Christ.

GLORY → GLORIFIED, GLORIFY, GLORIOUS
Ex 24:16 The **g** of the LORD settled
33:18 said, "Please let me see your **g**!"
40:34 and the **g** of the LORD filled
1 Sm 4:21 "Gone is the **g** from Israel,"
1 Kgs 8:11 since the **g** of the LORD had filled
1 Ch 29:12 Riches and **g** are from you, and you
1 Mc 1:40 As her **g** had been, so great was her
Ps 8:6 god, crowned him with **g** and honor.
19:2 The heavens declare the **g** of God;
24:7 portals, that the king of **g** may enter.
Is 6:3 All the earth is filled with his **g**!"
40:5 Then the **g** of the LORD shall be
Bar 5:4 of justice, the **g** of God's worship.
Ez 44:4 and the **g** of the LORD filled
Hos 4:7 I will change their **g** into shame.
Mt 25:31 the Son of Man comes in his **g**,
Lk 2:14 "**G** to God in the highest
Jn 1:14 us, and we saw his **g**, the **g** as
12:41 Isaiah said this because he saw his **g**
Rom 3:23 and are deprived of the **g** of God.
8:18 compared with the **g** to be revealed
9:4 the adoption, the **g**, the covenants,
1 Cor 10:31 do, do everything for the **g** of God.
2 Cor 4:17 weight of **g** beyond all comparison,
Heb 1:3 who is the refulgence of his **g**,
2 Pt 1:17 came to him from the majestic **g**,
Rev 4:11 to receive **g** and honor and power,
21:23 for the **g** of God gave it light, and its

GLUTTON → GLUTTONS
Mt 11:19 'Look, he is a **g** and a drunkard,

GLUTTONS → GLUTTON
Prv 23:21 drunkards and **g** come to poverty,

GNAT
Mt 23:24 who strain out the **g** and swallow

GO
Ex 5:1 Let my people **g**, that they may hold
Dt 6:14 You shall not **g** after other gods,
Jos 1:9 God, is with you wherever you **g**.
Ru 1:16 "Do not press me to **g** back
1:16 Wherever you **g** I will **g**,
Mt 28:19 **G**, therefore, and make disciples
Jn 14:3 if I **g** and prepare a place for you,

GOAT → GOATS
Lv 16:9 The **g** that is determined by lot
Dn 8:21 The he-**g** is the king of the Greeks,

GOATS → GOAT
Ps 50:13 of bulls or drink the blood of he-**g**?
Mt 25:32 separates the sheep from the **g**.
Heb 10:4 blood of bulls and **g** take away sins.

GOD → GOD'S, GODDESS, GODLESS, GODLY, GODS
Gn 1:1 when **G** created the heavens
1:27 **G** created mankind in his image;
1:27 in the image of **G** he created them;
3:5 **G** knows well that when you eat
17:1 I am **G** the Almighty.
Ex 3:4 **G** called out to him from the bush:
15:2 This is my **G**, I praise him; the **G** of my father, I extol him.
20:5 LORD, your **G**, am a jealous **G**,
34:6 LORD, a **G** gracious and merciful,
Nm 23:19 **G** is not a human being who speaks
23:19 Is **G** one to speak and not act,
Dt 4:7 our **G**, is to us whenever we call
6:5 your **G**, with your whole heart,
Jos 22:34 among them that the LORD is **G**.
1 Sm 2:2 there is no Rock like our **G**.

1 Kgs 8:27 "Is **G** indeed to dwell on earth?
18:24 The **G** who answers with fire is **G**."
2 Kgs 17:7 their **G**, who had brought them
Ezr 6:16 of this house of **G** with joy.
Neh 8:18 book of the law of **G** day after day,
Tb 4:19 your **G**, and ask him that all your
Ps 19:2 The heavens declare the glory of **G**;
22:2 My **G**, my **G**, why have you
46:2 **G** is our refuge and our strength,
46:11 "Be still and know that I am **G**!
47:8 For **G** is king over all the earth;
53:2 says in his heart, "There is no **G**."
68:21 Our **G** is a **G** who saves;
90:2 from eternity to eternity you are **G**.
136:2 Praise the **G** of gods; for his mercy
145:1 I will extol you, my **G** and king;
Eccl 12:13 all is heard: Fear **G** and keep his
Sir 32:14 Whoever seeks **G** must accept
Is 12:2 **G** indeed is my salvation;
40:28 The LORD is **G** from of old,
44:6 I am the last; there is no **G** but me.
Jer 10:10 The LORD is truly **G**, he is
10:10 he is the living **G**, the eternal King,
Bar 4:8 forgot the eternal **G** who nourished
Ez 28:2 you say, "I am a **g**! I sit
28:2 But you are a man, not a **g**;
28:2 you pretend you are a **g** at heart!
Dn 14:4 but Daniel worshiped only his **G**.
Hos 12:6 The LORD is the **G** of hosts,
Am 4:12 prepare to meet your **G**, O Israel!
Mi 6:8 and to walk humbly with your **G**.
Hb 3:18 LORD and exult in my saving **G**.
Mal 2:10 Has not one **G** created us?
Mt 1:23 which means "**G** is with us."
4:4 forth from the mouth of **G**.' "
4:7 the Lord, your **G**, to the test.' "
4:10 your **G**, shall you worship and him
6:24 You cannot serve **G** and mammon.
27:40 if you are the Son of **G**, [and] come
Mk 1:1 of Jesus Christ [the Son of **G**].
2:7 Who but **G** alone can forgive sins?"
10:9 Therefore what **G** has joined
12:30 You shall love the Lord your **G**
Lk 2:14 "Glory to **G** in the highest
18:19 No one is good but **G** alone.
22:70 "Are you then the Son of **G**?"
Jn 1:1 and the Word was with **G**, and the Word was **G**.
1:18 No one has ever seen **G**. The only Son, **G**, who is
3:16 For **G** so loved the world that he
5:18 but he also called **G** his own father, making himself equal to **G**.
20:28 said to him, "My Lord and my **G**!"
Acts 5:29 "We must obey **G** rather than men.
Rom 4:3 "Abraham believed **G**, and it was
6:23 the gift of **G** is eternal life in Christ
8:31 If **G** is for us, who can be against
1 Cor 10:31 do, do everything for the glory of **G**.
2 Cor 4:4 in whose case the **g** of this age has
4:4 of Christ, who is the image of **G**.
6:16 agreement has the temple of **G**
6:16 we are the temple of the living **G**;
Eph 4:6 one **G** and Father of all, who is over
Phil 2:6 though he was in the form of **G**,
2:6 regard equality with **G** something
Ti 2:13 of the glory of the great **G**
Heb 4:12 Indeed, the word of **G** is living
10:31 to fall into the hands of the living **G**.
12:29 For our **G** is a consuming fire.
Jas 2:23 "Abraham believed **G**, and it was
2:23 he was called "the friend of **G**."
4:8 Draw near to **G**, and he will draw
1 Jn 1:5 **G** is light, and in him there is no
4:16 to believe in the love **G** has for us.
4:16 **G** is love, and whoever remains in love remains in **G**
5:2 we love the children of **G** when we love **G**
Jude 1:21 Keep yourselves in the love of **G**
Rev 4:8 holy is the Lord **G** almighty,
19:13 his name was called the Word of **G**.
22:5 for the Lord **G** shall give them light,

***GOD → *LORD**
Gn 15:2 "Lord **G**, what can you give me,
2 Sm 7:18 I, Lord **G**, and what is my house,
Is 25:8 The Lord **G** will wipe away
61:1 spirit of the Lord **G** is upon me,

GOD'S → GOD
1 Cor 3:9 For we are **G** co-workers; you are **G** field, **G** building.
1 Jn 3:2 Beloved, we are **G** children now;

GODDESS → GOD
1 Kgs 11:5 Astarte, the **g** of the Sidonians,
Acts 19:27 of the great **g** Artemis will be of no

GODLESS → GOD
Jb 8:13 so shall the hope of the **g** perish.
1 Tm 1:9 lawless and unruly, the **g** and sinful,
2 Pt 3:7 and of destruction of the **g**.

GODLY → GOD
Sir 44:1 I will now praise the **g** our ancestors,
Mal 2:15 does the One require? **G** offspring!
2 Cor 7:10 For **g** sorrow produces a salutary

GODS → GOD
Ex 12:12 judgment on all the **g** of Egypt—
20:3 shall not have other **g** beside me.
Jgs 2:17 themselves by following other **g**,
2 Kgs 17:7 They venerated other **g**,
Jn 10:34 your law, 'I said, "You are **g**" '?
1 Cor 8:5 even though there are so-called **g**
8:5 many "**g**" and many "lords"),

GOG
Ez 38:18 day, the day **G** invades the land
Rev 20:8 corners of the earth, **G** and Magog,

GOLD
Ex 20:23 you make for yourselves gods of **g**.
25:17 shall then make a cover of pure **g**,
25:31 make a menorah of pure beaten **g**—
28:6 ephod they shall make of **g** thread
32:31 making a god of **g** for themselves!
1 Kgs 6:21 the interior of the house with pure **g**,
6:21 sanctuary, and covered it with **g**.
Tb 12:8 to give alms than to store up **g**,
Jb 28:15 Solid **g** cannot purchase her, nor can
Sir 31:5 The lover of **g** will not be free
Is 60:17 Instead of bronze I will bring **g**,
Acts 3:6 "I have neither silver nor **g**,
1 Pt 1:7 faith, more precious than **g** that is
Rev 21:21 the street of the city was of pure **g**,

GOLGOTHA
Mt 27:33 to a place called **G** (which means

GOLIATH
Giant killed by David (1 Sm 17; 21:9; Sir 47:4).

GOMORRAH
Gn 19:24 down sulfur upon Sodom and **G**,
Is 1:9 Sodom, would have resembled **G**.
Jude 1:7 Sodom, **G**, and the surrounding

GOOD → BEST, BETTER, GOODNESS
Gn 1: 31 he had made, and found it very **g**.
2: 9 delightful to look at and **g** for food,
2: 9 the tree of the knowledge of **g**
3: 22 like one of us, knowing **g** and evil!
50: 20 God meant it for **g**, to achieve this
Dt 6: 18 and **g** in the sight of the LORD,
6: 18 in and possess the **g** land
30: 15 today set before you life and **g**,
2 Ch 7: 3 "who is so **g**, whose love endures
Ps 34: 9 Taste and see that the LORD is **g**;
84: 12 The LORD withholds no **g** thing
Eccl 12: 14 hidden qualities, whether **g** or bad.
Is 52: 7 the feet of the one bringing **g** news,
Dn 3: 89 who is **g**, whose mercy endures
Mt 5: 45 his sun rise on the bad and the **g**,
25: 21 done, my **g** and faithful servant.
Mk 10: 18 him, "Why do you call me **g**? No one is **g** but God alone.
Lk 2: 10 I proclaim to you **g** news of great
6: 43 "A **g** tree does not bear rotten fruit,
6: 43 nor does a rotten tree bear **g** fruit.
Jn 10: 11 I am the **g** shepherd. A **g** shepherd
Rom 7: 16 not want, I concur that the law is **g**.
12: 2 what is **g** and pleasing and perfect.
12: 21 by evil but conquer evil with **g**.
Eph 2: 10 in Christ Jesus for the **g** works
1 Tm 4: 4 For everything created by God is **g**,
Heb 10: 1 has only a shadow of the **g** things
1 Pt 3: 17 For it is better to suffer for doing **g**,

GOODNESS → GOOD
Ps 23: 6 **g** and mercy will pursue me all

GOSHEN
Gn 45: 10 You can settle in the region of **G**,

GOSPEL
Mk 8: 35 sake and that of the **g** will save it.
Rom 1: 16 For I am not ashamed of the **g**.
1 Cor 9: 16 If I preach the **g**, this is no reason
2 Cor 4: 3 And even though our **g** is veiled,
Gal 1: 6 grace [of Christ] for a different **g**
Phil 1: 27 in a way worthy of the **g** of Christ,
1: 27 together for the faith of the **g**,

GOSSIP
2 Cor 12: 20 selfishness, slander, **g**, conceit,

GRACE → GRACIOUS
Wis 3: 9 Because **g** and mercy are with his
Jn 1: 14 only Son, full of **g** and truth.
1: 16 have all received, **g** in place of **g**,
Acts 15: 11 we are saved through the **g**
Rom 3: 24 by his **g** through the redemption
6: 1 we persist in sin that **g** may abound?
6: 14 are not under the law but under **g**.
11: 6 otherwise **g** would no longer be **g**.
1 Cor 15: 10 But by the **g** of God I am what I am,
15: 10 his **g** to me has not been ineffective.
2 Cor 12: 9 to me, "My **g** is sufficient for you,
Gal 5: 4 you have fallen from **g**.
Eph 2: 5 Christ (by **g** you have been saved),
2 Thes 2: 16 and good hope through his **g**,
Ti 2: 11 For the **g** of God has appeared,
Heb 4: 16 confidently approach the throne of **g**
4: 16 mercy and to find **g** for timely help.
Jas 4: 6 But he bestows a greater **g**;
4: 6 proud, but gives **g** to the humble."
1 Pt 5: 10 The God of all **g** who called you
Jude 1: 4 who pervert the **g** of our God
Rev 22: 21 The **g** of the Lord Jesus be with all.

GRACIOUS → GRACE
Ex 34: 6 the LORD, a God **g** and merciful,
Nm 6: 25 shine upon you, and be **g** to you!
Ps 116: 5 **G** is the LORD and righteous;
Col 4: 6 Let your speech always be **g**,

GRAFTED
Rom 11: 17 were **g** in their place and have come

GRAIN
Dt 25: 4 muzzle an ox when it treads out **g**.
Mk 2: 23 he was passing through a field of **g**
2: 23 a path while picking the heads of **g**.

GRAPES
Nm 13: 23 with a single cluster of **g** on it,
Is 5: 2 Then he waited for the crop of **g**, but it yielded rotten **g**.
Jer 31: 29 "The parents ate unripe **g**,
Mt 7: 16 Do people pick **g** from thornbushes,
Rev 14: 18 the earth's vines, for its **g** are ripe."

GRASS
Is 40: 6 "All flesh is **g**, and all their loyalty
Mt 6: 30 If God so clothes the **g** of the field,
1 Pt 1: 24 "All flesh is like **g**, and all its glory
1: 24 the **g** withers, and the flower wilts;

GRATIFY
Gal 5: 16 you will certainly not **g** the desire

GRAVE → GRAVES
Ps 49: 15 Straight to the **g** they descend,
Is 53: 9 was given a **g** among the wicked,

GRAVES → GRAVE
Ez 37: 12 I am going to open your **g**;
37: 12 make you come up out of your **g**,
Lk 11: 44 You are like unseen **g** over

GRAY
Prv 16: 31 **G** hair is a crown of glory;

GREAT → GREATER, GREATEST
Gn 1: 16 God made the two **g** lights,
12: 2 I will make of you a **g** nation,
12: 2 I will make your name **g**,
Ex 32: 11 of the land of Egypt with **g** power
Dt 10: 17 the Lord of lords, the **g** God,
Neh 8: 6 blessed the LORD, the **g** God,
Jdt 16: 13 O Lord, **g** are you and glorious,
Ps 95: 3 For the LORD is the **g** God, the **g**
Jer 10: 6 you are **g**, **g** and mighty is your
Lam 3: 23 **g** is your faithfulness!
Dn 9: 4 Lord, **g** and awesome God, you who
Jl 2: 11 How **g** is the day of the LORD!
Mt 4: 16 sit in darkness have seen a **g** light,
13: 46 When he finds a pearl of **g** price,
20: 26 to be **g** among you shall be your
Eph 2: 4 because of the **g** love he had for us,
Ti 2: 13 of the glory of the **g** God and of our
Heb 2: 3 if we ignore so **g** a salvation?
12: 1 we are surrounded by so **g** a cloud
13: 20 the dead the **g** shepherd of the sheep
Rev 14: 8 fallen is Babylon the **g**, that made

GREATER → GREAT
Mt 12: 6 something **g** than the temple is here.
Mk 12: 31 other commandment **g** than these."
Jn 14: 12 I do, and will do **g** ones than these,
15: 13 No one has **g** love than this, to lay
1 Jn 4: 4 is in you is **g** than the one who is

GREATEST → GREAT
Mt 22: 38 This is the **g** and the first
Lk 9: 48 all of you is the one who is the **g**."

1 Cor 13: 13 but the **g** of these is love.

GREECE → GREEK, GREEKS
1 Mc 1: 1 in his place, having first ruled in **G.**

GREED → GREEDY
Lk 12: 15 “Take care to guard against all **g**,
Col 3: 5 evil desire, and the **g** that is idolatry.

GREEDY → GREED
Prv 28: 25 The **g** person stirs up strife,
1 Cor 6: 10 thieves nor the **g** nor drunkards nor
Ti 1: 7 aggressive, not **g** for sordid gain,

GREEK → GREECE
Jn 19: 20 written in Hebrew, Latin, and **G.**
Rom 1: 16 for Jew first, and then **G.**
Gal 3: 28 There is neither Jew nor **G**, there is

GREEKS → GREECE
1 Cor 1: 22 signs and **G** look for wisdom,

GREEN
Gn 1: 30 I give all the **g** plants for food.
Ps 23: 2 In **g** pastures he makes me lie down;

GREW → GROW
1 Sm 2: 21 while young Samuel **g**
Is 53: 2 He **g** up like a sapling before him,
Lk 1: 80 The child **g** and became strong
2: 40 The child **g** and became strong,

GRIEVE → GRIEVED
Eph 4: 30 And do not **g** the holy Spirit of God,
1 Thes 4: 13 so that you may not **g** like the rest,

GRIEVED → GRIEVE
Is 63: 10 they rebelled and **g** his holy spirit;

GRINDING
Lk 17: 35 will be two women **g** meal together;

GROAN
Rom 8: 23 **g** within ourselves as we wait
2 Cor 5: 2 For in this tent we **g**, longing to be

GROUND
Gn 2: 7 the man out of the dust of the **g**
3: 17 it, Cursed is the **g** because of you!
Ex 3: 5 the place where you stand is holy **g.**
Mt 13: 5 Some fell on rocky **g**, where it had

GROW → GREW, GROWTH
Ez 47: 12 river every kind of fruit tree will **g**;
2 Pt 3: 18 But **g** in grace and in the knowledge

GROWTH → GROW
1 Cor 3: 7 but only God, who causes the **g**.
Col 2: 19 achieves the **g** that comes

GUARANTEE → GUARANTEED
Heb 7: 22 become the **g** of an [even] better

GUARANTEED → GUARANTEE
Rom 4: 16 and the promise may be **g** to all his

GUARD → GUARDIAN, GUARDS
Prv 2: 11 over you, understanding will **g** you;
2 Thes 3: 3 you and **g** you from the evil one.
2 Tm 1: 12 is able to **g** what has been entrusted

GUARDIAN → GUARD
1 Pt 2: 25 to the shepherd and **g** of your souls.

GUARDS → GUARD
Mt 28: 4 The **g** were shaken with fear of him

GUIDANCE → GUIDE
Prv 11: 14 For lack of **g** a people falls;

GUIDE → GUIDANCE
Is 58: 11 the LORD will **g** you always
Lk 6: 39 a blind person **g** a blind person?
Jn 16: 13 of truth, he will **g** you to all truth.

GUILT → GUILTY
Ps 32: 5 my sin to you; my **g** I did not hide.
32: 5 and you took away the **g** of my sin.
Zec 3: 9 I will take away the **g** of that land

GUILTY → GUILT
Ex 23: 7 to death, for I will not acquit the **g**.
Nm 14: 18 not declaring the **g** guiltless,
Dn 13: 53 and freeing the **g**, although the Lord
Mk 3: 29 but is **g** of an everlasting sin.”

H

HABAKKUK
Prophet to Judah (Hb 1:1; 3:1; Dn 14:33-39).

HADASSAH → See ESTHER

HADES
Rev 20: 14 **H** were thrown into the pool of fire.

HAGAR
Servant of Sarah, wife of Abraham, mother of Ishmael (Gn 16:1-6; 25:12). Driven away by Sarah while pregnant (Gn 16:5-16); after birth of Isaac (Gn 21:9-21; Gal 4:21-31).

HAGGAI
Post-exilic prophet who encouraged rebuilding of the temple (Ezr 5:1; 6:14; Hg 1–2).

HAIL → HAILSTONES
Ex 9: 19 will die when the **h** comes down
Rev 8: 7 there came **h** and fire mixed

HAILSTONES → HAIL
Jos 10: 11 these **h** than the Israelites killed
Rev 16: 21 Large **h** like huge weights came

HAIR → HAIRS
Jgs 16: 22 the **h** of his head began to grow as
Lk 7: 44 her tears and wiped them with her **h**.
Jn 12: 3 of Jesus and dried them with her **h**;
1 Cor 11: 6 she may as well have her **h** cut off.

HAIRS → HAIR
Ps 40: 13 They are more numerous than the **h**
Mt 10: 30 Even all the **h** of your head are

HALF
Est 5: 3 Even if it is **h** of my kingdom,
Mk 6: 23 of me, even to **h** of my kingdom.”
Lk 19: 8 “Behold, **h** of my possessions,

HALLOWED
Mt 6: 9 Father in heaven, **h** be your name,

HAM
Son of Noah (Gn 5:32; 1 Ch 1:4), father of Canaan (Gn 9:18; 10:6-20; 1 Ch 1:8-16). Saw Noah's nakedness (Gn 9:20-27).

HAMAN
Agagite nobleman honored by Xerxes (Est 3:1-2). Plotted to exterminate the Jews because of Mordecai (Est 3:3-15). Forced to honor Mordecai (Est 5–6). Plot exposed by Esther (Est 5:1-8; 7:1-8). Hanged (Est 7:9-10).

HANANIAH → =SHADRACH
1. False prophet; adversary of Jeremiah (Jer 28).
2. Original name of Shadrach (Dn 1:6-19; 2:17).

HAND → EMPTY-HANDED, HANDED, HANDS
Ex 15: 6 in power, your right **h**, O LORD,
Dt 19: 21 tooth for tooth, **h** for **h**, and foot
1 Kgs 18: 44 a cloud as small as a man's **h** rising

Jdt 9: 10 their arrogance by the **h** of a female.
Ps 110: 1 "Sit at my right **h**, while I make
Prv 3: 16 Long life is in her right **h**, in her left
Is 5: 25 he stretches out his **h** to strike them;
5: 25 back, his **h** is still outstretched.
Dn 5: 5 the fingers of a human **h** appeared,
5: 5 When the king saw the **h** that wrote,
Hb 2: 16 the LORD's right **h** shall come
Mt 3: 12 His winnowing fan is in his **h**.
Mk 9: 43 If your **h** causes you to sin, cut it
Lk 20: 42 said to my lord, "Sit at my right **h**
Jn 10: 28 No one can take them out of my **h**.
Rom 8: 34 who also is at the right **h** of God,
1 Cor 12: 15 I am not a **h** I do not belong
Heb 10: 12 seat forever at the right **h** of God;
Rev 1: 16 In his right **h** he held seven stars.
5: 1 in the right **h** of the one who sat

HANDED → HAND
Mt 27: 26 he **h** him over to be crucified.
Rom 4: 25 who was **h** over for our

HANDS → HAND
Ps 115: 7 They have **h** but do not feel,
Is 49: 16 palms of my **h** I have engraved you;
Lk 23: 46 into your **h** I commend my spirit";
24: 40 he showed them his **h** and his feet.
Acts 8: 18 by the laying on of the apostles' **h**,
Rom 10: 21 I stretched out my **h** to a disobedient
Heb 6: 2 about baptisms and laying on of **h**,
10: 31 to fall into the **h** of the living God.

HANNAH
Wife of Elkanah, mother of Samuel (1 Sm 1). Prayer at dedication of Samuel (1 Sm 2:1-10). Blessed (1 Sm 2:18-21).

HAPPY
Tb 13: 14 **H** are those who love you,
13: 14 **H** too are all who grieve over all
Prv 3: 13 **H** the one who finds wisdom,
Is 30: 18 of justice: **h** are all who wait for him!

HARD → HARDEN, HARDENED, HARDENING, HARDSHIPS
Ex 1: 14 life bitter for them with **h** labor,
Mt 19: 23 it will be **h** for one who is rich

HARDEN → HARD
Ps 95: 8 Do not **h** your hearts as at Meribah,
Heb 3: 8 '**H** not your hearts as

HARDENED → HARD
Mk 8: 17 Are your hearts **h**?
Rom 11: 7 the elect attained it; the rest were **h**,

HARDENING → HARD
Rom 11: 25 a **h** has come upon Israel in part,

HARDSHIPS → HARD
2 Cor 12: 10 weaknesses, insults, **h**, persecutions,

HARM
Gn 50: 20 Even though you meant **h** to me,
Neh 6: 2 They were planning to do me **h**.
Prv 12: 21 No **h** befalls the just, but the wicked
1 Pt 3: 13 Now who is going to **h** you if you

HARP → HARPS
Ps 150: 3 the horn, praise him with **h** and lyre.
Rev 5: 8 Each of the elders held a **h** and gold

HARPS → HARP
1 Ch 15: 16 to play on musical instruments, **h**,
Neh 12: 27 hymns and the music of cymbals, **h**,
Ps 137: 2 in its midst we hung up our **h**.

HARVEST
Gn 8: 22 earth, seedtime and **h**, cold and heat,
Ex 23: 16 of the grain **h** with the first fruits
23: 16 of the grain **h** with the first fruits
Mt 13: 39 The **h** is the end of the age,
Mk 4: 29 sickle at once, for the **h** has come."
Lk 10: 2 "The **h** is abundant but the laborers
10: 2 so ask the master of the **h** to send
Rev 14: 15 "Use your sickle and reap the **h**,
14: 15 because the earth's **h** is fully ripe."

HASTENING
2 Pt 3: 12 and **h** the coming of the day of God,

HATE → HATED
Ps 45: 8 You love justice and **h** wrongdoing;
97: 10 You who love the LORD, **h** evil,
Eccl 3: 8 A time to love, and a time to **h**;
Am 5: 15 **H** evil and love good, and let justice
Mal 2: 16 For I **h** divorce, says the LORD,
Mt 5: 43 your neighbor and **h** your enemy.'
Lk 6: 27 do good to those who **h** you,
Jn 7: 7 The world cannot **h** you, but it hates
Rom 7: 15 do what I want, but I do what I **h**.

HATED → HATE
Jn 15: 18 hates you, realize that it **h** me first.
Rom 9: 13 "I loved Jacob but **h** Esau."

HATES → HATE
Prv 6: 16 There are six things the LORD **h**,
Sir 15: 13 wickedness the LORD **h** and he
Jn 15: 23 Whoever **h** me also **h** my Father.

HAUGHTY
Prv 6: 17 **H** eyes, a lying tongue,
16: 18 disaster, and a **h** spirit before a fall.

HAY
1 Cor 3: 12 precious stones, wood, **h**, or straw,

HEAD → BEHEADED, HEADS
Is 59: 17 victory as a helmet on his **h**;
Mt 8: 20 of Man has nowhere to rest his **h**."
Mk 6: 28 He brought in the **h** on a platter
1 Cor 11: 3 that Christ is the **h** of every man,
11: 3 and a husband the **h** of his wife, and God the **h** of Christ.
Eph 1: 22 gave him as **h** over all things

HEADS → HEAD
Ez 11: 21 their conduct down upon their **h**—
Rev 12: 3 dragon, with seven **h** and ten horns,
12: 3 and on its **h** were seven diadems.

HEAL → HEALED, HEALING, HEALS, HEALTH
Dt 32: 39 I who inflict wounds and **h** them,
Eccl 3: 3 A time to kill, and a time to **h**;
Is 57: 19 says the LORD; and I will **h** them.
Jn 12: 40 be converted, and I would **h** them."

HEALED → HEAL
Is 6: 10 understand, and they turn and be **h**.
53: 5 us whole, by his wounds we were **h**.
Jas 5: 16 for one another, that you may be **h**.
1 Pt 2: 24 By his wounds you have been **h**.

HEALING → HEAL
Prv 12: 18 but the tongue of the wise is **h**.
1 Cor 12: 9 another gifts of **h** by the one Spirit;

HEALS → HEAL
Ps 103: 3 all your sins, and **h** all your ills,

HEALTH → HEAL
Sir 30: 15 rather have bodily **h** than any gold,
3 Jn 1: 2 in every respect and are in good **h**,

HEAR → HEARD, HEARERS, HEARING, HEARS
Dt 6: 4 **H**, O Israel! The LORD is our
31: 13 shall **h** and learn to fear the LORD,
Is 59: 1 to save, nor his ear too dull to **h**.
Jer 5: 21 not see, who have ears and do not **h**.
Ez 37: 4 bones, **h** the word of the LORD!
Mt 13: 17 and to **h** what you **h** but did not **h** it.
Mk 12: 29 "The first is this: '**H**, O Israel!
Lk 7: 22 the deaf **h**, the dead are raised,
Heb 3: 7 that today you would **h** his voice,

HEARD → HEAR
Is 40: 21 Have you not **h**? Was it not told you
Rom 10: 17 Thus faith comes from what is **h**,
10: 17 what is **h** comes through the word
1 Cor 2: 9 and ear has not **h**, and what has not
1 Jn 1: 3 seen and **h** we proclaim now to you,
Rev 22: 8 I, John, who **h** and saw these things,

HEARERS → HEAR
Jas 1: 22 doers of the word and not **h** only,

HEARING → HEAR
Am 8: 11 but for **h** the word of the LORD.
1 Cor 12: 17 were an eye, where would the **h** be?
12: 17 If the whole body were **h**,

HEARS → HEAR
Ps 69: 34 For the LORD **h** the poor,
Prv 15: 29 wicked, but **h** the prayer of the just.
Jn 5: 24 whoever **h** my word and believes
1 Jn 5: 14 according to his will, he **h** us.
Rev 22: 18 warn everyone who **h** the prophetic

HEART → BROKENHEARTED, HEART'S, HEARTLESS, HEARTS
Gn 6: 6 on the earth, and his **h** was grieved.
Dt 6: 5 with your whole **h**, and with your
30: 14 in your mouth and in your **h**, to do it.
Jos 22: 5 serve him with your whole **h**
1 Sm 16: 7 The LORD looks into the **h**.
Ps 19: 15 the thoughts of my **h** before you,
51: 12 A clean **h** create for me, God;
Prv 3: 5 Trust in the LORD with all your **h**,
7: 3 write them on the tablet of your **h**.
Sir 37: 17 The root of all conduct is the **h**;
Ez 36: 26 I will give you a new **h**, and a new
36: 26 I will remove the **h** of stone
36: 26 your flesh and give you a **h** of flesh.
Dn 3: 39 with contrite **h** and humble spirit let
Mt 5: 8 Blessed are the clean of **h**, for they
5: 28 adultery with her in his **h**.
Mk 12: 30 the Lord your God with all your **h**,
Lk 12: 34 treasure is, there also will your **h** be.
Rom 2: 29 and circumcision is of the **h**,
10: 9 in your **h** that God raised him
Heb 10: 22 let us approach with a sincere **h**

HEART'S → HEART
Rom 10: 1 my **h** desire and prayer to God

HEARTLESS → HEART
Rom 1: 31 are senseless, faithless, **h**, ruthless.

HEARTS → HEART
Ps 95: 8 Do not harden your **h** as at Meribah,
Jer 31: 33 them, and write it upon their **h**;
Mk 7: 6 lips, but their **h** are far from me;
Jn 14: 1 "Do not let your **h** be troubled.
Rom 2: 15 of the law are written in their **h**,
5: 5 into our **h** through the holy Spirit
Eph 3: 17 may dwell in your **h** through faith;
Col 3: 15 the peace of Christ control your **h**,
Heb 3: 8 'Harden not your **h** as
10: 16 'I will put my laws in their **h**, and I
2 Pt 1: 19 and the morning star rises in your **h**.
1 Jn 3: 20 in whatever our **h** condemn, for God is greater than our **h**
Rev 2: 23 to know that I am the searcher of **h**

HEAVEN → HEAVENLY, HEAVENS
Gn 14: 19 High, the creator of **h** and earth;
Ex 16: 4 to rain down bread from **h** for you.
Dt 31: 28 so may call **h** and earth to witness
Jb 16: 19 Even now my witness is in **h**,
Jer 10: 11 gods that did not make **h** and earth—
23: 24 Do I not fill **h** and earth?—
Mt 3: 2 for the kingdom of **h** is at hand!"
6: 9 Our Father in **h**, hallowed be your
24: 35 **H** and earth will pass away, but my
26: 64 and 'coming on the clouds of **h**.' "
Mk 10: 21 and you will have treasure in **h**;
Lk 19: 38 Peace in **h** and glory
24: 51 from them and was taken up to **h**.
Jn 3: 13 to **h** except the one who has come down from **h**,
Acts 1: 11 you into **h** will return in the same
1: 11 as you have seen him going into **h**."
Rom 10: 6 your heart, 'Who will go up into **h**?'
2 Cor 12: 2 was caught up to the third **h**.
Phil 3: 20 But our citizenship is in **h**,
1 Thes 1: 10 and to await his Son from **h**,
Heb 9: 24 one, but **h** itself, that he might now
2 Pt 1: 18 voice come from **h** while we were
Rev 4: 1 I had a vision of an open door to **h**,
21: 1 Then I saw a new **h** and a new earth.
21: 1 The former **h** and the former earth

HEAVENLY → HEAVEN
Mt 5: 48 just as your **h** Father is perfect.
2 Cor 5: 2 further clothed with our **h** habitation
Heb 3: 1 sharing in a **h** calling,

HEAVENS → HEAVEN
Gn 1: 1 when God created the **h**
28: 12 with its top reaching to the **h**;
Dt 10: 14 Look, the **h**, even the highest **h**,
28: 23 The **h** over your heads will be like bronze
1 Kgs 8: 27 If the **h** and the highest **h** cannot
Ps 57: 6 Be exalted over the **h**, God;
115: 16 The **h** belong to the LORD, but he
Eccl 3: 1 a time for every affair under the **h**.
Is 14: 12 How you have fallen from the **h**,
65: 17 See, I am creating new **h** and a new
Eph 4: 10 who ascended far above all the **h**,
Heb 4: 14 priest who has passed through the **h**,
2 Pt 3: 10 the **h** will pass away with a mighty

HEAVY
Mt 23: 4 They tie up **h** burdens [hard

HEBREW → HEBREWS
Jon 1: 9 "I am a **H**," he replied; "I fear
Jn 19: 20 and it was written in **H**, Latin,
Phil 3: 5 of Benjamin, a **H** of **H** parentage,

HEBREWS → HEBREW
Ex 3: 18 the God of the **H**, has come to meet
Jdt 10: 12 "I am a daughter of the **H**, and I am
2 Cor 11: 22 Are they **H**? So am I.

HEBRON
Gn 13: 18 the oak of Mamre, which is at **H**.
2 Sm 2: 11 David was king in **H** over the house

HEEL
Gn 3: 15 head, while you strike at their **h**.
25: 26 brother came out, gripping Esau's **h**;
Jn 13: 18 food has raised his **h** against me.'

HEIGHT → HIGH
Rom 8: 39 nor **h**, nor depth, nor any other
Eph 3: 18 breadth and length and **h** and depth,

HEIGHTS → HIGH
Ps 148: 1 praise him in the **h**.
Hb 3: 19 and enables me to tread upon the **h**.

HEIR → HEIRS
Gn 15: 4 No, that one will not be your **h**;
15: 4 your own offspring will be your **h**.
Gal 4: 7 a child, and if a child then also an **h**,
Heb 1: 2 whom he made **h** of all things

HEIRS → HEIR
Rom 8: 17 then **h**, **h** of God and joint **h**
Ti 3: 7 become **h** in hope of eternal life.
1 Pt 3: 7 since we are joint **h** of the gift

HELMET
Is 59: 17 victory as a **h** on his head;
Eph 6: 17 And take the **h** of salvation

HELP → HELPER, HELPS
1 Sm 7: 12 this place the LORD has been our **h**."
Jdt 6: 21 called upon the God of Israel for **h**.
Ps 33: 20 the LORD, he is our **h** and shield.
46: 2 an ever-present **h** in distress.
Sir 2: 6 Trust in God, and he will **h** you;
Mk 9: 24 out, "I do believe, **h** my unbelief!"
Heb 2: 18 able to **h** those who are being tested.
4: 16 and to find grace for timely **h**.

HELPER → HELP
Jdt 9: 11 **h** of those of little account, supporter
Ps 30: 11 mercy on me; LORD, be my **h**."
Heb 13: 6 "The Lord is my **h**, [and] I will not

HELPS → HELP
Ps 37: 40 The LORD **h** and rescues them,

HERBS
Ex 12: 8 with unleavened bread and bitter **h**.

HERMON
Dt 3: 8 from the Wadi Arnon to Mount **H**
Ps 133: 3 Like dew of **H** coming down

HEROD → HERODIANS
1. King of Judea; tried to kill Jesus (Mt 2; Lk 1:5).
2. Son of 1. Tetrarch of Galilee who arrested and beheaded John the Baptist (Mt 14:1-12; Mk 6:14-29; Lk 3:1, 19-20; 9:7-9); tried Jesus (Lk 23:6-15).
3. Grandson of 1. King of Judea who killed James (Acts 12:2); arrested Peter (Acts 12:3-19). Death (Acts 12:19-23).

HERODIANS → HEROD
Mk 3: 6 took counsel with the **H** against him
12: 13 and **H** to him to ensnare him in his

HERODIAS
Wife of Herod the Tetrarch who persuaded her daughter to ask for John the Baptist's head (Mt 14:1-12; Mk 6:14-29; Lk 3:19).

HEWN
Mk 15: 46 in a tomb that had been **h**

HEZEKIAH
King of Judah (Sir 48:17-25). Restored the temple and worship (2 Ch 29–31). Sought the LORD for help against Assyria (2 Kgs 18–19; 2 Ch 32:1-23; Is 36–37). Illness healed (2 Kgs 20:1-11; 2 Ch 32:24-26; Is 38). Judged for showing Babylonians his treasures (2 Kgs 20:12-21; 2 Ch 32:31; Is 39).

HID → HIDE
Gn 3: 8 and his wife **h** themselves
Ex 2: 2 he was, she **h** him for three months.
3: 6 Moses **h** his face, for he was afraid
Jos 6: 17 because she **h** the messengers we
1 Kgs 18: 13 that I **h** a hundred of the prophets
Is 49: 2 arrow, in his quiver he **h** me.
54: 8 for a moment I **h** my face from you;

HIDDEN → HIDE
Prv 2: 4 and like **h** treasures search her out,
Is 40: 27 "My way is **h** from the LORD,
Mk 4: 22 there is nothing **h** except to be made
Col 3: 3 your life is **h** with Christ in God.
Rev 2: 17 I shall give some of the **h** manna;

HIDE → HID, HIDDEN
Dt 31: 17 them and **h** my face from them;
Ps 13: 2 How long will you **h** your face
17: 8 **h** me in the shadow of your wings

HIGH → HEIGHT, HEIGHTS, HIGHEST, HIGHLY
Gn 14: 18 He was a priest of God Most **H**.
1 Kgs 3: 2 were sacrificing on the **h** places,
Ps 91: 1 dwell in the shelter of the Most **H**,
Mt 4: 8 took him up to a very **h** mountain,
17: 1 and led them up a **h** mountain
Mk 5: 7 me, Jesus, Son of the Most **H** God?
Eph 4: 8 "He ascended on **h** and took
Heb 2: 17 and faithful **h** priest before God
7: 26 that we should have such a **h** priest:

HIGHEST → HIGH
1 Kgs 8: 27 the **h** heavens cannot contain you,
Mt 21: 9 of the Lord; hosanna in the **h**."
Lk 2: 14 "Glory to God in the **h** and on earth

HIGHLY → HIGH
Rom 12: 3 of himself more **h** than one ought

HILL
Is 40: 4 every mountain and **h** made low;
Lk 3: 5 mountain and **h** shall be made low.

HINDERED
1 Pt 3: 7 so that your prayers may not be **h**.

HIRAM
King of Tyre; helped David build his palace (2 Sm 5:11-12; 1 Ch 14:1); helped Solomon build the temple (1 Kgs 5; 2 Ch 2) and his navy (1 Kgs 9:10-27; 2 Ch 8).

HITTITE → HITTITES
Gn 23: 10 So Ephron the **H** replied
2 Sm 11: 3 and wife of Uriah the **H**,

HITTITES → HITTITE
Dt 20: 17 the **H**, Amorites, Canaanites,
Ezr 9: 1 Canaanites, **H**, Perizzites, Jebusites,

HOLD → HOLDS
Ps 73: 23 you take **h** of my right hand.
Col 1: 17 and in him all things **h** together.

HOLDS → HOLD
Ps 37: 24 fall, for the LORD **h** his hand.
Rev 2: 1 " 'The one who **h** the seven stars

HOLES
Hg 1: 6 worker labors for a bag full of **h**.

HOLINESS → HOLY
Ps 89: 36 By my **h** I swore once for all:
Rom 1: 4 the spirit of **h** through resurrection
1 Tm 2: 15 persevere in faith and love and **h**,
Heb 12: 14 that **h** without which no one will see

HOLOCAUST → See BURNT (OFFERING)

HOLOFERNES
Assyrian general (Jdt 2:4). Beguiled and beheaded by Judith (Jdt 10–13).

HOLY → HOLINESS
Ex 3: 5 place where you stand is **h** ground.
15: 11 like you, magnificent among the **h** ones?
20: 8 the sabbath day—keep it **h**.
26: 33 which divides the **h** place from the **h**
Lv 11: 44 and keep yourselves **h**, because I am **h**.
Jos 5: 15 on which you are standing is **h**."
1 Sm 2: 2 There is no **H** One like the LORD;
1 Mc 1: 15 and abandoned the **h** covenant;
Ps 2: 6 my king on Zion, my **h** mountain."
11: 4 The LORD is in his **h** temple;
Is 6: 3 "**H**, **h**, **h** is the LORD of hosts!
40: 25 me as an equal? says the **H** One.
Dn 9: 24 for your people and for your **h** city:
9: 24 and a **h** of holies will be anointed.
Mt 1: 18 with child through the **h** Spirit.
3: 11 He will baptize you with the **h** Spirit
24: 15 in the **h** place (let the reader
Mk 1: 24 who you are—the **H** One of God!"
3: 29 blasphemes against the **h** Spirit will
Lk 3: 22 the **h** Spirit descended upon him
11: 13 in heaven give the **h** Spirit to those
Jn 14: 26 the **h** Spirit that the Father will send
Acts 2: 4 they were all filled with the **h** Spirit
2: 27 nor will you suffer your **h** one to see
5: 3 heart so that you lied to the **h** Spirit
Rom 12: 1 sacrifice, **h** and pleasing to God,
Eph 1: 4 to be **h** and without blemish before
4: 30 do not grieve the **h** Spirit of God,
Heb 6: 4 gift and shared in the **h** Spirit
1 Pt 1: 16 is written, "Be **h** because I [am] **h**."
1 Jn 2: 20 that comes from the **h** one, and you
Jude 1: 14 has come with his countless **h** ones
Rev 4: 8 "**H**, **h**, **h** is the Lord God almighty,
21: 2 I also saw the **h** city, a new
22: 11 still do right, and the **h** still be **h**."

HOME → HOMELESS
Dt 6: 7 Recite them when you are at **h**
Ps 68: 7 God gives a **h** to the forsaken,
2 Cor 5: 8 leave the body and go **h** to the Lord.

HOMELESS → HOME
Is 58: 7 afflicted and the **h** into your house;
1 Cor 4: 11 roughly treated, we wander about **h**

HONEST
Lv 19: 36 weights, an **h** ephah and an **h** hin.

HONEY
Ex 3: 8 a land flowing with milk and **h**,
Jgs 14: 8 of bees in the lion's carcass, and **h**.
Ps 19: 11 than **h** or drippings from the comb.
Mt 3: 4 His food was locusts and wild **h**.

HONOR → HONORABLE, HONORED, HONORS
Dt 5: 16 **H** your father and your mother,
Tb 4: 3 **H** your mother, and do not abandon
Ps 8: 6 god, crowned him with glory and **h**.
Mal 1: 6 a father, where is the **h** due to me?
Mt 13: 57 "A prophet is not without **h** except
15: 4 '**H** your father and your mother,'
Jn 12: 26 The Father will **h** whoever serves
Rom 13: 7 respect is due, **h** to whom **h** is due.
Eph 6: 2 "**H** your father and mother."
1 Tm 5: 17 who preside well deserve double **h**,
Heb 2: 7 you crowned him with glory and **h**,
Rev 4: 11 to receive glory and **h** and power,

HONORABLE → HONOR
Phil 4: 8 true, whatever is **h**, whatever is just,

HONORED → HONOR
1 Cor 12: 26 if one part is **h**, all the parts share its

HONORS → HONOR
Mal 1: 6 A son **h** his father, and a servant
Mt 15: 8 'This people **h** me with their lips,

HOOFS
Lv 11: 3 Any animal that has **h** you may eat,

HOOK → HOOKS
Mt 17: 27 drop in a **h**, and take the first fish

HOOKS → HOOK
Is 2: 4 and their spears into pruning **h**;

HOPE → HOPED, HOPES
Jb 17: 15 Where then is my **h**, my happiness,
Ps 62: 6 alone, from whom comes my **h**.
146: 5 of Jacob, whose **h** is in the LORD,
Prv 23: 18 and your **h** will not be cut off.
Jer 14: 8 **H** of Israel, LORD, our savior
Dn 13: 60 God who saves those who **h** in him.
Lam 3: 21 will call to mind; therefore I will **h**:
Mt 12: 21 in his name the Gentiles will **h**."
Rom 5: 5 and **h** does not disappoint,
12: 12 Rejoice in **h**, endure in affliction,
1 Cor 13: 13 So faith, **h**, love remain, these three;
Col 1: 27 it is Christ in you, the **h** for glory.
1 Thes 5: 8 the helmet that is **h** for salvation.
Heb 7: 19 other hand, a better **h** is introduced,
1 Pt 1: 3 a living **h** through the resurrection
1 Jn 3: 3 Everyone who has this **h** based

HOPED → HOPE
Heb 11: 1 is the realization of what is **h**
1 Pt 3: 5 how the holy women who **h** in God

HOPES → HOPE
1 Cor 13: 7 believes all things, **h** all things,

HOREB → =SINAI
Ex 3: 1 he came to the mountain of God, **H**.
Dt 5: 2 God, made a covenant with us at **H**;
1 Kgs 19: 8 nights to the mountain of God, **H**.

HORN → HORNS
Ps 18: 3 shield, my saving **h**, my stronghold!
Dn 7: 8 a little **h**, sprang out of their midst,
7: 8 This **h** had eyes like human eyes,
Jl 2: 15 Blow the **h** in Zion! Proclaim a fast,

HORNS → HORN
Gn 22: 13 ram caught by its **h** in the thicket.
Ex 27: 2 At the four corners make **h** that are
Dn 8: 3 by the river a ram with two great **h**,
Rev 5: 6 He had seven **h** and seven eyes;
9: 13 the [four] **h** of the gold altar before
17: 3 names, with seven heads and ten **h**.

HORSE → HORSES
Ex 15: 1 **h** and chariot he has cast
Ps 33: 17 Useless is the **h** for safety;
Zec 1: 8 on a red **h** standing in the shadows
Rev 6: 2 and there was a white **h**, and its
19: 11 opened, and there was a white **h**;

HORSES → HORSE
2 Kgs 2: 11 and fiery **h** came between the two
Ps 20: 8 others on **h**, but we on the name
Jl 2: 4 Their appearance is that of **h**;
Rev 9: 7 was like that of **h** ready for battle.
19: 14 mounted on white **h** and wearing

HOSANNA
Mk 11: 10 that is to come! **H** in the highest!"
Jn 12: 13 out to meet him, and cried out: "**H**!

HOSEA
Prophet whose wife and family pictured the unfaithfulness of Israel (Hos 1–3).

HOSHEA → =JOSHUA
1. Original name of Joshua (Nm 13:8, 16).
2. Last king of Israel (2 Kgs 15:30; 17:1-6).

HOSPITABLE → HOSPITALITY
1 Tm 3: 2 decent, **h**, able to teach,
Ti 1: 8 but **h**, a lover of goodness,
1 Pt 4: 9 Be **h** to one another without

HOSPITALITY → HOSPITABLE
Rom 12: 13 needs of the holy ones, exercise **h**.
1 Tm 5: 10 practiced **h**, washed the feet
Heb 13: 2 Do not neglect **h**, for through it

HOST → HOSTS
Dt 4: 19 whole heavenly **h**, do not be led astray
2 Kgs 17: 16 bowed down to all the **h** of heaven;
Lk 2: 13 of the heavenly **h** with the angel,

HOSTILE
Col 1: 21 and **h** in mind because of evil deeds

HOSTS → HOST
1 Sm 1: 3 to the LORD of **h** at Shiloh,
Ps 46: 8 The LORD of **h** is with us;
Is 48: 2 whose name is the LORD of **h**.

HOT
Rev 3: 15 that you are neither cold nor **h**. I wish you were either cold or **h**.

HOUR
Mt 24: 36 of that day and **h** no one knows,
Jn 2: 4 My **h** has not yet come."
17: 1 and said, "Father, the **h** has come.

HOUSE → HOUSEHOLD, HOUSES, HOUSETOP, HOUSETOPS, STOREHOUSE
Ex 20: 17 shall not covet your neighbor's **h**.
2 Sm 7: 11 the LORD will make a **h** for you:
Ezr 1: 5 up to build the **h** of the LORD
Ps 69: 10 zeal for your **h** has consumed me,
127: 1 Unless the LORD build the **h**,
Prv 9: 1 Wisdom has built her **h**, she has set
Is 56: 7 make them joyful in my **h** of prayer;
Mt 7: 24 be like a wise man who built his **h**
21: 13 'My **h** shall be a **h** of prayer,'
Mk 3: 25 And if a **h** is divided against itself,
3: 25 that **h** will not be able to stand.
Jn 2: 17 for your **h** will consume me."
14: 2 In my Father's **h** there are many
1 Pt 2: 5 a spiritual **h** to be a holy priesthood

HOUSEHOLD → HOUSE
Jos 24: 15 As for me and my **h**, we will serve
Mi 7: 6 enemies are members of your **h**.
Mt 10: 36 enemies will be those of his **h**.'
Eph 2: 19 ones and members of the **h** of God,
1 Tm 3: 4 He must manage his own **h** well,
3: 15 how to behave in the **h** of God,
1 Pt 4: 17 to begin with the **h** of God;

HOUSES → HOUSE
Ex 12: 27 who passed over the **h**
12: 27 Egyptians, he delivered our **h**.' "
Mt 19: 29 everyone who has given up **h**

HOUSETOP → HOUSE
Mt 24: 17 a person on the **h** must not go down

HOUSETOPS → HOUSE
Mt 10: 27 hear whispered, proclaim on the **h**.

HULDAH
Prophetess inquired by Hilkiah for Josiah (2 Kgs 22; 2 Ch 34:14-28).

HUMAN → HUMANKIND
Jdt 8: 16 God is not like a **h** being to be
Dn 5: 5 the fingers of a **h** hand appeared,
Hos 11: 4 I drew them with **h** cords,
Mt 15: 9 as doctrines **h** precepts.' "
1 Cor 2: 13 not with words taught by **h** wisdom,
Phil 2: 7 of a slave, coming in **h** likeness;
2: 7 and found **h** in appearance,
1 Tm 2: 5 between God and the **h** race, Christ Jesus, himself **h**,
Rev 4: 7 had a face like that of a **h** being,

HUMBLE → HUMBLED, HUMBLY, HUMILITY
Ps 25: 9 He guides the **h** in righteousness,
25: 9 and teaches the **h** his way.
Zep 2: 3 the LORD, all you **h** of the land,
Mt 11: 29 me, for I am meek and **h** of heart;
Jas 4: 10 **H** yourselves before the Lord and he
1 Pt 5: 5 proud but bestows favor on the **h**."

HUMBLED → HUMBLE
Lk 14: 11 who exalts himself will be **h**,
Phil 2: 8 he **h** himself, becoming obedient

HUMBLY → HUMBLE
Mi 6: 8 and to walk **h** with your God.

HUMILITY → HUMBLE
Prv 15: 33 wisdom, and **h** goes before honors.
Zep 2: 3 Seek justice, seek **h**;
Col 3: 12 kindness, **h**, gentleness,
1 Pt 5: 5 clothe yourselves with **h** in your

HUNDRED
Gn 17: 17 born to a man who is a **h** years old?
Is 65: 20 at a **h** years shall be considered
65: 20 of a **h** shall be thought accursed.
Rom 4: 19 (for he was almost a **h** years old)

HUNG
Ps 137: 2 in its midst we **h** up our harps.

HUNGER → HUNGRY
Dt 8: 3 therefore let you be afflicted with **h**,
Mt 5: 6 Blessed are they who **h** and thirst
Rev 7: 16 They will not **h** or thirst anymore,

HUNGRY → HUNGER
Ps 50: 12 Were I **h**, I would not tell you,
146: 7 oppressed, who gives bread to the **h**.
Prv 25: 21 If your enemies are **h**, give them
Mt 12: 1 His disciples were **h** and began
Rom 12: 20 "if your enemy is **h**, feed him;

HUSBAND → HUSBANDS
Gn 3: 6 and she also gave some to her **h**,
3: 16 Yet your urge shall be for your **h**,
Prv 31: 28 her **h**, too, praises her:
Sir 26: 1 Happy the **h** of a good wife;
Is 54: 5 For your **h** is your Maker;
1 Cor 7: 10 wife should not separate from her **h**
Eph 5: 23 For the **h** is head of his wife just as
Rev 21: 2 as a bride adorned for her **h**.

HUSBANDS → HUSBAND
Jn 4: 18 For you have had five **h**,
Eph 5: 25 **H**, love your wives, even as Christ
Col 3: 18 be subordinate to your **h**, as is
Ti 2: 4 train younger women to love their **h**
1 Pt 3: 7 you **h** should live with your wives

HUSHAI
Wise man of David; foiled Absalom's revolt (2 Sm 15:32-37; 16:15–17:16).

HYMN → HYMNS
Mt 26: 30 after singing a **h**, they went

HYMNS → HYMN
Eph 5: 19 one another [in] psalms and **h**
Col 3: 16 singing psalms, **h**, and spiritual

HYPOCRISY → HYPOCRITE, HYPOCRITES
Mt 23: 28 but inside you are filled with **h**
Mk 12: 15 Knowing their **h** he said to them,

HYPOCRITE → HYPOCRISY
Lk 6: 42 You **h**! Remove the wooden beam

HYPOCRITES → HYPOCRISY
Mt 6: 5 do not be like the **h**, who love
23: 13 to you, scribes and Pharisees, you **h**.
Mk 7: 6 did Isaiah prophesy about you **h**,

HYSSOP
Ex 12: 22 Then take a bunch of **h**, and dipping
Nm 19: 6 **h** and scarlet yarn and throw them
Ps 51: 9 Cleanse me with **h**, that I may be
Jn 19: 29 soaked in wine on a sprig of **h**

I

IDLE
Eccl 11: 6 at evening do not let your hand be **i**:

IDOL → IDOLS
Ex 20: 4 You shall not make for yourself an **i**
Is 40: 19 An **i**? An artisan casts it, the smith
1 Cor 10: 19 Or that an **i** is anything?

IDOLS → IDOL
1 Mc 1: 43 they sacrificed to **i** and profaned
Ps 115: 4 Their **i** are silver and gold, the work
1 Cor 8: 1 in regard to meat sacrificed to **i**:

IGNORANCE → IGNORANT
Acts 17: 30 God has overlooked the times of **i**,
1 Pt 2: 15 doing good you may silence the **i**

IGNORANT → IGNORANCE
Heb 5: 2 is able to deal patiently with the **i**
2 Pt 3: 16 things hard to understand that the **i**

ILL
1 Cor 11: 30 That is why many among you are **i**

ILLEGITIMATE
Jn 8: 41 they said to him, "We are not **i**.

IMAGE → IMAGES
Gn 1: 26 Let us make human beings in our **i**,
1 Cor 15: 49 Just as we have borne the **i**
15: 49 also bear the **i** of the heavenly one.
Col 1: 15 He is the **i** of the invisible God,
Rev 20: 4 or its **i** nor had accepted its mark

IMAGES → IMAGE
Nm 33: 52 destroy all their molten **i**,

IMITATE → IMITATORS
Heb 13: 7 of their way of life and **i** their faith.
3 Jn 1: 11 Beloved, do not **i** evil but **i** good.

IMITATORS → IMITATE
1 Cor 11: 1 Be **i** of me, as I am of Christ.
Eph 5: 1 So be **i** of God, as beloved children,

IMMORAL → IMMORALITY
1 Cor 5: 9 letter not to associate with **i** people,
Heb 12: 16 that no one be an **i** or profane

IMMORALITY → IMMORAL
2 Cor 12: 21 have not repented of the impurity, **i**,

IMMORTAL → IMMORTALITY
Rom 1: 23 exchanged the glory of the **i** God

IMMORTALITY → IMMORTAL
1 Cor 15: 53 is mortal must clothe itself with **i**.
1 Tm 6: 16 who alone has **i**, who dwells

IMPERISHABLE
1 Cor 9: 25 a perishable crown, but we an **i** one.
1 Pt 1: 4 to an inheritance that is **i**, undefiled,

IMPORTANCE
1 Cor 15: 3 handed on to you as of first **i** what I

IMPOSSIBLE
Zec 8: 6 if this should seem **i** in the eyes
8: 6 should it seem **i** in my eyes also?—
Mt 17: 20 Nothing will be **i** for you."
Mk 10: 27 "For human beings it is **i**, but not
Heb 11: 6 without faith it is **i** to please him,

IMPURE → IMPURITY
Eph 5: 5 this, that no immoral or **i** or greedy
1 Thes 2: 3 was not from delusion or **i** motives,

IMPURITY → IMPURE
Gal 5: 19 immorality, **i**, licentiousness,
1 Thes 4: 7 For God did not call us to **i**

INCENSE → FRANKINCENSE
Ex 25: 6 anointing oil and for the fragrant **i**;

INCREASE → INCREASED
Lk 17: 5 said to the Lord, "**I** our faith."
Jn 3: 30 He must **i**; I must decrease."

INCREASED → INCREASE
Rom 5: 20 where sin **i**, grace overflowed all

INDEPENDENT
1 Cor 11: 11 Woman is not **i** of man or man

INFANTS
Ps 8: 3 with the mouths of babes and **i**.
Mt 21: 16 the text, 'Out of the mouths of **i**
1 Cor 14: 20 In respect to evil be like **i**,

INFIRMITIES
Mt 8: 17 "He took away our **i** and bore our

INHERIT → INHERITANCE
Lk 10: 25 what must I do to **i** eternal life?"
1 Cor 6: 9 the unjust will not **i** the kingdom
Heb 1: 14 sake of those who are to **i** salvation?

INHERITANCE → INHERIT
Col 1: 12 to share in the **i** of the holy ones
Heb 9: 15 may receive the promised eternal **i**.

INIQUITIES → INIQUITY
Lv 16: 22 The goat will carry off all their **i**
Rom 4: 7 are they whose **i** are forgiven

INIQUITY → INIQUITIES
Hos 14: 2 you have stumbled because of your **i**.

INJURY
Lv 24: 20 The same **i** that one gives another

INJUSTICE
Rom 9: 14 Is there **i** on the part of God?

INN
Lk 2: 7 there was no room for them in the **i**.
10: 34 took him to an **i** and cared for him.

INNER → INWARDLY
Mt 24: 26 say, 'He is in the **i** rooms,' do not
2 Cor 4: 16 our **i** self is being renewed day

INNOCENCE → INNOCENT
Ps 26: 6 I will wash my hands in **i** so that I
Hos 8: 5 long will they be incapable of **i**

INNOCENT → INNOCENCE
Prv 6: 17 tongue, hands that shed **i** blood,
Mt 27: 24 saying, "I am **i** of this man's blood.

INQUIRE
Dt 12: 30 Do not **i** regarding their gods,

INSCRIBED → INSCRIPTION
Rev 19: 12 He had a name **i** that no one knows

INSCRIPTION → INSCRIBED
Mk 15: 26 The **i** of the charge against him
2 Tm 2: 19 bearing this **i**, "The Lord knows

INSIGHT
Dn 12: 3 But those with **i** shall shine brightly
Eph 1: 8 In all wisdom and **i**,

INSPIRED
2 Tm 3: 16 All scripture is **i** by God and is

INSTALL
Ex 29: 9 thus shall you **i** Aaron and his sons.

INSTITUTION
1 Pt 2: 13 every human **i** for the Lord's sake,

INSTRUCT → INSTRUCTED, INSTRUCTION
1 Cor 14: 19 mind, so as to **i** others also, than ten

INSTRUCTED → INSTRUCT
Is 40: 13 LORD, or **i** him as his counselor?

INSTRUCTION → INSTRUCT
Prv 8: 10 Take my **i** instead of silver,
15: 5 The fool spurns a father's **i**,
Mi 4: 2 For from Zion shall go forth **i**,
Rom 15: 4 previously was written for our **i**,
1 Tm 1: 5 The aim of this **i** is love from a pure

INSULTS
2 Cor 12: 10 I am content with weaknesses, **i**,

INTEGRITY
Ti 2: 7 respect, with **i** in your teaching,

INTELLIGENT
Prv 11: 12 lacks sense, but the **i** keep silent.

INTERCEDES → INTERCESSION
Rom 8: 26 the Spirit itself **i** with inexpressible

INTERCESSION → INTERCEDES
Heb 7: 25 he lives forever to make **i** for them.

INTERMARRY → MARRIAGE
Dt 7: 3 You shall not **i** with them,

INTERPRET → INTERPRETATION, INTERPRETATIONS
Gn 41: 15 a dream but there was no one to **i** it.
41: 15 'If he hears a dream he can **i** it.' "
1 Cor 12: 30 Do all speak in tongues? Do all **i**?

INTERPRETATION → INTERPRET
1 Cor 12: 10 to another **i** of tongues.
2 Pt 1: 20 that is a matter of personal **i**,

INTERPRETATIONS → INTERPRET
Gn 40: 8 to them, "Do **i** not come from God?

INVISIBLE
Col 1: 15 He is the image of the **i** God,
1 Tm 1: 17 ages, incorruptible, **i**, the only God,

INVITE → INVITES
Lk 14: 13 you hold a banquet, **i** the poor,

INVITES → INVITE
1 Cor 10: 27 If an unbeliever **i** you and you want

INVOKE
1 Pt 1: 17 if you **i** as Father him who judges

INWARDLY → INNER
Rom 2: 29 one is a Jew **i**, and circumcision is

IRON
Ps 2: 9 an **i** rod you will shepherd them,
Prv 27: 17 **I** is sharpened by **i**;
Dn 2: 33 its legs **i**, its feet partly **i** and partly
Rev 19: 15 He will rule them with an **i** rod,

IRREVOCABLE
Rom 11: 29 the gifts and the call of God are **i**.

ISAAC

Son of Abraham by Sarah (Gn 17:19; 21:1-7; 1 Ch 1:28). Abrahamic covenant perpetuated with (Gn 17:21; 26:2-5). Offered up by Abraham (Gn 22; Heb 11:17-19). Rebekah taken as wife (Gn 24). Inherited Abraham's estate (Gn 25:5). Father of Esau and Jacob (Gn 25:19-26; 1 Ch 1:34). Nearly lost Rebekah to Abimelech (Gn 26:1-11). Covenant with Abimelech (Gn 26:12-31). Tricked into blessing Jacob (Gn 27). Death (Gn 35:27-29). Father of Israel (Ex 3:6; Dt 29:13; Rom 9:10).

ISAIAH

Prophet to Judah (Is 1:1). Called by the LORD (Is 6). Announced judgment to Ahaz (Is 7), deliverance from Assyria to Hezekiah (2 Kgs 19; Is 36–37), deliverance from death to Hezekiah (2 Kgs 20:1-11; Is 38). Chronicler of Judah's history (2 Ch 26:22; 32:32).

ISCARIOT
Mt 10: 4 and Judas **I** who betrayed him.
Lk 22: 3 Judas, the one surnamed **I**, who was

ISHBAAL

Son of Saul; would-be king (2 Sm 2:8–4:12).

ISHMAEL

Son of Abraham by Hagar (Gn 16; 1 Ch 1:28). Blessed, but not son of covenant (Gn 17:18-21; Gal 4:21-31). Sent away by Sarah (Gn 21:8-21). Children (Gn 25:12-18; 1 Ch 1:29-31). Death (Gn 25:17).

ISRAEL → ISRAELITE, ISRAELITES, =JACOB

1. Name given to Jacob (Gn 32:28; 35:10).

2. Corporate name of Jacob's descendants; often specifically Northern Kingdom.

Gn 49: 28 All these are the twelve tribes of **I**,
Ex 28: 11 with the names of the sons of **I**
Nm 24: 17 and a scepter shall rise from **I**,
Dt 6: 4 Hear, O **I**! The LORD is our God,
Ps 125: 5 with the evildoers. Peace upon **I**!
Jer 31: 31 a new covenant with the house of **I**
Hos 11: 1 When **I** was a child I loved him,
Mt 2: 6 is to shepherd my people **I**.' "
Mk 12: 29 "The first is this: 'Hear, O **I**!
Lk 22: 30 judging the twelve tribes of **I**.
Acts 1: 6 going to restore the kingdom to **I**?"
Rom 9: 6 For not all who are of **I** are **I**,
Heb 8: 8 a new covenant with the house of **I**

ISRAELITE → ISRAEL
Jn 1: 47 and said of him, "Here is a true **I**.
Rom 11: 1 For I too am an **I**, a descendant

ISRAELITES → ISRAEL
Ex 2: 23 The **I** groaned under their bondage
29: 45 I will dwell in the midst of the **I**

ISSACHAR
Son of Jacob by Leah (Gn 30:18; 35:23; 1 Ch 2:1). Tribe of blessed (Gn 49:14-15; Dt 33:18-19), numbered (Nm 1:29; 26:25), allotted land (Jos 19:17-23; Ez 48:25), assisted Deborah (Jgs 5:15), 12,000 from (Rev 7:7).

ITCH
Dt 28:27 the **i**, from none of which you can be cured.

J

JACKALS
Jgs 15:4 Samson went and caught three hundred **j**,

JACOB → =ISRAEL
1. Son of Isaac, younger twin of Esau (Gn 26:21-26; 1 Ch 1:34). Bought Esau's birthright (Gn 26:29-34); tricked Isaac into blessing him (Gn 27:1-37). Fled to Haran (Gn 28:1-5). Abrahamic covenant perpetuated through (Gn 28:13-15; Mal 1:2). Vision at Bethel (Gn 28:10-22). Served Laban for Rachel and Leah (Gn 29:1-30). Children (Gn 29:31–30:24; 35:16-26; 1 Ch 2–9). Flocks increased (Gn 30:25-43). Returned to Canaan (Gn 31). Wrestled with God; name changed to Israel (Gn 32:22-32). Reconciled to Esau (Gn 33). Returned to Bethel (Gn 35:1-15). Favored Joseph (Gn 37:3). Sent sons to Egypt during famine (Gn 42–43). Settled in Egypt (Gn 46). Blessed Ephraim and Manasseh (Gn 48). Blessed sons (Gn 49:1-28; Heb 11:21). Death (Gn 49:29-33). Burial (Gn 50:1-14).
2. Corporate name of Jacob's descendants; often specifically Northern Kingdom.
1 Mc 1:28 all the house of **J** was clothed
Ps 135:4 For the LORD has chosen **J**
Mi 7:20 You will show faithfulness to **J**,
Rom 9:13 "I loved **J** but hated Esau."

JAEL
Woman who killed the Canaanite general, Sisera (Jgs 4:17-22; 5:6, 24-27).

JAIRUS
Synagogue ruler whose daughter Jesus raised (Mk 5:22-43; Lk 8:41-56).

JAMES
1. Apostle; brother of John (Mt 4:21-22; 10:2; Mk 3:17; Lk 5:1-10). At transfiguration (Mt 17:1-13; Mk 9:1-13; Lk 9:28-36). Killed by Herod (Acts 12:2).
2. Apostle (Mt 10:3; Mk 3:18; Lk 6:15).
3. Brother of Jesus (Mt 13:55; Mk 6:3; Lk 24:10; Gal 1:19) and Judas (Jude 1). With believers before Pentecost (Acts 1:13). Leader of church at Jerusalem (Acts 12:17; 15; 21:18; Gal 2:9, 12). Author of epistle (Jas 1:1).

JAPHETH
Son of Noah (Gn 5:32; 1 Ch 1:4-5). Blessed (Gn 9:18-28). Sons of (Gn 10:2-5).

JAR → JARS
1 Kgs 17:14 The **j** of flour shall not go empty,
Mk 14:3 She broke the alabaster **j** and poured
Lk 22:10 a man will meet you carrying a **j**

JARS → JAR
Jn 2:6 there were six stone water **j** there

JEALOUS
Ex 34:14 for the LORD—"**J**" his name—is a **j** God.
Nm 25:13 because he was **j** on behalf of his God
Dt 4:24 God, is a consuming fire, a **j** God.
Rom 10:19 "I will make you **j** of those who are

JEBUSITES
Ex 3:8 Girgashites, the Hivites and the **J**.
Jos 15:63 But the **J** who lived in Jerusalem

JECONIAH → See JEHOIACHIN

JEHOAHAZ
1. Son of Jehu; king of Israel (2 Kgs 13:1-9).
2. Son of Josiah; king of Judah (2 Kgs 23:31-34; 2 Ch 36:1-4).

JEHOASH → =JOASH
1. Son of Ahaziah, king of Judah (2 Kgs 12). See Joash, 1.
2. Son of Jehoahaz; king of Israel. Defeat of Aram prophesied by Elisha (2 Kgs 13:10-25). Defeated Amaziah in Jerusalem (2 Kgs 14:1-16). See Joash, 2.

JEHOIACHIN → =JECONIAH
Son of Jehoiakim; king of Judah exiled by Nebuchadnezzar (2 Kgs 24:8-17; 2 Ch 36:8-10; Ez 1:2). Status improved (2 Kgs 25:27-30; Jer 52:31-34).

JEHOIADA
Priest who sheltered Joash from Athaliah (2 Kgs 11–12; 2 Ch 22:11–24:16).

JEHOIAKIM → =ELIAKIM
Son of Josiah; made king of Judah by Nebuchadnezzar (2 Kgs 23:34–24:6; 2 Ch 36:4-8; Jer 22:18-23). Burned scroll of Jeremiah's prophecies (Jer 36).

JEHORAM → =JORAM
1. Son of Jehoshaphat; king of Judah. Prophesied against by Elijah; killed by the LORD (2 Ch 21). See Joram, 1.
2. Son of Ahab; king of Israel (2 Ch 22:5). Joined Jehoshaphat against Moab (2 Kgs 3). See Joram, 2.

JEHOSHAPHAT
1. Son of Asa; king of Judah. Strengthened his kingdom (2 Ch 17). Joined with Ahab against Aram (2 Kgs 22; 2 Ch 18). Established judges (2 Ch 19). Joined Joram against Moab (2 Kgs 3; 2 Ch 20).
2. Valley of judgment (Jl 3:2, 12).

JEHU
1. Prophet against Baasha (2 Kgs 16:1-7).
2. King of Israel. Anointed by Elijah to obliterate house of Ahab (1 Kgs 19:16-17); anointed by servant of Elisha (2 Kgs 9:1-13). Killed Joram and Ahaziah (2 Kgs 9:14-29; 2 Ch 22:7-9), Jezebel (2 Kgs 9:30-37), relatives of Ahab (2 Kgs 10:1-17; Hos 1:4), ministers of Baal (2 Kgs 10:18-29). Death (2 Kgs 10:30-36).

JEPHTHAH
Judge from Gilead who delivered Israel from Ammon (Jgs 10:6–12:7). Made rash vow concerning his daughter (Jgs 11:30-40).

JEREMIAH
Prophet to Judah (Jer 1:1-3). Called by the LORD (Jer 1). Put in stocks (Jer 20:1-3). Threatened for prophesying (Jer 11:18-23; 26). Opposed by Hananiah (Jer 28). Scroll burned (Jer 36). Imprisoned (Jer 37). Thrown into cistern (Jer 38). Forced to Egypt with those fleeing Babylonians (Jer 43).

JERICHO
Jos 6:2 I have delivered **J**, its king, and its
1 Kgs 16:34 his reign, Hiel from Bethel rebuilt **J**.
Lk 18:35 as he approached **J** a blind man was

JEROBOAM
1. Official of Solomon; rebelled to become first king of Israel (1 Kgs 11:26-40; 12:1-20; 2 Ch 10). Idolatry (1 Kgs 12:25-33; Tb 1:5; Sir 47:23); judgment for (1 Kgs 13–14; 2 Ch 13).
2. Son of Jehoash; king of Israel (2 Kgs 14:23-29).

JERUSALEM
2 Sm 5:5 **J** he was king thirty-three years over
15:29 took the ark of God back to **J**
2 Kgs 25:10 down the walls that surrounded **J**,
Ezr 2:1 and who came back to **J** and Judah,
Neh 2:17 how **J** lies in ruins and its gates
2:17 let us rebuild the wall of **J**,

1 Mc 1: 29 he came to **J** with a strong force.
Is 40: 2 Speak to the heart of **J**,
Lam 1: 8 **J** has sinned grievously,
Dn 9: 25 of the word that **J** was to be rebuilt
Mi 4: 2 and the word of the LORD from **J**.
Zec 1: 14 I am jealous for **J** and for Zion
14: 8 fresh water will flow from **J**,
Mt 23: 37 "**J**, **J**, you who kill the prophets
Lk 4: 9 Then he led him to **J**, made him
Gal 4: 25 it corresponds to the present **J**,
Heb 12: 22 the heavenly **J**, and countless angels
Rev 21: 2 city, a new **J**, coming down

JESSE

Father of David (Ru 4:17-22; 1 Sm 16; 1 Ch 2:12-17).

JESUS

1. Jesus the Messiah.

LIFE: Genealogy (Mt 1:1-17; Lk 3:21-37). Birth announced (Mt 1:18-25; Lk 1:26-45). Birth (Mt 2:1-12; Lk 2:1-40). Escape to Egypt (Mt 2:13-23). As a boy in the temple (Lk 2:41-52). Baptism (Mt 3:13-17; Mk 1:9-11; Lk 3:21-22; Jn 1:32-34). Temptation (Mt 4:1-11; Mk 1:12-13; Lk 4:1-13). Ministry in Galilee (Mt 4:12–18:35; Mk 1:14–9:50; Lk 4:14–13:9; Jn 1:35–2:11; 4; 6), Transfiguration (Mt 17:1-8; Mk 9:2-8; Lk 9:28-36), on the way to Jerusalem (Mt 19–20; Mk 10; Lk 13:10–19:27), in Jerusalem (Mt 21–25; Mk 11–13; Lk 19:28–21:38; Jn 2:12–3:36; 5; 7–12). Last supper (Mt 26:17-35; Mk 14:12-31; Lk 22:1-38; Jn 13–17). Arrest and trial (Mt 26:36–27:31; Mk 14:43–15:20; Lk 22:39–23:25; Jn 18:1–19:16). Crucifixion (Mt 27:32-66; Mk 15:21-47; Lk 23:26-55; Jn 19:28-42). Resurrection and appearances (Mt 28; Mk 16; Lk 24; Jn 20–21; Acts 1:1-11; 7:56; 9:3-6; 1 Cor 15:1-8; Rev 1:1-20).

MIRACLES. *Healings:* official's son (Jn 4:43-54), demoniac in Capernaum (Mk 1:23-26; Lk 4:33-35), Peter's mother-in-law (Mt 8:14-17; Mk 1:29-31; Lk 4:38-39), leper (Mt 8:2-4; Mk 1:40-45; Lk 5:12-16), paralytic (Mt 9:1-8; Mk 2:1-12; Lk 5:17-26), cripple (Jn 5:1-9), shriveled hand (Mt 12:10-13; Mk 3:1-5; Lk 6:6-11), centurion's servant (Mt 8:5-13; Lk 7:1-10), widow's son raised (Lk 7:11-17), demoniac (Mt 12:22-23; Lk 11:14), Gadarene demoniacs (Mt 8:28-34; Mk 5:1-20; Lk 8:26-39), woman's bleeding and Jairus' daughter (Mt 9:18-26; Mk 5:21-43; Lk 8:40-56), blind man (Mt 9:27-31), mute man (Mt 9:32-33), Canaanite woman's daughter (Mt 15:21-28; Mk 7:24-30), deaf man (Mk 7:31-37), blind man (Mk 8:22-26), demoniac boy (Mt 17:14-18; Mk 9:14-29; Lk 9:37-43), ten lepers (Lk 17:11-19), man born blind (Jn 9:1-7), Lazarus raised (Jn 11), crippled woman (Lk 13:11-17), man with dropsy (Lk 14:1-6), two blind men (Mt 20:29-34; Mk 10:46-52; Lk 18:35-43), Malchus' ear (Lk 22:50-51). *Other Miracles:* water to wine (Jn 2:1-11), catch of fish (Lk 5:1-11), storm stilled (Mt 8:23-27; Mk 4:37-41; Lk 8:22-25), 5,000 fed (Mt 14:15-21; Mk 6:35-44; Lk 9:10-17; Jn 6:1-14), walking on water (Mt 14:25-33; Mk 6:48-52; Jn 6:15-21), 4,000 fed (Mt 15:32-39; Mk 8:1-9), money from fish (Mt 17:24-27), fig tree cursed (Mt 21:18-22; Mk 11:12-14), catch of fish (Jn 21:1-14).

MAJOR TEACHING: Sermon on the Mount (Mt 5–7; Lk 6:17-49), to Nicodemus (Jn 3), to Samaritan woman (Jn 4), Bread of Life (Jn 6:22-59), at Feast of Tabernacles (Jn 7–8), woes to Pharisees (Mt 23; Lk 11:37-54), Good Shepherd (Jn 10:1-18), Olivet Discourse (Mt 24–25; Mk 13; Lk 21:5-36), Upper Room Discourse (Jn 13–16).

PARABLES: Sower (Mt 13:3-23; Mk 4:3-25; Lk 8:5-18), seed's growth (Mk 4:26-29), wheat and weeds (Mt 13:24-30, 36-43), mustard seed (Mt 13:31-32; Mk 4:30-32), yeast (Mt 13:33; Lk 13:20-21), hidden treasure (Mt 13:44), valuable pearl (Mt 13:45-46), net (Mt 13:47-51), house owner (Mt 13:52), good Samaritan (Lk 10:25-37), unmerciful servant (Mt 18:15-35), lost sheep (Mt 18:10-14; Lk 15:4-7), lost coin (Lk 15:8-10), prodigal son (Lk 15:11-32), dishonest manager (Lk 16:1-13), rich man and Lazarus (Lk 16:19-31), persistent widow (Lk 18:1-8), Pharisee and tax collector (Lk 18:9-14), payment of workers (Mt 20:1-16), tenants and the vineyard (Mt 21:28-46; Mk 12:1-12; Lk 20:9-19), wedding banquet (Mt 22:1-14), faithful servant (Mt 24:45-51), ten virgins (Mt 25:1-13), talents (Mt 25:14-30; Lk 19:12-27).

DISCIPLES see APOSTLES. Call (Jn 1:35-51; Mt 4:18-22; 9:9; Mk 1:16-20; 2:13-14; Lk 5:1-11, 27-28). Named Apostles (Mk 3:13-19; Lk 6:12-16). Twelve sent out (Mt 10; Mk 6:7-11; Lk 9:1-5). Seventy sent out (Lk 10:1-24). Defection of (Jn 6:60-71; Mt 26:56; Mk 14:50-52). Final commission (Mt 28:16-20; Jn 21:15-23; Acts 1:3-8).

Acts 9: 5 "I am **J**, whom you are persecuting.
1 Cor 8: 6 and one Lord, **J** Christ,
Phil 2: 10 name of **J** every knee should bend,
2 Thes 2: 1 to the coming of our Lord **J** Christ
1 Tm 1: 15 Christ **J** came into the world to save
Heb 12: 2 while keeping our eyes fixed on **J**,
13: 8 **J** Christ is the same yesterday,
1 Jn 1: 7 the blood of his Son **J** cleanses us
Rev 1: 1 The revelation of **J** Christ,
22: 20 Amen! Come, Lord **J**!

2. Disciple, also called Justus (Col 4:11).

3. Writer of Sirach (Sir Pr:1; 50:27; 51:1).

JETHRO

Father-in-law and adviser of Moses (Ex 3:1; 4:18; 18). Also known as Reuel (Ex 2:18).

JEW → JEWS, JUDAHITE, JUDAISM

Est 10: 3 The **J** Mordecai was next in rank
Rom 1: 16 for **J** first, and then Greek.
2: 29 Rather, one is a **J** inwardly,
1 Cor 9: 20 To the Jews I became like a **J** to win
Col 3: 11 Here there is not Greek and **J**,

JEWS → JEW

Est 3: 13 kill and annihilate all the **J**,
Mt 2: 2 is the newborn king of the **J**?
27: 11 him, "Are you the king of the **J**?"
Jn 4: 22 because salvation is from the **J**.
Rom 3: 29 Does God belong to **J** alone?

JEZEBEL

Sidonian wife of Ahab (1 Kgs 16:31). Promoted Baal worship (1 Kgs 16:32-33). Killed prophets of the LORD (1 Kgs 18:4, 13). Opposed Elijah (1 Kgs 19:1-2). Had Naboth killed (1 Kgs 21). Death (1 Kgs 21:17-24; 2 Kgs 9:30-37). Metaphor of immorality (Rev 2:20).

JEZREEL

2 Kgs 10: 7 baskets, and sent them to Jehu in **J**.
Hos 1: 4 Give him the name "**J**,"
1: 4 house of Jehu for the bloodshed at **J**

JOAB

Nephew of David (1 Ch 2:16). Commander of his army (2 Sm 8:16). Victorious over Ammon (2 Sm 10; 1 Ch 19), Rabbah (2 Sm 11; 1 Ch 20), Jerusalem (1 Ch 11:6), Absalom (2 Sm 18), Sheba (2 Sm 20). Killed Abner (2 Sm 3:22-39), Amasa (2 Sm 20:1-13). Numbered David's army (2 Sm 24; 1 Ch 21). Sided with Adonijah (1 Kgs 1:17, 19). Killed by Benaiah (1 Kgs 2:5-6, 28-35).

JOASH → =JEHOASH

1. Son of Ahaziah; king of Judah. Sheltered from Athaliah by Jehoiada (2 Kgs 11; 2 Ch 22:10–23:21). Repaired temple (2 Ch 24). See Jehoash, 1.

2. Son of Jehoahaz, king of Israel (2 Kgs 13; 2 Ch 25:17-25). See Jehoash, 2.

JOB

Wealthy man from Uz; feared God (Jb 1:1-5). Integrity tested by disaster (Jb 1:6-22), personal affliction (Jb 2). Maintained innocence in debate with three friends (Jb 3–31), Elihu (Jb 32–37). Rebuked by the LORD (Jb 38–41). Vindicated and restored to greater stature by the LORD (Jb 42). Example of righteousness (Ez 14:14, 20; Sir 49:9).

JOEL

1. Son of Samuel (1 Sm 8:2; 1 Ch 6:28).

2. Prophet (Jl 1:1; Acts 2:16).

JOHANAN

1. First high priest in the temple (1 Ch 6:9-10).

2. Jewish leader who tried to save Gedaliah from assassination (Jer 40:13-14); took Jews, including Jeremiah, to Egypt (Jer 40–43).

JOHN

1. Son of Zechariah and Elizabeth (Lk 1). Called the Baptist (Mt 3:1-12; Mk 1:2-8). Witness to Jesus (Mt 3:11-12; Mk 1:7-8; Lk 3:15-18; Jn 1:6-35; 3:27-30; 5:33-36). Doubts about Jesus (Mt 11:2-6; Lk 7:18-23). Arrest (Mt 4:12; Mk 1:14). Execution (Mt 14:1-12; Mk 6:14-29; Lk 9:7-9). Ministry compared to Elijah (Mt 11:7-19; Mk 9:11-13; Lk 7:24-35).

2. Apostle; brother of James (Mt 4:21-22; 10:2; Mk 3:17; Lk 5:1-10). At transfiguration (Mt 17:1-13; Mk 9:1-13; Lk 9:28-36). Desire to be greatest (Mk 10:35-45). Leader of church at Jerusalem (Acts 4:1-3; Gal 2:9). Elder who wrote epistles (2 Jn 1; 3 Jn 1). Prophet who wrote Revelation (Rev 1:1; 22:8).

3. Cousin of Barnabas, co-worker with Paul, (Acts 12:12–13:13; 15:37; see Mark).

4. Son of Simon Maccabeus (1 Mc 13:53; 16).

JOIN → JOINED
Ez 37: 17 **J** the two sticks together so they

JOINED → JOIN
Mt 19: 6 what God has **j** together, no human

JOINT → JOINTS
Rom 8: 17 heirs of God and **j** heirs with Christ,

JOINTS → JOINT
Heb 4: 12 soul and spirit, **j** and marrow,

JONAH

Prophet in days of Jeroboam II (2 Kgs 14:25). Called to Nineveh; fled to Tarshish (Jon 1:1-3). Cause of storm; thrown into sea (Jon 1:4-16). Swallowed by fish (Jon 1:17). Prayer (Jon 2). Preached to Nineveh (Jon 3). Attitude reproved by the LORD (Jon 4). Sign of (Mt 12:39-41; Lk 11:29-32).

JONATHAN

1. Son of Saul (1 Sm 13:16; 1 Ch 8:33). Valiant warrior (1 Sm 13–14). Relation to David (1 Sm 18:1-4; 19–20; 23:16-18). Killed at Gilboa (1 Sm 31). Mourned by David (2 Sm 1).

2. Brother and successor of Judas Maccabeus (1 Mc 2:5; 9:28-31).

JOPPA
Jon 1: 3 He went down to **J**, found a ship
Acts 9: 43 And he stayed a long time in **J**

JORAM → =JEHORAM

1. Son of Jehoshaphat; king of Judah (2 Kgs 8:16-24). See Jehoram, 1.

2. Son of Ahab; king of Israel. Killed with Ahaziah by Jehu (2 Kgs 8:25-29; 9:14-26; 2 Ch 22:5-9). See Jehoram, 2.

JORDAN
Gn 13: 10 watered the whole **J** Plain was as far
Nm 34: 12 boundary will descend along the **J**
Jos 3: 17 had completed the crossing of the **J**.
Mt 3: 6 in the **J** River as they acknowledged

JOSEPH → =BARNABAS

1. Son of Jacob by Rachel (Gn 30:24; 1 Ch 2:2). Favored by Jacob, hated by brothers (Gn 37:3-4). Dreams (Gn 37:5-11). Sold by brothers (Gn 37:12-36). Served Potiphar; imprisoned by false accusation (Gn 39). Interpreted dreams of Pharaoh's servants (Gn 40), of Pharaoh (Gn 41:4-40). Made greatest in Egypt (Gn 41:41-57). Sold grain to brothers (Gn 42–45). Brought Jacob and sons to Egypt (Gn 46–47). Sons Ephraim and Manasseh blessed (Gn 48). Blessed (Gn 49:22-26; Dt 33:13-17). Death (Gn 50:22-26; Ex 13:19; Heb 11:22). 12,000 from (Rev 7:8).

2. Husband of Mary mother of Jesus (Mt 1:16-24; 2:13-19; Lk 1:27; 2; Jn 1:45).

3. Disciple from Arimathea; buried Jesus in his tomb (Mt 27:57-61; Mk 15:43-47; Lk 24:50-52).

4. Original name of Barnabas (Acts 4:36).

JOSHUA → =HOSHEA

1. Son of Nun; name changed from Hoshea (Nm 13:8, 16; 1 Ch 7:27). Fought Amalekites under Moses (Ex 17:9-14). Servant of Moses on Sinai (Ex 24:13; 32:17). Spied Canaan (Nm 13). With Caleb, allowed to enter land (Nm 14:6, 30). Succeeded Moses (Dt 1:38; 31:1-8; 34:9).

Charged Israel to conquer Canaan (Jos 1). Crossed Jordan (Jos 3–4). Circumcised sons of wilderness wanderings (Jos 5). Conquered Jericho (Jos 6), Ai (Jos 7–8), five kings at Gibeon (Jos 10:1-28), southern Canaan (Jos 10:29-43), northern Canaan (Jos 11–12). Defeated at Ai (Jos 7). Deceived by Gibeonites (Jos 9). Renewed covenant (Jos 8:30-35; 24:1-27). Divided land among tribes (Jos 13–22). Last words (Jos 23). Death (Jos 24:28-31).

2. High priest during rebuilding of temple (Hg 1–2; Zec 3:1-9; 6:11). See Jeshua.

JOSIAH

Son of Amon; king of Judah (2 Kgs 21:26; 1 Ch 3:14). Prophesied (1 Kgs 13:2). Book of the Law discovered during his reign (2 Kgs 22; 2 Ch 34:14-31). Reforms (2 Kgs 23:1-25; 2 Ch 34:1-13; 35:1-19; Sir 49:1-4). Killed in battle (2 Kgs 23:29-30; 2 Ch 35:20-27).

JOTHAM

1. Son of Gideon (Jgs 9).

2. Son of Azariah (Uzziah); king of Judah (2 Kgs 15:32-38; 2 Ch 26:21–27:9).

JOY
Jb 20: 5 is short and the **j** of the impious
Prv 10: 1 A wise son gives his father **j**,
21: 15 justice is done it is a **j** for the just,
Is 12: 3 With **j** you will draw water
35: 10 singing, crowned with everlasting **j**; They meet with **j** and gladness,
Lam 2: 15 in beauty and **j** of all the earth?"
Bar 5: 9 For God is leading Israel in **j**
Mk 4: 16 the word, receive it at once with **j**.
Lk 1: 44 the infant in my womb leaped for **j**.
2: 10 good news of great **j** that will be
Jn 16: 22 no one will take your **j** away
Rom 14: 17 peace, and **j** in the holy Spirit;
Gal 5: 22 the fruit of the Spirit is love, **j**,
Phil 4: 1 I love and long for, my **j** and crown,
Heb 12: 2 the **j** that lay before him he endured
Jas 1: 2 Consider it all **j**, my brothers,

JUBILEE
Lv 25: 10 It shall be a **j** for you, when each
Nm 36: 4 the Israelites celebrate the **j** year,

JUDAH → JUDAHITE, JUDEA

1. Son of Jacob by Leah (Gn 29:35; 35:23; 1 Ch 2:1). Did not want to kill Joseph (Gn 37:26-27). Among Canaanites, fathered Perez by Tamar (Gn 38). Tribe of blessed as ruling tribe (Gn 49:8-12; Dt 33:7), numbered (Nm 1:27; 26:22), allotted land (Jos 15; Ez 48:7), failed to fully possess (Jos 15:63; Jgs 1:1-20).

2. Name used for Southern Kingdom.
2 Sm 2: 4 David king over the house of **J**.
Lam 1: 3 **J** has gone into exile,
Mt 2: 6 land of **J**, are by no means least among the rulers of **J**;
Heb 7: 14 is clear that our Lord arose from **J**,
Rev 5: 5 The lion of the tribe of **J**, the root

JUDAHITE → JUDAH
Zec 8: 23 hold of the cloak of every **J** and say,

JUDAISM → JEW
Acts 13: 43 were converts to **J** followed Paul
Gal 1: 13 heard of my former way of life in **J**,

JUDAS → =JUDE, =THADDAEUS, MACCABEUS

1. Apostle; son of James (Lk 6:16; Jn 14:22; Acts 1:13). Probably also called Thaddaeus (Mt 10:3; Mk 3:18).

2. Brother of James and Jesus (Mt 13:55; Mk 6:3), also called Jude (Jude 1).

3. Christian prophet (Acts 15:22-32).

4. Apostle, also called Iscariot, who betrayed Jesus (Mt 10:4; 26:14-56; Mk 3:19; 14:10-50; Lk 6:16; 22:3-53; Jn 6:71; 12:4; 13:2-30; 18:2-11). Suicide of (Mt 27:3-5; Acts 1:16-25).

5. Leader of the Maccabean revolt (1 Mc 2:4, 66). Recaptured Jerusalem and rededicated the temple and altar (1 Mc 4:36-61). Death of (1 Mc 9).

JUDE → See JUDAS, 2

JUDEA → JUDAH
Mt 2: 1 Jesus was born in Bethlehem of **J**,
Lk 3: 1 Pontius Pilate was governor of **J**,
Acts 1: 8 throughout **J** and Samaria,

JUDGE → JUDGED, JUDGES, JUDGMENT, JUDGMENTS
Ex 2: 14 appointed you ruler and **j** over us?
Is 11: 3 Not by appearance shall he **j**,
Ez 34: 17 I will **j** between one sheep
Jn 7: 24 by appearances, but **j** justly."
18: 31 and **j** him according to your law."
Rom 3: 6 For how else is God to **j** the world?
1 Cor 6: 2 that the holy ones will **j** the world?
2 Tm 4: 1 who will **j** the living and the dead,
Heb 12: 23 and God the **j** of all, and the spirits
Jas 5: 9 the **J** is standing before the gates.

JUDGED → JUDGE
Mt 7: 1 judging, that you may not be **j**.
Jas 3: 1 that we will be **j** more strictly,
Rev 20: 12 The dead were **j** according to their

JUDGES → JUDGE
Jgs 2: 16 the LORD raised up **j** to save them
1 Sm 2: 10 the LORD **j** the ends of the earth.
Sir 16: 12 he **j** people, each according to their
Lk 11: 19 Therefore they will be your **j**.
Acts 4: 19 you rather than God, you be the **j**.
Jas 4: 11 **j** his brother speaks evil of the law and **j** the law.
Rev 19: 11 He **j** and wages war

JUDGMENT → JUDGE
Ex 6: 6 arm and with mighty acts of **j**.
Ps 1: 5 the wicked will not arise at the **j**,
Eccl 12: 14 God will bring to **j** every work,
Jer 25: 31 he enters into **j** against all flesh:
Dn 7: 22 **j** was pronounced in favor
Mal 3: 5 I will draw near to you for **j**, and I
Mt 11: 24 on the day of **j** than for you."
Rom 14: 10 we shall all stand before the **j** seat
2 Cor 5: 10 we must all appear before the **j** seat
Heb 9: 27 beings die once, and after this the **j**,
10: 27 a fearful prospect of **j** and a flaming
Jas 2: 13 For the **j** is merciless to one who has
2: 13 mercy triumphs over **j**.
1 Pt 4: 17 it is time for the **j** to begin
1 Jn 4: 17 on the day of **j** because as he is,
Rev 18: 10 In one hour your **j** has come."

JUDGMENTS → JUDGE
Rom 11: 33 How inscrutable are his **j** and how
Rev 19: 2 for true and just are his **j**.

JUDITH

Virtuous widow and heroine of the deuterocanonical book of Judith (Jdt 8–16).

JUST → JUSTICE, JUSTIFICATION, JUSTIFIED, JUSTIFY
Dt 32: 4 without deceit, **j** and upright is he!
Tb 3: 2 Lord, and all your deeds are **j**;
1 Jn 1: 9 he is faithful and **j** and will forgive
Rev 15: 3 **J** and true are your ways, O king

JUSTICE → JUST
Jb 37: 23 abundant in **j**, who never oppresses.
Ps 33: 5 He loves **j** and right. The earth is
Prv 21: 15 When **j** is done it is a joy
Is 30: 18 For the LORD is a God of **j**:
42: 4 be bruised until he establishes **j**
Am 5: 24 Rather let **j** surge like waters,

JUSTIFICATION → JUST
Rom 4: 25 and was raised for our **j**.
Gal 2: 21 for if **j** comes through the law,

JUSTIFIED → JUST
Rom 3: 24 They are **j** freely by his grace
5: 1 since we have been **j** by faith,
10: 10 believes with the heart and so is **j**,
1 Cor 6: 11 you were **j** in the name of the Lord
Gal 2: 16 know that a person is not **j** by works
2: 16 Jesus that we may be **j** by faith
Jas 2: 24 See how a person is **j** by works

JUSTIFY → JUST
Rom 3: 30 will **j** the circumcised on the basis
Gal 3: 8 that God would **j** the Gentiles

K

KADESH → KADESH-BARNEA
Nm 20: 1 month, and the people stayed at **K**.
Dt 1: 46 had to stay as long as you did at **K**.

KADESH-BARNEA → KADESH
Nm 32: 8 I sent them from **K** to reconnoiter

KEEP → KEEPER, KEEPS, KEPT
Gn 17: 9 you must **k** my covenant throughout
Ex 19: 5 me completely and **k** my covenant,
Nm 6: 24 The LORD bless you and **k** you!
Dt 5: 10 love me and **k** my commandments.
Neh 1: 5 you and **k** your commandments.
Prv 7: 2 **K** my commands and live, and my
Eccl 3: 6 a time to **k**, and a time to cast away.
12: 13 Fear God and **k** his commandments,
Sir 1: 26 wisdom, **k** the commandments,
Jude 1: 24 the one who is able to **k** you
Rev 22: 9 of those who **k** the message of this

KEEPER → KEEP
Gn 4: 9 Am I my brother's **k**?"

KEEPS → KEEP
Jas 2: 10 For whoever **k** the whole law,

KEPT → KEEP
Jn 17: 6 to me, and they have **k** your word.
2 Tm 4: 7 finished the race; I have **k** the faith.

KEY → KEYS
Is 22: 22 I will place the **k** of the House
Lk 11: 52 You have taken away the **k**
Rev 3: 7 the true, who holds the **k** of David,

KEYS → KEY
Mt 16: 19 I will give you the **k** to the kingdom
Rev 1: 18 I hold the **k** to death

KIDRON
2 Sm 15: 23 the king crossed the Wadi **K** with all
Jn 18: 1 his disciples across the **K** valley

KILL
Ex 4: 23 to let him go, I will **k** your son,
Eccl 3: 3 A time to **k**, and a time to heal;

Mt 10:28 afraid of those who **k** the body but cannot **k** the soul;

KIND → KINDNESS, KINDS
Gn 6:20 Of every **k** of bird, of every **k** of animal,
1 Cor 13:4 Love is patient, love is **k**. It is not
Eph 4:32 [And] be **k** to one another,

KINDNESS → KIND
Rom 2:4 that the **k** of God would lead you
Gal 5:22 joy, peace, patience, **k**, generosity,

KINDS → KIND
Lv 19:19 yours with two different **k** of seed;
19:19 with two different **k** of thread.

KING → KINGDOM, KINGS
Ex 1:8 Then a new **k**, who knew nothing
Dt 17:14 "I will set a **k** over me, like all
1 Sm 8:7 They are rejecting me as their **k**.
2 Sm 2:4 anointed David **k** over the house
Jdt 9:12 waters, **K** of all you have created,
Ps 2:6 "I myself have installed my **k**
10:16 The LORD is **k** forever;
Is 6:5 and my eyes have seen the **K**,
Jer 10:10 the eternal **K**, Before whose anger
Mt 2:2 "Where is the newborn **k**
27:37 This is Jesus, the **K** of the Jews.
Lk 19:38 "Blessed is the **k** who comes
Jn 1:49 you are the **K** of Israel."
1 Tm 1:17 To the **k** of ages, incorruptible,
Rev 19:16 "**K** of kings and Lord of lords."

KINGDOM → KING
Ex 19:6 You will be to me a **k** of priests,
2 Sm 7:12 your loins, and I will establish his **k**.
1 Kgs 11:31 to tear the **k** out of Solomon's hand
Wis 10:10 Showed him the **k** of God and gave
Mt 4:17 for the **k** of heaven is at hand."
5:3 spirit, for theirs is the **k** of heaven.
6:10 your **k** come, your will be done,
13:24 "The **k** of heaven may be likened
Mk 1:15 The **k** of God is at hand.
6:23 ask of me, even to half of my **k**."
10:24 how hard it is to enter the **k** of God!
12:34 are not far from the **k** of God."
13:8 rise against nation and **k** against **k**.
Lk 17:21 the **k** of God is among you."
22:16 there is fulfillment in the **k** of God."
Jn 3:5 you, no one can enter the **k** of God
18:36 "My **k** does not belong to this
Acts 1:6 going to restore the **k** to Israel?"
Rom 14:17 For the **k** of God is not a matter
1 Cor 6:9 the unjust will not inherit the **k**
Eph 5:5 any inheritance in the **k** of Christ
Col 1:13 us to the **k** of his beloved Son,
1 Thes 2:12 of the God who calls you into his **k**
Heb 12:28 the unshakable **k** should have
2 Pt 1:11 entry into the eternal **k** of our Lord
Rev 11:15 "The **k** of the world now belongs

KINGS → KING
Gn 17:6 **k** will stem from you.
Ps 2:2 **K** on earth rise up and princes plot
138:4 All the **k** of earth will praise you,
Prv 8:15 By me **k** reign, and rulers enact
Is 52:15 nations, **k** shall stand speechless;
Dn 7:24 The ten horns shall be ten **k** rising
7:24 him, who shall lay low three **k**.
Acts 4:26 The **k** of the earth took their stand
1 Tm 6:15 the King of **k** and Lord of lords,
Rev 19:16 "King of **k** and Lord of lords."

KISS
Sg 1:2 Let him **k** me with kisses of his
Mt 26:48 "The man I shall **k** is the one;
2 Cor 13:12 Greet one another with a holy **k**.

KNEE
Is 45:23 To me every **k** shall bend;
Rom 14:11 Lord, every **k** shall bend before me,
Phil 2:10 name of Jesus every **k** should bend,

KNEEL → KNELT
Ps 95:6 let us **k** before the LORD who

KNELT → KNEEL
2 Ch 6:13 it, Solomon **k** in the presence

KNEW → KNOW
Dt 34:10 whom the LORD **k** face to face,
Jer 1:5 I formed you in the womb I **k** you,
Mt 7:23 to them solemnly, 'I never **k** you.
Rom 1:21 for although they **k** God they did not

KNOCK
Lk 11:9 **k** and the door will be opened

KNOW → FOREKNEW, KNEW, KNOWING, KNOWLEDGE, KNOWN, KNOWS
Gn 22:12 For now I **k** that you fear God,
Ex 6:7 and you will **k** that I, the LORD,
1 Kgs 8:39 their ways, you who **k** every heart;
Jb 19:25 for me, I **k** that my vindicator lives,
Eccl 8:16 I applied my heart to **k** wisdom
Is 1:3 But Israel does not **k**, my people has
Jer 31:34 and relatives, "**K** the LORD!"
31:34 from least to greatest, shall **k** me—
Mt 6:3 let your left hand **k** what your right
24:42 For you do not **k** on which day your
Lk 11:13 **k** how to give good gifts to your
22:34 deny three times that you **k** me."
Jn 10:14 and I **k** mine and mine **k** me,
13:35 This is how all will **k** that you are
21:24 and we **k** that his testimony is true.
Acts 1:7 "It is not for you to **k** the times
Rom 8:28 We **k** that all things work for good
1 Cor 8:2 he does not yet **k** as he ought to **k**.
13:12 At present I **k** partially; then I shall
13:12 then I shall **k** fully, as I am fully
Eph 3:19 to **k** the love of Christ that surpasses
Phil 3:10 to **k** him and the power of his
Ti 1:16 They claim to **k** God, but by their
Heb 8:11 and kinsman, saying, '**K** the Lord,' for all shall **k** me, from least to greatest.
1 Jn 2:4 Whoever says, "I **k** him," but does
3:16 The way we came to **k** love was
Rev 3:3 you will never **k** at what hour I will

KNOWING → KNOW
Gn 3:22 like one of us, **k** good and evil!
Jn 18:4 **k** everything that was going
Phil 3:8 good of **k** Christ Jesus my Lord.

KNOWLEDGE → KNOW
Gn 2:9 the tree of the **k** of good and evil.
Ps 94:10 one who teaches man not have **k**?
Prv 1:7 of the LORD is the beginning of **k**;
8:10 silver, and **k** rather than choice gold.
Eccl 1:18 whoever increases **k** increases grief.
Is 11:2 a spirit of **k** and of fear
Hos 4:6 My people are ruined for lack of **k**! Since you have rejected **k**,
Lk 11:52 You have taken away the key of **k**.
Rom 11:33 riches and wisdom and **k** of God!
1 Cor 8:1 we realize that "all of us have **k**";
Eph 3:19 the love of Christ that surpasses **k**,
Col 2:3 all the treasures of wisdom and **k**.

1 Tm 6: 20 and the absurdities of so-called **k**.
2 Pt 1: 5 your faith with virtue, virtue with **k**,
1 Jn 2: 20 the holy one, and you all have **k**.

KNOWN → KNOW
Lk 6: 44 For every tree is **k** by its own fruit.
1 Cor 2: 16 For "who has **k** the mind
Eph 1: 9 he has made **k** to us the mystery

KNOWS → KNOW
Ps 1: 6 the LORD **k** the way of the just,
103: 14 For he **k** how we are formed,
Mt 6: 8 Your Father **k** what you need before
24: 36 "But of that day and hour no one **k**,
Rom 8: 27 who searches hearts **k** what is
2 Tm 2: 19 "The Lord **k** those who are his";
1 Jn 4: 7 loves is begotten by God and **k** God.

KORAH → KORAHITES
Levite; led rebels against Moses (Nm 16; Jude 11).

KORAHITES → KORAH
Psalms of: Ps 42; 44–49; 84; 85; 87; 88.

L

LABAN
Brother of Rebekah (Gn 24:29), father of Rachel and Leah (Gn 29:16). Received Abraham's servant (Gn 24:29-51). Provided daughters as wives for Jacob in exchange for Jacob's service (Gn 29:1-30). Provided flocks for Jacob's service (Gn 30:25-43). Pursued and covenanted with Jacob (Gn 31).

LABOR → LABORER
Ex 1: 11 to oppress them with forced **l**.
20: 9 Six days you may **l** and do all your
1 Cor 15: 58 that in the Lord your **l** is not in vain.

LABORER → LABOR
Lv 19: 13 overnight the wages of your **l**.
Lk 10: 7 you, for the **l** deserves his payment.

LACKING
Col 1: 24 filling up what is **l** in the afflictions

LAID → LAY
Is 53: 6 the LORD **l** upon him the guilt
Mk 16: 6 Behold the place where they **l** him.
1 Jn 3: 16 love was that he **l** down his life

LAMB → LAMBS
Is 53: 7 Like a **l** led to slaughter or a sheep
Mk 14: 12 when they sacrificed the Passover **l**,
Jn 1: 29 "Behold, the **L** of God, who takes
1 Cor 5: 7 For our paschal **l**, Christ, has been
1 Pt 1: 19 as of a spotless unblemished **l**.
Rev 5: 12 "Worthy is the **L** that was slain
19: 7 the wedding day of the **L** has come,
21: 23 gave it light, and its lamp was the **L**.

LAMBS → LAMB
Ex 12: 21 and procure **l** for your families,
Is 40: 11 in his arms he gathers the **l**,
Jn 21: 15 He said to him, "Feed my **l**."

LAME
Is 35: 6 Then the **l** shall leap like a stag,
Zep 3: 19 I will save the **l**, and assemble
Mt 11: 5 blind regain their sight, the **l** walk,

LAMP → LAMPS, LAMPSTAND, LAMPSTANDS
Ps 18: 29 For you, LORD, give light to my **l**;
119: 105 Your word is a **l** for my feet,
Pr 13: 9 but the **l** of the wicked goes out.
31: 18 her **l** is never extinguished at night.
Mt 5: 15 Nor do they light a **l** and then put it
6: 22 "The **l** of the body is the eye.
Rev 21: 23 and its **l** was the Lamb.
22: 5 nor will they need light from **l**

LAMPS → LAMP
Ex 25: 37 You shall then make seven **l** for it
25: 37 set up the **l** that they give their light
Mt 25: 1 be like ten virgins who took their **l**

LAMPSTAND → LAMP, MENORAH
1 Mc 4: 50 altar and lighted the lamps on the **l**,
Zec 4: 2 I replied, "I see a **l** all of gold,

LAMPSTANDS → LAMP
Rev 1: 20 right hand, and of the seven gold **l**:
1: 20 the seven **l** are the seven churches.
11: 4 the two **l** that stand before the Lord

LAND
Gn 1: 10 God called the dry **l** "earth,"
12: 7 your descendants I will give this **l**.
Ex 3: 8 lead them up from that **l** into a good and spacious **l**,
20: 2 brought you out of the **l** of Egypt,
Nm 13: 2 men to reconnoiter the **l** of Canaan,
Jos 11: 23 Thus Joshua took the whole **l**,
11: 23 And the **l** had rest from war.
2 Kgs 17: 5 of Assyria occupied the whole **l**
25: 21 death in Riblah, in the **l** of Hamath.
2 Ch 7: 14 pardon their sins and heal their **l**.
Jer 22: 29 O **l**, **l**, **l**, hear the word
Dn 11: 41 He shall enter the glorious **l**

LANGUAGE
Acts 2: 6 heard them speaking in his own **l**.

LASHES
2 Cor 11: 24 Jews I received forty **l** minus one.

LAST → EVERLASTING
2 Sm 23: 1 These are the **l** words of David:
Is 44: 6 I am the first, I am the **l**; there is no
Mt 19: 30 But many who are first will be **l**, and the **l** will be first.
Mk 9: 35 first, he shall be the **l** of all
1 Cor 15: 26 The **l** enemy to be destroyed is
15: 52 the blink of an eye, at the **l** trumpet.
2 Tm 3: 1 will be terrifying times in the **l** days.
Heb 1: 2 in these **l** days, he spoke to us
1 Jn 2: 18 Children, it is the **l** hour; and just as
2: 18 Thus we know this is the **l** hour.
Rev 1: 17 I am the first and the **l**,

LAUGH → LAUGHINGSTOCK, LAUGHTER
Gn 18: 13 "Why did Sarah **l** and say, 'Will I
Eccl 3: 4 A time to weep, and a time to **l**;
Lk 6: 21 are now weeping, for you will **l**.

LAUGHINGSTOCK → LAUGH
Lam 3: 14 I have become a **l** to all my people,

LAUGHTER → LAUGH
Ps 126: 2 Then our mouths were filled with **l**;
Jas 4: 9 Let your **l** be turned into mourning

LAW → LAWFUL, LAWLESSNESS
Dt 1: 5 Moses undertook to explain this **l**:
31: 9 Moses had written down this **l**,
Jos 1: 8 Do not let this book of the **l** depart
1 Mc 2: 48 They saved the **l** from the hands
Ps 1: 2 the **l** of the LORD is his joy;
1: 2 on his **l** he meditates day and night.
Jer 31: 33 I will place my **l** within them,
Mt 5: 17 that I have come to abolish the **l**
23: 23 the weightier things of the **l**:
Lk 24: 44 written about me in the **l** of Moses
Jn 1: 17 because while the **l** was given

Rom 2: 15 the demands of the **l** are written
6: 14 since you are not under the **l**
10: 4 the end of the **l** for the justification
Gal 2: 19 For through the **l** I died to the **l**,
Heb 10: 1 Since the **l** has only a shadow
Jas 2: 10 For whoever keeps the whole **l**,

LAWFUL → LAW
Mt 12: 12 So it is **l** to do good
1 Cor 6: 12 "Everything is **l** for me," but not
10: 23 "Everything is **l**," but not

LAWLESSNESS → LAW
2 Thes 2: 7 the mystery of **l** is already at work.
1 Jn 3: 4 who commits sin commits **l**, for sin is **l**.

LAY → LAID
Mt 28: 6 Come and see the place where he **l**.
Jn 10: 15 I will **l** down my life for the sheep.
1 Cor 3: 11 no one can **l** a foundation other than

LAZARUS
1. Poor man in Jesus' parable (Lk 16:19-31).
2. Brother of Mary and Martha whom Jesus raised from the dead (Jn 11:1–12:19).

LAZY
Ex 5: 17 He answered, "**L**! You are **l**!

LEAD → LEADER, LEADERS, LEADS, LED
Ex 32: 34 **l** the people where I have told you.
Rom 2: 4 of God would **l** you to repentance?

LEADER → LEAD
1 Ch 28: 4 For he chose Judah as **l**, then one

LEADERS → LEAD
Is 3: 12 My people, your **l** deceive you,
Lk 19: 47 and the **l** of the people, meanwhile,
Heb 13: 7 Remember your **l** who spoke

LEADS → LEAD
Rom 6: 16 either of sin, which **l** to death,
6: 16 which **l** to righteousness?

LEAH
Wife of Jacob (Gn 29:16-30); bore six sons and one daughter (Gn 29:31–30:21; 34:1; 35:23; Ru 4:11).

LEAPED → LEAPING
Lk 1: 41 greeting, the infant **l** in her womb,

LEAPING → LEAPED
1 Ch 15: 29 and when she saw King David **l**

LEARN → LEARNED, LEARNING
Dt 4: 10 that they may **l** to fear me as long as
Is 1: 17 **l** to do good. Make justice your aim:

LEARNED → LEARN
Phil 4: 11 for I have **l**, in whatever situation I

LEARNING → LEARN
Acts 26: 24 much **l** is driving you mad."

LEAST → LESS
Mt 2: 6 are by no means **l** among the rulers
5: 19 one of the **l** of these commandments
5: 19 do so will be called **l** in the kingdom
Lk 9: 48 the one who is **l** among all of you is

LEAVE → LEFT
Nm 11: 20 'Why did we ever **l** Egypt?' "
Mk 10: 7 this reason a man shall **l** his father
Jn 14: 18 I will not **l** you orphans; I will come

LEAVEN → LEAVENS
Ex 12: 15 will have your houses clear of all **l**.

LEAVENS → LEAVEN
Gal 5: 9 A little yeast **l** the whole batch

LEAVES
Gn 3: 7 so they sewed fig **l** together
Ez 47: 12 their **l** will not wither, nor will their
47: 12 for food, and their **l** for healing."
Rev 22: 2 the **l** of the trees serve as medicine

LEBANON
Dt 11: 24 from the wilderness and the **L**,
Is 40: 16 **L** would not suffice for fuel, nor its

LED → LEAD
Is 53: 7 Like a lamb **l** to slaughter or a sheep
Mt 4: 1 Jesus was **l** by the Spirit
27: 31 and **l** him off to crucify him.
Rom 8: 14 For those who are **l** by the Spirit

LEFT → LEAVE
Dt 28: 14 either to the right or to the **l**,
Mt 6: 3 do not let your **l** hand know what
25: 33 on his right and the goats on his **l**.
Lk 17: 34 one will be taken, the other **l**.

LEGION
Lk 8: 30 He replied, "**L**," because many

LEGS
Jn 19: 33 dead, they did not break his **l**,

LENDER
Prv 22: 7 the borrower is the slave of the **l**.

LEPER → LEPERS
Mt 8: 2 And then a **l** approached, did him
26: 6 Bethany in the house of Simon the **l**,

LEPERS → LEPER
Lk 7: 22 the lame walk, **l** are cleansed,

LESS → LEAST
Ex 30: 15 nor shall the poor give **l**,
Ezr 9: 13 have made **l** of our sinfulness than it

LETTER
Mt 5: 18 not the smallest **l** or the smallest part of a **l** will pass
2 Cor 3: 6 new covenant, not of **l** but of spirit;
3: 6 for the **l** brings death, but the Spirit

LEVI → LEVITES, LEVITICAL, =MATTHEW
1. Son of Jacob by Leah (Gn 29:34; 46:11; 1 Ch 2:1). With Simeon avenged rape of Dinah (Gn 34). Tribe of blessed (Gn 49:5-7; Dt 33:8-11), chosen as priests (Nm 3–4), numbered (Nm 3:39; 26:62), given cities, but not land (Nm 18; 35; Dt 10:9; Jos 13:14; 21), land (Ez 48:8-22), 12,000 from (Rev 7:7).
2. See Matthew.

LEVIATHAN
Ps 74: 14 You crushed the heads of **L**,

LEVITES → LEVI
Nm 1: 53 but the **L** shall camp around
1: 53 The **L** shall keep guard over
Jos 14: 4 But the **L** were given no share
Neh 8: 9 and the **L** who were instructing

LEVITICAL → LEVI
Heb 7: 11 came through the **l** priesthood,

LIAR → LIE
Prv 19: 22 rather be poor than a **l**.
Jn 8: 44 because he is a **l** and the father
Rom 3: 4 though every human being is a **l**,

1 Jn 2:22 Who is the **l**? Whoever denies

LIARS → LIE
1 Tm 1:10 sodomites, kidnapers, **l**, perjurers,

LIBERTY
Lv 25:10 You shall proclaim **l** in the land
Is 61: 1 To proclaim **l** to the captives,
1 Cor 8: 9 make sure that this **l** of yours in no

LICENTIOUSNESS
Mk 7:22 malice, deceit, **l**, envy, blasphemy,
Gal 5:19 immorality, impurity, **l**,
Jude 1: 4 pervert the grace of our God into **l**

LIE → LIAR, LIARS, LIES, LYING
Is 11: 6 the leopard shall **l** down
1 Jn 2:21 because every **l** is alien to the truth.

LIES → LIE
Phil 3:13 forgetting what **l** behind
3:13 straining forward to what **l** ahead,

LIFE → LIVE
Gn 2: 7 blew into his nostrils the breath of **l**,
2: 9 with the tree of **l** in the middle
9: 5 demand an accounting for human **l**.
Ex 21:23 injury ensues, you shall give **l** for **l**,
Dt 12:23 for blood is **l**; you shall not eat that **l**
30:19 I have set before you **l** and death,
30:19 Choose **l**, then, that you and your
Ps 34:13 Who is the man who delights in **l**,
Prv 18:21 and **l** are in the power of the tongue;
Eccl 7:12 is profitable because wisdom gives **l**
Sir 4:12 Those who love her love **l**;
Is 53:10 By making his **l** as a reparation
Mt 7:14 constricted the road that leads to **l**.
10:39 Whoever finds his **l** will lose it,
10:39 whoever loses his **l** for my sake will
20:28 to give his **l** as a ransom for many."
Mk 10:30 and eternal **l** in the age to come.
Jn 1: 4 through him was **l**, and this **l** was
3:15 in him may have eternal **l**."
6:35 said to them, "I am the bread of **l**;
11:25 "I am the resurrection and the **l**;
14: 6 am the way and the truth and the **l**.
Acts 3:15 The author of **l** you put to death,
Rom 5:21 eternal **l** through Jesus Christ our
8:11 the dead will give **l** to your mortal
8:38 that neither death, nor **l**, nor angels,
2 Cor 3: 6 brings death, but the Spirit gives **l**.
Phil 4: 3 whose names are in the book of **l**.
1 Jn 3:14 to **l** because we love our brothers.
5:20 He is the true God and eternal **l**.
Rev 2: 8 who once died but came to **l**,
20: 4 They came to **l** and they reigned
20:12 scroll was opened, the book of **l**.
22: 2 of the river grew the tree of **l**

LIFT → LIFTED
Ps 119:28 **l** me up acccording to your word.

LIFTED → LIFT
Jn 3:14 just as Moses **l** up the serpent
3:14 so must the Son of Man be **l** up,

LIGHT → ENLIGHTENED, ENLIGHTENS, LIGHTS
Gn 1: 3 Let there be **l**, and there was **l**.
Ex 13:21 of a column of fire to give them **l**.
Ps 27: 1 The LORD is my **l** and my
Prv 4:18 the path of the just is like shining **l**,
Eccl 2:13 over folly as **l** has over darkness.
Is 42: 6 for the people, a **l** for the nations,
60: 1 for your **l** has come, the glory
Mt 4:16 sit in darkness have seen a great **l**,
4:16 by death **l** has arisen."
5:14 You are the **l** of the world.
11:30 my yoke is easy, and my burden **l**."
Jn 1: 9 The true **l**, which enlightens
8:12 saying, "I am the **l** of the world.
8:12 but will have the **l** of life."
Rom 13:12 [and] put on the armor of **l**;
2 Cor 11:14 Satan masquerades as an angel of **l**.
1 Pt 2: 9 out of darkness into his wonderful **l**.
1 Jn 1: 7 if we walk in the **l** as he is in the **l**,
Rev 22: 5 nor will they need **l** from lamp
22: 5 for the Lord God shall give them **l**,

LIGHTNING
Ex 19:16 there were peals of thunder and **l**,
Dn 10: 6 his face shone like **l**, his eyes were
Lk 10:18 "I have observed Satan fall like **l**
Rev 4: 5 From the throne came flashes of **l**,

LIGHTS → LIGHT
Gn 1:16 God made the two great **l**,
Jas 1:17 coming down from the Father of **l**,

LIKE → LIKENESS
Gn 3: 5 be opened and you will be **l** gods,
Ex 15:11 Who is **l** you among the gods,
15:11 Who is **l** you, magnificent among
2 Sm 7:22 There is no one **l** you, no God
Ps 113: 5 Who is **l** the LORD our God,
Is 46: 9 I am God, there is none **l** me.
Jer 10: 6 No one is **l** you, LORD, you are
Lk 13:18 "What is the kingdom of God **l**?
Rev 1:13 the lampstands one **l** a son of man,
10: 1 his face was **l** the sun and his feet
10: 1 and his feet were **l** pillars of fire.
16:15 ("Behold, I am coming **l** a thief."

LIKENESS → LIKE
Gn 1:26 beings in our image, after our **l**.
Rom 8: 3 his own Son in the **l** of sinful flesh
Phil 2: 7 form of a slave, coming in human **l**;

LINEN
Ex 26: 1 of ten sheets woven of fine **l** twined
Dn 10: 5 I saw a man dressed in **l** with a belt
Rev 19: 8 to wear a bright, clean **l** garment."
19: 8 (The **l** represents the righteous

LION → LION'S, LIONS'
1 Sm 17:34 whenever a **l** or bear came to carry
Eccl 9: 4 live dog is better off than a dead **l**."
Is 11: 7 the **l** shall eat hay like the ox.
Dn 7: 4 The first was like a **l**,
Rev 4: 7 The first creature resembled a **l**,
5: 5 The **l** of the tribe of Judah, the root

LION'S → LION
2 Tm 4:17 I was rescued from the **l** mouth.

LIONS' → LION
Dn 6:20 morning and hastened to the **l** den.

LIPS
Is 6: 5 For I am a man of unclean **l**,
6: 5 living among a people of unclean **l**,
Mt 15: 8 'This people honors me with their **l**,
Heb 13:15 the fruit of **l** that confess his name.

LISTEN → LISTENS
Jos 24:24 our God, and will **l** to his voice."
2 Kgs 17:40 But they did not **l**; they continued
Mk 9: 7 is my beloved Son. **L** to him."
Lk 16:31 'If they will not **l** to Moses

Acts 3:22 to him you shall **l** in all that he may

LISTENS → LISTEN
Jn 18:37 belongs to the truth **l** to my voice."
1 Jn 4:6 and anyone who knows God **l** to us,

LITTLE
Ex 16:18 a small amount did not have too **l**.
Ps 8:6 Yet you have made him **l** less than
Prv 15:16 Better a **l** with fear of the LORD
Sir 29:23 Whether **l** or much, be content
Mt 8:26 are you terrified, O you of **l** faith?"
2 Cor 8:15 whoever had **l** did not have less."
Gal 5:9 A **l** yeast leavens the whole batch

LIVE → ALIVE, LIFE, LIVES, LIVING
Ex 1:16 but if it is a girl, she may **l**."
33:20 my face, for no one can see me and **l**.
Dt 8:3 not by bread alone that people **l**,
Wis 5:15 But the righteous **l** forever,
Hb 2:4 is righteous because of faith shall **l**.
Mt 4:4 'One does not **l** by bread alone,
Jn 11:25 in me, even if he dies, will **l**,
Rom 1:17 who is righteous by faith will **l**."
14:8 For if we **l**, we **l** for the Lord,
14:8 so then, whether we **l** or die, we are
2 Cor 5:15 that those who **l** might no longer **l**
Gal 3:12 one who does these things will **l**

LIVES → LIVE
Gn 3:22 of life, and eats of it and **l** forever?
Tb 13:1 Blessed be God who **l** forever,
Jb 19:25 I know that my vindicator **l**,
Ps 18:47 The LORD **l**! Blessed be my rock!
Jn 11:26 everyone who **l** and believes in me
Rom 6:10 as to his life, he **l** for God.
1 Jn 3:16 to lay down our **l** for our brothers.
Rev 15:7 fury of God, who **l** forever and ever.

LIVING → LIVE
Gn 2:7 life, and the man became a **l** being.
3:20 she was the mother of all the **l**.
6:19 all **l** creatures you shall bring two
Dt 5:26 the voice of the **l** God speaking
Jer 2:13 forsaken me, the source of **l** waters;
Mt 16:16 the Messiah, the Son of the **l** God."
Jn 4:10 he would have given you **l** water."
6:51 I am the **l** bread that came down
Rom 12:1 to offer your bodies as a **l** sacrifice,
2 Cor 6:16 For we are the temple of the **l** God;
Heb 4:12 the word of God is **l** and effective,
1 Pt 2:4 Come to him, a **l** stone,

LOAVES
Mk 6:41 broke the **l**, and gave them to [his]
8:6 taking the seven **l** he gave thanks,

LOCK
Mt 23:13 You **l** the kingdom of heaven before

LOCUST → LOCUSTS
Jl 2:25 what the swarming **l** has eaten,

LOCUSTS → LOCUST
Ex 10:4 tomorrow I will bring **l** into your
2 Ch 6:28 mildew, or **l** swarm, or caterpillars;
Mt 3:4 His food was **l** and wild honey.
Rev 9:3 **L** came out of the smoke onto

LONG → LONGING
Ex 20:12 you may have a **l** life in the land
Ps 13:2 How **l** will you hide your face
Prv 3:16 **L** life is in her right hand, in her left
1 Cor 11:14 man wears his hair **l** it is a disgrace
1 Pt 2:2 **l** for pure spiritual milk so
Rev 6:10 in a loud voice, "How **l** will it be,

LONGING → LONG
2 Cor 5:2 **l** to be further clothed with our

LOOK → LOOKED, LOOKS
Ex 3:6 face, for he was afraid to **l** at God.
Ps 80:15 **l** down from heaven and see;
Lk 24:39 **L** at my hands and my feet, that it is

LOOKED → LOOK
Gn 19:26 But Lot's wife **l** back, and she was

LOOKS → LOOK
1 Sm 16:7 The LORD **l** into the heart.
Ps 14:2 The LORD **l** down from heaven
Mt 5:28 everyone who **l** at a woman

LORD → LORD'S, LORDS
Gn 18:27 I am presuming to speak to my **L**,
Ex 4:10 to the **L**, "If you please, my **L**,
Dt 10:17 the God of gods, the **L** of lords,
Jdt 6:19 "**L**, God of heaven, look at their
Ps 16:2 I say to the **L**, you are my **L**,
110:1 The LORD says to my **l**: "Sit at my
Sir 1:1 All wisdom is from the **L**
Is 6:1 I saw the **L** seated on a high
Dn 2:47 is the God of gods and **L** of kings
3:57 Bless the **L**, all you works of the **L**,
Mi 1:2 Let the **L** GOD be witness against
Mt 7:22 Many will say to me on that day, '**L**, **L**, did we not prophesy
12:8 Son of Man is **L** of the sabbath."
Mk 1:3 'Prepare the way of the **L**,
12:29 The **L** our God is **L** alone!
Lk 2:11 born for you who is Messiah and **L**.
10:27 "You shall love the **L**, your God,
19:38 who comes in the name of the **L**.
Jn 20:28 said to him, "My **L** and my God!"
Acts 2:34 'The **L** said to my **L**, "Sit at my
Rom 4:24 the one who raised Jesus our **L**
10:12 the same **L** is **L** of all, enriching all
1 Cor 2:16 "who has known the mind of the **L**,
8:6 we exist, and one **L**, Jesus Christ,
12:3 "Jesus is **L**," except by the holy
2 Cor 3:17 Now the **L** is the Spirit, and where
Eph 4:5 one **L**, one faith, one baptism;
Phil 2:11 confess that Jesus Christ is **L**,
4:5 be known to all. The **L** is near.
Col 3:13 as the **L** has forgiven you, so must
1 Thes 4:15 are left until the coming of the **L**,
1 Tm 6:15 the King of kings and **L** of lords,
Heb 12:14 without which no one will see the **L**.
Jas 4:10 Humble yourselves before the **L**
1 Pt 3:15 sanctify Christ as **L** in your hearts.
2 Pt 3:9 The **L** does not delay his promise,
Jude 1:4 who deny our only Master and **L**,
Rev 4:8 holy is the **L** God almighty,
19:16 "King of kings and **L** of lords."
22:20 Amen! Come, **L** Jesus!

***LORD** → *GOD, *LORD'S
Gn 2:7 the **L** God formed the man
13:4 and there Abram invoked the **L**
18:14 too marvelous for the **L** to do?
22:14 the mountain the **L** will provide."
Ex 3:15 The **L**, the God of your ancestors,
5:2 "Who is the **L**, that I should obey
5:2 I do not know the **L**, and I will not
6:7 the **L**, am your God who has freed
15:3 The **L** is a warrior, **L** is his name!
34:6 So the **L** passed before him
34:6 The **L**, the **L**, a God gracious
Lv 19:2 for I, the **L** your God, am holy.

Nm 6:24 The **L** bless you and keep you!
14:18 'The **L** is slow to anger
Dt 6:4 The **L** is our God, the **L** alone!
Jos 24:15 household, we will serve the **L**."
1 Sm 2:2 There is no Holy One like the **L**;
1 Kgs 8:11 glory of the **L** had filled the house of the **L**.
18:21 If the **L** is God, follow him;
1 Ch 16:11 Rely on the mighty **L**;
Ezr 7:10 practice of the law of the **L**
Neh 8:10 for today is holy to our **L**.
8:10 in the **L** is your strength!"
Jb 1:21 The **L** gave and the **L** has taken
1:21 blessed be the name of the **L**!"
42:12 Thus the **L** blessed the later days
Ps 1:2 Rather, the law of the **L** is his joy;
10:16 The **L** is king forever;
18:2 I love you, **L**, my strength,
23:1 The **L** is my shepherd;
33:12 is the nation whose God is the **L**,
84:12 For a sun and shield is the **L** God,
84:12 The **L** withholds no good thing
110:1 The **L** says to my lord: "Sit at my
113:5 Who is like the **L** our God,
125:2 the **L** surrounds his people both
128:1 Blessed are all who fear the **L**,
145:18 The **L** is near to all who call
150:6 has breath give praise to the **L**!
Prv 1:7 Fear of the **L** is the beginning
3:5 Trust in the **L** with all your heart,
19:23 The fear of the **L** leads to life;
21:2 but it is the **L** who weighs hearts.
Is 2:11 and the **L** alone will be exalted,
6:3 holy, holy is the **L** of hosts!
33:22 For the **L** is our judge, the **L** is our lawgiver, the **L** is our king;
53:6 the **L** laid upon him the guilt of us
64:8 Do not be so very angry, **L**, do not
Jer 4:4 Be circumcised for the **L**,
31:34 and relatives, "Know the **L**!"
32:27 I am the **L**, the God of all
Lam 3:25 The **L** is good to those who trust
Ez 3:23 of the **L** was standing there like
10:18 the glory of the **L** left the threshold
37:4 Dry bones, hear the word of the **L**!
44:4 of the **L** filled the LORD's house!
48:35 of the city is "The **L** is there."
Jl 1:15 For near is the day of the **L**,
Am 5:6 Seek the **L**, that you may live,
Ob 1:15 day of the **L** against all the nations!
Na 1:3 The **L** is slow to anger, yet great
1:3 the **L** will not leave the guilty
Zep 1:14 Near is the great day of the **L**,
Zec 14:9 The **L** will be king over the whole
14:9 that day the **L** will be the only one,
Mal 3:6 For I, the **L**, do not change,

LORD'S → LORD
Rom 14:8 whether we live or die, we are the **L**.
1 Cor 10:26 earth and its fullness are the **L**."

***LORD'S** → *LORD
Nm 11:23 Is this beyond the **L** reach?
Dt 32:9 But the **L** portion was his people;
Ps 24:1 The earth is the **L** and all it holds,
Ob 1:21 and the kingship shall be the **L**.

LORDS → LORD
Dt 10:17 gods, the Lord of **l**, the great God,
Ps 136:3 Praise the Lord of **l**; for his mercy
1 Cor 8:5 sure, many "gods" and many "**l**"),
Rev 19:16 "King of kings and Lord of **l**."

LOSE → LOSS, LOST
Mk 8:35 wishes to save his life will **l** it,
Heb 12:3 may not grow weary and **l** heart.
2 Jn 1:8 that you do not **l** what we worked

LOSS → LOSE
1 Cor 3:15 is burned up, that one will suffer **l**;
Phil 3:8 consider everything as a **l** because
3:8 his sake I have accepted the **l** of all

LOST → LOSE
Ps 119:176 I have wandered like a **l** sheep;
Jer 50:6 **L** sheep were my people,
Ez 34:16 The **l** I will search out, the strays I
Mt 10:6 Go rather to the **l** sheep of the house
Lk 15:6 because I have found my **l** sheep.'
19:10 to seek and to save what was **l**."

LOT → LOT'S, LOTS

1. Nephew of Abraham (Gn 11:27; 12:5). Chose to live in Sodom (Gn 13). Rescued from four kings (Gn 14). Rescued from Sodom (Gn 19:1-29; 2 Pt 2:7). Fathered Moab and Ammon (Gn 19:30-38).

2. Object cast to make decisions.

Nm 33:54 the land among yourselves by **l**,
33:54 Wherever anyone's **l** falls, there
Est 3:7 or **l**, was cast in Haman's presence
Prv 16:33 Into the bag the **l** is cast,
Acts 1:26 and the **l** fell upon Matthias, and he

LOT'S → LOT, 1
Gn 19:26 But **L** wife looked back, and she

LOTS → LOT, 2
Ps 22:19 for my clothing they cast **l**.
Jon 1:7 let us cast **l** to discover on whose
Mt 27:35 divided his garments by casting **l**;

LOVE → BELOVED, LOVED, LOVER, LOVERS, LOVES
Ex 20:6 showing **l** down to the thousandth generation of those who **l** me
Lv 19:18 You shall **l** your neighbor as
Dt 6:5 Therefore, you shall **l** the LORD,
Neh 1:5 of mercy with those who **l** you
1 Mc 4:33 by the sword of those who **l** you,
Ps 18:2 I **l** you, LORD, my strength,
116:1 I **l** the LORD, who listened to my
119:97 How I **l** your law, Lord! I study it
Prv 5:19 whose **l** you will ever have your fill,
8:17 Those who **l** me I also **l**, and those
Eccl 3:8 A time to **l**, and a time to hate;
Sg 1:2 for your **l** is better than wine,
8:6 For **L** is strong as Death, longing is
Sir 2:15 those who **l** him keep his ways.
4:12 Those who **l** her **l** life;
7:30 With all your strength **l** your Maker
Is 54:8 with enduring **l** I take pity on you,
Dn 9:4 show mercy toward those who **l** you
14:38 not forsaken those who **l** you."
Hos 11:4 with human cords, with bands of **l**;
Mal 1:2 I **l** you, says the LORD; but you say, "How do you **l** us?"
Mt 5:44 But I say to you, **l** your enemies,
6:24 will either hate one and **l** the other,
Mk 12:31 'You shall **l** your neighbor as
Lk 6:32 Even sinners **l** those who **l** them.
10:27 said in reply, "You shall **l** the Lord,
Jn 13:34 a new commandment: **l** one another.
14:15 "If you **l** me, you will keep my
15:13 No one has greater **l** than this, to lay
21:16 son of John, do you **l** me?"
21:16 Lord, you know that I **l** you."
Rom 5:5 because the **l** of God has been

5: 8 God proves his **l** for us in that while
12: 9 Let **l** be sincere; hate what is evil,
13: 8 to anyone, except to **l** one another;
1 Cor 8: 1 inflates with pride, but **l** builds up.
13: 4 **L** is patient, **l** is kind.
13: 13 So faith, hope, **l** remain, these three;
13: 13 but the greatest of these is **l**.
Gal 5: 6 but only faith working through **l**.
5: 22 the fruit of the Spirit is **l**, joy, peace,
Eph 2: 4 because of the great **l** he had for us,
3: 19 and to know the **l** of Christ
5: 25 Husbands, **l** your wives, even as
Col 3: 14 And over all these put on **l**, that is,
1 Thes 5: 8 on the breastplate of faith and **l**
1 Tm 6: 10 For the **l** of money is the root of all
Ti 2: 2 sound in faith, **l**, and endurance.
Heb 10: 24 how to rouse one another to **l**
13: 5 Let your life be free from **l**
Jas 2: 8 "You shall **l** your neighbor as
1 Pt 1: 8 you have not seen him you **l** him;
2 Pt 1: 7 affection, mutual affection with **l**.
1 Jn 2: 15 Do not **l** the world or the things
2: 15 the **l** of the Father is not in him.
3: 1 See what **l** the Father has bestowed
3: 16 The way we came to know **l** was
4: 7 Beloved, let us **l** one another, because **l** is of God;
4: 8 Whoever is without **l** does not know God, for God is **l**.
5: 3 For the **l** of God is this, that we keep
2 Jn 1: 6 For this is **l**, that we walk according
Jude 1: 21 Keep yourselves in the **l** of God
Rev 2: 4 you have lost the **l** you had at first.

LOVED → LOVE
Jer 31: 3 With age-old love I have **l** you;
Hos 11: 1 When Israel was a child I **l** him,
Jn 3: 16 For God so **l** the world that he gave
13: 1 He **l** his own in the world and he **l**
Gal 2: 20 in the Son of God who has **l** me
Eph 5: 2 as Christ **l** us and handed himself
1 Jn 4: 19 We love because he first **l** us.

LOVER → LOVE
Ps 99: 4 O mighty king, **l** of justice,
1 Tm 3: 3 not contentious, not a **l** of money.

LOVERS → LOVE
Jer 3: 1 played the prostitute with many **l**,
2 Tm 3: 2 be self-centered and **l** of money,

LOVES → LOVE
Ps 33: 5 He **l** justice and right. The earth is
Prv 3: 12 whom the LORD **l** he reproves,
Mt 10: 37 "Whoever **l** father or mother more
10: 37 and whoever **l** son or daughter more
Lk 7: 47 to whom little is forgiven, **l** little."
Rom 13: 8 the one who **l** another has fulfilled
Eph 5: 28 He who **l** his wife **l** himself.
Heb 12: 6 for whom the Lord **l**, he disciplines;
1 Jn 4: 7 everyone who **l** is begotten by God
Rev 1: 5 To him who **l** us and has freed us

LOW → LOWER, LOWLY
Is 40: 4 up, every mountain and hill made **l**;
Lk 3: 5 mountain and hill shall be made **l**.

LOWER → LOW
Heb 2: 7 for a little while **l** than the angels;

LOWLY → LOW
Jdt 9: 11 You are God of the **l**,
Lk 1: 52 from their thrones but lifted up the **l**.
Rom 12: 16 be haughty but associate with the **l**;

LOYAL
Dn 11: 32 but those who remain **l** to their God

LUKE
Associate of Paul (Col 4:14; 2 Tm 4:11; Phlm 24).

LUKEWARM
Rev 3: 16 because you are **l**, neither hot nor

LUST → LUSTS
Mt 5: 28 **l** has already committed adultery

LUSTS → LUST
Rom 1: 24 impurity through the **l** of their hearts

LYDIA
Acts 16: 14 them, a woman named **L**, a dealer

LYING → LIE
1 Kgs 22: 23 the LORD has put a **l** spirit
Prv 6: 17 Haughty eyes, a **l** tongue,
Wis 1: 11 and a **l** mouth destroys the soul.
Hos 4: 2 Swearing, **l**, murder,

LYRE
Ps 33: 2 on the ten-stringed **l** offer praise.

M

MACCABEUS → JUDAS
1 Mc 2: 66 And Judas **M**, a mighty warrior

MACEDONIA
Acts 16: 9 "Come over to **M** and help us."

MADE → MAKE
Gn 1: 31 God looked at everything he had **m**,
3: 21 The LORD God **m** for the man
15: 18 day the LORD **m** a covenant
Ex 20: 11 six days the LORD **m** the heavens
20: 11 the sabbath day and **m** it holy.
36: 8 doing the work **m** the tabernacle
Ps 8: 6 Yet you have **m** him little less than
118: 24 This is the day the LORD has **m**;
139: 14 you, because I am wonderfully **m**;
Jer 27: 5 It was I who **m** the earth,
Mk 2: 27 them, "The sabbath was **m** for man,
Acts 2: 36 that God has **m** him both Lord
Rev 14: 7 Worship him who **m** heaven

MADNESS
Dt 28: 28 the LORD will strike you with **m**,
Eccl 9: 3 and **m** is in their hearts during life;

MAGDALENE
Mt 27: 56 Among them were Mary **M**

MAGICIANS
Ex 7: 11 and they also, the **m** of Egypt,
Dn 2: 2 So he ordered that the **m**,

MAGNIFY
Ps 34: 4 **M** the LORD with me; and let us

MAJESTIC → MAJESTY
2 Pt 1: 17 came to him from the **m** glory,

MAJESTY → MAJESTIC
1 Ch 29: 11 are greatness and might, **m**, victory,
Ps 93: 1 The LORD is king, robed with **m**;
Heb 1: 3 at the right hand of the **M** on high,
2 Pt 1: 16 we had been eyewitnesses of his **m**.

MAKE → MADE, MAKER
Gn 1: 26 Let us **m** human beings in our
2: 18 I will **m** a helper suited to him.
12: 2 I will **m** of you a great nation,
12: 2 I will **m** your name great,
Ex 32: 1 **m** us a god who will go before us;

Is 61: 8 an everlasting covenant I will **m**
Jer 31: 31 when I will **m** a new covenant
Mt 28: 19 and **m** disciples of all nations,
Mk 1: 17 and I will **m** you fishers of men."

MAKER → MAKE
Jb 4: 17 be more blameless than their **M**?
Is 54: 5 For your husband is your **M**;

MAKING → MAKE
Gn 6: 6 the LORD regretted **m** human beings
Is 66: 22 heavens and the new earth which I am **m**

MALACHI
Post-exilic prophet (Mal 1:1).

MALE
Gn 1: 27 **m** and female he created them.
17: 10 every **m** among you shall be
Lv 20: 13 If a man lies with a **m** as
Mt 19: 4 the Creator 'made them **m**
Rev 12: 5 She gave birth to a son, a **m** child,

MALICE
Rom 1: 29 of wickedness, evil, greed, and **m**;
1 Cor 5: 8 the yeast of **m** and wickedness,

MAN → MEN
Gn 2: 7 the LORD God formed the **m**
2: 7 and the **m** became a living being.
2: 18 It is not good for the **m** to be alone.
1 Sm 13: 14 sought out a **m** after his own heart
Ps 8: 5 What is **m** that you are mindful of him, and a son of **m** that you care
Mt 9: 6 the Son of **M** has authority on earth
Lk 6: 5 them, "The Son of **M** is lord
Jn 9: 35 "Do you believe in the Son of **M**?"
1 Cor 11: 3 that Christ is the head of every **m**,
Rev 1: 13 the lampstands one like a son of **m**,
14: 14 one who looked like a son of **m**,

MANAGE
1 Tm 3: 4 He must **m** his own household well,
5: 14 and **m** a home, so as to give

MANASSEH
1. Firstborn of Joseph (Gn 41:51; 46:20). Blessed by Jacob but not as firstborn (Gn 48). Tribe of blessed (Dt 33:17), numbered (Nm 1:35; 26:34), half allotted land east of Jordan (Nm 32; Jos 13:8-33), half west (Jos 16; Ez 48:4), failed to fully possess (Jos 17:12-13; Jgs 1:27), 12,000 from (Rev 7:6).
2. Son of Hezekiah; king of Judah (2 Kgs 21:1-18; 2 Ch 33:1-20). Judah exiled for his detestable sins (2 Kgs 21:10-15). Repented (2 Ch 33:12-19).

MANGER
Lk 2: 12 clothes and lying in a **m**."

MANNA
Ex 16: 31 house of Israel named this food **m**.
Jos 5: 12 produce of the land, the **m** ceased.
Jn 6: 49 Your ancestors ate the **m**
Rev 2: 17 I shall give some of the hidden **m**;

MANTLE
2 Kgs 2: 8 Elijah took his **m**, rolled it

MANY
Is 53: 12 give him his portion among the **m**,
53: 12 Bore the sins of **m**, and interceded
Mt 22: 14 **M** are invited, but few are chosen."
Mk 10: 45 to give his life as a ransom for **m**."
Jn 20: 30 Now Jesus did **m** other signs
Rom 12: 5 though **m**, are one body in Christ

MARAH
Ex 15: 23 Hence this place was called **M**.

MARK → MARKED, MARKS
1. Cousin of Barnabas (Acts 12:12; 15:37-39; Col 4:10; 2 Tm 4:11; Phlm 24; 1 Pt 5:13), see John.
2. Brand or symbol:
Gn 4: 15 So the LORD put a **m** on Cain,
Rev 14: 9 or accepts its **m** on forehead
19: 20 astray those who had accepted the **m**

MARKED → MARK
Ez 9: 6 do not touch anyone **m** with the X.

MARKET → MARKETPLACE
1 Cor 10: 25 Eat anything sold in the **m**,

MARKETPLACE → MARKET
Jn 2: 16 making my Father's house a **m**."

MARKS → MARK
Gal 6: 17 for I bear the **m** of Jesus on my

MARRIAGE → INTERMARRY, MARRIED, MARRIES
Mt 22: 30 neither marry nor are given in **m**
Heb 13: 4 Let **m** be honored among all and the **m** bed be kept undefiled,

MARRIED → MARRIAGE
Mal 2: 11 has **m** a daughter of a foreign god.
Mk 12: 23 For all seven had been **m** to her."
1 Tm 3: 2 be irreproachable, **m** only once,
Ti 1: 6 a man be blameless, **m** only once,

MARRIES → MARRIAGE
Mk 10: 11 **m** another commits adultery against
1 Cor 7: 28 an unmarried woman sin if she **m**;

MARTHA
Sister of Mary and Lazarus (Lk 10:38-42; Jn 11; 12:2).

MARVELOUS
Ps 98: 1 LORD, for he has done **m** deeds.

MARY
1. Mother of Jesus (Mt 1:16-25; Lk 1:27-56; 2:1-40). With Jesus at temple (Lk 2:41-52), at the wedding in Cana (Jn 2:1-5), questioning his sanity (Mk 3:21), at the cross (Jn 19:25-27). Among disciples (Acts 1:14).
2. Magdalene; former demoniac (Lk 8:2). Helped support Jesus' ministry (Lk 8:1-3). At the cross (Mt 27:56; Mk 15:40; Jn 19:25), burial (Mt 27:61; Mk 15:47). Saw angel after resurrection (Mt 28:1-10; Mk 16:1-9; Lk 24:1-12); also Jesus (Jn 20:1-18).
3. Sister of Martha and Lazarus (Jn 11). Washed Jesus' feet (Jn 12:1-8).
4. Mother of James and Joses; witnessed crucifixion (Mt 27:56; Mk 15:40) and empty tomb (Mk 16:1; Lk 24:10).

MASTER → MASTERS
Mal 1: 6 his father, and a servant fears his **m**;
1: 6 And if I am a **m**, where is the fear
Mt 25: 21 His **m** said to him, 'Well done,
Jn 15: 20 'No slave is greater than his **m**.'
2 Pt 2: 1 and even deny the **M** who ransomed

MASTERS → MASTER
Mt 6: 24 "No one can serve two **m**.

MATTANIAH → See ZEDEKIAH

MATTATHIAS
Priest who started the Maccabean revolt (1 Mc 2).

MATTHEW → =LEVI
Apostle; former tax collector (Mt 9:9-13; 10:3; Mk 3:18; Lk 6:15; Acts 1:13). Also called Levi (Mk 2:14-17; Lk 5:27-32).

MATTHIAS
Disciple chosen to replace Judas (Acts 1:23-26).

MATURE
1 Cor 2: 6 speak a wisdom to those who are **m**,
Phil 3: 15 who are "perfectly **m**" adopt this
Heb 5: 14 But solid food is for the **m**, for those

MEAN → MEANING
Ex 12: 26 'What does this rite of yours **m**?'
Jos 4: 6 'What do these stones **m** to you?'

MEANING → MEAN
Gn 40: 5 and each dream with its own **m**.

MEASURE
Mk 4: 24 The **m** with which you **m** will be
Lk 6: 38 For the **m** with which you **m** will

MEAT
Rom 14: 21 it is good not to eat **m** or drink wine

MEDIATOR
Gal 3: 19 by angels at the hand of a **m**.
1 Tm 2: 5 There is also one **m** between God
Heb 8: 6 more excellent a ministry as he is **m**

MEDIUM
Lv 20: 27 man or a woman who acts as a **m**

MEEK
Mt 5: 5 Blessed are the **m**, for they will

MEET → MEETING
Ex 30: 36 tent of meeting where I will **m** you.
Am 4: 12 prepare to **m** your God, O Israel!
1 Thes 4: 17 the clouds to **m** the Lord in the air.

MEETING → MEET
Ex 27: 21 before the LORD in the tent of **m**,
40: 34 the cloud covered the tent of **m**,

MELCHIZEDEK
Gn 14: 18 **M**, king of Salem, brought out bread
Ps 110: 4 priest forever in the manner of **M**."
Heb 7: 1 This "**M**, king of Salem and priest

MELT
Ps 97: 5 The mountains **m** like wax before

MEMBERS
Rom 7: 23 I see in my **m** another principle
7: 23 the law of sin that dwells in my **m**.
1 Cor 6: 15 that your bodies are **m** of Christ?
6: 15 make them the **m** of a prostitute?

MEMORIAL
Jos 4: 7 are to serve as a perpetual **m**

MEN → MAN
Gn 18: 2 he saw three **m** standing near him.
Dn 3: 92 "I see four **m** unbound and unhurt,
Lk 9: 30 two **m** were conversing with him,

MENAHEM
King of Israel (2 Kgs 15:14-23).

MENE
Dn 5: 25 **M**, TEKEL, and PERES.

MENORAH → LAMPSTAND
Ex 25: 31 You shall make a **m** of pure beaten gold

MEPHIBOSHETH
Son of Jonathan shown kindness by David (2 Sm 4:4; 9; 21:7). Accused of siding with Absalom (2 Sm 16:1-4; 19:24-30).

MERCIFUL → MERCY
Dt 4: 31 is a **m** God, he will not abandon
Ps 111: 4 gracious and **m** is the LORD.
Sir 2: 11 the Lord is compassionate and **m**;
Jer 3: 12 For I am **m**, oracle of the LORD,
Mt 5: 7 Blessed are the **m**, for they will be
Lk 6: 36 Be **m**, just as [also] your Father is **m**.
Heb 2: 17 that he might be a **m** and faithful

MERCY → MERCIFUL
1 Ch 21: 13 the LORD, whose **m** is very great,
Ps 136: 1 he is good; for his **m** endures forever;
Lam 3: 22 The LORD's acts of **m** are not exhausted,
Zec 1: 12 how long will you be without **m**
Mt 9: 13 words, 'I desire **m**, not sacrifice.'
23: 23 judgment and **m** and fidelity.
Rom 9: 15 "I will show **m** to whom I will,
Eph 2: 4 who is rich in **m**,
Ti 3: 5 we had done but because of his **m**,
Heb 4: 16 the throne of grace to receive **m**
Jas 2: 13 to one who has not shown **m**;

MERIBAH
Ex 17: 7 place was named Massah and **M**,
Ps 95: 8 Do not harden your hearts as at **M**,

MESHACH → =MISHAEL
Hebrew exiled to Babylon; name changed from Mishael (Dn 1:6-7). Refused defilement by food (Dn 1:8-20). Refused to worship idol (Dn 3:1-18); saved from furnace (Dn 3:19-30).

MESSAGE → MESSENGER
1 Cor 1: 18 The **m** of the cross is foolishness
2 Cor 5: 19 to us the **m** of reconciliation.

MESSENGER → MESSAGE
Is 42: 19 servant, or deaf like the **m** I send?
Mt 11: 10 I am sending my **m** ahead of you;

MESSIAH → CHRIST, MESSIAHS
Mt 16: 16 "You are the **M**, the Son
Lk 2: 11 has been born for you who is **M**
Acts 2: 36 has made him both Lord and **M**,
Rom 9: 5 according to the flesh, is the **M**.

MESSIAHS → MESSIAH
Mk 13: 22 False **m** and false prophets will arise

MICAH
1. Idolater from Ephraim (Jgs 17–18).
2. Prophet from Moresheth (Jer 26:18-19; Mi 1:1).

MICAIAH
Prophet of the LORD who spoke against Ahab (1 Kgs 22:1-28; 2 Ch 18:1-27).

MICHAEL
Archangel (Jude 9); warrior in angelic realm, protector of Israel (Dn 10:13, 21; 12:1; Rev 12:7).

MICHAL
Daughter of Saul, wife of David (1 Sm 14:49; 18:20-28). Warned David of Saul's plot (1 Sm 19). Saul gave her to Paltiel (1 Sm 25:44); David retrieved her (2 Sm 3:13-16). Criticized David for dancing before the ark (2 Sm 6:16-23; 1 Ch 15:29).

MIDDLE
Gn 3: 3 the tree in the **m** of the garden
Rev 22: 2 down the **m** of its street.

MIDIAN → MIDIANITES
Ex 18: 1 the priest of **M**, heard of all

MIDIANITES → MIDIAN
Gn 37: 36 The **M**, meanwhile, sold Joseph
Nm 31: 2 Avenge the Israelites on the **M**,

MIDWIVES
Ex 1: 17 The **m**, however, feared God;

MIGHT → ALMIGHTY, MIGHTY
1 Ch 29: 11 Yours, LORD, are greatness and **m**,
2 Ch 20: 6 In your hand is power and **m**,

Zec 4: 6 Not by **m**, and not by power,

MIGHTY → MIGHT
Gn 49: 24 the power of the **M** One of Jacob,
1 Ch 16: 11 Rely on the **m** LORD; constantly seek
Ps 99: 4 O **m** king, lover of justice, you have
Lk 1: 49 The **M** One has done great things
Rev 18: 8 **m** is the Lord God who judges her."

MILE
Mt 5: 41 press you into service for one **m**,

MILK
Ex 3: 8 a land flowing with **m** and honey,
Heb 5: 12 You need **m**, [and] not solid food.
1 Pt 2: 2 pure spiritual **m** so that through it

MILLSTONE → STONE
Lk 17: 2 him if a **m** were put around his neck

MIND → MINDFUL, MINDS
Mt 22: 37 all your soul, and with all your **m**.
Rom 1: 28 their undiscerning **m** to do what is
1 Cor 2: 16 But we have the **m** of Christ.
2: 16 "who has known the **m** of the Lord,

MINDFUL → MIND
Ps 8: 5 What is man that you are **m** of him,
Heb 2: 6 is man that you are **m** of him,

MINDS → MIND
2 Cor 4: 4 of this age has blinded the **m**
Eph 4: 23 be renewed in the spirit of your **m**,
Phil 4: 7 your hearts and **m** in Christ Jesus.

MINISTER → MINISTERS, MINISTRY
Ex 28: 43 or approach the altar to **m**

MINISTERS → MINISTER
2 Cor 3: 6 who has indeed qualified us as **m**
11: 15 masquerade as **m** of righteousness.

MINISTRY → MINISTER
2 Cor 5: 18 and given us the **m** of reconciliation,
Eph 4: 12 the holy ones for the work of **m**,
Heb 8: 6 so much more excellent a **m** as he is

MIRACLES → See JESUS: MIRACLES

MIRIAM
Sister of Moses and Aaron (Nm 26:59). Led dancing at Red Sea (Ex 15:20-21). Struck with leprosy for criticizing Moses (Nm 12). Death (Nm 20:1).

MIRROR
1 Cor 13: 12 as in a **m**, but then face to face.
Jas 1: 23 who looks at his own face in a **m**.

MISHAEL → See MESHACH

MOAB
Gn 19: 37 birth to a son whom she named **M**,
Ru 1: 1 sons to reside on the plateau of **M**.
Is 15: 1 Oracle on **M**: Laid waste in a night,

MOANING
Ex 2: 24 God heard their **m** and God was mindful

MOCK → MOCKED
Ps 22: 8 All who see me **m** me;
Mk 10: 34 who will **m** him, spit upon him,

MOCKED → MOCK
Gal 6: 7 God is not **m**, for a person will reap

MOLECH
Lv 18: 21 your offspring for immolation to **M**,

MOMENT → MOMENTARY
Ex 33: 5 up in your company even for a **m**,
Ps 30: 6 For his anger lasts but a **m**;
Is 54: 7 For a brief **m** I abandoned you,
66: 8 or a nation be born in a single **m**?

MOMENTARY → MOMENT
2 Cor 4: 17 this **m** light affliction is producing

MONEY
Eccl 10: 19 but **m** answers for everything.
Mk 11: 15 the tables of the **m** changers
1 Tm 3: 3 not contentious, not a lover of **m**.
6: 10 the love of **m** is the root of all evils,
Heb 13: 5 Let your life be free from love of **m**

MONTH
Ex 12: 2 you will reckon it the first **m**
Ez 47: 12 Every **m** they will bear fresh fruit
Rev 22: 2 twelve times a year, once each **m**;

MOON → MOONS
Gn 37: 9 the **m** and eleven stars were bowing
Dt 17: 3 the **m** or any of the host of heaven,
Jos 10: 13 The sun stood still, the **m** stayed,
Acts 2: 20 and the **m** to blood,
Rev 6: 12 and the whole **m** became like blood.
21: 23 no need of sun or **m** to shine on it,

MOONS → MOON
2 Ch 8: 13 at the new **m**, and on the fixed

MORALS
1 Cor 15: 33 "Bad company corrupts good **m**."

MORDECAI
Benjamite exile who raised Esther (Est 2:5-15). Mordecai's dream (Est 11; 10:4-13). Exposed plot to kill Xerxes (Est 2:19-23; 12:1-6). Refused to honor Haman (Est 3:1-6; 5:9-14). Mordecai's prayer (Est 13). Charged Esther to foil Haman's plot against the Jews (Est 4). Xerxes forced Haman to honor Mordecai (Est 6). Mordecai exalted (Est 8–10). Established Purim (Est 9:18-32).

MORE → MOST
Ps 19: 11 **M** desirable than gold, than a hoard
69: 32 please the LORD **m** than oxen,
Mk 4: 25 the one who has, **m** will be given;
Lk 12: 23 For life is **m** than food and the body
1 Cor 12: 31 show you a still **m** excellent way.
Rev 21: 4 and there shall be no **m** death

MORIAH
Gn 22: 2 you love, and go to the land of **M**.
2 Ch 3: 1 LORD in Jerusalem on Mount **M**,

MORNING
Gn 1: 5 Evening came, and **m** followed—
Lam 3: 23 They are renewed each **m**—
Lk 24: 22 they were at the tomb early in the **m**
2 Pt 1: 19 and the **m** star rises in your hearts.
Rev 22: 16 of David, the bright **m** star."

MORTAL
1 Cor 15: 53 which is **m** must clothe itself
2 Cor 5: 4 so that what is **m** may be swallowed

MOSES
Levite; brother of Aaron (Ex 6:20; 1 Ch 6:3). Put in basket into Nile; discovered and raised by Pharaoh's daughter (Ex 2:1-10). Fled to Midian after killing Egyptian (Ex 2:11-15). Married to Zipporah, fathered Gershom (Ex 2:16-22).

Called by the LORD to deliver Israel (Ex 3–4). Pharaoh's resistance (Ex 5). Ten plagues (Ex 7–11). Passover and Exodus (Ex 12–13). Led Israel through Red Sea (Ex 14). Song of deliverance (Ex 15:1-21). Brought water from rock (Ex 17:1-7). Raised hands to defeat Amalekites (Ex 17:8-16). Delegated judges (Ex 18; Dt 1:9-18).

Received Law at Sinai (Ex 19–23; 25–31; Jn 1:17). Announced Law to Israel (Ex 19:7-8; 24; 35). Broke tablets because of golden calf (Ex 32; Dt 9). Saw glory of the LORD (Ex 33–34). Supervised building of tabernacle (Ex 36–40). Set apart Aaron and priests (Lv 8–9). Numbered tribes (Nm 1–4; 26). Opposed by Aaron and Miriam (Nm 12). Sent spies into Canaan (Nm 13). Announced forty years of wandering for failure to enter land (Nm 14). Opposed by Korah (Nm 16). Forbidden to enter land for striking rock (Nm 20:1-13; Dt 1:37). Lifted bronze snake for healing (Nm 21:4-9; Jn 3:14). Final address to Israel (Dt 1–33). Succeeded by Joshua (Nm 27:12-23; Dt 34). Death and burial by God (Dt 34:5-12). Praise of (Sir 45).

Law of (1 Kgs 2:3; Ezr 3:2; Mk 12:26; Lk 24:44). Book of (2 Ch 25:12; Neh 13:1). Song of (Ex 15:1-21; Rev 15:3). Prayer of (Ps 90).

MOST → MORE
Gn 14:18 He was a priest of God **M** High.
Ps 91:1 dwell in the shelter of the **M** High,
Mk 5:7 me, Jesus, Son of the **M** High God?
Col 4:5 making the **m** of the opportunity.
Jude 1:20 yourselves up in your **m** holy faith;

MOTH
Mt 6:19 earth, where **m** and decay destroy,

MOTHER → MOTHER'S, MOTHERS
Gn 2:24 why a man leaves his father and **m**
3:20 because she was the **m** of all
Ex 20:12 Honor your father and your **m**,
Jgs 5:7 arose, when I arose, a **m** in Israel.
Tb 4:3 Honor your **m**, and do not abandon
Prv 31:1 the instruction his **m** taught him:
Sir 3:6 who obey the Lord honor their **m**.
Is 66:13 As a **m** comforts her child, so I will
Mt 10:37 or **m** more than me is not worthy
Lk 14:26 me without hating his father and **m**,
Jn 2:3 ran short, the **m** of Jesus said to him,
19:27 to the disciple, "Behold, your **m**."
Gal 4:26 above is freeborn, and she is our **m**.
Eph 5:31 [his] **m** and be joined to his wife,
Rev 17:5 the great, the **m** of harlots

MOTHER'S → MOTHER
Jb 1:21 I came forth from my **m** womb,
Prv 1:8 and reject not your **m** teaching;
Jn 3:4 he cannot reenter his **m** womb

MOTHERS → MOTHER
Mk 10:30 and sisters and **m** and children

MOUNT → MOUNTAIN, MOUNTAINS
Ex 19:20 LORD came down upon **M** Sinai,
Dt 11:29 **M** Gerizim you shall pronounce the blessing, on **M** Ebal, the curse.
Ps 78:68 of Judah, **M** Zion which he loved.
Mi 4:7 shall be king over them on **M** Zion,
Zec 14:4 feet will stand on the **M** of Olives,
14:4 The **M** of Olives will be split in two
Mk 13:3 the **M** of Olives opposite the temple
Heb 12:22 you have approached **M** Zion
Rev 14:1 was the Lamb standing on **M** Zion,

MOUNTAIN → MOUNT
Ex 3:1 he came to the **m** of God, Horeb.
24:18 He was on the **m** for forty days
Is 2:2 The **m** of the LORD's house shall be established as the highest **m**
Dn 2:45 from the **m** without a hand being put
Mt 4:8 devil took him up to a very high **m**,
17:20 you will say to this **m**,
2 Pt 1:18 we were with him on the holy **m**.

MOUNTAINS → MOUNT
Gn 7:20 cubits higher than the submerged **m**.
Ps 125:2 As **m** surround Jerusalem,
Is 52:7 beautiful upon the **m** are the feet
1 Cor 13:2 if I have all faith so as to move **m**
Rev 16:20 island fled, and **m** disappeared.

MOURN → MOURNFUL, MOURNING
Eccl 3:4 a time to **m**, and a time to dance.
Sir 7:34 who weep, but **m** with those who **m**.
Zec 12:10 they will **m** for him as one mourns
Mt 5:4 Blessed are they who **m**, for they

MOURNING → MOURN
Ps 30:12 You changed my **m** into dancing;
Is 61:3 them oil of gladness instead of **m**,
Rev 21:4 there shall be no more death or **m**,

MOUTH → MOUTHS
Dt 8:3 forth from the **m** of the LORD.
Ps 19:15 the words of my **m** be acceptable,
Mt 4:4 comes forth from the **m** of God.' "
15:11 It is not what enters one's **m**
15:11 out of the **m** is what defiles one."
Jas 3:10 From the same **m** come blessing
Rev 19:15 Out of his **m** came a sharp sword

MOUTHS → MOUTH
Ps 115:5 They have **m** but do not speak,

MUCH
Eccl 12:12 in **m** study there is weariness
Lk 12:48 **M** will be required of the person entrusted with **m**,
Jn 12:24 but if it dies, it produces **m** fruit.

MULTIPLY
Gn 1:28 Be fertile and **m**; fill the earth
9:7 Be fertile, then, and **m**;

MULTITUDE
Jas 5:20 death and will cover a **m** of sins.
1 Pt 4:8 because love covers a **m** of sins.

MURDER → MURDERER, MURDERERS
Hos 4:2 lying, **m**, stealing and adultery break

MURDERER → MURDER
Nm 35:16 that person is a **m**, and the **m** must
Jn 8:44 He was a **m** from the beginning

MURDERERS → MURDER
Rev 21:8 the depraved, **m**, the unchaste,

MUSTARD
Mt 17:20 you have faith the size of a **m** seed,
Mk 4:31 It is like a **m** seed that, when it is

MUTUAL
Rom 12:10 love one another with **m** affection;
Heb 13:1 Let **m** love continue.

MYRRH
Mt 2:11 gifts of gold, frankincense, and **m**.
Mk 15:23 gave him wine drugged with **m**,

MYSTERY
Dn 2:19 During the night the **m** was revealed
Rom 11:25 want you to be unaware of this **m**,
1 Cor 15:51 Behold, I tell you a **m**. We shall not
Eph 3:4 my insight into the **m** of Christ,
1 Tm 3:9 holding fast to the **m** of the faith
Rev 17:5 which is a **m**, "Babylon the great,

MYTHS
2 Pt 1:16 did not follow cleverly devised **m**

N

NAAMAN

Aramean general whose leprosy was cleansed by Elisha (2 Kgs 5; Lk 4:27).

NABAL
Wealthy Carmelite the LORD killed for refusing to help David (1 Sm 25). David married Abigail, his widow (1 Sm 25:39-42).

NABOTH
Jezreelite killed for his vineyard (1 Kgs 21). Ahab's family punished (1 Kgs 21:17-24; 2 Kgs 9:21-37).

NADAB
1. Firstborn of Aaron (Ex 6:23); killed with Abihu for offering unauthorized fire (Lv 10; Nm 3:4).
2. Son of Jeroboam I; king of Israel (1 Kgs 15:25-32).

NAHUM
Prophet against Nineveh (Na 1:1; Tb 14:4).

NAILING → NAILS
Col 2:14 it from our midst, **n** it to the cross;

NAILS → NAILING
Jn 20:25 I see the mark of the **n** in his hands

NAKED → NAKEDNESS
Gn 2:25 The man and his wife were both **n**,
Jb 1:21 "**N** I came forth from my mother's womb, and **n** shall I go back there.
2 Cor 5:3 taken it off, we shall not be found **n**.

NAKEDNESS → NAKED
Rom 8:35 or famine, or **n**, or peril,

NAME → NAMES
Gn 2:19 each living creature was then its **n**.
4:26 began to invoke the LORD by **n**.
12:2 I will make your **n** great, so that you
Ex 3:15 This is my **n** forever; this is my title
20:7 anyone who invokes his **n** in vain.
34:5 him there and proclaimed the **n**,
Dt 12:11 place for his **n** you shall bring all
Ps 9:11 Those who know your **n** trust
Prv 18:10 The **n** of the LORD is a strong
Is 42:8 I am the LORD, LORD is my **n**;
Zec 14:9 and the LORD's **n** the only one.
Mt 1:21 a son and you are to **n** him Jesus,
6:9 in heaven, hallowed be your **n**,
28:19 them in the **n** of the Father,
Jn 1:12 God, to those who believe in his **n**,
20:31 belief you may have life in his **n**.
Acts 4:12 is there any other **n** under heaven
Phil 2:9 bestowed on him the **n** that is above every **n**,
Rev 13:17 the stamped image of the beast's **n** or the number that stood for its **n**.
19:13 his **n** was called the Word of God.
22:4 and his **n** will be on their foreheads.

NAMES → NAME
Gn 2:20 The man gave **n** to all the tame
Ex 28:9 engrave on them the **n** of the sons
Mt 10:2 The **n** of the twelve apostles are
Rev 21:14 were inscribed the twelve **n**

NAOMI
Wife of Elimelech, mother-in-law of Ruth (Ru 1:2, 4). Left Bethlehem for Moab during famine (Ru 1:1). Returned a widow, with Ruth (Ru 1:6-22). Advised Ruth to seek marriage with Boaz (Ru 2:17–3:4). Cared for Ruth's son Obed (Ru 4:13-17).

NAPHTALI
Son of Jacob by Bilhah (Gn 30:8; 35:25; 1 Ch 2:2). Tribe of blessed (Gn 49:21; Dt 33:23), numbered (Nm 1:43; 26:50), allotted land (Jos 19:32-39; Ez 48:3), failed to fully possess (Jgs 1:33), supported Deborah (Jgs 4:10; 5:18), David (1 Ch 12:34), 12,000 from (Rev 7:6).

NARROW
Lk 13:24 "Strive to enter through the **n** door,

NATHAN
Prophet and chronicler of Israel's history (1 Ch 29:29; 2 Ch 9:29). Announced the Davidic covenant (2 Sm 7; 1 Ch 17). Denounced David's sin with Bathsheba (2 Sm 12). Supported Solomon (1 Kgs 1).

NATHANAEL → =BARTHOLOMEW?
Apostle (Jn 1:45-49; 21:2). Probably also called Bartholomew (Mt 10:3).

NATION → NATIONS
Gn 12:2 I will make of you a great **n**, and I
Ex 32:10 Then I will make of you a great **n**.
Ps 33:12 Blessed is the **n** whose God is
Prv 14:34 Justice exalts a **n**, but sin is
Is 2:4 One **n** shall not raise the sword
66:8 or a **n** be born in a single moment?
Mt 24:7 **N** will rise against **n**, and kingdom
1 Pt 2:9 a holy **n**, a people of his own,

NATIONS → NATION
Gn 18:18 and all the **n** of the earth are to find
2 Kgs 17:15 the surrounding **n** whom
Ps 47:9 God rules over the **n**; God sits
Is 2:2 All **n** shall stream toward it.
42:1 he shall bring forth justice to the **n**.
Am 9:12 and all **n** claimed in my name—
Mt 28:19 and make disciples of all **n**,
Rom 4:18 become "the father of many **n**,"
Rev 22:2 the trees serve as medicine for the **n**.

NATURAL → NATURE
Rom 11:21 if God did not spare the **n** branches,

NATURE → NATURAL
2 Pt 1:4 may come to share in the divine **n**,

NAZARETH
Mt 2:23 went and dwelt in a town called **N**,
Jn 1:46 anything good come from **N**?"

NAZIRITE
Nm 6:2 women solemnly take the **n** vow

NEAR
Dt 30:14 No, it is something very **n** to you,
Is 55:6 found, call upon him while he is **n**.
Zep 1:14 **N** is the great day of the LORD,
Jas 4:8 Draw **n** to God, and he will draw **n**
Rev 22:10 book, for the appointed time is **n**.

NEBUCHADNEZZAR
Babylonian king, also spelled Nebuchadrezzar. Subdued and exiled Judah (2 Kgs 24–25; 2 Ch 36; Jer 39). Dreams interpreted by Daniel (Dn 2; 4). Worshiped God (Dn 3:28-29; 4:34-37).

NECK → STIFF-NECKED
Prv 3:22 soul, and an adornment for your **n**.
Mt 18:6 a great millstone hung around his **n**

NECO
Pharaoh who killed Josiah (2 Kgs 23:29-30; 2 Ch 35:20-22), deposed Jehoahaz (2 Kgs 23:33-35; 2 Ch 36:3-4).

NEED → NEEDY
Mt 6:8 knows what you **n** before you ask
1 Cor 12:21 head to the feet, "I do not **n** you."
1 Jn 2:27 you do not **n** anyone to teach you.

NEEDLE
Lk 18:25 pass through the eye of a **n** than

NEEDY → NEED
1 Sm 2:8 He raises the **n** from the dust;
Ps 113:7 He raises the **n** from the dust,

NEGLECT
1 Tm 4:14 Do not **n** the gift you have,

NEHEMIAH

Cupbearer of Artaxerxes (Neh 2:1); governor of Israel (Neh 8:9). Returned to Jerusalem to rebuild walls (Neh 2–6). With Ezra, reestablished worship (Neh 8). Prayer confessing nation's sin (Neh 9). Dedicated wall (Neh 12). Story of the miraculous fire (2 Mc 1).

NEIGHBOR

Lv	19:18	You shall love your **n** as yourself.
Dt	5:20	dishonest witness against your **n**.
Mt	19:19	shall love your **n** as yourself.' "
Jas	2:8	shall love your **n** as yourself,"

NESTS

Mt	8:20	dens and birds of the sky have **n**,

NEVER

Ps	15:5	acts like this shall **n** be shaken.
Dn	2:44	a kingdom that shall **n** be destroyed
Mt	7:23	to them solemnly, 'I **n** knew you.
Jn	10:28	eternal life, and they shall **n** perish.
1 Cor	13:8	Love **n** fails. If there are prophecies,
Heb	13:5	"I will **n** forsake you or abandon

NEW

Ex	1:8	Then a **n** king, who knew nothing
Ps	33:3	Sing to him a **n** song;
Eccl	1:9	Nothing is **n** under the sun!
Is	43:19	See, I am doing something **n**!
	65:17	See, I am creating **n** heavens and a **n** earth;
Jer	31:31	I will make a **n** covenant
Ez	36:26	I will give you a **n** heart, and a **n** spirit I will put within you.
Mt	9:17	People do not put **n** wine into old
	9:17	Rather, they pour **n** wine into fresh
Mk	1:27	A **n** teaching with authority.
Lk	22:20	"This cup is the **n** covenant in my
Jn	13:34	I give you a **n** commandment:
2 Cor	3:6	us as ministers of a **n** covenant,
Col	3:10	and have put on the **n** self, which is
Heb	8:8	I will conclude a **n** covenant
1 Pt	1:3	his great mercy gave us a **n** birth
2 Pt	3:13	we await **n** heavens and a **n** earth in which righteousness
1 Jn	2:7	I am writing no **n** commandment
Rev	21:1	Then I saw a **n** heaven and a **n** earth.
	21:2	saw the holy city, a **n** Jerusalem,
	21:5	said, "Behold, I make all things **n**."

NEWS

Is	52:7	the feet of the one bringing good **n**,
Mt	11:5	poor have the good **n** proclaimed

NICODEMUS

Pharisee who visted Jesus at night (Jn 3). Argued for fair treatment of Jesus (Jn 7:50-52). With Joseph, prepared Jesus for burial (Jn 19:38-42).

NIGHT → NIGHTS

Gn	1:5	and the darkness he called "**n**."
Ex	13:21	at **n** by means of a column of fire
	13:21	they could travel both day and **n**.
Jos	1:8	Recite it by day and by **n**, that you
Mt	24:43	the house had known the hour of **n**
1 Thes	5:2	the Lord will come like a thief at **n**.
Rev	22:5	**N** will be no more, nor will they

NIGHTS → NIGHT

Gn	7:12	forty **n** heavy rain poured down
Ex	24:18	mountain for forty days and forty **n**.
1 Kgs	19:8	and forty **n** to the mountain of God,
Mt	4:2	He fasted for forty days and forty **n**,
	12:40	of the whale three days and three **n**,
	12:40	of the earth three days and three **n**.

NINEVEH

Jon	1:2	Set out for the great city of **N**,
Na	1:1	Oracle concerning **N**. The book
Mt	12:41	the men of **N** will arise with this

NOAH

Righteous man (Ez 14:14, 20) called to build ark (Gn 6–8; Heb 11:7; 1 Pt 3:20; 2 Pt 2:5). God's covenant with (Gn 9:1-17). Drunkenness of (Gn 9:18-23). Blessed sons, cursed Canaan (Gn 9:24-27). Praised (Sir 44:17-18).

NOISE

Ex	32:17	Joshua heard the **n** of the people

NOON

Mk	15:33	At **n** darkness came over the whole

NORTH

Jer	4:6	Disaster I bring from the **n**,
Dn	11:6	to the king of the **n** to carry

NOTHING

Eccl	1:9	**N** is new under the sun!
Sir	39:20	To him, **n** is small or insignificant,
	39:20	and **n** too wonderful or hard
Jer	32:17	**n** is too difficult for you.
Mt	17:20	**N** will be impossible for you."
Jn	15:5	because without me you can do **n**.
1 Cor	13:2	but do not have love, I am **n**.

NULLIFY

Rom	3:3	Will their infidelity **n** the fidelity
Gal	2:21	I do not **n** the grace of God;

NUMBER → NUMBERED, NUMEROUS

Rom	11:25	part, until the full **n** of the Gentiles
Rev	13:18	who understands can calculate the **n**
	13:18	His **n** is six hundred and sixty-six.

NUMBERED → NUMBER

2 Sm	24:10	David regretted having **n** the people.

NUMEROUS → NUMBER

Ex	1:9	and become more **n** than we are!
Zec	10:8	and they will be as **n** as before.

O

OATH

Dt	7:8	his fidelity to the **o** he had sworn
Ps	132:11	The LORD swore an **o** to David
Heb	7:20	not without the taking of an **o**—
	7:20	others became priests without an **o**,

OBADIAH

1. Believer who sheltered 100 prophets from Jezebel (1 Kgs 18:1-16).

2. Prophet against Edom (Ob 1).

OBEDIENCE → OBEY

Rom	5:19	so through the **o** of one the many
Heb	5:8	he learned **o** from what he suffered;

OBEDIENT → OBEY

Phil	2:8	himself, becoming **o** to death,

OBEY → OBEDIENCE, OBEDIENT, OBEYED

Acts	5:29	"We must **o** God rather than men.
Eph	6:1	**o** your parents [in the Lord], for this

OBEYED → OBEY

Heb	11:8	faith Abraham **o** when he was called

OBSERVE

Lv	20:8	careful, therefore, to **o** my statutes.

OBSTACLE
1 Cor 9:12 so as not to place an **o** to the gospel

OBTAIN → OBTAINED
2 Tm 2:10 they too may **o** the salvation that is

OBTAINED → OBTAIN
Heb 8:6 Now he has **o** so much more

ODOR
Gn 8:21 the LORD smelled the sweet **o**,

OFFENSE
Mk 6:3 And they took **o** at him.

OFFER → OFFERING, OFFERINGS
Ps 4:6 **O** fitting sacrifices and trust
Heb 9:25 that he might **o** himself repeatedly,

OFFERING → OFFER
Gn 4:4 with favor on Abel and his **o**,
Ps 40:7 Sacrifice and **o** you do not want;
Eph 5:2 over for us as a sacrificial **o** to God
Heb 10:14 one **o** he has made perfect forever

OFFERINGS → OFFER
Mk 12:33 is worth more than all burnt **o**

OFFSPRING
Gn 3:15 and between your **o** and hers;

OHOLIAB
Craftsman who worked on the tabernacle (Ex 31:6; 35:34; 36:1-2; 38:23).

OIL
Ex 25:6 **o** for the light;
25:6 spices for the anointing **o**
Dt 14:23 wine and **o**, as well as the firstlings
Ps 23:5 You anoint my head with **o**;
Heb 1:9 anointed you with the **o** of gladness
Jas 5:14 anoint [him] with **o** in the name

OLD
Gn 21:7 have borne him a son in his **o** age."
Ps 74:12 are my king from of **o**,
Dn 13:61 They rose up against the two **o** men,
Mk 2:22 pours new wine into **o** wineskins.
Rom 4:19 he was almost a hundred years **o**)
Eph 4:22 you should put away the **o** self

OLIVE → OLIVES
Zec 4:3 And beside it are two **o** trees,
Rom 11:17 a wild **o** shoot, were grafted in their
11:17 to share in the rich root of the **o** tree,
Rev 11:4 These are the two **o** trees

OLIVES → OLIVE
Zec 14:4 feet will stand on the Mount of **O**,
14:4 The Mount of **O** will be split in two
Mt 24:3 he was sitting on the Mount of **O**,

OMEGA
Rev 1:8 "I am the Alpha and the **O**,"

OMRI
King of Israel (1 Kgs 16:21-26).

ONCE → ONE
Ex 30:10 **O** a year Aaron shall purge its
Rom 6:10 death, he died to sin **o** and for all;
Heb 7:27 he did that **o** for all when he offered
9:27 appointed that human beings die **o**,

ONE → FIRST, ONCE
Gn 2:24 and the two of them become **o** body.
Zec 14:9 day the LORD will be the only **o**,
14:9 and the LORD's name the only **o**.
Jn 10:30 The Father and I are **o**."
1 Cor 12:13 in **o** Spirit we were all baptized into **o** body,
12:13 were all given to drink of **o** Spirit.
Gal 3:28 for you are all **o** in Christ Jesus.
Eph 4:5 **o** Lord, **o** faith, **o** baptism;

ONLY
Gn 22:2 Take your son Isaac, your **o** one,
1 Kgs 18:22 "I am the **o** remaining prophet
Jn 1:14 the glory as of the Father's **o** Son,
Jn 3:16 the world that he gave his **o** Son,
1 Tm 1:17 invisible, the **o** God,
1 Jn 4:9 God sent his **o** Son into the world so

OPEN → OPENED, OPENS
Is 53:7 he submitted and did not **o** his mouth;
Rev 5:2 "Who is worthy to **o** the scroll

OPENED → OPEN
Gn 3:7 the eyes of both of them were **o**,
Dn 7:10 convened, and the books were **o**.
Lk 11:9 knock and the door will be **o** to you.
Heb 10:20 living way he **o** for us through
Rev 20:12 the throne, and scrolls were **o**.
20:12 Then another scroll was **o**, the book

OPENS → OPEN
Rev 3:7 who **o** and no one shall close,

OPPORTUNITY
Mt 26:16 he looked for an **o** to hand him over.
Gal 5:13 do not use this freedom as an **o**

OPPRESS → OPPRESSED, OPPRESSION
2 Sm 7:10 nor shall the wicked ever again **o**

OPPRESSED → OPPRESS
Gn 15:13 and **o** for four hundred years.
Ex 1:12 Yet the more they were **o**, the more
Ps 146:7 secures justice for the **o**, who gives

OPPRESSION → OPPRESS
Ez 45:9 Put away violence and **o**, and do

ORDER
Heb 5:10 according to the **o** of Melchizedek.

ORIGIN
Mt 21:26 'Of human **o**,' we fear the crowd,
Acts 5:38 or this activity is of human **o**, it will

ORNAMENTS
Ex 33:6 the Israelites stripped off their **o**.

ORPHANS
Jas 1:27 to care for **o** and widows in their

OTHER → OTHERS
Ex 20:3 shall not have **o** gods beside me.
Jgs 2:19 their ancestors, following **o** gods,
2 Kgs 17:7 They venerated **o** gods,
Is 45:5 there is no **o**, there is no God
Mt 6:24 will either hate one and love the **o**,
6:24 be devoted to one and despise the **o**.

OTHERS → OTHER
Lk 6:31 Do to **o** as you would have them do
Phil 2:3 humbly regard **o** as more important

OTHNIEL
Nephew of Caleb (Jos 15:15-19; Jgs 1:12-15). Judge who freed Israel from Aram (Jgs 3:7-11).

OUTSIDE
Lk 11:39 Although you cleanse the **o**
Heb 13:12 Jesus also suffered **o** the gate,
Rev 22:15 **O** are the dogs, the sorcerers,

OUTSTRETCHED → STRETCH
Ex 6: 6 I will redeem you by my **o** arm
Ps 136: 12 With mighty hand and **o** arm, for his
Jer 27: 5 by my great power, with my **o** arm;

OVERCOME
Jn 1: 5 and the darkness has not **o** it.

OVERSEERS
Acts 20: 28 the holy Spirit has appointed you **o**,

OVERSHADOW
Lk 1: 35 power of the Most High will **o** you.

OWE
Mt 18: 28 demanding, 'Pay back what you **o**.'
Rom 13: 8 **O** nothing to anyone, except to love

OWN
Is 53: 6 like sheep, all following our **o** way;
Jer 31: 30 shall die because of their **o** iniquity:
Jn 1: 11 He came to what was his **o**, but his **o** people did not accept him.
10: 18 from me, but I lay it down on my **o**.
1 Cor 6: 19 God, and that you are not your **o**?

OX → OXEN
Dt 25: 4 You shall not muzzle an **o** when it
Is 65: 25 and the lion shall eat hay like the **o**—
Ez 1: 10 the face of an **o**, and each had
1 Tm 5: 18 "You shall not muzzle an **o** when it

P

PAGANS
1 Cor 12: 2 how, when you were **p**, you were

PAIN → PAINS
Gn 3: 16 in **p** you shall bring forth children.
Is 53: 4 our **p** that he bore, our sufferings
1 Pt 2: 19 For whenever anyone bears the **p**
Rev 21: 4 wailing or **p**, [for] the old order has

PAINS → PAIN
Rom 8: 22 groaning in labor **p** even until now;
1 Thes 5: 3 them, like labor **p** upon a pregnant

PALM → PALMS
Jn 12: 13 they took **p** branches and went
Rev 7: 9 holding **p** branches in their hands.

PALMS → PALM
Is 49: 16 the **p** of my hands I have engraved

PARABLE → PARABLES
Mt 13: 18 "Hear then the **p** of the sower.

PARABLES → PARABLE; See also JESUS: PARABLES
Mt 13: 35 "I will open my mouth in **p**, I will

PARADISE
Lk 23: 43 today you will be with me in **P**."
2 Cor 12: 4 was caught up into **P** and heard

PARALYTIC → PARALYZED
Mt 9: 2 he said to the **p**, "Courage,

PARALYZED → PARALYTIC
Acts 8: 7 many **p** and crippled people were

PARCHMENTS
2 Tm 4: 13 papyrus rolls, and especially the **p**.

PARDON
Ex 34: 9 yet **p** our wickedness and sins,

PARENTS
Eph 6: 1 Children, obey your **p** [in the Lord],

PARTAKE
1 Cor 10: 17 body, for we all **p** of the one loaf.

PARTIALITY
Prv 24: 23 To show **p** in judgment is not good.
Rom 2: 11 There is no **p** with God.

PARTNERSHIP
2 Cor 6: 14 For what **p** do righteousness

PASHHUR
Priest; opponent of Jeremiah (Jer 20:1-6).

PASS → PASSED, PASSING
Ex 12: 13 Seeing the blood, I will **p** over you;
33: 19 make all my goodness **p** before you,
Am 5: 17 when I **p** through your midst,
Mt 24: 35 Heaven and earth will **p** away,
24: 35 but my words will not **p** away.
2 Pt 3: 10 then the heavens will **p** away

PASSED → PASS
Gn 15: 17 which **p** between those pieces.
Ex 12: 27 who **p** over the houses
33: 22 you with my hand until I have **p** by.
2 Cor 5: 17 the old things have **p** away;
1 Jn 3: 14 We know that we have **p** from death
Rev 21: 4 [for] the old order has **p** away."

PASSING → PASS
1 Cor 7: 31 world in its present form is **p** away.
1 Jn 2: 17 and its enticement are **p** away.

PASSIONS
Gal 5: 24 have crucified their flesh with its **p**

PASSOVER
Ex 12: 11 it in a hurry. It is the LORD's **P**.
Dt 16: 1 by keeping the **P** of the LORD,
Mk 14: 12 when they sacrificed the **P** lamb,
14: 12 and prepare for you to eat the **P**?"

PASTORS
Eph 4: 11 others as **p** and teachers,

PASTURES
Ps 23: 2 In green **p** he makes me lie down;

PATH → PATHS
Ps 16: 11 You will show me the **p** to life,
119: 105 lamp for my feet, a light for my **p**.
Mt 13: 4 some seed fell on the **p**, and birds

PATHS → PATH
Prv 3: 6 and he will make straight your **p**.
Mt 3: 3 the Lord, make straight his **p**.' "
Heb 12: 13 Make straight **p** for your feet,

PATIENCE → PATIENT
Mi 2: 7 of Jacob, "Is the LORD short of **p**;
Rom 2: 4 and **p** in low esteem,
Gal 5: 22 joy, peace, **p**, kindness, generosity,
2 Pt 3: 15 And consider the **p** of our Lord as

PATIENT → PATIENCE
1 Cor 13: 4 Love is **p**, love is kind. It is not
2 Pt 3: 9 but he is **p** with you, not wishing

PATTERN
Ex 25: 40 them according to the **p** shown you
Heb 8: 5 according to the **p** shown you

PAUL → =SAUL
Also called Saul (Acts 13:9). Pharisee from Tarsus (Acts 9:11; Phil 3:5). Apostle (Gal 1). At stoning of Stephen (Acts 8:1). Persecuted Church (Acts 9:1-2; Gal 1:13). Vision of Jesus on road to Damascus (Acts 9:4-9; 26:12-18). In Arabia (Gal 1:17). Preached

in Damascus; escaped death through the wall in a basket (Acts 9:19-25). In Jerusalem; back to Tarsus (Acts 9:26-30).

Brought to Antioch by Barnabas (Acts 11:22-26). First missionary journey to Cyprus and Galatia (Acts 13–14). Stoned at Lystra (Acts 14:19-20). At Jerusalem council (Acts 15). Split with Barnabas over Mark (Acts 15:36-41).

Second missionary journey with Silas (Acts 16–20). Called to Macedonia (Acts 16:6-10). Freed from prison in Philippi (Acts 16:16-40). In Thessalonica (Acts 17:1-9). Speech in Athens (Acts 17:16-33). In Corinth (Acts 18). In Ephesus (Acts 19). Return to Jerusalem (Acts 20). Farewell to Ephesian elders (Acts 20:13-38). Arrival in Jerusalem (Acts 21:1-26). Arrested (Acts 21:27-36). Addressed crowds (Acts 22), Sanhedrin (Acts 23:1-11). Sent to Caesarea (Acts 23:12-35). Trial before Felix (Acts 24), Festus (Acts 25:1-12). Before Agrippa (Acts 25:13–26:32). Voyage to Rome; shipwreck (Acts 27). Arrival in Rome (Acts 28).

PAVEMENT
Jn 19:13 bench in the place called Stone **P**,

PAY → REPAY
Dt 24:15 day you shall **p** the servant's wages
Mt 22:17 Is it lawful to **p** the census tax
Rom 13:7 **P** to all their dues, taxes to whom

PEACE → PEACEMAKERS
Lv 26:6 I will establish **p** in the land,
Ps 122:6 For the **p** of Jerusalem pray:
Is 26:3 With firm purpose you maintain **p**; in **p**, because of our trust
57:19 creating words of comfort. **P**!
57:21 There is no **p** for the wicked!
Jer 6:14 "**P**, **p**!" they say, though there is no **p**.
Lk 2:14 and on earth **p** to those on whom his
Jn 14:27 **P** I leave with you; my **p** I give
Rom 16:20 of **p** will quickly crush Satan under
1 Cor 14:33 is not the God of disorder but of **p**.
Gal 5:22 of the Spirit is love, joy, **p**, patience,
Eph 4:3 of the spirit through the bond of **p**:
Phil 4:7 Then the **p** of God that surpasses all
2 Tm 2:22 and **p**, along with those who call

PEACEMAKERS → PEACE
Mt 5:9 Blessed are the **p**, for they will be

PEARL → PEARLS
Mt 13:46 When he finds a **p** of great price,
Rev 21:21 of the gates made from a single **p**;

PEARLS → PEARL
Mt 7:6 or throw your **p** before swine,

PEKAH
King of Israel (2 Kgs 15:25-31; 2 Ch 28:6; Is 7:1).

PEKAHIAH
Son of Menahem; king of Israel (2 Kgs 15:22-26).

PENALTY
Rom 1:27 their own persons the due **p** for their

PENTECOST
Acts 2:1 When the time for **P** was fulfilled,

PEOPLE → PEOPLES
Ex 5:1 Let my **p** go, that they may hold
33:13 this nation is indeed your own **p**.
Dt 4:20 that you might be his **p**, his heritage,
Ru 1:16 Your **p** shall be my **p** and your God,
2 Sm 5:2 You shall shepherd my **p** Israel;
Ps 29:11 the LORD give might to his **p**; may the LORD bless his **p**
125:2 LORD surrounds his **p** both now
Is 40:1 give comfort to my **p**, says your
42:6 and set you as a covenant for the **p**,
53:8 living, struck for the sins of his **p**.
Jer 50:6 Lost sheep were my **p**,
Dn 9:24 weeks are decreed for your **p**
Zec 13:9 "They are my **p**," and they will
Mt 1:21 because he will save his **p**
Jn 11:50 one man should die instead of the **p**,
18:14 man should die rather than the **p**.
Rom 9:25 who were not my **p** I will call 'my **p**,'
Heb 8:10 their God, and they shall be my **p**.
1 Pt 2:9 a holy nation, a **p** of his own,

PEOPLES → PEOPLE
Gn 17:16 and rulers of **p** will issue from her.
Ps 117:1 Extol him, all you **p**!

PERFECT → PERFECTER
Ps 19:8 The law of the LORD is **p**,
Mt 5:48 So be **p**, just as your heavenly Father is **p**.
Rom 12:2 what is good and pleasing and **p**.
2 Cor 12:9 for power is made **p** in weakness."
Heb 5:9 and when he was made **p**,
1 Jn 4:18 **p** love drives out fear because fear
4:18 and so one who fears is not yet **p**

PERFECTER → PERFECT
Heb 12:2 on Jesus, the leader and **p** of faith.

PERISH → PERISHABLE
Jos 23:13 until you **p** from this good land
Est 4:16 contrary to the law. If I **p**, I **p**!"
Jn 3:16 who believes in him might not **p**
2 Pt 3:9 not wishing that any should **p**

PERISHABLE → PERISH
1 Cor 9:25 They do it to win a **p** crown, but we
1 Pt 1:23 not from **p** but from imperishable

PERSECUTE → PERSECUTED, PERSECUTION
Mt 5:44 and pray for those who **p** you,
Rom 12:14 Bless those who **p** [you],

PERSECUTED → PERSECUTE
Jn 15:20 If they **p** me, they will
2 Cor 4:9 **p**, but not abandoned;
2 Tm 3:12 religiously in Christ Jesus will be **p**.

PERSECUTION → PERSECUTE
Mt 13:21 or **p** comes because of the word,
Rom 8:35 or distress, or **p**, or famine,

PERSEVERE
Rom 12:12 endure in affliction, **p** in prayer.

PERSIA
Ezr 1:1 spirit of Cyrus king of **P** to issue

PESTILENCE
Dt 32:24 and consuming fever and bitter **p**,
Ps 91:6 Nor the **p** that roams in darkness,

PETER → =CEPHAS, =SIMON
Apostle, brother of Andrew, also called Simon (Mt 10:2; Mk 3:16; Lk 6:14; Acts 1:13), and Cephas (Jn 1:42). Confession of Christ (Mt 16:13-20; Mk 8:27-30; Lk 9:18-27). At transfiguration (Mt 17:1-8; Mk 9:2-8; Lk 9:28-36; 2 Pt 1:16-18). Caught fish with coin (Mt 17:24-27). Denial of Jesus predicted (Mt 26:31-35; Mk 14:27-31; Lk 22:31-34; Jn 13:31-38). Denied Jesus (Mt 26:69-75; Mk 14:66-72; Lk 22:54-62; Jn 18:15-27). Commissioned by Jesus to shepherd his flock (Jn 21:15-23).

Speech at Pentecost (Acts 2). Healed beggar (Acts 3:1-10). Speech at temple (Acts 3:11-26), before Sanhedrin (Acts 4:1-22). In Samaria (Acts 8:14-25). Sent by vision to Cornelius (Acts 10). Announced salvation of Gentiles in Jerusalem (Acts 11; 15). Freed from prison (Acts 12). Inconsistency at Antioch (Gal 2:11-21). At Jerusalem Council (Acts 15).

PHARAOH → PHARAOH'S
Gn 41:14 **P** therefore had Joseph summoned,

Ex 3: 11 "Who am I that I should go to **P**
14: 17 I will receive glory through **P**
Rom 9: 17 For the scripture says to **P**, "This is

PHARAOH'S → PHARAOH
Heb 11: 24 be known as the son of **P** daughter;

PHARISEE → PHARISEES
Lk 11: 37 a **P** invited him to dine at his home.
Jn 3: 1 there was a **P** named Nicodemus,
Acts 5: 34 But a **P** in the Sanhedrin named
Phil 3: 5 in observance of the law a **P**,

PHARISEES → PHARISEE
Mt 5: 20 surpasses that of the scribes and **P**,
16: 6 beware of the leaven of the **P**
23: 13 you, scribes and **P**, you hypocrites.

PHILEMON
Phlm 1: 1 brother, to **P**, our beloved and our

PHILIP
1. Apostle (Mt 10:3; Mk 3:18; Lk 6:14; Jn 1:43-48; 14:8; Acts 1:13).
2. Deacon (Acts 6:1-7); evangelist in Samaria (Acts 8:4-25), to Ethiopian (Acts 8:26-40).

PHILISTINE → PHILISTINES
1 Sm 17: 37 me from the hand of this **P**."

PHILISTINES → PHILISTINE
Gn 26: 1 Abimelech, king of the **P** in Gerar.
1 Sm 5: 1 The **P**, having captured the ark
17: 1 The **P** rallied their forces for battle
2 Sm 8: 1 David defeated the **P** and subdued
Am 1: 8 and the last of the **P** shall perish,

PHILOSOPHERS → PHILOSOPHY
Acts 17: 18 Stoic **p** engaged him in discussion.

PHILOSOPHY → PHILOSOPHERS
Col 2: 8 seductive **p** according to human

PHINEHAS
1. Grandson of Aaron (Ex 6:25; Jos 22:30-32). Zeal for the LORD (Nm 25:7-13; Ps 106:30).
2. A wicked priest (1 Sm 1:3; 2:12-17; 4:1-19).

PHOEBE
Rom 16: 1 I commend to you **P** our sister,

PHYSICAL
1 Tm 4: 8 while **p** training is of limited value,

PHYSICIAN
Mt 9: 12 who are well do not need a **p**,
Col 4: 14 Luke the beloved **p** sends greetings,

PIECES
Gn 15: 17 which passed between those **p**.
Lk 20: 18 on that stone will be dashed to **p**;

PIERCED
Jn 19: 37 look upon him whom they have **p**."
Rev 1: 7 will see him, even those who **p** him.

PIG
Dt 14: 8 And the **p**, which indeed has

PILATE
Governor of Judea. Questioned Jesus (Mt 27:1-26; Mk 15:15; Lk 22:66–23:25; Jn 18:28–19:16); sent him to Herod (Lk 23:6-12); consented to his crucifixion when crowds chose Barabbas (Mt 27:15-26; Mk 15:6-15; Lk 23:13-25; Jn 19:1-10).

PILLAR
Gn 19: 26 and she was turned into a **p** of salt.

PIT
Ps 103: 4 Who redeems your life from the **p**,

PITY
Dt 7: 16 You are not to look on them with **p**,
Hos 1: 6 I will no longer feel **p** for the house

PLACE → PLACES
Ex 26: 33 divides the holy **p** from the holy
Ps 24: 3 Who can stand in his holy **p**?
Jn 14: 3 And if I go and prepare a **p** for you,

PLACES → PLACE
Lv 26: 30 I will demolish your high **p**,
Ps 78: 58 They enraged him with their high **p**,

PLAGUE → PLAGUES
Zec 14: 12 this will be the **p**
Rev 11: 6 with any **p** as often as they wish.

PLAGUES → PLAGUE
Hos 13: 14 Where are your **p**, O death!
Rev 15: 1 seven angels with the seven last **p**,
22: 18 to him the **p** described in this book,

PLAIN
Gn 13: 12 settled among the cities of the **P**,
Is 40: 4 The rugged land shall be a **p**,

PLANNED
Is 46: 11 I have **p** it, and I will do it.

PLANT → PLANTED
Gn 1: 29 I give you every seed-bearing **p**
Eccl 3: 2 a time to **p**, and a time to uproot the **p**.

PLANTED → PLANT
Gn 2: 8 The LORD God **p** a garden
Ps 1: 3 He is like a tree **p** near streams
1 Cor 3: 6 I **p**, Apollos watered, but God

PLEASE → PLEASED, PLEASES, PLEASING, PLEASURE
Ps 69: 32 will **p** the LORD more than oxen,
Sir 2: 16 who fear the Lord seek to **p** him;
Rom 8: 8 who are in the flesh cannot **p** God.
15: 3 For Christ did not **p** himself;
1 Cor 10: 33 just as I try to **p** everyone in every
1 Thes 4: 1 conduct yourselves to **p** God—
Heb 11: 6 faith it is impossible to **p** him,

PLEASED → PLEASE
Mi 6: 7 Will the LORD be **p**
Mt 3: 17 Son, with whom I am well **p**."
Col 1: 19 him all the fullness was **p** to dwell,
2 Pt 1: 17 beloved, with whom I am well **p**."

PLEASES → PLEASE
1 Jn 3: 22 commandments and do what **p** him.

PLEASING → PLEASE
Ps 104: 34 May my meditation be **p** to him;
Eph 5: 10 Try to learn what is **p** to the Lord.
Phil 4: 18 an acceptable sacrifice, **p** to God.

PLEASURE → PLEASE
Prv 21: 17 The lover of **p** will suffer want;
Ez 18: 32 For I find no **p** in the death
2 Tm 3: 4 lovers of **p** rather than lovers

PLOWSHARES
Is 2: 4 They shall beat their swords into **p**

PLUNDERED
Ez 39: 10 plundering those who **p** them,

POISON
Jas 3: 8 It is a restless evil, full of deadly **p**.

POLE
Nm 21: 8 Make a seraph and mount it on a **p**,

POOR → POVERTY
1 Sm 2: 8 from the ash heap lifts up the **p**,
Jb 29: 16 I was a father to the **p**; the complaint
Ps 113: 7 dust, lifts the **p** from the ash heap,
Prv 19: 22 rather be **p** than a liar.
Mt 5: 3 "Blessed are the **p** in spirit,
Mk 10: 21 give to [the] **p** and you will have
12: 42 A **p** widow also came and put
Jn 12: 8 You always have the **p** with you,
2 Cor 6: 10 as **p** yet enriching many;
8: 9 sake he became **p** although he was
Jas 2: 5 Did not God choose those who are **p**

PORTION
Dt 32: 9 But the LORD's **p** was his people;
Ps 142: 6 my **p** in the land of the living.
Lam 3: 24 The LORD is my **p**, I tell myself,

POSSESS → POSSESSED, POSSESSION, POSSESSIONS
Is 60: 21 for all time they will **p** the land;

POSSESSED → POSSESS
Mt 8: 16 they brought him many who were **p**

POSSESSION → POSSESS
Ex 19: 5 will be my treasured **p** among all
Jos 1: 11 your God, is giving as your **p**.' "
Ps 2: 8 and, as your **p**, the ends of the earth.

POSSESSIONS → POSSESS
Lk 12: 15 one's life does not consist of **p**."

POSSIBLE
Mt 19: 26 but for God all things are **p**."
26: 39 if it is **p**, let this cup pass from me;

POTIPHAR
Egyptian who bought Joseph (Gn 37:36; 39:1-6), sent him to prison (Gn 39:7-30).

POTTER → POTTER'S
Sir 33: 13 Like clay in the hands of a **p**, to be
Rom 9: 21 does not the **p** have a right over

POTTER'S → POTTER
Jer 18: 2 Arise and go down to the **p** house;
Mt 27: 7 it to buy the **p** field as a burial place

POUR → POURED
Dt 12: 16 but must **p** it out on the ground like
Is 44: 3 I will **p** out my spirit upon your
Ez 39: 29 once I **p** out my spirit upon the house of
Acts 2: 17 'that I will **p** out a portion of my
Rev 16: 1 **p** out the seven bowls of God's fury

POURED → POUR
Acts 2: 33 Spirit from the Father and **p** it forth,
Rom 5: 5 the love of God has been **p**
Ti 3: 6 whom he richly **p** out on us through

POVERTY → POOR
Prv 30: 8 me, give me neither **p** nor riches;
Sir 11: 14 evil, life and death, **p** and riches—
Mk 12: 44 from her **p**, has contributed all she
2 Cor 8: 9 by his **p** you might become rich.

POWER → POWERFUL, POWERS
Ex 9: 16 to show you my **p** and to make my
15: 6 magnificent in **p**, your right hand,
Jdt 9: 14 are God, the God of all **p** and might,
Ps 68: 35 Confess the **p** of God,
68: 35 Israel, whose **p** is in the sky.
Prv 18: 21 and life are in the **p** of the tongue;
Mt 22: 29 know the scriptures or the **p** of God.
Mk 13: 26 coming in the clouds' with great **p**
Rom 1: 20 his invisible attributes of eternal **p**
1 Cor 15: 24 and every authority and **p**.
Eph 1: 19 of his **p** for us who believe,
Phil 3: 10 him and the **p** of his resurrection
2 Tm 3: 5 a pretense of religion but deny its **p**.
2 Pt 1: 3 His divine **p** has bestowed on us
1: 3 called us by his own glory and **p**.
Rev 20: 6 second death has no **p** over these;

POWERFUL → POWER
1 Cor 1: 26 not many were **p**, not many were

POWERS → POWER
Rom 8: 38 things, nor future things, nor **p**,
Eph 6: 12 with the **p**, with the world rulers

PRACTICE → PRACTICES
Sir 50: 29 If they put them into **p**, they can
Mt 23: 3 For they preach but they do not **p**.

PRACTICES → PRACTICE
Col 3: 9 have taken off the old self with its **p**

PRAISE → PRAISED, PRAISES
Ex 15: 2 This is my God, I **p** him; the God
Ps 56: 5 I **p** the word of God; I trust in God,
150: 6 has breath give **p** to the LORD!
Prv 27: 2 Let another **p** you, not your own
31: 31 let her deeds **p** her at the city gates.
Mt 21: 16 you have brought forth **p**'?"
1 Cor 14: 15 I will sing **p** with the spirit, but I will also sing **p** with the mind.
Rev 19: 5 "**P** our God, all you his servants,

PRAISED → PRAISE
Ps 48: 2 and highly **p** in the city of our God:

PRAISES → PRAISE
Sir 24: 1 Wisdom sings her own **p**,

PRAY → PRAYED, PRAYER, PRAYERS, PRAYING, PRAYS
1 Sm 12: 23 the LORD by ceasing to **p** for you
2 Ch 7: 14 humble themselves and **p**, and seek
Ps 5: 3 For to you I will **p**, LORD;
122: 6 For the peace of Jerusalem **p**:
Sir 37: 15 **p** to God to make your steps firm
Mt 5: 44 and **p** for those who persecute you,
6: 5 "When you **p**, do not be like
6: 5 to stand and **p** in the synagogues
Lk 11: 1 **p** just as John taught his disciples."
Rom 8: 26 do not know how to **p** as we ought,
1 Cor 14: 15 I will **p** with the spirit, but I will also **p** with the mind.
1 Thes 5: 17 **P** without ceasing.
Jas 5: 16 one another and **p** for one another,

PRAYED → PRAY
Mk 1: 35 off to a deserted place, where he **p**.
14: 35 **p** that if it were possible the hour

PRAYER → PRAY
Ps 6: 10 the LORD will receive my **p**.
Prv 15: 29 wicked, but hears the **p** of the just.
Is 56: 7 make them joyful in my house of **p**;
56: 7 house shall be called a house of **p**
Mt 21: 13 'My house shall be a house of **p**,'
Mk 11: 24 all that you ask for in **p**,
Rom 12: 12 endure in affliction, persevere in **p**.
Jas 5: 16 The fervent **p** of a righteous person

PRAYERS → PRAY
Mk 12: 40 and, as a pretext, recite lengthy **p**.
Heb 5: 7 he offered **p** and supplications
Rev 5: 8 which are the **p** of the holy ones.

PRAYING → PRAY
2 Mc 15: 12 was **p** with outstretched arms

PRAYS → PRAY
2 Mc 15: 14 Jews and fervently **p** for the people

PREACHING
1 Tm 5: 17 especially those who toil in **p**

PRECEPTS
Ps 19: 9 The **p** of the LORD are right,
119: 15 I will ponder your **p** and consider
Mt 15: 9 teaching as doctrines human **p**.' "

PRECIOUS
Ps 72: 14 for **p** is their blood in his sight.
Prv 3: 15 She is more **p** than corals, and no
Is 28: 16 tested, A **p** cornerstone as a sure
1 Pt 1: 19 with the **p** blood of Christ as
2: 6 chosen and **p**, and whoever believes

PREDESTINED
Rom 8: 30 And those he **p** he also called;

PREPARE → PREPARED
Mal 3: 1 he will **p** the way before me;
Mt 3: 3 the desert, '**P** the way of the Lord,
Jn 14: 2 that I am going to **p** a place for you?

PREPARED → PREPARE
1 Cor 2: 9 what God has **p** for those who love

PRESENCE
Ps 139: 7 From your **p**, where can I flee?

PRESENT
Rom 6: 13 do not **p** the parts of your bodies
6: 13 **p** yourselves to God as raised
1 Cor 3: 22 life or death, or the **p** or the future:
Eph 5: 27 he might **p** to himself the church
2 Tm 2: 15 Be eager to **p** yourself as acceptable

PREVAIL
1 Sm 2: 9 for not by strength does one **p**.

PRICE
Mt 27: 9 value of a man with a **p** on his head,
1 Cor 6: 20 For you have been purchased at a **p**.

PRIDE → PROUD
Prv 16: 18 **P** goes before disaster,
Sir 10: 7 Odious to the Lord and to mortals is **p**,

PRIEST → PRIESTHOOD, PRIESTS
Gn 14: 18 He was a **p** of God Most High.
Ex 2: 16 Now the **p** of Midian had seven
Ps 110: 4 "You are a **p** forever in the manner
Mk 14: 63 At that the high **p** tore his garments
Heb 3: 1 and high **p** of our confession,
5: 10 God high **p** according to the order
7: 3 Son of God, he remains a **p** forever.
10: 21 we have "a great **p** over the house

PRIESTHOOD → PRIEST
Ex 29: 9 Thus shall the **p** be theirs
Heb 7: 24 has a **p** that does not pass away.
1 Pt 2: 5 to be a holy **p** to offer spiritual

PRIESTS → PRIEST
Ex 28: 1 Israelites, that they may be my **p**:
Dt 31: 9 it to the levitical **p** who carry the ark
Mi 3: 11 for a bribe, the **p** teach for pay,
Mk 15: 3 The chief **p** accused him of many
Heb 7: 27 as did the high **p**, to offer sacrifice
Rev 20: 6 they will be **p** of God and of Christ,

PRINCE → PRINCES
Ez 37: 25 David my servant as their **p** forever.
Dn 10: 21 these except Michael, your **p**,

PRINCES → PRINCE
Dn 8: 25 he rises against the Prince of **p**,

PRISCILLA
Wife of Aquila, also called Prisca; co-worker with Paul (Acts 18; Rom 16:3; 1 Cor 16:19; 2 Tm 4:19); instructor of Apollos (Acts 18:24-28).

PRISON → PRISONER, PRISONERS
Mt 14: 10 and he had John beheaded in the **p**.
Acts 12: 5 Peter thus was being kept in **p**,

PRISONER → PRISON
Mk 15: 6 to them one **p** whom they requested.
Eph 3: 1 I, Paul, a **p** of Christ [Jesus] for you

PRISONERS → PRISON
Ps 146: 7 The LORD sets **p** free;
Is 61: 1 to the captives, release to the **p**,

PRIZE
1 Cor 9: 24 in the race, but only one wins the **p**?
Phil 3: 14 goal, the **p** of God's upward calling,

PROCLAIM
Ps 97: 6 The heavens **p** his justice;
Mt 10: 27 hear whispered, **p** on the housetops.
Mk 16: 15 and **p** the gospel to every creature.
Lk 4: 19 to **p** a year acceptable to the Lord."

PRODUCE → PRODUCES
Jos 5: 11 they ate of the **p** of the land
Prv 3: 9 wealth, with first fruits of all your **p**;

PRODUCES → PRODUCE
2 Cor 7: 10 For godly sorrow **p** a salutary
7: 10 regret, but worldly sorrow **p** death.
Jas 1: 3 testing of your faith **p** perseverance.

PROFANE
Lv 22: 32 Do not **p** my holy name,
1 Mc 1: 45 to **p** the sabbaths and feast days,

PROFIT
Sir 29: 11 that will **p** you more than the gold.
Mt 16: 26 What **p** would there be for one

PROMISE → PROMISED, PROMISES
Acts 2: 39 For the **p** is made to you and to your
Eph 2: 12 and strangers to the covenants of **p**,
1 Tm 4: 8 since it holds a **p** of life both
2 Pt 3: 9 The Lord does not delay his **p**,

PROMISED → PROMISE
Dt 1: 11 times over, and bless you as he **p**!
Eph 1: 13 were sealed with the **p** holy Spirit,

PROMISES → PROMISE
Ps 12: 7 The **p** of the LORD are sure,
2 Cor 1: 20 For however many are the **p** of God,
Heb 8: 6 better covenant, enacted on better **p**.

PROOFS
Acts 1: 3 by many **p** after he had suffered,

PROPHECIES → PROPHESY
1 Cor 13: 8 If there are **p**, they will be brought

PROPHECY → PROPHESY
Acts 21: 9 four virgin daughters gifted with **p**.
1 Cor 12: 10 to another **p**; to another discernment
2 Pt 1: 20 that there is no **p** of scripture that is

PROPHESY → PROPHECIES, PROPHECY, PROPHET, PROPHETS
Mt 7: 22 Lord, did we not **p** in your name?
1 Cor 13: 9 know partially and we **p** partially,

Rev 11: 3 commission my two witnesses to **p**

PROPHET → PROPHESY
Ex 7: 1 Aaron your brother will be your **p**.
Dt 18: 18 for them a **p** like you from among
18: 18 my words into the mouth of the **p**;
1 Mc 4: 46 of a **p** who could determine what
Lk 4: 24 no **p** is accepted in his own native
20: 6 are convinced that John was a **p**."
Rev 16: 13 and from the mouth of the false **p**.
20: 10 the beast and the false **p** were.

PROPHETS → PROPHESY
Nm 11: 29 the people of the LORD were **p**!
1 Kgs 18: 40 said to them, "Seize the **p** of Baal.
1 Mc 9: 27 had not been since the time **p** ceased
Ps 105: 15 ones, to my **p** do no harm."
Mt 5: 17 come to abolish the law or the **p**.
22: 40 law and the **p** depend on these two
Lk 24: 44 and in the **p** and psalms must be
1 Cor 12: 28 second, **p**; third, teachers;
Eph 2: 20 the foundation of the apostles and **p**,
4: 11 others as **p**, others as evangelists,
Rev 11: 10 because these two **p** tormented
18: 20 you holy ones, apostles, and **p**.

PROSPERITY → PROSPERS
Ps 73: 3 when I saw the **p** of the wicked.

PROSPERS → PROSPERITY
Ps 1: 3 whatever he does **p**.

PROSTITUTE → PROSTITUTES
1 Cor 6: 15 and make them the members of a **p**?

PROSTITUTES → PROSTITUTE
Mt 21: 31 **p** are entering the kingdom of God
1 Cor 6: 9 adulterers nor boy **p** nor sodomites

PROTECTION → PROTECTS
Eccl 7: 12 For the **p** of wisdom is as the **p** of money;

PROTECTS → PROTECTION
Ps 116: 6 The LORD **p** the simple;

PROUD → PRIDE
Ps 94: 2 give the **p** what they deserve!
Prv 21: 4 Haughty eyes and a **p** heart—
Sir 10: 9 Why are dust and ashes **p**?
Jas 4: 6 "God resists the **p**, but gives grace

PROVERBS
Prv 1: 1 The **p** of Solomon, the son
Eccl 12: 9 scrutinized and arranged many **p**.

PROVIDE → PROVIDES
Gn 22: 8 "God will **p** the sheep for the burnt
1 Cor 10: 13 the trial he will also **p** a way out,

PROVIDES → PROVIDE
1 Tm 6: 17 who richly **p** us with all things

PROVOKE → PROVOKED
Dt 32: 21 with a foolish nation I will **p** them.
Jer 25: 6 do not **p** me with the works of your

PROVOKED → PROVOKE
Ps 78: 41 God, **p** the Holy One of Israel.

PRUNES
Jn 15: 2 does he **p** so that it bears more fruit.

PSALMS
Lk 24: 44 prophets and **p** must be fulfilled."
Eph 5: 19 addressing one another [in] **p**

PUBLIC
Col 2: 15 he made a **p** spectacle of them,

PUNISH → PUNISHMENT
Ex 32: 34 When it is time for me to **p**, I will **p**
Jer 21: 14 I will **p** you—

PUNISHMENT → PUNISH
Gn 4: 13 "My **p** is too great to bear.
Mt 25: 46 And these will go off to eternal **p**,
1 Jn 4: 18 fear because fear has to do with **p**,

PURE → PURIFICATION, PURIFIED, PURITY
Ps 19: 10 The fear of the LORD is **p**,
Hb 1: 13 Your eyes are too **p** to look
Phil 4: 8 whatever is **p**, whatever is lovely,
1 Jn 3: 3 hope based on him makes himself **p**, as he is **p**.

PURIFICATION → PURE
Heb 1: 3 he had accomplished **p** from sins,

PURIFIED → PURE
Dn 12: 10 Many shall be refined, **p**, and tested,
1 Pt 1: 22 Since you have **p** yourselves

PURIM
Est 9: 26 so these days have been named **P**

PURITY → PURE
2 Cor 6: 6 by **p**, knowledge, patience,

PURPLE
Ex 25: 4 violet, **p**, and scarlet yarn;
Mk 15: 17 They clothed him in **p** and,

PURPOSE
Rom 8: 28 who are called according to his **p**.
Eph 3: 11 the eternal **p** that he accomplished

PURSUE → PURSUED, PURSUES
Ps 34: 15 and do good; seek peace and **p** it.
Rom 14: 19 Let us then **p** what leads to peace
1 Tm 6: 11 Instead, **p** righteousness, devotion,

PURSUED → PURSUE
Ps 18: 38 I **p** my enemies and overtook them;

PURSUES → PURSUE
Prv 21: 21 Whoever **p** justice and kindness will
Sir 31: 5 whoever **p** money will be led astray

PUT
Is 42: 1 Upon him I have **p** my spirit;
Ez 36: 27 I will **p** my spirit within you so
Eph 6: 11 **P** on the armor of God so that you

Q

QUARRELED
Ex 17: 7 because the Israelites **q** there

QUEEN
1 Kgs 10: 1 The **q** of Sheba, having heard
Est 2: 17 and made her **q** in place of Vashti.
Mt 12: 42 the judgment the **q** of the south will
Rev 18: 7 said to herself, 'I sit enthroned as **q**;

QUESTIONS
2 Ch 9: 1 Jerusalem to test him with subtle **q**,
Mt 22: 46 anyone dare to ask him any more **q**.

QUICK → QUICKLY
Jas 1: 19 everyone should be **q** to hear,

QUICKLY → QUICK
Jn 13: 27 "What you are going to do, do **q**."
Rom 9: 28 **q** will the Lord execute sentence
Gal 1: 6 you are so **q** forsaking the one who

QUIET
1 Tm 2: 2 that we may lead a **q** and tranquil

QUIVER
Is 49: 2 sharpened arrow, in his **q** he hid me.

R

RABBI
Mt 23: 8 As for you, do not be called '**R**.'
Jn 1: 38 him, "**R**" (which translated means

RACE
Eccl 9: 11 under the sun that the **r** is not won
1 Cor 9: 24 in the stadium all run in the **r**,
Heb 12: 1 in running the **r** that lies before us
1 Pt 2: 9 But you are "a chosen **r**, a royal

RACHEL
Daughter of Laban (Gn 29:16); wife of Jacob (Gn 29:28); bore two sons (Gn 30:22-24; 35:16-24; 46:19). Stole Laban's gods (Gn 31:19, 32–35). Death (Gn 35:19-20).

RAHAB
Prostitute who hid Israelite spies (Jos 2; 6:22-25; Heb 11:31; Jas 2:25). Mother of Boaz (Mt 1:5).

RAIN → RAINED, RAINS
Gn 7: 4 now I will bring **r** down on the earth
1 Kgs 17: 1 be no dew or **r** except at my word."
Is 45: 8 like gentle **r** let the clouds drop it
Mt 5: 45 and causes **r** to fall on the just
Rev 11: 6 so that no **r** can fall during the time

RAINED → RAIN
Gn 19: 24 and the LORD **r** down sulfur
Ex 9: 23 the LORD **r** down hail

RAINS → RAIN
Jas 5: 7 it receives the early and the late **r**.

RAISE → RISE
Dt 18: 15 **r** up for you from among your own
2 Mc 7: 9 the King of the universe will **r** us
Jn 2: 19 and in three days I will **r** it up."
2 Cor 4: 14 who raised the Lord Jesus will **r** us

RAISED → RISE
Mt 17: 23 and he will be **r** on the third day."
Acts 2: 24 But God **r** him up, releasing him
Rom 4: 25 and was **r** for our justification.
1 Cor 15: 4 that he was **r** on the third day

RAM → RAMS
Gn 22: 13 saw a single **r** caught by its horns
22: 13 and took the **r** and offered it up as
Ex 29: 22 from this **r** you shall take its fat:
29: 22 since this is the **r** for installation;
Dn 8: 3 the river a **r** with two great horns,

RAMS → RAM
1 Sm 15: 22 to listen, better than the fat of **r**.

RANSOM → RANSOMED
Mt 20: 28 to give his life as a **r** for many."
1 Tm 2: 6 who gave himself as **r** for all.

RANSOMED → RANSOM
Is 35: 10 the **r** of the LORD shall return,

RAVENS
1 Kgs 17: 6 **R** brought him bread and meat
Lk 12: 24 Notice the **r**: they do not sow

READ → READING
Ex 24: 7 he **r** it aloud to the people,
Jos 8: 34 were **r** aloud all the words
Neh 8: 8 Ezra **r** clearly from the book
8: 8 all could understand what was **r**.
Lk 4: 16 on the sabbath day. He stood up to **r**
2 Cor 3: 15 whenever Moses is **r**, a veil lies

READING → READ
Acts 8: 30 and heard him **r** Isaiah the prophet
8: 30 you understand what you are **r**?"

READY
Rev 19: 7 come, his bride has made herself **r**.

REAP
Gal 6: 7 a person will **r** only what he sows,
Rev 14: 15 "Use your sickle and **r** the harvest,
14: 15 for the time to **r** has come,

REBEKAH
Sister of Laban, secured as bride for Isaac (Gn 24). Mother of Esau and Jacob (Gn 25:19-26). Taken by Abimelech as sister of Isaac; returned (Gn 26:1-11). Encouraged Jacob to trick Isaac out of blessing (Gn 27:1-17).

REBEL → REBELLED, REBELLION
Ex 23: 21 Do not **r** against him, for he will not
1 Sm 12: 14 and do not **r** against the LORD's

REBELLED → REBEL
Nm 20: 24 because you both **r** against my

REBELLION → REBEL
1 Sm 15: 23 For a sin of divination is **r**,

REBUILD → BUILD
Neh 2: 17 let us **r** the wall of Jerusalem,
Acts 15: 16 return and **r** the fallen hut of David;
15: 16 from its ruins I shall **r** it and raise it

REBUKE
Prv 27: 5 Better is an open **r** than a love
Zec 3: 2 "May the LORD **r** you,
Mk 8: 32 took him aside and began to **r** him.

RECEIVE → RECEIVED
Jn 3: 27 said, "No one can **r** anything except
16: 24 ask and you will **r**, so that your joy
20: 22 and said to them, "**R** the holy Spirit.
Acts 2: 38 you will **r** the gift of the holy Spirit.
20: 35 more blessed to give than to **r**.' "
1 Cor 4: 7 you boasting as if you did not **r** it?
Rev 4: 11 to **r** glory and honor and power,

RECEIVED → RECEIVE
Mt 6: 2 say to you, they have **r** their reward.
1 Cor 11: 23 For I **r** from the Lord what I

RECONCILE → RECONCILED, RECONCILIATION
Acts 7: 26 and tried to **r** them peacefully,
Col 1: 20 through him to **r** all things for him,

RECONCILED → RECONCILE
Mt 5: 24 go first and be **r** with your brother,
1 Cor 7: 11 single or become **r** to her husband—

RECONCILIATION → RECONCILE
Rom 5: 11 whom we have now received **r**.
2 Cor 5: 18 and given us the ministry of **r**,

RED
Ex 15: 4 officers were drowned in the **R** Sea.
Mt 16: 3 for the sky is **r** and threatening.'
Rev 12: 3 it was a huge **r** dragon, with seven

REDEEMED → REDEMPTION
2 Sm 7: 23 whom you **r** for yourself
Ps 107: 2 that be the prayer of the LORD's **r**,

REDEEMER → REDEMPTION
Ps 19: 15 you, LORD, my rock and my **r**.
Is 48: 17 your **r**, the Holy One of Israel:

REDEMPTION → REDEEMED, REDEEMER
Lk 21: 28 raise your heads because your **r** is

Rom 3: 24 by his grace through the **r** in Christ
Eph 1: 7 In him we have **r** by his blood,
Heb 9: 12 own blood, thus obtaining eternal **r**.

REFINE → REFINED
Zec 13: 9 I will **r** them as one refines silver,

REFINED → REFINE
Dn 12: 10 Many shall be **r**, purified,

REFUGE
Prv 30: 5 a shield to those who take **r** in him.
Jer 16: 19 fortress, my **r** in the day of distress!

REGARD
Phil 2: 6 of God, did not **r** equality with God

REGRET
Nm 23: 19 nor a mortal, who feels **r**. Is God

REGULATIONS
Col 2: 20 why do you submit to **r** as if you
Heb 9: 10 **r** concerning the flesh,

REHOBOAM
Son of Solomon (1 Kgs 11:43; 1 Ch 3:10). Harsh treatment of subjects caused divided kingdom (1 Kgs 12:1-24; 14:21-31; 2 Ch 10–12).

REIGN
Ex 15: 18 May the LORD **r** forever and ever!
Ps 146: 10 The LORD shall **r** forever,
1 Cor 15: 25 For he must **r** until he has put all his
2 Tm 2: 12 persevere we shall also **r** with him.
Rev 11: 15 and he will **r** forever and ever."
22: 5 and they shall **r** forever and ever.

REJECT → REJECTED
Is 30: 12 Because you **r** this word, And put

REJECTED → REJECT
Ps 60: 3 O God, you **r** us, broke our
118: 22 stone the builders **r** has become
Mt 21: 42 that the builders **r** has become
1 Pt 2: 4 **r** by human beings but chosen

REJOICE → REJOICING
Ps 118: 24 let us **r** in it and be glad.
Is 62: 5 his bride so shall your God **r** in you.
Zep 3: 17 Who will **r** over you with gladness,
Lk 6: 23 **R** and leap for joy on that day!
Phil 4: 4 **R** in the Lord always. I shall say it again: **r**!

REJOICING → REJOICE
2 Cor 6: 10 as sorrowful yet always **r**;

RELEASE
Is 61: 1 to the captives, **r** to the prisoners,
Mt 27: 15 the governor was accustomed to **r**

RELENT
Jl 2: 14 Perhaps he will again **r** and leave

RELIGION
Jas 1: 27 **R** that is pure and undefiled before

RELY
Prv 3: 5 on your own intelligence do not **r**;
Sir 5: 1 Do not **r** on your wealth, or say,

REMAIN → REMAINS
1 Cor 7: 20 Everyone should **r** in the state
Heb 1: 11 They will perish, but you **r**;

REMAINS → REMAIN
Heb 7: 3 Son of God, he **r** a priest forever.
10: 26 there no longer **r** sacrifice for sins

REMEMBER → REMEMBERED, REMEMBERS
Ex 20: 8 **R** the sabbath day—keep it holy.
Dt 8: 18 **R** then the LORD, your God,
Jb 10: 9 **r** that you fashioned me from clay!
Eccl 12: 1 **R** your Creator in the days of your
Jer 31: 34 iniquity and no longer **r** their sin.
2 Tm 2: 8 **R** Jesus Christ, raised from the dead,
Heb 8: 12 evildoing and **r** their sins no more."

REMEMBERED → REMEMBER
Ps 78: 35 They **r** that God was their rock,
106: 45 For their sake he **r** his covenant
Rev 16: 19 But God **r** great Babylon, giving it

REMEMBERS → REMEMBER
Ps 111: 5 fear him, he **r** his covenant forever.

REMNANT
Gn 45: 7 of you to ensure for you a **r** on earth
Is 10: 21 A **r** will return, the **r** of Jacob,
Jer 50: 20 for I will forgive the **r** I preserve.
Rom 9: 27 of the sea, only a **r** will be saved;

RENEW → RENEWED
Is 40: 31 in the LORD will **r** their strength,

RENEWED → RENEW
2 Cor 4: 16 our inner self is being **r** day by day.
Eph 4: 23 and be **r** in the spirit of your minds,

REPARATION
Lv 5: 15 to the sanctuary shekel, as a **r** offering.

REPAY → PAY
Ps 28: 4 **R** them for their deeds, for the evil
Rom 12: 17 Do not **r** anyone evil for evil;

REPENT → REPENTANCE
Jb 42: 6 I have said, and **r** in dust and ashes.
Jon 3: 9 God may again **r** and turn from his blazing
Mt 3: 2 [and] saying, "**R**, for the kingdom
Acts 2: 38 [said] to them, "**R** and be baptized,
Rev 16: 9 but they did not **r** or give him glory.

REPENTANCE → REPENT
Mk 1: 4 desert proclaiming a baptism of **r**
Lk 3: 8 good fruits as evidence of your **r**;
Rom 2: 4 of God would lead you to **r**?
2 Cor 7: 10 produces a salutary **r** without regret,
2 Pt 3: 9 perish but that all should come to **r**.

REPROVE
Rev 3: 19 Those whom I love, I **r** and chastise.

RESCUE → RESCUED, RESCUES
Ps 22: 9 if he loves him, let him **r** him."
2 Pt 2: 9 the Lord knows how to **r** the devout

RESCUED → RESCUE
Prv 11: 8 The just are **r** from a tight spot,

RESCUES → RESCUE
Ps 37: 40 The LORD helps and **r** them,

RESIST
Jas 4: 7 **R** the devil, and he will flee

RESPECT
Rom 13: 7 toll is due, **r** to whom **r** is due,

REST → RESTED
Ex 31: 15 day is the sabbath of complete **r**,
2 Sm 7: 11 I will give you **r** from all your
Ps 95: 11 "They shall never enter my **r**."
Mt 11: 28 are burdened, and I will give you **r**.
Heb 4: 10 And whoever enters into God's **r**,

RESTED → REST
Gn 2: 2 he **r** on the seventh day from all
Ex 20: 11 but on the seventh day he **r**.

RESTORE
Ps 51: 14 **R** to me the gladness of your
Mt 17: 11 will indeed come and **r** all things;

RESURRECTION
Mt 22: 30 At the **r** they neither marry nor are
Mk 12: 18 who say there is no **r**, came to him
Jn 11: 25 told her, "I am the **r** and the life;
1 Cor 15: 12 some among you say there is no **r**
Phil 3: 10 the power of his **r** and [the] sharing
Rev 20: 5 years were over. This is the first **r**.

RETAIN
Jn 20: 23 and whose sins you **r** are retained."

RETURN
Gn 3: 19 eat bread, Until you **r** to the ground,
3: 19 you are dust, and to dust you shall **r**.
Dt 30: 2 and **r** to the LORD, your God,
Mal 3: 7 **R** to me, that I may **r** to you,

REUBEN

Firstborn of Jacob by Leah (Gn 29:32; 46:8; 1 Ch 2:1). Attempted to rescue Joseph (Gn 37:21-30). Lost birthright for sleeping with Bilhah (Gn 35:22; 49:4). Tribe of blessed (Gn 49:3-4; Dt 33:6), numbered (Nm 1:21; 26:7), allotted land east of Jordan (Nm 32; 34:14; Jos 13:15), west (Ez 48:6), failed to help Deborah (Jgs 5:15-16), supported David (1 Ch 12:37), 12,000 from (Rev 7:5).

REVEAL → REVEALED, REVELATION, REVELATIONS
Mt 11: 27 to whom the Son wishes to **r** him.

REVEALED → REVEAL
Is 40: 5 the glory of the LORD shall be **r**,
Mt 16: 17 and blood has not **r** this to you,
Lk 17: 30 be on the day the Son of Man is **r**.
Rom 1: 17 in it is **r** the righteousness of God
1 Jn 3: 2 what we shall be has not yet been **r**.
3: 2 when it is **r** we shall be like him,

REVELATION → REVEAL
1 Cor 14: 6 if I do not speak to you by way of **r**,
Eph 3: 3 was made known to me by **r**, as I
Rev 1: 1 The **r** of Jesus Christ, which God

REVELATIONS → REVEAL
2 Cor 12: 1 go on to visions and **r** of the Lord.

REVERENCE
Eph 5: 21 to one another out of **r** for Christ.

REWARD → REWARDED, REWARDS
Ps 19: 12 obeying them brings much **r**.
Is 40: 10 Here is his **r** with him,
Mt 6: 5 to you, they have received their **r**.
Lk 6: 23 your **r** will be great in heaven.

REWARDED → REWARD
2 Sm 22: 21 **r** my clean hands.

REWARDS → REWARD
Heb 11: 6 and that he **r** those who seek him.

RIB
Gn 2: 22 built the **r** that he had taken

RICH → RICHES
Mt 19: 23 one who is **r** to enter the kingdom
Lk 12: 21 is not **r** in what matters to God."
2 Cor 8: 9 he became poor although he was **r**,
8: 9 by his poverty you might become **r**.
Eph 2: 4 But God, who is **r** in mercy,
1 Tm 6: 18 good, to be **r** in good works, to be
Jas 1: 10 and the **r** one in his lowliness, for he

RICHES → RICH
Prv 30: 8 me, give me neither poverty nor **r**;
Lk 8: 14 are choked by the anxieties and **r**
Rom 11: 33 the depth of the **r** and wisdom

RID
1 Pt 2: 1 **R** yourselves of all malice and all

RIDER → RIDES, RIDING
Rev 19: 11 its **r** was [called] "Faithful

RIDES → RIDER
Dt 33: 26 who **r** the heavens in his power,
33: 26 who **r** the clouds in his majesty;

RIDING → RIDER
Zec 9: 9 and **r** on a donkey, on a colt,

RIGHT → BIRTHRIGHT
Ex 15: 6 magnificent in power, your **r** hand,
Dt 6: 18 Do what is **r** and good in the sight
Jb 4: 17 anyone be more in the **r** than God?
Ps 110: 1 "Sit at my **r** hand, while I make
Prv 14: 12 Sometimes a way seems **r**,
Mt 25: 33 He will place the sheep on his **r**
Acts 2: 34 said to my Lord, "Sit at my **r** hand
Heb 1: 13 "Sit at my **r** hand until I make your

RIGHTEOUS → RIGHTEOUSNESS
Jer 23: 5 I will raise up a **r** branch for David;
Mk 2: 17 I did not come to call the **r**
Rom 1: 17 "The one who is **r** by faith will
5: 19 of one the many will be made **r**.
1 Jn 2: 1 the Father, Jesus Christ the **r** one.
Rev 19: 8 (The linen represents the **r** deeds

RIGHTEOUSNESS → RIGHTEOUS
Gn 15: 6 attributed it to him as an act of **r**.
Mt 5: 6 are they who hunger and thirst for **r**,
Jn 16: 8 the world in regard to sin and **r**
Rom 3: 22 the **r** of God through faith in Jesus
Gal 3: 6 and it was credited to him as **r**."
Eph 6: 14 truth, clothed with **r** as a breastplate,
1 Pt 2: 24 free from sin, we might live for **r**.
2 Pt 3: 13 and a new earth in which **r** dwells.
Rev 19: 11 He judges and wages war in **r**.

RIPE
Jn 4: 35 and see the fields **r** for the harvest.
Rev 14: 15 the earth's harvest is fully **r**."

RISE → ARISE, RAISE, RAISED, ROSE
Nm 24: 17 and a scepter shall **r** from Israel,
2 Mc 12: 44 not expecting the fallen to **r** again,
Ps 94: 2 **R** up, O judge of the earth;
Dn 12: 13 you shall **r** for your reward
1 Thes 4: 16 and the dead in Christ will **r** first.

RIVER → RIVERS
Ps 46: 5 Streams of the **r** gladden the city
Is 48: 18 your peace would be like a **r**,
Ez 47: 12 Along each bank of the **r** every kind
Mt 3: 6 the Jordan **R** as they acknowledged
Rev 22: 1 Then the angel showed me the **r**

RIVERS → RIVER
Ps 137: 1 By the **r** of Babylon there we sat
Rev 8: 10 It fell on a third of the **r**

ROAD → CROSSROADS
Mt 7: 13 the **r** broad that leads to destruction,

ROARING → ROARS
1 Pt 5: 8 around like a **r** lion looking

ROARS → ROARING
Hos 11:10 the LORD, who **r** like a lion;
11:10 When he **r**, his children shall come
Jer 25:30 The LORD **r** from on high,
25:30 Mightily he **r** over his sheepfold,

ROB → ROBBER
Mal 3: 8 Can anyone **r** God? But you are
3: 9 for you, the whole nation, **r** me.

ROBBER → ROB
1 Cor 5:11 or a **r**, not even to eat with such

ROBE → ROBED, ROBES
Ex 28: 4 an ephod, a **r**, a brocade tunic,
Lk 15:22 'Quickly bring the finest **r** and put it
Rev 6:11 Each of them was given a white **r**,

ROBED → ROBE
Ps 93: 1 The LORD is king, **r** with majesty;
93: 1 the LORD is **r**, girded with might.

ROBES → ROBE
Mk 12:38 who like to go around in long **r**
Rev 22:14 are they who wash their **r** so as

ROCK
Ex 17: 6 Strike the **r**, and the water will flow
Nm 20: 8 forth water from the **r** for them,
1 Sm 2: 2 there is no **R** like our God.
Ps 19:15 LORD, my **r** and my redeemer.
Is 44: 8 There is no other **R**, I know of none!
Mt 16:18 upon this **r** I will build my church,
Mk 15:46 that had been hewn out of the **r**.
1 Pt 2: 8 and a **r** that will make them fall."

ROD
2 Sm 7:14 I will reprove him with a human **r**
Ps 2: 9 an iron **r** you will shepherd them,
23: 4 your **r** and your staff comfort me.
Prv 13:24 Whoever spares the **r** hates
Rev 2:27 He will rule them with an iron **r**.

ROLL
Mk 16: 3 "Who will **r** back the stone for us

ROOF
Jos 2: 6 Now, she had led them to the **r**,
2 Sm 11: 2 the **r** he saw a woman bathing;
Mk 2: 4 they opened up the **r** above him.

ROOM
Mk 14:15 show you a large upper **r** furnished
Rom 12:19 revenge but leave **r** for the wrath;
Eph 4:27 and do not leave **r** for the devil.

ROOT → ROOTED
Is 11:10 On that day, The **r** of Jesse,
Rom 11:16 and if the **r** is holy, so are
15:12 "The **r** of Jesse shall come,
1 Tm 6:10 love of money is the **r** of all evils,
Rev 5: 5 of the tribe of Judah, the **r** of David,

ROOTED → ROOT
Eph 3:17 that you, **r** and grounded in love,

ROSE → RISE
1 Thes 4:14 if we believe that Jesus died and **r**,

ROUGH
Is 40: 4 land shall be a plain, the **r** country,
Lk 3: 5 and the **r** ways made smooth,

ROYAL
Jas 2: 8 you fulfill the **r** law according
1 Pt 2: 9 are "a chosen race, a **r** priesthood,

RUBBISH
1 Cor 4:13 We have become like the world's **r**,
Phil 3: 8 and I consider them so much **r**,

RUINS
Ezr 9: 9 house of our God and restore its **r**,
Neh 2:17 how Jerusalem lies in **r** and its gates
Acts 15:16 from its **r** I shall rebuild it and raise

RULE → RULER, RULERS, RULES
Rev 19:15 He will **r** them with an iron rod,

RULER → RULE
Ex 2:14 "Who has appointed you **r**
Wis 8: 3 with God; even the **R** of all loved her.
Mt 2: 6 since from you shall come a **r**,
Rev 1: 5 dead and **r** of the kings of the earth.

RULERS → RULE
Is 40:23 makes the **r** of the earth as nothing.
Eph 6:12 the world **r** of this present darkness,

RULES → RULE
Ps 66: 7 who **r** by his might forever,
Is 40:10 GOD, who **r** by his strong arm;
2 Tm 2: 5 by competing according to the **r**.

RUN → FORERUNNER, RUNNERS
Is 40:31 They will **r** and not grow weary,
Gal 2: 2 not be running, or have **r**, in vain.

RUNNERS → RUN
1 Cor 9:24 that the **r** in the stadium all run

RUTH
Moabitess; widow who went to Bethlehem with mother-in-law Naomi (Ru 1). Gleaned in field of Boaz; shown favor (Ru 2). Proposed marriage to Boaz (Ru 3). Married (Ru 4:1-12); bore Obed, ancestor of David (Ru 4:13-22), Jesus (Mt 1:5).

S

SABBATH
Ex 20: 8 Remember the **s** day—keep it holy.
1 Mc 1:43 to idols and profaned the **s**.
Mt 12: 1 through a field of grain on the **s**.
Mk 2:28 Son of Man is lord even of the **s**."

SACKCLOTH
Dn 9: 3 petition, with fasting, **s**, and ashes.
Mt 11:21 would long ago have repented in **s**

SACRED
Ex 28: 2 you shall have **s** vestments made.
34:13 smash their **s** stones, and cut down

SACRIFICE → SACRIFICED, SACRIFICES
Ex 12:27 'It is the Passover **s** for the LORD,
1 Sm 15:22 Obedience is better than **s**, to listen,
Ps 40: 7 **S** and offering you do not want;
Prv 15: 8 The **s** of the wicked is
Dn 9:27 Half the week he shall abolish **s**
Hos 6: 6 not **s**, and knowledge of God rather
Mt 9:13 of the words, 'I desire mercy, not **s**.'
Phil 4:18 an acceptable **s**, pleasing to God.
Heb 13:15 let us continually offer God a **s**

SACRIFICED → SACRIFICE
1 Cor 5: 7 paschal lamb, Christ, has been **s**.
8: 1 Now in regard to meat **s** to idols:

SACRIFICES → SACRIFICE
Mk 12:33 than all burnt offerings and **s**."

SADDUCEES
Mt 16: 6 the leaven of the Pharisees and **S**."
Mk 12:18 Some **S**, who say there is no

SAFE
Prv 18:10 the just run to it and are s.

SALT
Gn 19:26 and she was turned into a pillar of s.
Mt 5:13 "You are the s of the earth. But if s

SALVATION → SAVE
Ps 27:1 The LORD is my light and my s;
51:14 to me the gladness of your s;
Is 12:3 draw water from the fountains of s,
52:7 news, announcing s, saying to Zion,
Lk 3:6 all flesh shall see the s of God.' "
Acts 4:12 There is no s through anyone else,
2 Cor 6:2 and on the day of s I helped you."
6:2 behold, now is the day of s.
Phil 2:12 work out your s with fear
Heb 2:3 we escape if we ignore so great a s?
2 Pt 3:15 the patience of our Lord as s, as our
Rev 19:1 S, glory, and might belong to our

SAMARIA → SAMARITAN
1 Kgs 16:24 then bought the mountain of S
16:24 the mountain the city he named S,
2 Kgs 17:6 the king of Assyria took S,
Jn 4:4 He had to pass through S.
Acts 1:8 throughout Judea and S,

SAMARITAN → SAMARIA
Lk 10:33 But a S traveler who came upon him

SAME
Rom 10:12 the s Lord is Lord of all,
1 Cor 12:4 of spiritual gifts but the s Spirit;
Heb 13:8 Jesus Christ is the s yesterday,

SAMSON
Danite judge. Birth promised (Jgs 13). Married a Philistine, but his wife given away (Jgs 14). Vengeance on the Philistines (Jgs 15). Betrayed by Delilah (Jgs 16:1-22). Death (Jgs 16:23-31). Feats of strength: killed lion (Jgs 14:6), 30 Philistines (Jgs 14:19), 1,000 Philistines with jawbone (Jgs 15:13-17), carried off gates of Gaza (Jgs 16:3), pushed down temple of Dagon (Jgs 16:25-30; Heb 11:32).

SAMUEL
Ephraimite judge and prophet (Heb 11:32). Birth prayed for (1 Sm 1:10-18). Dedicated to temple by Hannah (1 Sm 1:21-28). Raised by Eli (1 Sm 2:11, 18-26). Called as prophet (1 Sm 3). Led Israel to victory over Philistines (1 Sm 7). Asked by Israel for a king (1 Sm 8). Anointed Saul as king (1 Sm 9–10). Farewell speech (1 Sm 12). Rebuked Saul for sacrifice (1 Sm 13). Announced rejection of Saul (1 Sm 15). Anointed David as king (1 Sm 16). Protected David from Saul (1 Sm 19:18-24). Death (1 Sm 25:1). Returned from dead to condemn Saul (1 Sm 28).

SANCTIFICATION → SANCTIFIED
Rom 6:19 as slaves to righteousness for s.

SANCTIFIED → SANCTIFICATION
1 Cor 6:11 you were s, you were justified

SANCTUARY
Ex 25:8 They are to make a s for me, that I
1 Ch 22:19 to build the s of the LORD God,
1 Mc 1:21 He insolently entered the s and took
4:36 let us go up to purify the s
Ez 37:26 and put my s among them forever.
Dn 9:26 shall destroy the city and the s.
Heb 9:24 Christ did not enter into a s made

SAND
Mt 7:26 like a fool who built his house on s.

SANDALS
Ex 3:5 Remove your s from your feet,
Mt 3:11 I am not worthy to carry his s.

SARAH
1. Wife of Abraham, originally named Sarai; barren (Gn 11:29-31; 1 Pt 3:6). Taken by Pharaoh as Abraham's sister; returned (Gn 12:10-20). Gave Hagar to Abraham; sent her away in pregnancy (Gn 16). Name changed; Isaac promised (Gn 17:15-21; 18:10-15; Heb 11:11). Taken by Abimelech as Abraham's sister; returned (Gn 20). Isaac born; Hagar and Ishmael sent away (Gn 21:1-21; Gal 4:21-31). Death (Gn 23).
2. Daughter of Raguel, wife of Tobias (Tb 3; 6–8; 10–12).

SATAN
1 Ch 21:1 A s rose up against Israel, and he
Jb 1:6 the s also came among them.
Mt 4:10 Jesus said to him, "Get away, S!
12:26 And if S drives out S, he is divided
16:23 said to Peter, "Get behind me, S!
2 Cor 11:14 for even S masquerades as an angel
Rev 12:9 who is called the Devil and S,
20:7 S will be released from his prison.

SATISFY
Is 55:2 your wages for what does not s?

SAUL → =PAUL
1. Benjamite; anointed by Samuel as first king of Israel (1 Sm 9–10). Defeated Ammonites (1 Sm 11). Rebuked for offering sacrifice (1 Sm 13:1-15). Defeated Philistines (1 Sm 14). Rejected as king for failing to annihilate Amalekites (1 Sm 15). Soothed from evil spirit by David (1 Sm 16:14-23). Sent David against Goliath (1 Sm 17). Jealousy and attempted murder of David (1 Sm 18:1-11). Gave David Michal as wife (1 Sm 18:12-30). Second attempt to kill David (1 Sm 19). Anger at Jonathan (1 Sm 20:26-34). Pursued David: killed priests at Nob (1 Sm 22), went to Keilah and Ziph (1 Sm 23), life spared by David at En Gedi (1 Sm 24) and in his tent (1 Sm 26). Rebuked by Samuel's spirit for consulting witch at Endor (1 Sm 28). Wounded by Philistines; took his own life (1 Sm 31; 1 Ch 10). Lamented by David (2 Sm 1:17-27). Children (1 Sm 14:49-51; 1 Ch 8).
2. See Paul.

SAVE → SALVATION, SAVED, SAVIOR
Ps 54:3 O God, by your name s me.
Is 59:1 of the LORD is not too short to s,
Mt 1:21 because he will s his people
16:25 wishes to s his life will lose it,
Lk 19:10 to seek and to s what was lost."
Heb 7:25 s those who approach God through

SAVED → SAVE
Mt 10:22 endures to the end will be s.
Mk 15:31 themselves and said, "He s others;
Lk 13:23 will only a few people be s?"
Acts 2:21 everyone shall be s who calls
16:30 "Sirs, what must I do to be s?"
Rom 10:13 on the name of the Lord will be s."
Eph 2:8 grace you have been s through faith,

SAVIOR → SAVE
Is 49:26 LORD, am your s, your redeemer,
Hos 13:4 do not know; there is no s but me.
Lk 2:11 the city of David a s has been born
Acts 13:23 has brought to Israel a s, Jesus.
1 Tm 4:10 the living God, who is the s of all,
Ti 2:13 great God and of our s Jesus Christ,
2 Pt 3:18 of our Lord and s Jesus Christ.

SCARLET
Is 1:18 Though your sins be like s,
Mt 27:28 threw a s military cloak about him.

SCATTER → SCATTERED
Dt 4:27 The LORD will s you among

SCATTERED → SCATTER
Dt 30: 3 the LORD, your God, has s you.
Jer 31: 10 The One who s Israel, now gathers

SCEPTER
Gn 49: 10 The s shall never depart from Judah,
Heb 1: 8 and a righteous s is the s of your

SCOFFERS
Ps 1: 1 sinners, nor sit in company with s.
2 Pt 3: 3 the last days s will come [to] scoff,

SCRIBES
Mt 7: 29 having authority, and not as their s.
23: 13 "Woe to you, s and Pharisees,

SCRIPTURE → SCRIPTURES
Lk 4: 21 "Today this s passage is fulfilled
Jn 10: 35 came, and s cannot be set aside,
2 Tm 3: 16 All s is inspired by God and is

SCRIPTURES → SCRIPTURE
Mt 22: 29 because you do not know the s
Lk 24: 45 their minds to understand the s.
Jn 5: 39 You search the s, because you think
1 Cor 15: 3 our sins in accordance with the s;

SCROLL
Lk 4: 17 and was handed a s of the prophet
4: 17 He unrolled the s and found
Rev 5: 2 "Who is worthy to open the s

SEA
Gn 1: 26 dominion over the fish of the s,
Ex 15: 1 and chariot he has cast into the s.
Dt 30: 13 "Who will cross the s to get it
Ps 95: 5 The s and dry land belong to God,
Mi 7: 19 into the depths of the s all our sins;
Rev 4: 6 resembled a s of glass like crystal.
13: 1 come out of the s with ten horns
21: 1 away, and the s was no more.

SEAL → SEALS
2 Cor 1: 22 he has also put his s upon us
Rev 7: 3 or the trees until we put the s
22: 10 "Do not s up the prophetic words

SEALS → SEAL
Rev 5: 2 to open the scroll and break its s?"

SEARCH → SEARCHES
Dt 4: 29 indeed find him if you s after him
1 Ch 28: 9 If you s for him, he will be found;

SEARCHES → SEARCH
Rom 8: 27 the one who s hearts knows what is

SEASON → SEASONS
Ps 1: 3 of water, that yields its fruit in s;

SEASONS → SEASON
Gal 4: 10 days, months, s, and years.
1 Thes 5: 1 Concerning times and s, brothers,

SEAT → SEATED
Rom 14: 10 shall all stand before the judgment s
2 Cor 5: 10 all appear before the judgment s

SEATED → SEAT
Lk 22: 69 of Man will be s at the right hand

SECOND → TWO
Mt 22: 39 The s is like it: You shall love your
Rev 20: 14 (This pool of fire is the s death.

SECURITY
1 Thes 5: 3 "Peace and s," then sudden disaster

SEE → SEEN, SIGHT
Ex 33: 20 But you cannot s my face, for no one can s me and live.
Ps 115: 5 but do not speak, eyes but do not s.
Jn 9: 25 is that I was blind and now I s."
1 Cor 13: 12 At present we s indistinctly,
1 Jn 3: 2 like him, for we shall s him as he is.
Rev 1: 7 and every eye will s him, even those

SEED → SEEDS
Mt 17: 20 have faith the size of a mustard s,
1 Pt 1: 23 perishable but from imperishable s,

SEEDS → SEED
Mk 4: 31 the smallest of all the s on the earth.

SEEK
Ps 34: 11 but those who s the LORD lack no
119: 10 With all my heart I s you; do not let
Is 55: 6 S the LORD while he may be
Sir 2: 16 Those who fear the Lord s to please
Lk 19: 10 For the Son of Man has come to s
Heb 11: 6 that he rewards those who s him.

SEEMS
Prv 16: 25 Sometimes a way s right,
Heb 12: 11 all discipline s a cause not for joy

SEEN → SEE
Jn 1: 18 No one has ever s God.
14: 9 Whoever has s me has s the Father.
20: 29 to believe because you have s me?
20: 29 Blessed are those who have not s
1 Pt 1: 8 you have not s him you love him;

SELF-CONTROL → SELF-CONTROLLED
1 Cor 7: 5 tempt you through your lack of s.
2 Pt 1: 6 knowledge with s, s with endurance,

SELF-CONTROLLED → SELF-CONTROL
Ti 1: 8 temperate, just, holy, and s,
2: 5 to be s, chaste, good homemakers,

SELFISH → SELFISHNESS
Phil 1: 17 proclaim Christ out of s ambition,
Jas 3: 14 and s ambition in your hearts,

SELFISHNESS → SELFISH
2 Cor 12: 20 jealousy, fury, s, slander, gossip,

SELL
Prv 23: 23 Buy truth and do not s:
Mk 10: 21 Go, s what you have, and give

SEND → SENT
Ex 33: 2 I will s an angel before you
Is 6: 8 the Lord saying, "Whom shall I s?
6: 8 "Here I am," I said; "s me!"
Jn 3: 17 God did not s his Son into the world
14: 26 that the Father will s in my name—

SENNACHERIB
Assyrian king; siege of Jerusalem was overthrown by the LORD following prayer of Hezekiah and Isaiah (2 Kgs 18:13–19:37; 2 Ch 32:1-21; Is 36–37).

SENT → SEND
Ex 3: 14 I AM has s me to you.
Lk 10: 16 me rejects the one who s me."
Jn 17: 18 As you s me into the world, so I s
20: 21 As the Father has s me, so I send
1 Jn 4: 10 s his Son as expiation for our sins.

SEPARATE → SEPARATED
Mt 19: 6 together, no human being must s."
Rom 8: 35 What will s us from the love
1 Cor 7: 10 A wife should not s from her

SEPARATED → SEPARATE
Heb 7:26 undefiled, s from sinners,

SERPENT → SERPENTS
Nm 21: 9 Accordingly Moses made a bronze s
21: 9 and whenever the s bit someone,
2 Cor 11: 3 that, as the s deceived Eve by his
Rev 20: 2 the ancient s, which is the Devil

SERPENTS → SERPENT
Mt 10:16 so be shrewd as s and simple as

SERVANT → SERVANTS
Ps 19:12 By them your s is warned;
Is 42: 1 Here is my s whom I uphold,
53:11 My s, the just one, shall justify
Zec 3: 8 I will surely bring my s the Branch.
Acts 3:13 has glorified his s Jesus whom you
Heb 3: 5 in all his house" as a "s" to testify

SERVANTS → SERVANT
2 Kgs 17:23 as he had declared through all his s,
Rev 7: 3 the foreheads of the s of our God."

SERVE
Ex 20: 5 not bow down before them or s them.
Jos 24:15 choose today whom you will s,
24:15 household, we will s the LORD."
Ps 100: 2 s the LORD with gladness;
Mt 6:24 "No one can s two masters.
6:24 You cannot s God and mammon.
Mk 10:45 to s and to give his life as a ransom
1 Pt 4:10 it to s one another as good stewards

SETH
Gn 4:25 birth to a son whom she called S.

SETTLE
Nm 33:53 possession of the land and s in it,

SEVEN → SEVENTH
Gn 7: 2 take with you s pairs, a male and its
Ex 25:37 You shall then make s lamps for it
Jos 6: 4 s priests carrying ram's horns ahead
6: 4 day march around the city s times,
Dn 9:25 ruler, there shall be s weeks.
Mt 18:22 say to you, not s times but s times.
Rev 1:12 I turned, I saw s gold lampstands
5: 1 sides and was sealed with s seals.
8: 2 the s angels who stood before God
8: 2 before God were given s trumpets.
12: 3 dragon, with s heads and ten horns,
12: 3 and on its heads were s diadems.
15: 1 s angels with the s last plagues,

SEVENTH → SEVEN
Gn 2: 2 the s day God completed the work
2: 2 he rested on the s day from all
Ex 20:10 the s day is a sabbath of the LORD
23:11 the s year you shall let the land lie
Heb 4: 4 God rested on the s day from all his

SEVENTY → SEVENTY-SEVEN
Gn 46:27 Egypt amounted to s persons in all.
2 Ch 36:21 have rest while s years are fulfilled.
Jer 25:12 but when the s years have elapsed,
Dn 9:24 "S weeks are decreed for your

SEVENTY-SEVEN → SEVENTY
Mt 18:22 to you, not seven times but s times.

SHADOW
2 Kgs 20:11 He made the s go back the ten steps
Ps 17: 8 hide me in the s of your wings

SHADRACH → =HANANIAH
Hebrew exiled to Babylon; name changed from Hananiah (Dn 1:6-7). Refused defilement by food (Dn 1:8-20). Refused to worship idol (Dn 3:1-18); saved from furnace (Dn 3:19-30).

SHALLUM
King of Israel (2 Kgs 15:10-16).

SHALMANESER
King of Assyria; conquered and deported Israel (2 Kgs 17:3-4; 18:9; Tb 1:2).

SHAME → ASHAMED, SHAMEFUL
1 Cor 1:27 foolish of the world to s the wise,
1:27 weak of the world to s the strong,
Heb 12: 2 despising its s, and has taken his
1 Jn 2:28 not be put to s by him at his coming.

SHAMEFUL → SHAME
2 Cor 4: 2 we have renounced s, hidden things;
Eph 5:12 for it is s even to mention the things

SHAMGAR
Judge; killed 600 Philistines (Jgs 3:31; 5:6).

SHARE
Lk 3:11 "Whoever has two tunics should s
Rom 15:27 the Gentiles have come to s in their
Col 1:12 who has made you fit to s
Heb 12:10 in order that we may s his holiness.

SHARP → SHARPENS, SHARPER
Prv 5: 4 as s as a two-edged sword.
Rev 19:15 his mouth came a s sword to strike

SHARPENS → SHARP
Prv 27:17 one person s another.

SHARPER → SHARP
Heb 4:12 s than any two-edged sword,

SHEBA
1. Benjamite; rebelled against David (2 Sm 20).
2. Queen of Sheba (1 Kgs 10; 2 Ch 9; Mt 12:42; Lk 11:31).

SHECHEM
1. Raped Jacob's daughter Dinah; killed (Gn 34).
2. City where Joshua renewed the covenant (Jos 24). Abimelech as king (Jgs 9).

SHED → BLOODSHED, SHEDDING
Gn 9: 6 being shall that one's blood be s;
Prv 6:17 tongue, hands that s innocent blood,
Mt 23:35 you all the righteous blood s
Rev 16: 6 For they have s the blood

SHEDDING → SHED
Heb 9:22 without the s of blood there is no
12: 4 yet resisted to the point of s blood.

SHEEP → SHEEPFOLD
1 Kgs 22:17 like s without a shepherd,
Is 53: 6 We had all gone astray like s,
Ez 34:15 I myself will pasture my s;
Zec 13: 7 that the s may be scattered;
Mt 9:36 like s without a shepherd.
Lk 15: 4 man among you having a hundred s
Jn 10: 7 I say to you, I am the gate for the s.
10:15 I will lay down my life for the s.
Heb 13:20 great shepherd of the s by the blood
1 Pt 2:25 For you had gone astray like s,

SHEEPFOLD → SHEEP
Jn 10: 1 does not enter a s through the gate

SHELTER
Ps 91: 1 dwell in the s of the Most High,
Rev 7:15 who sits on the throne will s them.

SHEM
Son of Noah (Gn 5:32; 6:10). Blessed (Gn 9:26). Descendants (Gn 10:21-31; 11:10-32; Lk 3:36).

SHEOL
Ps 139: 8 if I lie down in S, there you are.

SHEPHERD → SHEPHERDS
Ps 23: 1 The LORD is my s;
Is 40: 11 Like a s he feeds his flock;
Mt 2: 6 who is to s my people Israel.' "
26: 31 'I will strike the s, and the sheep
Jn 10: 11 I am the good s. A good s lays down
Heb 13: 20 the dead the great s of the sheep
1 Pt 5: 4 And when the chief S is revealed,

SHEPHERDS → SHEPHERD
Ez 34: 2 prophesy against the s of Israel.
34: 2 Should not s pasture the flock?
Lk 2: 8 Now there were s in that region

SHIELD → SHIELDS
Gn 15: 1 I am your s; I will make your
Ps 7: 11 God is a s above me saving
Eph 6: 16 hold faith as a s, to quench all

SHIELDS → SHIELD
Jdt 9: 14 no other who s the people of Israel

SHILOH
1 Sm 1: 24 at the house of the LORD in S.

SHIMEI
Cursed David (2 Sm 16:5-14); spared (2 Sm 19:16-23). Killed by Solomon (1 Kgs 2:8-9, 36-46).

SHINE → SHINES, SHINING
Nm 6: 25 The LORD let his face s upon you,
Is 60: 1 Arise! S, for your light has come,
Dn 12: 3 with insight shall s brightly like
Mt 5: 16 your light must s before others,

SHINES → SHINE
Jn 1: 5 the light s in the darkness,

SHINING → SHINE
2 Pt 1: 19 as to a lamp s in a dark place,
1 Jn 2: 8 away, and the true light is already s.

SHOFAR
Ex 19: 16 mountain, and a very loud blast of the s,

SHORT
Is 59: 1 of the LORD is not too s to save,

SHOUT
Ps 47: 2 s to God with joyful cries.
Zec 9: 9 S for joy, O daughter Jerusalem!

SHOW → SHOWED
Gn 12: 1 house to a land that I will s you.
Ps 85: 8 S us, LORD, your mercy;
Jn 14: 8 "Master, s us the Father,
1 Cor 12: 31 I shall s you a still more excellent
Rev 4: 1 and I will s you what must happen

SHOWED → SHOW
Dt 34: 1 and the LORD s him all the land—
Jn 20: 20 he s them his hands and his side.

SHUT
Is 22: 22 opens, no one will s, what he shuts,

SICK → SICKNESS
Mt 8: 16 spirits by a word and cured all the s,
9: 12 not need a physician, but the s do.
Jas 5: 14 Is anyone among you s?

SICKLE
Rev 14: 14 his head and a sharp s in his hand.

SICKNESS → SICK
Ex 23: 25 I will remove s from your midst;

SIDE → ASIDE
Ps 91: 7 Though a thousand fall at your s,
Jn 19: 34 soldier thrust his lance into his s,

SIFT
Lk 22: 31 behold Satan has demanded to s all

SIGHT → SEE
Ps 72: 14 for precious is their blood in his s.
Mt 11: 5 the blind regain their s, the lame
2 Cor 5: 7 for we walk by faith, not by s.
1 Pt 3: 4 which is precious in the s of God.

SIGN → SIGNS
Gn 9: 12 This is the s of the covenant that I
Is 7: 14 the Lord himself will give you a s;
Mt 24: 3 what s will there be of your coming,
Mk 8: 12 does this generation seek a s?
8: 12 say to you, no s will be given to this

SIGNS → SIGN
Ex 7: 3 despite the many s and wonders
Mt 16: 3 you cannot judge the s of the times.]
Jn 20: 30 Now Jesus did many other s
1 Cor 1: 22 For Jews demand s and Greeks look
Rev 16: 14 demonic spirits who performed s.

SILAS
Prophet (Acts 15:22-32); co-worker with Paul on second missionary journey (Acts 16–18; 2 Cor 1:19). Co-writer with Paul (1 Thes 1:1; 2 Thes 1:1); Peter (1 Pt 5:12).

SILENT
Is 53: 7 or a sheep s before shearers, he did
Mk 14: 61 But he was s and answered nothing.
1 Cor 14: 34 women should keep s

SILVER
Ps 66: 10 us, O God, tried us as s tried by fire.
Prv 8: 10 Take my instruction instead of s,
Is 48: 10 See, I refined you, but not like s;
Zec 13: 9 I will refine them as one refines s,
Mt 26: 15 They paid him thirty pieces of s,
Acts 3: 6 "I have neither s nor gold, but what
1 Cor 3: 12 on this foundation with gold, s,

SIMEON → =SIMON
1. Son of Jacob by Leah (Gn 29:33; 35:23; 1 Ch 2:1). With Levi killed Shechem for rape of Dinah (Gn 34:25-29). Held hostage by Joseph in Egypt (Gn 42:24–43:23). Tribe of blessed (Gn 49:5-7), numbered (Nm 1:23; 26:14), allotted land (Jos 19:1-9; Ez 48:24), 12,000 from (Rev 7:7).
2. Godly Jew who blessed the infant Jesus (2:25-35).
3. See Peter (Acts 15:14; 2 Pt 1:1).

SIMON → =PETER, =SIMEON
1. See Peter.
2. Apostle; the Zealot (Mt 10:4; Mk 3:18; Lk 6:15; Acts 1:13).
3. Samaritan sorcerer (Acts 8:9-24).

SIMPLE
Ps 19: 8 trustworthy, giving wisdom to the s.

SIN → SINFUL, SINNED, SINNER, SINNERS, SINS
Gn 4: 7 but if not, s lies in wait at the door:
Ex 32: 32 if you would only forgive their s!
Nm 32: 23 of your s will overtake you.
1 Kgs 8: 46 "When they s against you (for there is no one who does not s),
Tb 12: 10 those who commit s and do evil are
Ps 119: 11 that I may not s against you.

Wis 10:13 was sold, but rescued him from s.
Dn 9:20 confessing my s and the s of my
Mt 5:29 If your right eye causes you to s,
Jn 1:29 who takes away the s of the world.
Rom 5:12 as through one person s entered the world, and through s, death,
6:23 For the wages of s is death,
2 Cor 5:21 him to be s who did not know s,
Heb 4:15 tested in every way, yet without s.
1 Jn 1:7 his Son Jesus cleanses us from all s.

SINAI → =HOREB
Ex 19:20 LORD came down upon Mount S,
Ps 68:18 S the Lord entered the holy place.
Gal 4:25 Hagar represents S, a mountain

SINFUL → SIN
1 Mc 1:10 sprang from these a s offshoot,
Lk 5:8 from me, Lord, for I am a s man."
Rom 8:3 own Son in the likeness of s flesh

SING → SINGERS, SONG, SONGS
Ex 15:1 I will s to the LORD, for he is
Jdt 16:13 "I will s a new song to my God.
Ps 47:7 S praise to God, s praise; s praise
Is 5:1 Now let me s of my friend,
1 Cor 14:15 I will s praise with the spirit, but I will also s praise with the mind.

SINGERS → SING
Ezr 2:70 the s, the gatekeepers,

SINGLE
Mt 6:27 by worrying add a s moment to your
Rev 21:21 of the gates made from a s pearl;

SINNED → SIN
Ps 51:6 Against you, you alone have I s;
Lam 5:7 Our ancestors, who s, are no more;
Dn 9:5 We have s, been wicked and done
Rom 3:23 all have s and are deprived
1 Jn 1:10 "We have not s," we make him

SINNER → SIN
Lk 15:7 heaven over one s who repents than
Jas 5:20 whoever brings back a s

SINNERS → SIN
Ps 1:1 Nor stand in the way of s, nor sit
Prv 23:17 Do not let your heart envy s,
Lk 6:33 is that to you? Even s do the same.
Rom 5:8 while we were still s Christ died
1 Tm 1:15 Jesus came into the world to save s.

SINS → SIN
1 Sm 2:25 If someone s against another,
2:25 but if anyone s against the LORD,
2 Ch 7:14 pardon their s and heal their land.
Ps 103:10 has not dealt with us as our s merit,
Sir 2:11 forgives s and saves in time
Is 1:18 Though your s be like scarlet,
53:12 transgressors, Bore the s of many,
Ez 18:4 Only the one who s shall die!
Mi 7:19 into the depths of the sea all our s;
Mt 9:6 authority on earth to forgive s"—
Mk 1:5 River as they acknowledged their s.
Lk 11:4 forgive us our s for we ourselves
Acts 3:19 that your s may be wiped away,
1 Cor 15:3 Christ died for our s in accordance
Heb 9:28 once to take away the s of many,
1 Jn 1:9 If we acknowledge our s, he is
1:9 will forgive our s and cleanse us
Rev 1:5 freed us from our s by his blood,

SISTER
Gn 12:13 that you are my s, so that I may fare
20:2 of his wife Sarah, "She is my s."
Prv 7:4 Say to Wisdom, "You are my s!"
Mk 3:35 the will of God is my brother and s

SIT → SITS
Ps 1:1 nor s in company with scoffers.
Mt 20:23 but to s at my right and at my left [,
Heb 1:13 "S at my right hand until I make

SITS → SIT
Is 28:6 for the one who s in judgment,

SIX
Ex 20:9 S days you may labor and do all
Prv 6:16 There are s things the LORD
Is 6:2 each of them had s wings:
Rev 4:8 each of them with s wings,

SKILL
Ex 28:3 whom I have endowed with s

SKIN
Jb 2:4 the LORD and said, "S for s!
Jer 13:23 Can Ethiopians change their s,

SKULL
2 Kgs 9:35 they found nothing of her but the s,
Mt 27:33 (which means Place of the S),

SKY
Mt 16:3 for the s is red and threatening.'
16:3 to judge the appearance of the s,
Rev 6:14 the s was divided like a torn scroll

SLANDER → SLANDERED
Ps 15:3 Who does not s with his tongue,
1 Pt 2:1 deceit, insincerity, envy, and all s;

SLANDERED → SLANDER
1 Cor 4:13 when s, we respond gently.

SLAUGHTER → SLAUGHTERED
Prv 7:22 like an ox that goes to s; Like a stag
Is 53:7 Like a lamb led to s or a sheep
Acts 8:32 "Like a sheep he was led to the s,

SLAUGHTERED → SLAUGHTER
Zec 11:4 Shepherd the flock to be s.
Rev 6:9 those who had been s because

SLAVE → ENSLAVE, SLAVERY, SLAVES
Gn 21:10 "Drive out that s and her son!
21:10 son of that s is going to share
Mk 10:44 be first among you will be the s
Jn 8:34 everyone who commits sin is a s
Gal 3:28 there is neither s nor free person,
Phil 2:7 taking the form of a s,
Phlm 1:16 no longer as a s but more than a s,

SLAVERY → SLAVE
Ex 20:2 land of Egypt, out of the house of s.
Rom 7:14 but I am carnal, sold into s to sin.
8:15 you did not receive a spirit of s
Gal 5:1 do not submit again to the yoke of s.

SLAVES → SLAVE
Rom 6:16 to someone as obedient s, you are s
6:20 For when you were s of sin,
2 Pt 2:19 though they themselves are s

SLEEP → ASLEEP, SLEEPER, SLEEPING, SLEEPS
Gn 2:21 So the LORD God cast a deep s
Dn 12:2 Many of those who s in the dust

SLEEPER → SLEEP
Eph 5:14 O s, and arise from the dead,

SLEEPING → SLEEP
Mt 9:24 The girl is not dead but s."

SLEEPS → SLEEP
Ps 121:4 of Israel never slumbers nor s.

SLING
1 Sm 17:50 triumphed over the Philistine with s

SLOW
Ex 34:6 s to anger and abounding in love
Nm 14:18 'The LORD is s to anger
Ps 145:8 s to anger and abounding in mercy.
Na 1:3 The LORD is s to anger, yet great
Lk 24:25 How s of heart to believe all

SMALL → SMALLEST
Jas 3:5 same way the tongue is a s member
3:5 Consider how s a fire can set a huge

SMALLEST → SMALL
Mk 4:31 is the s of all the seeds on the earth.

SMOKE → SMOKING
Ex 19:18 was completely enveloped in s,
Is 6:4 and the house was filled with s.
Rev 15:8 filled with the s from God's glory

SMOKING → SMOKE
Gn 15:17 there appeared a s fire pot
Ex 20:18 of the shofar and the mountain s,

SNAKE
Gn 3:1 Now the s was the most cunning of all
Lk 11:11 among you would hand his son a s

SNARE
Jgs 2:3 for you, and their gods a s for you.

SNOW
Ps 51:9 me, and I will be whiter than s.
Is 1:18 they may become white as s;
Dn 7:9 His clothing was white as s, the hair
Rev 1:14 was as white as white wool or as s,

SOBER
1 Thes 5:6 rest do, but let us stay alert and s.

SODOM
Gn 19:24 LORD rained down sulfur upon S
Is 1:9 We would have become as S,
Lk 10:12 it will be more tolerable for S
Rev 11:8 which has the symbolic names "S"

SOLDIERS
Mt 28:12 gave a large sum of money to the s,
Jn 19:23 When the s had crucified Jesus,

SOLID
1 Cor 3:2 I fed you milk, not s food,
Heb 5:14 But s food is for the mature,

SOLITARY
Lam 1:1 How s sits the city, once filled

SOLOMON
Son of David by Bathsheba; king of Judah (2 Sm 12:24; 1 Ch 3:5, 10). Appointed king by David (1 Kgs 1); adversaries Adonijah, Joab, Shimei killed by Benaiah (1 Kgs 2). Asked for wisdom (1 Kgs 3; 2 Ch 1). Judged between two prostitutes (1 Kgs 3:16-28). Built temple (1 Kgs 5–7; 2 Ch 2–5); prayer of dedication (1 Kgs 8; 2 Ch 6). Visited by Queen of Sheba (1 Kgs 10; 2 Ch 9). Wives turned his heart from God (1 Kgs 11:1-13). Jeroboam rebelled against (1 Kgs 11:26-40). Death (1 Kgs 11:41-43; 2 Ch 9:29-31).

Proverbs of (1 Kgs 4:32; Prv 1:1; 10:1; 25:1); psalms of (Ps 72; 127); song of (SS 1:1).

SON → SONS
Gn 21:2 bore Abraham a s in his old age,
Ex 4:23 Let my s go, that he may serve me.
4:23 I will kill your s, your firstborn.
2 Sm 7:14 to him, and he shall be a s to me.
Ps 2:7 he said to me, "You are my s;
Is 7:14 pregnant and about to bear a s,
Mt 1:23 shall be with child and bear a s,
2:15 "Out of Egypt I called my s."
3:17 "This is my beloved S, with whom
12:8 For the S of Man is Lord
16:16 Messiah, the S of the living God."
Mk 10:45 For the S of Man did not come to be
Lk 1:35 will be called holy, the S of God.
20:44 him 'lord,' how can he be his s?"
Jn 1:34 testified that he is the S of God."
3:16 the world that he gave his only S,
Rom 8:29 be conformed to the image of his S,
1 Thes 1:10 and to await his S from heaven,
Heb 1:2 he spoke to us through a s, whom he
1:5 "You are my s; this day I have
1:5 to him, and he shall be a s to me"?
2 Pt 1:17 glory, "This is my S, my beloved,
1 Jn 4:9 God sent his only S into the world
Rev 12:5 She gave birth to a s, a male child,
14:14 the cloud one who looked like a s

SONG → SING
Ex 15:1 and the Israelites sang this s
Dt 31:21 them, this s will speak to them as
Ps 40:4 And puts a new s in my mouth,
Rev 15:3 and they sang the s of Moses,
15:3 of God, and the s of the Lamb:

SONGS → SING
Col 3:16 and spiritual s with gratitude in your

SONS → SON
Gn 6:2 the s of God saw how beautiful
35:22 The s of Jacob were now twelve.
Dt 7:3 to their s nor taking their daughters for your s.
Acts 2:17 Your s and your daughters shall
2 Cor 6:18 you shall be s and daughters to me,

SOON
Rev 22:20 says, "Yes, I am coming s." Amen!

SORCERERS → SORCERY
Rev 22:15 are the dogs, the s, the unchaste,

SORCERY → SORCERERS
Gal 5:20 idolatry, s, hatreds, rivalry,

SORROW → SORROWFUL
Est 9:22 was turned for them from s into joy,
Eccl 1:18 in much wisdom there is much s;
Is 35:10 gladness, s and mourning flee away.

SORROWFUL → SORROW
2 Cor 6:10 as s yet always rejoicing;

SOUL → SOULS
Ps 16:9 my heart is glad, my s rejoices;
25:1 To you, O LORD, I lift up my s,
42:2 of water, so my s longs for you,
Sir 7:29 With all your s fear God and revere
Mi 6:7 fruit of my body for the sin of my s?
Mt 10:28 kill the body but cannot kill the s;
10:28 of the one who can destroy both s
Heb 4:12 penetrating even between s
Jas 5:20 his way will save his s from death
3 Jn 1:2 health, just as your s is prospering.

SOULS → SOUL
1 Pt 2:25 the shepherd and guardian of your s.

SOUND
Ez 1:24 Then I heard the s of their wings,
1 Cor 15:52 For the trumpet will s, the dead will
2 Tm 4:3 will not tolerate s doctrine but,
Ti 1:9 able both to exhort with s doctrine
Rev 1:15 his voice was like the s of rushing

SOW → SOWED, SOWER, SOWS
Ex 23:10 For six years you may s your land
Eccl 11:6 In the morning s your seed,
Hos 10:12 "S for yourselves justice,
Mt 13:3 "A sower went out to s.
1 Cor 15:36 What you s is not brought to life

SOWED → SOW
Mt 13:24 a man who s good seed in his field.

SOWER → SOW
Mk 4:14 The s sows the word.

SOWS → SOW
Jn 4:37 the saying is verified that 'One s
2 Cor 9:6 whoever s sparingly will also reap
9:6 and whoever s bountifully will

SPAN
Is 40:12 marked off the heavens with a s,
Mt 6:27 add a single moment to your l-s?

SPARE
Rom 11:21 God did not s the natural branches,
11:21 [perhaps] he will not s you either.
2 Pt 2:4 God did not s the angels when they

SPARROWS
Lk 12:7 You are worth more than many s.

SPEAK → SPEAKING, SPEECH, SPOKE
Gn 18:27 "See how I am presuming to s
Nm 12:8 face to face I s to him,
12:8 fear to s against my servant Moses?
Dt 18:20 if a prophet presumes to s a word
18:22 it is a word the LORD did not s.
Jb 13:3 But I would s with the Almighty;
Eccl 3:7 a time to be silent, and a time to s.
Mt 13:13 This is why I s to them in parables,
Acts 2:4 and began to s in different tongues,
1 Cor 12:30 Do all s in tongues?
Jas 1:19 to hear, slow to s, slow to wrath,

SPEAKING → SPEAK
1 Cor 14:39 and do not forbid s in tongues,

SPEAR → SPEARS
1 Sm 19:10 to pin David to the wall with the s,
19:10 and the s struck only the wall,

SPEARS → SPEAR
Mi 4:3 and their s into pruning hooks;

SPECTACLE
1 Cor 4:9 since we have become a s

SPEECH → SPEAK
Ex 4:10 but I am slow of s and tongue."
Sir 4:29 Do not be haughty in your s, or lazy
1 Tm 4:12 for those who believe, in s, conduct,
1 Jn 3:18 let us love not in word or s

SPICES
Ex 25:6 s for the anointing oil
Jn 19:40 with burial cloths along with the s,

SPIES
Jos 2:1 secretly sent out two s from Shittim,

SPIRIT → SPIRITS, SPIRITUAL
Gn 6:3 My s shall not remain in human
Nm 11:25 Taking some of the s that was
11:25 and as the s came to rest on them,
2 Kgs 2:9 receive a double portion of your s."
Neh 9:20 Your good s you bestowed on them,
Jb 33:4 For the s of God made me,
Ps 31:6 Into your hands I commend my s;
51:19 My sacrifice, O God, is a contrite s;
Prv 16:18 and a haughty s before a fall.
Is 42:1 Upon him I have put my s;
Ez 36:26 and a new s I will put within you.
Mt 1:18 found with child through the holy S.
5:3 "Blessed are the poor in s, for theirs
12:31 blasphemy against the S will not be
26:41 The s is willing, but the flesh is
Mk 1:8 will baptize you with the holy S."
Jn 3:5 without being born of water and S.
4:24 God is S, and those who worship him must worship in S
6:63 It is the s that gives life,
6:63 words I have spoken to you are s
14:26 the holy S that the Father will send
Acts 2:4 they were all filled with the holy S
2:4 as the S enabled them to proclaim.
2:38 will receive the gift of the holy S.
Rom 8:9 you are in the s, if only the S of God
8:26 the S too comes to the aid of our
8:26 but the S itself intercedes
1 Cor 6:19 is a temple of the holy S within you,
12:4 of spiritual gifts but the same S;
2 Cor 3:6 new covenant, not of letter but of s;
3:6 brings death, but the S gives life.
Gal 4:6 God sent the s of his Son into our
5:22 the fruit of the S is love, joy, peace,
Eph 1:13 sealed with the promised holy S,
2:18 have access in one S to the Father.
4:30 do not grieve the holy S of God,
5:18 debauchery, but be filled with the S,
1 Thes 5:19 Do not quench the S.
Heb 4:12 even between soul and s,
1 Jn 4:1 do not trust every s but test
Rev 1:10 caught up in s on the Lord's day

SPIRITS → SPIRIT
Nm 16:22 God of the s of all living creatures,
Dt 18:11 consults ghosts and s, or seeks
Lk 4:36 power he commands the unclean s,
1 Cor 12:10 to another discernment of s;
Rev 1:4 from the seven s before his throne,

SPIRITUAL → SPIRIT
Rom 7:14 We know that the law is s; but I am
1 Cor 2:13 describing s realities in s terms.
12:1 Now in regard to s gifts, brothers,
14:1 but strive eagerly for the s gifts,
15:46 But the s was not first;
15:46 rather the natural and then the s.
Eph 1:3 Christ with every s blessing
Col 1:9 of his will through all s wisdom
1 Pt 2:2 long for pure s milk so that through
2:5 let yourselves be built into a s house
2:5 to offer s sacrifices acceptable

SPIT
Mk 14:65 Some began to s on him.
Rev 3:16 cold, I will s you out of my mouth.

SPLENDOR
Eph 5:27 present to himself the church in s,

SPOKE → SPEAK
Mk 4:33 many such parables he s the word
Heb 1:1 God s in partial and various ways
2 Pt 1:21 the holy Spirit s under the influence

SPOT
Eph 5: 27 without s or wrinkle or any such
2 Pt 3: 14 be eager to be found without s

SPRING
Is 45: 8 let righteousness s up with them!
Jn 4: 14 become in him a s of water welling
Rev 21: 6 gift from the s of life-giving water.

SPRINKLE → SPRINKLED
Nm 8: 7 S them with the water
Ez 36: 25 I will s clean water over you

SPRINKLED → SPRINKLE
Lv 8: 11 he s some of the oil seven times
Heb 10: 22 with our hearts s clean from an evil

STAFF
Ex 4: 4 of it, and it became a s in his hand.
Ps 23: 4 your rod and your s comfort me.
Zec 11: 10 I took my s Delight and snapped it

STAND → STANDING
Ex 14: 13 S your ground and see the victory
Jb 19: 25 he will at last s forth upon the dust.
Mt 12: 25 house divided against itself will s.
Rom 14: 4 for the Lord is able to make him s.
14: 10 we shall all s before the judgment
Eph 6: 11 be able to s firm against the tactics

STANDARDS
1 Cor 1: 26 many of you were wise by human s,

STANDING → STAND
1 Cor 10: 12 thinks he is s secure should take
Jas 5: 9 the Judge is s before the gates.

STAR → STARS
Nm 24: 17 A s shall advance from Jacob,
Is 14: 12 O Morning S, son of the dawn!
Mt 2: 2 We saw his s at its rising and have
2 Pt 1: 19 the morning s rises in your hearts.
Rev 9: 1 I saw a s that had fallen
22: 16 of David, the bright morning s."

STARS → STAR
Gn 1: 16 one to govern the night, and the s.
Jb 38: 7 While the morning s sang together
Ps 148: 3 praise him, all shining s.
Dn 12: 3 to justice shall be like the s forever.
Rev 1: 16 In his right hand he held seven s.
12: 4 away a third of the s in the sky

STATUE
Dn 2: 31 O king, you saw a s, very large

STATUTES
Dt 4: 1 hear the s and ordinances I am
Neh 9: 13 laws, good s and commandments;

STEADFAST
Ps 57: 8 My heart is s, God, my heart is s.
1 Pt 5: 9 Resist him, s in faith,

STEAL
Ex 20: 15 You shall not s.
Mt 6: 19 destroy, and thieves break in and s.
Jn 10: 10 A thief comes only to s

STEPHEN
Early church leader (Acts 6:5). Arrested (Acts 6:8-15). Speech to Sanhedrin (Acts 7). Stoned (Acts 7:54-60; 8:2; 11:19; 22:20).

STEPS
Prv 16: 9 way, but the LORD directs the s.

STIFF-NECKED → NECK
Ex 32: 9 seen this people, how s they are,
Acts 7: 51 "You s people,

STILL
Ex 14: 14 you have only to keep s."
Jos 10: 13 The sun stood s, the moon stayed,
Ps 46: 11 "Be s and know that I am God!
Mk 4: 39 Be s!" The wind ceased and there
Rom 5: 8 while we were s sinners Christ died
Heb 11: 4 this, though dead, he s speaks.

STING
1 Cor 15: 55 Where, O death, is your s?"

STONE → CORNERSTONE, MILLSTONE, STONED, STONES
Gn 28: 18 the next morning Jacob took the s
Ex 28: 10 six of their names on one s,
28: 10 of the remaining six on the other s,
31: 18 the s tablets inscribed by God's own
1 Sm 17: 50 over the Philistine with sling and s;
Ps 118: 22 The s the builders rejected has
Is 28: 16 See, I am laying a s in Zion, a s
Mt 4: 6 you dash your foot against a s.' "
Mk 12: 10 'The s that the builders rejected has
16: 3 "Who will roll back the s for us
Rom 9: 32 They stumbled over the s
2 Cor 3: 3 not on tablets of s but on tablets
1 Pt 2: 4 a living s, rejected by human beings

STONED → STONE
2 Ch 24: 21 at the king's command they s him
Acts 14: 19 They s Paul and dragged him
Heb 11: 37 They were s, sawed in two,

STONES → STONE
Jos 4: 3 "Take up twelve s from this spot
1 Sm 17: 40 David selected five smooth s
Mt 3: 9 children to Abraham from these s.
Lk 19: 40 they keep silent, the s will cry out!"
1 Cor 3: 12 gold, silver, precious s, wood, hay,
1 Pt 2: 5 like living s, let yourselves be built

STORE → STOREHOUSE, STORING
Mt 6: 19 "Do not s up for yourselves

STOREHOUSE → HOUSE, STORE
Mal 3: 10 Bring the whole tithe into the s,

STORING → STORE
Rom 2: 5 you are s up wrath for yourself

STRAIGHT
Prv 3: 6 him, and he will make s your paths.
Sir 2: 6 make your ways s and hope in him.
Is 40: 3 Make s in the wasteland a highway
Mt 3: 3 of the Lord, make s his paths.' "
Acts 9: 11 go to the street called S and ask

STRANGE → STRANGER, STRANGERS
Dt 32: 16 With s gods they incited him,
1 Cor 14: 21 "By people speaking s tongues

STRANGER → STRANGE
Mt 25: 35 drink, a s and you welcomed me,

STRANGERS → STRANGE
Eph 2: 12 and s to the covenants of promise,
Heb 11: 13 acknowledged themselves to be s

STRAW
Ex 5: 10 'I will not provide you with s.
1 Cor 3: 12 precious stones, wood, hay, or s,

STRAY → ASTRAY
Ps 119: 10 do not let me s from your

STREAM → STREAMS
Is 2: 2 All nations shall s toward it.

Am 5:24 righteousness like an unfailing s.

STREAMS → STREAM
Ps 1:3 He is like a tree planted near s
42:2 As the deer longs for s of water,

STREET
Prv 1:20 Wisdom cries aloud in the s,
Mt 6:5 on s corners so that others may see
Rev 21:21 the s of the city was of pure gold,

STRENGTH → STRONG
Ex 15:2 My s and my refuge is the LORD,
Neh 8:10 rejoicing in the LORD is your s!"
Jdt 9:11 "Your s is not in numbers, nor does
1 Mc 3:19 but on s that comes from Heaven.
Ps 46:2 God is our refuge and our s,
Prv 31:25 She is clothed with s and dignity,
Is 40:31 in the LORD will renew their s,
Mk 12:30 all your mind, and with all your s.'
1 Cor 1:25 of God is stronger than human s.

STRENGTHEN → STRONG
Jgs 16:28 S me only this once that I may
Lk 22:32 back, you must s your brothers."
Heb 12:12 So s your drooping hands and your

STRETCH → OUTSTRETCHED, STRETCHED
Mk 3:5 said to the man, "S out your hand."

STRETCHED → STRETCH
2 Sm 24:16 the angel s forth his hand toward

STRIFE → STRIVE
Prv 23:29 Who have s? Who have anxiety?

STRIKE
Gn 3:15 They will s at your head, while you
3:15 your head, while you s at their heel.
Ex 17:6 S the rock, and the water will flow
Zec 13:7 S the shepherd that the sheep may
Mk 14:27 'I will s the shepherd, and the sheep
Rev 19:15 came a sharp sword to s the nations.

STRIVE → STRIFE
1 Cor 12:31 S eagerly for the greatest spiritual

STRONG → STRENGTH, STRENGTHEN, STRONGHOLD
Ex 6:1 For by a s hand, he will let them go;
Ps 140:8 my master, my s deliverer,
Prv 18:10 name of the LORD is a s tower;
Rom 15:1 We who are s ought to put
1 Cor 1:27 weak of the world to shame the s,
2 Cor 12:10 for when I am weak, then I am s.

STRONGHOLD → STRONG
Ps 9:10 The LORD is a s for the oppressed, a s in times of trouble.

STRUGGLE
Eph 6:12 For our s is not with flesh and blood
Heb 12:4 your s against sin you have not yet

STUBBORN
Hos 4:16 For like a s cow, Israel is s;

STUDY
Ezr 7:10 Ezra had set his heart on the s
Eccl 12:12 in much s there is weariness

STUMBLE → STUMBLING
Ps 37:24 May s, but he will never fall,
Prv 4:12 and should you run, you will not s.
Rom 9:33 in Zion that will make people s
1 Pt 2:8 "A stone that will make people s,
2:8 They s by disobeying the word, as is

STUMBLING → STUMBLE
Rom 11:9 a s block and a retribution for them;
1 Cor 8:9 in no way becomes a s block

STUMP
Is 11:1 shall sprout from the s of Jesse,

SUBDUE
Gn 1:28 fill the earth and s it.
1 Ch 17:10 And I will s all your enemies.

SUBJECTED
Rom 8:20 but because of the one who s it,
1 Cor 15:28 When everything is s to him,
15:28 be s to the one who s everything

SUBMIT
Gal 5:1 and do not s again to the yoke

SUCCEED
Prv 15:22 but they s when advisers are many.

SUDDENLY
Mal 3:1 the lord whom you seek will come s
Mk 13:36 May he not come s and find you

SUFFER → SUFFERED, SUFFERING, SUFFERINGS, SUFFERS
Lk 22:15 this Passover with you before I s,
24:46 is written that the Messiah would s
Rom 8:17 if only we s with him so that we
Heb 9:26 he would have had to s repeatedly
1 Pt 3:17 For it is better to s for doing good,

SUFFERED → SUFFER
1 Pt 2:21 because Christ also s for you,

SUFFERING → SUFFER
Jb 2:13 for they saw how great was his s.
Is 53:3 by men, a man of s, knowing pain,

SUFFERINGS → SUFFER
Rom 8:18 that the s of this present time are as
1 Pt 4:13 that you share in the s of Christ,

SUFFERS → SUFFER
1 Cor 12:26 If [one] part s, all the parts suffer

SUFFICIENT
2 Cor 12:9 said to me, "My grace is s for you,

SULFUR
Rev 21:8 is in the burning pool of fire and s,

SUMMED
Rom 13:9 there may be, are s up in this saying,

SUN
Jos 10:13 The s stood still, the moon stayed,
Ps 84:12 For a s and shield is the LORD
Eccl 1:9 Nothing is new under the s!
Mt 5:45 for he makes his s rise on the bad
Acts 2:20 The s shall be turned to darkness,
Rev 1:16 and his face shone like the s at its
19:17 I saw an angel standing on the s.
22:5 will they need light from lamp or s,

SUPERIOR
Heb 1:4 as far s to the angels as the name he

SUPPLICATION → SUPPLICATIONS
Eph 6:18 With all prayer and s, pray at every
6:18 and s for all the holy ones

SUPPLICATIONS → SUPPLICATION
1 Tm 2:1 then, I ask that s, prayers, petitions,
Heb 5:7 offered prayers and s with loud cries

SUPPORT
Ps 18: 19 distress, but the LORD was my **s**.
Rom 11: 18 consider that you do not **s** the root;

SURE
Nm 32: 23 you can be **s** that the consequences
Is 28: 16 cornerstone as a **s** foundation;
Heb 6: 19 as an anchor of the soul, **s** and firm,

SURPASSES → SURPASSING
Sir 25: 11 Fear of the Lord **s** all else.
Eph 3: 19 the love of Christ that **s** knowledge,
Phil 4: 7 **s** all understanding will guard your

SURPASSING → SURPASSES
2 Cor 9: 14 because of the **s** grace of God

SURPRISED
1 Pt 4: 12 do not be **s** that a trial by fire is

SURROUNDED → SURROUNDS
Lk 21: 20 you see Jerusalem **s** by armies,
Heb 12: 1 since we are **s** by so great a cloud
Rev 20: 9 and **s** the camp of the holy ones

SURROUNDS → SURROUNDED
Ps 125: 2 the LORD **s** his people both now

SURVIVORS
Ez 14: 22 there will still be some **s** in it who

SUSA
Neh 1: 1 year, I was in the citadel of **S**
Est 1: 2 throne in the royal precinct of **S**,

SUSANNA
Righteous woman wrongly accused of immorality (Dn 13:1-44); vindicated by Daniel (Dn 13:45-64).

SUSTAINS
Heb 1: 3 who **s** all things by his mighty word.

SWALLOW → SWALLOWED
Mt 23: 24 strain out the gnat and **s** the camel!

SWALLOWED → SWALLOW
Gn 41: 7 and the thin ears **s** up the seven fat,
Nm 16: 32 earth opened its mouth and **s** them
1 Cor 15: 54 "Death is **s** up in victory.

SWEAR → SWORE, SWORN
Dt 10: 20 fast and by his name shall you **s**.
Mt 5: 34 But I say to you, do not **s** at all;

SWEAT
Gn 3: 19 By the **s** of your brow you shall eat
Lk 22: 44 that his **s** became like drops

SWEET → SWEETER
Ps 119: 103 How **s** to my tongue is your promise,
Ez 3: 3 it was as **s** as honey in my mouth.
Rev 10: 10 In my mouth it was like **s** honey,

SWEETER → SWEET
Jgs 14: 18 said to him, "What is **s** than honey,
Ps 19: 11 **S** also than honey or drippings

SWIFT
Eccl 9: 11 sun that the race is not won by the **s**,
2 Pt 2: 1 them, bringing **s** destruction

SWINE
1 Mc 1: 47 to sacrifice **s** and unclean animals,
Mt 7: 6 or throw your pearls before **s**,
Mk 5: 12 with him, "Send us into the **s**.

SWORD → SWORDS
Gn 3: 24 and the fiery revolving **s** east
1 Sm 17: 47 shall learn that it is not by **s** or spear
1 Ch 21: 30 he was fearful of the **s** of the angel
Sir 21: 3 lawlessness is like a two-edged **s**;
Is 2: 4 shall not raise the **s** against another,
49: 2 my mouth like a sharp-edged **s**,
Mt 10: 34 come to bring not peace but the **s**.
Lk 2: 35 you yourself a **s** will pierce) so
Eph 6: 17 of salvation and the **s** of the Spirit,
Heb 4: 12 sharper than any two-edged **s**,
Rev 1: 16 A sharp two-edged **s** came
19: 15 his mouth came a sharp **s** to strike

SWORDS → SWORD
Is 2: 4 They shall beat their **s**

SWORE → SWEAR
Ex 6: 8 into the land which I **s** to give
32: 13 and how you **s** to them by your own
Ps 132: 11 The LORD **s** an oath to David
Heb 6: 13 whom to swear, "he **s** by himself,"

SWORN → SWEAR
Ps 110: 4 The LORD has **s** and will not
Heb 7: 21 "The Lord has **s**, and he will not

SYMPATHIZE
Heb 4: 15 have a high priest who is unable to **s**

SYNAGOGUE → SYNAGOGUES
Lk 4: 16 into the **s** on the sabbath day.
8: 41 an official of the **s**, came forward.
Acts 18: 26 He began to speak boldly in the **s**;

SYNAGOGUES → SYNAGOGUE
Mt 4: 23 teaching in their **s**,

T

TABERNACLE
Lv 26: 11 I will set my **t** in your midst,

TABITHA → See DORCAS

TABLE → TABLES
Ex 25: 23 shall also make a **t** of acacia wood,
Ps 23: 5 You set a **t** before me in front of my

TABLES → TABLE
Mk 11: 15 He overturned the **t** of the money

TABLETS
Ex 31: 18 Sinai, he gave him the two **t**
31: 18 the stone **t** inscribed by God's own
2 Cor 3: 3 not on **t** of stone but on **t** that are

TAKE → TAKEN, TAKES
Mt 11: 29 **T** my yoke upon you and learn
Mk 8: 34 must deny himself, **t** up his cross,

TAKEN → TAKE
Sir 44: 16 walked with the LORD and was **t**,
Heb 11: 5 By faith Enoch was **t** up so that he
11: 5 no more because God had **t** him."

TAKES → TAKE
Jn 1: 29 who **t** away the sin of the world.
10: 18 No one **t** it from me, but I lay it
Rev 22: 19 if anyone **t** away from the words

TALENT
Mt 25: 25 off and buried your **t** in the ground.

TAMAR
1. Wife of Judah's sons Er and Onan (Gn 38:1-10). Children by Judah (Gn 38:11-30; Mt 1:3).
2. Daughter of David, raped by Amnon (2 Sm 13).

TASTE → TASTED
Mt 16: 28 here who will not **t** death until they
Col 2: 21 Do not **t**! Do not touch!"

TASTED → TASTE
Heb 6: 4 enlightened and t the heavenly gift
1 Pt 2: 3 for you have t that the Lord is good.

TAUGHT → TEACH
Is 40: 14 Who t him the path of judgment,
Jn 6: 45 'They shall all be t by God.'

TAX → TAXES
Mt 11: 19 a friend of t collectors and sinners.'
Lk 18: 10 and the other was a t collector.

TAXES → TAX
Rom 13: 7 all their dues, t to whom t are due,

TEACH → TAUGHT, TEACHER, TEACHERS, TEACHING
Ps 90: 12 T us to count our days aright,
Jer 31: 34 They will no longer t their friends
Jn 14: 26 he will t you everything and remind
Col 3: 16 richly, as in all wisdom you t
1 Tm 2: 12 I do not permit a woman to t
1 Jn 2: 27 you do not need anyone to t you.

TEACHER → TEACH
Mt 10: 24 No disciple is above his t, no slave
Jn 1: 38 (which translated means T),

TEACHERS → TEACH
Ps 119: 99 I have more insight than all my t,
1 Cor 12: 28 third, t; then, mighty deeds;
Eph 4: 11 evangelists, others as pastors and t,
Jas 3: 1 Not many of you should become t,

TEACHING → TEACH
Mk 1: 27 A new t with authority.
Ti 1: 11 are upsetting whole families by t
2 Jn 1: 9 in the t of the Christ does not have
1: 9 remains in the t has the Father

TEAR → TORN
Mk 2: 21 from the old, and the t gets worse.
Rev 7: 17 God will wipe away every t

TEETH → TOOTH
Mt 8: 12 will be wailing and grinding of t."

TEKEL
Dn 5: 27 T, you have been weighed

TELL
Ps 50: 12 I would not t you, for mine is
1 Cor 15: 51 Behold, I t you a mystery.

TEMPERATE
1 Tm 3: 2 irreproachable, married only once, t,
Ti 2: 2 that older men should be t,

TEMPLE
1 Sm 3: 3 in the t of the LORD where the ark
1 Mc 4: 48 the interior of the t and consecrated
Ps 11: 4 The LORD is in his holy t;
Mt 4: 5 him stand on the parapet of the t,
12: 6 something greater than the t is here.
Jn 2: 21 speaking about the t of his body.
1 Cor 3: 16 not know that you are the t of God,
Eph 2: 21 grows into a t sacred in the Lord;
Rev 21: 22 I saw no t in the city, for its t is

TEMPTATION → TEMPTED, TEMPTER
1 Tm 6: 9 who want to be rich are falling into t
Jas 1: 12 is the man who perseveres in t,

TEMPTED → TEMPTATION
Mk 1: 13 the desert for forty days, t by Satan.
Gal 6: 1 so that you also may not be t.

TEMPTER → TEMPTATION
Mt 4: 3 The t approached and said to him,

1 Thes 3: 5 fear that somehow the t had put you

TEN → TENTH
Ex 34: 28 words of the covenant, the t words.
Dn 7: 24 The t horns shall be t kings rising
Mt 25: 1 will be like t virgins who took their
Rev 17: 12 The t horns that you saw represent t

TENDER
Lk 1: 78 because of the t mercy of our God

TENT
Ex 27: 21 the LORD in the t of meeting,
2 Sm 7: 2 but the ark of God dwells in a t!"
2 Cor 5: 1 dwelling, a t, should be destroyed,

TENTH → TEN
Gn 14: 20 Abram gave him a t of everything.
Is 6: 13 If there remain a t part in it,

TERROR
Ps 91: 5 You shall not fear the t of the night

TEST → TESTED, TESTING
Dt 6: 16 God, to the t, as you did at Massah.
Lk 4: 12 the Lord, your God, to the t.' "
10: 25 of the law who stood up to t him
2 Cor 13: 5 you are living in faith. T yourselves.
13: 5 unless, of course, you fail the t.
1 Jn 4: 1 but t the spirits to see whether they

TESTED → TEST
Ps 78: 41 Again and again they t God,
Heb 4: 15 but one who has similarly been t

TESTIFIED → TESTIFY
Jn 1: 15 John t to him and cried out, saying,
1 Pt 1: 11 them indicated when it t in advance

TESTIFIES → TESTIFY
1 Jn 5: 6 The Spirit is the one that t,

TESTIFY → TESTIFIED, TESTIFIES, TESTIMONIES, TESTIMONY
Jn 15: 26 from the Father, he will t to me.
1 Jn 5: 7 So there are three that t,

TESTIMONIES → TESTIFY
Ps 119: 2 Blessed those who keep his t,

TESTIMONY → TESTIFY
Mk 14: 59 Even so their t did not agree.
Rev 1: 9 God's word and gave t to Jesus.

TESTING → TEST
Jas 1: 3 that the t of your faith produces

THADDAEUS → =JUDAS
Apostle (Mt 10:3; Mk 3:18); probably also known as Judas son of James (Lk 6:16; Acts 1:13).

THANK → THANKS, THANKSGIVING
2 Ch 29: 31 and t offerings for the house
29: 31 the sacrifices and t offerings and all

THANKS → THANK
1 Ch 16: 8 Give t to the LORD, invoke his
Ps 107: 1 "Give t to the LORD for he is
Rom 1: 21 him glory as God or give him t.
1 Cor 11: 24 after he had given t, broke it
2 Cor 9: 15 T be to God for his indescribable
Rev 4: 9 t to the one who sits on the throne,

THANKSGIVING → THANK
Lv 7: 12 If someone offers it for t,
Ps 100: 4 Enter his gates with t,
Phil 4: 6 with t, make your requests known
Rev 7: 12 and glory, wisdom and t, honor,

THEFT → THIEF
Mt 15: 19 adultery, unchastity, **t**, false witness,

THIEF → THEFT, THIEVES
Ex 22: 1 If a **t** is caught in the act
Jn 10: 10 A **t** comes only to steal
1 Thes 5: 2 the Lord will come like a **t** at night.
Rev 16: 15 ("Behold, I am coming like a **t**."

THIEVES → THIEF
Mt 6: 19 destroy, and **t** break in and steal.

THINK → THINKING, THOUGHT, THOUGHTS
Rom 12: 3 I tell everyone among you not to **t** more highly than one ought to **t**,

THINKING → THINK
1 Cor 14: 20 stop being childish in your **t**.
14: 20 like infants, but in your **t** be mature.

THIRD → THREE
Hos 6: 2 on the **t** day he will raise us up,
Mt 26: 44 withdrew again and prayed a **t** time,
Lk 18: 33 him, but on the **t** day he will rise."
2 Cor 12: 2 was caught up to the **t** heaven.

THIRST → THIRSTY
Mt 5: 6 who hunger and **t** for righteousness,
Rev 7: 16 They will not hunger or **t** anymore,

THIRSTY → THIRST
Mt 25: 35 I was **t** and you gave me drink,

THOMAS
Apostle (Mt 10:3; Mk 3:18; Lk 6:15; Jn 11:16; 14:5; 21:2; Acts 1:13). Doubted resurrection (Jn 20:24-28).

THORN → THORNS
2 Cor 12: 7 a **t** in the flesh was given to me,

THORNS → THORN
Gn 3: 18 **T** and thistles it shall bear for you,
Mt 13: 7 Some seed fell among **t**, and the **t**
Jn 19: 2 the soldiers wove a crown out of **t**

THOUGHT → THINK
2 Cor 10: 5 take every **t** captive in obedience

THOUGHTS → THINK
Is 55: 8 For my **t** are not your **t**, nor are your
1 Cor 3: 20 "The Lord knows the **t** of the wise,
Heb 4: 12 reflections and **t** of the heart.

THOUSAND → THOUSANDS
Ps 90: 4 A **t** years in your eyes are merely
2 Pt 3: 8 the Lord one day is like a **t** years
3: 8 a **t** years and a **t** years like one day.
Rev 20: 4 reigned with Christ for a **t** years.

THOUSANDS → THOUSAND
1 Sm 18: 7 "Saul has slain his **t**, David his tens of **t**."
Dn 7: 10 **T** upon **t** were ministering to him,

THREE → THIRD
Gn 18: 2 up, he saw **t** men standing near him.
Ex 23: 14 **T** times a year you shall celebrate
Mt 18: 20 **t** are gathered together in my name,
26: 34 crows, you will deny me **t** times."
Mk 8: 31 and be killed, and rise after **t** days.
2 Cor 12: 8 **T** times I begged the Lord
1 Jn 5: 7 So there are **t** that testify,

THRONE → THRONES
2 Sm 7: 13 I will establish his royal **t** forever.
Ps 45: 7 Your **t**, O God, stands forever;
Is 6: 1 Lord seated on a high and lofty **t**,
Jer 33: 21 descendant to act as king upon his **t**,
Mt 19: 28 of Man is seated on his **t** of glory,
Heb 4: 16 So let us confidently approach the **t**
12: 2 his seat at the right of the **t** of God.
Rev 4: 10 before the one who sits on the **t**
4: 10 down their crowns before the **t**,
20: 11 Next I saw a large white **t**

THRONES → THRONE
Dn 7: 9 **T** were set up and the Ancient
Rev 4: 4 the throne I saw twenty-four other **t**

THROW → THROWN
Ex 1: 22 "**T** into the Nile every boy that is
Mt 7: 6 or **t** your pearls before swine,

THROWN → THROW
Rev 20: 10 Devil who had led them astray was **t**

THUMMIM
Ex 28: 30 you shall put the Urim and **T**,

THUNDER → THUNDERS
Ex 9: 23 the LORD sent forth peals of **t**
Rev 4: 5 lightning, rumblings, and peals of **t**.

THUNDERS → THUNDER
Rev 10: 3 out, the seven **t** raised their voices,

TIBNI
King of Israel (1 Kgs 16:21-22).

TIE
Mt 23: 4 They **t** up heavy burdens [hard

TIME → TIMES
Est 4: 14 perhaps it was for a **t** like this
Eccl 3: 1 and a **t** for every affair under
Rom 5: 6 at the appointed **t** for the ungodly.
2 Cor 6: 2 "In an acceptable **t** I heard you,
6: 2 Behold, now is a very acceptable **t**;
Gal 4: 4 when the fullness of **t** had come,
Rev 22: 10 book, for the appointed **t** is near.

TIMES → TIME
Jos 6: 4 day march around the city seven **t**,
Mt 16: 3 you cannot judge the signs of the **t**.]
18: 22 you, not seven **t** but seventy-seven **t**.
Mk 14: 30 twice you will deny me three **t**."

TIMOTHY
Believer from Lystra (Acts 16:1). Joined Paul on second missionary journey (Acts 16–20). Sent to settle problems at Corinth (1 Cor 4:17; 16:10). Led church at Ephesus (1 Tm 1:3). Co-writer with Paul (1 Thes 1:1; 2 Thes 1:1; Phlm 1).

TITHE
Dt 12: 17 partake of your **t** of grain or wine
Mal 3: 10 Bring the whole **t**

TITUS
Gentile co-worker of Paul (Gal 2:1-3; 2 Tm 4:10); sent to Corinth (2 Cor 2:13; 7–8; 12:18), Crete (Ti 1:4-5).

TOBIAH
Enemy of Nehemiah (Neh 2:10-19; 4; 6; 13:4-9).

TOBIT
Tb 1: 1 This book tells the story of **T**,

TODAY
Dt 30: 15 See, I have **t** set before you life
Ps 2: 7 are my son; **t** I have begotten you.
Lk 23: 43 **t** you will be with me in Paradise."
Heb 13: 8 Jesus Christ is the same yesterday, **t**,

TOGETHER
Mt 19: 6 what God has joined **t**, no human

TOIL
Gn 3: 16 I will intensify your **t** in childbearing;

TOLA
A judge of Israel (Jgs 10:1-2).

TOMB
Mk 15:46 laid him in a **t** that had been hewn
15:46 a stone against the entrance to the **t**.
Lk 24: 2 the stone rolled away from the **t**;

TOMORROW
Is 22:13 "Eat and drink, for **t** we die!"
Mt 6:34 Do not worry about **t**; **t** will take
Jas 4:14 no idea what your life will be like **t**.

TONGUE → TONGUES
Ex 4:10 but I am slow of speech and **t**."
Ps 139: 4 Even before a word is on my **t**,
Prv 18:21 and life are in the power of the **t**;
Is 45:23 by me every **t** shall swear,
1 Cor 14:19 also, than ten thousand words in a **t**.
Phil 2:11 every **t** confess that Jesus Christ is
Jas 3: 8 but no human being can tame the **t**.

TONGUES → TONGUE
Acts 2: 3 there appeared to them **t** as of fire,
1 Cor 12:10 to another varieties of **t**; to another interpretation of **t**.
14: 5 I should like all of you to speak in **t**,
14: 5 is greater than one who speaks in **t**,

TOOTH → TEETH
Ex 21:24 eye for eye, **t** for **t**, hand for hand,
Mt 5:38 'An eye for an eye and a **t** for a **t**.'

TORCHES
Dn 10: 6 his eyes were like fiery **t**, his arms
Rev 4: 5 Seven flaming **t** burned in front

TORMENTED
Rev 20:10 There they will be **t** day and night

TORN → TEAR
1 Sm 28:17 he has **t** the kingdom from your
Lk 23:45 the temple was **t** down the middle.

TORTURED
Heb 11:35 Some were **t** and would not accept

TOUCH
Gn 3: 3 'You shall not eat it or even **t** it,
Mt 9:21 "If only I can **t** his cloak, I shall be
Lk 24:39 **T** me and see, because a ghost does
Col 2:21 Do not taste! Do not **t**!"

TOWER
Gn 11: 4 a city and a **t** with its top in the sky,
Prv 18:10 name of the LORD is a strong **t**;

TRADITION
Mt 15: 2 "Why do your disciples break the **t**
Col 2: 8 philosophy according to human **t**,

TRAIN → TRAINING
Prv 22: 6 **T** the young in the way they should
1 Tm 4: 7 **T** yourself for devotion,

TRAINING → TRAIN
1 Tm 4: 8 while physical **t** is of limited value,
2 Tm 3:16 and for **t** in righteousness,

TRAITOR
Lk 6:16 and Judas Iscariot, who became a **t**.

TRANSFIGURED
Mt 17: 2 And he was **t** before them;

TRANSFORMED
Rom 12: 2 be **t** by the renewal of your mind,
2 Cor 3:18 are being **t** into the same image

TRANSGRESSION
Dn 9:24 Then **t** will stop and sin will end,
Gal 6: 1 even if a person is caught in some **t**,

TRAP
Lk 20:20 to be righteous who were to **t** him
Rom 11: 9 their table become a snare and a **t**,

TREAD → TREADING, TREADS
Rev 19:15 and he himself will **t** out in the wine

TREADING → TREAD
Mi 7:19 on us, **t** underfoot our iniquities?
1 Cor 9: 9 shall not muzzle an ox while it is **t**

TREADS → TREAD
Dt 25: 4 not muzzle an ox when it **t** out grain.

TREASURE → TREASURES
Ps 119:11 In my heart I **t** your promise, that I
Mt 6:21 For where your **t** is, there also will
2 Cor 4: 7 we hold this **t** in earthen vessels,

TREASURES → TREASURE
Col 2: 3 in whom are hidden all the **t**

TREE → TREES
Gn 3:24 to guard the way to the **t** of life.
Dt 21:23 shall not remain on the **t** overnight.
Mt 12:33 "Either declare the **t** good and its
12:33 or declare the **t** rotten and its fruit is
Acts 5:30 him killed by hanging him on a **t**.
Rom 11:24 what is by nature a wild olive **t**,
11:24 grafted back into their own olive **t**.
Rev 22: 2 side of the river grew the **t** of life

TREES → TREE
Ps 96:12 Then let all the **t** of the forest rejoice
Zec 4:11 "What are these two olive **t**,
Rev 11: 4 These are the two olive **t**

TREMBLE → TREMBLED, TREMBLING
Ps 114: 7 **T**, earth, before the Lord,
Hb 3: 6 he looked and made the nations **t**.

TREMBLED → TREMBLE
Ex 20:18 smoking, they became afraid and **t**.

TREMBLING → TREMBLE
Ps 2:11 exult with **t**, Accept correction lest
Phil 2:12 out your salvation with fear and **t**.

TRESPASSES
2 Cor 5:19 not counting their **t** against them

TRIAL → TRIALS
2 Pt 2: 9 how to rescue the devout from **t**
Rev 3:10 safe in the time of **t** that is going

TRIALS → TRIAL
Jas 1: 2 when you encounter various **t**,
1 Pt 1: 6 have to suffer through various **t**,

TRIBE → TRIBES
Nm 1: 4 there shall be a man from each **t**,
Ps 78:68 God chose the **t** of Judah,
Rev 5: 5 The lion of the **t** of Judah, the root

TRIBES → TRIBE
Gn 49:28 All these are the twelve **t** of Israel,
Ex 24: 4 stones for the twelve **t** of Israel.
Mt 19:28 judging the twelve **t** of Israel.
Rev 21:12 of the twelve **t** of the Israelites.

TRIUMPHS
Jas 2:13 mercy **t** over judgment.

TROUBLE → TROUBLED
Jb 14: 1 woman is short-lived and full of **t**.
Ps 9: 10 a stronghold in times of **t**.
Sir 51: 10 Do not abandon me in time of **t**,
Is 33: 2 morning, our salvation in time of **t**!

TROUBLED → TROUBLE
Jn 14: 1 "Do not let your hearts be **t**.

TRUE → TRUTH
Jn 1: 9 The **t** light, which enlightens
21: 24 and we know that his testimony is **t**.
Rom 3: 4 God must be **t**, though every human
1 Jn 5: 20 to know the one who is **t**. And we are in the one who is **t**,
5: 20 He is the **t** God and eternal life.
Rev 3: 14 the faithful and **t** witness, the source
19: 11 rider was [called] "Faithful and **T**."
22: 6 "These words are trustworthy and **t**,

TRUMPET → TRUMPETS
1 Cor 15: 52 in the blink of an eye, at the last **t**.
15: 52 For the **t** will sound, the dead will
1 Thes 4: 16 an archangel and with the **t** of God,

TRUMPETS → TRUMPET
Nm 10: 2 Make two **t** of silver, making them
Rev 8: 2 before God were given seven **t**.

TRUST → ENTRUSTED, TRUSTED, TRUSTS, TRUSTWORTHY
Nm 14: 11 How long will they not **t** me, despite
Ps 9: 11 Those who know your name **t**
37: 3 **T** in the LORD and do good
119: 42 with a word, for I **t** in your word.
Prv 3: 5 **T** in the LORD with all your heart,
Sir 2: 6 **T** in God, and he will help you;
Jer 17: 7 Blessed are those who **t** in the LORD; the LORD will be their **t**.
Heb 2: 13 and again: "I will put my **t** in him";

TRUSTED → TRUST
Ps 22: 5 In you our fathers **t**; they **t** and you
Dn 3: 95 to deliver the servants that **t** in him;
13: 35 she **t** in the Lord wholeheartedly.

TRUSTS → TRUST
Ps 86: 2 save your servant who **t** in you.

TRUSTWORTHY → TRUST
1 Cor 7: 25 as one who by the Lord's mercy is **t**.
Rev 22: 6 to me, "These words are **t** and true,

TRUTH → TRUE
Prv 23: 23 Buy **t** and do not sell:
Jn 1: 17 and **t** came through Jesus Christ.
4: 23 worship the Father in Spirit and **t**;
8: 32 and you will know the **t**, and the **t**
14: 6 "I am the way and the **t** and the life.
14: 17 the Spirit of **t**, which the world
16: 13 the Spirit of **t**, he will guide you to all **t**.
Eph 4: 15 Rather, living the **t** in love,
1 Tm 3: 15 God, the pillar and foundation of **t**.
2 Tm 2: 15 the word of **t** without deviation.

TUNIC
Lk 9: 3 and let no one take a second **t**.
Jn 19: 23 They also took his **t**, but the **t** was

TURN
Is 6: 10 and they **t** and be healed.
45: 22 **T** to me and be safe, all you ends
Lk 1: 17 of Elijah to **t** the hearts of fathers

TWELVE
Gn 49: 28 All these are the **t** tribes of Israel,
Ex 24: 4 and **t** sacred stones for the **t** tribes
Jos 4: 3 "Take up **t** stones from this spot
Mt 10: 1 he summoned his **t** disciples
Lk 9: 17 up, they filled **t** wicker baskets.
Rev 21: 12 with **t** gates where **t** angels were
21: 12 [the names] of the **t** tribes
22: 2 that produces fruit **t** times a year,

TWO → TWO-EDGED
Gn 1: 16 God made the **t** great lights,
6: 19 all living creatures you shall bring **t**
Ex 31: 18 he gave him the **t** tablets
Dt 17: 6 Only on the testimony of **t** or three
Mt 6: 24 "No one can serve **t** masters.
19: 5 and the **t** shall become one flesh'?

TWO-EDGED → TWO
Heb 4: 12 effective, sharper than any **t** sword,
Rev 1: 16 A sharp **t** sword came out of his

TYRE
Ez 28: 12 raise a lament over the king of **T**,
Mt 11: 22 it will be more tolerable for **T**

U

UNBELIEF → UNBELIEVER, UNBELIEVERS
Mk 9: 24 out, "I do believe, help my **u**!"
Rom 11: 20 They were broken off because of **u**,
1 Tm 1: 13 I acted out of ignorance in my **u**.

UNBELIEVER → UNBELIEF
1 Cor 10: 27 If an **u** invites you and you want
2 Cor 6: 15 a believer in common with an **u**?

UNBELIEVERS → UNBELIEF
2 Cor 6: 14 with those who are different, with **u**.

UNCIRCUMCISED → UNCIRCUMCISION
Ex 12: 48 But no one who is **u** may eat of it.
1 Mc 1: 48 to leave their sons **u**, and to defile
Acts 7: 51 people, **u** in heart and ears,
Rom 4: 11 through faith while he was **u**.
4: 11 the father of all the **u** who believe,

UNCIRCUMCISION → UNCIRCUMCISED
1 Cor 7: 19 nothing, and **u** means nothing;
Gal 5: 6 neither circumcision nor **u** counts

UNCLEAN
Lv 5: 2 it, touches any **u** thing, such as
5: 2 creature, and thus is **u** and guilty;
Is 52: 11 go out from there, touch nothing **u**!
Mk 3: 11 whenever **u** spirits saw him they
Rev 21: 27 but nothing **u** will enter it,

UNDER
Acts 4: 12 any other name **u** heaven given
Rom 6: 14 since you are not **u** the law but **u**

UNDERSTAND → UNDERSTANDING
Jb 42: 3 I have spoken but did not **u**;
Prv 2: 5 will you **u** the fear of the LORD;
Mt 13: 15 with their ears and **u** with their heart
Lk 24: 45 their minds to **u** the scriptures.
Acts 8: 30 "Do you **u** what you are reading?"
Eph 5: 17 try to **u** what is the will of the Lord.

UNDERSTANDING → UNDERSTAND
Ex 36: 1 **u** in knowing how to do all the work
Prv 2: 6 his mouth come knowledge and **u**;
Is 40: 14 or showed him the way of **u**?
Lk 2: 47 heard him were astounded at his **u**
Phil 4: 7 that surpasses all **u** will guard your
2 Tm 2: 7 for the Lord will give you **u**

UNFAITHFUL
Rom 3: 3 What if some were **u**?

UNGODLY
Rom 5: 6 died at the appointed time for the **u**.

UNITY
Eph 4: 3 preserve the **u** of the spirit through

UNJUST
Rom 3: 5 Is God **u**, humanly speaking,
Heb 6: 10 God is not **u** so as to overlook your

UNLEAVENED
Ex 12: 17 the custom of the **u** bread, since it
Mt 26: 17 first day of the Feast of **U** Bread,

UNPRODUCTIVE
1 Cor 14: 14 spirit is at prayer but my mind is **u**.
Ti 3: 14 needs, so that they may not be **u**.

UNRIGHTEOUS
2 Pt 2: 9 to keep the **u** under punishment

UPHOLD
Is 42: 1 Here is my servant whom I **u**,

UPRIGHT
Jb 1: 1 a blameless and **u** man named Job,

UR
Gn 15: 7 LORD who brought you from **U**

URIAH
Hittite husband of Bathsheba, killed (2 Sm 11).

URIM
Ex 28: 30 of decision you shall put the **U**

USE → USEFUL
Gal 5: 13 But do not **u** this freedom as
2 Tm 2: 20 for lofty and others for humble **u**.

USEFUL → USE
2 Tm 3: 16 by God and is **u** for teaching,

UZZIAH → =AZARIAH
Son of Amaziah; king of Judah also known as Azariah (2 Kgs 15:1-7; 1 Ch 6:24; 2 Ch 26). Struck with leprosy because of pride (2 Ch 26:16-23).

V

VAIN → VANITY
Lv 26: 16 You will sow your seed in **v**,
Ps 2: 1 and the peoples conspire in **v**?
Mt 15: 9 in **v** do they worship me, teaching as
Phil 2: 16 that I did not run in **v** or labor in **v**.

VALLEY
Ps 23: 4 Even though I walk through the **v**
Is 40: 4 Every **v** shall be lifted up,
40: 4 plain, the rough country, a broad **v**.
Lk 3: 5 Every **v** shall be filled and every

VALUE
Rom 3: 1 Or what is the **v** of circumcision?
1 Tm 4: 8 physical training is of limited **v**,

VANITY → VAIN
Eccl 1: 2 **V** of vanities, says Qoheleth,
1: 2 **v** of vanities! All things are **v**!
12: 8 **V** of vanities, says Qoheleth,
12: 8 says Qoheleth, all things are **v**!

VASHTI
Persian queen replaced by Esther (Est 1–2).

VEIL
Ex 34: 33 with them, he put a **v** over his face.
2 Cor 3: 15 is read, a **v** lies over their hearts,

VENGEANCE → AVENGE, AVENGER, AVENGING
Is 34: 8 For the LORD has a day of **v**,
Na 1: 2 The LORD takes **v** on his

VICTORY
Prv 21: 31 day of battle, but **v** is the LORD's.
1 Cor 15: 54 "Death is swallowed up in **v**.
1 Jn 5: 4 the **v** that conquers the world is our

VINDICATED → VINDICATION
Mt 11: 19 But wisdom is **v** by her works."
1 Tm 3: 16 in the flesh, **v** in the spirit,

VINDICATION → VINDICATED
Is 48: 18 your **v** like the waves of the sea,

VINE → VINEYARD
Ps 80: 9 You brought a **v** out of Egypt;
Jer 2: 21 But I had planted you as a choice **v**,
2: 21 so obnoxious to me, a spurious **v**?
Jn 15: 1 "I am the true **v**, and my Father is the **v** grower.

VINEYARD → VINE
1 Kgs 21: 1 Naboth the Jezreelite had a **v**
Is 5: 1 my beloved's song about his **v**.
Mt 21: 33 was a landowner who planted a **v**,

VIOLENCE
Hb 2: 17 For the **v** done to Lebanon shall
2: 17 and **v** done to the land, to the city

VIPERS
Mt 23: 33 you brood of **v**, how can you flee

VIRGIN
Jer 31: 21 Turn back, **v** Israel, turn back
Mt 1: 23 the **v** shall be with child and bear
2 Cor 11: 2 present you as a chaste **v** to Christ.

VISION → VISIONS
Is 22: 1 Oracle on the Valley of **V**:
Dn 8: 26 As for the **v** of the evenings
8: 26 But you, keep this **v** secret: it is
Acts 26: 19 not disobedient to the heavenly **v**.

VISIONS → VISION
Nm 12: 6 you, in **v** I reveal myself to them,
Ez 1: 1 opened, and I saw divine **v**.—
Dn 1: 17 to Daniel the understanding of all **v**
Acts 2: 17 your young men shall see **v**,

VOICE
Is 40: 3 A **v** proclaims: In the wilderness
Jn 1: 23 "I am 'the **v** of one crying
10: 3 and the sheep hear his **v**, as he calls
Heb 3: 7 that today you would hear his **v**,
Rev 3: 20 If anyone hears my **v** and opens

VOW → VOWS
Eccl 5: 4 better not to make a **v** than make it
Sir 18: 23 Before making a **v** prepare yourself;

VOWS → VOW
Ps 22: 26 my **v** I will fulfill before those who

W

WAGES
Rom 6: 23 For the **w** of sin is death, but the gift

WAIT
Ps 27: 14 **W** for the LORD, take courage;
27: 14 be stouthearted, **w** for the LORD!
Sir 2: 7 that fear the Lord, **w** for his mercy,
Hb 2: 3 If it delays, **w** for it, it will surely
Rom 8: 23 groan within ourselves as we **w**

WALK → WALKED, WALKING
Gn 17: 1 **W** in my presence and be blameless.
Ps 23: 4 Even though I **w** through the valley
Is 2: 5 let us **w** in the light of the LORD!
40: 31 grow weary, **w** and not grow faint.
Jer 6: 16 and **w** it; thus you will find rest
6: 16 But they said, "We will not **w** it."
Jn 8: 12 Whoever follows me will not **w**
2 Cor 5: 7 for we **w** by faith, not by sight.
Rev 21: 24 The nations will **w** by its light,

WALKED → WALK
Gn 5: 24 Enoch **w** with God, and he was no

WALKING → WALK
Mt 14: 26 the disciples saw him **w** on the sea

WALL
Jos 6: 20 The **w** collapsed, and the people
Neh 2: 17 let us rebuild the **w** of Jerusalem,
Eph 2: 14 and broke down the dividing **w**

WAR → WARRIOR, WARS
Eccl 3: 8 a time of **w**, and a time of peace.
Ps 24: 8 and mighty, the LORD, mighty in **w**.
Dn 9: 26 until the end of the **w**, which is
Rom 7: 23 my members another principle at **w**
Rev 19: 11 and wages **w** in righteousness.

WARRIOR → WAR
Ex 15: 3 The LORD is a **w**, LORD is his

WARS → WAR
Mt 24: 6 You will hear of **w** and reports of **w**;

WASH → WASHED
Ps 51: 9 **w** me, and I will be whiter than
Jn 13: 5 began to **w** the disciples' feet
Rev 22: 14 are they who **w** their robes so as

WASHED → WASH
1 Cor 6: 11 but now you have had yourselves **w**,

WATCH
Lk 2: 8 keeping the night **w** over their flock.
Heb 13: 17 for they keep **w** over you and will

WATER → WATERS
Ex 17: 1 But there was no **w** for the people
Nm 20: 2 Since the community had no **w**,
Jer 2: 13 broken cisterns that cannot hold **w**.
Ez 36: 25 I will sprinkle clean **w** over you
Mk 1: 8 I have baptized you with **w**;
Jn 2: 9 the headwaiter tasted the **w** that had
2: 9 who had drawn the **w** knew),
3: 5 of God without being born of **w**
4: 10 he would have given you living **w**."
1 Jn 5: 6 This is the one who came through **w**
5: 6 not by **w** alone, but by **w** and blood.
Rev 22: 1 me the river of life-giving **w**,

WATERS → WATER
Gn 7: 7 ark because of the **w** of the flood.
Eccl 11: 1 your bread upon the face of the **w**;

WAY → WAYS
Ps 1: 6 Because the LORD knows the **w**
1: 6 the **w** of the wicked leads to ruin.
86: 11 your **w** that I may walk in your
Prv 12: 15 The **w** of fools is right in their own
22: 6 the young in the **w** they should go;
Is 40: 3 the wilderness prepare the **w**
Mal 3: 1 he will prepare the **w** before me;
Mt 3: 3 desert, 'Prepare the **w** of the Lord,
Jn 14: 6 "I am the **w** and the truth
Acts 9: 2 or women who belonged to the **W**,
1 Cor 12: 31 show you a still more excellent **w**.
Heb 10: 20 living **w** he opened for us through

WAYS → WAY
Dt 10: 12 to follow in all his **w**, to love
Sir 2: 15 those who love him keep his **w**.
Ez 22: 31 bringing down their **w** upon their heads—
Rev 15: 3 Just and true are your **w**, O king

WEAK → WEAKNESS, WEAKNESSES
Mt 26: 41 spirit is willing, but the flesh is **w**."
Rom 14: 1 Welcome anyone who is **w** in faith,
1 Cor 1: 27 and God chose the **w** of the world
2 Cor 12: 10 for when I am **w**, then I am strong.

WEAKNESS → WEAK
Rom 8: 26 Spirit too comes to the aid of our **w**;

WEAKNESSES → WEAK
2 Cor 12: 10 I am content with **w**, insults,
Heb 4: 15 is unable to sympathize with our **w**,

WEALTH
Ps 49: 7 Of those who trust in their **w**
Prv 19: 4 **W** adds many friends, but the poor
Sir 5: 1 Do not rely on your **w**, or say,

WEAPONS
2 Cor 6: 7 with **w** of righteousness at the right

WEAR
Mt 6: 31 or 'What are we to **w**?'

WEARY
Is 40: 31 They will run and not grow **w**,
Heb 12: 3 in order that you may not grow **w**

WEDDING
Jn 2: 1 the third day there was a **w** in Cana

WEEKS
Ex 34: 22 You shall keep the feast of **W**
Lv 23: 15 you shall count seven full **w**;
Dn 9: 24 "Seventy **w** are decreed for your

WEEP → WEEPING
Eccl 3: 4 A time to **w**, and a time to laugh;
Rom 12: 15 who rejoice, **w** with those who **w**.

WEEPING → WEEP
Ps 30: 6 At dusk **w** comes for the night;
Mt 2: 18 Rachel **w** for her children, and she

WEIGHED
Dn 5: 27 you have been **w** on the scales

WELL
Mt 3: 17 Son, with whom I am **w** pleased."
17: 5 Son, with whom I am **w** pleased;
2 Pt 1: 17 with whom I am **w** pleased."

WEST
Ps 103: 12 As far as the east is from the **w**,
Is 43: 5 from the **w** I will gather you.

WHEAT
Mt 13: 25 and sowed weeds all through the **w**,
Lk 22: 31 demanded to sift all of you like **w**,
Jn 12: 24 you, unless a grain of **w** falls
12: 24 dies, it remains just a grain of **w**;

WHIRLWIND → WIND
2 Kgs 2: 11 and Elijah went up to heaven in a **w**,

WHITE → WHITER
Dn 7: 9 His clothing was **w** as snow, the hair
Mt 5: 36 for you cannot make a single hair **w**
Rev 1: 14 hair of his head was as **w** as **w** wool
20: 11 Next I saw a large **w** throne

WHITER → WHITE
Ps 51: 9 wash me, and I will be **w** than snow.

WHOLE
Dt 6: 5 love the LORD, your God, with your **w** heart, and with your **w** being, and with your **w** strength.

WICKED → WICKEDNESS
Gn 13: 13 the inhabitants of Sodom were **w**,
Ps 1: 5 Therefore the **w** will not arise
73: 3 when I saw the prosperity of the **w**.
Is 48: 22 There is no peace for the **w**,
Ez 18: 23 find pleasure in the death of the **w**—
Dn 12: 10 tested, but the **w** shall prove **w**;

WICKEDNESS → WICKED
Gn 6: 5 the LORD saw how great the **w**

WIDE
Mt 7: 13 for the gate is **w** and the road broad

WIDOW → WIDOWS
Ps 146: 9 to the aid of the orphan and the **w**,
1 Tm 5: 4 if a **w** has children or grandchildren,
Rev 18: 7 I am no **w**, and I will never know

WIDOWS → WIDOW
1 Tm 5: 3 Honor **w** who are truly **w**.
Jas 1: 27 for orphans and **w** in their affliction

WIFE → WIVES
Gn 2: 24 and mother and clings to his **w**,
Ex 20: 17 shall not covet your neighbor's **w**,
Tb 8: 6 you made his **w** Eve to be his helper
Prv 18: 22 To find a **w** is to find happiness,
Sir 26: 3 A good **w** is a generous gift
Mt 5: 32 whoever divorces his **w** (unless
19: 3 a man to divorce his **w** for any cause
Eph 5: 28 He who loves his **w** loves himself.
Rev 21: 9 you the bride, the **w** of the Lamb."

WILD
Ex 32: 25 were running **w** because Aaron had
Mk 1: 13 He was among **w** beasts,
Rom 11: 17 off, and you, a **w** olive shoot,

WILDERNESS
Is 40: 3 In the **w** prepare the way of the LORD!

WILL → WILLING
Ps 40: 9 I delight to do your **w**, my God;
143: 10 Teach me to do your **w**, for you are
Is 53: 10 it was the LORD's **w** to crush him
Mt 6: 10 kingdom come, your **w** be done,
Lk 22: 42 still, not my **w** but yours be done."
Jn 4: 34 to do the **w** of the one who sent me
Rom 9: 19 For who can oppose his **w**?"
Eph 6: 6 doing the **w** of God from the heart,
1 Jn 5: 14 we ask anything according to his **w**,

WILLING → WILL
Mt 26: 41 The spirit is **w**, but the flesh is
Lk 22: 42 if you are **w**, take this cup away

WIND → WHIRLWIND
1 Kgs 19: 11 violent **w** rending the mountains
19: 11 but the LORD was not in the **w**;
Ps 1: 4 They are like chaff driven by the **w**.
Eccl 1: 14 all is vanity and a chase after **w**.
Jn 3: 8 The **w** blows where it wills, and you
Acts 2: 2 sky a noise like a strong driving **w**,

WINE
Dt 7: 13 your soil, your grain and **w** and oil,
Ps 104: 15 **w** to gladden their hearts,
Prv 20: 1 **W** is arrogant, strong drink is
Sg 1: 2 for your love is better than **w**,
Sir 40: 20 **W** and strong drink delight the soul,
Mt 9: 17 People do not put new **w** into old
9: 17 the skins burst, the **w** spills out,
9: 17 Rather, they pour new **w** into fresh
Jn 2: 9 tasted the water that had become **w**,
Eph 5: 18 And do not get drunk on **w**,
Rev 18: 3 all the nations have drunk the **w**

WINGS
Ex 19: 4 how I bore you up on eagles' **w**
Ps 17: 8 hide me in the shadow of your **w**
Lk 13: 34 a hen gathers her brood under her **w**,

WIPE → WIPED
Is 25: 8 Lord GOD will **w** away the tears
Rev 21: 4 He will **w** every tear from their

WIPED → WIPE
Acts 3: 19 that your sins may be **w** away,

WISDOM → WISE
Dt 4: 6 for this is your **w** and discernment
1 Kgs 7: 14 He was endowed with **w**, understanding,
Jb 11: 6 And tell you the secrets of **w**,
Prv 1: 20 **W** cries aloud in the street,
9: 10 The beginning of **w** is fear
Eccl 1: 13 investigate in **w** all things that are
Wis 6: 12 Resplendent and unfading is **W**,
Sir 1: 1 All **w** is from the Lord and remains
24: 1 **W** sings her own praises, among her
Mt 13: 54 "Where did this man get such **w**
Lk 2: 52 And Jesus advanced [in] **w** and age
Rom 11: 33 the depth of the riches and **w**
1 Cor 1: 19 "I will destroy the **w** of the wise,
Col 2: 3 are hidden all the treasures of **w**
Jas 3: 17 the **w** from above is first of all pure,
Rev 5: 12 power and riches, **w** and strength,

WISE → WISDOM
Dt 4: 6 "This great nation is truly a **w**
Prv 3: 7 Do not be **w** in your own eyes,
13: 20 Walk with the **w** and you become **w**,
Eccl 12: 11 The sayings of the **w** are like goads;
Mt 25: 2 them were foolish and five were **w**.
1 Cor 1: 26 of you were **w** by human standards,
Eph 5: 15 live, not as foolish persons but as **w**,

WITHER → WITHERED, WITHERS
Ps 1: 3 Its leaves never **w**; whatever he does

WITHERED → WITHER
Mt 13: 6 scorched, and it **w** for lack of roots.
21: 19 And immediately the fig tree **w**.

WITHERS → WITHER
1 Pt 1: 24 the grass **w**, and the flower wilts;

WITHOUT
2 Ch 18: 16 mountains, like sheep **w** a shepherd,
Prv 19: 2 Desire **w** knowledge is not good;
Mt 9: 36 abandoned, like sheep **w** a shepherd.
Eph 2: 12 were at that time **w** Christ,
2: 12 **w** hope and **w** God in the world.
Heb 4: 15 been tested in every way, yet **w** sin.

WITNESS → EYEWITNESSES, WITNESSES
Dt 19: 15 One **w** alone shall not stand against
Jb 16: 19 Even now my **w** is in heaven,
Rom 2: 15 also bears **w** and their conflicting
Rev 1: 5 the faithful **w**, the firstborn

WITNESSES → WITNESS
Mt 26: 60 though many false **w** came forward.
Heb 12: 1 surrounded by so great a cloud of **w**,
Rev 11: 3 I will commission my two **w**

WIVES → WIFE
1 Kgs 11: 3 He had as **w** seven hundred
Eph 5: 22 **W** should be subordinate to their
1 Pt 3: 1 you **w** should be subordinate to your

WOE
Mt 23: 13 "**W** to you, scribes and Pharisees,
Rev 8: 13 cry out in a loud voice, "**W**! **W**!

WOLF → WOLVES
Is 11: 6 the **w** shall be a guest of the lamb,
Jn 10: 12 sees a **w** coming and leaves
10: 12 and the **w** catches and scatters them.

WOLVES → WOLF
Mt 7: 15 but underneath are ravenous **w**.

WOMAN → WOMEN
Gn 2: 22 he had taken from the man into a **w**.
3: 15 put enmity between you and the **w**,
Prv 11: 16 A gracious **w** gains esteem,
31: 30 the **w** who fears the LORD is to be
Dn 13: 2 a very beautiful and God-fearing **w**,
Jn 19: 26 he said to his mother, "**W**, behold,
Gal 4: 4 born of a **w**, born under the law,
Rev 12: 1 in the sky, a **w** clothed with the sun,

WOMB
Jb 1: 21 I came forth from my mother's **w**,
Ps 139: 13 you knit me in my mother's **w**.
Jer 1: 5 I formed you in the **w** I knew you,
Lk 1: 42 and blessed is the fruit of your **w**.
1: 44 the infant in my **w** leaped for joy.

WOMEN → WOMAN
Ezr 10: 2 by taking as wives foreign **w**
Mt 24: 41 Two **w** will be grinding at the mill;
Lk 1: 42 "Most blessed are you among **w**,
23: 55 The **w** who had come from Galilee
1 Pt 3: 5 how the holy **w** who hoped in God

WONDERS
Ps 136: 4 Who alone has done great **w**, for his
Jn 4: 48 you people see signs and **w**,
2 Thes 2: 9 deed and in signs and **w** that lie,

WOOD
Dt 28: 64 serve other gods, of **w** and stone,
1 Cor 3: 12 silver, precious stones, **w**, hay,

WORD → BYWORD, WORDS
1 Kgs 8: 56 Not a single **w** has gone unfulfilled
Ps 119: 105 Your **w** is a lamp for my feet,
Prv 30: 5 Every **w** of God is tested; he is
Is 40: 8 the **w** of our God stands forever."
55: 11 So shall my **w** be that goes forth
Mk 4: 14 The sower sows the **w**.
Lk 1: 38 done to me according to your **w**."
Jn 1: 1 In the beginning was the **W**, and the **W** was with God, and the **W**
1: 14 And the **W** became flesh and made
14: 23 loves me will keep my **w**, and my
17: 17 them in the truth. Your **w** is truth.
Rom 9: 6 it is not that the **w** of God has failed.
2 Tm 2: 15 imparting the **w** of truth without
Jas 1: 22 Be doers of the **w** and not hearers
1 Jn 2: 5 But whoever keeps his **w**, the love
Rev 19: 13 his name was called the **W** of God.

WORDS → WORD
Dt 4: 13 the ten **w**, which he wrote on two stone
11: 18 take these **w** of mine into your heart
Ps 5: 2 Give ear to my **w**, O LORD;
Prv 30: 6 Add nothing to his **w**, lest he
Hos 6: 5 I killed them by the **w** of my mouth;
Mt 24: 35 away, but my **w** will not pass away.
Lk 6: 47 listens to my **w**, and acts on them.
1 Cor 2: 13 them not with **w** taught by human
2: 13 but with **w** taught by the Spirit,
Rev 22: 19 from the **w** in this prophetic book,

WORK → WORKS
Gn 2: 2 God completed the **w** he had been
Ex 20: 10 You shall not do any **w**, either you,
Ps 8: 4 your heavens, the **w** of your fingers,
Jn 6: 27 Do not **w** for food that perishes
Phil 1: 6 the one who began a good **w** in you
2: 12 **w** out your salvation with fear
2 Tm 3: 17 equipped for every good **w**.
Heb 6: 10 not unjust so as to overlook your **w**

WORKS → WORK
Ps 8: 7 You have given him rule over the **w**
92: 6 How great are your **w**, LORD!
Gal 2: 16 a person is not justified by **w**
2: 16 in Christ and not by **w** of the law,
2: 16 because by **w** of the law no one will
5: 19 Now the **w** of the flesh are obvious:
Eph 2: 9 it is not from **w**, so no one may
1 Tm 6: 18 to be rich in good **w**, to be generous,
Jas 2: 17 itself, if it does not have **w**, is dead.

WORLD
Ps 9: 9 It is he who judges the **w**
Mt 5: 14 You are the light of the **w**. A city set
16: 26 there be for one to gain the whole **w**
Jn 1: 10 He was in the **w**, and the **w** came
1: 10 him, but the **w** did not know him.
3: 16 God so loved the **w** that he gave his
8: 12 saying, "I am the light of the **w**.
16: 33 In the **w** you will have trouble,
16: 33 courage, I have conquered the **w**."
1 Tm 6: 7 For we brought nothing into the **w**,
Jas 4: 4 to be a lover of the **w** means enmity
4: 4 of the **w** makes himself an enemy
1 Jn 2: 2 only but for those of the whole **w**.
2: 15 Do not love the **w** or the things of the **w**.
Rev 11: 15 kingdom of the **w** now belongs

WORM
Ps 22: 7 But I am a **w**, not a man,
Mk 9: 48 where 'their **w** does not die,

WORRY
Mt 6: 25 I tell you, do not **w** about your life,
10: 19 over, do not **w** about how you are

WORSHIP → WORSHIPED
Mt 4: 9 will prostrate yourself and **w** me."
Jn 4: 24 those who **w** him must **w** in Spirit
Rom 12: 1 pleasing to God, your spiritual **w**.
Rev 22: 3 be in it, and his servants will **w** him.

WORSHIPED → WORSHIP
Rev 5: 14 and the elders fell down and **w**.

WORTHY
Mt 10: 38 and follow after me is not **w** of me.
Eph 4: 1 in a manner **w** of the call you have
Heb 3: 3 But he is **w** of more "glory" than
Rev 4: 11 "**W** are you, Lord our God,
5: 12 "**W** is the Lamb that was slain

WOUND → WOUNDS
Ex 21: 25 burn for burn, **w** for **w**,
Rev 13: 3 but this mortal **w** was healed.

WOUNDS → WOUND
Ps 147: 3 and binding up their **w**.
1 Pt 2: 24 By his **w** you have been healed.

WRAPPED
Mk 15:46 **w** him in the linen cloth and laid
Lk 2: 7 She **w** him in swaddling clothes

WRATH
Ps 2: 5 his anger, in his **w** he terrifies them:
6: 2 LORD, nor punish me in your **w**.
Prv 15: 1 A mild answer turns back **w**,
Sir 16:11 and forgives, but also pours out **w**.
Lam 4:11 his anger, poured out his blazing **w**;
Zep 1:15 A day of **w** is that day, a day
Mt 3: 7 you to flee from the coming **w**?
Rom 1:18 The **w** of God is indeed being
Eph 2: 3 we were by nature children of **w**,
1 Thes 1:10 who delivers us from the coming **w**.
Rev 6:17 the great day of their **w** has come

WRITE → WRITING, WRITTEN, WROTE
Ex 34:27 **W** down these words,
Dt 6: 9 **W** them on the doorposts of your
Prv 7: 3 **w** them on the tablet of your heart.
Jer 31:33 them, and **w** it upon their hearts;
Heb 8:10 and I will **w** them upon their hearts.
Rev 21: 5 he said, "**W** these words down,

WRITING → WRITE
Dn 5: 7 "Whoever reads this **w** and tells me

WRITTEN → WRITE
Jos 23: 6 observe all that is **w** in the book
Dn 12: 1 everyone who is found **w**
Lk 24:44 that everything **w** about me
Jn 21:25 contain the books that would be **w**.
Rev 21:27 those will enter whose names are **w**

WRONG → WRONGDOING
Nm 5: 7 person shall confess the **w** that has
Acts 23: 9 "We find nothing **w** with this man.

WRONGDOING → WRONG
1 Jn 5:17 All **w** is sin, but there is sin that is

WROTE → WRITE
Ex 24: 4 **w** down all the words of the LORD
34:28 he **w** on the tablets the words
Jn 5:46 me, because he **w** about me.

Y

YEAR → YEARS
Ex 23:14 Three times a **y** you shall celebrate
Heb 10: 1 that they offer continually each **y**.

YEARS → YEAR
Gn 1:14 the seasons, the days and the **y**,
Ex 12:40 was four hundred and thirty **y**.
Nm 14:34 one year for each day: forty **y**.
2 Ch 36:21 rest while seventy **y** are fulfilled.
Ps 90: 4 A thousand **y** in your eyes are
Jer 25:12 when the seventy **y** have elapsed,
Dn 9: 2 was to lie in ruins for seventy **y**.
Gal 4:10 days, months, seasons, and **y**.
2 Pt 3: 8 Lord one day is like a thousand **y**
3: 8 **y** and a thousand **y** like one day.
Rev 20: 2 and tied it up for a thousand **y**

YEAST
Gal 5: 9 A little **y** leavens the whole batch

YESTERDAY
Heb 13: 8 Jesus Christ is the same **y**, today,

YOKE
Mt 11:30 For my **y** is easy, and my burden
Gal 5: 1 not submit again to the **y** of slavery.

YOUNG → YOUTH
Ps 119: 9 How can the **y** keep his way without
Acts 2:17 your **y** men shall see visions,

YOUTH → YOUNG
Ps 71: 5 my trust, GOD, from my **y**.
Eccl 12: 1 your Creator in the days of your **y**,

Z

ZACCHAEUS
Lk 19: 2 Now a man there named **Z**, who was

ZEAL → ZEALOUS
1 Mc 2:26 Thus he showed his **z** for the law,
Ps 69:10 Because **z** for your house has
Is 37:32 The **z** of the LORD of hosts shall
Jn 2:17 "**Z** for your house will consume
Rom 10: 2 to them that they have **z** for God,
Phil 3: 6 in **z** I persecuted the church,

ZEALOUS → ZEAL
1 Kgs 19:10 "I have been most **z**
Ez 39:25 of Israel; I am **z** for my holy name.

ZEBULUN
Son of Jacob by Leah (Gn 30:20; 35:23; 1 Ch 2:1). Tribe of blessed (Gn 49:13; Dt 33:18-19), numbered (Nm 1:31; 26:27), allotted land (Jos 19:10-16; Ez 48:26), failed to fully possess (Jgs 1:30), supported Deborah (Jgs 4:6-10; 5:14, 18), David (1 Ch 12:33), 12,000 from (Rev 7:8).

ZECHARIAH
1. Son of Jeroboam II; king of Israel (2 Kgs 15:8-12).
2. Post-exilic prophet who encouraged rebuilding of temple (Ezr 5:1; 6:14; Zec 1:1).

ZEDEKIAH → =MATTANIAH
1. False prophet (1 Kgs 22:11-24; 2 Ch 18:10-23).
2. Mattaniah, son of Josiah (1 Ch 3:15), made king of Judah by Nebuchadnezzar (2 Kgs 24:17–25:7; 2 Ch 36:10-14; Jer 37–39; 52:1-11).

ZEPHANIAH
Prophet; descendant of Hezekiah (Zep 1:1).

ZERUBBABEL
Descendant of David (1 Ch 3:19; Mt 1:3). Led return from exile (Ezr 2:2; Neh 7:7). Governor of Israel; helped rebuild temple (Ezr 3; Hg 1–2; Zec 4).

ZIMRI
King of Israel (1 Kgs 16:9-20).

ZION
2 Sm 5: 7 captured the fortress of **Z**, which is
Ps 2: 6 myself have installed my king on **Z**,
48: 3 Mount **Z**, the heights of Zaphon,
78:68 of Judah, Mount **Z** which he loved.
Is 28:16 I am laying a stone in **Z**, a stone
Mi 4: 2 from **Z** shall go forth instruction,
Zec 9: 9 Exult greatly, O daughter **Z**!
Mt 21: 5 "Say to daughter **Z**, 'Behold,
Rom 11:26 "The deliverer will come out of **Z**,
1 Pt 2: 6 "Behold, I am laying a stone in **Z**,
Rev 14: 1 was the Lamb standing on Mount **Z**,

ZIPPORAH
Daughter of Reuel; wife of Moses (Ex 2:21-22; 4:20-26; 18:1-6).

ZOPHAR
One of Job's friends (Jb 2:11; 11; 20; 42:9).

MAP 1

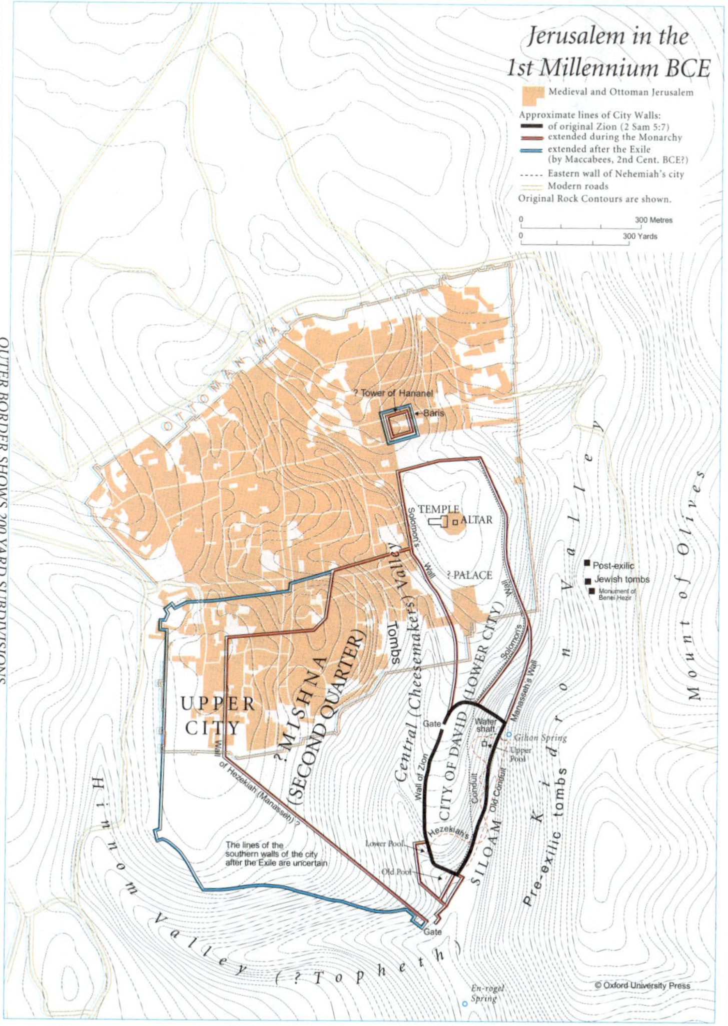
Jerusalem in the 1st Millennium BCE
Medieval and Ottoman Jerusalem
Approximate lines of City Walls:
of original Zion (2 Sam 5:7)
extended during the Monarchy
extended after the Exile (by Maccabees, 2nd Cent. BCE?)
Eastern wall of Nehemiah's city
Modern roads
Original Rock Contours are shown.
0 300 Metres
0 300 Yards
OTTOMAN WALL
? Tower of Hananel
Baris
TEMPLE
ALTAR
? PALACE
Solomon's Wall
Central (Cheesemakers') Valley
Tombs
?MISHNA (SECOND QUARTER)
UPPER CITY
Wall of Hezekiah (Manasseh) ?
CITY OF DAVID (LOWER CITY)
Gate
Wall of Zion
Water shaft
Upper Pool
Gihon Spring
Manasseh's Wall
Conduit
Old Conduit
Hezekiah's
SILOAM
Lower Pool
Old Pool
Gate
The lines of the southern walls of the city after the Exile are uncertain
Pre-exilic tombs
Kidron Valley
Post-exilic Jewish tombs
Monument of Benei Hezir
Mount of Olives
Hinnom Valley (?Topheth)
En-rogel Spring
© Oxford University Press

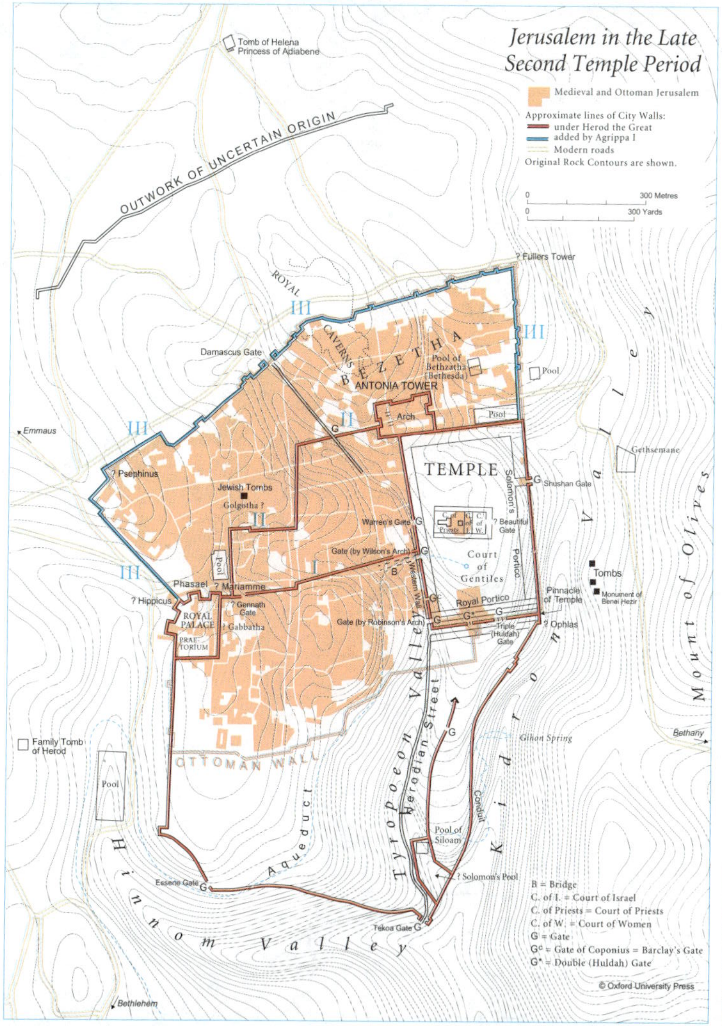
Jerusalem in the Late Second Temple Period
Medieval and Ottoman Jerusalem
Approximate lines of City Walls:
under Herod the Great
added by Agrippa I
Modern roads
Original Rock Contours are shown.
0 300 Metres
0 300 Yards
Tomb of Helena Princess of Adiabene
OUTWORK OF UNCERTAIN ORIGIN
ROYAL CAVERNS
? Fullers Tower
Damascus Gate
BEZETHA
Pool of Bethzatha (Bethesda)
ANTONIA TOWER
Arch
Pool
Emmaus
? Psephinus
Jewish Tombs
Golgotha ?
TEMPLE
Solomon's Portico
Shushan Gate
Gethsemane
Warren's Gate
? Beautiful Gate
Gate (by Wilson's Arch)
Court of Gentiles
Western Wall
Phasael
? Mariamme
? Hippicus
ROYAL PALACE
PRAETORIUM
? Gennath Gate
? Gabbatha
Royal Portico
Pinnacle of Temple
Gate (by Robinson's Arch)
Triple (Huldah) Gate
? Ophlas
Tombs
Monument of Benei Hezir
Mount of Olives
OTTOMAN WALL
Family Tomb of Herod
Pool
Aqueduct
Tyropoeon Valley
Herodian Street
Gihon Spring
Conduit
Pool of Siloam
? Solomon's Pool
Kidron Valley
Essene Gate
Tekoa Gate
Hinnom Valley
Bethany
Bethlehem
B = Bridge
C. of I. = Court of Israel
C. of Priests = Court of Priests
C. of W. = Court of Women
G = Gate
G^c = Gate of Coponius = Barclay's Gate
G* = Double (Huldah) Gate
© Oxford University Press

OUTER BORDER SHOWS 200 YARD SUBDIVISIONS

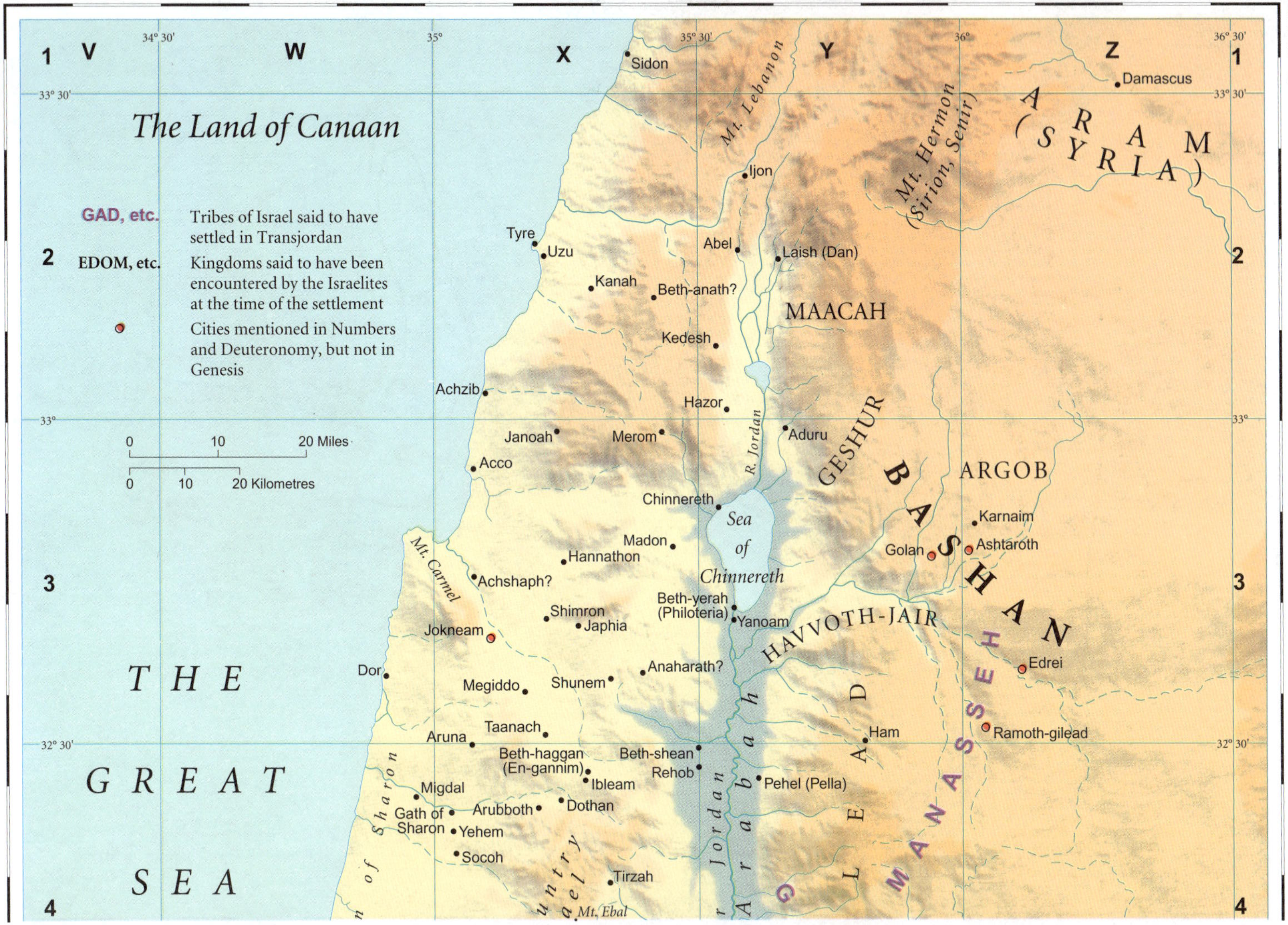
The Land of Canaan
GAD, etc. Tribes of Israel said to have settled in Transjordan
EDOM, etc. Kingdoms said to have been encountered by the Israelites at the time of the settlement
Cities mentioned in Numbers and Deuteronomy, but not in Genesis
0 10 20 Miles
0 10 20 Kilometres
V W X Y Z
1 2 3 4
34° 30'
35°
35° 30'
36°
36° 30'
33° 30'
33°
32° 30'
THE GREAT SEA
Sidon
Damascus
ARAM (SYRIA)
Mt. Lebanon
Mt. Hermon (Sirion, Senir)
Ijon
Tyre
Uzu
Abel
Laish (Dan)
Kanah
Beth-anath?
MAACAH
Kedesh
Achzib
Hazor
R. Jordan
Aduru
GESHUR
Janoah
Merom
Acco
ARGOB
BASHAN
Chinnereth
Sea of Chinnereth
Karnaim
Golan
Ashtaroth
Madon
Hannathon
Mt. Carmel
Achshaph?
Beth-yerah (Philoteria)
Yanoam
Shimron
Japhia
HAVVOTH-JAIR
Jokneam
Dor
Anaharath?
Edrei
Megiddo
Shunem
Taanach
Aruna
Ham
Ramoth-gilead
Beth-haggan (En-gannim)
Beth-shean
Rehob
Ibleam
Pehel (Pella)
Migdal
Gath of Sharon
Arubboth
Dothan
Yehem
Socoh
Tirzah
Mt. Ebal
Arabah
Jordan
Sharon
GILEAD
MANASSEH
GAD

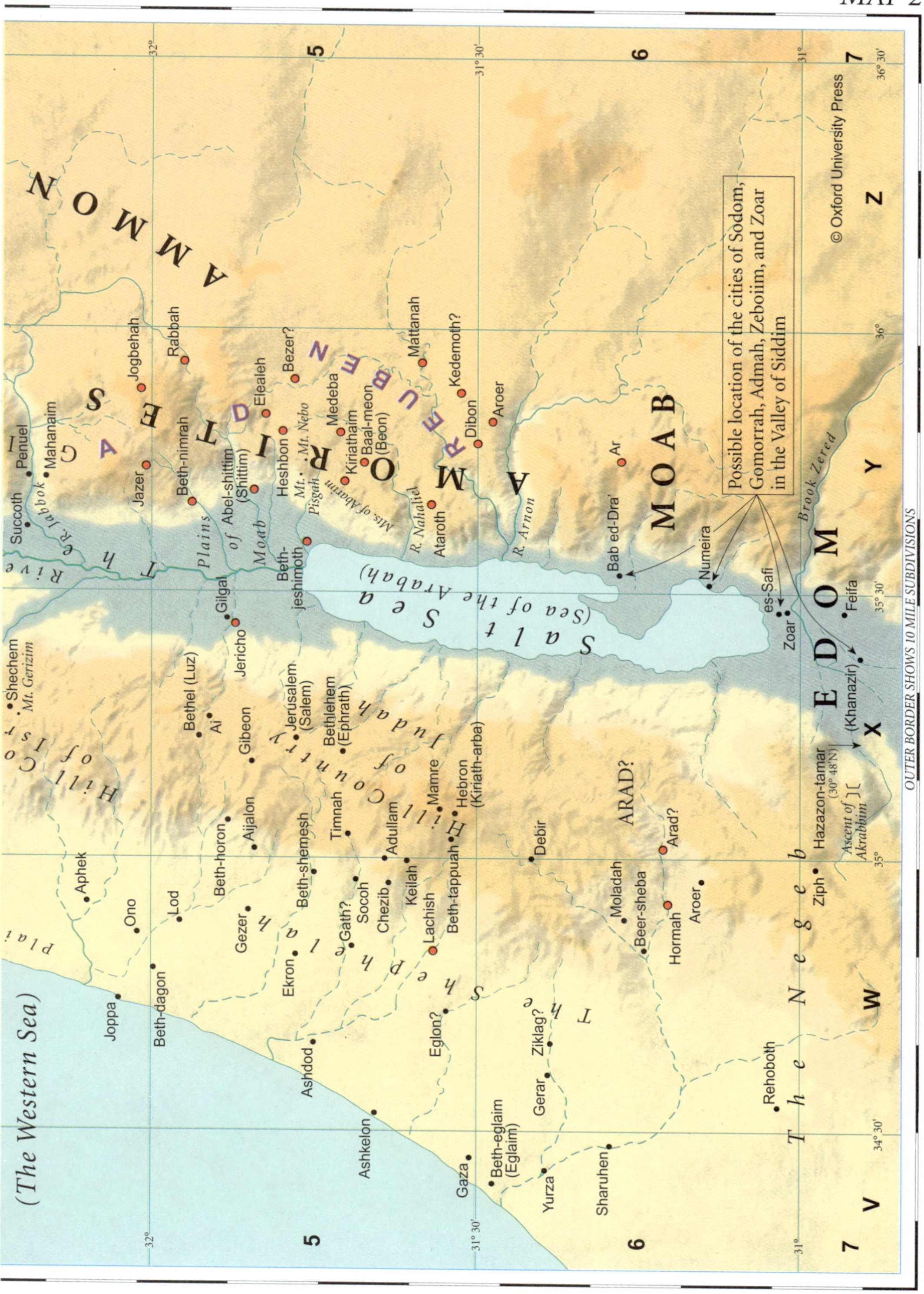

(The Western Sea)
AMMON
GADITES
AMORITES
REUBEN
MOAB
EDOM
Salt Sea
(Sea of the Arabah)
The River Jordan
R. Jabbok
Plains of Moab
Mts. of Abarim
Mt. Nebo
Mt. Pisgah
R. Nahaliel
R. Arnon
Brook Zered
Hill Country of Israel
Hill Country of Judah
The Shephelah
The Negeb
The Plain
Mt. Gerizim
Penuel
Mahanaim
Succoth
Jogbehah
Rabbah
Jazer
Beth-nimrah
Abel-shittim (Shittim)
Elealeh
Heshbon
Bezer?
Beth-jeshimoth
Medeba
Kiriathaim
Baal-meon (Beon)
Mattanah
Kedemoth?
Dibon
Aroer
Ataroth
Bab ed-Dra'
Ar
Numeira
es-Safi
Zoar
Feifa
(Khanazir)
Possible location of the cities of Sodom, Gomorrah, Admah, Zeboiim, and Zoar in the Valley of Siddim
Shechem
Bethel (Luz)
Ai
Gilgal
Jericho
Gibeon
Jerusalem (Salem)
Bethlehem (Ephrath)
Aijalon
Beth-horon
Aphek
Ono
Lod
Gezer
Beth-shemesh
Timnah
Adullam
Mamre
Hebron (Kiriath-arba)
Socoh
Chezib
Keilah
Beth-tappuah
Gath?
Ekron
Lachish
Eglon?
Debir
ARAD?
Arad?
Moladah
Beer-sheba
Hormah
Aroer
Ziph
Hazazon-tamar (30° 48'N)
Ascent of Akrabbim
Joppa
Beth-dagon
Ashdod
Ashkelon
Gaza
Beth-eglaim (Eglaim)
Gerar
Ziklag?
Yurza
Sharuhen
Rehoboth
32°
31° 30'
31°
34° 30'
35°
35° 30'
36°
36° 30'
5
6
7
V
W
X
Y
Z
OUTER BORDER SHOWS 10 MILE SUBDIVISIONS
© Oxford University Press

MAP 3

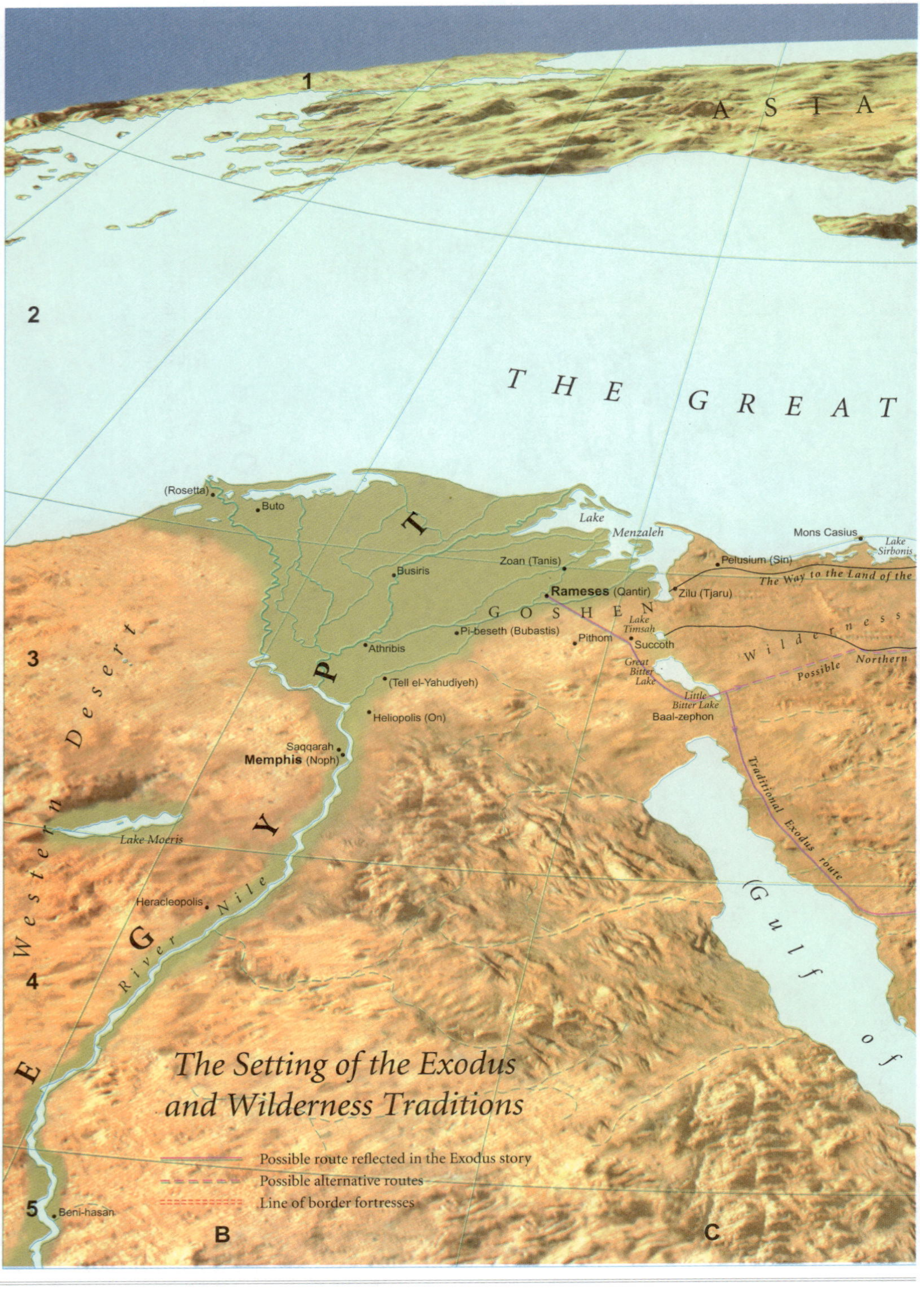
The Setting of the Exodus and Wilderness Traditions
Possible route reflected in the Exodus story
Possible alternative routes
Line of border fortresses
ASIA
THE GREAT
EGYPT
Western Desert
GOSHEN
(Rosetta)
Buto
Busiris
Lake Menzaleh
Zoan (Tanis)
Rameses (Qantir)
Mons Casius
Lake Sirbonis
Pelusium (Sin)
The Way to the Land of the
Zilu (Tjaru)
Lake Timsah
Pi-beseth (Bubastis)
Pithom
Succoth
Athribis
Wilderness
Northern
Possible
Great Bitter Lake
Little Bitter Lake
Baal-zephon
(Tell el-Yahudiyeh)
Heliopolis (On)
Saqqarah
Memphis (Noph)
Traditional Exodus route
Lake Moeris
(Gulf of
Heracleopolis
River Nile
Beni-hasan
1
2
3
4
5
B
C

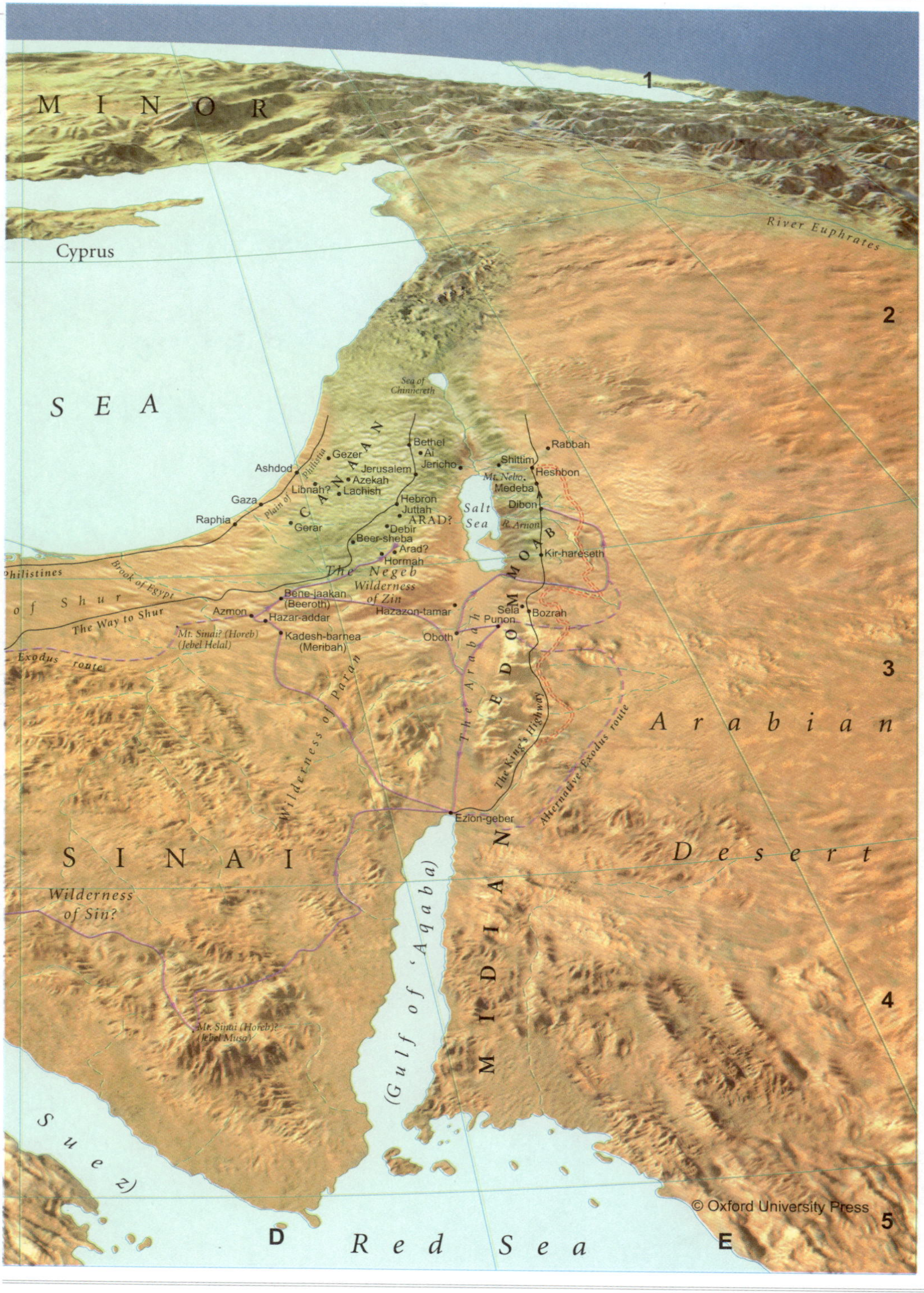
MINOR
Cyprus
SEA
River Euphrates
Sea of Chinnereth
CANAAN
Plain of Philistia
Ashdod
Gezer
Bethel
Ai
Jericho
Jerusalem
Azekah
Libnah?
Lachish
Gaza
Hebron
Juttah
ARAD?
Raphia
Gerar
Debir
Beer-sheba
Arad?
Hormah
Philistines
Brook of Egypt
The Negeb
Wilderness of Zin
of Shur
The Way to Shur
Bene-jaakan (Beeroth)
Azmon
Hazar-addar
Kadesh-barnea (Meribah)
Mt. Sinai? (Horeb) (Jebel Helal)
Exodus route
Hazazon-tamar
Rabbah
Shittim
Mt. Nebo
Heshbon
Medeba
Dibon
Salt Sea
R. Arnon
MOAB
Kir-hareseth
Sela
Bozrah
Punon
Oboth
EDOM
The Arabah
The King's Highway
Alternative Exodus route
Wilderness of Paran
Ezion-geber
Arabian
Desert
SINAI
Wilderness of Sin?
MIDIAN
(Gulf of 'Aqaba)
Mt. Sinai (Horeb)? (Jebel Musa)
(Suez)
Red Sea
1
2
3
4
5
D
E
© Oxford University Press

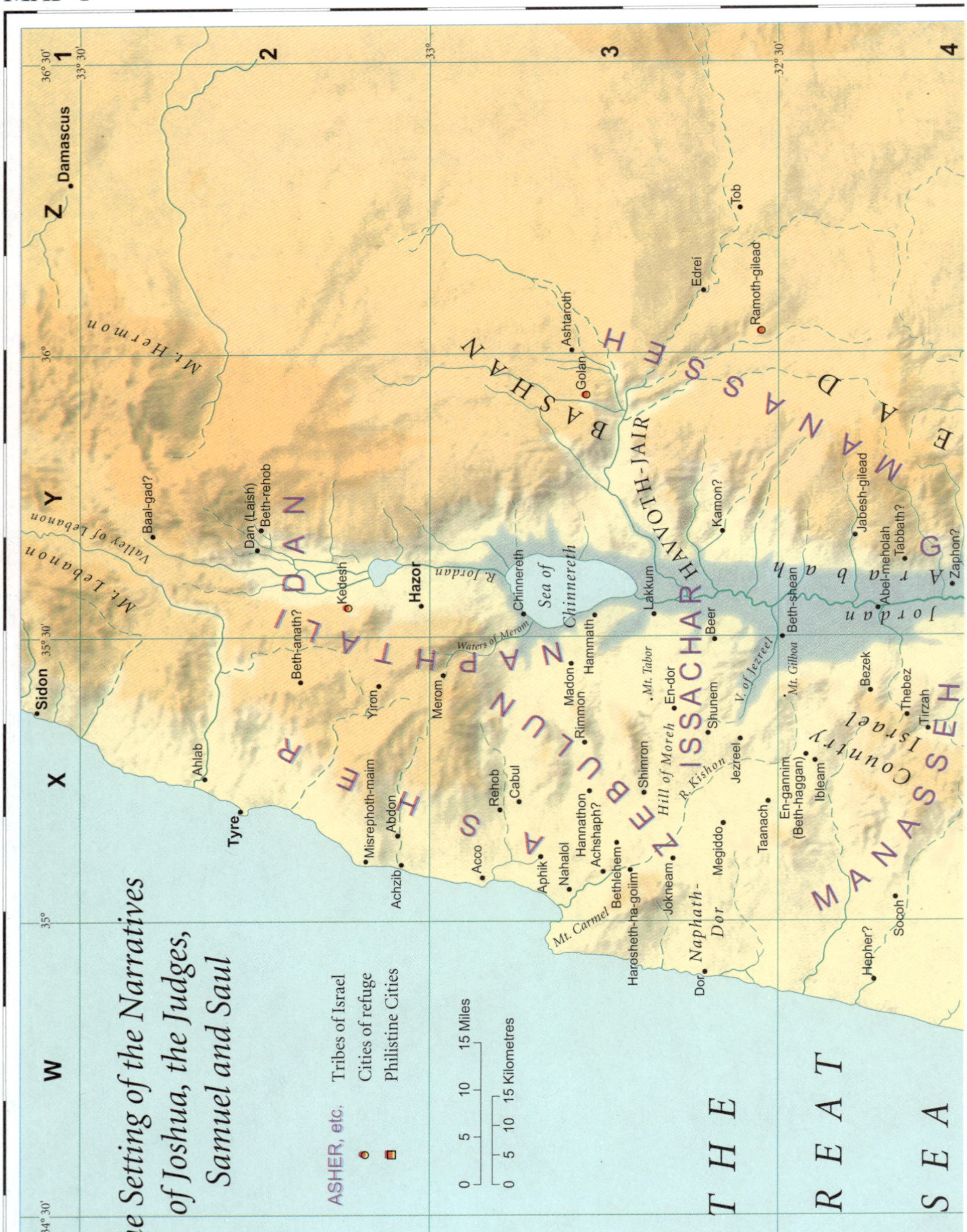

The Setting of the Narratives of Joshua, the Judges, Samuel and Saul

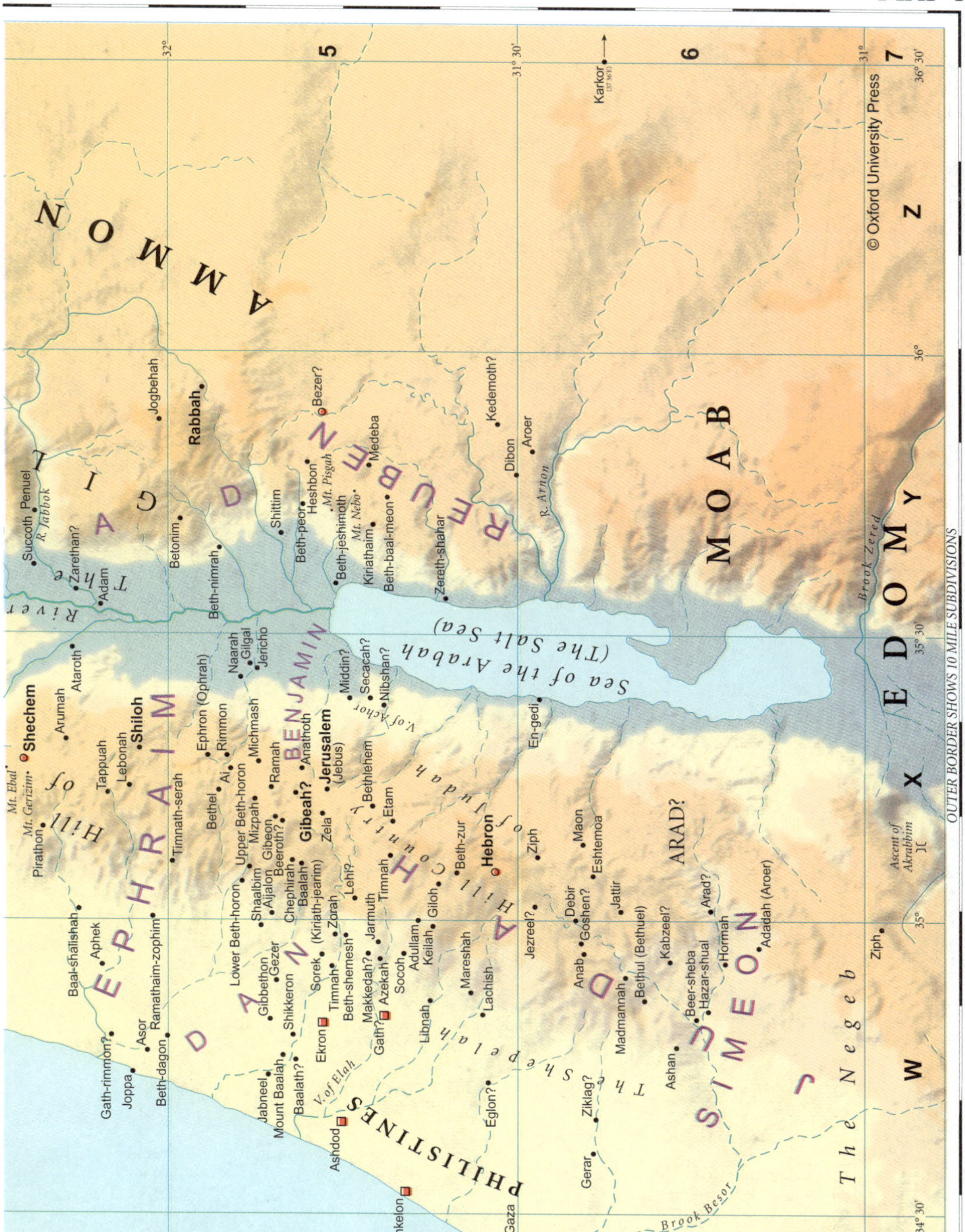
AMMON
GILEAD
GAD
REUBEN
MOAB
EDOM
EPHRAIM
BENJAMIN
DAN
JUDAH
SIMEON
PHILISTINES
ARAD?
Sea of the Arabah
(The Salt Sea)
The River
Hill of Ephraim
Hill Country of Judah
The Shephelah
The Negeb
R. Jabbok
R. Arnon
Brook Zered
Brook Besor
V. of Elah
V. of Achor
Ascent of Akrabbim
Mt. Ebal
Mt. Gerizim
Mt. Pisgah
Mt. Nebo
Shechem
Shiloh
Jerusalem
(Jebus)
Hebron
Rabbah
Gibeah?
Jericho
Gilgal
Naarah
Bethel
Ai
Rimmon
Ephron (Ophrah)
Michmash
Ramah
Anathoth
Mizpah
Gibeon
Beeroth?
Upper Beth-horon
Lower Beth-horon
Timnath-serah
Tappuah
Lebonah
Arumah
Ataroth
Pirathon
Baal-shalishah
Aphek
Ramathaim-zophim
Gath-rimmon?
Joppa
Asor
Beth-dagon
Gibbethon
Gezer
Shaalbim
Aijalon
Chephirah
Baalah
Zela
Kiriath-jearim
Zorah
Lehi?
Sorek
Timnah
Beth-shemesh
Shikkeron
Ekron
Jabneel
Mount Baalah
Baalath?
Ashdod
Ashkelon
Gaza
Makkedah?
Azekah
Gath?
Jarmuth
Timnah
Bethlehem
Etam
Socoh
Adullam
Keilah
Giloh
Beth-zur
Libnah
Mareshah
Lachish
Eglon?
Jezreel?
Ziph
Maon
Eshtemoa
Debir
Goshen?
Anab
Jattir
Madmannah
Bethul (Bethuel)
Kabzeel?
Beer-sheba
Hazar-shual
Arad?
Hormah
Adadah (Aroer)
Ashan
Ziklag?
Gerar
Ziph
En-gedi
Middin?
Secacah?
Nibshan?
Succoth
Penuel
Zarethan?
Adam
Betonim
Jogbehah
Beth-nimrah
Shittim
Beth-peor
Heshbon
Bezer?
Medeba
Beth-jeshimoth
Kiriathaim
Beth-baal-meon
Zereth-shahar
Dibon
Aroer
Kedemoth?
Karkor
© Oxford University Press
OUTER BORDER SHOWS 10 MILE SUBDIVISIONS
32°
31° 30'
31°
34° 30'
35°
35° 30'
36°
36° 30'
5
6
7
V
W
X
Y
Z

MAP 5

The Setting of the Narratives of David and Solomon
SYRIA, etc. Non-Israelite peoples
Places fortified by Solomon
I–XII Solomon's administrative districts (1 Kgs. 4. 7-19)
0 10 20 Miles
0 10 20 Kilometres
THE GREAT SEA
SIDONIANS
SYRIA (ARAM)
ZOBAH
Damascus
BETH-REHOB
MAACAH
ARGOB
GESHUR
BASHAN
HAVVOTH-JAIR
GILEAD
AMMON
ISRAEL
Arabah
Mt. Hermon
Mt. Lebanon
Sidon
Tyre
Abel-beth-maacah
Dan
Beth-rehob
Hazor
Merom
Cabul
Acco
Mt. Carmel
R. Kishon
Jokneam (Jokmeam)
Megiddo
Taanach
Jezreel
Mt. Gilboa
V. of Jezreel
Beth-shean
Dor
Sharon
Plain of Sharon
Hepher?
Socoh
Arubboth
Thebez
Mt. Ebal
R. Jordan
Sea of Chinnereth
Helam
Tob
Ramoth-gilead
Rogelim
Jabesh-gilead
Abel-meholah
I
II
III
IV
V
VI
VII
VIII
IX
X
V
W
X
Y
Z
1
2
3
4
33° 30'
33°
32° 30'
34° 30'
35°
35° 30'
36°
36° 30'

AMMON
GILEAD
MOAB
EDOM
JUDAH
ISRAEL
PHILISTINES
AMALEKITES
Rabbah (Rabbath-ammon)
R. Jabbok
Mahanaim
Succoth
Zarethan?
Lo-debar?
Jazer
The River
Heshbon
Medeba
Dibon
Aroer
R. Nahaliel
R. Arnon
Kir-hareseth
Brook Zered
Salt Sea
(Sea of the Arabah)
Wilderness of Judah
Shechem
Mt. Gerizim
Pirathon
Shiloh
Baal-hazor
Ephraim
Gilgal
Jericho
Bethel
Upper Beth-horon
Gibeon
Geba
Beeroth?
Anathoth
Jerusalem
Gibeah?
Elon
Beth-hanan
Lower Beth-horon
Shaalbim
Gezer
Makaz
Kiriath-jearim
Sorek
Beth-shemesh
Ekron
Baalath?
Bethlehem
Netophah
Tekoa
Timnah
Hebron
Carmel
Arad
Giloh
Adullam
Libnah?
Debir
Kabzeel?
Valley of Salt
Gath?
The Shephelah (Lowland)
Zeredah
Gath-rimmon
Joppa
Ashdod
Ashkelon
Gaza
Gerar
Ziklag?
Beer-sheba
The Negeb
Brook Besor
Tamar
(30° 48′N)
I
II
XI
XII
© Oxford University Press
OUTER BORDER SHOWS 10 MILE SUBDIVISIONS

The Kingdoms of Israel and Judah
ISRAEL, JUDAH Hebrew kingdoms
ASHER, etc. Tribal areas
SYRIA, etc. Non-Israelite peoples
Approximate boundary between Israel, Judah and Philistia
0 10 20 Miles
0 10 20 Kilometres
1 V W X Y Z 1
2
3
4
34° 30'
35°
35° 30'
36°
36° 30'
33° 30'
33°
32° 30'
THE GREAT SEA
SYRIA (ARAM)
ZOBAH
Damascus
R. Abana
R. Pharpar
Mt. Hermon
Entrance to Hamath
Mt. Lebanon
Sidon
Zarephath
SIDONIANS
Tyre
Ijon
Abel-beth-maacah (Abel-maim)
Dan
ASHER
NAPHTALI
Kedesh
Yiron
Hazor
Merom
Janoah
GALILEE
Acco
R. Jordan
Chinnereth
Sea of Chinnereth
BASHAN
MANASSEH
Karnaim
Ashtaroth
Aphek
Rumah
Hannathon
ZEBULUN
Gath-hepher
Mt. Carmel
R. Kishon
Mt. Tabor
Jokmeam
ISSACHAR
HAVVOTH-JAIR
HAURAN
Edrei
Dor
Megiddo
Shunem
Jezreel
V. of Jezreel
Beth-arbel
Ramoth-gilead
Taanach
Beth-haggan
Ibleam
Borim
Dothan
Tishbe
Brook Cherith
Abel-meholah
of Sharon
ISRAEL
Socoh
Yazith
Samaria
Tirzah
Siphtan
Mt. Ebal
MANASSEH
Jordan
Arabah
GILEAD
AMMON

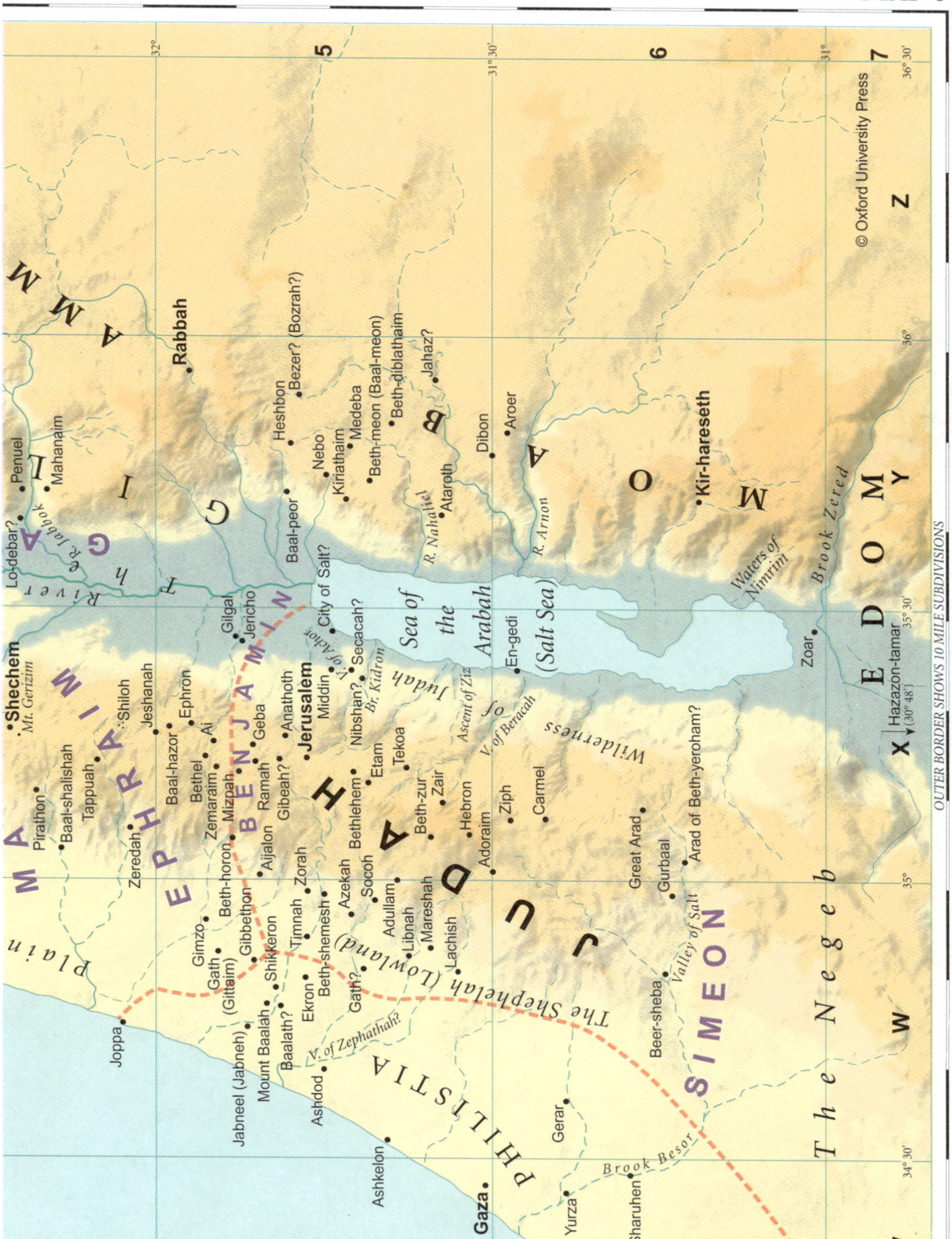

OUTER BORDER SHOWS 10 MILE SUBDIVISIONS
© Oxford University Press
V
W
X
Y
Z
5
6
7
32°
31° 30'
31°
34° 30'
35°
35° 30'
36°
36° 30'
GILEAD
AMMON
MANASSEH
EPHRAIM
BENJAMIN
JUDAH
SIMEON
PHILISTIA
MOAB
EDOM
The Negeb
Plain of Sharon
The Shephelah (Lowland)
Wilderness of Judah
River Jordan
R. Jabbok
R. Nahaliel
R. Arnon
Brook Zered
Waters of Nimrim
Sea of the Arabah (Salt Sea)
V. of Achor
Br. Kidron
Ascent of Ziz
V. of Beracah
Valley of Salt
V. of Zephathah?
Brook Besor
Shechem
Mt. Gerizim
Penuel
Mahanaim
Lo-debar?
Rabbah
Heshbon
Bezer? (Bozrah?)
Medeba
Beth-meon (Baal-meon)
Beth-diblathaim
Jahaz?
Nebo
Kiriathaim
Baal-peor
Ataroth
Dibon
Aroer
Kir-hareseth
Zoar
Hazazon-tamar (30° 48')
Pirathon
Baal-shalishah
Tappuah
Shiloh
Jeshanah
Zeredah
Baal-hazor
Ephron
Bethel
Ai
Zemaraim
Mizpah
Beth-horon
Ramah
Geba
Gibeah?
Anathoth
Gilgal
Jericho
City of Salt?
Middin
Secacah?
Nibshan?
Jerusalem
Aijalon
Gimzo
Gibbethon
Gath (Gittaim)
Shikkeron
Timnah
Zorah
Beth-shemesh
Azekah
Socoh
Bethlehem
Etam
Tekoa
Adullam
Libnah
Mareshah
Lachish
Beth-zur
Zair
Hebron
Adoraim
Ziph
Carmel
En-gedi
Great Arad
Gurbaal
Arad of Beth-yeroham?
Beer-sheba
Joppa
Jabneel (Jabneh)
Mount Baalah
Baalath?
Ekron
Gath?
Ashdod
Ashkelon
Gaza
Gerar
Yurza
Sharuhen
Raphia

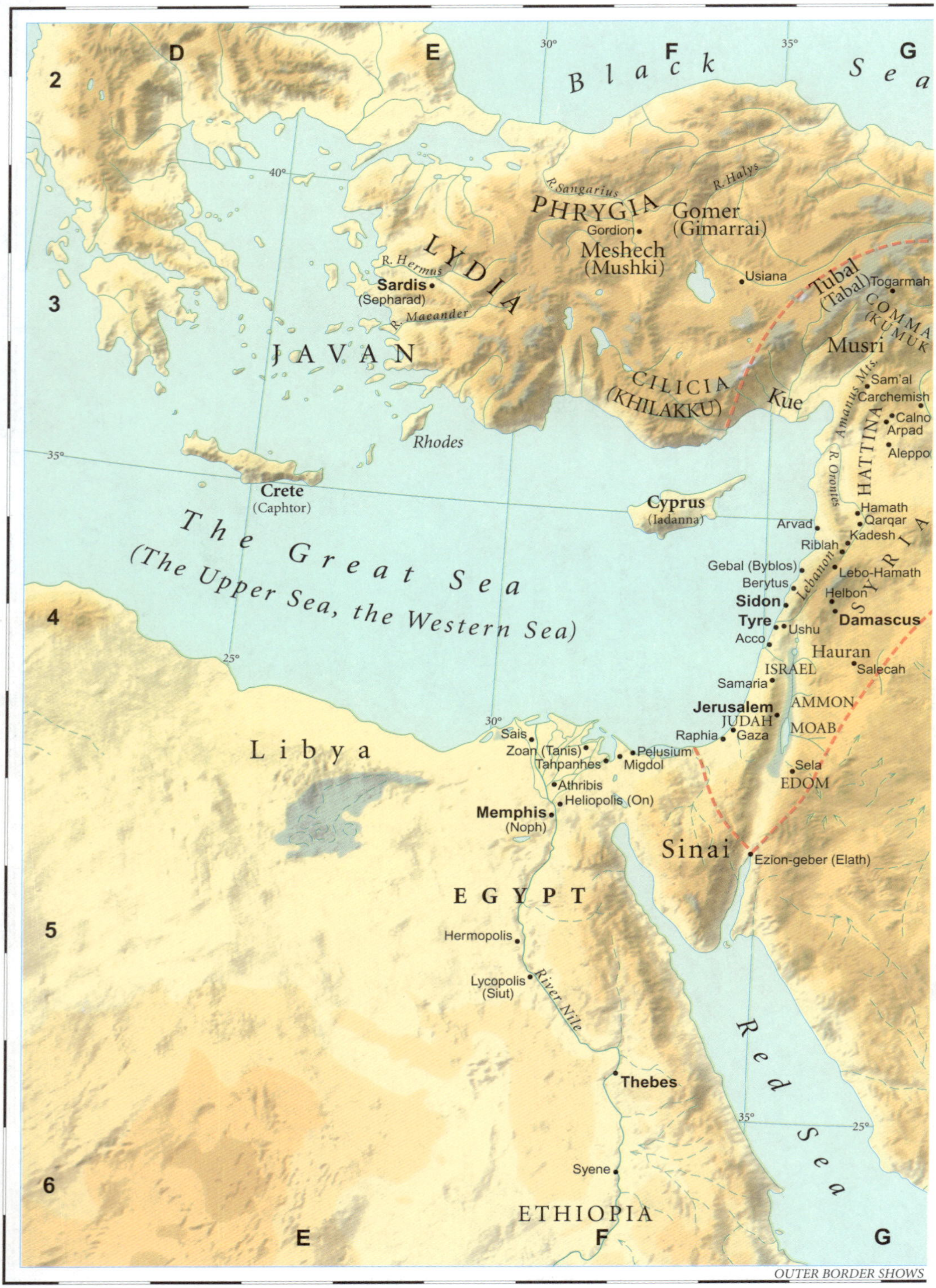

OUTER BORDER SHOWS

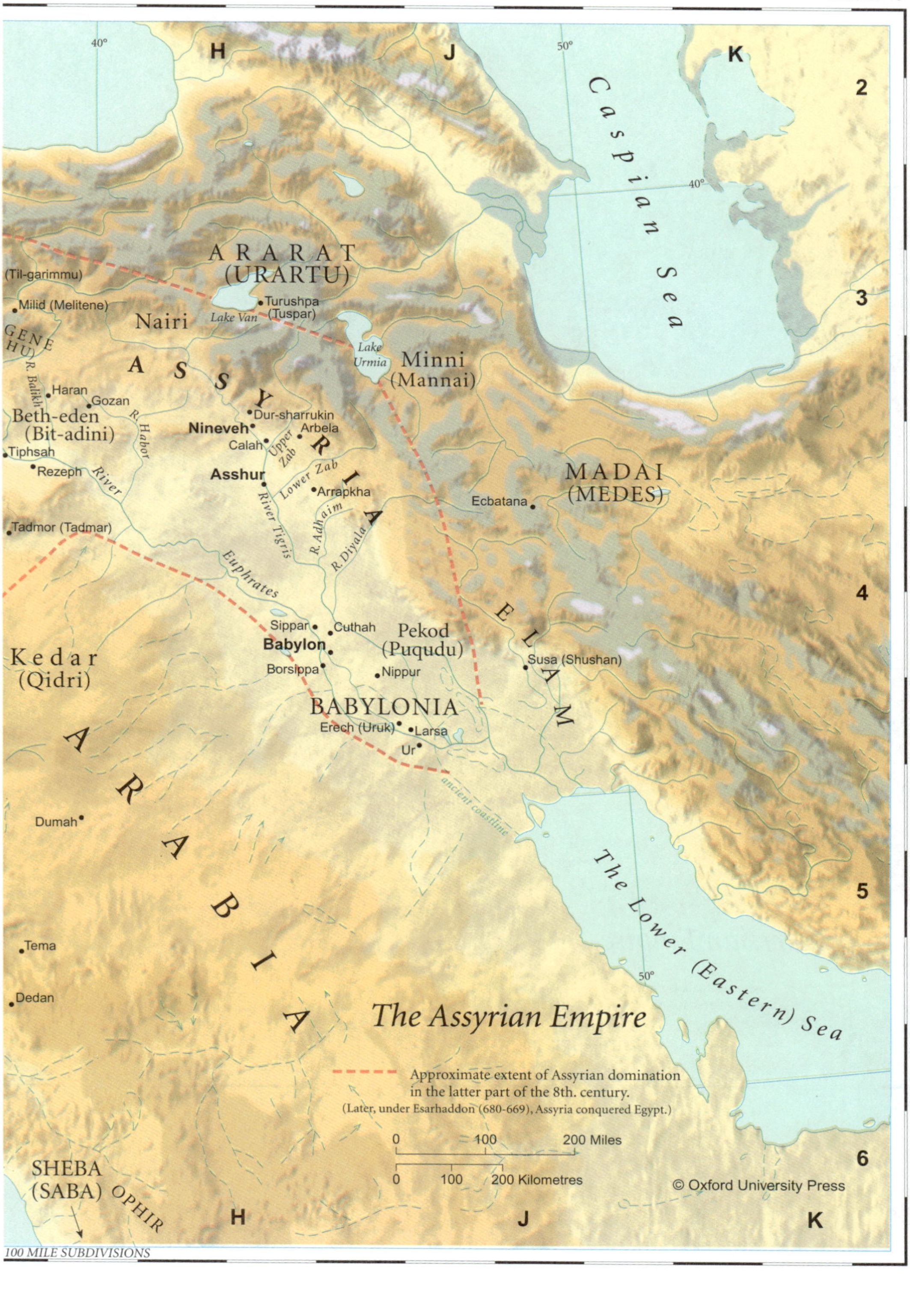
The Assyrian Empire
H
J
K
2
3
4
5
6
40°
50°
Caspian Sea
ARARAT (URARTU)
(Til-garimmu)
Milid (Melitene)
Turushpa (Tuspar)
Lake Van
Nairi
GENEHU
Lake Urmia
Minni (Mannai)
ASSYRIA
R. Balikh
Haran
Gozan
Beth-eden (Bit-adini)
R. Habor
Dur-sharrukin
Nineveh
Arbela
Calah
Upper Zab
Tiphsah
Rezeph
River
Asshur
Lower Zab
Arrapkha
MADAI (MEDES)
Ecbatana
River Tigris
R. Adhaim
R. Diyala
Tadmor (Tadmar)
Euphrates
Sippar
Cuthah
Pekod (Puqudu)
Babylon
Kedar (Qidri)
Borsippa
Nippur
Susa (Shushan)
ELAM
BABYLONIA
Erech (Uruk)
Larsa
Ur
ARABIA
ancient coastline
Dumah
The Lower (Eastern) Sea
Tema
Dedan
Approximate extent of Assyrian domination in the latter part of the 8th. century.
(Later, under Esarhaddon (680-669), Assyria conquered Egypt.)
0 100 200 Miles
0 100 200 Kilometres
SHEBA (SABA)
OPHIR
100 MILE SUBDIVISIONS

MAP 8

OUTER BORDER SHOWS

Hyrcanian
Sea
(Caspian Sea)
CHORASMIA
SAKA (SCYTHIANS)
Cyropolis
(Bokhara)
SOGDIANA
R. Oxus
R. Cyrus
R. Araxes
Margiana
(Margus)
R. Margus
Bactra
BACTRIA
GANDHARA
Astrabad (Gorgan)
Zadrakarta (Turang Tepe)
Tesmes (Mashhad)
(Damghan)
HYRCANIA
E M P I R E
MEDIA
Rages (Rhagae)
PARTHIA
Artacoana
R. Areius
ARIA
(Ghazni)
SATTAGYDIA
Ecbatana
(Achmetha)
Behistun (Bisutun)
SAGARTIA
DRANGIANA
(Kandahar)
ELAM
(SUSIANA)
Gabae (Isfahan)
Susa (Shushan)
ARACHOSIA
Anshan
(Tall-i Malyan)
Parsagarda (Pasargadae)
(Kerman)
Persepolis
PERSIS
(PERSIA)
ancient coastline
HINDUSH
(INDIA)
R. Indus
GEDROSIA
(MAKA)
CARMANIA
(Gulashkird)
Pura
Pattala
Lower Sea (Persian Gulf)
Erythraean
Sea
A
© Oxford University Press
J K L M N
2 3 4 5 6
50°
40°
55°
25°
60°
65°
200 MILE SUBDIVISIONS

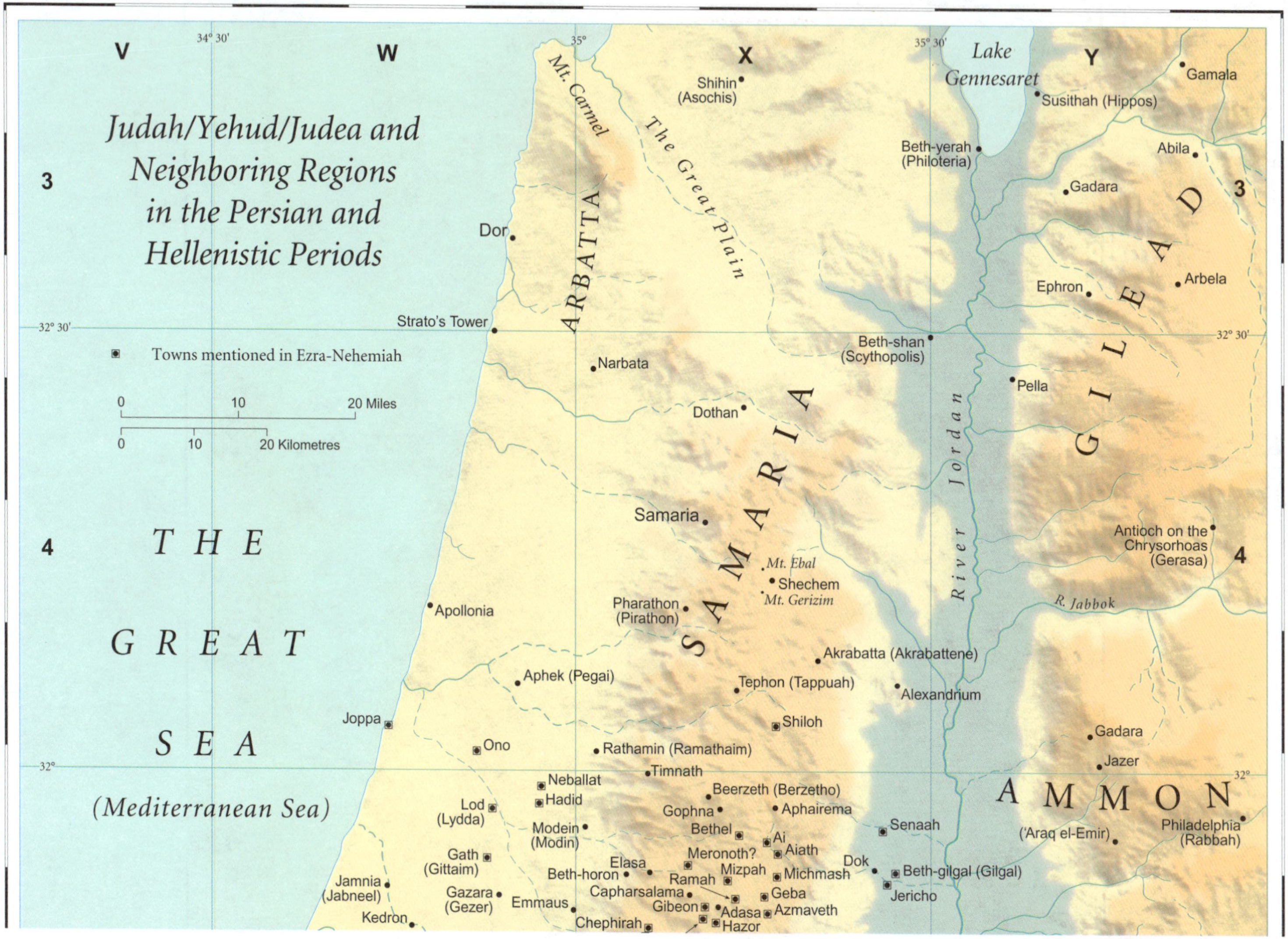

Judah/Yehud/Judea and Neighboring Regions in the Persian and Hellenistic Periods

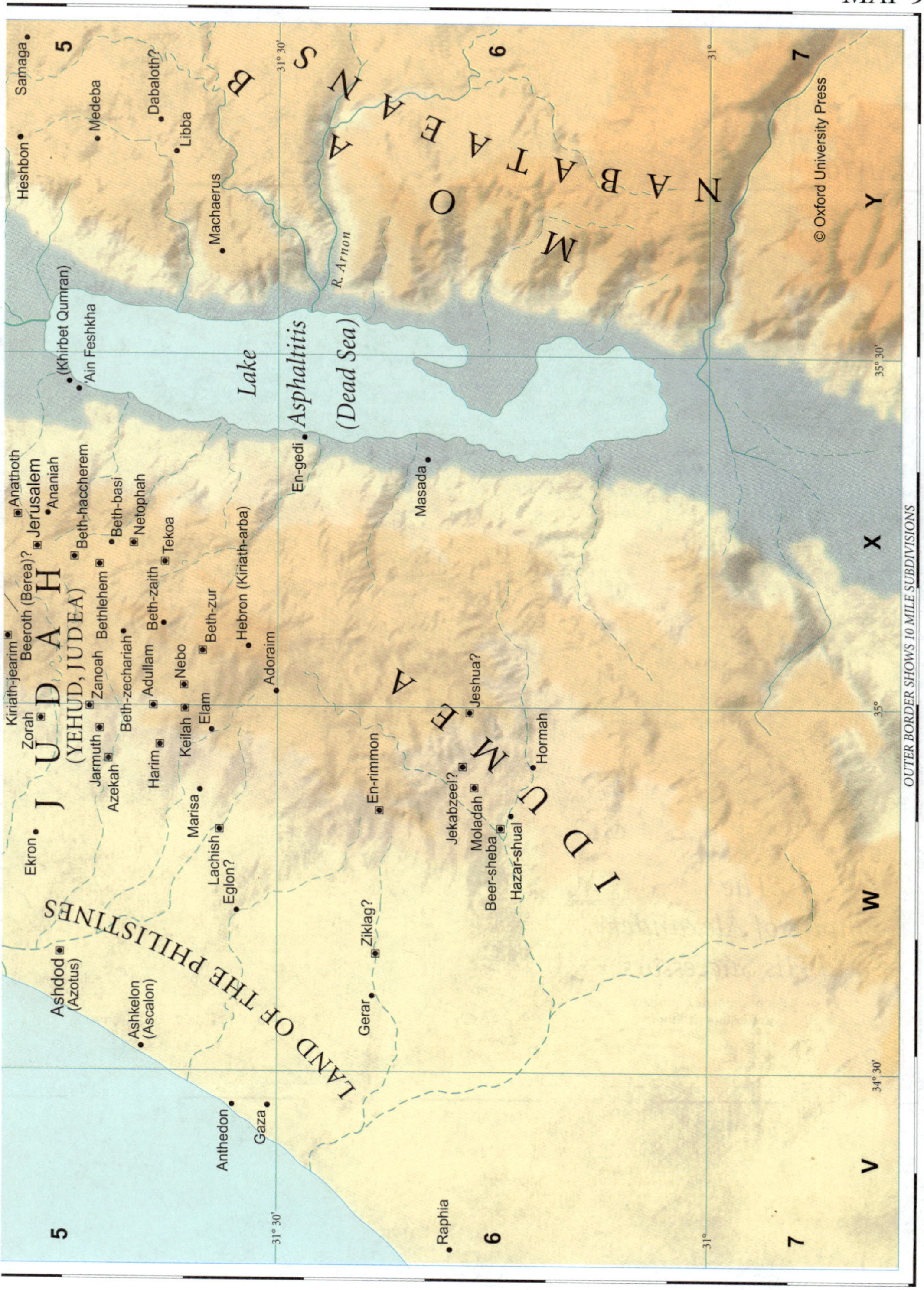

JUDAH
(YEHUD, JUDEA)
IDUMEA
MOAB
NABATAEANS
LAND OF THE PHILISTINES
Lake
Asphaltitis
(Dead Sea)
R. Arnon
Samaga
Heshbon
Medeba
Dabaloth?
Libba
Machaerus
(Khirbet Qumran)
'Ain Feshkha
En-gedi
Masada
Anathoth
Jerusalem
Ananiah
Beth-haccherem
Beth-basi
Netophah
Tekoa
Kiriath-jearim
Beeroth (Berea)?
Bethlehem
Beth-zaith
Beth-zur
Hebron (Kiriath-arba)
Zorah
Zanoah
Beth-zechariah
Adullam
Nebo
Adoraim
Jarmuth
Azekah
Harim
Keilah
Elam
Ekron
Marisa
Lachish
Eglon?
Jeshua?
Hormah
En-rimmon
Jekabzeel?
Moladah
Beer-sheba
Hazar-shual
Ziklag?
Gerar
Ashdod
(Azotus)
Ashkelon
(Ascalon)
Anthedon
Gaza
Raphia
V
W
X
Y
5
6
7
31° 30'
31°
34° 30'
35°
35° 30'
© Oxford University Press
OUTER BORDER SHOWS 10 MILE SUBDIVISIONS

MAP 10

OUTER BORDER SHOWS

200 MILE SUBDIVISIONS

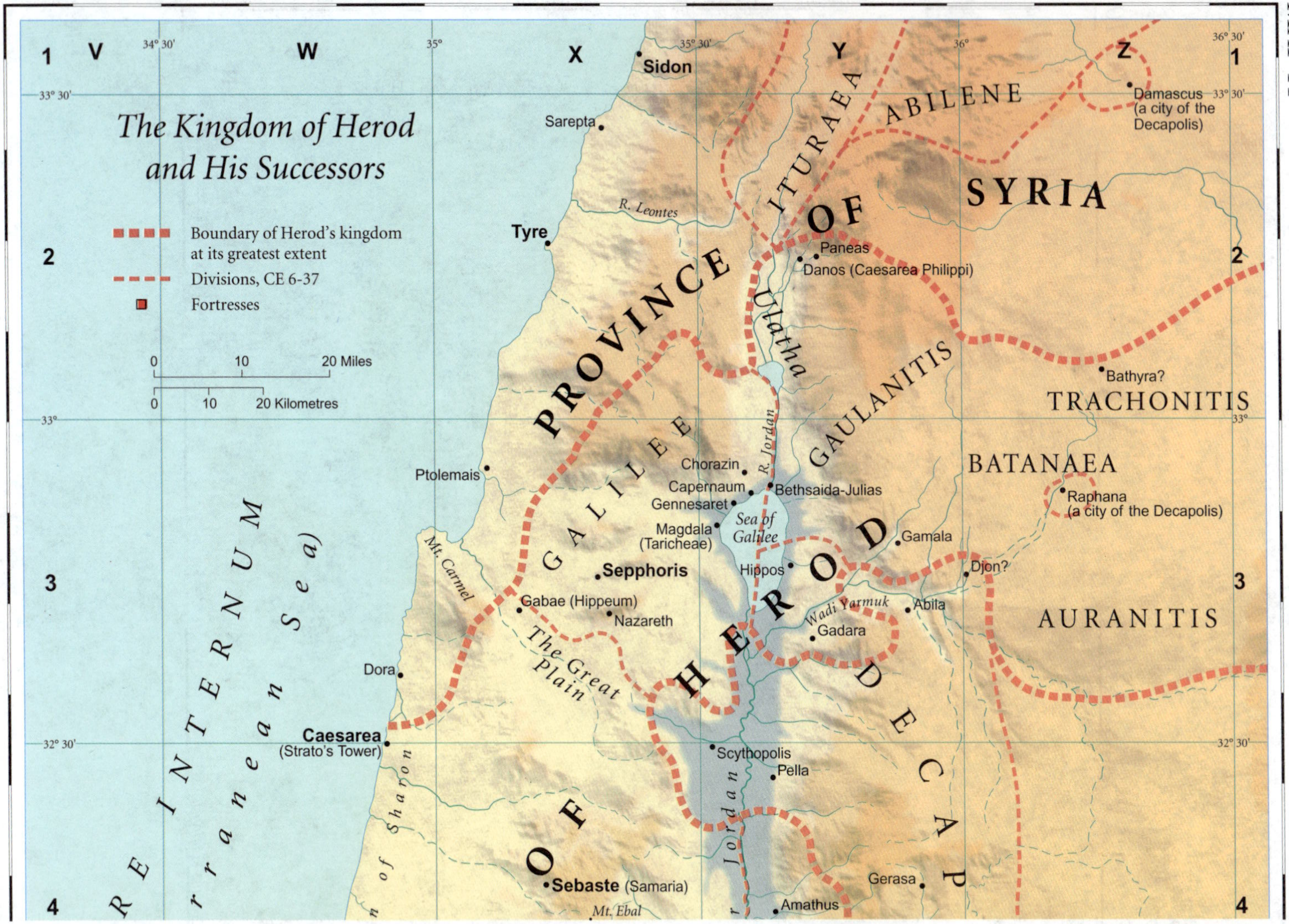
The Kingdom of Herod and His Successors
Boundary of Herod's kingdom at its greatest extent
Divisions, CE 6-37
Fortresses
0 10 20 Miles
0 10 20 Kilometres
V
W
X
Y
Z
1
2
3
4
34° 30'
35°
35° 30'
36°
36° 30'
33° 30'
33°
32° 30'
Sidon
Sarepta
Tyre
R. Leontes
ITURAEA
ABILENE
PROVINCE OF SYRIA
Damascus (a city of the Decapolis)
Paneas
Danos (Caesarea Philippi)
Ulatha
GAULANITIS
Bathyra?
TRACHONITIS
BATANAEA
Raphana (a city of the Decapolis)
AURANITIS
Djon?
GALILEE
R. Jordan
Chorazin
Capernaum
Bethsaida-Julias
Gennesaret
Magdala (Taricheae)
Sea of Galilee
Gamala
Hippos
Sepphoris
Gabae (Hippeum)
Nazareth
Wadi Yarmuk
Abila
Gadara
The Great Plain
Ptolemais
Mt. Carmel
Dora
Caesarea (Strato's Tower)
Plain of Sharon
Scythopolis
Pella
Jordan
Gerasa
Amathus
Sebaste (Samaria)
Mt. Ebal
OF HEROD
DECAPOLIS
MARE INTERNUM (Mediterranean Sea)

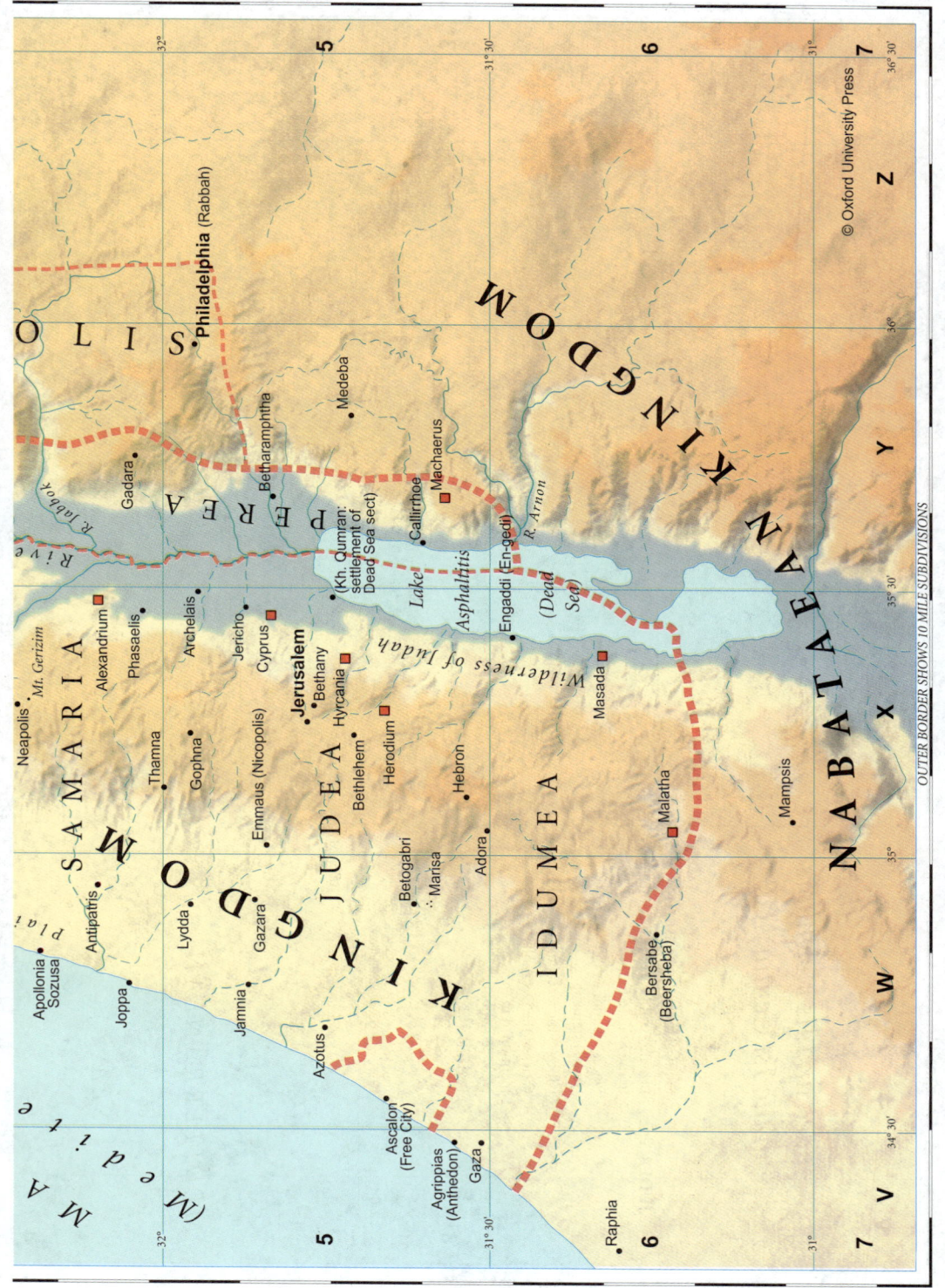

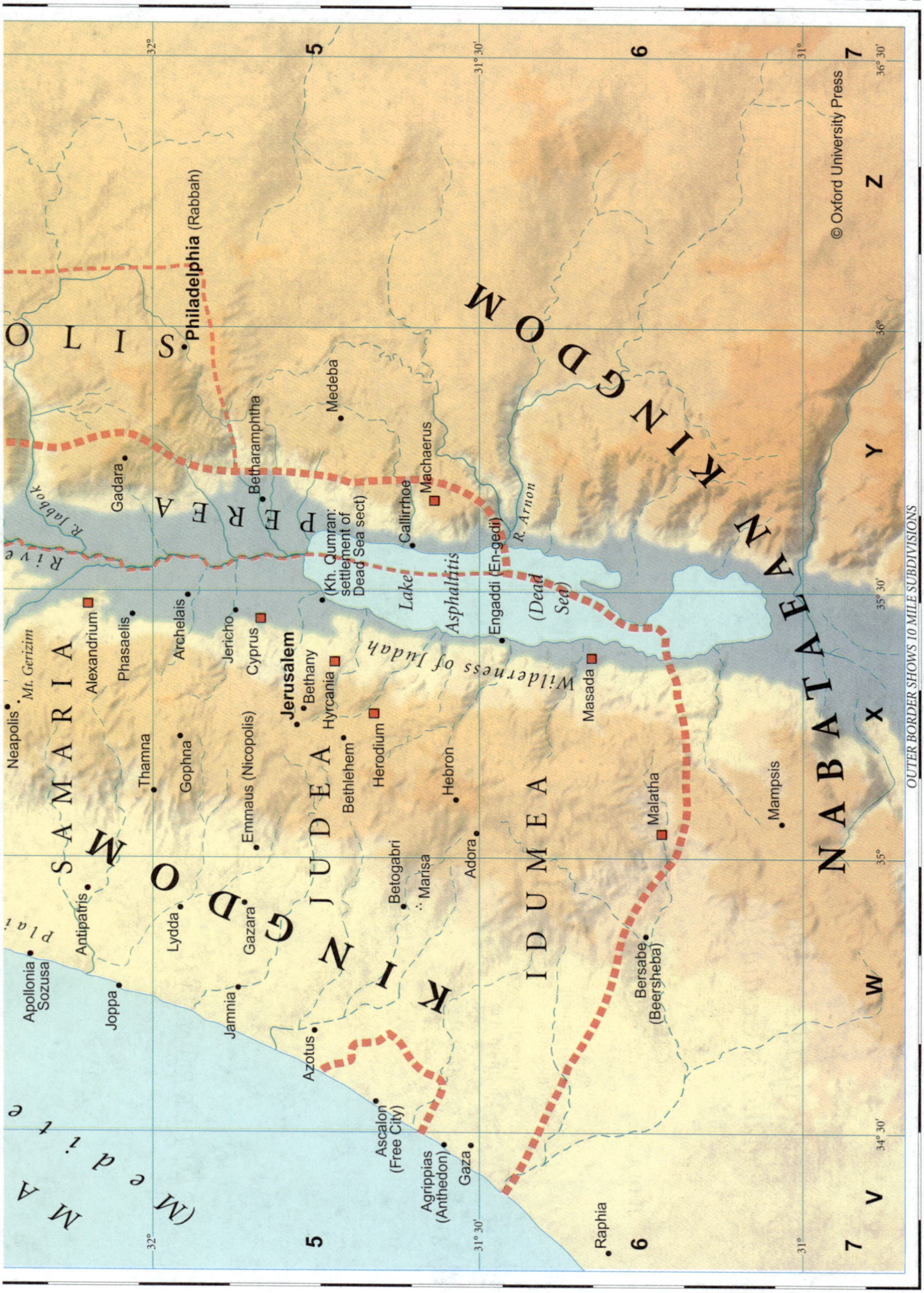
KINGDOM
SAMARIA
JUDEA
IDUMEA
PEREA
NABATAEAN KINGDOM
OLIS
Philadelphia (Rabbah)
Gadara
Betharamphtha
Medeba
Machaerus
Callirrhoe
R. Jabbok
River
R. Arnon
(Kh. Qumran: settlement of Dead Sea sect)
Lake Asphaltitis
(Dead Sea)
Engaddi (En-gedi)
Wilderness of Judah
Masada
Malatha
Mampsis
Neapolis
Mt. Gerizim
Alexandrium
Phasaelis
Archelais
Jericho
Cyprus
Jerusalem
Bethany
Hyrcania
Herodium
Bethlehem
Hebron
Adora
Thamna
Gophna
Emmaus (Nicopolis)
Betogabri
Marisa
Antipatris
Lydda
Gazara
Apollonia Sozusa
Joppa
Jamnia
Azotus
Ascalon (Free City)
Agrippias (Anthedon)
Gaza
Raphia
Bersabe (Beersheba)
Plai
(Mediterranean Sea)
5
6
7
V
W
X
Y
Z
32°
31° 30'
31°
34° 30'
35°
35° 30'
36°
36° 30'
© Oxford University Press
OUTER BORDER SHOWS 10 MILE SUBDIVISIONS

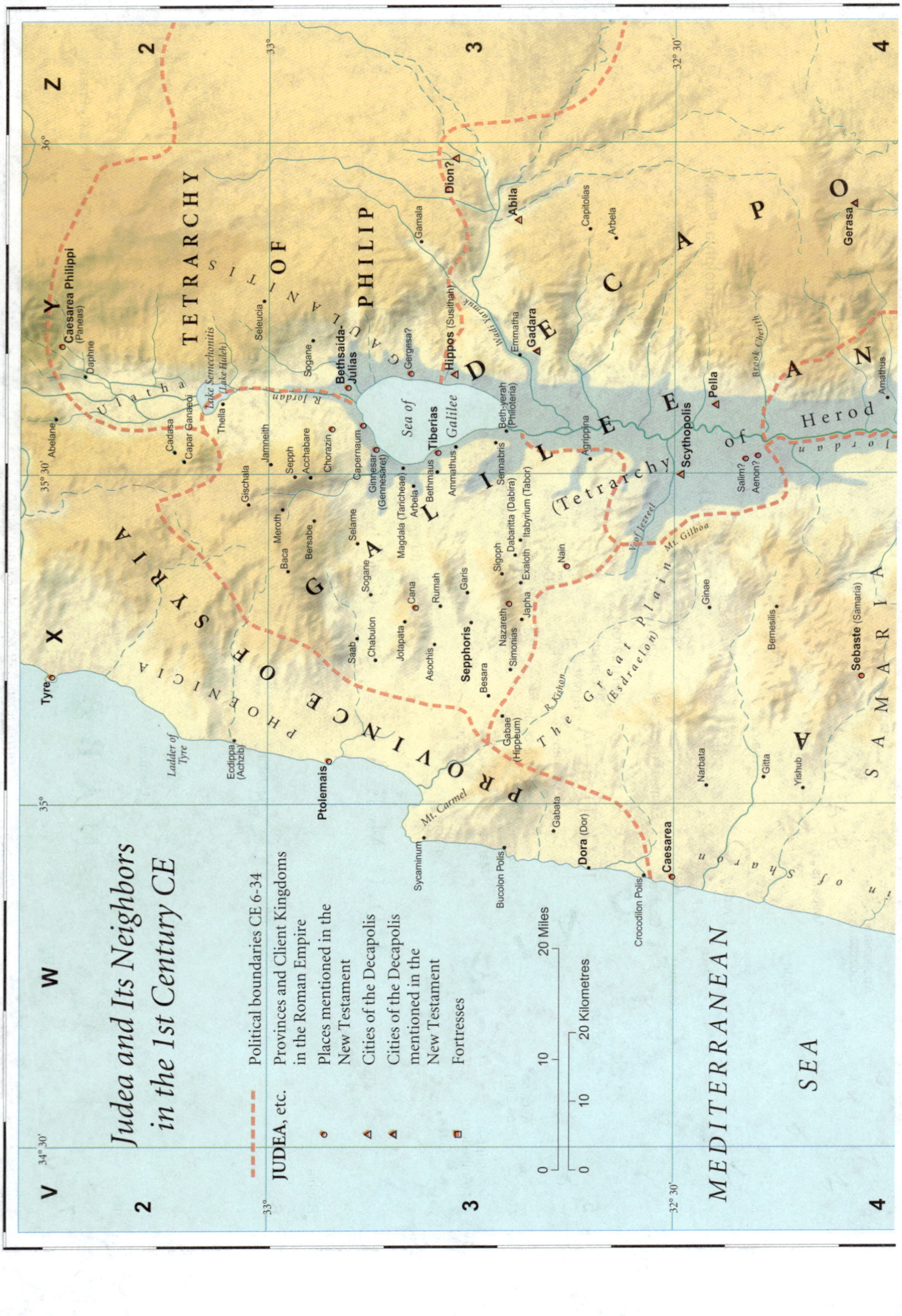
Judea and Its Neighbors in the 1st Century CE
Political boundaries CE 6-34
JUDEA, etc. Provinces and Client Kingdoms in the Roman Empire
Places mentioned in the New Testament
Cities of the Decapolis
Cities of the Decapolis mentioned in the New Testament
Fortresses
0 10 20 Miles
0 10 20 Kilometres
V
W
X
Y
Z
2
3
4
34° 30'
35°
35° 30'
36°
33°
32° 30'
MEDITERRANEAN SEA
PROVINCE OF SYRIA
PHOENICIA
TETRARCHY OF PHILIP
GAULANITIS
Ulatha
GALILEE
DECAPOLIS
(Tetrarchy of Herod
SAMARIA
Tyre
Ladder of Tyre
Ecdippa (Achzib)
Ptolemais
Mt. Carmel
Sycaminum
Bucolon Polis
Gabata
Dora (Dor)
Crocodilon Polis
Caesarea
Sharon
Gabae (Hippeum)
R. Kishon
The Great Plain (Esdraelon)
Mt. Gilboa
V. of Jezreel
Narbata
Gitta
Yishub
Ginae
Bemeselis
Sebaste (Samaria)
Abelane
Caesarea Philippi (Paneas)
Daphne
Cadasa
Capar Ganaeoi
Lake Semechonitis (Lake Huleh)
Thella
Seleucia
Sogane
Gischala
Jamneith
Meroth
Sepph
Acchabare
Chorazin
Baca
Bersabe
Selame
Capernaum
Bethsaida-Julias
R. Jordan
Gergesa?
Gennesar (Gennesaret)
Magdala (Taricheae)
Arbela
Sea of Galilee
Tiberias
Bethmaus
Ammathus
Hippos (Susithah)
Gamala
Dion?
Abila
Wadi Yarmuk
Emmatha
Gadara
Beth-yerah (Philoteria)
Sennabris
Agrippina
Dabaritta (Dabira)
Itabyrium (Tabor)
Exaloth
Sigoph
Nain
Saab
Chabulon
Sogane
Jotapata
Cana
Rumah
Garis
Asochis
Sepphoris
Nazareth
Simonias
Japha
Besara
Scythopolis
Pella
Salim?
Aenon?
Capitolias
Arbela
Gerasa
Brook Cherith
Amathus
Jordan

P E R E A
Antipas)
River
N A B A T A E A N K I N G D O M
I D U M E A
J U D E A
(under Roman administration)
Philadelphia
(Rabbah)
Medeba (Madaba)
Esbus
Betharamphtha
(Livias Julias)
Gadara
Zia
R. Jabbok
Areopolis (Rabbathmoab)
© Oxford University Press
Callirrhoe
Machaerus
R. Nahaliel
R. Arnon
Lake
Asphaltitis
(Dead Sea)
Masada
Engaddi (En-gedi)
Wilderness of Judea
(Kh. Qumran:
settlement of
Dead Sea sect)
Hyrcania
Kidron
Jericho
Cyprus
Taurus
Archelais
Phasaelis
Alexandrium
Coreae
(Wadi Farah)
Neapolis
Sychar
Tirathana
Mt. Gerizim
Mt. Ebal
Mahnayim
Pharaton
Acrabbein
Anathu Borcaeus
Selo (Shiloh)
Ephraim (Aphairema)
Aialon?
Michmash
Capharsalama?
Anathoth
Mt. Scopus
Bethphage
Bethany
Jerusalem
Colonia Amasa
(Emmaus?)
Gabath Saul
Gabaon
Adasa
Berea?
Upper Beth-horon
Lower Beth-horon
Bethel
Gophna
Berzetho
Tephon
Arus
Thamna (Timnath)
Ilon
Modein
Sappho
Emmaus
(Nicopolis)
Rathamin
(Arimathea?)
Adida
Tower of Aphek
Antipatris (Pegai)
Capparetaea
Capnarsaba
Brook of Kanah
Lydda
Gazara
Cariathiareim
R. Belus (Kedron)
Accaron
(Ekron)
Kedron
Jamnia
Apollonia Sozusa
Joppa
Iamnitarum Portus
(Jamnia Harbour)
Azotus
Azotus Paralius
(Azotus-on-Sea)
Ascalon
(Free city)
Maiumas Ascalon
(Baths of Ascalon)
Agrippias (Anthedon)
Gaza
To Province of Syria
Brook Besor
Bersabe
(Beersheba)
Malatha
Mampsis
(31°01')
Betogabri
(Wadi Qubeiba)
Capharabis
Gemmaruris
Bethletepha
Beth-zechariah
Beth-zaith
Caphartobas
Adora
?Caparorsa
Bethsura (Beth-zur)
Alulos
Terebinthus (Mamre)
Hebron
Aristobulias
Thecoa (Thekoa)
Herodium
Etam
Bethlehem
Beth-basi
W. Murabba'at
5
6
V
W
X
Y
Z
32°
31° 30'
34° 30'
35°
35° 30'
36°
OUTER BORDER SHOWS 10 MILE SUBDIVISIONS

MAP 13

B
C
D
E
2
3
4
5
PANNONIA
DACIA
Siscia
Sirmium
Singidunum
Viminacium
ILLYRICUM (DALMATIA)
R. Danube
Oescus
Novae
Odessus
Niassus
MOESIA
Sardica
Mesembria
Philippopolis
THRACE
Scodra
Scupi
Dyrrhachium
Apollonia
MACEDONIA
Philippi
Neapolis
Egnatian Way
Beroea
Thessalonica
THESSALY
Larissa
Genua
R. Po
45°
Portus Veneris
Luca
Florentia
Bononia
Ravenna
Pola
Ariminum
Ancona
Arretium
Perusia
Apennine Mts
R. Tiber
CORSICA
ROME
ITALY
Ostia
Three Taverns
Forum of Appius (Appii Forum)
Antium
Tarracina
Capua
Beneventum
Canusium
Puteoli
Neapolis
Pompeii
Appian Way
Paestum
Capreae (Capri)
Tarentum
Brundisium
SARDINIA
40°
Tyrrhenian Sea
Sea of Adria
Salonae
Sybaris
Croton
Corcyra
Nicopolis
Actium
Panormus
Messana
Rhegium
SICILY
Catana
Agrigentum
Syracuse
Utica
Carthage
Thapsus
St. Paul's Bay
Malta (Melita)
35°
ROMAN EMPIRE
Corinth
Cenchreae
Athens
Olympia
ACHAIA
Sparta (Lacedaemon)
Aegean Sea
40°
Cyzicus
Troas (Alexandria)
Assos
Adramyttium
Lesbos
Pergamum
Thyatira
Sardis
Chios
Smyrna
Philadelphia
Ephesus
Miletus
Cnidus
Rhodes
Rhodes
CRETE
Phoenix
Salmone
Fair Havens
Lasea
Cauda
Lesser Syrtis
Mediterranean Sea
(Mare Internum, Mare Nostrum)
Sabratha
Oea
TRIPOLITANIA
Lepcis Magna
15°
AFRICA
Greater Syrtis
20°
Cyrene
CYRENAICA
25°
LIBYA
Alexandria
EGY
Sahara Desert
C
D
E
OUTER BORDER SHOWS

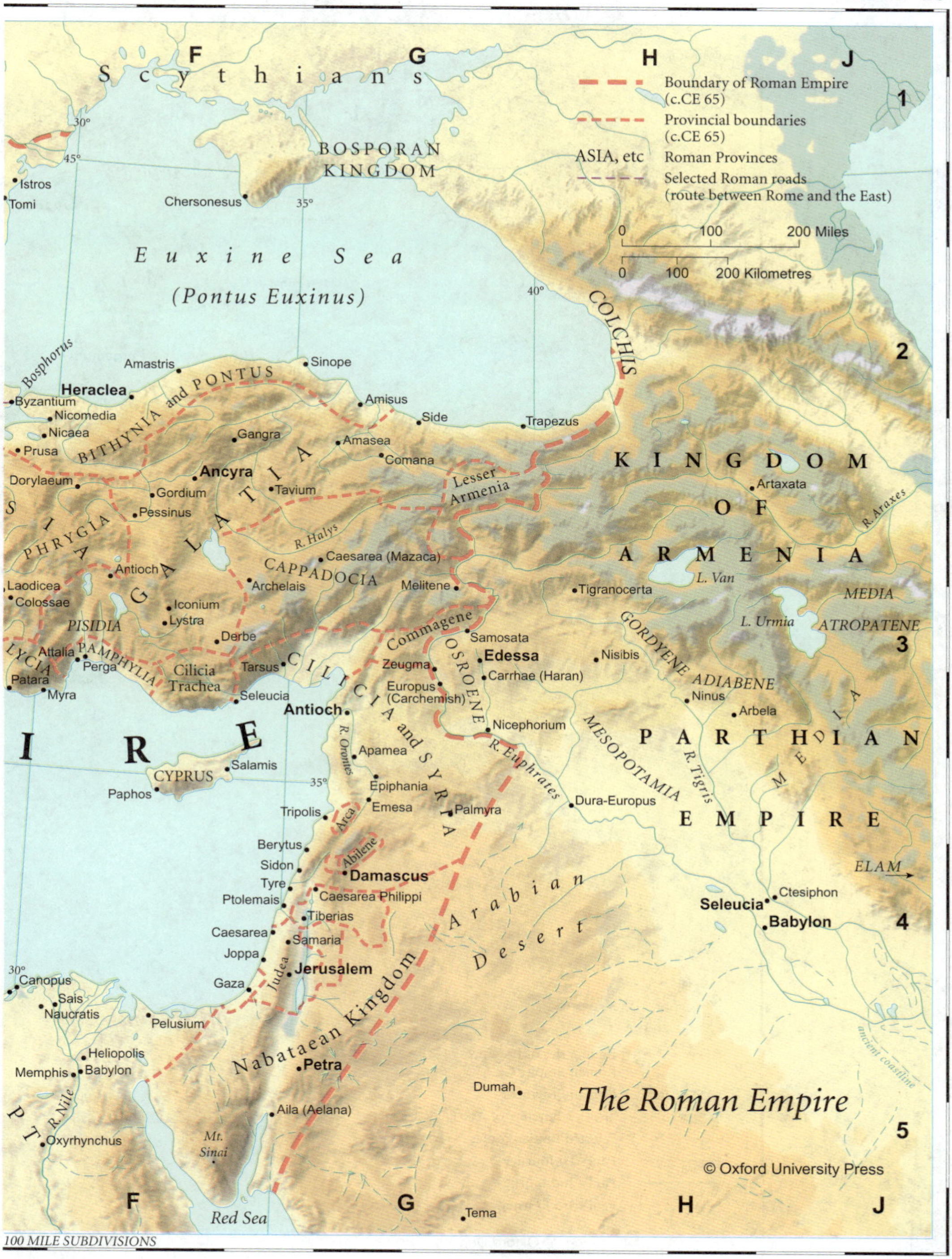

F
G
H
J
1
2
3
4
5
Scythians
Boundary of Roman Empire (c.CE 65)
Provincial boundaries (c.CE 65)
ASIA, etc
Roman Provinces
Selected Roman roads (route between Rome and the East)
0
100
200 Miles
0
100
200 Kilometres
30°
45°
35°
40°
BOSPORAN KINGDOM
Istros
Tomi
Chersonesus
Euxine Sea
(Pontus Euxinus)
COLCHIS
Bosphorus
Amastris
Sinope
Heraclea
Byzantium
Nicomedia
Nicaea
Prusa
BITHYNIA and PONTUS
Amisus
Side
Trapezus
Gangra
Amasea
Comana
KINGDOM OF ARMENIA
Artaxata
R. Araxes
Lesser Armenia
Dorylaeum
Ancyra
Gordium
Tavium
Pessinus
GALATIA
PHRYGIA
R. Halys
CAPPADOCIA
Caesarea (Mazaca)
Archelais
Melitene
Antioch
Laodicea
Colossae
Iconium
Lystra
Derbe
PISIDIA
L. Van
L. Urmia
MEDIA ATROPATENE
Tigranocerta
GORDYENE
Commagene
Samosata
Edessa
Nisibis
Carrhae (Haran)
ADIABENE
Ninus
Arbela
Attalia
PAMPHYLIA
Perga
LYCIA
Patara
Myra
Cilicia Trachea
Tarsus
CILICIA and SYRIA
Zeugma
Europus (Carchemish)
OSROENE
Seleucia
Antioch
Nicephorium
MESOPOTAMIA
R. Tigris
PARTHIAN EMPIRE
MEDIA
IRE
CYPRUS
Salamis
Paphos
R. Orontes
Apamea
Epiphania
Emesa
Palmyra
R. Euphrates
Dura-Europus
Tripolis
Arca
Abilene
Berytus
Sidon
Damascus
Tyre
Ptolemais
Caesarea Philippi
Tiberias
Caesarea
Samaria
Joppa
Jerusalem
Judea
Gaza
Arabian Desert
ELAM
Ctesiphon
Seleucia
Babylon
Canopus
Sais
Naucratis
Pelusium
Nabataean Kingdom
Heliopolis
Memphis
Babylon
Petra
R. Nile
Dumah
ancient coastline
The Roman Empire
Aila (Aelana)
Oxyrhynchus
Mt. Sinai
© Oxford University Press
Red Sea
Tema
100 MILE SUBDIVISIONS

MAP 14

OUTER BORDER SHOWS

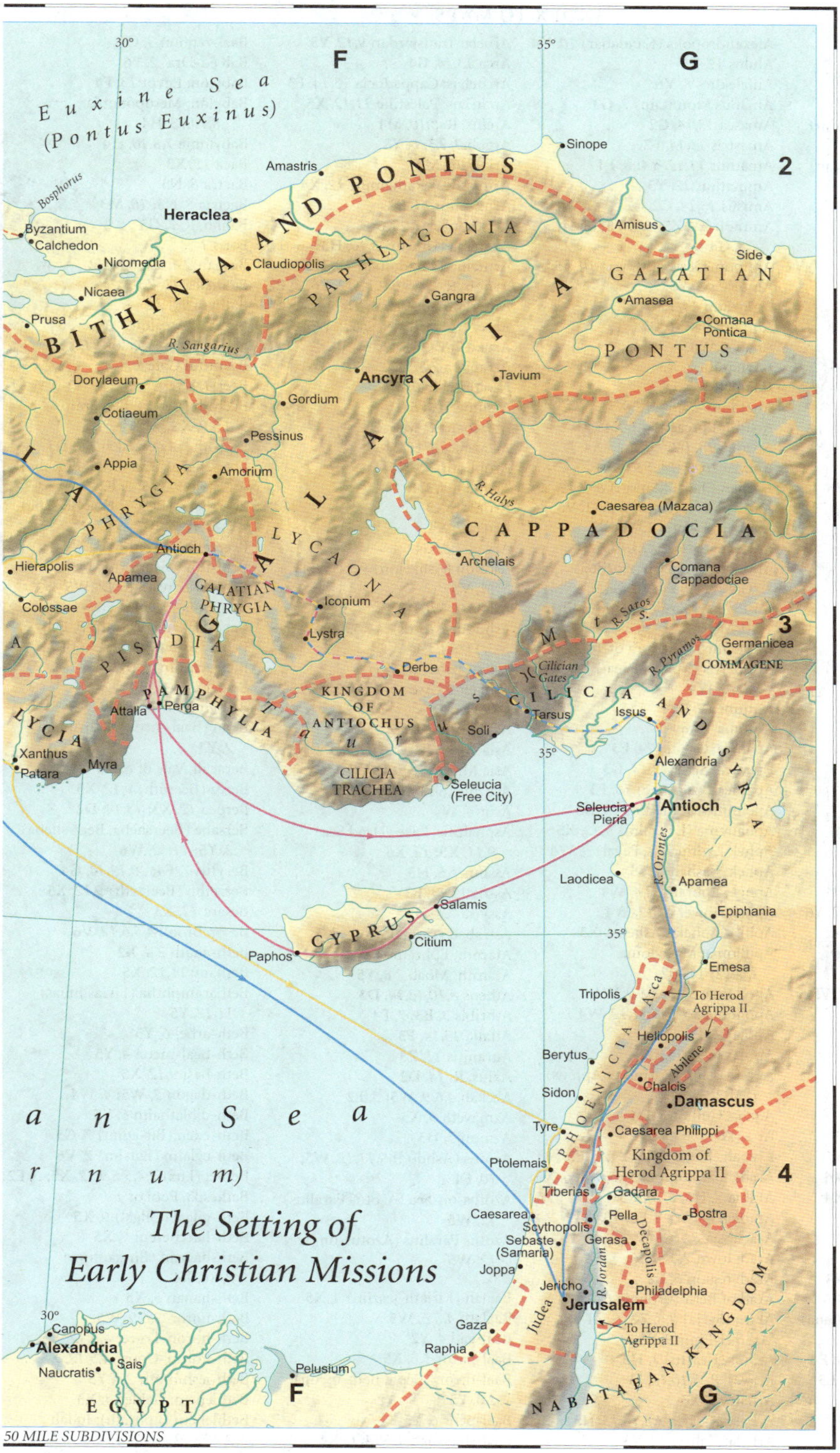
The Setting of
Early Christian Missions
Euxine Sea
(Pontus Euxinus)
Bosphorus
Byzantium
Calchedon
Heraclea
Amastris
Sinope
Amisus
Side
Nicomedia
Nicaea
Prusa
Claudiopolis
BITHYNIA AND PONTUS
PAPHLAGONIA
GALATIA
GALATIAN
PONTUS
Gangra
Amasea
Comana
Pontica
R. Sangarius
Dorylaeum
Cotiaeum
Ancyra
Tavium
Gordium
Pessinus
Appia
Amorium
PHRYGIA
R. Halys
Caesarea (Mazaca)
CAPPADOCIA
LYCAONIA
Antioch
Hierapolis
Apamea
Colossae
GALATIAN
PHRYGIA
Iconium
Lystra
Archelais
Comana
Cappadociae
R. Saros
PISIDIA
Derbe
KINGDOM
OF
ANTIOCHUS
Taurus Mts.
Cilician
Gates
CILICIA
Tarsus
R. Pyramos
Germanicea
COMMAGENE
PAMPHYLIA
Attalia
Perga
LYCIA
Xanthus
Patara
Myra
Soli
Issus
CILICIA
TRACHEA
Seleucia
(Free City)
Alexandria
SYRIA
Seleucia
Pieria
Antioch
R. Orontes
Laodicea
Apamea
Epiphania
Salamis
CYPRUS
Citium
Paphos
Emesa
Tripolis
Arca
To Herod
Agrippa II
Heliopolis
Abilene
Berytus
Chalcis
Sidon
PHOENICIA
Damascus
Tyre
Caesarea Philippi
Kingdom of
Herod Agrippa II
Ptolemais
Tiberias
Gadara
Caesarea
Scythopolis
Pella
Bostra
Sebaste
(Samaria)
Gerasa
Decapolis
Joppa
Jericho
R. Jordan
Philadelphia
Jerusalem
Judea
To Herod
Agrippa II
Gaza
Raphia
NABATAEAN KINGDOM
Canopus
Alexandria
Sais
Naucratis
EGYPT
Pelusium
...an Sea
...rnum)
F
G
2
3
4
30°
35°

50 MILE SUBDIVISIONS

INDEX TO MAPS

Abana, R. *6,* **Z1**
Abarim, Mts. of *2,* **Y5**
Abdon *4,* **X2**
Abel *2,* **Y2**
Abel-beth-maacah (Abel-maim) *5,* **Y2;** *6,* **X2**
Abel-maim (Abel-beth-maacah) *6,* **X2**
Abel-meholah *4,* **X4;** *5,6,* **Y4**
Abel-shittim (Shittim) *2,* **Y5**
Abelane *12,* **Y2**
Abila *9,11,12,* **Y3**
Abilene *11,* **Y2;** *13,14,* **G4**
Abydos *8,* **F5;** *14,* **E2**
Accaron (Ekron) *12,* **W5**
Acchabare *12,* **X3**
Acco *2,5,6,* **X3;** *7,* **F4**
Achaea *10,* **D3**
Achaia *13,* **D3;** *14,* **E3**
Achmetha (Ecbatana) *7,* **J3;** *8,* **J4**
Achor, Valley of *4,6,* **X5**
Achshaph *2,4,* **X3**
Achzib (Chezib): Judah *2,* **W5**
Achzib (Ecdippa): Phoenicia *2,4,12,* **X2**
Acrabbein *12,* **X4**
Actium *13,14,* **D3**
Adadah (Aroer) *4,* **W6**
Adam *4,* **Y4**
Adasa *9,12,* **X5**
Adhaim, R. *7,* **H4**
Adiabene *13,* **H3**
Adida *12,* **W5**
Admah *2,* **Y6**
Adora *11,* **W5;** *12,* **X5**
Adoraim *6,9,* **X5**
Adramyttium *13,14,* **E3**
Adria, Sea of *13,* **B2**
Adullam *2,9,* **X5;** *4,5,6,* **W5**
Aduru *2,* **Y3**
Aegean Sea *8,10,13,14,* **D3**
Aelana (Aila) *13,* **G5**
Aenon *12,* **Y4**
Aeropolis (Rabbathmoab) *12,* **Y6**
Aetolia *10,* **D3**
Africa *13,* **B4**
Agrigentum *13,* **B3**
Agrippias (Anthedon) *11,12,* **V5**
Agrippina *12,* **Y3**
Ahlab *4,* **X2**
Ai *2,4,6,9,* **X5;** *3,* **E2**
Aiath *9,* **X5**
Aialon *12,* **X5**
Aijalon: Dan *2,4,6,* **X5**
Aila (Aelana) *13,* **G5**
'Ain Feshkha *9,* **X5**
Akrabatta (Akrabattene) *9,* **X4**
Akrabattene (Akrabatta) *9,* **X4**
Akrabbim, Ascent of *2,4,* **X7**
Aleppo *7,8,10,* **G3**
Alexandria Arion *10,* **M4**
Alexandria Arachosion *10,* **N4**
Alexandria Kapisa *10,* **N3**
Alexandria (Antiochia-Margiana) *10,* **M3**
Alexandria: Egypt *8,10,13,14,* **E4**
Alexandria (Gulashkird) *10,* **L5**
Alexandria: Syria *10,14,* **G3**
Alexandria (Troas) *13,14,* **E3**
Alexandrium *9,11,12,* **X4**
Alexandropolis (Kandahar) *10,* **N4**
Alulos *12,* **X5**
Amalekites *5,* **V6**
Amanus Mountains *7,* **G3**
Amasea *13,14,* **G2**
Amastris *13,14,* **F2**
Amathus *11,12,* **Y4;** *8,* **F4**
Ammathus *12,* **Y3**
Amisus *13,14,* **G2**
Ammon *2,4,* **Z5;** *5,9,* **Y5;** *6,* **Z4;** *7,8,* **G4**
Ammon, Oasis of (Siwa) *10,* **E5**
Amorites *2,* **Y5**
Amorium *14,* **F3**
Amphipolis *14,* **D2**
Anab *4,* **W6**
Anaharath *2,* **X3**
Ananiah *9,* **X5**
Anathoth *4,5,6,9,12,* **X5**
Anathu Borcaeus *12,* **X4**
Ancona *13,* **B2**
Ancyra *10,13,14,* **F3**
Anshan (Tall-i Malyan) *8,* **K4**
Anthedon (Agrippias) *9,11,* **V5**
Antioch: Galatia *13,14,* **F3**
Antioch: Syria *10,13,14,* **G3**
Antioch on the Chrysorhoas (Gerasa) *9,* **Y4;** *10,* **G4**
Antiochia-Margiana (Alexandria) *10,* **M3**
Antiochus, Kingdom of *14,* **F3**
Antipatris (Aphek, Pegai) *11,12,* **W4**
Antium *13,* **B2**
Antonia Tower *1*
Apamea: Galatia *14,* **F3**
Apamea: Syria *13,14,* **G3**
Apamea (Calaenae) *10,* **F3**
Apennine Mountains *13,* **B2**
Aphairema (Ephraim) *9,12,* **X5**
Aphek (Antipatris, Pegai) *9,* **W4**
Aphek: Bashan *6,* **Y3**
Aphek: Ephraim *2,4,* **W4**
Aphek, Tower of *12,* **W4**
Aphik (Aphek): Asher *4,* **X3**
Apollonia: Macedonia *13,* **C2;** *14,* **D2**
Apollonia: Samaria *9,* **W4**
Apollonia Sozusa *11,12,* **W4**
Appia *14,* **F3**
Appian Way *13,* **C2**
Appii Forum (Forum of Appius) *13,* **B2**
Aqaba, Gulf of *3,* **D4**
Ar *2,* **Y6**
Arabah, The *2,4,5,6,* **Y4;** *3,* **E3**
Arabah, Sea of the *2,4,5,* **X6;** *6,* **X5**
Arabia *7,* **H5;** *8,10,* **G5**
Arabian Desert *3,* **E3;** *13,* **G4**
Arachosia *8,10,* **M4**
Arad: town *2,4,5,* **X6;** *3,* **E2**
Arad: region *3,* **E2**
Arad of Beth-yeroham *6,* **X6**
Aram (Syria) *2,6,* **Z2;** *5,* **Z1**
'Araq el-Emir *9,* **Y5**
Ararat (Urartu) *7,* **H3**
Araxes, R. *8,10,13,* **J3**
Arbatta *9,* **X3**
Arbela: Assyria *7,8,10,13,* **H3**
Arbela: Galilee *12,* **X3**
Arbela: Transjordan *9,12,* **Y3**
Arca *13,14,* **G4**
Archelais: Cappadocia *13,14,* **F3**
Archelais: Palestine *11,12,* **X5**
Areius, R. *8,10,* **M4**
Argob *2,* **Z3;** *5,* **Y3**
Aria *8,10,* **M4**
Arimathea (Rathamin) *12,* **X4**
Ariminum *13,* **B2**
Aristobulias *12,* **X6**
Armenia (Urartu) *8,10,* **H3**
Armenia, Kingdom of *13,* **H2**
Arnon, R. *2,4,5,6,9,11,12,* **Y6;** *3,* **E2**
Aroer: Moab *2,4,5,6,* **Y6**
Aroer (Adadah): Negeb *2,* **W6;** *4,* **Y4**
Arpad *7,8,* **G3**
Arrapkha *7,8,* **H3**
Arretium *13,* **B2**
Arsinoe *10,* **F5**
Artacoana *8,* **M4**
Artaxata *13,* **H2**
Arubboth *2,5,* **X4**
Arumah *4,* **X4**
Aruna *2,* **X3**
Arus *12,* **X4**
Arvad *7,8,* **G4**
Ascalon (Ashkelon) *9,12,* **W5;** *11,* **V5**
Ashan *4,* **W6**
Ashdod (Azotus) *2,4,5,6,9,* **W5;** *3,* **D2;** *8,* **F4**
Asher: tribe *4,6,* **X3**
Ashkelon (Ascalon) *2,4,5,9,* **W5;** *6,* **V5**
Ashtaroth *2,4,6,* **Z3**
Asia *13,14,* **E3**
Asia Minor: region *3,* **B1**
Asochis (Shihin) *9,12,* **X3**
Asor *4,* **W4**
Asphaltitis, Lake (Dead Sea) *9,11,* **X5;** *12,* **X6**
Asshur *7,8,* **H3**
Assos *13,14,* **E3**
Assyria *7,8,* **H3**
Astrabad (Gorgan) *8,10,* **K3**
Ataroth: Ephraim *4,* **X4**
Ataroth: Moab *2,6,* **Y5**
Athens *8,10,13,14,* **D3**
Athribis *3,* **B3;** *7,* **F4**
Attalia *13,14,* **F3**
Auranitis *11,* **Z3**
Axius, R. *14,* **D2**
Azekah *4,6,9,* **W5;** *3,* **E2**
Azmaveth *9,* **X5**
Azmon *3,* **D3**
Azotus (Ashdod) *9,11,12,* **W5;** *10,* **F4**
Azotus-on-Sea (Azotus Paralius) *12,* **W5**
Azotus Paralius (Azotus-on-Sea) *12,* **W5**

Baalah (Kiriath-jearim) *4,* **X5**
Baalath *4,5,6,* **W5**
Baal-gad *4,* **Y2**
Baal-hazor *5,6,* **X5**
Baal-meon (Beon, Beth-meon) *2,6,* **Y5**
Baal-peor *6,* **Y5**
Baal-shalishah *4,* **W4;** *6,* **X4**
Baal-zephon *3,* **C3**
Bab ed-Dra' *2,* **Y6**
Babylon: Egypt *13,* **F4**
Babylon: Mesopotamia *7,8,10,13,* **H4**
Babylonia *7,8,10,* **H4**
Baca *12,* **X3**
Bactra *8,* **N3**
Bactria *8,* **N3;** *10,* **M3**
Balikh, R. *7,* **G3**
Baris *1*
Bashan *2,4,* **Y3;** *5,6,* **Y2**
Batanaea *11,* **Z3**
Bathyra *11,* **Z2**
Baths of Ascalon (Maiumas Ascalon) *12,* **V5**
Beautiful Gate *1*
Beer *4,* **Y3**
Beeroth (Berea): Benjamin *4,5,9,* **X5**
Beeroth (Bene-jaakan) *3,* **D3**
Beer-sheba (Beersheba, Bersabe) *2,4,5,6,9,* **W6;** *3,* **E2**
Beersheba (Beer-sheba, Bersabe) *2,11,12,* **W6**
Beerzeth (Berzetho) *9,* **X5**
Behistun (Bisutun) *8,* **J4**
Belus (Kedron), R. *12,* **W5**
Bemesilis *12,* **X4**
Bene-jaakan (Beeroth) *3,* **D3**
Benei Hezir, Monument of *1*
Beneventum *13,* **B2**
Beni-hasan *3,* **B5**
Benjamin: tribe *6,* **X5**
Beon (Baal-meon, Beth-meon) *2,* **Y5**
Beracah, Vale of *6,* **X6**
Berea (Beeroth) *9,12,* **X5**
Beroea *12,* **X3;** *13,14,* **D2**
Bersabe (Beersheba, Beer-sheba) *2,* **Y5;** *11,12,* **W6**
Berytus *7,* **F4;** *10,13,14,* **G4**
Berzetho (Beerzeth) *9,12,* **X5**
Besara *12,* **X3**
Besor, Brook *4,5,6,12,* **V6**
Beth-anath *2,4,* **X2**
Bethany *11,12,* **X5**
Betharamphtha (Livias Julias) *11,12,* **Y5**
Beth-arbel *6,* **Y3**
Beth-baal-meon *4,* **Y5**
Beth-basi *9,12,* **X5**
Beth-dagon *2,* **W5;** *4,* **W4**
Beth-diblathaim *6,* **Y5**
Beth-eden (Bit-adini) *7,* **G3**
Beth-eglaim (Eglaim) *2,* **V6**
Bethel (Luz) *2,4,5,6,9,12,* **X5;** *3,* **E2**
Bethesda, Pool of *1*
Beth-gilgal (Gilgal) *9,* **X5**
Beth-haccherem *9,* **X5**
Beth-haggan (En-gannim) *2,4,6,* **X4**
Beth-hanan *5,* **X5**
Beth-horon *2,6,9,* **W5**
Beth-horon, Lower *4,5,12,* **X5**
Beth-horon, Upper *4,5,12,* **X5**
Beth-jeshimoth *2,4,* **Y5**
Bethlehem: Galilee *4,* **X3**
Bethlehem (Ephrath): Judah *2,4,5,6,9,11,12,* **X5**

Bethletepha *12,* **W5**
Bethmaus *12,* **Y3**
Beth-meon (Baal-meon) *6,* **Y5**
Beth-nimrah *2,4,* **Y5**
Bethphage *12,* **X5**
Beth-peor *4,* **Y5**
Beth-rehob: region *5,* **Y2**
Beth-rehob: town *4,5,* **Y2**
Bethsaida-Julias *11,12,* **Y3**
Bethsura (Beth-zur) *12,* **X5**
Beth-shan (Beth-shean) *2,* **X4**
Beth-shan (Scythopolis) *9,* **X4**
Beth-shean (Beth-shan) *2,5,* **X4;** *4,* **Y4**
Beth-shemesh: Judah *2,4,5,6,* **W5**
Beth-tappuah *2,* **W5**
Beth-yerah (Philoteria) *2,9,* **X3**
Bethul (Bethuel) *4,* **W6**
Beth-yerah (Philoteria) *12,* **Y3**
Beth-zaith *9,12,* **X5**
Beth-zechariah *9,* **W5;** *12,* **X5**
Beth-zur (Bethsura) *4,6,9,12,* **X5**
Betogabri *11,12,* **W5**
Betonim *4,* **Y5**
Beyond the River *8,* **G4**
Bezek *4,* **X4**
Bezer (Bozrah) *2,4,6,* **Y5**
Bezetha *1*
Bit-adini (Beth-eden) *7,* **G3**
Bithnia & Pontus *13,* **F2;** *14,* **E2**
Black Sea *7,8,10,* **F2**
Bokhara *8,* **M2**
Bononia *13,* **B2**
Borim *6,* **X4**
Borsippa *7,8,* **H4**
Bosphorus *13,14,* **E2**
Bosporan Kingdom *13,* **G1**
Bostra *14,* **G4**
Bozrah (Bezer) *6,* **Z5;** *3,* **E3**
Brundisium *13,* **C2**
Bubastis (Pi-beseth) *3,* **B3;** *10,* **F4**
Bucolon Polis *12,* **W3**
Busiris *3,* **B3;** *8,* **F4**
Buto *3,* **A2**
Byblos (Gebal) *7,* **F4;** *10,* **G4**
Byzantium *8,10,13,14,* **E2**

Cabul *4,5,* **X3**
Cadasa *12,* **Y2**
Caesarea (Strato's Tower): Palestine *11,* **W3;** *12,* **X4;** *13,14,* **F4**
Caesarea (Mazaca) *13,14,* **G3**
Caesarea Philippi (Danos) *11,* **Y2**
Caesarea Philippi (Paneas) *12,* **Y2;** *13,14,* **G4**
Calah *7,* **H3**
Calchedon *10,14,* **E2**
Callirrhoe *11,12,* **Y5**
Calno *7,* **G3**
Cana *12,* **X3**
Canaan *3,* **E2**
Canopus *13,14,* **F4**
Canusium *13,* **C2**
Capar Ganaeoi *12,* **Y2**
Caparorsa *12,* **X6**
Capernaum *11,* **X3;** *12,* **Y3**
Capharabis *12,* **W5**
Capharsalama *9,12,* **X5**
Caphartobas *12,* **X5**
Caphtor (Crete) *7,* **E4**
Capitolias *12,* **Y3**
Capparetaea *12,* **W4**
Capnarsaba *12,* **W4**
Cappadocia *8,* **F2;** *10,13,14,* **F3**
Capreae (Capri) *13,* **B2**
Capri (Capreae) *13,* **B2**
Capua *13,* **B2**
Carchemish (Europus) *7,8,10,13,* **G3**
Caria *8,10,* **E3**
Cariathiareim *12,* **W5**
Carmania *8,10,* **L5**
Carmel *5,6,* **X6**
Carmel, Mt. *2,4,5,6,9,11,12,* **W3**
Carrhae (Haran) *13,* **G3**
Carthage *13,* **B3**
Caspian Sea (Hyrcanian Sea) *8,* **K2**
Catana *13,* **B3**
Caucasus Mountains *8,* **H2**
Cauda (Gaudos) *13,14,* **D4**
Cenchreae *13,14,* **D3**
Chabulon *12,* **X3**
Chalcis *14,* **G4**
Chephirah *4,9,* **X5**
Cherith, Brook *6,12,* **Y4**
Chersonesus *13,* **F2**
Chezib (Achzib) *2,* **W5**
Chinnereth *2,6,* **X3;** *4,* **Y3**
Chinnereth, Sea of *2,4,5,6,* **Y3;** *3,* **E2**
Chios *13,14,* **E3**
Chroasmia *8,* **K3;** *10,* **L2**
Chorazin *11,12,* **Y3**
Cilicia (Khilakku) *7,8,* **F3**
Cilicia *10,* **F3**
Cilicia & Syria *13,14,* **G3**
Cilicia Trachea *13,14,* **F3**
Cilician Gates *8,10,* **G3**
Cimerians *8,* **F3**
Citium *8,10,14,* **F4**
City of David *1*
City of Salt *6,* **X5**
Claudiopolis *14,* **F2**
Cnidus *13,14,* **E3**
Coele-Syria *10,* **G4**
Colchi *8,* **H2**
Colchis *13,* **H2**
Colonia Amasa (Emmaus) *11,12,* **X5**
Colossae *13,14,* **E3**
Comana *13,* **G2**
Comana Cappadociae *14,* **G3**
Comana Pontica *14,* **G3**
Commagene *7,8,10,13,14,* **G3**
Coptos *8,* **F5**
Corcyra *13,* **C3**
Coreae *12,* **X4**
Corinth *8,10,13,14,* **D3**
Corsica *13,* **A2**
Cos: island *14,* **E3**
Cos: town *14,* **E3**
Cotiaeum *14,* **F3**
Court of Gentiles *1*
Court of Israel *1*
Court of Priests *1*
Court of Women *1*
Crete *7,10,* **E4;** *8,13,14,* **E3**
Crocodilon Polis *12,* **W3**
Crocodilopolis *10,* **F5**
Croton *13,* **C3**
Ctesiphon *10,* **H4;** *13,* **J4**
Cush (Ethiopia) *7,* **F5;** *8,* **F6**
Cuthah *7,* **H4**
Cydonia *10,* **D3**
Cyprus (Iadanna): island *3,* **D1;** *7,10,* **F3;** *8,13,14,* **F4**
Cyprus: Palestine *11,12,* **X5**
Cyrenaica *10,13,* **D4**
Cyrene *8,10,13,* **D4**
Cyropolis *8,10,* **N2**
Cyrus, R. *8,10,* **J2**
Cyzicus *13,14,* **E2**

Dabaloth *9,* **Y5**
Dabaritta (Dabira) *12,* **X3**
Dabira (Dabaritta) *12,* **X3**
Dacia *13,* **D1**
Dalmatia (Illyricum) *13,* **C2**
Damascus *2,4,5,6,11,* **Z1;** *7,8,10,13,14,* **G4**
Damascus Gate *1*
Damghan *8,* **K3**
Dan (Laish) *2,4,5,6,* **Y2**
Dan: tribe *4,* W5, **Y2**
Danos (Caesarea Philippi) *11,* **Y2**
Danube, R. *13,* **D2**
Daphne *12,* **Y2**
Dascylium *8,10,* **E2**
Dead Sea (Lake Asphaltitis) *9,11,12,* **X6**
Debir: Judah *2,4,5,* **X6;** *3,* **E2**
Decapolis *11,12,* **Y3;** *14,* **G4**
Dedan *7,8,* **G5**
Delos *10,14,* **E3**
Delphi *8,10,14,* **D3**
Der *8,* **J4**
Derbe *13,14,* **F3**
Dibon *2,4,5,6,* **Y5;** *3,* **E2**
Didyma *10,14,* **E3**
Dion *12,* **Y3**
Diyala, R. *7,* **H4**
Djon *11,* **Z3**
Doberus *14,* **D2**
Dok *9,* **X5**
Dor (Dora) *2,4,5,6,9,12,* **W3**
Dora (Dor) *11,12,* **W3;** *10,* **F4**
Doriscus *8,10,14,* **E2**
Dorylaeum *13,14,* **F3**
Dothan *2,6,9,* **X4**
Drangiana *8,10,* **M4**
Dumah *7,* **G5;** *8,13,* **G4**
Dura-Europus *10,13,* **H4**
Dur-sharrukin *7,* **H3**
Dyrrhachium *13,* **C2;** *14,* **D2**

Eastern Sea *7,* **K5**
Ebal, Mt. *2,4,5,6,9,11,12,* **X4**
Ecbatana (Achmetha) *7,* **J3;** *8,10,* **J4**
Ecdippa (Achzib) *12,* **X2**
Edessa *13,* **G3**
Edfu *8,* **F5**
Edom *2,4,5,6,* **X7;** *3,* **E3;** *7,* **G4**
Edomites *8,* **G4**
Edrei *2,4,6,* **Z3**
Eglaim (Beth-eglaim) *2,* **V6**
Eglon *2,4,9,* **W5**
Egnation Way *13,* **E2;** *14,* **D2**
Egypt *3,* **A4;** *7,8,10,* **F5;** *13,* **E4;** *14,* **F4**
Egypt, Brook of *3,* **D2**
Ekron (Accaron) *2,4,5,6,9,12,* **W5**
Elah, Valley of *4,* **W5**
Elam (Susiana) *9,* **W5;** *7,8,13,* **J4**
Elasa *9,* **X5**
Elath (Ezion-geber) *7,* **G5**
Elealeh *2,* **Y5**
Elephantine (Yeb) *8,* **F6**
Eleusis *14,* **D3**
Elon *5,* **X5**
Emesa *10,13,14,* **G4**
Emmatha *12,* **Y3**
Emmaus (Nicopolis or Colonia Amasa) *9,12,* **W5;** *11,* **X5**
En-dor *4,* **X3**
Engaddi (En-gedi) *11,12,* **X6**
En-gannim (Beth-haggan) *2,4,* **X4**
En-gedi (Engaddi) *4,6,9,11,* **X6**
En-rimmon *9,* **W6**
En-rogel Spring *1*
Ephesus *8,10,13,14,* **E3**
Ephraim: tribe *4,* **W4;** *5,* **X5;** *6,* **X4**
Ephraim (Aphairema) *12,* **X5**
Ephrath (Bethlehem) *2,11,* **X5**
Ephron: Gilead *9,* **Y3**
Ephron (Ophrah) *4,6,* **X5**
Epiphania *13,14,* **G3**
Epirus *10,* **D2;** *14,* **D3**
Erech (Uruk) *7,8,* **H4**
Erythraean Sea *8,* **L6;** *10,* **M6**
Esbus *12,* **Y5**
Esdraelon (Great Plain), Plain of *12,* **X3**
Eshnunna *8,* **H4**
Eshtemoa *4,* **X6**
Es-Safi *2,* **X6**
Etam *4,6,12,* **X5**
Ethiopia (Cush) *7,* **F5;** *8,* **F6**
Euboea *14,* **D3**
Euphrates, R. *3,* **G2;** *7,* **H4;** *8,* **H3;** *10,13,* **G3**
Europus (Carchemish) *13,* **G3**
Euxine Sea *13,* **F2;** *14,* **E2**
Exaloth *12,* **X3**
Ezion-geber *3,* **E3;** *7,* **G5**

Fair Havens *13,14,* **D4**
Farah, Wadi *12,* **X4**
Feifa *2,* **X7**
Florentia *13,* **B2**
Forum of Appius (Appii Forum) *13,* **B2**
Free City (Ascalon) *12,* **W5**
Free City (Seleucia) *14,* **F3**
Fullers' Tower *1*

Gabae (Hippeum) *11,12,* **X3**
Gabae (Isfahan) *8,10,* **K4**
Gabaon *12,* **X5**
Gabata *12,* **W3**
Gabath Saul *12,* **X5**
Gad: tribe *2,4,6,* **Y4**
Gadara: Decapolis *9,11,12,* **Y3;** *14,* **G4**
Gadara: Perea *9,11,12,* **Y4**
Galatia *10,13,14,* **F3**
Galatian Phrygia *14,* **F3**
Galatian Pontus *14,* **G2**
Galilee *6,11,* **X3**
Galilee and Perea *12,* **X3**
Galilee, Sea of *11,12,* **Y3**
Gamala *9,11,12,* **Y3**
Gandhara *8,* **N4;** *10,* **P4**
Gangra *13,14,* **F2**

Garis *12,* **X3**
Gate by Robinson's Arch *1*
Gate by Wilson's Arch *1*
Gath (Gittaim): Benjamin *6,9,* **W5**
Gath: Philistia *2,4,5,6,* **W5**
Gath of Sharon *2,* **W4**
Gath-hepher *6,* **X3**
Gath-rimmon *4,5,* **W4**
Gaudos (Cauda) *14,* **D4**
Gaugamela *10,* **H3**
Gaulanitis *11,12,* **Y3**
Gaza *2,4,5,6,9,11,12,* **V5;** *3,* **D2;** *7,8,10,13,14,* **F4**
Gazara (Gezer) *9,11,12,* **W5**
Geba *5,6,9,* **X5**
Gebal (Byblos) *7,* **F4;** *8,* **G4**
Gedrosia (Maka) *8,10,* **M5**
Gemmaruris *12,* **W5**
Gennath Gate *1*
Gennesaret *11,* **X3**
Gennesaret, Lake *9,* **Y3**
Genua *13,* **A2**
Gerar *2,4,5,6,9,* **W6;** *3,* **D2**
Gerasa (Antioch on the Chrysorhoas) *9,11,12,* **Y4;** *10,14,* **G4**
Gergesa *12,* **Y3**
Gerizim, Mt. *2,5,6,9,11,12,* **X4**
Germanicea *14,* **G3**
Geshur *2,5,* **Y3**
Gethsemane *1*
Gezer (Gazara) *2,4,5,9,* **W5;** *3,* **E2**
Ghazni *8,* **N4**
Gibbethon *4,6,* **W5**
Gibeah *4,5,6,* **X5**
Gibeon *2,4,5,9,* **X5**
Gihon Spring *1*
Gilboa, Mt. *4,* **X4;** *5,12,* **X3**
Gilead *2,4,5,9,* **Y4;** *6,* **Y5**
Gilgal (Beth-gilgal), nr. Jericho *2,4,5,6,9,* **X5**
Giloh *4,5,* **X5**
Gimarrai (Gomer) *7,* **F3**
Gimzo *6,* **W5**
Ginae *12,* **X4**
Ginnesar (Gennesaret) *12,* **Y3**
Gischala *12,* **X2**
Gitta *12,* **X4**
Gittaim (Gath) *6,9,* **W5**
Golan *2,4,* **Y3**
Golgotha *1*
Gomer (Gimarrai) *7,* **F3**
Gomorrah *2,* **Y6**
Gophna *9,11,12,* **X5**
Gordion (Gordium) *7,8,10,* **F3**
Gordium (Gordion) *10,13,14,* **F3**
Gordyene *13,* **H3**
Gorgan (Astrabad) *8,10,* **K3**
Gortyna *8,10,* **D3**
Goshen: Egypt *3,* **B3**
Goshen: Palestine *4,* **W6**
Gozan *7,* **G3**
Granicus, R. *8,10,* **E2**
Great Arad *6,* **X6**
Great Bitter Lake *3,* **C3**
Greater Syrtis *13,* **C4**
Great Plain, The *9,11,12,* **X3**
Great Sea, The *2,4,9,* **V4;** *5,* **V3;** *6,* **W3;** *3,* **B2;** *7,* **E4**
Gulashkird (Alexandria) *8,10,* **L5**
Gurbaal *6,* **W6**

Habor, R. *7,* **H3**
Hadid *9,* **W5**
Halicarnassus *10,14,* **E3**
Halys R. *7,* **F2;** *8,10,13,* **G3;** *14,* **F3**
Ham *2,* **Y3**
Hamath *7,8,* **G3**
Hamath, Entrance to *6,* **Y2**
Hammath *4,* **X3**
Hananel, Tower of *1*
Hannathon *2,4,6,* **X3**
Haran (Carrhae) *7,8,13,* **G3**
Harim *9,* **W5**
Harmozeia *10,* **L5**
Harod, Spring of *4,* **W3**
Hattina *7,* **G3**
Hauran *6,* **Z3;** *7,* **G4**
Havvoth-jair *2,4,5,6,* **Y3**
Hazar-addar *3,* **D3**
Hazar-shual *4,9,* **W6**
Hazazon-tamar *2,6,* **X7;** *3,* **E3**
Hazor: Benjamin *9,* **X5**
Hazor: Galilee *2,* **X2;** *4,5,6,* **Y2**
Hebron *4,5,12,* **X5;** *3,* **E2**
Hebron (Kiriath-arba) *2,6,9,11,* **X5**
Hecatompylus *10,* **K3**
Helam *5,* **Z3**
Helbon *7,* **G4**
Helena Princess of Adiabene, Tomb of *1*
Heliopolis (On) *3,* **B3;** *7,8,13,* **F4;** *10,* **F5;** *14,* **G4**
Hellespont *8,14,* **E3**
Hepher *4,5,* **W4**
Heraclea *10,14,* **F2**
Heracleon *14,* **E3**
Heracleopolis *3,* **B4**
Hermon, Mt. *2,4,5,6,* **Y2**
Hermopolis *7,8,10,* **F5**
Hermus, R. *7,14,* **E3**
Herod, Family Tomb of *1*
Herod, Kingdom of *11,* **W5**
Herodian Street *1*
Herodium *11,12,* **X5**
Heshbon *2,4,5,6,9,* **Y5;** *3,* **E2**
Hezekiah's Conduit *1*
Hezekiah, Wall of *1*
Hierapolis *14,* **E3**
Hindush (India) *8,10,* **N5**
Hinnom Valley *1*
Hipppeum (Gabae) *11,* **X3**
Hippicus *1*
Hippos (Susithah) *9,11,12,* **Y3**
Horeb, Mt. (Mt. Sinai) *3,* **D3, D4**
Hormah *2,4,9,* **W6;** *3,* **E2**
Huleh, Lake (Lake Semechonitis) *12,* **Y2**
Hyrcania *11,12,* **X5;** *8,10,* **K3**
Hyrcanian Sea (Caspian Sea) *8,* **K2;** *10,* **J2**

Iadanna (Cyprus) *7,* **F3**
Iamnitarum Portus (Jamnia Harbour) *12,* **W5**
Ibleam *2,4,6,* **X4**
Iconium *13,14,* **F3**
Ida, Mount *8,* **E3**
Idumea *9,11,12,* **W6**
Ijon *2,6,* **Y2**
Ilium (Troy) *10,* **E3**
Ilon *12,* **X5**
Illyricum (Dalmatia) *13,* **C2**
India (Hindush) *8,* **N5**
Imbros *14,* **E2**
Indus, R. *8,10,* **N5**
Ionia *8,10,* **E3**
Ioniacaria *14,* **E3**
Ipsus *10,* **F3**
Isfahan (Gabae) *8,* **K4**
Israel *5,6,* **X4;** *7,* **G4**
Israel, Hill Country of *2,4,* **X4**
Issachar: tribe *4,6,* **X3**
Issus *8,10,14,* **G3**
Istros *13,* **E2**
Itabyrium (Tabor) *12,* **X3**
Italy *13,* **B2**
Ituraea *11,* **Y2**

Jabbok, R. *2,4,5,6,9,11,12,* **Y4**
Jabesh-gilead *4,5,* **Y4**
Jabneel (Jabneh, Jamnia): Judah *4,6,9,11,* **W5**
Jabneh (Jabneel, Jamnia) *6,* **W5**
Jahaz *6,* **Y5**
Jamneith *12,* **Y3**
Jamnia (Jabneel, Jabneh) *9,11,12,* **W5**
Jamnia Harbour (Iamnitarum Portus) *12,* **W5**
Janoah *6,* **X3**
Japha *12,* **X3**
Japhia *2,* **X3**
Jarmuth: Judah *4,9,* **W5**
Jattir *4,* **X6**
Javan *7,* **E3**
Jazer *2,5,9,* **Y4**
Jebel Helal (Mt. Sinai) *3,* **D3**
Jebel Musa (Mt. Sinai) *3,* **D4**
Jebus (Jerusalem) *4,* **X5**
Jekabzeel *9,* **W6**
Jericho *2,4,5,6,9,11,12,* **X5;** *3,* **E2;** *14,* **G4**
Jerusalem *2,4,5,6,9,11,12,* **X5;** *3,* **E2;** *7,8,10,13,14,* **F4**
Jeshanah *6,* **X4**
Jeshua *9,* **X6**
Jezreel: Judah *4,* **W6**
Jezreel: Valley of Jezreel *4,5,6,* **X3**
Jezreel, Valley of *4,5,6,12,* **X3**
Jogbehah *2,4,* **Y4**
Jokmeam (Jokneam) *5,6,* **X3**
Jokneam (Jokmeam) *2,4,5,* **X3**
Joppa *2,4,5,6,9,11,12,* **W4;** *13,14,* **F4**
Jordan, R. *2,4,5,6,9,11,12,* **Y4;** *5,12,* **Y3;** *14,* **G4**
Jotapata *12,* **X3**
Judah: Kingdom & region *6,9,* **W6;** *7,8,* **F4**
Judah: tribe *4,* **W6**
Judah, Hill country of *2,4,* **X5**
Judah, Wilderness of *5,6,* **X6**
Judea: region *9,12,* **X5;** *11,* **W5;** *13,14,* **F4**
Judea, Wilderness of *11,12,* **X5**
Judea: Roman Empire *12,* **W5**
Juttah *3,* **E2**

Kabul (Ortospana) *10,* **N3**
Kabzeel *4,5,* **W6**
Kadesh *7,* **G4**
Kadesh-barnea (Meribah) *3,* **D3**
Kamon *4,* **Y3**
Kanah *2,* **X2**
Kanah, Brook of *12,* **W4**
Kandahar (Alexandropolis) *8,10,* **N4**
Karkor *4,* **Z6**
Karnaim *2,6,* **Z3**
Kedar (Qidri) *7,8,* **G4**
Kedemoth *2,4,* **Y5**
Kedesh *2,* **X2;** *4,6,* **Y2**
Kedron *9,12,* **W5**
Kedron (Belus), R. *12,* **W5**
Keilah *2,4,9,* **W5**
Kerman *8,* **L4**
Khanazir *2,* **X7**
Khilakku (Cilicia) *7,* **F3**
Khirbet Qumran *9,12,* **X5;** *11,* **Y5**
Kidron, Brook *6,12,* **X5**
Kidron Valley *1*
King's Highway, The *3,* **E3**
Kir-hareseth *5,6,* **Y6;** *3,* **E3**
Kiriathaim *2,4,6,* **Y5**
Kiriath-arba (Hebron) *2,9,* **X5**
Kiriath-jearim *4,5,9,* **X5**
Kishon, R. *4,5,6,12,* **X3**
Knossos *10,* **E3**
Kue *7,* **G3**
Kumukhu (Commagene) *7,* **G3**
Kyrenia *8,* **F3**

Lacedaemon (Sparta) *13,14,* **D3**
Lachish *2,4,6,9,* **W5;** *3,* **E2**
Laish (Dan) *2,* **Y2**
Lakkum *4,* **Y3**
Laodicea: Anatolia *13,14,* **E3**
Laodicea: Syria *10,14,* **G3**
Larissa *13,14,* **D3**
Larsa *7,* **J4;** *8,* **H4**
Lasea *13,* **E4;** *14,* **D3**
Lebanon *7,* **G4**
Lebanon, Mt. *2,4,5,6,* **Y2**
Lebanon, Valley of *4,* **Y2**
Lebo-Hamath *7,* **G4**
Lebonah *4,* **X4**
Lehi *4,* **X5**
Lemnos *14,* **E3**
Leontes, R. *11,* **X2**
Lepsis Magna *13,* **B4**
Lesbos *8,13,14,* **E3**
Lesser Armenia *13,* **G2**
Lesser Syrtis *13,* **B4**
Libba *9,* **Y5**
Libnah *4,5,6,* **W5;** *3,* **E2**
Libya *7,* **E4;** *8,13,* **D4**
Little Bitter Lake *3,* **C3**
Livias Julias (Betharamphtha) *12,* **Y5**
Lo-debar *5,6,* **Y4**
Lod (Lydda) *2,9,* **W5**
Lower Beth-horon *4,* **X5**
Lower Sea (Persian Gulf) *7,8,* **K5**
Lowland, The *6,* **W5**
Luca *13,* **B2**
Luz (Bethel) *2,* **X5**
Lycaonia *14,* **F3**
Lycia *10,13,14,* **E3**
Lycopolis (Siut) *7,10,* **F5**
Lydda (Lod) *9,11,12,* **W5**
Lycia *8,* **E3**
Lydia *7,8,14,* **E3**
Lysimachia *10,* **E2**

Lystra *13,14,* **F3**

Maacah *2,5,* **Y2**
Macedonia *8,10,13,14,* **D2**
Machaerus *9,11,12,* **Y5**
Madaba (Medeba) *12,* **Y5**
Madai (Medes) *7,* **J3**
Madmannah *4,* **W6**
Madon *2,4,* **X3**
Maeander, R. *10,14,* **E3**
Magdala (Taricheae) *11,12,* **X3**
Magnesia *8,10,14,* **E3**
Magnesia on Maeander *8,* **E3**
Mahanaim *2,5,6,* **Y4**
Mahnayim *12,* **X4**
Maiumas Ascalon
(Baths of Ascalon) *12,* **V5**
Maka (Gedrosia) *8,* **M5**
Makaz *5,* **W5**
Makkedah *4,* **W5**
Malatha *11,12,* **X6**
Malta (Melita) *13,* **B3**
Mampsis *11,12,* **X6**
Mamre (Terebinthus) *2,12,* **X5**
Manasseh: tribe *2,4,* **Y4;** *4,6,* **X4;**
6, **Y3**
Manasseh's Wall *1*
Mannai (Minni) *7,* **J3**
Maon *4,* **X6**
Marathon *8,* **D3**
Marathus *10,* **G4**
Mare Internum *11,* **V4;** *13,* **C4;**
14, **D4**
Mare Nostrum *13,* **D4**
Mareshah *4,6,* **W5**
Margus, R. *8,10,* **M3**
Margus (Margiana) *8,* **M3**
Margiana (Margus) *8,* **M3**
Mariamme *1*
Marisa *9,11,* **W5**
Masada *9,11,12,* **X6**
Mattanah *2,* **Y5**
Mazaca (Caesarea) *13,14,* **G3**
Mashhad (Tesmes) *8,* **M3**
Medeba (Madaba)
2,4,5,6,9,11,12, **Y5;** *3,* **E2**
Medes (Madai) *7,* **J3**
Media *8,10,13,* **J3**
Media Atropatene *13,* **J3**
Mediterranean Sea *9,* **V5;**
11,12, **V4;** *8,* **E4;** *10,14,* **D4;**
13, **C3**
Megiddo *2,4,5,6,* **X3**
Melita (Malta) *13,* **B3**
Melitene (Milid) *7,8,10,13,* **G3**
Mempis (Noph) *3,* **B3;**
7,8,10,13, **F5**
Menzaleh, L. *3,* **B2**
Meribah *4,* **X3;** *3,* **D3**
Merom *2,5,6,* **X3**
Merom, Waters of *4,* **X3**
Meronoth *9,* **X5**
Meroth *12,* **X3**
Mesembria *13,14,* **E2**
Meshech (Mushki, Moschi)
7, **F3;** *8,* **G2**
Mesopotamia *13,* **H3**
Messana *13,* **C3**
Michmash *4,9,12,* **X5**
Middin *4,6,* **X5**
Midian *3,* **E4**
Migdal *2,* **W4**
Migdol *7,* **F4**
Miletus *8,10,13,14,* **E3**
Milid (Melitene) *7,* **G3**
Minni (Mannai) *7,* **J3**
Mishna *1*
Misrephoth-maim *4,* **X2**
Mizpah *4,6,9,* **X5**
Moab *2,4,5,6,9,* **Y6;** *3,* **E3;** *7,8,* **G4**
Moab, Plains of *2,* **Y5**
Modein (Modin) *9,* **W5;** *12,* **X5**
Modin (Modein) *9,* **W5**
Moeris, Lake *3,* **A4**
Moesia *13,* **D2**
Moladah *2,9,* **W6**
Mons Casius *3,* **C2**
Moreh, Hill of *4,* **X3**
Moschi (Meshech, Mushki) *8,* **G2**
Mount Baalah *4,6,* **W5**
Murabba'at, Wadi *12,* **X5**
Mushki (Meshech) *7,* **F3**
Musri *7,* **G3**
Mycale, Cape *8,* **E3**
Myra *14,* **F3**
Mysia *14,* **E3**
Mytilene *8,10,14,* **E3**

Naarah *4,* **X5**
Nabataean Kingdom *11,* **X7;**
12, **X6;** *13,* **F4;** *14,* **G4**
Nabataeans *9,* **Y6;** *10,* **G5**
Nag Hammadi *10,* **F5**
Nahaliel, R. *2,5,6,12,* **Y5**
Nahalol *4,* **X3**
Nain *12,* **X3**
Nairi *7,* **H3**
Naphath-Dor *4,* **W3**
Naphtali: tribe *4,6,* **X3**
Narbata *9,12,* **X4**
Naucratis *13,14,* **F4**
Nazareth *11,12,* **X3**
Neapolis: Italy *13,* **B2**
Neapolis: Macedonia *13,14,* **D2**
Neapolis: Palestine *11,12,* **X4**
Neballat *9,* **W5**
Nebo: Judah *9,* **X5**
Nebo: Moab *4,6,* **Y5**
Nebo, Mt. *2,* **Y5;** *3,* **E2**
Negeb, The *2,4,5,* **W6;** *6,* **W7;** *3,* **E3**
Netophah *5,9,* **X5**
Niassus *13,* **D2**
Nibshan *4,6,* **X5**
Nicaea *10,* **F2;** *13,14,* **E2**
Nicephorum *13,* **G3**
Nicomedia *13,14,* **E2**
Nicopolis (Emmaus) *11,* **X5**
Nicopolis: Greece *13,14,* **D3**
Nile, R. *3,* **B4;** *7,8,10,13,* **F5**
Nimrim, Waters of *6,* **Y6**
Nineveh *7,8,* **H3**
Ninus *13,* **H3**
Nippur *7,8,* **J4;** *10,* **H4**
Nisibis *10,13,* **H3**
Noph (Memphis) *3,* **B3;** *7,* **F4**
Novae *13,* **E2**
Numeira *2,* **Y6**

Oboth *3,* **E3**
Odessus *13,* **E2**
Oea *13,* **B4**
Oescus *13,* **D2**
Olives, Mt. of *1*
Olympia *10,13,14,* **D3**
On (Heliopolis) *3,* **B3;** *7,* **F4**
Ono *2,9,* **W4**
Ophlas *1*
Ophrah (Ephron) *4,* **X5**
Orontes, R. *7,13,14,* **G3**
Ortospana (Kabul) *10,* **N3**
Osroëne *13,* **G3**
Ostia *13,* **B2**
Ottoman Wall *1*
Oxus, R. *8,10,* **M3**
Oxyrhynchus *13,* **F5**

Paestum *13,* **C2**
Palmyra *10,13,* **G4**
Pamphylia *8,10,13,14,* **F3**
Paneas (Caesarea Philippi)
11,12, **Y2;** *10,* **G4**
Pannonia *13,* **C1**
Panormus *13,* **B3**
Paphlagonia *10,14,* **F2**
Paphlagonians *8,* **F2**
Paphos *10,13,14,* **F4**
Paraetonium *10,* **E4**
Paran, Wilderness of *3,* **D3**
Parsagarda (Pasargadae) *8,10,* **K4**
Parthia *8,10,* **L4**
Parthian Empire *13,* **H3**
Pasargadae (Parsagarda) *8,* **K4**
Patara *13,14,* **E3**
Patmos *14,* **E3**
Patrae *14,* **D3**
Pattala *8,10,* **N5**
Pekod (Puqudu) *7,* **J4**
Pegai (Antipatris, Aphek)
9,12, **W4**
Pehel (Pella) *2,* **Y4**
Pelusium (Sin) *3,* **C2;**
7,8,10,13,14, **F4**
Pella (Pehel) *2,9,11,12,* **Y4;**
10, **D2;** *14,* **G4**
Pelloponnesus *8,* **D3**
Peniel (Penuel) *2,4,* **Y4**
Penuel (Peniel) *2,6,* **Y4**
Perea *11,* **Y5**
Perga *10,13,14,* **F3**
Pergamum *10,13,14,* **E3**
Persepolis *8,10,* **K5**
Persia (Persis) *8,* **K5**
Persian Empire *8,* **D4, N4**
Persian Gulf (Lower Sea) *7,8,* **K5;**
10, **J5**
Persis (Persia) *8,10,* **K5**
Perusia *13,* **B2**
Pessinus *13,14,* **F3**
Petra *10,* **G5;** *13,* **G4**
Pharathon (Pirathon) *9,* **X4**
Pharaton *12,* **X4**
Pharpar, R. *6,* **Z2**
Pharsalus *14,* **D3**
Phasael *1*
Phasaelis *11,12,* **X4**
Phaselis *10,* **F3**
Philadelphia: Asia *13,14,* **E3**
Philadelphia: Decapolis *14,* **G4**
Philadelphia (Rabbah,
Rabbath-ammon): Ammon
9,11,12, **Y5;** *10,* **G4**
Philip, Tetrarchy of *12,* **Y2**
Philippi *10,13,14,* **D2**
Philippopolis *13,14,* **D2**
Philistia *6,* **V6**
Philistia, Plain of *3,* **D2**
Philistines *4,* **W5;** *5,* **V6**
Philistines, Land of the *9,* **W5**
Philoteria (Beth-yerah) *2,9,* **X3;**
12, **Y3**
Phoenicia *12,* **X3;** *8,14,* **G4**
Phoenix *13,14,* **D3**
Phrygia *7,14,* **F3;** *8,10,13,* **E3**
Pi-beseth (Bubastis) *3,* **B3**
Piraeus *14,* **D3**
Pirathon (Pharathon) *4,5,6,9,* **X4**
Pisgah, Mt. *2,4,* **Y5**
Pisidia *10,13,14,* **F3**
Pithom *3,* **B3**
Po, R. *13,* **B2**
Pola *13,* **B2**
Pompeii *13,* **B2**
Pontus *10,* **G2**
Pontus Euxinus *13,* **F2;** *14,* **E2**
Portus Veneris *13,* **A2**
Praetorium *1*
Propontis *14,* **E2**
Prusa *13,14,* **E2**
Psephinus *1*
Pteria *8,10,* **F2**
Ptolemaic Empire *10,* **D5**
Ptolemais: Egypt *10,* **F4**
Ptolemais: Palestine *11,12,* **X3;**
13, **F4;** *14,* **G4**
Punon *3,* **E3**
Puqudu (Pekod) *7,* **J4**
Pura *8,10,* **M5**
Puteoli *13,* **B2**
Pyramos, R. *14,* **G3**

Qantir (Rameses) *3,* **B3**
Qarqar *7,* **G3**
Qidri (Kedar) *7,* **G4**
Qubeiba, Wadi *12,* **W5**
Qumran, Khirbet *9,* **X5;** *11,* **Y5**

Rabbah (Philadelphia,
Rabbath-ammon): Ammon
2,4,5,6,9,12, **Y5;** *3,* **E2**
Rages (Rhagae) *8,10,* **K3**
Ramah: Benjamin *4,6,9,* **X5**
Ramathaim (Ramathaim-zophim,
Rathamin) *9,* **X4**
Ramathaim-zophim
(Ramathaim, Rathamin) *4,* **W4**
Rameses (Qantir) *3,* **B3**
Ramoth-gilead *2,4,5,6,* **Z3**
Raphana *11,* **Z3**
Raphia *6,9,11,* **V6;** *3,* **D2;**
7,10,14, **F4**
Rathamin (Arimathea) *12,* **X4**
Rathamin (Ramathaim,
Ramathaim-zophim) *9,* **X4**
Ravenna *13,* **B2**
Red Sea *3,* **D5;** *7,8,10,* **G5;** *13,* **F5**
Rehob *2,* **X4;** *4,* **X3**
Rehoboth *2,* **W6**
Reuben: tribe *2,4,* **Y5**
Rezeph *7,* **G3**
Rhagae (Rages) *8,* **K3**
Rhegium *13,* **C3**
Rhodes: island *7,8,13,14,* **E3**
Rhodes: town *10,13,14,* **E3**
Riblah *7,* **G4**
Rimmon: Benjamin *4,* **X5**
Rimmon: Galilee *4,* **X3**

Rogelim *5,* **Y3**
Roman Empire *13,* **B2**
Rome *13,* **B2**
Rosetta *3,* **A2**
Royal Caverns *1*
Royal Palace *1*
Royal Portico *1*
Rumah *6,12,* **X3**
Royal Road *8,* **G3**

Saab *12,* **X3**
Saba (Sheba) *7,* **G6**
Sagartia *8,* **L4**
Sabratha *13,* **B4**
Sahara Desert *13,* **C5**
Sais *7,8,10,13,14,* **F4**
Saka (Scythians) *8,10,* **N2**
Salamis: Cyprus *8,10,13,14,* **F3**
Salamis: Greece *8,* **D3**
Salecah *7,* **G4**
Salem (Jerusalem) *2,* **X5**
Salim *12,* **Y4**
Salmone (Sammanion) *13,14,* **E3**
Salonae *13,* **C2**
Salt, Valley of *5,6,* **W6**
Salt Sea *2,4,5,6,* **X6;** *3,* **E2**
Samaga *9,* **Y5**
Sama'l *7,* **G3**
Samaria: region *9,11,12,* **X4**
Samaria (Sebaste) *6,9,11,12,* **X4;** *7,8,* **F4;** *10,13,14,* **G4**
Sammanion (Salmone) *14,* **E3**
Samos *8,10,14,* **E3**
Samosata *13,* **G3**
Samothrace *14,* **D2**
Sangarius, R. *7,8,10,14,* **F2**
Sappho *12,* **X5**
Saqqarah *3,* **B3**
Sardica *13,* **D2**
Sardinia *13,* **A2**
Sardis *7,8,10,13,14,* **E3**
Sarepta *11,* **X2**
Sattagydia *8,* **N4**
Saros, R. *14,* **G3**
Scodra *13,* **C2**
Scopus, Mt. *12,* **X5**
Scupi *13,14,* **D2**
Scythians (Saka) *8,10,* **N2;** *13,* **F1**
Scythopolis (Beth-shan) *9,* **X4;** *11,12,* **Y4;** *14,* **G4**
Sebaste (Samaria) *9,11,12,* **X4;** *14,* **G4**
Secacah *4,6,* **X5**
Sela *3,* **E3;** *7,8,* **G4**
Selame *12,* **X3**
Seleucia: Cilicia *13,* **F3**
Seleucia: E. of R. Jordan *12,* **Y2**
Seleucia (Free City) *14,* **F3**
Seleucia: Mesopotamia *10,13,* **H4**
Senaah *9,* **X5**
Senir (Mount Hermon) *2,* **Y2**
Seleucia Pieria *14,* **G3**
Seleucid *10,* **F3**
Selo (Shiloh) *12,* **X4**
Semechonitis, Lake (Lake Huleh) *12,* **Y2**
Sennabris *12,* **Y3**
Sepharad (Sardis) *7,* **E3**
Sepph *12,* **X3**
Sepphoris *11,12,* **X3**
Shaalbim *4,* **X5;** *5,* **W5**
Sharon, Plain of *2,5,6,11,12,* **W4**
Sharuhen *2,6,* **V6**
Sheba (Saba) *7,* **G6**
Shechem *2,4,5,6,9,* **X4**
Shephelah, The (The Lowland) *2,5,6,* **W6;** *4,* **Y4**
Shihin (Asochis) *9,* **X3**
Shikkeron *4,6,* **W5**
Shiloh (Selo) *4,5,6,9,12,* **X4**
Shimron *2,4,* **X3**
Shittim (Abel-shittim) *2,4,* **Y5;** *3,* **E2**
Shunem *2,4,6,* **X3**
Shur, Wilderness of *3,* **C3**
Shushan Gate *1*
Shushan (Susa) *7,8,* **J4**
Sicily *13,* **B3**
Siddim, Valley of *2,* **Y6**
Side *13,14,* **G2**
Sidon *2,4,5,6,11,* **X1;** *7,8,* **F4;** *10,13,14,* **G4**
Sidonians *5,6,* **X2**
Sigoph *12,* **X3**
Siloam: Jerusalem *1*
Siloam, Pool of *1*
Simeon: tribe *4,* **Y4;** *6,* **W6**
Simonias *12,* **X3**
Sin (Pelusium) *3,* **C2**
Sin, Wilderness of *3,* **D4**
Sinai: region *3,* **D3;** *7,8,* **F5**
Sinai, Mt. (Jebel Helal, Jebel Musa, Mt. Horeb) *3,* **D3, D4;** *13,* **F5**
Singidunum *13,* **D2**
Sinope *8,10,13,14,* **G2**
Siphtan *6,* **W4**
Sippar *7,8,* **H4**
Sirbonis, L. *3,* **C2**
Sirion (Mount Hermon) *2,* **Y2**
Sirmium *13,* **C2**
Siscia *13,* **C1**
Siut (Lycopolis) *7,* **F5**
Skudra (Thrace) *8,* **E2**
Smyrna *13,14,* **E3**
Socoh: Israel *2,5,6,* **X4;** *4,* **W4**
Socoh (Soco): Judah *2,4,6,* **W5**
Sodom *2,* **Z6**
Sogane: E. of R. Jordan *12,* **Y3**
Sogane: Galilee *12,* **X3**
Sogdiana *8,10,* **N3**
Soli *8,10,14,* **F3**
Solomon's Pool *1*
Solomon's Portico *1*
Solomon's Wall *1*
Sorek *4,5,* **W5**
Sparta (Lacedaemon) *8,10,13,14,* **D3**
St Paul's Bay *13,* **B3**
Strato's Tower (Caesarea) *9,* **W3;** *11,* **W4**
Strymon, R. *14,* **D2**
Succoth: Egypt *3,* **C3**
Succoth: Palestine *2,4,5,* **Y4**
Suez, Gulf of *3,* **C4**
Susa (Shushan) *7,8,10,* **J4**
Susiana (Elam) *7,8,10,* **J4**
Susithah (Hippos) *9,12,* **Y3**
Sybaris *13,* **C3**
Sycaminum *12,* **W3**
Sychar *12,* **X4**
Syene *7,* **F5;** *8,* **F6**
Syracuse *13,* **C3**
Syria (Aram) *2,6,* **Z2;** *5,* **Z1;** *7,* **G4;** *10,* **G3**
Syria, Province of *11,* **X2;** *12,* **X3**

Taanach *2,4,5,6,* **X3**
Tabal (Tubal) *7,* **G3**
Tabbath *4,* **Y4**
Tabor (Itabyrium) *12,* **X3**
Tabor, Mt. *4,6,* **X3**
Tadmor (Tadmar) *7,8,* **G4**
Tahpanhes *7,8,* **F4**
Tall-i Malyan (Anshan) *8,* **K4**
Tamar *5,* **X7**
Tanis (Zoan) *3,* **B3;** *7,* **F4**
Tappuah (Tephon) *4,6,9,* **X4**
Tarentum *13,* **C2**
Tarichaea (Magdala) *11,* **X3**
Tarracina *13,* **B2**
Tarsus *8,10,* **G3;** *13,14,* **F3**
Taurus *12,* **X5**
Tavium *13,14,* **F3**
Tekoa *5,6,9,* **X5**
Tell el-Yahudiyeh *3,* **B3**
Tema *7,8,13,* **G5**
Temple: Jerusalem *1*
Tephon (Tappuah) *9,12,* **X4**
Terebinthus (Mamre) *12,* **X5**
Tesmes (Mashhad) *8,* **M3**
Thamna (Timnath) *11,12,* **X4**
Thapsacus *8,10,* **G3**
Thapsus *13,* **B3**
Thasos *10,* **D2**
Thebes: Egypt *7,8,10,* **F5**
Thebes: Greece *7,* **F5;** *8,10,14,* **D3**
Thebez *4,5,* **X4**
Thecoa (Thekoa) *12,* **X5**
Thekoa (Thecoa) *12,* **X5**
Thella *12,* **Y2**
Thermopylae *8,* **D3**
Thessalonica *10,13,14,* **D2**
Thessaly *8,10,13,14,* **D3**
Thrace (Skudra) *8,* **E2;** *10,13,14,* **D2**
Three Taverns *13,* **B2**
Thyatira *13,14,* **E3**
Tiber, R. *12,* **Y3;** *13,* **B2**
Tiberias *13,14,* **G4**
Tigranocerta *13,* **H3**
Tigris, R. *7,10,* **H4;** *8,13,* **H3**
Til-garimmu (Togarmah) *7,* **G3**
Timnah: Hill Country of Judah *2,* **X5;** *4,* **W5**
Timnah: Dan *4,5,* **X5;** *6,* **W5**
Timnath (Thamna) *9,* **X5;** *12,* **X4**
Timnath-serah (Timnath) *4,* **X5**
Timsah, Lake *3,* **C3**
Tiphsah *7,* **G3**
Tirathana *12,* **X4**
Tirzah *2,4,6,* **X4**
Tishbe *6,* **Y4**
Tjaru (Zilu) *3,* **C3**
Tob *4,5,* **Z3**
Togarmah (Til-garimmu) *7,* **G3**
Tomi *13,* **E2**
Topheth: Jerusalem *1*
Trachonitis *11,* **Z2**
Trapezus *8,* **H2;** *10,13,* **G2**
Triple (Huldah) Gate *1*
Tripolis *10,13,14,* **G4**
Tripolitania *13,* **B4**
Troas (Alexandria) *13,14,* **E3**
Trogyllium *14,* **E3**
Tubal (Tabal) *7,* **G3**
Turang Tepe (Zadrakarta) *8,10,* **L3**
Turushpa (Tuspar) *7,* **H3**
Tyana *10,* **F3**
Tyre *2,4,5,6,11,12,* **X2;** *7,8,* **F4;** *10,13,14,* **G4**
Tyre, Ladder of *12,* **X2**
Tyropoeon Valley *1*
Tyrrhenian Sea *13,* **B3**

Ulatha *11,12,* **Y2**
Upper Beth horon *4,* **X5**
Upper Sea, The *7,8,* **E4**
Ur *7,8,* **J4**
Urartu (Armenia) *8,* **H3**
Urartu (Ararat) *7,* **H3**
Urmia, Lake *7,* **J3;** *8,10,13,* **H3**
Uruk (Erech) *7,* **H4;** *8,10,* **J4**
Ushu *7,* **G4**
Usiana *7,* **F3**
Uzu *2,* **X2**
Utica *13,* **B3**

Van, Lake *7,8,10,13,* **H3**
Viminacium *13,* **D2**

Warren's Gate *1*
Western Desert *3,* **A4**
Western Sea, The *2,* **W4;** *7,* **E4**

Xanthus *8,10,14,* **E3**

Yanoam *2,* **Y3**
Yarmuk, Wadi *11,12,* **Y3**
Yazith *6,* **X4**
Yeb (Elephantine) *8,* **F6**
Yehem *2,* **X4**
Yehud: region *9,* **W5**
Yiron *4,6,* **X2**
Yishub *12,* **X4**
Yurza *2,6,* **V6**

Zab, Upper & Lower *7,* **H3**
Zadrakarta (Turang Tepe) *8,10,* **L3**
Zair *6,* **X5**
Zanoah *9,* **X5**
Zaphon *4,* **Y4**
Zarephath *6,* **X2**
Zarethan *4,5,* **Y4**
Zeboiim *2,* **Z6**
Zebulun: tribe *4,6,* **X3**
Zela *4,* **X5**
Zemaraim *6,* **X5**
Zephathah, Vale of *6,* **W5**
Zered, Brook *2,4,6,* **Y7;** *5,* **Y6**
Zeredah: Ephraim *5,6,* **X4**
Zereth-shahar *4,* **Y5**
Zeugma *13,* **G3**
Zia *12,* **Y4**
Ziklag *2,4,5,9,* **W6**
Zilu (Tjaru) *3,* **C3**
Zin, Wilderness of *3,* **E3**
Zion, Wall of *1*
Ziph: Hill Country of Judah *4,6,* **X6**
Ziph: Negeb *2,4,* **W7**
Ziz, Ascent of *6,* **X5**
Zoan (Tanis) *3,* **B3;** *7,8,* **F4**
Zoar *2,6,* **X6**
Zobah *6,* **Z1**
Zorah *4,9,* **W5;** *5,* **Z1;** *6,* **X5**